W9-CPV-248

COWLES VOLUME LIBRARY

For over 50 years—a practical and authoritative reference. Written clearly and concisely for use in home, office, and library. Compiled with special attention to the needs of students.

TOPICALLY ARRANGED

THOROUGHLY INDEXED

FULLY ILLUSTRATED

SPECIAL 64-PAGE ATLAS

COWLES EDUCATION CORPORATION

A division of Cowles Communications

488 MADISON AVENUE   NEW YORK, N.Y.   10022

COWLES VOLUME LIBRARY

Copyright © 1968
by COWLES EDUCATION CORPORATION
a division of Cowles Communications
488 Madison Avenue, New York, N.Y. 10022

All rights reserved. This volume may not be
reproduced in whole or in part in any form without
written permission from the publishers.

Published simultaneously in the United States and Canada.
Copyright under the International Copyright Convention.

The Cowles Comprehensive Encyclopedia—The Volume Library
Copyright © 1967, 1966, 1965, 1964, 1963 by Cowles Education
Corporation. Copyright 1962, 1961, 1960, 1959, 1958, 1957, 1956,
1955, 1954, 1953, 1952, 1951, 1950, 1949, 1948, 1947, 1946, 1945,
1944, 1943, 1942, 1941, 1940, 1939, 1938, 1937, 1936, 1935, 1934,
1933, 1932, 1931, 1930, 1929, 1928, 1927, 1926, 1925, 1924, 1923,
1922, 1921, 1920, 1919, 1918, 1917 by Educators Association, Inc

Printed in the United States of America

Library of Congress Catalog Number 67-11920

PREFACE

WHAT IS COWLES VOLUME LIBRARY?

Cowles Volume Library is a distillation of the knowledge gathered through the ages. Centuries ago, one great scholar could master all the learning and academic disciplines of his time. Today, the vastly increased information in every area makes such a total mastery impossible. Yet the ambitious student and the responsible citizen have an ever-growing need for an understanding of countless subjects. It is the Volume Library's task to serve this need clearly, accurately, and comprehensively.

FOR WHOM IS COWLES VOLUME LIBRARY DESIGNED?

Cowles Volume Library, famous for over fifty years, has been expressly created for the student. It is designed to meet his four fundamental requirements: 1) the need for a complete, authoritative reference work covering a broad range of subjects; 2) the need for supplementary sources, readily available, that can eliminate long hours of exhausting searching; 3) the need for clarity, conciseness, and ease of use; 4) the need for economy. The student, whatever his scholastic level or age, will find this single volume indispensable.

Cowles Volume Library is also geared to the intellectual needs of persons long out of school who wish to brush up on their knowledge in particular fields. It has proved especially valuable to those who have been unable to complete their formal education, but are determined through self-education to make up the lack.

HOW DOES COWLES VOLUME LIBRARY MEET THESE NEEDS?

First of all, it is comprehensive. This means that within its covers the student will find factual answers to almost any question. Completely indexed information on a multitude of subjects is instantly at hand—set forth by experts in informal, easy-to-understand language.

Second, Cowles Volume Library presents in only one volume all the major subjects taught from kindergarten through high school and into college. It is topically organized into twenty-seven major sections, including History, Geography, Mathematics, Science, Literature, Government and Law, and many others. There is no need to thumb back and forth from one letter of the alphabet to another; all related facts are grouped together. The student finds not only the information he seeks, but dozens of related details and articles in a complete textbook on the same subject.

Third, this one-volume library of textbooks can be kept conveniently at the student's desk or reading table, constantly available for immediate reference.

Fourth, by limiting its format to one volume, Cowles Volume Library not only is practical, but it places the educational advantages of encyclopedia ownership within the means of every student and his family.

WHAT SPECIAL FEATURES DOES COWLES VOLUME LIBRARY PROVIDE?

In addition to its basic textbook sections, Cowles Volume Library includes: a complete, up-to-date, full-color chart of the flags of all the nations of the world; a special Conquest of Space supplement; a striking, 8-page visual projection of Human Anatomy; brilliant full-color reproductions of the world's most famous paintings; bright portfolios on Hunting and Fishing and many other subjects; an International Atlas with the latest maps; and concise dictionaries of terms and references used in particular subject areas.

HOW TO USE COWLES VOLUME LIBRARY

If you wish to increase your knowledge of politics, for example: turn to the minutely detailed Index—the key which unlocks every subject in Cowles Volume Library. There, listed under politics, you will find specific entries with page numbers directing you to various places in the book. One Index reference guides you to the section on Government and Law, with its descriptions of party government and legal procedure. Another, in the volume on Careers, offers a discussion of politics as a career. A third leads to the Parallel Outlines of American History and to detailed accounts of each presidential election and administration. A further reference is to political institutions, covered by the Sociology chapter in the volume devoted to Social Science.

A person making a systematic study of the subject or a student preparing for a comprehensive examination need not rely on the Index alone. He should turn to an appropriate text book section, such as Government and Law or History and work straight through it. He will find a complete review course, plus an extensive bibliography for further reading.

Finally, Cowles Volume Library is ideal for the general reader to browse through, following wherever his interests may lead him in the pursuit of a broader understanding of his world.

Because it is carefully updated every year, you can be certain that your Cowles Volume Library is as current, accurate, and thorough as modern research can make it. Remember that more than fifty years of scholarship and editorial experience enrich its pages. Use it to the fullest advantage.

COWLES VOLUME LIBRARY

Managing Editor
ROBERT J. FELDMAN

Art Editor
JAMES T. ANDREWS

Assistant Editors
STEVEN P. DALBER, STEPHANIE L. DRANOFF,
M. T. v. GERLOFF, SARA DULANEY GILBERT, PHYLLIS G. ROSEN,
HILARY ROSS, JUDITH C. TARTELL

Editorial Assistants
SUZANNE L. RINGER, SIMONE Y. SONG, D. D. WHEELOCK

Published by
COWLES EDUCATION CORPORATION

DAVID C. WHITNEY
President and Editor

FRANCINE KLAGSBRUN
Executive Editor

RONALD GILBERT
Art Director

ROBERT F. HIRSCH
Production Manager

A division of
COWLES COMMUNICATIONS

GARDNER COWLES
Editorial Chairman

WILLIAM ATTWOOD
Editor in Chief

ADVISORS

DONALD T. CLARK . . . A.B., B.S., M.B.A. University Librarian, University of California, Santa Cruz.

HENRY STEELE COMMAGER . . . Ph.B., A.M., Ph.D. Professor of History and American Studies, Amherst College.

ABRAHAM FISCHLER . . . A.B., A.M., Ed.D. Associate Professor of Education, University of California, Berkeley.

JULIUS H. HLAVATY . . . B.A., Ph.D. President, National Council of Teachers of Mathematics.

PHILIP JOHNSON . . . B.S., M.S., Ph.D. Professor of Science Education, Cornell University.

MELVIN KRANZBERG . . . A.B., A.M., Ph.D. Associate Professor of History, Case Institute of Technology.

GAINES POST . . . A.B., A.M., Ph.D. Professor of History, Princeton University.

JOHN WARD STUDEBAKER . . . A.B., A.M., LL.D. Former U.S. Commissioner of Education; Chairman of the Editorial Board, *Scholastic Magazine.*

WALTER TRATTNER . . . B.A., M.E., Ph.D. Associate Professor of History and Social Welfare, University of Wisconsin, Milwaukee.

LEONARD ZOBLER . . . B.A., M.A., Ph.D. Professor of Geology and Geography, Barnard College, Columbia University.

CONTRIBUTORS

ABBOTT, ROBERT E. . . . B.S.M.E. Mechanical engineer; managing editor, *Product Engineering.* PHYSICS: MECHANICS.

ALEXANDER, GEORGE W. . . . B.S.E.E. Manager, High Voltage Laboratory, General Electric Company. ENERGY AND POWER SOURCES: TRANSFORMER.

ALLEGRI, LINDA . . . Ph.D. Associate Professor, Hunter College; instructor, Teachers College, Columbia University; assistant editor, *Mathematical Education in the Americas.* HISTORY OF MATHEMATICS.

ASHBURN, ANDERSON . . . B.S.E. Editor, *American Machinist.* MACHINES AND PROCESSES: INDUSTRIAL CONTROL, MACHINE TOOLS, QUALITY CONTROL.

BAHLMAN, DUDLEY W. R. . . . Ph.D. Professor of History and Dean of the Faculty, Williams College, COUNTRIES OF THE WORLD-HISTORY: UNITED KINGDOM.

BAINER, ROY . . . M.S. Dean of Engineering, University of California. FOOD AND AGRICULTURE: AGRICULTURAL ENGINEERING.

BAKER, LAURENCE H. . . . Ph.D. Director, Computing Department, Pioneer Hi-Bred Corn Company; consultant, United States Feed Grain Council, Japan. FOOD AND AGRICULTURE: ANIMAL BREEDING, PLANT BREEDING, CORN OR MAIZE.

BALAMUTH, LEWIS . . . Ph.D. Vice-President, Research and Development, Cavitron Corporation. ENERGY AND POWER SOURCES: ULTRASONIC MOTOR.

BARTHOLD, LIONEL O. . . . B.S. Manager, AC Transmission Engineering, General Electric Company. ENERGY AND POWER SOURCES: ELECTRIC POWER TRANSMISSION.

BARZANTI, SERGIO . . . Ph.D. Associate Professor of Social Sciences, Fairleigh Dickinson University. UNITED NATIONS; COUNTRIES OF THE WORLD — HISTORY: EUROPE, MIDDLE EAST.

BATTISON, EDWIN A. . . . Associate curator, Division of Mechanical and Civil Engineering, Museum of History and Technology, Smithsonian Institution. COMMUNICATIONS AND TRANSPORTATION: CLOCKS AND WATCHES.

BENBEN, JOHN S. . . . Ph.D. Professor of Educational Administration, New York University. HISTORY OF EDUCATION.

BERKEBILE, DONALD H. . . . Museum specialist, Division of Transportation, Smithsonian Institution. COMMUNICATIONS AND TRANSPORTATION: MOTOR VEHICLE, ROADS AND HIGHWAYS.

BERKNER, LLOYD V. . . . Late director, Southwest Center for Advanced Studies. INTRODUCTION TO INDUSTRY AND TECHNOLOGY.

BERRY, E. WILLARD . . . Ph.D. Professor Emeritus of Geology, Duke University. GEOLOGY: PHYSICAL GEOLOGY.

BRAYNARD, FRANK O. . . . M.A. Editor, *Tow Line Magazine*. COMMUNICATIONS AND TRANSPORTATION: LIGHTHOUSE, MARINE ENGINEERING, MARINE SIGNALING, SHIP.

BROOKS, MARVIN C. . . . Ph.D. Commercial development manager, United States Rubber Tire Company. MACHINES AND PROCESSES: RUBBER MANUFACTURE.

BROWN, L. CARL . . . Ph.D. Associate Professor of Oriental Studies, Princeton University. COUNTRIES OF THE WORLD-HISTORY: AFRICA.

BROWN, ROBERT U. . . . B.A. President, Editor and Publisher Company. COMMUNICATIONS AND TRANSPORTATION: NEWSPAPER.

BRUA, LYNN A. . . . B.A. Director, Client Services, EBS Management Consultants, Inc. ADMINISTRATIVE SERVICES.

BUCHTA, J. W. . . . Ph.D. Late president, Minnesota Academy of Science. PHYSICS: INTRODUCTION, PROPERTIES OF MATTTER.

BURNLEY, ROSE MARIE . . . M.S. Home economist. MACHINES AND PROCESSES: HOUSEHOLD APPLIANCES, SEWING MACHINE.

BURR, HOWARD O. . . . Assistant to the president, Cambridge Instrument Company, Inc. MACHINES AND PROCESSES: VOTING MACHINE.

BUSHNELL, DAVID . . . Ph.D. Associate Professor of History, University of Florida. COUNTRIES OF THE WORLD-HISTORY: SOUTH AMERICA.

BUTTFIELD, HELEN . . . A.M. American Museum of Natural History. PLANT LIFE.

BYAM, GUY R. . . . M.A. Vice-president and Director of Personnel, Bankers Trust Company. PERSONNEL AND HUMAN RELATIONS.

BYERLY, THEODORE C. . . . Ph.D. Administrator, Cooperative State Research Service, United States Department of Agriculture. FOOD AND AGRICULTURE: AGRICULTURAL SCIENCE.

BYRNES, ROBERT F. . . . Ph.D. Distinguished Professor of History, Indiana University: COUNTRIES OF THE WORLD — HISTORY: EASTERN EUROPE.

CAMPBELL, JEROME . . . LL.B. Textile marketing consultant; Assistant Corporation Counsel of the City of New York. MATERIALS AND STRUCTURES: SYNTHETIC FIBERS.

CAREY, GEORGE W. . . . Ed.D. Associate Professor of Geography, Teachers College, Columbia University. COUNTRIES OF THE WORLD — GEOGRAPHY: CENTRAL AMERICA.

CARMICHAEL, LEONARD . . . Ph.D. Vice-president of Research and Exploration, National Geographic Society. PSYCHOLOGY AND PSYCHIATRY.

CHAMBERLIN, ROBERT H. . . . B.S. Account executive, Beaumont, Heller & Sperling, Inc. MATERIALS AND STRUCTURES: ALUMINUM.

CHAPELLE, HOWARD I. . . . Senior Historian, Museum of History and Technology, Smithsonian Institution. MACHINES AND PROCESSES: SHIPBUILDING.

CLARK, DONALD T. . . . M.B.A. University Librarian, University of California. BUSINESS GLOSSARY.

COHEN, MARSHALL H. . . . M.A. Economist. FOOD AND AGRICULTURE: CACAO, COFFEE, TEA.

COLEMAN, JOHN W. . . . Ph.D. Engineering leader, Scientific Instruments Engineering, Radio Corporation of America. MACHINES AND PROCESSES: ELECTRON MICROSCOPE.

COMMAGER, HENRY STEELE . . . Ph.D. Professor of History and American Studies, Amherst College. INTRODUCTION TO HISTORY.

COON, CARLETON S. . . . Ph.D. Professor Emeritus, Harvard University and University of Pennsylvania; Research curator, University Museum, University of Pennsylvania. ANTHROPOLOGY.

CUNNINGHAM, DONALD E. . . . Ph.D. Professor of Physics, Adelphi University. PHYSICS: NUCLEAR PHYSICS.

DABOLL, H. DAVIS . . . B.S. Former New York branch manager. Columbia Rope Company. MACHINES AND PROCESSES: ROPE.

DALRYMPLE, DANA G. . . . Ph.D. Economist, Federal Extension Service, United States Department of Agriculture. FOOD AND AGRICULTURE: FRUIT, GRAPE, VEGETABLE.

DASMANN, RAYMOND F. . . . Ph.D. Director, Environmental Studies, The Conservation Foundation. BIOLOGICAL RELATIONSHIPS.

DAVIS, FRANCIS K. . . . Ph.D. Head, Physics Department, Drexel Institute of Technology. INTRODUCTION TO METEOROLOGY.

DETWILER SAMUEL B., Jr. . . . M.A. Assistant to Deputy Administrator for Nutrition, United States Department of Agriculture. FOOD AND AGRICULTURE: AGRICULTURAL CHEMISTRY.

DIRKS, J. EDWARD . . . Ph.D. Professor, Yale University Divinity School; founder and editor, *Christian Science Quarterly*. RELIGION.

DIRKSEN, EVERETT M. . . . United States Senator; member, 73rd to 90th Congresses; Minority Whip; Minority Leader. CHOOSING A CAREER: A POLITICAL CAREER.

DUNBAR, ROBERT G. . . . Ph.D. Professor of History, Montana State University. FOOD AND AGRICULTURE: ALFALFA, SOILS, WHEAT.

DUPREE, LOUIS . . . Ph.D. Research Associate in Anthropology, American Museum of Natural History. COUNTRIES OF THE WORLD — AFGHANISTAN.

EDGAR, ROBERT F. . . . M.S. Electrical engineer, General Electric Company. PHYSICS: ELECTRICITY AND MAGNETISM.

EMBREE, AINSLIE T. . . . Ph.D. Associate professor, Columbia University. COUNTRIES OF THE WORLD — HISTORY:INDIA.

ENGLEBARDT, STANLEY L. . . . B.S. Free-lance science writer. COMMUNICATIONS AND TRANSPORTATION: DATA PROCESSING SYSTEMS, DUPLICATION MACHINES; MACHINES AND PROCESSES: AUTOMATION, CALCULATING MACHINES, COMPUTER.

ENNIS, THOMAS E. . . . Ph.D. Late professor of Far Eastern History, West Virginia University. COUNTRIES OF THE WORLD — HISTORY: ASIA.

EPPERT, RAY R. . . . D.Sc., LL.D. Chairman and chief executive officer, Burroughs Corporation. BUSINESS AND THE COMPUTER.

FEINBERG, SAMUEL . . . Columnist, *Women's Wear Daily*. MACHINES AND PROCESSES: CLOTHING INDUSTRY.

FINCH, JAMES K. . . . D.Sc. Late Dean of Engineering, Columbia University. MATERIALS AND STRUCTURES; MACHINES AND PROCESSES.

FISCHMAN, JEROME . . . Ph.D. Associate professor, Adelphi University. COUNTRIES OF THE WORLD — HISTORY: CENTRAL AMERICA.

FISHER, DOUGLAS A. . . . Former public relations writer, United States Steel Corporation. Materials and Structures: Iron and Steel; MACHINES AND PROCESSES: IRON AND STEEL PRODUCTION.

FITTS, JAMES W. . . . Ph.D. Chairman, Department of Soil Science, North Carolina State College; president, Soil Science Society of America. AGRONOMY.

FOREMAN, WILMER L. . . . Director of public relations, National Cotton Council of America. FOOD AND AGRICULTURE: COTTON.

FOSBURG, PHILIP L. . . . B.S. Regional engineering services manager, Westinghouse Electric Corporation. COMMUNICATIONS AND TRANSPORTATION: ELEVATOR, ESCALATOR, MOVING WALK.

FOX, JOHN C. . . . B.Sc. Secretary, Society of Mining Engineers of AIME. MACHINES AND PROCESSES: ASSAYING, MINING, ORE TREATMENT.

FREEMAN, JAMES M. . . . B.J. Director of Press Relations, American Telephone and Telegraph Company. COMMUNICATIONS AND TRANSPORTATION: TELEPHONE, TELETYPWRITER.

FUSSELL, GEORGE E. . . . Formerly in the British Ministry of Agriculture. Food and Agriculture: ALCOHOLIC BEVERAGES, BARLEY, CLOVER, RYE.

CONTRIBUTORS

GARVIN, CLIFTON C. Jr., . . . M.S. Director and Vice-president, Standard Oil Company. MATERIALS AND STRUCTURES: PETROCHEMICALS; MACHINES AND PROCESSES: PETROLEUM REFINING.

GIFFORD, RICHARD P. . . . A.B. General Manager, Communication Products Department, General Electric Company. COMMUNICATIONS AND TRANSPORTATION: FUTURE COMMUNICATIONS.

GILLESPIE, PHILIP R., Jr. . . . B.S. Manager, Transportation Systems Sales, Westinghouse Electric Corporation. COMMUNICATIONS AND TRANSPORTATION: ELECTRIC TRANSIT.

GILLETT, CHARLES A. . . . M.F. Consultant, American Forest Products Industries, Inc. MACHINES AND PROCESSES: LUMBER INDUSTRY, PAPER.

GIORDANO, FELIX M. . . . Ph.D. Editor, *The Tool and Manufacturing Engineer*. MACHINES AND PROCESSES: ELECTROPLATING, ENGRAVING, ETCHING, METAL COATING, WELDING.

GLEAZER, EDMUND J., Jr. . . . Ed.D. Executive director, American Association of Junior Colleges; chairman, United States Defense Advisory Committee of Education in the Armed Forces. COLLEGE PROFILE: JUNIOR COLLEGES – CHOICE AND CHANCE.

GLICKSMAN, ABRAHAM M. . . . M.A. Teacher of mathematics, Bronx High School of Science and Polytechnic Institute of Brooklyn. TRIGONOMETRY.

GORDON, MATTHEW . . . B.S., Director of information, Communications Satellite Corporation. COMMUNICATIONS AND TRANSPORTATION: COMMUNICATIONS SATELLITE.

GRAHAM, GORDON F. . . . B.A. Secretary, National Association of Wool Manufacturers. FOOD AND AGRICULTURE: WOOL.

GRANDELIS, DORIS D. . . . B.A. Vice-president, Shaner-Grandelis Associates. GEOLOGY: MINEROLOGY, HISTORICAL GEOLOGY, ECONOMIC GEOLOGY.

GREENE, MAXINE . . . Ph.D. Professor of English and Editor of *The Record*, Teachers College, Columbia University. PHILOSOPHIES OF EDUCATION.

GUNNELS, L. O. . . . B.A. Senior Information Specialist, Columbus Laboratories, Battelle Memorial Institute. ENERGY AND POWER SOURCE: NUCLEAR REACTOR.

HAMBURG, MORRIS . . . Ph.D. Professor of Statistics and Operations Research, University of Pennsylvania. SCIENTIFIC DECISION – MAKING TOOLS.

HANFORD, GEORGE H. . . . M.B.A. Executive vice-president, College Entrance Examination Board. COLLEGE PROFILE: SELECTING A COLLEGE.

HANSEN, VIGGO P. . . . Ph.D. Associate professor, San Fernando Valley State College. ARITHMETIC.

HAY, THOMAS R. . . . E.E. Former associate editor, Dictionary of American History and Collier's Encyclopedia. HISTORY: WORLD WAR I, WORLD WAR II, KOREAN WAR.

HEIMSATH, CHARLES H. . . . Ph.D. Professor of South Asian Studies, School of International Service, The American University. COUNTRIES OF THE WORLD – HISTORY: BHUTAN, NEPAL, PAKISTAN, SIKKIM.

HELMERS, RAYMOND A. . . . Editor, *Furniture Design and Manufacturing*. MACHINES AND PROCESSES: FURNITURE MANUFACTURING, WOOD FINISHING, WOODWORKING TOOLS.

HESS, CARL W. . . . Ph.D. Chief, Poultry Research Branch, United States Department of Agriculture. Food and Agriculture.

HESTER, ALBERT S. . . . B.S. Market research analyst, American Cyanamid Company. Food and Agriculture: Fertilizer.

HILL, CHARLES G., Jr. . . . Sc.D. Assistant Professor, University of Wisconsin. PHYSICS: HEAT.

HIRSCH, CHARLES J. . . . E.E. Former engineering consultant, Radio Corporation of America. COMMUNICATIONS AND TRANSPORTATION: TELEVISION.

HLAVATY, JULIUS H. . . . Ph.D. President, National Council of Teachers of Mathematics. ANALYTIC GEOMETRY, CALCULUS.

HUGHES, HUNTER . . . B.M.E. Office manager, The Kuljian Corporation. ENERGY AND POWER SOURCES: MACHINES AND PROCESSES.

HUNTER, LOUIS N. . . . B.A.Sc. Managing director, Air-Conditioning and Refrigeration Institute. MACHINES AND PROCESSES: REFRIGERATION.

INABA, M. G. . . . Ph.D. Chairman, Department of Geography, Hofstra University. COUNTRIES OF THE WORLD – GEOGRAPHY: ASIA.

ISSAWI, CHARLES . . . M.A. Ragnar Nurkse Professor of Economics, Columbia University. COUNTRIES OF THE WORLD – HISTORY: MIDDLE EAST.

JACOBUS, WILLIAM W., Jr. . . . Senior editor, Water Resources Section, *Engineering News-Record*. COMMUNICATIONS AND TRANSPORTATION; MACHINES AND PROCESSES; MATERIALS AND STRUCTURES.

JAHN EDGAR A. . . . B.M.E. Assistant director, Utilization Bureau, American Gas Association. MATERIALS AND STRUCTURES: GAS.

JANOWSKY, OSCAR I. . . . Ph.D. Professor Emeritus of History, City College of the City University of New York; visiting professor of history, Brandeis University. COUNTRIES OF THE WORLD – HISTORY: ISRAEL.

JOHNSON, ARTHUR M. . . . Ph.D. Professor of Business History, Harvard Graduate School of Business Administration. INTRODUCTION TO BUSINESS AND ECONOMICS.

JOHNSTON, S. PAUL . . . B.S. Director, National Air and Space Museum, Smithsonian Institution. COMMUNICATIONS AND TRANSPORTATION: AIRSHIP, AVIATION.

JONES, CHARLES J. . . . M.A. Dean of Manhattan Tutoring School. PHILOSOPHY.

KAREL, MARCUS . . . Ph.D. Associate professor of food engineering, Massachusetts Institute of Technology. FOOD AND AGRICULTURE: FISH AND SEAFOOD, FOOD ADDITIVES, FOOD MANUFACTURING, FOOD PRESERVATION.

KARPEL, BERNARD . . . M.A. Librarian, Museum of Modern Art, New York. FURNITURE: TWENTIETH CENTURY FURNITURE.

KELLEHER, JOSEPH J. . . . B.S. Mechanical engineer; associate editor, *Product Engineering*. COMMUNICATIONS AND TRANSPORTATION; ENERGY AND POWER SOURCES; MACHINES AND PROCESSES; MATERIALS AND STRUCTURES; PHYSICS: MECHANICS.

KEPPEL, FRANCIS . . . L.H.D., Chairman of the Board and President of General Learning Corporation; former United States Commissioner of Education. INTRODUCTION TO EDUCATION.

KILGOUR, FREDERICK G. . . . A.B. Director, The Ohio College Library Center. MACHINES AND PROCESSES: INTRODUCTION.

KISH, GEORGE . . . Ph.D. Professor of Geography, University of Michigan. COUNTRIES OF THE WORLD — GEOGRAPHY: EASTERN EUROPE.

KLINE, HIBBERD V. B., Jr. . . . Ph.D. Professor and Chairman, Department of Geography, University of Pittsburgh. COUNTRIES OF THE WORLD — GEOGRAPHY: AFRICA.

KNIGHT, ARTHUR . . . B.A. Professor, Cinema Department; University of Southern California; contributing editor, *Saturday Review*. COMMUNICATIONS AND TRANSPORTATION: MOTION PICTURE INDUSTRY.

KOCZY, FRIEDRICH F. . . . Ph.D. Professor and Chairman, Physical Science Division, Institute of Marine Science, University of Miami. OCEANOGRAPHY.

KOFF, RICHARD M. . . . M.M.E. Administrative editor, *Playboy*. PHYSICS: SOUND; ADVANCED MATHEMATICS.

KOMINUS, NICHOLAS . . . B.S. Director of Information, United States Cane Sugar Refiners' Association. MACHINES AND PROCESSES: SUGAR PROCESSING; FOOD AND AGRICULTURE: ARTIFICIAL SWEETENERS, SUGAR.

KREN, GEORGE M. . . . Ph.D. Associate Professor of History, Kansas State University. COUNTRIES OF THE WORLD – HISTORY: EUROPE.

LAPORT, EDMUND A. . . . Former director, Communications Engineering, Radio Corporation of America. COMMUNICATIONS AND TRANSPORTATION: RADIO.

LEARY, JOHN S., Jr. . . . Chief Staff Officer, Pharmacology, United States Department of Agriculture. FOOD AND AGRICULTURE: PESTICIDES.

LEITH, JAMES A. . . . Ph.D. Associate Professor of French History, Queen's University, Ontario. COUNTRIES OF THE WORLD — HISTORY: FRANCE.

LEVY, ALAN D. . . . B.S. Senior Associate Programming Writer/Analyst, Systems Development Division, IBM Corporation. HISTORY OF CHEMISTRY.

LEY, WILLY . . . L.H.D. Professor, Long Island University. Machines and Processes: GUIDED MISSILE; ASTRONAUTICS; SPACE BIOLOGY.

LOHMAN, PHILIPP H. . . . Ph.D. Vice-president, Walston & Company, Inc.; adjunct professor, Graduate School of Business Administration, Pace College. FINANCE.

LYNCH, REV. JOSEPH J. . . . Director, Seismic Observatory, Fordham University. MACHINES AND PROCESSES: SEISMOGRAPH.

MACKAY-SMITH, ALEXANDER . . . LL.B. Editor, *The Chronicle of the Horse*. FOOD AND AGRICULTURE: HORSE.

MACKEY, EDWARD F. . . . M.S. Electro-optical equipment project engineer, General Electric Company. PHYSICS: LIGHT.

MacKENZIE, VERNON G. . . . B.S. Assistant Surgeon General, Bureau of Disease Prevention and Environmental Control, Public Health Service. MACHINES AND PROCESSES: AIR POLLUTION.

MAURO, JAMES A. . . . Op.D. Consulting optics engineer, General Electric Company. PHYSICS: LIGHT.

MAYHEW, ZEB . . . B.A. President, Esso Exploration, Inc. MATERIALS AND STRUCTURES: PETROLEUM.

McBEE, RICHARD H. . . . Ph.D. Dean, College of Letter and Science, Montana State University. MICROBIOLOGY.

McCANN, HIRAM . . . B.A. Late editorial consultant, Society of Plastics Engineers. MATERIALS AND STRUCTURES: PLASTICS.

McCARTHY, E. JEROME . . . Ph.D. Professor of Marketing, Michigan State University. MARKETING.

McGANNON, HAROLD E. . . . Technical editor, Research and Technology, United States Steel Corporation, MATERIALS AND STRUCTURES: ALLOYS; MACHINES AND PROCESSES: ELECTRIC FURNACE.

McGREGOR, SAMUEL E. . . . M.S. Chief, Apiculture Research Branch, United States Department of Agriculture. FOOD AND AGRICULTURE: BEEKEEPING OR APICULTURE.

McGUIRE, ROBERT L. . . . B.S. Promotion Coordinator, R.R. Donnelley & Sons Company. COMMUNICATIONS AND TRANSPORTATION: PRINTING; MACHINES AND PROCESSES: BOOKBINDING.

McLELLAN, GEORGE W. . . . B.A. Director, Technical Information Service, Corning Glass Works. MATERIALS AND STRUCTURES: GLASS.

McNEIRNEY, FRANCIS A. . . . B.A. Editor, *American Dyestuff Reporter Magazine*. MACHINES AND PROCESSES: DYEING.

MELAMID, ALEXANDER . . . Ph.D. Professor of Economics, New York University. COUNTRIES OF THE WORLD — GEOGRAPHY: MIDDLE EAST.

MIEL, ALICE . . . Ed.D. Professor of Education, Teachers College, Columbia University; consultant, Curriculum Programs of Tennessee, New Jersey, New York. CURRICULUM.

MILLER, HERBERT F., Jr. . . . M.S. Product Planning Engineer, Deere & Company. MACHINES AND PROCESSES: FARM MACHINERY.

MILLER, STANLEY L. . . . Ph.D. Associate Professor of Chemistry, University of California. ORIGIN OF LIFE.

MILNE, LORUS J. . . . Ph.D. Professor of Zoology, University of New Hampshire. ANIMAL LIFE; PLANT LIFE.

MILNE, MARGERY J. . . . Ph.D. Lecturer in Nature Recreation and Zoology, University of New Hampshire. ANIMAL LIFE; PLANT LIFE.

MITCHELL, JOHN W. . . . Ph.D., D.Sc. Leader, Plant Hormone and Regulator Pioneering Research Laboratory, United States Department of Agriculture. FOOD AND AGRICULTURE: GIBBERELLIC ACID.

MONROE, DANIEL . . . M.D. Physician. PHYSIOLOGY.

MUREN, JAMES F. . . . Ph.D. Medicinal Research Chemist, Charles Pfizer & Company, Inc. CHEMISTRY: ORGANIC CHEMISTRY.

MUSHRUSH, R. S. . . . B.S. Manager, Direct Energy Conversion Operation, General Electric Company. ENERGY AND POWER SOURCES: FUEL CELL.

NICHOLSON, THOMAS D. . . . Ph.D. Assistant Director, The American Museum of Natural History. ASTRONOMY: ASTRONOMICAL INSTRUMENTS.

NOWELL, CHARLES E. . . . Ph.D. Professor of History, University of Illinois. COUNTRIES OF THE WORLD — HISTORY: EUROPE.

O'BRINE, JOHN . . . Senior staff writer, Radio Corporation of America. COMMUNICATIONS AND TRANSPORTATION: PHONOGRAPH.

OLIVER, JOHN E. . . . M.A. Instructor in Geography, Columbia University. WORLD: CITIES; NATURAL FEATURES.

OLIVER, PETER N. . . . A.M. Lecturer, York University. COUNTRIES OF THE WORLD — HISTORY: CANADA.

OSLIN, GEORGE P. . . . B.A. Former public relations director, Western Union. COMMUNICATIONS AND TRANSPORTATION: STOCK TICKER, TELEGRAPH.

PAVELIS, GEORGE A. . . . Ph.D. Chief, Water Resources Branch, United States Department of Agriculture. FOOD AND AGRICULTURE: IRRIGATION.

PETERSON, HAROLD L. . . . M.A. Chief Curator, National Park Service, United States Department of the Interior. MACHINES AND PROCESSES: FIREARMS.

PHILLIPS, C. J. . . . M.A. Professor of Ceramics, Rutgers University. MATERIALS AND STRUCTURES: CERAMICS, POTTERY; MACHINES AND PROCESSES: KILN.

PIZZUTO, ANTHONY E. . . . B.A. Advertising Manager, Water Treatment Products, Calgon Corporation. MACHINES AND PROCESSES: WATER TREATMENT.

POWELL, REED M. . . . Ph.D. Head, Management Sciences and Professor of Business Organization and Research, College of Administration, Ohio State University. PURCHASING.

PRESSLEY, RICHARD B. . . . Senior editor, *Textile World*. MACHINES AND PROCESSES: TUFTING, WEAVING.

PRICE, JOHN . . . B.A. Associate editor, *Chemical Week*. CHEMISTRY: ANALYTICAL CHEMISTRY, PHYSICAL CHEMISTRY, NUCLEAR CHEMISTRY; MACHINES AND PROCESSES: PHARMACEUTICAL INDUSTRY; MATERIALS AND STRUCTURES.

RAISBECK, GORDON . . . Ph.D. Director of Systems Engineering, Arthur D. Little, Inc. RESEARCH AND DEVELOPMENT.

RASMUSSEN, WAYNE D. . . . Ph.D. Chief, Agricultural History Branch, United States Department of Agriculture. MACHINES AND PROCESSES: CANNING AND PRESERVING; FOOD AND AGRICULTURE: INTRODUCTION.

REGENSBURG, ALICE . . . Director, National Shoe Institute. MACHINES AND PROCESSES: SHOE MANUFACTURE.

REID, ROBERT C. . . . M.S., Sc.D. Professor of Chemical Engineering, Massachusetts Institute of Technology. PHYSICS: HEAT.

RICHARDSON, DEUEL . . . B.A. Public Relations Manager, National Fire Protection Association. MACHINES AND PROCESSES: FIRE DETECTION, FIRE PREVENTION.

ROBERTS, KENNETH . . . Advertising Manager, Mosler Safe Company. MACHINES AND PROCESSES: SAFES.

ROBERTSON, VIRGINIA L. . . . A.B. Consultant, *American Heritage Dictionary*. HOME MANAGEMENT.

ROGERS, CHARLES E. . . . Ph.D. Former Head, Department of Journalism, Kansas State University. FOOD AND AGRICULTURE.

ROTBERG, ROBERT I. . . . D.Phil. Associate Professor of History and Political Science, Massachusetts Institute of Technology. COUNTRIES OF THE WORLD — HISTORY: AFRICA.

ROWNEY, DON KARL . . . Ph.D. Assistant Professor of History, Bowling Green State University. COUNTRIES OF THE WORLD — HISTORY: SOVIET UNION.

RUEBENSAAL, CLAYTON F. . . . B.Sc. Director of Corporate Planning, Uniroyal, Inc. MATERIALS AND STRUCTURES: RUBBER.

SCHLEBECKER, JOHN T. . . . Ph.D. Curator in charge, Division of Agriculture and Forest Products, Smithsonian Institution. FOOD AND AGRICULTURE; MATERIALS AND STRUCTURES: FUR AND LEATHER.

SCHLUMPF, LESTER W. . . . M.S. Principal, John Adams High School, New York City. ALGEBRA.

SHAW, DAISY K. . . . M.A. Director, New York City Bureau of Educational and Vocational Guidance; editor, *Guidance News*. CHOOSING A CAREER.

SHAW, FREDERICK . . . Ph.D. Acting Director, Bureau of Educational Program Research and Statistics, Board of Education of the City of New York. CHOOSING A CAREER.

CONTRIBUTORS

SHERIDAN, EUGENE T. . . . B.S. Mineral Specialist, Bureau of Mines, United States Department of the Interior. MATERIALS AND STRUCTURES: COAL, COAL TAR, COKE.

SHILEN, RONALD . . . Ph.D. Independent consultant on education; education advisor, COWLES VOLUME LIBRARY; staff writer, *Columbia Encyclopedia*. EDUCATIONAL STRUCTURE.

SIGFORD, JOHN V. . . . B.E.E. President, Sigford and Associates. MACHINES AND PROCESSES: AUTOMATIC CONTROL SYSTEMS.

SILAGI, SELMA . . . Ph.D. Assistant Professor of Genetics, Cornell University Medical College. GENETICS.

SITOMER, HARRY . . . M.A. Adjunct Associate Professor, C. W. Post College. GEOMETRY.

SMITH, DAVID A. . . . Ph.D. Associate Professor of Geography, State University of New York at Buffalo. COUNTRIES OF THE WORLD — GEOGRAPHY: AUSTRALIA, NEW ZEALAND, WESTERN SAMOA.

SMITH, WILLIAM V. . . . Ph.D. Manager, Physics, IBM Corporation. PHYSICS: MASERS AND LASERS.

SNIVELY, HOWARD D. . . . B.S. Manager, Advance Engineering, Medium AC Motor Department, General Electric Company. ENERGY AND POWER SOURCES: ELECTRIC GENERATOR, ELECTRIC MOTOR.

SPARLING, DOROTHY K. . . . B.S. Merchandise Coordinator, Belgian Linen Association. MATERIALS AND STRUCTURES: LINEN.

SPENCER, MARTIN E. . . . M.A. Associate editor, *Encyclopedia International*. PHYSIOLOGY.

SPORN, PHILIP . . . E.E. Director and Consultant, American Electric Power Company. ENERGY AND POWER SOURCES: INTRODUCTION.

STILES, WILLIAM W. . . . M.D., M.P.H. Professor of Public Health, University of California. PUBLIC HEALTH.

STUART, NEIL W. . . . Ph.D. Research Plant Physiologist, United States Department of Agriculture. FOOD AND AGRICULTURE: HYDROPONICS.

THOMPSON, JOHN M. . . . Ph.D. Professor of History, Indiana University. COUNTRIES OF THE WORLD — HISTORY: SOVIET UNION.

TRATTNER, WALTER I. . . . Ph.D. Associate Professor of History and Social Welfare, University of Wisconsin. HISTORY OF THE UNITED STATES.

TUGMAN, JAMES L. . . . Ph.B. Former publicist, General Electric Company. ENERGY AND POWER SOURCES: LIGHTING.

TURNER, WILLIAM J. . . . Ph.D. Manager, Research Staff Operations, IBM Corporation. PHYSICS: SEMICONDUCTORS.

UDALL, STEWART L. . . . LL.B. Secretary of the Interior, United States Department of the Interior; member, 84th to 86th Congresses. CONSERVATION.

VACZEK, LOUIS C. . . . B.Sc. Senior editor, Science, *Encyclopedia Britannica*. CHEMISTRY: INORGANIC CHEMISTRY.

VALENTINE, MARGOT . . . A.B. Editor, technical papers, The Babcock & Wilcox Company. MACHINES AND PROCESSES: BOILER.

Van den HAAG, ERNEST . . . Ph.D. Professor of Social Philosophy, New York University; lecturer, New School for Social Research. SOCIOLOGY.

VAN RIPER, JOSEPH E. . . . Ph.D. Professor and Chairman, Department of Geography, State University of New York at Binghamton. GEOGRAPHY: MAPS, PHYSICAL GEOGRAPHY.

VATERLAUS, HANS . . . Executive Vice-president, International Silk Association, Inc. MATERIALS AND STRUCTURES: SERICULTURE.

VERGARA, WILLIAM C. . . . B.E.E. Director, Physical Electronics Department, Bendix Communication Division, Bendix Corporation. COMMUNICATIONS AND TRANSPORTATION; ENERGY AND POWER SOURCES; MACHINES AND PROCESSES; MATERIALS AND STRUCTURES.

VINCENT, EMIL P. . . . Product Manager, Audio Systems, Visual Electronics Corporation. COMMUNICATIONS AND TRANSPORTATION: SOUND RECORDING AND REPRODUCTION.

VOLK, OLIVER R. . . . B.S. Staff Chemist, E.I. duPont de Nemours & Company, Inc. MATERIALS AND STRUCTURES: PAINT.

WAHBA, ISAAC J. . . . Ph.D. Research food technologist, General Mills, Inc. FOOD AND AGRICULTURE: GELATIN.

WALLINGTON, G. GRANTLY . . . Free-lance writer and consultant. COMMUNICATIONS AND TRANSPORTATION: PHOTOGRAPHY; MACHINES AND PROCESSES: CAMERA, CAMERA ACCESSORIES.

WATSON, HOWARD C. . . . B.S. Director of Public Relations, Magazine Publishers Association, Inc. COMMUNICATIONS AND TRANSPORTATION: MAGAZINES.

WEBB, KEMPTON E. . . . Ph.D. Associate Professor of Geography, Columbia University. COUNTRIES OF THE WORLD — GEOGRAPHY: SOUTH AMERICA; GEOGRAPHY: CULTURAL GEOGRAPHY.

WESTBROOK, WILMER C. . . . Technical writer, Saco-Lowell Shops. MACHINES AND PROCESSES: SPINNING.

WHATMORE, MARVIN C. . . . L.H.D. President, Cowles Communications, Inc. COMMUNICATIONS AND TRANSPORTATION: XOGRAPH.

WHEELER, DONALD H. . . . Ph.D. Principal scientist, General Mills Central Research Laboratories. FOOD AND AGRICULTURE: FATS AND OILS.

WHITE, JOHN H., Jr. . . . B.A. Curator of Transportation, Smithsonian Institution. COMMUNICATIONS AND TRANSPORTATION: RAILROAD, RAILROAD ENGINEERING, RAILROAD SIGNALING.

WHITE, ROBERT M. . . . Ph.D. Chief, United States Weather Bureau; chief, Meteorological Development Laboratory; research associate, Massachusetts Institute of Technology. METEOROLOGY: THE WEATHER BUREAU.

WILLIAMS, L. PEARCE . . . Ph.D. Professor of the History of Science, Cornell University. HISTORY OF SCIENCE.

WILSON, WALLACE E. . . . B.S. Vice-president in Charge of the Manufacturing Staff, General Motors. MANUFACTURING AND PRODUCTION.

WOLMAN, WILLIAM . . . Ph.D. Economics editor and member of the Board of Editors, *Business Week Magazine*. ECONOMICS.

WOOTON, ROGER O. . . . M.S.E. Nuclear Engineer, Battelle Memorial Institute. ENERGY AND POWER SOURCES: NUCLEAR ENGINEERING, NUCLEAR POWER.

YOUNG, ROBERT W., Jr. . . . M.B.A. Vice-president, Marketing Department, Colgate Palmolive Company. INTERNATIONAL OPERATIONS.

ZELINSKY, WILBUR . . . Ph.D. Professor of Geography, Pennsylvania State University. COUNTRIES OF THE WORLD — GEOGRAPHY: CANADA; UNITED STATES: GEOGRAPHY.

ZOBLER, LEONARD . . . Ph.D. Professor and Chairman, Department of Geology and Geography, Barnard College, Columbia University. EARTH SCIENCE.

ZOLBERG, VERA L. . . . B.A. Assistant Professor of Sociology and Anthropology, St. Xavier College. COUNTRIES OF THE WORLD — HISTORY: AFRICA.

TABLE OF CONTENTS

VOLUME

1

ANIMALS	1
Animal life	3
Animals	13
Bibliography	68

VOLUME

2

ARTS	69
Architecture	73
Painting	82
Sculpture	113
Ceramics	126
Glass	133
Graphic arts	136
Printing	142
Music	154
Dance	180
Bibliography	185

VOLUME

3

BIOGRAPHY	187

VOLUME

4

CAREERS	369
Choosing a career	371
Occupations	373
Bibliography	394

VOLUME

5

CHILD DEVELOPMENT	395
Modern kindergarten methods	397
Educational playthings	406

Mother Goose rhymes	408
Favorite poems	412
Songs and singing games	418
Stories	424
Fables	442
Bibliography	444

VOLUME

6

EARTH SCIENCE	445
Geology	447
Oceanography	461
Meteorology	468
Dictionary of earth sciences	479

VOLUME

7

ECONOMICS AND BUSINESS	521
Introduction	523
Economics	528
Finance	541
Scientific decision-making tools	547
Research and development	550
Purchasing	553
Manufacturing and production	555
Marketing	560
International operations	565
Business and the computer	569
Administrative services	576
Personnel and human relations	578
Economics and business glossary	582

VOLUME

8

EDUCATION	607
Introduction to education	609
History of education	612
Philosophies of education	622
Educational structure	625
Curriculum	638
Educational statistics	644
Bibliography	647

College profile	648
Junior colleges	711

VOLUME

9

FOOD AND AGRICULTURE	717
Food and agriculture	719
Agronomy	749

VOLUME

10

GEOGRAPHY	755
Physical geography	757
Cultural geography	767
Economic geography	771
Conservation	776
Maps	779
Bibliography	780

VOLUME

11

GOVERNMENT AND LAW	781
Theory of government	783
Government of the United States	785
Declaration of Independence	802
Articles of Confederation	804
Constitution of the United States	806
Law	812
Legal procedure	817
Labor legislation	827
Legal holidays in the United States	841
Parliamentary law	842
Government and legal glossary	849
Bibliography	914

VOLUME

12

HEALTH	915
Physiology	917
Human anatomy	929

Diseases	940
Space biology	949
Public health	954

VOLUME

13

HISTORY	961
Study of history	963
Archaeology	967
Ancient civilizations	972
Oriental civilizations	976
The Middle Ages	982
Modern Europe	986
The United Nations	990
History glossary	994
Chronological history of the world	1027
Parallel outlines of American history	1060
Major wars	1071
Chronological tables of rulers	1078
Bibliography	1081

VOLUME

14

HOMEMAKING	1083
Homemaking	1085
Furniture	1093
Interior decoration	1102
Etiquette	1112

VOLUME

15

INDUSTRY AND TECHNOLOGY	1121
Introduction	1123
Energy and power sources	1129
Communications and transportation	1151
Materials and structures	1189
Machines and processes	1228
Bibliography	1290

VOLUME

16

LANGUAGE AND GRAMMAR	1291
Nature of language	1293
Learning to read, write, and spell	1298
Grammar	1303
Punctuation	1311
Figures of speech	1314
Writing and composition	1316
Importance of correct English	1320
Words and phrases often misused	1322
Public speaking and debate	1326
The study of foreign languages	1329
Classification of languages	1333
Dictionary of abbreviations	1338
Bibliography	1340

VOLUME

17

LITERATURE	1341
General aspects of literature	1343
Literature of power	1347
History of literature	1350
Dictionary of literary allusions	1393
Mythology, legend, and folklore	1421
Books, persons, and places of the Bible	1450
Weights, measures, and distances of the Bible	1460
Dictionary of sobriquets and pseudonyms	1461
Great libraries	1463
Parallel outlines of world literature	1463
Grade reading list	1483

VOLUME

18

MATHEMATICS	1499
History of mathematics	1501
Arithmetic	1508
Algebra	1532
Geometry	1556
Trigonometry	1581

Analytic geometry	1590
Calculus	1594
Advanced mathematics	1596
Mathematics glossary	1601
Bibliography	1608

VOLUME

19

PHILOSOPHY AND RELIGION	1609
Philosophy	1611
Religion	1621
Bibliography	1634

VOLUME

20

PLANTS	1635
Plant life	1637
Plants	1648
Bibliography	1700

VOLUME

21

RECREATION	1701
Activities	1703
Associations	1742

VOLUME

22

SCIENCE	1747
History	1749
Astronautics	1763
Astronomy	1780
Chemistry	1798
Life science	1839
Physics	1869

VOLUME

23

SOCIAL SCIENCE	1921
Anthropology	1923
Sociology	1938
Psychology and Psychiatry	1947

VOLUME

24

UNITED STATES	1959
Geography	1961
Census	1970
States	1974
Territories	2000
Cities	2005
Features	2016
History	2021

VOLUME

25

WORLD	2083
Countries of the world	2085
Colonies and dependencies	2306
Natural features	2325
Cities	2344
Bibliography	2377

VOLUME

26

ATLAS	2379

VOLUME

27

INDEX	2445

VOLUME ONE

ANIMALS

Animal life   3
Animals   13
Bibliography   68

COPYRIGHT 1967 BY EMMY HAAS

Animal Life

ANIMAL LIFE

The branch of science that deals with animals is called Zoology. Although it deals with the structures and functions of animals, perhaps its best-known aspect is the orderly classification of animal life, from the simplest to the most complex.

Although it is easy to see that a bear is an animal and that a pine tree is a plant, some of the smaller animals and plants are not obviously members of their respective kingdoms. Most animals can be distinguished by movement; yet there are microscopic water plants that swim as freely as animals do.

All animals large enough to be seen with the naked eye obtain energy by eating plants or other animals. Surprisingly, a few microscopic animals are like green plants in that through the process of photosynthesis they can capture energy from sunlight and can use simple chemical compounds dissolved in water as food.

Thus, it is obvious that methods must be found to distinguish animals from plants and to separate one kind of animal from another. One way to do this is an analysis of food habits. Another way is by studying habitat, or where an animal lives. The most important factors, however, are structure and function—how an animal moves, digests its food, breathes, and reproduces.

FOOD HABITS. The food habits of an animal will give information concerning its structure and function, some of the animals related to it, and a general idea of the environment in which it lives. Sometimes a broad category of food habits will cover a wide variety of creatures.

Herbivores. Any animal that eats only vegetable matter is a *herbivore,* or plant-eater. Herbivores eat grasses, leaves, twigs, succulent plants, and other types of vegetation. The classification encompasses such different creatures as caterpillars and cows.

Carnivores. Animals that eat the flesh of other animals are called *carnivores,* or meat-eaters. Animals as different as lions and ladybird beetles are in this category. When a cat pounces on a mouse, kills it, and eats it, the cat becomes a predatory carnivore, or *predator.*

Animals such as the vulture and hyena are also carnivores, although they usually prefer to feed on dead animals; this makes them *scavengers.* Domestic animals also become scavengers at times, such as when they rummage through refuse.

Omnivores. The most familiar *omnivores,* creatures that eat both animal and vegetable matter, are man himself and the domestic pig. There are, however, less familiar omnivores that are far more numerous.

The *aquatic omnivores* subsist on food so small that they must strain it from the water. Clams and oysters do so by producing a current within the shell, filtering out the food, and expelling the water. Worms that burrow in the ocean floor build U-shaped tubes, then wiggle in order to draw water in at one end; after they have strained the food from the water, they force the water from the other end of the tube.

Even the giant whales, which may be as long as 110 feet, filter their food. They swim, mouth opened, until small crustaceans, plankton, and other types of food are caught between thin plates known as whalebone that hang down in the mouth cavity. Then they close their mouths and swallow the contents.

Symbionts. Animals that form a beneficial partnership with animals of some other kind or a similar partnership with a living plant are *symbionts.* If both partners in a symbiotic arrangement benefit equally, the relationship is *mutualistic.* If one benefits without harming the other, it is a *commensal* relationship; if one gains at the expense of the other, it is *parasitic.*

Many termites illustrate mutualism. They chew and swallow wood but cannot digest the wood fibers until they are predigested by minute animals that inhabit the termites' digestive tract. These minute animals could not obtain wood fibers without the termites; the termites could not utilize wood fibers if the minute animals did not first digest them.

The shark sucker, also called pilot fish or remora, has a commensal relation with sharks. It attaches itself to the shark by means of a suction disk and is carried from place to place to share the shark's food. The shark sucker detaches itself while the shark is feeding, eats, and reattaches itself, to be carried elsewhere. Occasionally a shark sucker will be found attached to a sea turtle or a small boat.

Most parasites are harmless unless they have become numerous. One chicken louse will cause a bird mild discomfort; hundreds will cause a bird to scratch itself constantly, weaken, and grow ill. Such parasites as lice, fleas, ticks, and mosquitoes are called *ectoparasites.*

There are also *endoparasites,* which are internal parasites. They include tapeworms, which inhabit the digestive tract; flukes, which inhabit the lungs; and malaria parasites, which attack the red cells in the blood.

Certain minute insects parasitize plants by producing chemicals that irritate the plants into forming unnatural swellings on the leaf or stem, producing deformed terminal buds. These *galls* provide a place for the insects to live while they suck sap from the plant. Each type has a distinctive shape and inner structure.

HABITAT. The oceans are the home of the greatest variety of animals. Near the sea's surface, sunlight penetrates and enables the small, drifting plants called *phytoplankton* to carry on photosynthesis. Swimming weakly through the phytoplankton and feeding on them are *zooplankton.* Larger animals, called *nekton,* swim strongly and feed on the smaller forms of life. The largest of the nekton are the whales, which may migrate from the Arctic to the Antarctic and back again in a period of a single year.

Deep-sea Dwellers. Many inhabitants of the dark ocean depths are scavengers, dependent on material that sinks from the surface; a few are predators. Even in the muddy ooze that covers the sea floor at the greatest depths, there are animals utilizing the organic materials in the ooze. Many of them eat the bacteria that decompose material that sinks from the surface. Some animals at the deepest levels produce their own light; its function is not certain.

Coastal Dwellers. Much animal life is found near the shores, where the seaweeds are larger and more plentiful because the water is rich in minerals washed from the land. Wave action incorporates air bubbles in the water, thus providing more oxygen for the animal life.

The main danger to coastal dwellers is that of being thrown ashore by the waves. Some, like the sea urchins and sea stars, attach themselves to rocks by means of suction disks. Others burrow, or they live only in areas protected from wave action.

Marsh Dwellers. Animals that live in salt marshes and river estuaries must be able to tolerate great fluctuations of the water's salt content—from very low after a heavy rain to very high after a long drought. This is also true of the plants and animals on which they feed.

Freshwater Dwellers. Fresh water, whether flowing or still, supports fewer forms of life than salt water because it contains fewer dissolved minerals. It is often muddy, however, from undissolved particles. These reduce the amount of light penetrating the water and thus reduce the amount of plant food available to animals.

Fresh waters change level rapidly during floods and droughts, thereby altering the habitat of many creatures. They also freeze over in the winter, thereby greatly reducing the available oxygen and forcing some creatures, such as frogs and turtles, to hibernate.

Land Dwellers. There are many types of habitats to be found on the land, and various types of animals live in each. In the soil there are, among others, earthworms, moles, and many insects. Such animals as bears and deer choose forests or their edges. The "edge" may grade off into willow or alder swamp, or into grassy field or pasture. In either case, there will be plants for herbivores, small herbivores for medium-sized carnivores, and large herbivores, such as deer, for large carnivores, for example, pumas.

Open plains, covered chiefly by grasses, have inhabitants like antelope, prairie dogs, rabbits, prairie chickens, and vast numbers of grasshoppers and ants. Wolves, coyotes, badgers, and snakes formerly were the main carnivores, but the spread of civilization has greatly reduced their numbers. Summer droughts have also served to curb predators, as well as to keep the herbivores from overgrazing the range.

Water is so scarce in deserts that few animals live there; those that do are generally small and have bodies specially adapted to their habitat. Only a few insects can live in ice or in hot springs. One or two kinds of flies have even been found living at the bottoms of shallow petroleum pools in oil fields, feeding on insects that happen to fall in.

Caves also have special animals that exist as external parasites on bats or eat the mold that grows on the bat droppings. Some of these animals prey on other cave creatures.

STRUCTURE AND FUNCTION. Any animal that is to continue to exist must at some time in its life perform the activities common to all animals: movement; food handling, that is, digestion, absorption, and excretion; respiration; coordination, both chemical and nervous; and reproduction, followed by the growth to maturity of new individuals able to carry on the same activities as the parents.

Structure. *Unicellular* (single-celled) marine animals are believed to have been the first form of life. Today there are about 30,000 species of animals that carry on all of their life processes within the one cell.

Most modern animals are *multicellular* (composed of many cells). Among these, the sponges are unique in that any cell can take over the function of any other cell. A sponge may evolve into a different kind of sponge, but it can never become any other kind of organism.

Function. All multicellular animals except sponges have their cells arranged in layers called *tissues;* each tissue is composed of cells with a definite structure and function. In the higher animals, the tissues are connected in *organ systems.*

A man is composed of organ systems, such as the digestive system; this system in turn is composed of such organs as the esophagus, stomach, intestines, and colon. The stomach is composed of a lining layer, muscle layers, and a covering layer; each tissue layer is composed of a definite type of cell. All multicellular animals have the same general types of tissues.

Contractile tissue, composed of tissues that shorten and lengthen, does the work of the body. This type of tissue forms either muscles moving the body or continuous sleeves around cavities, such as the digestive organs or the blood vessels.

Connective and *supporting tissue* is composed of cells that produce nonliving secretions between themselves. The tissue may be a solid mass in cartilage or bone; or tough strands in tendons, which connect bones; or it may be in ligaments, which connect muscle and bone. Connective tissues form the walls of capsules that hold the lubricant in each joint, as well as fine fibers resembling cobwebs that hold organs in place.

Epithelial tissue is composed of thin tilelike, cuboidal, or close-packed columnar cells that are on the surface of the body or are the lining layer of body cavities, ducts, and tubes. Epithelial cells produce such important nonliving substances as shells, hair, antlers, feathers, milk, sweat, and digestive juices. Some epithelial cells have microscopic extensions called *cilia,* which pulsate and propel fluids over the tissues.

Circulating tissue, or *blood,* is a fluid made of blood cells suspended in plasma. It is circulated by the pulsation of the heart muscles and of the blood vessel walls; it may also move incidentally when the body moves.

Endocrine tissue consists of cells that secrete hormones into the blood, to be carried throughout the body in order to coordinate its activities. The pituitary and thyroid glands are endocrine glands, or glands of internal secretion. *Exocrine* glands, or glands of external secretion, such as sweat glands, are epithelial tissue.

Conducting tissue is characteristic of the nervous system. Its individual cells, known as *neurons,* conduct impulses of electrochemical charge and help to coordinate the body by linking *receptors,* such as the light-sensitive cells of the eye, to *effectors,* the muscle cells or glands that respond. Large units of conducting tissue are *ganglia,* which are clusters of neurons, and such centers as the brain and spinal cord, from which many neurons extend in bundles known as *nerves.*

Reproductive tissue consists of egg cells produced in the female's *ovaries* and sperm cells produced in the male's *testes.* An egg is normally fertilized only by union with a sperm cell, becoming a new individual.

CLASSIFICATION

Animals are identified and grouped into a scheme of classes on the basis of their physical structure and the development of the body parts.

BINOMIAL NOMENCLATURE. The system of naming animals by specifying two names was developed in 1758 by Karl von Linné, a Swedish physician and naturalist. He is better known by his Latin signature, Carolus Linnaeus.

Under von Linné's system, a *species* is a group of creatures that can interbreed with complete fertility; several species may be included in a *genus* if they are very similar in structure, but crosses between two species either result in no offspring or in offspring with incomplete fertility. A familiar example is the mule, which is comparatively sterile. It is produced by a mating between a horse (*Equus caballus*) and a donkey (*Equus asinus*).

Von Linné also filled the need for levels of classification between the animal kingdom and the binomial nomenclature of the individual creature. He therefore set within the animal kingdom, in descending order, the *phylum,* the *class,* the *order,* and the *family,* which is composed of the *genus* and the *species.*

For example, the full classification of man is: phylum *Chordata* (vertebrates and near kin), class *Mammalia* (mammals), order *Primates* (mammals with nails and opposable thumbs or big toes or both), family *Hominidae* (man and manlike primates), genus *Homo,* species *sapiens.*

In some cases, additional levels of classification are added to show differences that are considered important. These include *subphyla,* each with one or more classes; *subclasses,* each with one or more orders; *suborders,* each with one or more families; and *subfamilies.*

TRINOMIAL CLASSIFICATION. Geographical divisions of a species are *subspecies,* also called *races.* The distinction among the members of a species is made by using *trinomial nomenclature.* Thus, for example, the white-footed mouse of Vermont is *Peromyscus maniculatus gracilis;* the white-footed mouse found in Canada north of Lake Superior is *Peromyscus maniculatus maniculatus,* the "typical" or "standard" member of the species. These and all other races of the species will interbreed freely if brought together.

EVOLUTION. The idea of evolution received little attention for more than a century after von Linné established the binomial classification. In 1859 Charles Darwin's *On the Origin of Species by Means of Natural Selection* gave evidence and explanation of change in body form over time.

Darwin pointed out that all animals reproduce faster than is necessary merely to maintain a stable population. Competition develops for food and habitat, and the weaker members of the species, unable to compete effectively, are likely to die before being able to reproduce. Only the fittest survive, and they pass on to their offspring any inheritable advantages.

Gradually a species adapts, splits into races, or dies out. Many extinct species, known only through their fossil records, have been classified through their similarities to living animals. All the animals of today are descended from those of the past and are ancestors of all future animals.

PHYLA

Of the more than one million species that have been named, all but 2 percent are classified in 14 phyla. Small additional phyla have been established for the remaining 2 percent, most of them inconspicuous deep-sea dwellers or parasites.

PHYLUM PROTOZOA. There are about 30,000 species of unicellular "first animals," most of them too small to be seen with the naked eye. They are commonly called *protozoans*.

Class Mastigophora. Because they propel themselves through the water by means of one or more whiplike projections from the body, these "whip-carriers" are called *flagellates*. Some, such as *Euglena*, have a single extension, or *flagellum*. Others have two or as many as ten.

Euglena is a large genus, including many species that contain chlorophyll and carry on photosynthesis. Some of these are so numerous in still water that after a period of heat and drought, the water appears bright green. Many colorless flagellates feed on bacteria. Still others are symbionts of termites, living in their digestive tracts and predigesting the wood fibers the insect swallows.

African sleeping sickness is caused by a parasitic flagellate, *Trypanosoma gambiense*, which is transmitted to man through the bite of the tsetse fly. Ordinarily the parasite lives in various wild animals, which seem to be unaffected.

Class Sarcodina. The most famous sarcodinians are the *amoebas*, the *radiolarians*, and the *foraminiferans*. All move about by extending lobes or networks of protoplasm, called *pseudopodia*, or false feet. Amoebas are extraordinary in that they have no definite shape; they flow into one pseudopodium after another as they travel in fresh water or in the digestive tract of an animal.

Radiolarians and foraminiferans, which live on bacteria and microscopic green plants, produce minute skeletons or chambered shells of either silica or lime, from the surface waters of the oceans. When these sarcodinians die, their skeletons sink to the bottom and build up great thicknesses of ooze. Radiolarian ooze becomes an inert powder suitable for making filters and bonding material in dynamite. Foraminiferous ooze gradually becomes a type of limestone.

Class Sporozoa. All sporozoans are parasites of multicellular animals and absorb their food in dissolved form directly from the *host*, the animal to which they attach themselves. They have no means of moving by themselves but must be transferred from one host to another by the activities of *carriers*, such as mosquitoes.

Perhaps the best-known sporozoan is *Plasmodium falciparum*, the cause of the most dangerous type of malaria

in man. It penetrates the red blood cells, reproduces, and causes the cells to break open, releasing more parasites to attack other red cells. *Plasmodia* are spread by mosquitoes of the genus *Anopheles*, which feed on blood. If an *Anopheles* consumes infected blood, the parasites undergo changes and then migrate to its salivary glands. If the mosquito bites a healthy person, the *Plasmodia*, which go with the saliva into the victim's blood stream, start a new infection.

Class Ciliata. Ciliates are named for the many hairlike *cilia* that project from their microscopic bodies, beating in rhythmic waves and driving the cell through the water. The animals are unique in possessing two different kinds of cell nuclei—*macronuclei* and *micronuclei*.

Ciliates live in water and feed on bacteria and small protozoans. Among the best-known are the slipper-shaped *Paramecium*, the bell-shaped *Vorticella*, and the trumpet-shaped *Stentor*. In a strong light, all of these *animalcules* are large enough to be seen without a microscope.

PHYLUM PORIFERA. Phylum *Porifera* contains some 4,500 species of colonial animals that remain attached to the bottom of the sea or to other solid objects, while cells, known as *flagellated collar cells*, draw water and minute particles of food through small holes that lead to a central chamber or system of chambers. After the collar cells have caught the food particles, the water is released through one or more large openings.

Most of these animalcules, commonly known as *sponges*, are marine; a few live in fresh water.

Class Calcarea. *Calcarea* are marine sponges whose cells secrete needle-shaped or branching *spicules* of lime. The spicules usually project from the surface of the colony and mesh, giving it structural support; however, they are regarded as an internal skeleton. Common genera of this class include *Grantia* and *Leucosolenia*, some of whose species grow to an inch in length.

Class Hyalospongiae. *Hyalospongiae* are deep-sea sponges, often of great beauty, that produce a skeleton of silica. *Euplectella* is the Venus' flower basket sponge.

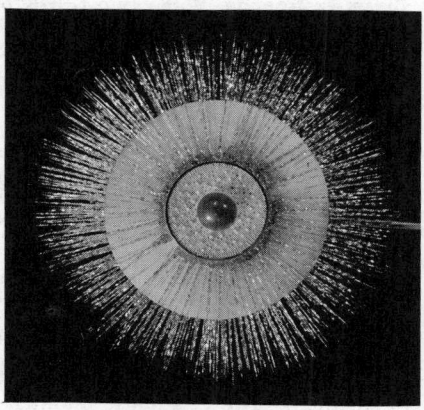

AMERICAN MUSEUM OF NATURAL HISTORY

THE RADIOLARIA has an inner skeleton of silica that houses the spherical nucleus.

Class Demospongiae. *Demospongiae*, the commonest sponges, either lack a skeleton or have one composed of a plastic-like secretion called *spongin*. Most of them live in relatively shallow seas, but one family lives in fresh water. The old-fashioned bath sponge is *Spongia*.

The freshwater sponges belong to the genus *Spongilla*; they are usually bright green or golden-green because they have microscopic plants as mutualistic symbionts.

PHYLUM COELENTERATA. The phylum *Coelenterata* is composed of some 9,600 species of aquatic animals, most of them marine, that have a saclike digestive cavity with a mouth opening at one end. The bodies of the coelenterates are radially or biradially symmetrical, with a ring of tentacles surrounding the mouth. On the tentacles, and often elsewhere, there are unique cells with which smaller animals are stung and paralyzed before they are thrust into the digestive cavity of the coelenterate.

Class Hydrozoa. Hydrozoans are characterized by their method of reproduction. Usually a *polyp* (hydroid) stage reproduces by asexual budding and releases free-swimming *medusae* (jellyfishes), which reproduce sexually; the embryos resulting from this mating settle to the bottom, become attached as polyps, and repeat the cycle.

Colonial hydroids include *Obelia* and *Plumularia*, also known as sea firs, and *Millipora*, or stinging coral. Freshwater hydras have no medusa stage, and some of the larger marine hydrozoan medusae have no known hydroid stage. Freshwater medusae are usually *Craspedacusta*.

Hydrozoans also include such free-floating colonies as the Portuguese man-of-war (*Physalia*), the by-the-wind sailor (*Velella*), and the porpita (*Porpita*).

Class Scyphozoa. *Scyphozoa*, the larger marine medusae, have armlike tentacles extending from the four corners of the pendant, tubular mouth. *Aurelia*, the moon jelly, is commonly found near shore; it is usually about eight inches in diameter. *Cyanea*, a giant medusa of the open ocean, may be seven feet across.

Class Anthozoa. All *anthozoans*, which are marine, lack a medusa stage; many are colonial. The most familiar are the sea anemones, the true corals, the sea fans, and the sea whips. They differ from other coelenterates in that they have additional cells in the usually noncellular *mesoglea*, or jelly, that separates the outer epithelium (epidermis) and the inner epithelium (gastrodermis). This additional cellular material makes the anthozoans' bodies firmer than those of other coelenterates.

The reef-forming corals obtain lime from seawater through their symbiotic relationship with microscopic green plants. Since reef-making corals depend on green plants, they occur only where sunlight penetrates warm seas.

PHYLUM CTENOPHORA. About 80 species of free-swimming marine animals with transparent, biradially symmetrical bodies make up the phylum *Ctenophora*. Comb jellies, as they are also known, swim by rhythmically beating eight lengthwise rows of paddle-like comb plates.

Ctenaphores feed on small planktonic animals that they usually capture by means of tentacles studded with adhesive cells. Many, such as *Mnemiopsis*, are thimble-shaped and glow in the dark when disturbed. *Cestus*, known as Venus' girdle, is ribbon-shaped and can be three feet long and two inches wide.

PHYLUM PLATYHELMINTHES. *Platyhelminthes* phylum, which is commonly known as flatworms, is composed of 15,000 species of flat-bodied animals that are bilaterally symmetrical and have well-organized muscle bands and muscle sheets. Flatworms also have a distinct nervous system consisting of at least one anterior ring of nerve fibers and lengthwise nerve cords.

Class Turbellaria. Turbellarians are free-living flatworms that glide on a ciliated lower epidermis or swim by bodily undulations. Most of these scavengers have a straight, Y-shaped, or multibranched blind digestive cavity. Although they are chiefly marine, *turbellarians* are also found in fresh water and in very moist soil. Freshwater turbellarians are known as *planarians*.

Class Trematoda. Trematodes are cilialess, parasitic flatworms that have one or more circular suckers with which to attach themselves to a host animal. The blind digestive tract is Y-shaped; the mouth, anterior.

Class *Trematoda* includes the flukes, such as the destructive liver fluke (*Fasciola*) found in sheep; intestinal and pulmonary parasites; and the dangerous African blood fluke *Schistosoma*. Some of the flukes, including *Schistosoma*, undergo a series of complex bodily changes that requires a sequence of hosts, one of which is usually a freshwater snail.

Class Cestoda. Cestodes, also known as *tapeworms*, are parasitic flatworms without digestive systems. They attach themselves to the intestine or body cavity of a vertebrate and absorb food directly.

Most tapeworms consist of an anterior individual (*scolex*) with suckers and hooks, and a series of posterior individuals. The latter are produced asexually by the anterior individual but can develop sex organs and produce fertilized eggs and embryos before breaking away from the oldest part of the chain and emerging from the host's body with the wastes.

Taenia solium, the tapeworm that attacks man when he eats improperly cooked, infected pork, can reach a length of 25 feet.

PHYLUM NEMATODA. The phylum *Nematoda* consists of about 10,500 species of cylindrical, unsegmented animals with a straight digestive tube from anterior mouth to posterior anus. Between the outer body wall, which has only lengthwise muscles, and the digestive tract is a bloodlike fluid that churns back and forth as the animal moves.

Some of these *roundworms* are free-living in moist soil and all aquatic situations, including hot springs and glaciers. However, parasitic nematodes are the best known. *Necator* and *Ancylostoma* are hookworms that attack man; *Euterobius* is the pinworm; *Trichinella* is a dangerous parasite acquired by eating infected, improperly cooked pork. *Filaria* causes elephantiasis.

PHYLUM ROTIFERA. Some 1,500 species of unsegmented aquatic animals, none over 1/16 inch long, compose the phylum *Rotifera*. The head region has a mouth with a muscular grinding mill nearby; two whorls of cilia move food particles toward the mouth and aid in swimming. Posterior to the anus, the wheel animalcule usually has a two-toed foot with cement glands that temporarily anchor the rotifer to a solid object.

Most rotifers are free-living freshwater dwellers. Although they are multicellular, rotifers are about the same size as the larger protozoans.

PHYLUM MOLLUSCA. There are about 100,000 living and 40,000 extinct species in the phylum *Mollusca*. All mollusks have a soft, muscular, usually unsegmented body with a dorsal mantle that generally secretes a limy shell. Usually the anterior head has a unique rasping instrument, called the *radula*, inside the mouth.

Class Amphineura. The class *Amphineura* consists of the *chitons*, all of which are marine. Most have a dorsal shell consisting of eight transverse overlapping plates. In dangerous situations, *chitons* curl up to protect the muscular ventral foot, exposing only the hard shell. The class name refers to the two pairs of ventral nerve cords that extend lengthwise from a nerve ring around the chiton's mouth.

Class Scaphopoda. Belonging mainly to the genus *Dentalium* and known as tooth shells, scaphopods are marine mollusks that have a slender, slightly tapered, tubular shell open at both ends. They use their muscular foot, somewhat resembling a horse's foot, to dig themselves into the ocean floor, leaving only the smaller opening of the shell exposed. Through this opening they draw in and expel water and minute particles of food.

Indians on the western coast of North America once used tooth shells as money; natives of New Guinea often wear them as ornaments in pierced ears, noses, and lips.

Class Gastropoda. Some two-thirds of the known species of mollusks are gastropods, known as snails if they have coiled shells, or slugs if they lack shells. All of them creep or cling on a flat, bilaterally symmetrical ventral foot; above the foot is a spiral body covered by the mantle.

Most gastropods are marine herbivores; but some, such as the whelk *Busycon* and the oyster drill *Urosalpinx*, are carnivorous predators.

Physa is a freshwater snail; *Helix pomatea* is the edible garden snail that has been cultivated in Europe for centuries.

Class Pelecypoda. Pelecypods are the *bivalves*, which have limy shells hinged and controlled by strong muscles between them. These aquatic mollusks are chiefly marine; they are unique in that they lack a head region and a radula. The best-known genera include the scallop *Pecten*; the mussel *Mytilus*; the oyster *Ostraea*; the freshwater clam *Unio*; and *Tridacna*, the huge bear's-paw clam of the South Pacific reefs.

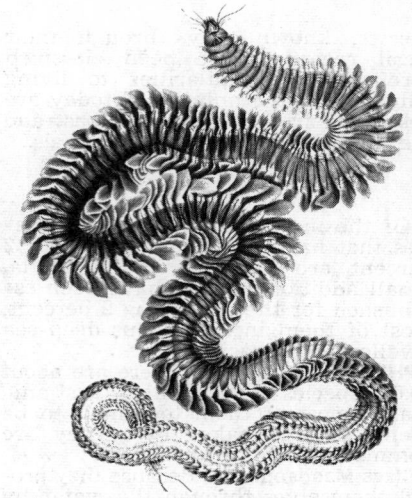

AMERICAN MUSEUM OF NATURAL HISTORY

CLAMWORM, *Neries virens*, shows an evolutionary link between mollusks and annelids.

Class Cephalopoda. Cephalopods are marine mollusks that are "head-footed" in the sense that from eight or ten to as many as ninety tentacles extend from the part of the foot that contains the mouth; the rest of the animal is almost hidden by a high, conical mantle. Among fossil cephalopods a chambered shell was common; today, however, only the pearly *Nautilus* of the East Indies produces such a shell, in whose outermost chamber it lives.

Other living cephalopods have a greatly reduced shell, such as the "cuttlebone" of the cuttlefish *Sepia*, or none at all, as in the eight-tentacled *Octopus*. Most modern cephalopods have a pair of very large, camera-style eyes, much like those of vertebrates, and a highly developed brain.

All cephalopods are predators, most of them grasping their victims with suction disks on the tentacles, then rasping out flesh with the radula. Others are equipped with a special pair of concealed horny jaws, like the beak of a parrot, used for biting their prey.

Class Monoplacophora. Monoplacophorans, discovered alive for the first time in 1957, differ from all other mollusks in that they show signs of segmentation. A low, conical, one-piece shell characterizes and names this class, and is attached to the animal by from eight to twelve pairs of muscles. The sides of the flat foot bear a corresponding number of paired gills and excretory organs; the latter resemble those of the segmented worms.

Living species of *Monoplacophora* are members of the genus *Neopilina*. Regarded as "living fossils" because they show an evolutionary link between mollusks and annelids, they are found in the deep waters of the eastern Pacific. Fossils of this class have been found in stratified rocks of the early Paleozoic Era, covering a period from the Ordovician Age to the Devonian Age.

PHYLUM ANNELIDA. Some 7,000 species of cylindrical or flattened segmented worms are included in the phylum *Annelida.* The body cavity of annelids is transversely divided into definite segments, each of which usually contains a portion of the straight digestive tract that extends from anterior mouth to posterior anus.

The body cavity also contains a ganglion of the ventral nerve cord; branches of the closed blood-vessel system; a pair of excretory organs, called *nephridia;* and a set of bristles used in locomotion.

Class Polychaeta. Most members of the class *Polychaeta* are marine worms with a distinct head and a fleshy paddle on each side of most body segments. The paddles are supported and moved by the body bristles embedded in them, and both paddles and bristles are controlled by muscles within the body wall.

Many of these annelids, such as the clam worm *Nereis,* are free-swimming predators and scavengers. Others build U-shaped burrows in the bottom mud and use their paddles to create a current that brings a constant supply of food and oxygen through the burrow. Polychaetes include the lugworm *Arenicola* and the parchment worm *Chaetopterus.*

Class Oligochaeta. The best-known oligochaetes are the terrestrial earthworms, which burrow and scavenge in the soil for decaying plant material. Earthworms have no distinct head and no lateral paddles; they creep or cling by means of bristles that can be extended from each body segment.

The body usually has a swelling, the *clitellum,* about one-third of the way along the body from the head. The clitellum provides a sheathlike case for the eggs.

The most common earthworms are *Lumbricus, Allolobophora,* and *Eisenia,* which can be distinguished by the location of the paired pores that connect to the sex organs. Other smaller oligochaetes live in fresh water, where they burrow into bottom sediments.

Class Hirudinea. The class *Hirudinea* is made up of predatory bloodsuckers whose bodies are composed of exactly 34 segments that are concealed among transverse wrinkles. All these annelids have a large posterior sucker; many also have an anterior one surrounding the mouth, which has three horny jaws to capture prey or to cut through the skin of a victim in order to reach the blood vessels.

Most leeches live in fresh water, but a few are marine; there is also one that lives in the rainy Malayan jungles. The medicinal leech, *Hirudo medicinalis,* has long been used in the bloodletting thought to be a remedy for many diseases in various parts of the world.

PHYLUM ARTHROPODA. There are more than 770,000 species of arthropods, of which about 700,000 are insects. Typically, each arthropod has a segmented body enclosed by an external skeleton containing the polysaccharide *chitin;* this *exoskeleton* is shed periodically. Many of the body segments have a pair of jointed appendages, from which the phylum takes its name.

Almost 80 percent of the known animals are included in this phylum, which includes marine, freshwater, and terrestrial creatures of many types: free-living, *sessile* (attached by the base), commensal, and parasitic.

Class Onychophora. The onychophores are the "velvet worms" or "walking worms" of humid climates, chiefly the tropics. Their cylindrical bodies, which may be as much as eight inches long, have from 15 to 43 pairs of soft legs, each ending in two claws. The anterior head region is indistinct and bears a pair of simple eyes, a pair of short, flexible tentacles, and a pair of blunt *papillae* through which large salivary glands open near the mouth.

Distinct impressions of onychophorans have been found among the oldest fossils, and those species alive today are referred to as "living fossils" because they show features of both arthropods and annelids.

Like other arthropods, they have the periodically shed exoskeleton of chitin; the reduced body cavity, which is mainly replaced by large *sinuses,* or cavities, through which blood flows in an open circulatory system; the system of fine *tubules* through which air reaches inner organs; and claw-tipped legs.

Like annelids, they have paired excretory organs (nephridia) and simple eyes; they also lack a distinct head (or head plus thorax). The best-known members of *Onychophora* belong to the genus Peripatus.

Class Trilobita. Extinct marine arthropods, of which over 2,000 species are known from Paleozoic times, compose the class *Trilobita.* Each had a flattened, elliptical body marked by lengthwise furrows that separated a central lobe and two lateral lobes (the three lobes gave the class its name).

Transversely, the body was divided into a head with a pair of joined antennae, four pairs of jointed *maxillae* (mouth parts), and a pair of compound eyes; a thorax of 2 to 29 segments, each with a pair of jointed appendages used in swimming and creeping; and an abdomen made up of several segments fused into one plate.

All trilobites, the longest of which were 26 inches long, seem to have been scavengers. Their numbers decreased when fishes with jaws, their natural enemies, proliferated.

Class Crustacea. Although generally marine, crustaceans can also be found in fresh water and on land. A few are parasites that attach themselves to fishes. All crustaceans have a head region with two pairs of *antennae,* a pair of *mandibles* (jaws), and at least two other pairs of maxillae. Both the thorax and the abdomen may have paired appendages for swimming and walking.

Familiar genera of these creatures include *Artemia,* the brine shrimp of alkaline lakes; *Balanus,* the acorn barnacle of seacoasts; *Lepas,* the goose barnacle; *Oniscus* and *Porcellio,* terrestrial pillbugs; *Homarus* the Atlantic lobster; and *Callinectes,* the blue crab.

Class Diplopoda. The diplopods are the *millipedes,* or "thousand-legged worms." Each has a pair of antennae, a pair of jaws, and a pair of maxillae on the head; four segments and three pairs of legs on the thorax; and from nine to more than a hundred segments on the trunk. Each of these segments is really two that have been fused in the course of evolution; thus, as the class name indicates, each segment has two pairs of legs.

Most diplopods are harmless terrestrial scavengers that inhabit moist places.

Class Chilopoda. Terrestrial predators commonly known as *centipedes,* chilopods have flattened bodies and only one pair of legs per segment—there may be from 15 to 181 pairs of legs. The head has a pair of jointed antennae; a pair of jaws; and two pairs of maxillae, the second pair partially joined to form a lower lip that gives the class its name.

The first pair of legs are hooklike and have poison glands that open at the sharp tip of each; these poisonous hooks inflict painful or dangerous wounds.

Class Insecta. More than 700,000 species of insects, the only flying animals without backbones, are known today; and more are discovered every year. Insects are primarily terrestrial arthropods whose body is distinctly divided into head, thorax, and abdomen.

The head has a pair of jointed antennae, a pair of mandibles, a pair of jointed maxillae, and a *labium* (lower lip) that evolved from another pair of maxillae; the maxillae may be modified for chewing, sucking, or lapping. Typically, each of the three thorax segments has a pair of legs, in adult insects the second and third segments may also have a pair of wings apiece.

Insects may be classified by structure and by development. Structurally, the details of the maxillae and the wings are considered. The ancient insects are wingless, and change little in body form from hatching to maturity. The modern insects undergo indirect metamorphosis, a spectacular transformation from a specialized *larva* that spends most of its time eating and growing, to a quiet, nonfeeding *pupa* that encases the larval body while it is becoming an adult, to an adult that reproduces.

Intermediate insects experience direct metamorphosis, an incomplete transformation that lacks a pupal stage; the animal progresses from immature stage to mature stage. The wings of intermediate insects develop as pads on the back; the wings of modern insects develop internally, in the pupal stage.

Of the 16 orders described here, the first two are ancient, the next nine are intermediate, and the last five are modern.

Order *Collembola* is made up of the *springtails,* minute insects that are rarely more than ⅛ inch long and have chewing mandibles. They leap by flipping a special ventral springing organ on the fourth abdominal segment from under a hook on the third segment. The order includes

GEORGE A. SMITH

THE MONARCH BUTTERFLY is one of roughly 122,000 species of *Lepidoptera*. The butterfly shown is just emerging from its chrysalis.

some 2,000 species that live on land, in soil, and over water.

Order *Thysanura* is composed of about 700 species of *bristletails*, including the silverfish *Lepisma*. They grow to 1¼ inches long, and their bodies are covered with overlapping scales. Thysanurans have chewing mandibles and long, threadlike antennae. There is also a pair of antenna-like structures on the posterior end, and the last body segment of thysanurans may extend as a third antenna-like "tail."

Order *Dermaptera* includes the *earwigs*, which may grow to two inches in length and have chewing mandibles and, at the end of the abdomen, a pair of strong forceps. Some are wingless; others have a short pair of leathery wings that, when the animal is at rest, cover a large pair of membranous, semicircular hind wings. Order *Dermaptera* includes about 1,100 species, some of them harmful to crops.

Order *Orthoptera* includes some 23,000 species of insects, including cockroaches, stick insects, short-horned grasshoppers (locusts), long-horned grasshoppers (including katydids), and crickets. Some of these insects reach a length of 12 inches.

Most of them have as adults a pair of narrow forewings that cover the hind wings when the animal is at rest. The hind wings are folded fanwise. Certain species of the order *Orthoptera* cause considerable damage to crops.

Order *Isoptera* is made up of the social insects called *termites* or "white ants." All of the some 1,800 species of this class have chewing mandibles and may reach a length of two inches. Only adult sexual individuals have wings, of which there are two narrow membranous pairs. The wings lie flat on the back when the termite is at rest and are detached after the nuptial flight. The thorax and abdomen are joined broadly; there is no "waist" like that of a true ant.

Termites that eat wood depend upon intestinal flagellates to predigest the fibers. Some tropical termites cultivate fungus plants on chewed vegetation, then eat the fungi.

Order *Odonata* contains about 6,000 species of damselflies and dragonflies, which in their immature stages are freshwater predators. Members of the order have chewing mandibles and may reach a length of six inches, with a wingspread up to one foot—fossil dragonflies had wingspreads of as much as 28 inches. Adults have two pairs of membranous wings crisscrossed with many veins; a head with huge compound eyes; and a long, slender abdomen.

Order *Ephemeroptera* consists of the mayflies, of which there are approximately 1,500 species. They have chewing mandibles in the immature aquatic stages, but these become only vestigial at maturity. Mayflies reach a length of as much as two inches but may look longer because the abdominal tip has two or three filamentous "tails."

Members of the order *Ephemeroptera* are unique in that the flying creature that emerges from the immature aquatic stage is not yet an adult; it must shed its skin once more —even over the wings. The wings consist of a large forepair and a small hind pair, both pairs membranous and crisscrossed with veins. Mayflies rarely survive more than a day as an adult, but may require a year or more to reach this stage.

Order *Mallophaga* is composed of the biting lice, which grow to ¼ inch long and have chewing mandibles. Their bodies are flat and wingless, and they have either no eyes or small eyes. There are about 2,700 species of biting lice, all of them external parasites on birds and mammals. The genus *Menopon* includes the hen lice.

Order *Anoplura* includes some 200 species of sucking lice, whose flat, wingless bodies may be up to ¼ inch long. These lice have sucking mouthparts and small eyes—or no eyes. *Pediculus capitis* is the head louse, or "cootie," which transmits typhus fever and other diseases; *Haematopinus suis* is the hog louse.

Order *Heteroptera* is the order of the true bugs, which may grow to a length of four inches and have piercing, sucking mouthparts that arise far forward on the head. Some *Heteroptera* are wingless as adults; those

with wings have a forepair that is thick and horny at the base but membranous at the tips, where they overlap when held flat and slightly crossed at rest. The hind wings are membranous and fold slightly below the forewings.

Among the order's approximately 45,000 species are such water striders as *Gerris*, the stinkbugs *Pentatoma*, the milkweed bug *Lygaeus*, and wingless bedbug *Cimex*.

Order *Homoptera* contains the cicadas and their kin, about 25,000 species in all. These insects, many of them injurious to plants, grow to five inches long and have piercing, sucking mouthparts that rise far back on the head. Winged adults have forewings larger than the hind wings; both sets are membranous and at rest are held in tent fashion over the back. Some of the better-known *Homoptera* are the cicadas, aphids (plant lice), scale insects, leaf hoppers, and the spittle bugs.

Order *Lepidoptera* consists of the moths and butterflies, insects that may have a length of four inches and a wingspread of almost one foot. A caterpillar usually has biting mandibles, three pairs of thoracic legs, up to four pairs of soft abdominal prolegs, and labral openings of silk glands, used in spinning the cocoon. Adults have maxillae joined to form a coiled sucking tube, or *proboscis*. They also usually have two pairs of broad, membranous wings covered by overlapping scales.

There are roughly 122,000 species of *Lepidoptera*, including many that, as caterpillars, eat man's crops or possessions.

Order *Diptera* is composed of the two-winged, or "true," flies. These insects may attain a length of two inches and have a wingspread of three inches. The larval stages are usually legless maggots, some of which have chewing mouthparts. The adults have piercing and sucking, or lapping, mouthparts and one pair of membranous wings; the hind wings are represented by a pair of short, knobbed balancers.

Some of the roughly 90,000 species in the order are the mosquitoes *Anopheles*, *Aedes*, and *Culex*; the

FULLY EMERGED from its pupa case, the butterfly is in the final stage of its metamorphosis from egg to larva and finally to butterfly.

black flies *Simulium;* the beneficial tachinid flies that parasitize caterpillars; the fruit fly *Drosophila;* the housefly *Musca domestica;* and the wingless sheep tick or sheep ked *Melophagus.*

Order *Coleoptera* is made up of the beetles and weevils, which have biting mandibles in both larval and adult stages and may grow to six inches in length. The larvae are usually wormlike creatures with well-developed legs. Adults have a pair of thick, veinless forewings that, at rest, meet along the midline above the membranous hind wings, whose tips are folded when the wings are not in use.

Coleoptera is the largest order of insects, containing some 260,000 species. Many, such as the lady bug beetle *Coccinella,* are beneficial to man; others, such as the boll weevil *Anthonomus grandis,* are destructive.

Order *Siphonaptera* includes the fleas, which in the adult stage are external parasites on birds and mammals. The minute, legless larvae are scavengers with biting mandibles. The adults, about ¼ inch long, have laterally compressed, wingless bodies; their mouthparts are adapted for piercing and sucking.

Of the approximtely 300 species, two of the best known are *Pulex irritans,* which attack rats and humans, and *Xenopsylla cheopis,* the Indian rat flea, which transmits bubonic plague.

Order *Hymenoptera* takes in the ants, bees, wasps, and their kin, some 103,000 species. Some hymenopterans grow to three inches in length and may have a five-inch wingspread. Their larvae may be either legless maggots or caterpillar-like creatures; the latter are distinguished from caterpillars of the order *Lepidoptera* by having more than four pairs of fleshy prolegs. Some larvae are parasitic, usually attaching themselves to other insects.

Adults usually are solitary, but some species build colonies and organize societies that show distinct castes. Those adults that can fly have membranous forewings longer than the hind wings; the latter are hooked together in flight. The female's ovi-

positor is commonly modified as a saw, drill, or stinger.

Among the better-known species of the order are sawflies, with herbivorous, caterpillar-like larvae; beneficial *ichneumon* flies and *chalcids,* which parasitize harmful insects; gall wasps, ants, such as *Formica;* wasps, such as *Vespa* and *Polistes;* bees, such as the bumblebee *Bombus* and domesticated honeybee *Apis mellifera.*

Class Merostomata. Only four "living fossil" species of horseshoe crabs remain of the ancient "divided mouth" class, Merostomata. All of them dwell in shallow, offshore seas, where they scavenge on seaweeds, sea worms, and young mollusks.

Merostomates are armored creatures with an unsegmented *cephalothorax* joined broadly to an abdomen that ends in a bayonet-like tail spine; they lack antennae and true jaws. Food is chewed between the spiny bases of the four pairs of walking legs that flank the elongated mouth slit. Also near the mouth are two pairs of appendages, the usually pincer-like *chelicerae* and the *pedipalpi.*

Perhaps the best-known species is *Limulus,* of the American eastern coast, which comes to shore each spring to lay its eggs in beaches from Maine to Yucatan.

During the Paleozoic Era, the merostomates included sea scorpions, up to six feet long, whose clearly segmented, flexible, tapering abdomens suggest that they may have been the ancestors of land scorpions. Horseshoe crabs, by contrast, have an abdomen fused into a single unit; however, like the sea scorpions, they have a ventral series of five or six pairs of plates that are used in swimming and as protection for the gills.

Class Arachnida. The class *Arachnida* includes some 30,000 species of spiders and their kin. Each species has a cephalothorax and an abdomen, a pair of chelicerae, a pair of pedipalpi, and four pairs of legs, but lacks antennae, jaws, and paired appendages on the abdomen.

The class arachnida includes the scorpion *Scorpio,* the house spider *Theridion,* the orb-web spider *Argiope,* the harvestman *Phalangium,* the tick *Dermacentor,* and the spider

mite *Tetranychus.* Scorpions, spiders, and many of the mites are predators; ticks and the rest of the mites are external parasites of animals or plants and may transmit diseases from infected hosts to healthy ones.

PHYLUM BRACHIOPODA. Brachiopods, known as lamp shells because of a resemblance between one type of shell and ancient oil lamps, are marine bivalves that secrete the dorsal half and the ventral half of the shell from the mantle. There are 260 living species and over 5,000 fossil species.

Most adult brachiopods remain permanently attached to their surroundings by means of a short posterior stalk that emerges through an opening in the ventral valve of the shell, near the hinge. The unsegmented body has two *lophophores,* spiral or V-shaped arms, from which the phylum takes its name; the lophophores bear ciliated tentacles that create currents to bring oxygen and microscopic food particles into the shell.

One class of brachiopods has a largely chitinous shell and no hinge teeth; these animals include *Lingula* and *Crania,* genera known longer than any others in the animal kingdom. A second class has a limy shell and teeth that keep the halves of the shell in alignment. These include *Terebratulina* and *Rafinesquina.*

PHYLUM ECHINODERMATA. There are roughly 5,700 species of echinoderms (or "spiny skins"), which begin life as bilaterally symmetrical embryos, then take on a false radial symmetry, and still later may become conspicuously biradial or even bisymmetrical; the symmetry usually has five parts.

If the creature has a skeleton, it is internal, composed of limy spicules or plates. Part of the large body cavity is separated to form a unique water-vascular system with special tube-like feet used in feeding and locomotion.

Echinoderms include the sea lilies and feather stars (class *Crinoidea*); sea cucumbers (class *Holothuroidea*); sea urchins, heart urchins, and sand dollars (class *Echinoidea*); sea stars, or starfishes (class *Asteroidea*); and serpent stars, or brittle stars (class *Ophiuroidea*).

PHYLUM CHAETOGNATHA. Roughly 50 species of arrow worms, all of them very slender, cylindrical, and unsegmented, compose the phylum *Chaetognatha.*

The lateral cranial lobes of these three-inch marine predators have chitinous bristles with which prey is captured and pushed into the mouth (hence the phylum name of "bristle jaws"). The digestive tract is straight, and the anus is just anterior to the tail. A pair of lateral fins, supported by fine chitinous rods, give the creature better stability and allow it to dart after minute crustaceans.

The arrow worms' remarkable transparency often causes them to be overlooked. They are plentiful, however, and provide an important source of food for whalebone whales.

PHYLUM CHORDATA. Chordates, of which there are some 45,000 species, are distinguished from all other animals by the development of a flexible supporting rod, called the *notochord.* This lies immediately below the hollow dorsal nerve cord and gives the phylum its name.

At some stage in development, gill slits connect the pharyngeal area to the outside of the body. Usually the body is bilaterally symmetrical and has a complete digestive tract, a closed circulatory system, and a tail posterior to the anus. Four subphyla are recognized.

Subphylum *Tunicata* is composed of about 1,600 marine species that have a notochord and a nerve cord only during the larval stage; the adult is a degenerate form surrounded by a secreted tunic, usually of cellulose.

The most familiar members of this subphylum are the sea squirts (class *Ascidiacea*). They are small and tadpole-shaped as larvae. The adult is permanently attached to the sea floor, where it draws in water, filters out microscopic food and absorbs oxygen, and expels the water.

Subphylum *Cephalochordata* includes about thirty marine species that retain the notochord and the nerve cord; both extend the full length of the body. Cephalochordates are the lancelets, or *amphioxi,* of the class *Leptocardii* and mainly of the genus *Brachiostoma.* They are slender, pointed at each end, and laterally compressed; they swim freely or make shallow burrows in the sandy sea floor near shore.

Subphylum *Agnatha* originally contained the earliest vertebrates, which are known through the fossilized covering of armor-like, bony scales over the head and much of the body; these members of the class *Ostracodermi* apparently were freshwater bottom dwellers during Ordovician, Silurian, and Devonian times.

Class Cyclostomata. Modern agnathans have a cartilaginous troughlike skull and a series of cartilaginous bars protecting the nerve cord. These smooth-skinned, cylindrical, unarmored creatures have horny teeth in their cup-shaped mouths, but no paired fins. They propel themselves by sinuous swimming movements of the whole body.

The hagfishes or slime eels, such as *Myxine,* are direct-developing marine scavengers that eat dead and dying fishes; the lampreys, such as *Petromyzon,* spend at least their larval stage in fresh water and then may move out to sea, where they attack living fishes. *Petromyzon marinus* spread through the Great Lakes in recent years and almost destroyed commercial fishing until recent efforts.

Subphylum *Gnathostomata* consists of chordates with an upper and lower jaw and blocks of cartilage or bone that serve as *vertebrae* and largely or completely replace the notochord in stiffening and supporting the body.

Usually these creatures have paired appendages—a pectoral pair of fins, legs, wings, or arms, and a pelvic pair of fins or legs. If the appendages are fins, the chordate is a fish; if they are limbs, it is a *tetrapod.* Six of the seven classes in the subphylum are represented by living species, the familiar vertebrates.

Class Placodermi. Placoderms (skin of plates) are extinct, jawed fishes that usually had an armor of bony plates or bony scales and two or more pairs of fins. These ancient fish are known from both freshwater and marine fossils of Upper Silurian to Devonian times; the best-known are *Dinichthys* and *Acanthodes.*

Class Chondrichthys. About 275 living species, all primarily marine, compose this class of cartilaginous fishes that includes the sharks, skates, rays, and chimeras. All of them have cartilaginous rather than bony skeletons (hence the class name); in some, the cartilage is calcified. The scales are minute and usually have an enamel covering over a dentine base, similar to that of teeth.

Class Osteichthys. A skeleton at least partly of true bone rather than of cartilage characterizes the approximately 25,000 marine or freshwater bony fishes in this class. Their bony scales either fit together in a diamond pattern or overlap like shingles.

Included in the class are the sturgeon *Acipenser,* whose eggs are caviar; the herring *Clupea;* the eel *Anguilla;* the sea horse *Hippocampus;* the cod *Gadus;* the freshwater perch *Perca;* the lungfish *Protopterus;* and the coelacanth *Latimeria,* sole known survivor of the lobe-fin fishes that are close to the ancestral line from which the tetrapods sprang.

Class Amphibia. Most of the nearly 2,000 species of amphibians transform from a gill-breathing immature stage (such as a tadpole) in fresh water to a lung-breathing, terrestrial adult stage. Most adults have forelegs and hind legs, the latter linked by way of a pelvic girdle to a specialized sacral vertebra. Unlike fishes, which have a two-chambered heart, adult amphibians have a three-chambered heart.

Common genera include the mud puppy *Necturus,* the salamander *Ambystoma,* the frog *Rana,* and the toad *Bufo.*

Class Reptilia. Some 5,000 living species of tetrapod chordates that have a dry skin, usually covered with overlapping scales, belong to the class *Reptilia* (creepers). Their skeletons are completely bony, and the pelvic girdle, if present, is linked to two sacral vertebrae.

These turtles, snakes, lizards, and crocodilians all obliterate the gill slits while developing within the egg; at no stage do they possess gills. Special membranes extend from the embryo to the eggshell and enable the embryo to breathe while surrounded by a watery egg "white" provided by the mother. Presumably the dinosaurs and all other extinct reptiles, including some that flew, were similar in general structure and development to modern reptiles.

Class Aves. More than 8,600 living species of birds are known, all of them warm-blooded and covered with feathers. They have a four-chambered heart and a system of blood vessels that carries all blood from the heart to the lungs for aeration before pumping it through the body again.

Other characteristics of birds are a mouth with a specialized beak; one pair of wings; and one pair of legs, which are linked to several vertebrae by way of a light but strong pelvic girdle. All birds lay eggs. Most can fly, but some—such as the ostrich *Struthio,* the kiwi *Apteryx,* and the penguin *Spheniscus*—are flightless and apparently had completely flightless ancestors.

Some well-known genera of class *Aves* are the domestic duck *Anas,* the fowl *Gallus,* the pigeon *Columba,* the crow *Corvus,* and the sparrow *Passer.*

Class Mammalia. There are more than 4,500 species of living mammals, all of them warm-blooded and at least partly covered with hair. The four-chambered heart pumps the blood through the lungs before it is circulated through the body. The pelvic girdle is fused to five vertebrae. Mothers secrete milk from special *mammary glands,* from which the newborn young gain nourishment. Twelve of the eighteen orders are of special interest.

Order *Monotremata* is composed of the egg-laying mammals. Some five genera belong to this order, all being found in Tasmania, New Guinea, and Australia; they include the duckbill or platypus *Ornithorhynchus* and the spiny anteater *Tachyglossus.* Only the young have teeth; adults have a horny beak. The large, yolky eggs are unique among mammals, as is the practice of incubating them.

The order is named to draw attention to the single body opening (cloaca) that serves the digestive, urinary, and reproductive tracts.

Order *Marsupialia* is made up of the pouched mammals, of which all but the American opossums inhabit Australasia. Unlike class *Monotremata,* the adult marsupials have teeth. The females have a pouch on the undersurface of the abdomen; the extremely immature newborn young creep in, attach themselves to a nipple, and remain attached until fully formed.

In all other orders of mammals (except *Monotremata*), the young are linked to the mother by a special membrane *(placenta)* formed by the embryo and used to transfer food and oxygen from the mother to the embryo, and wastes, including carbon dioxide, from the embryo to the mother. Such mammals are placental mammals.

Order *Insectivora* contains the insect-eating moles and shrews and their kin. These small mammals have pointed snouts and sharp teeth that are less specialized than those of other orders. The upper jaw has six to eight incisors, one pair of canine teeth, and three to four pairs of grinding teeth (molars and premolars); the lower jaw has no canines and often has fewer incisors.

Widely known genera are the mole *Talpa*, the shrews *Sorex* and *Blarina*, and the European hedgehog *Erinaceus*.

Order *Chiroptera* is composed of the bats, the only mammals that are capable of flapping flight. They fly by using their modified forelimbs, whose second to fifth toes are greatly elongated and support a thin, leathery membrane that extends to the hind legs, and usually to the short tail as well. The upper jaw often has one pair of incisors; the lower jaw, three.

Order *Primates* includes the monkeys and apes and their kin. Usually there are fewer incisors on both upper and lower jaws. Nails, rather than claws, are found on at least some fingers and toes. Characteristically, either the thumbs or great toes—or both—are opposable, and the shoulder girdle is linked to the breastbone by a collarbone on each side.

Modern man, *Homo sapiens*, and species of fossil man belong to this order, along with the chimpanzee *Pan*, the gorilla *Gorilla*, the orangutan *Pongo*, the rhesus monkey *Macacus*, the capuchin monkey *Cebus*, and the lemur *Lemur*.

Order *Edentata* includes the anteaters, sloths, and armadillos, about 30 different kinds of which live in tropical and warm-temperate America. The name means "without teeth," but actually only the anteaters are toothless. No kind has incisor or canine teeth, and there is no enamel on the premolar and molar teeth with which sloths and armadillos chew their plant food.

Order *Pholidota* consists of seven different kinds of pangolins, or scaly anteaters, of tropical Africa and Southeast Asia. These mammals are also toothless. They capture insects, particularly ants and termites, with a long, slender, sticky tongue and swallow the prey whole.

Order *Lagomorpha* includes rabbits and their kin. These animals may be distinguished by their teeth: two pairs of incisors in the upper jaw, one pair behind the other; one pair of incisors in the lower jaw; no canine teeth. The lower jaw can move from side to side but not from front to back; the jaws are not opposable. The tail is short. Some common genera are the pika or coney *Ochotona*, the hare *Lepus*, and the cottontail rabbit *Sylvilagus*.

Order *Rodentia* is made up of gnawing mammals that have only two incisors in the upper jaw and two in the lower; they have no canine teeth. Rodents have opposable jaws, and their lower jaws move forward and backward as well as from side to side.

Common rodents include the squirrel *Sciurus*, the marcot *Marmoto*, the rat *Rattus*, the mouse *Mus*, the beaver *Castor*, the porcupines *Hystrix* and *Erethizon*, and the South American capybara *Hydrochaerus* (the largest rodent, which grows to four feet in length).

Order *Carnivora* comprises land mammals with well-developed canine teeth used in tearing the flesh of their animal food. They have six small incisors above and below. Included in the order are the dog, wolf, and coyote *Canis*, the bear *Ursus*, the cat *Felis*, and weasel *Mustela*.

Order *Pinnipedia* consists of swimming mammals similar in many ways to carnivores, such as the seal *Phoca*, walrus *Odobenus*, and sea lion *Zalophus*.

Order *Tubulidentata* contains only the aardvark *Orycteropus* of Africa south of the Sahara. It resembles a large-size pig with teeth of a strange, tabular form found only in the sides of the mouth.

Order *Proboscidae* is now represented by only one type of animal, the elephant. These massive, thick-skinned mammals have a nose and upper lip that extend into a trunk tipped with nostrils.

The two upper incisors are elongated as tusks, and only one or two molars at a time are on each side of the upper and lower jaws; there are no canines or premolars. The teeth are large and have many folded rows of enamel.

An elastic pad behind the toes bears the animal's weight; the toes have nail-like hoofs on three to five digits, depending on the species.

Order *Artiodactyla* contains the even-toed hoofed mammals. These animals have two or four toes; on each toe is a horny hoof that reaches the ground. *Sus*, the boar or pig, and *Hippopotamus* have four toes on each foot. They also have a simple stomach.

Other artiodactyls have two toes on each foot and a four-part stomach; they chew regurgitated food in the form of a cud. Included in this second group are the camel, the caribou, the deer, the cow, the giraffe, the antelope , the sheep, the goat, and the musk ox.

Order *Hyracoidea* contains nine kinds of African and Near Eastern animals known as conies, dassies, or hyraxes, whose toes bear flattened nails resembling hoofs—four on the front feet and three on the rear. The

BIRTH OF AN OSTRICH. The egg, which is the largest laid by any living bird, is deposited in the sand and incubated by the heat of the sun. The ostrich, a flightless bird, lives in many parts of Africa.

EARL THEISEN

soles of the feet have special suction cups that help the animals climb on rocks and trees.

Order *Sirenia* is composed of four kinds of sea cows, large animals of the seacoasts that are said to have confused homesick sailors into believing in mermaids.

Order *Perissodactyla* is composed of the odd-toed hoofed animals. They bear their weight on either the middle toe or the three middle toes; there is a hoof on each functional toe. There are no canine teeth, but there are incisors and molars in both jaws. The stomach is simple, so no cud is formed. The best-known genera include the horse and zebra *Equus*, the tapir *Tapirus*, and the rhinoceros *Rhinoceros*.

Order *Cetacea* contains the whales and their kin. Toothed whales, such as the sperm whale *Physeter*, the killer whale *Orcinus*, and the dolphin *Delphinus*, have identical enamel-less teeth and are carnivorous, preying on fishes, squids, and other marine animals.

Toothless (whalebone) whales, such as the great blue whale *Balaenoptera* (which, at 110 feet and 150 tons, is the largest animal of all time) and the right whale *Balaena*, strain food from the sea between parallel fringed plates of whalebone that hang from the inside of the upper jaw.

Both types of whale have a body highly adapted for swimming and diving: the forelimbs are reduced to flippers, the hind limbs have disappeared (although a pelvic girdle remains), and the tail is flattened into a pair of transverse fleshy flukes.

ZOOLOGY IN PERSPECTIVE

The scientific study of animals, with information carefully arranged, began with the works (336–323 BC) of Aristotle—the "Father of Zoology"—a Greek physician and naturalist who studied under Plato and served as tutor to the prince who later became Alexander the Great. Through his works, Aristotle showed himself eager for knowledge for its own sake and ready to relate his knowledge of non-human creatures to man.

For some 1,800 years after Aristotle, few people realized that the ideas and information in his works were incomplete and erroneous, and that new discoveries could be important. Among the first to correct Aristotle's mistakes was Andreas Vesalius (1514–1564), a Belgian physician, whose illustrated work on human anatomy appeared in 1543 and earned him the reputation of the "Father of Modern Anatomy." A Swiss contemporary of Vesalius, the naturalist Konrad von Gesner (1516–1565), compiled information on the known kinds of animals in a five-volume encyclopedia he published between 1551 and 1587.

In the 1600s, 1700s, and 1800s, discoveries came so quickly that it was hard for zoologists to fit them all together, and some facts remained unappreciated for many years. Even details visible through the microscope did not lead to immediate understanding.

Milestones in this period included William Harvey's (1578–1657) proof that the human heart circulates blood (1628), Robert Hooke's (1635–1703) discovery and naming of cork cells (1665), Jean Baptiste de Lamarck's (1744–1829) conclusion that living things are evolving (1801—his theory that evolution came about through use and disuse was disproved), and Mattias Schleiden (1804–1881) and Theodor Schwann's (1810–1882) theory that all living things are either cells or composed of cells. Many zoologists after 1760 were content to improve upon the classification system established by Karl von Linné (1758).

EVOLUTION. Just as Schleiden and Schwann's cell theory provided a unifying concept among living things, so the theory of evolution provided an explanation for Sir Richard Owen's (1804–1892) principles of homology and analogy, set forth in 1843. Overwhelming evidence that evolution had occurred and a theory of its method through natural selection was provided in 1859 when Charles Darwin (1809–1882) published his book *On the Origin of Species*.

Darwin's lack of information on genetics forced him to assume that the visible variations he saw in each species followed an inheritable pattern. This first book and his later works stimulated zoologists all over the world to fresh research, which uncovered a wealth of new evidence supporting the theory of organic evolution.

The first experimental work to support Darwin's work came during his lifetime, in the statistical studies of inheritance in garden peas by the Austrian monk Gregor Mendel (1822–1884). This work, published in 1865, was not "discovered" until 1900, when three different research scientists brought it to the world's attention. In the meantime, W. Kuhne had discovered the nature of enzyme action (1878), W. Flemming had gained a consecutive understanding of the events in the cell division (1882), E. Van Beneden had discovered *meiosis* (1887), and Henry F. Osborne (1857–1935) had recognized the evolutionary principle of adaptive radiation.

MOLECULAR STUDIES. Many recent discoveries and theories have drawn attention to chemical similarities among animals, among plants, and between plants and animals. They have focused attention at the molecular level, leading to a greater appreciation of the steps in organic evolution—particularly those that occurred before the animals that have left fossils.

In 1916, Thomas H. Morgan (1866–1945) presented his theory of the gene; in 1953, the nature of the genetic code, in terms of the molecular structure of the DNA in the chromosomes, was visualized from the work of M. H. F. Wilkins, F. H. C. Crick, and J. D. Watson; today the fine details of the code are being worked out.

In 1929, K. Lohmann discovered ATP, the carrier of energy in living systems; in 1937, Sir Hans Krebs accounted for the citric acid cycle in the mitochondria of each cell as it

carries on respiration, using oxygen and producing ATP.

Wendell Stanley (1904–   ) discovered in 1935 that a virus can be purified until it becomes a nonliving crystal without losing its ability to cause a disease; this reopened the question of the line between the living and the nonliving and led to new considerations of the origin of life and the chemical evolution that preceded the appearance of recognizable plants and animals. In 1953, in Harold Urey's laboratory, Stanley L. Miller demonstrated that organic compounds can form spontaneously under conditions very similar to those that geologists envision for the Earth during the Archeozoic Era.

NEW PERSPECTIVES. With all of this information, the zoologist is able to interpret the range of animal life, both extinct and living, in a new way. He sees the first long period after life began as one during which chemical systems evolved. To survive, each system had to meet the fundamental requirements for life: the ability to absorb from its environment the chemical substances and energy it needed and the ability to reproduce. The zoologist assumes that an almost infinite number of combinations was tried and that each successful one progressed by adding slight variations that improved its chances of survival.

Until a modern form of photosynthesis released quantities of oxygen into the atmosphere, it is believed that there was no basis for *aerobic respiration* on Earth. It is possible that some ancestors of protozoans lived without oxygen, and the same may be true of unicellular ancestors of other phyla.

Predatory animals could not have existed until oxygen was present, for only aerobic respiration allows rapid expenditure of energy for more than a few seconds. Multicellular parasites can thrive without oxygen, but only so long as they have larger, multicellular hosts that carry on aerobic respiration.

Since the Cambrian Age, which began some 550 million years ago, when animals reached a size and firmness of body that made fossils possible, essentially all the phyla—and many of the classes—are represented. Each ancestral line is of about the same length, but some animals have changed more in structure than others. To a great extent, the ones that have changed most have spread from the sea to fresh water and onto the land, into deserts, hot springs, and petroleum pools; today, the seas hold most of the animals that have changed least.

Although all animals have become more specialized in structure and function, some have become too specialized to survive a change in environment. An example is the dinosaurs, which became extinct with the advent of the Ice Age. Thus, the phyla of modern animals are regarded as alternative ways of living, all equally successful in their respective environments and all incorporating general features of life that evolved before the Cambrian Age.

—Lorus J. Milne and Margery Milne

AARDVARK, an insect-eating mammal of Africa south of the Sahara and the Sudan. The aardvark (Dutch for earth pig) is about 5 feet long, including the tail. It uses its strong claws to burrow into the ground and to tear down the nests of termites (white ants). It licks up the termites with its long, sticky tongue. Although often called ant boar or earth pig, its small eyes and long snout are its only piglike features. Order Tubulidentata, specifically *Orycteropus afer.*

ABALONE, a sea snail of rocky coasts, which produces a low oval shell as much as 12 inches across. Abalones eat seaweeds, foraging for them while clinging to rocks by means of a large flat muscular foot. Only the edges of the foot project beyond the shell, which shows a slight spiral and usually a series of breathing holes near one side.

When disturbed, an abalone holds on like a suction cup, by contracting a strong muscle from the center of its foot to the center of its shell. This muscle has a high commercial value because of its delicate flavor. For their flesh and for the shells, which are lined attractively with mother-of-pearl, they are harvested in large numbers. Order Prosobranchiata, various species of genus *Haliotis.*

ADDER. See *Viper.*

AGOUTI, any of about 24 different rabbit-sized mammals native to the West Indies, South and Central America, and southern Mexico, For the most part, agoutis live on the ground eating roots, fruits, and foliage. They do not climb or dig to any great depth. When at rest or eating, they commonly sit on their haunches and hold food between their paws. They are considered good to eat and are sometimes domesticated. Agoutis can damage crops by eating the plant roots. Order Rodentia, member of genus *Dasyprocta.*

ALBATROSS, any of 13 different kinds of giant petrel-like sea birds. The extended wingspread may measure up to 12 feet, and the weight may exceed 20 pounds, making it the largest of all aquatic birds. Its plumage is white with black bands on the wings and back.

It has a strong, hard, long bill of a pale-yellow color with its nostrils near the tip; the flesh-colored feet are short and webbed, and the wings are long, narrow, and strong. Many species are frequently encountered in the South Pacific. Others have great nesting grounds on Laysan, an islet in the Hawaiian Islands Bird Reservation. Still another kind of albatross is seen in immense flocks about Bering Strait, in early summer, attracted by vast schools of migrating fish. Order Procellariiformes, the tube-nosed birds; members of genus *Diomedea.*

ALEWIFE, or sawbelly, a valuable herringlike fish as much as 15 inches long, with sharp projecting scales along its undersurface. Alewives are common near land along the western side of the North Atlantic Ocean from the Gulf of St. Lawrence to the Gulf of Mexico. Some are landlocked in Lake Ontario and lakes in New York State.

In spring, alewives from the ocean enter coastal shallows and streams in large numbers to spawn. The young, hatched from the eggs, remain in fresh water until they are about 4 inches long (usually by autumn), at which time they go downstream to the sea and mature there. Order Isospondyli, specifically *Pomolobus pseudoharengus.*

ALLIGATOR. See *Crocodile.*

ALPACA, the domesticated South American camel, which stands about 2 feet high at the shoulder, native to the higher portions of the Andes.

The Peruvians keep vast flocks of alpacas and esteem the silky luster and fineness of their wool. Order Artiodactyla, specifically *Lama huanaco.*

AMEBA, any of several different microscopic one-celled animals, or protozoans, which move by flowing slowly. An ameba has no head end, covering, or skeleton. Freshwater amebas (chiefly of genus *Amoeba,* from a Greek word meaning change) flow around and digest smaller animals and plants. A few kinds of parasitic amebas, such as the dysentery ameba (*Entamoeba histolytica*) of man, found in contaminated water, reach the intestine and cause severe inflammation. Class Sarcodina, order Amoebida.

ANACONDA. See *Boa.*

ANCHOVY, a bony fish about 4 inches long, belonging to the herring family. It abounds in the Mediterranean, particularly along the coasts of Italy, Greece, Spain, and France. It is bluish brown on the back and silvery white on the belly. Order Isospondyli, specifically *Engraulis encrasicholus.*

ANGELFISH, any of several different kinds of tropical bony fishes in which the body is so narrow and high that they can hide easily behind a plant stem. Their dorsal and anal fins are usually elongated, giving the body the appearance of having a long wing above and below. Marine angelfishes as much as 2 feet long are conspicuous in the shallow waters of coral reefs, where they display their bright colors

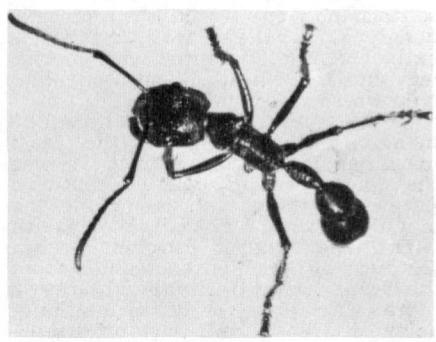

AMERICAN MUSEUM OF NATURAL HISTORY

ANT

and gay stripes when not busy reaching with their small mouths among the crevices for food.

The freshwater angelfish (*Pterophyllum scalare*) has long been a favorite for tropical aquariums, but it is active mostly at night, very nervous by day, and fights with others of its own kind; it is a native of the Amazon River. Order Acanthopteri; various genera in family Cichlidae.

ANT, a social insect of the order Hymenoptera, family Formicidae, found in most temperate and tropical regions. Small and powerful, these insects have long been noted for their remarkable activities and interesting habits. Theirs is a well-defined community consisting of males, breeding females (much larger than the males), and sterile females called neuters, workers, or nurses.

The workers are wingless, and the males and breeding females acquire wings only for the nuptial flight, after which the males and females divest themselves of their wings and either return to established nests or found new colonies. The workers perform all the labor of the anthill, the community abode; they excavate the galleries, procure food, and feed the larvae or young ants, which have no organs of locomotion.

Some ants live on animal food, picking clean the skeletons of dead animals. Others live on saccharine matter, being very fond of the sweet substance called *honeydew,* which exudes from the bodies of aphids, or plant lice. These the ants keep in their nests or tend on the plants where the aphids feed; sometimes they even superintend their breeding. By stroking the aphids with their antennae, they cause them to emit the sweet fluid. Other insects are found living with ants in different types of association.

In temperate climates most of the male and female ants survive until cold weather. The next brood of ants appears in the spring from eggs laid the preceding summer. In colder climates the workers pass the winter in a state of torpor and require no food. They need food only during the season of activity, when they have a vast number of young to feed. Some species have stings as weapons, others have only their powerful mandibles or an acrid and pungent fluid (formic acid) that they emit.

ANTEATER, any of three different tropical mammals related to armadillos and sloths, which capture insects as food by means of their long, slender, sticky tongues, extensible over a considerable distance. All three have powerful front legs with strong hooked claws, which they use in climbing and in ripping apart the nests of termites and ants. They walk on the sides of their feet, with the claws incurved. Anteaters live in South and Central America.

The great anteater (*Myrmecophaga tridactyla*), which lives in humid forests from northern Argentina to southern British Honduras, weighs up to 50 pounds and is almost 7 feet long, counting the long bushy tail. The collared anteater (*Tamandua tetradactyla*) and the silky 2-toed anteater (*Cyclopes didactylus*) are smaller, with short hair, and a long naked tail which is used like a fifth hand in climbing; both are found mostly in trees, from southern Mexico to Brazil and Bolivia, and become most active at night. Order Edentata.

ANTELOPE, any of more than 100 kinds of graceful, plant-eating, cud-chewing mammals, which resemble deer but have permanent hollow horns instead of solid antlers that are shed annually. Africa south of the great deserts is the home of most antelopes—the various gazelles, gnus, hartebeests, and the springbok (*Antidorcas euchore*) and two kinds of elands (species of *Taurotragus*). Europe and Asia have two species: the chamois (*Rupicapra rupicapra*), which inhabits the Alps; and the saiga (*Saiga tartarica*) in the Soviet Union.

Antelopes have a timid and restless disposition and are among the swiftest runners in the animal kingdom. Most are gregarious, associating in herds. Order Artiodactyla, family Bovidae.

ANT LION, or doodle bug, any of several dozen kinds of larval insects with soft, egg-shaped bodies and large flat heads, equipped with sickle-shaped projecting jaws. An ant lion digs a funnel-shaped pit in the driest and finest sand it can find, using its big head to toss out the sand. When the pit is about an inch deep, with smoothly sloping sides, the ant lion buries itself at the bottom, projecting only its jaws. If an ant or other luckless insect stumbles into the pit, it skids down the sides into the jaws of the ant lion.

Generally the ant lion reacts to the sandslide produced by the skidding insect, confusing its victim by tossing still more sand. A full-grown ant lion pupates in the sand, and transforms to a flying insect resembling a dragonfly. Order Neuroptera; various members of genus *Myrmeleon*.

APE, the most highly developed wild members of the mammalian order Primates. All inhabit the Old World. They include baboons, mandrills, macaques, orangutans, chimpanzees, and gorillas. The nostrils of an ape are separated by a narrow septum; both fore- and hind-feet have opposing thumbs; the callosities on the rump are generally naked; some species have cheek pouches.

APHIDS, or plant lice, any of several hundred different kinds of small, soft-bodied insects with slender, sucking mouthparts. They are found all over the world, sucking the juices from the buds, leaves, flowers, young stems, or tender roots of plants. Growing rapidly, they attain adulthood by direct development and generally reproduce by parthenogenesis (virgin birth).

In the late summer, aphids develop wings and fly feebly to new locations. Toward winter, males are produced. Mated females lay eggs that can survive cold weather, whereas all young and adults die when frozen.

Generally an aphid reaches into the veins or conducting tubes where the plant is transporting sugary solutions and other organic substances. Excess water and sugar are excreted by the aphid in droplets, known as *honeydew*.

To get honeydew to eat, some ants carefully carry the aphids to suitable locations on plants, as though these "ants' cows" were domestic animals. Aphids that ants place in underground chambers on the roots of crop plants often cause serious loss to farmers, without being seen. Order Homoptera; various genera in family Aphididae.

ARMADILLO, any of about 20 different kinds of burrowing mammals encased by an armor of bony material divided into small, separate bands. The bands are connected by a membrane, except on the forehead, shoulders, and haunches, rendering the armor flexible and enabling the animal to roll itself into an armored ball.

Armadillos live mostly in Central and South America. They burrow in the earth, where they lie in the daytime, seldom going out except at night. They subsist chiefly on fruits and roots, sometimes on insects and flesh. They are inoffensive and can be eaten.

The largest (*Priodontes giganteus* of eastern South America) is 3 feet in length, with an 18-inch tail; the smallest (*Chlamyphorus truncatus* of Argentinean deserts) is 6 inches long with a 1-inch tail. The nine-banded armadillo (*Dasypus novemcinctus*), more than 2 feet long with a 12-inch tail, has spread recently through Mexico into Oklahoma and Florida. Order Edentata; various species in 9 genera.

ASS, either of two horselike mammals with conspicuous ears, an erect mane, a dark stripe along the back, and hair covering the hind legs where a horse has bare, horny areas. The African wild ass, or donkey or burro (*Equus asinus*), is native to Ethiopia, Somaliland, and adjacent areas of East Africa. It is easily domesticated.

The Asian wild ass (*E. hemionus*), which once ranged over the deserts and high plains from Asia Minor to Central Mongolia, has small differences in color and markings that can be used to distinguish the Syrian wild ass (Syrian deserts) from the onager (Iran to Turkestan), the Indian wild ass (western India and Baluchistan), the kiang (Tibet), and the kulan (Central Mongolia). Of these, the Syrian wild ass is almost extinct.

The long-legged and slender-headed tarpan, from which the domestic horse (*E. caballus*) was derived, is extinct. A related animal with shorter legs and thick head is the Mongolian wild horse (*E. przewalskii*).

Of the zebras, or striped horselike mammals, the one with the least markings is already extinct. It was the quagga (*E. quagga*) of southern Africa. Surviving zebras include the mountain zebra (*E. zebra*) of South Africa and Angola; Burchell's zebra (*E. burchelli*), which is common from the Transvaal to Uganda; and Grévy's zebra (*E. grevyi*) of Somaliland, northern Kenya, and parts of Ethiopia. Order Perissodactyla; family Equidae.

AUK, any of more than 20 different kinds of heavy-bodied sea birds of the Northern Hemisphere. They fly and swim many miles out to sea, feeding mainly on fishes, squids, crustaceans, and sea worms. Auks are most numerous in Atlantic waters from Newfoundland to Iceland and south to Scotland, and in the Pacific from northern California to Bering Strait and southeast along the Soviet coast. They come to land only in times of bad weather and during the breeding season.

The great auk (*Plautus impennis*) is now extinct; the last survivors were killed about 1845. It stood about 3 feet tall. The great auk could not fly, but used its wings to guide its underwater swimming. Like all auks, it propelled itself by paddling with its webbed feet.

Among the smaller auks still alive, the razor-billed auk (*Alca torda*) stands about 16 inches tall. Various auklets (genus *Aethia*) are barely 6 inches high. Other auks, all of which belong to family Alcidae, include the guillemots and the puffins. Order Charadriiformes.

AVOCET, any of 4 different kinds of long-legged shore birds, about 18 inches in length with a peculiar upcurved beak. The avocet of Eurasia and Africa is black and white; the two avocets of North America and Australia have a tan head and neck; the fourth species lives around salt lakes in the Andes of Chile and Bolivia. All of these birds wade sedately, swinging their slender beaks from side to side in shallow water to capture aquatic insects and small mollusks. Order Charadriiformes; species of genus *Recurvirostra*.

BABOON, any of eight different kinds of powerful apes distinguished by having an elongated, abrupt, doglike muzzle, fairly long tail, and naked pads on the buttocks. All but one kind—the most famous—are restricted to Africa. The exception, whose range extends from northeastern Africa to Arabia, is the Arabian baboon (*Comopithecus hamadryas*), which was sacred to the ancient Egyptians, who depicted it on their monuments, and mummified and entombed it. Old males have a heavy mane around the neck and shoulders.

More widespread in Africa are the Chacma, or pigtailed, baboon (*Chaeropithecus ursinus*) of eastern and southern areas; the yellow baboon (*C. cynocephalus*) of central and southern parts of the continent; the western baboon (*C. papio*) of central and western Africa; and the Doguera baboon (*C. doguera*) of Kenya and Ethiopia. West African forest areas are the preferred territories for the bearded mandrill (*Mandrillus sphinx*) and drill (*M. leucophaeus*), which have particularly colorful skin on the face and buttocks. Ethiopian mountains have the distinctive Gelada baboons (*Theropithecus gelada*), whose nostrils open on the sides of the nose.

All of these animals run and sit on the ground. They rarely climb trees or stand upright. They travel by day in troops of 25 to 300 individuals of all ages hunting for edible roots, fruits, eggs, reptiles, and insects. Sometimes they attack sheep or vege-

U.S. DEPARTMENT OF THE INTERIOR
BEARS

table crops, despite the efforts of herders and farmers. If pursued, they defend themselves, often by throwing stones and dirt. Order Primates, family Cercopithecidae, which includes also the monkeys of the Old World.

BADGER, any of 9 different short-legged mammals, related to weasels and skunks, which dig for their food with large forepaws armed with strong claws. The American badger (*Taxidea taxus*), found in dry open country from southwestern Canada to central Mexico, is somewhat smaller than the Eurasian badger (*Meles meles*) of wooded country from Scandinavia to southern China, which attains a weight of as much as 40 pounds and a length up to 3 feet.

The hog-badger (*Arctonyx collaris*) of China, India, and Malaya, is equally large but more slender and has a long naked snout. Three kinds of ferret badgers (genus *Melogale*) and two of stink badgers (genera *Mydaus* and *Suillotaxus*) are found in the East Indies and adjacent parts of Southeast Asia. A honey badger, or ratel (*Mellivora capensis*), ranges over most of Africa and in Asia from Arabia to Turkestan and India.

Badgers feed on roots, fruits, insects, frogs, and ground squirrels. Most species have anal glands that secrete a malodorous fluid. Order Carnivora, family Mustelidae.

BARNACLE, any of about 800 different kinds of marine crustaceans that spend most of their lives permanently attached to rocks, submerged timbers, steel pilings, and ship bottoms. Their eggs hatch as free-swimming larvae, which feed, grow, and change their form. Soon each attaches itself to a firm support and begins to produce its limy shell of overlapping plates.

Shells of acorn barnacles (chiefly of the genus *Balanus*) are fixed directly to the support. Those of goose barnacles (genus *Lepas*) enclose the major parts of the body, which is held away from the support on a flexible, rubbery stalk.

Barnacles of all kinds cease feeding when exposed to air or when the water around them is muddy. In clear water, even during the crash of a wave, they extend from a gap in the shell several feathery extensions from their feet. In a combing motion, the barnacle captures minute sea animals as food and sweeps them into its shell, where it can get them into its mouth. Ships' hulls and wharf pilings often must be treated to prevent growth of barnacles on them. Order Cirripedia.

BASS, edible, perchlike bony fishes found throughout the world, most of them valued as food. Sports fishermen prize the American striped bass (*Roccus saxatilis*), which is native to the entire Atlantic coast from Florida north, and has been introduced successfully from California to Washington; it often reaches a weight of 60 to 70 pounds.

Almost as prominent among game fishes of freshwater are the small-mouthed and the large-mouthed black bass (species of *Micropterus*), which attain record weights of from 12 to 22½ pounds. The small-mouthed bass is sturdily built and dark in color; it frequents rivers and clear, cold water, and it is more active than the much heavier large-mouthed bass, which prefers quiet water and attains its greatest weight in semitropical regions. Order Percomorphi, the sea basses in family Serranidae, the freshwater basses in family Centrarchidae.

BAT, any of about 770 different kinds of mammals capable of flapping flight through use of wings formed from a thin webbing of skin stretched between the body and the elongated toes of the forelegs. Almost all land areas of the world, including remote islands, have their native bats or are visited by bats on migration. Most of these animals live in the tropical and subtropical regions, but a few kinds travel in season as far from the Equator as Scotland and Alaska.

Most bats are covered with short fur, have a pair of mammary glands in the chest region, and show their most distinctive features in the head—small eyes, small and numerous teeth, large ears, and nostrils often equipped with sensory lobes of peculiar shapes. Bats find their way about at night and in the dark places they choose for sleeping during the day by listening to the echoes of their own ultrasonic chirping. They can avoid obstacles as small as a stretched wire 1/16th of an inch in diameter, and pass through narrow openings without touching by the most dexterous use of their wings.

The majority of bats use the same type of echolocation to find flying insects and capture these as food. Tropical bats include a large number of kinds that seek out flowers that offer nectar at night, and unwittingly attend to pollination; others locate ripe fruits and crush them to get the juices. The largest of all bats is an Australian fruit-eating bat (the flying "fox" or kalong, *Pteropus giganteus*) weighing nearly 2 pounds and with a wing span of about 5 feet; it does much mischief in orchards.

Far more feared are the small vampirebats (*Desmodus* species) of tropical America, which use their razor-sharp front teeth to cut through the skin of sleeping people and large animals, add a saliva that prevents clotting of the blood, and lap up the blood as food. Still other bats in tropical America fly back and forth over the surface of quiet water, finding fishes of small size within reach of their long-clawed hind legs; these fish-eating bats (*Noctilio* species) either eat the fish in flight, or carry it home to the roost cave.

In caverns where many kinds of bats take shelter, each species clusters by itself, every bat suspended upside down. In cold regions, the bats either spend the winter hibernating where the temperature will always be above the freezing point, or they migrate toward the equator, where they can still be active and find food. All bats can bite in self-defense, and may be carriers of rabies. Order Chiroptera.

BEAR, any of 9 different mammals with large heads, large heavy bodies, short strong legs, and short tails. All except one (the polar bear, *Thalarctos maritimus*) live in temperate or tropical regions and tend to be active at night, sleeping by day.

All except one (the spectacled bear, *Tremarctos ornatus*, of northern South America) are animals of the Northern Hemisphere. The giants are the Alaskan brown bear (*Ursus arctos*) of the mainland and adjacent islands, which grows to almost 8 feet long with a weight of over 1,700 pounds, and the slightly smaller grizzly bear (*U. horribilis*) of the Rocky Mountains. Formerly, grizzlies ranged over much of western North America.

The Kodiak bear (*U. middendorffi* is a brown bear larger than the grizzly, found only on Kodiak Island, Alaska. American black bears (*Euarctos americanus*), which may be chocolate-brown, cinnamon-brown, blue-black, or even white, live in the forests all over North America except where they have been eliminated.

Asia has a black bear (*Selenarctos thibetanus*) in forests of the Himalayas, China, Japan, and Formosa; usually it has a white, crescent-shaped mark on the chest. The sloth bear (*Melursus ursinus*) lives in forests of Ceylon and of India as far as the foothills of the Himalayas, whereas the Malayan sun bear (*Helarctos malayanus*) is found in wooded areas of Southeast Asia from Burma to Indonesia.

All of these animals feed on fruits, roots, insects, and whatever small mammals they can catch. Grizzlies and the giant Alaskan brown bear are experts at flipping salmon out of streams during the annual spawning run. Polar bears eat seaweeds and carrion when other food is scarce; they swim readily, often from one ice floe to another in pursuit of seals. Unlike the other bears of the far northern regions they do not hibernate.

Hibernation, for a bear, consists of lying quietly, sleeping but capable of instantly being aroused, in a den of some kind during the winter months. The one or two young are ordinarily born at the end of this period of inactivity. Order Carnivora, family Ursidae.

BEAVER, either of two different gnawing mammals of the North Temperate Zone, with a broad flat naked tail and webbed hind feet. The European beaver (*Castor fiber*) and the American one (*C. canadensis*) are closely similar; both now occupy a small fraction of their previously wide range. In escaping from the attention of people who want to kill beavers for their fur, these animals have become nocturnal.

The European species makes its home inconspicuously in burrows along the banks of rivers, whereas the American beaver continues to construct a lodge of sticks and mud in the pond behind a special dam of the same construction. Beavers dive into the water for safety, propelling themselves with the hind feet while using the tail as a rudder, front paws folded against the chest.

Their food is exclusively vegetable matter, particularly the young twigs and thin bark of trees such as aspen and willow. A supply of this food is ordinarily collected during late summer and pushed into the muddy bottom of the beaver pond, where the beavers can go for it under the ice during the coldest weather. Order Rodentia, family Castoridae.

BEDBUG, a flat-bodied wingless insect that hides in cracks and bedding until night and then crawls out to suck human blood. Its saliva is poisonous to some people, its odor objectionable to almost everyone. It can live without a meal for as much as a year.

Related insects attack bats, swallows, and poultry, emerging from crevices in roosting sites to feed in darkness on their victim's blood. Order Heteroptera, specifically *Cimex lectularius*.

BEE, any of several thousand different wasplike insects with 4 membranous wings, the second pair much smaller than the first pair. The bee differs from the wasp in having a hairy body and mouthparts specialized for sucking as well as biting. Bees of many kinds inhabit virtually all land areas.

The bees eat and store honey made from the nectar of flowers and a material called "bee bread" made from pollen. On these nourishing materials the female bees feed the maggotlike larvae that hatch from their eggs.

Full-grown larvae transform to a pupa stage, during which their bodies are converted into the structure of the adult insect. While visiting flowers to gather nectar and pollen, bees unwittingly attend to pollination—usually cross-pollination—and hence are responsible for the efficient production of seeds and many kinds of fruits.

Bees differ greatly in their nesting habits. A majority of these insects make solitary nests, and are comparatively inconspicuous. Carpenter bees (of genus *Xylocopa*), which are as big as bumblebees, cut tunnels in timber, stock them with food and an egg in each of many chambers, and close up the opening afterwards. Leaf-cutter bees (of genus *Megachile*) snip out almost circular pieces of leaves and petals, particularly of roses, with which they line the burrows and construct the partitions separating one egg and its food store from the next.

Mason bees (such as the metallic green, bluish or purplish insects of genus *Osmia*) construct earthen cells under stones, in small holes in decaying wood, in deserted snail shells, and elsewhere. The cuckoo bees (species of *Nomada*) lack a means to collect pollen, and place their eggs in the nests of other kinds of bees. Social nesting is characteristic of bumblebees (of the genus *Bombus*) and honeybees (genus *Apis*). The bumblebees include about 50 different kinds in the North Temperate Zone and the Arctic, where they are the only bees present; they are rare in the Tropics.

Usually a bumblebee is about 1 inch long, heavier and larger than a honeybee, and covered with golden and black hair. Females build small separate cells on the ground, each one called a honeypot. Generally a few dozen bumblebees nest close together, building 200 to 300 honeypots.

Like most female bees, the female bumblebee has an effective sting. She can use it repeatedly until her supply of venom is temporarily exhausted, whereas a worker honeybee can sting only once because the act of stinging tears the stinger out of the honeybee's body. Bumblebees differ also from the honeybee in that the females of one colony never try to destroy one another; they do not swarm, and are regarded as showing only a simple social habit.

Few bees show so complex a social organization as the domesticated honeybee (*A. mellifera*). The most distinctive feature of this bee is its habit of continuing to store honey and bee bread not only for the breeding season but also to sustain the hive during the winter.

During the greater part of the year, the population of a honeybee hive is composed exclusively of two sorts of individuals—the mother, or queen bee, and the workers, or neuter bees, which are sterile females. The males, or drones, generally appear in May and are all dead by the end of July. The queen lives for several years, the workers only 1 to 2 months in seasons of activity, and the drones 1 to 2 months.

The queen has a longer body and shorter wings than the workers. She can use her sting repeatedly without rupturing herself, and normally will use it within minutes after escaping from her pupal cell. She will explore the hive thoroughly and sting to death all other queens present, even those that have not yet emerged as adults.

The old queen, with a large number of worker bees, has already left in a swarm, to find a new place for a colony. The young queen soon goes out on her nuptial flight, pursued by dozens of drones. Within 2 days, she is back in the hive, prepared to lay eggs at the rate of about 200 a day for the rest of her life. She lays each egg in a separate cell in the brood region of the hive, a short distance away from cells in which honey or bee bread is stored.

Development and hatching of the eggs, growth of the larva, pupation and transformation into an adult ready to emerge take an average of 24 days for the unfertilized eggs that mature into drones, 21 days for the fertilized eggs that mature into sterile workers on a low-protein diet, and 15½ days for the fertilized eggs that mature into new queens on a high-protein diet.

The life of a worker follows a regular schedule, with tasks changing to match development of various glands in her body. She produces saliva as a varnish for the cells in which the queen will lay eggs. She visits the honey stores and cells with bee bread to get food she can regurgitate for the larvae of different ages. The wax glands below her abdomen begin to secrete, and she takes wax scales in her jaws to work them into a material with which she builds new cells in the comb. Eventually, she

crawls to the doorway of the hive and uses her wings there to create a current of air to ventilate the hive.

After a few days of this chore and of guarding the doorway from intruders, such as spiders or bees from other hives (which have the wrong "hive odor"), she becomes a field bee. Until their wings wear out, field bees daily gather nectar, pollen, resinous materials for sealing cracks in the hive, and water in hot weather when the inside temperature must be lowered by evaporation. A single hive may contain 60,000 workers at one time.

Only the workers possess special features on each of their 3 pairs of legs, which make these efficient tools in collecting and transporting pollen. The hind pair of legs—longer than the others—have on the outer surface a triangular depression (the palette) surrounded by stiff hairs; this forms a "pollen basket," into which the insect presses pollen combed from the surface of the body. The first segment of the feet on these legs is larger than the others, and bears on its inner surface a large number of short stiff bristles, forming a "pollen brush." The front pair of legs have notches through which the feelers are drawn carefully to clean them of pollen grains; an "eye brush" is on each front foot. Most of these and other special features are used by the bee while hovering in flight.

Worker honeybees appear to change their behavior according to the amount of a "queen substance" produced by their queen, and the amount of food stored in the hive. They communicate with one another in the darkness of the hive by special dances and sounds that tell other workers the direction and approximate distance to food they have found, as well as some measure of its abundance. Order Hymenoptera, suborder Apoidea, and more than a dozen families.

BEETLE, any of more than 300,000 different kinds of insects in which the first pair of wings are hard, tough, and capable of meeting along the midline over the back to protect the membranous second pair of wings, which are used for flying. Beetles outnumber in variety all other insects, and are found on every continent, from forest to desert and fresh water.

Each beetle has a pair of strong jaws. Its eggs hatch to active larvae, which feed on living and dead parts of plants or on the remains of dead animals. Some bore in wood or live in tunnels eaten from the inner bark of trees. Upon reaching full size, a beetle larva pupates and transforms to the adult insect. Order Coleoptera.

BIGHORN, or mountain sheep, a wild sheep of the western mountain ranges of North America from New Mexico and California northward to British Columbia. It stands about 3 feet high at the shoulder; its horns are curved and spiraled back and outward, often to a full circle, and may measure from 32 to 40 inches in length. Its color varies from white to buffy brown to black with a large whitish rump patch. Order Artiodactyla, specifically *Ovis canadensis*.

BIRD OF PARADISE, any of 43 different kinds of perching birds related to crows, in which the adult male develops extraordinary feathers on the tail, wings, back, or head, used in courtship display. Females and young birds are inconspicuous and plain. Birds of paradise inhabit the remote forests of New Guinea and neighboring islands, and northeastern Australia. Field research has not yet provided full information on these magnificent birds. Order Passeriformes, family Paradisaeidae.

BISON, either of 2 kinds of large, cud-chewing mammals, remarkable for the great hump or projection over the fore shoulders, at which point the adult male is almost 6 feet high, and for the long shaggy rust-colored hair over the head, neck, and forepart of the body. In summer, from the shoulders backward, the surface is covered with very short, fine hair, soft and smooth as velvet. The tail is short and tufted at the end.

One, called the wisent (*Bison bonasus*), was once widespread in forested parts of Europe but survives now only in captivity. The other, the American bison (*B. bison*), was formerly numerous on the western plains of North America but is now present only in a few herds protected by law. The American bison is often incorrectly called a buffalo. Bison breed readily with domestic cattle, and their issue are fertile among themselves. Order Artiodactyla, family Bovidae.

BLACKBIRD, any of several American perching birds, related to orioles and meadowlarks. The red-winged blackbirds (*Agelaius phoeniceus*), which nest in marshes, often congregate in great flocks; the genus name *Agelaius* means gregarious. The related grackles are often called blackbirds. The unrelated European blackbird and the New Zealand blackbird are both songbirds of the thrush family. Order Passeriformes, family Icteridae.

BLACK DUCK, a common water bird of eastern North America, and a favorite with hunters. It is about 2 feet long and has dark-brown plumage with an iridescent bluish patch on the wings, and bright orange feet. It breeds from the Middle Atlantic States north to Labrador. The black duck and the closely related mallard are the two most abundant species of U.S. ducks. The nest of the black duck is a large structure made of weeds and grass; the 6 to 12 eggs are a pale greenish color. Order Anseriformes, family Anatidae, specifically *Anas rubripes*.

BLACK WIDOW, or hourglass spider, a small black spider with a black globular abdomen; a scarlet mark the shape of an hourglass on the abdomen's underside; and slender legs, the first and last pairs longer than the second and third. It is found in damp places from New England to Patagonia, more commonly in eastern North America and the far west.

The ¼-inch male is too small to be venomous, but the ½-inch female can puncture human skin where it is thin and soft, and inject a dangerous poison. She does so chiefly while guarding her 3 or 4 cocoons, each containing about 300 eggs, hung in a loose web in dark places such as cellars and outhouses. No deaths have been reported from such a bite in a healthy adult person. Related spiders with a similarly dangerous venom are found in Australia and New Zealand. Order Araneae, family Theridiidae, specifically *Latrodectes mactans*.

BLUEBIRD, any of 3 small perching birds of North America, with a soft twittering call and with blue feathers on much of the body. The eastern bluebird (*Sialia sialis*) was formerly much more common and was widely regarded as the harbinger of spring. Its breast and throat are earthy red, the rest of the body a solid blue. The western bluebird (*S. mexicana*) is similar except that the black is rusty red. The mountain bluebird (*S. currucoides*) is found from Mexico to Canada in high country; the male is azure blue, and the female is dull brownish with a blue rump, tail, and wings.

Bluebirds catch insects on the wing, but generally descend to the ground to eat them. They also eat fruits in season. Order Passeriformes, family Turdidae.

BLUEFISH, a mackerel-like marine fish, steely blue in color and beautifully shaped for speed and strength. It is widely distributed and abundant along the eastern coast of the United States.

Some individuals up to 20 pounds have been taken, but the average weight is from 3 to 8 pounds, and the length 20 to 30 inches. In addition to its food value, the fish is notable for the tremendous schools in which it congregates and for its feeding capacity. Young bluefish, called snappers, weigh about half a pound. Order Acanthopteri, family Pomatomidae, specifically *Pomatoma saltatrix*.

BLUE JAY. See *Jay.*

BOA, any of several dozen different nonvenomous snakes that resemble pythons in the way they capture and kill their prey, and in the possession of two functional lungs, not just the right lung as in snakes of other families. Unlike pythons, which lay eggs and are found only in the Old World, boas bear active young and most kinds inhabit the tropics of America.

In most boas and all pythons, a remnant of a hip girdle is attached to the backbone; in the male, further evidence of vestigial hind legs can be seen in a pair of protruding claws, one on each side of the vent. Like pythons, the boas lie in wait for prey, trying to capture mammals and birds far larger in diameter than the snake's head. Holding firmly with its mouth, the snake throws two or three coils of its body tightly around the victim and tightens still more every time the animal exhales. Prevented from breathing, the victim suffocates.

The snake swallows its prey whole, then seeks out some secluded spot in which to rest for a week or more while digesting its huge meal. Snakes with this habit are called constrictors. One referred to often as "the boa constrictor" is common from coastal Mexico to northern Argentina; it rarely exceeds 10 feet in length, but bears the name *Constrictor constrictor*.

The giant among boas is the anaconda (*Eunectes murinus*) of northern South America, which is reported to attain a length of 29 feet. It waits to prey along riverbanks, catching mammals and birds as they come to drink.

Beyond the New World, boas are represented in North Africa, Madagascar, the Mascarene Islands of the Indian Ocean, New Guinea, and on some islands of the South Pacific. Order Serpentes, family Boidae.

BOBOLINK, an American perching bird of southern Canada and the northern United States, except the west coast. It is related closely to the oriole, the blackbird, and meadowlark, and is known also as reedbird or ricebird in the southern states, through which it migrates to and from its winter home in central and southern South America.

The male bobolink is almost 7½ inches long. In spring and summer he is black and white on top and solid black underneath. By mid-summer, when bobolinks start south, and through the fall and winter, his plumage becomes buffy olive streaked with black, and the underparts olive or yellowish. Throughout the year the smaller female resembles the male in autumn plumage.

Order Passeriformes, family Icteridae, specifically *Dolichonyx oryzivorus*.

BOBWHITE, a quail native to the United States and Canada, named for its clear, loud two-part whistle. Both Rhode Island and Oklahoma have chosen the bobwhite as state bird. It has a conspicuous white patch on the throat and a pale mark from the beak over the eye and down the neck. At maturity the bird may be 11 inches long, including the short tail, and weigh 9 ounces.

Bobwhites benefit man by eating insects in summer and weed seeds in winter. They seldom fly far, but may

U.S. DEPARTMENT OF THE INTERIOR
BUFFALO

attain more than 50 miles per hour. Order Galliformes, family Perdicidae, specifically *Colinus virginianus.*

BOLL WEEVIL. See *Weevil.*

BONY PIKE. See *Gar.*

BOTFLY, a parasitic fly often mistaken for a honeybee buzzing about the head and front legs of horses, mules, or donkeys. The female botfly keeps the tip of her long pointed abdomen curled under her until she alights, usually on a leg, and begins attaching her yellowish eggs to hairs of a horse. The horse gets the eggs into its mouth when it licks the hairs; the eggs hatch quickly, releasing legless maggots called bots. These find their way to the horse's stomach and attach themselves to the lining.

For about 8 to 10 months of the year the bots absorb what they need of the horse's food, grow to maturity, and pass through the digestive tract. From the manure they enter the ground, where they pupate and transform into adult flies. Related flies attack deer, moose, rabbits, squirrels, and other mammals. Order Diptera, family Gastrophilidae, specifically *Gastrophilus intestinalis.*

BRISTLETAIL, any of several similar wingless insects in which the head bears two long, slender feelers and three similar appendages extend from the opposite end of the body; these are the "bristles" for which the animals are named. Best known are the cosmopolitan silverfish, or fishmoth, *(Lepisma saccharina)* and the Europaen firebrat *(Thermobia domestica),* which inhabit human homes.

Like the firebrat, the bristletail uses its biting mouthparts in scavenging for food. Not content with crumbs, it dines on the glue that holds books together, or the sizing on coated paper, or the starch in clothes—often eating holes in garments and causing extensive damage. Lacking any transformation in body form as they mature, the bristletails are regarded as among the most primitive of insects. Order Thysanura.

BROWN THRASHER, a handsome songbird slightly larger than a robin and with a longer tail, a dark cinnamon-colored back, and rows of brown spots on its gray breast. Native to North America east of the Rockies, it hunts for insects, spiders, and worms among the fallen leaves below shrubs and woodland trees. Related to the mockingbird and catbird, the brown thrasher often sings loudly, mimicking other birds, usually repeating each phrase twice in quick succession.

For the winter, the brown thrasher migrates to the southeastern United States and eastern Mexico. Order Passeriformes, family Mimidae, specifically *Toxostoma rufum.*

BUFFALO, wild cattle of marshy places in the Old World tropics and subtropics. They are about 5 feet high at the shoulder. Some have been domesticated and used as beasts of burden.

The Indian or water buffalo *(Bos bubalus)* has been domesticated throughout Asia. The Cape or Kafir buffalo *(B. caffer)* of southern Africa is a larger, more powerful animal with a deserved reputation for being dangerous because it will charge and attempt to kill anyone who wounds it or threatens its young. The name buffalo was transferred by the early explorers to the bison of North America, a very different kind of animal. Order Artiodactyla, family Bovidae.

BUFFLEHEAD, or butterball, one of the diving ducks of North America, seen on lakes, rivers, and ocean bays, where it flies into and out of the water, pursuing fish and aquatic insects. In flight it displays conspicuous white patches on each wing. On the water, the dark back is often invisible and the body appears all white. The male's head is blackish green except for a large white area on the top. The female has a small slanting white patch on each cheek.

Buffleheads nest to the west and north of Hudson Bay, but spend the winter in most of the United States and Mexico. During migration, when they are hunted, each bird weighs 1 pound or less. Order Anseriformes, family Anatidae, specifically *Glaucionetta albeola.*

BULLHEAD. See *Catfish.*

BUNTING, any of several sparrow-sized birds with plump bodies and conical beaks. Europe has about a dozen different members of the genus *Embiriza,* including the corn bunting, the reed bunting, and the yellowhammer. In Eurasia and North America, the name "bunting" is used also for the snow bunting *(Plectrophenax nivalis),* which is the whitest of small land birds.

North America has 3 kinds of native buntings *(Passerina),* all spending the winter in Mexico but flying to separate nesting areas each spring. The indigo bunting *(P. cyanea)* goes to the central and eastern United States and Canada, where the males are the only all-blue birds; the mate is brown, faintly streaked below. The lazuli bunting *(P. amoena)* stays west of the Great Plains; the male is sky blue above and on his throat, but has a chestnut breast band and white wingbars; his mate is brown, sparrowlike. The painted bunting *(P. ciris)* nests in the Gulf States and as far north as Missouri; the male is red, purple, and green, his mate all green. Order Passeriformes, family Fringillidae.

BURRO. See *Ass.*

BUSHMASTER. See *Pit Viper.*

BUTTERFLY, any of a large group of scaly-winged insects with knobbed or hook-tipped feelers (antennae). They are closely related to moths, and develop in comparable stages: from an egg, to a plant-eating caterpillar, to a pupa, and to an adult with 2 pairs of wings and sucking mouthparts. The most conspicuous and useful of the

mouthparts is a tube, which is coiled up like a watchspring when not in use.

Butterflies are active by day, and rest usually with the wings folded together vertically over the back, whereas moths are usually active at night, and rest with the wings more horizontal and to the rear. Most butterflies lay a single egg or a few in a place, and leave them unprotected. The caterpillars that hatch out are usually hairless, and pupate exposed, with no cocoon.

Of the 11 families of butterflies, 2 are composed of large insects found in the American Tropics: the brilliant iridescent blue *Morpho* butterflies (family Morphoidae), which conceal their display color when they close their wings; and the owl butterflies *(Caligo,* family Brassolidae), which have enormous eyespot markings on the underside of the rear wings, conspicuous when the insect is at rest.

Much more cosmopolitan are the skippers (most in family Hesperiidae), which are unique in having hooked, rather than knobbed, feelers, and of pupating in a cocoon; the swallowtails and their relatives (family Papilionidae), which include the giant birdwing butterflies of the Far East *(Troides)* and the familiar swallowtails *(Papilio);* the sulphurs, oranges, and whites (family Pieridae), including the cabbage butterfly *(Pieris rapae);* the blues, coppers, and hairstreaks (family Lycaenidae); the metalmarks (family Riodinidae); the huge family of brush-footed butterflies (Nymphalidae), such as the painted lady or thistle butterfly *(Vanessa cardui),* whose front legs, hairy and brushlike, are useless as legs; the wood-nymphs and satyrs (family Satyridae); the milkweed butterflies (family Danaidae), such as the migratory monarch *(Danaus plexippus)* of the Americas; and the heliconiids (family Heliconiidae), such as the zebra butterfly *(Heliconius charithonius)* of Florida, most of which are found in tropical America. Order Lepidoptera, suborder Rhopalocera.

BUZZARD. See *Vulture.*

BY–THE–WIND SAILOR, a colonial marine coelenterate, resembling an oblong floating jellyfish but related to the Portuguese man-of-war. Native to warm waters of the Atlantic and Pacific oceans, by-the-wind sailors are often carried north and south to temperate latitudes and cast ashore, where they die. Unlike the Portuguese man-of-war, by-the-wind sailors are harmless to people.

Each colony is supported by a thin purple float containing gas chambers and bearing a low upright sail diagonally across the top. From below a healthy colony, a central tube hangs down, ending in a mouth. Around the rim of the float, small individuals of the colony bear many tentacles with which they capture food. This consists of miniature crustaceans and other small marine animals that drift in surface waters. The food is passed to the mouth, where it enters the diges-

UNITED NATIONS

CAMEL

tive cavity. Additional individuals below the float attend to reproduction. Class Hydrozoa, order Siphonophora, specifically *Velella mutica.*

CADDISFLY, any mothlike adult insect with 4 hairy wings and soft nonfunctional mouthparts. Caddisflies are found in great numbers near lakes and streams because their caterpillar-like larval stages, called caddisworms, are all aquatic. Caddisworms usually are less than 1 inch long, are important food for fish, and are used as bait by anglers. The worms build cylindrical, portable cases of mineral or plant material or spin nets in swift waters to catch food particles carried by the current. Order Trichoptera.

CAMEL, a large cud-chewing mammal of North Africa and the Near East. There are two kinds — the Asiatic camel (*Camelus bactrianus*), which is about 9 feet tall and has two humps; and the African camel, or dromedary (*C. dromedarius*), which has only one hump. Camels can go for a long time without water but will lose weight and strength. When they are well fed, the hump is erect and plump, but when the camel is inadequately fed, the hump shrinks and falls over.

Fossil camels have been found in North America. The alpaca and llama of South America are closely related to the camels of the Old World. Order Artiodactyla, family Camelidae.

CANARY, a small songbird related to the sparrow, native to the Canary, Azores, and Madeira islands but domesticated in many countries for 300 years. Their acceptance of life in a cage and their sweet and powerful song have made canaries popular as household pets. The best singers, notably those raised in the Harz Mountains, bring high prices. Cage birds are usually yellow (canary color is a brilliant reddish yellow, named from the bird), but wild birds are a dull green with brown streaks. Order Passeriformes, family Fringillidae, specifically *Serinus canarius.*

CANKERWORM, either of 2 kinds of North American moth caterpillars that attack shade trees, orchard trees, and other woody plants. Both are described as measuring worms or inchworms because they move along by holding to the support alternately with the legs at the forward and the rear end of the body. When full grown, they let themselves down to the ground on long fine strands of silk, and burrow 1 to 4 inches into the earth before transforming into the adult stage—the moth.

Male moths have a wingspan of 1 to 1½ inches; the females are practically wingless, and merely crawl out of the ground, up a stem or tree trunk, and wait for a male to find them. Adults of the fall cankerworm (*Alsophila pometaria*) emerge in October or on warm days through the winter to as late as April. Adults of the spring cankerworm (*Palaeacrita vernata*) may appear as early as February or as late as May. The eggs of both species, laid in masses containing as many as 400, hatch about the time the leaves appear. Order Lepidoptera.

CANVASBACK. See *Duck.*

CARDINAL, or redbird, one of the most beautiful of American songbirds, the adult male being brilliant red, like a cardinal's hat, with a sharp crest of vermilion. The female and young are yellowish brown with some red, and with the same crest and heavy, red beak, which is black around the base. Its beautiful whistling song has given it the name, Virginia nightingale. The cardinal nests in bushes and thickets and constructs its nest of bark and twigs. Its food is almost equally divided among weed seeds, fruits, and insects. Order Passeriformes, family Fringillidae, specifically *Richmondena cardinalis.*

CARIBOU. See *Reindeer.*

CARP, a coarse bony fish of the minnow family. Carp are native to freshwaters in Europe and Asia, where they are raised in ponds as a source of protein for human use. In American streams and lakes, to which the carp was introduced many years ago, it causes serious damage by muddying the water, uprooting vegetation, and devouring the young of native fishes.

Usually a carp is brown in color, darker along the back. Close to its mouth are 4 soft projections, called barbels, which help the carp find vegetable food in muddy water. It also eats snails, worms, insects, and eggs and young of other fishes.

The carp attains maturity when about 12 inches long, and the female lays as many as 2 million eggs during the late spring. In ponds fertilized with farm manure, carp sometimes grow to 40 inches long and a weight of 60 pounds. Order Evantognathi, family Cyprinidae, specifically *Cyprinus carpio.*

CAT, any of several different mammals with retractile claws, teeth specially adapted for cutting, and vertically elongated pupils of the eyes. The name is used particularly for members of the genus *Felis,* which includes the domestic cat, the jaguar, leopard, lion, ocelot, and puma, and the genus *Lynx,* which includes the Canada lynx and the bobcat. Order Carnivora, family Felidae.

Domestic Cat. The common cat (*Felis domestica*) is probably a native of Egypt. Domesticated there, it was an object of worship and was frequently mummified. It was not known to the ancient Greeks and Romans who used domesticated martens to destroy rats and mice.

Domestic cats are fastidious animals, constantly washing their fur and paws. Different breeds vary widely in color, markings, size, shape, and length of tail. Notable are the tailless Japanese and Manx cats (coming from the Crimea as well as from the Isle of Man), the Angora or Persian cats with long silky fur, and the Siamese variety, a semialbino with blue eyes, a long pointed head, slender legs, and a long thin tail. The nose, ears, paws, and tail are darker than the body. The ancestor of the domestic cat was probably marked with black bars on a ground of tawny and white, these colors rendering it inconspicuous among the grasses and shrubbery where it ranged.

Wildcat. The name wildcat is applied in America to almost any cat (other than the domestic house cat). The lynx and puma are most commonly called wildcats. The true wildcat (*Felis catus*), however, is found only in Northern Europe and Asia. It is a striped animal, similar to other members of the cat family.

In the New World, the ocelot (*Felis pardalis*) is native to tropical America and has a limited range in the southern United States. Large specimens are about 3 feet long, excluding the 1-foot tail. The color is generally tawny-gray, barred or spotted with brown or black, with chin and underparts almost white. The ocelot preys mostly on birds in the deep forests. Individuals have been partly domesticated and trained for hunting, like the Asian cheetah.

The puma (*Felis concolor*), a little larger than the ocelot, is also native to America. It has a 2-foot tail. Slender, with long legs and small head, the puma is a fairly uniform tawny brown. This is the species referred to as mountain lion in the western United States, where it is notorious as a predator of young cattle and sheep. Elsewhere it is known as panther, painter, catamount, or cougar but the correct name is puma.

Leopard. The leopard (*Felis pardus*) is native to both Africa and Asia. The body of this fierce and rapacious animal is about 4 feet long. It is a superlative leaper, can swim and climb trees. The larger leopards are often called panthers, as are the American puma and jaguar. The leopard differs from the jaguar in having small spots thickly set; the jaguar's are large and open, making a beautiful pattern of dark rosettes on a tan or brown skin.

Jaguar. The jaguar (*Felis onca*), somewhat larger than the leopard, is one of the most formidable beasts of prey found on the American continent. It is typically South American but is found as far north as Texas. The banks of rivers are its favorite haunts, where it preys on such animals as the tapir and water hog or capybara. It kills by leaping on its victim's back, then twisting the neck with its heavy powerful paws until it breaks.

A noisy, heavy animal, it roams abroad at night, especially before the approach of bad weather. It is an expert climber and swimmer and sometimes catches fish for food.

Lion. The lion (*Felis leo*) is the most majestic member of the cat family. It is nearly a uniform tawny or yellowish, paler on the underparts; but the immature lions show stripes like a tiger's and some spots like a leopard's. The male usually has a great shaggy flowing mane and a long tufted tail. The whole frame is extremely muscular, and the foreparts, in particular, are remarkably powerful. The heavy shoulders, large head, bright eye, and copious mane give the animal a noble appearance that has led to its being called the king of beasts.

A lion of the largest size is not so big as a tiger. It measures about 8 feet from the nose to the tail, and the tail measures about 4 feet more. The lioness is smaller, has no mane, and is of a lighter color on the underparts.

The strength of the lion is such that it can carry off a heifer as a cat carries a rat. It is chiefly an inhabitant of Africa, although it is found also in Asia, particularly in certain parts of Arabia, Persia, and India. It was anciently much more common in Asia and was found in some parts of Europe (Macedonia and Thrace), according to Herodotus and other authors. The lion is an inhabitant of open plains in which the shelter of occasional bushes and thickets may be found. It hunts mostly at night and has a terrifying roar. It is easily tamed if it is taken young and abundantly supplied with food.

Tiger. The tiger (*Felis tigris*) is the largest and most dangerous of the cats, slightly exceeding the lion in size but far surpassing it in destructiveness. An Asian animal, the tiger reaches its highest development both in size and color on the hot plains of India. The full-grown male Indian tiger measures from 9 to 12 feet, and the tigress from 8 to 10 feet, from the nose to the tip of the tail, which has no tuft. The ground color is rufous or tawny yellow, white on the ventral surface, with vertical black stripes or elongated ovals and brindlings.

Although possessed of immense strength and ferocity, the tiger rarely attacks armed men, unless it is provoked, but often carries off women and children. When it is pressed by hunger or enfeebled by age and incapable of dealing with larger prey like buffalo, the tiger prowls around villages and, if it learns what easy prey humans are, it often becomes a habitual man-eater. Two varieties are the Bengal, or southern, type with short hair, and a northern variety, ranging as far north as Siberia, which has longer, softer hair. See also *Lynx*.

CATBIRD, a well-known American songbird, about 9 inches long, dark slate gray in color except for a rusty red area under the tail. During the summer it is found throughout the Middle Atlantic and New England States. During the winter it inhabits the extreme south of the United States, and is found also in Mexico and Central America. Order Passeriformes, family Mimidae, specifically *Dumetella carolinensis*.

CATERPILLAR, the wormlike immature stage in the development of a moth or butterfly. The name is said to be from the Latin *cata pilosa* (hairy cat), referring to the many caterpillars that are covered with hair. Most butterfly caterpillars are hairless.

Usually the head of the caterpillar, with its biting jaws, is followed by a portion of the trunk with 3 pairs of jointed legs. More posteriorly, the cylindrical body is generally supported on 6 pairs of stumpy, soft prolegs with many minute hooks; the last pair of prolegs are at the hind end of the caterpillar.

Some kinds of caterpillars do great damage to crops and other vegetation. An exception is the silkworm, which feeds on mulberry and grows to 1 inch long; it is economically valuable because commercial silk can be unwound from the cocoon it spins before pupating. Order Lepidoptera.

CATFISH, any of about 2,000 kinds of scaleless bony fishes with large, toothless mouths. Usually two or more long, soft, slender projections, called barbels, arise from the underjaw or from both jaws near the mouth. They help the catfish find food in muddy water.

Some kinds of catfishes have bony, platelike armor; other kinds are soft skinned. Generally the dorsal and pectoral fins have a stiff strong spine at the leading edge, which can serve as a dangerous weapon for self-defense. A species of catfish native to the Nile River and tropical Africa is capable of discharging an electric shock reaching 100 volts.

Most catfishes can live out of water for a few hours. Their flesh, which may be dark in color, is highly regarded in many parts of the world for human food. A common kind, attaining 20 inches long in American waters, is called the bullhead or horned pout (*Ameiurus nebulosus*), of order Ostariophysi, family Ameiuridae.

CATTLE, any of several kinds of large cud-chewing mammals useful to mankind as a source of power, meat, milk, hides, and horns. In India and other southern Asian countries, the zebu (*Bos indicus*) is used much as domestic cattle are in Europe or the United States. Zebus are humped animals with a great tolerance for hot weather. For meat, milk, and hides, they are less desirable than European and North African cattle (*B. taurus*), which have been bred into many particularly valuable lines of inheritance.

European cattle are especially productive of high-quality milk, and form the basis of the dairy industry. Among the dairy cattle, the Holstein breed (black and white) is perhaps the most important. Holstein cattle are great milk producers, but the percentage of its butter fat is somewhat less than in milk from other cattle. This variety originated in Holland, but has been imported to a considerable extent to the United States and now forms an important part of the milk industry.

Jersey cattle yield milk rich in butter fat. This breed originated in the Isle of Jersey, off the coast of France. Guernsey cattle are reddish, with white markings. They also originated on one of the Channel Islands. Their milk is probably the richest in fat, but the quantity is not so great as in other breeds.

Of the beef cattle, the English Shorthorns are a very sturdy breed. These vary from red to almost pure white. Shorthorns orginated in England, but later were introduced into North America, South America, and to Australia. Another valuable beef animal is the Hereford. This has a red body and white head. Herefords are not so widely distributed as Shorthorns.

Sometimes male cattle are castrated to render them more amenable for draft or agricultural work. These are called oxen. When this is done to improve the quality of the beef for eating, the cattle are known as steers. Order Artiodactyla, family Bovidae, genus *Bos*.

CAVY. See *Guinea Pig*.

CAYMAN. See *Crocodile*.

CENTIPEDE, literally "hundred legged," any of about 2,000 different kinds of segmented terrestrial arthropod animals with biting jaws, one pair of feelers (antennae) on the head, and one pair of walking legs on each of 14 to 180 segments of the body. Centipedes are found on all continents and most major islands. North American kinds are mostly small and inconspicuous, living under stones or in and under decaying logs. In the tropics they often attain great size, some growing to 10 inches in length.

Most centipedes have the first pair of legs modified into poison claws. With them they can inject venom, which kills their prey. It causes considerable pain but rarely death to a person. Centipedes can run forward or backward with almost equal ease. Several orders of class Chilopoda.

CHAMELEON, any of about 80 different Old World lizards with independently roving eyes, a long tongue that can be shot out to capture insect prey, grasping feet, and a curled, prehensile tail. Half of the species are confined to the island of Madagascar, the rest living in Africa south of the Sahara, except one (*Chameleo chamaeleon*) found from Spain across North Africa to Asia Minor.

Chameleon is a Greek word meaning lion-on-the-ground, that is, a low or dwarf lion. These animals are famous for changing their color either in accordance with the environment or when disturbed. The change is due to the presence of clear or pigment-bearing contractile cells placed at various depths in the skin, their contractions and dilations being under the influence of the nervous system.

Chameleons can fast for weeks. When disturbed they inflate themselves with air. These habits gave rise to the fable that they live on air. In general they are slow-moving and completely harmless.

Unrelated lizards show less spectacular but still surprising changes of color, and the name chameleon has been applied also to them, especially the American chameleon (*Anolis carolinensis*) of the iguana family in the southeastern states. Order Sauria, family Chamaeleonidae.

CHAMOIS, a goatlike cud-chewing mammal closely allied to antelopes, native to high, inaccessible mountains in Europe and western Asia. A chamois stands 25 to 30 inches high at the shoulders, and wears horns 6 or 7 inches long, which are round, almost smooth, perpendicular and straight until near the tip, where they suddenly terminate in a hook directed backward and downward.

The hair is brown in winter, fawn in summer, and grayish in spring. The head is pale yellow, and a black band from the nose to the ears surrounds the eyes. The tail is black.

Its agility, the nature of its haunts, and its powers of smell render the pursuit of the chamois an exceedingly difficult and hazardous occupation. It can jump 20 feet and is proverbially sure-footed. A very soft yellow leather for linings and cleaning cloths is made from chamois skin and from inferior and less expensive hides. Order Artiodactyla, family Bovidae, specifically *Rupicapra rupicapra*.

CHEETAH, or hunting leopard, a large catlike mammal with nonretractable claws, and circular pupils in the eyes. It is native to the high plains and savannas of Africa and Iran. Longer legged than true cats, cheetahs race after antelopes and other prey; the world's fastest runners, they often attain a speed of 60 miles an hour.

Generally, however, a cheetah watches a herd of antelopes for an hour or more to select the weakest member as prey. During this time, the cheetah remains almost invisible because its sand-colored short fur and pattern of small black spots let it blend with its surroundings.

Unlike other cats, a cheetah cannot retract its claws. It growls, snarls, spits, mews, and makes a birdlike chirp, but can neither roar like a lion nor purr like a house cat. In Africa, cheetahs are often kept as pets. Order Carnivora, family Felidae, specifically *Acinonyx jubatus*.

CHICKADEE, any of several small plump active songbirds named from the sound of its cheerful call, *chicka-dee-dee*. The common black-capped chickadee (*Parus atricapillus*) of Canada and the northern United States occurs also in Europe and Britain, where it is called the willow tit. Like the closely related titmice (singular, titmouse), chickadees eat many kinds of small insects, which make up about two-thirds of their diet, and various wild fruits. When offered suet, peanut butter, or sunflower seeds at a window feeder, chickadees become very tame.

All chickadees nest in small holes, such as in a decayed tree or branch,

and lay 5 to 8 eggs finely spotted with reddish brown. Order Passeriformes, family Paridae, members of genus *Parus*.

CHICKEN. See *Fowl*.

CHIMNEY SWIFT, a fast-flying North American bird related to hummingbirds. It spends most of its life in the air and is often mistaken for a swallow. Its slender, cigar-shaped body is supported by narrow curved wings that seem very far forward because the beak is so short. The mouth is wide, and the bird uses it to catch insects and to drink while flying.

Originally, chimney swifts roosted for the night and built their nests in hollow trees and caves. With the arrival of Europeans in Canada and the United States, they changed to using chimneys and wells that are open.

The nests are of twigs, collected on the wing, held in place by a gluelike saliva. The birds cling with sharp claws, propping themselves up with their short stiff tail feathers. At the approach of cold weather, they migrate to a remote area of Peru.

Order Micropodiformes, family Micropodidae, specifically *Chaetura pelagica*.

CHIMPANZEE, a great ape with large conspicuous ears and short forearms, native to west and central Africa. A full-grown chimpanzee is almost 5 feet tall and weighs up to 150 pounds. It is not so large or powerful as a gorilla. The chimpanzee walks erect better than most apes, but not so well as the gorilla; when walking on all fours the feet are flat, whereas the fingers touch the ground with the knuckles.

The chimpanzee is more a tree-dweller than the gorilla. It feeds on fruits, often robs the gardens of the natives, and constructs a sort of nest among the branches of the trees. Order Primates, family Pongidae, specifically *Pan troglodytes*.

CHINCH BUG, a sucking insect less than ¼ inch long, with a black or dark gray body and white wings, if mature. Chinch bugs suck so much juice from corn and grain crop roots that they annually destroy thousands of dollars worth of crops. The adults seek protection near the roots and spend the winter under the soil. They emerge in the spring and lay eggs, which hatch in about 2 weeks.

When the young hatch, they start to feed at once. In about 3 months the adult stage is reached, and the insects lay eggs for a second brood. The young are yellow at first, then red, and later black. They are killed by heavy rains but survive from one year to the next in dry places. Order Heteroptera, family Lygaeidae, specifically *Blissus leucopterus*.

CHINCHILLA, a small South American rodent, strongly resembling a ground squirrel. The chinchillas inhabit the Andes of Chile and Bolivia, where they live gregariously in deep burrows, feeding on roots. They are more

than 10 inches long and are highly prized and hunted for their lustrous gray pelts, which can be made into costly garments. An attempt has been made to domesticate them on fur farms in the United States. Order Rodentia, family Chinchillidae, specifically *Chinchilla laniger*.

CHIPMUNK, any of about 18 different kinds of small ground squirrels marked above with 5 lengthwise black or dark brown stripes separated by 4 paler stripes. One (*Tamias striatus*) inhabits most of the eastern United States and southeastern Canada. Another, the Siberian chipmunk (*Eutamias sibiricus*), is familiar from northern Japan westward through the northern Soviet Union.

The 16 others of this genus are denizens of forests and brushlands in western North America. Each chipmunk generally lives in a burrow, which it enlarges at intervals to make storage rooms for nuts, acorns, and seeds of many kinds. Four to 6 young are born in the burrow in early spring. Order Rodentia, family Sciuridae.

CICADA, any of about 1,500 different kinds of sucking insects with a short, heavy body and, when adult, 2 pairs of strong wings, the first pair much larger than the second. At rest, the wings are held tentlike over the body. Every continent and most large islands have cicadas; about 75 kinds are found in the United States, and 1 in Britain.

The call is among the most characteristic sounds of hot summer days in temperate zones, and a daily feature of the tropics. These loud sounds are produced by male cicadas, by means of a special pair of drumlike organs with resonators about midway back in the body. Females are attracted to the source of the sound and, after mating, lay eggs in slits cut into the bark of twigs on trees by means of a sawlike organ below the tip of the abdomen.

When the young cicadas hatch, they drop to the ground and spend the next 3 to 17 years (depending on the species) feeding on the sap from underground roots of trees and shrubs. Eventually the fully grown young

AMERICAN MUSEUM OF NATURAL HISTORY
CHIMPANZEE

cicadas climb to the soil surface, walk up a tree trunk or other support, and shed their skins to emerge as winged adults. Order Homoptera, family Cicadidae.

CIVET CAT, any of about 21 different kinds of weasel-like mammals related to mongooses, with a slender body and long tail, and a head suggesting that of a cat, with short rounded ears and sharp muzzle. The various kinds are widespread in the Old World, but one (the African civet, *Civettictis civetta*) from Africa south of the Sudan and the great deserts is best known for the musky substance it secretes in a sac near the anus. This substance, called civet, is used in making perfumes. Probably the civet cat uses the substance for marking out its territorial boundaries. The animal feeds on reptiles, small mammals, birds' eggs, and large insects. Order Carnivora, family Viverridae, several different genera.

CLAM, any of about 11,000 different kinds of bivalve mollusks, known in British countries simply as bivalves. Mostly they live on sandy or muddy bottoms, in both salt and fresh water, all over the world. They create a current of water containing oxygen and microscopic food particles, which enters the gaping shell at one opening, is used for respiration and feeding, and then passes out carrying wastes through a second opening.

In the United States, an important industry has grown up around freshwater clams (species of genera *Lampsilis*, *Margaritana*, and *Unio*), from whose hard shells are manufactured such articles as buttons and knife handles. Many marine clams are of considerable economic importance, chiefly for food.

Along the U.S. Atlantic coast, a favorite is the Venus clam (or little neck, or quahog, *Mercenaria mercenaria*), which is rounded and thick shelled, a source of wampum, which formerly was used as money among Indians; another is the soft-shelled or sand clam (*Mya arenaria*), oval in shape, about 2½ inches long, with shells that are almost paper thin. The soft-shell has been introduced on the Pacific coast, and now rivals in popularity the native Pismo clam (*Tivela stultorum*).

Other clams include the giant bear's-paw clam (*Tridacna*) of coral reefs in the South Pacific, which is the largest shelled mollusk; and the edible cockle (*Cardium*) of British and European shore waters, which provides food for man and bait for fish; a cockle can jump several inches by using its long powerful foot. Class Pelecypoda, various orders.

COBRA, any of several different venomous snakes of the Old World, with fixed fangs at the front of the mouth and a more or less distensible neck region. Best known is the Oriental common cobra (*Naja naja*), which ranges throughout Africa and tropical Asia; it can spread its "hood" in the neck region more widely than any other cobra. It has been used extensively by snake charmers during the

day largely because at that time it strikes (if at all) with its mouth shut, and hence does not bite.

The king cobra (*Naja Ophiophagus hannah*), native to Asia from India to the Philippines, attains a length of 12 feet and often stands its ground when disturbed; it eats other snakes as well as lizards, small mammals, and birds. South Africa has spitting cobras (of genus *Hemachatus*), which can discharge their venom with astonishing accuracy to a distance of 6 to 10 feet, apparently aiming for the eyes of prey or of people, and causing temporary blindness.

The asp of Egypt is a small deadly cobra (*Naje haje*), whose likeness is the dominant part of the headdresses for ancient Egyptian royalty. Order Serpentes, family Elapidae.

COCKATOO. See *Parrot*.

COCKLE. See *Clam*.

COCKROACH, any of a large number of different flat-bodied insects with long threadlike feelers (antennae), biting jaws, long spiny legs used in running rapidly, and usually a pair of short, sensitive projections from near the hind end of the body. Winged adults have two pairs of thin membranous wings, held flat over the back at rest.

Primarily tropical insects, they occur also in temperate woodlands. A few have adopted a life in human dwellings, stores, and factories where they can find food of many kinds. They require moderate or high humidity and are rare in very dry situations. Household pests include the 1-inch European cockroach (*Blatella germanica*), the 2-inch Oriental cockroach (*Blatta orientalis*), and the 3-inch American cockroach (*Periplaneta americana*). Order Orthoptera, family Blattidae.

COD, a marine bony fish with a projecting lower jaw, a barbel on the chin, a ductless air bladder, and soft-rayed fins. Formerly abundant in cold waters near shore on both sides of the North Atlantic Ocean, cod are still found in great numbers off the coast of Newfoundland.

The back of the cod is olive-green with darker spots, and the belly is white. At 4 years of age, the fish is about 2 feet long; at 5 years, it begins to mate and reproduce, a female laying as many as 9 million eggs.

The average length of cod caught for commerce is about 3 feet. Until about 1950, large quantities of oil were extracted from cod livers for medical use, because of the rich supply there of vitamins A and D. Now artificial vitamins can be made more cheaply and reliably.

Closely related to the cod (*Gadus callarias*) is the whiting (*G. merlangus*), a silvery fish with a black mark on the base of its pectoral fin but with no barbel on the chin. It is harvested from Norway to the Mediterranean and in Atlantic waters from Maine to Florida. Also lacking the barbel is the North Atlantic pollack (*G. pollachius*), which is greenish and has a jutting lower jaw. The coalfish (*G. virens*) is blackish and has a bar-

AMERICAN MUSEUM OF NATURAL HISTORY
COYOTE

bel but otherwise resembles the pollack.

A freshwater member of the cod family is the burbot (*Lota lota*), a slender fish of cold deep water found in the Great Lakes in North America, in Europe from the Arctic to mountain lakes in Italy, and in the far north of Asia. Order Anacanthini, family Gadidae.

CONCH, any of the large marine snails with heavy shells, which are powerful predators, seizing and eating the flesh of smaller snails, oysters and other bivalves, and sea urchins. Among the largest are the king conch (*Strombus gigas*) and the queen conch or cameo shell (*Cassis cameo*) of the Gulf of Mexico and warm waters of the Atlantic and Caribbean. A five-pound animal of this kind may have a shell 12 inches long.

The shells of the queen conch are shipped to Europe, particularly Italy, as the material from which cameo jewelry is carved. The trumpet shell (*Charonia tritonis*) is similar but more slender, with a higher spire and a long taper at the opposite end; it is sometimes made into a trumpet or shown as the musical instrument of the Greek sea demigods called Tritons. Class Gastropoda, order Prosobranchiata.

CONDOR. See *Vulture*.

CONE SHELL, any of a large number of different sea snails with smoothly conical chinalike shells. The spire of the shell is a short cone, and the opening is narrow. Cone shells live as vigorous predators in coastal waters of the tropics and the temperate zones, and are particularly numerous among the coral reefs of the South Pacific.

One of the most valued shells in the world is that of the fabulous glory-of-the-sea cone (*Conus gloria maris*) of the South Pacific, which combines beauty with extreme rarity. A collector of living cones must handle a snail with great care because it can jump part way out of its shell and drive into a person's hand a venomous organ, which normally is used to subdue fishes and other prey. A cone is very alert, watching with two eyes on long stalks for prey to come within reach. Order Prosobranchiata, family Conidae, various species of genus *Conus*.

CONY (known also as coney, cunny, and cunney), an ancient European name for a rabbit, a rabbitlike animal, or rabbit fur. The European rabbit (*Oryctolagus cuniculus*) has a diminutive, Latinized form of the word as its species name. The "coney" of the Bible (Leviticus 11:5) was probably the rabbit-sized hyrax or dassie (*Heterohyrax syriacus*) of Asia Minor and Africa, which are hoofed animals of order Hyracoidea, although they do not chew a cud and do not have a cloven hoof.

The rock cony or pika of northern Asia and the western mountains in North America (*Ochotona* species), which has no visible tail, and ears about as wide as they are high, is a member of the same order (Lagomorpha) as rabbits, but does not hop. The word is also used by fishermen for the burbot (*Lota* species), a codlike fish, and for a reef fish, the red hind (*Petrometopon cruentatus*) of the West Indies.

COOT, any of 10 different plump, short-tailed wading birds about 1½ feet long, whose individual toes have webbing on each side instead of between adjacent toes. Seven of the species are South American. Of the remaining 3, one breeds in southern Europe and winters in Africa south of the great deserts, another nests across Eurasia from Japan to the British Isles, and the third is found from southern Canada to northern South America.

All are expert swimmers and divers, inhabiting ponds and open water in marshes and swamps where they can find vegetable food. They pile up masses of vegetation in the water as the base for a nest. Coots are poor food, unsuspicious, and easily shot. This has led to the expressions "silly coot" or "queer as a coot" applied to persons who appear simple. Order Gruiformes, family Rallidae, members of genus *Fulica*.

COPPERHEAD. See *Pit Viper*.

COQUINA, or pompano shell, or butterfly shell, or variable wedge shell, a small marine bivalve 1 inch or less in length, living in sandy beaches from North Carolina to Florida and Texas. Rays of color mark the shell, diverging from the hinge region, often crossed by eccentric bands of the same or a different hue, in pink, yellow, green, blue, or lavender.

People collect them wholesale by scooping up the sand just below the edge of the tide, and passing it through a sieve. The coquinas are then cooked in their shells to make coquina soup. Other persons gather particularly colorful shells in pairs for use in jewelry. Order Teleodesmacea, family Donacidae, specifically *Donax variabilis*.

CORAL, any of a large number of lime-secreting, colonial marine coelenterates, or the limy external skeleton they secrete. Coral animals are mostly tropical. When the animals die, their skeletons remain so abundant and massive as to build up into the form of coral reefs and islands. The precious coral of the Mediterranean and of Japan is very solid and takes a high polish. Class Anthozoa.

CORMORANT, or shag, any of about 30 different large water birds which resemble geese when flying and loons while swimming. They are found all over the world, seldom out of sight of land, chiefly along coasts, inland lakes, and rivers. They dive and swim underwater in pursuit of fish, or to escape. Most kinds nest on cliffs and offshore islands in great colonies.

Most famous are the guanay birds (the white-breasted Peruvian cormorant, *Phalacrocorax bougainvillei*) off the Pacific coast of South America, whose nest areas provide guano as agricultural fertilizer. In China and Japan, trained cormorants are used for fishing, a brass ring being placed around their necks to prevent them from swallowing the fish.

Closely related are the 4 different kinds of snakebirds (*Anhinga* species) in which the beak is straight and sharp, not hooked at the tip. They are the original spear fishermen, impaling the fish or frog they catch on the closed beak, then tossing the victim into the air and catching it in the opened mouth. Both snakebirds and cormorants lack the usual waterproofing on their feathers, and must hold out their wings to dry after emerging from water. Order Pelecaniformes, families Phalacrocoracidae and Anhingidae.

CORNBORER, or corn-ear worm, the caterpillar of a moth native to Europe and now an introduced pest in America. It eats into the corn and makes it unsalable. Fermentation of the cornstalks in silos kills the overwintering insect; otherwise it lives through the winter in the plant, and emerges to reproduce the following summer. Order Lepidoptera, family Pyralidae, specifically *Pyrausta nubilalis*.

COTTONMOUTH. See *Pit Viper*.

COUGAR. See *Cat*.

COW. See *Cattle*.

COWBIRD, any of about 6 different kinds of dark-colored birds of medium size, which associate commonly with buffalo and cattle, eating insects disturbed by the grazing mammals. Most cowbirds lay their eggs in the nests of other birds (more than 90 species) and leave them there to be hatched and raised by the foster parents. Order Passeriformes, family Icteridae, chiefly members of genera *Molothrus* and *Tangavius*.

COWRIE, any of a large number of different sea snails with an egg-shaped shell, whose narrow aperture extends almost the full length. Through this opening, the animal puts out its foot and two short feelers, and two extensive folds of its soft mantle then expand, completely covering the shell.

Most cowries are tropical, living in shallow water. Each kind has a distinctive color pattern on its glossy shell, hence a collection of different cowries is particularly attractive. One of the smaller kinds in the South Pacific (*Cypraea moneta*) has been used for centuries as a kind of money by the inhabitants. Order Pectinibranchiata, family Cypraeidae, members of genus *Cypraea*.

COYOTE, a medium-sized wolflike mammal of the western plains in North America. It eats chiefly rabbits, ground squirrels, and other small mammals, but occasionally attacks domestic sheep, particularly when lambs are being born or are very young and helpless. Order Carnivora, family Canidae, specifically *Canis latrans*.

CRAB, any of several hundred different crustaceans that spend their larval stages in the sea and then transform to possess 5 pairs of legs and a small abdomen folded under the anterior part of the body (the cephalothorax). The vast majority are marine, but a few come out on land after transforming and, as land crabs, return to the water only in breeding season to lay their eggs in the sea.

The edible blue crab (*Callinectes sapidus*) of the Atlantic coast of America south of Cape Cod is often kept captive until it sheds its hard outer covering, molting to grow larger. It is then a "soft-shell crab" for a few hours, and much easier to open for the table.

A similar crab of the Pacific coast is *Cancer magister*, with rounded sides to the cephalothorax instead of extended sharp spines there. Among land crabs, those with a huge pincer on one side in the male sex are called fiddlers (*Uca* species); at low tide they emerge from their burrows in the beach and search for small particles of food, often in armies of several thousand 1-inch individuals.

Hermit crabs differ in having a soft abdomen, which they conceal in the empty shell of a snail, carrying this shelter around with them wherever they go. A giant hermit crab (*Birgus latro*) of tropical islands in the South Pacific grows larger than any snail shell it can find; thereupon its abdomen becomes hardened, and the crab begins climbing coconut trees to feed on the fruit. Some of these coconut crabs weigh 20 pounds. Order Decapoda, several families and many different genera. See also *Horseshoe Crab*.

CRANE, any of 14 different long-legged birds that fly with the neck extended, not curved over the back in an *S* as among herons, and that stand on 3 toes on each foot because the fourth toe is raised well above the ground; herons have all 4 toes at the same level. The windpipe (trachea) of a crane is extensively convoluted, giving the voice resonance and letting the birds' calls be heard for great distances.

MAINE DEPARTMENT OF ECONOMIC DEVELOPMENT
DEER

Cranes are native to all continents and major islands except South America, Malaya, New Zealand, and the Pacific Islands. They frequent large plains and marshes, where they can find insects, frogs, worms, mollusks, reptiles, fishes, and even small mammals. Cranes everywhere are becoming scarce. Those of North America are the rare whooping crane (*Grus americana*) of Great Slave Lake region, which winters in Texas, and the sandhill crane (*G. canadensis*) of northwestern and southeastern prairie country.

The European crane (*G. grus*) breeds in northern Europe and Siberia, but migrates south in winter, far into Africa. Order Gruiformes, family Gruidae.

CRAYFISH, or crawfish, a freshwater crustacean related to and resembling the North Atlantic lobster, but smaller (3 to 6 inches in length) and with claws proportionately smaller. The second syllable of the name was not originally fish, as the word is derived from French écrevisse and is like our word crevice—possibly from the burrows it digs. Originally applied to only one kind in Europe (*Astacus fluviatilis*), the name now refers to all fresh-water relatives in America. Crayfishes in the southern United States are considered a table delicacy. Their extensive burrowing causes considerable damage to levees and dams. Blind crayfishes are found in the river of Mammoth Cave, in Kentucky. Order Decapoda, family Astacidae.

CRICKET, any of more than 900 different insects related to grasshoppers, with long threadlike feelers (antennae) and cylindrical bodies; those adults that have wings hold the fore pair flat over the back, with the sides turned down sharply. Females with long ovipositors seem to have thick needles projecting from the rear of their bodies; the ovipositors are never

bladelike, as in the longhorned grasshoppers.

Only adult males produce the familiar chirping sounds, by rubbing together the bases of their forewings. Crickets are found all over the world, generally hiding during the day but emerging at night to feed on decaying plant material. The American black cricket (*Gryllus assimilis*) occasionally enters houses in cold weather. The European kind (*G. domesticus*) is the "cricket-on-the-hearth," which prefers living indoors on crumbs, and hiding in little chinks in the masonry of fireplaces.

Tree crickets (*Oecanthus* species) are slender, pale green, and stand on bushes while trilling continuously. Mole crickets (species of genus *Gryllotalpa*) have the front legs adapted for burrowing in soft soil. Cave crickets, known also as camel crickets because of their humped backs, are wingless members of a different family (Tettigoniidae), and remain permanently wingless; often they are found under bark or in cellars. Order Orthoptera, family Gryllidae.

CROCODILE, any of about 13 different formidable lizardlike reptiles whose long jaws gape widely and display strong teeth in bony sockets. They include the largest of living reptiles, and are found in tropical and subtropical shore waters and rivers in both hemispheres. They prepare nests of sticks and mud on shore, and guard their eggs until the young hatch.

Little crocodiles feed on insects and other small animals, but gradually change, as they grow, to larger food, often gorging on carcasses in a state of putrefaction. The nostrils at the end of the snout can be closed to prevent ingress of water.

Often a crocodile floats just below the surface, with only its prominent eyes and nostrils protruding into air. The long compressed tail forms a strong swimming organ. The legs are short, with 5 toes on the front pair and 4 on the hind, which are somewhat webbed. The skin is armored with square bony plates.

Best known is the Nile crocodile (*Crocodilus niloticus*), which was worshiped and embalmed by the ancient Egyptians. Today it has been exterminated from the Nile except in the Sudan and Uganda, but it is present in other rivers, such as the Congo and the Zambezi, and in Madagascar. The longest measured specimen was 16 feet; presumably it was old. The saltwater crocodile (*C. porosus*) of Indian, Malayan, East Indian, and north Australian coasts, is more dangerous and generally larger, the biggest known being 20 feet long. It swims from island to island, and often becomes a man-eater. Like other adult crocodiles, it seizes large prey in shallow water and then rolls over and over to subdue it, often drowning it in the process.

The American crocodile (*C. acutus*) of southern Florida, the West Indies, and northern South America often enters salt water. It and the long-snouted Orinoco crocodile (*C. intermedius*) have been measured at 23

feet long, which is the maximum that can be regarded as authentic for any of these animals.

The closest relatives of crocodiles (family Crocodilidae) are the alligators and caymans (family Alligatoridae) and gavials (family Gavialidae), all of which have cavities or pits in the upper jaw into which the long canine teeth of the lower jaw fit. Alligators and caymans have broadly rounded snouts, whereas the snout of a crocodile is pointed, and that of a gavial is very long, narrow, and ends in a soft tip that can be expanded at will. Alligators have a relatively soft skin, easily distinguished by touch from the skin of caymans, which have hard bony plates below the surface.

Of the two kinds of alligators, the larger is the now scarce American species (*Alligator mississippiensis*), which has been nearly exterminated for its hides, and a Chinese representative (*A. sinensis*). Of the 5 kinds of caymans, all inhabit swamps of northern South America and Central America. The sole species of gavial (*Gavialis gangeticus*) is a fish-eater of Indian rivers. Order Crocodilia.

CROW, any of about 10 different large perching birds about 20 inches long, with mostly black feathers and beaks. They are distributed throughout the world. The common North American crow (*Corvus brachyrhynchos*) is remarkable for its gregarious and predatory habits, as well as for its intelligence and cunning.

Crows pair in March; the old repair their nests, the young frame new ones; but they are such thieves that while the one is fetching materials the other must keep watch to prevent the rising fabric from being plundered by crow neighbors. As soon as the nest is finished and five bluish-green eggs with dark blotches are laid, the male starts to provide for his mate; he continues this during the period of incubation.

Crows frequent the same rookeries for years, but allow no intruders into their community. They feed chiefly on worms and the larvae of insects, consequently during outbreaks of insects the crows are beneficial; but they also eat grain and seeds and are thus injurious to the farmer. Chiefly because they destroy beneficial wild birds and their eggs, crows are often regarded as enemies of mankind.

The raven (*Corvus corax*) is the largest of perching birds and the most widespread of crows in the Northern Hemisphere. Because they destroy so many different crops, they have been driven out of the whole of the United States except the western region.

The fish crow (*C. ossifragus*) frequents the Atlantic and Gulf coasts of the United States. The carrion crow (*C. corone*) and the hooded crow (*C. cornix*) are closely related European birds. Most gregarious are the somewhat smaller rooks (*C. frugilegus*), which lose most of the feathers on the face as they mature. Well-populated nest sites in Britain and northern Europe have been used continuously for centuries. Order Passeriformes, family Corvidae, members of genus *Corvus*.

CUCKOO, any of about 200 different kinds of slender-bodied, long-tailed birds with downcurved beaks and pointed wings. They are widely distributed on land, and are of diverse habits. Literary references are generally to the common Eurasian and African cuckoo (*Cuculus canorus*) which has the familiar call of a striking cuckoo-clock. Like many other cuckoos, it is a parasite, laying its eggs in the nests of other birds.

Among the 40 kinds of cuckoos in the New World, the most familiar are the black-billed (*Coccyzygus erythrophthalmus*) and yellow-billed (*C. americanus*) cuckoos, which are shy, inconspicuous, about 1 foot long, and grayish-brown above, white below. They build their own nests, look after their own young, and make guttural, unmusical calls that have earned them the name of "rain crows," because some farmers claim that the sound generally precedes a rain. The cuckoos of both the Old and the New World are regarded as helpful to farmers, because they consume large numbers of caterpillars and other crop-damaging insects.

Ten of the 13 different ground cuckoos are American birds, the others living in Malaya and nearby Southeast Asia. One is the roadrunner bird, or chaparral cock (*Geococcyx californianus*), of the southwestern deserts in the United States and Mexico, where it runs about in search of lizards and snakes to eat.

Also related are the most sociable of the cuckoos, the three different coal-black anis (*Crotophaga* species) of the American Tropics, which make communal nests. Even immature anis appear to help in incubation and feeding of nestlings. Order Cuculiformes, family Cuculidae.

CUTTLEFISH, a squidlike cephalopod mollusk with 10 arms around the mouth and an enclosed, limy shell called a cuttlebone. Cuttlefishes are abundant in the Indian Ocean, and common in the Mediterranean Sea. They prey on fishes and grow to a length of 18 inches. Many persons in southern Europe eat cooked cuttlefish or use pieces for fish bait. When disturbed, a cuttlefish can discharge a black ink from an inkbag, clouding the water around its body. The pigment sepia originally was obtained from this source. Order Dibranchiata, specifically *Sepia officinalis*.

DADDY LONGLEGS. See *Harvestman*.

DAMSELFLY, any of a large number of extremely slender adult insects with four slender membranous wings, ordinarily folded together at rest above the long abdomen, while the insect clings to some support, such as a plant stem. Damselflies are found near freshwater on most continents and large islands. Their flight is weak, yet rapid enough to capture some other small insects, such as plant lice and midges.

Damselflies lay their eggs under the surface film of ponds and streams. When full grown, each immature damselfly (called a naiad) creeps up a stem or a rock out of the water and then transforms into the adult. Order Odonata, suborder Zygoptera, several families and genera.

DEER, any of more than 50 different kinds of long-legged, cud-chewing mammals with long necks, small heads carried high, large ears, and large prominent eyes. Usually the male produces solid, branching antlers that fall off annually and are replaced.

Deer are native to the Northern Hemisphere and as far south in South America as Uruguay, in Africa to the great deserts, and in Asia to the East Indies. They have been introduced in New Guinea, Australia, New Zealand, Hawaii, and reintroduced into the British Isles, where they had been exterminated.

Largest of existing deer is the American moose (*Alces americanus*), which is very similar to the smaller European animal (*Alces alces*) called an elk. Both have broad blades with tines as antlers, and inhabit spruce bogs.

The large wapiti or American elk (*Cervus canadensis*) and the smaller European red deer (*C. elaphus*) are similar animals with heavy antlers and many upturned tines on mature bulls. Eastern North America is the home of the white-tailed or Virginia deer (*Odocoileus virginianus*), which has as western counterparts the large-eared mule deer (*O. hemionus*) in the Rocky Mountain states, and the blacktail (*O. columbianus*) near the Pacific coast.

The Old World has small roe deer (*Capreolus capreolus*), which can bark like dogs, and fallow deer (*Dama dama*), which retain their juvenile pattern of pale spots for life. The only deer in which both sexes wear antlers are the reindeer (*Rangifer tarandus*) of the Eurasian Arctic, where it is domesticated and herded by nomads, and the caribou (*R. caribou*) of the Far North in Canada and Alaska, which form herds that wander continually. Order Artiodactyla, family Cervidae.

DINGO. See *Dog*.

DOBSONFLY, a North American insect, of which the larval stage is an aquatic predator known as a hellgrammite. The eggs are laid at the edge of a stream or river, which the larvae enter as soon as they hatch. They need 3 years to attain full size, at which time the mature larvae creep out of the water and pupate among fallen leaves or in the upper levels of the soil, there transforming into the winged adult.

The dobsonfly's wings are gray, with many veins, and spread to as much as 6 inches, making this the largest member of the order Neuroptera in the United States and Canada. The male has enormously extended jaws, held crossed in front of the head. The female has much smaller and more powerful jaws, similar to those of the larva.

Fishermen collect hellgrammites as a favorite bait for trout and other fishes of running water. Order Neuroptera, family Corydalidae, specifically *Corydalis cornuta*.

DOG, any of about 12 different kinds of wolflike mammals popularly regarded as distinct from wolves, jackals, and foxes. The domesticated dog (*Canis familiaris*) is presumed to have been derived from tamed wolves, and now is remarkable for the almost infinite variety in size, shape, color, and hair.

A domestic dog will live on cooked vegetables, but prefers meat. To drink, it laps with its tongue. It never perspires, but loses heat through its moist nose and by panting with its dripping tongue hanging from the mouth. The female (bitch) goes with young 63 days, and usually has 6 to 8 puppies in a litter. Blind at birth, they do not acquire sight until the tenth day. A dog is full grown at the end of its second year, is old at 15, and seldom lives beyond 20 years.

The main types of domestic dogs are: Eskimo, sheep dogs, greyhounds, mastiffs, terriers, hounds, spaniels, and poodles. In Australia, the dingo (*C. dingo*), which has yellowish brown fur, is semiwild. It was probably introduced in prehistoric times by the aboriginal people. Asia has a single kind of raccoon dog (*Nyctereutes procyonoides*), which is valued for its meat and fur but has become rare in Japan and adjacent parts of the mainland, and a red dog (or Indian dhole, *Cuon alpinus*) which associates into hunting packs in Java, Sumatra, Malaya, India, and parts of east Asia far into Siberia. Similar habits are shown by the small African hunting dogs (*Lycaon pictus*), which hunt game animals systematically over most of the continent south of the great deserts.

South America has bush dogs (*Speothos venaticus*) on the savanna areas of Paraguay northward to the Guianas and Panama, and small-eared dogs (*Atelocynus microtis*) in tropical forest areas of the Amazon basin, but both are short-legged, nocturnal, secretive animals about which little is known. Order Carnivora, family Canidae.

DOGFISH, any of several different small sharks that swim in schools along seacoasts, often destroying fish that have been caught in nets and tearing the nets as well. Dogfish rarely grow longer than 5 feet, or heavier than 30 pounds. They seldom attack bathers along beaches. But the spiny dogfish (*Squalus acanthias*) of North Atlantic coasts often severely wounds fishermen who are freeing dogfishes from tangled nets.

This dogfish has a strong sharp spine with a venom gland at the leading edge of each of its two dorsal fins, and while struggling to escape, may drive these spines into a human limb. Order Selachii, several families.

DOLPHIN, any of about 41 different kinds of small sea mammals with pointed noses, many teeth, streamlined bodies, flippers as forelimbs, a distinct fleshy dorsal fin, and transverse tail fin, or flukes, whose total length does not exceed 13 feet. They are found in all oceans.

Frequently dolphins accompany ships, displaying by leaping singly or in groups, coming out of the water in a graceful arc and plunging in again with scarcely a splash. Sometimes they ride the bow wave of a ship for hours at a time. Best known is the bottle-nosed dolphin (*Tursiops truncatus*) of the eastern coast of North America, which feeds on a variety of fishes and squids.

Formerly caught commercially as a source of fine oil for clocks and chronometers, they are now being studied in detail to discover how they navigate, echolocate food and obstacles underwater, and communicate with one another. Order Cetacea, family Delphinidae.

DONKEY. See *Ass*.

DOVE. See *Pigeon*.

DRAGONFLY, any of nearly 4,000 different strong-flying predacious insects with biting mouthparts, prominent compound eyes, four similar membranous wings with many crossveins, and a slender abdomen. They are found near freshwater all over the world. They lay their eggs in water where the young hatch and live as predators. The fully grown young crawl up the stem of an aquatic plant and transform into the adult dragonfly.

The adults destroy mosquitoes and other small insects. Some of the larger kinds are reputed able to fly at a speed of about 60 miles an hour. Popularly called "devil's darning needles" and thought to be dangerous, they are in fact harmless. Order Odonata, suborder Anisoptera.

DROMEDARY. See *Camel*.

DUCK, any of about 115 kinds of web-footed, swimming birds related to geese and swans, but of smaller size and with necks shorter than the body. Most gooselike are the whistling or tree ducks, of Central America and the Southern Hemisphere, of which one from Mexico and Brazil called the Muscovy duck (*Cairina moschata*) has been domesticated as the largest of barnyard ducks.

Some of the shelducks, native to the Old World, are large enough to be called geese; they include the Egyptian goose (*Alopochen aegyptica*) of the Nile valley and Africa south of the great deserts. Most familiar are the smaller ducks of rivers and ponds, which tip their bodies tail up to reach food on the bottom; they include the mallard duck (*Anas platyrhynchus*) of northern North America and Eurasia, from which the all-white peking duck (*A. platyrhynchus*) became a favorite domestic breed. The tipping or dipping ducks are often called "true ducks," or freshwater ducks; they include also black ducks, pintails, shovelers, widgeons, and various kinds of teal.

The larger bay ducks, which include the canvasback and scaup ducks, dive for their food. The perching ducks, such as the handsome wood duck of North America and the decorative mandarin duck of Japan and eastern Asia, generally nest in a hollow tree or on a horizontal limb high above the water. The eider ducks nest in communities along arctic and sub-arctic rocky coasts, covering their eggs and young in the nest with a heavy layer of down feathers that have been pulled from the mother's winter coat.

The sea ducks, which include the mergansers, scoters, and goldeneyes, are fish eaters whose meat is generally considered inedible. Now extinct, the Labrador duck was formerly abundant along shores of the North Atlantic Ocean.

Most ducks and geese are expert fliers and highly migratory. But the stiff-tailed ducks, such as the ruddy duck (*Oxyura jamaicensis*), tend to be labored in flight, to be residents, and nonmigratory. Yet they swim and dive superbly and perform distinctive courtship displays with the tail stiffly upright, moving the head quickly up and down. Order Anseriformes, family Anatidae.

DUCKBILL, or platypus ("broad foot"), an Australian web-footed mammal whose toothless jaws have the form of a beak, like that of a duck. This animal lives in streams, feeding on worms and insects from the mud at the bottom. At maturity, a duckbill is about 1 foot long. The male has a horny spur on each heel, connected to a poison gland. The female lays eggs with a soft shell in a burrow dug from a stream bank, and takes the young that hatch out into a pouch. She has no nipples on her mammary glands, but the young lap the milk as it oozes out onto her fur. Order Monotremata, specifically *Ornithorhynchus anatinus*.

EAGLE, any of 27 different large birds of prey with broad rounded wings, feathers over most of the head and face, and well down on the feet almost to where the strong toes spread apart. Eagles fly and used to nest in most parts of the continents.

Largest and most widespread is the golden eagle (*Aquila chrysaetus*) of the Northern Hemisphere, which soars high above mountainous terrain, watching with sharp eyes for rabbits, marmots, woodchucks, ground squirrels, and other prey upon which to dive and snatch aloft. The spread of its wings is nearly 10 feet, although the length of the bird from beak to tail tip is only 33 inches. The eagle was the symbol of power of the Roman Empire, and it was trained like a falcon by Jirghiz Tatars to hunt antelope.

The emblem of the United States, the bald eagle (*Haliaeetus leucocephalus*, the "white head"), is actually a sea eagle, close relatives of which live in Africa, in Madagascar, in Malaya and the East Indies, the South Pacific islands, and in the northern regions from Siberia to Iceland and on to Greenland. Tropical jungles have their eagles in the powerful crested birds known as the harpy eagle (*Harpia harpyja*), which hunts for sloths and large parrots in southern Mexico, Central America, and south to the Argentine, and the monkey-eating eagle (*Pithecophagus jefferyi*) of the Philippines.

The harrier eagles, which specialize in catching reptiles, are native to Eurasia, Africa, and Madagascar; they include the splendid, short-tailed bataleur eagle (*Terathopius ecaudatus*) of African highlands. Almost all of these birds are in need of protection to keep them from becoming extinct. Order Falconiformes, family Accipitridae.

EARTHWORM, any burrowing segmented worm that swallows soil and digests out the organic matter before discharging the inert mineral particles as castings. These worms are found in practically all land areas of the world, with the exception of Madagascar and Antarctica.

Earthworms lack eyes and appendages, but are sensitive over their entire body surface and hold to the substratum by means of bristles under muscular control. They work through and loosen the soil, aiding the agriculturalist. In winter they burrow beneath the frost line.

Because they are used as bait by fishermen, earthworms are sometimes called angleworms. The common earthworms (usually *Allobophora foetida* or *Lumbricus terrestris*) are 3 to 5 inches long; in some tropical countries giant earthworms are 5 or more feet long. Class Oligochaeta, order Megadrili, family Lumbricidae.

EARWIG, any of about 1,100 different kinds of insects with biting mouthparts, a slender and somewhat flattened body, and a prominent pair of pincers at the posterior end. They live in temperate and tropical areas, subsisting chiefly on plant material, for which they scavenge at night. By day, earwigs hide among fallen leaves, under boards, in beach drift, or even in clothing that can provide shade. They use their pincers in self-defense, and to help adult earwigs in folding their transparent hind wings to fit under the opaque and horny forewings.

The European earwig (*Forficula auricularia*) has become established along both coasts of North America and in other parts of the world, where it often feeds on fruits, flowers, and garden plants. Females of the European and some other earwigs commonly guard their eggs and newly hatched young, which are called nymphs. Order Dermaptera.

EEL, any of about 350 different kinds of slender, bony fishes of snakelike form, the best known of which mature in brackish estuaries or fresh water but reproduce in the depths of the sea. The common eel of the North Atlantic coasts (*Anguilla anguilla*) is a valuable food fish 2 to 5 feet long. For breeding and egg laying they migrate from Europe and America to deep water near the Bahama Islands, where the spawning takes place.

The infant is a ¼-inch-long, ribbon-like creature so unlike the adult that it was long considered a different fish. When they are large enough, the young eels swim up and westward until they are carried along in the Gulf Stream. Young American eels leave to enter rivers along the coast. European eels remain longer in the Gulf Stream, until they can easily reach Europe's river mouths. Six to 12 years later these eels are mature,

PREHISTORIC ANIMALS

PHOTOGRAPHS FROM THE PRIMEVAL WORLD AT DISNEYLAND. ©WALT DISNEY PRODUCTIONS

FIN-BACKED EDAPHOSAURUS, a giant, plant-eating reptile, roamed through forests of exotic plants more than 300 million years ago.

TRIO OF ORNITHOMIMUSES, *left,* called "ostrich dinosaurs," around a drying water hole as the rain forests give way to desert lands.

GIANT PTERANODONS, *right,* flying lizards with leathery 25-foot wings and three-foot beaks, lived over 150 million years ago.

BIRDS

© WALT DISNEY PRODUCTIONS

YOUNG TOUCANS

© WALT DISNEY PRODUCTIONS

FRIGATE BIRDS

© WALT DISNEY PRODUCTIONS

SANGUE-DE-BOIS

© WALT DISNEY PRODUCTIONS

JANDAIA

B. A. LEERBERGER, JR.

PENGUINS

© WALT DISNEY PRODUCTIONS

RED-FOOTED BOOBY CHICK

© WALT DISNEY PRODUCTIONS

HARPY EAGLE

INSECTS

© WALT DISNEY PRODUCTIONS

TARANTULA

© WALT DISNEY PRODUCTIONS

WOLF SPIDER

© WALT DISNEY PRODUCTIONS

SCORPION

© WALT DISNEY PRODUCTIONS

HORNED BEETLE

RICHARD PARKER FROM NATIONAL AUDUBON SOCIETY

RED-BANDED LEAFHOPPER

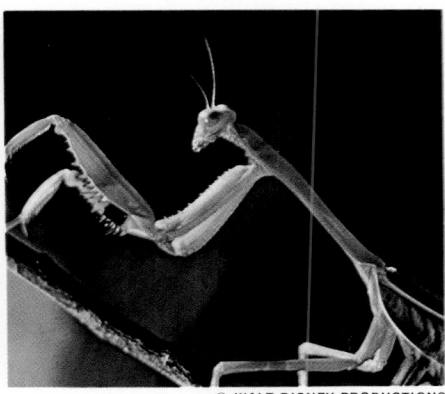

© WALT DISNEY PRODUCTIONS

PRAYING MANTIS

© WALT DISNEY PRODUCTIONS

BEE AT FLOWER

DENNIS BROKAW FROM NATIONAL AUDUBON SOCIETY

GRASSHOPPER ON THISTLE

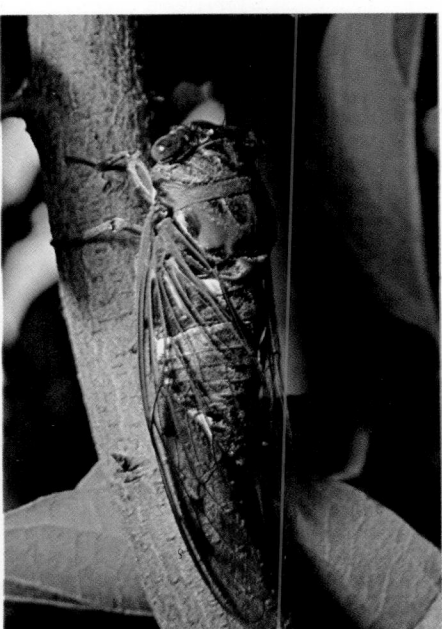

RICHARD PARKER FROM NATIONAL AUDUBON SOCIETY

CICADA

PHOTOS © WALT DISNEY PRODUCTIONS

JAGUAR

RHINOCEROSES

KOALA

BEARS

MAMMALS

BIGHORN MOUNTAIN SHEEP

PHOTOS © WALT DISNEY PRODUCTIONS

GIRAFFES

RACCOON

ANTEATER

RINGTAIL CAT

MUSTACHED TAMARING

REPTILES

PHOTOS © WALT DISNEY PRODUCTIONS

CORAL SNAKE

BRAZILIAN HORNED TOAD

LAND IGUANA

GILA MONSTER

MUSSERANA

RATTLESNAKE

TEJU LIZARD

and return to the spawning place and apparently die there.

Eels usually have minute scales, but the conger eel (*Conger conger*), a larger, strictly salt-water fish, is quite scaleless; it sometimes grows 8 feet long. Lampreys are sometimes called lamprey eels. Order Apodes, several families, especially Anguillidae.

EGRET. See *Heron.*

EIDER, any of 4 different kinds of large sea ducks, strikingly marked in the male with black and white. They are found in northernmost Europe, Asia, and America, going south beyond the limits of sea ice only in winter. Most species live wholly in the water and go to land only for breeding.

The female lines her nest with her own soft, downy breast feathers. In Iceland and many other arctic areas, people gather these feathers as soon as the nest is deserted, and use them to line pillows and quilts. Order Anseriformes, family Anatidae.

ELEPHANT, either of two gigantic land mammals in which the nose is greatly elongated to form a cylindrical prehensile trunk with the nostrils at the tip. Once widespread, the Asiatic (Indian) elephant (*Elephas indicus*) is now confined to forested regions of tropical India, Burma, the Malay Peninsula, and adjoining islands; and the African elephant (*Loxodonta africanus*) to Africa south of the Sahara.

The Indian elephant has a concave forehead and small ears; the African elephant has a convex forehead and large ears and is chiefly hunted for its ivory. A pygmy race of elephants (4 or 5 feet high, half the size of the regular African elephant) is found in the Congo.

In both species the two upper incisors or front teeth are often enormously developed, constituting long tusks. The lower incisors are lacking, and there are no other teeth in the jaws except the molars, or grinders, of which two are usually in use at one time on each side of each jaw. The molars are very large and expose a number of transverse plates or enamel united by dentine. As each molar is worn out another succeeds it. The feet have five toes, but these are barely indicated externally; the animal walks on the soles of its feet, each cushioned by a thick pad of skin.

Elephants are vegetable feeders, living almost entirely on the foliage of shrubs and trees, which they strip off by means of the prehensile trunk. As the tusks prevent the animal from drinking in the ordinary way, the water is sucked up by the trunk, which is then inserted in the mouth, where the contents are emptied.

Many species of extinct elephants are known, the most familiar of which are the mammoth and the mastodons. The mammoth (*Elephas primigenius*) formerly ranged over much of North America, Europe, and Siberia. In Siberia whole carcasses have been found preserved in the ice. Unlike the elephants of today, the mammoth was covered by long, thick hair. Its tusks reached a length of 15 feet, some weighing 250 pounds. The young of the Indian elephants have a hairy covering that sometimes lasts for several years—a vestigial remain of their remote ancestors which lived in colder climates.

The mastodons (*Mammut* species) at one time spread into South America. Some mastodons had a small pair of tusks on the lower jaw in addition to the large pair on the upper jaw. Order Proboscidea.

ELK. See *Deer.*

EMU, a flightless Australian running bird, similar in habits and appearance to the ostrich and second only to the ostrich in size, sometimes standing 7 feet high. The emu grazes in small groups on the level plains, relying upon keen vision and long legs to escape from danger. Order Casuariiformes, family Dromiceidae, specifically *Dromiceius novae-hollandiae*.

ERMINE. See *Weasel.*

FALCON, any of 58 different birds of prey with long-pointed wings, bare shanks and feet, loose-looking feathers on the thighs and, usually, a notch in the cutting edge of the upper beak. They are found on all major continents and large islands except New Zealand.

Largest of falcons is the powerful gyrfalcon (*Falco rusticolus*) of arctic tundras in both hemispheres; smallest is the Philippine falconet (*Microhierax erythrogonys*), which resembles a swallow. Most famous, and perhaps the most skilful flier, is the peregrine falcon (*F. peregrinus*), known in America as a duck hawk; the male is called a tercel. These falcons are the favorites of falconers, men who catch and train the birds to pursue and capture wild game. Order Falconiformes, family Falconidae.

FER–DE–LANCE. See *Pit Viper.*

FINCH, any of several hundred small seed-eating perching birds with heavy beaks, related closely to sparrows. Those of family Fringillidae are of New World origin and include the cardinal of the United States, Darwin's finches of the Galápagos Islands, and the Saffron finch of the West Indies and South America. Those of family Ploceidae come from the Old World, and include the bullfinch, goldfinch, house finch, and weaver finch.

The sexes may or may not be differently colored. Finches are to be found in all types of places, but especially in forests and open meadows. Seeds, insects, and fruits form the greater part of their food. Order Passeriformes.

FIREFLY, a nocturnal beetle with light-producing organs on the lower side of the abdomen used to bring potential mates together. The light is described as "cold" bioluminescence, since it includes little energy in the form of heat. It is caused by the oxidation of a secretion called *luciferin*. The larvae are luminous and called *glowworms*. In some species the eggs are luminous. Order Coleoptera, family Lampyridae.

FISHER. See *Marten.*

FLAMINGO, any of 4 different kinds of wading birds with longer legs and necks than any others. Their beaks have an angular downward turn, adapted to their use in filtering minute particles of food from shallow saline or alkaline water in which the birds stand.

Most widely distributed is the greater flamingo (*Phoenicopterus ruber*) of southernmost Florida, the Bahamas, Yucatan, northern South America, and the Galápagos Islands, and locally in Eurasia and Africa; those of tropical America have the brightest pink color. The Andean and James' flamingos inhabit alkaline marshes at high altitudes in South America. The lesser flamingo is found only in Africa south of the great deserts.

Flamingos nest in colonies of 4,000 to 5,000, on small isolated islands. They build volcano-shaped mud nests about 1-foot high, patting them into shape with feet and beak. One or 2 eggs are laid in the crater. For a time the young birds wear grayish white down and have difficulty standing up. Order Ciconiiformes, family Phoenicopteridae.

FLATFISH, any of a large number of bony fishes that swim or lie on the bottom with one side of the body regularly downward. During their development from symmetrical hatchlings, these fishes grow distorted. Both eyes come to be situated on the upper side of the head.

Flatfishes are found to moderate depths in all oceans, and ascend estuaries into almost freshwater. The one side that becomes the "belly" of the flatfish is usually white; the other side ("the back") often possesses remarkable powers of changing color and pattern. The fish matches the color of its surroundings so well that it is overlooked by small fishes of other kinds that it eats.

Largest of the flatfishes are the halibuts, the name meaning holy fish; they commonly weigh 50 to 120 pounds, and sometimes up to 720 pounds; much of this is white flesh of excellent flavor. Flounders are smaller and possess teeth in their twisted mouths; soles are still smaller and generally lack teeth. Order Heterosomata.

FLEA, a wingless jumping insect with a body strongly flattened from side to side, and mouthparts fitted for piercing flesh and sucking blood. Fleas are found all over the terrestrial world, as external parasites on particular kinds of warm-blooded animals. They lay eggs on the host or in its vicinity. Larval fleas hatch out, and scavenge for food, often in the bedding or nests of the host, or among organic matter in cracks. After transforming during a pupal stage, the adult flea emerges.

The human flea (*pulex irritans*) is about ¹⁄₁₀-inch long. Fleas of cats and dogs (*Ctenocephalus* species) sometimes bite people when very hungry.

In the West Indies and other tropical areas, a small flea called the chigoe (*Tunga penetrans*) burrows into human skin, freeing her eggs and breathing through a small hole reaching the body surface. Order Siphonaptera.

FLOUNDER. See *Flatfish*.

FLUKE, any of about 5,800 different kinds of parasitic flatworms that are found all over the world and that cling to their host animals by means of two or more suckers. About 700 different kinds have a simple life history, attacking only a single host animal. They usually attach themselves externally to the skin or the gills of fishes. But some flukes have become adapted to living in the mouth, the nasal cavities, or the urinary bladder of amphibians and aquatic reptiles, such as turtles.

More than 5,000 different kinds of flukes have complex life histories, involving two or more hosts. Generally they live in the intestine of a vertebrate animal or in organs, such as the liver, that are connected to it.

The Chinese liver fluke (*Opisthorchis sinensis*), which reaches a size of ¾-inch in the bile passages of the human liver, lays eggs that reach the outside world in the feces. If an egg gets into freshwater and is eaten by an aquatic snail of the correct kind, the egg hatches into a parasite of a slightly different form, which goes through several larval stages. In the last larval stage it escapes from the snail and swims actively in the water, ready to penetrate the body of a fish in which it can go dormant.

Man becomes infected with the parasite by eating the dormant stage of the fluke in the flesh of fish that has been inadequately cooked. In many tropical countries a more serious parasitic fluke enters the human skin and reaches maturity in the blood vessels of the intestine. It is known as a blood fluke (*Schistosoma* species). Various orders of class Trematoda.

FLY, any of about 85,000 different kinds of insects in which the adult has 1 pair of membranous wings and 1 pair of knobbed balancers (halteres). Flies live on all land areas of the world. Most lay eggs that hatch into active maggots, which grow until they can pupate to transform to adult flies. Some, such as the flesh flies (species of *Sarcophaga*), whose maggots feed on carrion, and the biting tsetse flies (species of *Glossina*) of Africa, deposit active larvae that have hatched inside the body of the mother.

The larvae of mosquitoes, called wrigglers, are active aquatic insects, feeding on microscopic animals and plants. The floating pupae, called bullheads, can swim when disturbed.

Fly maggots of many kinds serve importantly as decomposers of dead plants and animals. Those of the tachina flies (members of family Tachinidae) are internal parasites of caterpillars, and help control infestations upon crop plants. The house fly (*Musca domestica*) and others that eat and drink food used by humans can transmit diseases; they can pick up infections because they seek out manure and other wastes as the places in which their maggots can find food for growth. Order Diptera.

FLYCATCHER, any of a large number of small to medium-sized perching birds with weak feet, which dart from perches on tree branches to capture insects on the wing. Flycatchers of the New World include 365 different kinds from northern Canada to Patagonia, including the eastern kingbird (*Tyrannus tyrannus*) of eastern and central North America, the tail-wagging phoebe (*Sayornis phoebe*) of the eastern United States and Canada, the spectacular scissor-tailed flycatcher (*Muscivora forficata*) of south central United States, the brilliant red vermilion flycatcher (*Pyrocephalus rubinus*) of Mexico, Central America, and the southwestern United States, and the great kiskadee (*Pitangus Sulphuratus*) which calls out its name from southern Texas to Brazil.

Flycatchers of the Old World include 378 different kinds, chiefly tree-dwellers, of Africa, Europe, Southeast Asia, and Australia, among them the 5 friendly gray birds with a reddish breast that Australians call robins (*Petroica* species). Order Passeriformes, families Tyrannidae (New World) and Muscicapidae.

FLYING FISH, any of many specially adapted bony fishes that can glide for considerable distances in air, either with the aid of enlarged pectoral fins (the "two-winged flying fishes") or with both pectoral and pelvic fins expanded (the "four-winged flying fishes"). All have the lower lobe of the tail fin enlarged as a sculling organ.

Flying fishes probably take to the air to escape from larger sea animals that are pursuing them in the water. Order Synentognathi, family Exocoetidae.

FLYING LEMUR, or colugo, either of 2 kinds of gliding mammals about 15 inches long with a 9- or 10-inch tail with a gliding membrane linking the neck to the tips of fingers, toes, and tail. They live in the forests of Malaya and the East Indies, where they climb slowly but skilfully head up, or cling suspended by their front claws.

They feed on seeds, fruit, buds, flowers, and leaves. Although quite helpless on the ground, they are active in the trees, leaping from branch to branch with remarkable agility, and gliding as much as 450 feet for each 40-foot loss in altitude. Order Dermoptera, family Cynocephalidae, specifically *Cynocephalus volans* in the Philippines and *C. variegatus* in Southeast Asia and the East Indies.

FOWL, a term originally referring to any bird, but now generally restricted to members of the Order Galliformes, which includes the domestic fowl (rooster and hen), the peafowl (peacock and peahen), the pheasant, turkey, partridge, grouse, quail, and the moundbuilder of Australia. Most of these are rather heavy in the body, with short wings and an ability to fly short distances only. Generally they run on the ground, using their strong feet to scratch for food. Most nest on the ground, laying numerous eggs, which the hen bird incubates alone.

Wildfowl, however, are now regarded as ducks, geese, and swans, all members of the Order Anseriformes. Waterfowl include pelicans and all other swimming birds, but not the herons and other wading birds.

FOX, any of about 15 different kinds of small to medium-sized doglike mammals with a sharp muzzle, long bushy tail, and a "foxy" odor arising from special glands near the base of the tail. They inhabit most of Africa, Eurasia, and the Americas. The pupil of a fox's eye is generally elliptical in strong light; ears are usually triangular and pointed.

The red fox (*Vulpes fulva*) inhabits most parts of Europe and America and extends also into northern Asia. Its senses are extremely acute, and it has learned to use them to avoid man. It usually remains concealed in a burrow during the day and ventures abroad chiefly at night in search of food.

It is one of the principal predators on voles and mice, but eats also insects, eggs, fruit, grass, and whatever small birds and mammals are easy to catch.

The arctic, or white, fox (*Alopex lagopus*) is remarkable for changing its color with the season, being brown or bluish in summer and white in winter. The soles of its feet are hairy. The gray fox (*Urocyon cinereoargenteus*) is common from southern Canada to northern South America, and often climbs trees when pursued, or to rest inconspicuously. The furs of all foxes are valuable, especially the silver foxes and blue mutant strains of arctic foxes now raised for the market on fox farms. Order Carnivora, family Canidae.

FRIGATE BIRD, or man-of-war bird, any of 5 different tropical, web-footed birds with a long hooked beak, very long wings that are bent at an angle while soaring or flying, and a deeply forked tail. The magnificent frigate bird (*Fregata magnificens*) ranges from the Bahamas and Baja California to Brazil and Ecuador; the male is solid black, except for the brilliant red chest pouch that he inflates at mating season; the female has a white neck and throat.

The great frigate (*F. minor*), also measuring 40 inches from beak tip to tail tip, and whose wingspan is about 7 feet, patrols coasts of the western South Atlantic, and the central and western Pacific, and the Indian Ocean.

Smallest is the 32-inch long lesser frigate bird (*F. ariel*) of the South Pacific, Australian shorelines, Madagascar, and the coast of Brazil. These birds are all expert fliers, but can scarcely walk or swim. They pick food from the ocean surface, or snatch unguarded chicks from the nests of other sea birds, or like pirates attack any gull, booby, or cormorant that has caught a fish, forcing it to give up its prey. Order Pelecaniformes, family Fregatidae.

FROG, the common name for adult tailless amphibians that have smooth skin and webbed hind feet. Frogs inhabit moist places, near freshwater, all over the world. Females lay their eggs in long strings in the water. From these, fishlike larvae called tadpoles or polliwogs hatch out, each with a broad, swimming tail and gills on the sides of its head.

Tadpoles feed upon small aquatic plants that they scrape from sticks and stone with their horny jaws. As they increase in size, the legs grow out and the tail is absorbed. The anterior pair of legs forms first but remains concealed beneath the skin until the hind pair is well developed and conspicuous. With the growth of legs and the loss of tail, the gills disappear and the lungs come into use; nevertheless most species always remain in close proximity to water throughout life.

Adults live on animal food such as insects, mollusks, and small fishes. Some do not hesitate to eat members of their own species. Frogs are useful to man in keeping down certain species of insects. They are caught for the flesh in their hind legs, which is white meat of mild flavor.

The largest North American frog is the bullfrog (*Rana catesbiana*), 5 to 8 inches long, found almost everywhere east of the Rocky Mountains. The pickerel frog (*R. palustris*) is brown with green spots, and the leopard frog (*R. pipiens*) is brilliantly marked with black spots outlined in white on its bright-green skin. Order Salientia, family Ranidae.

FRUIT FLY, any of nearly 1,000 different kinds of 2-winged insects less than ¼-inch long, commonly found around bananas and other fruits in which its maggots can develop, feeding on yeasts in the fermenting juice. The Mediterranean fruit fly (*Ceratitis capitata* of family Trypetidae) is a destructive pest, especially on citrus fruits. Much that we know today about heredity has been learned from a study of fruit flies of the genus *Drosophila* (literally "honey-lovers"), of family Drosophilidae. Order Diptera.

GALLINULE, a marsh bird closely related to the coots and rails, with a plump body, suggesting that of a domestic fowl. Gallinules are found in many parts of the world, usually close to freshwater, in which they often swim about. Except on migration, they seldom fly far. They nest on platforms built of vegetation in the middle of marshes.

The common, or Florida, gallinule (*Gallinula chloropus*) of eastern North America and Central America is native also to Europe and Britain, where it is called a moorhen. The larger, purple gallinule (*Porphyrula martinica*) is a more conspicuous bird, with a purple breast and a blue shield on the forehead contrasting with a bright red, yellow-tipped beak, and with lemon-yellow legs.

Gallinules live along the Atlantic and Gulf coasts and in Central and northern South America. Similar, but flightless, birds in New Zealand are the pukeko (*Porphyrio melanotus*) of marsh edges and the rare takahe (*Notornis mantelli*) of valley tussock land, which until recently was believed to be extinct. Order Gruiformes, family Rallidae.

GAR (from an Anglo-Saxon word meaning pike or spear), any of about 8 different kinds of armored fishes with cylindrical bodies and needle-sharp teeth. They inhabit rivers and lakes of North America east of the Rockies and southward to the Isthmus of Panama.

Their covering is of rhomboidal scales, each with an enamel surface so hard that a fish spear will scarcely penetrate. The common gar, or bony pike (*Lepisosteus osseus*), sometimes attains a length of 5 feet and is easily distinguished by the long beaklike extension of the mouth region. The alligator gar of the lower Mississippi and of Mexico (*L. spatula*) is larger than the common gar, occasionally reaching 12 feet in length and a weight of 350 pounds. Order Ginglimodi, family Lepisosteidae.

GAZELLE, any of about 12 different exceedingly slender and long-legged antelopes, renowned for their long necks and graceful movements. They inhabit Africa, Asia Minor, and as far east as northern India and Mongolia. They include the dibatag or Clark's gazelle (*Ammodorcas clarkei*) of Somaliland, the gerenuk or Waller's gazelle (*Litocranius walleri*) of East Africa, the springbok (*Antidorcas marsupialis*) of South Africa and Angola, the Mongolian gazelles (species of *Procapra*), and various gazelles (genus *Gazella*) in which lyre-shaped horns develop in both sexes.

The common gazelle (*G. dorcas*), 3 to 4 feet tall, is fawn or dun colored on the back; a brown or black line separates this coloration from the white hair on the belly. The horns, stronger in the male than in the female, were used for lyre frames in early days.

The gazelle inhabits the large plains and the Saharan region of northern Africa, as well as Arabia and Syria, and lives in herds. Order Artiodactyla, family Bovidae.

GECKO, any of about 300 kinds of slender lizards, with special suction discs on its toes, permitting it to creep on smooth vertical surfaces or even ceilings in pursuit of insects as food. Geckos sometimes bask in the sun, watching for danger through slit pupils suggesting those of a cat. Like cats, they prefer to hunt in twilight and darkness, capturing their food by sudden extension of a long, sticky tongue with an extended tip. Often geckos produce loud calls, which may sound like geck'-oh or like the chirp of an insect.

The banded gecko (*Coleonyx variegatus*) of the North American southwest, from Texas to California, is pale brownish gray, banded or speckled with dark reddish brown, and attains a length of 4 inches. Like all geckos it is harmless, despite superstitions to the contrary. Order Sauria, family Gekkonidae.

GIBBON, any of about 7 kinds of tailless anthropoid apes with extremely long arms and legs, enabling them to exceed all other mammals in the agility with which they swing through the tree tops from branch to branch. They

ROTHSTEIN/LOOK

GIRAFFE

are native to southeastern Asia and the East Indies.

Rarely more than 3 feet high when standing erect, a gibbon usually balances itself by stretching its arms overhead. Let hang for a moment, the hands almost touch the ground. Gibbons have buttock pads and long canine teeth. They eat mostly fruit, leaves, buds, and whatever birds, eggs, and insects they can catch. By day they are active, but by night gibbons sleep upright in little groups, leaning on one another and some crouch in a big tree. Order Primates, family Pongidae.

GILA MONSTER. See *Lizard*.

GIRAFFE, the tallest mammal, a solid-horned cud-chewer with extraordinarily long neck and long legs. It inhabits African highlands, where it browses on the sides and tops of thorny trees. Formerly it was called the camelopard, because the neck was thought to resemble that of a camel, and the pattern of the skin the spots of a leopard. Actually it is related both to the antelopes, which have hollow horns, and the deer, which have solid antlers. In the giraffe the antlers are never shed, but continue to grow slowly under the hairy skin atop the head.

The giraffe uses its unusually long cylindrical tongue for stripping off the leaves from the trees on which it feeds. When the giraffe drinks it must spread its front legs wide apart to get its mouth to the water. Order Artiodactyla, family Giraffidae.

GNU, or wildebeest, either of 2 kinds of hollow-horned, cud-chewing African antelopes with a conspicuous beard, mane, tuft of hairs between the forelegs, and tuft of long hairs at the tip of the tail. Commonest and widespread on the African savannas is the brindled gnu or blue wildebeest (*Connochaetes taurinus*) which often forms mixed herds with zebras, each benefiting from the association. The white-tailed gnu (*C. gnou*), which has been exterminated except in South Africa, is about the size of a horse and has structural features suggesting a bison and a deer.

In both male and female the horns taper to points, curving forward from the skull and turning up at the ends. Order Artiodactyla, family Bovidae.

GOAT, any of 5 different hairy cud-chewing mammals, similar to sheep but differing in that the forehead is convex, rather than concave; in the possession of a beard and scent glands on the body of the male; and in the absence of scent glands on the feet of both sexes.

Goats inhabit Eurasia from Spain to Siberia, south to the Sudan, Ethiopia, and the Arabian peninsula. Mostly they are found in wild mountainous countries where they scramble among the high rocks. The domestic goat (*Capra hircus hircus*) may have been derived in ancient times from the bez-var goat (*C. hircus aegagrus*) of Asia Minor. It has been bred into many distinctive lines, such as the Angora, whose hair is woven into the fabric called mohair, and the Kashmir goat, whose hair becomes fine cashmere for India shawls.

The flesh, especially that of the kid or young goat, is used as food, despite its rather poor quality. The milk is very rich and nutritious, and, because it is free from tuberculosis germs, it is often fed to tubercular and other patients. Many cheeses are made from goats' milk. Some goats yield about 2 quarts. The skin is dressed as leather for many uses, particularly for gloves and other fine kinds of shoes. The horns, which are worn by both sexes, are used to make knife handles, and the fat to make candles.

The Rocky Mountain goat (*Oreamnos americanus*) is really a closer relative to the European chamois, intermediate between the antelope and the goat. It is about as big as an ordinary sheep, and it looks like a sheep of the Merino breed with long straight hair and spiky horns. Order Artiodactyla, family Bovidae.

GOLDENEYE, or whistler, a diving duck that nests in tree holes in the northern United States, Canada, Scandinavia, and northern areas of Europe and Asia. When feeding, it frequents lakes, broad rivers, and bays of the ocean, in which it can dive for crustaceans, plants, and aquatic insects. In flight, its wings make a characteristic high-pitched whistling sound.

Goldeneyes are dark colored toward the tip, with white patches above and below toward the body. In both sexes the body itself is white below and dark above. The male has a black head with a white spot between eye and beak, and a white neck. His mate has a brown head and a gray neck with a white collar. In the common goldeneye (*Bucephala clangula*), the white patches on the head of the male and the beak in both sexes are smaller than in Barrow's goldeneye (*B. islandica*), which nests farther north and at higher altitudes in North America, and only in Iceland in the Old World. Order Anseriformes, family Anatidae.

GOLDFINCH, a small songbird with a short, strong beak suited to opening seeds, and a quick, undulating flight. The American goldfinch (*Spinus tristis*) is common over most of settled Canada and all except the southernmost states of the Union in summer; it ranges down into eastern Mexico for the winter.

In summer the male goldfinch is often called a "wild canary," because he is then brilliant golden yellow with a black forehead, a black forked tail, and black wings marked with a white bar. His coloration in autumn and winter more closely resembles that of his mate and young goldfinches, which are brownish olive-yellow, darker above, with black tail and black wings similarly marked.

The European goldfinch (*Carduelis carduelis*), introduced into America in 1852 on Long Island, New York, is even more brightly colored, and equally in both sexes. Its face is brilliant red, snow-white at the sides; the crown of the head is jet-black, as are the nape of the neck, most of the forked tail, and the wings except for a broad band of bright yellow and white spots along the trailing edge. The body is brown except on the rump and belly, which are white. The call of the European goldfinch is usually a canarylike twitter.

In Europe and Asia, goldfinches are permanent residents of gardens, orchards, and cultivated land. They are rare or absent in Iceland, northernmost Scotland, and similar latitudes across the great continent of Eurasia. Order Passeriformes, family Fringillidae.

GOOSE, any of about 14 different kinds of web-footed birds related to swans, which are bigger and have longer necks, and to ducks, which are smaller and have shorter necks in proportion to the body. With the exception of the Australian magpie goose (*Anseranas semipalmata*), which is black and white, they are birds of the Northern Hemisphere. The legs of a goose are farther forward than a duck's, and thus better adapted for walking.

Geese spend much of their time on land, feeding on grass and other herbage, berries, seeds, and various kinds of vegetable food. Although large and bulky, they have great powers of flight. They strike with their wings in fighting; at the bend of the wings there is a hard callous knob or tubercle, which in some species becomes a spur.

Gray geese of 5 kinds include the domestic goose (*Anser domesticus*), which probably originated from the European gray-lag goose (*A. anser*), which is almost 3 feet long from the tip of the bill to the extremity of the short tail; the wingspread is about 5 feet. The weight of the largest bird is about 10 pounds. The other gray geese are the lesser white-fronted goose, the bean goose and the swan goose of Eurasia and the greater white-fronted of the North American arctic.

Three white geese are the snow goose (*Anser caerulescens*) of northern Asia and the American arctic, the blue goose of Baffin Land, and Ross' goose which comes from the Arctic Circle to winter in California.

The black geese include the Canada goose (*Branta canadensis*) and the smaller brant of North America, the barnacle goose of far northern Europe, the bar-headed goose of the Himalayas, and the rare nene of Hawaii.

Geese are kept for their eggs, for their flesh (a favorite Christmas dish), and for their feathers that are used for pillows and beds. Quill pens were made from goose feathers. Order Anseriformes, family Anatidae.

GOPHER, any of 21 different kinds of squirrel-like burrowing rodents of the open plains in the Northern Hemisphere. The name is from the French *gaufre* (honeycomb), alluding to the burrow.

Gophers search by day for seeds, nuts, roots, soft stems and leaves, insects, bird eggs, and whatever mice and birds they can catch. Near cultivated fields, they may raid by night, making themselves troublesome pests in some localities. They carry home dry foods to storage chambers, but also become very fat by midsummer and often go early into winter dormancy. Order Rodentia, family Sciuridae, species of genus *Citellus*.

GORILLA, the largest of the manlike apes, which may reach a height of 5½ feet and a weight of 400 pounds. Gorillas live in the bamboo forests of tropical West Africa. Their arms in relation to the body are shorter than those of any other ape. Gorillas are very strong, but they usually retreat before man. When grown to more than 100 pounds, they rarely climb. Usually they make beds of leaves and boughs.

Little was known of them until 1859 when Paul Du Chaillu, a French-American explorer, brought skins and skeletons to Europe. He brought back to the United States the first gorillas ever seen there. Order Primates, family Pongidae, specifically *Gorilla gorilla*.

GRACKLE, either of 2 large blackbirds, about 14 to 17 inches long, including the long tail, found in Canada and the United States east of the Rocky Mountains. The bronzed grackle (*Quiscalus quiscula*), sometimes called crow blackbird, nests as far north as Great Slave Lake and Newfoundland, and winters in the southeastern United States. The boat-tailed grackle (*Cassidix mexicanus*), which is slightly larger (up to 16 inches long), is a bird of Atlantic coastal states and Mexico. Order Passeriformes, family Icteridae.

ROTHSTEIN/LOOK

GORILLA

GREBE, any of 18 different kinds of diving water birds, each of whose toes has horny flaps at the sides, like individual webbing, used particularly in swimming underwater. Grebes are found on all continents as inhabitants of slow streams and ponds. When disturbed, grebes usually dive below the surface where they swim long distances. They are good flyers, however, but have some difficulty in leaving the surface of the water because of their small-sized wings.

They feed mainly on small fish, frogs, crustaceans, and insects. They build nests near or on the water and the matted plant material sometimes actually floats. Grebes carry their young pick-a-back, sometimes even diving to escape with the young birds still hanging on. Order Podicepediformes, family Podicepedidae.

GROSBEAK, any of several songbirds with a conical, heavy beak well adapted to opening thick-shelled seeds. They are distinctly larger than sparrows, and frequent trees and brush, seldom coming to the ground. They are birds of the Northern Hemisphere. Generally the two sexes are unlike in coloration; the males are much more brilliantly marked. Many individuals associate together in winter, often showing little fear of man.

Among the grosbeaks of North America are the cardinal (*Richmondena cardinalis*), which has a crest; the rose-breasted grosbeak (*Pheucticus ludovicianus*); the black-headed grosbeak (*P. melanocephalus*); the blue grosbeak (*Guiraca caerulea*); the evening grosbeak (*Hesperiphona vespertina*); and the pine grosbeak (*Pinicola enucleator*), which is found also in coniferous forests of northern Europe, where a much smaller bird (*Carpodacus erythrinus*) is called the scarlet grosbeak, although it is a close relative of the American purple finch (*C. purpureus*). Order Passeriformes, family Fringillidae.

GROUSE, any of 18 different kinds of the fowl-like birds with thick soft feathers, usually brown and reddish in inconspicuous patterns. Grouse are widely distributed in the Northern Hemisphere. Their short wings beat very rapidly in flight with a whirring sound, giving them great speed and agility over distances up to a few hundred yards. In general grouse prefer the deep woods and spend most of their lives on the ground where they find seeds, fruits, buds, and insects.

The ruffed grouse (*Bonasa unbellus*), sometimes called partridge in the northern states, is regarded as the finest of all upland game birds over its whole area of distribution, coast to coast in Canada, and southward to Georgia and northern California.

During the mating season, the male ruffed grouse drums with his wings at some open spot on or near the ground, the sound sometimes carrying more than a mile, and serving as a call to the female or as a challenge to combat for other males.

Spruce grouse (*Canachites canadensis*) occupy much the same area in coniferous woods rather than in cutover forests. Most beautiful is the black grouse (*Lyrurus tetrix*) of forests in northern Eurasia, and largest among grouse the capercaillie (*Tetrao urogallus*) of Scandinavia, which is almost as large as a turkey. The heath hen (*Tympanuchus gallo*), which became extinct on the American mainland about 1835 and on Martha's Vineyard Island in 1932, was an eastern race of the prairie chicken (same name) which is growing scarce over its range from the Canadian prairies to the Appalachians and Arkansas. Order Galliformes, family Tetraonidae.

GUINEA FOWL, any of 7 different kinds of short-tailed, pheasantlike birds that run, rather than fly. They are native to Africa and Madagascar. Because of their tasty meat they are now widely domesticated even though they are almost too noisy to be raised on a small farm. They are mainly vegetarian, digging and scratching for seeds and roots. The common domestic guinea fowl (*Numida meleagris*) prefers grassy areas in which to hunt for seeds, fruits, slugs, and insects, but it needs trees in which to roost at night. In Africa, flocks sometimes number 2,000. Order Galliformes, family Numididae.

GUINEA PIG, or cavy, any of about 20 different kinds of stout-bodied, tailless, vegetarian rodents about 10 inches long. They are native to brushlands in mountainous South America, where one kind (*Cavia cobaya*) was domesticated in pre-Columbian times by the Incas as a convenient source of meat. In the wild, this guinea pig produces small litters, but in captivity it is extremely prolific: it begins to breed when 10 months old, and produces several families in a year, each family consisting of about 8 young. The popular name is inappropriate; the animal is not a pig and it does not come from Guinea. Order Rodentia, family Caviidae.

GULL, any of 43 different kinds of web-footed, scavenging birds, larger than terns, with a hooked tip on the upper beak and the habit of directing the beak forward, not down, while in flight. Gulls are common along seacoasts and large bodies of inland water, and on garbage dumps all over the world. They are usually white below with the upper parts varying from a light gray to black.

They can run and walk readily and often help in controlling plagues of grasshoppers and crickets. The Pacific gull (*Larus pacificus*) patrols the shores of Australia and the Great Barrier Reef for young turtles as they hatch and scamper over the beach toward the water. The herring gull (*L. argentatus*) and others of North and Central America drop mussels and sea urchins on rocks, paved areas, and parked cars to break open the shells and get at the meat inside. Order Charadriiformes, family Laridae.

GUPPY, or mosquito fish, a small top minnow from freshwaters of northern South America and the islands of the West Indies. It is named for Robert J. L. Guppy, who in 1866 discovered fishes of this kind in Trinidad.

At 1 inch in length the male guppy attains full size, and develops a long anal fin that shows his sex. The female grows twice as large, with an anal fin of normal size. During courtship, the male uses his special fin to transfer sperm cells to the female. Fertilization is internal, and the embryos develop into active little fish before emerging from their mother. From a single mating, a female guppy may produce 200 young in a month, and 200 more each month thereafter for about 8 months.

Because young fish can take care of themselves if the parents do not eat them, and reach maturity quickly, guppies have become popular as the "million fish" for tropical aquariums in the home. Supposedly a pregnant female guppy could give rise to 1 million descendants in a year or less, if the offspring were supplied with enough food and space that includes vegetation wherein the young can hide from older fish.

The common name mosquito fish refers to the readiness of the guppies to eat small aquatic insects. In captivity they may be supplied with water fleas (*Daphnia*) or young brine shrimp raised for the purpose. Order Cyprinodontes, family Poeciliidae, specifically *Gambusia affinis*.

HADDOCK, a marine bony fish resembling a cod in having the dorsal fin divided into 3 parts and the anal fin into 2, but with only a white line along the side instead of a pattern of markings. Haddocks are common in cold waters of the North Atlantic, where they eat virtually anything edible, especially mollusks. Haddock is one of the most important of the food fishes, and exceeds all other fishes in tonnage caught and sold annually. It is often smoked for sale as "finnan haddie." Order Anacanthinae, family Gadidae, specifically *Melanogrammus aeglefinus*.

HAKE, any of several different marine food fishes differing from cod in details of the skull bones and ribs; the dorsal fin consists of a long forward part and a shorter rear part (not three parts, as in the cod), and the lower jaw bears no projections (barbels) with which to detect smaller fishes and other animals as prey upon the sea bottom.

Despite this lack, hake, which are widely distributed, catch fishes, crustaceans, and squids in large numbers. Apparently they do so with little exertion, for their flesh remains soft. Like the cod, hakes have soft fins and an air bladder with no connection to the outside world.

The European hake (*Merluccius merluccius*) inhabits deep water in the Mediterranean Sea and along Atlantic coasts from Norway to northwestern Africa; it attains a weight of 20 pounds, and is fished for at depths as great as 2,400 feet. The silver hake (*M. bilinearis*) along the Atlantic coast of North America and the Pacific hake (*M. productus*) are of smaller size. The South African hake, or stockfish (*M. capensis*), grows to as much as 4 feet in length, and is caught at depths to 1,800 feet by trawling, as the most valuable single commercial fish of that region. Order Anacanthini, family Merluccidae.

HAMSTER, any of several different kinds of small burrowing rodents from Mediterranean countries and Asia. The common, or black-bellied, hamster *(Cricetus cricetus)* is a short-tailed species, which makes extensive burrows in which to spend the day and the winter. A hamster may store as much as 200 pounds of grass seeds, dry small fruits, and even potatoes in its burrow. In summer these animals eat large numbers of insects as well as frogs, worms, and other smaller animals.

In some areas of Europe and Asia Minor, hamsters are trapped for their furry skins, which are usually light brown above, marked with white on the sides, and black below. During recent years, large numbers of common hamsters have been raised in captivity on a diet of dog biscuits, corn, and lettuce. They make interesting pets, and have become a valuable experimental animal for medical science. Order Rodentia, family Cricetidae.

HARE, any of about 30 different kinds of short-tailed, long-eared, jumping mammals with a short palate and the habit of bearing young that are fully haired, open-eyed, and ready to run with the mother. Native to North America and Eurasia as far south as Malaya, they have now been introduced into South America, Australia, New Zealand, islands off the northwest coast of Africa, and the northeastern United States.

The popular names hare and rabbit are often incorrectly used interchangeably. For example "jack rabbits" and "snowshoe rabbits" are not rabbits, but hares, whereas the "Belgian hare" is a rabbit.

Most kinds of hares live in open grassy country, but the varying hare *(Lepus americanus)* inhabits evergreen forests, where its fur is white in winter and dark brown in summer; its large feet make huge prints in the snow, hence the name "snowshoe rabbit" for this animal. The arctic hare *(L. arcticus)* is not found south of Hudson Bay. The black-tailed jack rabbit *(L. californicus)* occupies the U.S. southwest and Mexico.

All of these animals supply important food for the larger predators, and might contribute important meat and fur for mankind if raised in captivity, as is the European hare *(L. europaeus)* in many parts of Europe, to keep the animals free of disease. In the wild, they carry tularemia, a severe bacterial disease to which people who handle infected hares are susceptible. Order Lagomorpha, family Leporidae.

HARVESTMAN, or daddy longlegs, a spiderlike land animal with extremely slender long legs and a small, compact, often hard body bearing a pair of eyes on an elevated turret on its back.

Harvestmen are abundant in field and forest in all parts of the world from May to October. Eggs are laid in the fall and hatch the following spring. A few species sleep through the winter, but the majority of the adults die each fall after the breeding season. Their food consists mainly of small insects and other minute animals. They are harmless, but may produce an unpleasant odor when molested. Order Phalangida of class Arachnida.

HAWK, any of about 80 different medium-sized birds of prey, larger than falcons, smaller than eagles, kites, and vultures. Hawks are found in all parts of the world except New Zealand and Oceania. They are almost wholly carnivorous and rarely take food that has not recently been killed. The plumage is usually brown or white, although gray is not uncommon. The nests are built in trees and on rocky cliffs; occasional ground nests are found.

The principal kinds are the sharp-winged members of genus *Accipiter,* and the broad-winged hawks of genus *Buteo*. The sharp-shinned hawk *(A. velox)* is small, measuring only 11 to 13 inches in length, grayish on the back with bars of brown, whitish underneath, and with yellow legs and feet. Cooper's hawk *(A. cooperi)* is similar in plumage to the sharp-shinned, but larger.

The goshawk, originally goosehawk *(A. gentilis)*, is circumpolar and a great favorite with falconers for hunting marsh birds and rabbits. The marsh hawk *(Circus hudsonius)*, one of the harriers, is a highly beneficial and almost cosmopolitan bird which kills such pests as rats, mice, and grasshoppers; it rarely feeds on birds.

The broad-winged hawks prefer reptiles, amphibians, and small mammals no larger than a rabbit; they include the red-shouldered hawk *(Buteo lineatus)* of eastern North America, which winters in southern Florida and Cuba, and the birds called buzzards *(Buteo buteo* and *B. lagopus)* in Europe. Order Falconiformes, family Accipitridae.

HEATH HEN. See *Grouse*.

HEDGEHOG, any of about 12 different small mammals bearing barbless spines among the fur on the back and sides, and able to roll up into a ball surrounded by spines when disturbed. They are Eurasian and African animals, which feed on animal matter, live or dead, although they willingly eat bread and milk or other food put out for cats and dogs.

Hedgehogs measure from 10 to 12 inches in length; the legs are short; the snout is long; and the spines are usually about 1 inch long. They are nocturnal in habits; during the day they hide in logs and stumps. In winter hedgehogs hibernate in protected places. Their flesh is sometimes eaten in Europe. There are no true hedgehogs native to the northern hemisphere: the North Amercian porcupine *(Erethizon)* is sometimes erroneously called a hedgehog. Order Insectivora, family Erinaceidae, particularly the Eurasian *Erinaceus europaeus*.

ROTHSTEIN/LOOK

HIPPOPOTAMUS

HERON, any of the long-legged wading birds that have straight or slightly downcurved beaks, toothlike points on the side of the claw on each middle toe, and carry the head and neck in an S curve, particularly during flight. They are widespread, and commonly seen standing on one leg in shallow water, although they fly when disturbed.

Herons are generally subdivided into the bitterns (12 kinds), the tiger herons (6 kinds), the night herons (9 kinds), the day herons (35 kinds), and the agami heron of central and northern South America. Egrets are day herons with snowy plumes, the aigrettes of the milliner. The snowy, the white, and the reddish egrets live in the southern United States.

There are 2 American blue herons —the great blue *(Ardea herodias)*, sometimes called blue crane, about 50 inches high, with a black crest; and the little blue heron *(Hydranassa caerulea)*, only about 24 inches high. The European heron *(A. cinerea)* is so swift and strong that it was the favorite prey of trained falcons. Herons nest in high trees, in structures built of grass and twigs, sometimes in communities called heronries. The bitterns live in marshy places and the British species are becoming rare as marshy grounds are reclaimed.

The Old World bittern *(Botaurus stellaris)* is about 30 inches in length and about 44 inches in wingspread. Its usual color is a dull yellowish brown, with spots and bars of black or dark brown. It has long, loose breast feathers, a short tail, and a bill about 4 inches long. It is remarkable for its booming or bellowing cry, from which come the provincial names, miredrum, butterbump, and stakedriver. The eggs are 4 or 5 in number.

The North American bittern *(Botaurus lentiginosus)* resembles the common European bittern, and is 26 inches long. The little bittern *(Ixobrychus minutus)* of Eurasia to New Zealand and South Africa is not more than 15 inches in length. Order Ciconiiformes, family Ardeidae.

HERRING, any of about 175 different kinds of small, soft-finned, bony fishes with deciduous scales and a knifelike ridge along the undersurface of the compressed body. Some live in the freshwaters of Africa and the Amazon basin, but most are marine and commonly come to river mouths at spawning time.

These fishes occur in large schools; they swim through the sea with open mouths, scooping up the minute life for food. Immense numbers are caught. The young herring, also taken in quantity, are preserved as American sardines. Order Isospondyli, family Clupeidae.

HIPPOPOTAMUS (Greek for river horse), either of 2 kinds of large mammals with a broad snout, large mouth, bulky body, and short stout legs ending in 4 toes. The large hippopotamus (*Hippopotamus amphibius*) is a river dweller of many parts of Africa, whereas the pygmy hippo (*Choeropsis liberiensis*) lives only in swamp forests of West Africa.

The large hippo adult weighs about 4 tons, the pygmy about 550 pounds. Both feed on shrubs, grasses, and other vegetation, and spend most of each day almost submerged in a favorite water hole. The stomach is 3-parted, but the animal does not chew a cud. Order Artiodactyla, family Hippopotamidae.

HOG. See *Swine*.

HONEYBEE. See *Bee*.

HOOKWORM, any of several different small parasitic intestinal roundworms, which have special attachment spines around the mouth. They attain maturity while firmly anchored in the wall of the human small intestine where they often cause severe bleeding, with consequent anemia and weakness. Their eggs pass out with undigested wastes, and hatch if exposed to air on the soil.

The active larvae can bore through bare human skin, particularly along the sides of the foot, between the toes, and around the ankles, thus reaching the bloodstream. The blood carries them to the lungs where they bore through into the air cavities, opening an avenue for infection by tuberculosis bacteria and other diseases. The larval hookworms ride the mucous film up to the throat, are swallowed, and thus reach the intestine.

Millions of persons are infected by hookworms, primarily in warm countries where sanitary conditions are poor and bare feet are usual. Order Rhabditida, particularly genera *Ancylostoma duodenale* and *Necator americanus*.

HORNET, any of a number of wasplike insects about 1 inch long with conspicuous white or yellow markings on a brown or gray body. The name hornet is loosely applied to a number of stinging wasps, but referred originally to the European brown kind (*Vespa crabro*), which is justly noted for the virulence of the sting and the irritability of the female insects so equipped.

The widely distributed European hornet, now introduced accidentally near New York City, builds com-

munal nests in hollow trees, constructing the nest itself of wood fibers chewed to form a gray papery material.

The large gray hornet (*V. maculata*) found in eastern North America builds a similar "carton" nest, but suspends it from the limbs of trees. Inside the nest are cells like those of a honeycomb. The smaller yellowjackets (*V. communis* and *V. diabolica*) usually nest underground.

Hornets eat sweets of all kinds and steal honey from bees; they also feed on other insects. Order Hymenoptera, family Vespidae.

HORSE, either of 2 kinds of large herbivorous mammals that stand or run on a horny hoof capping the single elongated toe on each foot. Compared with the related asses and zebras, horses have small ears; they grow long hairs from the outer half of the tail, not at all from the end of the tail in a tuft as in these related animals.

Living horses are native to Africa north of the great deserts, and to central and eastern Asia. The only wild horses today are Mongolian, named *Equus przewalskii* after their discoverer the Russian explorer Nikolai Przhewalski; they are short-legged, thick-headed, stocky horses with an erect mane. The domesticated horse (*E. caballus*) is longer legged, more slender in the head, and graceful in body and legs. It probably is the descendant of an extinct horse of the same scientific name, the tarpan, which was an important source of food for mankind in prehistoric times.

Like other domestic animals, the horse has been developed into many special breeds, such as the Arabians for riding, the perchorons for draft use, thoroughbreds for racing, and ponies for work in mine passageways. Order Perissodactyla, family Equidae.

HORSESHOE CRAB, or king crab, any of 4 different marine arthropod animals, in which the heavily armored body as seen from above shows conspicuous subdivisions into a front division that is the shape of a horse's hoof and as much as 22 inches wide, a rear division that is roughly triangular, and a terminal long tapering tail spine.

The front division of the body bears a large compound eye on each side, and 2 small simple eyes near the midline far forward. Below this portion of the body are 4 pairs of walking legs, arising from the sides of the mouth, and 2 pairs of special appendages used for tasting and handling food, anterior to the mouth.

The rear division of the body bears below it a series of hinged plates to which the leaflike gills are attached. Waving these hinged plates and beating with its legs, a horseshoe crab swims upside down. After swimming, it often sinks to the bottom back downward and must turn over to walk along in search of worms and other soft food. It uses its tail spine to turn itself over onto its feet. Order Xiphosura of class Merostomata, family Limulidae.

One kind of horseshoe crab (*Limulus polyphemus*) lives along Atlantic and Gulf coasts of North America. The other 3 are found along coasts of Southeast Asia and the East Indies. These animals are not true crabs, but distant kin of scorpions and spiders (Class Arachnida); all of their nearest relatives, the sea scorpions, have been extinct for more than 200 million years.

HOUSE SPIDER, a small dust-colored spider not over ¼ inch long with slender legs 3 times the length of the body and several dark chevron markings on both the upper and lower surfaces of the egg-shaped abdomen. House spiders seldom live outdoors, having adopted human dwellings. They spin loose silken webs that catch small insects as well as dust; the spider flings strands of silk at its prey, using a special comb on its last pair of legs to handle the silk. Order Araneae, family Theridiidae, mostly *Theridion tepidariorum*.

HUMMINGBIRD, any of 319 different kinds of small day-active birds, with long slender bills and very small feet, which hover while sipping nectar from flowers and produce a humming sound by rapidly vibrating their wings. They are natives to the New World from southern Alaska and northern Nova Scotia to Tierra del Fuego. They are represented by the largest variety in tropical South America.

About 18 species are found in the United States, many of them only on the borders of the country. Only one species, the ruby-throated *Archilochus colubris*, is found east of the Mississippi River. It is 3¼ inches long and beautifully colored. Their beaks are long and curved allowing the birds to reach into deep-throated flowers, many of which they pollinate. Order Apodiformes, family Trochilidae.

HYDRA, any of several freshwater coelenterate polyps with a cylindrical, contractile body some ¾ inch long and about the diameter of the lead in an automatic pencil. It is ordinarily attached at one end to underwater vegetation; from the free end, which bears the mouth, 8 or more long threadlike tentacles extend into the water like fishing lines waiting for minute animals. Each tentacle is studded with microscopic nettling cells, which discharge when suitable prey touches them. Some of these cells inject a poison that quiets the prey, such as a water flea (*Daphnia*), while lassolike extensions of other cells hold on to the victim.

Slowly the hydra pushes the prey animal into its mouth, which opens into a sac-shaped digestive cavity. After all digestible materials have been absorbed, indigestible remains are ejected through the mouth in a spitting movement.

Well-fed hydras may develop from the side of the body new small individuals called buds, or produce sex cells in simple sex organs. Fertilized eggs grow to become swimming embryos, which eventually attach themselves somewhere and transform into the polyp form of the adult hydra.

The name hydra refers to a monster in Greek mythology, which grew new heads when old heads were cut off. The name was given to these polyps because of their powers of regeneration when mutilated. Class Hydrozoa, order Hydroidea, species of *Hydra* and other genera.

HYENA, any of 3 kinds of doglike mammals with disproportionately large head and forequarters but weak hindquarters. They inhabit the semi-arid portions of Africa and Asia, the spotted or laughing hyena (*Crocuta crocuta*) being widespread in Africa south of the great deserts, the brown hyena (*Hyaena brunnea*) in southern Africa, and the striped hyena (*H. hyaena*) from Asia Minor to West Pakistan.

The hyena is covered with coarse, bristly hair, short over most of the body, but forming a mane along the ridge of the neck. The hind legs are shorter than the forelegs, giving the body a slope from the withers to the haunches. The hyena is somewhat larger than a shepherd dog. The cheek muscles are greatly developed, and the large grinding teeth have great conical crowns that enable them to smash the thighbones of animals as large as the horse.

All hyenas are nocturnal in their habits. They are useful scavengers. Order Carnivora, family Hyaenidae.

IBIS, any of 23 different kinds of medium-sized, long-legged wading birds, which have no feathers on the face. Some lack feathers on the entire head and neck. Ibises are found in all warm and temperate regions except Oceania.

The sacred ibis (*Threskiornis aethiopica*) of Africa and Madagascar was worshiped in ancient Egypt; many legendary powers were ascribed to it. Today the bird has been virtually exterminated north of the great African deserts, although it is still common to the south. Far more widely distributed is the glossy ibis (*Plegadis falcinellus*) of southern Eurasia, Africa, Madagascar, Australia, the West Indies, and southern Florida.

The white ibis (*Eudocimus albus*), whose face and long down-curved beak and legs are reddish orange, is over 2 feet long with pure white plumage and a few black wing feathers. It nests generally by the thousands in immense rookeries in Florida, the West Indies, central and northern South America.

The scarlet ibis (*E. rubes*) of South and Central America has bright scarlet wings tipped with black. The American bird called a wood ibis is actually a kind of stork. Order Ciconiiformes, family Threskiornithidae—literally birds of worship, referring to the sacred ibis.

IGUANA, any of a number of tropical herbivorous lizards with a laterally compressed body and tail, and a number of soft spines that extend from the head to the tip of the tail, giving a crested appearance.

Iguanas are native to tropical America, including islands of the West Indies. A Galápagos iguana (*Amblyrhynchus cristatus*) lives on the lava rocks along the seashore and is partly aquatic, feeding on seaweeds, and growing to be 4 feet long. Even larger is the common green tree iguana (*Iguana iguana*) of Central and South America, which is sometimes 6 feet long.

Iguanas resemble more the legendary Chinese dragons than real animals. Their flesh has a delicate flavor, and their eggs, almost all yolk, are eaten in Latin America. Order Sauria, family Iguanidae.

JACKAL. See *Dog.*

JAY, any of about 50 different kinds of perching birds, smaller and more brightly colored than the closely related crows and magpies. They are found throughout the temperate and tropical zones, except in New Zealand and some oceanic islands. The common blue jay (*Cyanocitta cristata*) of eastern and central North America has beautiful bright-blue plumage, a conspicuous crest on its head, and a very harsh cry.

The Canada jay (*Perisoreus canadensis*) has sooty plumage, a black cap, white forehead, throat, and collar, but no crest. It is an accomplished thief, frequenting hunters' and prospectors' camps; it is called moose bird and whisky jack. Steller's jay (*Cyanocitta stelleri*) of America west of the Rockies is dark blue and black, with a crest, and inhabits coniferous forests. If they have a chance, nearly all jays will eat nestlings of smaller birds and their eggs. Otherwise they live on a wide variety of food, preponderantly of vegetable origin. Order Passeriformes, family Corvidae.

JELLYFISH. See *Medusa.*

JUNCO, any of several different sparrow-sized birds, characteristically slate-gray above, white below, and with white along each side of the tail. The feathers show no streaks or spots, but in some species provide red or pink color to the sides and some areas of the back. All are North American. Most widespread is the slate-colored junco (*Junco hyemalis*), which has a pink beak; it nests in Canada and the northern United States and winters throughout the United States and northern Mexico.

The western yellow-pine forests of the American Southwest are the sole home for the white-winged junco (*J. aikeni*), which has 2 white wing bars. Dry mountain forests and adjacent plains of the southwestern United States and northwestern Mexico have a gray-headed junco (*J. caniceps*), which has a gray head and a red-brown back. More widespread along the provinces and states of the Pacific slope and over the Rocky Mountain area into northern Mexico is the Oregon, or pink-sided, junco (*J. oreganus*).

All juncoes are often called "snowbirds," because they hop around on the winter snow while searching for dry seeds. During the summer they

AUSTRALIAN NEWS AND INFORMATION BUREAU
KANGAROO

eat large numbers of insects and feed their young exclusively on insects until the young birds leave the nest. Order Passeriformes, family Fringillidae.

JUNE BUG, or May Beetle, any of several kinds of flying adult beetles, which often fly to lights in late spring. Some are scarabs, such as *Phyllophaga* and *Cotinus;* others are stag beetles (*Pseudolucanus*). These types emerge from the ground where their larvae, called white grubs, pass a year or more feeding upon roots of grasses, vines, and trees. The adults, usually about an inch long, often chew vegetation; they are, however, most noticed when they fly through open windows and tumble to the floor. Order Coleoptera, chiefly families Scarabaeidae and Lucanidae.

KANGAROO, any of about 52 different kinds of mammals with a particularly strong, long tail serving as a third leg or as a prop while seated, with large, strong hind legs and small forelegs, and with a small head bearing a deerlike snout and large ears. Kangaroos and tree kangaroos, rat-kangaroos, wallabies, and wallaroos are found in Australia, Tasmania, New Guinea, and some adjacent islands. Females carry their young in a pouch (marsupium).

The largest kangaroo is the great gray (*Macropus giganteus*), which may stand 8 feet tall and weigh 150 pounds. Formerly plentiful over Australian plains, it is being eliminated to make space for cattle. While grazing, kangaroos walk on all fours. When alarmed or in a hurry, they leap along on their hind legs, 10 to 15 feet at a hop, the body being carried in a nearly horizontal position, and the tail extended to balance it. The forepaws are chiefly used for handling, and with these the females lift their young and place them in the pouch. The kangaroo skin is very soft and pliable and is used in making shoes and gloves. Order Marsupialia, family Macropodidae.

KATYDID, the popular American name for several different, large long-horned grasshoppers, which are active and make distinctive calls at night. In many parts of the country their loud, persistent "katy-did" notes are the most familiar sounds of a summer evening, being audible for ¼ mile or more on quiet nights. The sound is produced by the male rubbing the base of one forewing against the other. The katydids resemble common field grasshoppers in structure but are larger—almost 3 inches long—with bright-green bodies. Order Orthoptera, family Tettigoniidae.

KINGBIRD, any of several tyrant fly-catcher birds of North America, about 9 inches long. The common eastern kingbird (*Tyrannus tyrannus*) is crested, dark gray with white under-parts, and has a white band across the end of its black tail. It is famous for fighting off any attacker at its nest, and in chasing crows from the vicinity.

Yellow underparts are distinctive of the western or Arkansas kingbird (*T. verticalas*) and of Cassin's kingbird (*T. vociferans*) of the American south-west. Kingbirds are commonly seen on bare limbs of trees from which they dart to catch flying insects. The call note is rather harsh and shrill. Order Passeriformes, family Tyrannidae.

KINGFISHER, any of 84 different kinds of stout carnivorous birds with long strong beaks, large heads, short necks, short tails, and short legs on which the front toes are joined for more than half their length. Kingfishers are found all over the world, except in the Arctic and on some oceanic islands. Europe has only one kind, the Eurasian kingfisher (*Alcedo atthis*) of northern Africa, and from Portugal eastward to the Solomon Islands. Only the belted kingfisher (*Megaceryle alcyon*), a crested blue and white bird, lives in America north of Mexico.

Kingfishers eat mainly small fish, which they get by diving. Sometimes they also eat insects. Their nests are usually built in tree trunks or in the banks of streams.

The laughing jackass, or kooka-burra (*Dacelo gigas*), of eastern and southern Australia is a kingfisher as large as a crow, feeding chiefly on reptiles and insects and seldom going near water. The popular name comes from the bird's loud braying cry, which is like a noisy laugh. Order Coraciiformes, family Alcedinidae.

KINGLET, a very small plump bird of the forest, with a brilliant streak of feathers on its crown when mature. In the golden-crowned kinglet (*Regulus satrapa*) of North America and the goldcrest (*R. regulus*) of Britain and Europe the crest is bright orange-yellow bordered with black. In the ruby-crowned kinglet (*R. calendula*) of North America and the firecrest (*R. ignicapillus*) it is red.

All kinglets build nests in cone-bearing trees other than pine, suspending the nest below a branch or twig. In summer, these birds flit quickly through the dark evergreen forests, hunting for insects for themselves and their young. In winter, kinglets are more often seen on bare trees and evergreens around suburban homes. Order Passeriformes, family Sylvidae.

KINKAJOU, a tropical American mammal with a rounded head, short face, sharp claws, and a strong, prehensile tail. It lives in trees, hunts by night, eats insects, eggs, and honey, and is sometimes called a honey bear. A kinkajou is about as big as a house cat; it has soft wooly fur and is easily tamed. Order Carnivora, family Procyonidae, specifically *Potos flavus*.

KITE, any of about 25 different kinds of long-winged birds of prey with weak feet, which restricts their diet to small prey and carrion. All are strong fliers, graceful in the air.

Largest of the four kinds in the United States is the swallow-tailed kite (*Elanoides forficatus*), about 25 inches long, which spends most of its life on the wing, often in flocks of 20 or so. It hovers before pouncing on snakes, lizards, frogs, and other small reptiles, as well as grasshoppers, caterpillars, and grubs.

The other American kites, which differ in plumage but are similar in form and habits, are the white-tailed kite (*Elanus leucurus*), the Mississippi kite (*Ictinia mississippiensis*), and the Everglade kite (*Rostrhamus sociabilis*), which is dwindling toward extinction—perhaps because it feeds almost exclusively on one kind of snail. Order Falconiformes, family Accipitridae.

KITTIWAKE, a middle-sized gull of the open sea, which nests in colonies on steep rocky cliffs of Britain, Scandinavia, Iceland, and arctic Canada as far south as Gaspé peninsula of Quebec. Adults are distinctive because each wingtip appears to have been dipped in black ink, and the feet are black, not brown as in the immature bird.

Kittiwakes are rare inland, but common far out at sea, where they frequent the northern fishing areas. Often they pick food from the waves without stopping. At times they swim on the surface or dive deeply, apparently swimming underwater in pursuit of fishes. Order Charadriiformes, family Laridae, specifically *Rissa tridactyla*.

KIWI, any of 3 different plump-bodied flightless birds with virtually no wings and with a long slender beak at the tip of which the nostrils open. All kiwis are New Zealand birds, about the size of a domestic hen. They use the beak to reach into soft forest soil for earthworms and insects, locating them by scent. The wing stubs end in a claw; the feathers are hairy. The legs are strong, and used both for running and defense.

The female lays 2 eggs, each weighing about a third as much as she does after her laying is completed; her eggs are larger relative to her body than those of any other bird. Order Apterygiformes, family Apterygidae, species of genus *Apteryx* ("wingless").

KOALA, an Australian mammal as much as 33½ inches long, 33 pounds in weight, with a large head, big rounded hairy ears, a black bare nose, strong legs with opposable claw-bearing toes, and a vestigial tail. Native only to eucalyptus forests in eastern Australia, it feeds on about 12 different kinds of these trees, eating foliage, buds, and flowers. It clings tightly, using remarkable hands with thumb and forefinger both opposable to the other three fingers.

The young koala is carried in the mother's pouch for about 6 months and then on her back until it is a year old. Both appeal to people as living toylike "teddy bears." Order Marsupialia, family Phalangeridae, specifically *Phascolarctos cinereus* ("the ash-gray pouched bear").

KUDU, either of 2 African antelopes, second in size only to the eland. They frequent forests, where they browse on shrubbery. Unlike most other antelopes, they are heavy and rather ungainly.

The greater kudu (*Tragelaphus strepsiceros*, meaning twisted horn) inhabits southern Africa from Angola to Ethiopia, and stands almost 5 feet at the shoulder, 8 feet long not counting the long tufted tail; the male has massive horns up to more than 4 feet long, spirally twisted and beautifully curved.

Both sexes are grayish brown with a white stripe down the middle of the back and numerous vertical white stripes on the sides. The lesser kudu (*Strepsiceros imberbis*) of Somalia and East Africa is about 3½ feet tall at the shoulder, and its horns grow to more than 2 feet long. Order Artiodactyla, family Bovidae.

LAC BUG. See *Scale Insect*.

LACEWING, or goldeneye, or green fly, any adult insect that develops from an aphis lion. Lacewings are worldwide on land areas. Their 4 broad wings are pale green, with many cross veins, held at rest like a tent over the body; when spread, their span is about 1 inch. The head bears two large, bulging, golden-colored compound eyes and a pair of long threadlike antennae (feelers), as well as a pair of strong small jaws with which the insect attacks and devours aphids (plant lice).

Female lacewings lay their white eggs singly atop ½-inch slender stalks, seemingly to prevent the first larva that emerges from eating all unhatched eggs. The larva, called an aphis lion, devours large numbers of aphids. It attains full size in about 2 weeks, and spins a cocoon in which to transform to the winged adult lacewing. Often winter is spent in the cocoon. Because aphids cause so much damage to plant crops, lacewings are regarded as extremely beneficial insects. Order Neuroptera, families Chrysopidae and Hemerobiidae, members of *Chrysopa* (literally "golden eye").

LADYBEETLE, or ladybird beetle, or ladybug, a small hemispherical beetle, often orange or red with black spots, and ½ inch or less in diameter. It is a harmless beetle found in temperate and tropical climates. Lady beetles lay eggs on plants. The larvae that hatch out are usually black with a flattened pear-shaped body, the head with biting jaws, and six legs at or near the larger end.

In the Middle Ages, when it was seen that these insects and their larvae destroyed aphids (plant lice) and scale insects, they were dedicated to the Virgin and became "Beetles of Our Lady," hence ladybeetles. Most ladybeetles benefit agriculture, although a few kinds, when adult, such as the Mexican bean beetle (*Epilachua varivestis*) eat plants.

An Australian ladybeetle (*Vedalia cardinalis*) was introduced in California to control the cottony cushion scale, a mealy bug (also from Australia), which threatened the orange orchards. The countless descendants from 500 ladybeetles checked the pest in a few years. Order Coleoptera, family Coccinellidae.

LAMPREY, a cylindrical, jawless fish with a circular sucking mouth and no paired fins. Most lampreys live in the sea but ascend freshwater streams to lay eggs. They make nests by moving rocks on the pebbly bottom. The young hatch as small slender larvae, called *ammocoetes*. For 3 or 4 years, each larva burrows shallowly in mud or sand, drawing in water for respiration and filtering out microscopic particles of food. When ready to transform to the adult shape of body, it migrates to salt water to finish growing. Finally it returns to a stream to mate and die.

At maturity, a sea lamprey (*Petromyzon marinus*) is nearly 3 feet long. It uses the horny teeth in its mouth and suction to fasten itself as an external parasite on larger fishes, on whose blood and flesh it feeds. It has a single nostril and seven gill openings on the side of the neck.

Allied to the lampreys are the scavenging hagfishes or slime eels (genus *Myxine*), which sometimes burrow into the body of a dead or dying fish and eat it from the inside. Hagfishes, although uncommon along the Atlantic coast of North America, are abundant in European and Californian waters. Orders Petromyzontia and Myxinoidia Hyperoartia of class Cyclostomata.

LANCELET, or amphioxus, any of about 30 kinds of slender marine animals 2 to 3 inches long, about the shape of a willow leaf, sharp, pointed, and thin like a lance at both ends. Lancelets live near shore along temperate coasts all over the world, usually burrowing shallowly in sandy bottom materials during the day and emerging to swim about rapidly at night. The sexes are separate, but fertilization occurs in the open sea. Fertilized eggs develop into free-swimming larvae, which are distributed widely by water currents before they settle to the bottom and transform slightly to adult form.

At one end of the adult body is a narrow oval mouth opening into an extensive throat region (pharynx), which has multiple slits through which sea water passes. These slits allow the lancelet to filter from the water microscopic particles of food, and to absorb oxygen and get rid of carbon dioxide. The food, caught in sticky mucus, proceeds onward through a straight intestine.

Lancelets in some features resemble vertebrate animals in their embryonic development. They have a hollow dorsal nerve cord, a lengthwise supporting rod called a notochord, slits in the side walls of the pharynx that resemble gill slits in fishes, a closed circulatory system with arteries, capillaries, and veins, and a body cavity lined by a thin layer of cells called a peritoneum. But there are no indications of head or brain, nor of the blocks of cartilage or bone that form the internal skeleton of a vertebrate animal. Presumably lancelets represent an ancestral form of chordate animal, relatively unchanged for the last 600 million years or more. Subphylum Cephalochordata of phylum Chordata.

LARK, any of about 75 different kinds of songbirds the size of a large sparrow, noted for the song flights of the males. Most larks are African, but the group is represented in Eurasia, Australia, and North America.

The skylark of temperate Eurasia and North Africa (*Alauda arvensis*) begins its song early in the spring and continues to sing the whole summer. It is quietly colored in brown, buff, and creamy white, and in many countries is prized as food. The horned lark (*Eremophila alpestris*) of the same areas and the New World as far south as Colombia, has a black collar, yellowish throat, black tail, and black head "horns."

Meadowlarks of North America are about the size of a robin, with a black V on the yellow breast. They thrive, as the Old World larks do, on developed farmland and are highly regarded as destroyers of insect pests. The western meadowlark (*Sturnella neglecta*) is slightly smaller than the eastern (*S. magna*), and its whistled call is lower in pitch and less shrill. Meadowlarks are, however, totally different from true larks; they are related to blackbirds in family Icteridae, whereas the true larks comprise family Alaudidae, both families of order Passeriformes.

LAUGHING JACKASS. See *Kingfisher*.

LEAFHOPPER, any of more than 2,000 kinds of small insects resembling miniature cicadas, with a short head (often pointed) and compact body, and the 4 wings held tentlike lengthwise above them at rest.

They are found in all terrestrial parts of the world. With sucking mouthparts, they get nourishing juices from leaves, young stems, flower buds, and soft fruits, often doing much damage by introducing the carriers of disease.

The largest leafhopper is less than an inch long when mature, and most do not exceed ¼ inch in length. The eggs hatch into small wingless insects of the same body form and similar habits. Development is direct, with no pupal stage.

In some species, such as the rose leafhopper (*Empoa rosea*), two generations attain maturity in vast numbers each year, the first generation attacking one kind of plant (in this case almost any type of rose) and the second generation a quite different plant (in this case apples). Adults of the second generation generally fly back to plants suitable as food for members of the first generation, there to lay eggs that will survive the winter. Order Homoptera, family Cicadellidae.

LEECH, a flattened segmented worm with a sucker surrounding the mouth at the front end, where the animal has 3 knifelike jaws, and usually a second sucker at the hind end. Leeches mostly inhabit freshwater shallows, where they catch small crustaceans and snails, and have a chance to attach themselves to fish, turtles, or a mammal that is drinking or wading. With their jaws, leeches can cut through the skin and reach blood, making a quick meal of it before dropping off.

Half a century ago freshwater leeches (*Hirudo medicinalis*) 2 or 3 inches long were used extensively by physicians to relieve certain diseases by bloodletting, but since it was found that the human system is weakened by bloodletting, the use of leeches has diminished.

A few kinds of leeches live in the ocean, attacking fishes and turtles. In wet forests of Southeast Asia, one kind of leech waits for victims along game trails on land. Several orders of class Hirudinea, phylum Annelida.

LEMMING, any of about 12 kinds of small, short-eared, short-tailed rodents found in tundras, coniferous forests, and mossy bogs of northern Eurasia and North America. The lemming (*Lemmus lemmus*) of Scandinavia and northwestern Russia, about 5 inches long with a heavy, rounded body, short legs, and a large head, is famous for its periodic migrations suddenly every 8 to 10 years. At these times, huge numbers of lemmings travel downhill from overpopulated and food-scarce high country. If their migratory urge persists, they do not stop even when they reach the ocean but plunge in and drown.

Normally lemmings eat reindeer moss (a lichen) and other plants, and serve as the principal food of predatory animals in the Far North. Order Rodentia, family Cricetidae.

LEMUR, any of about 16 kinds of long-tailed monkeylike mammals, from 5 to 17 inches long not including the tail. They are native to Madagascar and the Comoro Islands. Most are arboreal, associating in troops of up to 20 individuals. Their very large eyes, staring appearance, and nocturnal habits earn them their name—*lemures* is Latin for ghosts. Lemurs eat fruit and insects. Lemurlike but unrelated animals (order Demoptera) that glide from tree to tree are known as flying lemurs. Order Primates, family Lemuridae.

LEOPARD. See *Cat*.

LIMPET, any of a large number of marine gastropod mollusks having a low, conical shell widely open below, where the body of the animal expands into a large flat foot with which it clings by suction to solid supports. They are common along rocky shores between high-tide mark and a few feet below low tide. Those most abundant in this location around Britain and Europe belong to genus *Patella,* named for a fancied resemblance to the bone in the tendon of the human knee; the most familiar limpets along American shores belong to genus *Acmaea.* Keyhole limpets, which have a hole at the tip of the shell and use it for discharge of water from which they have taken their oxygen, often belong to genus *Fissurella.*

All limpets browse on the film of minute seaweeds that grow on rocks along coasts, and resist both the pounding of waves and the combination of dry air and sun when exposed by the tide. They arch the central portion of the soft muscular foot to create a vacuum like that in a suction cup; they can be dislodged easily by pressing a thin knife blade between the rock and the foot, thus releasing the vacuum. Large numbers of limpets are collected along British and European coasts for use as food and fish bait. Order Aspidobranchia.

LING, or lingcod, a large marine bony fish resembling the closely related cod in having short soft projections (barbels) from the lower jaw, used to detect small fishes, crustaceans, worms, and other food on the sea bottom. Ling are caught in the North Atlantic Ocean off the coasts of Europe and Greenland. Like a hake, a ling has a dorsal fin divided into a small forward part and a much more extensive hind part, whereas a cod has a three-part dorsal fin.

Ling is a term derived from a Middle English word, meaning long, and refers to the proportions of the body. In some parts of the world remote from Europe, the same name is given to quite different fishes in which the body appears longer in proportion to height than is customary among familiar fishes. Order Anacanthini, family Gadidae, specifically *Molva molva.*

LION. See *Cat.*

LIZARD, any of about 3,140 different kinds of scale-covered reptiles in which the 2 sides of the lower jaw are joined together, not merely linked by a flexible ligament as among snakes. Usually the eyelids are movable and an external opening of the ear can be found; most commonly a lizard has 4 legs with distinct toes, but a few are legless and often mistaken for snakes.

Lizards live in temperate and tropical countries all over the world. Largest are the monitor lizards of Africa and tropical Asia to Australia; one, the Komodo dragon (*Varanus komodoensis*) discovered in 1912 on the small Komodo island in the East Indies, grows to a length of 9½ feet and is a formidable predator. Only the 2 kinds of beaded lizards in deserts of southwestern North America are venomous: the Gila monster (*Heloderma suspectum*) of Arizona and Mexico, and the Mexican beaded lizard (*H. horridum*) have a poisonous saliva that seeps into wounds made when the animal bites.

The tree iguanas (*Iguana iguana* and near relatives) of tropical America eat foliage high among the tall trees of the rain forest. Most other lizards are insectivorous or eat small invertebrate animals. This is the habit of the nocturnal geckos, the horned lizards (or horned "toads"), the fence lizards, the chameleons, and most of the legless lizards known as "worm" lizards or as "glass snakes" from their habit of breaking off the tip of the tail into separate twitching fragments when handled. Order Squamata, suborder Sauria (or Lacertilia).

LLAMA, a deer-sized, cud-chewing mammal of the Andes of South America. Although lacking a hump, it is related most closely to camels and, like them, has been domesticated as a beast of burden, capable of carrying 200 pounds for 17 miles in a day over mountain trails.

When annoyed, a llama spits and bites. From its long hairy coat, fine cloth can be made. The Andean Indians depend greatly on the llama for milk and meat. Order Artiodactyla, family Camelidae, specifically *Lama peruana.*

LOBSTER, a large marine "long-tailed" crustacean whose strong abdominal muscles are sought for food. At the front of the head are two pairs of sensitive feelers (antennae) and a pair of eyes on the end of short stalks.

The North Atlantic lobster (*Homarus americanus*) along coasts of both the Old and New World is distinguished by the exaggerated size of the front pair of legs, each ending in pincers, and one being larger than the other. Lobsters scavenge for decaying fish, and may be caught in large traps called *lobster pots,* made of lath and baited with decaying fish.

The number of lobsters taken is enormous, but overfishing has so greatly reduced their numbers that laws have been enacted almost everywhere to protect them. The annual catch on the New England coast is estimated at about 30,000,000 pounds, the weight of an average lobster being between 2 and 3 pounds.

The spiny, or rock, lobster, or sea crayfish (*Palinurus*), has no pincers on its 5 pairs of legs, but defends itself with antennae that are particularly thick and strong. They generally project from the rock crevices where the animal takes shelter. In the Mediterranean is found *P. vulgaris,* the langouste of French menus; similar animals are caught in the West Indies, southern Florida, Bermuda and the Bahama Islands, and along the coast of South Africa. Order Decapoda.

LOCUST, a loosely used word applied to (1) short-horned grasshoppers, (2) cicadas, and (3) several kinds of trees with edible seeds, belonging to the pea family. No one is sure which of these is referred to in the Bible as a food approved for Israelites (Leviticus 11:22) and as the food eaten with wild honey by John the Baptist (Matthew 3:4; Mark 1:6). Those that came in swarms and ate the crops were certainly the migratory grasshoppers (*Schistocerca peregrina*) of North Africa and Asia Minor.

BRANIFF INTERNATIONAL

LLAMA

A similar habit is shown by the smaller short-horned grasshoppers (*Melanoplus spretus*) of prairies near the Rocky Mountains in North America. Order Orthoptera, families Locustidae and Acrididae.

LOON, or diver, any of 4 large, handsome, fish-eating water birds whose legs are enclosed within the body all the way to the ankle joint. They normally come ashore only to nest, for their long, heavy body and short neck, as well as the position of the legs, make them clumsy and awkward on land. They cannot take flight from land at all, and even from the water they must run along the surface, frantically flapping their short wings.

Loons frequent coastal salt water and inland lakes, particularly far north in the Northern Hemisphere. They are rather solitary birds, and their favorite haunts are mostly in wild places unfrequented by man.

Most widespread is the red-throated loon (*Gavia stellata*) which nests around small arctic pools and winters as far south as Formosa and California around the Pacific, and the Gulf of Mexico and Mediterranean Sea around the Atlantic Ocean. The arctic loon (*G. artica*) and the yellow-billed loon (*G. adamsi*) are circumpolar but rarely come near human communities even in winter. The common loon (*G. immer*) of northern North America, Greenland, and Iceland is best known for its eerie calls, sometimes likened to the laughter of the insane. Order Gaviiformes, family Gaviidae.

LOUSE, any of a large number of wingless parasitic animals that cling to the body of a host animal or plant and feed from the surface. The blood-sucking lice that attack man and other mammals are classified in the insect order Anoplura. They include the worldwide head louse (*Pediculus humanus*), or cootie, which has often been the principal carrier of typhus fever, trench fever, and relapsing fever; and the hog louse (*Haematopinus suis*), which infests uncared-for domestic pigs, and occasionally spreads to people who walk among the pigs, causing intense itching but no harm.

The biting lice that feed on the feathers of birds are insects of the order Mallophaga; they include the common chicken louse (*Menopon gallinae*). So numerous do the chicken lice often become that the tickling by their feet of a fowl so distracts the bird from eating, sleeping, and social activities that its health declines. The whale lice that crawl over the surface of whales, feeding on the skin, are crustaceans of order Amphipoda.

These diverse parasites show remarkable adaptations in their legs, which help them hold to hairs or among feathers. Most lice are highly specialized to feed on one or a few closely related kinds of animals; they soon die if they cannot find the correct host.

Plant lice, or aphids, are insects that feed by placing their beaks into leaves and stems and sucking the juices; they are members of the family Aphididae in order Homoptera.

LOVEBIRD, any of several kinds of small plump parrots (*Agapornis*) of Africa and Madagascar, so named because they apparently choose a mate for life at a very early age and thereafter stay close together in pairs, giving frequent evidence of affection for one another.

In their native countries, lovebirds fly in large flocks, and generally nest close together. Like other members of the parrot family, they feed principally upon seeds and soft fruits, and produce a great deal of noise by their frequent chirps and calls and by the whir of their short wings as they fly from one branch to the next.

Each kind of lovebird has its distinctive color pattern, which usually is almost identical in the two sexes, and its own method for making a nest from plant fibers collected or cut with the beak in the forest.

The name lovebird is sometimes applied also to the Australian budgerigar (*Melopsittacus undulatus*) and to various South American parakeets (*Psittacula* species), all of which are attractive as cage birds. Order Psittaciformes, family Psittacidae.

LUNGFISH, any of about 5 different kinds of bony fishes in which the nostrils connect with the mouth cavity, instead of ending as blind pits, and the long slender body contains a pair of lunglike air sacs opening into the throat region. They are river fishes of Australia, South America, and Central Africa, living where the water dries up for part of the year. When the dry period comes, the fish burrow into the damp earth and breathe by means of air bladders that are similar to lungs. When water again appears in the river, the fish leave the burrow, and the gills function as in other fish.

Only the Australian lungfish, called the barramunda (*Neoceratodus forsteri*), has leaflike fins; the South American one (*Lepidosiren*) and the African kinds (*Protopterus*) possess only filamentous paired fins. Order Dipnoi, families Ceratodontidae and Lepidosirenidae.

LYNX, any of 4 different kinds of short-bodied, strong-legged, short-tailed, catlike mammals with conspicuous tufts of fur on the ears. Formerly these powerful predators ranged more widely in Europe and North America, and in Africa and Southern Asia. The European lynx (*Lynx lynx*) and the North American lynx, or catamount (*L. canadensis*), are forest animals, which attain a length of 3 feet and weigh as much as 40 pounds. The northern variety, larger and darker in color than its southern relative, is trapped in large numbers for its fur.

The bobcat, or bay lynx (*L. rufus*), which is pale brown with black streaks and spots, differs from other lynxes in having a slightly longer tail (6 inches, instead of 4) with a black mark only above at the tip; it occurs in southern Canada, northern Mexico, and most of the United States. The caracal lynx (*L. caracal*) of Africa and southern Asia prefers hilly country and scrub-covered plains. All lynxes are efficient killers of rodents, but sometimes attack poultry and livestock. Order Carnivora, family Felidae.

LYREBIRD, either of 2 different shy, solitary songbirds about the size of a domestic hen. The mature male possesses a spectacular array of showy tail-covert feathers as much as 25 inches long; in a courtship display, he turns them forward over his back and head in the shape of a graceful lyre. The female has a long straight tail and no special covert feathers.

Lyrebirds are forest dwellers in eastern Australia, the superb lyrebird (*Menura novaehollandiae*) occurring farther south than the Albert's lyrebird (*M. alberti*). They live on the ground, scratching among the leaf litter for insects, centipedes, snails, and other small animals as food. Lyrebirds whistle sweetly, and mimic expertly the calls of many other birds. Order Passeriformes, family Menuridae.

MACKEREL, any of about 10 different tunalike marine bony fishes with smoothly contoured bodies, widely forked tails efficiently linked to the last part of the backbone, and a series of dorsal and ventral finlets just in front of the tail. They are found in all oceans, from cold to tropical; many migrate along routes well known to fishermen.

Most important economically is the North Atlantic mackerel (*Scomber scombrus*), weighing up to 4 pounds, which is caught on hooks and with seine nets. A mackerel fleet from Gloucester, Mass., follows these fish yearly from Chesapeake Bay in April to the St. Lawrence River, which they reach in May. Among Spanish mackerels (species of *Scomberomorus*) in the North Atlantic, the largest is the king mackerel, or kingfish (*S. cavalla*), which grows to 100 pounds and a length of more than 5 feet. Frigate mackerels, such as the common *Auxis thazard* found in tropical seas around the world, are less valuable because their meat is dark. Order Acanthopteri, family Scombridae.

MAGPIE, or pie, any of a number of medium- to large-sized birds with predominantly black-and-white plumage in a bold design, and long oval tails. The name is given to birds of this appearance on all continents, following an old English tradition. There the black-billed magpie, or pie (*Pica pica*), of Eurasia and western North America long ago became a favorite cage bird, enjoyed because of its crafty behavior and its ability to imitate words; they were called Margaret or Mag (just as a parrot is Polly), hence magpie.

Wild magpies take a wide variety of food, animal and vegetable, often robbing other birds' nests of eggs and young. The Old World has also red-billed blue magpies, Ceylon blue magpies, and in Australia black-and-white magpies that are actually crow shrikes (*Gymnorhina* species). Western North America has a yellow-billed magpie (*P. nuttalli*), chiefly in the central valleys of California. Order Passeriformes, chiefly family Corvidae.

MALLARD, a large handsome dabbling duck with a glossy green head (purplish in some lights), a broad yellowish-green beak, a white ring around the neck, a brown back, and a whitish tail; the underparts are mottled gray, and the feet an orange red. Mallards are among the commonest ducks of the Northern Hemisphere, often flocking with black ducks in North America.

Mallards feed on plant rootlets, mussels, snails, small fish, frogs, fruits, and grain and other seeds. They nest inconspicuously in marshland near water, laying 6 to 10 olive-colored eggs. Domesticated mallard ducks have given rise to a number of hardy and prolific breeds for the barnyard. Order Anseriformes, family Anatidae, specifically *Anas platyrhynchos* (meaning broad-beaked duck).

MAMMOTH. See *Elephant.*

MANATEE. See *Sea Cow.*

MANDRILL. See *Baboon.*

MAN–OF–WAR. See *Portuguese man-of-war.*

MANTA. See *Ray.*

MARLIN, any of about 5 different kinds of spearfishes, in which the head is prolonged into a slender, sharp beak with a fancied resemblance to a marlinspike—a pointed metal tool used to splice rope. They are giant fishes of temperate and tropical seas, the largest being the black marlin (*Istiompax marlina*) of the Indo-Pacific, which grows to as much as 14½ feet long and 1,560 pounds. The striped marlin (*Makaira mitsukuri*) of the Pacific and blue marlin (*M. ampla*) of both the Pacific and Atlantic are slightly smaller. Order Percomorphi, family Istiophoridae.

MARMOSET, any of about 33 different kinds of small, monkeylike mammals in which the great toe is opposable and bears a flat nail, but the thumb is not opposable and, like the other fingers and toes, bears a sickle-shaped claw. They live in the forests of tropical South America and Panama, where they climb and leap jerkily from branch to branch in small groups, hunting for insects, spiders, and fruits. They have long, silky fur, elongated hind legs but short arms, and generally tufts of hair on their ears.

The one most often kept as a pet, called the common marmoset (*Callithrix jacchus*), has gray fur and produces a variety of birdlike chirps. Order Primates, family Callithricidae.

MARMOT, or woodchuck, or ground hog, any of about 16 different kinds of large burrowing rodents with pointed heads, small ears, short legs, and a tail about one third as long as the rest of the body. They inhabit cooler parts of the Northern Hemisphere, at lower elevations in the north and higher in the south.

When numerous in any area, woodchucks are the bane of the farmer. They devour many garden crops and are very fond of alfalfa and red clover. The burrow is deep and has several compartments in which the woodchuck hibernates from September to March. February 2, Candlemas, is known as Ground-hog Day or Woodchuck Day from the popular belief that then the animal comes out of his burrow and if he sees his shadow runs back again—cold weather will continue. Order Rodentia, family Sciuridae, species of genus *Marmota*.

MARTEN, any of 8 different kinds of tree-climbing, weasel-like mammals with a long bushy tail. In the New World they are denizens of coniferous and mixed forests; in the Old World they are found from the northern limits of forests to the Mediterranean and Malaya and the East Indies. Martens eat mice and squirrels, which they pursue relentlessly, and carrion, insects, and fruit. They have been trapped extensively for their fine fur.

In the New World, the larger of two kinds is the fisher, or pekan (*Martes pennanti*), sometimes 3 feet in length; the smaller is the pine marten (*M. americana*). Old World martens are often called sables, although one (*M. zibellina*), resembling the pine marten, is the only true sable; it is found chiefly in Siberia and Kamchatka where it is hunted for its fur, the darker shades being the most desired. Order Carnivora, family Mustelidae.

MASTODON. See *Elephant*.

MAY BEETLE. See *June Bug*.

MAYFLY, or shadfly, any of about 1,500 different kinds of adult flying insects with 2 or 3 long filamentous "tails" from the tip of the abdomen, and ordinarily 2 pairs of membranous wings, the front pair much larger than the rear pair. Mayflies are found near freshwater on all continents and major islands. Very few of them have functional mouthparts or live beyond a few days, during which they fly about, find mates, and deposit eggs.

The immature mayflies that hatch out are naiads or, incorrectly, nymphs. They have biting mouthparts, but feed principally on minute plant matter adhering to underwater vegetation or to rocks, or buried in the bottom sediments among which they burrow.

After a period of growth that lasts from 1 to 5 years according to the species, the naiad comes to the surface of the water and molts, freeing into air a flying individual that still is not mature. No other kind of insect includes in its development this winged stage, called subimago, which has wings but must molt again. Mayfly subimagoes and adults are consumed in great numbers by bats, swallows, and other insect-eating birds; the naiads form an important food for fish. Order Ephemeroptera.

MEDUSA, or jellyfish, any of several hundred different kinds of solitary, free-swimming coelenterates, whose soft body has a jellylike consistency and the shape of a bell with a pendant tube where the tongue of the bell would be. These animals are widespread in the oceans; a few live in freshwater.

The mouth, at the end of the pendant tube, leads into a digestive cavity which branches out toward the edges of the domed body. Around the rim of the bell are pendant tentacles, studded with nettling organs used to subdue or kill small animals as prey. These writhing tentacles led to the use of the name medusa, from the mythical Greek Gorgon whose hair consisted of writhing snakes.

The venom of some medusae can cause severe irritation to human skin. Medusae produce eggs that hatch into minute swimming larvae. The larvae settle to the bottom and there transform into colonial polyps (in class Hydrozoa) or special reproductive individuals (in class Scyphozoa) from which new medusae arise by asexual budding. After becoming free, they transform into little medusae, and swim away by expelling water from under the bell through muscular contractions.

MENHADEN, a large marine fish with a large head and special strainers on the gills used to filter from sea water the minute plankton animals and plants that form its diet. Menhaden live in coastal waters of the Atlantic Ocean from Nova Scotia to Brazil.

Mature fish, which average about 12 inches in length, are generally caught in the fall of the year while they are migrating to spawning grounds that remain unidentified. Their eggs float up to the surface and are carried along by oceanic currents, as are also the young fish when they hatch out.

Adult menhaden form large schools and are easily caught, but they are little used for human food because the flesh is very oily. The oil and eggs are often made into poultry food; the flesh from which the oil has been extracted is used for fertilizer. Order Clupeiformes, family Clupeidae, specifically *Brevoortia tyrannus*.

MERGANSER, any of several fish-eating ducks with a slender beak that is hooked at the tip, and saw-toothed along the sides. They are waterfowl of the Northern Hemisphere, along coasts and in freshwaters. The bird (*Mergus merganser*), known as the American merganser in the New World and as the goosander in the Old World, is slightly larger than a mallard duck, and has a conspicuously red bill and feet; unlike other mergansers, it lacks a crest; it prefers freshwater lakes, reservoirs, and large rivers, and builds its nest in proximity to water, usually in a hollow tree or a hole in the bank, chiefly in Canada and northern Eurasia to beyond the tree-growth limit.

The red-breasted merganser (*M. serrator*) is smaller, with a rakish crest, and red or pink low on the neck; it generally remains close to the ocean, nesting among grass or trees near water in Canada, Alaska, Eurasia, Iceland, and Ireland. A hooded merganser (*Lophodytes cucullatus*) in many of the same regions lives more often along slow streams, and nests in wooded areas, generally in a hollow tree or stump; its diet includes fish, but also frogs, tadpoles, crayfish, insects, and vegetable matter. Order Anseriformes, family Anatidae, subfamily Merginae.

MIDGE, in general any small, 2-winged fly of feeble flight. More specifically, a member of the family Chironomidae, especially those of *Chironomus*, which resemble mosquitoes but do not bite. Midges often form immense swarms over shrubs or over water, within which the individual flying insects seek out mates; the combined humming of their wings can sometimes be heard for a considerable distance.

Generally midges lay their eggs in large masses at the edge of the water, into which the cylindrical larvae go. Some of these larvae are bright red with hemoglobin, and are known as "bloodworms."

Most midges are scavengers; some live so successfully where there is an almost complete lack of dissolved oxygen that they are indicators of organic pollution. After 1 or 2 years of growth as larvae, these insects transform into a pupal stage that floats near the water surface until the adult insect is ready to emerge, using the floating pupal case as a raft while escaping into air.

Midge larvae are an important food for many kinds of fish, and the adults provide nourishment to bats, swallows, and other insect-eating birds. Order Diptera.

MINNOW, a popular name for small fishes that swim in schools, are easily netted, and serve as live bait for fishing. Scientists reserve the word minnow for about 1,200 different kinds of fishes from 1½ to 110 inches long, found in all watery habitats in the temperate and tropical regions except South America, Madagascar, and Australia.

Minnows lack teeth in the jaws, but have teeth in the throat; they have soft rays in their fins, and lack an adipose fin (between the dorsal fin and the tail fin on the back). Among the more familiar minnows are the silvery-scaled shiners (genus *Notropis*), and the goldfish (*Carassius auratus*) and carp (*Cyprinus carpio*) of Eurasia. Order Ostariophysi, family Cyprinidae.

MITE, or spider mite, any minute globular arthropod with 3 or 4 pairs of legs and an apparently unsegmented body. They are found all over the world as predators on microscopic animals in the soil or on the surface of plants, or as parasites on or in many kinds of animals and plants. Like the larger and closely related ticks, mites hatch from eggs as active creatures with 3 pairs of legs; at the first molt they gain another pair; the 4 pairs of legs are characteristically present for the rest of their lives.

In the itch mite (Sarcoptes scabiei) and similar species, the first two pairs of legs on the female are adapted into the form of suckers with which she pulls herself into a hair follicle on a person or other mammal. Protected within the skin, she extends her mouthparts to draw blood as food. In this position she can be reached for mating by male mites, which creep over the skin surface, and can extrude oval eggs, which she forces into furrows cut into the skin.

The skin develops an intense itching, and often scales off in large areas, partly from being scratched. The condition is commonly called sarcoptic mange or scab disease. It can be transferred easily to other individuals by contact or by infected cloth, since the mites themselves are less than 1/50 inch long and easily overlooked. Order Acarina of class Arachnida.

MOCCASIN. See *Pit Viper*.

MOCKINGBIRD, an inconspicuous ash-gray songbird slightly larger than a catbird, showing white on its wings when it flies. It is native to the southern United States, where it rivals the Eurasian nightingale in the variety of its song both day and night. It mimics other birds with special skill, but has a song of its own as well, full and varied. Order Passeriformes, family Mimidae, specifically *Mimus polyglottos*.

MOLE, any of about 40 different kinds of burrowing mammals with a pointed nose, small eyes, many tiny teeth, powerful forelegs, a cylindrical body, and usually a short tail or none. About half of them are golden moles (family Chrysochloridae) of Africa, with a metallic luster to their fine fur; they burrow by pushing their noses into the soil. The remaining moles (family Talpidae) live in Eurasia and North America, and dig with their front feet; they are grayish black.

For all moles, earthworms and insects provide the main diet. Moles build amazing subterranean fortresses or nests, consisting of an intricate system of chambers connected by tunnels at varying depths.

Largest of moles is the Eurasian desman (Desmana moschata), as much as 8½ inches long with a tail of equal length; except for the long flexible nose, it might be mistaken for a muskrat. The common Eurasian mole (Talpa europaea) is less than 6 inches long, as is the American star-nosed mole (Condylura cristata), which burrows in damp or muddy soil. The eastern mole of North America (Scalopus aquaticus) has partly webbed feet, but seldom swims. Order Insectivora.

MONGOOSE, any of about 30 different kinds of weasel-like mammals with pointed muzzles, mostly about the size of a house cat. They are persistent predators of the Old World, roaming alone or in small groups by day or night.

The Indian mongoose (Herpestes griseus), a 15- to 18-inch animal with a furry tail of almost equal length, has thick reddish-gray fur, and special agility used in killing poisonous snakes such as cobras. It was introduced as a rat- and snake-killer into Jamaica, Hawaii, and many other islands. In those places, it turned its attention to reptiles that were easier to catch and to native birds, often endangering the survival of rare kinds. In 1902 a law was enacted to forbid the bringing of a live mongoose into the United States.

The ichneumon (H. ichneumon) is a mongoose of North Africa and Asia Minor, that was kept like a house cat in ancient Egypt because of its efficiency in devouring rats, mice, crocodile eggs, and other pests. Order Carnivora, family Viverridae.

MONKEY, any of a large number of small tropical mammals with long tails, having opposable thumbs and great toes, and nails instead of claws. Most New World monkeys can support themselves by their tails; they have widely separated nostrils that open sidewise. Old World monkeys do not have prehensile tails; their nostrils open forward and downward, as in man.

Most monkeys anywhere choose fruits and soft greenery for their diet; however, they also eat insects, young birds, and eggs whenever they can. Order Primates, superfamilies Cercopithecoidae in Africa and Asia, and Ceboidae in America.

MOOSE. See *Deer*.

MOSQUITO, any of about 1,500 different kinds of delicate flies with long, slender sucking mouthparts. They are found in most parts of the world, feeding on sap from plants and blood from vertebrate animals.

Only the females "bite" animals. Usually they lay their eggs on the surface of water or in it, where larvae called wrigglers hatch out. These are unusual among fly larvae, in that they have eyes, well-developed biting mouthparts, and the ability to swim by wriggling until they can suspend themselves from the water's surface film while inhaling a fresh supply of air. With their mouthparts, mosquito wrigglers collect small particles of food from the water.

When fully grown, the wrigglers transform into pupae called bullheads, which are buoyant and float at the surface with breathing tubes reaching the air. If disturbed, a bullhead swims downward, but soon rises again. Inside the bullhead skin, the insect continues its transformation (metamorphosis) until it can break through into air as an adult mosquito, winged and ready to fly.

Males live on plant juices. Females of some species seek blood meals only and cause irritation and transmit disease. As a lubricant, anesthetic, and anticoagulant, a small amount of saliva is pumped into the wound made with the mosquito's mouthparts. The saliva contains proteins that later cause itching and often induce local swelling of the skin. Often the saliva contains live parasitic agents, such as the protozoan of malaria, the bacteria of myxomatosis (a disease fatal to European rabbits), the virus of yellow fever, and the filaria worm causing elephantiasis. Each of these diseases is carried only by a particular kind of mosquito; eradication of the disease can be achieved by elimination of the carrier mosquitoes, or by preventing the mosquitoes from becoming infected by "biting" people with the disease. Order Diptera, family Culicidae.

MOTH, any adult insect with 2 pairs of wings covered with overlapping scales and during flight linked together (as those of butterflies are not) by a special bristle or group of bristles on the leading edge of the hind wing. Moths are found on all habitable land areas of the world. They are usually recognized by having threadlike or feathery feelers (antennae), not knobbed or hooked ones as among butterflies; in folding their wings horizontally over the back at rest, not vertically as do butterflies; and in being active by night, rather than by day.

Like butterflies, however, moths lay eggs that hatch into caterpillars, most of which feed on foliage and other parts of plants. A large number of moths are regarded as major pests because of the damage their caterpillars do. After the caterpillar pupates, however, it no longer eats. Usually moth pupae lie in cocoons spun by the full-grown caterpillar. The moth that emerges from the pupa generally uses its long tongue to sip nectar from flowers that are open at night, and thus pollinates many of these plants, ensuring that seeds will form. Order Lepidoptera, suborder Heterocera.

MOUSE, the popular name for any small rodent. Mice are native to all continents except Australia and Antarctica, and of many islands, but not New Zealand. The house mouse (Mus musculus) of Eurasia has adopted man and gone with his belongings everywhere; in captivity the albino genetic strain has proved valuable in medical research. In Britain, most of Europe and parts of Asia, the wild harvest mouse (Micromys minutus) lives among tall undergrowth, while the various wood or field mice (species of Apodemus) frequent grasslands and open woods.

In North America the deer or white-footed mice (Peromyscus species) with very large eyes, occupy the woodland areas, while the short-tailed, short-nosed meadow mice or voles (species of Microtus) live in pasturelands and grain fields. Order Rodentia, family Muridae.

MULE, a hybrid bred from the horse and the ass, differing in size, strength, and beauty, according to the predominance of its parental species. Hybrids from a male ass and a mare are far superior to those from a she-ass and a horse, which are sometimes called hinnies to distinguish them from the other mules.

WIDE WORLD

MULES

In mountainous countries mules are highly serviceable, for no beast of burden is more sure-footed or more capable of enduring fatigue. In beauty of form they fall short of the horse, and usually cannot reproduce. The mule has a large, clumsy head, long erect ears, a short mane, and a thin tail. Order Perissodactyla, family Equidae.

MULLET, the popular name given to several types of fishes that are unrelated. In Britain, fishmongers distinguish between gray mullets of family Mugilidae, and red mullets of family Mullidae. In the western United States, plain mullets are actually suckers, of family Catostomidae.

Gray mullets are bottom feeders, living close to shore along seacoasts or in brackish estuaries. Most of them are small, weighing 3 pounds or less, with small mouths and a special muscular gizzardlike stomach used in grinding up the vegetable matter they swallow. The striped mullet (*Mugil cephalus*) reaches a weight of 15 pounds and length of 3 feet, growing faster than other mullets and supporting commercial fisheries at many places around the world — chiefly where the water is warm.

Red mullets are generally called goatfish because they have two tactile projections (barbels) under the chin. The common red mullet (*Mullus barbatus*) of the Mediterranean and Atlantic coasts northward was once a great favorite among Romans, who kept them in salt ponds and trained them to respond to the sound of a bell or a voice at feeding time. Orders: Percomorphi (Mullidae) and Mugiloidae (Mugilidae).

MUSK OX, a hairy arctic cud-chewing mammal about the size of a small ox but with shorter legs, a shaggy brown coat of long hair hanging almost to the ground, and thick hollow horns that curve and taper down and forward below the eyes. Its range in glacial times was over the whole of Europe and in the United States as far south as Kentucky; now it is confined to the arctic regions of Greenland and North America, where the steadily decreasing herds are hunted by Eskimos.

The animal is named for its musky odor, which—apparently not emitted by scent glands—is noticeable at a considerable distance from a herd and also in the flesh, which the Eskimo eats. The musk ox has gregarious habits, runs in herds of 30 to 40, and feeds on grass, shoots, moss, and lichens. Order Artiodactyla, family Bovidae, specifically *Ovibos moschatus*.

MUSKRAT, or musquash, a medium-sized rodent with a small round head, close-set ears, short neck, and bulky body covered with soft dense fur, brown on the back and gray below; the feet are partially webbed, the tail bare, round, and tapering. A marsh animal of North America, the muskrat has been introduced in Europe with mixed results. The fur, called Hudson seal, is useful. But the animal digs holes in dikes and shows a liking for vegetable gardens near water.

Normally muskrats eat aquatic roots, fish, worms, mollusks, vegetables, insects, and fruits. They are especially fond of apples and mussels, often traveling a considerable distance to procure them. Mostly nocturnal in habits, muskrats are not often seen, but their abundance is proved by the millions that are annually trapped for their skins. They do not seem to be on the decrease despite constant persecution by man and natural enemies.

The muskrat's home is built near water, usually burrowed into the bank of a stream with the entrance under the surface of the water. Order Rodentia, family Cricetidae, specifically *Ondatra zibethica*.

MUSSEL, a name loosely applied to members of 2 unlike types of bivalved mollusks. Marine mussels attach themselves to solid objects or to one another by means of strong threads of secretion. Often they form a wave-resistant "scalp" over sandbars and other soft bottom sediments, preventing erosion by storms.

In Europe the edible mussel (*Mytilus edulis*) is harvested from natural mussel beds, and also cultivated by driving leafless trees into the sea bottom to give mussels a place to cling.

Freshwater mussels, of which nearly 1,000 kinds are known, are widely distributed. Some are abundant in tributaries of the Mississippi River, attaining a length of 8 inches. They are used less for their meat and as a source of occasional pearls than as shells from which pearl buttons can be cut; shell waste is ground up to make lime fertilizer. Order Filobranchia, family Mytilidae, and order Eulamellibranchia, family Unionidae.

NAUTILUS, any of several shell-bearing cephalopod mollusks, distantly related to the octopus and squids. They live in the warm waters of the Indian and Pacific oceans close to the Equator, propelling themselves by squirting out sea water through a special nozzle. A nautilus has 4 gills instead of the 2 on all other cephalopods, and a large number of tentacles for capturing food. Unlike the tentacles or arms of an octopus or a squid, however, those of a nautilus lack suction cups which would give it a stronger grip.

The shell of a nautilus is a flat spiral, divided at intervals by curved partitions into a number of chambers. The animal lives in the outermost and largest chamber, but maintains control of the mixture of sea water and gas in the smaller chambers, using the mixture as a flotation device with which to rise or sink through the tropical sea in search of food.

The eyes of a nautilus lack a lens, and resemble a pinhole camera. Unlike most other cephalopod mollusks, the animal lacks an ink sac, and consequently cannot cloud the water about it while escaping from a predatory fish. About 300 different fossil species of nautilus are known, but only 4 remain alive today. Order Tetrabranchiata, genus *Nautilus*.

NEWT, or eft, any of several small aquatic, tailed amphibians or salamanders, with narrow compressed tails. The giant newt (*Triturus torosus*) of humid western parts of North America grows to be 6 inches long; it has red or orange underparts. The red eft (*T. viridescens*) is brick-colored with red and black spots. It is found in ponds and damp woodlands of eastern North America. A crested newt (*T. cristatus*) and a spotted one (*T. vulgaris*) are common in similar sites in Britain and Europe. Eft and newt are the same word; "an eft" was misdivided to "a neft" and rewritten "a newt." Order Caudata.

NIGHTHAWK, or bullbat, a medium-sized bird of the United States and Canada, allied to the whippoorwill and the nightjars. It has a short beak, an enormous mouth with which it catches flying insects while on the wing, pointed wings with a white spot near the tip, and a forked tail. The feet are so small and weak that the bird seldom walks. Instead it flutters to a stop on the ground, or a rooftop, or the tip of a fencepost, or a horizontal branch of a tree. On a branch it turns parallel, and appears to be only a swelling of the wood, its mottled brown feathers matching bark of many kinds of trees.

Nighthawks build no nest; they lay their 2 eggs in some open area where they can see any animal or person approaching. On dull days, in twilight and at night, nighthawks fly erratically in search of food, often beating their wings 3 times in quick succession and uttering a harsh *peenk*. At intervals, a bird closes its wings for a sudden dive, then, with a loud *zing-g-g*, spreads them again to check its descent. For the winter, nighthawks migrate to South America, some of them as far as Argentina. Order Caprimulgiformes, family Caprimulgidae, specifically *Chordeiles minor*.

NIGHTINGALE, either of 2 different small, inconspicuous brown thrushes of Europe, whose sweet melodious song from dense cover is enjoyed by night and by day. The nightingale (*Luscinia megarhyncha*) that visits Britain in summer is widespread in Europe south of Scandinavia. The thrush nightingale (*L. luscinia*), which has a few streaks on its underparts, visits eastern Denmark and southern Sweden in summer, but it is an eastern European and western Asian bird. The song resembles that of the American hermit thrush, which is a distantly related bird.

Nightingales build a nest of dry leaves, lined with grass, fine roots, and hair, and lay 4 or 5 eggs of olive-brown color. Order Passeriformes, family Turdidae.

NIGHTJAR, any of several kinds of Eurasian birds related to the whippoorwill of America with short beaks, enormous mouths, and long wings. The nightjar is active only at night, feeding in flight, eating large moths and smaller insects, which are caught in the widely open mouth as though the bird were trawling through the sky. By day the nightjars crouch motionless on the ground or on a tree branch, their mottled brown feathers camouflaging them well.

They build no nest, laying their eggs on the bare ground. The name refers to the loud jarring night song that rises and falls continuously for as much as 5 minutes at a time. Order Caprimulgiformes, family Caprimulgidae, members of genus *Caprimulgus*.

NUTHATCH, any of several small perching birds with strong beaks like those of woodpeckers, and large powerful feet, used in climbing down and up the bark of trees while searching for hidden insects to eat. Nuthatches do not use their short stubby tail as a prop the way a woodpecker does. They live principally in the coniferous forests of Eurasia (as far south as Malaya) and North America.

Nuthatches get their name from the habit of pecking at nuts that are wedged in the bark, probably to reach insects inside the nut. They do eat some fruits and many seeds; especially in winter, and will often visit a feeding shelf to get sunflower seeds.

Nuthatches nest in holes such as the abandoned cavities cut by woodpeckers, sometimes making their own holes by excavating the rotting wood in a dead tree. The female, whose size and coloration are closely similar to those of the male, attends to most or all of the incubation of the eggs; both sexes, however, bring insects as food for the nestlings.

Often the owner of the nest can be guessed before the bird is seen, because nuthatches commonly smear resin from coniferous trees or mud around the 1-inch opening to their nest. Order Passeriformes, family Sittidae, members of genus *Sitta*.

NUTRIA, or coypu, a South American rodent resembling a large rat, with a body weighing as much as 20 pounds; it is about 22 inches long and bears a 14-inch tail covered by scales and short hairs. The fur is long, grayish or brownish when seen at a distance, but thick because of a dense yellowish underfur visible when the outer guard hairs are parted. The large incisor teeth are bright orange-yellow. Only the hind feet are webbed. With them a nutria swims well. These animals dig burrows in the banks of rivers and marshes, and emerge principally at night to feed on many kinds of vegetation. Order Rodentia, family Myacastoridae, specifically *Myacastor coypus*.

OCELOT. See *Cat*.

OCTOPUS, or devilfish, any of a number of soft-bodied, shell-less marine cephalopod mollusks with 8 sucker-studded arms. These animals are found along most of the world's seacoasts, where they catch crabs and other animals as food. The common octopus (*Octopus vulgaris*) of the Mediterranean Sea, which is caught for food, often grows arms that can stretch 8 feet tip to tip. One (*O. apollyon*), found along the Pacific coast of North America from northern California to Alaska, is almost twice as large. Small ones are surprisingly abundant in tide pool and reef crannies in the tropics.

When it senses danger, the octopus squirts a dark inkish substance from a sac. It seems to have a high-domed head, although this actually is its body—above the head. The mouth is below, where the arms come together; in it is a pair of horny jaws and also a rasping organ *(radula)* with which an octopus can make a hole right through a heavy conch shell to reach the meat inside. Order Dibranchia, family Octopodidae.

OKAPI, a large cud-chewing mammal standing 4 feet high at the withers, with head and ears like those of a giraffe but a much shorter neck. It is found only in humid forests of Africa's Congo River basin. Its body is a curious mixture of deep red and black; the legs are cream-colored below and striped black and white where they join the body.

Sir Harry Johnston discovered the okapi in 1900. Order Artiodactyla, family Giraffidae, specifically *Okapia johnstoni*.

ONAGER. See *Ass*.

OPOSSUM, or possum, any of about 101 different kinds of short-legged, long-tailed marsupial mammals, most of which have a clawless, opposable big toe and a prehensile tail. All but one of the New World representatives live in the Tropics or in temperate South America; the exception is the Virginia opossum (*Didelphis marsupialis*), which is about the size of a housecat, occurring now from Florida north to eastern Canada and west to the Missouri River. When disturbed, it "plays possum," going into a sort of trance and giving no sport to animals that want live prey.

Possum is the official spelling for the Old World representatives, all members of family Phalangeridae, inhabiting Australia and New Guinea. The brush-tailed possum (*Trichosurus vulpecula*), which occurs in all humid forests of Australia, was introduced into New Zealand in 1900 as a fur bearer; too late was it recognized as a serious defoliater of native New Zealand trees.

All except 7 of the New World opossums belong to family Didelphidae. The 7 are small "rat" opossums from western South America, which have claws on their big toes and cannot grasp objects with their feet or their very long tails; they are grouped in family Caenolestidae. In these 7, as in some representatives among opossums and possums, a distinct pouch (marsupium) is lacking; the young must cling to the underside of the mother between two lengthwise folds of skin. Order Marsupialia.

ORANGUTAN, the Malay name (meaning man-of-the-woods) for a large manlike ape with dark brown skin and scanty reddish-brown hair. It is found in lowland swamps and forests of Borneo and Sumatra, where it grows to a height of slightly more than 4 feet. The arms of one big male, 4 feet 2 inches tall, spread 7 feet 9 inches; and when he stood erect, his hands nearly touched the ground. Such an orangutan weighs 250 to 300 pounds.

Orangutans live almost entirely in trees. They eat fruits, flowers, buds, and insects, and build for each night a new nest of leaves and boughs. The animal never jumps, but progresses through the forest by swinging itself from limb to limb. Order Primates, family Pongidae, specifically *Pbngo pygmaeus*.

ORIOLE, any of about 65 different kinds of starling-sized birds that frequent tree tops, build saucer-shaped or sac-like nests suspended from high branches, and are brightly colored, with yellow or orange generally conspicuous on the plumage. Oriole is a variant spelling of aureole, from the Latin *aureus* for golden. In Europe, Asia, and parts of Africa, more than 30 kinds of such birds are found, all members of the Old World family Oriolidae. Only the golden oriole (*Oriolus oriolus*), which winters in Africa, is common in Europe and comes as far as Britain. Australia has 2 members of this family, called figeaters (*Sphecotheres* species).

Curiously, unrelated birds in the New World show similar body form, coloring, and nesting habits. They are the 30 kinds of American orioles, including the Baltimore oriole (*Icterus galbula*), the male of which is bright orange with a black head and throat; this bird nests over much of the eastern United States and Canada, and winters in southern Mexico and Central America. However, American orioles are related closely to the blackbirds, grackles, and cowbirds, in family Icteridae. Order Passeriformes.

OSPREY, or fish hawk, a large hawk with a wingspread of as much as 72 inches, which eats fish exclusively, catching them by a spectacular plunge into the water and then grasping the prey in its strong feet. Ospreys were at one time numerous about large rivers and lakes and along coasts of North America, Central America, parts of South America (Peru, Chili, Paraguay), Asia, Australia, Europe, and Greenland. Now their numbers are reduced; and the bird is disappearing or has disappeared from many of these regions.

Ospreys generally return year after year to nest at the same site, adding sticks to a bulky mass built atop a dead tree, a utility pole, or even on the ground. Both parents defend the nest and tend the 2 to 4 eggs, the young that hatch out blind and helpless, and the young birds that grow rapidly on fishes brought to them all day long.

The female osprey is larger than her mate, weighing between 4 and 5 pounds; a male bird rarely is heavier than 3 pounds 3 ounces. In flight, both appear to hold their wings in a bent position. Often an osprey with a fish in its grasp is robbed of its prey by an eagle that attacks it in mid-air. Order Falconiformes, family Pandionidae, specifically *Pandion haliaëtus*.

OSTRICH, the largest of living birds, males growing 8 feet tall and reaching 250 pounds in weight. They graze on grasses and other low plants on African savannas south of the great deserts.

Ostriches are flightless because of their great size, but not wingless although their wing muscles are small and weak. Feathers from wings and tail formerly were used for decorating hats, but today the chief uses for ostrich plumes are in feather dusters and feather boas for stage costumes. To supply these, and ostrich meat and ostrich eggs, ostrich farms have been developed in South America, South Africa, and California.

A hen ostrich lays 10 to 12 eggs on the sand. Two or 3 hens of a single male may lay eggs in the same nest. The male stands guard over them by day, shielding them from the sun or warming them with his body, depending on the temperature. At night the females take turns incubating the eggs. Each egg has about the volume of 24 eggs of domestic fowl. Order Struthioniformes, family Struthionidae, specifically *Struthio camelus*.

OTTER, any of about 17 different kinds of short-legged, heavy-bodied, swimming mammals with durable, valuable fur. Most are river otters (species of *Lutra*), playful animals that live on fish in the Americas, much of Africa and Eurasia, including East Indian islands. They slide down mud banks and snow banks, headfirst into streams. One kind is the rare sea otter (*Enhydra lutris*) of kelp beds along North Pacific coasts from California to Alaska and Kamchatka, where it feeds on sea urchins, sea snails, and mussels. The mother sea otter plays with her pups for hours and sometimes is seen asleep on a tangle of seaweed in the water, lying on her back with the little otter in her front paws. Order Carnivora, family Mustelidae.

OWL, any of about 123 different kinds of predatory birds with extremely large heads; huge eyes directed forward; short, stout beaks hooked at the tip; and very large ear openings. Owls have feathered legs and 4 toes, the outer one capable of being directed backward to make a clutching fist. Their plumage is remarkably soft, and the feathers of the face form disks around the eyes.

Owls are found over the whole globe. Species vary in size from 5 inches to 2 feet in length. They feed

on small mammals, birds, fishes, and insects, swallowing the prey whole. Afterward they disgorge the hair, bones, feathers, and scales in the form of pellets. They nest on the ground, among rocks, in hollow trees and in buildings; some resort to the old nests of other birds. They lay from 2 to 5 roundish, white eggs.

Several species have feathered tufts of either side of the top of the head and are called horned owls or catowls — notably the eagle owl (*Bubo bubo*) of Europe and Asia and the North American great horned owl (*B. virginianus*), both about 25 inches long. The snow owl or snowy owl (*Nyctea scandiaca*), despite its scientific name meaning nocturnal, hunts in the long daylight of the Arctic in both hemispheres; it occasionally winters in northern United States; it has no horns and is almost snow-white.

One of the smallest owls is the 5½-inch elf owl (*Micropallas whitneyi*) of the American Southwest and Mexico, which often nests in abandoned

LOOK MAGAZINE

OWL

woodpecker holes in large saguaro cactuses. The burrowing owl (*Speotyto cunicularia*) of the American plains lives in the deserted holes of prairie dogs and viscachas. It is 9 or 10 inches long, and its legs are longer and barer than those of other owls. Order Strigiformes, family Strigidae.

OX. See *Cattle.*

OYSTER, any of a number of different marine bivalved mollusks that, at an early age, cease swimming and attach themselves by the left shell valve to the ocean bottom or a mangrove root or a wharf piling. Oysters live near shore along most coasts. Most valuable as a source of luxury food is the Atlantic-coast oyster (*Ostraea virginica*) of the United States from Cape Cod to the Gulf of Mexico. Formerly it extended to the coast of Maine, and even now there are scattered beds in the Gulf of St. Lawrence.

The European oyster (*O. edulis*) is smaller than the American and has a coppery taste. Both sexes are united in the same individual, whereas in the American species the sexes are separate.

In tropical waters, divers seek pearl oysters, *Avicula* and *Pinctada*, which are especially abundant around Cey-

lon, and *Margaritophora* near Bermuda. These oysters habitually secrete mother-of-pearl, which is the ordinary lining material for their shells, around sand grains, small worms, or other foreign particles that get between the body and shell. Layer after layer is added until a hard lump is formed; if it is spherical or of some interesting shape and suitably lustrous, the lump is a precious pearl. Order Prionodesmacea, family Ostreidae.

PANTHER. See *Cat.*

PARROT, any of about 315 different kinds of brightly colored birds in which both upper and lower beak are hinged movably to the skull, and the foot grasps strongly with 2 toes forward and 2 in back. Parrots live in all countries and major islands in the Tropics and also in some adjacent temperate lands.

In the southeastern United States there formerly lived a Carolina paroquet (*Conuropsis carolinensis*), but it was exterminated before 1910; tropical American parrots include 25 kinds of large macaws (species of *Ara*) with long slender tails, and another 25 of green parrots with short tails (species of *Amazona*), as well as numerous conures, parakeets, and parrotlets.

Africa is the home of the gray parrot (*Psittacus erithaceus*) with a red tail, which is particularly desirable as a cage bird because it excels in imitating human speech; other African relatives are the small colorful lovebirds (*Agapornis* species) of many kinds. Australia and New Guinea have numerous kinds of cockatoos, lorikeets, and the popular budgerigars (*Melopsittacus undulatus*) that now rival canaries as house pets.

New Zealand parrots include three plump kinds that are almost as big as a chicken: the flightless owl parrot, or kakapo (*Strigops habroptilus*), a rare ground bird of forest glades; the equally rare kaka (*Nestor meridionalis*), which feeds on fruit, nectar, and insects; and the mountain kea (*N. notabilis*), which now stays near camps and sheep-butchering stations, feeding on scraps and waste fat from sheep carcasses. No other parrot seems to have changed thus far from a diet of seeds and fruits in the treetops. Order Psittaciformes, family Psittacidae.

PARTRIDGE, any of several fowl-like birds with short beak, short legs, and short tail, and which produce a loud whirring sound when frightened into flying away.

Originally the word partridge referred to particular birds of Eurasia and Africa, specifically the Hungarian, or European, gray partridge (*Perdix perdix*), and the red-legged, or Chukar, partridge (*Alectoris rufa*) of Europe, Corsica, and the Canary Islands; both have been introduced widely into North America, New Zealand, and elsewhere as upland game birds that offer good targets and good eating.

In North America, the word partridge is often applied to quail in the southern states, and to the ruffed grouse farther north. Order Galliformes, family Phasianidae.

PEAFOWL, any of 3 different large pheasantlike birds with a slightly curved beak, a small distinctive crest on the head, short wings, long stout legs and, in the male, a magnificent set of long gold and green tail coverts that the peacock during courtship raises vertically like a semicircular screen extending from the ground on one side to the ground on the other.

The domesticated peafowl (*Pavo cristatus*) is native to India and Ceylon; both peacock and peahen have a blue neck and crest feathers with the little vanes only at the tips; the tail-covert feathers of the male are elaborately patterned with large eyespots, which show even when the plumes are lowered to make a "train" behind the bird. White peafowl, with no markings, are not uncommon in domestic flocks.

A Javanese peafowl (*P. muticus*) with a green neck and crest feathers with vanes the whole length lives in humid forests of Java and adjacent Southeast Asia. A Congolese peafowl (*Afropavo congensis*) is a glossy black bird with a patch of white in its crown. Order Galliformes, family Phasianidae.

PECCARY, either of 2 different kinds of New World wild pigs, whose tusks point downward instead of outward or upward, whose 2-chambered stomach shows special complexity, and whose long slim legs are peculiar in that the hind feet have only 3 toes, instead of the usual 4 among pigs.

Native to the New World, peccaries are forest animals, usually seen in bands containing both sexes and all ages. The larger white-lipped peccary (*Tayassu pecari*), which associates in groups of 50 to 100 or more, may if threatened, counterattack, slashing effectively with its sharp tusk.

Peccaries live from Paraguay to southern Mexico. The collared peccary (*T. tajacu*), found from Arizona and Texas to Patagonia, travels in bands of 5 to 15, often roaming desert regions as well as tropical forests.

Members of both species use their snouts to dig for vegetable food, grubs, snakes, and other small animals; sometimes they raid cultivated fields and inflict damage. Generally the presence of peccaries in an area is indicated by the strong-smelling substance their musk glands secrete whenever they are excited. Order Artiodactyla, family Tayassuidae.

PELICAN, any of 6 different kinds of fish-eating, swimming birds with a large pouch of skin between the halves of the lower jaw.

In the New World, the brown pelican (*Pelecanus occidentalis*) ranges along coasts from the southern United States to Venezuela and Chile; the white pelican (*P. erythrorhynchus*) is an inland bird, nesting from British Columbia to Ontario, and migrating to Mexico and the Gulf States in winter. Old World pelicans are largely white and venture far inland in Africa, southern Europe, southern Asia, to southeastern Australia.

All pelicans can hover, fold their wings, and plunge into water after fish. Sometimes they fish in groups. They scoop the fish into the pouch and swallow it while flying again or after returning to the shore. Order Pelecaniformes, family Pelecanidae.

PENGUIN, any of 15 different short-tailed swimming birds of the Southern Hemisphere, in which the strong wings lack flight feathers and are stiff, moving only at the shoulder as paddles for underwater propulsion or as weapons in self-defense. Except for the Galápagos penguin (*Spheniscus mendiculus*), which lives on the Equator surrounded by icy water, they are birds of the Antarctic and the southernmost coasts of Africa, Australia, New Zealand, South America, and remote islands.

Tallest is the emperor penguin (*Aptenoides forsteri*), 4 feet high, which lays its eggs and raises its chicks on Antarctica during the winter night there. The only other penguins on Antarctica are the Adélies (*Pygoscelis adeliae*), 30 inches tall. Of medium size and with a call like a donkey's bray is the jackass penguin (*Spheniscus demersus*) of South America and South Africa. The smallest is the fairy penguin (*Eudyptula minor*) of Australia and New Zealand, 16 inches tall.

Newly hatched penguins are covered with down, but the grown birds have stiff scalelike feathers. Their food consists chiefly of fish and squids. Order Sphenisciformes, family Spheniscidae.

PERCH, either of 2 small, edible, fresh-water fishes in which the pelvic fins are far forward, close to the pectoral fins, the dorsal fin has its spiny and its soft portions separated from one another, and there are 3 anal spines instead of 2, as in sunfishes.

The European perch (*Perca fluviatilis*), found through most of Europe to Siberia and in brackish waters of the Black Sea, sometimes grows to weigh 6 pounds. The yellow perch (*P. flavescens*) of North America lived only east of the Rocky Mountains until it was introduced elsewhere; a 15-inch fish weighing 2 pounds is a large one. Its orange-yellow sides have 6 to 8 dark vertical stripes, and its pelvic fins are reddish. Order Percomorphi, family Percidae.

PERIWINKLE, or winkle, any of several different kinds of small snails of the seacoast, with a compact top-shaped shell and a horny plate on the side of its foot with which to block the shell opening after the animal has withdrawn inside. Originally native to European coasts, periwinkles have now been introduced widely around the world. Periwinkles feed almost exclusively on small seaweeds, and their meat is delicately flavored.

Unlike many snails, a periwinkle has its foot divided into a right side and a left, and creeps by swinging alternately from side to side with a peculiar rolling gait. To reach its food, a periwinkle extends its tonguelike rasping organ (radula), which sometimes is twice as long as the 1-inch foot of the animal. Order Aspidobranchia, family Littorinidae, members of genus *Littorina*.

PETREL, any of 26 different kinds of small, web-footed sea birds, which have their nostrils opening at the end of a tubelike part of the upper beak. Four are plump-bodied diving petrels (family Pelecanoididae), resembling auks, flying with rapidly whirring wings, which they use also in swimming underwater in pursuit of fish. The others are slender-bodied storm petrels (family Hydrobatidae), which flutter over the sea surface but seldom alight, while feeding on squid, floating mollusks, surface shrimp and other crustaceans, or the galley scraps from passing ships.

Petrels are found far out at sea on all oceans, except at nesting time, when they return to offshore islands or the slopes of coastal mountains, generally coming in at dusk or after dark to burrows 2 to 3 feet deep or crannies under loose rocks. Leach's petrel (*Oceanodroma leucorhoa*) of the North Atlantic and North Pacific has a forked tail, the storm petrel (*Hydrobates pelagicus*) of European coasts, a rounded or square tail; both have become well known from their habit of following ships day after day, and are called Mother Carey's chickens—from the Latin *mater cara*, the divine virgin, referring to the Virgin Mary who is guardian of all seafarers. Petrel is believed to be a diminutive of St. Peter, alluding to the apparent ability of petrels to walk on water.

The name petrel is often given also to a shearwater, the giant fulmar, or giant petrel (*Macronectes giganteus*) of southern oceans, a bird 3 feet long with an 8-foot wingspan. No true petrel is longer than 10 inches; they are the smallest of all pelagic birds. Order Procellariiformes.

PEWEE, or wood pewee, a small inconspicuous woodland flycatcher whose olive-gray body blends with the shadows while it perches on a branch, awaiting a flying insect. The pewee flits out quickly, catches the insect, and returns to the same or another branch, often calling *pee'-a-wee'* or *pee'-wee* in a plaintive way.

The bird has a forked tail, 2 pale wing bars, and often raises the feathers on its head to form a low crest. It builds its nest on an outstretched branch of a deciduous tree, constructing it of rootlets and other plant fibers, frequently covering it with lichens as though for camouflage.

For the winter, pewees migrate to northwestern South America, where they mingle with closely related birds from western North America. The western wood pewee (*C. sordidulus*), which inhabits more open woodlands and calls *dear* or *dear-me*, often sings at night. Order Passeriformes, family Tyrannidae, specifically *Contopus virens*.

PHALAROPE, any of 3 different shore birds of the Arctic, resembling large sandpipers, in which the female is larger than the male, with a wingspread from 14 to 16 inches, and does the courting; she is more brightly colored but often leaves the building of the nest and incubation of the eggs she lays in it to her mate. All nest in the Arctic, their small pear-shaped eggs hatching in about two weeks, and the young birds hiding themselves among grasses near the simple nest.

The northern phalarope (*Lobipes lobatus*), known as the red-necked phalarope in Britain and Europe, flutters over salt water, using its long beak to catch minute crustaceans and other small plankton animals as food. The red phalarope (*Phalaropus fulicarius*), called the gray phalarope in the Old World, swims more frequently in freshwater and performs characteristic spinning movements that appear to disturb insects, snails, and other prey into moving and being seen.

The Wilson's phalarope (*Steganopus tricolor*) of Arctic America nests farther south, to California and Indiana, feeding itself and young on terrestrial insects, crustaceans, spiders, and snails found near the marshlands where it nests. As soon as their young are ready to fly, all phalaropes migrate far south to cold waters off the coasts of South Africa and South America, particularly where ocean currents from the Antarctic enrich the surface waters and support large numbers of plankton, crustaceans, and small fishes. Order Charadriiformes, family Phalaropodidae.

PHEASANT, any of about 50 different kinds of large, long-tailed, grouselike birds. They are native to central and southern Asia and the East Indies, but many of them have been introduced elsewhere. The ringneck, or English or Mongolian pheasant (*Phasianus colchicus*) probably reached Britain during Roman times; it is a well-known and popular game bird. The argus pheasant (*Argusianus argus*) of Southeast Asia is almost as big as a peacock. Female pheasants are dull and plain compared to the males. In some parts of the United States, the name pheasant is used loosely for grouse and quail. Order Galliformes, family Phasianidae.

PHOEBE, a medium-sized flycatcher, is olive-gray in color, slightly paler below; continually wagging its tail up and down, it frequently calls its name *phee'-be* or (more insistently) *phee'-beee'*. Like other flycatchers it perches on bare branches where it can see flying insects coming, and dart out to catch them. It builds its nest under a cover, such as alongside an overhanging bank above a stream or under a bridge or porch roof.

In winter it migrates to Florida, the Gulf States, and Mexico. It was a nestful of young phoebes that John James Audubon marked along a stream in Pennsylvania, using loose bracelets of silver wire, in the first experimental study to determine whether birds return after a winter's absence to the region where they were hatched. Of 5 phoebes marked in this way, 3 returned the following spring to nest along the same stream. Order Passeriformes, family Tyrannidae, specifically *Sayornis phoebe*.

PICKEREL. See *Pike*.

PIG. See *Swine*.

PIGEON, any of almost 300 different kinds of small-headed, stout-bodied birds with short, rounded beaks topped by a fleshy part (the cere) through which the nostrils open. They are represented on every continent and most islands. Generally the term pigeon refers to birds with square or rounded tails, and the term dove to more slender-bodied related birds with pointed tails.

Domesticated and city pigeons are derived from the common rock pigeon (*Columba livia*), about 13 inches long, native to southern Eurasia and north Africa. Careful breeding has produced from this bird distinctive strains excelling in racing speed, homing ability, aerial acrobatics, showy feathers, and quick production of meat for people who enjoy eating young birds (squabs) that have just reached full growth.

The extinct passenger pigeon (*Ectopistes migratorius*) that vanished in the wild about 1899 had occupied vast oak and beech forests in central and eastern North America. Colonists destroyed their habitat, and also netted, shot, and trapped the birds for shipment to market until there were no more.

The giants are the 3 kinds of crowned pigeons in New Guinea, as much as 33 inches long. They have a crest of lacy feathers, and 16 instead of the usual 12 tail feathers. Nearby Australia has big, metallic-colored pigeons called bronzewings (the common one is *Phaps chalcoptera*), which eat so many seeds from a poisonous plant that their bones and internal organs are deadly to predatory animals, although their flesh is unharmed and edible. Order Columbiformes, family Columbidae.

PIKE, any of about 8 different kinds of predatory fishes of northern freshwaters, with a long pointed head, large mouth with formidable teeth, no spines in any of the fins, the dorsal fin far back—behind the pelvic fins and above the anal fin—and with a body slender and spear-shaped, as the name pike suggests.

Most widespread is the northern pike (*Esox lucius*) of Eurasia and the northern United States and Canada, a fish that has been recorded as attaining 54 inches in length and a weight of 46 pounds. It is exceeded in both ways by the muskellunge (*E. masquinongy*) of the upper Great Lakes and adjacent waters, which may grow to 102 pounds.

Smaller relatives of these large fish are called pickerels ("little pikes"), and differ in details of the scale pattern on the head and body, as well as in distribution and habits. Aside from the northern pike, the only member of this group in Eurasia is the black-spotted pike (*E. reicherti*) of Siberia. Order Haplomi, family Esocidae.

The fish called a walleyed pike (*Stizostedion vitreum*), found in eastern North America, and the pikeperch (*Lucioperca lucioperca*), found in Eurasia, are members of the perch family.

U.S. ARMY SIGNAL CORPS

PIGEON

PINTAIL, a dabbling duck of freshwaters, in which the male has 2 long middle tail feathers 5 to 9 inches long stretching out behind his 28-inch body. Pintails breed in northern Eurasia, Canada, and the northwestern United States, migrating southward and to the Pacific coast in winter.

The male has a reddish-brown head, gray back, and white throat and underparts. The female is smaller and is streaked with brown. They nest on the ground, concealed in bunches of grass or weeds, usually near water. Seven to 10 greenish eggs are laid in March or April. Order Anseriformes, family Anatidae, specifically *Anas acuta*.

PIRANHA, any of several South American freshwater fishes 7 to 24 inches long, with elliptical bodies, strong lower jaw, and many razor-sharp teeth. Four kinds of piranha are greatly feared in their native rivers and lakes, because they attack in large numbers any person or mammal that enters the same water—particularly if it falls in and splashes about.

Most widely distributed is the 4-inch *Serrasalmus nattereri* of the Brazilian river systems, particularly the Amazon, whose normal diet consists of other fishes. This piranha might be mistaken for a small sunfish until it darts at a victim and uses its incredibly strong jaws and sharp teeth to cut out pieces of flesh and bone. Fishermen seek piranhas, an excellent food, but use strong wire leaders on fishing lines to prevent the piranha from cutting itself loose and swimming away with the baited hook. Order Ostariophysi, family Characidae, species of *Serrasalmus*.

PIT-VIPER, any of several poisonous snakes, which possess between nostril and eye a distinctive pit that is sensitive to radiant heat. They live in eastern Asia and the New World. Using its paired pits, the snake even in complete darkness, can find animals as prey because these are warmer than their surroundings—as a sleeping bird or a mammal would be, or cooler—as a frog would be because of evaporation from its wet skin. The pit-viper strikes its prey with two erectile fangs in its upper jaw, within which venom canals are connected to large glands that secrete the poison.

Most feared of these snakes is the bushmaster (*Lachesis muta*) of northern South America, Panama, and parts of Costa Rica, which lies in wait for small mammals along their trails through forest and scrubland where its mottled brown color makes it almost invisible. No less deadly is the smaller fer-de-lance (*Bothrops atrox*) which sometimes attains a length of 8 feet and frequents coconut plantations from southern Mexico to southern Peru, through all of northern South America. Like most pit-vipers, but unlike the bushmaster which lays eggs, the fer-de-lance mother brings forth active young, as many as 71 at a birth, each with its sensory pits and venom apparatus fully developed.

Far less dangerous are the copperhead (*Ancistrodon contortrix*) of forest regions in eastern North America, the cottonmouth moccasin (*A. piscivorus*) of swamplands in the southern United States, and related members of the same genus in Mexico and the Old World from the southern edge of the Russian steppes to Ceylon, Malaya, and Japan.

Rattlesnakes (*Crotalus* and *Sistrurus*), which are exclusively North American, represent a more venomous group of pit-vipers. In these snakes, only part of each old skin is shed at molting time, and the remainder contributes to the accumulated loose sections of the "rattle" at the end of the tail. Because the terminal "button" and additional parts of the rattle commonly break away and the snake may shed its skin more than once a year, it is impossible to learn the age of a rattlesnake by counting the pieces in its rattle.

The amount of venom that a rattlesnake can inject, and hence the danger offered by the snake, is roughly proportionate to the length of the animal. This varies from one species to another, the giant being the eastern diamondback rattlesnake (*C. adamanteus*), one of which was found to be 98 inches long. Next in size, so far as known, are the western diamondback (84 inches), the western Mexican rattlesnake (80 inches), and the South American rattlesnake (78 inches).

The famous timber rattlesnake (*C. horridus*), which was the first kind encountered by the English colonists, sometimes reached a length of 75 inches. It is still found in many parts of the area from northern New England to northern Florida, west to eastern Texas and north to Wisconsin. From this territory westward to the Pacific coast and northward into Canada, the prairie rattler (*C. viridis*) takes its place, sometimes becoming as much as 60 inches long. Order Serpentes, family Crotalidae.

PLATYPUS. See *Duckbill*.

PLOVER, any of 38 different kinds of shore birds with legs of moderate length and beaks no longer than the head, slightly enlarged toward the tip. They are found almost all over the world, nesting on open beaches and fields, where their spotted eggs blend inconspicuously and are easily overlooked. In England and on the Continent plovers' eggs are a great delicacy.

As a group, plovers are noted for covering enormous distances on their migratory flights. The golden plover (*Pluvius dominica*), about 11 inches long, a beautiful but fast-diminishing species, breeds on the Arctic coasts but winters in southeastern Brazil and Argentina; its annual southern flight takes it many hundreds of miles out to sea, although it takes an overland route flying north.

One of the most familiar plovers is the killdeer of North America (*Charadrius vociferus*), so called because the Latin word *vociferus* (loud) describes its noisy, reiterated cry. Killdeers, often found in the uplands many miles from water, are recognizable by their brown back, tail and wings. They are 10 inches long, brownish above and with 2 black bands on the white breast and 2 on the head.

The pole-backed, 7-inch piping plover (*C. meloda*) is nearly always found on the beach where it is often difficult to distinguish from the sand whose color it matches; it has a plaintive, melodious whistle, as indicated by its name. Order Charadriiformes, family Charadriidae.

POLECAT, any of several weasel-like predatory mammals in which the anal musk glands are well developed, producing a fetid secretion when the animal is threatened. Native to northern Africa and Eurasia, they have contributed one member which can be domesticated—the ferret, which is usually an albino and is valuable in driving rabbits from burrows or in destroying rats.

The wild form of the ferret is the most widespread polecat (*Mustela putorius*); it grows to 20 inches long with a 7-inch tail, is dark brown to black in color with a yellow patch on each side of the head between ear and eye. Its pelt is sold in the fur trade as "fitch." A marbled polecat (*Vormela peregusna*) lives in steppes of southeastern Europe and across to Mongolia, differing markedly from other polecats in its mottled dark and pale coloration. Order Carnivora, family Mustelidae.

POLLOCK. See *Cod*.

PORCUPINE, any of about 43 different kinds of rodents in which the back, and often the head and tail as well, bear large hollow barbed quills that pull out easily from among the shorter fur. In the Old World, 20 kinds in family Hystricidae live mostly on the ground, eating carrion and plant materials, in Africa, southern Europe to southern China, Indonesia, and the Philippines. In the New World, 23 kinds in family Erethizontidae are more tree-dwellers, as vegetarians, ranging from coast to coast and from the Arctic to southern South America.

When disturbed, a porcupine tries to hide its unprotected and sensitive nose, while presenting its quills by raising them at right angles from the body. The North American porcupine

AMERICAN MUSEUM OF NATURAL HISTORY
PORCUPINE

(*Erethizon dorsatum*) may back up, swatting vigorously with its quill-studded tail. Porcupines in Central and South America have prehensile tails that help them hold on while eating leaves high in the trees. The porcupines of Europe and Africa are as much as 32 inches long, weigh as much as 56 pounds, and have some quills 12 inches long. At birth, the quills are soft, but they harden in a few hours. Order Rodentia.

PORPOISE (from old French for hogfish), any of about 7 different kinds of small-toothed whales less than 6 feet long, with a blunt nose. Almost all of the world's coasts, estuaries, and harbors are visited by these animals as they hunt for unarmed fishes of modest size, squid, and crustaceans; sometimes they are seen following schools of fish, singly or in pairs or in groups of nearly 100. Unlike dolphins, they rarely follow ships.

Formerly they were caught in Europe for meat and an oil useful for lubrication and for burning. Porpoise fisheries still operate along the coasts of some Oriental countries. Order Cetacea, family Delphinidae, chiefly genus *Phocaena*.

PORTUGUESE MAN–OF–WAR, a dangerous colony of marine coelenterate animals, 1 member of which at a time grows to become a pinkish blue, gas-filled balloon as much as 8 inches long and 5 high. The float provides buoyant support for the colony; floating high in the sea surface, it catches the wind and hence pulls the colony along. Below it dozens of other members of the colony extend slender contractile tentacles, deep blue in color and as much as 60 feet long.

The tentacles hang down like fishing lines, waiting for fishes and other edible animals to bump into them. Special nettling cells on the tentacles can inject poison into a victim, stunning or killing it, while other cells cling to the prey and the whole tentacle (or group of tentacles) shortens to haul up the victim right under the float. There other individuals with soft flexible mouths begin digesting the prey. The digested food is then shared throughout the colony. In season, special reproductive individuals are formed, providing eggs and sperms for sexual multiplication.

The Portuguese man-of-war is common in tropical American waters, and is often carried northward by the Gulf Stream, to be blown ashore. Even dead colonies on the beach can sting painfully if their tentacles are touched, and live ones in water can sting a human swimmer worse than a nestful of wasps. Order Siphonophora, family Physalidae, specifically *Physalia pelagica*.

PRAIRIE CHICKEN. See *Grouse*.

PRAIRIE DOG, any of 5 different kinds of short-tailed, short-legged burrowing squirrel-like mammals. They live sociably in prairie-dog "towns" where bison used to roam, on the plains east of the Rocky Mountains, from the Canadian prairie provinces to northern Mexico. Like their relatives, the marmots, prairie dogs have well-developed claws on all the toes of the forefeet and shallow cheek pouches. They feed on herbs and grasses but store little.

The best-known species is the plains prairie dog (*Cynomys ludovicianus*), about 1 foot long with a 4-inch tail, reddish-brown above, variegated with gray. The name refers to their alarm cry, which suggests the barking of a small dog. Order Rodentia, family Sciuridae, all members of genus *Cynomys*.

PRAYING MANTIS, any of about 1,500 kinds of predatory insects with special grasping forelegs, thought to be the only insect with a neck so flexible it can turn its head and look backward. For hours a praying mantis may remain motionless or may sway slightly on the 4 long slender legs that support it, waiting for some other insect to come within snatching distance. Victims are held firmly by the forelegs, which are folded once again in a prayerful attitude, while the head is moved and the jaws are brought into play.

A female mantis may even eat her mate and incorporate his nourishment into the mass of eggs she will lay. As many as 1,000 eggs go into each mass, which is affixed to a plant stem or other support and coated with a brown froth that hardens as it dries. In the spring, miniature praying mantises emerge and are distributed by the wind. Those that survive will grow slowly, molt by molt, until they acquire wings and become mature—usually by autumn.

The largest mantises in the United States are the kind introduced from China (*Paratenodera sinensis*), of which females may be nearly 6 inches long. The introduced European mantis (*Mantis religiosa*) is rarely more than 2 inches long. There is only 1 mantis (*Stagmomantis carolina*) native to the United States. Order Orthoptera, family Mantidae.

PRONGHORN, a handsome antelope-like mammal, which differs from all true antelopes in possessing on the head of both sexes an unusual kind of armament—a pair of horns with a bony core, covered by a horny sheath that is shed each year. This is the swiftest mammal of the New World, able to run at least 65 miles per hour and to "cruise along" at 48 mph, often traveling 20 miles a day in its native western North America.

A full grown male (buck) pronghorn weighs about 125 pounds and stands 3 feet high at the shoulder. A female (doe) may reach 90 pounds. Both are marked alike, the back, 3 collars, and a streak down to each leg being reddish brown, the hind-quarters shining white, and the rest of the animal sand-colored.

Pronghorns feed on a wide variety of vegetation in open country, in herds and as individuals at short distances from one another. When alarmed they flash their white rumps in many directions, alerting all pronghorns in sight. Order Artiodactyla, family Antilocapridae, specifically *Antilocapra americana*.

PTARMIGAN, any of 4 different kinds of grouselike birds with feathers all the way down the legs and out on the toes. They live in the Arctic and on high mountains, nesting in thickets on the ground, eating buds, insects, berries, and roots.

Ptarmigans, with one exception, are reddish-brown in the summer, but turn snow-white in winter—a remarkable example of protective coloration. The exception is called the red grouse (*Lagopus scoticus*), and is found now only in Ireland and England. Britain has also the rock ptarmigan (*L. mutus*) and the willow ptarmigan (*L. lagopus*), both of which are circumpolar. A distinctive white-tailed ptarmigan (*L. leucurus*) living above the snowline in Alaska and the Rocky Mountains retains the white color of its tail in summer. Order Galliformes, family Tetraonidae.

PUFFIN, or sea parrot, any of 3 kinds of sea birds with heavy bodies, short tails, short-pointed wings, short necks, and enormous triangular beaks marked with red, yellow, and blue. At the end of the breeding season, the bright covering of the beak is shed, and a new one grown, bearing an extra ridge and colored stripe by which the age of a puffin can be estimated. A puffin feeds mostly on fish, crustaceans, and small mollusks.

Nesting in colonies on offshore islands along northern coasts, these birds produce a single large egg, then tend the single young in a hole in the ground or a natural crevice among boulders. The young bird becomes enormously fat, heavier than the parents, and is then deserted. It completes its development, taking on adult form, finds its way to the coast, and dives into the sea to get its food.

The Atlantic puffin (*Fratercula arctica*) is abundant in Iceland and breeds in smaller numbers as far south as Maine and Britain. Pacific puffins of the Far North include the horned puffin (*F. corniculata*) which has a small, fleshy appendage like a horn on its upper eyelid, and the tufted puffin (*Lunda cirrhata*), named for the yellow plume of feathers extending backward like a great eyebrow on each side of the head. Order Charadriiformes, family Alcidae.

PUMA. See *Cat*.

QUAIL, any of about 40 different kinds of small, grouselike birds with short beaks, wings, and tails, but strong legs and plump bodies. The 33 in the New World are nonmigratory, lack spurs, and have a notch in the cutting edge of the upper bill. They include the 4 different bobwhite quails (*Colinus* species) that live in fields and woodland edges from Canada to South America, whistling loudly the 2-note call for which they are named; and the valley quail (*Lophortyx californicus*) of the American Southwest and Mexico, in which the male has a fancy little recurved plume over his forehead.

The 7 kinds of quails in the Old World are migratory, lack the notch in the beak, and mostly have spurs. One is the European quail (*Coturnix coturnix*), which ranges widely over Eurasia and Africa. Three others have spread from Southeast Asia all the way to Australia and New Zealand: the Australian brown quail (*Synoicus ypsilophorus*), the Chinese painted quail (*Excalfactoria chinensis*) no bigger than a sparrow, and the stubble quail (*Coturnix novae-zealandiae*) which vanished in New Zealand in 1870. Order Galliformes, family Phasianidae.

QUETZAL. See *Trogon*.

RABBIT, any of about 18 different kinds of long-eared, long-legged, short-tailed mammals similar to hares but differing in being born naked, blind, and helpless in a nest prepared by the mother. They are generally smaller than the hares and live only on grasses or other herbaceous matter.

In the New World they are represented by 13 kinds of cottontails, marsh rabbits, and tropical forest rabbits (all in genus *Sylvilagus*) from southern Canada to Argentina and by the volcano rabbit (*Romerolagus diazi*) of highland Mexico, trotting instead of hopping.

In the Old World, the most widespread kind of rabbit is the European rabbit (*Oryctolagus cuniculus*), which makes extensive burrows in the wild, and is raised for food, fur, experimental medicine, and for esthetic purposes; the "Belgian hare" is one true-breeding strain.

Additional kinds of rabbits are found locally in the Ryukyu Islands near Japan, in the foothills of the Himalayas, in forests of Sumatra, and in African equatorial forests. Order Lagomorpha, family Leporidae.

RACCOON, or coon, any of several different kinds of doglike forest mammals with a black masklike mark across the eyes, fore paws that are almost as flexible and versatile as a monkey's, hind feet that make footprints like a child's, and a well-furred tail marked with 5 to 10 black rings.

Raccoons are forest dwellers from southern Canada to northern South America. They climb and swim well, and prefer food found close to water, in which they habitually manipulate it, perhaps to free it of grit. From this comes the name of the most widespread species, *Procyon lotor*—the

AMERICAN MUSEUM OF NATURAL HISTORY

STING RAY

washer. During the day the raccoon curls up in a tree to sleep. Order Carnivora, family Procyonidae, all members of genus *Procyon*.

RAIL, any of about 100 different kinds of running, swimming, and wading birds of marshes and tussock land, distinguished from the closely related coots and gallinules by the narrowness of their bodies, which helps when they run through thick marsh vegetation. They are "thin as rails."

Rails are found throughout the world except in polar regions. Living almost exclusively in marshlands, they are shy and use their wings only as a last resort, when they fly feebly for a short distance, immediately settling back into the swamp grass from which they were flushed.

Long-billed rails include the largest kind, the king rail (*Rallus elegans*) of the eastern United States. It grows to about 19 inches long, is dusky brown in color, and similar to the 11-inch Virginia rail (*R. virginianus*). Short-billed rails, called crakes in Europe, include the common American sora rail (*Porzana carolina*), 9 inches long, brown above and gray below. Rails are largely nocturnal in habits, and so elusive by day that gunners generally try to approach them silently by boat. Order Gruiformes, family Rallidae.

RAT, a vague term applied to almost any medium-sized rodent with a pointed nose, unspecialized legs, and long, usually naked tail. New World rats include rice rats, water rats, climbing rats, vesper rats, Andean rats, web-footed rats, cotton rats, pack rats, wood rats, fish-eating rats, mole rats, maned rats, and sand rats, all in family Cricetidae. Old World rats include climbing rats, spiny rats, tree rats, thick-tailed rats, shaggy-haired rats, bush rats, swamp rats, soft-furred rats, water rats, pouched rats, prehensile-tailed rats, cloud rats with bushy tails, shrewlike rats, and the two most destructive rats—the Norway rat (*Rattus norvegicus*) and the black rat (*Rattus rattus*).

The Norway rat probably is native to Japan and eastern Asia, and reached Europe about 1730 and America by 1775, to both by ship. The black rat comes from Asia Minor, and came to Europe with the returning Crusaders. It is a better climber than the Norway rat, and lives better under tropical conditions. Both kinds harbor and carry bubonic plague, typhus fever, trichinosis, rabies, tularemia, and other diseases deadly to man. The laboratory white rat is a domesticated variety of the black rat. Order Rodentia, family Muridae.

RAVEN. See *Crow.*

RAY, any of about 340 different kinds of cartilaginous marine fishes in which the body is flattened or extended to the sides, the pectoral fins greatly enlarged, the gill slits on the lower surface, the pelvic fins small, and the tail often long and whiplike.

Rays are most abundant and varied in the Tropics, but are found also along cold coasts and in the great abysses. The giant manta rays, or devilfishes, measure as much as 22 feet from side to side, and probably weigh more than 3,500 pounds; they cruise slowly near the surface, using a special pair of feeding fins to drive small crustaceans and other food toward the cavernous scooplike mouth.

Sawfishes have the head prolonged into a flat "saw," studded on each side with sharp teeth; they use this strange tool to dislodge edible animals from sandy bottoms, and to slash sideways through schools of fishes, maiming and impaling many victims, which they can then eat at a leisurely pace. Rays of 2 different families have venom spines on their tails, and are called stingrays. Perhaps 25 different kinds of rays can discharge jolts of electricity in self-defense or to stun prey; they are called torpedoes or electric rays. Most rays, however, are relatively harmless, feeding on mollusks, crustaceans and small fishes they catch along the sea bottom and crush with teeth that have flat surfaces fitting together like tiles in a mosaic.

All rays swim with special grace, undulating their large pectoral fins (which form the edges of the body) as though they were the wings of a bird in leisurely flight. In Europe, some of the smaller and flattest rays, called skates, are sought as food. Order Batoidea, several different families.

REDSTART, any of several small, active dark-colored birds in the Northern Hemisphere. Redstarts in Eurasia are members of the thrush family (Turdidae), related closely to the nightingale; they continually flicker their rust-colored tails and display a rusty rump patch; they are classified in genus *Phoenicurus*.

Colonists to America, who were used to seeing Eurasian redstarts transferred the name to American birds of similar size, color, and behavior, without realizing that those of the New World were essentially different, being wood warblers of family Compsothlypidae. The common American male redstart (*Setophaga ruticilla*) is mostly black, with bright orange areas on wings and tail, and a white belly; the female is olive-brown where the male is black, and yellow where he is orange.

Members of both sexes continually droop their wings and display their colorful tail feathers while they hunt among the foliage for small insects. In the Southwest, a painted redstart (*S. picta*) is found in high mountains; it is black with white patches on the wings and tail, and a bright red patch on the breast. Order Passeriformes.

REINDEER. See *Deer.*

RHINOCEROS (from Greek words meaning nose horn), any of four kinds of massive, thick-skinned, 3-toed, hoofed mammals. Equatorial and South Africa have the largest two kinds, both with 2 nose horns: the square-lipped or white rhino (*Ceratotherium simus*), which is slate-gray and a grazer, and the slightly darker black rhino (*Diceros bicornis*)—both names mean two-horned—with a more pointed, prehensile lip, used in browsing. Next to the elephants, these are the largest land animals.

The Asian rhinos are smaller: the one-horned Indian rhino (*Rhinoceros unicornis*), often seen in zoos, comes from marshes of Southeast Asia and Java, and is threatened with extinction; the two-horned Asiatic rhino (*Didermocerus sumatrensis*), which is the smallest, is rare now in Southeast Asia, Sumatra, and Borneo, where it inhabits dense forests near streams. Order Perissodactyla, family Rhinocerotidae.

ROBIN, any of several different kinds of plump-bodied birds that are dark on the back, red or orange on the chest, and seen commonly near homes. The European bird (*Erithacus rubecula*), for which all the others were named, is about 5½ inches long; it is distinguished from the native redstart mostly by appearing neckless and having dark brown instead of chestnut-colored feathers in the tail. The British introduced "their" robin in Africa, India, Australia, and North America; it became naturalized in all except North America.

The New World robin (*Turdus migratorius*) is a bigger bird, 10 inches long, gray on the back, reddish on the breast, with the outer corners of the tail white; it nests throughout Alaska, Canada, the continental United States, Mexico, and the West Indies, migrating south well into the continent for the winter, except in regions along the coasts.

The European and American robins are both members of the thrush family (Turdidae). The Pekin robin (*Leiothrix lutea*), 6 inches long, in southern China and the Himalayan foothills, and five Australian robins (of genus *Petroica*) are unrelated babblers (Timaliidae) and flycatchers (Muscicapidae), respectively. Order Passeriformes.

SABLE. See *Marten.*

SALAMANDER, any of about 240 different kinds of Eurasian and North American amphibians with a distinct head, a trunk, and permanent tail, usually with clawless-toed limbs of about equal size. The young have gills and resemble the adults, having teeth in both jaws. From the characteristically moist cool skin has come the superstition that a salamander can live in fire, and the use of the name "salamander furnaces" for heating buildings during construction.

The common European spotted salamander (*Salamandra maculosa*) is 6 to 8 inches long, black with yellow or orange patches, sluggish, very shy, and perfectly harmless. The olm (*Proteus anguinus*) of caves in southeastern Europe is pink, unpigmented, and blind, its eyes covered by skin. The related mud puppy, or water dog (*Necturus maculosus*), of eastern North America grows to 17 inches long in rivers, but never loses its gills, although at maturity it develops lungs.

North America also has many kinds of lungless salamanders, mostly under 6 inches long, that respire through their moist skins after they lose their larval gills. The axolotl (*Ambystoma mexicanum*) of Mexican lakes and marshes is sought as food, and interests scientists because in places where water is permanent it becomes sexually mature and reproduces while still a larva in body form—8 to 10 inches long, with gills on each side of the neck region. Given hormone treatment, it transforms and develops adult body pattern and other features not normally acquired.

The giants among salamanders are the Japanese *Cryptobranchus maximus*, sometimes over 5 feet long, and the related hellbender (*C. alleganiensis*) about 18 inches long in streams of the Ohio Valley. Various orders in subclass Caudata.

SALMON, any of a number of different kinds of edible carnivorous fishes with a small soft adipose fin between the dorsal fin and the tail, directly above the anal fin, with pink or red flesh, and with a habit of migrating at spawning time. They are native to the Northern Hemisphere, particularly along seacoasts and in landlocked lakes that once were connected to the oceans by rivers up and down which the salmon could swim.

Atlantic salmon (species of genus *Salmo*) are large trout, which make seasonal spawning runs into rivers of eastern North America and western Europe, returning to the sea afterward. Pacific salmon (6 species of genus *Oncorhynchus*) enter rivers on the west coast of North America and the east coast of Asia, and die there after mating and laying eggs. All of these salmon commonly attain a length of 3 to 4 feet, and a weight of about 30 pounds; record individuals weigh 100 pounds or more. The king, or chinook, salmon (*O. tschawytscha*) has been successfully introduced into New Zealand, where it has set up a new migration pattern.

Only the landlocked salmon feed in freshwater. The others enter rivers full fed and in fine condition, but fast while they swim and leap past rapids and small waterfalls to reach the headwaters where they lay their large eggs.

The hatchling salmon, known as parr, feed in freshwater for various lengths of time from 1 to 7 years, depending upon the species and the latitude. They descend to the ocean, losing their crossbands and becoming silvery as they go, and are known as grilse when the change is completed; they are almost indistinguishable, except for size, from full-grown salmon.

The remainder of their feeding is done in the ocean, over a period of 6 to sometimes more than 7 years, and while traveling 1,000 to 2,500 miles away from the coast. Eventually, many of them find their way back to the same tributaries of the identical streams in which they spent their immature lives. Order Isospondyli, family Salmonidae.

SAND DOLLAR. See *Sea Urchin.*

SANDERLING, a small, active, 3-toed sandpiper, seen virtually wherever in the world waves break against sandy shores. Feeding in small flocks on mollusks, worms, crustaceans, and insects, it follows each receding wave onto the wet sand, probing for food until the last moment before being overwhelmed by the next wave.

A conspicuous white stripe shows on the wing when the bird flies, helping give it a common name of *whitey.* The sanderling lays its eggs in a slight hollow, lined with grass or leaves, on the upper beach. Usually there are 4 eggs, which hatch to downy chicks that hide among the nearby grasses. Order Charadriiformes, family Scolopacidae, specifically *Crocethia alba.*

SANDPIPER, any of 23 different kinds of small wading birds in which the slender, straight, or slightly downcurved beak is as long or longer than the head; all except the sanderling have 4 toes on each foot. Almost all breed in the Northern Hemisphere, mostly in the arctic and subarctic barren grounds. They seldom are found far from water, even on their long migrations, which take them to the limit of land in the Southern Hemisphere.

Largest is the 10-inch knot (*Calidris canutus*), sometimes called the robin sandpiper because its breast is red in spring and summer; it nests in the arctic and antarctic barrens, visiting western Europe and the North American Atlantic and Gulf coasts on migration.

Smallest is the least sandpiper, or stint (*Erolia minutilla*), a 6-inch bird seen frequently on marshes and along the open beach; it nests from Newfoundland to Alaska, and winters in the southernmost United States, Mexico, Central and northern South America.

The best-known in America is the spotted sandpiper (*Actitis macularia*), a 7-inch bird that teeters its tail up and down, bobbing its head at the same time. The Eurasian common sandpiper (*A. hypoleucos*) has the same habit. Order Charadriiformes, family Scolopacidae.

SAPSUCKER. See *Woodpecker.*

SARDINE. See *Herring.*

SAWFISH. See *Ray.*

SAWFLY, any adult insect with 4 membranous wings, the fore pair larger than the hind pair, and biting mouthparts, differing from the ant, bee, and wasp in that its abdomen is broad where it joins the thorax portion of the body, never constricted to a narrow waist. Female sawflies possess a sawlike egg-laying organ, with which they produce narrow slits in plant stems that hold the eggs securely.

From the eggs, larvae resembling caterpillars emerge. They are leafeaters, and usually can be distinguished by having soft paired appendages (prolegs) on almost every body segment, not just 4 pairs in the middle region of the abdomen and a pair at the rear, as in a caterpillar. Commonly the full-grown larva of a sawfly creeps down into the soil to pupate, and emerges for a relatively brief period of adult life. Order Hymenoptera, family Tenthredinidae.

SCALE INSECT, any of a large number of soft-bodied sucking insects that secrete over themselves a hard protective scale or a series of fluffy projections that fend off ants and hungry birds. Found on all continents and most islands, scale insects attach themselves to plant stems while sucking the juices. For most of the year they produce young by the process of parthenogenesis, one female often giving birth to thousands of offspring during one summer season. Generally the young remain for a while close to the mother, benefiting from her shelter; they they go off on their own to grow quickly.

The pernicious San José scale insect (*Aspidiotus perniciosus*), which attacks citrus and shade trees, is individually only about 1/16-inch long; it produces infestations so dense that the bark of the tree appears covered with dark-gray scurfy patches of overlapping sucking insects. The cottony scale of maple, Virginia creeper, and other plants (*Pulvinaria innumerabilis*) places its eggs in a mass of cottony secretion.

The cochineal insect (*Coccus cacti*) of tropical America sucks the juice from stems of prickly pear cactus, and was the source of a famous red dye called cochineal, now replaced by synthetic colors from coal tar. The lac insect (*Tachardia lacca*) of Asia secretes a substance from which shellac and also several dyes can be prepared.

In the Near East, the manna scale insect (*Gossyparius manifera*) on tamarisk trees produces an edible secretion, which is said to have been the food called manna, used by the Israelites as described in Exodus 16. Order Homoptera, many genera of family Coccidae.

SCALLOP, any of more than 100 different kinds of marine bivalved mollusks, in which the shell valves are shallowly saucer-shaped, almost circular, and serve in swimming to expel jets of water from the ends of the hinge at the back. Scallops live along most of the world's seacoasts, below low-tide mark and to depths of about 100 feet.

Around the edge of a scallop's shell, minute eyes look out, attached to the edge of the soft mantle. Generally the shell has ridges radiating from hinge to edge, which is wavy in the pattern said to be scalloped, from the name of the mollusk. Scallops are caught with nets and dredges, chiefly during July and August, after their spawning is completed. The edible part is the strong muscle that pulls the two valves together. Order Filobranchia, family Pectinidae.

SCAUP, either of 2 very similar ducks of northern latitudes in America and Eurasia, feeding and swimming along seacoasts except when nesting in the far north.

The distinctive markings of the male scaup include a pale blue beak, dark head, neck, and tail, and pale gray back and wings. The female is brown where the male is black, and has a white face. The greater scaup (*Aythya marila*) is 19 inches long, the lesser scaup (*A. affinis*) 17 inches, with a more angular head and less white on the wing.

Scaups fly swiftly and erratically in large flocks; they are often seen sitting on the water in so-called *rafts* that number several thousand; many are shot each year by hunters. Order Anseriformes, family Anatidae.

SCORPION, any of a large number of terrestrial arthropod animals walking on 4 pairs of legs, with a pair of pincers on the most anterior appendages, and with a slender elongated jointed portion of the flexible abdomen ending in a venomous stinger.

They live in tropical and warm lands, on all continents, preying upon insects and spiders, holding them in their pincers and often stinging a struggling captive to subdue it before bringing it to the mouth. Like spiders, scorpions lack both jaws and feelers (antennae). They crush their animal prey, squeezing out drops of liquid they can take in through the small, sucking mouth.

After an elaborate courtship and mating ceremony, female scorpions give birth to as many as 60 young of identical appearance, and carry them about on their backs for a week or so until the growing youngsters become independent. Scorpions are active chiefly at night, and often hide by day in shoes and clothing. Particularly in the tropics, where scorpions are often large and venomous, it is wise to shake out every garment before putting it on. Order Scorpionida of class Arachnida, family Scorpionidae.

SEA ANEMONE, any of about 1,000 flowerlike, marine, coelenterate animals found attached to piles and floating timber. Sea anemones usually do not have a free-swimming jellyfish stage. From their attached positions they extend arms or tentacles in all directions to find food, which consists of microscopic organisms. When a sea anemone is irritated, it contracts violently, expelling water from its central digestive cavity. Several orders in subclass Zoantharia of class Anthozoa.

SEA COW, any of 4 different massive aquatic mammals with a rounded head, small mouth, short neck, paddlelike forelimbs, no hind limbs, and a tail that is horizontally flattened. They are found in tropical waters along coasts, estuaries, and marsh-bordered rivers on both sides of the Atlantic and Indian oceans, from the Red Sea to the Philippines and the northwest coast of Australia.

The Indian Ocean representative is the dugong (*Dugong dugon*), which usually feed in groups of 2 or more, eating marine plants in shallow waters; they grow to 9 feet in length and a weight of nearly 400 pounds.

The Atlantic Ocean sea cows, called manatees, include one (*Trichechus manatus*), which inhabits the coast from Florida and the West Indies to northern South America; another (*T. inunguis*) in the Amazon and Orinoco River drainage areas of South America; and one (*T. senegalensis*) in West Africa. Manatees have a rounded tail, rather than a notched one, and feed mostly at night.

Sea cows are hunted in many areas for their tasty flesh and for a clear oil that does not turn rancid. Order Sirenia, families Dugongidae and Trichechidae.

SEA CUCUMBER, or bêche-de-mer, or trepang, any of about 500 different kinds of sausage-shaped, soft-bodied echinoderms that maintain their shape through hydraulic pressure of liquid in their voluminous body cavities. They are exclusively marine and occur in all oceans, but most commonly in the tropics. Their only skeletal support consists of tiny limy plates in the outer part of the body wall.

Many sea cucumbers are regarded as food; others are used as the source of a fish poison with which to force edible fishes in tide pools to come out of hiding, anesthetized and helpless. Many orders of class Holothurioidea.

SEA FAN, a colonial coelenterate animal of shallow warm seas, attached to a rock or some dead coral or other solid support, and growing upward in the form of a branching tree with all the branches in one plane. In the large sea fans (*Gorgonia*) of semitropical waters, the branches grow together to form a lacy network, upon the surface of which the individual polyps live. Each is a tiny, soft-bodied sac with a microscopic mouth at the center of a ring of tentacles.

Nettling cells on the tentacles help the sea fan catch and subdue equally small swimming animals in the nearby water, and to pull each victim into the mouth for digestion inside the body. Each polyp contributes toward the growth of the tough, hornlike protein which forms the core of the fan, and toward secreting the surface coating of limy spicules, which may be pastel yellow, lavender, pink, or purple.

In season, sea fans produce reproductive cells and liberate free-swimming larvae that eventually settle to the bottom where they may begin new colonies. Each colony grows toward whatever currents come regularly in the water, letting the polyps on both sides of the fan benefit equally from food in the passing water. Order Gorgonacea of class Anthozoa.

SEA HORSE, any of about 50 kinds of small, marine, bony fishes with a head strongly resembling that of a horse or the knight chessman. The mouth is round, at the end of a tubular snout, and used for sucking in minute animals and plants for food. The whole body is covered with bony plates. Generally a sea horse swims in an almost vertical position. It prefers quiet brackish waters and coils its long, prehensile tail around seaweeds and sea grasses to keep from being swept away by the currents.

The female sea horse lays her eggs in a pouch on the belly of the male, where they develop to the hatching stage, at which time he expels them. The common sea horse of the east coast of North America (*Hippocampus hudsonius*) is about 5 inches long; the Pacific coast sea horse (*H. kuda*) grows almost twice as large. Order Solenichthyes, family Syngnathidae.

SEAL, any of 18 different kinds of fin-footed marine mammals with only a wrinkle to show where the ear opens, with a tail of moderate length that is inconspicuous between hind legs so specialized for sculling through water that they cannot be folded forward, but merely drag when the animal hauls out on land. The harbor seal (*Phoca vitulina*), found along Pacific and Atlantic coasts of the Northern Hemisphere, sometimes follows shad and other fishes far into rivers. Leopard seals (*Hydrurga leptonyx*), which grow to 11½ feet long, prey on penguins and other birds. Order Pinnipedia, family Phocidae.

SEA LILY, any of about 630 different kinds of marine echinoderms in which the body is cup shaped, protected by limy plates that fit together closely just under the skin, and bearing 5 arms that divide close to the base into 2 equal feathery extensions. Almost all sea lilies live at great depths in temperate and tropical oceans, but those of polar seas live in shallower water.

All of the deep-water sea lilies seem permanently attached by long cylindrical armored stalks with rootlike clasping parts that can hold to firm objects on the sea bottom. Some shallow-water sea lilies, called feather stars, live in the Tropics on coral reefs, where they soon free themselves from their short stalks and move about from time to time; some can even swim feebly. Fossil sea lilies of the Paleozoic era are found in great numbers. Several orders of class Crinoidea.

SEA LION, any of about 12 different kinds of fin-footed marine mammals with a small protruding ear, a short tail, and hind legs sufficiently flexible to be folded forward and used for awkward walking or running on land. They live along coastlines of western North America and South America, Australia, New Zealand, some oceanic islands, and southern Africa.

The trained "seals" of circuses and vaudeville shows are California sea lions (*Zalophus californianus*), which are found also along the shores of the Galápagos Islands and Japan. Related are the fur seals (*Callorhinus ursinus*) of the Aleutian Islands and Alaska, of which about 90,000 of an estimated 2 million are harvested annually for their fur; and the Antarctic fur seals (6 species of genus *Arctocephalus*), of which about 30,000 are taken each year. Order Pinnipedia, family Otariidae.

SEA SQUIRT. See *Tunicate*.

SEA STAR, or starfish, any of about 2,000 different kinds of marine echinoderms in which the body is star-shaped, 5-angled, and generally extended into from 5 to 50 flexible arms below which are grooves containing tubefeet used for locomotion and for holding to the substratum. Sea stars are found in all oceans, and some kinds tolerate being exposed to air a few hours while the tide is out. Most are predatory, feeding on mollusks and sand dollars. Many orders of class Asteroidea.

SEA URCHIN, any of about 860 different kinds of marine echinoderms in which the body is made firm by interlocking limy plates just beneath the skin, and protection is given by movable spines operated by muscles and located on ball-and-socket joints on the limy plates. These animals are found in all oceans, at many depths, but rarely where they are exposed by the receding tide.

A sea urchin holds on and moves about by means of a large number of fine flexible tube feet. Its mouth, on the surface next to the substratum, has 5 hard, sharp limy jaws with which it can bite out pieces of seaweed to swallow. Most sea urchins are circular, and their shells show impressive detail in a radially symmetrical pattern. Some urchins, mostly burrowing kinds, are heart shaped. Others, known as sand dollars, are very flat-bodied and live in the surface ooze over sand bars below low-tide level. Many orders of class Echinoidea.

SECRETARY BIRD, a long-legged, fast-running hawk about 4 feet high, with a crested head that gives the bird its popular name—as if it were a secretary with several pencils stuck in her hair. It is common in Africa south of the great deserts, and protected because of its fearless attacks on snakes, even large and poisonous varieties, which it kills with its talons and wings. It is sometimes domesticated as a snake-killer. Order Falconiformes, family Sagittariidae, specifically *Sagittarius serpentarius*.

SHAD, any of several edible, herring-like fishes about 2 feet long, which in spring seek out freshwater shallows to mate and lay their eggs. Many, such as the American shad (*Alosa sapidissima*) of the Atlantic coast, return to the sea, where they feed on plankton. Others, such as the Ohio shad (*A. ohiensis*), are restricted to river life.

Although the meat is full of small bones, shad are caught in large numbers for table use. Their eggs (roe) are also a delicacy. Order Isispondyli, family Clupeidae.

Related gizzard shad (6 kinds in genus *Dorosoma*, family Dorosomidae) live in salt water and freshwaters as forage fish. Their name refers to the specially modified muscular stomach with which they grind up their food.

SHARK, any of more than 250 different kinds of cartilaginous fishes with a torpedo-shaped body, a wide mouth underneath the head, separate gill slits on the sides, and a two-lobed tail of which the upper lobe is much the longer. They are found in all seas, and occasionally ascend rivers into freshwater, as in Lake Nicaragua.

The giants among sharks are the whale shark (*Rhincodon typus*), sometimes 45 feet long, and the giant basking shark (*Cetorhinus maximus*), which is nearly as big; both eat only tiny sea animals. The slender blue shark (*Prionarce glauca*), 12½ feet long, and the great white shark (*Carcharodon carcharias*, named from Greek words meaning sharp tooth because its teeth are shaped like arrowhead flints), up to 36½ feet long, is a fast-swimming predator of open oceans, and the most famous of the man-eaters. It can swallow a 100-pound sea lion, a 50-pound seal, or a Newfoundland dog at a single gulp.

Almost as dangerous to skin divers and men overboard (or in flimsy life rafts) are the tropical Atlantic, 18-foot, mackerel shark, or porbeagle (*Lamna ditropis*), which is sharp-snouted, and the hammerhead shark (species of genus *Sphyrna*), whose head is extended on both sides like the top of a T, with the eyes at the extreme corners. Many tales of man-eating sharks are exaggerated and overdrawn.

Small sharks include some called dogfishes, which destroy fish caught in fishnets; spiny dogfishes, with a spine in front of each of the 2 dorsal fins, include many species of the genus *Squalus*. Smooth dogfishes lack these spines, and may be species of genus *Mustelis*. Both are caught for sale in Europe and the Orient, often as "grayfish" with edible flesh. Order Selachii, many families.

SHEEP, any of 9 different kinds of hollow-horned, cud-chewing mammals with narrow noses and pointed ears, distinguished from goats by the lack of a scent gland at the base of the tail. They are native to northern mountains of Eurasia and North America, and to Sardinia and Corsica, North Africa and the Sudan across to the north bend of the Niger River. The largest are the African aoudads, or Barbary sheep (*Ammotragus lervia*), which have a mane of long hairs on the throat, chest, and upper parts of the forelegs.

Slightly smaller are the Rocky Mountain sheep, or bighorns (*Ovis canadensis*) and Dall sheep (*O. dalli*) of western North America, and the argali, or Marco Polo sheep (*O. ammon*), of the central U.S.S.R. to Nepal and western China. The massive horns

MONTANA HIGHWAY COMMISSION
SHEEP

on the males reach impressive size, and are used in ceremonial butting activity at mating season. The mouflon (*O. musimon*) of Mediterranean islands has been introduced widely.

The original of the domestic sheep (*O. aries*) is no longer known in the world. It probably originated in Asia, and has been bred into many distinctive races. The Shropshire is a popular breed in the Middle States and is a good mutton sheep. The most important wool sheep is the Merino breed, Spanish in origin but found today largely in America and Australia, where its fine wool is a product of great importance.

In addition to their furnishing of wool and meat products, sheep are of considerable importance to farming because of the manure that they produce. Order Artiodactyla, family Bovidae.

SHINER. See *Minnow*.

SHIPWORM, any of several highly specialized marine bivalve mollusks that settle on wood soaked with seawater and spend most of their lives burrowing into this material. They are found in most parts of the world, doing great damage to wooden ships and pilings by weakening their structure.

The shipworm, also called teredo, uses its small valves as boring tools, while its elongated siphon (part of the mantle) extends to the surface of the wood to get seawater containing microscopic food and oxygen, and to discharge wastes, carbon dioxide, and reproductive cells. A thin limy tube is secreted around the wormlike siphon. Order Eulamellibranchia, family Teredinidae, chiefly members of genus *Teredo*.

SHREW, any of more than 200 different kinds of small, short-legged mouselike mammals with long-pointed noses and many small teeth; only the upper middle incisors are enlarged, and they are not fitted for gnawing. Shrews are found in most land areas, but not on arctic islands, the West Indies, Australia, Tasmania, New Zealand, or South Pacific islands. They include the smallest known mammal, the dwarf shrew (*Suncus etruscus*) of Mediterranean coastal countries, 1½ to 2 inches long with a 1-inch tail, weighing about 1/15 ounce.

Except in breeding season, shrews are solitary, voracious predators, spacing out their meals on insects, snails, and worms with seeds and other plant materials. The commonest shrew in the United States and Canada is the short-tailed *Blarina brevicauda*, which might be mistaken for a mole except for its delicate legs and feet. Order Insectivora, family Soricidae.

SHRIKE, or butcherbird, any of 73 different kinds of small to medium-sized birds with large heads, stout beaks hooked and notched at the tip, strong legs, short rounded wings, and, usually, long tails. They are found in both hemispheres, with 39 bush shrikes and 9 helmet shrikes in Africa.

Only 2 of the other shrikes live in America; one (the loggerhead shrike, *Lanius ludovicianus*) migrating from southern Canada to Mexico and central America, the other (the northern shrike, *L. excubitor*) ranging farther north and also across Eurasia. Like many shrikes, they are gray above, white below, black and white on wings and tail, and have a mask mark across the eyes.

Shrikes have the peculiar habit of impaling insects, frogs, and small birds on thorns or barbed wire fences, perhaps because the shrike's feet are not strong enough to hold its prey while its powerful bill tears the food apart. Order Passeriformes, family Laniidae.

SHRIMP, or prawn, any of a number of different aquatic crustaceans, 6 inches or less in length, with laterally compressed bodies or abdomens. Most shrimps are marine, and some 1½ to 3 inches long are caught in enormous numbers for human food. Those from the Gulf of Mexico (especially *Penaeus setifer*) are a delicate gray-green color spotted with brown; when cooked they turn pink and white. Order Decapoda.

The name shrimp is given to unrelated crustaceans: brine shrimps (*Artemia salina*) of salt lakes and fairy shrimps (*Eubranchipus vernalis*) of freshwater ponds in early spring belong to order Anostraca; freshwater shrimps, or scuds (species of *Gammarus*), live in shallows of streams and ponds, and belong to order Amphipoda; opossum shrimps, most of which are marine (species of *Mysis*), belong to order Mysidacea.

SILKWORM, any of a number of different moth caterpillars that spin a viscous secretion from their salivary glands into a single, continuous, fine silk strand with which to construct the egg-shaped cocoon that is to protect them during their pupal transformation.

Only one, the oriental silkworm (*Bombyx mori* of family Bombycidae), has achieved commercial importance. It supports an industry where cheap labor is available to keep captive caterpillars fed with fresh mulberry leaves, and to unravel and wind up the silk strands from the finished cocoons.

The caterpillar itself is yellowish gray, about 3 inches long when fully grown, with a hornlike projection on the last segment of the body. After the cocoon is complete and has hardened, it is plunged into hot water to kill the enclosed pupa and to free the silk fibers. As reeled, the raw silk fiber may be bright orange, tan, or almost white. Order Lepidoptera.

SILVERFISH. See *Bristletail*.

SKATE. See *Ray*.

SKIMMER, any of 3 coastal birds in which the lower bill is longer than the upper and used in a peculiar method of fishing. The black skimmer (*Rhynchops nigra*), which ranges along the Atlantic coast of North America from Long Island southward, and down both sides of Central and South America, is the largest. Its wingspan may be as great as 50 inches, and its red beak 4½ inches long from the lower jaw and 3 inches from the upper.

The African skimmer, found along the coasts and larger rivers of Africa, has a bright yellow beak. The Indian skimmer, with a bill black at the base and yellow at the tip, patrols the rivers of India and Southeast Asia.

All skimmers cruise low over the water by steady beating of their long-pointed wings, while they lower the underbill into the water. If the tip of the bill encounters an obstacle, such as a fish or a crustacean at the surface, the bird quickly bends its head and closes its mouth, picking up the trophy as food. Skimmers feed mostly in the early evening and before dawn, when the water is calm and prey tend to come to the surface.

By day, skimmers roost in flocks on open beaches, and withstand the intense light by closing to a narrow slit their unusual pupils, which suggest those of a cat. Their nests are mere unlined depressions in a sandflat or beach near the water, with 4 eggs blotched with brown. The young birds have both bills equal until almost full grown. Order Charadriiformes, family Rhynchopidae.

SKUNK, any of 10 different kinds of short-legged, bushy-tailed mammals marked strikingly in black and white, and armed with a special gland under the tail, secreting an ill-smelling fluid that can be squirted to 10 to 15 feet with fair accuracy.

Skunks live only in the Americas, where they seek under logs and stones for insects, and catch mice and frogs; occasionally skunks attack birds, including poultry. Hog-nosed skunks (6 species of *Conepatus*) are the only ones in South America; their range extends to the southern United States. Spotted skunks (*Spilogale* species) are found from British Columbia to Central America, and striped skunks (*Mephitis* species) from eastern Canada to Central America. Order Carnivora, family Mustelidae.

SLIPPER SHELL, or boat shell, or quarterdeck, any of several kinds of marine snails that increase the surface area for attaching themselves to their

oval shells by producing one half a horizontal shelflike platform.

Boat shells feed on minute animals and plants that become stuck in a film of mucus over the gills on each side of the foot. At intervals of about 4 minutes, the snail twists its head to right or left and sucks up the loaded mucus into its mouth. It swallows large particles at once but stores larger ones in a pouch for a later meal. The snail can feed on these at low tide when it must clamp its shell down tightly and hold on.

Often slipper shells are found holding on to horseshoe crabs or larger snails, or even to other slipper shells in a cluster of several dozen, all rolling together on the sea bottom. Female boat shells produce about 50 membranous egg cases, each containing about 250 eggs, and stand guard over these until the young hatch out. The young swim freely for about 2 weeks, then settle on some firm surface where they can become more or less permanently attached. Order Prosobranchiata, family Crepidulidae, species of genus *Crepidula*.

SLOTH (meaning slowness, laziness), any of 7 different kinds of tropical mammals with round heads, ears that are barely visible, eyes directed forward, and all feet with long, curved strong claws from toes not exceeding 3 in number, bound together for most of their length. Sloths live only in the Americas.

Sloths hang by their claws below horizontal branches, progressing slowly while feeding upon the leaves. The young, only 1 at a birth, holds tight to the mother's back and is almost hidden by her long hair.

There are 2 genera: *Bradypus* (which means slow foot), having 3 claws on the front feet; and *Choloepus* (lame foot), having 2 claws on the front feet. On the ground, sloths are practically helpless. They are usually 1½ to 2 feet long. Order Edentata, family Bradypodidae.

SLUG, any snail-like mollusk that is unprotected by a limy shell. Some of the land slugs that are classified in Order Pulmonata because they breathe air through a lunglike organ, have concealed a small shell that they secreted at a very early age and then outgrew. These slugs glide about on a large flat foot, chiefly at night or during rains when they are in less danger of desiccation. If attacked, they eject a thick slime that discourages birds and insects from coming closer.

Eating vegetable matter, both living and decaying, some land slugs (such as *Limax maximus* of the Olympic National Park forest in Washington state) grow to a length of 8 inches. Sea slugs lack a shell altogether, and are classified in Order Opisthobranchiata. They also lack gills and breathe by means of highly decorative plumes upon the back.

Sea slugs commonly creep over corals, sea fans, and other coelenterates, browsing on the polyps; they also crawl among seaweeds, eating the moss animals (bryozoans). One kind (*Glaucus eucharis*) has a deep blue color, and creeps along the underside of the surface film on the warm water of tropical oceans, capturing minute crustaceans and other animals as food.

SMELT, any of 13 different kinds of slender, bony, salmon-shaped fishes, with a small soft adipose fin in front of the tail, directly above the large anal fin. Smelt are fish of the Northern Hemisphere, especially Pacific Ocean coasts.

Tons of Sacramento smelt (*Spirinchus thaleichthys*) are caught annually in San Francisco Bay and the mouth of the Columbia River. The small surf smelt (*Hypomesus pretiosus*), which lives mostly close to shore, is a favorite bait for both surf fishermen and commercial operators.

The 1-foot Atlantic smelt (*Osmerus mordax*) of the American east coast was introduced into the Great Lakes in 1912 and is thriving in fresh water. The Atlantic smelt, or sparling, of Europe (*O. eperlanus*) is a valuable fish of northern waters, reaching a length of 8 inches. Order Isospondyli, family Osmeridae.

SNIPE, any of 25 different kinds of small- to medium-sized shore birds with short legs, and long beaks used for probing for small edible animals in muddy shores. They nest in arctic muskegs and freshwater marshes of all continents except Australia.

The circumpolar common snipe (*Capella gallinago*) nests over the northern United States, most of Canada, and much of northern Eurasia, but winters in the Americas from the middle United States to southern Brazil, and in the Southern Hemisphere of the Old World. The Japanese snipe (*Gallinago hardwicki*), which nests only on the northern islands of Japan, winters in New Zealand and eastern Australia, where it is called the Australian snipe. Order Charadriiformes, family Scolopacidae.

SOLE. See *Flatfish.*

SOWBUG, or slater, any of a large number of terrestrial crustaceans with a jointed oval body. On all continents, they scavenge in damp places, under fallen logs, stones, and the bark on rotting trees, eating principally decaying vegetation.

Some sowbugs, such as members of the common genus *Armadillidium*, are able to curl up into a ball when disturbed. In this position, their delicate legs and the vestigial gills with which they breathe in air are well protected by the hard armor of the body's upper surface. These particular sowbugs are often called "pill bugs."

Other kinds are unable to curl so tightly. Sometimes one that does not curl is seen to be a female carrying a batch of eggs with her, in a brood sac formed by flat projections from her legs. The young that hatch out are of the same body form as the parents. Order Isopoda.

SPARROW, or bunting, any of about 265 different kinds of 4½- to 8-inch perching birds, usually of a dark brown inconspicuous color and with a beak smaller than that of a finch. Found all over the world but most commonly in the American tropics, they generally frequent grasslands or open woodlands, hunting for seeds and insects on or near the ground. They nest on the ground or in low bushes. The snow bunting (*Plectrophenax nivalis*) and several kinds of longspurs (species of *Calcarius*) are circumpolar, nesting southward in mountain regions.

Temperate North America has about 50 different kinds of native sparrows, of which the largest is the fox sparrow (*Passerella iliaca*), 7 inches long, with a streaked breast and a reddish brown tail; it nests across Canada and in the western United States, wintering in the southern states. Its pleasant song is heard only in spring and fall, while the bird is migrating. The song sparrow (*Melospiza melodia*) is more widespread and sings much of the year; its white underparts have brown markings that fuse in the center of the breast to form a large blotch.

The white-throated sparrow (*Zenotrichia albicollis*), which nests in Canada and New England and winters in the southern United States, has a particularly sweet, clear whistle. The chipping sparrow (*Spizella passerina*), 5 inches long with a rusty stripe on the top of the head, nests near houses.

None of these native sparrows damages crops or drives away other birds as does the house sparrow (*Passer domesticus*), which was introduced into the United States in 1850, supposedly to eat insect pests. House sparrows spread to all parts of the continent, and became pests themselves. In their native northern Eurasia, they appear helpful to farmers, devouring insects and weed seeds.

Eurasia and Africa have 30 different kinds of very similar birds, which are called buntings (*Emberiza* species), and the most common sparrow of all—the chaffinch (*Fringilla coelebs*). All are primarily seedeaters, although the name seedeater is ordinarily reserved for about 30 kinds of birds in tropical America (species of *Sporophila*). Order Passeriformes, family Fringillidae.

SPRINGTAIL. any of a large number of widely distributed minute, wingless insects in which the hind-most abdominal segments (the "tail") are held in a curled position, turned forward under the more anterior abdominal segments. There the tip of the tail is held by a sort of catch, under voluntary muscular control. When alarmed, a springtail tenses its abdomen as though to straighten it out, then slips the catch. The tail strikes the surface, land or water, on which the springtail is standing, with enough force to toss the insect itself high in the air. It falls somewhere else and may be able to scurry away before being discovered.

Often large numbers of springtails scavenge for microscopic particles of food along the edge of a stream, on the water surface, giving the combined appearances of a gray-blue line ¼ inch or more in width. At the slightest disturbance, all of these insects toss themselves into the air, and the line vanishes as though by magic. Order Collembola.

SQUETEAGUE, or sea trout, or weakfish, any of several different kinds of marine bony fishes related to the croakers, with a triangular front dorsal fin and long rear dorsal fin. Squeteagues travel in schools along both the Atlantic and Pacific coasts of North America, attracting both commercial fishermen and sportsmen. The name weakfish refers to the ease with which the jaws can be torn from the head with a fisherman's hook while the fish is fighting for its life.

The Atlantic kinds attain lengths to 32 inches and weights to 17½ pounds. The closely related California sea bass (*Cynoscion nobilis*) is larger; largest is the totuava (*C. macdonaldi*) of the Gulf of California, which grows to 225 pounds. Order Percomorphi, family Sciaenidae, members of genus *Cynoscion*.

SQUID, any of about 300 different kinds of free-swimming, predatory, marine, cephalopod mollusks with 10 long arms projecting from the head end of the barrel- or cigar-shaped body. Squids are common in all oceans from the surface down to the greatest depths. They have 2 well-developed eyes, quite similar in form to those of vertebrate animals.

When disturbed, a squid gives off an inky substance that provides an underwater smokescreen and apparently dulls the sense of smell for fishes that are pursuing the squid. Squid themselves eat smaller fishes, young fishes, and crustaceans of many kinds; in turn, squid are eaten in large numbers by large fishes, seals, and toothed whales. Most squids are less than 2 feet long, but a giant squid (*Architeuthis harveyi*) of the North Atlantic attains a length of 52 feet, including both body and arms. Order Dibranchia.

SQUIRREL, any of about 280 different kinds of active rodents, mostly with bushy tails and tree-dwelling habits. They are found in most land areas except southern South America, Madagascar, Australia and New Zealand, and major deserts. Many are ground

U.S. NATIONAL PARK SERVICE
SQUIRREL

squirrels with less conspicuous tails, living underground except while hunting for food. All except the flying squirrels, which do not fly but glide by means of a parachute of skin extending between the legs of each side, are active during the day and sleep at night.

Squirrels eat seeds and fruits, as well as some insects and snails, and occasionally birds' eggs. When numerous and hungry, they may attack corn and other crop plants. In the United States and Canada, red squirrels (2 species of *Tamiasciurus*) are common in evergreen coniferous forests, whereas the gray (*Sciurus carolinensis*) and fox (*S. niger*) squirrels live among hardwoods. Gray squirrels are larger and drive away red squirrels when the two meet.

The fur of a number of larger kinds of squirrels is valuable, and their meat is delicious. In both North America and Eurasia, ground squirrels (*Citellus* species) are plains animals, whereas chipmunks (*Tamias* in eastern North America and *Eutamias* in the West as well as in Asia) inhabit brush land and growing forests. Order Rodentia, family Sciuridae.

STARFISH. See *Sea Star*.

STARLING, any of about 106 different kinds of Old World perching birds with short tails, strong beaks and legs, and stout bodies. Most of them walk, instead of hopping. Starlings are chiefly African and Oriental birds of open country, but one of the Eurasian kinds is known as the common starling (*Sturnus vulgaris*). A vigorous, 8½-inch bird with a yellow beak, black iridescent feathers, and pointed wings, it provides important control over insect pests in its native regions.

Introduced into New York around 1890, it has spread over almost the entire United States and become a major menace, descending in enormous flocks to eat cereal crops, cultivated fruits, and berries. It competes for food and nesting places with many native birds, nearly all of which are more beneficial to man than the introduced starling. In many cities, the clamor of roosting starlings and the filth from their droppings have led to campaigns to destroy these birds, never with any success. Order Passeriformes, family Sturnidae.

STICK INSECT, any of a large number of biting insects with a long slim cylindrical body, long feelers (antennae), long slender legs, and wings (if any) similar to those of grasshoppers. Most stick insects, and all of the large ones—some to a length of 10 inches—live in the Tropics.

Stick insects move very slowly, eating green leaves on shrubs and trees, and remain motionless or slightly swaying if alarmed. In this way they resemble dead sticks or twigs and are overlooked by animals that eat insects. In the middle and northern United States and southern Canada, a completely wingless stick insect (*Diapheromera femorata*) is fairly common, and grows to a length of 4 to 5 inches, larger in the female. Order Orthoptera, family Phasmidae.

STICKLEBACK, any of several small fishes of the Northern Hemisphere. The 3-spine stickleback (*Gasterosteus aculeatus*), which has 2 or 3 sharp stiff spines on its back in front of its dorsal fin, occurs in both freshwater and salt water in North America and Eurasia. The brook stickleback (*Eucalia inconstans*), which rarely exceeds 2½ inches in length, has 4 to 6 spines and is restricted to fresh waters in the northernmost United States and southern Canada, coast to coast.

In breeding season, the male stickleback builds an elaborate globular nest with a front and back door. He courts a female and induces her to lay her eggs in his nest. After fertilizing the eggs, he stands guard over them and aerates them by fanning water through them with his fins. After the eggs hatch, he tries to keep the young fish together near the nest but they soon wander off. Despite their spines, many sticklebacks are eaten by birds. Order Thoracostei, family Gasterosteidae.

STILT, either of 2 shorebirds, related to avocets, with long, slender, straight beaks and very long legs. Only flamingos have legs longer in proportion to the body. In temperate and tropical regions all over the world, the black-necked, or pied stilt (*Himantopus mexicanus*) wades with a peculiar gait, as though skating on the water. Its back is black, its belly white, and its legs blood red.

The banded stilt (*Cladorhynchus leucocephalus*) of Australia and Tasmania stands slightly taller, and is white except for a brown band across the wing; its belly is light brown, and its legs red. Stilts swim if necessary and are strong fliers. All of them migrate to the Tropics for the winter. Order Charadriiformes, family Recurvirostridae.

STOAT. See *Weasel*.

STONEFLY, any insect (more than 200 kinds in North America) with biting mouthparts, 2 pairs of similar wings held flat over the back at rest, 2 "tails" (cerci) at the end of the abdomen, and aquatic young. The adults mate soon after emerging from the water, and live only a few days. Females deposit masses of eggs in the water of streams and rivers, where they hatch into immature stoneflies, called naiads or nymphs.

The naiads are carnivorous, preying upon smaller water animals found while prowling along the bottom. Each naiad has strong jaws, strong legs, visible gills in pads just behind the base of the legs, and two tails. It may need 1 to 3 years to reach full size. Both naiads and adults are favorite food of trout and other fishes. Order Plecoptera.

STORK, any of 17 different kinds of large heronlike birds with comparatively short toes, which are partially webbed, and no voice. They communicate by gestures and by clapping the beak together. Storks live in most temperate and tropical countries, but not in northern North America, New Zealand, and islands of the South Pacific. They inhabit the vicinity of marshes and rivers, where they find food consisting of frogs, lizards, fishes, and even young birds.

The white stork (*Ciconia alba*) is migratory, arriving at nesting areas from the Mediterranean to Scandinavia, departing for the winter to warm areas of Africa all the way to the Cape of Good Hope. The black stork (*C. nigra*) is a swamp bird of Europe and Asia. The adjutant birds, or marabou, storks (*Leptoptilus* species) of tropical Africa and Asia, 60 inches tall, feed on carrion and snakes and are protected as useful scavengers by Indian law.

The wood stork, often misnamed an ibis (*Mycteria americana*), of the Gulf coast of the United States and as far south as Argentina, sometimes migrates after the breeding season to both California and Canada. It is one of the most striking of the group; it stands 4 feet high, is white with black tail and wing-tips, and has long, bluish legs and a long probing bill; the head and neck of the adult are entirely bare. Order Ciconiiformes, family Ciconiidae.

STURGEON, any of 21 different kinds of large fishes whose elongated body is clad in 5 rows of platelike scales, each with a raised ridge down the center; the upper half of the tail is longer than the lower, and the snout bears 4 barbels, somewhat resembling whiskers, beside the small sucking mouth. Sturgeons are native to the Northern Hemisphere, some in the ocean but entering fresh water to spawn, others in lakes and streams for their entire lives.

The American lake sturgeon (*Acipenser fulvescens*), once plentiful in the Great Lakes, reaches a weight of 200 pounds; it has blotched, reddish sides. The common sturgeon (*A. sturio*), a marine fish found on both sides of the North Atlantic Ocean, grows to 10 feet long and a weight of 500 pounds. The largest in North America is the white sturgeon (*A. transmontanus*) of freshwaters along the Pacific coast, weighing as much as 1,800 pounds. In Eurasia, the giant is the famous beluga (*Huso huso*) of the Caspian Sea, Black Sea, and Volga River, where it is believed to attain an age of 200 years; the record for size is 28 feet long and 2,860 pounds.

All sturgeons are sluggish fish, resting on the bottom, and sucking in vegetable matter plus any animals in it from the debris around marshes and near shore. Smoked sturgeon meat is widely appreciated as a delicacy. The eggs, preserved with salt, form caviar; the best quality comes from a small Russian sturgeon, the sterlat (*A. ruthenus*), usually 2 to 3 feet long. Air bladders from sturgeons were formerly sold as transparent plastic, called isinglas. Order Chondrostei, family Acipenseridae.

SUCKER, any of about 100 different kinds of minnowlike freshwater bony fishes in which the thick-lipped mouth is set low in the head and is toothless.

The fish was named from its habit of sucking mud and organic matter from the bottom. Most are North American fishes. The commonest, the white sucker (*Catostomus commersonnii*), is 28 inches long, with soft, bony, edible flesh. Order Eventognathi, family Catostomidae.

SUNFISH, any of more than 25 different kinds of small- to medium-sized freshwater fishes and 3 of enormous oceanic fishes, which have compressed bodies that appear oval or almost circular from the side. Freshwater sunfishes are all native to North America, although they have been introduced into Europe and elsewhere to delight fishermen. They differ from perches in having the spiny and soft-rayed portions of the dorsal fin continuous or separated by no more than a narrow notch, never as entirely separate fins.

Some sunfishes, such as the pumpkinseed (*Lepomis gibbosus*) which is common in ponds and streams from Maine to Florida and the Mississippi valley, have an earlike lobe from the rear edge of the gill cover, blood red in the pumpkinseed and bright blue in some other species. Largest is the largemouth bass (*Micropterus salmoides*), recorded at 22½ pounds and 32½ inches in length, which eats smaller sunfishes, including the bluegill (*L. macrochirus*). In the southeastern United States, two kinds of sunfishes called crappies (species of *Pomoxis*) are favorites with fishermen. All freshwater sunfishes are edible, and belong to family Centrarchidae of order Acanthopteri.

Ocean sunfishes include one (*Mola mola*) as much as 11 feet long, weighing a ton; as a young fish, it swims in the normal vertical position, but as it ages it lazily cruises with one side up, swallowing medusae and other slow animals of the sea surface. Order Plectognathi, family Molidae.

SWALLOW, any of 79 different kinds of small, slender, long-winged birds with 12 tail feathers and short, broad beaks that open widely, surrounded by stiff facial bristles. Swallows are almost cosmopolitan over land, being absent chiefly from polar regions, oceanic islands, and New Zealand. All are noted for their graceful flight, and for their regular migrations in great flocks. They feed almost exclusively on insects, which they catch on the wing.

The name swallow is often mistakenly applied to the swifts, which have 10 tail feathers and no facial bristles. The American barn swallow (*Hirundo rustica*), 7½ inches long and with a deeply forked "swallow tail," is known in Britain as "the swallow" and elsewhere in Europe as "the chimney swallow"; it builds a nest of mud and grass atop the rafters of barns.

The cliff swallow (*Petrochelidon pyrrhonota*), 6 inches long, of America from Canada to central Mexico, constructs bottle-shaped nests of mud under eaves or cliffs; those nesting at the San Juan Capistrano Mission in California have earned a reputation for returning, generally on the same date each spring. Largest of the swallows in America is the sociable purple martin (*Progne subis*), 8 inches long, which alternately soars and flies rapidly. Order Passeriformes, family Hirundinidae.

SWALLOWTAIL, any of a number of large butterflies found all over the world, in which the hind wings are abruptly extended into a "tail" as much as ½ inch long. The eggs of swallowtails are laid on plants, where they hatch into caterpillars that eat the leaves.

Generally, swallowtail caterpillars are able to repel birds by suddenly extending from the head region a pair of long soft tentacles that release a disagreeable odor and probably a bad taste. When full grown, each caterpillar spins both a button of silk in which to anchor its posterior end and an open loop of silk to give extra support to the body after it transforms into a chrysalis (pupa). Within its loop, the chrysalis remains head up, leaning back like a professional window washer into his safety belt.

Among the best-known swallowtail butterflies of America, where it is widespread except along the West Coast, is the tiger swallowtail, or lilac butterfly (*Papilio glaucus*), which has a wingspan of about 5 inches, and a caterpillar that feeds on foliage of ash, birch, cherry, and poplar; it spends the winter in the chrysalis stage, and emerges in late spring, seemingly just in time to visit lilac flowers for nectar. Order Lepidoptera, family Papilionidae.

SWAN, any of 7 different large, long-necked water birds, with webbed feet and a beak about as long as the head. All but 2 swans are white birds of the Northern Hemisphere. The black swan (*Cygnus atratus*) of Australia has a little white on the wings; the black-necked swan (*C. melanocoryphus*) of South America is white except for the black neck.

European swans include the Polish swan (*C. olor*) of Eurasia which is the domesticated species, the whooping swan (*C. cygnus*) and the smaller Bewick's swan (*C. bewicki*), both of which nest in the Arctic. The domesticated swan is often called the mute swan, although it does make several different calls. In the United States there are 2 wild species: the whistling swan (*C. columbianus*) of arctic barrens, which winters southward along the Atlantic coast and the trumpeter (*C. buccinator*) of Montana

AMERICAN MUSEUM OF NATURAL HISTORY
SWAN

and Wyoming, which does not migrate. Trumpeter swans were on the verge of extinction when they were made a protected species, and in their sanctuary their number has begun to increase.

The legend that the swan sings before it dies—a farewell song—is not true. Formerly swans were bred for the table but they are now raised solely as ornamental birds for lakes and pools. Order Anseriformes, family Anatidae.

SWIFT, any of 67 different kinds of small, fast-flying, insect-eating birds in which the tail contains only 10, not 12, feathers, and the short beak and wide mouth have no fringe of bristles such as distinguish the swallows. Swifts are primarily tropical and subtropical birds. Even the American chimney swift (*Chaetura pelagica*) journeys to Colombia, South America, for each winter.

Swifts are usually seen in groups. Nests are placed in inaccessible places, such as the sides of rocks, chimneys, and caves and are fastened in place by the birds' saliva. The edible birds' nests of Asia, especially China, are built by small swifts, particularly *Collocalia inexpectata*; and these nests are almost entirely composed of a salivary secretion. Order Apodiformes, family Apodidae.

SWINE, any of about 9 different medium-sized, thick-skinned mammals with barrel-shaped bodies, short necks, long heads ending in a flat snout, and a 2-chambered stomach. They are native to Eurasia, Africa, and Madagascar. The Eurasian wild hog (*Sus scrofa*) was hunted for centuries for sport and meat, and to prevent it from destroying crops; later it was domesticated, and true-breeding strains were selected for smallness of tusks, large production of meat, and other qualities.

In the wild form, the young are marked with brown stripes that remain for several months after birth. The African wart hog (*Phacochoerus aethiopicus*) received its name from the large facial growths that resemble warts. In this species there is a growth of long hair down the middle of the back, and the tusks are well developed in both jaws. Order Artiodactyla, family Suidae.

SWORDFISH, a very large bony fish in which the head is prolonged into a sharp, straight projection one-third as long as the body. These fishes are widely distributed in open waters of both the Atlantic and the Pacific oceans. The body itself is cylindrical in form, tapering toward the strongly notched tail. There are no scales, the sides being naked and grayish in color. This fish has no teeth and no ventral fins, and the dorsal fin is very long, often projecting above the surface of the water when the fish is sunning itself. The maximum weight of specimens is about 800 pounds, but the average is about half that size.

The beak of the swordfish can be a dangerous weapon and there are instances on record of its having been thrust through the planking of ships, so crippling them that they were forced to turn home for repairs. In feeding, the swordfish, capable of great speed, swims in among a school of fishes, lashing out from side to side with its beak, crippling or killing its food. Order Percomorphi, family Xiphiidae, specifically *Xiphias gladius*.

SWORDTAIL, a handsome freshwater fish with an extraordinary extension (the "tail") shaped like a sword, from the lower portion of the normal tail on the male fish; females are swordless. These fishes live in rivers along the Atlantic slope of southern Mexico and Guatemala. The body is shining olive-brown above, shading to blue or green on the sides, marked lengthwise and often vertically with red brown.

As a popular aquarium fish, a male swordtail will mate with 4 to 6 females, who produce living young in 6 to 8 weeks. The parents are likely to eat their own young if the 100 to 200 little fishes cannot find hiding places among tangled vegetation in the aquarium. Female swordtails are generally larger than males, and may attain a length of 4 inches. Order Cyprinodontes, family Poeciliidae, specifically *Xiphophorus helleri*.

TANAGER, any of about 200 different kinds of small- to medium-sized perching birds with a slightly downcurved conical beak that is notched in the cutting edges just before the slightly hooked tip. All live in tropical and subtropical America, except 4 that have become migratory and have spread as far north as Canada.

The best-known tanager is the handsome scarlet tanager (*Piranga olivacea*), 7 inches long, which nests from the Atlantic coast to Manitoba and Oklahoma, migrating for the winter to western South America. The male in summer is flaming red with jet-black wings and tail, but in fall and winter changes the red to olive-green shading to yellow underneath; the female resembles the winter male except that she is brownish gray where he is black.

The summer tanager (*P. rubra*), which migrates from the southern United States to Cuba, Mexico, and Central America for the winter, is slightly larger; the male is a uniform, dull red, and the female is yellowish green above, dull yellow below. In the western tanager (*P. ludoviciana*), which prefers open woodlands from the Rocky Mountains to the Pacific coast, the male is variegated yellow, black, and red; the female is undistinguished except that she has 2 yellow wing bars which are lacking in other similar birds.

The hepatic tanager (*P. flava*) nests as far north as Arizona and New Mexico, south to Guatemala. Many of the tropical tanagers belong to the genera *Tanagra* and *Tangara*, names derived from the language of the Tupi Indians of the Amazon basin. Order Passeriformes, family Thraupidae.

TAPEWORM, any of a large number of parasitic flatworms living in the digestive tract of vertebrate animals, each worm consisting of a single anchoring individual (the scolex), which holds to the wall of the intestine by means of hooks or suckers or both, and an indefinite number of flat individuals that appear to be mere segments of the tapeworm, called proglottids. The scolex individual absorbs food from the intestinal contents, and reproduces asexually, forming one proglottid after another from the free end by the process of budding.

The proglottids remain connected to one another and to the scolex for a long while, and give the appearance of a continuous ribbon, constricted at intervals where one proglottid joins the next younger or next older one. The proglottids also absorb food and grow, becoming sexually mature and mating within the intestine. Eventually each proglottid is old and full of fertilized eggs that have already developed through many embryonic stages. The old proglottid breaks free and is carried out with the feces.

The embryos hatch into larvae which can wait a few days or weeks to be swallowed by a host of another kind, such as a cow or a fish. In this secondary host, the larvae move to the muscles and become dormant. If the beef or fish flesh is eaten uncooked, the dormant larvae of the tapeworm become active and soon attach themselves to the lining of the digestive tract in the meat-eating animal (the primary host), growing there into the scolex stage that can produce a whole tapeworm. Nine different orders in class Cestoda.

TAPIR, any of 4 different large tropical mammals somewhat resembling donkeys with close-clipped fur, short tails, and a long flexible nose bearing the nostrils at the tip. The Brazilian tapir (*Tapirus terrestris*) inhabits water edges in rain forests from northern South America to Paraguay. The mountain tapir (*T. roulini*) travels in its search for vegetable food even higher than the limit of forest in the Andes. Baird's tapir (*T. bairdi*) is found northward from Ecuador through Central America into southeastern Mexico.

Largest of all is the Malayan tapir (*T. indicus*), 6 to 8 feet long, which, unlike the dull reddish or brownish black animals of the New World, is white on the back and sides. All young tapirs are striped and spotted with yellow and white. Tapirs have 3 toes reaching the ground on both the fore and hind feet. Order Perissodactyla, family Tapiridae.

TARANTULA, originally the name given to a moderately poisonous wolf spider (*Lycosa tarentula*) of Taranto in southern Italy, with a striped tan and brown body about 1 inch long and legs spreading about 2½ inches. In North America, tarantula became the name for large and relatively harmless hairy spiders (*Avicularia* and *Eurypelma* species particularly), which arrived in shipments of tropical fruit. Order Araneae.

TARPON, either of 2 different kinds of marine bony fishes with a large bony plate under the head between the two sides of the lower jaw, and a long filamentous extension from the last ray of the dorsal fin. The smaller Pacific tarpon (*Megalops cyprinoides*), which ranges from Guam to the east coast of Africa, rarely exceeds 40 inches in length.

The Atlantic tarpon (*M. atlanticus*), which is caught from Cape Cod in summer to Brazil, grows as much as 8 feet long and to 240 pounds or more. The large overlapping silver scales of such a fish are more than 3 inches across.

No fish fights harder for its freedom than a hooked tarpon; it often makes explosive leaps as much as 8 feet out of the water, 15 to 20 times in succession before becoming exhausted. At each leap, its greenish blue upper back and shining silver sides gleam in the light. Order Isospondyli, family Elopidae.

TEAL, any of about 15 different kinds of small diving ducks with particularly rapid flight. They are found in the Americas, Eurasia, Africa, Australia, New Zealand, Hawaii, and other oceanic islands. One of the world's vanishing birds is the little teal of Laysan Island (*Anas laysanensis*), which nests nowhere else. The common teal in Eurasia (*A. crecca*), 14 inches long, is Europe's smallest duck; it visits North American coasts regularly. The Hottentot teal (*A. punctata*) of Ethiopia is Africa's smallest duck.

North American teals come in several sizes: the 14-inch green-winged teal (*A. carolinensis*), which has a chestnut-brown head, nests across Canada and in the northwestern United States; the 15-inch blue-winged teal (*A. discors*), which has chalky blue patches on the wings, nests over most of Canada and the United States; and the 16-inch cinnamon teal (*A. cyanoptera*), with a cinnamon-colored head and body, nests in the western provinces of Canada and states southward into Mexico. Order Anseriformes, family Anatidae.

TENT CATERPILLAR, the destructive larval stage of a North American moth (*Malacosoma americana*) found commonly east of the Rocky Mountains. Tent caterpillars hatch in early spring from thick, crusty masses of about 200 eggs which surround the twigs of trees, particularly apple and cherry. At once the caterpillars set about spinning an unsightly protective tent of silk, into which they retire by day. At night, when birds are less active, the caterpillars walk out of their tent and feed on the foliage, often stripping a tree in a few days.

When fully grown, a tent caterpillar is about 2 inches long, with a continuous white stripe down its black back, and with blue and white spots on each side. After about 6 weeks of feeding, the larvae spin cocoons, often on the bark of the same tree, and pupate. In about 3 weeks the moths emerge, each rather heavy bodied, with a wingspread of 1¼ inches in the male to 2 inches in the female.

A related moth and caterpillar (*M. disstria*) which is widespread in forested areas of Canada, the United States, and Mexico, is often called a "forest tent caterpillar" moth, although its caterpillars produce silken carpets only—never a voluminous tent in which to hide. Order Lepidoptera, family Lasiocampidae.

TERMITE, or white ant, any of about 1,800 different kinds of insects with biting mouthparts, the thorax of the soft body broadly joined to the abdomen, and 2 pairs of similar, narrow membranous wings carried flat over the back and detached after the nuptial flight. Termites are mostly tropical, social insects, living in social communities with an elaborate system of castes and functional varieties.

Immature individuals of both sexes assist in the work of the colony, gathering and sharing food. The queen lays millions of eggs, sometimes 4,000 in a day. Many termites eat wood, which they digest with the help of single-celled protozoans in their intestines. Their damage to wooden buildings, books, and other human possessions causes enormous losses in tropical countries and, until extermination methods were improved recently, in many temperate regions of the United States.

In Africa and Australia, certain termites build huge nests, or termitaries, 20 to 40 feet high, piled up a grain of earth at a time. The earth is cemented by saliva. Order Isoptera.

TERN, or sea swallow, any of 39 different kinds of slender, gull-like seabirds 8 to 23 inches long, with slender pointed beaks, webbed, weak feet, and a pattern of feather coloration that is usually gray above and white below, with black markings on the head; some kinds are pure white.

Although all terns are migratory, the circumpolar Arctic tern (*Sterna paradisaea*), which is grayish white with a red beak and red legs, is probably the champion migrant. Most of the Arctic terns breed in the Arctic in summer, and winter in the Antarctic, 11,000 miles away. They travel more than 25,000 miles a year; many cross the Atlantic Ocean in their migration. Order Charadriiformes, family Laridae.

TERRAPIN. See *Tortoise.*

THRUSH, any of 306 different kinds of medium-sized perching birds, 8 to 12 inches long, many of them renowned for their melodious song. They are native to all temperate and tropical lands except New Zealand and some oceanic islands. Thrushes include the nightingale (*Luscinia megarhynchos*) of Europe and southwestern Asia, the song thrush (*Turdus ericetorum*) of Eurasia, the familiar and widespread North American robin (*T. migratorius*), and the smaller, more slender wood thrush (*Hylocichla mustelina*) of the eastern United States, and the widely distributed hermit thrush (*H. guttata*).

Opinion is divided as to whether the nightingale, the hermit thrush, or the shama thrush (*Kittacincla macrura*) of India has the sweetest song. All are birds of the underbrush, eating insects and fruits, and raising young whose breast feathers are spotted. Order Passeriformes, family Turdidae.

TICK, any of about 2,000 different kinds of external parasitic arthropods larger than mites, which attach themselves to vertebrate animals and suck the blood, often becoming greatly engorged before voluntarily dropping off. They are found all over the world. Immature mites have 3 pairs of legs, but add a fourth pair at the molt that brings them to mature form. Several different diseases, such as tularemia in rabbits and Texas fever in cattle, are transmitted from infected animals to uninfected ones by ticks. Order Acarina of class Arachnida.

The name tick is used also for several degenerate kinds of insects that are external parasites, such as the sheep tick (*Melophagus ovinus*) of Order Diptera, family Hippoboscidae.

TITMOUSE, any of about 65 different kinds of small, active songbirds similar to chickadees. Most are Eurasian, but several live in Africa and in America south to Guatemala. In Britain and Europe they are called tits. All are extremely energetic and trusting, as they hunt for insects in bark crevices and on foliage; they also eat some small fruits and seeds. The tufted titmouse (*Parus bicolor*) of the southeastern United States, which has a crest and is about 6 inches long, often visits feeding shelves around homes for suet, peanut butter, and sunflower seeds. Order Passeriformes, family Paridae.

TOAD, any of several hundred different kinds of amphibians that, like frogs, develop from aquatic tadpoles, have a protusible tongue fitted for catching insects, and large hind legs fitted for leaping. Toads differ from frogs in having a rough skin, more suited for life on land far from water. Toads are common in most parts of the world except the Australasian region, living even in some deserts. Many kinds have glands in the skin that secrete an acrid or poisonous fluid, which protects them from attack. They cannot cause warts. Several orders in subclass Salientia.

AMERICAN MUSEUM OF NATURAL HISTORY
TURTLE

TOOTH SHELL, or tusk shell, any of about 200 kinds of marine mollusks that produce a slightly curved and gradually tapered conical shell open at both ends. The common tooth shell (*Dentalium entale*) found on both sides of the Atlantic Ocean below low tide in sandy bottoms attains a length of about 2 inches.

The precious tooth shell (*D. pretiosum*) of the Pacific coast of North America served until recently as a form of money and status symbol among west coast Indians; the abundant 1-inch shells had little value, but a 2-inch specimen had the buying power of a shilling, and a 3-inch shell could be owned only by a major chief, who generally wore it around his neck on a loop of woven plant fiber. In New Guinea, mountain people still use large tooth shells for personal adornment, pushed through holes made in lower lip, nose, and ear lobes.

A living tooth shell keeps the small end of its shell above the sediments of the bottom, to breathe water in and out through the hole at the end; it has no gills. The body is extended from the lower, larger opening of the shell to extend the foot—shaped like a horse's hoof—and a number of threadlike tentacles. The tentacles push among the sand particles, find and capture small bits of organic matter as food, and bring it back to the mouth. Class Scaphopoda, family Dentalidae.

TORTOISE, or turtle, any of about 265 different kinds of broad-bodied, slow-moving reptiles with horny jaws instead of teeth, and usually with some vertebrae and ribs fused to a shell-like armor consisting of an upper, convex carapace and a lower, flat plastron, which are joined at the sides. The shell protects the head, legs, and tail when these are retracted into special cavities.

Tortoises are found worldwide, except for western South America and New Zealand. Some are marine, coming ashore only to lay their eggs; others live in arid lands and deserts; most live near freshwater or frequent moist forests. Most tortoises eat both plant and animal food, including small dead animals.

Among the largest are the giant tortoises of the Galápagos Islands and islands in the Indian Ocean, where individuals attain a length of 4 feet and a weight of 400 pounds. Notable among the sea turtles are the green (*Chelonia midas*) of tropical Atlantic and Gulf of Mexico coasts, the loggerhead (*Caretta caretta*) of the Atlantic, and the hawksbill (*Eretmochelys imbricata*) of all tropic seas, which provides the best quality of horny plates from the shell, known commercially as "tortoise shell." All of these large sea turtles are sought for meat, and their eggs are collected for people to eat.

In the southeastern United States, the diamondback terrapin (*Malaclemys centrata*) was formerly raised in pens as one of the most expensive luxury foods; this turtle of muddy marshes, both brackish and salt, grows to 5½ inches long in about 9 years, then more slowly; for a while, a 7-inch terrapin brought $7 on the market, with an extra dollar for each ½ inch additional length.

Painted turtles (*Chrysemys marginata* and related species), 5 to 6 inches long, are common in freshwater ponds of eastern North America; the box turtle (*Terrapene carolina*), on the other hand, frequents open woodlands in the same area. This turtle can draw its body completely within its shell and close the ends by raising hinged portions of the plastron. Order Testudinata.

TOUCAN, any of 37 different kinds of tropical, fruit-eating birds with a beak nearly as long as the body, not including the tail. They are birds of forests and clearings from southern Mexico to Paraguay. Although the beak is strong, it is lightweight and does not make the bird awkward. Toucans use their beaks to pick fruit and in elaborate courtship displays. They fly with beak ahead, almost like woodpeckers—flapping vigorously 8 to 10 times, then gliding with wings stiffly spread. They nest in holes in trees.

The toco (*Ramphastos toco*) of the Guianas and Brazil is 25 inches long, of which 8 inches is beak and 8 inches is tail; its black plumage is set off by a white throat, red under the tail, and an orange-red, black-tipped beak. Many smaller toucans are called araçaris (species of *Pteroglossus*), and live in large flocks. In the Andes they are found to 10,000 feet elevation. Order Piciformes, family Ramphastidae.

TRAP-DOOR SPIDER, any of a number of black or brown spiders with long stout legs, on which the third pair bear a claw used in digging. They live in the western and southern United States and Latin America, and on other continents.

Most are 1 inch or more in length, and dig vertical burrows 6 inches or more deep, topped with neatly fitted trapdoors made of mud and silk. Below the doors, the spiders rest, ready to jump out and seize passing insects, then drag them back into the burrow and close the door again. New Zealand trapdoor spiders make similar lairs in the thick bark of trees. Order Araneae, family Ctenizidae, many different genera.

TROGON, any of 34 different kinds of brightly colored tropical birds with long tails or tail-covert feathers. The New World has 20 kinds from the southwestern United States to northern Argentina. Africa has 3 kinds south of the great deserts. Asia has the others, chiefly in Malaya and the islands of Sumatra, Java, and the Philippines.

The most famous trogon is the quetzal (*Pharomachrus moccino*), the national symbol of Guatemala and the name used for their coin. It is now almost extinct there. In former times the native chiefs used the long, green tail-covert feathers of the male for decorations. The bird was worshiped by the Aztecs and Mayas in the cult of Quetzalcoatl, the mythical king, part bird and serpent (coatl).

The female trogon is brownish except for green back and wings and red under the tail; the male is brilliant green on head, chest, and wings, blue on the back, and scarlet underneath. Order Trogoniformes, family Trogonidae.

TROUT, a common name for several bony fishes closely related to salmon, with soft, rayed fins and a small soft adipose fin without rays on the back behind the large dorsal fin. They have very small scales. All are excellent eating and are regarded as game fish.

The North American brook trout (*Salvelinus fontinalis*) thrives in the coldest and clearest streams, laying its eggs in December or January. Other species in North America are the lake trout (*Cristivomer namaycush*) and the salmon trout (species of *Salmo*) in the East, and the rainbow and Dolly Varden trout in the West. Sea trout is a general term for any salt-water trout that enter freshwater only to spawn.

All species belong to the Northern Hemisphere, but they have been introduced into Australia and New Zealand. Order Isospondyli, family Salmonidae.

TUBE-NOSED BIRD, any of the large or medium-sized sea birds in which the beak provides a tubular extension for the nostrils, making these breathing holes open separately almost at the tip of the beak or open together as a single hole above the tip of the beak. They include the albatrosses, shearwaters (or mutton birds), the storm petrels, and the diving petrels. All of these birds remain at sea, feeding on fishes and squids from the surface water, except during the breeding season. Order Procellariiformes.

TUNA, any of about 10 large marine bony fish, resembling the smaller but closely related mackerels in having a streamlined body that narrows to a slender stalk just before the large tail, which is almost T-shaped. Tunas are found in all oceans, and are hunted by both sportsmen and commercial fishermen; tuna flesh is valuable food.

Largest of tunas is the great bluefin (*Thunnus thynnus*), which reaches a length of 14 feet and weight of 1,800 pounds, following a migration pattern from the Tropics to far northern waters off Norway. The albacore (*T. alalunga*), which has particularly long pectoral fins, is a favorite because its meat is white.

Yellowfin tunas (*T. albacares*) of the Indian and Pacific oceans grow as much as 60 pounds in a year; those at 90-pound size are sought for canning. They feed in great schools and are netted or caught with a short line on heavy poles. Of recent years this fish has become recognized by sportsmen for its strength and fighting ability, and specimens weighing around 800 pounds have been landed by rod and reel. One of the favorite grounds for tuna fishing is off Nova Scotia. Order Acanthopteri, family Scombridae.

TUNICATE, or sea squirt, any of about 1300 kinds of soft-bodied marine animals that attach themselves to solid objects in sea water and secrete a stiffening tunic of cellulose within the skin. They are found along most seacoasts in water to 200 feet deep. Most of the space in the body of a tunicate is occupied by an enormous throat region (pharynx) of the digestive tract.

Water entering the mouth passes out through a large number of pores in the pharyngeal wall, while oxygen is exchanged for carbon dioxide and particles of food are captured in a film of mucus. The loaded mucus goes on to the intestine. If a tunicate is disturbed, it contracts suddenly, expelling water from its mouth in a forceful jet, hence the name sea squirt.

In season, tunicates develop reproductive organs and release into the sea small larvae that resemble tadpoles. Each has a pharynx with gill openings, a hollow dorsal nerve cord, and a supporting rod called a notochord in the propulsive tail.

These features indicate that tunicates are degenerate members of the same phylum to which the vertebrate animals belong. Degeneration occurs when the larva settles to the bottom, attaches itself permanently, and absorbs its tail, its notochord, its propulsive muscles, and transforms into the form of the adult. Order Tunicata of the chordate subphylum Urochordata.

TURKEY, either of 2 different large pheasantlike birds with naked heads. They are native to woodlands in America from Canada to Central America, where they search along the ground for food by day and roost each night in trees.

The common turkey (*Meleagris gallopavo*), a 48-inch bird of southeastern United States and Mexico, was domesticated in Mexico at least 500 years before Columbus discovered America. Spanish conquistadores introduced them into Europe, and colonists brought them to New England. The tame birds differ somewhat in appearance from the birds in a wild state. In Yucatan, British Honduras, and Guatemala, the ocellated turkey (*Agriocharis ocellata*) still runs wild; it is a 36-inch bird, which lacks the beardlike chest tuft of feathers characteristic of the male common turkey. Order Galliformes, family Meleagrididae.

TURTLE. See *Tortoise*.

VAMPIRE, any of several different kinds of blood-sucking bats in which the incisor and canine teeth are shearlike, specialized for cutting through the skin of warm-blooded animals. Vampire bats alight gently on sleeping mammals such as horses, cattle, and even man, or creep along to a vantage point from which they can use their teeth to get blood flowing. They then lap the fresh blood with the tongue.

The teeth are so sharp that often considerable blood is lost and the bat has departed before the victim becomes aware that anything has happened. Order Chiroptera, family Desmodontidae.

VIPER, any of a large number of poisonous, stout-bodied Old World snakes in which the venom is discharged through 2 erectile fangs at the front of the upper jaw. They are widespread in Eurasia and Africa, and differ from the pit-vipers of America in lacking the heat-sensitive pits between eye and nostril.

The adder, or common viper (*Vipera berus*), widely distributed in Eurasia, is the only British venomous snake. Its bite rarely proves fatal. It attains a length of 25½ inches, is brown with a black zigzag line down the back, feeds chiefly upon mice and, like most vipers, is viviparous (bears young alive —not from eggs).

The puff adders (*Bitis arietans*) of Africa south of the great deserts lie in wait for rat-sized rodents, which they strike with incredible speed and then slowly pursue for the few seconds needed until the victim dies of the poison. Largest is the Gaboon viper (*B. gabunica*), nearly 6 feet long and 6 inches in diameter, which rarely bites people, even to defend itself. Order Serpentes, family Viperidae.

VOLE, or meadow mouse, a small, short-tailed rodent (*Microtus pennsylvanicus*) of orchards and pasturelands in North America. The head and body are chestnut-brown above, gray beneath, marked with black above and cinnamon color below. A vole eats approximately its own weight daily of many kinds of plants, and cuts down a great deal that it does not eat.

Since a female vole begins producing young when only a month old, and may bear 13 litters of 4 to 8 young within a year, the population can increase spectacularly if not controlled by foxes, hawks, and other predators. Voles are the basic food for most of these flesh-eaters. Order Rodentia, family Cricetidae.

VULTURE, any of 6 different carnivorous, scavenging birds of the New World, and of 4 in the Old, all capable of soaring for hours with no apparent motion of their wings. With incredibly keen eyesight, they watch from high up for carcasses of dead animals or mammals that are dying or badly injured. Circling down, they alight near the carcass, then, using their strong hooked beaks, tear it into strips small enough to swallow.

Largest is the Andean condor (*Vultur gryphus*), 52 inches long with a wingspan of 10 to 12 feet and a weight of 20 to 25 pounds; it is one of the world's largest flying birds, and is be-

coming increasingly rare although it nests and perches from 10,000 to 15,000 feet above sea level on inaccessible cliffs. Under stress of hunger, it descends to the plains in search of sick and dead domestic animals, and is shot by ranchers.

A somewhat similar bird, the California condor (*Gymnogyps californianus*), is threatened with extinction in its last retreat—some relatively inaccessible mountain regions of California.

In the Old World, the only vulture of comparable size is the bearded vulture, or lammergeier (*Gypaetus barbatus*), named for a tuft of bristly feathers on its chin, which has the reputation of stealing lambs over the mountains from the Pyrenees and North Africa to eastern India. However, its feet are too weak to hold a struggling animal and it ordinarily waits until other scavengers have cleaned a carcass before descending to get the bones; it can crush these or drop them on crags and pick up the pieces to get at the marrow inside.

The griffin vulture (*Gyps fulvus*), a 41-inch bird with a ruff of white feathers into which it can withdraw its bare head and neck, watches over the same area surveyed by the lammergeier for animals to die; flocks of griffin vultures stand near the burning ghats in India, waiting to feast on the remains of human corpses that are thrown into the sacred Ganges. The smaller, white, Egyptian vulture (*Nephron percnopterus*), sometimes called pharaoh's chicken, ranges all over countries bordering the Mediterranean, often staying close to villages to eat whatever meat scraps it can find.

In the New World, the turkey vulture, or turkey buzzard (*Cathartes aura*), is the common scavenger from southern Canada to Tierra del Fuego. It gets its name from the reddish color of the naked head and upper neck; its body plumage and wings are drab gray-brown, but its wingspan of 6 feet lets it soar gracefully all day. Its services as a scavenger have earned it rigorous legal protection.

The black vulture, or black buzzard, or carrion crow, or urubu (*Coragyps atratus*), is a heavier bird of smaller size, residing in the southern United States and southward to Argentina. From southern Mexico southward it competes to some exent with the king vulture (*Sarcorhamphus papa*), a 32-inch bird whose naked head and neck bear many bright colors—white, yellow, red, and black— in a pattern made more startling by the bird's white eye.

New World vultures all belong to family Cathartidae, distinguished by longitudinal instead of round nostrils, lack of a voice, beaks so weak they cannot tear flesh until it rots, slightly webbed toes, and the hind toe somewhat elevated. Old World vultures belong to family Vulturidae. All vultures are classified in order Falconiformes.

WALLABY, any of about 35 different kinds of small- and medium-sized grazing and browsing marsupial mammals similar to but smaller than

kangaroos. They inhabit Australia, New Guinea, and adjacent islands, often taking refuge among boulders. Often they emerge to sunbathe, but they feed mostly at night. The many genera are classified in order Marsupialia, family Macropodidae.

WALRUS, an arctic marine mammal (*Odobenus rosmarus*), closely related to seals and sea lions, distinguished by its bristly whiskers and enormous, down-turned tusks, or canine teeth, projecting from the upper jaw. Those of the male are larger and longer and sometimes reach a length of 16 inches beyond the sockets. The generic name means tooth walking, for it was once supposed that the walrus used its tusks to help drag its heavy body along land and ice. Actually, the tusks are used by the walrus to free mollusks from the sea bottom when feeding. The female walrus has smaller tusks.

Walruses have a heavy body, deepest at the shoulders, and limbs that are adapted for swimming. They reach a length of 12 feet or more, and a weight of 2,200 pounds. They are hunted for their hides, their tusks, and their blubber that produces 25 to 30 gallons of oil from each walrus. Order Pinnipedia, family Odobenidae.

WARBLER, any of 300 different kinds of small birds, mostly dull colored, in the Old World, all members of family Sylviidae, and nearly 120 of small, mostly bright-colored birds in the New World, all members of family Parulidae. To prevent confusion, the New World warblers are now referred to often as wood warblers. The name warbler is deceptive, in that very few of them are singers of any ability. In spite of this, the warblers are among the most charming and useful citizens of our wildlife. Their insect- and larvae-destroying activities are worth millions of dollars yearly.

Widespread in Eurasia are the grasshopper warbler (*Locustella naevia*), whose song is more distinctive than its plumage; the reed warbler (*Acrocephalus scirpaceus*) of reed beds and waterside shrubbery; the sedge warbler (*A. schoenobaenus*) of similar habitats; the blackcap (*Sylvia atricapilla*) of woodlands; the garden warbler (*S. borin*) of bramble patches; the whitethroat (*S. communis*) of more open country; and the chiffchaff (*Phylloscopus collybita*) of evergreen woodlands.

Familiar warblers in North America include the black-and-white warbler (*Mniotilta varia*) that creeps around tree trunks searching for insect food in crevices; the yellow warbler or yellowbird (*Dendroica petechia*), yellowish green above and bright yellow beneath; the myrtle warbler (*D. coronata*), slate gray, with conspicuous yellow patches at the base of the tail, the crown, and on either side of the breast; the redstart (*Setophaga ruticilla*), with brilliant red wing and tail marks contrasting with its jet-black plumage; and the yellowthroat (*Geothlypis trichas*), olive above and bright yellow below, with a black mask over its face. Order Passeriformes.

AMERICAN MUSEUM OF NATURAL HISTORY
VULTURE

WASP, a member of any of several families of insects that, as adults, have biting mouthparts, 2 pairs of membranous wings of which the fore pair is much the larger, a narrow waist between thorax and abdomen, and in females and sterile workers, a well-developed stinger and poison gland at the hind end of the body.

Wasps differ from bees in having slenderer bodies and no pollen-gathering specialized apparatus on the hind legs. Some are solitary; others form colonies in which the individuals work together for the common good. Solitary wasps include the digger wasps (family Bembecidae), which excavate holes in the soil or in wood and there store insects that they have paralyzed with their stinger, as food for the maggotlike young that will hatch from their eggs.

The thread-waisted wasps (family Sphecidae) include mud daubers (genus Sceliphron), which collect spiders to fill the cells of nests built by sticking mud to beams in barns or similar places. The social wasps, chiefly members of family Vespidae, are commonly called simply wasps, or hornets.

Some wasps make a nest in the earth; others make paper nests from bits of decaying wood that they chew into a real paper pulp. In the colonies the male wasps die when winter approaches; but the females live to start a new colony in the spring. Order Hymenoptera.

WATER BOATMAN, any of a large number of aquatic insects (Corixa) ¾ inch long or less that swim actively in fresh and stagnant water, propelling themselves with oarlike hind legs. They are found all over the world. The front legs are adapted for scraping microscopic algae from leaves, stones, and other firm surfaces. Females lay top-shaped yellow eggs on submerged objects. The immature water boatmen that emerge have the same blunt, boat-shaped body as the adults, but gain wings only at the final molt when they are mature.

Water boatmen often fly to lights, as well as to colonize new bodies of freshwater, including bird baths and public fountains. The adults are eaten by many kinds of birds, and the aquatic individuals by fishes and water birds. Order Heteroptera, family Corixidae.

WATER FLEA, a small crustacean of fresh and brackish water, not more than ⅛ inch long, which appears to dance as it swims by lashing its 2 feathery antennae. Most water fleas belong to genus Daphnia. They are found all over the world.

The sides of the flattened body of the water flea are extended ventrally to provide protection for the gills and for clusters of developing eggs. For favorable parts of the year, sexual reproduction is unnecessary; females reproduce by parthenogenesis, freeing a new brood of minute young with the same body form every 7 to 11 days.

Males develop toward the end of the summer or when a pond becomes too stagnant; the fertilized eggs have a heavy shell and can survive desiccation or frost. In this dormant condition, water fleas pass periods of drought, of winter, and get carried from one pond to another in mud on the feet of wading birds. Water fleas are raised in enormous numbers by fanciers of tropical fish, as a suitable food to add to aquariums. Order Branchiopoda, suborder Cladocera.

WATER STRIDER, or pond skater, any of a large number of insects with a compact, canoe-shaped body that support themselves on 4 long outstretched slender legs atop the surface film over ponds and streams. They are found in the Americas, Eurasia, and Africa, but not in Australasia or most oceanic islands.

Waxy hairs of microscopic size prevent the water from wetting the feet of a water strider. The insect holds its body well above the surface film as it sculls along with its middle pair of legs, riding its slight weight on the long hind legs and short front legs, which are held close together below the head.

Water striders are scavengers, investigating as possible food all objects of modest size that float up to the water film from below or that float in it after falling from above. In winter and during rain storms, most striders crawl out on the shore and hide under leaves. One that cannot often do so is the sea-going water strider (Halobates) that is common among the mangroves on quiet tropical lagoons, but ventures also far out at sea. It is believed to lay its eggs on the floating feathers dropped by sea birds. No one knows how it survives during storms. Order Heteroptera, family Gerridae.

WATER THRUSH, either of 2 short-tailed wood warblers (Seiurus), closely related to the ovenbird, which seem nervous as they teeter while walking along the edges of streams and rivers in North America and northern South America.

The northern water thrush (S. noveboracensis) is slightly smaller than the Louisiana water thrush (S. motacilla), and differs in that it has a yellowish line above the eye rather than a white one, and dark streaks on the greenish yellow breast instead of none. The northern water thrush prefers northern bogs and swamps or near quiet water as a nesting site; the Louisiana water thrush prefers flowing streams and rivers.

Both birds eat insects and crustaceans picked up along the edge of the water but, unlike the water ouzel, they do not venture into the water itself. Order Passeriformes, family Parulidae.

WAXWING, any of 3 different kinds of sleek, crested, fruit-eating, tree-dwelling birds 6 to 8 inches long, which have a yellow band across the end of the tail and red tips to the secondary flight feathers that show when their wings are folded at rest. The largest is the Bohemian waxwing (Bombycilla garrulus), found from northern Eurasia into the western United States.

The cedar waxwing (B. cedrorum) nests from coast to coast in Canada and the northern United States, flying south into Central America and the West Indies for the winter. A Japanese waxwing (B. japonica) has red-tipped wing feathers, but not the small pellets of waxy bright-red material found in the New World birds. Order Passeriformes, family Bombycillidae.

WEASEL, or stoat, any of 10 different kinds of short-legged predatory mammals so slender that they can follow a mouse to the end of its burrow or pass through a knothole into a chicken coop. They are found in North Africa, Eurasia, and America as far south as the rim of the Amazon basin. The longtailed weasel (Mustela frenata) of southernmost Canada southward into South America has brown feet even in winter when, in northern latitudes, its coat becomes completely white except for the feet and the black tip of the tail.

The ermine (M. erminea) of the northern United States, Canada, and northern Eurasia similarly has a black tip to its tail, turns white elsewhere in winter, and brown on the back in summer. Its pelt has been sought for centuries to line the robes of royalty and magistrates and, more recently, to make expensive fur coats for wealthy people.

Closely related are the two semi-aquatic minks, the European (M. lutreola) being found from Scandinavia into Siberia, and the American (M. vison) over all of North America except the southwestern states and Mexico. Unlike other weasels, minks have some webbing between their toes and a white patch on the chin; otherwise they are dark brown or black. Young minks are sometimes kept as pets and used like ferrets for hunting. Order Carnivora, family Mustelidae.

WEEVIL, or snout beetle, any of a large number of beetles, in which the forward part of the head is prolonged into the form of a snout, with the jaws at the tip. They are found all over the world, often as pests causing extensive damage to fruits and grains. With its jaws, a weevil cuts a cylindrical hole the length of its snout into fruits of many kinds, both to obtain food and to prepare a deep pit in which it can have some protection for the eggs it lays there. Order Coleoptera, family Curculionidae.

WHALE, any of about 34 different kinds of large marine mammals in which the forelimbs have the form of flippers, the hind limbs are completely concealed within the body or absent, and the tail is expanded widthways into flukes used in sculling along. Only the little white whale (Delphinapterus leucas) of shallow waters and large rivers in the Arctic, and the narwhal (Monodon monoceros)— named for the single long spirally-twisted tusk that grows straight forward from the male's head—of Arctic seas are less than 15 feet long; these two mature at 11 to 12 feet in length, and are placed in the same family (Monodontidae).

Twenty other kinds of whales have teeth of some kind, and are referred to as "toothed whales." They include the gregarious pilot whales, or blackfish (species of *Globicephala*), which are harvested off Newfoundland for oil and for meat to feed foxes on fur farms; and the dreaded killer whale, or orca (*Orcinus orca*), of all seas but especially the Arctic and Antarctic, which attack in packs, often tearing even the biggest whales to pieces; these are members of family Delphinidae. Beaked whales of 14 different kinds (family Ziphiidae) and of all oceans are less famous than one of the 2 kinds of sperm whales—the cachalot (*Physeter catodon*) made familiar by Melville's *Moby Dick*; it attains a length of 60 feet, a weight of 50 tons, provides the teeth carved by sailors and called "scrimshaw," and is placed in family Physeteridae.

The whalebone, or baleen whales, which have row upon row of fringed horny plates ("whalebone") hanging from the roof of the enormous mouth, include the gray whales of the North Pacific (*Eschrichtius glaucus*), many of which migrate within sight of the California coast to calving and breeding areas along the coasts of Baja California and mainland Mexico; and 5 different "right" whales (family Balaenidae) represented in all oceans, so named because they floated and could be flensed by old-time whalers, whereas "wrong" whales—the 6 kinds in family Balaenopteridae—sank when harpooned. The latter include the largest of whales: the blue or sulphur-bottom (*Sibbaldus musculus*), to 100 feet long and 100 tons—the largest mammal that ever lived; 4 kinds of finback whales (members of genus *Balaenoptera*); and the humpback whale (*Megaptera novaeangliae*) that often swims near coasts and inlets on its migration between tropical and polar seas north and south. Whalebone whales use their strange plates to strain from the water the 1- to 2-inch crustaceans and the squids and fishes that form their food. The blubber of whales, which underlies the smooth shining skin, is rich in oil and serves both to insulate the body from losing heat too rapidly in icy water and to buoy up the whale, saving it from expending extra effort to stay near the water's surface.

All whales dive, holding their breath for many minutes. The champion diver is the sperm whale, which dives to such great depths that it sometimes is caught and drowned by becoming entangled with transoceanic telephone cables. To these depths the sperm whale plunges in pursuit of the giant squid that form its favorite food. Undigestible beaks from these squids may irritate the lining of the whale's digestive tract until it forms a cheesy material called ambergris, which is much sought as a fixative for perfumes. Order Cetacea.

WHIPPOORWILL, an American bird (*Caprimulgus vociferus*) related to the nighthawk and the European nightjar, or goatsucker, named for its loud cry that sounds like "whip poor Will" with the last syllable heavily accented. The bird is not often seen, although it is abundant in damp woods of the eastern United States. It usually rests on the ground during the day and searches for insects at early nightfall.

It is about 10 inches long and of plain colors, being grayish, much variegated with black and buff. Its bill is very broad, its mouth large (hence the genus name meaning cave mouth) and provided with a tuft of long bristles. It builds no nest but deposits its eggs on leaves or in a slight depression in the ground. Order Caprimulgiformes, family Caprimulgidae.

WHITEFISH, any of several freshwater fishes (*Coregonus*) of cool clear lakes and deep rivers in the Northern Hemisphere, distantly related to shad and herring. Whitefishes have few or no teeth, possess a pair of flaps between the nostrils, and are characteristically meaty and clad in silvery scales. They feed principally on insects and bottom animals, but come to shallow water to lay their eggs on rocks. These eggs are often gathered for sale as edible fish roe. The Great Lakes whitefish (*C. clupeiformis*) was formerly an important commercial species, attaining a length of 24 inches and a weight to 23 pounds. Invasion of the lakes by sea lampreys has ruined the fishery. Order Isospondyli, family Coregonidae.

WHITING. See *Cod.*

WIDGEON. See *Duck.*

WILDEBEEST. See *Gnu.*

WOLF, either of 2 different kinds of doglike, flesh-eating mammals, 42 to 54 inches long, with a tail 12 to 22 inches in length that is held high when the animal runs. Formerly, wolves were widespread in Eurasia and in North America from the Arctic to south of Mexico. Now the small, tawny red wolf (*Canis niger*) is restricted to a few areas of Oklahoma and Texas. The formerly widely distributed timber wolf, or gray wolf (*C. lupus*), has been restricted to parts of the United States and eastern Canada. In the northernmost parts of its range, it remains white most or all of the year. Farther south it is usually gray, sprinkled with black.

A wolf differs from other members of the genus *Canis* in its larger size, longer legs, narrower but deeper and heavier body, and wider nose pad. Wolves can be crossed successfully with some breeds of domestic dogs, especially Eskimo sled dogs. Probably the preference for sled dogs that are part wolf has continued for thousands of years, keeping the fertility high despite the fact that the domestic dog has a separate, Asian origin. Order Carnivora, family Canidae.

WOLVERINE, or glutton, a heavy-bodied weasel-like mammal with a squarish head, short legs, and bushy tail, and very dark brown except for a pale stripe along each side and across the back at the base of the tail. It inhabits the northern coniferous forest

AMERICAN MUSEUM OF NATURAL HISTORY
WOLF

near the arctic tundra of Eurasia and North America. Usually solitary, it lives in dens or burrows, emerging when hungry to seek carrion or to feed on live animals, birds' eggs and nestlings in spring, and fruits in autumn. It is notorious for its skill in robbing traps of the meat used to bait them, without getting caught despite the most ingenious devices set for that purpose.

On a full-grown wolverine, nearly 3 feet long, the fur is coarse. Yet, better than any other fur, it repels condensation of moisture in freezing weather and, for that reason, is in large demand to trim parkas and reduce the formation of frost from moisture in the breath. Order Carnivora, family Mustelidae, specifically *Gulo gulo.*

WOMBAT, either of 2 different kinds of bearlike marsupial mammals, 2 to 3 feet long, with small eyes, short legs, and chisel-like incisor teeth that continue growing like those of rodents. Wombats live in Australia and Tasmania, hiding in burrows by day and feeding on grasses and roots in the forest by night. Both the coarse-haired wombat (*Phascolomis ursinus*) and the soft-furred wombat (*Lasiorhinus latifrons*) compete with livestock, and are in danger of being exterminated by stock raisers. Order Marsupialia, family Phascolomidae.

WOODCHUCK. See *Marmot.*

WOODCOCK, either of 2 different kinds of heavy-bodied birds with extraordinary adaptations to concealment on the ground against a pattern of fallen leaves, making a strange whirring courtship flight in twilight, and probing in the soft soil of swamps for earthworms. The Eurasian woodcock (*Scolopax rusticola*), 14 inches long, migrates from temperate regions southward for the winter. The American woodcock (*Philohela minor*), an 11-inch bird known also as the timberdoodle, nests in eastern Canada and the United States, and winters in the southeastern States.

Both kinds arrive in their nesting territories in early spring, and prepare a place for their eggs on the ground close to an alder swamp, into which they lead the young as soon as these hatch out. All during the mating and nesting season, the male wood-cock performs at twilight his rapid, whizzing flights, rising high into the air and descending again close to his mate. She seems so confident that her soft mottled brown feathers match her background that she will not move if approached on the nest, until actually touched.

A woodcock's beak is well adapted to probing for and catching worms and insects deep down in the soft soil of the swamp. At all times when the beak is down, the bird can see in all directions because its large eyes are positioned unusually high on its head. The flesh of woodcock is delicious, and the birds are challenging targets, for they ascend almost vertically when flushed from the thick cover of vegetation, and fly off at high speed, dodging branches in a zigzag flight path. Many gunners swear a wood-cock can fly sideways. Order Chara-driiformes, family Scolopacidae.

WOODPECKER, any of 210 different kinds of birds with strong, straight, pointed beaks, long extensile tongues having barbs at the tip, short legs with 2 long toes forward, 2 backward and sharp curved toenails, and tail-feathers that are stiff, strong, and pointed at the tip. Woodpeckers live on all major land areas where there are trees, except Madagascar, Aus-tralia, and the oceanic islands. They fly strongly, undulating by beating their wings 4 or 5 times in quick succession to gain altitude, then closing the wings and curving downward like a projectile until the next series of wingbeats.

Most woodpeckers perch on tree trunks and branches, clinging to the bark while propping themselves with their special tail feathers. They ham-mer with the beak to expose insects, then spear each on the barbed tongue. Flickers, which often stand on the ground to pick up ants, and sapsuck-ers, which drill for sap and also eat nuts and fruits, match their food sup-ply by migrating regularly. Other woodpeckers rarely fly far or on a schedule corresponding to the seasons. All except the South African ground woodpecker (Geocolaptes olivaceus) use the beak to make nest cavities in large trees.

The largest woodpeckers, which feed on carpenter ants in large, dead standing trees, are in danger of ex-tinction because suitable forests are getting fewer: the imperial wood-pecker (Campephilus imperialis), a 22-inch bird with a crest in Mexico; the ivory-billed (C. principalis), which once made the chips fly in the southeastern United States and Cuba; and the magellanic woodpecker (C. magellanicus) of southern South America. The sparrow-sized wood-peckers, such as the downy (Dendro-copos pubescens) of North America and the lesser spotted woodpecker (D. minor) of Europe are much more widespread and common.

The yellow-bellied sapsucker (Sphyrapicus varius), an 8½-inch bird of temperate North America, and the 6 kinds of flickers (genus Co-laptes) of America from Alaska to southern Chile are seen as transients in many regions between their nesting and wintering grounds. Two North American woodpeckers show peculiar habits, the red-headed (Melanerpes erythrocephalus) often pursuing in-sects on the wing in the manner of a flycatcher, and the California wood-pecker (Balanosphyra formicivora) often embedding acorns in telephone poles. Order Piciformes, family Picidae.

WREN, any of 59 different kinds of small brownish birds with slender, slightly downcurved, pointed beaks, short, rounded wings, and compara-tively large strong legs and feet. They fly fast, straight, and with a buzzing sound, and stand characteristically with tail upright. All but one are birds of the New World. The one (Troglodytes troglodytes), called the winter wren in America, is found in Eurasia from Iceland to Siberia, south to northern India and northwest Af-rica. The house wren (T. aedon), a 4½- to 5½-inch bird that nests readily in bird houses close to people, is dis-tributed all the way from southern Canada to Tierra del Fuego.

The song of the wren is very melo-dious but exasperatingly repetitious and amazingly loud for so small a bird. The male is a good protector for nesting territory and young, often at-tacking birds much larger than itself, such as a bluebird and swallow. Most wrens live on or near the ground, feeding on insects and worms that they find in the dense underbrush. Order Passeriformes, family Troglo-dytidae.

YAK, or grunting ox, a long-haired, heavy-bodied, cud-chewing mammal (Bos grunniens) native to the high regions of Tibet. A full-grown male may be 6 feet high at the shoulder and weigh nearly a ton, with wide-spreading horns. Wild yaks are black-ish brown with a pale mark over the eye that gives them a sleepy appear-ance. Domesticated yaks are more varied in color, and serve docilely as beasts of burden; they are also a source of meat and milk. Yak hair is woven into fabrics and rope, and the tails are used for fly swatters. Order Artiodactyla, family Bovidae.

YELLOWLEGS, either of 2 American shorebirds with long, yellow legs. They are seen most often on migration or near the water of coastal marshes during the winter, for their breeding territory extends in a narrow band from Alaska across the southern end of Hudson Bay to southern Labrador and Newfoundland.

The greater yellowlegs (Totanus melanoleucus) winter along both oceanic coasts of the United States around the Gulf of Mexico and well down into the West Indies and Latin America. The lesser yellowlegs (T. flavipes), which have a straight rather than an upturned beak and are 11, not 15 inches long as are the greater yellowlegs, spend the cold months around the Gulf coast and in the West Indies southward to Patagonia. In flight, these birds extend beak and long neck forward, and their legs stretch out behind. They wade about, capturing mollusks, aquatic insects, crustaceans, and some small fishes among water plants near shore. Order Charadriiformes, family Scolopacidae.

YELLOWTHROAT, an active olive-brown wood warbler with a yellow throat and a buff-colored breast, of which the male has a distinctive black mask on the face; both sexes differ from similar birds in having a whitish belly. Yellowthroats live in North America, frequenting the edges of swamps, marshes, and streams. They build a large cup-shaped nest of grasses and leaves, usually under a bush in a marsh.

The northern yellowthroat (Geo-thlypis trichas), formerly called the Maryland yellowthroat, has a loud song, witchity-witchity-witch, heard over most of the United States and Canada; it winters in the Gulf States, California, Latin America, and the West Indies. A Mexican bird that does not migrate, the Rio Grande yellow-throat (Chamaethlypis poliocephala) is larger and vireolike; the black mask of the male is so small that it does not reach beyond the eye. Order Pas-seriformes, family Parulidae.

ZEBRA. See Ass.

BIBLIOGRAPHY

ALLEN, GLOVER M. Birds and Their Attributes. Peter Smith, 1962.
BELLAIRS, ANGUS D'A. Reptiles. Har-per & Bros., 1960.
BUCHSBAUM, RALPH M. and L. S. Lower Animals: Living Inverte-brates of the World. Doubleday & Co., Inc., 1960.
BURTON, MAURICE. A Systematic Dic-tionary of Mammals of the World. Thomas Y. Crowell Co., 1962.
COCHRAN, DORIS M. Living Amphibi-ans of the World. Doubleday & Co., Inc., 1961.
GLASS, BENTLEY, OWSEI TEMKIN, and WILLIAM L. STRAUS, JR. Forerunners of Darwin, 1745–1859. The Johns Hopkins Press, 1959.
HERALD, EARL STANNARD. Living Fishes of the World. Doubleday & Co., Inc., 1961.
MILNE, LORUS J. and MARGERY. Ani-mal Life. Prentice-Hall, Inc., 1959.
PALMER, EPHRAIM LAURENCE. Field-book of Natural History. McGraw-Hill, Inc., 1949.
ROTHSCHILD, NATHANIEL MEYER. Clas-sification of Living Animals. John Wiley & Sons, Inc., 1961.
STORER, TRACY IRWIN and ROBERT L. USINGER. Elements of Zoology. Mc-Graw-Hill, Inc., 1961.
SUSSMAN, MAURICE. Animal Growth and Development. Prentice-Hall, Inc., 1960.
TEALE, EDWIN WAY. Grassroot Jun-gles: A Book of Insects. Dodd, Mead & Co., 1953.
WALKER, ERNEST P., and ASSOCIATES. Mammals of the World. The Johns Hopkins Press, 1964.

Introduction   71   Printing   142
Architecture   73   Dictionary of
Painting   82   printers' terms   150
Sculpture   113   Music   154
Ceramics   126   Dictionary of music   172
Glass   133   Dance   180
Graphic arts   136   Bibliography   185

VOLUME TWO

ARTS

THE METROPOLITAN MUSEUM OF ART, ROGERS FUND, 1941

Arts

The division that man can make of what he sees about him is nature and art. A thing is either natural or artificial; either God made it or man made it. The things that man makes may be either useful or beautiful or both. Usually there is the combination of beauty and utility, as in architecture, the handicrafts and the new machine-age industrial art. The arts in which utility is considered secondary to the creation of formal beauty are called the *fine arts* and are usually listed as architecture, painting, sculpture, music and poetry. Of these the most nearly related are architecture, painting and sculpture, which are the major *visual* arts.

It seems as if all the wise men through the ages have tried to answer the question, *What is art?* But it is still impossible to tell in simple intelligible language what art is or what it means. Esthetes used to say that "art is the creation of the beautiful"; but nowadays such a definition seems dangerously like an evasion of the whole difficulty, because *beautiful* is just as impossible to explain as *art;* and *beautiful* applies to many natural things that are not art.

A few modern definitions hint at the essence of art and so may be useful in affording us an inkling of its meaning. A common one is that "art is the expression of an emotion." Since art has more to do with emotions than with intellectual knowing and logical statement, there is at least a valuable clue in this definition.

Some of the moderns, in referring to the visual arts, have given this basic statement: "Art is the expression of a conceived image." This reminds us that the artist has conceived or imagined something in his inner being: he has seen it uniquely and then has given it concrete expression in terms of the materials and methods of the particular art he has chosen as his medium.

At the end of any attempt to explain the theory of art or esthetics, one might as well say: Do not worry too much if you do not discover a simple definition. If you will take the pains to go where actual art is and expose yourself to it, you will find yourself enjoying it; and that *experience* of art will give you a better notion of its essence and characteristics than all the definitions ever penned.

Art is surely an evidence of the divine in man. It is something that distinguishes him from all the rest of creation. The work of art carries a message that the artist receives from his Creator, and it is his duty and joy to pass it on to humanity. This is the reason why the artist has been revered at many times during the course of civilization.

There are other fine arts, such as the dance and the drama, and there are those industries where the arts of painting and sculpture are closely intermingled with the handicrafts, such as ceramics, leaded and stained glass, jewelry, weaving, cabinetmaking and many others.

The general terms that divide art into chronological or historical divisions are unfortunately very loose and uncertain. Usually they are listed: prehistoric, ancient, Byzantine, medieval, Renaissance and Modern. These divisions leave out of account the magnificent manifestations of art in India, later Persia, Java, China and Japan, and the student should keep in mind that hardly one-half of world achievement is told in the story of western art alone.

Prehistoric Art.—It is only during the last 50 years that we have discovered that a truly great and noble pictorial art existed among our ancestors perhaps 50,000 years ago. The Cro-Magnon men, who lived in caves in Europe in the Paleolithic or Old Stone Age, left drawings and carvings of animals that compare very favorably with the work of the foremost modern artists. This work we call *prehistoric* art, and so also can be classified the work of any race produced before the dawn of its recorded history; such was the art of the lake dwellers of Switzerland and of the mound builders and cliff dwellers of America.

Ancient Art.—Not long after 5,000 B.C. the Egyptians built the first of their tombs and invented the system of picture-writing or hieroglyphics. This affords a convenient date for beginning the study of ancient art. The course of ancient art continues through the lives of the inhabitants of Babylonia, Assyria, ancient Persia, Phoenicia, Crete, Greece (where in the 6th and 5th centuries B.C. it reached its greatest glory) and Rome. The art of Greece and Rome is termed *classic,* and on it alone is based a great deal of the subsequent art of Europe and even of the art of today. At the fall of Rome and the Western Empire in 476 A.D., ancient art may be considered to have ended.

Byzantine and Medieval Art.—Medieval is the name given to the period of a thousand years that followed the fall of Rome—the time when modern western nations began to rise out of the wreck of the ancient Roman Empire, and the northern barbarian hordes that had overthrown Rome gradually became civilized. Its most important phenomenon was the rise and increasing power of Christianity as exemplified in the Roman Catholic Church, with its head, the Pope, in Rome. This was the romantic period of chivalry and of the feudal system, of King Arthur and his Round Table, of knights and ladies, of castles and dungeons. During the late Middle Ages occurred the Crusades, the long-drawn-out struggle of the Christian nations to recover the Holy Land from the Moslems. Christianity triumphed over Mohammedanism in the struggle for the possession of Europe. England was won by William the Conqueror. Although the Middle Ages had the usual share of ignorance, poverty, cruelty and wretchedness, it was glorified by the highest examples of chivalry, ecstatic faith and courage, and it saw the creation of some of the most magnificent architecture and sculpture of all time. The Christian monasteries nurtured the minor arts through the period of the Dark Ages and developed crafts and traditions that were to lead to the building and ornamentation of the Gothic cathedrals. The monastic system had grown up first in the Eastern churches, and it is to the East that we must look for the origins of a good deal that went into both Romanesque and Gothic art.

Even before the fall of Rome the *Byzantine* style had taken form in Asia. It is essentially an eastern Christian art. Its background is Persian, Syrian and Egyptian (Coptic), with also some post-classic Greek strains. It is the one European style marked by the frank formalism and the opulent decorativeness of the Oriental peoples. It was brought to Ravenna and Venice and Palermo in its purest types of expression, especially in the 5th, 6th and 11th centuries. It went to France, Spain and Lombardy in only slightly modified forms. Finally it deeply influenced the Romanesque, the western medieval style, and indeed is so mingled with it that no dividing line between the two can be found.

The *Romanesque* style is often said to mark the survival or revival of classic Roman elements as Europe came back to civilized living and expression after the Dark Ages. It is really the most impure of the major styles: Roman methods of building and classic motives are mixed with the distinctive patterning, rich color and abstract formalization brought westward by the Byzantine craftsmen. Romanesque as a style had its beginnings about the 6th century and flourished especially in the 10th and

11th. It disappeared finally in the *Gothic* style in the 12th century. From that time until 1500 Gothic expression ruled in all the northern countries. The outstanding monuments and the culminating glory of the entire Middle Ages are the Gothic cathedrals.

The Renaissance.—Renaissance means rebirth and refers to a rebirth of classic ideals—the ideals of Greece and Rome. The term Renaissance in a strict sense covers the period from 1420 to 1500. In a broad sense, it includes the entire period up to the emergence of modern styles in architecture, sculpture and painting in the early 20th century. In architecture Europe, beginning with Italy in the early 15th century, began to use again the ancient forms and methods of Rome. In sculpture Italian artists had initiated the revival of classic methods as early as the 13th century, although the culmination came in the 15th. There was a corresponding interest in Greek and Roman literature, and this intellectual activity spread to science and exploration. Perspective was discovered, and there was a great interest in anatomy; these studies gave birth to the Renaissance painting that is still considered the finest in European history. Printing, the telescope, the circulation of the blood, the Copernican theory of the universe, the discovery of America—all are Renaissance gifts, where "Man discovers himself and the world."

The middle years of the Renaissance were concerned with spreading the new arts over Europe and with wars determining the boundaries of European nations; the later years, generally speaking, were concerned with the development of science and industry. An outstanding event of the Renaissance was the discovery of America and the spread of the European neoclassic culture on the new continent.

Modernism.—We are so close to modern events and modern art that it is difficult properly to appraise their significance. There is no doubt that vital changes, social and artistic, were taking place in the decades just preceding the World War; and the world we live in today is a very different one from that of 1890. In fact, there are many reasons for believing that we are seeing the birth of a new era in culture and art—an era that future historians will classify as opening a new epoch as different from the Renaissance as that was different from the Middle Ages. Within a single generation we have seen the overturning of the standards of art that had prevailed from the beginning of the Renaissance until the opening of our century. Thus is born Modernism.

Divisions of the Fine Arts.—Architecture has been called the *mother of the arts*. In her sheltering arms painting and sculpture have been nourished and protected. It is architecture, therefore, that best shows in its development the chronology of art described above, but all the other arts to a greater or less degree keep step with architecture in their march through the centuries.

Sculpture, the eldest, is ever pres-

ALINARI-ART REFERENCE BUREAU

THE VIRGIN WITH ST. ANNE, JESUS, AND ST. JOHN, a crayon drawing by Leonardo da Vinci, is a good example of the artist's use of *chiarscuro*, or juxtaposition of light and shade.

ent from the days of the caveman-artist. Egyptian sculpture appears with the earliest ruins of buildings, and the art has a noble history through 4,000 years of recorded civilization on the Nile. In Greece, in the age of Pericles, sculpture reached a height that in perfection of craftmanship, beauty of transcribed natural form and logical conception has seldom been surpassed. In the Middle Ages sculpture shared, side by side, the fortunes of architecture: they begged by the roadside in the Dark Ages but were the hosts of popes and kings in the portals of magnificent cathedrals of the 12th and 13th centuries. From the time of the Renaissance sculpture strayed away from architecture. But now when the possibilities of freestanding sculpture seem almost exhausted, there are tremendous opportunities opening up for the sculptural adornment of mighty modern buildings.

If we go back to the adornment of the Pleistocene caves, the art of the Cro-Magnons—a combination of painting and engraving—appears to antedate architecture, although obviously anything in the nature of a structure could not have survived the enormous stretch of the centuries. We know much of the pictorial and painted art of the Egyptians, which is found chiefly in the abundant and engaging mural paintings in the tomb-temples. Greek painting we know at firsthand only in miniature forms, but if the murals and easel pictures described by Greek writers were as fine as the surviving works of the early vase painters, the art flourished then. In medieval times painting appeared in new forms garbed in the gorgeous beauty of stained and leaded glass, in the dignity of Byzantine mosaics and in the countless varieties of the art of the weaver and the illuminator. Painting and its sister arts, drawing and engraving of various kinds, did not come to full flower in Europe until the Renaissance. First, in late medieval times, came the fresco and altarpiece; and in the 15th century appeared the use of perspective, painting in oils, development of the easel picture and engraving. Painting was no longer the handmaid of architecture and of the Church; it became the independent and splendid interpreter of a new era. The painting of the Renaissance is comparable to the sculpture of Greece in the Periclean Age.

The *graphic arts* are, with the possible exception of music and the dance, the most popular and widely distributed of all arts. Besides the various forms of painting in oils on canvas (such as murals, portraits, still life and landscapes), there are water colors, wash drawings, line drawings of many kinds, etching, aquatints and dry points, mezzotints, steel and copperplate engraving, woodcuts and woodblocks, lithography and the many commercial and mechanical forms of reproduction, such as half-tones, zinc etchings and color reproduction.

(NOTE: Sometimes the term *graphic arts* is limited to printing, etching, engraving and the other arts that reproduce and manifold copies of an original work of art.)

Interior decoration and the design of furniture are and always have been more closely allied to architecture than have any other arts. So true is this that characteristic ornament often occurs simultaneously in furniture and architecture. Choir stalls, if they are movable, would be regarded as furniture; if they are connected to the structure, they become a part of the architecture. The same is true of other decoration.

The fine arts, in graphic form, have never been with us and about us more than they are today. If science and the machine have crowded them out of the position closest to our hearts, they are nevertheless as indispensable to a happy and healthy life as they ever were. It is our duty and should be our joy to know and love them.

ARCHITECTURE

The art of building beautifully is architecture. Temples and cathedrals, palaces and public buildings have taken major space in histories of the art, but houses and shops, factories and garages are equally subject to treatment that will endow them with architectural beauty. Recently men have tended to think of all fine art as in the monumental fields, but today we know that the shed and the silo no less than the skyscrapers have their own appropriate artistic character if the architect is both able engineer and imaginative designer.

Architecture from the dawn of history has so constantly touched and mingled with human life in the home, the shop and the temple that often it is the best history and commentary we have of the life of its creators. On account of its universality and its ancient origin, it is often called *the mother of the arts.* It is the most useful of the fine arts and the noblest of the useful arts.

CONSTRUCTION

Twenty years ago students used to be told that there are three elemental types of construction that (alone or in combination) control the form of all architecture:

First, the lintel or lintel-and-post system, in which openings are spanned by a flat slab or beam supported at each end by uprights;

Second, the arch with the opening covered by a number of pieces of masonry arranged usually in a curved form (the vault and the dome are forms of the arch);

Third, the truss, in which pieces of wood or metal are joined together in triangular formation, the main cross member being relieved of a portion of the down-pressing weight by a scientific method of bracing. More accurately speaking, a truss is a framework substituted for the lintel and designed with true regard to compression and tension.

These elementary principles, formerly the three Rs of the building art, continue to be important, and any student will do well to study them in practice wherever building projects are currently going forward. But modern building in its creative development since 1890 has brought in so many new methods and materials, and they are so commonly used in conjunction with the old, that the simple historic approach no longer brings full understanding. Steel framing is today almost universal in monumental structures and is the basic invention making possible our most spectacular form of building, the skyscraper. In relation to the lintel and arch, steel framing is an utterly revolutionary step, for it provides a sort of birdcage frame upon which walls, roof and floors are hung. Finally concrete came in to displace masonry, particularly concrete reinforced with steel bars to form monolithic floors, roofs or wall sections. Glass also has been developed in new forms and for a great variety of new uses.

The lintel system was used exclusively by the Egyptians and the Greeks. The arch and the vault were Eastern inventions and were probably brought to Europe by the Etruscans. From the Etruscans the Romans took the device, and the Roman engineers used the arch to erect some of the grandest structures known to history. Extension of the arch principle was responsible for the great medieval cathedrals. It is said that the truss was not invented until the 16th century, when it made possible the roofing of great areas not easily compassed by the dome; but as a device or principle it failed to give rise to major styles of building. The steel frame and concrete, however, have made it possible for contemporary architects to initiate a totally new stylistic cycle.

HISTORY OF ARCHITECTURE

Architectural Styles.—Styles properly grow out of materials, methods of construction and building uses. Elaboration in the direction of accent and ornament arose from structural forms.

TRANS WORLD AIRLINES

THIS EIGHTH-CENTURY B.C. complex of stones—a few supporting huge 40-ton lintels—placed in concentric circles, is Stonehenge, which went unexplained until 1964. Then calculations suggested it had been a sun and moon calendar capable of predicting eclipses.

The Greek, Byzantine and Gothic are most notable in the Western world of a very few fundamental styles. But many different countries and different races, different climates and different periods have developed styles or substyles more or less distinctive and logical. Thus one meets such varieties as English Perpendicular, a sort of Gothic; baroque Renaissance (a variation of a variation); Norman and Spanish Colonial.

Historically, the outstanding family of styles is the *classic*, born and matured in Greece, adapted in ancient Rome, revived in Renaissance Italy, from there disseminated to all parts of Europe and America and with us still in our Georgian Colonial architecture.

Egyptian Architecture.—Egypt is an extraordinary country in many ways and particularly in its architecture. The earliest Greek architecture dates from about 650 B.C., but in Egypt thanks to its climate and isolated position there are buildings in excellent preservation that were built more than 2,000 years earlier, between 4,000 and 5,000 years ago. Notwithstanding the vastness and sublimity of Egyptian architecture, it had almost no effect on the architecture of Greece and has none at all on ours. In that sense it is a dead art, whereas Greek art served as a model and inspiration to architects of Europe (and finally America) at intervals down to the opening of the 20th century.

The Egyptian buildings that have come down to us are tombs and temples. The temples were probably palaces as well. They employed exclusively the lintel type of construction. The buildings were built of stone or granite blocks, usually of huge size, and the walls were covered with word pictures or hieroglyphics and figures of men and gods in low-relief sculpture, which were usually colored. The great pyramids built, perhaps, about 3500 B.C., are the most impressive of the tombs. They have been admired through the ages as masterly examples of simple, monumental architecture. There were other rock-cut tombs, such as that of Tutankhamen, which have given us not only the mummified bodies of the royal occupants themselves but their furniture, jewelry, toys and even food. Besides the tombs there were obelisks, sphinxes and great figures of the kings, who were regarded as gods. The temple-palaces were equally extraordinary. That of Karnak is a vast assemblage of pylons, colonnades and the hypostyle hall, covering in all an area 1,215 feet long by 376 feet wide. The great columns are 70 feet high and 12 feet in diameter. Other great temples are at Edfu, Luxor, Dendera and Philae.

Egyptian art was practiced until about 300 A.D., long after the conquest by Rome, and maintained its character to the last.

Sumer and Babylonia.—Recent excavations in Sumeria, the land later known as Babylonia and then as Chaldea, indicate that the art and culture of the Mesopotamian region are as ancient as those of Egypt. The dwellers in the Fertile Crescent of Mesopotamia were greatly handicapped by having little but mud to build with; but they made the mud into bricks and with these they built low buildings with immensely thick walls on the top of stupendous terraces of brick and clay. Decorative effects were secured by applying glazed colored tiles and carved slabs of precious alabaster to the face of the walls. Since they had no stone or even wood of large sizes, their rooms were very narrow; possibly some rooms were vaulted, for the Babylonians seem to have understood the use of the arch. No evidence of windows has been discovered, and these strange hall-like rooms probably reflected from their tiled walls only the flickering light of lamps and the daylight that entered the single door. Today many houses in the same locality dispense with windows as a protection against the terrific heat. The principal remains of art and architecture are found in excavations at the sites of the Sumerian city-states, especially Ur and Lagash, and in the ruins of Babylon. The Sumerian buildings were blocklike affairs, built in terraces, with dominating towers. The present ruins of Babylon date from a comparatively late rebuilding, of the 6th century B.C. At that time the great Chaldean King Nebuchadnezzar built an immense palace (near the Tower of Babel), and it was he who had the vast hanging gardens, one of the Seven Wonders of the World.

Assyria.—To the north of Babylonia, in the valley of the Euphrates, was its rival Assyria. The Assyrians possessed stone and wood in limited quantities and understood well the arch and vault. Nevertheless they copied the uncomfortable plans of the Babylonians and their ornament seems to have been derived equally from Babylonia and Egypt. They seem never to have made use of the column. The remains of architecture in Assyria are extensive owing to their use of stone, and the great palace of Sargon at Khorsabad and palaces at Nineveh and Nimrud are notable.

Persia.—From 536 to 525 B.C. the Persians under Cyrus the Great and Cambyses became masters of ancient Assyria and of Chaldea and Egypt as well. At Persepolis and Susa they built great palaces from the remains of which we can form excellent conceptions. The Persians continued the building traditions of Assyria and Chaldea in the use of glazed brick and tile on terraces and thick walls; but they added the use of the column, thereby attaining vast rooms in which slender columns of stone of a curious design supported timber roofs. The arts which they borrowed from the conquered countries were modified by their Eastern inheritance, but it is doubtful whether they advanced far beyond the Babylonians in developing a style of building. The truer architecture of Persia was to follow typically Oriental designing with arch and dome and colorful ornamentation. It was to father both the Byzantine and the Mohammedan styles.

Solomon's Temple.—About the architecture of Biblical times our knowledge comes almost solely from the Bible, which contains a detailed description of the Temple built by Solomon. Added to and rebuilt by different rulers it presented, during the lifetime of Christ, an extraordinary combination of Egyptian, Assyrian and classic elements and must have been one of the most magnificent buildings of its day. The great contribution of the Hebrews to civilization is in the realms of religion, literature and law and not in the visual arts.

Greek Classic Architecture.—The mind of the Greek was sharply distinguished from that of the Egyptian, the Assyrian or the Hebrew. Joined to a love of nature, of whose attributes he created deities, was a highly intellectual and analytical mind. A Greek lived close to the sea (a circumstance which made him a trader and traveler) and in a land rich in structural, if not ag-

Corinthian

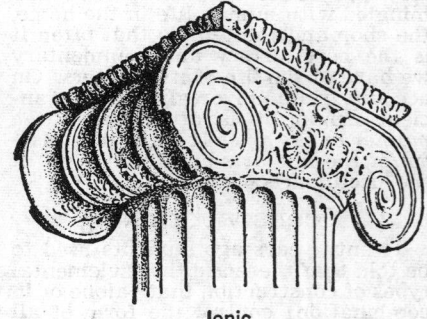

Ionic

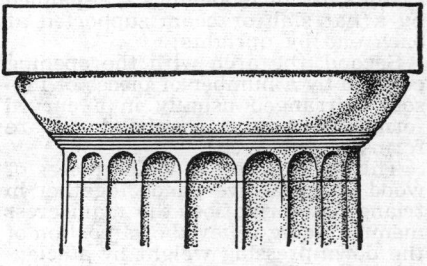

Doric

THE STYLE of a Greek building, as well as its columns, is called the *order*. Shown are the characteristic *capitals*, the ornamental tops of columns. The Doric is the oldest and simplest; the Ionic is marked by spirals or volutes. The ornate Corinthian is the latest and was used more extensively by the Romans than by the Greeks.

ricultural, resources. The Egyptian had granite; the Assyrian, clay; the Greek, marble. The beginnings of Greek art are original, vivid and human. There was some borrowing of methods and motives from earlier and alien cultures, chiefly of Egypt and Babylonia. But most authorities find the foundation materials in the relics of earlier occupants of the same lands, the Mycenaeans on the Peloponnesus and their kinsfolk, the Minoan peoples of nearby Crete.

It is with the invention of the orders, about 700 B.C., that Greek architecture takes a definite stamp. The type of construction adopted by the Greeks was exclusively of the lintel form; the arch and vault, even if they were not unknown, were never used. The lintels were upheld by posts or columns. These columns with the lintels they supported were of three distinct varieties, called *orders*. The first had sturdy columns from 5 to 7 diameters in height, without any base, and with a cap of great simplicity and beauty composed of a square block (*abacus*) above a curved molding (*echinus*). The lintel, more properly in this case called the *entablature,* was composed of three members, the *architrave, frieze* and *cornice,* each arranged in a characteristic fashion. This is the *Doric* order, apparently invented by a vigorous northern tribe of Greeks called Dorians.

The Ionians from across the Aegean gave us the second order, the *Ionic.* The curious and beautiful capital has delicate spirals (*volutes*) as its characteristic feature. The entablature is divided into three parts but is differently ornamented from the Doric. The columns have bases as well as caps and are more widely spaced. The Doric was likened in its vigor, even by the ancients, to the masculine form; and the Ionic, in its grace, represented the feminine. The third order is the *Corinthian,* little used among the Greeks and the last in origin. It is the same as the Ionic except for the capital, an inverted bell in form, richly decorated with acanthus leaves arranged below four small protruding volutes. The shafts of all these columns were lined vertically with delicate grooves (*flutes*); and temples, particularly in the Doric style, were highly colored. One of the orders was generally used exclusively in a building, but they were sometimes combined.

The Greek solved his problem perfectly, but we must admit it was very simple. Buildings that have come down to us were chiefly of two kinds, temples and theaters. The temples were composed of a rectangular room, to which in various ways was attached a colonnaded portico often embellished with sculpture. The theaters were usually semicircular, uncovered and occupying a natural depression in a hill. The noblest period of Greek architecture is the age of Pericles, 460-410 B.C. To it belong the three gems of Greek architecture—the Parthenon, the Erectheum and the Propylaea. Greek architecture became florid in the years after Alexander the Great, 300-100 B.C., but lasted as a recognizable style through the

Roman domination, from about 100 B.C. to 200 A.D.

Roman Classic Architecture.—The 500 or 600 years in which the western world was under Roman domination, from about 100 B.C. to the fall of Rome, saw the erection of many great monuments of engineering but the decline rather than advance of the classic style, decoratively considered. The Roman was ambitious, hardheaded, a great organizer and builder. He was not the artist or the individualist that the Greek was. His outward architectural expression is based on the three Greek orders which he altered and elaborated. His favorite was the Corinthian, which became the principal vehicle for the "grandeur that was Rome."

In engineering the Roman made great and original contributions. He developed the arch, the vault and the dome from the primitive arched construction of the Etruscans, and these he united with the column and lintel of the Greeks. He used concrete for vaults and walls, facing it with stone and marble. Where the Greeks had but one or two types of building, the Romans had a dozen and often on an enormous scale. Temples, basilicas, theaters, amphitheaters, circuses, triumphal arches, vast baths, palaces and houses in their ruins attest the might and skill of the Romans. In every Roman city, from Italy to Britain, was a forum or civic center adorned with statues, colonnades and monumental buildings. The greatest of these that have come down to us are the Pantheon, the Baths of Diocletian and of Caracalla, the Colosseum, the Forum and many arches—all in Rome; the Maison Carrée, a temple at Nimes in France, and the nearby aqueduct known as the Pont du Gard; ruined temples in Timgad, Algeria, and Palmyra and Baalbek in Syria; and, perhaps most interesting of all, the entire city of Pompeii at the foot of Mount Vesuvius in Italy. In 79 A.D. this Roman suburban city was entirely engulfed by mud and ashes from the volcano, and has thereby been preserved through the ages. The excavated houses and other buildings show us in minute detail the daily life and surroundings of a Roman citizen in the century in which Christ lived.

The great pagan Roman Empire became Christian by an edict of Constantine in 313 A.D., and hardly more than 100 years later, in one of the most extraordinary cataclysms in history, it fell before the onrush of vast hordes and tribes of northern barbarians. Civilization was almost snuffed out, and in the following period of a thousand years, called the Dark Ages, a new culture slowly emerged from the ruins of the mighty Roman Empire.

Romanesque and Byzantine Architecture.—The architecture and art of Europe between 500 and 1100 A.D. are called *Romanesque,* which of course means like Roman or derived from Roman. Though the style was derived in part from Roman art, it soon developed characteristics that made it very distinct.

There was very little building after the fall of the Empire. Temples and

villas lay empty and forlorn. The artists and artisans had been killed or dispersed, and their knowledge had died with them. The small amount of construction was done with fragments of imperial buildings. The only type of building the Romans had not built in profusion was the church. The early Christians refused to use pagan temples, but had no objection to using the law courts or basilicas. These were low, oblong buildings, usually divided by two parallel rows of columns into a central space or *nave* and an aisle on either side. At the end oppo-

METROPOLITAN MUSEUM OF ART

ROMANESQUE doorway. Thirteenth century.

site the entrance was a bay or *apse* that held the judge's seat. The Christians replaced the seat with an altar, and the basilica made an excellent church. Many of our own churches today can be traced back, step by step, to the basilica. The great Christian basilicas of St. Paul, St. John Lateran and others in Rome have come down to us. Romanesque art is almost entirely concerned with the building of churches and monasteries, although utilitarian fortifications and castles took on some of the same forms of expression. Columns soon took a secondary place, and Romanesque buildings are usually attempts, often crude, to use the arch in decorative design and some kind of vault or dome to cover the aisles and nave. Heavy walls, deep shadows, recessed doors and windows often gave the buildings a gloomy aspect. But the portals and sometimes full façades were enriched with sculptural compositions as opulently patterned as those of Asia.

In the Eastern Christian Empire there developed a style corresponding to the Romanesque, in the same centuries or earlier, known as the *Byzantine* (from Byzantium, the old name of Constantinople, capital of the Eastern emperors). It seemed to appear suddenly, fully developed, in one magnificent building in Constantinople—Santa Sophia, built during 532-37 A.D. under the Emperor Justinian—but in reality it had prototypes, both structurally and in decorative idioms, in the Oriental Christian countries, Mesopotamia, Syria, Persia and Egypt. But Santa Sophia is the masterpiece in the style, and certainly it ranks as one of the most precious buildings in the world, perhaps next to the Parthenon in importance. Except

FRENCH GOVERNMENT TOURIST OFFICE

THE CATHEDRAL OF CHARTRES spans the development of the Gothic in France. The façade and right tower, completed about 1150, show the difference between the massive Romanesque and the lighter Gothic on the left. The circular rose window is a perfect example of that widely used motif in Gothic architecture. The spire (*left*) dates from the fifteenth century

for certain Mohammedan disfigurements it still exists in its pristine splendor.

Justinian's architects, Anthemius and Isodorus, supported the great dome on the tops of four mighty arches, the support taking the form of four spherical triangles (*pendentives*). This became the method used thereafter in the building of domes, as it made possible the roofing of a square plan by a dome. The Byzantine dependence on color by the use of inlays of marble and mosaic continued as the basis of all Mohammedan and Near-Eastern decoration. The exquisite arabesques and inlays of the Alhambra, built by the Moors in Spain, are similar expressions of the Eastern genius for delicate but rich ornamentation. In Venice St. Mark's is an outstanding Byzantine monument, and there are other notable examples at Ravenna and in and near Palermo, Sicily.

The principal monuments of the Romanesque in Europe are: in Italy, the leaning tower, cathedral and baptistery at Pisa; in France, many vaulted churches that vary in their constructional scheme according to their locality; in England, all the Norman churches and cathedrals, such as those at Durham and parts of Canterbury; along the Rhine, a number of fine brick churches of which the Cathedral of Mainz is a good example; and in Spain, many churches (such as that at Salamanca), which were often altered into the succeeding Gothic.

The Gothic Style.—The 5th century B.C. in Greece and the 13th century A.D. in France are usually regarded as marking the highest peaks to which architecture as a fine art has attained. In the 13th century were built the great cathedrals that have immortalized the Middle Ages. Their style is called *Gothic*—not a very appropriate name but one too firmly entrenched to be uprooted.

Romanesque architecture rather suddenly developed into Gothic through the invention or adaptation of three architectural devices. The first was the *ribbed vault;* the second, the *flying buttress;* the third, the *pointed arch.* Combination of these devices made it possible to build naves of great height (Beauvais is 165 feet in the clear); but it is the pointed arch that gives the style its characteristic appearance, because this form was uniformly used in ornamental as well as in structural features.

Whereas the Romanesque found its limited opportunity in the abbey church, the monastery and the fortress, the Gothic found a broader and more magnificent field in the great cathedral and later in secular buildings of various kinds, such as town halls, palaces and college buildings. The Gothic style owed much to the arts of sculpture, stained glass and even painting. The cathedral with its piers, buttresses and towers leading heavenward, its niches filled with statues of saints and kings, its great windows glowing with the fires of stained and leaded glass, its altars hung with rare fabrics and painted with scenes from the Scriptures, became a symphony of beauty and exaltation. No wonder they thrill us today! The Gothic style can usually be dated by its window tracery, which progressively became more complicated and ornate.

Some of the great cathedrals are: in France—Chartres, Amiens, Reims, Paris; in England—Salisbury, Westminster Abbey, York, Canterbury; in Germany—Cologne, Strasbourg, Freiburg; in Belgium—Antwerp; in Spain—Seville, Burgos, Toledo. The Italian Gothic cathedrals are less pure in style; but Giotto's Tower in Florence is uniquely beautiful, and Milan cathedral is impressive in some aspects. Other examples of Gothic occur in Belgium's town halls and Italy's civic buildings.

The Classic Renaissance.—The meaning of the Renaissance has already been suggested, and its architectural peculiarity—the abandonment of medieval forms and the return to the Classic (the architecture of Greece and Rome)—has been pointed out. Architecturally the Renaissance began later than in sculpture and painting. In 1420 Filippo Brunelleschi used Classic forms in the addition of the great dome to the cathedral of Florence. Classic art became the fashion; Gothic was looked upon with contempt. We know the names of very few ancient or medieval architects. With the Renaissance they became important personalities. Alberti, Bramante, Peruzzi, Raphael, Michelangelo, Palladio, Vignola—all followed the example of Brunelleschi and developed the application of Classic art to contemporary problems.

About 1500 the Renaissance, partly through French conquest but mostly through fashion, spread to France. Here it became associated with the reigns of brilliant kings, each of whom developed it in some characteristic fashion and gave his name to a period, such as Francis I, Henry II, Henry IV, Louis XIV, Louis XV, Louis XVI. Napoleon is represented

ALINARI ART REFERENCE BUREAU

THE FARNESE PALACE in Rome epitomizes Renaissance architecture. The style emphasizes a monumental formality where logic, reason, and symmetrical design are the expressive aims. The palace was begun in 1514 and was completed a few years later by Bramante and Michelangelo; the latter designed the third story with its sculptured "cap," or cornice.

by a further variation, known as Empire.

The English work in its early stages was less sophisticated and much cruder than the Italian models. Here the periods are named from the reigning families or rulers, such as Tudor, Elizabethan, Jacobean and Georgian. England has given us one of the best known of architects, Sir Christopher Wren, the builder of Saint Paul's Cathedral.

Partly through the influence of native artists who had traveled in Italy, partly through rulers who wished to have the latest thing in palaces, Germany adopted a good deal of the Renaissance architectural language. Here it developed in a manner somewhat similar to that of England. Spain produced in the plateresque and churrigueresque styles the most fantastic variations of classic motives that are to be found.

The American colonies, before our government was founded, were active participants in the Renaissance. Our beautiful Colonial style is an importation of the English Georgian, tastefully adapted to our needs and materials.

Renaissance buildings, particularly in Italy, were often embellished with the most beautiful painting and sculpture. The art of the landscape architect was a new development; and great palaces, such as those at Versailles in France, owe much of their effect to the gardens, fountains and trees. Though the architects of this period borrowed the orders and most of their constructional features from ancient Rome, they used great ingenuity and a high degree of skill to con-

form these to the complexities of contemporary life. By the invention of the true truss they added a great structural principle to architecture.

The amount of building in the Renaissance vastly exceeded that of all the preceding periods, and almost all of it exists today. Only the briefest summary of outstanding examples can be made here.

Italy, which had so woefully lagged behind in the Gothic period, inaugurated and predominantly led in the Renaissance. The Medici, Rucellai and Strozzi palaces, the Pazzi Chapel, and the loggia of the Foundling Hospital in Florence; the library of Saint Mark's in Venice; palaces and churches almost without number in such cities as Siena, Milan, Verona, Vicenza, Genoa; and especially the Farnese Palace, the Vatican and Saint Peter's in Rome, the largest church in Christendom, culminated one of the most brilliant architectural epochs in history.

In France we find the chateaux of the pleasure-loving monarchs, such as Blois and Fontainebleau; great churches, like the Invalides and St. Sulpice in Paris; and the magnificent palaces of Versailles and the Louvre.

England gives us many manor houses, the palace of Whitehall by Inigo Jones and the famous churches and Saint Paul's Cathedral from the hand of Sir Christopher Wren.

In Germany the buildings are fewer, comprising town halls of picturesque design, the ruined castle of Heidelberg and a number of minor palaces.

The architecture of Spain varies between the greatest exuberance, as at Salamanca, and the frigidity of the

Escorial, the palace and tomb of Philip II.

Town halls and churches were built in lesser degree in Holland, Belgium and the Scandinavian countries.

Later Architecture in Europe.—About 1800 for the first time the Greek buildings of the Acropolis in Athens became widely known. This gave rise to an architectural fashion known as the Greek Revival. Its best monuments in England are St. George's Hall, Liverpool, and the British Museum, London. Germany built its art museums and the Brandenburg Gate; France, the beautiful Madeleine Church. Towards the middle of the century there was a Gothic revival in England that produced the Houses of Parliament; and in France, under Napoleon III, an ostentatious variation of regal Renaissance that has given us the Opera House in Paris. *Eclectic* design—that is, revivals and adaptations of the historic styles—ruled in the decades from 1860 to 1920 in all of Europe and the Americas, producing a crop of buildings in direct imitation of the monuments of Greece, Rome, medieval France and Italy.

Before the end of the century, pioneering architects, especially in America but notably also in Holland and Austria, laid the groundwork for a totally new architecture, known now as the *Modern* style; but it was 1920 before it was brought into extensive practice. Based on honest expression of machine-age materials and method

BRITISH TRAVEL ASSOCIATION

ST. PAUL'S CATHEDRAL, London (1675–1710), designed by Sir Christopher Wren. One of the most famous churches in the world, it is noted for its superb dome.

of building and on perfect fitness to use, this latest style derives its appearance values out of function and thus out of the life of these times. The actual buildings erected so far should be considered as only the early, experimental expressions of the mode, but there can be no doubt that an epochal and revolutionary style has been born.

Original and interesting work has been done in Germany and the northern countries, especially in Finland and in Sweden; and Holland, Austria, France and Italy are progressively substituting in most new building this essentially machine-age art for the borrowed historic or eclectic forms. At present Modernism is everywhere growing apace. In the direction particularly of engineering and planning America is exerting an increasing influence upon Europe. Further discussion of the Modern style and particularly of its most striking form, the skyscraper, will be found at the close of the section dealing with American architecture.

Mohammedan Architecture.—From the the 8th century A.D. onward for a thousand years, a characteristic and often magnificent type of architecture was practiced at varying times in the great stretch of territory from Spain on the west along the southern shores of the Mediterranean to northern India on the east. The style, like the Byzantine, is based on the architecture of the Near East, particularly Persia. Structurally it depends on the dome and vault; decoratively, on elaborate geometrical surface ornament and on color for effect. Its buildings are principally mosques, palaces, tombs and city gates. Its great centers are in the Moorish cities of Spain, where the Alhambra, the Mosque of Cordova and the Giralda Tower furnish magnificent examples; in the Arabic city of Cairo, with its many mosques, of which the mosques of Omar and of Sultan Hassan are characteristic; in Constantinople, where the Turks built the great Mosque of Solyman; in Persia, with the famous tomb at Sultaniyeh, and finest and noblest of all, the buildings of the great Mogul Empire in northern India. The Taj Mahal at Agra, the gem of the style, was built as a tomb by Shah Jahan about 1650. In beauty of material, proportion, workmanship and setting it is hardly surpassed by any building in the world.

Oriental Architecture.—The Hindu and Buddhist styles of India and the architecture of China and Japan are so remote, and their contact with our arts so slight that a description of them must be very brief. Indian architecture dates as far back as 279 B.C. It has various manifestations, and the buildings are either circular shrines to Buddha (called *topes*), rock-cut temples or monasteries. Use was made of both domes and columns, and surfaces were elaborately carved with ornament and allegorical figures. Horizontal emphasis predominates. Monuments are scattered over the whole land, but predominate in the South.

Chinese and Japanese Architecture.—The architecture of China and Japan has been chiefly of wood and perishable material. Within the limits adopted it has a consistent beauty, unappreciated in the West because of the unfamiliarity of the structural and decorative forms, but enjoyed and praised by those who have got beyond its strangeness. With the exception of towerlike pagodas, the temples are low and unimpressive and are usually aggregations of small buildings. It is remarkable that the splendid sense of beauty in decoration in both these peoples has not led to a monumental architecture. Perhaps this is partially responsible for the fact that European architecture is appearing beside the native styles, although there is a determined effort in some places to return to the local tradition.

Architecture in the United States.—Architecture in the United States used to be dismissed with a paragraph or two. But the extraordinary development and expansion of building in the last 35 years has raised America to world leadership, and its architectural development has become a thrilling story that all should know.

Colonial Style (1630-1800). Our colonists looked to England for their models in building; so the American houses built before 1700 were small, crude, very simple and without enriching detail, very like houses of the reign of Elizabeth in England. Such is the Capen house, Topsfield, Massachusetts, or the Paul Revere house in Boston. Under stress of new economic and climatic conditions, the variation sometimes known as *Founders' Colonial* or merely as *Early American* was created by invention builders. About 1730, safety, prosperity and regular intercourse with England were established, and thereafter the decorative features of the architectural style of the mother country were freely imported.

This is the *Georgian* style, a form derived by the English architects from the Italian Renaissance. It makes great use of the orders and classic detail. With excellent taste the orders were altered in proportion to fit American material, which was for the most part good white pine. For the greater part of the century the style was vigorous and robust—the influence, doubtless, of Sir Christopher Wren, whose London churches in particular were models for the familiar New England churches. After the Revolution the style became delicate and attenuated, following the mode dictated in London by the Adam brothers, famous architects and designers. Buildings were limited to houses, churches and a few town halls.

Founders' Colonial and the simplified Georgian house, which we are likely to visualize as typical Colonial, developed especially in New England. The central seaboard colonies and especially New York saw the creation of the beautiful and distinctive Dutch Colonial variation. In the Southern colonies a more dignified and pretentious, even monumental, type evolved, which was based on English Renaissance models. There was an unrelated development in the Southwest from Texas to California of Spanish Colonial forms, also neoclassic, brought in from Mexico.

Post-Colonial (1790-1820). Thomas Jefferson, on his return from France, where he had been the U. S. minister for four years, turned our eyes from England to France. He designed three important buildings—Monticello, his home; the capitol at Richmond and the University of Virginia. Professional architects began to appear, notably Charles Bulfinch (1763-1844), a native of Boston and one of the architects of the Capitol at Washington. The old City Hall in New York city was built in the French manner. At Washington the Capitol was under construction, and the White House was built. The architecture of this period is sometimes labeled *Republic*.

Greek Revival (1820-1850). We have mentioned the Greek Revival in Europe. It was introduced into America by a famous architect, Benjamin Henry Latrobe (born in England and educated in Germany) and, curiously enough, it flourished in the second quarter of the 19th century. The Greek style was used for every kind of building from the Atlantic Ocean to the Great Salt Lake and throughout the southern states. Arlington, Va., the home of Robert E. Lee, is a fine example; one of the best is Girard College, Philadelphia.

Eclecticism (1850-1920). Our attitude toward architecture was decidedly provincial in the years immediately preceding and following the Civil War. These years mark the low ebb of taste in America. We attempted to borrow the architectural fashions of the hour from England and from France. The first exists in many examples of a debased form of Gothic made popular in England by John Ruskin; and the second in the fashionable and elaborate Classic style, popular in Paris under Napoleon III. Houses with cupolas and mansard roofs belong to this period. The Centennial Exposition (Philadelphia, 1876) marked the high point of this era.

After 1876 and up to 1920, there was a succession of able designers, equipped with taste and wide knowledge, who clothed their buildings in one or another of the historic styles. H. H. Richardson built Trinity Church, Boston, in 1877. This caused a sudden and extraordinary vogue for building in the Romanesque style, second only in popularity to the rage for Greek art of 50 years before. The Chicago World's Fair of 1893, of which Daniel H. Burnham was architect in chief, put an end to the Romanesque Revival and re-established the Classic style in its several forms. Thereafter there were adaptations from the Greek on bank fronts and for libraries and college buildings. Then, in what is sometimes called the *American Imperial* age, the architects turned to Rome and built monuments like the Pennsylvania Station in New York (a vast building modeled after the Baths of Caracalla in Rome) and Columbia University Library (after the Pantheon). McKim, Mead and White took leadership with the building of the Boston Public Library (an

BALTAZAR KORAB

STRUCTURAL and decorative uses of aluminum characterize this Detroit office designed by Minoru Yamasaki & Associates for Reynolds Metals Co.

Modern architecture: Technology and design combine with nature to create new settings for contemporary life.

CURVING IN SPACE, a continuous spiral ramp leads the visitor past the works of art on exhibit in New York's Guggenheim Museum—a totally new concept of museum design by the late architect Frank Lloyd Wright.

THE SOLOMON R. GUGGENHEIM MUSEUM

JULIUS SHULMAN

CLEAN, TRANSPARENT geometry of Richard Neutra's "Desert House" contrasts with rugged landscape at Palm Springs, Calif.

OFFICES designed by Skidmore, Owings & Merrill for Connecticut General Life Ins. open into the New England countryside.

EZRA STOLLER ASSOCIATES

NEWMAN SCHMIDT

JOHN EBSTEL

FALLING WATER, by Frank L. Wright (1938), shows some of his innovations: use of native materials and adapting the building to its surroundings. Similar thinking—though less concerned with nature—underlies Louis Kahn's brick and concrete medical research building in Philadelphia (1958–1960): the forms are not superficial but rigorous and inventive, and spring logically from the demands of laboratory scientists. The repeated T-shaped parts of the window wings are frankly exposed; the brick towers enclose fume exhausts, fresh-air intakes, and stairs. Excellent use is made of concrete, a material beginning to be used with understanding.

adapted Renaissance palace) about 1895, and that firm held top rank for a considerable period, due to its tasteful Eclectic works. Ralph Adams Cram and Bertram Goodhue, however, achieved the finest work in Gothic Revival, erecting such monuments as St. Thomas's Church, New York, the chapel of West Point Military Academy and buildings in the Princeton University group. Yale and other universities also adopted the revived Gothic style. In Italian Renaissance style, beautiful villas were built at Newport, R. I., Santa Barbara, Calif., and Lake Forest, Ill.

The greater number of existing architectural monuments in America are, of course, survivals from this Eclectic era. It is often pointed out that they well represent the vast wealth and power of our country as developed between the Civil War and the World War. But they also symbolize America's dependence upon Europe for artistic standards and models. It is increasingly recognized that our architects then were practicing tastefully in every style except one that might be termed American. The buildings showed excellent taste in selection but no originality; intelligent imitation but a lack of creativeness.

Modernism. The great revolution that has taken place in American architecture in the past decade, during which a true machine-age style has emerged, was, as a matter of fact, foreseen and to a small extent practiced 50 years ago. It was during the late 80s that the steel-frame skeleton for tall buildings was invented in Chicago. Soon throughout the country the architects were struggling with the problem of the skyscraper. In mechanical invention it developed with marvelous rapidity, and the towers soared higher and higher. But the architects failed to find any outward artistic expression of the new materials and the exciting new engineering feats that made the towers possible. Mostly they clothed the new tall structures in patches and shreds taken from the exterior garments of the ancient buildings that had so long been their models—Greek temples, Roman stadiums, medieval fortresses and Gothic cathedrals. The best of these "masked" skyscrapers—the least illogical, the Moderns would say—are perhaps the Woolworth Building in New York and the Chicago Tribune Tower, both Gothic-decorated.

The first bold American to face the facts of the future was Louis H. Sullivan of Chicago, who proclaimed that "form must follow function." His efforts expressed in the verticals and horizontals of a skyscraper's form the space-volumes enclosed by its steel skeleton. For this there was no historic precedent. This style is best seen in the Wainwright building in St. Louis built in 1890. This archaic example of the new architecture prepared the way for such skyscrapers as the Chicago Daily News Building, The Philadelphia Saving Fund Society Building, and, in New York, the Rockefeller Center and United Nations groups.

But the skyscrapers are merely the most spectacular phase of the new architecture. The same kind of study of human needs and economic and structural resources they require has brought into being in twentieth-century Europe and America whole communities of low-cost homes which are already paying dividends in improved health and reduced crime.

These and other astonishing developments in flexible planning for human needs have grown up during the lifetime of one man, Frank Lloyd Wright. Once one of Sullivan's draftsmen Wright could speak sixty years later of the "great master and of the pencil in his hand—myself." It was Wright rather than Sullivan who was acclaimed by European innovators soon after 1910 as the prophet of the new architecture. By 1920 foreign-trained American architects, who had "discovered" the style in Austria and Germany and Holland and finally, France, paved the way to popular and professional recognition of the two American pioneers and joining with them helped to create the increasing flood of machine-age building. Among this group that came to America in the 1920's, '30's, and '40's, were such outstanding men as Lescaze, Saarinen, Aalta, Neutra, Mendelssohn, Miës van der Rohe, Gropius, and Breuer. These last two have contributed especially to the experiments on prefabricated houses.

The tremendous changes in architectural tastes makes it possible to assert that any building built in America from this time on, that is reminiscent of the ancient Greek, Roman or Byzantium style will be already out-of-date, as a somewhat meaningless imitation of past accomplishment. In other words, it is clear that the modern world, machine-powered and scientific-minded, has found its own forms of architectural expression. That there are already masterpieces of design in the new style is open to question. More likely we have seen merely the primitive, starkly expressive phase. But architects are today feeling for richer expression in innumerable houses and business buildings, factories and clubs, even churches. Each year sees the ranks of the Eclectics dwindling, the Moderns gaining new ground and new adherents.

The aspect of the new architecture is utterly different from that of any style out of the past, as should be the case, considering that within a half-century mankind has experienced the most revolutionary change in ways of living known to human history. The architect has at his disposal engineering methods undreamed of in earlier eras, and there is a bewildering range of new materials: steel and chromium; glass in sheets of unprecedented size, as well as glass bricks;

concrete in precast blocks and poured concrete reinforced with steel bars. These materials alone give new appearance values to the building, an exterior flash and gleam, long unbroken lines and solidity of mass. New ways of fabricating these materials find external expression, such as in the unimpeded lift of the skyscraper and the horizontal spread of planned communities and their individual building units. Above all there is the extreme simplification, the shearing off of all ornament, the creating of proportion and mass and the playing of sheer surfaces against patterned window complexes. Essential also, is the use of each building expressed in its outward appearance. Banks and railway terminals no longer need masquerade as temples or public libraries as royal palaces.

This is all expressed in the one word *functionalism*. The best architects are bringing in also that other indefinable quality of vision and imagination, which lifts the utilitarian structure to the plane of universal art, to a truely creative architecture. Frank Lloyd Wright is still the greatest figure

among the architects in America. The foremost opponents of the functional or severely simple school are William Lescaze working in New York and Philadelphia and Richard J. Neutra in California. Other architects are scattered through out the country.

It is an exciting era in architecture with the foundations of the epochal new style thus laid, with a new and dynamic way of living to be expressed and with visionary creators working all round us. The next half century is likely to see an immense expansion of engineering and building, and, we hope and believe, the creation of masterpieces comparable to those of Egypt and Greece, of Italy and France, but in our own unmistakable architectural language. It is the hardest part of history to write, but for you, the reader, it should be the most fascinating bit in the whole account of the world's ways of building. You can look through the nearest window and actually see history fresh-made or in the making—can find actual illustration of these words in your own immediate surroundings. For architecture is the art nearest to every man's everyday life.

PAINTING

The art of painting is expression on a flat surface of forms in space, accomplished by the major means of line, color and light and shade, often aided by texture and other minor devices. Painting is thus a two-dimensional art (as distinguished from sculpture), but is concerned with three-dimensional effects, every picture affording the impression of volumes in space or at least of planes or areas receding from the surface of the painter's paper or canvas.

The visual form that constitutes a painting has two aspects—*representation* and *design*. Representation as a term covers the objects and events depicted from outward nature, their shapes, make-up, relationships and meanings—for instance, a body, a flower, a spacious landscape, a trait of character or a story. Design refers to the arrangement or organization of the abstract elements—color, line and the like—as such, and with the creation of that unexplainable element known as order or rhythm or formal beauty. Design and representation cannot be separated; they grow together in the creative mind of the artist. Artists vary in their emphasis. Some are greatly interested in representation, in which case they add to the world's store of realistic, naturalistic and documentary art. Others, more visionary and imaginative, care more for the fine organization of their color, light and line, in which case they add to the art that is highly formalized or decorative.

There are various ways in which order is manifested in a work of art: in balance, in similarity or repetition, in easy sequence or clearly felt gradation and in that final unity, like that of a living organism, in which every

part is essential to every other part. These are so-called principles of design, but no great painting was ever achieved merely by following them. The life or order of a great work of art is so complex and so subtle that it eludes our crude attempts at analysis. As one critic has said, artists can only work for order and hope for beauty.

ANCIENT PAINTING

Old Stone Age.—The oldest paintings that we know were painted thousands of years ago by men of the Paleolithic or Old Stone Age on the walls and ceilings of caves in southern France and northern Spain. These men were hunters and painted their familiar world, a world of animals—the reindeer, wild horse and mammoth, the bison, wolf and wild boar. Sometimes they were shown at rest or grazing, but more often they were depicted running, galloping, fighting. They were painted with the most astonishing keenness of vision and with a line that was swift and sure.

There was a development covering thousands of years, from the early drawings cut into the rock with a sharp flint or sketched in red or yellow ocher to the great polychrome period when the strong contour lines were filled in with shaded color masses of red, yellow, brown and black, earth colors mixed wth animal oil or fat. The polychrome period may have been 15,000 B.C. or 30,000 or even 60,000.

Later, perhaps about 10,000 B.C., a different people in the south and east of Spain left in caves and under overhanging rocks some remarkable paintings of human figures. These people had the bow and arrow, and

their paintings were largely of bowmen in action—in the hunt, fight or war dance. Occasionally there were other scenes, such as a man taking honey from a tree while the angry bees fly about him. There was no such realism or form or rhythm of line as was shown by the animal painters, but there was a great aptitude for expressing movement. Recent discoveries have indicated that these people went from southern Europe into Africa, where their rock pictures

SATOUR

THIS PRIMITIVE ROCK PAINTING from South Africa depicts a fight over a herd of cattle between Bushmen and neighboring Kaffirs.

are found in many localities. The art of the African Bushmen of the last 500 years seems to be a survival of this Old Stone Age painting.

New Stone Age.—By 10,000 B.C. it is supposed that the climate and geography of Europe was about the same as it is today; and with this change the Paleolithic men disappeared. The people of the Neolithic or New Stone Age were a different people with a very different art. Neolithic man learned to cultivate grain and domesticate animals; he built houses, wove cloth and made pottery. In Europe his painting was confined to geometric designs on pottery—lines, zigzags, curves, spirals—with rarely any suggestion of the human figure.

Egyptian Painting.—In the years between 4000 and 3000 B.C., when Europe was still in the Stone Age, Egypt had discovered metal, invented a system of writing and started to build up a high civilization. Before 2000 B.C., paintings were not very numerous, and we must trace the pictorial tradition in painted low reliefs. But after that there is a continuous history of painting down to the Christian era. The Egyptian loved the out-of-doors so much that he brought it into his house, painting the floors with lotus, ducks, birds and fishes, the walls with trees and the ceiling with stars in a blue sky. But the houses have perished, and only fragments of such painting remain. There were also paintings in temples, in papyrus manuscripts and on the coffins of the dead; but most surviving Egyptian painting is found on the walls of tombs.

This tomb painting is not a gloomy art; far from it. There are pictures of the Egyptian's gods, of his adventures in war but especially of his own intimate little world. He loved life and all its hard-won luxury, and he wanted depicted on the walls of his tomb all the good things of his life on earth as reassurance that they would continue in the life hereafter. We see him gliding in his reed boat in the marshes hunting ducks, perhaps accompanied by his wife and daughter, who are gathering lotus; or harpooning fish or feasting at a banquet where dancing girls sway to the music of harps. We see his butchers cutting, his masons building, his slaves reaping and threshing the grain, picking grapes and making wine.

The Egyptian painter worked in outlines and flat color tones: long, swift, continuous lines and strong harmonies of vivid blue, green, red and yellow. Since he ignored light and shade, volume and distance, his painting is flat and decorative.

Exact representation is not his strong point. He did not see in his imagination the figure as a whole, from a single point of view. He drew the face in side view, eye front, shoulder front; and then, by a mysterious twist he drew the body below the waist in side view again. This rendering became traditional and scarcely changed through the centuries. By the XVIII Dynasty (1580–1350 B.C.) considerable progress had been made; greater freedom in pose and movement, more flowing line, overlapping of figures, an occasional face in front

METROPOLITAN MUSEUM OF ART

EGYPTIAN TOMB PAINTING depicted a splendid afterlife that magically assured the deceased continuance of luxuries he enjoyed in life. In this tomb of 1250 B.C., at Thebes, a slave works a garden well and thus guarantees an eternal water supply for his master.

view. In the time of Ikhnaton (1375–1358), the great king who believed in one god, there was a great advance in the direction of naturalism; but with his son-in-law Tutankhamen came a reversion to the old forms in art as in religion.

There is no deep space in Egyptian painting. If an object is to appear as behind another, it is placed above. A pool of water is drawn in floor plan and not as it appears to the eye. The flesh of men is always dark; that of women, light. But in spite of these unnatural conventions the Egyptian tells his story well, with expert craftsmanship and a feeling for fine design.

Aegean Frescoes.—In Europe it was the part nearest Egypt that first emerged from the Stone Age—the lands around the Aegean Sea: Greece, Asia Minor and the nearby islands, especially Crete. Apparently it was in Crete that the first important European culture developed, marked by monumental architecture, refined pottery, exquisite metalwork and some small achievement in sculpture and in painting. Excavations of the great palace at Knossos (built about 1500 B.C.) have revealed a series of frescoes in vivid colors that tell a story of luxury and splendor and of an amazing art.

We see a strangely modern-looking people with irregular European features, pinched waists, elaborate coiffures, tight bodices and flounced skirts. A youth marches in procession bearing a silver vase, a naked boy picks crocuses, women in low-cut gowns watch a bull fight from a balcony, and youths and maidens engage an angry bull. A vivacious young girl, with a curl in the middle of her forehead, presents her profile with a large front-view eye—for the Cretans hardly advanced beyond the Egyptians in mastery of anatomical detail. A fresco from Melos made about 1600 B.C. shows flying fish darting through the water in rhythmic movement.

Cretan paintings, like Egyptian, are in outlines and flat color tones; they have no distance, neither have they light and shade; and the same convention of brown for the skin of men, white for that of women is seen. But their line is less continuous; it has a quicker and more lively tempo, and the contours have more individuality. From Crete supremacy in the arts, as in other activities of life, passed to the Myceneans of the Peloponnesus, and the ruins of their palaces yield fragments of similar frescoes.

Greek Vase Painting.—It was an invasion of barbarians from the North that finally destroyed the Aegean civilization. About 1400 B.C. the palace of Knossos was burned; by 1100 the whole of Aegean culture had been overturned. Gradually this new people, known as Dorians, joining with the Ionians, developed into the Greeks of historic times, and the Cretan world lived only in Greek myth and legend.

The earliest Greek painting (1100–800) consisted of geometric designs on pottery, with human figures and animals almost as geometric as the bands and zigags. The 8th- and 7th-century pottery showed contacts with the Near East in its rows of animals and backgrounds filled with rosettes. In the 6th century further progress foretold the glory of the 5th. Athens began to manufacture wares of great refinement of shape and beauty of decoration. There were water jars, mixing bowls, drinking cups, wine pitchers and oil flasks. In the 6th century they were black-figured, the decoration being painted in black glaze on the natural red of the clay, with details of features and drapery scratched into the glaze, disclosing the clay beneath.

Toward 500 B.C. this style was gradually supplanted by the red-figured, in which the background was painted with black glaze and the figures and decoration were left in the reddish clay. Now all the details, instead of being cut into the glaze, could be freely executed with the brush. All through the black-figured period the Greeks made progress in realistic representation. They learned not only how to draw a consistent profile but also how to show three-quarters and front views. The figure becomes flexible; it bends and twists; its contours suggest volume and solidity; stiff draperies change to flowing folds. Progressively, however, the artists lost the virtues of stylized drawing and spirited decorativeness that characterized the vases of certain 6th-century masters.

The vase pictures tell the stories of the Greek gods—those very human gods made in the image of man and enjoying all that he enjoyed—and of the heroes, the labors of Hercules and the adventures of the Trojan War. And they give a very remarkable picture of Greek daily life; we see children at school, women weaving, athletes at their games. There is still no deep space—a mountain is indicated by a tree and the sea by dolphins. But there is, until the late and decadent periods, a splendid sense of pattern in line and mass.

Greek Murals.—The humble vase paintings, which flourished until the 4th century B.C., are one of our best clues to the mural and panel painting of Greece, all of which has perished. This loss is a great tragedy in art history, for we know that the Greeks esteemed their painting as highly as their sculpture. Literature tells us about the famous painters, such as Polygnotus (active 480–450 B.C.), who still painted in outlines and flat color tones, but who introduced the new freedom in representation that is reflected by the vases; and it tells us about the painters of the middle of the century who were interested in deep space and perspective and about Apollodorus (5th century B.C.), who introduced light and shade and thus helped to determine the future of European painting.

In the 4th century, murals for the home as well as for temple and public building became popular. Panel paintings increased. Portraits and scenes of everyday life were painted beside illustrations of the ancient myths and national wars. The conquests of Alexander were of tremendous importance in the history of art. After his death in 323 B.C. Greek culture was spread over all his vast empire. Athens yielded to new art centers in Asia Minor and in Egypt. In this Hellenistic period (323–146 B.C.) painting rapidly became more expressive of emotion, of movement and of individual character; costumes grew realistic, landscape appeared—all this, however, often at the cost of great design.

Roman Painting.—Rome in the second and first centuries B.C. became mistress of nearly all the countries bordering on the Mediterranean and of western Europe as well. Even earlier her victorious generals had collected works of Greek art and pillaged conquered provinces. But the first centuries B.C. and A.D. saw a golden age of art production in Rome herself. There are many paintings of this period, some in and about Rome, but most from the excavated cities of Pompeii and Herculaneum, buried by Vesuvius in 79 A.D. The artists were mostly Greek or Greek-trained. Some of the paintings were copies of Greek works of the 5th and 4th centuries, others were in the Hellenistic mode of the day. Design often suffers, but there is convincing expression of the volume and weight of the modeled figures and variety in pose and action.

These pictures, framed by painted architecture, give the Roman house, with its few windows, the effect of opening out on gardens and spacious vistas. They give an impression of bright color in subdued light, and they are filled with garlands of fruits and flowers, gods and goddesses, half-veiled dancers. Cupids play at being merchants, goldsmiths, wine dealers; they race in chariots on land and on crabs and dolphins on the sea.

Landscape backgrounds had probably originated at Alexandria in Egypt, but on Roman soil they ceased to be mere backdrops and began to give the illusion of real space in which the figures took their proper places. This was a Roman contribution to Hellenistic naturalism.

Early Christian Painting.—From the early years of the Christian era we have paintings in the catacombs of Rome—those galleries below the ground where the members of the new faith, forced to secrecy, buried their dead and held religious services. These frescoes were made from the 2d to the 4th centuries, most of them probably in the 4th. The beginnings of Christianity caused no more upheaval in Roman art than in Roman life. Early Christian artists were Roman or Alexandrian artists working in the Hellenistic style. Decorative settings were quite Pompeian. Only the subject matter was new—the Greek and Roman story was supplanted by the Jewish, and many of the old pagan forms were used as symbols to express new Christian meanings. The great change was in the quality of the painting; it became very poor. Design fell apart, and figures lost their relation in space as well as in meaning.

In the 4th century, when Christianity was made a legal religion, Christians emerged from the catacombs and began to build churches. The 5th century was a period of rich decoration of Christian buildings, mostly in mosaic with great splendor of color and gold. Ravenna was the chief center in Italy, and the artists came largely from the Eastern Empire rather than from Rome. The early frescoes and mosaics in Roman churches had been distinctly classical; but in the 6th century, when the new

style came in, it was called *Byzantine* because it was brought from Byzantium (capital of the Eastern Roman Empire) and the Near East.

Byzantine Painting.—Byzantine was really an old Greek style that had been orientalized. When this style traveled to the Near East, the Asiatic artists gradually flattened the rounded figures of the Greeks and turned their light and dark into a decorative pattern. They also added an oriental opulence of color. We can trace the flattening out of the Greek forms through Asia Minor and Syria and even down to Egypt. Christian illuminated manuscripts best tell the story. These are the early Christian books written by hand on vellum, lavishly illuminated in gold and colors and illustrated with pictures called *miniatures*. They were lettered and decorated by monk artists in specially established studios at the monasteries, at first in Egypt and Syria, perhaps, then throughout the Eastern Christian lands and finally in Italy and other parts of Europe.

In the 6th century, when the mosaicists of Byzantium came to decorate the churches of Ravenna with pictures of Christ and the Virgin, solemn processions of apostles and of saints, gorgeous portraits of the emperor and his court; they brought with them this new Eastern style, and it became so popular that it dominated mural art in Italy for centuries. Although highly decorative and emotional in its rich color, gold ground and rhythmic pattern, it was from the start quite lacking in any physical reality. Gradually it declined into mere lifeless repetition in which the fine qualities of Byzantine pattern finally were lost.

In the 11th century there came a new period of building, and decoration received a fresh wave of influence from the Near East. This was the developed Byzantine style, still highly decorative and other-worldly but not so flat, not so unnatural. Gold backgrounds are occasionally pierced by a clump of trees; figures show considerable modeling and are sometimes in vigorous movement. It was still, however, an unrealistic art, solemn and gorgeous, well planned to inspire the awe and reverence that the medieval church desired and, through color and line, to create a spiritual mood. It remained the style of Italy until the 13th century.

EARLY ITALIAN PAINTING

In the last years of the medieval period there came the changes that ushered in a new culture and a new art—the Renaissance or rebirth, which began in the 13th century and reached its climax in the 16th century. The crusades, the growth of the cities, the fervent religious revivals, all played their part in the tremendous stir of thought and feeling that characterized the 13th century. Men no longer looked to a future life as the only one of value but enjoyed their part in the present world.

A new naturalistic art was the result of two discoveries: the naturalism of exhumed Greek and Roman art, now considered *classic,* and a fresh vision of the world of nature and of simple human things. In this new vision there was no greater influence than that of St. Francis of Assisi who brought man back to nature. St. Francis praised the Lord for the earth and all its creatures, for the sun and moon and stars, for his brother wind, for his sister water and brother fire. In 1226 he died, and immediately there grew up about him a cycle of picturesque stories with a local Italian background that furnished the artist with a new and very human world of figures, events and meanings.

The Early Florentine School.—The great church erected over the tomb of St. Francis at Assisi has been called the cradle of Italian painting, for on its walls we find the seed of almost all that was to come. There Cimabue, first of the Florentine school, tried to make the old Byzantine forms express the new fire and passion. There the colder Cavallini of Rome drew his solid forms. And there Giotto, their young assistant, learned from them both and then created a new form of expression that was to determine the whole future of the art of Florence.

We are not certain as to what his

METROPOLITAN MUSEUM OF ART

PAINTED ON WOOD in tempera, a medium using yolk of egg to bind pigments, this Sienese Madonna and Child represents the stylized Byzantine tradition that gave way to the naturalism of the Renaissance.

share was in the fine series of St. Francis stories at Assisi—*St. Francis Preaching to the Birds, The Miracle of the Spring* and many others. But in the Arena Chapel at Padua, Giotto told the story of the Virgin, her birth and childhood, her suitors and her marriage; there, also, he told the story of Christ, from his birth and the flight into Egypt through all the episodes of his life to that final scene of the women mourning over his pale body, while the men stand by in silent, helpless grief, and frantic little angels fly about the sky. He turned the whole of the Arena Chapel into a gallery of such pictures, all in soft,

bright colors against an azure ground that suggests the sky.

His figures are rounded, sculptural. Solid bodies underneath the clothes are suggested by the simplest line and light and shade. There is little depth —a tree stands for a landscape, a stone portal for a town. There is no perspective, in the later scientific sense, but this passes unnoticed in the dramatic telling of the story and the unity of the designs.

In 1337 Giotto died. After that most of the painters of Florence adopted his manner, but throughout the 14th century not one approached his stature. At most they made progress in representation. As religious intensity lessened, the Bible stories tended to become events of the day, rich in incident and detail. So naturally there was improvement in showing landscape, architecture and objects of everyday life.

Sienese Painting.—The first master of the Sienese School was Duccio di Buoninsegna, who lived about the same time as Giotto. In Siena the new naturalism never did away with old Byzantine ideals. Painters still delighted in rhythmic pattern of line, in rich color, brocaded stuffs, inlay and ornament. They began to care very much for spatial organization. Figures were purposely flattened, and even when they were highly modeled, they had not the solidity of Giotto's. Space, harmonious line and lack of insistence on the physical gave Sienese painting a spiritual feeling akin to that of Byzantine but tempered with a distinctive sweetness of expression.

Duccio's altarpiece executed for the cathedral of Siena contains the elements of all later Sienese painting. On the front is the Virgin with the Child, enthroned in majesty, encircled by angels. At her feet kneel the patron saints of Siena; beside her extend long lines of girl martyrs and bearded evangelists. It is a flat decorative pattern of gold, deep color and flowing line. But on the back are 38 scenes from the life of Christ and the Virgin, each a lively narrative, not so simple and dramatic as in Giotto but with more definition and a clearer rhythm. In *Christ Entering Jerusalem* the city towers stretch into the distance; an orchard appears beyond a wall, with people in the trees; a great crowd of diverse types streams from the city gate.

Sienese painting developed along these two lines; decoration in line and color and increased narrative and pageantry. Simone Martini of the next generation was a master of enrichment by pattern and melodious line; he was chiefly the artist of the decorative altarpiece as shown in his exquisite *Annunciation* in the Uffizi Gallery in Florence. Ambrogio Lorenzetti, however, was more accomplished as a storyteller. Sienese art had considerable influence on individuals in other Italian schools and even influenced French art when Simone Martini was called to Avignon in 1339 to paint at the court of the exiled Pope. But for the most part it could not withstand the pressure of other schools, and although Siena con-

tinued, even in the 15th century, to produce artists devoted to the old ideal, such as Sassetta, it was an ideal so little congenial to the spirit of the Renaissance that it finally died away or merged with other tendencies.

The 15th Century in Florence.—Masaccio came at the beginning of the 15th century and lived only 27 years. As one critic has said, he was Giotto born again and instantly making his own all that had been gained in the years that came between. His figures are majestic in their breadth and mass; they look like real people, and one can move around and among them. Both architecture and landscape assume a more normal relation to the figures; there is deep space and atmosphere—objects become increasingly blurred as they retreat. Lighting has logical direction, and tonal shadowing begins. There is interest in the nude and in facial expression; and the storytelling is as simple and direct as Giotto's.

As far as the religious subject is concerned, Masaccio is a true child of the approaching Renaissance. He converted legendary materials into intimate stories of man and his immediate world. At times he even let religious meaning be obscured by some human element, such as the powerful realism of a naked man shivering with cold in his *St. Peter Baptising the Heathen.* As the century advanced, the religious subject yielded more and more to other interests. Portraits became common, with plain or landscape background. There were battles, tournaments, historical scenes and finally many subjects from ancient Greek and Roman literature, then being eagerly read in the great revival of classical learning that was the dominating characteristic of the Renaissance.

All through the 15th century painters thought about the same things as did Masaccio. There were exceptions, it is true. The monk, Fra Angelico, for instance, somewhat older than Masaccio, showed in certain works that he was not unaffected by the new realism; but he preferred a pattern of rhythmic line and of bright harmonious colors. He is always deeply religious and has something in common with the spirit of Siena and also with the earlier illuminators of manuscripts. He recently has gained in stature, as art lovers during the 20th century have returned to appreciation of formal and spiritual values as against realistic; and he now takes a place with Duccio and Giotto among the foremost masters of the early Renaissance.

LATER ITALIAN PAINTING

Early Renaissance in Florence.—For the most part, however, 15th-century painters carried forward the interests of Masaccio. They were not content with expressing the large essentials of form, movement and decoration. They studied anatomy because they wanted to be able to show the body in every variety of posture and of movement. They studied perspective to help them in showing the changes that objects undergo as they appear at increasing

ALINARI ART REFERENCE BUREAU

PAULO UCCELLO (1397–1475) painted *The Rout of San Romano* in 1435. Early Renaissance Florentine painters at this time were discovering the nature of man and investigating the secrets of science. Uccello's preoccupation with perspective is typical of the new interests. He took great pains to foreshorten the broken lances and armor: all point toward common vanishing points. Some critics object to this work's decorative nature as well as to the background, which they say is unrelated to the front "stage"; others disagree, finding it one of the most well-ordered and decorative—in the best sense of the word—canvases of this period.

distance from the eye. They were ambitious to represent deep space, the vista of a long room, the far-sweeping Tuscan landscape. Sometimes they were so intent upon what they were representing that they quite forgot design and became recorders of facts instead of artists. But this was not true of the greatest men of the school. Their ability to show deep space and movement and three-dimensional form only added to the richness and variety of their expression and design,

Uccello (1396–1475) had a passion for perspective and is sometimes rather amusing in his exaggeration of the rate at which his distant hills recede, and in those battle scenes where he fills the ground with broken lances, armor, dead cavaliers—all directed toward the "vanishing point." But he used the new lines and spaces to make very rich pageantlike pictures.

Most powerful of all the realists was Andrea del Castagno (1390–1457) who knew all the secrets of bone and muscle and built up three-dimensional forms of tremendous vigor and powerful design. Antonio Pollaiuolo (1429–98) made a systematic study of anatomy. He contributed an extraordinary knowledge of movement, especially of the nude figure fighting, wrestling or in other violent action.

Piero della Francesca (c. 1420–92), although an Umbrian (the Umbrian school derived originally from Siena), was in spirit Florentine. He wrote a treatise on perspective, but apparently his scientific interests only helped him as an artist for he became one of the greatest designers of his day.

However, not all painters made contributions of this sort. Many, notably Fra Filippo Lippi and Ghirlandaio, were content with illustrating the stories and depicting the panorama of the Florentine life of their time and humanizing further the Christian stories. Especially do individual Florentines live for us in the amazing portraits of Ghirlandaio.

High Renaissance in Florence.—Botticelli and Leonardo da Vinci both lived into the 16th century. Botticelli (c. 1447–1510) springs from Fra Filippo Lippi and Pollaiuolo, and his early work is what one might expect from an accomplished painter with his training. But he turned aside to indulge a passion for movement, not only of moving figures and fluttering draperies but also of pure line—long and quiet or swiftly changing as a flame. He was quite willing to distort the figure, twist and bend it, lengthen legs and arms, if thereby he might weave his lines into a more living arabesque. He gives us idylls of the ancient world. Venus, born of the sea, sails shoreward, lightly poised upon a shell and wafted by the winds; or she watches the coming of Spring, blown in by the West Wind, while Flora scatters flowers and the Graces dance for Mercury. But these visions of the ancient world are seen through Tuscan eyes and are tinged with melancholy, even though the scenes are dressed in the rich trappings of Florentine court life.

Leonardo da Vinci (1452–1519) cared for light and shade as Botticelli cared for line, not only for the sake of form but for its own sake, for the pure melody of its gradations. Leonardo without a trace of effort exploited all that the Florentines had achieved in representation since the days of Giotto. His figures surpass any before in delicate modulations of light and shade that suggest flesh as well as bone and muscle. His outlines waver in a veil of atmosphere. Landscape backgrounds, filled with air, recede into a luminous distance. Oil painting, which had come in during the 15th century, made possible a softer edge than tempera. His religious subjects are very human. His Christ Child is a real baby. His *Last Supper* is a dramatic rendering of the effect on the Twelve of one startling sentence, "One of you shall betray me."

High Renaissance in Rome.—Michelangelo (1475–1564) was unlike Leonardo. He was chiefly a sculptor and wanted no lost edges or veil of air to soften the massive bulk and structure of his figures. He bends them back and forth in space in splendid balanced designs and stops at no exaggeration that would increase the solid weight or rhythm of their forms. His great work in painting is the ceiling decoration of the Sistine Chapel in Rome. A multitude of gigantic figures are held together by moving line and a subdued color tone of gold and violet. The subject is the drama of Genesis, the Creation and Fall and man's continued struggle. Painted architectural motives and nude figures connect the paintings, and supporting this framework are great seated sibyls and prophets. Michelangelo is the culminating figure in Florentine expression of form and surpasses all his predecessors in imaginative vision.

Raphael (1483–1520) was not a Florentine but went to Florence in 1504 and fell under the spell of Leonardo and Michelangelo. He was Umbrian and reflects all the influences of the Umbrian school—Sienese line and pattern, sweetness of facial expression and fondness for space—modified by Florentine realism. Raphael was always the skilful adapter of traits of other men, but he did create a combination that was quite his own. In 1508 he was called to Rome to decorate certain rooms in the Vatican, and it is in his great murals there and in his masterly portraits rather than in his storytelling pictures and long series of Madonnas that his real achievement lies. He went farther than had any earlier artist in detailed naturalistic representation, and he had an extraordinary sense of balanced surface composition. He was, too, the culminating figure in the refinement of the technical means of the painting art; his religious pictures have attained unrivaled popularity.

Early Renaissance in Venice.—In Venice there was such close relation to the East that the Byzantine influence toward formalism lasted longer than elsewhere in Italy. In the 14th century it was softened by a new realism more suited to this gay, luxurious, nature-loving people. But it was not until the early years of the 15th century that Venetian painting was really stirred into new life. Then Sienese and Florentine traditions were brought to Venice through the visiting Umbrian painter, Gentile da Fabriano, and his Verona follower, Vittore Pisano.

The movement was carried on by Jacopo Bellini, the so-called father of Venetian painting, and his sons Gentile and Giovanni. Jacopo's daughter married Andrea Mantegna of Padua, and this brought a fresh outside influence into Venice. Padua more than any other Italian city was under the spell of antiquity. Mantegna studied Francisco Squarcione's famous collection of ancient sculpture, and whenever possible he used in his paintings Roman architecture, costumes and details of every sort. His fine form did not come from the antique alone—he knew also the frescoes of Giotto in the Arena Chapel and other work from Florence.

The early works of Giovanni Bellini echo the Paduan style of Mantegna with its hard linear documentation and its accentuation of contours. But gradually Giovanni begins to modulate his light and dark, to clothe with

METROPOLITAN MUSEUM OF ART

RAPHAEL'S majestic *The Holy Family with St. Elizabeth and St. John the Baptist.*

flesh the skeleton. His style broadens; rich color takes on the beginning of Venetian glow; pastoral backgrounds foretell Giorgione's poetic landscapes. Giovanni lived to be 90 years old and took part in the whole development of Venetian painting from the Paduan influence to the triumph of those broad, simplified surfaces of light and color, with edges lost in atmosphere, that were created by his great pupils, Titian and Giorgione.

Venetian painting stands primarily for glorious color and masterly formal organization. It never deserted the solid structure of the body but saw it in terms of light and color. It did not emphasize line as Florentine painting did. Line, color and strong rhythms of dark and light entered together into Venetian design. Oil technique was very helpful in producing effects of light and space. Venetian art was not religious; it was quite worldly and delighted in depicting the joy of living. The Venetian loved beautiful textures, picturesque costumes, architecture, processions and pageants, civil or religious. He treated religious subjects in an intimate, everyday fashion. Vittore Carpaccio's *Vision of St. Ursula* becomes a detailed picture of a Venetian room in early morning light, with a young girl asleep, and the visiting angel is merely introduced in one corner. The altarpieces of Madonnas and saints are in reality pictures of happy,

healthy Venetians. Symmetry of design disappears in favor of an equally well-balanced but more natural grouping. There is new emphasis on the nude and on landscape. But most notably there are more opulent color, richer pageantry and a certain symphonic grandeur of design.

High Renaissance in Venice.—Giorgione (*c.* 1478–1511) abolishes the edge, discovers the color in deep shadows, builds his forms in broad masses of rich, glowing color. In his *Sleeping Venus* (probably completed by Titian) he also weaves his lines into fine rhythmic pattern. Landscape is a natural outcome of feeling for color and light. It is not so much a mere background as in Florentine painting; the figures are not in front of it but often in it. Giorgione made the greatest progress up to this time in landscape—luminous distance, luxuriant trees or bare trees patterned against the sky, the heat of a summer day or the cool of evening, the lightning flashes of a coming thunderstorm. His portraits have a mood of reverie, his Arcadian idyls belong to some past golden age.

With Titian we reach the climax of the Venetian school. He was born a year before Giorgione and outlived him 66 years, dying in 1576, aged 99. At first he resembles his master Bellini, then Giorgione. But gradually his own personality asserts itself—he changes from the lyrical to the

METROPOLITAN MUSEUM OF ART

TITIAN shows the nude with a new sensuality. *Venus and the Lute Player*, detail.

more dramatic style shown in the vigorous action and exuberance of his *Bacchus and Ariadne*. His work is more elaborated and more powerful than that of Giorgione, more solid and real and still more splendid in color. His range is vastly greater. He left a huge number of works of all kinds, portraits, altarpieces, nudes, classic myths and great decorations. He can be thoughtful and profound, as in the splendid *Entombment* of the Louvre; his portraits are intense and vivid studies of character. His large altarpieces, although often grandiose, are always rich designs in line, light and color. But perhaps most typical and most popular are the allegorical and pastoral pieces in which the nude figure is presented with unparalleled dignity, opulence and even nobility.

Il Tintoretto's style is quite different. There is no trace of calm and serenity. All is tremendous energy, movement and drama, due largely to the brilliant lighting of parts and their dramatic contrast with shadow. Tintoretto achieves a sense of deep space within his canvas, and he manipulates swirling lines, receding planes and figures touched by flamelike lights in a sort of symphony of movement. He also uses his brush in a new way, with evident delight in the strokes as such.

Veronese, who came from Verona to Venice in 1528, painted enormous canvases of great decorative richness—usually very spectacular pictures with imposing architectural backgrounds giving the illusion of great space. He turns the *Last Supper* and the *Marriage at Cana* into contemporary Venetian banquets. He does not retain the Venetian glow but paints in cooler tones, and he is a lesser master of plastic design.

Decadence in Italy.—The decline of painting was not so rapid in Venice as elsewhere in Italy. Even in the 17th century Venice produced sound painters and in the 18th had a brief but brilliant renaissance of which Tiepolo, Canaletto and Guardi were the masters. The decline everywhere began with the imitation and exaggeration by lesser men of the obvious

traits of the great masters of their time: Michelangelo's muscles and twisted torsos, Raphael's "ideal" figures and grace of line, Correggio's light and shade. Correggio's influence was especially destructive. He was a north Italian painter who lived in the first half of the 16th century. In certain churches he actually painted away the architecture, giving an illusion of real figures soaring into clouds with hosts of angels. He also did a series of illustrations of the Greek myths, with charming rhythmic figures of exceptional sensuous charm. His light and shade, derived from Leonardo but carried further, lent itself to very sentimental and exaggerated treatment by his followers.

The Eclectics (meaning "choosers") tried to revive art by combining "the line of Angelo, the color of Titian and the grace of Raphael," but their ambition was not rewarded. There was one new movement in the 16th century in revolt from the artificiality of the decadence—that of the Realists headed by Caravaggio of Naples, who painted murders, quarrels and the like and used even for his religious paintings Neapolitan types of the day. These he painted with striking effects of narrow streaks of light coming out of dense shadows and with very limited color. His treatment by emphasized light was later to influence Rembrandt and Velásquez and thus be passed down to modern art.

MEDIEVAL PAINTING IN THE NORTH

By northern painting we mean chiefly that of England, France, Germany, the Netherlands and Spain. Not many mural and panel paintings of the period before the 15th-century Renaissance have survived. But there are many paintings in illuminated manuscript books throughout the Middle Ages and also considerable stained and painted glass of Gothic period in which we can trace a continuous history of the art.

The manuscript books were the product of the monasteries, written and illuminated by the monks who civilized and Christianized the men of the North and preserved for them the remains of ancient culture. Some were copies of old Greek and Roman manuscripts, but most of them were religious books: Bibles, lives of the saints, books of devotion, service books for the church. The paintings in them were a mixture of the native art of the North and the traditions brought from Rome and Byzantium.

Celtic Painting.—The chief quality of native northern art was linear movement. In Ireland and England this was most developed. Irish painting is entirely unrealistic, mostly pure ornament. Ribbons and spirals are elaborated with animal features; birds, dragons and serpents are stretched into patterns, their tongues and tails prolonged into ribbons interlaced and tied with wonderful dexterity. Human beings become purely geometrical figures very much like the kings and queens of playing cards. The unity lies in the continuous, rhythmic movement. The most important man-

uscripts preserved belong to the **7th** century A.D.

Continental Painting.—When Charlemagne restored the Roman Empire (800 A.D.), he wanted to make his court at Aix-la-Chapelle (now Aachen in Germany) the home of all the ancient culture that had survived and the center of a new culture that would radiate to all parts of his empire. To that end he gathered scholars and artists from Italy, England and Spain. The pictures in the magnificent volumes executed at his court show a curious mixture: Celtic ornament combined with classical and Byzantine, stiff Byzantine portraits of Evangelists in frames of architecture or perhaps with a perspective background that hints of Hellenistic sources.

Away from Aix, especially at Reims, we find the old Hellenistic naturalism preserved. This is especially true of illustrations in the *Utrecht Psalter* (9th century). It shows an immense number of small, restless figures in the most lively action, draperies fluttering wildly, in a spacious landscape that looks like windswept dunes.

The style of the *Utrecht Psalter* had an enlivening influence on painting after Charlemagne's time, and when it was imported into England in the 10th century, its rhythmic linear movement proved so agreeable to Anglo-Saxon artists that it became the favorite style for 2 centuries. And when England was brought into the fold of the continent by the Norman invasion of the 11th century, the linear style returned to the continent and influenced Romanesque painting and sculpture in France.

Gothic Painting.—For the arts the 12th and 13th centuries are periods glorious and unique. Architecture dominated, but sculpture, painting, illumination, stained glass, tapestry, embroidery and all the allied crafts were joined in an amazing unity. Its center was no longer the monastery but the town and the cathedral. The artists were laymen instead of monks. Subject matter was no longer exclusively religious; manuscripts, for instance, included historical, literary and scientific subjects. As the cathedral rose to dizzy heights, and the openings grew larger, painting was transferred from the walls to the glass of the windows. More splendid color has never been produced, and the French cathedrals particularly are still visited by art pilgrims from all parts of the world.

The colors are luscious shades of rich reds and deep blues, yellows and greens in smaller quantity. The pieces of colored glass are very small, and when from a distance the difference between the colors is lost, the whole becomes a purple of wonderful richness. Details were painted in brown enamel on the colored glass and then fired, thus fusing enamel with the glass. The figures, always small in the early 12th-century glass, were used in a series of medallions, each one telling some sacred or legendary story. Thirteenth century glass was much the same except that some larger figures appeared. In the 14th century large figures were predominant, and shadows and relief appeared as did a whole range of delicate half tones; but the glory of the earlier centuries had vanished.

The Thirteenth Century.—For painting proper our chief source is still the manuscript. Books became small in this century and pictures delicate and minute. Books were resplendent with burnished gold and rich colors, especially blue and red, reflecting the brilliance of stained glass—black outlines even suggesting the leading of the glass. Backgrounds were commonly of gold, blue or red, with no suggestion of surroundings other than perhaps a tower or patterned tree. Later in the century the little figures became supple and delicate in body and feature, slightly modeled in color and took on a certain gentle gayety—in form and spirit they resembled Gothic sculpture.

Fourteenth Century.—Naturalism increased. Drawing became more flexible, lines more flowing, the figure elastic and swaying, the narrative more lively. Colors were still rich but more varied. Modeling created an effect of third dimension. Backgrounds became elaborate with stippled gold and patterns. Occasionally they were broken to admit a bit of landscape or interior view. By the 15th century the formal background yielded entirely, and the figures took their place in natural surroundings, interior or landscape. The range of subject matter became broader.

In the late 14th and 15th centuries literary and historical works increased, and manuscript books of all sorts were made in great numbers, not only for churches and monasteries but especially for the magnificent libraries of the princes and nobles. In the 14th century we can trace the gradual changes that mark off English, French, Flemish, Dutch and Spanish manuscripts as the life of the different countries takes on distinct national character. In general we may say that illuminated manuscripts, with their rich imagination, fine craftsmanship, brilliant colors and lavish gold upon the silken texture of fine vellum, are among the most exquisite remains of the Middle Ages.

NORTHERN RENAISSANCE PAINTING

Paris was the great artistic and intellectual center of the 14th century, and a brilliant French Renaissance was about to unfold there when civil war and later disasters plunged France into misery. The Renaissance of northern painting took place in Flanders and in Burgundy at the hands of Flemish artists. In the 15th century the dukes of Burgundy had united under their peaceful and prosperous rule all the Netherlandish provinces. Netherlandish art flourished, and even the manuscripts of the great French patrons were done by Flemish painters. (Flemish is a time-honored term for the art of the whole Netherlands until the 17th century when the term Dutch is used for the separated provinces—Holland—in the north.)

Panel paintings had been increasing in the 14th century, but the 15th was their real flowering period. Paintings were now made for the home, guild hall and town hall as well as for church and chapel. Religious feeling was still fervent but no longer dominated. Art tended to become a record of the splendor and great wealth of princely merchants and manufacturers.

Flemish Painting, 15th Century.—The earliest important Flemish painters were the brothers Hubert and Jan van Eyck, whose altarpiece at Ghent, *The Adoration of the Lamb,* was all—and more—to the painting of the North that Masaccio's frescoes were to that of Italy. In this painting all the interests of the Flemish school are revealed. When the wings are opened, the color has the blazing splendor of stained glass. Above a great figure of God in jeweled robes is enthroned with Mary (a Flemish Virgin, fair and blonde) and John beside him. On either side are singing and playing angels in rich brocades heavy with gold embroidery and with jewels. Beyond are naked figures of Adam and Eve shown in stark realism. Below is a Paradise of green with violets, cowslips, daisies, roses and purple flags; in the far distance are the towers of a Gothic city and snowcapped mountains against a blue sky. In the meadow the angels with rainbow wings surround the Lamb on the altar. Hosts of worshipers stand and kneel—popes and cardinals, poets and philosophers—while from either side hermit, pilgrim and warrior saints wind through a wooded country toward the scene of adoration. On the outside of the wings are portraits of the donor of the altarpiece and his wife, solid, weighty forms, full of character.

These were the qualities handed down to northern painting of the 15th century by Hubert and Jan van Eyck: brilliant color; a painstaking realism; delight in the texture of stuffs, of jewels, wood and stone; a tendency to angular line pattern instead of curves; an enthusiasm for portrait and landscape. Jan van Eyck's little portraits are powerful renderings of individual character, unified in design in spite of their exact detail. Landscape was very spacious, with a high horizon giving what is often called *bird's-eye perspective* because the point of view is from a height. It was an assembled landscape in the sense that many bits studied from nature were put together in an imaginary whole.

The Van Eycks have been credited with the invention of oil painting. It was not oil painting in the modern sense but the use of an oil varnish mixed with the white or yolk of egg (or both) as a medium for the ground pigments. Probably the Van Eycks perfected this method, and it became the traditional technique of the North just as tempera was in the South before the introduction of real oil painting in the 16th century.

A quite different personality was Roger van der Weyden (*c.* 1400–64), whose home was in the southern part of the country and who was more French in temperament. His religious pictures express intense emotion and are bound together by a rhythmic flow of line. Dirk Bouts of Haarlem contributed to the color and light of landscape. Hugo van der Goes made further contributions to realism in his study of light and of everyday types of people.

Hans Memling, who lived some 50 years after Jan van Eyck, brought in more delicate transitions of light and dark. His figures have little weight or solidity—they are ethereal and otherworldly. His line is flowing, and his design is beautifully patterned. On the panels of a little shrine he tells the story of the martyrdom of St. Ursula and her 11,000 virgins in the spirit of a medieval fairy tale against a background of castles and cities and the swelling sails of boats. He is never dramatic, but he does impart a definite spiritual quality to his religious pictures even when he must introduce in the foreground careful portraits of the donor and his five sons and the donor's wife and her 11 daughters.

Flemish Painting, 16th Century.—Quentin Matsys, a transitional painter between the 15th and 16th centuries, played a role similar to that of Leonardo in Italy in humanizing and dramatizing the religious story, in his enthusiasm for light and dark and in his creation of form by softly modulated tones. Sometimes the genre element overwhelmed the religious sentiment, as in the case of a martyrdom of St. John in which the fiendish stokers are obviously of more interest to the painter than is the exalted saint in the caldron of boiling oil. The next step was to paint the genre subject for its own sake, and in this Matsys was the pioneer. Matsys has the color of the earlier men with more variety, shimmer and sparkle.

Bosch and Pieter Breughel were both from the Holland country. Bosch (*c.* 1462–1516) was the inventor of a world of nightmares and monstrous beings, of caricature and satire, but he was also a master of pictorial construction and carried on the splendid color tradition of his school. From him descended Breughel (*c.* 1525–69), humorist, satirist of the vices and foibles of humanity but a painter of such broad interests that he could turn from the most involved allegory to the depiction of a village fair, a peasant dance or a landscape more natural than any seen before. With Breughel landscape becomes truly local and believable instead of an imaginary assemblage of bits. Often he lowers the horizon line so that his perspective is from the normal point of view. He is distinguished for his light and color and for his spatial pattern. Recently he has been elevated by critics to a place close to the foremost masters of western painting. Expressionistic values were discovered in his paintings that were not recognized during the realistic centuries. Beyond his achievement of masterly formal organization, Breughel repays study for his typical Flemish characterization and human feeling.

Bosch died early in the 16th century; Breughel lived through the middle. Both men were the natural outgrowth of the Van Eyck tradition. But in the early years of the century there had developed a new and elaborate style that reflected the changing taste of the time. In this new painting there was an abundance of impossibly fanciful architecture, and saints and Virgin appeared in the latest fashions of the day. This extravagance was further complicated by Italian influence.

In the 15th century the Italians had been eager to learn the secrets of Flemish craftsmanship, but after the Florentine Renaissance had culminated in the achievements of Leonardo, Michelangelo and Raphael, the situation was quite different. Early in the 16th century the Flemings were fired with enthusiasm for Italian art, and there was a pilgrimage of artists to Italy with the most unfortunate results. They could not make their natures Italian, and the outcome was a strange mixture that sometimes reached the grotesque. They imitated the great compositional schemes of the Italians and especially their treatment of the nude; it became the height of ambition to be known as the Flemish Raphael. Probably the leading artists were Jan Gossart (otherwise known as Mabuse) and Bernard van Orley.

No period is wholly decadent, and there was some progress made, chiefly in greater breadth and freedom in representation. Pictures of contemporary life and portraits flourished. Landscape became of more importance than figure interest, thus pointing the way to the 17th-century development of landscape for its own sake with no figure interest at all. In this development, besides Breughel, Joachim de Patinir was important. He is accounted by some, indeed, as the first great western master of landscape. (In China this branch of painting had been practiced beautifully for many centuries.)

French Painting.—In France in the 15th century there are few famous names. There are a few outstanding anonymous paintings such as the great *Virgin of Pity* from Villeneuve, now in the Louvre, which illustrates perfectly the French style with its northern realism modified by feeling for line, its emotion and masterly arrangement. Ever since Simone Martini went to Avignon during the exile of the popes, there had lingered a Sienese influence very agreeable to the French temperament. In the course of the 15th century this yielded to realistic Flemish influence as shown in the work of Nicholas Froment. Jean Fouquet is the greatest French name of the century, a painter of simple and direct portraits and also of miniatures in manuscripts, some of which give intimate pictures of his country and his time.

In the 16th century France, like Flanders, was in the grip of Italianism. Italian artists were brought to the court to cover palace walls with paintings in the southern manner. Pictures of allegory and mythology with many nude figures grew common,

but at the same time there was an intense enthusiasm for portraits. Jean Clouet, who was of Flemish origin, and his son François were the most famous of the portrait painters. Their portraits are light, delicate, with few colors and few lines, but they express the personalities of the aristocracy of the time with great vitality.

German Painting, 15th Century.—In the 14th century a school of painting had emerged from manuscript illumination, supposedly under the leadership of a Master Wilhelm of Köln. The style of this school was not expressive of ceremony but rather of private devotion. There were small Madonna pictures for private oratories and Paradise pictures with Virgin and Child surrounded by saints in a medieval garden.

In 1430 Stephan Lochner, a stranger from Swabia, came to Köln and became the leading master of the school. Lochner quite lacked the force and grandeur of the Van Eycks; he is simple and human with no trace of the austere realism of the Flemings. The Virgin sits in a garden, eyes lowered, smiling and ecstatic, holding the Child; small angels gather around her, painted in clear tones of red, blue, green and rose. Flesh tones are luminous, and the bright colors have a soft modulation.

As the century advanced the religious story took on the flavor of everyday life; painting deserted the mystic garden and told new stories in the spirit of naturalistic observation. After 1450 Flemish influences, especially from Bouts and Van der Weyden, turned the school from 14th-century idealism and fondness for line to realism and modeling in light and dark.

From about 1480 Flemish influence, especially that of Van der Weyden, came to predominate in the South also. The most influential painter of this epoch was Martin Schongauer. In general the German schools may be distinguished from the Flemish by their heavier color, their angularities of gesture and attitude and their more crowded designs.

German Painting, 16th Century.—In the 16th century came the same Italianism that had overwhelmed the other countries. But several great artists learned from Italy and still maintained their German spirit. Chief of these was Albrecht Dürer (1471–1528), the learned artist of the time, curious, theoretical. He worked for a time in Italy and developed from the Venetians an absorbing interest in light. In spite of their extraordinary amount of detail his compositions are held together by a lighting that is emotionally expressive—somber gloom, unearthly glitter, soft sunshine. He absorbed all Italian progress in representation. He tried to carry his expression even to the point of symbolizing abstract ideas. He advanced from a very complicated style to the simple broad unity of his last powerful work, the *Four Apostles, John, Peter, Mark and Paul.* Today his brilliant and lifelike portraits are most appreciated among his paintings. He is even more celebrated for

his engravings and ranks as Europe's foremost master of engraving on both copper and wood.

Contemporary with Dürer was Lucas Cranach, who as a painter was a more versatile master. He was an accomplished portraitist and painted some of the most distinctive and imposing of German religious pictures and (what is exceptional among northern artists) a series of naively charming nude Eves and Venuses.

Among others of the period Mathias Grünewald stands out as an exceptional colorist and a master of emotional expression. His colors and his dramatic forms can be agitating and harrowing, tragic and ecstatic. Grünewald as well as Dürer influenced Albrecht Altdorfer, who is known for the development of landscape for its own sake, though in a technique more fitting for a draughtsman than for a painter. Hans Baldung (known oftener as Hans Baldung Grün because he so loved the color green) was one of the greatest of German painters but left very few works that can be confidently identified as his.

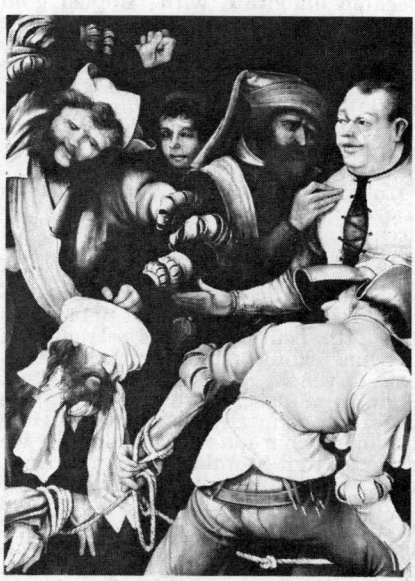

ALTE PINAKOTHEK, MUNICH

GRÜNEWALD was the great German master of color. *The Mocking of Christ* (early sixteenth century) displays the intense emotional forces that characterize his work.

Hans Holbein the Younger early fell under Italian influence and produced religious pictures in the southern manner. He was a second-rate painter in all but portraiture. In that field he became a master with an international reputation. After working in Germany and Switzerland he went to England and became court painter to Henry VIII. His gallery of painstaking and sensitive likenesses of notables of the time is endlessly interesting as a revelation of character and as an example of sustained craftsmanship. If his work lacked imagination, if it erred often in overdetail, Holbein is yet foremost among the world's realistic portraitists. One

REMBRANDT'S *Lady with a Pink* shows his characteristic working of light and shade, which unifies this masterful portrait.

must go to the Orient to find artists who could outline a contour of cheek or lip with equal delicacy and grace.

THE SEVENTEENTH CENTURY

In this century we find certan changes that contain all the germs of 18th- and 19th-century art. Interest in landscape led to a great interest in space. Il Tintoretto had carried his figures back into space; but beyond the figures space tended to lose reality. Certain painters of the 17th century carried their realization of depth even to the horizon. Space stretched out as never before, not in parallel planes as was usual with Renaissance painters, but through great diagonals or curves that led attention in and out of the picture field. Space existed between objects. Design was no longer a matter of the surface in relation to the rectangle of the picture but moved in and out of depth.

At the same time an absorbing interest in light and color tended to break down expression of space and volume in favor of a mosaic of light and color that anticipated the 19th-century impressionists.

Flemish Painting.—With the giant Rubens a new golden age of Flemish painting emerged from the 16th-century decline. Peter Paul Rubens, born in 1577, about the time of Titian's death, went to Italy and was able to assimilate Italian ideals without damage to his Flemish traditions and to pass on to later centuries the elements of both. He has Venetian feeling for color masses, with Florentine sense of form and expressive line; but Venetian glow becomes reddish with Rubens, the strong modeling is softened, line grows atmospheric and turns to shorter curves and double curves, and Venetian composition becomes more florid.

Whether he painted myths, battles, animals, markets, peasant fetes, altarpieces, landscapes, portraits, still life —everything is in movement; if it is not a drama of human beings in movement, it is a drama of moving color, light and dark and line. One

has the impression of a great energy in continual transformation but of a controlled and ordered energy, for Rubens is a great designer—a designer in space—even to the smallest unit of his great canvases. His chief followers were Jakob Jordaens and Sir Anthony Van Dyck, the latter a very great master of portraiture; and after them came the Flemish decadence.

Dutch Painting.—In the 17th century the southern part of the Netherlands, modern Belgium, was still Catholic and was under the rule of Spain; but the northern Netherlands, modern Holland, had become Protestant and independent. There were no palaces for which the Dutch could paint and no churches, for Protestantism disapproved of the decoration of churches. Instead they painted for the private house, the town hall, the homes of the various guilds and institutions. There was great enthusiasm for paintings of everything that had to do with their own people and their own country, now especially dear to them in their new and hard-won independence. Artists began to specialize as painters of portraits, of landscapes, of genre.

Frans Hals, next to Rembrandt, was the greatest of the portrait painters. He has left us a transcription of the Dutch people, the merchants and their wives, the archers of the civic guard, directors of the poorhouse, a laughing servant, a jolly toper, an old witch with her owl. He is known for his vivid expression of life, due partly to catching his subject in a lively mood, partly to his vigorous and dashing brush strokes.

Rembrandt van Rijn (1606–69), the greatest genius of the Dutch school, painted not only portraits but scenes of everyday life, landscapes, still life and a vast number of religious subjects. These were not monumental paintings for the church but stories of the Old Testament, told with splendor of imagination and with feeling for the ancient East, and pictures of the New Testament in the simple spirit of the Gospels. He treats of all ages, all emotions and all conditions of people. Most of his early paintings were executed with a sober realism and attention to form in minute detail. But in 1642 in his *Sortie of the Civic Guard* he allowed himself, in his passion for light and dark, to forget the careful representation of form so dear to the Dutch heart. Only a few figures emerge clearly from the moving light and shadow—and the result was his immediate decline in popularity. Rembrandt's light is not natural but a glow that is all his own, with which he brings volumes from the shadows into golden light and then lets them retreat again into gloom. Sometimes his fascination with light so dominated that his lights and darks mass into patterns that quite obscure objects and foretell the complete visual impressionism of the 19th century.

The Dutch of the 17th century gave genre painting a distinct character. Their works are small, minute in technique, splendid in craftsmanship; placid little pictures that repeat over and over again favorite themes of peasant life, such as the fete, dance or market, or scenes from the home life of the rich burghers, as the music

RUBENS went south to Italy to learn firsthand from the Renaissance masters. He brought back to Flanders the monumentality of Michelangelo's nudes and the glowing color of the Venetians. In addition, he developed a characteristic love of movement, liveliness, attention to realistic detail, and dramatic spacing of his subjects, as is seen in this *Venus and Adonis*, from the first half of the seventeenth century.

lesson and card party. The story is of little importance; the real concern is with color, texture and the decorative whole. The chief men were Gerard Ter Borch, Jan Steen, Jan Vermeer and Pieter de Hooch. The last two were fascinated with natural light, air-filled space, effects of sunlight. Vermeer could show the most delicate differences in value (amount of light) of every spot of color.

Of the Dutch landscapists, Meyndert Hobbema and Jacob Ruisdael were the greatest. Ruisdael studied the forms of trees and their manner of growth, the solid ground and vastness of the sky; his clouds have bulk and carrying power. Sometimes it is the country around his native Haarlem; again, with romantic imagination, he treats of strange rocks and hills and waterfalls.

Realism did not extend to color; Dutch landscape, with few exceptions, transposed the colors of nature into a scheme of browns and brown-greens, sparingly enlivened with blue and red.

French Painting.—Italianism was less disastrous to France than to other countries. It continued even into the 17th century with happy results in the work of Nicolas Poussin and Claude Lorrain. Poussin, who preferred to live in Rome rather than in Paris, admired Raphael and ancient sculpture, and his work shows the spirit of the Italian Renaissance through French eyes. His sculptural figures are tied together in varied and rhythmical arrangements. His favorite subjects were stories of classical antiquity against a background of landscape carefully studied for its clouds, tree forms and the solid structure of the ground.

Claude Lorrain was primarily a landscape painter, although he always introduced some small and unimportant figure interest, biblical or classical. His special contribution lay in light and atmosphere. His landscapes are romantic, majestic, with great tree masses placed against a vast and mist-filled distance. Color is secondary, being submerged in a warm or silvery light enveloping the whole. For his fondness for introducing classical architecture he is often called the father of classical landscape. It is an assembled landscape, built on the study of nature but entirely imaginary in its final form.

Spanish Masters.—The history of Spanish painting during the Renaissance is largely one of foreign influences but of influences that immediately took on a Spanish character. They were Flemish in the 15th century—Jan van Eyck visited Spain—and Italian in the 16th. A distinguishing feature of Spanish style in the 15th century was the primitive fondness for gold backgrounds—plaster relief covered with gold. The eclectic Italians dominated the 16th century with their twisted torsos, exaggerated muscles, striking darks and lights.

In the late 16th century there came to Spain a foreign painter, Domenico Theotocopuli. He came from Crete and was popularly called *El Greco* (The Greek). He had studied with Titian and knew the works of Michel-

FRICK COLLECTION

BOUCHER'S *Spring* is typical of the pictorial refinement in the court of Louis XVI.

angelo. In Spain his warm Venetian colors cooled, became dulled with black, and his whites became silvery. More than any other painter he expresses the religious emotion of the Spanish temperament. He is unique in the restless, flamelike rising of his forms, the flickering lights, the elongated, undulating bodies that he does not hesitate to bend at will. From these he created formal organizations, dynamic and powerful, unsurpassed in the whole range of world art.

El Greco worked into the 17th century. Quite unlike him were the realists, Francisco de Zurbarán and Velásquez, who lived some 50 years later. Velásquez began as the accomplished student of all the traditions of his time. Later in his life he became court painter of Philip IV of Spain, and in the long series of portraits of the king and queen, the

FRICK COLLECTION

EL GRECO'S elongations and the dramatic rhythms of light and shade give *St. Jerome* a dramatic and vibrant individuality.

infantas, dwarfs and the whole nobility of the Spanish court, he revealed himself in a new and individual manner. In the cool, diffused light of the Spanish palace there were no strong shadows to throw forms into relief; instead they tended to appear as color masses of various degrees of light. Velásquez became engrossed with purely visual impressions. So sensitive was he to the exact relations of values that at times he produced an uncanny illusion of space; but he did it solely with his color and not with line or shadow. He was never a mere reproducer of nature's light and color but achieved a decorative unity by arranging his masses of color and light in finely balanced patterns. He grew fond of low-toned colors, casting aside the warm glow of the Italians for cool subtleties of blacks and whites and silver grays, with notes of rose, red, blue and yellow. Velásquez's color-studies had some influence two centuries later upon French painting, particularly through Manet, and he is sometimes called one of the fathers of Impressionism.

THE EIGHTEENTH CENTURY

English Painting.—Painting was still on its downward slope in Italy and in Germany; Holland and Flanders, after the brilliant 17th century, had not a single great name. In England and France, however, there was an art founded on that of Rubens. England had not developed a national school since the Middle Ages. In the 16th century she had imported Holbein from Germany as court painter; in the 17th, Van Dyck from Flanders. The first important English painter was William Hogarth, a portraitist and storytelling painter who satirized the social life of his day, notably in his famous series *Marriage à la Mode*.

About the middle of the century, chiefly under the influence of Rubens and Van Dyck and the Venetians, there grew up a school of English portrait painters with Sir Joshua Reynolds and Thomas Gainsborough as leading masters. Compared with the older masters whose secrets they sought to recapture, they have only surface charm; but their portraits of David Garrick, Sarah Siddons, Dr. Samuel Johnson and of the English aristocracy are a valuable record of the artificial elegance of the England of their day. Reynolds was a more academic painter than Gainsborough, but Gainsborough had a better grasp on the deeper elements of design. He had too a special charm of light and texture and of vivacity and movement, with an undercurrent of romantic melancholy. The school ended with the superficially brilliant portraiture of the early 19th century.

French Painting.—The painter who brought into France something of the color, light and movement of Rubens and of the Venetians was Jean Antoine Watteau. He painted fairylike fetes of lovers in romantic landscapes and the Harlequins, Columbines and other actors of French and Italian comedy. He is slight as compared with Rubens, light and vivacious; but within his scope he is a master. His

FRICK COLLECTION

FRICK COLLECTION

EARLY NINETEENTH CENTURY painting took two directions. The conventional neoclassicism was best represented by Ingres, who idealized the aristocratic personality. This portrait, 1845, is expertly drawn, and color is used classically. By contrast, Goya's use of light and dark and his concern with the common people is shown in *The Forge*, 1818–1820.

delicately modulated light and dark move rhythmically in and out of space, his color breaks into jewellike and iridescent bits. His fairyland art degenerated in the hands of his followers into shallow and frivolous imitation.

The ingenious decoration of salon walls and ceilings with make-believe shepherdesses, dairymaids and classical divinities had a special vogue in the 18th century. Painters like François Boucher tried to merge the classical art of Poussin with the tradition of Rubens with resulting weakness but decorative charm. Jean Honoré Fragonard was more successful. Jean Marc Nattier was the painter of many portraits, artificial but decorative, of the French aristocracy posing as classical divinities.

Jean Chardin, following a path directly away from the fashionable, make-believe art of Watteau and Fragonard, was perhaps the finest painter of the century. He was a genre painter who turned the most trivial subjects into poetry. He painted his wife and children, their kitchen, the vegetables, meats, pots and pans; and he achieved a triumph in texture of materials, color and design.

About the middle of the 18th century came the first important discoveries among the ruins of Pompeii and Herculaneum. French taste of the day turned to the classical subject. Jacques Louis David inaugurated a classical movement in painting that successfully put an end to the frivolities of the salon decorators but at the same time destroyed the whole tradition of northern art. David succeeded in imposing his style upon almost the whole of Europe—the classical subject, figures like marble statues in their clear-cut contours and hard texture, flat tones of lifeless color,

stafuesque rigidity instead of movement.

The Spanish Goya.—Goya, who like David lived through the first quarter of the 19th century, stands out in vivid contrast, as a realist with exceptional human warmth and a brilliant technical method. His style descended from Velásquez, and he likewise was a painter of the Spanish court. He is distinguished for his character portrayal, his fine patterns of light and dark and his color harmonies. In

another aspect, in his illustration and satire of the corruptions and weaknesses of his day, he suggests the Englishman Hogarth.

THE NINETEENTH CENTURY

Classical Movement.—David's classical art proved to be only a curious break in the chain of tradition. Jean Ingres, his greatest follower, also subordinated color to line; but his classical works had much more life, and there was movement and vitality in his linear patterns. Pierre Paul Prud'hon was even romantic in his veiling of classical forms and his emotional use of light and dark.

French Romanticism.—Classical art could not hope to express the emotion and passion for liberty let loose by the French Revolution. Swift on the heels of classicism came the Romantic movement—life and color, play of light and shadow, the atmospheric edge, emotional expression, the tradition of Rubens reinstated. Subject matter changed to heroic events of the day or, in reaction against the classical subject, to the medieval story—the crusades, tales from Dante, Shakespeare or Byron. Eugène Delacroix was the leader. His special contribution lay in color, which he used to express emotion and to contribute to the drama of the situation. Sometimes he let color dominate so that we see his pictures as a pattern of color masses before we can distinguish what the patches of color represent. In this he anticipated Impressionism.

Naturalism in England.—Revolt against the idea that only subjects strange or remote in time or place were suitable for painting brought about a new naturalism—painters insisted upon expressing their fresh impressions of the world about them. This is some-

METROPOLITAN MUSEUM OF ART

JOHN CONSTABLE (1776–1837), *Salisbury Cathedral*. He was very much interested, as was Goya, in the effect of light on color variation. He was the first of the nineteenth-century painters to work outdoors, trying to depict the changes of light at different times of day. These were sketches, which he proposed to finish as paintings. His experiments with color and light in nature strongly influenced the Impressionists.

times called a new aspect of romanticism because of the sentimental attitude toward nature. The greatest impetus came from England in the work of John Constable who painted intimate scenes of his own England with the same love that the Dutch had lavished on the Holland countryside. He dared to cast away their green-brown scheme of color and paint nature's greens, making them more vital by painting what he called a *multitude of greens* in separate strokes instead of mixing them upon the palette. Constable painted only in the English summer, but he caught its exact character, its breezes, heat and heavy coloring, lowering storm clouds, rainbows and sudden bursts of sunshine.

Constable is a great contrast to his contemporary, Turner, who began by painting landscapes in the tradition of Claude Lorrain—vast, majestic, artificial—but developed an individual style of his own, marked by great luminosity and brilliance of color. His technique for achieving this was like Constable's, and the two men are considered forerunners of the French school of Impressionists.

The Barbizon School.—Paintings by Constable shown at the Paris Salon in 1824 stimulated Delacroix to further study of color and inspired a little group of revolutionary spirits who were founding a new school of French landscape painting. Theodore Rousseau settled in the little village of Barbizon on the edge of the Forest of Fontainebleau and began to paint intimate scenes of the French countryside. The permanence and strength of nature appealed to Rousseau; he built up the solid structure of his trees and placed them against a blue sky or flaming sunset. Charles François Daubigny, Diaz de la Peña and Jules Dupré were also at work in the forest—all different personalities but filled with the same sincere desire to express their vision of the world about them.

Jean François Millet (1814–75) added to the new landscape. He had a great reverence for Poussin and Michelangelo, and this appears in his simple paintings of the French peasant when he seizes just the essential lines to indicate a movement or to create the solid volume of a figure against a far-reaching plain.

Corot never lived at Barbizon, but he was allied in spirit to the group. His art was descended directly from Claude and Poussin. He introduced small classical figures into his landscapes and like Poussin created arabesques of line and mass. He was especially the painter of morning light, of the cool blue-green of foliage, of vanishing distance half-hidden by mist. He was even more important as a figure painter although less known as such.

Realism.—It was not Millet but a more aggressive personality, Gustave Courbet, who came to Paris in 1839 and succeeded in putting to rout the historic-romantic subject. He painted such subjects as a *Funeral at Ornans* and the *Stonebreakers* and many landscapes and marines of great vigor and breadth but photographically detailed.

His professed aim was to transcribe nature unadorned.

Honoré Daumier, who was also important in the cause of realism, was descended from Michelangelo, Rembrandt and Bosch. He painted in rich, somber color, giving only the essential volumes of his figures and binding them into strong spatial designs. Expressive line is important in the part of his work devoted to satire and character studies. He seems destined to live on—with Goya—as one of the two very great realists of the 19th century, because he added to his gifts as observer and reporter a genius for formal organization.

Impressionism.—Courbet had painted his out-of-door figures with the colors and shadows of the studio. Édouard Manet, who had discovered Velásquez, wanted to show the natural subject in natural light. Both his figures and background tended to become flat color masses. These he simplified so that they appeared to have almost no modeling and bound them into a decorative whole.

Light, as Manet once said, became the principal person in the picture. But Manet never went so far as his landscapist friends, Claude Monet and Camille Pissarro, who dissolved all form into atmosphere and broke up Manet's simple color masses into a wealth of changing hues. About 1870 Monet and Pissarro in their desire to add to Manet's light the brilliance of out-of-door color adopted a special technique of broken or divided color, based on the fact that a blue and red, for instance, placed side by side on the canvas, will produce a more luminous and brilliant violet than when mixed upon the palette. The stained-glass painters of the 12th century had understood this; so to some extent had Watteau, Constable and Turner. But the color impressionists made a scientific study of this technique; its possibilities stimulated new observation of nature and suddenly a whole new world of color was revealed, not the artificial jewellike gleam of the Flemish or the suffused glow of the Venetians but splendid in quite another way—in the shimmer, glitter and radiance of the light and atmosphere of out-of-doors.

Impressionism took the final step in freedom of subject matter, for when light and color became the chief interests no subject was too commonplace to interest the painter.

Postimpressionism.—Certain artists at first allied with the Impressionists, notably Manet, Degas and Whistler, created novel patterns in line and color, partially under the influence of Japanese prints, which were then coming into vogue. But most of the painters continued to imitate the momentary appearance of some fragment of nature in some particular light.

The reaction from Impressionism had two aspects, first a desire to recover the solider subject elements that the Impressionists had lost, and second, a conscious endeavor to push forward into new fields of plastic and decorative design. The new artists arose within the ranks of the Impressionist group. Renoir, one of the less radical insurgents, became interested

in recovering volume and structure and at the same time was inspired by the voluptuousness and fragile decorativeness of Boucher and the court painters. In his nude studies in particular he arrived at a sensuous loveliness and a feminine grace seldom paralleled in the history of painting.

Georges Seurat turned in the opposite direction and hardened rather than softened composition. He carried on the scientific study of color and has been called a *Neoimpressionist*. But it is clear from his too rare pictures that he is to be marked as a pioneer in the search for abstract and plastic values and is therefore a forerunner of the 20th-century *Expressionists*.

But the real father of Postimpressionism was Paul Cézanne, who said that he wanted to make something solid of Impressionism. He wanted volume and depth as well as color. He began to use color to intensify his form, painting not the accidental surface patches of light and dark and color but studying the way in which hues change as they advance into light and recede into gloom and using such advancing and receding colors to help build up his formal structure. Volume in itself has no artistic merit. but Cézanne's paintings, whether of apples and dishes on his kitchen table or of the far-reaching plains and distant mountains of his home in southern France, have their volumes composed, ordered in some compelling relationship.

THE TWENTIETH CENTURY

The ferment of change, which began in the France of the 19th century and which was realized by the exploration of Cézanne into the structural aspects of painting, gained new impetus with the rise to prominence of artists of such divergent natures as Vincent Van Gogh, Paul Gauguin, Henri Matisse, Georges Braque, and Pablo Picasso. They brought to art an almost volcanic outpouring of ideas, impelling in many directions an art which had been content for a century or more to imitate only the fleeting aspects of nature.

The impetus thus initiated brought to the fore a series of schools of painting: cubism, surrealism, expressionism, futurism, vorticism, synchronism and, of course, the continuing current of realism and naturalism. The urge to abstraction and away from realism was one of the outstanding characteristics of the first half of the twentieth century. A real interest in the visual reality of the academic school has not, however, languished. The untrained layman still prefers that which he understands, and his limited background and training confine his preference, for the most part, to the realistic school. With the growth of reproductions of paintings, a wider appreciation of abstractions ensued. This seeming confusion in art—resulting from the many schools and cults—was brought about by the insistent and prevalent scientific urge to know as much about the painter's craft as possible. A profound change in painting with international reverberations has resulted from this

Giotto di Bondome (1266-1337), St. Francis Breaks With His Father, Upper Church of San Francesco, Assisi, Italy

Botticelli, Sandro (1444-1510), Primavera (detail), Uffizi Gallery, Florence

Bruegel, Pieter (1525/1530—1569), The Beggars, the Louvre, Paris

Flemish, Italian
and Dutch
masters each
express character
differently
by variations in
composition,
light and texture

Leonardo da Vinci (1452-1519), The Madonna of
the Rocks (detail), the Louvre, Paris

Rembrandt van Rijn (1606-1669), Self-Portrait,
Wallraf-Richartz Museum, Cologne, Germany

Velazquez, Diego (1599-1660), Juan, a servant, Earl of Radnor's Collection, Salisbury, England

A Spaniard, two French Post Impressionists dramatize figures in their own lives: a Moorish servant, a Bohemian cousin, Tahitian women

Gauguin, Paul (1843-1890), Maternity, A Private American Collection

Toulouse-Lautrec, Henri de (1864-1901), G. Celeyran, Cousin, Musee Toulouse-Lautrec, Albi, France

Van Gogh, Vincent (1853-1890), Self-Portrait, Musee du Jeu de Paume, Louvre, Paris

Impressionists experimented with pastel to effect subtle changes of light, color

Degas, Edgar (1834-1917), The Tub, The Hill-Stead Museum, Farmington, Conn.

Klee, Paul (1879-1940), Fish Magic, Arensburg Collection, Philadelphia Museum of Art

Modigliani, Amedeo (1884-1920), Jeanne Hebuterne, Collection of Mr. and Mrs. Sidney F. Brody, Beverly Hills, California

Roualt, Georges (1871-1958), The Holy Face, Gallery Umeda, Osaka, Japan

Picasso, Pablo (1881-   ), Portrait of Madame Z, Home of the Artist

METROPOLITAN MUSEUM OF ART

CÉZANNE reworked impressionism's atmospheric light and color to create dynamic relationships between all connected elements of the picture. An abstract design forms the structure of *The Card Players*, 1890–1892, and results in a strong, "simplified" realism.

quest for forms. Political implications stem from the official favor gained by the realists in Nazi Germany, Fascist Italy and especially in Soviet Russia where only Socio-realistic art was officially permitted. Art, however, in the main has continued much as in past centuries to be free of entanglements. The search for the truth goes on. The leaders in the field continue to be little understood and little appreciated by the average person, since most people like what they know and do not really know what they like.

Dissatisfaction with surface realism forced the artist into an inquiry of all phases of structure and craft. The mechanical imitation of nature was foreordained to pass, since the invention and perfection of the camera gave the artist a tool which was at once a blessing and an evil. It was a blessing, for with the camera, the artist found both his superficial and inadequate observation of nature to be lacking, and explored fascinating unknowns. Creative painting gained much from the invention of such other scientific tools as the electronic microscope and x-rays. These tools permitted him to view minutia never before suspected and, in turn, hastened him to revaluate his world. Speculation into these strange and never-before explored areas forced the artist to seek new means of expressing himself, because the old proved insufficient. The camera was an evil, since the impact of new ideas affected a quickening of the departure from realism as it was known in the 19th century and produced a further widening of the gap between the truly creative artist and his audience. In truth, the scientific urge to view his world humanistically impinged upon the artist. He was impelled to translate this new consciousness, and his terms were inadequate. It is little wonder, then, that he had to turn to abstraction.

Picasso, Braque and Matisse, the great figures of cubism, continued the analysis begun by Cézanne. Picasso, as the great innovator, gave more impetus to this research than most, for his facile mind and quick Gallic spirit penetrated the surface into the hidden facets. He remains a commanding figure in the increasing ranks of the non-realistic group of artists. Matisse and Braque have held to a more constant style, content to perfect their chosen way of expression. de Chirico, Léger, and Rouault followed other paths. Rouault, much admired for his medieval mysticism, gave to contemporary art crushed jewel-like color which some have likened to the stained glass windows of the Medieval cathedrals he loves. To de Chirico has been assigned the title of surrealist inventor, a title which he did not seem to relish, since he later returned to rigid imitation of nature. Léger has lent to painting brightness of color, a boldness of solution, and an almost over-simplified concern for structural and surface design.

Miro, Kandinsky, Klee, Mondrian and a myriad of other painters have continued to search for the real into the remote fastness of the mind. These four are much admired by the younger group of abstractionists and, in the restless search for a means of articula-

tion, have been instrumental in contributing new expressiveness to the painter's language.

Vuillard, Vlaminck, Utrillo, and Chagall—to name a few—have gone their independent ways to contribute to the surge of internationalism in art. Each has a very personal way of expression. Each has his devoted followers, each his influence upon the younger painters. Vuillard, refined and finely characterized the cubistic tendencies. Vlaminck and Utrillo personalized and revitalized the realistic motifs. Chagall re-emphasized the mystical charm of the spirit.

Two and three-dimensional structural design has been brought to a high degree of perfection. Knowledge of these aspects of painting is greater than ever before, but it has not brought with it any greater painting. All things considered, there has, perhaps, been less great painting than in previous centuries, although production has been greater than at any other time in history.

Time will prove what many hold to be true, that world leadership in art has finally found residence in the United States of America. Painters of the stature of leaders in European art, such as Amadee Ozenfant, Max Beckmann, Salvador Dali, George Grosz, Max Ernst, and Eugene Berman, have forsaken Europe. Others have visited and painted in the U. S. because they found their readiest market there. Some artists, however, have professed to find the U. S. way of life to be alien to their best production.

PAINTING IN THE UNITED STATES

Painting in America has undergone some profound changes since Colonial days. From the early "limner", or face painter, to the contemporary abstractionist is indeed a far step. It has been said that a culture takes many centuries to develop, but, concerning the unfolding of American art, some variance from the normal pattern appears. It is not true, as generally believed, that the Puritans and the Quakers denied art a place in their life. The early art of real consequence in this country was developed in New England and in Pennsylvania, although their religions caused them to look with disfavor upon images and color; and certainly, in the normal religious existence, they did shun such things.

Not because of religious prejudice, but because of the material difficulties in a raw and undeveloped land, we were natively poor in artistic matters. Much of the labor was, of necessity, pledged to the development of industry, trade, and agriculture. As a well-to-do class emerged, we find the Puritans and Quakers importing much artistic furniture and, with it, paintings.

The influence of European culture on our own has been a mixed blessing. It has contributed mightily and yet has proven to be a curiously retarding fac-

METROPOLITAN MUSEUM OF ART

ROMANTICISM was the predominant mood of nineteenth-century American painting. George Caleb Bingham's *Fur Traders Descending the Missouri* is a celebration of the natural world.

tor in our growth. We, in a sense, have been in cultural bondage to Europe. Even so, in a period of two centuries, we have managed a definite withdrawal from European influence to become one of the most powerful forces in the shaping of future world art.

Since our main body of citizenry was of English stock, England was our natural source of cultural nutriment in colonial days. Nearly all of the early artists received their training there. England, however insular she may have been in other respects, owed much of her eminence in the arts to Italy and France. It was only natural that Renaissance and Baroque influences should be felt there as well as in other European countries. These influences were vicariously passed on to the colonies, since Benjamin West, Gilbert Stuart, Copley and others were directly inspired by such English painters as Gainsborough, Romney, Reynolds, Lawrence, and Raeburn. West remained perhaps the greatest influence, for, after his initial training in Italy, he elected to stay in London when the powerful Sir Joshua Reynolds was practically dictator of the arts in England. There he taught, and came to know a steady stream of American students. Thus he confirmed a close affiliation with the English school of painting.

For a long period the only real painting was being effected by the portrait painters, both those trained in Europe and the local "limners". The "limners" were more important than their trained colleagues who brought the more highly refined techniques to portraiture. The former endowed their work with an honesty of approach that had a rugged simplicity and great dignity. It was the habit of the "limner" to prepare his portraits in advance except for the face; thus he was termed a "face painter" and his work had a quality of planned design.

Along with the popularity of the portrait, historical and mythological sub-

jects became important through the influence of West. These continued to be the only real painting of importance for some time, although there were other native painters who preferred to depict similar subject matter. Among these were such painters as Edward Hicks, William S. Mount, Eastman Johnson, and George Caleb Bingham. Some, like George Catlin, wandered far into new territory to depict the life of the Indian and, in doing so, showed an adventurous spirit matched by later American artists in intellectual rather than physical departures.

The keen interest in the appearance of a remote and mysterious America ushered in a period of landscape painters who had much to do with the westward movement of our population. Thomas Moran and Bierstadt painted magnificent panoramic views of the west, exciting the eastern part of the country to pride in the land. The Hudson River school of landscape painting —Thomas Doughty, Thomas Cole, Asher B. Durand and John Frederick Kensett—gave a realistic turn to painting which found popular response here and in England. It may be said that these early painters contributed to the popularity of realistic painting today, for their influence has come down to us directly through such strong figures as George Innes, Winslow Homer, and Thomas Eakins.

Toward the end of the 19th century, more and more of our young painters flocked to Europe, especially to Paris, although some went to Munich and Düsseldorf. This division of loyalty between the French and German capitals of art and the waning of the English influence laid the basis for the controversy that now rages between the so-called schools of academic and abstract art. In Paris, the young American in the atliers of the academic painters learned subject matters and techniques chiefly concerned with realistic visual perception. In Düsseldorf and Munich, they learned a more direct approach

given to strong brush work and dominant contrast in design, of dark and light. In the main, however, both their arts were much concerned with the same kind of accurately visual rendering of nature. Later, the Paris school of Impressionism began to influence some of our painters; Childe Hassam, John Twatchman, Maurice Prendergast among others. This influence, in part at least, seems to have spurred the younger artist to more personal experiments. The final process of crystallization was accomplished by the famous Armory show of 1913 where young Americans exhibited side by side with Cézanne, Maillol, Brancusi, and Lehmbruck.

Those currents, which are prevalent abroad, do somehow seem to have their counterparts at home. We match a mystic like Rouault with an Albert Ryder, a realist like Manet with an Eakins, an abstractionist like Kandinsky with a Marin. There are many such comparisons that could be made, for individuals have their counterparts everywhere. Although we have not as yet produced figures of the stature of Picasso and Matisse, they will come.

The contemporary scene in America is filled with cross currents eddying out of the past. All the influences mentioned above are at work. The main question, however, seems to concern how abstract our art will become. Some fight for retention of realism since the public seems to prefer this type to all others. Others have gone to abstraction. Still others find much of value in both.

Edward Hopper and Charles Burchfield typify the best of the realist tradition, with youngster Andrew Wyeth contributing to the Homer realistic tradition. Max Weber, Abraham Rattner, Karl Zerbe, Max Beckmann, George Grosz, Jack Levine, and a host of others who give American art prestige, are highly competent painters retaining something of representation while gaining much from abstraction. In the tradition of Ryder we have men of the calibre of Morris Graves, Mark Tobey, and Kenneth Callahan of the Northwest, where a fusion of oriental and occidental influences is taking place.

The seeds of the impressionist, the realist, the cubist, the surrealist, and the abstractionist are not only firmly planted but crops are already being harvested. Hybrids of all sorts have been produced and we seem well on our way toward producing a genuine American art. Or, we might claim a real leadership in international art.

In this vast land there are so many painters of merit that it would be impossible to mention even the smallest fraction of them. Suffice it to say, that there is a stirring in the land that will produce great painters. Our youngsters are well trained in the techniques. They have achieved a degree of intellectual maturity and they are becoming increasingly more conscious of their own strength and of the realization that they are at last finding a place in the fabric of everyday life. They are being more and more accepted at home, and they will fully enrich the cultural pattern of America.

THE REALIST TRADITION is firmly rooted in America. Thomas Eakins' *The Gross Clinic* (*far right*) is reality arrested and defined. Edward Hopper's *Second Story Sunlight* imbues the ordinary daylight world with an unspoken and haunting intensity.

WHITNEY MUSEUM OF AMERICAN ART

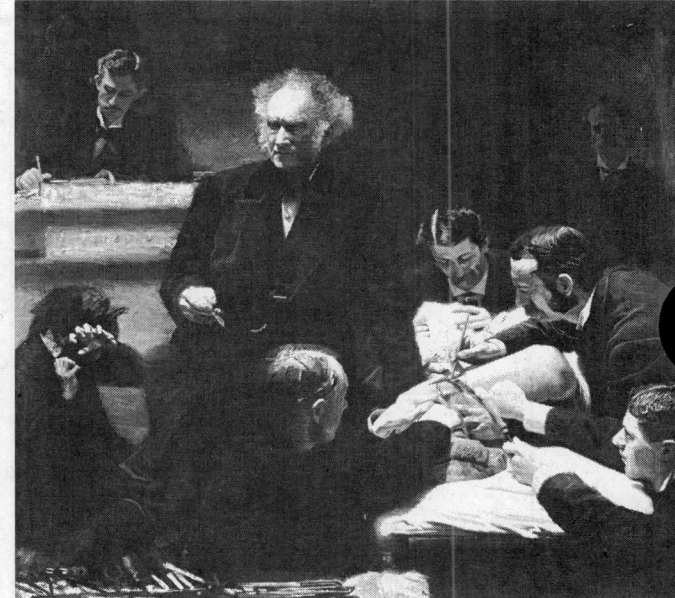

JEFFERSON MEDICAL COLLEGE

LITERAL DESCRIPTION of the outside world is no longer possible or desirable. The impact of Freud's discoveries, the social and political upheavals of two world wars, and new scientific advances have so changed man's understanding of the world that it is no longer enough to paint what the eye sees. As the camera takes over the task of representation, contemporary artists turn inward. Adolph Gottlieb, in *Blasts I* (*right*), shows two opposing natural forces. Morris Graves' *Blind Bird* (*far right*), enmeshed in threads of light, evokes Man's distress in a harsh world. Arshile Gorky's *Agony* is an abstraction, expressing emotion through the direct impact of form and color. Other artists, such as Robert Rauschenberg, (*far right*) turn away from classical contemporary art to "pop art," using the ordinary and the castoff, together with paint and canvas, in an attempt to show the modern world in terms of its own images.

MUSEUM OF MODERN ART

MUSEUM OF MODERN ART
MUSEUM OF MODERN ART

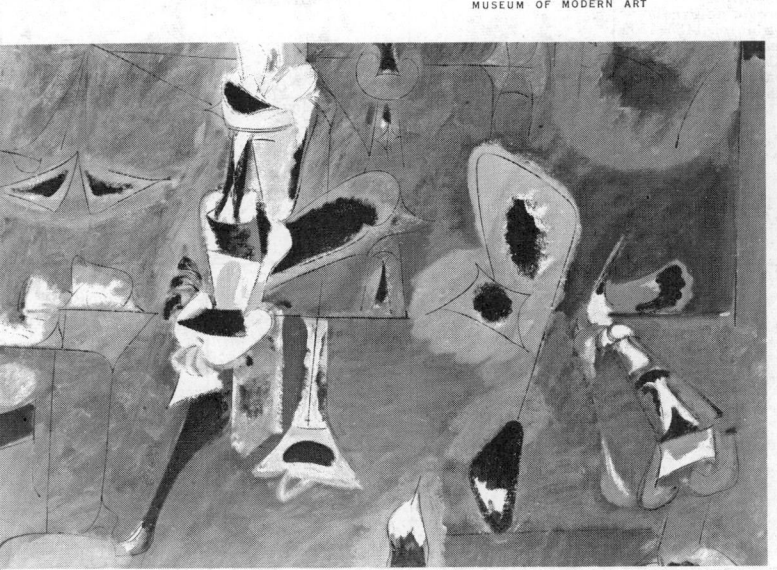

LEO CASTELLI GALLERY

GREAT PAINTERS

	ITALY			NETHERLANDS	GERMANY	FRANCE
	FLORENTINE	SIENESE				
Thirteenth and Fourteenth Centuries	Cimabue *c.* 1240–1302 Pietro Cavallini (Rome) 1250–1330 Giotto *c.* 1276–*c.* 1337 Taddeo Gaddi *c.* 1300–1366 Andrea Orcagna 1308?–1368 Spinello Aretino *c.* 1330–1410	Guido da Siena 13th century Duccio di Buoninsegna *c.* 1260–1319 Simone Martini *c.* 1283–1344 Pietro Lorenzetti active 1305–1348 Ambrogio Lorenzetti active 1323–1346?				Jean d'Orleans 1305–1408 André Beauneveu active 1360–1403 Jacquemart de Hesdin active 1384–1400
	FLORENTINE	UMBRIAN	VENETIAN AND NORTH ITALIAN			
Fifteenth Century	Masolino da Panicale *c.* 1383–*c.* 1447 Fra Angelico 1387–1455 Andrea del Castagno *c.* 1390–1457 Paolo Uccello 1396–1475 Masaccio 1401–1428 Fra Filippo Lippi 1406–1469 Benozzo Gozzoli 1420–1498 Alessio Baldovinetti *c.* 1425–1499 Antonio Pollaiuolo 1429–1498 Andrea Verrocchio 1435–1488 Cosimo Rosselli 1439–1507 Piero Pollaiuolo 1443–1496 Sandro Botticelli *c.* 1447–1510 Domenico Ghirlandaio 1449–1494 Leonardo da Vinci 1452–1519 Filippino Lippi *c.* 1457–1504 Lorenzo di Credi 1459–1537	Gentile da Fabriano *c.* 1370–1427 Sassetta (Siena) 1392–1450 Giovanni da Paolo (Siena) *c.* 1403–1483 Piero della Francesca *c.* 1420–1492 Melozza da Forli 1438–1494 Fiorenzo di Lorenzo *c.* 1445–1525 Luca Signorelli 1441–1524 Pietro Perugino 1446–1523 Bernardino Pinturicchio 1454–1513	Francesco Squarcione (Padua) 1394–1474 Vittore Pisano 1397–1455 Vincenzo Foppa (Pavia) *d.* 1462 Jacopo Bellini *c.* 1400–1470 Antonio Vivarini *d. c.* 1470 Giovanni Bellini *c.* 1426–1516 Gentile Bellini *c.* 1427–1507 Antonello da Messina *c.* 1430–1479 Cosimo Tura (Ferrara) *c.* 1430–*c.* 1495 Andrea Mantegna (Padua) 1431–1506 Francesco Cossa (Ferrara) 1438–1480 Bartolommeo Vivarini 1450–1499 Carlo Crivelli *c.* 1430–*c.* 1493 Francia (Bologna) 1450–1518 Ambrogio de Predis (Milan) *c.* 1455–1506 Cima da Conegliano *c.* 1459–*c.* 1517 Lorenzo Costa (Ferrara) 1460–1535	Hubert van Eyck *c.* 1370–1426 Robert Campin 1375–1444 Jan van Eyck *c.* 1390–1440 Jacques Daret active 1427–1468 Roger van der Weyden *c.* 1400–1464 Petrus Christus *c.* 1400–1473 Dirk Bouts (Dutch) *c.* 1410–1475 Justus van Ghent *b.* 1410 Hans Memling 1430–1495 Aelbert van Ouwater (Dutch) active *c.* 1450–*c.* 1480 Hugo van der Goes *d.* 1482 Gheerardt David *c.* 1450–1523 Jerome Bosch *c.* 1462–1516 Geertgen van Haarlem (Dutch) *c.* 1465–*c.* 1493 Quentin Matsys 1466?–1530	Stephan Lochner *d.* 1451 Michael Wolgemut 1434–1519 Martin Schongauer *c.* 1445–1491 Bartholomäus Zeitblom *c.* 1450–1517 Hans Holbein the Elder 1460–1524	Engverrand Charonton 15th century Henri Bellechose active *c.* 1415–1440 Jean Fouquet *c.* 1415–*c.* 1480 Jean Bourdichon 15th century Nicolas Froment active 1476
	FLORENTINE	VENETIAN				
Sixteenth Century	Mariotto Albertinelli 1474–1515 Fra Bartolommeo 1475–1517 Bernardino Luini *c.* 1475–*c.* 1533 Michelangelo Buonarroti 1475–1564 Il Sodoma (Siena) 1477–1549	Vittore Carpaccio *c.* 1450–*c.* 1522 Marco Basaiti *c.* 1470–1527 Titian 1477–1576 Giorgione da Castelfranco 1478–1511		Jan Gossaert (Mabuse) *c.* 1470–*c.* 1541 Jan Mostaert (Dutch) 1475–*c.* 1556	Albrecht Dürer 1471–1528 Lucas Cranach the Elder 1472–1553 Hans Burgkmair 1473–1531 Hans Baldung (Grün) *c.* 1476–1545	Jean Clouet 1485–1545

GREAT PAINTERS—Continued

Sixteenth Century—Cont.

ITALY — FLORENTINE—Cont.	ITALY — VENETIAN—Cont.	SPAIN	NETHERLANDS	GERMANY	FRANCE
Raphael (Umbria) 1483–1520 Andrea del Sarto 1486–1531 Giulio Romano (Rome) 1492–1546 Jacopo da Pontormo 1494–1557 Il Moretto (Brescia) c. 1498–1554 Bronzino, Il 1502–1572 Daniele da Volterra (Rome) 1509–1566 Alessandro Allori 1535–1607 Agostino Carracci (Bologna) 1557–1602 Annibale Carracci (Bologna) 1560–1609 Caravaggio (Naples) 1569–1609	Marcantonio Raimondi c. 1480–1534 Palma Vecchio 1480–1528 Lorenzo Lotto c. 1480–1556 Sebastiano del Piombo c. 1485–1547 Correggio (Parma) 1494–1534 Tintoretto 1518–1594 Giambattista Moroni (Brescia) c. 1525–1578 Paul Veronese 1528–1588	Luis de Morales c. 1509–1586 El Greco c. 1548–1614	Joachim de Patiner c. 1485–1524 Bernard van Orley c. 1491–1542 Lucas van Leyden (Dutch) 1494–1533 Jan van Scorel (Dutch) 1495–1562 Pieter Pourbus (Dutch) c. 1510–1584 Antonio Moro (Dutch) 1519–1576 Pieter Breughel the Elder c. 1525–1569	Albrecht Altdorfer 1480–1538 Matthias Grünewald c. 1480–c. 1530 Hans Holbein the Younger c. 1497–1543 Christopher Amberger c. 1500–1562	Corneille de Lyon 1500–1575 François Clouet c. 1510–c. 1572

Seventeenth Century

ITALY	SPAIN	HOLLAND	HOLLAND	FLANDERS	FRANCE

Guido Reni 1575–1642
Francesco Albani 1578–1660
Domenichino 1581–1641
Sassoferrato 1605–1685
Salvator Rosa 1615–1673
Carlo Dolci 1616–1686
 	
ENGLAND
Nicholas Hilliard 1537–1619
Isaac Oliver 1556–1617
Sir Peter Lely 1618–1680
	Francisco de Herrera 1576–1656
	José Ribera 1588–1656
	Francisco de Zurbarán 1598–1662
	Diego Velásquez 1599–1660
	Bartolome Murillo 1618–1687
		Frans Hals c. 1581–1666
		Jan van Goyen 1596–1656
		Rembrandt van Rijn 1606–1669
		Gerard Douw 1613–1675
		Gerard Ter Borch 1617–1681
		Philips Wouwerman 1619–1668
		Aalbert Cuyp 1620–1691
		Jan Steen 1626–1679
		Pieter de Hooch 1629–1677
		Nicolaas Maas 1631–1693
		Willem Van de Velde 1633–1707
			Adrian Van Ostade 1610–1685
			Ferdinand Bol 1616–1680
			Gonzales Coques 1618–1684
			Paul Potter 1625–1654
			Jacob Ruysdael c. 1628–1681
			Jan Vermeer 1628–1691
			Gabriel Metzu 1630–1667
			Ludolf Bakhuisen 1631–1709
			Meyndert Hobbema 1638–1709
				Peter Paul Rubens 1577–1640
				Frans Snyders 1579–1657
				Jakob Jordaens 1593–1678
				Anthony Van Dyck 1599–1641
				Adriaen Brouwer c. 1605–1638
				David Teniers the Younger 1610–1690
					Simon Vouet 1590–1649
					Jacques Callot 1592–1635
					Le Nain Brothers (3)
					  Antoine, c. 1588–1648
					  Louis, c. 1593–1648
					  Mathieu, 1607–1677
					Nicolas Poussin 1594–1665
					Claude Lorrain 1600–1682
					Pierre Mignard 1610–1695
					Charles Lebrun 1619–1690

Eighteenth Century

ITALY	UNITED STATES	ENGLAND	GERMANY / SPAIN	FRANCE	FRANCE
Giovanni Battista Tiepolo 1696–1770 Canaletto 1697–1768 Pietro Longhi 1702–1785 Francesco Guardi 1712–1793 Giambattista Piranesi 1720–1778 Bernardo Bellotti 1724–1780	Gustavus Hesselius 1682–1755 John S. Copley 1738–1815 Benjamin West 1738–1820 Charles Willson Peale 1741–1827 Gilbert Stuart 1755–1828 John Trumbull 1756–1843	William Hogarth 1697–1764 Richard Wilson 1714–1782 Sir Joshua Reynolds 1723–1792 Thomas Gainsborough 1727–1788 George Romney 1734–1802 Valentine Green 1739–1813 Sir Henry Raeburn 1756–1823 William Blake 1757–1827 John Hoppner 1758–1810 John Crome 1768–1821	**GERMANY** Anton Raphael Mengs 1728–1779 **SPAIN** Francisco de Goya y Lucientes 1746–1828	Nicolas Largillière 1656–1746 Antoine Coypel 1661–1722 Jean Baptiste Chardin 1699–1779 Jean Nattier 1685–1766 François Lemoine 1688–1737 François Boucher 1703–1770 Joseph Vernet 1714–1789 Jean Baptiste Greuze 1725–1805 Jean Honoré Fragonard 1732–1806 Gabriel Moreau 1740–1806	Hyacinthe Rigaud 1659–1743 Antoine Watteau 1684–1721 Nicolas Lancret 1690–1743 Jean Baptiste Pater 1696–1736 Maurice Quentin de La Tour 1704–1788 Joseph Vien 1716–1809 Clodion (Claude Michel) 1738–1814 Jacques Louis David 1748–1825

GREAT PAINTERS—Continued

	UNITED STATES		ENGLAND	FRANCE		OTHER COUNTRIES
Nine- teenth Century and Early Twen- tieth Century	John Vanderlyn 1775–1852 Edward Malbone 1777–1807 Washington Allston 1779–1843 Thomas Sully 1783–1872 Samuel F. B. Morse 1791–1872 Chester Harding 1792–1866 Henry Inman 1801–1846 Thomas Cole 1801–1848 Emanuel Leutze 1816–1868 George Fuller 1822–1884 William Hart 1823–1894 J. F. Crapsey 1823–1900 George Inness 1825–1894 James Abbott McNeill Whistler 1834–1903 A. H. Wyant 1836–1892 Winslow Homer 1836–1910 Thomas Moran 1837–1926 Robert S. Gifford 1840–1905 Thomas Eakins 1844–1916 Albert Ryder 1847–1917 Frank Duveneck 1848–1919 D. W. Tryon 1849–1925 Charles M. Dewey 1849–1937 Theodore Robinson 1852–1896 Edwin A. Abbey 1852–1911 Benjamin Foster 1852–1926 John Twachtman 1853–1902 Henry W. Ranger 1853–1916 L. Birge Harrison 1854–1929 George de F. Brush 1855–1941 John W. Alexander 1856–1915 John Singer Sargent 1856–1925 Willard Metcalf 1858–1925 Harry S. Mowbray 1858–1928 Childe Hassam 1859–1935 Frederick J. Waugh 1861–1940 Arthur B. Davies 1862–1928 Cecilia Beaux 1863–1942 Robert Henri 1865–1929 Max Bohm 1868–1923 William S. Kendall 1869–1938 William J. Glackens 1870–1938 John Marin 1870–1953 Frederick B. Williams 1871–1956 Charles W. Hawthorne 1872–1930 John Johansen 1876– Paul Dougherty 1877–1947 Maurice Sterne 1877–1957 Jonas Lie 1880–1940	Thomas Doughty 1793–1856 Asher B. Durand 1796–1886 Charles L. Elliott 1812–1868 Daniel Huntington 1816–1906 John F. Kensett 1818–1872 William Morris Hunt 1824–1879 Eastman Johnson 1824–1906 Frederic E. Church 1826–1900 James Hart 1828–1901 Edward Moran 1829–1901 Albert Bierstadt 1830–1902 John La Farge 1835–1910 Homer Martin 1836–1897 Elihu Vedder 1836–1923 Mary Cassatt 1845–1926 Ralph Blakelock 1847–1919 Edwin Blashfield 1848–1936 William Chase 1849–1916 Abbott H. Thayer 1849–1921 J. Alden Weir 1852–1919 Edward E. Simmons 1852–1931 J. F. Murphy 1853–1921 Will H. Low 1853–1932 Emil Carlsen 1853–1932 Leonard Ochtman 1854–1934 Kenyon Cox 1856–1919 Douglas Volk 1856–1935 Charles H. Davis 1857–1933 John Elliott 1858–1925 Elliott Daingerfield 1859–1932 Gari-Melchers 1860–1932 Frank Benson 1862–1951 Alfred Stieglitz 1864–1946 George Luks 1867–1933 Edward Redfield 1869– H. Breckenridge 1870–1937 John Sloan 1871–1951 Lyonel Feininger 1871–1956 Ernest Lawson 1873–1914 B. Robinson 1876–1952 Marsden Hartley 1877–1943 Daniel Garber 1880– Walt Kuhn 1880–1949	Thomas Lawrence 1769–1830 Joseph Mallord William Turner 1775–1831 John Constable 1776–1837 John Cotman 1782–1842 William Etty 1787–1849 Richard Bonington 1801–1828 Edwin Henry Landseer 1802–1873 George F. Watts 1817–1904 Alfred Stevens 1818–1875 Francis Haden 1818–1910 William Holman-Hunt 1827–1910 Dante Gabriel Rossetti 1828–1882 John Millais 1829–1896 Sir Edward Burne- Jones 1833–1898 Philip Steer 1860–1942 Maurice Prendergast 1861–1924 James Shannon 1862–1923 Charles Shannon 1865–1937 David Cameron 1865–1945 Frank Brangwyn 1867–1956 William Rothenstein 1872–1945 Sir William Orpen 1878–1931 Augustus John 1879–	Pierre Prud'hon 1758–1823 Antoine Jean Gros 1771–1835 Jean Dominique Ingres 1780–1867 Jean Theodore Gericault 1791–1824 H. Paul Delaroche 1797–1856 Paul Huet 1803–1864 Constant Troyon 1810–1865 Jules Dupre 1812–1889 Jean Francois Millet 1814–1875 Charles Daubigny 1817–1878 Theodore Chasseriau 1819–1856 Rosa Bonheur 1822–1899 Eugene Boudin 1824–1898 Gustave Moreau 1826–1898 Edouard Manet 1832–1883 Edgar Degas 1834–1917 Ignace Fantin-latour 1836–1904 Paul Cezanne 1839–1906 Alfred Sisley 1840–1899 Auguste Renoir 1841–1919 Eugene Carriere 1849–1906 Georges Seurat 1859–1891 Paul Signac 1863–1935 Pierre Bonnard 1867–1947 Georges Rouault 1871–1958 Raoul Dufy 1877–1953 Georges Braque 1881–	Georges Michel 1763–1843 Jean Camille Corot 1796–1875 Eugene Delacroix c. 1799–1863 Narcisso Diaz de la Pena 1808–1876 Honore Daumier 1808–1869 Theodore Rousseau 1812–1867 Thomas Couture 1815–1879 Gustave Courbet 1819–1877 Pierre Puvis de Cha- vannes 1824–1898 Jean Gerome 1824–1904 Jules Breton 1827–1906 Camille Pissarro 1813–1903 Claude Monet 1840–1926 Berthe Morisot 1840–1895 Odilon Redon 1840–1916 Paul Gauguin 1848–1903 Jeanne Lucien Simon 1861–1945 Henri Toulouse- Lautrec 1864–1901 Henri Matisse 1869–1954 Maurice de Vlaminck 1876–1958 Andre Derain 1880–1954 Fernand Leger 1881–1955	**GERMANY** Adolf Menzel 1815–1905 Franz von Lenbach 1836–1904 Hans von Marees 1837–1887 Wilhelm Leibl 1844–1900 Max Liebermann 1847–1935 Franz Marc 1880–1916 **SWITZERLAND** Arnold Bocklin 1827–1901 Ferdinand Hodler 1853–1918 Paul Klee 1879–1940 Andre Hofer active 1912–1930 **SWEDEN AND NORWAY** F. Thaulow (Norway) 1847–1906 Carl Larsson (Sweden) 1853–1919 Anders Zorn (Sweden) 1860–1920 Edward Munch (Norway) 1863–1944 **SPAIN** Mariano Fortuny y Carbo 1839–1874 Joaquin Sorolla y Bas- tida 1863–1923 Ignacio Zuloaga 1870–1945 Pablo Picasso 1881– Salvador Dali 1904– **HOLLAND** Johann Jongkind 1819–1891 Joseph Israels 1824–1911 Hendrik Mesdag 1831–1902 Jacob Maris 1837–1899 Anton Mauve 1838–1888 Vincent van Gogh 1853–1890 **ITALY** Adolphe Monticelli 1824–1886 Giovanni Segantini 1858–1899 Amedeo Modigliani 1884–1920 **MEXICO** Jose Clemente Orozco 1883–1949 Diego Rivera 1886–1957

GREAT PAINTERS—Concluded

	UNITED STATES		ENGLAND	FRANCE		OTHER COUNTRIES
Twen-tieth Century	Max Weber 1881–1961 Edward Hopper 1882– Charles Demuth 1883–1935 Leon Kroll 1884– Henry McFee 1886–1953 Thomas Hart Benton 1889– Charles Burchfield 1893– George Grosz 1893–1959 Stuart Davis 1894– Georg Hartmann 1894– William Gropper 1897– Reginald Marsh 1898–1954 Alexander Brook 1898– Bradley Walker Tomlin 1899–1953 Yves Tanguy 1900–1955 Morris Graves 1910– Willem de Kooning 1904– Jackson Pollack 1912–1956	Joseph Stella 1880–1946 George Bellows 1882–1925 Rockwell Kent 1884–1950 Bernard Karfiol 1884–1950 Marcel Duchamp 1887– Georgia O'Keeffe 1887– Grant Wood 1892–1942 Yasuo Kuniyoshi 1893–1953 Niles Spencer 1893–1952 Franklin C. Watkins 1894– John Steuart Curry 1897–1946 Ben Shahn 1898– Robert Brachman 1898– Pavel Tchelitchew 1898–1957 Arshile Gorky 1904–1948 Peter Blume 1906– Loren MacIver 1909– Mervin Jules 1912– Andrew Wyeth 1917–	Wyndham Lewis 1884–1957 Duncan Grant 1885– Henry Lamb 1885– Paul Nash 1889–1946 C. R. Nevinson 1889–1946 Gilbert Spencer 1892– Stanley Spencer 1892–1959 John Nash 1893– Ben Nicolson 1894– John Tunnard 1900– John Piper 1903– Graham Sutherland 1903–	Jacques Villon 1875–1963 Maurice Utrillo 1883–1955 Robert Delaunay 1885–1941 Jean (Hans) Arp 1888–1966 Moise Kisling 1891–1952 André Masson 1896– Christian Bérard 1902–1949	Raoul Dufy 1877–1953 André Dunoyer de Segonzac 1884– Marc Chagall 1887– Max Ernst 1891– Chaim Soutine 1894–1943 Jean Dubuffet 1901– Nicolas de Staël 1914–1955	James Ensor (Belgium) 1860–1942 Piet Mondrian (Holland) 1872–1944 Paul Klee (Swiss) 1879–1940 Ludwig Kirchner (Germany) 1880–1938 Giorgio de Chirico (Italy) 1888– Joan Miro (Spain) 1893– Candido Portinari (Brazil) 1903–1962 Rufino Tamayo (Mex.) 1900– Vasili Kandinsky (Russian) 1866–1944 Carlo Carrà (Italy) 1881– Max Beckmann (Germany) 1884–1950 Juan Gris (Spain) 1887–1927 Otto Dix (Germany) 1891– David Alfaro Siqueiros (Mex.) 1898– Sebastian Antonio Matta (Chile) 1912–

FAMOUS PAINTINGS IN IMPORTANT GALLERIES

I. In the Rijks Museum, Amsterdam

TITLE OF THE PAINTING	PAINTER	SCHOOL	COMMENTS
THE BUTTERY	Pieter de Hooch (1629–c. 1677)	Dutch	A study of light and space in the characteristic Dutch rectilinear pattern
WILLIAM II OF ORANGE AND HIS BRIDE	Van Dyck (1599–1641)	Flemish	The betrothal of William of Orange and Mary Stuart executed by the artist when he was painter at the Court of England
THE MILL	Jacob Ruysdael (c.1628–1681)	Dutch	Fine cloud structure and dramatic play of light and dark
GIRL READING A LETTER	Vermeer of Delft (1628–1691)	Dutch	Masterly in values of light, balance of spaces and harmony of color
SORTIE OF THE CIVIC GUARD	Rembrandt (1606–1669)	Dutch	In this picture, usually called the *Night Watch*, Rembrandt presented the members of this company not as sober portraits but for the rich play of light and shade
SYNDICS OF THE CLOTH HALL			Holds in one unified impression six powerful and individual portraits
VIRGIN AND CHILD	Fra Angelico (1387–1455)	Florentine	The gold curtain and the pattern suggest illuminated manuscripts

II. In the Royal Museum, Antwerp

ENTOMBMENT	Quentin Matsys (1466–c. 1530)	Flemish	Shows realism of types and brilliance and diversity of color
THE SEVEN SACRAMENTS	Roger van der Weyden (c. 1400–1464)	Flemish	Blends daily life of the people with medieval mysticism
THE MANDOLIN PLAYER	Ter Borch (1617–1681)	Dutch	Intimate home life of the Dutch aristocracy of his day
THE DAUPHIN OF FRANCE	François Clouet (c. 1510–c. 1572)	French	Every stroke of the brush counts in the simple, vivid characterization
SASKIA	Rembrandt (1606–1669)	Dutch	Portrait of his wife in one of the elaborate costumes he designed
ST. BARBARA	Jan van Eyck (1390–1440)	Flemish	An unfinished panel revealing the method of painting in the 15th century; pigment used as a glaze after the picture had been completely drawn and modeled in monotone
ADORATION OF THE MAGI	Rubens (1577–1640)	Flemish	Of his third period when light and color reached the peak
THE CRUCIFIXION			The majesty of Christ is contrasted with the violence of the thieves
CHRIST AND ANGEL MUSICIANS	Memling (1430–1495)	Flemish	Figures stand out in soft, light tones against a gold background

III. In the Walters Art Gallery, Baltimore

MADONNA AND CHILD	Mantegna (1431–1506)	Venetian	Pioneer effort at perspective rendering; classic theme
IMMACULATE CONCEPTION	Murillo (1618–1687)	Spanish	Showing his favorite subject in charming pattern and color
MADONNA OF THE CANDELABRA	Raphael (1483–1520)	Umbrian	Masterly skill and human feeling in his favorite subject
JUGURTHA BEFORE THE CONSUL	Tiepolo (1696–1770)	Italian	Delicate coloring in a spirited vigorous style

IV. In the Kaiser Friedrich Museum, Berlin

HIERONYMUS HOLZSCHUER	Dürer (1471–1528)	German	A powerful characterization of a man of impressive personality
MADONNA OF THE GOLDFINCH			Showing the influence of Venetian light and color
PORTRAIT OF A LADY			Lady against the sea. Executed with breadth of light and shadow
YOUNG LADY WITH PEARL NECKLACE	Vermeer of Delft (1628–1691)	Dutch	A splendid relation of tones and of color—blue and gold against gray
ALTAR OF JOHN THE BAPTIST	Roger van der Weyden (c. 1400–1464)	Flemish	A very small altarpiece showing the Baptism of Christ in the center
ADORATION OF THE CHRIST CHILD	Fra Filippo Lippi (1406–1469)	Florentine	A decorative background the Virgin adores the Child
THE CONCERT	Ter Borch (1617–1681)	Dutch	An example of the perfect color craftsmanship of the Dutch Little Masters
THE PROPHET ELIJAH	Dirk Bouts (c. 1410–1475)	Dutch	Shows the characteristic jewellike color, stiff figures and angular pattern
MAN WITH THE PINK	Jan van Eyck (1390–1440)	Flemish	Powerful and uncompromising realism in depiction of age and character

FAMOUS PAINTINGS IN IMPORTANT GALLERIES—Continued

IV. In the Kaiser Friedrich Museum, Berlin—Concluded

Title of the Painting	Painter	School	Comments
St. John Baptist in Wilderness	Geertgen (c. 1465–1493)	Dutch	Brooding figure of St. John in a spacious and decorative landscape
Madonna and Child	Quentin Matsys (1466–c. 1530)	Flemish	A very human mother kissing her child
Étienne Chevalier & St. Stephen	Jean Clouet (1485–1545)	French	Portrait of the king's treasurer and his patron saint
Hille Bobbe	Frans Hals (c. 1581–1666)	Dutch	The rollicking soothsayer of Haarlem painted in loose, bold brush strokes
Portrait of Child with Nurse			Showing a minute technique in rendering flesh but no sacrifice of lifelike quality
The Utrecht Canons as Pilgrims	Antonio Moro (1519–1576)	Flemish	Two impressively truthful portraits
Portrait of Titian's Daughter, Lavinia	Titian (1477–1576)	Venetian	The daughter of Titian; showing his usual skill in the treatment of flesh and sumptuous fabrics
Adoration of the Shepherds	Hugo van der Goes (d. 1482)	Flemish	Shows the realism of daily life
The Bladelin Altarpiece	Roger van der Weyden (c. 1400–1464)	Flemish	The Nativity, the Christ Child and a vision of the Virgin and Child

V. In the Museum of Fine Arts, Boston

Title of the Painting	Painter	School	Comments
Catalonian Fresco	(12th century)	Byzantine	Byzantine decoration of the apse of a little Romanesque church in Spain
Infanta Maria Theresa	Velásquez (1599–1660)	Spanish	Showing mastery of color values and relations, texture and brush
St. Luke Painting the Virgin	Roger van der Weyden (c. 1400–1464)	Flemish	Shows influence of the Italians
Hunting Scene	Gustave Courbet (1819–1877)	French	Hunting the roebuck in the high Jura
Emma and Her Children	George Bellows (1882–1925)	American	A portrait in bold technique, design and color
Portrait of George Washington	Gilbert Stuart (1755–1828)	American	Painted from life in 1796; considered the standard likeness

VI. In the Art Institute of Chicago

Title of the Painting	Painter	School	Comments
Retable and Altar Frontal	(14th century)	Spanish	Scenes from the life of Christ and the Virgin in the style of an enlarged miniature
Assumption of the Virgin	El Greco (1548–1614)	Spanish	This altarpiece of the soaring Virgin shows his own vivid coloring
Life of St. John the Baptist	Giovanni da Paolo (c. 1403–1483)	Sienese	Showing dramatic quality and fantastic treatment of landscape
Wings of Altarpiece	School of Amiens (15th Century)	French	Seven panels of great decorative quality
Virgin and Child	Roger van der Weyden (c.1400–1464)	Flemish	Brilliant jewellike color and texture
Rinaldo and Armida	Tiepolo (1696–1770)	Venetian	A great decoration in a brilliant style telling an idyllic love story
Two Little Circus Girls	Renoir (1841–1919)	French	Two jugglers, notable in design as well as in color and radiant light
Stoke-by-Nayland, Suffolk	Constable (1776–1837)	English	A landscape in his most spontaneous and vigorous manner
Sunday at the Grande Jatte	Seurat (1859–1891)	French	Illustrating his pointillist technique and vigorous design
The Bedroom at Arles	Van Gogh (1853–1890)	Dutch	The artist's own room; showing his emotional intensity
The Basket of Apples	Cézanne (1839–1906)	French	An achievement in design and in expression of form through color
The Interrupted Reading	Corot (1796–1875)	French	Showing Corot's treatment of the figure
The Home of the Heron	Inness (1825–1894)	American	Sensitive romantic treatment of mood in landscape

VII. In the Dresden Gallery

Title of the Painting	Painter	School	Comments
The Sistine Madonna	Raphael (1483–1520)	Umbrian	The Virgin and Child float forward in the clouds. World famous
Sleeping Venus	Giorgione (c.1478–1511)	Venetian	Brilliant color and golden glow—a Venetian nude Venus
Tribute Money	Titian (1477–1576)	Venetian	The story is told by two figures sharply contrasted in character and color
The Cheat	Caravaggio (c. 1609)	Neapolitan	An example of Caravaggio's realism and of his experiments in light
Lady Washing Her Hands	Ter Borch (1617–1681)	Dutch	A sensitive treatment of the intimate scene, especially fine in textures
Nativity	Correggio (c. 1494–1534)	Venetian	Movement among the figures and a dramatic light contrasted with night
Finding Moses	Veronese (1528–1588)	Venetian	A splendid design in swinging curves. The figures wear gorgeous costumes
Virgin, Child and Four Saints	Titian (1477–1576)	Venetian	A painting of beautiful texture and brilliant color

VIII. In the Pitti Gallery, Florence

Title of the Painting	Painter	School	Comments
The Concert	Giorgione (c. 1478–1511)	Venetian	Some critics attribute this to Giorgione; others to Titian
Pope Julius II	Raphael (1483–1520)	Umbrian	One of Raphael's greatest character interpretations
Granduca Madonna			One of his many treatments of this theme
Portrait of Ippolito de' Medici	Titian (1477–1576)	Venetian	A superb portrait of Ippolito in Hungarian hunting dress of rich purple velvet
Portrait of Cardinal Bentivoglio	Van Dyck (1599–1641)	Flemish	A distinguished portrait, in a scheme of brilliant reds
Madonna and Child	Fra Filippo Lippi (1406–1469)	Florentine	The design is a circular panel

IX. In the Uffizi, Florence

Title of the Painting	Painter	School	Comments
Birth of Venus	Botticelli (1447–1510)	Florentine	Born of the sea foam, the goddess is wafted ashore by the breath of the Winds
Adoration of the Magi			The group includes three of the de' Medici family
Spring			The goddess of Love presides over a springtime festival
Madonna Enthroned	Cimabue (c. 1240–c. 1302)	Florentine	One of the first efforts to revive the art of painting
The Annunciation	Simone Martini (1283–1344)	Sienese	An exquisite decoration on a background of gold
Heracles and Hydra	Antonio Pollaiuolo (1429–1498)	Florentine	A pioneer representation of the body in violent movement
Madonna of the Harpies	Andrea del Sarto (1486–1531)	Florentine	So named from the harpies which are carved on the pedestal
Portrait of the Duke of Urbino	Piero della Francesca (c. 1420–1492)	Umbrian	Remarkable for realism of characterization and for unity of linear pattern
Madonna of the Goldfinch	Raphael (1483–1520)	Umbrian	Raphael's characteristic pyramidal grouping against a spacious landscape
Altar of the Portinari Family	Hugo van der Goes (d. 1482)	Flemish	One of the most important Flemish altarpieces, so called because it was ordered by Tommaso Portinari
Holy Family	Michelangelo (1475–1564)	Florentine	The interest is in the composition and form of his figures
Coronation of the Virgin	Fra Filippo Lippi (1406–1469)	Florentine	Painted for the nuns of St. Ambrosio—radiantly informal, joyous and exciting
Deposition	Fra Angelico (1387–1455)	Florentine	Showing broad, panoramic treatment in pure sparkling color
Adoration of the Magi	Leonardo da Vinci (1452–1519)	Florentine	A rich, complicated, beautifully ordered picture

X. In the Hermitage, Leningrad

Title of the Painting	Painter	School	Comments
Evening	Claude Lorrain (1600–1682)	French	Expressing the mood of evening in imaginative and classical style
The Swamp	Jacob Ruysdael (c. 1628–1681)	Dutch	Sunlight playing through twisted trees, showing romantic attitude
Return of the Prodigal Son	Rembrandt (1606–1669)	Dutch	Showing the intense feeling with which Rembrandt interpreted the Old Testament stories and his dramatic use of light and dark to give accent and mystery
Sacrifice of Abraham			
Danae	Titian (1477–1576)		One of this artist's few essays in the nude figure
Old Woman in Black Head-dress	Rembrandt (1606–1669)		No one before Rembrandt so well realized the picturesque possibilities for play of light and dark on wrinkled face and knotted hands
Old Man with White Beard			
Card Player	Chardin (1669–1779)	French	Charm of subject together with a color, texture and pattern that delight the eye

FAMOUS PAINTINGS IN IMPORTANT GALLERIES—Continued

XI. In the Haarlem Museum, Haarlem

TITLE OF THE PAINTING	PAINTER	SCHOOL	COMMENTS
OFFICERS OF ST. GEORGE	Frans Hals (c. 1581–1666)	Dutch	Ruddy flesh tones set off by black costumes with crimson sashes
BANQUET OF OFFICERS OF ST. GEORGE			One of Hals' earliest known pictures. A vivid portrayal of a group
OFFICERS OF ST. ADRIEN			A wonderful canvas in which the subjects are completely characterized
REGENTS OF ST. ELIZABETH'S HOSPITAL			A portrait group with natural attitudes and gestures
LADY GOVERNORS OF ST. ELIZABETH'S			Every figure is a remarkably individualized portrait

XII. In the Royal Museum, The Hague

TITLE OF THE PAINTING	PAINTER	SCHOOL	COMMENTS
ROBERT CHESEMAN	Holbein (c. 1497–1543)	German	Portrait of the king's falconer richly dressed, showing superb textures
ANATOMY LESSON	Rembrandt (1606–1669)	Dutch	A group of excellent portraits in Rembrandt's earlier manner
ISABELLA BRANT	Rubens (1577–1640)	Flemish	Portrait of Rubens's first wife, suggestive of his Venetian inheritance
HELENA FOURMENT			A seated portrait of Rubens's second wife
VIEW OF HAARLEM	Jacob Ruysdael (c. 1628–1681)	Dutch	Dramatic play of light and dark on a linen bleaching scene near Haarlem
ANNA WAKE	Van Dyck (1599–1641)	Flemish	Showing splendid portrayal of texture and interesting pattern

XIII. In the National Gallery, London

TITLE OF THE PAINTING	PAINTER	SCHOOL	COMMENTS
AVENUE AT MIDDELHARNIS	Meyndert Hobbema (1638–1709)	Dutch	Shows splendid expression of distance
JAN ARNOLFINI AND HIS WIFE	Jan van Eyck (1390–1440)	Flemish	Minute detail with a new realism of light in every part
MAN WITH RED TURBAN			The great red turban contributes to the vitality of the portrait
MADONNA OF THE ROCKS	Leonardo da Vinci (1452–1519)	Florentine	Believed to be a copy of the Virgin in the Louvre
CHAPEAU DE PAILLE	Rubens (1577–1640)	Flemish	Portrait of the sister of Rubens's second wife
JUDGMENT OF PARIS			An example of mastery of form and rendering of golden flesh
CHÂTEAU STEEN			The country place of the Dutch painter, Jan Steen
DOGE LEONARDO LOREDANO	Giovanni Bellini (c. 1426–1516)	Venetian	A direct, forceful portrait; beautiful play of color—white, gold and orange against the old blue of the background
ORIGIN OF THE MILKY WAY	Tintoretto (1518–1594)	Venetian	Figures lightly poised in air, subdued harmony and luminous shadows
BACCHUS AND ARIADNE	Titian (1477–1576)		The effect of impetuous movement is carried through the whole group
THE TAILOR	Moroni (c. 1525–1578)	Brescian	Designed in a cool color scheme suggestive of the Spanish
LORD HEATHFIELD	Sir Joshua Reynolds (1723–1792)	English	One of his best works; a complete picture of English characteristics
LADY HAMILTON	Romney (1734–1802)	English	A delicate portrait free from sentimentality
VALLEY FARM	Constable (1776–1837)	English	An exhilarating, fresh, unaffected study of light in a landscape
THE SHRIMP GIRL	Hogarth (1697–1764)	English	Spontaneous, live painting; fresh color and bold handling
CANON AND PATRON SAINTS	Gheerard David (c. 1450–1523)	Flemish	Strongly individualistic portrait in a simple unified composition
MYSTIC MARRIAGE OF ST. CATHERINE			Shows delicate treatment of light
CORNELIUS VAN DER GEEST	Van Dyck (1599–1641)	Flemish	Strong interpretation of character and masterly drawing
COURT OF DUTCH HOUSE	Pieter de Hooch (1629–c. 1677)	Dutch	A study of a bright day without direct sunshine
MRS. SIDDONS	Gainsborough (1727–1788)	English	The face with its brilliant painting of flesh holds the interest
PHILIP IV OF SPAIN	Velásquez (1599–1660)	Spanish	Extremely simple and subtle in its rendering of form by color values
A FRANCISCAN	Zurbaran (1598–1662)	Spanish	A study of an impressive figure of simple and powerful design
ARTIST'S FATHER	Dürer (1471–1528)	German	The most minute detail, dominated by the intense vitality of the eyes
SELF PORTRAIT	Rembrandt (1606–1669)	Dutch	Simple in representation but subtle in its pattern of light and dark
THE FIGHTING TEMERAIRE	Turner (1775–1851)	English	Turner's brilliant color. The ship is being towed to her last berth

XIV. In the Prado, Madrid (before the Spanish Revolution)

TITLE OF THE PAINTING	PAINTER	SCHOOL	COMMENTS
THE YOUNG CARDINAL	Raphael (1483–1520)	Umbrian	Striking portrait of Cardinal Alidoro in brilliant-red robe and cap
FAMILY OF CHARLES IV	Goya (1746–1828)	Spanish	Ruthless characterization in the richest color and sparkling light
MARIE LOUISE OF PARMA			An unusually live portrait, a full-length figure in blues and greens
THE ENTOMBMENT	Titian (1477–1576)	Venetian	The emotional effect is achieved by movement of figures and the play of light
CHARLES V ON HORSEBACK			A portrait imaginative rather than realistic, but expressive of character
CRUCIFIXION	El Greco (1548–1614)	Spanish	Elongated forms and swift contrasts of light heighten the emotion
DON RODERIGO VAZQUEZ			Subdued color harmony in yellows and greenish blacks
PORTRAIT OF A MAN	Dürer (1471–1528)	German	A portrait, strong in characterization, of a Nuremberg banker
MARTYRDOM OF ST. BARTHOLOMEW	Ribera (1588–1656)	Spanish	Striking treatment of light and of various movements of the body
MARIE DE' MEDICI	Rubens (1577–1640)	Flemish	Painted to decorate the galleries of the Luxembourg
MAIDS OF HONOR	Velásquez (1599–1660)	Spanish	Picture of the Infanta Margarita with her maids, dwarfs and dogs
INFANTA MARIA THERESA			The Infanta, in rose and silver against a red curtain, stands facing the light
THE TAPESTRY WEAVERS			The figures in the sunlight are cleverly differentiated from those of the tapestry
THE TOPERS			The amazing life and realism of Velásquez' early manner
THE SURRENDER OF BREDA			Often called The Lances. The general receives the keys of the city
QUEEN MARY OF ENGLAND	Antonio Moro (1519–1576)	Flemish	A gorgeous court portrait of the determined queen
ADORATION OF THE MAGI	Jerome Bosch (c. 1462–1516)	Flemish	The artist's satiric fancy is shown in the actions of the rustics
DONOR AND ST. JOHN THE BAPTIST	Robert Campin (1375–1444)	Flemish	Two panels of a triptych in which the furniture and accessories are treated with extraordinary minuteness
ST. BARBARA			

XV. In the Alte Pinakothek, Munich

TITLE OF THE PAINTING	PAINTER	SCHOOL	COMMENTS
THE FOUR APOSTLES	Dürer (1471–1528)	German	Life-sized, intense and powerful figures showing breadth and grandeur
DAUGHTERS OF LEUCIPPUS	Rubens (1577–1640)	Flemish	Extraordinary rendering of form and movement in an allegory
THE LION HUNT			The dramatic struggle of wild animals organized into fine design
LANDSCAPE WITH CATTLE			Showing command over representation of space and of design in depth
ELEVATION OF THE CROSS	El Greco (1548–1614)	Spanish	Swift contrasts of light and dark heighten the emotional effect
DEPOSITION OF CHRIST	Rembrandt (1606–1669)	Dutch	Rembrandt manipulates his light for drama, emotional expression and the revealing of significant forms
SEVEN JOYS OF THE VIRGIN	Memling (1430–1495)	Flemish	An altarpiece, depicting events in the life of the Virgin

XVI. In the Frick Gallery, New York

TITLE OF THE PAINTING	PAINTER	SCHOOL	COMMENTS
ROMANCE OF LOVE AND YOUTH	Fragonard (1732–1806)	French	His masterpiece; an allegory in light decorative coloring
PORTRAIT OF COMTESSE D'HAUSSONVILLE	Ingres (1780–1867)	French	A serious color study in the classic technique
SAINT JEROME	El Greco (1548–1614)	Spanish	Cardinal's red robe gives color to serious character study
SIR THOMAS MORE	Holbein (c. 1497–1543)	German	A portrait unsurpassed for character and color harmony
MISTRESS AND MAID	Vermeer (1628–1691)	Dutch	Harmonious arrangement; remarkable shadow luminosity
LADY HAMILTON AS NATURE	Romney (1734–1802)	English	Shows grace and charm in brilliant color technique
CHOICE OF HERCULES	Veronese (1528–1588)	Venetian	Allegorical portraits, superbly drawn but weakly characterized
THE FORGE	Goya (1746–1828)	Spanish	Vivid color contrast and shadow technique with simple theme
THE POLISH RIDER	Rembrandt (1606–1669)	Dutch	An equestrian portrait of subdued color but studied grace
COLOGNE, EVENING	Turner (1775–1831)	English	Unusual golden color richly applied to a river scene
SAINT FRANCIS IN ECSTASY	Giovanni Bellini (c. 1426–1516)	Venetian	A pioneer use of landscape as a major interest in the theme

FAMOUS PAINTINGS IN IMPORTANT GALLERIES—Continued

XVII. In the Metropolitan Museum, New York

TITLE OF THE PAINTING	PAINTER	SCHOOL	COMMENTS
VILLE D'AVRAY	Corot (1796–1875)	French	A river with trees "drenched with light," in the cool of early morning
ABDUCTION OF REBECCA	Delacroix (c. 1799–1863)	French	A spirited and romantic illustration of Scott's *Ivanhoe*
PORTRAIT OF PHILIP IV	Velásquez (1599–1660)	Spanish	Known as the Villahermosa portrait
WHEATFIELDS	Jacob Ruysdael (c. 1628–1681)	Dutch	Extraordinary illusion of moving light with clouds scudding across the fields
YOUNG WOMAN WITH A WATER JUG	Vermeer of Delft (1632–1675)	Dutch	An effect of diffused light throughout the picture
WOMAN WITH A PARROT	Manet (1832–1883)	French	Subtle color study in tones of yellow-rose showing broad areas of light
PORTRAIT OF MADAME X	John Singer Sargent (1856–1925)	American	The brilliant style of Sargent at his simplest and best
ADORATION OF THE SHEPHERDS	El Greco (1548–1614)	Spanish	Flamelike movement throughout the canvas
DON SEBASTIAN MARTINEZ	Goya (1746–1828)	Spanish	Range of color and economy in rendering contrasted with detail
JAMES STUART, DUKE OF RICHMOND	Van Dyck (1599–1641)	Flemish	Has the characteristic rendering of varied textures
YONKER RAMP AND HIS SWEETHEART	Frans Hals (c. 1581–1666)	Dutch	A lively picture of a tavern scene in rich and varied color
THE MAINE COAST	Winslow Homer (1836–1910)	American	By the American realist whose marines are known for depth and power
CHRIST APPEARING TO HIS MOTHER	Roger van der Weyden (c. 1400–1464)	Flemish	The third panel of a famous triptych
HOLY FAMILY WITH ST. FRANCIS	Rubens (1577–1640)	Flemish	Life-sized figures of Virgin and Child with infant St. John
LANDSCAPE	Poussin (1594–1665)	French	Showing depiction of far distant space
MADAME CHARPENTIER & CHILDREN	Renoir (1841–1919)	French	In the cool delicate color of Renoir's early period
ARISTOTLE CONTEMPLATING THE BUST OF HOMER	Rembrandt (1606–1669)	Dutch	Dramatic juxtaposition of shadow and light; rich tonal values

XVIII. In the Louvre, Paris

MONA LISA	Leonardo da Vinci (1452–1519)	Florentine	Often called La Gioconda. The most subtle interpretation of character and an equally subtle modeling of form
MADONNA OF THE ROCKS			An original and intense conception in a romantic setting
MADAME RÉCAMIER	Louis David (1748–1825)	French	The classical portrait at its best—a finely organized pattern of flowing line
THE GLEANERS	Millet (1814–1875)	French	Powerfully constructed figures in rhythmic movement against a vast plain
MARRIAGE AT CANA	Veronese (1528–1588)	Venetian	The Bible story converted into a gorgeous banquet of the Renaissance
MAN WITH THE GLOVE	Titian (1477–1576)	Venetian	One of the great portraits of all time, in the lyrical spirit of youth
THE ENTOMBMENT			A dramatic and poignant rendering rich in color and in arabesque
THE LACE MAKER	Vermeer of Delft (1628–1691)	Dutch	A broad and simple treatment of light in a scheme of blue and yellow
OLYMPIA	Manet (1832–1883)	French	The delicacy of flesh set off by varied whites
SHEPHERDS IN ARCADIA	Poussin (1594–1665)	French	A French version of the classical tradition of the Italian Renaissance
SUPPER AT EMMAUS	Rembrandt (1606–1669)	Dutch	Use of light and dark to create deep religious feeling
HENDRICKJE STOFFELS			Splendid modeling, characteristic illumination, suggestive treatment
BANKER AND HIS WIFE	Quentin Matsys (1466–c. 1530)	Flemish	One of the earliest examples of *genre* painting for its own sake
GIPSY GIRL	Frans Hals (c. 1581–1666)	Dutch	An impression of movement and dashing use of the brush
MYSTIC MARRIAGE OF ST. CATHERINE	Correggio (c. 1494–1534)	Venetian	A study in light and in brilliant transparent color, like that of Venetian glass
PASTORAL SYMPHONY	Giorgione (c. 1478–1511)	Venetian	Showing romantic quality and warm glow of color
LA BELLE JARDINIÉRE	Raphael (1483–1520)	Umbrian	One of the finest of Raphael's series of the Madonna and Child
VIRGIN AND CHILD WITH CHANCELLOR ROLIN	Jan van Eyck (1390–1440)	Flemish	Showing Jan van Eyck's jewellike color, his portrayal of character, of texture, and of the intimate and picturesque details of Flemish life
PORTRAIT OF ERASMUS	Holbein (c. 1497–1543)	German	Powerful characterization has seldom been carried so far as in this portrait
EMBARKATION FOR CYTHERA	Watteau (1684–1721)	French	The light suffusing the canvas moves in rhythmic pattern
LA SOURCE	Ingres (1780–1867)	French	The simple modeling, the delicacy and truth of line reveal classical qualities
LA KERMESSE	Rubens (1577–1640)	Flemish	Realistic and exuberant portrayal of Flemish peasant life
LANDING OF MARIE DE MÉDICIS AT MARSEILLE			One of the series of twenty-one decorative canvases of episodes in the life of Marie de Médicis
INFANTA MARGARITA	Velásquez (1599–1660)	Spanish	Exquisite color and subtle tone values in satin dress and silky hair
CHARLES I	Van Dyck (1599–1641)	Flemish	An achievement in color and clever subordination of unimportant figures
MOTHER	Whistler (1834–1903)	American	A subtle characterization called *An Arrangement in Gray and Black*
THE BURIAL AT ORNANS	Courbet (1819–1877)	French	This sincere and vigorous painting initiated the realistic movement
DANTE AND VIRGIL	Delacroix (c. 1799–1863)	French	The intensity and emotional color are significant of the new Romanticism
THE BLUE VASE	Cézanne (1839–1906)	French	A still-life resolved into perfect order of line and color and space
MADONNA	Memling (c. 1430–1495)	Flemish	Showing the artist's seductive color and polished technique

XIX. In the Huntington Gallery, San Marino, Calif.

MRS. SIDDONS AS TRAGIC MUSE	Reynolds (1723–1792)	English	One of the world's most-loved portraits in superb color harmony
THE MISSES BECKFORD	Romney (1734–1802)	English	Superficial characterization in brilliant, transparent coloring
LADY BEAUCHAMP	Hoppner (1758–1810)	English	Portrait of a lady of fashion in the best taste of the age
PINKIE: MARY MOULTON-BARRETT	Lawrence (1769–1830)	English	Restraint and idealism in a gay informal portrait study
MASTER WILLIAM BLAIR	Raeburn (1756–1823)	English	Realism in vivid style and graceful portrait technique
THE BLUE BOY	Gainsborough (1727–1788)	English	Masterly portrait composition with startlingly massed blues

XX. In the Villa Borghese, Rome

SACRED AND PROFANE LOVE	Titian (1477–1576)	Venetian	Richness of color and texture of nude forms and sumptuous fabrics
THE ENTOMBMENT	Raphael (1483–1520)	Umbrian	A serious theme in a confused style and arrangement
DIANA AND HER NYMPHS	Domenichino (1581–1641)	Bologna	Spirited nude girls in a landscape setting
DANAE	Correggio (c. 1494–1534)	Venetian	Showing illusion of depth and imaginative treatment of the Greek myth

XXI. In the Vatican Gallery, Rome

TRANSFIGURATION	Raphael (1483–1520)	Umbrian	Good example of space design and use of gesture to unite figures
MADONNA DI FOLIGNO			With portrait of Sigismondo Conti as donor
THE ENTOMBMENT	Caravaggio (1569–1609)	Naples	One of his most important paintings; drastic contemporary tragedy
MADONNA IN GLORY WITH SIX SAINTS	Titian (1477–1576)	Venetian	Below the Mother, Child and angels are the six saints
PORTRAIT OF SIXTUS IV	Melozzo da Forli (c. 1438–1494)	Umbrian	Historical portrait group of Sixtus IV, his librarian and attendant cardinals
ST. ANTONIO AND SAINTS	Antonio Vivarini (d. c. 1470)	Venetian	Characteristic of conservative tendencies in Venetian painting before advances of the remarkable Bellini family

XXII. In the Royal Gallery of Fine Arts, Venice

MADONNA OF THE TWO TREES	Giovanni Bellini (c. 1426–1516)	Venetian	Showing breadth of modeling and life and vitality
THE DREAM OF ST. URSULA	Carpaccio (c. 1450–1522)	Venetian	The angel offers to the dreaming Ursula the martyr's palm
PRESENTATION OF CHRIST IN TEMPLE			Ruskin considered this the most beautiful baby Christ in all Venetian art
MIRACLE OF ST. MARK	Tintoretto (1518–1592)	Venetian	Irresistible rhythm of movement in space and golden brilliance of color
CAIN KILLING ABEL			Dramatic expression; superbly balanced masses of light and shade
PROCESSION IN PIAZZO OF SAN MARCO	Gentile Bellini (c. 1427–1507)	Venetian	A procession, showing the artist's capacity as painter of light and air

FAMOUS PAINTINGS IN IMPORTANT GALLERIES—Concluded

XXIII. In the Imperial Gallery, Vienna

TITLE OF THE PAINTING	PAINTER	SCHOOL	COMMENTS
MADONNA OF THE CUT PEAR	Dürer (1471–1528)	German	The German type of Madonna painted with minute precision
MADONNA WITH CHERRIES	Titian (1477–1576)	Venetian	The more mature type of Virgin and informal composition
GIPSY MADONNA			This picture foreshadows the splendor of his later coloring
PORTRAIT OF JANE SEYMOUR	Holbein (c. 1497–1543)	German	Portrait of the third wife of King Henry VIII in miniaturelike style
PORTRAIT OF HELENA FOURMENT	Rubens (1577–1640)	Flemish	Portrait of Rubens's second wife, nude with only a fur coat about her
MIRACLE OF ST. ILDEFONSO			A mature work in which light and color had become major interests
INFANTA MARGARITA THERESA	Velásquez (1599–1660)	Spanish	A portrait in a color scheme of silver, black and coral
HUNTERS IN THE SNOW	Breughel (c. 1525–1569)	Flemish	An innovation in landscape and representation of great space
THE RUSTIC WEDDING			Red caps, white coifs and yellow omelettes in an unusual color harmony
PORTRAIT OF HIS MOTHER	Rembrandt (1606–1669)	Dutch	Rembrandt was probably the first artist to interpret old age with sympathy
MADONNA OF THE MEADOW	Raphael (1483–1520)	Umbrian	Painted in 1506 under the influence of Leonardo da Vinci
BIRTH OF CHRIST	Gheerard David (c. 1450–1523)	Flemish	Remarkable for its effect of light which emanates from the Child's body
VIRGIN AND DONOR	Memling (1430–1495)	Flemish	Depicting the Virgin and worshiping donor in the central panel

XXIV. The National Gallery (Mellon Foundation), Washington

TITLE OF THE PAINTING	PAINTER	SCHOOL	COMMENTS
ADORATION OF THE MAGI	Botticelli (c. 1447–1510)	Florentine	One of several subjects done in the traditional classic method
SALISBURY CATHEDRAL	Constable (1776–1837)	English	Masterpiece of perspective and charming color harmony
MARQUESA DE PONTEJOS	Goya (1746–1828)	Spanish	Characteristic brilliant color contrast and vivid style
OFFICER WITH RED SASH	Hals (c. 1581–1666)	Dutch	A vigorous character study
LA FERME AU SOLEIL	Hobbema (1638–1709)	Dutch	Simple realistic study in superb lights and shadings
ALBA MADONNA	Raphael (1483–1520)	Umbrian	A simple study full of character and grace
ISABELLA BRANT	Rubens (1577–1640)	Flemish	Blending of Venetian and Flemish color techniques
TOILET OF VENUS	Titian (1477–1576)	Venetian	Unsurpassed rich golden flesh tones and human feeling
LORD PHILIP WHARTON	Van Dyck (1599–1641)	Flemish	Sensitive portraiture and finished technique
LACE MAKER	Vermeer (1628–1691)	Dutch	Distinguished by luminous color and harmony of design

This list is merely an introduction to the great galleries of the world and some of their treasures. It does not include all of the accepted masterpieces nor does it include all the museums. Some of the smaller museums may be very important because of the paintings housed there. Many of the most famous paintings of the world are not in museums, but rather in churches and buildings for which they were originally painted. For instance, the paintings of Giotto are in the Arena Chapel at Padua; the greatest paintings of Rome are not in galleries, but in the apartments of the Vatican decorated with the great frescoes of Raphael, and in the Sistine Chapel where Michelangelo spread upon the ceiling his great drama of creation.

Since the second World War many of the famous paintings listed above are missing from their accustomed places on the walls of museums, particularly in Germany and Austria. Whether or not they will soon reappear is not known.

SCULPTURE

Sculpture in the strict sense of the word refers only to works carved or cut by hand in some solid substance; but the term is commonly extended to include all three-dimensional figuring, whether carved, molded, hammered, cast or engraved.

MATERIALS AND METHODS

Almost every imaginable material has been used—gold, silver, bronze, ivory, marble and other stones, wood, clay, wax and plaster. Sometimes several materials are combined.

Polychromy.—We are so accustomed to a colorless sculpture in stone that we forget how large a part was played in the past by polychromy, the art of giving a colored surface to sculpture. This was particularly the practice among the Babylonians, Egyptians, Assyrians and early Greeks. It survived through the best Greek periods and was used by Etruscan, Roman, medieval and Renaissance artists. As most of this color gradually wore off when exposed to the weather, it is difficult to understand exactly how a great deal of the sculpture appeared when it came from the sculptor's hand. On the colored and glazed terra cottas the color was permanent. The lions and other animals and figures built up of enameled tiles in relief, found at Babylon, Susa and Khorsabad, show how familiar this method

ALINARI ART REFERENCE BUREAU

THE ANCIENT ART of coloring sculpture is seen in Della Robbia's fifteenth-century glazed relief of the Madonna and Child now in the National Museum, Florence.

was to the ancient Orient. The most famous later examples are the terra cottas of the Italian Renaissance, called *Robbia ware* because they were made by the Della Robbia family.

The remains of polychromatic Greek sculpture are enough to show that brilliant and heavy coloring was used at an early date, especially in architectural sculptures. As soon as marble replaced other stone it was not necessary to stucco and paint the entire surface, and the polychromy was gradually restricted to patterns and borders and to shading the eyes, the hair and other details. Statues of women found on the Acropolis, after being buried there since about 480 B.C., show the most exquisite of the early coloring. We are told that Nicias, a famous painter, was accustomed to color the masterpieces of the sculptor Praxiteles.

Surface Treatment.—There is great variety in the treatment of surfaces, from sculpture in the round at one end to intaglio or incised design below the surface, used particularly in precious and semiprecious stones. In intaglio the design is often reversed. Sometimes the design is merely scratched or outlined on the surface, as in Greek and Etruscan bronze mirrors and jewel cases, but this is really more like engraving than sculpture. Next comes work in which the background is but slightly lowered, and the figures are left standing in slight relief, sometimes in connection with figures in higher relief in the same composition. The Romans combined figures on different planes in a single composition with the figures in the foreground nearly detached and held by only one or two members of the figures behind them. This gives practically the effect of statuary.

In statuary or sculpture in the round, the figure is freestanding on all sides, as in statues that stand upon pedestals, to be viewed from any angle.

Objectives of Sculpture.—Sculpture of the human figure has a triple aim: to express plastic beauty of form, to embody thought and feeling and to act as a chronicler of facts. Naturally it is impossible to accomplish this triple aim with equal emphasis on the three parts, and different civilizations have stressed one or another aspect. In general it may be said that the Oriental countries have magnified plastic or abstract values or as we say, have formalized their sculpture; but in Greece, Rome and Renaissance Italy factual or naturalistic representation prevailed.

The special character of sculpture gave it certain limitations. Sculpture cannot tell a story with the same detail as painting. But it can embody a natural or idealized representation of typical humanity better than painting.

At the other extreme is sculpture turned into pictorial channels; this was mainly in relief work, especially after the Romans had used a multiplicity of figures in several planes. The reliefs of Greco-Roman art with their backgrounds of landscape and architecture and the spiral narrative of Trajan's Column lead up to such elaborate compositions as the bronze doors of the baptistery of Florence, the work of Lorenzo Ghiberti (c. 1378–1455). In this sort of relief, modern critics believe, sculptors were trying unwarrantedly to do the work of painting, and the trend is to appreciation of the solider and less involved types of work. If one part of the mission of sculpture is to express plastic beauty of form, they say, the expression should be obviously sculptural and therefore to an extent heavy and rocklike, not light and painty.

HISTORY OF SCULPTURE

Bird's-Eye Views.—Sculpture has had a history of at least 6,000 years. Aside from the crude statuettes of the Old Stone Age and similar works found in many parts of the world from the time when mankind was emerging from prehistory into the earliest phases of civilization, the first flowering of sculpture came about 3000 B.C. when Egyptian culture began to take shape. During the next 300 years the Egyptians produced some of the noblest examples of sculptural art known to history. Even earlier the Mesopotamian culture of the Sumerians or early Babylonians was assuming definite form; but in that region sculpture was not an outstanding accomplishment until many centuries later, when the Assyrians and later

Babylonians developed the art of relief carving to a notable degree.

In the light of modern archeological findings, it is safe to say that magnificent sculpture had been achieved long before the advent of the Greeks. Explorers and scholars are still reconstructing our knowledge of the little-known Scythians and other steppe peoples of Asia, who left beautiful relics in small metal sculpture; but we do not know whether it was before or after the Greek flowering. The early history of Chinese sculpture also is veiled in doubt.

By 500 B.C. the Greeks had already produced that portion of their art known as *archaic.* At this time a tide of realism and idealization got underway that set the standard in Europe for many centuries to follow. The immediate result of the Greek devotion to a clear, natural art was the creation of a long series of *classic* masterpieces dating from the time of the Parthenon artists.

With the fall of Rome there came something of a dark age for sculpture. Before the last Roman monuments had been erected, however, the Byzantine style had developed in small sculpture in the Near East and Egypt. Sculpture flowered again with the emergence of the Romanesque style of building. There is no real dividing line between Romanesque and Gothic work, and the abundant and gorgeous sculptures that are still to be seen on the great Gothic cathedrals are best studied with the Romanesque under the general name *medieval.* They represent one of the major achievements of the art.

Contemporary with the Gothic development in the north of Europe, Italian artists were reviving the ideals of Rome. By the end of the 13th century the seed of the Renaissance had been sown. Thenceforward the revival of classic forms shaped the course of sculpture in the western world except for the work of the nonconformist genius, Michelangelo. From the time of the mid-Renaissance, when naturalistic and pictorial sculpture reached again the pitch of perfection touched by the Romans, the art gradually declined and grew artificial. In their better manifestations these artificial and involved forms are called *baroque.* Towards the end of the 19th century there was a further revival of realism, this time scientifically and even photographically exact; and this gave way to the Modernism of the 20th century, which is frankly antirealistic and akin to the efforts and aims of Oriental sculpture.

In the Far East sculpture has from earliest times taken a course directly away from the naturalism and idealism of the West. In the countries of most importance in Asiatic art, Persia, India, Java, Cambodia, China and Japan, the ideals have been formal and decorative. Indian, Cambodian and Chinese sculpture may be said to have been expressionistic through all history. China especially is rich in monuments that look strange and even abnormal if one limits appreciation to the Greek conception; but in the wider view of sculpture the Chi-

nese have produced a greater and more varied body of beautiful works than any other people.

Egyptian Sculpture.—In Egypt sculpture ranges over more than 3,000 years. In that time the changes are many, but a recognizable character runs through the nation's achievement from beginning to end. In general Egyptian sculpture is massive, solid and dignified. The best of it is nobly monumental, impersonal and serene, as befits an art closely related to religious beliefs and customs. On the other hand there are works as graceful, charming and intimate as any to be encountered in Europe or Asia.

Three main periods of creativeness are generally marked. In the *Old Kingdom,* which began about 2980 B.C., the sculptors produced some of the outstanding masterpieces of monumental art. The subjects are usually kings (portrayed perhaps as gods), nobles and officials. In these there is the characteristic Egyptian amplitude, massiveness and dignity. The bodies are in general standardized, appearing in a few conventional poses. But the heads are likely to be realistically individual, with as fine a combination of exact rendering and sculptural stylization as one can find

METROPOLITAN MUSEUM OF ART

IN ANCIENT EGYPT rank and importance were shown by size; this official was more important than his wife or daughter.

in the whole annals of the art. In other words the statue becomes at once an unmistakable likeness of the sitter and a formal creation of inescapable beauty. Such particularly is one of the best-known of the large rock-cut works, the *Seated Figure of King Khafre* (c. 2800 B.C.). This and the statue in wood called *The Village Magistrate* should be known to well-informed art lovers as favorably as the Parthenon marbles and the later Greek *Venuses* and *Victories.*

The realism of *The Village Magistrate* and of a great number of less masterly works is explained by a very special intention on the part of the artists, growing out of the Egyptian

METROPOLITAN MUSEUM OF ART

BREAD, WINE, FRUIT, and meat are among the offerings the Pharaoh Rameses and his wife are shown presenting to the god Osiris in this relief from the Temple of Abydos, Egypt.

religion. It was believed that the soul of the deceased would return at intervals to inhabit the body and in case anything should have happened to the body portrait statues were provided with heads so realistic that the soul would be sure to recognize it. Hence the pains to reproduce every smallest peculiarity and the filling of the chamber tombs of Egypt with such statues.

In the figures of the god-kings, such as the *Khafre,* there was an effort to add to the likeness a feeling of grandeur and majesty. The quality becomes at times one of aloofness and other-worldliness; the supreme example of this being the famous *Sphinx* near the pyramids at Giza, near Cairo, where a natural outcropping of rock is carved into a colossal statue, having a body of a lion and the head of a man, the face bearing an enigmatic expression.

In later eras the sculpture of the Old Kingdom was freely copied, sometimes beautifully, oftener with loss of the finer characteristics. A true renaissance occurred during the Middle Kingdom, about a thousand years after the time of King Khafre, and some of the most magnificent regal statues date from the period. It was, however, after another lapse of centuries, in the so-called New Kingdom, that a totally different sort of excellence was accomplished. Under King Ikhnaton, a ruler who brought a new freedom in the arts, there were produced portrait statues which combined amazing character portrayal with solid sculptural virtues. The faces are so clear a revelation of the inner man or woman that we of today find these studies, 33 centuries old, modern in our sense of the word. The finest examples are heads and busts of Ikhnaton, of Nefretete his queen and of their daughters.

In all the forms of monumental and portrait sculpture, the Egyptians must

be ranked as among the three or four foremost peoples of all times. To this should be added the fact that they have left more masterly relief art, literally untold miles of it, than any other nation. The relief sculptures that line the tomb walls of important personages tell amazingly full and engaging stories of the life of these pleasure-loving and pious people. And in the tombs have been found exceptionally beautiful craftwork enriched with miniature forms of sculpture: household utensils, jewelry and jewel boxes, combs and decorated furniture.

Babylonia, Assyria, Persia.—There is reason to believe, from latest excavations, that the history of the arts will be carried back to an earlier date in Babylonia or Sumer as the original civilization on the Euphrates is

known, than in Egypt. Certainly the Sumerian and Babylonian artists never approached in artistry the workers on the Nile. The most successful and typical pieces from the earlier periods are some comparatively crude statues and statuettes of gods, reliefs for architectural decoration in metal and a few attractive little figures of animals found in the grave of Queen Shub-ad (*c.* 3100 B.C.). Lack of stone suitable to easy carving may have hindered the development of sculpture.

Assyria was Babylonia's successor in artistic leadership in western Asia. Numerous quarries of soft limestone gave an opportunity to develop relief sculpture and to illustrate on the inner palace walls the exploits of the Assyrian kings. Although this sculpture was chiefly narrative and at first bound by some rather wooden conventions, one gets a distinct impression of force from the muscular and energetic Assyrian warriors and of animal vitality from the hybrid monsters that guard the portals of the palaces. The Assyrians were great sportsmen and hillmen; they knew and studied animal life and could picture animals far more faithfully than men. The lions, wild asses, deer and hounds that we see in the royal hunts— wounded, slain or led—are full of character and realism. In fact in the opinion of some critics the depiction of animals in action has never been accomplished with more sensitive artistry. One Assyrian reproduction of a wounded lioness, with paralyzed spine, dragging herself along, is famous.

All the other peoples of the Near East practiced sculpture to a certain extent; but there are only a few important recovered works of the Hittite and Phoenician artists. With the conquest of Babylonia, Persia began the development of a distinctive type of sculpture based at first on Assyrian, Hittite and Babylonian models but with a touch of Oriental formal-

METROPOLITAN MUSEUM OF ART

THE ASSYRIAN ARTISTS were among the most skillful portrayers of animal forms. Although their human figures were often stiff and awkward, the animals that they carved in clay, stone, and ivory show an extraordinary lifelike quality both in form and expression. This ivory plaque of a doe, only six and a half inches long, dates from the eighth century B.C.

ization and ornamentalism that came from Persia's own Iranian background. The reliefs in the royal audience hall of the palace at Persepolis, built by the Persian kings at about 500 B.C., exhibit a better sense of stylization than do the Babylonian reliefs, and the so-called bull capitals in the palace at Susa similarly illustrate a superior sculptural conception. There are also some marvelously spirited animal figures, apparently in the tradition of the Scythian or steppe art. From these Persia was to go on to a foremost place as a homeland of the design styles of the Near East. She was to influence deeply the later Byzantine and Mohammedan cultures and to recapture at intervals her own deeply creative impulse as in the celebrated reliefs in silver of the Sassanian period and the later Persian-Islamic decorated metalwares.

The Sculpture of Greece.—Greek sculpture may be divided into four periods: *the archaic style,* before 480 B.C.; the *grand style* of the 5th century; the more relaxed and *realistic* style of the 4th century; the *dramatic* and *picturesque* style of the Hellenistic Age.

Archaic Period. A few statuettes and considerable gold ware and silverware with pictorial-sculptural reliefs of an ancient Aegean art have been preserved, chiefly from the Minoan period in Crete and from the Mycenaean civilization in the Peloponnesus. The Dorian invasion seems to have wiped out this civilization, and it is not until the 6th century B.C. that sculpture of importance reappears. Two distinct racial schools had then formed: the *Ionic,* originating in Asia Minor, and the *Doric* with its center in Greece in the Peloponnesus. We are accustomed to these styles in architecture; they were quite as real in sculpture. The Ionian school developed relief work and the draped female figure, and showed imagination in types of gods, heroes, legends and myths. The Dorian school studied particularly the nude male figure and perfected the athletic type. Both schools made attempts at portraiture and realism in details, and that is interesting to remember in connection with the ancient Minoan and Mycenaean work which also showed a gift for observation, as contrasted with the Oriental gift for imagination and decoration. The most interesting sculptures of this early or archaic Greek period are the fascinating priestesses from the Athenian Acropolis, each a different character study, and the long series of type figures that are known as *Apollos* though they more likely represent athletes.

The famous statues of the gables of the Temple of Aegina, now at Munich, are the best works of the pure Doric school. The discoveries at Delphi have given notable works of both schools to this age: the unique bronze *Charioteer,* purely Doric, and a series illustrating the development of relief sculpture during the century preceding the Parthenon (550-450 B.C.).

The reaction against the archaic stiffness of the early athletic figures, with arms glued to their sides, already evident at Aegina, is emphasized in

METROPOLITAN MUSEUM OF ART

GREEK tombstone with sphinx, sixth-century B.C. Note stylized hair of this period.

the group of the tyrant killers, *Harmodius and Aristogiton,* carved by Critius and Nesiotes, of which a copy is in Naples. They are rushing forward vehemently to strike the tyrant Hipparchus. This vehemence is itself eliminated in the works of Myron, in which mastery of physical form in action is complete and yet repressed. His two masterpieces, of which copies remain, are the *Discobolus* (discus thrower), bending low for the throw, and the *Marsyas* (a god of nature, resembling Pan), starting back as he sees the flutes of Athena. The *Marsyas* is in the Lateran at Rome. All traces of the archaic have disappeared except in such minor details as the hair.

Another masterly work was the gable sculpture at the Temple of Zeus at Olympia. It represented, at one end of the building, a fight between the Lapithae and Centaurs, and at the other a chariot race. The grouping and posing are freer than at Aegina. Apparently the artists, said by Pausanias to be Paeonius and Alcamenes, relied considerably on polychromy and distance. The stately Apollo in the center is still somewhat archaic, but the reclining seer is a realistic portrait. This archaic art was supple and human before the full advent of the Phidian types.

Grand Style. The decorations of the Parthenon are sometimes considered the greatest works of sculpture of any age. They are nearly all collected in the British Museum. It is impossible to say that Phidias himself actually handled any part of them or that he did more than merely plan them; but as all his known masterpieces, such as the colossal statues of *Athena Parthenos* and the *Olympian Zeus,* have disappeared, the Parthenon decorations are our only clue to his style. The two pediments pictured the *Birth of Athena* and the *Contest between Athena and Poseidon for Athens.* The most wonderful of the remaining male nude figures are the *Theseus* and the *Cephisus* or *Ilissus,* both reclining. Of the females, the group of the *Three Fates* is perhaps the grandest in its majestic beauty; in the drapery, minute yet broad, free yet clinging; in the full yet supple forms, showing so richly in Ionic softness.

The frieze representing the Panathenaic procession in honor of Athena had an average relief of only one inch and a half, but the extraordinary modeling makes the figures appear to project much farther, and this effect is increased by the skilful overlapping managed through inclining the planes. The most beautiful of the figures in repose is the group of the three gods from the east frieze, still in Athens; but it is difficult to select one slab as more perfect than another among the graceful groups of Athenian horsemen and maidens. They are the embodiment of idealized humanity expressed by an art as subtle in the rendering of personality as in that of form and texture.

There was another great master of realism in the 5th century, Polyclitus. He was Dorian, not Attic, and he naturally excelled in athletic figures. His masterpieces are the *Diadumenos,* a young victor binding the fillet around his head, and the *Doryphoros,* an ath-

BRITISH MUSEUM

THE THREE FATES, from the Parthenon, c. 435 B.C., is a masterpiece of the grand style. Here, the entire group is united by the rhythms and movements of the robes and limbs.

lete with a spear. In his massive build this javelin thrower embodies the law of proportions for the human body that Polyclitus established as a rule to be followed by all sculptors.

Realistic Period. Praxiteles, about 350 B.C., introduced a new ideal of grace and beauty, a different feeling for textures and postures, a more humanized and less lofty esthetic ideal. The most beautiful of Praxiteles' statues was considered by antiquity to be the *Aphrodite of Cnidus.* Of the lost original, the best copy is in the Vatican. It was the most famous of Greek nude Aphrodites: soft and voluptuous, yet broadly developed; shrinking, yet conscious of her beauty. There remains one original by the hand of Praxiteles himself which, though less famous in antiquity, is far more precious to us because it gives his own handling, which was so great a part of his art. It is the statue of Hermes holding the infant Dionysus, found at Olympia, a pretty combination of strength and tenderness, of structure and finish.

Another sculptor, quite as great as Praxiteles and as dramatic as Praxiteles was self-poised, was Scopas. His is the spirit that heralds the coming age. He took part in the most ambitious sculptural work of the times, the Mausoleum of Halicarnassus, built after 351 B.C. Many characteristic pieces are in the British Museum, especially the majestic colossal statue of Mausolus himself and the frieze of the Amazons, which is interesting to compare with 5th-century work. It is less crowded, more delicate and lithe. The museums are full of the statues of the schools of Scopas and Praxiteles: gods and goddesses (particularly Eros and Aphrodite), satyrs and fauns, as well as various portrait statues of poets and philosophers. This period was the golden age for well-poised, calm and humanistic types. There was also, however, the dramatic and pathetic side to this art, represented especially by Scopas.

Latest of the 4th-century masters is Lysippus, a prolific and popular artist who headed the Dorian or Sicyonian school. The best copy of his masterpiece, the *Apoxyomenos* (athlete cleaning himself with a scraper) with its light pose and agile strength, indicates a further advance in naturalism. Alexander the Great so admired Lysippus that he decreed that no other sculptor could make portraits of him, and several notable busts of Alexander may be Lysippus's work.

The most famous work of the end of this age, and the best preserved work of Greek sculpture, is the so-called *Sarcophagus of Alexander* from Sidon, in Constantinople. Its hunting and battle scenes between Greeks and Persians are even more picturesque than the Amazon frieze of Halicarnassus; and the effect is enhanced by the perfect condition of the surface, on which every detail of the delicate polychromy remains to show us how the late Greek sculptors strove to eliminate the hard whiteness of the marble.

Picturesque Hellenistic Period. Alexander's conquests assisted in the spread of Hellenic sculpture through-

out the East and changed its character by creating new centers of artistic production. Athens and even Greece itself ceased to lead. The principal schools were at Alexandria, Rhodes, Pergamum and other cities of Asia Minor. Sculpture became more pictorial, dramatic and sentimental. Landscape, portraiture, genre, colossal figures and groups, historic scenes and theatrical episodes became the fashion. The placidity and grace of the previous age were lost. Many among the best-known Greek originals and copies belong to this period.

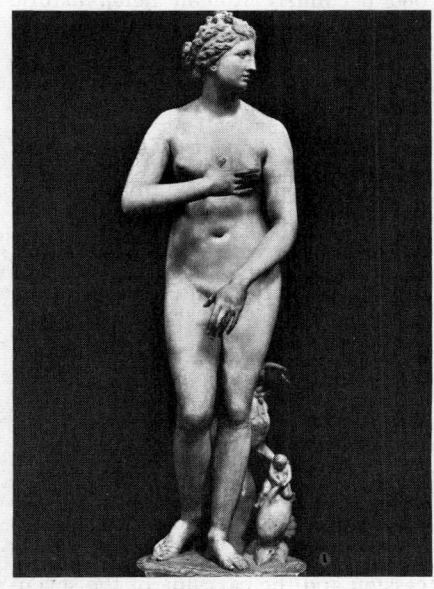

ALINARI ART REFERENCE BUREAU

THIS MARBLE ATHENA from the realistic school of classical Greece is more human than the Olympian ideal of the grand style.

Conspicuous is the *Apollo Belvedere,* a Roman copy in marble of a bronze Greek original of Apollo as an archer —a graceful figure which became famous at a time when few Greek originals were known.

Of the figures of Venus or Aphrodite, the foremost and the only Greek original is the celebrated *Venus de Milo* (Louvre), which is considered to stand on a level with even the sculpture of the Parthenon. The exquisite handling of flesh and drapery and the grace of the pose are subordinated to the artist's conception of the goddess as superwoman.

A Greek original dating from the very beginning of this age (306 B.C.) is the Nike (goddess of victory) found at Samothrace and now in the Louvre, a nobly exultant work adorned with flying drapery.

Pergamum, in Asia Minor, was the seat of the Attalid kings. Its greatness was due to Attalus (241 B.C.), whose victories over the hordes of Gauls were commemorated in a group of bronze statues. The intensely dramatic figure of *The Dying Gaul* in the Capitoline Museum at Rome is an early marble copy of one of these masterpieces and a realistic study of a barbarian hero. Another copy from this series is the Gaul slaying himself

and his wife in preference to falling a captive (Terme Museum, Rome). Eumenes, the direct successor of Attalus, built at Pergamum the great Altar of Zeus, one of the Seven Wonders of the Ancient World. It was surrounded by an enormous carved frieze, 430 feet long. The subject is *The Battle of the Gods and Giants.* It is for the Hellenistic age what the Parthenon sculptures are for the 5th century. The two most dramatic sections are those where Zeus and Athena are engaged in combat. There is an exuberant and massive vigor about the figures, a restlessness and intricacy, a contrast of light and shade, a clashing of lines in the composition that combines with the size of the figures to make it quite overpowering. The relief is so high that the figures are almost detached. For nearly three centuries this great Pergamene altar influenced art.

This influence is shown in the spectacular group of Laocoön and his sons, by Agesander, Polydorus and Athenodorus. They were of the Rhodian school, and completed their work about 100 B.C. We see in this struggling and writhing mass a decadent form of the art of the earlier Pergamenians, in which everything is sacrificed to technical display and melodramatic emotion. To the same school and date belong the group of the *Farnese Bull* in Naples, representing the punishment of Dirce, fastened to a bull's horns by her stepsons, the last word in naturalistic, pictorial, theatrical sculpture.

Portraiture also was developed. There are the characteristic heads of Alexander, conspicuous for his leonine locks, his deep-set eyes and his neck drawn down to one side. In the Naples Museum are many bronze heads from Herculaneum of this age, some supposed to be portraits of the Ptolemies; others, of the famous Greek philosophers and poets. The *Boy with a Goose,* in the Louvre, after Boethus (2d century), and similar pieces in the Vatican show the genre work that was so popular in Alexandria.

Roman Sculpture.—Before Rome became great, there had already been a notable development of sculpture on Italian soil. The Etruscans had produced beautiful works, not unrelated to the art of western Asia and of archaic Greece. A number of terra cotta sarcophagi or coffins have formalized figures, and others in stone have carved relief panels. Most distinctive and beautiful are the Etruscan statuettes in bronze, particularly the figures of warriors.

As the Roman conquerors subdued neighboring peoples, they took over certain cultural elements, and for a time Etruscan sculptors helped shape early Roman expression. But soon generals, whose armies had overrun and plundered the western and eastern Greek colonies and then Greece itself, brought back Hellenistic Greek works of art as spoils, and thereafter Etruscan works and ideals were lost to sight, and naturalistic late Greek statuary became fashionable.

Rome's contribution to the art of sculpture is not original or important and cannot be compared with Greek or Egyptian or Indian. But in certain departments Rome added new elements to the art, chiefly in *portraiture, historic reliefs, equestrian* statuary and *decorative relief* sculpture.

Portraiture. In almost any of the large museums one is impressed by some characteristic Roman bust or portrait statue. Ancestor worship and the use of realistic wax figures and painted terra cotta portraits in Republican Rome explain why portraiture in marble and bronze under the Empire attained a perfection never equaled before or since. It is a realistic art that approaches photography from nature in its exact rendering of detail;

HELEN BUTTFIELD

GIGANTIC HEAD of late Roman period. As Empire declined art was exaggerated.

but in the best examples attains to a revelation of inner character. This art kept its excellence for nearly three centuries. To compare the seamed and gnarled old man with nearsighted eyes in the marvelous head of the time of Cicero with the serene countenance of Augustus from his statue in the Vatican, is to see the two sides of this art in its earliest stage. One can gain a clearer idea of Roman character from these heads than from reading Latin literature. The equally rotund and unintellectual emperors, Vitellius and Vespasian, are amazingly characterized. And before the art begins to stiffen, these are followed by numerous excellent portraits of Trajan and Hadrian. Even then there are remarkable exceptions, such as a head of Caracalla, a masterly transcript of unbalanced fury and a return to a vicious primitive type. How different all this is from the Greek ideal of concealing the emotions under a serene and perfectly balanced exterior and of giving to sculpture the form of types instead of the form of individuals!

Many of the portraits belong not to busts but to life-size or colossal statues, in which Hellenic and Roman peculiarities were combined. The emperors were represented often as gods and as nude or slightly draped figures of Hellenic type. They were also shown as orators and benefactors in statues like those of Sophocles or Demosthenes produced by Hellenistic art. They also appear as generals in full military panoply like the Vatican Augustus, and this form is typically Roman. There never was a time in the history of sculpture when so many portrait statues of persons of every sort, men and women, were erected. The squares of every town, the basilicas and porticos, the villas, the baths, the theaters and hippodromes were all peopled with hundreds of these works.

Historic Relief Sculpture. The second peculiarly Roman field, historic relief sculpture, was made possible by new advances in technique. Roman artists revolutionized the art. Their realism seized on relief sculpture as a medium for expressing national and political life as well as mythological scenes. They did this at first without breaking away radically from the Greek methods. We see this in the reliefs covering the marble parapet that encircled the famous Altar of Peace, which was erected in the Campus Martius at Rome in 12 A.D. to celebrate the pacification of the world by Augustus. In contrast with the Hellenic symbolism that left out personalities entirely, we see in certain panels of the *Ara Pacis* the imperial family headed by Augustus on their way to the commemorative sacrifice.

It took a century to develop out of this graceful semi-Hellenic Augustan style what was more characteristically Roman—forceful, picturesque and storytelling. A halfway stage was marked in 81 A.D. by the relief on the Arch of Titus, with its triumphal procession and the carrying of the seven-branched candlestick. It was in 114 A.D., in the reliefs of the Arch of Trajan at Beneventum, that the final stage was reached and perfectly expressed. Here nearly all the principal events of Trajan's reign were represented: his triumph over the Dacians, his Eastern wars, his army reforms, his efforts to restore prosperity by the encouragement of agriculture and commerce.

To tell all of these stories effectively the sculptor placed his figures in three planes in perspective, one behind the other, and so rivaled, perhaps inappropriately, the painters of the time. The figures in the front plane are sometimes almost detached, being held by an arm so that they have almost the effect of freestanding statues; but the figures in the background are almost flat and sink back. This gave the sculptor the opportunity for the greatest variety of pose and direction, of groupings and composing. There is great play of light and shade, and this helps to give dramatic effect. So carried away were the Romans of this time with the storytelling possibilities of relief sculpture that the same men who decorated this arch carved a continuous spiral band that winds around the Column of Trajan at Rome, which tells the entire history of his two Dacian wars. It is in very low relief, and local touches are given by details of architecture and landscape. Originally its effectiveness was increased by brilliant coloring.

Equestrian Statues. Equestrian statues were used by Greek sculptors before the time of Alexander, whose figure on a prancing steed, engaged in battle, is known to have been a work often copied by Roman artists. The colossal bronze *Marcus Aurelius* in the square of the Capitol at Rome is one of the most famous equestrian statues in the world, and served as a model for artists during the Renaissance and later.

Decorative Sculpture. Another interesting innovation was the increased use of decorative sculpture, lavishly employed and fantastically varied, as an embellishment of architecture. Encouraged by late Hellenistic suggestions, there developed a rank exuberance, a richness of decorative work, a charming mingling of figures and ornament. Nothing could be more exquisite than some of the carved marble vases and altars in the Vatican Museum, or the continuous friezes or separate wall panels or pilaster decorations on buildings.

Even figures alone were made to serve a decorative purpose, as in the stuccoes in the walls of certain tombs on the Via Latina and in the Terme Museum at Rome. The artist would sketch in the wet stucco on the walls little genre scenes that have never been surpassed in light effectiveness.

During and after the reign of Septimius Severus there came a gradual decline. At the close of the 3d century, under Diocletian, figure sculpture had become lifeless and almost puppetlike.

Early Christian and Byzantine Sculpture.—It was the natural result of the decay of Roman society rather than enmity to sculpture that eliminated it from the field of art at about the time when Christianity became the religion of the state under Constantine. The friezes of the Arch of Constantine— about the only parts of its sculpture that were not robbed from earlier monuments—and the figures of consuls of this time found in the Roman Forum show that the growing incapacity of sculptors is a sufficient explanation, and that it is not necessary to suppose that the Christian Church prohibited the art because it so frequently represented the idols of paganism. The decay was general throughout Roman territories except where they had contact with the Orient. For a short time the Christian tombs in their reliefs could tell in a mechanical way the story of Christian belief in the Bible and immortality; but even this phase came to an end in the 5th century.

After this sculpture remained in eclipse in Europe for several centuries, while the world went through many changes: the crumbling of the old Roman civilization, the invasion of the northern races, the rise of Mohammedanism and the gradual growth of the nationalities and the culture of European peoples under the guidance of the Church. Architecture and painting ebbed but survived. In the midst of the Dark Ages the rich art of mosaic murals developed in the Eastern Roman Empire, especially at Byzantium, which has become the modern Istanbul.

The next great flowering of sculpture also is Byzantine and is seen first in the Eastern Christian lands—Syria, Greece, Constantinople and its surrounding region—and in Egypt where a special form known as Coptic is notable. Gradually the style pushed westward and became the standard sculpture of Christian Europe until the Romanesque type emerged in the 11th century. Byzantine sculpture is typically Oriental in its denial of the Western realistic canons and in its rich ornamental patterning. Large statuary is almost unknown. The most characteristic product is high- or low-relief, especially in miniature ivory panels which were often hinged together as a triptych, a picture that can be opened to show three related compositions and can be closed to protect the sculptured portions.

Some of the finest reliefs in ivory were carved for the adornment of book covers, altar fronts and caskets. One of the best-known examples of Byzantine carving is the cathedra or bishop's chair of Maximian at Ravenna. The chair is covered with a great number of intricately carved panels in ivory imbedded with innumerable exquisite independent compositions, beautiful arabesquelike designs of leaves and branches, birds and animals. As in so much Eastern sculpture, the human figure is an incidental rather than dominating motive. The commonest Byzantine sculptures are smaller ivory reliefs treating religious subjects.

Byzantine influences seeped into western Europe, and examples of Byzantine work were imported or were actually produced in Spain, Italy, and France. At various times Byzantine artists and workmen emigrated from the Eastern to the Western Empire, and their ideas and craftsmanship became part of the background of Romanesque art. In Ravenna, Venice and Sicily there are the magnificent architectural monuments erected under imported Byzantine designers, and in conception and execution many sculptures in the medieval churches of France may be considered more Eastern than Roman. Before the end of the 11th century Byzantine influences had fused with those surviving from old Rome. This period marked the beginning of the Romanesque style. Romanesque sculpture was influenced by the stone crosses of early Celtic Ireland, the finest decorative sculpture of the northern peoples up to that time, and to some extent by the art of other northern peoples.

Romanesque Sculpture.—Romanesque sculpture is marked by two types. The first is illustrated by examples surviving on the porch of the Church of St. Trophime at Arles in southern France. Byzantine ancestry is shown in the massing of figures in panels for pattern effect, in the close relationship of sculpture and architecture with no freestanding figures and in a flat rounding of the figures. The sculpture is mixed with typically classic architectural detail, and the symmetry of arrangement is Roman rather than Eastern. Other fine examples are to be seen in Spanish and

Italian churches, especially Lombardian.

Before 1150 the marvelous church sculptures at Moissac, Vézelay and Autun, all of the 12th century, had been produced. They represent the second type of Byzantine sculpture and are among the foremost sculptural monuments in all Europe. They are rich in motives repeated in pat-

VANGUARD PRESS

METROPOLITAN MUSEUM OF ART

HIRMER FOTOARCHIV

tern effects, and the single figures are treated with unprecedented freedom and vigor. The sculptor's art has seldom been so fitted to its decorative place within an architectural organism. Similar works existed in abundance in other countries, especially in England, but destruction of religious images during the struggles between the Catholic and Reformed

METROPOLITAN MUSEUM OF ART

SMALL IVORY RELIEF CARVINGS (*center left*), c. 700 A.D., are typical Byzantine sculptures: solemn poses, flat decorative patterns are characteristic. The style slowly merged with that of Western Christianity and, influenced by northern invaders, was known as Romanesque. Eve (*top*), a twelfth-century wall relief, reveals barbarian influence. Architectural embellishment (*center right; below*) shows origins of medieval manuscripts.

churches left those countries with hardly more than broken fragments.

Gothic Sculpture.—If it is difficult to find a dividing line between Byzantine sculpture and Romanesque, the change from Romanesque to Gothic is even more obscure. Almost insensibly the formalism, distortion and rhythmic patterning of the earlier style were modified, and more natural and humanistic works were substituted. More emphasis was put upon the single figure, as against the group composition, and increasingly the statue began to stand out independent of the architecture.

Chartres cathedral affords an instructive lesson in the change of methods and aims. The west portal figures, set back stiffly in their niches on the columns, are obviously more important as parts of an architectural whole than for their own sake; and the tympanums (arched spaces over the doors) are filled with richly composed story scenes of the sort noted at Moissac and Vézelay. But in later doorways of the same cathedral the statues take on individual character and importance, and the story scenes in the panels become at once more real and more literary. At Chartres these changes took place over a period of more than a century, from 1145 to the mid-13th century.

At this time occurred the very culmination of the Gothic development, when Amiens, Reims and Paris are being built. All through the 13th and 14th centuries the drift to a more intimately realized humanity and a more believable reality can be traced. Nevertheless the sculpture of the finest Gothic cathedrals of the early and middle periods remains beautifully integrated in the architectural fabric, and today the French cathedrals afford the richest firsthand experience of sculptural art to be had in the Western world.

France. France not only was the birthplace of the Gothic style but established its purest forms as well. The cathedrals were the one place where all the people congregated not only for worship but for plays, for fairs, for public and political meetings; the cathedrals were used as the means for instructing the masses. Their walls and portals were carved with figures and reliefs that systematically summed up all the teaching and knowledge of the time. The sculptor was once more a man with a mission as he was in Greece in the 5th century B.C. Each cathedral is a museum of masterpieces, beginning at Notre Dame in Paris and continuing at the cathedrals of Bourges, Chartres, Reims, Amiens and others.

The perfection of French Gothic sculpture is shown in the 530 figures that decorate the west façade of Reims cathedral. We have here breadth of style, a grand treatment of drapery and majesty of pose. At the same time there is the greatest variety. A sense of humor is shown in many heads, as in the *St. Joseph,* and a capacity for grotesque effects appears in many of the corbel masks. One of the apostles recalls an antique philosopher or poet—a Sophocles or

METROPOLITAN MUSEUM OF ART

METROPOLITAN MUSEUM OF ART

IN THE EARLY GOTHIC French prophet from the twelfth century (*left*), the nobility of the face is heightened by the abstract treatment of the drapery. The fifteenth century St. Barbara (*right*) is more naturalistic, with dignity giving way to curvilinear sweetness.

Aeschines. St. Elizabeth is like a Juno.

Although it is true that most of the heads are types rather than portraits, there is an evident study of nature. This is seen, for instance, in the charming youthful head of the Virgin and the piquant angel at Reims. Some of the finest statues are those dividing the main portal. The *Beautiful Christ* at Amiens and the severer one at Chartres, the dignified *Virgin* at Notre Dame, the smiling and coquettish *Virgin* at Amiens and the rather self-conscious *Grande Dame* at Reims are all masterpieces. As a composition one of the most symmetrical and artistic is the tympanum of the left doorway at Notre Dame with the *Resurrection and Coronation of the Virgin.* Mannerisms and studied richness in drapery appeared later in the century, as in the apostles at the Sainte Chapelle. And the sculptors became more and more artificial as the 14th century advanced, until from the North, especially Flanders, came a wave of detailed realism and character study, notable in the school of Burgundy, in the monuments of Dijon, in the tombs of the dukes of Burgundy and in Claus Sluter's fountain called the *Well of Moses.*

Spain. French artists carried to Spain their decorative system and subjects. There are fine portals of Burgos, León and Toro of the 13th century, and sculpture was more abundant here than in Italy or Germany; but though the designs were good, we seldom find the sensitive beauty of French work.

Germany. An interesting use of monumental sculpture had begun in the Romanesque age, especially in Saxony and neighboring provinces; and it is in Germany in the middle of the 13th century that one finds the first works of real genius, with a

mastery of technique and expression to rival the French works. These are the Golden Gates of the cathedral of Freiburg, the portals of Magdeburg cathedral and especially the statuary and portals of Bamberg. The most famous single figure is the equestrian statue of the Emperor Conrad III at Bamberg. There is little of the French idealism, little of creation of types; but rather a strong individuality and directness of expression. This art reaches great force in certain figures in the choir of the cathedral at Naumburg, especially the 12 statues of the great nobles. Bold, free, strong and full of life, they have all the virtues and none of the defects of German naturalism and are the most perfect embodiments of the feudal pride of the Saxons. Perhaps the finest are the Margrave Eckardt and his wife Uta. Their date is about 1260.

At Strasbourg cathedral we find other great German masterpieces of a few years later, though in this Rhenish school French influence is much more dominant. The earliest part is the extraordinary *Angels' Pillar* inside the transept, which is still archaic; and the most perfect are the two famous statues of *The Church* and *The Synagogue,* outside the south transept. On the main façade the statues of the *Wise Virgin* and the *Foolish Virgins* and of the *Prophets* are less masterly but very striking and dramatic.

Besides architectural sculpture there are also many German sepulchral monuments and shrines, which are better preserved than in France, where the Revolution destroyed so much. Terra cotta and wood were more generally used than in France, and here we can see more traces remaining of the polychromy originally in Gothic sculpture. The tradition of sculpture in wood continued for two centuries longer, and some of the minor religious figures of the 14th and 15th centuries are among the masterpieces of wood carving.

The Pre-Renaissance.—We usually speak of the *revival* of art, in the sense of an early Renaissance, as beginning in Italy during the 13th century with Giotto in painting and Niccola Pisano in sculpture. Yet Italy was far inferior to France during the Gothic age in the amount and quality of her sculpture. Niccola Pisano (*c.* 1220–1278) was her first great sculptor, and the famous pulpit in the baptistery at Pisa, completed in 1260, was his earliest masterpiece. In its bas-reliefs we see an interesting adaptation of Roman, Byzantine and French Gothic models. In *The Adoration of the Magi* the Virgin is a Juno, and the angel seems taken from some work of the time of the Emperor Justinian. The figures have none of the Gothic vivacity and slenderness, but are majestic and heavy, and an occasional nude figure indicates plainly the study of the antique. Another pulpit, at Siena, is the work of the master with the help of his son Giovanni and several scholars. Here enters a dramatic element that was developed by Giovanni (1245–*c.* 1320) who is far more of a typical Gothic artist than is his father: his pulpit in Sant' Andrea at Pistoia is his best. Giovanni became overdramatic in his later works, but several of his statues of the Virgin and Child are full of dignity.

This school of the Pisani spread over the entire peninsula. At Bologna is the shrine of St. Domenico, and the royal tombs in Naples prove how quickly the new movement conquered the south. In Florence and Orvieto are the school's two most extensive undertakings. The façade of the cathedral of Orvieto is unique in Italy. Four broad piers flank the portals and are covered with a series of low reliefs representing a vast Christian poem in four groups of scenes, from Genesis to the Last Judgment. This epitome of the Biblical world is given in a charmingly poetic and at times dramatic style.

Giotto's tower at Florence has many reliefs on five-sided panels (54 in all), which were planned by Giotto himself, mainly in the spirit of allegory—the virtues and vices, the arts and sciences, the glorification of labor, commerce, industry and organized society. Of greater grace are the reliefs in the bronze doors of the baptistery by Andrea Pisano (? –1348), mainly devoted to the life of John the Baptist. These charming framed and grouped scenes lie midway between the typical formalized work of medieval times and the work of those Renaissance sculptors who were to surrender completely to the pictorial and illustrational ideals of the 15th century. The last notable master of this school was Orcagna (*c.* 1308–*c.* 68), whose famous tabernacle at Or San Michele in Florence is an extraordinary combination of Gothic architectural forms with lavish examples of the new picture-book or story-telling sculpture.

The Renaissance.—Italy now wrests the leadership from France. The Renaissance comes to its fullest flowering in Florence during the 15th century. Three men take the lead in the field of sculpture: Donatello, Ghiberti and Jacopo della Quercia.

Italian Renaissance Sculptors. Donatello (1386-1466) occupies a key position in the history of the Renaissance and was undoubtedly one of the world's greatest realistic sculptors. His *St. George* is one of the famous statues of the era, standing solidly and earnestly, a masterpiece of simplification. But nothing more rollicking and joyous can be imagined than his dances of merry children as depicted on reliefs designed for the singing gallery of the cathedral of Florence. His portraits are startlingly vivid. He hewed great figures out of the rock, and he modeled tiny reliefs of exquisite delicacy. He created in his *Gattamelata* (1453) the first great equestrian statue since the *Marcus Aurelius.*

Lorenzo Ghiberti (*c.*1378–1455), a contemporary of Donatello, is chiefly famous for the bronze gates of the baptistery at Florence. In the first gate he imitates closely the neighboring gate of 1336 by Andrea Pisano, with its small simple compositions. A few years later he adopted an absolutely opposite scheme for his second gate. Here the scenes were few and large and the figures numerous and small. These reliefs with their vanishing planes, their picturesqueness and elaborate scenario struck an entirely new note in sculpture.

Jacopo della Quercia (1378–1438), the third in this early trio, was the forerunner of Michelangelo in his dramatic power. He was superior to all other sculptors of his time in the achievement of a largeness appropriate to this art, an amplitude of forms and a massive simplicity. This is especially evident in his work at San Petronio in Bologna in the reliefs of the portals in the façade and the group of the Virgin holding the Child. He was at the same time master of a delicate and penetrating charm, which he shows in the exquisite reclining figure of Ilaria del Caretto on her tomb at Lucca, on a cenotaph decorated with children holding a long wreath, the most beautiful instance of a favorite motive suggested by some Roman original. As the culminating work of the early Florentine school came the greatest equestrian statue the world has seen, the *Bartolommeo Colleoni* in Venice by Andrea del Verrocchio, the faultless ideal of a fearless Renaissance adventurer. Horse and man are one and full of force and life.

The latter part of the 15th century is so crowded with talent not only of Florentines and other Tuscans but also of Lombards that it is difficult to single out special men and works. Mino da Fiesole's bust of Bishop Salutati, with its keen, ascetic face, naturalistically realized, is a highly finished example of Tuscan skill. Among the numerous sepulchral monuments, in which decoration and figures were more happily combined than in any other class of works, the Carlo Marsuppini tomb by Desiderio da Settignano and the tomb of Leonardo Bruni by Bernardo Rossellino, rank high. Among the pulpits the most characteristic of this period is that in Santa Croce in Florence by Benedetto da Majano.

Robbia School. Luca della Robbia (*c.*1400–82) a serene religious artist, is most noted as the creator of that form of relief sculpture in polychromatic glazed terra cotta known as

ALINARI ART REFERENCE BUREAU

DONATELLO brought a totally new attitude to the art of sculpture. In this high relief from the Museum of Santa Maria del Fiore in Florence, his fascination with perspective is readily apparent, and the singing angels are presented as lively, natural human children.

ALINARI ART REFERENCE BUREAU

MICHELANGELO'S figure of Night, from the Medici Chapel in Florence, expresses the human futility of man, who faces a harsh world of frustration and disillusionment.

Robbia ware. It was extremely popular throughout Tuscany and farther south. His nephew, Andrea, almost equaled him in talent and productiveness. Later the coloring became more and more elaborate until under Andrea's son Giovanni it was at times crude. The Robbia school was the great popular religious medium in the Italian sculpture of the Renaissance.

Michelangelo (1475–1564) was essentially a plastic genius, a sculptor by first intention. It is evident even in his works of architecture and painting. He cut himself loose from traditions and schools. At first he steeped himself in classic sculpture and imitated it so well in his *Faun's Mask* as to deceive the best critics. Then he passed through a phase of normal religious themes, as is evidenced in his *Pietà* at St. Peter's. This work of art, with its highly finished surface, presents a magnificent group completed before its author was 26 years old. Michelangelo reached the full realization of his colossal talent in two works: the tomb of Pope Julius II, which was never completed, and of which the famous statue of Moses was a detail; and the monuments of the Medici at San Lorenzo in Florence, of which the tombs of Giuliano and Lorenzo were almost finished. We have in these works primitive, elemental sculpture used to convey general ideas of life and death. The mystery that has enveloped the reclining figures that we call *Dawn* and *Twilight, Day* and *Night,* has been continuous since the day of their execution. The *Lorenzo,* popularly called *Il Pensieroso,* is far more than a portrait; it is brooding introspection. No artist before Michelangelo had so habitually played with the human form, and yet none had been so completely an idealist. His heads, especially the *David,* the *Brutus* and the *Lorenzo,* make an undying appeal.

After Michelangelo came a decline. Benvenuto Cellini, to be sure, was an extraordinary technician. His *Perseus with the head of Medusa* shows that he could produce things other than the miniature works of delicate and decorative beauty for which he was famous. Baccio Bandinelli and Bartolommeo Ammanati were inflated and debased followers of Michelangelo's tempestuous mood. Giovanni da Bologna had better taste and in his bronze statuettes created works that are pleasing and competent. But with him the spirit of the Italian Renaissance is all but spent.

The French Renaissance. Though Italy certainly overshadowed the rest of Europe during the Renaissance, some interesting sculpture was produced in France, and its national character is now being more clearly seen. Its greatest representative in the 16th century was Jean Goujon (*c.*1510–*c.*64), whose influence transformed the French school, combining with it characteristics both Italian and Flemish. His most famous figures are the *Water Nymphs* for the Fountain of the Innocents in Paris and the *Diana of the Fountain* for the chateau at Anet. In the latter, really a portrait of Diane de Poitiers in the guise of the goddess Diana, one finds the strange combination of naturalism of detail and artificiality of pose and conception that will be evident in so much European sculpture until the end of the 19th century. The work of Goujon's predecessor, Michel Colombe (*c.* 1431–1512), though it is quite different from the Italian style, is more closely related to it. There is a great deal of picturesqueness in his relief of *St. George Fighting the Dragon,* made for the chateau of Gaillon. Germain Pilon made masterpieces of the tombs of Francis I and Henry II at St. Denis.

The German Renaissance. The German Renaissance failed to reach in sculpture the high level it attained in painting. Something seemed to prevent its sculptors from passing beyond a vigorous naturalism. One great exception was Peter Vischer (*c.* 1455–1529). His exquisite shrine of St. Sebaldus at Nuremburg with its beautiful apostles shows Italian influence; his colossal bronze statues of Kings Arthur and Theodoric at Innsbruck are quite original and deserve to take their places beside the Gothic *St. Theodoric* at Chartres and Donatello's *St. George.*

It is somewhat remarkable that in all Germany, Austria and the Netherlands there is so little during the 16th century that is at all notable, considering that so much was produced in mere quantity: carved portals, stations of the cross, altarpieces, sepulchral monuments. Curiously, the German sculptors seem to have stepped from the formalism and naïveté of a lingering medievalism direct into the light decorativeness of the baroque style; with little pause between for the intellectual and realistic triumphs of the true Renaissance artists.

Baroque and Neoclassic Sculpture.— The 17th and 18th centuries were a rather futile period for sculpture everywhere in Europe. The spirit of the Renaissance was dead, the modern spirit not yet born. There was nothing real or simple in art; all was artificial and exaggerated and designed to display technical skill. Giovanni Lorenzo Bernini led the baroque style in Italy; François Girardon and Pierre Puget in France, Andreas Schlüter in Germany. Draperies were inflated, attitudes twisted, compositions overdramatic. The *Vision of St. Theresa* by Bernini is more characteristic of him and of the religious sentimentality of the age than are his classic pieces, and the same is true of Girardon's monument to Richelieu. Puget's *Milo of Crotona* and *Alexander and Diogenes* introduced the manner even into classic themes. The climax of theatrical art so characteristic of the age of Louis XV is embodied in such works as the extravagant monument for Marshal Maurice of Saxony by Jean Baptiste Pigalle at Strasbourg.

One may perhaps date the real beginning of the next phase at the French Revolution and preface it with Jean Antoine Houdon's vivacious figure of *Voltaire,* its prophet—though Houdon carried on certain mannerisms of the baroque. The change was at first characterized by a classic revival, necessarily artificial because it had no connection with the age. Canova, a Venetian, and Thorvaldsen, a Dane, were its leaders. Canova's influence became universal. Rome and the excavated marbles of antiquity inspired them all.

Antonio Canova (1757–1822) was an unusually prolific artist. Of his many works the early *Cupid and Psyche* and *Pauline Borghese* represented as Venus are especially famous and illustrate his charm of line and smoothness of texture. The essential coldness of his style, however, kept his art from becoming great.

Albert Thorvaldsen (1770–1844) showed even more dependence on the antique. His frieze at the Quirinal in Rome proves that he was as accomplished in reliefs as in statuary. Johann von Dannecker (1758–1841) spread the new style in Germany as in his *Ariadne* at Frankfort. John Flaxman (1755–1826) did the same in England, though his design was better than his modeling.

Sculpture as the real reflection of the age had, however, its representatives and grew stronger with the years. On the Arc de Triomphe in Paris, the stupendous group commemorating the French Revolution, known as *The Marseillaise,* is a work of vital drama bordering on melodrama by François Rude (1784–1855). A similar quality appears in his pupil, Jean Baptiste Carpeaux (1827–75) whose nervous force is best expressed in the group of *The Dance* at the Opera in Paris. Antoine Louis Barye (1795–1875) came also with his spirited and faithful representations of animal life, so familiar to Americans. In Germany, Johann Schadow (1764–1850) created many public monuments and graceful works. Toward the end of the century Adolf von Hildebrand (1847–1921) was important, partly for his teaching; and Louis Tuaillon (1862–1919) created some of the finest equestrian monuments of recent times.

Auguste Rodin.—In sculpture as in painting France retained her leadership during the last half of the 19th century. National styles were no longer to be discovered, but the outstanding artists and talented students of other countries flocked to the famous Latin Quarter in Paris. A strong insurgent current was present, unrecognized under the realistic sculpture of the moment. It was Auguste Rodin (1840-1917) who summed up the several phases of both scientific and impressionistic realism and then, at the end of his life, stepped over into Modern art, that of the expressionists.

With Rodin, in other words, we reach the ultimate break with tradition and with all recurrences to past types. He

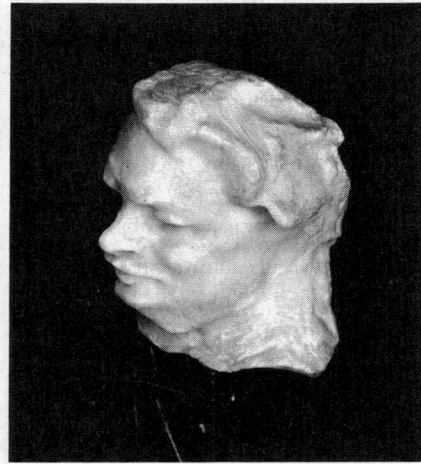

LEGION OF HONOR

HEAD OF BALZAC, Auguste Rodin, marble.

was at times as naturalistic as Donatello in his beginnings; as primeval as Michelangelo, if less bridled, in largeness and power. His *The Kiss* is an embodiment of passion; his *The Thinker,* the ruminating spirit of brute force; his *The Age of Bronze,* a perfect photographic impression. The group *The Burghers of Calais* is extraordinarily original and full of power. Rodin's extreme individualism made his works very uneven, but finally his innate originality carried him on to creation of striking works in the field beyond realism, most notably the powerful and thought-provoking monument to Balzac.

As time passes and the aims of one generation give way to those of another, a choice of sculpture which can be regarded as "modern" must continue to change. From a position midway through the twentieth century, such sculpture would seem to be that which began to develop about 1905 in reaction to the kind created by Auguste Rodin (1840-1917). The younger sculptors at the beginning of the century came to regard the French master's techniques of modelling in clay as too facile, too pictorial in effect. They came to feel that he depended too much upon literary and symbolical appeal, and too little upon genuine sculptural qualities. They objected to the importance which he attached to the titles of his works—

The Gate of Hell, for example, or *The Hand of God,* or *Thought.*

It is true that the first leaders of the "modern" movement failed to rid themselves completely of the influence of Rodin, but they succeeded despite that influence in making important contributions of their own. Aristide Maillol remained like Rodin indifferent to materials but he did manage to create a fresh, new sculpture, strong in its appeal to touch and massive in its forms. Antoine Bourdelle found like Rodin many of his ideas in the art of the past, but he did succeed in achieving through bold oppositions of mass and thrust, great power of expression.

Carl Milles remained tinged with a Roden-like storyteller's intent, but he did find his way to forms expressive of the materials composing them. The Swedish sculptor's compactly rounded *Sea God,* which he proposed as one of a series of mooring posts for Stockholm's waterfront, could only have been carved from granite. His *Folkunga Fountain* in Linköping is a granite-bound horse trough above which rears amid sprays of water a horse-and-rider the restlessness of whose pose is appropriately conceived in bronze. His forty-foot high *Peace Monument* in St. Paul's City Hall uses the translucency of Mexican onyx to suggest the spiritual presence of the Indian God of Peace with his pipe, summoned from the smoke of the council fire around which kneel a circle of braves.

Emphasis on materials and techniques has been a ruling objective of many sculptors. Some, like Georg Kolbe in bronze, Ernst Barlach in wood, or Jacob Epstein in clay, have followed traditional conventions of representation. Others, like Henry Moore, have been drawn by technique of direct carving and a sensitive responsiveness to materials to create forms of unprecedented character. The works of the English sculptor seem to live, not so much by resemblance to the human form as by a vivified realization of the stuff of which they are made: stone, dense and resistant; wood, light and open, calling for stronger accents, deeper penetrations; and clay, when the artist occasionally resorts to modelling, with all its plastic "give" and bulge.

Much talked about but still rarely realized save in the occasional works of Milles and Moore and a few others is the ideal of direct relationship between a sculpture and a building or a sculpture and a public place. Parallel to a corresponding development in architecture, however, has been the growth of new qualities of expression in sculpture which seem to promise some closer future relationship. A pioneer in this new trend had been in the Rumanian, Constantin Brancusi. By reducing his forms to "lowest common denominators," Brancusi was able to abstract the essence of their very movement, not to mention their mass. His *Bird in Flight* is one example, his *Bird at Rest,* another example.

At the hands of such later artists as the two Russian brothers, Naum Gabo and Anton Pevsner, the Polish Jacques Lipchitz, the Hungarian László Mo-

holy-Nagy, and the American Alexander Calder, sculpture has gone through transformation akin to those in architecture. New materials and techniques have been adopted: hammering metals, folding papers, twisting wires, moulding plastics, perforating glass. Much forging, drilling, soldering, and welding have been employed—to create compositions which are totally non-representational. Many such works depend for their effect upon actual, rather than apparent, movement. They make volumes of open space as much a part of their compositions as volumes of mass; they permit this space to interpenetrate the mass and merge with the space surrounding. It is these *constructions, mobiles,* and *space modulators* which give sculptural expression to the same state of mind that made possible the splitting of the atom.

American Sculpture.—Horatio Greenough (1805-52) was one of America's earliest professional sculptors and the first to study abroad. Like his contemporary, Hiram Powers, he was not

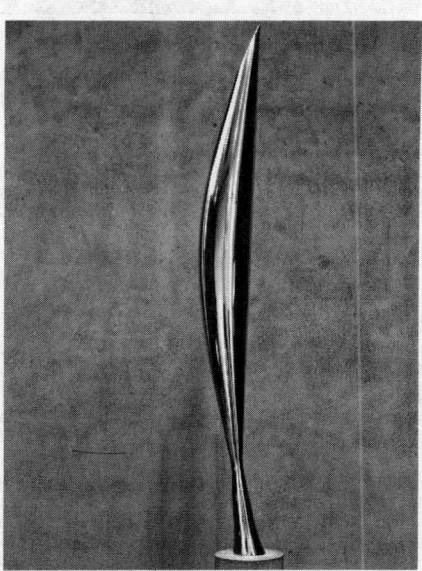

MUSEUM OF MODERN ART

BRANCUSI'S *Bird in Space,* (1919), bronze.

influenced by the neoclassic vogue of his day, and his *Washington,* like Powers' *Greek Slave,* might have been carved in the workshop of Canova. Thomas Crawford made a grandiose pediment for the national Capitol, an equestrian *Washington* for Richmond. Other pioneers were Thomas Ball, Henry Kirke Brown, John Rogers, William Wetmore Story, Erastus D. Palmer and William H. Rinehart. John Q. A. Ward was long the ideal of American sculptors and will be remembered for his *Henry Ward Beecher* in Brooklyn. Our greatest sculptor up to the opening of the 20th century was Augustus Saint-Gaudens (1848-1907) who, from his *Admiral Farragut* to his second *Lincoln,* produced a series of noble works. Among these are the standing *Lincoln,* the *Puritan,* the *Shaw Memorial, Adams Memorial* and *General Sherman.* Daniel Chester

MUSEUM OF MODERN ART

MUSEUM OF MODERN ART

THE HUMAN FIGURE is the theme of both these bronze statues. Epstein's *Portrait of Oriel Ross* (*left*) suggests the animation of the person through surface modeling. The simplified, rhythmic forms of Lipchitz' *Figure*, 1926–1930 (*right*), have the power of a primitive totem.

French likewise created a host of widely appreciated works, like *Death and the Young Sculptor* and the great *Lincoln* in the Lincoln Memorial at Washington. Frederick MacMonnies has won a great name both at home and abroad. He lived in France for many years and there he modeled his *Nathan Hale, Shakespeare, Bacchante* and his fountain at the Columbian Exposition at Chicago in 1893. Equally well known abroad was Paul Bartlett whose *Columbus, Michelangelo* and *Law* for the Library of Congress are typical. His equestrian *Lafayette* stands in the court of the Tuileries in Paris. George Grey Barnard was characterized by originality and vigor. His large groups for the State House of Pennsylvania are among the most remarkable of American sculptures. Herbert Adams has modeled female heads of exquisite beauty. Hermon MacNeil, Gutzon Borglum, Cyrus Dallin, Adolph Weinman and James Fraser are a few among an army of well-trained artists. Malvina Hoffman, a pupil of Rodin, is known for her figures of ballet dancers, for studies of Paderewski and for the 100 studies of racial types in the Field Museum, Chicago.

Such artists continued far into the 20th century to act on the idea that sculpture is an illusionary art to which interest can be added by borrowing from styles of the past. Only gradually did a new idea come to replace it, that sculpture is an art of "pure form." We can follow the changes through such works as A. Stirling Calder's *Fountain of Energy* at the Panama-Pacific Exposition in San Francisco (1915), Paul Manship's *Dancer and Gazelles* (National Academy of Design award, 1917), and Gaston Lachaise's various versions of the *Standing Woman* (1912-1927). By simplifying surfaces, sharpening edges, and opposing masses, the creators of such sculptures gave their compositions a significance beyond that of the subject by itself.

The New York Armory Show of 1913, which introduced the most advanced European art of the time to American sculptors, was followed after the First World War by the actual arrival of leading European sculptors. Quickened by the presence of great artist-teachers like Carl Milles, Ivan Mestrovic, and Alexander Archipenko, the younger sculptors reached such a degree of expressive freedom, even to non-representation, as to make the earlier works of the century seem still tradition-bound. Direct carving at the hands of William Zorach, John B. Flannagan, or José de Creeft has found unexpected qualities in a block of stone or wood. New industrial techniques of metal-working and-joining have led others like Alexander Calder (son of Stirling Calder), or David Smith, or Peter Grippe, into hitherto unexplored realms of actual movement where once there was stability, of interpenetrating line, plane and hollow where once there was mass.

Mayan, African and Oriental Sculpture. —Some of the greatest sculptors ever to live on the American continent were the anonymous artists of the Mayan civilization of Mexico and Central America. As early as the 6th century the Mayans were creating idols and architectural figures and sculptural potteries worthy to stand beside the finest works produced in the Old World. From monumental to miniature figures an amazing range of expressive and beautiful works has recently been uncovered by archeologists.

Modern interest in nonrealistic forms of art has resulted in opening up to appreciation other national or racial bodies of sculpture neglected by earlier histories because they were considered exotic and crude. Especially popular in the last decade have been the small wooden idols of the negro carvers of Africa, examples of intuitive feeling for rhythm, and impeccably craftsman-like. Even stranger to the eye are the fine masks and idols discovered among the peoples of the South Sea Islands.

But the greatest step accomplished in the broadening of appreciation during the recent reappraisal of world art has been embraced in the rediscovery of the arts of the Far East and the bringing of Eastern works to our Western museums. Histories of Indian, Chinese and Japanese art cannot be included in a brief review such as this, nor can the consecutive periods and changes in styles mean a great deal without knowledge of the background of life in the several countries. But at least it should be said that China leads all the countries of the world in the amount and variety of sculpture produced and surviving. The whole gamut is run from gorgeously spirited monumental works in stone to the most sensitive and exquisite miniature figures in the metals and clay and jade. Japan has contributed rather less of original work in sculpture, but Cambodia is rich in masterpieces (mostly religious works grown out of the Buddhist faith), and Java has architectural monuments as richly ornamented with vitalized sculpture as the great medieval churches of Europe.

AMERICAN MUSEUM OF NATURAL HISTORY

THE MAYANS, though often severe and cruel, had great imagination and vigor, as seen in this Mexican fired-clay incense holder (600–900 A.D.), which is powerful in its mastery of two-dimensional design.

LEADING SCULPTORS

	ITALY	FRANCE	GERMANY	OTHER COUNTRIES
Thirteenth and Fourteenth Centuries	Giovanni Pisano 1245–c. 1320 Nicola Pisano c. 1220–1278 Andrea Pisano c.1270–1348 Andrea Orcagna 1308–1368			
Fifteenth Century	Jacopo della Quercia 1378–1438 Filippo Brunelleschi 1377–1446 Lorenzo Ghiberti 1378–1455 Donatello 1386–1466 Bernardo Rossellino 1409–1464 Agostino di Duccio 1418–1498 Luca della Robbia 1400–1482 Desiderio da Settignano 1428–1464 Antonio Pollaiolo 1429–1498 Mino da Fiesole 1431–1484 Antonio Rossellino 1427–1479 Mateo Civitali 1436–1501 Andrea del Verrocchio 1434–1488 Benedetto da Maiano 1442–1497 Andrea della Robbia 1437–1528	Michel Colombe c. 1455–1529	Veit Stoss c. 1440–1533	Claus Sluter (Flemish) c. 1400
Sixteenth Century	Andrea Sansovino 1460–1529 Michelangelo 1475–1564 Jacopo Sansovino 1486–1570 Baccio Bandinelli 1493–1560 Benvenuto Cellini 1500–1571 Bartolommeo Ammanati 1500–1592 Giovanni da Bologna c. 1524–1608	Jean Goujon c. 1510–1568 Germain Pilon c. 1535–1590	Peter Vischer c. 1455–1529	Gasparo Becerra (Spanish) 1520–1570
Seventeenth Century	*ITALY:* Giovanni Bernini 1598–1680 *UNITED STATES:* —	Pierre Puget 1622–1649 Francois Girardon 1628–1715 Antoine Coysevox 1640–1720	Andreas Schlüter 1664–1714	Juan Montanes (Spanish) 1568–1649 Alonso Cano (Spanish) 1601–667 Grinling Gibbons (English) 1648–1720
Eighteenth Century	*ITALY:* Antonio Canova 1757–1822 *UNITED STATES:* Patience Wright 1728–1785; William Rush 1756–1833	Nicolas Coustou 1658–1733 Guillaume Coustou 1677–1746 Jean Baptiste Pigalle 1714–1785 Jean Antoine Houdon 1741–1828		
Early Nineteenth Century	*UNITED STATES:* John Frazee 1790–1852; Hiram Powers 1805–1873; Horatio Greenough 1805–1852; Thomas Crawford 1813–1857	Francois Rude 1784–1855 Pierre Jean David 1788–1856 Antoine Louis Barye 1795–1875	Johann von Dannecker 1758–1841 Johann Schadow 1764–1850 Christian Rauch 1777–1857	John Flaxman (English) 1755–1826 Albert B. Thorwaldsen (Danish) 1770–1844
Late Nineteenth and Early Twentieth Centuries / **Late Twentieth Century**	*UNITED STATES:* Henry Kirke Brown 1814–1886 William Rimmer 1816–1879 William Wetmore Story 1819–1895 William H. Rinehart 1825–1874 John Rogers 1825–1904 J. Q. A. Ward 1830–1910 Augustus Saint-Gaudens 1848–1907 Edward C. Potter 1857–1923 Cyrus E. Dallin 1861–1944 Frederick MacMonnies 1863–1937 Hermon MacNeil 1866–1947 Solon Borglum 1868–1922 Adolph Weinman 1870–1952 James E. Fraser 1876–1953 Anna H. Huntington 1876– Warren Wheelock 1880–1960 Chester Beach 1881–1956 Jose de Creeft 1884– Malvina Hoffman 1887– Chaim Gross 1904– Theodore J. Roszak 1907– Clark Mills 1815–1883 Erastus Palmer 1817–1904 Thomas Ball 1819–1911 Randolph Rogers 1825–1892 Harriet Hosmer 1830–1908 Olin Warner 1844–1896 Daniel C. French 1850–1931 Herbert Adams 1858–1945 A. Phimister Proctor 1862–1950 Paul W. Bartlett 1865–1925 Karl Bitter 1867–1915 Furio Piccirilli 1868–1949 Lee Lawrie 1877–1963 John Gregory 1879–1958 Gaston Lachaise 1882–1935 Hunt Diederich 1884–1953 Paul Manship 1885–1956 William Zorach 1887– Carl Jennewein 1890– Henry Kreis 1899– Heinze Warneke 1895– Albert Stewart 1900– Emma Lu Davis 1905– Leo Amino 1911– Peter Grippe 1912– Lorado Taft 1860–1936 George Grey Barnard 1863–1938 John B. Flannagan 1863–1952 Gutzon Borglum 1867–1941 Attilio Piccirilli 1868–1945 Janet Scudder 1873–1940 Mahonri Young 1877–1957 Robert Aitken 1878–1949 Leo Lentelli 1879–1961 Elei Nadelman 1885–1946 Jo Davidson 1883–1952 Alfeo Faggi 1885– Robert Laurent 1890– Oronzio Maldarelli 1892– Edgar Miller 1899– Alexander Calder 1898– Isamu Noguchi 1904– David Smith 1906– Charles Umlauf 1911–	*FRANCE:* Emmanuel Fremiet 1824–1910 Paul Dubois 1829–1905 Henri Chapu 1833–1891 Aguste Rodin 1840–1917 Louis Barrias 1841–1905 Jean Baptiste Carpeaux 1827–1875 Alexandre Falguière 1831–1900 Jules Dalou 1838–1902 Rene de Saint-Marceaux 1915–1945 Antonin Mercie 1845–1916 Antoine Bourdelle 1861–1929 Aristide Maillol 1861–1944 Charles Despiau 1874–1945 Henri Bouchard 1875– Raymond Duchamp-Villon 1876–1918 Henri Laurens 1885–1954 Jean (Hans) Arp 1888–1966 Henri-Gaudier-Brzeska 1891–1915 Jacques Lipchitz 1891–	Reinhold Begas 1831–1911 Rudolf Siemering 1835–1905 Emil Hundreiser 1846–1911 Adolf von Hildebrand 1847–1921 Max Klinger 1857–1920 Louis Tuaillon 1862–1919 Ernst Barlach 1870–1938 Georg Kolbe 1877–1947 Wilhelm Lehmbruck 1881–1919 Oskar Schlemmer 1888–1943 Renee Sintenis 1888– Gerhard Marcks 1889–	Alfred Stevens (English) 1818–1875 Constantin Meunier (Belgian) 1831–1905 Hamo Thornycroft (English) 1850–1925 Franz Metzner (Austrian) 1870–1919 Carl Milles (Swedish) 1875–1955 Constantin Brancusi (Rum.) 1876–1957 Jacob Epstein (English) 1880–1959 Pablo Gargallo (Spanish) 1881–1934 Julio Gonzalez (Spanish) 1881–1942 Umberto Boccioni (Italian) 1882–1916 Eric Gill (English) 1882–1940 Ivan Mestrovic (Jugoslav) 1883–1962 Georges Vantongerloo (Belgian) 1886– Alexander Archipenko (Russian) 1887–1964 Naum Gabo (Russian) 1890– Ben Nicholson (English 1894–) Laszlo-Moholy-Nagy (Hungar.) 1895–1946 Henry Moore (English 1898–) Alberto Giacometti (Swiss) 1901–1966 Marino Marini (Italian 1901–) Barbara Hepworth (English) 1903–

CERAMICS

In the broadest sense the term ceramics includes the whole field of the compounds and mixtures of which the foundation is silica and to which solidity and permanence are given by the action of fire. In this term, therefore, are included not only pottery and porcelain but bricks, tiles, terra cotta, stoneware, glass, the hydraulic cements and enamels for steel ware and for use in jewelry. The practical production in each case involves mixing or preparation, shaping or application and firing or fusion.

The study of ceramics may be approached from many sides. The historical view concerns itself with the gradual development of the nations as expressed in fictile ware; the artistic is founded upon the historical and deals with clay, glaze and color as means of art expression; the technical and scientific considers the methods by which results are produced and the industrial or utilitarian view deals with the production of wares upon a large scale and as a commercial proposition.

Materials Employed.—Certain rocks and minerals are the foundation of all ceramic work. Clays of various kinds, feldspars, quartz, limestone, steatite, cryolite and fluorspar are used more or less, and with them, for glazing, the compounds of lead, zinc, barium, boron, potash and soda. Some of these substances are easily fusible, others resist the action of very high temperatures and the remarkable variety of ceramic products is due to

the possibility of wide variation in the nature of the compounds. Two things are, in the main, necessary—a sufficient resistance to the action of fire and a sufficient yielding to produce the solidity due to partial fusion. Some clays, such as those used for brick or terra cotta, possess both these properties naturally balanced; others, such as the white clays used for porcelain and fine earthenware, possess only the refractory nature, the yielding to heat must be induced by an admixture. Thus all white wares are more or less artificial in that the material is not found in nature ready for use. In fact almost the only wares that are made from unmixed clays are bricks, roofing tile, pipes for drainage and conduits for wiring.

DEVELOPMENT OF CERAMICS

The development of clay working among the nations has been through similar phases in all parts of the world although in some cases the beginning has been with the brick, in others with the pot. Broadly speaking the brick was evolved from adobe and was manufactured only under climatic conditions such as made sun-dried clay a possibility. The pot was evolved from the basket, leather or bark vessel and was made by primitive peoples in many parts of the world. Possibly sun-dried pots were made at the first but no specimens remain. The origin of burning or baking the clay is unknown. The Britons placed pots in the funeral pyre and afterward collected the bones and buried them in one of the vessels, using others to contain food and water.

Though the earliest pottery was shaped by hand alone, numerous examples formed on the potter's wheel have been found in settlements dating from 4000 B.C. The wheel of that period was very crude, but the evidence of its use is definite.

The Greeks.—As producers of pottery from natural clays the Greeks were supreme. Thousands of their vases are now to be seen in museums. The work is classified under certain well-marked styles. The earliest wares were plain or simply decorated with bands; then came the geometric style in which, as the name implies, the pieces were covered, more or less completely, with lines arranged in angular patterns. This was succeeded by the black-figured ware in which animals, birds and human figures were painted in black silhouette upon the brown or red clay. The finest period was that of the red-figured ware in which the black pigment was used as a background, and the figures were reserved in the natural red. All these wares are fired only once, the pigment being laid upon the unburned clay.

The Romans.—The Roman potters carried their art into many lands using often local clay. The black ware commonly known as *Upchurch* from the locality in England where much of it has been found was made of a common red clay and was turned

METROPOLITAN MUSEUM OF ART

CHINESE JAR WITH COVER, made of porcelain, is from the Ming dynasty, the Wan Li period, which dates back to 1573–1620.

black in the burning by the action of smoke. Castor ware is a variety that is characterized by painting in white clay upon a black or brown body. Arretine ware was molded from a bright red clay and glazed. None of these ancient wares has been perpetuated with the possible exception of the Castor ware that may have been the remote ancestor of the early English slip-decorated wares. The treatment is similar though there does not seem to have been any continuity of production.

Chinese Influence.—The whole trend of the pottery idea was changed by the influence of Chinese porcelain upon the western world. Up to about the 13th century dark-colored wares from natural clays had been made exclusively; but as soon as the porcelains of the Chinese became known through the channels of trade the whole ceramic world strove for the production of white pottery. In the Near East the expedient was adopted of coating the dark clay with a white veneer of ground quartz mixed with a little pipe clay. The knowledge of this process was confined to the Persians, Arabs and Moors.

Majolica.—Upon the invasion of Spain by the Moors the ware known as *majolica* was originated. The characteristic feature of this is a glaze rendered opaque by the use of tin oxide that serves, as did the earlier white veneer, to conceal the dark-colored clay of the body. Nearly every country in Europe participated in this development. The majolica of Italy, delftware of Holland, and the different styles of faïence made at Nevers, Rouen, Moustiers and other places in France are technically almost identical. Wide differences are, of course, apparent in design and form, but the essential technique is the opaque tin enamel.

The name *majolica* is from that of the island of Majorca in the Mediterranean, whence these wares were exported. The term was first applied only to the lustered pottery that originated in Spain and was afterward made with such great success

METROPOLITAN MUSEUM OF ART

RED-FIGURED AMPHORA of fifth-century Greece. This Athenian, two-handled vase, attributed to the Suessula painter, is believed to have come from Suessula. This side shows a maenad pursuing a satyr.

METROPOLITAN MUSEUM OF ART

CERAMIC DISH of fifteenth-century Florence. This dish bearing the emblem of the Visconti-Sforza family of Milan is known as Majolica. The characteristic is an opaque glaze used to cover the dark clay.

in Italy; but it is now generally used for all wares with the stanniferous enamel or tin glaze. Whether the knowledge of this was carried from Spain to Italy or was communicated to the Italian potters by Oriental workmen is a debatable point. In any case it was in Italy that the art reached its fullest perfection. The names of Luca della Robbia, Giorgio Andreoli and even Michelangelo are connected with this product. It is from the name of the town of Faenza that the word *faïence* is derived. The world is fortunate in possessing a manual of the potter's art in Italy during the 16th century by Piccolpasso, a contemporary writer. In this most exhaustive work detailed information is given as to the production of the wares of the time and every modern writer has drawn liberally upon this source.

Soft Porcelain.—Ware of soft body may be said to have grown naturally from majolica, first in Italy where the rare Medici porcelain was made about the year 1580, and afterward in France at St. Cloud in 1695, at Chantilly in 1725 and at Vincennes, the forerunner of Sèvres. The aim of the early porcelain makers was to produce a translucent white ware that would approach the Chinese masterpieces in appearance. No pure white clay had then been discovered in Europe, so that it had to be accomplished · by artificial means. A mixture was made of sand, gypsum, salt, alum and niter and was fused in crucibles to a solid slag known as *frit*. This was then ground to a fine powder and to it was added a small portion of a plastic calcareous clay. This clay tended to darken the color, so that it was not possible to use enough to impart a working plasticity to the mass. Hence the porcelain makers were driven to use such emollients as soap and mucilage before the paste could be shaped. So tender was this ware in its resistance to fire that heavy losses were experienced in the kilns and it was eventually superseded by the hard porcelain that now constitutes the staple European product. No more beautiful ware than the French *pâte*

tendre has ever been made. The glaze was a very fusible glass composed largely of lead oxide and, consequently, the paintings, which were executed with consummate skill by artists of repute, sank into the glaze in the burning and acquired lustrous beauty. To this fact is also to be attributed the superb quality of the ground colors, the inimitable turquoise, the apple green, the *rose du Barry* and the *bleu du Roi*.

Progress in France.—France gave birth, in the 16th century, to two notable departures from established pottery methods. These were the faïence known as Henri II and the ware of Bernard Palissy. The former has been the subject of much discussion as to its place of origin. It was first attributed to Hélène de Hangest, who was a woman of refined taste, the chatelaine of the Château d'Oiron. It was said that she and her librarian together made this pottery as a labor of love. Only 53 pieces are now known to exist. The characteristic feature of the ware is that a light, yellowish clay is inlaid, somewhat after the method of a bookbinder, with clays of darker color, the whole being covered with a transparent glaze. Other locations have been given to this ware but the name Henri Deux (Henry II)

METROPOLITAN MUSEUM OF ART

FRENCH CERAMICS of the eighteenth century. Sèvres ware is a soft porcelain (*pâté tendre*) with a glass glaze made in a national factory at Sevres, France. This sugar bowl was made about 1761.

is accepted as the most satisfactory.

Bernard Palissy was born in 1510, and his life has inspired many a theme. His aim was to make a perfect white-enameled pottery, and though he struggled for 15 years he never realized his purpose. He made, however, the beautiful colored glazes that will always be associated with his name. Being a devoted student of nature he modeled reptiles and fishes on his platters and covered the clay with glazes in the natural colors.

Neither of these two French wares had any appreciable effect upon the ceramic industry and neither is made at the present time.

Hard Porcelain.—Chinese porcelain is generally conceded to be the criterion, as it is the prototype of this class of ware. The ingredients are the pure clay, known as *kaolin,* and

feldspar and quartz. The glaze is composed of lime, clay, feldspar and quartz. Both body and glaze are burned together at a very high temperature. The perfection of the work of the Chinese potters was reached between the 14th and the 17th centuries to which period most of the finest pieces are referred. It was this porcelain that inspired the European connoisseurs as already stated. France led the way at St. Cloud with a purely artificial ware; but the first hard porcelain made in Europe must be accredited to Saxony. In the year 1709 one Johann Friedrich Böttger, being employed as chemist by the Elector of Saxony, was shown some infusible, white earth. He had become interested in porcelain through the fine collection of Chinese and Japanese wares in the possession of the Elector and at once essayed its production. The result was the famous porcelain of Meissen (near Dresden) now known as Dresden china. The production of porcelain now became the passion of princes. One after another the rulers of the German states established studios or small factories in which the fashionable art could be pursued. Vienna, Höchst, Berlin, Nymphenburg and many other places became centers of production; but in the majority of cases the work ceased upon the death of the patron, Meissen, Vienna and Berlin still flourish, together with a large number of modern manufactories that are successfully producing commercial wares.

Kaolin (porcelain clay) was discovered in France in the year 1768 and after some experiments the manufacture of hard porcelain was begun. For some years both wares were produced at Sèvres, but in 1804 making the soft paste was finally abandoned.

English Porcelains

England soon became involved in the passion for porcelain, three manufactories being established within a very brief period. These were Bow (1744), Chelsea (1748) and Worcester (1751). The work of each was in close imitation of the French in technical treatment but influenced by the Chinese as to motive. The china made at Bow contained as one of the ingredients a white earth that was imported from America, from the "back of Virginia," a locality whence china-clays are now procured. There was a factory in Derby that was flourishing in 1756, though the exact date of its origin is unknown. Worcester, now known as *Royal Worcester* is the only one of these establishments that survives, though a new factory has been set up at Derby.

Hard porcelain in England has had but two exponents. When, in 1756, William Cookworthy discovered china clay in the country at Cornwall, he set up a factory at Plymouth, the nearest important town, for the purpose of using the clay. He made a kaolinic porcelain after the manner of the Chinese, but so imperfect were his methods that a piece of Plymouth porcelain without a flaw is unknown. The venture did not succeed and in

1770 the factory was removed to Bristol where Richard Champion was already engaged in making a similar porcelain. The works at Bristol are now engaged in the manufacture of earthenware only.

About this time the characteristic English china was perfected. This is known as *bone china* from the fact that the paste contains about 40 per cent calcined bone. This ware differs from both soft and hard porcelains and may be regarded as a compromise. It is not as tender as the French soft paste and is glazed with a compound that is much softer than that necessary for hard porcelain. Much of the success of English tablewares may be attributed to the quality of this china.

General Types.—Although the manufacture of porcelain came to England as an alien art, the production of pottery is indigenous to the soil. From the days of the ancient Britons there were potters in the land. They wrought the native clays and evolved the slip-painted wares, the combed and marbled wares, the tortoise-shell, the agate and the mottled wares of modern museums. They also made a

METROPOLITAN MUSEUM OF ART

MEISSEN porcelain of the eighteenth century. This chocolate pot is decorated in Chinese style in gilt, over a blue underglaze.

beautiful white stoneware, glazed with salt, after the German fashion, and decorated with transparent colors. From the ranks of these potters arose Dwight and Toft and Astbury and Whieldon to be topped in turn by Josiah Wedgwood. The potters foregathered in North Staffordshire, where clays and coal were abundant, and thus were founded the Staffordshire potteries, a federation of small towns that have separate entities but one interest. Here are the famous Minton, Copeland, Wedgwood, Doulton, Meakin, Johnson and a hundred other flourishing factories whose wares are on every table. Nearly all the English potters make both china and earthenware. The latter is a white ware, light and porous, which is much cheaper than

china. Native clays are almost exclusively employed, but feldspar is imported from Sweden.

The type of ware known as *grès de Flandres* originated in Germany and was exported from the low countries, hence the name. From its hardness it was also known as *stoneware* and was the forerunner of the recent wares of this type. The first glazing was by a unique and previously unknown process. When the pottery was in the kiln and at a glowing heat a quantity of common salt was thrown upon the fire. This was vaporized by the heat and the fumes attacked the hot clay forming a glassy coating over the surface. This process, while still in demand for decorative wares, has been superseded in the manufacture of common jars by a cheaper method.

Pottery in America

The aboriginal pottery of America constitutes a rich field of study to those who are specially interested in the historical and artistic growth of this industry. The primitive craftsmen of ancient Maya produced ornamented, utilitarian and religious objects of unglazed clay. Quantities of such articles have been unearthed, some in an excellent state of preservation, and authentically dated as having been made as early as 95 B.C. Pottery making in the countries of Central America reached its highest peak by the year 500 A.D. It has a distinct relation to present-day potting as there is every indication to prove that many of these early objects were mold-made. Original clay molds have been discovered from which many pieces had been either pressed or cast in clay. Native potters are still producing domestic utensils in the Middle American countries much in the same manner as their ancestors.

In 1600 glazed pottery was being made in Puebla, Mexico, by native workmen who were trained by Dominican friars from Spain. Consequently the wares produced were very similar to the Spanish tin-enameled majolicas. It is interesting to note that pottery of nearly the same character is still being made in Puebla.

The mound builders in many sections of the United States made crude vessels of clay, many of which are to be found in museums in all parts of the country and offer an interesting field of research. The industrial aspect of pottery making in America, however, is evidenced by the work of the early settlers in Virginia and Pennsylvania. Brick and roofing tile were probably the first to be made, for there is evidence that in Virginia brick were burned in the year 1612, and Professor Morse states that the German immigrants in Pennsylvania introduced the manufacture of roofing tile after the German pattern. Very early in the settlement of the country, white or light-colored wares were made by those who brought with them a knowledge of the potter's art. Native clays were used, but at that time the country had been so little explored that the

finer clays were unknown. Naturally the potters settled where clays were found and in those places the pottery centers were established. The exact location of the earliest pottery is not known, although from the middle of the 17th century local clays were being used in Virginia, Massachusetts, New Jersey, Pennsylvania and South Carolina. These early efforts in all cases were influenced by Dutch and English potters. Jugs, crocks and even dinnerware were made. A stoneware with decorations mostly in blue, covered with a salt glaze, and redclay ware with slip decorations were the main types manufactured. Very few specimens of this earliest colonial pottery remain today.

As a foil to the importation of American clays by English potters it is related that Josiah Wedgwood was greatly exercised in mind over the fact that an English workman named Bartlem emigrated to South Carolina in 1766 and attempted to establish a pottery there. Wedgwood, in a private letter, deplored this, stating that "an amazing quantity of white stoneware" was being exported to the "continent of North America" and expressing fear that if English potters should begin to practice their art in the colonies the trade of the mother country would suffer. Recent developments have shown that his fears were without foundation.

Eighteenth-Century Wares.—During the 18th century a number of small potteries were established in the eastern counties of Pennsylvania, mainly by the German settlers. Dr. E. A. Barber has made a special study of the wares produced in this district and has written a good deal upon the subject. He thus describes the process of sgraffito as practiced by the Pennsylvania potters:

The decorative process consisted in covering the red clay with a thin layer of lighter-colored slip, through which designs were scratched with a style to expose the darker [clay] below. A coating of transparent glaze, slightly clouded with green and yellow oxides, was then applied to the surface, and, after the final firing, the ware presented the appearance of a rich red intaglio beneath a greenish or mottled-yellow ground.

The slip decoration that was a contemporary of this process consisted in using a fluid clay as a pigment. It was usually a light clay painted upon a darker surface, but the reverse also was used. Some fine earthenware, fairly white and decorated domestic utensils were made in this period in both Pennsylvania and New York. Besides these, the red clay Dutch tulip ware and fine stonewares were very prominent. Many interesting pieces of these wares are to be seen in most museums, some of which are splendid examples of artistic merit.

Nineteenth-Century Developments.—During the opening years of the 19th century attempts were made in many places in the eastern states to establish the industry of pottery manufacture. At first the potters paid but little heed to the location of the clays, thus departing from the practice of their predecessors. Stoneware was attempted in more than one place in

METROPOLITAN MUSEUM OF ART

CHOCOLATE SET (*left*) of eighteenth-century England. This pottery is known as Wedgwood. The white cameo-like decorations on blue (with reliefs of groups of children) are taken from Lady Templetown's drawings. At right is a coffee-and-tea set of nineteenth-century England.

New York state where little or no stoneware clays are to be found. Gradually, however, the matter of raw materials prevailed and segregation began. The first pottery in East Liverpool, Ohio, now one of the most important seats of the industry, was built in 1839 by James Bennett, who selected this location on account of the superior quality of the clay for the manufacture of yellow ware. As evidence of the progress of the art it is interesting to note that, though this clay is still used, the bulk of East Liverpool wares are now made from clays found elsewhere. Mr. Bennett was joined by his three brothers, one of whom, the late Edwin Bennett of Baltimore, in 1851 was the originator of the well-known teapot with the

bas-relief of Rebecca at the Well, a design that has been copied by teapot-makers all over the world. The next few years saw some important developments. Men bearing the now well-known names of Harker, Taylor, Goodwin, Knowles, Vodrey and Lee settled along the Ohio River and built their kilns until there are now in East Liverpool nearly 50 establishments engaged in the manufacture of clay products.

Likewise in the early part of the 19th century hard-paste porcelain, of excellent body and glaze and decorated with gold as a rule, was being manufactured in Jersey City, N. J., as a commercial product. Other factories soon opened for the manufacture of porcelain in Philadelphia,

Penn., and Bennington, Vt., many of which employed artisans from the well-known establishments in France, Germany and England. In 1842 quite a distinct type of ware was developed in America, statuary porcelain, used for making miniature reproductions of famous pieces of sculpture called *Parian ware* because it looks like Parian marble. It is a special kind of hard-paste biscuit porcelain, made of finely ground clays and mellowed somewhat by the use of bone ash. Parian china was made eventually by most all the larger factories of this era, although Bennington, Vt., appears to have been the first to make it in any quantity.

The first kiln in Trenton, N. J., was set up in the year 1852 by Taylor and

METROPOLITAN MUSEUM OF ART

AMERICAN CRAFTSMEN'S COUNCIL

SPILWARE PLATE of nineteenth-century America (*left*). From Pennsylvania, it bears a sgraffito decoration, which consists of covering red clay with a lighter color and scratching the design to expose the darker clay. At right, a modern speckled stoneware tea set and casserole.

Speeler. As in the Ohio field the first product was yellow ware made from local clay. In order to improve the quality of the wares extensive search was made for better materials, and kaolin deposits were found in Delaware and Pennsylvania, feldspar in Pennsylvania and quartz in Maryland. The potters had difficulty in adjusting themselves to the new materials and lost heavily. Gradually, however, the obstacles were overcome and distinctive wares were developed. One of these, known as *hotel china* is a fine earthenware that closely approaches hard porcelain in character, being white and translucent. This ware is in constant demand wherever severe usage is expected, and it has no superior for service under such conditions. The body is composed of kaolin (porcelain clay), a plastic clay known also as *ball clay,* feldspar and quartz. The glaze is a compound of lead oxide, lime, potash, soda, boron sesquioxide, alumina and silica. When the ingredients are melted, they form a hard glass that protects the body and offers great resistance to wear. The decoration is usually printed beneath the glaze and therefore lasts as long as the china itself.

Belleek Ware.—Another development was the soft porcelain known as *Belleek.* The name is that of a village in Ireland where a porcelain of similar character was originally made. Not finding any natural substance that would fuse at a sufficiently low temperature, the experimenters, Messrs. Brewer and Bromley, constructed an artificial feldspar or *frit* to which they added a sufficient amount of plastic clay, thus following the plan of the early workers in France. Belleek ware is of a soft-yellow color and is usually made extremely thin. It is much in demand for decorative pieces but is too tender for severe use on the table.

In the latter part of the 19th century the manufacture of pottery in this country began to come into its own. Man-power for turning the potter's wheel was being supplanted by steam, and in our present generation has given way to the scientifically constructed and delicately balanced potter's wheel or *jigger,* as it is termed in the industry, driven by electricity. Many changes also took place with regard to the processes of hardening the clay to make the ware more durable, such as the addition of synthetic fluxes to the body, and more scientific heat treatment through the use of controlled firing processes in muffle and tunnel kilns.

By the year 1880 several well-established potteries were making a high grade of ware. A short list of some of these that are still working include such centers as East Liverpool, Ohio, Syracuse, N. Y., Beaver Falls, Penn., and Trenton, N. J. From this time on the bulk of the pottery industry seems to have grown up around centers of the larger markets and nearness of skilled labor, rather than in locations of clay deposits. The potteries mentioned above were making certain types of dinnerware,

TABLE OF POTTERY AND EARTHENWARE

Country	Date	Nature of Product	Remarks
Egypt	B.C. 3000	Unglazed pottery	Household vessels, mostly wheel-made
Egypt	1900	Glazed stoneware	Rich blue glaze. Figures and charms molded
Greece	1800	Pottery, Minoan	Primitive decoration. Wheel-made
Assyria	800	Unglazed pottery	Utensils both hand- and wheel-made
Assyria	700	Inscribed tablets	Cylinders and slabs with impressed letters
Greece	700	Polished pottery; called *Mycenaean*	Geometric style. Interlaced lines in dark color. Wheel-made
Greece	600	Polished pottery; called *Mycenaean*	Wheel-made. Archaic style Birds and animals in black silhouette, the details scratched in
Greece	500	Polished pottery. Red figured ware. Finest period	Wheel-made. Background in black, figures in natural color of clay. Faces and eyes in profile. Drapery in detail
Greece	400	Polished and ornamental ware. Decadent period	Figures and embossments in color
England	400	Primitive hand-formed pottery	Used in funeral ceremonies and found in burial mounds
Rome	100	Black and gray ware, called *Upchurch* from the English locality where much is found. Found also in France and Germany	Wheel-made. Lines polished. Black color produced by smoke in burning
North America (Maya)	95	Unglazed pottery. Crude red clays	Hand-built and mold-made. Domestic utensils and religious idols
Rome	A.D. 40	Dark ware with white decoration. Called Castor from the English locality	The beginning of slip painting. Hunting scenes and scrolls
Japan	200	Common pottery glazed and unglazed	The art introduced by Korean potters
England	490	Anglo-Saxon pottery	Crude and unglazed
China	c.800	The first hard porcelain	Porcelain was a gradual development. The first undoubted product appears in the Sung dynasty
India	900 *et seq.*	Pottery of natural clay with with colored glazes	Wheel-made. Decorated with floral arabesques under the glaze
England (Malvern; other places)	1250	Encaustic tiles. Particolored clays	Made for church use, by the monks
Persia	1300	Engobe or slip-coated pottery	A natural dark clay covered or veneered with a white coating, colored and glazed
Spain	1320	Tin-enameled ware, known as *majolica*	Elaborately decorated with rich paintings in color. Lustered and sometimes with a brilliant overglaze
China	1368	Ming dynasty. The finest period	The works of this time constitute the crowning glory of Chinese porcelain
Syria; Arabia	1400	Engobe ware of the same general type as the Persian	Decorated under the glaze with fine arabesques in color
Persia	1400	Called *Gombroon ware.* Attributed to Chinese influence	A porcelaneous earthenware of fine quality. Perforated and filled in with semitransparent glaze. Sometimes decorated in blue
Italy (Luca della Robbia)	1450	Architectural modeled work coated with the characteristic tin enamel	Luca della Robbia is believed to have greatly improved the quality of the enamel
Italy (Giorgio Andreoli)	1520	Ruby pots, dishes and platters	Maestro Giorgio, worked at Gubbio; his ruby lusters are unique
France	1520	Glazed cream-colored pottery, inlaid with dark clays	Called *Faience d'Oiron* from the supposed place of origin. A very rare and valuable ware; only 53 pieces are known
Mexico	1532	Unglazed pottery. Utilitarian wares	Made by native workmen. Hand built
France (Rouen)	1540	Tin-enameled wares of superior quality	The style is entirely French. Figures and conventional ornament
Germany	1540	Salt-glazed stoneware	Brown, gray or cream clays, embossed and sometimes decorated in blue
England (Fulham, Mortlake, Staffordshire)	1550	Salt-glazed ware	Knowledge of the process was derived from Germany
France (Palissy)	1560	Light-colored earthenware with richly toned glazes	Modeled embossments of natural objects glazed in proper colors. Also some modeled figures
France (Nevers)	1580	Tin-enameled wares in Italian style	The maker of these wares came from Faenza, Italy; hence the term *faience*
Italy (Florence)	1580	A semihard porcelain with blue decoration	The famous and rare Medici porcelain. Only 26 pieces are known
Holland	1600	Tin-enameled pottery decorated in blue	The well-known delftware, made in Delft
England (Staffordshire)	1610	Lead-glazed pottery on colored clays	Primitive in character. Wheel-made or shaped by hand
United States	1612	Brick and hollow tile	Crude clays. Made in Virginia and Pennsylvania
England (Wrotham, Staffordshire)	1620	Slip-decorated ware	A characteristic English product. Dark clay with ornamentation in light-colored slips
England (Lambeth, Staffordshire, Liverpool)	1635	Tin-enameled wares	Introduced from Holland
United States	1641	Wheel-made red wares with slip decoration. Stoneware with underglaze decoration and salt glaze	Exact location of earliest potteries not known. Early efforts influenced by English and Dutch potters.

Table of Pottery and Earthenware—Continued

Country	Date	Nature of Product	Remarks
Mexico (Puebla)	1650–1750	Glazed pottery. Mexican majolica tiles, tin-enameled wares. Finest period	Introduced from Spain by Dominican friars. Spanish style of painting. Blue monochrome and polychrome, on-glaze decoration
China	1661	*Famille vert* (Jacquemart)	Porcelain finished and glazed in the usual way, then decorated in black and covered with a fusible green enamel
England (Staffordshire)	1680	Combed and marbled wares in particolored clays	A domestic pottery largely made in cottage homes
France (St. Cloud)	1695–1773	Soft porcelain	The first French porcelain
Germany (Meissen or Dresden)	1709	Hard porcelain, called *Dresden china*	No porcelain was made in Germany until the discovery of kaolin. Böttger was the first man to make hard porcelain in Europe
Germany (Vienna, Anspach, Bayreuth, Höchst, Fürstenberg, Berlin, Frankenthal, Nymphenburg, Ludwigsburg)	1718–58	Hard porcelain	Nearly every German prince desired a porcelain works during this period. There is not much to choose between the wares as regards quality, but the decoration, largely overglaze, has different characteristics. Few such factories now exist
China	1723	*Famille rose* (Jacquemart)	Overglaze decoration in which rose-color made from gold is the characteristic feature
Italy (Capo di Monte, near Naples)	1743	Soft porcelain	Modeled figures colored over the glaze
England (Bow)	1744	Soft porcelain	Bow was at one time called *New Canton*. It is believed that bone ash was here first used in English china. The factory closed in 1776 when William Duesbury removed the equipment to Derby
France (Vincennes)	1745	Soft porcelain	Vincennes was the forerunner of Sèvres. In 1753 the king of France purchased one-third the stock and gave the title *Royal* to the factory
England (Chelsea)	1745	Soft porcelain, called *Chelsea ware*	Patronized by the king and by the duke of Cumberland. The style of treatment was French. Purchased in 1769 by Duesbury and the equipment removed to Derby
England (Derby)	c. 1750	Soft porcelain	Derby was concerned in making china probably as early as 1745. In 1769 Duesbury combined with the Derby works the resources of Chelsea. Hence the term *Chelsea-Derby* for the product from 1770–84
United States	1750–1850	Mostly earthenware with underglaze slip decoration. Some stoneware and porcelain	Pennsylvania Dutch tulip ware, puzzle jugs, domestic utensils and Rockingham ware are of this period
England (Worcester)	1751	Soft porcelain. Ivory porcelain. Bone porcelain	Founded by Dr. Wall and for a time occupied chiefly in producing Chinese patterns. Consolidated with Chamberlains in 1840. The present company, formed in 1862, now manufactures the famous Royal Worcester wares
France (Sèvres)	1756	Soft porcelain (*pâte tendre*), called *Sèvres ware*	Removed from Vincennes. In 1759 Louis XV became sole proprietor; now national factory
England (Lowestoft)	1757	Soft porcelain; blue-and-white product	Outgrowth of the Bow works. None made after 1802.
Spain (Buen Retiro)	1760	Soft porcelain	Removed from Capo di Monte, Italy, when King Charles of Naples became King Charles III of Spain
Denmark (Copenhagen)	1760	Soft porcelain	This factory was closed in 1768. The paste is good and the painting of excellent quality
England (Etruria)	1762–76	Wedgwood wares, queensware and jasper	The beginning of modern manufacture
England (Etruria)	1762 (still working)	Bone porcelain and earthenware	The original House of Wedgwood has developed all the modern styles with success
England (Bristol)	1768	Hard porcelain	Champion began to make porcelain in Bristol and in 1771 purchased the Plymouth patent. The works still exist, but produce earthenware only
England (Plymouth)	1768	Hard porcelain	This, the first factory in England for the manufacture of hard porcelain, was established by Cookworthy as a consequence of the discovery of porcelain clay in Cornwall. Removed to Bristol in 1771
France	1769	Hard porcelain (*pâte dure*)	Kaolin (porcelain clay) was discovered at St. Yrieix-la-Perche in 1768 and the production of hard porcelain followed. The *pâte tendre* was finally discontinued in 1804. The factory still exists as the most important national porcelain works in the world
United States	1769	Earthenware, white and decorated. Fine stoneware. Bone china	Domestic utensils. Some slip-decorated stoneware

for the most part. These types included hotel china, Belleek, semivitreous ware and both hard and soft porcelains.

American Decorative Wares.—In pottery that claims to be decorative and ornamental, America has achieved some notable results. The general type of wares made is best defined as faience, that is, glazed earthenware produced at a low or moderate temperature. The glazes are both brilliant (glossy) and matt (dull) and the decorations are either beneath the glaze or consist in colors added to the glaze itself. A pioneer in this field has been the Rookwood Pottery of Cincinnati, Ohio, which was founded in 1880. Several other potteries making decorative wares of an individual nature have had careers equally fascinating and instructive as that of Rookwood. The background of purpose and intention of these smaller companies was the feeling of a need in America for rare and beautiful products made by individual craftsmen rather than on the commercial basis of mass production. The fact that many of these early projects have survived and kept to their standards of technical and artistic excellence attests their importance in the ceramic developments in America. Two other potteries of this type are the Newcomb Pottery, founded in 1897 at Newcomb College, New Orleans, La., and the Van Briggle Pottery, Colorado Springs, Colo., founded by Artus Van Briggle in 1899. The above-mentioned potteries alone cover a geographically wide area and point out that interest in pottery-making was not confined solely to established centers.

Some very important works in interior decoration have been carried out in several cities by some of these smaller potteries. Tiles and architectural faience have been made for use in fireplace mantels, fountains and decorative panels. Another type of pottery being made in America, classed as art ware, is the stoneware garden pottery. Since the advent of architectural landscaping of gardens a fair demand for pottery to be used outdoors has arisen. It is usually made of stoneware clays and may be either glazed or unglazed. The pieces consist in large ornamental jars, flower pots, bird baths and lawn benches.

The growth of small potteries and clay products made by individual craftsmen all over America increased by leaps and bounds in the early part of the 20th century. Nearly all these enterprises were producing a representative art ware, characteristic of the taste of the founders or of their particular section of the country. A list of a few of this type includes Marblehead, Fulper, Weller, Haeger, Jugtown, Conestoga, Inwood, Cowan, Appletree Lane, Pewabic, Niloak, Shearwater and Camark located in as many different states. Besides these a great many studio potteries are operating as individuals making unique pieces that are always in demand by collectors and for use in attractive homes. Most museums contain at least a few pieces of some of these contemporary art potteries. In 1931 there was inaugurated an annual exhibition of contemporary American ceramics, founded as a memorial to Mrs. Adelaide Robineau, and opened each year at the Syracuse Museum of Fine Arts, Syracuse, N. Y. Here one may find a representative collection of the creative work of individual potters from all over the United States.

Structural Clay Products.—The structural clay products include brick, roofing tile, hollow tile and terra cotta. A résumé of the development of ceramics in America would not be complete unless mention was made of these products and the many others made partly or entirely of clay. Great progress has been made in the structural clay products in this country since 1900. Technical improvements have been made in their manufacture in recent years. These products are generally thought of as unglazed objects, although in the last few years even brick have been glazed for architectural color effects. Many alluvial clays are used in the manufacture of common brick, which are used as backers in all types of structural work. Bricks are made in regular or special shapes and for different purposes, such as in building, paving and firebrick for furnace linings, gas retorts and in general wherever a high-temperature refractory is needed. Architectural terra cotta is an excellent fireproof building material and is also used for ornamental effects on some structures. In the latter case terra cotta is usually glazed and perhaps decorated in colors. For the most part the coal-measure clays are the best for the manufacture of terra cotta because the demand is for light colors. These clays are buff-colored when burned and therefore do not destroy the light surface tints as red clays would. The unglazed terra cotta is coated with a thin film of prepared clay that secures both uniformity of tint and the desired color effect. The surface is impervious to water and is easily cleaned. The weight of the piece makes it impossible to dip them in the liquid coating, so this is sprayed on by means of compressed air.

Electrical Porcelain.—Recent advances in the use of electric power have made it necessary to transmit high-tension currents for long distances. This has created a large demand for insulators capable of resisting the strain. Glass, though suitable for currents of low voltage will not, on account of the irregularities of structure caused by rapid cooling, stand the heating that is inseparable from the transmission of currents at high pressure and recourse has been had to porcelain. The body structure is the same as that used for all porcelain wares except that color is not of great importance. It is found, however, that the white porcelains are the best because they can be burned at a higher temperature than those of impure color; in fact the color of the ware is an indication of the purity of the clay. The wares are glazed with the lime-feldspar compound already mentioned and are burned at an intense heat, approximately 1400° C. They are tested under an enormous voltage for the detection of flaws.

The automobile and airplane industries have created a large demand for porcelain spark plugs. These and other porcelain specialties in several varieties are made according to requirements. The operations have been so standardized as to be almost entirely automatic and great mechanical perfection has been attained.

Glass and Enamel.—Glass and enameled products are not closely related but both are important in the field of ceramic industry. The growth of both fields in the last 20 years has been phenomenal. Window glass and ordinary glass containers are not new but structural glass bricks, ornamental glass and many specialties, such as heat-resistant glass are the products of more recent scientific development. Vitreous enamels are applied to steel and iron and increase the durability and appearance of the metal to a great extent. These enamels have been applied to copper and some of the finer metals for decorative objects, such as bowls, boxes, trays and desk accessories.

Table of Pottery and Earthenware—Concluded

Country	Date	Nature of Product	Remarks
England (Leeds)	1770	White earthenware	Perforated and glazed
Denmark	1772	Hard porcelain	Became a royal factory in 1779. Is now noted as one of the first in the world
England (Stoke on Trent)	1779 (still working)	Bone porcelain, ironstone china and other wares, such as Spode	Copeland was the successor to Spode. All kinds of tablewares. Also ornamental wares
France (Limoges)	1779 et seq.	Hard porcelain	The famous works of Haviland, Guerin, Pouyat and others now manufacture very large quantities of the well-known French china
England (Staffordshire)	1784	Willow pattern, introduced by Spode	Spode was the forerunner of the House of Copeland
England (Stoke on Trent, Mintons)	1793 (still working)	Bone porcelain, earthenware and pottery	Begun as a factory of earthenware, the House of Minton, under the leadership of Campbell and Arnoux, took the lead in the well-known Staffordshire potteries. The wares are of the finest
England (Cauldon Place, Brown-Westhead, Moore & Co.)	1794 (still working)	Bone porcelain and earthenware	The present house is the successor to Ridgway & Sons. They are noted for china dinnerware
England (Coalport)	1814	Soft porcelain. Bone porcelain	The successor of Jackfield and Caughley. This factory is still in existence and produces fine wares
England (Lambeth, Doulton)	1818 (still working)	Stoneware	A salt-glazed ware, decorated in sgraffito and otherwise commonly known as *Doulton ware*
England (Staffordshire, Furnivals)	Date of origin of these factories is unknown. They developed from 17th century domestic industry.		A fine quality of earthenware for table use; blue-and-white
England (Staffordshire, Meakin's)			An excellent earthenware, largely in demand for table services
England (Staffordshire, Johnson's)			One of the best of the English earthenwares
United States	1841	Cream-colored and Rockingham wares	Domestic untensils. Hound-handled pitchers
United States	1850–58	Slip-decorated and sgraffito wares. Red earthenware and coarse stoneware	Some agate wares and ironstone china. Hard-paste wares. Parian china in Vermont
England (Derby)	1877	Bone porcelain and other wares	Royal Crown Derby porcelain. Still among the foremost in England
United States (Rookwood; Newcomb, Van Briggle)	1880–1900	Ornamental tiles and decorative wares. Earthenware and faience	Unique pieces made by individual craftsmen. Pottery of excellent artistic merit for this period
United States (Ohio, New Jersey, Pennsylvania)	1880	White wares. Yellow and Rockingham wares	Whitewares called ironstone china and white granite. Several of these factories are still working although not necessarily making the same kind of wares
England (Burslem, Doulton)	1880 (still working)	Bone porcelain and other wares	The factory of Pindar, Bourne & Co. was purchased by the firm of Doultons, Lambeth, and the work now produced ranks with the finest English wares
United States (Lenox, Onondaga, Harker, Homer-Laughlin, Knowles, Taylor, Sebring, Mayer)	1890	Porcelain, earthenware, semi-vitreous ware	These factories and many others are the largest producers of tablewares in America. They manufacture but one type of product in one factory, such as porcelain or hotel china
United States (Jugtown, Marblehead, Shearwater, Fulper, Weller, Niloak)	1900	Decorative art ware. Faience and stoneware	These smaller potteries are still working and along with numerous others have been in production between 1900 and the present; some actually were begun after 1900, although in the first quarter of the century

GLASS

Glass is properly included among ceramic products because it results from treatment of earthy materials by fire. The main difference between clay wares and glass is in the effect of the fire or heat, which brings the glassmaking mixture to a completely liquid condition, whereas clay wares contain a great deal of crystallized material bound together by a glassy matrix.

The various kinds of glass commercially produced are made up of a few oxides dissolved together by fusion in a relatively wide range of proportions. Essentially, glass contains silica, an alkali and lime or lead oxide. Silica is the vitally necessary glass-forming oxide. The alkali is the flux that makes the mixture melt at temperatures not too high. The lime or lead oxide gives the glass resistance to attack by water and changes its physical and optical properties.

Pure silica can be melted at temperatures above 3100° F. to a very viscous liquid that will cool without crystallizing. This fused silica is the remarkable *quartz glass* that finds many important uses because it is so durable and so indifferent to sudden changes of temperature; and because it transmits all colors and wavelengths of light—including the ultraviolet—remarkably well.

Silica retains this glass-forming character when it is combined with alkalis such as soda and potash. The resulting silicates melt much more readily. Soda and potash, which hasten the process, are called *fluxes.* But the alkali silicates are quite soluble in water. Tons of silicate of soda are annually made, dissolved in water to form the syrupy liquid known as *water glass* and used to cement together corrugated paper boxes, to preserve eggs and in many other ways.

In order to make glass that will be durable, some oxide whose silicate is insoluble must be included in the composition. Lime is the most important of these oxides and is used in all common glass, as for windows, bottles and tableware. Magnesia is commonly found in American limestones and thus gets into a great many mixtures, behaving like lime. Lead oxide is used instead of lime in many optical glasses and in fine tableware and art glass. It makes the glass softer to cut, easier to work and more brilliant and sparkling (refractive). Barium oxide and zinc oxide appear in some special glasses. Boron oxide—also a glass former by itself—gives glass a lower expansibility and is used in laboratory ware, cooking ware and thermometers. Alumina is always accidentally present as an impurity and is often added to increase durability.

Commercial glasses contain, as an average, about three-quarters silica, with the remaining quarter divided more or less equally between alkalis and earthy oxides. At a bright red heat glass is gathered on iron tools or flowed in cut-off gobs to machines, where it behaves like stiff molasses.

METROPOLITAN MUSEUM OF ART

EGYPTIAN GLASSWARE of the 20th dynasty from Thebes. The center vase is a typical four-inch perfume jar made by building up layers of glass around a removable earthen core.

It can still be shaped as long as it is hot enough to show redness. In special ovens called *leers* or *lehrs,* the glassware is cooled slowly, because rapidly cooled glass develops internal strains that may cause it to fly to pieces.

The raw materials for the common glasses are sand, soda, ash and lime. Glass sand consists of fine grains of quartz and is almost chemically pure silica. Soda ash (the dry carbonate) may be replaced in part by sodium sulphate or sodium nitrate. Lime may also be introduced as raw limestone or as the hydrate. For large-scale melting, these granular materials are mixed into a batch and fed into a tank. This is a huge receptacle 3 or 4 feet deep, as large as a living room, built of thick blocks of fire clay and roofed with silica brick. Here the furnace fire plays directly upon the glass and the new batch, producing a dazzling white heat of perhaps 2700° F.—so hot that it melts the materials into a uniform liquid and makes the glass fluid for the bubbles of carbon dioxide and other gases to escape.

When fine glassware is being made, potassium carbonate, saltpeter and red lead are mixed with the sand, and the batch is melted in covered pots that hold a ton or more. The temperatures inside the pots may reach 2500° F.

All materials used in glassmaking must be oxides or yield oxides when they are exposed to heat in the presence of silica. Borax is used to introduce both boron oxide and soda. Feldspar is a convenient mineral for putting in alumina and, with it, alkalis and silica. Reagents such as arsenic oxide are added in small quantities to help remove the bubbles.

All the raw materials, especially limestone and sand, contain as an impurity iron oxide, which colors glass green. In order to produce glass that will be colorless or crystal, this green or yellowish-green color from the iron must be covered up or masked by producing a complementary color in the glass. This is done by using manganese dioxide in pot glasses or a combination of selenium and cobalt oxide in tank glasses. The best crystal glass requires exceptionally pure raw materials and much skill in the use of these decolorizers.

Larger quantities of manganese give a purple or violet color; selenium makes the glass pink; and cobalt oxide, a rich blue. The best greens are obtained with chromium oxide, and uranium oxide gives a peculiar greenish yellow. Copper oxide was used by the Egyptians for making blue glasses and glazes. Iron oxide in quantity gave the color to the antique green glass and is used for window glass and bottle glasses today. Ruby glasses owe their color to exceedingly small particles of gold or copper or a combination of selenium and cadmium sulphide. Yellow or amber glasses are colored by sulphur or sulphides. Black glass is made by loading the glass with such a quantity of several colorants that all the light is prevented from passing through it. White or opal glasses contain very small crystals of fluorides, phosphates, tin oxide or antimony oxide. The intensity of coloration of a piece of glass depends on the quantity of coloring material it contains and its thickness.

Interesting effects are produced upon glass surfaces by the slow processes of weathering. No glass is completely insoluble or unaffected by water. Glass made in ancient medieval times was so susceptible to the action of the moisture and carbonic acid of the atmosphere that the surface of much old glassware has been strongly corroded. When this weathering or corrosion penetrated far enough to make a laminated or scaled surface, the play of light on this surface produces an iridescent effect that at times is very beautiful. This is seen in many museum pieces, such as tear bottles, taken from ancient tombs in Cyprus and elsewhere.

Old cathedral windows were made of glass so imperfectly melted and refined that it would seem crude today; they were worked by processes that gave them irregular thickness and uneven surfaces, and they have been weathered to a dimmed or iridescent surface so that they have a softness and rich variety of color tones that cannot be duplicated by the processes now in use for colored window glass. The modern glass is too clear, too uniform and too perfect in its surface. In a few small establishments art glass for windows is now being made by processes that imitate those in use in the Middle Ages and that give artistic color effects; but only time can give the patina that is a part of the charm of the old cathedral glass. Stained-glass making is not a lost art —except as modern methods have eliminated some of the charm of colored glass for windows by making it too faultless. John LaFarge and Louis C. Tiffany promoted the art of the stained-glass window in America, and Tiffany Furnaces, Flushing, L. I., produce the Favrile iridescent glass that originated there. Opal glass is much used in windows.

HISTORY

Glassmaking is an art so ancient that its beginnings can no more be traced than the beginnings of the use of iron. Anyone who is familiar with the formation of clinkers in a coal fire or glassy, stuck-together masses where a hot wood fire has burned can readily imagine the accidental discovery of crude glass. In nature it is as old as the earliest rocks. Obsidian is a volcanic glass rock, and a great cliff of this solid glass may be seen in Yellowstone Park. Many volcanic lavas are glassy, especially pumice, which is glass that was filled with fine bubbles while it was molten. The glazes and enamels of early Egypt are remarkable for their quality and exquisite coloring.

While glass for table and household use was made quite extensively in the Near East during the Middle Ages there was no great improvement or development until the 16th century when all the arts were stimulated by the great Renaissance. Venice took the lead. It is said that the purity of the sand on the island of Murano led to the establishment there of the industry. Venetian glass has long been regarded as the finest example of the art. Every attempt was made to keep Venetian methods a secret. A law of 1474 pronounced a sentence of death on any glassblower who left Venice and refused to return. The republic paid an executioner to track him down and kill him. The Venetian experts were lured to all parts of Europe and were protected in their new homes. As the industry developed in Germany, France and England it was generally more utilitarian than it had been in Venice. Bohemian table glass is unexcelled, and of late years the English factories in

METROPOLITAN MUSEUM OF ART

STIEGEL GLASSWARE, eighteenth-century America. The sugar bowl and its cover are blue flint glass, and the flask is amethyst. Both pieces were probably pattern-molded. Clear Stiegel glassware is considered to be the most beautiful glass blown in America.

London and Stourbridge have produced some beautiful examples.

Glassmaking began in America about 1611 when the Virginia colonists made colored beads for the Indian trade and later made bottles. Other factories were opened in southern New Jersey and in Massachusetts where supplies of good sand offered advantages. Later, as settlement spread to the west, the abundant coal of Pennsylvania and West Virginia and the natural gas found in these states and still farther west encouraged the location of the principal American factories in a broad belt between the Allegheny Mountains and the Mississippi River.

AMERICAN GLASS

The chief American contribution to glassworking is the art of pressing. Cast-iron molds can be made in many different shapes and any sort of surface design or marking can be cut in them. When hot glass is dropped into one of these molds and forced by a plunger to conform to mold outlines, shapes and designs can be duplicated in any desired number. Sometimes further shaping of pressed ware is done by reheating the pieces as they are held on hot iron rods and by polishing their surfaces with the aid of wooden tools. Sometimes the surface designs are more carefully finished by smoothing and polishing after the ware is cold. Stiegel glass, a treasured American flint product made in Manheim, Pa., by Henry W. Stiegel after 1768, is superior in color, form and quality.

The pressed glass made at Sandwich, Mass., as early as 1827, and called *Sandwich glass* is much prized by collectors as an early example of this American development. It has its direct descendants in many examples of modern tableware excellent in crystal and colors. By no means all these shapes and patterns have any artistic merit, but the fault does not lie with the quantity production made possible by pressing, but in the lack of artistry in the original designs.

This democracy in production, resulting from mechanical methods and producing glassware in quantity for all to possess, has given rise to a few excellent items designed for purely utilitarian purposes. Naturally the business of shaping glass in a mold rather than by hand tools has been extended to ware that is blown either on a pipe by mouth or by a machine using compressed air. The graceful flasks and retorts of the laboratory,

METROPOLITAN MUSEUM OF ART

ITALIAN GLASS of the sixteenth century. This magnificent Venetian goblet is colorless, with two blue glass wing handles.

copied as they are from the more or less natural forms produced by blowing the glass free in the air, the bulbs that serve as envelopes for electric lamps, bottles and containers of countless shapes and sizes have all a certain honesty of design and a fitness for their purpose that gives them a simple type of beauty, although their purely ornamental value is slight.

One of the centers where artistic glasswares are now being made is the Corning Glass Works, the Steuben Division of which produces many lovely handmade pieces. Architectural panels and applications of glass to illumination have been highly developed at Corning. Such tableware factories as Fostoria, Heisey and Cambridge produce lovely stemware and dishes by hand blowing and pressing in molds in fairly large quantities. Numerous small plants make novelties and knickknacks that occasionally include pieces of surprising merit. Many large factories with automatic machinery turn out by the million pieces that make up in their perfection of workmanship and finish and their excellent quality for any lack of individuality in their design.

The modern trend especially in America has been toward more and more automatic mechanical production of glassware. Though we have lost the skilled craftsmanship that

STEUBEN GLASS

STEUBEN GLASSWARE designed by Donald Pollard—liqueur service decanter with a teardrop stopper and slender liqueur glass.

could make a few finely executed pieces for the possession of the very rich, we have gained in the abundance of fairly good glassware for everyone.

It remains for us to apply better designing and to develop in all the people a better artistic taste that will demand the abolition of ugliness in our pieces of glassware. The modern window pane, drawn as a smooth, flat sheet directly from the bath of glass, is so clear and perfect that we forget its presence when we look through a window. Still more perfect is plate glass, formed by the careful grinding and polishing of thick rolled sheets. Optical glass, compounded with extreme care and stirred to a high degree of homogeneity, supplies us with spectacles, telescopes, opera glasses and microscopes, which are not only indispensable to the scientist, but which enable us to perceive beauties which would otherwise be hidden from us forever as a result of our own visual inadequacy.

The opportunity for the artist of today lies not in any attempt to develop hand craftsmanship but rather in the development of original designs that will be not only useful but beautiful and that through mass production will bring this beauty within the reach of all the people. Glassmaking today must be both a science and an art.

GLASS

Country	Date	Nature of Product	Remarks
Egypt	B.C. circa 2400	Dark-blue glass. Semiopaque	The earliest dated specimens known are of this era
Egypt	1450	Transparent green glass	A bead found at Thebes is the oldest clear glass known
Nineveh	712	Pale green transparent	A small vase in the British Museum bears the name of Sargon, King of Assyria
Greece or Phoenicia	circa 400	Colored glass. Waved, striated and sometimes carved	Numerous small bottles. Beads and ornaments. The Phoenicians claimed the invention of glass
Rome	circa 30 B.C. to 309 A.D.	Common green glass. Colored and ornamental glass, carved, cut and woven glass	Enormous quantities of glass of every description, even including window glass, were produced
China	circa 140 B.C.	Small vessels ornamented and embossed	The statements regarding early glass in China are very uncertain. Few specimens remain
Constantinople (Byzantium)	A.D. 800 to 1200	Heavy molded glass in dark colors. Some window glass	Classic models were followed, but the wars of the period caused much interchange of plunder, and the origin of many specimens is doubtful
Damascus and the East	1200 to 1400	Vessels of clear glass often richly ornamented	Many lamps and vessels for religious use are found in mosques
Italy (Venice and Murano)	1090	Every description of fancy glass	Glass mosaics preceded the general manufacture of glass in Venice. The furnaces were removed to Murano probably about 1300. Venetian glass is the model for the world
Italy (Murano)	1490	Mille-fiore (thousand-flowers) glass	This had been made by the Romans. Canes of colored glass were cut into short lengths and these, with the cut ends showing, were fused into the body of the vessel
Italy (Murano)	1500	Vitro-di-trina (lace glass)	Threads of opaque white glass were fused in a geometric pattern into the clear glass of the vessel
France	1400 to 1600	Utensils of various sorts colored and decorated. Window glass	Small manufactures of glass existed in many parts of France, but most of the product was unimportant
Spain	circa 500 to 800	Cups, vials and bottles	As in the case of France, the Roman influence was felt in Spain
Spain	1400 to 1600	Utensils and drinking cups	Some Spanish glass bears evidence of Venetian influence. Colored and reticulated forms are found
Germany	1400 et seq.	Steins and goblets. Window glass	The stein was even then a feature in Germany. A great variety of form and treatment is found. Some highly ornate pieces are preserved
Great Britain	circa 600	Beads, crude cups, window glass	Both Roman and Saxon specimens are found. The original tumbler was a glass drinking horn which could not be set down until empty
Great Britain	1300 to 1600	Cathedral glass. Vessels of many sorts	English stained glass for church windows is unsurpassed. The vessels were generally plain and useful

Modern Productions

Country			
Italy (Venice and Murano)			The glass is much on the old style. Every description of colored, blown, woven and reticulated glass is produced. The material is still of the lime-soda mixture
France			A great deal of modern French glass is crystal of the lead-potash compound. The molded glass is very fine. Some French craftsmen have produced wonderful effects in colors
Bohemia			This glass is well known in the small and inexpensive bric-a-brac of the stores. A good deal of it is decorated in color and gold
Germany (Jena)			In optical and chemical glass the Jena works led the world for many years. All varieties of commercial glass are produced
England			The English glassmakers are surpassed by none. Table glass of pure crystal, cut glass and ornamental pieces are made in great variety
America			Much of the American glass is molded in the form of tumblers and household vessels. Fine cut glass is made at Corning, Toledo and other places. Plate glass is an important part of the industry. Fine optical glass and heat-resisting glasses have been developed here

In general the term graphic may be applied to any fine art that represents figures and appeals to the eye. In the more limited sense the graphic arts are printing, engraving, etching and the like—the duplicating and manifolding arts.

There are two steps in any graphic art: first, making a design on copper, zinc, stone or wood; and second, printing impressions of the design with ink on paper, vellum or fabric. The first step is creative—what we call artistic; the second is largely mechanical but to a considerable degree artistic too, and the particularly important thing about it is that it makes it possible to duplicate the design many times.

Although few of us are able to collect paintings and sculpture, and we may be far from museums, we are not wholly excluded from owning and seeing superlatively fine examples of the visual arts. Through *prints* we may share in the treasures left by the great artists of the past; and in a few well-chosen woodcuts and etchings and lithographs we may find our deepest and most intimate pleasure in the art of today. These are, indeed, the arts that touch the common man most closely. They afford, too, the best approach to an understanding of the *fine arts*.

The advantage of the graphic arts over painting and sculpture lies, of course, in the wide dissemination of pictures at a moderate cost. Great paintings and sculpture are found in art galleries, museums and private collections where but limited numbers have the opportunity to study them. There are reproductions of these masterpieces; but they are usually reduced in size and lack the full richness and sensitive detail of the originals.

In the graphic arts the number of prints may run up to hundreds, each print an exact duplicate of the first impression from the plate of metal, stone or wood. Each is therefore an original—not a reproduction of the artist's work, but a duplication.

The commoner graphic arts, named for the methods employed, are etching, soft-ground etching, dry point, copper engraving, aquatint, mezzotint, woodcut and lithograph. Making prints by any of these processes involves the use of ink. Ink is usually black, but methods of printing have been developed to such a high degree of perfection as to present a full range of color, and the graphic arts have the range of color possible to painting. This is accomplished chiefly through lithography but also by colored etchings and colored woodcuts—as in the well-known *Japanese prints*. On the other hand many collectors and lovers of prints believe that etching, copper engraving and wood engraving, because they are essentially *arts of line,* are at their best when the artist limits his work to black and white.

An additional factor in the enjoyment and possession of the graphic arts is the fact that prints are usually limited to a size for easy handling.

They range from plates no larger than a postage stamp through the average size that comprises most collections in portfolios, coming within the range of 15 by 20 inches, up to much larger sizes, for example, the large lithographic posters on billboards.

Rare printed pictures may equal paintings in cost, but first published prices are usually nominal and within the reach of moderate purses. Enthusiastic collectors of prints enjoy a hobby that brings deep satisfaction and the power to share it with others.

ETCHING

Chronologically etching belongs at the end of the list of graphic arts; but because it is now receiving more attention in America than it has in 50 years and has become more popular for the home and portfolios than lithography or line engraving, it will be considered first.

The history of etching begins late in the 15th century, and the first very great practitioner is Albrecht Dürer (1471–1528). Only a few of his finest plates are in etching (as compared with his engravings on both wood and copper); and for a long time after him there are only lesser masters, of whom the German Albrecht Altdorfer and the French Jacques Callot are most notable. Then comes the superlative artist Rembrandt van Rijn, who carried on his work between the years 1628 and 1661. In him the art reached its greatest perfection and found its widest expression. Before him etching had often been used as a mere adjunct of engraving with no separate existence of its own until he raised it to a high art; and afterward many print makers combined the two meth-ods, so that there are great numbers of prints that cannot with certainty be labeled etchings or engravings. After the death of Rembrandt (1669) the art suffered periodical decadence and restoration to favor, coincident with the rise and fall of specialized interest in art. It was only in the late 19th century that etchers again appeared who are now considered worthy to rank with the great masters. Most appreciated is Whistler, an American-born artist who spent most of his later life in England. Charles Méryon (French) and Sir Francis Seymour Haden (English) are other great modern figures. In the 20th century a number of proficient artists have turned to the medium, and never have etchings of sterling quality been so plentiful, although no living etcher seems quite so inspired as those named.

The method of etching is suggested by its name translated from the Dutch (where it was first used): *etsen,* like the German *essen,* means eat; applied specifically, it denotes the eating or corrosive action of acids on metal; to use the etcher's own laboratory term, the *biting* of the acid into the metal. Etchings are printed from a metal plate, usually copper or zinc, upon which the lines have been etched or deepened by acid.

Preparation of the Plate.—The plate of polished metal is about 1/16 of an inch thick, cut to the dimensions required. In order to subject it safely to the action of acid, usually nitric, the plate must be covered with a protecting substance. This is found in a preparation of wax, asphaltum and pitch called a *ground,* which is melted and spread thin by roller or dabber over the entire surface of the hot plate.

METROPOLITAN MUSEUM OF ART

REMBRANDT, in his middle years, increasingly probed the underlying character of people. This etching, *Girl with Hair Falling on Her Shoulders,* 1635, is from that period.

When cold, this thin covering forms a smooth, hard surface that is made black by smoking over a candle flame. Through this black surface lines are drawn by a steel needle.

Making the Drawing.—Some artists work from nature directly upon their plates with the needle, just as they would sketch with pencil on paper. In this case the drawing, when printed, will be in reverse. Others make careful drawings with ink or pencil on paper and transfer them by various methods to the plate in reverse. The transferred lines are visible on the wax grounds and may be followed with the needle. This insures greater accuracy in drawing and placing, inasmuch as corrections may be made before the transfer; but a print produced by this careful procedure is not so likely to convey that spontaneity or freshness of inspiration that is apparent when a well-directed needle records the impressions of the moment upon the metal itself. Such a picture, when printed, will be a positive of the original drawing—but a negative of the reverse on the metal.

As the lines are drawn by the needle in the wax only, they must be made permanent upon the plate by being bitten into the copper. This is accomplished by applying acid, usually nitric, nitrous fuming, Dutch mordant or perchloride of iron, in one of two ways: either by dropping it on the plate and moving it about with a feather or by entirely submerging the plate (held by waxed strings) in a glass or porcelain dish. The strength of the acid to be used is determined by the atmosphere. If the air is warm, it calls for a weak solution, say three parts of water to one of acid. Cold makes chemical action sluggish, and the solution must be strengthened accordingly.

If the lines have been drawn with a fine needle, they may be varied in strength and depth by submitting them to the acid through longer or shorter periods. Delicate lines representing distance should be exposed only a short time, probably a minute or two. The plate is then taken out of the solution, washed carefully in cool water and dried, and the finest lines are covered by a small brush with stopping-out varnish. When it is dry, the plate may be returned to the acid and exposed for the next grade of lines for a period of several minutes or more, after which the process of washing, drying and stopping out is repeated. In this way the work is carried forward until the lines desired to be heaviest have been bitten. Some etchers vary their lines by using fine and coarse needles and give the plate only one biting; but this is an exceptional method, and those who use it are certain to lose variety and delicacy of line. Others work on the plate while it lies in the acid, putting the heaviest lines in first and ending with the lightest. There is no way of determining, except approximately, what the acid is doing until the wax ground is removed. This is done by kerosene or turpentine after the plate has been warmed.

There are three distinct chances for failure in making an etching: in the drawing, the biting and the printing. An artist may be an excellent draftsman and draw lines on the copper faultlessly, but the etching will not be a success unless he possesses the knowledge of how to bite lines into the copper. Again he may have the skill to draw and bite, but his plate will be useless if it is not well printed. Many etchers do not attempt the printing themselves but leave it to experienced craftsmen who make that their profession. The most satisfactory results are obtained when the artist does his own work from the first drawing to the final print, but the expense of the necessary equipment is so great as almost to prohibit etching as a pastime. The practice involved in acquiring skill in printing plates is such as to put it out of the hands of most etchers for anything but the simplest working proofs of their work.

The chief joy of an etching is its spontaneity. In the hands of a skilful worker, it may be rushed through to completion, and the etcher may look upon the moist print from his copper plate before his enthusiasm cools. This joy is unknown to the artist who must send his plate to a professional printer for a proof. So the etcher who can take his plate out of the acid, wash and dry it for the last time, warm and remove the wax ground and turn at once to his press is the only one to taste the full fruition of pleasure in his work.

Printing.—A thoughtful etcher will have prepared his paper by dampening it before it is time to print, dipping it in clean water or sponging it and putting it in piles between blotters upon which are heavy weights. If he grinds his own ink, which is made of a fine black powder and plate oil, he will have that ready also.

With a smooth roller or dabber the thick ink that stands up in a shiny heap is forced into the lines. The whole surface of the plate is solidly blacked. Then with a pad of open-meshed cloth—tarlatan is best—the ink lying on the surface of the plate is carefully wiped off, leaving the sunken lines full. At this point it would be possible to list the many methods of manipulation that result in the production of various special effects; but an explanation of these would be interesting and comprehensible only to a printer. Both bare hand and cloth may be used to clean the plate of superfluous ink and yet leave what is necessary to produce the effect desired.

The plate, which should be warm, is now laid on the steel bed of the press; over it is laid a sheet of paper moistened with water until it is limp and soft but not wet. Over this are placed several fine white blankets woven for the purpose. Then the bed passes between two heavy steel rollers, as clothes are fed into a wringer, coming out and stopping on the other side. The pressure should be even and as heavy as it can be and still allow the bed to pass between the rollers.

The soft blankets force the moist paper into the lines, and the sheet takes up all the ink it finds there. When the blankets are lifted and the paper is peeled off the metal plate, permanently embossed upon the paper will be the ridges of ink that filled the etched lines, together with any tone left on the surface. For the artist this is the crucial moment in the whole work of etching. Up to this time there has been no certainty of what has been accomplished. The lines may be clearly seen upon the plate, but it is not enough merely to make a line; there should be fine lines, heavy lines, black, gray, rich and ragged lines. The success of the biting lies in the quality of the lines. Hence it is a staid heart that does not quicken when the first proof of an etched plate is lifted.

Alterations.—If the proof is satisfactory, the plate is ready for further printing. If some lines are too heavy, the copper surface around them is scraped with a sharp-edged scraper, burnished with a smooth polished burnisher and rubbed down with fine charcoal and a buffer, reducing the depressions to the desired depth. If the lines are too light, the plate may again be covered with a wax ground and the lines bitten deeper. Lines may be added or erased, but never with ease; it is a slow and tedious process to make alterations on a plate.

Color.—The color of an etching results from, and corresponds with, the color of the ink with which it is printed. There may be light color on the print where there are no lines; this is a thin film of ink left on the surface of the plate. Wiping a plate clean puts the whole burden of the story on the lines. If they are not expressive and full of quality, the picture may as well have been drawn with pen and ink. But a printer with a painter's touch knows how to make hard lines sympathetic and draws them all together with a bond of tone. A plate, however well it may be etched, is not complete nor desirable unless it is well printed. Although etching is primarily a linear process, colors other than black are sometimes used; but they are always put on the plate and never on the paper, except in the way described above.

Paper.—Both paper and ink are large factors in the success of an etching. Any plate that can stand the test of white paper and black ink can be considered well done, for it is a severe combination. Ink that is slightly warmed by brown, printed on paper of a creamy tone, is generally more pleasing. Soft Japan paper is still more mellow but not brilliant. All Japanese papers are likely to grow wooly with handling and are difficult to clean. The Western handmade papers are desirable for their texture and lasting qualities. Most attractive of all are the precious sheets of handmade paper made in early centuries, some of which are still discoverable in old shops in Italy, Germany, France and Holland. A rare proof may be seen on a worm-eaten sheet of paper, on the other side of which are found accountant's notes of three centuries ago. But with its very age has come a tone and quality that cannot be duplicated in modern paper.

Perfect tonality is difficult to attain in an etching, except with great labor and skill, and labor is the one thing

METROPOLITAN MUSEUM OF ART

REMBRANDT'S *Jacob Haaring,* dry point.

that should not be apparent in an etching. The action should appear effortless and spontaneous, just as one would pen a letter to a friend. This is why etching is called the most autographic of all arts. Its strong points are brevity, freedom, precision and power; but coarseness of line is not to be confused with strength. Etching is the intimate art—the art of the home and of the hand. Poring over a portfolio of master prints is a recreation that never palls, because the final word is never said; there is always a new impression to meet a different mood.

DRY POINT

Dry point is so frequently confused with etching, both as to method and result, that only those familiar with the actual steps of production may be expected to define the term correctly. The name *dry-point etching,* although it is essentially incorrect, has come into such wide use that a special explanation is necessary.

An etching is etched with acid, as its name implies; a dry point, on the other hand, is a method of incising lines on metal with a sharp cutting needle or diamond point without the intervention of acid, hence the term *dry point.* The work is different and the result is different from etching, as the student will quite readily detect and understand with observation.

With a sharp steel point or—even better—with a ruby or diamond set in a handle that is held in a slanting position, lines are cut directly into the metal plate lightly or deeply, doing at once what the acid takes longer to do. As the cutting edge acts much like a plow throwing a furrow, the edge of a dry-point line holds a *burr* that, unless it is removed with a scraper, is the one distinguishing characteristic of the method. When the plate is

wiped and inked, the burr catches extra ink and spreads it like the edge of a tiny feather along the line, thereby producing a rich, velvety appearance not known to the lines in any other graphic-art process. The possibility of achieving the lightest and subtlest of lines and at the same time the heaviest and richest, makes dry point a desirable medium for portraits and subjects in which great variation and delicacy are required. It lacks the freedom of the etched line because, in its making, it must be guided with pressure sufficient to furrow the metal. Moreover, a dry-point plate yields fewer proofs than an etched one because the delicate burr quickly wears away with the manipulation of inking and wiping the plate. Since the mechanical work of biting a plate is the greatest stumbling block in etching, the omission of grounding and biting and the directness of the method lead many artists to dry point; but the preference is not without its drawbacks, especially the extra difficulties in printing.

SOFT-GROUND ETCHING

The artist employing the soft-ground process does not use the usual etcher's needle. The copper plate is covered with ordinary etching ground mixed with tallow in such proportions that whether it is used in summer or winter, it does not become hard. Over the plate coated with this soft ground is stretched a sheet of thin, grained paper upon which a drawing is made with a lead pencil. When the paper is removed, it will be found that the ground has adhered to it wherever the pencil was used, leaving the lines exposed on the copper. These lines are bitten with acid in the regular way, producing varied depths by stopping out, just as in regular etching. The principle of printing is the same. The

result looks somewhat like a pencil drawing or a lithograph.

AQUATINT

Aquatint is the art of etching upon metal *in tones* (as distinct from lines) with acid or, as it is technically called, *aquafortis.* The result printed in black or brown, strongly resembles a water color or wash drawing; hence the name *aqua tinto* or *aquatint.* There are several ways of preparing a ground for this process, all of them designed to leave on the copper plate a multitude of tiny globules of resin with minute interstices between. The simplest preparation is by a coating with *spirit ground,* a mixture of alcohol and resin being applied, and the alcohol permitted to evaporate. Preferable to this is the *dust ground,* which is produced by powdering dry resin particles uniformly over the copper surface and then heating the plate to melt the particles into a secure ground. There are elaborate devices for spreading the dust, such as boxes with a fan to set the dust flying or screens of cloth through which the dust is sifted on the plate. But the simplest way of all is to put powdered resin in a small bag of fine mesh that can be held in the hand and that may be struck lightly with a ruler, thus causing the particles to drop. The disadvantage of this method is that the particles may not be distributed as evenly as if they are allowed to settle from the air in a box.

The plate must be carefully handled while it is being put on a heater where each grain of resin is crystallized, forming a hard but porous surface. Where no color on the plate is desired, the highest lights are painted out with stopping-out varnish before the first immersion of the plate in the acid, and succeeding steps are followed as in biting etched lines: short

WILLIAM H. SCHAB GALLERY

AN ETCHING with aquatint, *May God Repay You for This,* sums up the principal aspects of Goya's thinking: the poet, not blind but with eyes closed, is still entranced by poetic inspiration as the bull, symbol of irrational brute force, lifts him and carries him off.

METROPOLITAN MUSEUM OF ART

THE MOST BRILLIANT ENGRAVINGS come from the German and Dutch masters working around the turn of the sixteenth century. Dürer was perhaps the most significant, but the Dutch Lucas van Leyden (1494–1533) was a great master of decorative and ornamental composition. His drawing is always sensitive in feeling as well as technique. The influence of Dürer can be seen in this engraving, *The Milk Maid*, done in 1510. Van Leyden's later work took on a definite italianate spirit and its opulence and humor stands in sharp contrast to the angularity of the Gothic style.

Engraving originated in the 15th century with the work of goldsmiths, who cut designs in gold and silver plates and filled in the lines with black alloy for ornaments called *nielli* (from Latin *nigelli*, little blocks). The black substance in the design made it possible to get an impression on paper. This discovery eventually developed into engraving for the sake of the printed picture. From a mere record of a *niello* design, engraving passed into an art that became lucrative for the translation and interpretation of paintings and other work. The work of the artist lapsed into laborious and tedious copying that, although resulting in superlative technique, furnished the world, except in a few notable instances, with no masterpieces. But between 1460 and 1550 came that culmination of the art that gave to the world the most brilliant engravings known to history. The earliest great independent engravers, creators rather than copyists, were the Italian Andrea Mantegna (1431–1506) and the German Martin Schongauer (*c.* 1445–91). Transcending all others, were Dürer's copper-plate prints. They are rich and full, yet drawn with a felicitous touch and sensitive restraint. After him the German "Little Masters" created many beautiful prints, with a special miniature delicacy; but the next outstanding master was the Dutch artist Lucas van Leyden (1494–1523). At a later period France took over leadership, especially in portrait engraving, a field in which Robert Nanteuil (1623–78) was supreme. But the art never again touched the heights attained by the 15th-and 16th-century group of Germans.

intervals for shallow spaces and longer intervals for deep ones. The removal of the ground and the printing are the same as with etching, except that the tiny sections of copper that stand up will not yield as many impressions as the depressed lines. Aquatint is capable of many gradations of tone, and the artist conceives his picture from the painter's point of view rather than the etcher's.

MEZZOTINT

This is another method of engraving in tone not in lines, but the work is done with tools and without acid. A metal plate is uniformly roughened by means of a toothed instrument called a *rocker* or *cradle*—a method that dates back, as far as records tell us, to 1611. There may be from 40 to 120 fine teeth to the inch of the tool. It is rocked over the copper in every direction, either by hand or by machinery, to produce tiny indentations, each with a slight burr on its edge like a shallow volcanic crater. If it is inked and printed at this stage, the plate yields a rich solid black surface. The object is to let the lights of the design through this dense black, which is done by means of a bayonet-shaped scraper and a burnisher. Where a clear surface is desired, all indentations must be removed and the surface polished with a burnisher; this takes that part of the plate back to its first state. From this point to the deepest, blackest shadows, it is a question of controlling the scraper in the leveling process to produce varying gradations of tones. The complete result, when the plate is inked, wiped and printed as already described, is the richest combination of light and shade that can be produced. But like dry point, which depends upon burr for its richness, and like aquatint, which has shallow indentures, the yield of proofs is limited. Were it not for an invention called *steel facing*, which has been in use since 1857, much of the fine work would have been limited to very few proofs. Steel facing consists in laying on the copper plate by electroplating methods a thin film of steel that protects the soft copper and preserves a uniformity of excellence in the prints for whatever larger edition the artist determines. Without steel facing, the wearing of the plate determines the number of proofs that may be taken; for as it loses its fine values, it is no longer printable and should be canceled or destroyed.

ENGRAVING

Practically all engraving work on metal before 1820 was on copper. At about that time steel came into use because very much larger editions of prints could be taken from steel plates without loss of delicate nuances or brilliancy. The art was widely popularized, and the name *steel engravings* came into common currency. This name still incorrectly persists in some quarters. As a matter of fact, engraving on steel flourished through only one generation. Then, with the invention of the process of steel facing metals softer than steel, engravers returned to the more sympathetic copper. *Copper engraving* is the correct term today, as it had been up to 1820—that is, through the greater part of the history of the art.

Each artist has his own way of indicating or sketching on the copper plate design that is to be cut. The incised lines themselves are carved with a tool called an *engraver* or *burin*. It is a steel rod about 4 inches long, lozenge-shaped and sharpened by being cut obliquely at the end. The wooden handle is shaped like half of a mushroom to fit the palm of the hand, while the rod is held between the thumb and second finger and is pushed forward, cutting a clear V-shaped furrow without burr. Such a laborious method cannot approach the etched line in its freedom and spontaneity; it results in stiffness and formality. Stipple engraving makes use of dots instead of lines, although it is sometimes used with line. The printing of engravings, in principle, is like that of all incised metal plates as described in the paragraphs about etching. With line engraving, however, the impressions are taken with a view to keeping the lines clear, and less tone is employed than in printing etchings. Indeed one of the cardinal virtues of an engraving is considered to be a clean-cut, almost severe quality of line, without *drag* or blur.

WOODCUTS

Broadly speaking, *engraving* may be applied to an incision made in any material; but the word *engravings* when used alone is the more likely to mean prints from *metal* plates, as some authorities would restrict the

METROPOLITAN MUSEUM OF ART

ALBRECHT DÜRER (1471–1528) raised the graphic arts of woodcutting, engraving, and etching to major art forms, and was the first—and probably the greatest—master of these techniques In *The Adoration of the Magi*, a woodcut of 1511, the Magi, bearing gifts, and the Holy Family are shown in the costumes of sixteenth-century Germany.

grain; but many engravers have preferred other woods and blocks cut with the grain. Because woodcuts have been so generally used with type for illustration of book texts, the blocks are usually prepared type high —meaning 0.918 inch (about 11/12). The artist's design is drawn on the block in reverse.

In white-line engraving the artist conceives his design in terms of white lines on black, and the strokes of his cutting tool appear in white. He carves away the high lights and secures half lights with white lines or white cross-hatching or white stippling on areas originally black. Some connoisseurs consider white-line engraving superior to black-line, since the toolmarks are shown more directly for what they are; a certain spontaneity results, not easily attainable by a process in which the lines have to be "worked around."

Working around the lines is just what the artist does when he produces the more common black-line woodcut. He carves away the white spaces, to leave a design in black lines standing on the surface of the block. Beautiful work has been done in this technique, and if it is less characteristic of the woodcutting process than white-line, it nevertheless has been practiced far more by the outstanding masters of the art—perhaps because the draughtsman who made the drawing on the block was often an artist renowned in painting and pen work, and the engraver merely a craftsman translating the other's design, making possible its duplication by printing.

The history of the art in Europe is concerned at first with a great number of anonymous designs indicating masterly ability. These are partly from the *block books* that were designed to give the common people stories in picture form, at a time when painting and illuminated manuscripts were reserved for the very wealthy classes; and partly from early printed and illustrated books. The first masters of the woodcut whose names we know and perhaps the greatest of all time were the Germans. Again Dürer must be put down as the master of all masters, and Hans Baldung, Lucas Cranach and Hans Holbein the Younger deserve mention in even the shortest list. Much later, in England, Thomas Bewick, William Blake and Edward Calvert were important innovators. Timothy Cole in America was the last but not the least of the wood engravers of the older period.

For a long period woodcutting became a reproductive art, craftsmen trying only to reproduce the characteristic effects of pen-and-ink drawing and wash drawing, chiefly for magazine and book illustration. But in our own time creative woodcutting has known a renaissance, and very beautiful work is being done in the medium in most European countries and in Mexico and the United States.

Block Prints.—The name *block prints* is reserved by some authorities for woodcuts of a broad sort cut on *planks* instead of the cross-grained boxwood block, with knives instead of burin. This is the process employed

term. Nevertheless it is logical and not unusual to speak of wood engravings. It is just as well, however, to adopt here the word *woodcuts* for all sorts of prints from negatives cut on wood. Woodcuts may be produced by either one of two processes: white-line or black-line.

There is one basic distinction between woodcuts whether white-line or black-line and all types of hand engraving or etching on metal, a distinction that the student of the subject should hold in mind from the outset. The parts of the wood block that print are *in relief;* they stand up on the block, and the hollows between and around them produce whites in the final product. This is the exact opposite of intaglio or incised processes on metal, for in them the lines to be

printed are cut *into* the metal, indented below the surface, and the parts that are not etched away do not print in the final product. Woodcut prints are *contact* prints; they can be produced from the block exactly as fine books are printed from set type— the paper merely touches the block face or type face. But copper engravings and etchings can be properly printed only with sufficient pressure to force the dampened paper down into the ink-filled incisions.

The tools used by the woodcut artist are knives and an engraving tool like that of the copperplate engraver, the *burin*. In general it may be said that knives are used to produce the broader effects, and the burin for delicate work. The block most commonly used is of boxwood, sawed across the

by the Japanese artists for their famous color prints; and indeed the method is standard wherever polychrome prints are made from wood.

In polychrome work a block is made for each color, and the designs superimposed. The artist begins by drawing his outlines on very thin paper that is pasted, face down, on the first or key block. With knives and gouges lines are cut standing up with sloping sides like dikes, to give solidity, and large spaces are gouged out more deeply. At each of two opposite corners there is a triangular mark for registering, that the Japanese call *kento*. In turn a block for each additional color is cut, and each one is provided with corresponding register marks. There may be 5 or 6 blocks or (more rarely) as many as 16 or even 18. Finally the dampened paper is laid on the face of the first block, which has been charged with color by short brushes. Over this is gently rubbed a flat disk about 4 inches in diameter called a *baren*, which presses the paper to the block and absorbs

WILLIAM H. SCHAB GALLERY

VAN GOGH'S only graphic work is this etching of Dr. Gachet done in 1890 at Auvers.

the color. One by one the colored parts of the picture from each of the remaining blocks are superimposed. The resulting color prints, as produced by the Japanese, constitute one of the most wonderful instances in all history of a popular and a cheap art with the highest artistic values. Every one should know the names and works of Utamaro, Hokusai and Hiroshige, masters of the Japanese block print.

LITHOGRAPHY

Metal plate lines are in itaglio. Wood plates are in relief. Printing from the surface or plane is lithography. A lithograph is a crayon drawing on stone, done in the manner of a crayon or charcoal drawing on paper, the difference being that by means of inking and a press the drawing on stone may be multiplied.

Lithographic stone is a form of calcium carbonate cut in slabs 2 or 3

MUSEUM OF MODERN ART

JEALOUSY, lithograph by Edward Munch.

inches thick. The best stone comes from Solnhofen, Bavaria. The crayon is composed of a greasy substance that sinks into the stone wherever it is touched by the crayon. When the drawing is finished, the stone is moistened with water. As water and grease do not combine, the parts that have drawing on them repel the water, but the parts not drawn upon absorb it. A roller charged with greasy ink is then passed over the surface; the ink is repelled by the wet parts and adheres to every part that is not wet and that was drawn upon by the crayon. A sheet of paper is next placed upon the stone, which is passed under a heavy roller. The ink is transferred to the paper and produces an exact facsimile of the original drawing. These are the principles of lithography, though there are mechanical details connected with the printing of interest only to workers.

Drawings may be made on prepared paper and sent to lithograph printers who transfer them to stone. This process (called *transfer lithography*) permits making drawings where large and cumbersome stones may not be taken; such, for instance, as the large drawings of Panama Canal subjects made by one of the best lithographers, Joseph Pennell (1857–1926). The drawing transferred to the stone is exactly as it was made by the artist, but some critics insist that the resulting lithograph is less artistic than the one drawn on the stone itself by the artist. Nevertheless certain very delicate gradations and textural subtleties are possible where the draughtsman works directly on the stone—effects not possible to the transfer process of lithography.

No other graphic art possesses as immense scope or has been called upon for such a variety of purposes as lithography. It has been used for the most delicate of book illustrations and for such miniature designs as pictorial calling cards and bookplates; and at the other extreme it has produced commercial posters in full color of huge size.

There is no other multiplying medium as sensitive to the artist's touch. The most delicate grays as well as the strongest blacks may be reproduced exactly as the artist made them. It was discovered in 1798 by Aloys Senefelder, a Bavarian, and was introduced into the United States

about 1835. In the early 19th century some of the most eminent artists of Germany and France turned to the new medium, and the French painter and caricaturist Honoré Daumier is considered the greatest of all lithographers.

PRINT COLLECTING

The fascination of collecting prints is such that a whole library of books has been written on the subject, and print dealers and print galleries are to be found even in small cities. The latest historian of print making, Carl Zigrosser, opens his *Six Centuries of Fine Prints* with a quotation from an anonymous author of two centuries ago; and this passage may, more fitly than any more recent expression, serve to close the present brief review of the graphic arts:

"When I reflect on the Usefulness of this Art, I am surprized to find so few Gentlemen professed Admirers of it. It requires a large Fortune to make a fine Collection of Paintings, and great Judgement to avoid Imposition, and understand their Beauties; but Prints are adapted to all Ages, all Ranks of Men, and all Fortunes; . . .

"Prints are also as useful as entertaining; they represent absent things to us, as if they were present; they convey us instantly, without Hazard or Expence, into the most distant Countries, and make us as well acquainted with them as with our own; they communicate to us the Knowl-

JANET MEVI

COLOR LITHOGRAPH, Toulouse-Lautrec.

edge of many beautiful Objects in those Countries, which we must have been ignorant of, without their Assistance; and make us Contemporaries (in a manner) with the greatest Men of past Ages by giving us their lively Resemblance . . .

"Lastly, there is hardly any Subject, with Regard to which we cannot either acquire some Knowledge, or enlarge what we already have, by the Help of this noble Art."

PRINTING

Letterpress printing, the oldest and best-known way of transferring impressions of type and engravings to paper, is often called *relief* printing because only the raised surface of the type or engraving receives the ink, which is then transferred to the paper by pressure. Nearly all newspapers, books and magazines, as well as numerous other forms of printed matter, are produced by this method.

The Historical Background.—Letterpress printing in the western world began about 1440 when Johann Gutenberg of Mainz invented movable types. This invention was the final link in a long series of previous developments: the alphabet; a surface to write on; a liquid and an instrument to write with. The next and final step was a method of duplicating, quickly and economically, the written page and its illustrations.

The Alphabet.—Prehistoric man drew pictures of animals and other objects on various surfaces—the walls of caves, flat rocks, bones, metals, the skins of animals. He supplemented his primitive language with gestures or signs, from which were evolved pictographs, a crude sort of picture writing. From these pictographs were evolved ideographic writing such as is used by the Chinese and various alphabets, notably the Roman that we use.

Writing Materials.—It is probable that one of the first materials used for writing was the tanned skins of animals. As skins were often difficult to obtain, the Egyptians made from the papyrus reed a crude form of paper that was far from satisfactory. It was so brittle that it could not be folded or creased. The only way to bind a papyrus book was to wind it around a stick of wood. Split, tanned and bleached animal pelts proved to be far better. Calfskin made a very satisfactory product known as *vellum.* Sheepskin or goatskin made into parchment was less expensive. The Chinese produced the first satisfactory paper—about 105 A.D., and this invention was transmitted to Europe by the Arabs after their conquest of Samarkand in 751. But it was four centuries later that the first paper was made in Europe—in Spanish mills. Before 1270 paper was being made in Germany. There is no authentic record when writing ink was discovered or when brushes and pens came into use. Probably it was long before papyrus was first used.

Manuscript Books.—Sheets of vellum or parchment, folded to make two leaves or more, and a number of sheets bound together to form a book by 400 A.D., had largely supplanted the papyrus or parchment rolls that had been used for so many centuries. During the next thousand years these manuscript books became more and more elaborate. On many were lavished the utmost skill of the penman, the illustrator, the illuminator, the binder. They were very expensive, and a grave fault was the inaccuracy of the texts. It was impossible for the copyist to avoid repeating the errors in the book he was copying or to escape making new errors. What was needed was a method of producing books at much less cost that would also reduce the number of errors.

Movable Types.—As early as 1050 A.D. the Chinese were using movable types. Centuries before this and long before the idea of printing from movable types dawned on Gutenberg, men had been cutting letters on stone, wood and various metals. These letters were often in relief (above the surface). In the early times slaves and cattle were branded by burning with hot irons, the letters or signs used being forged or cut in relief on the ends of iron rods. Potters stamped

JOHANN GUTENBERG, inventor of movable type. A 42-line Bible, the Gutenberg Bible, was first book printed with movable type.

their names or marks in the soft clay of their wares, which was afterward hardened by baking. Engraved dies and molds had long been used for making coins and seals. The Assyrians preserved their records on clay cylinders that had been stamped from engravings. From stamping on these materials it was but a step to stamping on vellum or parchment. Some manuscript books are decorated with large initial capitals that were cut in relief on wood or metal and then impressed on the parchment. The letters were more uniform, and there was a tremendous saving in labor.

Then crude pictures were stamped from designs cut in relief on wood. The first extensive use of this method of printing was for playing cards; and about the same time, early in the 15th century, pictures of sacred personages began to be made in large quantities by wood-block printing. At first the titles of these pictures were added with pen or brush. Soon they were made part of the picture, being cut in relief on the engraved block.

Obviously, the next step was to bind a number of these pictures into the form of a book, adding a cover of some kind to protect the leaves. These first printed books with crude engravings poorly printed on inferior paper could not compare with the magnificent handwritten books blazing with brilliant colors and with elaborate gold-stamped leather bindings. But all that was required to produce a book equal to the handwritten volume (and at much less expense) was better paper, better ink, better presswork and some method that would obviate the excessive labor of cutting on wood the many letters of the text. In Paris in 1470 a copy of Gutenberg's 42-line Bible could be bought for 2,000 francs; a few years before, the same book handwritten cost five times as much.

To improve the paper was not difficult. All that was needed was better ingredients and more care in manufacture. Lacking a satisfactory paper, vellum or parchment could be used. To obtain better ink it was only necessary to adapt the new linseed-oil paints then popular with artists and use them instead of the weak watercolor inks that had been used for printing block books. Nor did better presswork present a problem. The screw press was then in general use for pressing grapes and olives, for removing moisture from the sheets in making paper and for printing textiles. All Gutenberg had to discover was a method of producing quickly, cheaply and accurately letters that could be combined into one page of text and then could again be assembled into another page of text with different words.

We shall never know how Gutenberg solved this problem, but it would seem that he must have devoted years to study and experiment before he hit on the solution. It is easy to picture him as testing and rejecting letters cut on wood as being too laborious to produce; as cutting letters on lead or other metals and rejecting them for the same reason; as placing one of the wooden letters in a recess and filling the cavity with molten lead. The great discovery was now almost within his grasp. From the reversed letter thus produced it was only necessary to obtain a reversed duplicate. What, then, could be more natural than to place this duplicate in the recess and again fill the cavity with metal? When the metal had cooled, and the letter was removed from the cavity, Gutenberg held in his hand his first type cast in a mold. The possession of books was no longer to be confined to a few persons, and their cost was soon to be reduced until they were within the means of nearly everybody.

The Mold.—It would seem that Gutenberg's first problem was devising a mold that would cast type with one unvarying dimension but would be adjustable for the dimensions that do vary—the widths of the different letters. The principle of the mold he evolved was very simple and was in use for centuries. Probably the first one constructed was two **L-**

shaped blocks of brass, copper or iron, shaped thus: ⊓ With one of the blocks held stationary, moving the other in either direction left one dimension of the opening unchanged but made it possible to vary the other to any size within the limit of the mold. Thus from a single mold letters of various widths could be cast, yet all would be of uniform size from top to bottom of the printing surface. The other dimension, the distance from the printing surface to the base of the type, was not of great importance, except it was necessary that all the types be of the same length. This was doubtless obtained by the thickness of the blocks, which controlled the depth of the cavity, and the final degree of accuracy was obtained with a file or plane.

The Matrix.—In operating the mold the reversed type (known at the *matrix*) was accurately positioned at the bottom of the opening in the mold, and the recess was filled with molten lead. It is probable that the first matrices were cast in lead from letters cut on wood. It was soon discovered that they had but a short life. Doubtless it was not long before Gutenberg evolved the method used today, cutting the letter in relief on the end of a rod of soft iron or steel that was then hardened and driven into a block of copper or brass. Matrices of this kind are almost indestructible.

The Press.—The claim has been made that Gutenberg *invented* the first printing press, since the block books already mentioned seem to have been printed by laying the paper on the inked block and rubbing or brushing the back of the sheet until the ink was transferred to the paper. It would be better to say that he adapted the press. Probably what Gutenberg did was to build a stronger and heavier press than those then in use for pressing grapes and printing textiles, so that it was powerful enough to give an even impression to a large page of heavy-face type when printed on parchment or vellum. It was difficult to devise a method of applying an even coat of thick ink to the type page. It is probable that he used two leather balls stuffed with hair and obtained a more or less even coating of ink on the balls by rotating them together by hand and then rolling the balls over the type page. Obviously this was a task that required much skill. It is not known if ink balls were invented by Gutenberg. They may have been devised by the printers of block books.

Did Gutenberg Invent Movable Types?—The claim that Gutenberg was the first European to cast metal type from matrices and the first to use such types for the printing of books is based on evidence that is scanty and inconclusive but is more conclusive than the proof for any other claimant. Gutenberg, born in Mainz about 1400, was living in Strasbourg in 1439. Records of a lawsuit in that year contain obscure references that may mean he was then engaged in making type or printing books. The records of a lawsuit in 1455 show that Gutenberg had borrowed 800 gulden

from a goldsmith named Johann Fust to "finish the work;" and in 1452 Fust had advanced another 800 gulden so he could share as a partner in the profits of the enterprise. Here there is definite proof that the enterprise was making books. Fust won the suit and obtained possession of Gutenberg's printing equipment. In 1465 Archbishop Adolph appointed Gutenberg one of the gentlemen of his court, and in 1468 a Dr. Konrad Humery gave the archbishop recompense for certain materials used in printing that Gutenberg had left after his death.

Besides we know that the goldsmith Fust and his son-in-law and partner Peter Schoeffer in 1457 completed a magnificent Psalter. This book bears a colophon in Latin that says it was printed by Fust and Schoeffer in 1457. Even if these men printed this book, there is strong presumptive evidence that it was planned by Gutenberg, and that he had it well under way when his connection with Fust was brought to an end by the 1455 lawsuit.

The Gutenberg Bibles.—These Bibles are perhaps the most convincing proof that Gutenberg was the inventor of movable types; at the time they appeared he was the only man who had the knowledge and the experience to produce such magnificent books. The best-known is the 42-line, so called because there are 42 lines to a column on many of the pages. So far as known, only 32 perfect copies are in existence. It was printed before the Fust and Schoeffer Psalter, for the Mazarin 4-volume copy of the 42-line Bible in a Paris library has a notation that the binding and rubrication were completed on August 15, 1456. Not so well known is the 36-line Bible, only eight copies of which are in existence, and

not all of these are perfect. It is conjectured that Gutenberg had this Bible under way when he secured the first loan from Fust; that it was then laid aside to bring out the 42-line work; and that he completed it with Albrecht Pfister as his financial backer after his partnership with Fust ceased in 1455. If this conjecture is correct, then the 36-line Bible has the best claim to being the first printed book.

Early German Printers.—Printing was not long confined to Mainz, but soon spread to other near-by towns. Early German books are noted for their woodcut illustrations. At Bamberg, in 1460, Albrecht Pfister, already mentioned as the reputed financial backer of Gutenberg, began printing a long series of illustrated books. At Cologne, about 1478, Heinrich Quentell printed a magnificent Bible with over a hundred woodcut illustrations. At Nuremberg, the great wood engraver, Albrecht Dürer, served his apprenticeship.

Printing Spreads Over Europe.—After Fust won his lawsuit against Gutenberg, the firm of Fust and Schoeffer prospered for several years, printing a considerable number of fine books. It is probable that their plant was either wrecked or closed when the town of Mainz was sacked in 1462. Their workmen then emigrated to other countries, taking with them all the knowledge required to make type and print books. The best-known of these men were Konrad Sweynheim and Arnold Pannartz, who began to print near Rome in 1464. At Strasbourg Johann Mentelin was printing huge volumes by 1460. Three German printers, probably from the Fust and Schoeffer printing shop, established a press at the Paris Sorbonne in 1469. Their names were Freiburger, Kranz,

NEW YORK PUBLIC LIBRARY

GERMAN BIBLE, printed in Cologne in 1478. This is the ninth leaf from the end of this beautifully illustrated Bible. Along the bottom is shown the adoration of the Magi.

Gering. At Bruges in 1474 William Caxton printed the first book in English. Two years later he set up the first press in England. He was long the only printer in that country and though he was not a finished workman, he was an excellent scholar and translated into English more than a score of the books he printed. The type he used was an unusual but readable form of black letter, more graceful that Gutenberg's.

Venice, the Center of Early Printing.— Venice noted for its sea-borne commerce and many industries, was famous for its printers, and the number of books printed there soon exceeded that of any other city in Europe. One of the first printers and perhaps the best-known was the Frenchman Nicolas Jenson, the first great type-designer, who made the first Roman lower-case types. Next was the Italian Aldo Manuzio, better known by his Latinized name, Aldus Manutius, not a printer but a great scholar and publisher and the first to issue small and inexpensive books. He was much interested in the literary treasures of antiquity and published a number of the Greek classics, as well as Greek grammars and dictionaries. He also printed many correct texts of the Latin classics. He died in 1515, but the business he established did not end until 1597.

Early French Printers.—The 16th-century Estienne family (also known by the Latinized form, Stephanus) is perhaps the best known. Henri, who married the widow of a printer, specialized on Greek and Latin classics. One of his proofreaders was the celebrated Geoffroy Tory, spelling reformer and type-designer, best known for his remarkable wood engravings and his ability to teach that difficult art to others. When Henri Estienne died, his widow married another famous printer, Simon de Colines, who frequently employed Tory to design the initials, borders and diagrams for the books he printed. Robert Estienne, who was the son of the widow Estienne and Henri, and his learned wife edited scores of the Greek and Latin classics they printed. Robert was also famous for the Latin, Greek and Hebrew dictionaries he compiled, aided by others. Distinguished as a scholar, he attained equal fame as a printer, and his books were noted for their correct design and careful workmanship. Several other members of the Estienne family gained fame as scholars, publishers or printers.

Early Printers in Holland and Belgium.—There is reason to believe that a crude form of printing was practiced in Holland before Gutenberg printed his famous Bibles, but the first dated books produced in that country were printed at Utrecht in 1473. Perhaps the best known of the early printers in Belgium was the Frenchman Christophe Plantin (1514–89). His masterpiece, which almost ruined him, was his great eight-volume Polyglot (many-language) Bible. His printing house in Antwerp, in existence for many years after his death, is now a museum. Another celebrated family of printers and publishers in Holland in the 17th century were the Elzevirs.

JOHN WYCLIF translated Bible into English.

Their claim to fame rests on the many small and inexpensive books they produced.

The Spanish Polyglot Bible.—Although printing in Spain had been introduced at an earlier date, perhaps the first great masterpiece was a Polyglot Bible, printed by Brocar at Alacalá in 1514–18. The languages were Hebrew, Greek, Latin and Chaldee. Another notable figure was Ibarra, remembered for his Spanish and Latin editions of Sallust. In one of his

MANUALE

TIPOGRAFICO

DEL CAVALIERE

GIAMBATTISTA BODONI

———

VOLUME PRIMO.

PARMA

PRESSO LA VEDOVA

MDCCCXVIII.

MANUAL contains samples of type faces.

many existing letters Benjamin Franklin expressed admiration of the Sallust and a fine edition of *Don Quixote.*

The New Craft in England.—Caxton, the first English printer, was succeeded by an Alsatian, Wynkyn de Worde (d. *c.* 1534). Other early printers were Thomas Berthelet, Richard Grafton, John Day. Little notable work was produced, however, until William Caslon (1692–1766) cut the types that have since borne his name and that ended the importing of inferior types from Holland. The next great name in English type design and printing is that of John Baskerville (1706–75), erstwhile footman and master penman, who made a fortune as a japanner and lost the greater part of it as a publisher and maker of fine books. In return, however, he gained a great measure of fame and the acquaintance and friendship of many famous men. Of his first production, a Vergil over which he labored for years, Macaulay said it "went forth to astonish all the librarians of Europe." Benjamin Franklin, who never forgot he was a printer or any of the details of the printer's craft, purchased six copies, one of which he presented to Harvard College. Samuel Johnson hastened to buy a copy and present it to Trinity College, Oxford, as a recompense for the extensive use he had been permitted to make of its library. Cambridge University recognized what Baskerville had accomplished by electing him printer to the University for 10 years. Oxford University commissioned him to design and cast a font of great primer Greek, for which he was paid 200 guineas. During the next 20 years he produced scores of beautiful volumes, one of the most magnificent being his Folio Bible. Long out of fashion and bitterly criticised when they first appeared, Baskerville's types are now having extensive use. This penniless youth, who started life without education or friends, belongs in the second rank of the world's printers.

Baskerville's Disciples.—The fame of Baskerville spread all over Europe, and others began to print books more or less in the style he had created, notably that energetic Italian Giambattista Bodoni (1740–1813). Baskerville accentuated the light and heavy strokes of the letters he designed, and Bodoni increased the difference, avoiding any suggestion that his letters were the offspring of pen or brush, and made it clear that they were produced solely with the square and compass. Like Baskerville, in his later books Bodoni avoided all decoration but paid great attention to paper and presswork.

A French family of printers and type founders, the Didots, also were disciples of Baskerville. François, printer, publisher, bookseller, produced a number of well-printed volumes before he died in 1757. One of his sons, François Ambrose, was an able type founder who perfected Fournier's point system of measuring type bodies, which continues to be the basis of the French method. Among other books he printed is a collection of French classics sponsored by Louis

XVI. It was with this family that Benjamin Franklin placed his grandson, young Bache, that he might master the type founder's trade. One of the sons of this family, Pierre, *l'aîné*, took over the printing office and printed a long series of magnificent editions, perhaps the finest being one of Racine. The other brother, Firmin, succeeded to the type-foundry branch, and the many handsome types he produced, reminiscent of Baskerville, retain their popularity in France.

Early American Printing.—It is probable that the first printing in North America was in Mexico City. In 1539 an Italian, Giovanni Paoli, was sent there with printing equipment. The first printing in what is now the United States was at Cambridge, Mass. Jose Glover, a clergyman, interested in establishing a college in Massachusetts Bay Colony, decided that a printing office would be a worth-while adjunct to the proposed institution. In addition to the equipment for printing, when he sailed from England in 1638, Glover brought with him Stephen Day, a locksmith, and two of Day's sons; one, Matthew, 18 years old, was a printer. Glover died during the voyage and his widow purchased a house in Cambridge and later married Rev. Henry Dunster, the first president of Harvard College. Meanwhile the management of the college provided a dwelling for Stephen Day and his family, and in this house the printing plant was established. It was probably in operation by October, 1638. The first work produced was a small broadside, "The Freeman's Oath," no copy of which is in existence. The first book, the *Bay State Psalm Book*, appeared in 1640. Matthew Day died in 1649 and was succeeded by Samuel Green, who was connected with the Cambridge Press for nearly half a century. Green's greatest work was the printing, with the help of Marmaduke Johnson, of Eliot's Indian Bible, in the language of the Natick Indians.

Ben Franklin, Printer.—No mention of early printing in the United States would be complete unless something was said about that public-spirited citizen, great statesman, scientist and diplomat, the genial old philosopher who thus began his last will and testament: "I, Benjamin Franklin, Printer . . ." At the age of 12 he was apprenticed to his half-brother James, a printer. At 16 his name appeared as editor and publisher of a newspaper that his brother had started but that the authorities had forbidden to appear under the brother's name. After a quarrel with his brother, young Ben left Boston for Philadelphia. He worked as a printer in London for a time. Returning to Philadelphia, he soon embarked in the printing business and then started the profitable *Pennsylvania Gazette* and the even more profitable *Poor Richard's Almanack*. Twenty years later he was able to retire with a comfortable fortune.

The Deterioration of Printing.—Unlike other great discoveries, the first printed book, the 42-line Bible, was an almost perfect example of correct design and fine workmanship. But it was not long before the high standards set by Gutenberg began to deteriorate. There were revivals from time to time, but it is not too much to say that by 1888, all over the world, the average quality of printing had fallen to a very low level. William Morris, a many-sided genius, must be given credit for arousing interest in the production of better books, as well as all forms of printed matter. It was in 1889 that he started to design a type-face he termed the Golden, which was first used in a book he

THE PENNSYLVANIA GAZETTE, the most widely read paper in the colonies, was started by Samuel Keimer in December 1728. Benjamin Franklin purchased interest in the *Gazette*, and it was first issued under his name as publisher October 2, 1729. Franklin also edited the four-page weekly, which became the most influential newspaper of the time. Ben had been apprentice to his brother and set type for *The New England Courant*. He worked as a printer in London and, upon his return to Philadelphia, set up a printing business. The *Gazette* was noted for its fine appearance, superior news presentation, and notable writing. From the same press came *Poor Richard's Almanack* (1732) and many pamphlets concerned with public issues.

wrote himself, *The Story of the Glittering Plain* (1891). This volume, as well as the later issues of the Kelmscott Press, attracted much attention, so perfect were they in every detail. Not since the days of Gutenberg had such magnificent volumes been produced. *The Works of Geoffrey Chaucer* is considered the masterpiece among the Kelmscott books. But it is not so much by what Morris accomplished in the field of fine bookmaking that he will be long remembered. Rather, it is by the many talented men whom he inspired to make better books.

Fine Printing of Today.—In the United States the two veterans who should be

mentioned first are Bruce Rogers and D. B. Updike, who both made fine books for 40 years or more. Another veteran is Carl Rollins, an unusually fine workman with exquisite taste. Updike will be best remembered for his monumental *Printing Types*, a scholarly two-volume production that probably will never be supplanted by a more accurate and comprehensive study. The fame of Rogers rests chiefly on the Lectern Bible, printed at the Oxford University Press under his direction in his Centaur type. Frederic W. Goudy, American type-designer, produced more and better typefaces than any other man since movable types were invented. Aided

by his gifted wife, the late Bertha Goudy, who composed in such faultless style the type matter in the books bearing the imprint of the Village Press, Goudy composed books treasured by many collectors. A fifth veteran is John Henry Nash of San Francisco, who produced many fine books that are notable for their good composition, excellent presswork and faultless bindings.

How Printing Is Produced.—It is only within the last century that there has been any great improvement in the methods used to produce printing. Many of the chief labor-saving devices are less than 50 years old. Others came into existence within the last 25 years. The last 10 years have witnessed a number of other remarkable advances. Judging the future by the past, it would seem safe to predict a continual improvement in quality, as well as a reduction in the cost of printing.

Casting Type.—The hand mold Gutenberg invented for casting type was in use for centuries. Not until about 1840 with the advent of the Bruce type-caster did casting type by machine come into general use.

Setting Type.—Today type is set by hand in about the same way it was 500 years ago. With a shallow wooden tray before him, termed a *case,* and holding in his left hand a device known as a *stick,* with the thumb and two fingers of his right hand, the compositor picks up the types, letter by letter and places them in the stick. With the thumb of his left hand he holds the types upright until the line is almost completed. Between each word he places a shorter piece of metal known as a *space.* As he approaches the end of the line and finds that he has either too many or too few words to make a line the right length, he substitutes thinner or thicker spaces between the words until the length of the line is correct. This is known as *justification.* When the stick is full of composed types, they are placed on a galley, a shallow tray; and when the galley is full, a proof is made of the composition. The proof is read by comparison with the copy; the type matter is corrected and revised; and it is then ready to be made up into pages. The pages are then locked in a steel frame (a *chase*).

Sizes of Types.—Types are made in many sizes, the smallest in general use being about 12 lines to the inch; larger sizes may be but a single line to the inch or less. Type cut on wood, used for posters, may measure a foot to the line or more. The early printers had names for the various sizes of type—diamond, agate, pearl, minion, brevier, long primer, pica and others. These picturesque terms are now seldom used. A more accurate system of measurement was devised about 50 years ago. This is based on a unit known as a *point,* which is .013837 of an inch; 72 points measure approximately one inch or .996. The body of 6-point type (nonpareil) measures .083 or a trifle less than a twelfth of an inch.

Machine Composition.—Setting type by hand is now seldom practiced. To set type by machine was long the goal

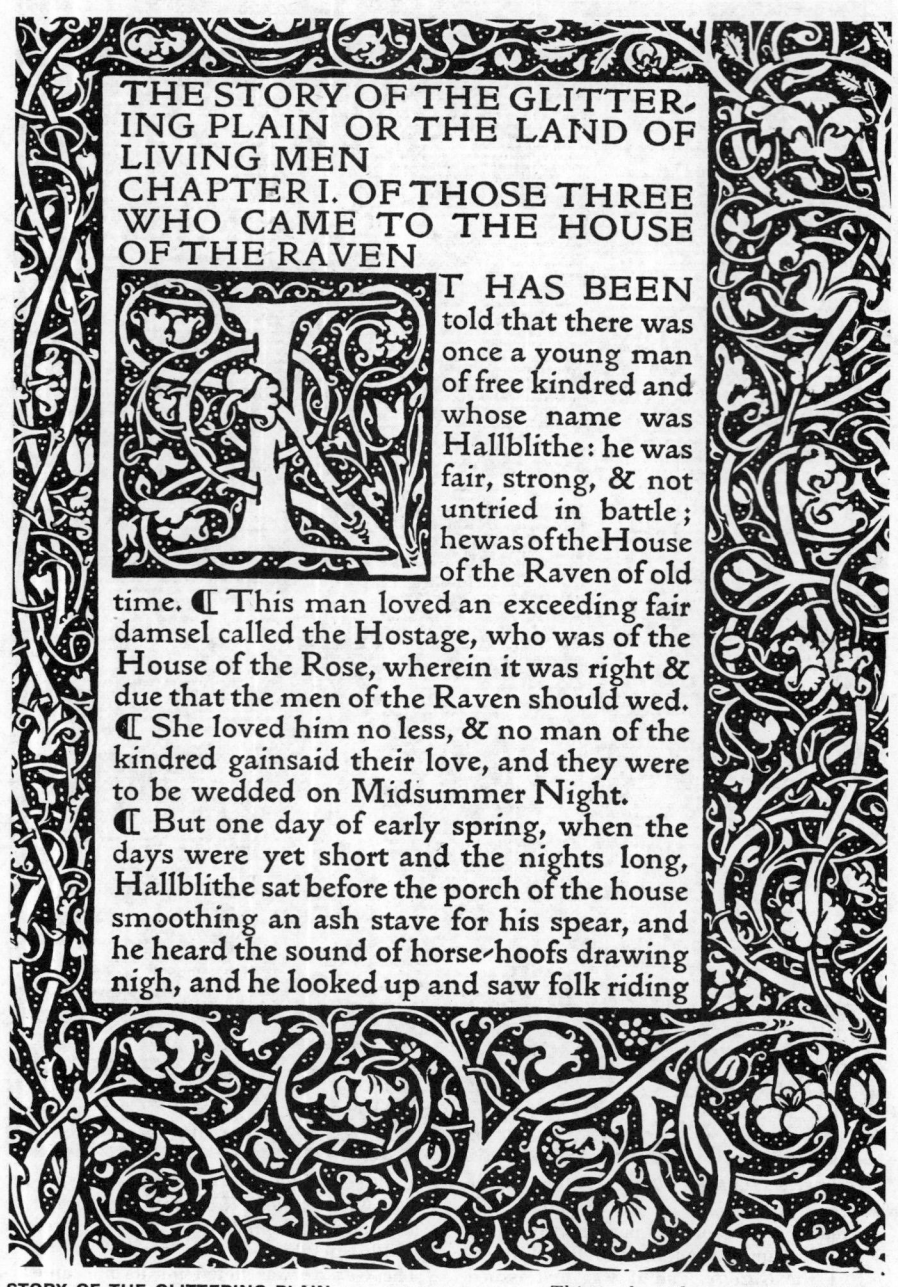

STORY OF THE GLITTERING PLAIN was a prose romance. This is the title page from William Morris' book, written in 1891 and published by his own firm, Kelmscott Press. Morris revived fine printing and bookmaking with his introduction of the Golden type face, illustrated in this book. Elaborate borders and initial letters are characteristic of Morris' style.

of many inventors; one of the first devices patented was that of William Church in 1822. Mark Twain, a compositor in his youth, sunk a considerable fortune in financing an attempt to perfect the Paige composing machine. The inventors who tried to make machines for setting the types used by hand compositors encountered two unsurmountable obstacles—justifying the lines to even length and distributing the type after it was used. A German, Ottmar Mergenthaler (1854-1909), overcame the difficulty when he approached the problem from a different angle—casting all the characters of a line in a single cast and from matrices assembled by the operator, using wedges between the words to justify the line. Tolbert Lanston (1844-1913), with his Monotype, gained the same end by a different and more complicated method.

The Linotype.—The first practical Linotype, a crude machine, was used in 1886 in the office of the *New York Tribune.* Constantly improved, the Linotype is now capable of producing nearly every kind of type composition. The machine is operated from a keyboard, the touching of a key releasing a matrix from the magazine, located directly over the keyboard. A revolving belt transfers the matrix to an assembly box. When enough matrices to fill a line are thus assembled, depressing a lever causes the line of matrices, with its wedge-shaped spaces between the words, to be presented to the mold. There a cast is made from a pot of molten metal, and the product is a slug, on one of the narrow surfaces of which is an impression of the matrices. The machine now automatically shaves the slug to correct size, delivers it to a galley and returns the matrices to the machine, each being housed in its proper channel, ready to be released again by the touch of a key. While these operations are taking place, the operator is assembling another line of matrices.

This description also applies to the Intertype, a machine almost identical with the Linotype. A third machine that produces a slug is the Typograph, used to a large extent in Germany.

The Monotype.—Unlike the Linotype, the Monotype produces individual types. They are automatically assembled and after they are corrected and made up into pages, they are ready for the press or to be electrotyped. Two units are required, a keyboard and a caster. The keyboard has keys like those of a typewriter, but there are five alphabets and no shift key. Striking a key does not produce a type but makes perforations in a strip of paper ribbon. When the ribbon is completed, it is placed in a power-driven casting machine, the operations of which are controlled by the perforations in the ribbon and cause the matrix case to present to the mold in correct sequence the matrices required to cast the letters indicated by the perforations. The justification of the lines is accomplished automatically. By means of certain attachments the casting machine can also be used to cast large type for hand composition,

as well as rules, borders and spacing material.

The Ludlow Typograph.—With this machine, matrices are set by hand and the line is cast in the form of a slug. It is much used for setting large type, such as newspaper headings and advertisements.

Other Type Casters.—The All-Purpose Linotype is operated in much the same way as the Ludlow, its product also being a slug cast from matrices set by hand. The Thompson casts type for hand composition as large as 48-point. The Monotype Giant Caster casts individual type to be set by hand as large as 72-point.

Proofs and the Proofreader.—Proofreaders are a necessary part of printing because authors make many errors, and errors are also made by machine operators and compositors, all of which the proofreader is supposed to detect. With what is known as the first proof, the copyholder reads the copy while the proofreader follows the proof and corrects any errors or deviations, marking them by symbols. Many more proofs may be required before all concerned are agreed that the type composition is without error.

Make-up, Imposition, Lockup.—*Make-up* is the assembling of the various sizes and kinds of type, as well as engravings, and placing them in correct positions on the page. *Imposition* is placing in correct position

Marks	Explanation	Marginal Marks	Errors Marked
id	Take out letter, letters, or words indicated.		He marked the proof.
#	Insert space where indicated.		He marked theproof.
9	Turn inverted letter indicated.		He maяked the proof.
r	Insert letter as indicated.		He maked the proof.
lc	Set in lower-case type.		He Marked the proof.
wf	Wrong font.		He marked the proof.
×	Broken letter. Must be replaced.		He marked the proof.
ital	Reset in italic type the matter indicated.		He marked the proof.
rom	Reset in roman (regular) type the matter indicated.		He marked the proof.
bf	Reset in bold-face type word, or words, indicated.		He marked the proof.
⊙	Insert period where indicated.		He marked the proof
tr	Transpose letters or words as indicated.		He the proof marked.
stet	Let it stand as it is. Disregard all marks above the dots.		He marked the proof.
/=/	Insert hyphen where indicated.		He made the proofmark.
eq. #	Equalize spacing.		He marked the proof.
[or]	Move over to the point indicated.		[He marked the proof.
	[if to the left; if to the right]		He marked the proof.]
⊔	Lower to the point indicated.		He marked the proof.
⊓	Raise to the point indicated.		He marked the proof.
⸲	Insert comma where indicated.		Yes he marked the proof.
ꝰ	Insert apostrophe where indicated.		He marked the boys proof.
❝ ❞	Enclose in quotation marks as indicated.		He marked it proof.
≡	Replace with a capital the letter or letters indicated.		he marked the proof.
sc	Use small capitals instead of the type now used.		He marked the proof.
⊥	Push down space which is showing up.		He marked the proof.
⌒	Draw the word together.		He ma rked the proof.
2̂	Insert inferior figure where indicated.		Sulphuric Acid is HSO.
2̌	Insert superior figure where indicated.		a² + b² = c.
Out, see copy	Used when words left out are to be set from copy and inserted as indicated.		He proof.
æ	The diphthong is to be used.		Caesar marked the proof.
fi	The ligature of these two letters is to be used.		He filed the proof.
spell out	Spell out all words marked with a circle.		He marked the ②d proof.
¶	Start a new paragraph as indicated.		reading. The reader marked
No ¶	Should not be a separate paragraph. Run in.		marked. The proof was read by
②	Query to author. (Encircled in red.)		The proof read by
?	This is the symbol used when a question is to be set. Note that a query to author is encircled in red.		Who marked the proof
═	Out of alignment. Straighten.		He marked the proof.
1-em dash.			He marked the proof.
2-em dash.			He marked the proof.
En dash.			He marked the proof.
□	Indent 1 em.		He marked the proof.
□□	Indent 2 ems.		He marked the proof.
□□□	Indent 3 ems.		He marked the proof.

Proofreader's Marks

DOUGLAS MCMURTRIE, THE BOOK

PAPYRUS, the first writing paper, is here being harvested in Egypt (from a 1475 B.C. inscription). Papyrus was very brittle and could not be folded. It proved unsatisfactory.

all the pages that are to be printed on one sheet at one impression. *Lockup* is locking in a steel frame all the pages that are to be printed on a sheet of paper.

Printing Presses.—Over a century elapsed before the screw type of wooden press that Gutenberg used was improved to any great extent. Late in the 18th century the English earl of Stanhope constructed the first iron printing press. Though it would print a larger sheet than the presses then in use, there was little or no increase in the output. A German, Friedrich König (1774–1833), aided by Andrew Bauer, developed a machine that made the impression from a continually revolving cylinder. The type rested on a flat bed, and the machine was operated by steam power. Later it was improved to print both sides of the sheet before the sheet was delivered. The first machine was used to print *The Times* of London in 1814. Meanwhile, George Clymer had improved the hand press, greatly increasing its output by substituting a compound-lever movement for the screw method of making the impression. The hand press was further improved and the output increased by the use of a toggle joint to make the impression. Daniel Treadwell of Boston in 1882 brought out a press that was operated by power but used the principle of the hand press. This press was improved by Isaac Adams, and a few Adams presses are still in use at the Riverside Press in Cambridge, Mass.

There is not space to enumerate other early presses, nor to mention the huge newspaper and magazine presses in use today, or the many large and small presses used by book and commercial printers. Some of these print as many as five or more colors from a roll of paper and at unbelievable speeds.

Modern Methods of Making Paper.—Printing presses could not be operated to advantage if paper were not made by machine. Until about 1805 all paper was made by hand, the sheets seldom being larger than 22 by

JOHN CLYDE OSWALD. PRINTING IN THE AMERICAS

WOODEN HAND PRESS at Montpelier, Vermont. It is thought to be the press brought to America by Mrs. Jose Glover in 1638 and used by Matthew Day at Cambridge for the *Bay Psalm Book.*

28 inches, and much of it was of very poor quality, quite unlike the beautiful handmade and machine papers now obtainable. A Frenchman named Louis Robert in 1798 invented a machine that made paper in a continuous roll. The Fourdrinier brothers greatly improved Robert's machine and built a mill in England in 1803. Another invention was necessary before the Fourdrinier machine could be successful. It was soon found that the supply of cotton and linen fibers (or even of straw and fibrous grasses) was not equal to the demand or was too expensive. Henry Voelter in 1860 devised a method of making paper from pine and hemlock pulp. Nearly all modern papers are made from wood fibers.

Related Processes.—The present low cost and high quality of printing has been made possible by a number of interrelated processes; electrotyping, stereotyping, half-tone and line engraving and the use of machines for so many of the operations required for binding printed matter.

Electrotyping and Stereotyping.—These processes make possible the rapid and economical duplicating of type pages or engravings. They are used to avoid wear or damage to the originals, to avoid keeping pages in type for future editions, to reduce the number of impressions by printing more than one copy at a single impression and for producing curved plates that make it practicable to print from a rotating cylinder.

By the electrotype process, the duplicate is obtained by depositing with an electric current a thin film of copper on the face of a wax impression of the type matter or engraving. This film is then strengthened with a backing of lead. When it is heated, it can be curved for clamping to the cylinder of a rotary press; or it can be used as a flat plate for printing on a flat-bed press. Half-tone engravings are frequently molded in lead, and the copper is deposited on the lead.

Instead of wax, the stereotype method uses a flexible matrix of papier-mâché, and the cast is made by bringing the molten stereotype metal in contact with the matrix. Curved plates are cast in curved boxes, and flat casting boxes are used to produce flat plates.

Half-tone and Line Photoengraving.—Few illustrations appeared in newspapers, magazines and books until this century. Those that did appear were usually wood engravings. These ranged from the masterpieces of great engravers, such as Timothy Cole, to the crude productions of less

skilled workmen. An expensive book might have steel or copperplate engravings, but the ordinary volume was usually without pictures of any kind. Some of the illustrated weekly publications, *Puck* and *Judge* being typical examples, depended on lithography, then a comparatively slow and expensive process. There was a great need of a better, faster, more accurate and less expensive method of reproducing photographs and other subjects. This need had long been recognized, and there were many attempts to solve the problem. The first experiments were probably made by Fox Talbot in 1852. His idea, a sound one, was to resolve an image into dots of various sizes, and from that to make a printing plate. It was based, as is all photoengraving, on a previous discovery that gelatin or albumen impregnated with chromate or bichromate salts, when it is exposed to light, becomes insoluble in water. But evidently he could not solve the dot problem; that had to await the experiments of Frederic Eugene Ives, who produced the first satisfactory half-tone screen in 1885–86. As it is used today, this screen is two plates of glass, each ruled with very fine opaque lines that may be as close together as 400 to the inch, or as coarse as 65 to the inch. When the plates are cemented together with a transparent adhesive, the lines cross each other. (The number of lines to the inch gives the size of the screen—a 100-line half tone is one that has 100 lines to the inch. A 65-line half tone is used in newspapers; 120-line, for magazine illustration.)

This screen is interposed between the lens and the sensitized plate when the photographic negative is made, thus breaking up the subject into very small dots. The sizes of these dots are dependent on the amount of light passing through the lens, and then through the screen. But little light is transmitted from the dark parts of the image, hence those parts of the negative have very large dots. More light is transmitted from the lighter parts of the image. This means that when they are developed and fixed, those parts of the negative will have very small dots. When the negative is developed, those parts that receive the most light are the most transparent. Obviously, then, when a print is made from this screened negative to a bichromated metal plate, it has the appearance of a photograph, the dots being so small that they can be detected only when magnified. Before the print is made, the negative must be reversed because there will be another reversal when the plate is printed.

The metal plate, having been coated with a bichromatic solution of fish glue, is washed in water. Parts of the glue are dissolved and disappear, while the remainder are not affected. It is now only necessary to protect the remaining glue with something that will resist the acid used to etch the plate. Asphaltum is generally used with copper plates, as it resists the chloride of iron used for etching. If the plate is zinc, a resinous powder is required to resist the nitric acid used to etch the plate. In either case the action of the acid etches away all the parts of the plate not to be printed from, leaving the printing surface in relief. After various hand operations, the plate is ready for the printing press.

A line plate, made from a pen-and-ink drawing or any other subject that does not have continuous tones, is produced in much the same way as a half tone only there is not a screen between the lens and the negative.

The photoengraving method of producing printing plates is largely a mechanical process. It has now been so perfected and organized that little handwork is required. Aside from the faithfulness of the reproduction, it is a very fast process. the production of a newspaper half tone requiring but a few minutes.

Color Reproductions by Photoengraving.—Before the half-tone process was perfected, experimenters were endeavoring to make reproductions in color. It had already been established that all the colors of the spectrum could be obtained from the three primaries. In addition to the half-tone screen a *color filter* must be placed between the subject and the sensitized plate. This filter permits the passage of all the colors in the subject except one of the primaries. As that color does not pass through the filter, it later becomes the printing surface of the plate. This method is used with the other two primaries, a different filter being used for each. An etched copper plate is made from each of these three negatives, and when they are printed with yellow, red and blue inks in register (that is with accurate matching or superimposition of the plates), a result approximating the original is obtained. This was the method used by the first color engravers. It has since been found that better results are gained by the addition of a black plate.

PLANOGRAPHIC PRINTING

In *planographic* printing the printing surface is a flat plane. Alois Senefelder, a German, discovered this new way of printing in 1796. Near his home in Bavaria he found a porous stone that would absorb both grease and water. The legend is that he happened to write on a flat surface of the stone with a greasy crayon. Curious to know what would happen, he dampened the stone with water and then endeavored to cover it with printing ink. As he expected, he found that the ink would adhere only to the greasy writing; it was impossible to make it stick to the damp surface of the stone. Applying pressure to a sheet of paper placed on the stone, he found the ink would transfer to the paper. Thus lithography came into existence, and during the next hundred years it developed into a huge and complex industry. One of its chief uses was for illustrations in color. The Currier & Ives prints, millions of which were printed, and specimens of which now frequently command good prices, are typical examples of early color lithography.

But measured by present-day standards, lithography was far from being a perfect reproductive process. With the development of photoengraving for letterpress printing, inventive minds began to seek a way to apply that process to lithography. First, however, a way had to be found to eliminate the heavy and fragile lithographic stones, their use preventing a high production speed. While others had been working on the problem, the discovery of the offset method of lithographic printing was made in 1904 by Ira W. Rubel, a New Jersey lithographer. He had made some reproductions through a screen on a lithographic stone and was endeavoring to print them on a flat-bed lithographic press, the impression cylinder of which he had covered with a rubber blanket. When the press feeder omitted to send a sheet of paper through the press, the image on the stone was printed on the rubber blanket. With the next impression, the sheet of paper was printed on both sides, on one side being the direct impression of the image on the stone and on the other side the previous impression on the rubber blanket. When Rubel saw the back of the double-printed sheet, he was so impressed with the clearness and sharpness of the result that the feeder and he spent the remainder of the day making further experiments. Rubel later designed a press to print by this *offset* method, and as its merits were soon apparent, several concerns began to manufacture the presses. Unfortunately for Rubel, no basic patent could be obtained, because the same principle of printing had long been used for printing on tin. Furthermore, it had been previously discovered that thin, light sheets of zinc or aluminum grained so as to retain a certain amount of moisture could be substituted for lithographic stones, thus making it possible to use a rotating cylinder as a printing surface instead of the slow reciprocating movement the lithographic stone requires.

The principle of offset printing is very simple. Instead of printing direct from the printing cylinder to the paper, as with letterpress work, another cylinder is interposed, covered with a yielding rubber blanket, which receives the inked impression of the printing cylinder. This impression is then transferred or *offset* to a third cylinder, to which is attached a sheet of paper. As the three cylinders are geared to turn in unison, the offset press is capable of high speed.

Photography and the principle of the letterpress half tone have now been adapted to placing on the zinc

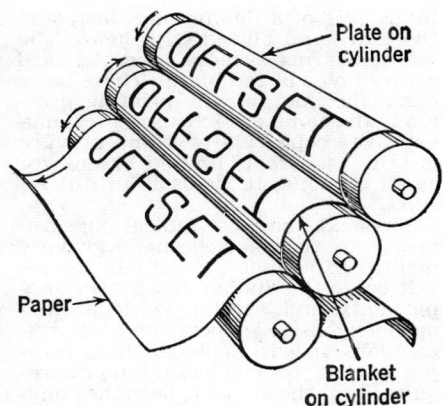

Plate on cylinder

Paper

Blanket on cylinder

HARRIS-SEYBOLD-POTTER COMPANY

OFFSET PRINTING operates on the indirect rotary principle. The impression first passes from a curved zinc plate to a rubber blanket, is then transferred onto the paper.

or aluminum sheets reproductions of type matter, drawings and photographs. As a consequence, the use of the offset method is rapidly expanding. A rubber blanket is used to receive the impression of the printing plate and then transfer it by pressure to the paper. This makes it possible to use rough-surface papers for printing half tones, which is almost impossible with letterpress. Larger and better presses and the perfecting of details have greatly increased production and improved the quality of the work. Remarkable results are also being obtained with photo-color reproductions, made possible by the use of two-color and four-color presses.

THE GRAVURE METHOD

The discovery of the gravure method of printing has been attributed to an early Italian goldsmith, Tommaso Finiguerra (1426–64). It is assumed that he was the first to incise a design on a metal plate, fill the lines with ink, remove the surplus ink from the flat surface and then impress on the plate a sheet of paper, using a soft packing and considerable pressure to force the paper into the incisions and transfer the ink to the paper. This is the basic principle of all gravure processes.

Dissatisfied with the results obtained with woodcuts, early printers often made use of copperplate engravings, the subjects being incised on copperplates and printed by the method just outlined. The steel engravings of a later period were identical with the copperplates, except for the use of steel, the method of printing being the same. Though copper and steel engravings are still used for the more expensive forms of announcements and stationery and paper currency, they are seldom used for book illustrations, having been superseded by the gelatin process or the hand photogravure. Hand photogravure is etching with acid positives of photographs or wash drawings that have been printed on sensitized tissue and transferred to copper. No screen is used, for the acid bites through the interstices of a fine powder dusted on the plate and affixed with heat. The powder forms a resist, and the acid etches holes in the plate. These holes carry the ink, and the printing process is the same as that used for hand-engraved copperplates. Hand gravure is still used to a limited extent for small editions; it yields beautiful results.

The next and most radical improvement was to adapt the hand gravure method to volume production, the result being the Sunday newspaper supplements and similar work printed on inexpensive papers and at tremendous speeds. This method, *rotogravure* or *rotary photogravure,* requires that the subjects be etched on a copper cylinder. Web-feed and sheet-feed presses are used. The paper is fed between a plate cylinder and an impression cylinder. The resiliency of the rubber surface of the impression cylinder forces the paper into the cavities of the plate cylinder and thus transfers the ink to the paper. As the plate cylinder revolves, and before it comes in contact with the printing cylinder, it receives a coating of almost liquid ink, but all the surplus ink is then scraped off the surface of the cylinder by a steel bar called a *doctor,* and the ink remains only in the etched cells that represent the design.

Etching the cylinder is the most difficult task, but anything that can be photographed can be used as a subject. The negative is photographed in the usual way, and a positive is made from the negative. From the positive is printed the *resist,* a film of chromated gelatin mounted on carbon tissue. The resist is next exposed under a special screen that breaks up the image into a series of black dots. The various pieces of resist are now placed in exact position on the copper cylinder and are then soaked in water until the carbon can be peeled off. This leaves the gelatin attached to the cylinder. The cylinder is now developed by rotating in hot water. When it is dry, it is etched with perchloride of iron. When it has been developed, those parts of the gelatin exposed to the most light, being insoluble, are the thickest and offer the most resistance to the acid. The parts that received less light, especially those protected by the tiny opaque squares of the screen, retain little or no coating of the gelatin. Here the acid penetrates deepest into the copper, and the result is that these parts have many fine holes of various depths and will retain various amounts of ink.

Minor Printing Processes and Binding Methods.—A description of every method of placing type or pictures on paper would be an endless task, as new methods are being continually devised. The following are some of the more important:

Collotype.—This is a lithographic process using a gelatin plate as a printing surface. It is adapted only to small editions, but so far as faithfulness of reproduction is concerned it is superior to any other. It is used particularly for making copies of famous originals, like first editions.

Thermography.—When the cost prohibits the use of copper or steel engraving, but an embossed effect is desired, this method will give a pleasing result. The letterpress method is used, but a special ink is required, and while the ink is still wet on the sheet, it is dusted with a powder that adheres to the ink. The sheets are then baked, and this causes the particles of powder to fuse together and give a raised effect.

Embossing requires a female die, usually of brass, and a male die formed on the press. If the design is large and requires great pressure, a special press is necessary. Best results are obtained if the female die is heated.

Bronzing is accomplished by printing an adhesive size on the paper and dusting with a metallic powder while it is still wet. In recent years there has been a great improvement in metallic inks applied direct to the paper like ordinary inks. While the results are not always as satisfactory, these inks are frequently used in preference to bronzing, because of the greater cost of the latter.

Die Cutting strictly speaking is not a printing process, but the work is frequently done on printing presses. The work is cutting paper or cardboard to some irregular shape and is usually accomplished with steel cutting rules, a brass plate being used to receive the pressure of the die after it has cut through the substance.

Binding.—Printing has become a highly specialized industry and today few printers do their own binding. Binding has also become specialized. In nearly every large city there are a few small shops binding books by hand and by methods used for centuries. There are also *edition binderies,* turning out every day thousands of sewed and case-bound books. This is made possible by the use of machinery. The sheets are folded, collated, sewed and trimmed by machine and nearly every succeeding operation is also done by machine. The boards, forming the front and back of the binding, are cut by special cutters; the rolls of cloth are split by cloth cutters; the cloth is glued to the boards by glueing machines; casing-in machines attach the covers to the books; and the covers of the books are stamped with power presses. These mechanical methods of manufacturing make it possible for books to be made at lower cost and therefore increase their range of usefulness.

Pamphlet binderies have different equipment for folding sheets. Their collating machines have wire-stapling attachments; and they have punching, perforating, numbering and ruling machines. Other plants use round-cornering, eyeleting, varnishing, pebbling and gumming machines.

DICTIONARY OF PRINTERS' TERMS

agate, the old name for 5½-point type.

agate line, a unit for measuring advertisements. In an advertisement a column wide and an inch deep, there are 14 agate lines; if it is *two* columns wide and an inch deep, it contains 28 agate lines.

alive, type composition until it is no longer of use. It then becomes *dead* matter.

ampersand, the type character that represents the word *and;* printers usually call it the *short and.*

ascenders, the seven tall letters of the lower-case alphabet—b, d, f, h, k, l, t—and the parts of these letters that go above the height of other letters.

author's alterations, changes or corrections in type composition not the fault of the printer and so subject to an extra charge.

author's proof, the proof sent to the author with the manuscript; the same proof after it has been corrected and returned by the author or editor.

backed-up, printed on both sides.

backing, the molten lead poured over the back of the copper shell to strengthen it in electrotyping. Afterward it is shaved to the desired thickness. In bookbinding, backing is preparing and shaping the back to fit the cover. Books may be *backed flat,* which means little or no *round* or the back may be rounded.

back margin, that part of the blank paper between the type impression and the binding edge of the leaf. On right-hand pages this margin is at the left of the type page.

bastard title, the title only of the book; printed on a right-hand page preceding the regular title-page; also called *half title* or *mock title.*

batter, the damaged part of a page of type, engraving or plate that will not print properly.

Ben Day, a process invented by Ben Day that makes it possible to produce tone on any part of a line drawing by using gelatin films. These films have their designs in relief, and when they are inked, the design is printed on the plate before it is etched.

bevel, the sloping edge of a printing plate that makes it possible to attach the plate to a wood or metal base.

Bible paper, a very light book paper, usually thicker than India paper.

binding edge, that part of a folded sheet where the pages are stitched together.

black letter, a pointed Gothic typeface used by Gutenberg to produce the first printed book. It was designed to imitate the letters then used in Germany for hand-written books and was later called *black letter* to distinguish it from the lighter, more open and more rounded letters designed by Nicolas Jenson, which are now the more popular form of the roman alphabet.

bleed, an illustration that projects beyond the trimmed size of the leaf. When the leaf is trimmed, part of the illustration is cut away or *bled.* The bleed allowance is usually ⅛ inch. For example the size of the plate for a 6-by-9-inch booklet cover that is to bleed on all but the binding edge should be 6⅛ by 9¼ inches.

body type, that used for reading matter, usually sizes smaller than 18 point, to distinguish it from the larger type used for headings and other display purposes.

bold face, a heavier, blacker type than that used in a text. **This is bold face.**

book paper, the paper principally used for books—antique and smooth finish stocks; not newsprint, writing or coated papers.

botched, printing badly or carelessly executed.

box head, a type heading enclosed with a rule or ornamental border.

bronzing, printing with an adhesive size, to which a metallic powder is applied while the size is still wet.

capitals or **caps,** the large letters in printing used at beginning of sentences, proper names and so forth. In printers' parlance, *upper case.*

caption, title for article, chapter or illustration.

case, the compartments in which type is kept for hand composition. The old arrangement of the case had small letters nearer the compositor's hand in the lower case; so *lower case* (abbreviated *l.c.*) is the printer's term for small letters. *Upper case* (*u.c.*) means capital letters. Nowadays both large and small letters are kept in one case.

casting off copy, estimating the space required for type set from given copy.

chase, an iron or steel frame in which type matter is locked.

composition, type setting by hand or machine.

cut, a wood engraving; also (less correctly) any engraving or illustration.

cylinder press, a printing press with a continuously rotating cylinder. The blank sheet of paper is fed to the cylinder, where one edge is seized by the grippers attached to the cylinder. The sheet now comes in contact with the printing form, attached to a flat bed with a reciprocating movement, and the impression is made. With the completion of the impression, the printed sheet is transferred to a mechanism that transfers it to the delivery table.

dagger, symbol (†) used as a reference mark.

dead, type composition that has served its purpose and will not be used again.

deckle edge, the irregular edge left on paper as manufactured without trimming.

descenders, those letters that go below the regular line—g, j, p, q, y; and the part that goes below the line.

devil, a printer's youngest apprentice.

display, emphasizing certain words by using larger or heavier type, often in shorter and centered lines, as in heads or advertising headlines.

display type, heavy-faced types of any size or design; all types larger than 14-point used for emphasis or in headings and seldom used for ordinary reading.

distribute, to return types to their proper locations in cases after they have been used.

double leaded, placing two 2-point leads between lines of type. With machine composition this is usually avoided by casting the types or slugs on larger bodies. For example, 8-point type cast on 12-point body.

dummy, the assembled sketched or pasted layout giving the intended arrangement for a book or periodical.

edition, the first press run of a publication or book and subsequent printings that vary from the first or one another. Additional unchanged printings are properly called *impressions.*

electrotyping, a process for making duplicate printing plates of type composition or engravings. A wax impression is made of the form to be duplicated. A thin shell of copper is then deposited electrically on the wax. This shell is then backed up or strengthened by a coating of molten metal. After the plate has been made the proper thickness and attached to a wood or metal block, it is ready for use.

em, the square of a type body of any size; the unit of measure for type matter, originally the letter *m* (formerly square). The size of the em, of course, varies with the size of type. In 6-point matter, there are 144 ems to the square inch; in 12-point, only 36; 500 ems of 10-point (52 to the square inch) occupy an area of nearly 10 square inches. Column widths are expressed in pica ems, each 1/6 of an inch; so that a 12-pica column is 2 inches wide. The em dash is the single type or its imprint showing a line the length of the *m* in that size of type and used as a mark of punctuation; it is doubled or tripled in length as desired—2-em and 3-em dashes are used to indicate elision, between body type and footnotes and in charts and tables.

embossing, stamping with dies to form letters or ornaments in relief.

en, in English usage, the unit of measuring type matter; it is one-half the em. An *en* dash is a dash half as long as the *em* dash.

fillet, a decorative band or border.

folio, the page number, always beginning with a right-hand (*recto*) page, thus causing the even numbers to be on left-hand (*verso*) pages; a *dropped folio* appears at the bottom of the page. The term also applies to a sheet of paper folded once.

font (older form, still used in England, *fount*), a full assortment in proper proportion (*e*'s and *a*'s occur more frequently than other letters in English) of all the letters and symbols of a given size and face of type, as 12-point Caslon. It includes the requisite number for limited work of capitals, small capitals, lower-case letters, figures, punctuation marks, accents, signs and logotypes. A font may be in either roman or italics.

NOTE. Specimens of the complete font of the body type of this book are printed below:

A B C D E F G H I J K L M N O P Q R S
T U V W X Y Z
A B C D E F G H I J K L M N O P Q R S
T U V W X Y Z
A B C D E F G H I J K L M N O P Q R S
T U V W X Y Z
a b c d e f g h i j k l m n o p q r s
t u v w x y z

a b c d e f g h i j k l m n o p q r s
t u v w x y z
a b c d e f g h i j k l m n o p q r s
t u v w x y z
A B C D E F G H I J K L M N O P Q R S T U
V W X Y Z
1 2 3 4 5 6 7 8 9 0
& , . : ; - ( ) ! ? ' ' * $
fi fl ff ffi ffl

fonted, printed, taken from a font.

foolscap, sheets of paper about 13 inches wide and 16 or 17 inches long. The name comes from the fool's cap and bells that were used as a watermark by early papermakers.

foolscap and half, sheets of paper 13 by 24 inches.

foolscap and third, sheets of paper 13 by 21½ inches.

foot, the lower part of a type block, opposite the face or printing surface of the type.

foot line, the name given to the line at the foot of a page; it usually refers specifically to the blank line, below the type page, where the page number is sometimes put.

footnote, a line or a paragraph in smaller type than the text, placed at the foot of the page and giving a reference or an explanation for matter referred to in the text.

fore edge, the front of a page in a book, that is, the edge opposite the bound edge.

form, (1) type matter, engravings, electrotypes or stereotypes locked in a chase ready to be printed from. Job forms may be a single page; book forms are usually some multiple of four—4, 8, 16, 32, 64 pages. (2) A printed sheet or several sheets with blank spaces left for dates, names, amounts, descriptions and the like.

format, an indefinite term generally used to describe the form of a book, including size, paper, types, illustrations and the like.

forwarding, rounding, backing and other work in bookbinding after the sewing and before casing or attaching the cover.

foundry, place where metal is cast or where the electros and the printing plates are made.

foundry form, a page of type, or several pages of type or engravings, surrounded with type-high pieces of metal about ¼-inch thick and locked in an iron chase, ready to be sent to the foundry and electrotyped or stereotyped.

foundry proof, a proof of a page after the type has been locked in a chase for electrotyping. It is usually scanned carefully by the proofreader to detect damaged letters and errors that have been overlooked, since it is expensive to make corrections in an electrotype and impossible with a stereotype.

full bound, having a binding of all leather.

furniture, strips of wood or metal used around type matter to fill the extra space and make it possible to lock all tightly in the form.

galley, narrow, shallow metal tray, to hold type matter after it is set; also abbreviation for *galley proof,* the impression taken while type is in the galley.

gothic, a square-faced letter with no serifs.

grain, with machine-made paper, the direction the fibers run. Paper folds easier with the grain but has greater strength across the grain. With work requiring the paper to be folded, the fold is usually with the grain. Due to the method of manufacture, handmade papers have no grain, the fibers being equally matted or crossed in every direction.

guards, strips of type-high metal, ¼-inch or less thick, placed around type composition or engravings to prevent the spreading of the wax when the electrotyper makes a mold of the form.

gutters, the blank spaces between the pages of a type form.

hair line, the finest possible printed line.

half tone, an engraving on either copper or zinc, produced by the photoengraving process.

hanging indention, see *indention.*

head or **heading,** display phrase or caption used to gain attention, inform, summarize or suggest; usually named according to the position occupied on the page or in the column, as *center heads,* placed in the center of the column; *side heads,* at the beginning of a paragraph; *cut-in heads,* next to the outside margin in a space created by indenting several lines; *box heads,* enclosed by rules in the margin. *Running heads* are the book and chapter titles on the top of opposite pages in a book or other publication.

height to paper, the standard height of type, that is, its upright dimension as it stands on the press. All sizes have the same height, 0.9186 inch.

hellbox, printer's box for broken type and type-metal discards.

hot embossing, the usual process of producing raised effects on paper by means of male and female dies. With heavy papers, such as cover stocks, better results are obtained if the female die is heated.

imposition, placing the pages in the form on a table or stone (called imposing stone) in the order necessary to insure their proper sequence when the signatures (pages on a single sheet) are folded to be sewn.

indention or **indent,** white space at the beginning of a paragraph; or in the *hanging indention,* such as this paragraph shows, where the first line is set full measure, and those that follow are indented 1 em.

India paper, a very thin book paper used mainly for Bibles and prayer books and developed to perfection by Oxford and Cambridge University presses.

inferiors, characters cast low on the face of a type body and standing at the bottom of the line as in chemical symbols.

inserts, illustrations or type matter printed separate from the signatures and inserted and pasted between the pages during binding operations; also called tip-ins.

inside form, those pages that when printed are on the inside of the folded sheet, that is, with a 16-page form, pages 2, 3, 6, 7, 10, 11, 14, 15.

intaglio (in tal' yō), incised, cut in, as distinct from relief printing. Intaglio engraving is used in photogravure.

intertype, a composing machine almost identical with the linotype. The matrices of Intertype and Linotype machines are interchangeable.

italic, a sloped letter; used in words to be emphasized, book titles and foreign phrases; first used by Aldus in Venice, in imitation of the Italian handwriting of the 15th century.

jacket, the paper slip cover of a book used to protect the cloth cover and to attract attention; also called *dust jacket* and *wrapper.*

job press, any of a number of small presses used for various purposes. At one time the term was applied only to platen presses, but it is now used to describe small cylinder presses, such as the Miehle vertical.

justify, to equalize the spacing to fill a line properly. Composing machines justify automatically.

kern, in such letters as the *f* the beak that frequently projects beyond the body of the type.

keyplate, in process color work the plate with which all the other plates must register.

kill, to cancel portions of copy or type matter.

layout, sketched or pasted plan or arrangement for an advertisement, section or full page.

leaders, dots or dashes in a row to connect related parts—in bills, price lists, tables, formulas and on content pages—as a convenience to carry the eye from the name of an item to its price or page number; also used to indicate a full-line omission.

lead mold, an impression in lead of a half tone in the process of making electrotype duplicates to be used in printing. The lead impression is separated from the original and is faced with a shell of copper, deposited by electroplating. The first deposit may be nickel, followed by copper, or when extreme durability is required, the copper may be given a chromium plating. The other method of molding is with wax. The lead mold makes a plate that yields as good impressions as the original; it is preferable to wax for fine-screen half tones.

leads, thin strips of metal between lines of type, used for spacing.

legend, title or description printed under an illustration.

letterpress, typography or relief printing; type matter as distinct from illustrations.

line drawing, a pen-and-ink, dry-brush or other drawing without tone that can be photoengraved without the use of a screen.

linotype, a composing machine whose product is a slug bearing on one of its surfaces a cast of a line of matrices assembled by the operator so that a whole line of type is cast in a single unit.

lithography, a method of printing based on the physical law of repulsion between grease and water.

logotype, a type on which is cast more than a single letter, either letters tied together—*ligatures* like *æ, œ, fi, ff, fl, ffi, ffl,* found in all fonts of type and set as a single character; or a whole word cast as a single character—like such frequent words as *the, and, of;* or a peculiar setting of a trade name, such as *Ford* in the distinctive script used in Ford advertising.

low-to-paper, type composition or any printing surface less than the standard height of .9186 of an inch.

TAgerta
CASLON 540 — 42 PT.

TAgerta
GARAMOND — 48 PT.

TAgertai
GOUDY OLDSTYLE — 36 PT.

TAgerta
BOOKMAN — 36 PT.

TAgerta
NICHOLAS COCHIN BOLD — 48 PT.

TAgerta
FUTURA DEMIBOLD — 48 PT.

TAgerta
BERNHARD TANGO — 48 PT.

TAgerta
CENTURY EXPANDED — 42 PT.

TAgertas
WEISS ROMAN — 48 PT.

TAgerta
BODONI — 48 PT.

TAgerta
CHELTENHAM BOLD — 48 PT.

TAgerta
STYMIE BOLD — 48 PT.

TAgerta
TIMES ROMAN — 48 PT.

TAgerta
COMMERCIAL SCRIPT — 48 PT.

TAgerta
GOUDY TEXT — 48 PT.

TAgerta
MELIOR — 48 PT.

TYPE SETS are classified as black letter, old-style roman, old-style roman italic, modern roman italic, cursive, and sans-serif. According to width, it is standard, condensed, extra-condensed, or extended. The weight of the type, light or dark, is indicated as light, medium-bold, or extrabold. Most widely used are Caslon, Futura, Bodoni, and Times Roman.

lower case, the small letters of the alphabet. See *case.*

make-up, arrangement of type and illustrations in pages according to dummy, with running heads, captions and folio, ready for imposition (or placing in the form); also the planned arrangement in the dummy.

margins, blank area surrounding the printed part of a page.

masthead, statement as to the name and place of publication, editors and subscription rate, published in every issue of a newspaper or periodical.

matrix, any impression from which metal is molded and cast for relief printing. Type is cast from matrices of brass, hard copper or (for large sizes) aluminum alloy. Stereotypes for newspaper printing are made by pouring molten metal into papier-mâché or composition matrices (usually called *mats*) that have been molded from original type metal or engravings or both. The matrix is a positive, that is, the letter or illustration is seen on its face as it appears when it is printed and is not reversed as it is in type or actual printing plate.

matter, copy or type set for printing, before which it is *live matter,* after which it is *dead matter* or if it is kept for further use, *standing matter.*

modern typefaces, a new form of the roman alphabet late in the 18th century designed by the celebrated Italian printer and punch-cutter Giambattista Bodoni. His types were characterized by marked differences between the widths of the light and heavy strokes of the letters and by long and slender serifs. Since then all types with these characteristics have been termed *moderns.*

monotype, a composing machine whose product is individual types automatically cast in a machine. The machine is controlled by a ribbon perforated at another machine by the operator. Corrections are easier to make on matter set by monotype as the whole line need not always be reset as in linotype.

mortising, making an opening through a cut to receive type so that a legend or caption may be inserted where the part was removed.

multicolor press, a press for printing several colors at one operation.

nickeltype, an electrotype in which the first deposit in the mold is nickel, followed by the copper deposit. Nickeltypes are not affected by mercury inks.

offset, a mark or smudge made by the wet ink of a printed sheet when it comes in contact with another sheet.

offset printing, a recent development of lithography by which the image is printed on a rubber-covered cylinder and then offset or transferred to the paper attached to another cylinder.

old style, roman types distinguished by short, stubby serifs and comparatively uniform weight of light and heavy strokes. Caslon type is a good example. Old style is contrasted with modern roman, which has more contrast in light and heavy strokes.

overmatter, matter in excess of allotted space.

overrun, surplus printing—printed copies or sheets above the number ordered.

photoengraving, a printing plate produced by a combination of chemical and photographic processes. Also the print made from a photoengraved plate.

photogravure, the photographic process of intaglio engraving; and the print from such a plate.

pi, type matter that has been upset and disordered.

pica, 12-point type; the pica em (1/6 × 1/6 in.) is the standard unit of type measurement, matter or column being so many picas (*ems* is dropped but understood) in width, whatever size of type is used.

plates, electrotypes, stereotypes, female embossing, dies and so on. The term is also applied to half tones and line engravings. *Plating* is making a page or other unit of type or illustration into one piece of metal from which it can be printed. Matter that is electrotyped or stereotyped is *plated.*

point, the unit for measuring type sizes, approximately 1/72 inch. The measurement is the depth of the type body—in other words, the vertical measure on the page. If nine lines of type set solid occupies one inch (up and down the page) it is 8-point type. *Pointwise* is measure of type vertically, up and down the page.

proofs or **proof sheets,** impressions pulled by hand of printed matter after it has been set so that it may be read for alterations and corrections before it goes to press. The first proofs are called *galley proofs,* and most changes are made on them. Revised galleys

are checked before the matter is made-up into pages. Then *page proof* is pulled, and further comparison and corrections are made. *Foundry proof* is final and comes from the composing room before the type is cast for electrotyping.

punch, the die for a type matrix.

quad, a square shaft of type metal, not quite type high, used for wide spacing between words, before and after paragraphs and for blocking out wherever necessary in charts, tables and similar short-line composition. The em-quad is the size of the type for the letter *m;* the en-quad, the size of the letter *n* in the different points or sizes. To avoid misunderstanding the similar sounds of em and en in speaking, printers use the terms *mutton quad* and *nut quad,* respectively.

quad folder, a folding machine that folds four signatures from one sheet of paper at a single operation.

query, a question mark on the margin of a proof to call attention to an error in the copy or to a doubtful point.

quire, a measured quantity of paper, 24 sheets of coarse paper, 25 of fine.

quoin, originally a wooden wedge, now usually a wedge-shaped metal device operated with a key, used between furniture and iron or steel chases to tighten the type securely within the form for safe removal from imposing stone to press or to the electrotyper.

ream, formerly 20 quires of 24 sheets each—or 480 sheets; now 500 sheets of paper.

recto, right-hand page of a book.

reference marks, marks inserted in reading matter to call attention to footnotes in smaller type at the bottom of the page or at the end of the chapter. The names of the marks and the order in which they should be placed are:

* Asterisk
† Dagger
‡ Double Dagger
§ Section
‖ Parallel
¶ Paragraph

Reference marks are now seldom used; superior figures are preferred.

register, correct correspondence of parts, as columns or lines printed on both sides of one sheet or page, or the superimposition of the several plates in multicolor printing.

resist, a protective acid-proof coating used to cover the printing area of a plate, the parts to be etched being left exposed to the acid. Dragon's blood, which is a palm-tree resin, or some asphaltic substance is commonly used for resist.

revise, a corrected proof or the act of checking a proof to see if all errors marked on a previous proof have been corrected.

roman, name of the most used, upright style of type. The capitals are based on the letters on Trajan's Column in Rome, but the small letters were derived from those used in Italian manuscript books at the time printing came into use.

rotary, a printing press that prints from curved plates attached to a printing cylinder. Sheet-feed rotaries print from single sheets; web-feeds from a continuous web of paper.

rotogravure, printing from intaglio-etched cylinders.

routing, cutting away by hand or machine any part of a zinc or copper etching or half tone not wanted to print.

rules, strips of type-high brass or type metal used for tabular composition, borders and so on. Steel rules are used for die-cutting.

run in, to omit paragraphing or add new matter without setting new paragraph.

running head, a line appearing at the top of a page of type, usually with the number of the page. Although newspapers and books usually carry the running head at the top, some magazines have it at the bottom of the page.

sans serif, types without serifs. What is known in this country as Gothic types are sans serifs, as well as the popular imported types, such as the Kabel and Futura.

screen, etched glass interposed between the lens and the negative of a camera with diagonal lines drawn close together and crossing at right angles. These lines break up the photographic image into fine dots. When these dots are printed on metal and the metal is etched with acid, the dots become the printing surface of a half-tone photoengraving. In the gravure method, they become holes in the plate, and the holes are filled with ink before the impression is made.

script, any type face designed to reproduce handwriting with letters that join; they may be upright or slanting.

Cursive type, which has similar characteristics, is somewhat more fluent.

serif, a fine line on letters of certain faces, especially cross strokes at the top or foot of a letter. Gothic letters are square cut with no serifs.

set, arrangement and spacing in composition. *Setwise* means in the direction that the type is set, that is, width—distinguished from *pointwise,* the vertical dimensions, up and down the page.

sheetwise, printing one side of a sheet of paper at a time, the other side of the sheet to be printed at another operation.

short letters, the characters (capitals, small capitals and lower case letters, either roman or italics) so formed that each occupies only the central part of a type; they are a, c, e, m, n, o, r, s, u, v, w, x, z.

signature, a printed sheet containing a number of pages and folded as one unit, usually 8, 16 or 32 pages.

slipsheeting, placing sheets of paper, usually waste, between printed sheets as they are delivered from the press, to prevent offset of the ink. It is not necessary when the wax-spray device is used, as the minute particles of transparent wax prevent close contact of the sheets.

small caps, letters having the capital-letter outlines but the same size as lower case letters. They are used for emphasis or cross reference. THESE LETTERS ARE SMALL CAPS.

stereotype, a printing plate made from type or engraving (or both) by taking an impression (matrix) in plaster or wood pulp and then filling this mold with type metal. It is used in newspaper printing.

stick, a small adjustable metal tray used in setting type by hand. It is held in the left hand, and the thumb and first two fingers of the right hand are used to pick up the type and transfer it to the stick. It will contain about two inches of type Long sticks for setting widths 12 inches or more are usually of wood.

superiors, letters, figures and signs, smaller than the text type and cast high on the body of the type. They are used as exponents or algebraic symbols—in x^2 the 2 is superior; and as references to footnotes.

swash letters, italic capitals that display decorative flourishes at top or bottom; used as ornamental initial letters.

take, any part of copy that is divided among various typesetters.

tint laying, a mechanical method of shading a line drawing for engraving, usually called by the name of its inventor Ben Day.

turtle, the half-cylinder plate used on a rotary press; an imposing stone on rollers.

type family, all the variants of one parent design, such as the Cheltenham family. This family includes light, medium, bold, extra bold; as well as wide, normal, condensed, extra condensed, in both roman and italic. The Goudy type family is also quite extensive, and all the variants are based on a single design conceived by Frederic W. Goudy.

type height, the standard height for type from foot to printing surface, 0.9186 inch.

upper case, abbreviated *u.c.,* capital letters.

verso, the left-hand page of a book.

wax engraving, the process in which a design is incised on a metal plate coated with wax, the incisions being cut through to the metal base. An electrotype is then made from the matrix thus formed. The process was once used to a considerable extent for map-making.

wax mold, one method of taking an impression from an original half-tone or line engraving in the process of making electrotype duplicates to be used in printing. The wax impression is separated from the original and is faced with a shell of copper, deposited by electroplating. The wax mold is more economical than the lead mold for making reproductions of line engravings; but it is not so good as lead for fine-screen half-tone engravings.

widow, a closing word or line of a paragraph left standing alone in the make-up; to be avoided because it mars the general appearance of a page.

wood engraving, picture or design engraved upon a boxwood block.

work-and-turn, printing both sides of a sheet of paper at one operation. This necessitates that the sheet be double size. The first time through the press the front and back pages are printed on one side of the sheet. The sheet is then backed up with a second impression, and when cut in half two complete signatures are obtained.

zinc etching or **zinc,** a photoengraving upon a zinc plate much used for reproducing line drawings and lettering, and for coarse-screen half tones.

MUSIC

EARLY HISTORY OF MUSIC

Music is sometimes classed with Literature as an *immaterial* art, whereas Architecture, Painting and Sculpture are termed *material* arts. These three arts of the second group seek expression through visible, tangible means. Literature and Music, though they may have a visible record in the form of certain arbitrary symbols, speak more immediately and directly from one mind to another. Hence they are to a certain extent allied and they may be combined in a variety of ways. But Music speaks even more directly and immediately than does Literature. Schopenhauer said that Music differs from other arts in that it is not the image of an idea but is itself idea. Other arts, he said, are shadow, but Music is substance.

So nearly universal is music, even if only in rude form, that it has been said that wherever human life is, there is music. Owing to its nature it has, however, been slower in development than the other arts. Because it is subjective, it could not look to physical nature for patterns as did painting and sculpture. Any musical system had to be based on tones, which had to be arranged in a certain order or *scale*. Yet such an arrangement, without which musical art forms could not exist, has no prototype in physical nature; nor does physical nature afford originals for the intervals of the scale. It is not surprising, therefore, that mythologies so often ascribed the invention of music to the gods, who bestowed this noble gift upon mankind.

The origin of music remains obscure. From the study of the music existing today among primitive peoples, we have gained some hints of what the music of races now civilized may once have been. In such study the use of recording by phonograph has been of aid. Something has been learned also from the music of the peoples of Asia. The examination of actual instruments and of instruments as pictured in wall paintings and pottery has helped scholars in tracing stages of advancement from crude beginnings; for, in a general way, the extending scope of these instruments and the increasing skill in their making point to the use of a wider range of tones, the arrangement of those tones in scales and a developing technique on the part of the performers. Yet in many cases we are limited to theories about which the learned disagree. At best our knowledge is only fragmentary.

Still more obscure is the fundamental nature of music. Science has gained practical knowledge of the action and effects of the force we call electricity and has devised means for utilizing that force, but scientists do not know what electricity really is. In somewhat the same way we say that music is divided into three basic elements: *rhythm, melody* and *harmony.* We determine the relations of tones, one to another, and have the means for producing them; we are conscious of musical effects. But why and how music speaks to us in a manner difficult to interpret in words—this we cannot fathom.

Primitive Music.—The element of rhythm was undoubtedly the first to be appreciated by primitive man. Gradually tones were chosen. Then small groups of tones, repeated over and over, were used to form *melodies.* Next *melodic design* was introduced; instead of repeating one group or *phrase,* contrasting groups or phrases were used alternately. Then tones were arranged in different scales. Common among primitive peoples was the *pentatonic* or five-toned scale. This had the same series of tones as may be produced by striking the black keys of a piano in regular succession, no white keys being struck. The reason for this was that music was at first wholly *vocal.* Half-tones were found more difficult to sing than whole or primary tones, and the pentatonic scale did not contain half-tones. Primitive music lacked *tonality;* there was no central tone to which all the other tones were referred; and it was also without *modulation* from one scale into another. Probably no attempts were made to combine tones into *chords,* groups of tones produced simultaneously instead of successively—the element of *harmony* was lacking. According to our present-day idea, the beginning not only of harmony but of musical art is in the chord—three or more concordant tones sounded simultaneously.

The first musical instruments were of the *percussion* (or *drum*) type. Their resonance was employed to accent rhythm. Next came instruments of the *wind* type, first made of reeds or of the horns of animals. Horns were later wrought of metal, and the reeds were replaced by more durable wood. Last in order of development were instruments of the *lyre* or string type. Possibly these had their inception in the taut bowstring. And just as the string instrument appeared last in order, so today the musical culture and appreciation of a people are found to be higher in proportion as instruments of the string type are given precedence over those of the percussion type.

Through the study of the condition of music among savage and semi-barbarous peoples of today, it has been possible to gain some idea of what the music of primitive man must have been. In the United States musicians and students of music have learned something of primitive musical forms through investigation of the music of the southern Negro and the American Indian. Some have thought that in this way a basis might be found for a distinctive national school. Others, though regarding it as necessarily outside the line of the white man's musical development, have valued it for its tonal coloring and emotional content and have drawn upon it as source material.

FOLK MUSIC

The first musical impulse in every nation springs from the people, and it is natural to look to folk music for the germ of all that later will be found in the great musical compositions of every nation. Yet in considering folk music, there are several points to remember.

First, there is the influence of actual geographical conditions. All dwellers in the mountains lift or lower their voices in song to correspond to the peaks rising above them, while those on the vast plains show a monotony in their songs quite as apparent as that of the landscape; and people living by the sea reflect the rocking of the waves in the rhythm of their songs.

Second, there is the difference in racial characteristics; for example, all the music of the Slavic race has points of striking similarity, whether it be found in Russia, Poland, Serbia or Czechoslovakia. The fiery music of the Slav is in direct contrast with the more stolid, plodding type of Teutonic music found among the German and Scandinavian peoples. All Latins, whether they live in Italy, Spain, France or Rumania, show similar musical characteristics, and their music is unlike that of other races. Interesting examples of racial similarity are to be found in the music of Scotland and Ireland, for both these lands have inherited many melodies from the Gaelic race. The folk airs of the Welsh and of the people of northern France are similar, which is not strange when one recalls that both are of the Celtic race. Probably the most striking instance of racial influence is found in the music of the Hungarians and the Finns, both coming from the Magyar race.

Third, political conditions have influenced the folk music of the world. Thus Germany claims many folk airs belonging to Austria, to Poland, to Lithuania, to Alsace, to Lorraine, to Bohemia and to Switzerland. Russia has usurped many folk airs of the Ukraine, of Georgia, of Poland, of Lithuania, of Latvia, of Estonia and of Finland.

Historical events have left their mark on folk music. Many of the greatest patriotic airs were born during war days.

Five Classes of Folk Music.—Folk music is usually divided into the following classes:

1. Folk Dance Songs, the earliest type of folk music, sung by the people as an accompaniment to their simple games and dances.

2. Legendary Folk Songs, airs sung for so many generations that the composer's name, if it ever was known, has long since been forgotten.

3. Composed Folk Songs, usually of a later period; the name of the composer is known.

4. Patriotic Songs, reflecting a love for native land and a desire to serve it. There are many patriotic songs of the legendary type, though the composer is generally known.

5. National Compositions, musical works in which folk themes have been used. Sometimes the composer uses folk music from a land other than his own, an outstanding example being the opera *Carmen,* which uses Spanish characteristics, though the opera was written by a Frenchman, Georges Bizet.

A study of the folk music of every land will give one an amazing understanding of geographical and historical facts. Our modern music has been greatly influenced by folk music, and much of the national music of the past 50 years has been founded on nationality.

MUSIC OF THE ORIENT

Chinese Music.—As civilization advanced, definite musical systems arose, scales were established and beginnings were made in musical theory. Instruments were more skilfully made and more proficiently used. This was particularly true in Oriental countries.

A system existed in China from very early times. So old, indeed, was it that even in Confucius's day it was growing obsolescent; and three centuries later it had disappeared. We learn from Chinese books that the first scale was the pentatonic. The octave was later divided into 12 semitones similar to ours, and 84 scales were fixed. The Chinese regard these scales as descending, whereas we think of ours as ascending. In Chinese music the interest lies not in the progression of individual tones but in the tone color. Eight kinds of tone color are recognized, depending on the material used in producing them, whether baked earth, bamboo, gourd, metal, silk, skin, stone or wood. From these materials instruments are made such as the *king,* in which 16 stone plates are suspended from a frame, tones being produced by striking the plates with a mallet. Similar instruments employ bells instead of stone plates. The *sheng* is constructed by inserting into a gourd bamboo pipes, each of them with a metal reed; the performer blows into a mouthpiece resembling the spout of a teapot, and vibrations in the bamboo pipes create the tones. Hence the *sheng* is a forerunner of the reed organ once found in nearly every American parlor. Among the Chinese instruments, the greater number are of the percussion type. There are many sorts of drums, and the tone of a drum is sometimes modified by placing rice inside. Save for the music used in religious ceremonies, the most characteristic Chinese melodies are met with in the folk songs of sailors and peasants.

Music in Japan and Thailand. In Japan, Java, and Thailand, the pentatonic scale is common, though often very modified. Among Japanese instruments of the string type are the *koto,* in the style of an elaborate zither: the *samisen,* like a small guitar, and the *kokiu,* a kind of rude violin.

Women are frequent performers. Sometimes Japanese music is based upon a scale approximating in form our own chromatic scale. Music in the native style is still considered an important feature of religious worship, but it is in some danger of being superseded for secular use by the European system, which has been generally adopted for instruction in the public schools.

In Thailand the characteristic instrument is the *ranat,* in which metal or wooden bars are sounded with a hammer. Orchestras are common among the Thais.

The Music of India.—The origin of Hindu music was ascribed to the gods, and a well-developed system appears in the sacred books known as the *Vedas.* The scale was originally pentatonic, but it was in time so modified that it consisted of 21 minute portions termed *srutis,* separated from one another by only a third or quarter tone. From these an extensive collection of scales was developed. There are numerous instruments, among which those of the string type are in the majority. These include two rudimental violins: the *magoudi,* a four-stringed, long-necked guitar, and the *vina,* which may be called the national instrument. The *vina* is a long, hollow tube, with seven metal strings stretched over no less than 19 movable bridges. Attached to the tube are two hollow gourds for reinforcing the volume of tone.

Hindu melodies are full of embellishments, and the rhythms are greatly varied. The Brahmins composed songs called *ragas,* celebrating various special occasions and of highly formal character. Religious music of a strictly prescribed nature and frequently combined with dancing has an important place in the life of the Hindu. Music dramas are performed, and musical fare is also provided by orchestras and by strolling minstrels.

Burmese instruments include gong and bell organs, each with 21 tones.

Arabian Music.—The Arabs divided the octave into 17 equal parts, each being one-third of a tone, and from these they derived 34 scales. With such minute intervals as a basis and with delicately adjusted instruments they produced melodies of a chantlike sort. They were used principally for social diversion, for Mohammed frowned on the use of music in connection with religion. Of all Oriental music that of the Arabs sounds least unfamiliar to our ears.

Arabian instruments are especially worth noting because they were the precursors of many of our own. Such was the *rabab* or *rebab,* kin to the medieval viol in its several forms; such was a mandolin-shaped instrument called *al'ud,* the type of pear-shaped instruments having strings stretched over resonant bodies and played by snapping, plucking or twanging. Of this there were no less than 32 varieties with a varying number of strings. It was known to medieval Europe as the *lute.* Modern representatives of this type are the *banjo,* the *guitar* and the *mandolin.* The Arabs had also three varieties of

lyres and several kinds of *dulcimers,* instruments placed on a table and struck with hammers. When under the influence of Mohammedanism the Arabs overran North Africa and Spain, they naturally took with them their music; and thus, as well as through the Crusades, European civilization came in contact with it.

Egyptian Music.—Egyptian music, like Egyptian civilization in general, was of ancient origin, at least antedating 3000 B.C. From the first it was closely connected with religion. By the time it reached its golden age (1500–1200 B.C.), it was also employed for social diversion. It was performed by trained singers, players and dancers—professionals who formed choruses and orchestras. In bas-reliefs and paintings these orchestras are always shown with a leader, and stringed instruments predominate. From the size of the orchestras it is surmised that some kind of harmony must have existed.

The national instrument was the *harp,* which was made in a variety of sizes, from the huge, superbly decorated specimens used in temples to those that were easily portable. It was characteristic of these harps that they were invariably constructed without the supporting pillar in front to which we are accustomed in the modern harp. Lyres and lutelike instruments also were used. Chief among the wind instruments were flutes and both single and double pipes. For military music there were drums, trumpets and a distinctive instrument called the *sistrum.* This was a horseshoe-shaped affair of metal with metal bars mounted loosely on it, so that they rattled when it was shaken. Such knowledge as we have of Egyptian music has been derived wholly from the paintings and bas-reliefs already mentioned and from hieroglyphics and the actual remains of instruments discovered by archeologists. From the structure of the instruments it has been supposed that the scale was diatonic; but whatever records of the Egyptian system may have existed have unfortunately disappeared.

Assyrian Music.—In Assyria flourished a system no less ancient than that of Egypt—a part of the culture of Babylonia, which was merged with the Assyrian empire. Some of the Assyrian remains show that although the Assyrians had instruments similar to those of Egypt, these instruments were so made that they might be suspended from the body and borne in processions. Drums, tambourines, trumpets, double pipes, dulcimers, harps—all were portable, thus reflecting the warlike character of the people.

Hebrew Music.—It is probable that the Hebrews derived their music from Egypt, Babylonia and Assyria. They had but two distinctively national instruments—the *shofar* and the *kerem,* which were ram's horns employed in the Temple worship. We encounter nothing similar among the other races of antiquity. Most of their other instruments were taken over from the Egyptians—for example, the *harp,* which was smaller than its

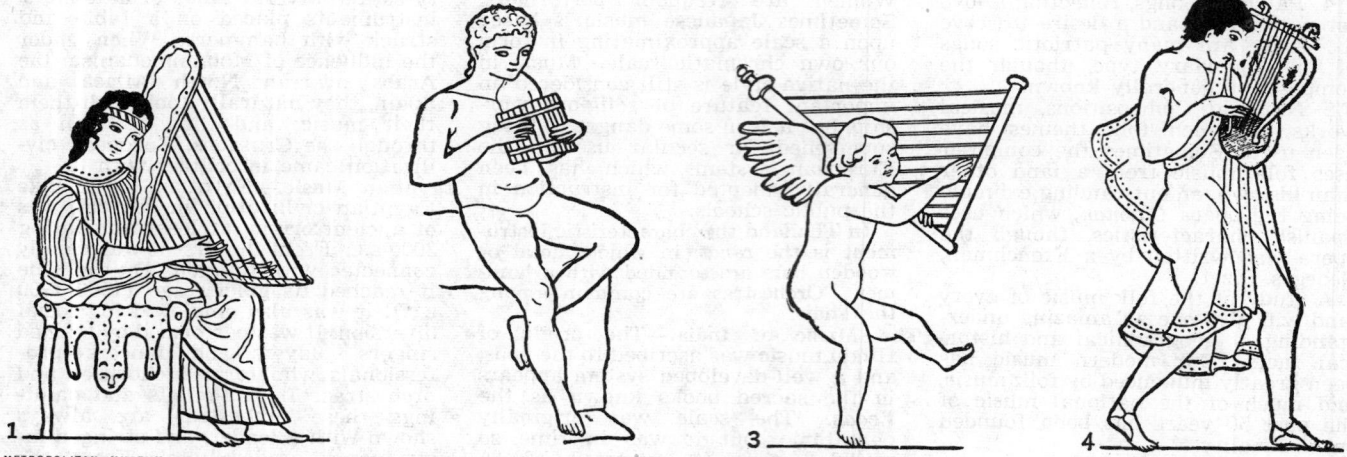

METROPOLITAN MUSEUM OF ART

Musical Instruments of Ancient Greece and Rome

1, Harp from a Greek vase dating from the time of Alexander the Great (356–323 B.C.). *2,* Panpipe from a bas-relief in the Albani Villa at Rome. *3,* Trigon (*trigonos*) from Herculaneum. *4,* Lyre (*phorminx*) from the interior of an Etruscan tomb (*c.* 400 B.C.)

common Egyptian prototype, and the four-stringed *nebel* (or psaltery). Most of the wind instruments mentioned in the Hebrew Scriptures had likewise an Egyptian origin. Nor can it be said that the Hebrews contributed much to music on its purely artistic side. But they exalted it by regarding it as an aid to direct communication with deity. When Elisha was about to prophesy before King Jehoshaphat, he said: "Now bring me a minstrel." "And it came to pass," says the account (II Kings 3:15–16), "when the minstrel played, that the hand of Jehovah came upon him [Elisha]."

Music assumed a prominent place in the Temple, especially in the reign of Solomon, although the figures given for the number of singers and instrumentalists are so prodigious that they may be taken as exaggeration. The book of Ecclesiasticus includes in its types of famous men (44:5):

"Such as sought out musical tunes,
And set forth verses in writing."

It is considered probable that the melodies were of narrow compass (though much embellished) and sung in unison, no matter how large the number of performers may have been. The most distinctive and interesting feature of Hebrew singing resulted from the use of the parallel couplets of Hebrew poetry, for example:

"Who shall ascend into the hill of the Lord?
Or who shall stand in his holy place?"

These balancing couplets seem to have been sung either by opposite sides of a choir or by a choir giving response to a leader. This antiphonal style of chanting was borrowed by the early Christians and became a feature of Christian worship.

It is impossible to draw from the present music of the Jewish synagogue any conclusions as to ancient Hebrew music. In music, as in other arts, the Jews have been wont to adapt themselves to the forms prevailing among the peoples with whom they lived. It has been said that in certain Gregorian chants we may perhaps more truly distinguish traces of the ancient Hebrew style. That this style had a special character among Oriental systems is evidenced by the invitation of the Babylonians to their Hebrew captives: "Sing us a song of Zion!" To which the significant response was: "How shall I sing the Lord's songs in a strange land?" In 70 A.D. the Temple was destroyed. The Hebrews lost their national focus and their national culture. Dispersed about the world, they became artistic rivals of the races with whom they tarried. The *shofar* continues to be used in synagogues on holy days; and the *cantor* (precentor or leader of the singing) has a post of dignity next to that of the rabbi.

MUSIC AMONG THE GREEKS

The Greeks and Ourselves.—It is true that Greek music had a considerable influence upon our own. This statement demands, however, some explanation. It is a truism that in the case of our plastic art and our poetry we cannot construct an outline of development that ignores Greek influence. From the very beginning of the Christian era we discover them existing under this influence, though at times it may not be plainly evident; and apart from it, European cultural remains have little significance. With the Renaissance began a definite awakening of what was called the Greek spirit. The recovered works of Greek plastic art and Greek poetry were a wellspring of modern art among all European peoples. It was then that Greek music first took on real importance with respect to ours. No doubt it had long before had a direct effect on early Christian music, but it was not until the Renaissance that any actual study of it was attempted. At the close of the 16th century, the union of drama and music in an independent art form was undertaken, with the ancient Greek drama as a model. But whereas in the case of the plastic and literary arts surviving examples furnished a direct working pattern, in the case of the music there was nothing but a theoretical basis from which to start—a basis fashioned from principles arrived at purely by reasoning from inadequate data. Theory was forthwith discarded, and the new art form proceeded along its own line of development. Of this we shall learn more when we consider *opera* and *oratorio.*

Fragments of Greek music have since been discovered by archeologists. For example, in October 1893 the French School unearthed at Delphi two stones bearing the words of a hymn to Apollo with the Greek musical notation attached. By a strange coincidence it celebrated a victory over the Gauls in 279 B.C. But it cannot be said that even if rich finds of such music were made, they would ever have for us a significance comparable to that of Greek poetry and plastic art. They would never contribute to a musical renaissance. For the Greek concept of music was quite different from our own. The Florentines of the Renaissance and Wagner in the 19th century alike had the ideal of an art form in which poetry and music should be combined—in which, so to say, each should permeate the other. Have we not here a connecting link between Greek music and the music of today? The rejoinder must be: What is the nature of the music with which poetry is to be joined? In its means of expression, in its *timbre,* in its entire character the music of Wagner is as remote from the music of the Greeks as are the symphonies of Beethoven.

With the Greeks music was absolutely subject to poetry in much the same way that their painting was subservient to plastic design. Both mimicry and music were but the attendants of poetry and employed only to heighten its effect. The connection between music and poetry was maintained, whereas in certain instances, as in the epic and the lyric, the dance was dispensed with. The emphasis given to the text helps to explain the lack of *polyphony* in Greek music; for all polyphony (as well as free instrumental accompaniments) must unavoidably render more difficult a ready comprehension of the words. From the statements of Greek writers on musical theory, we gather that to the Greek, *melody,* as contrasted with *rhythm,* was more material in character, and rhythm appeared more spiritual. To us, on the other hand, the express soul of music lies in melody; melody seems to be the essence of music because it is peculiar to music, whereas rhythm is operative also in poetry and the dance.

The Course of Greek Music.—For convenience, the history of Greek music may be divided into three periods, as follows:

1. *From about 1000 B.C. to about 660 B.C.* This is largely the period of mythology. Hermes invents the *lyre,* and to the sound of the lyre Amphion builds the walls of Thebes. The lyre becomes an attribute of Apollo, who, when the flute-playing Marsyas challenges him, wins the contest and flays the presumptuous Marsyas alive —thus asserting the supremacy of strings over wind instruments. Pan devises the *syrinx* or shepherd's pipe. Orpheus receives the lyre from Apollo and with it enchants beasts, trees and rocks, so that they follow him. To the accompaniment of the lyre the bards chanted heroic poetry, of which we have examples in the *Iliad* and the *Odyssey.*

2. *From 660 B.C. to the Macedonian conquest, 338 B.C.* Intercourse with Egypt gave fresh impetus to music at the beginning of this period. Terpander of Sparta increased the strings of the lyre from four to seven and established the first Grecian system or school of music. Pythagoras, the celebrated mathematician and philosopher of Samos, studied musical principles and wrote about them, and advanced the famous doctrine of the *music of the spheres,* to which Lorenzo refers in The Merchant of Venice (V, 1) when he says:

"There's not the smallest orb which thou behold'st
But in his motion like an angel sings,
Still quiring to the young-eyed cherubins."

A well-known story told how Pythagoras fixed the mathematical relations of the original Greek scales by chancing to hear the different tones produced by striking hammers of varying weights upon an anvil. He then suspended weights corresponding to those of the several hammers. Unfortunately for the story, different hammers do not produce different tones from the same anvil any mcre than do different clappers from a given bell.

The most important expression of music during this period was in the Attic drama, which flourished at Athens during the 5th century B.C. In works of this type the chief use of music was in accompanying the *chorus,* which to the notes of flutes and lyres marched or danced about an altar and voiced a commentary upon the action of the piece. The post of *choragus* or leader of the chorus was considered one of high honor. One *choragus* was elected from each tribe, and he was expected to provide

the funds for rehearsing and equipping his chorus.

Plato and Aristotle both wrote on musical esthetics; and Aristoxenus (*c.* 320 B.C.) of Tarentum, a pupil of Aristotle, was a voluminous writer on musical topics. Portions of two of his works have survived; and *On Music,* by Plutarch (or attributed to him), owes much of its value to the copious extracts from Aristoxenus.

3. *The period of decline.* Everything now ran to elaboration and to empty displays of virtuosity. Whereas one flute player had once sufficed, orchestras of six hundred musicians were now assembled. Lyres had 40 strings, ten times their original number. Upon certain virtuosi were heaped honors exceeding those accorded in modern times to our coloratura sopranos.

Greek Modes.—The subject of the Greek *modes,* as the scales were called, is an involved and difficult one. The Greek tonal system was based not upon the *octave,* as is ours, but on the *tetrachord.* That is, each mode consisted of four notes, corresponding to the four strings of the primitive Grecian lyre. Tones were not, as in our system, determined by their relation to *tonic* (or *keynote*) and dominant (or fifth note of the scale) but purely by intervals. The difference between one mode and another lay in the different arrangements of the intervals (for only the highest and lowest tones were uniformly the same distance apart); and in the *pitch* of the perfect fourth that comprised them. Like the Chinese scales, the Greek modes were thought of as descending. They were of three sorts:

(*a*) *Diatonic,* the most important and the most favored by the purists (two whole tones and one half tone);

(*b*) *Chromatic* (two half tones and one minor third);

(*c*) *Enharmonic* (two quarter tones and one major third).

Today our ear no longer distinguishes quarter-tones. Even among the Greeks themselves enharmonic modes were in only transient use. Our notion of *chromatic* is different from theirs. A five-toned scale seems to have been the most ancient form used by them. In their musical *notation* the words were cut on stone, with letters placed above them as symbols to indicate the pitch.

Greek Instruments.—The Greeks had string and wind instruments. The native lyre (*phorminx*) and *kithara* were in course of time added to by string instruments introduced from Asia. Each string served for but one tone, to which it was tuned. In playing, the finger or a *plektron* was used. Wind instruments (*auloi*) were of many kinds—chiefly they remind us of our own *clarinet, oboe* or *flute.* The *Panpipe* was a later addition. It was a kind of mouth organ, with seven reeds fastened together, each reed producing a different tone of the scale. Homer and Hesiod mention only the string instruments. The Homeric heroes and minstrels sing to the accompaniment of the phorminx, and it is only from within the Trojan lines that we hear the sound of flutes and pipes. Wind instruments

seem to have reached the Greeks by way of Phrygia. As a rule the Greeks used a double flute—two blown at the same time, but the single flute (*monaulos*) was introduced from Egypt. Among the foreign string instruments taken over by the Greeks were the *trigonos,* or three-sided harp, from Syria; the *magadis* and *pektis* from Lydia; and the *barbiton.* In no other field were the Greeks more influenced from without than they were in music. The terms *Phrygian* and *Lydian* were used in naming some of the diatonic modes.

In general it may be said that among the Greeks the knowledge and cultivation of music were deemed essential to the character of a free man. Music was fundamental in the education of youth, a necessary part of all liberal training.

Roman Music.—The Romans borrowed instruments from Greece and from Asia. With the extension of Roman conquests and the founding of the Empire, alien music of many sorts became familiar. Trumpets (*tuba, buccina*), introduced from Lydia, suited the Roman military turn of mind. There was much rather vulgar affectation of art, even by the emperors. Nero is a classic example of the idle, shallow dilettante. During his reign the *hydraulic organ* (a Greek development from the Panpipe), in which air was forced into pipes by water pressure, became popular. Hadrian and, still later, Justinian, made unavailing attempts toward musical reforms. Though contributing to music almost nothing that was original, the Romans did help to disseminate musical ideas. The late Roman philosopher Boëthius (*c.* 500 A.D.) wrote, when the antique world was already passing, five books *De Musica* (*On Music*) that had a remarkable influence throughout the Middle Ages as a textbook of the musical art.

MUSIC OF THE MIDDLE AGES

In a survey of the music of the Middle Ages, we must follow the progress of two different styles, the *churchly* or *ecclesiastical* and the *lay* or *secular.* The first grew up and developed in connection with the ritual or form of public worship of the Christian Church. Following the division of the Roman Empire (395 A.D.) into the empires of the East and the West, church history also began to be divided, although the final separation into Eastern and Western churches did not take place until 1054 A.D. In tracing the formation of our musical system, our interest lies with the progress of music in the Western or Roman Church. The second style, the secular, developed from *folk music,* the expression of the people; from the music of strollers—singers and also instrumentalists, playing fiddles, clarinets, flutes, trumpets, pipes and harps; from the art songs of *troubadours* and *trouvères, minnesinger* and *Meistersinger;* from music of a religious or devotional nature with words not in the ecclesiastical Latin of ritual but in the vernacular or common speech.

Early Church Music.—The Romans did not take over into Latin the Greek word *hymnos* (hymn), by which the Greeks meant a poem in honor not only of their gods but also of heroes or distinguished men. It happens, however, that we have from the classic age of Latinity a few poems that in both their form and their general character are nearer to modern ideas of hymnody than is anything we have in Greek. Such, for example, are Horace 1,21: "Sing to Diana, gentle maids," and Catullus xxxiv: "We are Diana's votaries." It is nevertheless to the Greek-speaking churches that we must look for the first use of Christian hymnody. Paul (Coloss. 3:16) refers to "psalms and hymns and spiritual songs" and to "singing with grace in your hearts unto God." In I Cor. 14:26, he says, "When ye come together, each one hath a psalm," the context plainly showing that he alludes to meetings for worship. It is told that Paul and Silas sang hymns in their jail at Philippi (Acts 16:25). James (5:13) says: "Is any cheerful? let him sing praise." In Acts 4:24–30 we read of a group of Christians who "lifted up their voice to God with one accord" in a passage of hymnlike character; and elsewhere in the New Testament are passages that have sometimes been regarded as quotations from hymns of the Apostolic period. The modern distinction between hymns and psalms must be viewed as purely arbitrary; such a distinction appears to have been unknown to the early Church. St. Augustine's definition of *hymn* was "praise to God with song."

Although the word *hymn* is from the Greek, it is to Hebrew sources that we must look for the origin of Christian hymn singing. Psalm tones (or psalm tunes) in Christian use at a very early date are found to be adapted not to Greek prosody but to the peculiar construction of Hebrew verse—the parallel couplets that we have already noted. This points to the *antiphonal* style of chanting, a characteristic Hebrew form. Pliny's famous letter to the Emperor Trajan (Epist. 97) reveals that in Bithnia at the end of the 2d century A.D., when Pliny was governor there, antiphonal singing was already well established. Christianity came to the West through Greek channels, and it was therefore quite natural that the West should follow Greek authority and practice. Even in Latin-speaking assemblies the hymns long were sung in Greek. This Greek hymnody was not imitated in the West until the 4th century, when Latin hymnody had its beginnings with Hilary of Poitiers (d. 367 A.D.) and Ambrose of Milan (d. 397 A.D.). St. Augustine, one of Ambrose's converts, explains how it was appointed that "after the manner of the Eastern churches, hymns and songs should be sung lest the people should grow weary and faint through sorrow." Of himself, as he listened, he says: "The voices flowed into my ears; the truth distilled into my heart."

Ambrose of Milan, to prevent the loss of the ancient melodies, which had been preserved by vocal tradition only and had suffered many changes, compiled the Ambrosian Breviary—

a *breviary* being a collection of hymns proper to the season and the week. The hymns it contained by Ambrose himself were lofty in expression, brief and readily singable. Pope Gregory I (Pope, 590–604) has been credited with another revision of Church music, the compilation of an *antiphonary* and the establishment at Rome of a *schola cantorum* (singing school) in which teachers were prepared to form other schools elsewhere. So in addition to the Ambrosian style of ecclesiastical music another and different style arose known as *Gregorian*. The Gregorian style came to be accepted as the sanctioned Roman use, and the Ambrosian was almost wholly restricted to the diocese of Milan.

It is a mistake to suppose that the Gregorian *modes* (or scales) were derived from the ancient Greek modes, though Greek names were given to them. Between the two *tonalities* no connection whatever existed. The melodies of the Gregorian *chant* or plain chant (*cantus firmus*) are written not in the major and minor scales of present-day music but in one of 12 modes, the intervals of each mode being based on a fundamental starting note paradoxically known as the *final* and corresponding to the *tonic* (or keynote) of present-day scales. Each mode comprises eight sounds. The compass of the first series of six, known as *authentic* modes, runs to the octave above the final; that of the second series of six, known as *plagal* modes, extends from the fourth note below the final to the fifth note above it. Of the several distinct classes of plain-chant melodies, the oldest and most interesting is that including the psalm tones sometimes known as *Gregorian tones*. Following these in antiquity are the *antiphons*, *graduals*, *introits* and *offertoria* that are employed at High Mass.

Originally notation was by means of symbolic letters, as in the ancient Greek system; but later, in place of letters, a series of signs called *neumes* was devised. These were written over the words of the text, to indicate the melodic trend. Eight of these (with Latin names) were of particular importance, and from these, in some cases, combinations were formed. Letters prefixed to indicate the pitch evolved into *clef* or *key* signs, and a four-line *staff* was adopted, this being sufficient for the compass of Gregorian modes. To a Benedictine monk, Guido d'Arezzo (*c.* 990–*c.* 1050), is usually attributed the invention of *solmisation*—the way of reading scales by the syllables *ut, re, mi, fa, sol, la.* It was said that he took these syllables from the initial words of successive lines of an ancient hymn to John the Baptist:

> *Ut* queant laxis
> *Re*sonare fibris,
> *Mi*ra gestorum
> *Fa*muli tuorum,
> *Sol*ve polluti
> *La*bii reatum,
> Sancte Ioannes.

At any rate, the syllables are certainly there; and when a seventh note

was added to the scale, the syllable *si* was formed from the initial letters of "Sancte Ioannes." The ingenious Guido divided the scale into seven interchangeable groups of six notes each (*hexachords*). Of these the lowest started from a foundational G (Greek *gamma*) below *ut*. From this conjunction of *gamma* and *ut* came the word *gamut,* meaning the whole scale of tones.

Gradually the use of the classical metres (for congregational singing the *iambic* dimeter was a favorite) yielded to that of accentual rhythm, and this was aided by *rhyme*. Ultimately intricate rhyme patterns were employed. The greater the freedom of melody from metrical quantities, the more were experiments made with prolonging tones, with embellishments, with developing fantastic *motifs* on a single syllable. It is recorded that in the Roman Church the Alleluia in the Mass was anciently sung "with the *pneuma*"— that is, the *coloratura* was sustained so long as the singer had breath (Greek *pneuma*). In the ritual of the Coptic Church to the present day, it is said, a single Alleluia is often prolonged for a quarter of an hour. In the Roman Church, the *gradual* was the anthem that followed the *epistle* and preceded the *gospel* in the office of the Mass. The gradual ended with an Alleluia, and the extension of this was known as a *sequence*. The sequence was originally metrical—a "musical jubilation" was prolonged through a certain number of tones. Notker Balbulus of St. Gall (d. 912 A.D.) wrote new words to go with the old *motifs*. These Notkerian sequences (or *proses*) were not metrical but rhythmical, fitted exactly to the tones they were designed to accompany. From this it was but a step to the composition of new motifs also. The sequence became the favorite form of composition in the earlier Middle Ages, and numerous examples have survived. Five still have place in the Roman missal: *Victimae paschali laudes; Veni Sancte Spiritus; Lauda Sion Salvatorem; Stabat mater; Dies irae.* Originally the congregation had been permitted to take up the sequence as a response, but afterward the tendency of the Church was set against this. But sequences became the means through which the music of the Church most influenced secular music. The Gregorian chant also had its influence. Hymns continued to be written—to the Trinity, for the holy seasons, to the Virgin, for private devotions and for other uses; but Latin hymnody had reached its finest development. The subsequent revival of learning led to an extensive revision of the hymns of the breviary (or abridgment of the daily offices for the use of those in major orders), by which the medieval Latin was much altered to conform to that of classical writers.

Early Secular Music.—From a period so remote that it is lost in obscurity, folk music and folk dancing characteristic of different nationalities are known to have existed. The songs were of simple literary form and often, because of their combination

DAS STANDEBUCH (114 WOODCUTS BY JOST AMMAN WITH RHYMES BY HANS SACHS), LEIPZIG.

MUSICIANS of the Middle Ages with various instruments of that period. On the left is a lute maker playing one of his lutes; in the center, three men (*left to right*) play a lute, a trombone, and a harp; on the right, a guitar-fiddler is accompanied by an organist.

with dancing, had strongly marked rhythms. The folk music of Germany and France won particular importance. That of Germany was marked by a concise form and a freedom from ornamental embellishment. That of France was a source of *themes* for the musicians who developed *counterpoint* in the Netherlands. To furnish accompaniment for voices, many different instruments were used; and these contributed to the rise of our modern *tonalities* and *harmonies*.

In the earlier Middle Ages we encounter two classes of *minstrels*—the *bards,* found principally in the northern countries, where their recitals of mighty deeds of the heroic past were esteemed as a means to arouse patriotism; and the *itinerant* entertainers who roamed through Europe. At first, though their music was welcomed at village festival and town fair (where they were accustomed to show their versatility by exhibiting trained beasts and performing tricks), they were regarded as vagabonds of the road, outside the pale of the law. In time laws dealing with them were enacted; but the Church that had frowned on them admitted them to some part in its miracle plays. They were particularly numerous in France, where they were styled *jongleurs* (literally, jugglers). Massenet's charming opera *Le Jongleur de Notre Dame* has to do with one of these strollers. In the towns, *guilds* of minstrels were commonly formed, and these guilds, like the trade guilds, endeavored to fix certain standards for their members. Some minstrels became musicians in the private orchestra of a nobleman or in a military band. For a time the minstrels were the most faithful custodians of the *folk song,* and the evolution of instrumental music depended wholly upon them. Then there were traveling clerics, *vagantes* and goliards, who used mostly Latin rather than the vernacular. One of their songs is "Meum est propositum," attributed to a Gualterus who is variously identi-

fied. Some songs of a folk character have Latin words and rhyming lines—such as the *Festum asini* (or *Prose de l' âne*), which was known as early as the 12th century and was sung at festivals in France.

The Age of Chivalry that had its beginnings in the 12th century led to a study of Provençal music and poetry and an imitation of Provençal customs. A group or school of courtly musicians and poets arose; and during the 12th and 13th centuries these poets and musicians, aided by the professional services of *jongleurs,* wrote *chansons, pastorelles, serenades* and the like in praise of their ladies. The rendition of these was usually supplied by the *jongleurs.* The Church modes were used, though somewhat simplified. These compositions, at first natural and sincere in manner, later became thoroughly artificial. In some cases the melodies were made the basis of works for the Church or were adapted to folk songs. In Germany a similar movement was carried on by the *minnesinger,* though with differences. The *minnesinger* were usually but not always of rank; they less frequently sought the aid of the minstrels; and they had a greater variety of topics, nature, patriotism or even piety. Their compositions were written in the Gregorian modes but were sung more in the recitative manner, and greater attention was paid to the instrumental accompaniment. Prominent representatives of this school were Walther von der Vogelweide and Wolfram von Eschenbach in the first quarter of the 13th century.

The *Minnelied* became increasingly formalized and was succeeded by the *Meistergesang.* The *Meistersinger* took their work very seriously. Most of them were worthy artisans and honest citizens of German towns, who, usually of a Sunday afternoon, gathered at the church, the town hall or the guild house to study singing. Many of them not only were unfamiliar with the melodies of the *minnesinger,* to

whom they believed themselves to be the successors, but did not even understand musical notation. To them, for the most part, the writing of poetry was a purely formal job, the skill for which was to be acquired by learning the rules. The gay science of the *troubadours,* the *trouvères* and the *minnesinger* had now become a handicraft. One worked his way up through the grades of *Schüler, Schulfreund, Dichter* and *Sänger* to become *Meister.* One figure stands out from these surroundings—Hans Sachs (1494–1576), the cobbler-poet of Nuremberg, 13 of whose melodies we have. He appears in Wagner's *Die Meistersinger von Nürnberg,* which gives a livelier and truer picture than could any mere description, however lengthy. From this we may learn that although from a strictly musical point of view the *Meistersinger* may have little significance for us, they did perform a service in endeavoring to preserve a native musical art at a time when German princes and nobles were turning their backs upon it.

Secular Instruments.—As a result of the Crusades a number of Oriental instruments were added to the instruments already in use, and these were adapted to accompaniments for Western dances and songs. Percussion instruments were not much in favor. Of wind instruments, *pipes* of various sorts (including both whistle and reed types) were popular; for military uses, horns and trumpets served. Stringed instruments were especially preferred, and were of two leading sorts: (*a*) those that were struck or plucked; and (*b*) those that were bowed. In the first group were *guitars, harps, lutes* and *psalteries.* Lutes, though to our notions difficult to tune and play, were prime favorites and appeared in a wide variety of shapes and sizes. In the second group were *viols* of many designs; the viol had the Arabian *rabab* (with the Welsh *crwth*) as its supposed prototype and was itself the prototype of the violin family of today. As the compass of instruments increased, a corresponding extension became necessary in the system of notation. Hence arose various schemes of *tablatures,* specially adapted to different kinds of instruments. For example, the tablature for the lute represented by lines the strings of the instrument itself, and symbols on these lines indicated the various positions of the fingers on the strings for producing the desired tones.

Contrapuntal Schools.—We pass now in the history of medieval music from unison singing to vocal polyphony. *Counterpoint* has to do with the arrangement of a musical composition into a number of separate and distinct *parts.* As we have already seen, *harmony* implies that several concordant tones are heard at the same time. The art of counterpoint consists in the arrangement of these several tones in such a way that each may belong to a different part, which is throughout capable of being performed by a separate and distinct voice or instrument. Each of the parts must in itself form a kind of melody, but the combination of them all must be so arranged as to produce, when they are heard together, a satisfactory harmony. It is chiefly in vocal composition that counterpoint is used, although it appears in instrumental works, as in *chamber music* (*quartets, quintets*) and sometimes also in orchestral pieces—though in these not all the parts are *real,* that is, perfectly separate and distinct one from another. Counterpoint is found in organ works by Johann Sebastian Bach, though these are to be played upon a single instrument.

The exponents of strict counterpoint, which flourished in the period we have now reached, added to a given melody or *cantus firmus* one or more other melodies, the relations of which to the given melody were determined by rule. Ever since that time a knowledge of counterpoint has been part of a thorough study of composition, although the art has often been greatly neglected and the rules governing it have been much relaxed in modern times. A school, directed by the organists of Notre Dame, grew up in Paris; another at Tournai. This activity spread northward—to the north of France, to Belgium, to the Netherlands. For a long time, musicians of the Netherlands were highly considered all over Europe as composers, performers and teachers. They surpassed all others in the involved technique of their contrapuntal arrangements. Prominent among them were Johannes Okeghem and Josquin des Prés, but the greatest of the school was undoubtedly Orlando di Lasso (*c.* 1532–1594), who wrote a vast number of compositions and was known as the Prince of Musicians. Schools were busy also at Venice and in Rome. Most distinguished of the Roman school was Palestrina (*c.*1515–1594), who became organist and later director of music at St. Peter's and developed an individual style in his contrapuntal works, which include his famous Mass dedicated to Pope Marcellus.

The system of neumes no longer sufficed for musical notation. It had been adequate for chanting in unison; but when counterpoint arrived and different singers had different melodies with a differing number of notes, it was necessary to the harmony that the duration of each note be known. So *mensural* notation was introduced—clumsily at first, to be sure, but marking a great advance.

MUSIC OF THE REFORMATION

As early as 1476 Ulrich Hahn of Ingolstadt printed a missal in which he used movable types for the notes. This was at Rome, and there the process was developed by Ottaviano Petrucci (1466–1539), who employed two impressions (one for the lines, the other for the notes), and who was the foremost music printer of his day. Before this innovation, the printing of music had been done with plates cut from wood. By the new method, compositions could be published much less expensively. This resulted in an increased circulation of music and helped musical art eventually to have its share in the general movement of the Renaissance.

Music in Protestant Churches.—Luther's purpose was to reform, not wholly to discard, the old forms of service. He therefore retained many of their features, introducing the modifications he felt to be required by new conditions. In conformity with his insistence upon the natural right of the individual to communicate directly with God, he had much of the old liturgy rendered into the vernacular. He also made a point of restoring the custom of hymn singing by the congregation that had prevailed in the early Church. In order to provide suitable music, he enlisted the aid of prominent musicians, and not only Gregorian melodies but German religious and secular folk tunes were arranged for the new vernacular hymns.

A highly dignified strophic or rhythmic form was developed, known as the *Choral.* This came to take in the Lutheran services a place very similar to that of the Gregorian chant in Roman services. In the beginning, chorales were sung in unison, unaccompanied, by the entire congregation. After a while additional parts were written in the contrapuntal style. These were sung by the choir while the congregation sang the chant (*cantus*). But whereas the old way of counterpoint was to build an ornate vocal structure upon the *cantus firmus* as basis, this new style put more emphasis on the basis, with a resultant effect of greater simplicity. Plain chords came much into use, and the leading part was, for greater convenience in harmonizing, transferred from the *tenor* to the *soprano.* Modern music was beginning; and it should here be clearly stated that modern music is greatly simplified from the highly wrought polyphony of medieval music, written in accordance with a set of rules often subtilized to the point of absurdity. Subsequently the Choral lost its vital character and grew rather tedious. Because, as was the custom of the time, the music was written without

bars, the original rhythmic movement gave way to *polyrhythm*—frequent change of rhythm within the same composition. This was opposed to the earlier simplicity and unity and to the idea of congregational singing with a text that should be readily intelligible.

The *motet* (a word that has been explained as a diminutive of *motus*) was also much in favor. The older *a capella* motet was a kind of contrapuntal anthem in which the tenor part carried a Gregorian melody, and against it the other voices sang another Latin text. It was not divided for stanzas but had continuous movement. It might be secular as well as ecclesiastical. The new variety of motet had instrumental accompaniment and was written with greater freedom. Such motets were sometimes called *cantiones sacrae.* The older unaccompanied motet was not, however, entirely supplanted. The *cantata,* which had originated in Italy and been developed by Giacomo Carissimi and others, also became popular for the new church music. It had been made up of chorus passages varied by *arias* (solos) with accompaniment. The new style of cantata used texts drawn from hymnals, expanded by the interpolation of passages from the Bible. It showed less use of the aria and greater development of the choruses.

Among the leading German composers of this period were Heinrich Finck, Heinrich Isaac (*c.* 1450–1517), Ludwig Senfl (1492–1555) and Johann Walther (1496–1570). But these were only a few out of many, for there was a veritable flood of texts and melodies.

The Swiss Reformation adopted a musical usage not greatly different from the Lutheran but putting a special emphasis on the singing of metrical psalms. These were collected in volumes known as *psalters.* In England a well-developed school of music must have existed as early as the 13th century, for King Sigismund and the Duke Philip of Burgundy after their stay in England were loud in their praises of the English art and sought to introduce it into their own lands. English musicians and singers by hundreds visited the Continent and were welcomed there. Among them the best-known was John Dunstable (*d.* 1453), composer and theorist, whose pupils included founders of the Netherlands school of counterpoint.

Music of the English Reformation.—As consequences of the English Reformation, the Bible was translated into English and the liturgy was both translated and adapted, appearing in authorized form in the Book of Common Prayer (1549). Three kinds of musical setting were used: (*a*) for the portions intoned by the clergy or used for responses; (*b*) for the chanting of Psalms; (*c*) for the *canticles* (such as the *Te Deum*) prescribed for use in the different services. In addition to the music of the liturgy, there were anthems set to words from the prayer book or from the Bible and congregational hymns. At the outset Gregorian melodies were employed, but in time distinctive new styles based on harmonic forms arose. Thomas Tallis (d.1585) and Tallis's pupil William Byrd (1540–1623), both organists of the Chapel Royal; Dr. John Bull (1562–1628), also organist of the Chapel Royal and later at the Antwerp Cathedral; and Orlando Gibbons (1583–1625) were distinguished members of the contrapuntal group that still relied mainly on vocal effects in their works.

Secular Music in England.—Throughout England folk dances and folk songs were abundant. Many of the most characteristic of the songs were in the form of *ballads,* recounting at length some episode or glorifying some deed. Among art compositions, *madrigals* were especially popular. The madrigal was a kind of motet, simple, tuneful and gay. It had its origin in Italy. Thomas Morley (1557–1603), a pupil of William Byrd, and John Dowland (1562–1626) wrote numerous madrigals. Among fashionables the six-stringed lute was a favorite instrument, and concerted pieces in madrigal form, known as *fancies,* were written for it. The *virginal,* a quadrangular, boxlike, legless kind of *spinet,* was supposed to be particularly an instrument for young ladies. Queen Elizabeth I, who liked to be regarded as a patron of secular music, performed on the virginal; and at Cambridge is preserved a manuscript volume of compositions, known as *Queen Elizabeth's Virginal Book,* in which are short pieces by composers of her day—some variations on popular tunes, others dances, but all in counterpoint and very like works written for the organ during the same period.

Instruments with Keyboards.—It has already been noted that the hydraulic organ had some popularity among the Romans of Nero's day. In the earlier Middle Ages the organ went out of use. After some hundreds of years its use was revived, and three varieties of the instrument were made: (a) the *portative*—small enough to be carried about quite readily or to be held on the lap; (b) the *positive,* larger than the portative—often designed for being wheeled about and sometimes even installed in churches; (c) the *great organ*—large, powerful instruments, for the most part built into churches. These great organs were at first exceedingly clumsy; the keys were six inches in width and were struck with the fist. Narrowed until the performer's hand could span a fifth, they were finally brought down to their present dimensions. Gradually, too, the compass was extended from the original 12 diatonic tones and was filled in by adding chromatics, beginning with the middle register; then other *manuals* (keyboards) were introduced; the positive organ was attached to the great and became the *choir organ* (so called, probably, because used in the first place for accompaniments to the choir); and *pedals* (a keyboard to be played with the feet) were devised. The great organ must by itself have been unsuited to accompaniments, and probably its chief use was to announce the Gregorian tone for the singers. But prior to the invention of the wind chest, even greater trouble was had with the matter of air supply. In some cases so many bellows were needed that one organ took seventy men to blow it.

The organ had a series of *claves* (keys; from the Latin *clavis,* a key), levers that opened valves (otherwise closed) to admit air from the windchest into the respective pipes. The assembly of these *claves* was known as a *claviarium.* Hence came the name of a type of instrument quite different from the organ—the *clavier* type. In German a pianoforte is still termed *Klavier.* It is the key and its associated mechanism that form the characteristic distinction between instruments of the clavier type and other stringed instruments. These claviers were adapted to domestic and social use and were of two main types, *clavichords* and *harpsichords.* Harpsichords, derived from the psaltery, plucked the strings by means of quills attached to the keys. Clavichords, originating in the dulcimer, used brass tangents raised and held against the strings. Among the instruments of the harpsichord type were the *clavecin,* the *spinet* and the *virginal.* A larger form was developed, called the *harpsichord,* in shape like the modern grand piano but smaller and suited to use with orchestras of the period. From this the type derived its name.

THE RISE OF OPERA

Beginnings in Italy.—The high point of the music of the Middle Ages had been reached in unaccompanied choral music. In its *polyphonic* style all the voices had an equal importance. It was contemplative music, quite without anything of what we know as dramatic quality. Within its own limits it did reach a high development—some, indeed, have described its expression as perfect. The limits were, however, decided. With the Renaissance a demand was made upon the musical art that it express, as other arts had begun to do, the new assertion of the rights of the individual that characterized the Renaissance spirit. A means was found through *homophony* (or monody), in which paramount importance was given to one melody and the other melodies were subordinated to it. One natural result was that contrapuntal design gave place to *harmonic* design. In *polyphony, chords* were purely matters of chance, happening at times as the melodies progressed. But in homophony, chords, both individually and in their relations with one another, ceased to be mere chance affairs and took a leading place in the writing of music. Harmonic design had existed to a certain extent in secular dance music, derived mainly from folk sources; but now it began to be a subject of experiment and study. With this change in musical form, *opera* and *oratorio* (and also the instrumental *suite*) really had their start.

Opera (the word is Italian, meaning *work*) was launched by amateurs who, in the closing years of the 16th century, met in Florence at the house of Giovanni Bardi, philosopher and poet. The first public performance of opera was *Euridice* (1600), music by Jacopo Peri, book by Ottavio Rinuccini. In this, certain quieter passages were sung with half-spoken tones to a subdued accompaniment; and here was the origin of dramatic *recitative.* Some composers who had been trained in polyphony endeavored to write opera (*dramma per musica,* it was at first called) on a polyphonic, strictly vocal basis with choruses in madrigal style. The works of Claudio Monteverde (1567–1643), who had been well schooled in the polyphonic style, made a definite break and prevented a further development in the choral art of the 16th century. His *Orfeo* (1607), *Arianna* (1608) and *Il Combattimento di Tancredi e Clorinda* (*The Combat of Tancred and Clorinda,* 1624) had in their day a truly impressive effect, particularly in the development of the resources of the orchestral instruments. Formal melody began to supplant recitative; pauses in the action were used for vocal displays, which by the time of Alessandro Scarlatti (1659–1725) had established the *aria* or solo tune. From Scarlatti until the works of Gluck appeared, opera was virtually aria and little else, with two exceptions. The first was that of Giovanni Lully (1633–1687), a Florentine who became conductor at the court of Louis XIV and who introduced into opera of the Italian sort spectacular *ballets* in the French manner. The second was that of Henry Purcell (1658–1695), an Englishman who at 21 composed his *Dido and Aeneas,* a work much in advance of its time. Italian opera reached England in 1707.

THE EARLY ORATORIO

The first oratorio was Emilio del Cavalieri's *Rappresentazione di Anima e di Corpo* (*Representation of Soul and Body*), which was produced in the oratory of the church of Santa Maria at Vallicella, Italy, in 1600—the same year in which the first opera was performed. In fact there is, as has been pointed out by historians, practically nothing that distinguishes it from Peri's *Euridice* except its religious subject. Giacomo Carissimi (1604–1674), a pioneer of the cantata, was also known as an oratorio writer. He and other Italians composing in this field during his general period wrote in the manner of serious Italian opera, although to a Latin text; and their oratorios were presented with dramatic action and stage accessories. Later the oratorio passed from Italian composers to those of Germany and England, where it became a significant art form.

English Church Music.—The English Puritans officially discouraged the singing of anything but the most austere psalm tunes, sung in unison and unaccompanied. Psalmbooks were issued with tunes severe and cheerless in melody, having the simplest rhythms and set to metrical versions that detracted from the poetry of the Scripture originals. During the Commonwealth (1649–1660) Puritan influence had full sway. Milton's lifelong fondness for music is always referred to as something exceptional for those days. Church organs were destroyed by iconoclasts. The ecclesiastical music of an earlier period was kept alive chiefly at Oxford. After the Restoration the new harmonic forms began to be adopted. Purcell wrote anthems. Croft and Boyce were learned musicians but not of Purcell's quality. Anthems were now written with elaborate instrumental accompaniments by orchestra or organ. A new method of chanting, the *Anglican* chant, consisted of a single tune (seven measures) or a double tune (fourteen measures), each preceded by a varying group of words called the recitation, which was made on a reciting-note. These tunes, harmonized in plain chords, were introduced for antiphonal chanting of the Psalter, but similar ones were adapted to the *canticles*. Until the 18th century hymns continued without musical decoration.

DEVELOPMENT OF ORGAN MUSIC

It was through the organ that instrumental music, which had existed as an auxiliary to vocal music, achieved its independence. Compositions written specially for the organ as an independent instrument find their earliest date in the works of a group of musicians, who all served as organists of St. Mark's, Venice. Two of them were from the Netherlands: Adrian Willaert (1480–1562)—"Messer Adriano" the Italians styled him—, and Cyprian de Rore (1516–1565). Two were Italians: Andrea Gabrieli (c. 1510–1586) and his nephew, Giovanni Gabrieli (1557–1612?). Girolamo Frescobaldi (1583–1644), whom some have called Italy's greatest organ virtuoso, was organist at St. Peter's, Rome, except for a brief interval, from 1608 until 1643. Such was his reputation as a performer that his audiences often numbered 30,000. He took over existing forms—*canzone, fantasia, fugue, passacaglia, toccata*—but gave them all an irregular turn, sometimes a dash of the fantastic and bizarre. Subsequently, he has been esteemed less for his compositions than for the strong impetus he gave to the technique of the organ (and also of the claviers) and for his activity as a teacher. Jan Sweelinck of Amsterdam (1562–1621) was considered the greatest organ instructor of his day. In Germany at the beginning of the 17th century the organ had begun to furnish accompaniment for the *Choral*. In this way the organists to a certain extent directly inherited the vocal art of the past. Counterpoint was appropriated and was adapted to instrumental technique. On the technical side, several composers did much to pave the way for Bach. Prominent among these were: Samuel Scheidt (1587–1654); Johann Froberger (c. 1605–1667), Frescobaldi's most important pupil; and the Danish Dietrich Buxtehude (1637–1707), organist of the Marienkirche in Lubeck, to hear whom Bach, then aged 19 and organist at Arnstadt, walked from Arnstadt to Lubeck, overstayed his leave, and nearly got himself into trouble with his church.

MUSIC OF THE 18TH CENTURY

In music the earlier 18th century has three pre-eminent and commanding figures: Handel, Bach and Gluck —all Germans, although Handel spent so much of his life in England that he is identified with English music. Handel and Bach were born in the same year; Gluck was born 30 years later. Handel was a cosmopolitan, versed in music of many origins and sorts, much before the public, seeking to reach that public with genuine music cast in a brilliant and popular form. Handel wrote for the vocalist, aiming at beauty of melodic line and some vocal flourish. Bach wrote as an organist, though in a highly characteristic idiom. He wrote reflective music, wrote to please himself and to satisfy his own ideals of art. In his own day he was little understood and had far less influence than did Handel. Since that day he has increased in stature until in the 20th century his compositions, though not appealing to a superficial taste, are regarded as standards of musical expression. Gluck, like Handel and Bach, sought to lead music away from the trite, the banal, the trivial; for into these it had begun to lapse. Having gained success in Italian opera, he turned from it to find a new path. He was a militant, publishing expositions of his theories and writing works to exemplify them. He was accepted in France, but elsewhere the Italian style continued to prevail. It has been asserted that only because there was a lack in the tonal resources available did he fail of a place similar to that of the later Wagner, to whom he was certainly prior in the field of music drama.

Handel.—Georg Friedrich Händel (1685–1759), who became George Frederick Handel to the England in which he spent two-thirds of his life and who was known in Italy as Hendel or *Il Sassone* (*The Saxon*), was born in Halle-an-der-Saale, Lower Saxony. Though destined for a lawyer, the boy by surreptitious practice in the attic upon an instrument variously called a clavichord, a harpsichord or a spinet, acquired a skill that amazed the court musicians of the duke of Saxe-Weissenfels. At 10 he wrote six trios, still extant, for two oboes and bass, which give him as a youthful prodigy a niche close beside that of Mozart. He was a pupil of Zachau, organist of the Hauptkirche (cathedral) in Halle, studying clavier instruments, organ, violin, oboe and composition. In 1702 he became organist of the Schlosskirche in Halle; in 1703 went to Hamburg, where opera was coming into some prominence and where the first of his 42 operas, *Almira*, was performed with great success. At the end of 1706 he left for Italy. There he was active in Florence, Naples, Rome and Venice; was welcomed by such musicians as Domenico Scarlatti (1685–1757), the foremost Italian representative of clavier music, whose harpsichord technique had significance for the works of Haydn and Beethoven and thus for the modern pianoforte. In Italy Handel produced two operas

GEORGE FREDERICK HANDEL

and two oratorios; and during this sojourn, with the ready power of assimilation that always characterized him, he developed the smoothness of vocal style that was a consistent feature of his subsequent work.

Appointed *Kapellmeister* (conductor) to the elector of Hanover in 1709, he went on leave of absence to England in 1710; and in February 1711 his opera *Rinaldo*, which Addison reviewed for the *Spectator*, had a highly successful première at the London Haymarket. Though he went back to his post in Hanover when the opera season was over, he paid a second visit to England in 1712, wrote a *Te Deum* for Queen Anne and was still in the vicinity of London when the elector arrived in 1714 as George I. Pardoned for his breach of contract, he was naturalized in 1726. In 1720 he became impresario of the Italian opera at the Haymarket, which he managed until 1728. He directed other companies and went on writing Italian opera until 1741, when *Deidamia*, his last work in that genre, was produced. None of his many Italian operas continues to be performed in its entirety, but arias from most of them (like "Lascia ch'io pianga" from *Rinaldo*) are still prized. He now turned his back on opera and devoted his attention particularly to the oratorio. In this field he had already made a successful beginning and in it he wrote his best works and made his most significant contributions to music. His subjects were both secular and Biblical. Between the two kinds is no discernible difference in method and treatment. His method was in fact operatic, and the Biblical oratorios originally served as a kind of Biblical opera that might be patronized during Lent. He began to use English texts in 1733 with an augmented version of *Esther*. Transferred from the strict conditions of stage production to the freedom of the concert, the Handelian oratorios increasingly emphasized the choruses. In so doing they greatly aided the development of the English art of chorus singing. The best-known to

JOHANN SEBASTIAN BACH

modern audiences is *The Messiah* (1742), although Handel himself preferred *Samson* (1744). Others are *Belshazzar* (1745), *Judas Maccabaeus* (1747), *Joshua* (1748), *Jephtha* (1752). Handel also wrote music for Dryden's "Ode for St. Cecilia's Day" and Milton's "L'Allegro." Among his instrumental compositions are harpsichord suites, organ concertos and violin sonatas. A suggestion of his vast output may be given in the statement that one edition of his complete works fills a hundred volumes. His indebtedness to other composers for material has been a subject of much discussion. From May 1752 his eyesight was affected, but he continued to labor.

Bach.—Johann Sebastian Bach (1685–1750) was born in Eisenach, almost in the shadow of the Wartburg, where singers of the Middle Ages once had competed, and Luther had translated the Bible. The Bachs were a musical clan, and Sebastian was taught from an early age. In 1700 he became a student in the St. Michael's school at Luneburg, where he had been appointed a chorister. His earlier development in music was due chiefly to his study of the works of earlier composers, such as Frescobaldi, and those of his contemporaries, for example, Dietrich Buxtehude (1637–1797) and Johann Reinken (1623–1722). He made copies of all the worth-while music he could find. After a brief stay at Weimar as a violinist in the orchestra of Prince Ernst, he took the post of organist at the new church in Arnstadt in 1703. There the consistory reprimanded him for astonishing the congregation "by introducing many remarkable variations into the *Choral*, mingled with many strange tones." For about a year (1707–1708) he was organist at Muhlhausen; then he returned to the court of Saxe-Weimar, where he spent nine happy, busy years—composing some of his finest organ works, as well as cantatas. From 1717 to 1723 he was *Kapellmeister* to Prince Leopold of Anhalt-Köthen, having neither

organ nor church services but writing and directing chamber music. After 1723 the remainder of his life was passed at Leipzig as cantor of the Thomasschule, where he was often enough annoyed by the town councilors, who were able to understand neither the independence of the man nor the genius of the composer. There, however, such works were written as his *Passion According to St. Matthew* and the *Mass in B-minor*. His last days were passed in blindness. The Germany that was afterward so eager to claim him as an expression of the German spirit did not at all realize what it had lost. His grave was unmarked, its place was long unidentified; his widow was allowed to fall into such want that she died a pauper. Such was the gratitude of the world toward one who caused Beethoven to exclaim: *Nicht Bach, Meer sollte er heiszen!*—"His name should be not Bach [the German for brook] but Ocean!"

Neglected by his smart young contemporaries, his works waited until the first half of the 19th century to be rediscovered. In the past he was appreciated by only the more significant composers—by Mozart, whose style was greatly enriched by study of manuscript copies of Bach scores; by Beethoven, who devoted much thought to Bach's harpsichord and other works, so far as accessible; by Mendelssohn, who learned from the *St. Matthew Passion* a great deal about the oratorio. The critics have traced Bach's influence in the styles of such diverse composers as Chopin, Wagner and Brahms. It has been said that Bach towers, a gigantic landmark, between two eras. All that music had achieved before him, converges in him. "In the genius of the amazing Bach," declared Tieck, "reposed all the subsequent development of music."

Gluck.—Christoph Wilibald von Gluck (1714–87), born at Weidenwang in the Palatinate, studied music first at Prague and later as a pupil of Sammartini (1704–1774) at Milan. In Italy he wrote several operas in the conventional Italian style; they were so well received that he was invited to London to supply works in that vein for the Haymarket company, which at that time (1745) had declined from the excellence it had known in the days of Handel. In 1746 he quit London for Paris, where he made a first-hand study of the traditions and style of French opera, although for several years these appeared to have had no effect upon his own methods of composition. Appointed *Kapellmeister* at the court of Maria Theresa in 1754, he settled in Vienna in 1756 and there gradually developed his ideas for a reform of opera. To advance these ideas, he produced at Vienna three works, *Orfeo ed Euridice* (1762), *Alceste* (1767) and *Paride ed Elena* (1769). Feeling that these had not been received by the Viennese with the proper interest, he departed in 1773 for Paris, where he had earlier become familiar with the works of Lully and of Jean Rameau (1683–1764). In the French capital, as Gluck was aware, a controversy

had for years been in progress as to the true nature of the music drama. Italian opera had won many successes, but French national opera, in which the rights of the dramatic action and the libretto had been respected, had also held its ground. Though it had thus far remained a long way from true music drama, Gluck felt that the best elements in it coincided with his own views. With the aid of Marie Antoinette, who had been his pupil in Vienna and now was dauphiness of France, his *Iphigènie en Aulide* was produced at the Academie de Musique on April 19, 1774. Thereupon burst out one of those violent musical wars that have been so characteristic of Europe. Niccolo Piccini (1728–1800), a well-known composer, was summoned from Rome and put forward by the Italian party as its champion. Piccini's works in the field of *opera buffa* (*opéra bouffe*, comic opera of a rather extravagant sort) are said to show

CHRISTOPH W. GLUCK

spontaneity and humor; but in the rivalry that followed, engineered by the partisans of the Italian school, Gluck, following the stormy reception of his *Armide* (1777), won an unquestioned artistic and popular triumph with *Iphigènie en Tauride*. In 1780 he returned to Vienna.

Gluck, in expounding his theories, carefully stated his purpose. He wrote: "I shall try to reduce music in opera to its real function, that of seconding poetry by intensifying the expression of sentiments and the interest of situations without interrupting the action by needless ornament." He gave more character to the orchestra; represented different moods by varied tone colors; restricted the aria and made the recitative more free.

Gluck will sometimes be met with as the Chevalier Gluck or Ritter von Gluck because a papal knighthood was bestowed on him. His name is often incorrectly spelled Glück.

Special attention has been given to Handel, Bach and Gluck for their individual importance and for their position in musical history. Their immediate influence determined the character of modern music as we know it today. Furthermore, though earlier art music holds interest for the antiquary or the professional and may even in some cases, if skilfully and persuasively rendered, be enjoyed by average present-day audiences, the compositions of these men are the earliest that keep an assured place in répertoires and in the regard of listeners.

INSTRUMENTAL MUSIC PROGRESSES

Haydn.—Franz Joseph Haydn (1732–1809), born in the little market town of Rohrau in lower Austria, was favored by the appreciation and support of the Esterhazys of Hungary, and remained in the service first of Prince Paul Anton, then of Prince Nicholas, for 33 years. During most of this time he was director of an excellent orchestra and leader of a group of well-trained singers. Pensioned from 1790, honored both on the Continent and in England, he devoted the remainder of his life to composition. He was the friend of Mozart, who came to live in Vienna in 1781. Beethoven went to Vienna in 1792 in order to be his pupil. Both these composers were indebted to him, and he in turn enriched his own style through a study of Mozart's works, which he greatly admired. A simple, sunny, kindly, unselfish soul, his temperament was clearly reflected in his work.

His services to music were many and varied. He developed the *symphony,* the *string quartet* and the *sonata* forms as they are today understood. His clavier sonatas number 54; his symphonies (which in a general way follow the form of the sonata, but with increased scope), no less than 125, about 18 of which have been designated as representative of his finest style. His string quartets, of which he wrote 77, are of all his chamber music the most important.

BETTMANN ARCHIVE
FRANZ JOSEPH HAYDN

The skill with which the separate parts are contrapuntally treated never gets in the way of the melody. In one of these string quartets are found the variations on the theme of the Austrian Hymn ("Gott erhalte Franz den Kaiser"), which he wrote and which is familiar in church hymnals. He also ignored the formalists of his day by his use of folk tunes and by fashioning many of his own tunes in the manner of folk music. His instrumental works also include 30 string trios. None of his 24 operas has continued to hold the stage, but his oratorio *The Creation* (with descriptive passages rather in the style of Handel) has maintained a place, especially in England. This includes the well-known chorus, "The heavens are telling."

Mozart.—Another figure of high importance in the development of instrumental polyphony was Wolfgang Amadeus Mozart (1756–1791), probably the most outstanding example of precocious genius yet known. At the age of 5 he was an accomplished harpsichord player and was composing little pieces. One day, without having had any instruction on the violin, he played faultlessly the second violin part in a trio. Born in Salzburg, known to us for its music festivals in our own day, at the age of 6 he was taken on tour with his sister Maria Anna, 5 years older. They appeared with much success in Munich, Vienna, Paris and London. Following his return to Salzburg, Wolfgang was appointed (1769) *Konzertmeister* to the archbishop of Salzburg, by whom and by the members of whose court he was treated with a brutal tyranny. From this unpleasant job he departed in 1777 and went to Paris, where the controversy was in full swing between the supporters and the opponents of Gluck, and where Mozart had ample opportunity to study Gluck's method. From it he received a certain stimulus, but he was himself too much of an eclectic to adopt it wholeheartedly or to identify his art with Gluck's reforming ideals. His opera *Idomeneo* was produced at Munich in January 1781, and he went to Vienna to live. There in July 1782 was produced his opera *Belmonte und Konstanze, oder die Entführung aus dem Serail* with a German text. But his most important operas belong to the last 5 years of his life: *Le Nozze di Figaro* (1786; to a libretto by Lorenzo da Ponte), *Don Giovanni* (1787; book also by da Ponte) and *Die Zauberflöte* (1789; text by Emanuel Schikaneder). These have all kept the stage, and *Don Giovanni* has been an especial favorite. Mozart did not live to finish a requiem mass, which was completed from his notes by his pupil Süszmayer. His other vocal works include *Lieder,* of which the best-known is probably *Das Veilchen (The Violet),* with words by Goethe; and a quantity of church music.

His instrumental compositions, written with a remarkable facility, comprise sonatas, in the form established by Haydn but individual in treatment; piano concertos; string quartets (six

of them dedicated to Haydn) and quintets and symphonies, of which at least three—the *E-flat,* the *G-minor,* and the *C* (with fugue), popularly styled "the Jupiter"—are ranked with the world's greatest. His melodic style was always full of beauty and his skill unfailing, especially in the handling of orchestral effect. Through Haydn and Mozart the symphonic orchestra took on its present organization, and they furnished it with its earliest means of adequate expression.

Beethoven.—Probably the most striking personality in the history of music was Ludwig van Beethoven (1770–1827). Born at Bonn, he too was a prodigy; for at 8 years he played the violin well; at 12 was an accomplished pianist; and at 13 was a composer. In 1792 he went to Vienna, where he was a pupil of Haydn, and where he made his debut as a concert pianist,

WOLFGANG AMADEUS MOZART

playing his own *C-minor Concerto.* What is termed his first period as a composer extended to 1803, and works of that period include numerous sonatas for piano, the first three piano concertos and the first two symphonies. During the second period, 1803–1815, were written his only opera, *Fidelio* (first produced in November 1805), piano concertos, sonatas and his third symphony (known as the *Eroica*). This symphony was originally dedicated to Napoleon, but Beethoven trampled on its title page when he learned that Napoleon had become emperor. During this period the composer's deafness increased. The third period, from 1815, was marked by the later piano sonatas, the *Missa solemnis (Solemn Mass),* and the *Ninth Symphony.* In 1822 Beethoven became completely deaf. When the *Ninth Symphony* was presented in 1824, he was quite unable to hear the storm of applause. Karoline Unger, one of the soloists, turned him toward the audience that he might see the waving of handkerchiefs and hats.

An eminent pianist, as was Mozart, Beethoven was able to avail himself

NEW YORK PUBLIC LIBRARY
FRANZ PETER SCHUBERT

of improvements in the construction of the piano, and thus obtained in his piano works an extended compass, greater body and richness and a sustained tone. He took the sonata where Haydn and Mozart had left it and went on to treat it in his own fashion, subordinating form to an often intense style of personal expression. His piano concertos, though they show an extraordinary command of technical resources, keep the musical content steadily in mind. He enlarged the possibilities of the symphony orchestra and in his symphonies (written with four movements) continued to disregard conventional boundaries until in the great *Ninth* he introduced a chorus to supplement the orchestra. In fact he was ruggedly original, both as a person and in his work. He composed most readily for the orchestra, and his compositions other than the symphonic abound in traces of his predilection for using orchestral terms.

THE ROMANTIC MOVEMENT

Beethoven forms the real starting point of 19th century music. Between the formal style of the 18th century and the romantic movement he was a kind of connecting link. It is not easy to give to this romantic movement an exact definition. In general it may be said that it emphasized the subjective—the altering or discarding of traditional restrictions, so that a composer might express his own thoughts in his individual way. With this went the alliance of music and poetry, folklore, legend, the development of descriptive music (or what we today call *program music*) and the carrying of instrumental brilliance to a point of extreme difficulty and often of utter irrelevance.

Schubert.—Living in Vienna at the same time as Beethoven, though the two never met, was one of the most spontaneous musicians ever known. Exquisite melody flowed from his pen and he wrote in many forms. This great genius was Franz Schubert (1797–1828)—a man who in his short life wrote over 600 songs (*Lieder*); twenty-four piano sonatas; nine symphonies, of which that in C-major and that in B-minor (known as the *Unfinished*) are generally ranked with Beethoven's; besides choral works, violin pieces and short piano compositions (*impromptus, moments musicals*). Many of Schubert's compositions he never heard; they were found after his death by Robert Schumann. The collected edition of his works fills forty volumes.

Schubert's songs are his outstanding contribution to music. His accompaniments are of as great importance as is the voice part in reflecting the meaning of the text. To Beethoven he owed more artistically than to anyone else. "Truly, in this Schubert lives the divine spark," said the dying Beethoven.

Weber.—Contemporaneous with Beethoven and Schubert was another German, Karl Maria von Weber (1786–1826). *Der Freischütz*, Weber's first opera, produced in 1821, gave to Germany her first national opera, telling a German folk story through the medium of German folk music. It retained the spoken dialogue of the 18th century *Singspiel*, and by its supernatural element and its descriptive music, as well as its folk character, it exemplifies the romantic movement. His *Oberon* was produced at London in 1826. The romantic opera he thus established led directly to Wagner.

Also identified with the romantic movement in Germany was Ludwig Spohr (1784–1859), who wrote chamber music, nine symphonies, ten operas and several oratorios. His best work was in his violin concertos. He was among the finest violinists of his day, and his method was continued for years through the activities of his numerous pupils. His general style was more or less in the manner of the classical school, but his romantic tendencies were evidenced in his increase of tone color in the orchestra and his leaning toward the supernatural. He was among the few elder musicians who recognized the significance of Wagner; and his opera *Die Kreuzfahrer* (*The Crusaders,* 1845) shows the influence of Wagnerian ideas.

Mendelssohn and Schumann.—The two greatest composers associated with the German Romantic School are Felix Mendelssohn-Bartholdy (1809–1847) and Robert Schumann (1810–1856). Both were highly educated and brought a rich background of historical and literary associations to their music. Mendelssohn possessed a greater melodic gift, but Schumann was more dramatic. Mendelssohn wrote in all forms except opera, although his incidental music for Shakespeare's *A Midsummer Night's Dream* ranks with any operatic work. His greatest oratorios were *St. Paul* and *Elijah*. His further works include symphonies, concert overtures, two piano concertos (D-minor and G-minor), a violin concerto (universally a favorite), string quartets and other compositions for chamber combinations; 48 piano numbers in the form of tone pictures, known as *Songs Without Words;* vocal solos, and six sonatas for organ. (Bach and Mendelssohn were the only composers of foremost rank to write distinctly for the organ.)

Schumann was not only a great

ROBERT SCHUMANN

FELIX MENDELSSOHN

KARL MARIA VON WEBER

composer but the first great music critic. His praises introduced to the musical world Berlioz, Chopin, Liszt, Wagner and Brahms and made known the true greatness of Bach and Schubert.

As a composer Schumann excelled in short but exquisite compositions for the piano. For orchestra he left concert overtures and symphonies. His other works include the piano concerto in A-minor; a secular oratorio, *Das Paradies und die Peri* (1841), based on Moore's *Lalla Rookh,* and many chamber-music compositions. His opera *Genoveva* (1850) was not successful. A few of Schumann's songs (such as "Ich grolle nicht" and "Die Lotosblume") have been ranked close to Schubert's.

At this time a new form the concert overture came into existence. It bore a title and was program music inasmuch as it was descriptive and told a definite story; it was a free adaptation of the sonata-form pattern.

Chopin.—Frédéric Chopin (1810–1849) came to Paris from his native Poland in 1831, and his poetic genius attracted the attention of the musical world. With the exception of a few songs and a trio for piano and strings, Chopin wrote only for the piano. His two concertos are his largest works. He also wrote sonatas, but his best-known compositions were his small pieces for his chosen instrument. Chopin was the first great composer to use the folk-dances of his native land; and his mazurkas, polonaises, nocturnes and waltzes are among his most popular works. Other groups (the individual pieces being without title) were the préludes, études, ballades, rondos, scherzi. Chopin developed new resources in the piano and made it speak an individual language. As a *salon* pianist he played with magnetic charm. Schumann greeted him by writing: "Hats off, gentlemen—a genius!"

The Romantic Movement in France.— In France the ideals or romanticism were carried to a far greater extreme than in Germany. The Court of Louis Philippe attracted to Paris all the greatest artists of the day,

NEW YORK PUBLIC LIBRARY
FRÉDÉRIC CHOPIN

while the French public, satiated with the horrors of the recent Revolution, demanded that their literature and art should all be extremely sensational. To Paris came not only Chopin but also the great violinist Nicolo Paganini (1782-1840), whose dazzling technique laid the foundation for the present-day school of violin playing, and Franz Liszt, the brilliant Hungarian pianist. The greatest French composer of the day was Hector Berlioz (1803–1869), called by Schumann the "uncompromising champion of programme music." Berlioz wrote almost exclusively for the orchestra. He possessed a dazzling virtuosity in orchestral composition, and his uses of the instruments were always startling and unusual. All his compositions were descriptive, and he frequently used a definite theme, which he called "the fixed idea," to designate certain characters. His operas are rarely given today. His greatest works are his dramatic symphonies: *Harold en Italie, La Damnation de Faust* and *Roméo et Juliette.*

Franz Liszt.—Franz Liszt (1811–1886), who was a Hungarian by birth, went to Paris to pursue his education as a composer. His pianistic ability attracted such attention that he soon became the center of the artistic group of the French capital and was recognized as the most dazzling pianist of his day. His tours were continuous ovations. For some time he lived with the gypsies, studying their music. In 1847 he accepted the position of court music director at Weimar, where he remained for 10 years, and from that time was known chiefly as a composer. In 1865 he was made an abbé. From 1873 he divided his time between Pesth, Weimar and Rome. Wherever he was, a crowd of pupils surrounded him. Liszt used Hungarian melodies in the same remarkable manner that Chopin had used those of Poland. His fourteen *Hungarian Rhapsodies* are still his most popular works. He wrote with great dramatic intensity for orchestra, all his works following the lines of program music. His greatest symphonies are based on Dante's *Divine Comedy* and Goethe's *Faust,* and his symphonic poems (such as *Les Préludes*) were inspired by various literary and historical works. Liszt created a new form in the symphonic poem (an adaptation of the sonata form), a work which bore a title and followed a definite dramatic program. There were two main subjects, but these were so developed that frequently the entire character of the work itself was changed. Liszt also wrote vocal works, including two oratorios. He did much to aid the musicians of his time, and his help to Wagner was chiefly responsible for the development of the Wagnerian music drama.

Writers of French Grand Opera.—The French Romantic School brought forward the French grand opera, which supplanted the earlier *opera seria* of Händel's day. Many of the great names associated with this form are of Italian composers, who came to Paris at this time.

FRANZ LISZT

Luigi Cherubini (1760–1842) was for many years head of the Paris Conservatory. Among the better-known Italians who rejuvenated Italian opera in Paris were: Gasparo Spontini (1774–1851) who cultivated the style of Gluck; Gioacchino Rossini (1792–1868), whose *Barber of Seville* and *William Tell* are still popular; Gaetano Donizetti (1797–1848), composer of *Lucia di Lammermoor, La Fille du Régiment* and *Don Pasquale;* and Vincenzo Bellini (1801–1835), whose *Norma* and *Sonnambula* are the joy of coloratura sopranos.

The most spectacular opera composer of the day was a German who took the Italian name of Giacomo Meyerbeer (1791–1864). His works were all written to dazzle and amaze. His operas *Les Huguenots* and *Le Prophète* are still given all over the world.

There were also a few French composers of opera at this period, among them being Méhul (1763–1817), Boieldieu (1775–1834), Auber (1782–1871), Hérold (1791–1833), and Halévy (1799–1862). Although they wrote excellent operas, these men were completely overshadowed by the more spectacular works of their foreign competitors.

Richard Wagner and the Music Drama.— A great change came at the end of the Romantic School through the advent of the mighty Richard Wagner (1813–1883)—a figure who stands in the same relation to the music drama that Beethoven does to the symphony. Conductor successively at Magdeburg, Königsberg and Dresden, he took some part in the revolutionary movement of 1848. A writ was issued against him, and he fled to Switzerland where he lived an exile until 1859. His earlier operas, *Rienzi* (1842) and *Der fliegende Holländer* (1843), were in the spectacular vein of Meyerbeer. But he had begun to feel that the only right principles for dramatic composition were those which had been held by Gluck in his attempted reforms. In *Tannhäuser* (1845) and still more fully in *Lohengrin* (completed in 1848) he began to set forth his ideas, which, although based on principles before attempted, were still new. Wagner used for each character, as well as for many inanimate objects, a definite characteristic musical figure or *leitmotiv* and, although "fixed" numbers (arias, duets) are still present, the tendency is toward a more continuous dramatic action. His other works, for which he continued to write his own libretti, were: *Die Meistersinger von Nürnberg;* the cycle *Der Ring des Nibelungen* (usually known as the Ring cycle), comprising *Das Rheingold, Die Walküre, Siegfried* and *Die Götterdämmerung; Tristan und Isolde* and *Parsifal.*

In these developed operas, preludes (*Vorspiele*) are used instead of overtures; the melody is carried by the orchestra; the music is a kind of running commentary on the action and the text; *leitmotivs* are more prominent; the action is viewed throughout from the viewpoint of poetry and drama instead of from that of musical form; vocal or instrumental ornament is extremely rare; the brasses are placed on equality with the strings and the woodwind; new effects are introduced.

Feeling that these great works needed an ideal performance, Wagner and his friends, aided by the generosity of Ludwig II of Bavaria, erected in Bayreuth, Germany, an opera

RICHARD WAGNER

house devoted exclusively to the production of Wagner's works and opened in 1876. His influence on the composers who have followed him is far greater than that of any other writer of music. Every composer since his day has reflected Wagner's principles. This is particularly noticeable in the operas of the great Italian Verdi, whose early works had been modeled after the Italian operas of the period.

Verdi.—Giuseppe Verdi (1813–1901), became organist of his native Roncole (Italy) and in the period from 1836 to 1849 composed ten operas— expressive of the trend toward national unity, and all successful, *Ernani* (1844) being at once the best and the most popular. *Rigoletto* (1851), *Il Trovatore* (1853) and *La Traviata* (also 1853) marked a decided advance; for though they were cast more or less in the routine mold of Italian opera, they showed power of characterization and of drama, and in *La Traviata* the little chorus and long passages are in the *parlando* manner. These were followed by *Un Ballo in Maschera* (1859), in two versions, the second of which had its scene in Boston; and *Don Carlos* (1867). His third period produced his greatest works (which clearly show Wagner's influence). *Aida* (1871), a perennial favorite, written for the khedive of Egypt to celebrate the opening of the Suez Canal; *Otello* (1887), and *Falstaff* (1893), written when the composer was 80, are regarded as the most significant Italian operas. The libretti to *Otello* and *Falstaff* were by Arrigo Boito, himself a composer.

HARPER'S WEEKLY
GIUSEPPE VERDI

Brahms.—Johannes Brahms (1833–1897) has been called the greatest modern master of *absolute music*— that is, music in which formal pattern is of greater importance than descriptive program. As a matter of fact his opposition to programme music was considerably exaggerated. Ranked by some with Bach and Beethoven, Brahms is considered one of the greatest symphonic writers in the history of music. He wrote no operas, his largest choral work being the *Deutsches Requiem,* in cantata form. He left many short piano compositions, which included the Hungarian Dances; exquisite songs; a piano quintet (op. 34); two concertos, and four great symphonies, each considered a masterpiece.

Other modern masters of absolute music in Germany were: Joseph Rheinberger (1839–1901); Anton

Bruckner (1824–1896); Max Bruch (1838–1920); Gustav Mahler (1860–1911); Georg Schumann (1866–1952); Max Reger (1873–1916).

MODERN SCHOOLS OF MUSIC

Italian Opera After Verdi.—Following Verdi in the modern operatic school of Italy were Arrigo Boito (1842–1918), whose greatest work was *Mefistofele;* Amilcare Ponchielli (1834–1886), with *Gioconda;* Ruggiero Leoncavallo (1858–1919, *I Pagliacci* and *Zaza;* Pietro Mascagni (1863–1945), *Cavalleria Rusticana* and *Iris;* Baron Alberto Franchetti (1860–1942), *Germania;* Umberto Giordano (1867–1948), *Andrea Chénier, Fedora* and *La Cena della Beffe;* Gia-

JOHANNES BRAHMS

como Puccini (1858–1924), *La Bohème, Tosca, Manon Lescaut, Madama Butterfly* and *The Girl of the Golden West;* Ermanno Wolf-Ferrari (1876–1948), *Il Segreto di Susanna* and *I Gioielli della Madonna;* Riccardo Zandonai(1883–1944), *Conchita* and *Francesca da Rimini,* and Italo Montemezzi (1875–1952), *L'Amore dei Tre Re.*

In the United States the popular Leoncavallo and Mascagni are each known for only one opera. This, in spite of the fact that they both wrote many others. The *Cavalleria* and *Pagliacci* are usually done on the same program and are part of the permanent repertoire of every operatic company. Puccini was one of the most prolific of operatic composers and because of this has often been compared with Verdi. His works also have had a phenomenal, continued success.

Italian Instrumental Composers.—There was practically no instrumental school in Italy from the 17th century until that founded by Giovanni Sgambati 1841–1914), a pupil of Liszt. Among his followers were Martucci (1856–1909), the pianist Busoni (1866–1924) and the organist Bossi 1861–1925). Lorenzo Perosi (1872–1956) composed fine church music in the style of Palestrina. Among the more recent masters in Italy are Ottorino Respighi (1879–1936), famous for his transcriptions; Alfredo Casella (1883–1947); Gian Malipiero (1882–); Mario Castelnuovo-Tedesco (1895–) who has written many movie scores; Stefano Donaudy (1879–1925), most famous for his songs; and Umberto Giordano (1867–1948) and his famous opera "André Chenier."

Modern German Composers.—German writers who followed after Wagner and Liszt were: Karl Goldmark (1830–1915, a Hungarian by birth, whose best-known opera is *Die Königin von Saba* (1875) and whose orchestral works include the *Rustic Wedding Symphony;* Engelbert Humperdinck (1854–1921), whose *Hänsel and Gretel* is among the popular

BETTMANN ARCHIVE
CESAR FRANCK

operas of today; and Hugo Wolf (1860–1903), who was one of the greatest masters of song writing. A modern German who experimented in new musical forms was Arnold Schönberg (1874–1951). Among his followers were Franz Schreker (1878–1934), Ernst Křenek (1900–), Erich Korngold (1897–1957) who has done outstanding scores for the movies; and Alban Berg (1885–1935). Paul Hindemith (1895–1963) was considered an intellectual contrapuntalist.

The French School.—In France the operatic genius following Meyerbeer was Charles Gounod (1818–1893), whose *Faust* is among the prime favorites of opera.

Also popular is the opera *Mignon* by another French composer, Ambroise Thomas (1811–1896), whose other works for the operatic stage are not often presented. George Bizet (1838–1875), who showed Wagnerian influence, wrote music for Daudet's *L'Arlésienne,* and his *Carmen* (1875) is one of the most popular operas. Contemporaneous with Brahms was the organist César Franck (1822–1890), a distinctive spirit in the French music of his time. Franck wrote in the polyphonic (many-

voiced) style of Bach, and all his compositions were filled with poetic mysticism. His greatest choral work was *Les Béatitudes.* He wrote many compositions for piano and organ, exquisite works for chamber-music combinations, songs, symphonies and symphonic poems. His *Symphony in D-minor* ranks with the greatest works in that form.

Franck had many followers, among them being his pupils Vincent d'Indy (1851–1931) and Ernest Chausson (1855–1899). Other French composers of that period were Alexis Chabrier (1841–1894); Alfred Brunean (1857–1934), the great organists, Alexandre Guilmant (1837–1911), whose organ method was taught in the United States by his pupil William C. Carl (1865–1936) and Charles Widor (1845 –1937); Théodore Dubois (1837–1924); Gabriel Fauré (1845–1924).

Camille Sainte-Saëns (1835–1921) was one of the most prominent of modern French composers. He wrote in all forms, his greatest works being the opera *Samson et Dalila* and his symphonic poems (especially the *Danse Macabre*).

Unique among modern composers was Claude Debussy (1862–1918), who returned to the pentatonic (five-tone) scale. Debussy left many short pieces for piano, equisite songs, orchestral pieces and chamber-music compositions. He also wrote the music drama, *Pelléas et Mélisande.* Following Debussy was Maurice Ravel (1875–1937). Cécile Chaminade (1861–1944) became famous for her graceful *Scarf Dance.*

Some of the modern French composers who have written primarily for the voice are Poulenc ,1899–1963), Reynaldo Hahn (1874–1947) and Georges Hüe (1858–1948). Milhaud (1892–) and Honegger (1892–1953) have both written outstanding orchestral compositions.

Music of Scandinavia.—The founder of the Scandinavian school of music was Nils Gade (1817–1890), a Dane who was greatly influenced by the romanticism of Schumann and Mendelssohn. The great Norwegian violinist, Ole Bull (1810–1880), was exceedingly fond of the folk tunes of his native land and played them all over the world. He encouraged Edvard Grieg (1843–1907) in his musical work, and Greig became the most popular of the composers of Norway. Greig wrote no symphonies and but few large orchestral works; yet his shorter compositions for piano and violin and his many lovely songs won for him world recognition. The incidental music for Ibsen's drama, *Peer Gynt,* as arranged in two orchestral suites, is Grieg's best-known work. Also popular are his great piano concerto and his sonatas for violin and piano. All Grieg's works are in the Norwegian musical idiom and are outstanding examples of modern national composition. Other Norwegian composers are Johann Svendsen (1840 –1911), Christian Sinding (1856–1941) and Johan Halvorsen (1864–1935).

Sweden's outstanding composers have been August Södermann (1837–1876), Emil Sjögren (1853–1918), Tor Aulin (1866–1914), Lars-Erik Lars-

son (1908–), and Niels Bjorkander (1893–). They have all used folk songs in their works.

In Denmark, Jacob Gade (1879–1963) and Bernhard Christensen have written in the modern medium, but from Finland has come the mighty master of present-day Scandinavian music. Jean Sibelius (1865–1957) is known throughout the musical world for such masterpieces as the tone poem *Finlandia.* He has imbued all of his compositions, the small, delicate songs and orchestral works as well as the large symphonic forms, with a certain mysticism and exotic beauty of his homeland. Selim Palmgren, Armas Järnefelt, and Urjo Kilpinen are recent Finnish song composers.

Bohemian Composers.— Bohemia, as it was known before World War I, has always been regarded as a most musical country, distinguished for the musical aptitude of its people; but

EDVARD GRIEG

it has only been in the modern day that this land has possessed its own school of music. Bedřich Smétana (1824–1884), a pupil of Liszt, was the first to write a Bohemian opera. His *Bartered Bride* (1866), a gem of lighter opera, tells a folk tale in the Bohemian language with Bohemian folk tunes.

The greatest Bohemian composer was Anton Dvořák (1841–1904), who wrote in all forms and is regarded as the greatest modern master of national composition. He used original themes, but always in such a characteristic manner that they seemed to have been born of the people. Dvořák lived in America for several years and was the first to bring to the attention of the musical world the importance of America's native folk music. His symphony *From the New World* (op. 95) contains reminiscences of the manner of American Negro spirituals. Dvořák's other works include the *Slavonic Dances;* four other symphonies; symphonic poems; many charming chamber-music compositions and equally charming songs. Leoš Janáček (1854–1928), Josef Suk (1874–1935), Josef Bohuslav Förster (1859–1951) and the light-opera composer Rudolph Friml (1884–), were also excellent.

Other Bohemian composers were Wilhelm Blodek (1834–1874) and Zedenko Fibich (1850–1900).

The Russian School.—The feeling for national expression that came into music with the Romantic School has developed and increased among modern composers of every country. The latter half of the 19th century saw the development of great national schools not only in Scandinavia and Bohemia but also in Russia. Italian and French opera received a welcome there but not until the 19th century was attempt made toward a Russian school. The early native composers were men of other professions, who gave up their work for the cause of Russian music.

The first great Russian composer was Mikhail Glinka (1804–1857), whose *A Life for the Czar* was the first Russian opera. Associated with Anton and Nikolai Rubinstein in the Russian Musical Society were César Cui (1835–1918); Alexander Borodin (1834–1887); Nikolay Rimski-Korsakov (1844–1908); Modest Moussorgski (1839–1881); Mili Balakirev (1837–1910); and Petr Tchaikovsky (1840–1893). The last ranks as one of the popular modern composers. He wrote in all forms. His operas *Eugen Onégin, Jeanne d'Arc* and *Pique Dame* are regarded as his best. He left six great symphonies (including the *Pathétique*), piano concertos, many dramatic concert overtures, ballet suites, much chamber music and many short piano compositions and songs. As in the case of other Rus-

NEW YORK PUBLIC LIBRARY

PETR TCHAIKOVSKY

sian musicians, many of his compositions are based on Russian folk songs. He used the orchestra always in a striking and unusual manner, his characteristics being excessive melancholy or extreme gayety. Rimski-Korsakov was a popular, brilliant master of orchestration and had many followers, chief among them being Alexandr Glazunov (1865–1936), Anton Arensky (1861–1906) and Sergei Rachmaninov (1873–1943), a great pianist as well as a composer, who came to live in the United States.

Anton Rubinstein (1830–1894), the distinguished piano virtuoso, though he did so much for Russian music,

especially as director of the St. Petersburg Conservatory and the instructor of a large group of pupils, has, as a composer, been regarded as more German than Russian. He wrote operas and symphonies as well as concertos and piano pieces. The pianist Alexandr Scriabin (1872–1915) began the revolt against established restrictions in composing and was followed by Sergei Prokofiev and Igor Stravinski (1882–) who gave the new music beauty, form and meaning. Other recent Russian composers are Ippolitov-Ivanov (1859–1935), Glière (1875–1956), Gretchaninov (1864–1956), Rebikov (1866–1920), Medtner (1879–1951), Viktorovich Jelobensky (1911–) Dmitri Kabalevsky (1904–), Nicolai Tcherepinin (1873–1945), Aram Khachaturian (1904–) and Dmitri Shostakovich (1906–). All of these composers use folk melodies in modern tonal combinations.

Modern Spanish Composers.—The founder of the modern school in Madrid was Isaac Albeniz (1860–1909). He used Spanish folk airs as the basis for his compositions. One of his pupils was Enrique Granados (1867–1916), who died in World War I. Manuel de Falla (1876-1946) had the remarkable ability to combine folk melodies with modernism. He died in World War II.

Modern English Composers.—One of England's outstanding composers was Sir Edward Elgar (1857–1934). He wrote many large compositions such as oratorios, symphonies, concertos, chamber music, organ works, and several songs.

Samuel Coleridge - Taylor (1875–1912) used African and American Negro melodies in most of his compositions. Sir Arthur Sullivan (1842–1900) wrote many beautiful serious compositions, such as the *Lost Chord*, but he became most famous for his collaboration with Sir W. S. Gilbert. Together they gave to the world the wonderful comic operas *Pinafore, The Pirates of Penzance, Iolanthe, The Mikado, The Yeomen of the Guard,* and many others.

Other composers are Arthur Goring Thomas (1850–1892), Sir Edward German (1862–1936), Liza Lehmann (1862–1918) and Sir Granville Bantock (1868–1946).

An outstanding personality in the music field has been Percy Grainger 1882–). He was born in Australia, became a naturalized American and used English folk tunes in his ultramodernistic compositions.

Cyril Scott (1879–1945) was known as "the English Debussy," because of his delicate shadings and early imitation of Debussy. Ralph Vaughan Williams (1872–1958) also was influenced by the French master.

More recently, the following English composers have become well known: Fredrick Delius (1862–1934); Sir Arnold Bax (1883–1953); Arthur Bliss (1891–) and Richard Addinsell (1904–) for their film music; Peter Warlock (1894–1930); Eric Coates (1886–1958); Noel Coward (1899–) known not only as a composer but also as an actor, dancer, singer, and playwright; and Benjamin Britten (1913–) who is most famous for his operas

and songs.

Modern Hungarian School.—Hungary has for many years been an outstanding contributor to the musical life of Europe. Among the more famous composers of that country are Jenö Hubay, a violin virtuoso, known as Hubay von Szalatna; Zoltán Kodály (1882-), Ernest Dohnányi (1877–1960), and Béla Bartók (1881–1945).

AMERICAN MUSIC

Music in the Colonies.—The Puritans brought to New England their psalmody. At first they had no books with musical notation and not many with even the words; so the psalms were "lined" (or "deaconed")—a deacon read a line and then (occasionally with the aid of a pitch pipe) "raised" the tune. Later, instrumental music (before organs were introduced) accompanied the singing. Singing was natural to the Dutch of New Amsterdam and to the Germans of Pennsylvania. The first performances of Haydn's *Creation* and *Seasons* in this country were by the Moravians of Bethlehem. In the North religious music was popular, but the South leaned more toward the secular. Companies of singers from London, like Hallam's and Kean and Murray's, toured in the South. Charleston in 1735 had the first performance of opera in the colonies, the piece being the ballad opera *Flora*. In Charleston was established (1762) the first musical society, the St. Cecilia, which continued in existence until 1912. With the exception of the Quakers, the early Americans were generally fond of singing. Singing schools grew up everywhere. Cooper in his *Last of the Mohicans* gives us David Gamut, the singing teacher who delivered "sacred song" in "full, sweet and melodious tones."

The Revolution and Afterwards.—Among the earliest composers were Francis Hopkinson (1737–1791), author of the satirical "Battle of the Kegs" and one of the signers of the Declaration; James Lyon (1735–1795) and William Billings (1746–1800). Immigration after the Revolution helped to encourage and develop music, especially in New York and Philadelphia. National airs arose—"Hail, Columbia" (Joseph Hopkinson); "Adams and Liberty" (Samuel Arnold); and patriotic ballads like "The Death of Warren" (Epes Sargent) and "The Sword of Bunker Hill" (Bernard Covert). Lowell Mason (1792–1872) was a force in awakening musical interest. He traveled about, particularly in New England, organizing music festivals, holding teachers' conventions (the predecessors of the summer normal schools of today) and introducing the teaching of music in public schools. Other composers were Thomas Hastings (1784–1872), George J. Webb (1803–1887) and William B. Bradbury (1816–1868). The choral Handel and Haydn Society was founded in 1815; the Musical Fund Society in Philadelphia in 1820; the New York Philharmonic Society in 1842, furnishing the first professional orchestra in the United States.

Stephen Collins Foster.—In Stephen C. Foster (1826–1864), America had a, musical genius, a natural composer unschooled in his art, whose airs both plaintive and comic are known over the world; a melodist who has been ranked with Schubert, though his simple accompaniments lack the harmonic richness of the Viennese. It was Foster who wrote both words and music of such irresistible songs in the folk manner as "Old Dog Tray," "My Old Kentucky Home," "Massa's in de Cold, Cold Ground," "Camptown Races," "Oh! Susannah" (favorite of the pioneers that crossed the plains), "I Think of Jeanie" and "Old Folks at Home" (Suwanee River). He wrote a greater number of popular songs than any other American—songs of which it has been said, "We have yet to hear one which is devoid of meaning in the words or beauty in the air." Louis M. Gottschalk (1829–1869), the first American pianist of note, was one of the most popular performers of his day (he gave no less than 80 recitals in New York during the winter of 1855–1856) and made transcriptions of Creole melodies with much originality.

With the German invasion of 1848 and the development of a national consciousness in the Civil War period, American music had an impetus that led to an increasing spread of musical culture. Composers to be mentioned are Anton Heinrich (1781–1861), William H. Fry (1815–1864), George F. Bristow (1825–1898) and William Mason (1829–1908), who had much influence as a piano teacher. Prominent among those who did effective work in improving public taste were Leopold Damrosch (1832–1885) and Theodore Thomas (1835–1905), active as conductors. n 1881 the Boston Symphony Orchestra was established. Other orchestras of excellent quality began to be maintained. John K. Paine (1839–1906, professor of music at Harvard from 1875 to 1906; Dudley Buck, William Gilchrist, Frederick Gleason—these all were leaders; Buck doing much, both as organist and composer, for American organ music. Then we pass to the "Boston group"—George W. Chadwick (1854–1931), head of the New England Conservatory; Horatio Parker (1863–1919), director of music at Yale and composer of the opera, *Mona;* Arthur Foote and Mrs. H. H. A. Beach, foremost among American women composers.

MacDowell and Later Composers.—One of the most individual geniuses in American music was Edward MacDowell (1861–1908). He used native American tunes in most of his compositions. In addition to his lovely little pieces and songs, for which he is most remembered today, he also composed symphonic poems, orchestral suites, concertos, and sonatas for the piano. Ethelbert Nevin (1862–1901) wrote graceful little piano pieces and some songs. One of these, "The Rosary," became very popular. He was followed by Reginald De Koven (1859–1920) and Henry Hadley (1871–1937). Victor Herbert (1859–1924) endeared himself to the people of his generation with charming operettas which are still revived today. John Phillip Sousa

(1854–1932) won fame throughout the world as the "March King."

Among German-Americans in music are Charles Martin Loeffler (1861–1935), Walter Damrosch (1862–1950), Frank Damroscn (1859–1937), Frederick Stock (1872–1942). Some of the more modern composers who adhered to the traditional harmonic style were Charles Wakefield Cadman (1881–1946); John Alden Carpenter (1876–1951); Deems Taylor (1885–1966); Leo Sowerby (1895–); best known for his religious and choral music; Roy Harris (1898–); Paul Creston (1906–) also famous as a musicologist; Norman Dello-Joio (1913–); Nathaniel Dett (1882–1943), one of the best-known arrangers of Negro folk songs; Arthur Foote (1853–1937); Morton Gould (1913–); David Guion (1895–) who made several arrange-

LOOK MAGAZINE

LEONARD BERNSTEIN, composer-conductor.

ments of native cowboy and hillbilly tunes; Richard Hagemann (1882–); and Virgil Thompson (1896–) who is also a prominent music critic.

A unique figure in modern American music is George Gershwin (1898–1937). He was one of the first so-called jazz composers who adapted this style to conventional forms. His importance lies, to a large extent, on his influence on contemporary composers. Since Gershwin, America has begun to produce a distinctive musical style. Among the more harmonically-revolutionary composers are Marc Blitzstein (1905–1964); Aaron Copland (1900–) who has worked continuously on behalf of American Composers, has written outstanding music for ballets and for several movies; Samuel Barber (1910–) who has written in all forms but is best known for his vocal compositions; Leonard Bernstein (1918–) hailed as a "boy genius" since he not only has written wonderful musical-comedy scores, symphonies, and individual songs, but has also done outstanding conducting of symphony orchestras; Gian-Carlo Menotti (1911–), who has combined a rather traditional style with melodramatic texts and produced on Broadway several successful operas, the latest of

which "The Saint of Bleeker Street," won a Pulitzer Prize in 1955; Ernest Bloch (1880–1959) a naturalized Swiss, whose music is conscientiously Jewish. Some young modern composers are Leon Kirchner (1919–   ), master of complex music; Harold Shapero (1920–   ), known for his robust style; Alan Hovhaness (1911–   ), producer of Oriental-sounding music; Peter Mennin (1923–   ) and Robert Kurka (1922–   ).

American Folk Music.—American music is only now receiving recognition throughout the world. The United States' emergence as a world power helped to carry its music to the older nations of the world. In the past our musicians were trained in foreign schools or were of foreign birth, we had much native talent which was unrecognized.

The music of the American Indian is of far greater importance to American music than many of us realize. Each tribe had its own music as it had its own language. The savage tribes, constantly on the warpath, used the drums or tom-toms with reiterated rhythms; but among the peace-loving tribes, the flute songs were the most popular, the flute being the most cherished possession of the Indian chief. The Navajos, outstanding lovers of peace, are said to possess more than 15,000 different songs. All the Indian songs have legendary stories, for they recall the important ceremonies and history of the different tribes. Indian mothers sing lullabies to their babies, sometimes using as a refrain the flute love-call theme which was sung as a wooing song during the days of the father's courtship. Many tribes have work songs, while the medicine men use songs and dances for the cures for all diseases. Indian themes have been used as the basis of musical works by many American composers, including Charles Wakefield Cadman, Thurlow Lieurance, Arthur Farwell and Charles Sanford Skilton.

The music of the American Negro is more interesting than any other American folk expression. It was but natural that, during the days of slavery, a distinctive musical expression should come into being. All people who are oppressed or denied political freedom reflect in their rhythmic expression their desire for liberty. This breaking-over of rythmic laws is called *syncopation.* Singing always binds closely any oppressed people and the high, close harmonies heard when Negroes sing together is an outstanding characteristic of their music. Like other primitive peoples, the Negro always showed his religious enthusiasm by his personal appeal to his Maker, and the Negro spirituals are rightly regarded as the most beautiful "folk songs of sorrow" found in musical literature. There are two types of spirituals: those of the "Lower South" being intensely sad and reflecting the dread of being sold into deeper slavery "down river," while the "Upper South" spirituals are of a happier character, frequently using dance rhythms and reflecting the carefree nature of the Negro whose life on the plantation was a fairly contented one.

Negroes have always sung as they have worked, and many of their work songs are characteristic of the occupation of the singers. The dance and play songs are very gay and lively. Among the Louisiana Negroes many of the songs are tinged with French feeling and Spanish rhythms. Many American composers have used Negro themes and there have also developed in recent years a distinctive group of composers of Negro blood, among them being Henry Burleigh and Nathaniel Dett.

Another distinctive folk expression of America is the music of the cowboys. Just as in medieval days the singing of ballads by the bard or minstrel was the chief entertainment of any large group, so in the old ranch houses, after a hard day's work, the cowboys used to meet and sing songs telling of their various adventures. Some of the airs were old ballad tunes which they had known in their homes in the East; others they made up as they sang.

Another distinctive type of American folk song is to be found among the mountaineers of the Appalachian range. Many of these were originally old folk songs of Great Britain. The words of these songs were changed by the different conditions under which the singer was living. Also, entirely new songs have developed. The young people of the mountains loved to dance to the old fiddle tunes of their ancestors and many of our simple pioneer dance tunes, like "Turkey in the Straw," "Arkansas Traveler" and others came into being from the old mountain fiddlers.

From the beginning of America's first settlements, music has been coming to our land from other countries, and much of this has been assimilated and made our own. The Puritans did not believe in singing and dancing, and they chanted their hymns and psalms in a monotonous drone. Yet some fine old hymn tunes developed from the Puritans. When the early Scotch and Irish colonists came into New England, they brought their love of song with them.

The first English settlers of Virginia brought their old ballads and their homes were filled with the stately dance tunes they had known at home. But when the Negro musicians began to play for their masters minuets and gavottes and the gayer country dances popular in England, the character of these compositions changed most decidedly and they became the "Virginia Reel" and the old jig tunes so popular in Colonial America.

The French colonists brought many interesting songs, which are to be found, not only in French Canada but all through the Great Lakes region and down the Mississippi to New Orleans. When the French Canadian pioneer ventured forth into the wilderness, he was called a *voyageur*, and as many of these brave men were identified with America's lumber industry, their songs became identified with the logging camps. The voyageur songs are another important addition to the folk music of America.

"Modern" Folk Songs. Since the Second World War, interest in American folk music has increased considerably. Peter Seeger became a disciple of two earlier folk singers, Woodie Guthrie and Hudie Ledbetter ("Leadbelly"). In the 1950's, Harry Belafonte came to the United States from the Caribbean Islands and made calypso songs popular. During this period, many new folk-singing groups were organized and won great popularity among high school and college students. These groups, such as The Kingston Trio, The Brothers Four, The New Lost City Ramblers, and The Serendipity Singers, perform regularly before large audiences and have recorded many songs.

GREAT NAMES IN MUSIC
4th TO 13th CENTURIES
France
St. Hilary of Poitiers..................(c. 300–67)
Italy
St. Ambrose..........................(c. 340–97)
St. Augustine.........................(354–430)
Boëthius...........................(c. 480–524)
St. Gregory........................(c. 540–604)
Guido of Arezzo.....................(990–1050)
Switzerland
Notker Balbulus........................(d. 912)
Netherlands
Hucbald of Flanders...............(c. 840–930)
Germany
Franco of Cologne...................(c. 1200)
Early Secular School
Troubadours.........(12th and 13th centuries)
Richard I of England.................(1157–99)
Chatelain de Coucy................(12th century)
Thibaut, King of Navarre............(1201–53)
Adam de la Hale..................(c. 1238–88)
Minnesingers
Wolfram von Eschenbach........(c. 1165–c. 1220)
Gottfried von Strassburg..........(13th century)
Walter von der Vogelweide.........(1198–1228)
Heinrich von Meissen.............(c. 1250–1318)
Mastersingers
Hans Sachs.........................(1494–1576)

14TH AND 15TH CENTURIES
Gallo-Belgic School
Guillaume de Machaut................(1300–77)
Guillaume Dufay....................(c. 1400–74)
England
John Dunstable....................(15th century)
Netherlands
Johannes Okeghem................(d. c. 1495)
Italy
Ulrich Hahn..........................(d. 1478)
Ottaviano Petrucci.................(1466–1539)

16TH CENTURY
Italy
Gioseffo Zarlino....................(1517–90)
Andrea Gabrieli...................(c. 1510–86)
Giovanni Gabrieli................(1557–c. 1612)
Giovanni Pierluigi Palestrina.........(d. 1594)
Filippo Neri........................(1515–95)
Emilio del Cavalieri...............(c. 1550–c. 99)
Germany
Heinrich Finck.......................(d. 1527)
Martin Luther......................(1483–1546)
Ludwig Senfl.........................(d. 1555)
Johann Walther.....................(1496–1570)
Sethus Calvisius...................(1556–1615)
Hans Leo Hasler...................(c. 1564–1612)
England
Thomas Tallis.....................(c. 1510–85)
Thomas Morley...................(c. 1557–1603)
Thomas Weelkes......................(d. 1623)
Netherlands
Heinrich Isaac...................(c. 1450–1517)
Josquin des Prés..................(1450–1521)
Adrian Willaert....................(1480–1562)
Cyprian de Rore....................(1516–65)
Jacob Arcadelt...................(c. 1514–75)
Claude Goudimel...................(1510–1572)
Orlando di Lasso...................(1532–94)

17TH CENTURY
Italy
Giulio Caccini...................(1558–c. 1615)
Felice Anerio......................(1560–1614)
Jacopo Peri........................(1561–1633)
Claudio Monteverde.................(1567–1643)
Gregorio Allegri..................(c. 1580–1652)
Girolamo Frescobaldi...............(1583–1644)
Pietro Francesco Cavalli........(c. 1599–1676)
Giacomo Carissimi................(c. 1604–74)
Marcantonio Cesti..................(1618–69)
Alessandro Stradella...............(1645–81)
Arcangelo Corelli..................(1653–1713)

Alessandro Scarlatti................(1659–1725)
France
Pierre Perrin........................(d. 1680)
Robert Cambert.....................(1628–77)
Giovanni Lully (Italian born).......(1633–87)
Germany
Heinrich Schütz...................(1585–1672)
Samuel Scheidt....................(1587–1654)
Johann Froberger...................(1605–67)
Johann Kaspar Kerl.................(1628–93)
Dietrich Buxtehude.................(1637–1707)
England
William Byrd......................(1540–1623)
John Dowland......................(1562–1626)
John Bull........................(c. 1562–1628)
William Lawes........................(d. 1645)
Orlando Gibbons...................(1583–1625)
Henry Lawes........................(1596–1662)
Henry Purcell....................(c. 1658–95)
Netherlands
Jan Sweelinck.....................(1562–1621)

18TH CENTURY
Italy
Giovanni Battista Bononcini......(b. c. 1672)
Antonio Lotti...................(c. 1667–1740)
Antonio Vivaldi...................(1675–1743)
Francesco Durante..................(1684–1755)
Domenico Scarlatti.................(1685–1757)
Benedetto Marcello.................(1686–1793)
Niccolò Porpora....................(1686–1766)
Guiseppe Tartini...................(1692–1770)
Nicola Logroscino..............(c. 1700–c. 63)
Giovanni Sammartini................(1704–74)
Baldassare Galuppi.................(1706–85)
Giovanni Pergolesi.................(1710–36)
Niccolò Jommelli...................(1714–74)
Niccolò Piccini...................(1728–1800)
Antonio Sacchini...................(1734–86)
Giovanni Paisiello.................(1741–1816)
Luigi Boccherini...................(1743–1805)
Domenico Cimarosa.................(1749–1801)
Muzio Clementi....................(1752–1832)
Giovanni Viotti...................(1753–1824)
Antonio Salieri...................(1750–1825)
France
Jean Philippe Rameau...............(1683–1764)
Jean Jacques Rousseau..............(1712–78)
François Philidor Danican..........(1726–95)
Pierre Alexandre Monsigny.........(1729–1817)
François Gossec...................(1734–1829)
André Grétry......................(1741–1813)
Étienne Méhul.....................(1763–1817)
Jean François Lesueur.............(1760–1837)
Luigi Cherubini (Italian born)...(1760–1842)
Germany
Johann Kuhnau.....................(1660–1722)
Friedrich Wilhelm Zachau...........(1663–1712)
Johann Reinken......................(d. 1722)
Johann Mattheson..................(1681–1764)
Georg Philipp Telemann.............(1681–1767)
Johann Sebastian Bach..............(1685–1750)
Georg Friedrich Handel.............(1685–1759)
Johann Adolph Hasse................(1699–1783)
Karl Heinrich Graun................(1701–59)
Karl Philipp Emanuel Bach.........(1714–88)
Christoph Wilibald von Gluck.......(1714–87)
Franz Joseph Haydn................(1732–1809)
Karl von Dittersdorf...............(1739–99)
Wolfgang Amadeus Mozart ....(1756–91)
England
Henry Carey..........................(d. 1743)
John Pepusch (German born) ....(1667–1752)
William Croft.....................(1678–1727)
Thomas Arne.......................(1710–78)
William Boyce.....................(1710–79)

19TH CENTURY
Italy
Gasparo Spontini ....(1774–1851)
Nicolò Paganini...................(1782–1840)
Gioacchino Rossini.................(1792–1868)
Gaetano Donizetti..................(1797–1848)
Vincenzo Bellini...................(1802–35)
Giuseppe Verdi...................(1813–1901)
Amilcare Ponchielli................(1834–86)
France
François Adrien Boïeldieu..........(1775–1834)
Daniel François Auber.............(1782–1871)
Louis Joseph Hérold...............(1791–1833)
Jacques Fromental Halévy..........(1799–1862)
Adolphe Adam......................(1803–56)
Louis Hector Berlioz...............(1803–69)
Felicien David....................(1810–76)
Ambroise Thomas...................(1811–96)
Friedrich von Flotow
  (German born)...................(1812–83)
Charles François Gounod............(1818–93)
Jacques Offenbach (German born)...(1819–80)
César Franck......................(1822–90)
Édouardo Lalo.....................(1823–92)
Léo Delibes.......................(1836–91)
Alexandre Guilmant................(1837–1911)
Georges Bizet.....................(1838–75)
Alexis Chabrier...................(1841–94)
Jean Robert Planquette.............(1848–1903)
Benjamin Godard...................(1849–95)
Ernest Chausson....................(1855–99)

Germany
Ludwig van Beethoven (1770–1827)
Ludwig Spohr (1784–1859)
Karl Maria von Weber (1786–1826)
Giacomo Meyerbeer (1791–1864)
Heinrich Marschner (1795–1861)
Johann Carl Loewe (1796–1869)
Franz Peter Schubert (1797–1828)
Gustave Lortzing (1803–59)
Felix Mendelssohn-Bartholdy (1809–47)
Robert Schumann (1810–56)
Ferdinand David (1810–73)
Richard Wagner (1813–83)
Joachim Raff (1822–82)
Peter Cornelius (1824–74)
Anton Bruckner (1824–96)
Johann Strauss (1825–99)
Johannes Brahms (1833–97)
Max Bruch (1838–1920)
Karl Goldmark (1830–1915)
Engelbert Humperdinck (1854–1921)
Hugo Wolf (1860–1903)
Gustav Mahler (1816–1911)
Ludwig Thuille (1861–1907)

England
Sir Julius Benedict (1804–84)
Michael Balfe (1808–70)
Sir Arthur Sullivan (1842–1900)
Arthur Goring Thomas (1850–92)

Czechoslovakia (Bohemia)
Bedrich Smétana (1824–84)
Wilhelm Blodek (1834–74)
Anton Dvorák (1841–1904)
Zedenko Fibich (1850–1900)

Hungary
Franz Liszt (1811–86)

Poland
Frédéric François Chopin (1810–49)

Denmark
Niels Gade (1817–90)

Norway
Ole Bull (1810–80)
Halfdan Kjerulf (1815–68)
Edvard Grieg (1843–1907)

Sweden
August Sodermann (1837–76)

Russia
Mikhail Glinka (1804–57)
Aleksandr Serge Dargomyzhsky (1813–69)
Anton Rubinstein (1830–94)
Aleksandr Porfirevich Borodin (1834–87)
Nikolai Rubinstein (1835–81)
Modest Moussorgski (1839–81)
Petr Ilich Tchaikovsky (1840–93)
Nikolay Rimski-Korsakov (1844–1908)
Anton Arensky (1861–1906)

Spain
Isaac Albeniz (1860–1909)

20TH CENTURY

Italy
Arrigo Boito (1842–1918)
Giovanni Sgambati (1841–1914)
Giuseppe Martucci (1856–1909)
Giacomo Puccini (1858–1924)
Ruggiero Leoncavallo (1858–1919)
Pietro Mascagni (1863–1946)
Ferruccio Busoni (1866–1924)
Arturo Toscanini (1867–1957)
Ermanno Wolf-Ferrari (1876–1948)
Ottorino Respighi (1879–1936)
Gian Francesco Malipiero (1882–)
Alfredo Casella (1883–1947)
Mario Castelnuovo-Tedesco (1895–)
Vittorino Rieti (1898–)
Goffredo Petrassi (1904–)
Gianandrea Gavazzeni (1909–)
Gino Gorini (1914–)

France
Camille Saint-Saëns (1835–1921)
Jules Massenet (1842–1912)
Gabriel Faure (1845–1924)
Vincent d'Indy (1851–1931)
Claude Debussy (1862–1918)
Gabriel Pierne (1863–1937)
Paul Dukas (1865–1935)
Erik Satie (1866–1925)
Florent Schmitt (1870–1958)
Maurice Ravel (1875–1937)
Jacques Ibert (1890–1962)
Darius Milhaud (1892–)
Francis Poulenc (1899–1963)
Arthur Honegger (1892–1955)
Olivier Messiaen (1908–)
Jean Francaix (1912–)

Germany
Richard Strauss (1864–1949)
Max Reger (1873–1916)
Arnold Schönberg (1874–1951)
Franz Schrecker (1878–1934)
Alban Berg (1885–1935)
Ernst Toch (1887–)
Paul Hindemith (1895–1963)
Ernst Křenek (1900–)
Kurt Weill (1900–1950)

England
Sir Charles Hubert Parry (1848–1918)
Sir Charles Villiers Stanford (1852–1924)
Sir Edward Elgar (1857–1934)

Frederick Delius (1862–1934)
Sir Granville Bantock (1868–1946)
Ralph Vaughan Williams (1872–1958)
Gustav Hoist (1874–1934)
Cyril Scott (1879–1945)
Frank Bridge (1879–1941)
Sir Arnold Bax (1883–1953)
Arthur Bliss (1891–)
Eugene Goossens (1893–1962)
Peter Warlock (1894–1930)
Edmund Rubbra (1901–)
William Walton (1902–)
Constant Lambert (1905–1951)
Michael Tippett (1905–)
Benjamin Britten (1913–)

Czechoslovakia
Josef Suk (1874–1924)
Bohuslav Martinu (1890–1959)

Hungry
Ernst von Dohnányi (1877–1960)
Bela Bartok (1881–1945)
Zoltán Kodály (1882–)

Poland
Ignace Jan Paderewski (1841–1690)
Karol Szymanowski (1883–1937)
Alexandre Tansman (1897–)

Norway
Johan Svendsen (1840–1911)
Christian Sinding (1856–1941)
Karstein Valen (1887–1952)
Harald Saeverud (1897–)

Sweden
Tor Aulin (1865–1914)
Hugo Alfven (1872–1960)

Denmark
Carl Nielsen (1864–1931)
Knudage Riisager (1897–)

Finland
Jean Sibelius (1865–1957)
Edvard Armas Jarnefelt (1869–1954)
Selim Palmgren (1878–1951)

Russia
Cesar Cui (1835–1918)
Mili Balakirev (1837–1910)
Alexander Gretchaninov (1864–1956)
Alexander Glazunov (1865–1936)
Alexander Scriabin (1872–1915)
Sergei Rachmaninov (1873–1943)
Reinhold Gliere (1875–1956)
Igor Stravinsky (1882–)
Sergei Prokofiev (1891–1953)
Aram Khatchaturian (1903–)
Dmitri Kabalevsky (1904–)

Dmitri Shostakovitch (1906–)
Spain
Felipe Pedrell (1841–1922)
Enrique Granados (1867–1916)
Manuel de Falla (1876–1946)
Oscar Esplà (1886–)
Rodolfo Halffter (1900–)
Ernesto Halffter Escriche (1905–)

Latin-America
Heitor Villa-Lobos (1886–1959)
Carlos Chavez (1899–)
Camargo Guarnieri (1907–)
Alberto Ginastera (1916–)

AMERICA—FROM 1700 TO THE PRESENT
Francis Hopkinson (1737–1791)
Joseph Hopkinson (1770–1842)
Dr. Lowell Mason (1792–1872)
Stephen Foster (1826–1864)
William Mason (1829–1908)
Theodore Thomas (1835–1905)
Dudley Buck (1839–1909)
Arthur Foote (1853–1937)
John Philip Sousa (1854–1932)
George W. Chadwick (1854–1931)
Victor Herbert (1859–1924)
Edward MacDowell (1861–1908)
Charles Martin Loffler (1861–1935)
Walter Damrosch (1862–1950)
Henry K. Hadley (1871–1937)
Frederick Stock (1872–1942)
Edward Burlingame Hill (1872–1960)
Daniel Gregory Mason (1873–1953)
Charles Ives (1874–1955)
John Alden Carpenter (1876–1951)
Ernest Schelling (1876–1939)
Ernest Bloch (1880–1959)
Charles Wakefield Cadman (1881–1946)
Charles Tomlinson Griffes (1884–1920)
Deems Taylor (1885–1966)
Douglas Moore (1893–)
Walter Piston (1894–)
Virgil Thompson (1896–)
Howard Hanson (1896–)
Roger Sessions (1896–)
Roy Harris (1898–)
George Gershwin (1898–1937)
Randall Thompson (1899–)
Aaron Copland (1900–)
Samuel Barber (1910–)
William Schuman (1910–)
Gian-Carlo (1911–)
Leonard Bernstein (1918–)
Leon Kirchner (1919–)

DICTIONARY OF MUSIC

A cappella (It.) (ä käp pel'lä), in the old church style; vocal music unaccompanied, especially those pieces of the Italian school.

A capriccio (It.) (ä kä prēt' chō), at will; according to the individual taste.

Accelerando or **Accelerato** (It.)(ak sel ēr an'dō or ät chä lä rän'dō), gradually increasing the speed.

Accent, a stress or emphasis upon a certain note or passage to mark its position in the bar, or its relative importance in regard to the composition. The first beat of each measure has *primary* accent. In 4/4 time, the third beat has *secondary* accent; in 9/8 time the fourth has secondary accent, the seventh *tertiary*. Notes especially accented are marked with the sign ∧, called *sforzando,* abbreviated *sf., sfz.* or *fz.*

Accessory Notes, small embellishing notes which are located one degree above or one degree below the principal note.

Accidentals, sharps, flats, double sharps, double flats and naturals which are not provided for in the signature.

Accompaniment, a separate part or parts, for voices or instruments, added to a solo or concerted piece, to enrich or support the general effect, or to produce such effects as would be otherwise unattainable.

Accordion (a kôr'di un), a small, portable wind instrument, perhaps the most popular in the world. It consists of a pair of hand bellows to which is attached a keyboard having from five to fifty keys, according to the size of the instrument. As the player presses a key a valve opens and the air is admitted to the metal reeds, one sounding when the air is expanded and the other when it is compressed. The right hand plays the keys and the left hand works the bellows.

Acoustics (a kōōs'tiks), the science which treats of the nature and laws of sound.

Action, the mechanism attached to the keys of piano or organ; also the mechanism attached to the pedals of a harp, which changes the pitch of the strings by shortening them.

Adagio (It.) (a dä'jō), slowly; quicker than *largo* but slower than *andante;* also, a name given to a movement written in that time.

Ad libitum (Lat.) (ad lib'i tum), at will; in passages so marked, the time may be altered at the will of the performer; also, the part so marked may be omitted.

Agitato (It.) (ä jē tä'tō), an agitated or restless style of playing or singing, in which the time and expression are broken and hurried.

Air, in its modern sense, a tune, or the tune, or melody, with or without words; the part of the composition which carries the melody.

Alla breve (It.) (ä'lä brä'vä), a direction that the notes are to be made shorter, that is, the pace taken quicker than usual. Expressed in the signature by ¢.

Allegretto (It.) (al e gret'ō), (1) rather light, cheerful and quick; slower than allegro; (2) a movement in this time.

Allegro (It.) (ä lā'grō), quick, lively; sometimes used to describe a whole movement of a quartet, sonata or symphony.

Allegro con brio (It.) (ä lā'grō kōn brē'ō), quickly and with spirit.

Alto (al'tō), one of the chief divisions of the human voice; female altos are more properly called contraltos. In mixed chorus, it is the next part below the soprano sung by the low female voice; a tenor violin, or viola; term formerly given to the highest male voice or part.

Andante (It.) (än dän'tä or an dan'tē) (literally, walking), moderately slow, but flowing easily; often qualified by other words, as *con moto, largo, maestoso.*

Andantino (It.) (än dän tē'nō), a diminutive of andante, by some understood to mean *not so slow* as andante; by others, rather *slower than* andante.

Anthem, a vocal composition, the words of which are usually selected from the Bible, used in church either with or without accompaniment.

Apassionato (It.) (ä päs syō nä'tō), with feeling, passion or affection.

Appoggiatura (It.) (a poj'a tōō'ra), an accessory note, placed before a principal note. If it is marked with a diagonal line through the stem and hook, it is called *short* and is played with the least possible duration; if it is without a diagonal line, it is called *long* and has definite time value as indicated.

Arabesque, Arabesk (ar *a* besk'), an embellished work.

Aria (It.) (ä'ri *a* or âr'i *a*), (1) an air; (2) a vocal solo with instrumental accompaniment, generally threefold in form. The words consist frequently of two sentences.

Arioso (It.) (ä ryŏ'so), in the style of an air; the direction that the music to which it refers is to be performed tunefully, sweetly, in the style of an aria.

Arpeggio (It.) (är pej'ō), playing the notes of a chord in succession instead of striking them together; marked with a wavy line before the chord.

Articulation, (1) in singing, the art of distinct pronunciation; (2) in instrumental music, the art of producing proper tone by a right adjustment of the fingers, or the lips.

Augmentation, the introduction of a subject of a fugue or canon, in the course of its progress, in notes of longer duration.

Authentic Cadence, a final close, in which the common chord of the tonic is immediately preceded by the common chord of the dominant.

Auxiliary Notes, notes not essential to the harmony, introduced for the sake of breaking monotony, or of giving freedom of motion to one or more of the parts. They may occur on either the accented or the unaccented part of the bar, and if introduced below the melody should be only a semitone from the proper note of that melody, but if above they may be either a tone or a semitone as the position in the scale would warrant, or taste suggest.

Ave Maria (Lat.) (ä vä' mä rē'ä or ä've ma rī'a), Hail! Mary, the angel's salutation of the Blessed Virgin Mary, used in the Roman Catholic Church as an Antiphon, etc.

Bagatelle (Fr.) (bag a tel'), sketch, short piece, trifle.

Bagpipe, wind instrument. It is still found in a primitive form among the shepherds of the countries of Europe; the Scotch and Irish bagpipes are well known. The bellows, held under the player's arm, force the air into the bag, while the pipes, fitted into the side, give out various tones as they are set in vibration by the player's breath. The "chanter pipe" has eight holes in the side, which are operated by the player's fingers.

Balalaika (bal a lī'kä), a Russian stringed instrument, played like the mandolin with a plectrum held in the player's right hand while the strings are stopped with his left. The balalaika is triangular in shape, having

UNITED PRESS INTERNATIONAL

BAGPIPES

a very long neck over which the two, often three, strings are stretched.

Ballad, a short, simple song of natural construction, usually in the narrative or descriptive form.

Ballet (Fr.) (bal'ä or ba lä'), a theatrical representation of some story by means of dances or pantomimic action, accompanied by music.

Banjo, a stringed instrument of African origin which has reached a high state of development in the United States. Over its tambourine-like body parchment is stretched like a drumhead. A long neck is attached to this, and in it are fitted pegs for five tornine strings which are plucked with the fingers or plectrum. The banjo is a favorite instrument of American Negroes.

Bar, a line drawn from the top to the bottom of the stave to denote the division of the time in a piece of music, and the place of the strong accent.

Barcarolle (Fr.) (bär ka rōl'), a song or air sung by the Venetian gondoliers, or boatmen, while at work.

Baritone, a male voice intermediate between bass and tenor; also applied to any musical instrument between bass and tenor.

Bass, the lowest part in a musical composition, the lowest male voice; the lowest of a family of instruments.

Bassoon (ba sōōn'), the largest and deepest-voiced of the wood wind instruments. Its long tube, bent double for convenience, has a long curved mouthpiece. The bassoon is the bass of the double reed family. Although its tone is deep, the instrument possesses such agility of execution that its tones often sound grotesque; therefore it is frequently called "the clown of the orchestra." Yet it possesses a lovely pastoral singing voice in its upper registers. The deepest wood wind instrument is the double bassoon or contra bassoon.

Baton (Fr.) (bà tôn' or bat'un), stick used by a leader in beating time.

Beat, a single motion of the band, or baton, in beating time. A division of a bar, or measure.

Bell, the lower termination of any tubular musical instrument which by the outward turning of the rim assumes the form of a bell.

Bells, percussion instruments of various kinds, such as the gong, glockenspiel and celesta.

Berceuse (Fr.) (ber sŭz'), a cradle song.

Binary Form (bī'n*a* ri fôrm), the form of a movement which is founded on two principal themes or subjects.

Bolero (Sp.) (bō lâr'ō), a Spanish dance in triple measure with strongly-marked accent, similar to the cachucha. It is accompanied by singing and castanets.

Bowing (bō'ing), the art of managing the bow; the proper manner of using the bow, indicated by certain marks; ⊓ for *down* bow; ∧ for *up* bow; two dots over a note for *spiccato* or *bounding bow.*

Brass Wind Instruments, in the modern orchestra the trumpet, horn, trombone and tuba. The lips of the players act as the reeds of the brass instruments, each tone being produced by a different lip pressure.

Break, (1) the point of junction in the quality of tenor, soprano and alto voices. A genuine bass voice has no break. (2) Break in an organ stop is the sudden alteration of the

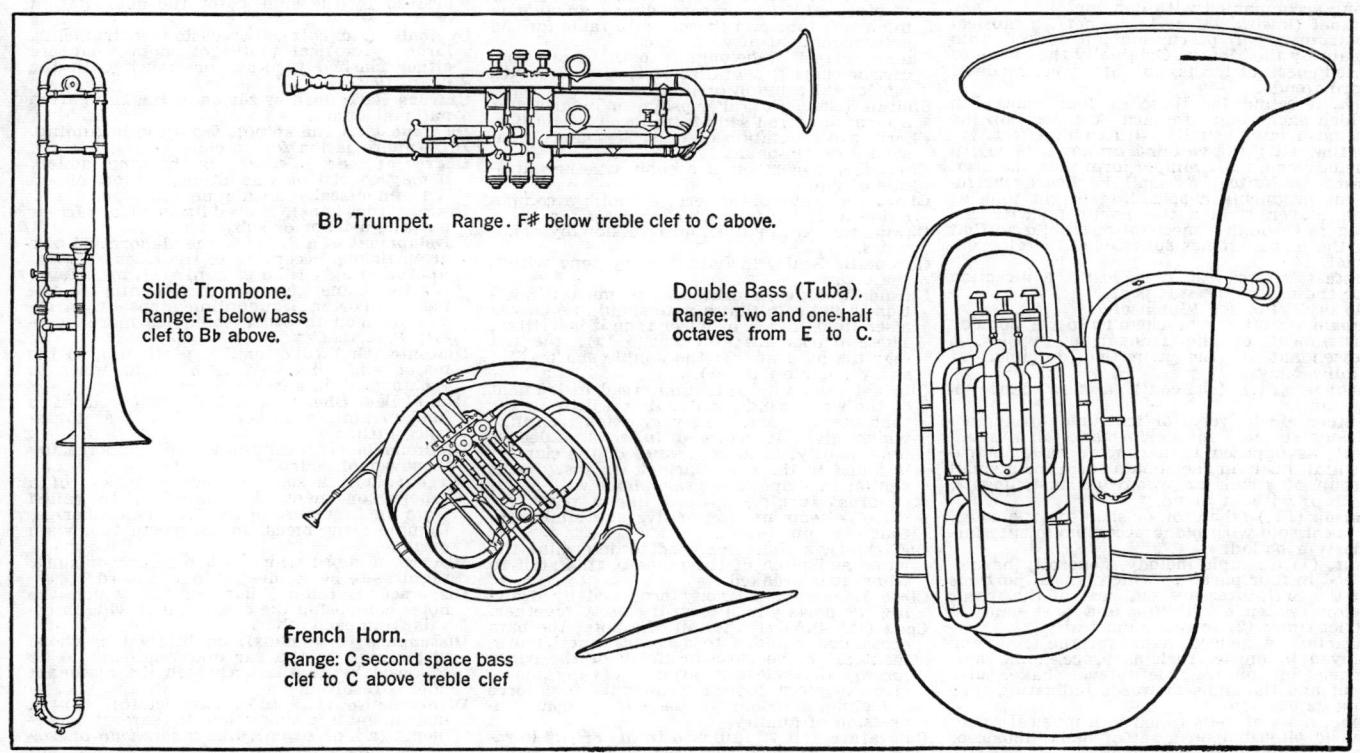

Bb Trumpet. Range. F# below treble clef to C above.

Slide Trombone.
Range: E below bass clef to Bb above.

Double Bass (Tuba).
Range: Two and one-half octaves from E to C.

French Horn.
Range: C second space bass clef to C above treble clef

RUDOLPH WURLITZER COMPANY: G. SCHIRMER, INC.

Important Brass-Wind Instruments of the Orchestra

proper scale-series of the pipes by returning to those of an octave lower in pitch.

Bridge, a piece of wood which, on instruments having a resonance box, performs the double duty of raising the strings above the belly and of terminating at one end their vibrating portion.

Brindisi (It.) (brin′dē zē), a drinking song.

Burden, the chorus or refrain of a song.

Cachucha (Sp.) (ka chōō′cha), a Spanish dance, resembling the bolero.

Cadence, (1) a close in melody or harmony, dividing it into numbers or periods, or bringing it to a final termination; (2) the end of a phrase, formerly called fall, either in melody or harmony.

Cadenza (It.) (ka dent′sa or ka den′za), a florid ornamental passage introduced before the cadence of a song or instrumental solo.

Canon, a contrapuntal composition in which the melody is taken by the leading voice, and then taken up in turn by the second, third and fourth voices at intervals of a definite number of beats or measures.

Cantabile (It.) (kän tä′bē lä), in a singing manner.

Cantata (It.) (kán tä ta), a short oratorio, frequently entirely secular. Bach wrote a coffee-cantata (a humorous protest against drinking too much), as well as many religious cantatas; Haydn selected a Greek subject, *Ariadne at Naxos;* Mozart composed a Masonic cantata.

Canticle (kan′ti kl), a song or hymn in honor of God, or of some special sacred event.

Canto (It.) (kan′tō), the upper voice part in concerted music, so called because it has the melody or air.

Cantor (Lat.) (kan′tôr or tēr), a singer; a precentor.

Cantus firmus (Lat.) (kan′tus fûr′mus), (1) the *tenor* or chief melody; (2) a fragment of plain song, to which counterpoint has been added; (3) any subject chosen for contrapuntal treatment, generally a short diatonic passage of semibreves or other long notes.

Canzone (It.) (kän tsō′nä), a short song, the music being more important than the words.

Capellmeister (Ger.) (kä pel′mīs′tēr), (1) the musical director of a church or chapel; (2) a conductor of a band or an opera: usually spelled **kapellmeister.**

Capriccio (It.) (kä prēt′chō), a freak; whim; fancy. A composition irregular in form.

Carillon (Fr.) (kar′i lon or ka rē yôn′), a set of bells upon which a melody can be played; an instrumental piece in the style of carillon music.

Carol, a song of praise, applied to a species of songs sung at Christmastide; originally a song accompanied with dancing.

Castanet (kas ta net′ or kas′ta net), a musical instrument of percussion introduced into Spain by the Moors. Originally they were of dried chestnut husks, but later were made of hard wood.

Catch, a round for three or four voices, in which each singer in turn "catches" up the melody; later usually with comic effect.

Cavatina (It.) (kä vä tē′nä or kav a tē′na), a melody or a more simple form than the *aria.*

Celesta (sē les′ta), a small keyboard instrument producing a sparkling bright tone as the player strikes the hammers with his fingers through a mechanism similar to that of the piano. It has superseded the glockenspiel.

Celeste (Fr.) (sä lest′ or sē lest′), a direction for the use of the soft pedal.

Cello or **'Cello,** see **Violoncello.**

Cembalo (sem′ba lō or chem′ba lo), a popular instrument of the Hungarian gypsies, a descendant of the primitive dulcimer of Biblical days.

Chaconne (Fr.) (shä côn′), a slow dance in 3/4 time.

Chamber Music, vocal or instrumental compositions suitable for performance in a small hall, as opposed to a concert hall; instrumental music in the sonata form for a small group of string or woodwind instruments, with or without piano.

Chanson (Fr.) (shan′son or shän′son′), a song; a vocal solo with piano accompaniment; formerly a ballad.

Chant, (1) a simple melody, generally harmonized in four parts, to which lyrical portions of the Scriptures are set, part of the words being recited *ad libitum* and part sung in strict time; (2) to recite musically.

Characters, a general name for the signs employed in music, such as brace, bind, bar, sharp, flat, natural, clef, stave, shake, turn, beat and the signs of words indicating time and expression.

Chime, a set of bells tuned to a musical scale; music played upon a set of bells; music or melody; to sound in harmony.

Choir (kwīr), a group of singers, usually connected with a church; that part of a church edifice set apart for the singers.

IGOR STRAVINSKY

Choir Organ, in a large pipe organ, that group of pipes and the corresponding manual having a soft tone and therefore suitable for the accompaniment of vocal music.

Choral, (1) of or belonging to the choir, concert or chorus; choral service, a service with music; (2) a hymn or psalm tune.

Chorale (Ger.) (kō räl′), psalm or hymn tune; a form of sacred song introduced by Luther.

Chord, a combination of musical sounds, consonant or dissonant.

Chorister, a member of a choir whether juvenile or adult.

Chorus, a group of singers; a choir; a composition intended for a chorus; a refrain.

Chromatic (krō mat′ik), progression by semitones.

Chromatic Scale, including every tone within the octave.

Chromatic Signs, marks used in musical notation to indicate that a note should be played a semitone higher or lower than it is written. These marks are: the sharp (♯); the flat (♭); the natural (♮); the double sharp (𝄪); and the doble flat (♭♭).

Clarinet (klar i net′), a single reed instrument of the wood wind family. It is a little larger than the oboe and has a very extensive range which gives its voice a fuller and deeper tone quality. The deep voice of the clarinet is found in the bass clarinet, an instrument similar in shape to the saxophone with a bell of brass turning upward like a pipe. Its voice is deep and impressive and similar to that of a pipe organ.

Clef (klef), a character used to determine the name and pitch of the notes on the staff to which it is prefixed.

Close Harmony, harmony produced by drawing the parts which form it closely together.

Coda (It.) (kō′da), the tail of a note; the bars occasionally added to a contrapuntal movement after the close or finish of the *canto fermo;* that closing adjunct of any movement, or piece, especially intended to enforce a feeling of completeness and give an impression of finality.

Coloratura (It.) (kul ēr a tu′ra or kō lō rä-tōō′ra), ornamental passages, runs, trills, embellishments, in a vocal or instrumental solo; a high soprano voice of great flexibility and unusual brilliancy.

Common or **Double Time,** time with two beats in a bar, or any multiple of two beats in a bar.

Compass, the whole range of sounds capable of being produced by a voice or instrument.

Composition, (1) a piece of music, for voices or instruments, or a combination of both effects, constructed according to the rules of art; (2) the act and the art of writing original music.

Concert, a public performance of music, in which a number of singers or instrumentalists, or both, take part.

Concertina (kon sēr tē′na), an instrument similar to the accordion. It has a keyboard at each end, the bellows being between. The same tone is produced when the bellows are compressed as when they are expanded. The compass of the concertina is much greater than that of the accordion, and as it is possible to play very intricate harmonies, the concertina is a popular instrument.

Concertmeister (Ger.) (kōn tsert′mīs tēr), the leader of the band, the conductor; the leader of the first violins, who is next in rank to the conductor.

Concerto (It.) (kōn cher′tō or kon sûr′tō), (1) a concert; (2) an extended composition in sonata form for a solo instrument with orchestral accompaniment.

Conductor, the director or leader of an orchestra or chorus.

Con sordino (It.) (kōn sōr dē′nō), with the mutes on; with the soft pedal at the pianoforte held down.

Contra (It.) (kon′tra), against; in compound words this signifies an octave below.

Contrabass (It.) (kon′tra bäs), the double bass; the deepest toned stringed instrument played with a bow.

Contralto (It.) (kon tral′to), the voice of deepest tone in females.

Cornet (kôr′net or kôr net′), a brass wind instrument similar to the trumpet.

Cotillion or **Cotillon** (Fr.) (kō til′yun or kō tē-yôn′), a lively, spirited dance, introducing a great variety of figures, such as the pyramid, the two flowers, the coquette, a quadrille.

Counterpoint. The art of adding one or more parts to a given theme or subject.

Courante (Fr.) (kōō ránt or kōō ränt′), "running." A dance of French origin in triple time; the second part in the old *suites des danses.*

Cremona (krē mō′na), (1) a violin made in the town of Cremona; (2) a reed stop in the organ.

Crescendo (It.) (kre shen′dō), increasing, a gradual increase in the force of sound expressed by the sign <, or the abbreviation *cresc.*

Cymbals (sim′balz), percussion instruments, large cylindrical plates of metal that are either clashed together or struck with the drumstick.

Czardas (chär′däsh or zär′das), the Hungarian national dance.

Da Capo (It.) (dä kä′pō), from the beginning.

D.C., abbreviation for da capo.

Degree of a Scale, a stop in the tone ladder; it may consist of a semitone, a tone, or—in the minor scale—an augmented tone.

Descant (des′kant), the addition of a part or parts to a tenor or subject.

Development of a Subject, the elaboration of a given theme, according to the rules of art.

Diapason (Eng.) (dī a pā′zun), (1), an octave; (2) the name given in this country to the most important foundation stops of an organ, termed in other countries more properly *Principal.*

Diatonic (Gr.) (dī′a ton′ik), pertaining to the major and minor scales of eight tones to each octave, in any key.

Diminished Chord, a chord composed of a fundamental, a minor third and a diminished fifth.

Diminuendo (It.) (di min ū en′dō), decreasing in power of sound.

Dirge (dûrj), a solemn piece of music, of a funeral or memorial character, so called from the first word of the Antiphon, "Dirige, Domine Deus meus, in conspectu tuo, viam meam."

Discord, a chord which, when struck or sung, requires to be resolved into a concord.

Dispersed Harmony, harmony in which the notes composing the chord are at wide intervals from each other.

Dissonance (dis′ō nans), an interval or chord displeasing to the ear and requiring to be followed by another in which the dissonant note is resolved.

Divertimento (It.) (dē ver tē men′tō), (1) an instrumental composition in several movements (six or seven), like a *serenada* or *cassation;* (2) a potpourri.

Divisi (It.) (dē vē′zē), a direction that instruments playing from one line of music are to separate and play in two parts. The reunion of the parts into unison is directed by the words *a due.*

Dominant, the fifth degree of the scale; the reciting note of Gregorian chants.

Double Bar, a sign formed of two single bars showing (1) the end of a piece; (2) the end of a movement of a work; (3) the end of a portion to be repeated; (4) the commencement of a change of key; (5) the commencement of a change of time; (6) the end of a line of words set to music as in a hymn tune.

Double Bass, the largest of the stringed instruments played with a bow. Like the viola and cello it is a descendant of the viol family. Until Beethoven's time it was used chiefly to double the bass parts by the cello, but modern composers have used it as an important individual voice.

Double Flat, a sign (♭♭) used before a note already flatted in the signature, which depresses the note before which it is placed another half tone. It is contradicted by a natural and a flat.

Double Octave, the interval of a 15th.

Double Sharp, a sign (✕) used before a note already sharp, to indicate that it is desired to raise the pitch by a semitone. It is contradicted by a natural and a sharp.

Down Beat, the first beat in each bar is so called because in counting time the hand or conducting stick is allowed to fall at that place.

Doxology (Gr.) (doks ol'ō ji), the hymn or song of praise—the Gloria in Excelsis and the Gloria Patri as sung in the Christian church; also any metrical form of the same.

Drone, the largest pipe of the bagpipe, sounding only one note, which serves as a bass for every tune; the chorus or burden of a song.

Drums, in the modern orchestra the tympani or kettledrums, the side or snare drum and the bass drum. (See *Kettledrums.*) The snare drum is cylindrical. It has thin pieces of gut (snares) stretched under the vellum on one side which, as the player beats upon it, produces a sharp, incisive tremolo frequently needed in military music. The bass drum is the largest instrument of the group. In military music it is played *fortissimo;* played *pianissimo,* it is very impressive in funeral marches.

Duet, a composition for two voices or instruments, or for two performers upon one instrument, or for two instruments of the same kind.

Dynamics (dī nam'iks), that part of musical science which deals with differences and contrasts in loudness of tones.

Echo, a sound produced by reverberation.

Eighth, the interval of an octave: *Eighth note,* a note whose value is ⅛ that of a whole note.

Encore (Fr.) (äng kōr' or -kôr'), again; more; a demand for the reappearance of a performer, as by applause; the performance given in response to such a demand.

English Horn, see *Oboe.*

Enharmonic (en här mon'ik), (1), one of the three genera of Greek music, the other two being the Diatonic and Chromatic; (2) having intervals less than semitone; (3) an enharmonic modulation is a change as to notation, but not as to sound.

Ensemble (Fr.) (än'som'bl), together; the whole; (1) the general effect of a musical performance; (2) the union of the whole company of performers in a concerted piece.

Entr'acte (Fr.) (än tract' or än'träkt'), music played between the acts or divisions of an opera, drama or other stage performance.

Episode, a term in fugue writing, applied to those phrases which are supplemental to the main subjects or their answers.

Etude (Fr.) (ā tüd'), a study, exercise or lesson.

Euphony (ū'fō ni), sweet sound; an agreeable combination of sounds.

Exercise, (1) preparatory practice in order to obtain skill; (2) a composition intended for the improvement of the singer or player; (3) a composition or thesis, required of candidates for degrees in music in the universities.

Expression, the power or act of rendering music so as to make it the vehicle of deep and pure emotion; the *spirit* of music as opposed to the mere mechanical production of sound. Expression marks are given in compositions to aid the performer in the proper interpretation of the number.

Extemporize, to play *extempore,* that is, to create melody and harmony without premeditation.

Extravaganza (eks trav *a* gan' za), a composition in burlesque style.

Falsetto (It.) (fôl set'ō), the artificial or supplementing tones of the voice, higher than the chest or natural voice.

Fandango (Sp.) (fan dang'gō), a lively Spanish dance in triple time, derived from the Moors. It is danced by two persons, male and female, and accompanied by the sounds of a guitar.

Fanfare (Fr.) (fan'fâr), a flourish of trumpets, a call.

Fantasia (It.) (fan t*a* zē'*a* or fan tä'zi *a*), a composition in a style in which form is subservient to fancy.

Fermata (It.) (fer mä'tä), a pause—from *fermare,* to stay or stop.

Fife, a small flute used with the drum in military bands.

Fifth, a diatonic interval of five notes. The interval between a fundamental tone and the fifth tone above.

Figure, a form of melody or accompaniment maintained throughout the phrase in which it is suggested. In a melody figure is called sequence. In harmony a figure relates to the rhythmical observance of a certain form in all the accompanying chords to the melody; (2) a musical phrase; (3) a florid melody.

Finale (It.) (fē nä'lā or lē), the conclusion; the last piece of any act of an opera; the concluding number of a concert; the last movement of a composition in the sonata form.

Fine (It.) (fē'nā), the end; used to show the end of a piece or movement; often a repeat, or partial repeat.

Fingering, the art of placing and using the fingers properly in performing upon a musical instrument.

Flat, the sign (♭), which directs the lowering of the tone to which it is prefixed by one semitone; singing or playing is said to be *flat* when the sounds produced fail to reach the true pitch.

Flute, a wind instrument used in various forms since ancient Greece. The flute is a cylindrical tube, closed at one end, and blown at a lateral opening called the embouchere. Its compass is about three octaves above middle C. The flute is extremely agile, well adapted to serve as a coloratura voice, and is useful in light, graceful passages. Other flutes are the fife and piccolo.

Foot, (1) a metrical measure; (2) a drone bass; (3) the chorus of a song; (4) the part of an organ pipe below the mouth; (5) to foot, to dance.

Form, the pattern or design in which musical ideas are presented.

Forte (It.) (fôr'tā), loud; powerful.

Fortissimo (It.) (fôr tis'i mō), very loud.

Forzando (It.) (fôr tsän'dō), forced; emphasis upon one note or chord; marked >.

Fourth, an interval of four notes.

Free Style, composition not absolutely according to the strict rules of counterpoint.

French Horn, see *Horn.*

Fugue (fūg), a fugue is a composition in which a melody is chosen that may be accompanied by a perfect imitation of itself. It is hard to explain it without using terms that must themselves be explained; but everybody has sung *"Three Blind Mice"* or some other *round* in which different voices come in with the same tune at different points. On such a principle of imitation is built up what is called a *canon.* A fugue is a freer and more elaborate canonical structure.

Full Score, a score in which all the parts for voices and instruments are displayed.

Fundamental, the lowest element of a tone, the other elements being its harmonics; applied also to the lowest note of a chord when the chord is founded upon that note.

Fundamental Tones, the tones from which harmonics are generated; that is, the first, fifth and fourth tones of any diatonic scale.

Galop (Fr.) (gal'up), a lively dance in 2/4 time, originally a separate and independent dance, but now also forming a portion of a set of quadrilles.

Gavotte or **gavot** (g*a* vot' or gav'ot), a dance tune of a lively yet dignified character, said to be of French origin, and to take its name from the Gavots; in quick common time, introduced at the French Court in the 16th century, the step characterized by raising the feet instead of sliding; a composition in gavotte style.

Gigue, see *Jig.*

Glee, a vocal composition of three or four more or less independent parts, not necessarily gleeful; popular in England between 1760 and 1830.

Glissando (It.) (glē sän'dō), slurred; in a gliding manner.

Glockenspiel (glok'en spēl), a percussion instrument, either flat metal bars fastened to a frame, or bells tuned to the diatonic scale, played by hammers or by means of a keyboard.

Gong, a bronze, copper or tin disc hanging from a bar and struck with a padded stick. It is occasionally used in orchestras.

Grace Notes, Graces, ornamental notes or short passages, introduced as embellishments into vocal or instrumental music, not actually essential to its harmony or melody. Grace notes are written small and are not counted as part of the measure.

Gregorian Chant, a style of church music without definite rhythm, written in one of the eight church modes or scales, formerly attributed to Pope Gregory. It is now believed that he did not originate it, but merely arranged and edited such music as already existed.

Guitar (gi tär'), a stringed instrument with a flat back and curved sides, made in several sizes. The Spanish guitar of present-day use has six strings, giving the instrument a range of about three and a half octaves. The tone is produced by plucking the strings with the fingers of the right hand, while the left hand stops the string on the frets of the neck.

Half Note, a note having half the time value of a whole note and twice that of a quarter note.

Half Rest, a pause equal in duration to a half note.

Harmonic Modulation, the change from one key to another in a succession of chords.

Harmonics, higher partial tones present in practically every musical sound, which can also be sounded separately upon many musical instruments.

Harmonium, see *Reed Organ.*

Harmony, a combination of tones which, sounded simultaneously, produce a pleasing effect; the structure of music with respect to the composition and progression of its chords, as contrasted with melody and rhythm; music consisting of a progression of chords, as distinguished from counterpoint, which consists of melody added to melody.

Harp, a stringed instrument of triangular form, furnished with gut strings. It has a compass varying from three to six octaves and a half, according to the size of the instrument.

Head-voice, the sounds produced above the chest-register, but not in falsetto.

Hold, an old English name for the sign of a pause (𝄐).

Homophony (Gr.) (hō mof'ō ni or hom'ō fō ni), unison of voices or instruments of the same character.

Horn, a general term for wind instruments of brass or metal, wood or animal horn. The French horn has perhaps one of the most exquisite voices in the modern orchestra. It is a long brass tube bent into a number of circular curves ending in a flaring bell and provided by pistons, making it a chromatic instrument.

Hymn, a lyric for use in worship.

Imitation, the repetition of a short subject by another part.

Impresario (It.) (im prā sä'ri ō), a designer, conductor or manager of a concert or opera party. This term is often applied to a man who trains singers, or obtains them for public performances.

Impromptu (Fr.) (im promp'tū), a piece of music written or played without previous preparation of the subject.

Improvisation (im prō vī zā'shun or im prov i-za'shun), the act and the art of composing and rendering music without previous preparation.

Inflection, any change in the pitch of the voice.

Interlude, a piece of music either impromptu or prepared, played between the acts of a drama, the verses of a canticle or hymn or between certain portions of a church service.

Intermezzo (It.) (in tēr med'zō), an interlude; a short movement in the symphony; one of the parts of the old suite.

Interval, the distance between any two sounds; *harmonic,* if between two tones sounded together and *melodic,* if between two tones sounded in succession. The intervals of the diatonic scale are do, *unison* or *primo;* do-re, *second;* do-mi, *third;* do-fa, *fourth;* do-sol, *fifth;* do-la, *sixth;* do-si, *seventh;* do-do, *eighth* or *octave.* Of these, the *unison, fourth, fifth* and *octave* are classified as *perfect.* The *second, third, sixth* and *seventh* are *major* in the major scale. The *minor intervals* are a chromatic half step smaller than the major intervals of the same name. *Augmented intervals* are a chromatic half step larger than perfect and major intervals. *Diminished intervals* are a chromatic half step smaller than perfect and minor intervals. Intervals not exceeding an octave are called *simple;* those greater than an octave, *compound.*

Intonation, the method of producing sound from a voice or an instrument; correctness of pitch; the method of chanting certain portions of the church services.

Introduction, an opening strain or short movement which prepares the way for the main body of a composition.

Inversion, changing the position of notes forming intervals, chords or themes.

Jig or **Gigue** (Fr.), a lively dance which may be performed by one or more dancers.

Kettledrums, important percussion instruments of the modern orchestra, used usually in pairs, threes or fours: also called timpani. They are kettle-shaped drums of brass or copper having parchment coverings. The drummer uses two sticks. It is the only drum which can be tuned to a definite pitch; this is done by tightening or loosening the head by means of key screws or foot pedals.

Key, (1) in its modern sense, it is the starting point of the definite series of sounds which form the recognized scale. Different starting points require the relative proportion of the steps of the scale to be maintained by means of sharps or flats in the signature. The key of C requires no flats or sharps for this purpose, hence it is called the *normal* key; (2) mechanical contrivance for closing or opening ventages, as in flutes, clarinets, etc.

Keyboard, the range of keys upon a pianoforte or organ. Keys played by the fingers are called *manuals;* those by the feet are called *pedals.*

Keynote, the note which, according to the signature, forms the starting point of the scale. The tonic, or first note of the scale, as "do."

Keys, Related, those differing by not more than one accidental in their respective signatures.

Larghetto (It.) (lär get'ō) (dim, of *largo*), at a slow pace but not so slow as *largo.*

Largo (It.) (lär'gō); slow; broadly.

Larynx, the organ by means of which we produce vocal sounds. It is situated at the top of the trachea or windpipe, of which it forms a continuation, and its position is known popularly by that of the "Adam's apple," the prominence of one of the cartilages or masses of gristle which form it.

Leading Note, the seventh degree of ascending major scale. It is called *leading* because of its tendency to rise or lead up to the tonic.

Ledger Lines, short lines drawn above or below the ordinary stave at the relative distances at which the whole lines would be placed.

Legato (It.) (lā gä'tō or lē gä'tō), smooth and connected, opposite of *staccato.*

Leitmotiv or **Leitmotif** (Ger.) (līt'mō tēf'), a guiding theme associated with a special person, act or sentiment in an extended composition.

Libretto (It.) (li bret'ō), literally, little book; the text of an opera or oratorio.

Lied (Ger.) (lēt), a song, but the word is especially applied to that class of song which owes its origin and evolution to the German temperament, poetic leanings and national tastes.

Ligature (lig'*a* tūr), a slur; a group of notes sung to one syllable or in one breath, or bowed with one stroke.

Litany (lit'*a* ni), a prayer, or supplication; in particular, that early form of prayer in which a minister recites a petition and the people answer "Lord, have mercy."

Lullaby, a cradle song.

Lyre (līr), one of the most ancient stringed instruments.

Madrigal (mad'ri gal), an unaccompanied song, usually a love song, for three or more voices, often six or eight, making use of counterpoint and imitation; perfected about 1450 in the Netherlands.

Major, greater; a major third consists of four semitones, a minor third of three; used to signify standard or normal as opposed to minor, diminished and augmented; applied to intervals, chords and keys.

Major Mode or **Scale,** the ordinary diatonic scale, having semitones between the third and fourth, and the seventh and eighth degrees.

Mandolin (man'dō lin), a lute-like stringed instrument. It has four to six pairs of strings, tuned in fifths with the same tonality as the violin. These strings are of wire and vibrate as they are plucked by a plectrum with a thin, sweet tone. The player stops the strings with his left hand, the pitch being indicated by frets on the long-necked keyboard.

Manual, a key or digital of a keyboard; the keyboard of an organ played by the hands, as opposed to the pedal board played by the feet.

Marcato (It.) (mär kä'tō), marked, or emphasized.

March, a musical composition so arranged as to be suitable for accompanying troops in marching. There are quick and slow marches, in double and triple time, besides marches peculiar to certain nationalities.

Marimba (m*a* rim'b*a*), see **Xylophone.**

Mass, name given to the Communion Office, Eucharist Service or Liturgy, from the words *Ite, missa est* (Depart; the congregation is dismissed), sung by the priest or minister just before the end of the service. The subdivisions are Kyrie, Gloria, Credo, Sanctus, Benedictus and Agnus Dei.

Mazurka (Pol.) (m*a* zûr'k*a* or m*a* zōōr'k*a*), a Polish dance of lively, grotesque character, the music of which is in 3/8 or 3/4 time, with a peculiar rhythm; a composition in the rhythm of this dance.

Measure, time; pace; rhythm; the contents of a bar; also the space lying between two adjoining bars. In England the name used for a very stately dance, slow in movement, supposed to be somewhat like the minuet and once in favor on occasions of high court functions, somewhat like our grand march.

Mediant, the third degree of any scale.

Medley, a mixture; a composition made up of detached passages from other compositions; usually applied to vocal music.

Meistersinger (Ger.) (mīs'tēr sing ēr), a title given to the most renowned musician of a township or district in Germany during the Middle Ages.

Melodeon (mē lō'de un), see *Reed Organ.*

Melodrama, a dramatic piece in which the interest is heightened by the character of the vocal or instrumental music accompanying certain situations.

Melody, an agreeable succession of simple sounds, produced by a single voice or instrument, and so regulated as to give a pleasing effect, or to be expressive of some kind of sentiment; opposed to harmony, which consists of two or more tones sounded simultaneously; the leading part of a composition.

Meter, Metre, the grouping of notes or beats into units of measure to form rhythm; the distribution of long and short, accented and unaccented notes in the measure.

Metronome (Gr.) (met'rō nōm), an instrument said to have been invented in 1816 by J. B. Maelzel for the purpose of measuring the relative duration of the notes in a piece of music. The machinery is of clock work, and the various grades of time are measured on a balance rod serving the purpose of a pendulum, the speed being regulated by a shifting or sliding weight. To be correct, the metronome should beat seconds when set at 60.

Mezzo (It.) (med'zō) or **Mezza** (med'zä), medium, half, as *mezzo bravura*—semi bravura style.

Mezzo-Soprano (It.) (med'zō-sō prä'nō or -pran'ō), a female voice, the range of which lies between the soprano and the alto.

Middle C, the note standing on the first ledger line above the bass stave and the first ledger line before the treble stave.

Minor (Lat.), less; smaller; applied to intervals and to chords, scales, and keys having intervals a semitone less than major.

Minor Scale, a scale having its third and sixth minor. There are three forms: *Normal* or *natural minor* which has half steps between 2 and 3, and 5 and 6. *Harmonic minor* which is the same except that the 7th tone is raised a semitone. This makes it a scale with half steps between 2 and 3, 5 and 6, 7 and 8, and one step and a half between 6 and 7. The *melodic minor* has half steps between 2 and 3, and 7 and 8 ascending, while in descending it usually has the form of the normal minor.

Minuet (min'ū et' or min'ū et), a slow, graceful dance in triple rhythm, said to have been invented in Poitou, France, about the middle of the 17th century; a composition in the rhythm of this dance.

Missa (Lat.) (mīs'*a*), a mass; as *missa pro defunctis,* a requiem mass.

Mode, a scale; a species of scale, as *major mode, minor mode;* a church scale.

Modulation, going from one key to another, by a certain succession of chords, either in a natural and flowing manner or sometimes in a sudden and unexpected manner; inflecting the voice musically.

Moll (Ger.) (mol), minor.

Molto (It.) (mōl'tō), much; very; as *molto adagio,* very slow.

Monody (Eng.) (mon'ō di), a song for a single voice, generally of a plaintive character. The term was originally applied to vocal solos in the church service.

Monotone (mon'ō tōn), to recite words on a single note without inflections.

Motet (mō tet'), a vocal composition in harmony, set to words generally from the Scriptures, or to paraphrases of the sacred writing.

Motion, melodic progression; (1) motion of a single part, *conjunct* if by single degrees, *disjunct* if by skips; (2) of two parts, *contrary* or *opposite* if one ascends while the other descends; *oblique* if one remains stationary while the other ascends or descends; *parallel* if both ascend or descend together; (3) of several parts, *mixed* if two of these motions occur at the same time.

Motive, a musical figure or phrase which serves as the germ from which a composition or a movement is developed.

Moto (It.) (mō'tō), motion; movement, as *con moto* with spirited movement, keeping up the interest of the music.

Movement, same as *Motion;* style of rhythm, as waltz movement; a distinct division of a composition having its own key, rhythm, themes and general character.

Mute, a small instrument of brass, wood or ivory, so made that it can be readily fixed upon the bridge of a violin or violoncello, to muffle or deaden the sound. The direction for its use is written *con sordini,* or *muta,* its discontinuance by *senza sordini.*

Natural, a sign (♮) which restores a note to its position in the natural scale. It has the effect of sharpening a note previously flatted, or of flatting a note previously sharpened.

Natural Keys, those having no sharps or flats in the signature, as C major and A minor.

Neapolitan (nē *a* pol'i tan) **Sixth,** a name, apparently without much reason, given to a chord occurring on the subdominant of a minor key, and consisting of a minor third and minor sixth.

Nocturne (nok'tûrn or nok tûrn'), originally a kind of serenade, or night piece; now a piece of music of gentle and quiet character.

Notation, the act and the art of representing music by means of notes and other symbols; these notes and other symbols taken collectively.

Obbligato (It.) (ob li gä'tō), an instrumental part or accompaniment of such importance that it cannot be dispensed with.

Oboe (It.) (ō'bō or ō'boi), hautbois, Fr.; hautboy, Eng., from the French word literally translated "high-wood," a wood wind instrument with a mouthpiece having a double reed. The oboe is the soprano of the double reed family and is essentially a pastoral instrument. Its voice is more reedy in quality than that of the clarinet, and, although it may play soft, tender passages, its tone is always penetrating. The alto oboe is the English horn, an instrument larger and longer than the oboe, and bell-shaped at the end. The tone of the English horn is always sad and plaintive.

Octave (ok'tāv or -tiv), the interval of an eighth—major, minor or augmented; the whole series of tones within the interval.

Offertory (ôf'ēr tō ri), in the Roman Catholic Church an anthem or instrumental piece performed while the bread and wine are "presented" to God before consecration, and at this time a collection may be taken; in Protestant churches, music performed while an offering is being taken.

Open Score, when each part has a separate line assigned to it, music is said to be in *open score.* When more than one part is written, in *close* or *short score.*

Opera (op'ēr *a*), a drama set to music, for voices and instruments, and with scenery, decorations and action.

Operetta (op ēr et'*a*), a little opera, generally of a light and playful character.

Opus (Lat.) (ō'pus), a work; a composition, as opus No. 1, the first work of a composer. Properly the number of an opus refers to the order of publication, not of the composition. May include several numbers or may consist of a single piece.

Oratorio (or *a* tō'ri ō), a sacred work analogous to an opera, but without action, scenery or costume.

Orchestra (ôr'kes tr*a*), (1) a band of musicians performing upon various instruments; the modern orchestra employs four kinds of instruments: (a) *stringed*—belonging to the violin family; (b) *woodwind*—flutes, oboes, clarinets and bassoons; (c) *brass*—trumpets, horns, and trombones; (d) *percussion*—kettledrums, cymbals, triangle and bells; (2) the space in a theater occupied by the band or orchestra.

Organ (ôr'gan), the largest, most intricate and one of the oldest of musical instruments. It was developed from the ancient Panpipe. The tone of the modern organ is produced from a graduated series of pipes by means of compressed air, the player controlling the tone through a system of keyboards similar to a piano keyboard. The instrument is entirely in the control of a single player, the organist, who sits at the console. The wind pressure and pneumatic devices, which make the keyboard of the organ as easy to manipulate as that of the piano, are controlled by electricity. No effect of the modern orchestra is impossible of imitation on the organ.

Organ Point or **Pedal Point,** a tone sustained by one part through a succession of harmonies of which it forms no part.

Ornamental Notes, unessential notes introduced for the purpose of embellishment, such as *acciaccatura, appoggiatura, grace notes, trill, turn.*

Overture (Eng.) (ō'vēr chūr), an introduction to an oratorio, opera or other large composition.

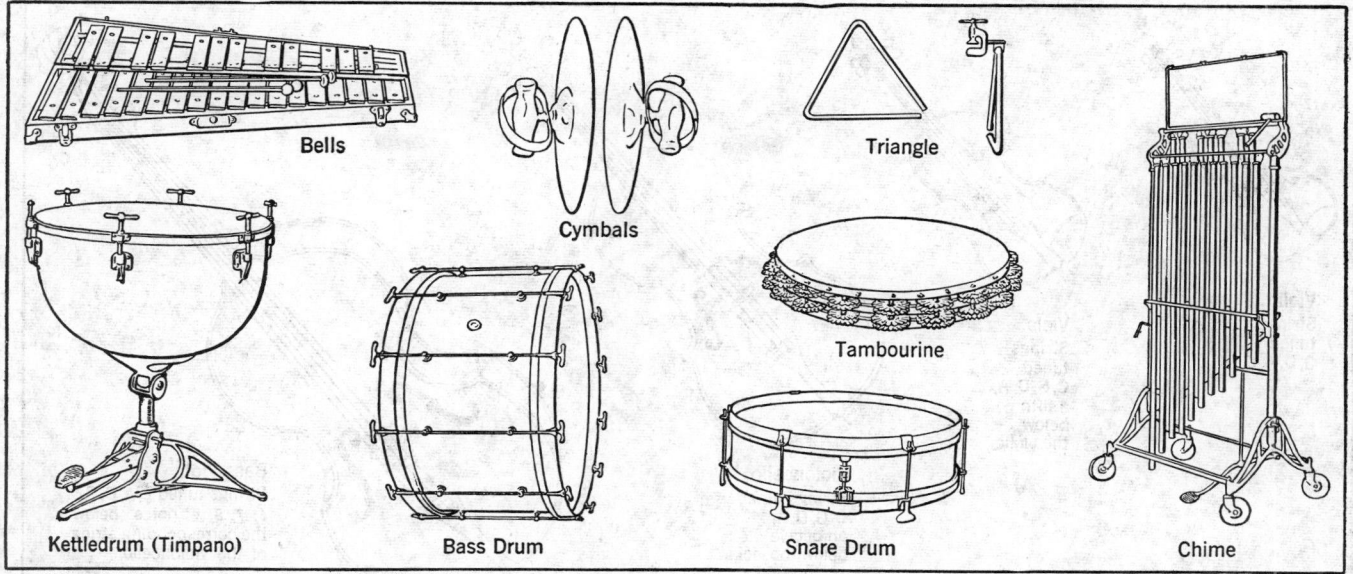

Important Percussion Instruments of the Orchestra

RUDOLPH WURLITZER COMPANY; C. G. CONN, LTD.; G. SCHIRMER, INC.

Parallel Motion, the motion of two or more parts at fixed intervals as thirds, sixths. Parallel fifths are under certain limitations forbidden.

Paraphrase, the rearrangement of a composition for some other instrument than that for which it was originally written.

Part, the music for any one voice or instrument; division of a work.

Partita (It.) (pär tē'ta), a composition consisting of a collection of dance tunes, which came into vogue about 1700; also called *suite.*

Part Song, an unaccompanied song for three or four voices, which originated in Germany.

Passage, a phrase of music; a figure; a run.

Passion Music, music set to the narrative of our Lord's Passion in the Gospels, similar to a cantata or an oratorio.

Pastorale (pás tō rä'lā or pas tō rä'lē), a simple melody in 6/8 time in a rustic style; a cantata, the words of which are founded on pastoral incidents; a complete symphony, wherein a series of pastoral scenes is depicted by sound-painting, without the aid of words.

Patetico (It.) (pä tä'tē kō), pathetic.

Pause, a rest or pause; a bar's rest.

Pedal, a foot lever, as piano pedal, organ pedal, harp pedal.

Pedal Keys, a set of pipe organ keys played by the feet.

Pedal Point, see *Organ Point.*

Pentatonic (pen ta ton'ik) **Scale,** a name given by Carl Engel to the ancient musical scale which is easiest described as that formed by the black keys of the pianoforte. It consists of the 1st, 2d, 3d, 5th and 6th degrees of a modern diatonic scale.

Percussion (pēr kush'un), an ingenious contrivance whereby a hammer strikes the tongue of a reed and sets it in motion simultaneously with the admission of air from the windchest, thus securing the rapid speech of the reed.

Percussion Instruments, in the modern orchestra those instruments sounded by striking, as drums, cymbals, triangles, tambourines, bells, chimes and castanets.

Period, a complete musical sentence; it is composed of two or more phrases usually of four measures each, and closes with a cadence.

Phrase (fräz), a musical clause, corresponding to a line of a poem.

Phrasing, a musical punctuation; in piano music, it refers to varieties of touch; in violin music, to bowing; in singing, to breathing places.

Phrygian (Gr.) (frij'i an), one of the Greek modes; the name of a cadence.

Piano (pi an'ō), less commonly, **pianoforte** (pi an o fōr'te), the most popular and important keyboard stringed instrument. The modern piano was developed in the early 18th century by Bartolomeo Cristofori, an instrument-maker of Florence, from the older keyboard forms of virginals, harpsichords and clavichords. The chief difference between the modern piano and those earlier instruments is that in the pianoforte the tones are produced by vibrating strings struck by hammers, which are controlled by a keyboard. The mechanism is so constructed that the force of the blow struck by the hammers is under the control of the player's fingers, therefore the tone may be very soft or very loud; hence the name pianoforte.

Piano (It.) (pi än'ō), softly; *pianissimo,* as softly as possible.

Piccolo (pik'ō lō), a small flute an octave higher than the ordinary flute.

Pitch, the position of a sound with reference to the number of vibrations which cause it; as standard of pitch as *international pitch,* now used in all civilized countries except England, in which the A above middle C has 435 vibrations a second.

Pizzicato (It.) (pit sē kä'tō), a direction to violinists to produce the tone by plucking the string with the finger instead of using the bow.

Plagal (plā'gal), church modes beginning a fourth below the authentic and distinguished by the word hypo; also the name of a cadence formed when a subdominant chord immediately precedes the final tonic chord.

Plain Song, a nonmetrical chant in one of the ecclesiastical modes, common in early church music; such a melody serving as *cantus firmus* in a contrapuntal composition; any simple tune or melody.

Plectrum (plek'trum), a small thin piece of horn, metal or wood, used for playing certain stringed instruments, as the mandolin, banjo, etc. In Greek the word was *plectron.*

Polacca (It.) (pō lä'ka), Polish. A title applied to melodies written in imitation of Polish dance tunes. Synonymous with the French word polonaise.

Polonaise (Fr.) (pō lō näz' or pol'ō näz), see *Polacca.*

Polyphony (pō lif'ō ni or pol'i fō ni), music in which the parts or voices are melodically independent while at the same time in harmony; contrapuntal music; opposed to *homophony,* in which one part carries the melody.

Position, a chord is said to be in its *original position* when the ground note is in the bass, in other *positions* when the relative arrangement of the component notes is changed; a *position.*

Postlude (pōst'lūd), a concluding voluntary; a piece played at the end of the service.

Potpourri (Fr.) (pō pōō rē' or pot poor'i), a medley, a collection of various tunes linked together.

Precentor (prē sen'tēr), the leader of a church choir or of congregational singing.

Prelude (prel'ūd or prē'lūd), a movement played before, or an introduction to, a musical work or performance.

Presto (It.) (pres'tō), quick; rapid.

Program Music, music intended to portray or suggest a definite series of objects or events; first applied to Beethoven's "Pastoral Symphony."

Progression, *melodic progression* is a succession of sounds forming a tune or melody; *harmonic progression* is the movement of one chord to another, and is diatonic or chromatic.

Psalm (säm), a sacred song.

Quadrille (Fr.) (kwo dril' or ka dril'), a French square dance of five figures in 6/8 or 2/4 time; the music for such a dance.

Quartet (kwôr tet'), a composition in four parts, or for four performers; part of a movement sung by four voices *soli* as opposed to *coro;* the four performers rendering the quartet.

Quintet (kwin tet'), a composition in five parts, or for five performers.

Recitative (It.) (res i tä tēv'), musical declamation.

Reed Instruments, those in which the sound is produced by the vibration of one or more reeds in the mouthpiece.

Reed Organ, an organ in which the air is forced over free metal reeds, as in the vocalion, harmonium, melodeon and cabinet organ.

Refrain, the *burden* or *chorus* of a song, repeated at the end of each stanza.

Register, an organ stop; the range of voice or musical instrument.

Relative Key, a key whose tonic chord is a relative chord; that is, a key whose first, third and fifth degrees form a common chord made up of notes of the key to which it is related.

Repeat, a sign that a movement or part of a movement is to be twice performed. That which is to be repeated is generally included within the sign of two or four dots in the spaces of the staff.

Requiem (Lat.) (rē'kwi em or rek'wi em), a mass for the dead; a musical setting for the same.

Rests, signs enjoining the silence of a performer for a given length of time.

Rhapsody (rap'sō di), a composition of irregular form, and in the style of an improvisation.

Rhythm (rith'm or rith'm), movement characterized by regular, measured or harmonious recurrences of stress or impulse, beat, sound accent or motion.

Ritardando (It.) (rē tär dän'dō or -dan'dō), with gradually increasing slowness of pace.

Romance (rō mans'), a vocal or instrumental composition of a romantic character, without a fixed form.

Rondo (It.) (ron'dō), a vocal or instrumental composition in which the first strain recurs after each of the other strains.

Root, called also fundamental note, generator and ground note. The lowest note if the chord is in its natural position, but some other if the chord is inverted.

Round, a composition in which several voices starting at stated distances of time from each other, sing each the same music, the combination of all the parts producing correct harmony.

Rubato (It.) (rōō bä'tō), literally, robbed; some notes are held for more, and others for less than their strict duration.

Run, a rapid succession of notes.

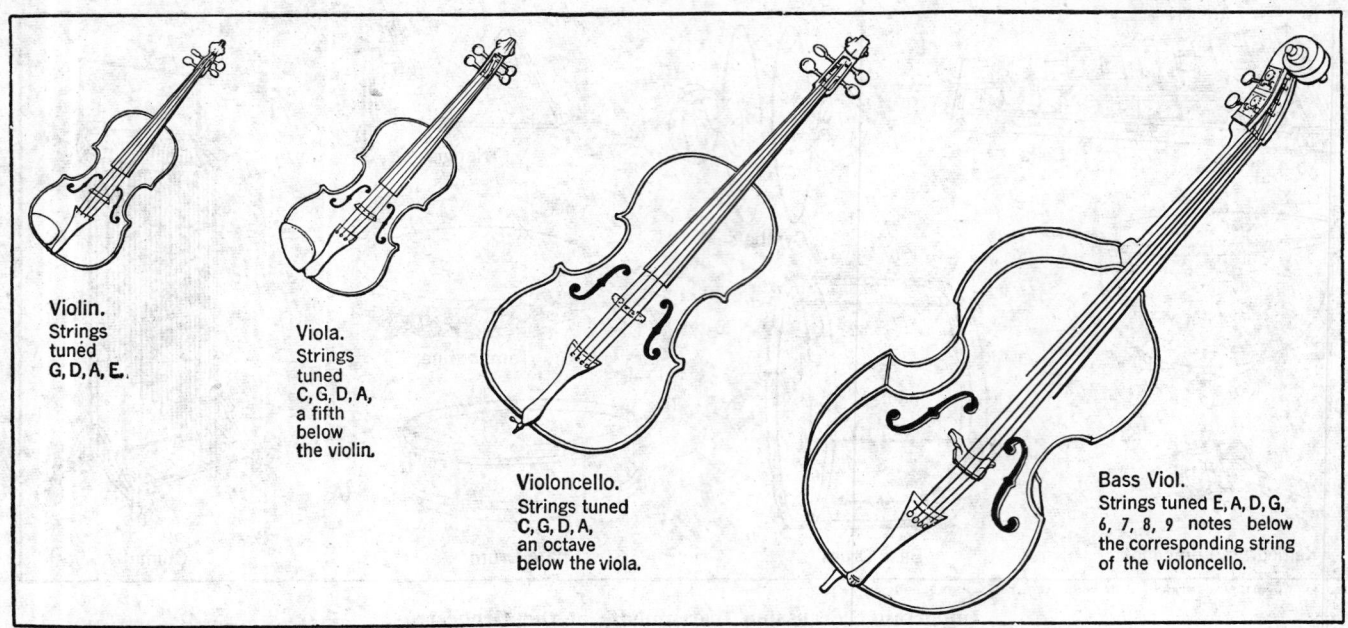

Violin.
Strings tuned G, D, A, E.

Viola.
Strings tuned C, G, D, A, a fifth below the violin.

Violoncello.
Strings tuned C, G, D, A, an octave below the viola.

Bass Viol.
Strings tuned E, A, D, G, 6, 7, 8, 9 notes below the corresponding string of the violoncello.

RUDOLPH WURLITZER COMPANY: G. SCHIRMER, INC.

Important Stringed Instruments of the Orchestra

Other stringed instruments often used in orchestral compositions are the *piano* and the *harp*.

Saraband (sar′*a* band), Spanish dance of Moorish origin, for a single performer, who accompanies himself with the castanets, in triple rhythm.

Saxhorn (saks′hôrn), a group of brass wind instruments made in seven different keys.

Saxophone (sak′sō fōn), a wind instrument with a clarinet mouthpiece and a bent conical tube of metal with finger keys: it is made in six sizes. The saxophone and the saxhorn were the inventions of Adolph Sax. The former is an important instrument in jazz orchestras and military bands.

Scale, a ladder; a series of tones ascending by regular intervals, and descending, usually in the same order. The interval scheme of the modern scale is the octave. The standard and most common form is called *major*. The three *minor* scales are the *normal, harmonic* and *melodic*. Another variant form is the *chromatic*.

Scena (It.) (shā′nä), the largest vocal solo form, usually part of an opera, but sometimes an independent composition.

Scherzo (It.) (sker′tsō), literally, jest; instrumental composition of a humorous, playful or whimsical character.

Schottische (Ger.) (shot′tish), literally Scotch; a slow dance of modern introduction, written in 2/4 time; the music for such a dance.

Score, a copy of a musical work in which all the component parts are shown, either fully, or in a compressed form.

Second, the interval between a fundamental tone and the next diatonic tone above.

Secondo (It.) (sā kōn′dō), second; as *violino secondo*—second violin.

Semitone, a half a tone, or an approximate half a tone.

Sequence (Eng.) (sē′kwens), the recurrence of a harmonic progression or melodic figure at a different pitch or in a different key to that in which it was first given.

Serenade (Fr.) (ser ē näd′), originally a vocal or instrumental composition for use in the open air at night, generally of a quiet, soothing character; now any composition of that general character.

Seventh, the seventh diatonic tone above a fundamental; the interval between a keynote and the seventh step.

Sextet (seks tet′), a composition for six voices or instruments; the performers of such a composition.

Sforzando (sfôr tsän′dō) or **sforzato** (sfôr tsä′tō), emphasis upon a certain note or chord, marked *sf.* or (∧) or (>).

Shake, an ornament produced by the rapid alternations of two notes, either one tone or a semitone apart, as the case may be. The sign of the shake is *tr.*, the first two letters of the word trillo placed over the chief note.

Sharp, the sign (♯) which raises a note one semitone above the normal or natural pitch; above the proper pitch, as one sings or plays sharp.

Signature, the signs placed at the commencement of a piece of music. There are two kinds of signature, the time-signature and the key-signature—the latter requiring a clef to show the pitch.

Sixth, Chord of the, the first inversion of the common chord; it consists of a note with its third and sixth.

Slur, a curved line placed over notes directing that they are to be played or sung legato.

Solfeggio (It.) (sol fej′ō), a singing exercise in which a single vowel or the syllables do, re, mi, fa, sol, la, si are used.

Solo, alone; as *voci soli*—voices alone.

Sonata (It.) (sō nä′ta), an instrumental composition made up of three or four movements in different though related keys and in different forms and moods. The word *sonata* originally meant something played, as contrasted with cantata, something sung. Sonatas have been written not only for the piano but for almost every other instrument in combination with it. A *string quartet* is a sonata for two violins, a viola and a cello. An *overture* is only an orchestral work based on the same form as the first movement of a sonata. A *concerto* is a brilliant sonata for some instrument, as piano or violin, with orchestral accompaniment. A *symphony* is simply a sonata for the full orchestra with the enlargements natural to the enlarged resources.

Sonatina (It.) (sō nä tē na), a short sonata. One in which the subjects are not developed at length.

Song, a short poem intended for music; a musical setting of a short poem or portion of prose.

Soprano (It.) (sō prä′nō or sō pran′ō), the highest kind of female or boy's voice; also the singer possessing that voice.

Sotto Voce (It.) (sōt′tō vō′chä), in an undertone.

Space, the degree or interval between two lines of the staff.

Stabat Mater (Lat.) (stä′bät mä′tēr or stä′bat mä′tēr), a well-known Latin hymn on the Crucifixion, sung during Passion Week in the Roman Catholic Church.

Staccato (It.) (sta kä′tō or stäk kä′tō), detached; taken off; separated. Sometimes a dot over a note is called a staccato mark, but it is more properly the sign of a spiccato.

Staff (stȧf), the five horizontal lines, on and between which music is written.

Stop, the pressure by the fingers of the strings upon the finger board of a stringed instrument; a fret upon a guitar or similar instrument; a collection, register or row of pipes in an organ.

Strain, a musical subject forming part of, and having relation to, a general whole; a complete period, its close being indicated upon the staff by a double bar.

Stringed Instruments, musical instruments in which the tone is produced by the vibration of strings. The violins, violas, violoncellos and double basses are the strings of the modern orchestra. Stringed instruments are divided: (1) strings plucked by the fingers —harp, guitar, etc.; (2) strings struck by plectra—mandolin, zither, etc.; (3) strings vibrated with a bow—violin, violoncello, etc., and (4) strings struck with hammers—piano, dulcimer, etc.

String Quartet, music written for four stringed instruments, usually two violins, a viola and a cello; the performers of such music.

Style, character; form or temperament of music with reference to the result of individual influence; the conformity of music to the purpose for which it was written; the conventional or national method of performance, or its construction.

Subdominant (sub dom′i nant), the dominant below; the fourth tone of the diatonic scale, which is in the same relation to the keynote from below as the dominant is from above.

Subject, the theme or principal phrase of any movement from which all the subordinate ideas spring or are developed.

Submediant (sub mē′di ant), the sixth of the scale.

Subtonic, the seventh tone of the diatonic scale.

Suite (Fr.) (swēt), a set; series; or succession of movements in music; a large orchestral composition consisting of a series of movements in any one of a number of forms and in different keys; sometimes a collection of distinct compositions.

Supertonic, the tone one degree above the tonic in the diatonic scale.

Suspension, the holding or prolongation of a note in any chord which follows, thereby often producing a discord or dissonance which is resolved by moving the discordant tone into the chord tone which it had displaced.

Symphony (sim′fō ni), a composition for an orchestra, similar in construction to the sonata, which is usually for a single instrument. See *Sonata*.

Syncopation (sing ko pā′shun), suspension or alteration of rhythm by driving the accent to that part of a bar not usually accented.

Tambourine (tam boo rēn′), percussion instrument similar to a small drum, often used to accompany dancing. It consists of a hoop of wood or metal about two inches deep with a covering of parchment; jingles are attached to the frame. The tambourine is held in the left hand and struck by the right.

Tarantella (It.) (tar′an tel′*a*), a rapid Neapolitan dance in triplets, so called because it was popularly thought to be a remedy against the supposed poisonous bite of the tarantula spider. Others say that the bite of the spider causes this delirious dance, which ends fatally.

Technic (tek′nik), technique.

Technique (tek nēk′), manner of execution; musical skill.

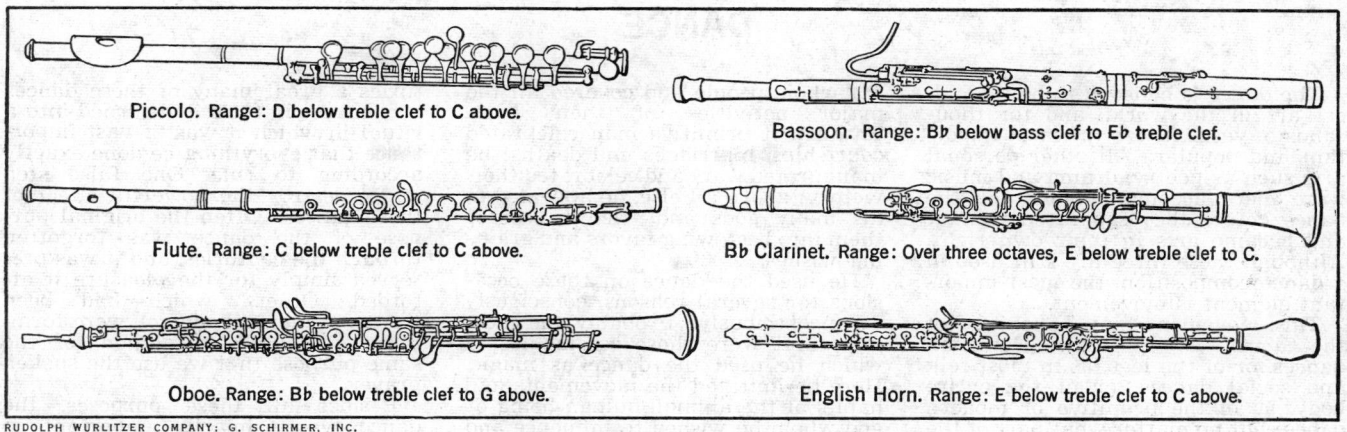

Piccolo. Range: D below treble clef to C above.

Bassoon. Range: B♭ below bass clef to E♭ treble clef.

Flute. Range: C below treble clef to C above.

B♭ Clarinet. Range: Over three octaves, E below treble clef to C.

Oboe. Range: B♭ below treble clef to G above.

English Horn. Range: E below treble clef to C above.

RUDOLPH WURLITZER COMPANY; G. SCHIRMER, INC.

Important Wood-Wind Instruments of the Orchestra

The *alto clarinet* and the *bass clarinet* are other wood-wind instruments often used in orchestral compositions.

Tema (tä'mä), theme; subject.

Tempo (It.) (tem'pō), time or measure; the rate of speed at which a composition should be played. Indicated at the beginning by such terms as *tempo rubato*—robbed or stolen time; *tempo di marcic*—in marching time.

Tenor, the third of the four kinds of voices arranged with regard to their compass; a musical instrument, the range of which corresponds to the high male voice.

Tetrachord (Gr.) (tet'ra kôrd), a scale-series of four notes; half an octave.

Theme, one of the divisions of a subject in the development of sonata form; the *cantus firmus* on which counterpoint is built; the subject of a fugue; a simple tune on which variations are made.

Theremin, a musical instrument invented in 1920 by the Russian electrical engineer and musician Professor Leon Theremin (b. 1896). The instrument is based on the principle of high frequency oscillations produced by electronic (radio) vacuum tubes. It is played by movement of the hands and fingers in free space without touching anything, through the electrical capacity influence of the human body on two metal rods attached to high-frequency circuits. The right hand, through approach to the vertical rod, controls the pitch, while the left hand through raising and lowering toward the locklike bent rod, controls the volume. The Theremin produces a sound similar to the singing human voice, string-bow instruments or wind instruments, depending on the character of the movements of the musician's hands. The usual range is four and one-half octaves. About 1,000 of the instruments have been distributed by the Radio Corporation of America.

Thesis (thē'sis), the downward wave of the hand to denote the absence of accent.

Tie, a curved line placed over two or more notes in the same position on the stave, indicating they should be played as one.

Timbre (Fr.) (tim'bēr or tan'br'), literally, texture; the quality of tone or sound.

Time, the rate of speed at which a piece of music should be played.

Timpani (tim'pa nē), see *Kettledrums.*

Toccata (It.) (tō kä'ta or tōk kä'tä), a prelude or overture; a composition for the organ or harpsichord, popular in the 16th century, free in style, resembling the cappriccio.

Tom-tom (tom'tom'), a Chinese gong; a percussion instrument used for producing harsh effects.

Tone, sound; quality of tone; a sound whose vibrations are sufficiently regular to give it a definite pitch.

Tonic Sol-fa, a letter system of notation, and of teaching vocal music, employing the syllables *do, re, mi, fa, sol, la* and *si,* with modifications for sharps and flats.

Touch, the resistance made to the fingers by the keys of a pianoforte or organ; the peculiar manner in which a player presses the keyboard, whether light, heavy, firm, etc.

Transition, a modulation; a passing; a change from one theme to another.

Transposition, a change of key; an inversion of parts in counterpoint.

Treble, the highest vocal or instrumental part, sung by women or boys, or played by violins, flutes, oboes, clarinets or other instruments of acute tone.

Treble Clef, the G clef on the second line of the stave used for treble voices and instruments of high and medium pitch, such as flutes, oboes, etc.

Tremolo (It.) (trem'ō lō), the rapid repetition of a note or chord which produces the effect of trembling or quivering; the stop of a pipe organ, which, when brought into use, causes the tones to tremble or flutter.

Triad (trī'ad), a chord of three notes; a common chord composed of a fundamental tone and the third and fifth above.

Triangle, a percussion instrument consisting of a bent piece of steel shaped like a triangle. It is struck with a steel rod and gives out a clear bell-like tone.

Trill, see *Shake.*

Trio (trē'ō or trī'ō), a composition for three voices or instruments; a part of a minuet, march, etc.

Triplet, a group of three notes performed in the time of two. The triplet is always indicated by a slur and the figure 3. (3̄).

Trombone (trom'bōn), a brass wind instrument consisting of a long cylindrical tube bent back upon itself; its tubes slide into each other, contracting its length and regulating its tone. The voice of the trombone is of great majesty and beauty and adds dignity and solemnity to the full orchestra.

Trumpet (trum'pet), a brass wind instrument consisting of a long twice curved metal tube ending in a bell. Tone variations are secured by the force of blowing and by means of finger holes and keys. The trumpet is the highest voice of the brasses. Its noble, brilliant tone quality is one of the most penetrating in the orchestra.

Tuba (tū'ba), a brass wind instrument resembling a large horn and with from three to five valves. The tuba is the bass of the brasses, giving impressive strength to the brass choir.

Tuning, the adjustment of the sounds naturally produced by any instrument to some standard pitch and to their proper relation to each other.

Tuning Fork, an instrument of steel with two prongs, which, when set in vibration, gives out a musical sound varying in pitch according to the thickness of the metal or the length or width apart of the prongs; useful as a standard of pitch in tuning musical instruments.

Turn, an embellishment following a note, which consists of rapid alternation between the principal note, the note a step above and the note a half step below, indicated by the sign (∽).

Tutti (It.) (tōō'tē), all; the whole, as *tutta forza*—the full power or force.

Ukelele (ū ku lā'lē), the Hawaiian adaptation of the guitars and mandolins brought to the South Seas by Spanish and Portuguese sailors. A miniature guitar in shape, the tiny metal strings of the ukelele are capable of many new and interesting chord combinations.

Unison, having the same number of vibrations; identical in pitch; another name for the interval *prime.*

Variations, certain modifications with regard to the time, tune and harmony of a theme proposed originally in a simple form.

Verse, those portions of an anthem or service intended to be sung by a single voice to a part; a separate stanza of a song or a ballad.

Vibrato (It.) (vē brä'tō), a tremulous quality of tone as opposed to a pure equal production.

Viol (vī'ul), a stringed instrument, shaped like the violin but of larger size.

Viola (vē ō'la), a tenor violin, slightly larger than the violin, but tuned a fifth lower. Its tone is not as brilliant or penetrating as that of the violin, but possesses a lovely quality.

Violin (vī ō lin'), a four-stringed instrument of the viol class, played with a bow. The violin has the first place in the orchestra. It is divided into two groups; the second violins play the second soprano or contralto voice to the first violin.

Violoncello (vē ō lon chel'ō), a stringed instrument, the modern Viola da Gamba. It has four strings and is played with a bow. The cello is tuned in fifths like the viola, but an octave lower in pitch. In the string quartet the cello serves as the bass; in the orchestra it is used as the baritone, and sometimes as the tenor. Its tone is more like the human voice than any other instrument. Violoncello is commonly shortened to *cello.*

Virtuoso (It.) (vûr chū ō'sō), a skilled performer on some particular instrument, especially the violin.

Vivace (It.) (vē vä'chä), quickly; sprightly.

Vocal, for or by the voice; music intended to be sung.

Voice, sound produced by the vocal organs in singing or speaking; the faculty of uttering sound.

Voicing, the regulation of the tone and power of an organ pipe.

Volume, a term applied to the power and quality of the tone of a voice or instrument, or of a combination of sounds.

Voluntary, an organ prelude; an organ solo played before, during or after an office of the Church.

Waltz (wôlts), a round dance in triple rhythm, performed by couples whirling around and advancing around the room; music in the rhythm of this dance.

Whole Note, the longest note in common use. Shorter notes are timed as parts of the whole note.

Whole Rest, a rest equal in duration to a whole note.

Whole Step, a major second; the interval between a fundamental tone and the next diatonic tone above.

Wind Instruments, in the modern orchestra the wood-wind and brass-wind instruments (*q.v.*).

Wood-wind Instruments, in the modern orchestra the flute, oboe, bassoon and clarinet.

Xylophone (zī'lō fōn or zil'ō fōn), a percussion instrument consisting of strips of wood graduated to produce the diatonic scale. They rest on belts of straw or felt and are struck by hammers held one in each hand. The primitive African xylophone, also its modern form, is called the marimba.

Zither (zith'ēr), a stringed instrument, a descendant of the cithara of ancient Greece. The zither consists of a flat box, which lies on a table. Across this are stretched five metal strings which pass over frets. The melody is played by a plectrum attached to the player's right thumb; this plucks the string as the tones are stopped by the player's left hand. In addition to the five melody strings there are from 25 to 40 open strings; these are played as an accompaniment to the melody, being struck harp-fashion by the fingers of the right hand.

DANCE

The dance is believed to be the oldest art in the world, and for thousands of years it was the most important and popular. All other personal arts such as poetry, drama and music were mere accompaniments for the dance before they separated from it and became arts in their own right. Although these three are still used in a dance composition, the most important element is movement.

This movement may be chiefly of the arms, as in some Hawaiian dances, or of the legs, as in most folk and social dances, or of the entire body, as in the primitive or modern dance; but no matter what part of the body is used the movements are always rhythmic. They are accented, repeated and varied, and they are composed in the same manner as words are composed in poetry so as to express an emotion or an idea.

The dance is the most immediate and most personal expression that we can give of the great rhythms that run through all things and bind them together. Each place and each thing has a rhythm peculiar to itself, and each of these is a variation on a larger rhythm that contains them all. We walk differently in the city from the way we walk at the seashore because each place has a rhythm that affects us differently. We breathe in a rhythm of inhalation, hold and exhalation that becomes faster or slower, accented or distorted according to our excitement or calm. The waves along the seashore also have a rhythm. At first they seem monotonous, but as we watch them we find that there are several small waves in succession followed by two or three large waves, which are stronger and faster, like an accent in poetry. These will be followed again by smaller ones. Certain birds and mammals during the mating season step out a rhythmic dance to attract the attention of their mate.

We dance, then, largely because we are compelled to. Rhythmic movement satisfies equally two conflicting desires that all men have. One is the desire to make themselves outstanding. The other is the desire to feel themselves as part of a social group. In dancing, almost alone of the arts, we can perform to our best ability as individuals and at the same time feel ourselves one with all others in the common rhythm. The dance gives us ease, strength and self-assurance. When man lived closer to nature than he does now, and when he was less burdened with the laws, ideas, traditions and scientific facts that govern us, he was more aware of the value of the dance and gave it more spontaneous expression.

Primitive Dance.—Among primitive peoples the dance was used at all times of social significance and was performed by all the people, young and old. It made use of movement employing all parts of the body. Rarely, if ever, was there an audience in the way that we conceive of audiences at a theater today. It was a dance of the whole people and covered all the major activities of their lives. Through it primitive man celebrated courtships, marriages and deaths; he inaugurated wars and celebrated their victory; above all else, he appealed to his many gods and tried to coerce them into bestowing favors and granting wishes.

He used the dance on these occasions for several reasons, consciously or unconsciously. Probably the most important were those ceremonies in which he used the dance as magic. Here he imitated the movements and habits of the animal, human being or god whom he wished to influence and control. His human enemies were mimicked so that they might be more easily vanquished. The buffalo was mimicked so that it might increase in numbers and be easily killed. The

SATOUR

YOUNG MAIDENS from the Bavenda tribe in the South African Transvaal perform the Python Dance, raising and lowering a huge "snake" made by grasping each other's forearms.

gods were mimicked so that they might be favorable to him and give him the things he needed.

In other dances he abandoned himself to wild, excited movement that was used to intoxicate and hypnotize the dancer. The movement often mounted to a frenzy at the peak of which he became "possessed." In the mimetic dances mentioned above he tried to secure control, to influence and coerce his gods through magic, but in this dance he himself became the god with all the god's strength and divine power. By this wild abandonment he became for a time more powerful than he would ordinarily be and was therefore able to accomplish greater things. These dances were often used in preparation for war so that he might become bolder and more daring.

Still other dances were used for courtship and marriage. In many ways these are similar to dances performed by birds and other animals wherein they exhibit themselves to their best ability and advantage so that they may appeal to their mates. Many of our social dances are, in a lesser degree, this form of personal exhibition.

Through repetition over many centuries a great many of these dances became set in form and turned into a ritual in which it was of vast importance that everything be done exactly according to rule. One false step might destroy the powerful effect of these dances. Often the original purpose of the dance was forgotten through the centuries, and it was preserved simply for the pleasure it afforded. Others, which had been dances of magical control, were formalized and used in religion for the same purpose that we use the spoken prayer.

Besides all these purposes, the dance was primarily important in achieving social unity. All persons are in some degree afraid of solitude and the dance was the best means of releasing them from themselves and their fears and bringing them into the stream of life. That is why, even when the purpose of a dance had been lost or when its value as a means of coercing the gods and influencing enemies was no longer believed, it still had its use as a means of social communication.

The primitive dance contained all the elements by which a work of art is composed, whether it be dance, poetry, drama or painting.

Primitive man used movement to express things that he felt deeply but for which he had no words. That is the purpose of all the arts: to say things that can be said in no other way. He found that it was not enough to use a certain movement or phrase once. It had to be repeated several times to be sure that its meaning was understood. Furthermore in mimicking some subject, he found that he must concentrate on some things and leave out others, for if he mimicked everything, he would never be done, and in the second place he would give no emphasis to what he felt was most important. At times some elements were so important that he found it necessary to emphasize them even more, so that he clapped his hands, stamped his feet, drummed with a stick, sang or increased the volume of the musical accompaniment.

In doing these things, he was using elements which have become the basis of all art form. They are: repetition, accent, contrast and distortion, the first three of which together constitute rhythm.

Transition.—We have a great deal of information on the primitive dance because primitive tribes still exist almost as they were centuries ago, preserving the same habits and customs, which are easily studied. The next period of which we have extensive information begins in the 1400s, but there was a period of many centuries between this and the primitive period during which great dancing, on which information is sparse, was performed in Egypt and Greece. Apparently no one at this time thought of inventing a method of signs by which the dances might be written down and preserved for the use of people ages later. Even the written descriptions do not tell us much about the actual form of the dance.

As religion gradually replaced magic, the divine powers that had belonged to everyone became concentrated in a few people, the priests. Likewise the dance, which had been a communal activity, became concentrated in certain groups, and the professional dancer appeared. As the complexities of life increased, more and more people became specialized in particular things and that specialization continues to the present day. In primitive times man was killer of game, tiller of the soil, weaver, dancer, artist and builder; then he began to specialize in only one of these things in which he excelled, and the rest of the things he was required to trade, buy or merely look at and admire. From this point onward the separation between dancer and audience grew ever wider, and the dance itself began to break up into different types for different classes of people: the aristocracy (nobleman and ruler), the middle class (merchant and business man) and the lower classes (worker, artisan and peasant).

The first great center that influenced the western world was Egypt, where there were now religious and secular dances. The secular dances, which employed a wide range of movement for all parts of the body, became more personal and were carried at the height of Egypt's power across to all the Mediterranean countries and profoundly influenced the dances of Spain and Greece.

Eventually Egypt declined and Greece was in the ascendancy. Here the dance was held in greater esteem than it has ever been held before or since. It was practiced by all types of people both for religious purposes and for sheer enjoyment. Great philosophers taught it as a necessity in order to have a healthy mind in a healthy body. It was widely used in the training of soldiers to give them greater poise, co-ordination and strength. As in primitive times it was used to commemorate great events and to celebrate the sowing and the harvest. It was employed by professional dancers and buffoons. Very probably the

LEGONG DANCE of Bali, performed by two Balinese girls in rich costumes. In many of the Oriental dances, the upper part of the body and the arms and hands are used symbolically.

dance was the mother of that other art in which Greece excelled, the drama. Even after the spoken word became of greater importance than the movement, large choruses of dancers were still used.

When Greece's power fell, the dance center moved to Rome. There the art became degenerate and obscene, and the Romans themselves contributed nothing to its development. Later it was taken under the protection of the Christian church and was widely used in religious services until the reformers eventually banished it as indecent and immoral. Nothing further was contributed to the art until the birth of the ballet in Italy in the late 1400s.

Folk and Social Dances.—But the desire to dance could not be banished. There has been no time in the history of the world when it has not been practiced assiduously at some place. It was widespread in India and the Orient, where great dancing may still be seen, but the dances of these countries, although they have often influenced the dance of the western world momentarily, have not had a sufficiently profound effect on the dances of Europe and America to be discussed here. We turn instead to the common people of the West, the slaves, workers and peasants, to find the dances that were later to be adapted in the court and in the beginnings of the ballet.

The folk dance is generally gay and is performed mainly with the feet and legs, although there are exceptions to this in such countries as

Spain where effective use is made of the whole body. It expresses the national characteristics of the people who create it, and the number of folk dances practiced by a given nation will often tell us of its vitality or weakness. After hours of hard work it was these dances that gave amusement and release to the great working classes. The movement in them is usually large, open and free, full of exuberance and gusto.

The movement of the social dance, on the other hand, is usually restrained, refined and close to the body. Its origin is almost invariably a folk dance that has found favor with the ruling classes and has been polished and refined for use in their gala occasions. The animal gusto and vigor of the upper classes seems to have been weakened and effeminized so that they are unable to participate in the dance as do the lower classes. Even in our own day the wild dances borrowed from the Negro have been only fads, eventually disappearing and giving place to the staid, dignified and monotonous fox trot.

Among some of the better-known folk dances that are still being practiced we have, from Scotland, the *sword dance* and the *Highland fling,* both vigorous and spirited in execution and angular in movement. England gives us the *sailor's hornpipe* and the more ordinary *morris dances;* Ireland, the clog and shuffle dances, such as the *jig,* the *reel* and the *hornpipe,* all with complicated foot movement. Some of the best composed dances come from Russia and Poland, such as the *czardás,* the *mazurka,* the *Cossack dance* and the *obertass.* These are full of violent changes in rhythm and are performed with quick, brilliant movement. Italy is best known for its *tarantella,* which is said to have been used originally to cure the bite of the Tarantula spider.

The country richest in dances is Spain. Cadiz, under the influence of dancers from Egypt, became one of the great dance centers of the world. The dances of Gypsy origin are called *flamenco* dances and include *la farruca, el tango* and *el garrotin,* all wild and exuberant and full of violent contrasts in rhythm. The more dignified and stately dances that were cultivated by the court are called Iberian or Classic dances, the most famous of which are the *bolero, las seguidillas* and the *fandango.*

To trace the progressive history of the dance from primitive times until today, we must turn to France. The French invented very few dances themselves, but they are of great importance for two reasons: they served as a melting pot for the national dances of other countries, and they established the first terminology and rules and regulations for the dance. It is to France that we are indebted for the first accurate descriptions of social dances and for the analysis of movement and the setting up of rules that resulted in an Academy of dancing and governed the later history of the ballet. All terminology of any importance, up to the present day, describing steps and series of movements, is of French origin. The French people, although poor at invention and creation, were excellent at systematizing and cataloguing and describing.

One of the most important dance books in the world is the *Orchesography* of an elderly clergyman, under the assumed name of Thoinot Arbeau, describing the social dances that were prominent in the 1500s. It was the first book of its kind to give sufficiently accurate descriptions so that the dances can be recreated today. The most popular dance during the 1500s was the *gaillarde,* a lively dance for a man and woman, of which there were innumerable varieties. Others of importance were the *volte,* the *allemande,* the *pavane* and *sarabande,* both borrowed from Spain, the *courante,* from which the *minuet* and *waltz* were partly derived, and the *gavotte.* It was these social dances of the 16th century that were first used in the ballet.

As court manners became more stiff and formalized, the popular *gaillarde* was replaced during the late 1600s and early 1700s by the *minuet,* which was the essence of the artificiality of that age. It in turn was replaced by the *waltz,* which remained the most popular dance until 1900.

Other dances that were popular in Europe and America up to the 20th century were the *quadrille,* the *lancers,* the *polka,* the *galop,* the *barn dance,* the *Paul Jones,* the *Washington Post,* the *polka-mazurka,* the *polonaise,* the *schottisch,* the *Sir Roger de Coverley* and the *cotillion.*

The Ballet.—Let us suppose that, in celebration of some famous event, we wish to have as festive an entertainment as possible. The committee will choose a rambling theme or story to serve as framework. Then they will hire troupes of masked actors to parade down the aisles, other actors and dancers to form striking tableaux in brilliant costume, musicians and singers to accompany this with a medley of tunes and songs, and possibly even large floats to be drawn across the stage. Interspersed in all this activity there will be occasional dances performed by various troupes. These dances will be ballroom displays of the *waltz,* the *tango,* the *fox trot,* the *rumba* and the *Charleston.* At the end of the entertainment both performers and audience will join in a concluding dance.

It was in such a way as this that the ballet was born in Italy in the late 1400s as a spectacular pageant designed to amuse the nobility. The *gaillardes, gavottes* and other dances that were used were as modern at that time as the *rumba* or the *Susy-Q* were in 1938. In its general form the ballet was at first influenced by the mime and the pantomime, which came to be known as the mummery or masque, and by the great circuses and pageants that were dominant during the height and decline of the Roman Empire.

New Interests and Ideas. There were many influences at work in society that eventually shaped the ballet, and we may stress two in particular. The first was man's interest in himself and his own adventures, whereas previously all of his art works had been concerned solely with gods and supernatural beings. Some things that contributed to this interest were the fact that he had become a Christian and believed in a personal God and a future life, that printing had been invented and that sciences were coming into being whereby things could be more accurately measured, tested and explained.

The second was the increasing interest in time and space that came as a result of the first. Previously he had known little of the world beyond the small town or village in which he lived. He believed that the world was flat and was surrounded by unknown monsters. It was as though he were standing within a small, walled-in arena beyond whose circumference he could not see, then slowly that arena was enlarged and came to include more and more things.

At the time the ballet was created, Leonardo da Vinci, the great Italian painter, was interested in flying machines; Gutenberg had printed the first book; Columbus was bold enough to declare that there should be a land to the west and requested money and ships to find it; the clock and the mirror came into general usage; and perspective, a method of creating depth on a flat surface, was introduced into painting.

All these interests were reflected at first in the subject matter of the ballet. It danced about moons and stars, Indians and tobacco, legendary heroes and nymphs, but it still used an earthy movement, performed almost exclusively by the feet and legs close to the ground.

The Court Masques, which were pageants with interludes of dancing, attracted the attention of Catherine de' Medici, Queen of France. It was not long before the ballet declined in Italy and its center was established in France where it remained until its decline in the late 1800s. Louis XIV established the first Royal Academy of the Dance in 1661, and he himself danced in the ballets invented by Beauchamps and Pécour to the music of Lully.

In the Renaissance. The Renaissance in Italy had focused attention

MINUET, a dance of the seventeenth and eighteenth centuries, in ¾ time. It reached its height in the French court, with Louis XIV introducing it at one of his imperial balls.

upon man as an individual, and it was during the reign of Louis XIV that attempts were being made on all sides to organize this new knowledge and to establish fully the importance and nobility of man. This was also a time of scheming, planning and rationalizing. Everything was to be explained by mechanical and mathematical laws The gardens were laid out in geometric patterns and the hedges and trees clipped into geometric shapes. Fantastic costumes and headdresses prevented one from ever knowing what the human being actually looked like. Even metal rods were worn under the coat up one's spine, partly to prevent one from tiring, since no one sat down but the king, and partly to make one seem as noble as possible. It was natural, then, that movement also should be explained mathematically and mechanically.

Beauchamps described the Five Positions of the feet, which are still used by the ballet today, with the feet turned out at a certain degree of angle and moved precisely only in certain established directions. Symmetrical movements for the arms also were invented, and much attention was given to the correct manner of entering a room, standing, bowing and saluting a lady. It was at this time also that the curve became predominant and afflicted the ballet until the 1900s, as it afflicted everything else. Curves and spirals and circles were so profusely applied to everything from clocks to architecture that their real structure was completely hidden.

The whole life of the period was best expressed in the *minuet*, which was one of the dances used in the ballets. It combined correct, systematic, strictly regulated steps with a certain gaiety and lightness. It was both pompous and delightful, full of affectation yet suffused with charm. The stiff-jointed action of the marionette was considered more beautiful than any possible human movement.

Greater Freedom and Grace. While these rules and regulations were being formulated, the interest in time and space was again felt in the gradual increase during the next two hundred years in aerial movement. The jumps, leaps and toe-dancing defied the laws of gravity. They were used to free the body from the earth and make it as close to a light, ethereal spirit as possible.

In 1681 female dancers were introduced into the ballets for the first time, and they grew increasingly important until the male dancers were often reduced to mere props used to hold them up during difficult elevations or to increase the length of a linear design that could not be done without the male dancer's help. The introduction of the female dancer, coupled with current notions of her supposed fragility and delicacy, added to the ethereal quality of the movement and made the whole of ballet dancing more feminine. (Women, of course, had danced in primitive times in Egypt and Greece and in folk and social dances, but they had not before been allowed to dance on the stage in Europe.)

Each dancer in turn made contri-

butions to the vocabulary of movement, but it was not until the advent of Jean Georges Noverre that revolutionary changes were made. Dancing up to his time had been used as *divertissement* and had become increasingly stilted, partly through the cumbersome costumes and masks that were worn. In 1760 in his book *Letters on the Dance* he pled for reform in costume and took the first steps toward the creation of the *ballet d'action* in which a good, consistent plot was to be expressed entirely in dancing and mime. His purpose was "to break hideous masks, to indicate a manner of dress more noble, to demand action and expression in dancing, to demonstrate the immense distance which lies between mechanical technique and the genius which places

dancing beside the imitative arts."

Noverre himself was not very successful in realizing his aims, but his work was carried on by Dauberval and finally achieved by Salvatore Vigano, who was active in the early 1800s. The *ballet d'action* remained the accepted form until the early 1900s. After this step forward the ballet again declined, and no new movements or other developments have come from France since that time.

Birth of the Modern Ballet. It was the visit of Isadora Duncan, American dancer, to Russia in the first decade of the 20th century that finally caused the revolution in the ballet academy. Michel Fokine was the dancer who led this revolt, inspired by the new, free dancing of Duncan. He

ALLEGRA KENT as Titania, and Jacques d'Amboise as Oberon, in "Midsummer Night's Dream," play by Shakespeare and music composed by Mendelssohn. Ballet, dancing of a drama set to music, was first part of opera. It came into its own in Paris, 1581, when the *Ballet comique de la Reine* coordinated action, music, and decoration.

wished to free the classical ballet from its restrictions, to broaden its scope, to add new steps derived from unexplored folk material, to make fuller use of the entire body and above all to make the ballet a true expression of the Russian spirit.

Fokine was joined by such famous dancers as Mlles. Pavlova, Lopoukowa and Karsavina, Adolph Bolm and the great Nijinsky. Léon Bakst designed costumes and sets, and such composers as Glazunov, Tcherepnin and Rimski-Korsakov provided the musical setting. The Russian Government, which sponsored the academy, disapproved of this revolt and banished them, but fortunately they found a brilliant director in Diaghilev, and in 1909 the Diaghilev Ballet was storming Europe.

They turned to the legends of Russia, Persia and Egypt for subject matter, dispensed with the restrictions of the ballet slipper and the traditional costume and recreated the mimetic drama wherein the designer, the musician and the choreographer (dance composer) worked closely together. The dance was no longer a *divertissement* but grew out of the subject matter itself. Traditional technique was still maintained as a basis.

Brilliant as it was, there remained two problems that could not be solved. One was that the real form of the ballet was not the dance itself but the story upon which dances were hung as beads on a string. Pantomime filled in the intervening places. The other was not able to express the great drama of contemporary life, since the foundations of that technique were laid several centuries before, when people thought and lived differently.

Two of the greatest dancers of the period were Anna Pavlova and Nijinsky. They were followed by such choreographers as Leonide Massine, George Balanchine, and, later, Anthony Tudor and Jerome Robbins. The Diaghilev company finally disbanded. Among today's leading ensembles are the New York City Ballet, London's Royal Ballet, and the Bolshoi Ballet in Moscow.

The classical ballet has recently invaded the field of musical comedy. Here it has become more than just a series of dances arranged on a thread of dramatic narrative. It has become an integral part of the plot.

Ballet today often is designed as a show case for individual technical brilliance. The newer choreographers are, however, supplementing this by making ballets an expression of an actual story or mood. Quite often the music for these new ballets is taken from classical composers.

The Modern Dance.—In rebellion against the mechanical precision of the ballet and its emphasis on perfection of form, a new concept developed in America and came to be known as *The Modern Dance* in contrast to the classic and romantic forms in vogue until that time. Although primarily American in conception, it expressed so well the individualistic movement of the 19th century of which it was a part, that it was readily adopted by European countries, particularly Germany.

The Modern Dance differs from other and older forms primarily because it is expressionistic in nature and does not rely for its acceptance upon its entertainment values or its ritualistic form. Those who follow this form of dance insist, however, that it is not new but merely a continuation of the primitive tribal dances in which man sought to express, without exhibitionism, his personal relationship to the forces which surrounded him. In such a dance form there can be no imitation, no rationalization, and no conventionalization. It is based on movements dictated by what the individual dancer has to impart and not a preconceived principle of design—it is completely unfettered by convention, precise physical disciplines and shuns the usual limitations imposed by musical accompaniment. The dancer usually performs with a background of sounds specifically designed for this presentation, often consisting of a single piano, percussion, gourds, or similar sounds. Under usual circumstances, it would not be possible to perform such a dance to music of a melodic nature unless it had been composed for the specific presentation. The costume and scenic decor are usually simple and functional. Color and lighting are employed for the emotional support they give the dancers rather than for their decorative value.

While the rebellion was general and widespread it was the personality of Isadora Duncan which brought it into focus and made of it a cause. There had been other revolutionaries in dance before her. Noverre, 18th-century ballet master, had advocated taking patterns of conduct and movements from life and developing the dance along realistic lines rather than by means of standardized and overfamiliar material. However, Noverre probably did not perceive the ultimate development which would result one hundred and fifty years later as Isadora Duncan, unshod and clothed in a simple Greek styled tunic, began her evangelism for dancing from the "soul" as an expression of one's own individuality. Duncan sought the "divine expression of the human spirit through the medium of the body's movement". This interest in individualism was typical of her entire life not only artistically but politically and socially as well.

Unfortunately for the new form she advocated, Duncan was equally outspoken and unconventional in her attitude toward religion and society and her dance movement was branded by the unsympathetic as a cult. This charge has often been brought against modern dance because it has no specific vocabulary. It is primarily emotional and as such its only language is movement of a kind that is within itself.

After Isadora Duncan, there came a number of highly creative individuals each of which left a strong imprint in the historical structure of this dance. Ruth St. Denis and Ted Shawn combined forces to form the Denishawn company devoted to the popularization of the form by concert tours and appearances with professional revue-style stage productions. Ruth St. Denis, preoccupied with oriental forms and her "visualization" of musical themes, gave some support to the charges of mysticism. It is to be expected in a dance form placing such a high premium on individuality, that its principal proponents would be individuals or pairs rather than large groups. Three recent artists who constitute the principal shaping forces of this dance are, Martha Graham, Doris Humphrey and Charles Weidman. Humphrey and Weidman were at one time members of the Denishawn group but withdred from it to establish themselves as separate artists. Humphrey's greatest contribution is in the field of composition. Her trilogy "Theatre Piece," "With My Red Fires," and "New Dances" is one of the finest examples of the imaginative work possible in this form of dance. Weidman was for a time a partner of equal status with Humphrey. He brought to their work an incomparable gift of miming and a perfect grasp of formal abstractions. On several occasions, Weidman carried his talent into revue-style Broadway productions but he found as did others who followed him that modern dance is not essentially theatrical. However, its basic vitality and originality have been borrowed by modern theatre dance and overlaid on its form by such splendid teachers and artists as Hanya Holm and Agnes DeMille. In these instances, it has produced a hybrid that is vigorous and dynamic. The older form of ballet has borrowed conspicuously from modern dance and disregarding their fundamental differences the two now freely exchange ideas, methods and personnel. Martha Graham was the supreme technician of the group that was constantly seeking to extend the range of expressional movement beyond any limit hitherto known. These qualities were particularly evident in her "Frontier." Mary Wigman, another of the early leaders, brought from Germany the conviction that her expression could have no finality, no crystallization and that the dance must constantly seek the complete statement of selfhood in which new elements and new principals tend to validate older ones.

Doris Humphrey's death in 1959 removed from the modern dance scene one of its most distinguished figures. However, her influence remains, particularly in the work of her protege and long-time collaborator, Jose Limon. This Mexican-born artist is perhaps best known for his enormously impressive "The Moor's Pavanne," a modern dance adaptation of *Othello*, to the seventeenth-century music of Henry Purcell.

Other artists deserving special recognition are Helen Tamiris, Glück-Sandos, Felicia Sorel and Valerie Bettis. In their work and elsewhere, modern dance continues its dynamic evolution as something truly evocative and individual. Most recently it has begun to incorporate jazz motifs and other elements of popular art, as in some of Jerome Robbins' more uninhibited works. But it has not forsaken its more austere, introspective path.

BIBLIOGRAPHY

ART

General Aspects: History and Theory

BARR, ALFRED H., JR. (ed.). *Masters of Modern Art.* Museum of Modern Art, 1961.

BAUR, J. I. H. *Revolution and Tradition in Modern American Art.* Harvard University Press, 1951.

BILZER, BERT and others. *The Praeger Picture Encyclopedia of Art.* Frederick A. Praeger, Inc., 1958.

BRION, MARCEL. *Romantic Art.* McGraw-Hill, Inc., 1960.

CANADAY, JOHN. *Mainstreams of Modern Art.* Simon & Schuster, Inc., 1959.

CLARK, KENNETH. *The Nude: A Study in Ideal Form.* Bollingen Foundation, 1962.

DOVER, CEDRIC. *American Negro Art.* New York Graphic Society, 1963.

FRANKFORT, HENRI. *The Art and Architecture of the Ancient Orient.* Penguin Books, Inc., 1954.

FRASER, DOUGLAS. *Primitive Art.* Doubleday & Company, Inc., 1962.

GARDNER, HELEN. *Art Through the Ages* (4th ed.). Harcourt, Brace & World, Inc., 1962.

GOETZ, HERMANN. *India: Five Thousand Years of Indian Art.* Crown Publishers, Inc., 1959.

GOMERICK, E. H. *The Story of Art.* Oxford University Press, Inc., 1950.

GRAY, CHRISTOPHER. *Cubist Aesthetic Theories.* The Johns Hopkins Press, 1962.

HAGGAR, REGINALD C. *A Dictionary of Art Terms.* Hawthorn Books, Inc., 1962.

HAJEK, L. *Chinese Art.* Tudor Publishing Co., 1962.

HERBERTS, KURT. *The Complete Book of Artists' Techniques.* Frederick A. Praeger, Inc., 1958.

HOLT, ELIZABETH G. *Literary Sources of Art History.* Princeton University Press, 1947.

HUXLEY, ALDOUS. *On Art and Artists.* Meridian Books, 1963.

KAYSER, WOLFGANG. *The Grotesque in Art and Literature.* Translated by Ulrich Weisstein. Indiana University Press, 1963.

LANGE, K. and HIRMER, M. *Egypt: Architecture, Sculpture, Painting in Three Thousand Years* (c. 3000–30 B.C.). Phaidon Publishers, Inc., 1957.

LEUZINGER, ELSY. *Africa: The Art of the Negro People.* McGraw-Hill, Inc., 1960.

MCCLINTON. *Christian Art Through the Ages.* The Macmillan Co., 1963.

MUNSTERBERG, HUGO. *The Arts of Japan.* Charles E. Tuttle Co., Inc., 1963.

NOTT, STANLEY. *Chinese Jade Throughout the Ages.* Charles E. Tuttle Co., Inc., 1963.

OLSCHKI, LEONARDO. *The Genius of Italy.* Cornell University Press, 1954.

PANOFSKY, ERWIN. *Studies in Iconology.* Oxford University Press, Inc., 1939.

READ, HERBERT. *Art and Industry.* Horizon Press, Inc., 1954.

READ, HERBERT. *The Meaning of Art.* Faber & Faber, Ltd., 1936.

RICE, DAVID TALBOT. *The Art of Byzantium.* Harry N. Abrams, Inc., 1959.

RICE, TAMARA TALBOT. *Russian Art.* Penguin Books, Inc., 1949.

ROBB, DAVID M. and GARRISON, J. J. *Art in the Western World* (4th ed.). Harper & Bros., 1960.

SCHODER, RAYMOND V. *Greek Art.* New York Graphic Society, 1960.

TAYLOR, FRANCIS H. *Fifteen Centuries of Art.* Harper & Bros., 1960.

UPJOHN, E. M. and others. *History of World Art* (2nd ed., rev.). Oxford University Press, Inc., 1958.

WILLETTS, WILLIAM. *Chinese Art.* 2 vols. Penguin Books, Inc., 1958.

WOLDERING, I. *The Art of Egypt* (Art of the World Library). Crown Publishers, Inc., 1963.

WOLFFLIN, H. *Principles of Art History.* Dover Publications, Inc., 1961.

YASHIRO, YUKIO. *2000 Years of Japanese Art.* Harry N. Abrams, Inc., 1958.

Architecture

ANDREWS, WAYNE. *Architecture in America: A Photographic History from the Colonial Period to the Present.* Atheneum Publishers, 1960.

BLAKE, PETER. *The Master Builders.* Alfred A. Knopf, Inc., 1960.

BURCHARD, JOHN and BUSH-BROWN, ALBERT. *The Architecture of America.* Little, Brown & Co., 1961.

CARVER, NORMAN. *Form and Space in Japanese Architecture.* Charles E. Tuttle Co., Inc., 1962.

CONRADS, ULRICH and SPERLICH, HANS. *The Architecture of Fantasy.* Frederick A. Praeger, Inc., 1963.

HAMLIN, TALBOT F. *Architecture Through the Ages.* G. P. Putnam's Sons, 1953.

MORRISON, HUGH. *Early American Architecture.* Oxford University Press, Inc., 1952.

PEVSNER, NIKOLAUS. *An Outline of European Architecture.* Penguin Books, Inc., 1960.

SANFORD, TRENT E. *Story of Architecture in Mexico.* W. W. Norton & Co., Inc., 1947.

SHORT, ERNEST HENRY. *A History of Religious Architecture.* W. W. Norton & Co., Inc., 1951.

SMITH, G. E. KIDDER. *The New Architecture of Europe.* Meridian, 1963.

WATTERSON, JOSEPH. *Architecture: Five Thousand Years of Building.* W. W. Norton & Co., Inc., 1950.

ZEVI, BRUNO. *Architecture as Space: How to Look at Architecture.* Horizon Press, Inc., 1963.

Painting

BARNES, ALBERT C. *The Art in Painting* (3rd ed.). Harcourt, Brace & World, Inc., 1962.

BERENSON, BERNARD. *The Italian Painters of the Renaisssance.* Oxford University Press, Inc., 1959.

CRAVEN, THOMAS. *Treasury of Art Masterpieces from the Renaissance to the Present Day.* Simon & Schuster, Inc., 1952.

FRIEDLAENDER, WALTER. *David to Delacroix.* Translated by Robert Goldwater. Harvard University Press, 1952.

GRABAR, ANDRÉ. *Byzantine Painting.* Skira International Corp., 1954.

HAZAN, F. (ed.). *Dictionary of Modern Painting.* Tudor Publishing Co., 1962.

HUNTER, SAM. *Modern French Painting: Fifty Artists from Manet to Picasso.* Dell Publishing Co., Inc., 1956.

LAKE, CARLTON and MAILLARD, ROBERT (eds.). *A Dictionary of Modern Painting.* Tudor Publishing Co., 1956.

LEMAITRE, HENRI. *The English School of Painting.* Universe Books, Inc., 1955.

McCOUBREY, JOHN W. *American Tradition in Painting.* George Braziller, Inc., 1963.

MYERS, BERNARD S. (ed.). *Encyclopedia of Painting.* Crown Publishers, Inc., 1955.

RELOUGE, I. E. (ed.). *Masterpieces of Figure Painting.* The Viking Press, Inc., 1959.

RICHARDSON, EDGAR P. *A Short History of Painting in America.* Thomas Y. Crowell Co., 1963.

ROSTEN, LEO and the editors of LOOK. *The Story Behind the Painting.* Doubleday & Co., Inc., 1963.

SEUPHOR, M. (ed.). *Dictionary of Abstract Painting.* Tudor Publishing Co., 1962.

SUANN, PETER C. *Chinese Painting.* Universe Books, Inc., 1958.

VASARI, GIORGIO. *Vasari's Lives of the Painters.* (4 vols.) E. P. Dutton & Co., 1927.

WILENSKI, R. H. *Flemish Painters: 1430–1830.* The Viking Press, Inc., 1960.

WILENSKI, R. H. *French Painting.* Charles T. Branford Co., 1962.

WILENSKI, R. H. *Modern French Painters.* Harcourt, Brace & World, Inc., 1954.

Graphic Arts and Printing

BLAND, DAVID. *History of Book Illustrations: The Illustrated Manuscript and the Printed Book.* The World Publishing Co., 1958.

CHRISTENSEN, ERWIN O. *The Index of American Design.* The Macmillan Co., 1950.

HANSLER, ROLF. *Great Drawings of the Masters.* G. P. Putnam's Sons, 1962.

IVINS, WILLIAM M. JR. *How Prints Look.* Metropolitan Museum of Art, 1943.

LANE, RICHARD. *Masters of the Japanese Print: Their World and Their Work.* Doubleday & Co., Inc., 1962.

McMURTRIE, D. C. *Story of Printing and Bookmaking.* Oxford University Press, Inc., 1943.

MARINACCIO, ANTHONY. *Exploring the Graphic Arts*. D. Van Nostrand Co., Inc., 1959.

MICHENER, JAMES. *The Modern Japanese Print: An Appreciation*. Charles E. Tuttle Co., Inc., 1963.

NEWHALL, BEAUMONT. *The History of Photography from 1839 to the Present Day*. Museum of Modern Art, 1961.

ROSENBERG, J. *Great Draughtsmen from Pisanello to Picasso*. Harvard University Press, 1959.

SACHS, PAUL J. *Modern Prints and Drawings*. Alfred A. Knopf, Inc., 1954.

STEINBERG, S.H. *Five Hundred Years of Printing*. Penguin Books, Inc., 1962.

WECHSLER, HERMAN J. *Prints and Printmaking*. Hearthside Press, 1962.

ZAIDENBERG, ARTHUR. *New Encyclopedia of Drawing, Painting, and the Graphic Arts*. A. S. Barnes & Co.

Sculpture

BERTRAM, ANTHONY. *Michelangelo*. E. P. Dutton & Co., 1964.

BUSCH, H., and B. LOHSE. *Renaissance Sculpture*. Macmillan Co., 1964.

DERAMBEZ, PIERRE. *Greek Sculpture*. Tudor Publishing Co., 1962.

ELISOFON, ELIOT. *Sculpture of Africa*. Frederick A. Praeger, Inc., 1958.

HAZAN, F. (ed.). *Dictionary of Modern Sculpture*. George Wittenborn, Inc., 1962.

HURLMANN, MARTIN, and ERIC NEWTON. *Masterpieces of European Sculpture*. Harry N. Abrams, Inc., 1959.

JOHNSON, LILLIAN. *Sculpture*. David McKay Co., Inc. 1960.

POPE-HENNESSY, JOAN. *Italian Renaissance Sculpture*. Phaidon Publishers, Inc., 1958.

READ, HERBERT. *The Art of Sculpture* (2nd ed.). Bollingen Foundation, 1962.

RICHTER, G. M. A. *Sculpture and Sculptors of the Greeks*. Yale University Press, 1950.

SEUPHOR, MICHEL. *The Sculpture of This Century*. George Braziller, Inc., 1960.

WILENSKI, R. *The Meaning of Modern Sculpture*. Basic Books, Inc., 1963.

YALOURIS, NICHOLAS. *Classical Greece: The Elgin Marbles*. New York Graphic Society, 1962.

Ceramics

EBERLEIN, HAROLD D., and ROGER W. RAMSDELL. *The Practical Book of Chinaware*. J. B. Lippincott Co., 1948.

FORD, BETTY D. *Ceramic Sculpture*. Reinhold Publishing Corp., 1964.

HYMAN, NORMAN R. *Ceramics Handbook*. Arco Publishing Co., 1953.

KINGERY, W. O. *Introduction to Ceramics*. John Wiley & Sons, 1960.

LEE, WILLIAM. *Ceramics*. Reinhold Publishing Corp., 1961.

MATSON, F. R. (ed.). *Ceramics and Man*. Aldine Publishing Co.

RADA, PRAVOSLOV. *Book of Ceramics*. Tudor Publishing Co., 1960.

MUSIC

BERNSTEIN, LEONARD. *Joy of Music*. Simon and Schuster, Inc., 1959.

BRIGGS, THOMAS H. *Opera and its Enjoyment*. Teachers College Press, Columbia University, 1960.

BURIAN, K. V. *The Story of World Opera*. Tudor Publishing Co., 1962.

CORBETT, WALTER WILLSON, and COLIN MASON (eds.). *Corbett's Cyclopedic Survey of Chamber Music* (2nd ed.). Oxford University Press, Inc., 1964.

COOPER, MARTIN (ed.). *Concise Encyclopedia of Music and Musicians*. Hawthorn Books, Inc., 1958.

COPLAND, AARON. *Music and Imagination*. Harvard University Press, 1952.

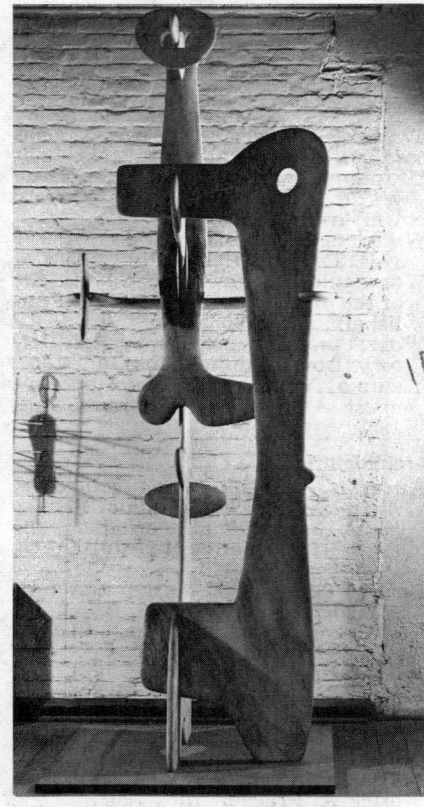

MODERN SCULPTURE by Isamu Noguchi.

COPLAND, AARON. *What to Listen for in Music*. McGraw-Hill, Inc., 1939.

DONINGTON, ROBERT. *The Instruments of Music*. Barnes and Noble, Inc., 1962.

EWEN, DAVID. *Ewen's Musical Masterworks*. Arco Publishing Company, Inc., 1963.

FERGUSON, DONALD N. *Image and Structure in Chamber Music*. University of Minnesota Press, 1964.

GRANT, DONALD J. *History of Western Music*. W. W. Norton & Co., Inc., 1960.

GREEN, BENNY. *The Reluctant Art: The Growth of Jazz*. Horizon Press, Inc., 1963.

GROVE, GEORGE. *Dictionary of Music and Musicians* (5th ed.). 10 vols. St. Martin's Press, Inc., 1954.

HALL, JAMES. *The Art of Song*. University of Oklahoma Press, 1953.

HENTOFF, NAT, and ALBERT McCARTHY. *Jazz*. Holt, Rinehart & Winston, Inc., 1959.

HOWES, FRANK. *Music and its Meanings*. Oxford University Press, Inc., 1958.

LUBBOCK, MARK, and DAVID EWEN. *The Complete Book of Light Opera*. Meredith Publishing Co., 1963.

MACHLIS, JOSEPH. *The Enjoyment of Music*. W. W. Norton & Co., Inc., 1963.

MILLER, WILLIAM HUGH. *Everybody's Guide to Music*. Chilton Company, 1961.

ROBERTSON, ALEX (ed.). *Chamber Music*. Penguin Books, Inc., 1957.

SACHER, JACK. *Music, A to Z*. Grosset & Dunlap, Inc.

SALTER, LIONEL. *Going to a Concert*. Penguin Books, Inc., 1950.

SARGENT, SIR MALCOLM, and MARTIN COOPER (eds.). *The Outline of Music*. Arco Publishing Company, Inc., 1963.

SCHRADE, LEO. *Tragedy in the Art of Music*. Harvard University Press, 1964.

SCHROEDER, IRA. *The Listener's Handbook: A Guide to Music Appreciation*. Iowa State University Press, 1962.

THOMPSON, OSCAR (ed.). *International Cyclopedia of Music and Musicians*. Dodd, Mead & Co., 1958.

ULRICH, HOMER. *Chamber Music: The Growth and Practice of an Intimate Art*. Columbia University Press, 1948.

ULRICH, HOMER. *Music: A Design for Listening*. Harcourt, Brace & World, Inc., 1962.

ULANOV, BARRY. *History of Jazz in America*. The Viking Press, Inc., 1953.

WEINSTOCK, HERBERT. *Music as an Art*. Harcourt, Brace & World, Inc., 1953.

WOODWORTH, G. WALLACE. *The World of Music*. Harvard University Press, 1964.

DANCE

ATKINSON, M. F., and M. HILLMAN. *Dancers of the Ballet*. Alfred A. Knopf, Inc., 1955.

CHUJOY, ANATOLE, (ed.). *Dance Encyclopedia*. A. S. Barnes & Co., 1949.

COHEN, SELMA (ed.). *Dictionary of Modern Ballet*. Tudor Publishing Co., 1962.

O'DOUBLER, MARGARET. *Dance: A Creative Art Experience*. University of Wisconsin Press, 1959.

LLOYD, MARGARET. *The Borzoi Book of Modern Dance*. Alfred A. Knopf, Inc., 1949.

SACHS, CURT. *World History of the Dance*. W. W. Norton & Co., Inc., 1937.

TERRY, WALTER. *Dance in America*. Harper & Row, Publishers, Inc., 1956.

TURNER, M. J. *Dance Handbook*. Prentice-Hall, Inc., 1959.

VOLUME THREE

Concise biographies of more
than three thousand key historical and contemporary figures.

BIOGRAPHY

NYU

Biography

A

Aalto, Alvar (1899–), Finnish architect and designer of furniture. In 1927 he won the competition for the municipal library at Viipuri. The clergy opposed his modern design, and the library was not built until 1934. The Finnish Pavilion at the Paris Exposition won him an international award. His first chair, exhibited in 1932, was made of plywood and was based on a study of sitting postures. His furniture designs became popular. While research professor in architecture at Massachusetts Institute of Technology, he designed its dormitory.

Abbas I or **Abbas the Great** (1557–1628), shah of Persia (1586–1628), succeeding his father, Shah Mohammed. When he ascended the throne, the administrative system was in a state of chaos; the country was threatened by enemies from within and by Tatars and Turks from without. Through successful military campaigns he extended his rule from the Tigris to the Indus. Building bridges and roads to unify and expand his realm and to encourage commerce, he is remembered for a reign that was prosperous and, for his time, extremely enlightened.

Abbey, Edwin Austin (1852–1911), American illustrator and painter. His best-known works are *Quest of the Holy Grail*, for the Boston Public Library, and a series for the capitol at Harrisburg. His pen-and-ink illustrations for editions of Herrick, Shakespeare, and Goldsmith are also famed. He was commissioned as official painter at the coronation of Edward VII of England.

Abbott, Grace (1878–1939), American social worker. Born at Grand Island, she studied at the universities of Nebraska and Chicago and then taught high school. She was head (1921–1934) of the Children's Bureau, U.S. Department of Labor. She wrote on immigration, labor laws, and child welfare.

Abbott, Jacob (1803–1879), American Congregational clergyman and author of children's books. Born in Hallowell, Maine, he graduated from Bowdoin, then studied theology at Andover. He founded in Boston a school for girls based not on stern methods but on kindness and trust. He won popularity with his *Rollo* books and the *Franconia Stories*.

Abbott, Lyman (1835–1922), American Congregational clergyman, editor, and writer, son of Jacob Abbott. In association with Henry Ward Beecher, he edited *Christian Union*, and in 1881 he became editor in chief of this publication, later known as *The Outlook*. Among his many books are *The Theology of an Evolutionist* (1897), *Henry Ward Beecher* (1903), *The Spirit of Democracy* (1910), and *Reminiscences* (1915).

Abdul-Hamid II (1842–1918), sultan of Turkey (1876–1909). Within two years of his accession, Turkey was badly defeated by Russia and lost more than half of its European possessions by the Treaty of San Stefano (1878). Following a long period of misrule, the Young Turks forced him to grant a constitution, then deposed him.

Abdullah ibn-Husein (1882–1951), first king of Jordan, formerly Transjordan (1946–1951). Born in Mecca, in 1908 he became the representative of Mecca in the Turkish chamber of deputies and was later elected vice-president. He cooperated with the British in World War I; in 1919 Abdullah was proclaimed king of Iraq. In 1946, Transjordan became independent, Abdullah was made king, and a treaty of alliance was signed with Great Britain. He helped form the Arab League in 1945, and opposed creation of the state of Israel. In 1949 he took the title "King of Hashemite Jordan."

Abélard or **Abailard, Pierre (Peter Abelard)** (1079–1142), French scholar and theologian, born at Pallet near Nantes. In 1113 he was appointed lecturer at the cathedral school of Notre Dame in Paris, where he taught many who later became famous. He fell in love with and seduced Héloïse, the niece of Canon Fulbert, and they were married secretly. The marriage angered her uncle, who instigated a brutal attack upon Abélard in which he was castrated. He became a monk, Héloïse a nun. In 1140 Abélard was condemned for heresy; he died in 1142 on his way to Rome to present his defense. An important figure in the history of scholastic philosophy, he helped establish the authority of Aristotelian doctrine.

Acton, John Emerich Edward Dalberg-Acton, 1st Baron (1834–1902), English historian. He was a member of Parliament for five years. As leader of the liberal Catholics in England, he opposed the doctrine of papal infallibility. Honored by many universities, he was appointed professor of modern history at Cambridge, where he planned the *Cambridge Modern History;* he died soon after the first volume appeared. His lectures and articles were collected and printed in *Lectures on Modern History*.

Adam, Robert (1728–1792), Scottish architect and designer, born in Kirkcaldy. Architect to George III from 1762 to 1768, he designed the University of Edinburgh and with brothers James and William developed the Adelphi section of London. Robert and James built many public structures and private mansions. The Adam style has wreaths, honeysuckle, and fan ornaments.

Adams, Brooks (1848–1927), American historian, son of Charles Francis Adams. He graduated from Harvard in 1870 and started the practice of law; later he turned to the writing of history. His books include *The Emancipation of Massachusetts* (1887), *The Law of Civilization and Decay* (1895), and *The New Empire* (1902).

Adams, Charles Francis (1807–1886), American statesman, son of John Quincy Adams. In the Massachusetts legislature (1840–1845) he led the conservative antislavery group. He was elected to Congress for two terms. As minister to Great Britain (1861–1868) Adams served with distinction, aiding in the settlement of the *Alabama* claims and helping to prevent England's recognition of the Confederacy. He edited and printed *Works of John Adams* (1850–1856) and *Memoirs of John Quincy Adams* (1874–1877).

Adams, Charles Francis (1835–1915), American historian and railway official, son of Charles Francis Adams (1807–1886). He was chairman (1872–1879) of the Massachusetts board of railway commissioners, and president (1884–1890) of the Union Pacific Railroad. Adams wrote several volumes on railroads but his chief interest was in historical subjects. Among his works are *Richard Henry Dana, A Biography* (1890), *Life of Charles Francis Adams* (1900), and *Studies: Military and Diplomatic* (1911).

Adams, Franklin Pierce, known as **F.P.A.** (1881–1960), American humorist, author, and radio personality. Three New York newspapers ran his column, "The Conning Tower," and he was a charter member of the witty radio program "Information Please." Among his works are *Tobogganing on Parnassus* (1910), *In Other Words* (1912), *Christopher Columbus* (1931), and *The Diary of Our Own Samuel Pepys* (1935).

Adams, Henry (1838–1918), American historian, son of Charles Francis Adams and grandson of John Quincy Adams. He became secretary to his father, who was diplomatic minister to the Court of St. James (1861–1868). From 1870 to 1877 he taught history at Harvard. The outcome of lengthy study was his nine-volume *History of the United States During the Administrations of Thomas Jefferson and James Madison* (1889–1891). Adams' *Mont-Saint-Michel and Chartres* (1904), an interpretation of the medieval spirit, and *The Education of Henry Adams* (1906), an autobiography, reveal a genuine literary artistry.

Adams, John (1735–1826), second president of the United States (1797–1801). He was born in Braintree (now Quincy), Massachusetts. After he graduated from Harvard in 1755, he became a teacher; later he studied law and was admitted to the bar in 1758. A strong advocate of American independence, Adams used every opportunity to press his view. He represented Massachusetts in the First and Second Continental Congresses. Here he counseled several states on preparing their constitutions, and drafted the Plan of Treaties establishing the foreign policy of the new nation. It was Adams who was largely responsible for the selection of Washington as commander in chief.

Adams served with distinction in Europe. In 1782 he obtained a loan from Holland as well as recognition of American independence. As one of the commissioners negotiating the peace treaties with Great Britain, and as U.S. minister there from 1785 to 1788, he ably protected American interests.

After returning home, Adams was chosen as the first vice-president of the United States; in 1792 he was reelected. At the end of Washington's second term in 1796, he was elected president. Jefferson, though he belonged to another party, was elected vice-president. In the election of 1800, Adams was defeated and retired to private life. His writings, published 1850–1856 in ten volumes, included *A Defence of the Constitutions of Government of the United States* and his letters.

Adams, John Couch (1819–1892), British astronomer and mathematician. He was born in Cornwall and graduated from Cambridge, where in 1858 he became professor of astronomy and geometry. In 1845 he computed the position of a hypothetical planet to account for changes in the motion of Uranus. The new planet, named Neptune, was later observed by J. G. Galle to be within one degree of this position. Adams also did valuable research on lunar motions and on the great meteor shower of 1866.

Adams, John Quincy (1767–1848), sixth president of the United States (1825–1829), eldest son of John Adams and Abigail Smith Adams. He accompanied his father, who was pursuing the cause of American independence, to France and Holland. Returning to America, he attended Harvard, graduated in 1788, and began the study of law. In 1794 he was minister to the Netherlands.

Adams became U.S. senator in 1803; when he voted for the Louisiana Purchase and the Embargo Act, irate Federalists forced him to resign by naming his successor prior to elections. He was appointed minister to Russia by President Madison, was one of the commissioners who negotiated the Treaty of Ghent that concluded the War of 1812, and was minister to Great Britain

BETTMANN ARCHIVE

ABÉLARD as a monk with Héloïse as a nun.

from 1815 to 1817. As President Monroe's secretary of state (1817–1825) he was required to handle the negotiations that resulted in the acquisition of Florida, the settlement of a fisheries dispute with Great Britain, and resolution of Russian claims to land adjoining Alaska. He also formulated the policy known as the Monroe Doctrine.

In 1824 Adams was the only Northern candidate for the presidency. Since none of the four candidates—Adams, Andrew Jackson, Henry Clay, William H. Crawford—received a majority vote, the election passed to the House of Representatives. Clay supported Adams and the latter was elected. Adams' appointment of Clay as secretary of state brought accusations of a political bargain. Jackson and his followers were so embittered that little constructive legislation was passed. Adams' unimpressive record as president made his reelection impossible, and the presidency went to Jackson.

Adams is the only president to have accepted a lesser public office after leaving the White House: from 1831 until his death he represented Massachusetts in the U.S. House of Representatives. He spoke frequently against the slaveholders and was tireless in his efforts to contain slavery.

Adams, Samuel (1722–1803), American Revolutionary patriot and statesman, born in Boston. He was a delegate to the Continental Congresses (1774–1781), signed the Declaration of Independence, took an active part in framing the constitution of Massachusetts, and was an influential figure in the U.S. Congress. From 1794 to 1797 he was governor of the state of Massachusetts. One of the leaders of the Revolution, Adams was especially notable for his persuasive articles urging separation from England.

Adams, Will, Japanese title **Anjin Sama,** meaning "Mr. Pilot" (c.1575–1620), navigator, first Englishman to reach Japan. He was engaged in 1598 as pilot major for a Dutch fleet, but only his ship survived the voyage and managed to reach Kyushu in 1600. The shogun at Osaka spared his life because of his knowledge of shipbuilding and navigation. Rising in favor, in 1613 he obtained a trading station for the English at Hirado.

Adams, William Taylor. See *Optic, Oliver.*

Addams, Jane (1860–1935), American social worker, author, and advocate of international peace. She was born in Cedarville, Illinois, and graduated from Rockford College in 1881. For more than four decades she presided over the social settlement in Chicago known as Hull House, which she and Ellen Gates Starr had founded in 1889. Hull House became the model for similar enterprises. She was prominent in movements for social reform, woman suffrage, and international peace. In 1931 she shared the Nobel Peace Prize. Her career in social work is described in her *Twenty Years at Hull House* (1910) and its sequel, *The Second Twenty Years at Hull House* (1930).

Addison, Joseph (1672–1719), English essayist, poet, and statesman. He was educated at Charterhouse School and at Oxford, where he became known as a skillful writer of Latin verse. Having won official favor by his poem *The Campaign* (1704), celebrating Marlborough's victory at Blenheim, Addison became under secretary of state in 1706, and, from 1708 on, was a member of Parliament. He wrote essays in Richard Steele's *Tatler,* and with Steele co-authored the nonpolitical *Spectator.* He also wrote 53 essays for Steele's *Guardian,* a journal started after the *Spectator* was discontinued.

Ade, George (1866–1944), American humorist and playwright, born in Kentland, Indiana. He graduated from Purdue and took up newspaper work. His early sketches, especially in the Chicago *News* (later called *Record*), were read for their pungent comments on everyday life. Notable for his *Fables in Slang,* written in the vernacular, he also wrote the operetta *The Sultan of Sulu* (1902). Other works include *The Girl Proposition* (1902), *The County Chairman* (1903), and *Father and the Boys* (1907).

Adenauer, Konrad (1876–1967), German statesman, chancellor of the Federal Republic of Germany (1949–1963). Born in Cologne; studied law at Bonn, Munich, and Freiburg universities; and became mayor of Cologne in 1917. In 1933 Nazis ousted him from government. He lived in retirement for about 12 years. Cooperating with the West, he succeeded in restoring West German sovereignty in 1955. Died in Rhondorf, near Bonn, Apr. 19, 1967.

Adler, Alfred (1870–1937), Austrian psychologist and psychiatrist, founder of the school of Individual Psychology. He was born and educated in Vienna, and in 1895 graduated from the University of Vienna Medical School. Adler joined Sigmund Freud in 1902, but, disagreeing with Freud's stress on sex as a basis for neurosis, broke with him in 1911 to found his own school. Adler originated the term "inferiority complex." His books include the classic *Understanding Human Nature* (1927), *The Practice and Theory of Individual Psychology* (trans. 1927), and *The Science of Living* (1929).

Adler, Cyrus (1863–1940), American Jewish educator, curator, and historian. He was born in Van Buren, Arkansas, and received degrees from Pennsylvania and Johns Hopkins universities. For many years he was with the Smithsonian Institution as librarian, then assistant secretary. Adler founded the American Jewish Historical Society (1892), became president of Dropsie College (1908), and was president of the Jewish Theological Seminary of America (1924–1940) and of the American Jewish Committee (1929–1940). Author of several books, he served as editor of the *Jewish Encyclopedia,* the *American Jewish Year Book,* and the *Jewish Quarterly Review,* and as editorial board chairman for the New Jewish Translation of the Bible.

Adler, Felix (1851–1933), American educator and ethical reformer. He was born in Alzey, Germany, and was brought to America in 1857. In 1870 he graduated from Columbia College, and, after additional studies at Berlin and Heidelberg, was appointed professor of Hebrew and Oriental literature at Cornell University. In 1876 he established the New York Society for Ethical Culture, designed for those who desired spiritual fellowship outside the orthodox churches.

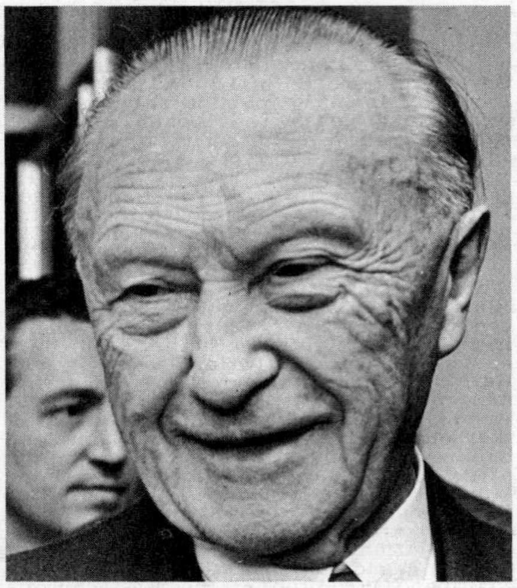

UNITED PRESS INTERNATIONAL

KONRAD ADENAUER

This society strongly influenced educational methods and social reform movements. Adler became professor of social and political ethics at Columbia in 1902, and for more than a quarter of a century was chairman of the National Child Labor Committee. Among his books are *An Ethical Philosophy of Life, Incompatibility in Marriage,* and *The Reconstruction of the Spiritual Ideal.*

Adrian IV (c.1100–1159), pope (1154–1159). Born at Langley, he was the only Englishman ever elected to the papacy. His name was Nicholas Breakspear. Successively abbot of St. Rufus (near Avignon) and cardinal bishop of Albano, he was elected pope in 1154. Documents reveal that he granted Henry II authority to conquer Ireland.

Aeschylus (525–456 B.C.), Greek dramatic poet, born at Eleusis, Attica. He was the earliest of the great tragic dramatists of Greece. He distinguished himself as a soldier at the Battle of Marathon and at Salamis prior to his success as a playwright. In the annual competitions at Athens, he first gained the prize for tragedy in 484 B.C. *The Persians,* earliest of his extant works, formed part of a trilogy that won the prize again in 472. In 468 he was defeated by Sophocles and is said to have gone to the court of Hiero, king of Syracuse.

Altogether, Aeschylus composed 70 tragedies, winning 13 first prizes. However, only seven of his tragedies remain: *The Persians, Seven Against Thebes, The Suppliants, Prometheus Bound* (only surviving drama of the Prometheus trilogy), *Agamemnon, Choephoroe,* and *Eumenides* (the last three forming the trilogy *Oresteia,* based on the story of Orestes). Prior to Aeschylus' plays, only one actor appeared on the stage at a time; by bringing on a second, he in effect originated dramatic dialogue. The splendor of his poetry as well as his innovations in drama justify his recognition as creator of Greek tragedy.

Aesop (c.620–c.560 B.C.), storyteller, reputedly the Greek author of *Aesop's Fables.* Nothing is actually known of his life, but it is thought that he was born a slave, received his freedom, and then attached himself to the court of Croesus, king of Lydia. It is supposed the tales were transmitted orally. Aesop's fables, mentioned by Aristophanes and Plato, were put into Greek verse by Babrius (c.1st century A.D.), and soon Phaedrus translated them into Latin.

Aëtius, Flavius (c.396–454), Roman general. He fought successfully against the Franks and the Gauls. His greatest victory was that over Attila the Hun at Châlons-sur-Marne in 451. Jealous of Aëtius, the emperor Valentinian III stabbed him to death.

Aga Khan, hereditary title of the spiritual leaders of the Ismaili Muslim community. **Aga Khan I,** original name **Hasan Ali Shah** (1800–1881), traced his descent from rulers of Egypt and Persia, and from Fatima, daughter of the Prophet Mohammed. He was governor-general of the province of Kerman in Persia, but left after a quarrel with the shah and went to India. As a spiritual leader in India he greatly aided the British government; for these services he received the title "His Highness the Aga Khan" and a large pension. His work was carried on by his son, **Aga Khan II,** who died in 1885; then, at the age of eight, his grandson, **Aga Khan III,** real name **Aga Sultan Sir Mohammed Shah** (1877–1957), became imam. He was educated in England at Eton and Cambridge. A leader in the establishment of the All-India Muslim League (1906) as well as its first president, he worked to advance Indian independence. Immensely wealthy, he founded and subsidized the Muslim university at Aligarh. **Aga Khan IV,** original name **Karim al Hussaini Shah** (1936–), succeeded, in 1957, his grandfather, Aga Khan III, as imam. He was educated at Le Rosey in Switzerland and attended Harvard University. While at Harvard he was recalled to Pakistan to assume the role of Aga Khan IV.

Aga Mohammed Khan. See *Agha Mohammed Khan.*

Agassiz, Alexander (1835–1910), Swiss-American scientist and author, born in Neuchâtel, Switzerland, son of Louis Agassiz. He studied at Harvard and at its Lawrence Scientific School, and became an assistant in the U.S. Coast Survey in 1859. From 1860 until his death he was associated with the Museum of Comparative Zoology at Harvard. Development of the Calumet and Hecla mines in Michigan brought him wealth, and he gave generously to Harvard and other institutions. Agassiz went on many explorations of coastal waters and reefs and became one of the foremost authorities on marine zoology. He wrote *North American Starfishes* (1877) and other studies.

Agassiz, Louis, in full **Jean Louis Rodolphe Agassiz** (1807–1873), Swiss-American naturalist, born in Môtier, Switzerland. He studied at Zurich, Heidelberg, and Munich universities, eventually becoming interested in general scientific research, especially in connection with fossil fishes. He was made professor of natural history at the University of Neuchâtel (1832–1845), where he wrote a five-volume treatise, *Recherches sur les poissons fossiles* ("Researches on Fossil Fishes"), 1833–1834. From 1835 to 1845 his summers were spent examining Alpine glaciers; in 1840 his *Etudes sur les glaciers* ("Studies of Glaciers") was published. Agassiz came to the United States in 1846 to lecture for the Lowell Institute. In 1848 he was appointed professor of natural history at Harvard and founded there the famous Museum of Comparative Zoology. He was an inspiring teacher whose lectures served to popularize science; his summer school on Penikese Island in Buzzards Bay led to the establishment of biological stations and greatly influenced the teaching of natural history. Among his other works are *Fresh Water Fishes of Central Europe* (1839–1842) and *Contributions to the Natural History of the United States* (1857 ff.).

Agee, James (1909–1955), American novelist, poet, motion-picture critic, and script writer. He was born in Knoxville, Tennessee, and was educated at Philips Exeter Academy and Harvard. His first volume of poetry was *Permit Me Voyage* (1934). A study of the life of Alabama sharecroppers produced *Let Us Now Praise Famous Men*

(1941). During the years 1939 to 1948 he wrote reviews of motion pictures for *Time* and *The Nation*. After 1948 he worked primarily on scripts and adaptations for both screen and television, notably such outstanding films as *The Quiet One, The African Queen*, and *Night of the Hunter*. Published posthumously, his best-known novel, *A Death in the Family*, won the Pulitzer Prize in 1958, and again in 1961 in its dramatized form, *All the Way Home*.

Agesilaus II (c.444–360 B.C.), king of Sparta (c.400–360 B.C.). He brilliantly defended his country against the Corinthian league of Greek states. His victory at Coronea in Boeotia (394) forced the allies to make a peace treaty favorable to Sparta. He also saved his country from disaster after the Spartans met defeat at Leuctra in 371.

Agha Mohammed Khan (1720–1797), shah of Persia (1794–1797) and founder of the Kajar Dynasty. He overthrew the reigning Zand Dynasty (1779–1794) and its chief ruler, Karim Khan. When he was assassinated, his nephew Fath Ali became shah.

Agricola, Gnaeus Julius (37–93), Roman governor and general, father-in-law of the historian Tacitus. While Agricola was governor of Britain, the island was completely subjugated by the Romans for the first time, and was ruled with great integrity and administrative ability. He defeated the Caledonians of Scotland but could not consolidate his gains. He is the subject of Tacitus' *Agricola*, a remarkable biographical sketch.

Agrippa, Marcus Vipsanius (63–12 B.C.), Roman general and statesman. As naval commander at the Battle of Actium (31), he led the force that routed the fleets of Antony and Cleopatra, thus helping to establish Octavian (Augustus) as sole ruler of the Roman world and first Roman emperor. Agrippa became the trusted subordinate of the emperor and held many responsible offices. As chief magistrate he did much to improve and beautify Rome.

Aiken, Conrad Potter (1889–), American poet and novelist. He was born in Savannah, Georgia, and graduated from Harvard in 1911. Aiken wrote poems, short stories, and some long prose works. He won the 1930 Pulitzer Prize for his *Selected Poems*, the 1954 National Book Award for *Collected Poems*, and the 1956 Bollingen Award for *A Letter from Li Po*. Other works are the novels *Blue Voyage* (1927) and *King Coffin* (1935) and his autobiographical *Ushant* (1952). From 1950 to 1952 he was consultant in poetry for the Library of Congress.

Airy, Sir **George Biddell** (1801–1892), English mathematician, astronomer, physicist, and engineer. He was born at Alnwick and graduated from Trinity College, Cambridge, in 1823. Soon after, he published his *Mathematical Tracts* on lunar theory and other subjects. As astronomer royal at Greenwich, he introduced many improvements and carried on investigations in lunar theory, the magnetism of iron ships, density of the earth, and a variety of problems.

Akbar, known as **Akbar the Great** (1542–1605), Mogul emperor (1556–1605) of India who actually began his rule in 1560. He was an excellent administrator, and built roads, established a uniform system of weights and measures, introduced legal and social reforms, encouraged art and education, and was tolerant toward all religions. During his reign the empire was extended to include all of Hindustan north of the Deccan.

Akeley, Carl Ethan (1864–1926), American taxidermist, naturalist, sculptor, and author. He was born on a farm in Orleans County, New York. From 1895 to 1909 he was associated with the Field Museum in Chicago, and after 1909 with the American Museum of Natural History. He was a taxidermist of great skill, as his extraordinarily lifelike bronzes and habitat groupings in American museums bear witness, raising taxidermy to a fine art; his methods have been widely adopted by museums. In 1926 he created a wild-game sanctuary, Parc Albert, in the Belgian Congo. He died of tropical fever.

à Kempis, Thomas. See *Thomas à Kempis*.

Alaric I (c.370–410), king of the Visigoths (West Goths). After his invasion of Greece (395–396), he was appointed prefect of Illyricum by Arcadius, emperor of the East. Spurred on by this prize, he penetrated northern Italy (c.400) but was checked by the Roman general Stilicho and persuaded to shift allegiance to Honorius, emperor of the West. Believing himself betrayed, Honorius had the general executed (408), whereupon Alaric stormed Rome. He entered into an agreement with Honorius by which he was to receive a huge sum of gold. The emperor failed to keep his promise and Alaric's troops plundered the city three days, sparing only the Christian churches.

Alba, Duke of. See *Alva or Alba, Duke of*.

Albee, Edward Franklin (1928–), American playwright. He was born in Washington, D.C., and attended Trinity College. He wrote his first play, *Aliqueen*, at the age of 12. In 1959 his one-act play *The Zoo Story* was produced for the first time in Germany; it premiered in New York in 1960 and has since been often produced in off-Broadway theaters. *The Death of Bessie Smith*, a one-act play, was produced in Berlin in 1960 and in New York in 1961. His *Who's Afraid of Virginia Woolf?* appeared on Broadway in 1962; it won the Drama Critics' Circle Award of 1963 as well as a number of other notable awards. In 1960 Albee received the Vernon Rice Award for outstanding achievement of an off-Broadway production, and in 1961 he won the Lola D'Annunzio Award for "sustained accomplishments in playwriting." Albee's other works include *The American Dream* (1960), *The Sandbox* (1960), *The Ballad of the Sad Cafe* (1963), and *Tiny Alice*, which appeared on Broadway in 1965 and aroused much controversy as to its interpretation.

Albéniz, Isaac (1860–1909), Spanish pianist and composer, born in Catalonia. He made concert tours of Europe and the United States, gaining fame as a brilliant pianist. His compositions, notably the suite *Iberia* (1906–1909), draw heavily on Spanish folk themes and rhythms.

Albers, Josef (1888–), abstract painter, glass designer, photographer, and typographer. Born in Westphalia, Germany, he obtained his schooling in Berlin, Essen, and at the Bauhaus, where he subsequently taught (1925–1933) after the institution moved to Dessau. From 1933 to 1950 Albers was a professor at Black Mountain College, North Carolina, and since 1955 has taught at Yale University. A highly esteemed pedagogue, he has exercised a strong influence on twentieth-century art. He is most noted for his refinement of color theory and its application to achieve highly subtle effects within the simplest rectilinear framework. Much of his painting is done on glass; the sandblasting of designs on the glass surfaces is accomplished by a process invented by him.

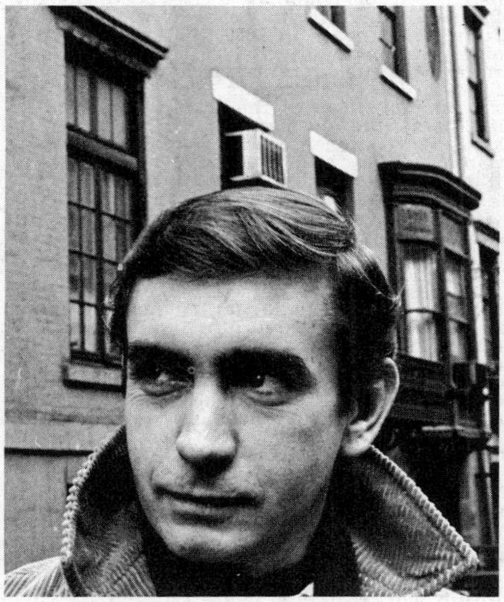

LOOK MAGAZINE

EDWARD ALBEE

Albert I (1875–1934), king of the Belgians (1909–1934), son of Philip, count of Flanders. He was born in Brussels and attended the Military Academy. Traveling extensively, he toured the United States in 1898, and made a study of American railways. In 1900 he married Elizabeth, a duchess of Bavaria, and in 1909 became king. Albert's dedication to social reform and to the commercial and industrial development of his country won him great popularity. He was active in the military campaigns of World War I. After the war, he devoted himself to the rehabilitation of the devastated regions of the country. While mountain climbing near Namur, Albert fell to his death. His eldest son reigned next, as Leopold III.

Albert, Prince (1819–1861), prince consort of England, husband of Queen Victoria. He was a son of the hereditary duke of Saxe-Coburg-Gotha (Germany). In 1840 he married Victoria, and in 1857 the formal title "Prince Consort" was conferred upon him. He was a man of culture and progressive ideas. Their marriage was a happy one, and Victoria owed much of her success to the good judgment of her husband. He was not, however, popular with the English, who claimed he interfered in national politics.

Alberti, Leon Battista (1404–1472), Italian architect and humanist, born in Florence. Like many Renaissance artists, his versatility encompassed a wide range of activities: painting, music, literature, the sciences. He wrote treatises on such diverse subjects as family life, law, care of horses, and moral virtue, as well as love poems, fables, and satirical works. However, he is best remembered as the first Renaissance architect to identify the fundamental elements of classic design and to adapt Roman forms and Greek principles of design to Renaissance buildings. Two of his most distinguished works are the Rucellai Palace at Florence and the Church of San Francesco at Rimini. His *De re aedificatoria* ("On the Art of Building") was highly esteemed and was translated into many languages.

Albertus Magnus or **Albert the Great,** also known as "Doctor Universalis" (1206?–1280), medieval scholastic, theologian, and natural scientist. He was born in Lauingen, Germany, and studied at Padua. Having entered the newly founded Dominican order, he taught in the schools of Hildesheim, Regensburg, and Cologne, and at the University of Paris. His most distinguished pupil was Thomas Aquinas. Commenting extensively on the writings of Aristotle, Albertus served to popularize these works. He sought to reconcile Aristotelianism with theology and the natural sciences, of which he had a vast fund of knowledge, and in so doing spurred the development of the natural sciences.

Albuquerque, Affonso de (1453–1515), Portuguese admiral. His career was extremely successful. He extended Portuguese power over the Malabar coast, Ormuz, and the peninsula of Malacca, and made the Portuguese name respected throughout India.

Alcaeus (fl.600 B.C.), Greek lyric poet, born in Mytilene, Isle of Lesbos. He wrote hymns, love songs, drinking songs, and political odes, of which only fragments remain. Alcaeus invented a form of stanza called, in his honor, the Alcaic, which was successfully used by the Latin poet Horace.

Alcibiades (c.450–404 B.C.), Athenian general. He was for a time a pupil of Socrates, by whose virtues he seems to have been little influenced. He was handsome and talented, but thoroughly unprincipled. His career as a soldier began and ended with the Peloponnesian War (431–404 B.C.) between Athens and Sparta. Chosen to lead an expedition against Syracuse, in Sicily (415), he was accused of the strange mutilation of all the Hermae (busts of Hermes) in Athens. He escaped trial by fleeing to Sparta, where he plotted against Athens. Distrusted by the Spartans, he fled to Asia Minor (412), where he allied himself with the Persians. Recalled to Athens, Alcibiades defeated the Spartan fleet at Abydos and Cyzicus (411, 410), and then returned to Athens; but after the final defeat of Athens, he fled to Phrygia, and there he was murdered.

Alcock, Sir **John William** (1892–1919), English aviator. He received his aviation certificate in 1912, and from the outbreak of war in 1914 until 1917 he was an instructor in the Royal Naval Air Force. He then distinguished himself in active combat duty, leaving the Air Force in 1919. On June 14–15, 1919, with Lieutenant Arthur Whitten Brown as navigator, Alcock made aviation history by flying from St. John's, Newfoundland, to Clifden, Ireland—a distance of 1,960 miles—in 16 hours 12 minutes, the first nonstop transatlantic flight. He was knighted for this heroic accomplishment.

Alcott, Amos Bronson (1799–1888), American educator and author, father of Louisa May Alcott. He was born near Wolcott, Connecticut, and received a meagre education. First a farmhand, then book peddler, he was inspired by the Quakers to become a teacher. From 1828 to 1833 he directed schools in Boston and in Germantown; in 1834 he established in Boston a school based on new methods. It was far in advance of its time, and although it demonstrated the value of his methods, it was misunderstood and misrepresented; he closed it in 1839. In 1844 he was the moving spirit in the communal experiment at Fruitlands, near Harvard; this, too, failed. Subsequently he traveled widely, delivering lyceum addresses or conducting "conversations" with special groups on a variety of topics. He was an exponent of that American transcendentalism that found in Emerson its literary spokesman. In 1879 Alcott founded the Concord Summer School of Philosophy and Literature. His writings include *Principles and Methods of Infant Instruction* (1830), *The Doctrine and Discipline of Human Culture* (1836), *Orphic Sayings*, contributed to *The Dial* of Boston

(1839–1842), *Ralph Waldo Emerson* (1865–1882), and *Tablets* (1868).

Alcott, Louisa May (1832–1888), American author, daughter of Amos Bronson Alcott, born in Germantown, Pennsylvania. She lived at Concord, Massachusetts, in Orchard House, which is pictured in *Little Women* and which has been preserved as a memorial. *Hospital Sketches* (1863) was inspired by her experiences as a volunteer nurse during the Civil War. Miss Alcott is at her best in juvenile stories, and these books are still read and loved. Among her other works are *An Old-Fashioned Girl* (1870), *Little Men* (1871), *Eight Cousins* (1875), and *Jo's Boys* (1886). *Little Women* (1868–1869), possibly the most popular girls' book ever written in English, was successfully dramatized for the stage and for motion pictures.

Alcuin or **Albinus** (735–804), English scholar. Born in York and educated at the archbishop's school there, he later became principal of this school. From 781 to 790 he was in residence at Charlemagne's court at Aachen, where he directed the academy of the palace. In 796 he was made abbot of St. Martin's at Tours. He left, in addition to poems and letters, extensive writings on theology, philosophy, philology, rhetoric, and mathematics.

Alden, John (1599–1687), one of the founders of Plymouth Colony. He was born in England, and came to America on the *Mayflower* in 1620; he was a signer of the Mayflower Compact. He settled at Duxbury, Massachusetts, married Priscilla Mullens, and had a long and honored record as a magistrate in the colony. He also served as governor's assistant and deputy governor. Alden is best remembered as the hero of Longfellow's poem *The Courtship of Miles Standish*, though the story is fictional.

Aldhelm (c.640–709), English scholar and cleric, abbot of Malmesbury (c.675–709), and first bishop of Sherborne (705–709). He founded schools and built several churches. He wrote a treatise on Latin prosody containing his famous 101 riddles, a treatise on the saints, and poems in English.

Aldington, Richard (1892–1962), English poet and novelist. Born in Hampshire and educated at the University of London, he became a leader of the Imagist school of English verse writing. In 1919 Aldington worked on the London *Times* literary supplement. He served in World War I (1916–1918) and lived in Europe until the outbreak of World War II; in 1939 he became a resident of the United States. His works include translations from Greek, French, and medieval Latin; a life of Voltaire (1926); and his verse: *Images* (1915), *Images of War* (1919), *Images of Desire* (1919), *A Fool i' the Forest* (1925), *A Dream in the Luxembourg* (1930), *Life Quest* (1935), and *The Crystal World* (1938). He also wrote the novels *Death of a Hero* (1929), *All Men Are Enemies* (1933), *Very Heaven* (1937), and *Rejected Guest* (1939); short stories; an autobiography *Life for Life's Sake* (1941).

Aldrich, Nelson Wilmarth (1841–1915), American politician and financier. He was born in Foster, Rhode Island. Successful in business, he entered the arena of politics and was elected to Congress in 1878; he was a member of the Senate from 1881 to 1911. His name is associated with tariff and currency legislation. He was co-author of the Payne-Aldrich Tariff Act of 1909 and chairman of a monetary commission that published recommendations for changes in U.S. banking that led to the Federal Reserve System.

Aleichem, Sholem or **Sholom**, pseudonym of **Solomon Rabinowitz** (1859–1916), Yiddish author and humorist. Born in Pereyaslav, Russia, he received the traditional Hebrew schooling. His name means "Peace be unto you." At the outset he wrote poems and stories in Russian and Hebrew but in 1883 turned to Yiddish. He founded (1888) and edited *Die Yiddishe Folksbibliotek*, to which eminent writers contributed, and raised the prestige of Yiddish as a literary language. By 1914, when he took up residence in the United States, he was known as "the Jewish Mark Twain." Through such beloved characters as Tevye the Dairyman (dramatized in the Broadway success *Fiddler on the Roof*, 1964), Sholem Aleichem recreated Jewish small-town life in Russia with remarkable perceptiveness, warmth, and humor. There have been many translations of his works.

Alemán Valdés, Miguel (1902–   ), Mexican president. He was born in Sayula, in the state of Veracruz, and was educated in the public schools; he studied law, especially labor law, and began practice in 1928. Because of his knowledge of agrarian law, in 1930 he was appointed a consulting attorney for the Department of Agriculture. Later

he became a justice of the Superior Court. He was elected senator from Veracruz, and then was governor of the province from 1936 to 1940. From 1940 to 1945 he served as minister of the interior. He was elected president of Mexico and took office December 1, 1946, to serve a six-year term. His accession meant for Mexico a break with the past and the beginning of a new era of progress, economically and socially.

Alessandri Palma, Arturo (1868–1950), Chilean lawyer and statesman, president (1920–1925, 1932–1937). He was born near Linares, of Italian lineage. A leader of the Liberal group, Alessandri was minister of finance (1913–1918), and of the interior (1918–1920). In 1920 he ran for president of Chile as a member of the Liberal Alliance, an anti-Conservative coalition party, and was elected. He attempted many social and political reforms, but was forced out of office by the depression and by an army revolt in 1924. He was again elected president in 1932 and served through 1937.

Alexander I (1777–1825), czar of Russia (1801–1825), son of Paul I and grandson of Catherine the Great. Alexander began his reign with a show of liberal ideas: he encouraged literature, established a council, and began to codify the laws. Later he became more conservative and was influenced by the reactionary Metternich of Austria. He was temporarily an ally of Napoleon, but it was during his reign that Napoleon's Grand Army was destroyed (1812) while invading Russia. In 1815 Alexander formed a league with the rulers of Austria and Prussia known as the Holy Alliance.

Alexander II (1818–1881), czar of Russia (1855–1881), son of Nicholas I. He came to the throne during the Crimean War. After the humiliating peace of 1856, the emperor gave his attention to internal reforms: serfs and state peasants were freed and given land. Though land allotments were inadequate, the emancipation of the serfs, completed in 1861, was the outstanding achievement of his reign. Later Alexander adopted a reactionary policy and repressive measures. He was assassinated by the Nihilists in 1881.

Alexander III (1845–1894), czar of Russia (1881–1894), son of Alexander II, whom he succeeded. Openly opposed to the liberal policies of his father, he vigorously repressed the Nihilists and other dissenters, and was a harsh persecutor of the Jews. During his reign the gentry became more powerful in local government. However, his ministers of finance established policies that improved the financial condition of the country. He terminated Russia's bonds with Germany and initiated an alliance with France. He was succeeded by his son, Nicholas II, last of the czars.

Alexander III, called **Alexander the Great** (356–323 B.C.), king of Macedonia (336–323 B.C.), and conqueror of the Persian empire, son of Philip II. As a youth, Alexander displayed uncommon ability and astuteness; for a time Aristotle was his preceptor and taught him philosophy, natural science, and literature. In 338 he fought at Chaeronea. Philip was assassinated in 336, and Alexan-

der had scarcely taken the throne when he had to curb a revolt by Balkan tribes. He was more severe with rebellious Thebes and razed all but the temples and the house of Pindar. In 334 he defeated a Persian force at the Granicus. A year later he was victorious at Issus, capturing the Persian army treasure, his first wealth. Advancing to Phoenicia, he took Tyre and Gaza, then occupied Egypt. Here, in 332, he founded Alexandria, considered his greatest monument.

In control of the eastern Mediterranean coast, Alexander next renewed his assault on Persia, shattering Darius' army in the Battle of Arbela (331) and capturing Babylon, Susa and Persepolis (with their fabulous royal wealth), and the Median capital, Ecbatana. Macedonian hegemony stretched from the Adriatic to the distant borders of India, an unknown and mysterious land.

In 327 Alexander began his campaign to invade India. However, his soldiers refused to go farther. They were weary after a long year's marching and combat, and their recent bizarre experience of fighting at the Jhelum against armored elephants had shaken them. Moreover, they resented Alexander's attitude toward the conquered Asians, for he treated them as equals, not subjects. Thus compelled to turn back (326), Alexander followed the Indus. At the river mouth he dispatched a fleet, commanded by Nearchus, to explore the Persian Gulf for a West-East waterway, while he continued on land. Despite severe hardships, the fleet succeeded, and rejoined the army at Babylon (324). The new route served to stimulate trade with India.

To shape his newly expanded empire into a commonwealth of peoples, the young king commanded mass intermarriages (himself wedding Roxana, a Bactrian princess), and insisted that administrative office be held by Orientals as well as by Greeks; he planted colonies along trade routes and reorganized the army as an allied police force. Alexander fell ill at Babylon, and within a few days died, more from exhaustion than from fever; he was only 33 years old.

The great empire of Alexander was divided among his chief generals, and their successors continued for centuries. But his impact on history goes beyond military conquest. In his aspiration to fuse the many peoples of the empire and to bring them the fruits of Greek civilization, Alexander carried the language and much of the culture of Greece over immense expanses of the ancient world, and by so doing, inaugurated the rich Hellenistic culture.

Alexander, Grover Cleveland (1887–1950), American baseball player. He pitched more games (696) than any other player in the National League and also won more (373). He spent twenty years in the major leagues and pitched 90 shutout games, including 16 in one year (1916). Alexander was elected to the baseball Hall of Fame in 1938.

Alexander Nevski (c.1220–1263), Russian ruler and national hero, born in Vladimir. In the absence of his father, Prince Yaroslav of Novgorod, Alexander fought bravely to keep

CHARLES PHELPS CUSHING

ALEXANDER THE GREAT, Greek conqueror.

BETTMANN ARCHIVE

ALEXANDER NEVSKI, Russian national hero.

out the Swedes and Teutonic Knights, earning the surname "Nevski" in recognition of his victory over the Swedes on the Neva River (1240). In 1252 he was made grand duke of Vladimir.

Alexander Severus (c.208–235), Roman emperor (222–235), adopted son of Heliogabalus, whom he succeeded. The loftiness of his personal character was not matched by administrative ability, and he was unable to enforce military discipline. In 235, while leading a campaign against the Germans in Gaul, he was killed by order of Maximinus, a legionary who succeeded him to the throne.

Alexis I Mikhailovich (1629–1676), second Romanov czar of Russia (1645–1676), son of Michael (Mikhail). By treaty with Chmielnicki (1654), eastern Ukraine came under Russian rule. In the period 1654 to 1667 he fought against Poland, acquiring possession of Smolensk. But his war with Sweden proved unsuccessful, and he also had difficulty subduing the revolt led by Stenka Razin. He extended his conquests eastward in Asia. Alexis promulgated a revised legal code, and took the first step toward Westernization of Russia—thus easing the way for the work of his son, Peter the Great.

Alexius I, known as **Grand Comnenus** (c. 1180–1222), emperor of Trebizond (1204–1222), grandson of the Byzantine emperor Andronicus I. At the capture of Constantinople in 1204, he made himself master of Trebizond, and later raised it from the position of a province of the Byzantine Empire to that of an independent empire. He later launched an attack against Theodore I of Nicaea, but was unsuccessful.

Alexius I Comnenus (1048–1118), Byzantine emperor (1081–1118), born in Constantinople. In 1081 he deposed his predecessor, Nicephorus III, and undertook the rule of an empire ringed with hostile forces. Alexius skillfully exploited the antagonisms of his enemies, setting Turkish tribes against each other. An alliance with Venice helped to offset the Norman threat. He persuaded the soldiers of the First Crusade who had invaded his land to go on to Asia Minor.

Alfieri, Conte **Vittorio** (1749–1803), Italian dramatic poet, born in Asti, Piedmont. He began to write at the age of 25 and produced 19 tragedies, several comedies, lyric verse (including odes on American independence), and an autobiography. He wrote in the classic Tuscan dialect. His patriotic ardor helped to arouse a desire for Italian national unity. *Saul* (1782) and *Maria Stuarda* (1804) are among the best known of his works, most of which have been translated into English.

Alfonso V (1385–1458), king of Aragon and of Sicily (1416–1458) and of Naples (1443–1458). He was called "the Magnanimous," and his patronage of art and letters made him a notable figure of the Renaissance.

Alfonso X, called **Alfonso the Wise** (c.1226–1284), king of Castile and León (1252–1284), son of Ferdinand III. As a political and military leader, he was unsuccessful. However, as a man of great learning, his achievements lay in his determination to compile and to unify all human knowledge. He encouraged the study of astronomy and other branches of learning, had many Arab scientific treatises translated, and directed the compilation of laws into a unified code. This code and the two chronicles, *Crónica general,* a history of Spain, and *General estoria,* a history of the world, were written in the vernacular. Alfonso's court became one of the intellectual centers of Europe.

Alfonso XII (1857–1885), king of Spain (1874–1885), son of Isabella II. In 1870 his mother abdicated in his favor, and in 1874 he proclaimed himself monarch of Spain. He suppressed the Carlist revolutionaries (1876), followers of the pretender Don Carlos, established order, and stabilized finances.

Alfonso XIII (1886–1941), king of Spain (1886–1931), posthumous son of Alfonso XII. His mother, Queen María Cristina of Austria, acted as regent until 1902. In 1906 Alfonso married Princess Victoria Eugenia of Battenberg, granddaughter of Queen Victoria of England. During World War I, Alfonso kept Spain neutral. He supported the dictatorship of Primo de Rivera. The economic crisis of 1929, Rivera's downfall in 1930, and the huge vote for a republic in the election of 1931 forced Alfonso into exile (1931).

Alfred the Great (849–899), king of the West Saxons (871–899) and overlord of several other English kingdoms, born in Wantage, Berkshire, England. Alfred succeeded his brother Ethelred in 871, at a time when Danish invasions were threatening to sweep the land. In 876 a new invasion of Wessex was begun by the Danes, who had already made themselves masters of the eastern and southern coasts and of Northumbria and northern Mercia. Alfred was forced to retire in 878 to the Isle of Athelney and there reorganized his forces. After a few weeks he defeated the Danes at Ethandun (supposedly the modern Edington, in Wiltshire), and peace was concluded at Wedmore between Alfred and Guthrum, the Danish king. This great victory did not end the harassment; other invasions followed at intervals, but in 896 Alfred decisively defeated his foes.

Alfred's organizational and administrative talents were no less extraordinary than his military ability. He reorganized and reinforced military units, improved the fighting capability of his ships, and consolidated the many petty kingdoms into one unified realm. He divided the country into efficient administrative districts, codified and simplified the existing laws, and, though he did not, as has been claimed, institute trial by jury, he did make justice for rich and poor alike the rule in the kingdom. He established a court school to which he invited the best scholars of the time, translated into the language of the people such Latin works as Bede's *Ecclesiastical History,* and probably ordered the compilation of the *Saxon Chronicle,* a valuable source of early English history. Alfred is a greatly beloved figure in legend as well as in history.

Algardi, Alessandro (1602–1654), Italian baroque architect and sculptor, born in Bologna. His best sculpture, *Retreat of Attila,* over the altar of St. Leo in St. Peter's, is an alto-relievo. He ranks among the leading artists of his time.

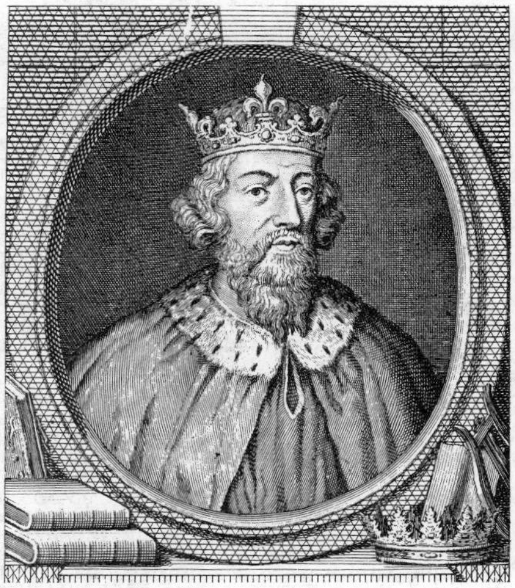

BETTMANN ARCHIVE

KING ALFRED THE GREAT

Alger, Horatio (1834–1899), American author of books for boys. He was born in Revere, Massachusetts, and graduated from Harvard in 1852. For a time he was a Unitarian preacher, then entered social service. From 1866 on, he wrote more than a hundred volumes. He enjoyed great popularity with such stories as *Ragged Dick* (1867) and *Tattered Tom* (1871), about poor boys who became rich and famous.

Alger, Russell Alexander (1836–1907), American soldier and public official, born in Lafayette, Ohio. He was admitted to the bar in 1859, became colonel of a Michigan cavalry regiment in the Civil War, and was brevetted to major general of volunteers. Alger was governor of Michigan, 1885–1887; secretary of war, 1897–1899; and U.S. senator from 1902 until his death. Severely criticized for his conduct of the War Department, he wrote *The Spanish-American War* (1901).

Ali, Mehemet. See *Mehemet Ali.*

Alighieri, Dante. See *Dante.*

Allegri, Gregorio (c.1582–1652), Italian composer, born in Rome. He studied with Nanini, friend of Palestrina, and from 1629 on was a member of the choir of the Sistine Chapel. His famous *Miserere,* sung there annually during Holy Week, was long kept unpublished, but in 1769 the boy Mozart wrote it down after a single hearing.

Allen, Ethan (1738–1789), American Revolutionary soldier, leader of the Green Mountain Boys, born in Litchfield, Connecticut. So daring and effective was his harassment of the British that he was outlawed. He is remembered chiefly for his surprise capture of Fort Ticonderoga in 1775. He was a prisoner-of-war in Canada from 1775 to 1778 and after his exchange became brigadier-general of the Vermont militia. Allen was a picturesque figure of the Revolution.

Allen, Florence Ellinwood (1884–1966), Jurist, the first woman to become a state supreme court judge and a federal judge. Born in Salt Lake City; graduated Western Reserve University (1904); studied law at New York University; began practice in Cleveland, Ohio, in 1913. Before elevation to the Ohio supreme court in 1922, she was an assistant county prosecutor and judge of the court of common pleas. In 1934 Pres. Franklin D. Roosevelt appointed her to the U.S. Circuit Court of Appeals. Died Sept. 12, 1966 in Waite Hill, O.

Allen, Grant, in full **Charles Grant Blairfindie Allen** (1848–1899), British author of scientific books and novels. He was born in Kingston, Ontario, and graduated from Oxford in 1871. His scientific works include *Physiological Aesthetics* (1877), *The Color Sense* (1879), and *The Evolutionist at Large* (1881). *The Woman Who Did* (1895) is the best-known work among his 30 novels.

Allen, (William) Hervey (1889–1949), American poet, novelist, and biographer. He was born in Pittsburgh, Pennsylvania, and graduated from the University of Pittsburgh in 1915. He was wounded in France in World War I and was sent home. He collaborated with DuBose Heyward on a volume of verse published in 1922; in 1926 Allen completed a two-volume biography of Edgar Allan Poe. His greatest work is the 600,000-word novel, *Anthony Adverse* (1933).

Allen, James Lane (1849–1925), American novelist. Born near Lexington, Kentucky, he was educated at Transylvania College. He taught at Bethany College, West Virginia, from 1880 to 1883, and subsequently devoted all his time to writing. Allen won wide recognition as a sympathetic interpreter of Kentucky life. Typical books include *Flute and Violin* (1891), *A Kentucky Cardinal* (1894), *The Choir Invisible* (1897), and *The Reign of Law* (1900).

Allenby, Edmund Henry Hynman Allenby, 1st Viscount (1861–1936), British general. He served in several African campaigns from 1884 to 1902. As chief of the Third Army in World War I, he fought on the Somme, and served with distinction. He was appointed commander in chief in Egypt and Palestine. His army took Jerusalem from the Turks in December, 1917, and afterward occupied Syria. He was raised to viscount in 1919.

Allison, William Boyd (1829–1908), U.S. senator, born in Perry, Ohio. He graduated from Western Reserve College, Cleveland, in 1849, and was admitted to the bar in 1850. Elected in 1862, Allison went to Congress and served four terms; in 1872 he was elected U.S. senator, and was reelected five times. He was co-author of the Bland-Allison Act of 1878, which required the government to purchase a specified amount of silver bullion each month to maintain parity between gold and silver.

Allston, Washington (1779–1843), American painter and author, born in Waccamaw, South Carolina. He graduated from Harvard in 1800 and studied at the Royal Academy in London under Benjamin West, then in Paris, Florence, and Rome. As a painter, Allston won renown both in America and in Europe. His use of color shows the influence of the Venetian masters. Among his paintings are *The Dead Man Revived, The Deluge,* and a portrait of Benjamin West. He was also author of *The Sylphs of the Seasons with Other Poems* (1813).

Almqvist, Karl Jonas Ludvig (1793–1866), Swedish author. He was born in Stockholm, and graduated from the University of Uppsala in 1815. After a restless career in many occupations, he was implicated in a murder and fled to the United States in 1851. He returned to Europe in 1865 and went to Bremen as Professor Westermann, retaining the assumed name until his death. Almqvist's novel *Det går an* (1839), defending extramarital relations, provoked widespread comment. His best-known writings consist of the novels, plays, and poems which were published serially as *The Book of the Thorn-Rose* (1832–1835).

Alströmer, Jonas (1685–1761), Swedish industrial reformer. He made a fortune in the shipping business in England and returned to Sweden in 1724. There he established woolen factories, improved the breed of sheep, and introduced efficient methods in many industries. In appreciation of his services, he was made chancellor of commerce and his statue was erected in Stockholm.

Altdorfer, Albrecht (c.1480–1538), German engraver, landscape painter, and architect for the city of Regensburg. Altdorfer was one of the "Little Masters" (a name given to a group of sixteenth-century painters, all of them followers of Dürer). His works include the *Holy Family* (at Vienna) and *Alexander's Victory at Arbela* (at Munich).

Alva or **Alba, Fernando Álvarez de Toledo,** Duke of (1508–c.1582). Spanish general. As governor of the Netherlands (1567–1573), he quelled a revolt against Philip II of Spain with unsparing severity, and during his term executed 18,000 persons. In 1573, after the destruction of his fleet, he was recalled. In 1580 he conquered Portugal with characteristic cruelty.

Alvarado, Pedro de (1495?–1541), Spanish conquistador, born in Badajoz. He sailed for the West Indies in 1510. He was chief lieutenant under Cortés, and became commander of the city of Mexico and later governor of Guatemala and Honduras. He was killed in battle soon after his return to Mexico. Alvarado published *An Account of the Conquest of Guatemala in 1524* (trans. 1924).

Amadeo or **Omodeo, Giovanni Antonio** (1447?–1522), Italian sculptor and architect of the Renaissance, born in Pavia. Among his greatest works are the decoration of the Colleoni Chapel in Bergamo, the sculpture on the pulpit of the Cathedral of Cremona, and the façade of the Certosa in Pavia.

Amanullah Khan (1892–1960), deposed king of Afghanistan. He came to the throne in 1919, after the assassination of his father, later changing his title from "Amir" to "King." In 1928, after a tour of Europe, he instituted reforms in dress, social customs, and government. The people were not ready for these reforms and forced Amanullah to abdicate in 1929; he then lived in Europe.

Amati, family name of celebrated sixteenth- and seventeenth-century violin makers of Cremona, Italy. **Andrea Amati** (c.1530–c.1611) founded the school, the traditions of which were carried on by his two sons, **Antonio** (c.1550–c.1638) and **Geronimo,** also known as **Hieronymus** or **Girolamo** (c.1556–1630). Surpassing all of them was **Nicolò** (1596–1684), the son of Geronimo. Nicolò taught Antonio Stradivari, the greatest violin maker of all time, as well as Andrea Guarnieri. Nicolò's son **Geronimo** (1649–1740) was the last of the family to continue the craft with distinction.

Ambrose, Saint (c.340–397), Roman Catholic theologian, born at Treves (modern Trier, Germany). Although a layman, he was chosen bishop of Milan in 374 by popular demand. He then took up religious studies, becoming a power in the Church. Ambrose forced the emperor Theodosius to do penance for his massacre of the Thessalonians (390) and was instrumental in the conversion of Saint Augustine. He wrote a number of dogmatic treatises, such as *De mysteriis* (387) and *De paenitentia* (c.384), as well as commentaries and hymns.

Amenhotep I, Egyptian pharaoh (c.1546–1526 B.C.) of the 18th dynasty, succeeding his father, Amasis I (Ahmose I). He extended his dominions by successful military campaigns against Libya and Syria, and beautified Thebes.

Amenhotep II, Egyptian pharaoh (c.1447–1420 B.C.) of the 18th dynasty, succeeding his father, Thutmose III. He suppressed uprisings in Palestine and Syria, maintaining Egyptian rule. He built many notable structures in Memphis and Heliopolis.

Amenhotep III, Egyptian pharaoh (c.1411–1375 B.C.) of the 18th dynasty, succeeding his father, Thutmose IV. He consolidated the empire carved out by his predecessors, maintained peace with Asia, and encouraged trade with other nations, thereby ushering in a period of great prosperity. A distinctive architecture emerged under Amenhotep: monuments, statues, and temples of great beauty and unsurpassed workmanship were erected. A noteworthy example is the famed temple to Amon at Luxor. Amenhotep was last of the great Middle Kingdom rulers.

Amerigo Vespucci or **Americus Vespucius.** See *Vespucci, Amerigo.*

Ames, James Barr (1846–1910), American educator and teacher of law. Born in Boston, he received his undergraduate and law degrees from Harvard. There he returned to replace Henry Adams as instructor in medieval history; he later became professor, then dean (1895–1910) of the Law School. One of the founders of the *Harvard Law Review* in 1897, Ames wrote *Lectures on Legal History and Miscellaneous Legal Essays* as well as a number of case books. He is noted for his adaptation of Langdell's method of teaching by case study.

Ames, Joseph Sweetman (1864–1943), American physicist and college president, born in Manchester, Vermont. He graduated from Johns Hopkins University in 1886, received his doctorate there in 1890, and subsequently returned to teach at the university. He was chairman of the National Advisory

NEW YORK PARKS DEPARTMENT

HANS CHRISTIAN ANDERSEN monument.

Committee for Aeronautics in the period 1927 to 1939; from 1929 to 1935 he was president of Johns Hopkins. His researches in electrodynamics gained wide recognition; his writings include *Manual of Experiments in Physics* (1898) and other books on physics.

Amherst, Jeffrey Amherst, Baron (1717–1797), British officer. During the French and Indian War he was in command at the surrender of Louisburg in July, 1758, and in September of that year he replaced Abercrombie as commander in chief of the British army in North America. He captured Ticonderoga and Crown Point (1759) and Montreal (1760). From 1760 to 1763 he served as governor-general of British North America, and in 1776 was made a baron. Amherst College was named in his honor.

Amici, Giovanni Battista (c.1786–c.1863), Italian optician and astronomer, born at Modena. He developed the achromatic microscope which bears his name, and made important improvements in the mirrors of reflecting telescopes.

Amontons, Guillaume (1663–1705), French physicist, born in Paris. In 1687 he invented the hygrometer, for determining the moisture content of the air. His experiments with telegraphy were also important. About the same time as Halley, he found that the boiling point of water varies with elevation and hence with pressure.

Ampère, André Marie (1775–1836), French mathematician and physicist, born near Lyons. He was for a time a professor of mathematics at the Lycée at Lyons; afterward he taught in the Ecole Polytechnique in Paris. Ampere's researches in the field of electricity laid the foundations of electrodynamics. His name is perpetuated in the word "ampere," the unit of measurement of electric currents.

Amundsen, Roald (1872–1928), Norwegian explorer, born in Borge, Norway. At the age of 25 he went as first mate on the Belgian Antarctic Expedition of 1897–1899. In 1903 he set sail in the *Gjöa* on an expedition that resulted in the discovery of the Northwest Passage and a relocation of the magnetic North Pole. In the summer of 1910 he departed from Norway in the *Fram* with four companions, and in December, 1911, discovered the South Pole.

With Lincoln Ellsworth and General Umberto Nobile, Amundsen flew over the North Pole in 1926 in the dirigible *Norge*. Nobile organized a second flight over the pole in 1928 in the dirigible *Italia*, but the airship crashed on ice, north of Spitsbergen. Amundsen led a rescue party in a seaplane; his expedition was never heard from again, but a part of the plane was found. Amundsen published *The North West Passage* (1908) and *The South Pole* (1912), as well as *My Life as an Explorer* (1927).

Anacreon (c.572–c.488 B.C.), Greek lyric poet, born at Teos in Asia Minor. He was at one time tutor to Polycrates of Samos, where he became a court favorite. He was called to Athens on Polycrates' death by Hipparchus, the patron of Simonides and other literary figures, but probably returned to Teos after Hipparchus was assassinated in 514. Anac-

reon's verse concerns itself primarily with love and wine. The short facile lyrics made him extremely popular and he was widely imitated in the Alexandrian period. A form of verse, Anacreontics, is named for him.

Anastasius I (c.430–518), Byzantine emperor (491–518). He suppressed the degrading gladiatorial fights between men and wild beasts, abolished the sale of offices, and built a wall on the west of Constantinople to defend it against the Bulgars and Slavs.

Anaxagoras (500?–428 B.C.), Greek philosopher, born in Clazomenae. He settled in Athens and became the teacher of Pericles, Euripides, and perhaps Socrates. Anaxagoras introduced the idea that mind operates on matter and controls all material phenomena. Because his explanation of natural events was opposed to the religious ideas of the day, the enemies of Pericles sought to have him executed for impiety. However Pericles was very influential, and Anaxagoras was only sentenced to banishment; he died in Mysia, Asia Minor.

Anaximander (c.611–c.547 B.C.), Greek philosopher, mathematician, and astronomer, born in Miletus, Asia Minor. He succeeded Thales as head of the Ionian school of philosophy. Anaximander taught that the path of the sun is oblique, estimated the sizes and distances of the planets, and considered the earth to be a cylinder on the top of which men live. He wrote a dissertation on geometry and is said to have invented a sundial and a celestial globe.

Anaximenes of Lampsacus (4th century B.C.), Greek rhetorician and historian. He wrote histories of Philip of Macedon and of Greece, as well as an epic on Alexander, and is the probable author of *Rhetorica ad Alexandrum,* once credited to Aristotle.

Andersen, Hans Christian (1805–1875), Danish writer of fairy tales, poems, and dramas. Born of poor parents at Odense, he had little formal education, but studied theater and at one time tried to be an actor. Through influential friends of Hans in Copenhagen, King Frederick became interested in the boy, sent him to school, and then granted him a pension. His first novel was favorably received, but he is remembered for his simple fairy tales, loved the world over. The best known of his tales are *The Ugly Duckling, The Fir Tree, The Tinder Box,* and *The Red Shoes.*

Anderson, Carl David (1905–), American physicist, born in New York City. He studied at the California Institute of Technology. At the age of 31 he shared the Nobel Prize in physics with Victor F. Hess for his studies of cosmic rays, in particular for his discovery of the positron (1932).

Anderson, Marian (1902–), American concert contralto, born in Philadelphia. In 1925 she won first prize in a contest with 300 other singers for an appearance with the New York Philharmonic Orchestra. She was awarded a scholarship by the National Association of Negro Musicians, and in 1933 was sent to Europe for an extensive concert tour, and was highly acclaimed. Thereafter she made several successful tours of the

LOOK MAGAZINE

MARIAN ANDERSON, American contralto.

United States and in 1936 sang at the White House. The Spingarn Medal for "highest achievement" by one of the Negro race was awarded to her in 1939. In 1955 she made her debut at the Metropolitan Opera in New York, the first Negro ever to sing with the company. In 1958 President Eisenhower named her delegate to the United Nations.

Anderson, Maxwell (1888–1959), American playwright. He was born in Atlantic, Pennsylvania, and was educated at the University of North Dakota and at Stanford. For a time he worked on the editorial staff of various newspapers. He then collaborated with Laurence Stallings in writing the play *What Price Glory?*, which was produced with great success in 1924. He received the Pulitzer Prize for the political satire *Both Your Houses* in 1933; his *Winterset* (1935) and *High Tor* (1937) won him New York Drama Critics' Circle Awards. Among his other well-known plays are *Saturday's Children* (1927), *Elizabeth the Queen* (1930), *Mary of Scotland* (1933), and *Anne of the Thousand Days* (1948).

Anderson, Sherwood (1876–1941), American author and editor, born in Camden, Ohio. The son of poor parents, he received little formal schooling; he went to work at 12, became a soldier in Cuba, managed a paint shop, and did newspaper work. Late in life he settled in Marion, Virginia, and became the editor of two weekly newspapers of opposing political views. Anderson's first novel, *Windy McPherson's Son* (1916), marked him as a realist. *Winesburg, Ohio* (1919) and *The Triumph of the Egg* (1921) are collections of short stories. His novels include *Marching Men* (1917), *Many Marriages* (1922), and *Dark Laughter* (1925).

André, John (1751–1780), British officer and spy, born of Franco-Swiss parents. He served in the British army in America, was a member of Sir Henry Clinton's staff, and became a major. He conducted negotiations with Benedict Arnold for the betrayal of West Point but was discovered, arrested, and hanged as a spy. A gallant young man, he was mourned by Britons and Americans. A tablet to his memory is in Westminster Abbey; another was placed by Americans on the spot where he was arrested.

Andrea del Sarto. See *Sarto, Andrea del.*

Andrée, Salomon August (1854–1897), Swedish scientist and aeronaut. He was born in Grenna, Sweden, and received a technical education. Andrée was attached to the Swedish meteorological expedition of 1882. In July, 1897, with two companions, he attempted a balloon flight from Spitsbergen to the North Pole; he never returned. Thirty-three years later, the three bodies, logbook, diaries, and instruments were discovered by seamen on White Island, near Greenland.

Andreev or **Andreyev, Leonid Nikolaevich** (1871–1919), Russian novelist and playwright, born in Orel, Russia. He graduated from the Moscow University School of Jurisprudence but, unsuccessful as a lawyer, he became a police-court reporter. His writing talent was recognized by Gorki, who encouraged and aided him. Andreev suffered much from poverty and melancholia, and attempted suicide three times. His stories are characterized by stark realism verging on the morbid, his plays permeated with symbolism and mysticism. His most successful play, *He Who Gets Slapped* (1916), was produced in Europe and America and was made into a motion picture.

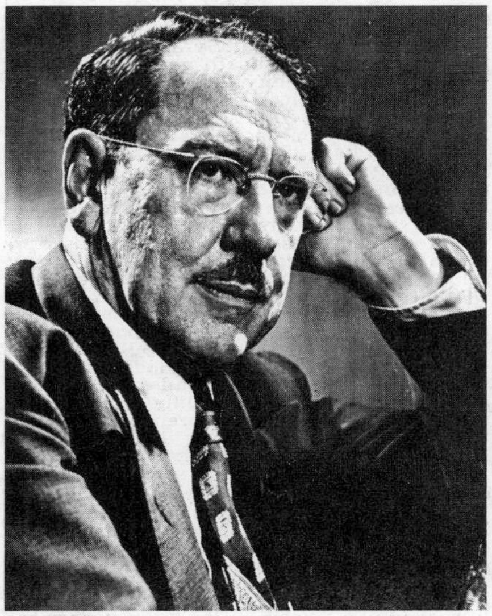

ASSOCIATED PRESS

MAXWELL ANDERSON, American playwright.

Andrews, Elisha Benjamin (1844–1917), American educator. He was born in Hinsdale, New Hampshire, and graduated from Brown University. Andrews was successively president of Denison (1875–1879) and Brown (1889–1898) universities, superintendent of schools in Chicago, and chancellor of the University of Nebraska (1900–1908). Among his published works is the six-volume *History of the United States* (1913).

Andrews, Roy Chapman (1884–1960), American naturalist and explorer. He was born in Beloit, Wisconsin, and was educated at Beloit College and Columbia University. In 1916 he headed the American Museum of Natural History's first expedition to secure data on prehistoric life in Asia. He explored Tibet, China, Mongolia, Central Asia, and the Gobi Desert, and made many valuable finds, including fossilized dinosaur eggs. He was director of the American Museum of Natural History from 1935 to 1941. Andrews is author of *Ends of the Earth* (1929), *The New Conquest of Central Asia* (1932), *This Amazing Planet* (1940), and *An Explorer Comes Home* (1947).

Andronicus of Rhodes (1st century B.C.), Greek Peripatetic philosopher in Rome. An expounder of Aristotelian philosophy, he compiled, catalogued, and published the works of Aristotle about 70 B.C.

Andros, Sir **Edmund** (1637–1714), English colonial governor. He was appointed governor over all of New England in 1686. His strict enforcement of the navigation acts, his introduction of the English landholding system and opposition to land speculation, and his encouragement of religious freedom antagonized various segments of the colonial population. In 1689 Andros was arrested and sent to England to stand trial. However he was soon released, and from 1692 to 1697 he served as governor of Virginia.

Angelico, Fra, popular name of **Giovanni da Fiesole,** originally **Guido di Pietro** (1387–1455), early Italian Renaissance painter, born at Vecchio. He joined the Dominican order at Fiesole in 1407, lived later in Foligno and Cortona, and again at Fiesole. In Florence (1436–1445) he did the exquisite frescoes for the Convent (now Museum) of San Marco. While in Rome (1445–1455) he painted *The Life of St. Lawrence and St. Stephen* in the Vatican and the famed frescoes at Orvieto (1447). "Angelic" he was indeed, not only in personality but in his art, which, blending medieval serenity with Renaissance naturalism, offers a delicacy of color, grace, and quiet spirituality that have remained unique.

Angell, James Rowland (1869–1949), American educator and psychologist, son of James Burrill Angell. He was born in Burlington, Vermont, and was educated at Michigan, Harvard, and several universities abroad. In 1894 he began his long association with the University of Chicago, where he started as assistant professor of psychology. He was director of research in functional psychology, and in 1906 was president of the American Psychological Association. In 1911 he became dean of the university faculties, and served as president (1921–1937) of Yale University. Thereafter he took an interest in the educational possibilities of broadcasting. His better-known works are *Psychology* (1904), *Chapters in Modern Psychology* (1912), and *American Education* (1937).

Angell, Sir **Norman,** original name **Ralph Norman Angell Lane** (1874–1967), British economist and author. Spent his early years in the United States as a cowboy and prospector, then as a reporter. Returned to Europe in 1898, continuing in journalism as a correspondent and editor. In 1929 he was Labor Party candidate for Parliament and was elected. Knighted in 1931. Angell achieved wide acclaim as author of *The Great Illusion, 1933,* a book dedicated to proving the futility of war. Received the Nobel Peace Prize for 1933. Died Oct. 7, 1967 in Croydon, England.

Angevin or **Anjou,** a French noble family, established in the ninth century, the name being derived from Anjou, a county in western France. There have been several houses of Anjou: Fulk or Foulques; the Plantagenet kings of England, especially the first three—Henry II, Richard I, and John; and the kings of Naples and Sicily.

Angström, Anders Jonas (1814–1874), Swedish astronomer and physicist. He studied at the University of Uppsala, where he later became a member of the faculty. A pioneer spectroscopist, he made a number of spectral analyses, particularly of the sun and the aurora borealis; in 1862 he identified hydrogen in the solar atmosphere. The angstrom, a unit for measuring the wavelengths of light, is named after him.

Anna Comnena (1083–c.1148), Byzantine princess and historian, daughter of the emperor Alexius I Comnenus. During the eleventh century the empire was constantly beset by invaders, first the Turks and Scythians, later the Normans and Franks. Anna accompanied her father and her husband on their military campaigns and gained firsthand experience. In 1118 she attempted to overthrow her brother, John II, but was unsuccessful and retired to a convent. Here she wrote the *Alexiad,* in praise of her famous father and family. This work has value in the light it sheds not only on the leading figures of the time but on morality then; in addition, her account of military tactics and weapons is detailed and knowledgeable.

Anne (1665–1714), queen of Great Britain and Ireland (1702–1714), second daughter of James II and successor to William III. In 1683 she married Prince George of Denmark. Since none of her seventeen children survived childhood, she was the last of the Stuarts. Anne was the first English sovereign to use the term "Great Britain" in her title, for it was during her reign, in 1707, that the union of England and Scotland occurred. Anne's reign was notable for the victories won by Marlborough in the War of the Spanish Succession. The queen's character was essentially weak, and the duke and duchess of Marlborough were long the power behind the throne. Alienated by their Whig sympathies, Anne came under the influence of Mrs. Masham, who helped bring to power a Tory ministry.

Anne of Austria (1601–1666), queen of France, daughter of Philip III of Spain and great-granddaughter of the emperor Maximilian II. Anne married Louis XIII of France in 1615, and their son, Louis XIV, was born in 1638. The queen was estranged from her husband during most of their married life because of the enmity of his minister, Richelieu, who feared the influence of her family connections. On the king's death in 1643, Anne assumed the regency and followed the advice of her own minister, Mazarin. In 1661 she transmitted royal authority to her son Louis, and went into retirement.

Anne of Cleves (1515–1557), queen of England, daughter of the German duke of Cleves. In January, 1540, Anne became the fourth wife of Henry VIII of England—a match urged by Thomas Cromwell as a means of associating the king's policies with German Protestantism. In July of the same year, partly because he thought her homely and partly because a change in events made the match no longer important politically, Henry had the marriage nullified. Anne spent the rest of her life in England, supported by an annuity from Henry.

Annunzio, Gabriele D'. See *D'Annunzio, Gabriele.*

Anouilh, Jean (1910–), French dramatist. He was born in Bordeaux and attended the Collège Chaptal and, for a time, the University of Paris. During World War I, when Paris was occupied by the Nazis, Anouilh, like other contemporary dramatists, turned to classical themes as his literary vehicles, for example *Eurydice* (1941) and *Antigone* (1942). His first real success in Paris was *Le Voyageur sans bagages*, 1937 (*Traveler Without Luggage*, 1964), a play about a war veteran suffering from amnesia who is forced to seek his family and learn the truth about himself. Anouilh's dramas had little appeal for New York audiences, and it was not until 1955 that he achieved his first popular success on Broadway with *The Lark* (*L'Alouette;* adaptation by Lillian Hellman, starring role by Julie Harris). Other notable plays are *Léocadia*, 1939 (*Time Remembered*, 1954); *L'Invitation au château*, 1947 (*Ring Round the Moon*, 1950); *La Valse des toréadors* (1952); and *Pauvre Bitos* (1956). The recurring theme in his dramas is the conflict between the individual and society, between the innocence of youth and the pressures of life that corrupt. Anouilh is distinguished primarily for his magnificent sense of theater, his mastery of dramatic construction, dialogue, and style, and for the sardonic humor that frequently illumines his somber themes.

Anselm, Saint (1033–1109), theologian and archbishop of Canterbury. He was born in Aosta, Italy, and studied in France. He became prior (1063) at the Abbey of Bec, then abbot (1078). Later he succeeded Lanfranc as archbishop of Canterbury. He was canonized in 1494 by Pope Alexander VI. Anselm was an expositor of Augustinian doctrine and of the priority of faith over reason, and in this he anticipated the thought of later scholastics. He is most noted for his ontological arguments, and is author of *Monologion* and *Proslogion* (on God) and *Cur Deus Homo* (on atonement).

Ansermet, Ernest (1883–), Swiss orchestral conductor, born at Vevey, Switzerland. He taught mathematics while studying music. In 1915 he became the principal conductor of Diaghilev's Ballet Russe. Three years later he established the Orchestre de la Suisse-Romande at Geneva and became its permanent director. He is best known for his interpretations of modern music, especially that of Stravinsky.

Anspacher, Louis Kaufman (1878–1947), American playwright, born in Cincinnati, Ohio. Among his works are the poetical drama *Tristan and Isolde* (1904), *Embarrassment of Riches* (1906), *The Glass House* (1912), and *A Way of Life* (1937).

Anthony, Saint (c.251–c.350), founder of Christian monastic institutions, born in Egypt. Giving up all his property at the age of 20, he retired to the desert and lived as a hermit. Yielding to the pleas of his followers, he returned to instruct them, thus founding at Fayum (c.305) the first monastery.

Anthony, Susan Brownell (1820–1906), American author, lecturer, and organizer, a leader in woman suffrage and other reform movements. She was born in Adams, Massachusetts, of Quaker parentage, and received a good education. At the age of 15 she was already teaching school. Becoming convinced that women could not achieve equal rights without first obtaining the right to vote, Miss Anthony campaigned vigorously for woman suffrage. Championing other causes as well—coeducation, temperance, abolition of slavery—she was constantly active. With Mrs. Elizabeth Cady Stanton she founded the National Woman Suffrage Association in 1869 and was its president from 1892 to 1900. She was co-author of *History of Woman Suffrage*.

Antigonus I, called **Antigonus Cyclops** (382–301 B.C.), king of Macedonia (306–301) and general under Alexander the Great. After Alexander's death, the empire was divided among his generals, and Antigonus became governor of Phrygia, Lycia, and Pamphylia. He sought to reunite the empire under his control and waged many wars. His rivals joined forces, and, in battle with Lysimachus and Seleucus at Ipsus, he was killed.

Antiochus III, called **Antiochus the Great** (242–187 B.C.), Syrian king (223–187). His reign was largely one of wars. He curbed uprisings in Persia and Media (220) and subdued the governor of Asia Minor, but suffered defeats by Egypt, Phoenicia, and Palestine. From 212 to 198 the tide turned; he conquered Armenia, regained Phoenicia, Palestine, and other lands, and defeated Egypt. However, his pact with Philip of Macedon to divide Egypt's maritime lands and his invasion of Thrace provoked the Romans—with disastrous results. Victors at Thermopylae and Magnesia (191, 190), the Romans stripped Antiochus of all his dominions west of the Taurus. From then on, the Seleucids ceased to be a power.

Antiochus IV, called **Antiochus Epiphanes** (c.215–163 B.C.), Syrian king (175–163), son of Antiochus III, succeeding his brother, Seleucus IV. In the war against Egypt (171–168) he defeated Ptolemy VI and VII. He captured Jerusalem twice, in 170 and in 168, and by harsh methods sought to impose there the worship of Greek gods, declaring Judaism illegal. This incited the Jews to a successful insurrection under Mattathias and his sons, the Maccabees.

Antipater (c.398–319 B.C.), general under Philip of Macedon and his son Alexander the Great. When Alexander went to conquer the East, he made Antipater governor of Macedonia, and the latter ruled well. After Alexander's death, he was reassigned to Macedonia. Frequently at war with the Greek states, Antipater managed to suppress all revolts.

Antoinette, Marie. See *Marie Antoinette*.

Antoninus, Marcus Aurelius. See (1) *Caracalla*, (2) *Marcus Aurelius*.

Antoninus Pius, in full **Titus Aurelius Fulvus Boionius Arrius Antoninus** (86–161), Roman emperor (138–161). In 120 he was made consul; afterward Hadrian, then emperor, sent him as proconsul into Asia, where his wise and gentle rule won him a high reputation. He defended Roman dominion in Britain by building a new wall from the Firth of Forth to the Firth of Clyde to stop invasions of the Picts and Scots. Acceding to Hadrian's wishes, he adopted the future emperors Marcus Aurelius and Lucius Verus. In 138 Antoninus was adopted by Hadrian and succeeded him. His reign was peaceful.

Antony, Mark or **Marc,** Latin name **Marcus Antonius** (c.83–30 B.C.), Roman politician and soldier, born of a patrician family. A capable and ambitious leader, he early attached himself to Caesar and, in 48, helped him defeat Pompey at Pharsalus. In Caesar's absence, Antony was left in charge of Italy. After Caesar was assassinated, Antony made an eloquent funeral oration and so stirred the people that the murderers fled. In 43 Antony allied himself with Octavian (the future Caesar Augustus) and Lepidus to form the Second Triumvirate. The triumvirs made themselves supreme in Italy by defeating Brutus and Cassius at Philippi in 42.

Antony visited Asia Minor in order to strengthen Roman power. There, in 41, he met Cleopatra, queen of Egypt, and spent months with her in idleness and dissipation. Upon defeat of his brother by Octavian, he returned to Italy in 40 and married the sister of Octavian in order to strengthen his bonds with the latter. He entered into a new pact whereby he was to be ruler of the East, but again succumbed to the lure of Cleopatra in Egypt. Octavian declared war against the queen. In 31 the Roman fleet engaged Cleopatra's ships off Actium and routed them, whereupon she fled. With his own forces defeated, Antony then followed Cleopatra to Egypt where, believing her dead, he committed suicide.

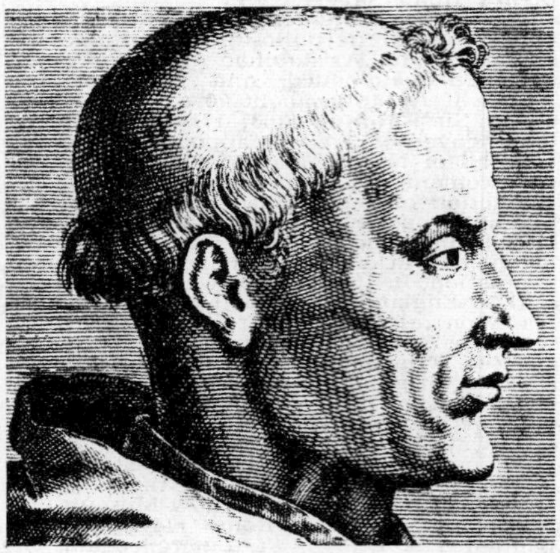

SAINT THOMAS AQUINAS

Apelles (4th century B.C.), Greek artist, regarded as the greatest painter of antiquity. Court painter to Philip of Macedon, Alexander the Great, and others, he produced his greatest works under Alexander: Aphrodite rising from the sea and his portrait of Alexander with a thunderbolt in his hand. His paintings, with their delicate coloring and accuracy of drawing, were described by Lucian and inspired later artists. None of his paintings, unfortunately, survived.

Apollinaire, Guillaume, real name **Guillaume de Kostrowitski** (1880–1918), French poet, novelist, and playwright. He was born in Rome of Polish parentage, and in 1898 went to Paris. Here he emerged as an art critic and writer, associated with the avant-garde. Among his works are the manifestoes *Les Peintres cubistes* (1913) and "L'Esprit nouveau" (in the *Mercure de France*, December, 1918); two important collections of poems, *Alcools* (1913) and *Calligrammes* (1918); the novels *Le Poète assassiné* (1916) and *La Femme assise* (1920); and the plays *Les Mamelles de Tirésias* (1917) and *Couleur du temps*, published posthumously in 1920.

Apollodorus of Damascus (2d century A.D.), Greek architect. He designed the Forum and the Column of Trajan at Rome, the remains of both of which still stand. He also built a great stone bridge over the Danube. Hadrian, Trajan's successor, executed Apollodorus for criticizing his architectural plans.

Apollonius of Perga, called "the Great Geometer" (3d century B.C.), Greek mathematician of Asia Minor. He wrote a celebrated treatise on conic sections in eight books, seven of which are extant.

Apollonius of Rhodes (c.305–235 B.C.), Greek epic poet, probably born in Alexandria. He became a citizen of Rhodes and established a school of rhetoric there. He succeeded Zenodotus as head of the Alexandria Library. His only extant poem is *Argonautica*.

Appleseed, Johnny. See *Chapman, John*.

Apuleius or **Appuleius, Lucius** (2d century A.D.), Roman satirical writer, born in Africa. He studied philosophy in Athens, traveled widely, and made a firsthand investigation of religious mysteries. Later he wrote the novel *Metamorphoses*, or *The Golden Ass*, in which the hero Lucius is transformed into an ass with human comprehension. His adventures in all strata of society were a rich source for subsequent writers.

Aquinas, Saint **Thomas,** often called "Doctor Angelicus" (c.1225–1274), foremost philosopher and theologian of the Middle Ages and founder of Thomism. Born near Aquino, Italy, he received his early education from the Benedictine monks at Monte Cassino, studied liberal arts at the University of Naples, and, in about 1243, entered the Dominican order. He was a pupil of Albertus Magnus, first at Paris (1245–1248) and later at Cologne (1248). Here he started a theological school and began his teaching career. Important recognition came after his return to Paris (1252–1256, 1268–1272), for it was there that he brilliantly disputed the interpretation which Siger de Brabant and the Averroists advanced on Aristotelian ideas.

Aquinas' principal contributions were to formulate the doctrines of Thomism and to systematize theology so definitively that in 1879 the Roman Catholic Church pronounced his teachings to be official. Among his voluminous writings are a commentary (1254–1256) on Peter Lombard's *Sentences;* commentaries (1265–1273) on Aristotle's *Physics, Metaphysics, De Anima,* and *Ethics;* and a treatise reconciling reason with faith, *Summa de Veritate Catholicae Fidei contra Gentiles* (1258–1260). The *Summa Theologica* (1267–1273), however, was Aquinas' greatest achievement and continues to remain one of the most influential philosophic-religious documents of all time. In 1323 he was canonized by Pope John XXII and in 1567 was made a doctor of the church.

Arago, Dominique François Jean (1786–1853), French physicist and astronomer. As early as 1809 he was elected to the Academy of Sciences and appointed professor of analytic geometry at the Ecole Polytechnique in Paris. He became director of the Royal Observatory in 1830. Arago built a polariscope and, with A. J. Fresnel, developed the wave theory of light as well as the laws of polarization. His discovery of the magnetic properties of nonferrous substances won him the Copley Medal. Arago participated in the July revolution (1830) and was elected to the Chamber of Deputies. Minister of war and marine (1848), he improved conditions for the sailors and abolished Negro slavery in the French colonies.

Arbuthnot, John (1667–1735), Scottish writer and wit, physician to Queen Anne. He counted among his friends such notables as Swift and Pope. It was Arbuthnot and Pope who assisted John Gay in writing the farce *Three Hours After Marriage*. Utterly careless of literary fame, he was one of the founders of and chief contributor to the brilliant *Memoirs of Martinus Scriblerus*, first published in Pope's works. He also wrote the five tracts published under the title *The History of John Bull*.

Archimedes (c.287–212 B.C.), Greek mathematician and inventor. Little is known of his personal life other than that he was born in the Greek city-state of Syracuse, in Sicily, and that he met his death at the hands of a soldier when the city fell to the Romans. Archimedes' greatest achievements were in the field of pure and applied mathematics. His discovery of a basic law of hydrostatics was said to have been made in a bath when he observed that his body displaced its own weight in water. He applied geometric principles to the invention of simple machines, such as levers and pulleys, as well as the Archimedean screw, which was used to pump water for irrigation. Among his many scientific treatises are *On the Sphere and the Cylinder* and *On the Measurement of the Circle*, concerned with proof of theorems on areas and volumes of figures bounded by curved lines or surfaces; *On the Equilibrium of Planes* and *On Floating Bodies*, dealing with problems in statics and hydrostatics; and *On the Method*, revealing Archimedes' methods of discovering theorems. References to Archimedes' discoveries in Greek and Arabic writings reveal the extent of the impact of his work on later scientists.

Archipenko, Aleksandr Porfirievich (1887–1964), Russian sculptor. He was born in Kiev and studied in Moscow. In 1908 he moved to Paris and spent many years there, coming under the influence of the cubists. After several years in Berlin, in 1923 he made his residence in the United States, eventually becoming a citizen. A leader in twentieth-century art, Archipenko was one of the first to recognize the value of negative forms. He explored the concept of voids, concentrating on abstract forms. Another innovation was the use of plastic, lighted from within.

Aretino, Guido. See *Guido d'Arezzo*.

Aretino, Pietro (1492–1556), Italian writer and satirist. He was born in Arezzo but lived most of his life in Rome and Venice. His sharp wit was at the service of Pope Leo X, the Marquis of Mantua, Pope Clement VII, and the famed Medici warrior, Giovanni delle Bande Nere. A threat against his life caused him to flee, in 1527, to Venice, where he remained until his death. Here he became undisputed master of the artistic community. Feared for his satirical thrusts against his powerful contemporaries—popes, kings, and artists alike—he earned the epithet "Scourge of Princes." Most of his voluminous writings were published while he was in Venice. They include *La Cortigiana* (1534), a lively comedy; *Ragionamenti* (1532–1534); and six volumes of his letters (1537–1557). The tragedy *Orazio* (1546) is one of his finest plays.

Argand, Aimé (1755–1803), Swiss physicist and chemist. He invented the circular wick for oil lamps which permitted a larger area of burning space and a greater intensity of light, obtained by the circulation of air inside the wick. The Argand lamp was first used in England in 1782.

Argyll, Archibald Campbell, 1st Marquis and 8th Earl (1598–1661), Scottish soldier and statesman, member of the famed family, the Campbells of Argyll. Leader of a clan of 20,000 disciplined men, he was an important figure in the conflict involving church and state. In the long dispute between Charles I and the Scottish Presbyterians, he supported the Covenanters. Campbell was defeated by Montrose in 1645. The execution of Charles I by Cromwell caused Campbell to turn his allegiance to Charles II. After almost a year he was taken by Cromwell's troops; at the Restoration he was executed.

Ariosto, Lodovico or **Ludovico** (1474–1533), Italian poet, born in Reggio Emilia. He studied under Gregorio da Spoleto. In 1503 he entered the court of the powerful Ippolito, Cardinal d'Este, and later went into the service of his brother, Alfonso d'Este, duke of Ferrara. His fame rests chiefly on his metrical romance *Orlando furioso* (1516), a sequel to Boiardo's *Orlando innamorato*. Ariosto also wrote comedies and satires.

Aristarchus of Samos (fl.280–264 B.C.), Greek astronomer. According to Copernicus and Archimedes, Aristarchus was the first to maintain that the earth rotates about its own axis and moves around the sun. His treatise on the magnitude and distance of the sun and the moon included a scientific method for calculating these measurements.

Aristarchus of Samothrace (c.217–c.145 B.C.), Greek grammarian and critic, a leading Homeric scholar of antiquity, now considered one of the greatest philologists of the ancient world. He was a student of Aristophanes of Byzantium, and later took his place as librarian at Alexandria. He edited and commented on Hesiod, Pindar, Aeschylus, Sophocles, and other Greek writers. His arrangement of the *Iliad* and *Odyssey* into 24 books is the basis of many modern texts.

Aristides, called **Aristides the Just** (c.530–c.468 B.C.), Athenian statesman and general. He was one of the leaders at the Battle of Marathon (490), and a year later became chief archon. Aristides opposed Themistocles on naval policies so vehemently that the citizens of Athens ostracized him. In the second Persian War, Aristides, profiting by a general amnesty, fought for Athens at Salamis (480) and Plataea (479). Later he was entrusted with the organization of the Delian League (a confederation of Greek states), a task he performed with great integrity.

Aristippus (c.435–c.356 B.C.), Greek philosopher, born in Cyrene, Africa. He was founder of the Cyrenaic school of philosophy. Aristippus was a pupil of Socrates, but developed his own system of thought involving the assertion that happiness is the highest good when its pursuit is wisely controlled.

Aristophanes (c.448–c.380 B.C.), Greek dramatist, considered one of the greatest writers of comedy ever to have lived. Little is known of his life except that he lived in Athens, a contemporary of Socrates and other eminent men whom he ridiculed in his plays, and that his plays were enormously successful. His life spanned the golden age of Pericles, the destruction of the Athenian empire, and the fall of democracy at the end of the Peloponnesian War. Hence his satires on the politics, philosophy, literature, and educational practices of the day, while in themselves excellent pieces of literary criticism, have served also to contribute substantially to our knowledge of Athenian culture. Of the 54 comedies credited to him, only 11 remain: *The Acharnians* (425), *The Knights* (424), *The Clouds* (423), *The Wasps* (422), *The Peace* (421), *The Birds* (414), *Lysistrata* (411), *The Thesmophoriazusae* (411), *The Frogs* (405), *The Ecclesiazusae* (c.393), *The Plutus* (388).

Aristotle (384–322 B.C.), Greek philosopher and scientist, one of the world's greatest intellects. He was born in Stagira, Macedonia, and was the son of Nicomachus, personal physician to King Amyntas. At the age of 17 he went to Athens, where for 20 years he was a member of Plato's Academy. When Plato died, he joined a group of Platonists in Asia Minor under the aegis of King Hermeias, whose niece he married; here he taught and conducted research in biology. In 343 Philip of Macedon appointed Aristotle tutor to his son, the future Alexander the Great. When Alexander set forth to acquire new dominions in Asia, Aristotle returned to Athens and founded the Peripatetic school—so named from the Greek word for a covered court, *peripatos*, in the garden of the school. Alexander financed Aristotle's research, and even had specimens of plants and animals collected for him during the military campaigns. Following the death of Alexander (323), Aristotle was caught up in the wave of anti-Macedonian feeling, was accused of impiety, and was forced to flee to Chalcis, where he died within a year.

Aristotle probed all aspects of human knowledge, among them philosophy, logic, the natural sciences, politics, and literature. His philosophy taught the concept of moderation: conduct must be founded on virtue, which lies in a mean between two extremes, and the correct mean must be ascertained through experience and common sense. Concerning matter and form, he believed that everything has an internal impulse toward development of its own specific form, as the seed develops into the plant, or the embryo into the adult. It is a process from potentiality into actuality. At the apex of development exists pure form, the perfect being (God), who has no part in matter or potentiality. God's existence sustains the whole world order by activating the internal impulses toward form. God is pure mind, and man is fulfilled through his intellectual life.

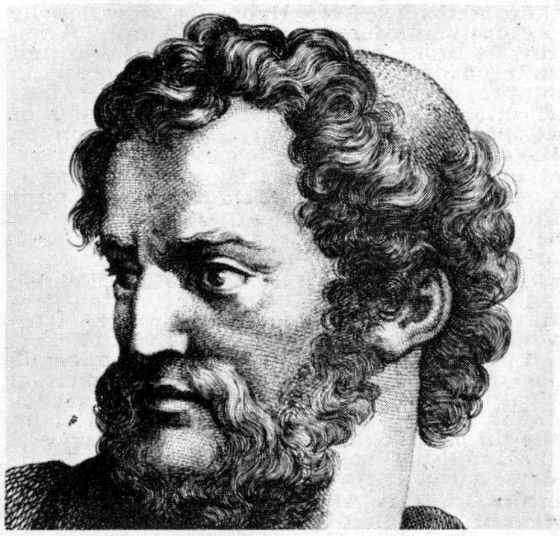

NEW YORK PUBLIC LIBRARY

ARISTOTLE

Aristotle developed and systematized logic, as can be seen in the *Organon*, and is considered the founder of formal logic.

In the natural sciences, Aristotle's achievements are impressive. Through his investigations he amassed a considerable body of new information. More important, however, than the substance of his findings was his method—a system of carefully organized surveys, descriptions, classifications, and comparisons that laid the foundations for the scientific method. Aristotle used this procedure in a wide range of subjects. He made the first thorough study of geometry, clarifying old definitions and introducing new concepts; his examination of meteorology resulted in the first textbook ever written on the subject; his work on anatomy produced the beginnings of the study known as comparative anatomy; and he wrote the first treatise on chemistry. His primary aim throughout was to make clear the fundamental principles of each science.

Among the works that have survived, largely in fragmented form, are the *Organon*, *Nicomachean Ethics*, *Politics*, *Physics*, *On the Heavens*, *On Beginning and Perishing*, *On the Soul (De Anima)*, *On the History of Animals*, *Rhetoric*, *Poetics*, and his greatest philosophical work, *Metaphysics*.

It is recognized that in the area of the natural sciences Aristotle made errors—errors that persisted for centuries precisely because of his great prestige. Not even these, however, can diminish the stature of this intellectual titan, whose genius reshaped into orderly, logical form the discrete knowledge of the past and enriched with new concepts the heritage of future generations.

Arius (c.280–336), Alexandrian priest whose name is given to the doctrine called Arianism, later the Arian heresy. This involved a belief that Christ was a combination of divine word and human body, that he was neither perfect God nor perfect man. This contradicted the Catholic view that Christ and God are of one substance. Arius was deposed and excommunicated in 321 by the provincial synod at Alexandria. The controversy spread; in 325 he defended his views before the Council of Nicaea but they were condemned as heresy. The Nicene Creed, then adopted, is still Catholic doctrine.

Arkwright, Sir Richard (1732–1792), English inventor. In 1768 he produced the model of his famous cotton-spinning frame, by which thread could be spun at great speed to any fineness and strength required. Backed by inventor Jedediah Strutt, he soon had in operation a horse-driven machine (patented 1769). Despite harassment by other manufacturers, including a lengthy lawsuit, he continued to improve and refine textile-processing techniques. Arkwright was first to substitute machinery on a large scale for hand labor. He was knighted in 1786.

Arminius or **Armin**, German name **Hermann** (c.17 B.C.–21 A.D.), German chieftain of the Cherusci. He became a Roman soldier and citizen, but soon devoted himself to the cause of German independence. His defeat of the three Roman legions under Varus at the Teutoburg Forest in 9 A.D. ended Roman rule and determined the course of cultural development of the Germanic peoples along Teutonic rather than Latin lines. Arminius became a German national hero.

Arminius, Jacobus, real name **Jacob Harmensen** (1560–1609), Dutch theologian. A leading interpreter of Calvinism, he was called upon, during a controversy on predestination, to defend its doctrines. In his studies his own views changed. He found the doctrine and content of Dutch Calvinism too rigid and scholastic. Outstanding theologians took sides in the dispute. After Arminius died, his followers presented in a Remonstrance five articles essential to an understanding of Calvinism, including conditional predestination and universal redemption. His doctrines, condemned by the synod at Dort (1619), are the basis for the Arminian, or Remonstrant, sect in Holland, the Methodists in America, and the Wesleyans in Great Britain.

Armstrong, (Daniel) Louis, nicknamed **"Satchmo"** (1900–), American Negro trumpet player, composer, and band leader. Born in New Orleans, he learned the bugle and cornet at the Waif's Home, and played in the streets and saloons of Orleans and on the riverboats. In 1917 he joined "Kid" Ory's band, in 1922 Joe "King" Oliver's group in Chicago, changing from cornet to trumpet. He formed his own band in 1929.

Armstrong has to his credit more than a thousand records, as trumpeter and singer; such songs as *Satchel Mouth Swing*, *Sugar Foot Stomp*, and *Wild Man Blues;* several motion pictures, among them *Cabin in the Sky;* two books, *Swing That Music* and *Horn of Plenty*, and an autobiography, *Satchmo* (from *Satch*el *Mouth*), 1954; and several jazz concerts. He has toured the United States, Europe, and, under State Department auspices, Africa and South America. Distinguished for his technical mastery, original and exciting phrasing, and above all his imaginative improvisation, he has been hailed as the world's greatest jazz trumpeter.

Armstrong, Nellie. See *Melba*.

Armstrong, William George, Baron **Armstrong of Cragside** (1810–1900), English engineer and inventor, born in Newcastle upon Tyne. Abandoning the practice of law for mechanical engineering, he invented the hydroelectric generator, the hydraulic crane, and a breech-loading field gun (1855) bearing his name. He donated his patents to the government. Armstrong expanded his plants to include a shipyard, building the first modern armored cruiser. He was knighted, and in 1887 was created 1st Baron Armstrong of Cragside. His best-known scientific work is *Electric Movement in Air and Water* (1897).

Arnauld, Antoine, called "the Great Arnauld" (1612–1694), French theologian. His *De la fréquente communion* expounded Jansenist doctrines and sharply criticized the Jesuits. He was censured and expelled from the Sorbonne, and in 1656 retired. With Pierre Nicole he wrote *Logique de Port-Royal*, and with Dom Claude Lancelot *Grammaire générale et raisonnée*. He published tracts against the Protestants, but in 1677 resumed his attacks on the Jesuits and fled to Belgium.

Arndt, Ernst Moritz (1769–1860), German poet. During the Napoleonic Wars his poems helped arouse the national spirit and unite Germany against the French. While professor of history at Greifswald he wrote *Der Geist der Zeit* (1806), boldly attacking Napoleon. Twice he fled the country. His fiery *Was ist des Deutschen Vaterland?* was put to music and was sung by the soldiers.

Arnold, Benedict (1741–1801), American officer, born in Norwich, Connecticut. Early in the Revolution he fought under Ethan Allen at Ticonderoga, under Montgomery in Canada, and, in 1777, rendered invaluable service at the second Battle of Saratoga, which resulted in Burgoyne's surrender. Arnold was severely wounded. Congress gave him a delayed promotion to major-general, and in 1778 he was put in command at Philadelphia.

Disputes with the civil authorities led to his court-martial, where he was acquitted of deliberate misdemeanors but was reprimanded. Embittered by this as well as by congressional slights, Arnold engaged in treasonable negotiations with Sir Henry Clinton for betrayal of West Point, a key defense position which he commanded. The plan was exposed with the capture of Major John André, and Arnold fled to the British lines. He was made a brigadier-general in the British army, and in 1781 took his family to England. He died in poverty and despair.

Arnold, Henry Harley, nicknamed **"Hap"** (1886–1950), American aviator and officer, a leader in developing American military aviation. He set records for altitude, for distance, and for continuous flying, and was first to fly air mail. Recipient of many awards, among them the Distinguished Flying Cross (1934), Arnold was placed in command of the U.S. Army Air Corps in 1938 and organized the fleets of planes that bombed Germany and Japan; in 1944 he was made a general of the army, continuing to command all air forces until he retired in 1946. He wrote *Air Men and Aircraft* (1929).

Arnold, Matthew (1822–1888), English poet, essayist, and critic, eldest son of Thomas Arnold, headmaster of Rugby. He was educated at Winchester, Rugby, and Oxford. In 1845 Arnold was elected fellow of Oriel College and was professor of poetry at Oxford for two terms (1857–1867). As inspector of schools (1851–1886) he traveled throughout England and did much to improve the primary education of students. His poetry, touching frequently on the loneliness of individuals and the healing quality of nature, is dignified and intellectual. Among his best-known volumes are *The Strayed Reveller and Other Poems* (1849) and *Empedocles on Etna and Other Poems* (1852); single poems include *The Scholar-Gipsy*, *Thyrsis*, *Dover Beach*, and the lengthy *Sohrab and Rustum*.

His fame rests chiefly on critical works such as *On Translating Homer* (1861); *Essays in Criticism: First Series* (1865), wherein he first defines the nature of criticism, and *Second Series* (1888), which contains essays on Milton, Keats, Wordsworth, Byron, Shelley, and other poets; and *On the Study of Celtic Literature* (1867). He also wrote on education, religion, and social problems.

Arnold, Thomas (1795–1842), English educator. He was born on the Isle of Wight and was educated at Winchester and Oxford. After entering the church, he spent nine years at Laleham preparing young men for the universities. As headmaster of Rugby (1828–1842) he brought fame to the school. He set up a new, fair code of conduct aimed at a better relationship between master and pupil, introduced a number of modern courses into the curriculum, and urged greater independence of thought. On the whole he revitalized the English public school system. Best known of his works are an edition of Thucydides and his *History of Rome*.

Arrhenius, Svante August (1859–1927), Swedish chemist. He graduated from the University of Uppsala in 1881 and submitted his doctoral thesis on electrolytic dissociation in 1884. This theory, revised and extended, was published three years later and met for the most part with hostility and ridicule. Arrhenius became rector of the University of Stockholm in 1887, and professor of physics in 1895. From 1905 on, he was director of the Nobel Institute for Physical Chemistry. His theory on electrolysis won him the Nobel Prize for chemistry in 1903. Also noteworthy are his studies of toxins.

Arrian, Latin name **Flavius Arrianus** (fl.2d century A.D.), Greek historian. He was born in Nicomedia, and studied with the Greek Stoic philosopher Epictetus, whose teachings he later published. He was governor of Cappadocia (c.131–137) under Hadrian, and archon of Athens (c.147) under Antoninus Pius. He wrote, in the style of Xenophon, such valuable historical works as the *Anabasis* of Alexander, recounting the victories of Alexander the Great; *Periplus of the Euxine* (Black Sea); and *Indica* (India).

Artaxerxes I, surnamed **Longimanus** (d.424 B.C.), king of Persia (464–424), succeeding his father, Xerxes I. He put down the rebellion during which his father and elder brother had been assassinated. Thereafter, with the exception of an unsuccessful revolt in Bactria and in Egypt, his reign was peaceful and prosperous. Judaism flourished: the Jews were allowed to rebuild Jerusalem and to restore the Temple, and in 445 he appointed the Jewish leader Nehemiah governor of Judea. His sons were Xerxes II, Sogdianus, and Darius II.

Artaxerxes II, surnamed **Mnemon** (d.359 B.C.), king of Persia (404–359), succeeding his father, Darius II. His brother Cyrus the Younger early attempted to seize power but was defeated and killed in the ensuing battle at Cunaxa (401). Artaxerxes was constantly harassed by rebellious satraps.

Artaxerxes III, surnamed **Ochus** (d.338 B.C.), king of Persia (359–338), succeeding his father, Artaxerxes II. Upon his accession he promptly murdered most of his family. When revolts broke out in his kingdom, he at first suffered defeats; he succeeded, however, in suppressing with great cruelty the uprisings of cities in Phoenicia and Cyprus and of Egypt. He was murdered by the eunuch Bagoas and was succeeded by his son Arses.

Artemisia, queen of Caria (c.353–350 B.C.), succeeding her husband, Mausolus. She built the mausoleum at Halicarnassus, one of the seven wonders of the ancient world, as a memorial for her husband.

Artevelde, Jacob van (c.1290–1345), Flemish statesman, born in Ghent. During the hostilities between England and France, Artevelde, recognizing the dependence of Flemish textiles on English wool, formed a league for neutrality and signed a commercial treaty (1338) with Edward III. He abandoned neutrality, urging that Edward claim the throne of France. But when he proposed the English Black Prince as count of Flanders, a riot ensued in which he was killed.

Arthur, Chester Alan (1830–1886), 21st president of the United States (1881–1885). He was born in Fairfield, Vermont. Graduating from Union College, Schenectady, in 1848, he studied law and practiced successfully in New York City. Though married to a Southerner, Arthur was firmly opposed to slavery, and engaged actively in building the Republican Party in New York. He served on the governor's staff during the Civil War and became quartermaster general of the state. Appointed by Grant, he was collector of the port of New York from 1871 to 1878. When Arthur refused to reduce the number of his employees, Hayes, bent on abolishing the spoils system, removed him from office.

The Republican National Convention of 1880 nominated Garfield for president, Arthur for vice-president. Garfield's assassination soon after inauguration brought Arthur to the White House. He surprised former political associates by supporting the Civil Service Reform Bill (passed 1883), vetoing a fat pork-barrel harbor-improvement bill, and by serving honestly and well.

Asbury, Francis (1745–1816), English clergyman, first Methodist Episcopal bishop ordained in America. At 18 he became a Wesleyan preacher, and in 1771 was sent as a missionary to Philadelphia. The conference in Baltimore elected him superintendent in 1784; the title "bishop" came later. Disturbed by the reluctance of his colleagues to carry Methodism beyond the cities, he initiated the practice of circuit riding, himself riding thousands of miles each year along frontier trails. He organized conferences, founded schools, and set up a publishing house; he can be credited with the unusual growth of Methodism in America.

Asch, Sholem, also **Sholom** or **Shalom**, meaning "peace" (1880–1957), American novelist and playwright, noted for works in both Yiddish and English. He was born in Kutno, near Warsaw, and was trained for the rabbinate in religious schools of his town. In 1914 he moved to the United States and became a citizen in 1920. He traveled frequently to Europe and made four trips to Palestine. Asch is author of the plays *Mottke the Thief* (1917) and *The God of Vengeance* (1918), and other fiction: *The Mother* (1930), the famous trilogy *Three Cities* (1933), *The War Goes On* (1936), *Song of the Valley* (1939), and *East River* (1945). Well versed in Christian and classical traditions, Asch considered Judaism and Christianity "one culture and one civilization," and gained world renown with his series on Biblical lives, *The Nazarene* (1939), *The Apostle* (1943), *Mary* (1949), and *Moses* (1951).

Ascham, Roger (1515–1568), English scholar and writer, educated at St. John's College, Cambridge. He was tutor (1548–1550) to Princess Elizabeth, secretary (1550–1553) to Edward VI's ambassador to the emperor Charles V, and Latin secretary (1553–1565) to Mary Tudor and Elizabeth I. One of the first masters of modern English prose, Ascham wrote *Toxophilus* (1545), a treatise on archery in dialogue form, still a classic; and *The Scholemaster* (1570), on education, notable for its method of teaching Latin.

Asclepiades of Bithynia (fl.100 B.C.), Greek physician. In caring for the ill, he urged simple treatments such as diet, bathing, and exercise, and, for the insane, music. He is credited with being the first to distinguish between acute and chronic diseases.

Ashburton, 1st Baron. See *Baring, Alexander*.

Ashurbanipal or **Assurbanipal**, last great king of Assyria (669–626 B.C.). Under him the empire achieved its greatest expansion, encompassing Assyria, Babylonia, Syria, Palestine, and Egypt. Of the many uprisings, only the revolt of the Egyptians (c.660–654), led by Psamtik I of Saïs, was successful. Ashurbanipal suppressed the Babylonian rebellion (c.668–648) under his brother, defeated the Cimmerians who had invaded Asia Minor (c.652), and conquered Elam (642–639). Despite the atrocities he committed in reprisals against the insurrectionists, Ashurbanipal was a man of education and a patron of culture. The period of his reign became the golden age of Assyrian art, architecture, and literature. He collected in his palace at Nineveh an immense and valuable library of cuneiform literature which yielded much of our knowledge of Assyrian culture.

Asoka or **Ashoka**, called **Asoka the Great** (d.232 B.C.), king of Magadha (273–232), of the Maurya Dynasty of India. He became emperor after four years of war with his brothers. He conquered the Kalingas (modern Orissa), expanding his domain to nearly all of modern India, Afghanistan, and Baluchistan. Shaken, however, by the carnage of the Kalinga campaign, he converted from Brahmanism to Buddhism, making it the state religion. He convoked great Buddhist councils, sent missionaries as far west as Syria, Egypt, and Greece, built thousands of Buddhist temples, and had edicts on Buddhism engraved on rocks and pillars throughout India to instruct the people.

Asquith, Herbert Henry, 1st Earl (1852–1928), British statesman, leader of the Liberal Party, and prime minister (1908–1916). Born in Morley, Yorkshire, he graduated from Oxford and practiced law. In 1886 he was elected to Parliament. He served as home secretary from 1892 to 1895 and as chancellor of the exchequer from 1905 to 1908, when he became prime minister. Under his leadership, social reform measures were enacted, the absolute veto power of the House of Lords was abolished (1911), and the Irish Home Rule Bill was passed (1914). However, the home rule bill met with intense opposition and the threat of civil war in Ulster, and was not enforced. After a political crisis in 1916, Asquith resigned and was succeeded by Lloyd George. He was created the 1st Earl of Oxford and Asquith in 1925.

Assisi, Saint **Francis of**. See *Francis of Assisi*.

Aston, Francis William (1877–1945), British physicist and chemist. He was born in Harborne, near Birmingham, and was educated at Malverne College and Birmingham University. He did researches with gases, electric discharges, and radioactive materials. Aston invented the mass spectrograph, and with it proved (1920) that many elements contain isotopes—atoms that are chemically identical but different in mass. For instance, he demonstrated that chlorine has two types of atoms, one with a mass of 35, the other, 37. He received many awards, among them the Nobel Prize for chemistry in 1922. He is author of *Isotopes* (1922) and *Mass Spectra and Isotopes* (1933).

Astor, John Jacob (1763–1848), American merchant and capitalist, founder of the Astor fortune. Immigrating to America in 1784, he invested his small capital in furs, establishing lucrative fur-trading posts in upper New York and in Canada. About 1800, he began trade with China, Europe, and regions of the Mediterranean. Astor acquired large holdings in Manhattan farmlands that proved to be immensely valuable. By 1827 he had won a monopoly of the fur trade and had amassed great wealth. The Astor Li-

brary, now part of the New York Public Library, was endowed by him. The family interests were administered by four descendants, all named John Jacob Astor.

Atahualpa or **Atabalipa** (c.1500–1533), last Inca ruler of Peru. After the death of his father, Huayna Capac, in 1525, Atahualpa defeated his half brother Huáscar and became sole ruler. In 1532 the Spanish conquistador Pizarro pretended to invite the emperor to a friendly meeting, then treacherously imprisoned him. Though a vast ransom in gold was collected for Atahualpa's release, Pizarro had him strangled, thus assuring subjugation of the Inca empire by the Spaniards.

Athanasius, Saint (c.295–373), Greek theologian, born in Alexandria. From 328 until his death he served as bishop of Alexandria. Intransigent in his rejection of Arianism—the doctrine that Christ is not coequal with God—he endured exile five times. Long known as *Athanasius contra mundum* ("Athanasius against the world"), he was ultimately successful and is today honored as the "Father of Orthodoxy." Among his numerous writings are *Defense Against the Arians* and *Discourses Against the Arians.*

Atkinson, (Justin) Brooks (1894–), American journalist and drama critic. He was born in Melrose, Massachusetts, and graduated from Harvard in 1917. From 1925 on, he was distinguished as drama critic for the New York *Times,* also serving the newspaper as foreign correspondent from 1942 to 1946. Among his writings are *Skyline Promenades* (1925), *Henry Thoreau, the Cosmic Yankee* (1927), *East of the Hudson* (1931), and *Once Around the Sun* (1951).

Attalus I, surnamed **Soter** (269–197 B.C.), king of Pergamum (241–197). Refusing to pay tribute to the Gauls of Galatia, he decisively defeated them, earning the name Soter, meaning "Saviour." Attalus aided the Aetolian League against Philip V of Macedon, then gave support to Rome in the first and second Macedonian wars (211–196). He was considered to be a patron of the arts.

Attalus II, surnamed **Philadelphus** (220–138 B.C.), king of Pergamum (c.160–138), succeeding his brother, Eumenes II. Attalus continued the pro-Roman policy. Also a patron of the arts, he spurred the artistic and architectural enrichment of Pergamum.

Atticus Herodes. See *Herodes Atticus, Tiberius Claudius.*

Attila, also known in legend as **Etzel** or **Atli** (c.406–453), king of the Huns (c.433–453), ruling jointly with his brother Bleda over the barbarian tribes of northern Asia and Europe until Bleda's death (c.445). Attila's cruelty in warfare and widespread destruction of cities earned him the name "the Scourge of God." He extended his realm, penetrating the Balkans and Italy, devastating their lands, and exacting tribute. Roman troops under Aëtius allied with the Visigoths under Theodoric I inflicted a major defeat on Attila at the Battle of Châlons (451). He again invaded Italy (452) but spared Rome—a decision more likely induced by the famine and plague there than the pleas of the pope.

Attlee, Clement Richard, 1st Earl (1883–1967), British political leader and prime minister (1945–1951). Born in London; educated at Oxford. He left law practice to do social work in East London. After World War I service, elected mayor of Stepney (East London) in 1919, and member of the House of Commons in 1922. From 1935 to 1940 led the Labor opposition. In World War II he was deputy prime minister in Churchill's coalition government. With the victory of Labor in 1945 he became prime minister.

Attlee directed Britain's transition to a peacetime, welfare-state economy along the lines of the Labor Party program. Social security, health, and welfare measures were enacted. Most of Britain's basic industries, such as coal mining, iron and steel, transportation, and communications, were nationalized. His party was defeated in 1951, but the victorious Conservatives retained much of Labor's program. In 1955 Attlee was created an earl. Died Oct. 8, 1967 in London.

Auden, Wystan Hugh (1907–), poet, playwright, and literary critic. He was born in York, England, and studied at Gresham's School and at Christ Church, Oxford. He joined a circle of leftist writers, who felt deeply the impact of the depression and became the social conscience of the times. His first book, *Poems* (1930), reflected his hopes for a better society. His poem *The Dance of Death* (1933) and two plays, *The Dog Beneath the Skin* (1935) and *The Ascent of F. 6* (1936), both written in collaboration with Christopher Isherwood, also contain social criticism. Succeeding works, however, show concern for the gifted individual rather than the masses. *Spain* (1937), one of the finest of the many poems inspired by the Spanish Civil War, is also considered Auden's best political poem. Jointly with Louis MacNeice he wrote *Letters from Iceland* (1937). He was editor of the *Oxford Book of Light Verse* (1938). In 1939 he came to the United States, where his poems became increasingly religious. *The Age of Anxiety* (1947) won the Pulitzer Prize for poetry in 1948. Auden is considered one of the most influential poets of his generation.

Audubon, John James (1785–1851), American ornithologist and artist. Born in Haiti, the son of a French lieutenant and a Creole mother, he was educated in France. He left for the United States at 17, settling for a while near Philadelphia, then in Louisville and other cities. Through the years Audubon devoted himself exclusively to the study and illustration of birds. The result was a series of business failures that impoverished his family and led him to the debtors' prison. He managed, on the other hand, to accumulate an impressive mass of information and illustrations of birdlife never before seen.

Unable to interest a publisher in America, in 1826 he sailed to England, where he was warmly received. His notable *Birds of America* (4 vols., 1827–1838), consisting of hand-engraved, hand-colored copper plates made from his own drawings, and his *Ornithological Biography* (5 vols., 1831–1839), containing detailed histories, were published and aroused great interest in wild birds. His last project was the finely illustrated *Viviparous Quadrupeds of North America,* in which he was assisted by John Bachman and his own two sons. He drew birds in their environment—nesting, feeding, fighting. His work gave an impetus to ornithology and inspired the creation of numerous Audubon Societies for the preservation of wildlife.

BETTMANN ARCHIVE

SAINT AUGUSTINE

CHARLES PHELPS CUSHING

AUGUSTUS CAESAR

Auenbrugger, Leopold (1722–1809), Austrian physician. He originated the method of examining the chest by percussion. The sound produced by such tapping enables the physician to diagnose the condition of the lungs.

Auer, Leopold (1845–1930), Hungarian violinist and teacher. He became concertmaster in Düsseldorf (1863) and Hamburg (1866), and for half a century was professor of violin at the Imperial Conservatory in St. Petersburg. In 1918 he took up permanent residence in New York. Auer became world-famous as the teacher of the distinguished violinists Heifetz, Zimbalist, and Elman.

Auerbach, Berthold (1812–1882), German author and poet. He was born at Nordstetten, a village in Württemberg, in the Black Forest, and studied at Tübingen, Munich, and Heidelberg. Becoming deeply interested in Spinoza, he edited and translated Spinoza's works and wrote his biography (1841). Auerbach is famed for his portrayal of peasant life in the Black Forest in *Schwartzwälder Dorfgeschichten,* 1843 (*Village Tales from the Black Forest,* 1846), *Barfüssele* (1856), and *Auf der Höhe* (1856).

Augustine, Saint, Latin name **Aurelius Augustinus** (354–430), early Christian church father and theologian. Born in Tagaste, Africa, a son of the pagan Patricius and Monica, a devout Christian, he was raised as a Christian. To complete his education he was sent to Carthage, where he excelled at rhetoric but otherwise neglected his studies for the riotous living then prevalent in the city. His reading of Cicero's *Hortensius* stimulated a desire for serious study, and he turned to the Bible. Finding it unintelligible, he espoused Manichaeanism for nine years.

In 384, while teaching rhetoric, he met St. Ambrose, bishop of Milan, who urged him to return to the Christian faith. His conversion (387) is described in his *Confessions.* He was chosen for the priesthood by the people of Hippo, and in 396 became bishop of Hippo. Augustine's monastery was the training ground for many who later set up schools and convents in Africa.

A man of great dedication, Augustine zealously defended Christian orthodoxy against the Manichaeans, the Donatists, and the Pelagians. He wrote widely on grace, free will, predestination, and other aspects of disputed Christian doctrine. Fundamental is his emphasis upon both the inherent freedom and weakness of human will, which consequently must rely upon divine grace for strength, illumination, and salvation. A key distinction exists between inability to sin and ability *not* to sin: man does not possess the latter and can only arrive at the former after gaining the grace of God. The precondition for such an experience is faith: unless one believes, one cannot understand.

His works, especially *The City of God, Confessions,* and *De Trinitate,* exerted great influence throughout the Christian world.

Augustine, Saint (d.604), first archbishop of Canterbury. In 596, while a prior of St. Andrew's at Rome, he was sent by Pope Gregory I to Britain, along with 40 other missionaries, to convert the Anglo-Saxons to Christianity. With conversion of Ethelbert, king of Kent (597), Christianity spread rapidly on the island. In 601 Augustine was made archbishop of Canterbury.

Augustus (63 B.C.–14 A.D.), first Roman emperor (27 B.C.–14 A.D.), imperial name of Gaius Julius Caesar Octavianus (Octavian). He was the grandnephew of Julius Caesar, who adopted him and made him his heir. Caesar's assassination occurred while Octavian was studying in Illyricum. Octavian hastened to Rome in 44 and was able to take possession of his property only after raising an army and defeating Antony, then consul. Later he and Antony became allies and in 43, with Lepidus, they formed the Second Triumvirate. They defeated Brutus and Cassius at Philippi in 42, and held joint control.

Forced into a subordinate role, Lepidus soon retired; Antony became ruler of the East. Antony's infatuation for Cleopatra, queen of Egypt, alienated Roman support; the senate deprived him of all authority and declared war on Cleopatra. In 31 Octavian defeated the forces of Antony and Cleopatra off Actium, remaining in sole command of Rome. In 27 the senate proclaimed him Augustus, meaning "exalted" or "sacred."

Augustus ruled with a strong hand. His legions were victorious in Asia and Europe until checked by Arminius at the Battle of Teutoburg Forest in 9 A.D. He founded cities, beautified Rome, and encouraged the arts. Horace, Vergil, and others flourished under his aegis, and the period came to be known as the Augustan Age, signifying an era of literary and artistic splendor.

Aurangzeb, Aurungzeb, or **Aurangzib,** surnamed **Alamgir,** meaning "Conqueror of the

World" (1618–1707), Mogul emperor of Hindustan (1658–1707), third son of Shah Jahan. He imprisoned his father and had his elder brothers killed, ascending the throne in 1658. Aurangzeb conquered the Mohammedan kingdoms of Bijapur and Golconda, and extended his empire to the outermost limits of India. Himself a pious Muslim, he was intolerant of other faiths. The Marathas rebelled and were defeated, but continued their harassment. His order (1669) to destroy Hindu schools and temples and the imposition (1680) of a poll tax on non-Muslims further increased hostility. At his death signs of the future disintegration of the Mogul empire were already apparent.

Aurelian, Latin name **Lucius Domitius Aurelianus** (c.212–275), Roman emperor (270–275), justly famed as the "Restorer of the Roman Empire." Of peasant birth, he became a common soldier, but was so highly regarded for his military exploits that upon Claudius' death the army elected him emperor. Aurelian drove the Juthungi out of Italy and restored order at home. In the east he humbled Queen Zenobia of Palmyra, and won back Syria, Mesopotamia, and Egypt; attacking the Gallic empire in the west, he regained Spain, Gaul, and Britain. Aurelian's wall, 40 feet high and 12 miles long, encircling Rome, is still preserved.

Austen, Jane (1775–1817), English novelist, born in Steventon, Hampshire, where her father was a clergyman. Having little formal education, she read omnivorously. At the age of 14 she was already composing amusing skits and parodies, and by 23 had completed *Pride and Prejudice*. Her novels depict the everyday routine of the typical English town with realism and quiet humor. In the words of Scott, she had "the exquisite touch which renders ordinary commonplace things and characters interesting." Her other novels are *Sense and Sensibility* (1811), *Mansfield Park* (1814), *Emma* (1816), and *Persuasion* and *Northanger Abbey*, both published posthumously in 1818.

Averroës or **Averrhoës,** Latin name of **Abu al-Walid ibn-Rushd** (1126–1198), Arab philosopher, physician, and lawyer, born in Córdoba, Spain. He was a gifted pupil, and his education encompassed the entire range of knowledge of his time. While serving as judge and as physician to the court of the caliphs, he wrote treatises on law, grammar, astronomy, theology, and philosophy. His valuable commentaries on Aristotle's works won him great prestige among Jewish and Christian philosophers alike, and he became known as "the Commentator." With the Latin translation of his *Great Commentary* on Aristotle's *Metaphysics*, Averroës' influence was strongly felt in medieval Europe. Also notable was his *General Medicine*, the standard text in Islam and in Europe.

Averroës argued for separation of philosophy and science from theology, a concept advanced by fourteenth-century Averroists as separation of church and state.

Avicenna, Latin name of **Abu Ali ibn-Sina** (980–1037), Arab philosopher and physician, born near Bukhara. Exceptionally gifted, at the age of 19 he had mastered almost every field of science. Early demonstrating his medical skill, he became court physician and scientific adviser to many princes of Iran, and traveled extensively. His most famous work is the *Canon of Medicine*, regarded for many centuries as the authority on the subject. *Shifa* contains an account of Aristotelian thought, from which Avicenna's own philosophy was largely derived. Author of more than a hundred treatises, Avicenna's works were widely read by medieval scholars in the Orient and, translated, in Europe.

Avogadro, Count **Amedeo** (1776–1856), Italian chemist and physicist, born in Turin. He became professor of physics at Vercelli in 1809, and professor of mathematical physics at Turin in 1820. In 1811 he formulated the hypothesis, now known as Avogadro's law, that under the same temperature and pressure, equal volumes of gases contain equal numbers of molecules.

Azaña y Díez, Manuel (1880–1940), Spanish statesman, president of the Spanish Republic (1936–1939), and leader in the overthrow of the monarchy. A lawyer and prominent literary figure, he edited liberal periodicals and was active politically. In 1930 Azaña organized the Republican Action Party which helped depose Alfonso XIII. He became minister of war, then premier (1931), in the first Republican ministry. He attempted many reforms which were unpopular with the conservative army and clergy, and he was forced to resign. A leader of the Republican Left, he became premier, later president (1936). Civil war erupted, and Azaña went into exile. Upon recognition of the fascist Franco regime by Britain and France, he resigned (1939) as president.

B

Babbage, Charles (1792–1871), English mathematician and mechanical genius. Babbage is known for his work on the calculating machine, to which he devoted 37 years of his life. He also invented an ophthalmoscope in 1847, but failed to make it known. He is the author of *On the Economy of Machinery and Manufactures* and the *Ninth Bridgewater Treatise*. Babbage was also a founder of the Royal Astronomical Society.

Babbitt, Isaac (1799–1862), American inventor of the alloy known as Babbitt metal. He was born in Taunton, Mass., and trained to be a goldsmith. In 1839, while working in Boston, he developed an antifriction alloy of tin, antimony, and copper, and proved its effectiveness in bearings and other industrial uses. For his invention, he was awarded $20,000 by Congress. Later, he set up his own manufacturing company.

Babur or **Baber,** nickname of **Zahir ud-Din Muhammad** (1483–1530), Turkish founder of the Mogul dynasty in India. A descendant of Tamerlane and Genghis Khan, he succeeded his father as ruler of Fergana (in west Central Asia) in 1495. He inherited a weak empire, and spent the next 20 years strengthening it. In the 1520's he began a series of raids into India, and after a few years founded an empire in northern India, which his successors consolidated.

Baccio della Porta. See *Bartolommeo, Fra*.

Bach, Johann Sebastian (1685–1750), German composer, regarded as the greatest of the Baroque period that flowered in the eighteenth century. Born in Eisenach of a family of musicians, he studied violin and organ as a boy. By 1708 he had become court organist at Weimar. In 1714 he was made concertmaster to the Duke of Anhalt-Köthen, with the additional duty of composing vocal music for the ducal chapel. From 1723 he was director of music in Leipzig and cantor of St. Thomas School.

Although Bach is now known as the father of German music, his greatness was not recognized until 50 years after his death, when the composer Felix Mendelssohn championed his cause. Bach's important compositions include the *Mass in B Minor*, the *St. John Passion*, and the *St. Matthew Passion*, large-scale vocal works that are still regularly performed. In addition, he also composed some 200 church cantatas. His instrumental music includes *The Well-Tempered Clavier* (48 preludes and fugues), the *Goldberg Variations*, the *Inventions*, and numerous chamber music pieces. Several of Bach's sons were musicians and composers of note.

Bacon, Francis, 1st Baron Verulam (1561–1626), English statesman, philosopher, and essayist. Born in London, he was educated at Trinity College, Cambridge and admitted to the bar in 1576. He spent the next three years in France, returning to England after his father's death. From 1584 to 1614 he was a member of Parliament, afterwards serving as attorney general and lord chancellor. In 1620 Bacon was accused of accepting bribes. He confessed and was condemned by his

SIR FRANCIS BACON

peers, fined, and deprived of office. Later, he was pardoned by King James I but was prohibited from returning to politics. He spent his last years in retirement, devoting all his attention to writing.

Bacon's fame rests upon his philosophical writings and his essays. In general, he was a leading figure in the transition between medieval and modern thought. Bacon published his first series of *Essays* in 1597, which he rewrote and augmented for the editions of 1612 and 1625. In his great philosophical works, the *Advancement of Learning* (1605) and *Novum Organum* (1620), Bacon took a new look at science and nature, seeking to correct previous errors in observations of the natural world. Essentially, Bacon's philosophy was a forerunner of modern scientific thought.

Bacon, Henry (1866–1924), American architect who designed the Lincoln Memorial in Washington, D.C. Born in Watseka, Ill., he attended the University of Illinois, and studied in Europe. He worked ten years for an architectural firm in New York City, and then opened his own office. Bacon specialized in designing memorials and public buildings, and was a leader in the revival of the classical Greek style. The Lincoln Memorial, commissioned in 1911, was completed in 1920.

Bacon, Roger (c.1214–1294), English philosopher and scientist. After studies at Oxford and Paris, he entered the Franciscan monastery at Oxford, where he built a microscope and telescope for investigations of bacteria and nebulae. For these pursuits he was suspected of witchcraft by his superiors, who transferred him to Paris, where he was kept in virtual imprisonment for many years. In Bacon's major work, *Opus majus* (1268), he sought to reform university studies by introducing science into the curricula. During his day, Bacon's researches in optics, astronomy, and alchemy were considered revolutionary.

Baden-Powell, Robert Stephenson Smyth (1857–1941), British soldier and founder of the Boy Scouts and Girl Guides. Born in London, he chose a military career, serving in India and Africa. During the Boer War, he became a national hero when his troops withstood a seven-month siege in 1899–1900. He was appointed inspector general of the South African police force in 1903, and developed training principles for recruits. He then adapted these methods for training boys, and set up an experimental camp in 1907. His pioneer handbook, *Scouting for Boys*, was published in 1908. The movement became popular in England, and soon throughout the world. He resigned from the army in 1910 to devote his full time to the Boy Scouts, and in the same year, with his sister Agnes founded the Girl Guides. He was made a baronet in 1922 and a baron in 1929.

Badoglio, Pietro (1871–1956), Italian general who led Italy's invasion of Ethiopia (1935). As a young man he entered the Italian army and by World War I had risen to the rank of general. After the war he became chief of the general staff and was given the rank of field marshal. From 1928 to 1933 he was governor general of Libya. When Mussolini decided to invade Ethiopia

BADEN-POWELL, founder of the Boy Scouts.

in 1935, Badoglio was put in command of all armed forces, and after the subjugation of that country was made viceroy of Ethiopia. During World War II he was chief of staff for most of 1940, but resigned in protest when Italy invaded Greece. After Mussolini's fall in 1943, Badoglio became prime minister, and in 1944 he dissolved the Fascist party and declared war on Germany. He resigned as prime minister in June, 1944.

Baedeker, Karl (1801–1859), German publisher of guidebooks for travelers. His first guidebook, to the Rhine, Belgium, and the Netherlands, was issued in 1839; by the time of his death he had published guidebooks for most of Europe. In these works Baedeker provided practical information on places to visit, reliable hotels, and geographical details. Baedeker's sons carried on the business after his death. So successful were these books that "Baedeker" has become a synonym for guidebook.

Baeyer, Adolf von, in full **Johann Friedrich Wilhelm Adolf von Baeyer** (1835–1917), German chemist who won the Nobel Prize (1905) for his contributions to organic chemistry. He was professor of chemistry at the University of Strasbourg, and later at Munich, where he founded the Chemical Institute. Baeyer synthesized many drugs and dyes, and was the first to produce indigo artificially. His scientific papers were collected and published in 1905.

Baffin, William (1584–1622), English navigator who discovered Baffin Bay and Baffin Island in northern Canada. Beginning in 1612, he was chief pilot of several expeditions to find the Northwest Passage. In 1616 he entered the great bay that bears his name. Later he took part in expeditions to India and the Middle East. He was the first navigator on record to measure longitude at sea by lunar observations.

Bailey, Liberty Hyde (1858–1954), American botanist and horticulturist who was a pioneer in scientific agriculture. Born in South Haven, Mich., he graduated from Michigan Agricultural College, and taught horticulture there for a few years. From 1888 to 1913 he was professor of horticulture at Cornell University, serving from 1903 as director of its College of Agriculture. Also at Cornell, he founded (1920) the world's first center for identifying cultivated plants. A leading authority on botany, horticulture, and agriculture, he published many reference works and textbooks considered the best in their fields.

Bainbridge, William (1774–1833), American naval officer who commanded the frigate *Constitution*, known popularly as "Old Ironsides." Born in Princeton, N.J., he became a captain in the merchant service. When the U.S. navy was organized in 1798 he was appointed a lieutenant. In the War of 1812 he commanded the *Constitution* in its capture of the British frigate *Java*. After the war he served as a member of the board of naval commissioners.

Baker, Newton Diehl (1871–1937), American statesman who was secretary of war in Pres. Wilson's cabinet during World War I. Born in Martinsburg, W.Va., he graduated from Johns Hopkins University (1892) and became a successful lawyer. Turning to politics, he was city solicitor (1902–1912), then mayor (1912–1916) of Cleveland. Appointed secretary of war in 1916, Baker initiated plans for universal military conscription, which prepared the U.S. for its entry into the war in 1917. After the war he returned to law practice in Cleveland, and in 1928 was U.S. representative to the Permanent Court of International Justice at The Hague.

Baker, Sir Samuel White (1821–1893), English explorer who was one of the discoverers of the sources of the Nile River. After spending several years in Asia and the Near East, he went to Africa in 1861 and explored the tributaries of the Nile. Joining forces with John Hanning Speke, he discovered Lake Albert in 1864. Baker mapped the interior of Africa, opening up the country for trade. He also helped suppress the slave trade in many areas. Baker wrote several books describing his explorations. He was knighted in 1866.

Bakunin, Mikhail Aleksandrovich (1814–1876), Russian anarchist who founded the political philosophy known as Nihilism. Born of an aristocratic family, he served in the Imperial Guard for a few years, but resigned his commission in 1838 to study philosophy. His studies took him to many parts of Europe, where he became active in radical movements. In 1847 he refused an order to return to Russia, and his property was confiscated. For his activities in the German revolutions of 1848–1849, he was arrested and sentenced to death, but was sent back to Russia and exiled to Siberia. In 1861 he escaped and went to London, where he became known as a militant anarchist. A violent foe of Marxism, Bakunin also renounced all other political philosophies, and advocated the destruction of all forms of government.

Balanchine, George (1904–), Russian-American choreographer who founded the New York City Ballet. Born in St. Petersburg, Russia, he was trained at the Imperial Ballet School and in 1924 was appointed choreographer to Sergei Diaghilev's ballet troupe in Paris. Balanchine came to the U.S. in 1933 and organized a ballet company that became (1948) the New York City Ballet. The creator of most of the company's repertoire, he has been acclaimed in particular for his settings of dances to the music of Igor Stravinsky.

Balboa, Vasco Núñez de (1475–1517), Spanish explorer who discovered the Pacific Ocean. In 1500 he joined an expedition to the Americas, and settled on the island of Hispaniola. In 1510 he went to Colombia, then to Darien (in modern Panama), where he established a settlement. While on an expedition in 1513, he led the first party of white men across the Isthmus of Panama and discovered the Pacific Ocean. Always a controversial political figure, he became an enemy of Pedrarias, governor of Panama, who had him arrested and tried for treason. Convicted on false testimony, Balboa was beheaded.

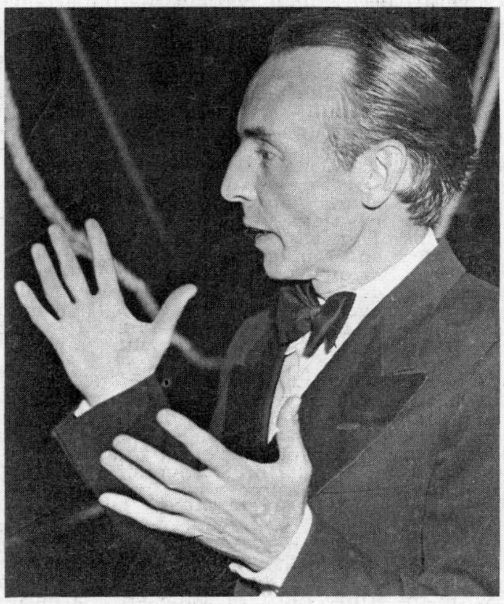

WIDE WORLD

GEORGE BALANCHINE, choreographer.

Baldwin, Matthias William (1795–1866), American locomotive manufacturer, born in Elizabethtown, N.J. He was a jeweler and a toolmaker in Philadelphia, and was the first in the U.S. to produce tools for bookbinding and rolls for calico printing. In 1832 he built his first locomotive (called "Old Ironsides") for the Philadelphia and Germantown Railway. He later founded the Baldwin Locomotive Works, which, in his lifetime, produced more than 1,500 locomotives. Baldwin supported a number of philanthropic causes, especially in aid of Negroes.

Baldwin, Stanley, 1st Earl **Baldwin of Bewdley** (1867–1947), British prime minister (1923–1924, 1924–1929, 1935–1937). Born in Worcestershire and educated at Cambridge, he was first elected to Parliament in 1908 as a Conservative, and rose steadily in political life. During World War I he was secretary of the treasury, and when England was sorely pressed for money, Baldwin gave one-fourth of his private fortune to the government. In 1920 he was appointed to the privy council and in the following year was president of the Board of Trade, a cabinet post. In 1923 he succeeded Bonar Law as prime minister.

Only a few months later the Labour party triumphed in a national election and Ramsay MacDonald replaced him. In 1924 the Labourites lost power, and again Baldwin became leader of the House of Commons. At the next general election the Labourites were returned to power and from 1929 to 1931 Baldwin led the Conservative opposition to the government. With the British financial system threatened in 1931, Baldwin joined MacDonald's national coalition government as lord president of the council. In 1935 the two leaders again changed places, and Baldwin was prime minister until the summer of 1937, when he accepted a peerage. His handling of the abdication crisis of 1937 saved the principle of constitutional monarchy. The speech he made in the House of Commons, after King Edward VIII (later the Duke of Windsor) announced his final determination to renounce the throne, represented his greatest parliamentary effort, and when he retired in 1937 his prestige was high.

Balfe, Michael William (1808–1870), Irish composer remembered for his light opera *The Bohemian Girl* (1843). In his early career he was well known as a singer in Italian operas. He composed his first few operas with Italian librettos. His first English opera, *The Siege of Rochelle,* was produced in 1835. But *The Bohemian Girl,* with its familiar air "I dreamt I dwelt in marble halls," was his only work to gain an international reputation.

Balfour, Arthur James, 1st Earl (1848–1930), British statesman and Conservative leader who was prime minister of England from 1902 to 1905. Born in Scotland, he was educated at Eton and Trinity College, Cambridge. During his 50-year career, he rose from a private secretary to his uncle, Lord Salisbury, to his country's highest post. Before succeeding Salisbury as Conservative leader in the House of Commons, he was secretary for Scotland (1886–1887) and chief secretary for Ireland (1887–1891). At the outbreak of World War I he reentered political life as first lord of the admiralty, and later was secretary of state for foreign affairs. In 1917 he issued the Balfour Declaration, which established the principle of a Jewish national homeland in Palestine. After the war he headed the British delegation to the Washington Naval Disarmament Conference (1921–1922). He was created an earl in 1922. At his death he was called "the last of the great Victorians."

Baliol or **Balliol, John de** (1249–1315), king of Scotland (1292–1296). In 1290 Queen Margaret of Scotland died, leaving no direct heirs. Baliol claimed the throne through a distant blood relation to the royal line, but so did Robert Bruce. Edward I of England, called upon to settle the matter, elected in favor of Baliol. The new king soon fell out of favor with Edward, who drove him from the throne in 1296 and seized it for himself. Baliol was imprisoned briefly in the Tower of London, but was released in 1299. He spent his last years in France.

Baltimore, Lord, See *Calvert, George.*

Balzac, Honoré de (1799–1850), French novelist, the first and perhaps greatest French writer of realistic novels. He was educated at the college of Oratorians at Vendôme (which he described in *Louis Lambert)* and in Paris. He studied law for three years, and worked for a time as a lawyer's clerk, where he learned much about the underside of life that he used later in his novels. During this time he published several novels under assumed names or anonymously, without financial gain; and he became almost penniless. The turning point in his career came in 1829 with the publication of *Le Dernier Chouan,* a historical novel with Brittany as its background. He was then 30, and for the next few years he wrote constantly, steadily mastering his craft. Among his acquaintances were Victor Hugo, George Sand, and Lamartine; he also fell under the spell of Mme. Evelina Hanska, a wealthy Polish woman whom he married a few months before his death.

Balzac's great *La Comédie Humaine,* a vast cycle consisting of about 97 novels and short stories, was written between 1831 and 1850. This major work deals with all phases of contemporary French society. Among his works are *la Physiologie du mariage* (1829) *La Peau de chagrin* (1830), *Louis Lambert* (1832), *Eugénie Grandet* (1833), *La Recherche de l'absolu* (1834), *Le Père Goriot* (1834), and *Seraphita* (1835). The last-named appeared in 1849, dedicated to Mme. Hanska, to crown his devotion of 15 years. His chief works have been translated into English.

Bancroft, George (1800–1891), American historian and diplomat, noted for his ten-volume *History of the United States.* Born in Worcester, Mass., he graduated from Harvard and spent five years studying and traveling in Europe. After returning to America in 1822, he taught Greek at Harvard for a year, and for seven years conducted a boys' school. He became active in Democratic party affairs, and in 1836 Pres. Martin Van Buren appointed him collector of the port of Boston. He was named secretary of the navy by Pres. James K. Polk in 1845, and minister to England from 1846 to 1849. Bancroft spent 40 years writing his *History of the United States*, a monument of historical research; the first volume appeared in 1834, the tenth in 1874.

Bandinelli, Baccio or **Bartolommeo** (1493–1560), Italian sculptor, born in Florence. He was trained as a goldsmith before turning to sculpture. Among his best works are the statue *Hercules and Cacus* in Florence and his bas-reliefs in the Florence cathedral. Although Bandinelli was overshadowed by his great contemporary Benvenuto Cellini, his works were esteemed by the Medici family, who were his patrons.

Banks, Sir **Joseph** (1743–1820), English naturalist and patron of the natural sciences. He inherited a fortune from his father, which he used to support scientific expeditions. On trips to Newfoundland, Labrador, and Iceland he collected plant and insect specimens. He financed Capt. James Cook's first voyage of discovery (1768–1771), which he accompanied as naturalist. Banks was president of the Royal Society from 1778 until his death, and he left his natural history collection and library to the British Museum. He was created a baronet in 1781.

Banks, Nathaniel Prentiss (1816–1894), American politician and Civil War general. Born in Waltham, Mass., he was self-educated. He served in the Massachusetts legislature (1849–1852) and in the U.S. Congress (1853–1857). In his second term he was speaker of the House. After a term as governor of Massachusetts, he was appointed major general of volunteers at the start of the Civil War, during which he commanded Union troops in Virginia, Louisiana, and Texas. After the war he was reelected to Congress and served three two-year terms between 1865 and 1891.

Banting, Sir **Frederick Grant** (1891–1941), Canadian physician and scientist who was a codiscoverer of insulin. Born in Ontario, he received his medical degree at the University of Toronto. After serving in World War I, he returned to the university to do research. In 1921 he and Dr. Charles H. Best isolated the hormone insulin for the treatment of diabetes. Banting and Dr. J. J. R. Macleod, director of the university research laboratory, shared the 1923 Nobel Prize for physiology and medicine. Banting was created a knight commander of the British Empire in 1934.

Barbarossa. See *Frederick I.*

Barber, Samuel (1910–), American composer whose opera *Antony and Cleopatra* (1966) inaugurated the opening season of the Metropolitan Opera at Lincoln Center in New York. Born in West Chester, Pa., he graduated from the Curtis Institute of Music in Philadelphia in 1932, afterwards devoting his full time to composing. Barber has been noted for his lyrical, romantic compositions, more conservative than modern in technique. Among his best-known works are the *Overture to "The School for Scandal"* (1933), *Adagio for Strings* (1936), *Piano Sonata* (1948), the ballet *Medea* (1946), the opera *Vanessa* (1958), and *Piano Concerto* (1962); the last two works won Pulitzer Prizes.

Barbirolli, Sir **John** (1899–), English orchestral conductor, born in London of an Italian father and a French mother. He was a cellist with the International String Quartet from 1920 to 1924 and was the conductor of opera companies in England and Scotland. From 1936 to 1943 he was conductor of the New York Philharmonic, succeeding Arturo Toscanini. He then returned to England, where he conducted the Hallé Orchestra until 1958. Barbirolli has also been guest conductor with many of the world's great orchestras. He was knighted in 1949.

Barclay de Tolly, Prince **Mikhail** (1761–1818), Russian general who was largely responsible for the rout of Napoleon's army after its invasion of Russia. A descendant of a Scottish family that had settled in Russia, he joined the army and served in several campaigns before the French invasion. In 1812 he was put in command of one of two armies fighting Napoleon's forces, but his tactics of avoiding direct battle and sacrificing land to the French caused much criticism. He resigned his command but returned in 1813 and was made commander in chief of Russian forces. In 1814 and 1815 he led Russian troops in invasions of Germany and France. At the end of this war, he was made a prince and a field marshal. During France's invasion of Russia, it was his delaying tactics that did more than anything else to exhaust the French army.

Baring, Alexander, 1st Baron **Ashburton** (1774–1848), English statesman and financier. He extended the financial operations of his father's banking house in the United States and Canada. From 1806 to 1835 he was a member of Parliament. In 1842 he was appointed ambassador to the United States; in this capacity he negotiated the Webster-Ashburton Treaty (1842).

Barkley, Alben William (1877–1956), vice-president of the United States (1949–1953) under Pres. Harry S. Truman. Born in Graves County, Ky., and educated at local colleges, he studied law at the University of Virginia and was admitted to the bar in 1901. From 1913 to 1927 he represented Kentucky in the U.S. Congress, and was a senator from 1927 to 1949 (majority leader from 1937–1947). As vice-president, Barkley was enormously popular with both political parties, earning the affectionate nickname "Veep." He was reelected to the Senate in 1954 and served until his death.

Barlach, Ernst (1870–1938), German sculptor, noted for his neo-Gothic wood and bronze figures. A member of the Expressionist school that flourished in Germany during the 1920's, Barlach first achieved fame with a series of monumental war memorials in German cities. When the Nazis came to power Barlach fell into disfavor, and his works were removed from museums. After World War II, however, his genius was once again recognized. Barlach also wrote several successful plays, but his importance rests chiefly on his sculpture.

Barlow, Joel (1754–1812), American poet and diplomat. Born in Redding, Conn., he was educated at Yale, and became a lawyer and newspaper publisher in Hartford. With John Trumbull, Timothy Dwight, and others, he became a member of the Hartford Wits, a group that worked to establish an independent American literature. Barlow is best remembered for his mock-pastoral poem, *The Hasty Pudding* (1796). A more ambitious but less successful work was his *The Vision of Columbus* (1787), enlarged and published as *The Columbiad* (1807). Barlow went on several diplomatic missions for the U.S. government, also serving as consul to Algiers (1795–1797), and as minister to France (1811–1812). He died on his way to a conference with Napoleon in Russia.

Barnard, Edward Emerson (1857–1923), American astronomer who, through celestial photography, discovered many comets and stars. Born in Nashville, Tenn., he studied photography as a boy and graduated from Vanderbilt University in 1887. As assistant astronomer at Lick Observatory in California (1887–1895), he discovered the fifth satellite of Jupiter and took photographs of the Milky Way. From 1895 until his death, he was chief astronomer at Yerkes Observatory, and was associated with the University of Chicago. Barnard's Star, a 10th magnitude star, which he discovered in 1916, was named for him.

Barneveldt or **Barneveld, Jan van Olden** (1547–1619), Dutch statesman who was a leader in his country's fight for independence. As grand pensionary of Holland, he controlled the nation's civil affairs. Much of his career was spent in a struggle with Maurice of Nassau, head of Holland's military forces. Barneveldt won Spain's recognition of the independence of Holland and in 1609 concluded a truce for 12 years, thus keeping Holland out of the Thirty Years' War. His enemies had him arrested for treason in 1618, and he was tried and condemned to death. Prevented as he was from exercising full right of defense, his trial and sentence amounted in substance to judicial murder.

Barnum, Phineas Taylor (1810–1891), American showman and impresario, regarded as the greatest of his time. Born in Bethel, Conn., he entered show business at an early age. He first became prominent in 1841, when he purchased a museum in New York City, where he exhibited freaks, rare animals, and other sensational acts. Barnum introduced and made famous the dwarf "General Tom Thumb," the Swedish opera singer Jenny Lind, and the circus elephant Jumbo. In 1871 Barnum formed his own circus, which he called "The Greatest Show on Earth." Ten years later, he joined forces with his chief rival, James Anthony Bailey, to form the Barnum and Bailey Circus. Barnum is often considered the inventor of modern publicity techniques. Famous for his quips, he coined the phrase "There a sucker born every minute."

Barras, Vicomte **Paul François Jean Nicolas de** (1755–1829), French revolutionist who contributed to Napoleon Bonaparte's rise to power. Although a nobleman, he sympathized with the masses. In the French Revolution he took part in the storming of the Bastille and the attack on the royal palace. He was elected to the National Convention and voted for the execution of King Louis XVI. His zeal made him president of the Convention and as one of the members of the Directory he was largely responsible for ending the Reign of Terror. It was he who called upon young Napoleon Bonaparte to repel the Royalists about to storm the Directory.

Saving the Directory marked the beginning of Napoleon's rise to power. By 1799 Napoleon had become first consul of the new republic. Suspected of intrigue and corruption, Barras was forced to leave Paris to avoid the consequences of opposing the ambitions of the new leader. Barras retired to his estate near Paris, constantly watched by Napoleon's aides. He returned after the monarchy was restored, but never regained his influence.

Barrie, Sir **James Matthew** (1860–1937), British dramatist and novelist noted for his sentimental plays and stories. Born in Kirriemuir, Scotland, he graduated from Edinburgh University, chose a writing career, and moved to London in 1885. His first novel *Better Dead* (1887), was about a Scot's attempt to make a living in London. This was followed by *Auld Licht Idylls* (1888), sketches about his native village, and the novel *The Little Minister* (1891, dramatized in 1897). His greatest play, *Peter Pan* (1904), a sentimental fantasy about a "boy who wouldn't grow up," has been beloved by generations of theatergoers, young and old. Barrie's other dramatic successes include *The Admirable Crichton* (1902), *What Every Woman Knows* (1908), and *Dear Brutus* (1917). He was made a baronet in 1913, and from 1930 until his death was chancellor of Edinburgh University.

Barry, Sir **Charles** (1795–1860), English architect who designed the Houses of Parliament in London. The former was begun in 1840, when the foundation of the House of Lords was laid; the House of Commons was begun in 1852. Barry died before the entire structure was completed. Other great buildings planned and erected by him are the Travellers' (1831) and Reform clubs (1837) in London.

Barry, John (1745–1803), American naval officer noted for his victories over the British during the Revolutionary War. Born in Ireland, he emigrated to America in 1760 and settled in Philadelphia. He built up a fleet of sailing vessels and made a fortune in shipping. When the Revolutionary War began, he was one of the first naval officers commissioned by Congress, and the first to be given the rank of commodore. In command of the *Lexington*, he captured the British *Edward*, the first enemy vessel taken by an American commissioned officer. After the war, Barry devoted himself to the development of the navy, and until his death he was its ranking officer.

Barrymore, Ethel, real name **Ethel Blythe** (1879–1959), American actress remembered for her distinctive style and wit. Born in Philadelphia, the daughter of an actor and actress, she made her debut in 1894 as a member of a company managed by John Drew, her uncle. Under Charles Frohman's direction, she became one of America's leading actresses, starring in *A Doll's House* (1905), *Alice-Sit-by-the-Fire* (1906), *Déclassé* (1919–1921), and *The Corn is Green* (1940–1943). She also appeared in many films, including *None But the Lonely Heart* and *Portrait of Jennie.*

Barrymore, John, real name **John Sidney Blythe** (1882–1942), American actor noted for his interpretation of Hamlet and other Shakespearean roles. He was born in Philadelphia, the brother of Ethel and Lionel Barrymore. After making his stage debut in *Magda* (1903), he quickly became a star, notably for such plays as *Glad of It, The Dictator, A Stubborn Cinderella, Uncle Sam, The Jest,* and *Peter Ibbetson.* His long run in *Hamlet* at the Haymarket Theater, London, was a record. As a motion picture actor he is remembered for his roles in *Grand Hotel, Bill of Divorcement,* and *Twentieth Century.*

Barrymore, Lionel, real name **Lionel Blythe** (1878–1954), American actor noted for his character roles. Born in Philadelphia, the elder brother of Ethel and John Barrymore, he made his debut in 1893 and soon became a leading actor in such plays as *Peter Ibbetson* (1917) and *The Copperhead* (1918). With his brother John he played in *The Mummy and the Humming-bird* (1898) and *The Jest* (1919). In 1921 he appeared in *Macbeth*. He became a motion picture director and actor of silent and talking films. For his role in *A Free Soul* (1931), he won an Academy Award. His yearly interpretation of Scrooge in Dickens' *A Christmas Carol*, first performed in 1934, was a Yuletide radio favorite for nearly 20 years.

Barth, Karl (1886–), Swiss Protestant theologian, one of the greatest of the twentieth century. Born in Basel, he taught theology in Switzerland and Germany for many years. In 1919 the publication of his commentary on St. Paul's *Epistle to the Romans* established his reputation. Rejecting liberal theology, Barth contended that God, not man, is the center of the universe, and that God's grace is the key to man's life. According to Barth, true knowledge of God comes from one source—Jesus Christ, through whom God manifested himself.

Bartholdi, Frédéric Auguste (1834–1904), French sculptor whose most famous work is the Statue of Liberty in New York harbor. This colossal bronze, which he called *Liberty Enlightening the World*, was unveiled on Bedloe's Island in New York harbor in 1886. For this work, he was awarded the French Legion of Honor. Bartholdi's huge *Lion of Belfort*, executed (1880) in Belfort, France, is considered his masterwork. He also did statues of the marquis de Lafayette and George Washington.

Bartók, Béla (1881–1945), Hungarian composer regarded as one of the greatest of the twentieth century. For many years Bartók taught at the Royal Academy of Music in Budapest. His compositions reveal a strikingly original style based on the subtle interplay of haunting melody and sweeping tonal range of Hungarian folk music. Among his most frequently performed works are the opera *Duke Bluebeard's Castle* (1911), the ballet *The Miraculous Mandarin* (1919), the collection of piano pieces called *Mikrokosmos* (1926–1937), and the *Concerto for Orchestra* (1943). Bartók lived in the United States after 1940.

Bartolommeo, Fra, originally **Bartolommeo di Pagolo del Fattorino,** called **Baccio della Porta** (1475–1517), Italian painter, noted for his religious subjects. A native of Florence, he was influenced by Leonardo da Vinci, Michelangelo, Bellini, and Giorgione. When his friend Savonarola met a tragic death, Bartolommeo became a monk. After four years, however, Raphael visited Florence and persuaded him to resume his work. Bartolommeo learned much about perspective from Raphael, and Raphael's art was in turn enriched by advice from Bartolommeo on the use of color. Most of his work was on religious subjects, the best of which are *Saint Sebastian* and *Saint Mark* (1517), in Florence. His *Marriage of St. Catherine* (1511) is in the Louvre, Paris; and Lucca Cathedral has his *Madonna with Saints John and Stephen* (1509).

Barton, Clara, in full **Clarissa Harlowe Barton** (1821–1912), American nurse who founded the American Red Cross. Born in Oxford, Mass., she taught school for many years, and in 1854 went to Washington, D.C., as a civil service clerk. When the Civil War broke out, she organized relief for wounded soldiers, on her own initiative.

She worked in France and Germany for the International Red Cross during the Franco-Prussian War. In 1881 the American Red Cross was founded and she served as its first president until 1904. Originally the Red Cross was empowered to serve only in war, but she brought about a change that authorized its services in behalf of the victims of calamities. Miss Barton personally supervised relief at the Johnstown (Pa.) flood of 1889, during the Russian famine (1892), in Armenia at the time of the massacre of 1896, and in Cuba (1898) during the Spanish-American War.

Bartram, John (1699–1777), American botanist, often called the "father of American botany." Born near Philadelphia, Pa., he was self-educated, and soon became an authority on plant life. At Kingsessing, near Philadelphia, he set up the first botanical garden in the U.S., and stocked it with many plants that he found in his travels in the eastern part of the country. He exchanged seeds with many European botanists and thus introduced many new varieties to this country. His garden was a national point of interest and is still part of Philadelphia's park system.

Baruch, Bernard Mannes (1870–1965), American financier and presidential advisor. Born in Camden, S. C., he graduated from the College of the City of New York in 1889. He became a stock speculator and amassed a fortune by the age of 30. Just before World War I, Baruch entered public life at the request of Pres. Woodrow Wilson, who appointed him to the Council of National Defense. Later he became chairman of the War Industries Board. In 1919 he was economic advisor to Pres. Wilson at the Versailles peace conference. For the next three decades Baruch was an advisor to virtually every president. Particularly notable were his efforts on behalf of economic mobilization during World War II. A noted philanthropist, Baruch gave millions of dollars in support of medical and educational institutions.

Basil or **Basilius,** Saint, called **Basil the Great** (c.330–c.379), one of the most illustrious saints of the Greek Church. He lived when the churches of the East and West were hostile to each other, and he made heroic but unsuccessful attempts to unite them. As bishop of Caesarea, he organized some of the first monasteries, dedicated to public service instead of private asceticism. Many of his treatises and letters survive. His feast day is June 14th.

Bassano, originally **Ponte, Jacopo** or **Giacomo da** (1510–1592), Italian painter noted for his landscapes. A leader of the late Renaissance school in Venice, he was much influenced by Titian. In addition to landscapes, his favorite subjects were peasants, animals, and scenes of village life. He was also successful as a portrait painter.

Bateson, William (1861–1925), English biologist who founded the science of genetics. Born in Whitby, he graduated from Cambridge. His theories on the evolution of vertebrates came to be the foundation of modern genetics. His most influential books are *Mendel's Principles of Heredity—A Defence* (1902) and *Problems of Genetics* (1913). He was director of the John Innes Horticultural Institution in Surrey (1910–1925).

Battani, al-, Arabic name **abu-'Abdullāh Muhammad ibn-Jābir al-Battāni,** Latin name **Albategnius** (c.850–929), Arab astronomer and mathematician. He founded (c.877) an observatory at Antioch, and compiled tables that corrected many earlier statistics. In addition, he determined with greater accuracy the inclination of the ecliptic and the length of the seasons. He is also credited with the introduction of sines in mathematics. His principal work was translated into Latin (c.1100) as *De motu stellarum,* and published in Nuremberg, Germany, in 1537.

Battenberg, a princely family of German extraction recreated in 1851 by Prince Alexander of Hesse (its original branch having died out in 1314). Various members were influential in several European countries. The oldest son of Prince Alexander and Countess von Haucke was **Louis Alexander Mountbatten** (1854–1921; surname adopted after 1917), who was naturalized as a British subject, joined the navy, became first sea lord in 1912 and admiral of the fleet in 1921. The second son was Prince **Alexander Joseph** (1857–1893). He was chosen to rule Bulgaria in 1879 as Alexander I. In 1886 a Russian-inspired conspiracy overthrew him; he was restored to the throne, but abdicated shortly afterward. The third son, Prince **Henry Maurice** (1858–1896), entered the British royal family by his marriage to Princess Beatrice, a daughter of Queen Victoria. His daughter Princess Victoria became queen of Spain in 1906.

Baudelaire, Charles Pierre (1821–1867), French poet, considered one of the greatest of the nineteenth century. Although from a prosperous family and a university graduate, he chose a bohemian existence in Paris, where he wrote poetry and articles for numerous journals, and translated many works by Edgar Allan Poe. A collection of poems, published in 1857 as *Les Fleurs du Mal (Flowers of Evil),* was regarded as scandalous by his contemporaries, dwelling as it did on decadence and eroticism. At his death, much of his work remained unpublished. Not until the twentieth century did his genius receive recognition. His *Les Fleurs du Mal* exerted an unparalleled influence on the French symbolists and a number of modern poets.

Baudouin I (1930–), king of Belgium since 1951. The elder son of King Leopold III and Queen Astrid, he was in exile during the German occupation in World War II. In 1950 the Belgian parliament granted him authority to assume royal prerogatives when the Belgians rose in protest against the reinstatement of his father, who allegedly sympathized with the Nazis during the war. When his father abdicated in 1951, Baudouin became king.

Baum, Lyman Frank (1856–1919), American writer who created the popular Wizard of Oz stories. Born in Chittenango, N.Y., he was a newspaper editor for several years. In 1899 he published *Father Goose: His Book,* the first of a series of humorous fantasies. Baum's finest book, the *Wonderful Wizard of Oz* (1900), was an immediate success. It was adapted for a musical comedy in 1901 and in 1939 was made into a motion picture.

Baumgarten, Alexander Gottlieb (1714–1762), German philosopher who founded the science of aesthetics and coined the word itself. For many years he was a professor of philosophy at Frankfort an der Oder. His unfinished *Aesthetica acromatica* (1750–1758) laid the foundation for much of modern art criticism and appreciation.

Bayard, Seigneur de, originally **Pierre Terrail** (c.1473–1524), French soldier known as *Chevalier sans peur et sans reproche* ("the knight without fear and above reproach"). He was knighted for valor in 1495, after winning the battle of Fornovo. He is said to have defended a bridge alone against 150 Spaniards in 1503. He led the French to victory at Marignano in 1515; on that battlefield he knighted his king, Francis I. Bayard was fatally wounded in the battle of Sesia River, but the victorious Spaniards returned his body to France. Throughout his life he was so admired for his knightly virtues, that even when he was captured by the enemy, he was released unconditionally.

Bayard, Thomas Francis (1828–1898), American statesman who was secretary of state (1885-1889) and the first U.S. ambassador to Great Britain (1893–1897). Born in Wilmington, Del., of a family prominent in politics, he had little formal education, but studied law in his father's office. A leader in Democratic party circles, he was a U.S. senator from Delaware from 1869 to 1885. After serving as secretary of state under

METRO-GOLDWYN-MAYER

THE BARRYMORE FAMILY: actors John (*left*) and Lionel (*right*) with their sister, Ethel.

Pres. Grover Cleveland, he was appointed U.S. ambassador to Great Britain, the first minister to hold that rank.

Bayazid, Bayezid or **Bajazet I** (1347–(1403), sultan of the Ottoman Empire (1389–1403), known as *Yilderim* (Lightning) for the speed of his victories. He succeeded his father, Murad I, and won a series of wars against Hungary, Bulgaria, Greece, and several other countries. Later he sent his armies to fight in Asia Minor, but his soldiers were reluctant to oppose fellow Muslims. In 1402 Bayazid was defeated by Tamerlane at Angora.

Bayle, Pierre (1647–1706), French philosopher whose controversial encyclopedia of philosophy criticized the orthodox thought of his time. Born a Protestant, Bayle became a convert to Catholicism, but later returned to his original faith. Appointed professor of philosophy at Rotterdam (1681), he defended liberty of thought and urged religious tolerance; for these and other controversial views he was dismissed in 1693. In his great work, *Dictionnaire historique et critique* (1697), his comments upon accepted philosophical and historical doctrines created a furor among his contemporaries. His philosophy is considered the foundation of eighteenth-century rationalism.

Bazaine, Achille François (1811–1888), marshal of France who capitulated to the Germans in the Franco-Prussian War. Before becoming a marshal in 1864, he had served over 30 years in the French army, notably in the Crimean War and in campaigns against Spain and Austria. Shortly after the war with Germany started, Bazaine surrendered at Metz with an army of 173,000 men, after a siege of seven weeks in 1870. He was denounced as a traitor, tried by a military court, and sentenced to death. His sentence was commuted to 20 years in prison on the island of Sainte-Marguerite. He escaped in 1874, went to Italy and then to Spain, where he died in exile.

Beard, Charles Austin (1874-1948), American historian who stressed the role of economics in shaping history and political policy. Born near Knightstown, Ind., he graduated from De Pauw University and took his Ph.D. at Columbia where he taught from 1907 to 1917. His best-known work (written with his wife, Mary R. Beard), *The Rise of American Civilization* (1927), was an influential textbook for over 20 years. A prolific writer, he produced and edited over 30 books on American history, many of which were controversial. In an earlier book, *The Economic Basis of Politics* (1922), he championed liberalism and the importance of national planning. In later books on foreign policy, Beard was critical of Pres. Franklin Roosevelt, and was accused of being an isolationist.

Beardsley, Aubrey Vincent (1872–1898), English artist and illustrator, noted for his decorative black and white drawings. With little formal training, he moved from a career in architecture to one in book illustration. His strikingly original drawings for books such as Oscar Wilde's *Salomé* (1894) evoked high praise from some critics and cries of outrage from others. Always a controversial artist, closely associated with the end-of-the-century trend to decadence in literature, Beardsley did much of his best work for the periodicals *Yellow Book* and *The Savoy*.

Beaton, Cecil Walter Hardy (1904–), English photographer and stage designer. By the 1930's he was a world-famous photographer, and was appointed photographer to the British royal family. In World War II he served with the British Ministry of Information and published several noteworthy volumes of war photographs. Beaton has been acclaimed in the theater for his elegant sets and costumes, notably for plays set in the Victorian and Edwardian periods.

Beatty, David, 1st Earl of the **North Sea** and of **Brooksby** (1871–1936), British admiral who commanded the fleet at the Battle of Jutland, a key naval engagement in World War I. Born in England, he entered the navy in 1884, becoming a captain in 1900 and a rear admiral in 1910. On May 31, 1916, he encountered the German fleet at Jutland. Although he sustained losses, Beatty achieved his primary objective of drawing the German fleet into the North Sea, so that a larger force led by Admiral John Jellicoe could engage it. From 1919 to 1927 Beatty served as first sea lord of the English fleet, and in 1921 was a delegate to the disarmament conference in Washington.

Beaumarchais, Pierre Augustin Caron de (1732–1799), French dramatist and adventurer whose plays *The Barber of Seville* (first performed in 1775) and *The Marriage of Figaro* (1784) exemplify French comic drama of the eighteenth century. During a crowded career, Beaumarchais was a watchmaker, a music master (he taught the daughters of Louis XV), a secret agent, and a strong supporter of the American Revolution. His two most famous plays provoked much controversy by mocking the nobility and championing the cause of liberty. Later, both plays were set to music, *The Marriage of Figaro* by Mozart in 1786 and *The Barber of Seville* by Rossini in 1816.

Beaumont, Francis (1584-1616), English dramatist who, chiefly with John Fletcher, wrote some 50 highly popular plays. From about 1606 to 1614 he and Fletcher collaborated in such dramas as *Philaster*, *The Maid's Tragedy* (1610), and *A King and No King* (1611). Basically these plays were characterized by idyllic settings, intricate and melodramatic plots, and emotional rhetoric. They were highly successful in their time and influenced several generations of English playwrights. Beaumont also wrote several plays without Fletcher.

Beaumont, William (1785–1853), American physician noted for his contributions to the physiology of human digestion. Born in Lebanon, Conn., he studied medicine and was an army surgeon during the War of 1812. In 1822, while treating a wounded Canadian trapper, Alexis St. Martin, he became interested in the digestive processes. St. Martin's gunshot wound had left a hole in his abdomen, exposing part of his stomach. During the next year Beaumont made daily observations of its functions and set forth the chemical nature of digestion. His classic work, *Experiments and Observations on the Gastric Juice and the Physiology of Digestion* (1833), reported his findings.

Beauregard, Pierre Gustave Toutant de (1818–1893), American Confederate general, born near New Orleans, La. He served in the Mexican War (1846–1847) and in 1860 was appointed superintendent of the military academy at West Point. He resigned the next year and became a brigadier general in the Confederate army. He commanded the troops that bombarded Fort Sumter, S.C. After the Battle of Bull Run he was made a full general. His military career ended (April 26, 1865) with his surrender to Gen. W. T. Sherman.

Beaverbrook, 1st Baron, born **William Maxwell Aitken** (1879–1964), British newspaper publisher and statesman, born in Ontario, Canada. He became a stockbroker and, before he was 30, amassed a fortune by amalgamating the entire cement industry in Canada. Moving to England in 1910, he became a Conservative member of Parliament. In 1916 he secured control of the London *Daily Express*, which he developed into one of the world's largest newspapers, and eventually built the largest newspaper chain in Britain. He was minister of information during World War I, and in World War II held several important posts in Winston Churchill's cabinet. He was created Lord Beaverbrook in 1917.

Bebel, August (1840–1913), German socialist leader In 1869 (with Wilhelm Liebknecht) he founded the German Social Democratic party. For some 40 years, Bebel was the leading spokesman for socialism, serving his party in the Reichstag and as an editor of socialist publications. One of his works, *Die Frau und der Sozialismus* (*The Women and Socialism,* 1883), is considered a classic in socialist writing. By 1912 Bebel's party was the largest group in the Reichstag.

Becket, Thomas à, also Saint **Thomas Becket** (1118–1170), English cleric and martyr whose stormy relations with King Henry II led to his murder. Appointed (1155) royal chancellor to Henry II, he achieved prominence both in diplomacy and in war. In 1162 Henry helped secure him the post of archbishop of Canterbury. Henceforth, he upheld the rights of the Church against the royal prerogative. When Becket showed greater loyalty to the pope than to Henry, relations between the two steadily deteriorated. Henry dismissed Becket, who then left for Rome. The pope ordered Henry to reinstate Becket, but on his return, late in 1170, he was murdered by four of Henry's overzealous knights. He was canonized in 1173; his feast day is December 29.

Becquerel, Antoine Henri (1852–1908), French physicist who discovered radioactivity. Born in Paris, he became a physicist and, like his distinguished father (Alexandre Edmond) and grandfather (Antoine César), was a professor at the Museum of Natural History in Paris. In 1896 he discovered that uranium emits an invisible radiation that can penetrate many dense and opaque substances. In 1903 he shared the Nobel Prize for physics with Pierre and Marie Curie.

Bede, Baeda, or **Beda,** Saint, called **the Venerable Bede** (673–735), English historian whose chronicles of Anglo-Saxon England earned him the title "Father of English History." He spent his whole life in a monastery in Durham County. His *Historia ecclesiastica gentis Anglorum* (*Ecclesiastical History of the English People*, 731), written in Latin, is the source of nearly everything known about England before that time. In the book he referred to his other writings: lives of the saints, hymns, and commentaries on books of the Bible. Bede was canonized in 1899.

Beebe, Charles William (1877–1962), American naturalist, explorer, and writer. He was born in Brooklyn, N.Y., and graduated from Columbia University. In 1899 he was appointed curator of ornithology (birds) at the New York Zoological Society and director of its department of scientific research. An authority on deep-sea life, he made many underwater explorations in diving apparatus. He also explored jungles in little-known parts of the world, writing much on the animal life found there. Beebe published many scientific papers and more than a dozen books, notably *Jungle Peace* (1918), *The Arcturus Adventure* (1925), *Galápagos, World's End* (1923), and *Half Mile Down* (1934).

Beecham, Sir **Thomas** (1879–1961), English conductor, noted for his interpretations of Mozart and Handel. Born in Saint Helens, Lancashire, he made his debut in London in 1905. Five years later he began conducting opera, notably the works of Richard Strauss and Frederick Delius, whom he introduced to British audiences. In 1947 he founded the Royal Philharmonic Orchestra, and thereafter devoted himself more to orchestral music. In later years he was a guest-conductor of orchestras throughout the world, including the Houston Symphony Orchestra. He was knighted in 1916.

Beecher, Henry Ward (1813–1887), American clergyman famed for his oratory. Born in Litchfield, Conn., he became a Presbyterian minister and held pastorates in Indiana for 10 years. For 40 years (1847–1887) he was pastor of Plymouth Congregational Church in Brooklyn, N.Y., where he achieved national renown for his oratory. In 1875 one of the most sensational trials of the century took place when Beecher was accused of immorality in a case involving the wife of a former friend. The charges were not substantiated, and the majority of his church officers and members supported him. In addition to his church activities, Beecher also edited religious publications for many years, and wrote several popular inspirational books.

Beecher, Lyman (1775–1863), American evangelist, father of Henry Ward Beecher and Harriet Beecher Stowe. Born in New Haven, Conn., he graduated from Yale in 1797. As pastor of several churches in Massachusetts, he became famous for his revival meetings. In 1832 he became president of Lane Theological Seminary in Cincinnati, Ohio, a post he held until 1852, when he was tried

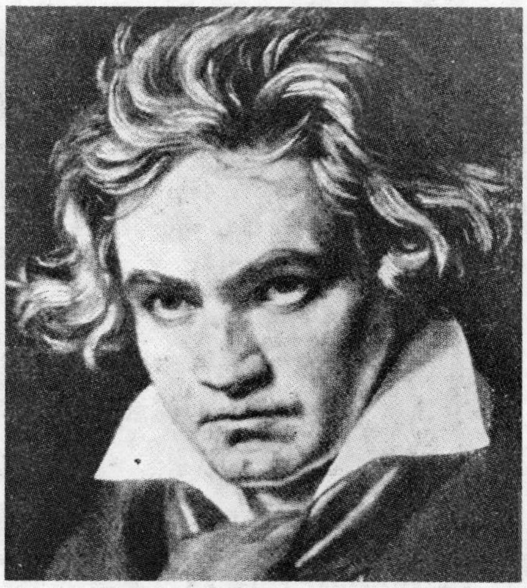

GERMAN INFORMATION CENTER

LUDWIG VAN BEETHOVEN

for heresy but exonerated. Of his 13 children, six sons became clergymen, and one of his five daughters, Harriet, became the celebrated author of *Uncle Tom's Cabin.*

Beerbohm, Sir **Max** (1872–1956), English author and caricaturist. As a parodist and cartoonist he was unmatched in his unerring ability to catch the essential nature of his subject. Born in London, he studied at Oxford, where he gained a reputation for wit and elegance. He contributed essays and cartoons to the *Yellow Book* and other magazines and in 1898 was appointed drama critic of the *Saturday Review,* succeeding G. B. Shaw. Beerbohm's literary output includes a novel *Zuleika Dobson* (1911), a satire on college life; *A Christmas Garland* (1912), parodies of contemporary writers; and several volumes of caricatures. He also had a regular radio program in England for several years.

Beethoven, Ludwig van (1770–1827), German composer generally regarded as the greatest of the Romantic period. Born in Bonn, he showed exceptional talent for the violin and piano as a boy, and his father, determined to make him a Mozartian child prodigy, sought the best teachers for him. At the age of 10 he became a student of Christian Gottlieb Neefe, the elector's court organist. He soon became assistant on the piano to Neefe in the elector's chapel. At the age of 17 he was sent to Vienna to study under Mozart and later under Haydn. Vienna became his home (from 1792) and the scene of his later triumphs. He established himself as a professional pianist, performing his *Concerto in C Major* at his public debut in 1795. In the same year he published three pianoforte trios (*Opus I*). He gave his own first public concert in 1800. Before becoming totally deaf (c.1814) he produced more than twenty-five sonatas for the piano, numerous quartets, and trios, and eight symphonies (1800–1814). His last work was the *Ninth Symphony* (1823), one of the greatest of his compositions with its last choral movement set to Friedrich Schiller's *Ode to Joy.* He labored for five years on the *Mass in D* (*Missa solemnis;* 1818–1823). One of the most popular of his compositions is the *Moonlight Sonata* (*Opus 27;* c.1802); in this form he perfected the beginnings made by Haydn and Mozart. In addition to many songs, Beethoven wrote one opera, *Fidelio,* in 1805.

Behring, Emil Adolf von (1854–1917), German bacteriologist, often regarded as the founder of the science of immunology. He studied medicine in Berlin and served several years in the German army medical corps. As director of the Hygienic Institute at Marburg, he conducted research on infectious diseases, notably lockjaw and diphtheria. In this work, he furthered Louis Pasteur's theory that injections of weak viruses promote immunity against strong ones, and gradually developed the science of toxins and antitoxins. As a result of his work, diphtheria antitoxin soon came into general use. In 1901 von Behring was awarded the Nobel Prize for medicine.

Behrman, Samuel Nathaniel (1893–   ), American dramatist, noted for such plays as *The Second Man* (1927), *Biography* (1933), *No Time for Comedy* (1939), *Jacobowsky and the Colonel* (1944, with Franz Werfel), and *Fanny* (1954, with Joshua Logan). Born in Worcester, Mass., and educated at Harvard, he collaborated on several plays before striking out on his own. His most successful plays were social comedies, marked by sophisticated dialogue and subtle characterization. Behrman has also achieved renown as an essayist (notably in the *New Yorker* magazine) and a film writer. In addition, he wrote a well-received biography of Max Beerbohm, entitled *Portrait of Max* (1960).

Belasco, David (1853–1931), American playwright and producer, remembered for his spectacular theatrical productions. Born in San Francisco, Calif., he became a child actor and later a stage manager and play adapter. In 1880 he moved to New York, where he gained a reputation for meticulously detailed productions with lavish settings and unique mechanical effects. Among the many plays that he wrote or adapted were *Madame Butterfly* (1900), *Du Barry* (1901), *The Girl of the Golden West* (1905), and *Lulu Belle* (1926).

Belisarius (c.505–565 A.D.), Byzantine general who served under Emperor Justinian I of the Eastern Roman Empire. He suppressed an insurrection in Constantinople (532), drove the Vandals out of North Africa (533–534), and recaptured Rome from the Goths (536). In 562 his enemies succeeded in bringing him to trial for conspiracy against Justinian, and he was imprisoned for seven months. He was restored to favor when the emperor was convinced of his innocence.

Bell, Alexander Graham (1847–1922), American scientist who invented the telephone. Born in Edinburgh, Scotland, he moved in 1870 with his parents to Canada, where his father developed ways of teaching deaf-mutes to speak. Alexander went to Boston in 1872 to train teachers of the deaf, and in 1873 he became professor of vocal physiology at Boston University, continuing the work that his father had begun.

As early as 1865 Bell had experimented with speech transmission; ten years later, while he was working with a harmonic telegraph, the idea of reproducing and sending speech by electric wires came to him, resulting in 1876 in the invention of the telephone. It was exhibited at the Philadelphia Centennial Exhibition in that year, but was considered little more than a toy.

Elisha Gray also claimed to have invented the telephone, but Bell won against Gray and all other claimants after years of litigation. He also invented the photophone, wax recorders for phonographs, and instruments for the deaf. In 1883 he founded the magazine *Science.*

Bell, Sir **Charles** (1774–1842), Scottish anatomist who made notable contributions to knowledge of the brain and nervous system. Born in Edinburgh, he studied anatomy there under the direction of his brother, a surgeon. In 1804 he went to London, where he became a distinguished lecturer on anatomy and surgery. From 1812 to 1836 he was a surgeon and lecturer at Middlesex Hospital and the Royal College of Surgeons. Bell was the first to show the relation between the nerves and the brain—how some nerves control sensation, others motion, and still others both sensation and motion. Bell was knighted in 1833 and in 1836 accepted the chair of surgery at the University of Edinburgh.

Bell, Clive in full **Arthur Clive Howard Bell** (1881–1964), English art critic, famed as the champion of modern art. Educated at Trinity College, Cambridge, he became a member of the Bloomsbury group of writers and artists. The publication of his book *Art* in 1914 helped gain public recognition of the "modern" art of the time. Bell asserted that form is the significant thing in painting and sculpture, rather than subject matter and realistic description. Notable among his other works are *Since Cézanne* (1922); *Proust* (1929), a literary study; and *An Account of French Painting* (1931).

Bell, Henry (1767–1830), Scottish engineer who introduced steam navigation to Europe. In 1812 he launched on the River Clyde his 30-ton vessel *Comet,* a paddle-boat equipped with a three-horsepower engine that reached a maximum speed of about seven miles per hour. There is a monument to him on the banks of the Clyde.

Bell, John (1797–1869), American politician who tried to keep Tennessee out of the Civil War. Born near Nashville, Tenn., he represented his state in Congress for six terms (1827–1841), and served in the Senate from 1847 to 1859. A moderate and a conservative, he was the presidential candidate of the Constitutional Union party in 1860, but received only 39 electoral votes. He opposed secession, but when the Civil War broke out he joined the Confederates.

Bellamy, Edward (1850–1898), American social reformer and author, remembered for his utopian novel *Looking Backward* (1888). Born in Chicopee Falls, Mass., he became a journalist and wrote articles and stories critical of contemporary American civilization. In *Looking Backward,* Bellamy depicted a future society (c.2000), based on brotherhood and the sharing of industrial wealth. A sequel, *Equality* (1897), dealt with similar social themes.

Bellarmine, Saint **Robert,** Italian **Roberto Francesco Romolo Bellarmino** (1542–1621), Italian cardinal who was the leading defender of Roman Catholicism during the sixteenth century. In 1560 he entered the Society of Jesus (Jesuits), where he became known for his lectures on controversial religious subjects. Spurred by the challenge of Protestantism, he produced several important works that defined the Church's position on various subjects. In an age noted for its bigotry, he displayed tolerance toward social and scientific ideas. He was made a cardinal in 1599. In 1930 he was canonized; his feast day is May 13.

Bellini, Giovanni (c.1430–1516), Italian painter who, with his brother, **Gentile Bellini** (c.1429–1507), founded the Venetian school of painting. The brothers studied under their father, **Jacopo Bellini** (c.1400–1470), and specialized in religious paintings that are noted for richness of color and depth of feeling. Titian and Giorgione were among Giovanni's most distinguished students. Giovanni Bellini's altarpieces and madonnas are considered among the finest that have ever been done.

Bellini, Vincenzo (1801–1835), Italian operatic composer, noted for the purity and beauty of his vocal melodies. Born in Sicily, he studied music in Naples. His first important opera, *Il Pirata,* was produced at La Scala in 1827. His other operas include *La Sonnambula* (1831); his masterpiece, *Norma* (1831); and *I Puritani* (1835). While his operas lack the drama and elaborate orchestration of such later composers as Verdi and Wagner, Bellini composed some of the most beautiful melodies in all of music.

Belloc, Hilary, in full **Joseph Hilary Pierre Belloc,** pen name **Hilaire Belloc** (1870–1953), English writer of essays, light verse, novels, and biographies. Born in St. Cloud, France, and educated at Oxford, he wrote chiefly from a Roman Cathtolic point of view, which involved him in several controversies with other English writers. Among his chief works are biographies of Richelieu, Napoleon, Danton, and Wolsey; a four-volume history of England; several volumes of light verse; and several travel books.

Bellow, Saul (1915–   ), American author. Born in Lachine, Quebec, he grew up in Montreal and Chicago, and graduated from Northwestern University in 1937. In his most representative novels, *The Adventures of Augie March* (1953) and *Herzog* (1964), Bellow depicts with humor and irony the trials of the Jewish intellectual in modern America. For these novels he received the National Book Award in 1954 and 1965. Bellow's other works include the novels *Dangling Man* (1944), *Seize the Day* (1956), and *Henderson the Rain King* (1959).

Bellows, George Wesley (1882–1925), American painter and lithographer, noted for his realistic paintings and drawings. He was born in Columbus, Ohio, and educated at Ohio State University. He went to New York in 1904 and in 1913 was one of the organizers of the famous Armory Show. In a series of prize-fight paintings, Bellows captured the violent action and ruggedness of the participants in a unique way. His best-known painting, *Stag at Sharkey's* (1907), is a prize-fight scene. Bellows was noted for his portraits and his bold, vivid city scenes. In later years he turned to lithography and won acclaim for his prints.

Benavente y Martínez, Jacinto (1866–1954), one of the leading Spanish dramatists of the twentieth century. In his realistic early plays he departed drastically from the melodramatic drama that dominated the Spanish stage. Among his best dramas are *Saturday Night* (1903), *The Bonds of Interest* (1907), and *The Passion Flower* (1913). His collected plays were translated into English in 1917. Benavente was awarded the Nobel Prize for literature in 1922.

Ben Bella, Ahmed (1919–   ), first premier of the Republic of Algeria. Born in western Algeria, he became a leader in his country's quest for independence from France. On July 22, 1962, he and his supporters formed a seven-man bureau to assume political control of Algeria. On September 26, 1962, he became the country's first premier, and in 1963 he was elected president. However, he was ousted from office by a military coup in 1965.

Benchley, Robert Charles (1889-1945), American author famed for his short humorous essays on the foibles of mankind. Born in Worcester, Mass., he graduated from Harvard in 1912. By 1920 he was a drama critic, and he began to gain popularity for his monologues and humorous skits. From 1929 to 1940 he was drama critic for the *New Yorker* magazine. The humorous essays he wrote were collected in some 15 books, including *My Ten Years in a Quandary* (1936) and *Benchley Beside Himself* (1943). He also achieved renown as a motion-picture actor, specializing in roles of men confused by the common experiences of everyday life. One of his films, *How to Sleep* (1936), is still a favorite.

Benedict XIII, born **Pietro Francesco Orsini** (1649–1730), Roman Catholic pope (1724–1730). A member of the celebrated Orsini family, he became pope at the age of 75. During his pontificate he tried unsuccessfully to unite all Christian sects under the Catholic banner. Pious and scholarly, he was concerned with ecclesiastic reforms and left the secular matters to his ministers.

Benedict XIV, born **Prospero Lambertini** (1675–1758), Roman Catholic pope (1740–1758). One of the most scholarly and enlightened of all popes, he advanced learning in Rome by establishing chairs in science and mathematics. He set up boards to examine all candidates for high office in the Church, to assure himself of their exalted moral character. In the papal states he reduced taxation, supported industry, and encouraged agriculture. He was remarkably conciliatory in foreign relations.

Benedict XV, born **Giacomo della Chiesa** (1854–1922), Roman Catholic pope (1914–1922). He succeeded Pius X only a month before the outbreak of World War I; consequently, most of his affairs were related to the war. He made strong efforts to bring about a peace, and many of his proposals were adopted in the Fourteen Points of Pres. Woodrow Wilson.

Benedict of Nursia, Saint (c.480–c.543), Italian monk who founded the Benedictine Order. Sent as a young man to Rome for an education, he became dissatisfied with the superficiality and sins of the time. He retired to a remote spot, where he lived for three years in a cave, and by his austerity and devotion attracted many followers. Within a few years he established several monasteries, most notably (c.529) the famous one at Monte Cassino, halfway between Rome and Naples. There he wrote his *Holy Rule*, describing the regulations and duties of his order. In time, this work was adopted as the basis of all monastic life in the West. His feast day is March 21.

Beneš, Eduard (1884–1948), president of Czechoslovakia (1935–1938, 1940–1948). Born in Kožlany, Bohemia, he taught political science in Prague. When World War I broke out, he joined forces with Tomás G. Masaryk in a movement to free Czechoslovakia from Austrian rule. When the new republic of Czechoslovakia was formed in 1918, he became its first foreign minister, and its prime minister in 1921. He succeeded Masaryk as president in 1935, resigning three years later under pressure from Nazi Germany. During World War II he was president of the Czech government in exile, returning to his native land in 1945. Three years later he resigned his office after refusing to sign the new constitution that had been pushed through by the Communists.

Benét, Stephen Vincent (1898–1943), American poet and novelist whose *John Brown's Body* is considered one of the finest narrative poems written by an American. Born in Bethlehem, Pa., he studied at Yale where he published two volumes of verse before graduating in 1919. For *John Brown's Body* (1928), an epic poem on the Civil War, he received the Pulitzer Prize in 1929. Notable among his other works are *A Book of Americans* (1933); the well-known short story *The Devil and Daniel Webster* (1937); and the posthumous *Western Star* (1943), for which he received a second Pulitzer Prize in 1944.

Ben-Gurion, David (1886–   ), Israeli statesman who in 1948 became Israel's first prime minister. Born in Plonsk, Poland, he became interested in Zionism at an early age. In 1906 he went to Palestine, where he became active in the labor movement and helped organize defense units that protected Jewish settlers against Arab raids. Exiled by the Turkish government in 1915, he went to the United States, where he organized the Jewish Legion of World War I. For over 30 years he led the drive to establish the state of Israel, achieved in 1948. As both prime minister and minister of defense, he was chiefly responsible for Israel's successful defense against Arab attacks. He served as prime minister until his retirement in 1953. He was returned to office in 1955 and remained as head of the government until his resignation in 1963.

Benjamin, Judah Philip (1811–1884), American statesman who was Confederate secretary of state during the Civil War. Born in the West Indies, he emigrated to the U.S., graduated from Yale, and practiced law in New Orleans. From 1852 to 1861 he served in the U.S. Senate, then joined the Confederate cause. As attorney general and secretary of state, he became known as the "brains of the Confederacy." When the South surrendered, he left the U.S. and settled in London, where he practiced law until his retirement in 1883.

Bennett, Arnold, in full **Enoch Arnold Bennett** (1867-1931), English novelist, noted for his realistic portrayals of middle-class life in England. A prolific writer, he produced over 50 books, notably *The Old Wives' Tale* (1908), *Clayhanger* (1910), and *Riceyman Steps* (1923). In his best work he described life in the Staffordshire towns where he had lived as a boy. These novels show the influence of the French realistic and naturalistic tradition. He also wrote several plays and scores of articles and reviews. Bennett's *Journal* (1933) is a detailed account of his literary life from 1896.

Bennett, James Gordon II (1841–1918), American newspaper publisher, son of **James Gordon Bennett** (1795–1872), founder of the New York *Herald*. Born in New York City, he became managing editor of the *Herald* in 1866 and its owner and publisher in 1872. He spent much of his time in Europe, where he established editions of the *Herald* in London and Paris. It was Bennett who sent Henry M. Stanley to Africa to hunt for David Livingstone. At his own expense he equipped the *Jeannette* for a polar expedition, headed by George W. De Long. Bennett was one of the organizers of the cable service between America and Europe. He also promoted sports and offered the Gordon Bennett cups in automobile, balloon, and airplane races.

Bentham, Jeremy (1748–1832), English philosopher, noted as the founder of utilitarianism. Born in London, he graduated from Oxford and became a lawyer, but soon left his practice to devote himself to writing on social reform and philosophy. In his masterwork, *An Introduction to the Principles of Morals and Legislation* (1789), Bentham defined utility as that which gives the greatest pleasure or good to man. Accordingly, the object of all legislation should be to create the greatest good for the greatest number of people. The ideas in this work, as well as those in many other books he wrote, were very well received throughout Europe and the U.S.

Benton, Thomas Hart (1782–1858), American senator who was influential in pre-Civil War politics. Born near Hillsboro, N.C., he became a lawyer in Nashville, Tenn., and served as a colonel in the War of 1812. After the war, he settled in St. Louis, Mo., where he practiced law and edited the St. Louis *Enquirer* (1818-1820). As a Democratic U.S. senator from Missouri (1821–1851), he strongly advocated the use of both gold and silver as money, voted for the bill to annex Texas, opposed the spread of slavery from the South to the West, and championed agrarian principles. His autobiography, *Thirty Years' View* (1854–1856), is a valuable source for the political history of his period.

Benton, Thomas Hart (1889–   ), American painter noted for his realistic portraits, scenes, and murals on American subjects. Born in Neosho, Mo., he studied art in Chicago and Paris, and taught at the Art Students League in New York. He first achieved renown after World War I with his paintings and murals of farm scenes and the day-to-day activities of mid-westerners. During much of his creative life, Benton was a teacher, first in New York and later in Kansas City. A colorful, controversial figure, he published his autobiography, *An Artist in America*, in 1937.

Berenson, Bernard (1865–1959), American art critic who was a leading authority on Italian Renaissance art. Born in Lithuania, he grew up in Boston, Mass., and graduated from Harvard in 1887. He then settled at a villa near Florence, Italy, where he became recognized as an expert on Renaissance art. Dealers and collectors from all parts of the world sought his advice. Among his many books perhaps the most influential are *Italian Painters of the Renaissance* (1932) and *Aesthetics and History in the Visual Arts* (1949). A discriminating collector of art himself, Berenson left his collection, together with his villa *I Tatti* outside Florence, to Harvard University as an art study center. Selections from his diaries under the title *The Passionate Sightseer* were published in 1960.

Berg, Alban (1885–1935), Austrian composer best known for his opera *Wozzeck*. Born in Vienna, he studied under Arnold Schönberg, who developed the 12-tone technique of composition. In *Wozzeck*, finished in 1921, Berg combined the radical approach of Schönberg with more traditional methods of composition; the result was a work so "modern" that it was only rarely performed until long after the composer's death. A second opera, *Lulu*, was unfinished when Berg died, but has since been performed with increasing frequency. Not a prolific composer, Berg also wrote a piano concerto, a string quartet, and some songs and orchestral pieces.

Bergh, Henry (1811–1888), American humanitarian who founded the American Society for the Prevention of Cruelty to Animals (ASPCA). Born in New York City and educated at Columbia University, he served for a time in the diplomatic service, then gave his full attention to the campaign against cruelty to animals. The ASPCA was formed in 1866. At his death 39 states and many foreign nations had passed legislation to protect animals. Bergh also was a founder (1875) of the Society for the Prevention of Cruelty to Children.

Bergman, Ingmar, full name **Ernst Ingmar Bergman** (1918–   ), Swedish film writer and director, noted for his psychological studies of sex and human guilt. After writing the screen play for *Torment* (1943) and directing the film *Crisis* (1945), he did two comedies, *A Lesson in Love* (1953) and *Smiles of a Summer Night* (1955). For the latter, he won the Cannes Film Festival Award (1956), an honor which he received again in 1957 and 1958 for *The Seventh Seal* and *Brink of Love*. One of Bergman's most famous films is *Wild Strawberries* (1958). Later films include *The Virgin Spring* (1960), *Through a Glass Darkly* (1961), and *The Silence* (1963). Bergman has also directed plays and operas.

Bergson, Henri (1859–1941), French philosopher, born in Paris, one of the most influential thinkers of his time. In his philosophy he taught that change is the basis of all reality, and that man's intellect alone is not sufficient to grasp the meaning of change. Therefore, he argued, man must rely on his intuition as well as his intellect to grasp the *élan vital* (creative force). A lucid, imaginative writer, Bergson's works include *Matière et Memoire*, *Essai sur les rapports du corps à l'esprit* (1896; *Matter and Memory*, 1911), *Le rire* (1900; *Laughter*, 1911), and *L'Évolution créatrice* (1907; *Creative Evolution*, 1911). He won the Nobel Prize for literature in 1927.

Bering, Vitus (1680–1741), Danish navigator and explorer. Born in Jutland, he joined the Russian navy and fought against Sweden. He was appointed (1724) by Czar Peter the Great to lead an expedition to northeastern Siberia. His explorations gave his name to the sea and strait between Siberia and America. He discovered in 1728 what Simon Dezhnev, a Cossack, in 1648 had already proved by sailing through the strait, that Siberia and Alaska are not a continuous land mass. Just before his death he traced the western shore of North America from the Bering Sea down to latitude 69°. Russia's claim to Alaska rested upon his exploration.

Berkeley, Sir **William** (1606–1677), English man and philosopher noted for his philosophy of idealism. Born near Kilkenny, he was educated at Trinity College, Dublin, where he remained as a fellow for 20 years. He traveled widely and wrote voluminously before settling down in Ireland to oversee his bishopric. His idealist philosophy rests on the belief that material things exist only when they are perceived by men. A vigorous prose stylist, Berkeley produced a number of works on religion, morality, and the natural world. His works include *A Treatise Concerning the Principles of Human Knowledge* (1710) and *Three Dialogues between Hylas and Philonous* (1713).

Berkeley, Sir **William** (1606–1677), English colonial administrator in America. He was twice governor of the Virginia Colony, first by royal appointment in 1641, second by election by the general assembly of the colony in 1660. When Oliver Cromwell came to power in England, Berkeley resigned (1651) but remained in the colony. During his second term as governor (1660–1676), Bacon's Rebellion occurred. Berkeley took stern measures with those who had defied his authority. In recalling Berkeley to England, Charles II said, "The old fool has taken more lives in that naked country than I did for the murder of my father."

Berlin, Irving, real name **Israel Baline** (1888–   ), American composer of popular songs. Born in Russia, he was brought to the U.S. when he was five. He began his musical career in 1904 as a singing waiter in New York City. A few years later he began composing the simple, melodic songs that were to make him famous: *Alexander's Ragtime Band, God Bless America, White Christmas, Always, Oh, How I Hate to Get Up in the Morning*, and hundreds of others. Berlin composed the music for many motion pictures and Broadway musicals.

Berlioz, Louis Hector (1803–1869), French composer of the Romantic school. Born in La Côte-Saint-André, he was sent by his father, a physician, to study medicine in Paris. He soon gave up his medical studies in favor of a musical career. After studies at the Paris Conservatory, he began producing the great variety of compositions for which he is famous. Among his greatest achievements are the operas *Benvenuto Cellini* (1838) and *Les Troyens* (1858); the religious works *Requiem* (1837) and *Te Deum* (1849); the dramatic oratorios *The Damnation of Faust* (1846), *The Childhood of Christ* (1854), and *Romeo and Juliet* (1839); and the symphonic works *Harold in Italy* (1834) and *Symphonie Fantastiquel* (1830). Although his works were not fully appreciated during his lifetime, Berlioz is recognized today as one of the creators of program music.

IN THE GRAVEDIGGER SCENE, Shakespeare's Hamlet muses upon the skull of "poor Yorick."

Creators of world literature

Hans Christian Andersen
(1805-75) Denmark

Maurice Maeterlinck
(1862-1949) Belgium

Gerhart Hauptmann
(1862-1946) Germany

Molière (1622-73)
France

Anton Pavlovich Chekhov
(1860-1904) Russia

William Shakespeare
(1564-1616) England

Sir James Matthew Barrie
(1860-1937) Scotland

Robert Louis Stevenson
(1850-94) Scotland

Edwin Markham
(1852-1940) United States

John Milton (1608-74)
England

Honoré de Balzac
(1799-1850) France

Harriet Beecher Stowe
(1811-96) United States

Alexandre Dumas, pere
(1802-70) France

Miguel de Cervantes
Saavedra (1547-1616) Spain

Giovanni Boccaccio
(1313-75) Italy

Count Lev Tolstoy
(1828-1910) Russia

Victor Hugo (1802-85)
France

Nathaniel Hawthorne
(1804-64) United States

Washington Irving
(1783-1859) United States

Sir Walter Scott
(1771-1832) Scotland

Masters of prose and drama

Henrik Ibsen (1828-1906)
Norway

William Makepeace Thack-
eray (1811-63) England

Friedrich von Schiller
(1759-1805) Germany

Paul von Heyse
(1830-1914) Germany

American and European poets

Heinrich Heine (1797-1856)
Germany

Oliver Wendell Holmes
(1809-94) United States

Henry Wadsworth Longfel-
low (1807-82) United States

Alfred de Musset
(1810-57) France

Robert Browning (1812-89)
England

Robert Burns (1759-96)
Scotland

Johann Wolfgang von Goe-
the (1749-1832) Germany

Dante Alighieri
(1265-1321) Italy

Aleksandr Pushkin
(1799-1837) Russia

John Greenleaf Whittier
(1807-92) United States

Thomas Moore (1779-1852)
Ireland

Edgar Allan Poe
(1809-49) United States

Bernadette of Lourdes, real name **Marie Bernarde Soubirous** (1844–1879), French saint whose series of visions led to the establishment of the shrine at Lourdes, France. When she was 14, she claimed to have been visited on several occasions by the Virgin Mary, who told her that the waters at Lourdes were to be given miraculous healing powers. Despite the doubts of local citizens, Bernadette stoutly defended her original story of the visions. She joined the Sisters of Charity in 1866 and spent the rest of her life in a convent. She was beatified in 1925 and canonized in 1933.

Bernadotte, Jean. See *Charles XIV.*

Bernard of Clairvaux, Saint (1091–1153), French religious leader. Born of a noble family in Burgundy, he entered the Cistercian order and founded (1115) the abbey at Clairvaux, serving as its first abbot. Soon his influence extended beyond the monastery, and eventually he exercised power over many secular authorities in France and Italy and, in some affairs, even over the pope. He was one of the greatest of the Latin hymn writers. In addition, he wrote more than 400 epistles and 340 sermons. He was canonized in 1174.

Bernardin de Saint-Pierre, Jacques Henri (1737–1814), French author remembered for his romantic novel *Paul et Virginie* (1788). As a young man he traveled and served with the military before beginning his literary career in 1773 with a work describing his travels on the island of Mauritius in the Indian Ocean, *Voyage a l'Ile de France.* He was a friend of Jean Jacques Rousseau, whose influence is apparent in *Paul et Virginie,* which stresses the close relationship between man and nature.

Bernhardt, Sarah, original name **Rosine Bernard** (1844–1923), celebrated French actress, known as "the Divine Sarah" of the stage for more than 50 years. Born in Paris, she made her stage debut in *Iphigenie en Aulide* in 1862. In the next few years her appearances in classical French roles, both at the Comédie Française and at other theaters, established her reputation. After her first performance in England (1879), she made several tours of other European countries as well as the United States and Canada. In all, her troupe made nine tours of the United States. Besides her appearances in the plays of Racine, Hugo, and Shakespeare (playing the title role in *Hamlet*), she also had great success in the dramas of contemporary playwrights, notably the *Tosca* and *Fédora* of Victorien Sardou. A tireless worker, she had a leg amputated in 1915, but continued to appear on the stage for seven more years.

Bernini, Giovanni Lorenzo (1598–1680), Italian architect and sculptor, regarded as the leading architect of the Baroque period. Born in Naples, he studied sculpture with his father, Pietro, and before he was 25 had created his first masterpieces. Most of his important sculptures are in Rome, where he also designed outdoor fountains. As an architect, Bernini designed the enormous square in front of St. Peter's in Rome, as well as several palaces and churches. His famous statues include *Apollo and Daphne* and *David.*

Bernstein, Leonard (1918–   ), American conductor and composer. Since 1958 he has conducted the New York Philharmonic Orchestra. Born in Lawrence, Mass., he graduated from Harvard (1939) and the Curtis Institute of Music (1941). He became a protégé of Serge Koussevitsky, and in 1943 was appointed assistant conductor of the New York Philharmonic. After years as a guest conductor, he became the first American-born conductor of the New York Philharmonic. A prolific composer of both serious and popular music, Bernstein has written such works as the *Jeremiah Symphony* (1942) and *The Age of Anxiety* (1949). For Broadway, he wrote the scores for *On the Town* (1944), *Candide* (1956), and *West Side Story* (1957).

Berthollet, Comte **Claude Louis** (1748–1822), French chemist who was the first to analyze ammonia and to discover the bleaching power of chlorine. With Antoine Laurent Lavoisier, he established the system of chemical nomenclature, which has survived with little change. For his work in developing improved methods of making gunpowder and steel, he was created a count and senator by Napoleon Bonaparte.

Bertillon, Alphonse (1853–1914), French criminologist who developed a system for identifying criminals by their physical measurements. Based on a pattern of bodily measurements and photographs, the Bertillon system (introduced in 1880) was widely used until the more practical system of fingerprinting was devised. As head of the identification department of the Paris police, Bertillon experimented with his system.

Berzelius, Baron **Jöns Jacob** (1779–1848), Swedish chemist whose work with atomic weights and the elements makes him one of the founders of modern chemistry. Between 1807 and 1818, he analyzed some 2,000 compounds to determine their exact compositions. Later his work on the atomic weight of elements led to his discovery of the elements cerium, thorium, and selenium. He was also the first to isolate such elements as silicon, tantalum, and columbium in their pure states. Berzelius introduced the present system of abbreviations for elements and the method for writing chemical formulas.

Bessemer, Sir **Henry** (1813–1898), English engineer who invented the process for converting pig iron into steel by a cheaper means than was possible before. In the Bessemer process, a blast of air is blown through molten pig iron, thus speeding up the conversion of iron into steel by decarburization. Bessemer also perfected a method for compressing carbon into a solid, thus simplifying the marking of lead pencils. Among his other inventions was a new method of casting type. He was knighted in 1879.

Bethmann-Hollweg, Theobald von (1856–1921), chancellor of Germany (1909–1917), the first to be appointed from the civil service. Conservative and bureaucratic, he was no match for the German military. Though he opposed World War I, he supported German militarism. But by 1917 his domestic policies had fallen into disfavor, and he was forced to resign.

Bevan, Aneurin (1897–1960), British political leader, who as a Labourite was one of Britain's most powerful politicians. A miner's son, he worked several years as a miner and was active in mine unions. He was elected to Parliament in 1929 as a Labourite. In 1945 he joined the postwar Labour government of Clement Attlee, and formulated the controversial national health service that still exists in Britain. Resigning from the cabinet in 1951 over a policy split, he became the leader of a leftwing faction within the Labour party. A few years later he resolved his differences with the majority in his party and was elected deputy leader after the general election of 1959. Soon afterward, however, he became fatally ill. His wife, Jennie Lee Bevan, was a Socialist and Labourite member of Parliament for many years.

Bevin, Ernest (1884–1951), British Labour leader who was foreign secretary from 1945 to 1951. He was a dock worker in Bristol, and in 1910 became a leader of the Docker's Union. In 1922 he was chosen secretary of the Transport and General Workers Union. From 1925 to 1940 he was a member of the Trades Union Congress, serving as chairman in 1936–1937. In 1940 he became minister of labor and national service in Churchill's coalition government. When the Labour government took office in July, 1945, Bevin was appointed foreign secretary in the cabinet of Clement Attlee. He retired in 1951.

Beyle, Marie Henri. See *Stendhal.*

Bhartrihari (seventh century A.D.), Hindu poet and philosopher, celebrated as one of the greatest writers of Sanskrit verse. He wrote three works called *Satakas* (meaning centuries), each containing 100 stanzas on the subjects of *Good Conduct, Passion of Love,* and *Renunciation.* He also wrote a philosophy of grammar.

Bhavabhuti (eighth century A.D.), Hindu dramatist who wrote in Sanskrit. Of his three known plays, two are concerned with the great Indian hero Rama, and the third, *Malatimadhava,* is a love story that has been called the Hindu *Romeo and Juliet.* He spent most of his life in the court of a central Indian ruler.

Bibulus, Marcus Calpurnius (d.48 B.C.), Roman politician who opposed the policies of Julius Caesar. Supported by the conservative aristocratic faction in Rome, he became Caesar's colleague in the consulship of 59 B.C. He unsuccessfully opposed Caesar's agrarian proposals in the Senate and later sided with Pompey against Caesar. In 49 B.C. Pompey appointed him commander of the fleet in the Ionian Sea, to prevent Caesar from reaching Greece. He was unsuccessful in this also, and died shortly afterward.

Bidault, Georges (1899–   ), French statesman who played a key role in the government of France immediately after World War II. A Resistance leader during the war, he was appointed foreign minister in 1944 by Gen. Charles de Gaulle. In 1946, he founded a new party, the Mouvement Républicain Populaire (MRP), became a deputy in the French parliament, continued to serve as foreign minister, and was prime minister from June to December of 1946.

In 1947–1948 he was foreign minister again, and in 1949–1950 became prime minister again for seven months. In 1958 he formed a party of Christian Democrats, which worked to preserve French control of Algeria. He went into exile in 1962 to continue his anti-Gaullist policies.

Biddle, John (1615–1662), English theologian who founded Unitarianism in England. He was imprisoned several times and banished once for his religious writings and preachings. In particular, he denied the divinity of the Holy Ghost, and with this, the doctrine of the Trinity. His followers first called themselves Biddellians, later taking the name of Unitarians.

Bienville, Sieur de **Jean Baptiste Lemoyne,** (1680–1768). French explorer who founded the city of New Orleans in Louisiana. The son of an early French colonist in Canada, he founded and set up capitals at Biloxi (1699), Mobile (1710), and New Orleans (1718). At different times, he served as governor and lieutenant governor of various French colonies along the Gulf of Mexico.

Bierce, Ambrose Gwinett (1842–c.1914), American journalist and satirist, noted for his caustic, pessimistic tales. Born in Meigs County, Ohio, he served in the Civil War and became a journalist in San Francisco. The best of his stories are in such collections as *Tales of Soldiers and Civilians* (1891), *Can Such Things Be?* (1893), and *Fantastic Fables* (1899). His *The Cynic's Word Book* (1906) was reprinted as *The Devil's Dictionary* (1911) and has remained a popular favorite. Noted for his mordant wit, Bierce specialized in bitter, ironic short stories, of which the well-known *An Occurrence at Owl's Creek Bridge* is representative. In 1913 he went to Mexico to report for his newspaper on the Mexican Revolution, and some time afterwards disappeared under still-unknown circumstances.

Billy the Kid. See *Bonney, William H.*

Bion (fl. second century B.C.), Greek pastoral poet noted for his simple love lyrics. Born in Smyrna (modern western Turkey), he reportedly lived in Sicily as an adult. Little of his work has survived, except for a few fragments from a collection called *Bucolica.* Attributed to Bion is the *Lament for Adonis;* consisting of 98 hexameters, which is notable for its simplicity and emotional strength. Percy Bysshe Shelley's poem *Adonais* is based on this work.

Bismarck in full **Bismarck-Schönhausen, Prince Otto Eduard Leopold von** (1815–1898), Prussian statesman who founded the German Empire and served as its first chancellor. After several years in the Prussian civil and military service, he became (1847) a member of the United Diet of Prussia. As the Prussian ambassador to the Germanic Diet at Frankfurt (1851–1858), he challenged Austria's right to control German affairs. He was ambassador to Russia (1859–1862), and then became ambassador to France, but after a few months in Paris he was made president of the Prussian cabinet and foreign minister (1862).

Bismarck worked unceasingly to strengthen the confederation of German states and to exclude Austrian influence. By 1867 he had become the most popular man in Germany and was the only candidate for the post of chancellor of the North German Confederation. When it became evident that war with France was near, Bismarck made full preparations for the struggle. In the war that followed (1870–1871), Germany was the victor; it annexed the French provinces of Alsace and Lorraine and received an indemnity of one billion dollars.

As the leader of the newly-formed German Empire, Bismarck became chancellor, a prince, and Europe's strongest statesman. In 1872 he alienated the Roman Catholic party by promoting adverse legal measures (the anti-papal Falk or May laws of 1873), which he later repealed for political reasons. He instituted many social and economic reforms, including universal suffrage, a protective tariff, and a reformed coinage. In 1878 he presided at the Congress of Berlin. In March, 1890, he disagreed with the new young emperor, Wilhelm II, and resigned from office.

Bizet, Georges, originally **Alexandre César Léopold Bizet** (1838–1875), French composer of the opera *Carmen.* A musically precocious youth, he composed the famous *First Symphony in C* when he was 17 years old. After studies in Paris and Rome, he settled in Paris as a composer and music teacher. During the 1860's Bizet experienced some difficulties in getting his music performed, although the operas *Les pêcheurs de perles* (*The Pearl Fishers,* 1863) and *La jolie fille de Perth* (*The Fair Maid of Perth,* 1867) were produced with some success. In the last years of his brief career

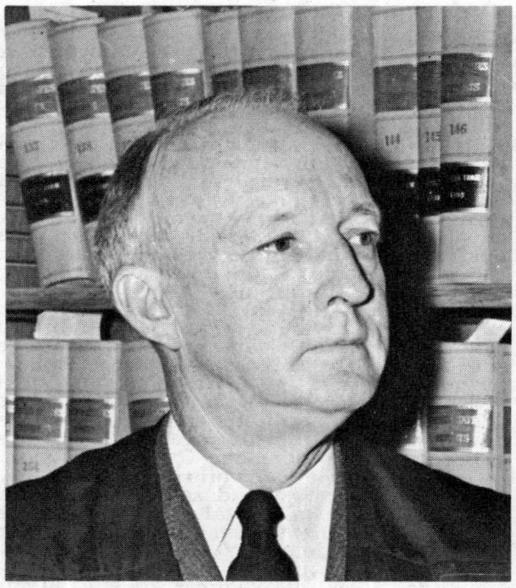

WIDE WORLD

HUGO BLACK, U.S. Supreme Court justice.

he produced his finest music, notably the piano suite *Jeux d'enfants* (1871) and the incidental music to Alphonse Daudet's *L'Arlésienne* (1872). His fame, however, rests with *Carmen* (1875), a masterpiece of tuneful melodies, rich orchestral color.

Björnson, Björnstjerne (1832–1910), Norwegian novelist, dramatist, and poet, regarded as his country's greatest novelist, and surpassed as a dramatist only by Ibsen. He established his reputation as a novelist with a series of peasant tales, including the much-admired *Arne* (1858). The best of his plays, noted for social and political criticism, include *Sigurd the Bastard* (a trilogy, 1862), *Mary Stuart in Scotland* (1864), *A Bankruptcy* (1875), *A Gauntlet* (1883), and *Paul Lange and Tora Parsberg* (1898). He also wrote many novels and poems. An ardent nationalist, he wrote the words of the Norwegian national anthem. He won the 1903 Nobel Prize for literature.

Black, Hugo La Fayette (1886–), American Supreme Court justice, noted for his liberal interpretations of the Constitution. Born in Harlan, Ala., he graduated from the University of Alabama in 1906 and practiced law in Birmingham. He served two terms in the U.S. Senate, where he directed investigations of ship subsidies and airmail contracts. When Pres. Franklin D. Roosevelt appointed him to the Supreme Court in 1937, a nation-wide controversy arose over Black's membership in the Ku Klux Klan. Nevertheless, his appointment was approved by the Senate, and he made a record as one of the most liberal of justices. His efforts in behalf of freedom of the individual under the Bill of Rights and in support of racial equality are noteworthy.

Black Hawk, Indian name **Ma-ka-tae-mish-kia-kiak** (1767–1838), American Indian chief of the Sac and Fox Indians, who fought to check the westward expansion of white settlers during the 1830's. As tribal chief in Illinois, he joined the British against the Americans in the War of 1812. Some 20 years later he started what has come to be known as the Black Hawk War (1832). After some early victories, his forces were routed by federal troops and were virtually annihilated at the battle of Bad Axe River. Black Hawk escaped, but was soon captured and put in prison. In 1834 he was given as a hostage to Keokuk, a rival chieftain, with whom he lived until his death. In his *Autobiography of Black Hawk* (1833) he attempted to explain and defend his actions.

Blackmore, Richard Doddridge (1825–1900), English novelist best known as the author of *Lorna Doone*. Educated for the law, he gave up his practice to become a writer. A highly regarded craftsman, he wrote some 14 novels, of which *Clara Vaughan* (1864) and *The Maid of Sker* (1872) were well received in his time. *Lorna Doone* (1869), notable for its theme of romantic adventure and delineation of character, has been hailed as a minor classic.

Blackstone, Sir **William** (1723–1780), English jurist whose legal commentaries set the standard for the English-speaking world. Born in London, he eventually became a judge, a member of Parliament and a law professor at Oxford University, his alma mater. His lectures attracted national attention and resulted in the publishing of his great book *Commentaries on the Laws of England* (4 vols., 1765-1769), which ever since has been a guide to jurisprudence. He was appointed king's counsel in 1761 and solicitor general to the queen in 1763. He was knighted in 1770. When he declined the post of solicitor general he was made a justice of common pleas in 1770.

Blackwell, Elizabeth (1821–1910), American physician, the first woman in the U.S. to receive the degree of doctor of medicine. Born in England, she was brought to the U.S. at the age of 11. After being refused admission by two medical schools, she was accepted at the medical school in Geneva, N.Y., from which she graduated in 1849. Four years later she established, with her sister Emily, the New York infirmary for Women and Children, with a medical college for women. In 1869 she returned to London and joined the staff of the London School of Medicine for Women, which she had helped found.

Blaine, James Gillespie (1830–1893), American statesman and presidential candidate in 1884. Born in West Brownsville, Pa., and educated at Washington and Jefferson College, he taught school for a few years before becoming a newspaper editor in Augusta, Me. He began his political career in the Maine Legislature, and in 1863 was elected to the U.S. Congress. Serving until 1876, he was speaker of the House for six years. At the Republican national convention of 1876, Blaine narrowly missed becoming his party's presidential nominee. In the same year, he was elected to the U.S. Senate. In 1884 Blaine was the Republican nominee for president, but lost a close race to Grover Cleveland. In 1889 he became secretary of state in the cabinet of Benjamin Harrison, resigning in 1892 because of failing health. Known to his followers as the "plumed knight," Blaine was very influential in the Republican Party

Blake, Robert (1599–1657), English admiral who reorganized the British navy and made it the strongest in the world. In 1652 he fought the Dutch commanders Tromp, De Ruyter, and De Witt four times and destroyed the supremacy of Holland. Under appointment by Cromwell (1654) he made the English flag respected in the Mediterranean area. In 1657 he gained one of his most important victories by defeating the Spaniards at Tenerife.

Blake, William (1757–1827), English poet and artist noted for his mystical poems and his allegorical paintings and engravings. Born in London, he was trained to be an engraver. A poet from childhood, he published his first collected poems in 1783. His engraving shop afforded Blake a meager living for 20 years, but he was able to print and illustrate his own works, all of them mystical, lyrical, and boldly conceived. His best-known literary efforts are *Songs of Innocence* (1789), the *Prophetic Books* (1793–1804), and *Songs of Experience* (1794). Among his art works, his illustrations for the *Book of Job* (1820–1826) and Dante's *Divina Commedia* are especially noteworthy. Blake died in obscure poverty, his strange visions and religious symbolism being little admired by his contemporaries.

Blanc, Louis, in full **Jean Joseph Charles Louis Blanc** (1811–1882), French political leader and journalist who strongly influenced the development of socialism. Born in Spain of French parents, he founded a socialistic journal in 1839 and became famous the following year with an essay, *The Organization of Work,* in which he set down his theories on labor and the equalization of wages. He became a member of the provisional government that followed the revolution of 1848, and pushed through a plan that forced the government to guarantee employment to workers. His actions aroused the conservative opposition and Blanc was forced to flee to England, where he remained until 1870. When he returned to France in 1871, he was elected to the Chamber of Deputies, serving until 1879. Blanc wrote many political pamphlets and books on the French Revolution and English politics.

Blasco-Ibañez, Vicente (1867–1928), Spanish novelist, born in Valencia. He achieved an international reputation for *The Four Horsemen of the Apocalypse* (1916) and *Mare Nostrum* (1918), colorful adventure novels of World War I. Many critics, however, regard his earlier naturalistic stories of Spanish life as superior, notably *The Cabin* (1898), *Reeds and Mud* (1902), and *Blood and Sand* (1908). He also served eight terms in the Spanish legislature. For his leftist views and outspoken criticism of King Alfonso XIII, he was imprisoned several times and finally exiled.

Blennerhassett, Harman (1765–1831), American adventurer who conspired with Aaron Burr to set up an independent government in the Southwest. Born in Hampshire, England, he came to the U.S. in 1796 and built an estate on an island on the Ohio River, near Parkersburg, W. Va. In 1805 he joined with Burr in the scheme to seize northern Mexican territory in America. He and Burr were arrested for conspiracy in 1806, but were acquitted. He returned to England and died on the Island of Guernsey.

Blériot, Louis (1872–1936), French aviator who was the first to fly across the English Channel. Born in Cambrai, he studied engineering in Paris. A pioneer in the development of early aircraft, he produced an efficient monoplane. On July 25, 1909, he crossed the Channel, flying from Calais to Dover. For his flight, he received a prize of £1000. During World War I, Blériot helped build aircraft for the French government.

Bligh, William (1754–1817), English naval officer who commanded the H.M.S. *Bounty* at the time of its famous mutiny. In 1787 he commanded the *Bounty* on an expedition to Tahiti, where he was to secure breadfruit trees to replant in the West Indies. On April 28, 1789, the crew mutinied under the leadership of Fletcher Christian, the master's mate, and Bligh and 18 men were set adrift in the open sea. After drifting for some 4,000 miles, Bligh and his men reached land, and finally made their way back to England. A warship was sent to capture the mutineers, although Christian and a few others escaped to Pitcairn Island. The mutiny had little effect on Bligh's career, and he was a vice admiral when he retired. The story is told in *Mutiny on the Bounty* (1932) by J.M. Hall and C.B. Nordhoff.

Bloch, Ernest (1880–1959), American composer, noted for his works on Jewish themes. Born in Geneva, Switzerland, he came to the U.S. in 1916. He was founder and director of the Cleveland Institute of Music (1920–1925) and director of the San Francisco Conservatory of Music (1925–1930). In 1939 he was appointed professor of music at the University of California. In *Three Jewish Poems* (for orchestra) and *Schelomo* (for cello and orchestra), Bloch produced uniquely modern works based on traditional Jewish themes. His other compositions include the operas *Macbeth* and *Jezebel,* symphonic poems, sonatas, and concertos.

Bloomer, Amelia Jenks (1818–1894), American pioneer in social reform and woman's rights. Born in Homer, N.Y., she became a writer and lecturer on education, woman's suffrage, and temperance. Today she is remembered chiefly for her promotion of the "bloomer costume," which consisted of Turkish trousers beneath a short skirt.

Blow, John (1648–1708), English organist and composer. He was organist at Westminster Cathedral from 1669 to 1679, when he was succeeded by his pupil Henry Purcell. Renowned for his church music, he produced 14 services and more than 100 anthems, which are still in use in English churches. His *Venus and Adonis* (1680–1685) was the first English opera in which the entire text was set to music.

Blücher, Gebhard Leberecht von, Prince of **Wahlstatt,** nicknamed **Marschall Vorwärts** (1742–1819), Prussian field marshal during the Napoleonic wars. Born in Rostock, he entered the Swedish army as a young man, but later transferred to the Prussian army. In the Waterloo campaign he commanded the Prussian army in Belgium and was severely defeated by Napoleon at Ligny. By outmaneuvering the French Marshal Emmanuel de Grouchy, however, he was able to arrive at Waterloo in time to decide the victory for the allies and pursue the routed French army. It was on this occasion that the duke of Wellington prayed for the coming of "Blücher or night." Had his army failed to arrive, Napoleon might have won at Waterloo.

Blum, Léon (1872–1950), French political leader, the first Socialist premier of France. Born in Paris, he studied literature and law at the Sorbonne. Early in his career he supported Jean Jaures in the defense of Alfred Dreyfus (1894). In 1895 he entered the Conseil d'Etat (the French equivalent of the U.S. Supreme Court). After World War I, as an active member of the Socialist party opposing the occupation of the Ruhr, he was elected to the Chamber of Deputies. When the Herriot and Poincaré governments needed the support of the Socialists, Blum, as their leader, had considerable power in France. The sweeping gains made by Socialists and Communists throughout the country elected him premier in 1936. The following year he resigned after the Senate refused him power to remedy an alarming financial situation, but he was reelected premier in 1938 and in 1946. He wrote books, poems, and essays, and enjoyed a reputation as a literary critic.

Boadicea or **Boudicca** (d.62 A.D.), queen of the Iceni, an ancient tribe that inhabited eastern Britain. Her husband, Prasutagus, willed his kingdom jointly to his family and to Nero, emperor of Rome, hoping that Nero would offer protection against all enemies. The Romans, however, desired no joint rule, and their soldiers ravaged the country, defying Boadicea and her daughters. She raised an army of 200,000 and made war upon the Romans. In a spot of their own choosing they met her in battle, killed possibly 180,000 of her soldiers and lost only 400 of their own. Rather than submit to the conqueror, Boadicea committed suicide.

Boccaccio, Giovanni (1313–1375), Italian writer and humanist, famous for his collection of tales called the *Decameron* (1353). In 1350 he formed an intimate friendship with Petrarch, whose influence on his career was great. It is said that he was the first Italian to have obtained from Greece copies of the *Iliad* and the *Odyssey*. While in Naples, about 1334, he fell in love with a young woman whom he called Fiammetta, an illegitimate daughter of King Robert of Naples. She returned his love and to please her he wrote *Il Filocolo*, a prose romance, and afterwards *La Teseide*, the first attempt at romantic epic poetry, of which Boccaccio may be considered the inventor. The *Decameron*, however, is his most outstanding work. The stories are remarkable for their realistic treatment of classic human themes, although they were once attacked as licentious.

Boccherini, Luigi (1743–1805), Italian composer, noted for his instrumental works. Born in Lucca, the son of a musician, he became proficient on the cello at an early age and gave concerts throughout Europe. For several years he was composer of chamber music to the Spanish Infante Don Luis. From 1785 to 1797 he was at the court of Friedrich Wilhelm II in Berlin. He lived in Spain for the remainder of his life, dying in poverty. In addition to his religious music, symphonies, and concertos, Boccherini composed more than 100 quartets and quintets, and some 50 trios. The bulk of his work is marked by warmth, elegance, and delicacy.

Bode, Johann Elert (1747–1826), German astronomer, born in Hamburg. His determinations of the relative distances of the planets from the sun became known as Bode's Law. In 1774 he founded the *Astronomical Yearbook* and personally edited the first 51 volumes. In 1801 he published *Uranographia*, his most important work. This book listed 17,240 stars, exceeding by 12,000 the number that had previously been charted. From 1786 to 1825, Bode was director of the Berlin Observatory.

Bodhidharma, also called **Tamo** (d. about 530 A.D.), Buddhist monk who founded a contemplative school of Buddhism. Born in southern India, he went (c.520) as a Buddhist missionary to China, where his philosophy became popular. Bodhidharma is recognized as the first patriarch of Buddhism in China.

Bodoni, Giambattista (1740–1813), Italian printer and type designer, born in Saluzzo. The son of a printer, he became head of the printing house of the duke of Parma, and made it one of the most famous in Europe. Five years after his death (1818), his *Manual of Typography* appeared. Today many types of his design are still in use and many others are based on these.

Boethius, Anicius Manlius Severinus (c.480–c.524 A.D.), Roman philosopher remembered for his work *De Consolatione Philosophiae (The Consolation of Philosophy)*. Under Theodoric, king of the Ostrogoths, he held several high offices, but about 522 he was accused of conspiring against the king and was imprisoned; two years later he was executed. In *The Consolation of Philosophy*, written while he was in prison, Boethius argued that philosophy is the source of the highest happiness since it leads man to greater knowledge of the highest good, God. His other works include treatises on theology, logic, geometry, music, and astronomy.

Bohr, Niels Henrik David (1885–1962), Danish physicist who made outstanding contributions to theories of nuclear energy. His theories on the structure of atoms and the nature of radiation were vital to the development of the atomic bomb. Born in Copenhagen, he was educated there and did research in England. In 1920 he was appointed director of the Copenhagen Institute for Theoretical Physics. He was awarded the Nobel Prize for physics in 1922. During World War II Bohr was an adviser to the Manhattan Project, which developed the first atomic bomb. He wrote *Atomic Physics and Human Knowledge* (1958).

Boito, Arrigo (1842–1918), Italian composer, born in Padua. He is perhaps best known as the librettist for Verdi's *Otello* and *Falstaff* and Ponchielli's *La Gioconda*. As a composer, he produced only two operas. The first, *Mefistofele* (1868), on which he worked 20 years, is considered one of the finest of late romantic operas. *Nerone* (1918), his second opera, was less successful. In his compositions Boito sought to combine elements of German music (especially that of Richard Wagner) with those of traditional Italian style. His collaborations with Verdi resulted in two of opera's masterpieces.

Bok, Edward William (1863–1930), American editor, born in Helder, the Netherlands. He was brought to the U.S. as a child and educated in the public schools of Brooklyn, N.Y. In 1886, he organized the Bok Syndicate Press, which distributed special features to newspapers. From 1889 until 1919 he edited the *Ladies' Home Journal*. For his autobiography, *The Americanization of Edward Bok* (1920), he was awarded the Pulitzer Prize. In 1923 he offered a prize of $100,000 for the best plan for assuring the peace of the world. As a tribute to the country in which he found opportunity and wealth, he established a bird sanctuary at Lake Wales, Fla., and erected there the Singing Tower, a marble structure containing a carillon, beneath which is his tomb.

Boleyn, Anne (1507–1536), queen of England (1533–1536), the second wife of Henry VIII and the mother of Elizabeth I. She went to France at the age of 12 with Mary Tudor, who was to be the wife of Louis XII, and remained in that court for three years. On her return to England, she became maid of honor to Queen Catherine. Courted by King Henry VIII, she became his mistress before Catherine was divorced (May, 1533). As soon as the divorce was pronounced, Henry publicly married Anne (a secret marriage had already taken place), and she was crowned queen amid great splendor. In September, 1533, she gave birth to a daughter who became Queen Elizabeth I. Henry soon tired of Anne and charged her with adultery. The Privy Council heard her plea of innocence but condemned her. She was imprisoned in the Tower of London and beheaded.

Bolingbroke, 1st Viscount, title of **Henry St. John** (1678–1751), English statesman, one of the most influential politicians of his time. He was born in Surrey and educated at Eton. He entered Parliament in 1701 and in 1704 was appointed secretary of war. Later, as secretary of state for foreign affairs, he negotiated the Treaty of Utrecht (1713), by which much of Canada was ceded to Great Britain. Upon the accession of George I (1714), Bolingbroke's enemies brought a charge of treason against him, and he fled to France. His estate was confiscated, but when he was permitted to return to England in 1725, it was restored. However, he was banned from Parliament.

Bolívar, Simón (1783–1830), South American patriot, known as *El Libertador* (the Liberator). Born in Caracas, Venezuela, and educated in Spain, he became a legend during his lifetime, and was responsible for the overthrow of Spanish rule in a large part of the continent. His native Venezuela was first to rebel against Spain; he joined the revolution in 1810 but had to flee to save his life. He returned with a sufficient force to defeat the enemy and take Caracas, but was again forced to flee, and it was not until 1821, after several more attempts, that Venezuelan independence was finally achieved. He also led in the liberation of Colombia and Peru from Spanish rule. Southern Peru was made a separate republic and named Bolivia in his honor. Near the close of his career, he was chosen president of the Republic of Colombia and became dictator of Peru. He spent his very considerable fortune in carrying on the struggle for South American independence.

Boltzmann, Ludwig (1844–1906), Austrian physicist who made important contributions to the laws of thermodynamics and mechanics. Born in Vienna, he spent much of his life teaching at various universities. Boltzmann applied the concepts of atomic physics to already established laws of physics, and contributed especially to the mechanics of energy and radiation. His work helped lay the foundation for later discoveries in atomic physics. He is noted especially for the Stefan-Boltzmann law, which relates to the radiation from a black body.

Bonaparte, Joseph (1768–1844), elder brother of Napoleon Bonaparte. He was king of Naples and Spain in his brother's empire. After Napoleon had tested him in minor posts, Joseph was sent to conclude a treaty of friendship with the United States. When Napoleon became emperor he made Joseph commander of the Naples garrison, in 1805 ruler of the Two Sicilies, and in the next year king of Naples. In 1808, to Joseph's regret, Napoleon placed him on the throne of Spain. After the Battle of Waterloo, Joseph escaped to the United States. In 1841 he was permitted to rejoin his wife, who had lived in Italy after 1815.

Bonaparte, Louis (1778–1846), brother of Napoleon Bonaparte, king of Holland, and the father of Charles Louis Napoleon Bonaparte, who became emperor of France as Napoleon III. Louis's marriage to the stepdaughter of Napoleon, Hortense Beauharnais, Josephine's daughter by her first marriage, preceded his appointment as king of Holland. He was only a nominal ruler, for he reigned under his brother's direction. He resigned this post in 1810, because of hostility to Napoleon's policies, and lived mostly in Italy after Napoleon's downfall.

Bonaparte, Lucien (1775–1840), younger brother of Napoleon Bonaparte and a disciple of Robespierre during the French Revolution. After Robespierre's fall, Lucien was imprisoned for a time, but Napoleon's influence secured his release. Before Napoleon's power was recognized, Lucien was president of the Council of Five Hundred and used his power to advance his brother's interests. He opposed Napoleon's imperial ambitions, however, not wishing him to become emperor. As a consequence he was exiled from France. After Napoleon's fall he lived in Rome.

Bonaparte, Napoleon. See *Napoleon*.

Bonaventura or **Bonaventure**, Saint, original name **Giovanni di Fidanza** (1221–1274), Italian philosopher. Known as "the Seraphic Doctor," he was one of the most famous medieval writers and mystics. Born in Tuscany, he entered the Franciscan order about 1242 and studied in Paris. In 1273 he was made bishop of Albano, and in the same year was created a cardinal. Venerated during his lifetime, he appears as a saint in Dante's *Paradiso*. He was canonized in 1482 and was made a doctor of the church in 1587.

Bonheur, Rosa, full name **Marie Rosalie Bonheur** (1822–1899), French painter noted for her studies of horses and other animals. Born in Bordeaux, the daughter of an art teacher, she studied in Paris. Her best-known work, *Horse Fair* (1853), is in New York's Metropolitan Museum of Art. In 1894 she became the first woman to be awarded the Grand Cross of the Legion of Honor.

Boniface VIII, original name **Benedetto Caetani** (c.1235–1303), pope of the Roman Catholic Church (1294–1303). During his pontificate, relations between the church and European monarchies became strained; several countries, especially France, openly rejected papal authority. As a result, Boniface issued a papal bull directed at Philip IV of France, who had imposed taxes on the French clergy, declaring that no church official should pay tribute to a secular government without papal approval. Other bulls, issued later, asserted the temporal as well as the spiritual supremacy of the pope. Imprisoned in 1303 by allies of Philip, he survived only a short while afterwards.

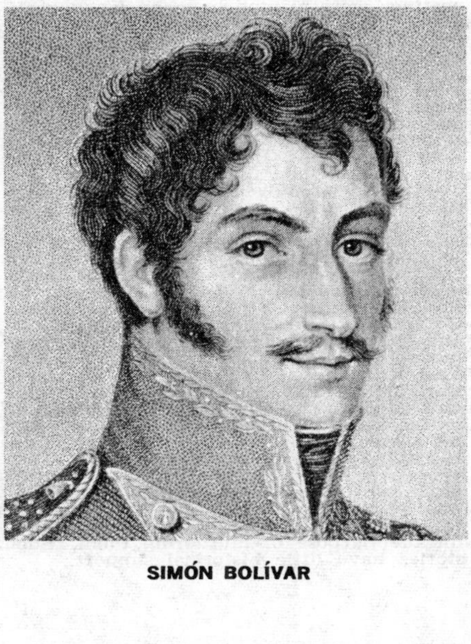

SIMÓN BOLÍVAR

Bonnard, Pierre (1867–1947), French painter of the Impressionist school. He was born near Paris and studied at the École des Beaux-Arts. He specialized in landscapes and still lifes, which are characterized by bright, warm colors. Among those who influenced his work were Paul Gauguin and Jean Vuillard, who was his associate in founding the "intimist" school of painting.

Bonney, William H., known as **Billy the Kid** (1859–1881), American outlaw in the Southwest. He was born in New York City, and after his father died, he moved with his mother to Kansas. While living in New Mexico, and still only 12 years old, he reportedly stabbed a man to death. By the time he was 18, he supposedly had killed 11 other people. One of the few verified facts of his legendary career is that he was shot at Fort Sumner, N. M., by Pat Garrett, a sheriff and former acquaintance. Subsequent research has proved that he was a great deal less heroic than he has been depicted in dramatized versions of his life.

Boone, Daniel (1734–1820), American pioneer, explorer, and hunter, born near Reading, Pa. As a boy he moved to North Carolina with his father. He married and tried farming, but preferred the life of a hunter and guide, for which he became famous in Tennessee. In 1775 he established the first permanent settlement in Kentucky. About 1799 he moved to Missouri, then a possession of Spain. A legendary figure during his lifetime, Boone was an influential leader in the settlement, expansion, and defense of the American frontier.

Booth, Edwin Thomas (1833–1893), American actor famed for his interpretations of Shakespearean roles. He was born in Bel Air, Md., the son of the actor **Junius Brutus Booth** (1796–1852), and the brother of John Wilkes Booth. After touring with his father's company, Booth emerged in the 1850's as a major actor, notably in such tragic roles as Hamlet, King Lear, Romeo, Iago, Brutus, and Othello. A more natural performer than many of his bombastic contemporaries, he had commanding stage presence and a controlled voice. In 1869 he opened the Booth Theater, and in 1888 he founded the Players' Club for actors, both in New York City.

Booth, John Wilkes (1829–1865), American actor who assassinated Pres. Abraham Lincoln. Born in Bel Air, Md., the brother of Edwin Booth, he became famous as a Shakespearean actor. During the Civil War, he sympathized with the South, and joined in a conspiracy to murder Lincoln and several cabinet officers. On April 14, 1865, he shot and killed Pres. Lincoln during a performance at Ford's Theather in Washington, D.C. During the turmoil he escaped, but was discovered and shot 12 days later in a nearby town.

Booth, William, known as **General Booth** (1829–1912), English religious leader who founded the Salvation Army. He was born in Nottingham and became a Methodist minister in 1852. He resigned in 1861 to do evangelistic work, and in 1865 founded a mission. Booth continued this work until 1878, when its scope was broadened into an organization which he called the Salvation Army. By 1880 there were branches throughout the world. As general of the Salvation Army, Booth repeatedly visited America, South Africa, and Australia, and his writings were printed in many languages.

Borgia, Cesare (c.1476–1507), Italian cardinal, military leader, and diplomat. The son of Pope Alexander VI, he was made a cardinal in 1493, but renounced his title five years later to enter politics. He was sent as papal legate to the court of Louis XII at Paris and while serving there married the daughter of the king of Navarre. In a campaign with King Louis, Borgia believed he could set up a kingdom in Italy for himself and by treachery and murder nearly accomplished his purpose. When his father, the pope, died, Borgia's influence waned. In 1504 Pope Julius II sent him as a prisoner to Spain. He escaped, joined the forces of his father-in-law, and was killed in battle.

Borgia, Lucrezia (1480–1519), daughter of Pope Alexander VI and sister of Cesare Borgia. Her evil deeds, some based on fact and others embellished by legend, have made her name synonymous with wickedness in woman. Her first two marriages were arranged by her father; the one to the lord of Pisaro he annulled; and the second, to the son of king of Naples, ended with his murder by order of her brother Cesare. Her third marriage was to Alphonso d'Este, who became duke of Ferrara. Lucrezia practiced most of the vices of her day. She was alleged to have mixed fatal poisons, which she would offer to her guests, invited for the purpose of murdering them. Such stories have little historical support.

Borglum, Gutzon, full name **John Gutzon de la Mothe Borglum** (1867–1941), American sculptor and painter who executed the colossal reliefs at Mount Rushmore in the Black Hills of South Dakota. Born near Bear Lake, Idaho, he studied art in San Francisco and Paris. In 1901 he settled in New York City, where he received many commissions, including the head of Abraham Lincoln in the Capitol rotunda at Washington, D.C. At Mount Rushmore, his heads of Washington, Jefferson, Lincoln, and Theodore Roosevelt represent his major works.

Boris Godunov. See *Godunov, Boris.*

Borodin, Aleksandr Porfirevich (1833–1887), Russian composer and scientist, remembered especially for his nationalistic opera *Prince Igor.* Born in St. Petersburg (Leningrad), he was a professor of chemistry and devoted his leisure time to the composition of music. Never a prolific composer, Borodin wrote two symphonies, two string quartets, and several songs. *Prince Igor,* begun in 1869, was completed in 1889 by Nikolai Rimsky-Korsakov and Alexander Glazunov.

Bosch, Hieronymus (c.1450–1516), Dutch painter famous for his fantastic, grotesque paintings. Little is known of his life, and none of his works is dated. His paintings often depict sin and evil through allegorical subjects. Many are filled with grotesque beings—half human, half animal—in the throes of agony. Due to the interest that Philip II took in his work, many of his masterpieces are in Spain.

Boswell, James (1740–1795), Scottish barrister whose life of Samuel Johnson is considered one of the finest biographies ever written. His journals, rediscovered long after his death and published in the twentieth century, reveal him to have been also one of the greatest of diarists. Born in Edinburgh and educated for the law, Boswell first met Johnson in 1763, when Johnson was 54 and he was only 23. Ten years later they voyaged together to the Hebrides Islands, and Boswell published his interesting *Journal* of the trip. In 1791, after Johnson's death, Boswell published his celebrated *Life of Johnson.* Filled with anecdotal reportage and transcripts of conversations, it has been hailed as a monument of English biography.

Botha, Louis (1862–1919), South African soldier who was the first prime minister of the Union of South Africa. In the Boer War (1899–1902), he besieged British forces at Ladysmith, defeated them at Colenso, and was made commander in chief of the Boer army. He headed a delegation to London to secure the organization of the Union of South Africa. After his election (1910) as the first prime minister of the Union, he became a loyal British subject. In World War I he commanded the South African troops in the conquest of German Southwest Africa.

Botticelli, Sandro originally **Alessandro di Mariano dei Filipepi Botticelli** (c.1444–1510). Italian painter, one of the foremost artists of the Renaissance. Born in Florence, the son of a tanner, he studied painting under Fra Filippo Lippi. His reputation was established by the *Adoration of the Magi* (Uffizi) painted for Santa Maria Novella. He gained the patronage of the great Florentine families, especially the Medici, for whom he painted many portraits as well as the famous *Pallas and the Centaur* (Uffizi), *The Birth of Venus,* and *Primavera* (Uffizi). Botticelli went to Rome (1481) to paint in the Sistine Chapel for Pope Sixtus IV and returned to Florence the following year. The influence of the great reformer Savonarola led Botticelli to restrict himself to religious paintings, two of the most important of these being *The Magnificat* (c. 1482), and *Virgin with the Pomegranate* (1487), both in the Uffizi Gallery in Florence.

Boucher, Francois (1703–1770), French painter, born in Paris. He was a favorite of Mme. de Pompadour, whose portrait he painted, and in 1763 he was appointed painter to the court of Louis XV. Boucher was also director of the Gobelins tapestry factory, where he produced striking designs for tapestries. He painted portraits, landscapes, and even theatrical sets, but his most typical works are allegorical paintings of mythical figures.

Bougainville, Louis Antoine de (1729–1811), French navigator and soldier prominent in the early history of Canada. Born in Paris, he gave up law for the army. In the French and Indian War he was aide-de-camp to Gen. Louis de Montcalm, who assigned to him the defense of Canada against the British. He was the first Frenchman to sail around the world (1766–1769), and rediscovered the Solomon Islands, the largest of which was named in his honor.

Bouillon, Godefroy de. See *Godfrey of Bouillon.*

Bourbon, an ancient French family that gave three royal dynasties to France, Spain, and Italy. The first of the line was Adhemar, lord of the Bourbonnais (now Allier) at the beginning of the tenth century. The power and possessions of the family increased until 1272, when Beatrix, daughter of Agnes of Bourbon and John of Burgundy, married Robert, sixth son of Louis IX of France. Their son Louis became the first duke of Bourbon. The elder line of the dukes of Bourbon became extinct in 1527. From the younger line descended Anthony of Bourbon, duke of Vendôme, who by marriage acquired the kingdom of Navarre, and whose son Henry of Navarre became Henry IV of France. The Spanish Bourbon dynasty originated in 1700, when Louis XIV placed his grandson Philip, duke of Anjou, on the Spanish throne to become Philip V of Spain. The royal line of Naples, or the Two Sicilies, arose when in 1735 Don Carlos, the younger son of Philip V of Spain, obtained the crown of Sicily and Naples (then attached to the Spanish monarchy) and reigned as Charles III.

Bowditch, Nathaniel (1773–1838), American mathematician and astronomer whose *New American Practical Navigator* (1802) was a standard text for generations of seagoing navigators. Born in Salem, Mass., he went on several long voyages as a young man, serving as navigator and later commander of various vessels. His book was officially adopted by the U.S. navy.

Bowen, Elizabeth (1899–), Irish novelist, born in Dublin. She is noted for her sensitive portrayals of modern women. Her novels include *The Hotel* (1927), *To the North* (1932), *The Death of the Heart* (1939), *The Heart of Day* (1949), and *A World of Love* (1955).

Boyle, Robert (1627–1691), British physicist and chemist who made valuable contributions to early science. Today he is remembered chiefly as the formulator of Boyle's law, which states that the pressure of a gas is inversely proportional to its volume at constant temperature. Born in Ireland, he studied in England, where he settled permanently in 1644 to devote his life to scientific research. During his active career he investigated a wide range of subjects, including metallurgy, chemical compounds, optics, and sound. Boyle was also one of the leading religious thinkers of his time.

Braddock, Edward (1695–1755), British general who commanded British troops in North America in the French and Indian War. After assuming command in 1755, he led a force of some 3000 men (including Col. George Washington) that was to lay siege to Fort Duquesne (now Pittsburgh, Pa.). Just before reaching the target, his troops were ambushed by French and Indian forces (July 9, 1755). Braddock was severely wounded and died four days later.

Bradford, William (1590–1657), one of the Pilgrim Fathers in America. He was governor of the Plymouth Colonoy for 30 years between 1621 and 1656. Born in Yorkshire, England, he sailed from Holland on the *Mayflower,* and in 1621 was elected governor of Plymouth Colony. Reelected 30 times to this one-year office, he governed democratically and wisely. A self-educated man, Bradford kept a journal from 1620 to 1647, later published (1856) as *A History of Plimmoth Plantation,* which is the most detailed account of Pilgrim life available today.

Bradley, Omar Nelson (1893–), American general who was one of the leading officers of World War II. He was born in Clark, Mo., and graduated from West Point in 1915. During World War II, his first notable victory came in North Africa. Transferred to England in 1943, he began planning for the invasion of France, and in 1944 led the largest force that participated in the invasion. He was administrator of Veterans' Affairs (1945–1947) and chief of staff of the U.S. army (1948–1949). After the armed services were unified in 1949, he became the first chairman of the Joint Chiefs of Staff, holding this post until 1953. Before his retirement, he was promoted to the rank of general of the army.

Brady, James Buchanan, known as **Diamond Jim Brady** (1856–1917), American financier, famed for his ostentatious display of wealth. Born in New York City, he held a number of minor jobs until he amassed a fortune as a financier. Called Diamond Jim because of his enormous jewel collection, he was one of the most famous of café society figures. In 1912 he endowed the Brady Urological Institute at Johns Hopkins University.

Brady, Mathew B. (c.1823–1896), American photographer, born in Warren County, N.Y. As a young man, he learned how to make daguerreotypes, and about 1845 he began an ambitious program to photograph famous people. When the Civil War broke out, he received permission to accompany and photograph the Union troops. Although the venture ruined him financially, he produced over 3,500 valuable photographs, many of them taken on the battlefield.

Bragg, Braxton (1817-1876), Confederate general in the American Civil War. He was born in Warrenton, N.C., and educated at West Point. He served with distinction under Gen. Zachary Taylor in the Mexican War, and retired to private life in 1856. When the Civil War began (1861), he joined the Confederate army and was made a brigadier general. He succeeded Gen. Pierre Beauregard in command of the army in Mississippi, with the rank of major general, in 1862. After his defeat by Gen. Ulysses S. Grant, he was relieved of his command and made military adviser to Jefferson Davis.

Bragg, Sir **William Henry** (1862-1942), English physicist, noted for his work in crystal structure. With his son **William Lawrence Bragg** (1890-   ), he investigated the structure of crystals by means of X-ray diffraction. For this work, the two shared the Nobel Prize for physics in 1915. Bragg also did much research in radioactivity. His writings include *The World of Sound* (1920), *Concerning the Nature of Things* (1925), and *The Universe of Light* (1933).

Brahe, Tycho (1548-1601), Danish astronomer, born in Knudstrup. He settled at an observatory built for him by King Frederick II, but had to flee the country in 1597 after the king died. Under the protection of Rudolf II, he moved in 1599 to Prague, where he was joined by Johannes Kepler. Brahe was more precise in astronomical measurements than any preceding scientist, and it was his accuracy that enabled Kepler later to formulate the fundamental laws of motion of planetary bodies. In 1572 he discovered a brilliant star in the constellation Cassiopeia, named Tycho's star.

Brahms, Johannes (1833-1897), German composer, one of the greatest of the nineteenth century. Born in Hamburg, the son of a musician, he began making public appearances as a pianist when he was only 14. In 1853 he met Robert Schumann, who, after hearing his music, publicly proclaimed that Brahms would be the great composer of the future. It was not until the 1860's, however, that Brahms became a towering figure in music. After moving to Vienna, which he adopted as his native city, he achieved a great success with his *German Requiem* (1868). During the next 25 years, Brahms secured his reputation with a series of masterworks, including the four symphonies that are familiar to every music lover. Other well-known works include a violin concerto, two piano concerti, several string quartets, and many songs.

Braille, Louis (1809-1852), French teacher of the blind, born in Coupvray. At the age of three, he was accidentally blinded, and at ten he went to study at the National Institute for the Young Blind in Paris. Later, as an instructor at the school, he invented a method of teaching the blind to read. For his alphabet, he developed a system of dots and dashes embossed on thin cardboard, which could be differentiated by touch. Braille was also an accomplished church organist and was considered to be one of the best in Paris.

Bramante, Donato d'Agnolo or **d'Angelo** (1444-1514), Italian architect, one of the leaders of Renaissance architecture. He was born in Urbino and studied painting, but gave it up for architecture. After designing several buildings in Milan, he went to Rome (1499), where he was employed by two popes in designing the reconstruction of St. Peter's Cathedral. He died before construction was completed, and many of his ideas were altered. Bramante was influenced by ancient Greek and Roman architectural design.

Brancusi, Constantin (1876-1957), Romanian sculptor, one of the leading influences of twentieth-century art. A native of Bucharest, he went to Paris (1904) where he spent most of his life. A traditional sculptor at first, he became increasingly abstract, influenced by modern art and also by primitive sculpture. In his major works, Brancusi emphasized simple, streamlined geometric forms, usually with a highly polished finish. The Museum of Modern Art in New York City owns many of his most important pieces.

Brandeis, Louis Dembitz (1856-1941), American jurist who, as a member of the U.S. Supreme Court, was noted for his liberal interpretations of the Constitution. He was born in Louisville, Ky., and educated at Harvard. As an attorney in Boston (1879-1916), he was known as "the people's counsel" because of his work in behalf of the

NASA

WERNHER VON BRAUN, missile scientist.

public interest. He represented several states in cases involving minimum wage laws and working hours. He was appointed an associate justice of the U.S. Supreme Court in 1916 by Pres. Woodrow Wilson. Always a liberal, for many years he was almost alone on the Supreme Court bench in his championship of liberal legislation. His writings include *Other People's Money* (1914) and *The Curse of Bigness* (1934). Brandeis University in Waltham, Mass., is named for him.

Braque, Georges (1882-1963), French painter who, with Pablo Picasso, founded the school of cubism. Born in Le Havre, he studied in Paris and produced many works that were influenced by the leading artists of the day. About 1910, however, he and Picasso began experimenting with what has become known as cubism. Painting mostly in shades of gray and tan, Braque began executing still lifes and portraits broken up into the series of angular planes that is characteristic of cubism. At the same time, he originated the technique of collage painting, in which cutouts from newspapers and other sources are pasted on canvas. His later work, less angular and geometric, nevertheless was a natural outgrowth of his cubist period.

Braun, Wernher von (1912-   ), German scientist who, after World War II, was a leading figure in the development of American missile programs. He was born in Berlin and studied at the University of Berlin. Von Braun was technical director of the liquid-fuel rocket and guided-missile center at Peenemuende, Germany (1937-1945). He was instrumental in developing the V-2 rocket—the first step in the rocket and space age. In 1946 von Braun came to the U.S. as project director of the rocket center at White Sands, N.M. Von Braun was made technical director of the guided

GROVE PRESS

BERTOLT BRECHT, modern German author.

missile group, an important post at a crucial time. He also headed the Army Ballistics Missile Agency, which later became the civilian National Aeronautics and Space Administration.

Brecht, Bertolt (1898-1956), German playwright, noted for his stark, compelling dramas on social themes. Born in Augsburg, he studied medicine but gave it up for writing. After World War I he made his reputation as the author of realistic plays, but his biggest commercial success came in 1928 with *The Threepenny Opera*, set to music by Kurt Weill. When the Nazis came to power in the 1930's, Brecht went into exile and eventually settled in the United States. Among his leading plays of this period are *Mother Courage* (1941), *Galileo* (1943), and *The Caucasian Chalk Circle* (1948). A lifelong Socialist, Brecht moved to East Germany in 1948, where he founded a repertory company that presented his plays. In his best work, Brecht relies heavily on irony and satire to achieve his effects.

Breshkovsky, Catherine (1844-1934), Russian revolutionist, called "the Little Grandmother of the Russian Revolution." Born near Vitebsk into a wealthy family of nobles, she left home in her twenties to promote revolutionary causes, eventually becoming a follower of Mikhail Bakunin. She spent many years in prison, returning to revolutionary activities during periods of freedom. When the Bolsheviks seized control in Russia, she disapproved of their policies and was forced into exile. She spent her last years in Czechoslovakia.

Breuer, Marcel Lajos (1912-   ), Hungarian-American architect, noted for his stark functional designs. He studied and later taught at the influential Bauhaus School in Weimar, Germany. While in Germany he became known for his tubular-steel and plywood furniture. After practicing architecture in London, he came to the U.S. in 1937, where he taught at Harvard under Walter Gropius. One of his special interests has been the low-cost prefabricated house. He has also designed many large buildings, notably the UNESCO building in Paris.

Breughel. See *Brueghel.*

Brewster, Sir **David** (1781-1868), Scottish physicist noted for his work in light and optics. He invented the kaleidoscope (1816), and with Wheaton devised the stereoscope (1817). Brewster made many contributions to the knowledge of polarized light and the reflection and absorption of light. He was knighted in 1832. Among his books is a biography of Sir Isaac Newton (1855).

Brezhnev, Leonid Ilyich (1906-   ), Russian political leader who, on October 14, 1964, replaced Nikita Khrushchev as first secretary of the Communist party of Russia. A native of the Ukraine, he first became active in Communist politics in the late 1930's, and during World War II served as a political commissar at the front with the rank of major general. After holding a series of increasingly important posts, he was elected to the Soviet Central Committee in 1952. In 1960 he was elected chief of state. Before his elevation to first secretary, he served briefly as a secretary of the Central Committee.

Brian, known as **Brian Boru** (926-1014), king of Ireland from 1002 to 1014, when he was slain at Clontarf (near Dublin) while battling the Danes. Too old to fight, Brian was murdered in his tent by a small group of Danes who had escaped the victorious Irish forces. An outstanding leader and diplomat, be became one of the great national heroes of the Irish.

Briand, Aristide (1862-1932), French statesman who was premier of France eleven times. Born in Nantes, he studied law and became a Socialist. Before becoming prime minister (1909), he served as minister of education and religion. At the outbreak of World War I, he was a leader in the mobilization of French manpower. In the following years he repeatedly assumed the premiership to restore political tranquility to an unstable country. A firm supporter of antiwar measures, Briand shared the Nobel Peace Prize with Gustav Stresemann and Austen Chamberlain in 1926.

Bridges, Robert Seymour (1844-1930), English poet, critic, and poet laureate. Born in Walmer, he graduated from Oxford and studied medicine in London. In 1882 he gave up his practice to devote himself to writing. A superb poetic craftsman, Bridges is noted especially for his short lyrics. His major work, *The Testament of Beauty* (1929), presents his aesthetic principles. In 1913 he was appointed poet laureate, succeeding Alfred Austin.

Bright, John (1811-1889), English orator and statesman who was a leading liberal in Victorian politics. He was born in Lancashire, of Quaker parents, and as a youth worked in his father's cotton mill. Bright entered Parliament in 1843, and except for a few months out of office because of his opposition to the Crimean War, held his seat for the rest of his life. With Richard Cobden, he was instrumental in the defeat of the corn laws (1838–1846). As an ally of William E. Gladstone, Bright was a leading agitator for parliamentary reform. During the American Civil War he was a friend of the North, even though his opposition to the South injured his cotton-mill interests.

Britten, Benjamin (1913–), English composer, born in Lowestoft. His first major work, the opera *Peter Grimes* (1942), was an immediate success. His other operas include *The Rape of Lucretia* (1946), *Billy Budd* (1951), *The Turn of the Screw* (1954), and *A Midsummer Night's Dream* (1960). Britten has also produced many orchestral pieces, as well as choral music with religious settings. His *War Requiem* (1964) has been widely acclaimed and performed.

Brontë, Charlotte (1816–1855), English novelist, born in Yorkshire, sister of Emily Brontë. She is best remembered as the author of *Jane Eyre* (1847), a melodramatic novel with brilliant characterization, vivid description, and an exciting plot. Her other novels include *Shirley* (1849) and *Villette* (1853). An early novel, *The Professor*, was refused by every publisher and was not printed until after her death. Her life was dreary and almost without a stirring event. She married the Rev. Arthur Nicholls, her father's assistant pastor, a year before her death.

Brontë, Emily (1818–1848), English novelist and poet, sister of Charlotte Brontë. She is best known as the author of *Wuthering Heights* (1848), a vivid, dramatic novel set on the Yorkshire moors.

Brooks, Van Wyck (1886–1963), American literary critic and essayist noted for his five-volume work, *Makers and Finders: A History of the Writer in America, 1800–1915*. Published between 1944 and 1952, the series attempted to recapture what Brooks called the usable past in American literature. It is considered one of the finest, most penetrating analyses of American thought. For one of these volumes, *The Flowering of New England* (1936), he won the Pulitzer Prize in 1937. Brooks also wrote many other books, including biographies and critical studies of Mark Twain, Ralph Waldo Emerson, Henry James, and John Sloan.

Brown, John (1800–1859), American abolitionist leader, born in Torrington, Conn. He had little formal education as a youth but he developed strong religious convictions against the institution of slavery. After an unsuccessful career in a number of vocations, he organized his own abolitionist movement and traveled about the country with his sons in a crusade to free the slaves. Convinced that he was doing God's work, he often adopted violence in pursuit of his aims. In a number of skirmishes with slaveholders or sympathizers of slavery in Kansas, he was known to have taken many innocent lives. As he progressed in his campaign he grew increasingly fanatical and violent. On October 16, 1859, with 17 white men and 5 Negroes, he attacked a Federal arsenal at Harpers Ferry in Virginia, captured it and took a number of citizens as prisoners. Had he retired promptly to the mountainous country nearby, he might have found at least temporary safety, but he lingered all day. By night a strong company of militia entered the town and captured Brown and his followers. He was tried for treason and executed on December 2, 1859. The treasonable act produced momentous results. People in the North generally approved it, and within a year the song *John Brown's Body* was prophetic of the coming crisis between the North and the South.

Browne, Sir **Thomas** (1605–1682), English writer, scholar, and physician, one of the greatest prose stylists of his age. Born in London, he was a physician. In his major work, *Religio Medici* (*A Doctor's Religion*, 1642), Browne issued a plea for religious tolerance. A lifelong student of natural history and an antiquarian, he also wrote *Pseudodoxia Epidemica* (*Vulgar and Common Errors*, 1646), in which he debunked popular myths and superstitions concerning the natural world, and *Hydriotaphia: Urne-Buriall* (1658), a treatise on death and immortality. In these and other writings, Browne displayed a lofty, cadenced, and sonorous style that established him as one of the major prose writers in English.

Browning, Elizabeth Barrett (1806–1861), English poet, wife of Robert Browning, remembered for her romantic love lyrics. Born near Durham, she was a frail child and virtually an invalid until her marriage in 1846. Her reputation as a poet was established with the publication of *The Seraphim and Other Poems* in 1838. Two years later, she was near death from a burst blood vessel and did not leave her room for seven years thereafter; but her literary work did not cease. During this time, a book of poems containing *The Cry of the Children* and *Lady Geraldine's Courtship* appeared. In the latter she praised Robert Browning's poetry. The two met in 1845 and were married the next year, over the protests of her pious but selfish and despotic father. The Brownings went to Italy to live. Mrs. Browning published another volume of verse in 1850, in which *Prometheus Bound* appeared, and in 1856 *Aurora Leigh*. Her last books, published shortly before her death, were *Poems Before Congress* and *A Curse for a Nation*. Her love for her husband generated the romantic lyrics of her collection *Sonnets from the Portuguese*, written during their engagement and published privately.

Browning, Robert (1812–1889), English poet, considered one of the finest poets of the late Romantic period. Born near London, he was educated by private tutors and at University College, London, after which he traveled in Italy and Russia. His first book of poems, *Pauline* (1833), attracted little attention, but it contained strong and beautiful passages. Then followed *Paracelsus*

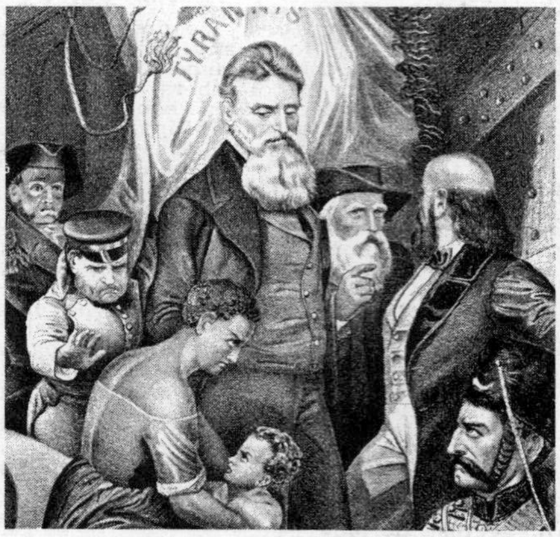

LIBRARY OF CONGRESS

JOHN BROWN

(1835), widely acclaimed; the historical drama *Strafford* (1837); and *Sordello* (1840), a narrative poem. *Bells and Pomegranates* (1841–1846), a collection of poems beginning with *Pippa Passes*, drew praise from Elizabeth Barrett, whom he afterwards married. Browning's masterpiece is *The Ring and the Book* (1868–1869), an epic poem of more than 21,000 lines that presents an account of a murder trial from the point of view of the characters. *A Blot in the 'Scutcheon*, a drama; *Evelyn Hope, Fra Lippo, How They Brought the Good News from Ghent to Aix, The Flight of the Dutchess, The Lost Leader*, and *A Soul's Tragedy* are but a few of his poems worthy of special mention. Browning's poetry, famous for its optimism, is often difficult to read. Much of it seems obscure, with passages heavy and ponderous; he ignored accepted forms of expression at times to give emphasis to the strength of his thought.

Broz or **Brozovich, Josip.** See *Tito*.

Bruce, Robert, later **Robert VIII** (1274–1329), king of Scotland (1306–1329), known as "the Bruce," and the liberator of Scotland. As a young man he paid homage, as had his father, to Edward I of England, but he later joined others in an attempt to secure independence for Scotland. After his father died, Bruce killed John Comyn, one of the regents, declared himself king of Scotland, and gathered an army to defend his position. The royal English forces defeated him, and he fled to Ireland, returning to do battle as soon as new supporters could be brought together. In 1306, after a succession of victories and defeats, his right to reign was acknowledged. His rule was beset by trouble with the English. At the battle of Bannockburn (1314), in which Bruce commanded in person, he was forced to withdraw. When Edward III became king of England, hostilities began again, and it was not until 1328 that Scotland's independence was definitely acknowledged. Bruce contracted leprosy and spent the last two years of his life in retirement.

Bruckner, Anton (1824–1896), Austrian composer who, with Gustav Mahler and Richard Strauss, led in the flowering of late Romantic, post-Wagnerian music. He was born in Ansfelder and spent much of his early life in obscurity; his genius did not blossom until he was in his forties. A devout Catholic, Bruckner produced somber works of grandeur, including nine symphonies, several masses and other choral works, and a string quintet. Heavily influenced by the music of Richard Wagner, his works were not universally acclaimed until after his death.

Brueghel, Bruegel, or **Breughel, Pieter** (c.1525–1569), Flemish painter, born in Brueghel, in the Dutch province of Limburg. In 1551 he entered the Antwerp painters' guild, and in the following year went to Rome to study art. Returning to Antwerp, he established himself as a leading painter. Brueghel's most famous works, bold and original in their mastery, depict robust peasants at work, dancing, or resting—all displayed in lively color with humorous and satirical overtones. He was also a landscapist of note. Among his celebrated works are The *Harvesters* (1565) and *Peasant Wedding* (1568).

Brummell, George Bryan, known as **Beau Brummell** (1778–1840), English fashion leader, born in London. He was known as the prince of dandies and was patronized by the prince of Wales (afterwards George IV). He spent a fortune in sumptuous living, and in matters of etiquette and dress his opinions were considered indisputable. He eventually quarreled with the prince and fled from his creditors to Calais, where, reduced to destitution, he lived some years.

Brunelleschi or **Brunellesco, Filippo** (c.1377–1446), Italian architect, often called the founder of Renaissance architecture. He was born in Florence, where he produced all his major works. Originally a sculptor, he took a deep interest in perspective, and can be said to have made it a science in the perfectly proportioned buildings he designed. Among his major designs are the Pitti Palace, the dome of the Cathedral of Florence, the church of San Lorenzo, and the Pazzi Chapel.

Brunetto Latini. See *Latini, Brunetto*.

Bruno, Giordano (c.1548–1600), Italian philosopher, born in Nola. He joined the Dominican Order in 1566, became a priest, but was expelled in 1576 because of his heretical views. Between 1580 and 1591 he wandered about Europe in continual danger of arrest and condemnation. In 1591 he went to Venice, where he was betrayed by a false friend and delivered over to the Roman Inquisition. He was imprisoned for eight years and finally burned at the stake. His condemnation was on religious grounds and not because of his support of the Copernican doctrine in astronomy. His writings were very influential in the late seventeenth century and were particularly admired by Spinoza and Leibniz.

Bruno of Cologne, Saint (c.1030–1101), German monk who founded the Carthusian Order. He became rector of the cathedral school at Rheims but, oppressed by the wickedness of his time, withdrew in 1804 to the wilds of Chartreuse, near Grenoble. Here with six friends he founded the austere Carthusian Order. In 1094 he established a second Carthusian monastery at Della Torre in Calabria. He was canonized in 1628, and his feast day is October 6.

Brutus, Marcus Junius (c.85–42 B.C.), Roman politician who supported Pompey in his wars against Julius Caesar. The victorious Caesar pardoned Brutus and made him governor of Cisalpine Gaul, but when the Senate conspiracy against Caesar took form, Brutus joined in the plot. After Caesar's assassination, the story of which is familiar through Shakespeare's play *Julius Caesar*, Brutus fled from Rome to Athens and raised a force with the intention of establishing a new power in Macedonia. He was defeated by Octavius at Philippi and, realizing his cause lost, killed himself by falling on his sword.

Bryan, William Jennings (1860–1925), American political leader and orator who was nominated three times for the presidency. Born in Salem, Ill., he lived in Nebraska after 1887. He was elected to Congress for the first time in 1891. As an alternate delegate to the Democratic convention in Chicago in 1896, he secured the seat of a colleague at one session and made a speech advocating free silver, which so electrified the convention that he was nominated for the presidency. His opponent, William McKinley, on a gold standard platform, easily won the election. In 1900 and again in

1908 he won the Democratic nomination, but each time was defeated. During his years of ascendancy he published *The Commoner*, a weekly paper, in which his policies were given wide publicity. In 1912 he so dominated the Democratic convention that he forced the nomination of Woodrow Wilson for the presidency. When Wilson was elected and formed his cabinet, he appointed Bryan secretary of state. In this office he negotiated 30 treaties setting up machinery for arbitration of international disputes. In 1915 he resigned because of his opposition to the administration's attitude toward Germany in World War I. His last public appearance was as one of the prosecutors of J. T. Scopes, a Tennessee teacher accused of teaching evolution contrary to a state law. He died suddenly at the end of the trial. Though it was successfully concluded from his point of view, Bryan was subjected to merciless cross-examination by Clarence Darrow, the attorney for the defense.

Bryant, William Cullen (1794–1878), American poet and editor chiefly remembered for his nature poetry. Born in Cummington, Mass., the son of a doctor, he entered Williams College at 16, but after a year left to study law privately. He was admitted to the bar in 1815 and practiced law for ten years. His most famous poems are *Thanatopsis, To a Waterfowl,* and *To the Fringed Gentian*. Bryan collaborated in writing a history of the United States and also translated the *Iliad* and the *Odyssey*. In addition to his collected poems, he published *Letters of a Traveler* (1850) and *Letters from the East* (1869), both embodying his observations in Europe, and *Orations and Addresses* (1873). From 1826 until his death he was editor in chief of the New York *Evening Post*. Through his editorials, Bryant wielded a great deal of political influence.

Buber, Martin (1878–1965), Israeli scholar and philosopher whose work considerably influenced modern Jewish thought. Born in Vienna, Austria, he studied there and in Germany. He was editor of the Vienna *Welt*, and later *Der Jude*, and from 1924 to 1933 was professor of religion and ethics at the University of Frankfurt am Main. In 1938 he was appointed professor of social philosophy at the Hebrew University in Jerusalem. A leader in the Zionist movement, he worked for the revival of Hasidism, which encouraged spontaneity, immediacy, openness before God, and the cultural significance of Judaism. Besides his famous *I and Thou*, his works include *The Tales of the Hasidim, Between Man and Man, Eclipse of God, The Legend of Baal-Shem*, and *Two Types of Faith*.

Buchanan, James (1791–1868), fifteenth president of the United States (1857–1861). Born near Mercersburg, Pa., he graduated from Dickinson College in 1809, studied law, and was admitted to the bar in 1812. He served five terms in Congress (1821–1831), was minister to Russia (1831–1833), and returned to the U.S. in 1834 to fill a vacancy in the Senate. Twice reelected, he resigned in 1845 to become secretary of state under Pres. James K. Polk. During the administration of Pres. Franklin Pierce, Buchanan was minister to Great Britain. As the political campaign of 1856 approached, Buchanan proved the only man who could unite the Democratic party. He was opposed by John C. Frémont (Republican) and Millard Fillmore (Know-Nothing). After his election to the presidency, Buchanan attempted to steer a middle course between rival northern and southern factions, but was unable to stop the drift toward open war.

Buck, Pearl Sydenstricker (1892–), American novelist who won the Nobel Prize for literature in 1938. Born in Hillsboro, W. Va., she spent her youth in China, where her parents were missionaries. After graduating from Randolph-Macon College (Lynchburg, Va.), in 1914, she returned to China, where she married Dr. John Buck, a missionary. She wrote a number of novels about China, one of which, *The Good Earth* (1931), earned her the Pulitzer Prize (1932) and international acclaim. In 1934 she returned to the U.S., divorced her husband, and remarried (but continued to write under the name Pearl Buck). She wrote some 40 books, of which her novels about China are her best. These include *Sons* (1932), *A House Divided* (1935), *Dragon Seed* (1942), and *Pavilion of Women* (1946). Her autobiography, *My Several Worlds*, appeared in 1954.

Buddha. See *Gautama Buddha*.

Buffalo Bill. See *Cody, William Frederick*.

Bulganin, Nikolai Alexandrovich (1895–), Russian Communist leader who was premier of the Soviet Union from 1955 to 1958. Born in Nizhni Novgorod, he joined the Communist party in 1917. After Joseph Stalin came into power, Bulganin held many important posts, including that of minister of armed forces during World War II. When Stalin died, Bulganin became a deputy premier, and succeeded Georgi Malenkov as premier in 1955. In March 1958 he resigned as premier, and in September he was ousted from the Communist Party presidium.

Bülow, Prince **Bernhard von** (1849–1929), German statesman who was imperial chancellor of Germany from 1900 to 1909. Born in Holstein, he entered the German foreign service in 1873. He held a variety of diplomatic posts until 1897, when he was named secretary of state for foreign affairs. When Prince Chlodwig Hohenlohe resigned in 1900, Bülow succeeded him as chancellor. During the early years of his leadership, he was successful in both domestic and foreign affairs, but he estranged himself from Kaiser Wilhelm II, who forced him to resign in 1909.

Bunche, Ralph Johnson (1904–), American statesman who in 1950 became the first Negro to win the Nobel Peace Prize. He was born in Detroit, Mich., graduated from the University of California at Los Angeles in 1927 and received a Ph.D. from Harvard in 1934. After teaching at Howard College (Washington, D.C.) for several years, he joined the government's Office of Strategic Services in 1941 and was transferred to the state department in 1944. There, he helped draft the trusteeship

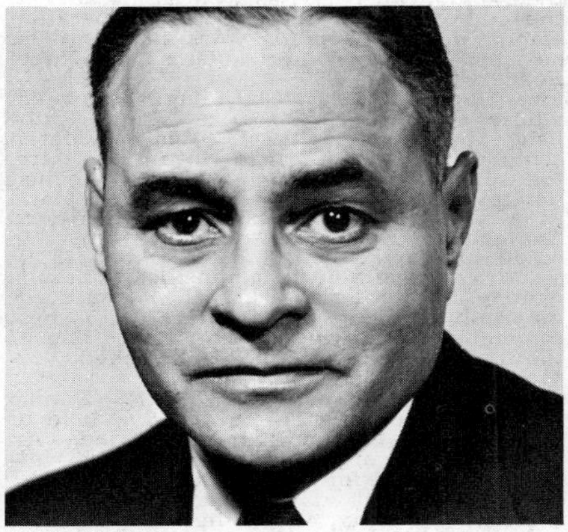

UNITED NATIONS

RALPH BUNCHE

clauses of the United Nations charter, and in 1946 was appointed director of the trusteeship division of the UN. In 1948 he was named mediator in the dispute between Israel and the Arab states; it was for this work that he was awarded the Nobel Prize. In 1955 he was appointed UN undersecretary, and in 1967 he became Under Secretary-General for special political affairs.

Bunin, Ivan Alekseevich (1870–1953), Russian novelist and poet who in 1933 became the first Russian to win the Nobel Prize for literature. Born in Voronezh, he was a journalist for several years. He then turned to literature and won acclaim for his poetry and translations of American and European writers. His greatest success came, however, with his short stories, many of which have been translated into English. Perhaps the best known to English readers is *The Gentleman from San Francisco*, which first appeared in English in 1922. Bunin is considered one of the finest Russian stylists. Opposed to communism, he left Russia in 1919 and spent most of his life in France.

Bunsen, Robert Wilhelm Eberhard von (1811–1899), German chemist famed for his inventions and his researches in spectrum analysis. He was born in Göttingen, educated there, and taught chemistry at several universities in Germany. He was professor of chemistry at the University of Heidelberg from 1852 until his death. Best known as the inventor of the Bunsen burner, he also was the first to produce magnesium in large quantities. In 1860 he invented the magnesium light, formerly widely used in photography. His greatest contribution, however, was the development of spectrum analysis in collaboration with Gustav Kirchhoff. It was through this work that he discovered the elements cesium and rubidium.

Bunyan, John (1628–1688), English Puritan minister who wrote *Pilgrim's Progress* (1678). Born in Bedfordshire, he became a tinker, as was his father. He married at 19 and joined the Baptists, later becoming a preacher. After the Restoration in 1660 a law forbade any ministerial work outside the established Church of England. For his persistent preaching, he was thrown into Bedford jail and held there for nearly 12 years. During this time he wrote his great work, an allegory of a common man making his way to heaven. Bunyan also wrote *Grace Abounding to the Chief of Sinners* (1666) which was autobiographical, and *Holy War* (1682), an allegory.

Burbank, Luther (1849–1926), American naturalist and horticulturist, famed for his work in producing new varieties of plants. Born in Lancaster, Mass., he took up his life work when he was only 21. In 1875, needing better climate and soil for his work, he moved to Santa Rosa, Calif. There he devoted his life to improving plants. He developed not only larger varieties but also entirely new ones. Among these are the Burbank potato, two new varieties of apples, new and larger plums and prunes (one of them stoneless), three new roses (peach-blow, Burbank, and Santa Rosa), the Shasta daisy increased to four inches in diameter, a spineless cactus, a large form of amaryllis, and the white blackberry. One of his creations was the plumcot, produced by crossing the apricot with the Japanese plum. His autobiography, *Harvest of the Years*, appeared in 1927, one year after his death.

Burgoyne, John (1722–1792), British general who served in America during the American Revolution. It was his task to drive south from Canada into the colonies and cut New England off from communication with its more southerly neighbors. His expedition, after minor successes, failed at the battle of Saratoga (1777). His command of the campaign displeased the home authorities, and he was recalled to England, where he subsequently resigned. He spent his later years as a playwright. One of his plays, *The Heiress* (1786) was a great success.

Burghley, Baron. See *Cecil, William*.

Burke, Edmund (1729–1797), British statesman, orator, and writer who had a profound influence on the political affairs of his time. Born and educated in Dublin, he went to London in 1750. He exhibited literary ability and published a number of highly influential works, notably *The Sublime and Beautiful* (1756). He then became private secretary to the chief secretary for Ireland and later to the premier, Lord Rockingham. At the age of 37 he entered Parliament and for 28 years was an influence in that body. He early evinced an interest in American colonial affairs, but it was not until 1775 that he made his great speech *On Conciliation with America*. It made a profound impression and shocked the Tory mind, but did not avert the conflict. He was not in sympathy with the French Revolution and bitter feeling on that subject severed many friendships. He fought for native rights in India as against the oppression and greed of officials sent to govern there.

Burne-Jones, Sir **Edward Coley** (1833–1898), English artist, noted for his neo-medieval paintings and his stained-glass windows. Born in Birmingham, he studied at Oxford, where he met William Morris, with whom he worked for some years. Another friend was John Ruskin, with whom he spent a year in Italy. Greatly influenced by these two men, Burne-Jones produced paintings that were a blend of romantic and medieval themes, nearly all of them richly decorative. In addition to his work in stained glass, he designed tapestries and mosaics.

Burnett, Frances Eliza Hodgson (1849–1924), American novelist who wrote *Little Lord Fauntleroy* (1886). Born in Manchester, England, she came to the U.S. as a child. Author of some 40 novels, she was most successful with children's themes, notably *The Little Princess* (1905) and *The Secret Garden* (1909).

Burnham, Daniel Hudson (1846–1912), American architect and city planner, born in Henderson, N.Y., and educated in Chicago. The firm of architects that he headed was commissioned to plan the World's Columbian Exposition in Chicago (1893), and this gigantic task made Burnham famous. He was later chairman of the committee charged with beautifying Washington, D.C. Notable among his designs are the Flatiron Building in New York, the old Masonic Temple in Chicago, and the Union Passenger Station in Washington, D.C. He had a large share in the rebuilding of San Francisco after the 1906 earthquake and fire.

Burns, Robert (1759–1796), the most famous Scottish poet. Born in Alloway, he was the son of a small farmer, and was brought up in poverty. He received a common-school education, though most of his learning was gained from the books he read, among which were *The Spectator*, the works of Alexander Pope, and the poems of Allan Ramsay. When he was 16 years of age he fell in love, and his feelings, as he tells us, at once burst into song. His first volume of poetry was issued in 1786, from Kilmarnock, and at once became popular. The success of this volume, which was speedily republished in Edinburgh, induced him to take the farm of Ellisland, near Dumfries, where he married his "bonny Jean." He moved to Dumfries in 1791 and, having been appointed as exciseman through the influence of a friend and admirer, lived on the $350 a year that office paid. In 1792 he wrote about a hundred songs as accompaniments to the melodies of Scotland. His health failed, partly because of intemperance, and he died at 37. Though imprudent, he was an honest, proud, warm-hearted man, combining sound understanding with high passions and a vigorous imagination. He was a poet who, alive to every emotion, excelled in humor and tenderness.

Burr, Aaron (1756–1836), American political leader, one of the most controversial figures in U.S. history. Born in Newark, N.J., he was educated at Princeton. He was a colonel in the American Revolution, attorney general of New York (1789), and a U.S. senator (1791–1797). In 1801 he was elected vice-president on the ticket with Thomas Jefferson. Enmity existed between Burr and Alexander Hamilton, for Burr believed Hamilton had conspired to defeat him for the governorship of New York. This bitterness led to a duel in Weehawken, N.J., in which Hamilton, who fired his weapon into the air, was killed (July 11, 1804). Burr's career, once so promising, was now doomed. In 1805 Burr engaged in an enterprise that seemed to aim at the formation of a new government in the Southwest. He confided his plan to Gen. James Wilkinson of the army, who promptly notified Pres. Jefferson of the treasonable design. Burr was arrested and tried (Henry Clay was his attorney), but he was not convicted. Two later arrests resulted in acquittals. Broken, he went to London and Paris. Unable to establish himself there, he returned to New York in 1812 to practice law.

Burroughs, John (1837–1921), American naturalist and author, born in Roxbury, N.Y. He taught school as a young man and was later a clerk in the treasury department at Washington (1864–1873). While a treasury clerk, he wrote *Notes on Walt Whitman as Poet and Person* (1867), based on firsthand knowledge of Whitman. Burroughs wrote a large number of books and essays, among the most important being *Birds and Poets, Bird Enemies, Winter Neighbors, An Idyll of the Honey-Bee, Squirrels and Other Fur-*

Bearers, Field and Study, and *Under the Apple Trees*. His later writings tended to be less about nature and more about philosophy, though they continued to be as widely read as his earlier works.

Burton, Sir Richard Francis (1821–1890), English explorer and diplomat, noted for his translations of Arabic literature. Born in Torquay, he joined the East India Company in 1842. This gave him many opportunities to travel in eastern countries and to learn and record languages — Persian, Afghan, Hindustani, and Arabic. He also explored widely in Africa and South America and wrote about his travels. His best-known work is a literal translation of the *Arabian Nights* from the Arabic, called *The Thousand Nights and a Night* (16 vols., 1885–1888).

Burton, Robert (1577–1649), English clergyman and scholar, whose *Anatomy of Melancholy* (1621), is considered one of the most unusual books in the English language. A church vicar most of his life, Burton devoted most of his time to writing. The *Anatomy*, which he revised five times after its first appearance, is a curious mixture of humor, philosophy, and classical lore. Later writers used it as source material.

Butler, Nicholas Murray (1862–1947), American educator, born in Elizabeth, N.J. He was educated at Columbia University, taking his Ph.D. in 1884. As a young man, Butler challenged traditional methods of education, and in 1902, when he was named president of Columbia, he got the chance to put his theories into action. One result was founding of the Teachers College at Columbia. Later he became nationally prominent in the Republican party, as well as a leader in the drive for international cooperation among nations. For his work in this field, he shared with Jane Addams the Nobel Peace Prize for 1931.

Butler, Samuel (1835–1902), English novelist whose novel *The Way of All Flesh* (published posthumously in 1903) is considered a modern classic. Born in Nottinghamshire, the son of a minister, he rebelled against his father and emigrated to New Zealand as a young man. In 1864 he returned to England to devote himself to writing. He made his reputation with *Erewhon* (1872), a satirical treatment of a nonexistent utopia. Among his other works, the semi-autobiographical *The Way of All Flesh* is best remembered, chiefly because it was one of the first books that openly attacked Victorian customs and morals.

Buxtehude, Dietrich (c.1637–1707), Danish composer and organist, regarded as one of the greatest of the Baroque period. An accomplished organist, he composed important works for the organ. In 1668 he became organist at St. Mary's Church in Lubeck, Germany, where he remained the rest of his life. Later composers influenced by his work include Bach and Handel. In addition to his organ music, Buxtehude composed many cantatas and other vocal pieces. Much of his work was lost until it was rediscovered in the twentieth century.

Byrd, Richard Evelyn (1888–1957), American naval officer and polar explorer who commanded the first flights over the North and South Poles. Born in Winchester, Va., he graduated from Annapolis in 1912. He retired from the navy after three years, but soon reentered the service to become a naval aviator. About 1924, after an Arctic expedition, Byrd began plans to fly over the North Pole. Two years later (1926), he and copilot Floyd Bennett accomplished this feat, the first men to do so. In 1929, during an Antarctic expedition, Byrd and three companions were the first men to fly over the South Pole. During succeeding years, Byrd led several expeditions to Antarctica. He wrote *Little America* (1930), *Discovery* (1935), *Exploring With Byrd* (1937), and *Alone* (1938).

Byron, George Gordon, 6th Baron (1788–1824), English poet whose flamboyant personality and striking verse caused him to become the popular image of the Romantic poet. He became Lord Byron at the age of ten, when his great-uncle died. His first volume of poems, *Hours of Idleness* (1807), appeared while he was at Cambridge. After leaving school, Byron traveled throughout Europe for a time, and then returned to England in 1811, where the first two cantos of his first great success, *Childe Harold's Pilgrimage*, appeared. After the publication of *Manfred* (1817) and *Don Juan* (first canto, 1819), he became famous throughout Europe. At this time he also produced the poems *Beppo* (1818), *The Lament of Tasso* (1817), and *The Prophecy of Dante* (1821), as well as a number of dramas. Always a liberal in politics, Byron went to Greece in 1823 to help in its struggle for independence. In the following year his health failed and he died after a short illness.

ADMIRAL RICHARD E. BYRD is best known for his many exploratory and scientific expeditions to the continent of Antarctica.

C

CHARLES PHELPS CUSHING

EMPEROR of Rome, Gaius Julius Caesar.

Cabot, John, original name **Giovanni Caboto** (1450–1498), Italian navigator and explorer whose exploits are a part of the early history of America. He was born in Genoa, and eventually became a citizen of Venice, where his son was born. About 1484 the Cabot family moved to Bristol, England. Two years later, the news of the discovery of America stirred the European continent, and in 1497 Cabot secured permission from King Henry VII authorizing him to seek new lands for England. The Cabot expedition sailed from Bristol and landed near Cape Breton Island on June 24, and unaware that he was in America, he took possession in the name of the king of England. On a second voyage, in 1498, Cabot explored the east and west coasts of Greenland, Baffin Land, and Newfoundland. He died shortly after his return to England.

Cabot, Sebastian (c.1476–1557), son of John Cabot, continued the explorations begun by his father. It is not known if Sebastian accompanied his father on his voyages; the only authentic accounts connected with his career date from after his father's death. He led a Spanish expedition to Brazil in 1526 under the patronage of Charles V, and discovered the river that he named La Plata, but because he stayed three years in the district, he returned to Spain in disgrace. His later years were spent in the service of England. As governor of the Company of Merchant Adventurers, he helped to advance English trading in various parts of the world.

Cabrini, Saint Frances Xavier (1850–1917). Italian-American missionary who was the first American citizen to be canonized by the Roman Catholic Church. Born in Sant'Angelo, Lombardy, she was refused membership in religious orders because of poor health. Turning to charity work, she became the superior of an orphanage in Codogno, Italy, and about 1874 founded the Missionary Sisters of the Sacred Heart. Known as Mother Cabrini, she came to the United States with a small group of sisters in 1889. She was naturalized in 1909. Much of her work in the U.S. went into setting up missionary houses and caring for Italian immigrants. She was canonized in 1946. Her feast day is December 22.

Cadillac, Sieur Antoine de la Mothe (1658–1730), French soldier and explorer who founded the city of Detroit. Born in Gascony of a noble family, he served as a captain in the French army in Acadia (now Nova Scotia). In 1694 he became commander of the fort at Mackinac, Mich. Seven years later (1701) he established a fort at Detroit, with 50 soldiers and 50 settlers. He was governor of Louisiana from 1713 to 1716.

Caesar, Gaius Julius (100–44 B.C.), Roman general and statesman under whose leadership Rome became the greatest power in the world. When he was 17 he married Cornelia, the daughter of Lucius Cinna, friend of the democratic leader Marius.

This connection gave offense to the dictator Sulla, who was the political enemy of Marius, and upon Caesar's refusal to divorce his wife, Sulla confiscated his property and threatened his life. Caesar felt that he could not submit to him, and in 81 B.C. he went into military service in Asia. On the death of Sulla (78 B.C.), Caesar returned to Rome and began to plead in the courts. Desiring to improve his oratory, he studied under Apollonius Molor at Rhodes. Caesar was pontifex maximus in 63 B.C., praetor in 62 B.C., and governor of Spain in 61 B.C. On his return to Rome, having united with Pompey and Crassus in the First Triumvirate, he became consul and then obtained the government of Gaul with the command of four legions. Caesar's military career was rapid and brilliant. He compelled the Helvetii, who had invaded Gaul, to retreat to their native country; subdued Ariovistus, who at the head of a German tribe had attempted to settle in the country of the Aedui; and conquered the Belgi. In nine years he subdued all Gaul, crossed the Rhine twice (55 and 53 B.C.), and twice invaded Britain. The Senate had continued his rule in Gaul for another period of five years, while Pompey was to have the command of Spain, and Crassus that of Syria for five years. The death of Crassus in his campaign against the Parthians dissolved the triumvirate; and about the same time the friendship between Caesar and Pompey cooled.

The Senate, influenced by Pompey, ordered Caesar to resign his offices and command within a certain time or be proclaimed an enemy of the state, and appointed Pompey general of the army of the Republic. Caesar urged his soldiers to defend the honor of their leader and in 49 B.C. crossed the Rubicon, a small stream separating his province from Italy. This was an act of war, but he made himself master of Italy without striking a blow, for Pompey fled to Greece, and the people hailed the hero of Gaul as a deliverer. Caesar then took an army into Spain, which he reduced to submission without coming to battle with Pompey's generals. He next conquered Massilia (now Marseilles), and returned to Rome, where he was appointed dictator. He followed Pompey into Greece and defeated him at Pharsalia (48 B.C.), from which Pompey escaped, only to be assassinated in Egypt. Before he returned to Rome, Caesar went to Egypt, where he won back the crown for the dethroned queen Cleopatra.

In Rome the Senate and the people strove eagerly to gain the favor of Caesar, who, without changing the ancient forms of government, ruled with almost unlimited power. In 46 B.C. he crossed to Africa, defeated the Pompeians—Scipio and Cato—at Thapsus, and on returning to Rome was received with high honors. The term of his dictatorship was prolonged, the office of censor was conferred on him alone, his person was declared inviolable, and his statue was placed beside that of Jupiter in the Capitol. Soon afterward, Caesar was honored with four triumphs, made perpetual dictator, and given the title of *imperator* with full powers of sovereignty. In February, 44 B.C., he declined the diadem which Antony publicly offered him, and the next morning his statues were decked with diadems. His glory, however, was short-lived, for a conspiracy against him was organized by his enemy Cassius, joined by many of his supposed friends, including Brutus. Notwithstanding the danger, he attended a meeting of the Senate on the Ides (the 15th) of March, 44 B.C., and was stabbed to death. As an orator, Caesar was second only to Cicero, and as a writer he is noted for his *Commentaries* on the Gallic wars and civil war. He is also known for reforming the calendar (46 B.C.).

Cagliari. See *Veronese, Paolo.*

Calder, Alexander (1898–   ), American sculptor who developed the moving free-form construction known as the mobile. Born in Philadelphia, Pa., the son and grandson of well-known sculptors, he was educated as an engineer, but as a young man turned to wire and sheet-metal sculpture. In 1932 he constructed his first mobile —pieces of sheet metal, delicately balanced by wires, which move with air currents. Calder has also specialized in monumental, abstract sculpture, chiefly in metal.

Calderón de la Barca, Pedro (1600–1681), Spanish dramatist and poet, recognized as one of the greatest playwrights of his age. Born in Madrid, he graduated from the University of Salamanca in 1619. He had begun to write plays at the age of 13, and within the next two decades won a reputation as the foremost Spanish writer of the sacred allegorical drama, known as *autos*

sacramentales. After a brief military career, he resumed his writing, and in 1650 joined the third Order of Saint Francis. Ordained a priest in 1651, he continued his literary work. Among his best-known plays are *La vida es sueño* (*Life is a Dream*), *El magico prodigioso* (*The Wonder-Making Magician*), and *La devoción de la cruz* (*The Devotion of the Cross*).

Caldwell, Erskine Preston (1903–   ), American author noted for his realistic novels and stories about white southerners. Born in White Oak, Ga., he worked at a number of jobs before becoming a writer. His first success came with *Tobacco Road* (1932), which showed the plight of poor southerners with humor and pathos. His other novels include *God's Little Acre* (1933) and *A House in the Uplands* (1946).

In *North of the Danube* (1938) and *Say! Is This the U.S.A.?* (1941), illustrated by his wife, photographer **Margaret Bourke-White,** he reported on living conditions in the U.S. and the U.S.S.R.

Calhoun, John Caldwell (1782–1850), American statesman who was the South's leading spokesman before the Civil War. Born in Abbeville County, S.C., he graduated with high honors from Yale in 1804 and was admitted to the bar in 1807. After a term in the North Carolina legislature, he was elected to Congress in 1811. In 1817 he was appointed secretary of war in the cabinet of Pres. James Monroe. He served during both of Monroe's terms and made a strong impression as an administrator and organizer. Elected vice-president in 1824, serving under Pres. John Quincy Adams, Calhoun was also elected vice-president under Pres. Andrew Jackson in 1828. In the following year Calhoun declared that a state had a right to nullify any law which it considered unconstitutional. When in 1832 a South Carolina convention passed an ordinance nullifying the tariff, Calhoun resigned the vice-presidency and entered the Senate fully prepared to uphold the action of his state. Henry Clay brought about a compromise, but the question of states' rights remained an issue. Calhoun remained in the Senate until 1843, when he declined reelection. In the following year he became secretary of state under Pres. John Tyler. In the meantime he had become a strong advocate of slavery, and his desire to see the slave-holding territory increased led to his active support of the annexation of Texas. Though this move brought on the Mexican War, Calhoun tried his best to prevent that struggle. In 1845 he was back in the Senate, where, until his health failed, he fought unceasingly for the interests of the South. His *Disquisition on Government,* regarded as a classic in political writing, explains his theories concerning federal and state responsibility.

Caligula, real name **Gaius Caesar** (12–41 A.D.), Roman emperor (37–41 A.D.) the younger brother of Nero. He succeeded Tiberius as emperor in 37 A.D. The third emperor of Rome, he was the youngest son of Germanicus Caesar and Agrippina. Extremely cruel, tyrannical, and extravagant, he at first masked his real character by ruling with tolerance and generosity. After a serious illness had weakened his mind, he let his lowest passions have full sway and no act of cruelty or of senseless barbarity was too atrocious for him. He was finally assassinated by one of the tribunes.

LOOK MAGAZINE

ARTIST Alexander Calder with his mobiles.

NEW YORK PUBLIC LIBRARY

THEOLOGIAN of Reformation, John Calvin.

Calvert, George, 1st Baron **Baltimore** (c. 1580–1632), English statesman and explorer whose son founded the American province of Maryland. He entered Parliament in 1609, became Lord Baltimore by knighthood in 1617, and two years later became secretary of state and a member of the privy council. He sent colonists to Newfoundland and visited there for two years with his family. Because of the severe climate he sailed southward to find a more congenial location for a colony and chose a spot in what is now Maryland. To settle disputes with Virginia, he sailed home to secure a new charter but soon died, and his plans were carried out by his son, **Cecilius Calvert,** 2d Baron **Baltimore** (1605–1675), who became colonial proprietor of Maryland. The present city of Baltimore was named in the son's honor.

Calvin, John, originally **Jean Chauvin** or **Cauilyn** (1509–1564), French theologian and reformer. Next to Martin Luther, he was the most influential figure in the Protestant Reformation. He was born in Noyon, Picardy, where his father was a diocesan secretary. At the age of 12 he was presented with a church office. The income enabled him to go to Paris for study, but he soon became dissatisfied with the teaching of the Roman Catholic Church and took to the study of law in Orléans. In 1533 he returned to Paris and found that church reformers were still being prosecuted. As a result, he retired to Basel, where he published his great work, *Institutio religionis christianae* (*The Institutes of the Christian Religion,* 1536). In 1538, in company with Guillaume Farel, he was expelled from Geneva because of the strict reforms they tried to introduce there. Calvin went first to Bern and then to Strasbourg. His friends in Geneva succeeded in having him recalled, and finally in 1541 his proposed laws about church discipline were accepted and published. His college of pastors and doctors and his court of discipline formed a sort of dictatorship with himself at the head. This group tried to manage all municipal matters and control the social and individual life of the people. Michael Servetus, passing through Geneva in 1553, was arrested; Calvin was instrumental in having him burned alive because he had attacked the mystery of the Trinity in a book, which had been neither written nor printed at Geneva. This has been regarded as the great blot on Calvin's career. Up to 1561 the Lutherans and the Calvinists were as one, but in that year Calvin rejected, among other things, the tenth article of the Confession of Augsburg, the Lutheran creed. From this time, his followers were known as Calvinists. Calvin retained his personal influence to the last, although he was broken in health for a year or two before his death.

As a theologian Calvin was equal to any of his contemporaries in his profound knowledge and acute mind. As an author he merits great praise. His Latin works are written with much method, dignity, and correctness. His collected works were published in English by the Calvin Translation Society of Edinburgh in 52 volumes (1844–1856).

Cambyses II (d.522 B.C.), king of the Medes and Persians (522–529 B.C.), succeeded his father, Cyrus the Great. After establishing his rule in Persia, he undertook the conquest of Egypt, which his father had planned. In 525 B.C. he defeated King Psamtik III of Egypt, and in the following year he captured Memphis. He then subdued the Nubians, but failed to overcome the Ethiopians and Carthaginians. Having learned of a revolt in Persia, in which a usurper named Gaumata was impersonating his murdered brother Smerdis, Cambyses started home but died in Syria, supposedly of an accidental wound.

Camoes, in English **Camoëns, Luiz Vaz de** (1524–1580), most celebrated poet in Portuguese history. Born in Lisbon of a distinguished but impoverished family, he specialized in literature at the University of Coimbra and early began writing love sonnets. He was banished from Lisbon in 1546 because he expressed his affection for a court lady too openly; thereafter, he lived the life of an adventurer. After spending many turbulent years abroad, he published *Os Lusiadas* (*The Lusiads,* 1572), a spirited narrative of Portuguese history. Written in the exalted style of the heroic epics of Greece, it is one of the earliest epics written in a modern language. Camoes was also an important lyric poet and dramatist.

Campbell, Alexander (1788–1866), American clergyman who founded the Protestant sect known as the Disciples of Christ. He was born in County Antrim, Ireland, the son of a Protestant minister. The father emigrated to America in 1807; Alexander followed him two years later and first settled in Washington, Pa. Campbell soon became the leader of a movement to unite the Christian sects of that region. His followers adopted immersion as the approved form of baptism and sought to unite with the Baptists. Difficulties arose, however, and the separate organization, called Disciples of Christ, was formed about 1827. In 1840 he founded Bethany College in Bethany, W. Va., of which he was president until his death.

Camus, Albert (1913–1960), French novelist and essayist, one of France's leading writers and intellectuals after World War II. He was born in Algeria of French-Spanish parentage. Raised in poverty, Camus attended the public schools of Algeria and worked his way through the University of Algiers. The author of several plays, he began his artistic life as a theatrical actor-manager and then turned to the writing of novels and essays. He produced three novels: *L'étranger* (1942; *The Stranger,* 1946), *La peste* (1947; *The Plague,* 1948), and *La chute* (1956; *The Fall,* 1957). His philosophical essays are *Le mythe de Sisyphe* (1942; *The Myth of Sisyphus and Other Essays,* 1955) and *L'homme révolté* (1951; *The Rebel,* 1954). Camus founded and edited the underground newspaper *Combat* during the wartime occupation of France. Once identified with Jean-Paul Sartre and existentialism, Camus later broke with this group, adopting a philosophy that, briefly stated, holds that within an absurd, Godless universe, moral alternatives remain whereby man may be defined. In 1957 he received the Nobel Prize for literature.

Canova, Antonio (1757–1822), Italian sculptor who founded the Neoclassical school of sculpture that succeeded Baroque art. Born in Possagno of a family of stone masons, he became famous at an early age for his works in Venice and Rome. Revolting against the ornateness of Baroque sculpture, he took his inspiration from Greek and Roman classical works. Later, he became a favorite artist of Napoleon Bonaparte, for whom he executed several commissions. After Napoleon's fall, Canova headed a group sent to France to recover art works that had been seized by the French.

Canute II, known as **Canute the Great** (c. 994–1035), king of Denmark, Norway, and England. He succeeded his father, Sweyn Forkbeard, King of the Danes, in 1014. At the outset of his rule in England, he was opposed by the partisans of King Ethelred and his son, Edmund Ironside. In 1016, after several months of fighting, Canute and Edmund agreed to divide the realm, Ethelred having died. Edmund was killed soon after and Canute became the sole king. Cruel and tyrannical at first, he later ruled with moderation and wisdom, restoring order and granting justice to all. At his death, he was king of England, Denmark, and Norway. He made his eldest son, Sweyn, king of Norway and his youngest son Hardecanute, ruler of Denmark and England; but his middle son, Harold, seized the English throne.

Caracalla, real name **Marcus Aurelius Antoninus,** originally **Bassianus** (188–217 A.D.), Roman emperor from 211 to 217. He succeeded his father, Lucius Septimius Severus, in 211. Much of his reign was spent in bitter rivalry with adherents of his brother Geta, who had been declared joint emperor in 211, but whom Caracalla had slain in 212. Giving full rein to his depraved nature, Caracalla ordered a wholesale massacre of his brother's adherents. He himself was murdered five years later. In order to increase the revenue from taxes, Caracalla in 212 gave citizenship to all free inhabitants of the empire. The ruins of the enormous baths he built can still be seen in Rome.

Caravaggio, Michelangelo Amerighi da (c.1573–c.1610), Italian painter famed for his revolutionary use of light and color. Born in Lombardy, he went to Rome as a young man, where he created a sensation with his altarpieces and canvases. Here he brought the art of *chiaroscuro* (literally, light-dark) to a new high with his strong contrasts of light and dark. Always a forceful personality, Caravaggio killed a companion in a duel (c.1606) and was forced to flee Rome. During the next few years he moved from town to town, painting as he went. Although he painted many portraits, it is his religious paintings that reveal his genius most clearly. These include *Calling of St. Matthew, Death of the Virgin Mary, Doubting of Thomas,* and *Supper at Emmaus.*

Cardano, Geronimo or **Girolamo** (1501–1576), Italian mathematician whose treatise *Ars Magna* contains the solution of the cubic equation. This famous problem of algebra was first published in 1545, but its reputed author did not originate it; the solution was stolen from Nicola Tartaglia, a contemporary. Cardano was highly versed in philosophy, medicine, mathematics, and astrology. He also wrote *De subtiliate rerum* (1551) and *De rerum varietate* (1557).

Cardozo, Benjamin Nathan (1870–1938), American jurist, born in New York City and educated at Columbia. He was admitted to the bar in 1891. After practicing law for 22 years, he was elected to the New York supreme court. Shortly afterwards he was appointed to the court of appeals and in 1926 was made chief justice. In 1932, Pres. Herbert Hoover appointed him an associate justice of the U.S. Supreme Court, succeeding Oliver Wendell Holmes. Justice Cardozo was a liberal in opinion and advocated restating and simplifying the law. Although he supported the New Deal measures of Pres. Franklin D. Roosevelt, he opposed the extension of presidential powers.

Carducci, Giosue (1835–1907), Italian poet who won the Nobel Prize for literature in 1906. Born in Valdicastello, Tuscany, he was a professor at the University of Bologna (1860–1904), and one of the most popular poets in Italy. As a young man he rejected Romantic poetry and tried to reintroduce classical metrical schemes. In addition to verse, Carducci wrote historical studies and literary criticism. He is considered the national poet of modern Italy.

Carlyle, Thomas (1795–1881), Scottish essayist and historian, one of the leading men of letters of the Victorian period. Born in Ecclefechan, he was educated at the University of Edinburgh, and for five years was a schoolteacher. In 1818 he returned to Edinburgh as freelance writer. In 1823 his series of biographical articles for the *London Magazine* were well received and became the basis of his *Life of Schiller.* A translation of Goethe's *Wilhelm Meister* appeared in 1824; though severely criticized on its publication, in time it won favorable judgment. Two years later Carlyle married Jane Welsh. They moved in 1828 to a lonely farmhouse on the Craigenputtock moors, and for six years Carlyle devoted himself to strenuous writing, producing the famous *Sartor Resartus (The Tailor Done Over),* essays on Burns and Voltaire, Boswell's *Life of Johnson,* and other critical and biographical articles.

In 1834 they moved to London, and in the following years Carlyle published *The French Revolution, Chartism, Past and Present, Heroes and Hero Worship,* and *History of Frederick the Great,* the last a work he labored on for 14 years. In 1865, while Carlyle was in Scotland being appointed lord rector of Edinburgh University, Jane Carlyle died. After that he wrote nothing of great importance. Carlyle is known today as one who fought against sham, hypocrisy, and the fetters of tradition. His rugged style, his stimulating criticism, and his truthfulness give him an honored place in British literature.

Carnegie, Andrew (1835–1919), American industrialist and philanthropist, who was one of the richest and most generous men in the world. Born in Dumfermline, Scotland, he emigrated with his family to America in 1848 and settled near Pittsburgh. Carnegie

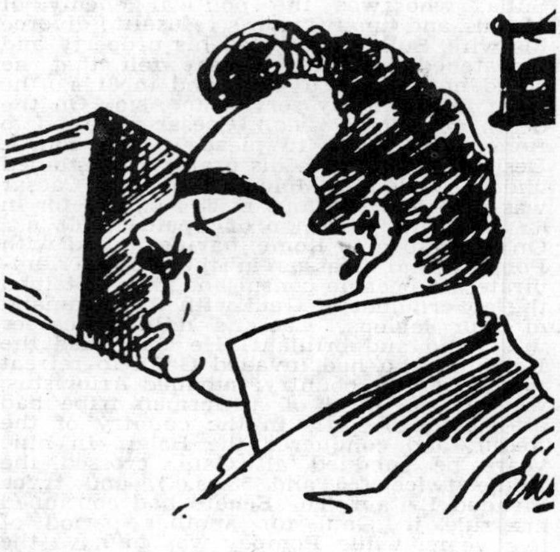

RCA

ENRICO CARUSO drew this self-caricature.

went to work in a cotton factory, which also employed his father, his wages being $1.20 a week. At 15 he became a telegraph messenger boy, learned telegraphy, and was engaged as an operator. Successively railroad clerk, train dispatcher, and division manager for the Pennsylvania Railroad, Carnegie was a successful business man at the age of 24. He had invested his savings and was on the road to fortune.

During the Civil War he supervised military railways and government telegraph lines, and after the war he became an iron manufacturer, foreseeing the arrival of the steel age. In 1868 he introduced the Bessemer process into the industry. Thirty-three years later, after the merger of the Carnegie Steel Company with the United States Steel Corporation, he retired with a fortune of $500 million.

The rest of his life was devoted to the distribution of great sums for philanthropy, education, and public welfare. Hundreds of Carnegie libraries in English-speaking countries, the Institute of Technology in Pittsburgh, endowments to Scottish universities, the Peace Palace in The Hague, the ground and building of the Pan-American Union in Washington, D.C., the Endowment for International Peace, the Foundation for the Advancement of Teaching, the Institution for Research,—these are a monument to his industry and generosity.

Carnot, Nicolas Léonard Sadi (1796–1832), French physicist who helped found the modern science of thermodynamics. Born and educated in Paris, he served in the French army engineering corps (1814–1828), and devoted his remaining years to research. He was the first to see clearly the nature of the connection between heat and mechanical work. He also developed the theory of the reversible heat engine. In this engine, gas absorbs heat, expands to do work and is compressed, giving up the absorbed heat. This series of operations is known as Carnot's cycle.

Carracci or **Caracci,** the name of three Italian painters of Bologna. **Lodovico Carraci** (1555–1619), together with his cousins **Agostino Carraci** (1557–1602) and **Annibale Carraci** (1560–1609), founded an academy in Bologna, where they taught the principles of composition, perspective, correct use of color, and the use of live models. Their own works included landscapes as well as religious and mythological subjects. Agostino was also a highly talented engraver; he and Annibale executed the famous frescoes of the Farnese Palace in Rome.

Carrel, Alexis (1873–1944), French surgeon famed for his work on blood vessels and blood transfusions. He was born in Sainte-Foy-lès-Lyon and studied at the University of Lyon. He came to the U.S. in 1905 and joined the staff of the Rockefeller Institute for Medical Research in 1906. In 1912 he was awarded the Nobel Prize for physiology and medicine for his successful work in suturing blood vessels and transplanting organs. During World War I Carrel engaged in surgical work in French hospitals. He carried on many experiments in cultivating living tissue outside the body. Carrel was regarded as one of the great surgeons of his day. He wrote *The Preservation of Tissues, The Transplantation of Limbs,* and *The Transplantation of Veins and Organs.*

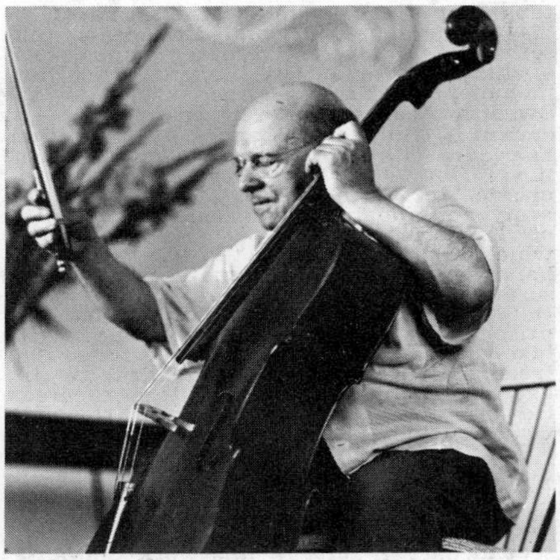

LOOK MAGAZINE

PABLO CASALS, great contemporary cellist.

His philosophical book *Man the Unknown* (1935) was popular for many years.

Carroll, Charles (1737–1832), American Revolutionary leader and a signer of the Declaration of Independence. Born in Annapolis, Md., he was a wealthy landowner and gave generously of his riches to advance the cause of the colonies. Carroll sat in the Continental Congress and was Maryland's first senator under the Federal Constitution. He always signed his name as "Charles Carroll of Carrollton."

Carroll, Lewis. See *Dodgson, Charles.*

Carson, Christopher, known as **Kit Carson** (1809–1868), American frontiersman, born in Madison, Ky. He became famous successively as a hunter, trapper, explorers' guide, and Indian agent. He was associated with John C. Frémont on two expeditions; was federal agent to the Apache and Utah Indians; and received the brevet grade of brigadier general for his work as scout in the Union Army during the Civil War.

Cartier, Jacques (1491–1557), French explorer in Canada who discovered the St. Lawrence River. In 1534 he led an expedition to the New World, commissioned by Francis I, to find a new passage to the Far East. Cartier reached the Gulf of Saint Lawrence, landed at Cape Gaspé (on the coast of what is now Quebec province), and took possession of the land in the name of his king. On a return trip in 1535, he discovered and sailed up the St. Lawrence River, anchoring his ships near the site of the present city of Quebec. He then led a small band inland to an Indian village. He had named the hill overlooking the village "Mount Royal," which became the name of the city now known as Montreal.

Cartwright, Edmund (1743–1823), English inventor who devised the power loom, which revolutionized textile manufacture. Born in Marnham, he was rector of a church in Leicestershire (1779–1808). He produced his first crude loom in 1785. Later, he set up 400 improved machines in a factory, but it was burned by workmen who feared the loss of their jobs. Cartwright also patented a wool-carding machine and a steam engine that burned alcohol.

Caruso, Enrico (1873–1921), Italian tenor, regarded by many as the greatest of the twentieth century. He was born in Naples, where he sang in clubs and churches as a boy soprano. After his first appearances in *Traviata* (1896) and *La Bohème* (1898), he was in great demand on both sides of the Atlantic. His debut in *Rigoletto* was an outstanding success at the Metropolitan Opera House, New York, in 1904, and he built up an almost unprecedented reputation. His repertoire of 40 operas included *Aïda, Il Trovatore, Cavalleria Rusticana, The Girl of the Golden West,* and *Madam Butterfly.* Caruso's voice was sweet, powerful, and of wide range. He was one of the first singers to record for the phonograph.

Carver, George Washington (c.1864–1943), American Negro botanist and educator acclaimed for his researches in agriculture. He was born in Diamond Grove, Mo., the son of slaves. He graduated from Iowa State College (1894), taught there, and went to Tuskegee Institute in 1896. There, as director of agricultural research, he gave special attention to the culture of sweet potatoes and peanuts, developing many byproducts from them. In 1940 he established the Carver Foundation at Tuskegee Institute.

Carver, John (c.1576–1621), one of the Pilgrim Fathers in America. He was chosen first governor of Plymouth Colony by the signers of the Compact of Government in the cabin of the *Mayflower* (1620). Carver had been one of the leaders of the little band of dissenters who fled to Holland from England, and it was he who secured a patent for the new colony from the Virginia Company and chartered and provisioned the ship in which they voyaged. He died in the spring of 1621, a few months after the colonists landed in Massachusetts.

Casals, Pablo (1876–), Spanish cellist regarded as the greatest of the twentieth century. Born in Vendrell, Tarragona, he became first cellist of the Paris Opéra before he was 20, then built a notable career as a solo performer. When the Spanish Civil War ended, he refused to return to Spain, settling at Prades, France, where he organized a world-famous summer festival. In 1956 he moved to Puerto Rico, where the following year he established another summer festival. Casals is famed for his interpretations of the music of Bach.

Casanova or **Casanova de Seingalt, Giovanni Jacopo** (1725–1798), Italian adventurer whose candid memoirs shocked the society of his time. Born in Venice, the son of an actor, he was educated for the priesthood, but was expelled from the seminary because of scandalous conduct. Thereafter he worked at a number of jobs (preacher, alchemist, gambler, violin player) before he was arrested for practicing magic and imprisoned in 1755. The following year he escaped and went to Paris. During the next few years he traveled throughout Europe, engaging in all kinds of intrigues. Among his leading works are *The History of My Flight* (1788), telling of his escape from prison, and *Memoires écrits par lui-même* (12 vols., 1826–1838).

Cassander (c.350–297 B.C.), king of Macedonia (305–297 B.C.). He was the son of Antipater, who had been named regent after the death of Alexander the Great. When he failed to be named successor after Antipater's death in 319, he decided to wage war against Polyperchon, the new regent. Aided by several Greek states, he was successful. He seized and put to death Olympias, mother of Alexander, and in the same year (316) married Alexander's half sister Thessalonica. The rest of his reign was marked by warfare with Antigonus I (a general of Alexander's), who aspired to power.

Cassatt, Mary (1844–1926), American artist noted for her Impressionistic portraits of mothers and children. Born in Pittsburgh, Pa., she attended the Pennsylvania Academy of Fine Arts (1861–1865), then went to Europe to study. Settling in Paris, she became associated with Edgar Degas and the Impressionist group of painters. Beginning in 1879, she exhibited with them in several shows. Recognition came early to her in France, but much later in the United States. Today she is generally considered the foremost woman painter produced by America.

Cassius, in full **Gaius Cassius Longinus** (d. 42 B.C.), Roman political leader, one of the group that conspired to assassinate Julius Caesar. Though Cassius was opposed to Caesar during the conflict with Pompey, Caesar pardoned him after the battle of Pharsalia and made him foreign praetor in 44 B.C. Cassius, however, became disgruntled because a younger man was made city praetor, and he persuaded Brutus and others to join him in the conspiracy to assassinate Caesar. When popular feeling was roused to a high pitch by Mark Antony's funeral oration, the conspirators fled. After the defeat at Philippi (42 B.C.), Cassius commanded his freedman Pindarus to kill him.

Castro, Fidel (1927–), Cuban revolutionary who in 1959 seized control of Cuba and became its prime minister and dictator. Born in Mayari, Oriente Province, he received a law degree from the University of Havana (1950), and became active in movements to overthrow the government of dictator Fulgencio Batista. Arrested in 1953, he received an amnesty in 1955, and left for Mexico to organize a plot to invade Cuba. At the end of 1956 he landed in Cuba and began a guerrilla campaign that culminated in victory. At once he began a program of drastic social and economic reforms along Marxist lines. In foreign relations he sided with the Soviet Union against the United States. Under his direction, attempts to promote communism in all of Latin America have continued.

Cather, Willa Sibert (1873–1947), American novelist, born in Winchester, Va. She was raised in Nebraska and graduated from the state university. She taught English in a high school in Pittsburgh, Pa., and was managing editor of *McClure's Magazine* (1906–1912). Her first novel, *Alexander's Bridge,* appeared in 1912. Her reputation derives from her novels with a frontier setting, notably *O Pioneers!* (1913), *My Antonia* (1918), and *A Lost Lady* (1923). Her later works—*The Professor's House* (1925), *Death Comes for the Archbishop* (1927), and *Sapphira and the Slave Girl* (1940)—are marked by a strong sense of disillusion. For her novel *One of Ours* (1922), about World War I, she won a Pulitzer Prize.

Catherine II, called **Catherine the Great,** Russian name **Ekaterina Alekseevna** (1729–1796), empress of Russia (1762–1796). The daughter of a German prince, she married Prince Peter of Russia in 1745 and was baptized with Greek Orthodox rites. In 1762 her husband succeeded to the throne as Czar Peter III. After about six months, he was murdered by conspirators acting under her orders, and she became the sole ruler of Russia. Although her personal life often scandalized her contemporaries, Catherine worked zealously to improve Russian life — in literature, in education, and in commerce. During her reign, Russia acquired the Crimea and a part of Poland. She greatly enhanced the prestige of Russia in foreign eyes, but her dependence on the Russian nobles made it impossible for her to improve the lot of the serfs.

Catherine de Médicis, Italian name **Caterina de'Medici** (1519–1589), queen of France (1547–1559), the wife of Henry II. Born in Florence, Italy, she married the duc d'Orléans (1533) who became Henry II in 1547. When her eldest son, Francis II, became king in 1559, she assumed a measure of authority that increased to full control when her second son, the weak Charles IX, ascended the throne in 1560. It was her plotting that led to the terrible Massacre of St. Bartholomew. Continuing her intrigues after the ascension of her third son, Henry III, in 1574, she was the most feared and hated figure in France.

Catherine of Aragon (1485–1536), queen of England (1509–1533), the first wife of Henry VIII. She was the youngest daughter of Ferdinand II and Isabella of Spain. The wife of Arthur, prince of Wales, (1501–1502, when he died) she married his brother Henry in 1509 when he succeeded to the throne. By 1526 Henry was in love with Anne Boleyn; eager to have a male heir, he began proceedings to obtain a divorce from Catherine. His grounds were that their marriage was incestuous because Catherine had been previously married to his brother. Although the Pope Clement VII ruled against the divorce, the Archbishop of Canterbury had already given his consent to Henry. It was his failure to get the pope's consent that led Henry to pronounce the Act of Supremacy (1534), by which he declared himself the sole head of religious rule and paved the way for the separation of the English church from Rome. Catherine died two years later. She was the mother of Queen Mary of England.

Catherine of Siena, Saint (1347–1380), Roman Catholic patron saint of Italy and author of numerous religious works. Renowned for her unusual devoutness, she dedicated her life to helping reform the Church and unifying a badly divided Italy. She succeeded in persuading Pope Gregory XI of Avignon to return to Rome in 1377. During the Great Schism she struggled against anti-papal forces to preserve recognition of Gregory's successor, Urban VI. She was canonized in 1461 and declared patron saint of Italy in 1939; her feast day is April 30.

Catiline, full name **Lucius Sergius Catalina** (c.108–62 B.C.), Roman political leader who in 63 B.C. attempted to overthrow the Roman government. Although he had previously held several important posts, he acquired an unsavory reputation, which caused Cicero to speak out against him in the Senate. After learning of Catiline's plot, Cicero made a series of speeches, forcing Catiline to leave Rome. He made his way north, where he was defeated and killed by the senatorial army.

Cato, Marcus Porcius, called **Cato the Elder** or **Cato the Censor** (234–149 B.C.), Roman orator and statesman and one of the first important Latin writers. In his youth he lived and worked on a small farm where he learned to value the simple customs of the early republic. Later, in Rome, he severely disapproved of the Grecian influence that he believed was corrupting the citizens, and when he assumed the office of censor (184 B.C.), he performed his duties so rigidly that "the Censor" became a permanent part of his name. A visit to Carthage in 175 B.C. convinced Cato that this city was a dangerous rival of Rome. Thereafter he concluded every one of his speeches in the Senate with the words, "Carthage must be destroyed."

Cato, Marcus Porcius surnamed **Uticensis,** called **Cato the Younger** (95–46 B.C.), Roman statesman, the great-grandson of Cato the Elder. He is remembered for his attempts to preserve Roman tradition against the encroachment of newcomers such as Julius Caesar. He held, successively, the offices of quaestor, tribune, and praetor. A rigid moralist, like his distinguished ancestor, he failed to appreciate that Rome needed leaders who could be dictators if necessary. Eventually he took sides with Pompey and opposed Julius Caesar as an enemy of the state. As tribune he had even accused Caesar of being implicated in the conspiracy of Catiline. After the defeat of Pompey's forces at Pharsalia, Cato sailed for Africa. He undertook command of the opposition forces at Utica, but committed suicide when he was convinced that further effort was useless.

Catt, Carrie Lane Chapman (1859–1947), American leader in the movement for woman suffrage. She was born in Ripon, Wis., and educated at Iowa State College. She was an organizer of the National American Woman Suffrage Association and became its president in 1900, succeeding Susan B. Anthony. She led in the campaign to win the vote for women through a constitutional amendment. After the amendment was ratified in 1920, she organized the League of Women Voters to educate women in politics. She devoted the rest of her life to various peace movements.

Catullus, Gaius Valerius (c.84–54 B.C.), Roman lyric poet, regarded with Horace as the finest lyric poet of ancient Rome. Little is known of his life, except that he was born at Verona and as a young man went to Rome. He left 113 poems, most of them heavily influenced by Greek poetry. Among his most outstanding odes are those addressed to "Lesbia." His best work has a passion and vigor that many critics consider unmatched in Roman literature.

Cavell, Edith Louisa (1865–1915), English nurse who was executed by the Germans in World War I. She was born in Swardeston, Norwich, and studied nursing in London. When the war broke out, she was first matron of a training school for nurses in Brussels. The school became a Red Cross Hospital and she remained on duty. On August 5, 1915, she was arrested by the Germans on the charge of having assisted Allied soldiers to escape from Belgium. She was convicted and shot on October 11. The affair served to intensify popular feeling against Germany. Her body was removed to Norwich Cathedral in 1919, and in 1920 a monument to her was erected in London.

Cavendish, Henry (1731–1810), English chemist and physicist who made important contributions to knowledge of electricity, gases, and heat. Born in Nice, France, he was educated in London. A wealthy man, he became a recluse and devoted all his time to research. He discovered the specific heat of many substances, as well as the chemical composition of air and water, and described the properties of hydrogen (which he called inflammable air). Cavendish also determined the density of the earth.

Cavour, Conte **Camillo Benso di** (1810–1861), Italian statesman who led the struggle to unify modern Italy, and was its first prime minister. Born in Turin, he was an army officer as a young man, but resigned in 1831 to travel and study new agricultural techniques. In support of the unification of Italy, he founded a newspaper in 1847. In the following year he was elected to the parliament serving the united districts of Sardinia, Piedmont, and Savoy. In 1852 he became head of the government, and two years later, during the Crimean War, forced Sardinia into an alliance with France and England against Russia. Sardinia was thus qualified to sit at the Paris peace congress in 1856, and its status as the probable nucleus of an independent Italy was brought to the attention of the powers.

Cavour next devoted himself to preparing for a struggle with Austria, then dominant in Italy. He brought about an alliance with Napoleon III, and in 1859 Austria was defeated. Napoleon, however, made peace with Austria without freeing Italy, and Cavour, overcome with disappointment and humiliation, resigned his position as minister of war. In 1860 he returned to office as premier, the hero and spokesman of the Italian people. By consenting to the cession of Savoy and Nice to France, he secured French aid. Early in 1861, after Garibaldi had conquered Sicily and overthrown the kingdom of Naples, all Italy except Rome and Venetia acknowledged Victor Emmanuel as king. Cavour died that year, but not before he had witnessed the assembling of the first Italian parliament at Turin.

Caxton, William (c.1422–1491), the first English printer. Born in Kent, he came to London at the age of 16 and became a clothier's apprentice. In 1441 he went to Bruges, Flanders, and during a long stay abroad became a prosperous merchant. He also studied languages and learned the art of printing. In 1474 at either Bruges or Cologne, he printed the first book in English, a translation from the French of a history of Troy. In 1476 Caxton set up a wooden printing press in an almonry near Westminster Abbey, where the first book to be printed in England, *Dictes and Sayings of the Philosophers*, was issued in 1477. Caxton later printed works by Sir Thomas Malory, Chaucer, and Cicero.

Cecil, Edgar Algernon Robert, 1st Viscount **Cecil of Chelwood** (1864–1958), British statesman who was a leading figure in the founding of the League of Nations. Born in London, he entered Parliament in 1906, and as a Conservative held positions as minister of blockade and lord privy seal. After World War I he helped draft the Covenant of the League of Nations. He received the Nobel Peace Prize in 1937 for his efforts to promote international good will. From 1918 to 1945 he was chancellor of Birmingham University. He was made a viscount in 1924.

Cecil, William, Baron **Burghley** or **Burleigh** (1520–1598), chief minister to Queen Elizabeth I of England, the son of Richard Cecil, master of the robes under Henry VIII. At the age of 21, Cecil entered Gray's Inn as a barrister. He first rose to power when Henry VIII appointed him secretary of state. When Mary I came to the throne he resigned his appointment but was reappointed to office by Elizabeth. For 40 years he advised Elizabeth in the many difficulties she encountered in her reign. She made him lord high treasurer and raised him to the peerage as Lord Burghley. At times Burghley acted with great skill and prudence, but he was ruthless to his enemies.

Cecilia, Saint (d. about 230), Christian martyr, revered as the patron saint of church music. According to legend, she was born of a noble Roman family and vowed to remain a virgin. Forced against her will to marry, she told her husband of her vow. Respecting her wishes, he became a convert when he saw her talking to an angel. After she had distributed all her belongings to the poor, she was ordered to be burned to death. When the flames did not harm her, she was beheaded. She has been the subject of many paintings, and is often portrayed playing the organ. Her feast day is November 22.

Celestine III, born **Giacinto Bobone** (c.1106–1198), Roman Catholic pope (1191–1198), succeeded Clement III. During his pontificate, his most important act was to crown Henry VI Holy Roman emperor. Later, however, he threatened to excommunicate Henry for imprisoning Richard I of England and holding him for ransom; but he never carried out this threat. Both men died a few months apart, and the struggle of each for control over the other was unresolved.

Celestine V, Saint, born **Pietro di Murrone** (1215–1296), Roman Catholic pope for five months during 1294, voluntarily relinquished his papacy. At the age of 79, after years of the severest asceticism, he was elevated to the papacy in August, 1294, only to relinquish it in December in order to resume his old life of discipline and penance. He himself had issued a decree permitting voluntary abdication. His successor, Boniface VIII, kept him prisoner in order to prevent disunion in the church. Celestine died ten months later. He was canonized in 1313; his feast day is May 19.

Cellini, Benvenuto (1500–1571), Italian sculptor and the most renowned goldsmith of the Renaissance. Born in Florence, he had a high temper and a quarrelsome disposition, which made his life a hectic one. He described his life in a celebrated autobiography, first printed in Italy in 1728 (first English edition 1771). The chief authentic relic of Cellini's art as a goldsmith is a magnificent salt cellar of embossed gold and enamel, made for Francis I of France, and now in the Metropolitan Museum of Art, New York. Of surviving pieces of statuary, the most famous is his bronze *Perseus with the Head of Medusa,* in a public square of Florence. The Louvre, in Paris, possesses another bronze figure, *Nymph of Fontainebleau.* He was a prodigious worker, was seldom without commissions from popes and royalty, and was long at the court of Francis I, in France.

Celsius, Anders (1701–1744), Swedish astronomer who invented the centigrade thermometer. He was born in Uppsala and taught at the University of Uppsala (1730–1744), where he built and directed the observatory. Among his research projects was a study of the aurora borealis. His thermometer was first described in 1742 to the Swedish Academy of Sciences.

Cervantes, full name **Miguel de Cervantes Saavedra** (1547–1616), Spanish author whose novel *Don Quixote* is a recognized world classic. In 1571 he joined John of Austria's army and fought the Turks. In the Battle of Lepanto (1571) he received a wound which deprived him of the use of his left hand and arm. He remained in active service until 1575, when, on his way from Italy to Spain, he was captured and imprisoned by the Moors in Algiers. In 1580 his relatives and friends purchased his freedom. He returned to Madrid at the age of 34 and began his literary career. He produced there his pastoral romance, *Galatea,* and several plays for the stage.

From 1598 to 1603 all trace of him is lost, but he is supposed to have spent the interval in La Mancha, where he is said to have begun *Don Quixote* in prison. The first part was published in 1605 and the second part in 1615. In this work Cervantes satirized chivalry and all of the mummeries of knight errantry. Although it won great praise for him, it also aroused bitterness from those who felt that Cervantes's satire was aimed at them. Cervantes returned to Madrid and published his *Novelas ejemplares (Cautionary Tales,* 1613), most of which had been written earlier. In 1614 he published *Viaje al Parnaso (Journey to Parnassus),* a collection of poems.

When the second part of *Don Quixote* appeared it was received with universal enthusiasm. This work immortalized the name of Cervantes as one of the greatest writers of all time. He had been living in great poverty, which the sale of this work relieved. However, his health began to fail, and he had a presentiment of his death. This is indicated in the preface of his *Persiles y Sigismunda,* a serious romance that he prepared for the press at the beginning of 1616, though it was not published until 1617 by his widow. On April 19 he dictated to his wife a letter addressed to his friend Lemos, to whom he dedicated the work. He died on April 23, 1616, the same day as Shakespeare.

Cézanne, Paul (1839–1906), French painter, one of the major figures in the development of abstract art. Born in Aix-en-Provence, the son of a wealthy banker, he studied law briefly but decided to pursue painting. He was encouraged by his good friend Émile Zola to join him in Paris (1861), where he was introduced to Édouard Manet, Camille Pissaro, and other members of the Impressionist school. He exhibited with the Impressionists in 1874 and 1877; however, his work was severely attacked. After 1892 he began to be recognized and his fame constantly increased, particularly after his death. Cezanne's paintings now hang in many great museums.

Chabrier, Alexis Emmanuel (1841–1894), French composer noted for his colorful, impressionistic music. He was born in Ambert and was in the civil service until he was nearly 40. He taught himself musical composition, in which he experimented in

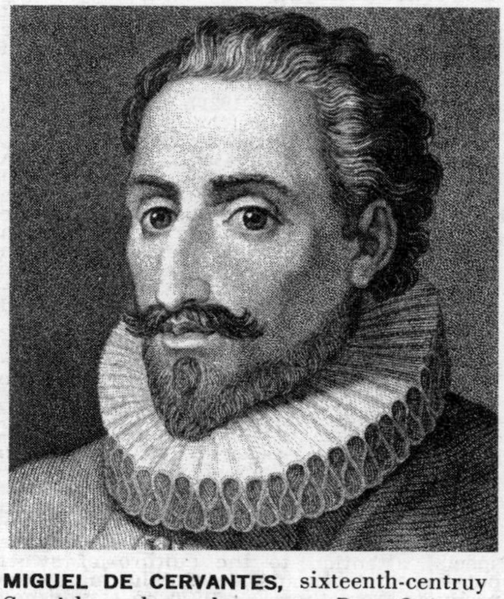

MIGUEL DE CERVANTES, sixteenth-centruy Spanish author who wrote *Don Quixote.*

his spare time. He left the government service to devote himself entirely to music. His best-known works include *España* (1883), the opera *Le Roi malgré lui* (1887), and *Bourrée fantasque* (1891). For much of his music, Chabrier drew upon folksongs and popular Parisian melodies of the day.

Chagall, Marc (1887–), Russian painter, famed for his colorful, neo-primitive works. He was born in Vitebsk and studied art in Paris (1910–1914), where he became known for his paintings of life in a Russian-Jewish village. During World War II, he lived in the United States, returning to France in 1948. His major works include a striking series of stained-glass windows for a synagogue in Israel, as well as a ceiling mural for the Opera House in Paris. Among his works are *The Wedding* (1910), *I and the Village* (1911), *The Green Rabbi* (1914), *The Birthday* (1915), and *Time Is a River Without Banks* (1939).

Chaliapin, Feodor Ivanovich (1873–1938), Russian operatic basso whose interpretation of the title role in *Boris Godounov* is one of the legends of opera. Born in Kazan, Russia, he joined an opera company in the early 1890's. After his debut in St. Petersburg in 1894, he sang leading basso roles throughout Europe. In 1922 his appearance at the Metropolitan Opera in New York caused a sensation. In such parts as Boris Godounov and Ivan the Terrible, his singing, stage presence, and characterization were extraordinary.

Chamberlain, Joseph (1836–1914), British statesman noted for his efforts to unify the British Empire and for his work on tariff reform. As a young man he entered business with his father as a screw manufacturer and by 1874 had become wealthy. In 1873 he was elected mayor of Birmingham, and in 1876 his constituents sent him to Parliament. He became president of the Board of Trade under William Gladstone in 1880, and in 1886 president of the local government board. Not liking Gladstone's Irish policy, he resigned and organized the Liberal-Unionist party. In 1895 he became secretary for the colonies in the Conservative (Unionist) cabinet of the Marquis of Salisbury, a position that he retained under Arthur Balfour. Although the country was divided on his conduct of the negotiations preceding the Boer War, in the "Khaki" election of 1900 he triumphed. In 1906 he forced an election on the tariff issue, but his party was defeated by the Liberals, and Chamberlain retired.

Chamberlain, Neville, full name **Arthur Neville Chamberlain** (1869–1940), British prime minister (1937–1940) who was linked with the policy of "appeasement" that preceded World War II. Born in Birmingham, the son of Joseph Chamberlain, he entered Parliament in 1918 and for four years remained an undistinguished figure. In 1922 his political career was really launched when Bonar Law made him postmaster general. In the posts of minister of health and chancellor of the exchequer under Stanley Baldwin, Chamberlain began to show supreme competence as an administrator. He balanced the budget and persuaded the depression-struck country to abandon free trade for tariffs. In 1937 Chamberlain as leader of the Conservative party became prime minister when Baldwin retired. He worked for a peaceable agreement with Germany and Italy and in 1938 agreed to the Munich Pact, which gave Germany a part of Czechoslovakia.

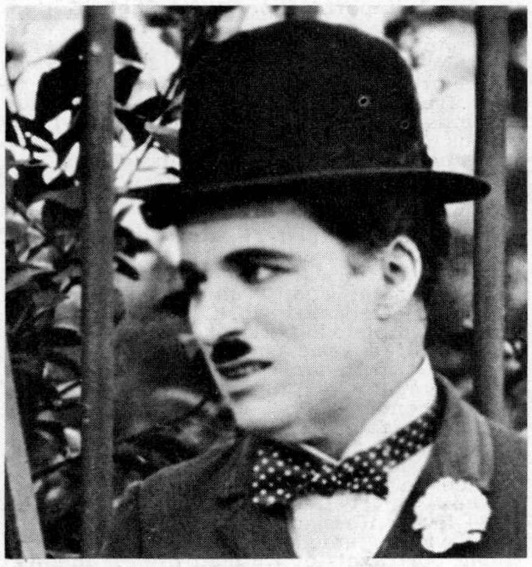

UNITED ARTISTS

CHARLES CHAPLIN, film actor and director.

Champlain, Samuel de (c.1567–1635), French explorer of Canada, known as the "Father of New France." After a period in the French army, he took command of the *Saint-Julien* and started on a cruise to the West Indies (1599), which lasted two years. He visited the Spanish settlements in South America and Mexico and, in a report to King Henry IV, suggested the feasibility of a canal across the Isthmus of Panama. In 1603 he undertook the first of many voyages to the northern part of North America, exploring the St. Lawrence River as far as the Lachine Rapids and the Saguenay for nearly 40 miles. During the next few years he explored the coast of what is now New England and helped to found a settlement at Port Royal, Nova Scotia. This colony was abandoned, however, and in 1608, when Champlain assumed his duties as lieutenant governor of New France, he established and named the town of Quebec.

He made friends with the Algonquins and Hurons and in 1609 discovered Lake Champlain while helping these Indians in a raid against the Iroquois. In 1611 he built a trading post on the site of Montreal and returned to France to obtain a grant of the fur trade monopoly. Returning to New France, he went with the Hurons to Lake Huron and Lake Ontario and mapped them. In 1629, when Quebec was captured by the English, Champlain was carried captive to England. There he wrote his *Voyages in New France*. Two years before his death, he returned to Canada.

Champollion, Jean François (1790–1832), French archaeologist regarded as the founder of Egyptology. He studied under his brother, a famous archeologist, and in 1809 became professor of history at the Grenoble Lyceum. The discovery of the Rosetta Stone (1799) had aroused worldwide interest in hieroglyphics, and he applied himself to deciphering them for many years. His success in establishing the alphabetic character of the hieroglyphs made it possible to translate a great deal of ancient Egyptian writing.

Channing, William Ellery (1780–1842), American clergyman and author, known as the "Apostle of Unitarianism." He was born in Newport, R.I., and graduated from Harvard in 1798. In 1819 he set forth the aims of Unitarianism and had a tremendous influence on the public thereafter. In 1822 he visited Europe and made the acquaintance of several authors, notably Wordsworth and Coleridge. He wrote essays and treatises, all vigorous, eloquent, and openminded. In his views on public education, his denunciation of war, and his solution of labor problems, he was well in advance of his time. Though not allied with the Abolitionists, his speeches and writings against slavery were a great help to Pres. Abraham Lincoln. His published *Works* in six volumes passed through 11 editions.

Chaplin, Charles Spencer (1889–), English motion-picture actor famed for his comic roles. He was born in London and as a youngster appeared in music halls with his father. He came to the United States with an English company in 1910. Engaged by Mack Sennett to make films, he adopted the eccentric makeup and costume that were to make him the best known entertainer in the world. In 1918 he organized his own company and produced such masterpieces of the silent screen as *The Kid*, *The Gold Rush*, and *The Circus*. For some years after the advent of talking pictures, he continued to act in pantomime, notably in *City Lights* (1931) and *Modern Times* (1936). Later Chaplin abandoned the tramp character he had created, producing and starring in such films as *The Great Dictator* (1940), *Monsieur Verdoux* (1947), and *Limelight* (1952). In 1966 he came out of retirement to direct the movie *A Countess From Hong Kong*.

Chapman, John, known as **Johnny Appleseed** (1774–1845), American frontier figure remembered for the orchards he seeded during early settlement days in the Midwest. Born in Leominster, Mass., he went to western Pennsylvania about 1800, where he began planting apple-tree seedlings. To help pioneers, he collected apple seeds from the waste of cider presses and gave them to settlers who were heading westward. Then for some 40 years he walked through Ohio, Indiana, and Illinois, tending his trees and teaching frontier settlers how to plant and care for orchards. Soon after his death, he became an almost legendary character, the subject of many folk stories.

Chardin, Jean Baptiste Siméon (1699–1779), French painter, noted for his studies of people in everyday life. Born in Paris, he was largely self-taught, achieving recognition in 1728 after an exhibition for young painters. In his best work Chardin portrayed common people doing ordinary household tasks. He was also an accomplished painter of still lifes.

Charlemagne or **Charles the Great** (c.742–814), king of the Franks (768–814) and Holy Roman emperor (800–814), the first to bear this title. He was the elder son of Pepin the Short, the first Frankish king of the Carolingian dynasty. On the death of Pepin (768), the Frankish kingdom was divided between Charlemagne and his younger brother Carloman, Charlemagne receiving the eastern part. Carloman died three years later, and Charlemagne ruled the whole realm. Master of Gaul and western Germany, he then entered upon a brilliant career of conquest. In becoming the sole king, he had excluded the sons of Carloman, and when his brother's widow sought the aid of Desiderius, king of the Lombards, Charlemagne declared war. The result was that Charlemagne conquered the kingdom (774), placing the iron crown of the Lombards upon his own head and forcing Desiderius to retire to a monastery. It was not until 787, however, that the last traces of revolt were crushed. Meanwhile, Charlemagne had confirmed his father's grant of certain lands to the pope, thus setting up the papal claim to temporal power. More severe was the struggle with the Saxons, a contest that Charlemagne inherited from his father and grandfather. The war went on intermittently from 772 to 804 and was marked by repeated Saxon invasions and, in one instance, a Frankish massacre of more than 4,000 Saxon prisoners. Finally the stubborn resistance was overcome, the people accepted Christianity by force, and their chiefs became vassals of the Frankish conqueror.

In 778 Charlemagne crossed the Pyrenees to make war upon the Moors. The country was taken as far as the Ebro, but on his return his rear guard was destroyed by the Basques at Roncesvalles. Roland, hero of a medieval cycle of romantic tales, was among the slain. The design of Duke Tassilo of Bavaria to unite the enemies of Charlemagne against him failed, and that country was placed under Frankish governors. War was waged against the Slavic tribes on the Baltic, and the subjection of the Avars was completed in 796. The territories of Charlemagne were thus extended from the Ebro to the Eider and Volturno, and his aim of restoring the western Roman Empire was achieved. On Christmas Day, 800, he was crowned at Rome by Pope Leo III and thenceforth styled himself "Emperor of the West," regarding himself as the successor of Augustus, Trajan, and Marcus Aurelius. This event was the actual beginning of the Holy Roman Empire.

Charlemagne tried to set up a strong central government in his motley empire. Laws were discussed by great national assemblies, and the edicts known as capitularies evince Charlemagne's wisdom. The whole dominion was divided into counties, governed by earls, who were placed under imperial delegates. He increased the power of the clergy, but kept them under his control; he encouraged trade and industry and established a uniform currency. Competent men were invited from all countries to diffuse learning in his empire.

Charlemagne himself was a diligent scholar and a patron of art. He was also an active, frugal, and temperate man. His favorite residence was Aix-la-Chapelle, and there he was buried. He was survived by one son who succeeded him, Louis the Pious, upon whose death in 843 the great empire was divided into three parts. Charlemagne's work, however, lived after him. He was the chief constructive force during the Dark Ages, and he helped prepare the way for the revival of learning.

Charles I (1600–1649), king of England, Scotland, and Ireland (1625–1649), the second son of James I. His reign was mainly a struggle with Parliament over royal rights and privileges. When his third Parliament (1628) presented the *Petition of Right*, instead of yielding, he dissolved that body and ruled for eleven years without a legislature. An insurrection in Scotland in 1640 forced him to summon a new Parliament to obtain funds, but he dissolved it in three weeks. This so-called "Short Parliament" was followed by the "Long Parliament," equally hostile to him. Finally, in 1641, Charles' attempt to arrest five parliamentary leaders within the walls of the House of Commons brought on a war. After some early successes the royal forces were completely defeated by Oliver Cromwell's army at Naseby (1645). The king sought refuge in Scotland but was brought to England for trial and beheaded in 1649.

Charles II (1630–1685), king of England, Scotland, and Ireland (1660–1685). The son of Charles I, he ascended the throne after the defeat of the Puritans led by Oliver Cromwell. This event is known historically as the Restoration. Charles became nominal king of Great Britain at his father's death but accepted the throne of Scotland, where he went in 1651. He invaded England, but his army was defeated at Worcester, and he managed to get to France. After nine years in exile he returned to England as king (1660) and reigned for 25 years, meeting difficulties with a great deal of wisdom. He died without legitimate issue. Six of his illegitimate sons were made dukes. Among the events of his reign were the fire and plague of London and the passage of the Habeas Corpus Act.

Charles V, known as **Charles the Wise** (1337–1380), king of France (1364–1380). The son of John the Good, he ruled as regent after 1356, when the English captured his father, and assumed the throne in 1364. He himself carried on the war against England successfully. Among other things, he erected the Bastille in Paris, founded a national library, and advanced the arts, literature, and science.

Charles VII, known as **Charles the Victorious** (1403–1461), king of France (1422–1461). When he ascended the throne, the English claimed it for the infant Henry VI and continued their invasions of France. Charles was incapable of resisting, and when the city of Orléans was besieged in 1428, France was apparently doomed. At the darkest hour Joan of Arc saved her country. In May, 1429, the siege of Orléans was raised, and Charles was crowned king at Rheims in July. A period of development followed, and France gradually won back all its lost territory except Calais. Charles' record is marred by his lack of decision and his abandonment of Joan of Arc to her fate.

Charles X (1757–1836), king of France (1824–1830) who attempted to restore much of the royal power lost in the French Revolution. In his brief reign of six years he sought in every way to restore the absolutism that had brought on the Revolution, for he was a true Bourbon, one who "remembered everything and learned nothing." In 1830 his attempt to destroy all freedom of the press and to dissolve the Chamber of Deputies led to a revolution, and he was forced to abdicate. He died in exile, the last of the older line of Bourbons.

Charles V (1500–1558), Holy Roman emperor (1519–1556) and king of Spain (1516–1556). He was the elder son of Philip of Burgundy (Philip I of Spain), son of Emperor Maximilian I, and Johanna, daughter of Ferdinand and Isabella of Spain. Charles inherited the Netherlands, and in 1516 he became king of Spain by right of his mother, and with that crown secured possession of Italy. In 1519 he inherited the Austrian duchies from his grandfather, Maximilian. As ruler of this immense realm, he was elected emperor, thus becoming the most powerful man in Europe. Although not a great soldier, he organized several successful campaigns. He crushed Francis I of France, who had been his great rival, but he could not solve the differences of the warring parties that the Reformation had created in Germany. Charles preferred toleration to a civil war, but he had established his supremacy in Spain and in the Netherlands, and he decided to establish it in the empire also.

Charles easily broke the power of the Protestant princes and made prisoners of their leaders. He then renewed his efforts to reconcile the Catholics and Protestants, and to this end issued the Augsburg Interim (1548), but quite suddenly Maurice of Saxony turned on him, and Charles, completely surprised, had to flee for his life. Maurice and his party were able to impose their own terms, which restricted the emperor's authority. Charles was forced to agree to the Treaty of Passau (1552) and to the Peace of Augsburg (1555), which acknowledged the existing conditions and established Protestantism over a great part of Germany. The Peace of Augsburg was the culmination of his reign. Disappointed in his ambitions and broken in health, he gave his son Philip the sovereignty over the Netherlands in 1555 and, a year later, over his Spanish dominions. He abdicated as emperor in 1556 in favor of his brother, Ferdinand, but the latter was not formally recognized until 1558. Charles retired to a monastery at San Yuste in Spain, two years before his death.

Charles X Gustavus (1622–1660), king of Sweden (1654–1660). He succeeded his cousin, Queen Christina, who abdicated. Trained as a fighter by arduous military service in the Thirty Years' War, he invaded Poland soon after his accession in order to eliminate King John Casimir as a claimant to the Swedish throne. With the enforced aid of Frederick William of Brandenburg, he defeated the Poles at Warsaw in 1656. Subsequently, he carried on a war with Denmark that resulted in great additions to Swedish territory. Charles won wide renown for his boldness in taking his army across the ice-bound straits between the islands and mainland of Denmark in the winter of 1657–1658.

Charles XII, called **Madman of the North** (1682–1718), king of Sweden (1697–1718). In 1697 he succeeded his father, Charles XI, and found that the security of his kingdom was menaced by the jealousy of three other rulers—Frederick IV of Denmark, Augustus II of Poland, and Peter the Great of Russia. By attacking the Danes and Russians separately, the young Swedish king defeated both in 1700, and in 1704 he overran Poland and dethroned its king. There then followed a rash invasion of Russia in 1708, and the annihilation of the Swedish forces at the battle of Poltava (1709). For five years Charles remained a virtual prisoner in Turkey, where he had fled. In 1714 he escaped to Sweden, foolishly attempted to recoup his losses, and in 1718 was killed during an invasion of Norway.

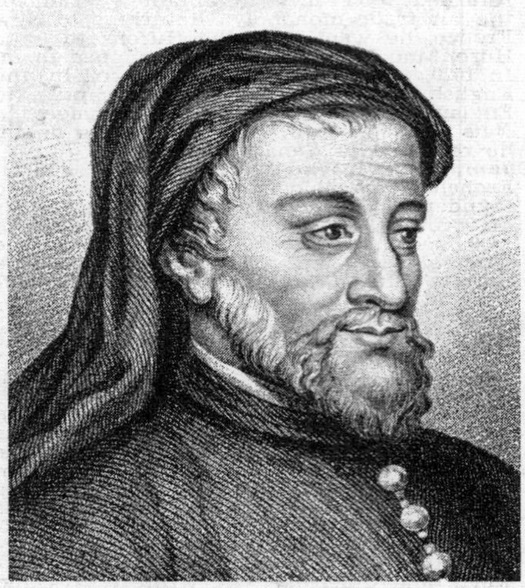

GEOFFREY CHAUCER, medieval English poet.

Charles XIV John, born **Jean Baptiste Jules Bernadotte** (c.1763–1844), king of Norway and Sweden (1818–1844). Born in France, the son of a lawyer, he saw much service as a soldier under Napoleon, became a general, was Napoleon's ambassador at Vienna (1798), and his war minister (1799). When the Empire was established he was made a marshal and governor of Hanover. He took part in other campaigns, and in 1810, just after his appointment as governor of Rome, his popularity in Sweden led to the offer of the Swedish crown and adoption by the aged Charles XIII. He accepted and took the name Charles John. He made an alliance with Russia and England against Napoleon and helped to defeat the French army at Leipzig. Leading his army into Denmark, he forced her to cede Norway to Sweden in 1815. Charles took the throne in 1818, and much peaceful progress was made during his reign. His son, Oscar I, succeeded him.

Charles Martel (c.690–741), grandfather of Charlemagne who, under the title mayor of the palace, virtually ruled the Frankish kingdom from 717 until his death. He gained fame at the battle of Tours (732) by defeating the Saracens and saving western Europe from Muslim domination. This victory won him the title *Martel*, or the Hammer. His sons Pepin the Short (Charlemagne's father) and Carloman were the first rulers of the Carolingian dynasty.

Charpentier, Gustave (1860–1956), French composer, remembered for his opera *Louise*. A student of Jules Massenet, he composed many vocal and orchestral works. But it is *Louise*, with its sentimental view of Paris working-class people, that remains his most popular work. First staged in 1900, it had been performed almost a thousand times in Paris before he died.

Chase, Salmon Portland (1808–1873), American statesman, born in Cornish, N.H. Educated at Dartmouth College, he was admitted to the bar in 1829, and practiced for many years in Ohio, where he became famous as the defender of fugitive slaves. As a U.S. senator from Ohio (1849–1855) he fought persistently against the extension of slavery. Chase subsequently served two terms as governor of Ohio and was one of the first members of the Republican party. As secretary of the treasury under Pres. Abraham Lincoln, he rendered invaluable service until his resignation in 1864. Though he had disagreed with Lincoln over war policies, the president appointed him chief justice of the Supreme Court, and in that capacity Chase presided over the impeachment trial of Pres. Andrew Johnson. His most notable service to the government during the Civil War emergency had to do with the establishment of the national bank system in 1863.

Chase, Samuel (1741–1811), American Revolutionary War leader, signer of the Declaration of Independence, and justice of the U.S. Supreme Court. Born in Somerset County, Md., he served for more than 20 years in the Maryland legislature, before becoming a member of the Continental Congress. In 1796 Pres. George Washington appointed him an associate justice of the U.S. Supreme Court, a post he held until his death. In 1804 he was impeached because of his partisan conduct at trials and because of his unfavorable remarks about Pres. Thomas Jefferson's administration. The following year he was acquitted. His trial established the view that Supreme Court justices can be removed only if their conduct has been criminal.

Chateaubriand, Vicomte François René de (1768–1848), French politician and author, one of the first Romantic writers in France. He visited the United States in 1791 but hastened back to France on hearing of the arrest of Louis XVI. He joined the royalist army, which was defeated at Thionville (1792). Although wounded, he escaped to England, where he lived until 1800. In 1797 he published his first book, *Essai historique, politique et moral sur les révolutions anciennes et modernes*, and in 1801 the love story *Atala*, which established his literary reputation. His *René* (1805) made him the greatest romantic writer of his time in France. Chateaubriand became an enemy of Napoleon, supported the Bourbons, and was made a peer of France. From 1822 to 1824 he was ambassador to Great Britain.

Chatterton, Thomas (1752–1770), English poet and early romantic remembered as the author of the Rowley poems. Although he claimed that they were the work of Thomas Rowley, a monk of the fifteenth century, he himself had written them, beginning when he was 12. He was a youth of rich imagination and rare creative ability, and his poetry was a source of inspiration to Coleridge, Keats, D. G. Rossetti, and William Morris. Chatterton's extraordinary genius netted him so little in the way of earnings that, upon failure to obtain patronage from Horace Walpole, he killed himself at the age of 18 rather than die by starvation or accept charity.

Chaucer, Geoffrey (c.1340–1400), English poet, the greatest in Middle English, and one of the most important poets in English literature. Born in London, the son of a wine merchant, he served in the army of Edward III that invaded France in 1359, and was taken prisoner. For the next ten years he was frequently employed on diplomatic missions abroad, and his affairs were prosperous. After sitting in the Parliament of 1386, he was deprived of his offices and reduced to comparative poverty. It was not until 1398 that he received an annual pension. Chaucer's first poem, a translation of *Le Roman de la Rose*, was written about 1369. Between 1370 and 1386 he produced *The House of Fame, The Legend of Good Women*, and *Troilus and Criseyde*. His most celebrated work, *The Canterbury Tales*, completed between 1386 and 1389, consists of a series of tales in verse (except for two in prose), supposed to be told by a company of pilgrims to the shrine of Saint Thomas à Becket at Canterbury. In its pages fourteenth-century English life is portrayed as nowhere else in literature. The first collected edition of his works was printed in 1532.

Chekhov or **Tchekov, Anton Pavlovich** (1860–1904), Russian playwright and short-story writer, famed for his half-comic, half-tragic portrayals of Russian life. A medical student, he supported himself by writing short stories. These made him famous, and about 1885 he began to devote himself entirely to writing. Chekhov soon turned to the stage, achieving his first success with *Ivanov* in 1887. Later came the plays that were to make him famous throughout the world: *The Seagull* (1896), *Uncle Vanya* (1897), *The Three Sisters* (1901), and *The Cherry Orchard* (1903). The theater had never seen dramas quite like those of Chekhov. There was little in the traditional way of plot; rather, the plays represented cross sections of life as Chekhov saw it, full of human loneliness and pathos.

Chénier, André Marie de (1762–1794), French poet and revolutionist, remembered for his classical verse and his role in the French Revolution. Born in Constantinople (Istanbul), where his father was in the French consular service, he was trained to be a soldier, but elected to become a writer. When the Revolution began (1789), he was in London with the French embassy. Returning to France in 1790, he wrote political articles protesting the excesses of the Reign of Terror. Because of his writings, he was arrested by Robespierre and guillotined in 1794. One of the finest French poets of the century, Chénier wrote many poems in a classical vein and also produced some of the greatest political satires in verse in French literature.

Ch'ên Tu-hsiu (1879–1942), Chinese scholar and Communist leader, regarded as the chief founder of the Communist party in China (1924). Educated in Japan and France, he was for a time editor of the magazine *New Youth* and started a movement to make *pai-hua* (vernacular Chinese) the national language. He was a member of the Central Executive Committee of the Kuomintang (1925-1928); after he was expelled he was arrested (1932) and imprisoned. He later spent several years in exile.

Cheops. See *Khufu*.

Cherubini, Maria Luigi Carlo Zenobio Salvatore (1760–1842), Italian composer and leader in the development of French opera. Born in Florence, he was thoroughly grounded in the traditions of Italian music when he went to London in 1785 to become composer to King George III. A year later he settled permanently in Paris, where his operas *Medée* (1797) and *Les Deux Journées* (1800) were well received. Besides his operas, Cherubini also composed string quartets and two requiems. In 1822 he became the first director of the newly-founded Paris Conservatoire, and in this position he had a great influence on the development of French music. Beethoven admitted his debt to Cherubini, as did many other composers.

Chiang Kai-shek, in Peking dialect **Chiang Chieh-shih,** real name **Chiang Chung-cheng** (1886–), Chinese soldier and statesman who ruled China from 1928 to 1949, when he was defeated by the Chinese Communists. After 1949 he became head of the Chinese government-in-exile on Formosa. A follower of Sun Yat Sen, he became commander of the Nationalist forces in 1925. Chiang led these forces to the capture of Peking and to other victories. In 1928 he was chosen president of the republic and ruled as a dictator. Two years later he conducted campaigns against the Communists in the south and against the northerners who still refused to accept his rule. Japanese attempts to secure control of China assumed tremendous proportions in the 1930's. Chiang, attempting to bring order into Chinese affairs, was hindered by the Japanese and by dissension and corruption among his own followers. The Japanese gained control of north China and in 1934 set up the state of Manchukuo. In 1937 an "incident" began the long undeclared war with Japan. Chiang moved the capital to Chungking in southwest China, where it remained until 1945. The United States sent money, arms, and military advisers, one of whom was Gen. Joseph W. Stilwell. The two men differed on policy and Stilwell went to Burma. Chiang was visited by other American advisers in the hope that an aggressive campaign could be got under way. The foundation of the Nationalist government was so corrupt that no positive action could be taken.

The war's end brought the defeat of Japan and forced her evacuation of China. The Communists, after Chiang had refused to join them in a coalition government, had moved into north China. Chiang's military position deteriorated over the years and the Communists turned southward again. By the summer of 1949 they were in Nanking, Chiang's government having moved first to Chengtu and then to Chungking. On January 28, 1949, Chiang resigned his office of president of Nationalist China, but on April 19, 1949, he was reelected. In December, 1949, Chiang moved the Nationalist capital to the island of Formosa.

Chippendale, Thomas (c.1718–1779), English furniture maker, one of the greatest and most widely copied. He started in the cabinetmaking business in London about 1750 and soon had a reputation for excellence. He borrowed ideas from France, but gradually developed his own distinctive style, which stressed lightness and grace of line. Later furniture makers have produced chairs and cabinets modeled after Chippendale's. His *Gentleman and Cabinet Maker's Director* (1754) is illustrated with his own drawings.

Chopin, Frédéric François (1810–1849), Polish composer whose works for the piano are standard concert fare the world over. Born near Warsaw of French-Polish parentage, he was a child prodigy whose feats at the piano made him the pet of Polish society. His debut in Vienna was an immense success, and in Paris, where he finally settled, he was acclaimed a master of the piano. He published his first piano composition in 1825. Chopin's love affair with the writer George Sand is famous in history. It was during their association (1837–1845) that he write his major compositions, including 3 sonatas, 2 concertos, 4 ballades, 4 scherzos, 19 nocturnes, 27 études, and a set of 24 preludes. His melancholy compositions, romantic and harmonically original, reflect his brooding nature.

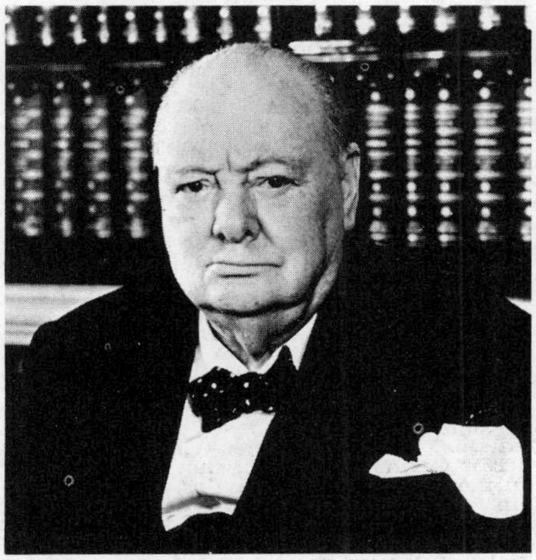

BRITISH INFORMATION SERVICES

WINSTON CHURCHILL, British statesman.

Chou En-lai (c.1898–), Chinese Communist leader who was one of the founders of the Chinese Communist party. As a young man he studied in France, returning in 1924 to become a follower of Sun Yat Sen. When the Communist party and the Kuomintang separated in 1927, he became one of the most active Communist leaders. During the 1930's and 1940's, he continued as a leader in the Communist struggle to oust the forces of Chiang Kai-shek. When the Communist victory came, Chou became premier and foreign minister (1949). Because of his experience outside China, which few of the other Communist leaders had, Chou was often called upon to make diplomatic trips to various foreign countries.

Chrétien de Troyes (d. about 1190), French poet whose romances on courtly love and Arthurian legend were among the earliest written. Little is known of his life, except that he probably (judging by his name) came from the French town of Troyes, in the Champagne district. In his romances, with their accounts of the deeds of knights such as Lancelot and Perceval, he recounted chivalrous adventures intermixed with love stories. His stories were very popular, and formed the basis of many later interpretations of Arthurian legends.

Christ, Jesus. See *Jesus*.

Christian II (1481–1559), king of Denmark and Norway (1513–1523), and of Sweden (1520–1523). His cruel massacre of prominent persons in Sweden led to a revolt under Gustavus Vasa, and in 1523 Christian fled to the Netherlands, after being spurned by his Danish countrymen. He made an unsuccessful attempt to recover his crown in 1531, and was kept in prison until his death.

Christian IV (1577–1648), king of Denmark and Norway (1588–1658). He engaged in various wars and was defeated by the count of Tilly at Lutter in 1626. A war with Sweden from 1643 to 1645 was equally unsuccessful. Christian was an enlightened ruler in civic affairs and furthered industry, science, and commerce. He founded the Norwegian city of Christiania (now Oslo).

Churchill, John, 1st Duke of **Marlborough** (1650–1722), English general whose military victories over the French during the early 1700's made him the power behind the English throne. After a series of striking military successes as a young man, he joined forces with William of Orange in the 1680's and was elevated to the earldom of Marlborough. Under Queen Anne, he became commander in chief of the British armies and won a dukedom for his leadership in the War of the Spanish Succession. Between 1704 and 1713 he won a series of notable victories over the French, which culminated in the Treaty of Utrecht in 1713. At length his fortunes were undermined by political intrigue in England, and he was dismissed from office on the charge that he had embezzled public funds. When George I ascended the throne in 1714, Churchill was restored to full honors.

Churchill, Sir **Winston Leonard Spencer** (1874–1965), English statesman who as prime minister led his nation to victory in World War II. The elder son of Lord Randolph Churchill (himself a notable politician), he entered the army at the age of 21, served in India and Egypt, and was a newspaper correspondent in the Boer War, in which he later took part as an officer after being captured and making his escape. In 1900 he entered Parliament as a Conservative but altered his viewpoint and joined the Liberals. In 1911, when Prime Minister Herbert H. Asquith felt an approaching conflict with Germany, Churchill, as first lord of the admiralty, prepared the fleet to resist an attack by Germany. When World War I broke out he took a naval force to try to save Antwerp from the Germans. When the Liberal government fell in 1915, he went to France to command a regiment. He returned to England to be appointed minister of munitions by Lloyd George in 1917, and secretary of war and air in 1918. Churchill was chancellor of the exchequer from 1924 to 1929.

Through the 1930's he opposed appeasement of Hitler's Germany and urged preparedness. He was prime minister of Great Britain during most of World War II and by his inspiring leadership helped achieve victory. Because of the defeat of his government by the Labour party in July, 1945, he resigned and became leader of the opposition. Churchill always worked closely with the United States and was prominent in his opposition to nazism and communism. He led the attack on the Labour government's socialization program, becoming prime minister again from 1951 to 1955. His writings include *The World Crisis* (4 vols., 1923–1929; 1942), *Marlborough, His Life and Times* (6 vols., 1933–1938), a personal history, *The Second World War* (6 vols., 1948–1953), and *A History of the English-Speaking Peoples* (4 vols., 1956–1958). In 1963 he was made an honorary citizen of the United States by a special act of Congress.

Chu Teh (1886–), Chinese Communist general whose armies, in 1948 and 1949, defeated Nationalist forces in northern China. After graduation from military school, he joined Sun Yat Sen's revolutionary movement and by 1916 was a brigade commander. In Germany (1922) he was converted to communism and he went to Moscow for training. When Chiang Kai-shek began his Communist purge in 1927, Chu Teh joined Mao Tse-tung, leader of the Chinese Communists. With Mao, he led the "Long March" of 6,000 miles from Kiangsi to Yenan in 1935.

Cicero, Marcus Tullius (106–43 B.C.), Roman scholar, orator, and statesman, remembered for his writings and speeches and for his unsuccessful efforts to preserve the Roman republic. Born in the province of Campania of a cultured and well-to-do family, he received excellent training in literature, law, oratory, and philosophy, and at the age of 26 began to plead in the public courts. In 70 B.C. he won wide fame as the prosecutor of Verres, governor of Sicily, where Cicero himself had served as quaestor in 75 B.C. So convincing was his first oration that Verres fled into exile without attempting a defense. Within the next few years, Cicero attained the offices of praetor and consul (63 B.C.). As consul, he made a sensational attack on the conspiracy headed by Catiline and was acclaimed the "father of his country." This triumph was later turned into defeat when Clodius, his personal enemy, charged him with having executed the Catilinian conspirators without a formal trial. Public feeling was so aroused that Cicero fled to Thessalonica (58 B.C.) and remained in exile for 16 months.

After his return to Rome, Cicero sided

with Pompey in his final struggle against Caesar. When Pompey was defeated at Pharsalia (48 B.C.), Cicero abandoned politics. He enjoyed a few years of quiet devotion to writing until Caesar's assassination (44 B.C.). At first inclined to sympathize with the conspirators, he decided finally to lend his support to Octavian later Emperor Augustus). He delivered a series of orations against Mark Antony, so fiery that they suggested the denunciation of Philip of Macedon by Demosthenes, and so have been called *Philippics*. When Antony joined Octavian in the Second Triumvirate, Cicero was killed by hired agents. As long as Latin literature is read, among its foremost examples of masterly prose will be Cicero's great works — *On Old Age*, *On Friendship*, the four *Orations against Catiline*, and the 14 against Antony. His style has influenced writers of the West for 2,000 years.

Cid, the or **el Cid Campeador,** real name **Rodriguez Díaz de Bivar** (c.1040–1099), Spanish medieval hero famed for his valor in battle. He was a Castilian soldier who spent his life fighting battles both for and against the Moors, who were then masters of a great part of Spain. His exploits, often highly romanticized, are set forth in Spanish poetry, in a play of Corneille, and in an opera by Massenet.

Cimabue, Giovanni (c.1240–c.1302), Italian painter whose work marks a transition from Byzantine to early Renaissance art. Little is known of Cimabue's life, except that he was born in Florence and worked in Pisa and Rome. He was a great mosaicist as well as a painter, and his mosaic figure of Saint John in the apse of the cathedral at Pisa is famous. His paintings are represented by frescoes in the Church of St. Francis of Assisi and *The Madonna of Santa Trinita* in the Academy of Florence.

Cimon (c.507–449 B.C.), Athenian statesman and general who, after the wars with Persia, took a leading role in the development of the Greek empire. The son of Miltiades (the victorious general at the battle of Marathon), he was a co-officer with Aristides in command of the Athenian naval unit in the war with Persia in 477 B.C. At the river Eurymedon (466 B.C.), he was victorious over the naval and land forces of the Persians. His policy of peace with Sparta, later opposed by the Athenians, helped Athens to conserve its strength and become a major power. He died while besieging a Persian garrison on Cyprus.

Cincinnatus, Lucius Quinctius (c.519–c.439 B.C.), Roman dictator and hero. In 469 B.C. he was elected consul, and two years later, in a national crisis, was chosen dictator. Notified by messengers of the honor, he was found behind the plow. He dropped his work, rescued Lucius Minucius, the consul, from the Aequi, and returned to his farm after 16 days. At the age of 80 he again assumed the dictatorship in order to suppress a plebian uprising. A patriotic American organization, the Society of the Cincinnatus, is named in his honor.

Cinna, Lucius Cornelius (d.84 B.C.), Roman statesman, leader of the opposition to the senatorial party of Sulla. After Sulla had driven Marius from Rome, and before setting out against Mithridates, he allowed Cinna to be elected consul on his vow not to disturb the existing constitution. No sooner, however, had Cinna taken office (87 B.C.) than he impeached Sulla and agitated for Marius's recall. Cinna and Marius next declared themselves consuls after a cruel massacre of the Roman citizens. Marius died a few days later and Cinna prepared to meet Sulla but was slain by his own rebellious troops at Brundisium. During his fourth consulate his daughter Cornelia married Julius Caesar.

Clark, George Rogers (1752–1818), American frontier soldier whose victories were a major factor in the opening up of western lands to settlers. Born near Charlottesville, Va., he was a delegate to the Virginia legislature from the Kentucky district in 1776. Clark brought about the organization of Kentucky as a separate county. In 1778, having secured the approval of Gov. Patrick Henry, he raised an armed force to protect the frontier against both Indians and the British during the Revolutionary War. His capture of Kaskaskia, Cahokia, and Vincennes enabled the United States to gain title to the Northwest Territory. He served as Indian commissioner after the war, and in 1783 the Virginia legislature voted him a large tract in the present state of Indiana.

Clark, William (1770–1838), American soldier and explorer who, with Meriwether Lewis, led a famous expedition to the Pacific Northwest. Born in Caroline County, Va., he was a brother of George Rogers Clark. In 1794, as lieutenant of infantry, William Clark fought under Gen. Anthony Wayne against the Indians. He resigned from the army in 1796 because of ill health but resumed military life in 1803 as a second lieutenant. From May, 1804, until September, 1806, he was the companion of Lewis on the famous expedition from St. Louis to the Pacific coast and back. Clark was governor of the Missouri territory (1813–1821) and was superintendent of Indian affairs thereafter. He kept a complete dairy with maps and drawings, which became part of *History of the Expedition under the Commands of Captains Lewis and Clark.*

Claude Lorrain. See *Lorrain, Claude.*

Claudian, full name **Claudius Claudianus** (c.365–c.408 A.D.), last of the Roman classical poets. He came from Alexandria to Rome in 395 A.D. and was in favor at court through the influence of Stilicho. His extant works include two epic poems, *Rape of Proserpine* and the unfinished *War of the Giants*, besides panegyrics on Honorius and Stilicho, and *Epigrammata.*

Claudius I, full name **Tiberius Claudius Drusus Nero Germanicus** (10 B.C.–54 A.D.). He was the youngest son of Drusus, the stepson of Augustus. Claudius lived the life of a student until the praetorian guard made him emperor in the year 41, after the murder of Caligula. Claudius was kindly and liberal-minded but was under the influence of two cruel and unscrupulous wives —Messalina and Agrippina. He had the former executed, and the latter poisoned him in 54 in order to place her son Nero on the throne. During his reign the conquest of Britain was begun and the Claudian aqueduct completed.

Clausewitz, Karl von (1780–1831), Prussian general whose theories on land warfare influenced modern war strategy. Entering the Prussian army in 1792, he advanced steadily until 1812, when he resigned his commission and entered the Russian army to help in the war against Napoleon. In 1814 he returned to the Prussian army and served in the Waterloo campaign. In 1818 he was made a general and administrative head of the Allemeine Kriegsschule (German War School). During the next few years he wrote his major work, *Vom Kriege* (*On War*). Perhaps his most significant contribution to the theory of warfare was his belief that war and politics are inextricably bound—that war is merely an extension of politics.

Clausius, Rudolf Julius Emanuel (1822–1888), German scientist who was a pioneer in modern molecular physics. Born in Koslin and educated at Berlin, he taught physics at Zürich, Würzburg, and Bonn. He is famous for his mathematical investigations of the kinetic theory of gases and for the first clear statement of the second law of thermodynamics. "Heat cannot pass of itself from a cool body to a warm one." He published many works on physics.

Clay, Henry (1777–1852), American statesman, known as the "Great Compromiser," during the pre-Civil War period. Born in Hanover County, Va., he was admitted to the bar in 1797, and began his career at Lexington, Ky. After three years in the Kentucky legislature, he was appointed (1806) to an unexpired term of one year in the U.S. Senate and in 1810 to another unexpired term of one year. In 1811 he was elected to the House of Representatives, where he was chosen speaker. There Clay became famous as the author of the Missouri Compromise, restricting the spread of slavery. In 1824 he was an unsuccessful candidate for the presidency, but was made secretary of state by Pres. John Quincy Adams. He then entered the Senate, in which he played a leading part for many years, especially in the tariff compromise of 1833. Clay was again a presidential candidate before the first Whig national convention in 1839, but Benjamin Harrison was nominated and elected. He had in 1842 bidden farewell to the Senate, but returned to it in 1849, when the nation was again divided over the slavery issue. The following year Clay brought about the Compromise of 1850, his greatest achievement.

Clay, Lucius Dubignon (1897–), American general, born in Marietta, Ga., and a graduate of West Point (1918). At the outset of World War II he was in charge of the army procurement program. In 1945 he was appointed deputy military governor of Germany, and in 1947 became commander in chief of the U.S. occupation forces in Germany. During his administration, he set up the air lift that supplied Berlin during the Russian blockade of that city. He resigned from the army in 1949 to take a position in industry, serving from time to time on government commissions.

Clemenceau, Georges (1841–1929), French statesman who as premier led his country to victory in World War I. He studied medicine in Paris, and after a period of travel and journalistic writing, part of which was spent in the United States, he returned to France and became mayor of Montmartre, Paris, in 1870. In 1876 he began his career as a member of the Chamber of Deputies. In 1902 Clemenceau was elected to the Senate from the department of the Var. He was appointed minister of the interior in March, 1906, and became prime minister the following October. His vigorous use of soldiers to break a miners' strike marked his definite severance from the Socialist party, but he was always more interested in social reform than in party organization. He had opposed Georges Boulanger and supported Alfred Dreyfus, and fought several duels over his political views.

Clemenceau's ministry remained in office until 1909. His term was notable for the establishment of the Entente Cordiale, following the trouble with Germany in 1908, and the separation of church and state. He was an opposition leader from 1909 to 1917, when he again became premier and minister of war. Recognized as the strongest man in France, he brought the war to a successful conclusion and presided over the peace conference at Versailles in 1919. He resigned in 1920 and lived in retirement. Clemenceau completed *In the Evening of My Thought* shortly before he died, and an autobiography, *Grandeur and Misery of Victory*, was published after his death.

Clemens, Samuel Langhorne, pen name **Mark Twain** (1835–1910), American novelist, short-story writer, and essayist whose *Adventures of Huckleberry Finn* is considered an American classic. Born in Florida, Mo., he worked as a printer for a while, then as a Mississippi River pilot before going West in 1861, where he was an unsuccessful gold miner in Colorado. For two years he edited the Virginia City *Territorial Enterprise* before moving to San Francisco in 1864. In 1867 he published his first collection of short stories, *The Celebrated Jumping Frog of Calaveras County and Other Sketches.* That same year he toured Europe, gathering material for his second book, *Innocents Abroad* (1869). In 1871 he settled in Hartford, Conn., as a fiction writer, producing such works as *Roughing It* (1872), *The Gilded Age* (1873), and *The Adventures of Tom Sawyer* (1876), which gained him a vast following. With the publication of *Life on the Mississippi* (1883) and *Huckleberry Finn* (1885) his reputation was further enhanced. Most of Twain's early works were in a humorous, gentle vein. As time went on, however, his writing took on a bitter tone, notably in such works as *What Is Man?* (1906) and *The Mysterious Stranger* (1916). Today, however, he is remembered for his humor and for the immensely believable characters he created.

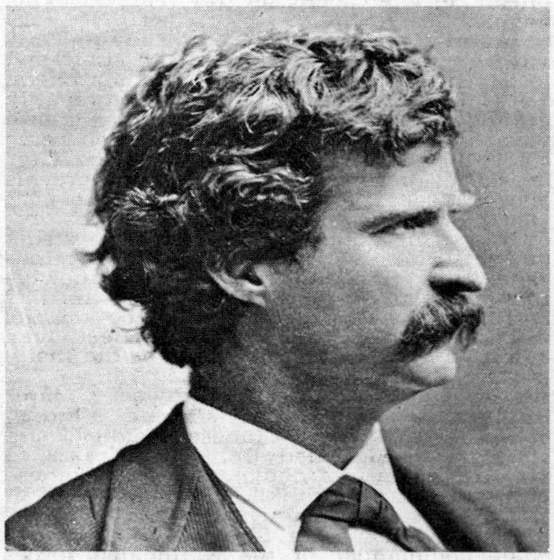

INTERNATIONAL NEWS

SAMUEL CLEMENS

Cleopatra (69–30 B.C.), Egyptian queen whose love affairs with Julius Caesar and Mark Antony are among the most celebrated in history. As Cleopatra VII, she and a brother, Ptolemy XIV, succeeded their father, Ptolemy XIII (Auletes), in 51 B.C. In the third year of their reign, Ptolemy's friends dethroned Cleopatra, but she won Caesar to her cause and was reinstated by his influence. Ptolemy was killed, and

Caesar proclaimed Cleopatra queen of Egypt. Another brother having been made co-ruler, the queen accompanied Caesar in 46 B.C. to Rome, where they had a son, Caesarion.

After Caesar's assassination in 44 B.C., Cleopatra returned to Egypt, poisoned her brother, and made her young son her colleague. Because she failed to announce her support of the triumvirs who had partitioned the Roman world, Mark Antony, ruler of the East, summoned her to meet him at Tarsus, in Cilicia. Dazzled by her beauty, he threw away honor and career, and eventually divorced his wife Octavia, the sister of his colleague Octavian (afterwards Emperor Augustus) for her. In a war with Octavian, Anthony's fleet was defeated at Actium (31 B.C.), and he fled to Egypt. Deceived by a report that Cleopatra had died, he killed himself. The queen soon learned that Octavian was indifferent to her charms, and preferring death to enslavement, she too committed suicide. Plutarch wrote an account of her, and Shakespeare, a play.

Cleveland, Grover, full name **Stephen Grover Cleveland** (1837–1908), twenty-second and twenty-fourth president of the United States (1885–1889, 1893–1897). He was born in Caldwell, N.J., where his father was a Presbyterian minister. The family moved to Fayetteville, N.Y., when Grover was only four years old, and later went to Clinton, where the boy was prepared for college. After his father's death Cleveland became a teacher at Batavia, N.Y. Subsequently, he studied law in Buffalo and began to practice there in 1859. He was

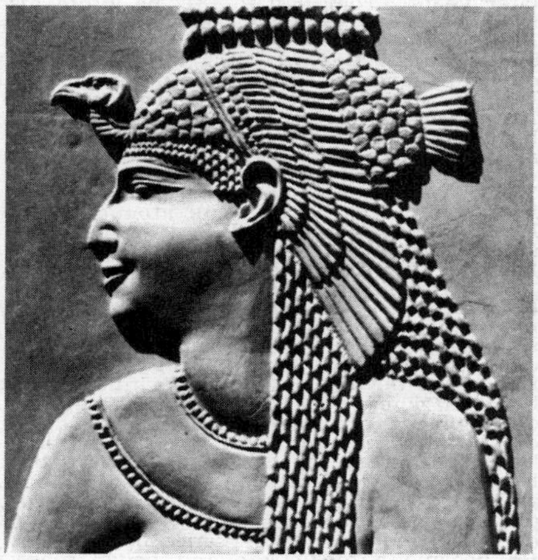

BETTMAN ARCHIVE

CLEOPATRA

appointed assistant district attorney in 1863, and elected sheriff of the county in 1870. Elected mayor in 1881, his record for honesty and efficiency brought him the Democratic nomination for governor of New York in 1882, followed by his election. As mayor he reorganized the city government; as governor he put through a strong civil service law. In 1884 the Democratic national convention at Chicago nominated him for the presidency, and he was elected.

Cleveland's first administration was notable for the extension of the civil service, much labor unrest, the use of federal military forces to maintain order in Utah and Panama, a drastic policy of vetoing pension bills and the passage of several important acts, including the Presidential Succession Act of 1886 and the Interstate Commerce Act of 1887. The tariff was the leading issue of the campaign of 1888, and the country was apparently in a mood for return to a high-protection policy. Renominated by the Democrats, Cleveland lost to the Republican candidate, Benjamin Harrison of Indiana, who carried Cleveland's own state in the election.

After an interval of four years at his law practice, Cleveland was returned to office in 1892 on a wave of dissatisfaction with the McKinley Tariff Act. In this administration he ordered federal troops to Chicago to protect the mails during the riotous Pullman strike of 1894; he repealed the silver legislation; and he insisted on arbitration of the Great Britain-Venezuela boundary dispute involving British Guiana and Venezuela. After expiration of his second term of office he lived at Princeton, N.J., was a trustee of Princeton University for ten years and occasionally lectured there. Cleveland gained a high place in public estimation for his unflinching honesty and for his diligent efforts to promote the best interests of the country.

Cliburn, Van, full name **Harvey Lavan Cliburn, Jr.** (1934–), American pianist who in 1958 became world-famous when he won an international competition in Moscow. A native of Texas, he graduated with highest honors from the Juilliard School of Music, New York City, in 1954. He made his concert debut with the Houston Symphony Orchestra at the age of 13 in 1947; seven years later, he appeared with the New York Philharmonic. Since winning the international Tschaikovsky competition in Moscow, he has toured extensively and has made many recordings.

Clinton, DeWitt (1769–1828), American political leader, who sponsored construction of the Erie Canal. Born in Little Britain, N.Y., he graduated from Columbia College in 1786. He was admitted to the New York bar in 1788 and became active in politics as an Antifederalist. From 1797 until 1802, he served in the state legislature, and in 1802 was elected to the U.S. Senate. Resigning in the same year to become mayor of New York, he held this office most of the time between 1803 and 1815. He was the presidential choice of the Democratic-Republican party in 1812, but was defeated by James Madison. Afterward he was a leader in various civic movements in his state and was elected governor in 1817, 1820, and 1824.

Clive, Robert Baron **Clive of Plassey** (1725–1774), British soldier and statesman who helped England gain control over India. In 1743 he went to Madras as a clerk in the East India Company. This trading company was Britain's sole representative in India, where at the time France was enjoying authority and prestige. In 1747 war broke out, and soon Clive's daring and resourcefulness made him a leader. In 1751, with only a few men, he captured Arcot, which he held during a long siege. From 1753 to 1755 Clive was in England, where he was hailed as a conqueror. Returning to India, he exacted revenge for the Black Hole outrage, recaptured Calcutta, and in 1757, by winning at Plassey against heavy odds, put an end to French rule. Clive placed a friendly native on the throne of Bengal, but he himself ruled the country until 1760, when he returned to England, entered Parliament, and in 1762 was made a peer. In 1765 he went back to India to straighten out the affairs of the East India Company. In 1772 charges of dishonesty were made against him in Parliament, and an investigation followed. The report gave him credit for his services but did not fully exonerate him, and he committed suicide.

Clovis I (c.465–511), founder of the Frankish kingdom. In 481, on the death of his father, Childeric I, Clovis became king of the Salian Franks, with headquarters in what is now Belgium. In 486 he defeated the Gallic Romans at Soissons and subsequently took possession of the territory now included in northwestern France. He made Paris his capital, and at his death he was ruler of a united Frankish kingdom. In 496 he defeated the Alammani and in accordance with a vow made to the Christian God of his wife Clotilda, was baptized on Christmas Day at Reims.

Cobb, Tyrus Raymond, known as **Ty Cobb** (1886–1960), American baseball player, often called "the Georgia Peach." In his career, he established more records than any other ball player in history. Born in Narrows, Ga., he joined the Detroit team of the American League in 1905, and for 21 years was the most feared batter and base runner in baseball. He batted over .300 for 21 consecutive seasons, with a lifetime average of .367 and 12 batting championships. He played 2,805 games and stole 866 bases. He managed the Detroit team (1921–1926), played one season with the Philadelphia Athletics, and retired in 1928. He was the first player elected to the Baseball Hall of Fame (1936).

Cocteau, Jean (1889–1963), French poet, novelist, playwright, and film writer, regarded as one of the geniuses of modern literature. He wrote several novels, including *Thomas l'imposteur* (1923; *Thomas the Imposter,* 1925), and several volumes of poetry as a young man, then turned to writing opera libretti, essays on art, and stage and film plays. His best-known drama is *Les parents terribles* (1938), translated into English as *Intimate Relations* in 1951. Cocteau also made several films, including *Le sang d'un poète* (*Blood of a Poet,* 1932), *L'eternal retour* (*The Eternal Return,* 1944), and *La belle et la bête* (*Beauty and the Beast,* 1945).

Cody, William Frederick, known as **Buffalo Bill** (1846–1917), American scout, Indian fighter, and showman, born in Scott County, Iowa. He was a rider at the age of 14 for the Pony Express, which was established in 1860 to carry the mails overland. He was a Union scout and guide during the Civil War and also served in the Seventh Kansas Cavalry. In 1876 he fought in the war with the Sioux Indians, killing Chief Yellow Hand in a hand-to-hand fight. Cody organized the original "Wild West Show" in 1883, and in 1887 exhibited its Indians, cowboys, and animals in Europe. His grave is on a mountain near Denver. Cody won the name "Buffalo Bill" by killing buffaloes to supply meat for crews of railway workers.

Cohan, George Michael (1878–1942), American actor, song writer, dramatist, and producer, known as the "Yankee Doodle Dandy." He was born in Providence, R.I., and as a child appeared in numerous plays and on the vaudeville stage. Later he wrote, produced, and acted in many plays and musical comedies and wrote popular songs. He was particularly successful in *Get-Rich-Quick Wallingford, Seven Keys to Baldpate, The Miracle Man,* and *I'd Rather be Right.* Among his songs are *Mary's a Grand Old Name, Over There, Give My Regards to Broadway,* and *You're a Grand Old Flag.*

Coke, Sir **Edward** (1552–1634), English jurist and statesman, noted for his defense of common law against the encroachment of royal power. In 1593 he was elected to Parliament and became speaker of the House of Commons. The following year he was chosen attorney general, in which capacity he prosecuted the earl of Essex, Sir Walter Raleigh, and the conspirators in the Gunpowder Plot. Coke was appointed chief justice of Common Pleas in 1606, and in 1613 chief justice of the King's Bench. In 1617 he was removed from office by James I because he insisted on maintaining the supremacy of the law. Later, as a member of Parliament, Coke helped to frame the *Petition of Right* (1628), which caused Charles I to dissolve his third Parliament and rule without one for eleven years. Coke's treatises, including *Coke upon Littleton,* are among the greatest of all writings in the field of English law.

Colbert, Jean Baptiste (1619–1683), French statesman who, as minister of finance to Louis XIV, effected wide-reaching financial and economic reforms. When he took office in 1665, he found the finances of France in such a deplorable condition that he instituted an entirely new system, bringing about economies and reforms in many fields. With enlarged powers he promoted art, science, and literature as well as industry and commerce; built up the French navy; beautified Paris; and revised the laws. Colbert's services, however, were offset to some degree by Louis' military policies.

Cole, Thomas (1801–1848), American landscape painter, one of the founders of the Hudson River school of painting. Born in England, he began his career in Philadelphia as a wood engraver but soon turned to painting. After studying at Philadelphia Academy he established himself in New York in 1825. His small canvases depicting the beauty of New York and New England have been praised for their fidelity to nature. Among his other works are several large allegorical pictures, a series called *Course of Empire* (New York Historical Society), and *Oxbow,* a Connecticut River scene (Metropolitan Museum of Art).

Coleridge, Samuel Tayor (1772–1834), English poet, critic, and philosopher, famous for his poem *The Rime of the Ancient Mariner.* Born in Devonshire, as a young man he met William Wordsworth, with whom he wrote *Lyrical Ballads* (1798), *The Ancient Mariner* being Coleridge's main contribution. Issued anonymously, this small book definitely marked the end of English conventional poetry of the eighteenth century and ushered in an era of verse in which richness of imagination and freedom of expression had full sway. The Romantic spirit that transformed both prose and poetry during the next three decades owes much to the work of the two friends. At this time Coleridge also wrote the first part of *Christabel* and *Kubla Khan.*

Through the generosity of friends, he went with the Wordsworths to Germany. He studied German and translated Schiller's *Wallenstein.* Coleridge settled in the English Lake district after his return, with Robert Southey and Wordsworth as neighbors, and there "the Lake Poets" wrote memorable verse. Unfortunately for Coleridge the damp climate of the north gave him rheumatism, and his custom of relieving pain with opium led him into the habitual use of the drug. From 1816 until he died he was under the care of a physician in London, but he recovered enough to produce *Biographia Literaria*, which contained autobiographical material and his views on a variety of subjects. Coleridge's philosophy, criticism, and poetry had a great influence on English literature.

Colette, Sidonie Gabrielle Claudine (1873–1954), French novelist, famed for her accounts of Paris life. Prompted by her husband, she published her first works (1900–1903) under the pen name Willy. Divorcing her husband in 1906, she embarked on a music-hall career that lasted for many years. After World War I she devoted most of her time to writing, producing such well-received novels as *Chéri* (1920), *La Maison de Claudine* (1922), and *Gigi* (*1945*). In 1953 she was named grand officer of the Legion of Honor.

Colfax, Schuyler (1823–1885), American statesman who was vice-president of the United States (1869–1873). Born in New York City, he was editor of an Indiana newspaper. He served in Congress from 1855 to 1869, was elected speaker of the House in 1863, and served as vice-president during Pres. Ulysses S. Grant's first term. In 1873 charges of corruption were made against the administration, and Colfax's name was connected with the Crédit Mobilier scandal. Although the charges were never substantiated, he was forced to retire from active politics.

Coligny or **Coligni, Gaspard de** (1519–1572), French admiral who led the Huguenots in their struggle against the Roman Catholics. He fought under Francis I and Henry II, and in 1552 was appointed admiral of France. As the actual leader of the Huguenots in 1557 (Louis I, prince of Condé being a figurehead), he fought against the Catholic forces in the religious war, carrying on after Condé's death and arranging terms of peace in 1570. Coligny's growing influence with Charles IX aroused the enmity of the queen mother, Catherine de Medicis, and in 1572 Coligny died in the Massacre of St. Bartholomew, which Catherine had planned.

Collins, Michael (1890–1922), Irish revolutionary leader, the chief figure in the creation of the Irish Free State. The son of a farmer, he had a common-school education and at 15 became a clerk in the civil service in Dublin. Later he worked in a bank in London. He was imprisoned in 1916 for participating in the Easter uprising and was again jailed in 1918. After his release he became director of Irish armed resistance to England and showed himself remarkably skillful in guerrilla warfare. Collins believed that Ireland's interests lay in accepting the status defined by the Irish Free State Constitution, and he became premier of the provisional government in 1922. In August of that year, he was murdered.

Collodi, Carlo. See *Lorenzini, Carlo*.

Colt, Samuel (1814–1862), American inventor of the Colt revolver. Born in Hartford, Conn., he began designing guns about 1831. He secured the first patent for a revolving-breech pistol in 1835 but was unable to manufacture it profitably until 1847, when he contracted to supply a thousand of the weapons for Gen. Zachary Taylor's use in the Mexican War. An armory for their manufacture was established in Hartford in 1852. Colt also invented a battery for submarine harbor defense, and made the first successful submarine cable.

Columbus, Christopher (c.1446–1506), Italian navigator and explorer who discovered America. Born in Genoa, he followed his father's trade of weaver until early manhood. Early documents say that Columbus started on a Genoese ship for England in 1476. The ship was attacked by pirates, and Columbus found refuge in Lisbon, where in 1477, he settled and married the daughter of a Portugese navigator. Certain maps and charts to which he had access, as well as Marco Polo's tales of the Far East, intensified his interest in foreign countries.

Columbus was one of the few persons of his era who believed that the earth is round, and he decided that it was possible to reach Asia by sailing westward. After making a vain appeal for funds to the senate of his native state, Genoa, he turned to John II, king of Portugal, but without result. He appealed to Henry VII of England and to the dukes of Medina Sidonia and Medina Celi, who advised him to ask Isabella of Castile. After seven years of delays, Columbus' proposals were finally accepted by the Spanish monarchs, Isabella and Ferdinand. Columbus was given the rank of admiral and the promise that he was to be viceroy of such lands as he should discover and take possession of for the sovereigns of Spain.

On August 3, 1492, he set sail with one small ship, the *Santa Maria*, and two caravels, the *Pinta* and the *Niña*, the whole expedition including only 120 men. His real voyage of discovery began when he sailed westward from the Canary Islands on September 6. On October 7 the ships were turned to the southwest, and flocks of land birds guided them to an island in the Bahamas, probably the one now called Watlings, but named San Salvador by Columbus. Soon Cuba was discovered and then Haiti, which was named Hispaniola. Columbus believed it to be Cipango (Japan); to the day of his death he did not know that he had discovered not an Asian outpost, but a new world.

A storm having wrecked the *Santa Maria*, Columbus returned to Spain in the *Niña*, leaving Hispaniola on January 4, 1493, and casting anchor at Palos, Spain, on March 15. The Spanish sovereigns received him with enthusiasm and provided the equipment for a return journey. On September 25, with 17 ships and 1,500 men, Columbus set out again and on November 3 the fleet reached the island of Dominica. The admiral was discouraged in his attempts to organize a government for Hispaniola, but he had help from his brother Bartholomew, who arrived at the island in 1494. When Columbus departed for Spain in 1496, he left his brother in charge of the colony, and the latter founded the city of Santo Domingo. On May 30, 1498, Columbus left Spain on a third voyage with a fleet of six vessels. He discovered the mainland of South America, skirted its coast for some distance, and then proceeded to Santo Domingo, where his incapacity for administration soon became apparent. Unable to restore order, he was sent back to Spain (1500) by Francisco de Bobadilla, the new governor.

In 1503, with four ships, Columbus sailed from Spain on his fourth and last voyage, hoping to find a short route to India. He arrived at Santo Domingo, refitted his ships, and coasted along the shores of Central America. His ships were unseaworthy, and he was forced to abandon his hopes when he reached the Gulf of Darien. Worn out by hardships and sickness, he managed to get back to Spain in 1504. He died at Valladolid on May 20, 1506.

Commager, Henry Steele (1902–), American historian, author, and educator. He was born in Pittsburgh, Pa., and educated at the universities of Chicago and Copenhagen. From 1931 to 1938 he was professor of history at New York University, and in 1939 was appointed professor of American history at Columbia. Since 1956 he has been professor of history and American studies at Amherst College. Commager is best known for his books of historical and contemporary import, some of which have been published abroad in French, German, and Italian editions. For his contributions to the fields of education and history, Commager has received numerous awards, including honorary doctoral degrees from fourteen universities in America and Europe. His principal works include *The Growth of the American Republic* (with S.E. Morison; 1931), *Documents of American History* (1934), *Majority Rule and Minority Rights* (1943), *Blue and Gray* (1950), *The American Mind* (1951), *Freedom, Loyalty, Dissent* (1954), *The Spirit of Seventy-Six* (1958), and *Nature and Problems of History* (1965).

Compton, Arthur Holly (1892–1962), American physicist who discovered the "Compton effect," the change in wave lengths of X rays when they are scattered by electrons. Born in Wooster, Ohio, he was educated at Wooster College and received his Ph.D. from Princeton in 1916. He taught in a number of colleges and universities and held research appointments in industry. Much of his research work was with X rays, for which he shared the Nobel Prize for physics in 1927. He worked also on specific heats. While he was professor of physics at the University of Chicago (1923–1945), he helped organize the atomic bomb project. He was chancellor of Washington University in St. Louis from 1945 to 1953. He wrote *Secondary Radiations Produced by X Rays*.

Comstock, Anthony (1844–1915), American reformer, born in New Canaan, Conn. He fought in the Union army during the Civil War, then joined the Young Men's Christian Association in New York City. In the 1870's he decided to devote his life to crusading against immorality. He served without pay as a special agent of the U.S. Post Office Department, drafted the law forbidding the transmission of obscene matter through the mails, and was active in suppressing lotteries and the sale of immoral books. He also helped establish the Society for the Suppression of Vice.

Comte, Auguste, in full **Isidore Auguste Marie François Comte** (1798–1857), French philosopher, founder of the philosophical

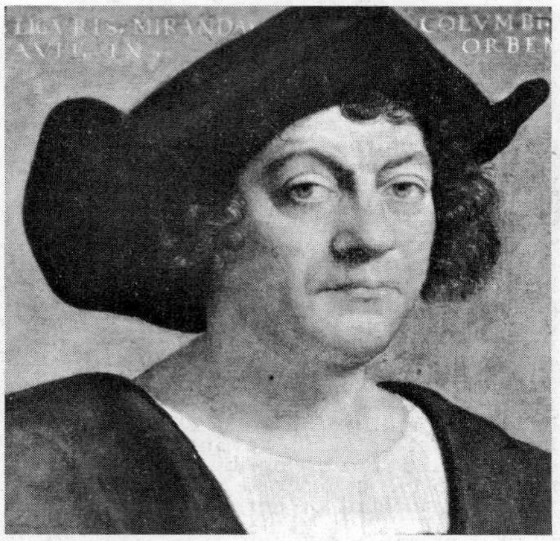

BETTMANN ARCHIVE

CHRISTOPHER COLUMBUS

system known as positivism. He studied at the École Polytechnique in Paris and was early a pronounced skeptic, though he believed in a religion of humanity. Intense application to study and writing brought on an attack of insanity at the height of his career. He accepted a position as examiner at the École Polytechnique in 1836; voluntary gifts from admirers supported him in later years. From 1830 to 1842 he wrote his monumental work, *The Course of Positive Philosophy*.

Conant, James Bryant (1893–), American educator and scientist, distinguished for his roles in education and government service. Born in Dorchester, Mass., he obtained his Ph.D. at Harvard in 1916 and stayed on as a chemistry teacher. In 1933 he was named president of Harvard. Shortly before World War II, he became a leading figure in the move to develop the atomic bomb. In 1953 he was named U.S. high commissioner for West Germany. He was ambassador to West Germany from 1955 to 1957. After returning to the U.S., he undertook an intensive study of elementary and high-school education, publishing several significant books on this subject.

Confucius, Chinese name **K'ung Fu-tzŭ** or **Kung Fu-tse** (c.551–479 B.C.), Chinese philosopher whose ideas deeply influenced the development of Asian thought. A native of the province of Shantung, he became keeper of granaries at the age of 20, but later turned to studies and became famous as a teacher. He taught veneration for old laws and records and insisted upon decorum and strict observance of all rites. He became a magistrate and began many administrative reforms until envious officials forced him out. From 496 to 483 he was in voluntary exile, wandering about with a group of disciples and teaching his ideas. At the age of 68 he returned to his native province and devoted himself to editing the classics and writing.

He never taught Confucianism as a religion, but the people took it up as such. As a result Confucius' name is always associated with ancestor worship in China. This came about through his insistence on respect for superior persons and things. He taught that the five fundamental human relationships are between sovereign and subject, father and son, elder and younger brother, husband and wife, and friend and friend. In each case, the younger or inferior was to defer to the other, but at the same time the superior person had certain obligations to the inferior.

Congreve, William (1670–1729), English playwright whose comedies mark the high point of Restoration comedy. His first comedy, *The Old Bachelor* (1693) was an immediate success. During the next few years he wrote two more comedies, *The Double Dealer* (1693) and *Love for Love* (1695), and a tragedy, *The Mourning Bride* (1697). In 1700 his masterpiece, *The Way of the World*, was produced; at its initial performances, it was a failure, but today it is Congreve's most frequently revived play. Regarded as a master of wit in dialogue, Congreve's plays ridiculed the artificial conventions of his age.

Connaught, Duke of, Prince **Arthur William Patrick Albert** (1850–1942), English general, the third son of Queen Victoria of England. From his youth he showed great ability as a soldier. He fought in Egypt, commanded the Bombay army in India, and served as chief commander in Ireland and in the Mediterranean. He was a popular and efficient governor-general of Canada (1911–1916). During World War I a Canadian regiment adopted the name of his daughter Patricia and was popularly known as "the Princess Pat's." In 1920 Connaught was the king's representative at the legislative councils of Madras, Bengal, and Bombay.

Conrad, Joseph originally **Józef Teodor Konrad Naecz Korzeniowski** (1857–1924), English novelist, born in Poland, famous for tales of the sea. He went to sea as a youth and for many years his life was a series of adventures. Not until he was 20 did he learn to speak English; yet he became an acknowledged master of style when writing in that language. Conrad was 37 when his first novel, *Almayer's Folly* (1895), was published. Reflecting his own picturesque experiences in the East, it was a definite success and was followed by others, including *The Nigger of the "Narcissus"* (1897), *Lord Jim* (1900), and (1902) *Typhoon*.

Constable, John (1776–1837), English painter, often considered the father of modern landscape painting. Born in Suffolk, he studied art at the Academy School in London, but he claimed to have learned more by painting from nature. His first canvases showed such variation from accepted standards that from 1803 to 1814 he could sell them only to his friends. However, after three pictures were exhibited in the French Salon in 1824, his work was better appreciated. In his treatment of atmospheric effects and his subordination of form to color, Constable laid down new principles of landscape art.

Constantine I, in full **Flavius Valerius Aurelius Constantinus,** known as **Constantine the Great** (c.280–337), the first Roman emperor to join the Christian faith. He succeeded his father, Constantius Chlorus, as emperor of the West in 306. The claims of various aspirants to both the Eastern and Western empires led to years of fighting, but Constantine defeated all who opposed him and in 325 became the sole ruler of the Roman world. In 329 he began to rebuild Byzantium on the Bosporus, making it his capital and renaming it Constantinople (now Istanbul). Constantine adopted Christianity in 313, after a battle near Rome in which he defeated his rival Maxentius. Soon after, he issued the Edict of Milan, granting toleration to Christians in the Western empire.

Constantine I (1868–1923), king of Greece (1913–1917, 1920–1922) succeeding his father, George I. He was educated in Germany and in 1889 married Sophie, sister of the former emperor William II of Germany. His sympathies, therefore, were with the Germans in World War I, and he steadfastly opposed the efforts of Prime Minister Eleutherios Venizelos, a pro-Ally, to bring Greece into the struggle. In 1917 he was forced into exile. A reaction against Venizelos restored him to the throne in 1920, but after the defeat of his armies in the Turkish War in Asia Minor, he was again forced to abdicate (1922). He died in Palermo, Sicily.

Cook, James, known as **Captain Cook** (1728–1779), English navigator famed for his explorations and discoveries in the Pacific Ocean. He became mate for a shipping company in 1755 and in 1759 obtained a master's warrant in the British navy with an appointment as master of the *Mercury*. His published reports on Newfoundland and Labrador induced the Royal Society to send him on an expedition to Tahiti in 1769 to observe the transit of Venus. On the return voyage, Cook charted the coasts of New Zealand and Australia and obtained other important data; in 1771 he was promoted to commander. Subsequently he explored the Antarctic region from New Zealand to Cape Horn and was made a captain. In command of the *Resolution* (1776–1778), he rediscovered the Sandwich (Hawaiian) Islands and surveyed the American coast north to Bering Strait. On his return to the islands, he was killed in a fight with the natives.

Coolidge, Calvin (1872–1933), thirtieth president of the United States (1923–1929). Born on a farm near Plymouth, Vt., he attended the village school and received a high school education at neighboring academies. In 1895 he graduated from Amherst College. He then studied law, was admitted to the bar in 1897, and began practice in Northampton, Mass., which became his home.

His election as councilman was followed by a succession of local victories: he was city solicitor, clerk of courts, member of the general court of Massachusetts, mayor of Northampton, member of the Massachusetts senate and its president (1914–1915), lieutenant governor of Massachusetts (1916–1918), and, for two terms (1919–1920), governor of his state. The policemen's strike in Boston (1919) brought him into national prominence through his firm and expert handling of the trouble.

In the Republican convention of 1920 Coolidge was nominated for the vice-presidency by acclamation and shared in Warren G. Harding's victory over James M. Cox and Franklin D. Roosevelt. Pres. Harding's death, on August 2, 1923, occurred while Coolidge was visiting his father at his Vermont farmhouse. On August 3 Calvin Coolidge took the oath of office as president; his father, a notary public, officiated. A second oath was taken two weeks later in Washington. No changes were made in the cabinet until the Teapot Dome investigation began, following which Edwin L. Denby, secretary of the navy, and Harry M. Daugherty, attorney general, were forced to resign. During this administration, the war veterans demanded adjusted compensation and the Soldiers' Bonus Act was passed over the president's veto. Coolidge also vetoed a pension bill in behalf of veterans of the Civil and Spanish-American wars and a bill increasing the pay of postal employees. He restricted immigration and reduced the income tax, and as he had the confidence of the people, his nomination for a full term seemed inevitable. In 1924 he was reelected with Charles G. Dawes as vice-president.

The term beginning in 1925 was notable for an international agreement renouncing war, the continued reduction of the public debt, the funding of debts owed to the United States by foreign nations, a wave of prosperity with attending speculation in stocks and the development of aviation. Coolidge was considered a strong candidate for a second elected term, but in the summer of 1927 he announced his refusal to seek reelection in a message marked by his usual brevity: "I do not choose to run for president in 1928." Coolidge retired from the presidency popular with the general public. He reopened his law office in Northampton and for a time engaged in journalistic work.

Cooper, James Fenimore (1789–1851), American novelist, remembered for his Leatherstocking novels. Born in Burlington, N.J., he studied at Yale and served in the merchant marine before settling down as a writer. In 1820 he produced his first novel, *Precaution*. It was a failure because it dealt with the English aristocracy, about which he knew nothing. His next novel, *The Spy* (1821), was a pronounced success and proof that his strength lay in adventure stories about the young America. Thereafter Cooper wrote books in rapid succession. Not all of them were up to the standard of his best novel—*The Last of the Mohicans* (1826)—but he produced a number that give him rank with the foremost writers of fiction. *The Pioneers* and *The Pilot* (1823), *The Praire* (1827), *The Red Rover* (1828), *The Pathfinder* (1840), and *The Deerslayer* (1841) are robust stories of power and imagination. The author preserved for future generations a phase of life that was soon to pass, and he added a few genuine characters to American fiction—Harvey Birch, the spy; Natty Bumppo or "Leatherstocking," the hero of the pioneer romances called "Leatherstocking tales"; Long Tom Coffin; and Uncas, the Indian. Besides his novels he wrote *A History of the Navy of the United States* (1839).

Cooper, Peter (1791–1883), American manufacturer and philanthropist who founded Cooper Union in New York City. A native of New York, at 17 he became apprentice to a coach maker, and a few years later he invented a machine for shearing cloth that was used in the War of 1812. Cooper began the manufacture of glue and isinglass in 1824 and maintained that business for half a century. He also made iron products and in 1830 built the first steam locomotive used on an American road, the *Tom Thumb*. The laying of the Atlantic cable was due in part to his efforts. In 1859 he founded Cooper Union, a day and evening school for the working people of New York. He was nominated for president by a group of independents (1876), and received nearly 100,000 votes.

Copernicus, Nicolaus Latinized form of **Mikolaj Kopernik** or **Niklas Koppernigk** (1473–1543), Polish astronomer, famed for his publication of the theory upon which modern astronomy is based—that the planets revolve about the sun. Having studied medicine and theology at Cracow and law at Bologna, he was made a canon of Frauenburg in 1497. In 1500 he went to Rome, where he taught mathematics and astronomy. He studied medicine at Padua and in 1505 left Italy for Prussia, where he carried out his life's work.

Doubting that the motions of the heavenly bodies could be so confused and complicated as the Ptolemaic system made them, he brought out the simpler hypothesis that the Sun was the center around which Earth and the other planets revolve. Besides announcing this fundamental truth, Copernicus stated other facts of astronomical science, such as the rotation of the Earth on its axis and the immense distance of the stars, which made their apparent position the same from any part of the Earth's orbit. His general theory also enabled him to explain for the first time many of the important phenomena of nature, such as the variations of the seasons and the precession of the equinoxes.

The great work in which Copernicus explained his theory, *De Revolutionibus Orbium Coelestium* (*On the Revolutions of the Celestial Orbs*), was completed in 1530, but the author delayed publishing it until 1543, because the public was not ready for a theory so opposed to religious teaching.

Copland, Aaron (1900–), American composer, noted for his musical interpretation of American scenes. He was born in Brooklyn, N.Y., and studied music privately in New York and Paris. In his early works, such as *Music for the Theater* (1925) and his concerto for piano and orchestra (1927), his incorporation of jazz elements into serious music gained him a high reputation. During the 1930's and 1940's he composed the works that are frequently played today: *El Salón Mexico* (1936), *Billy the Kid* (1938), *Rodeo* (1942), and *Lincoln Portrait* (1942). His opera *The Tender Land* was produced by the New York City Opera Company in 1954.

Copley, John Singleton (1738–1815), leading American portrait painter of the pre-Revolutionary period. Born in Boston, he painted his first portrait at the age of 15. By the mid-1760's he had become well known for his portraits. In 1774 he went to Italy to study for two years, and then settled in London permanently, where he became renowned for his paintings. In 1779 he was elected to membership in the Royal Academy.

Corbusier, Le. See *Le Corbusier*.

Corday, Charlotte (1768–1793), French revolutionary, remembered for her assassination of Jean Paul Marat. At first she sympathized with the Revolution, but after the fall of the moderate Girondist party, she turned from the Revolutionists who had inaugurated the Reign of Terror. Convinced that France would be saved only by the death of Marat, she forced her way into his house, and pretending that she could give him the names of certain Girondist enemies, stabbed him while he was in his bath. She was guillotined a few days later.

Corelli, Arcangelo (1653–1713), Italian composer, famed for his chamber music. After studying music in Bologna, he settled down permanently in Rome about 1675. A noted violinist, he composed some 60 sonatas for violin, violoncello, organ, and harpsichord. He also wrote a set of *concerti grossi* that is still popular among musicians. During his lifetime his music was immensely popular throughout Europe.

Corneille, Pierre (1606–1684), French dramatist, considered the founder of tragedy in the French theater. He was born in Rouen and educated for the law, but the success of his first play, *Mélite* (1629), encouraged him to take up writing as a profession. He wrote a number of mildly successful comedies, but when *Le Cid* appeared in 1636, his greatness was seen. This play, part tragedy and part comedy, is regarded as the beginning of modern French drama. Not all of Corneille's subsequent plays were in a class with this masterpiece, but at least three of his tragedies—*Horace* (1640), *Cinna* (1640), and *Polyeucte* (c.1642)—are among the great examples of dramatic literature.

Cornelia (2d century B.C.), Roman matron, celebrated as the mother of Tiberius and Gaius Gracchus. When someone asked to see her jewels, she pointed to her sons and said, "These are my jewels." Upon her death a statue was erected to her memory, on the base of which were the words "Cornelia, Mother of the Gracchi."

Cornelius, Peter von (1783–1867), German painter, remembered for his revival of fresco painting. In Rome, which he visited in 1811 to study, he became associated with German painters called "Nazarenes," whose aim was to restore simplicity and sincerity to painting. Cornelius and some of the Nazarenes were asked to decorate a room in the Prussian consulate, and in carrying out this commission they revived the art of fresco painting. In 1825 Cornelius was appointed director of the Academy of Munich. His frescoes for the Glyptothek in Munich, representing Greek myths, are representative of his best work, noble in conception and excellent in composition. The actual painting was done by pupils from their teacher's masterly cartoons.

Cornell, Katharine (1898–), American actress, born in Berlin, Germany, and educated in New York. She began her stage career in 1917 as one of the Washington Square Players and performed with the Jesse Bonstelle Stock Company (1919–1921). She traveled with *The Man Who Came Back* in 1920 and the same year played in London in *Little Women.* Under the able direction of her husband, Guthrie McClintic, she starred in many notable successes. These include *A Bill of Divorcement, The Green Hat, Candida, Saint Joan The Barretts of Wimpole Street,* and *The Three Sisters.*

Cornwallis, Charles, 1st Marquis (1738–1805), English general who surrendered to Gen. George Washington at Yorktown, Virginia (October 19, 1781). After completing his education at Cambridge, Cornwallis entered the army, participated in the Seven Years' War, and became a major general in 1775. He commanded British forces in America against the revolutionary colonies, acting under generals William Howe and Henry Clinton. In 1781, after a siege at Yorktown, Va., he surrendered to Gen. Washington. This marked the end of the Revolutionary War and indicated victory for the American colonies. Back in England, Lord Cornwallis was appointed governor general of India, a post in which he served with distinction from 1786 to 1793.

Coronado, Francisco Vásques de (1510–1554), Spanish explorer of the American Southwest. He went to Mexico in 1535 and led an expedition northward in 1540 in search of legendary Quivira, a town reputedly rich in gold. Going up the Colorado River, he discovered the Grand Canyon. He also explored the California peninsula, followed the course of the Rio Grande, and traveled north across what is now the Texas Panhandle and Oklahoma into eastern Kansas (1540–1542).

Corot, Jean Baptiste Camille (1796–1875), French painter of the Barbizon school. His art was unique, an expression of his desire to show the beauty of nature in delicate and tender forms and moods. Soft colors and misty backgrounds were his delight. In his later years, honors and riches made up for an early lack of recognition. Among his paintings are *Bridge of Narni, Chartres Cathedral, Dance of the Nymphs, Woman With the Pearl* (Louvre, Paris); and *Ville d' Avray* (Metropolitan Museum, N. Y.). He also executed some religious and historical paintings.

Correggio, original name **Antonio Allegri da Correggio** (c.1494–1534), Italian painter, one of the leading Italian Renaissance artists. Little is known of his early life, but it is believed that he came under the influence of many prominent artists of his time and that he did excellent work before he was 20. Correggio was a master of technique; in his handling of light and shade, his use of perspective, and his ability to impart an effect of dramatic action he is an outstanding figure. Masterly, too, is his handling of color. His frescoes on the cupola of San Giovanni, together with those in the convent of San Paolo and the cathedral, all in Parma, are the summit of Correggio's achievements. Other famous works are *Marriage of St. Catherine* (Louvre, Paris), *Holy Night* (Dresden), and *Danaë* (Borghese Gallery, Rome).

Cortés, Hernan, or **Hernando Cortez** (1485–1547), Spanish explorer who conquered Mexico. In 1504 he departed for Santo Domingo, where he helped to suppress a native revolt. Under Diego Velásquez he displayed remarkable ability in the conquest of Cuba and in November, 1518, before his chief could stop him, he set out for the mainland in command of seven vessels. The following spring, after many adventures, Cortés and his company founded a town on the site of Vera Cruz, renounced all allegiance to Velásquez, and leaving a small garrison behind, started inland for Mexico. The capital city of the Aztecs was entered on November 8, 1519. The visitors were at first unmolested. Later, when Cortés learned that the natives were plotting to drive him out, he seized Montezuma, the Aztec chief, and kept him as a hostage. While Cortés was absent on an expedition against Narvaez, who had been sent by Velásquez to arrest him, fighting broke out between the natives of Mexico City and the Spaniards under Alvarado. On his return, Cortés was permitted to enter the city but was at once attacked. Montezuma was killed and the Spaniards were driven out by a new emperor. After being harried by the Aztecs for six days, Cortés in desperation gave battle at Otumba and won a decisive victory (July, 1520). Within a year the conquest of Mexico was completed, colonists were brought over from Spain, and Mexico City was practically rebuilt. Through the intrigues of his enemies at home, Cortés was deprived of civil authority in Mexico. In 1539 he returned to Spain, where he died neglected and poor. During his sojourn in Mexico, he discovered Lower California (1536).

Cosgrave, William Thomas (1880–1965), Irish stateman, president of the Irish Free State (1922–1932). An active leader of the Sinn Fein movement, he was imprisoned and for a time under sentence of death. When Britain offered Ireland the status of a self-governing member of the empire, Cosgrave agreed to cooperate, and in August 1922 became head of a provisional government. In December 1922, after ratification of a constitution, he was elected president of the executive council and held that position until 1932, when he was defeated by Eamon de Valera. Died Nov. 16, 1965 in Dublin, Ireland.

Coulomb, Charles Augustin de (1736–1806), French physicist who pioneered in research on electricity. When the French Revolution broke out in 1789, he retired to a country estate to do research. In addition to doing important original work in the field of electricity and magnetism, he invented the torsion balance for verifying electrical and magnetic laws. The coulomb, a unit to measure quantity of electricity, was named in his honor.

Couperin, François (1668–1733), French musician, regarded as the first great composer for the harpsichord. He was the most renowned of a family of musicians associated with the Church of Saint Gervais in Paris. Between 1713 and 1733 he published his harpsichord compositions in four volumes. He also wrote sacred music and chamber music.

Courbet, Gustave (1819–1877), French painter who was a leader in the movement toward realism. In 1841 he went to Paris to study, afterwards visiting Holland to study the Dutch masters. Around 1850 he became the leader of a school of realistic painters that, coming a generation before the Impressionistic school, had a deep influence on such artists as Cezanne, Manet, and Renoir. His liberal political views led to his imprisonment in 1871, when he joined the Commune and led the destruction of a column in the Place Vendôme. After six months in jail, he was released and went to Switzerland, where he spent his remaining years.

Coverdale, Miles (c.1488–1568), English clergyman who translated the first printed English Bible. Originally a Catholic monk of the Augustinian order, he accepted the Reformed faith about 1526 and brought out his translation of the Bible in 1535. The psalms of this version are those used in the Book of Common Prayer. He became bishop of Exeter in 1551 but was removed from office and imprisoned by Mary I. A year later he was released, and lived abroad until 1559. Coverdale wrote a number of tracts in support of the Reformation.

Coward, Noel (1899–), English playwright, composer, and actor, famed for his sophisticated comedies and songs. In the 1920's he became known as the most versatile man in British and American theaters, writing plays and revues, acting in many of them, and producing some. His successes include *Hay Fever, On with the Dance* (revue), *Bitter Sweet* (operetta), *Private Lives, Design for Living, Tonight at Eight-Thirty* (a series of one-act plays) and *Blithe Spirit.* Films include *Brief Encounter, In Which We Serve, This Happy Breed,* and *The Astonished Heart.* His autobiography, *Present Indicative,* appeared in 1937.

Cowles, Gardner (1903–), American publisher, noted as the founder of *Look* magazine (1936) and as a staunch supporter of research and experimentation throughout the field of communications. He was born in Algona, Iowa, and educated at Phillips Exeter Academy and Harvard University. Cowles began his journalistic career as a reporter for the Des Moines *Register and Tribune.* He was subsequently named to executive and editorial positions, becoming executive editor (1931), associate publisher (1939), and then president (1943). As both an editor and a businessman, he was largely responsible for the success of *Look* magazine. In 1965 he became chairman of the board and editorial chairman of Cowles Communications, Inc., an enterprise encompassing *Look, Family Circle, Venture,* radio and television stations, newspapers, and an educational books corporation.

Cowley, Abraham (1618–1667), English poet and essayist. Inspired by reading Spenser's *Faerie Queene,* he wrote poems in boyhood and won renown at Cambridge as a translator and the author of an epic on the life of David. Because of his royalist sympathies, Cowley was expelled from college during the Civil War and lived away from England for a decade. After the Restoration he retired to an estate in Surrey. His best work includes his elegies on William Harvey and Richard Crashaw, his Pindaric odes, *To Light* (a hymn), and a number of gracefully written essays.

Cowper, William (1731–1800), English poet, remembered for his unpretentious verse celebrating country life. Early in his career he began to show signs of mental stress; in 1763, having grown increasingly despondent about an appointment as clerk of the journals of the House of Lords, he tried to commit suicide and was put in a private asylum. After recovering, he turned to poetry, collaborating with John Newton on *Olney Hymns* (1779). Cowper also wrote verse, of which *Poems* (1782), *John Gilpin* (1782), *The Task* (1785), and *The Castaway* (1798) are representative examples.

Cranach, Kranach, or **Kronach, Lucas** (1472–1553), German painter of the Renaissance. About 1505 he moved to Wittenberg, where he was court painter to the electors of Saxony, a post he held for the rest of his life. An exceptionally accomplished painter, engraver, and woodcut artist, in his long career he produced hundreds of works of art. Many of his paintings are religious scenes, but he also was noted for his portraits and his female nudes. In his woodcuts he approached the genius of his contemporary, Albrecht Dürer.

Crane, Hart, in full **Harold Hart Crane** (1889–1932), American poet, remembered for his epic work *The Bridge* (1930). Born in Garrettsville, Ohio, he published the first of his two works, *White Buildings,* in 1926. In his more ambitious *The Bridge* (1930), Crane attempted to capture the essence of the American spirit in a series of poems whose focal point was the Brooklyn Bridge in New York. In 1932, returning by ship from Mexico where he had gone to gather material for a book on Montezuma, Crane was drowned.

Crane, Stephen (1871–1900), American writer whose war novel, *The Red Badge of Courage* (1895), is regarded as a classic. Born in Newark, N. J., he studied at Lafayette College and Syracuse University. Moving to New York in 1891, he published his first novel, *Maggie: a Girl of the Streets,* in 1893. Two years later, with appearance of *The Red Badge of Courage* and *The Black Riders* (his first book of poems), he became famous immediately. During the next few years spent as a newspaper correspondent, he covered the Greco-Turkish War. He spent the last three years of his life chiefly in England. Crane's short stories appeared in such collections as *The Little Regiment* (1896), *The Open Boat and Other Tales of Adventure* (1898), and *The Monster and Other Stories* (1899). A second book of poems, *War Is Kind,* appeared in 1899.

Cranmer, Thomas (1489–1556), English clergyman who became the first archbishop of Canterbury in the Reformed Church of England. He first came to the notice of Henry VIII when he suggested that Henry submit to the European universities the question of the legality of his marriage to Catherine of Aragon. In 1533 he was made archbishop of Canterbury and was Henry's agent in divorcing Anne Boleyn and Anne of Cleves. He worked for the establishment of the Reformed faith during Henry's reign and that of his successor, Edward VI. On the accession of Queen Mary, Cranmer was accused of treason, sentenced to death, and burned at the stake in 1556.

Crassus, Marcus Licinius, surnamed **Dives** (c.115–53 B.C.), Roman financier and statesman who played an important role in the Roman republic before Julius Caesar's coming to power. When Gaius Marius captured Rome in 87 B.C., Crassus escaped to Spain, but returned with the victorious Sulla. In 71 B.C. he was appointed praetor and crushed the revolt of the slaves led by Spartacus. He was consul with Pompey in 70 B.C. and in 65 B.C. served as censor. Crassus joined Pompey and Caesar in organizing the First Triumvirate, for which he was the financial backer. Again consul with Pompey in 55 B.C., he became governor of Syria the following year and undertook a campaign against the Parthians, but was defeated and executed.

Credi, Lorenzo di, surnamed **Barducci** (1459–1537), Italian artist, remembered for his paintings of the Madonna. Born in Florence, he became an apprentice (as did

Leonardo da Vinci) in the workshop of Andrea del Verrocchio. Most of his work was done in oils, rather than in frescoes. Many museums own his studies of Madonna and Child and other ecclesiastical paintings.

Crittenden, John Jordan (1787–1863), American statesman remembered for his efforts to reach compromises just before the Civil War. Born in Versailles, Ky., he was elected a U. S. senator in 1817, serving almost continuously for the rest of his life, except for two years as governor of Kentucky and a year as attorney general in the cabinet of Pres. William Henry Harrison. His name is perpetuated in the Crittenden Compromise (1860), which he offered in the Senate to prevent the secession of the South. When war came, Crittenden was consistently loyal to the Union.

Croce, Benedetto (1866–1952), Italian philosopher, critic, and aesthetician. He became a senator in 1910 and was minister of public instruction (1920–1921). During this time, he became famous for his philosophical, historical, and literary writings, published in a periodical *La Critica* that he founded in 1903. He wrote several volumes of literary essays on Italian, European, Latin, and Greek authors and the important works *Goethe* (1919) and *Ariosto, Shakespeare, e Corneille* (1920). A distinguished scholar of aesthetics and a liberal political thinker, he had a profound influence on European literature and thought.

Crockett, David, known as **Davy Crockett** (1786–1836), American frontiersman who was virtually a legend in his lifetime. Born near Rogersville, Tenn., he had practically no schooling, yet he was twice elected to the state legislature (1821–1823), and three times to the U. S. Congress (1826, 1828, and 1832). In the war between Texas and Mexico, Crockett fought with the Texans and was one of the defenders of the Alamo. The exact manner of his death at the time of the final assault, March 6, 1836, is uncertain. He may have died then or soon after. His *Autobiography,* written in a racy backwoods style, is one of the valued documents in American literature.

Croesus (r. 560–546 B.C.), the last king of Lydia (now part of Asia Minor) and a monarch so wealthy that his name is now a symbol of great riches. An oracle having told him that he would destroy a great empire, Croesus attacked the Persians under Cyrus the Great and suffered a crushing defeat. His magnificent capital Sardis was surrendered, and he saw the oracle's prophecy fulfilled in the loss of his own empire. It is believed that his life was spared by his conqueror, Cyrus.

Crompton, Samuel (1753–1827), English inventor of the spinning mule, which revolutionized the production of yarn. In his youth he was engaged in weaving at home. Dissatisfied with the machines then in use, he perfected a device in 1779 that could spin a yarn suitable for weaving muslin. Many people were made rich by the invention, but Crompton realized only about $350 from his machine. In 1812 Parliament voted him a grant of about $25,000.

Cromwell, Oliver, nicknamed **Old Noll** (1599–1658), lord protector of England (1653–1658). Born in Huntingdon, he went to a free school there, and in 1616 entered Sidney Sussex College at Cambridge but remained there less than a year. Having early experienced a "saving change," he emerged from a period of gloom a stern, convinced Puritan and Calvinist and a determined rebel against the authority of the Established Church. Cromwell sat as a member for Huntingdon in the Parliament of 1628 and during his earlier years in public life seems to have been more interested in opposing ecclesiastical tyranny than in fighting the political despotism of Charles I. His opportunity came when civil war began in England. He fought at Edge Hill (1642) and there perceived the weakness of the parliamentary troops against the spirit and dash of the royalist cavaliers. He saw that a counter-motive was required to meet the gallant traditions inspiring the king's soldiers, and this he found in the stern godliness of the English yeoman. Having organized his famous cavalry regiments from this class, he demonstrated the superiority of his troops, the "Ironsides," at Marston Moor (1644) and Naseby (1645) and stood forth as the greatest English military leader of the time.

Cromwell early attached himself to the independent party in the army and the state and was its representative in the struggles with Parliament, which, after Naseby, wished to disband the army. War was renewed and the opening battle was a great victory over the Scottish royalists near Preston (1648). Cromwell took an active part in the trial of Charles I, whose life the army had demanded, and was one of the signers of his death warrant. After Cromwell's return from a ruthless expedition against the royalists in Ireland, he was summoned to Scotland, where he won a decisive victory at Dunbar in 1650. A year later he ended his military career by winning a victory at Worcester, England, over the Scottish army that had crossed the border with Charles II.

Although his military supremacy was unquestioned, Cromwell met serious difficulties as England's "uncrowned king." The Rump Parliament (remnant of the Long Parliament) showed itself so incompetent that Cromwell dismissed it (1653). Its successor, the Little, or Barebones, Parliament, was no better and dissolved itself voluntarily. At this point, the committee of officers drew up, in written form, the Instrument of Government, which made Cromwell practically a dictator; created for him the title lord protector of the Commonwealth of England, Scotland, and Ireland; and provided for the election of a Parliament of one chamber. The first assembly summoned showed no comprehension of the needs of the country. A second, called in 1656, drew up a new constitution providing for an upper house and offering Cromwell the title of king. He refused the honor and in 1658 dissolved Parliament for the last time. Thenceforth he ruled without a legislature. Meanwhile he had been upholding England's prestige abroad. He wanted his country to be the champion of Protestantism and so brought to an end an undesired war with Holland. He humbled Spain on the seas and allied England with France in an attack against the Spanish Netherlands. At home, Cromwell's stern military rule kept peace and order in the demoralized country. Puritanism was tolerated but Catholicism and all tendencies toward Episcopalianism were resented. After the lapse of nearly three centuries, Cromwell stands out as one of the commanding figures in English history.

Cromwell, Thomas, Earl of **Essex** (c.1485–1540), English statesman who planned the reformation of the English Church under Henry VIII. Of humble birth and little education, he rose to positions of influence through natural ability. He entered Parliament as a protégé of Cardinal Wolsey, and became private secretary to Henry VIII. In 1540, after receiving a succession of appointments, he attained the title of earl of Essex. Meanwhile, he had forced the Act of Supremacy by suppressing monasteries and had given the king valuable aid in establishing the Reformed faith in England. Cromwell arranged Henry's marriage to Anne of Cleves. Shortly afterward, he was convicted of treason and executed.

Crookes, Sir **William** (1832–1919), English chemist and physicist who discovered the element thallium. Born in London, he studied at the Royal College of Chemistry and held positions at the Radcliffe Observatory, Oxford, and the Chester Training College. After 1854 he devoted most of his time to original research and to editing scientific journals. He shared in the Nobel Prize for chemistry in 1907. Crookes discovered the element thallium (1861) and computed its atomic weight; he originated the radiometer for measuring the intensity of radiant energy; introduced a new method of spectroscopic investigation; and discovered a process for separating gold and silver from their ores. The Crookes Tube, his chief invention, is a glass bulb that has two electrodes, cathode and anode. Crookes also discovered the rays that appear when a high-voltage electrical current is used.

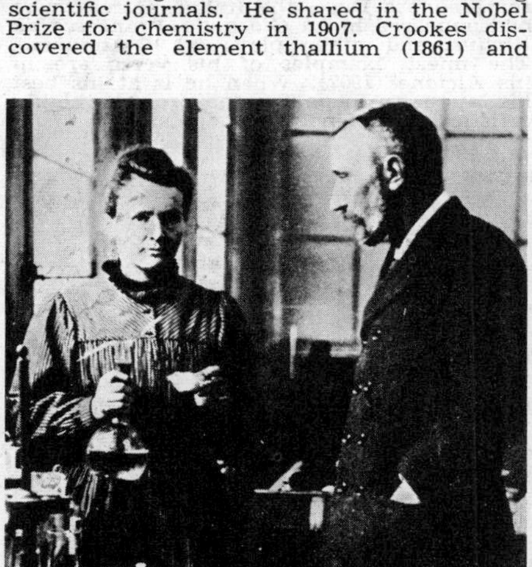

FRENCH EMBASSY PRESS & INFORMATION

PHYSICS pioneers, Marie and Pierre Curie.

Cruikshank, George (1792–1878), English artist and caricaturist, famed for his book illustrations and satirical political cartoons. The son of an artist, he followed his father's profession but early developed great skill as an etcher. His famous book illustrations are in the works of Dickens, Scott, Defoe, Goldsmith, Fielding, Smollett, and Ainsworth. His drawings on political subjects are of great historical value.

Cummings, Edward Estlin, known as **e. e. cummings** (1894–1962), American poet, remembered for his original, experimental poems. He was born in Cambridge, Mass., and graduated from Harvard in 1915. During World War I a misunderstanding led the French to imprison him as a spy; he was released within six months. His experiences in the internment camp are recorded in his novel *The Enormous Room* (1922). In his verse Cummings often resorted to odd typography (he never used capital letters) and exhibited an exaggerated sense of humor, although he also wrote lyric verse of a high order. His many volumes of collected poetry include *Tulips and Chimneys* (1923), *XLI Poems* (1925), *One Times One* (1944), *Poems 1923–1954* (1954), *95 Poems* (1958), and *73 Poems* (1963).

Cunard, Sir **Samuel** (1787–1865), English shipowner who founded the steamship line that bears his name. A native of Halifax, Nova Scotia, he engaged in lumbering, whaling, and banking enterprises, and in 1838 he moved to England. The Cunard Line, established in 1878, was the outgrowth of the Royal Mail Steam Packet Company, founded in 1839 by Cunard with Nova Scotian and British backers. In 1840 its first vessel crossed from Liverpool to Boston in 14 days, 8 hours.

Curie, Marja Sklodowska (1867–1934), French scientist, born in Poland, the wife of Pierre Curie. Together they discovered radium and shared the Nobel Prize for physics (1903) with A. H. Becquerel. After her husband's death she was appointed his successor in the chair of physics at the Sorbonne. In 1911 she received the Nobel Prize for chemistry, and in 1919 she was appointed professor of radiology at Warsaw. The French government founded the Curie Institute, with Mme. Curie as its director, for research work in the treatment of cancer. Mme. Curie's daughter Irene (Mme. Curie-Joliot) succeeded her as director of the Institute.

Curie, Pierre (1859–1906), French scientist, born in Paris, husband of Marie Curie, and co-discoverer of the element radium. Inspired by A. H. Becquerel's discovery of radioactivity, the Curies began their research for radioactive substances in 1896 and in 1898 announced their epoch-making discovery of radium and polonium. In 1903 they shared the Nobel Prize for physics with Becquerel.

Curtis, George Ticknor (1812–1894), American jurist and historian, noted for his works on U.S. constitutional history. He was born in Watertown, Mass., and educated at Harvard. Admitted to the bar in 1836, he practiced law for the rest of his life, first in Worcester and Boston, and later in New York City and before the U.S. Supreme Court. His many notable cases included those involving Dred Scott, legal tender, and the Colt revolver patents. He was an acknowledged authority on U.S. constitutional history.

Curtiss, Glenn Hammond (1878–1930), American pioneer in the development of aviation. Born and educated in Hammondsport, N.Y., he showed mechanical ingenuity from boyhood and as early as 1902 had started a motorcycle factory in Hammondsport. He gave the first public airplane flights in America (the Wright brothers conducted their work in secret). In 1908 he won the *Scientific American* trophy for the first public flight of one mile, piloting the *June Bug,* a plane of his own construction. After winning the Gordon Bennett Cup and the New York *World* prize of $10,000 for flights in Curtiss-designed biplanes, he made the first public demonstration of the hydro-airplane in 1911. In 1912 his flying boat (an airplane equipped with pontoons) won the prize of the Aero Club of America. In 1914 Curtiss built for Rodman

Wanamaker the *America*, the first heavier-than-air flying craft designed for overseas flight. The first Atlantic crossing achieved by any kind of aircraft was made by a Curtiss machine in 1919. During World War I, Curtiss built all types of planes for the United States and the Allies.

Custer, George Armstrong (1839–1876), American soldier, best known as the leader of a band of cavalry annihilated in a battle with the Sioux Indians. Custer was born in New Rumley, Ohio, and graduated from West Point (1861) just in time to participate in the first battle of Bull Run. He served with distinction throughout the war, rising to the rank of brevet major general of volunteers. As lieutenant colonel of the Seventh Cavalry he became an Indian fighter in 1867 and in 1873 was ordered to Dakota Territory to help suppress a revolt of the Sioux under Sitting Bull and Crazy Horse. In June, 1876, on the Little Big Horn River, Custer and five companies of his regiment (about 250 men) were suddenly attacked by a superior force of Indians and massacred. A national cemetery occupies the site of the battle.

Cuvier, Baron **Georges Léopold Chrétien Frédéric Dagobert** (1769–1832), French naturalist, born in Montbéliard. He moved to Paris in 1800 and became professor of natural history at the Collège de France. Two years later, he was appointed professor of comparative anatomy at the Jardin des Plantes. Known as the founder of the science of paleontology and comparative anatomy, he wrote *Leçons d'anatomie comparée* (5 vols., 1800–1805) and *Règne animal distribute d'après son organisation* (1816–1829), stating the essentials of his theory of comparative anatomy. His interest was in the relationships that prevail among the various parts of the body. He proposed the idea that the function of any one part can be determined simply by noting such characteristics as size and shape. Thus, by examining one fossil bone, Cuvier could determine a great deal about the animal to which it belonged.

Cyrano de Bergerac, Savinien de (1619–1655), French poet, soldier, and freethinker whose life became a legend after he died. After being severely wounded in battle, he devoted himself to study. His works include *Le pédant joué* (a comedy, 1654) and *La mort d'Agrippine* (a tragedy, 1664). *Histoire comique des États et Empires de la Lune* (1656) and *Histoire comique des États et Empires du Soleil* (1662) are accounts of imaginary voyages—the first to the moon, the second to the sun. Written in 1649 and published posthumously, they have been compared to the works of Rabelais. The tragedy *Cyrano de Bergerac*, by Edmond Rostand, takes his name but has little factual basis in the events of the life of this French soldier-poet.

Cyrus the Great (c.600–529 B.C.), founder of the Persian Empire. According to cuneiform records he was the son of the Persian King Cambyses. Herodotus called him the grandson of the Median King Astyages, whose vassal he was. Few rulers have been so often the subject of legend, but we know that Cyrus defeated Astyages in 549 B.C., and then reigned over the Medo-Persian realm. He subdued Croesus of Lydia in 546 B.C., thus becoming ruler of practically all Asia Minor. In 539 B.C. Cyrus brought his career to a climax by conquering the city of Babylon, whose king, Nabonidus, was in exile. Cyrus permitted the captive Jews to return to Jerusalem to rebuild their temple, as told in the Book of Ezra. Ten years later, the conqueror fell in battle while fighting a nomad people to the north. Cyrus was a humane and enlightened ruler.

Cyrus the Younger (c.424–401 B.C.), son of Darius II, remembered for his attempts to seize the throne from his older brother, Artaxerxes II. In 404 B.C., Cyrus plotted against his older brother who had ascended the throne. When his scheme was disclosed, he was saved from death only by the plea of his mother. Though made a governor of Asia Minor, Cyrus continued his plotting, and in 401 B.C. left Sardis, the Lydian capital, with a great army that included 13,000 Greek mercenaries. This army met defeat at Cunaxa, where Cyrus was killed. The retreat of 10,000 Greeks, who fought their way out, is the subject of Xenophon's *Anabasis*.

Czerny, Karl (1791–1857), Austrian pianist and composer whose works are still popular with piano teachers. Born in Vienna, he was for a time a student of Beethoven. Later he became a teacher (one of his students was Franz Liszt). During his years as a teacher, he published almost 1,000 works. He was especially adept at transcribing orchestral works for the piano.

D

Dana, Charles Anderson (1819–1897), American journalist, born in Hinsdale, N.H. His first editorial experience was with the *Harbinger*, the organ of Brook Farm. He was one of the founders of the New York *Tribune* and was on its staff from 1847 to 1862, resigning after a disagreement with Horace Greeley about war politics. From 1863 to 1864 Dana served as assistant secretary of war, and from 1868 until his death he was editor in chief of the New York *Sun*. The simple, clear, literary style that he advocated had a great influence upon American journalism. Dana edited the *New American Cyclopaedia* (with George Ripley) and its successor, the *American Cyclopaedia*.

Dana, James Dwight (1813–1895), American geologist and educator, born in Utica, N.Y. He studied at Yale (1830–1833), traveled abroad as instructor in the U.S. navy, and returned to Yale to teach. He was mineralogist and geologist with the Wilkes Exploring Expedition (1838–1842), and the permanent records of his investigations are today valuable governmental reports. Dana held the chair of natural history at Yale University from 1849 to 1892. From 1840 until his death he served as editor of the *American Journal of Science*. His various books on mineralogical and geological subjects are standard authorities.

Dana, Richard Henry, Jr. (1815–1882), American lawyer and author, born in Cambridge, Mass. He is best known for his book *Two Years Before the Mast* (1840), which Dickens called "about the best sea book in the English language." A record of a two-year voyage on the Pacific in the brig *Pilgrim*, it portrays his own experiences as a common sailor; he had made the voyage when he was compelled to leave Harvard because of impaired eyesight. Upon his return in 1836, Dana resumed his studies at Harvard, graduating in 1837. He was admitted to the bar in 1840 and specialized in admiralty cases.

D'Annunzio, Gabriele, Prince of **Monte Nevoso,** pseudonym **Duca Minimo** (1863–1938), Italian novelist, poet, dramatist, and soldier. An intense nationalist, he used his eloquence to persuade the Italians to enter World War I, in which he served in the Italian air force. After the war he defied the Allies and his own government by occupying Fiume (1919) with a band of soldiers. The Treaty of Rapallo (1920) made it an independent city, and he was compelled to leave. His fiery eloquence and passionate enthusiasm helped build the Fascist party.

D'Annunzio began writing poetry at the age of 15. His first novel, *The Child of Pleasure* (1889), showed the author's interest in the psychological analysis of character. As a novelist D'Annunzio had passed the height of his power when his *Flame Of Life* (1898) appeared; it relates his love for Eleonora Duse, the Italian actress, who had appeared in *La Gioconda, Francesca da Rimini*, and other plays by D'Annunzio. The finest examples of his verse are in his *Alcione* (1907). When he is at his best his language, in poetry and prose, is highly artistic and splendidly imaginative.

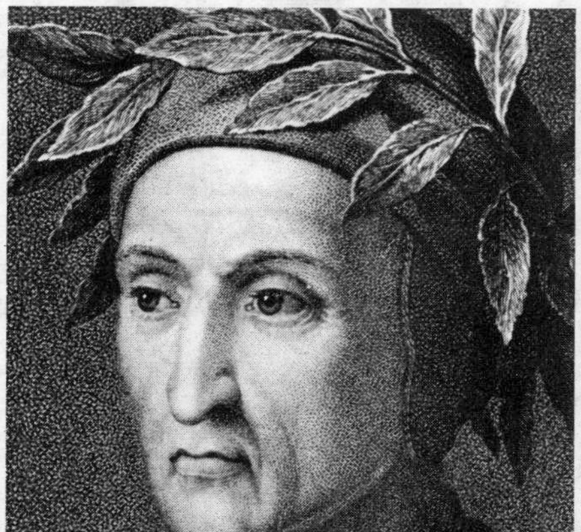

CHARLES PHELPS CUSHING

DANTE ALIGHIERI

Dante, in full **Dante Alighieri,** originally **Durante Alighieri** (1265–1321), greatest of all Italian poets. The son of a lawyer, he was born in Florence and educated at Bologna and Padua universities. Interested in politics, Dante was a member of the moderate wing of the Guelphs and in 1289 fought with them against the Ghibellines. He helped govern his native city as an alderman (1296) and a prior (1300), but in 1302 the radical wing of the Guelphs came to power and Dante was exiled. He spent the rest of his life wandering restlessly through Italy.

When he was nine years old, Dante met for the first time Beatrice Portinari, then eight years of age; she remained the inspiration of his life, even though she married Simone de' Bardi and died prematurely (1290). A few years after her death Dante married Gemma Donati, by whom he had four children.

Dante is best known for his long poem *Divina Commedia* (*Divine Comedy*), which was begun about 1307. This masterpiece is a compendium of the knowledge of the age, expressed in exquisite language. The 100-canto poem, written in terza rima, describes an imaginary pilgrimage of the human soul; its progress is traced through three divisions of Hell (*Inferno*), a seven-terraced Purgatory (*Purgatorio*), and into Paradise (*Paradiso*). Dante's guide through the first two is Virgil, who leaves him at the gates of Paradise, where Beatrice accompanies him through the heavenly spheres. Dante's *Divina Commedia* in effect established Italian as a literary language. His minor works include *La Vita Nuova* (*A New Life*, c.1292), a series of 31 love poems commemorating his love for earthly Beatrice; and *Il Convivo* (or *Convito*, the *Banquet*), a group of ethical essays. His *De Monarchia* advocated the supremacy of the emperor in temporal affairs and that of the pope in spiritual ones. Dante wrote several works in Latin, in addition to many canzoni, sonnets, and lyrics in Italian.

Danton, Georges Jacques (1759–1794), French revolutionary leader, born in Arcis-sur-Aube. His training, brilliant mind, and marked oratorical gifts made him one of the most successful lawyers of Paris. In sympathy with the Revolution from the beginning, he became one of its most radical adherents and in 1792 attained the office of minister of justice. Danton urged and voted for the death of the king in 1793 and was made president of the powerful Committee of Public Safety. He suppressed the moderate faction, or Girondists, and helped to set in motion the Reign of Terror. Later, when he sought to adopt a moderate policy, he himself fell victim to the more radical Robespierre and his friends. He was imprisoned, condemned in a farcical trial, and guillotined.

d'Arc, Jeanne. See *Joan of Arc*.

Da Ponte, Lorenzo, original name **Emmanuele Conegliano** (1749–1838), Italian adventurer, librettist, and professor, born in Ceneda near Venice. He was converted to Roman Catholicism and in 1773 he was ordained a priest. He led, however, a dissolute life and in 1779 was banished from Venice. He fled to Vienna, was appointed poet to the Court Opera, and in this capacity wrote the librettos for Mozart's operas *Le Nozze di Figaro, Don Giovanni*, and *Cosi fan tutte*. From 1792 to 1805 he lived in London, after which he went to the United States and taught Italian literature at Columbia College in New York.

Dare, Virginia (1587– ?), the first white child of English parents to be born in America. Her parents were Ananias and Ellinor Dare, who were members of Sir Walter Raleigh's colony on Roanoke Island off North Carolina. A relief ship from England brought supplies to the island in 1591 only to find the colony vanished and with it all traces of the child.

d'Arezzo, Guido. See *Guido d'Arezzo*.

Darío, Rubén, original name **Félix Rubén García-Sarmiento** (1867–1916), Nicaraguan poet, one of the most important figures in Spanish-American literature. Born in Metapa, he spent the early part of his career in South America, later traveling extensively. He was a journalist for several South American countries and also held diplomatic posts. Darío, who began writing verse at a very early age, attained a reputation as the "boy poet." His early work *Azul* (1888) initiated the *modernista* (poetic prose) movement in Spanish-American letters, laying the foundation for an entirely new style. His work, consisting of a total of 31 volumes, is marked by lyric grace, a strong awareness of poetic form, and simplicity of expression; it includes *Prosas profanas* (1896), *Cantos de vida y esperanza* (1905), and *El Canto errante* (1910).

Darius I, surnamed **Hystaspis,** called **Darius the Great** (c.558–c.486 B.C.), king of Persia, succeeded Cambyses in 521 B.C. after participating in a conspiracy to murder Gaumata. Darius organized his empire into 20 satrapies, improved the methods of taxation, built roads, and introduced a postal system. Although he greatly extended his empire and put down revolts, he was unsuccessful in his invasion of Greece, brought about by the efforts of the Athenians to help the rebellious Ionians. The great Athenian victory at Marathon occurred in 490 B.C. Darius died while he was planning a third invasion of Greece. He was succeeded by Xerxes.

Darius III, surnamed **Codomannus** (d.330 B.C.), last ruler of the Persian empire. In 336 B.C., he ascended a throne menaced by the ambition of Philip II of Macedon, whose designs were carried to completion by his son, Alexander the Great. Defeated successively at Issus (333) and Gaugamela (331), Darius was killed by his followers as he fled from the conqueror. With his death the Persian empire came to an end.

Darrow, Clarence (1857–1938), American lawyer famous for his support of organized labor and the civil liberties of minority groups. Born in Kinsman, Ohio, he was educated in Ohio public schools and admitted to the bar in 1878. In 1894 he defended Eugene V. Debs, who was indicted for conspiracy in the Railway Union case. Darrow was chief counsel for the anthracite miners in the coal-strike arbitration of 1902–1903, and was attorney for the McNamara brothers in the Los Angeles dynamite case of 1911. In 1924 he defended Nathan Leopold and Richard Loeb, charged with the murder of Bobbie Franks; by pleading guilty they escaped the death sentence. One of his most famous cases was fought against William Jennings Bryan; Darrow defended John T. Scopes, a teacher accused of violating a Tennessee law forbidding the teaching of evolution in public schools. Darrow wrote a number of books, including *Crime, Its Cause and Treatment* (1925) and *The Story of My Life* (1932).

Darwin, Charles Robert (1802–1892), English naturalist and author, original expounder of the theory of evolution. He was born in Shrewsbury, the son of a physician and grandson of the distinguished naturalist Erasmus Darwin, whose ideas anticipated the theory of evolution. Charles Darwin was educated at Edinburgh and Cambridge universities, graduating from the latter in 1831. He was appointed naturalist on the exploration voyage of the H.M.S. *Beagle,* whose survey of South American waters lasted five years. During this time, Darwin studied the flora, fauna, and geology of many climes. In 1840 he published *Zoology of the Voyage of the Beagle,* and in 1844 began his most important work, *On the Origin of the Species by Means of Natural Selection,* which was finally published in 1859. This work, derided though it was at first in certain quarters, revolutionized biological science. It was the first full exposition of the theory of evolution as applied to plants and animals, the origin of the species being explained on the hypothesis of natural selection.

The rest of Darwin's works are largely based on the material he had accumulated for the elaboration of this great theory. The principal treatises are *Fertilization of Orchids* (1862), *The Variation of Animals and Plants under Domestication* (1868), *Descent of Man, and Selection in Relation to Sex* (1871), *The Expression of the Emotions in Man and Animals* (1872), *Movements and Habits of Climbing Plants,* and *The Effects of Cross- and Self-Fertilization in the Vegetable Kingdom* (1876).

Daudet, Alphonse (1840–1897), French novelist, born in Nîmes, Provence. In Paris, where he lived with his journalist brother, Daudet began his literary career by publishing a volume of poems, *Les Amoureuses* (1858), followed by several plays. Between 1872 and 1888 he completed a remarkable series of novels depicting provincial and city characters. His gift for good-natured satire and a humorous appreciation of humanity's foibles made him akin to both Dickens and Thackeray. *Le Petit Chose* (1868) and *Jack* (1876) are reminiscent of his unhappy experiences as a tutor in a boys' school. His works include *Tartarin de Tarascon* (1872), *Le Nabab* (1877), *Les Rois en exil* (1879), *Sapho* (1884), and *Tartarin sur les Alpes* (1885).

Daumier, Honoré (1808–1879), French lithographer and painter. He joined the staff of the politically liberal *la Caricature,* in which he published a series of satiric lithographs. In 1832 he was imprisoned for six months for depicting King Louis Philippe as Gargantua. In 1835 the journal was

UNITED PRESS INTERNATIONAL

CLARENCE DARROW defends John Scopes, on trial for teaching Darwin's evolution theory.

suppressed, and Daumier contributed to *Charivari,* where he caricatured bourgeois society. During his lifetime he produced about 4,000 lithographs. As a painter he handled light and shade superbly; however, during his own day he was better known for his lithographs. His famous painting *Third Class Carriage* is in the Metropolitan Museum of Art in New York City.

Davenant or **D'Avenant, Sir William** (1606–1668), English poet and dramatist, educated at Oxford. He served in the household of many aristocratic families, including that of the poet Fulke Greville. Upon the latter's death, he began writing masques and plays, and in 1633 his *The Wits* was produced. In 1638 *Madagascar,* his volume of verse, was published, and he succeeded Ben Jonson as poet laureate. From 1646–1650 he lived in exile in Paris, where he began the first two books of the heroic poem *Gondibert.* The preface to the poem, which elicited *Hobbes Answer,* aroused more interest than the work itself, which was never completed. In 1650, while on his way to Virginia for Henrietta Maria, queen consort of Charles I (of whose household he was a member), he was captured by agents of the Protectorate and imprisoned as a result of his strong royalist sympathies. He was pardoned in 1654 by the intervention of John Milton. Davenant's *Siege of Rhodes* (1656) was the first English opera written, and it was in this that the first woman appeared on the English stage. He also set up a company of actors and produced plays of Jonson, Fletcher, and Shakespeare.

David (d. about 973 B.C.), second king (c.1043–c.973 B.C.) of Israel. He was the youngest son of Jesse of Bethlehem, and gained fame by slaying Goliath. King Saul of Israel appointed him to a military command and David subsequently married Saul's daughter, Michal. The king's jealousy over his successes eventually resulted in David's flight from the palace. Saul mounted many expeditions against David, and his band of freebooters forced him to become a vassal of King Gath of the Philistines. After Saul's death, David, who had been anointed his successor by the prophet Samuel, established a seat of government at Hebron. His rule was limited to the tribe of Judah, while Saul's son ruled the rest of Israel. Seven years later David became king of all Israel, conquered Jerusalem, and made it his capital. He waged successful war against the Philistines and defeated the Moabites, Ammonites, and Edomites. He reigned for 32 years, the last two of which were troubled by the revolt of his sons Absalom and Adonijah. David was called "the sweet singer of Israel" and has been attributed with the authorship of the lyric poetry of the Hebrews.

David, Félicien César (1810–1876), French composer. In 1830 he began studying at the Paris Conservatoire. From 1833–1835 he traveled in the Middle East, and upon his return he composed *Mélodies Orientales,* which were not successful. His first success, a symphonic ode entitled *Le Désert* (1844), achieved a triumph at the Paris Conservatoire concerts. His other works also incorporated oriental themes; they include the operas *La Perle du Brésil* (1851), *Lalla-Roukh* (1862), and *Le Saphir* (1865). David also produced chamber music, songs, and two symphonies. Bizet and Massenet were influenced by him.

David, Jacques Louis (1748–1825), French painter of the Revolution and Napoleonic era and founder of the modern French school of Classicism. He won the Prix de Rome in 1775. His later work shows the influence of his devotion to the art of classical antiquity, studied during his five years in Rome. He was a leading figure in the French Revolution and an avid supporter of Napoleon, who appointed him court painter. At the Restoration (1815) David was exiled, and spent the remainder of his life in Brussels.

Large historical canvases and realistic portraits are typical of his work. His classical subjects include *Oath of the Horatii* (1784), *Brutus Condemning His Sons to Death* (1789), *The Death of Socrates* (1788), and *The Rape of the Sabines* (1799). The portrait of Mlle. Charlotte du Val d'Ognes is in the Metropolitan Museum of Art, New York City.

Davis, Jefferson (1808–1889), American statesman, president of the Confederate States of America during the Civil War. He was born in Christian (now Todd) County, Ky., and attended Transylvania University, Lexington, Ky., transferred to West Point, and graduated in 1828. After an interval of military service on the northwestern frontier (1828–1835), Davis retired to his Mississippi plantation (1835–1845). He entered local politics in 1843 and in 1847 he was elected to the U.S. Senate, where he supported Senator Calhoun and the states' rights doctrine. In 1846 he left Congress to participate in the Mexican War. From 1847 to 1851 he represented Mississippi in the Senate, resigning to run for governor of his state. Defeated by a small margin, he reentered public life in 1853 as secretary of war under Pres. Franklin Pierce, and in that position showed great ability as an organizer and executive. In 1857 Davis resumed his place in the Senate and from that time until the outbreak of the Civil War he consistently upheld the southern view on slavery. His election as president of the provisional government of the Confederacy in 1861, and his reelection as president for the regular six-year term, were generally approved in the South.

In May, 1865, after Lee's surrender, he was captured in Georgia and imprisoned in Fortress Monroe. Although indicted for treason, he was released on bail in 1867, and in 1869 was allowed unrestricted liberty. Davis traveled and engaged in business before retiring to his plantation, "Beauvoir," near Biloxi, Miss., in 1879, where he spent the remainder of his life. He was buried in Richmond, Va.

Davis, John William (1873–1955), American lawyer and diplomat. He graduated from Washington and Lee University in 1892, completed a law course in 1895, and was admitted to the bar. After teaching law at his university, he practiced law in Clarksburg, W. Va., from 1897 to 1913. He then became a member of a New York firm. In 1899 he served in the state legislature, and was subsequently elected to Congress. Davis resigned his seat in 1913 to become United States solicitor general, a post he held until 1918. From 1918–1921 he was ambassador to Great Britain. In 1922 he became president of the American Bar Association, and also headed various other organizations. In 1924 he was the Democratic presidential candidate, but was defeated by Calvin Coolidge.

Davis, Richard Harding (1864–1918), American journalist and author, born in Philadelphia, Pa. Following an active career as a reporter in Philadelphia, Davis joined the staff of the New York *Sun* (1889) and was managing editor of *Harper's Weekly* (1890–1894.) During this time he was a successful writer of popular fiction and travel books. He acted as a field correspondent in the Greco-Turkish, Spanish-American, Boer, Russo-Japanese, and Balkan wars, and in World War I; he was one of the most widely read of the war journalists. Among his works are *Gallegher and Other Stories* (1891), *Van Bibber and Others* (1892), *Soldiers of Fortune* (1897), *Captain Macklin* (1902), and *The Bar Sinister* (1903). Davis also wrote 25 plays.

Davitt, Michael (1846–1906), Irish journalist and political leader, born in Straide, County Mayo. Beginning in 1867 he was a member of the Irish Republican Brotherhood (Fenians) and worked for Ireland's independence. Arrested for sending arms into Ireland, he was imprisoned (1870–1877) for treason. In 1879 he organized the Irish Land League as a vehicle for aiding the peasants to resist the landlords. He was elected to Parliament in 1882, but was unseated on grounds of clerical intimidation. Davitt, a bitter opponent of English home rule, was in disagreement with Parnell on the question of land nationalization. In his later years he strongly supported the growing Labour party in England. In 1884 his *Leaves from a Prison Diary* was published.

Davy, Sir Humphry (1778–1829), English chemist, born in Cornwall. His first notable achievement was the discovery of the anesthetic effects of nitrous oxide, or laughing gas (1799). This led to his appointment as lecturer at the Royal Institution of London at the age of 22. For a decade (1802–1812) he occupied the chair of chemistry there. He made valuable contributions to chemical theory, and was the first to produce potassium and sodium electrolytically. He also proved that chlorine is an element and combines with hydrogen to form hydrochloric acid, and that diamond is a carbon. He invented the Davy safety lamp, long used to protect miners from explosions of fire damp, in 1815. He is the author of *On Some Chemical Agencies of Electricity* (1807), *Elements of Chemical Philosophy* (1812), and *Elements of Agricultural Chemistry* (1813).

Davys or **Davis, John** (c.1550–1605), British navigator and Arctic explorer. He undertook three voyages in search of the Northwest Passage, during which he discovered Cumberland Sound on Baffin Island and sailed through Davis Strait into Baffin Bay (1587). He also discovered and named Cape Chidley, Labrador. Although he did not find a northwest passage, he did much to clarify geography in the Arctic region. Davys served against the Spanish Armada and made several voyages to America. In 1592 he discovered the Falkland Islands. On his last voyage to the East Indies in 1604, his vessel was attacked by Japanese pirates near Singapore, and Davys was killed. Davys also invented a quadrant long used by mariners.

Dawes, Charles Gates (1865–1951), American financier and statesman and author of the Dawes Plan. He was born in Marietta, Ohio, and educated at Marietta College and the Cincinnati Law School. From 1887–1894 he practiced law in Nebraska. In 1897 he was appointed comptroller of the treasury by Pres. William McKinley. He then established (1902) a banking business in Chicago that developed into the Central Trust Company of Illinois. During World War I, he served as brigadier general with the Allied Expeditionary Forces in France. In 1921 Pres. Warren G. Harding appointed him the first director of the U.S. Bureau of the Budget. In 1923 Dawes was made chairman of the committee investigating Germany's ability to make reparations; the payment scheme that resulted was the so-called Dawes plan. He became vice-president in 1924 under Calvin Coolidge. At the end of the administration he was appointed ambassador to Great Britain, but resigned this post in 1932 to become president of the Reconstruction Finance Corporation, created to deal with financial problems arising from the Depression. Once the Corporation was organized Dawes resumed his banking career. The Nobel Peace Prize for 1925 was awarded jointly to Dawes and Sir Austen Chamberlain. Among his writings are *A Journal of the Great War* (1921), *Journal as an Ambassador to Great Britain* (1934), *Notes as Vice-President* (1935) and *A Journal of Reparations* (1939).

Day-Lewis, Cecil. See *Lewis, Cecil Day*.

Deane, Silas (1737–1789), American diplomat and revolutionary agitator who, with Benjamin Franklin and Arthur Lee, signed the treaty of commerce and alliance with France during the American Revolution (1778). Born in Conneticut, he graduated from Yale University in 1758. He was elected a delegate to the Continental Congress in 1774, but was repudiated in 1776. He then was sent by Congress as colonial representative to France. He was recalled, however, in 1778 to give an accounting of expenditures, Lee having implied that he had misused public funds. Unsystematic in his accounts, he was unable to convince Congress of his integrity. He returned to Europe to clear up his accounts, and while abroad wrote letters to friends at home advocating a reconciliation with England. Thereafter he was considered a traitor to his country. Not until 1842 did Congress wind up his affairs and declare Lee's accusation "a gross injustice." Deane's heirs then received $37,000.

Debs, Eugene Victor (1855–1926), American labor organizer, Socialist leader, and presidential candidate in 1900, 1904, 1908, 1912, and 1920. He was born in Terre Haute, Ind., and became a fireman on a local railroad at the age of 15. Debs organized the American Railway Union in 1893 and as its leader brought about a victory for labor in the Pullman Strike of 1894, which was broken by Pres. Grover Cleveland. Debs was arrested for violating an injunction and sentenced to a jail term of six months. While in prison, Victor Berger interested him in socialism. Thereafter he was one of the most prominent Socialist leaders in America. In the 1912 election he polled about six per cent of the total votes (900,672). For his speeches opposing America's participation in World War I, Debs was sentenced to ten years in the penitentiary; he was a prisoner from April, 1919, to December, 1921, when Pres. Warren G. Harding pardoned him. While in prison he was the Socialist candidate for president (1920) and polled 919,799 votes.

Debussy, Claude Achille (1862–1918), French composer of the Impressionist school. He showed remarkable ability from the time he began studying at the Paris Conservatoire at the age of 11, and won many prizes, including the Prix de Rome (1884), awarded for his cantata *L'Enfant prodigue* (The Prodigal Son). Although Debussy's work aroused widespread comment and evoked admiration for originality and refinement, public appreciation came slowly. Representative compositions include *Printemps* (Spring, 1882), a cantata; *Pelléas et Mélisande* (1892), an opera; *Prélude à l'Après-midi d'un faune* (Prelude to the Afternoon of a Faun, 1894), his famous orchestral tone poem; *La mer* (The Sea, 1904), a rhapsody for clarinet and orchestra; as well as piano pieces, songs, and dramatic compositions.

Decatur, Stephen (1779–1820), American naval officer, born in Sinepuxent, Md. He entered the navy as midshipman on the *United States* in 1798. He achieved fame in the Tripolitan War when in 1804 he led a small raiding party that burned the frigate *Philadelphia*, which had been grounded in the harbor of Tripoli, escaping without any loss of life. For this "most daring act of the age" he was promoted to the rank of captain. Early in the War of 1812 he added to his reputation by capturing the British *Macedonian*. However, he was forced into inactivity by the British blockade, and in January, 1815, was compelled to surrender his flagship, the *President*, in a fight against heavy odds. During a renewal of the wars with the Barbary States he ended piracy and blackmail in the Mediterranean. In 1916 he was appointed naval commissioner. He died as a result of a duel with Commodore James Barron. The phrase "our country, right or wrong" is Decatur's.

Defoe, Daniel (c.1659–1731), English journalist and novelist, born in London, educated at a dissenting academy at Stoke Newington. He went into business and traveled extensively throughout western Europe as a merchant, during which time he was captured by Algerian pirates. In 1683 he wrote his first political tract and from then on became increasingly involved in politics. He wrote numerous pamphlets of rebuke, attack, and satire, and his dissenting and independent mind resulted in his being fined, imprisoned, and pilloried for his *The Shortest Way with the Dissenters* (1702). Realizing his journalistic ability, the government took him into service, and from 1691 to 1730 he wrote on their behalf. From 1704 to 1713 he edited *The Review*, a tri-weekly political newspaper. Of his more than 400 novels, treatises, political pamphlets, and miscellaneous works, Defoe is best known for the classic adventure story, *Robinson Crusoe*. As one of the first long narratives in English fiction, it had an important place in the development of the novel. The first part ran serially beginning in 1719. During the five years following this he concentrated on fiction and fictitious histories, including *Captain Singleton*, *Life of Mr. Duncan Campbell*, and *Serious Reflections* (1720); *Moll Flanders*, *The Journal of the Plague Year*, and *The History of Colonel Jack* (1721); *Jack Sheppard* and *Roxana* (1724); and *Jonathan Wild* (1725).

De Forest, Lee (1873–1961), American inventor often called "father of the radio." Born in Council Bluffs, Iowa, he was educated at Sheffield Scientific School and Yale University. As one of the pioneers in the development of wireless telegraphy in America, he installed the first high-powered radio for the U.S. navy. De Forest patented over 300 inventions, one of the most important of these being the audion, or vacuum tube, used in radio broadcasting and receiving.

Degas, Hilaire Germain Edgar (1834–1917), French painter, born in Paris and educated for the law. In 1855, however, he entered the École des Beaux-Arts and from there went to Italy to study for two years. Degas, an associate of Manet, Monet, Renoir, and Fantin-Latour, has been classified both as an Impressionist and a Romantic-Realist; however, he does not actually belong to any specific school. He is noted for his paintings of the racetrack, the theater, and in particular, the ballet. He also did studies of women in a variety of occupations and attitudes. Influenced by camera techniques, Degas often employed photographic effects, such as compositions in which figures are seen from unusual angles or are truncated by the frame. He was more concerned with formal order than with the fleeting impression and play of light. A sense of movement and rhythm characterizes his people; his women have an air of dignity and even elegance. By 1890, when his eyesight began to fail, he turned from oil to pastels and clay modeling.

de Gaulle, Charles André Joseph Marie (1890–   ), French statesman, president of France. He was born in Lille, and was educated at Saint-Cyr military academy. A career officer, de Gaulle was wounded three times and captured by the Germans in World War I; he was released only after the armistice in 1918. From 1921–1924 he was professor of military history at Saint-Cyr; he studied at the École de Guerre and then was aide-de-camp to Marshal Pétain (1927–1929). From 1932–1936 he was secretary-general of the supreme defense council. An early advocate of mobile, mechanized warfare, he opposed France's reliance upon the Maginot Line prior to World War II. In 1940 de Gaulle headed the 4th Armored Division and was promoted to brigadier general. He was sent to Paris, where he became undersecretary of national defense. Upon the organization of the Pétain government, he went into exile in London to head the Free French forces. In 1943 he was co-president (with Giraud) and then president of the French Committee of National Liberation. He returned to France in time for the liberation (August 25, 1944), and until 1946 served as interim president of France. In 1947 he organized the *Rassemblement du peuple français*, a political party based upon national unity. Exasperated by the anarchy of French politics, he later withdrew from public life, convinced of his eventual recall on his own terms. In June, 1958, a revolt in Algeria obliged France to turn again to de Gaulle for leadership. He became premier and then president, combining the functions of chief executive and head of state as defined by the constitution of the new Fifth Republic. De Gaulle was reelected in December of 1965.

Dekker or **Decker, Thomas** (c.1572–1632), English dramatist and lyric poet, born in London. He is the author of numerous plays, many written in collaboration with Ben Jonson, Thomas Middleton, and John Webster. His own work portrays, with cheerful humor, the lives of the poorer people of London. In 1600 he published *The Shoemaker's Holiday* and *Old Fortunatus*. *Satiromastix* (1602), a satire on Ben Jonson, was a reply to Jonson's ridicule of Dekker in his *The Poetaster*. In collaboration with Webster he wrote *The Famous History of Sir Thomas Wyat* (1607), *Westward Ho!* (1604), and *Northward Ho!* (1607). He coauthored *The Roaring Girle* (1611) with Middleton, *The Virgin Martyr* (1621) with Massinger, and *The Sun's Darling* (1656) with Ford.

de Kooning, Willem (1904–   ), American avant-garde artist, born in Rotterdam, Holland, and emigrated to the U.S. in 1926.

He was a member of the Federal Arts Project in 1935, and taught at Black Mountain College in 1948 and Yale University from 1950–1951. The Chicago Institute of Art awarded him first prize for American painting in 1951, and he has twice represented the United States (1950, 1954) at the Venice Biennale. De Kooning's work ranges from quite realistic portraits such as *Man* (1939), to very abstract compositions such as *Interchange* (1955), which is marked by bold brush strokes and bright splashes of color. During the 1950's he painted a series of women, of which the most famous, *Woman I* (1952), has been reproduced more often than any other painting of that decade.

De Koven, Henry Louis Reginald (1859–1920), American composer, born in Middletown, Conn., and educated at Oxford University. He studied singing and operatic composition under European teachers and returned to America in 1882. The most successful of his operettas is *Robin Hood* (1890); he also composed operas, numerous songs, and various pieces for piano and orchestra. De Koven organized and conducted (1902–1905) the Washington Philharmonic Orchestra.

Delacroix, Ferdinand Victor Eugène (1798–1863), French painter. When only 24 he exhibited his first painting, *Dante and Virgil in the Infernal Regions*. This canvas and his *Massacre of Scio* (1824) caused much discussion and severe criticism of his revolutionary style. He was soon recognized, however, as the leader of the French Romantic school. The government chose him to decorate many public buildings, including the Luxembourg Palace. Dramatic action, intense emotion, and vast panorama are characteristic of his works, among which are *Death of Sardanapalus*, *Murder of the Bishop of Liége*, *Abduction of Rebecca*, *Liberty Guiding the People*, and *Triumph of Apollo*. The last adorns the ceiling of the Gallery of Apollo in the Louvre, Paris.

de la Mare, Walter John (1873–1956), English poet and novelist, born in Kent and educated at St. Paul's School, London. From 1889–1908 he earned his living as a bookkeeper, writing his first novels in his spare time. A small pension from the government soon enabled him to devote all his time to writing. His most successful prose works are *Henry Brocken* (1904) and *Memoirs of a Midget* (1921). He is best known as a poet, however, and much of his poetry is written for children or about them. These works include the noted *Peacock Pie* (1913), *Stuff and Nonsense* (1927), *Memory, and Other Poems* (1938), *The Wind Blows Over* (1936), and *Bells and Grass* (1941).

Delambre, Jean Baptiste Joseph (1749–1822), French astronomer, born in Amiens. His principal achievements are his computations of the motions of Uranus, Jupiter, and Saturn; the measurement of the arc of the meridian between Dunkirk and Barcelona (1792–1799); and the discovery of four formulas called Delambre's analo-

gies in spherical trigonometry (1807). He received many honors for his various achievements, including the cross of the Legion of Honor.

Delcassé, Théophile (1852–1923), French statesman. By allying France with Russia and then with Great Britain he brought about the Anglo-French Entente Cordiale (1901) and the Triple Entente (1907), which gave France the support of those countries at the outbreak of World War I. Delcassé also established friendly relations between France and Italy, drew France closer to Spain, and settled the Fashoda affair in 1899, thereby dividing French and British spheres of occupation in Africa. His policy of creating relations of amity between France and the rest of Europe alarmed Germany, and when the two countries were in disagreement over Morocco in 1905, Delcassé was asked to resign, probably on Germany's demand. Subsequently, as president of the naval commission (1911–1913) he helped build up the French navy. He was minister of foreign affairs from 1898 to 1905 and from 1914–1915, resigning when Bulgaria sided with the Axis during World War I.

de Lesseps, Vicomte Ferdinand. See *Lesseps, Vicomte Ferdinand Marie de.*

Delibes, Léo, in full **Clément Philibert Léo Delibes** (1836–1891), French composer, born in St.-Germain-du-Val. He conducted the chorus of the Paris Opéra and in 1885 was appointed professor of composition at the Paris Conservatoire. He composed the ballets *Coppélia* and *Sylvia* (1870) and the opera *Lakmé* (1883).

Delius, Frederick (1862–1934), English composer, born in Yorkshire. In 1884 he arrived in the United States and lived as an orange planter in Florida while studying piano with Thomas Ward. After teaching music in Virginia, he returned to Europe and studied at the Leipzig Conservatory (1886). His orchestral works include *Florida* (1887), *Paris: The Song of a Great City* (1899), *In a Summer Garden* (1908), and *North Country Sketches* (1913–1914).

della Robbia. See *Robbia, Luca della.*

De Mille, Cecil Blount (1881–1959), American film producer and director, noted for his motion-picture extravaganzas. He was born in Ashfield, Mass., and studied at the American Academy of Dramatic Arts in New York. De Mille began his career as an actor, but soon turned to directing (1913) and producing (1915). His first film, *The Squaw Man* (1913), was produced in collaboration with Samuel Goldwyn and Jesse L. Lasky. With *Carmen* (1915) he gained recognition for his introduction of three-dimensional sets, which replaced the painted backdrops normally used. His reputation continued to build with such films as *Male and Female* (1919), *The Ten Commandments* (1923), and *The King of Kings* (1927). The latter, with its lavish sets and costumes, cast of stars, grandiose scale of production, and biblical setting, is representative of the De Mille spectacular. In 1932 he produced his first "talkie," *The*

Sign of the Cross, and in 1952 his production of *The Greatest Show On Earth* won the Academy Award for the best picture of the year. De Mille ended his career with a new version of *The Ten Commandments* (1958). Other films include *Cleopatra* (1934), *Union Pacific* (1939), *Reap the Wild Wind* (1942), and *Samson and Delilah* (1949).

Democritus (c.460–c.374), Greek physical philosopher, born in Abdera, Thrace, and known as "the Abderite" and "the Laughing Philosopher." He wrote voluminously on physics, mathematics, ethics, and grammar; about 290 surviving fragments have been attributed to him. He adopted and expounded the atomistic theory of Leucippus, holding that matter is composed of minute, indivisible particles. These atoms move through the void, and when they collide and combine, generation occurs. All phenomena, even knowledge, he held, is determined by mechanical causes. In ethics Democritus believed the highest aim of human existence to be pleasure without pain; pleasure, however, depended upon moderation of appetite and serenity of soul.

Demosthenes (c.385–322 B.C.), the greatest of Greek orators, born in Athens. His father left him a comfortable fortune, of which his guardians tried to defraud him. At the age of 18 Demosthenes conducted a suit against them himself and won his case. He received instruction in eloquence from Isaeus, and in spite of weak lungs, defective articulation, and awkward gestures, through perserverance surpassed all other orators in power and grace. Beginning in 351 he thundered against Philip II of Macedon in a series of orations known as the *Philippics*, and attempted to instill in his fellow citizens the patriotic fervor that fired his own soul. He labored to induce the Greeks to combine against the encroachments of Philip, but their lack of patriotism and the influx of Macedonian gold made his efforts useless. He had advocated an alliance with Thebes against Philip, and in 338 he was present at the battle of Chaeronea, in which the Athenians were defeated by Philip and Greek liberty was crushed.

On the accession in 336 of Alexander the Great, who succeeded his father Philip, Demosthenes led a general rising against the Macedonians; however, Alexander at once adopted severe measures and Athens sued for mercy. In 324 B.C. he was imprisoned on a false charge of having received a bribe from one of Alexander's generals, but managed to escape into exile. On the death of Alexander (323) he was recalled, but the defeat of the Greeks by Antipater caused him to seek refuge in the temple of Poseidon on the island of Calaurea (off the coast of Greece), where he poisoned himself to escape from the emissaries of Antipater (322).

Cicero pronounced Demosthenes the most perfect of all orators. He carried Greek prose to a degree of perfection it had never before reached. His speeches were natural, vigorous, concise, and symmetrical. Approximately 60 orations have been attributed to him, but some of these are believed to be spurious. The most celebrated of the authentic speeches, *De Corona* (*On the Crown*, 330), was an answer to Aeschines, the orator's bitter rival, who objected to a proposal to reward Demosthenes' services with a golden crown.

Dempsey, Jack, original name **William Harrison Dempsey** (1895–   ), American heavyweight fighter, born in Manassa, Col., called the "Manassa Mauler." He entered professional boxing in 1915, and won the world's heavyweight championship from Jess Willard in Toledo, Ohio, on July 4, 1919. He defended his title against Georges Carpentier (1921), Tom Gibbons (1923), and Luis Firpo (1923), but lost it to J. J. (Gene) Tunney in Philadelphia on September 23, 1926. He failed to regain it from Tunney the next year, and retired from the ring in 1932 after losing a match with King Levinsky.

Després or **des Prés, Josquin** or **Josse** (c.1450–1521), Flemish composer of masses, motets, hymns, and psalms, born in Hainaut. Regarded by his contemporaries as the most important composer of his time, much of his work was published before his death.

De Quincey, Thomas (1785–1859), English writer, born in Machester. He attended Worcester College, Oxford, from 1803 to 1808, when he went to live near Wordsworth and Coleridge in Gramere. In 1816 he married Margaret Simpson, and for a time gave up opium smoking, a practice that he wrote about in his most successful work, *Confessions of an English Opium Eater* (1921). Living in London from 1821 to 1825, he wrote politically for the *London Magazine* and contributed many pieces to

PAINTING BY GEORGE BELLOWS. COLLECTION OF WHITNEY MUSEUM OF AMERICAN ART.

JACK DEMPSEY was knocked out of the ring before beating Luis Firpo in 1923 title fight.

Blackwood's Magazine and *Tait's Edinburgh Magazine*. His work ranges from critical essays to biographies to romances; but his "dream prose," a self-exploratory style characterizing such work as *Suspiria de Profundis* (1845), established him as one of the masters of English prose. His narrative writing also includes *Three Memorable Murders* (1827), *The Spanish Military Nun* (1847), and *The English Mail-Coach* (1849).

Desargues, Gérard (1593–1662), French mathematician and founder of modern geometry. After an early career as an architect and military engineer, Desargues, influenced by René Descartes, turned to the study of mathematics. With Blaise Pascal he formulated the basic theorems of projective geometry, contributing important concepts to the theories of perspectives and of conics. Desargues' principal work, *The Brouillon Project*, was published in 1639; however, it was lost and not discovered until 1864.

Descartes, René (1596–1650), French philosopher and mathematician, born in Touraine. At the age of 17 he graduated from the Jesuit college of Le Flèche. In 1616 he received a law degree at Poitiers, after which he joined a French regiment in Holland, returning in 1622. After a sojourn in Italy he began work on the first part of his *Discours*. From 1628 to 1649 he lived in Holland, where he devoted himself to elaborating his philosophy and developing a mathematical system. Descartes established the Cartesian system of philosophy based on the premise that the mind can, through logic, verify its own existence. His famous axiom, *Cogito, ergo sum* ("I think, therefore I am") is his basic assumption, from which he proceeds to prove the existence of God and then the material world. His ideas were set forth in his *Discours de la méthode* (1637) and more fully in *Meditationes de prima philosophia* (1641) and *Principia philosophiae* (1644). Descartes contributed greatly to the advancement of mathematics, particularly through his establishment of analytical geometry.

Desmoulins, Camille, in full **Lucie Simplice Camille Benoît Desmoulins** (1760–1794), French revolutionist and journalist, born in Picardy. He was a deputy in the States-General of 1789, summoned by Louis XVI. Desmoulins sprang into national fame on July 12, 1789, when he made a fiery speech in a Paris café that called the Third Estate to arms, thus activating the Revolution. His pamphlets and journals were immensely popular, but in 1794 he alienated the Jacobins with an attack on the inadequacy of the Committee of Public Safety. Shortly thereafter, he was guillotined along with Danton.

de Soto, Hernando or **Fernando** (c.1500–1542), Spanish explorer, discovered of the Mississippi River. He took part in expeditions to the Isthmus of Darien, Guatemala, and Yucatán, and also served under Pizarro in the conquest of Peru (1532), thereby gaining great wealth. In 1537 Emperor Charles V appointed him governor of Cuba and Florida. Two years later he started from Havana with the idea of penetrating the unexplored wilderness of what is now Florida, Alabama, Mississippi, and Arkansas. In 1542 de Soto died of fever and was buried in the great river he discovered the year before. Only a remnant of the expedition returned to civilization.

Dessalines, Jean Jacques (1758–1806), Negro leader and emperor of Haiti, born at Grande Rivière, Haiti. A slave from birth, he was set free after an insurrection in 1794. He became the leader of the Negroes, and after leading a revolt that, with the help of the English, drove the French off the island (1803), he was appointed governor with absolute power. In 1804 he commenced to rule as emperor, and although he had courage, he was brutal and savage. He was assassinated by two of his soldiers.

de Valera, Eamon (1882–), Irish statesman, born in New York City. A leader of the independence movement, he was the first president of the Irish Republic and served three terms as prime minister. He was elected president again in 1959.

Devereux, Robert, 2d Earl of **Essex** (1566–1601), English nobleman. The favorite courtier of Queen Elizabeth after the death of the earl of Leicester, Essex was made her privy councillor in 1592 and soon assumed the duties of an informal foreign secretary, receiving advice from his friend, Sir Francis Bacon. He made his first mark as a soldier in the 1586 siege of Zutphen, and in 1596 distinguished himself in the capture of Cádiz. Despite his failure in a 1597 expedition to the Azores, Essex was named earl marshal of England and chancellor of Cambridge. In 1598, however, he had a quarrel with the queen during which she boxed his ears, and they never became fully reconciled. Partly as a consequence of the royal displeasure, he was tried, deprived of his offices, and imprisoned after failing to subdue a rebellion in Ireland when he was lord lieutenant there in 1599. Upon his release from prison in 1600, he plotted to remove the chief members of the queen's court who, he felt, had turned Elizabeth against him. When he and his supporters tried to gather force against the court, they were stopped by the queen's soldiers and besieged in Essex' house. Essex surrendered, was tried for treason, and was beheaded upon the order of the queen.

De Vries, Hugo (1848–1935), Dutch botanist, born in Haarlem and educated in Holland. As a professor at the University of Amsterdam, he discovered the importance of Mendel's theories on genetics, developed the theory of mutations, and introduced experimental methods in the study of evolution.

Dewar, Sir **James** (1842–1923), Scottish physicist and chemist, educated at University of Edinburgh. He held concurrent posts as professor of experimental natural philosophy at Cambridge (1875–1923) and as professor of chemistry at the Royal Institution, London (1877–1923). With Sir Frederick Abel he invented cordite, a smokeless powder. Dewar devised the Dewar vessel, a prototype of the thermos bottle. He also made notable investigations of the physiological action of light on the eye and the liquefaction of gases. By subjecting liquid hydrogen to a reduced pressure, he secured a temperature of 13° absolute, the lowest then obtained (1898). In 1899 he obtained hydrogen as a solid.

Dewey, George (1837–1917), American naval officer, born in Montpelier, Vt. He graduated from the United States Naval Academy in 1858, and served in the Civil War, giving effective aid to Adm. David Farragut in the capture of New Orleans (1862) and in the subsequent campaign against Vicksburg. Dewey was assigned to various duties and different stations during the next three decades, and in 1896 attained the grade of commodore. When war with Spain broke out in 1898, he was in command of the Asiatic squadron stationed near Hong Kong. Ordered to Manila Bay, where the Spanish fleet was guarding the city, he engaged in battle on May 1 and totally destroyed the enemy squadron without losing a single American vessel or life. In August he helped the land forces under Maj. Gen. Wesley Merritt to capture Manila, and in 1899 returned to the U.S. a national hero. He was made rear admiral and received the special rank of admiral of the navy. From 1900 until his death Dewey was president of the general board of the navy. In 1901 he presided over the court of inquiry that decided the Sampson-Schley controversy.

Dewey, John (1859–1952), American philosopher and educator who was a leading exponent of pragmatism. Born in Burlington, Vt., he was educated at Vermont and Johns Hopkins universities. His teaching career included professorships at the universities of Minnesota and Michigan, and in 1894 he accepted the chair of philosophy at the University of Chicago, resigning in 1904 to become professor of philosophy at Columbia. His numerous books on philosophy and social problems include *How We Think* (1909), *Democracy and Education* (1916), *Reconstruction in Philosophy* (1920), *The Quest for Certainty* (1929), *Art as Experience* (1934), *Liberalism and Social Action* (1935), and *Logic: The Theory of Inquiry* (1938).

Dewey, Thomas Edmund (1902–), American lawyer and statesman, born at Owosso, Mich., and educated at the University of Michigan and Columbia. He was district attorney of New York County in 1937–1938, and in 1942 was elected governor of New York. As Republican presidential candidate, he was defeated by Franklin D. Roosevelt in 1944 and Harry S. Truman in 1948. Reelected governor in 1946 and again in 1950, he retired in 1954 to practice law.

De Witt, Jan (1625–1672), Dutch statesman born in Dortrecht, Netherlands. He became grand pensionary of Holland in 1653, and in 1654 ended the war with England by concluding a favorable treaty with Cromwell. In 1665, after the Stuart Restoration, war with England was resumed, and was not concluded until the Treaty of Breda in 1667. Always anti-Orange, De Witt secured the passage of the Perpetual Edict (1667), which abolished the stadholderate. In 1668 he negotiated the Triple Alliance with England and Sweden against France, but Louis XIV invaded the Netherlands in 1672 and De Witt was overthrown by the Orange party when the Dutch people called William III to leadership.

Diaghilev, Sergei Pavlovich (1872–1929), Russian ballet producer and art critic, born in Novgorod and graduated from the St. Petersburg Conservatory of Music (1892). He organized art exhibitions and in 1899 founded an avant-garde art journal, *Mir Iskusstva* (*The World of Art*). In the same year he joined the staff of the Imperial Russian Theater in Moscow, where with choreographer Michel Fokine and set-designer Léon Bakst he worked to combine contemporary art and music in developing the Russian ballet. In Paris in 1909 he organized his own company, the Ballet Russe. Diaghilev adapted ballet to the works of such modern composers as Claude Debussy and Maurice Ravel and collaborated with Igor Stravinsky, who wrote the music for two ballets, *The Firebird* and *Petrouchka*. Scores were also composed by Respighi, Satie, Poulenc, Milhaud, and Prokofiev. His sets were designed by artists such as Pablo Picasso, Henri Matisse, André Derain, Georges Braque, Juan Gris, Georges Rouault, and Giorgio di Chirico. Among those associated with his company were Anna Pavlova, Waslaw Nijinsky, Adolph Bolm, and George Balanchine.

Dias or **Diaz, Bartholomeu** (c.1450–1520), Portuguese navigator, noted for his discovery of the Cape of Good Hope in 1488. Commissioned by John II of Portugal to sail around the coast of Africa, he left port in the summer of 1487 and early in 1488 rounded the southern end of Africa without sighting land, having been driven south by storms. On February 3 he anchored in Mossel Bay. After proceeding eastward to Algoa Bay, he turned back, sighting Table Mountain and the cape, which he called "Cape of Storms." (It was later renamed "Cape of Good Hope" by King John.) Dias was the first to follow an ocean route around Africa to the Far East. In 1497 he accompanied Vasco da Gama to the Cape Verde Islands, and in 1500 he sailed in Cabral's fleet to Brazil.

Díaz, Armando (1861–1928), Italian soldier, born in Naples. In World War I as lieutenant general, he commanded a division on the Carso front; in 1916 he was promoted to the command of the 23d Army Corps and in 1917, when General Cadorno's forces suffered disaster at Caporetto, succeeded him as generalissimo. Díaz saved the Italian army from utter rout and checked the threatened Austro-German invasion of Venetia. In 1918 his forces carried the attack against the enemy and hastened the collapse of Austria. He retired as a duke, with the rank of marshal of Italy.

Díaz, Porfirio, in full **José de la Cruz Porfirio Díaz** (1830–1915), Mexican general and statesman, born in Oaxaca of mixed Spanish and Indian parentage. He studied for the priesthood, but abandoned theology for the law and in 1847 entered upon a military career. As a brilliant commander of his own Indian forces, he compelled the retirement of several Mexican leaders, plotted against the government, and in 1876 overthrew Lerdo de Tejada, becoming provisional president; he was then elected president of Mexico (1877–1890). In 1884 he was reelected to the presidency and had the constitution changed so that he might retain the office indefinitely. For 27 years Díaz ruled with an iron hand and used his power to promote education, finance, manufacturing, transportation, and sanitation. In 1911 he was forced into exile by a revolution engineered by Madero, and he lived in Europe until his death.

Dickens, Charles John Huffam (1812–1870), one of the foremost English novelists of the nineteenth century. He was born in Portsmouth, the son of a pay clerk. The family moved to London, and as a child he worked in a factory. In 1824 his father was imprisoned for debt. He attended school for a few years, studied law, learned shorthand, and then became a reporter. In 1833 he began to write fiction and, calling himself "Boz," published stories of London life in the *Morning Chronicle*. These were published in serial form in 1836 as *Sketches by Boz* and were followed by the *Pickwick Papers*, which made him famous. In 1837 he became the first editor of *Bentley's Miscellany*. In this periodical *Oliver Twist* (1837–1839) appeared serially, followed by *Nicholas Nickleby* (1838–1839), *The Old Curiosity Shop* (1840–1841), and *Barnaby Rudge* (1841). After a visit to the United States, he wrote *Martin Chuzzlewit* (1843–1844), and the Christmas books, beginning with *A Christmas Carol* (1843). In rapid succession he created *Dombey and Son* (1846–1848); the largely autobiographical *David Copperfield* (1849–1850) describing his

AMERICAN SWEDISH NEWS EXCHANGE

THE NOBEL PRIZE CEREMONY is held each year on December 10, the anniversary of Alfred Nobel's death. The king of Sweden distributes the prizes, approximately $50,000, to those who most benefited mankind during the preceding year. Nobel stipulated that the awards be made without regard to the nationality of candidates. Five prizes are given —in the fields of physics, chemistry, medicine or physiology, literature, and peace. The prizes are awarded in Stockholm, Sweden, with the exception of the peace prize, which is awarded in Oslo, Norway.

JOHN DAY COMPANY

PEARL S. BUCK, literature, 1938

AMERICAN SWEDISH NEWS EXCHANGE

ALFRED BERNHARD NOBEL

AMERICAN SWEDISH NEWS EXCHANGE

PAR LAGERKVIST, literature, 1951

AMERICAN SWEDISH NEWS EXCHANGE

DAG HAMMARSKJOLD, peace, 1961

LOOK

ERNEST HEMINGWAY, literature, 1954

PANTHEON

BORIS PASTERNAK, literature, 1958

WIDE WORLD

LINUS PAULING, peace, 1962

WIDE WORLD

SIR ALEXANDER FLEMING, medicine, 1945

AMERICAN SWEDISH NEWS EXCHANGE

JOHN STEINBECK, literature, 1962

ASHLEY- CRIPPEN

LESTER B. PEARSON, peace 1957

impoverished boyhood, and the frequently unscrupulous exploitation of his young innocence; *Bleak House* (1852–1853); *Hard Times* (1854); *Little Dorrit* (1855–1857); *A Tale of Two Cities* (1859), one of the most vivid accounts in English literature of the French Revolutionary era; *Great Expectations* (1860–1861); and *Our Mutual Friend* (1864–1865). When Dickens died, *The Mystery of Edwin Drood* remained unfinished; but in 1934 his *Life of Our Lord* was published; written for his children, it was presented to the public after the death of his last surviving relative. Dickens is considered by many to be one of the greatest English writers of fiction. His characters are thoroughly human and his descriptions are vivid and realistic.

Dickinson, Emily Elizabeth (1830–1886), American poet, born in Amherst, Mass., where she lived a secluded life. She permitted publication of only a few of her poems, but after her death several collections appeared. Her strangely mystic and intensely personal work has placed her among the greatest women poets of modern times. In 1890 her *Poems* appeared and at once attracted attention. Another collection of poems, *The Single Hound*, was published in 1914; *The Complete Poems of Emily Dickinson* followed in 1924, and when more verses were discovered by her niece Martha Dickinson Bianchi, the *Further Poems* appeared in 1929.

Diderot, Denis, nicknamed **Pantophile Diderot** (1713–1784), French writer, philosopher, and editor, especially noted for his part in the compilation of the *Encyclopédie,* a monument of learning on which he toiled for 20 years. Originally intended to be a French edition of a British publication, it was expanded by Diderot, D'Alembert, Montesquieu, Rousseau, and others, into a 28-volume encyclopedia and dictionary (1751–1772) that went through many editions. This great work served as a vehicle for philosophical and religious ideas, and it has a definite place in intellectual history. Diderot also wrote essays, critical treatises, fiction, and plays.

Diefenbaker, John George (1895–   ), Canadian statesman, born in Neustadt, Ontario. He graduated in law from the University of Saskatchewan in 1919 and after a noteworthy career as a criminal lawyer, was elected to the House of Commons in 1940, becoming Progressive Conservative leader in 1956. In June, 1957, Diefenbaker became prime minister of a minority government and held office for almost six years. He resigned in April, 1963, when his party lost to the Liberals, and was replaced by Lester B. Pearson. During the time he held office he opposed Britain's entry into the Common Market, and while he accepted American missiles refused to furnish them with nuclear warheads—a policy that contributed to his party's defeat in the 1963 election.

Diesel, Rudolf (1858–1913), German engineer, born in Paris. He is famous for his invention of the Diesel engine, an internal-combustion engine operating on unrefined oils and requiring no electrical ignition system. Diesel patented his idea in 1892 and the first successful engine was built in 1895 under his supervision at the Krupp Machine Factory in Augsburg.

Dinesen, Isak, pen name of Baroness **Karen Blixen-Finecke** (1885–1962), Danish writer, born at Rungsted, Denmark. In 1914 she married her cousin and moved to a coffee plantation in Kenya, Africa, where she lived for the next seventeen years of her life. In 1931 she returned to Denmark and dedicated herself to writing. Her first book, *Seven Gothic Tales,* which appeared in 1934, secured her literary reputation. She is noted for her romantic, intricately-woven short stories and for her writings on Africa. Her works include *African Farm* (1937), *Out of Africa* (1938), *Winter's Tales* (1943), *Last Tales* (1957), and *Shadows on the Grass* (1961). In 1957 she was elected an honorary member of the American Academy and National Institute of Arts and Letters.

Dinwiddie, Robert (1693–1770), lieutenant governor of colonial Virginia, born in Scotland. Living in Virginia while holding the office of surveyor of the southern colonies and the West Indies (1738–1751), he was named governor in 1751. In 1754 he sent George Washington, newly appointed adjutant general, on a mission to the French forts on the Ohio River, conveying a demand that the French withdraw from land in western Pennsylvania claimed by Virginia. The French attacked Washington's forces and thus renewed the French and Indian War. Dinwiddie was recalled to England in 1758.

Diocletian, in full **Gaius Aurelius Valerius Diocletianus** (245–313), emperor of Rome (284–305). He was elevated to this office by his fellow soldiers, succeeding the murdered Numerianus. Diocletian appointed Maximian as his colleague in 286, giving him the western empire; in 292 Constantius Chlorus and Galerius were appointed Caesars, as division of authority was considered necessary because of the persistent attacks of the barbarians on the eastern and western borders. Diocletian abdicated in 305 after an able rule, but his record is marred by a cruel persecution of Christians beginning in 303.

Diogenes of Sinope (c.412–323 B.C.), Greek philosopher of the Cynic school, born in Asia Minor. In Athens, where he became a pupil of Antisthenes, he adopted a mode of life remarkable for simplicity. Believing that in order to be happy a man must shun riches, comfort, and all other pleasures of life, he wore little clothing, slept in a tub, and ate only the coarsest food. On a voyage to Aegina he was captured by pirates. Eventually he was sold as a slave to a rich man of Corinth, who freed him and made him the tutor of his children. Diogenes left no formal statement of his philosophy but set an example of upright and simple living. Many anecdotes are told of him, the most familiar one being the story of his going about with a lantern in search of an honest man.

Dionysius of Halicarnassus (d. about 7 B.C.), Greek literary critic, rhetorician, and historian who lived in Rome the last 22 years of his life. He wrote a history entitled *Roman Antiquities,* the history of Rome to about 264 B.C. in 20 volumes, of which the first ten have survived in their entirety. This work, though not based wholly on historic facts, is a valuable source of information on the life of the early Romans.

Dionysius the Areopagite, a first-century Athenian converted by Saint Paul. He has been credited with the authorship of certain Greek treatises on mystical subjects (*On the Heavenly Hierarchy, On the Ecclesiastical Hierarchy, On Divine Names, On Mystical Theology*), but they were probably written by an unknown fifth-century author, now usually styled "the Pseudo-Areopagite." These works were highly regarded in the Middle Ages and their authenticity was not challenged until the fifteenth century; since then they have continued to be a subject of controversy among ecclesiastical scholars.

Disney, Walt, in full **Walter Elias Disney** (1901–1966), American producer of animated motion picture cartoons, born in Chicago, where he studied at the Art Institute. After a brief career as a commercial artist in Kansas City, Disney went to Hollywood, Cal., and began producing animated cartoons. For some years he experimented with various types of characters and finally originated Mickey Mouse, who immediately became popular. A second success, *Silly Symphonies,* soon followed. In 1937 he produced the first full-length animated cartoon feature picture, *Snow White and the Seven Dwarfs.* Later he produced the full-length pictures *Pinocchio* (1939), *Fantasia* (1940), *Bambi* (1942), *Alice in Wonderland* (1951), *Cinderella* (1950), and *Lady and the Tramp* (1955). He also produced the feature-length nature films *The Living Desert* (1953), *Vanishing Prairie* (1955), and *The African Lion* (1955). In 1955 he opened Disneyland, an amusement park. He died Dec. 15, 1966 in Los Angeles, Cal.

Disraeli, Benjamin, 1st Earl of **Beaconsfield** (1804–1881), British statesman, prime minister, and author, born in London, the son of Isaac D'Israeli, poet and novelist. The family was Jewish but Disraeli's parents adopted the Christian faith, and all their children were baptized in the Church of England. Benjamin was educated under his father's direction and before entering politics traveled in Europe for three years. In 1826 he published his first novel, *Vivian Grey.* He was determined to enter Parliament, however, and in 1837 was elected. With a program of social and political reform, Disraeli was soon a notable figure. He held his first cabinet post—chancellor of the exchequer under Lord Derby—in 1852, and was reappointed in succeeding ministries in 1858 and 1866. He sponsored the reform bill, passed in 1867, enlarging the franchise, and in 1868 he became prime minister. Though his ministry was defeated within a year, he assumed office again in 1874 and for six years guided the nation through one of the most brilliant administrations of its history.

The keynote of Disraeli's policy was aggressive imperialism. In domestic affairs he was a friend of the poor; in foreign matters he labored to exalt the British empire. He bought enough shares in the Suez Canal to gain its control by Britain; advised Queen Victoria to assume the title of Empress of India; withheld from Russia the spoils of victory in its clash with Turkey; and acquired Cyprus for Britain. Queen Victoria honored him by creating him earl of Beaconsfield in 1876. In 1878 he was English plenipotentiary at the Congress of Berlin. In 1880 his ministry was overthrown. Disraeli was the author of *Vindication of the British Constitution* (1835) and the novels *The Young Duke* (1831), *Henrietta Temple* (1837), *Coningsby* (1844), *Sybil* (1845), *Tancred* (1847), *Lothair* (1870), and *Endymion* (1880).

Döbereiner, Johann Wolfgang (1780–1849), German chemist. He developed what is known as Döbereiner's lamp, a piece of platinum sponge that ignites a jet of hydrogen in the presence of oxygen. This was in use before the introduction of sulfur matches. He also discovered furfural, a compound now used in making plastics. His recognition and classification of the relationships between the properties of elements and their atomic numbers prepared the way for the periodic law.

Dodgson, Charles Lutwidge, pseudonym **Lewis Carroll** (1832–1898), English mathematician and author, educated at Rugby and Oxford. Dodgson lectured in mathematics at Oxford from 1855 to 1881, but he is remembered as the author of the children's classics *Alice's Adventures in Wonderland* (1865) and *Through the Looking Glass* (1872), which were illustrated by Sir John Tenniel. He also wrote *The Hunting of the Snark* (1876) and *Sylvie and Bruno* (1889).

Dole, Sanford Ballard (1844–1926), American lawyer and political leader in Hawaii, born in Honolulu, where his parents, Americans, were engaged in missionary work. Graduated from Williams College, he studied law in Boston and began practice in Honolulu. From 1887 to 1893 he was an associate justice in the Hawaii supreme court. In 1893 he headed the provisional government that replaced the rule of the deposed Queen Liliuokalani, and in 1894 he was elected constitutional president of the republic. Pres. Grover Cleveland's opposition postponed the annexation of Hawaii to the United States until 1898, after which a plan of government was worked out. From 1900 to 1903 Dole served as the first governor of the Territory of Hawaii; from 1904 to 1915 he was a judge in the United States district court for Hawaii.

Domenichino, Il, real name **Domenico Zampieri** (1581–1641), Italian painter, born in Bologna. He studied in Bologna and in 1602 went to Rome with Guido Reni, a fellow student, and studied at the Carracci Academy. Here he assisted in decorating many buildings, including the Farnese Palace. In 1617 he returned to Bologna. In 1621 Pope Gregory XV appointed him chief architect of the Vatican, and in 1630 he was commissioned to do work in the cathedral of Naples. His works include the *Communion of St. Jerome* (the Vatican), *Pieta, St. Cecilia, Ascension of Magdalen,* and *Adam and Eve.*

Dollfuss, Engelbert (1892–1934), Austrian statesman, educated at the universities of Vienna and Berlin. During World War I he was an officer in a Tyrolean regiment. He then entered public life as secretary of a league of peasants. In 1931 he became minister of agriculture and forestry in the Austrian cabinet; in 1932 he was named chancellor of Austria. He proclaimed a dictatorship in 1933, abolishing freedom of speech, press, and assemblage. He was assassinated by Nazi rebels.

Dominic, Saint (1170–1221), Spanish monk, founder of the Dominican order. He became canon of the cathedral at Osma in Castile in 1195, and was sent by Pope Innocent III to preach to the dissenting Albigenses in southern France. Out of this crusade arose his order of friars, which Pope Honorius III confirmed in 1216. Dominic lived austerely and devoted himself to arduous toil in behalf of the order. He was canonized in 1234.

Donatello, real name **Donato di Niccolo di Betto Bardi** (c.1386–1466), Italian sculptor of the early Renaissance, born in Florence. Breaking away from the ideals of the Classic school, he introduced intense realism and dramatic action into his work. He was an associate of Brunelleschi, Ghiberti, and Michelozzo; Cosimo de' Medici was his friend and patron.

Donatello's scores of figures in bronze and marble adorn the galleries and churches of Florence, Rome, and Venice. Among his works in Florence are *John the Evangelist, St. George, St. Peter* and *St. Mark, Magdalen,* a colossal *David,* the monument of Pope John XXIII (in the Baptistery), and *Judith and Holofernes.* Among his sculptures in Rome is *Burial of Christ* in St. Peter's.

Donizetti, Gaetano (1797–1848), Italian operatic composer, born in Bergamo. Between 1819 and 1843 he composed a total of 64 operas, the best known being *Lucia di Lammermoor* (1835), based on Sir Walter Scott's *The Bride of Lammermoor*. The sparkling quality of the famous sextet from this opera is typical of Donizetti's work. In his comic operas *Don Pasquale* (1843) and *La fille du régiment* (*Daughter of the Regiment*, 1840), he showed a natural gift for comedy. *Lucrezia Borgia* (1833) ranks after *Lucia* among his tragic operas. He also wrote *Linda di Chamounix* (1842).

Donne, John (1572–1631), English poet and divine. Reared as a Roman Catholic, Donne was educated at Oxford, Cambridge, and Lincoln's Inn. He traveled on the Continent and accompanied the earl of Essex to Cádiz and the Azores (1596-1597). On his return he became secretary to Sir Thomas Egerton, the lord keeper, and it was at this time that most of his satires and love poems, including the *Songs and Sonnets*, were written. These were highly original, cynical, and frankly sensual. His career was ruined in 1601 when his secret marriage to Ann More, Egerton's niece, was discovered. For the next 14 years he lived in poverty, largely dependent on patronage. It was for one of his patrons, Sir Robert Drury, that he wrote *An Anatomie of the World* (1611) and *The Progresse of the Soul* (1612). In 1615, at the instigation of James I, Donne entered the church. He became dean of St. Paul's in 1621 and gained a reputation as the greatest preacher of his day. Thereafter, his poetry was essentially philosophical and religious. After a serious illness (1623–1624), he produced the *Devotions*, which were published during his lifetime, as were some sermons. Most of his work, however, appeared posthumously in 1633. Recognized by his contemporaries as the first and most prominent metaphysical poet, Donne was long neglected, but his work has been rediscovered in the twentieth century.

Dono, Paolo di. See *Ucello, Paolo*.

Doolittle, Hilda, pen name **H.D.** (1886–1961), American poet, born in Bethlehem, Pa. She attended Bryn Mawr for two years but left because of ill health. After writing for periodicals for a short time, she went to England (1911), where through the encouragement and guidance of Ezra Pound, she developed into a leading Imagist poet. In 1913 she married Richard Aldington, an English poet and novelist; the marriage ended in divorce in 1938. Among her many books of poetry are *Sea Garden* (1916), *Hymen* (1921), *Heliodora and Other Poems* (1924), *The Walls Do Not Fall* (1944), *Tribute to the Angels* (1945), and *The Flowering of the Rod* (1946). She also wrote several novels, including *Palimpsest* (1926), *Hedylus* (1928), and *The Hedgehog* (1937).

Doré, Paul Gustave (1833–1883), French illustrator and painter, born in Strasbourg. After a few years' study in Paris, he made his first series of sketches for the *Journal pour rire* in 1848 and gained immediate recognition. In 1861 he was decorated with the cross of the Legion of Honor. He illustrated many literary classics included among them are the works of François Rabelais, Honoré de Balzac's *Contes drolatiques*, Cervantes' *Don Quixote*, John Milton's *Paradise Lost*, and the Bible. He was less successful as a painter, but among his better-known works are *Christ's Entry into Jerusalem*, *Christ Leaving the Praetorium*, and *Retreat from Moscow*; the latter is in the Metropolitan Museum of Art in New York City.

Dorr, Thomas Wilson (1805–1854), American political leader, born in Providence, R.I. He was elected governor of Rhode Island in 1842 by the Rhode Island Suffrage Association, a party organized to oppose the law that limited the vote to landholders. A regularly-elected governor, inaugurated at the same time, received the support of the federal authorities, and Dorr fled to Connecticut. In 1844 he was sentenced to imprisonment for life but was released within a year. The adoption of a liberal constitution in 1842 was a direct result of "Dorr's Rebellion."

Dos Passos, John Roderigo (1896–), American author, born in Chicago, Ill., and graduated from Harvard in 1916. During World War I he served as a volunteer in the ambulance corps and then in the medical corps. In his novels he introduced innovating techniques, such as "newsreels," and montages of newspaper headlines, popular songs, and sketches of important figures; these paralleled or contrasted with the action of his characters. His work includes *Three Soldiers* (1921); *Manhattan Transfer* (1925); a trilogy called *U.S.A.*, which includes *The 42nd Parallel* (1930), *1919* (1932), and *The Big Money* (1936); *Adventures of a Young Man* (1939); *Number One* (1943); and *The Grand Design* (1949). Dos Passos has also written several plays and historical studies.

Dost Mohammed Khan (1793–1863), ruler of Afghanistan and founder of the Barakzai dynasty, which ruled until 1929. As khan of Kabul, Dost Mohammed gained control of Afghanistan in 1826 and assumed the title of amir in 1835. In 1834 he lost Peshawar to Ranjit Singh, the Sikh ruler of Punjab, and upon the refusal of the British in 1837 to help him regain it, he turned to Russia for aid. As a result, the British invaded Afghanistan, beginning the First Afghan War (1839–1842). Dost Mohammed was defeated and taken prisoner. Shah Shuja was then named amir but was assassinated in 1842 by Dost Mohammed's followers. When the British withdrew, they released Dost Mohammed, who reassumed the throne. He sided with the Sikhs in their war against the British (1845–1849), but in 1855 he signed a treaty with Britain and joined in the war against Persia (1857), winning Herat (1863).

Dostoevski, Fëdor Mikhailovich (1821–1881), one of the most important Russian novelists of the nineteenth century, born in Moscow, the son of a physician. He graduated from the Military School of Engineering in 1843 and served in the army, resigning to devote himself to literature. Dostoevski produced his first work, a long story called *Poor Folk*, in 1846. In 1849 he was arrested, tried, and sentenced to death for allegedly conspiring against the government. At the last moment the sentence was commuted to imprisonment in Omsk, Siberia. Dostoevski was pardoned in 1855 and four years later returned to St. Petersburg (Leningrad). There he resumed writing, publishing almost immediately *The House of Death* (1861)—a long story based on his experiences in prison. Dostoevski's other novels include *The Insulted and Injured* (1863), *Notes from the Underground* (1864), *Crime and Punishment* (1866), *The Idiot* (1869), *The Possessed* (1871), and *The Brothers Karamazov* (1880). These novels reveal Dostoevski's profound interest in psychology; he explores the psyche of the intellectual man, the evil man, and the "saint"—the godly man of pure spirit.

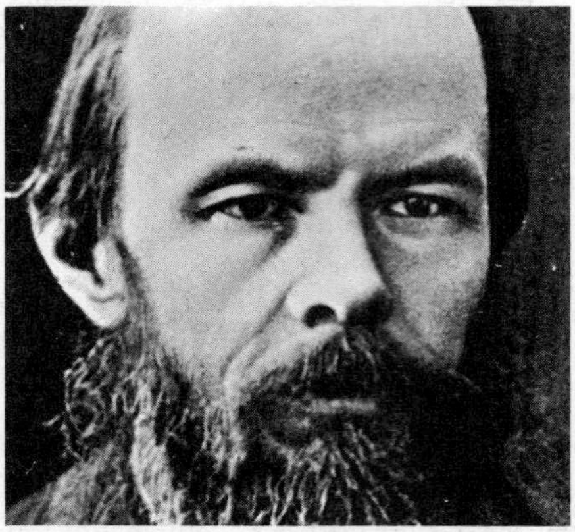

BETTMANN ARCHIVE

FËDOR DOSTOEVSKI

Douglas, John Sholto, 8th Marquis of **Queensberry** (1844–1900), English sporting enthusiast and a patron of boxing. In 1895 he defended in court a libel action brought against him by Oscar Wilde, who was a friend of his son, Lord **Alfred Bruce Douglas** (1870–1945). Douglas was acquited.

Douglas, Stephen Arnold (1813–1861), American statesman, born in Brandon, Vt. He spent his youth in the East; in 1833 he settled in Jacksonville, Ill., where, in 1834, he began practicing law. After a career as a state legislator and judge of the state supreme court, Douglas was elected to the House of Representatives in 1843 and served there until 1847. From 1847 until his death, he was a United States senator and a leading figure in the Democratic party. In 1854 he sponsored the Kansas-Nebraska Act through Congress; the bill reflected Douglas' belief in "popular sovereignty"—the right of each territory or state to decide the slavery question for itself. During his successful campaign for reelection to the Senate in 1858, he engaged his rival, Abraham Lincoln, in a series of debates. These famous Lincoln-Douglas debates established Douglas as an impressive public speaker and an adroit political leader. He left the party in 1860 when Pres. James Buchanan, a Democrat, refused to recognize the "popular sovereignty" principle. Running for president on an independent ticket, Douglas split the Democratic vote, thus enabling the Republican candidate, Abraham Lincoln, to win. However, when the threat of civil war was imminent, Douglas gave Lincoln and the Union his vigorous support. Douglas died of typhoid fever while on a speaking campaign for the Union.

Doumergue, Gaston (1863–1937), French statesman, born in Aignes-Vives, France. After a career as colonial magistrate in Indochina and Algiers, he became active in the Radical-Socialist party and was elected to three terms in the Chamber of Deputies, meanwhile holding various executive positions. In 1910 Doumerge was elected to the Senate. He was premier from December, 1913, to June, 1914, and in August, 1917, served as foreign minister. Forced to resign in 1914, he became minister of the colonies at the outbreak of World War I and in 1917 reentered the Senate, becoming its president in 1923. The following year Doumergue succeeded Miller as president of France, and served the full term of seven years. In 1934 he was called to the premiership in the midst of the Stavisky scandal. After nine months in office he resigned.

Doyle, Sir **Arthur Conan** (1859–1930), British novelist and physician, born in Edinburgh, educated at Stonyhurst and in Germany. From 1882 until 1890 he practiced medicine at Southsea, during which time he wrote *A Study in Scarlet* (1887), in which there appeared a private detective called Sherlock Holmes and his assistant Dr. Watson. During this time, he also wrote *Micah Clarke* (1888), *The Sign of the Four* (1889), and *The White Company* (1890). The success of these led to his final abandonment of medicine for literature. Other works include *The Adventures of Sherlock Holmes* (1891), *The Memoirs of Sherlock Holmes* (1894), *The Hound of the Baskervilles* (1902), and *The Return of Sherlock Holmes* (1904). He volunteered for medical service in the Boer War, and wrote *The Great Boer War* (1900) and *The War in South Africa* (1902) for which he was knighted. He also wrote a series of historical romances and a *History of the British Campaign in France and Flanders* (6 vols., 1915–1920).

Draco (7th century B.C.), Athenian legislator, who, in 621 B.C., codified and put into writing the common laws. Because even the smallest crimes were punishable by death, the Draconian code in later times was said to have been written in blood, not in ink. Draco, however, did not originate these harsh laws; on the contrary, he had set up a court of appeal to prevent injustice. Years later Solon modified the severity of the Draconian code.

Drake, Sir **Francis** (c.1540–1596), English navigator, born in Devonshire. He served as a sailor in a coasting vessel and afterwards joined Sir John Hawkins, a relative, in his last expedition against the Spaniards. As Drake grew older, he turned to privateering and enriched English coffers at the expense of Spanish shipping. His swift raids with two small ships on the Spanish Main bewildered his enemies and made him Spain's most feared and respected antagonist. In 1577 Drake made the most famous of his voyages. With five ships he plundered along the coasts of Peru and Chile and captured a galleon laden with jewels and gold. He then sailed north to about 48°, seeking a passage to the Atlantic, touched San Francisco, which he called New Albion, then steered for South Africa and England, the first Englishman to sail around the world. He arrived laden with treasure, and Queen Elizabeth knighted him in 1580. Five years later Drake was again attacking the Spaniards in the West Indies. His greatest triumph came in 1588, when the Spanish Armada, the most powerful flotilla ever assembled, set sail to invade England. Drake led the counterattack and, displaying superb seamanship, scattered and burned the Spanish fleet. This victory broke the power of Spain and made England mistress of the seas.

Dreiser, Theodore Herman Albert (1871–1945), American novelist and editor, born in Terre Haute, Ind. He began newspaper work on the Chicago *Daily Globe* in 1892, was soon connected with both the St. Louis *Globe-Democrat* and *Republic*, and in 1894 began an editor's career in New York. He was editor-in-chief of the Butterick publications from 1907 to 1910, and until 1934 he edited *The American Spectator*. During this time, he contributed stories and articles to various magazines and in

1900 published his first novel, *Sister Carrie,* which was censored and withdrawn from circulation. Other novels followed, and Dreiser's reputation soon became established. He is best known for *Jennie Gerhardt* (1911), *The Financier* (1912), *The Titan* (1914), and *An American Tragedy* (1925), his greatest success. A naturalist rather than a realist, one of his persistent themes is the oppression of the individual by the conventions of society and by external natural forces beyond his control. He also wrote verse, essays, and plays.

Drew, John, Jr. (1853–1927), American actor, born in Philadelphia, the son of John Drew, an Irish comedian, and actress Louisa Drew; uncle of John, Ethel, and Lionel Barrymore. He began his career in his parents' stock company, and in 1875 joined Augustin Daly's New York company. He soon became one of the foremost light comedians of the American stage, but was also noted for his Shakespearean roles. He appeared in such plays as *Taming of the Shrew, As You Like It, The School for Scandal,* and *Twelfth Night.* At the time of his death Drew was acting in an all-star revival of Pinero's *Trelawney of the Wells.* His portrayals were polished, intelligent, and touched with a flavor of the romantic.

Dreyfus, Alfred (1859–1935), French army officer, born in Alsace of Jewish descent, central figure in the Dreyfus affair. Dreyfus entered the army in 1882, reached the rank of captain of artillery in 1889, and in 1891 was appointed to the general staff. In 1894 he was accused of having sold military secrets to Germany; on the basis of the alleged similarity of his handwriting to that on the documents in question, he was arrested and charged with treason. After an unfair trial, throughout which he protested his innocence, he was sentenced to penal servitude for life and was sent to Devil's Island, off the coast of French Guiana. The case was reopened after disclosures that pointed to a gross injustice, and in 1899 a second court martial was held at Rennes. By a vote of five to two Dreyfus was again declared guilty "with extenuating circumstances" and condemned to ten years' imprisonment. He was pardoned, however, by Pres. Émile Loubet.

Supporters of Dreyfus included Georges Clemenceau, Anatole France, and Émile Zola. Zola, who published *J'accuse,* a summary of the evidence against the army, was imprisoned for a year. It was not until 12 years after the accusation was made that Dreyfus' name was vindicated (1906). He was reinstated in the army and promoted to the rank of major. In World War I, he commanded a fort protecting Paris and was promoted to a lieutenant colonel. He was given the cross of the Legion of Honor in 1919. However, the effects and implication of the scandal were far reaching and long lasting for the political, religious, social, and intellectual factions in France.

Drinkwater, John (1882–1937), English poet and playwright, born near London. He studied at Oxford High School and, at the age of 19, entered the insurance business. Long before he gave up business, he began writing verse and plays. He published his first volume, *Poems,* in 1903 and in 1911 his first play, *Cophetua.* This was performed in Birmingham by The Pilgrim Players, an amateur society he helped to found and which eventually became The Birmingham Repertory Theatre. His first successful play, *Abraham Lincoln,* was performed by this group in 1918. The plays, *Mary Stuart* (1919), *Oliver Cromwell* (1921), *Robert E. Lee* (1923) and *Robert Burns* (1925) followed. His comedy *Bird In Hand* was successfully produced in New York and London in 1928. Among Drinkwater's other works, are *Poems, 1908–1914;* literary monographs; biographies of Byron, Swinburne, and Shakespeare; and two autobiographical volumes, *Inheritance* (1931) and *Discovery* (1932).

Drummond, Henry (1851–1897), Scottish clergyman and biologist, noted for his attempts to reconcile the doctrines of Christianity with the theory of evolution. He was born in Stirling and educated at the University of Edinburgh. After studying for the ministry at New College, he was appointed lecturer of natural history and science at Free Church School, Glasgow, in 1877. In 1884 he was professor of theology in the New Jerusalem Church. His books include *Natural Law in the Spiritual World* (1883), *The Greatest Thing in the World* (1890).

Drusus, Nero Claudius Germanicus, called **Drusus Senior** (38–9 B.C.), Roman general and governor of Gaul (13–10 B.C.). He was the stepson and successor of the emperor Augustus and younger brother of Tiberius. Married to Mark Antony's daughter, Antonia, he was the father of the emperor Claudius and of Germanicus Caesar. His place in history is that of a brilliant military leader. Between 19 and 9 B.C., when he was killed in a fall from his horse, he subdued the Alpine tribes, the Gauls and their German allies, and several other barbarian peoples who were revolting against Roman supremacy. Drusus also promoted the construction of canals, bridges, and other public works.

Dryden, John (1631–1700), English poet, critic, and playwright, born in Northamptonshire. Upon graduating from Trinity College, Cambridge in 1654, he entered upon a literary career, succeeding Sir William Davenant as poet laureate in 1670. His *Essay of Dramatic Poesy* (1668), according to Dr. Johnson, created the school of English criticism. Of Dryden's plays, *Marriage-à-la-mode* (1673) and *All For Love* (1678) are the most memorable; but he was more successful with his poetry, the chief of which are his satires, notably *Absalom and Achitophel* (1681), an attack on Lord Shaftesbury. Other poems include *Mac Flecknoe* (1682), an attack on Thomas Shadwell; *The Hind and the Panther* (1687), written in defense of Roman Catholicism; and the remarkable short lyric *Alexander's Feast* (1697). In his old age he translated Virgil and Juvenal.

du Barry, Comtesse **Marie Jeanne Bécu** (1746–1793), French adventuress, daughter of Anne Bécu, and mistress of Louis XV of France, who was so under the sway of her beauty and charm that he let her dominate him and his court for five years. When Louis died in 1774, she was banished from court, but due to the intercession of the queen her château near Versailles was restored to her. She remained there until the French Revolution. In 1793 Robespierre had her tried and guillotined on charges of wasting public funds, conspiracy, and wearing mourning for the late king. Du Barry was her legal name, as she had married Comte Guillaume du Barry in 1768.

Duchamp, Marcel (1887–), French painter, born in Blainville, France, and brother of the sculptor Raymond Duchamp-Villon (1876–1918). Duchamp is best known for his *Nude Descending a Staircase* (1912), one of the most famous cubist paintings. An attempt to depict movement by a repetition of forms, the canvas caused a sensation when it was exhibited in New York at the 1913 Armory Show—the first major exhibit in the United States of contemporary European art. For the next four years Duchamp produced no major work, although he strongly influenced the Dadaists. In 1920 he gave up painting and devoted himself to chess and experiments in optics. Most of his paintings are in the Philadelphia Museum of Art.

Dudevant, Aurore. See *Sand, George.*

Dufy, Raoul (1877–1953), French painter, born in Le Havre. In 1900 he went to study art at the École des Beaux-Arts in Paris. There he was at first attracted by the work of the Impressionists Claude Monet and Camille Pissaro, but he turned Fauvist from 1905 to 1909. During the next four years his style was influenced by his study of the late works of Paul Cézanne. It was at this time he did the illustrations for Guillaume Apollinaire's *Le Bestiare* (1911), which first brought him to public attention. About 1920 Dufy developed a definite personal style, painting gay, brightly-colored canvases. Among his best-known works are *The Sea at Le Havre, Trouville, Boulevard at Nice, Regatta at Le Havre, Panorama of Paris, The Park at St. Cloud,* and *Antibes.*

Dukas, Paul (1865–1935), French composer, born in Paris. He studied at the Paris Conservatoire (1882–1889) and in 1888 won the second Prix de Rome with his cantata *Velléda.* He became known for his overture to Pierre Corneille's *Polyeucte* (1891), *Symphony in C* (1896), and *L'Apprenti-Sorcier* (*The Sorcerer's Apprentice,* 1897), his most popular work. Dukas' other work includes music for the opera *Airane et Barbe-Bleue* (*Ariadne and Bluebeard,* 1907), based on a text by Maurice Maeterlinck, and the ballet *La Péri* (1912).

Dulles, John Foster (1888–1959), American lawyer and statesman, born in Washington, D.C. He graduated from Princeton in 1908 and received a law degree from George Washington University in 1911; he then practiced law in New York. He served in World War I, was a member of the U.S. delegation at the Paris peace conference (1918–1919), and a member in 1919 of the German reparations committee. In 1945 he became an adviser to the U.S. delegation of the United Nations and urged Senate ratification of the UN charter. As the Republican party's expert on foreign policy, he was present as an adviser at important diplomatic conferences. In 1947 Dulles was appointed U.S. delegate to the UN General Assembly, where he advocated a bipartisan foreign policy and supported the Marshall plan and the ECA. Pres. Dwight Eisenhower appointed him secretary of state (1953–1959). Dulles played an important role in negotiating the Japanese peace treaty following World War II.

Dumas, Alexandre, called **Dumas père** (1802–1870), French novelist and playwright, born in Villers-Cotterets, the son of a general under Napoleon. His father's parents had been a French nobleman of Haiti and a Negress of the island. Educated by a priest, Dumas became a clerk in a local law office. In 1823 he went to Paris, found work as a secretary in the home of the future King Louis Philippe, and in 1829 had his play, *Henry III and His Court,* successfully produced. After a period of playwriting, during which he wrote *Christine* (1830), *Napoleon Bonaparte, Antony,* and *Richard Darlington* (all produced in 1831), he began a series of novels and narratives of adventure and romance that are still popular today. Such works as *The Count of Monte Cristo* (1844–1845), *The Three Musketeers* (1844), *Twenty Years After* (1845), and *The Vicomte de Bragelonne* (26 vols., 1848–1850) made Dumas famous and wealthy. He squandered his money, however, and in his last years, when ill and impoverished, was cared for by his son. Dumas permitted his name to appear on the title pages of about 300 novels, but some of these were written by hirelings whom he supplied with ideas, and some were merely revised by him. He left enough of his own work, however, to place him among the great writers of fiction.

Dumas, Alexandre, called **Dumas fils** (1824–1895), French playwright and novelist, illegitimate son of Dumas père. He is best known as the author of *La Dame aux camélias* (called *Camille* in English). Originally written as a novel (1848), it was dramatized in 1852 and proved very successful on the stage. Beginning in 1853 Dumas wrote a series of plays that evidenced his preoccupation with morality and ethics. They include *La Question d'argent* (1857), *Le Fils naturel* (1858), *Le Pere prodigal* (1859), *Les Idées de Madame Aubray* (1867), *La Femme de Claude* (1873), and *L'Etrangère.* His *Entr'actes* are four volumes of social essays.

Dumas, Jean Baptiste André (1800–1884), French chemist, born in Alais. In 1821 he served as tutor in the polytechnic school in Paris and then as professor of chemistry in the École de Médecine. His researches in organic chemistry, on atomic weights, sulfuric ether, and the law of substitution attracted the attention of the world of science. In 1875 he was elected to the Académie Francaise.

du Maurier, Daphne (1907–), English novelist, noted for her romantic and exciting tales. Born in London, she is the granddaughter of Georges du Maurier. Her fascinating family is brought alive in *Gerald, a Portrait* (1934) and *The du Mauriers* (1937), two clever and rather frank stories about them. Du Maurier first achieved popular recognition with the publication of *Jamaica Inn* (1936), a fast-moving adventure story. *Rebecca* (1938), her best-known work, is a gothic novel about a second wife who is haunted by the eerie experiences of her predecessor. Other works include *The Loving Spirit* (1931), *Frenchman's Creek* (1942), *My Cousin Rachel* (1952), and *Flight of the Falcon* (1965).

du Maurier, George Louis Palmella Busson (1834–1896), English artist and novelist, grandfather of Daphne du Maurier, born in Paris. At the age of 17 he went to London and began studying art. In 1865 he joined the staff of *Punch,* and for years his sketches of social life were a feature of its pages. He began writing late in life, illustrating and publishing *Peter Ibbetson* (1891) and *Trilby* (1894), both of which were dramatized for the stage. A third novel, *The Martian* (1896), appeared after his death.

Dunbar, Paul Laurence (1872–1906), American Negro poet, born in Dayton, Ohio, of parents who had been slaves. His first volume of poems was *Oak and Ivy* (1893), followed by *Majors and Minors* (1895) and *Lyrics of Lowly Life* (1896), which had an introduction by William Dean Howells and established his literary reputation. Many of his poems were written in dialect. Other volumes include *Lyrics of the Hearthside* (1899), *The Fanatics* (1901), and *The Sport of the Gods* (1902), one of his four novels.

Dunsany, Edward John Moreton Drax Plunkett, 18th Baron (1878–1957), Irish playwright and poet, served in the Boer War and World War I. His first play, *The Glittering Gate*, was produced in 1909 by W. B. Yeats in the Abbey Theatre, Dublin. Other plays followed, including *A Night at an Inn* (1916), *If* (1921), and *Alexander* (1925). Among his books are *The Gods of Pegana* (1905), *Evil Kettle* (1926), *Fifty Poems* (1929), and *Travel Tales of Mr. Joseph Jorkens* (1931). His autobiographical works are *Patches of Sunlight* (1938), *While Sirens Slept* (1944), and *The Sirens Wake* (1945).

Duns Scotus, John, known as **Doctor Subtilis** (c.1265–c.1308), Franciscan theologian and philosopher, born in Duns, Scotland. He studied at Oxford University where in 1301 he became professor of theology. Duns Scotus, one of the most eminent of the Franciscans, founded the scholastic system called Scotism and was the chief opponent of the Dominicans, who adhered to the theological teachings of Thomas Aquinas. The Thomists and the Scotists were particularly opposed on the issue of the Immaculate Conception of the Virgin Mary, which Duns Scotus brilliantly defended in Paris in 1304. He also contended that divine revelation is essential to an understanding of religious truths.

Dunstan, Saint (c.925–988), English philosopher and archbishop of Canterbury, born near Glastonbury, educated at the school connected with the monastery there. He was appointed abbot of Glastonbury by Edmund (c.943), and under both Edmund (r. 940–946) and Edred (r. 946–955) Dunstan enjoyed great influence in ecclesiastical and court circles; but he was banished by Edwy (r. 955–959) in 956 because he criticized the new king's attitude toward the Church and denounced his forthcoming marriage. On the accession of Edgar in 959 Dunstan was recalled, and in 961 he was created archbishop of Canterbury. He had much to do with the success of the king's reign. He retained his importance during the reign of Edward (975–978), but his influence declined upon the accession of Ethelred II in 978.

du Pont, a family of American manufacturers. The line starts with **Pierre Samuel du Pont de Nemours** (1739–1817), French statesman and economist. He was one of the diplomats who discussed American independence in 1783 and who drafted the treaty recognizing the United States. A member of the States-General in 1789, he was imprisoned in 1792 because of his reactionary views. He lived in the United States from 1799 to 1802, returning to France to become a member of the commission that negotiated the Louisiana Purchase. He published a number of works on commerce and politics; his correspondence with Pres. Thomas Jefferson from 1798 to 1817 has also been published. He lived in the United States after 1815.

His son, **Éleuthère Irénée du Pont** (1771–1834), born in Paris, was taken by Lavoisier into the royal powder works at the age of 17. He learned to make explosives, but in 1791 took over his father's printing plant. During the Revolution he was arrested three times; finally the Jacobins sacked the shop, and du Pont, with his father and a brother, **Victor Marie du Pont** (1767–1827), emigrated to America. In 1802 they set up a gunpowder mill near Wilmington, Del., that was instantly successful and that has since grown to be one of the largest industrial establishments in the world, producing chemicals, plastics, and dyes.

Three brothers were leaders in its development in the twentieth century: **Pierre Samuel du Pont** (1870–1954), **Irénée du Pont** (1876–1963), and **Lammot du Pont** (1880–1952). The descendants of the original family have now spread throughout the U.S., and many are active in the Du Pont Company.

Dupré, Jules (1811–1889), French landscape painter of the Barbizon school, born in Nantes. He studied in Paris, but his most valuable lessons were learned through study of the masters in the Louvre and personal contact with nature. Dupré excelled in depicting nature in her darker moods and melancholy aspects. The Metropolitan Museum, New York, possesses several of his canvases, including *Old Oak, Hay Wagon,* and *Summer*. Among Dupré's other notable pictures are *Interior of a Forest, Valley of Montmorency, Environs of Southampton,* and *Storm at Sea*.

Dürer, Albrecht (1471–1528), German painter, draftsman, and engraver, leader of the German Renaissance school. He was born in Nürnberg, the son of a goldsmith, and in boyhood learned his father's craft. In 1486, at his own request, he began the study of painting under Michel Wohlgemuth, with whom he studied for about three years. Then followed several years of travel and study, including two visits to Venice. Later he studied the works of the Flemish painters in The Netherlands. He returned to Nürnberg, and from 1505–1520 perfected his woodcuts, copper engravings, and drawings. Dürer was court painter to the emperors Maximilian I and Charles V. Among his paintings are his masterpiece *Four Apostles* (Munich), *Adoration of the Magi* (Uffizi, Florence), *The Feast of the Rose Garlands* (Prague), *Charles the Great* (Nürnberg), and numerous portraits. His genius as a copperplate engraver is represented by *Melancholia I, Knight, Death and the Devil, St. Jerome in His Study,* and *Adam and Eve. The Four Horsemen of the Apocalypse* is one of his famous woodcuts. Dürer is considered the inventor of etching.

Durrell, Lawrence (1912–), British novelist and poet, noted for his elaborate prose with its rich and complex imagery. He was born in Julundur, India and educated at the College of St. Joseph in Darjeeling, India, and at St. Edmund's School, Canterbury. He has held a number of jobs including those of jazz pianist and teacher. From 1941 until 1956, he served the British foreign office as a press attaché and public relations director, and lived in Cairo (1941–1944), Alexandria (1944–1945), Rhodes (1945–1947), Argentina (1947–1949), Yugoslavia (1949–1952), and Cyprus (1952–1956). The settings of Durrell's novels reflect the influence of these extensive travels and his acute sensitivity to atmosphere. *Justine* (1957), his best-known work, is particularly noteworthy for its exotic depiction of Alexandria. It is the first book of the *Alexandria Quartet*, which also includes *Balthazar* (1958), *Mounolive* (1959), and *Clea* (1960). Among Durrell's other works are *Prospero's Cell* (1945), *Bitter Lemons* (1957), *Esprit de Corps* (1957); *Cities, Plains and People*, a collection of poetry (1946); and *Sappho*, a play (1950).

Duse, Eleonora (1859–1924), Italian actress, born near Venice, the daughter of traveling players. She appeared on the stage when a child, and after a period of discouragement, won recognition in Naples in 1897. Thereafter her position as an actress of first rank was acknowledged throughout Europe and America. In 1895 she and Sarah Bernhardt both played in *Magda* in a contest to determine the best actress. A quarrel with Gabriele D'Annunzio, who wrote many of the plays in which she had the leading role, and his frank revelations of her private life in his *Flame of Life,* led to her retirement in 1902. In 1921 she reappeared on the stage in order to regain the fortune that she lost in World War I. Her great roles include the heroines in *La Dame aux camélias, La Tosca, La Gioconda, Cavalleria Rusticana, The Second Mrs. Tanqueray, Rosmersholm,* and *Hedda Gabler*. Duse was perhaps the greatest tragic actress of modern times.

Dvořák, Anton (1841–1904), Czech composer, born in Bohemia. When his early training in music was cut short by lack of funds, he found employment playing the viola in bands and orchestras. An engagement at the new Bohemian Theatre in Prague (1862) gave him an opportunity to study Beethoven's scores, and he later began a successful career as a composer of symphonies, operas, chamber music, sacred pieces, and instrumental music of a varied nature. Dvořák's compositions are national in spirit, vigorous, and original. He introduced two new forms—the dumka (elegy) and furiant (a scherzo). His chief works include *Stabat Mater* (1884), *Requiem Mass* (1891), *The Specter's Bride* (a cantata, 1885), *Slavonic Dances* (for the pianoforte, 1878), and *From the New World* (usually called *The New World Symphony,* 1893). His *Humoresque* for piano is his best-known short composition. He was engaged as director of the National Conservatory of Music in New York (1892–1895). After 1895 he lived in Prague where, from 1901 to 1904, he directed the Conservatorium.

Dykstra, Clarence Addison (1883–1950), American city manager and university president, born in Cleveland, Ohio, educated at the University of Iowa. He taught history and political science in a number of schools and universities, became known as an expert in civic affairs, and was often called into consultation and service in such matters. He served as city manager of Cincinnati, Ohio (1930–1937), and became internationally known for the efficiency of his administration in the flood of 1937. From 1937 to 1944 he was president of the University of Wisconsin. From 1944 he was provost of the University of California.

E

Eads, James Buchanan (1820–1887), American engineer and inventor, born in Lawrenceburg, Ind. He was a steamboat clerk before he mastered, largely on his own, the principles of engineering. His greatest achievements were the designing and construction of the three-span bridge at St. Louis that bears his name and the jetties at the mouth of the Mississippi River. He also built for the federal government seven ironclad gunboats, which were used in the capture of Fort Henry early in the Civil War.

Eakins, Thomas (1844–1916), American painter and sculptor, born in Philadelphia, Pa. He studied at the Pennsylvania Academy and taught there and in Paris. His paintings are notable for their plain, unadorned realism, and many have won wide acclaim. He painted portraits of Cardinal Martinelli, Dr. Gilbert L. Parker, Louis Kenton, Carroll Beckwith, and P. Hayes Agnew. Other works include *The Chess Players, The Cello Player, Clinic of Dr. Agnew,* and *The Crucifixion*. His sculptures include the horses on the Brooklyn Soldiers' and Sailors' Monument and two reliefs on the Trenton battle monument.

Earhart, Amelia (1898–1937), American aviator, born at Atchison, Kans., educated at schools in Atchison and Philadelphia; matriculated for medicine at Columbia University in 1919. On June 17, 1928, she flew from Newfoundland to Burry Point, Wales; in 1935 she flew from Honolulu to California—the first woman to fly the Atlantic and the Pacific oceans. In 1932 she received the Distinguished Flying Cross. On July 2, 1937, flying 2570 miles from New Guinea to Howland Island on a leg of her nearly completed round-the-world flight, she was lost in the Pacific with her navigator, Capt. F. J. Noonan. Her autobiography, *Last Flight*, edited by her husband, George Palmer Putnam, was published posthumously the following year.

Early, Jubal Anderson (1816–1894), American soldier, born in Franklin County, Va. After his graduation from West Point in 1837, he practiced law, sat in the state legislature, and served in the Mexican War as major of Virginia volunteers. Although he opposed the secession of his state, Early gave his services to the Confederacy and was in action at the first battle of Bull Run, Chancellorsville, Gettysburg, and the Wilderness, rising to the rank of lieutenant general. Despite his defeats by Sheridan in the Shenandoah Valley and by Custer at Waynesboro, he was one of the ablest of the Confederate generals.

Eastlake, Sir **Charles Lock** (1793–1865), English painter, born at Plymouth, studied under Haydon, in the Royal Academy school, and in Paris. In 1855 he was director of the National Gallery. He pro-

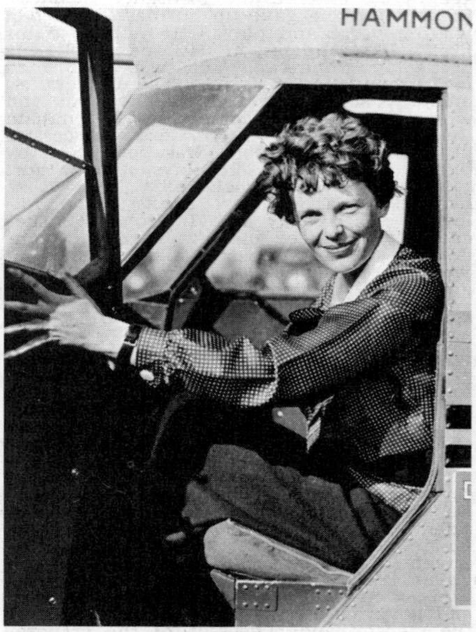

UNITED PRESS INTERNATIONAL

AMELIA EARHART

duced two full-length portraits of Napoleon. His other paintings are *Christ Blessing Little Children, Lord Byron's Dream, Pilgrims in Sight of Rome,* and *Christ Restoring Life to the Daughter of Jairus.* A style of machine-made furniture was named after him; it was similar to the William Morris style. He is also known for his *Materials for the History of Oil Painting* (1847). His wife, Lady **Elizabeth Rigby Eastlake** (1809–1893), author and art critic, edited many of his works.

Eastman, George (1854–1932), American inventor, born in Waterville, N.Y., and studied at Rochester, N.Y., where the large Eastman factories are now located. Out of amateur experiments he arrived at a process for making gelatin dry plates, and began their manufacture in 1880. He then devised and manufactured a small camera for amateurs that he named "Kodak," as well as a transparent rollable film. Eastman made generous use of his great fortune, donating about ninety million dollars to education and philanthropic enterprises. Eastman was the founder of the Eastman School of Music in Rochester.

Ebers, Georg Moritz (1837–1898), German novelist and Egyptologist, born in Berlin. He devoted many years to travel and study in connection with his favorite subject, Egyptology, and at various times was associate professor at Jena and Leipzig. His novels were written to describe ancient Egyptian life in a way that would appeal to public interest. They include *An Egyptian Princess* (3 vols., 1864), *Uarda* (1877), *The Sisters* (1880), and *Serapis* (1885). He also published stories of Dutch, German and Greek life. The *Papyrus Ebers* is a remarkable Egyptian medical treatise discovered and published by Ebers in 1875.

Ebert, Friedrich (1871–1925), first president of the German Republic (1919–1925), born in Heidelberg. He became a journeyman saddler, settled in Bremen, and was active there in the trades-union movement. The Social Democrats appointed him party leader in 1913 following his election to the Reichstag as party deputy in 1912. He was a liberal but not an extremist, and Germany owed much to his wise prudence during the upheavals of 1918. He helped form the first provisional government and was elected president of the Reich by the National Assembly in February, 1919. His term was extended to 1925, and he died in office.

Eck, Johann, original surname **Mayer** (1486–1543), German theologian, able opponent of Luther and the Reformation, born in Eck, Swabia, and educated at the leading German universities. He was a professor of theology at Ingolstadt in 1510. In 1519 he engaged in a famous disputation with Luther at Leipzig, and it was through his urging that Pope Leo X issued the bull of condemnation that Luther publicly burned. Doctor Eck took part in disputations at Baden and Basel and was present at the convocations at Worms (1540) and Ratisbon (1541). He made a German translation of the Old Testament.

Eckener, Hugo (1868–1954), German aeronaut, born in Flensburg. He joined the Zeppelin factory in 1908 and three years later was made a director. He brought the ZR 3 (later renamed the *Los Angeles*) to the United States from Germany in 1924, the first airship flight over the Atlantic. In 1929 he piloted the German dirigible *Graf Zeppelin,* which he built, on a round-the-world flight, and with the *Hindenburg* established regular commercial service between Germany and the United States.

Eckhart, Eckart or **Eckardt, Johannes,** called **Meister Eckhart** (c.1260–c.1327), German Dominican theologian, founder of German mysticism, born in Hochheim near Gotha. As a member of the Dominican order he taught and studied theology in Paris (1302), was appointed provincial of his order in Saxony (1303–1311), and vicar-general of Bohemia (1307). His preaching carried him to Paris, Strasbourg, and Cologne, where the archbishop accused him of heresy (1327). A few years after his death Pope John XXII condemned his writings, which consisted of treatises and sermons in Latin and German. His pantheistic philosophy, generating from Neoplatonism, scholasticism, and Arabic and Jewish concepts, later affected religious mysticism and speculative philosophy.

Eddington, Sir Arthur Stanley (1882–1944), English astronomer and physicist, born in Kendal, educated at Trinity College, Cambridge. He became a professor of astronomy at Cambridge in 1913 and director of its observatory a year later. He made many important contributions to knowledge of the evolution, motion, and structure of the stars and was an exponent of the theory of relativity. In his writings Eddington tried to reconcile science and religion, and to bring about a new understanding of the nature of the universe according to advanced theories. His most influential books were *Space, Time and Gravitation* (1920), *The Nature of the Physical World* (1928), *The Expanding Universe* (1933), and *New Pathways in Science* (1935). In 1939 Eddington was honored by the Order of Merit.

Eddy, Mary Morse Baker (1821–1910), founder of Christian Science, born in Bow, N.H. Severe injuries from a fall left Mary Eddy an invalid. She claimed that she overcame her invalid state not by physical means, but by discovering that disease is an illusion and can be cured by working on the mind—the doctrine of Christian Science. She wrote of her spiritual enlightenment in *Science and Health with Key to the Scriptures* (1875). Mrs. Eddy organized the "Church of Christ, Scientist," in Boston in 1879. Reorganized in 1892 as the First Church, it is recognized as the mother church by Christian Scientists. In addition to *Science and Health,* Mrs. Eddy wrote *Unity of Good* (1891), *Church Manual* (1895), and founded *The Christian Science Journal* and The Christian Science Publishing Society (1898), publishers of *The Christian Science Monitor* and *The Christian Science Quarterly.*

Eden, Sir **Anthony,** in full **Robert Anthony Eden,** Earl of **Avon** (1897–), English statesman, 7th baronet of Windlestone Hall, Durham, educated at Eton and Oxford. He served as a captain in World War I. Elected to Parliament in 1923, he served from 1926 to 1929 as private secretary to Sir Austen Chamberlain, who was then foreign secretary. From 1931 to 1933 he was undersecretary for foreign affairs; lord privy seal (1934–1935); and minister without portfolio for the League of Nations in 1935. Eden served as foreign secretary from 1935 to 1938, resigning after differences with Prime Minister Chamberlain over policy toward Fascist Italy. He served again under Winston Churchill, from 1940 until 1945. He was appointed foreign secretary and deputy prime minister in 1951. He became prime minister in 1955, but resigned because of ill health, in 1957 during the Suez crisis.

Edison, Thomas Alva (1847–1931), American inventor, born in Milan, Ohio, of mixed Dutch and Scottish descent. His formal schooling, in Port Huron, Mich., was slight; he gave his mother sole credit for his early instruction. When he was a boy of twelve, he sold newspapers on the Grand Trunk Railway; in 1862 he started a weekly paper, the *Grand Trunk Herald,* the first newspaper to be printed on a train. When a fire broke out in the section of the baggage car where he did the printing and which was a tiny experimental laboratory, Thomas was ordered off the train with a blow on the ear that eventually brought on permanent deafness. In later years Edison refused to have the trouble corrected, for he found that his world of silence was a help, rather than a hindrance, to a life of experiment and research. Another accident made him a railway telegrapher. He snatched a little boy out of the path of an oncoming train, and the child's father, a station master, offered to teach the youth telegraphy at the Mt. Clemens, Mich. office. Edison became a skilled operator and held positions at various stations in the United States and Canada. Meanwhile he continued studying and experimenting and by 1869 had become permanently interested in invention. In 1876 he set up a workshop in Menlo Park, N. J., but in 1887 transferred his activities to West Orange, N.J.

At the time he became a telegraph operator, only one message at a time could be sent over any single wire. He invented the duplex, the quadruplex, and then the sextuplex system that permits the transmission of six messages over the same wire at the same time. His carbon transmitter made the telephone much more efficient. He invented a phonograph with cylindrical records, creating thereby a new form of entertainment and a new industry, and later perfected a disk machine with a permanent diamondpoint needle. Edison was a pioneer in developing motion pictures, for the parent of the modern projection machine was the Edison kinetoscope in 1889, a peephole device that showed pictures in motion on a loop of film. He attempted talking pictures as early as 1913 but withdrew the combination of phonograph and camera because it was imperfect. The incandescent electric lamp is perhaps the most important of Edison's inventions. His inventions number in the hundreds and include the microphone, the electric pen and mimeograph, the alkaline storage battery, and the self-regulating dynamo for use on electric railways. He devised the first successful

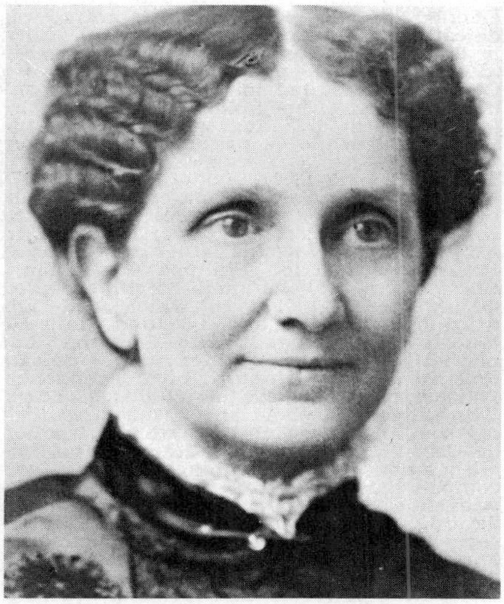

THE FIRST CHURCH OF CHRIST, SCIENTIST, BOSTON MASS.

MARY BAKER EDDY

carbon-filament lamp, and he perfected a system whereby current was properly divided among several circuits. After the outbreak of World War I he designed and operated chemical plants for making benzol and other materials required in industry.

Edmund or **Eadmund II,** called **Ironside** (c.980–1016), king of the English people (1016), the son of Ethelred the Unready. He rallied to his father's defense in 1015 when Canute, the Danish king, invaded England. In 1016 after Ethelred's death and Edmund's defeat at Assandun (Ashingdon in Essex), Canute and Edmund agreed to divide the kingdom between them, but Edmund died within a few weeks and the Danes took over all of England.

Edward or **Eadward,** called **the Confessor** (c.1002–1066), the last king of the Anglo-Saxon line (1042–1066), son of Ethelred the Unready and Emma of Normandy, born in Oxfordshire. He lived in Normandy until 1041, when he was invited to England by King Hardecanute, his half brother. (Edward's mother married Canute, the Dane, after Ethelred's death.) Edward was elected king in 1042 on Hardecanute's death and in 1045 married the daughter of Earl Godwin, leader of the Saxon party, who exercised more actual power than the quiet, monkish king. Edward the Confessor is renowned as the founder of Westminster Abbey. He was canonized in 1161 by Pope Alexander III, who bestowed on him the title Confessor.

Edward I, called **Longshanks** (1239–1307), king of England (1272–1307), eldest son of Henry III and Eleanor of Provence. In 1254 he married Eleanor of Castile, the half sister of the Spanish king. He became king in 1272, the first of eight rulers of England of that name. He succeeded in making Wales a part of the kingdom by 1284. The attempt to conquer the Scots cost Edward many years of fighting, and he died with Robert Bruce defying him as king of an independent Scotland. As an administrator Edward was one of England's great kings. He brought about greater democracy in Parliament by summoning to his Model Parliament in 1295 representatives of cities, boroughs, and towns, as well as churchmen and nobles. He established the principle that the monarch cannot levy taxes without the approval of Parliament.

Edward II (1284–1327), king of England (1307–1327), of the house of Anjou or Plantagenet, born in Caernarvon, Wales, the son of Edward I and Eleanor of Castile. As heir apparent he had been created Prince of Wales in 1301, a title to which the eldest son of each king has been eligible ever since. He succeeded his father in 1307. Against the wishes of his dying father, Edward created his Gascon favorite, Piers Gaveston, earl of Cornwall, and left him in command of his kingdom in 1308 when he departed for France to marry Isabella, Philip IV's daughter. The honors heaped upon Gaveston enraged the nobles and they demanded his banishment; twice he was compelled to leave England, and finally was captured and executed in 1312. Edward's reign was largely taken up by wars with Scotland and disputes with Charles IV of France over territory claimed by the English. His army was defeated by Robert Bruce at Bannockburn in 1314, and eventually Edward had to agree to a truce with Scotland. The trouble with Charles IV resulted in an uprising of banished nobles. The king was deposed by Parliament in 1327 and was murdered the same year while a prisoner in Berkeley Castle.

Edward III (1312–1377), king of England (1327–1377), of the house of Anjou or Plantagenet, born in Windsor, son and successor of Edward II. He was chosen king by Parliament in 1327, six days before his father was deposed. In 1328 he married Philippa of Hainault. His mother, Isabella, and Mortimer ruled as regents until 1330, at which time Edward banished her and executed him. He renewed the struggle with Scotland, but neither his invasions nor their defeats crushed the Scottish spirit of independence. In this reign began the Hundred Years' War between England and France, in which his son, the Black Prince, won distinction at Crécy and Poitiers. Although the English gained some advantage, Edward was compelled to agree to a truce in 1374, when both sides were too weakened to continue fighting. Edward's final years were also beset with difficulties at home. Public finance lapsed into ruin, Parliament disputed with him, and Edward, weakened by his defeats, yielded his power to his avaricious mistress, Alice Perrers, and his third son, John of Gaunt. The Black Prince died in 1376, and a year later the king passed away.

Edward IV (1442–1483), king of England (1461–1470; 1471–1483), of the house of York, the son of Richard, duke of York, and Cecily Neville, daughter of the first earl of Westmorland. Born in Rouen, he was given the title earl of March. He laid claim to the throne in 1461, two months after the death of his father at the battle of Wakefield (December, 1460) in the Wars of the Roses. Edward, as leader of the Yorkist faction, defeated the Lancastrians and was crowned king. When secretly he married Elizabeth, daughter of Richard Woodville (1464), his popularity diminished and he lost the allegiance of the earl of Warwick, who befriended the Lancastrian Queen Margaret and married his daughter Ann to her son Edward. King Edward's struggle with the Lancastrians continued, and in 1470 an uprising led by the earl of Warwick temporarily restored Henry VI, who had been imprisoned in London Tower. Edward again defeated the Lancastrians at Tewkesbury in 1471, murdered Prince Edward and probably Henry VI, and reigned until his death. During his reign Edward advocated the supremacy of the crown and paved the way for Tudor absolutism.

Edward V (1470–1483), king of England (April-June, 1483), of the house of York, son of Edward IV and Elizabeth Woodville, born in Westminster sanctuary. He succeeded his father in 1483 but never ruled. Before the date set for his coronation, he and his younger brother, the duke of York, were confined in the Tower by their paternal uncle, Richard, duke of Gloucester. The young princes were probably killed at Richard's command, for he ascended the throne as Richard III.

Edward VI (1537–1553), king of England and Ireland (1547–1553), of the house of Tudor, son of Henry VIII and Jane Seymour, born in Hampton Court. The boy prince was only ten when his father died (1547), and the young king's uncle, Edward Seymour, duke of Somerset, was the actual ruler for five years. Somerset was deposed and executed in 1552. His successor, John Dudley, duke of Northumberland, induced Edward, on his deathbed, to nominate Lady Jane Grey as his successor. After a reign of nine days she was executed. Mary I succeeded her.

Edward VII, in full **Albert Edward,** called **the Peacemaker** (1841–1910), king of Great Britain and Ireland (1901–1910), of the house of Saxe-Coburg, eldest son of Queen Victoria, born in Buckingham Palace. Created prince of Wales, he succeeded his mother in 1901. He was educated by private tutors and at the universities of Edinburgh, Oxford, and Cambridge, and in 1860 visited the United States and Canada. The year 1863 marked his entrance into the House of Lords and his marriage to Alexandra, eldest daughter of Christian IX of Denmark. They had six children; the eldest surviving son succeeded his father as George V in 1910. Prince Albert Edward was long the representative of Queen Victoria in social and public gatherings and was keenly interested in art, science, and charity, besides being an enthusiastic sportsman. His reign of nine years was notable for his efforts to promote friendly relations among the countries of the world, and he was popular throughout the British Empire.

Edward VIII, in full **Edward Albert Christian George Andrew Patrick David** (1894–), king of Great Britain and Ireland (1936), of the house of Windsor, eldest son of King George V and Queen Mary, born in White Lodge, Richmond, Surrey. He was prepared for the navy, entered Osborne in 1907, the Royal Naval College at Dartmouth in 1909, and in 1911 served as midshipman on H.M.S. *Hindostan.* His investiture as prince of Wales in July, 1911, was an innovation in that it took place in Wales. The prince enrolled as a student at Oxford in 1912 but left at the outbreak of World War I, in which he showed an eagerness to share all the hardships and dangers of the soldiers. After the war he visited all parts of the British empire, the United States, and South American countries. On the death of his father, January 20, 1936, he became king. On December 11, still uncrowned, he abdicated the throne to marry Mrs. Wallis Warfield Simpson, an American who, because she had been twice divorced, was unacceptable to the British government as the king's consort. Edward then left England and was made duke of Windsor. His brother succeeded him as King George VI.

Edward, Prince of **Wales,** known as **the Black Prince** (1330–1376), the eldest son of Edward III of England. His popular name, bestowed long after his death, was derived from the black armor worn by him at the battle of Crécy, where, as a lad of 16, he led an army division to victory. In 1356 at the battle of Poitiers, he captured the French king, John II, subsequently taking him to London for ransom. In 1361 he married Joan, the Fair Maid of Kent, who gave him two sons, one the future Richard II. Prince Edward's valor and his ability as ruler of Gascony and Aquitaine did not prevent the gradual decline of English power in France, and in 1371 he returned home an invalid.

Edwards, Jonathan (1703–1758), American theologian, born in East Windsor, Conn. He graduated from Yale in 1720 at the head of his class, and was pastor of a church in Northampton, Mass. from 1727 to 1750. A great exponent of evangelism and of strict Calvinism, Edwards aroused opposition in his parish by ruling that only those who had been converted should partake of the Lord's Supper. This stand led to his dismissal, and from 1751 to 1758, while he was a missionary to the Indians at Stockbridge, he wrote his famous book on theology, *An Inquiry into the Freedom of the Will* (1754). Edwards accepted the presidency of the College of New Jersey (now Princeton University) in 1758.

Egbert or **Ecgberht** (c.775–839), first king of Anglo-Saxon England (802–839) to become overlord of all other Saxon kings, the son of Ealhmund, a descendant of the early Wessex kings. Upon the death of Cynegils (786), Egbert laid claim to the Wessex kingdom, but had to flee to the court of Charlemagne to escape the hostility of the king of Wessex. In 802 he returned to England, became king of the West Saxons and subsequently conquered Cornwall, Mercia, Kent, and Northumbria. He became supreme overlord in 829. He successfully defended the country against an invading northern host in 837. Egbert left the throne to his son Ethelwulf.

Ehrenburg, Ilya Grigorievich (1891–1967), Russian writer, born in Kiev. In 1906 he joined the Bolshevik party, and two years later was arrested. In 1909 he escaped and fled to Paris. After the Bolshevik revolution he went back to Russia, but returned to Paris in 1921. His notable works include *Nicholas Kourbov* (1922), *Micheal Lykow* (1929), *Factory of Dreams* (1931), *The Adventures of Julio Jurento* (English translation 1930), and *The Fall of Paris* (1941). He died Sept. 2, 1967 in Moscow.

Ehrlich, Paul (1854–1915), German bacteriologist, born in Silesia, educated at the universities of Breslau, Strasbourg, Freiburg, and Leipzig. His standardized diphtheria antitoxin was widely used, and he did valuable research work in histology of the blood and in immunity. His most important discovery was the specific salvarsan, or "606," for the treatment of syphillis. In 1908 Ehrlich shared with Élie Metchnikoff the Nobel Prize for medicine.

Eichmann, Adolf (1906–1962), Nazi German official. During World War II Eichmann was in charge of the Gestapo's Bureau of Jewish Affairs. At the war's end he escaped from Germany, but was captured in Argentina in 1960 by Israeli agents. He was tried by a special court in Jerusalem, under Israeli law, for his responsibility for the deportation and death of millions of Jews in World War II. He was found guilty and executed.

Eiffel, Alexandre Gustave (1832–1923), French engineer, born in Dijon, famed as the designer and builder of the great tower in Paris that bears his name (1887–1889). He built the framework for the Statue of Liberty in New York harbor, made designs for the Panama Canal locks, and constructed several bridges and viaducts, including the iron bridge over the Garonne River, Bordeaux. His *Resistance of the Air and Aviation* (translated, 1913) is an authoritative discussion of aeronautic mechanics.

Einstein, Albert (1879–1955), American physicist, formulator of the theory of relativity. Born in Germany of Jewish parentage, he was educated in Munich and in Switzerland, where he became a naturalized citizen in 1894. While in Switzerland he announced his special theory of relativity (1905). In 1909 Einstein joined the faculty of Zurich University, in 1911 was professor of physics at Prague, and in 1912 returned to Zurich to become full professor of theoretical physics at the Federal Institute of Technology. In 1914 he received a research professorship at the Kaiser Wilhelm Physical Institute in Berlin, enabling him to devote his entire time to study. The publication of his paper on general relativity in 1916 and of one on the unity of gravitation, electricity, and magnetism in 1929 were sensational events in the world of science. He also published original papers elucidating the Brownian movement and Planck's quantum theory. In 1921 he received the Nobel Prize for physics. Einstein received acclaim on his

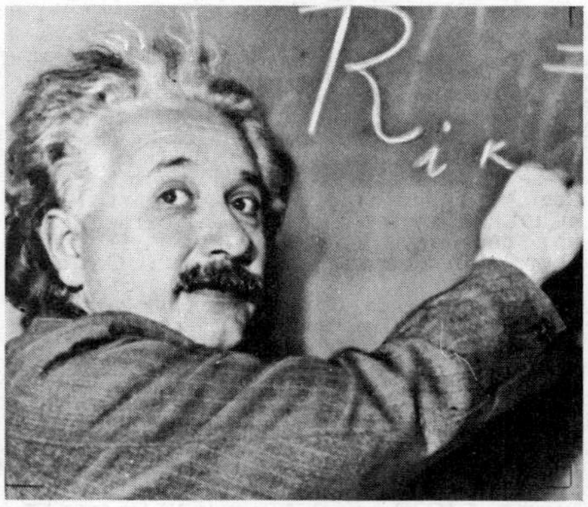

WIDE WORLD

ALBERT EINSTEIN

visits to the United States in 1930 and 1931. In 1933 he left Germany, and his property was confiscated; in 1934 he was deprived of his citizenship by the Nazi government. After offers from universities throughout the world, he finally came back to America as head of the school of mathematics at the Institute for Advanced Study at Princeton. He became a naturalized American citizen in 1940. In September, 1939, he wrote his famous letter to Pres. Franklin Roosevelt on the possible creation of a powerful bomb based on atomic fission, and the perils the world would face if Germany produced one before the United States. At the conclusion of the war, however, he campaigned for the international control of atomic weapons. In 1950 he announced completion of his new theory, a unification of his previous theories. His notable works include *The Meaning of Relativity* (1923), *On the Method of Theoretical Physics* (1933), *Why War?* (coauthored with Sigmund Freud, 1933), and *The World as I See It* (1934).

Eisenhower, Dwight David (1890–), thirty-fourth president of the United States (1953–1961), Allied commander in chief during World War II. Born in Denison, Tex., he was raised in Abilene, Kans. He graduated from West Point in 1915 and undertook tours of army duty until 1935, when he was assigned to the staff of Gen. Douglas MacArthur in the Philippines. Eisenhower was a lieutenant colonel when recalled to the United States in 1940, won quick promotions and recognition as he helped the army expand, and in 1942 was sent overseas as chief of the operations section in London, with the rank of lieutenant general. His tact and organizational powers in this position led to his appointment in 1942 as commander in chief of all Allied forces in North Africa, directing the invasion of Italy. In December, 1943, Eisenhower was called to London as supreme allied commander to plan and execute the cross-channel invasion of Europe. His inspiring leadership contributed greatly to the ultimate victory of the Allied Powers in World War II.

In 1945 Eisenhower succeeded George Marshall as army chief of staff. In 1948 he became president of Columbia University; but in December, 1950, Pres. Harry Truman asked him to become supreme allied commander for Europe, with the task of creating a European defense army composed of troops from the twelve-nation North Atlantic Treaty Organization. In 1952 and again in 1956 Eisenhower defeated Adlai Stevenson for the presidency of the United States. He fulfilled his campaign promise to terminate the war in Korea. During his administration, America strengthened its ties with the Southeast Asian countries by establishing the Southeast Asia Treaty Organization.

Eisner, Kurt (1867–1919), German politician and journalist, born in Berlin of Jewish parentage, educated at Marburg. He started his journalistic career on the staff of *Frankfurter Zeitung* (1892–1893); became an editor of *Vorwärts* in Berlin (1899), and was editor in chief of the Socialist paper *Fränkische Tagespost* in Nürnberg (1907–1910). During World War I he sympathized with the government, but in 1917 threw his support to the Independents. He lead the Bavarian revolution of 1918–1919 and became the first president of the Bavarian republic. He was assasinated by Count Arco-Valley, a German army official.

Elgar, Sir Edward (1857–1934), English composer, born in Broadheath near Worcester, son of an organist. Aside from violin lessons, his musical education was self-taught. He succeeded his father as organist of St. George's Roman Catholic Church in 1885, and was conductor of the Worcester Glee Club and the County Asylum Band. In 1891 he settled in Malvern, devoting himself to composition. He was the most prominent figure in English music at the turn of the century. His memorable works include the oratorios *The Dream of Gerontius* (1900), *The Apostles* (1903), and *The Kingdom* (1906); the concert overture *In the South* (1904); and symphonies and concertos for violin and cello.

El Greco, see *Greco, El.*

Eliot, Charles William (1834–1926), American educator, born in Boston and graduated from Harvard in 1853. He was professor of chemistry at Massachusetts Institute of Technology, and in 1869 became president of Harvard. During his administration (1869–1909), he developed the elective system in the undergraduate courses, organized the graduate school of arts and sciences, planned future graduate and professional schools, and played an instrumental role in the establishment of Radcliffe College (1894). He is the author of *The Happy Life* (1896), *Educational Reform* (1898), *The Religion of the Future* (1909), and *The Durable Satisfactions of Life* (1910).

Eliot, George, pseudonym of **Mary Ann** or **Marian Evans** (1819–1880), English novelist, born in Warwickshire, tutored in German, Italian, and music. She began her literary career by translating Strauss's *Leben Jesu,* and became in 1851 an assistant editor of the *Westminster Review.* During this time she formed the acquaintance of Herbert Spencer, Thomas Carlyle, and George Henry Lewes, with whom she lived as his common-law wife until his death. Lewes encouraged her to publish her first stories, which appeared in *Blackwood's Magazine* in 1857 and were then issued in book form in 1858 as *Scenes from Clerical Life.* This proved a signal success and was followed by a series of seven novels, beginning in 1859 with *Adam Bede,* which attained an immense success and at once secured her rank with the most eminent novelists of the day. This was followed in 1860 by *The Mill on the Floss* and in 1861 by *Silas Marner, the Weaver of Raveloe.* In 1863 *Romola* appeared; *Felix Holt* was published in 1866 and *Middlemarch* in 1872; *Daniel Deronda* and *Impressions of Theophrastus Such* appeared later. In 1878 Lewes died and George Eliot terminated her literary career. She married John Cross in 1880 but died that same year. Her novels are renowned for their realistic depiction of the lower middle class of the Midland counties.

Eliot, John (1604–1690), called "Apostle of the Indians," early American evangelist, born in England and educated at Cambridge. In 1631 he migrated to America for religious reasons, preached for a year in Boston, and then settled in nearby Roxbury. With this town as his headquarters he devoted his life to converting the Indians, learning their language so that he might preach to them in their own tongue. The author of four-

METROPOLITAN MUSEUM OF ART   WIDE WORLD

QUEEN Elizabeth I (*left*) ruled England, 1558-1603; Elizabeth II (*right*) reigns today.

teen works, including a translation in 1663 of the Bible into the Indian language (the first Bible printed in America), Eliot also helped prepare the famous *Bay Psalm Book* (1640), the first English-language book published in North America.

Eliot, Thomas Stearns (1888–1965), English poet, critic, and dramatist, born in St. Louis, Mo., and educated at Harvard and Oxford. After completing his doctoral dissertation at Oxford in 1915, Eliot decided to remain in England and in 1927 became a naturalized British subject. His first book of poems, *Prufrock and Other Observations* (1917), introduced to modern English poetry a voice of despair and doubt that was echoed in later poems, most notably in *The Waste Land* (1922), perhaps the most celebrated poem of modern times. In these works, Eliot's themes were the barrenness of the present, contrasted to the richness of the past; the decline of tradition and order; and the moral vacuity of the period that followed World War I. To present these ideas, Eliot adopted a poetic technique that differed radically from traditional verse forms. The tone of these poems was often conversational, reflecting the poet's belief that there is a strong relationship between poetry and actual speech. Much of the verse was irregular, in contrast to the precise metrical forms normally associated with poetry. To achieve an ironic effect, Eliot deliberately juxtaposed colloquial, banal language and scholarly references to mythology and literature. In his early critical essays, Eliot repeated his concern with the lack of order and tradition in modern society.

In the late 1920's, Eliot became a convert to the Anglican church, calling himself "an Anglo-Catholic in religion, a classicist in literature, and a royalist in politics." This concern with religion is an important element in his later work, particularly in the philosophical poem *Four Quartets* (1943) and in the verse plays *Murder in the Cathedral* (1935), *The Family Reunion* (1939), and *The Cocktail Party* (1950). One of the most influential and widely imitated poets of his time, Eliot himself was influenced by Dante, John Donne, the French Symbolist poets, and fellow poet Ezra Pound. In 1948 Eliot was awarded the Nobel Prize for literature.

Elizabeth I (1533–1603), queen of England and Ireland (1558–1603), the daughter of Henry VIII and Anne Boleyn. In 1536 her mother was executed for failing to produce a male heir; her father took little interest in his daughter, though he provided her with a well-rounded Renaissance education. After Henry's death in 1547, the throne was ascended by Edward VI, Elizabeth's younger half brother, who died in 1553 and was succeeded by her older half sister, Mary I (called Bloody Mary). Although Elizabeth was heir presumptive to the throne, her ties with Protestantism angered Mary, a devout Roman Catholic with Spanish sympathies. As a result, Elizabeth was briefly imprisoned in 1554 and later placed in protective custody until Mary died in 1558.

Upon ascending the throne, Elizabeth's first act was to release imprisoned Protestants and reestablish Protestantism. She proclaimed that the church service be read in English, eliminated the elevation of the host, and had Parliament establish the Act of Supremacy, making Protestantism and

patriotism synonymous in England. In short, the Reformation begun by Henry VIII was rendered permanent under the reign of Elizabeth. Very early in her reign she was troubled by the pretensions of the friends of Mary, Queen of Scots, who was now the next heir to the throne. As Mary was a most zealous Catholic, the counselors of Elizabeth were anxious that she should marry in order to secure the Protestant succession. Though she negotiated and coquetted with one person after another, she finally refused to marry, though it is believed that she would have accepted her favorite, the earl of Leicester, for a husband, if she had not been prevented by her other counselors. Twelve years after her accession, in 1570, Elizabeth was excommunicated by Pope Pius V. Sixteen years later, in 1586, the Babington conspiracy was formed, the object of which was to reestablish the papacy and to set Mary, Queen of Scots, on the throne of England. This plot led to Mary's execution after she had been imprisoned in England for 19 years. In 1588, two years after this conspiracy, Elizabeth had to contend with a more formidable enemy in Philip II of Spain, who avowed his resolution to annihilate Protestantism, but whose threatened invasion of the country was prevented by the defeat and destruction of his armada. The firmness and sagacity of Elizabeth's advisers, especially of Burghley, protected her against these dangers; and at the close of her reign England was stronger and greater than it had ever been before. Elizabeth was great mainly through her counselors, among whom were some of the most eminent statesmen that England has produced. The Elizabethan age was a period of glory in English history. Its literature alone would make it memorable, for writers of this period included William Shakespeare, Sir Philip Sidney, Edmund Spenser, and Sir Francis Bacon. The maritime discoveries of Drake, Hawkins, and Raleigh also belong to this period.

Elizabeth II, born **Elizabeth Alexandra Mary** (1926–   ), queen of Great Britain, Northern Ireland, and Head of the Commonwealth, daughter of the duke of York. When Edward VIII abdicated in 1936 in favor of Elizabeth's father, George VI, who had no sons, Elizabeth as the oldest daughter became heir presumptive to the throne. In 1947 she married Philip Mountbatten, formerly Prince Philip of Greece, who was given the title duke of Edinburgh on the eve of their wedding. Elizabeth succeeded to the throne February 6, 1952. Her first child, Prince Charles, duke of Cornwall, born in 1948 as heir-apparent, was called prince of Wales in 1958. A daughter, Princess Anne, was born in 1950. A second and third son, Prince Andrew and Edward, were born in 1960 and 1964.

Ellis, Havelock, in full **Henry Havelock Ellis** (1859–1939), English psychologist and writer, known for his writings on sexual psychology. Born in Croydon, Surrey, he was educated in a London boys' school and by private tutors. Ellis began his active career as a teacher in charge of a government school in New South Wales (1878–1880). He returned to England to study medicine at St. Thomas's Hospital in London, but abandoned his practice to pursue research in human biology and literary work. His studies in psychology and the sociology of sex, motivated by personal experiences, resulted in the seven-volume *Studies in the Psychology of Sex* (1897–1928). His literary skill is evident in his editing of the "Mermaid" series of Elizabethan and Jacobean dramatists. Other works include *The Nationalization of Health* (1892), *The Soul of Spain* (1908), *The World of Dreams* (1911), and *My Life* (1939), the latter an autobiography.

Ellsworth, Lincoln (1880–1951), American explorer and aviator, born in Chicago, Ill., studied for two years at Columbia University. He spent several years surveying the Canadian transcontinental railroad and gold prospecting in Canada and Alaska. In 1924 he organized a geological expedition to the Andes Mountains, sponsored by Johns Hopkins University. He conducted and navigated the *N 24* on the Amundsen-Ellsworth Polar Flying Expedition of 1925, but the explorers reached only 88° N latitude. The next year, however, Ellsworth, Amundsen, and Nobile flew across the Pole in the dirigible *Norge*. In 1933 and again in 1935–1936 Ellsworth explored the Antarctic by plane, covering 2,300 miles and claiming 300,000 square miles of new territory for the United States. On this last trip, with a disabled plane and a radio that failed, he was missing in the Antarctic for two months before being rescued.

Ellsworth, Oliver (1745–1807), American jurist and statesman, born in Windsor, Conn., educated at Yale and Princeton (then called the College of New Jersey), received a degree from the latter university in 1766. In 1771 he was admitted to the Connecticut bar. From 1778 to 1783 he was a member of the Continental Congress and he represented his state in the Constitutional Convention of 1787, in which he had an important part in the organization of the national legislative system. He was elected to the Senate in 1789 and as chairman of the judiciary committee drew up the plan for the present federal court system. In 1796 he was appointed chief justice, but resigned after three years due to ill health. In 1800 he served as one of three commissioners to France who negotiated a treaty with Napoleon which allowed the free passage of goods between France and America.

Emanuel or **Manuel I**, called **the Great** and **the Fortunate** (1469–1521), king of Portugal (1495–1521), born at Villa Dalcouchete. During his reign Portugal became the first naval power of the world. Emanuel promoted the expeditions of Vasco da Gama, Cabral, Corte-Real, and other famous explorers, and his reign is regarded as the golden age of Portugal. A religious fanatic, he expelled Jews and Moors from Portugal.

Emerson, Ralph Waldo (1803–1882), American essayist, poet, and philosopher, born in Boston, Mass., the descendent of a long line of clergymen. He was raised in a home of refinement and culture and received the traditional New England education, being graduated from Harvard in 1821. In 1829 he became pastor of the Second Unitarian Church of Boston. His congregation could not approve of his desire to dispense with the rite of the Lord's Supper, and he resigned his pastorate in 1832. The next year, when he made the first of three trips to Europe, he met several writers of note and formed a deep and lasting friendship with Thomas Carlyle. After his return to America Emerson settled in Concord, Mass., married, and began his lifelong career as writer and lecturer.

His first published book, *Nature* (1836), contains the essentials of his Transcendental philosophy, a philosophy which perceives the outer world of objects as a symbolic representation of the inner world of man, and stresses individual awareness and spiritual independence. In 1837 he delivered at Harvard the Phi Beta Kappa oration that he called *The American Scholar*. Again he sounded the note of self-confidence and individualism. In his controversial "Address before the Divinity Class, Cambridge, 1838," he urged the individual to be conscious of his ability to judge for himself in spiritual matters and divorce himself from the churches, bibles, and historical creeds. Emerson's *Essays* appeared in parts in 1841 and 1844, and between these dates he wrote several articles for the *Dial*, the periodical of the Transcendentalists of which he was editor for a brief period. His first book of poems was published in 1847. His poems tend to be meditative and intellectual; the *Concord Hymn* and a few others are often quoted and contain lines of deep beauty. In 1850 *Representative Men* appeared. This contains some of the lectures delivered on a second visit to England. Another outcome of this voyage was a book of travel, *English Traits* (1856). Then followed *The Conduct of Life* (1860), another collection of

poems and, in 1870, *Society and Solitude*. His last volume of essays *Letters and Social Aims* was published in 1876.

Emmet, Robert (1778–1803), Irish patriot, born in Dublin, and studied for a time at Trinity College. From 1800 to 1802 he was in Europe trying to get French support for an Irish revolution. He and his followers made the attempt in Dublin in 1803 but failed, and Emmet had to hide in County Wicklow. He was captured and hanged when he returned to Dublin to see his sweetheart, Sarah Arran. Emmet's whole plan was foolish and was known to the English authorities from its beginning. However, his daring appealed to the Irish people, who made him a national hero. His exploit is celebrated in the poetry of his friend Thomas Moore and several songs.

Empedocles (c.490–430 B.C.), Greek philosopher, poet, and statesman, born at Agrigentum, Sicily, disciple of Pythagoras and Parmenides. Renowned in Sicilian society as a physician and soothsayer, he used his influence to help establish a democratic form of government in his native city. He taught that matter consists of four primary elements: fire, air, earth, and water; and that change is the result of two primal forces, love and hate, or affinity and antipathy. The first he called the uniting force. Fragments of two of his poems have survived. Although conflicting theories concerning his death have been advanced by two other Greek writers, Aristotle and Lucien, legend has it that Empedocles leaped into the burning crater of Mt. Etna, hoping thereby to spread a belief that he had been transported alive to heaven. Matthew Arnold made this story the basis of his poem *Empedocles on Etna*.

Encke, Johann Franz (1791–1865), German astronomer, born in Hamburg. He studied at Göttingen, and served as director of the Observatory in Berlin from 1825 to 1863. He is best known for his computation of the period of the comet discovered in 1818 by the French astronomer Jean Louis Pons. It is now called Encke's comet and has the shortest period of any comet known; it revolves about the sun in about 1,200 days. Encke also determined the orbit of the brilliant comet of 1680 and computed a value of the sun's parallax long accepted as standard.

Endecott or **Endicott, John** (c.1588–1665), governor of Massachusetts Colony, born in Dorchester, England. He and five others bought a patent for land on Massachusetts Bay from the Plymouth Council in England. In 1628 he sailed to Massachusetts, and was acting governor until 1630, when John Winthrop took over. He held a number of administrative positions, becoming governor in 1649. He is chiefly known for the severe rules of personal conduct that he imposed on the colonists. In later years he persecuted the Quakers severely.

Enesco or **Enescu, Georges** (1881–1955), Romanian violinist, conductor, and composer, born in Dorohoiu, Romania. He studied at the Vienna Conservatorie, and in Paris with Massenet and Faure. In 1900 he began a tour of Europe, playing and conducting in many of the large cities. He also appeared in North America as a guest conductor. The two symphonies that Enesco composed are strongly nationalistic in tone. His other compositions include an opera, *Oedipe* (1936), two Romanian rhapsodies, and a *symphonie concertante* for cello and orchestra. Enesco was the teacher of violinist Yehudi Menuhin.

Engels, Friedrich (1820–1895), German Socialist, born in Barmen, in Rhenish Prussia, the son of a wealthy textile manufacturer. He served an apprenticeship in Germany and then went to work in his father's factory in Manchester, England, at which time he wrote *Condition of the Working Class in England* (1845). He is famous for his collaboration with Karl Marx in organizing an international Socialist movement and for his coauthorship with him of *The Communist Manifesto* (1848). His last years were spent editing and publishing Marx's works, including volumes two and three of *Das Kapital* (1885 and 1894).

Ennius, Quintus (239–c.169 B.C.), Roman poet, born in Rudiae, Calabria. He knew Greek, Latin, and the Italian dialect Oscan. Cato the Elder took him to Rome, where he taught Greek and Latin and befriended Scipio Africanus the Elder. He became a Roman citizen in 184 B.C. Ennius wrote tragedies and comedies, epigrams, satires, and an epic, *Annales;* however, nothing remains of his work but fragments quoted by other ancient authors. His satires were a peculiarly Latin form of literature; his Latin poetry, composed in hexameters, followed the Greek meter. He is considered the father of Roman literature.

Ensor, Baron James (1860–1949), Belgian painter and etcher. Born in Ostend, he studied at the Brussels Academy. The influence of the sixteenth-century painter Breughel is apparent in the early genre paintings of Ensor, while his later paintings and etchings, where macabre masks and ghosts dominate the scene, bear a similarity to the surrealistic works of Bosch. In 1929 Ensor was created baron by King Albert.

Enver Pasha, know earlier as **Enver Bey** (c.1881–1922), Turkish statesman and soldier, born in Constantinople. As an army officer he became associated with leaders of the Young Turk movement and himself became its leader. He had much to do with the overthrow of Sultan Abdul-Hamid in 1909. After that he assumed much power and was virtually dictator of Turkey during World War I. When turkey surrendered at the close of the war he fled to Russia and was killed in a skirmish with Russian revolutionists.

Epaminondas (c.418–362 B.C.), Theban statesman and general. By his superior generalship at the battle of Leuctra, 371 B.C., the Thebans defeated a larger Spartan force and saved Thebes from Spartan domination. From that time on Epaminondas devoted himself to weakening the power of Sparta, and in 362 B.C., while engaged in his fourth expedition against the enemy, overwhelmed the combined Spartan and Athenian forces at Mantineia. He himself fell in battle, and the power of Thebes soon waned.

Épée, Abbé Charles Michel de l' (1712–1789), French priest, born in Versailles, one of the pioneers in the education of deaf-mutes. After he entered the priesthood, he was obliged to leave his position at Troyes because of his beliefs and in 1755 began to develop a sign-language system for the deaf and dumb. The school that he founded in Paris (1770) became a government institution after his death. Épée also wrote a dictionary of manual signs.

Epictetus (c.50–c.130), Greek Stoic philosopher, probably born in Hieropolis, Phrygia. He became a slave in Rome during the reign of Nero; and Epictetus seems not to be his real name since in Greek it means "purchased" or "bought." After he was set free, he began his philosophic studies in Rome but was banished by the emperor Domitian; he then settled in Epirus. The Greek historian Arrian, his most famous pupil, published some of his master's teachings in his *Discourses* and the *Enchiridion*. Epictetus taught many principles later associated with Christ, such as the love of good and hatred of evil, and he exalted patience, temperance, and self-control.

Epicurus (c.342–270 B.C.), Greek philosopher, born in Samos of Athenian parentage. Epicurus settled in Athens in 306 B.C. and founded the Epicurean school in a garden, attracting pupils from all parts of Greece and Asia Minor. The central idea of his philosophy was that pleasure is good and pain is evil. By pleasure he did not mean sensual enjoyment, but the joy that comes from prudence, temperence, and justice. The happy person, he taught, is the one whose soul is free from fear and whose body is free from pain. In physics he taught the atomic theory of Democritus: that the universe was formed by combinations of atoms. Although little has survived of his voluminous writing, Cicero, Seneca, and Plutarch expounded his theories, and Lucretius embodied his philosophy in his great poem *De rerum natura*.

Épinay, Louise Florence Pétronille de la Live d', nee **Tardieu d'Esclavelles** (1726–1783), French writer, born in Valenciennes. In 1745 she formed a close intimacy with Rousseau. An unfortunate jealousy that Rousseau conceived for Grimm, another friend of Madame d'Épinay, was followed by an open rupture with his benefactress. In 1774 she wrote *Les Conversations d'Émilie*, a book for the education of her granddaughter, which was crowned by the Academy in 1783. Her *Mémoires et correspondance* (3 vols., 1818), consisting of letters of Rousseau, Grimm, Diderot, and others, throws a vivid light on the literary social life of the period.

Epstein, Sir Jacob (1880–1959), British sculptor, of Russo-Polish parentage. Born in New York he studied at the École des Beaux-Arts in Paris. He settled in London in 1905, where he remained for the duration of his life. In 1954 he was knighted. He produced massive creations in stone and bronze; with the latter medium he sculptured portraits of such eminent persons as Bernard Shaw, Joseph Conrad, Albert Einstein, and Emperor Haile Selassie of Ethiopia. By distorting the features and working the surface until it was rough and angular, he created fiery and expressionistic portraits. Many of his monumental works

UNITED PRESS INTERNATIONAL

MAO TSE-TUNG and **NIKITA KHRUSHCHEV**

WIDE WORLD

CHOU EN-LAI

INTERNATIONAL NEWS PHOTOS

SIR ANTHONY EDEN

WIDE WORLD

HAROLD WILSON

WIDE WORLD

SIR ALEC DOUGLAS-HOME

UNITED PRESS INTERNATIONAL

CHIANG KAI-SHEK and **MADAM CHIANG**

WIDE WORLD

SUKARNO

LOOK MAGAZINE

INDIRA GANDHI

FRENCH EMBASSY PRESS AND INFORMATION

JEAN-PAUL SARTRE

LOOK MAGAZINE

MARTIN LUTHER KING

LOOK MAGAZINE

LYNDON B. JOHNSON

EUROPRESS - PIX

CHARLES DE GAULLE

WIDE WORLD

HO CHI MINH

were criticized for being either excessively distorted, blasphemous, or indecent. Among his works are the Oscar Wilde memorial (1909) in the Père Lachaise Cemetery, Paris; the eighteen figures (1907–1908) that adorn the British Medical Association Building in London; *Genesis* (1931), a nude of a woman; and *Ecce Homo* (1933), a massive statue of Christ. His autobiography, *Let There Be Sculpture*, was published in 1940.

Erasistratus (c.304–c.245 B.C.), Greek anatomist, born on the island of Ceos. After a career as practicing physician, he settled in Alexandria, where he co-founded with Herophilus a school of anatomy. Erasistratus made original discoveries in the anatomy of the blood vessels and nerves and was the first to reveal the distinction between motor and sensory nerves and their common origin in the brain. He was also the first to trace the veins and arteries to the heart. He disagreed with Herophilus on the validity of the Hippocratic humoral theory, that the body consists of four fluids — blood, phlegm, black bile, and yellow bile. It is believed that he invented the catheter.

Erasmus, Desiderius, original name **Gerhard Gerhards** or **Geert Geerts** (c.1466–1536), Dutch scholar and Humanist of the Renaissance. He was born in Rotterdam, the illegitimate son of a physician's daughter and Gerard of Gouda, who became a priest, and was educated at the school of the Brethren of the Common Life in Deventer. He was induced by his guardian to become a monk but soon abandoned the monastery for the life of a scholar, teacher, and writer. Considering that Erasmus neither founded nor led a great movement and wrote no outstanding classic, his influence on his times was remarkable. In an age that produced Columbus, Thomas More, Luther, and Calvin, Erasmus was content to point out abuses, suggest reforms, and work for an increase of knowledge. He has been called the "apostle of common sense and of rational religion." He took no active part in the Reformation for he disapproved of a schism within the Church, believing war was the antithesis to the Christian way of life. Favoring moderate reform in the Catholic Church, he opposed many of the embellishments of the Church, which he outlined in his *Enchirdion militis christiani (The Handsome Weapon of a Christian Knight,* 1503). Erasmus visited many different countries, spending considerable time in England, where he became the friend of Thomas More and John Colet, and taught Greek at Cambridge. In addition to producing numerous works in Latin, he prepared a new edition of the Greek New Testament and made a parallel translation in Latin. His three thousand extant letters are regarded as valuable source material. Perhaps his greatest works are the *Colloquies* (1519), the *Encomium moriae (Praise of Folly,* 1509), a satire on the faults of the Church and its dignitaries, and the *Adagia,* a remarkable collection of proverbs (1500; enlarged in 1515). He also edited and translated many of the classics.

Eratosthenes (c.275–194 B.C.), Greek astronomer, geographer, and mathematician, born in Cyrene, Africa. He was a student of the Stoic philosopher Ariston, the Academician Arcesilans, the poet Callimachus, and the grammarian Lysanias. Ptolemy Euergetes asked him to take charge of the great library at Alexander, where Erastosthenes remained until his death. He knew that the earth is round, computed its circumference, and estimated the inclination of the axis with a very small degree of error; he also measured the obliquity of the ecliptic. Another notable achievement of his was the founding of scientific chronology, whereby he attempted to set important dates of ancient Greek political and literary history.

Erhard, Ludwig (1897–), German statesman and economist, born in Fürth, Bavaria, educated in Nürnberg, and the University of Frankfurt, where he received his doctorate in economics in 1928. He served as director of the Institute of Economic Studies at Nürnberg from 1928 until 1942, at which time he was commanded to establish the Institute for Industrial Research. In 1947 he was appointed professor of economics at the University of Munich; that same year Erhard was named chairman of a special agency for the preparation of a plan for currency reform (the Bizonal Council). In 1948 he was made director of the economic council of the United Economic Region, and in 1949 became minister of economic affairs of West Germany. Erhard played an instrumental role in the revitalization of the West German market; he provided incentives to increase production and exportation. In 1957 he was appointed vice-chancellor of West Germany. In 1963 he was elected as chancellor after a year-long dispute with Adenauer, who at first opposed Erhard's succession.

Eric the Red (fl. 10th century), Norwegian explorer and colonizer of Greenland. About 985 Eric brought a band of Norwegians to Greenland; his settlement there lasted about four hundred years, but no trace exists today. His adventures and that of his son Eric are related in the Icelandic sagas.

Ericson or **Ericsson, Leif,** Scandinavian explorer, son of Eric the Red and supposedly the discoverer of the North American continent. According to accounts in the Icelandic sagas (hero tales), about the year 1000 Leif discovered a land to the west of Greenland that he called Vinland. No one knows whether this was Labrador, Newfoundland, or a part of New England. Since nothing came of the discovery, Columbus has always been honored as the real discoverer of the Americas.

Ericsson, John (1803–1889), Swedish-American inventor, born in Varmland, Sweden. He was an army engineer before his removal to England in 1826. There he invented a new type of screw propeller for steamships. In 1839 he came to America to engage in construction work for the United States navy. In 1861 he designed the ironclad *Monitor;* it set a new precedent in naval engineering for it was propelled solely by steam, used a screw propeller, and had guns mounted in an armored tower that revolved.

Ernst, Max (1891–), German-French-American painter and writer. He was born in Brühl and studied philosophy at the University of Bonn (1909–1914). After serving in the German army during World War I he decided to become a painter, although he lacked formal training. In 1919 he founded the Dadaist movement in Cologne. He introduced the collage — an abstract composition consisting of a variety of materials, such as newspaper clippings, parts of advertisements, etc., pasted together along with the artist's own colors and lines. In 1922 he settled in Paris, where he joined André Breton's Surrealist movement. When World War II erupted Ernst was interned in a concentration camp in France. In 1941 he secured his release and came to the United States. Among his works are *Monument to Birds, Revolution in the Night,* and *Women Crossing a River Crying.*

Esarhaddon (d.669 B.C.), king of Assyria, the son of Sennacherib. He reigned 681–668 B.C. Esarhaddon, who was a great warrior, was successful in attacks against Chaldea, Sidon, and Egypt. He died while on an expedition against the Egyptians, who had rebelled. One of his most important acts was the rebuilding of Babylon, which his father had destroyed. He was succeeded by his son, Ashurbanipal.

Espy, James Pollard (1785–1860), American meteorologist, born in Washington County, Pa., and educated at Transylvania University. His *Philosophy of Storms,* published in 1841, was commended by the French Académie des Sciences. Appointed in 1842 to the Washington Observatory, Espy laid the basis of the Weather Bureau. He was the first to explain the cause of rain (1836) as accepted in modern meteorology.

Essex, 2d Earl of. See *Devereux, Robert.*

Estaing, Comte **Jean Baptiste Charles Henri Hector d'** (1729–1794), French admiral, commander of the fleet sent to America in 1778 during the American Revolution to help the colonies in their fight for independence. D'Estaing returned to France in 1780 after capturing two islands in the West Indies and taking part in the unsuccessful attack on Savannah. During the French Revolution he was in sympathy with the moderate faction, and in 1792 was appointed admiral of France. He testified in behalf of Marie Antoinette and in 1794 the extremists ordered that he be executed as a Royalist.

Ethelbert or **Aethelbert** (c.552–616), English king of Kent who came to the throne in 560. By 593 he had extended his rule over all the territory south of the Humber River. Through the influence of his wife Berta, daughter of Charibert, king of Paris, and Saint Augustine, Ethelbert was converted to Christianity in 597. A legal code issued by him in 600 is memorable as the first written compilation of Saxon laws.

Ethelred or **Aethelred II** (c.968–1016,, called "the Unready," king of England (978–1013; 1014–1016), son of King Edgar. He succeeded his half brother, Edward the Martyr, who was assassinated by his stepmother. His surname had reference to his lack of good *rede* or judgment. Ethelred married Emma, daughter of the duke of Normandy; one of their sons was Edward the Confessor. The king's energies had to be diverted from civic matters to fighting the Danes, with whom he finally concluded a peace treaty in the year 1000. War again broke out in 1002 because of a general massacre of the Danes in England. Ethelred frequently bought peace by money payments, but war continued intermittently until his death. In 1013, when Sweyn was declared king of England, Ethelred fled to Normandy, returning in 1014 upon Sweyn's death. He expelled Sweyn's son Canute and ruled until his own death.

Ethelwulf or **Aethelwulf** (d.858), king of Wessex and Kent (839–858), the son of Egbert. He married Judith, daughter of Charles the Bald of France, and was the father of Alfred the Great. While Ethelwulf was on a pilgrimage to Rome (855–856), his son Ethelbald fomented a rebellion; on his return Ethelwulf granted the son the throne of Wessex, and he himself ruled over Kent.

Eucken, Rudolf Christoph (1846–1926), German philosopher, born in Aurich and educated at Göttingen and Berlin. He held the chair of philosophy at Basel (1871–1874) and thereafter had a similar position at Jena. Eucken lectured at Harvard and in Japan. In 1908 he received the Nobel prize for literature. His philosophy of ethical activism emphasizes the worth of the inner life; all knowledge is faith and man with the aid of the divine struggles for the spiritual control of life. English translations of his works include *The Meaning and Value of Life, The Truth of Religion,* and *Collected Essays.* He defended Germany's role in World War I and signed a manifesto to this effect with other German intellectuals.

Euclid or **Euclides** (c.323–285 B.C.), Greek mathematician and physicist, called the "Father of Geometry." He founded a school in Alexandria during the reign of Ptolemy I (306–283 B.C.). His *Elements,* the basis of all later texts on geometry, consisted of thirteen books, of which only six are in use today. Euclid's fame as a mathematician rests not on his own research, for most of the theorems in the *Elements* are not his own. However, he was the first to compile and organize the mathematical knowledge of two and a half centuries into a single text. Only the Pythagorean theorem is definitely credited to him. It is said that when Ptolemy asked him if there were not an easier method of learning geometry than studying the *Elements,* Euclid replied, "There is no royal road to geometry."

Eudoxus (c.408–c.353 B.C.), Greek mathematician and astronomer of Cnidus, called by Cicero the "Prince of Astronomers." He studied under Plato and then under the Egyptain scholars. He founded a school in Cyzicus and spent his later years in Athens, where he had an observatory. It is claimed that he discovered the solar year to be six hours longer than 365 days, offered an explanation of the paths of the planets, and developed the part of geometry that is in Euclid's fifth book.

Eugénie, in full **Eugénie Marie de Montijo de Guzmán,** Comtesse **de Teba** (1826–1920), empress of France, wife of Napoleon III, born in Granada, Spain, and educated in France. Her father was a Spanish grandee and her mother was the daughter of an American-Scot. In 1853 Eugénie married the newly-crowned emperor, who was fascinated by her beauty and charm. In the days of her prosperity she set the fashions, and there have been modern revivals of "Empress Eugénie" styles. The empress was partly responsible for her husband's attempt to set up a French empire in Mexico and for his declaration of war against Germany in 1870. After Napoleon's surrender at Sedan, Eugénie fled to England, where her husband joined her in 1871. All hopes for her restoration to power were lost by Napoleon's death in 1873 and that of their only son in 1879. She died in Spain and was buried in England.

Euler, Leonhard (1707–1783), Swiss mathematician, born in Basel. He studied under Jean Bernoulli and is regarded as a founder of the science of pure mathematics. In 1727 Catherine I asked him to come to St. Petersburg, where he was appointed professor of physics (1730) and of mathematics (1733) at the Academy of Sciences. In 1741 he went to the Berlin Academy of Sciences at the request of Frederick the Great, and was made director of mathematics (1744). His eyesight failing, he returned to St. Petersburg in 1766, and soon became totally blind. A prolific writer, Euler published numerous works on mathematics, physics, astronomy, phydrodynamics, and optics. His *Introductio in analysin infinitorum* (1748) contributed as much to modern analysis as Euclid's *Elements* did to geometry.

Euripides (c.480–406 B.C.), youngest of the three Greek tragic poets who made Athens famous in literature, the others being Aeschylus and Sophocles. Euripides was born on the island of Salamis on the day, it was said, that the Greeks won the decisive battle over the Persians in the adjoining straits. He was of humble birth but received a good education and began his dramatic writing in youth. His first play, *The Daughters of Peleus,* was produced in Athens when he was 25; though it won only third place in the competition of that year, he was encouraged to go on. It was 14 years before he won first prize; he is thought to have attained that coveted honor five times in his career. In 408 B.C. he was invited to the court of Archelaus in Macedonia and died there two years later. Euripides was more appreciated in later times than in his own age, because his style was more modern than the earlier dramatists'. His characters are more sympathetic; they are not idealized figures who represent good or evil, but are ordinary people whose unchecked appetites and passions bring disasters to themselves and others. Unlike Aeschylus' tragic figures, who are victims of divine intervention, Euripides' protagonists are the cause of their own tragedies. In form Euripides' plays differ from the other two Greek tragedians' in their dependence on prologue and epilogue to set scenes, further actions, and change the fortunes of characters. Among his eighteen extant dramas are *Alcestis, Medea, Iphigenia in Tauris, Iphigenia in Aulis, Hippolytus, Hecuba, Andromache, Electra* and *Orestes.*

Eusebius of Caesarea, surnamed **Pamphili** after his teacher Pamphilus (c.260–c.340), Greek historian, often called the "Father of Ecclesiastical History," born in Palestine. He became bishop of Caesarea c.314 and enjoyed a wide reputation for learning and piety. As leader of the semi-Arian or moderate party, he attended the Council of Nicea; he supported the doctrine that Christ was a secondary deity. He later opposed this position and adhered to the Nicene Creed. His most important work is *Historia Ecclesiastica,* a ten-volume history of the Christian Church to the year 324. Another notable work of his is the *Chronicon,* a history of the world to 325.

Eustachio, Bartolommeo, Latin name **Eustachius** (c.1524–1574), Italian anatomist whose name was given to the tube between the upper part of the pharynx and the ear and to the valve in the heart, because he wrote the first accurate descriptions of that part of the ear and heart. He also made valuable discoveries in the anatomy of the thoracic duct, the teeth, and the kidneys.

Evans, Herbert McLean (1882–), American anatomist and embryologist. His discoveries include the number of chromosomes in man (1918), Vitamin E (1922), and the origin of the vascular trunk from the capillaries (1909). He experimented with the anterior hypophyseal hormone and was the first to produce gigantism by parenteral administration. He also did research on the physiology of reproduction.

Evans, Mary Ann. See *Eliot, George.*

Evans, Maurice (1901–), Englisn actor, born in Dorsetshire. He first gained recognition as an actor of high caliber in *Journey's End* in the role of Second Lieutenant (1929). He is best known for his Shakespearean roles. He played Romeo to Katherine Cornell's Juliet in a United States production in 1935–1936, and played *Richard II* (1937), Falstaff in *Henry IV* (part I; 1937–1938), and *Hamlet* (1938–1939).

Evans, Robley Dunglison (1846–1912), American naval officer, born in Floyd County, Va., graduated from Annapolis in 1863. During the Civil War he took part in the capture of Fort Fisher, where he was severely wounded. In 1891 he forced an apology from the commander of a Chilean war vessel in Valparaiso harbor for insults to Americans. The incident gave him the popular name of "Fighting Bob." In the battle of Santiago (1898), in the Spanish-American War, Evans commanded the *Iowa.* He was promoted rear admiral in 1901 and made commander of the Asiatic fleet in 1902. He retired in 1908. He wrote two autobiographical works, *A Sailor's Log* (1901) and *An Admiral's Log* (1910).

Evarts, William Maxwell (1818–1901), American lawyer and statesman, born in Boston. He rose steadily to a prominent place in law and politics and during the Civil War represented Lincoln in a diplomatic capacity in England. As senior counsel of Pres. Andrew Johnson he helped to win an acquittal for the chief executive in the impeachment trial (1868). In 1868–1869 Evarts was attorney general in Johnson's cabinet; in 1872 he was chief American counsel in the Geneva Court of Arbitration. He represented the Republicans before the electoral commission that decided the Hayes-Tilden contest (1877). Evarts was secretary of state under Hayes and from 1885–1891 served as senator from New York.

Evelyn, John (1620–1706), English diarist, author, and public official, born of wealthy parentage in Wotton, Surrey, England. He attended Balliol College, Oxford, and Middle Temple. Evelyn sympathized with King Charles II in his fight with Parliament to preserve an absolutist government, but was forced to leave England during the Civil War to avoid signing an oath of allegiance to Parliament. With the king's permission he traveled on the Continent for four years. At Paris in 1647 he married Mary Browne, the ambassador's daughter; in 1652 he established himself at Sayes Court, Deptford. After the Restoration, Evelyn was favored with several minor offices and was also an active member of the Royal Society. When his elder brother died in 1669 he inherited Wotton and resided there until his death. His copious works are on such varied subjects as architecture, numismatics, politics, landscape gardening, painting, engraving, education, and commerce. His three best works are *Fumifugium* (1661), a work dealing with the nullification of the smoke nuisance in London; *Sylva* (1664), a volume on the reforestation of England after the Civil War; and his celebrated *Diary,* a day-by-day account of seventeenth century England, covering seventy years. The *Diary* was discovered in 1817 in an old clothes basket.

Everett, Edward (1794–1865), American orator, statesman, and educator, born in Dorchester, Mass. After graduating from Harvard in 1811 he became a Unitarian minister, serving a congregation in Boston (1813–1815). He then traveled and studied to fit himself for the professorship of Greek literature at Harvard. He edited the *North American Review* (1820–1824) and then for ten years represented Massachusetts in Congress. Everett was governor of Massachusetts (1836–1840), minister to Great Britain (1841–1845), and for the years 1846–1849 was president of Harvard. In 1852 he succeeded to Webster's place as secretary of state, holding it for the remaining four months of Fillmore's term. From 1853 to 1854 he was a United States senator, but resigned because he was severely criticized for his moderate position on slavery. In 1860 Everett was nominee for vice-president with Bell on the Constitutional Unionist ticket, which received 39 electoral votes. He later gave Lincoln his undivided support and was the chief orator of the day at the dedication of the battlefield of Gettysburg. His long, polished address received much more attention at the time than Lincoln's short speech.

Ewell, Richard Stoddert (1817–1872), Confederate cavalry leader, born in Georgetown, D. C. He graduated from West Point, served in the Mexican War, and fought against the Apache Indians in 1857. When the Civil War began, Ewell joined the Confederate army. As major general he fought at Bull Run and Antietam, was severely wounded at Warrenton Turnpike, and succeeded to Stonewall Jackson's command after Jackson's death and was promoted to lieutenant general. Ewell's corps was captured by Sheridan at Sailor's Creek in 1865.

Eyck, Hubert or **Huybrecht van** (c.1366–1426) and his brother **Jan van Eyck** (c.1370–c.1440), Flemish painters, born in Maeseyck, founders of the Flemish school of painting. Although the van Eycks probably did not invent oil painting, they perfected its technique. They followed a secret method of mixing oils, and their colors were so brilliant and so skillfully applied that their work still retains its fresh beauty. Little is known about Hubert, except that he worked for years on a collossal altarpiece, *Adoration of the Lamb,* for the Church of St. Bavon in Ghent. This is the only work that is known positively to be his; he died before it was finished and his brother completed it. Some of the panels were removed to Berlin in 1816 but were restored to Ghent by provisions of the Treaty of Versailles, and the most outstanding work of Flemish art may now be seen there in its entirety. Unlike his brother's, Jan's life was not shrouded in mystery. In 1442 he was commissioned to paint decorations for John, duke of Holland, at The Hague, and he was reputed to have illustrated the manuscript of the duke's *Book of Hours.* In 1425 he was appointed court painter to Philip the Good, duke of Burgundy at Lille. He died in Bruges. Outstanding among his numerous signed and dated paintings are the triptych of the *Virgin and Child* (Dresden), the *Annunciation* (National Gallery, Washington, D. C.), and *St. Francis Receiving the Stigmata* (Philadelphia Museum).

F

Fabius Maximus Verrucosus, Quintus, surnamed **Cunctator,** the Delayer (d.203 B.C.), Roman general, consul, and censor, elected dictator in 217. He won his nickname by his tactics in the Second Punic War. Instead of engaging in open battle with Hannibal, the Carthaginian general, he cut off Hannibal's supplies and wore out his patience by indefinite marches and skirmishes. This "Fabian" policy, which Washington studied and adopted in the Revolutionary War, gave the Romans time to consolidate their strength and led to their ultimate victory.

Fabriano, Gentile da. See *Gentile da Fabriano.*

Fahrenheit, Gabriel Daniel (1686–1736), German physicist, born in Danzig. He lived in England for a time, where he became a manufacturer of instruments used in the study of the weather. He originated the thermometer scale that bears his name, brought the mercury thermometer into general use (1714), and discovered that other liquids besides water have a fixed boiling point.

Faisal I, also **Feisal** or **Feisul** (1885–1933), king of Iraq (1921–1933), son of **Husein ibn-Ali** (1856–1931), first king of Hejaz. Faisal was born in Mecca, and educated in Constantinople (now Istanbul). He was active in the revolt of the Arabs against the Ottoman Turks during World War I. He was proclaimed king of Syria (1920), but was ousted by the French after a few months in office. In 1921 the British appointed him king of Iraq (formerly Mesopotamia), which was a British mandate until it was admitted to the League of Nations as an independent state (1932). It was Faisal's reconstruction policy that convinced the British of Iraq's readiness to attain independent status.

Falkenhayn, Erich von (1861–1922), German general, born near Graudenz, Poland. He participated in the Chinese campaign (1899–1903), was promoted to general (1913), and served as Prussian war minister (1913–1915). Early in World War I he succeeded Count von Moltke as chief of the general staff but was replaced by Paul von Hindenburg in 1916 after the failure of the German attack on Verdun. Falkenhayn was then appointed commander in chief of the Ninth Army, composed of Austro-German divisions, which he directed in the opening drive against Romania. He was sent to the Turkish sector in 1917 but was replaced in 1918. Falkenhayn disagreed at times with Hindenburg and Ludendorff, but was considered a great strategist by many authorities.

Falkner, William. See *Faulkner, William.*

Falla, Manuel de (1876–1946), Spanish composer, born in Cadiz. He was a student of Felipe Pedrell, the composer responsible for reviving native Spanish music. He also studied in Paris, where he was encouraged by Maurice Ravel and Claude Debussy. Falla's music is a splendid fusion of Spanish folk and French impressionist music. His compositions include the opera *Life is Short* (1905); *Nights in the Gardens of Spain* (1914–1916), the ballets *Wedded by Witchcraft* (1915) and *The Three-Cornered Hat* (1919); and *Master Peter's Puppet Show* (1923), a marionette play.

Fallières, Clement Armand (1841–1931), French statesman and eighth president of France (1906–1913), born in Mézin, Lot-et-Garonne. He entered the Chamber of Deputies in 1876 as a radical Republican. Beginning as undersecretary in the department of the interior in 1880, he held a succession of cabinet positions. In 1890 he was elected to the Senate, of which he was president from 1899 to 1906. He was elected president of France in 1906 by the Republican Left. His administration was notable for its favorable attitude toward labor.

Fallopio, Gabriello, Latin name **Fallopius** (1523–1562), Italian anatomist, born in Modena. He studied medicine at Ferrara, and taught at Pisa and at Padua. He is remembered today for his anatomical descriptions, especially those of the inner ear and the organs of generation. The tubes that lead the human ovum from the ovary to the uterus, known as the Fallopian tubes, are named after him.

Fanfani, Amintore (1908–), Italian statesman and economist. In 1947 the republican constitution that he helped draft took effect, and from that time on he held many high government posts. He was minister of labor in the first postwar cabinet, and served four terms as prime minister (1954, 1958–1959, 1960–1962, and 1962–1964). A leader of the Christian Democratic party, Fanfani three times presided over coalition cabinets, the most notable of which he formed in 1962 by making an "opening to the Left" to admit the influential Italian Socialist party to power. In 1966, in the midst of a political controversy, Fanfani resigned his post as foreign minister, which he had held since 1964. As premier Fanfani worked for western European unity; he helped to bring prosperity to Italy through improvements in education, housing, land allotment, and the use of natural resources. Fanfani, who has a doctorate in political economy, began his career as a professor, and has continued his teaching activities during his political life, while also completing over forty books on politics and economics.

Fantin-Latour, Ignace Henri Joseph Théodore (1836–1904), French painter, born in Grenoble, and a student of Gustave Courbet. His most notable paintings are portraits and flower studies. *Homage to Delacroix* (showing the Spanish painter surrounded by Baudelaire, Manet, Whistler, Champfleury, and Duranty) and *Corner of the Table* (a group portrait of Verlaine, Rimbaud, and others) are two of this best-known works.

Farabi, al-, Latin name **Alfarabius** (c.870–950 A.D.), Arab philosopher, born in Farab, Turkestan, of Turkish parentage. Considered one of the greatest of Arab philosophers, he introduced the works of Aristotle and Plato to the Arab world and attempted to integrate Greek and Islamic thought. His translations of the Greek philosophers and his book *The Perfect City*, modeled on Plato's *Republic*, had a great influence on Avicenna and Averroës.

Faraday, Michael (1791–1867), English chemist and physicist, born in Newington Butts, Surrey. The son of a blacksmith, he received little formal education and at 13 was apprenticed to a bookseller. His keen interest in science led him to attend a series of lectures by Sir Humphry Davy, professor of chemistry at the Royal Institution. Davy was so impressed by Faraday's notes that he made him his assistant in 1812. Faraday was later appointed to the Institution, where he remained for over 50 years. Faraday's contributions to chemistry include a method to liquefy gases, and the discovery of benzene and two chlorides of carbon. In 1821 he published a paper on electromagnetism and demonstrated the revolution of a magnetic needle around an electric current. He discovered electrical induction, which in turn led to his invention of the electric generator. He formulated the laws of electrolysis and carried on valuable research in the use of polarized light, in addition to many other discoveries in electricity and chemistry. The farad, the unit of electrical capacity (as in a condenser), is named in his honor, and so is the faraday, the unit of electrical quantity. Faraday was an extremely religious man; frowning upon wordly vanity, he declined many awards and offices of honor, except his membership in the Royal Society. His *Chemical Manipulation*, published in 1827, is his only book. His published lectures include *Experimental Researches in Electricity* (1844–1855), *Experimental Researches in Chemistry and Physics* (1859), and *Lectures on the Chemical History of a Candle* (1861).

Farley, John Murphy (1842–1918), American cardinal, born in Newtown-Hamilton, Ireland. He came to the U.S. and after studies in New York City and Troy, N.Y., he was ordained in Rome, Italy, in 1870. He was appointed pastor of St. Gabriel's, in New York City (1884), and in 1891 was made vicar-general of the diocese. After promotion to auxiliary bishop of New York in 1902, he was made archbishop, and created cardinal in 1911. He was one of the founders of the *Catholic Encyclopedia*.

Farouk I. See *Faruk I.*

Farragut, David Glasgow (1801–1870), American naval officer, born near Knoxville, Tenn., the adopted son of the naval hero David D. Porter. He learned seamanship by service in the navy, which he entered as a midshipman at the age of nine. He participated in the War of 1812, traveled to all parts of the world, and in 1841 reached the rank of commander. During the Mexican War he commanded the *Saratoga*, and later helped to establish the Mare Island navy yard in San Francisco.

He offered his services to the Union when the South seceded, and late in 1861 was placed in command of the West Gulf Blockading Squadron, being ordered to cooperate with Commander Porter in the capture of New Orleans. The surrender of the city in April, 1862, was brought about by Farragut's dash past the forts and his destruction of the Confederate fleet in open battle. This exploit won for him the rank of rear admiral. In August, 1864, he won new laurels in the battle of Mobile Bay, where his tactics destroyed a Confederate fleet and silenced the protecting forts. At the close of the year, he was raised to the rank of vice admiral and in 1866 to that of admiral, grades created for him by special acts of Congress.

Farrar, Geraldine (1882–1967), American operatic soprano, born in Melrose, Mass. After studying in Berlin and Paris, she made her debut in 1901 at the Royal Opera House in Berlin as Marguerite in *Faust*. A great favorite with American audiences, she sang with the Metropolitan Opera Company in New York from 1906 to 1922. Her greatest roles were as Marguerite, Madame Butterfly, Manon, Tosca, Carmen, Juliet, and Gilda. She died Mar. 11, 1967 in Ridgefield, Conn.

Farrell, James Thomas (1904–   ), American novelist and critic, born in Chicago, Ill. He studied at the University of Chicago and was a newspaper reporter before his career as novelist. His naturalistic novels of middle-class life in Chicago, the most famous being the *Studs Lonigan* trilogy (1932–1935), show the influence of Theodore Dreiser. A prolific writer, Farrell's other novels include *No Star is Lost* (1938), *Father and Son* (1940), and *This Man and This Woman* (1951). An independent thinker with leftist leanings, Farrell as a critic wrote a number of illuminating studies on literary and political subjects in the 1940's.

Faruk I or **Farouk I** (1920–1965), king of Egypt (1936–1952), succeeding his father, Fuad I. He was educated in England. In 1938 he married Farida Zulficar, who bore him three daughters but no sons. Farouk divorced her in 1948, and in 1951 married Narriman Sadek, who bore him a son.

Under his leadership Egypt maintained a close military and economic relationship

WIDE WORLD

WILLIAM FAULKNER

with Britain until the start of World War II (1939) when it became apparent that Germans and Italians were penetrating his regime. In 1942 Britain ordered the reinstatement of Nahas Pasha, Faruk's former premier and leader of the Wafd party, a strongly nationalistic group. He severed diplomatic ties with Germany, Italy, and Japan, and in 1945 declared war on Germany and Italy. After the War, Faruk's excessive gambling and numerous love affairs lost him the respect of his subjects. In July, 1952, a *coup d' etat* headed by Naguib forced him to abdicate. He fled to Italy, and in 1959 became a citizen of Monaco, where he continued his hedonistic ways until his death in 1965. He was buried in Egypt.

Faulkner, William, originally **Falkner** (1897–1962), American novelist and short-story writer, born in New Albany, Miss., and educated at the University of Mississippi. He served with the British Royal Air Force during World War I. His first book, *Soldier's Pay* (1926), described World War I experiences. *Sartoris* (1929) was the first in a series of novels focusing on the social and racial problems of the fictional town of Jefferson (based on Oxford), Miss. It introduced a theme prominent in his novels—the disintegration of the old order in the South. Other novels include *The Sound and the Fury* (1929), where Faulkner experiments with a style reminiscent of James Joyce's, *As I Lay Dying* (1930), *Sanctuary* (1931), *Light in August* (1932), *Absalom, Absalom!* (1936), *The Hamlet* (1940), *Go Down, Moses* (1942), *Intruder in the Dust* (1948), *Requiem for a Nun* (1951), and *A Fable* (1954), which won him a Pulitzer Prize. Faulkner's penetrating depiction of the decaying South in his novels and short stories earned him the Nobel Prize for literature in 1949 and in 1963 (posthumously).

Fauré, Gabriel Urbain (1845–1924), French composer, noted for his exquisite technique and subtle harmony, which marked a departure from the influence of German Romantic music. He was born in Pamiers, and studied at the École Niedermeyer in Paris. He was an organist at the Madeleine Church in Paris and in 1896 was appointed professor of composition at the Paris Conservatoire. He was director from 1905 to 1920, when he retired to devote himself to composition. His works include a *Requiem* (1887); the musical dramas *Prométhée* (1900) and *Pénélope* (1913); short lyrical pieces for piano, violin and cello; a number of songs; and incidental music for Maeterlinck's *Pelléas et Mélisande* (1898).

Faust, Johann, Latin name **Johannes Faustus** (c.1480–1540), German magician and astrologer, born in Knittlingen, Württemberg. His name is associated with the well-known legend of a man who agrees to surrender at his death his soul to the devil in exchange for superhuman powers and wealth for a period of twenty-four years. Very little is known about Faust's life, except that he practiced astrology and necromancy, and was a schoolmaster in the university cities. He won the respect of some of the leading figures of his day, while others banished him from their cities and labeled him a charlatan. Certain members of the Reformed clergy, including Martin Luther and Melanchthon, believed in his magical prowess, and may be responsible for sustaining his legend after his death.

BURNDY LIBRARY

MICHAEL FARADAY

U.S. NAVAL ACADEMY MUSEUM

ADMIRAL DAVID FARRAGUT

The Faust legend was the basis of a play by Christopher Marlowe, a dramatic poem by Goethe, an opera by Charles Gounod, a musical drama by Hector Berlioz, a novel by Thomas Mann, and numerous other works in music and literature.

Fawkes, Guy (1570–1606), English conspirator, the principal figure in the famous Gunpowder Plot of November 5, 1605. After James VI of Scotland ascended the English throne as James I, Fawkes (originally a Protestant) and several other Catholics plotted to blow up the king, his ministers, and both houses of Parliament on the day it was to assemble, hoping thereby to set up a Catholic government. The plot was discovered and he and his confederates were executed. November 5 is still celebrated in parts of England by processions and the burning of Guy Fawkes effigies.

Feininger, Lyonel (1871–1956), American painter, born in New York City. A political cartoonist and caricaturist for American and German magazines in Berlin (1895–1910), Feininger started painting seriously in 1907. From 1919 until the Nazis came to power (1933) he taught at the Bauhaus at Weimar and Dessau, where he became associated with Kandinsky, Klee, and Jawelensky. Known as the *Blaue Reiter* (Blue Rider) group, they held exhibitions from 1925 to 1934. Feininger returned to the U.S. in 1936 and co-founded a school in Chicago with Walter Gropius and Mies van de Rohe. His work, with its clean angular lines, leans toward cubism, though it maintains an individualistic style of its own. His paintings are in the Museum of Modern Art (New York), the Detroit Institute of Arts, and the Walker Art Center in Minneapolis.

Ferber, Edna (1887–　), American novelist and short-story writer, born in Kalamazoo, Mich. While working as a reporter for the Milwaukee *Journal* and Chicago *Tribune*, she wrote a number of short stories, published in collections such as *Dawn O'Hara* (1911), *Buttered Side Down* (1912), and *Roast Beef Medium* (1913), which earned her a name and enabled her to make a career of fiction writing. Her novels, all very popular and successful, include *So Big* (1924), *Show Boat* (1926), *Cimarron* (1929), *Saratoga Trunk* (1941), *Giant* (1952), and *Ice Palace* (1958). *So Big*, *Cimarron*, and *Giant* were popular also as motion pictures, and *Show Boat* was produced by Florence Ziegfeld as a musical play. With George S. Kaufman, Miss Ferber wrote the successful plays *The Royal Family* (1927) and *Dinner at Eight* (1932). She received the Pulitzer Prize in 1925 for *So Big*.

Ferdinand I (1503–1564), Holy Roman emperor (1556–1564), the son of Philip I of Spain and the younger brother of Charles V. He received the hereditary Austrian possessions from Charles in 1521. In 1526, after the death of his brother-in-law, Louis II of Hungary and Bohemia, he succeeded to the throne of Bohemia but his claim to the kingship of Hungary was contested by John Zápolya. He fought Zápolya and his Turkish allies (1526–1538) and finally secured Hungary. He was elected king of Germany in 1531 and in 1556 succeeded Charles V as Holy Roman emperor, though his title was not fully recognized until 1558.

Ferdinand II (1578–1637), Holy Roman emperor (1619–1637), the grandson of Ferdinand I. He was king of Bohemia (1617–1619, 1620–1637), and of Hungary (1621–1637). A Catholic zealot, he was overthrown by the Protestants and lost the Bohemian kingship in 1619. With the Catholic League and Spain as his allies, he deposed Elector Palatine Frederick V of Bohemia, and was made Holy Roman emperor about 1619. Ferdinand's determination to stamp out Protestantism in his dominions led to the Thirty Years' War. In 1629 he issued the Edict of Restitution, which nullified almost all the rights of the German Protestants. His generals Wallenstein and Tilly attempted to carry out this edict, but were met by opposition from Cardinal Richelieu and Gustavus Adolphus of Sweden, and the Protestants regained their rights.

Ferdinand II, called King **Bomba** (1810–1859), king of the Two Sicilies, comprising Naples and Sicily (1830–1859), the son of Francis I, whom he succeeded in 1830. His obsequiousness to the Austrians after his marriage to the daughter of Archduke Charles of Austria, his reactionary policies, and the wretched economic condition of his subjects led to a series of rebellions. In 1848, a year of revolution in Europe, he was forced to grant his people a constitution. In the following year Ferdinand put down an uprising in Sicily by bombarding Messina, thereby earning the name "King Bomba." His despotism and political persecutions resulted in the intervention of Great Britain in 1858, and he was compelled to free thousands of people whom he had willfully imprisoned.

Ferdinand V of Castile or **Ferdinand II** of Aragon, known as **the Catholic** (1452–1516), Spanish king, son of John II of Aragon. As king of Sicily (1468–1516), Ferdinand married his cousin Isabella (1469), sister of Henry IV of Castile, and on the death of Henry in 1474 most of the nobles proclaimed Ferdinand and Isabella cosovereigns. Five years of civil war followed, and in 1479 when King John died, the kingdoms of Castile and Aragon were united. The prosperous rule of these monarchs, known as *los reyes católicos* (the Catholic kings), laid the foundation for the subsequent greatness of Spain. To fight the banditti, Ferdinand established the Santa Hermandad (1476), a kind of militia-police; in 1480 he organized the Inquisition. He defeated the Moors in 1492, and in the same year he conquered Granada and expelled the Jews from his kingdom. Ferdinand and Isabella aided Columbus, who sailed under their auspices and discovered the New World in 1492, but after 1499 they dishonored him. When Isabella died in 1504, Ferdinand placed his insane daughter Juana on the Castilian throne and proclaimed himself regent. He participated in the League of Cambrai (1508) against Venice and in 1512 conquered Navarre.

Fermat, Pierre de (1601–1665), French mathematician, born in Beaumont de Lomagne. While serving as councilor for the Toulouse parliament, he spent his spare time working on mathematical problems. He is noted for his contribution to the theory of numbers, published after his death in his *Varia Opera Mathematica* (1679). He formulated, with Blaise Pascal, the calculus of probabilities and is the reputed founder of the differential calculus.

Fermi, Enrico (1901–1954), Italian-American physicist, born in Rome, Italy. He studied at Pisa, Göttingen, and Leiden, and in 1927 was appointed professor of theoretical physics at the University of Rome. His studies were primarily on the structure and behavior of atomic particles. In 1934 he and his colleagues were able to produce artificial radioactivity by bombarding uranium with neutrons. He was awarded the Nobel Prize for physics in 1938. In 1939 he came to the U.S. as professor of physics at Columbia University. In 1942 he became the first scientist to create an atomic chain reaction, and in 1945 he was appointed professor at the Institute for Nuclear Studies. Two days before his death, the Atomic Energy Commission honored him with a special award for his outstanding work in atomic energy.

Ferrero, Guglielmo (1871–1942), Italian historian, born in Portici, and educated at Pisa and Turin. He favored Italian intervention on the side of the Allies during World War I and opposed fascism in the 1920's. Ferrero's best-known work is *Greatness and Decline of Rome* (5 vols., 1907–1909). His other writings include *Ancient Rome and Modern America* (1914), *A Short History of Rome* (with Corrado Barbagallo, 1918), and *Peace and War* (1933). He was professor of modern history at the University of Geneva from 1930 to 1942.

Fessenden, William Pitt (1806–1869), American statesman, born in Boscawen, N. H., and educated at Bowdoin College. He became prominent in law and politics in Portland, Me., and served in Congress as a Whig (1841–1843). Fessenden was a forceful orator against slavery. Elected to the Senate in 1854, and reelected as a Republican in 1859, he remained a leading figure until his death. For a brief period in 1864–1865 he served as secretary of the treasury, and helped to improve the country's financial condition.

Fichte, Johann Gottlieb (1762–1814), German philosopher, born of working-class parents in Rammenau, Upper Lusatia. Intellectually gifted as a boy, he received the patronage of a wealthy nobleman and prepared himself for entrance to the University of Jena. There and at Leipzig and for several years after his graduation, he supported himself by tutoring. An interview with Immanuel Kant at Königsberg (1791) proved eventful, for the older philosopher advised him to publish his *Critique of all Revelation*. This work made Fichte's reputation and won for him the chair of philosophy at Jena in 1793. Fichte embodied Kantian ideas in his philosophy, though he set forth his own "science of knowledge," whereby knowledge is dependent upon moral certainty and self-activity. He substituted Kant's "thing in itself" for the primitive conscious "ego." Deeply interested in theology, Fichte saw the objective world or the "non-ego" as the world of God, and he asserted that it was man's moral duty to devote himself to this world. In these terms, the "non-ego" is dependent on the "ego" for its reality, with man morally obligated to serve this objective world. In 1798 he published a magazine article that was regarded as atheistic, as a result of which he lost his position. Soon, however, he was lecturing to appreciative audiences in Berlin, and in 1805 he received a professorship in Erlangen. During the Napoleonic invasions Fichte stirred the nation by his patriotic addresses, which instilled in the German people a spirit of unity. In 1809 he was appointed to the chair of philosophy at the newly organized University of Berlin.

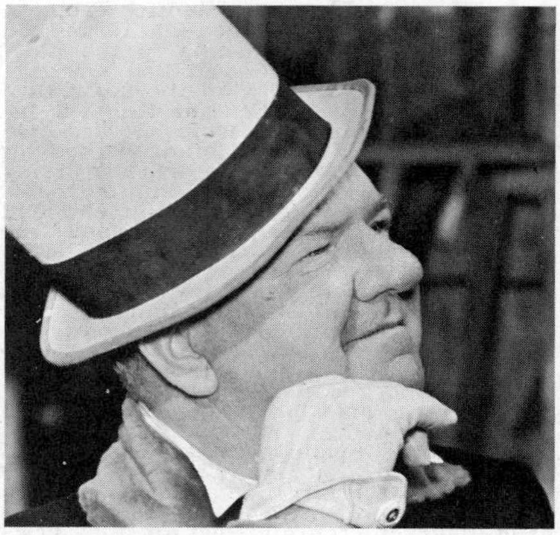

ASSOCIATED PRESS

W. C. FIELDS, comic actor, in costume.

Field, Cyrus West (1819–1892), American financier, noted for his part in the laying of the first Atlantic cable. Born in Stockbridge, Mass., he entered the business world at the age of 15 and retired at age 33 with a fortune of $250,000. In 1854 Field became interested in the idea of a transoceanic cable and organized the New York, Newfoundland, and London Telegraph, of which Peter Cooper was president. After many failures, a submarine line between Ireland and Newfoundland was put into operation in 1858, but the cable soon broke. This disaster, together with financial troubles, postponed the success of the venture until 1866. Field subsequently turned his attention to railroad development. He was one of the organizers of the elevated railway system of New York City.

Field, David Dudley (1805–1894), American jurist, born in Haddam, Conn. He entered Williams College (1821), studied law, and was admitted to the bar in 1828. He settled in New York and soon made his way into the front rank of his profession. In 1848 the New York state code of civil procedure, usually called the Field Code, was enacted—he had proposed the idea and had headed the commission to execute it. In 1867 he brought before the British Association for Social Science a proposition to frame an international code. This led him to prepare what was a complete work on international law, though entitled *Draft Outlines of an International Code* (1872, revised 1876).

Fielding, Henry (1707–1754), English novelist, born near Glastonbury. He studied at Eton and at the University of Leiden. On his return from Leiden he began writing for the stage and for ten years was a prolific playwright of comedies and farces such as *The Temple Beau* (1730), *Tom Thumb* (1730), *The Modern Husband* (1732), *Pasquin* (1736), and *The Historical Register* (1736). The latter two burlesques provoked the Licensing Act of 1737, and the Little Theatre in the Haymarket, which Fielding managed and wrote for, was closed. His dramatic career at an end, he studied law at the Middle Temple and in 1740 was admitted to the bar. A few years later he turned to the writing of novels with which his name is now principally associated: *Joseph Andrews* (1742), *Jonathan Wild* (1743), *Tom Jones* (1749), and *Amelia* (1751). *Joseph Andrews*, which began as a parody of Richardson's *Pamela*, fuses elements of the drama, mock epic, mock romance, and picaresque novel. *Jonathan Wild* is a biting satire on Robert Walepole, the creator of the Licensing Act that terminated Fielding's playwriting career. An outstanding example of Fielding's brilliant characterizations is the spirited title hero of *Tom Jones*, considered his finest work. Sophia Western in *Tom Jones* and the title character of *Amelia* are believed to be modeled after Fielding's first wife, Charlotte Craddock. Fielding's *Journal of a Voyage to Lisbon*, published posthumously in 1755, has much biographical interest.

Fields, W. C., originally **William Claude Dukenfield** (1880–1946), American actor and writer, noted for his vaudeville routine as the shabby but amiable drunkard with a quick wit. He was born in Philadelphia and ran away from home at the age of 11. While working as a newsboy, Fields taught himself to juggle and later made use of this skill as part of a comic routine in the *Ziegfeld Follies* (1915–1921). He made his first motion picture, *Sally of the Stardust*, in 1925. This was followed by many others, including *If I Had a Million* (1933), *Mrs. Wiggs of the Cabbage Patch* (1934), *The Man on the Flying Trapeze* (1935), and *You Can't Cheat an Honest Man* (1939).

Fiesole, Giovanni da (1387–1455), Italian painter known as **Fra Angelico** for the angelic figures that adorn his paintings and frescoes. Born in Vicchio, he joined the Dominican monastery in Fiesole (1407). In 1436 he joined the newly established monastery of San Marco in Florence, where many of his religious frescoes are to be found. At the invitation of Pope Eugenius IV, he came to Rome in 1445 and lived there until his death. Other frescoes by Fra Angelico are in the Nicholas Chapel of the Vatican and in Cortona and Fiesole. His well-known painting *The Coronation of the Virgin* is on exhibit at the Louvre and his *Glory* is at the London National Gallery.

Filarete, real name **Antonio di Pieto Averlino** or **Averulino**. (c.1400–c.1470), Italian architect and scultpor. He is best known for building the magnificent bronze doors of St. Peter's in Rome, and the Porta Giova of Sforzesco Castle in Milan.

Fillmore, Millard (1800–1874), thirteenth president of the United States (1850–1852), born in Locke, N.Y. At the age of 15 he was apprenticed to a clothier, but he was determined to become a lawyer and at 19 began to study in the office of a Cayuga County judge. In 1823 he was admitted to the bar and opened an office in East Aurora, N. Y., where he practiced until 1830. Beginning in 1928 he served three terms in the New York state legislature as an Anti-Mason, and in 1833 entered the U. S. Congress as a Whig. In Congress he favored the abolition of slavery in the District of Columbia and was the author of the tariff law in 1842. In 1847 Fillmore became comptroller of New York State and in 1848 was elected vice-president on the ticket with Zachary Taylor. He was called upon to preside over the Senate during the slavery arguments of 1850. When Pres. Taylor died suddenly in July, 1850, Fillmore became president, Although he opposed slavery, he signed the Compromise Act, for he feared that the South would otherwise secede. By signing the act for the surrender of fugitive slaves he brought about the utter defeat of the Whig party. He was an unsuccessful presidential candidate in 1852, and again in 1856, when he won only one state. Fillmore then retired from politics.

Finsen, Niels Ryberg (1860–1904), Danish physician who pioneered in the treatment of skin disease with light rays. He was born in Thorshavn, Faeroe Islands, and received his medical degree from the University of Copenhagen in 1890. The Danish government financed the establishment of his Medical Light Institute near Copenhagen, where he effected many remarkable cures of eczema, lupus, superficial cancer, and other skin ailments. In 1903 he received the Nobel Prize for medicine.

Firestone, Harvey Samuel (1868–1938), American industrialist, born in Columbiana County, Ohio. He entered the rubber business and in 1900, at Akron, Ohio, organizing the Firestone Tire and Rubber Company with 17 employees. During the next three decades the company increased its staff to more than 20,000, and as many native laborers were employed in Liberia, West Africa, where a million acres of rubber land were leased in 1926.

Fischer von Erlach, Johann Bernhard (1656–1723), Austrian architect, born in Graz. One of the foremost Baroque architects, he designed the palace of Prince Eugène in Vienna (1705), the Clam-Gallas Palace in Prague (1707), and the University Church in Salzburg. He also designed the Castle Schönbrunn (1695–1700) and the Royal Library in Vienna.

Fish, Hamilton (1808–1893), American statesman, born in New York City and educated at Columbia College. Admitted to the bar in 1830, he was elected to Congress as a Whig in 1843. Fish was governor of New York from 1849 until 1851, when he began a term in the U.S. Senate. During the Civil War he was instrumental in bringing about the exchange of Federal and Confederate prisoners. He served as secretary of state during Pres. Ulysses S. Grant's two terms (1869–1877). In this capacity he helped to negotiate the Treaty of Washington, providing for the arbitration of the Alabama Claims; and he brought about the settlement of the northwestern boundary dispute with Great Britain.

Fisher, John Arbuthnot, 1st Baron **Fisher of Kilverstone** (1841–1920), British admiral, born in Ceylon. He entered the naval service in 1854. From 1855 to 1882 he served in the Crimean, Chinese, and Egyptian wars. He became first sea lord of the admiralty, resigning in 1910, but he was recalled at the outbreak of World War I, finally resigning in 1915. In 1905 he received the Order of Merit.

Fisk, James (1834–1872), American financier, born in Bennington, Vt. During the Civil War he made a fortune by trading in cotton. Assisted by Daniel Drew, he set up a brokerage house, Fisk and Belden, in New York City in 1866, and thereafter became one of the most feared, hated, and admired of business buccaneers. With Jay Gould he carried on unscrupulous manipulations of Erie Railroad stock that wrecked the company but gave them millions. Other operations led to the famous "Black Friday" stock market crash in 1869, which ruined hundreds. He lived luxuriously and dabbled in the production of plays and operas. He was fatally shot by Edward S. Stokes, a former business partner.

Fiske, John, original name **Edmund Fisk Green** (1842–1901), American philosopher and historian, born in Hartford, Conn. He graduated from Harvard Law School (1865), and later returned as a lecturer in philosophy (1869–1871), instructor in history (1870), and assistant librarian (1872–1879). Thereafter he devoted his time to lecturing on philosophy and writing history books dealing mainly with the colonial period. He published such books as *Myths and Myth-Makers* (1872), *The Outlines of Cosmic Philosophy* (2 vols., 1874), *Darwinism and Other Essays* (1879), *The Beginnings of New England* (1889), *The American Revolution* (2 vols., 1891), *The Dutch and Quaker Colonies* (2 vols., 1899), and *The Origin of Evil* (1889). Fiske spent part of his life trying to popularize Spencerian evolution, and interpreting Darwinism.

Fitch, John (1743–1798), American inventor, born in Windsor, Conn. Before serving in a New Jersey regiment during the American Revolution, he formed a brass and silversmith business. While engaged in making a map of the northwest after the Revolution, he conceived the idea of navigating the American rivers with steamboats (1785), and he devoted most of his life to the application of steam power to navigation. After much difficulty he formed a company and built several boats equipped with steam engines, but financial difficulties forced him to drop the project. In 1793 he went to France to secure further aid, but was again disappointed. He then moved to Kentucky in the hope of claiming land there. Fitch preceded Fulton in designing a ship using steam, but his models were inferior to Fulton's as practical carriers of passengers and freight.

FitzGerald, Edward (1809–1883), English poet and translator, born near Woodbridge, Suffolk. He was educated at Cambridge. His fame rests chiefly on his translation from the Persian of the *Rubáiyát* of Omar Khayyám (published in 1859). FitzGerald did not translate slavishly but expressed the author's thoughts in exquisite poetry, taking whatever liberties he deemed necessary to preserve the quality of the famous quatrains. He also translated the *Agamemnon*, two dramas of Sophocles, and six plays of Calderón (1853); and authored *Euphranor: a Dialogue on Youth* (1851), and *Polonius: a Collection of Wise Saws and Modern Instances* (1852). His work was admired by the poets and writers of his day, and he was friendly with many of them, including William Makepeace Thackeray, Alfred Tennyson, Thomas Carlyle, and Bernard Barton, the Quaker poet, whose daughter FitzGerald was married to for a short time.

Fitzgerald, Francis Scott Key (1896–1940), American novelist and short-story writer, born in St. Paul, Minn. The life of F. Scott Fitzgerald, as well as his works, is said to epitomize the American "lost generation" of the period following World War I. He attended Princeton University from 1917 to 1919 and served in World War I. After the war he resided in New York City, where he wrote advertising copy. Upon selling his first short stories to a magazine, he turned his full attention to creative writing. After marrying Zelda Sayre, he went with her to France, residing there for several years. In 1920 his first novel, *The Beautiful and the Damned*, was published. *The Great Gatsby*, reputed to be Fitzgerald's finest novel, appeared in 1925. It is critically acclaimed for its excellent depiction of the twenties. Other works by him include the novels *This Side of Paradise* (1920), *The Beautiful and the Damned* (1921), *Tender is the Night* (1934), *Taps at Reveille* (1935), and *The Last Tycoon*, published posthumously in 1941; and the collections of short stories, *Flappers and Philosophers* (1920), *Tales of the Jazz Age* (1922), and *All the Sad Young Men* (1926). Three of his short stories, *Babylon Revisited*, *The Rich Boy*, and *The Diamond Big as the Ritz*, are particularly well known and have been reprinted in several short-story anthologies. *The Crack-Up*, published in 1945, contains some of his essays and letters and extracts from his journals.

Flagstad, Kirsten (1895–1962), Norwegian operatic soprano, noted for her performance of Wagnerian roles. She made her operatic debut in Oslo in 1913, but it was not until she made her United States debut at the New York Metropolitan Opera House in 1935, in the role of Sieglinde in *Die Walküre*, that she received international recognition. From 1935 until 1941 she remained with the Metropolitan, holding court there with her brilliant interpretation of Wagnerian roles; but when Germany occupied Norway, she returned to her native country (1941) to be with her second husband, Henry Johansen. Miss Flagstad's residence in Norway during Nazi occupation was severely critized, but her successful American concert tour in 1947 softened her critics and she was formally vindicated of her wartime activities. In 1952 she retired from the stage, and in 1958 was appointed director of the Norwegian Opera Company. She died Dec. 8, 1962 in Oslo, Norway.

Flaubert, Gustave (1821–1880), French novelist whose works, particularly *Madame Bovary*, were the connecting link between the dying Romantic school and the naturalistic fiction of the next era. Born in Rouen, he studied law in Paris, but failing his exams he gave up his studies to pursue a literary career. A nervous disease that afflicted him from childhood and a distaste for the masses made Flaubert spend most of his life in seclusion, although he befriended many of the great literary figures of his day. His correspondence with them, especially with George Sand, are of considerable interest because they contain much of his literary criticism. In addition to *Madame Bovary*, his first published and most controversial work (1857), other notable works of his are *Salammbô* (1862), *L'Education sentimentale* (1869), *La Tentation de sainte Antoine* (1874), and *Trois contes* (1877).

Flaxman, John (1755–1826), English sculptor and draftsman, born in York. The son of a moulder of plaster casts, he began to study at the Royal Academy in London in 1769, and within a few years became a designer for the famous pottery house of Josiah Wedgwood. In 1787 he went to Rome to study Greek and Roman art, and while there he executed drawings for the *Iliad* and *Odyssey*, Dante's *Divine Comedy*, and the plays of Aeschylus. He returned to London in 1794, and produced memorial monuments of Lord Mansfield, Robert Burns, and Lord Horatio Nelson. In 1810 he became professor of sculpture at the Royal Academy. He was considered one of the leaders of the Classical revival in English art.

Fleming, Sir Alexander (1881–1955), British bacteriologist who discovered the antibiotic penicillin. Born in Scotland, he graduated from St. Mary's Hospital Medical School at the University of London. While studying bacteria culture plates in his laboratory in 1928, he noticed that a mold had landed on one of the plates and was destroying the bacteria. Instead of throwing away the contaminated culture, he began to experiment with the mold and found it made a powerful and nonpoisonous antiseptic, thus discovering penicillin. Fleming also discovered the antiseptic lysozyme in 1929. In 1944 he was knighted, and the following year shared the Nobel Prize for medicine with Dr. Howard Florey and Ernest B. Chain, two Oxford scientists who succeeded in purifying the penicillin mold, thereby making it available for use in injections.

Fleming, Sir John Ambrose (1849–1945), English electrical engineer, born in Lancaster. Educated at the Royal College of Chemistry and Cambridge University, from 1885–1926 he was professor of electrical engineering at University College, London. He contributed to the development of the telephone, electric lighting, and wireless telegraphy, and is the inventor of the thermionic valve that made many electronic instruments possible. He wrote *Electric Lamps and Electric Currents* (1897), *The Principles of Electric Wave Telegraphy and Telephony* (1906), *Wireless Telegraphy* (1913), and *Electric Waves and Wireless Telephony* (1923).

Fleming, Sir Sandford (1827–1915), Canadian civil engineer, born in Scotland. He went to Canada in 1845, supervised the construction of the Intercolonial Railway (1867–1876), and as chief engineer for the Canadian Pacific Railway (1872–1880) surveyed the route followed by the present Canadian National Railway, including several well-known routes: Kicking Horse, Eagle, and Yellowhead passes. Fleming, who was knighted in 1897, devised the system of time zones (1879) used universally.

Fleury, André Hercule de (1653–1743), French cardinal and statesman, born in Lodève. He received favor and promotion from Louis XIV, and was appointed bishop of Fréjus. When the king's son ascended the throne as Louis XV in 1715, Fleury was appointed the boy's tutor. In 1726, at the age of 73, Fleury succeeded the duc de Bourbon as prime minister and soon after was appointed cardinal. He did much for the internal progress of France and was instrumental in bringing to completion the Bibliothèque Nationale.

Flexner, Simon (1863–1946), American pathologist, born in Louisville, Ky. After completing postgraduate studies at Johns Hopkins University, at universities abroad, and at the Pasteur Institute, he joined the faculty of Johns Hopkins University. Later he took up hospital work and in 1903 became director of the laboratories of the Rockefeller Institute for Medical Research in New York. Flexner is best known for his research work in the causes, transmission, and cure of infantile paralysis, and for his discovery of the serum for the treatment of epidemic cerebrospinal meningitis, which greatly reduced the death rate from that disease.

Flotow, Baron Friedrich von (1812–1883), German composer of light operas, born in Mecklenburg-Schwerin. Of his 18 operas only one, *Martha* (1847), is heard on the operatic stage today. The charm of its melodies, one of them being an interpolation of Moore's *Last Rose of Summer*, and a picturesque setting have made *Martha* a lasting favorite. It is sometimes found in the repertoire of grand opera companies, but more often is considered as an operetta to be sung in English. Flotow's *Stradella* (1844) was a success for some time but gradually waned in popularity.

Foch, Ferdinand (1851–1929), French marshal, born in Tarbes in the French Pyrenees. After his graduation from the École Polytechnique in 1873 he was commissioned a lieutenant in the artillery. In 1894 he was appointed professor of strategy at the École de Guerre, where he delivered a famous series of lectures that were later compiled into two volumes, *De la conduite de la guerre* (1897) and *Des principes de la guerre* (1899). When World War I broke out in 1914 Gen. Foch was commanding the 20th Army Corps at Nancy. His ability as a strategist was brilliantly displayed in 1914 in the defense of Nancy, the battle of the Marne, the battle in the Artois sector,

and in 1916 in the fighting on the River Somme. He strongly urged unity of command in 1917, and in March, 1918, was put in command of the Allied armies on the western front. He was made marshal of France in August, 1918, and framed the armistice terms in the fall of that year. Foch was present at the opening of the disarmament conference in Washington in 1921. He lies buried in Les Invalides in Paris, near Napoleon.

Fontaine, Jean de la. See *La Fontaine.*

Fontana, Domenico (1543–1607), Italian architect and engineer, born in Mili, near Lake Como. Among his important achievements are the completion of the dome and lantern of St. Peter's Basilica in Rome; in collaboration with Giacomo della Porta and following Michelangelo's plans, the setting up of the Egyptian obelisk in the piazza of the basilica; the construction of the Lateran Palace; and the building of the Vatican Library. Under Pope Sixtus V (who was Fontana's patron when he was Cardinal Montalto) Fontana was papal architect; after the pope's death he was employed by the king of Naples to build a royal palace.

Fontanne, Lynn, born **Lily Louise** (1887–), American actress, born in London. Her first stage appearance was as a child at the Drury Lane Pantomime. She made her debut on the London stage in 1909, and on the New York stage in 1910. Before coming to America, she performed with Beerbohm Tree and other notables on the London stage and in numerous English touring companies. In 1922 she married the American actor Alfred Lunt, and thereafter costarred with him in numerous American productions, the first being *The Guardsman* in 1924. Other plays that she and her husband have appeared in are *Goat Song, Strange Interlude, Pygmalion, Taming of the Shrew, Idiot's Delight, Amphytrion 38, The Great Sebastians,* and *The Visit.*

Fontenelle, Bernard Le Bovier de (1657–1757), French writer and philosopher, born in Rouen. The nephew of the great tragic poet Corneille, Fontenelle during his long career (he lived to be 100 years) attempted almost every literary genre, including satires, histories, dialogues, and critical essays. He exercised a powerful influence on the writers of his day, holding court in many of the literary salons. He was very interested in the scientific discoveries of the period, and in 1697 was appointed secretary of the Académie des Sciences, where he was later made president. In his works *Dialogues des morts* (*Dialogues of the Dead,* 1683) and *Digression sur les anciens et les modernes* (*Digression on the Ancients and the Moderns,* 1688) he attacks conventionalism, and criticizes members of the literary world of his day who worshipped the ancients and lacked faith or interest in their own period. His best-known works are *Entretiens sur la pluralité des mondes* (*Conversations on the Plurality of Worlds,* 1866), an examination of the philosophic consequences of the discoveries of Copernicus, and *L'historie des oracles* (*History of Oracles,* 1686), a study of the fables and myths of classical antiquity.

Fonteyn, Dame **Margot,** stage name of **Margaret Fonteyne Hookham de Arias** (1919–), English ballerina, born in Reigate, Surrey. She studied at the Sadler's Wells School, joining the school's professional company in 1934. Her first solo role was in *The Haunted Ballroom.* Her inter-

pretation of *Giselle,* which she first danced in 1937, has been critically acclaimed. As prima ballerina of the Royal Ballet (formerly the Sadler Wells), she has received many awards, among them the Commander Order of the British Empire (1951) and the D.B.E. (1956). In 1955 she married Panamanian diplomat Roberto E. Arias.

Forbes-Robertson, Sir Johnston (1853–1937), English actor, born in London. He received his education at Charterhouse, London; at Rouen; and at the Royal Academy of Arts. He made his first stage appearance in 1874 in *Mary Queen of Scots;* he subsequently played with Ellen Terry, Sir Henry Irving, the Bancrofts, Mrs. Patrick Campbell (in *Romeo and Juliet,* 1895, under his own management), with his wife, Gertrude Elliott, and with other celebrated actors. He made several tours of the United States, where he won general admiration for his work, especially in *Hamlet* (1898), *The Passing of the Third Floor Back* (1909–1911), *The Light That Failed,* and *Caesar and Cleopatra.* He was knighted in 1913 and retired after a farewell season in 1914. He is generally recognized as one of the greatest Shakespearean actors of all time.

Ford, Henry (1863–1947), American automobile manufacturer, born in Greenfield, Mich. He attended a district school, worked on his father's farm, and at the age of 16 began work as a machinist in Detroit, eventually becoming chief engineer of the Edison Illuminating Company. During his spare hours he began to experiment with horseless carriages run by steam, then turned his attention to gasoline power. In 1903, at Dearborn, Mich., he started the business that grew into the Ford Motor Company, and he soon became the largest manufacturer of motor cars in the world. He pioneered in installing mass-production methods, in lowering prices to extend the market, and in increasing wages to secure efficiency. During World War I Ford, a staunch pacifist, chartered a steamer, *The Peace Ship,* and led a group of pacifists to Europe to negotiate a peace conference (1915–1916).

Forrest, Nathan Bedford (1821–1877), American army officer, born in Bedford County, Tenn. He had little formal education but became a successful cotton planter and slave trader. When the South seceded, he entered the Confederate army as a private, and was soon asked to organize a cavalry battalion. He participated in the defense of Fort Donelson, but withdrew before the surrender. In 1864, as major general, he had charge of the cavalry of the Army of Tennessee; the following year, as lieutenant general in command of a larger force, he was forced to surrender at Gainesville, Ala. A brilliant cavalry officer, Forrest attributed his many victories in Tennessee, Kentucky, Alabama, and Mississippi in 1862–1864 to a military tactic that he conceived, which was to "get there first with the most men." The statement is more commonly known today in its misquoted form—"firstest with the mostest." Forrest is reputed to have been the commanding officer of the original Ku Klux Klan, which was organized during the Reconstruction period.

Forster, Edward Morgan (1879–), English writer, noted for his critical examination of conventional British mores. He was born in London and educated at Tonbridge School and King's College, Cambridge. The impact of Forster's extensive travels to Greece, Italy, Egypt, and India is apparent in much of his work. His best known novel, *A Passage to India* (1924), deals with the conflict between English colonists and their Indian subjects. More profoundly, it is a penetrating study of human relationships. For this work Forster was awarded the Prix Femina Vie Heureuse and the James Tait Black Memorial prize. His other novels include *Where Angels Fear to Tread* (1905), *Room With A View* (1908), and *Howard's End* (1910). He also wrote short stories and collaborated with Eric Crozier on the libretto for Benjamin Britten's opera *Billy Budd* (1951). In 1953 he was made a Champion of Honor.

Foscari, Francesco (c.1372–1457), doge of Venice (1423–1457). In this office he followed a military policy that brought most of northern Italy under the rule of Venice. Although successful in office, the doge suffered much from the political activities of his son Giacopo, who was banished three times and died in exile. About a week before his own death, Foscari was deposed for alleged treasonous activities. Byron based his tragedy *The Two Foscari* on the lives of the father and son.

Foscolo, Ugo, original name **Niccolò Foscolo** (1778–1827), Italian writer, born on the island of Zante. He studied at Spalato and Venice. His most notable work, an episto-

UNITED PRESS INTERNATIONAL

MARGOT FONTEYN in Cinderella ballet role.

HENRY FORD, American industrial innovator.

lary novel entitled *Ultime lettere di Jacopo Ortis* (*The Last Letters of Jacob Ortis,* 1802), expresses Foscolo's depressed state when Italy was placed under Austrian rule. He fought in the French armies, believing that Napoleon would liberate Italy; but when he realized that this was not the emperor's intentions, he retired to Milan, where he wrote his famous poem *I sepolcri*. Unwilling to remain in Italy while it was under Austrian domination, Foscolo went to Switzerland in 1815, and the following year journeyed to London, where he resided until his death. He also wrote the tragedies *Aiace* and *Ricciarda*, published in 1811; a translation of Sterne's *Sentimental Journey* (1813); and numerous essays, sonnets, and odes.

Foster, John Watson (1836–1917), American diplomat and statesman, born in Pike County, Ind. He studied at Indiana University, graduated from the Harvard Law School, and was admitted to the bar in 1857. He joined the Union army at the outbreak of the Civil War and rose to the rank of colonel. Foster entered the diplomatic service in 1873 when appointed minister to Mexico, and subsequently was sent to Russia (1880–1881), and to Spain (1883–1885). In 1892–1893 he was secretary of state and in 1894 was invited by the Chinese to participate in the peace negotiations terminating the Sino-Japanese War (1894–1895). In 1898 Foster was a member of the commission to settle controversies between the United States and Canada, and in 1903 participated in the settlement of the Alaska boundary dispute; in 1907 he acted as delegate from China to the Second Hague Conference. He wrote several books on diplomacy, among them *A Century of American Diplomacy, 1776–1876* (1900), *American Diplomacy in the Orient* (1903), and *Diplomatic Memoirs* (2 vols., 1909).

Foster, Stephen Collins (1826–1864), American song writer, born near Pittsburgh, Pa. He wrote both lyrics and music for most of his songs, although he had no formal music training. Many of his works, with their folk-song quality, were popular with the Negro minstrel troupes. Among the best known of his songs are *My Old Kentucky Home, O Susanna, Suwanee River, Nelly Bly, Old Dog Tray, Old Black Joe, Nelly Was a Lady, Old Uncle Ned, Massa's in the Cold, Cold Ground, Jeannie With the Light Brown Hair,* and *Come Where My Love Lies Dreaming*. He wrote about 125 songs, and although they sold well (over 400,000 copies of *My Old Kentucky Home* were sold in his lifetime), he was impoverished at his death.

Foucault, Jean Bernard Léon (1819–1868), French physicist born in Paris. He first studied medicine and then experimental physics. In one research project, he hung a 200-foot pendulum from the roof of the Pantheon in Paris (1851). Free to oscillate in any direction, it never traced the same path twice, but constantly varied to the right. This experiment showed that the floor was moving under the pendulum—that the earth was rotating. Foucault also proved that light travels faster in air than in water (1850). He invented the gyroscope (1852), the Foucault polarizing prism (1857), and the spheroid mirror for use in reflecting telescopes (1858). Foucault was appointed to the Paris Observatory in 1855 and in 1864 was made an officer of the Legion of Honor.

Fouquet or **Fouquet, Jean** (c.1416–1480), French artist, court painter to Charles VII and Louis XI. He was born in Tours, and studied there and in Paris and Italy. His style shows influences of both Florentine and Flemish masters. In addition to his works for the French Royal Court, he was commissioned by Étienne Chevalier, Marie de Clèves, and Philippe de Comines to do illuminations for various *Livres d' Heures* (*Books of Hours*). Other works include a lost portrait of Pope Eugenius IV, and illustrations for the French translation of Boccaccio and for Flavius Josephus' *Antiquities of the Jews*.

Fourier, François Marie Charles (1772–1837). French social philosopher, born in Besançon. He began his career as a traveling mercantile agent and later established a business of his own in Lyons. From 1794 to 1796 he served in the Revolutionary army. His most influential work is *Traité de l'Association domestique et agricole* (*Treatise on Domestic and Agricultural Association,* 1822). The sufferings of the poor and the injustices of the capitalistic system made a profound impression upon him in his earlier years. His system, known as Fourierism, was an outgrowth of the philosophy of Rousseau and taught that an entirely new social order was necessary; that men and women must be allowed to live as they like, free from the trammels imposed by civilization. The Brook Farm experiment in America was based on Fourier's ideas.

Fox, Charles James (1749–1806), English statesman and orator, born in London and educated at Eton and Oxford. He entered Parliament in 1768 at the age of 19 and rose rapidly to political prestige. His policies grew increasingly liberal and he advocated freedom for the American colonies. In 1789 he greeted the fall of the Bastille with great speeches and continued to be a firm supporter of the French Revolution, which led to a rupture of his long friendship with Edmund Burke. Fox's political life was mainly spent in opposition to the government, but when his great rival William Pitt formed his last administration, he asked Fox to join it. King George III, however, refused to give his approval. On Pitt's death in 1806 the king was at last obliged to admit Fox to office, and he became foreign secretary in Greenville's ministry. In that capacity, he tried to negotiate peace with France, and revealed a plot to assassinate Napoleon. His last motion in Parliament was directed against the slave trade; the measure founded upon it passed into law a few months after his death.

Fox, George (1624–1691), English founder of the Society of Friends, born in Leicestershire. He began preaching in his home neighborhood to the "Friends of Truth," for which he was frequently persecuted and imprisoned. He was convinced of the futility of learning for the work of the ministry, the presence of Christ in the heart as the "inner light," and the necessity of trying men's opinions and religions by the Holy Spirit and not by the Scriptures. He told a magistrate to "tremble at the word of God," hence the nickname "Quaker." His writings included *A Collection of Epistles* (1698), and *Gospel Truth* (1706), published posthumously.

Foxe, John (1516–1587), English author of a famous book on martyrs, born in Boston, Lincolnshire, and educated at Oxford. As an ordained deacon (1550) and priest (1560), he adopted the Reformed faith and fled to the Continent on the accession of Mary I. In Strasbourg he began in Latin his *Actes and Monuments*. First issued in English in 1563, it is now universally known as *The Book of Martyrs*.

Fra Angelico. See *Angelico, Fra.*

Fra Diavolo, real name **Michele Pezza** (c.1771–1806), Italian bandit who became a legendary figure. Reputedly expelled from a monastery, he organized a band of brigands and terrorized the countryside. He was later made a colonel in a war against France but was captured by the French and executed in Naples. His name was used as the title of an opera by Auber (1830).

Fragonard, Jean Honoré (1732–1806), French painter, born in Grasse. He began his art studies at the age of 18 under Jean Chardin, and François Boucher and in 1752 won the Prix de Rome. From about 1770 until the French Revolution, Fragonard was one of the most popular artists of his day. His work is representative of the so-called Rococo period, when classic simplicity was replaced by elaborate decoration and an atmosphere of gaiety. Among his principal works is the series, ordered by Mme. du Barry, now known as *Romance of Love and Youth*, in the Frick Collection, New York. Many of his studies of contemporary French life, such as *Instant Désiré, Heure du Bergen, Le Serment d'Amour,* and *Le Billet Doux*, are to be found in the museums and galleries of Europe.

France, Anatole, real name **Jacques Anatole François Thibault** (1844–1924), French novelist, poet, and critic, born in Paris. The son of a bookseller, he began his literary career by writing novels, which soon won him a reputation of one of the greatest men of letters in France. In 1897 he was elected to the French Academy. A socialistic free-thinker, he defended Capt. Alfred Dreyfus and wrote in support of France during World War I. He received the Nobel Prize for literature in 1921. His works include *Poèmes dorés* (1873), *Les Noces corinthiennes,* a verse play (1876), *Le Crime de Sylvestre Bonnard* (1881), *Thaïs* (1890), *Historic contemporaine* (4 vols., 1897–1901), *Les Dieux ont soif* (1912), and *La Vie en fleur* (1922).

Francesca da Rimini (died c.1285), Italian noblewoman, immortalized by Dante in the fifth canto of the *Inferno*. She was also the subject of numerous other works of art, including a play by Gabriele d'Annunzio, a symphonic poem by Tchaikovsky, and paintings by Jean Ingres and George Watts. She was born in Ravenna, where her father, Guido da Polenta, was a lord. Married to Giovanni Malatesta, she had an affair with his younger brother Paolo, himself a married man. Giovanni eventually discovered the illicit love, and killed his wife and brother.

Francesco di Giorgio, in full **Francesco Maurizio di Giorgio Martini Pollaiuolo** (1439–1502), Italian artist and engineer, born in Siena. He was military engineer to the duke of Urbino, and built the Church of the Madonna del Calcinai near Cortona. He designed civic buildings at Ancona and at Iesi, and was chief architect of the Cathedral of Siena.

Francis I (1494–1547) king of France (1515–1547), son of Charles, count of Angoulême and Louise of Savoy. In 1515, one year after his marriage to the dauphine Claude, he succeeded his father-in-law, Louis XII. The election of Charles V as Holy Roman emperor in 1519 started a long series of wars between Francis and Charles. Francis sought the aid of Henry VIII of England, and in 1520 the two kings met on the Field of the Cloth of Gold. Henry, however, decided to ally himself with Charles. In 1525 Francis was taken prisoner at Pavia and was kept captive for more than a year until he had ceded Burgundy and made other sizeable concessions in the Treaty of Madrid (1526). He waged two more wars before making peace with Charles V at Crespy, three years before his death. He is remembered as a patron of art and learning and for his love affairs with Diane de Poitiers and the Duchesse d' Étampes. He founded the Royal College of France in 1530.

Francis I, original name **Francis Stephen** (1708–1765), Holy Roman emperor (1745–1765), son of Leopold, the duke of Lorraine. He succeeded to his father's title in 1729, but in 1735 ceded the duchy to the king of Poland, in return for the right of succession to Tuscany, becoming grand duke in 1737. In 1736 he married Maria Theresa of Austria, who succeeded her father, Emperor Charles VI, in 1740. Francis had little to do with the government of his wife's realm; she herself assumed direction of the War of the Austrian Succession against Frederick (1740–1748) and the Seven Years' War (1756–1763). It was due to her efforts that Francis was elected Holy Roman emperor. Their son Joseph succeeded to the title in 1765 and their daughter became the ill-fated queen of France, Marie Antoinette.

Francis II (1768–1835), Austrian emperor (1804–1835), eldest son of Emperor Leopold II, and the last emperor of the Holy Roman empire (1792–1806). From 1797–1809 he waged war three times against France, losing to Napoleon, until in 1813 he joined the allies and assisted in the final defeat of Napoleon. In 1804 he proclaimed himself hereditary emperor of Austria; and two years later abdicated the crown of the Holy Roman empire, which was dissolved after an existence of ten centuries. Although Napoleon married Francis' daughter Maria Louisa in 1810, Francis joined the coalition against the conqueror. After Napoleon's defeat in 1815, the Austrian emperor became associated with Russia and Prussia in the Holy Alliance.

Francis Ferdinand (1863–1914). Austrian archduke, son of Archduke Charles Louis and nephew of Emperor Francis Joseph I. He became heir apparent to the crowns of Austria and Hungary on the deaths of his cousin Crown Prince Rudolf in 1889 and his own father in 1896. In 1900 Francis Ferdinand contracted a morganatic marriage with the Countess Chotek, duchess of Hohenberg, but children of the couple were barred from succession rights because the princess was not of royal blood. On June 28, 1914, the archduke and his wife were assassinated at Sarajevo, Bosnia. The events that ensued led to the outbreak of World War I.

Francis Joseph I, German name **Franz Josef** (1830–1916), ruler of the Austro-Hungarian monarchy at the outbreak of World War I. He became emperor of Austria in 1848 and king of Hungary in 1867, when the two countries were united in the dual monarchy. Francis Joseph succeeded to the Austrian throne on the abdication of his uncle, Emperor Ferdinand I. During his reign of 68 years Francis Joseph faced rebellion in his own country, domestic tragedy, and foreign wars, including the humilitating Seven Weeks' War with Prussia (1866), which ended Austria's long dominance in German affairs and lost Venetia to Italy. However, the emperor held fast and instituted political reforms. He took the fatal step of declaring war on Serbia after the assassination of his heir, Francis Ferdinand, in 1914. Francis Joseph died in the war and was succeeded by his grandnephew, the archduke Charles Francis Joseph, who ruled as Charles I until the end of the war, when the monarchy fell.

Francis of Assisi, Saint, born **Giovanni Francesco Bernadone** (1182–1226), founder of the Franciscan Order. He was born in Assisi, Italy. His father, a cloth merchant, named him Francesco ("the Frenchman") because of his fondness for France. In his youth Francis lived the life of a wealthy young man, interrupted by a spell of military service during which he was taken prisoner and held captive for a year at Perugia. During an illness he turned his thoughts toward religion and although he returned to the army, a second illness at Spoleto decided his career for life. At the age of 26 he resolved to fulfill literally the counsels of the Scriptures and decided to live in poverty. His father brought him before the bishop to have him legally disinherited. Francis left his native city as a pauper. He soon attracted a few followers and in 1210 went to Rome to obtain permission to found an order devoted to poverty, work, and service—the Franciscan Order. Saint Francis attracted many disciples, whom he sent in parties to different provinces of Italy. Five of the brotherhood, who had gone to Morocco to preach to the Moors, became the first martyrs of the order. But after Pope Innocent II approved the order in 1209, it increased with extraordinary rapidity. At the first general assembly (1219), 5,000 members were present. Francis himself inaugurated the future missionary character of his order by going to the East (1223).

Francis of Sales, Saint (1567–1622), Roman Catholic bishop and writer, born of noble parentage at the family seat in Savoy. Though he earned his Doctor of Laws in Padua (1591), he entered the priesthood out of love of religious work. He was ordained in 1593, and in 1594 was sent to chateaus in Savoy to convert the colonists to Catholicism. After his success there, he was appointed bishop of Geneva (1602). As priest, bishop, and writer, Francis was simple, earnest, and deeply pious. Patron saint of Catholic writers since 1922, his *Introduction to the Devout Life* is one of the most widely read of all religious books. In 1665 he was canonized by Pope Alexander VII. His feast day is January 29.

Francis Xavier, Saint. See *Xavier.*

Franck, César Auguste (1822–1890), French composer, born in Liège, Belgium. He established himself in Paris in 1844, where he won distinction as church organist at Ste. Clotilde and professor of organ at the Paris Conservatoire. His compositions were acclaimed by Franz Liszt and others and were studied by many contemporary musicians, but his general popularity as a composer developed slowly. His chief works include the oratorios *Les Béatitudes* (1880), *Ruth* (1846), *Rédemption* (1872), and *Rebecca* (1881); some chamber music; and one symphony, the Symphony in D Minor (1889).

Franco, Francisco, in full **Francisco Paulino Hermenegildo Téodulo Franco-Bahamonde** (1892–), Spanish general and revolutionary leader; Fascist dictator of Spain. He was born at the naval base at El Ferrol where his father was commandant. Franco began his military career in the Spanish army in Morocco, where he helped to organize the Spanish Foreign Legion and was liaison officer with the French army during the Riff uprising of 1925. At the age of 33 he became a brigadier general, the youngest in Europe; ten years later he was appointed chief of staff of the Spanish army.

For five years after the formation of the Spanish republic in 1931 the trend in elections was steadily toward the Left. In April, 1936, Manuel Azana became president and began a campaign against private property and the Church. Rightist elements had not been idle, and Franco led a revolt in Spanish Morocco and crossed into Spain with the Foreign Legion and thousands of Moorish troops. He became generalissimo of the Rebel forces during the Civil War (1936–1939), and after his victory became chief of state, commander in chief of the armed forces, and prime minister. He ruled Spain with a strong hand as absolute head of the Falange party. Franco kept Spain neutral during World War II, although his sympathies were with the Axis. In 1947 he was granted the life tenure as chief of state.

Franklin, Benjamin (1706–1790), American statesman, scientist, and writer, born in Boston, Mass. He was apprenticed to his older brother James, a printer, at the age of 12. When James started the *New England Courant,* Franklin secretly wrote some pieces for it and had the satisfaction of finding them well received. Soon after, he left his brother's employ and at the age of 17 found work in Philadelphia as a compositor. After an 18-month sojourn in

London, Franklin returned to Philadelphia and within a short time became owner of *The Pennsylvania Gazette;* in 1732 he started the popular *Poor Richard's Almanack.* In about 1727 he formed a discussion club, the "Junto," which in 1743 became the American Philosophical Society. By his efforts a public library, improved systems of education, and a scheme of insurance were established in Philadelphia.

An active member of the Pennsylvania Assembly, he was sent in 1757 to England as the agent of the province. So great was his reputation both at home and abroad, that he was appointed agent of Massachusetts, Maryland, and Georgia. Oxford and Edinburgh conferred on him their highest academic degrees, and the Royal Society elected him a fellow.

In 1762 he returned to America but only remained until 1764 when he was again appointed agent to bring to England a remonstrance against the project of taxing the colonies. He opposed the Stamp Act and in 1774 presented to the British king the petition of the First Continental Congress. On his return he was elected a member of the Second Continental Congress and exerted all his influence in favor of the Declaration of Independence, which he helped to draft and signed. In 1776 he was sent to France in behalf of the American colonies. After the surrender of British Gen. John Burgoyne he concluded with France the first treaty of the United States with a foreign power (1778) and was subsequently named one of the commissioners for negotiating peace with Great Britain. On his return to America he served as a delegate in the Constitutional Convention of 1787 and helped to draw up the Constitution of the United States in 1788.

During his busy career he spent some time in scientific research, particularly on electricity. Practical results were his inventions of the lightning rod, bifocal eye glasses, and the Franklin stove, a kind of open stove devised to preserve heat by placing the hearth out in the room and connecting it with the chimney by a flue. His last public act was to sign a bill before Congress (February 12, 1790) asking for the abolition of slavery. His works include his unfinished *Autobiography* and a great number of political, financial, economic, and scientific papers.

Franklin, Sir John (1786–1847), English explorer, born in Spilsby, Lincolnshire. He became a midshipman in the Royal Navy at the age of 14, fought under Admiral Horatio Nelson at Trafalgar in 1805, and became a lieutenant in 1808. He commanded two successful Arctic expeditions (1819–1822), (1825–1827). Franklin was promoted to captain, and in 1829 was knighted. After a period in the Mediterranean, Franklin served as lieutenant governor of Van Diemen's Land, now Tasmania (1836–1843). In 1845 he started on his last expedition, in command of the *Erebus* and *Terror* in search of the Northwest Passage. The party never returned, and it was not until 1859 that definite proof was found of the tragic end of the expedition.

Fraunhofer, Joseph von (1787–1826), German physicist and optician, born in Straubing, Bavaria. He made great improvements in optical glass for prisms and lenses and invented several valuable optical devices. His best-known discovery is that of the dark lines in the solar spectrum, known now as Fraunhofer lines, which he observed while investigating the refractive index of various kinds of glass. He is regarded as the founder of spectroscopy.

Frazer, Sir James George (1854–1941), Scottish anthropologist, born in Glasgow. He was educated in Glasgow and at Cambridge, and in 1907 was appointed professor of anthropology at the University of Liverpool. His chief work, *The Golden Bough* (2 vols., 1890, enlarged to 12 vols., 1900), is a definitive study of the development of primitive cults, myths, and religious rites. Among his numerous other works are *Totemism and Exogamy* (1910), *Man, God, and Immortaility* (1927), and *The Fear of the Dead in Primitive Religion* (3 vols., 1933–1936). He received the Order of Merit in 1925.

Frederick I, known as **Frederick Barbarossa** or **Redbeard** (c.1123–1190), Holy Roman emperor (1155–1190) and successor to his uncle, Conrad III, as king of Germany in 1152. His esteem among the Germans rests upon his patronage of learning, the arts, and commerce. After establishing order at home, he proceeded to Italy to carry out a plan of asserting his authority over the powerful Lombard cities. In 1155 Pope Adrian IV crowned him Holy Roman emperor, but the cities rebelled against him. He also had to contend with the hostility of Pope Alexander III, Adrian's successor.

Frederick set up several antipopes and destroyed Milan in 1162, but the Lombard League, formed in 1167, renewed the war and gained a decisive victory at the battle of Legnano (1176). In 1183 a compromise was agreed upon. The Peace of Constance gave the cities local autonomy, and Frederick returned to Germany. Having established peace in all his dominions, he started in 1189 on the third Crusade to the Holy Land but was drowned the following year while crossing a small river in Cilicia.

Frederick II (1194–1250), king of the Two Sicilies (1198–1250) and Germany (1215–1250) and Holy Roman emperor (1220–1250). The son of Emperor Henry VI and the grandson of Frederick I, he was a patron of learning and literature. He succeeded to the throne of Sicily in 1198 but was under the guardianship of Pope Innocent III until 1208. In 1212 he disputed Otto IV's claim to the imperial throne of Germany and in 1220 was crowned Holy Roman emperor. During most of his reign he was opposed by the Lombard cities and popes Gregory IX and Innocent IV, both of whom excommunicated him. In 1229, however, while on the fifth Crusade to Palestine, Frederick was crowned king of Jerusalem.

Frederick II, known as **Frederick the Great** (1712–1786), king of Prussia (1740–1786). He succeeded his father, Frederick William I, who had pursued a policy of stern economy. The young king fell heir to a well-filled treasury and a splendidly-trained army. His first act was to invade Silesia. He fought two wars (1740–1742, 1744–1745), for possession of this territory. The wars were concluded in 1745 by the Peace of Dresden, which put Silesia in Frederick's possession and brought him renown as a great military leader. This prestige reached its greatest height in the ensuing Seven Years' War (1776–1763), in which Frederick, allied with England, fought a coalition of five continental powers —Austria, France, Russia, Saxony, and Sweden—and emerged victorious. Prussia became one of the five great powers of Europe, and Frederick then devoted himself to undoing the suffering and devastation that were the price of victory. He reorganized the national economy, built roads and canals, promoted agriculture and industry, equalized taxation, and instituted justice for rich and poor alike. By taking part with Russia in the first partition of Poland (1772), Frederick added more territory to Prussia. In 1778 he again waged war on Austria and again enlarged his kingdom. He died without a male heir. His nephew, Frederick William II, succeeded him.

Frederick William (1620–1688), elector of Brandenburg, called the "Great Elector." When he became elector in 1640, his country was in the throes of the Thirty Years' War, finances were in disorder, and the towns and villages almost depopulated. By the Treaty of Westphalia (1648) he recovered the Brandenburg possessions that had been seized, and within a decade he had built a well-organized, standing army. After years of warfare against Poland, Sweden, and France, the elector was free to give his attention to internal reforms. Aided by his genius for finance, he encouraged immigration, promoted industry, opened up canals, organized a postal system, and promoted education, thus laying the foundation for the supremacy of Brandenburg-Prussia among the German states.

Frederick William I (1688–1740), king of Prussia (1713–1740), son of Frederick I. Early in his rule (1713) he entered the war waged by Sweden against Russia, Poland, and Denmark, at the end of which he acquired Pomerania and Stettin. The remainder of his reign was devoted to improving the internal condition of Prussia. Sternly practical and determined, he despised the arts and was rigidly economical and strict in his dispensation of justice. At his death in 1740, he left the country in a sound financial position and with an army of more than 80,000 men, one of the best disciplined forces in Europe. His son Frederick the Great succeeded him.

Frederick William III (1770–1840), king of Prussia (1797–1840) son of Frederick William II. When he succeeded his father in 1797, the Napoleonic Wars were in progress, and although the king at first refused to join the allies who were leagued against Napoleon, popular clamor brought Prussia into the coalition in 1806. For years after the Treaty of Tilsit (1807), Prussia was practically a French province, but the king and people, aided by the statesman Heinrich Stein and others, steadily prepared for a war of liberation. The battle of Leipzig (1813) liberated Germany, and Blüchers' success at Waterloo (1814–1815) reestablished Prussia's position. The king adopted a reactionary policy, joining Russia and Austria in the Holy Alliance that disappointed the German people. However, he established a customs union and otherwise advanced the material welfare of the country.

Frelinghuysen, Frederick (1753–1804), American Revolutionary leader, born in Somerset County, N.J. He graduated from Princeton (1770) and was admitted to the bar in 1774. He served on the Committee of Public Safety, was a major in the Minute Men, and as captain of artillery fought at the battle of Trenton. Later he was active as colonel of the New York militia. After the Revolution Frelinghuysen served in the Continental Congress and was a U.S. senator (1793–1796). In the Whisky Rebellion he served as major general of the New Jersey militia.

Frémont, John Charles (1813–1890), American explorer and army officer. Born of French parentage in Savannah, Ga., he was educated at Charleston College, S. C. He early became interested in railway surveying and in 1842 made his first government expedition to the West, leading a party of 21 men over the Oregon Trail to the Rocky Mountains. Fremont Peak (13,790 feet), named for him, was ascended on this trip. On his next expedition (1843–1844), he reached Fort Vancouver by way of the Columbia River and returned home by way of California. On a third expedition, which took him again to California (1845–1847), he became involved in the Mexican War and helped to wrest California from Mexico. Com. Robert F. Stockton assumed chief command there, and when Gen. Stephen W. Kearney arrived in 1846, he quarreled with Stockton, and Frémont refused to acknowledge his authority. A subsequent court-martial sentenced him to dismissal for mutiny. The sentence was remitted by Pres. James K. Polk, but he resigned from the army in 1848. He was elected California's first U. S. senator in 1850. In 1856 the new Republican party named him as its first presidential nominee, but he lost to James Buchanan. Frémont was given command of the department of the West in the Civil War, but, not wishing to subordinate his private feelings to army discipline, he resigned in 1862. He served as governor of the Arizona Territory (1878–1883), and in 1890 Congress placed him on the retired list with the rank of major general.

French, Daniel Chester (1850–1931), American sculptor, born in Exeter, N. H. He spent a year at the Massachusetts Institute of Technology, studied anatomy in Boston under William Rimmer, and worked for a time in the studio of J. Q. A. Ward. In 1875 he produced *The Minute Man of Concord,* his earliest statue and one of his best, for the town of Concord, Mass. After studying in Florence with Thomas Ball, French returned to America. His portrait and memorial statues and decorative pieces are noted for grace and beauty of technique. They include *John Harvard,* Cambridge, Mass; *Lewis Cass,* rotunda of the capitol in Washington; *The Angel of Death Staying the Hand of the Young Sculptor,* in Forest Hills Cemetery, Boston; the colossal *Statue of The Republic,* in Jackson Park, Chicago; and the bronze Lincoln for the Lincoln Memorial in Washington.

French, John Denton Pinkstone, 1st Earl of **Ypres** (1852–1925), British field marshal, born in Kent. He joined the army in 1874 and won distinction in the Boer War (1899–1901) as a commander of cavalry. He was promoted to general in 1907, and was made field marshal in 1913, but he resigned from the service in 1914 because of dissatisfaction with the government's Irish policy. When Britain entered World War I, he reported for duty and was sent to France at the head of the expeditionary forces. In the battle of Ypres he prevented the Germans from capturing Calais. After numerous disagreements with Lord Kitchener, he resigned his command (1915). The following year he was made commander in chief of the United Kingdom. His disclosures regarding ammunition supplies were partly responsible for the fall of Asquith's cabinet. From 1918 until his retirement in 1921 he served as lord lieutenant of Ireland. In 1821 he was created earl of Ypres.

Freneau, Philip Morin (1752–1832), American poet, known as "the Poet of the American Revolution." He was born in New York City of French parentage, and graduated from Princeton in 1771. In a varied career he was a teacher, law student, journalist, seaman, privateer, and editor. He is best known as the author of lyrics, including *The Indian Burying-Ground, The Wild Honeysuckle, Eutaw Springs,* and *A Poem on the Rising Glory of America.*

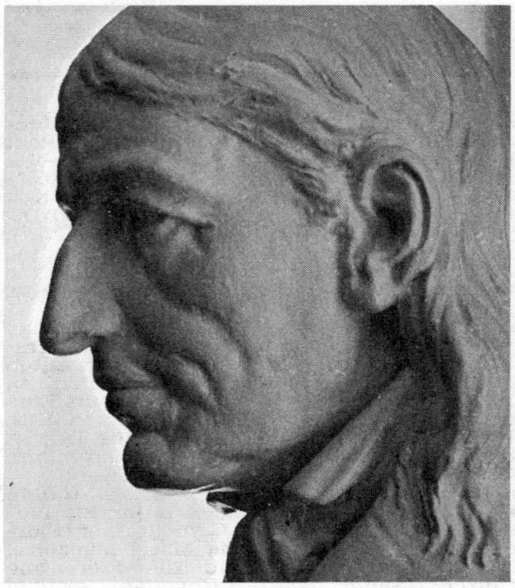

GERMAN INFORMATION CENTER

FRIEDRICH FROEBEL

Fresnel, Augustin Jean (1788–1827), French physicist, renowned for his research in the field of optics. He disproved Isaac Newton's corpuscular theory of light and demonstrated by actual experiment that light is a wave movement. Fresnel also showed that light waves have a transverse movement in ether. Among other achievements, he greatly improved lighthouse illumination by introducing the use of compound lenses.

Freud, Sigmund (1856–1939), Austrian physician and founder of psychonalysis, born in Freiberg, Moravia. He graduated in medicine from the University of Vienna. In 1884 he began work with Josef Breuer on the treatment of hysteria by hypnosis. Freud then studied in Paris under the neurologist Jean M. Charcot (1885–1886). He abandoned hypnosis for a method of "free association" that developed into the psychoanalytic method, which allows the patient to recall past emotional crises, recognize them as the cause of his conflicts, and release the emotion he has suppressed. Finding the major sources of emotional stress in suppressed conflicts and desires, Freud emphasized the importance of the unconscious mind to psychological stability. He built his psychological theory around the three forces he saw dominant in mental life: the *id,* the life force producing sexual and love drives; the *ego,* the conscious identity dealing with reality; and the *super-ego,* the conscience controlling the ego. Freud's studies concentrated on the development and interaction of these forces.

In 1902 he became professor of neuropathology at Vienna, a post he held until 1938. After the Nazi occupation of Austria in 1938 Freud was dispossessed of his property, but he was permitted to leave the country, and he settled in England. Among his writings are *The Interpretation of Dreams* (1900), *The Psychopathology of Everyday Life* (1904), *Totem and Taboo* (1910) *The Ego and the Id* (1923), *The Future of an Illusion* (1927), *Moses and Monotheism* (1939).

Freytag, Gustav (1816–1895), German novelist, dramatist, and critic, born in Kreuzburg, Silesia. He studied at Breslau and Berlin universities, lectured at Breslau on German literature (1848–1870), and was editor of the Liberal organ *Die Grenzboten.* His most successful comedy, *Die Journalisten* (1854, *The Journalists),* is still seen on the German stage. In 1855 he published his widely-translated novel *Soll und Haben* (*Debit and Credit*). Freytag's greatest effort went into a series of six novels, *Die Ahnen* (*The Ancestors*), written between 1872 and 1880. This work gives a picture of German life from the migrations of the early Germanic tribes to the Napoleonic Wars.

Frick, Henry Clay (1849–1919), American steel and coke magnate, born in West Overton, Pa. At the age of 22 Frick borrowed funds to form his first coke company, and by the time he was 30 he was a millionaire. His fruitful association with Andrew Carnegie began in the 1890's. As chairman of Carnegie Brothers and Company, he played a significant role in the creation of the Carnegie steel empire. In 1899 Frick broke with Carnegie. He then became director of the Pennsylvania Railroad and took part in the organization of the United States Steel Corporation in 1901. At his death, Frick bequeathed his mansion in New York City, with his famous art collection, to the public as a museum.

Frobisher, Sir **Martin** (c.1535–1594), English navigator. He made his first voyage to Guinea before he was 20. The first of his three unsuccessful expeditions in search of a northwest passage to China was made in 1576. He reached an inlet of Baffin Island of the Northwest Territories, Canada, which was named Frobisher Bay in his honor. In 1586 he sailed as vice-admiral in Drake's expedition to the West Indies, and in 1588 he was in command of the *Triumph,* a ship that helped to defeat the Spanish Armada. In that battle he so distinguished himself that he was knighted on board his own ship. After taking part in other expeditions and battles, he died of a wound received in an attack on Brest.

Froebel or **Fröbel, Fredrich** (1782–1852), German educator and founder of the kindergarten. He was born in Oberweissbach and at the age of 15 he was apprenticed to a forester. After working at various jobs, he decided to teach, and from 1807 to 1810 worked with Johann Pestalozzi at Yverdon, Switzerland. After active service in the War of Liberation (1814) he devoted himself to education. He founded a school at Griesheim (1816) in which he began to develop his ideas of child education. He encountered much opposition but continued to train teachers and in 1837 established at Blankenburg, Thuringia, the world's first kindergarten. This name, meaning children's garden, had flashed into his mind only the year before. Froebel died without realizing the far-reaching effects of his work. Educators regard the kindergarten system, with its emphasis on self-expression and the development of all phases of the child's nature, as one of the most important educational movements of the nineteenth century.

Froissart, Jean (c.1337–c.1400), French historian, best known for his *Chronicles,* a history of the main events of western Europe from 1325 to 1400. He went to England at the age of 18 and entered the household of Edward III. After a five-year leave of absence in France, he returned in 1361, bringing with him a rhymed account of the wars of the time. He then became one of the secretaries of Queen Philippa. For his *Chronicles,* he gathered material from King David of Scotland, Edward, the Black Prince, and many other personages who gave him their versions of historical events. Froissart's *Chronicles* was printed several times before 1510 and was widely read.

Fromm, Erich (1900–), American psychoanalyst, born in Frankfurt am Main, Germany. He studied at Heidelberg, Munich, and the Psychoanalytic Institute in Berlin. In 1934 he settled in the United States, where he set up practice and taught at the Institute for Social Research in New York (1934–1939), Columbia (1940–1941), Yale (1949), Michigan State (1957–1961), and, since 1962, New York University. In opposition to the Freudian theory of subconscious causation, Fromm believes that man is a product of his culture, and therefore emphasizes the individual's adjustment to the world. Among his writings are *Escape From Freedom* (1941), *Psychoanalysis and Religion* (1950), *The Forgotten Language* (1951), *The Sane Society* (1955), *The Art of Loving* (1956), and *The Heart of Man* (1964).

Frontenac, Comte **de Palluau et de, Louis de Buade** (1620–1698), governor of New France (Quebec). Before his appointment in 1672, he was a brigadier general. He was an able administrator, and the prosperity of early Canada owed much to him. He promoted French interests by aiding the expeditions of Jolliet, Marquette, and La Salle. Quarrels over religious matters led to his recall by Louis XIV in 1682, but when New France floundered in his absence, he was reappointed in 1689. His wars against the Iroquois Indians forced them to make peace in 1696.

Frost, Robert Lee (1875–1963), American poet, born in San Francisco, Calif., and educated at Dartmouth and Harvard. He remained in neither college long enough to earn a degree, leaving to work at various trades. He managed his own farm near Derry, N.H. (1900–1905), and was a teacher (1905–1912). In 1912 he sailed for England where he remained three years and published his volumes of poems, *A Boy's Will* and *North of Boston.* With his reputation as a poet established, he returned to America and became professor of English at Amherst College and at the University of Michigan. He won four Pulitzer Prizes in poetry: for *New Hampshire* (1923), *Collected Poems* (1930), *A Further Range* (1936), and

A Witness Tree (1942). He has been called "the voice and embodiment of rural New England."

Frye, William Pierce (1831–1911), American statesman, born in Lewiston, Me., and educated at Bowdoin College. In 1871 he entered the U. S. Congress, to which he was reelected five times. From 1881 till his death he was a U. S. senator. He was president pro tempore of the Senate in 1896 and its permanent presiding officer after the death of Vice-Pres. Garret Hobart in 1899. Frye again held that office in 1901, when after Pres. William McKinley's death Theodore Roosevelt became president. He was one of the peace commissioners at the conclusion of the Spanish-American War.

Fuller, Margaret, later Marchioness **Ossoli** (1810–1850), American essayist and critic, an associate of Emerson in the Transcendental movement. She was born in Cambridgeport, Mass., and educated by her father and in private schools. She edited the *Dial* (1840–1842) and became literary critic for the New York *Tribune* in 1844. In 1846 she went to Europe and a year later in Rome married the Marquis Angelo Ossoli. Together they participated in the Revolution of 1848, and fled to the mountains in 1849 during the French siege of the city. En route to New York with her infant son, the three were drowned after a shipwreck off Fire Island, New York. Her books include *Woman in the Nineteenth Century* (1845) and *Papers on Literature and Art* (1846).

Fuller, Melville Weston (1833–1910), American jurist, born in Augusta, Me. He was chief justice of the United States Supreme Court from 1888 until his death. He graduated from Bowdoin College, and began the practice of law in Augusta (1856). In the midst of a successful career he moved to Chicago and became influential in Illinois state politics. Pres. Grover Cleveland appointed him chief justice to succeed Morrison R. Waite in 1888. He was also one of the arbiters in the boundary dispute between Great Britain and Venezuela in 1899, and a member of the Permanent Court of Arbitration at The Hague (1900–1910).

Fulton, Robert (1765–1815), American inventor, engineer, and artist, born in Lancaster, Pa. He designed guns during the Revolutionary War and early in his career was a successful artist, doing portraits, landscapes, and mechanical drawing in Philadelphia. He became greatly interested in promoting canal building and in inventing machinery for dredging canals. The War of 1812 turned his attention to war devices, and he spent several years in Europe, developing fairly successful torpedoes and submarines.

In 1806 he returned to the United States, bringing with him an English steam engine. With Robert R. Livingston he built the steamboat *Clermont*, in which he installed the engine. The boat made its first successful trip in 1807, and in the next year Fulton and Livingston secured a monopoly on steamboat service on the Hudson. Fulton built many other ships, including the *Fulton*, the first steam-driven warship.

Funston, Frederick (1865–1917), American soldier, born in New Carlisle, Ohio. He fought with the Cuban insurgents in 1896 and at the outbreak of the Spanish-American War was sent to the Philippines as colonel of the 20th Kansas volunteers. He became a national hero in 1901 by his capture of Emilio Aguinaldo, leader of the Filipinos. He was promoted to brigadier general, served successively as commander of various departments, and in 1915 commanded the expedition to Vera Cruz, attaining the rank of major general. He also organized the operations that were led against Francisco (Pancho) Villa on the Mexican border (1916).

Furnivall, Frederick James (1825–1910), English philogist and Shakespearean scholar, born in Egham, Surrey, and educated at Cambridge. Furnivall founded societies for the publication of texts of early English writings, ballads, and the works of Chaucer, Shakespeare, Browning, Wycliffe, and Shelley. He prepared for publication 43 facsimilies of the quartos of Shakespeare's plays and was an editor of the Oxford English Dictionary.

Furtwängler, Adolf (1853–1907), German archaeologist and art critic. He took part in the excavations at Olympia (1878–1879), was a professor of archaeology at Berlin (1884) and Munich (1894), and in 1901 began a six-year series of expeditions to Aegina, Amyclae, and Orchomenus. His works, which deal with Greek art and ornaments, include *Masterworks of Greek Sculpture* (1893), *Greek Vase-Painting* (1900–1904), and *Description of the Munich Glyptothek of King Louis I* (1903).

G

Gabriel, family of French architects, **Jacques Gabriel** (1630–1686), designed the Pont Royal and the Château de Choisy-le-Roi for Louis XIII. **Jacques Gabriel** (1667–1742), royal architect to Louis XIV, best known for the city halls at Rennes and Dijon. **Jacques Ange Gabriel** (1698–1782), royal architect to Louis XV, designed the École Militaire, the Hôtel Crillon, and the favorite house of Queen Marie Antoinette, the Château du Petit Trianon.

Gabrilowitsch, Ossip (1878–1936), Russian pianist and conductor, born in St. Petersburg (Leningrad). He studied under Anton Rubinstein and won the Rubinstein Prize in 1894. After extended concert tours in Europe, he came to the United States in 1900. In 1918 he became conductor of the Detroit Symphony Orchestra. He married Clara Clemens, the daughter of Mark Twain.

Gaddi, family of Florentine artists, **Gaddo Gaddi** (1260–1332), was known for his mosaics, especially in the Cathedral of Florence, the basilica of Santa Maria Maggiore, the old St. Peter's, and the Florentine church, Santa Maria Novella. **Taddeo Gaddi** (c.1300–1366), son of Gaddo and a student of Giotto, continued his master's work of building the Campanile; he also designed the Ponte Vecchio and painted numerous Madonnas. **Agnolo Gaddi** (c.1333–1396), son of Taddeo, was known for the *Resurrection of Lazarus* and for frescoes in Pieve di Prato and in Santa Croce.

Gadsden, James (1788–1858), American diplomat, born in Charleston, S.C. He served in the War of 1812 and in the Seminole War (1818). As minister to Mexico (1853), he negotiated the purchase of the land that now comprises Arizona and New Mexico, known as the Gadsden Purchase. The acquisition of this area, totalling about 45,535 miles, enabled the building of the Southern Pacific Railroad.

Gagarin, Yuri Aleksevich (1934–1968), Soviet astronaut, born in Smolensk. On Apr. 12, 1961, he made the first flight around the earth in the spacecraft *Vostok*, which orbited the earth in 89.1 minutes. Gagarin was killed in March 1968 testing a new plane.

Gage, Thomas (1721–1787), British general and colonial governor of Massachusetts, born in Firle, Sussex. He served in the French and Indian War (1755–1763), after which he was commander of the British forces in America (1763–1773). After a year in England he returned as governor of Massachusetts and again commanded the British army. His severe measures in dealing with rebellious colonists precipitated the battles of Concord and Bunker Hill, which marked the beginning of the Revolutionary War. He was recalled to England in 1775 after the battle of Bunker Hill.

Gaillard, David Du Bose (1859–1913), American army engineer, born in Fulton, S.C. A graduate of West Point (1884), he made a reputation as an engineer on difficult hydraulic and channel dredging projects. He was in charge of building the central section of the Panama Canal, which included the excavation of the Culebra Cut, the most troublesome part of the entire canal. He succeeded at the cost of his health, and after his death the cut was renamed the Gaillard Cut.

Gainsborough, Thomas (1727–1788), English painter, born in Sudbury, Suffolk. He had some instruction in London but was essentially self-taught. Gainsborough spent 14 years in Ipswich and in 1759 went to Bath, a fashionable resort, where his services as a portrait painter were in great demand by socially prominent persons. After his return to London in 1774, he was summoned to court to paint the portraits of George III and his family. Gainsborough's portraits (more than 200 in number) are remarkable for their grace, beauty of coloring, and expression of personality. Among his most famous are *Mrs. Siddons* (National Gallery, London), *The Blue Boy* (Huntington Gallery, San Marino, Calif.), and *Duchess of Devonshire* (Metropolitan Museum, N.Y.). His most representative landscapes are *The Market Cart* and *The Harvest Waggon*.

Gaius or **Caius** (c.110–c.180 A.D.), Roman jurist, author of the *Institutes*, the earliest complete textbook of Roman law. This manual (4 books), was the basis of the *Institutes* of Justinian, the next great legal authority. The Gaius manuscript, lost for centuries, was discovered in 1816 in the cathedral library of Verona. Gaius wrote numerous other works on law, of which Justinian made extensive use, notably *Commentaries on the Twelve Tables* and *Edict of the Magistrates*.

Galba, Servius Sulpicius (5 B.C.–69 A.D.), Roman emperor, successor to Nero. He won a favorable reputation as a soldier and administrator in the provinces and was in military service in Spain when the Gallic legions revolted against Nero in the year 68. When he learned of Nero's death, he accepted the imperial office from the Praetorian Guard. His administration was a disappointment, for he proved to be greedy, partial, and harsh. In January, 69, he was killed by his rebellious soldiers.

Galen, Claudius (c.130–c.200 A.D.), Greek physician, born in Pergamum, Asia Minor. He studied in his native town and in other cities of the Greco-Roman world, including Alexandria. In his later years he practiced in Rome, where he was physician to Commodus, the heir of Marcus Aurelius. Galen demonstrated that the arteries contained blood and not air and was the first to understand the pulse. Although his diagnosis and methods of cure were often faulty, he emphasized the importance of studying anatomy by actual dissection and is considered the founder of experimental physiology. He wrote about 500 treatises, some of which are extant, which prove him to be, after Hippocrates, the greatest of Greek physicians.

Galileo, full name **Galileo Galilei** (1564–1642), Italian astronomer and mathematician, born in Pisa. He began the study of medicine at the university there, but soon turned to mathematics and natural science. At the age of 19 Galileo announced the fact that a simple pendulum takes a certain length of time to swing through its arc; the time is the same whether the arc is

N. D. GIRAUDON; BURNDY LIBRARY

GALILEO was tried by the Inquisition for holding heretical theories about the universe.

short or long. He discovered this by studying the movement of a hanging lamp in the cathedral in Pisa. While teaching mathematics at the University of Pisa he conceived the law of falling bodies. Galileo was primarily an experimental scientist; by dropping balls of varying weights from the leaning tower of Pisa he learned that freely falling bodies have a uniform velocity (in a vacuum) regardless of weight. Hampered by the ill will of the followers of Aristotle, whose theories he rejected, he resigned to accept a professorship in mathematics at the University of Padua (1592).

During the succeeding 18 years Galileo rose to his greatest heights as an astronomer. He completed a refracting telescope in 1609, the first instrument adapted to astronomical research. He observed first the roughened surface of the moon and determined that its illumination is the sun's light reflected by mountains and valleys. He saw that the Milky Way was composed of separate stars, and (1610) discovered the four satellites revolving about Jupiter. He detected the movable spots on the sun and deduced that the sun rotates on its axis. Among his inventions of this period were a proportional compass and a thermometer.

In 1610 he was invited to Florence by his patron Cosimo de'Medici, the duke of Tuscany, and became his official mathematician and philosopher. But Galileo was soon in difficulty with the Church authorities because he advocated the Copernican theory that the earth and other planets revolve about the sun. His career came to a climax in 1632 with the publication of his *Dialogue Concerning the Two Great World Systems*. He was summoned before the Inquisition which forced him to retract his theories. He was sentenced to prison, but was instead confined to his own house for the remainder of his life. His tomb and a memorial monument are in the church of Santa Croce.

Gall, Franz Joseph (1758–1828), German anatomist, the founder of phrenology, born in Tiefenbrunn, Baden. While practicing medicine in Vienna, he developed his theory that the mental and moral characteristics of a person are determined and indicated by the shape of the head, because of a direct relation between the brain and the outer appearance of the skull. He lectured on his theories in Vienna until he was forced to stop by the government (1802). In 1807 he established himself in Paris; a year later a committee of the Institute of France reported unfavorably on the system as presented by Gall and his associate, Johann Spurzheim.

Gallatin, Albert, in full **Abraham Alfonse Albert Gallatin** (1761–1849), American statesman, born in Geneva, Switzerland. He immigrated to the U.S. in 1780 and in 1789 was a delegate to the Pennsylvania constitutional convention. Elected to the state legislature (1790), he helped to avert the worst excesses of the Whisky Rebellion. In 1793 he was elected to the U.S. Senate, but was declared ineligible because only nine years had elapsed since he had taken the oath of citizenship. In 1795 he entered the House of Representatives, where he showed an aptitude for finance, and in 1801 was appointed secretary of the treasury by Pres. Thomas Jefferson. Gallatin held this post for 12 years and did much to systematize national expenditures. In 1814 he helped negotiate the Treaty of Ghent. He was minister to France (1815–1823), and minister to Great Britain (1826–1827). He was a founder of the American Ethnological Society in 1842.

Gallaudet, Thomas Hopkins (1787–1851), American educator of the deaf, born in Philadelphia, Pa., and educated at Yale and Andover Theological Seminary. In 1817, after a trip to Europe to study methods of teaching the deaf, Gallaudet and a teacher from Paris opened the first American deaf-mute school, at Hartford, Conn. Funds for the enterprise were secured from individuals and churches, and the movement spread to other states. Gallaudet College, Washington, D.C., was named for him.

Galle, Johann Gottfried (1812–1910), German astronomer, born in Pabsthaus, Saxony. While serving as an assistant at the Berlin Observatory, he discovered the planet Neptune (1846), basing his search on the calculations of the French astronomer Urbain Leverrier. In 1851 Galle was appointed director of the observatory and professor of astronomy at the University of Breslau.

Galli-Curci, Amelita (1889–1963), Italian operatic soprano. Born in Milan; in 1909 made her debut in Rome as Gilda in *Rigoletto*. She came to the United States in 1916, first appearing in Chicago and then joining the New York Metropolitan Opera Company in 1920. In 1930 she retired after having appeared in such roles as Lakmé, in *Lakmé*, Violetta in *La Traviata*, Juliette in *Roméo et Juliette*, and Lucia in *Lucia di Lammermoor*. She died Nov. 26, 1963 in La Jolla, Calif.

Gallieni, Joseph Simon (1849–1916), French general, born in St.-Béat. He served in the Franco-Prussian War, and in Africa and Martinique, after which he was an administrator in the Sudan, Madagascar, and other French colonies. In World War I, he sent troops into the First Battle of the Marne (September, 1914) from Paris in taxicabs and probably saved Paris from capture by the Germans. In 1915 he was minister of war in the cabinet of Aristide Briand.

Galois, Évariste (1811–1832), French mathematician, born in Bourg-la-Reine. While studying at the École de Louis-le-Grand and the École Normale, he published original papers on the theory of equations and the theory of numbers. He also developed a theory on the solubility of irreducible equations of prime degree by radicals, and helped to formulate the theories of groups and functions.

Galsworthy, John (1867–1933), English author, born in Coombe, Surrey, and educated at Harrow and Oxford. He gave up his law practice to write and in 1898 began his long literary career by publishing (under the pseudonym *John Sinjohn)* the novel *Jocelyn*. Thereafter, he wrote plays, novels, and essays of uniformly high quality. Galsworthy's plays, including *The Silver Box, Strife, Justice, Loyalties, The Skin Game,* and *Escape,* deal largely with social problems. His novels are remarkable for their lucid analysis of English life and character. Most famous is the series devoted to the Forsyte family, consisting of six novels and several short stories. The earlier ones were published together as *The Forsyte Saga*, the later ones as *A Modern Comedy*. For *The Forsyte Saga* he won the Nobel Prize for literature in 1932. In *Maid in Waiting* (1931), Galsworthy began another family narrative, which he did not finish.

Galton, Sir **Francis** (1822–1911), English anthropologist, founder of the science of eugenics, and author of the general law of ancestral inheritance. He was born in Birmingham, the grandson of Erasmus Darwin, and cousin of Charles Darwin. Galton spent several years in travel in the interests of anthropology and devoted himself to meteorology. He originated a method of map making followed today in weather forecasting. His fame rests chiefly on his development of biological theories applied to inheritance and the improvement of the race. In his book *Enquiries into Human Faculty and Its Development* (1883), he was the first to use the term eugenics. He was knighted in 1909.

Galvani, Luigi or **Aloisio** (1737–1798), Italian physiologist and discoverer of current electricity. Born in Bologna, he taught anatomy at the university where he performed a series of experiments that led to the invention of the electric battery by Alessandro Volta. Galvani studied the effects produced on the legs of a freshly killed frog by inserting a copper hook into the spine and placing it in contact with another metal. The twitching of the frog's legs he attributed to animal electricity; today we know that when the two different metals were moistened by the saline juices of the frog's body, an electric current was generated by chemical action. Galvanism, galvanic electricity, galvanizing and the galvanometer were named for him.

Gama, Vasco da (c.1469–1524), Portuguese navigator, born in Sines. He is noted for his discovery of a sea route to India by way of the Cape of Good Hope. In July, 1497, under commission from King Emanuel I, da Gama started with four ships from Lisbon, rounded the southern point of Africa in November, and anchored off Calicut, on the Malabar coast, in May, 1498. On a second expedition in 1502, he bombarded and sacked the town and destroyel the fleet of the hostile rajah. In 1524 da Gama was sent to India as viceroy by John III to correct abuses in the Portuguese possessions, but he died of fever soon after his arrival.

Gambetta, Léon (1838–1882), French statesman, born in Cahors. He began his career as a lawyer in Paris and was a member of the Chamber of Deputies when the Franco-German War began in 1870. During the siege of Paris he escaped from the city in a balloon and set up a dictatorship in Tours. To show his disapproval of the peace treaty, which he regarded as treasonable, he went to Spain, but he soon returned to France and became one of the most radical men in the newly-organized Republic. Gambetta was president of the Chamber of Deputies in 1879 and was premier of France for two months under Pres. Jules Grévy (1881–1882).

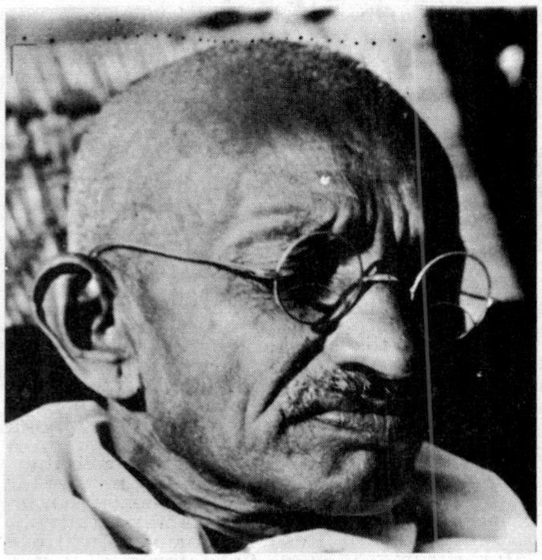

MOHANDAS GANDHI

Gandhi, Mohandas Karamchand (1869–1948), Indian nationalist and Hindu religious leader called *Mahatma* (great-souled) by his followers. Born in Porbandar, Western India, of a well-to-do family, he studied law in London and practiced in Bombay. He spent about 20 years in South Africa, handling legal affairs of Indians unjustly treated by the whites. After many hardships, Gandhi won social and legal rights for his countrymen in India. During World War I, he raised a volunteer ambulance corps in London. In 1919 Gandhi became the leader of a strong nationalist movement in India, in which he led millions of Muslims and Hindus in the movement known as noncooperation, and organized a boycott of British goods and a movement for economic independence. In 1922 he was arrested by the British for sedition and sentenced to a term of imprisonment; he was released in 1924. After a period of quiet he renewed agitation in 1930; his speeches urging the expulsion of the British from India led again to his arrest. He was, however, soon released, and at Delhi made an agreement with the viceroy to stop the boycott in return for a large measure of self-government for India. In 1931 he came to London to attend the Round Table Conference and demanded complete independence for India. He was imprisoned shortly after his return to India, but was again released. Gandhi wrote *Indian Home Rule* and *Young India*. He was assassinated in 1948.

Gandhi, Shrimati Indira (1917–), Indian political leader, born in Allahabad and educated at Somerville College, Oxford. The daughter of Pandit Jawarharlal Nehru, she married Feroz Gandhi in 1942. In 1938, at the age of 21, she became a member of the Indian National Congress; in 1955 she joined its Working Committee and in 1959 was elected its president. Mrs. Gandhi was appointed minister for information and broadcasting in 1964. On the death of Shri Lal Bahadur Shastri in January, 1966, she became prime minister of India.

Garcia, Manuel (1805–1906), Spanish musician, born in Madrid. He was taught by his father, a tenor singer and voice instructor. He traveled for a time with his father's opera company, but left the stage in 1829 and settled in Paris as a singing teacher, numbering Jenny Lind among his pupils. Garcia was professor of singing at the Royal Academy of Music in London from 1848 to 1895. He was still teaching privately when he died at the age of 101. He invented the laryngoscope, a device for viewing the interior of the larynx.

García Lorca, Federico. See *Lorca*.

García Iñiguez, Calixto (c.1836–1898), Cuban patriot and soldier, born in Santiago. He began his military career in 1868 as a rebel fighter in the Ten Years' War against Spain and eventually became commander of the revolutionary army in Oriente. He was captured and held a prisoner in Spain (1880–1895) but escaped to the United States, where he collected arms and munitions. He fought with distinction in the last Cuban insurrection and led a Cuban force at El Caney in the Spanish-American War (1898). He died in Washington, D.C., where he was attending a conference on Cuban affairs. He is believed to have been the inspiration for Elbert Hubbard's famous essay *A Message to Garcia*.

Gardiner, Samuel Rawson (1829–1902), English historian, born in Ropley, Hampshire, and educated at Oxford, Edinburgh, and Göttingen universities. He taught modern history at King's College, London (1877–1885) and was examiner in history at Oxford (1886–1889). His greatest achievement as a historian is the 10-volume *History of England* (1863–1882), covering the period from the accession of James I to the outbreak of the Civil War. His other works include *History of the Great Civil War* (1886–1891) and *History of the Commonwealth and Protectorate* (1895–1901). Three volumes of the last had been issued when the author died. He based his work on an exhaustive study of original sources and treated his subject with a remarkable lack of bias.

Garfield, James Abram (1831–1881), twentieth president of the United States (March-September, 1881), born in Orange, Cuyahoga County, Ohio. As a youth he worked on a farm and drove horses and mules on the towpath of the Ohio Canal; and at the age of 18 he entered the academy at Chester, Ohio, to prepare for teaching. After studying later at Western Reserve Eclectic Institute (later Hiram College), he entered Williams College and graduated with honors in 1856. He taught Latin and Greek at the Eclectic Institute and in 1857 was chosen president of the school.

He studied law privately and in 1861 was admitted to the Ohio state bar, but the Civil War prevented his entering practice. An abolitionist and one of the first members of the Republican party, Garfield offered himself for service when the war began. In 1861 he was commissioned lieutenant colonel in an Ohio volunteers regiment and served with distinction in Kentucky and at the battles of Shiloh, Corinth, and Chickamauga, rising to the rank of major general. His home district elected him to Congress in 1862, and he resigned from the army the following year. In the House he gave valuable service as a member of the military committee and in connection with the enforcement of the Draft Act. In the troubled days that followed Abraham Lincoln's assassination, Garfield was in the forefront of those who sought a constructive policy. He voted for Pres. Andrew Johnson's impeachment. He was a member of the house until 1880, when the Ohio legislature elected him to the U.S. Senate. Before taking his seat, however, he was elected president with Chester A. Arthur as his vice-president.

Garfield began his term with a serious handicap—the still smoldering hostility between the Republican factions — and he came to an open break with Senator Roscoe Conkling of New York over Federal patronage. On July 2, 1881, only four months after his inauguration, he was shot in Washington by Charles J. Guiteau, a mentally unbalanced lawyer, who had unsuccessfully sought a diplomatic post.

Garibaldi, Giuseppe (1807–1882), Italian patriot, born in Nice (then a part of Italy), the son of a sea captain. Contact with the Young Italy leaders, including Giuseppe Mazzini, inspired him with a zeal for Italian liberation. He took part in a futile uprising in Genoa in 1834 and was forced to flee to France. During the next few years Garibaldi led a roving, adventurous life and at one time helped the Uruguayans fight the dictator of Argentina. He returned to Italy in 1848, took part in the revolt of northern Italy against Austria, and was one of the defenders of Rome when it was besieged by the French. Again he was forced into exile and lived for a time on Staten Island, N.Y. In 1854 he settled on Caprera, an island off Sardinia, where he waited for the next great uprising. In 1859, under the leadership of Victor Emmanuel II of Sardinia and Camillo di Cavour, his prime minister, the crucial struggle began. Garibaldi's special contribution was leading a band of volunteers that conquered Sicily and Naples (1860), opening the way to the proclamation of Victor Emmanuel as king of a united Italy.

In 1862 and again in 1867 he made unsuccessful attempts to conquer Rome. He fought for the French Republic in the later phases of the Franco-German War and was elected to the Italian Parliament in 1874. He spent his last years on Caprera.

Garner, John Nance (1868–), vice-president of the United States, born in Red River County, Tex. He had little opportunity for formal schooling but studied law and was admitted to the bar in 1890. He served in the lower house of the Texas Legislature (1898–1902), after which he represented his district in the U.S. Congress until 1933. He became chairman of the important Ways and Means Committee in 1921, a stepping-stone to the speakership of the House, to which he was elected in 1931. Candidate for the Democratic nomination for the presidency in 1932, he threw his Texas votes to Franklin D. Roosevelt and won the vice-presidential nomination. He served two terms, often disagreeing with many of Roosevelt's policies. At the end of his second term in 1941, he retired to his farm in Texas.

Garrick, David (1717–1779), English actor and playwright, born in Hereford. He studied at Lichfield under Samuel Johnson, and the two went to London together in 1737. In 1741, after some preliminary theatrical experience, Garrick appeared in a London theater as Richard III. Thereafter, he enjoyed uninterrupted success until his retirement in 1776. He was especially identified with the historic Drury Lane Theater, which he managed from 1747 to 1776. His natural manner of acting, his ability to play almost any type of character, and his insistence on presenting Shakespeare's plays as he thought the author meant them to be produced and acted, were all noteworthy factors in his success. As a playwright he wrote several popular farces and collaborated with George Colman on *The Clandestine Marriage* (1766), a highly successful comedy.

Garrison, William Lloyd (1805–1879), American abolitionist, born in Newburyport, Mass. As a youth he was a printer's apprentice and wrote essays for local newspapers. In 1826 he became editor of the Newburyport *Free Press* and an advocate of the abolition of slavery. He founded the *Liberator* in Boston (1831), the chief organ of the abolitionist movement. At first he alone did all the writing, typesetting, printing, and distributing of his small paper. In 1835 he was attacked by a mob hostile to his views in the streets of Boston. Because the U.S. Constitution permitted slavery, he called it "a covenant with death and an agreement with Hell," and burned a copy of it publicly in 1854. He was president of the American Anti-Slavery Society for many years and wrote brilliant anti-slavery essays. After slavery was abolished, he worked for woman suffrage and better treatment of the American Indian.

Gary, Elbert Henry (1846–1927), American industrialist, born near Wheaton, Ill., and educated at Wheaton College and the University of Chicago. He was admitted to the Illinois bar in 1867, served two terms as county judge, and became a successful corporation counsel in Chicago, where he practiced for 25 years. When the United States Steel Corporation was founded in 1901, Gary was selected chairman of the board, a position he held until his death in 1927. Gary, Ind., the location of the main plant of the corporation, was named for him.

Gates, Horatio (1728–1806), American Revolutionary general, born in Maldon, England. He came to America in 1755 to take part in the French and Indian War and served under Generals Edward Braddock and Robert Monckton. At the outbreak of the Revolutionary War in 1775, he sided with the colonists and became a general in the Continental Army. In 1777 he was in command of the army that forced the surrender of Gen. John Burgoyne at Saratoga, the turning point of the war. The unsuccessful Conway Cabal against Gen. George Washington aimed to put Gates in supreme command in Washington's place. After an unsuccessful military command in Camden, S.C. (1780), Gates retired.

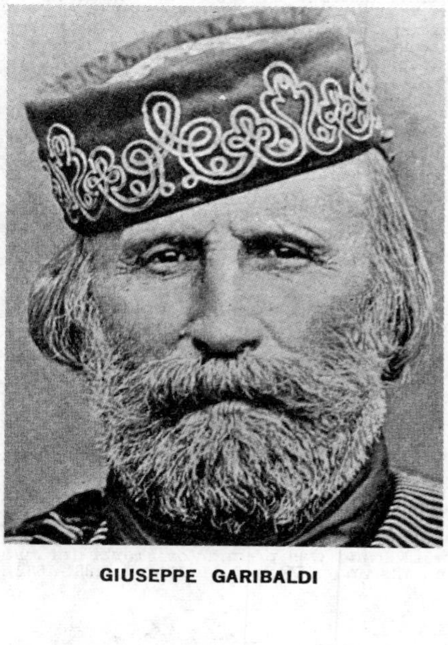

GIUSEPPE GARIBALDI

Gauguin, Paul, full name **Eugène Henri Paul Gauguin** (1848–1903), French painter, born in Paris. He took up painting as a hobby while he was a banker in Paris and after 1881 devoted all his time to art. He became attracted to Impressionism but soon abandoned it and at Port-Aven in Brittany became the leader of a group known as the Synthetic-Symbolists, whose work is characterized by pure colors, simple forms, and emotional force. After 1891 he lived in Tahiti, although he periodically returned to France. He found modern civilization degenerate, and felt that the fulfillment of his life was to be found painting among the simple islanders of Polynesia. Among his most characteristic works are *The Yellow Christ*, *The Day of God*, and *Where do we come from? What are we? Where are we going?*

Gaulle, Charles de. See *de Gaulle, Charles.*

Gauss, Karl Friedrich (1777–1855), German mathematician, born in Brunswick. He discovered the geometrical method of dividing a circle into 17 equal arcs, invented a new method for calculating the location of bodies on the celestial sphere, and is regarded as the founder of the mathematical theory of electricity. Important among his numerous writings is the discussion of the method of least squares. He was professor of mathematics and director of the observatory at the University of Göttingen from 1807 until his death.

Gautama Buddha or **Gotama Buddha,** original name Prince **Siddhartha,** called **Sakyamuni,** or "Sage of the Sakyas" (c.563–483 B.C.), Indian philosopher who was the founder of Buddhism. Buddha's father, Suddhodana, was ruler of the Sakyas and Buddha led a sheltered life amid the luxuries of the court. He was married at 16 to Yasodhara, and they had a son, Rahula. When he was 29, Buddha saw an old man, a sick man, and a corpse, and thus for the first time noted the existence of age, illness, and death in the world. After this realization he left his wife and son and set out to seek the truth, wandering for seven years through northern India. Finally, emancipation of the spirit came to him under a Bo tree at Buddh Gaya (hence his name Buddha, or "the Enlightened One"). Buddha spent the rest of his life teaching his faith in the Ganges valley. He founded an order of monks and one of nuns. He died at Kusinagara in Nepal.

Gautier, Théophile (1811–1872), French author, born in Tarbes. He began life as a painter, turned to poetry in 1830 and made a name for himself in verse, fiction, literary and art criticism. In 1830 he published *Albertus*, a narrative poem that was favorably received by the critics. Among the great number of his novels and travel books are *Madamoiselle de Maupin* (1835), *Le Capitaine Fracasse* (2 vols., 1861; 1863), and *Voyage en Espagne* (1843).

Gay, John (1685–1732), English poet and dramatist, born in Barnstaple. His *Beggar's Opera*, a ballad operetta, was a great success when first presented in 1728. About 200 years later it was revived and had a record run (three and a half years) in London. His pastoral play *The Shepherd's Week* (1714) was suggested to him by Alexander Pope. Gay began his literary career in 1708 and wrote a succession of plays, ballads, and other poems, of which the best known are his *Fables* (1727, 1738), tales in verse. He also wrote an opera, *Achilles*, which was produced in Covent Garden in 1733.

Gay-Lussac, Joseph Louis (1778–1850), French scientist, born in St. Léonard. He studied chemistry under Claude Berthollet and became his assistant. Gay-Lussac made studies of vapor densities and pressures, which were the subjects of his first memoirs. In collaboration with F.H.A. von Humboldt, he published (1804) the fact that hydrogen and oxygen, in the ratio of two to one (by volume), unite to form water. From this, Gay-Lussac was led to the discovery of the general law of volumes, a fundamental concept in chemistry. He was the first to isolate hydriodic and iodic acids and cyanogen.

Geber or **Jabir** (c.721–776 A.D.), Arab scholar and alchemist, often regarded as one of the founders of chemistry. He lived at Baghdad and seemed to have had some knowledge of nearly all the chemical processes in use in his time. His reputed writings describe various kinds of furnaces, distillation and other chemical processes, the properties of metals, and the functions of mercury, silver,

and arsenic. He thought that one metal could be transmuted into another, the assumption behind experiments in alchemy.

Geddes, Sir **Auckland Campbell** (1879–1954), British anatomist and diplomat, born in Edinburgh, Scotland. He studied medicine at Edinburgh, in London and in Freiburg, Germany. He was professor of anatomy at Edinburgh, Dublin, and McGill universities. Geddes served in the South African War and in 1916 had charge of recruiting in England. He served as minister of national service (1917–1919), president of the Board of Trade, and ambassador to the United States (1920–1924).

Gehrig, Henry Louis, known as **Lou Gehrig** (1903–1941), American baseball player, born in New York City, and educated at Columbia University. Gehrig, a first baseman, played 2,130 consecutive games for the New York Yankees (1923–1939), had a lifetime batting average of .339, and was voted the American League's most valuable player four times (1927, 1931, 1934, 1936). Afflicted by a rare form of paralysis, he retired in 1939 and served as a New York City parole commissioner until his death.

Gelon (died 478 B.C.), Sicilian ruler of Gela and Syracuse. In 491 Gelon succeeded Hippocrates as the tyrant of Gela, and in 485 became tyrant of Syracuse. He controlled more than half of Sicily and was highly regarded by his subjects as a just and benevolent ruler.

Geneviève, Saint (c.422–512), patron saint of Paris. Her name is associated with the threatened invasion of the city by Attila and his Huns (451), which Geneviève was said to have averted by prayers and fasting. Another story tells how she gathered food for the starving people of Paris during a famine. During the French Revolution her body was taken from its burial place (beneath the present Panthéon) and burned, but her relics may be seen in the Church of St. Étienne du Mont. Her feast day is January 3.

Genghis Khan, original name **Temujin** or **Temuchin** (1162–1227), Mongol conqueror. At the age of 13 he succeeded his father as tribal chief. By 1204 he had gained mastery of the Mongol and Tatar tribes. Entering upon a wider field of conquest, he brought northern China under his sway and captured Peking in 1215. Bokhara, Samarkand and other cities of Turkestan next yielded to him, and the Mongols soon swept over Persia, penetrated into northern India, and ravaged the land between the Volga and the Dnieper. His great empire was divided at his death among his three sons but the major portion eventually passed to his grandson Kublai Khan, the founder of the Mongol dynasty in China.

Genseric or **Gaiseric** (c.390–477 A.D.), Vandal king who won repeated victories from the Roman emperors in the last years of the Western Empire. Beginning his career of conquest in 429, he became sole king of the Vandals. He subjugated northern Africa and in 439 made Carthage his capital. In 455 he led his armies into Italy and captured Rome, which his followers were allowed to plunder for two weeks. In 460 the emperor of the West lost a naval battle to Genseric in the Bay of Cartagena, and a fleet of the emperor of the East was defeated in 468. When Genseric died in 477, his kingdom was still intact.

Gentile, Giovanni (1875–1944), Italian philosopher and statesman, born in Castelvetrano. He taught philosophy at several Italian universities, and was an editor of the critical journal *Giornale critico della filosophia italiano* and of the *Enciclopedia Italiana* (1922–1924). As a public figure, he was minister of education (1922–1924), president of the commission to reform the Constitution (1925), and a member of the Fascist Grand Council (1925–1929). In his writings he was a Fascist apologist, supporting the policies of the dictator, Benito Mussolini.

Gentile da Fabriano real name **Gentile Massi** (c.1370–1427), Italian painter, born in Fabriano. His greatest works were decorations for the Doge's palace in Venice, and frescoes for the Church of St. John Lateran in Rome, at the request of Pope Martin V. One of the greatest of his many paintings, the *Adoration of the Magi*, is in the Church of the Holy Trinity, Florence.

George, Saint (d. about 303), patron saint of England. According to tradition, he suffered martyrdom in Lydda, Palestine, probably before the reign of Emperor Constantine. The accounts of Saint George are all legendary. The English Crusaders brought back many stories of him, and in the fourteenth century Edward III made him patron of his new Order of the Garter.

George I (1660–1727), king of Great Britain and Ireland (1714–1727). He was the son

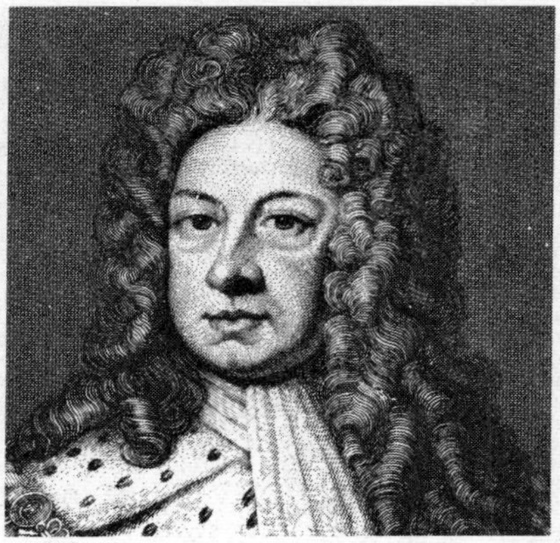

GEORGE I

of Ernest Augustus, elector of Hanover, and Sophia, granddaughter of James I of England. By the Act of Settlement (1701), which declared his mother next successor to the English throne, Prince George became the heir apparent. His mother died two months before the death of Queen Anne and he succeeded as George I in 1714. Educated in Germany and with only a slight knowledge of the English language, he left the actual government largely to his ministers, notably Sir Robert Walpole. During his reign the country experienced a financial panic through the collapse of the South Sea Company, and although Walpole was able to avert a complete disaster, many investors were ruined.

George II (1683–1760), king of Great Britain and Ireland (1727–1760), son of George I. He was born in Hanover and lived there until his accession. Although he had learned the English language, he did not participate in politics, especially while Sir Robert Walpole was his prime minister. However, in 1743 he personally led an army to victory against the French at Dettingen. George's 33 year reign was notable for the Jacobite uprising in 1745 and for war with France. His reign ended with major victories for England (1759). In America, England won Canada, and Clive's victory at Plassey laid the foundations for the British empire in India. Walpole continued as prime minister until 1742. Later in George's reign William Pitt was England's most influential statesman.

George III (1738–1820), king of Great Britain and Ireland, (1760–1820), born in England, the son of Frederick Louis, Prince of Wales, who died in 1751. George succeeded his grandfather, George II, in 1760, as the first Hanoverian king. Through his mother's influence he grew up with a definite conception of royal authority and set about at once to destroy the power of the Whigs, who had dominated the two preceeding kings. It was not until 1770 that he found in Lord Frederick North a prime minister who exactly suited him. During the administration of this Tory premier the United States won its independence. Other wars of this reign included those with the Revolutionary government in France, with Napoleon, and with the young American nation in the War of 1812. In 1801 the legislative union of Great Britain and Ireland was concluded. George III became blind in 1809 and insane in 1811.

George IV (1762–1830), king of Great Britain and Ireland (1820–1830), son of George III. He was crowned in 1820 but had ruled as prince regent from 1811. George, noted for his extravagance, occupied the throne for 10 years but had no great influence on public affairs. The later wars of his father's reign occurred during his regency. Late in his own reign an act was passed providing for Catholic emancipation. He was succeeded by his brother William IV.

George V (1865–1936), king of Great Britain and Northern Ireland and emperor of India (1910–1936). He was the second son of Edward VII of England and Alexandra of Denmark. As a prince, George received thorough training in the navy, rising from cadet to vice-admiral. In 1893 he married Princess Victoria Mary of Teck, who had been engaged to his elder brother, Prince Albert Victor (died 1892). The reign of George V was marked by recurring crises, for the country had to cope with World War I, the postwar problems of unemployment and economic adjustment, the settlement of the Irish question, and the nationalist movement in India. In 1917, during World War I, he renounced all his German titles and changed the name of the royal house from Saxe-Coburg-Gotha to Windsor.

George VI (1895–1952), king of Great Britain and Northern Ireland (1936–1952) and emperor of India (1936–1948). He was the second son of George V, born in London and named Albert Frederick Arthur George. He became earl of Inverness, Baron Killarney and the duke of York. In 1923 he married Lady **Elizabeth Bowes-Lyon** (1900–). Two daughters were born, **Elizabeth Alexandra Mary** (1926–) and **Margaret Rose** (1930–). On December 12, 1936, George was proclaimed king following the abdication of his brother, Edward VIII, who was made the Duke of Windsor.

George I (1845–1913), king of Greece or the Hellenes (1863–1913). He was born in Copenhagen, Denmark, the second son of Christian IX. He ascended the throne in 1863 after the revolution that deposed King Otto, and was made king of Greece with the consent of the European powers. He won the esteem of his subjects in spite of a disastrous war with Turkey (1897) and constitutional and financial difficulties. He married Princess Olga of Russia in 1867. While on a visit to Salonika during the Balkan War, King George was assassinated. His son Constantine I succeeded to the throne.

George II (1890–1947), king of Greece or the Hellenes (1922–1923, 1935–47). He was the son of Constantine I, whom he succeeded in 1922. In the next year there was so much hostility to the throne that he had to leave the country, but was restored to power in 1935 when a plebiscite was taken to decide whether Greece would continue as a monarchy or become a republic.

George, David Lloyd. See *Lloyd George, David.*

George, Henry (1839–1897), American economist, born in Philadelphia, Pa. From the time he was 14, when he left school, until 1865, when he attained some success as a journalist in San Francisco, George drifted from one employment to another and was usually close to poverty. While in California, where he witnessed a spectacular rise in land values, he evolved his theory of the single tax, the most important economic principle developed by an American. George first discussed this theory in *Our Land and Land Policy* (1871) but gave it more elaborate treatment in his famous *Progress and Poverty* (1879). In brief, he believed that a single tax on the rent of land and the unearned increase in land value was the most equitable form of taxation. George was an independent candidate for mayor of New York in 1886 and ran again in 1897 but he died before the election.

Géricault, Jean Louis André Théodore (1791–1824), French painter, born in Rouen. He studied under Carl Vernet and Pierre Guérin. His best-known paintings are *The Wounded Cuirassier*, *Heroic Landscapes*, and *Raft of the Medusa*. He also did many lithographs and watercolors.

Germanicus Caesar (15 B.C.–19 A.D.), Roman general, son of Nero Claudius Drusus and the adopted son of the Emperor Tiberius, his uncle. In 16 A.D. Germanicus gained renown by defeating Arminius, the German chieftain who had conquered Varus and his legions in the Teutoburg Forest in 9 A.D. Because of his nephew's popularity, which he considered dangerous to himself, Tiberius sent him on a mission to the East. Germanicus died near Antioch, supposedly poisoned at the command of the jealous emperor.

Geronimo (c.1829–1909), Apache Indian chief, born in New Mexico. He was notorious as a raiding leader and terrorist in the southwestern United States from 1884 to 1886. In 1886 he agreed to surrender to Gen. George Crook but escaped to the Mexican mountains with his followers and was not subdued until Gen. Nelson A. Miles took charge of the campaign. Geronimo died a prisoner in Fort Sill, Oklahoma.

Gerry, Elbridge (1744–1814), American statesman, born in Marblehead, Mass., and educated at Harvard. He began his public career in 1772 as a member of the General Court of Massachusetts and was a prominent member of the Continental Congress (1776–1781, 1782–1785). He signed the Declaration of Independence but refused to affix his signature to the Constitution, which he steadfastly opposed as a delegate to the Constitutional Convention. Gerry was elected from Massachusetts to the first two Congresses and in 1797 was one of three envoys sent to treat with the French Directory. Elected governor of Massachusetts in 1810 and 1811, he was criticized for signing a law to redistrict the state so as to give his own party a political advantage (a practice since named for him, *gerrymandering*). Gerry was elected vice-president of the United States on the ticket with James Madison in 1812, and died in office.

Gershwin, George (1898–1937), American composer, born in Brooklyn, N.Y. His parents were Russian-Jewish immigrants. He started as a young pianist with a firm of music publishers and soon began to write songs. At the age of 20 he wrote the musical comedy *La, La, Lucille*. A leader in the development of jazz, he is famous for his *Rhapsody in Blue*. He composed *Concerto in F* (1925), *Porgy and Bess* (1935), and *Of Thee I Sing* (1931). The latter musical won the Pulitzer Prize.

Gest, Morris (1881–1942), American theatrical producer, born in Vilna, Russia. He came to the U.S. in 1893 and attended the Boston public schools. With F. Ray Comstock as his partner, Gest produced such notable plays as *The Wanderer* (1917), *Chu Chin Chow* (1918), *Aphrodite* (1919), and *Mecca* (1920). His company also introduced to American audiences Nikita Baliev's *Chauve-Souris* (1922) and the artists from the Moscow Art Theater. Eleanora Duse played her farewell tour under Gest-Comstock auspices, and the partners sponsored *The Miracle* (1924).

Ghazzali or **Ghazali, al-** (1058–1111), Moslim theologian and philosopher. Born in Tus, Khurasan, a Persian city, he was educated by the theologian al-Juwayni at Nishapur. He taught at Baghdad (1091–1095) and after travels to Damascus, Jerusalem, Mecca, and al-Medina, he returned to his native province and entered a monastic order. Most of his writings were syntheses of various strands of Islamic religious thought.

Ghiberti, Lorenzo, real name **Lorenzo di Cione di Ser Buonaccorso** (c.1378–1455), Italian sculptor and goldsmith, born in Florence. His bas-reliefs on the two bronze gates of the baptistery in Florence are considered the finest of their kind in the world. It required over 20 years to complete the 28 panels of the north gates that picture scenes from the life of Christ and the evangelists. The east portals display Old Testament scenes. Ghiberti spent 27 years in doing this part of the work, the beauty of which inspired Michelangelo to exclaim that the portals were worthy to be the gates of Paradise. Ghiberti also designed some of the painted glass windows for the cathedral in Florence.

Ghirlandajo, Ghirlandaio, or **Grillandajo,** real name **Domenico di Tommaso Bigordi** (1449–1494), Italian painter, born in Florence. Most of his representative paintings may be seen in Florence, including his *Last Supper* and *St. Jerome* in the monastery and church of Ognissanti, the frescoes of Saint Francis for the Sassetti Chapel in the Sacred Trinity, and the frescoes in Santa Maria Novella that contain portraits of members of leading Florentine families. He also did a fresco of St. Peter and St. Andrew in the Sistine Chapel of the Vatican. At one time Michelangelo was a pupil of Ghirlandajo.

Gibbon, Edward (1737–1794), English historian, author of *The History of the Decline and Fall of the Roman Empire*. He was born in London and at 15 enrolled in Magdalen College, Oxford, but was dismissed after 14 months because he had become a convert to Catholicism. He pursued further study at Lausanne, Switzerland. The influence of a Calvinist minister, in whose house he lived, led to Gibbon's reconversion, but eventually he renounced all religious belief.

He returned to England in 1758 and continued to read and study. In 1763 he began a continued tour that took him to France, Switzerland, and Italy. While in Rome, contemplating the ruined monuments of the city's past, he resolved to write the history of its decline. A long period of research led to an expansion of the plan so that the work came to include the whole story of imperial Rome. The first volume appeared in 1776, the second and third volumes in 1781 and the concluding three in 1788. This monument of scholarship was Gibbon's life work, the culmination of vast reading and study. He also wrote an excellent autobiography that was published after his death as *Memoirs of My Life and Writings*. He was a member of Parliament (1774–1783) and commissioner of trade and plantations.

Gibbons, James (1834–1921), American Roman Catholic cardinal, born in Baltimore, Md. He studied for the priesthood at St. Mary's Seminary, Baltimore, and was ordained in 1861. He became archbishop of Baltimore (1887) and in 1886 was appointed cardinal by Pope Leo XIII. Cardinal Gibbons was the author of *Faith of Our Fathers* (1876), *Our Christian Heritage* (1889), *The Ambassador of Christ* (1896), and *A Retrospect of Fifty Years* (1916).

Gibbs, Josiah Willard (1839–1903), American mathematician and physicist, born in New Haven, Conn. A graduate of Yale, he also studied at Paris, Berlin, and Heidelberg. In 1871 he was appointed professor of mathematics and physics at Yale. His special field was thermodynamics, to which he contributed the Gibbs absorption equation, the Gibbs function, and the Gibbs-Helmholtz equation. He was elected to the Hall of Fame in 1950.

Gide, André (1869–1951), French novelist and man of letters. He was born in Paris of mixed ancestry, his father being a Huguenot and his mother a Protestant convert from Catholicism. He received a staunch puritanical education. Gide's early works such as *Les Cahiers d'André Walter* (1891) and *Traité du Narcisse* (1891) belong to the Symbolist school. However, after a prolonged illness and a trip to North Africa, he renounced this earlier style. In *Paludes* (1895) and *Les Nourritures Terrestres* (1897) Gide argues for freedom from conventionality in order to fully appreciate sensual pleasures. Each of his later protagonists is searching for a kind of fulfillment, but is eventually destroyed by the quest itself. In *L'Immoralist* (1902) Gide shows how the defiance of tradition and all of its restraints can grow into an uncontrollable obsession and, in *La Porte étroite* (1909), he shows how the opposite extreme, puritanism, can become equally dangerous when allowed to take over one's life.

Gide received the Nobel prize for literature in 1947. His other novels include *Le Prométhée mal enchaîné* (1899), *Le Retour de l'enfant prodigue* (1907), *Les Caves du Vatican* (1914), and *Les Faux-Munnayeurs* (1926). He is also one of the founders of *La Nouvelle Revue Française* (1909–1940), an influential magazine in the literary circles of its time.

Gielgud, Sir **John** (1904–), British actor, director and producer. He was born in London and studied at the Royal Academy of Dramatic Art. In 1921 he made his stage debut with the Old Vic Theatre in London. His earliest successes were as Lewis Dodd in *The Constant Nymph* (1926) and as Inigo Jollifant in *The Good Companion* (1930). However, it was for his portrayal of Richard II in his own production of *Richard of Bordeaux* that he first received recognition as a distinguished actor. Gielgud's reputation in the United States is built on his production of *The Importance of Being Earnest* (1947) in which he created the role of Ernest Worthing and his appearance as Valentine in *Love for Love*. These were followed by his production of *Medea* starring Judith Anderson and himself and his portrayal of Raskolnikov in Rodney Ackland's adaptation of *Crime and Punishment*.

The excellence of Gielgud's interpretation of Hamlet has won him international acclaim; he has appeared in the role over 500 times. Among the many other Shakespearean characters whom he has portrayed are Romeo, Macbeth, and King Lear. He has also been seen in several motion pictures and is the author of his autobiography, *Early Stages* (1939), and *Stage Directions* (1964). The famous Gielgud repertory theater was founded by him in 1938. He was knighted in 1953.

Gieseking, Walter Wilhelm (1895–1956), German pianist, known especially for his interpretations of Mozart and Debussy. Born in Lyon, France, he received his musical training at the Hanover Municipal Conservatory. He gave concerts throughout Europe and America (1920–1929) and returned to Germany in 1939. He remained there for most of the war and in the 1950's he again made concert tours in Europe and South America.

Gigli, Beniamino (1890–1957), Italian operatic tenor, born in Recanati. He studied at the Conservatorio di Musica in Rome, and made his debut (1914) as Enzo in *La Giaconda*, in Rovigo, near Venice. He was best known for the role of Faust in Arrigo Boito's *Mefistofele*. He also gave radio concerts and appeared in films.

Gilbert, Sir **Humphrey** (c.1539–1583), English explorer and colonizer, born in Compton and educated at Eton and Oxford. He was a half brother of Sir Walter Raleigh. From 1566 to 1568 he served with the army in Ireland and became governor of Munster in 1569. In support of his theory that there was a Northwest Passage to India, he published a book in 1576, which guided English exploration for two centuries. In 1583 he reached Newfoundland, which he claimed for England. He explored farther to the southwest, then turned back toward England. On the return trip he was drowned when his ship sank.

Gilbert, William (1540–1603), English physician and physicist, born in Colchester, and educated at Cambridge. He was president of the Royal College of Physicians and chief physician to Queen Elizabeth. Gilbert's fame rests on his discoveries in electricity and magnetism. Thales had recorded the attraction of light bodies by a piece of amber, and Gilbert showed that other bodies also possessed this property. To these he gave the name electrics from the Greek *elektron*, amber. This marked the beginning of the experimental study of electricity. In a treatise on magnetism, *De Magnete, Magneticisque Corporibus et de Magno Magnete Tellure, Physiologia Nova* (1600), he described the earth as being a great magnet with its magnetic poles, equator, and axis. As Gilbert was a staunch advocate of the Copernican theory, his work was admired by Galileo and Kepler but belittled by Francis Bacon.

Gilbert, Sir **William Schwenck** (1836–1911), British playwright and author, born in London. While practicing law he came into notice as a contributor to the magazine *Fun*, which printed his famous *Bab Ballads* (1869–1873). From 1871 to 1896 he collaborated with the musician Sir Arthur Sullivan in a number of comic operas, of which the best-known are *H.M.S. Pinafore* (1878), *The Pirates of Penzance* (1879), and *The Mikado* (1885).

Gildersleeve, Basil Lanneau (1831–1924), American philologist and classical scholar, born in Charleston, S.C., and educated at Princeton and in Europe. When Johns Hopkins University was founded in 1876 Gildersleeve was appointed to the chair of Greek and retained this post until 1915 when, at the age of 84, he retired. He founded and edited (1880–1920) the *American Journal of Philology*. Gildersleeve's contributions to the study and history of the classics include *Latin Grammar* (1867), *Syntax of Classical Greek from Homer to Demosthenes* (Part 1, 1901; Part II, 1911) with C. W. E. Miller and *Hellas and Hesperia* (1909).

Gillette, William Hooker (1855–1937), American actor and playwright, born in Hartford, Conn. He began as a stock company actor in 1877, after which he adapted and wrote plays with great success. He became a popular star in comedies, chiefly of his own authorship. He played the title role in *Sherlock Holmes* (1899) for which he is best known, and in J. M. Barrie's *The Admirable Crichton* (1903) and *Dear Brutus* (1919). He also wrote and appeared in *The Private Secretary* (1880), *Esmeralda* (1881), and *Secret Service* (1895).

Gilson, Étienne (1884–), French historian noted for his study of medieval philosophy and its influence on modern thought. He was born in Paris and studied at the Sorbonne. In 1913 he taught at Lille, in 1919 at Strasbourg, and from 1921 to 1932 he held the chair of medieval philosophy at the Sorbonne. Gilson came to the United States in 1928 as a guest professor at Harvard University and in 1929 was named director of the Institute of Medieval Studies at the University of Toronto.

Among his works are *Le Thomisme* (1922), *L'Esprit de la philosophie mediéval* (1932), *Dante et la philosophie* (1939), *God and Philosophy* (1941), and the *History of Christian Philosophy in the Middle Ages* (1955). He is also the founder of the Archives d'histoire doctrinale et litterature du moyenage (1926).

Ginsberg, Allen (1926–), American poet noted as the leader of the "beat" movement of the 1950's. He was born in Newark, N.J. and studied at Columbia University. Ginsberg popularized his poetry with readings in coffee houses in New York and San Francisco. In his poem *Howl*, which was banned for obscenity when first published, he claims to express the thoughts and feelings of his generation. Other works by Ginsberg include *Kaddish and Other Poems* (1960), *Journal of the Death Vine* (1963), and *Reality Sandwiches* (1963).

Giordano, Luca (1632–1705), Italian painter, born in Naples. He learned to paint under his father, who hurried him so persistently that the son became known as *Luca Fa Presto* (Luca the Speedy). In later years Giordano painted with incredible speed. Although he was a good colorist and used his brush with skill, his paintings show the effects of too rapid execution. As court painter to Charles II of Spain, Giordano decorated the grand staircase of the Escorial with the frescoes *Battle of Saint-Quentin* and *Taking of Montmorency*. He made use also of Biblical and mythological subjects and was one of the most popular artists of his day.

Giorgione Il, real name **Giorgio Barbarelli da Castelfranco** (c.1478–1511), Italian painter of the Venetian school. He was born in Castelfranco and studied under Giovanni Bellini. Comparatively little has remained that is undeniably his work, but he painted mostly landscapes and legendary scenes. Bathed in a soft diffused light, they have a lyrical, often mysterious, quality. Giorgione's work had a profound influence on his contemporaries, especially Titian. Among his works are *Three Philosophers, The Tempest, Sleeping Venus* and the *Castelfranco Madonna.*

Giotto, full name **Giotto di Bondone** (c.1276–c.1337), Italian painter, sculptor, and architect, born near Florence. Most of Giotto's paintings have either been lost or are so greatly repainted that their originality must be contested. However, his finest works are frescoes of religious subjects, notably the *Allegories of St. Francis,* in the Church of St. Francis at Assisi; the decorations of the Arena Chapel, Padua; and the frescoes in the Bardi and Peruzzi Chapels of Santa Croce, Florence. In the Gardner Collection, Boston, is the *Presentation of Christ in the Temple,* a good example of Giotto's panel pictures. His work established the basis for Renaissance painting with the monumentality and plasticity of its human forms, broad and simple execution, and emotional depth. Giotto also designed the Campanile (bell tower) of the cathedral at Florence.

Giraudoux, Jean (1882–1944), French writer and diplomat, born in Bellac, Haute-Vienne, and educated at the École Normale Supérieure. Beginning in 1910 he served for 30 years in the Ministry of Foreign Affairs in various capacities. In 1939 he was made propaganda director for the Vichy government. Although he wrote many novels, he is known for his plays, which include *Siegfried* (1928), *Amphitryon 38* (1929), *Electre* (1937), and *La Folle de Chaillot* (1943.)

Gladstone, William Ewart (1809–1898), English statesman, born in Liverpool of Scottish ancestry. At Oxford he distinguished himself in scholarship, oratory, and debating, receiving a double first degree in 1831. In 1832 he was elected to Parliament. At this time he was a Tory (Conservative) in his political thinking, and he became a follower of Sir Robert Peel, who was called upon to form a cabinet late in 1834. In Peel's short-lived ministry, Gladstone was undersecretary for the colonies for a few weeks in 1835. He did not attain a cabinet position until 1843, when he was made president of the Board of Trade in the Peel ministry of 1841–1846. In performing the duties of this office he showed a remarkable aptitude for finance. He was out of Parliament (1845–1847), when he served as colonial secretary, but this was the only period in which he did not hold a seat in a career of over 50 years. As chancellor of the exchequer in the Lord Aberdeen cabinet in 1853 Gladstone devised schemes for taxation to meet the new budget. He continued in this office in three succeeding cabinets, the third being that of the Liberal leader Lord Russell. Gladstone himself for several years had been gradually turning away from the Conservatives, and his enthusiastic support of Lord Russell's reform bill of 1866 for the broadening of the franchise marked his open espousal of Liberal principles. In 1867 he succeeded Russell as the party leader.

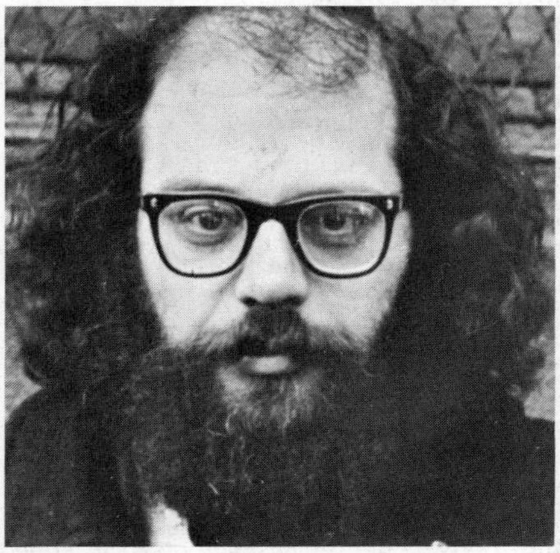

CITY LIGHTS BOOKS

ALLEN GINSBERG, modern American poet.

One year later Gladstone became prime minister on the issue of disestablishment of the Irish Church. After this measure was carried, he put through a bill in 1870 to give relief to the Irish tenants. In 1874 he relinquished the Government to Benjamin Disraeli when his party lost to the Conservatives in the general election of that year. After an interval of retirement Gladstone came back into political life as an opponent of Disraeli's foreign policy, and in 1880 his party was returned to power on this issue. In his second ministry (1880–1885), Gladstone was unfortunate in his handling of the Irish question, for his moderate policy pleased neither the English nor the Irish nationalists, so in 1885 the Cabinet resigned. In 1886 the Conservatives again gave way to the Liberals, but the failure of Gladstone's plans for home rule for Ireland again put him out of office. However, the election of 1892 saw him prime minister for the fourth time. A new Home Rule Bill passed the Commons in 1893, but when it failed to carry in the House of Lords, he resigned in 1894.

Glass, Carter (1858–1946), American statesman, a leader in national financial legislation. He was born and educated in Lynchburg, Va., learned the printing business, and became publisher and owner of the Lynchburg *Daily News* and *Daily Advance.* Glass entered public life in 1899 as a member of the Virginia senate and in 1902 was elected to the U.S. Congress. After successive reelections, he resigned in 1918 to become secretary of the treasury. He retired from this position in 1920 to accept appointment as senator from Virginia. He was subsequently elected to four full terms, serving in the Senate until his death in 1946. As chairman of the House Committee on Banking and Currency, Glass was active in the formulation of the Federal Reserve System. In the Senate he was coauthor with Henry B. Steagall of the credit relief bill of 1932. He opposed many of the New Deal measures of Franklin D. Roosevelt's administration.

Glauber, Johann Rudolf (1604–1668), German chemist, born in Karlstadt. He developed the process for preparing hydrochloric acid by the action of sulfuric acid on common salt. Glauber's salt (sodium sulfate) is named for him.

Glenn, John Herschel, Jr. (1921–), American astronaut, born in Cambridge, Ohio. Working with Project Mercury, he was the pilot of a Mercury-Atlas orbital space flight launched from Cape Kennedy, Fla., in February, 1962. He is the coauthor of *We Seven,* the story of Project Mercury and the seven original astronauts.

Glinka, Mikhail Ivanovich (1803–1857), Russian composer noted as the founder of the Russian national school. He was born in Novospasskoie. A self-taught pianist, violinist, and singer, Glinka went to Berlin to study theory with Siegfried Dehn. After returning to Russia he wrote his first opera, *A Life for the Czar* (1836), which was well received. His second opera, *Russlan and Ludmilla* (1842) was not a success, although it is considered musically superior to the first. Glinka also wrote several songs for piano and for orchestra and some chamber music.

Gluck, Christopher Willibald (1714–1787), German composer, born in Erasbach, Bavaria. He brought out his first opera *Artaserse* (1741) in Milan, Italy, and for 20 years as an operatic composer produced works modeled on the popular though frivolous Italian type. In 1762 he produced in Vienna the first of his reform operas, *Orfeo ed Euridice.* The presentation of *Iphigénie en Aulide* in Paris (1774) marked the definite acceptance of the new operatic form in which music and words were coordinated.

Glycon (c.50 B.C.), Athenian sculptor, who executed the famous colossal statue of the Farnese Hercules, modeled after the original of Lysippus.

Gobelin, family of French dyers of the fifteenth century, that founded the dye works in the Faubourg Saint Marcel near Paris. The founder of the factory was Jean Gobelin (died 1476). During the sixteenth century the company began to make the celebrated Gobelin tapestries. The works were purchased by Louis XIV in 1662, and converted into the royal tapestry and furniture works. The most important Gobelins are the 14 tapestries celebrating Louis XIV, and those designed after Raphael's Vatican frescoes.

Godfrey of Bouillion, French **Godefroy de Bouillon** (c.1061–1100), French leader of the First Crusade. He was duke of Lower Lorraine and a descendant of Charlemagne on his mother's side. For his valor and sagacity he was proclaimed king of Jerusalem at the time of its capture (1099), but he declined the honor. At Ascalon he defeated a superior force under the sultan of Egypt, then set for himself the task of organizing the government of Jerusalem. He drew up a code of laws that reflected the best in jurisprudence of the feudal period. In his epic poem *Jerusalem Delivered,* Tasso praised Godfrey's manifold virtues, and his valorous deeds are set forth in the *Chansons de Geste.*

Godiva or **Godgifu,** known as Lady **Godiva** (fl.1040–1080), wife of Leofric, earl of Mercia. All that is known of her life is her interest in the monastaries at Stow, Lincolnshire, and at Coventry, Warwickshire. According to legend, she rode naked on horseback through Coventry, in fulfillment of her vow to do so if her husband would relieve the taxes on the people of the town.

Godowsky, Leopold (1870–1938), American pianist and composer, born in Vilna, Lithuania. He played in public at the age of nine and later secured training in music in Paris under Saint-Saëns. Godowsky made his first American tour in 1884. He was director of the piano department of the Chicago Conservatory of Music (1895–1900). In 1909 he was appointed director of the Imperial School at Vienna. He composed many pieces for piano and stringed instruments.

Godoy, Manuel de, full name **Manuel de Godoy y Álvarez de Faria** (1767–1851), Spanish statesman, born in Badajoz. Favored by the royal family, he became prime minister in 1792. He waged war on France (1793) and negotiated the Treaty of Basel (1795). After an uprising by the people at Aranjuez forced King Charles IV of Spain to abdicate, Godoy was imprisoned, but was released by Napoleon's efforts in his behalf. He was granted asylum in France, where he lived in exile.

Godunov, Boris Fëdorovich (c.1551–1605), czar of Russia. He was regent to the demented Czar Theodore I, and in 1598 he was elected to the Imperial throne despite rumors that he had assassinated Crown Prince Dmitri in 1591. A liberal reformer, Boris secured the independence of the Russian Church from the Greek (1589), modernized serfdom by prohibiting the transference of peasants from estate to estate, began the resettlement of Siberia, and showed great favor to Western immigrants and merchants. He waged successful war against the Khan of the Crimean Tatars (1591) and against the Swedes (1595), who had previously annexed Russian territory. His life is the subject of an opera by Modest Mussorgsky.

Godwin or **Godwine** (d.1053), English statesman who was prominent in the reigns of Canute and Edward the Confessor. As earl of Wessex, wealthy and powerful, he wielded great influence during Edward's reign and was a consistent advocate of the Saxon or national party as opposed to the Norman courtiers. In 1051 he incurred the king's ill will and was outlawed, but in the following year won back his property and position through a show of force and the enthusiastic support of the people.

Godwin, Mary Wollstonecraft (1759–1797), English writer, wife of William Godwin. Among her books and pamphlets are *Vindication of the Rights of Women* (1792), *Historical and Moral View of the French Revolution* (1794), and *The Wrongs of Women* (published posthumously).

Godwin, William (1756–1836), English man of letters noted for his defense of the French revolution in England and for his anarchical political and social philosophy. He studied for the ministry, but soon left the Anglican Church to become a radical political reformer. His most important work, *Enquiry Concerning Political Justice and Its Influence on General Virtue and Happiness* (1793), is considered as one of the greatest treatises on purely philosophical radicalism. Godwin differs from the French revolutionaries in his attack on the smaller institutions of society. He believes that man is corrupted, not only by church and state, but also by the ties of marriage, school, work, and even private property. In his logic, man is basically good and, left to rely on pure reason, will maintain his virtue. However, society so poisons his character that vice cannot disappear until all institutions have been destroyed. These theories had a strong influence on the young thinkers of Godwin's time such as William Wordsworth, Samuel Coleridge, Robert Southey, and Percy Bysshe Shelley. His other works include the novels *Adventures of Caleb William* (1794) and *St. Leon* (1799), *Of Population* (1820), and a *History of the Commonwealth* (1824–1828).

Goebbels, Joseph Paul (1897–1945), German political leader, born near Düsseldorf, and educated at Heidelberg. He was lame and did not serve in World War I. He became politically prominent in 1926, when he was the Nazi leader in Brandenburg and editor of the official Nazi newspaper, *Der Angriff*. He rose to power with Adolf Hitler and was responsible for the election of many Nazis to Reichstag seats before Hitler became chancellor. Hitler placed him in charge of all education and propaganda, giving him complete control of radio, press, theaters, and the arts. Goebbels was believed to have originated many Nazi policies, especially persecution of Jews and supermilitarism. His rise was largely a result of his abilities as a writer and orator. He killed his wife, his children, and himself near the end of World War II.

Goes, Hugo van der (c.1440–1482), Dutch painter, born in Ghent. His chief work is an altarpiece, *The Adoration of the Shepherds*, which was painted for the hospital chapel of Santa Maria Nuova in Florence. It is now in the Uffizi Gallery in Florence.

Goethals, George Washington (1858–1928), American soldier and engineer, born in Brooklyn, N.Y. He graduated from West Point (1880), where he later taught military engineering. During the Spanish-American War he served with the volunteers as chief of engineers with the rank of lieutenant colonel. By successive promotions Goethals reached the grade of major general in 1915. He was selected by Pres. Theodore Roosevelt in 1907 as the best man to build the Panama Canal and was made chairman and chief engineer of the commission in charge. The completion of the project in August, 1914, several months ahead of schedule, was a matter of worldwide comment. Goethals was governor of the Canal Zone (1914–1916).

Goethe, Johann Wolfgang von (1749–1832), German poet, dramatist, novelist, and philosopher, born in Frankfurt am Main, where he received his early education. Goethe did not attend school regularly but studied under tutors and was greatly influenced by his mother. He learned quickly, assimilated much of art and music, and could speak several languages by the age of ten. At 16 he went to Leipzig to study law but devoted himself chiefly to art and classical literature. In the fall of 1768 a serious illness sent him back to Frankfurt. He had already begun to write; and two dramatic works, begun in Leipzig, were later finished in Frankfurt. On his recovery Goethe went to Strasbourg to complete his legal education and in 1771 took his degree. Through his friendship with Johann von Herder, Goethe fell under the spell of Shakespeare and German folksongs, and this stirring of the imagination bore fruit in the Romantic drama of a sixteenth-century robber knight *Götz von Berlichingen* (1773). It was followed by a novel, *The Sorrows of Young Werther* (1774), an expression of a melancholy period in his own life when he was hurt by both love and friendship.

For a decade after 1775 Goethe lived in Weimar under the patronage of Charles Augustus, the reigning duke of Saxe-Weimar. He held several administrative offices and studied geology, botany, anatomy, and morphology. He wrote little but found time to begin a masterpiece of fiction, *The Apprenticeship of Wilhelm Meister*. Then followed a sojourn in Italy (1786–1788), during which he resumed his dramatic writing, working on *Iphigenie*, *Egmont*, and *Tasso*. The literary beauty of these plays is unquestioned but none is especially suited to stage presentation.

Goethe returned to Weimar, and under the inspiration of a close association with Friedrich Schiller he finished *Wilhelm Meister's Apprenticeship* (1796) and wrote the pastoral epic *Hermann and Dorothea* (1797) in addition to several ballads. Later came his novel *Elective Affinities* (1809), followed by an autobiography, a sequel to *Wilhelm Meister*, lyrics, and scientific and critical writing. In the year before his death, the second part of his great poetic masterpiece *Faust* was completed. On this drama he had labored during the greater portion of his entire creative period. It was, as he said, his confession of what life had revealed to him, an expression of his belief that the soul finds the answer to its problems in continual striving.

Gogh, Vincent van (1853–1890), Dutch painter, born in Groot-Zundert. He left his work as an art dealer to become an evangelist among coal miners. In 1882 he took up painting, using conventional styles. Four years later he joined his brother Théo, an art dealer, in Paris. There he met followers of more unconventional practices in painting, and his whole point of view was changed. He spent several years in the south of France and there produced most of his work, including landscapes, still lifes and figure studies. His mind began to fail, and he spent his last years in an insane asylum. Van Gogh's paintings are done in rich colors and are full of light. Among his best-known works are *The Potato Eaters, Berceuse, The Bridge at Arles, Sunflowers, Gypsy Camp*, and a self-portrait.

Gogol, Nikolai Vasilievich (1809–1852), Russian novelist and playwright, born near Mirgorod, Poltava, of Cossack ancestry. His first literary work, sketches called *Evenings on a Farm near Dikanka* (1831), revealed a gift for realistic description of provincial life. Other stories followed, including *Taras Bulba* (1835), a tale of the Cossacks. His play *The Inspector General* (1836) satirizes official corruption. Gogol's masterpiece is *Dead Souls* (1842), about a rogue who attempts to make his fortune by buying the rights to dead souls. In this novel, Gogol presents a magnificent picture of a socially stratified Russia strangled by bureaucracy. Gogol has been regarded as the father of the Russian novel.

Goldberg, Arthur Joseph (1908–), American labor lawyer, noted for his successes in reconciling opposing unions. He was born in Chicago and studied law at Northwestern University. In 1948 Goldberg was named as general counsel for the Congress of Industrial Organizations (CIO) and the United Steelworkers of America. Having achieved national recognition for his role in the AFL-CIO merger of 1955 and in the formulation of its code of ethical standards, Goldberg was chosen as secretary of labor by Pres. John F. Kennedy in 1961 and then appointed to the Supreme Court in 1962. In 1965 Goldberg was appointed United States ambassador to the United Nations by Pres. Lyndon Johnson following the death of Adlai Stevenson.

Goldoni, Carlo (1707–1793), Italian playwright, born in Venice. He is regarded as the founder of modern Italian comedy. In 1761 he undertook to write for the Italian theater in Paris and was attached to the French court until the Revolution. Among the best of his many plays are *La bottega di caffé* (*The Coffee Shop*, 1750), *La donna di garbo* (*The Mistress of the Inn*, 1753), and *Il barbero benefico* (*The Beneficent Boor*, 1771).

Goldsmith, Oliver (1728–1774), Anglo-Irish novelist, poet, playwright, and essayist noted for his gay and witty style. He was born in County Longford, Ireland and studied at various local schools before entering Trinity College, Dublin. Most of his life was spent moving from one job to another, trying his hand at teaching, the church, law, clerking in an apothecary store, proofreading, and literary hack work. In 1752 he went to Edinburgh to study medicine, left there for Leiden, and eventually made a grand tour of Europe, supporting himself with his stories and his flute. During this period he sent home his first poem, *The Traveller* (1756), but still showed little interest in a literary career. In 1756 he returned to England and continued to float. He did practice medicine for a short while, but failed to pass an examination to be a hospital mate in the navy.

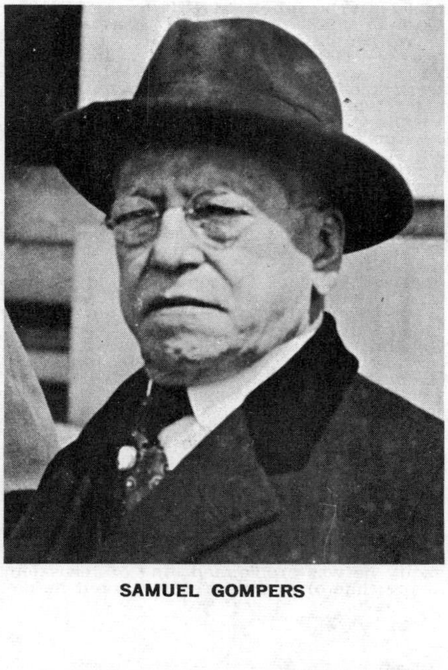

SAMUEL GOMPERS

As a hack writer Goldsmith wrote a quantity of works on diverse subjects, often historical. He first achieved recognition for his *Enquiry into the Present State of Polite Learning in Europe* (1759) and then for a series of essays subsequently collected in *The Citizen of the World; or Letter from a Chinese Philosopher Residing in London to his Friends in the East* (1762). However, it is for his one novel, *The Vicar of Wakefield* (1766); his long poem, *The Deserted Village* (1770); and his comedy, *She Stoops to Conquer* (1773); that Goldsmith is remembered today. The latter was distinguished by its break with the eighteenth century tradition of sentimental comedy. Although the plot, based on the mistaking of a gentleman's house for an inn, is ludicrous, the play itself is exceptional in its perceptive portrayal of character and its realistic rendering of atmosphere. Other works by Goldsmith include: *A History of England in a Series of Letters from a Nobleman to his Son* (2 vols., 1764), *The Traveller; or, a Prospect of Society* (1764), *The Good Natur'd Man* (1768), *A History of England* (1771), and *A History of Greece* (1774).

As one of the original members of the famous literary "Club" which included Dr. Samuel Johnson, Sir Joshua Reynolds, and James Boswell, Goldsmith's prodigal existence was the subject of much criticism. Still, Johnson mourned his death with the famous words: "Let not his frailties be remembered, he was a very great man."

Goldwater, Barry (1909–), American politician, noted for his uncompromising support of conservative policies. He was born in Phoenix, Ariz., and studied at the University of Arizona until his father's death, when he left to work in the family department store. He began his political career in the Phoenix city council in 1949 and in 1952 he was elected to the United States Senate, having defeated Ernest McFarland, the Senate Democratic majority leader. As a senator Goldwater was known for his opposition to any expansion of federal authority and for his support of national defense legislation. His nomination as the Republican candidate for the presidency in 1964 was followed by a highly controversial campaign which created much discord within the Republican party itself because of Goldwater's extremist views. Although defeated by Lyndon B. Johnson, Goldwater remains the spokesman for arch-conservatism in the United States. He has written *The Conscience of a Conservative* (1960) and *Why Not Victory?* (1962).

Goldwyn, Samuel (1882–), American film producer, born in Warsaw, Poland. He came to the U.S. in 1896, and became a citizen in 1902. A pioneer in the movie industry, he founded Goldwyn Pictures Corp., and after several mergers became head of Metro-Goldwyn-Mayer. He received an Academy Award for producing *The Best Years of Our Lives* (1947).

Gómez y Báez, Máximo (1826–1905), Cuban patriot, born in Santo Domingo. At first a soldier in the Spanish army, he joined the Cuban rebels in 1868 and was made a colonel. In the insurrection of 1895 he commanded the army of the Cuban republic, adopting the strategy of harassment rather than of fighting in the open Gómez cooperated with the Americans during the Spanish-American War and helped to organize the civil government of Cuba. He was governor of Santa Clara province under Pres. Estrada Palma.

Gompers, Samuel (1850–1924), American labor leader, born in London, England, of Jewish parents. He came to the U.S. in 1863, worked as a cigarmaker, his father's trade, and in 1864 helped to organize an international union of cigar workers. He took a prominent part in organizing the Federation of Organized Trades and Labor Unions, which became the American Federation of Labor in 1886, and of which he was president continuously until his death, except for the year 1895. His policy was always to improve the working conditions of labor through legislation.

Goncourt, Edmond Louis Antoine de (1822–1896) and **Jules Alfred Huot de** (1830–1870), two brothers noted for their remarkable collaboration as French novelists. Edmond was born in Nancy and Jules in Paris. They lived and worked together, rarely being separated until Jules died. After several unsuccessful attempts at playwriting and painting, they turned to historical studies of the eighteenth century such as *L'art du dix-huitième siècle* (1859–1870), which played an important part in the revival of the French rococo style. Their novels are studies of contemporary life based on their personal experiences. *Germinie Lacerteux* (1865), for example,

deals with the decadence of their housekeeper. Considered as the first French proletarian novel, the work is significant for its influence on the naturalistic style of Émile Zola. The writings of the Goncourts are characterized by looseness of structure and a manneristic use of language, the "écriture artiste" with its twisted syntax, playful rhythms, and extensive vocabulary.

Among the other products of this unusual partnership are *Histoire de la société française pendant la Révolution* (1854), *Portraits intimes du dix-huitième siècle* (1857–1858), *Charles Demailly* (1869), and *Manette Salomon* (1867). After the death of Jules, Edmund wrote *La fille Élisa* (1877), *Chérie* (1884), several studies of Japanese art, and completed the famous *Journal des Goncourts* (1887–1896). He also founded the Académie des Goncourt which awards annually the Prix Goncourt to an outstanding French author.

Goodman, Benny (1909–), American band leader and clarinet player, known as the "King of Swing". He was born in Chicago and studied at the Lewis Institute and under Franz Schoepp of the Chicago Symphony Orchestra. After playing for radio shows, New York clubs, and theater orchestras, Goodman organized his own jazz band (1934), which was responsible for much of the popularity of the "big band" sound of the late 1930's. He also started the *Let's Dance* radio program (1934), conducted swing concerts at such places as Carnegie Hall, New York, and Symphony Hall, Boston, and appeared as a clarinet soloist with the New York Philharmonic Orchestra. In 1959 he toured Europe and in 1962 visited the Soviet Union as a representative of American jazz. The movie, *The Benny Goodman Story*, appeared in 1956.

Goodrich, Benjamin Franklin (1841–1888), American physician and manufacturer noted for his prominent role in the rubber industry. He was born in Ripley, N.Y. and studied medicine at the Cleveland Medical College. After serving as a surgeon during the Civil War plus one year of private practice, Goodrich gave up his medical career to enter the real estate business. He soon became associated with the rubber industry and organized the firm of Goodrich, Tew, and Company (1870), which became the B. F. Goodrich Company (1880).

Goodyear, Charles (1800–1860), American inventor, born in New Haven, Conn. He experimented with crude rubber and accidentally discovered that a mixture of rubber and sulfur, when it is subjected to heat, becomes elastic and retains its elasticity under all conditions of temperature. He spent years in perfecting the process of vulcanization and patented it in 1844. It is the basis of the modern rubber industry.

Gordon, Charles George, also called **Chinese Gordon** and **Gordon Pasha** (1833–1885), British soldier, born in Woolwich. He graduated from the Royal Military Academy (1852) and fought in the Crimean War (1855). His leadership of the Chinese soldiers who suppressed the Taiping Rebellion (1863–1864) gained him the nickname of "Chinese" Gordon. At the request of the khedive he was sent in 1874 to organize the Egyptian Sudan, of which he was governor (1877–1880). He was sent to the Sudan again in 1884 to organize the withdrawal of troops before the Mahdi's advance, and was besieged for 10 months in Khartoum, where he was killed two days before help came.

Gorgas, William Crawford (1854–1920), American physician and sanitation expert, born in Mobile, Ala., and educated in New York at the Bellevue Hospital Medical College. Appointed army surgeon in 1880, he became widely known for the sanitary campaign that wiped out yellow fever in Cuba after the Spanish-American War. As chief sanitary officer of the Canal Commission, he made it possible to build the Panama Canal by eliminating yellow fever and checking malaria in the Canal Zone. In 1914 Gorgas went to South Africa to help combat pneumonia in the mines of the Rand. He became surgeon general of the U.S. army with the rank of brigadier general in 1914 and was promoted to major general in 1915.

Göring, Hermann (1893–1946), German political leader, born in Rosenheim, Bavaria. He was a distinguished aviator during World War I, and led the famous Richthofen squadron. He was early associated with Adolf Hitler and took part in the unsuccessful beer hall revolt in Munich in 1923. Göring escaped arrest and lived abroad for four years. In 1928 he entered the Reichstag and rose to power with Hitler, whose chief lieutenant he was from the beginning.

When Hitler became chancellor and virtual dictator in 1933, Göring was made a general, premier of Prussia, minister for aviation, speaker of the Reichstag, and head of the secret police. He put down opposition to his party by crushing it without compunction. He was Hitler's right-hand man in World War II. Sentenced to death at the Nürnberg trials, he committed suicide in jail.

Gorky, Maxim, also spelled **Maksim Gorki** (1868–1936), Russian novelist and playwright, born near Nizhni Novgorod. After the publication of his first short story, *Makar Chudra* (1892), Gorky became one of the most popular of contemporary Russian fiction writers. He stood for revolutionary doctrines and became one of the foremost figures in Soviet Russia, being a friend of Lenin and Stalin. Gorky's play *The Lower Depths* (1903) earned worldwide acclaim for its brutally frank picture of slum life. His other writings include *My Childhood, In the World, My University Days, Fragments from My Diary*, and *Reminiscences of My Youth*. Nizhni Novgorod in central Russia was renamed Gorky in his honor.

Gosnold, Bartholomew (d.1607), English navigator, born in Suffolk. In 1602 he left Falmouth with a ship and 20 colonists, attempting to cross the ocean in a direct line. Contrary winds took his vessel to the Azores, from where after a tedious voyage of seven weeks, he reached the coast of Maine. Following the land-line in a southwesterly direction, he discovered Cape Cod and Martha's Vineyard. In 1606 Gosnold and Captain John Smith brought the first settlers to Virginia. Through their joint efforts the settlement of Jamestown was established in 1607, the first permanent English colony in America. Gosnold, however, did not approve of placing the colony on the Jamestown site.

Gosse, Sir **Edmund William** (1849–1928), English writer, born in London. He served as translator to the Board of Trade (1875–1904), was professor of English literature at Trinity College, Cambridge (1885–1890), and librarian to the House of Lords (1904–1914). Among his writings are *Studies in the Literature of Northern Europe, History of Modern English Literature*, several volumes of verse, and a drama. To many, however, his greatest book is *Father and Son* (1907), (published anonymously), describing his father, Philip Gosse, a naturalist with an old-fashioned theology, who differed on many points with his literary son. Edmund Gosse was knighted in 1925.

Gottfried von Strassburg, German poet of the late twelfth century who wrote the chivalric epic *Tristan und Isolde*, regarded as the greatest work in German medieval literature. The legend, Celtic in origin, traveled by way of Brittany, through northern France, where it was eventually picked up by Gottfried. In his hands the romance became one of the greatest works of the Arthurian cycle.

Goujon, Jean (c.1510–c.1568), French sculptor, leader of the Renaissance school in France. His work as a sculptor was done chiefly in association with the architect Pierre Lescot. Beginning in 1547 the two decorated a new section of the Louvre in Paris. For one of the galleries Goujon made four caryatids of great classical beauty. His bas-reliefs for the Fountain of the Innocents are also outstanding.

Gould, Benjamin Apthorp (1824–1896), American astronomer, born in Boston, Mass., and educated at Harvard and Göttingen. He founded the *Astronomical Journal* in 1849 and edited it for many years. He was director of longitude determinations of the Coast Survey (1852–1867) and of Dudley Observatory at Albany, N.Y. (1855–1859). Gould determined the longitudinal relations between America and Europe telegraphically by use of the Atlantic cable. He made possible a wider knowledge of the Southern heavens by establishing the National Observatory at Córdoba, Argentina, in 1870.

Gould, George Jay (1864–1923), American financier, born in New York City, the eldest son of Jay Gould. He increased the Gould railway holdings to 50,000 miles and developed the Wabash into a transcontinental line, but by 1912 he had lost control of the Gould system. Gould was president of the Manhattan Elevated Railway, New York, from 1892 to 1913 and was a prominent clubman and sportsman.

Gould, Jay (1836–1892), American financier, born in Roxbury, N.Y. He attended public schools and an academy, while supporting himself as a blacksmith's helper and store clerk. Gould laid the foundations for his fortune by buying railroad stock after the panic of 1857 and selling when prices reached a higher level. He invested his profits in bonds of the Rutland and Washington Railroad and in 1859 moved to New York City. By following a system of buying stock at depressed values he acquired control of the Erie, Union Pacific, Missouri Pacific, Wabash, Texas & Pacific, St. Louis Southwestern and International & Great Northern railroads, representing about one-tenth of the railway mileage of the United States. In 1869 he and his partner, James Fisk, brought on the famous "Black Friday" panic of September 24 by a raid on the gold market. Gould also bought control of the Western Union Telegraph Company in 1881 and at his death left a huge fortune.

Gounod, Charles François (1818–1893), French operatic composer, born in Paris. He studied music at the Paris Conservatoire and in 1839 won the Grand Prix de Rome. He then visited Rome and Vienna and in 1849 became an organist in Paris. His best and most successful operas are *Faust* (1859) and *Roméo et Juliette* (1867). He wrote several other operas as well as church music, masses, and oratorios.

Goya y Lucientes, Francisco José de (1746–1828), Spanish painter, born near Saragossa, Aragon. His principal paintings include portraits of the Dutchess of Alba, Ferdinand VII and Charles IV of Spain, and other famous people of the day; the cupola frescoes of St. Anthony for the Church of San Antonio de la Florida; and numerous canvasses depicting the life and activities of the common people. Equally famous is his series of etchings, the *Disasters of War*, depicting the horrors he witnessed during Napoleon's peninsular campaign. Goya's influence was greatest on the work of later nineteenth-century painters, particularly that of Delacroix and Manet.

Graaf, Regnier de (1641–1673), Dutch physician and anatomist, born in Schoonhoven. He discovered the nature and function of pancreatic juice and generative organs. The Graafian follicles in the ovary were discovered by and named for him.

Gracchus, Gaius Sempronius (c.153–121 B.C.), Roman tribune, younger son of the Roman general and administrator Tiberius Sempronius Gracchus and Cornelia, daughter of Publius Scipio Africanus the Elder. Elected to tribune in 123 B.C., he enforced the agrarian laws drafted by his brother and introduced new reform legislation. He was reelected in 122 B.C., but his enemies prevented a second reelection and civil war resulted. Rather than fall into the hands of the aristocrats, Gaius ordered his slave to kill him. He and his brother Tiberius Sempronius are known as the Gracchi.

Gracchus, Tiberius Sempronius (c.162–133 B.C.), elder of the Gracchi. He began a military career in his youth and was present at the siege and storming of Carthage (146 B.C.). In the course of the next few years he became seriously concerned about the unequal distribution of public lands and the condition of the poor. Elected tribune of the people in 133 B.C., he forced the passage of laws that partly corrected the evils, and he offered himself for reelection at the end of his term. Riots ensued, in which he and many of his followers were killed.

Graham, Martha (1895–), American choreographer and dancer. She was born in Pittsburgh, Pa., and studied dance under Ruth St. Denis. In 1919 she made her dancing debut in Ted Shawn's *Xochitl* and by 1926 she was appearing in her own compositions. Among her dances are *Primitive Mysteries* (1931), *Letter to the World* (1940), *Cave of the Heart* (1947), and *Episodes* (1959), for which she collaborated with George Balanchine. She is also the founder of the Dance Repertory Theater of New York (1930) and head of the Martha Graham School for Contemporary Dance. From 1955 to 1956 she made a tour of the Far and Middle East sponsored by the U.S. state department.

Graham, William Franklin, known as **Billy Graham** (1918–), American Protestant evangelist, born in Charlotte, N.C. After being ordained a Baptist minister, his first church service was in Western Springs, Ill. His radio program *Songs in the Night* was aired from 1943 to 1945. In 1946 he began his nationwide evangelical missions. His books include *Calling Youth to Christ* (1947), *Revival of Our Times* (1950), *America's Hour of Decision* (1951), and *Korean Diary* (1953). He has produced many religious films, has made many European tours preaching his evangelical message. He has been very active in the civil rights movement.

Grahame, Kenneth (1859–1932), British author, born in Edinburgh, Scotland. He is best known for his charming and imaginative books, *The Golden Age* (1895), *Dream Days* (1898), about his own childhood, and *The Wind in the Willows* (1908), a children's classic. From 1898 to 1908 he was secretary of the Bank of England.

Grainger, Percy Aldridge (1882–1961), Australian pianist, noted for his performance of the words of Edvard Grieg. He was born in Brighton, Melbourne, and moved to the United States, becoming a citizen shortly after his American debut in 1915. Grainger toured through Great Britain, Australia, New Zealand, and South Africa. He also composed several piano pieces, including *Country Gardens* and *Shepherd's Hey*.

Grant, Ulysses Simpson (1822–1885), American general and eighteenth president of the United States. (1868–1877). He was born in Point Pleasant, Ohio, the son of a farmer, attended the public schools until he was 17, and graduated from West Point in 1843. He served under Gen. Zachary Taylor in the Mexican War (1846–1848) until the capture of Monterrey. In 1852 he served in Oregon but in 1854 resigned his commission and settled in St. Louis, Mo., from where in 1859, he moved to Galena, Ill., and worked in the leather trade. At the beginning of the Civil War (1861), he volunteered his services and was appointed colonel of an Illinois regiment. In August, 1861, he was appointed brigadier general, commanding the district around Cairo. He then occupied Paducah and led an expedition on the Mississippi. In February, 1862, he distinguished himself in the capture of Fort Donelson on the Tennessee River and was made a major general.

On April 6, 1862, after a preliminary defeat, he won a great battle over the Confederates at Pittsburg Landing, or Shiloh, Tenn. Succeeding Gen. Henry W. Halleck in the west, he commanded the land forces that, in conjunction with the navy, reduced Vicksburg on July 4, 1863. This was soon followed by the fall of Fort Hudson and the opening of the Mississippi. In 1864 he was appointed lieutenant general and commander in chief and personally directed the operations of the great final struggle in Virginia. The northern forces, though often repulsed with heavy losses, finally compelled the evacuation of Richmond, April 2, 1865, and on April 9 the Confederate army surrendered under Gen. Robert E. Lee. Congress, in recognition of his eminent services, passed an act reviving the grade of "general of the army of the United States," to which Grant was immediately appointed.

In 1868, as a Republican, he was elected president of the United States, defeating Horatio Seymour by an electoral vote of 214 to 80. His first term of office saw the passage of the fifteenth amendment to the Constitution and the settlement of the Alabama claims dispute. Scandals among high officials were discovered during Grant's second term of office (1873–1877). Although innocent of any actual corruption himself, he did delay and obstruct improvement of conditions at times by refusing to believe wrong of anyone who was his friend. He retired from public life in 1877, toured the world, and received enthusiastic welcomes in England and France.

Simple, reticent, earnest, and persevering in his character, he owed his military success not so much to strategy as to superior numbers and resources and hard fighting. Having lost his moderate fortune in an unfortunate speculation, Grant battled heroically with cancer to finish his *Personal Memoirs*, and thus provide an income for his family.

Grass, Günther (1927–), German writer, born in Danzig, and educated at the Berlin Academy of Fine Arts. His novels, for which he is best known, include *Die Blechtrommel* (*The Tin Drum*, 1959) and *Katz und Maus* (*Cat and Mouse*, 1961).

Grattan, Henry (1746–1820), Irish statesman and orator, born in Dublin and educated at Trinity College in that city. After studying at the Middle Temple in London, Grattan was admitted to the Irish bar in 1772. He was elected to the Irish Parliament in 1775 and held his seat during most of the next 25 years. From 1805 until his death, Grattan was a member of the British House of Commons, where he worked unceasingly for Catholic emancipation.

Graves, Robert (1895–), British poet, novelist, critic, and lecturer. He was born in London and studied at Charterhouse and at St. John's College, Cambridge. During World War I he served in the Royal Welsh Fusiliers, completing his education afterward. He taught at the University of Cairo for one year (1926), and then devoted all of his time to writing until 1961 when he was named professor of poetry at Oxford. Noted for his masterly prose style, Graves has produced such historical novels as *I, Claudius* (1934), *Wife to Mr. Milton* (1943), *Hercules My Shipmate* (1945), and *King Jesus* (1946). His poetry includes *Collected Poems* (1948 and 1959), *More Poems* (1961), and *New Poems* (1962). He is also the author of *White Goddess* (1948), an impressive study of poetic myth.

Gray, Elisha (1835–1901), American inventor, born in Barnesville, Ohio. He secured his first patent (1867) for a telegraphic switch and annunciator. The 70 patents for which he applied include those for multiplex telegraphy, a type-printing telegraph, and the telautograph, which was demonstrated at the Chicago World's Fair in 1893. Gray applied for a patent for the speaking telephone in 1876, but the rights were awarded to Alexander Graham Bell, and Bell's claims were upheld by the U.S. Supreme Court.

Gray, George (1840–1925), American jurist and senator, born in New Castle, Del., and educated at Princeton and Harvard Law School. He was admitted to the bar in 1863, became attorney general of Delaware in 1879, and held a Democratic seat in the U.S. Senate (1885–1899). He supported Pres. Grover Cleveland on tariff and financial questions. Gray was judge of the United States circuit court (1899–1914) and had a notable record as an arbiter. He was, at various times, a member of the Anglo-American Joint High Commission, the Paris Peace Commission, the Anthracite Coal Strike Commission, and the North Atlantic Fisheries Arbitration Board.

Gray, Robert (1755–1806), American explorer, born in Tiverton, R.I. Outfitted by Boston merchants in 1787, he set out in the sloop *Lady Washington* to trade with the Pacific Coast Indians. In 1790, in command of the *Columbia*, he set sail from Boston for a voyage around the world, returning in 1793 to become the first American to carry the U.S. flag around the globe. He discovered the Columbia River and Grays Harbor, an inlet of the Pacific Ocean in Washington. It was Gray's voyage that paved the way for the American colonization of Oregon.

Gray, Stephen (d.1736), English physicist who evolved the principle of the communication of electric power from native electrics to other bodies. He also noted the possibility of the insulation of conductors by cakes of resin and was the first to show that the human body is a conductor.

Gray, Thomas (1716–1771), English poet, most widely known for his *Elegy Written in a Country Churchyard* (1751). He was born in London and educated at Cambridge. Most of his life was spent in Cambridge as student and writer; though appointed professor of history and modern languages at the university in 1768, he never lectured. Gray's exquisite *Elegy* was written in the churchyard at Stoke Poges, his mother's home. He was buried there, near the church of the "ivy-mantled tower." His other poems, notably his odes, have much of the finish of his masterpiece. He was one of the transition poets who paved the way for the Romantics Wordsworth, Shelley, Keats, and their contemporaries.

Greco, El, real name **Kyriakos Theotokopoulos** (c.1548–1614), Greek painter who lived in Spain. He was born near Candia, Crete, studied under Titian in Venice, and for a time painted in Rome under the patronage of Cardinal Farnese. He is usually associated with the Castilian school of Spanish mystic mannerist artists. El Greco's style, which stresses elongated forms, sharp breaks and contrasts, and a metallic quality of color, has a dynamic quality that bridges the Classical, Renaissance, and Baroque schools of art. Among his numerous works, the best known are *View of Toledo, Adoration of the Shepherds, Assumption of the Virgin, Nativity,* and *The Burial of the Count of Orgaz.*

Greeley, Horace (1811–1872), American journalist, born in Amherst, N.H. At the age of 15 he was apprenticed to a newspaper publisher in East Poultney, Vt., and after some experience as a journeyman printer settled in New York in 1831. He made an unsuccessful attempt in 1833 to found a newspaper called the *Morning Post*, supposed to have been the first one-cent daily. He had better fortune with a weekly literary paper, the *New Yorker*, for which he wrote essays and verse, and which he published from 1834 to 1841. In 1841 he merged the *New Yorker* with the *Log Cabin*, issued during 1840 as a campaign organ for William Henry Harrison, and the merger resulted in the New York *Tribune*, which became one of the great newspapers of America. A weekly edition, started a few months later, was for years the most influential journal in the northern and western states.

From 1850 until the Civil War, Greeley and his editorial associates, Bayard Taylor, Charles A. Dana, George Ripley, and others, fought for the antislavery cause. Greeley himself was one of the delegates to the Republican convention that nominated Abraham Lincoln, and once the war was started he urged its vigorous prosecution. But he was sensitive to the horrors of the conflict and in 1864 tried to reach a compromise with Confederate agents in a conference in Canada. When the war ended, he favored a universal amnesty; his participation in the bail bond of Jefferson Davis was in accordance with his principles, though it brought keen censure from Northern extremists. Greeley made an unsuccessful attempt to win a seat in Congress in 1870 and in 1872 joined the Liberal Republicans as an opponent of the renomination of Ulysses S. Grant. He was nominated for the presidency by this faction and endorsed by the Democrats but carried only border and Southern states, six in all. He died soon after the election. Greeley's expression, "Go west, young man, and grow up with the country," has become famous.

Greely, Adolphus Washington (1844–1935), American explorer, born in Newburyport, Mass. He served in the Civil War, rising to the rank of brevet major of volunteers. After the war he was attached to the signal corps in the regular army, becoming chief officer in 1887. He commanded a government expedition to establish one of a chain of polar stations in 1881; his party reached latitude 83° 24′, the farthest point north attained up to that time, but only seven survivors were left when Capt. Winfield S. Schley's relief expedition reached them in 1884. Between 1898 and 1902 thousands of miles of telegraph and cable lines were laid under Greely's direction. Promoted to major general (1906), he was placed in command of relief operations in San Francisco to care for the victims of the earthquake and fire. In 1935 he was awarded the Congressional Medal of Honor.

Green, William (1873–1952), American labor leader, born in Coshocton, Ohio. He worked as a coal miner, joined the United Mine Workers of America, became subdistrict president in 1900, president of the Ohio District Mine Workers' Union in 1906, and secretary-treasurer of the United Mine Workers of America in 1913. In 1924 Green was elected president of the American Federation of Labor, succeeding Samuel Gompers. As a Democrat he served two terms in the Ohio senate. He advocated a 30-hour week as the only permanent solution to unemployment.

At the American Federation of Labor Convention in 1935 Green came into sharp conflict with John L. Lewis, president of the United Mine Workers of America, an affiliated union. Lewis wanted to organize the mass-production industries as units, according to "vertical unionism" principles. Green prevented Lewis from swinging the Federation to this plan. Lewis withdrew and organized his rival group, the Committee for Industrial Organization. Green held to more conservative labor policies and for several years fought a losing battle; the Federation was weakened by the secession of member groups and the growth of the C.I.O. under Philip Murray.

Greene, Graham (1904–), English novelist and playwright, born in Berkhamsted. His novels have as a foundation psychological studies in the tradition of Kafka and Dostoevski. His best-known novels are *The Power and the Glory* (1940), *Orient Express* (1942), *The Ministry of Fear* (1943), *The Heart of the Matter* (1948), *The End of the Affair* (1951), and *The Quiet American* (1955). His plays include *The Living Room* (1953), *The Potting Shed* (1957), and *The Complaisant Lover* (1959).

Greene, Nathanael (1742–1786), American Revolutionary general, regarded by many as second only to George Washington in ability. He was born in Potowomut (now Warwick), R.I. Enlisting as a private in 1774, Greene was appointed to the command of the Rhode Island division in 1775 with the rank of brigadier general, and was soon promoted to major general. He showed brilliant qualities of leadership at Trenton and Princeton and saved the Americans from rout at Brandywine. At Germantown he commanded the left wing. He won greater fame, however, as commander of the often defeated Army of the South, which he took over from Gen. Horatio Gates (1780). After reorganizing the dispirited forces Greene began a campaign to divide the British armies and to force them to win costly and fruitless victories. In this way he gained control of Georgia and the Carolinas and paved the way for the surrender of Gen. Charles Cornwallis.

Gregory I, Saint, known as **Gregory the Great** (c.540–604), bishop of Rome, elected pope in 590 as successor to Pelagius II. He was born in Rome of a well-to-do family and studied law; about 575, however, he voluntarily entered the monastery of St.

Andrew in Rome. According to the Venerable Bede, he was touched by the sight of some fair-haired Anglo-Saxon youths who were being sold as slaves and decided to go to Britain as a missionary. Pope Pelagius had other duties for him, but after Gregory became pope, he sent Saint Augustine to England. Gregory was one of the greatest administrators and organizers of the Catholic Church and the last of the four Latin fathers. The present forms of the ritual and sacred chants (Gregorian chants) are ascribed to him. His feast day is March 12.

Gregory VII, Saint, real name **Hildebrand** (c.1020–1085), bishop of Rome from 1073. Born in Tuscany, Italy, he passed his youth in a monastery in Rome. He won the friendship of Pope Leo IX, who made him a cardinal subdeacon in 1049, and during the years that followed he rose steadily in prestige and authority. On the death of Pope Alexander II in 1073 Gregory was unanimously elected to the papal chair but was not consecrated until he had secured confirmation of his election from Henry IV, king of Germany and Holy Roman emperor. The new pope at once applied himself to effecting reforms, ecclesiastical and political. He corrected abuses such as clerical marriage and simony (the buying of holy offices), but the general practice of secular investiture brought him into direct conflict with Henry. In 1075 he threatened to excommunicate anyone who received investiture from a layman. In 1076 Henry defied him by offering protection to Church officials thus punished; when summoned to Rome the emperor retaliated by having Gregory deposed by a decree of a diet at Worms. Gregory in turn excommunicated the emperor, who then promised to submit.

Early in 1077 Henry went to the pope's castle at Canossa, Italy, and for three days was forced to stand before the gates, barefoot in the snow and exposed to the severe cold. Absolution granted, he soon displayed the insincerity of his submission, for he made war on and defeated his rival, Rudolf of Swabia, and in 1080 deposed Gregory, setting up the antipope Guibert, archbishop of Ravenna. In 1084 Henry entered Rome and had himself crowned by his own pope, who had assumed the name Clement III. Gregory took refuge in the Castel Sant' Angelo and was rescued by Robert Guiscard, a Norman duke, but he could not maintain his position in Rome and died in retirement the following year. In 1728 he was canonized. His feast day is May 25.

Gregory, Lady **Augusta** (1852–1932), Irish playwright and director, noted for her significant role in the revival of the Irish national theatre. She was born in Roxborough, County Galway. As a result of her friendship with William Butler Yeats she became interested in the Irish literary movement and started translating old Gaelic folk stories. She was one of the founders of the Irish National Theater Society and contributed much to the development of the Abbey Theatre as both a playwright and a director. Among her works are translations of *Cuchlain of Muirthemne* (1902) and *Gods and Fighting Men* (1904), the plays *Spreading the News* (1904) and *The Rising of the Moon* (1907), and *Our Irish Theatre* (1913), the story of its birth and struggle for survival and recognition. Lady Gregory is the subject of several poems by Yeats and will be remembered as the aristocratic woman of *In Coole Park* (1929).

Grenville, Sir **Richard** (c.1541–1591), English naval hero, a cousin of Sir Walter Raleigh. He commanded a fleet that brought colonists to Virginia in 1585. He won his reputation in 1591 as commander of the *Revenge,* one of a fleet preying upon Spanish treasure ships. Grenville and the *Revenge* became separated from the other ships and fought a 15-hour engagement against 15 Spanish vessels before he was captured. Tennyson's ballad *The Revenge* tells the story.

Gresham, Sir **Thomas** (c.1519–1579), English financier for whom Gresham's Law was named. He was born in London and studied at Caius College, Cambridge. After working as an apprentice for his uncle, a merchant, he became a member of the Mercer's Company (1543). In 1551 he was appointed fiscal agent for Henry VIII and in 1558 was named to Queen Elizabeth's first council, serving as ambassador to the Netherlands (1559–1561). He also founded the Royal Exchange, which was built at his expense, and provided for the founding of Gresham College (1597).

Gresham's experience with foreign exchange led him to observe that if two currencies of unequal value are in circulation at the same time, the one of lesser worth will circulate freely, while the more valuable one will be hoarded. Although he is not the discoverer of this principle, Gresham is responsible for its recognition in England.

Grévy, François Paul Jules (1807–1891), French statesman born in Mont-sous-Vaudrey. He was a law student in Paris during the revolution of 1830 and from then on was an ardent Republican, giving legal aid to political prisoners after he was in practice. During the regime of Louis Napoleon he kept out of politics but was active in the National Assembly that met after the Franco-Prussian War. In 1876 he became president of the Chamber of Deputies. Grévy was elected president of France in 1879 and was reelected in 1885. He was forced to resign in 1887 because of a political scandal involving his son-in-law.

Grew, Nehemiah (1641–1712), English botanist and physiologist, born in Warwickshire, and educated at Cambridge and Leiden. His writings on the anatomy and physiology of plants were the first of their kind. In his *The Anatomy of Plants* (1682), he revealed the discovery of sexual organs and reproduction methods among plants.

Grey, Sir **Edward,** 1st Viscount **Grey of Fallodon** (1862–1933), British statesman, born in Northumberland, and educated at Winchester and at Balliol College, Oxford. He was a liberal member of Parliament (1885–1916) and as secretary of state for foreign affairs (1905–1916), was regarded as an outstanding figure in European diplomacy. The Triple Entente was formed by Great Britain, Russia, and France while he was in the Foreign Office, and he negotiated for peace in the Balkans in 1913. He endeavored to prevent World War I through arbitration. Grey guided British policy until the resignation of Herbert Asquith's coalition cabinet in 1916; he then retired and was created Viscount Grey of Fallodon. In 1919 he visited the United States on a peace mission and in 1928 was elected chancellor of Oxford University. Grey published his memoirs in 1925. He was a noted authority on fly-fishing and an excellent amateur naturalist with a special interest in birds.

Grey, Lady **Jane** (1537–1554), queen of England for nine days. She was the eldest daughter of Henry Grey, duke of Suffolk; her mother was a granddaughter of Henry VII. Late in the reign of Edward VI, the duke of Northumberland, who was Lord Protector, brought about the marriage of Lady Jane to his son Guilford Dudley. He then induced the king to declare the succession in favor of Lady Jane, hoping thus to transfer the crown from the Tudors to the Dudleys. Lady Jane, good and accomplished, was innocent of the conspiracy. After the king's death on July 6, 1553, she was proclaimed queen, but Mary's friends were too strong, and on July 19 Lady Jane was arrested. She was tried, sentenced to death for high treason, and on February 12, 1554, was beheaded with her husband.

Grey, Zane (1875–1939), American writer, born in Zanesville, Ohio. After a public school education, he completed a course in dentistry at the University of Pennsylvania and practiced in New York (1898–1904). He then turned to writing popular stories of the West and produced more than 60 novels, selling millions of copies. The best known of his books include *Riders of the Purple Sage* (1912), *The Light of Western Stars* (1914), *The Thundering Hero* (1925), and *The Vanishing American* (1926).

Grieg, Edvard (1843–1907), Norwegian composer of Scottish descent, born in Bergen. After some early instruction by his mother he continued his training in music in Leipzig and Copenhagen. In Copenhagen he became absorbed in the study of Norwegian folk music, which later influenced him greatly. His works have a national quality that classes him with composers such as Frédéric Chopin and Franz Liszt, who tried to express the character of their countries in their music. Grieg founded the Philharmonic Society of Christiania (Oslo) in 1871 and was its conductor until 1880. As a composer he produced numerous songs of great beauty, piano pieces, and a variety of orchestral works. The *Peer Gynt* suite (1876), which he wrote for Henrik Ibsen's play, is one of his best-known compositions.

Griffith, Arthur (1872–1922), Irish political leader, founder of the Sinn Fein. Born in Dublin, he worked for Irish independence as editor of a series of newspapers, and was second in command to Eamon De Valera throughout the early stages of the fight. When De Valera refused the treaty setting up the Irish Free State, Griffith became its first president (1922) but died after a few months in office.

Griffith, David Lewelyn Wark (1875–1948), American motion picture director, noted for his imaginative experimentation with camera effects. He was born in La Grange, Ky., and started an acting career at an early age. His first motion picture appearance was in *Rescued from an Eagle's Nest* (1907) A year later he directed his first film *The Adventures of Dolly,* for the Biograph Company. In 1913 Griffith became an independent producer in order to have more freedom in his directing. *Birth of a Nation* (1914), his most famous work, was one of the first films to depart from the 1,000-foot form and ran for an unheard of three hours. Other Griffith innovations include long vista shots and close-ups, the fade-in and fade-out, and cross-cutting. During his lifetime he directed almost 500 films; among the best known are *Intolerance* (1916), *Hearts of the World* (1918), *Broken Blossoms* (1919), *Way Down East* (1920), and *Orphans of the Storm* (1921). He was also one of the founders of the United Artists Corporation.

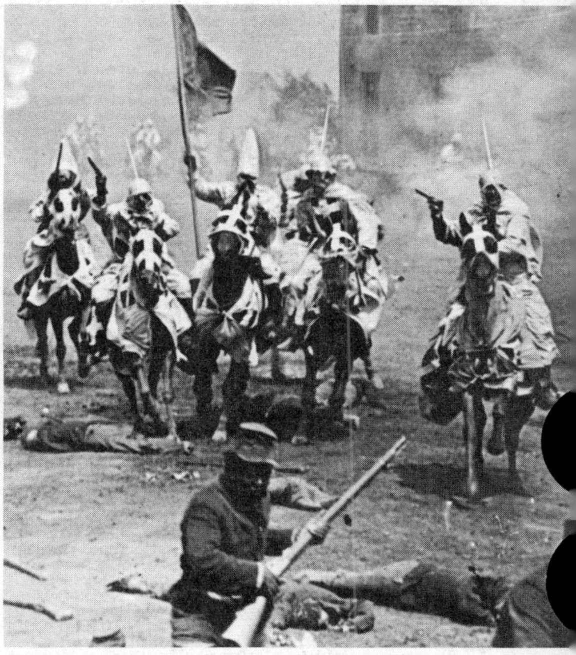

CULVER

D. W. GRIFFITH'S film, *Birth of a Nation.*

Grillparzer, Franz (1791–1872), Austrian playwright, born in Vienna. He studied law and in 1813 entered the civil service, in which he remained until 1856. He first attracted notice in 1817 by a tragedy *Die Ahnfrau,* which was followed by *Sappho* (1818), *Das goldene Vliess* (1821), *Des Meeres und der Liebe Wellen* (1831), and *Der Traum, ein Leben* (1834). He produced lyric poetry and two novels, *Das Kloster bei Sendomir* (1828) and *Der arme Spielmann* (1848).

Grimm, name of two brothers, German philologists, **Jakob** (1785–1863) and **Wilhelm** (1786–1859). Both studied law at the University of Marburg, and in 1840 both received professorships at Kassel. They are best known as the authors of *Grimms' Fairy Tales.* The first volume of this work was published in Germany in 1812 as *Kinder- und Hausmärchen.* The second volume appeared in 1815 and the third in 1822. The *Tales* have been translated into many languages. Jakob Grimm produced a four-volume German grammar that established Grimm's law, formulating the way different Indo-European languages changed their consonantal structure when they became part of the Germanic language group.

Gris, Juan (1887–1927), Spanish painter, born in Madrid. With Georges Braque in France, he was one of the leading figures of the cubist movement in art. His works include numerous portraits and still-lifes.

Gromyko, Andrei A. (1909–   ), Soviet economist and diplomat, born in Gromyki. Gromyko was counselor of the Soviet embassy in Washington, D.C., from 1939 to 1943, and from August, 1943 to April, 1946 he was Soviet ambassador to the United States. He was appointed permanent Russian delegate to the United Nations in March, 1946, and his famous "walkout" during the debate over the Iranian question brought him wide notoriety. In 1949 he was made chief deputy foreign minister of the

Soviet Union. He was ambassador to Great Britain from 1952 to 1953. Gromyko became chief deputy foreign minister in 1953 and foreign minister in 1957.

Gropius, Walter (1883–), German architect, noted for his use of the newest industrial techniques and, in particular, for his experimentation with glass. He was born in Berlin and studied at the Technische Hochschule in Munich and under Peter Behrens in Berlin. Gropius first achieved recognition for the Fagus factory at Alfeld and the Hall of Machinery at the Werkbund Exposition in Cologne (1914). In 1919 he undertook the reorganization of the grand ducal art schools at Weimar, which subsequently became the Staatliches Bauhaus at Dessau. Under Gropius' direction and housed in buildings of his design, the Bauhaus school of architecture, with its emphasis on functionalism, gained international renown. In 1934 Gropius moved to London, where he worked with Maxwell Fry. He came to the United States in 1937 to teach at Harvard University and was named chairman of the Harvard graduate School of Design the following year.

Gropius' works include the civic theater at Jena, the Harvard Graduate Center, and several industrial buildings and prefabricated homes. He is also the author of *Internationale Architektur* (1925), *The New Architecture and the Bauhaus* (1935), *Rebuilding Our Communities* (1945), and the *Scope of Total Architecture* (1955).

Grosz, George (1893–1959), American painter and cartoonist, born in Berlin, Germany. He was a leader of the German school of expressionism known as "The New Objectivity," and participated in the Dada movement. His works, which satirized the bourgeoisie, militarism, capitalism, and Germany during the 1920's, were censored by the Nazis. In 1932 he emigrated to the U.S., settled in New York, and became a citizen in 1938. Much of his later work, typified by *The Pit*, the *Stick Men* series, and *A Piece of My World*, is grim, satirical, highly critical of modern civilization.

Grote, George (1794–1871), English historical writer, born in Clayhill, Kent, and educated at the Charterhouse. At first a clerk in his father's bank, he was elected to Parliament in 1832, and served in the House of Commons until 1841. His interests in education eventually brought him the vice-chancellorship of the London University (1860) and the presidency of University College (1869). Among his works are a *History of Greece* (8 vols., 1846–1856) and *Plato and Other Companions of Socrates* (3 vols., 1865).

Grotius, Hugo, Dutch name **Huigh de Groot** (1583–1645), Dutch jurist, born in Delft, the son of the local burgomaster, who was also curator of the University of Leiden. A child prodigy, Grotius graduated from Leiden at the age of 15 and began his career as a practicing lawyer in The Hague. He was appointed pensionary (chief magistrate) at Rotterdam in 1613. At that time the Protestants of the Netherlands were involved in a bitter dispute over theology, being divided into two groups—the orthodox Calvinists and the more liberal followers of Jacob Arminius, called *Arminians* or *Remonstrants*. Grotius sided with John van Oldenbarneveldt, an Arminian, and narrowly escaped death on the scaffold as a heretic. Instead he was sentenced to life imprisonment in the fortress of Loevestein but escaped after 18 months when his wife contrived to have him carried out of the castle in a linen chest. Grotius at first sought refuge in France and there wrote his great work *De iure belli ac pacis (On the Law of War and Peace*, 1625). Originally published in Paris, it ranks as the first text on international law. After an absence of 12 years Grotius returned to his native country, relying on the protection of Frederick Henry, prince of Orange, who wrote him a sympathetic letter. His enemies, however, succeeded in having him banished, and in 1634 he entered the diplomatic service of Sweden. He was Swedish ambassador to the French court (1634–1645). Besides his work on law Grotius wrote verse in Latin and Dutch, histories, and theological treatises.

Grouchy, Marquis **Emmanuel de** (1776–1847), French general, born near Paris. He began his military career at the age of 14 and was rapidly advanced. He fought in the Republican army during the foreign wars of the French Revolutionary government and became one of Napoleon's most trusted officers. He especially distinguished himself at Hohenlinden and in the retreat from Moscow. When Napoleon returned from Elba, Grouchy entered his service again and was promoted to the rank of marshal. As commander of an army division he was ordered by Napoleon to engage Gebhard von Blücher's forces after their defeat at Ligny. Grouchy kept the Prussian rear guard in action but permitted the main body of German troops to move on to Waterloo, where they joined the British under the Duke of Wellington. Upon the restoration of the Bourbons, Grouchy went into exile and lived in Philadelphia, Pa., for five years but was permitted to return to France in 1819. After the revolution of 1830 his rank as marshal was restored.

Grove, Sir George (1820–1900), English engineer and writer on music, born in London. He erected the first two cast-iron lighthouses in the West Indies and assisted in the building of the Britannia tubular bridge, which unites Anglesey and Wales. He was knighted in 1883 on the opening of the Royal College of Music, of which he was director until 1895. As a musicologist, his *Dictionary of Music and Musicians* (1878–1889), a standard reference volume, and *Beethoven and His Nine Symphonies* (1884; rev. ed. 1886) are his best-known works.

Gruber, Max von (1853–1927), German bacteriologist. He developed the process for the agglutination of bacteria by a serum of an organism immune by nature to, or by contact with, such diseases as typhoid fever, cholera, and meningitis. Von Gruber's findings were used by Ferdinand Widal in the Widal test for diagnosis of typhoid fever.

Grüewald, Matthias or **Mathäus** (fl. 1500–1530), German painter, born near Würzburg. He worked under the patronage of Albert of Brandenburg, elector and cardinal of Mainz. His masterwork is the *Isenheim Altarpiece* (c.1516).

Guardi, Francesco (1712–1793), Italian painter, born in Venice, a pupil of Antonio Canaletto. His works, most of which depict Venice, are especially vivid in the use of color. Among his paintings are *Procession of the Doge, Grand Hall of the Palazzo Ducale,* and *Church and Piazza of San Marco.*

Guericke, Otto von (1602–1686), German physicist, born in Magdeburg. He traveled in England, Sweden, and France and returned to hold public office in his native town. In 1650 he invented a vacuum pump with which he pumped the air from two close-fitting hollow hemispheres. Atmospheric pressure held them together so tightly that eight horses attached to each could not pull them apart. He demonstrated this experiment in public. In the field of electricity he discovered conduction of current and electric sparks. He collected his most important observations and described them in his *Experimenta nova* (1672).

Guest, Edgar Albert (1881–1959), American poet, noted for his folksy, homespun verse. He was born in Birmingham, England, was brought to the U.S. at the age of ten, and in 1895 joined the editorial staff of the Detroit *Free Press.* His numerous works include *Home Rhymes* (1909), *A Heap o' Livin'* (1916), *Life's Highway* (1933), and *Living the Years* (1949).

Guggenheim, Daniel (1856–1930), American industrialist and philanthropist, born in Philadelphia, Pa. He engaged with his brothers in the mining and smelting business left them by their father, Meyer Guggenheim, but became most widely known as the donor of a $2,500,000 fund for the promotion of aviation. When the affairs of the fund were wound up in 1929, twice the original amount had been expended. Guggenheim also gave a million dollars as an endowment for an aviation school at New York University.

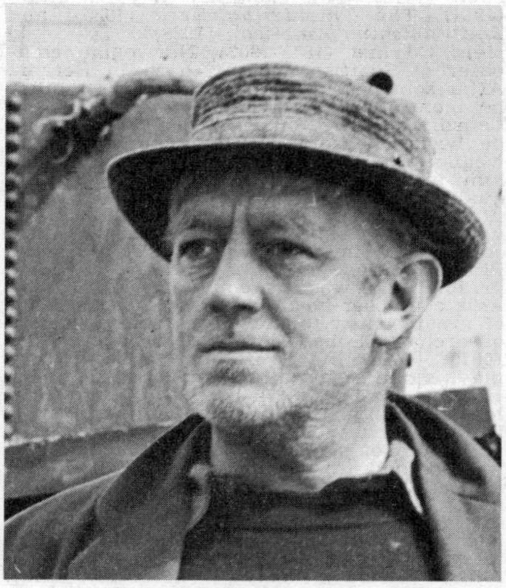

ALEC GUINNESS in *The Horse's Mouth* role.

Guggenheim, Simon (1867–1941), American industrialist and philanthropist, brother of Daniel. He went to Colorado in 1888 and, elected as a Democrat, represented the state in the U.S. Senate (1907–1913). In memory of his son he established in 1925 the John Simon Guggenheim Memorial Foundation with a capital of $3,500,000, which each year grants fellowships to deserving U.S. students for advanced study abroad.

Guido d'Arezzo or **Guido Aretino** (c.995–c.1050), Italian Benedictine monk who named the notes of the muscial scale and introduced other innovations, such as the four-line staff (previously only two lines were used). He was long thought to have been a native of Arezzo, Italy, but it is now believed he was born near Paris. His service in the field of music notation was recognized by Pope John XIX, who studied the new system and helped to popularize it. Guido became prior of the monastery of Avellano in 1029 and probably died there.

Guido Reni. See *Reni, Guido.*

Guillaume, Charles Édouard (1861–1938), French physicist, born in Fleurier, Switzerland, winner of the Nobel Prize for physics in 1920. In 1883 he was appointed assistant in the Bureau International of Weights and Measures in Paris and became its director in 1915. Guillaume first came into public notice in 1896 as the discoverer of Invar, a steel-nickel alloy that does not expand appreciably with heat. It greatly decreased the cost of geodetic measurements. He also discovered platinite, a nickel-iron alloy that cut the cost of electric light bulbs, since it replaced the expensive platinum as the material for the wire that carries current through the glass of the bulb.

Guillotin, Joseph Ignace (1738–1814), French physician, born in Saintes. He taught at the Jesuit College at Bordeaux and practiced medicine in Paris. He became a deputy to the States-General (1789) and secretary of the National Assembly (1790). The guillotine, a machine which he suggested be used in cases of capital punishment, was named for him.

Guise, 1st Duc **de,** title of **Claude I de Lorraine** (1496–1550), second son of the duke of Lorraine. He fought under Francis I at Marignano in 1515, thereby helping the French king to reconquer Milan. He then remained at home as a defender of France against the English and Germans. For suppressing the peasant revolt in Lorraine in 1527, Francis created him first duke of Guise, so called for the town of that name.

Guise, 2d Duke **de,** title of **François de Lorraine,** surnamed **Le Balafré** (1519–1563), son of 1st duc de Guise, one of the greatest generals of France. He and his brother Charles, a cardinal, managed to become all-powerful during the reign of Francis II. Guise and Montmorency won a victory over the Huguenots at Dreux in 1562, but Guise was assassinated by a Huguenot the following year during the siege of Orléans.

Guise, 3d Duke **de,** title of **Henry I de Lorraine,** surnamed **Le Balafré** (1550–1558), son of Francis. He fought on the Catholic side in the Wars of Religion in 1569, forced Gaspard de Coligny to raise the siege of Poitiers and was active in the Massacre of St. Bartholomew's Day. King Henry III feared his growing power and had him assassinated at Blois.

Guise, 5th Duke **de,** title of **Henry II de Lorraine** (1614–1664), grandson of Henry I of Guise. He abandoned his position as archbishop of Reims when his elder brother's death (1640) made him heir to the dukedom. Having joined the league against Cardinal Richelieu, he was condemned to death but escaped to Flanders. He put himself at the head of Masaniello's revolt in Naples as the representative of the Anjou family but was taken by the Spanish in 1647 and carried to Madrid, where he remained five years. After another attempt to win Naples (1654), he settled at Paris. The direct line of the dukes of Guise ended in 1667, three years after his death.

Guiness, Sir **Alec** (1914–), English actor. He was born in London and made his stage debut in 1934. Guiness appeared with John Gielgud's company and with the Old Vic for many years. He also played the leading role in T.S. Eliot's *The Cocktail Party* in New York (1950) and starred in several plays in Canada's first Stratford (Ontario) Shakespeare festival (1953). In the United States Guiness is best known for his motion pictures which include *Kind Hearts and Coronets* (1949), *The Lavendar Hill Mob* (1951), *The Horse's Mouth* (1958),

Our Man in Havana (1960), and *Lawrence of Arabia* (1962). In 1957 he received an Academy Award for his memorable portrayal of the stubborn British colonel in *Bridge on the River Kwai.* Guiness was knighted in 1959.

Guizot, François Pierre Guillaume (1787–1874), French historian and statesman, born in Nîmes. His father was guillotined in 1794 during the Terror, and François was educated in Geneva, Switzerland. He began his literary career in Paris, and his first publication (1809) was a dictionary of synonyms. In 1812 Guizot was appointed professor of modern history at the Sorbonne. From then to the July Revolution of 1830 he alternated writing with a political career. He was most prominent in French politics during the 18 years of Louis Philippe's reign, serving successively as minister of the interior, minister of public instruction, ambassador to London, and minister of foreign affairs in the cabinet of Nicolas Jean de Dieu Soult (1840–1847). During the last year of the king's reign, Guizot was prime minister and helped to bring on the crisis that overthrew the monarchy. Guizot escaped to England but returned in 1849 and devoted the rest of his life to historical research and writing.

Gunther, John (1901–), American journalist and author, born in Chicago, Ill. His books include *Inside Europe* (1936), *Inside Asia* (1939), *Inside Latin America* (1941), *Inside U.S.A.* (1947), *Inside Africa* (1955), and *Inside Europe Today* (1961).

Gustavus II, known as **Gustavus Adolphus** (1594–1632), king of Sweden, son of Charles IX, whom he succeeded in 1611. His efficient reorganization of the government and his victories over the armies of Denmark, Russia, and Poland made him an outstanding figure in 1630, when he entered the Thirty Years' War to assist the Protestants. He added further to his reputation as the first soldier in Europe by his victory at Breitenfeld (1631). A year later, on the field of Lützen, he overcame the forces of the German general Wallenstein but was mortally wounded.

Gustavus V (1858–1950), King of Sweden, the son of Oscar II, whom he succeeded in 1907. His education at the University of Uppsala was supplemented by European travel, and he secured training for his career by acting as regent at various periods when his father was ill or away from court. Gustavus was criticized in World War I and World War II for keeping Sweden neutral, but his policy kept his country prosperous and safe. Gustaf Adolf, eldest of his five sons, succeeded him. He was one of the most popular kings of the twentieth century.

Gutenberg, Johann (c.1400–1468), German printer, born in Mainz. His father's name was Gensfleisch, but Johann assumed the name Gutenberg, his mother's maiden name. He became a citizen of Strasbourg about 1420, where it appears he devoted many years to mechanical experiments. As early as 1438 he had a press, movable types, forms, and other appliances for printing. After 1444 there is no record of him until 1448, when he was again in Mainz. In 1450 he entered into a partnership with Johann Fust, a goldsmith, to carry on a printing business; Fust financing their undertaking. The partnership ended after five years, most of the materials being taken by Fust for his investment. Afterward, Gutenberg apparently carried on a successful business alone. In 1465 he abandoned printing and entered the service of Archbishop Adolph of Nassau, elector of Mainz. In his own and in modern times he shared with Fust and Peter Schöffer, Fust's son-in-law, the credit of his invention; but in the preface to a German translation of Livy (Mainz, 1505) it is distinctly declared by Schöffer that the "admirable art of printing was invented in Mainz, in 1450, by the ingenious Johann Gutenberg." The opinion of most modern writers seems to be that Gutenberg not merely invented the art but practiced it long before he became associated with Fust. The *Gutenberg Bible* was the masterpiece of his press.

Guyot, Arnold Henry (1807–1884), Swiss geographer and naturalist, born near Neuchâtel, and educated there and at the University of Berlin. In 1848 he came to the United States, where he became a lecturer at the Lowell Institute, Boston. From 1854 until his death he was professor of physical geography and geology at Princeton. Guyot's principal contributions to science include his investigation of the structure of glaciers, the organization of weather observations, and the preparation of meteorological tables, geographical texts, and wall maps. Many of his papers were published by the Smithsonian Institute.

H

Haakon VII (1872–1957), king of Norway (1905–1957), second son of King Frederick VIII of Denmark and a nephew of Queen Alexandra of Great Britain. Baptized Carl, he assumed the name of Haakon after Parliament unanimously elected him king on November 8, 1905, following Norway's declaration of independence from Sweden. A democratic, constitutional monarch known as "the people's king," Haakon in 1940 led a heroic resistance to the invading German army and sustained the movement's spirit while he and his government were in temporary exile in England. Upon his death, Haakon was succeeded by his son, Olaf V.

Hadrian (76–138), Roman emperor (117–138), success of Trajjan, his kinsman and guardian, whom he had assisted on many military and administrative missions across an empire threatened in many of its farthest reaches. Upon becoming emperor, Hadrian took immediate steps to limit and consolidate Roman power, both geographically and politically. He abandoned the wars of expansion of his predecessor in favor of a massive public works program, which won the approval of the Roman populace. A constant traveler who was absent from Rome 12 of the 20 years of his reign, Hadrian worked to strengthen the entire Roman empire. He abolished the distinction between Italy and the provinces, codified the law, and reorganized the army. Builder of roads, aqueducts, and entire cities, Hadrian was also expertly versed in mathematics, painting, and literature. Perhaps the most notable monument to him is his mausoleum in Rome, now known as the Castel Sant' Angelo.

Haeckel, Ernst Heinrich (1834–1919), German zoologist and philosopher who was an early advocate of Darwin's doctrine of organic evolution. Haeckel first advanced his views in a treatise (1862), after joining the faculty of the University of Jena, where he remained for the rest of his life. In 1867 he published a popular summary of evolutionary theory in *History of Creation.* He devoted his later work to the exposition of monism, the theory that all forms of matter, organic and inorganic, possess an essential unity. In *Riddle of the Universe* (1899), Haeckel explained the universe as the product of natural causes rather than divine power. Darwin himself held that Haeckel's vigorous support of the doctrine of organic evolution was chiefly responsible for its success in Germany. Well-known as a field naturalist, Haeckel was also the first to create a genealogical tree of relationships within the animal kingdom.

Hafiz, real name **Shams ud-din Mohammed** (c.1325–1390), Persian lyric poet who lived all his life at Shiraz, where as a court poet he enjoyed the patronage of rulers and dignitaries. The title "Hafiz" was bestowed in recognition of his having learned the Koran by heart. *Divan,* his principal work, is a collection of short lyric poems that celebrate love and wine. Enormously popular among Persian-speaking peoples. Hafiz' poems are noted for their simple language and proverbial expressions. Numerous translations of his poetry into English and other languages have been made.

Hagen, Walter (1892–), American professional golfer, born in Rochester, N.Y. In 1922, Hagen became the first American to win the British Open Championship (a feat that he repeated in 1924, 1928, and 1929). He also won the American Open Championship twice and the French once. A contemporary and chief rival of Bobby Jones, Hagen won many other national and regional titles. His autobiography, *The Walter Hagen Story,* was published in 1956.

Haggard, Sir **Henry Rider** (1856–1925), British novelist best known for romantic novels about Africa. From 1875 to 1880, he lived in South Africa on duty for the British government. After returning to England, he studied law and was admitted to the bar. Haggard wrote a number of imaginative, highly popular novels with African settings, including *King Solomon's Mines* (1885), *She* (1887), *Cleopatra* (1889), and *Red Eve* (1911). He was also interested in farming and served on several government commissions connected with agricultural matters. For these services he was knighted in 1912.

Haig, Douglas, 1st Earl (1861–1928), British field marshall who was commander in chief of British forces in France for most of World War I. Born in Edinburgh and a graduate of Oxford, Haig joined the army in 1885 and served in the Nile campaign (1898) and the South African War (1899–1902). After further service in India, he became a lieutenant general in 1910. At the outbreak of World War I, he went to France as commander of the First Army corps, and in December 1915 succeeded Sir John French as commander of the First Army corps, and He directed action at the battle of the Somme (1916) and in the indecisive engagements of 1917. In August 1918 his army's offensive drove back the enemy and led to the German plea for armistice. Early in 1919 he retired from active duty and was created an earl. In later years he devoted himself to the welfare of ex-servicemen.

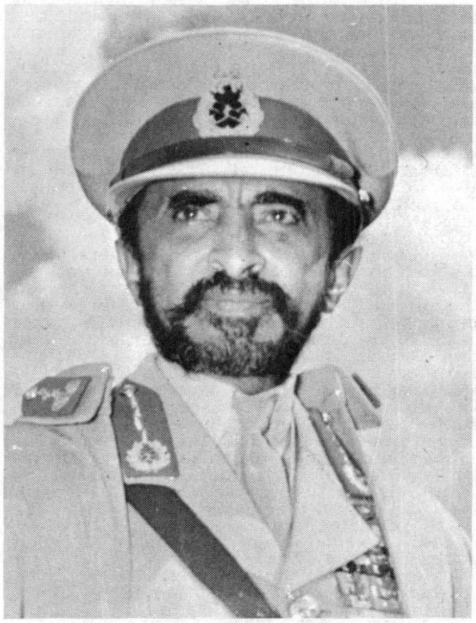

EMPEROR HAILE SELASSIE

Haile Selassie, title of Ras **Taffari** or **Tafari Makonnen** (1892–), emperor of Ethiopia since 1930, born in Harar. He became regent and heir to the throne in 1916, serving under Empress Zauditu as "King of the Kings of Ethiopia, Lion of Judah, the Elect of God." Following Zauditu's death in 1930, he formally became emperor with the title of Haile Selassie I. He gave his people their first written constitution, organized a bicameral legislature, and introduced a whole series of domestic reforms. When the Italian army invaded Ethiopia in 1935, he appealed unsuccessfully to the League of Nations for help and was forced into exile in 1936. After four years in England, he returned to Africa in 1940 and in May, 1941, reentered his capital, Addis Ababa. Haile Selassie's most notable accomplishment has been the transformation of a war-torn, backward land into a stable, modern nation.

Hakluyt, Richard (c.1552–1616), English geographer and author. Educated at Oxford, he took holy orders as a young man, but was chiefly interested in geography and exploration, particularly that of North America. In 1589 he published his great work, *Principal Navigations, Voyages, and Discoveries of the English Nation.* Reissued in expanded form (1598–1600), the work contains valuable source material on 16th-century explorations. Hakluyt interested himself in the colonization of Virginia and the search for a northwest passage to the Pacific. The Haklyut Society, named for him, was organized in 1846 to print and distribute records of discovery and exploration.

Haldane, John Burdon Sanderson (1892–1964), English biologist, noted for his contributions to biochemistry and genetics. Born in London, he was educated at Eton College and at Oxford, and taught genetics at London University and biometry at University College, London. In a career dedicated to research, Haldane investigated sex-linkage in chromosomes, developed a treatment for tetanus, and pioneered in the development of the heart-lung machine and high-pressure oxygen therapy. His most representative writings are *Science and Ethics* (1928), *The Outlook of Science* (1935), and *New Paths in Genetics* (1941). A Marxist until his later years, when he became a pacifist, Haldane in 1957 left England in protest against the presence of American troops on British soil. He emigrated to India, where he directed a genetics and biometry laboratory.

Haldane, Richard Burdon, Viscount **Haldane of Cloan** (1856–1928), British statesman born in Cloan, Scotland, and educated in Scotland and Germany. After a career as a lawyer, he entered Parliament as a Liberal in 1885 and was created a viscount in 1911. As secretary of state for war (1905–1912), he introduced much-needed reforms in the organization of the British army, including the creation of a general staff. In 1915, falsely accused of being pro-German, Haldane retired from active politics and did not return until 1924, when he served briefly as lord chancellor in the first Labour government. During his retirement Lord Haldane wrote *The Reign of Relativity* (1921) and *Philosophy of Humanism* (1922), as well as other philosophical works.

Hale, Edward Everett (1822–1909), American Unitarian clergyman and author, born in Boston and educated at Harvard. He was pastor of a church at Worcester, Mass. (1846) and of one at Boston (1856). In 1903, he became chaplain of the U.S. Senate. The author of more than 50 books on historical, literary, and religious subjects, Hale is best remembered for his story *The Man Without a Country* (1863). A liberal theologian and member of the "social gospel" movement, Hale and his writings inspired the formation of several youth groups and promoted such causes as workmen's housing, Negro education, and immigrant aid.

Hale, George Ellery (1868–1938), American astronomer, born in Chicago, Ill., and a graduate of the Massachusetts Institute of Technology (1890). After research work at Harvard and in Berlin, he became professor of astrophysics at the University of Chicago, where he organized the Yerkes Observatory. Hale made outstanding contributions to the science of spectroscopy, invented the spectroheliograph for the study of solar phenomena, and wrote of island universes and outer space in such books as *The New Heavens* (1922) and *The Depths of the Universe* (1924). The 200-inch Hale telescope at Mount Palomar, California, was named for him.

Hale, Nathan (1755–1776), American Revolutionary hero, born in Coventry, Conn., and educated at Yale. He joined a Connecticut volunteer regiment when war with England began, and in 1776 was commissioned a captain in the regular army. After the battle of Long Island, he volunteered to cross British lines to obtain information needed by Washington. Disguised as a Dutch schoolmaster, Hale carried out the plan but was recognized and arrested. On September 22, 1776, he was hanged as a spy by order of General Howe. His last words were "I only regret that I have but one life to lose for my country."

Halévy, name assumed by **Jacques François Fromental Élie Lévy** (1799–1862), French composer, born in Paris. Between 1827 and 1858 he wrote more than 30 operas. His best-known opera, *La Juive* (1835), was enormously popular and was a favorite vehicle for Enrico Caruso. The chief influence on Halévy was the composer Giacomo Meyerbeer, the leading exponent of grand opera during the mid-nineteenth century. Halévy was the father-in-law of the composer Georges Bizet.

Halévy, Ludovic (1834–1908), French dramatist and novelist, born in Paris. He began his career by writing satirical comedies in collaboration with Henri Meilhac, including *Fanny* (1868) and *Froufrou* (1869). The pair also created libretti for several operas, including Offenbach's *La Belle Hélène* (1864) and *La Périchole* (1868), as well as Bizet's *Carmen* (1875). As a fiction writer, Halévy is best remembered for *L'Abbé Constantin* (1882), a very popular novel. In 1884, he was elected to the French Academy.

Halifax, 1st Earl. See **Montague, Charles.**

Halliburton, Richard (1900–1939), American explorer and writer, born in Brownsville, Tenn. He graduated from Princeton in 1921 and the following year went on an expedition to western Tibet. In 1923 Halliburton scaled Mount Fujiyama, and subsequently climbed mounts Olympus, Etna, and Popocatepetl. Fond of duplicating historic journies, he traced on foot Cortes' route in the conquest of Mexico and Balboa's march across the Darien, as well as the routes of the first Crusade, of Hannibal from Carthage to Italy, and of Alexander the Great to India. He also did independent exploration in Yucatán, Peru, and Brazil. He was lost at sea while sailing in a Chinese junk from Hong Kong to San Francisco. Among his many books are *The Royal Road to Romance* (1925), *The Glorious Adventure* (1927), *The Flying Carpet* (1932), and *The Orient* (1937).

Hall, Charles Martin (1863–1914), American chemist, inventor, and manufacturer, born in Thompson, Ohio, and educated at Oberlin College. He devised, shortly after graduating, an electrolytic process for reducing aluminum from bauxite ore cheaply. This process became the basis for mass production of aluminum. In 1889 he received patent rights to his invention and became a vice-president of the Pittsburgh Reduction Company (later, the Aluminum Company of America), which produced aluminum in commercial quantities.

Hall, Granville Stanley (1846–1924), pioneer American psychologist, born in Ashfield, Mass. A graduate of Williams College (1867), he taught at several colleges, and received his doctorate from Harvard. In 1881 he became professor of psychology at Johns Hopkins, where he established the first psychological laboratory in the U.S. In 1888 Hall became the first president of Clark University, a position he held until 1920. In this role he became a vital force in national education, especially in the promotion of child study. Hall was the first president of the American Psychological Association, as well as the founder of the *Pedagogical Seminary* and the *American Journal of Psychology*, the first periodical of its kind in America. Among the most important of his many works are *Adolescence* (1904), *Youth* (1907), and *Senescence* (1922).

Hallam, Arthur Henry (1811–1833), son of the English historian Henry Hallam and a graduate of Cambridge. An essayist of some promise, Hallam was a close friend of Alfred Tennyson and at the time of his sudden death was engaged to Tennyson's sister Emily. He is the subject of Tennyson's poem *In Memoriam* (1850).

Hallam, Henry (1777–1859), English historian chiefly remembered for his *Constitutional History of England* (1827). After graduating from Oxford in 1799, he practiced law, but retired after securing a private income and a government position. Hallam's principal historical works, which are distinguished by factual accuracy and clarity of style, were published between 1818 and 1839.

Halleck, Henry Wager (1815–1872), American soldier who was commander in chief of the Union armies (1862–1864) during the Civil War. Born in Westernville, N.Y., he graduated from West Point and served in California during the Mexican War, but later resigned from the army to practice law. When the Civil War began, he returned as a major general in command of the western theater of war, and in 1862 was called to Washington as commander in chief. Halleck was a brilliant administrator but had little talent for military strategy; as a result, subordinate generals such as McClellan, Pope, and Burnside suffered a series of military defeats. In 1864 Halleck was replaced by Gen. Ulysses S. Grant and became chief of staff, a post he held until the end of the war. Halleck's *Elements of Military Art and Science* (1846) was an influential text for Union officers during the Civil War.

Haller, Albrecht von (1708–1777), Swiss physiologist and anatomist who made notable contributions to the understanding of living substances and the function of the nervous system. Born in Berne, he studied medicine at Tübingen and Leiden before becoming professor of anatomy, medicine, and botany at Göttingen in 1736. After 17 years he resigned and returned to Berne, where he wrote numerous medical works as well as philosophical romances. His findings in botany, surgery, and anatomy became the foundation for the next century of physiological research.

Halley, Edmund (1656–1742), English astronomer who in 1682 observed the comet that bears his name. His first notable achievement was a catalogue of 341 stars of the Southern Hemisphere, published in 1679 after a two-year stay on the island of St. Helena. After financing the publication of his friend Isaac Newton's *Principia*, Halley made use of Newton's theory as the basis for his own most famous accomplishment: correct orbital calculation of the great comet of 1682, since then known as Halley's Comet. In 1720 he became astronomer royal and devoted the next 18 years to studying the moon's behavior, as well as the motions of stars and planets. Halley was the author of numerous works on astronomy, and was the first astronomer to predict the exact time of return of a comet.

Hals, Frans (c.1580–1666), Dutch portrait painter, especially noted for his depiction of familiar, everyday life. A contemporary of Rembrandt, Rubens, and Van Dyck, Hals is today called "The Elder" to distinguish him from his son, "The Younger," also a painter of note. Born in Antwerp, he spent many impoverished years in Haarlem, where the largest single collection of his work still remains. Painting people from every level of society, often from the lowest, Hals created portraits memorable for their character penetration and robust vitality. Never a highly paid artist, nor fully respected during his life, Hals nevertheless had a substantial influence on subsequent Dutch painting. His zest for life, and the good humor that is often reflected on the faces of those he painted, have made him a favorite among museum-goers.

Hamilcar Barca or **Barcas** (c.270–228 B.C.), Carthaginian general, father of Hannibal. The Romans first met him in 247, during the First Punic War, when at the age of 23 he was given command of the Carthaginian forces in Sicily. Though the Romans controlled most of the island, Hamilcar constantly outwitted them and kept his supply lines open for several years. After peace was concluded in 241, he left Sicily and returned to Africa where, in 238, he crushed a revolt of his mercenary troops. The next year he led his forces to Spain, planning to conquer and use it as a base for waging war on Rome. He fought nine years in Spain and built up the power of Carthage before dying in battle.

Hamilton, Alexander (1755–1804), American statesman born in the West Indies and educated at King's College (now Columbia University). When the Revolutionary War began, he volunteered for service and became captain of an artillery company. In 1777 he was made aide-de-camp and confidential secretary to Gen. George Washington, a position he held with great success for the next four years. After the war, Hamilton returned to New York, married Gen. Schuyler's daughter Elizabeth, and began practicing law. In 1782 he became a member of the Continental Congress, where he was unsuccessful in several attemps to strengthen that body's powers. During the period under the Articles of Confederation, he was instrumental in bringing about the call for the Constitutional Convention, in which he sat as a delegate from New York. Hamilton's political philosophy advocated a strong central government at the expense of the states. To put across this philosophy he wrote (with James Madison and John Jay) a series of 85 essays called *The Federalist*, which defended the constitution and the central government. These essays (Hamilton wrote 51 of them) were widely read and had a great influence on the shaping of American politics.

Congress established the treasury department in 1789 and Hamilton was appointed its first secretary. Seeking to establish the nation's credit at home and abroad, as well as to strengthen the federal government, Hamilton arranged for the government to assume debts that the states had contracted during the Revolution and requested a system of taxation to pay for the debts. At the same time, asserting that the constitution gave the government implied powers as well as stated ones, he persuaded Congress and the president to charter a national bank as well as a mint. By these and other astute measures, Hamilton established the credit of the United States and stabilized the nation's financial structure.

As a proponent of a strong central government, Hamilton was opposed by Thomas Jefferson and others, who felt that power should rest more directly with the people. Out of these conflicting concepts arose the first two political parties, Federalist and Antifederalist. In 1795 Hamilton resigned from the cabinet, chiefly for financial reasons, and returned to law practice. Nevertheless, he remained an important influence in politics until, in 1804, he was killed by Aaron Burr in a duel that arose from a political quarrel.

Hamlin, Hannibal (1809–1891), American statesman who was vice-president of the United States during the first term of Abraham Lincoln (1861–1865). Born in Paris Hill, Me., Hamlin began practicing law in 1833 and entered politics with his election in 1836 to the Maine state legislature as a Democrat. In 1843 he was elected to Congress, sat in the Senate from 1848 to 1857, and then resigned to become governor of Maine. He was one of the founders of the Republican party. During his years as vice president, he was a strong proponent of antislavery measures; later, as a senator

(1869–1881) during the postwar period, he advocated radical reconstruction policies. In 1881–1882 he was U.S. minister to Spain.

Hammarskjöld, Dag Hjalmar Agne Carl (1905–1961), Swedish statesman, secretary-general of the United Nations (1953–1961), and posthumous recipient of the Nobel Peace Prize. The son of a former Swedish prime minister, Hammarskjöld studied law and economics at the universities of Uppsala and Stockholm. After lecturing for a short period at Stockholm, he became permanent undersecretary of finance in 1936, and, five years later, chairman of the board of the Bank of Sweden. He joined the Foreign Office as a financial expert and in 1951 entered the cabinet as a deputy foreign minister. In 1953, while serving as head of the Swedish delegation to the United Nations, he was elected to succeed Trygve Lie as secretary-general of the UN. Hammarskjöld increased the prestige of his office, and with "quiet diplomacy" augmented the influence of the United Nations. He personally conducted peace missions to Peking (1955) and to the Middle East—Suez (1956), Lebanon (1958), and Jordan (1959). In 1961, four years after establishing the UN emergency force in the Middle East, he arranged for another such force in the strife-torn Republic of the Congo. On September 18, 1961, while on a peace mission to the Congo, he was killed in a plane crash. *Markings*, a volume of selections from his diaries, was published posthumously.

Hammerstein, Oscar, 2d (1895–1960), American lyricist and librettist, born in New York City and a graduate of Columbia University. He was the grandson of Oscar Hammerstein, the German-American opera impresario. Hammerstein's career was characterized by a long series of commercially successful collaborations with the leading theatrical composers of the day. With Rudolf Friml he wrote *Rose Marie* (1924); with Sigmund Romberg, *The Desert Song* (1926) and *New Moon* (1927); with Jerome Kern, *Sunny* (1925) and *Show Boat* (1927); and with Richard Rodgers such musicals as *Oklahoma!* (1943), *Carousel* (1945), and *South Pacific* (1949). Hammerstein received academy awards for his songs *The Last Time I Saw Paris* (1945) and *It Might as Well Be Spring* (1946). In contrast to most musical-comedy writers of his time, who wrote conventional music-hall revues, Hammerstein in his plays strove to relate words to music in an integrated dramatic form.

Hammond, John Hays, Jr. (1888–1965), American inventor and electrical engineer, born in San Francisco and a graduate of Yale (1910). Hammond won renown as the inventor of military and radio-controlled devices. His many inventions include a wireless-controlled torpedo for coastal defense; a radio system for ship control; a system of selective radio telegraphy that carries eight messages on one wave; improvements in pipe-organ mechanisms; and a new reflecting modulator for pianos.

Hammurabi. Hammurapi or **Khammurabi** (c. 1955–1913 B.C., possibly two centuries earlier), the sixth and greatest king of the first dynasty of Babylon. He is celebrated as the originator of a code of civil laws that guaranteed justice for all and protected the poor against oppression by the rich. The Code of Hammurabi regulated such matters as rents, wages, and insurance, and established penalties for theft and other crimes. The criminal code was based on the "eye for an eye" principle. Hammurabi was responsible for the geographical expansion of his kingdom as well as for the building of religious and secular structures.

Hampton, Wade (1818–1902), American soldier and statesman who rose to prominence in the Confederate army. A native of Charleston, S.C., he was opposed to secession from the Union, but supported his state in the Civil War. Hampton's Legion, a company that he equipped at his own expense, followed his leadership at Bull Run, in the Peninsular campaign, and at Fair Oaks. In 1862 he joined J. E. B. Stuart's army of northern Virginia, saw action at Gettysburg, The Wilderness, and the Upper Shenandoah Valley, and in 1864 succeeded to the cavalry command that Stuart's death had left vacant. After the war he worked to reconstruct the South and in 1876 was elected governor of South Carolina. He served in the U.S. Senate from 1879 to 1891.

Hancock, John (1737–1793), American patriot, born in Braintree, Mass., and a graduate of Harvard (1754). Early in his career he was a selectman of Boston and member of the Massachusetts General Court. His later activities on behalf of the Colonial

cause brought him into disfavor with Governor Gage, whose attempt to arrest Hancock and Samuel Adams led to the battles of Concord and Lexington. In 1775 Hancock was elected president of the Continental Congress and was the first person to sign the Declaration of Independence. When Massachusetts became a state in 1780, he became its first governor, serving from 1780–1785 and again from 1787–1793.

Hancock, Winfield Scott (1824–1886), Union general during the Civil War. A West Point graduate in 1844, he fought against the Indians and served in the Mexican War. During the Civil War, he commanded troops in the Peninsular campaign, at Gettysburg, and in the final drive on Richmond, rising to the rank of major general. After the war he commanded occupation troops in Louisiana and Texas, where his "soft" policy on reconstruction endeared him to the Democratic Party, which nominated him for the presidency in 1880. After losing a close race to James A. Garfield, he returned to military life.

Hand, Learned, in full, **Billings Learned Hand** (1872–1961), American jurist, born in Albany, N.Y., and a graduate of the Harvard Law School (1896). He was a U.S. district judge from 1909 to 1924, when he was appointed to the U.S. circuit court of appeals. He served as presiding judge from 1939 until his retirement in 1951. Hand made notable decisions in the areas of free speech and monopolies. An authority on constitutional law, his speeches and articles were collected in *The Spirit of Liberty* (1952).

Handel, George Frederick (1685–1759), Anglo-German composer of operas, oratorios (most notably, *The Messiah*), and instrumental works. At the age of 18 he joined the orchestra of the Hamburg Opera House, which two years later produced his first opera, *Almira*. He then spent three years in Italy, where his works received great popular acclaim. In 1710 he returned to Germany and became chapelmaster to Elector George of Hanover (afterwards George I of England). Later that year he went to London, where his opera *Rinaldo* was successfully produced. After 1712 he made England his home, becoming a naturalized British subject in 1726.

Among the first works he composed in England were a *Te Deum* and *Jubilate* to celebrate the Peace of Utrecht (1713) and the birthday of Queen Anne, who rewarded him with a pension. George I, her successor, was even more generous (the story that Handel composed *The Water Music* to overcome George's resentment at his having left Hanover is unsubstantiated). During the next twenty years, Handel composed some twenty operas. An attempt at independent management brought financial disaster, but he recouped his losses by devoting part of his time to composing oratorios, including *Saul* (1739), *Israel in Egypt* (1738), *The Messiah* (1742), *Samson* (1741), and *Judas Maccabaeus* (1747). When *The Messiah* was first produced, the king and the audience rose as the strains of the "Hallelujah Chorus" began, establishing a tradition that continues today. Although Handel's oratorios overshadowed his operas during the eighteenth and nineteenth centuries, there has been a revival of interest in his operas during recent years.

Handy, William Christopher (1873–1958), American Negro composer who popularized that development of ragtime music known as the blues. Born in Florence, Ala., he was a schoolmaster in his youth, but later conducted his own orchestra (even though he became blind at the age of thirty). His two most popular works were *Memphis Blues* (1911), written as a campaign song for the mayor of Memphis, and *St. Louis Blues* (1914). Handy compiled several anthologies of Negro blues and spirituals and wrote *Negro Authors and Composers in the United States* (1935).

Hanna, Marcus Alonzo, known as **Mark Hanna** (1837–1904), American politician, born in Lisbon, Ohio. After amassing a fortune in coal, iron, and shipping, he became prominent in Republican politics in Ohio. His support of William McKinley in the gubernatorial elections of 1891 and 1893, as well as the presidential elections of 1896 and 1900, made him a figure of national interest. Hanna entered the Senate by appointment in 1897, was elected to the full term in 1898, and served until his death.

Hannibal (247–183 B.C.), Carthaginian general, the son of Hamilcar Barca. At the age of nine he was taken to Spain by his father, who made the boy swear eternal enmity to Rome. In 221 Hannibal was elected commander of the Carthaginian forces in Spain, and at once laid plans to crush his country's rival. He began by

laying siege to the Spanish city of Saguntum, an ally of Rome, and captured it after eight months. Rome retaliated by declaring war in 218, and so began the Second Punic War. Hannibal's plan was to invade Italy and eventually to march on Rome. In 218 he left Spain with 90,000 foot soldiers, 12,000 horsemen, and a band of elephants. Crossing the Pyrenees into southern Gaul, he defeated a Roman army in the Rhone Valley and then made his celebrated march across the Alps. With only a small part of his original army left, he defeated the Romans in a series of important battles over the next few years. But Hannibal no longer had the strength to march on Rome, and he was forced to remain on the defensive in the mountains for the next few years. In 203 he was called back to Carthage, then in danger of capture by the Romans. The following year, his unbeaten army was captured at last by Scipio Africanus, and the next year Carthage accepted a humiliating peace. Hannibal was made head of the Carthaginian government, but fled in 196 when the Romans accused him of attempting to renew hostilities. He then joined Antiochus the Great, king of Syria, in his war on Rome. The defeat of Antiochus in 190 was followed by a treaty that specified the surrender of Hannibal. Seeing no further possibility of escape, Hannibal committed suicide in 183 at the court of Bithynia, where he had sought refuge.

Hanson, Howard Harold (1896-   ), American composer and conductor, born in Wahoo, Neb. After spending three years in Italy as winner of the American Prix de Rome, he returned in 1924 as director of the Eastman School of Music in Rochester, New York, a position he held until 1965. During this time he organized and was conductor of the Eastman-Rochester Symphony Orchestra. His compositions include piano pieces, choral works, five symphonies, chamber music, and an opera, *Merry Mount* (1934), commissioned and produced by the Metropolitan Opera. In 1944 he was awarded the Pulitzer Prize for his Fourth Symphony.

Hanson, John (1721–1783), American patriot, born in Maryland, who was elected president of Congress in 1781, when the Articles of Confederation went into effect. Before this, he had a notable career in Maryland politics for many years. Because Hanson's title, as president of Congress, was "President of the United States in Congress Assembled," he is considered by some to have been the first President. He was not, however, the first president under the Constitution. After only a year in office, he resigned because of poor health.

Han Yü or **Han Wên-kung** (768–824), Chinese poet and philosopher, born in Honan. Han Yü held an official position during the T'ang dynasty until 819, when he was banished for criticizing the emperor. He regained his place at court in 820 and thereafter devoted himself to a literary career. He created the classic Chinese essay form, and his poems with their simplicity of language and lack of artificiality are considered examples of perfect Chinese style.

Harding, Warren Gamaliel (1865–1923), twenty-ninth president of the United States (1921–1923), born near Blooming Grove, Ohio. After college, Harding worked on a newspaper and in 1884 bought the Marion *Star*, which he developed into a prosperous daily that became a great influence in Republican politics in Ohio. Entering politics in 1900, Harding served as a state senator, lieutenant governor of Ohio, and in 1914 was elected to the U.S. Senate. In 1920 he became a "dark horse" candidate for the Republican nomination for the presidency, chiefly to break the deadlock between conservative and progressive factions at the nominating convention. With Calvin Coolidge as his running mate, he was elected by a large majority.

In domestic policies, Harding favored a "return to normalcy." Immigration was restricted, a national budget system was established for the first time, and a beginning of debt reduction was made. Although some progress was made in foreign policy, Harding's domestic policy soon fell under heavy criticism, culminating in the Teapot Dome scandal, in which a cabinet member was accused of taking bribes from oil interests. In the midst of impending disclosure of further irregularities in his administration, Harding died suddenly while on a transcontinental tour.

Hardy, Thomas (1840–1928), English novelist and poet who began his career as an architect but turned to literature in 1868. His first important novel was *Far from the Madding Crowd* (1874), followed by such works as *The Return of the Native* (1878), *The Mayor of Casterbridge* (1886), *Tess of the D'Urbervilles* (1891), and *Jude the Obscure* (1895). Hardy's novels are somber, and his characters are portrayed as victims of a predestined fate that they cannot escape. In contrast to other Victorian novelists, Hardy emphasized man's animal nature. In his later years Hardy turned to poetry, in which he had been absorbed as a youth. His masterpiece in verse is *The Dynasts* (1904–1908), a long epic drama about England during the Napoleonic Wars.

Hargreaves, James (d. 1778), English inventor, born in Lancashire, who developed the carding machine in 1760 and the spinning jenny in 1764. After he had sold a few of the jennies, which did eight times the work of the old machines, Hargreaves was attacked by fellow spinners, who broke into his house and destroyed his machines, because they feared they would lose their jobs. In 1768 he moved to Nottingham, where he built a spinning mill and went into the business of making yarn. In 1770, he received a patent on his jenny.

Harriman, Edward Henry (1848–1909), American financier and railroad administrator, born in Hempstead, N.Y. A member of the New York Stock Exchange at the age of 21, Harriman became vice-president of the Illinois Central Railroad in 1887. At that time he began to organize and consolidate railroads, eventually controlling more than 60,000 miles of track. His career was marked by struggles with other railroad men and with the government. In 1901 his fight with J. J. Hill over control of the Northern Pacific Railroad precipitated a stock exchange panic. After investigations in 1906 and 1907, the Interstate Commerce Commission condemned his operations.

Harris, Joel Chandler (1848–1908), American author best known for his "Uncle Remus" tales. Born in Eatonton, Ga., Harris worked on a series of southern newspapers (notably the Atlanta *Constitution*), establishing a reputation as a humorist. His first popular success, "The Tar-Baby Story," written in 1879 for a newspaper, immediately created a vogue for Negro dialect stories. This was followed by *Uncle Remus—His Songs and Sayings* (1880) and a series of similar works. Harris' writings are good examples of the "local color" school that flourished in American writing during the last decades of the nineteenth century.

Harris, William Torrey (1835–1909), American educator, born in Killingly, Conn., and educated at Yale. Connected with the St. Louis, Mo., public school system from 1857 to 1888, Harris became the most widely known school educator in the U.S., chiefly through his introduction of arts into school curricula. He was equally notable as an expounder of German philosophic thought, and a founder of the Concord School of Philosophy. From 1889 to 1906, he was U.S. Commissioner of Education.

Harrison, Benjamin (1833–1901), twenty-third president of the United States (1889–1893), born in North Bend, Ohio, a grandson of William Henry Harrison (ninth president). A graduate of Miami University (Ohio), he began practicing law in Indianapolis in 1854. He served in the Civil War as a colonel in a regiment he had helped to raise, and was promoted to brigadier general. After the war, he became prominent in national Republican politics and was instrumental in bringing about the nomination and election of James A. Garfield in 1880. A term in the U.S. Senate (1881–1887) increased his national reputation, and in 1888 he received the Republican nomination for the presidency. He won the election, defeating Grover Cleveland by an electoral vote of 233 to 168, although the latter received a larger popular vote. The tariff was the chief issue of the campaign.

Harrison's administration was marked by the passage of the Sherman Anti-Trust Act, reform of the civil service, and the admission of several new western states into the Union. Through the influence of his secretary of state, James G. Blaine, the first Pan-American Congress was held in Washington. The tariff was again an issue in the campaign of 1892, and again Harrison and Cleveland were the nominees. But public opinion had turned against the protectionist policy of the Republicans, and Cleveland won the election. Harrison returned to his private law practice.

Harrison, William Henry (1773–1841), ninth president of the United States (1841), born in Charles City County, Va., grandfather of Benjamin Harrison (twenty-third president). Early in his career he served in the army, but resigned in 1797 to become secretary of the Northwest Territory and, in 1799, the first territorial delegate in Congress. In this capacity, he secured the passage of the first homestead laws and was influential in having the Northwest Territory divided. He was governor of the Indiana Territory, the western part, from 1801 to 1813.

Harrison's success in securing a land cession from the Indians and his victory over the followers of Tecumseh at the battle of Tippecanoe (1811) made him a national hero. Shortly after the War of 1812 broke out, he was appointed commander of the army in the Northwest and promoted to major general in 1813. The climax of his military career was his victory over the Indians and British in the battle of the Thames (1813).

In 1814 Harrison retired from the army and went into politics. After serving in Congress and in the Senate, he was made the Whig presidential candidate in 1836. Although he was defeated by Martin Van Buren, the Democratic candidate, he was elected four years later after a rousing "log cabin and hard cider" campaign with the slogan "Tippecanoe and Tyler too." Harrison's personality was the deciding factor in the election, but he had no opportunity to test his abilities, for he died of pneumonia a month after inauguration.

Hart, Moss (1904–1961), American playwright and stage director, born in New York City. After collaborating with Irving Berlin in *Face the Music* (1932), he began a successful partnership with George S. Kaufman, which in 1936 produced *You Can't Take It With You*. Hart received the Pulitzer Prize for this play. His other plays include *I'd Rather Be Right* (1937), *The Man Who Came to Dinner* (1939), *Lady in the Dark* (1941), and *Winged Victory* (1943). In 1955 he directed the musical *My Fair Lady* and in 1960 was both producer and director of the musical *Camelot*. His autobiography, *Act One* (1959), tells of his early years in the theater.

Harte, Bret, originally **Francis Brett Harte** (1836–1902), American author, known for sketches and short stories describing nineteenth-century California life. Born in Albany, N.Y., he went to California at 18, when the first gold rush was still at its peak. In 1868, after a variety of jobs, including newspaper work, he became editor of a magazine, the *Overland Monthly*. For this journal he wrote some of his finest stories, including *The Luck of Roaring Camp* and *The Outcasts of Poker Flat*. Suddenly famous, Harte left California in 1870 for New York. After 1878 he lived abroad and was in the consular service until 1885. He spent his last years in England. *The Luck of Roaring Camp and Other Sketches* (1870) and (1875) represent his best work.

Harun al-Rashid (c. 764–809), caliph of Baghdad, the fifth and most famous Abbasid caliph, whose reign marked a high point in the flowering of Arab culture. As a youth and again as ruler, he conducted successful wars against the Byzantines, and his caliphate attained its greatest territorial and political powers. The brilliance of his court is revealed in stories in *The Arabian Nights*.

Harvard, John (1607–1638), English clergyman for whom Harvard University is named. Born in London, he immigrated to Charlestown, Mass., in 1637 and became assistant pastor of First Church, but died about a year later. In his will, he bequeathed a library of between 300 and 400 volumes and the sum of approximately £780 to a seminary situated in Cambridge, Massachusetts. On March 13, 1639, this college was named Harvard in his honor by the Massachusetts General Court.

Harvey, William (1578–1657), English physician who discovered the circulation of the blood. Born in Kent, and educated in England and Italy, he became a doctor of medicine in 1602. In 1616 he began a course of lectures in which he first expressed his views on the circulation of blood. Harvey served as physician to James I and later to Charles I. In 1628 his book *Exercitatio anatomica de motu cordis et sanguinis in animalibus* (*Treatise on the Motion of the Heart and Blood*) appeared. The work excited considerable controversy, but Harvey lived to see its general acceptance in England and on the Continent. Harvey also did pioneer work in the field of animal and human reproduction.

Hasdrubal, name borne by several Carthaginian generals. The Hasdrubal who was a son-in-law of Hamilcar Barca founded the city of New Carthage in Spain (c. 228 B.C) and conquered most of the tribes who lived on the Spanish peninsula. He was assassinated in 221 B.C., but his work was continued by Hannibal. Another Hasdrubal, the second son of Hamilcar Barca, was left in command of Spain when Hannibal went to Italy; he was ultimately defeated by the Romans in 207 B.C. After his death Carthaginian rule came to an end.

Hastings, Warren (1732–1818), English statesman, appointed by Parliament in 1773 to be the first governor general of India. Hastings held this position for twelve years and was instrumental in establishing the judicial and administrative systems upon which England built its Indian empire. His unscrupulous methods of raising money brought him severe censure on his retirement and return to England. In 1788 an impeachment trial was begun in the House of Lords. The proceedings called forth the eloquence of Burke, Fox, and Sheridan, and the trial dragged on for seven years. Hastings was finally acquitted in 1785.

Hathaway, Anne. See *Shakespeare, William*.

Hatshepsut, or **Hatshepset** also **Hatasu** (c.1540–1582 B.C.), queen of ancient Egypt during the Diospolite (18th) dynasty. The daughter of Thutmost I, she married and reigned with her half brother, Thutmost III. Hatshepsut's rule was peaceful and was marked by artistic and architectural achievement. She was the mother of Amenhotep II, who succeeded his father, Thutmose III.

Hauptmann, Gerhart (1862–1946), German dramatist, novelist, and poet. Born in Silesia, he studied sculpture before beginning his literary career with his first play, *Before Sunset* (1889), which established him as a leader of German naturalistic drama. In other early plays (*The Festival of Peace, Lonely Lives,* and *The Weavers*), all written in protest against social injustice and militarism, Hauptmann showed his debt to Ibsen, Zola, and Tolstoi. In later works Hauptmann wrote in a more idealistic manner, producing novels, plays, and poetry in which myth and mysticism are prevalent. In 1912 he received the Nobel Prize for literature.

Havelock, Sir Henry (1795–1857), British general, hero of the Sepoy Mutiny of 1857. He entered the army soon after the battle of Waterloo and in India served in the Afghan and Sikh wars. In 1857 he had command of a small force sent to relieve besieged cities. Havelock fought his way from Cawnpore to Lucknow and was able to hold the city until relief troops arrived. He died shortly afterward.

Hawkins, Sir John (1532–1595), English admiral who was chiefly responsible for building up the British navy that defeated the Spanish Armada. He was the first English slave trader, carrying slaves from Africa to the West Indies. Elected to Parliament in 1572, he was an efficient treasurer of the navy, and became a prosperous shipbuilder. In 1588, as rear admiral, Hawkins commanded the *Victory* in the battle with the Spanish Armada and was knighted for bravery. He died in 1595 while serving as second in command to Sir Francis Drake in a plundering expedition to the Spanish West Indies.

Hawthorne, Nathaniel (1804–1864), American novelist and short-story writer, born in Salem, Mass., and a graduate of Bowdoin College (1825). For the next two decades he wrote several volumes of short stories, including *Twice-Told Tales* (1837), *Grandfather's Chair* (1841), and *Mosses from an Old Manse* (1846). His first full-length novel, and his masterpiece, was *The Scarlet Letter*, published in 1850. Within a decade, he published three other novels: *The House of the Seven Gables* (1851), *The Blithedale Romance* (1852), and *The Marble Faun* (1860). A contemporary of Emerson and Longfellow, Hawthorne rejected their optimism and rosy view of mankind. His major themes were sin, especially the sin of pride, and the fallen state of man. To express these themes, he relied heavily upon allegory and symbolism. In later years Hawthorne spent five years (1853–1858) as U.S. consul in Liverpool, England.

Hay, John Milton (1838–1905), American statesman and author who was secretary of state under presidents McKinley and Theodore Roosevelt. Born in Salem, Ind., and educated as a lawyer, he accompanied Abraham Lincoln to the White House in 1861 as an assistant private secretary to the president. After a varied career as legation secretary, editor of the New York *Tribune*, assistant secretary of state, and writer, he was appointed ambassador to Great Britain in 1897. In 1898 he began his career as secretary of state to two presidents. Hay's greatest triumph lay in securing the open-door policy in China. He also negotiated the Hay-Pauncefote

Treaty of 1901, making possible construction of the Panama Canal. His ten-volume *Abraham Lincoln: A History* (written with John C. Nicolay) appeared in 1890. Other works include *Pike County Ballads* (1871), the novel *The Breadwinners* (1884), and *Poems* (1890).

Haydn, Joseph, in full **Franz Joseph Haydn** (1732–1809), Austrian composer who was the first great master of the symphony and who invented the modern string quartet. Haydn wrote prolifically as a young man, but his career blossomed when, in 1760, he became chapelmaster to Prince Miklós József Esterházy; he remained in that family's service for the rest of his life. During this period he composed an enormous number and variety of orchestral works, operas, string quartets, keyboard pieces, and church music. This period was memorable, too, for his close friendship with Mozart. A two-year stay in London (1790–1792), where his works were received with great success, was a high point in Haydn's artistic life. In 1798 the oratorio *The Creation* was performed in Vienna, followed by another oratorio, *The Seasons*, in 1801—one of the composer's last works. Haydn was a musical giant who spanned the world of baroque music, represented by Bach and Handel, and the Romantic period that began early in the nineteenth century with Beethoven.

Hayes, Helen, original name **Helen Hayes Brown** (1900–   ), American actress, born in Washington, D.C. She first appeared on the stage at the age of five. Later, her gift for portraying fine shades of pathos and comedy was brought out in such plays as *Pollyanna, Dear Brutus, What Every Woman Knows, The Good Fairy,* and *Mary of Scotland.* Her greatest critical success came with her portrayal of the title role in *Victoria Regina* (1935–1938). In 1932, she received an Academy Award for her acting in the movie *The Sin of Madelon Claudet.*

Hayes, Cardinal Patrick Joseph (1867–1938), American prelate, born in New York City. Ordained a priest in 1892, he became chancellor of the New York archdiocese in 1903, was president of Cathedral College from 1903 to 1914, and in 1914 was consecrated auxiliary bishop of New York. During World War I Bishop Hayes was Catholic chaplain bishop for the United States army and navy. He was elevated to the archbishopric of New York in 1919 and was created cardinal in 1924. As archbishop, he unified various Catholic charities into a central agency that became a model for other Catholic dioceses.

Hayes, Rutherford Birchard (1822–1893), nineteenth president of the United States (1877–1881), born in Delaware, Ohio. He received a law degree from Harvard in 1845, and practiced in several Ohio cities until the outbreak of the Civil War. After his discharge as a brevet major general, he represented his home district in Congress in 1865. Two years later the Ohio Republicans elected him governor, reelecting him in 1869 and in 1875. In 1876 he received the Republican nomination for the presidency. In the race that followed against Democrat Samuel J. Tilden, the vote was extremely close, with complications caused by disputes over the electoral votes of several states. Finally, after months of intense partisan feeling, an electoral commission decided that Hayes had won by an electoral vote 185 to 184. His term was marked by civil service reforms, the withdrawal of federal troops from the South, and the resumption of specie payments for greenbacks.

Hayne, Robert Young (1791–1839), American statesman who was a leading spokesman for the South and states' rights during the pre-Civil War period. Born in Colleton District, S. C., he became a lawyer in Charleston and rose to prominence in local politics. Hayne entered the U.S. Senate in 1823 as a states'-rights Democrat. In 1830 he engaged in a debate with Daniel Webster that became celebrated as a brilliant exposition of two theories of government. Hayne argued the states'-rights cause; Webster denied the right of a state to nullify a federal law. Hayne was governor of South Carolina from 1832 to 1834.

Haynes, Elwood (1857–1925), American inventor, born in Portland, Ind. In 1893, a few years after he had left teaching to go into business, he produced the first successful horseless carriage in the United States. Equipped with one-horsepower gasoline engine, the car traveled at speeds of six to nine miles an hour. Haynes also developed several metal alloys and discovered a process for making stainless steel. His first automobile, regarded as the oldest in the United States, is preserved in the Smithsonian Institution, Washington, D.C.

Hays, Will H. (1879–1954), American lawyer, born in Sullivan, Ind. After gaining prominence in local and national politics, in 1918 he became chairman of the national Republican committee. In 1921 President Harding appointed him postmaster general, a post he resigned one year later to become president of the newly organized Motion Picture Producers and Distributors of America. In this position he became censor of motion pictures and a virtual czar of the industry.

Hazlitt, William (1778–1830), English essayist and critic who wrote on politics, philosophy, literature, and the arts. Trained in the ministry, he later became an artist before turning in 1805 to writing. A friend of Coleridge, Wordsworth, and Lamb, Hazlitt produced his best essays in the books *Table Talk* (1821) and *The Plain Speaker* (1826). His penetrating comments on English writers, especially the Elizabethan dramatists, have withstood the test of time.

Hearn, Lafcadio, in full **Patricio Lafcadio Tessima Carlos Hearn** (1850–1904), writer and translator, born on Leukas, one of the Ionian Islands. Educated in Europe, he immigrated at 19 to the United States and worked on newspapers in Cincinnati and New Orleans. In New Orleans, his translations from French and Spanish authors, together with original sketches, attracted widespread attention, as did his first two novels, *Chita* (1889) and *Youma* (1890). He went to Japan in 1891, intending to become a newspaper correspondent, but instead became a professor of English at the University of Tokyo. Charmed by Japanese life, he married a native and became a Buddhist and a Japanese citizen. Hearn wrote several books on Japan, notably *Glimpses of Unfamiliar Japan* (1894).

Hearst, William Randolph (1863–1951), American publisher, born in San Francisco and educated at Harvard. In 1887, given control of the San Francisco *Examiner* by his wealthy father, he made it a successful newspaper within two years, then moved to New York and bought the *Morning Journal,* whose circulation he built up with sensational journalism. His success with sensational articles on crime and jingoism in foreign affairs (notably during the Spanish-American War) led him to form a nationwide chain of newspapers. He also acquired several magazines, including *Good Housekeeping* and *Harper's Bazaar.* Ambitious for public office, he was a member of Congress from 1903 to 1907, but was defeated in races for mayor of New York City (1905 and 1909) and governor of New York (1906). Hearst always dictated the editorial policies of his papers, which opposed the entry of the United States in World War I, fought against the League of Nations, and adopted a nationalistic attitude in postwar years. His estate at San Simeon, left to the state of California, has become a popular tourist attraction.

Hedin, Sven Anders (1865–1952), Swedish explorer, remembered for his expeditions to Asia. His book *Through Asia* (1899) contains an account of his travels in Turkestan, Tibet, China, and Siberia. On his next expedition, to the Gobi Desert and Tibet, he attempted unsuccessfully to enter the sacred city of Lhasa. A later trip to Tibet (1905–1908) resulted in the compilation of the first detailed map of that part of Asia. His other books include *Across the Gobi Desert* (1932), *A Conquest of Tibet* (1934), and *Chiang Kai-shek, Marshal of China* (1940).

Hegel, Georg Wilhelm Friedrich (1770–1831), German philosopher whose doctrine of an all-embracing absolute became the leading philosophical system during the nineteenth century. Hegel viewed the quest for truth as a dialectic, or discussion, between a *thesis* (orignal tendency or force) and its *antithesis* (opposing tendency or force); from this came a *synthesis* that resolved differences between opposites, hence a more absolute "truth." Many later philosophers were influenced by Hegel, most notably Karl Marx and the Russian dialecticians. A prolific writer, Hegel explained his system as a whole in his *Encyclopaedia of the Philosophical Sciences* (1817).

Heidegger, Martin (1889–   ), German philosopher who was a major influence on the development of twentieth-century existentialism. His major work, *Sein und Zeit* was published in 1927 but not translated into English (as *Existence and Being*) until 1949. In this work, his view of the individual is similar to that of Kierkegaard, although it lacks Kierkegaard's profoundly religious quality. In 1933 he became the first Nazi rector of the University of Freiburg. After World War II his Nazi affiliations caused him to lose favor, although his earlier philosophy remained popular.

Heifetz, Jascha (1901–   ), American violinist, born in Russia. A child prodigy, he began giving public concerts at the age of five. When the Russian Revolution of 1917 broke out, his family fled with him to the United States. Since that time, he has made regular tours of the principal countries of the world. His playing is considered remarkable for impeccable technique, purity of tone, and brilliance of interpretation. Unlike most other child prodigies, Heifetz reached his greatest artistic heights in his mature years.

Heine, Heinrich (1797–1856), German Romantic poet whose lyrics are regarded as among the finest in the German language. With his first book of poems, published in 1821, he became well known. With the appearance of *Buch der Lieder* (*Book of Songs*) in 1827, his reputation was assured. Though highly esteemed as a writer, his open admiration of Napoleon and satirical criticism of the Prussian government forced him to flee to Paris in 1831. He became an invalid in later life but continued to write poetry as well as essays. Heine's best poems were short love lyrics; many were set to music by Schubert, Schumann, and Wolf.

Heisenberg, Werner Karl (1901–   ), German physicist whose work on the quantum theory spurred the development of atomic and nuclear physics. After becoming a professor of theoretical physics at the University of Leipzig in 1927, Heisenberg began studying atomic structure and developing his theories of quantum mechanics. This led to his formulation of the uncertainty principle, an important postulate of modern physics. In 1932 he was awarded the Nobel Prize for physics. In 1946 he was appointed director of the Max Planck Institute for Physics at Göttingen.

Heliodorus (c.4th century A.D.), Greek writer, born in Syria. He was the author of *Ethiopica*, considered the best extant Greek romance. It is a romantic epic that clearly shows the influence of Homer and Euripides. This style was later imitated by Italian, French, and Spanish writers.

Helmholtz, Hermann Ludwig Ferdinand von (1821–1894), German scientist who developed the idea of the conservation of energy and made important contributions to the sciences of optics and acoustics. From 1849 until his death, he held a series of professorships at leading German universities, and his investigations covered almost every field of science. Later in life, he also wrote on philosophy and aesthetics.

Héloïse. See under *Abélard, Pierre.*

Helvétius, Claude Adrien (1715–1771), French philosopher noted for his philosophy of sensualism as expressed in *De l'esprit* (1758). Basic concepts in the work, which shocked most of his contemporaries, were that self-interest motivates all action, all man's faculties are physical, and that all intellects are equal. Though he later retracted his philosophical theories the work was publicly burned in 1759. He lived the rest of his life in seclusion in the country.

Hemingway, Ernest (1898–1961), American novelist and short-story writer whose bare, simple style exerted a profound influence on twentieth-century writing. Born in Oak Park, Ill., he made a worldwide reputation with three books about life in Europe during and after World War I: *The Sun Also Rises* (1926), *Men Without Women* (1927), and *A Farewell to Arms* (1929). These are highly realistic works, written in a vigorous, clipped style that has been widely imitated. In 1953, *The Old Man and the Sea* won a Pulitzer Prize, and in 1954 Hemingway was awarded the Nobel Prize for literature. His other books include *Death in the Afternoon* (1932), *The Green Hills of Africa* (1935), and *For Whom the Bell Tolls* (1940). In much of his work, Hemingway was chiefly concerned with violence whether in war or in nature, and with the dignity of individual man in his response to violence.

Hennepin, Louis (1640–c.1701), French Franciscan missionary and explorer, born in Belgium, who went to Canada in 1675. He began his mission work at Fort Frontenac and in 1678 accompanied La Salle on an exploring trip westward. By way of Niagara Falls, the Great Lakes, and connecting rivers, the explorers reached the region of Illinois. Early in 1680 Hennepin left the party and, joining another expedition, followed the Mississippi northward but was captured by the Sioux. Accompanying the Indians on hunting trips, he eventually reached St. Anthony Falls, where Minneapolis now stands. Rescued by a party of Frenchmen, he returned to

France where he wrote of his travels. Though marred by exaggerations, his writings are valuable source materials of seventeenth-century exploration in America.

Henry I (1068–1135), king of England (1100–1135), youngest son of William the Conqueror. Because of his learning he was called *Beauclerc* (Good Scholar). On the death of his brother William Rufus in 1100, he claimed the throne and was crowned at Westminster. Henry's brother Robert Curthose, duke of Normandy, disputed his claim to the throne, and war broke out in 1101. In 1106 Henry took Robert prisoner and seized Normandy. Henry's reign was notable for uniting of Saxon and Norman elements, the development of national sentiment, and a strengthening of royal power at the expense of the nobles.

Henry II (1133–1189), king of England (1154–1189), first of the Plantagenet line, son of Geoffrey Plantagenet, count of Anjou, and Matilda, daughter of Henry I of England. He succeeded Stephen of Blois, nephew of Henry I, after years of civil war. When Henry II became king, he ruled a vast French domain, acquired by inheritance and through his marriage to Eleanor of Aquitaine. He continued his grandfather's policy of building up royal power at the expense of nobles and the church, a policy that led to the assassination of Archbishop Thomas à Becket. During his reign he faced several rebellions, even by his own sons. An able administrator, Henry made notable legal reforms, and his expeditions to Ireland established lasting English influence in that country. His son, Richard I, (the Lionhearted) was his successor.

Henry III (1207–1272), king of England (1216–1272), the elder son of King John, whom he succeeded at age nine. Royal affairs were directed by regents until Henry was declared of age in 1227. His submission to foreign courtiers and the numerous relatives of his wife, Eleanor of Provence, as well as his weakness before ecclesiastical tyranny and the drains on the treasury for military projects, made him extremely unpopular. This resulted in civil war between the king and his barons, headed by Simon de Montfort, earl of Leicester. In 1264 Henry was defeated at Lewes and imprisoned, but was rescued by his son, Prince Edward (later Edward I), who became virtual ruler. Though his reign continued officially until 1872, he played only a minor part in governing England.

Henry IV, surnamed **Bolingbroke** (1367–1413), king of England (1399–1413), eldest son of John of Gaunt, duke of Lancaster. He ascended the throne when his cousin, Richard II, was forced to abdicate. Since Parliament authorized the abdication and the new king's claim to the crown, Henry IV may be considered England's first constitutional monarch. He was also the first king of the House of Lancaster. His reign was marked by frequent rebellions of the Scots and Welsh, which he vigorously suppressed. The story of these revolts was described by Shakespeare in *Henry IV, Part I*. Henry was succeeded by his son, Prince Hal (later Henry V), in 1413.

Henry V (1387–1422), king of England (1413–1422), eldest son and successor of Henry IV. Made prince of Wales in 1399, he aided his father in suppressing the revolts of the nobles. Upon gaining the throne, he set in motion a far-reaching design to conquer France and acquire the French crown, which he claimed through descent from his great-grandfather, Edward III. In 1415 came the great victory over the French at Agincourt. After seizing the whole of Normandy, Henry forced the French to sign the Treaty of Troyes (1420), by which he was recognized as regent and successor to Charles VI of France. He married Catherine of Valois, a daughter of Charles VI, in the same year. Henry died within two years and was succeeded by his son Henry VI. Shakespeare portrayed him as the ideal king.

Henry VI (1421–1471), king of England (1422–1461, 1470–1471), son of Henry V. He was proclaimed king on the day of his father's death, when he was only nine months old. A few weeks later he was proclaimed king of France, his rights in that country being entrusted to his uncles, the dukes of Bedford and Gloucester. In 1429 the French, united by the inspiration of Joan of Arc, crowned Charles VII at Reims, and refused to acknowledge any other king. After 1455, Henry was subject to attacks of insanity, and Richard Plantagenet, duke of York, was made protector 1454). Meanwhile the disputes between the houses of Lancaster and York led to the Wars of the Roses. In 1460 York was killed and in 1461 Henry was deposed in favor of York's son, who became Edward IV. Imprisoned by the Yorkists from 1465–1470, Henry, now an imbecile, was restored to the throne by Richard Neville, duke of Warwick. In the following year, Edward returned from exile, regained the crown, and had Henry VI murdered. His death marked the downfall of the Lancastrians.

Henry VII, often called **Henry Tudor** (1457–1509), king of England (1485–1509). The first of the Tudor line, he succeeded Richard III, the last Yorkist king, in 1485, after defeating Richard in the battle of Bosworth. Though his mother had been a Lancaster, he ended the rivalry by marrying Elizabeth of York, daughter of Edward IV. Henry maintained royal power at the expense of the nobles and was popular with the middle classes, because he kept the country at peace and furthered commerce. During his reign John Cabot discovered the continent of North America (1497), which laid the basis of England's claim to Canada. He was succeeded by his second son, Henry VIII, in 1509.

Henry VIII (1491–1547), king of England (1509–1547), and father of Queen Elizabeth I. Shortly after ascending the throne he married his brother's widow, Catherine of Aragon. Early in his reign he joined the Holy League formed by the pope and Spain against France, leaving affairs of state in the hands of his minister, Cardinal Wolsey. But when Wolsey failed to secure from the pope an annulment of his marriage to Catherine, Henry had him arrested for treason. Henry later secured a divorce and in 1533 secretly married Anne Boleyn. To obtain the divorce, Henry had to break openly with the pope, an act that at first was not so much a question of reforming the Church as of satisfying the king's personal interests. In 1536 Anne Boleyn was beheaded for crimes against the king, and Henry married Jane Seymour. Her death in 1537 left him free to marry the German princess Anne of Cleves (1540), the choice of Thomas Cromwell, who had risen to royal favor. But Anne did not please Henry, and he had the marriage annulled; this led to the execution of Cromwell. Henry's fifth wife, Catherine Howard, was beheaded for unfaithfulness, and in 1543 he married Catherine Parr, who outlived him. Henry's defiance of papal authority resulted in the separation of the Church of England from the Roman Catholic body. In 1547, Henry was succeeded by Edward VI, his son by Jane Seymour. Two of his daughters became English queens: Mary, daughter of Catherine of Aragon, and Elizabeth, daughter of Anne Boleyn.

Henry I (1008–1060), king of France (1031–1060), a grandson of Hugh Capet. The years of his reign were spent mainly in quieting rebellions within his kingdom, chiefly in Normandy and Burgundy. An early ally but later enemy was William, duke of Normandy, who became William I of England. He was succeeded by a son, Philip I, in 1060.

Henry II (1519–1559), king of France (1547–1559), the son of Francis I. In two wars with England, beginning in 1550 and in 1557, France recovered all its English-held territories, the last stronghold (Calais) being taken in 1558. Several later military campaigns were successful, until a stalemate with Spain after a series of costly battles forced the two countries to sign a peace treaty in 1559. During most of his reign, Henry vigorously prosecuted. Protestants in France. The husband of Catherine de Médicis, he was the father of three kings: Francis II, Charles IX, and Henry III. His daughter married Philip of Spain.

Henry III (1551–1589), king of France (1574–1589), third son of Henry II. During the reign of his brother, Charles IX, he commanded the royal army against the Huguenots and helped his mother, Catherine de Médicis, instigate the massacre of St. Bartholomew's Day (August 24, 1572). Elected king of Poland in 1573, he succeeded his brother Charles IX as king of France in 1574. During Henry's reign the religious wars between Catholics and Huguenots continued. Henry had a powerful enemy in the duke of Guise, head of the Holy League, which accused him of being too lenient with the Huguenots but was secretly working to secure the crown for the Guises. In 1588 Guise was killed by the king's guards. To defend himself against the League, Henry allied himself with Henry of Navarre. In 1589 the two Henrys lay siege to Paris, but before the city surrendered, Henry III was assassinated by a Jacobin friar. Henry of Navarre then became Henry IV.

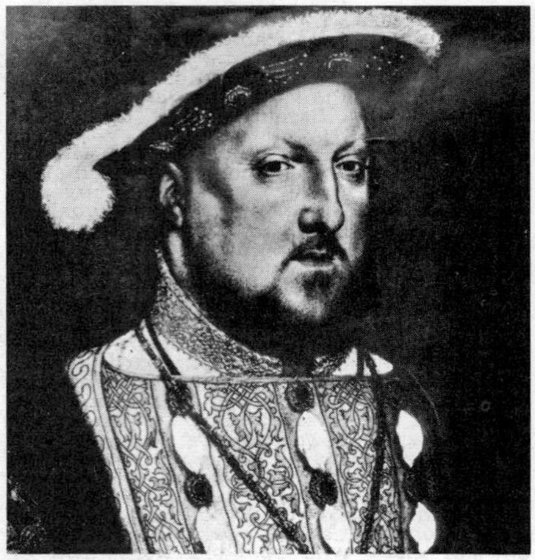

EARL SPENCER

HENRY VIII

Henry IV, earlier **Henry of Navarre** (1553–1610), king of France, (1589–1610), the son of Anthony of Bourbon and the queen of Navarre. In 1572 Henry became king of Navarre (an independent kingdom north of the Pyrenees). His marriage to Margaret of Valois, sister of Charles IX, took place shortly before the Massacre of St. Bartholomew. Although Henry had been raised as a Protestant, his life was spared when he promised to become a Roman Catholic. In 1576 he escaped from Paris and became the leader of a Huguenot army, joining forces with Henry III to besiege Paris in 1589. On the assassination of Henry III, he became the first Bourbon king of France, but was unable to assume royal power until he publicly recanted his Protestantism in 1593. A series of brilliant victories over Roman Catholic forces finally ended the war with the Holy League in 1596. Henry signed the Edict of Nantes (1598), which granted religious liberty to the Huguenots, and then turned his considerable energies to restoring order and prosperity to his kingdom. Divorcing Margaret in 1599, he married Marie de Médicis, by whom he had six children. He was assassinated by a religious fanatic.

Henry the Lion (1129–1195), duke of Saxony and Bavaria who was a leading figure in the civil wars throughout Germany during the twelfth century. As leader of the Guelph party against the Hohenstaufen party headed by Emperor Conrad III, Henry tried unsuccessfully to seize Bavaria, which had been taken from his father. But Emperor Frederick Barbarossa, Conrad's successor, restored Henry's rights to Bavaria, and the two formed an alliance that lasted for 20 years. In 1176, however, Henry refused to support the emperor's Italian wars and was banished. He was permitted to return to Germany, but was unable to restore his damaged fortunes. Noted for his encouragement of agriculture and colonization of Saxon cities, Henry nevertheless hindered Germany's recovery from the destructive civil wars of the twelfth century.

Henry III, called **Henry the Black** (1017–1056). German king, later Holy Roman emperor (1039–1056), son of Conrad II. He succeeded his father as king of Germany in 1039 and extended his authority as a feudal lord over portions of Poland, Bohemia. Hungary and Italy. In 1046 he was summoned to Italy to settle the conflicts of Benedict IX, Gregory VI, and Sylvester III, all claimants to the papal throne. Henry appointed a new pope, Clement II, and on Christmas Day, 1046, was crowned emperor. Henry continued to nominate papal candidates and attempted to check ecclesiastical abuses.

Henry IV (1050–1106), Holy Roman emperor, (1056–1106), son of Henry III. He became king of Germany, Italy, and Burgundy at the age of six, his mother acting as regent until he came of age. When he assumed control in 1065, he found a weak and disordered realm. After establishing his authority, he encountered opposition from Pope Gregory VII, who in 1075 forbade all prelates to accept appointments from secular rulers. In response, Henry called a council at Worms in 1076 to resist the pope, but a papal edict of excommunication caused him to submit in 1077. Civil war in

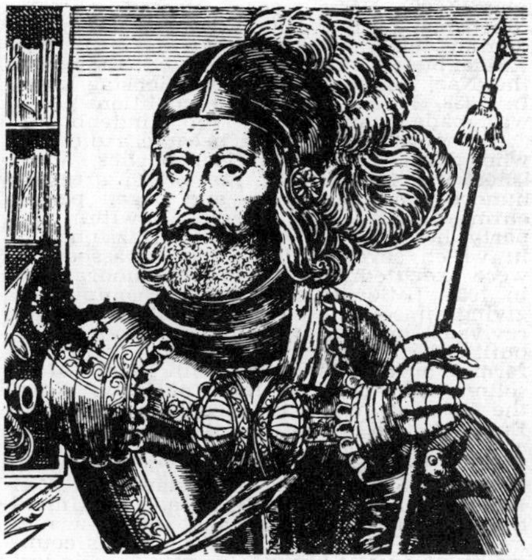

BETTMANN ARCHIVE

HENRY THE NAVIGATOR

Germany followed. In 1084 Henry captured Rome, established Clement III as pope, and was crowned emperor. In 1105 he was compelled to abdicate, and died in 1106 while preparing to regain his throne.

Henry the Navigator (1394–1460), Portuguese prince who sponsored naval explorations of the West African coast, although he himself made no voyages. Under his leadership, Portuguese seamen reached the Madeira Islands in 1420, and by the time of his death had extended Portuguese influence as far south along the West African coast as Sierra Leone. Besides his financial support of voyages, he also founded a school for navigation and erected an observatory. His pioneering work set the pace for later explorations by European countries.

Henry, Joseph (1797–1878), American physicist whose work in electromagnetism led to several important developments. Born in Albany, N.Y., he taught mathematics and natural philosophy at the Albany Academy, and in 1832 became professor of natural philosophy at Princeton. Henry developed the electromagnet to the point that it is still used in electric motors and dynamos. He discovered and operated the first electromagnetic telegraph, preparing the way for its widespread commercial use. For his discovery of electrical inductance in 1832, the International Congress of Electricians gave his name to the standard unit of inductive resistance. Another discovery, electromagnetic induction, was made independently by both Henry and Faraday, but the latter published his theory first and received the credit. From 1846, Henry served as the first secretary and director of the newly formed Smithsonian Institution.

Henry, O. See *Porter, William Sydney.*

Henry, Patrick (1736–1799), American statesman whose gift for oratory made him a leading spokesman for the Colonial cause during the American Revolution. Born in Hanover County, Va., his early life was marked by failures as a farmer and as a merchant. He entered law practice in 1760 and was later elected to the Virginia legislature. At the Virginia Provincial Convention of 1775, he made a speech containing the famous declaration. "I know not what course others may take, but as for me, give me liberty or give me death." Carried away by his oratory, the assembly voted to organize the Virginia militia. During and after the Revolution Henry held several important state posts, including two terms as governor.

Henty, George Alfred (1832–1902), English writer, born near Cambridge. During the Crimean War, he was a war correspondent for a London newspaper. Afterwards, in this capacity, he spent several years in adventurous travels, including exploits with Garibaldi, Lord Napier, and Lord Wolseley. In middle life, he wrote over 80 popular adventure novels for young readers, including *Out on the Pampas* (1868) and *With Clive in India* (1884).

Heraclitus (c.540–480 B.C.), Greek metaphysical philosopher known as the "weeping philosopher" because of his pessimism and called "the dark one" because of his obscurity. Essentially, Heraclitus maintained that change is the first principle of the universe, that all things are in a constant state of flux. To him, fire (identified with life and reason) was the fundamental substance of the universe, and man's soul was shared with the soul-fire of the universe. Heraclitus believed that life was a system of constantly changing opposites, and man's goal was to find their underlying connection.

Herbert, George (1593–1633), English metaphysical poet. Born in Montgomery, Wales, and educated at Cambridge, he entered the Anglican Church in 1625, in which he spent the remainder of his life as a parish priest. His poems, published posthumously in *The Temple,* are religious in nature. They are distinguished for their lyricism, serenity, and humble, quaint conceits. Herbert's poetry is often compared to that of his better-known contemporary, John Donne.

Herbert, Victor (1859–1924), Irish-American composer, born in Dublin. In 1886 he came to America as solo cellist at the Metropolitan Opera House in New York. Later he won fame as a conductor and as a composer of highly successful operettas, including *Babes in Toyland* (1903), *The Red Mill* (1906), *Naughty Marietta* (1910), and *Sweethearts* (1913). Herbert also composed orchestral works and two operas, *Natoma* (1911) and *Madeleine* (1914), as well as the music for the motion picture *The Fall of a Nation* (1916).

Herder, Johann Gottfried von (1744–1803), German critic and philosopher who exerted great influence on Goethe and the whole Romantic movement in Germany. Herder first made a reputation as a critic, poet, and translator of folk songs, but subsequently turned to philosophy. In his greatest work, *Ideas on the History of Mankind* (1784–1791), he advanced a theory of historical evolution, in which both nature and history obey a uniform system of laws.

Hero or **Heron of Alexander** (c.1st century A.D.), Greek scientist, mathematician, and inventor. Expert in mechanics and pneumatics, he invented numerous devices operated by compressed air, water, and steam, including a siphon, a fountain, and a primitive steam engine. He also established the optical principle that the angle of incidence equals that of refraction, and discovered a formula for finding the area of a triangle using the lengths of its sides.

Herod, the name of a line of rulers of Palestine near the beginning of the Christian Era (c.55 B.C.–93 A.D.). **Antipater the Idumaer** (d.43 B.C.) founded the family fortune, but his son **Herod the Great** (c.73–4 B.C.) gave the family its name. A friend of Mark Antony, who made him king of Judaea, Herod tried to mollify the Jews by showing them special favor. Herod married ten times and executed several of his own children for plotting against him. It was Herod the Great who was ruling at the time of Christ's birth and who ordered the slaughter of the innocents (Matthew 2.22). One of his sons, **Herod Antipas** (d. after 40 A.D.), was ruler of Galilee and Peraea at the time of Jesus' death.

Herodes Atticus, Latin name **Tiberius Claudius** (c. 101-177 A.D.), Greek rhetoritician, born in Marathon. He tutored young Roman emperors and became Roman consul in 143. A sophist, he wrote dialogues and orations, only two of which are extant.

Herodotus (5th century B.C.), Greek historian, called the father of history. Born in Asia Minor, he became a traveler who visited almost every part of the then known world, including Scythia, Syria, Palestine, Babylon, and Egypt. He first visited Athens in 447 B.C. From these travels came his *History,* whose main subject is the Persian Wars. In the book, Herodotus frequently digressed from his chief subject to introduce his historical, geographical, and antiquarian knowledge. His chief defect as a historian is an uncritical acceptance of the marvelous, but he is truthful and accurate whenever he writes from his own observations. The simple beauty of his style, the grandeur of his plan, and the charm of his narrative have delighted readers in all ages. Since his predecessor Homer wrote only in verse, Herodotus can be considered the first European writer of prose.

Herrick, Robert (1591–1674), English poet, noted for his short lyrics. Born in London, he spent most of his adult life as a church vicar. During the Commonwealth he was forced to retire because of his Royalist sympathies, returning upon the restoration of Charles II in 1660. In 1648 his poems were published under the titles *Hesperides* and *Noble Numbers.* Of some 1,400 poems, most were short lyrics, distinguished for their perfection of form and style, whose pagan tone and hedonistic philosophy can be traced to classical influences. Among his often-quoted single poems are *Gather Ye Rosebuds* and *Corinna's Going A Maying.* Although Herrick is remembered chiefly for his secular poems, he also wrote a number of sacred verses.

Herriot, Édouard (1872–1957), French statesman who as leader of the Radical Socialist party became premier of France in 1923 and again in 1932. Born in Troyes, and originally a university professor, he entered public life in 1905. When the Germans occupied France during World War II, he was placed in a prison camp, but in 1945 resumed his position as leader of the Radical Socialists. He became a member of the National Assembly in 1945 and served as its presiding officer from 1947 to 1953. In later years, he was a vigorous proponent of a united Europe.

Herschel, Sir **John Frederick William** (1792-1871), English astronomer, who specilized in studies of nebulae and star clusters, son of Sir William Herschel. In addition to enlarging his father's catalogue of northern nebulae and star clusters, he made a survey of the southern heavens from an observatory he established at the Cape of Good Hope. Herschel also made several important contributions to the development of photography. His *Outline of Astronomy* appeared in 1849.

Herschel, Sir William, originally **Friedrich Wilhelm Herschel** (1738–1822), German astronomer who lived in England after 1757. Between 1773 and 1786 he made a series of telescopes, culminating in a giant reflector with a four-foot mirror. In 1781 he discovered the planet Uranus, for which he was knighted by King George III. Among other achievements, he discovered the infrared rays of the solar spectrum, catalogued some 2,500 nebulae, decided the direction of motion of the solar system, and was the first astronomer who gave estimates of the universe's immensity.

Hersey, John Richard (1914–), American author, born of American parents in Tientsin, China, and educated at Cambridge and Yale. During World War II he was a magazine correspondent, and his first-hand experiences led to a novel about wartime Italy, *A Bell for Adano* (1944). Shortly after the war he published *Hiroshima* (1946), which described the effects of the atomic bomb upon the Japanese city and its people. Later novels include *The Wall* (1950), *The War Lover* (1959), and *The Child Buyer* (1960).

Herter, Christian Archibald (1895–1966), American statesman, born in Paris of American parents, educated at Harvard. From 1916 to 1924 he served in various diplomatic posts, then entered politics. He was a member of Congress (1943–1953) and a governor of Massachusetts (1953–1957). He was undersecretary of state (1957–1959), becoming secretary of state after John Foster Dulles died. After leaving that post in 1961, he was active in NATO. He died Dec. 31, 1966 in Washington, D.C.

Hertz, Heinrich Rudolph (1857–1894), German physicist who was the first to demonstrate the propagation and reception of radio waves. A professor of physics at several German universities during his lifetime, he discovered electromagnetic waves in 1885. Later, he demonstrated the properties of these waves, measuring their velocity and length and showing that their properties of refraction, reflection, and polarization made them similar to light waves. These discoveries were vital to the development of wireless telegraphy.

Herzl, Theodor (1860–1904), Hungarian founder of modern Zionism, born in Budapest. As a correspondent for a Viennese newspaper, he was sent to Paris to report on the Dreyfus affair, which deeply affected his outlook on life and began his connection with the Jewish cause. In 1896 he published *Der Judenstaat* (The Jewish State), in which he propounded his theories on the need for a separate Jewish state. He founded the World Zionist Organization, which he hoped would supply the political and economic foundation from which the state could be created. He died 44 years before his vision became a reality in Israel.

Hesiod (8th century B.C.), early Greek poet who was the founder of didactic poetry, which aims to instruct or to point a moral. Little is known of his life, but tradition has it that he was a wandering bard. Three of his works are extant: *Theogony,* a genealogy of the gods; *The Shield of Heracles,* also mythological in content; and *Works and Days,* his greatest and earliest poem. This poem is a kind of almanac, containing moral reflections on labor, rules for the farmer, and a religious calendar showing lucky and unlucky days for performing certain tasks. Though it lacks the vivid beauty of Homer's epics, Hesiod's poetry strongly influenced Greek education.

Hess, Rudolf, in full **Walther Richard Rudolf Hess** (1894–), German politician. In 1920 Hess joined the Nazi party and, after the Munich uprising of 1923, was imprisoned with Adolf Hitler. Deputy Führer in 1933, Hess later became second in line to the dictatorship. In 1941 Hess captured the world's attention with a sensational solo flight to Scotland, presumably to negotiate peace with England. Imprisoned in England for the remainder of the war, he was sentenced to life imprisonment at the Nürnberg trial in 1946.

Hess, Victor Francis (1883–), Austrian-American physicist who, together with Carl D. Anderson, discovered cosmic radiation. In 1918 he helped establish the number of alpha particles emitted by a gram of radium. In 1936, while professor at Innsbruck University, he shared the Nobel Prize for physics with Anderson. In 1938 he was appointed professor of physics at Fordham University, New York, and in 1944 became an American citizen.

Hesse, Hermann (1877–1962), German-Swiss poet and novelist, born in Germany, who received the Nobel Prize for literature in 1946. Particularly interested in problems of psychology and philosophy, Hess wrote a long line of novels, the most important of which are *Demian* (1919), *Peter Camenzind* (1904), *Der Steppenwolf* (1927), *Death and the Lover* (1930) and *Magister Ludi* (1943).

Hicks, Elias (1748–1830), American Quaker, founder of the division of the Society of Friends known as Hicksites. Born in Hempstead, N.Y., he became widely known as a traveling minister and antislavery orator. In 1811 he published his *Observations on Slavery,* and later helped to bring about abolition of slavery in New York State. Doctrinal differences between the orthodox Quakers and the followers of Hicks led to a split in 1828, for which Hicks was unjustly blamed. A liberal in theology, Hicks was one of the first proponents of progressive revelation.

Higginson, Thomas Wentworth (1823–1911), American clergyman, author, soldier, and abolitionist. Born in Cambridge, Mass., and educated at Harvard, he became a minister and actively participated in antislavery movements. During the Civil War, he served as colonel of the first Negro regiment in the Union army. After the war Higginson devoted himself to numerous social causes, and produced a large number of books, including essays, histories, and literary reminiscences.

Hildebrand. See *Gregory VII.*

Hill, James Jerome (1838–1916), American railroad magnate, born in Ontario, Canada. After leaving his father's farm for a business career in Minnesota, he established a steamship company in 1870, which operated to Winnepeg by way of the Mississippi and Red rivers. Hill next formed a syndicate that secured control of the St. Paul and Pacific Railroad, which in 1890 became part of the Great Northern Railway Company. Hill became president of the entire Great Northern system and before his death had developed a network of railroads that covered the American Northwest. He was also a leader in the building of the Canadian Pacific Railroad.

Himmler, Heinrich (1900–1945), German politician and police chief. Himmler joined the Nazi movement at its inception, and in 1929 was made head of the *Schutzstaffel* (known as the S.S.) by Hitler. He also commanded the *Gestapo,* or secret police, which carried out a campaign of political and anti-Semitic terror with the death of some six million Jews as one of its results. In 1943 Himmler was made minister of the interior and, in the following year, commander in chief of the home forces. When it became obvious that the Nazi effort was doomed, Himmler took poison in order to escape trial. As head of the Gestapo, Himmler bears the responsibility for many of the horrors that were perpetrated in the name of the Third Reich.

Hindemith, Paul (1895–1963), German composer who was a leading figure in the reaction against nineteenth-century romanticism. In much of his work. Hindemith superimposed modern harmony on early polyphonic and baroque styles. Much of his work is dissonant, but he never espoused the 12-tone system of his contemporary Arnold Schönberg, feeling that harmony should fundamentally be tonal. In 1938 he left Germany and came to the United States, where he taught at Yale, and became a citizen in 1946. A prolific composer in every area of music, Hindemith wrote such works as the opera *Mathis der Maler* (1938), the ballet *Nobelissma Visione* (1938), *The Philharmonic Concerto* (1932), and the requiem *For Those We Love* (1944).

Hindenburg, Paul von (1847–1934), German soldier, hero of World War I, and the second president of the Weimar Republic. After retiring as a general in 1911, he was recalled as World War I began to command the German Army in East Prussia. His success was phenomenal, and he succeeded Gen. Erich von Falkenhayn as chief of the general staff in 1916. He remained out of politics until 1925, when he was elected president of the Weimar Republic. In the election of 1932 he defeated Adolf Hitler, but Hitler's power was steadily growing. Yielding to Nazi pressure, he appointed Hitler chancellor in 1933, marking the virtual end of Hindenburg's power.

Hipparchus (c.160–125 B.C.), Greek astronomer and mathematician, born in Asia Minor. He discovered the precession of the equinoxes; compiled a catalogue of 1,080 stars, showing the celestial latitude and longitude of each; and calculated the length of the solar year, the distances of the sun and moon from the earth, and the orbital motions of the planets. Through his use of higher mathematics, he became one of the founders of trigonometry.

Hippocrates (460–c.377 B.C.), Greek physician, called "the Father of Medicine." He believed that human health was affected by climate, water, environment, food, and exercise, and he treated diseases by attending to a patient's diet and general regimen. Observing and recording symptoms with great care, he produced 87 medical treatises, comprising what is called the "Hippocratic Collection." The "Hippocratic Oath," an ethical code he is said to have devised, is still administered to those who are entering medical practice.

Hirohito (1901–), emperor of Japan since 1926. During the 1930's, dominated by the military leaders of his country, he permitted the aggression that led to the Sino-Japanese War (1937–1945) and to Japan's entry into World War II. After Japan's defeat, Hirohito publicly repudiated the doctrine of the emperor's divinity and relaxed much of the formality that had characterized the Japanese court.

Hiroshige, Ando (1797–1858), Japanese artist famous for his colored prints. He produced some 5,000 prints, including landscapes, seascapes, and flower and bird prints. His most successful series of prints was the *Fifty-Three Stages of the Tokaido,* which depicted scenes at each of the 53 stages or overnight stations on the road between Tokyo and Kyoto. His prints are marked by an economy of elements and a bold use of color. An exhibition of Hiroshige's prints in Paris, late in the nineteenth century, is said to have profoundly influenced many of the French Impressionist painters.

Hitler, Adolf (1889–1945), dictator of Germany (1933–1945), born in Austria. After serving in the German army during World War I, he formed the German National Socialist Workers' party (abbreviated "Nazi") in Munich in 1920. After leading the "Hitler Putsch," a 1923 revolt against the government, he was sentenced to five years in prison, but was released after a short time. While in prison, he wrote his major work, *Mein Kampf.* He reorganized his party but remained peaceful until 1930, when 107 Nazis were elected to the Reichstag. In 1932 Hitler entered the presidential election campaign against von Hindenburg, but was defeated; however, the Nazi party gained 230 Reichstag seats. In 1933, Hitler, leading a coalition party, was made chancellor by von Hindenburg.

Almost at once, Hitler became a dictator who purged other political parties, abolished the freedom of the press, arrested hundreds of clergymen, and began persecuting Jews. To quell a revolt within the party, he ordered the famous "Nazi purge," in which several of his closest associates were executed. When von Hindenburg died in 1934, Hitler ruled Germany completely, giving himself the title "Der Führer." Hitler revived compulsory military service and built a formidable military force. In 1937 he formed an understanding with Benito Mussolini, the Fascist dictator of Italy. When the German armies invaded Poland in 1939, England and France declared war. In successive campaigns, Hitler's armies captured Poland, Denmark, Norway, the Netherlands, Belgium, France, and Yugoslavia. In 1941 Hitler declared war on Russia and the United States, and the German and Italian armies swept into Africa. Hitler inspired his country to unusual accomplishments, but underestimated the strength of the Allied countries and overestimated his own resources. The tide of war turned against him in 1944, and as the Allies were entering Berlin, he committed suicide rather than submit to capture. An evil genius who hated non-Germans, especially Jews and Slavs, he brought disaster to Germany, irreparable damage to Europe, and death to 6 million Jews.

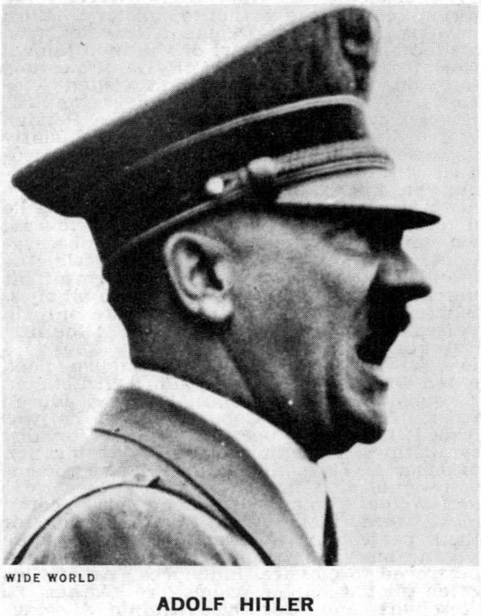
WIDE WORLD

ADOLF HITLER

Ho Chi Minh (1890–), Indochinese Communist leader, born in Vietnam. Always a revolutionist, he became an ardent Communist as a young man and later organized the Viet Minh in Indochina to harass the Japanese during World War II. After the Japanese surrender, the Viet Minh established Ho as their president and continued their guerrilla warfare against the French. When the French were defeated at Dienbienphu (1954), an armistice was signed and the Communists and Ho Chi Minh were given control of North Vietnam.

Hobbes, Thomas (1588–1679), English political philosopher, educated at Oxford. He published his first book, a translation of Thucydides, in 1628. From 1640 until 1651 he lived chiefly in Paris, his writings on political science having made him unpopular in England. Although Hobbes upheld the monarchical form of government, he believed that royal power was derived from the people and not based upon divine right. Hobbes' fame rests upon ideas stated in *The Leviathan, or the Matter, Form and Power of a Commonwealth* (1651). In its own day, the book was a major force that turned English philosophical thinking to social and utilitarian approaches.

Hobson, Richmond Pearson (1870–1937), American naval officer, born in Greensboro, Ala., and a graduate of Annapolis in 1889. As a lieutenant in the Spanish-American War, Hobson became a national hero by attempting to sink the collier *Merrimac* in order to blockade the harbor at Santiago, Cuba. Hobson resigned from the Navy in 1903 and represented an Alabama district in Congress from 1907 to 1915. Later he lectured on international peace, naval preparedness, and prohibition. In 1933 he was awarded the Congressional Medal of Honor.

Hoe, Richard March (1812–1886), American inventor who developed the rotary printing press. Born in New York City, he became a partner in his father's business, Hoe & Company, and greatly improved the company's products. In 1846 he discarded the flat-bed press and, placing the type on a moving cylinder, introduced the rotary press—the first of the kind used in modern newspaper printing. Afterwards, he refined his invention, developing a rotary press that printed on both sides of a roll of paper and cut, folded, and counted sheets simultaneously.

Hofer, Andreas (1767–1810), Tyrolese patriot and popular hero, who in 1796 headed a rebellion against the French and in 1809 uprisings against the Bavarians, French, and Italians. Fighting for the reunion of Tyrol with Austria, at first succeeded but later (1810) was captured and shot, allegedly by order of Napoleon.

Hoffa, James Riddle (1913–), American labor union executive, born in Brazil, Ind. A member at 20 of the International Brotherhood of Teamsters, Hoffa became vice-president in 1952, and was elected president in 1957. Under his leadership, the Teamsters Union became one of the most powerful unions in American history. Despite repeated government investigations on charges of fraud and corruption, he was returned to office in 1961.

Hofmann, Hans (1880–1966), German-American painter, teacher, and leading exponent of abstract expressionism. Trained in the art schools of Munich, Hofmann as a young man became interested in post-Impressionistic painting. The exuberant color of Fauvism, together with the structure of Cubism, became integral parts of his art. After moving to the U.S. he became a distinguished teacher of abstract painting.

Hofmannsthal, Hugo von (1874–1929), Austrian poet and dramatist who led a neo-Romantic movement that stressed aesthetics rather than naturalism. He wrote a great number of lyrical plays, including *Death and the Fool* (1913) and *Jedermann* (1911), based on the English morality play *Everyman*. Outside Germany, he is best known for librettos he wrote for several operas by Richard Strauss, including *Der Rosenkavalier* (1911), *Ariadne auf Naxos* (1912), and *Die Frau ohne Schatten* (1919). After World War I he and Max Reinhardt founded the Salzburg Festival, which annually gives performances of *Jedermann*.

Hogarth, William (1697–1764), English artist, born in London. Justly famed for his paintings, he is even more renowned for his satirical engravings. After several years of painting portraits, Hogarth had his first great success in 1732 with a series of six engravings called *The Harlot's Progress*. A similar series, *The Rake's Progress*, appeared in 1735. During the next three decades, Hogarth produced a steady stream of prints, in which satire and serious social comment are combined to expose the injustice and hardship of contemporary life in London. He was the first English-born artist to achieve an international reputation for his work.

Hohenstaufen, a royal house of Germany, members of which wore the crown from 1138 to 1208 and again from 1212 to 1254. The name was derived from a castle in Württemberg. The first Hohenstaufen was Conrad III. He was followed by Frederick I (called Barbarossa), Henry VI, Frederick II, and Conrad IV, the last of the line.

Hohenzollern, a royal family important in German history between 1701 and 1918. From Frederick I of Prussia (1701–1713) to Emperor William II, who abdicated in 1918, the Hohenzollerns furnished kings to Prussia and emperors to Germany (1871–1918) in unbroken succession. There were eight Hohenzollern kings of Prussia, three of whom reigned as emperors of Germany. The name was derived from the ancestral castle Zollern or Hohenzollern (High Zollern) in Swabia.

Hokusai, Katsushika (1760–1849), Japanese artist, famous as a wood engraver for his depiction of ordinary, everyday scenes in Japanese life. His important works include the *Manga*, sketches from life, which appeared in 15 volumes between 1812 and 1875; and the *Hundred Views of Mount Fuji* (1835). Hokusai's prints are noted for their technical perfection. Like his younger contemporary Hiroshige, he won great prestige abroad, particularly in Europe during the late nineteenth century.

Holbein, Hans, called **the Younger** (1497–1543), German painter and engraver who studied under his father (known as "the Elder"). After beginning his career as a painter in Switzerland, he went to England in 1526, carrying letters from his friend Erasmus to Sir Thomas More. Ten years later he was made court painter to Henry VIII. One of the world's great portrait painters, Holbein depicted many of the notables of his time. As an engraver, he is best known for a series of 58 woodcuts called *The Dance of Death*.

Holberg, Baron **Ludvig** (1684–1754), Danish author, recognized as the founder of the nation's literature. His masterpiece, *Peder and Paars*, a comic heroic poem, appeared in 1719, and by 1722 he had produced five plays in Danish. Until that time, only French and German had been used on the Danish stage. Besides writing in Danish for the theater, he also published many works in history, science, and philosophy. Almost singlehandedly, he made Danish a literary language, acceptable to his countrymen.

Holinshed, Raphael (d. about 1580), English chronicler from whom Shakespeare borrowed much of the material for his historical and other plays. He is remembered for one book, *Chronicles of England, Scotland and Ireland* (1577). The work, originally planned as a universal history, was begun by Reginald Wolfe, printer to Queen Elizabeth; Holinshed served as his translator. After Wolfe died, Holinshed completed and published the book.

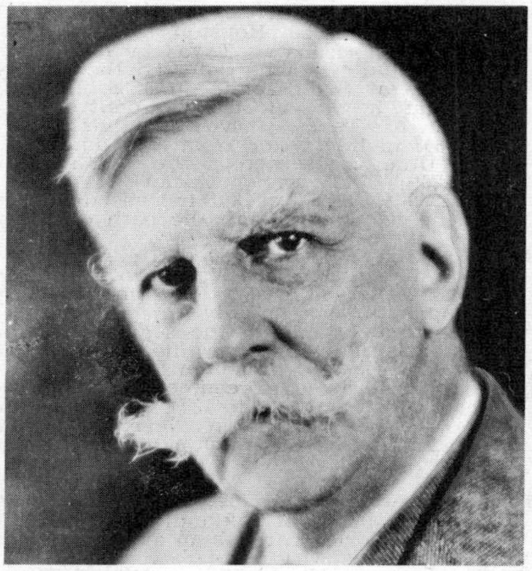

WIDE WORLD

JUSTICE OLIVER WENDELL HOLMES

Holland, John Philip (1840–1914), American inventor who developed the first submarine for the U.S. Navy. Born in Liscannor, Ireland, he came to America in 1872 and was a school teacher until 1879, when he built a small submarine that operated successfully. In 1900 the navy purchased its first submarine from him.

Holmes, Oliver Wendell (1809–1894), American poet and writer, born in Cambridge, Mass., and educated at Harvard. First a student of law, Holmes abandoned it for medicine but forsook active practice for teaching and writing. His well-received *The Autocrat of the Breakfast-Table* (1858), a collection of sketches that first appeared in the *Atlantic Monthly*, was followed by *The Professor at the Breakfast-Table* (1860). A novel, *Elsie Venner*, appeared in 1861. In addition to other novels and essays, Holmes wrote a great deal of serious and humorous verse, including *The Chambered Nautilus*, *Old Ironsides*, and *The Wonderful One-Hoss Shay*. A friend of Emerson, Longfellow, Lowell, and Whittier, Holmes was renowned for his wit and personality.

Holmes, Oliver Wendell (1841–1935), American jurist, born in Boston and named for his father, the poet and writer. A Harvard graduate, he was a captain in the Civil War. With a law degree from Harvard, he began practice in Boston in 1867. After a year on the Harvard law faculty, he became associate justice of the Massachusetts Supreme Court, serving as chief justice from 1899 to 1902, when he began 30 years of service as associate justice of the U.S. Supreme Court. In 1932 he completed one of the longest judicial careers in the history of the United States when he resigned at the age of 91. His interpretations of the U.S. Constitution, and his many decisions in common law, are among the most celebrated in the history of the Supreme Court.

Home, Sir **Alexander Frederick Douglas** 1909–   ), British prime minister (1963–1964). Home, who first became a member of Parliament in 1931, was secretary of state for commonwealth relations (1955–1960), lord president of the Council, leader of the House of Lords (1957–1960), and secretary of state for foreign affairs (1960–1963). He became prime minister in 1963 after Harold Macmillan retired. Originally an earl, he renounced his title in anticipation of the general elections of 1964; however, he lost his position as prime minister when his Conservatives lost to the Labour party.

Homer (9th century B.C.), most famous of the classical Greek poets, the author of the *Iliad* and the *Odyssey*. Little is known of his life; even his birthplace is not known. He is believed to have been blind and to have traveled about singing his poems. The *Iliad* describes the siege of Troy by the Greeks, and the *Odyssey* describes the wanderings of Ulysses (Odysseus) after the fall of that city. Both epics are written in the Ionic dialect, and each is divided into 24 books. There have been many English translations of the poems.

Homer, Winslow (1836–1910), American painter, famous for his marine paintings, born in Boston. A self-taught artist, he was field correspondent and artist for *Harper's Weekly* during the Civil War. In addition to sketches, he began to work in oil and produced several canvases depicting war scenes. In later life, after becoming an established artist, he made his home at Prout's Neck on the Maine coast, where he painted the New England village scenes and marine subjects for which he is famous.

Honegger, Arthur Oscar (1892–1955), French composer who rose to prominence after World War I as a member of the French school called Les Six, which included Darius Milhaud and Francis Poulenc. Outstanding examples of his work include the oratorios *King David* (1921) and *Joan of Arc at the Stake* (1936); and *Pacific 231* (1923), a musical portrait of a locomotive.

Honorius, Flavius (384–423), emperor of Western Rome (393–423) during the Gothic invasions. The second son of Theodosius the Great, Honorius received the western half of the realm when his father died in 395, his brother Arcadius becoming emperor of the East. During his reign Honorius failed to halt the invasions of the Gothic tribes, and by the time of his death Rome had lost several provinces.

Hood, Thomas (1799–1845), English poet and humorist, born in London, famous for his puns and figurative language. During a career as magazine editor, Hood published several collections of satirical works, including *Odes and Addresses to Great People* (1825) and *The Comic Annual* series, first published in 1830. Hood also wrote many serious poems, most notably *The Song of the Shirt*, which criticized social conditions of his time.

Hooker, Joseph (1814–1879), American general who held several important commands during the Civil War. Born in Hadley, Mass., he was a West Point graduate (1837). He retired in 1853 but was recalled as a brigadier general when the Civil War started, and fought with distinction in the Peninsular Campaign, as well as at Bull Run and Antietam. In 1862 at the battle of Fredericksburg, he commanded two army corps, and in the following year Lincoln gave him command of the Army of the Potomac. After criticism of his defeat at Fredericksburg, he resigned his command, but later served with distinction in the battles of Chattanooga and Atlanta.

Hooker, Thomas (1586–1647), American colonist and Congregational theologian, born in England. He preached in Holland for three years and in 1633 went to Massachusetts with John Cotton and established himself in Newtowne (now Cambridge). In 1636 he led a number of his parishioners to the Connecticut Valley, where they founded the city of Hartford. Hooker was a leader in the organization of New England settlements for protection against the French and Indians. He also helped found the United Colonies of New England (1643), the first union of the kind in America.

Hoover, Herbert Clark (1874–1964), thirty-first president of the United States (1929–1933). Born in West Branch, Iowa, and a graduate of Stanford (1895), Hoover became a mining engineer whose activities ranged all over the world. At the outbreak of World War I, he was appointed chairman of the American Relief Commission, during the war served as head of the Food Administration Bureau, and after the war gained fame as the director of relief in countries threatened with famine. In 1921 he served as Pres. Warren G. Harding's secretary of commerce until 1928, when he received the Republican nomination for president. In the election, he defeated Alfred E. Smith by 444 to 87 electoral votes. In the first year of Hoover's term, the stock market crash (October 29, 1929) was the first of several economic crises that led to much criticism of his administration. Hoover set up several measures to end the depression that followed, but in the election of 1932 he was defeated by Governor Franklin D. Roosevelt of New York, chiefly because the country was still in the grip of economic difficulties. After leaving the White House, Hoover served on many government and private committees, most notably as chairman of a committee organized in 1947 to study government reorganization.

Hopkins, Gerard Manley (1844–1889), English poet and Jesuit priest, now generally recognized as one of the major Victorian poets. None of his poems was published during his lifetime, and not until 1918 did a collected edition appear. Hopkins wrote highly personal verse, characterized by lyricism and tenderness but frequently obscure and difficult to interpret. In his best poems he delicately suggests the contrast between the sensuality of nature and the asceticism of his religious life. In metrics, Hopkins developed what he called "sprung rhythm," which depended on stress, not syllable count, to determine the line.

Hopkins, Harry Lloyd (1890–1946), American government official, born in Sioux City, Iowa and graduated from Grinnell College. He had directed a number of welfare organizations when, in 1931, he was chosen to head emergency-relief activities in New York. In 1933 he became head of the National Emergency Relief organization, and in 1935 director of the Works Progress Administration, where he was in charge of all unemployment relief activities during the Depression of the 1930's. Hopkins served as Pres. Franklin D. Roosevelt's emissary to Russia and Britain in 1941 and as special assistant to the president (1942-1945).

Hopkinson, Francis (1737–1791), American jurist, born and educated in Philadelphia. A member of the Continental Congress, he signed the Declaration of Independence in 1776 and helped to draft the Articles of Confederation. His best-known work, *Seven Songs* (1788), was the first book of music published by an American composer. Hopkinson also wrote a number of poems and political pamphlets.

Hopper, Edward (1882–1967), American painter, born in Nyack, N.Y. First gaining fame as an engraver, his paintings have established him as a major American painter. Hopper's work is realistic, with sharply contrasting areas of light and shade, often containing lonely figures. His paintings of New York City scenes and landscapes are widely represented in U.S. museums. He died May 15, 1967 in New York City.

Horace, in full **Quintus Horatius Flaccus** (65–8 B.C.), Roman poet and essayist, born in southern Italy and educated in Rome and Athens. In 38 B.C. his contemporary Vergil introduced him to Maecenas, and through this connection Horace gained an income, a home, and the friendship of Emperor Augustus, to whose reign he contributed much literary glory. His principal writings include *Odes* (four books), *Epodes* (short poems), *Satires* (two books), and *Epistles* (two books), the last epistle being the well-known *Art of Poetry*. He was Rome's greatest lyricist and is among the most widely read of all Latin poets.

Horowitz, Vladimir (1904–   ), American pianist born in Kiev, Russia. He made his American debut in 1928 after a highly successful career in Europe. Renowned for the technical perfection of his performances, he is best known for his interpretations of Chopin and Scarlatti. After a lengthy career, he retired from the concert stage in 1953 but returned with a notable performance in 1965 at Carnegie Hall, New York.

Hotspur. See *Percy, Sir Henry.*

Houdini, Harry, real name **Ehrich Weiss** (1874–1926), American magician who became famous for his escapes from locks, handcuffs, and sealed chests. At the same time, he campaigned against spiritualists and those who claimed supernatural powers. He wrote several books that exposed the tricks of spiritualists and mediums.

Houdon, Jean Antoine (1741–1828), French sculptor, famed for his busts and statues of celebrated figures of the eighteenth century, including Franklin, Rousseau, Napoleon, Molière, and Voltaire. He is known to Americans for his statue of Washington now in the capitol at Richmond, Va. Though he molded over 200 portrait busts, he was perhaps best known for his daring figure of Diana, the mythological goddess of the hunt.

House, Edward Mandell (1858–1938), American statesman, born in Houston, Tex., and educated at Cornell. As a member of the governor's staff in Texas, House acquired the title "Colonel." He was Pres. Wilson's personal representative to the European governments in 1914-1916 and a delegate to the Peace Conference in 1917. Colonel House also helped to formulate the Covenant of the League of Nations. As a confidential advisor to Pres. Woodrow Wilson, House wielded considerable influence in national politics. ·

Housman, Alfred Edward, known as **A. E. Housman** (1859–1936), English poet and scholar, educated at Oxford. As professor of Latin at Oxford and Cambridge, he was famous as a classical scholar. The world at large, however, remembers him for two volumes of verse, *A Shropshire Lad* (1896) and *Last Poems* (1922). The poems, most of them short lyrics, are noted for their simplicity of language, melodious verse, and pessimistic tone; their subject matter is friendship, the passing of youth, and human vanity.

Houston, Samuel, called **Sam Houston** (1793-1863), American soldier and statesman, born in Rockbridge County, Va. As a young man, his varied career included living with Indians, fighting in the War of 1812, and election to Congress from Ten-

nessee (1822). In 1827 he was elected governor of Tennessee. Houston took up the cause of Americans in Texas in 1832, and led the volunteers who defeated the Mexican army at San Jacinto in 1836. In the same year, he was elected president of the republic of Texas, served another term from 1841 to 1844. After Texas was admitted to the Union he served in the U.S. Senate (1846–1859) and was governor of Texas from 1859 to 1861. In 1861 he was deposed when he would not take the oath of allegiance to the Confederacy.

Howard, Oliver Otis (1830–1909), American general during the Civil War, born in Leeds, Maine. He participated in a number of campaigns, most notably in Sherman's march from Atlanta to the sea, where he was in command of the right wing. After the war, he served as commissioner of the Bureau of Refugees, Freedmen, and Abandoned Lands from 1865 to 1874. As a tribute to his active interest in Negro welfare, Howard University in Washington, of which he was a founder and president, was named for him.

Howard, Sidney Coe (1891–1939), American playwright, born in Oakland, Calif. After serving in World War I as an aviator, Howard began his writing career. His most famous play, *They Knew What They Wanted* (1925), won him the Pulitzer Prize. Other important plays include *The Silver Cord* (1926), *The Late Christopher Bean* (1932), and *Yellowjack* (1934). Howard also adapted several European plays for the American stage.

Howe, Elias (1819–1867), American inventor of the sewing machine, born in Spencer, Mass. While he was a machinist, he began the experiments that resulted in the invention of the sewing machine, for which he was given a patent in 1843. The first Howe sewing machines were marketed in England, where he received the financial backing that he had not been able to secure in the United States. His rights to the invention were established in a series of patent infringement suits (1849–1854), after which he received royalties on all sewing machines made in the United States.

Howe, Julia Ward (1819–1910), American poet who wrote *The Battle Hymn of the Republic.* Born in New York City, she married Dr. Samuel Gridley Howe, noted philanthropist and educator of the blind, in 1843. During a lengthy but very active career, she took part in movements for woman suffrage, prison reform, and international peace. She published many volumes of prose and verse.

Howe, Richard, Earl (1726–1799), British admiral who became one of England's greatest heroes by defeating the French in a battle off Ushant island on June 1, 1794. Active in England's fleet for 50 years, he served in the French and Indian wars, commanded the English fleet in America during the Revolutionary War, and in 1782 won a brilliant victory against the French and Spanish at Gibraltar.

Howe, William, 5th Viscount (1729–1814), British general, brother of Adm. Richard Howe, who was commander in chief of the British armies in America from 1776 to 1778. When the Revolutionary War broke out, he was sent to Boston, where he led the British forces at Bunker Hill (1775). Promoted to lieutenant general, he succeeded Gen. Thomas Gage as commander of troops in America. In 1776 he won the battles of Long Island and White Plains. Howe defeated Washington at Brandywine and Germantown in 1777. In 1778 he resigned his command and returned to England.

Howells, William Dean (1837–1920), American novelist and editor, born in Martin's Ferry, Ohio. As a young man Howells wrote a campaign biography of Abraham Lincoln, who rewarded him with a consulate post in Venice (1861–1865). Returning to America, he joined the staff of the *Atlantic Monthly* in 1866 and served as its editor from 1872 to 1881. He was the editor of *Harper's Magazine* from 1886 to 1891. A pioneer in introducing realism to American fiction, Howells was a close friend of Mark Twain and Henry James, and did much to promote the acceptance of their work. The best of his chief novels are *The Rise of Silas Lapham* (1885), *A Modern Instance* (1882), and *A Hazard of New Fortunes* (1890). The most influential critic of his day, Howells also produced many volumes of criticism, essays, travel sketches, and verse.

Hoxie, Vinnie Ream (1847–1914), American sculptor, born in Madison, Wis. When only 18 she won a $30,000 prize for her life-size statue of Abraham Lincoln, now in the rotunda of the Capitol at Washington. Later she received a government commission to make the statue of Adm. David G. Far-

ragut, in Farragut Square in Washington. Mrs. Hoxie was the first woman sculptor to be given a government commission.

Hoyle, Edmond (1672–1769), English authority on games. He spent many years in London as a teacher of whist and other card games. In 1742 he published his *Short Treatise on the Game of Whist,* followed by similar books on backgammon, piquet, quadrille, and chess. The expression "according to Hoyle" has come to mean the definitive word on the rules of a game.

Hsüan T'ung, personal name **Henry Pu-yi** (1906–1965), last emperor (1908–1912) of the Manchu dynasty in China. Elected emperor in 1908, with his father as regent, he was forced to abdicate in 1912 when the republic was proclaimed. In 1917 a coup d'état returned him briefly to the throne. In 1924 he was driven out of Peking and lived under Japanese protection until in 1934 he was made chief executive of Manchoukuo, the newly formed puppet state of the Japanese. In 1934 he was crowned emperor with the new name K'ang Teh. The Russians captured him in 1945, and in 1950 he was tried by the Chinese as a war criminal, receiving a pardon in 1959.

Hubbard, Elbert (1856–1915), American author and publisher, born in Bloomington, Ill. Inspired by the arts and crafts movement in England, Hubbard established the Roycroft Press at East Aurora, N.Y. in 1895 for issuing special editions of books. He and his associates also organized a handicraft group that made furniture and furnishings. Hubbard's essays and series of *Little Journeys* were widely read. His best-known work is the short story *A Message to Garcia* (1899). He was drowned in the sinking of the *Lusitania.*

Hudson, Henry (died 1611), English explorer, discoverer of the North American river, strait, and bay that bear his name. After making two voyages to Greenland, he was commissioned by the Dutch East India Company to find a northerly route to the Orient. Sailing from Amsterdam in 1609, he established the Dutch claim to what is now New York. In 1610 he sailed again to the New World, this time under English auspices, and through the strait now called Hudson entered the bay now named for him, claiming this territory for England. In 1611 Hudson and his son were cast adrift in an open boat by a mutinous crew, and disappeared without a trace.

Hudson, William Henry (1841–1922), British author, born in Argentina of American parents. He went to England in 1880 and became a naturalized subject ten years later. Hudson's best-known novel is *Green Mansions* (1904), a fantasy, laid in South America, that received great praise for its beautiful style and poetic prose. Hudson was also a naturalist of note, who wrote a number of delightful books on birds, small animals, and other outdoor subjects.

Hughes, Charles Evans (1862–1948), American jurist, born in Glens Falls, N.Y., and a graduate of Columbia Law School in 1884. He practiced and taught law until 1906, when his work as investigator of life-insurance companies brought him wide notice and the Republican nomination for governor of New York. Elected in 1907, he was reelected for a second term, but resigned in 1910 to become associate justice of the U.S. Supreme Court. In 1916, he was the Republican candidate for the presidency, but lost a close contest to Woodrow Wilson and returned to his law practice. In 1921 he became secretary of state in Pres. Warren G. Harding's cabinet and retained this post under Pres. Calvin Coolidge until 1925. Appointed chief justice of the Supreme Court by Pres. Herbert Hoover, he served from 1930 to 1940.

Hughes, Langston, in full **James Langston Hughes** (1902–1967), American Negro writer, born in Joplin, Mo.; educated at Columbia and Lincoln universities. Vachel Lindsay discovered his poetry in 1925. His first volume of poetry was *The Weary Blues,* (1926). Later collections of poetry include *Shakespeare in Harlem* (1942), *One Way Ticket* (1949), and *Selected Poems* (1959). His poems often contain dialect and jazz rhythms, and some have been set to music. He died May 22, 1967 in New York City.

Hugo, Victor Marie (1802–1885), French author, son of a general who fought under Napoleon. After publishing several novels as a youth, Hugo was recognized as the herald of Romantic drama with the appearance of his *Cromwell* in 1827. *Hernani* (1830) confirmed his position as a leader of the new school. During the next few years he wrote several more plays, notably *Le roi s'amuse* (*The King Amuses Himself* 1832), the basis of the opera *Rigoltto,* *Lucrèce Borgia* (1833), and *Ruy Blas* (1838).

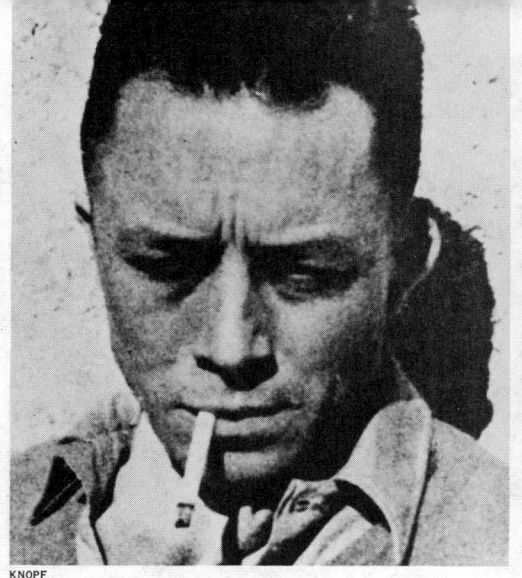

KNOPF

ALBERT CAMUS

CHARLE'S SCRIBNER'S SONS

JOHN GALSWORTHY

WIDE WORLD

T. S. ELIOT

MARK GERSON

LAWRENCE DURRELL

KNOPF

MIKHAIL SHOLOKHOV

RIE NISSEN

ISAK DINESEN

From the portrait by Sir Joshua Reynolds

Dr. Samuel Johnson (1709-84)

Samuel Johnson, the 18th-century poet, critic, oracle and wit, was the author of *A Dictionary of the English Language* published in two folio volumes in 1755. It was the first complete dictionary of the English language. As was the custom of the time, Johnson addressed his work to a wealthy nobleman, the earl of Chesterfield, who, contrary to the generous behavior of other patrons of literary men, rewarded this homage with hardly more than kind words. Although Johnson lacked a scholar's knowledge of derivations, his definitions were clear, precise and humorous, and he was the first to illustrate the meanings of words by use of literary quotations

From an engraving

Denis Diderot (1713-84)

The monumental French *Encyclopédie* issued in 28 volumes from 1751-80 is not a dictionary, but in any list of makers of great reference works, Diderot's name assuredly has a place. The *Encyclopédie* had an extraordinary influence on his time. It was a practical work treating science, industry and agriculture in the factual style of modern scholarship. The reactionary governing class was angered that his treatment of philosophic and religious subjects did not follow the conventional manner of the time, and the *Encyclopédie* was formally suppressed, but this did not halt Diderot from completing his enormous task alone, working in secret after his colleagues deserted.

From the portrait by S. F. B. Morse

Noah Webster (1758-1843)

In the years following the setting of the new republic, the books that Americans read and studied were almost all imported from England. Webster saw America's need for books and especially for a dictionary for Americans. His brief *Compendious Dictionary of the English Language* (1806) was preparation for his great work, *The American Dictionary of the English Language* (1828). He had spent the intervening years in study of English and foreign languages. Webster introduced encyclopaedic features into his dictionary, established the practice of recording nonliterary words and defined words of purely American origin that he considered worthy

Courtesy Oxford University Press

Sir James A. H. Murray (1837-1915)

In modern times scientific organization is applied to scholarship when the work of many minds is co-ordinated to produce a dictionary. Several hundred eminent scholars selected and transcribed the 1,827,306 illustrative quotations for use of words that resulted in *The New English Dictionary on Historical Principles*. This great work in 13 volumes published 1884-1928 is often called the *Oxford English Dictionary* because it was produced in close association with the scholars and resources of the English university. Sir James A. H. Murray was the guiding genius of this largest and most complete of English dictionaries, although he died before the work was finished

Hugo was elected to the French Academy in 1841 and made a peer in 1845. When Louis Napoleon (Napoleon III) became head of the republic, Hugo supported the new regime and was a member of the Constituent Assembly. When Napoleon overturned the republic in 1851, Hugo sought to organize a resistance and was forced into exile. He remained away from France until the beginning of the Franco-Prussian War, when he returned to become a member of the National Assembly.

Hugo's output was enormous. Probably the best known of his many works are the Romantic novels *Nôtre Dame de Paris* (1831) and *Les miserables* (1832). But in France he is chiefly remembered as a poet, with the volume *Les contemplations* (1856) containing his purest verse.

Huizinga, Johan (1872–1945), Dutch historian best known for his works on the history and culture of medieval and Renaissance Europe. In his most famous book, *The Waning of the Middle Ages*, written in 1919 and translated into English in 1924, he theorized that the Renaissance marked the death of the Middle Ages rather than the beginning of the modern world. Among his other works is a biography of Erasmus, published in 1924.

Hull, Cordell (1871–1955), American statesman and secretary of state in Pres. Franklin D. Roosevelt's cabinet (1933–1944). Born in Carthage, Tenn., and educated at Cumberland University, he was elected to the Tennessee legislature in 1893. After service in Cuba during the Spanish-American War, he was elected a circuit judge. In 1907 he was elected to Congress and, except for one two-year period, served continuously until 1931, when he was elected to the Senate. During his term as secretary of state, he negotiated many reciprocal trade agreements, particularly with the Latin American countries. In 1945 Hull was awarded the Nobel Peace Prize, and in 1948 he published his memoirs.

Hull, Isaac (1773–1843), American naval officer born in Shelton, Conn. After serving in the merchant marine, he was commissioned a lieutenant in the navy in 1798. Hull commanded the brig *Argus* in the war with Tripoli (1803–1804). He became a national hero by winning the first American naval victory in the War of 1812. In August of that year, as commander of the *Constitution* ("Old Ironsides"), Hull forced the surrender of the British frigate *Guerrière*. He continued in the naval service after the war and attained the rank of commodore.

Humbert I, in Italian **Umberto** (1844–1900), king of Italy (1878–1900). He succeeded his father, Victor Emmanuel II. His reign was marred by financial depression, the discontent of an overtaxed people, and a rising tide of republicanism. He was assassinated in 1900 by an anarchist, Pietro Acciarito.

Humboldt, Baron Alexander von (1769–1859), German naturalist, famed for his travels in the Americas. His first important work (1790) was based on geological investigations in Germany. In 1799 he went to Central and South America with Aimé Bonpland, a French botanist, on a five-year journey that included visits to the United States. Humboldt began publishing the results of their investigations in 1805, completing the 23d and final volume in 1834. The masterpiece of his later career was the five-volume *Kosmos*, a description of the physical universe.

Humboldt, Baron Karl Wilhelm von (1767–1835), German philologist and statesman. He represented Prussia at Rome and Vienna while in the diplomatic service, and had an important part in drawing up the treaties that grew out of the Napoleonic Wars. While serving as minister of education (1808–1810), he founded the University of Berlin. He pioneered in studies of Basque and other languages, making notable contributions to the science of philology.

Hume, David (1711–1776), Scottish philosopher and historian, the foremost exponent of empiricism who profoundly influenced later philosophical thought. Born at Edinburgh where he was trained for the law, he left Scotland in 1734 to reside in France and devote himself to philosophical writings. During his stay abroad he completed his most renowned philosophical work, *A Treatise of Human Nature* (1739). He then turned to subjects of political interest and wrote *Essays, Moral and Political* (1741–1742). In 1746 he accepted the post of judge advocate to Gen. James Sinclair, and two years later had his *Inquiry Concerning Human Understanding* published. In 1752 he was keeper of the Advocates' Library in Edinburgh, and in 1763 was again abroad, attached to the British embassy in

France; on his return he was undersecretary of state (1767–1769).

A skeptical philosopher, Hume stressed the limitation of human knowledge to empirical experience—ideas and sensation—and denied the possibility of obtaining ultimate truths, the reason being that the human mind is always bound to the world of experience. In keeping with his empiricism, Hume also negates causation, or the existence of a logical link between cause and effect. Other works are *Political Discourses* (1752), *Four Dissertations* (1757), *The History of England* (1754–1761), and *Dialogues Concerning Natural Religion* (1779).

Humperdinck, Engelbert (1854–1921), German composer, born at Siegburg, near Bonn, educated in Cologne. His education in music profited by an early association with Richard Wagner, who had the young composer assist him in preparing *Parsifal* for its first presentation at Bayreuth in 1882. Besides a number of operas, Humperdinck wrote ballads, chorale music, and incidental music for Shakespearian plays. He was at his best when composing for folk tales and fairy stories, and his best-known work is the opera *Hänsel und Gretel* (1893). Another popular work of his is *Die Königskinder (The Royal Children)*, produced at the Metropolitan Opera House, New York, in 1910.

Humphrey, Hubert Horatio, Jr. (1911–), thirty-eighth vice-pres. of the United States, born in Wallace, S. Dak. At first a student of pharmacy at the Denver College of Pharmacy he switched to political science, receiving his A.B. degree at the University of Minnesota (1939) and his M.A. from Louisiana State University (1940). His first public service position was with the Works Progress Administration (W.P.A.) in Minnesota in 1941. Humphrey, the Minnesota campaign manager of the Roosevelt-Truman Committee in 1944, was elected mayor of Minneapolis in 1945, a post he held until 1948, when he conducted a successful campaign for United States senator. As a member of the Democratic party, he was active in fusing the Democratic and Farmer-Labor parties. As one of the foremost liberal senators, he proposed medical care for the aged; his Medicare bill was passed in 1965 while he was vice-president. While assistant majority leader in 1961, he effectively won congressional ratification of the nuclear test-ban treaty of 1963 and the 1964 Civil Rights Act. In 1964, after two unsuccessful attempts to receive the vice-presidential nomination in 1956 and 1960, he was chosen the vice-presidential candidate to run with Lyndon B. Johnson.

Hunt, Leigh in full **James Henry Leigh Hunt** (1784–1859), English critic and poet. With his brother he edited *The Examiner* (1808), a liberal literary and political newspaper in which Keats and Shelley were first published. From 1813–1815 the Hunts were imprisoned for libeling the prince regent. In his journal *The Indicator* (1819–1821) he continued to introduce the Romantic poets to the public. Hunt was a close friend of Shelley, Keats, and Byron. After Keats' death, the Hunts went to Italy to edit Byron's *The Liberal* (1822–1823). The association with Byron was not a happy one, and in 1825 Hunt returned to England. His house at Hampstead attracted all the literary personages of the time. Among his works are *The Story of Rimini* (1816), the verse collection *Foliage* (1818), *Imagination and Fancy* (1844), and the prose work *The Town* (1848).

Hunt, Richard Morris (1827–1895), American architect, born in Brattleboro, Vt., the brother of William Morris Hunt. At 15 he began the study of architecture in Geneva, and received a diploma from the École des Beaux Arts in France. After a period of travel he helped a former teacher, Lefuel, in the construction of the new Louvre in Paris. He returned to the U.S. in 1855, drew plans for enlarging the Capitol in Washington, and then founded in New York the first American architectural training studio. Among the buildings Hunt designed are the Lenox Library, N.Y., the main section of the Metropolitan Museum of Art, N.Y., the naval observatory in Washington, and the pedestal of the Statue of Liberty.

Hunt, William Morris (1824–1879), American painter, born in Brattleboro, Vt., brother of Richard Morris Hunt. While studying in Paris he was influenced by the Barbizon school, particularly by Jean François Millet. In 1855 he established himself in Boston as a teacher and painter, and introduced French ideals and methods to American painters. Hunt was at his best

as a landscape artist, but he also painted many excellent figure subjects and portraits. Among his works are *Peasant Girl at Barbizon* and *Hurdy-Gurdy Boy* (Boston Museum), *The Bathers* (Metropolitan Museum, N.Y.), portrait of Chief Justice Shaw (Salem, Mass.), *Gloucester Harbor* and *Falls of Niagara*, and the mural decorations in the capitol at Albany, N.Y.

Hunter, John (1728–1793), English physiologist and surgeon, born in Glasgow. He began the study of anatomy in 1748 and became house surgeon at St. George's Hospital, London (1756). In 1762 he served as staff surgeon with the English army in Portugal, resuming practice in London in 1763 and becoming surgeon at St. George's in 1768. He was appointed surgeon extraordinary to George III in 1776 and deputy surgeon general to the army in 1786. His years of experimentation and study, including the dissection of more than 500 different animal species, yielded valuable scientific results. Hunter was accounted the best operating surgeon of his time, the most competent anatomist, and an unsurpassed zoologist. His collection of over 10,000 specimens was given to the Royal College of Surgeons (it was destroyed in World War II).

Hunyadi or **Hunyady, János,** in English **John Huniades** (c.1387–1456), Hungarian soldier and statesman, leader against the Turks. He fought in the army of King Sigismund from 1410; under his successor, Albert II, he was made head of Szöreny (1438), a district exposed to attack by the Turks. Turkish forces invaded the country during a period of civi war, but they were defeated by Hunyadi and forced to accept peace terms in 1443. In a renewal of the war, Hunyadi was defeated at Kosovo (1448), but he maintained Hungarian independence a few years later through his victory at Belgrade, which Mohammed II besieged in 1456. The defeated Turks lost 80,000 men and were compelled to raise the siege. Shortly thereafter Hunyadi died of plague. Hunyadi is a national hero of Hungary.

Huss, John or **Jan Hus,** (c.1369–1415), Bohemian religious reformer, born in Husinetz, Bohemia, of Czech parents. He took his name from his birthplace. Huss was educated at the University of Prague, where he was successively lecturer, dean of philosophy, and rector. In 1401 he was ordained a priest and became interested in the doctrines of the English theologian Wycliffe. His preaching of Wycliffe's doctrines aroused the anger of the authorities, and he and his followers were excommunicated in 1410. However, Huss, who had the support of King Wenceslaus IV, continued to write and speak against ecclesiastical abuses. In 1414 he was summoned to appear before the grand council in Constance. Within a month of his arrival he was arrested on orders from the antipope, John XXIII. In 1415 he was tried, convicted of heresy, and burned at the stake. His martyrdom brought on a political and religious revolution in Bohemia, and led to the Husserite War (1419–1434). He wrote religious works, including *De Ecclesia* (1413).

Hutchinson, Anne (1591–1643), American religious leader in the colonial period. Born in Lincolnshire, England, she married William Hutchinson in 1612 and emigrated with her family in 1634, settling in Boston. When she advocated religious beliefs that ran counter to the stern New England Calvinism and preached salvation by grace instead of by works, she was tried and convicted for heresy by the General Court of the Massachusetts Bay Colony (1637). The following year she was banished from the colony. First she took her followers to Rhode Island, but after her husband's death in 1642 she moved to Dutch territory just north of what is now New York City. In 1643 she and all but one member of her family were killed by the Indians.

Hutchinson, Thomas (1711–1780), American colonial administrator, born in Boston, educated at Harvard College (1727). He rose to prominence in the colony and was elected to the Massachusetts legislature (1737–1749), serving as speaker of the house for the last two terms. While serving as chief justice in 1761, he became unpopular by issuing writs of assistance, or search warrants, which inspired Otis' famous oration against the tyranny of taxation without representation. Later he attempted to enforce the Stamp Act, although he did not personally approve of it, and as a result his house was sacked and burned by a mob (1765). Hutchinson became acting governor in 1769 and governor in 1771. His unpopularity increased, and in 1774 he was replaced by Gen. Gage. He then sailed for England, where he died.

RALPH STEINER
ALDOUS HUXLEY

Huxley, Aldous Leonard (1894–1963), English novelist, essayist, and critic, the grandson of Thomas Henry Huxley. He was educated at Eton and Balliol College, Oxford. Because of defective vision, he abandoned his study of medicine. In 1919 he joined the staff of the London *Athenaeum*, and was drama critic for the *Westminster Gazette*. His first published work, *Limbo* (1920), a collection of poems, was followed by the novels *Chrome Yellow* (1921) and *Antic Hay* (1923). His two most noted works are *Point Counter Point* (1928), a study of modern literary and artistic society, and *Brave New World* (1932), which depicts a mechanized, dehumanized "utopia." Other works of this period are *Eyeless in Gaza* (1936) and *After Many A Summer Dies the Swan* (1939). Huxley settled in California in 1939, and his interests were taken up with history and mysticism. *The Perennial Philosophy*, an anthology of mysticism, appeared in 1945, and *The Doors of Perception*, describing the effects of mescalin, appeared in 1954. Other works include numerous essays and several biographies. He had a broad range of interests and employed a great variety of literary forms.

Huxley, Sir Julian Sorell (1887–), English biologist and writer, grandson of T. H. Huxley, and older brother of Aldous. He was educated at Eton and Balliol College, Oxford, and then served as research associate (1912–1913) and assistant professor (1913–1916) at Rice Institute, Houston, Tex. After serving in World War I, he taught zoology at New College, Oxford (1919–1928) and at King's College, London (1926–1927). In 1935 he was appointed secretary of the Zoological Society of London, resigning in 1942. From 1946 to 1948 Huxley served as the first director general of UNESCO. His voluminous writings include *What Dare I Think?* (1931), *Scientific Research and Social Needs* (1934), *The Living Thoughts of Darwin* (1939), *Evolution: The Modern Synthesis* (1942), *Heredity, East and West* (1949), *Religion Without Revelation* (1957), *Biological Aspects of Cancer* (1957), *Essays of a Humanist* (1963), and *The Human Crisis* (1964).

Huxley, Thomas Henry (1825–1895), English biologist and educator, early advocate of Darwin's theory of evolution. In 1842 he began studying at Charing Cross Hospital, and received his medical degree from the University of London in 1845. As assistant surgeon on the H.M.S. *Rattlesnake* (1846–1850), during a four-year survey of the Great Barrier Reef region of Australia, he collected and studied many forms of marine life, classifying them with his own system. While abroad Huxley sent various scientific papers to London to be published in the *Philosophical Transactions* of the Royal Society (1849). He was elected fellow of that organization in 1851. In 1854 he was appointed professor of natural history at the Royal School of Mines, where he taught for 31 years. He also held numerous other academic posts. When Darwin published his *Origin of Species* in 1859, Huxley immediately became his most avid supporter, engaging in debates with the clergy (notably Bishop Samuel Wilberforce), deans, and even Prime Minister

Gladstone. His essays *Man's Place in Nature* appeared in 1863. Huxley was accorded many honors during his life, and in 1881 he was elected president of the Royal Society, retiring in 1885 due to poor health. Among his works are *Science and Culture* (1881), *On the Causes of the Phenomena of Organic Nature* (1863), *Manual of the Comparative Anatomy of Vertebrate Animals* (1871), *Science and Culture* (1881), and *Evolution and Ethics* (1893).

Huygens or **Huyghens, Christian** (1629–1695), Dutch mathematician, astronomer, and physical scientist, born in The Hague and educated at Leiden and Breda. In 1663 he was invited to become a member of the Royal Society of London. In 1666 he went to Paris at the invitation of Louis XIV's minister Colbert and joined the new French Academy of Sciences, returning in 1681 to Holland. Huygens is famed as the originator of the wave theory of light, by which he was able to explain both refraction and reflection. He also discovered polarization of light, and made preliminary studies in the physics of moving bodies that were of great value to Newton. In 1665 he and his brother found a more accurate method of grinding and polishing lenses. With these lenses he discovered the ring and fourth satellite of Saturn (1665). In 1666 he perfected the first pendulum clock. His complete works (10 volumes) were published by the Holland Academy of Sciences.

Huysmans, the name of three seventeenth-century Flemish painters, all born in Antwerp. **Jacob** (1633–1696) went to London and became a fashionable portrait painter. His portraits of Queen Catherine of Braganza and of Izaak Walton now hang in the National Gallery, London. **Cornelis** (1648–1727) is best known for his brilliantly colored landscapes, although he painted many religious and historical subjects as well. His *Woodland With Chateau* is in the National Gallery. **Jan Baptist** (1654–1716), the brother of Cornelis, painted landscapes and figures.

Huysmans, Joris Karl, originally **Charles Marie Georges Huysmans** (1848–1907), French novelist, privately educated in Paris. In 1866 he became a clerk in the ministry of the interior, working there until his retirement in 1898. While working there he published his most famous novels. His first works, *Marthe* (1876), *Les sœurs vatard* (1879), and *En ménage* (1881), are naturalistic and reflect the influence of Flaubert and Zola. However, in 1884, with the publication of *À rebours*, (*Against the Grain*, 1922), a novel called "the breviary of the Decadents," Huysmans revealed his individual style and genius. Formally breaking with Zola, he went on to publish *En rade* (1887), a novel combining elements of naturalism and surrealism, and *Là-bas* (1891), a reflection of his interest in the supernatural. After he returned to the Roman Catholic Church, he published *En route* (1895), *La cathédrale* (1898), and *L'Oblat* (1903), on religious themes.

Hyde, Douglas known as **An Craoibhin Aoibhinn,** "the fair branch" (1860–1949), Irish scholar, statesman, and first president of Ireland under the 1937 constitution. The son of a Protestant minister, he was educated at Trinity College, Dublin, where he devoted himself to language and literature. He became associated with the Irish Nationalist movement from its inception. In 1893 he helped organize the Gaelic League, and served as its first president from that year until 1915. From 1909–1932 he was professor of modern Irish at the National University of Ireland. In 1925 and 1938 he served as a senator in the Irish parliament, and in 1938 he was chosen president of Ireland by the agreement of De Valera's party and the opposition led by W. T. Cosgrave. Among his works which include essays, histories, verse, and plays, are *Love Songs of Connacht* (1894), *Story of Early Irish Literature* (1897), and *A Literary History of Ireland* (1899).

Hyksos, dynasty of Egyptian kings who conquered Egypt in about 1700 B.C. and ruled c.1650–1580 B.C. The name "Hyksos" means either "foreign kings" or "shepherd kings." Under their leader, Salatis, the Hyksos came from the East and captured the city Memphis. They then subdued all of Egypt, setting up the fortress Avaris, on the border of the Nile delta, as their capital.

Hypatia (d.415), Greek philosopher of the Neoplatonic school. A teacher in Alexandria, she became the principal member of the Neoplatonists' school there. Her pagan beliefs and supposed opposition to the clergy incurred the hatred of Cyril, the archbishop of Alexandria, who incited a mob to murder her. Hypatia is the heroine of Kingsley's romantic novel *Hypatia* (1853).

I

Ibáñez, Vincente Blasco. See *Blasco-Ibáñez.*

Ibert, Jacques François Antoine (1890–1962), French composer, born in Paris. He studied under Gabriel Fauré at the Paris Conservatoire and won the Prix de Rome in 1919. Ibert is best known for his orchestral compositions, notably *Escales* (1922), *Ouverture de fête* (1942), and *Louisville Concerto* (1954). He also composed several popular ballets, including *Ballade de la geôle de Reading* (1920) and *Diane de Poitiers* (1934), and a number of operas, chamber works, and cantatas. Ibert was director of the French Academy in Rome (1937–1961).

Iberville, Pierre Lemoyne, Sieur d' (1661–1706), French-Canadian naval officer, founder of Louisiana province. Born in Montreal, he joined the navy and distinguished himself in several battles against the English, notably in Hudson Bay. In 1698 he founded a French colony at the mouth of the Mississippi and built a fort near the present site of Biloxi, Miss. The colonists suffered terrible sickness, and he moved most of them to Mobile (1702), which then became the center of the French foothold in Louisiana. In 1706 Iberville commanded an expedition to the West Indies that captured the English-held islands of Nevis and St. Christopher.

Ibn Ezra, in full **Abraham ben Meir ibn Ezra** (1092–1167), Jewish philosopher, poet, and astronomer, born in Toledo, Spain. One of the most distinguished scholars of medieval Spain, he traveled widely and wrote in Hebrew on a broad spectrum of subjects, including Biblical interpretation, astronomy, mathematics, philosophy, and grammar. He was the subject of Robert Browning's famous poem *Rabbi Ben Ezra.*

Ibn-Saud, Abdul-Aziz (1880–1953), king of Saudi Arabia (1932–1953), born in Riyadh, Nejd, and raised in Kuwait while his family was in exile. He succeeded his father as ruler of Nejd in 1901 and gradually extended his domain by the conquest of Hai and Hejaz. In 1927, with British recognition, he assumed the title of king of the Hejaz and Nejd. The kingdom and its dependencies became known as Saudi Arabia in 1932. By royalties from oil concessions granted to United States companies in 1936 and 1939, the national treasury was considerably enriched. Ibn-Saud maintained Saudi Arabian neutrality in World War II but remained friendly with the Allies.

Ibsen, Henrik (1828–1906). Norwegian playwright, born in Skien. He was an apothecary's assistant at Grimstad (1844–1850), and at the age of 22 went to Oslo to study. His first play, *Catilina* (1850), was a failure. After several other dramatic efforts while working as a journalist, he became director of the National Theater in Oslo (1857). His next plays, *The Warriors in Helgeland* (1858), *Love's Comedy* (1862), and *The Pretenders* (1864), placed him in the foremost rank of Scandinavian dramatists. When the National Theater went bankrupt (1862), Ibsen left Norway and lived for several years in Rome, Dresden, and Munich. Aided by a pension from the Norwegian government, he wrote the plays *Brand* (1866) and *Peer Gynt* (1867). Ibsen's greatest fame, however, rests on the powerful socio-psychological dramas that attacked

NORWEGIAN INFORMATION SERVICE
HENRIK IBSEN

the hypocrisy of contemporary European society. The greatest of his plays include *The Pillars of Society* (1877), *A Doll's House* (1879), *Ghosts* (1881), *An Enemy of the People* (1882), *The Wild Duck* (1884), *Rosmersholm* (1886), *The Lady From the Sea* (1888), *Hedda Gabler* (1890), *The Master Builder* (1892), *Littler Eyolf* (1894), *John Gabriel Borkman* (1896), and *When We Dead Awaken* (1899). In these plays Ibsen proved himself a master of dramatic development, symbolism, and stagecraft. Two particular themes recur throughout his work: the ultimate value of the individual, and the conviction that the denial of love constitutes the only true tragedy. Among the many writers who were profoundly influenced by Ibsen were Anton Chekhov, George Bernard Shaw, and James Joyce.

Ictinus (5th century B.C.), Greek architect during the age of Pericles. He designed the crowning achievement of Greek architecture, the Parthenon (447–432 B.C.), in association with Callicrates; Phidias supervised the sculpture. His other works include the shrine of Demeter and Persephone at Eleusis and the temple of Apollo Epicurius at Bassae (c.430–B.C.).

Ignatius, Saint, surnamed **Theophorus** (c.35–c.107), bishop of Antioch and one of the Apostolic Fathers. Little is known of his life. He is supposed to have been a disciple of the Apostle John and to have been martyred in Rome during the reign of Emperor Trajan. Tradition has it that on his way to martyrdom in the Roman Amphitheater he wrote seven important epistles to churches in Rome and Asia Minor. Known as the *Ignatian Epistles,* these letters stress the importance of the virgin birth and are an indictment of Docetism, the heresy that Christ did not have a mortal form. In these and other matters, the letters provide a valuable insight into the early Christian church.

Ignatius of Loyola, Saint. See *Loyola.*

Ikhnaton, also known as **Amenhotep IV,** Egyptian pharaoh (c.1375–1358 B.C.) of the 18th dynasty. A religious philosopher, he replaced polytheism with a kind of monotheism that established the sun, Aton, as the god to which all living matter owed its existence. He created a new capital, Akhetaton, in honor of Aton and developed an impressive program of artistic and architectural works. In his fanaticism, Ikhnaton caused the desecration of monuments to Amon, the previously dominent god, which outraged the priestly class and many common people and turned them against him. A decline in Egypt's political and territorial power added to his unpopularity, and the cult of Aton died with him.

Indy, Vincent d' (1851–1931), French composer, born in Paris. He was a student of César Franck, whom he succeeded (1890) as president of the Société Nationale de Musique. He was a founder of the Schola Cantorum in Paris (1894), of which he was director from 1911 until his death. D'Indy is best known for his highly romantic *Symphonie cévenole* (1886) for piano and orchestra, and the symphonic variations *Istar* (1896). With August Sérieyx, he published *Cours de composition musical* (3 vols., 1897–1903), and himself wrote biographies of Franck (1906), Beethoven (1911), and Wagner (1930).

Inge, William Motter (1913–   ), American playwright, noted for his four Broadway hits of the 1950's. He was born in Independence, Kans., and studied drama at the University of Kansas. He was a drama critic for the St. Louis *Star-Times* (1943–1946) and then taught English at the University of Washington at St. Louis (1946–1949). Inge's first play, *Farther Off From Heaven* (1947), was followed by *Come Back Little Sheba* (1950), *Picnic* (1953), *Bus Stop* (1955), and *The Dark at the Top of the Stairs* (1957). He won the Pulitzer Prize and the New York Drama Critics' Award for *Picnic* and an Academy Award for the screenplay *Splendour in the Grass* (1961).

Inge, William Ralph (1860–1954), English clergyman and author, born in Crayke, Yorkshire, and educated at Eton and Cambridge. He became vicar of All Saints' Church, London (1905), and was professor of divinity at Cambridge (1907–1911). He is best remembered as the dean of St. Paul's Cathedral, London (1911–1934). For his pointed and pessimistic criticism of contemporary life in his speeches and writings, he was called "the gloomy dean." Among his many works are *Outspoken Essays* (1919, 1922), *Lay Thoughts of a Dean* (1926), and *Our Present Discontents* (1938).

Ingersoll, Robert Green (1833–1899), American lawyer, orator, and writer, born in Dresden, N.Y. He practiced law in Illinois, was a colonel in the Union army during the Civil War, and served as attorney general of Illinois (1867–1869). Active in Republican party affairs, he was widely acclaimed for his eloquent speech nominating James G. Blaine, the "Plumed Knight," at the party's presidential convention in 1876. However, his attacks on Christianity, and religion in general, caused him to lose political favor. Among his writings are *Some Mistakes of Moses* (1879), *Why I Am An Agnostic* (1896), and *Superstition* (1898).

Ingres, Jean Auguste Dominique (1780–1867), French painter, leader of the Classical school. Born in Montauban, he studied with Jacques L. David in Paris and in 1801 won the Prix de Rome, which he accepted five years later. After 14 years in Rome and four in Florence, he returned to Paris in 1824. He was appointed a professor at the French Academy (1826) and became the acknowledged head of the Classical school. In 1834 he was made director of the French Academy in Rome. He returned to Paris in 1841 and lived there until his death. A draftsman of exceptional skill, Ingres held that "a thing well drawn is well enough painted." His paintings were tightly structured, classically linear, and often concerned with abstract form although some of his later works have significant Romantic qualities. Among Ingres' finest and most important works are *Le Grande Odalisque*, *The Spring*, *The Bather of Valpinçon*, *The Turkish Bath* and the portraits of M. Bertin, Mlle. Rivière, and La Comtesse d'Haussonville (Frick Collection, New York City). Ingres' influence was not restricted to the Academic school. Such distinguished figures as Degas, Renoir, Matisse, and Picasso have acknowledged their debt to him.

Inman, Henry (1801–1846), American painter, born in Utica, N.Y. He studied under the portrait painter John W. Jarvis. Among his well-known portraits are those of Chief Justice John Marshall, Martin Van Buren, John J. Audubon, William Wordsworth, and Thomas Macaulay. Of his landscapes, *Rydal Falls, England* is noteworthy. He was a founder of the National Academy of Design.

Inness, George (1825–1894), American landscape painter, born in Newburgh, N.Y. Essentially self-taught, he studied in Rome and Paris, and was considerably influenced by the French Barbizon painters. A leading member of the Hudson River school in the early part of his career, Inness subsequently turned from panoramic detail to a freer, more richly colored and more personal interpretation of nature. His works include *Autumn Oaks*, *Spring Blossoms*, *Delaware Valley* (Metropolitan Museum, New York), *Rainbow after a Storm*, and *Home of the Heron* (Chicago Art Institute). His son, **George Inness, Jr.** (1854–1926), was also a landscape artist.

Innocent III, born **Giovanni Lotario de Conti** (1161–1216), Roman Catholic pope, born in Anagni, Italy, and educated in Paris, Rome, and Bologna. In 1198 he succeeded Celestine III. He was responsible for the fourth crusade (1202–1204) and for the resulting capture of Constantinople. Innocent III later started another crusade, this time against the Albigenses (1208). It was his aim to continue the work of Gregory VII and establish the supremacy of church over state. Among his targets were Otto IV of Germany, whom he dethroned in 1215; Philip Augustus of France, upon whom he forced martial fidelity; King John of England, whom he excommunicated and in other ways humiliated; and England itself, which he made part of the Holy See. Under Innocent's orders, the historic fourth Lateran Council was convened in 1215, by which time the state was firmly in the power of the church. Among his voluminous writings is the treatise *Misery of the Condition of Man* and numerous letters and sermons.

Ionesco, Eugene (1912–   ), French playwright, born in Rumania. Heralding an entirely new form of drama, he wrote short, surrealistic plays utilizing material from his own dreams and proceeding on the Freudian premise that the turbulent world of dreams is common to all mankind. Characterized by paradoxes and bizarre twistings of reality, his highly controversial works include *The Bald Soprano* (1950), *The Chairs* (1952), *The Pictures* (1958), and *The Rhinoceros* (1960).

Irene (752–803), Byzantine empress who restored the use of ikons in the Eastern Church, born in Athens. Upon the death of her husband, Leo IV in 780, she became regent for their son Constantine VI and devoted herself to combatting the iconoclasts. She convoked the second Council of Nicea (787), which restored the worship of images. When Constantine became emperor in 790, she was forced to abdicate, but managed to have her title of empress confirmed in 792. For the next five years she plotted to regain power, and in 797 managed to have her son blinded and imprisoned. She ruled until 802, when the patricians turned against her in favor of Nicephorus, who had her exiled to the island of Lesbos.

Irving, Washington (1783–1859), American writer and diplomat, born in New York City. He studied law, and upon his return from a European tour (1804–1806) was admitted to the bar. During this time he had begun composing humorous sketches. With his brother William and James K. Paulding he published the satirical *Salmagundi* papers (1807–1808). In 1809, under the pseudonym Diedrich Knickerbocker, he wrote *A History of New York, From the Beginning of the World of the End of the Dutch Dynasty*, a burlesque chronicle that has sometimes been taken for an actual history. On a visit to England in 1815 he assumed control of the Liverpool line of his family's hardware business. After returning to New York, he published the ever-popular *Legend of Sleepy Hollow* and *Rip Van Winkle* (1819). Irving served as a staff member of the U.S. embassy in Madrid (1826–1829), as secretary of the U.S. legation in London (1829–1832), and as U.S. minister to Spain (1842–1846). His writings of this period included *A History of the Life and Voyages of Christopher Columbus* (1828), *A Chronicle of the Conquest of Granada* (1829), and *The Alhambra* (1832). In 1846 Irving returned to the U.S. and settled near Tarrytown, N.Y. Continuing his literary efforts, he produced such works as *Oliver Goldsmith* (1849), *Mahomet and His Successors* (2 vols., 1849–1850), and *Life of Washington* (5 vols., 1855–1859). Irving has often been called the father of the American short story and the first great American prose stylist.

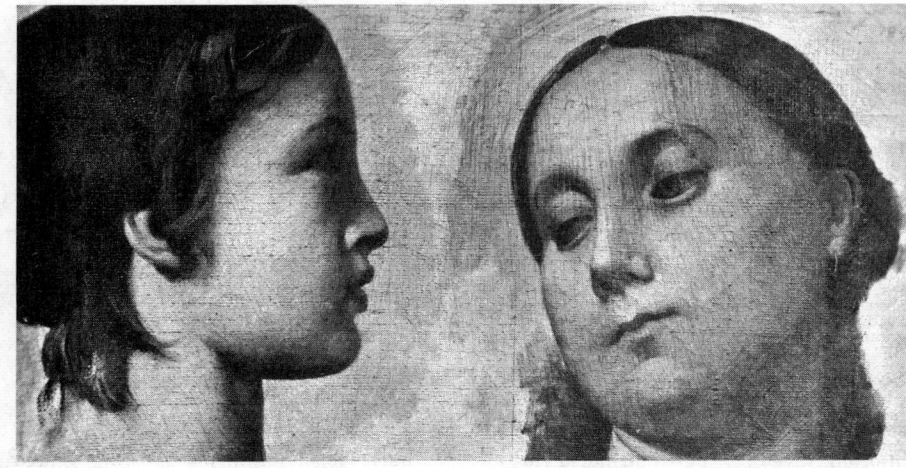

M. KNOEDLER

JEAN INGRES, the nineteenth-century French painter, did this study of his wife and son.

Isabella I, often called **Isabella the Catholic** (1451–1504), queen of Castile (1474–1504), daughter of John II. In 1469 she married Ferdinand of Aragon, with whom (1479) she began joint rule of Castile and Aragon—a reign of considerable contribution to Spain. She subsidized Columbus' voyage of discovery, encouraged church reform, and was a patron of education and the arts.

Isherwood, Christopher William Bradshaw (1904–), English novelist and playwright, born in Disley, Cheshire, and educated at Cambridge. Collaborating with W.H. Auden, he wrote the plays *The Dog Beneath the Skin* (1935), *Ascent of F. 6* (1936), *On the Frontier* (1938), and the travel study of China, *Journey to a War* (1939). His own most famous novels, *Mr. Norris Changes Trains* (1935) and *Goodby to Berlin* (1939), were the result of a four-year stay in Germany (1928–1932); they deal with the theme of tyranny, particularly the dilemma of the intellectual under dictatorship. Isherwood emigrated to the United States in 1939 and became a citizen in 1946. Fascinated with Hinduism, he became a yogi, and collaborated in various translations from the Sanskrit, including the *Bhagavad-Gita*. Among his later novels are *The World in the Evening* (1954) and *Down There on a Visit* (1962). He also wrote an autobiography, *Lions and Shadows* (1938).

Isidore of Seville, Latin name **Isodorus Hispalensis** (c.560–636), Spanish ecclesiastic and scholar, born in Seville or Cartagena. As archbishop of Seville (c.600) he had considerable influence in Church affairs. He was a leader in the second Council of Seville (619) and the fourth national Council of Toledo (633), from which the canons of Spanish constitutional law were derived. One of the leading scholars of his time, he worked to promote education and the founding of monasteries and schools. His *Originum seu etymologiarum libri XX* (c.622–633), a vast compendium of then-current knowledge, he has been regarded as the first universal encyclopedia.

Ismail Pasha or **Ismail I** (1830–1895), khedive of Egypt (1863–1879), born in Cairo, the son of Ibrahim Pasha. He succeeded his uncle, Said Pasha, as viceroy in 1863, and assumed the hereditary title of knedive in 1867. He encouraged the construction of the Suez Canal as well as of domestic roads, railways, and communication systems, and worked to increase Egyptian influence in the Sudan. Ismail's extravagance, however, led to severe financial difficulties and forced him to sell controlling interests in the canal to England and France. In 1879 he was deposed by the sultan of Turkey.

Isocrates (436–338 B.C.), Greek writer and teacher, born in Athens, a student of Socrates and the Sophists. Although he is often called an orator, Isocrates was not a particularly effective public speaker; instead, he wrote speeches and trained the budding orators of his day, notably Ephorus, Isaeus, and Lycurgus. Through these pupils his style strongly influenced the development of Greek prose. His great ambition was to unite all the Greeks against the Persians; to this end he wrote the famous *Panegyricus*, the most celebrated of his speeches. He is supposed to have committed suicide after the conquest of Greece by Philip of Macedon.

Ito, Marquis **Hirobumi** (1841–1909, Japanese statesman, born in Choshu province. From visits to the United States, England, and Europe, he became convinced of the value of Western civilization for the advancement of Japan. It was largely through his efforts that a uniform coinage system, extensive economic reforms, and a new constitution (1888–1889) were introduced. As prime minister (1885–1901), he led Japan to victories in wars with China and Russia. Ito later served as special adviser to Emperor Meiji, and planned the treaty by which Korea was made a virtual Japanese protectorate. He was assassinated in 1909 by a Korean while on a visit to Manchuria.

BETTMANN ARCHIVE

QUEEN ISABELLA

Iturbide, Agustín Cosme Damian de (1783–1824), Mexican revolutionist, born in Valladolid. In 1820 he joined the royalists and led an army against Vincente Guerrero. He negotiated the Plan of Iguala (1821). When the plan failed, Iturbide succeeded with the aid of the new Spanish viceroy to institute the Treaty of Córdoba (1821), establishing Mexican independence. In 1822 Iturbide was proclaimed Emperor Agustín I. Revolutions broke out and, under pressure by Antonio Santa Anna, he abdicated (1823) and went into permanent exile. When he returned to Mexico the next year, he was arrested and shot as an outlaw.

Ivan III Vasilievich, known as **Ivan the Great** (1440–1505), grand duke of Moscow (1462–1505), son of Basil II. Upon becoming grand duke, Ivan III commenced a campaign of conquest by which he annexed Novgorod (1478), drove out the Tartar "Golden Horde" (1480), and brought most of Russia under the rule of Moscow. In 1492 Ivan married Sophia, niece of the Byzantine emperor: the double eagle was added to the Russian arms, Byzantine customs were introduced, and Moscow came to be considered the "third Rome," the protector of Orthodox Christianity. Known for his wisdom and caution, Ivan III reformed the courts, codified the laws, encouraged art, and sponsored widespread architectural construction and renovation.

Ivan IV Vasilievch, known as **Ivan the Terrible** (1530–1584), Russian ruler (1533–1584), first to hold the formal title of czar (1547). He was the son of Basil III and the grandson of Ivan III. During his youth he had been horrified by the cruelties inflicted upon the common people by the boyars (nobles) and when he came into power he suppressed the aristocrats and initiated local self-government. In 1552 he began Russia's eastward expansion with the conquest of Kazan and Astrakhan; later in his rule Siberia fell under his control. The death of his first wife, Anastasia Romanovna (1560), marked a turning point in Ivan's character. He began to suspect treason, and seeing shadows of conspiracy everywhere, initiated a reign of terror, directed particularly at the boyars. Ivan ravaged Novgorod (1570) and killed his own son (1580); for these and other cruelties he earned the nickname "the Terrible." He did, however, destroy boyar rule and establish an unquestioned czarist aristocracy. He was succeeded by Boris Godunov.

Ives, Burl (1909–), American singer and actor, born in Hunt, Ill., and educated at Eastern Illinois State Teachers College and New York University. After a varied career, he became a highly popular folk singer. He then turned to the stage and screen and scored critical acclaim for his roles in *Cat on a Hot Tin Roof, Sierra, East of Eden, The Power and the Prize,* and *The Big Country,* for which he received an Academy Award. His publications include *Wayfaring Stranger* (1948), *Burl Ives Song Book* (1953), and *Song in America* (1961).

Ives, Charles Edward (1874–1954), American composer, born in Danbury, Conn., and educated at Yale. He supported himself by working as an insurance agent. He first became known as a composer in 1939 with the first performance of his piano sonata, *Concord*, an interpretation of American Transcendentalist thought of Emerson and Thoreau, who lived in Concord, Mass. Ives was awarded the Pulitzer Prize in 1947 for his *Third Symphony*. A prolific composer, his works include numerous organ, choral, and symphonic compositions. Often incorporating Negro folk music and utilizing unusual polytonality, many of Ives' compositions antedated the trend toward the abstract style introduced by Arnold Schönberg and Igor Stravinsky.

Ives, Frederick Eugene (1856–1937), American photographic inventor, born in Litchfield, Conn. He developed (1881) the first group of trichromatic plates, invented (1888) the first successful process of half-tone photoengraving, and devised a method by which natural colors could be used in motion pictures. His other inventions include the photochromoscope and the short-tube, single-objective binocular microscope. His son, **Herbert Eugene Ives** (1882–1953), was also an inventor; he contributed to the process of sending photographs over telephone lines and was a pioneer in the development of television.

J

Jackson, Andrew (1767–1845), seventh president of the United States (1828–1836), born in Waxhaw, S.C. He was admitted to the bar in Salisbury, N.C. (1787), and in 1788 he became public prosecutor of the territory that is now Tennessee. He was elected to Congress in 1796 and was judge of the Tennessee supreme court (1798–1804). In the War of 1812 he led the Tennessee militia to victories over the Creek Indians (1813) and was commissioned a major general in the regular army. He captured the British base at Pensacola, Fla., and moved on to New Orleans, where in January, 1815, he hastily built defenses and repulsed a much larger British force. Although the Treaty of Ghent had already ended the war, neither army had yet been informed, and the news of the victory made Jackson a popular hero. In 1818 he defeated the Seminole Indians in Florida, but due to a confusion of orders, Jackson executed two British citizens whom he accused of stirring up the Indians. This involved the United States in serious trouble with both Great Britain and Spain. However, Spain ceded Florida to the United States in 1819, and in 1821 Jackson became governor of the state. Elected to the U.S. Senate in 1823, Jackson in the following year was nominated for the presidency after the Tennessee legislature presented his name as its Democratic candidate. None of the candidates won a majority of the votes, and the contest was decided by the House of Representatives. Jackson, having led in the number of popular votes, deeply resented the election of John Quincy Adams, whom Henry Clay had supported. He resigned from the Senate in 1825 and opposed Adams until his own election to the presidency in 1828, with John C. Calhoun as his running mate. In 1832 he was reelected, defeating Clay by a decisive majority.

The period covered by Jackson's two terms was notable in many respects. He was accustomed to give rather than take advice, and his cabinet had little voice in affairs. He relied on the opinion of a few close friends who made up what was popularly called the "Kitchen Cabinet." Jackson introduced the spoils system and was the first president to build up a political machine composed of party members. One of his most important acts was a decisive rebuke to South Carolina for her attempt to nullify an unpopular tariff law. He went so far as to concentrate troops and warships near Charleston in order to make it clear that the federal union would be preserved at all costs. Jackson also showed stubborn reliance on his own judgment in vetoing a bill for rechartering the United States Bank. He ordered the government's funds removed (thus putting an end to the bank) and deposited them in state banks. This intensely controversial move was a major factor in his reelection in 1832. Three years later Jackson completely paid off the national debt. In his last year of office (1836) Jackson issued the famous Specie Circular, ordering payments for public lands to be made in gold or silver. It was this policy, combined with other factors, that brought on the Panic of 1837, which had to be dealt with by Jackson's successor, Martin Van Buren.

Jackson, Thomas Jonathan, known as **Stonewall Jackson** (1824–1863), American Confederate general, born in Clarksburg, Va. (now W. Va.). He graduated from West Point (1846), served with distinction in the Mexican War, and taught at Virginia Military Institute (1851–1861). He was appointed brigadier general after the Civil War broke out, and put up such a solid stand at Bull Run that he earned the nickname "Stonewall." Promoted to major general, he marched into the Shenandoah and drove the British south. More victories followed at Richmond, Cedar Run, and Manassas. On September 15, 1862, he took Harper's Ferry with 13,000 prisoners and on the following day rescued Gen. Robert E. Lee at Antietam. Promoted to lieutenant general, he crushed the Union army at Fredericksburg, and on May 1, 1863, defeated Gen. Joseph Hooker at Chancellorsville. He was shot accidentally after dark on the same day, by a patrol of his own men, and died nine days later.

Jacquard, Joseph Marie (1752–1834), French inventor, born in Lyons. He invented the Jacquard loom for highly intricate figured weaving. Napoleon recognized the importance of the device, which eventually revolutionized the weaving industry, and

BETTMANN ARCHIVE

WILLIAM JAMES (*left*) excelled in psychology; his brother Henry (*right*), in literature.

granted Jacquard an annuity as well as membership in the Legion of Honor. Jacquard also invented an apparatus for weaving nets.

Jahn, Friedrich Ludwig (1778–1852), German patriot, regarded as the father of German gymnastics, the initiator of the Turnplatz, or athletic field. Depressed by the plight of Germany, which had been crushed by Napoleon's tyranny, Jahn believed that gymnastic groups would help rally the country's morale. The movement spread rapidly, kindling a spirit of nationalism and the desire for a unified Germany. The excessively liberal political nature of the groups, however, caused their abolition in 1818 by the Prussian government; Jahn himself was imprisoned (1818–1825). He was elected to the national parliament in 1848.

James I (1566–1625), king of England (1603–1625), the son of Mary, Queen of Scots, and Lord Darnley. He was born in Edinburgh Castle, and succeeded to the throne of Scotland in 1567 as James VI. Until 1578 the kingdom was governed by a succession of regents—Moray, Lennox, Mar, and Morton. After 1581 he ruled Scotland with the assistance of the earl of Arran and the duke of Lennox, his two favorites. His reign was marked by constant and widespread discontent, as well as by friction with both Protestants and Catholics. In 1603, upon the death of Queen Elizabeth, he ascended the throne of England as James I. The most important events of his reign include the founding of the first English colony in America at Jamestown (1607), the establishment of Plymouth Colony (1620), and the publication of the *King James Version* of the Bible (1611). His religious ideas were anathema to both Puritans and Roman Catholics, and his harshness towards the latter provoked the Gunpowder Plot (1605). His foreign policy, essentially one of appeasement, was neither consistent nor wise, and was publicly regarded with considerable suspicion. He was a learned man and wrote several political, historical, and poetic works. He was succeeded by his son, Charles I.

James II (1633–1701), king of England, Scotland, and Ireland (1685–1688), son of Charles I. At the Restoration (1660) he was appointed lord high admiral of England (1660) and subsequently saw action in the Dutch Wars (1665, 1672). He converted to Catholicism (c.1668). Forced by the Test Act (1673) to resign as admiral, James II proceeded to incur the dislike of the Whigs and, in general, steadily began to lose popularity. In 1679 he was exiled after the Popish Plot revealed him to have been intriguing with the French, as well as with the Catholics. With renewed power, James returned to England in 1682 and three years later became king upon the death of his brother, Charles II. James immediately made his favoritism of the Catholics clear, provoking public fear of Catholic control; he simultaneously injected an unwanted influence upon local affairs. Finally, upon the call of Whig and Tory leaders, James' son-in-law, William of Orange, came to England and took over the throne after the Glorious Revolution of 1688. Exiled to Ireland, James in 1690 tried to regain the throne at the battle of the Boyne, but this, as well as several later attempts, was a failure.

James, Henry (1843–1916), American novelist, born in New York City, brother of William James. He spent most of his youth traveling and studying abroad, but returned to America at 19 to enter Harvard Law School. Although he was qualified to practice law, he continued the literary career that he had begun while he was in school and by the late 1860's was a steady contributor to *The Nation*, the *Atlantic*, and *Galaxy Magazine*. After 1876 he was a resident of London and became a British subject in 1915. During his European travels, he established close association with Ivan Turgenev and Gustave Flaubert. Keenly aware of the finest subtleties of human character, James was a stylist of extraordinary sophistication and devoted much of his writing to contrasting the conduct and characteristics of the typical American with his European counterpart. He wrote numerous novels, volumes of literary criticism, travel sketches, and plays. His novels include *The American* (1877), *The Europeans* (1878), *Daisy Miller* (1879), *The Portrait of a Lady* (1881), *The Bostonians* (1886), *The Wings of the Dove* (1902), *The Ambassadors* (1903), and *The Golden Bowl* (1904).

James, Jesse Woodson (1847–1882), American "Wild West" desperado, born in Clay County, Mo. He led a murderous band of train and bank robbers, and was finally cut down by one of them, believed to be Robert Ford. After his death, James was extolled as a modern Robin Hood and was favorably commemorated in songs, stories, and motion pictures.

James, William (1842–1910), American philosopher, born in New York City, brother of Henry James. He received his medical degree from Harvard (1869), joined the faculty in 1872 as a teacher of anatomy and physiology, and in 1881 was appointed professor of philosophy and psychology. The foremost American philosopher of his day, James in 1890 published *Principles of Psychology*, which quickly became a classic. A lucid and fascinating stylist, James has often been described as a psychologist who wrote like a novelist, whereas his brother, Henry, has been regarded as a novelist who wrote like a psychologist. William James was one of the founders of pragmatism—a philosophy that stresses the importance of experience and maintains, in essence, that something is true because (and only *if*) it works. Among his other works are *The Will to Believe and other Essays* (1897), *Varieties of Religious Experience* (1902), *Pragmatism* (1907), *A Pluralistic Universe* (1909), and *The Meaning of Truth* (1909).

Jameson, Sir Leander Starr, known as **Doctor Jameson** (1853–1917), British colonial administrator in South Africa. Born in Edinburgh, he received a medical education in London. In 1878 he settled in Kimberley, Cape Colony, where he practiced medicine and became an associate of Cecil Rhodes in various colonizing enterprises. Jameson was appointed administrator of Rhodesia in 1891. During a period of friction in Johannesburg between the Boer government and the Uitlanders, he headed the famous Jameson Raid (1895) into the Boer-controlled Transvaal. Surrounded and starved into surrender, Jameson and his officers were turned over to the British authorities, who sent them to England for trial. Jameson

served less than a year of a prison sentence. He returned to South Africa and carried on political efforts against the Boers. As prime minister of the Cape Colony (1904–1908), Jameson was instrumental in bringing about the union of the South African colonies. He later returned to England and was created a baronet in 1911.

Janáček, Leos (1854–1928), Czech composer, born in Moravia. He studied at Prague and Leipzig and settled in Brno, where he directed an organ school (1881–1920). Drawing upon the folksong tradition of his country, Janáček composed a number of vocal and symphonic works. He was, however, principally a composer of operas, notably *Jenufa* (1904), *Osul* (1904), and *From a House of the Dead* (1938).

Jansen, Cornelis (1585–1638), Dutch Roman Catholic theologian, founder of the Jansenist sect. He was born in Acquoi, near Leerdam, and educated at Utrecht, Louvain, and Paris. He was director of the College of St. Pulcheria, Louvain (1617), and professor at Louvain (1630), and in 1636 was appointed bishop of Ypres. In his treatise *Augustinus*, which was published posthumously in 1640 and condemned by Pope Urban VIII in 1642, Jansen argued that Saint Augustine's teachings were actually contrary to Jesuit dogma. The ensuing controversy (in which Jansen's banner was carried by Blaise Pascal, Antoine Arnauld, and the Port Royalists) raged throughout France for almost a century and ultimately was responsible for the emigration of many Jansenists to the Netherlands.

Jaspers, Karl (1883–   ), German existentialist philosopher, born in Oldenburg. He was first a physician and later taught psychology and philosophy at the University of Heidelberg and at Basel, Switzerland. As a philosopher, he stressed the importance of science but recognized its limitations as a guide to human values and action. Philosophy, in his view, should address itself to the individual and provide his total rational and nonrational being with an all-embracing framework for meaningful existence. Accordingly, it is man's responsibility to communicate with others and share his knowledge and experience. Among his most important works are *Psychology of World Views* (1919), *Man in the Modern Age* (1933), *Existentialism and Humanism* (1952), and *Reason and Existence* (1955).

Jay, John (1745–1829), American statesman and jurist, born in New York City. He graduated from King's College (now Columbia University) in 1764, and began to practice law in New York in 1768. Jay was active in various official capacities throughout the Revolutionary War and served as president of the Continental Congress (1778–1779). He was a minister to Spain and later to Paris, where (1782–1783) he helped negotiate the peace treaty that ended the Revolutionary War. From 1784 to 1789 he was secretary of foreign affairs for the Confederation. As an author of the *Federalist* papers, Jay helped to bring about ratification of the federal Constitution. After the U.S. government was established, he was the first chief justice of the Supreme Court (1789–1795). In 1794 he negotiated Jay's Treaty, which eased strained relations between the United States and England. A leader of the Federalist party, Jay was governor of New York (1795–1801).

Jeanneret, Charles Édouard. See *Le Corbusier.*

Jeans, Sir James Hopwood (1877–1946), English physicist, mathematician, and astronomer, born in London. He was educated at Cambridge, taught mathematics at Princeton (1905–1909) and Cambridge (1910–1912), and was a research associate at the Mount Wilson Observatory in California (1923–1944). He was also secretary of the Royal Society (1919–1929) and president of the Royal Astronomical Society (1925–1927). Renowned for his work on radiation and the kinetic theory of gases, he is equally famous for his popularization of science and scientific philosophy. His popular works include *The Universe Around Us* (1929), *The Mysterious Universe* (1930), *Through Space and Time* (1934), and *Physics and Philosophy* (1942). He was knighted in 1928.

Jeffers, Robinson, in full **John Robinson Jeffers** (1887–1962), American poet, noted for his dark allegories of human corruption. He was born in Pittsburgh, Pa., graduated from Occidental College, and studied medicine and forestry at the universities of Washington, Southern California, and Zurich. Jeffers moved to Carmel, Cal., and built a medieval tower there from which he could view the coast. The influence of this magnificent setting is apparent in much of his work. His poetry deals with the evil tendencies of man as opposed to the purity of nature. It is also characterized by classical overtones and a peculiar dithyrambic sprung rhythm. In 1954 he was awarded the Pulitzer Prize for *Hungerfield and Other Poems*. His work includes *Tamar and Other Poems* (1924), *The Roan Stallion* (1925), *Cawdor and Other Poems* (1928), *Thurso's Landing and Other Poems* (1932), and a free translation of Euripides' *Medea* (1947).

Jefferson, Thomas (1743–1826), third president of the United States (1801–1809), born in Shadwell, Albemarle County, Va. He graduated from William and Mary (1762), studied law, and was admitted to the bar in 1767. His political life began with his election to the Virginia House of Burgesses in 1769. In 1775 he was elected to the Continental Congress and in June, 1776, was appointed chairman of a committee to draw up the Declaration of Independence, signed on July 4. Jefferson wrote the first draft; it underwent only minor revision.

In 1779 Jefferson succeeded Patrick Henry as governor of Virginia, and in 1783 took his seat in the Continental Congress, where he both urged adoption of the decimal system of coinage and prepared a plan for the government of the Northwest Territory that was later the basis of the famous Ordinance of 1787. In 1785 Jefferson became U.S. minister to France and returned in 1789 to become the first secretary of state (1790–1793). A believer in the ability of the people to govern themselves, Jefferson came into conflict with Alexander Hamilton, Pres. George Washington's secretary of the treasury and a firm advocate of strong central government. Though the names of the parties have changed, the Democrats of today regard Jefferson as the chief founder of their party, while the Republicans honor Hamilton in much the same way. Jefferson served as vice-president under Pres. John Adams, a Federalist, and in 1801 was elected president by the House of Representatives after tying with Aaron Burr in the popular vote.

The outstanding events of his first term were the Louisiana Purchase, Ohio's admission to the Union, and the war against Tripoli. In 1804 Jefferson was reelected by an overwhelming majority of the popular vote. His second term, which saw rising discontent among the electorate, was particularly important for the Embargo Act of 1807, the Lewis and Clark Expedition, and abolition of the slave trade. Jefferson refused to run for a third term and retired in 1809 to Monticello, his plantation in Virginia. Architect, scientist, and distinguished man of letters, he devoted much time to education and both designed and helped found the University of Virginia, whose buildings remain one of the monuments of American architectural achievement and nobly express the essence of Jefferson's liberal and democratic political beliefs.

Jeffreys, George, 1st Baron **Jeffreys of Wem** (1644–1689), English jurist, born in Acton. Beginning his career as solicitor to the duke of York (1677), he rose quickly in politics and in 1683 became privy councilor. Ever ready to defer to the desires of the crown, he soon (1685) became lord chancellor. Notorious for his cruelty, his infamous judicial dealings included the execution of Algernon Sidney, the trials of Richard Baxter and Titus Oates, and the Bloody Assizes, which involved the brutal sentencing of hundreds who supported the duke of Monmouth's rebellion. When James II was overthrown and had fled in disguise, Jeffreys tried to follow but was captured and imprisoned in the Tower of London (1688) where he died a year later.

Jellicoe, John Rushworth, 1st Earl (1859–1935), British admiral, born in Southampton. He entered the navy in 1872, rose to rear admiral by 1907, and when World War I began was given command of the grand fleet. His direction of the battle of Jutland (May 31, 1916) provoked much controversy. Later that year, he was promoted to first sea lord and took charge of the antisubmarine campaign. He was appointed admiral of the fleet in 1919, and served as governor of New Zealand (1920–1924).

Jenghiz Khan. See *Genghis Khan.*

Jenks, Jeremiah Whipple (1856–1929), American economist, born in St. Clair, Mich., and educated at the University of Michigan and the University of Halle. He was professor of political economy and social science at Cornell University (1891–1912) and later taught government at New York University. As a political economist, Jenks rendered the U.S. government valuable service in the investigation of trusts, currency reform, taxation, labor, international exchange, and immigration. His principal publications include *The Trust Problem* (1900), *Principles of Politics* (1909), *Governmental Action for Social Welfare* (1910), and *The Immigration Problem* (1911).

Jenner, Edward (1749–1823), English physician, discoverer of vaccination. Born in Berkeley, Gloucestershire, he studied medicine in London. Settling in Berkeley (1773), he began to study cowpox as a preventive of smallpox, having heard in Gloucestershire that dairymaids who contracted cowpox never developed smallpox. After many years of experiment and investigation, Jenner performed his first public inoculation with vaccine in 1796. Two years later he published his findings in *Inquiry into the Cause and Effects of the Variolae Vaccinae.* Within a year, his discovery was internationally acclaimed.

Jerome, Saint (c.340–420), Christian biblical scholar, one of the first four Doctors of the Church. Born in Stridon, between Dalmatia and Pannonia, he was ordained in 379. He went to Rome in 382 and became secretary to Pope Damasus I. His extraordinary erudition and eloquence won him many devoted followers, some of considerable importance. Two of them, Lady Paula and her daughter, accompanied him to Bethlehem (386). There he entered a monastery, continued his brilliant writing and studies, and completed his Latin version of the Bible (the Vulgate). He is widely regarded as the most scholarly of the Latin fathers, and has been represented as such in numerous masterpieces of art. His feast day is September 20.

Jerome of Prague (c.1360–1416), Bohemian religious reformer, associated with John Wycliffe and John Huss as one of the forerunners of the Protestant Reformation. After studying at the universities of Prague and Oxford, he attracted attention by his defense of Wycliffe's ideas, became a champion of Huss, and zealously joined him in criticising papal doctrine. When he heard of Huss's arrest, Jerome started for Constance to defend him. He was arrested in Bavaria (1415) and imprisoned in Constance. He recanted, but withdrew his recantation, and was burned at the stake.

Jesus, Jesus Christ, or **Christ Jesus,** also called **Jesus of Nazareth** (c.4 B.C.–c.29 A.D.), founder of Christianity. Born in Bethlehem, Jesus is believed by some Christian sects to have been miraculously conceived by the Holy Ghost and the Virgin Mary. Jesus lived in Nazareth as a child and became a carpenter (the occupation of his legal father, Joseph). After being baptized by his cousin, John the Baptist, he went to Galilee, where he gathered twelve disciples and for several years conducted a phenomenal program of preaching, healing, and ministering to the poor. In the meantime, due to his repeated criticism of the rich and ruling class, he grew increasingly unpopular with officialdom. After several years in Galilee, he and his disciples returned to Jerusalem and carried on their work. Finally, during the famous Last Supper with his disciples, he was betrayed by one of them, Judas Iscariot. Jesus was arrested, tried, and found guilty of blasphemy; it was with reluctance that the Roman procurator, Pontius Pilate, passed the prescribed death sentence. Jesus was taken to Golgotha and crucified. On the third day, according to Christian dogma, he arose from the dead and ascended into heaven.

The life and teachings of Christ became the foundation of Christianity, a faith which empasizes the importance of love, personal sacrifice, repentance for sins, and the eternally redeeming power of God's love for all men. The only biographical sources for Christ are the four Gospels of the New Testament (Matthew, Mark, Luke, and John); additional references appear in Josephus, Tacitus, Suetonius, and certain other writings of the period. The principal Christian feasts, commemorating events of Christ's life, include Christmas, Epiphany, and Easter.

Jevons, William Stanley (1835–1882), English logician and economist, born in Liverpool. He studied metallurgy at University College, London, and was an assayer at the mint in Sydney, Australia (1854–1859). He was professor of logic at Owens College, Manchester (1866–1879), and of political economy at University College, London (1876–1880). His widely influential books propounded the original theory that utility determines value and that a mathematical relationship exists between the two. Jevons' major works include *Pure Logic* (1864), *The Coal Question* (1865), *Theory of Political Economy* (1871), and *The Principles of Science* (1874).

Jinnah, Mohammed Ali (1876–1948), Pakistani statesman, founder and first governor general of Pakistan. Born in Karachi, India, and educated in England, he became a member of the Viceroy's Legislative Council (1910), joined the Muslim League in 1913 and was elected its president in 1916. As head of the Muslim League, he set as his goal the establishment of an independent Pakistan. This was accomplished on August 15, 1947, when Pakistan was created. As its first governor general, Jinnah worked for a peaceful resolution of the many political and religious problems occasioned by the partition of India.

Joan of Arc, Saint, French name **Jeanne d'Arc,** called the **Maid of Orléans** (1412–1431), French national heroine and saint. Born in Domrémy of devout peasant parents, she began at the age of 13 to have visions and hear "voices." She was convinced that she was receiving divine messages urging her to go to the rescue of France, the northern part of which was held by the English and their Burgundian allies. When the city of Orléans seemed in danger of capture in 1429, Joan obtained an audience with the dauphin, Charles VII. She convinced him and the court theologians of her sincerity, donned a suit of armor, and led the French troops into battle with such spirit that the English were forced to raise the siege. After defeating the English at Patay, Joan persuaded Charles to go to Reims and be crowned (July 17, 1429) in defiance of the Treaty of Troyes. She then failed in several military efforts, including an attack on Paris, but she continued to lead the soldiers of France to battle. In May, 1430, she was captured by the Burgundians at Compiègne. Six months later they sold her to the English, who in turn avoided responsibility by turning her over to a French ecclesiastical tribunal at Rouen. After a prolonged and brutal trial, Joan was found guilty of sorcery and heresy, and on May 30, 1431, she was burned at the stake in Rouen. Fourteen years later, by belated order of Charles VII, the sentence was annulled, and Joan was proclaimed innocent. She was beatified in 1909 and canonized in 1920 by Pope Benedict XV. An immense literature has grown up around her, including works by Schiller, Voltaire, Mark Twain, and George Bernard Shaw.

Joffre, Joseph Jacques Césaire (1852–1931), French general, born in Rivesaltes. He entered the army in 1870 and fought in the Franco-Prussian War. He rose rapidly in positions of authority and at the outbreak of World War I was made commander in chief of the French armies. Although his strategy of attrition failed to check the German advance, he is credited with an important share in the victory of the Marne. After the battle of Verdun (1916) Joffre was replaced by Gen. Robert Nivelle. He was promoted to marshal of France (1916), made president of the Allied War Council (1917), and in 1918 was elected a member of the French Academy.

John, Augustus Edwin (1879–1961), British painter, born in Tenby, Wales. He studied at the Slade School of Art, London, and established a reputation as an etcher. John later became a portrait painter and was acclaimed for his studies of T. E. Lawrence, James Joyce, W. B. Yeats, George Bernard Shaw, Dylan Thomas, and Queen Elizabeth II. A member of the Royal Academy, John was awarded the Order of Merit in 1942. His autobiography, *Chiaroscuro*, was published in 1952.

John XXIII, born **Angelo Giuseppe Roncalli** (1881–1963), Roman Catholic pope

POPE JOHN XXIII

SAMUEL JOHNSON

(1958–1963). He studied in Bergamo and Rome, and was ordained a priest in 1904. After acting as secretary to the bishop of Bergamo, he became prominent in Church affairs throughout Italy. Elevated to archbishop in 1925, he subsequently served as apostolic delegate to Bulgaria, Turkey, and Greece. He was named papal nuncio to France (1944), created a cardinal (1953), and was patriarch of Venice (1953–1958). On November 4, 1958, he was elected the supreme pontiff of the Roman Catholic Church. Known for his imagination, progressiveness, and humanity, John XXIII expanded the membership of the College of Cardinals for the first time since 1586, and revised tradition by making frequent trips outside the Vatican. In 1961 he convoked the 21st ecumenical council for the purpose of investigating ways to strengthen the ties among the various Christian churches.

John, also called **John Lackland** (1167–1216), king of England (1199–1216), the youngest son of Henry II and Eleanor of Aquitaine. He succeeded his brother Richard I, Coeur de Lion. In 1203, at Rouen, he arranged the murder of his nephew Arthur. His refusal to acknowledge Stephen Langton's election as archbishop of Canterbury (1207) provoked a papal interdict against England (1208), his own excommunication (1209), and a papal bull ordering his deposition (1212). When Philip II of France was appointed executor, John hurried to placate the pope by accepting back his kingdom in fief and agreeing to a large annual tribute. In 1214 John invaded France, met defeat, and returned to England. At Runnymede (1215) he again met defeat, this time at the hands of the English barons, who forced him to sign the Magna Charta. The document became the foundation for the English constitution.

John II, called **John the Good** (1319–1364), king of France (1350–1364). He succeeded his father, Phillip VI of Valois, and began a reign of cruelty and corruption. Defeated by Edward the Black Prince at Poitiers in 1356, John was imprisoned in London (1356–1360) while his son (later Charles V) served as regent. He was released by the Treaty of Brétigny, after giving hostages and promise of ransom. When one of the hostages—John's second son, the duke of Anjou—broke parole in 1363, the king gallantly returned to England where he died a few months later.

John of Gaunt, Duke of **Lancaster** (1340–1399), English statesman, a son of Edward III of England. Born in Ghent, Belgium, he married Blanche of Lancaster (1359) and became duke in 1362. John aided his brother, Edward the Black Prince, in the Hundred Years' War. He also supported Peter the Cruel of Castile and took part in the battle of Nájera. After Blanche's death, he married Constance (1372), a Spanish princess, through whom he had a claim to the crown of Castile. Toward the end of his father's reign, he became the most powerful figure in the kingdom and had ambitions of taking the throne. The young king, Richard II, distrusted him and in 1386 sent him on an expedition to secure his Castilian kingdom. This resulted in a treaty of marriage by which John's daughter, Catherine, would become queen of Castile. Having himself become duke of Aquitaine (1390), John worked to support Richard II and in 1394 arranged for a truce with France. In 1396 he married his mistress, Catherine Swynford, and obtained legitimization for their sons, the eldest of whom became Henry IV. This last marriage introduced the Tudor line of English monarchs.

John III Sobieski (1624–1669), national hero and king of Poland (1674–1696). Born in Galicia, he rose to distinction in the military service and was appointed commander in chief of the Polish army in 1665. He defeated the Turks at Hotin in 1673. When the king died in 1674, John was elected to the throne by the Polish diet. He resumed his wars against the Turks, regaining much of the Ukraine. In 1683 he won a stunning victory for Christendom by forcing the Turks to raise the siege of Vienna.

Johnson, Andrew (1808–1875), seventeenth president of the United States (1865–1869). He was born in Raleigh, N.C. At the age of ten Johnson was apprenticed to a tailor and used his free time to educate himself. In 1826 he moved to Greenville, Tenn., where he opened a tailor shop and began to take an interest in local affairs. His political career was launched with his election as alderman (1828) and then as mayor (1830). In 1835 he was sent to the state legislature and in 1843 to the House of Representatives. During his ten years as a congressman he supported the Democratic party and took a particular interest in the Homestead Act, intended to aid homeless whites, which was vetoed by Pres. James Buchanan. In 1853 and again in 1855 he was elected to the U.S. Senate. He remained in the Senate even after Tennessee seceded from the Union and became its military governor in 1862.

As a Jacksonian Democrat supported by workingmen, Johnson was a good running mate for the Republican Abraham Lincoln. He was nominated for the vice-presidency in 1864 and became president on April 14, 1865, following Lincoln's assassination. Johnson tried to implement Lincoln's moderate plans for reconstruction, but was overwhelmed by the opposition of radical Republicans. His quarrel with Congress resulted in the nullification of most of his vetoes and the passage of several bills designed to restrict presidential authority. In 1868, because he ignored the new Tenure of Office Act (1867) and dismissed Edwin M. Stanton, secretary of war, impeachment proceedings were brought against him. Although the two-thirds majority necessary to remove him from office was not obtained, he was not renominated in 1869. Returning to Tennessee, he remained active in politics and returned to the Senate in 1875 shortly before his death.

Johnson, Hiram Warren (1866–1945), American politician and senator. Born in Sacramento, Calif., he attended the University of California, studied law, and practiced in Sacramento. In San Francisco (1908), he successfully prosecuted a famous case involving graft, which enhanced his reputation. Elected governor of California in 1911, he broke the statewide political stranglehold of the Southern Pacific Railroad. He was one of the founders of the Progressive party, and in 1912 was nominated for the vice-presidency on the ticket with Theodore Roosevelt. He was reelected governor of California (1914), but resigned in 1917 to enter the U.S. Senate. A powerful member of the isolationist faction, he opposed U.S. membership in the League of Nations and later in the United Nations.

Johnson, James Weldon (1871–1938), American Negro author, born in Jacksonville, Fla., and educated at Atlanta University. After practicing law in Jacksonville (1897–1901), he was appointed U.S. consul in Venezuela (1906) and Nicaragua (1909–1912). He helped found the National Association for the Advancement of Colored People (NAACP) and was its secretary, from 1916 to 1930. Of his many writings in poetry and prose, the best known is *The Autobiography of an Ex-Colored Man* (1912).

Johnson, Lyndon Baines (1908–   ), thirty-sixth president of the U.S. (1963–   ), born near Stonewall, Texas. He graduated from Southwest State Teachers College in Texas (1930) and was elected to the U.S. Congress in 1937. Serving in the Senate from 1949 to 1961, he was Democratic minority leader of the 83rd Congress and majority leader of the 84th-86th Congresses. In 1960 he received the Democratic vice-presidential nomination and was elected on the ticket with John F. Kennedy. When Kennedy was assassinated in Dallas, Texas (November 22, 1963), Johnson took the oath of office as president. In November, 1964, with Hubert Humphrey as running mate, Johnson won the presidential election by a landslide that crushed the Republican candidate, Sen. Barry Goldwater, and the party as well. With consummate political skill Johnson continued the basic policies of Kennedy, and pushed through Congress an unprecedented number of bills. Among the major measures directed toward creation of Johnson's "Great Society" were Medicare, reapportionment provisions, antipoverty acts, and the most liberal civil rights legislation in American history.

Johnson, Samuel (1709–1784), English writer, lexicographer, and critic, the foremost conversationalist and literary dictator of his day. Born in Lichfield, the son of a bookseller, Johnson attended Oxford (1728–1729) and married a widow twenty years his senior (1735). He started a school, which failed, although he established a lifelong friendship with one of his pupils, David Garrick. The two went together to London (1737), where Johnson began writing for the *Gentleman's Magazine*. In 1738 he published *London*, a poem imitative of the third satire of Juvenal. He wrote the parliamentary debates for the *Gentleman's Magazine* (1740–1743), composed his poem *The Vanity of Human Wishes* (1749), the verse tragedy *Irene* (1749), and wrote essays for the *Rambler* (1750–1752). By the time he published his famous *Dictionary of the English Language* (1755), he was already famous. Publications soon to follow were the novel *Rasselas* (1759) and essays for the *Idler* (1758–1760).

In 1762 the government awarded him an annual pension of £300. The following year Johnson established his friendship with James Boswell and in 1764 founded the Literary Club, whose charter membership included Oliver Goldsmith, Edmund Burke, Garrick, and Boswell. In 1765 Johnson received a doctor's degree from Trinity College, Dublin, and in the same year produced his eight-volume edition of Shakespeare with its critically significant preface. His later works include *A Journey to the Western Islands of Scotland* (1775) and his highly acclaimed *Lives of the English Poets* (1779–1781). From their meeting in 1763, Boswell had devotedly recorded Johnson's inimitable conversations and opinions, which he immortalized in his memorable *Life of Samuel Johnson* (1791).

Johnson, Walter Perry (1887–1946), American baseball player, born in Humboldt, Kans. In a 21-year career with the Washington Senators (1907–1927), he was the greatest fast-ball pitcher in the major league. He won 414 games, of which 113 were shutouts, and scored 3,497 strikeouts. He later managed Washington (1929–1932) and the Cleveland Indians (1933–1935). In 1936 he was elected to the Baseball Hall of Fame.

Johnston, Joseph Eggleston (1807–1891), American Confederate general, born in Prince Edward County, Va. He graduated from West Point (1829) and served in the Black Hawk and Seminole wars and in the Mexican War. In 1861 he joined the Confederate army and soon became a brigadier general. He fought in the first battle of Bull Run, opposed Gen. George McClellan in the Peninsular Campaign, and was wounded in the battle of Fair Oaks (1862). In 1863 he made an unsuccessful attempt to relieve the siege of Vicksburg. Commanding the army of Tennessee (1864), he failed to halt Gen. William T. Sherman's advance on Atlanta and was replaced by Gen. John Hood. Returned to command in 1865, Johnston resisted Sherman's march through North Carolina but finally, upon learning of Gen. Robert E. Lee's surrender to Grant, capitulated himself on April 26. One of the defensive geniuses of the Civil War, Johnston went on to show considerable talents as a civilian.

Joinville, Jean de (c.1224–1317), French historian, born in Champagne. He was seneschal of Champagne and accompanied Louis IX on the seventh crusade (1248–1254). In 1250 Joinville composed the *Credo* (confession of faith) and during the crusade recorded numerous valuable events and impressions. His *Histoire de Saint Louis* (1304–1309), based on a long personal contact with the king, is an invaluable and delightfully written historical document.

Jókai, Maurus or **Mór** (1825–1904), Hungarian novelist, born in Komárno. For taking part in the Hungarian revolution of 1848–1849, Jókai was imprisoned. When a constitutional government was formed, he served as a Liberal member of the Hungarian parliament (1861–1897). Jókai's novels combine narrative skill, subtle humor, and considerable political and social comment. Notable among these are *The Day of Wrath* (1856), *The New Landlord* (1868), *Black Diamonds* (1870), *The Modern Midas* (1875), and *Eyes Like the Sea* (1890).

Jolliet or **Joliet, Louis** (1645–1700), French-Canadian explorer, born in Quebec, Canada. With Father Jacques Marquette he explored the western territory in search of a legendary great river. They started west in May, 1673, found and floated down the Mississippi, passing the mouth of the Arkansas River and far enough south to determine that the Mississippi flowed into the Gulf of Mexico. On the way back, Marquette and Jolliet separated; Jolliet's canoe overturned and all records of the expedition were lost. From memory, however, along with Marquette's data, he was able to make a significant contribution to the geography of the Middle West.

Jones, Henry Arthur (1851–1929), English playwright, born in Grandborough, Buckinghamshire. His first melodrama was *Only Round the Corner* (1878), his first great success, *The Silver King* (1882)—after which, influenced greatly by Henrik Ibsen, he turned to writing dramas of social and moral import. Of these, the most important include *The Middleman* (1889), *Judah* (1890), *The Liars* (1897), *Mrs. Dane's Defence* (1900), and *Mary Goes First* (1913). Among his critical works are *The Renascence of the English Drama* (1895) and *The Theatre of Ideas* (1915).

Jones, Inigo (1573–1652), English architect who introduced the principles of the Italian Renaissance into England. Born in London, he established himself (1605) as a stage and costume designer for the courts of James I and Charles I. In Italy, he studied Roman architecture, particularly the classically porportioned Renaissance structures of Andrea Palladio. He was appointed surveyor-general to the king in 1615. Jones' first English building in the Palladian style was the Queen's house at Greenwich, Kent (completed 1635). It was followed by the banquet hall in Whitehall, London (1619–1621), which is widely held to be his masterpiece. His later works include designs for the Church of St. Paul, Covent Garden (1631–1638), the restoration of St. Paul's Cathedral (1634), and houses in and around London.

Jones, John Paul, original name **John Paul** (1747–1792), American naval hero, born in Scotland. He went to sea as a boy and, after some years as a mate on a merchant vessel settled in Fredericksburg, Va. (c.1773), and added *Jones* to his name. In 1775 he was commissioned as a lieutenant in the Continental navy, was promoted to captain in 1776, and in 1777 sailed for Europe and the British Isles on the *Ranger*. While in command of this ship, he captured the *Drake*, the first British warship taken by a Continental vessel. Jones then secured an old French ship that he reconditioned and named the *Bonhomme Richard*, in honor of Benjamin Franklin and his *Poor Richard's Almanack*. In September, 1779, he engaged the British *Serapis* in a spectacular battle off Scarborough, England. Jones captured the far more powerful British ship after heavy hand-to-hand fighting. His own vessel was so badly damaged that it sank two days later and he brought his crew to France on the *Serapis*. After the Revolution, Jones served in the Russian navy, and although he heroically beat the Turks in the Black Sea (1788), he was victimized by intrigues and received no credit. Granted a leave of absence by Catherine the Great, Jones went to Paris, where he lived from 1790 until his death. In 1905 his body was reburied at Annapolis with honors.

Jones, Robert Tyre, known as **Bobby Jones** (1902–   ), American golfer, born in Atlanta, Ga. He was educated at the Georgia Institute of Technology and Harvard, and studied law at Emory University. Admitted to the bar in 1928, he practiced in Atlanta. He won the National Amateur Golf championship five times (1924, 1925, 1927, 1928, and 1930), and the National Open championship four times (1923, 1926, 1929, and 1930). Jones was British open champion in 1926, 1927, and 1930, and British amateur champion in 1930. His greatest achievement was the "Grand Slam" in 1930, in which he won both the British and American amateur and open titles in a single year. He later retired from competition to practice law in Atlanta. Jones wrote *Down the Fairway* with O. B. Keeler (1927); *How to Play Golf* (1940), with H. E. Lowe; and by himself, *Golf Is My Game* (1960).

Jonson, Ben (1573–1637), English dramatist and man of letters whose name is linked with Shakespeare's and Marlowe's as one of the three great Elizabethan playwrights. He was born in the vicinity of London and studied at the Westminster school under William Camden, a renowned classical scholar and poet of his times. Jonson worked as a bricklayer, a soldier, and an actor before he turned to writing. His first success as a dramatist was in 1598 with the performance of *Every Man in His Humour*. The next few years were colored by the so-called "war of the theaters," literary quarrels which took the form of personal allusions hidden in plays. *Cynthia's Revels* (1600) and *Poetaster* (1601) are two such critical satires of Jonson's attacking John Marston and Thomas Dekker. In 1603 Jonson wrote an entertainment for the queen at Althrope. This was the beginning of his collaboration with Inigo Jones, which resulted in the great success of the court masque. However, Jonson is better known for his comedies *Volpone* (1606), *Epicoene* (1609), *The Alchemist* (1610), and *Bartholomew Fair* (1614). Each of these is an ingenious and witty exposé of man's weaknesses and, at the same time, is a sharp critique backed by an earnest moral. Jonson is also the author of many poems, including *To Celia,* a tribute to Shakespeare, and the classical tragedies *Sejanus* (1603) and *Catiline* (1611). Although his last years were spent in obscurity and poverty, he was buried in Westminster Abbey.

Jordaens, Jakob (1593–1678), Flemish Baroque painter, born in Antwerp. He studied under Adam van Noort, who was also Peter Paul Rubens' master. Through Rubens' influence, Jordaens received commissions from the courts of England and Sweden. His work is essentially Flemish, and his pictures of the people of his day are notable for a humor and realism that is sometimes coarse. He also painted religious and mythological subjects, portraits, and historical scenes. His masterpiece is the mural *Triumph of the Stadtholder*, painted for the palace of the widow of Frederick Henry of Orange, now in the House in the Wood, The Hague.

Joseph II (1741–1790), Holy Roman emperor (1765–1790), the son of Emperor Francis I and Maria Theresa of Austria. His mother remained the actual ruler until her death in 1780. Joseph then put various reforms into effect, but his domestic and foreign policies were unsuccessful. He quarreled with Pope Pius VI and declared himself independent of the papacy. The later years of his reign were troubled by an unsuccessful war with Turkey and a revolt in the Netherlands.

Josephus, Flavius (c.37–c.95 A.D.), Jewish historian and military commander, born in Jerusalem. In 67, while governor of Galilee, he was taken prisoner by Vespasian, who had been sent there by Nero to crush an uprising of the Jews. Because he prophesied that Vespasian would one day be emperor, Josephus received a considerable degree of liberty. He took the name Flavius, Vespasian's family name. He witnessed the capture of Jerusalem by Titus (70) and thereafter lived in Rome as a writer. His extant works include his *History of the Jewish War,* his most valuable contribution to historiography; *Jewish Antiquities;* and an autobiography.

Joubert, Petrus Jacobus, known as **Piet Joubert** (1834–1900), Boer general and statesman, born in Cape Colony of Dutch-Huguenot parents. He became a wealthy farmer and politically prominent in the South African Republic. As commander of the Boer forces (1880–1881), Joubert helped to win a war against the British. He acted as president (1883–1884) in the absence of Stephanus Kruger, and in 1893 was elected vice-president. Joubert was in command of the army that checked the Jameson raid into the Transvaal, and held the position of commandant general when the South African War began in 1899. He conducted the Natal campaign and had already laid siege to Ladysmith when his health failed and he died in Pretoria.

Joule, James Prescott (1818–1889), English physicist, born in Lancashire. An invalid, he was educated at home and studied under John Dalton. Taking up the study of electricity and magnetism, Joule developed several important theories. His great work was the investigation of problems of heat and energy, and he was the first to demonstrate the mechanical equivalent of heat (1847). The joule, named after him, is a unit of electrical energy.

Joyce, James Augustine Aloysius (1882–1941), Irish writer, born in Dublin and educated at Belvedere College and the Catholic University of Dublin. His variety of early interests—music, the theater, and journalism—are all reflected in *Ulysses,* his most famous work. Joyce's life was marked by a constant struggle against poverty and increasing blindness; literary recognition came slowly. *Ulysses,* which was for many years banned in America and in England, established him as one of the greatest and most influential literary artists of the twentieth century. Of particular significance is his development of the internal monologue and stream-of-consciousness technique. His works include *Dubliners* (1914), a book of short stories; *A Portrait of the Artist as a Young Man* (1916), his first novel; *Exiles* (1918), an Ibsenesque drama; *Ulysses* (1922); *Finnegan's Wake*

CULVER

JOHN PAUL JONES' *Bonhomme Richard* defeated the *Serapis* on September 23, 1779.

(1939); and the posthumous *Stephen Hero* (1944). In addition he wrote two volumes of poetry: *Chamber Music* (1907) and *Pomes Penyeach* (1927).

Juarez, Benito Pablo (1806–1872), Mexican statesman, born in Oaxaca of Indian parents. He gained prominence as governor of Oaxaca, and as leader of the Liberals became president of Mexico in 1858. A civil war followed, and Juarez did not establish himself in Mexico City until January of 1861. Re-elected in March, he tried to remedy Mexico's financial distress by suspending payments on the national debt, but this measure brought British, Spanish, and French troops into Mexico. War with France resulted and Archduke Maximilian became emperor. Juarez offered stubborn resistance but was driven to the north. Finally, through the influence of the United States, the French troops were withdrawn. Maximilian was captured and shot in 1867, and Juarez returned to be twice re-elected president. Although he instituted numerous reforms, his administration was marked by continuous revolutionary uprisings.

Jugurtha or **Iugurtha** (d. 104 B.C.), king of Numidia (113–104 B.C.). On the death in 118 of his uncle, King Micipsa, Jugurtha was given a share of the kingdom with his two cousins, one of whom he murdered. The other, driven out of the country, appealed to Rome. Jugurtha obtained the western and richer half of Numidia by bribery. He killed his surviving cousin and several Romans in 112, bringing on the Jugurthine

War. For years Jugurtha evaded capture by bribing the Roman generals. However, he was eventually defeated by Quintus Metellus. Captured by Sulla in 106, he was exhibited in a triumphal procession at Rome two years later. After this humiliating appearance with his two sons in the triumph of Marius, Jugurtha was imprisoned and died either of starvation or strangulation.

Julian, in full **Flavius Claudius Julianus** (331–363 A.D.), Roman emperor, the nephew of Constantine the Great. Born in Constantinople, he was raised as a Christian. He studied in Athens, where he converted to paganism and became a vigorous opponent of Christianity; hence he was called "Julian the Apostate." In 355 Constantine made him joint ruler and sent him to Gaul, where, as a leader popular with his army, he won several victories against the Germans. He became emperor in 361 upon the death of Constantine and was killed two years later in a battle against the Persians.

Julius II, born **Giuliano della Rovere** (1443–1513), Roman Catholic pope. His uncle Sixtus IV made him a cardinal in 1471, and in 1503 he succeeded Pius III as pope. Although he was a soldier and politician who, within his ten-year reign, restored the Papal States, drove the French out of Italy, and reformed Church rule, his more lasting significance is as a patron of the arts. He laid the cornerstone of the new St. Peter's, designed by Bramante in 1506. He commissioned Michelangelo to decorate the ceiling of the Sistine Chapel and to design his own tomb, and employed Raphael to decorate his private apartments.

Julius Caesar. See *Caesar, Gaius Julius.*

Jung, Carl Gustav (1875–1961), Swiss psychologist and psychiatrist, born in Basel. An early and brilliant disciple of Sigmund Freud, he broke with his mentor in 1912 and formulated his own theory of the libido, which he regarded as the will to live. Jung's system, which he called "analytical psychology," differs from Freudian psychology in its emphasis upon present problems of adjustment as opposed to the problems of early childhood. Jung's most original concept is his idea of the collective unconscious—those qualities inherited from ancestors. The unconscious, he maintained, includes both the personal unconscious of the individual and his ancestral unconscious. Jung gave modern psychology the terms extraversion and introversion. His works include *The Psychology of the Unconscious* (1916), *Theory of Analytical Psychology* (1917), *Psychological Types* (1923), *Modern Man In Search of a Soul* (1933), *Psychology and Religion* (1938), and *The Undiscovered Self* (1958).

Justin, Saint, known as **Justin the Martyr** or **the Philosopher** (c.100–c.165), early Christian writer, born in Flavia Neapolis, a Roman city in Samaria. Educated as a pagan, he studied the Stoic and Platonic philosophies and accepted the latter. After his conversion to Christianity in Ephesus (c.135), he made every effort to win converts to his adopted faith. Justin was the author of *Apologies for the Christians,* addressed respectively to the Roman emperor and the Senate, and of *Dialogue with Tryphon the Jew.* He is said to have suffered martyrdom in the reign of Marcus Aurelius. His feast day is April 14.

Justinian I, in full **Flavius Petrus Sabbatius Justinianus,** (known as) **Justinian the Great** (482–565), Roman ruler of the Byzantine empire, nephew and successor of Justin I. He ascended the throne in 527 and reigned for 38 years. His long reign was made brilliant by the military exploits of his generals Belisarius and Narses, who conquered the Vandal kingdom in Africa and reestablished Roman authority in northern Italy and in Spain. Justinian built the Church of Hagia Sophia (now a mosque) in Constantinople (Istanbul), and constructed aqueducts and other public works. However, his work as legislator and lawgiver gives him greater distinction. Under his direction a committee of eminent lawyers completed a codification of the Roman laws that became the basis of most of the European legal systems.

Juvenal, in full **Decimus Junius Juvenalis** (c.60–c.140 A.D.). Roman satirist. Little is known of his life except that he served in the army and visited Britain and Egypt. Juvenal is noted for his *Satires,* perhaps the most famous of their kind. The 16 known satires describe the manners and morals of Rome in his time, but his stories are now considered to be greatly exaggerated. Juvenal's third and tenth satires were imitated by Samuel Johnson in his poems *London* and *The Vanity of Human Wishes.* He had a profound influence on the development of satire as a literary form.

K

Kafka, Franz (1883–1924), Austrian novelist, born in Prague of Jewish parentage. His highly original and powerful novels *The Trial* (1925), *The Castle* (1926), and *America* (1927), are influenced by Freudian psychology and present the plight of modern man confronted with a hostile society. His central characters are invariably guilt-ridden and isolated from the mass of humanity. Kafka's style depends for its effects on a seemingly casual accumulation of details together with a matter-of-fact tone; it is marked by understatement and dependent on implication. Writers such as Albert Camus and Samuel Beckett have expressed their indebtedness to him. His short stories include *Metamorphosis* (1915) and *In the Penal Colony* (1919).

Kalakaua, David (1836–1891), king of the Hawaiian Islands, elected to the throne by the legislature in 1874. His reign was marked by quarrels with the more progressive political elements—especially after he tried to ignore a new constitution that had been ratified in 1887. He was succeeded by his sister, Liliuokalani.

Kandinski, Vasili (1866–1944), Russian painter and designer, born in Moscow. He spent his childhood in Italy, and as a young man moved to Paris, where he did his early work. In Munich, he was a cofounder of *Blaue Reiter* (Blue Rider), a group of abstract expressionist artists, whose aesthetic program is detailed in his book *The Art of Spiritual Harmony* (1914). He taught at the Bauhaus school at Weimar (1922–1933), where he exerted a profound influence on modern painting.

Kane, Elisha Kent (1820–1857), American explorer and scientist, born in Philadelphia, Pa. He received a medical degree from the University of Pennsylvania and in 1843 became an assistant surgeon in the U.S. navy. In 1850 Kane joined the First Grinnell Expedition to the Arctic in search of Sir John Franklin. He himself organized the Second Grinnell Expedition, which started northward in 1853. In command of the *Advance* he reached a latitude of 80°35′ north in June, 1854; this remained for 16 years the most northerly point reached by man. The *Advance* was abandoned in the spring of 1855, and the expedition used small boats to reach a rescue party. Kane's first published accounts of the expeditions gained much attention and he was honored by various European and American scientific groups.

Kano, a family of Japanese painters and a school of painting famous in Oriental art history. **Masanobu Kano** (c.1453–c.1540) was the founder of the family; he worked mostly in ink and did landscapes, birds, and figure compositions. **Motonobu Kano** (c.1476–1559), son of Masanobu and one of Japan's greatest artists. He is regarded as the actual founder of the Kano school, endowing it with its distinctive character: the subordination of color to design. His chief contribution to Japanese painting is that he freed the style of his time from Zen Buddhist influence, making aesthetic satisfaction its sole object, and thus established a new nationalized style. He painted landscapes, screens, and murals. **Eitoku Kano** (1543–1590), grandson of Motonobu. An official court painter, he decorated royal palaces and also painted screens and landscapes. **Morinobu Kano,** also called **Tanyu** (1609–1674), grandson of Eitoku and the last of the great Kano masters. Versatile and highly original, he practically founded a school of his own.

IMMANUEL KANT

Kant, Immanuel (1724–1804), German philosopher, born in Konigsberg, Prussia, the son of a Scottish saddlemaker. He graduated from the University of Konigsberg (1755) where he lectured on logic, metaphysics, mathematics, and several of the sciences. He was professor of logic and metaphysics at Konigsberg from 1770 to 1797. His famous *Critique of Pure Reason,* containing the fundamental doctrines of his system, appeared in 1781. This was followed by two supplementary works. *Critique of Practical Reason* (1788) and *Critique of the Power of Judgment* (1790).

Kant's ideas had a great influence on other thinkers. He maintained that knowledge begins when the senses transmit images made out of space and time. However, these images do not become knowledge until they have been unified by the inner power of understanding. The act of unifying follows twelve laws of thought that Kant called categories; these include such concepts as quantity, quality, cause, and effect. Thus all knowledge is made up of sensations joined together by the power of thought according to its own laws. Knowledge of good and evil, however, is not the result of experience or sensation but is part of the inner understanding.

Károlyi, Count **Mihály** (1875–1955), Hungarian statesman, born in Budapest. He entered the Hungarian parliament in 1905 as a liberal and in 1912 became a radical. After the outbreak of World War I he tried to bring about peace. Following the Hungarian revolution of 1918, he was made prime minister, and in 1919 he became president of the Hungarian republic. He resigned when revolutionists under Béla Kun established a Communist government. Károlyi went into exile after the conservative government was re-established. The High Court of Hungary found him guilty of treason because of his pacifist and radical views and confiscated his estates. After several years in exile, he returned to Hungary in 1946, and served as ambassador to France (1947–1949).

Karsh, Yousuf (1908–   ), Canadian portrait photographer, born in Mardin, Turkey. He was raised and educated in Canada, becoming a citizen in 1924. Among his portraits of eminent persons are those of George VI, Elizabeth II, Winston Churchill, Thomas Mann, Albert Schweitzer, Albert Einstein, and Pablo Picasso. Karsh's work is exhibited in the Museum of Modern Art (New York City), in the Chicago Art Institute, and in the Eastman House collection (Rochester, N.Y.)

Katsura, Prince **Taro** (1847–1913), Japanese statesman and soldier, three times premier of Japan. In his early twenties, he fought on the imperial side in the civil wars of the restoration period. His distinguished service in the war with China (1894–1895) won him a viscountcy. He served as minister of war from 1898 to 1900. During the Russo-Japanese War he became premier, but in protest against the Treaty of Portsmouth, resigned in 1906. Katsura was again premier from 1908 to 1911; he also held the office for two or three months in 1912–1913. In 1911 he was made a prince. The Anglo-Japanese alliance was formed during his first administration.

Kaufman, George Simon (1889–1961), American playwright, born in Pittsburgh, Pa. He studied law, worked as a salesman, and was drama critic for the New York *Times.* Most of his successful productions were the result of collaborations with Moss Hart, Marc Connelly, Alexander Woollcott, and Edna Ferber. Satire was Kaufman's forte, and his works enjoyed enormous popularity. He twice won the Pulitzer Prize: in 1932 for the musical comedy *Of Thee I Sing,* and in 1937 for *You Can't Take It with You.* Among his other notable productions, many of which he himself directed, are *The Man Who Came to Dinner* (1939), *Guys and Dolls* (1950), *The Solid Gold Cadillac* (1952), and *Silk Stockings* (1953).

Kaunitz, Count **Wenzel Anton von,** Prince **von Kaunitz-Rietberg** (1711–1794), Austrian statesman, born in Vienna. In 1735 he was appointed councillor to Charles VI, whose daughter and successor, Maria Theresa, he served for many years. Maria Theresa placed almost unlimited trust in Kaunitz. As chancellor and minister of foreign affairs he brought about the Austro-French alliance against Frederick the Great in 1756, which was followed by the Seven Years' War. He represented the empress in the partition of Poland (1772) and wrested Bucovina from Turkey (1775). After several years of service to Joseph II, Maria's successor, Kaunitz retired in 1792.

Kazantzakis, Nikos (1885–1957), Greek writer, born in Crete. He studied law in Athens and philosophy under Henri Bergson in Paris. He was minister of public welfare (1919–1927) and minister of state (1945–1946). Kazantzakis' literary output is marked by variety and quantity; he wrote fiction, poetry, translations, travel books, and philosophic essays. His greatest successes are his novels, which dramatize superbly the conflict between a life of action and a life of contemplation. Pessimism, which Kazantzakis considered heroic, pervades his writing and often seems close to nihilism. His most famous novels are *Zorba the Greek* (1952) and *The Greek Passion* (1953). His other works include *The Odyssey: a Modern Sequel* (1938), *The Last Temptation of Christ* (1951), and translations of *The Divine Comedy* and *Faust*.

Kean, Edmund (1787–1833), English actor, born in London. After 12 years as a member of traveling troupes, he achieved sensational success in London (1814) in the role of Shylock in Shakespeare's *Merchant of Venice*. He subsequently appeared in *Richard III*, *Hamlet*, *Othello*, *King Lear*, *Macbeth*, and other dramas. In 1820 and 1825 Kean visited the United States, where critics proclaimed him the greatest actor of his day.

Keats, John (1795–1821), English Romantic poet, born in London. He attended school in Enfield until 1811, when he was apprenticed to an apothecary-surgeon at Edmonton. Although he passed his medical examinations, he fell under the influence of Spenser's *Faerie Queen* and longed to become a poet. In London he made friends with William Hazlitt, Leigh Hunt, and Percy Bysshe Shelley and, owing to his increasing passion for literature, abandoned surgery. Hunt printed a sonnet for him in the *Examiner* in May, 1816. His first publication, *Poems by John Keats* (1817), was indifferently received. *Endymion* (1818) was savagely criticized in *Blackwood's Magazine* and in the *Quarterly Review*. In 1820 Keats published *Lamia and Other Poems*, his last book of verse. Seriously ill with consumption, he sailed for Italy in 1820 and died in Rome the following year.

Keats' longer poems include *Hyperion*, *Endymion*, the unfinished *Lamia*, *The Pot of Basil*, and *The Eve of St. Agnes*. It is, however, in his shorter poems that his true genius displays itself. Among these are the odes *On a Grecian Urn*, *To a Nightingale*, and *To Autumn*; the sonnets *On First Looking into Chapman's Homer* and *Bright Star*; and the ballad *La Belle Dame sans Merci*. Few English poets have so movingly expressed themselves on the subject of beauty, or have considered the subject of time and human mortality with greater feeling. Keats' collected letters, many of them written to his sweetheart, Fanny Brawne, are among the finest in English literature and suggest their author's sensitivity and bravery.

Keble, John (1792–1866), English poet and clergyman born in Fairford. He was educated at Corpus Christi College, Oxford, where he won several prizes. He was made a fellow of Oriel College in 1811 and was ordained five years later. In 1827 he published a volume of sacred poetry, *The Christian Year*, which was widely read and led to his appointment to the chair of poetry at Oxford in 1831. He was one of the leading spirits in the Tractarian movement in the English Church. For several years, with Dr. Edward Pusey and Cardinal John Henry Newman, he was engaged in issuing *Tracts for the Times*. The movement was essentially a defense of the Church against threats brought about by political changes and new habits of thought. Keble's sermon *National Apostasy* (1833) was regarded by Newman as responsible for the formation of the Oxford movement.

Keller, Helen Adams (1880–   ), American author, born in Tuscumbia, Ala. She became blind and deaf after a serious illness at the age of two. When she was eight, she became the pupil of Anne Mansfield Sullivan, a teacher at the Perkins Institution for the Blind. She learned to read Braille, type, and speak, and graduated with honors from Radcliffe in 1904. With Anne Sullivan, and later Polly Thompson, she has travelled widely in the United States and abroad, lecturing and visiting schools and hospitals. Her writings include *The Story of My Life* (1902), *The World I Live In* (1908), *Out of the Dark* (1913), *Midstream—My Later Life* (1930), and *Let Us Have Faith* (1940).

Kellogg, Frank Billings (1856–1937), American statesman, born in Potsdam, N.Y. He practiced law in Rochester and St. Paul, Minn., and became widely known as a special counsel for the United States in cases involving large corporations. He represented Minnesota in the U.S. Senate (1917–1923). In 1924 he was appointed ambassador to Great Britain and was secretary of state in the cabinet of Pres. Calvin Coolidge (1925–1929). He was the originator in 1928 of the treaty for the renunciation of war, commonly called the Kellogg-Briand Peace Pact, for which he was awarded the Nobel Peace Prize in 1929.

Kelvin, 1st Baron, title of **William Thomson** (1824–1907), British mathematician and physicist, born in Belfast, Ireland. He graduated from St. Peter's College, Cambridge, studied in Paris, and in 1846 became professor of natural philosophy at the University of Glasgow, a position he held for 53 years. In 1904 he was made chancellor of the university. His long career was remarkable for unceasing activity and achievement and won him many honors at home and abroad. He was knighted in 1866 and was created Baron Kelvin in 1892. His work as an electrical engineer for companies laying the Atlantic cables (1857–1858, 1865–1866) led to his invention of the mirror galvanometer for cable signaling and a siphon recorder for receiving signals. He invented a mariner's compass that is not affected by the iron of the ship and a sounding apparatus for use in deep water. Several forms of electrometer, the ampere balance, the electrostatic voltmeter, and electric-supply meters are the results of his original work in electricity and magnetism. He also worked in the fields of heat, sound, and light and formulated theories on the nature of ether and inertia.

Kemal Ataturk, also known as **Mustafa** or **Mustapha Kemal** (1881–1938), Turkish statesman, born in Salonika. He was given the name "Kemal," meaning perfection, because of his excellence in mathematics. Though of Spanish-Jewish descent, he was educated as a Muslim in Constantinople (now Istanbul). He fought in the Tripolitan and Balkan wars and commanded the Turkish armies on the Gallipoli peninsula in 1915. As the head of a group of nationalists he was strong enough in 1922 to establish the office of sultan. In 1923 Kemal won a diplomatic victory when the Treaty of Lausanne restored to Turkey much of the territory she had lost. He was chosen president of the republic in the same year, and Turkey rapidly became westernized. To hasten this process, Kemal abolished the Arabic alphabet in favor of a modified Latin alphabet. He was reelected in 1927, 1931, and 1935. He was awarded the family name "Atatürk," which means "father of the Turks" in 1934.

Kempis, Thomas A. See *Thomas a Kempis*.

Kennan, George Frost (1904–   ), American diplomat, born in Milwaukee, Wis. After graduating from Princeton (1925), he joined the foreign service of the state department and served in various diplomatic posts. He studied Russian culture and language, became an expert on Soviet affairs, and after 1947 was one of Pres. Harry S. Truman's top advisers on Communist containment. In 1952 he was appointed ambassador to Russia, but was recalled at the Soviet government's request because of his outspoken criticism of living conditions in Moscow. Kennan retired from diplomatic service in 1953 and received a professorship at the Institute for Advanced Study at Princeton in 1956. He was ambassador to Yugoslavia (1961–1963). For his book *Russia Leaves the War* he was awarded the Pulitzer Prize in 1957. His other books include *American Diplomacy 1900–1950* (1951); *Russia, the Atom and the West* (1958), and *Russia and the West Under Lenin and Stalin* (1961).

Kennedy, John Fitzgerald (1917–1963), thirty-fifth president of the United States (1961–1963), the first Roman Catholic and, at the age of 43, the youngest man ever elected to that office. He was born in Brookline, Mass., and educated at the Choate School and at Harvard University. In 1941 he joined the navy and during World War II achieved renown for the heroic rescue of his PT 109 crew after their boat was sunk by a Japanese ship.

Kennedy started his political career as representative of the 11th Massachusetts Congressional District (1946). He was reelected twice (1948; 1950) and in 1952 defeated Henry Cabot Lodge, Jr., for the Senate. His campaign for the presidential nomination began at the 1956 democratic convention. In 1958 he was reelected to the Senate and in 1960 was nominated for the presidency with Lyndon B. Johnson as his running mate. The theme of the Kennedy platform was established in his acceptance speech as he said, "We stand today on the edge of a new frontier." This was the beginning of a unique campaign that was highlighted by a series of television debates with the Republican candidate, Vice-president Richard M. Nixon.

At his inauguration (January 20, 1961) Kennedy gave a classic political address, which ended on the now famous phrase, "Ask not what your country can do for you—ask what you can do for your country." Once in office he had little success with his domestic program, but did play an active role in international affairs. In 1961 the Peace Corps was established and an Alliance for Progress was set up between the United States and Latin America, and in 1963 a limited nuclear test ban treaty was signed by the United States, Great Britain, and the Soviet Union. The most dramatic occurrence of Kennedy's presidency was the Cuban crisis of 1962 in which he ordered a quarantine on all ships carrying armaments to Cuba in order to halt a Russian missile build-up on that soil.

On November 22, 1963, Kennedy was assassinated while on a speaking tour in Dallas, Texas. He is buried in Arlington National Cemetery.

Kennedy is the author of *Why England Slept* (1940), a thesis, written while he was at Harvard, on the British appeasement policy which led to the Munich Pact; and *Profiles in Courage* (1956), a Pulitzer Prize winner about eight United States senators.

Kennedy, Robert Francis (1925–   ), American public official, born in Boston, Mass. He graduated from Harvard and the University of Virginia Law School. During the 1950's he served as an attorney in the department of justice and as counsel for Senate subcommittees on investigations and on improper activities in labor and management. He managed his brother John F. Kennedy's presidential campaign in 1960 and was appointed attorney general in 1961. In 1964 he was elected U.S. Senator from New York.

Kenny, Elizabeth, known as **Sister Kenny** (1886–1952), Australian nurse, born in Warialda, New South Wales. She graduated from St. Ursela's College (1902), became a nurse in the Australian bush country, and developed a treatment for infantile paralysis. During World War I she served as a nurse, after which she returned to Australia and in 1933 set up a clinic in Queensland. She lectured in England and elsewhere and in 1942 organized the Elizabeth Kenny Institute in Minneapolis, Minn., serving as director until April, 1949, when she became a consultant. Although her methods aroused controversy among some American doctors, her work was recognized by the National Foundation for Infantile Paralysis.

Kent, Rockwell (1882–   ), American painter, illustrator, and author, born in Tarrytown Heights, N.Y., and educated at Columbia University. He traveled in South America, Alaska, Greenland, and Labrador, and many of his paintings are of the people and scenes in the north. He is noted for his original and vigorous illustrations of literary classics such as *Moby Dick*, *The Decameron*, *The Canterbury Tales*, and *Candide*. Among his own books are *Wilderness* (1920), *Voyaging* (1924), *N by E* (1930), and *Salamina* (1935).

Kepler, Johannes (1571–1630), German astronomer, born in Weil, Württemberg. He studied theology and the classics at the University of Tübingen, but soon became interested in the teachings of Copernicus and the study of astronomy. In 1594 he was appointed professor of astronomy and mathematics at the University of Graz. Six years later, he became Tycho Brahe's assistant at the observatory near Prague. When Brahe died in 1601, Kepler took his place as imperial astronomer and mathematician, and continued the preparation of the new astronomical tables that he and Brahe had begun for Emperor Rudolph II. The Rudolphine Tables, with a catalogue of 1,005 stars, were published in Ulm in 1627. Meanwhile, in 1612, Kepler had become mathematician to the states of Upper Austria, with headquarters at Linz. In 1628 he accepted a similar position under Wallenstein. His greatest work, *Astronomia Nova* (1609), contains the first two of the celebrated planetary motion laws—those concerning elliptical orbits and equal areas. The third Kepler law, on the relations between periods and distances, was published in a treatise in 1619. These laws, on which Isaac Newton based his discoveries, modernized the science of astronomy.

Kerenski, Aleksandr Feodorovich (1881–), Russian revolutionary leader, born in Simbirsk. He studied law in St. Petersburg (Leningrad) and practiced in Moscow. Kerenski sat as a moderate Socialist in the last Duma (parliament) under Czar Nicholas II. He was minister of justice in the provisional cabinet set up in March, 1917, and in the ministry newly formed in May he dominated the cabinet as minister of war. In September he became president of the new republic and for a time ruled the country. However, the Bolsheviks proved too strong for him and in November, with the triumph of Lenin and Trotzky, Kerenski was forced to flee from Russia. His writings include *The Prelude to Bolshevism* (1919), *The Catastrophe* (1927), and *The Crucifixion of Liberty* (1934).

Kern, Jerome David (1885–1945), American composer, noted for his songs and musicals. Born in New York City, he studied at the New York College of Music and in Germany. With his musical *Show Boat* (1927), his greatest success, he influenced the development of American light opera. Among Kern's best-known scores are those for *Rock-a-Bye Baby* (1918), *Sally* (1920), and *Roberta* (1933). The best-known of his many songs include *Smoke Gets in Your Eyes, Ol' Man River*, and *The Last Time I Saw Paris.*

Kettering, Charles Franklin (1876–1958), American engineer, noted for his invention of the automobile self-starter. He was born in Loudonville, Ohio, and studied electrical engineering at Ohio State University. He first worked for the National Cash Register Company in Dayton where he invented an electric cash register. In 1909 he was named vice-president of Dayton Engineering Laboratories Company (Delco). He became general manager and president of General Motors Research Corporation in 1917, and two years later he was asked to organize and direct a central research lab for them. One of the top automotive engineers of his time, Kettering is responsible for such engineering advances as high-octane gasoline, electric refrigeration, and an improved diesel engine. He is also the founder of the Charles F. Kettering Foundation at Antioch College (1925) and the Sloan-Kettering Institute for Cancer Research in New York City (1945).

Key, Francis Scott (1779–1843), American lawyer, best known as the author of *The Star-Spangled Banner,* the U.S. national anthem. He was born in Frederick County, Md., studied law at St. John's College, Annapolis, and began practice in Frederick City in 1801. Later he lived in Washington and was appointed district attorney for the District of Columbia. During the War of 1812 he was sent on an errand under a flag of truce to the British fleet in the harbor of Baltimore. Kept on shipboard during the bombardment of Fort McHenry, he watched the battle throughout the night, and when the dawn revealed the American flag floating over the fort, he wrote the famous words to the anthem. Although known thereafter as the national anthem of the U.S. and adopted as such by the army and navy, it was not officially sanctioned by Congress until 1931.

Keynes, John Maynard (1883–1946), English economist, noted for his theory of economic aggregates, which led to the formation of a new school of macro-economics. He was born in Cambridge and educated at Eton and at King's College, Cambridge. From 1906 to 1908 he worked for the revenue department of the India Office. During both World War I and World War II he served the British treasury in an advisory capacity and in 1919 was sent as its delegate to the Paris Peace Conference. When his arguments against the reparations clause of the treaty were not recognized, he resigned and published his protest in *The Economic Consequences of the Peace* (1919). In 1941 he was named a director of the Bank of England and in 1944 was chosen to head the British delegation to the United Nations Monetary and Financial Conference at Bretton Woods, N.H., where he played a critical role in the formation of the International Bank for Reconstruction and Development and the International Monetary Stabilization Fund. His last service for the British government was to negotiate the Anglo-American loan of 1945.

In his most important work, *The General Theory of Employment, Interest, and Money* (1936), Keynes looks at the level of aggregate demand, total consumption, investment, and government spending as the cause of business cycles. He argues that the amount people spend on consumption and invest is determined by their income, and therefore the only way to increase aggregate demand and reverse a downward spiral is to increase government spending; this will directly raise the level of aggregate demand and generate new income, thereby giving more people more money to spend. These ideas were incorporated in the New Deal program of Pres. Franklin D. Roosevelt.

Keyserling, Count **Hermann Alexander** (1880–1946), German philosopher, born in Könno, Livonia (now Estonia). His property was confiscated during the Russian Revolution (1917), and he moved to Darmstadt, Germany, where he founded the School of Wisdom, a philosophical movement intended to reconcile differences in Eastern and Western thought. His philosophy stressed the idea of spiritual regeneration. Among his best-known works are *The Travel Diary of a Philosopher* (1925), *Creative Understanding* (1929), *Art of Life* (1937), and *Immortality* (1938).

Khayyám, Omar. See *Omar Khayyám.*

Khufu, also **Cheops** (r. 2590–2658 B.C.), Egyptian king of the 4th dynasty whose tomb, the Great Pyramid of Khufu, in Giza, is one of the seven wonders of the ancient world.

Kheraskov, Mikhail Matveevich (1733–1807), Russian poet, born in the Ukraine. He is best known for two epic poems: *Rossiada* (12 books, 1771–1779), which recounts Ivan the Terrible's campaign at Kazan; and *Vladimir Vozrozhdennyi* (18 books, 1785), which describes the conflict between pagan instincts and Christian faith.

Khrushchev, Nikita Sergeevich (1894–), Soviet political leader, who was first secretary of the Communist party and premier of the U.S.S.R. Born in Kalinovka, the son of a miner, he joined the Bolsheviks in 1918 and served as a soldier in the civil war. During World War II Stalin made him a lieutenant general and appointed him to the Presidium of the Communist party. When Stalin died in 1953, Khrushchev became first secretary. In 1958 he replaced Nikolai Bulganin as premier and served until October, 1964, when he was replaced by Leonid Brezhnev and Aleksei Kosygin.

Kidd, William, known as **Captain Kidd** (c.1645–1701), British pirate, born in Greenock, Scotland. He went to sea in his youth, settled in New York, and became a trader. During King William's War with France, Kidd was commissioned a captain to suppress piracy on the high seas, and in 1696 he sailed from Plymouth, England, in the galley *Adventure*. After taking on more men at New York he proceeded to Madagascar. He is believed to have taken up piracy himself in the course of his adventures. In 1699 he was arrested in Boston and charged with killing a mutinous gunner on the *Adventure*. Kidd was tried in England and hanged in 1701. Some of the treasure taken by him was dug up on Gardiners Island, N.Y., in 1699, and seized by colonial officials.

Kierkegaard, Sören Aabye (1813–1855), Danish existentialist philosopher and theologian, born in Copenhagen. Opposing Hegel's objective philosophy, he based his own on the subjective—faith, passion, and will. Religion was an individual matter for Kierkegaard, and the relation of the individual to God was one of suffering. His works include *Either/Or* (1843), *Fear and Trembling* (1843), *Philosophical Fragments* (1844), *Stages on Life's Way* (1845), and *Sickness Unto Death* (1849).

King, Martin Luther, Jr. (1929–1968), American Negro clergyman and civil rights leader, born in Atlanta, Ga. After graduating from Morehouse College, King obtained his bachelor of divinity degree from Crozier Theological Seminary and his doctorate from Boston University. He did much to further integration and brotherhood among Americans of all races. King wrote *Stride Toward Freedom* (1958) and *Why We Can't Wait* (1964). President of the Southern Christian Leadership Conference, a group dedicated to non-violence, Dr. King was awarded the Nobel Peace Prize in 1964. He was assassinated in Memphis, Tenn., on Apr. 4, 1968.

King, William Lyon Mackenzie (1874–1950), Canadian statesman, born in Kitchener, Ontario, and educated at the University of Toronto. In 1900 he became deputy minister of labor. He was elected to the House of Commons as a Liberal in 1908 and became first minister of the department of labor in 1909. Defeated in 1911, he devoted himself to economic research. He returned to political life in 1921 and, except for a brief period, headed the Liberal government as prime minister until 1930, when the Conservatives were returned to power. In 1935 he again became prime minister, an office he held until 1948. In 1945 he was one of the signers of the Washington Declaration on Atomic Energy and the UN Charter at San Francisco. He was chairman of the Canadian delegation to the San Francisco United Nations Conference on International Organization in 1945, the Conference of Paris in 1946, and the General Assembly of the United Nations held in Paris in 1948.

Kipling, Rudyard, in full **Joseph Rudyard Kipling** (1865–1936), English novelist and poet, born in Bombay, India. He was educated in England. His book *Stalky and Co.* (1899) is a group of stories about school life based on his experiences at the United Services College in Devonshire. In 1882 he returned to India, where he held editorial positions with the Lahore *Civil and Military Gazette* and the Allahabad *Pioneer*. His early verse and stories appeared in these periodicals. Between 1887 and 1889 he published *Plain Tales from the Hills, Soldiers Three, The Phantom Rickshaw, Wee Willie Winkie,* and other short stories that established his reputation as a writer of unique power. Before the end of the century he had produced the popular *Barrack-Room Ballards, The Light That Failed* (a novel), two *Jungle Books, Captains Courageous,* and other works of fiction.

After 1890 he spent several years traveling and during one period, having married an American in 1892, settled in Vermont. Kipling's *Kim, The Just-So Stories,* and *Puck of Pook's Hill,* written 1901–1906, were in the characteristic vein upon which his fame rests, but some of his later works seemed to lack the spontaneity and freshness his readers had learned to expect. He wrote busily, however, producing short stories, verse, political articles, essays, and a collection of his speeches, entitled *Book of Words* (1928). Kipling was the first British author to receive the Nobel Prize for literature (1907). In 1923 he succeeded James M. Barrie as lord rector of St. Andrew's University, Scotland, one of the many academic honors conferred on him. He was buried in Westminster Abbey.

Kirchhoff, Gustav Robert (1824–1887), German physicist, born in Königsberg. He is especially noted for his work with the spectroscope. With Robert Bunsen he discovered the elements cesium and rubidium and explained the Fraunhofer lines in the solar spectrum.

Kirchner, Ernst Ludwig (1880–1938), German painter and designer, born in Aschaffenburg. He studied art in Munich and architecture in Dresden. In 1905, with Erich Heckel and Karl Schmidt-Rottluff, Kirchner founded *Die Brücke* (The Bridge), the first school of German expressionist painters, which profoundly influenced modern German art. Kirchner's woodcuts and paintings are equally important. His work is characterized by intensity; Berlin street scenes are one of his recurring subjects. After World War I he settled in Davos, Switzerland. He committed suicide after his works were exhibited by the Nazis as examples of degenerate art.

Kitchener, Horatio Herbert, 1st Earl **Kitchener of Khartoum and of Broome** (1850–1916), British general, born in Ballylongford, Ireland. He was educated at the Royal Military Academy in England and joined the Royal Engineers in 1871. He did survey work in Cyprus (1878–1882), was assigned to the Egyptian army, and served in campaigns in Egypt and the Sudan. In 1892 he became sirdar (commander) of the Egyptian army and by his victories at the Atbara and Omdurman destroyed the power

INTERNATIONAL NEWS

RUDYARD KIPLING

of the Mahdi and restored Khartoum and the Sudan to British influence.

Kitchener left Egypt in 1899 and was appointed chief of staff to Lord Frederick S. Roberts in South Africa. He succeeded Roberts as commander in chief and was made a viscount in 1902 for his contribution to the victory over the Boers. After valuable service in India, he was promoted to field marshal in 1909. He was appointed consul general of Egypt (1911) and for his services there was made an earl (1914). On leave in England when World War I broke out, he assumed the position of secretary of state for war and with shrewd foresight made plans for a struggle of at least three years. While on a mission to Russia in 1916, Kitchener and his staff were lost in the North Sea. Their ship, the cruiser *Hampshire*, was mysteriously sunk, presumably by a mine.

Klee, Paul (1879–1940), Swiss painter, born in Bern, Switzerland. He studied at the Munich Academy, taught at the Bauhaus schools in Weimar and Dessau (1921–1931) and at the Düsseldorf Academy (1931–1933). He returned to Switzerland in 1933, when the Nazis came to power. With Vasili Kandinski and Franz Marc, he founded the German abstract school *Blaue Reiter* (Blue Rider). His work is an abstract interpretation of the subconscious and combines a variety of textures with delicacy of color and line.

Klopstock, Friedrich Gottlieb (1724–1803), German poet, born in Quedlinburg. His interest in theology characterizes his great epic poem *Der Messias* (The Messiah), which was influenced by Milton's *Paradise Lost*. The publication of the first three cantos at Leipzig in 1748 may be said to mark the beginning of the classical period of German literature; the last of the twenty cantos did not appear until 1773. He was invited to Copenhagen in 1751 by King Frederick V of Denmark, who provided him with a yearly pension. From 1770 until his death he lived chiefly in Hamburg, where he completed *Der Messias*. Klopstock also wrote odes, hymns, and poetic dramas.

Knox, Henry (1750–1806), American general, born in Boston, Mass. He joined the Revolutionary forces after the battle of Lexington, fought at Bunker Hill, and became one of George Washington's closest friends and advisors. He was commissioned brigadier general of artillery in 1776, saw distinguished service in every major battle from Princeton to Yorktown, and was made a major general in 1781. Knox was instrumental in the founding of West Point and was appointed its first commandant in 1782. He was the first secretary of war under the Confederation (1785–1789) and held this post in Pres. George Washington's cabinet (1789–1794).

Knox, John (c.1505–1572), Scottish Protestant reformer, who was one of the chief organizers of the Presbyterian Church in Scotland. Born near Haddington, he studied for the priesthood, became apostolic notary at Haddington (1540), but adopted the Reformed faith in about 1546. After Cardinal Beaton was murdered, Knox fled to the castle of St. Andrews for protection, but was captured by the French and imprisoned. Through the efforts of Edward VI he was released in 1549; he remained in England to work for the Reformation, but left in 1553 when Edward died. While he was pastor of the English church at Geneva (1555–1558), he met and was strongly influenced by John Calvin. In 1559 he returned to Scotland, where he became the leader of the reformers.

When Mary, Queen of Scots, returned from France (1561), Knox began preaching throughout Scotland against Roman Catholicism, which she sought to reestablish. For this he was forced into temporary retirement, but when Mary abdicated in 1567, Knox regained his former prestige. Before his death he saw Protestantism firmly established in Scotland. His chief work is *The History of the Reformation of Religioun Within the Realme of Scotland* (pub. 1584).

Knox, Philander Chase (1853–1921), American statesman, born in Brownsville, Pa., and educated at Mount Union College, Ohio. Admitted to the bar in 1875, he practiced in Pittsburgh and was an attorney for the Carnegie Steel Company. In 1901 Pres. William McKinley appointed him attorney general of the United States, a post he retained under Pres. Theodore Roosevelt. He was widely known for his prosecution of trusts. In 1904 he was appointed to the U.S. Senate to succeed Matthew S. Quay, and was elected for the term 1905–1911. In 1909 he resigned to become secretary of state under Pres. William H. Taft. Knox was reelected to the Senate

in 1916 and died in office. He was one of the leading opponents of the Treaty of Versailles and of the League of Nations.

Koch, Robert (1843–1910), German bacteriologist, born in Klausthal. He studied medicine at Göttingen and practiced in Wollstein, devoting most of his time to research. In 1882 he announced the discovery of the bacillus of tuberculosis and in 1883 that of Asiatic cholera. Koch spent considerable time in South Africa, where he discovered the causes of sleeping sickness and malaria, for which he prepared antitoxins. One of his most important discoveries was tuberculin, known as Koch's lymph, used in the test for diagnosis of tuberculosis. He was awarded the Nobel Prize for physiology and medicine in 1905.

Kodaly, Zoltan (1882–1967), Hungarian composer, born in Kecskemét; studied at the Budapest Academy of Music, where he was professor of composition from 1907 to 1942. With Béla Bartók he collected some 3,500 Hungarian folk songs. These influenced his own music. His best-known compositions include *Psalmus Hungaricus* (1923), a *Te Deum* (1936), the *Missa Brevis* (1945), and the opera *Háry János* (1926). He died Mar. 7, 1967 in Budapest Hungary.

Koestler, Arthur (1905–   ), Hungarian novelist and journalist. He was born in Budapest and received a scientific education at Vienna. In 1927 he became a foreign correspondent for a chain of German newspapers serving first in the Middle East, then in Paris, and finally in Berlin as foreign editor. Following his conversion to Communism in the 1930's, he spent a year traveling in the Soviet Union. In 1936 he was sent to Spain to report on the Spanish Civil War for the London *News Chronicle*. A year later he was in prison under death-sentence having been accused of spying by Franco. After three months he was released and began a record of his experiences, *Spanish Testament* (1937) or *Dialogue With Death* (1942) as it is called in the American edition. In 1938 Koestler returned to Paris and became editor of an anti-Nazi, anti-Communist German weekly. At the outbreak of the war he was again imprisoned and sent to a French concentration camp. He managed to escape and fled to England, where he later joined the British army. In 1951 he became a resident of the United States by act of Congress.

Koestler's best known work, *Darkness at Noon* (1941), is based on his own disillusionment with Communism following the Moscow purge trials (1936–1938) and his close brush with death in Spain. Koestler's other works include *The Gladiators* (1939), *Scum of the Earth* (1941), *Promise and Fulfillment* (1949), *The Age of Longing* (1951), *The Sleepwalkers* (1959), and *The Act of Creation* (1965).

Kokoschka, Oskar (1886–   ), Austrian painter, born in Pöchlarn. He studied in Vienna, where he later taught at an industrial school. He was a cavalry officer in the German army during World War I, and taught at the Dresden Academy of Art from 1918 to 1924. A leading Expressionist painter, he specialized in landscapes and portraits. His pictures were branded as degenerate by the Nazis and removed from German galleries.

Kollwitz, Käthe (1867–1945), German painter, etcher, and lithographer, born in Königsberg, Prussia. She studied in Berlin and Munich and settled in Berlin after her

marriage to a physician who deliberately chose to live and work among the proletariat. She is best known for her lithographs and woodcuts, which are eloquent protests against the hunger and misery of the poor and oppressed. In 1936 the Nazis banned the exhibition of her works.

Komura, Marquis Jutaro (1855–1911), Japanese statesman, born in Hyuga and educated at Harvard. He began his public career in 1877 as an official in the department of justice, was transferred to the foreign office in 1884, and later served as minister to the United States and Russia. As foreign minister he helped negotiate the Treaty of Portsmouth (1905), which ended the war with Russia. He was ambassador to England (1906–1908), after which he again served as foreign minister.

Kosciusko, Thaddeus, Polish name **Tadeusz Andrzej Bonawentura Kościuszko** (1746–1817), Polish patriot who served in the American Revolutionary War. Born in Lithuania, he received a military education in France. In 1776 he joined the American colonists in their fight for independence. He was a colonel under Gen. Horatio Gates and helped to construct the fortifications at West Point. He was later adjutant to Gen. George Washington. After the war Congress brevetted him brigadier general. Kosciusko returned to Poland in 1784, joined the Polish revolutionary forces, and distinguished himself in a number of battles against Russia. He became commander in chief of the army in 1794; fighting against heavy odds, he was severely wounded, captured, and taken to St. Petersburg (Leningrad). In 1796 he was released by order of the czar. He received a hero's welcome in England and the U.S., took up residence in France, and then retired to Solothurn, Switzerland.

Kossuth, Lajos (1802–1894), Hungarian patriot and statesman, born in Monok. He practiced law and became involved in reform movements. In 1837 he was imprisoned for illegally publishing a liberal newspaper. After his release in 1840, he continued his efforts as editor of the Pest *Journal*. In 1847 he was elected to the Diet of Hungary and became a leading spirit in the revolutionary activities of 1848. In the spring of 1849 the Diet proclaimed the independence of Hungary and appointed Kossuth governor with dictatorial powers. When the movement failed, he fled to Turkey, where he was imprisoned, but eventually released through the intervention of Britain and the United States. He spent the rest of his life in exile in England and Italy.

Kosygin, Aleksei Nikolayevich (1904–   ), premier of the Soviet Union, born in St. Petersburg (Leningrad). He was director of a textile factory in Leningrad and in 1939 was elected mayor of the city. In 1943 Stalin made him premier of the Russian republic, the most important of the Soviet states. He was appointed finance minister in 1948 and managed to survive the purge of 1949, but was demoted in 1952. He was made first deputy premier by Khrushchev in 1960, and in 1964 Kosygin succeeded him as premier of the Soviet Union.

Koussevitzky, Serge or **Sergei Alexandrovitch** (1874–1951), conductor of the Boston Symphony from 1924 to 1949. He was born in Vyshni Volotchok, Russia, and studied the double bass at the Philharmonic Music School of Moscow. Both as a conductor and as a bass player, Koussevitzky achieved re-

CHARLES PHELPS CUSHING

PATRIOTS: Kosciusko of Poland (*left*) aided Washington; Kossuth (*right*) defended Hungary.

nown in Russia and throughout Europe. In 1917 he moved to Paris, where he organized the "Concerts Koussevitzky" and conducted them until he was invited to come to the United States by the Boston Symphony. In 1934 he established the Berkshire Music Center at Lenox, Mass. (Tanglewood), famous for its summer festivals, and in 1940 he founded the Berkshire Music School.

Krafft-Ebing, Baron **Richard von** (1840–1902), German neourologist, noted for his work in the clinical analysis of paranoia. He was born in Mannheim and studied psychology at Heidelberg, Zurich, and Prague. In addition to holding professorships at Strasbourg (1872), Graz (1873), and Vienna (1889), he directed an electrotherapeutical clinic at Baden-Baden. He is the author of *Lehrbuch der gerichtlichen Psychopathologie* (1875), *Lehrbuch der Psychiatrie auf klinesche Grundlage* (1879), and *Psychosis Menstrualis (1902)*. His most famous work, *Psychopathia Sexualis* (1886; 17th edition, 1924), has been translated into seven languages.

Kranach, Lucas. See *Cranach.*

Kreisler, Fritz (1875–1962), American violinist and composer, born in Vienna, Austria. He studied in Vienna and at the Paris Conservatory. A virtuoso performer of his own and others' works, Kreisler made a number of extraordinarily successful European and American tours. As a composer he is best known for the violin pieces *Caprice viennois, Liebesfreud,* and *Liebeslied.* Kreisler also arranged classical music for the violin, wrote a string quartet, and an operetta, *Apple Blossoms* (1919). He became a U.S. citizen in 1943.

Krishna Menon, V.K. (1897–), Indian statesman born in Calicut, Malabar, and educated in India and at the University of London. He was a barrister and a history teacher in London and in 1929 he was made secretary of the India League and, thus, the spokesman for Indian nationalism in England. When India achieved dominion status (1947), he was appointed high commissioner. He also served as ambassador to Ireland. As leader of the Indian delegation to the United Nations (1952–1957), Krishna Menon was, in effect, the leader of the Asian "neutralist" nations. He served as India's minister of defense (1957–1962).

Kropotkin, Prince **Pëtr Alekseevich** (1842–1921), Russian revolutionary leader, born in Moscow. In 1862 he joined the Cossacks and served in the Amur region of Siberia, where he conducted several geographical surveys. He left the army, returned to St. Petersburg (Leningrad) in 1867, and made valuable geographical explorations in Siberia, Finland, and Manchuria (1871–1873). Kropotkin became associated with the radical workers' movement in Switzerland. He was imprisoned (1874) by the Russian authorities for spreading anarchist propaganda, but escaped (1876) and went to England. He returned to Switzerland (1877) but was expelled (1881) when Czar Alexander II was assassinated. After several years in England, he returned to Russia in 1917. Although critical of the Bolsheviks, he was allowed to remain in Moscow.

Kruger, Stephanus Johannes Paulus, known as **Oom Paul** (1825 1904), South African statesman, born in Colesberg, Cape Colony. In 1836 he trekked into the Transvaal with his family and became one of the founders of the Transvaal state. Active in the military and political history of the province, he was the leader of the revolt against British annexation. Following the war of 1880–1881 he was active in negotiating for Dutch independence north of the Vaal River and in 1883 Kruger was elected president of the newly-formed South African Republic, an office he held for four successive terms. Realizing that the South African War was inevitable, he made every possible preparation for it. In 1900, after the fall of Pretoria, he fled to Europe and spent most of his remaining years in The Netherlands.

Krupp, a family of German industrialists and manufacturers. **Friedrich Krupp** (1787–1826), founder of the family, invented a formula for making cast steel, and established a small plant in his native city of Essen, Prussia, in 1810. **Alfred Krupp** (1812–1887), son of Friedrich, established the present Essen steelworks. He was a brilliant metallurgist and the inventor of the weldless railway tie and the breech-loading rifle. **Friedrich Alfred Krupp** (1854–1902), son of Alfred, greatly expanded his father's steelworks, which became known throughout the world for its manufacture of heavy guns. In 1906 his daughter Bertha married **Gustave Krupp von Bohler und Halbach** (1870–1950), who adopted the Krupp name and assumed control of the company. The "Big Berthas," large German guns used during World War I, were named for his wife. Gustav Krupp made steam engines and agricultural machinery after the war. But when Hitler rose to power, Krupp gave financial support to the Nazi party and aided Hitler in the secret rearmament of Germany.

At the Nürnberg Trials (1945), Gustav was declared too senile to stand trial as a war criminal. His place was taken by his son **Alfred Krupp von Bohlen und Halbach** (1907–), who became head of the firm in 1942. An honorary member of Hitler's SS, Alfred was convicted of plunder in territories occupied by the Nazis and of employing concentration camp victims under slave-labor conditions. His twelve-year prison sentence was cancelled by an amnesty granted in 1951.

Kublai Khan, Kubilai Khan, or **Kubla Khan** (1216–1294), Mongol emperor of China, founder of the Mongol (Yüan) dynasty. A grandson of Genghis Khan, Kublai Khan succeeded his brother Mangu to the throne in 1259. Although his accession was disputed by another brother and a cousin, he maintained his hold on the khanate. In 1264 he founded his capital at Tai-tu (Peking); after it was completed, he proceeded with his plan to conquer all of China, a task to which he devoted 20 years. By 1280 China yielded to him, and he became the head of a great Mongol empire. The major portion of his empire was actually ruled by subchiefs, who recognized Kublai Khan as their overlord. In Tibet he set up the ruler of whom the Dalai Lama is a direct descendant. He was a patron of the arts, and under his rule Buddhism became the state religion. His empire lasted until 1368, when the Ming dynasty came to power. It was Kublai Khan who was the patron of Marco Polo.

Kuniyoshi, Yasuo (1893–1953), American painter, born in Okayama, Japan. He came to the United States in 1906, studied in Los Angeles and at the Art Students League in New York, and taught in several American art schools. His paintings, drawings, and prints combine Western techniques and Oriental ideas.

Kupka, Frantisek or **Frank** (1871–1957), Czech painter and illustrator, born in Dobruska. He settled in Paris, where he experimented with fauvism and pointillism. Kupka and Robert Delaunay were the earliest exponents of what Delaunay called "simultaneous color contrasts" and what Appollinaire later named *Orphism.*

Kuroki, Count **Tamemoto Tamesada** (1844–1923), Japanese soldier, born in Saga. He fought on the imperial side in the Satsuma uprising of 1877, won distinction in the Sino-Japanese War (1894–1895), and was commander of the First Army in the Russo-Japanese War (1904–1905). Kuroki fought in the battles of Yalu, Liaoyang Shaho, and Mukden, and in 1906 he was appointed inspector general of the army.

Kutuzov, Mikhail Ilarionovich, Prince of **Smolensk** (1745–1813), Russian field marshal, born in St. Petersburg (Leningrad). He served in Poland (1764–1769) and against the Turks (1770–1772; 1811–1812), where he distinguished himself and lost an eye. In 1787 he was made governor general of the Crimea and afterwards served successively as ambassador at Constantinople, governor general of Finland, ambassador at Berlin, and governor general of St. Petersburg. As an army commander in the wars against Napoleon, he suffered defeats by the French at Austerlitz (1805) and at Borodino (September, 1812), but won the greatest victory of his career at Smolensk (November, 1812) when, after forcing Napoleon to retreat, he cautiously followed the French, attacked them in full force, and annihilated them.

Kyd or **Kid, Thomas** (c.1557–c.1595), English dramatist, noted for his development of Elizabethan revenge tragedy. He was born in London and studied at the Merchant Taylor's School. After working as a scrivener, he turned to translating and writing plays. He was supported by a patron from 1587 until 1593, when he was arrested for blasphemy. Although he swore that the incriminating pamphlets were written by Christopher Marlowe, he was not freed until after Marlowe's death. Unable to find another patron, he died in poverty.

In his most important work, *The Spanish Tragedy,* (c.1585), a revenge play based on Senecan drama, Kyd employed the classical devices of the ghost and soliloquy, but placed the violence on stage instead of having it reported by messengers. Thus, he developed a whole new dramatic pattern, and his influence on Elizabethan popular tragedy is considerable. Most of Kyd's other work is either lost or unidentifiable, but Shakespeare's *Hamlet* is thought to be based on one of his plays.

L

LAFAYETTE: from portrait by S. F. B. Morse.

La Bruyere, Jean de (1645–1696), French writer and moralist. He was tutor to the duc de Bourbon, born and lived most of his life in the duke's household and is known for his book *Les Caractères de Théophraste, traduits du grec, avec les caractères ou les moeurs de ce siècle* (1688), a painstaking and witty description of the life and people of his time. It was enormously successful and remains a valuable source of historical information and a model of French style.

Lachaise, Gaston (1882–1935), American sculptor, born and trained in Paris. He came to the United States in 1906 and became an American citizen in 1916. Although he executed decorative sculpture in New York at Rockefeller Center and for the American Telephone and RCA buildings, he is chiefly known for his monumental single figures, which in their sensuous treatment convey powerful abstract rhythms.

La Farge, John (1835–1910), American painter, born in New York City. He was educated in the U.S. and studied art in Paris. In 1876–1877 he executed the mural decoration of Trinity Church, Boston, and in 1878 began glass painting and window designing. Among his numerous church murals are those in St. Thomas's, Church of the Ascension, Church of the Incarnation, and Church of the Paulist Fathers, all in New York. His commissions included mosaic windows for churches in Chicago and New York and for the Crane Memorial Library in Quincy, Mass. He also painted in oils and water colors, did book illustrations, and wrote art criticism.

La Farge, Oliver Hazard Perry (1901–1963), American writer and anthropoligist, born in New York City and educated at Harvard. He taught ethnology at Tulane University (1926–1928). Later he headed three archeological expeditions to Arizona for Harvard, two to Mexico and Guatemala for Tulane, and one to Guatemala for Columbia. He wrote *Laughing Boy* in 1929, a novel of Navaho Indian life for which he received a Pulitzer Prize. His story *Haunted Ground* won the O. Henry Memorial prize. In addition to several other novels, he wrote the text for a *Pictorial History of the American Indian* (1957).

Lafayette, Marquis **de,** in full **Marie Joseph Paul Yves Roch Gilbert du Motier de Lafayette** (1757–1834), French statesman and soldier, descended from an ancient family of Auvergne, born in the Château de Charaniac, Auvergne. He became a soldier and in 1777 came to America to fight on the side of the colonists in the Revolutionary War. Congress entrusted him with the defense of Virginia, where he rendered important services. He became acquainted with liberal principles in America and when he returned to France he tried to promote reform there. The extreme French Republicans came to dislike him because he advocated a constitutional kingdom; at the same time he was unpopular with the court party, especially the queen, because of his zeal for establishing a new order. Lafayette was a founder of the Club of the Feuillants. From 1789 to 1791 he was active in the National Assembly and Paris National Guard. In 1792 he was chosen to command an army fighting the Austrians. He lost his power and position in France through attacks by the Jacobins and was accused of treason but acquitted. After several efforts to maintain the cause of national liberty he left Paris for Flanders, but he was taken prisoner by the Austrians and held at Olmutz until Napoleon liberated him in 1797. He was in the Chamber of Deputies (1818–1824, 1825–1830). In 1824 he revisited America by invitation of Congress, which voted him a grant of $200,000 and a township of land. He took part in the French Revolution of 1830 as commander of the National Guard.

Laffite or **Lafitte, Jean** (c.1780–c.1826), French pirate, born in Bayonne. He and his brother Pierre were the leaders of a band of outlaws who had their headquarters on an island in Barataria Bay, off Louisiana. They preyed on shipping, engaged in smuggling, and terrorized traders in the Gulf of Mexico. In the War of 1812 he offered his services to Gen. Andrew Jackson and took part in the battle of New Orleans (1815). In recognition of his patriotism, Pres. James Madison pardoned Lafitte and his men. Laffite later returned to piracy, making his headquarters in Galveston, Texas, and, after they were destroyed, preyed on the Spanish main.

La Follette, Robert Marion (1855–1925), American statesman and political leader, born in Primrose, Wis. His name is associated with such doctrines as direct primaries, just taxation, pacifism, control of railroad rates, and government ownership. He graduated from the University of Wisconsin in 1879 and began to practice law the following year. He served four years as district attorney of Dane County and six years in the U.S. House of Representatives (1885–1891). Failing to be reelected, he resumed his law practice. During this period he attracted notice as a leader of those in revolt against the Republican machine in Wisconsin, and in 1900 was elected governor on a platform of political reform. Twice reelected, he resigned in 1906 to enter the U.S. Senate, and he remained there until his death. "Fighting Bob," as he was called, was an insurgent Republican throughout his senatorial career. Though his opposition to American participation in World War I temporarily lost him much prestige, he regained his standing and in 1924 was nominated for the presidency by the Progressive Party.

La Fontaine, Jean de (1621–1695), French poet, born in Château-Thierry. He studied for the priesthood, but gave it up to be a poet. After writing a series of tales based on Boccacio's *Decameron* and other sources, and several plays—all unsuccessful—he began in 1661 to compose his celebrated *Fabliaux* (*Fables*) in verse. In these fables his characters are beasts who behave like men. Although their simplicity and ingenuous charm make them appealing to children, the stories are essentially satires on the French society of his time. The series, totalling 238 fables in all, were collected in volumes that were published 1668, 1678, 1679, and 1694. La Fontaine was elected to the French Academy in 1683.

Lagerkvist, Pär Fabian (1891–). Swedish author, winner of the 1951 Nobel Prize for literature for *Barabbas* (1950). Lagerkvist's major works, which express in stark poetic prose his faith in man's goodness and his despair over intolerance and inhumanity, include *The Hangman* (1933), *The Dwarf* (1944), and *Pilgrims at Sea* (1963).

Lagerlöf, Selma Ottiliana Lovisa (1858–1940), Swedish author, born in Marbacka Manor, Värmland, and educated in Stockholm. She began writing novels while teaching at a girl's high school. Her first important novel, *Gösta Berling's Saga,* was published in 1891. Thereafter she was acclaimed as a writer of exceptional talent and in 1909 received the Nobel Prize for literature. In 1914 she became the first women to be elected to the Swedish Academy. Her other novels include *The Wonderful Adventures of Nils* (2 vols., 1906–1907), a children's book; *Jerusalem* (2 vols., 1901–1902); *The Girl From the Marsh Croft* (1908); and *The Outcast* (1918).

La Guardia, Fiorello Henry (1882–1947), American public official, born in New York City and educated at New York University. From 1901 to 1906 he was in the consular service and from 1907 to 1910 was interpreter at Ellis Island. He was deputy attorney general of the state of New York from 1915 to 1917. In 1917 he was elected to the U.S. House of Representatives, but during part of the term commanded the American air forces on the Italian-Austrian front. He was president of the Board of Aldermen of New York City in 1920 and 1921, and served in the U.S. Congress from 1923 to 1933. In 1934 he was elected mayor of New York City on a fusion ticket and served until 1945. He became nationally famous through his reforms, his relentless war on lawless elements, and his refusal to be governed by party politics.

WIDE WORLD

FIORELLO LAGUARDIA

Lalande, Joseph Jérôme Le Français de (1732–1807), French astronomer, born in Bourg-en-Bresse. The French Academy sent him to Berlin in 1751 to determine the moon's parallax and in 1753 elected him assistant astronomer. In 1762 Lalande became professor of astronomy at the Collège de France and in 1768 director of the Paris Observatory. In 1802 he founded an annual prize of 540 francs for special work in astronomy.

Lalo, Édouard Victor Antoine (1823–1892), French composer, born in Lille and educated there and in Paris. His works include the operas *Fiesque* (1867) and *Le roi d'Ys* (1888), a ballet *Namouna* (1882), and a violin concerto *Symphonie Espagnole* (1873), which became a concert favorite.

Lamarck, Chevalier **de,** in full **Jean Baptiste Pierre Antoine de Monet Lamarck** (1774–1829), French naturalist, born in Bazentin. He is regarded as the founder of invertebrate paleontology (study of fossils). Lamarck advanced a theory of evolution that was a notable advance in scientific thought, though later scientists would not accept his ideas about the inheritance of acquired characteristics. He is also remembered for his reform of the classification of animals, having added much to the system established by Carolus Linnaeus. In 1788 he was appointed keeper of the herbarium of the Jardin du Roi (now the Jardin des Plantes) and in 1793 became professor of invertebrate zoology at the Museum of Natural History. Lamarck's great work is his *Histoire naturelle des animaux sans vertèbres* (7 vols., 1815–1822). His evolutionary theories are contained in his *Philosophie zoologique* (1809). In a sense he was a forerunner of Charles Darwin, but he knew nothing of natural selection and the variation of types.

Lamartine, Alphonse Marie Louis de Prat de (1790–1869), French poet, historian, and statesman, born in Mâcon. His best-known work is *Méditations poétiques* (1820), which was an instant success and had a significant influence upon the Romantic revival in France. In 1848 Lamartine became a member of the executive committee of the provisional government and served as minister of foreign affairs. His *Histoire des Girondins* (1846), a defense of the Girondists, is noted for its articulate prose. His other poetic works include *Harmonies poétiques et religieuses* (1830), *Jocelyn* (1836), and *La chute d'un ange* (1838).

Lamb, Charles (1775–1834), English essayist and critic, born in London. He attended Christ's Hospital School, where he formed a lasting friendship with Samuel Taylor Coleridge. In 1792 he began his work in the accounting office of India House, where he remained for 33 years. It was during this period that he produced his most important literary work. Tragedy shadowed Lamb's life. His mother suffered from a streak of insanity, which appeared once in himself, though temporarily, but which affected his older sister, **Mary Ann Lamb** (1764–1847), throughout her life. In 1796 she stabbed their mother to death, and thereafter Lamb devoted himself to her, giving up thoughts of marriage and keeping her at his home during her intervals of sanity. Fortunately, she was able at times to assist him in his literary work.

In 1796 Lamb had four sonnets published in a book of poems by Coleridge. He continued to write but met with no real success until the publication of *Tales from Shakespeare* (1807), a children's version of the plays, written for William Godwin's *Juvenile Library*. Mary wrote the comedies for this series. Lamb's fame rests on his *Essays of Elia,* begun in 1820 for the *London Magazine*. These were collected in book form in two volumes, the second appearing in 1833 as *Last Essays of Elia*. They represent a wide variety of themes and are full of humor, imagination, and delicate charm. Among them are the well-known *Dissertation upon Roast Pig, Dream Children,* and *Old China*. Lamb retired from business life on a pension in 1825 and spent his last days in Edmonton. His sister died in 1847.

Lambert, Johann Heinrich (1728–1777), German mathematician and physicist, born in Mulhouse, Alsace. He was the son of a tailor and largely self-educated. He did valuable research on heat, light, and color. His first important paper, *Photometria* (1760), demonstrated how to measure the intensity of light. In addition, Lambert measured the coefficient of air expansion, constructed a color pyramid, formulated a theorem concerning planetary motion, and demonstrated the irrationality of π. The lambert (a unit of brightness) is named for him. Immanuel Kant developed a considerable interest in Lambert's *Neues Organon* (1764), a work concerning analytical logic, and corresponded with him.

Landis, Kenesaw Mountain (1866–1944), American judge and baseball commissioner, noted for his critical role in redeeming the integrity of major league baseball. He was born in Millville, Ohio, and studied at the University of Cincinnati and at Chicago's Union Law School. Landis practiced law until 1905, when he was named U.S. district judge for northern Illinois. His best known decision as a judge was a verdict of guilty with the record fine of $29,240,000 against Standard Oil of Indiana in the notorious rebate case. (The decision was later reversed in the appellate court.) Landis' reputation as a severe arbiter in the support of honesty led to his appointment as baseball's first commissioner after the "Black Sox" scandal of 1919. He resigned from the bench in 1922 in order to devote his full time to this position. In 1943 he was elected to the Baseball Hall of Fame.

Landor, Walter Savage (1775–1864), English poet and prose writer, born in Warwick and educated at Rugby and Oxford. He inherited a fortune on the death of his father, and squandered it. In 1808 he raised and led a force to help Spain in the Peninsular War. As a prose writer his fame rests chiefly on his *Imaginary Conversations* (5 vols., 1824–1829), consisting of a series of dialogues or literary and social topics. His other works are *Citation and Examination of William Shakespeare . . . Touching Deer-Stealing* (1834), *Pericles and Aspasia* (1836), and *The Pentameron* (1837). His best verse was published under the titles *Hellenics* (1847), *Simonidea* (1806), and *Collected Poems* (1795). Landor, a friend of Charles Dickens, was the model for Lawrence Boythorn in Charles Dickens' *Bleak House*.

Landowska, Wanda (1877–1959), Polish pianist and harpsichordist, born in Warsaw. She studied at the Warsaw Conservatory and in Berlin, then settled in Paris. After teaching at the Hochschule in Berlin (1912–1919), she returned to Paris, where she founded the École de Musique Ancienne in 1925. In 1940 she settled in the U.S. A foremost interpreter of early keyboard music, she is chiefly responsible for the revival of interest in the harpsichord.

Lang, Andrew (1844–1912), Scottish author, born in Selkirk and educated at St. Andrews and Oxford universities. He was a fellow of Merton College, Oxford (1868–1875) and then settled in London. Lang wrote almost constantly until a year or two before his death on subjects ranging from the Greek classics to physical phenomena, to primitive religion. He produced verse, fiction, literary criticism, biography, history and translations. Typical works include *Ballards and Lyrics of Old France* (1872), *Myth, Ritual, and Religion* (1887), *Life and Letters of John G. Lockhart* (1896), *The Mystery of Mary Stuart* (1901), and *Maid of France and Homer and His Age* (1908). Lang is also known for his collections of fairy tales; the first was *The Blue Fairy Book* (1889), followed by *The Red Fairy Book* (1890), *The Green Fairy Book* (1892), and others.

Langland or **Langley William** (c.1332–c.1400), English poet, a native of the Western Midlands and probably educated at the Monastery of Great Malvern. He is the author of *The Vision of Piers Plowman*, a satire that presents a vivid picture of fourteenth-century English life. Little is known about him except that he became a priest and spent most of his life in London as a singer of masses for the dead.

Langley, Samuel Pierpont (1834–1906), American astronomer and aviation pioneer, born in Roxbury, Mass. His formal education ended with high school. He became assistant at the Harvard Observatory (1865), assistant professor of mathematics at the United States Naval Academy (1866) and after 1887 served as secretary of the Smithsonian Institution. He invented the bolometer, an instrument for measuring radiant heat, and he established the Astrophysical Observatory and National Zoological Park at Washington. Langley devoted years of study to transportation by air and designed a motor-driven plane that performed successfully in the air in 1896. His machine embodied the correct principles of airplane construction, and he is generally credited with having proved the possibility of mechanical flight, although his machine failed to carry a man through the air. He wrote

voted himself exclusively to music and poetry. He was first flutist in the Peabody Symphony Orchestra in Baltimore. In 1875 he published his poem *Corn* in *Lippincott's Magazine*. His first volume of collected poems appeared in 1877. In 1879 he became lecturer on English literature at Johns Hopkins University. His lectures were published under the titles *The Science of English Verse* (1880), a study of the interrelationships between music and poetry, and *The English Novel* (1883). The melodious quality of Lanier's verse is evident in such poems as *The Song of the Chattahoochee, The Marshes of Glynn,* and *Sunrise.*

Lansdowne, Sir **Henry Charles Keith Petty-Fitzmaurice,** 5th Marquis (1845–1927), British statesman, educated at Eton and Balliol College, Oxford. In 1866 he succeeded to his father's seat in the House of Lords as a Liberal-Unionist, was lord of the treasury from 1869 to 1872, and in 1883 became governor general of Canada. His five-year term was notable for the completion of the Canadian Pacific Railway, the settlement of the fisheries dispute with the United States, and the suppression of the Riel Rebellion. Lord Lansdowne was viceroy of India from 1888 to 1893 and then returned to England, where he was prominent as Unionist leader in the House of Lords. After serving as minister without portfolio in Herbert Asquith's coalition cabinet he retired to private life in 1916. During World War I he advocated a peace with Germany and was repudiated by his government and by his party for having outlined peace terms in a letter written to the London *Daily Telegraph* in 1917.

Lansing, Robert (1864–1928), American statesman, born in Watertown, N.Y., and educated at Amherst College. He began the practice of law in 1889 and became

Laplace, Marquis **Pierre Simon de** (1749–1827), French mathematician and astronomer, born in Beaumont-en-Auge and educated at the College of Caen. His name is associated with the nebular hypothesis, a theory designed to account for the solar system. This hypothesis has long since been abandoned, but many remarkable discoveries make Laplace's fame secure. He was called "the Newton of France." In mathematics he developed the theory of probabilities and did brilliant research in integral calculus. In astronomy he extended knowledge of the motions of Jupiter and Saturn, the theory of the tides, and the stability of the solar system. His two chief astronomical works are *Celestial Mechanics* (1799–1825) and *Exposition of the World System* (1796), the latter containing the nebular hypothesis. In 1816 he became one of the "forty immortals" of the French Academy.

Lardner, Ring in full **Ringgold Wilmer Lardner** (1885–1933), American writer, born in Niles, Mich., and educated at Armour Institute of Technology in Chicago. He began his career in 1905 as a reporter for the South Bend (Ind.) *Times* and was later a sports writer for various newspapers, chiefly in Chicago. After 1919 he became a syndicated writer and contributed fiction to the *Saturday Evening Post* and other magazines. Lardner was noted for his humorous short stories written in a characteristic American vernacular. His books have been published under the titles *Bib Ballads* (1915), *You Know Me, Al* (1915), *Gullible's Travels* (1917), *Treat 'Em Rough* (1918), *How to Write Short Stories* (1924), *The Love Nest and Other Stories* (1926), and *Round Up* (1929).

La Rochefoucauld, Duc **François de** (1613–1680), French writer, best known for his widely translated *Maxims,* published anonymously in 1665 under the title *Réflexions ou sentences et maximes morales.* Another of his well-known works is *Les Memoirs sur la régence d' Anne d' Antriche* (1662). He was born in Paris of a noble and ancient family and at 16 joined the army. Active in the politics of his time, he fought in the wars of the Fronde. After being severely wounded in 1652 he retired to his country house. In later years, a prominent figure in the literary salon of Madame de Sablé, he counted Mme. de Sévigné and the Comtesse de La Fayette among his close friends.

La Salle, Robert Cavelier Sieur de, (1643–1687), French explorer, born in Rouen. He emigrated to Canada (1667), acquired a tract of land near Montreal, and became a fur trader. In 1669 he started westward on a tour of exploration that took him to the junction of the Ohio and the Mississippi or, according to some, as far as the Louisville rapids of the Ohio. When his men deserted, La Salle returned to Lake Erie alone. He immediately began to plan other expeditions and was aided by the Comte de Frontenac, governor of Canada. In 1682 he descended the Mississippi to its mouth and took possession of the great valley in the name of France, calling it Louisiana in honor of Louis XIV. After building a fort on the Illinois River, on the bluff now called Starved Rock, he went to France to organize a colonizing expedition. In 1684 four vessels carrying 400 men and stores of supplies set sail for the New World. By mistake the colonists were landed at Matagorda Bay at the mouth of the Colorado, and the captain of the fleet department for France before the error was discovered. After months of wandering in search of the Mississippi, during which the colony dwindled, La Salle started on foot for Canada and was murdered by his men.

Laski, Harold Joseph (1893–1950), British Socialist, noted for his important role in the growth of the British Labour movement. He was born in Manchester, England, and studied at New College, Oxford, where he became a member of the Socialist Fabian Society. Laski taught history at McGill University in Montreal (1914–1916) and at Harvard (1916–1920) before returning to England to work for the London School of Economics. In 1926 he became professor of political science at the University of London, a position he held until his death. Laski was a member of the executive committee of the Labour party from 1936 to 1949 and its chairman in 1945.

As a young Socialist, Laski believed in pluralism—that the rights of social groups could be attained through democratic means. He later altered his views in favor of the individual and, as he grew more and more disillusioned with the fruits of the democratic process, he became the advocate of a Socialist revolution. His works include *Authority in the Modern State*

CULVER

STEAM-POWERED AIRPLANE, built by Samuel P. Langley in 1896, flew for about a minute.

The New Astronomy (1888), *Experiments in Aerodynamics* (1891), and *Internal Work of the Wind* (1893).

Langmuir, Irving (1881–1957), American chemist, born in Brooklyn, N.Y., and educated at Columbia University and in Germany. In 1909 he became associate director of the General Electric Company's research laboratories. He developed several important theories involving atomic structure, introduced the use of hydrogen gas in welding (to prevent oxidation of the metals being welded), invented a gas-filled incandescent lamp in 1913, and contributed much to the development of the vacuum tubes used in broadcasting. He won the Nobel Prize for chemistry (1932) and the Faraday Medal (1943).

Langton, Stephen (d.1228), English theologian, educated in Paris. In 1207 he was appointed archbishop of Canterbury by Pope Innocent III, but King John refused to acknowledge the appointment until 1213. Langton was the first of the subscribing witnesses to the Magna Charta. He opposed the king after the reconciliation of the ruler and the church and was suspended from his office for two years. Reinstated at Canterbury in 1218 under Henry III, he held office until his death. He was responsible for the division of the Old Testament books of the Vulgate and was instrumental in the transition of the English church from a feudal to a national institution.

Lanier, Sidney (1842–1881), American poet and musician, born in Macon, Ga., and educated at Oglethorpe College. He fought in the Confederate army and after the Civil War became a lawyer. After 1873 he de-

prominent as counsel for the United States in the controversies with Great Britain involving the Alaska boundary and the Bering Sea and North Atlantic fisheries. In 1915 he succeeded William Jennings Bryan as secretary of state in Pres. Woodrow Wilson's cabinet, remaining in office until 1920. As secretary of state his knowledge of international law proved useful. He handled many critical situations incident to the World War I and attended the Peace Conference in Paris.

Lao-tzu, Lao-tse, or **Lao-tsze** (c.604–531 B.C.), Chinese philosopher, considered to be the founder of Taoism. He was a contemporary of Confucius, who visited him several times and was deeply impressed by his spirituality and humility. The precepts of Lao-tse are contained in his *Tao Tê Ching,* one of the sacred books of China. He taught the doctrine of the transmigration of souls according to Taoism, "All things originate from Tao, conform to Tao, and to Tao they at last return."

La Pérouse, Comte de, in full **Jean François de Galaup** (1741–1788), French navigator, born near Albi. He fought in the Seven Years' War and in the American Revolutionary War, in which he captured the British forts in Hudson Bay. In 1785 he sailed with two ships from Brest, France to look for the Pacific entrance to the Northwest Passage. At the same time he was supposed to study trade, and to explore coast lines bordering the Pacific. He actually finished much of the work and sent back records overland from Siberia. He was killed when both his ships were wrecked in the New Hebrides.

(1919), *A Grammar of Politics* (1925), *Liberty in the Modern State* (1930), *The State in Theory and Practice* (1935), and *The American Democracy* (1948).

Lassalle, Ferdinand (1825–1864), German Socialist, born in Breslau. He became an advocate of socialism and corresponded with Karl Marx and Fredrich Engels. In 1848 he was imprisoned for his outspoken criticism of the government. In later years he wrote political pamphlets that had considerable influence on members of the working classes. In 1863 he founded a revolutionary society dedicated to the overthrow of capitalism. A year later he was killed in a duel, the outcome of a love affair. This romance is the basis of George Meredith's novel *The Tragic Comedians.* Modern Socialists look to Marx as the exponent of their economic principles, but Lassalle was influential in giving the movement a political character.

Latimer, Hugh (c.1485–1555), English bishop, born in Leicestershire and educated at Cambridge. Through his preaching he popularized the principles of the Reformation. As a member of the ecclesiastical court that passed on the legality of the marriage of Henry VIII and Catherine of Aragon, Latimer upheld the king in declaring the marriage void. He was appointed bishop of Worcester in 1535. Dissatisfied with the progress of the Reformation, he resigned in 1539 and was imprisoned in the Tower of London in 1546. He was released when Edward VI took the throne and was again imprisoned when Mary became queen in 1553. After many months in the Tower he was tried, convicted, and burned at the stake.

Latini, Brunetto (c.1212–c.1294), Italian writer and statesman, born in Florence. He introduced French literature to Italy. A member of the Guelph party, he lived in exile in France from 1260 to 1269. He was chancellor of Florence in 1273. The prose encyclopedia *Li Livres dou trésor*, written in French, is the first vernacular encyclopedia and Latini's chief work. He was a friend of Dante, who referred to him in Canto XV of the *Inferno.*

La Tour, Georges de (1593–1652), French painter, born in Vic-sur-Seille. Although his works were well known to his contemporaries, they were neglected for centuries after his death. Little is known of his life except that he was one of the original members of the Royal Academy of Painting and Sculpture. His works, chiefly religious and genre subjects, show the influence of Caravaggio in their highly dramatic use of light (many are candlelight scenes) and simplicity of form. Among his fourteen extant pictures are *St. Joseph in the Carpenter's Shop, The Fortune Teller, The Newborn Child,* and *Adoration of the Shepherd.*

Latrobe, Benjamin Henry (1764–1820), American architect and engineer, born in Yorkshire, England. He came to the U.S. in 1796 and helped to build the James River - Appomattox Canal and supervised the building of the penitentiary in Richmond. In 1798 Latrobe settled in Philadelphia, where he designed the Bank of Pennsylvania, the old Academy of Art, and the Bank of the United States. As surveyor of public buildings in Washington under Pres. Thomas Jefferson, he had an influential part in designing the original Capitol and superintended its rebuilding after it was burned in 1814. He designed the Roman Catholic Cathedral in Baltimore, the first cathedral built (1805–1821) in the U.S.

Laud, William (1573–1645), English archbishop, born in Reading and educated at Oxford. Ordained a priest in 1601, he soon became chaplain to James I. His advancement was rapid: he became bishop of Bath (1626), bishop of London (1628), and archbishop of Canterbury (1633). A fierce opponent of Roman Catholicism and Puritanism, Laud established strict rules for worship and persecuted those who did not conform. This policy was the cause of much unrest, especially in Scotland. In 1641 he was arrested by order of the House of Commons, which had impeached him on a charge of high treason, and he was beheaded on Tower Hill, London.

Laurens, Henry (1724–1792), American statesman, born in Charleston, S.C. In 1776 he became a member of the Continental Congress, representing South Carolina, and in the following year was elected its president. In 1779 he was sent on state business to Holland but was captured on the way by a British ship-of-war and taken to London, where he was kept prisoner in the Tower of London for 15 months. When the Revolutionary War ended, he was freed and became one of the group that drew up the treaty of peace.

Laurier, Sir Wilfrid (1841–1919), Canadian statesman, the first French Canadian to become prime minister (1896–1911) of the Dominion. He was born in St. Lin, Quebec, and studied law at McGill University. He rose rapidly in his profession and in 1871 was elected as a Liberal to the Quebec Provincial Assembly. In 1874 he was elected to the Federal Assembly. When Edward Blake retired in 1891, Laurier was chosen leader of the Liberal party which he led to victory in the general election of 1896. His tariff legislation of 1897, giving Great Britain the benefit of preferential trade with Canada, was warmly received in both countries. In 1900 he again secured the approval of both the Dominion and the Empire by the prompt dispatch of Canadian troops to aid Britain in South Africa, and he led his party to another victory at the polls in November. He was again returned to office in 1904 and 1908. During World War I he urged the French Canadians to support the Allies.

Lavoisier, Antoine Laurent (1743–1794), French scientist, one of the founders of modern chemistry. He was born in Paris and educated at the Collège Mazarin, where he distinguished himself in mathematics, botany, and chemistry. In 1768 he was elected to the Academy of Sciences, and in 1769 was given a government office. The income from this position enabled him to carry on the original studies which made him one of the great pioneers of chemical research. Lavoisier was the first to use the quantitative method of solving chemical problems. By actual weighing he proved that matter may be altered but is never destroyed, and until recent times his theory was accepted without question. In experiments with combustion he showed that the combustible substance always combines with oxygen, which he named.

In addition, Lavoisier proved that water is a compound of two elements, hydrogen and oxygen, and he paved the way for the modern scientific classification of elements and compounds. The generally accepted system of chemical language is described in his *Méthode de nomenclature chimique*, (*Method of Chemical Nomenclature*, 1787). Lavoisier did much for scientific agriculture in France; improved the manufacture of gunpowder; introduced reforms in accounting, taxation, and banking; and helped to organize the metric system of weights and measures. During the French Revolution he was convicted of having aristocratic sympathies, and was guillotined.

Law, Bonar, full name **Andrew Bonar Law** (1858–1923), British statesman, born in New Brunswick, Canada. He was educated in Scotland, entered business and became a successful iron manufacturer in Glasgow. In 1900 he entered Parliament as a Unionist (Conservative) and was active in politics thereafter. In 1911 he succeeded Arthur J. Balfour as leader of the Conservative opposition, and he joined Herbert H. Asquith's war cabinet in 1916 as colonial secretary. He became chancellor of the exchequer under David Lloyd George in the crisis of December, 1916, and acted as leader of the House of Commons. In 1918 he gave up the exchequer post but remained colonial secretary until March of 1921, when he resigned because of poor health. In October, 1922, after the end of the war ministry, he became prime minister, but he resigned in the following May. He was buried in Westminster Abbey.

Law, John (1671–1729), Scottish financier and speculator, born in Edinburgh. After killing a man in a duel (1694), he fled to Amsterdam, where he studied banking. In 1716 he founded the Banque Générale, the first bank in France. In 1717 he developed the Mississippi Scheme, which began with the Compagnie d'Occident, an enterprise incorporated for the development of Louisiana. It merged in 1719 with the French East India Company and other firms to form the Compagnie des Indes. In the same year the Banque Générale became the royal bank. In 1712, when his scheme collapsed, Law was driven from France.

Lawrence, David Herbert, known as **D. H. Lawrence** (1885–1930), English novelist, poet, short-story writer, and essayist, known for his frank discussions of sexual relationships. He was born in Eastwood, Nottinghamshire, and by the age of 18 was teaching in the local schools at Croydon. The acceptance of his early verse by the *English Review* enabled Lawrence to publish his first novel, *The White Peacock,* in 1911. Although it was not a financial success, he decided to give up teaching in order to devote all of his time to writing. The publication of *The Rainbow* (1915), his first major work, created quite a scandal and the book was subsequently charged with obscenity and banned. This was the beginning of the heated controversy which was to accompany the appearance of each of his novels. Lawrence himself was not an immoralist, but he believed that society's repression of free sexual relationships was preventing man from leading a normal and fulfilled life. In *Women in Love* (1921), the best expression of this philosophy, Lawrence considers the sexual act as a polarization rather than a union, the man taking from the woman what is masculine in her and vice versa. He objects to the whole tradition of the devoted, self-sacrificing spouse, insisting that a woman in love should retain her independence and emerge from the relationship an even stronger individual.

Lawrence's other novels include *Sons and Lovers* (1913), *Aaron's Rod* (1922), *Kangaroo* (1923), *The Plumed Serpent* (1926), and *Lady Chatterly's Lover* (1928). He is also the author of *Psychoanalysis of the Unconscious,* several volumes of poetry, and some short stories and travel books.

Lawrence, Thomas Edward, known as **T. E. Lawrence** (1888–1935), British soldier, archaeologist, and explorer, called Lawrence of Arabia. He was born in Carnarvonshire, Wales, and educated in Jesus College, Oxford. Intense interest in oriental archaeology and native languages and customs kept him in Arabia, Syria, and Mesopotamia for several years. After the outbreak of World War I he joined the British intelligence service. In 1916 the British government sent him to Arabia, where he organized the Arab tribes for war, led them in battle, and was the mainspring of the campaign that destroyed Turkish influence in the region. A daring fighter whose specialty was train-wrecking, he won enormous respect and personal devotion from the Arabs. An account of his adventures, *The Seven Pillars of Wisdom,* was published in 1926. Disillusioned by the outcome of the postwar peace conference, Lawrence, by then a colonel, left the colonial office and enlisted as a mechanic in the RAF under the legally-adopted name of T. E. Shaw. He died in England in a motorcycle accident.

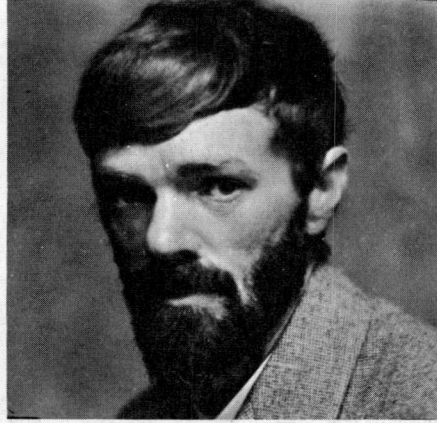

© MURRAY, BETTMANN ARCHIVE

D. H. LAWRENCE, controversial novelist.

N.Y. PUBLIC LIBRARY

T. E .LAWRENCE, called Lawrence of Arabia.

Lazarus, Emma (1849–1887), American poet, essayist, and philanthropist, born in New York City. Her literary works include *Admetus and Other Poems* (1871); *Alide* (1874), based on Goethe's autobiography; the poetic drama *The Spagnoletto* (1876); *Songs of a Semite* (1882); and *By the Waters of Babylon* (1887). Outraged by the persecution of Jews in Russia under Nicholas II, she devoted a considerable part of her last years to Jewish nationalism. Five lines from Emma Lazarus' sonnet *The New Colossus* are engraved on the pedestal of the Statue of Liberty, welcoming immigrants to America.

Lear, Edward (1812–1888), English artist and humorist, born in London. Although he was a successful painter of birds and landscapes, he is best known for his books of nonsense verse. These include *The Book of Nonsense* (1846), *Nonsense Songs, Stories, Botany, and Alphabets* (1871), and *More Nonsense* (1871). He traveled widely and wrote *Illustrated Journals of a Landscape Painter* about his experiences.

Le Brun or **Lebrun, Charles,** (1619–1690), French historical painter, born in Paris. After studying in Rome under Poussin, he returned to Paris and from 1642 until his death was the most influential painter and decorator in France. He founded the Académie Royale de Peinture (1648), designed the fountains and statues of the park at Versailles, superintended the adornment of the palace, and became first director of the Gobelin tapestry works. He produced numerous historical pictures and portraits, including Louis XIV's commissioned series now in the Louvre, based on the life of Alexander the Great.

Lecky, William Edward Hartpole (1838–1903), Irish historian and essayist, born near Dublin and educated at Trinity College, Dublin. He originally planned to become a priest but his interest in literature and history turned him toward writing. From the publication of his first book, *The Religious Tendencies of the Age* (1860), he was recognized as a writer of remarkable force, originality, and learning. The greatest monument to his scholarship is the *History of England in the Eighteenth Century* (8 vols., 1878–1890), written after ten years of research. Other works include *History of the Rise and Influence of the Spirit of Rationalism in Europe* (2 vols., 1865), *History of European Morals from Augustus to Charlemagne* (2 vols., 1869), and *Democracy and Liberty* (2 vols., 1896).

Le Corbusier, real name **Charles Édouard Jeanneret-Gris** (1887–1965), Swiss architect, born in La Chaux-de-fonds, one of the great innovators in modern architecture. After working for August Perret, a pioneer in reinforced concrete construction, and for Peter Behrens, a Berlin factory designer, he settled in Paris in 1917. During the 1920's he made an important contribution to the development of the international style in modern architecture. A pioneer in ferro-concrete frameworks, he introduced the idea of massive supporting stilts in his Swiss Pavillon at the Cité Universitaire in Paris. In addition, he employed the standing man as a unit of measurement in his apartment houses, which deal imaginatively with the problem of twentieth-century communal living. He was a vigorous advocate of architectural functionalism, and his influential *Vers une architecture* (*Toward a New Architecture,* 1923) includes some of the outstanding statements on modern architecture.

Lee, Charles (1731–1782), American Revolutionary general, born in Dernhall, Cheshire, England. He accompanied Edward Braddock to America in 1755 and later served in the Portuguese army against Spain. In 1773 he settled in America. Lee supported the patriot cause and in 1775 was appointed a major general in the Continental army. He accepted undeserved credit for the brilliant defense of Charleston, S.C., and in 1778 showed indiscretion by disobeying Gen. Washington's orders and failing to cross the Hudson, thereby nearly causing a severe American defeat. He was captured by the British but was exchanged. A court-martial suspended him and he was later dismissed for writing an impertinent letter to Congress.

Lee, Francis Lightfoot (1734–1797), American Revolutionary statesman and patriot, born in Westmoreland County, Va., a brother of Richard Henry Lee. As a member of the Virginia House of Burgesses (1758–1776) he boldly urged resistance to England. He was a member of the Continental Congress (1775–1779) and signed the Declaration of Independence. He served in the Virginia senate and later retired to his plantations in Virginia. He supported the Constitution, although his brother was opposed to it.

Lee, Henry, called **Light-Horse Harry Lee** (1756–1818), American Revolutionary general and statesman, born near Dumfries, Va., the father of Robert E. Lee. He graduated from Princeton at the outbreak of the Revolution and became a cavalry captain. His nickname was given him because of his quickness and energy in scouting and outpost duties. In 1780, at the head of "Lee's Legion," he covered Gen. Nathanael Greene's retreat through the Carolinas and fought brilliantly in several battles. He held various public offices after the war including the governorship of Virginia (1792–1795), and he was a member of the U.S. Congress (1799–1801). He was called upon to give a eulogy of George Washington, and delivered the oration that is remembered for the famous phrase, "First in war, first in peace, first in the hearts of his countrymen."

Lee, Richard Henry (1732–1794), American patriot, born in Westmoreland County, Va., and educated in England. As a leading member of the Continental Congress he introduced (June 7, 1776) the resolution declaring the colonies independent of Great Britain. This was adopted on July 2. Two days later the Declaration of Independence was adopted, and Lee later signed it. He was elected U.S. senator from Virginia after the ratification of the Constitution, and in spite of his opposition to the Constitution he supported the new regime and proposed the tenth amendment. Lee retired to private life in 1792 because of ill health.

U.S. ARMY SIGNAL CORPS

GENERAL ROBERT E. LEE

Lee, Robert Edward (1807–1870), American Confederate general, born in Westmoreland County, Va. He graduated from West Point (1829), second in his class, and was assigned to the engineer corps. In the Mexican War he was chief engineer of the central army in Mexico and was severely wounded at the storming of Chapultepec. As superintendent of the U.S. Military Academy (1852–1855) he greatly improved its efficiency. He was in command in Texas in 1860. At the outbreak of the Civil War, Pres. Abraham Lincoln offered him command of the Federal forces, but Lee refused. Resigning from the U.S. army, he offered his services to Virginia. Soon he became military adviser to Jefferson Davis and in 1862 was made commander of the forces around Richmond. There he won some success, turning the tide of war for a time in favor of the South.

In 1863 he won a great victory at Chancellorsville. Although defeated at Gettysburg, he managed to hold his own against superior forces. In February, 1865, Lee was put in command of all the southern forces, but by then they were too weak to make an impression on the strengthened northerners. On April 9, 1865, Lee surrendered his army to Gen. Ulysses S. Grant at Appomattox Court House, Va., and the war virtually ended. He frankly accepted the result and, although he had lost all his property, refused offers of money and accepted the presidency of what came to be called Washington and Lee University, at Lexington, Va., where he remained until his death. Many military critics regard Lee as the greatest military leader of the nineteenth century.

Leeuwenhoek or **Leuwenhoek, Anton van** (1632–1723), Dutch naturalist and microscopist, born in Delft. As a youth he used lenses in examining cloth in a factory in Amsterdam. In later years he assembled microscopes of great strength, some of them magnifying objects 270 times. He examined red blood cells and gave the first complete description of blood. In addition, he studied the anatomy of many insects and investigated the principle of male and female reproduction. The Royal Society of England honored him for being the first to see bacteria (1677).

Le Gallienne, Eva (1899–), American actress and producer. She was born in London, the daughter of the poet Richard Le Gallienne, and educated in Paris. In 1926 she founded the Civic Repertory Theater and ran it successfully until 1933. Notable productions were *Alice in Wonderland* and *The Cherry Orchard.* She played leading roles in many Broadway productions, including *Liliom* and *The Swan* by Ference Molnar; *The Master Builder* and *Hedda Gabler* by Henrik Ibsen; and *The Sea Gull* by Anton Chekhov.

Léger, Fernand (1881–1955), French painter, born in Argentan, Normandy, and educated at the École des Beaux-Arts in Paris. Originally trained as an architect, he became one of the leading painters of the Cubist movement and a popular teacher of painting in Paris and New York. His works have the sharpness and precision of a machine, whose beauty he celebrated. He also designed stained-glass windows.

Lehár, Franz (1870–1948), Hungarian operetta composer, born in Komarom, Hungary. He studied music with his father and at the Prague Conservatory of Music. Lehár's operetta *The Merry Widow* (1905) was presented in the Theater an der Wien in Vienna and had over 5,000 performances. In 1934 it was produced as a motion picture. Lehár's other works include *The Count of Luxemburg* (1909), *Gipsy Love* (1910), *Eva* (1911), and *Friederike* (1928).

Lehman, Herbert H. (1878–1963), American banker and politician who supported social and labor legislation and had concern for minority problems. He was born in New York City and studied at Williams College. After first working in the textile industry, in 1908 he became a partner in the family banking house. Lehman's political career did not begin until 1928, when he was elected lieutenant governor of New York. He was reelected in 1930, and in 1932 became governor, remaining in this office for four successive terms. Lehman was named head of the Office of Foreign Relief and Rehabilitation Operations by Pres. Franklin Roosevelt in 1942, and the following year was chosen to direct the United Nations Relief and Rehabilitation Administration (UNRRA), resigning in 1946. In 1949 he was elected to the U.S. Senate to finish the term of Robert F. Wagner. He was reelected in 1950 and retired in 1956.

Lehmbruck, Wilhelm (1881–1919), German Expressionist sculptor and etcher, born in Meiderich near Duisburg, the son of a miner. He studied in art schools in Düsseldorf as a scholarship student, lived in Paris from 1910 to 1914, and in Zurich during World War I. His early work shows the influence of the French sculptor Aristide Maillol. As his art developed, however, his single nudes began to appear as elongated figures, simply posed and expressing an agonized melancholy. Among his best-known sculptures are *Torso of a Woman, Standing Woman, The Kneeling Woman, Seated Youth,* and *Mother and Child.* The Art Museum at Duisburg and the Museum of Modern Art in New York have the two largest collections of Lehmbruck's works.

Leibniz or **Leibnitz,** Baron **Gottfried Wilhelm von** (1646–1716), German philosopher and mathematician, born in Leipzig. He studied law at the University of Leipzig, and although he was ready for his degree at the age of 20, the university authorities considered him too young for the honor and he received his doctor of law degree from the University of Altdorf (1666). He wrote several legal and theological treatises that showed his remarkable scholarly abilities and in 1670 entered the diplomatic service of the state of Mainz. In 1676 he was made librarian and privy councilor to the duke of Brunswick, at whose request he began a history of the House of Brunswick. For the rest of his life, Leibniz lived chiefly in Hanover. However, he visited Paris, London, and other centers of learning at various times and was on intimate terms with some of the leading intellectuals of the period.

He persuaded Frederick I, king of Prussia, to found the Academy of Sciences of Berlin in 1700 and Leibniz himself became its first president. He won distinction in many fields—history, theology, political science, engineering, and literature—but his most important work was in philosophy. He developed a theory in which substance consists of atoms or monads, each self contained and individual, the whole forming a perfect harmony with God, its center and creator. In mathematics Leibniz shares honors with Isaac Newton for the develpment of differential and integral calculus.

Leicester, 1st Earl, title of **Robert Dudley** (c.1532–1588), English courtier. In 1553 he was imprisoned in the Tower of London for participating in the plot to place Lady Jane Grey on the throne, and narrowly escaped the fate of his father, the duke of Northumberland, who was beheaded. After Elizabeth I came to the throne, he enjoyed many favors and was the queen's avowed suitor. She made him earl of Leicester. His first wife, Amy Robsart, died from a fall in 1560, and it was rumored that he was responsible for her death. The story is elaborated in Sir Walter Scott's *Kenilworth*. In 1573 he married Lady Shenfield and in 1578 he bigamously married Lettice Knollys, countess of Essex, but he remained Elizabeth's favorite until his death.

Lely, Sir Peter, real name **Pieter Van der Faes** (1618–1680), Dutch-English painter, born near Ubrecht, Netherlands. He went to England with William of Orange in 1641 and became famous for his portraits of important people. He was made court painter and was knighted by Charles II. His well-drawn pictures are of historical value, some of his subjects being Oliver Cromwell, Charles I, and Nell Gwynn. Two of his historical subjects are *Susannah and the Elders* and *Rape of Europa*.

L'Enfant, Pierre Charles (1754–1825), French army engineer and architect, born in Paris. He served with the French army but became filled with enthusiasm for the colonist's cause in the Revolutionary War. He came to America and joined the Continental army, rose to the rank of major, and was highly regarded by George Washington. When Congress decided to build a federal city, L'Enfant drew up the plans for it (1791). Wide avenues and large tracts set aside for parks and gardens were specified. He was appointed to carry out the work, but his disposition was such that nobody could work with him, and finally others built the city according to his plans.

Lenin, Nikolai, real name **Vladimir Ilich Ulyanov** (1870–1924), Russian Bolshevik leader, born in Simbirsk (now Ulyanovsk), on the Volga, the son of a government school official. He studied law at the universities of Kazan and St. Petersburg (Leningrad) and was admitted to the bar in 1891. His dominant interest, however, was in revolutionary politics. A brother had been executed in 1887 for conspiring against Czar Alexander III, and Lenin himself lived for a time in exile in Siberia (1895–1900); during this time he completed his economic study *The Development of Capitalism in Russia* (1899). He continued his radical activities in Russia and abroad and during the revolution of 1905 was editor of the first Socialist daily openly published in St. Petersburg. World War I gave Lenin his great opportunity. He was in Switzerland when the revolution of 1917 overturned the imperial government. Through the aid of the German secret

service he was permitted to go to Russia through Germany, and within a few months had triumphed over Aleksandr Kerenski and his associates, who could not counteract the propaganda of the Bolsheviks. In November, 1917, Lenin set himself up as the president of the Soviet of People's Commissars. He shaped the subsequent course of the revolution and established the Soviet Union and the system known as Bolshevism. Lenin has been regarded a brilliant revolutionary strategist.

Lenôtre, André, (1613–1700), French landscape architect who designed the gardens at Versailles, born in Paris. Louis XIV made him director of royal parks and gardens. Lenôtre's style, which emphasized spacious formality and the long, unbroken vista, dominated European landscape architecture until the nineteenth century. He designed, wholly or in part, the gardens at Versailles, Chantilly, Fountainebleau, the Tuileries, and St.-Cloud in France, and Kensington Gardens and St. James's Park in England.

Leo I, Saint, called **Leo the Great** (c.390–461), Roman Catholic pope (440–461), born in Tuscany. Leo upheld papal authority over the Roman Church, emphasizing its universal character. He also suppressed non-orthodox theories. In 452, when Attila the Hun invaded Italy, Leo persuaded him not to sack Rome. In addition, he was instrumental in saving the city from destruction by the Vandal hordes of Genseric (455). His feast day is April 11.

Leo X, born **Giovanni de' Medici** 1475–1521), Roman Catholic pope (1513–1521), son of Lorenzo the Magnificent, born in Florence. At the age of 13 he was created a cardinal by Pope Innocent VIII. Six years later he was expelled from Florence with other members of the Medici family and spent some time traveling. In 1513 he succeeded Pope Julius II. Leo's pontificate was remarkable for its patronage of art and learning. He encouraged Raphael and other artists of the Renaissance and welcomed to his court the finest scholars of the time. Abuses connected with raising funds to rebuild St. Peter's led to the reform movement under Martin Luther, who was excommunicated by Leo in 1520. Leo was drawn into the controversy between Francis I of France and Charles V, Holy Roman emperor. In 1516 he concluded a concordat with Francis, but later gave his support to Charles V.

Leo XIII, born **Gioacetino Vincenzo Pecci** (1810–1903), Roman Catholic pope (1878–1903), born in Carpineto, Italy. He studied for the priesthood, was ordained and became a domestic prelate under Gregory XVI (1837). In 1853 Pope Pius IX made him a cardinal as a reward for his years of service as archbishop of Damietta and of Perugia. Upon the death of Piux IX he was elected pope (1878) and entered upon one of the longest papal reigns in history. Leo XIII restored the hierarchy to Scotland, began one in India, settled religious difficulties in Germany, and maintained friendly relations with France. He regarded himself as a "prisoner of the Vatican", refusing to recognize the Italian government in Rome. Leo issued statements on capital and labor, Christian marriage, freemasonry, socialism (*Rerum Novarum,* 1891), and other controversial subjects. In 1883 he opened the Vatican archives to scholars interested in historical research. A man of scholary tastes, Leo wrote Latin prose and poetry of high merit.

Leonardo da Vinci. See *Vinci, Leonardo da.*

Leoncavallo, Ruggiero (1858–1919), Italian operatic composer, born in Naples, and educated at the Naples Conservatory. He spent a number of years trying to have an opera produced while supporting himself by playing at café concerts. His first and most famous opera, *I Pagliacci,* was performed at Milan in 1892. A later work, *Zazà* (1900), was moderately successful, but Leoncavallo's more ambitious pieces never managed to succeed. He was his own librettist.

Leonidas I (d.480 B.C.), king of Sparta (c.490–480 B.C.). He succeeded his half brother, Cleomenes I. In 480 B.C., when a great army of Persians under Xerxes threatened Greece, Leonidas went to the mountain pass of Thermopylae to hold back the invaders. For two days his 300 Spartans and 5,000 Thespians and Thebans successfully opposed the invading horde, but on the evening of the second day Ephlates, a traitor, told the enemy of a secret path at the rear. The next morning Leonidas sent his auxiliary forces home, and his small band of Spartans met the onslaught of the invaders alone, each man fighting till death.

Leopardi, Conte Giacomo (1798–1837), Italian poet and philologist, one of the foremost nineteenth-century Italian poets. Born in

BROWN BROTHERS

POPE LEO XIII

Recanati, he was plagued by physical deformity and chronic illness from early childhood. His family, distrusting his liberal religious and political ideas, kept him a virtual prisoner by depriving him of funds. His poems are characterized by intense patriotism, a romantic lyricism and feeling for nature, and a profound pessimism. His most important collection of poems is *Canti* (1836); others include *Canzoni* (1824) and *Versi* (1826). He also wrote poetic and prose satires and a number of philological studies.

Leopold II, originally **Louis Philippe Marie Victor** (1835–1909), king of the Belgians (1865–1905), eldest son of Leopold I, whom he succeeded in 1865. His reign was notable for the development of Belgian interests in Africa. In 1876 he organized the International African Association and in 1877 financed Sir Henry Morton Stanley's exploration of the Congo. In 1885 the Berlin Conference placed the Congo Free State under the personal sovereignty of Leopold. A system of forced labor and ruthless exploitation of the rubber and ivory industries caused an international scandal, Leopold being held responsible for the virtual enslavement of the natives. In 1908 the Congo Free State was turned over to the Belgian government. He was succeeded in 1909 by his nephew, Albert I.

Leopold III (1901–   ), king of the Belgians (1931–1951). After studying at Eton and training in the Belgian army, Leopold held a hereditary seat in the Belgian senate from 1926 until 1934, when his father, King Albert I, died and he became king. Strongly committed to neutrality, Leopold attempted to protect Belgium from German aggression by breaking all defensive alliances with England and France when the neighboring German Rhineland region was rearmed in 1937. In May, 1940, when Hitler's army did invade Belgium, the king surrendered soon after the first attack, bringing a heavy blow to Allied strategy and creating a storm of criticism upon himself from his senate, which voted to dethrone him. Having refused to go into exile, Leopold was interned in Belgium by the Nazis and was later sent to Germany, where he remained throughout the war, refusing to cooperate with the Nazis and obtaining aid for his people by appeals to Hitler. Between 1944 and 1950 the dethroned king remained in exile while his brother, Prince Charles, served as regent. In a 1950 plebiscite, slightly more than half the Belgian people voted to return Leopold to the throne; the senate obeyed the vote and Leopold was once more king. But the sharply divided national opinion created such severe disorders that, Leopold in 1951, abdicated in favor of his elder son, Baudouin, and since then has been only moderately active in public affairs.

Lepidus, Marcus Aemilius (d. about 13 B.C.) Roman politician prominent in the latter days of the republic. He was virtual dictator of Rome while Caesar was absent in Spain (49–48 B.C.) and was associated with him as consul in 46. After Caesar's assassination Lepidus joined Antony and Octavian (Augustus) in the Second Triumvirate and was given Gaul and Spain as

NOVOSTI PRESS AGENCY

NIKOLAI LENIN

his share of the Roman world (43). After the triumvirs defeated Brutus and Cassius at Philippi (42), they renewed their agreement and Lepidus was given Africa as his province. Because he felt neglected by his colleagues, he attempted to take Sicily by force. Having lost his army, his province, and his place in the triumvirate (c.32), he retired to obscurity.

Lermontov, Mikhail Yurievich (1814–1841), Russian poet and novelist, often called "the poet of the Caucasus," born in Moscow. After being dismissed for insubordination from the University of Moscow, he attended the cadet school in St. Petersburg (Leningrad) and became an officer in the guards. Stirred by Aleksander Pushkin's death, he addressed an impassioned poem to the czar (On the Death of the Poet, 1837), which resulted in his arrest, court-martial, expulsion from the guards, and brief exile to the Caucasus with a line regiment. Among his most famous poems are The Demon, Ismail Bey, The Novice, Hadji-Abrek, Valerik, and The Song of the Czar Ivan Vasilievich. His best-known novel is A Hero of Our Times (1839). He was killed in a duel with a schoolmate.

Lesage, Alain René (1668–1747), French novelist and dramatist, born in Sarzeau, Brittany. He studied law in Paris but receiving a pension on which he could live, he decided to write. His masterpiece, the novel L'Histoire de Gil Blas de Santillane appeared in four parts between 1715 and 1735. It is the story of the adventures of a rogue, Gil Blas, and is written in a realistic style that inspired numerous other authors. Lesage's other works include the novels Le Diable boiteux (The Devil on Two Sticks, 1707) and Tucaret (1708).

Lesseps, Vicomte Ferdinand Marie de (1805–1894), French engineer and diplomat, born in Versailles. He entered the consular service in 1825 and in 1828 was ambassador to Madrid. While on a visit to Egypt in 1832, he was impressed by the need of a canal across the Isthmus of Suez. Twenty-two years later Said Pasha, viceroy of Egypt, granted him a concession to build such a waterway, but work was not begun until 1859. De Lesseps was made president of the construction company that completed the Suez Canal in 1869. Ten years later he was asked to accept the presidency of a French company formed to construct a canal across the Isthmus of Panama. This project was abandoned in 1888 after the company became bankrupt. De Lesseps, financially ruined and discredited, was tried and sentenced to imprisonment.

Lessing, Gotthold Ephraim (1729–1791), German critic and dramatist, born in Kamenz, Saxony. He studied theology at the University of Leipzig but was much more interested in philosophy and the drama. In 1748 he settled in Berlin as a translator, literary critic, and author of verse and plays. Here Lessing associated with Voltaire and Moses Mendelssohn, among others. In 1755 he published a collection of his writings, including the drama Miss Sara Sampson (1755), the first German tragedy dealing with the common people. He is best known for the critical journal he helped to found, Briefe, die neueste Litteratur betreffend (24 vols., c.1759–1767). Among his other works are Laokoön (1766), a treatise on poetry and painting; Minna von Barnhelm (1767), regarded as his best play; Emilia Galotti (1772), and Nathan der Weise (1779).

Leucippus (5th century B.C.) Greek philosopher, said to be a native of Miletus. Little is known of his life; in fact his very existence is denied by Epicurus. There is evidence, however, that he studied under Zeno and founded a school at Abdera. Leucippus was considered by Aristotle to be the founder of the atomic theory in association with Democritus.

Leutze, Emanuel (1816–1868), American painter, born in Württemberg, Germany. He studied art in Philadelphia and in Europe. Leutze is best known for the popular Washington Crossing the Delaware, which is owned by the Metropolitan Museum of Art in New York. Another well-known work is the fresco Westward the Course of Empire Takes Its Way, in the Capitol at Washington, D.C. Other paintings include Columbus in Chains, Washington at Monmouth, and Cromwell's Visit to Milton.

Levant, Oscar (1906–) American pianist, actor, and composer, born in Pittsburgh, Pa. He was a close associate of George Gershwin, who greatly influenced him and his music. From 1935 to 1937 he studied composition with Arnold Schönberg. Levant became well known to the public through his acidly witty participation on the radio program Information Please from 1938 through 1942. He also gained fame for

his acting and piano playing in the movies, Rhapsody in Blue (1945) and An American in Paris (1951), as well as for his many recordings and frequent solo performances with symphony orchestras. After a prolonged illness in the 1950's, Levant returned to do his own television program on the west coast and has appeared as a performer in concerts. He is now a frequent guest on network television programs. His musical compositions include two string quartets, a piano concerto, a nocturne and many songs. He is the author of A Smattering of Ignorance (1940) and Memoirs of an Amnesiac (1965).

Leverrier, Urbain Jean Joseph (1811–1877), French astronomer, born in St. - Lô. He studied the motions of the planet Uranus and concluded that there must be another planet farther out in space. This resulted in discovery of the planet Neptune. The English astronomer J. C. Adams had come to the same conclusion a little earlier but had not announced his findings. Both men shared the honor. In 1854 Leverrier became director of the Paris Observatory.

Lewes, George Henry (1817–1878), English writer and critic, born in London. His knowledge of the literature and philosophy of Germany was reflected in his writings. He gave up medicine for literature, and in 1863 founded the Fortnightly Review, which he edited for fifteen years. His best-known book is his Life of Goethe (1855). He also wrote fiction, tragedies, and comedies. His long association with George Eliot had influence on her writings.

Lewis, Cecil Day, originally Cecil Day-Lewis (1904–), English poet and critic, born in Ballintogher, Ireland, and educated at Oxford University. During the 1930's Lewis, along with Stephen Spender and W. H. Auden, was an outspoken advocate of Marxist literary theories at Oxford; these ideas were expressed in A Hope for Poetry, published in 1934. By using contemporary ideas and symbols expressing the age, the three were credited with infusing a new life into poetry. In 1939 Lewis repudiated communism. From 1941 to 1946 he was editor of books and pamphlets for the British ministry of information. He was professor of poetry at Oxford from 1951 to 1956. Using the pseudonym of Nicholas Blake, he wrote several detective novels. His work includes From Feathers to Iron (1931), The Magnetic Mountain (1933), The Friendly Tree (1936), Overtures to Death (1938), Word Over All (1943), and Pegasus and Other Poems (1958).

Lewis, John Llewellyn (1880–), American labor leader, born in Lucas, Iowa. He worked in coal mines until he became an executive of the United Mine Workers' Union. In 1920 he became president of that union. During World War I, he was a member of the government committee that supervised coal production. In 1933 he was an adviser on labor problems to the NRA administration. Lewis became a national figure after the American Federation of Labor convention in the fall of 1935. The AFL was organized around the skilled trades, and Lewis suggested that the mass-production industries be organized as units —"vertical unionism." He was successfully opposed by William Green, president of the AFL. Lewis withdrew his union from the AFL and set about forming a rival organization called the Committee for Industrial Organization, later Congress of Industrial Organizations (CIO) of which he was elected the first president (1938). The CIO grew rapidly; its membership included not only the unions that seceded from the AFL but also a great many workers previously not unionized. Strikes were called in the motor, steel, and shipping industries. Lewis has at times led his United Mine Workers back to the AFL and at times he has led them as an independent union.

Lewis, Meriwether (1774–1809), American explorer, born near Charlottesville, Va. He was the leader of the expedition that charted the Louisiana county during Pres. Thomas Jefferson's administration. In 1803, when Jefferson decided to send an expedition into the West, he gave the leadership to Lewis, then his private secretary. Lewis chose his friend Capt. William Clark as associate leader, and the exploring party was gone until 1806. For his services Lewis received from Congress a tract of 1,500 acres. In 1807 Jefferson appointed him governor of Louisiana Territory. Lewis was mysteriously killed while traveling to Washington with records of the expedition.

Lewis, Sinclair (1885–1951), American novelist, born in Sauk Centre, Minn. He graduated from Yale in 1907 and he began his career as a reporter, working on newspapers in New Haven, Conn., and San Francisco. He was editor of Transatlantic

Tales, Volta Review, and Adventure, and for several New York book companies. In 1914, with the publication of Our Mr. Wren, he became well-known as a novelist. His first outstanding success was Main Street (1920), a satirical study of middle-class life in a small town in Minnesota. This was followed by Babbitt (1922), Arrowsmith (1925), Mantrap (1926), Elmer Gantry (1927), The Man Who Knew Coolidge (1928), Dodsworth (1929), Ann Vickers (1933), Work of Art (1933), It Can't Happen Here (1940), and The Prodigal Parents (1938). Lewis won the Nobel Prize for literature in 1930, the first American so honored. He had previously declined the Pulitzer Prize for Arrowsmith (1927).

Lie, Trygve Halvdan (1896–), Norwegian diplomat and United Nations official, born in Oslo. He studied law in Oslo, became legal adviser to the Norwegian Labor party, and was a member of its national council from 1926 to 1940. Lie served in the Labor government as minister of justice (1935–1939), minister of commerce (1939–1941), and characterized the United Nations of which he became secretary-general in 1946, as "the chief force that holds the world together against all the conflicting strains that are pulling it apart." In 1955 he was elected governor of Oslo.

Liebknecht, Wilhelm (1826–1900), German Socialist leader, born in Giessen. He was educated there and at Berlin and Marburg. He acquired radical views in his student days, was in Paris when the German revolution broke out in 1848, and led some volunteers to Baden in a vain attempt to establish a republic. Liebknecht then fled to London, where he came under the influence of Karl Marx. He wrote for several German newspapers and with the amnesty of 1861 returned to Germany, where he became editor of a newspaper. He was banished from Prussia in 1865 for his bitter opposition to Bismarck, and in 1872 he and Bebel were imprisoned for two years for libeling Bismarck. While in jail he was elected to the Reichstag. He became editor of Vorwärts, and in 1895 his written attack on the monarchy caused his arrest.

Li Hung-chang (1823–1901), Chinese statesman, born in Luchow and educated at Hanlin College, called "the Bismarck of Asia." In 1853, in the Taiping rebellion, he joined the imperial army as secretary. In 1862 he was appointed governor of the Kiangsu provinces and in 1870 viceroy of Chihli. He founded the Chinese navy and promoted a native mercantile marine. When war broke out with Japan in 1894, Li, in supreme command of the military and naval forces in Korea, was thwarted by the incompetence, dishonesty, and cowardice of inferior officers. The Chinese forces were swept out of Korea and Li, whose policy was that of peace, was deprived of his honors and summoned to Peking. Although he refused to obey, the emperor soon restored him to his post. Through his efforts the war was brought to an end in 1895.

Lilienthal, David Eli (1899–), American government official, born in Morton, Ill. He graduated from DePauw University in 1920 and from Harvard Law School in 1923. He practiced law in Chicago (1923–1931), then served for two years as a member of the Wisconsin Public Service Commission. He was appointed director of the Tennessee Valley Authority in 1933 and became its chairman in 1941. He was chairman of a commission whose report to the state department formed the basis for the United States' proposals for the establishment of the United Nations Atomic Energy Commission. This appointment aroused considerable opposition and confirmation by the Senate was delayed nearly six months. Charges of "incredible mismanagement" were leveled against the commission in general and against Lilienthal, as chairman, in particular. He resigned this post in 1949. Lilienthal urged public recognition of the importance of atomic science in nonmilitary projects, particularly in medicine, agriculture, and in the production of electricity.

Lilioukalani, Lydia Kamekeha (1838–1917), last queen of the Hawaiian Islands. She succeeded her brother Kalakaua in 1891 but was deposed in 1893 because she attempted to introduce reactionary measures and to rule without the constitution. A republic was established in 1894, but the plan to annex Hawaii to the United States failed at that time through Pres. Grover Cleveland's opposition. After annexation in 1898, the deposed queen retired to her estate but made several efforts to regain her throne.

Lincoln, Abraham (1809–1865), sixteenth president of the United States (1861–1865), born on a farm in Hardin (now Larue) County, Ky. He moved with his family in

1816 to Spencer County, Ind. For the next ten years he did manual labor of various kinds and was able to get only about a year's schooling. Twice he left farming to work on cargo boats that sailed down to New Orleans. He became a clerk at New Salem, Ill., joined a campaign against the Black Hawk Indians in 1832, and served for three months as captain of a volunteer company. Then he opened a country store, was appointed postmaster of New Salem, began to study law, and at the same time became a land surveyor. In 1834 he was elected to the Illinois legislature and was three times reelected to two year terms.

In 1846 he was elected a representative to the U.S. Congress from Illinois and, as a Whig, voted consistently with his party. The Republican party was formed to prevent any extension of the slaveholding area. Lincoln soon became its leader in Illinois and in 1858, supported by the new party, he campaigned for senator against Stephen A. Douglas, who was seeking reelection. The high point in the campaign was the series of debates to which Lincoln challenged Douglas. Although Douglas won the election, the debates had made Lincoln a national figure. In the Republican national convention held in Chicago in May, 1860, Lincoln was nominated for the presidency. The southern states, alarmed at the aggressive slavery policy declared by many of the leading Republicans, began to secede.

Lincoln was elected in November, 1860, and took office on March 4, 1861. It was his intention to conciliate the southern states if possible, but he was determined to preserve the Union even if he could not free the slaves. The southern Confederacy had been formed on February 4, and on April 14 the Civil War began when the Confederates captured Fort Sumter.

Lincoln announced the emancipation of the slaves in 1863 and was reelected in 1864. Gen. Ulysses S. Grant's victory over Robert E. Lee on April 2, 1865, was followed by Lee's surrender, and peace was in sight. On April 14, Lincoln was shot in Ford's Theater, Washington, by John Wilkes Booth. He died the next day.

Lincoln, Mary Todd (1818–1882), wife of Pres. Abraham Lincoln, born in Lexington, Ky. Married to Lincoln in 1842, she suffered much criticism during his presidency. After the deaths of her husband and three of her four sons, she became insane but recovered several years before her death.

Lind, Jenny (1820–1887), Swedish soprano, born in Stockholm and trained in Paris. In 1847 she appeared for the first time in London and later made her home in England where known as "the Swedish nightingale" she became very popular. She retired from the operatic stage in 1849 but was a concert favorite for many years. In 1850, under the management of P. T. Barnum, she made her first visit to the United States.

Lindbergh, Charles Augustus (1902–), American aviator, born in Detroit, Mich. In 1920 he entered the University of Wisconsin to study mechanical engineering but left in 1922 to enroll in a flying school in Lincoln, Neb. Lindbergh became an airmail pilot in 1926, making his first trip between Chicago and St. Louis. When he heard of the Raymond B. Orteig prize of $25,000 for the first nonstop flight from New York to Paris, he ordered a specially designed monoplane to be built in San Diego, Calif. He received financial backing from several residents of St. Louis and named his plane the Spirit of St. Louis. In this plane he took off from San Diego on May 11, 1927, reaching Curtiss Field, Long Island, in record time — 21 hours and 20 minutes. He took off from Roosevelt Field Long Island, on May 20 and landed at Le Bourget Field, Paris, 33½ hours later. This was the first solo flight across the Atlantic Ocean. When he returned to America he was officially welcomed by Pres. Calvin Coolidge, from whom he received the Distinguished Flying Cross and a commission as colonel in the Army Reserve Corps.

He then began a flying tour to 75 cities in the United States under the auspices of the Daniel Guggenheim Foundation for the Promotion of Aeronautics. Upon the invitation of Pres. Plutarco Calles of Mexico, Lindbergh flew from Washington to Mexico City. After completing a goodwill flight over Mexico, Central America, and the West Indies, and helping to inaugurate airmail service between these regions and South America, Lindbergh became an executive with a commercial aviation company. He continued his private flights, and in 1931 he and his wife (Anne Morrow Lindbergh), who herself had become a skilled pilot, flew to Japan by way of Alaska and Siberia. In 1932 the kidnaping of their son, Charles Augustus, Jr., shocked the nation; Bruno Hauptmann was executed in 1936 for this crime. During World War II he acted in an advisory capacity to the U.S. air force and was later made a brigadier general by Pres. Dwight D. Eisenhower. After his child's death Lindbergh lived abroad for a number of years. He returned to America from England in 1939 and made antiwar speeches for the America First Committee, an activity that prompted some to accuse him of pro-Nazi sympathies. Lindbergh is the author of *We* (1936), the story of the 1927 Paris flight. A later account, *The Spirit of St. Louis*, won the Pulitzer Prize in 1954.

Lindsay, Howard (1889–1968), American actor, director, and playwright, born in Waterford, N.Y. After one year at Harvard, Lindsay began his acting career in 1909, touring with repertory and vaudeville companies. With the distinguished Margaret Anglin repertory troupe (1913–1918), he gained experience in producing and directing. In 1921 he directed *Dulcy*, actress Lynn Fontaine's first success; in 1927 he produced and directed *Tommy*, a play he had written. Later, he wrote scripts for film and produced two successful movies, *Arsenic and Old Lace* (1941)) and *Detective Story* (1949).

During the 1920s Lindsay acted in a variety of Broadway productions. His best-known role was Clarence Day in *Life With Father* (1939), which he had written with Russell Crouse. Lindsay's association with Crouse began in 1934 with the musical *Anything Goes* and continued with many hits, including *State of the Union* (1945), which won a Pulitzer Prize; *Call Me Madame* (1950); and *The Sound of Music* (1960), for which Lindsay won an Antoinette Perry ("Tony") award. In 1959 Lindsay was awarded a special "Tony" citation for 25 years of excellence in the theater. He died Feb. 11, 1968, in New York City.

Lindsay, Vachel, in full **Nicholas Vachel Lindsay** (1879–1931), American poet, born in Springfield, Ill., and educated at Hiram College (Ohio), Chicago Art Institute, and New York School of Art. In 1912 he walked from Illinois to New Mexico, distributing verse and lecturing, a modern wandering minstrel trying to arouse a response to beauty among the people. In 1920 he became the first American poet to lecture at Oxford. His published poetry collections in which the influence of jazz is significant, include *General William Booth Enters Into Heaven and Other Poems* (1913), *The Congo and Other Poems* (1914), *The Chinese Nightingale* (1917), and *Collected Poems* (1923).

Lindsey, Benjamin Barr (1869–1943), American jurist, born in Jackson, Tenn. Admitted to the bar in 1894, he was appointed public guardian and administrator in Denver under the Colorado Juvenile Court Law of 1899. He served as judge of the juvenile court from 1900 to 1927, when he was removed from office for having accepted a bribe. After 1927 he became interested in an attempt to solve marriage problems, arousing wide discussion and much criticism for his advocacy of trial marriage. His writings include *The Beast and the Jungle* (1910), *The Revolt of Modern Youth* (1925), and *Companionate Marriage* (1927). He won an international reputation as a pioneer of the juvenile-court system.

Linnaeus, Carolus, Swedish name **Karl von Linné** (1707–1778), Swedish naturalist, the father of scientific botany and founder of scientific nomenclature, born in Rashult. He went to Vexiö for preparatory and college training and studied botany and medicine for a year at Lund. In 1728 he entered the University of Uppsala, later studied in Holland, and received his degree in medicine at the University of Harderwijk in 1735. For a few years he practiced medicine in Stockholm, and in 1741 he was appointed professor of medicine at Uppsala. A year later he began to teach botany there.

When Linnaeus began the study of botany, the method of classifying plants was so confused as to be almost worthless. He introduced a system based on the number of stamens and pistils that was the foundation of the modern method of classification. He is also famous as the father of the two-name method of naming plants, known as the Linnaean or binomial system, and for his simplification of plant description. Among the more important of his many books are *Systema naturae* (1735), *Fundamenta botanica* (1736), *Genera planatarum* (1737), *Philosophia botanica* (1751), and *Species planatarum* (1753).

Lin Piao (1907–), Red Chinese minister of defense, considered one of the prominent men in the succession to Mao Tse-tung. Lin Piao was born in central Hupei Province. After joining the Communist party at the age of 18, he decided on a military career and entered Chiang Kai-shek's Whampoa Military Academy at Canton. In 1927, when Chiang turned against the Communists, he led the guerilla rebellion and by 1932 was commander of the first Red Army corps. As a soldier Lin was highly respected for his courage. He led the famous march to Yenan (1934) which broke through the Nationalist encirclement, and after World War II he continued to effectively oppose Nationalist troops.

Lin first became involved in politics when he was elected to the Politburo in 1950. Then followed his rapid rise to power. In 1958 he became a member of the exclusive Standing Committee of the Politburo and in 1959 replaced the purged P'êng Têh-huai as marshal of the People's Liberation army. Lin was responsible for the political reorganization of the Chinese armed forces and for their increased intervention in civil affairs. In 1965 he published *Long Live the Victory of People's War*, considered the definitive expression of Chinese foreign policy. His army's newspaper played an important part in the 1966 purge and cultural revolution.

Lin Yutang, originally **Lin Yu-t'ang** (1895–), Chinese-American author and philologist, educated in Chinese mission schools and at Harvard and Leipzig. He taught English philology at Peiping University (1923–1926), invented the Chinese system of indexing, and collaborated in the official romanization plan. Since his settling in the United States in 1928, he has written in English. His works include *My Country and My People* (1935), *A Leaf in the Storm* (1941), *Between Tears and Laughter* (1943), and several novels.

Lippi, Filippino or **Lippino** (c.1457–1504), Italian painter, born in Prato, son of Fra Filippo Lippi. He was taught by his father and later by Botticelli. At the age of 23 he was commissioned to finish the frescoes begun by Masaccio in the Brancacci chapel in Florence. These and various other early works show his father's influence, but in later years he developed a taste for exaggerated poses and extreme decorativeness. Examples of this later style are his frescoes for the Strozzi chapel, Florence.

Lippi, Fra Filippo or **Lippo** (c.1406–1469), Italian painter. Fra Lippi was born in Florence and was raised in a Carmelite convent. In 1456 he became chaplain of the nunnery of Santa Margherita at Prato. According to Vasari, his biographer, he fell in love with a beautiful nun, whom he abducted and took to his house in the town. The two were permitted to marry after being released from their vows, and she became the mother of his son. Fra Lippi's paintings are noted for an exquisite blending of realism and spiritual beauty. Examples of his Madonnas may be seen in the Florentine Academy, the Louvre, the Pitti and Uffizi palaces, and in the Berlin and Munich museums. His frescoes from the lives of John the Baptist and St. Stephen in the cathedral at Prato are equally famous.

Lippmann, Gabriel (1845–1921), French physicist, born in Hollerich, Luxembourg. He taught experimental physics and was head of the research laboratory at the Sorbonne in Paris. He invented a process of color photography and did important research in thermodynamics and in the measurement of time. He won the Nobel Prize for physics in 1908.

Lippmann, Walter (1889–), American author and editor. He was born in New York City and educated at Harvard. He was associate editor of the *New Republic* for a time, but when the United States entered World War I he became assistant to Newton D. Baker, secretary of war, and later prepared data for the use of the American delegation at the Paris Peace Conference. He was on the editorial staff of the New York *World* from 1921 to 1931, serving as editor during the last two years. In 1931 he became a newspaper columnist for the New York *Herald-Tribune*, commenting on political and economic affairs. His books include *A Preface to Politics* (1913), *Public Opinion* (1922), *The Phantom Public* (1925), *A Preface to Morals* (1929).

Lister, Joseph, 1st Baron **Lister of Lyme Regis** (1827–1912), English surgeon and scientist, born in Upton, Essex. He graduated in medicine from the University of London in 1852. After hospital experience in London he became assistant surgeon at the Edinburgh Royal Infirmary and in 1860 was appointed professor of surgery at the University of Glasgow. Be became professor of clinical surgery at Edinburgh University in 1869 and was professor of surgery at King's College Hospital, London (1877–

1893). Lister was one of the greatest surgeons of his time, but is chiefly famous for his discovery of antiseptic surgery. He had seen that nearly every surgical case was complicated by suppuration and fever. He found the key to the difficulty in Louis Pasteur's discovery that microbes cause infection. In 1865 Lister made known his method of excluding pus-forming bacteria by sterilization of surgical instruments.

Liszt, Franz (1811–1886), Hungarian pianist and composer, born in Raiding. As a youth he showed so much ability that his education was financed by a group of Hungarian nobles. He studied in Vienna and Paris and soon performed on concert platforms appearing in London and other large cities. He was conductor of the Court opera at Weimar (1849–1861) and director of the Hungarian Academy of Music (1875). Liszt produced over 1,200 compositions, of which the best known are the *Hungarian Rhapsodies*. He was the creator of the term "symphonic poem", and left twelve examples of that musical form. In 1865 he joined the Franciscan order and after 1869 was known as the "Abbé-Liszt."

Littleton, Sir **Thomas** (c.1422–1481) English jurist, best known as the author of the *Tenures* (c.1481), the first printed treatise on English law, and the basis of the seventeenth-century commentary *Institutes of the Lawes of England* (1628, called *Coke upon Littleton*). Originally written in Norman French, it was printed in 1481.

Livingston, Edward (1764–1836), American lawyer and statesman, brother of Robert R. Livingston, born in Clermon, N. Y. He graduated from Princeton in 1781 and was admitted to the New York bar in 1785. He was a member of Congress from 1795 to 1801. In 1801 he became U.S. attorney for the district of New York and in 1804 was admitted to the bar in New Orleans. He soon rose to distinction as a lawyer in the South and compiled *A System of Penal Law*. He again served in Congress (1823–1829), entered the Senate in 1829 and in 1831 became secretary of state under Pres. Andrew Jackson. Two years later he was appointed minister to France, where he tried to get payment of U.S. claims for damage to shipping during the Napoleonic wars.

Livingston, Robert R. (1746–1813), American patriot and statesman. He was born in New York City and educated at King's College (Columbia University) in 1765. He became a member of the bar in 1773, developed a successful practice, and for a time was a partner of John Jay. Livingston was a delegate to the Continental Congress and served on the committee that drew up the Declaration of Independence. He helped draft the constitution of New York and as first state chancellor administered the oath of office when George Washington was inaugurated. In 1781 he became secretary of foreign affairs under the Confederation. He went to France as minister in 1801 and helped to negotiate the Louisiana Purchase. After his retirement from public life he devoted many years to scientific agriculture and steam navigation.

Livingstone, David (1813–1873) Scottish missionary and explorer, born in Blantyre. He studied medicine at Glasgow and in 1840 sailed for Africa as a missionary. He worked among the natives of Bechuanaland until 1849, when he left to explore the country to the north. Between 1849 and 1856 he discovered Lake Ngami, the Zambezi River, and Victoria Falls, having followed the Zambezi from its upper reaches to its mouth in the Indian Ocean. He published his *Missionary Travels and Researches in South Africa* after his return to London in 1856.

In 1858 he was appointed British consul for the east coast of Africa and commissioned to explore east and central Africa. He discovered Lakes Shirwa and Nyasa in 1859, and the results of the expedition were published in England in 1864–1865. He began his third and last journey to Africa late in 1865, to discover the source of the Nile and suppress slavery. The six years of this expedition were marked by hardship and privation. In 1871 he was rescued at Ujiji by Henry M. Stanley, sent by James Gordon Bennett, Jr., editor of the New York *Herald*, to find him.

Livy, in full **Titus Livius** (59 B.C.–17 A.D.) Roman historian, born in Patavium (Padua), in northern Italy. He was the most popular of the Roman historians. His work *The Annals of the Roman People*, was written partly at Rome and partly at Naples, under the patronage of Emperor Augustus. It consisted originally of 142 books, of which only 35 are wholly or partly extant. The history begins in 753 B.C. with the founding of the city and ends in 9 A.D. with the death of Drusus.

Lloyd George, David, 1st Earl of **Dwyfor** (1863–1945), British statesman, born in Manchester, England, of Welsh descent. He studied law and was admitted to the bar in 1884. He was elected to Parliament in 1890 as a Liberal. At that time he was regarded as radical in his views. He strongly opposed the Boer War in 1899. In 1905 he entered Sir Henry Campbell-Bannerman's cabinet as president of the Board of Trade. Three years later, as chancellor of the exchequer under Herbert H. Asquith, Lloyd George was responsible for important social legislation, including unemployment insurance, old-age pensions, and a financial policy that was adopted by the Liberal party. When World War I began, he prevented a financial collapse and maintained England's credit. He was appointed minister of munitions in the war cabinet of 1915 and became war minister on the death of Lord Kitchener. He was chosen prime minister late in 1916. Lloyd George led Britain through the war and represented the British government at the Paris Peace Conference. In 1922, unable to win support for his Irish and Greek policies, he had to dissolve his ministry. From then he became a leader of the Liberal opposition.

Locke, John (1632–1704), English philosopher, born in Wrington, Somersetshire. He was educated at Oxford and lectured there from 1661 to 1664 on Greek, rhetoric, and moral philosophy. He also studied medicine and became a physician. In 1666 Locke met Anthony Ashley Cooper, afterward earl of Shaftesbury, who later became his patron. For political reasons Shaftesbury sought refuge in Holland; Locke followed him into exile and remained abroad until the abdication of James II brought William and Mary to the throne (1689). Under the new government Locke was made commissioner of appeals, and in 1696 he was appointed commissioner of trade and plantations. This post he resigned in 1700 due to poor health.

Locke had organized the plan for his famous *Essay on Human Understanding* as early as 1670. He continued the work in exile and published it in complete form in 1690. In 1700, when a fourth edition was issued, he added a chapter on "association of ideas." He discussed the original sources and scope of human knowledge. His conclusions were that all knowledge is the result of experience and that beliefs in good or evil arise largely from the association of ideas; that the human mind is like a sheet of white paper (*tabula rosa*), upon which experience writes the impressions of the senses; and that sensation and reflection are the two sources of all our ideas. Among Locke's other works are his *Letters on Toleration, Two Treatises of Government* (1690), *Some Thoughts Concerning Education* (1693), and *The Reasonableness of Christianity* (1695).

Lockhart, John Gibson (1794–1854), Scottish biographer, editor, and novelist, best known as the author of a biography of his father-in-law, Sir Walter Scott. Lockhart was born in Cambusnethan and graduated from Oxford in 1813. Although admitted to the Scottish bar in 1816, he soon left law for journalism and general literary work. He contributed to *Blackwood's Magazine*, translated old Spanish ballads, and wrote novels. From 1825 to 1835 he edited the *Quarterly Review*. His principal work, *Memoirs of the Life of Sir Walter Scott*, appeared in seven volumes (1836–1838). He wrote biographies of Napoleon and Burns.

Lockyer, Sir **Joseph Norman** (1836–1920), English astronomer, born in Rugby. In 1868 he announced a method of studying the prominences of the sun in daylight. Under government auspices he took part in eight expeditions for the observation of eclipses. He was director of the Solar Physics Observatory at South Kensington in 1885 and 1913 was appointed to a similar office at the Hill Observatory, Devonshire. Lockyer wrote *Chemistry of the Sun* (1887) and *Sun's Place in Nature* (1897).

Lodge, Henry Cabot (1850–1924), American statesman and historian, born in Boston, Mass., and educated at Harvard, where he received degrees in law and philosophy. He lectured at Harvard and was editor of the *North American Review* and *International Review*, after which he entered political life. He represented Massachusetts in the House of Representatives (1887–1893) and in the Senate from 1893 until his death. Lodge was one of the most influential Republican leaders. He led the opposition to Pres. Woodrow Wilson's peace policies after World War I. Known as the "scholar in politics," he published biographies of Daniel Webster, Alexander Hamilton, and George Washington, and wrote *The Story of the Revolution* (2 vols., 1898) and *The Senate and the League of Nations* (1925).

Lodge, Henry Cabot, Jr. (1902–), American statesman, born in Nahant, Mass., grandson of Henry Cabot Lodge. After graduating from Harvard he worked on the editorial staff of the New York *Herald-Tribune* (1924–1936). He was elected to the U.S. Senate from Massachusetts in 1936 and reelected in 1942, whereupon he resigned to enter the army. He was reelected to a six-year term in 1946, but lost to John F. Kennedy in the senatorial race of 1952, the year in which he managed Dwight D. Eisenhower's first presidential campaign. Lodge served under Eisenhower as U.S. representative to the United Nations from 1953 to 1960. In 1963 he became U.S. ambassador to South Vietnam, a post to which he was reappointed in 1965 after resigning in 1964 to assist moderate Republican forces in the presidential campaign. He ran unsuccessfully for vice-president on the ticket with Richard M. Nixon in 1960.

Lodge, Sir **Oliver Joseph** (1851–1940), English physicist, born in Penkhull, Staffordshire. A graduate of University College, London, he became assistant professor of applied mathematics there in 1879, was professor of physics at University College, Liverpool (1881–1900), and from 1900 until 1919 was principal of the University of Birmingham. He won numerous honors and was knighted in 1902. Lodge made important investigations in the field of electricity. His researches on the nature of sound and electromagnetic waves were especially valuable and helped to make wireless telegraphy possible.

Loeb, Jacques (1859–1924), American biophysiologist, born in Mayen, Germany. He taught physiology at Würzburg and Strasbourg, and after 1891 he held professorships at Bryn Mawr College and at Chicago and California universities. In 1910 he was appointed director of the department of experimental biology at the Rockefeller Institute, New York. His researches on the origin of life convinced him that "life in all its branches is mechanistic." He exposed the eggs of sea urchins to ultra-violet rays and succeeded in developing them.

Lomax, Louis Emanuel (1922–), American Negro writer, born in Valdosta, Ga. He worked as a journalist from 1941 to 1958, after which he has been a free-lance writer and newscaster. He wrote *The Reluctant African* (1960) and *The Negro Revolt* (1962).

Lombroso, Cesare (1836–1909), Italian physician and criminologist, born in Verona. He was successively professor of psychiatry at Pavia, superintendent of the hospital for the insane at Pesaro, and professor of criminal anthropology at Turin. In his study *L'uomo delinquente* (*The Criminal*, 1875), Lombroso theorized that there is a definite criminal type, distinguished by a sloping skull, abnormal features, and a slight growth of beard. Although modern scientists do not accept this theory, Lombroso's researches initiated the science of criminology. He also discovered that pellagra is caused by faulty diet.

London, Jack, in full **John Griffith London** (1876–1916), American novelist, born in San Francisco. London's fiction was often based on his own experiences; he went to sea at seventeen, joined the gold rush to the Klondike, hunted seals in the Bering Sea, tramped through the United States and Canada, and became a newspaper correspondent in the Russo-Japanese War and the Mexican border troubles of 1914. London's first novel, *The Son of the Wolf*, appeared in 1900. Others include *The God of his Fathers* (1901), *The Call of the Wild* (1903), *The Sea Wolf* (1904), *Before Adam* (1906), *The Valley of the Moon* (1913), and *The Little Lady of the Big House* (1916).

Long, Crawford Williamson (1815–1878), American surgeon, born in Danielsville, Ga. He was the first to use ether for anesthetic purposes. Long graduated from Franklin College in 1835 and took his medical degree at the University of Pennsylvania in 1839. After experiments upon himself, he used ether vapor in 1842 in an operation for the removal of a neck tumor. In 1846 a Boston dentist, William T. G. Morton, made a public demonstration of the anesthetic properties of ether. As Long did not publish his findings until 1849, Morton received general credit for discovering the uses of ether.

Long, Huey Pierce (1893–1935), American lawyer and public official, born in Winnfield, La. He practiced law in Winnfield (1915–1928) and thereafter in Shreveport. He was governor of Louisiana (1928–1931) and U.S. senator (1931–1935), when he was assassinated by the son of one of his political enemies. Known as "the kingfish" and founder of the Long political dynasty, he received his strongest political support from Louisiana's backwoods districts. As governor he built roads and hospitals and provided schools with free textbooks; at the same time he established a virtually dictatorial regime in the state capital. A senator during the early years of the Depression, Long wrote *Every Man A King* (1933), a book advocating a share-the-wealth program.

Longfellow, Henry Wadsworth (1807–1882), American poet, born in Portland, Me. His mother traced her descent from John and Priscilla Alden, whose romantic story Longfellow told in *The Courtship of Miles Standish* (1858). He graduated from Bowdoin College in 1825 and was offered the chair of modern languages there. After three years of travel and study in France, Spain, and Italy, he took up his duties, which he varied by writing a book of travel sketches, *Outre-Mer* (1834). In 1835 he made a second trip to Europe to prepare for the Smith professorship of modern languages at Harvard. He settled in Craigie House, Cambridge, which he eventually bought for a permanent home. During that seventeen-year period at Harvard, Longfellow produced some of his best-known poetry. His mixture of sentimentality and didacticism made him extremely popular with the nineteenth- and early twentieth-century American reader; today he is less esteemed. Among his best-known poems are *Psalm of Life* (1839), *The Village Blacksmith* (1841), *The Wreck of the Hesperus* (1841), *Evangeline* (1847), *The Song of Hiawatha* (1855), *The Courtship of Miles Standish* (1858), and *Tales of a Wayside Inn* (1863), which includes *Paul Revere's Ride*. At his best, Longfellow exhibited a great gift for narrative.

Longstreet, James (1821–1904), American Confederate general, born in Edgefield, S.C. He graduated from West Point in 1842 and served against the Indians on the western frontier and later in the Mexican War. In the Civil War he joined the Confederacy, became a lieutenant general, took part in the first and second battles of Bull Run, commanded the Confederates left at Fredericksburg, and directed Pickett's charge at Gettysburg. He helped win the battle of Chickamauga and was severely wounded in the battles of the Wilderness, but returned to active service in 1864. After the war he became a Republican and held several government positions, including that of minister to Turkey.

Lope de Vega. See *Vega, Lope de*.

Lorca, Federico García (1898–1936), Spanish poet and dramatist, born in Fuente Vaqueros, Granada. He studied law at Granada and Madrid, but gave this up for literature. *Romancero gitano* (1928), his best-known work, and *Canciones* (1927) are both collections of gypsy songs. The central theme of his writings is death. Among his plays are *Bodas de sangre* (*Blood Wedding*, 1933), *Yerma* (1934), and *La Casa de Bernardo Alba* (1936). Lorca was killed, either deliberately or owing to a misunderstanding, soon after the outbreak of the Spanish Civil War.

Lorenzetti, the family name of two brothers, both Italian painters of the Sienese school. Little is known of the early lives of either. **Ambrogio Lorenzetti** (c.1300–c.1348), the more imaginative of the two brothers, fuses the styles of Florence and Siena in his work and shows the influence of Giotto and Giovanni Pisano. His greatest achievement is the cycle of frescoes of the *Good and Bad Government* in the Palazzo Pubblico at Siena (1337–1340). His panels of the *Presentation of Christ in the Temple* (1342) hang in the Uffizi. **Pietro Lorenzetti** (c.1280–c.1348), Ambrogio's teacher. Like Ambrogio, he is thought to have perished in the plague of 1348. He too shows the influence of both Giotto and Pisano in his works, which include the *Madonna* polyptych (1320), an altarpiece in Arezzo, and the *Nativity of the Virgin* (1335–1342) in the Museo dell' Opera del Duomo in Siena.

Lorenzini, Carlo, pen name of **H. Carlo Collodi** (1826–1890), Italian author and journalist, known for his series of didactic tales and adventures collected under the title *Le Avventure di Pinocchio* (1882). Pinocchio was translated into English in 1892; it was made into a film by Walt Disney in 1940.

Lorenzo, Monaco, also known as Don **Lorenzo** (c.1370–1425), Italian painter of the Sienese school, and a teacher of Fra Filippo Lippi. He became a Camaldolese monk in 1391 and spent the greater part of his life at the monastery of Santa Maria degli Angeli in Florence. The sophisticated use of line and delicate texture of Lorenzo's early work shows profound Sienese influence. Later he combines the rhythmic line of Siena with a Florentine feeling of the followers of Giotto. Only one signed work exists: *The Coronation of the Virgin* (1414), which hangs in the Uffizi Gallery in Florence. His other works include the *Annunciation* in the Church of Santa Trinità, Florence, and a *Madonna and Child* in the National Gallery of Art, Washington, D.C.

Lorenzo the Magnificent. See *Medici*.

Lorrain, Claude, real name **Claude Gelée** (1600–1682), French landscape painter and engraver, born in Chamagne, Lorraine. As a child he went to Rome, where he came to grind paints for Agostino Tassi, a painter of seaports. Later he studied in Naples and worked for a year in Nancy as assistant to the duke of Lorraine's painter. In 1627 he returned to Rome, where he remained until his death. Lorrain's works were much sought after (and often forged) following his commission of four landscapes by Pope Urban VIII in 1629.

Lorrain's harmonious and mellow colors create a soft atmosphere and golden light that capture the essential mood of the Italian landscapes. At the same time his forms are arranged in a stable, architectural fashion. A favorite with the early Romantics of the late eighteenth century because of his subjective rendering of nature, he is represented in the Louvre, the Prado, the National Gallery of Art in Washington, D. C., and the Doria Palace in Rome.

Loubet, Émile (1838–1929), French statesman and seventh president of France (1899–1906). He was born in Marsanne, studied law in Paris, and in 1870 was elected mayor of Montélimar, where he had established himself as a lawyer. In 1876 he was elected to the Chamber of Deputies and in 1885 was sent to the Senate. Between that date and his election to the presidency, Loubet held important ministries; he was prime minister in 1892. The agitation for the reinstatement of Capt. Alfred Dreyfus and for the passage of the law separating church and state occurred during his term. He was succeeded by Clément A. Falliéres.

Louis IX, known as Saint **Louis** (1215–1270), king of France (1226–1270). He succeeded his father, Louis VIII, in 1226 and enjoyed a long and relatively peaceful reign. He was trained by his mother, Blanche of Castile, who acted as regent. When he came of age he carried on a war against Henry III of England. In 1248, in fulfillment of a vow made during an illness, Louis led the sixth crusade. He was taken prisoner in Egypt by the Muslims, but continued his journey after the payment of a ransom. In 1270 he started on another crusade but died of the plague in Tunis. Louis did much to improve French law. He was canonized in 1297. His feast day is August 25.

Louis XII, called **Père du Peuple,** or Father of the People (1462–1515), king of France (1498–1515), son of Charles, Duc d'Orleans, and Marie de Clèves and successor of Charles VIII. During the early years of his reign, Louis tried to gain possession of Milan. In 1508 he joined the League of Cambrai against the Venetians, having as his allies Pope Julius II, the emperor Maximillian, and Ferdinand of Aragon. He defeated the Venetians at Agnadello in 1509, but in 1511 faced an alliance of his former allies and Henry VIII of England, who were united in the Holy League. Henry VIII defeated the French in 1513 in the battle of the Spurs, and peace was made the next year. Among the terms was a provision for the marriage of Louis and Mary Tudor, Henry's sister.

Louis XIII (1601–1643), king of France (1610–1643), son of Henry IV and Marie de Médicis. He succeeded to the throne in 1610 when his father was assassinated. His mother acted as regent until 1617. During most of his reign affairs of state were dominated by Cardinal Richelieu, who increased the royal power at the expense of the nobles and destroyed the political power of the Huguenots, capturing their stronghold, La Rochelle, in 1628. Louis had two sons by his wife, Anne of Austria; the elder son succeeded him as Louis XIV.

Louis XIV, called **the Great,** also **le Grand Monarque** and **le Roi Soleil** (1638–1715), king of France (1643–1715). He succeeded his father, Louis XIII, when he was five years old. On the death of Cardinal Mazarin (1661), the minister who had been all-powerful during his minority, Louis declared that he would be his own minister. In 1667 his army invaded the Spanish Netherlands and gained several victories until checked by a combination of Dutch, Swedish, and English troops. Louis retained possession of French Flanders in 1668 by the Treaty of Aix-la-Chapelle, but was forced to relinquish Franche-Comté. A renewal of the war made Louis dominant in Europe, but he suffered reverses when faced by a powerful coalition headed by William III of England. The wars were finally concluded by the Treaty of Utrecht (1713), under which France lost many of her conquests. Louis reigned for 73 years, the longest reign in European history, and was by far the most prominent figure of his day. His court, the most splendid and luxurious in Europe, influenced literature, art, politics, and fashion throughout the world.

FRENCH EMBASSY PRESS AND INFORMATION SERVICE

KING LOUIS XIV

Louis XV, called **the Well-Beloved,** or **le Bien-Aimé** (1710–1774), king of France (1715–1774), the son of the duke of Burgundy and the successor of his great-grandfather, Louis XIV. He reigned for nearly 60 years. From 1755 to 1763 France was at war with Great Britain. Under the terms of the peace treaty, signed in Paris in 1763, England took possession of Canada, Nova Scotia, and France's other North American colonies, in addition to Granada, Dominica, and Tobago, in the West Indies. During his later years Louis was governed wholly by his favorites, among whom were Madame de Pompadour and Madame Du Barry. Weak and sensual, the king had little influence in the affairs of state.

Louis XVI (1754–1793), king of France (1774–1792), the grandson of Louis XV, whom he succeeded. He married Marie Antoinette of Austria, daughter of Maria Thérèsa and sister of the emperor Joseph. Louis's first acts as king endeared him to his people, for he gave them new privileges and made many reforms in the administration. He was soon beset by financial troubles, however, and was not wise in his choice of ministers. The state of the country gradually became worse, and in 1789 the French Revolution began. In June, 1791, Louis escaped from Paris to Vincennes, but he was captured and brought back. Until September, 1792, he reigned as a constitutional king, but the office was then abolished, and Louis was tried and guillotined on January 21, 1793.

Louis XVII (1785–1795), king of France in name only. The second son of Louis XVI and Marie Antoinette, he became dauphin (title borne by the eldest son of kings of France) in 1789 upon the death of his eldest brother. In 1792 the little prince was imprisoned with his parents, but was separated from them and given over to the keeping of a brutal cobbler. In 1795 he was reported to have died of abuse and neglect. Several pretenders to the throne later pressed their claims as the lost dauphin, but all were imposters.

Louis XVIII, in full **Louis Xavier Stanislas,** called **Louis le Désiré** (1755–1824), king of France (1814–1824), a younger brother of Louis XVI. His title was comte de Provence. He fled from Paris on the same night that his brother made his unsuccessful attempt to escape, and reached the Belgian frontier. After the death of the dauphin he assumed the title of king and was living in England when Napoleon met his downfall in 1814. Soon afterward, Louis went to Paris and assumed the crown but fled when Napoleon returned from Elba. Reinstated by the allied powers after the battle of Waterloo, he reigned until 1824. His brother, Charles X, succeeded him.

Louis, Joe, originally **Joseph Louis Barrow** (1914–), American prizefighter and world heavyweight boxing champion, born in Lafayette, Ala. He began amateur boxing in Detroit, Mich., where in 1932 he won the Golden Gloves light-heavyweight championship. In 1937, only three years after his first professional bout, Louis won the heavyweight title from James Braddock and became the second Negro to hold the world championship. He kept the title for twelve years and defended it successfully 24 times before retiring from the ring in 1949. Louis returned, however, in 1950 to challenge champion Ezzard Charles, but lost the 15-round decision. He left boxing permanently after a defeat from Rocky Marciano in 1951. Louis is the author of *My Life Story* (1947).

Louis Philippé, known as **Roi citoyen,** or **Citizen King** (1773–1850), king of France (1830–1848), the eldest son of Philippe-Égalité, Duc d'Orleans. He had joined the cause of the French Revolutionists, repudiating his titles and fighting in the foreign wars of the period, but he fell under the suspicion of the government and in 1793, after the execution of his father during the Reign of Terror, escaped into Austrian territory. In 1814, upon the fall of Napoleon, Louis Philippe returned to Paris and recovered his estates. He lived in exile in England (1815–1817) and then returned to live in France. In 1830, after the abdication of Charles X, Thiers and other liberal monarchists selected him "citizen king." The popularity of his "July Monarchy" steadily decreased during his eighteen-year reign. The rising tide of unrest reached a climax in the revolution of 1848. Louis Philippe abdicated and fled to England, and a republic was declared. He died in London two years later.

Low, Juliette Gordon (1860–1927), American youth leader, founder of the Girl Scouts of America. Born in Savannah, Ga., she was educated in Virginia and New York, and married William Low of England. She divided her time among England, Scotland, and the U. S., with a home in each country. Through friendship with Sir Robert Baden-Powell and his sister, she became interested in their Boy Scout and Girl Guide movements. She gained experience by working with a Girl Guide group in Scotland and in 1912 organized her own Girl Guide group in her hometown of Savannah, Ga. The name was changed to Girl Scouts in 1913. She helped the movement spread to other U.S. cities and was elected president.

Lowell, Abbott Lawrence (1856–1943), American educator, successor to Charles W. Eliot as president of Harvard University. He was born in Boston and graduated from Harvard in 1877. After receiving his degree at the Harvard Law School he practiced law in Boston. In 1897 he was appointed lecturer on the science of government at Harvard and from 1900 to 1909 was full professor. In 1909 he became president of the university and served until his retirement in 1932. From 1900 he was the sole trustee of Lowell Institute and in 1910 was elected trustee of the Carnegie Foundation for the Advancement of Teaching. A recognized authority on government, Lowell wrote *Government and Parties in Continental Europe* (1896), *The Government of England* (1908), and *Conflicts of Principle* (1932).

ASSOCIATED PRESS

JOE LOUIS

Lowell, Amy (1874–1925), American Imagist poet, born in Brookline, Mass., of a distinguished family. Abbott L. Lowell of Harvard and Percival Lowell, the astronomer, were her brothers. Besides publishing many volumes of verse she lectured at the Brooklyn Institute of Arts and Sciences and at Yale and Brown universities. Her books include *Sword Blades and Poppy Seed* (1914), *Six French Poets: Studies in Contemporary Literature* (1915), *Tendencies in Modern American Poetry* (1917), *Fir Flower Tablets: Poems Translated from the Chinese* (1921), and the critical biography *John Keats* (2 vols., 1925).

Lowell, James Russell (1819–1891), American poet and critic, born in Cambridge, Mass. He graduated from Harvard in 1838, where he distinguished himself in literature. Lowell's first published volume was a collection of poems entitled *A Year's Life* (1841). In 1843 he became editor of a periodical of criticism, *The Pioneer,* to which Poe, Hawthorne, and Whittier contributed. *The Biglow Papers,* first printed in the Boston *Courier* in 1846, gave Lowell a reputation for shrewd humor; this rhymed satire on the Mexican War was enjoyed for its witty use of the New England dialect. Two other poems appeared in 1848—*Vision of Sir Launfal* and *A Fable for Critics.* He succeeded Henry Wadsworth Longfellow as professor of modern languages at Harvard (1855–1877) and was associate editor of the *North American Review* (1864–1872). In 1877 he became ambassador to Madrid and in 1880 to London. He left the diplomatic service in 1885. His best literary and critical essays were collected under the titles *Conversations on Some of the Old Poets* (1845), *Among My Books* (1870), and *My Study Windows* (1871). In the *Atlantic Monthly* appeared a second series of *Biglow Papers,* expressing his anti-slavery sentiments. Perhaps Lowell's finest single poem is the *Commemoration Ode,* which he delivered in 1865 in honor of the Harvard men who had fallen in the Civil War.

Lowell, Percival (1855–1916), American astronomer, founder of the Lowell Observatory at Flagstaff, Ariz. He was born in Boston, Mass., and graduated from Harvard in 1876. After several years of residence in Japan he returned to the United States and began work at Flagstaff in 1894. He was appointed professor of astronomy at Massachusetts Institute of Technology in 1902. Lowell became widely known for his study of the markings on Mars and wrote several books in support of his theory that living beings exist there. In 1905 he predicted, from mathematical calculations, the discovery of a new planet. It was discovered in 1930 and named Pluto.

Lowell, Robert (1917–), American poet, born in Boston and educated at Kenyon College. Lowell worked briefly as an editorial assistant and as consultant in poetry to the Library of Congress. During World War II he was an outspoken conscientious objector. His poetry is characterized by its complexity, rich symbolism, the influence of Roman Catholicism, to which he was converted, and a high level of technical virtuosity. His works include *Land of Unlikeliness* (1944), *Lord Weary's Castle* (1946), *The Mills of the Kavanaughs* (1951), *Life Studies* (1959), and *For The Union Dead* (1964). He was awarded the Pulitzer Prize for poetry in 1947.

Loyola, Saint **Ignatius,** real name **Íñigo de Oñez y Loyola** (1491–1556), Spanish saint, born in the province of Guipúzcoa, Spain, of a noble Basque family. He founded the Society of Jesus, commonly called the Jesuits. In his youth he was a page in the court of Ferdinand and Isabella, where he saw all the vices and frivolities of the age. As a young man he entered the army and was severely wounded in a war with the French. During his long convalescence he read books on devotion and lives of the saints, with the result that in 1522 he dedicated himself to the service of the Church. About this time he wrote the book of devotion called *Spiritual Exercises.* After entering the Church, Loyola made pilgrimages to Rome and Jerusalem and from 1524 to 1527 attended the schools and universities of Barcelona, Alcala, and Salamanca. In 1528 he went to Paris, where he completed a seven-year course of general and theological training. In 1534 he and six others took vows that marked the foundation of the Society of Jesus, which was dedicated to work for the conversion of the heathen. In 1540, when the order was formally founded by Pope Paul III, Loyola became its first superior. The rest of his life was spent in Rome organizing the society. He was canonized by Pope Gregory XV in 1622.

Lubbock, Sir **John,** 1st Baron **Avebury** (1834–1913), English naturalist, born in London and educated at Eton. He was a member of the House of Commons almost continuously from 1870 to 1900, when he was raised to the peerage as Lord Avebury. His fame rests chiefly on his work as a scientist. His *Prehistoric Times* (1865), the result of original research, was long a standard text on archaeology. Lubbock also specialized in the study of insects, and on this subject he wrote *Ants, Bees, and Wasps* (1882) and other books. While in the House of Commons he introduced a number of banking reform bills.

Lübke, Heinrich (1894–), German public official, elected president of the German Federal Republic in 1959. He was director of the Deutsche Bauernschaft, an agricultural organization (1926–1933), and a member of the Prussian Landtag (1931–1933). In 1933 the Nazis deprived him of his offices and imprisoned him. He was minister of food, agriculture, and forestry in the federal government from 1953 to 1959.

Lucas van Leyden, real name **Lucas Hugensz,** also known as **Lucas Jacobsz** (1494–1533), Dutch painter and engraver, the first Dutch genre painter, probably born in Leiden, Netherlands. He studied under Huygh Jacobsz and Cornelis Engelbrechtsen. A child prodigy who managed to produce more than 200 engravings, etchings, and woodcut designs during his life, he was influenced by Albrecht Dürer, whom he met in 1521. Van Leyden is, after Dürer, the most important engraver of the sixteenth century. His work is characterized by delicacy, painstaking craftsmanship, and dramatic force. Among his paintings are *Lot and His Daughters* (Louvre), *St. Jerome* (Berlin), *The Last Judgment* (Leiden), and *The Blind Man of Jericho Healed by Jesus Christ* (Moscow).

Luce, Henry Robinson (1898–1967), American publisher and editor, born in Shantung province, China, where his parents were missionaries. When he was 14, they returned to the U.S. After graduating from Yale (1920) and studying at Oxford, he took a reporting job on the Chicago *Daily News* (1921). Two years later he and Britton Hadden founded the weekly news magazine *Time* in New York City. The success of this venture led to the establishment of three more magazines: *Fortune* (1930), a monthly; *Life* (1936), a weekly specializing in pictorial reporting; and *Sports Illustrated* (1954). In 1935 he married Clare Boothe, an American writer, politician, and diplomat. He died Feb. 28, 1967 in Pheonix, Ariz.

Luce, Clare Boothe (1903–), American playwright and diplomat, born in New York City. She was on the editorial staff of *Vogue* (1930–1931) and *Vanity Fair* (1931–1934), the latter of which she was managing editor. In the 1930's four of Mrs. Luce's plays appeared on Broadway; three of them, *The Women* (1936), *Kiss the Boys Goodbye* (1938), and *Margin for Error* (1939), enjoyed successful runs. Her entry into politics occurred in 1940 when she supported the Republican presidential candidate, Wendell Wilkie. From 1943 to 1947 she represented Fairfield County, Conn., in the U.S. House of Representatives. Pres. Dwight D. Eisenhower appointed her ambassador to Italy in 1953, a post that she held until 1957. Mrs. Luce is the author of several books, including *Stuffed Shirts* (1933), *Europe in the Spring* (1940), and *Saints for Now* (1952), a Catholic anthology that she edited.

Lucretius, in full **Titus Lucretius Carus** (c.96–55 B.C.), Roman philosophical poet. He is famous for his philosophical poem *De rerum natura* (*On the Nature of Things*). In the six books of this work Lucretius set forth the materialistic philosophy of Epicurus on atomism and ethics. He discusses the Epicurean theory on the creation of the universe and the laws of nature, emphasizing that the universe is void of a divine being who creates and governs men's lives. He attacks religious belief, calling it man's greatest sorrow in that it enmeshes him in groundless fears and superstitions. Little is known of Lucretius' life, although there is a tradition that he died by suicide.

Lucullus, Lucius Licinius (c.110–57 B.C.), Roman general and epicure. He fought under the famous general Sulla in the Social War (90–89 B.C.) and won further honors in the wars with Mithridates, king of Pontus. At the start of the second Mithridatic War in 74, Lucullus, then a consul, was made chief commander of the Romans. In 71 he defeated Mithridates and in 69, Tigranes, king of Armenia. He instituted many reforms in Asia Minor, but was superseded in Asia by Pompey (66) when his soldiers mutinied. At Rome he tried to check the ambitious designs of Pompey but failed. He was extremely wealthy and thereafter lived in luxury in his town house and suburban villas. The opulence of his banquets have made the expression "Lucullan feast" applicable to expensive and elaborate gourmet dinners. He was the patron of artists and writers.

Ludendorff, Erich Friedrich Wilhelm (1865–1937), German general, born in the province of Posen, Prussia (now a part of Poland). He received a military education, and from 1904 to 1913 he was an officer on the general staff of the army. At the outbreak of World War I (1914), having reached the grade of quartermaster general, he took part in the invasion of Belgium. As Gen. Paul von Hindenburg's chief of staff, he contributed to the victories over the Russians at Tannenburg (August 26-31, 1914) and the defeat of the Serbians and Rumanians. After Gen. von Falkenhayn's failure at Verdun (1916), when Hindenburg was made chief of staff of all the armies, Ludendorff was appointed chief quartermaster general. He favored intensification of the submarine campaign and helped plan the drives of 1918, by which the Germans sought to end the war before the U.S. could take full part. In October, 1918, he was discharged, and after a stay in Sweden settled in Munich. In the 1920's he was active in German politics as a National Socialist (Nazi), and with Hitler led the unsuccessful Beer Hall Putsch (1923). He was active in the pagan anti-Christian movement and supported Hitler, but later deserted the Third Reich.

Ludwig, Emil, original surname **Cohn** (1881–1948), German writer, born in Breslau, but a long-time resident of Switzerland, of which he became a citizen in 1913. He received his education at the University of Breslau and the law school of the University of Heidelberg. He began his literary career by writing plays. He also produced some novels, including *Manfred und Helene* (1911) and *Diana* (1918), but his reputation rests on his biographies. Along with his contemporaries, André Maurois and Lytton Strachey, Ludwig upset the traditional approach to writing biographies. Instead of idealizing his subjects he often discussed in depth their passions and weaknesses, thus producing colorful, dramatic, and often controversial psychological studies. Some of his notable biographies are *Goethe* (1920), *Napoleon* (1924), *Wilhelm II* (1925), *Bismarck* (1927), *Lincoln* (1930), *Three Titans* (1930), and *Roosevelt: a Study in Fortune and Power* (1938).

Lully, Jean Baptiste, Italian name **Giovanni Battista Lulli** (1632–1687), French composer born in Florence, Italy. While still a boy he came to Paris, where he played in the band of the cousin of Louis XIV. He entered into the service of the king in 1652 first as a ballet dancer, then as a member of the violin corps of the royal orchestra, and finally as court composer; while in this capacity he wrote ballets and masques for the royal court. In 1672 he was appointed director of the Académie Royale de Musique (now the French national opera), for which, with Philippe Quinault as librettist, he composed about 18 operas, including *Alceste* (1674), *Thésée* (1675), *Atys* (1676), *Amadis de Gaule* (1684), and *Armide et Renaud* (1686). Lully contributed to the development of French opera and is also credited with introducing the French form of overture. In his operas he gave great importance to the ballet and, as opposed to Italian operas in which the arias are often embellished by the singers, he demanded that they be sung as written. Aside from composing operas, Lully wrote some 30 ballets, church music, and pastorales.

Lumière, Louis Jean (1864–1948), French chemist and industrialist, born in Besançon. He and his brother, **Auguste Marie Louis Nicolas Lumière** (1862–1954), also a chemist, manufactured photographic equipment. In 1895 they invented the cinematograph (a moving picture machine) and a process of color photography. Earlier (1884), they developed a more advanced type of photographic plate, which they manufactured at their factory in Lyons. Auguste was also involved in cancer research, and was mainly concerned with the treatment of the disease.

Lunt, Alfred (1893–), American actor, born in Milwaukee, Wis. He left Harvard to join the repertory company of the Castle Square Theatre in Boston, where he made his stage debut in *The Gingerbread Man* (1913). In 1917 he appeared in *Romance and Arabella*, playing his first leading role in New York. He first worked with the British-born actress Lynn Fontanne, whom he later married (1922), while doing stock together in the summer of 1919. The first of many plays that they co-starred in was *The Guardsman* in 1924. Thereafter they appeared together, except when Lunt starred in *Marco's Millions* in 1928, distinguishing themselves as one of the foremost husband and wife acting teams in the history of the theatre. Some of the plays that they played in are *Pygmalion, Caprice, Design for Living, Idiot's Delight, Amphitryon 38, The Great Sebastians,* and *The Visit*.

Luther, Martin (1483–1546), German religious reformer, born in Eislenben. The son of a miner, he attended the Latin schools of Magdeburg and Eisenach; in 1501 he entered the University of Erfurt, from which he received a master's degree in 1505.

Although his father had intended that he be a lawyer, Luther dropped from law school two months after enrolling and entered the monastery of the Augustines at Erfurt in 1505. Luther became an Augustinian monk and in 1507 was consecrated a priest; in 1508, through the influence of his patron, John Staupitz, who was provincial of the order, he lectured on philosophy and theology at the new University of Wittenberg.

He became doctor of theology in 1512 and

PAUL OCKRASSA, CONCORDIA HISTORICAL INSTITUTE

LUTHER nailed theses to this church door.

succeeded Staupitz as professor of Biblical literature at the university. Meanwhile, Luther was struggling with the religious doctrines that he had mastered so well, finding them unfulfilling in his search for salvation. It was probably during the winter of 1512–1513 that he discovered what he believed was the true approach to Christianity, which he preached as the doctrine of justification by faith rather than by works. The arrival in 1517 of John Tetzel in Wittenberg to sell indulgences for sins roused Luther and caused him to draw up his famous protest in 95 theses, which he nailed to the church door in Wittenberg. The result was that the sale of indulgences ceased, Tetzel fled, and a great religious reform spread rapidly through Germany.

Luther was summoned to Rome to explain his heretical proceedings but refused to go; nor were the efforts of Cardinal Legate Cajetan able to effect a reconciliation between him and the pope. His dispute with theologian Johann Eck at Leipzig in 1519, in which he denounced indulgences and questioned the authority of the pope, was followed in 1520 by the following series of pamphlets in which he furthers his arguments: *Address to the Christian Nobility of the German Nation, The Babylonian Captivity of the Church,* and the *Liberty of the Christian Man.* On June 15, 1520, a papal bull was issued to Luther, excommunicating him from the church — a document that Luther straight-way burned publicly in Wittenberg. This open defiance of Rome required that he defend himself before the German emperor, Charles V. When summoned to appear before him at the Diet of Worms (1521), Luther acknowledged his writings, made an eloquent defense but refused to recant. Subsequently, an edict was issued against Luther, banning him and his works. When he retired from Worms he was met by a friendly troop of soldiers belonging to Frederick, the Elector of Saxony, who took him to the castle of Wartburg, where he remained for nearly a year.

In 1525 he married Katharina von Bora, one of nine nuns who had renounced their religious vows under his teaching. During that same year Luther published *De servo arbitrio (On the Bondage of the Will)* in response to Desiderius Erasmus' *De libero arbitrio* (*On Free Will*, 1524).

From the year 1521 Luther had been busy translating the Bible from Greek into German with the aid of Melanchthon and others, and the great task was completed in 1534. This important work, taken in connection with the Augsburg Confession, drafted in 1530, served to establish the reformer's doctrines in Germany and closed the important part of his public life. He continued his private work of teaching, preaching, and writing until his death.

Lycurgus (9th century B.C.), lawgiver of ancient Sparta, reputed founder of that city state's constitution. All the facts of his life are in some doubt. Tradition says that as regent he governed wisely for his young nephew, King Charilaus, and then traveled in Crete, Ionia, and Egypt. On his return the citizens implored him to rescue the state from the disorder into which it had fallen. Lycurgus introduced a new social order and laid the foundations for the military supremacy that Sparta later enjoyed. He then went into voluntary exile, having made the people promise to maintain the new laws without change.

Lydgate, John (c.1370–c.1451), English poet, disciple of Chaucer, born in Lydgate, Suffolk. He took his vows as a Benedictine monk at Bury Saint Edmunds, where he formed a school for tutoring the sons of nobles in poetry. From 1423 to 1434 he was prior of Hatfield Broadoak, and was court poet during the reigns of Henry IV, V, and VI. An imitator of Chaucer, Lydgate considered his *Story of Thebes* (written c.1420, pub. 1500) as a supplement to *The Canterbury Tales;* the story is based on a French verse romance. He is also known for the *Troy Book* (written 1412–1420, pub. 1513), in which he pays tribute to Chaucer; *The Fall of Princes* (written 1430, pub. 1494); and two allegorical poems, *Complaint of the Black Knight* and *Temple of Glass.*

Lysander (d.395 B.C.), Spartan admiral, the son of Aristocritus. In 408 he assumed command of the Spartan fleet off the coast of Asia, but was replaced by Callicratidas in 406. As commander of the fleet again in 405, with the rank of vice admiral, Lysander defeated the Athenians at Aegospotami. The next year he captured Athens, and with the capture of the city the Peloponnesian War came to an end. This victory placed Lysander at the head of the Greek empire, and he exploited his prestigious position to strengthen the Spartan domain. He replaced the democratic governments of Greece with oligarchies, of which the most famous was the Thirty Tyrants of Athens, although it lasted only one year before the democracy was restored. Upon his return to Sparta he attempted to destroy the hereditary monarchy and to substitute for it an elective kingship. His action was prompted by Agesilaus' unwillingness to fall under his sway, although Lysander was responsible for his succession to the throne. He failed to change the monarchy and his prestige was greatly reduced. He was killed at Haliartus while commanding an army against the Boeotians.

Lysimachus (c.361–281 B.C.), Macedonian general who fought in the army of Alexander the Great. On Alexander's death (323 B.C.) Lysimachus received Thrace and the region bordering on the Danube, and in 306 assumed the title of king. By conquest he added a part of Asia Minor to his realm. In 288 B.C. he formed an alliance with Ptolemy, Seleucus, and Pyrrhus against Demetrius, by which he obtained control of Macedonia. To please his Egyptian wife, Arsinoe, he murdered his son Agathocles; this roused his Asian subjects, and with the aid of Seleucus they defeated and killed him at Corcorus.

Lysippus (4th century B.C.), Greek sculptor, the founder of a new school at Sicyon in the Peloponnesus. He was Alexander the Great's favorite sculptor, and he made many portrait busts of the conqueror. Of the 1,500 busts and statues attributed to him, only copies are in existence, notably the *Apoxyomenos* (an athlete scraping off oil) in the Vatican. Almost all of his works were done in bronze, and they are recognizable by the smallness of the heads, the elongation of the limbs, and the slenderness of the torsos. His statues were modeled in the round as opposed to the works of most of his predecessors, in which only a frontal view of the figure is given.

M

Mabuse, Jan, real name **Jan Gossaert** or **Jenni Gossart** (c.1478–1533), Flemish painter who was one of the first to introduce Italian Renaissance art to the Low Countries. His early works resembled those of his Dutch and Flemish contemporaries. In 1508, however, he spent a year in Italy with his patron, Philip of Burgundy, and returned with ideas that revolutionized the art of the Netherlands. Mabuse excelled at portraits and in later life was renowned as a painter of nudes. He also painted religious and mythological subjects.

McAdam, John Loudon (1756–1836), Scottish engineer who developed the macadam road. He made a fortune in America as a young man, and returned to Scotland, where he headed several road maintenance projects in Scotland and England. The method of paving he invented was first used in England in 1815. A macadam road is a thick layer of small broken stones, which become cemented by the action of water on stone dust. Although macadam is cheaper to construct than concrete or asphalt roads, it does not hold up as well under heavy traffic.

McAdoo, William Gibbs (1863–1941), American lawyer who was secretary of the treasury in Pres. Woodrow Wilson's cabinet (1913–1918) and director general of railways during World War I. He was born near Marietta, Ga., and was educated at the University of Tennessee. He first became prominent when, as president of the Hudson and Manhattan Railroad Company, he supervised the construction of the first Hudson River tunnels. In 1914 he married Pres. Wilson's daughter Eleanor. A candidate for the Democratic presidential nomination in 1920 and in 1924, McAdoo was elected U.S. senator from California in 1933, and remained in office until 1938.

MacArthur, Douglas (1880–1964), American general who commanded Allied forces in the Pacific during World War II. Born in Little Rock, Ark., and educated at West Point, he was the son of a distinguished army officer. He served in the Philippines (1903–1904), took part in the Vera Cruz expedition of 1914, and in World War I was commander of the famous Rainbow Division.

When Japan attacked the Philippines in 1941, MacArthur led his troops in a courageous defense, but was forced back by overwhelming numbers. As commander of Allied Forces in the southwest Pacific, he led troops that retook the Pacific islands in a number of brilliant strategic moves. After World War II he was made commander of the occupation troops in Japan.

In 1950 fighting broke out in Korea, and MacArthur was named commander in chief of all United Nations forces in Asia. The fighting was a series of offensive and defensive movements, which were generally successful. MacArthur was at variance with the UN plan of strategy and spoke out in opposition to it. As a result, in 1951 Pres. Harry Truman stripped him of all his commands. He was accorded a hero's welcome when he returned to the United States. MacArthur's later years were spent in retirement; his memoirs were published in 1964.

Macaulay, Thomas Babington (1800–1859), English historian and politician whose multivolume *History of England* was an enormous success during his lifetime. Elected to Parliament as a Whig in 1830, he afterwards held several important posts, including secretary of war (1839–1841) and paymaster general (1846–1847). But Macaulay was primarily interested in literature and history rather than politics. The first volumes of his great work, *History of England from the Accession of James II,* appeared in 1848, and two more volumes in 1855. The work was immensely popular among ordinary readers, who found that history could be made as interesting as fiction. Macaulay's prose style is esteemed for its clarity and balance. Besides his historical works, he also wrote essays on a wide variety of subjects. As a writer of verse, he is best remembered for *Horatius at the Bridge,* one of the poems in his *Lays of Ancient Rome.* He was buried in Westminster Abbey.

Macbeth (d. 1057), king of the Scots (1040–1057) and the title character of Shakespeare's drama *Macbeth.* As ruler of Moray province, Macbeth revolted against King Duncan in 1040 and killed him in battle (not, as in Shakespeare's play, in bed). He then ruled Scotland until he was killed in battle by Malcolm, Duncan's son. The story as told in Holinshed's *Chronicles* was the basis for Shakespeare's drama.

UNITED PRESS INTERNATONAL

DOUGLAS MACARTHUR (*left*) leaves landing craft to wade through the surf in the invasion of Leyte Island. Thus, he has fulfilled the dramatic vow he made to return to the Philippines. He is accompanied here by Lieutenant General Richard Sutherland (*center*).

McBurney, Charles (1845–1913), American surgeon, born in Roxbury, Mass. He studied medicine at the College of Physicians and Surgeons, New York City. He taught at the college from 1872 until his retirement in 1907, serving as professor of clinical surgery from 1892. Dr. McBurney gained an international reputation as operating surgeon, authority on appendicitis, and pioneer in asepsis. He discovered McBurney's Point, a pressure point important in the diagnosis of appendicitis. In 1894 he developed a surgical incision, later named for him.

Maccabees, also called **Hasmonaeans** (2nd and 1st centuries B.C.), family of Jewish patriots, prominent in Jerusalem, who fought for Jewish liberty. The most famous Maccabee was **Judas Maccabeus** (Judah the Hammer), son of **Mattathias,** a priest who founded the dynasty. At the death of Mattathias in 166 B.C., Judas took command of the Israelites, reconquered Jerusalem from the Syrians, and restored the holy service. After Judas' death, members of the family continued to rule, with varying degrees of success, for more than a century. In 37 B.C., the dynasty was dissolved when Antigonus, the last Maccabee ruler, was executed by Mark Antony.

McCarthy, Mary (1912–   ), American critic and novelist, born in Seattle, Wash. After gaining a solid reputation as a social and drama critic, she published her first novel, *The Oasis,* in 1949. Her other novels, marked by a detached, satirical approach to their subjects, include *The Groves of Academe* (1952) and *The Group* (1964). An autobiography of her early years, *Memories of a Catholic Girlhood,* appeared in 1957.

Macchiavelli. See *Machiavelli.*

McCauley, Mary, known as **Molly Pitcher** (c.1754–1832), American heroine of the Revolutionary War, born near Trenton, N.J. During the Battle of Monmouth (June 28, 1778), she brought water to wounded American soldiers, who nicknamed her *Molly Pitcher.* When her husband succumbed to the heat, she took over his cannon and fought for the remainder of the battle.

McClellan, George Brinton (1826–1885), American general who during the Civil War was commander of Union troops for a short period (November, 1861–March, 1862). Born in Philadelphia and educated at West Point, he resigned from the army in 1857 but returned in 1861 as major general of the Ohio Volunteers. After the Union defeat at Bull Run (July, 1861), he was appointed commander of the Army of the Potomac; in November, he replaced Gen. Winfield Scott as general in chief of the army. His indecisive command in the ensuing Peninsula campaign aroused much criticism, and in July, 1862, he was replaced by Gen. Henry W. Halleck. Reappointed commander of the Army of the Potomac, McClellan checked Lee at Antietam but again failed to make the most of the victory. As Democratic candidate in the presidential election of 1864, he was defeated by Lincoln. From 1878 to 1881 he was governor of New Jersey.

McCloskey, John (1810–1885), American prelate and the first American cardinal, born in Brooklyn. N.Y. He was ordained a priest in 1834 and in 1841 became the first president of St. John's College (later Fordham University), in New York. In 1864 he was created archbishop of New York and was elevated to cardinal in 1875. Cardinal McCloskey founded churches, seminaries, and missions, and also helped to complete St. Patrick's Cathedral in New York.

McCormick, Cyrus Hall (1809–1884), American inventor, born at Walnut Grove, Va. He is famous for his invention of the reaper, the first important contribution to mechanized agriculture. McCormick gave the first public demonstration of his machine in 1831 but did not patent it until 1834. The basic features of the modern reaper are practically unchanged from McCormick's first design. In 1847 he built a factory in Chicago. He built up an enormous fortune, much of which he dispensed in his many philanthropies.

McCullers, Carson Smith (1917–1967), American novelist, born in Columbus, Ga. A prominent member of the southern regional group, she won critical acclaim for her novels *The Heart is a Lonely Hunter* (1940), *Reflections in a Golden Eye* (1941), *The Ballad of the Sad Café* (1951), *Square Root of Wonderful* (1958), and *Clock Without Hands* (1960). Her novel, *The Member of the Wedding* (1946), was adapted for the Broadway stage in 1950 and later made into a motion picture. She died Sept. 29, 1967 in Nyack, New York.

NEW YORK PUBLIC LIBRARY

MACHIAVELLI, Renaissance political theorist.

MacDonald, James Ramsay (1866–1937), British statesman who was the first Labour prime minister of England. Born in Scotland of working-class parents, he joined the newly-formed Labour party in 1894. Elected to Parliament in 1906, he held office until 1918, when his pacifist ideas caused his defeat. Returned to Parliament in 1922, he led the Labour party and in 1924, after the Conservative party's defeat, became prime minister. His ministry fell within a year and did not return to power until 1929, when he again became prime minister. After the financial crisis of 1931, he joined with the Conservatives and Liberals to form a coalition government with himself as prime minister. In 1935 he resigned and was succeeded by Stanley Baldwin. MacDonald then became lord president of the council in Baldwin's cabinet, a post he held until May, 1937, when poor health and lack of public support forced him to resign.

Macdonald, Sir **John Alexander** (1815–1891), first premier of Canada (1867–1873). Born in Glasgow, Scotland, He went to Canada at an early age, where he was educated and admitted to the bar (1836). As a rising young lawyer he was elected in 1844 to the Legislative Assembly of Canada as a Conservative. In 1841 Upper and Lower Canada had been united under one legislature, but the union did not give full satisfaction. In the period between 1844 and confederation in 1867 Macdonald was one of the most influential leaders in the movement that brought about the formation of the Dominion of Canada. He held various minor offices until 1857 and during the next decade was several times head of the government. In 1867, after the passage of the British North America Act, he headed the first Dominion cabinet. Macdonald resigned in 1873 but once again became premier in 1878 and remained in office until his death.

MacDowell, Edward Alexander (1861–1908), American composer, born in New York City. He studied music in France and Germany, and after 1881 was well known as a teacher, composer, and pianist. Returning in 1888 to the United States, he continued to compose and perform his music. In 1896 he became head of the newly-formed music department at Columbia University, a post he held until 1904. MacDowell is considered one of the most original of American composers. *Woodland Sketches* and *Sea Pieces* for the piano, and the orchestral *Indian Suite* are typical of his best work, which is lyrical in the manner of Grieg and Schumann.

McGraw, John Joseph (1873–1934), American baseball player and manager, born in Truxton, N.Y. He played third base for the Baltimore Orioles, then became manager of the New York Giants. Known as a strict leader and keen strategist, he led the Giants to ten league pennants and three World Series championships between 1902 and 1932. McGraw is one of the original members of the Baseball Hall of Fame.

MacGregor or **Campbell, Robert,** known as **Rob Roy** (1671–1734), Scottish freebooter and rogue, by his own claim leader of the clan MacGregor. As a young man he formed an armed band that rustled cattle and exacted tribute for protection against thieves. Under the sponsorship of the duke of Argyll, he rebelled against the dukes of Montrose and Atholl and was captured, but was pardoned in 1727.

McGuffey, William Holmes (1800–1873), American educator, best remembered for his grammar school readers. Born near Claysville, Pa., he was a school and college teacher and president of two colleges. The first of his readers, known as McGuffey's *Eclectic Readers,* appeared in 1836, followed by five others over the next twenty years. The books were compilations of stories from many sources, and usually taught some moral lesson. Standard textbooks for two generations, more than 120 million copies of these readers were sold.

Machiavelli, Niccolò (1469–1527), Italian statesman and writer whose masterpiece, a study of realism in politics, is *The Prince* (written in 1513). He held several diplomatic posts in Florence, but was deprived of office when the Medicis returned to power in 1512. He retired to his estate, where he devoted himself to writing. In *The Prince,* Machiavelli attempted to show that a ruler is justified in taking any steps that will maintain his power, whether these steps be right or wrong. From this is derived the term "machiavellian," meaning expert, crafty, or cunning in politics.

Mack, Connie born **Cornelius McGillicuddy** (1862–1956), American baseball player and manager, born in East Brookfield, Mass. He became a big-league catcher in 1886, with the Washington Club of the National League. He was manager of the Philadelphia Athletics (American League) from 1901 to 1950, and won nine pennants and five World Series. He was an original member of the Baseball Hall of Fame.

Mackenzie, Sir **Alexander** (c.1764–1820), Canadian explorer and fur trader, born in Inverness, Scotland. In 1789, under the auspices of the Northwest Company, he made an expedition from Lake Athabasca to the Arctic Ocean and on this journey discovered the great river that bears his name. Three years later he went westward to the Pacific, ascending the Peace River and crossing the Rockies, to complete the first overland journey across the northern part of North America. His experiences are related in his *Voyages,* published in London in 1801. He was knighted in 1802.

MacKenzie, William Lyon (1795–1861), Canadian political agitator who in 1837 led an unsuccessful attempt to end British rule in Upper Canada. Born in Scotland, he emigrated to Canada in 1820. His radical speeches in the Legislative Assembly, to which he was elected from York (Toronto) in 1828, caused him to be expelled after each reelection, but he secured a seat in 1834 when his party gained a majority. He took part in the uprising of 1837 and proclaimed the establishment of a provisional government. When this was crushed he escaped to the United States, where he was arrested and imprisoned. He was permitted to return to Canada in 1849 and again sat in the legislature. During his career he organized and published several periodicals, mostly as a means of spreading his political views.

McKim, Charles Follen (1847–1909), American architect who was a leader in the neoclassical revival of the late nineteenth century in America. Born in Chester County, Pa., he opened offices in 1872 in New York City, where he was later associated with William R. Mead and Stanford White. McKim's special talent for combining massive effects with decoration was revealed in the Boston Public and Columbia University library buildings; the Pennsylvania Station, Morgan Library, and Bowery Savings Bank, in New York; and in the Agricultural Building at the Chicago World's Fair of 1893. He also helped to design the Washington Arch in New York, the Library and Hall of Fame of New York University, and several prominent club houses in Manhattan.

McKinley, William (1843–1901), twenty-fifth president of the United States (1897–1901), born in Niles Center, Ohio. A teacher at the outbreak of the Civil War, he resigned to enlist in the Union army. McKinley served with the 23rd Ohio Volunteers throughout the war and in 1865 was brevetted major of volunteers. He then studied law and was admitted to the bar in 1867. In 1869, while practicing law in Ohio, he was elected prosecuting attorney of Stark County.

McKinley showed his aptitude for politics during the campaign of 1875, when he helped Rutherford B. Hayes win reelection as governor of Ohio. He was elected to Congress in the following year, holding office until 1891 except for one brief interval. Appointed to the ways and means committee in 1880, he became its chairman in 1888. McKinley framed the tariff bill of 1890, which bore his name and won for him national prominence as an advocate of protection. His election as governor of Ohio followed in 1891 and reelection in 1893.

He was nominated for the presidency at the Republican convention of 1896. His Democratic opponent was the "boy orator of the Platte," William Jennings Bryan. McKinley conducted his campaign from the porch of his home in Canton and delivered many speeches denouncing Bryan's free-silver platform. He defeated Bryan by an electoral vote of 271 to 176. Though McKinley had at one time favored bimetallism, he had become a convert to the gold standard, and the election was won chiefly on that issue. He was reelected in 1900, again defeating Bryan. Notable events of the McKinley administration were the Spanish-American War, which made the Philippines, Puerto Rico, and Guam American possessions; the annexation of the Hawaiian Islands; the first conference of The Hague Tribunal; the Boxer Rebellion in China; and the passage of the tariff bill. On September 6, 1901, the president was shot by an anarchist, Leon Czolgosz, during a public reception at the Pan-American Exposition in Buffalo. He died eight days later.

MacLeish, Archibald (1892–), American poet, born in Glencoe, Ill., and educated at Yale and Harvard. After publishing several books of poetry during the 1920's, MacLeish gained renown with his long poem *Conquistador* (1932), which won the Pulitzer Prize in 1933. This was the first volume of what he called "public" poetry, devoted to political and social issues, which was followed by *The Fall of the City* (1937) and *Aid Raid* (1938), verse plays for radio and *America Was Promises* (1939). MacLeish was librarian of Congress (1939–1944), director of the Office of War Information (1942–43), and assistant secretary of state (1944). He won a second Pulitzer Prize in 1953 for his *Collected Poems 1917-1952.* A verse play, *J.B.,* written in 1957, was produced successfully on Broadway and won the 1959 Pulitzer Prize in drama.

MacLeod, John James Rickard (1876–1935), British physiologist who, together with Frederick G. Banting, discovered insulin for the treatment of diabetes. Born and educated in Scotland, he came to Cleveland, Ohio, in 1903 as professor of physiology at Western Reserve University. In 1917 he moved to the University of Toronto, where he and Banting discovered insulin. In 1923 the two shared the Nobel Prize for medicine.

MacMahon, Marie Edmé Patrice Maurice de (1808–1893), French marshal and second president of the Third Republic (1873-1879). In 1859 he defeated the Austrians at the battle of Magenta and was created marshal of France and duke of Magenta. In the Franco-Prussian War he was in command of the army that was defeated at Sedan. In 1871 he led the Army of Versailles in the battle that wrested Paris from the Commune; and in 1873 he was elected president of France to succeed Thiers. During his administration there was a constant struggle between the republican and monarchical factions, and his actions aroused a good deal of hostility. MacMahon resigned in 1879 and retired to private life.

MacMillan, Donald Baxter (1874–), American Arctic explorer, born in Provincetown, Mass., and educated at Bowdoin College and at Harvard. He became a member of the Peary North Pole Expedition of 1908 and organized many independent expeditions thereafter. His explorations covered the Hudson Bay region, the Kane Sea glaciers, Labrador, and Greenland. His 1925 expedition was the first to use airplanes in the far north. In 1944 he was awarded a special Congressional Medal.

Macmillan, Harold (1895–), English political leader, prime minister of England (1957–1963). The son of the publisher who founded Macmillan & Company, he was born in London and educated at Oxford. After assuming direction of his father's publishing house, he moved into political circles and served as British representative at Gen. Dwight D. Eisenhower's Allied Headquarters during World War II. He demonstrated his political acumen in a series of government posts and, in January 1957, following the Suez debacle, was chosen to replace Anthony Eden as prime minister. He effectively neutralized Labour opposition by middle-of-the-road domestic programs. His foreign policy was based upon close cooperation with the U.S., and upon Britain's entry into the European Common Market. In 1963 he resigned because of illness, to be succeeded by Douglas Home.

McNamara, Robert Strange (1916–), American secretary of defense, born in San Francisco and educated at the University of California, Harvard, and the University of Alabama. From 1940 to 1943, he taught business administration at Harvard. In 1946 he joined the Ford Motor Company, and became president in 1960. In 1961 named secretary of defense by Pres. Kennedy, retaining the post under Pres. Johnson until 1968, when he became president of the World Bank.

Macpherson, James (1736–1796), Scottish poet who wrote the so-called Ossian poems, which he claimed to have translated from a third-century poet named Ossian. The first collection of Ossian poems, published in 1765, were purportedly translations from the Gaelic or Erse language. Two other works in this vein were *Fingal* (1762) and *Temora* (1763). Subsequent studies have revealed that Macpherson combined translations of eleventh century (and later) works with his own poetry to produce his Ossian poems.

Madero, Francisco Indalecio (1873–1913), Mexican revolutionary who was president of Mexico from 1911 to 1913. Of aristocratic background, he sided with the poorer classes and organized a liberal movement against the dictatorship of Porfirio Díaz. Nominated in 1910 for president by the National Democratic party, he was imprisoned by Díaz' orders until after the election. After his release he issued a reform plan and urged the people to revolt. While he was in Texas to avoid arrest, his followers overthrew the government; on his return, he was elected president in 1911. Hampered by internal strife and a hostile Congress, he was overthrown by Gen. Victoriano Huerta in 1913. Madero was arrested and shot, supposedly by a group of Huerta's men.

Madison, James (1751–1836), fourth president of the United States (1809–1817) and a principal architect of the United States Constitution. Born in Port Conway, Va., he graduated in 1771 from the College of New Jersey (now Princeton University).

In 1776 he served on the Virginia constitutional committee with Jefferson and supported Jefferson's plea for religious toleration. He was elected to the first State Assembly in 1777 and in 1780 represented Virginia in the Continental Congress. He was reelected to Congress in 1787 and in that year was instrumental in calling the Constitutional Convention at Philadelphia. He was the author of the Virginia Plan, which formed the basis for many sections of the Federal Constitution drawn up by the Convention. He then wrote many pamphlets, urging ratification of the Constitution. About a third of the papers collectively known as *The Federalist* are his.

Madison was elected to the first House of Representatives as a Federalist and served throughout Washington's administration (1789–1797). He gradually drew away from his party and became a leader of the Jeffersonian group, called Republicans at that time. In the House he was prominent in securing the adoption of the first ten amendments. When John Adams was elected president, Madison retired to his home in Virginia. He wrote the Virginia Resolutions protesting against the Alien and Sedition Acts and in 1799–1800 served in the Virginia legislature. In 1801, after Jefferson became president, Madison entered the cabinet as secretary of state and in 1809 was himself elected president.

Madison lost many of his followers during the War of 1812, for he was essentially a man of peace and not very successful as a war president; however, he was reelected for a second term a few months after war was declared. American defeats on land and the burning of the Capitol in Washington increased his unpopularity. The war ended with the signing of the Treaty of Ghent (1814). Madison then adopted some of the Federalist principles. He supported the second Bank of the United States, proposed a protective tariff, and advocated a system of new roads and canals. At the close of his second term he retired to Montpelier, his estate in Virginia, where he devoted himself to education and agriculture.

LOOK MAGAZINE

ROBERT McNAMARA, appointed secretary of defense in 1961 by John F. Kennedy.

Madison, Dolley Payne Todd (1768–1849), wife of James Madison and famed as White House hostess. Born in North Carolina, she was the widow of John Todd, Jr., when she married Madison in 1794, seven years before her husband became secretary of state. Noted for her elegance and charm, she was the Capitol's official hostess, first for President Jefferson, who was a widower, and then for her husband.

Maecenas, Gaius (c.70–8 B.C.), Roman statesman and literary patron. After Julius Caesar's assassination (44 B.C.), Maecenas rose to prominence in the service of Octavian. When Octavian became Emperor Augustus and was occupied with foreign wars, Maecenas served as administrator of Italy. Seeking to glorify the regime, he sponsored such writers as Vergil and Horace. His name signifies a patron of the arts.

Maeterlinck, Maurice (1852–1949), Belgian dramatist and symbolist poet. Born in Ghent, he practiced law briefly but soon turned to writing. A distinctive feature of his work is a mystical and fatalistic viewpoint, presented in delicate, exotic language. In 1911 he received the Nobel Prize for such dramas as *Pelléas et Mélisande* (1892) and *The Blue Bird* (1909). A proficient naturalist, he wrote popular studies of bees, ants, spiders, and pigeons. During World War II, he lived in the United States, and spent the rest of his life in France.

Magellan, Ferdinand (1480–1521), Portuguese navigator, discoverer of the straits that bear his name, and the first European to cross the Pacific Ocean. In 1519, under the auspices of King Charles I of Spain, his fleet of five ships set sail for the New World. After sailing down the coast of South America, the fleet entered the Pacific Ocean in November, 1520. Crossing the Pacific, Magellan reached what are now called the Philippine Islands, where he was killed by natives in April, 1521. One vessel of his fleet, the *Victoria*, reached Spain in September, 1522, thus completing the first voyage around the world.

Mahan, Alfred Thayer (1840–1914), American naval officer whose writings on sea power influenced the growth of the modern American navy. Born in West Point, N.Y., and a graduate of Annapolis, he served in the navy for 40 years. His book *The Influence of Sea Power Upon History* was published in 1890 and immediately hailed as a classic. To Mahan, control of the sea was the decisive factor in military history. Until World War II, his doctrines on naval strategy were considered to be the most authoritative on the subject.

Mahler, Gustav (1860–1911), Austrian composer and conductor, a leading figure in post-Wagnerian music. He was director of the Imperial Opera in Vienna (1897–1907), then conductor of the New York Philharmonic for three years. In addition to writing ten symphonies (the last unfinished), Mahler wrote several song cycles, including *Das Lied von der Erde* (*The Song of the Earth*, 1908), which has become his best-known work. In his symphonies and songs, Mahler extended the traditions of romantic music, with touches of modern dissonance and ironic musical effects.

Mahomet. See *Mohammed*.

Maillol, Aristide (1861–1944), French sculptor famous for his figures of nudes. Trained as a painter, he turned to sculpture about 1900, being influenced by early Greek tradition. Maillol also produced terra-cotta statuettes and, toward the end of his life, many book illustrations.

Maimonides, or **Rabbi Moses ben Maimon,** known also as **Rambam** (1135–1204), Jewish philosopher and commentator on the scriptures. Born in Córdoba, Spain, he studied under the great Arab scholars and in 1177 became rabbi of Cairo. In his philosophical system, he attempted to reconcile Rabbinic Judaism with Aristotelian philosophy. His greatest work is *Guide of the Perplexed*, which contains the essence of his philosophy. Maimonides also wrote an Arabic *Book of Precepts* and a Hebrew work *Misneh Torah* (Second Law), as well as works on medicine, logic, and mathematics.

Maintenon, Françoise d'Aubigné, Marquise de (1635–1719), queen of France as second wife of Louis XIV. Her wit and grace led her to a favored position at the French court, and in 1669 she was appointed governess to the children of Louis XIV and Mme. de Montespan. In 1685 she was married to the widowed king in a private ceremony, thus becoming queen consort of France at the age of 50. She is looked upon favorably by historians, for she had not only charm and intelligence, but high moral values and great sympathy for the arts. She outlived the king by four years.

Malamud, Bernard (1914–), American author, born in Brooklyn, New York. He spent most of his mature life as a teacher in New York City high schools (1940–1949), at Oregon State University (1949–1961), and at Bennington College (1961-). Among his works are the novels *The Natural* (1952), *The Assistant* (1957), and *A New Life* (1961). He received the National Book Award for fiction in 1959.

Malenkov, Georgi Maximilianovich (1902–), Soviet Communist leader who served as premier from 1953 to 1955. Born in the Ural region, he joined the Red Army at the age of 17, became a member of the Communist party at 18, and in 1925 was appointed personal secretary to Joseph Stalin. He modeled himself, his behavior, even his clothing, after Stalin. In the 1930's, as the party's personnel chief, he built up his own personal following with his appointments. During World War II he was director of Soviet military production, achieving an output of arms hitherto unknown in Russian history; after the war, in charge of reconstruction, he demonstrated driving powers that were equally dynamic. When Stalin died in 1953, he was elected premier, but by 1955 his power had waned, and he was forced to resign after being denounced by Nikita Khrushchev.

Malevich, Kazimir (1878–1935), Russian painter who is generally accepted as the founder of abstract painting. Early in life, he was influenced by the French impressionists, but shortly before World War I he began painting abstract geometrical patterns, calling his approach suprematism. When the Soviet Union took a firm stand against abstract art, Malevich's career ended. He died in Leningrad.

Mallarmé, Stéphane (1842–1898), French poet who was the leader of the symbolist movement in French poetry in the late 1900's. Born in Paris, he spent a good portion of his life teaching English in various French schools. In his major works, notably *L'Après-midi d'un faune* (*The Afternoon of a Fawn*), Mallarmé produced sensuous evocative poetry that captured the feel of music.

Malory, Sir **Thomas** (d.1471), English writer famous for his *Morte d'Arthur*, the first account in modern English of King Arthur and his knights of the Round Table. Little is known of Malory's life, save that he himself was a knight who served the earl of Warwick. The *Morte d'Arthur* was first published in 1485 by the English printer William Caxton.

Malpighi, Marcello (1628–1694), Italian physiologist who founded microscopic anatomy. He taught medicine in several Italian cities before becoming, in 1691, physician to Pope Innocent XII. With his microscope, Malpighi was the first to prove the existence of capillary circulation. He also described the structure of the human lung and added to knowledge of the kidney, spleen, and brain. In addition, he studied the cell structure of plants and left excellent descriptions of all his findings in several memoirs.

Malraux, André (1901–), French novelist, critic, and statesman who first gained fame as a novelist, then as an art historian. As a young man he was in China during the revolutions of the 1920's. From this experience came his finest novel, *La Condition Humaine* (1933), published in English as *Man's Fate*. Later, he participated in the Spanish Civil War and in World War II as a member of the Resistance. After the war, Malraux became minister of information under de Gaulle (1945–1946), and returned as minister of culture under de Gaulle in 1958. In recent years, he has written several important books on art history, including the widely acclaimed *Les Voix du Silence* (*The Voices of Silence*), which first appeared in 1951.

Malthus, Thomas Robert (1766–1834), English economist noted for this theory that population tends to increase faster than production of food. A curate and college professor, in 1798 he published his *Essay on the Principle of Population*, a pessimistic study which warned that population growth, which is geometric, would eventually outstrip growth in food production, which is arithmetical. Population, he argued, will always grow to the limit of subsistence, being held in check only by famine, disease, and war.

Manet, Édouard (1832–1883), French painter who greatly influenced the development of the Impressionist school of painting. After studying in several European art centers, he settled in Paris, where his controversial paintings aroused much hostility, chiefly because of their realism and their unorthodox use of color and composition. Rejected in official circles, Manet and his followers organized their own exhibits. By the early 1880's he had achieved acceptance for his work. Today he is considered one of the leading French painters of all time.

Mann, Horace (1796–1859), American educator who has been called the father of American public-school education. Born in Franklin, Mass., he became a lawyer and then a member of the Massachusetts legislature (1827–1837), where he attracted notice with his criticism of the state public-school system. Afterwards, as secretary of the state board of education, he stirred the country to develop its school system and was influential in the establishment of the first normal school, at Lexington, Mass. Mann was in Congress from 1848 to 1853, where he was active in the antislavery movement. He was president of Antioch College from 1852 until 1859.

Mann, Thomas (1875–1955), German writer of philosophical and psychological novels and stories. His first novel, *Buddenbrooks* (1901), which traces the rise and fall of a German merchantile family, earned him a solid reputation as the chronicler of the Germany of his time. In a series of other novels, Mann closely examined the spiritual crisis of Europe. These works include *Tonio Kröger* (1903), *Death in Venice* (1912), and *The Magic Mountain* (1924)—the latter regarded as his masterpiece. He was awarded the Nobel Prize for literature in 1929. After Hitler's rise to power in 1933, Mann went to the United States, where he lived until his death. His work is characterized by a polished style, acute observation, and philosopical and psychological subtlety.

Mansart, François (1598–1666), French architect who specialized in the classical style. The roof style known as *mansard* derives from his name. During his lifetime he built a number of important houses in Paris and elsewhere, each of them marked by simple lines and restraint in design. From 1636 he was royal architect to Louis XIII.

Mansfield, Katherine (1890–1923), English short-story writer, regarded as one of the finest of the twentieth century. Born in New Zealand, she came to England at the age of 19. Among her published collections are *Bliss* (1920), *The Garden Party* (1922), and *The Dove's Nest* (1923). Her short stories, which depend more on atmosphere than on plot, are distinguished by their sensitive characterization and subtle insights.

ALFRED A. KNOPF

THOMAS MANN

Mantegna, Andrea (1431–1506), Italian artist, regarded as one of the greatest fresco painters of the fifteenth century. His chief works are in Padua (his native city), Mantua (where his patron was the duke of Mantua), and Rome (where he decorated a small chapel in the Vatican for Pope Innocent VIII). In addition to frescoes, Mantegna produced a number of smaller paintings. Most of his work has religious subjects.

Manutius, Aldus (1450–1515), Italian printer who founded the Aldine press, most celebrated of Renaissance publishers. Manutius founded his press in Venice around 1490. He knew Latin, Greek, and Hebrew, and published the classics of these languages. Perhaps his most famous book is his 1501 edition of Vergil, in which italic print appears for the first time. Also a scholar of note, Manutius compiled several dictionaries and grammatical texts on Latin and Greek.

Manzoni, Alessandro (1785–1873), Italian poet, dramatist, and novelist, whose novel *I Promessi Sposi* (*The Betrothed*, 1827), is considered one of the finest Italian novels. One of the leading personalities of his age, Manzoni wrote dramas and poetry in addition to novels. In much of his work, an underlying theme is the Italian struggle for independence. Always concerned with politics, he took part in the 1848 revolt in Milan, and in 1860 was made a senator of Italy. After his death, his friend Giuseppe Verdi wrote the *Manzoni Requiem* (1874) that honors his memory.

EASTFOTO

MAO TZE-TUNG

Mao Tze-tung (1893–   ), a founder of the Chinese Communist party and the leading Chinese Communist after the defeat of Chiang Kai-shek in 1949. Born in Hunan province, Mao became a revolutionary at an early age. After news of the Russian revolution reached China in 1917, he went about North China organizing workers and students. In 1921 he helped found the Chinese Communist party and later (1924–1925) served on the combined executive committee set up by the Communists and the Kuomintang, headed by Chiang Kai-shek. Mao broke with the Kuomintang in 1926 and returned to Hunan to organize the peasants. By 1931 he was political commissar of the Chinese Red Army, and throughout the Sino-Japanese War, which began in 1937, worked to consolidate the Communist forces. At the end of World War II, his army contained more than one million men. As the Nationalist government under Chiang became weaker, Mao's forces increased in cohesion and power. By the end of 1949, Mao controlled all of China and was head of state as well as chairman of the Communist party. In 1959 he relinquished the former position but retained his post as party chairman.

Marat, Jean Paul (1744–1793), French revolutionary leader and journalist. Born in Switzerland, he studied medicine and practiced in London, and in 1777 settled in Paris, where he published a political newspaper that attacked the French government. Forced to seek refuge in England in 1791,

COLUMBIA ARTISTS

MARCEL MARCEAU

he returned the following year and was elected to the Assembly. He then engaged in a bitter struggle with the Girondists that ended in the fall of that party. Charlotte Corday, a Girondist sympathizer, stabbed him to death in his bath.

Marceau, Marcel (1923–   ), French actor whose pantomime sketches have become classics in the theater. He has excelled in acting out, usually without words, the farces that are characteristic of mime theatrics. The director of his own company, Marceau led his troupe on a world tour from 1959 to 1963. Since then, the company revisited the United States and other countries on several occasions.

Marconi, Marchese Guglielmo (1874–1937), Italian physicist who developed a practical system of radiotelegraphy. Born in Bologna, he experimented with wireless communication in his youth, after Heinrich Hertz had announced his discovery of electromagnetic waves in 1888. By 1890 Marconi had made considerable progress in transmitting signals through the air but was unable to interest the Italian government in his ideas. He went to England in 1896 and received the first patent for wireless apparatus ever issued. In 1897 the Marconi Wireless Telegraph Company was organized in London, and in 1899 signals were transmitted across the English Channel. In that year wireless was first used for saving life at sea. Marconi's apparatus was so improved by 1901 that messages were being sent across the Atlantic. Transoceanic communication was placed on a commercial basis in 1903. In 1914 he began experiments with short waves, which led to the beam system of long-distance and directed wireless transmission. He shared the Nobel Prize for physics in 1909, was appointed a senator of Italy for life, and in 1929 received the hereditary title of marchese (marquis).

Marco Polo. See *Polo, Marco.*

Marcus Aurelius, surnamed **Antonius,** original name **Marcus Annius Verus** (121–180), Roman emperor (161–180), remembered for the book *Meditations,* which reflects the philosophy of stoicism. Adopted by Emperor Antoninus Pius at the age of 17, he was made consul in the year 140 and was a trusted official of the emperor, whom he succeeded in 161. Until 169 he administered the government with Lucius Verus. In 168 Marcus Aurelius led his legions to the Danubian provinces to put down a revolt; this was the first of a series of uprisings that kept the emperor on the field of battle much of the time. During his reign great strides were made in the codification of Roman law, and persecution of Christians, though carried out from time to time, was not so harsh as under his predecessors. His *Meditations,* which emphasizes the virtues of self-sacrifice and nobility, gives a good picture of the man himself.

Marcy, William Learned (1786–1857), American statesman, born in Southbridge, Mass. A graduate of Brown University in 1808, he practiced law in Troy, N.Y. He fought in the War of 1812 and subsequently became active in state politics. In 1831 Marcy was elected to the U. S. Senate as a Democrat. While defending Pres. Van Buren's use of Federal patronage, he uttered the now famous remark, "To the victor belong the spoils of the enemy." In 1832 he resigned his seat to become governor of New York, holding that office until 1838. He was secretary of war (1845–1849) under Pres. James K. Polk and secretary of state (1853–1857) under Pres. Franklin Pierce.

Margaret of Anjou (1430–1482), queen of Henry VI of England. She was remarkable for the energy that she put into her husband's cause during the Wars of the Roses. In 1461, however, the Yorkist party was triumphant at Towton, and Edward IV ascended the throne, though Henry VI was still alive. Margaret made several efforts to regain the crown for her family but her cause was finally lost with the defeat of the Lancastrians, her son being one of those killed. She was imprisoned in the Tower of London but was released after five years through the intercession of Louis XI of France. She then returned to France.

Margaret of Denmark (1353–1412), queen of Denmark, Norway, and Sweden, the daughter of Valdemar IV of Denmark. She married Haakon VI of Norway in 1363. Their son Olaf became king of Denmark when Valdemar died. When Haakon died, Olaf also ruled Norway under Margaret's regency. She claimed the Swedish throne as well, defeated the Swedes, and took Sweden in 1395. The next year she placed her grandnephew Eric on the Swedish throne. However, Margaret remained the real ruler of all three nations until her death, after which the union fell apart.

Margaret of Navarre (1492–1549), queen of Navarre, daughter of Charles of Orleans and sister of Francis I of France. In 1527 she became the wife of Henri d'Albret, king of Navarre. Their daughter, Jeanne d'Albret, was the mother of Henry of Navarre, who ruled France as Henry IV. Margaret wrote poetry and prose, and is noted for her *Memoirs* and *The Heptameron,* modeled after Boccaccio's *Decameron.*

Maria Theresa (1717–1780), empress of the Holy Roman Empire, daughter of Charles VI, Holy Roman emperor. Having no male heir, Charles secured a pledge from the leading European powers that his daughter would be recognized as heiress to the Hapsburg territories. When Charles died in 1740, Maria Theresa became queen of Hungary and Bohemia, and archduchess of Austria. Her claims to her father's possessions were disputed by several nations, in spite of their promises, bringing on the eight-year War of the Austrian Succession. The Hungarians supported their queen, and by the Peace of Aix-la-Chapelle (1748) Maria Theresa's titles were recognized, though she lost Silesia to Frederick II of Prussia. Aided by her minister, Count von Kaunitz, she developed her country's agriculture and commerce and introduced financial reforms. In 1756 she renewed the struggle with Frederick II, and the ensuing Seven Years' War (1756–63) exhausted the country without restoring the lost province of Silesia. Joesph II, son of Maria Theresa and Francis I, succeeded his father as Holy Roman emperor in 1765 and in 1772 persuaded his mother to take part in the first partition of Poland. Among the ten surviving children of the empress was Marie Antoinette, queen of France.

Marie, in full, **Marie Alexandra Victoria** (1875–1938), queen of Rumania (1914–1927), the daughter of Queen Victoria's second son and the Grand Duchess Marie, a Russian princess. In 1893 she married Crown Prince Ferdinand of Rumania, who succeeded to the throne in 1914 and ruled until his death (1927). In 1926 she made a widely publicized tour of the United States and Canada. Her eldest son assumed the crown in 1930.

Marie Antoinette (1755–1793), queen of Louis XVI of France, daughter of Holy Roman emperor Francis I and Maria Theresa. At the age of 15 she married the prince who later became Louis XVI. Soon after Louis' accession in 1774 stories were circulated about her gaiety and extravagance, and she became unpopular with the masses. In 1789 she was attacked by a crowd of infuriated women who stormed the Palace of Versailles. The royal family moved to the Tuileries in Paris. In June, 1791, she persuaded Louis to flee from France, but the fugitives were stopped at Varennes and returned to Paris. During the Revolution the king and queen barely escaped murder at the hands of a mob that attacked the Tuileries. They sought refuge in the Convention Hall but were shortly afterward placed in prison.

Marie was regarded as responsible for much of the misery in the land and as the evil genius of her husband, although by no stretch of the imagination could the terrible condition of France be charged against the queen. At her trial she defended herself with dignity and spirit, but sentence of death was passed October 16, 1793, and on the same day she was guillotined.

Marie de Médicis (1573–1642), wife of Henry IV of France and queen regent (1610–1614) after his death. The daughter of Francesco de Medici, grand duke of Tuscany, she married Henry in 1600. After her son, Louis XIII, came of age in 1614, she continued to rule for him until 1617, when he assumed control. Marie went into exile, but in 1619 began a revolt, assisted by Richelieu, whom she had made a cardinal in 1622. Reconciled with her son, she spent the next few years in attempting to unite France, Austria, and Spain against Protestantism. In 1630, however, her conspiracy against Richelieu (who had become her enemy) failed, and she was exiled, never to return to France.

Marie Louise (1791–1847), second wife of Napoleon I of France and daughter of Emperor Francis I of Austria. Napoleon married her in 1810 after divorcing Josephine, who had borne him no heirs. Their son, born in 1811, became Napoleon II. Marie Louise did not go with Napoleon in exile. The Congress of Vienna awarded her the duchies of Parma, Piacenza, and Guastalla. Twice remarried, she died in Parma, Italy.

Marin, John Cheri (1872–1953), American artist, best known for his vivid watercolors. Born in Rutherford, N.J., he studied painting in Philadelphia and New York, and spent six years in Europe, returning in 1911. In 1936, a retrospective showing of his work at the Museum of Modern Art in New York City established his reputation. Marin's best works are his Maine seascapes, in which bold coloring and slight distortion heighten the intensity of the subject matter without lapsing into abstraction.

Marion, Francis (1732–1795), American soldier during the Revolutionary War, called the "Swamp Fox" by the British because of his elusive tactics. Born near Georgetown, S. C., he was made a captain when the Revolution broke out, and in 1780 organized Marion's Brigade, a volunteer troop composed mainly of South Carolina mountaineers and hunters. Appointed a brigadier general in 1781, he led his troops in raids against the British in the Carolinas. After the war he served in the South Carolina senate from 1782 to 1790.

Maritain, Jacques (1882–), French philosopher noted for his writings on the thought of Saint Thomas Aquinas. Born in Paris, he studied there and in Heidelberg, and became a Roman Catholic convert in 1906. He spent much of his adult life as a teacher, including two periods in the United States, at Columbia University (1940–1944) and Princeton (1948–1953). After World War II, he was French ambassador to the Vatican from 1945 to 1948. His works, which often combine principles of Saint Thomas Aquinas and Aristotle, include *Art and Scholasticism* (1920), *Art and Poetry* (1935), and *Moral Philosophy* (1960). In 1958, the University of Notre Dame established a Jacques Maritain center.

Marius, Gaius (c.155–86 B.C.), Roman general and statesman who was consul seven times during a long career. Of lowly birth, his military exploits won him the title "Savior of Rome." He first became consul in 107 B.C. and ended the war against Numidia (now Algeria) by capturing its king. He next crushed the Teutonic tribes that had invaded the Roman provinces. In 88 B.C. he involved Rome in civil war and was forced to flee, but he obtained help from Lucius Cinna and captured Rome. Marius then ordered a terrible massacre of his enemies. He died a few days after he had been elected consul for the seventh time.

Markham, Edwin (1852–1940), American poet, best remembered for his poem, *The Man With the Hoe* (1899), inspired by the painting of Jean F. Millet. Born in Oregon City, Ore., he began to write poetry at an early age. When *The Man With the Hoe* appeared, he was a school teacher, but abandoned this calling to become a writer and lecturer. During the remainder of his life, he produced several other volumes of poetry—none of which, however, captured the public's fancy as the early poem did.

Marlborough, Duke of. See *Churchill, John.*

Marlowe, Christopher (1564–1593), English poet and dramatist, considered the finest English dramatist before Shakespeare. The son of a Canterbury shoemaker, he began his career in London as a writer of tragedies. The first of his plays, *Tamburlaine the Great,* was produced about 1587. Then followed *Doctor Faustus, The Jew of Malta,* and *Edward II.* Marlowe was the first to use blank verse, as we understand the form, and his poetry is noted for its power and beauty. His promising career was cut short when he was killed in a quarrel at the age of 29. The well-known phrase, "Marlowe's mighty line," is a tribute to the stateliness of his verse.

Marquand, John Phillips (1893–1960), American novelist noted for his portraits of New England aristocracy. Born in Wilmington, Del., he graduated from Harvard in 1915. After working as a newspaperman, he began writing short stories for magazines, and his famous series of "Mr. Moto" detective novels. Later, he produced the novels that brought him serious recognition as an artist: *The Late George Apley* (1937), *H. M. Pulham, Esq.* (1941), *Point of No Return* (1949), and *Melville Goodwin, U.S.A.* (1951). In these works, Marquand dwelt ironically but fondly on the passing of the old gentility and the emergence of new social forces.

Marquette, Jacques, known as **Père Marquette** (1637–1675), French explorer and Jesuit priest who in 1673 traveled down the Mississippi River with Louis Jolliet. In 1666 he went to Canada as a Jesuit missionary and in 1668 founded a mission at Sault Ste. Marie. After his expedition down the Mississippi, he worked among the Indians who lived near the Great Lakes. He died near the present town of Ludington, Michigan.

Marryat, Frederick (1792–1848), British naval officer who wrote a series of highly popular novels for young readers, including the well-known *Mr. Midshipman Easy* (1836). He entered the navy as a midshipman at the age of 14 and by 1830 reached the grade of captain. His many books, based on his experiences at sea, continue to be popular with boys. Among his better-known novels are *The King's Own* (1830), *Peter Simple* (1834), and *Poor Jack* (1840).

Marsh, Reginald (1898–1954), American painter, born in Paris, France, of American parents who were painters. A realistic painter, Marsh is remembered for his many paintings of New York City, which follow in the tradition of the so-called Ashcan school of the preceding generation. He was also a noted magazine illustrator. Two of his murals, *Sorting Mail* and *Transfer of Mail from Tugboat to Liner,* are in the U. S. Post Office Building, Washington, D.C.

Marshall, George Catlett (1880–1959), American general and statesman, Army chief of staff during World War II, and afterwards both secretary of state and secretary of defense. Born in Uniontown, Pa., he was educated at Virginia Military Institute. After a lengthy career in the army, he was made chief of staff in 1939, and supervised the army's activities throughout World War II. In 1945 he was sent as a special envoy to China. As Pres. Harry Truman's secretary of state (1947–1949), he implemented the Marshall Plan for aid to Europe. On his retirement he became president of the American Red Cross. When the Korean War broke out in 1950, he was recalled to active duty as secretary of defense, serving one year. In 1953 he was awarded the Nobel Peace Prize.

Marshall, John (1755–1835), fourth chief justice of the United States Supreme Court. Born in Germantown, Va., he fought in the Revolution under his father, Colonel Thomas Marshall, rising to the rank of captain. In 1781 he began practicing law in Virginia, and during the next few years served several terms in the state legislature. In 1797 he was sent as envoy to France with Charles Pinckney and Elbridge Gerry to settle problems created when France restricted American commerce. Marshall was elected to Congress in 1799 and in 1800 was appointed secretary of state by Pres. John Adams. In 1801 he began a 34-year career as chief justice of the Supreme Court. His decisions strengthened the role of the federal government and set a pattern that later courts followed.

Martel, Charles. See *Charles Martel.*

Martí, José Julian (1853–1895), Cuban patriot and writer, regarded as his country's greatest hero. As a young man, he sympathized with the cause of Cuban patriots against Spain. As a result, he spent much of his life in exile, where he became famous as a writer on Latin American revolutionary movements. In 1895 he led an invasion party to liberate Cuba, but was killed in battle shortly afterward. His writings are credited with doing much to promote better understanding between the United States and Latin America.

Martial, born **Marcus Valerius Martialis** (c.40–104), Roman writer, noted for his epigrams. He came to Rome in 64 and lived there for most of his life. Martial wrote more than 1,500 epigrams, which reveal a Roman society. In these short verses, he brought the Latin epigram to perfection.

Marvell, Andrew (1621–1678), English metaphysical poet and political writer, noted for his subtle and satirical wit. A staunch defender of Oliver Cromwell, he wrote many political satires against the Restoration government in England. For the last 18 years of his life, he was a member of the House of Commons. After his death, his wife published a collection of his poems, of which *To His Coy Mistress* and *The Garden* are among the best. Largely ignored during the eighteenth and nineteenth centuries, Marvell in this century has come to be recognized as one of the most important seventeenth-century poets.

Marx, Karl Heinrich (1818–1883), German philosopher whose *Das Kapital,* written with Friedrich Engels, is the most important document in the history of socialism. Born in Prussia and educated at universities in Bonn and Berlin, he received a doctor's degree in 1841 from the University of Jena. Shortly afterward, he became a newspaper editor in Germany, but his newspaper was suppressed and he left for Paris, where he first met Engels. In 1847, at a radical congress in Brussels, Marx and Engels issued the *Communist Manifesto,* which stated the aims of the Communist party. He returned to Germany in 1848, but was expelled the next year and went to England, where he spent the remainder of his life. The first volume of *Das Kapital* was published in 1867. In this work, Marx expressed his belief that all wealth, being produced by labor, should be returned to labor, and that capitalism would be abolished. The second and third volumes of *Das Kapital* were edited by Engels and published in 1885 and 1894.

Mary I or **Mary Tudor,** often called **Bloody Mary** (1516–1558), queen of England (1553–1558), the daughter of Henry VIII and Catherine of Aragon. She succeeded her half brother Edward VI in 1553 and the following year married Philip II of Spain, but the union was an unhappy one. Mary Tudor began her reign by repealing laws directed against Roman Catholics in England. Later she began the persecutions for which she was called "Bloody Mary." Through Philip's influence she waged a war with France, in which England lost Calais, its last foothold in France. She was succeeded by her half sister, Elizabeth I.

Mary II (1662–1694), queen of England (1689–1694) and wife of King William III. The daughter of King James II, she was married to her cousin William of Orange in 1677. Some ten years later, after a quarrel had broken out between her husband and her father, she supported her husband's successful invasion of England. She and Wil-

liam were made joint sovereigns on April 11, 1689. During the years of her reign, she was immensely popular with her subjects.

Mary, Queen of Scots, called **Mary Stuart** (1542–1587), the daughter of James V of Scotland. She was only a week old when her father died, but as heir to the throne was proclaimed queen of Scotland at once. Taken to France in childhood, she was married in 1558 to the heir to the French throne, who became Francis II in 1559. After her husband died in 1561, she returned to Scotland. Four years later, she married Lord Darnley, her cousin.

A staunch Roman Catholic, she was opposed to Calvinism, which had won many followers in Scotland through the teachings of John Knox. Gradually, she enlisted the support of Rome, Spain, and France against Protestant England. Meanwhile, Mary had personal trouble with her court. In 1567, only a year after her son (who became James I of England) was born, Lord Darnley was killed in an explosion. James Hepburn, earl of Bothwell, was suspected of plotting the explosion, and Mary herself aroused suspicion when she married Bothwell soon after. This reckless act caused a revolt among the nobles. They imprisoned Mary, but she escaped and fled to England, where her cousin Queen Elizabeth kept her a prisoner for 19 years. In 1587 Mary was tried for complicity in a plot to murder Elizabeth and was executed.

Masaccio, real name **Tommaso Guidi** (1401–1428), the first Florentine Renaissance painter, and one of the greatest of all Italian painters. A native of Tuscan, he was admitted to a Florentine art guild in 1422. Up to this time, the medieval style had dominated Italian painting. By introducing perspective and depth to his paintings, Masaccio created a new style that greatly influenced later masters such as Raphael and Michelangelo. His most important frescos are in a chapel of the Carmine Church in Florence. Only 27 when he died, Masaccio in a few years transformed Florentine art from medieval to Renaissance style.

Masanobu. See *Kano.*

Masaryk, Tomáš Garrigue (1850–1937), Czechoslovakian statesman who in 1918 became his country's first president. A blacksmith before he entered college, he soon became prominent in literary circles and in 1882 became a professor at the University of Prague. A member of the Austrian Parliament from 1891 to 1893, he was reelected in 1907 and opposed Germany's policy toward Austria, as well as the aggressive policy of Austria in the Balkans. After the outbreak of World War I, he organized the Czechoslovakian (Bohemian) movement for independence. When in 1918 the Allies recognized the Czechoslovakian government, he was elected president of the republic by acclamation. After holding this office for 17 years, he resigned in 1935. Masaryk had many friends in the United States, notably Pres. Woodrow Wilson. When he married an American girl, Charlotte Garrigue, he took her family name as his middle name. His son, Jan, later became foreign minister of Czechoslovakia.

Mascagni, Pietro (1863–1945), Italian composer, remembered chiefly for his opera *Cavalleria Rusticana* ("Rustic Chivalry"), composed in 1889. As a young man he took music lessons secretly while studying for the law. Some of his compositions aroused so much interest that he became a full-time composer, chiefly of operas. A leading exponent of the *verismo* (realistic) style of music, Mascagni wrote several other operas, including *L'amico Fritz* (1891) and *Iris* (1898), that are frequently performed in Italy. However, *Cavalleria Rusticana* is his only opera still regularly performed throughout the world.

Masefield, John (1878–1967), English poet who became poet laureate of England in 1930. When he was 14, he ran away to sea and was a common sailor for many years. His first work, *Salt-Water Ballads* (1902), reflecting his experiences at sea, contains his most popular poem, *Sea Fever.* He became famous after the publication in 1911 of *The Everlasting Mercy,* which shocked many by its use of coarse language. Besides many books of poetry, he produced numerous prose works. In general, his poetry is traditional rather than "modern." He died May 12, 1967 near Abingdon, England.

Massasoit (c.1580–1661), American Indian chief who ruled the Wampanoag Indians in southern Massachusetts when the Pilgrims arrived. In March, 1621, he visited the colony of Pilgrims and made a treaty of peace that lasted for half a century. His principal village was in what is now Rhode Island, where he befriended Roger Williams after Williams was banished from Massa-

chusetts. Massasoit was succeeded by his son Metacomet, known as King Philip.

Massenet, Jules Émile Frédéric (1842–1912), French composer, remembered for his romantic operas. Educated at the Paris Conservatory, he completed his first opera at the age of 25. In *Manon* (1884), his masterpiece, Massenet best revealed his gift for writing delicate, sensuous music. Other operas include *Werther* (1892), *Thaïs* (1894), *Le Jongleur de Notre-Dame* (1902), and *Don Quichotte* (1910). Although these works are performed regularly in France, it is *Manon* that has won worldwide fame. Massenet's *Élégie* (1873), a hauntingly melodic composition, is a popular concert piece for violin, cello, and piano.

Massys, Quentin (c.1455–1530), Flemish painter who was the first major artist of the Antwerp school. Originally a blacksmith, he became an important member of the guild at Antwerp and, through his art, came to know such painters as Dürer and Holbein. In addition to religious scenes and portraits, he specialized in portraits of contemporary bankers and merchants.

Masters, Edgar Lee (1869–1950), American poet and novelist, best known as the author of the *Spoon River Anthology* poems. Born in Garnett, Kansas, he attended Knox College in Illinois, and practiced law in Chicago. After a few years, he became active as a writer. *Spoon River Anthology* (1915), his greatest work, is a collection of some 200 tombstone epitaphs in free verse, purporting to be the honest confessions of those who had died. Masters also produced several novels.

Mather, Cotton (1663–1728), American clergyman who was the most famous of Puritan ministers. The son of Increase Mather, he was born in Boston and graduated from Harvard at the age of 15. Two years later, he became his father's assistant at North Church, Boston, assuming full charge during his father's absence in England. Mather was known as a linguist and published an enormous number of books. Among them are his *Ecclesiastical History of New England* and a book on witchcraft, which helped to bring on the persecution of "witches" in Salem. Interested in science, he advocated inoculation against smallpox. He helped to found Yale University.

Mather, Increase (1639–1723), American clergyman, born in Dorchester, Mass. He was graduated from Harvard College in 1656, followed his father's calling and for nearly 60 years was pastor of North Church, Boston. During the years 1685–1701 he also served as president of Harvard. He was important in matters of state. The people of Massachusetts sent him to England in 1688 to secure a charter, which William III granted. He was the author of books on colonial history and theology.

Matisse, Henri (1869–1954), French painter, generally recognized as one of the greatest artists of the twentieth century. After several years of conventional art study, he changed his approach radically when he discovered Impressionist painting, then considered revolutionary. Matisse then went beyond impressionism, taking his inspira-

SOVFOTO

MARX banner in Red Square on May Day.

CARL ZIGROSSER AND PHILADELPHIA MUSEUM OF ART

HENRI MATISSE in a rare self-portrait.

tion from primitive African art, Islamic art, and early Italian painting. Ridiculed at first, he became famous for his extraordinary use of color and his simple, primitive outlines. His output over the years was enormous. In addition to numerous paintings, he also produced lithographs and sculpture. Late in life, he designed the decoration for a chapel at Vence in southern France, which he considered to be his masterpiece.

Maugham, William Somerset (1874–1965), English writer and dramatist, a popular writer of the twentieth century. Educated to be a doctor, he never practiced, but his medical experiences are reflected in his best-known novel, *Of Human Bondage* (1915). A prolific writer, Maugham was prominent as a playwright before he turned exclusively to fiction. Among his other works are *The Moon and Sixpence* (1919), a fictional account of the painter Gauguin; *Cakes and Ale* (1930); and *The Razor's Edge* (1944). Widely traveled, Maugham used the Far East as the setting for much of his work. In *The Summing Up* (1938) and *A Writer's Notebook* (1949), Maugham expressed his philosophy of life and his experiences as a writer.

Maupassant, Guy de (1850–1893), French short-story writer and novelist, noted for his realistic, bittersweet tales. He began work as a clerk in the navy department, but was inspired to write through the influence of Flaubert. He became famous in 1880 when his short story *Boule de Suif* ("Ball of Fat") appeared in an anthology. After this, he published many books of short stories, as well as several novels, including the well-known *Bel-Ami* (1885). Maupassant's strength as a writer lies in his great powers of observation, realistic portrayal of all facets of French life, and his spare, laconic style. In poor health during the latter part of his life, he was pronounced insane shortly before his death.

Mauriac, François (1885–), French novelist, winner of the Nobel Prize for literature in 1952. A staunch Roman Catholic, his dominant themes are sin and redemption, reflected in such subjects as incompatible husbands and wives, domineering mothers, and religious hypocrites. In addition to his novels, Mauriac has also produced biographies and philosophical works. After World War II, he became one of France's foremost political essayists.

Maurois, André, pen name of **Emile Herzog** (1885–1967), French writer, noted for fictionalized biographies. In World War I he was a liaison officer with the British army. From his experiences came his first book, *Les Silences du Colonel Bramble* (1918), a satire on British military life. During the next 20 years he published biographies of writers and statesmen, including Shelley, Byron, Dickens, Voltaire, Disraeli, and Chateaubriand. After World War II, spent in the United States and North Africa, he published biographies of George Sand, Hugo, the Dumas family, and Balzac. In addition to biographies, he has also written histories of the United States, England, and France. He died Oct. 9, 1967 in Paris, France.

Maury, Matthew Fontaine (1806–1873), American naval officer whose oceanographic researches gained widespread recognition. Born in Spotsylvania, Va., he entered the navy as a midshipman in 1825. In 1841, after he had broken his leg and was permanently crippled, he was appointed supervisor of charts and instruments in the navy department, where he aided in organizing the Naval Observatory and the Hydrographic Office. Maury served the Confederate cause in the Civil War as head of coastal defenses. After the war, he was appointed commissioner of immigration by Emperor Maximilian of Mexico. In 1868 he became professor of meteorology at Virginia Military Institute. He published several textbooks and geographies.

Maximilian, in full **Ferdinand Maximilian Joseph** (1832–1867), archduke of Austria and emperor of Mexico (1864–1867). At the age of 25, he was made governor of Lombardy and Venetia, then Austrian possessions, by Emperior Francis Joseph. In 1863 Napoleon III laid plans to conquer Mexico and set up an empire there. He offered the throne to Maximilian, who was crowned in June, 1864. The empire fell apart after two years when the French army withdrew its support. Maximilian then tried to form a native army for his own defense, but was captured and shot by Mexican republicans.

Maximilian I (1459–1519), Holy Roman emperor (1493–1519), the eldest son of Emperor Frederick III of the Hapsburg dynasty. In 1477 he married Mary, daughter of Charles the Bold, duke of Burgundy. When Charles died, Maximilian was attacked by Louis XI of France, who claimed part of Mary's inheritance. By the Treaty of Arras (1482), Louis received Burgundy and other French territory, but Maximilian kept most of the Netherlands. He was elected king of the Romans in 1486 and succeeded his father in 1493. Much of his reign was occupied with warfare against the French and the Turks. When his son Philip married Juana of Spain, he brought about the succession of the Hapsburgs to the vast Spanish dominions. The marriage of his grandson Ferdinand to Anne of Hungary and Bohemia brought both countries under Hapsburg influence. His grandson Charles succeeded him.

Maxwell, James Clerk (1831–1879), British physicist who made important contributions to knowledge of electricity. After many years of teaching, he became first professor of experimental physics at Cambridge, where he published his greatest book, *Electricity and Magnetism* (1873). Maxwell is noted for his theoretical demonstration that light waves are electromagnetic. This theory, together with his ideas about electromagnetism in general, led to the discovery of radio communication. Maxwell also contributed much to knowledge of heat, color perception, and gases.

Mayo, Charles Horace (1865–1939) and **Mayo, William James** (1861–1939), brothers who founded the Mayo Clinic in Rochester, Minnesota, one of the leading medical centers in the United States. The sons of a well-known doctor, the brothers established the Mayo Foundation for Medical Education and Research in 1915. Later, the foundation became a part of the University of Minnesota. In World War I the Mayos were chief consultants in surgery to the U.S. army. Many modern surgical practices originated with the Mayo brothers.

Mazarin, Jules (1602–1661), Italian diplomat who, as chief minister to Louis XIII and Louis XIV, had great influence in the shaping of French power. Educated in Italy and Spain, he represented Pope Urban VIII on a diplomatic mission to Paris, where he attracted the notice of Cardinal Richelieu, who designated him his successor. Appointed chief minister to Louis XIII, he retained that position under Louis XIV, becoming the most powerful man in France. After becoming a French citizen, he was made a cardinal in 1641, and brought the Thirty Years' War to a successful conclusion with the Treaty of Westphalia in 1648. In his later career, Mazarin reconciled rival factions within France and negotiated international treaties to insure French power.

Mazzini, Giuseppe (1805–1872), Italian patriot who was a leader in the nineteenth-century drive for independence. Born in Genoa and educated as a lawyer, he turned to revolutionary activities at an early age. In 1830 he was expelled from Italy and lived for several years in France, Switzerland, and England, where he carried out plans for the unification of Italy. For 40 years (1830–1870) he kept in close touch with Italian patriots and vigorously supported Garibaldi and Cavour. He was one of the triumvirs of the short-lived Roman republic of 1849. In exile thereafter for most of his life, he nevertheless lived to see his dream of a united Italy come true.

Mc—Names beginning with this prefix are alphabetized as if spelled *Mac*.

Mead, Margaret (1901–), American anthropologist, born in Philadelphia. A graduate of Barnard College, she received her doctor's degree from Columbia in 1929. She was assistant curator of ethnology at the American Museum of Natural History, New York from 1926 and curator from 1942. In the 1920's and 1930's she made field trips to New Guinea, Bali, and Samoa, where she studied native customs. From this work came her authoritative books *Coming of Age in Samoa* (1928) and *Growing up in New Guinea* (1930). A member of the faculty of Columbia, she has also written *Male and Female* (1949) and *Growth and Culture* (1951), among other books.

Meade, George Gordon (1815–1872), American Civil War general, who led the Union army to victory over Gen. Robert E. Lee at the battle of Gettysburg (1863). Born in Cádiz, Spain, of American parents, he graduated from West Point in 1835 and saw service in the Mexican War. In the Civil War, he fought with distinction in several early battles and became a major general. Just before the engagement at Gettysburg, he replaced Gen. Joseph Hooker and went on to win perhaps the most crucial battle of the war. During the last year of the war, he served under Gen. Ulysses S. Grant. After the war he had a variety of military posts.

Meany, William George (1894–), American labor leader who, after the merger of the AFL and CIO unions in 1955, became head of the combined organization. Born in New York City, the son of a plumber, he himself became a plumber and active in union affairs. In 1923 he was elected secretary-treasurer of the New York Building Trades Council. Meany later became a state president of the American Federation of Labor, and in 1935 succeeded in getting union wages for WPA workers. In 1939 he became secretary-treasurer of the AFL, and president in 1952. After 1955 he became the most powerful union leader in the U.S.

Medici, Lorenzo I de', known as **Lorenzo the Magnificent** (1449–1492), ruler of the Florentine republic, great patron of the arts, and a prominent member of a celebrated family that exercised great influence in Italy and other European countries. Lorenzo and his brother Giuliano became leaders of the Florentine state in 1469. In 1478 a conspiracy was formed by the Passi, another powerful family, which resulted in Giuliano's assassination. Lorenzo was wounded but lived to crush his opponents. He fully earned the epithet *Lorenzo the Magnificent* by the way he spent his great wealth in beautifying Florence and encouraging artists and poets. The Laurentian Library, founded by his grandfather, was enriched with priceless classical manuscripts.

Mehemet Ali or **Mohammad Ali** (1769–1849), Turkish soldier who became pasha of Egypt in 1805 after he had taken a prominent part in expelling the French under Napoleon. Though forced to acknowledge the nominal authority of the sultan, he exercised independent power and did much to develop the country. In 1811 he crushed the Mamelukes by a general massacre at Cairo and for several years thereafter warred against the Wahabis in Arabia. He conquered a good part of Arabia and part of the Sudan and helped the Turks in their struggle with the Greeks. In Egypt he remained powerful until he became insane in 1848.

Meiji. See *Mutsuhito*.

Melba, Dame **Nellie,** stage name of **Helen Porter Mitchell** (1861–1931), Australian soprano who was a leading figure on the opera stage from 1887 to 1926. Born in Melbourne, she made her operatic debut in 1887 in Brussels under the name of *Melba*, after her home town. With her debut in London the following year, she was acclaimed the reigning coloratura singer of her time. During a long career, she sang roles in the principal opera houses of Europe and the United States. In 1918 she was created a Dame of the British Empire for her work with wounded soldiers.

Melchior, Lauritz (1890–), Danish tenor, generally recognized as the finest Wagnerian tenor of the twentieth century. Born in Copenhagen, he made his debut there in 1913 as a baritone. Becoming a tenor five years later, he sang in the major European opera houses. After his debut in 1926 at the Metropolitan Opera in New York, he became the leading tenor in Wagnerian operas, in which he appeared scores of times with the soprano Kirsten Flagstad. He became an American citizen in 1947 and continued to sing until his retirement in 1950.

Melville, Herman (1819–1891), American author whose novel *Moby Dick* is considered a classic in American literature. Born in New York City, he went to sea at 17 on a whaling ship. His first two novels, *Typee* (1846) and *Omoo* (1847), are based on his experiences in the South Seas. From a hitch in the U.S. navy came the material for *White Jacket* (1850). His greatest novel, *Moby Dick* (1851), is the story of a whaling captain's relentless pursuit of a legendary white whale. Melville also produced several short novels, such as *Benito Cereno* and *Billy Budd*, which are considered masterpieces of the genre. In most of his work, Melville explored philosophical themes, especially the nature of good and evil.

Memling, Hans (c.1430–1494), Flemish painter, noted for his religious paintings and portraits. Little is known of his life, except that he was chiefly active in Bruges, and that he was the pupil of Rogier van der Weyden. Of the paintings that still remain in Bruges, the most outstanding are in the museum of the Hospital of St. John.

Menander (c.343–291 B.C.). Athenian comic dramatist, considered by his contemporaries to be second only to Aristophanes. He studied drama under Alexis, his uncle, who was a leading writer. Menander was closely associated with the philosophers Theophrastus and Epicurus. He was awarded a prize for a comedy at the age of 21 and later won first prize for eight plays. He won a reputation for his comedies, of which only fragments survive. The Roman writers Plautus and Terence made adaptations of his plays.

Mencius (c.371–289 B.C.), Chinese moral teacher, born in what is now Shantung province. He was a traveling teacher and had many followers. The basis of his philosophic system was a belief in the ethical goodness of man's nature. He also taught advanced economic and political principles, advocating freedom of trade, the unseating of bad rulers, popular education, and the abolition of war. After he died, his disciples published his sayings and conversations as the *Book of Mencius*.

Mencken, Henry Louis (1880–1956), American editor and writer, noted for his satirical essays and his studies of the American language. Born in Baltimore, he began his literary career as a reporter on the *Morning Herald*. He was literary critic of *Smart Set* (1908–1923) and co-editor of this periodical (1914–1923). From 1924 to 1933 he edited the *American Mercury*, which he had helped to found. He became widely known as a critic of contemporary letters, politics, religion, and customs. His lifelong researches in American English were gathered in *The American Language*, a monumental work, published with revisions and supplements between 1919 and 1948. His essays appear in many books, notably in *Prejudices*.

Mendel, Gregor Johann (1822–1884), Austrian priest and botanist who developed the modern science of genetics. Born in Silesia, he became abbot of the monastery at Brünn and in 1856 began his experiments in the monastery garden. He grew many generations of garden peas, crossing and hybridizing them and keeping careful records. In this way he discovered what characteristics are passed on to offspring under varying environments and with various matings. Much modern research has been devoted to amplifying his original findings.

Mendeleev, Dmitri Ivanovich (1834–1907), Russian chemist who developed the periodic table for chemical elements, which he arranged according to their atomic weights. Born in Siberia, he was for many years professor of chemistry in the technological institute at St. Petersburg. His periodic table of the elements showed that all chemical elements have a definite relationship with one another; when arranged in a table according to their atomic weights, they reveal many valuable characteristics. Mendeleev's table showed some gaps, representing elements still to be discovered, yet he was able to predict what their characteristics would be. The 101st element, mendelevium, is named for him.

Mendelssohn, Felix (1809–1847), German composer, one of the leading figures in Romantic music. He was born in Hamburg of Jewish parents, who adopted the Christian faith and changed the name to Mendelssohn-Bartholdy. A child prodigy, he had the best instruction available, and at the age of 24 became director of music at Düsseldorf. Two years later, he was appointed director of public concerts in Leipzig, where he organized the now famous conservatory. Among his masterworks, still frequently performed, are his music for *A Midsummer Night's Dream* (written when he was only 17), the *Italian* and *Scottish* symphonies, the oratorio *Elijah*, and the piano pieces called *Songs Without Words*. Mendelssohn was also influential in reviving interest during his lifetime in the music of Bach and other earlier composers.

Mendès-France, Pierre (1907–   ), French statesman who was prime minister of France in 1954–1955. He entered the French parliament in 1932 as a member of the Radical party. In 1941 he joined the Free French Forces in England after escaping from a Vichy government prison. After the war, General de Gaulle appointed him minister for national economy, and in 1954 he became prime minister for national economy, and in 1954 he became prime minister. Though a strong and capable leader, he was forced to resign in 1955 when his North African policy was defeated. He remained in parliament as an outspoken critic of de Gaulle until he lost his seat in 1958.

Menelik II (1844–1913), emperor of Ethiopia (1889–1913) who created the modern Ethiopia. Called *Negus Negusti* (King of Kings), he succeeded his father, claiming direct descent from King Solomon and the queen of Sheba. During his reign he defeated the Italians in 1896, gained control over warring tribes within his realm, and introduced many needed social reforms.

Menon, V. K. Krishna. See *Krishna Menon.*

Menotti, Gian-Carlo (1911–   ), operatic composer, born in Italy, who emigrated to the United States when he was 17. He studied at the Curtis Institute of Music in Philadelphia and began composing operas shortly afterward. Among his successful operas are *The Medium, Amelia Goes to the Ball, The Consul,* and *The Last Savage.* His music is in the tradition of Verdi and Puccini rather than in the atonal style that is typical of many modern operas. His most popular work is *Amahl and the Night Visitors,* a Christmas opera written originally for television.

Menuhin, Yehudi (1916–   ), American violinist, born in New York City. A child prodigy, he made his formal debut at age seven as soloist with the San Francisco Symphony Orchestra, and in the following year gave a concert recital at the Manhattan Opera House in New York City. He went on to earn international acclaim as a violin virtuoso. In recent years he has lived mostly in England, where he has organized a successful chamber orchestra.

Mercator, Gerhardus (1512–1594), Flemish geographer whose maps are considered the finest examples of early mapmaking. His earliest known map, of the Holy Land, appeared in 1537. In his celebrated map of the world (1569), he introduced a system of map projection (known as *Mercator projection*), in which latitude and longitude lines are at right angles to each other at any point on the map. Such maps are valuable to navigators because the true direction from one point to another can be shown by a straight line.

NEW YORK PUBLIC LIBRARY

MICHELANGELO, shown (*left*) in a 1561 bronze relief, painted a self-portrait, as the tortured St. Bartholomew, into his *Last Judgment* fresco, a detail of which is at *right.*

Meredith, George (1828–1909), English poet and novelist, one of the major Victorian writers. Among his novels, noted for their wit and elegance, the best are *The Ordeal of Richard Feverel* (1859), *The Egoist* (1879), and *Diana of the Crossways* (1885). His best-known verse is contained in the volumes *Modern Love* (1862) and *Poems and Lyrics of the Joy of Earth* (1883).

Mérimée, Prosper (1803–1870), French writer, noted for his short stories and novels. *Colomba*, a story of Corsica, is his most popular tale, although it is not so well known to English readers as his *Carmen*, upon which Bizet based his opera. During much of his life Mérimée was a member of the French civil service. His appointment in 1831 as inspector of archeological monuments led to authoritative works on the archeology of France. In 1844 he was elected to the French Academy. Mérimée is noted for his simple, clear style and polished wit.

Mesmer, Franz (1733–1815), German physician, born in Switzerland and educated in Vienna. In 1778 Mesmer met with much success when he treated his patients with *mesmerism*, a method of sending a person into a trance or sleep by the use of suggestion and movements of the hands. Mesmer used these methods and other aids, such as a darkened room hung with mirrors and filled with scents. Modern research has shown that he could induce a state of trance identical to that of hypnotism.

Metternich, Prince Klemens Wenzel Nepomuk Lother von (1773–1859), Austrian statesman, presided at the Congress of Vienna (1815), which ended the power of Napoleon in Europe. He became Austrian ambassador at Dresden in 1801, was transferred to Berlin in 1803 and to Paris in 1806. As minister of foreign affairs he consistently worked for Austria's advancement. He was the dominant personality at the Congress of Vienna. From 1815 he became very powerful, and by his founding of the Holy Alliance and subsequent suppression of all popular movements he contributed largely to the growth of Austrian power in Europe.

Meyerbeer, Giacomo (1791–1864), German composer of spectacular Romantic operas. Born near Berlin, he began composing operas at an early age, but did not gain success until he moved to Paris in 1826. His fame rests on *Robert le Diable, Les Huguenots, Le Prophète,* and *L'Africaine,* produced between 1831 and 1864. Meyerbeer was enormously popular in his time, but today his operas are performed infrequently, because they are so difficult to sing. Yet his influence was great on later composers, notably Verdi.

Michelangelo, in full **Michelangelo Buonarroti** (1475–1564), Italian sculptor, painter, architect, and poet. He is considered the greatest sculptor since the time of the Greeks and one of the greatest painters of the Renaissance. Born in a mountain village of Tuscany, he grew up in Florence, where he received his first art lessons from the painter Ghirlandajo. He attracted the attention of Lorenzo de' Medici by the skill with which he restored the mutilated head of a laughing faun, and he was taken into the Medici household. During the next few years his art reached maturity. While on a visit to Rome about 1500 he carved the famous *Pietà* that now graces St. Peter's. A colossal *David*, the masterpiece of his early period, was completed in 1504 for the city of Florence.

In 1505 Michelangelo was called to Rome by Pope Julius II, who wanted plans for a tomb (for himself) to be erected in St. Peter's. The design called for so large a monument that the plan of the church itself was changed to accommodate it. Difficulties arose between the sculptor and his patron, and the work was interrupted (1506). The colossal *Moses* intended for the tomb was erected in a small church in Rome. Instead of finishing the Julian tomb, Michelangelo painted the ceiling of the Sistine Chapel in the Vatican. This task he began in 1508 and completed within four years. The decorations are frescoes depicting the Creation and other Biblical subjects and are among the outstanding paintings of all time. He later devoted several years to designing the tombs of the Medici for their memorial chapel in San Lorenzo, Florence.

At the age of 60 he painted *The Last Judgment* in the Sistine Chapel. This altarpiece is the largest fresco in the world, containing over 100 life-size figures and reaching a height of 70 feet. In his last years he turned to architecture, his most notable undertaking being the design for St. Peter's. Refusing all pay for his labor, he did not live to see the work completed. His sonnets are fine examples of Italian poetry.

Michelson, Albert Abraham (1852–1931), American scientist, famed for his research on the velocity of light. Born in Germany, he came with his parents to the United States in 1854. A graduate of Annapolis in 1873, he was an instructor there from 1875 to 1879. After resigning from the navy, he taught at several universities and then was appointed head of the physics department at the University of Chicago. Early in his teaching career, Michelson conducted a series of experiments to test the relative motion of the earth through space; its negative results suggested to Einstein the theory of relativity. With E. W. Morley he conducted an experiment to determine the effect of the earth's motion on the speed of light (1887). In 1925 he repeated the test, both results being negative. He invented the interferometer, a valuable astronomical instrument used to make measurements of the standard meter in terms of the wave length of the red radiation of cadmium. He received the Nobel Prize for physics in 1907.

Mickiewicz, Adam (1798–1855), Polish Romantic poet, considered to be his country's greatest poet. His first poems, published in 1822, attracted favorable notice. Two years later, he was arrested as a revolutionary for having formed a student secret society, and was banished to Russia, where he remained until 1829. After this, he spent much of his time in Paris and Italy, where he taught, wrote poetry, and worked for Polish national freedom. Mickiewicz is considered by the Poles to be their national poet and, next to Pushkin, the greatest Slavic poet. His works include the epic *Sir Thaddeus*, *Crimean Sonnets*, and several volumes of collected poems.

Mies van der Rohe, Ludwig (1886–   ), American architect, born in Germany, noted for his glass and steel structures. After a successful career in Europe, Mies came to the United States in 1938 as director of the department of architecture at the Illinois Institute of Technology, Chicago. Here he designed the campus and its buildings. In his most representative work, Mies combines steel and expanses of glass to produce light, airy buildings that are simple and functional in design. Among his outstanding works are the German pavilion in Barcelona, Spain (erected in 1929), and the steel-and-glass apartment towers on the lake front in Chicago. He became a United States citizen in 1944.

Mikoyan, Anastas Ivanovich (1895–   ), Russian statesman and politician, born in Armenia. Early in life he studied theology, but abandoned it to become a revolutionary. In 1915 he became a leader of the revolutionary movement in the Caucasus. Later he met Lenin and Stalin in Moscow, where he became an active Bolshevik. In 1922 he became a member of the Soviet Central Committee and, because he aided Stalin against Trotsky, was made minister of trade in 1926. In 1958 he became a first vice-chairman in the Council of Ministers and a member of the Supreme Soviet of the USSR. Under Nikita Khrushchev, Mikoyan became first deputy prime minister, and in 1964 rose to the position of chairman of the presidium of the Supreme Soviet (or nominal chief of state). In 1965 he retired because of ill health.

Milhaud, Darius (1892–   ), one of the leading French composers of the twentieth century. Milhaud was a member of "Les Six," a group of French composers that had considerable influence on music during the 1920's. In 1923 he visited the United States as a guest conductor, and returned in 1940 to teach at Mills College, California. His music is marked by bold dissonances and an ingenious use of folk themes. Among his works are the opera *Christopher Columbus*, the ballet music *The Creation of the World*, and the orchestral *Provincial Suite*.

Mill, John Stuart (1806–1873), English philosopher and economist whose writings influenced nineteenth-century thought. Born in London, he was a gifted child who was rigorously educated by his father, James Mill. In 1823 he entered India House as a clerk and eventually succeeded his father as head of the company.

In economics, philosophy, and logic he was one of the greatest thinkers of his age. In ethical philosophy he was a leading utilitarian, who held that public policy should be based on the idea of the greatest good for the greatest number. In logic he developed the principle of induction, and in economics he made clear the real meaning of value and its relation to supply and demand. Mill wrote *A System of Logic*, *Principles of Political Economy*, and *On Liberty*. His *Autobiography* has been hailed as a literary classic.

Millais, Sir John Everett (1829–1896), English artist and a leading figure in the Pre-Raphaelite movement in nineteenth-century English art. Born in Southampton, he studied art at the Royal Academy. In 1848, in association with Holman Hunt, Dante G. Rossetti, and others, he founded the Pre-Raphaelite Brotherhood, which sought to return to the simplicity and sincerity of the painters before Raphael. His earlier works were in this mood. As his art matured, Millais drew away from the strict tenets of the school, and his canvases became more conventional. He painted many portraits, including those of Gladstone, Carlyle, Tennyson, and other noted men. He was made a baronet in 1885 and, before his death, was president of the Royal Academy.

Millay, Edna St. Vincent (1892–1950), American poet, widely praised for her sonnets and dramatic verse. Born in Rockland, Me., she graduated from Vassar in 1917. In that year her first work, *Renascence and Other Poems*, established her reputation. Succeeding volumes included *Second April* (1921), *The Buck in the Snow* (1928), and *Huntsman, What Quarry?* (1939). Although her best works were short romantic lyrics, she wrote several successful plays, notably *Aria Da Capo* (1921) and *Conversation at Midnight* (1937). She also wrote the libretto for Deems Taylor's opera *The King's Henchman*, produced at the Metropolitan Opera of New York in 1927.

Miller, Arthur (1915–   ), American playwright, born in New York City. He won the Pulitzer Prize in 1949 for his drama *Death of a Salesman*, a probing study of success and failure, and their underlying causes. In this and other plays, Miller revealed his concern for the chief social and political issues of his time. His first success, *All My Sons* (1947), dealt with profiteering during wartime. In *The Crucible* (1953), he examined witchcraft hysteria in seventeenth-century New England. And in *Incident in Vichy* (1964) he wrote of religious persecution during World War II. Miller's play *After the Fall* (1963) was the first presented by the repertory theater of the Lincoln Center in New York City.

Miller, Henry (1891–   ), American author, born in New York City. During the 1930's he became a leading figure in the Paris-based school of American writers. Always a controversial writer, he produced a series of autobiographical works that were banned in the United States and England and had to be published in Paris. His outspoken views on life (notably man's sexual behavior) are expressed in the novels *Tropic of Cancer* (1934), *Tropic of Capricorn* (1938), and the trilogy *The Rosy Crucifixion*, first published in Paris in 1949. Not until the 1960's were Miller's books allowed to be published in the United States.

Millerand, Alexandre (1859–1943), French statesman who was premier and also president of the French republic from 1920 to 1924. As early as 1885 he was elected to the Chamber of Deputies, where as a Radical Socialist he became prominent as a social reformer. While serving in several cabinet posts, he was also an editor of Socialist papers and journals. In 1920 he succeeded Georges Clemenceau as premier and later in that year succeeded Paul Deschanel as president. He resigned in 1924 when his supporters lost control of the Chamber. Elected senator in 1925, he served until 1940.

Millet, Jean François (1814–1875), French painter of the Barbizon school, noted for his scenes of peasant life. Born in Normandy, he studied in Cherbourg, and the people of that town financed his studies in Paris. He settled at Barbizon and became known for his paintings. Among them are the famous *Angelus* and *The Gleaners* in the Louvre, Paris. The Metropolitan Museum, New York, possesses *The Sower* and *Water Carrier*, and the Museum of Fine Arts, Boston, his *Potato Planters*. *The Man with the Hoe*, which inspired Markham's poem of that title, is in the San Francisco Museum.

Millikan, Robert Andrews (1868–1958), American physicist who won the Nobel Prize in 1923 for his work in elementary electric charges. Born in Morrison, Ill., he studied at Oberlin College and at Columbia, Berlin, and Göttingen universities. He was on the faculty of the University of Chicago from 1896 to 1921. In 1921 he became chairman of the executive council of the California Institute of Technology and director of the Norman Bridge Laboratory. Through his famous "oil drop" experiments he measured fundamental electrical quantity and proved that all electrons are alike. His isolation and measurement of the electron and his achievement of exact photoelectric determination of the light quantum won him the Nobel Prize for physics in 1923. He received the Roosevelt Association medal in 1932 for his discovery of cosmic rays. He contributed to knowledge of X rays and many physical and electrical phenomena. He wrote and lectured much in an effort to reconcile science and religion.

Mills, Clark (1815–1883), American sculptor, born in Onondaga County, N.Y. He is best known for equestrian statues of Andrew Jackson and George Washington, both in Washington, D.C., and for the colossal statue of Liberty, from a design by Thomas Crawford, which crowns the dome of the Capitol, finished in 1863.

Milne, Alan Alexander (1882–1956), English writer of humorous children's stories. Born in London, he graduated from Trinity College, Cambridge, in 1903. During his early career as a writer, he was an assistant editor of *Punch* (1906–1914). All his work, verse and prose, has a charm that appeals to children and adults alike. His books for children, written especially for his son, Christopher Robin, include *When We Were Very Young* (1924), *Now We Are Six* (1927), *Winnie-the-Pooh* (1926), and *The House at Pooh Corner* (1928). Milne also wrote several successful comic plays.

Miltiades (5th century B.C.), Athenian general. He commanded the army that defeated the Persians at Marathon in one of the most decisive battles in history. After the battle the Persians took to their ships and sailed to attack Athens, expecting to find it undefended. However, Miltiades was there when they arrived and again repulsed them. He had driven his tired troops on a spectacular overland march. Later Miltiades attacked the Island of Paros to regain control of the Aegean but was defeated. He was ordered to pay a heavy fine for misleading the people as to his motive for attacking Paros. Unable to pay, he was put in prison.

Milton, John (1608–1674), English poet, considered second only to Shakespeare in the ranks of English poets. Born in London and educated at Christ's College, Cambridge, he obtained his master's degree in 1632 and then spent six years on his father's country estate, devoting himself to literature. His early poems, *L'Allegro*, *Il Penseroso*, and *Lycidas*, show the influence of country life, as well as the classical learning and the beauty of language that mark his later works. In this period he also wrote the masque *Comus*, first performed in 1634.

After a tour abroad Milton turned to politics and prose writing. Most of his prose works deal with theology, for Milton strongly opposed the doctrines of the Episcopal Church. His *Areopagitica* is the greatest plea for liberty of speech in the English language. In the Civil War he favored the Parliamentary cause. He became Latin secretary to the Commonwealth in 1649 and in 1655 secretary to Oliver Cromwell. During these years he wrote a few sonnets and some Greek and Latin verse.

In 1658, after losing his eyesight, he began work on a great poem that had long filled his mind. The restoration of Charles II in 1660 sent him into political retirement and permitted him to complete *Paradise Lost* in 1665. The blind poet dictated this to his three daughters. The greatness of its theme, the fall of man, and the stately beauty of its verse make it one of the great epic poems of the world.

In 1671 he published a second epic, *Paradise Regained*. Other well-known shorter works are his *Hymn on the Morning of Christ's Nativity*, *On Shakespeare*, and *To Cyriack Skinner*. The sonnet on his blindness, written in later years, is one of the finest inspirational poems in the English language. His last poem, *Samson Agonistes*, a Greek tragedy, was written three years before his death.

Minot, George Richards (1885–1950), American physician and pathologist who, in 1934, won the Nobel Prize for medicine for his researches on the value of liver in the treatment of anemia. Born in Boston and educated at Harvard, he later taught medicine at Harvard and Johns Hopkins before becoming director of Thorndike Memorial Laboratory in Boston. With W. P. Murphy and G. H. Whipple (with whom he shared the Nobel Prize), Minot developed the first successful treatment for pernicious anemia and conducted nutritional experiments.

Minuit or **Minnewit, Peter** (1580–1641), Dutch colonial governor of New Amsterdam and founder of what is now New York City. In 1625 he was appointed director-general of the Dutch West India Company's settlements in North America, and in the following year he purchased Manhattan Island from the Indians for goods and trinkets valued at 60 guilders (about $24). Recalled to the Netherlands in 1631, he later entered the employ of the Swedish West India Company and in 1638 built Fort Christina, near the site of Wilmington, Del.

Mirabeau, Honoré Gabriel Riqueti, Count **de** (1749–1791), French statesman, one of the leading figures in the Assembly at the beginning of the French Revolution. He spent his youth in wild living and was imprisoned and sentenced to death, but was pardoned in 1782. He then lived by writing until he was elected a delegate to the States-General. By refusing to accede to the king's request to adjourn the Third Estate, or commoners, he precipitated the French Revolution. Mirabeau tried by his great oratory to put the king at the head of the Revolution by forming a new government on the English plan, but he failed through the interference of Marie Antoinette. He was elected president of the Jacobin Club in November, 1790, and became president of the National Assembly a few months before he died.

Miró, Joan (1893–), Spanish painter, famous for his witty, abstract style. Born in Barcelona, he went to Paris in 1919 and within a few years was a leading figure of avant-garde painting. Miró's paintings are distinguished by their extreme, almost childlike, simplicity, their violent use of color, and their highly decorative qualities. Besides his painting, he has also done sculpture, engraving, and book illustration.

Mitchell, Margaret (1900–1949), American author whose only novel, *Gone With the Wind,* became one of the most popular novels of all time. Born and educated in Atlanta, Ga., she was a newspaper writer from 1922 to 1926, when she resigned because of ill health. In 1936 *Gone With the Wind,* a 1037-page novel of life in the South during the Civil War and Reconstruction days, appeared. The work was awarded the Pulitzer Prize in 1937 and was filmed in 1939. By 1949 over eight million copies, in 30 languages, had been sold.

Mithridates VI Eupator, called **The Great** (c.132–63 B.C.), king of Pontus (an ancient country in Asia Minor) from about 121 B.C. He fought three bitter wars with Rome between 88 and 65 B.C., and was finally defeated by Pompey. After the third war he retired to the Crimea. When his son Pharnaces led a rebellion against him, Mithridates took his own life. The Romans regarded him as their most formidable enemy.

Mitropoulos, Dimitri (1896–1960), Greek conductor, famed for his interpretations of late Romantic and modern music. After establishing a reputation in Europe as a conductor and pianist, he came to the United States in 1936. From 1937 to 1949 he was conductor of the Minneapolis Symphony Orchestra, and from 1951 to 1958 conducted the New York Philharmonic. Gifted with a remarkable memory, he conducted without a score. In later years he was also principal conductor at the Metropolitan Opera in New York. He became an American citizen in 1946.

Modigliani, Amedeo (1884–1920), Italian painter and sculptor, noted for his portraits of women. In 1906 he went to Paris, where he remained until his death. Modigliani's style is characterized by elongated, primitive faces and a candor in depicting nudes that caused his first exhibit (in 1918) to be closed by Parisian authorities.

Mohammed, Mahomet, or **Muhammad** (c. 570–632), founder of Mohammedanism or Islam, called "the Prophet." He was born in Mecca, Arabia, of a family of the tribe of Koreish. He was orphaned when he was young and was cared for first by his grandfather and later by an uncle. With his foster-father Mohammed made caravan journeys through Syria and Arabia and at the age of 25 entered the employ of a widow named Khadija, serving as her agent or possibly as her camel driver. He married Khadija, who was 16 years his senior; they had two sons, who died in infancy, and four daughters. Mohammed remained faithful to his wife until her death in 619, after which he established a harem.

For about ten years after his 30th birthday Mohammed made periodical visits to a solitary cave on Mount Hira, near Mecca, for religious contemplation. When he was 40, he told his wife of a vision in which he had received a revelation from the angel Gabriel. He felt assured, he said, that he was called by God to be the prophet of a faith that should reclaim the Arabs from the idolatry into which they had fallen. He went about seeking converts, at first with very little success, and he aroused such opposition that his uncle had him removed to a fortified castle outside of Mecca. There he remained for three years. Some of his adherents fled to Abyssinia, but at a critical moment he received help from the city of Yathreb (Medina), where he had a following made up of pilgrims who had been converted while in Mecca. They urged him to come to their city, and in 622 he and his friend abu-Bakr secretly left Mecca. This flight of the prophet, or *Hegira,* is the event with which the Mohammedan calendar begins. Mohammed established himself in Medina as the political and religious leader of the community and proceeded to make war on the tribesmen who remained hostile. In 630 Mecca was captured, other victories followed, and in a few years Mohammed had won all Arabia. In the last year of his life he made a final pilgrimage to Mecca at the head of 40,000 pilgrims. He left no son,

SAUDI ARABIA INFORMATION SERVICE

MOHAMMEDAN shrine, the Kaaba, in Mecca.

being survived only by his daughter Fatima, wife of Ali ibn-abu-Talib.

The doctrines of Mohammedanism are contained in the Koran, which is made up of the prophet's revelations as written down by his disciples. He taught that man must submit himself to the one God; that nations are punished for rejecting God's prophets; that heaven and hell await in the future life; and that the world will come to an end in a great judgment day. Mohammed offered himself to Jews and Christians as the successor of Jesus Christ.

Mohammed Ali. See *Mehemet Ali.*

Molière, pen name of **Jean Baptiste Poquelin** (1622–1673), greatest French writer of comedies and often considered the greatest of all French dramatists. Born in Paris, the son of a well-to-do upholsterer in the service of the court, he followed his father's trade for a while, but became a theatrical manager in 1643. He joined a troupe of actors in 1646 and toured the provinces. King Louis XIV saw him act in Paris in 1658 and was so pleased that "the king's comedians," as the Molière players were called, enjoyed the patronage of the court for 15 years.

Molière had already adapted plays and written two of his own, but the presentation of his *Affected Misses* in 1659 ushered in a new school of dramatic satire. Play followed play, holding up to ridicule the follies, affectations, and frailties of human nature, satirizing the miserly, the bores, the pedants, and the hypocrites. Typical of his plays are *The School for Husbands, The Bores, The School for Wives, The Misanthrope, The Hypocrite, The Miser,* and *The Imaginary Invalid.* The last named was the immediate cause of Molière's death, for he played the leading part while very ill.

Molnár, Ferenc (1878–1952), Hungarian playwright, famed for his witty dialogue and highly developed sense of irony. At first a journalist, he later became a highly successful playwright with such dramas as *Liliom* (1909), *The Swan* (1920), and *The Red Hill* (1923). In 1940 he moved to the United States and settled in New York, where he lived until his death. Translations of his plays were highly successful in the United States, both on the stage and as films. The musical version of *Liliom,* produced by Rodgers and Hammerstein as *Carousel,* has become a perennial musical-comedy favorite.

Molotov, Vyacheslav Mikhailovich (1890–), Russian Communist leader who from 1930 to 1956 was one of the most powerful men in Russia. Born and educated in St. Petersburg (now Leningrad), he changed his name from Skriabin to Molotov (meaning "hammer") in 1906, when he took the Communist oath of loyalty. During his youth he organized Bolshevik student groups and worked on the newspaper *Pravda.* At the time of the first Russian revolution of February, 1917, he worked with Stalin to prepare for the reception of Lenin who was then in exile. He played a major role in the October, 1917, revolution, and held a number of posts in the newly-constituted revolutionary government. In 1920 he was secretary of the Communist party of the Ukraine and the next year was appointed secretary of the entire USSR, becoming a member of the Politburo in 1926.

In 1930 he became president of the Soviet of Peoples' Commissars and held this office, the equivalent of premier, while also succeeding Maxim Litvinov as foreign commissar in May, 1939. In this capacity, on August 24, 1939, he signed the Nazi-Soviet nonaggression pact which set the stage for World War II.

On May 6, 1941, Molotov resigned as premier in favor of Stalin, took over the office of vice-premier, and retained that of foreign minister, in which capacity, on July 13, 1941, he signed the British-USSR mutual aid pact. He attended the Yalta conference in February, 1945, and was present in April, 1945, at the San Francisco meeting that laid the foundation for the United Nations.

After Stalin's death in 1953, he was reappointed foreign minister, but when Nikita Khrushchev gained power in 1957, Molotov was named ambassador to Outer Mongolia, thus ending his influence in Soviet politics.

Moltke, Count **Helmuth Karl Bernhard von** (1800–1891), Prussian field marshal who led the Germans to victory in the Franco-Prussian War. He was educated at a military school in Copenhagen and entered the Prussian army in 1822 as second lieutenant. Rising steadily in authority and rank, he was appointed chief of the general staff in 1857 and had much to do with the transformation of the army into the efficient machine that defeated Denmark (1864), Austria (1866), and France (1870–1871). In the Franco-Prussian War he planned the concentration on Metz, which resulted in the French defeat at Sedan.

Monck, George (1608–1670), English soldier and politician who helped bring about the restoration of the monarchy in 1660. Early in his career he served in the Spanish and Dutch armies. He fought for Charles I in the Civil War, was captured at Nanturich, and imprisoned in the Tower at London for two years. Released when he promised to support the Parliamentary cause, he made a brilliant record under Oliver Cromwell, conquering Scotland in 1651. Though he later supported Richard Cromwell, he realized the national demand for the restoration of the monarchy, and in 1660, as commander of the army, he brought about the return of the crown prince as Charles II. Charles made him duke of Albemarle.

Mondriaan, Pieter Cornelis or **Piet Mondrian** (1872–1944), Dutch nonobjective painter, noted for his brightly colored arrangements of squares and straight lines. In 1910 he went to Paris where he came under the influence of the Cubist school. Thereafter, he used straight lines instead of curved lines in most of his paintings. At the start of World War II, he came to New York City, where he lived until his death.

Monet, Claude (1840–1926), French painter who was one of the founders of the school of impressionism. As a young man he was influenced by the landscapes of Camille Corot, the Barbizon painters, and Édouard Manet. His insistence on working in the open air, where he could reproduce the subtle effects of light on the subject matter, had a beneficial influence on modern painting, although

Monet at first met with much hostile criticism. In 1874 his painting *Impression*, exhibited at the first large showing of Monet and his colleagues, gave the name to the new school of art. As his art developed, Monet concentrated on interpreting on canvas the play of light on landscape and water. Some of his studies of water lilies, painted late in life when his eyesight was failing, are among his masterpieces.

Monmouth, Duke of, original name **James Scott** (1649–1685), pretender to the English throne who led the rebellion against James II in 1685. The son of King Charles II's mistress, he enjoyed royal and popular favor at first, and was created duke of Monmouth in 1663. But acquiring a reputation for vice, he fell into disfavor and having joined the Whigs, was exiled for alleged complicity in the Rye House Plot (1683). This was a plot, inspired by several Whigs, to assassinate Charles II and the duke of York (later James II). When Charles died in 1685, Monmouth returned to England, where he led a Protestant rebellion against James II. In July, the rebels and his own forces were defeated, and Monmouth was captured, imprisoned, and later beheaded.

Monroe, James (1758–1831), fifth president of the United States (1816–1824), remembered for his promulgation of the Monroe Doctrine. Born in Westmoreland County, Virginia, he entered the College of William and Mary at the age of 16, but within two years the Revolution broke out, and he left to join a Virginia regiment. He took part in several battles in the campaign of 1777–1778, was promoted to lieutenant colonel in 1778, but saw no further active service. Through the influence of Thomas Jefferson, Monroe was elected to the Virginia assembly in 1782, and from 1783 to 1786 he was a delegate to the Continental Congress. When his last term expired, he hoped to retire to private life, but his state reelected him to the assembly and in 1788 sent him to the state convention called to ratify the federal Constitution. A determined anti-Federalist, he spoke vigorously against adoption but in 1790 was elected to the Senate under the document he opposed. There Monroe continued his opposition to Federalist policies as carried out by Washington and Hamilton. Thus he became, with Jefferson, a leader in the party that was formerly called Democratic-Republican and is today the Democratic party.

In 1794 Monroe went to France as minister, but his inability to improve relations between France and the United States brought about his recall in 1796. From 1799 to 1802 he served as governor of Virginia, and then, in turn, special envoy to France, minister to London, and envoy to Madrid. In Paris he arranged the purchase of Louisiana by the United States. When he returned home in 1807 he was again elected to the Virginia assembly. In 1811 he was again chosen governor, but he resigned within a few months when Pres. James Madison appointed him secretary of state. Monroe remained at the head of the state department until his own election to the presidency.

In 1820 he was reelected without opposition. The principal events of Monroe's administration were a war with the Seminole Indians, the passage of the Missouri Compromise, the acquisition of Florida, and the promulgation of the Monroe Doctrine. This doctrine warned European nations that the United States would not tolerate interference in the affairs of governments in the Western Hemisphere. At the end of his second term, Monroe retired to private life.

Montagu, Charles, 1st Earl of **Halifax** (1661–1715), English statesman and patron of the arts, who founded the Bank of England and served as prime minister. He entered Parliament in 1688 and became a lord of the treasury in 1692. Two years later, he founded the Bank of England and was appointed chancellor of the exchequer and privy councilor. In 1697 he became first lord of the treasury and prime minister, but lack of popular support forced him to resign in 1699. He was created Baron Halifax in 1700, which meant that he could no longer sit in Commons. In later years he was subjected to impeachment proceedings, but his loyal support of George I earned him an earldom and also another period as prime minister. Famed as a satiric wit, Montagu was the patron of such writers as Congreve, Addison, and Steele. With Matthew Prior, he wrote the satirical poem *The Country Mouse and the City Mouse.*

Montagu, Elizabeth Robinson (1720–1800), English writer and society leader. In 1742 she married Edward Montagu, 1st earl of Sandwich, and established the leading literary and social salon of her time. The term "blue-stocking," denoting female writer, was first applied to her and her group. Among her friends were Samuel Johnson, Sir Joshua Reynolds, David Garrick, and Horace Walpole.

Montagu, Lady **Mary Wortley** (1689–1762), English writer, especially remembered for her letters. As the wife of Edward Wortley Montagu, she was a favorite in court and literary circles during the reign of George I. In 1716 Montagu was appointed ambassador at Constantinople, and Lady Mary lived with him in Turkey until 1718. While in the East, she became interested in vaccination for smallpox, and introduced the practice in England after her return. As a writer she is remembered for her letters to various persons, which are regarded as among the best in the English language.

Montaigne, Michel Eyquem de (1533–1592), French writer who is regarded as the father of the literary essay. Deeply versed in classical literature, he was taught as a boy to speak Latin and Greek. He served as a parliamentary counselor at Bordeaux from 1554 to 1567, and later was a member of the court of Charles IX. In 1570 he resigned his judicial office and returned to the family estate at Montaigne, where he began to write the series of essays by which he is remembered today. The first two books of essays appeared in 1580 and were republished, together with a third, in 1588.

NEW YORK PUBLIC LIBRARY

MONTEZUMA, ruler of the Aztec kingdom.

Montaigne's essays cover a variety of topics and are notable for the grace and freshness of their style. Sentences and anecdotes from the ancients are mingled with the author's own remarks about himself and humanity in general. His writings greatly influenced later authors, and were known to Shakespeare through John Florio's translation of 1603.

Montcalm, Marquis **Louis Joseph de Montcalm de Saint-Véran** (1712–1759), French general who fought the British for control of Canada. He entered the army in 1721 and after service in Italy and Germany was sent to Canada (in 1756) to direct the king's forces in the last struggle for French supremacy in North America. In 1756 he captured Fort Ontario from the British; in 1757 he seized Fort William Henry and in 1758 warded off the attack on Ticonderoga. After the French had lost Louisbourg and Fort Duquesne, Montcalm met defeat on the Heights of Abraham at Quebec in 1759. Routed in battle by Wolfe on September 13, he was wounded trying to rally his forces, and died the next day. Quebec surrendered a few days later.

Montesquieu, Baron **de la Brède et de, Charles Louis de Secondat** (1689–1755), French political historian whose *The Spirit of Laws* is a classic in political science. Born near Bordeaux, he followed the family tradition by studying law and was president of the Bordeaux parliament from 1716 to 1726. His first published work, *Lettres Persanes* (1721), is a daring and subtle travesty on the follies of the day.

Though Montesquieu always ridiculed the French Academy in these letters, he was admitted to membership in 1728. He spent from 1729 to 1731 in travel, remaining for some time in England to study the British political system, which he greatly admired. After he returned to France, Montesquieu retired to his estate near Bordeaux and devoted himself to literature. In 1734 he published a survey of the greatness and decline of Rome. In 1748 appeared the work on which his fame chiefly rests, *The Spirit of Laws*. In this work Montesquieu carefully distinguished among political institutions, showing a marked preference for the independent freedom enjoyed by the legislative, executive, and judicial powers in England during his time. The book greatly influenced the framers of the Constitution.

Montessori, Maria (1870–1952), Italian educator who founded a system of child training, the Montessori Method, in which children are encouraged to learn according to their own instincts and creative ability. She was graduated with a medical degree from the University of Rome in 1894, the first woman so honored in Italy. As assistant in the university clinic she became interested in the needs of feeble-minded children and tested some of her ideas while principal of a school for the underprivileged (1898–1900). After further study Dr. Montessori opened the first "House of Childhood" in Rome in 1907. She also applied her method of self-education to the training of normal children.

Monteverdi, Claudio (1567–1643), Italian composer whose innovations in music, especially in opera, made him the leading composer of his time. From 1590 to 1612 he was a court musician in the service of the duke of Mantua, and from 1613 until his death he was head conductor of the choir at St. Mark's Cathedral in Venice. Monteverdi's importance to music lies not only in his works themselves, but in the innovations he brought to music, such as his unparalleled ability to translate human passions into dramatic music, his use of dissonance to create dramatic effects, and his novel orchestration. Among his works are the operas *Orfeo* (1607) and *L'Incoronazione di Poppea* (1642), in addition to madrigals, masses, cantatas, and motets.

Montezuma II or **Moctezuma II** (c.1480–1520), the last Aztec emperor of Mexico. He took the throne in 1503 and engaged in wars of conquest that added Honduras and Nicaragua to his realm. But he lost the favor of his people by despotic rule and oppressive taxation. The Spaniards under Cortes invaded Mexico in 1519, marched to the capital, and soon made the emperor a virtual prisoner. In 1520 Montezuma tried to prevent the Mexicans from attacking the Spaniards, but he was himself attacked by them, captured, and killed.

Montfort, Simon de, Earl of **Leicester** (c. 1208–1265), English statesman who led the revolts against King Henry III in medieval England. Born in France of French-English descent, he went to England in 1230 and in 1238 married Princess Eleanor, sister of Henry III. At first a great friend of Henry, who created him earl of Leicester, he afterward fell into disfavor. For many years he led the barons in attempts to make the king rule wisely and in 1265 called a parliament that was the forerunner of modern government. He was defeated that year at Evesham by Edward.

Montgolfier, Joseph Michel (1740–1810), French inventor who with his brother developed the first balloons for manned flight. He began experiments on balloons about 1782 with the aid of his brother **Jacques Étienne** (1745–1799); together they invented the first practical balloon. Louis XVI granted the brothers 40,000 francs so that they could give all their attention to aeronautics. Joseph also invented the parachute, hydraulic screw, and other devices.

Montgomery, Bernard Law, 1st Viscount **Montgomery of Alamein** (1887–), British field marshal who during World War II gained renown for his victories in Africa and Europe. Born in London, the son of a clergyman, he entered military service in 1908 and was twice wounded in France during World War I. In World War II he commanded the third division, which was evacuated from Dunkirk in June, 1940. As commander of the British 8th Army in 1943, he stopped the Germans under Rommel at El Alamein, thus saving the Suez Canal and Middle East. As commander of British ground forces under Gen. Dwight D. Eisenhower, he stopped the German breakthrough in Belgium and led the English to victory. In 1951 Montgomery was appointed deputy supreme commander of Atlantic Pact forces, a post he held until his retirement in 1958.

Moody, William Vaughn (1869–1910), American poet and dramatist whose *The Great Divide* (1906) is considered by many to be the first significant modern American drama. Born in Spencer, Ind., he graduated from Harvard in 1893. After teaching English at Harvard and Radcliffe, in 1895 he joined the faculty of the newly organized University of Chicago, where from 1901 to 1907 he was assistant professor of English and rhetoric. A second play, *The Faith-Healer*, appeared in 1909. Moody also wrote a lyrical drama, *The Masque of Judgment*, and several volumes of verse. *Ode in Time of Hesitation* is considered his best single poem. With Robert Morss Lovett he wrote a *History of English Literature* (1902).

Moore, George (1852–1933), Irish novelist, remembered for his novel *Esther Waters* (1894), one of the first naturalistic novels in English, and his autobiographical trilogy *Hail and Farewell* (1911–1914). As a young man he studied painting in Paris, but soon turned to poetry and fiction. In addition to *Esther Waters*, he wrote *The Mummer's Wife* (1885), *Evelyn Innes* (1898), *The Brook Kerith* (1916), and *A Story-Teller's Holiday* (1918), among other books.

Moore, Henry (1898–), English sculptor, considered one of the best of the twentieth century. Born in Yorkshire, a miner's son, he studied at the University of Leeds before becoming a teacher of sculpture. Primitive art and the surrealist art of contemporary France were the chief influences on his work. His reputation grew steadily after a major exhibition in 1946 at the Museum of Modern Art, New York, and an award from the Venice exhibition in 1948. Moore's major works are impressions of human figures, usually seated or reclining, characterized by their simplicity and suggestiveness. The statue at Lincoln Center in New York is representative of his best work.

Moore, Marianne Craig (1887–), American poet, noted for the originality, wit, and lyricism of her verse. Born near St. Louis, Mo., she graduated from Bryn Mawr College in 1909, and afterwards taught school and worked in the New York Public Library. Her first book of poems was published in England in 1915, and her first American volume, *Observations*, appeared in 1924. In 1951 her *Collected Poems* received the Pulitzer Prize. Some of her best-known poems are *In Distrust of Merit*, *Poetry*, and *The Fish*.

Moore, Thomas (1779–1852), Irish poet and satirist, best remembered for his songs. Born in Dublin, he went to London in 1799 to study law, but became a writer instead. In 1807 his songs, later collected under the title *Irish Melodies*, began to appear. Among them are *Believe Me if All Those Endearing Young Charms*, *The Last Rose of Summer*, *Oft in the Stilly Night*, and *Those Evening Bells*. His *Lalla Rookh*, an Oriental romance in verse, was very popular in his time. Moore also wrote *The Life of Byron*.

More, Hannah (1745–1833), English author of novels and tracts. The daughter of a schoolmaster, she began writing verse and prose in childhood, composing a pastoral drama when she was 17. In 1774 she went to London and became friendly with Johnson, Burke, Garrick, and other celebrities. Garrick produced her tragedy *Percy* in 1777, but after his death she renounced the theater and became a reformer. She wrote on moral and religious subjects, and her *Coelebs in Search of a Wife* (1809), which went through numerous editions, was her most popular work.

More, Sir Thomas (1478–1535), English scholar and saint, remembered for his work *Utopia* (1516) and for his opposition to Henry VIII's religious policies. Born in London and educated at Oxford, he was admitted to the bar in 1501 and rose to a position of favor under Henry VIII. The king entrusted him with confidential missions and in 1521 knighted him. More succeeded Thomas Wolsey as lord chancellor, but he resigned that office in 1532. He believed in church reform, opposed the extreme measures adopted by Martin Luther, and refused to recognize the king as head of the church. In 1535 he was accused of high treason, committed to the Tower, and beheaded. More was beatified in 1886 and canonized in 1935. His great book, *Utopia*, describes an ideal state; the word has since come to denote any ideal or idealized state.

Morgan, John Hunt (1825–1864), Confederate general, noted for his guerrilla attacks against Union forces during the Civil War. Born in Huntsville, Ala., at the outbreak of the Civil War he became colonel of a band of raiders—Morgan's Squadron—that perpetually harassed the enemy in Kentucky and Tennessee. He was promoted to brigadier general in 1862 and in that year made the famous "Christmas Raid" into Kentucky. In 1863 he and some of his followers were captured and placed in prison in Columbus, Ohio. Morgan escaped and resumed his guerrilla tactics, but in 1864 was surrounded by Union troops near Greeneville, Tenn., and was shot while attempting to escape.

Morgan, John Pierpont (1837–1913), American financier, born in Hartford, Conn. He studied at the University of Göttingen, Germany, and in 1857 entered the bank of Duncan, Sherman and Company in New York. In 1871 he became a member of a firm later known as J. P. Morgan and Company. He built up a railroad empire largely by reorganizing bankrupt lines and took part in many famous financial battles for railroad control. He formed the United States Steel Corporation in 1901 and built up other huge industrial combinations. Some of his operations were criticized, and in 1912 a congressional inquiry was held.

He made large donations to museums, churches, libraries, and colleges, especially in New York City. He founded the Morgan Library in New York to house his great collection of books, manuscripts, and art.

EDWARD STEICHEN

JOHN PIERPONT MORGAN, Jr.

Morgan, John Pierpont, Jr. (1867–1943), American financier, the son of John Pierpont Morgan. Born in Irvington, N.Y., he entered the London branch of the family banking business and took charge after the death of his father in 1913. The firm was important in World War I; it raised huge loans and financed many of the combatant nations. After the war, it sold more than 2 billion dollars' worth of foreign government and corporation securities and twice that amount of American securities. He continued many of his father's philanthropies.

Morgenthau, Henry, Jr. (1891–), American statesman who was secretary of the treasury in President Franklin D. Roosevelt's cabinet. Born in New York City and educated at Cornell University, he became a farm expert and the publisher of an agricultural journal. In 1930 Roosevelt, then governor of New York, appointed him to plan a farm-relief program for the state, and later Morgenthau became state conservation commissioner. When Roosevelt became president, he made Morgenthau chairman of the Federal Farm Board and later governor of the Farm Credit Administration. In 1933 he acted as secretary of the treasury when Secretary William H. Woodin fell ill, and when Woodin resigned, he took his place. One of Roosevelt's closest advisers, he favored a moderate cheapening of the dollar and a government-managed currency.

Morley, Christopher Darlington (1890–1957), American author, editor, and critic. He was born in Haverford, Pa., graduated from Haverford College, and was a Rhodes Scholar at Oxford, England (1910–1913). A bookish man of vast erudition and subtle wit, Morley was a popular college teacher, lecturer, and literary critic. A prolific writer of light verse and familiar essays, Morley is best remembered for his novel *Kitty Foyle* (1939), the sentimental story of an office girl in love with a man of higher social class. Notable among his other novels are *Parnassus on Wheels* (1917) and *The Haunted Bookshop* (1919), delightful for their excursions into the world of books and book-selling, and *The Trojan Horse* (1937), a modern version of the classic Troilus and Cressida story. Morley helped found the *Saturday Review of Literature* and was one of its leading editors from 1924 to 1940. He twice revised and expanded Bartlett's *Familiar Quotations*.

Morley, John, Viscount **Morley of Blackburn** (1838–1923), English statesman and writer, noted for his biography of William Gladstone. Born in Blackburn and educated at Oxford, he was (after 1859) editor, successively, of the *Literary Gazette*, *Morning Star*, *Fortnightly Review*, and *Macmillan's Magazine*. In 1883 he entered Parliament as a Liberal, supported Gladstone's Irish Home Rule policies, was chief secretary for Ireland (1886, 1892–1895) and secretary for India (1905–1910). In 1914 he resigned from the cabinet in opposition to the war policy. Morley also wrote a life of Edmund Burke.

Morris, Gouverneur (1752–1816), American statesman who served in several important posts in post-Revolution America. Born in New York City, he graduated from King's College (now Columbia University) in 1768 and was admitted to the bar in 1771. A member of the Continental Congress, Morris in 1778 presented the report calling on Great Britain to recognize the independence of the colonies before the opening of peace negotiations. He developed the decimal system of coinage used in the United States. In 1787 he represented Pennsylvania in the Constitutional Convention and was one of the committee that drew up the final draft of the Constitution. He was minister to France from 1792 to 1794 and U.S. senator from 1800 to 1803.

Morris, Robert (1734–1806), American financier who was a signer of the Declaration of Independence. He came from England to Philadelphia when he was 13, became a clerk in the countinghouse of Charles Willing, a Philadelphia merchant, and was a partner in the firm (1754–1793). He lent money to the government throughout the Revolutionary War, founded the Bank of North America and was superintendent of finance (1781–1784). Morris sat in the first U.S. Senate until 1795. He suffered serious financial losses in his last years and was in debtors' prison from 1798 to 1801.

Morris, William (1834–1896), English poet and designer who did much to change Victorian England's taste in the arts. Born in Walthamstow and educated as an architect, he later branched into the manufacture of furniture and household decorations. He did much to improve the public taste in wallpapers, fabrics, tapestry, and other house furnishings. In literature he is best known for his historical narratives in verse, including *Life and Death of Jason*, *The Earthly Paradise*, and *Sigurd the Volsung*. The Morris chair, a kind of easy chair, was named for him, though he did not invent it. Morris was a leader in the British Socialist movement.

Morse, Samuel Finley Breese (1791–1872), American inventor of the telegraph and one of the foremost U. S. portrait painters. Born in Charlestown, Mass., he graduated from Yale in 1810 and studied painting in England from 1811 to 1815. Returning to America, he became one of the best portrait painters in this country. In 1835 he was appointed professor of art history at New York University. Earlier, he had helped found the National Academy of Design, and served as its first president.

About 1835 Morse had developed a working model of the electric telegraph, but it was not until 1843, after many discouragements, that he was given $30,000 by Congress for an experimental line between Washington and Baltimore. On May 24, 1844, the first public message sent over the line was the historic "What hath God wrought?"

Morton, Levi Parsons (1824–1920), American banker who was vice-president (1889–1893) in the administration of Benjamin Harrison. Born in Shoreham, Vt., he entered the banking business in Boston in 1850, later moving to New York, where he became head of one of the best-known private banking firms in America. From 1879 to 1881 he sat in Congress as a Republican, then was minister to France (1881–1885) before becoming vice-president. Morton was governor of New York from 1895 to 1896.

Morton, William Thomas Green (1819–1868), American dental surgeon who was the first to publicly demonstrate the use of ether as an anesthetic. Born in Charlton, Mass., he studied dentistry in Baltimore and medicine in Boston. He first used ether on September 30, 1846, in the extraction of a tooth. Although it was later learned that ether had been used in an operation as early as 1842, it was Morton who made its value known to the medical world.

Moseley, Henry Gwyn-Jeffreys (1887–1915), British physicist whose studies of the X-ray spectra of the elements added to knowledge of the atom. He was born in Weymouth and educated at Oxford. In his early 20's, as an assistant to Ernest Rutherford, he studied the number of electrons emitted during the disintegration of radium. He later determined the number of positive charges in an atom of gold and in atoms of other elements. Studying the X-ray spectra of 38 elements, he found the number and order of the elements. This revised Mendeleev's Table and related it to atomic valency, thus specifying the characteristics of elements that have since been found. Moseley enlisted in the army during World War I and was killed at Gallipoli at the age of 28.

Moses, Anna Mary, known as **Grandma Moses** (1860–1961), American painter of farm scenes and country landscapes. Born in Greenwich, N.Y., she worked as a hired girl and for 40 years was married to a farmer. In her late seventies, crippled with arthritis in her hands, she began painting in oil, using old Currier and Ives prints as a guide. With no other formal guidance, she developed her own style for which she became known as a "modern primitive." As she was unable to paint outdoors, she did her work from memory. Her paintings reveal a sharp eye for details and a vivid sense of color.

Moses, Robert (1888–), American public official who, as park commissioner of New York City, directed some of the most extensive civic developments of all time. Born in New Haven, Conn., he began public service for New York State at the age of 25. In a series of state and city jobs, Moses developed parkways and beaches and directed the 1939 and 1964–1965 World's Fairs in New York City. In 1933 he was defeated in the race for mayor of New York City by Fiorello LaGuardia, who appointed him city park commissioner (1934–1960). He has served as both member and chairman of many city committees, including the Triborough Bridge and N.Y.C. Tunnel Authority, the N.Y.C. Parkway Authority, and the N.Y. World's Fair of 1964–1965.

Mosley, Sir Oswald Ernald (1896–), British politician who led the Fascist party in England during the 1930's. After serving in World War I, he was a member of Parliament from 1918 to 1931, when he resigned from the Labour party to form the British Union of Fascists, contending that it was the only alternative to socialism. Interned in 1940, he was released in 1943 because of ill health. After World War II he founded a new movement that called for a politically and economically united Europe.

Mossadegh, Mohammed (1881–1967), Iranian statesman, son of a Persian princess and the finance minister of Persia. He entered politics in 1906, and for the next four decades campaigned unceasingly against foreign influence (especially British) in his country. In 1951, after Iran's premier was assasinated, Mossadegh assumed the post and immediately nationalized Iran's oil. Production of oil stopped, and in the next two years Iran was almost bankrupt. In 1953 the Shah's personal intervention with army support forced Mossadegh's overthrow. He died Mar. 5, 1967 in Tehran, Iran.

Motonobu. See *Kano.*

Moultrie, William (1731–1805), American Revolutionary War general who successfully defended Sullivan's Island in South Carolina against British attack. Born in Charleston, he became colonel of a South Carolina regiment when war broke out. In 1776, as commander of the fort on Sullivan's Island (later named Fort Moultrie) near Charleston, he held it against heavy attack. After further successes, he was taken prisoner in 1780 when Charleston surrendered to the British. Two years later, he was exchanged for General John Burgoyne and was promoted to major general. Moultrie served as governor of South Carolina for two-year terms beginning in 1785 and 1794.

Mountbatten, Lord Louis, 1st Earl of **Burma** (1900–), English naval officer, the son of a German-born prince and a granddaughter of Queen Victoria. He entered the royal navy in 1913, serving in both world wars. In 1943 he was appointed supreme Allied commander in Southeast Asia and conducted the campaign against the Japanese

in Burma. In 1947 he was appointed viceroy of India, later transferring his power to the new country and becoming governor general of the Dominion of India. In July, 1948, he returned to duty with the British navy, becoming first sea lord in 1955. He was made viscount in 1946 and earl in 1947.

Moussorgsky. See *Mussorgsky.*

Mozart, Wolfgang Amadeus (1756–1791), Austrian composer, universally acclaimed as one of the great composers of all time. The son of a violinist, he was a child prodigy whose compositions and performances on the harpsichord astonished Europe. Leaving their native Salzburg, the Mozart family traveled throughout Europe for years. At the age of six Mozart was composing concertos, and when he was 11 had completed his first opera. A 15-month tour of Italy, begun in 1569, had a decided influence on his development as a composer. After 1771 he resided chiefly in Salzburg, but also visited other European cities.

In his short life, Mozart produced more than 600 compositions of all kinds, including operas, symphonies, quartets, masses, songs, and concertos. Of his operas, those still frequently performed include *The Abduction from the Seraglio* (1782), *The Marriage of Figaro* (1786), *Don Giovanni* (1787), *Così fan tutte* (1789), and *The Magic Flute* (1791). Many of his 41 symphonies, 30 string quartets, and numerous concertos are regular features of today's symphonic programs, and his *Requiem Mass,* which he left uncompleted, is considered one of the most beautiful of that genre. Historically, Mozart's music represents the Classical school.

Mühlenberg, Henry Melchior (1711–1787), German-American clergyman, born in Einbeck, Prussia, and educated at Göttingen and Halle. In 1742 he came to the U.S. as missionary to the Lutheran congregations in Pennsylvania. He founded the German Lutheran Church in America and organized the first Lutheran synod in 1748.

Muir, John (1838–1914), American naturalist and explorer who led in the campaign for forest conservation and the founding of national parks. Born in Scotland, he settled in Wisconsin in 1849, and studied at the state university. He then began a career of exploration that took him to every continent. He was a pioneer in the conservation movement in America; it was partly through his efforts that the Sequoia and Yosemite regions were made national parks. The Yosemite Valley was his headquarters for 10 years. He discovered 65 permanent glaciers in the Sierras and Muir Glacier in Alaska. His writings include *Our National Parks* (1901), *The Yosemite* (1912), and *Story of My Boyhood and Youth* (1913). He made a fortune from California vineyards.

Mumford, Lewis (1895–), American author, noted for his writings on architecture and city planning. Born in New York City, he was educated at Columbia and New York universities. Among his books on architecture, *Sticks and Stones* (1924) and *The Brown Decades* (1931) earned him a solid reputation not only as an architectural critic but as a social critic. *The City in History* (1961) sums up his thoughts on city planning. During much of his life, Mumford has taught at a number of universities.

Munch, Edvard (1863–1944), Norwegian painter, famed for the psychological and symbolic depth of his canvases. Educated in Oslo, he began painting landscapes, portraits, and interiors at an early age. His distinctive style, characteristic of the expressionistic school, began to appear in the early 1890's. Munch's mature paintings combine strong color, great sensitivity, and psychological undercurrents. In addition to his oils, he also achieved a reputation for woodcuts and lithographs. A retrospective exhibition at the Guggenheim Museum in New York City was held in 1965–1966.

Murat, Joachim (1771–1815), French officer who was made king of Naples by Napoleon in 1808. He enlisted in a cavalry regiment in 1787 and rose to distinction under Napoleon, whose sister he married in 1800. When the Empire was established, Murat was created a prince and marshal and grand admiral of France. His brilliant service in the Austrian campaigns won him the throne of Naples. Murat led the army in the disastrous retreat from Moscow (1812) and commanded the cavalry in the battle of Leipzig. He then allied himself with the Austrians, but returned to his former allegiance when Napoleon escaped from Elba. Murat lost his army and his throne through a severe defeat in northern Italy. He tried to recover his kingdom and landed on the coast of Calabria with a small army, but he was defeated, captured, tried by court-martial, and shot.

Murillo, Bartolomé Esteban (1617–1682), Spanish painter, known for his religious scenes and portraits of children. Born in Seville, he supported himself early in his career by painting crude, hastily drawn pictures for local merchants. Later he went to Madrid, where he was befriended by Diego Velázquez and learned much by copying the old masters. By 1650 he was recognized as the leader of the Sevillian school of art. He left about 400 canvases, principally religious subjects and studies of street children. Murillo's pictures of the little urchins he saw every day have always been popular favorites.

Murphy, William Parry (1892–), American physician who shared the Nobel Prize for medicine in 1934. Born at Stoughton, Wis., he studied at the University of Oregon and at Harvard. After serving in a number of hospitals, in 1924 he joined the medical faculty at Harvard. In 1934 he shared the Nobel Prize with G. R. Minot and G. H. Whipple for his discoveries in the use of liver for treating pernicious anemia.

Murray, Sir James Augustus Henry (1837–1915), Scottish lexicographer who was the editor of the *New English Dictionary.* His *Dialect of the Southern Counties of Scotland* made him well known as a philologist. The great work of his life, the editing of the *New English Dictionary* (later known as the *Oxford English Dictionary*) was begun in 1879 and continued at Oxford until its completion in the 1920's. Murray was knighted in 1908.

Murray, Lindley (1745–1826), American grammarian whose English grammar and spelling books were widely used in his time. Born in Swatara, Pa., he was educated in Philadelphia at a Quaker academy. As a lawyer in New York during the Revolutionary War, he amassed a fortune by selling merchandise to the British. In 1784 he went to England, where he devoted himself to writing and botany. Murray's *Grammar of the English Language, English Reader,* and *Spelling Book* became standard textbooks for thousands of nineteenth-century school children. He is also known for his religious tracts, including *The Power of Religion on the Mind* (1787).

Murray, Philip (1886–1952), American labor leader who helped organize the United Steel Workers of America and also the Congress of Industrial Organizations (CIO). Born in Scotland, he came to the United States in 1902, and went to work as a coal miner. Active in the United Mine Workers Union, he became a member of its national executive board in 1912 and served as international vice-president from 1920 to 1942. In 1936 Murray became chairman of the Steel Workers' Organization Committee and in 1942 was chosen president of the United Steel Workers of America. He helped found the Congress of Industrial Organizations and became president on November 22, 1940. He supported the government's wage control policy during World War II, but after the war he led the steelworkers in a round of demands for wage increases. In the fall of 1949 he obtained a grant of old age pensions for his union financed entirely by the employers.

Musset, Alfred de (1810–1857), French poet and dramatist, one of the leading figures of the French Romantic period. His first collection of poems, *Tales of Spain and Italy* (1830), excited notice for their passion, exotic settings, and controversial subjects. Musset fell in love with George Sand, and in 1833 accompanied her to Italy. Although their romance lasted but two years, it inspired some of Musset's best love poems, notably the lyrics entitled *Nuits* and *Souvenir.* As a dramatist, Musset's reputation rests with such plays as *Les Caprices de Marianne* (1833) and *Lorenzaccio* (1834).

Mussolini, Benito (1883–1945), Italian premier and dictator, founder of the Italian Fascist party. The son of a blacksmith, he was educated at a normal school and became a teacher but soon went to Switzerland as a journalist. Back in Italy he became a socialist editor and writer. He founded the paper *Il Popolo d'Italia* in Milan in 1914.

Conditions in Italy after World War I enabled Mussolini to emerge as a leader. In 1919 he organized the first group of Fascists or Black Shirts at Milan. When the Fascists marched on Rome, King Victor Emmanuel dismissed Prime Minister Facta and invited Mussolini to enter Rome, October 30, 1922. Mussolini became the dictator of Italy with the title of *Il Duce* (leader or chief). He was at once premier and minister of foreign affairs, interior, colonies, war, marine, air, and labor. Mussolini put down all opposition. In 1929 he arranged the treaty that reconciled the papacy, the pope becoming

ASSOCIATED PRESS

MUSSOLINI struts with the arrogance of power as he addresses the populace in 1935.

sovereign of the newly created state of Vatican City.

In 1938 he replaced the Italian Chamber of Deputies with a Chamber of Fasci and Corporations. Large private industries were also abolished, with a view to nationalizing them for war purposes. Mussolini announced the annexation of Ethiopia in May.

In 1940, when Germany was invading northern France, Mussolini brought Italy into the war by invading southern France. Italian armies also invaded Africa, but there, as in the Balkans, and finally in Italy itself, Mussolini's forces were defeated. The Fascist Grand Council had him imprisoned, but he was rescued by German parachutists and went into hiding behind German lines. He and his mistress were discovered near Lake Como by Italian underground troops. They were given a brief trial, shot to death, and their bodies hung by the heels in Milan.

A writer all his life, Mussolini's most important works are *My Diary* (1920) and *My Autobiography* (1928).

Mussorgsky, Moussorgsky, or **Musorgski, Modest Petrovich** (1835–1881), Russian Romantic composer, a leader of the nationalist school. He was educated at a military school in St. Petersburg and studied music under the composer Mili Balakirev. Although he was famous for his orchestral pieces and songs, Mussorgsky is best remembered for his opera *Boris Godunov* (1874), whose dramatic intensity and melodic inspiration have made it a world favorite. His piano suite *Pictures from an Exhibition* is a perennial concert favorite. He wrote three other operas, including the unfinished *Khovanshchina*. Among his numerous songs, the cycle *Songs and Dances of Death* is noteworthy.

Mutsuhito, known as **Meiji** (1852–1912), Japanese emperor (1867–1912) who led Japan from a feudal empire to a modern nation. He succeeded his father, Osahito, in 1867 and the following year assumed the name Meiji (meaning year of enlightened peace). He abolished feudalism, moved his capital from Kyoto to Yeddo (now Tokyo), and set up a parliamentary form of government. To support the new way of life, Mutsuhito had to put down three rebellions led by traditionalists. During his reign, Japan was successful in wars with China (1894) and Russia (1905). As emperor, he left a modernized empire.

Myron (5th century B.C.), Greek sculptor, noted for his bronzes. Although none of his original works is preserved, copies reveal that he had an original style of realism and great technical skill. Copies of his most famous work, the *Discobolus* (Discus Thrower), are in the Vatican and the British Museum.

N

Nabokov, Vladimir Vladimirovich (1899–). Russian-born writer of satirical novels. Born in St. Petersburg, he left Russia when the Revolution broke out and was educated at Cambridge, England. After writing a series of novels in Russian during the 1930's, he emigrated to the United States, where he became a citizen and taught at Wellesley College and Cornell University. In his best-known novel, *Lolita* (1955), he portrays a middle-aged intellectual who falls in love with a young girl. Nabokov abandoned teaching in 1955 to devote himself entirely to writing. Among his later works are the novels *Pnin* (1957) and *Pale Fire* (1962), and a translation of Pushkin's *Eugene Onegin* (1964).

Nansen, Fridtjof (1861–1930), Norwegian Arctic explorer and scientist. He made his first Arctic expedition to Greenland in 1882 and in 1888 crossed Greenland on foot with a party of six men—a feat that earned him international renown. In 1893 he set out to explore the whole polar region, and got as far north as 85°57', the most northerly point ever reached up to that time. On his return to Norway, he became professor of zoology at Christiania University and actively supported the separation of Norway from Sweden in 1905. During the next ten years, he made several oceanographic expeditions. After World War I, Nansen directed relief work during the famine in Russia. For this and his work with refugees on behalf of the League of Nations, he was awarded the Nobel Peace Prize in 1923. Nansen wrote several popular books and technical reports on his expeditions.

Napier, John (1550–1617), Scottish mathematician who invented logarithmic tables. In a treatise published in 1614, Napier showed the correspondence between arithmetic and geometric progressions, and demonstrated the use of logarithms as a means of facilitating computations. He was among the first to use the present system of decimal notation. Napier also originated several formulas in trigonometry, and invented mechanical devices similar to modern calculating machines.

Napoleon Bonaparte (1769–1821), emperor of the French (1804–1815), who led France to its greatest military and political power. Born in Corsica of Italian descent, he was educated in France, and joined the army as a junior lieutenant in 1788. He was in Paris in the early stages of the French Revolution, saw the mob invade the Tuileries and witnessed the overthrow of the monarchy. In 1793 he took a leading part

NEW YORK PUBLIC LIBRARY

in ousting the British from Toulon and in 1794 was appointed a general, commanding the French artillery in Italy. He married Joséphine de Beauharnais in 1796. Shortly thereafter, he left to command the army in Italy, where he won a series of victories over the Sardinians and the Austrians.

Bonaparte returned to Paris and got permission from the Directory to invade Egypt, by which he hoped to restore French supremacy in India. He conquered Egypt, but Nelson's victory on August 1, 1798, in the battle of the Nile was a bitter reverse, and the French fleet was destroyed. In 1799 Napoleon invaded Syria and returned to Egypt, where he defeated the Turks in the battle of Aboukir. Hearing of the successes of the second coalition in Europe, of the French loss of Italy, and of the condition of France, he returned home. The revolution of November 9, 1799, gave Napoleon autocratic power as first consul under a new constitution.

Austria and Britain then became the chief foes of France. Austria was quickly defeated. On March 27, 1802, the Peace of Amiens was signed with Britain; on August 1 Bonaparte was proclaimed consul for life. The concordat with the pope had already been signed, and Napoleon, as he was thereafter called, gave to the nation the Bank of France and the Code Napoléon, reformed its educational system, conciliated many of the old nobles, and instituted the Legion of Honor. During 1802–1803, however, Napoleon made preparations for a fresh development in foreign policy. He proposed to found one colonial empire in the New World and another in India. His schemes with regard to America were frustrated when fever destroyed his army in Haiti in 1803. In the same year he sold the territory of Louisiana to the United States for $15,000,000. He then determined to rearrange the map of Germany and to destroy Britain's commerce. Early in June, 1802, he became president of the Italian republics, and in September and October he annexed Piedmont, Parma, and Piacenza. In February, 1803, he reconstituted Switzerland and sent secret agents to stir up a rebellion in Ireland. In addition, he demanded the British evacuation of Malta. On May 18, 1803, war between France and England broke out.

In 1804 he became emperor as Napoleon I. Then followed a period of despotic government at home, with several campaigns abroad. In 1807 France and Spain agreed to conquer Portugal, and Junot entered Lisbon. No sooner had Napoleon made Joseph Bonaparte king of Spain, than the Spanish people rose, an English expedition landed in Portugal, and Wellington won the battle of Vimeiro. The Peninsular War proved to be one of the principal causes of the fall of Napoleon. War with Austria again broke

NAPOLEON appears at *left* in the dignity of battle dress. He is shown in the 1815 French cartoon at *right* in the guise of an acrobat or jester, leaping aboard an English ship for the trip to St. Helena with his servant, the only man, it is said, he could still command.

out; after the battles of Aspern and Wagram the Austrian emperor was forced to sign the humiliating treaty of Vienna (Schönbrunn), in October, 1809.

To strengthen his political position Napoleon divorced Josephine and in 1810 married Marie Louise of Austria. At the same time he renewed his efforts to ruin England by his "continental system," an agreement among France, her allies, and neutral nations not to trade with England. When the czar of Russia showed a desire to abandon the system, Napoleon resolved to invade Russia. His disastrous defeat at Moscow (1812) encouraged Europe to rise against him, and in 1813 the war of liberation began. Russia, Prussia, and Austria united against him, and the French were defeated at Leipzig.

The Allies invaded France; Napoleon abdicated (1814) and was exiled to Elba. He escaped and landed in France on March 1, 1815, and the famous Hundred Days began. The battle of Waterloo (June 18) completed the downfall of his hopes. After his surrender to the British he was exiled to St. Helena, where he died.

Napoleon II, born **François Charles Joseph Bonaparte** (1811–1832), son of Napoleon I and Marie Louise of Austria. Shortly after his birth he was given the title of king of Rome. When Napoleon I abdicated in 1814, he named his son as his successor, but Napoleon II never ruled because the Allies who had defeated Napoleon refused to accept him. Until his death, he lived in the court at Vienna, a virtual prisoner. In 1818 he was named Duke of Reichstadt by the Austrians. He died of tuberculosis.

Napoleon III, born **Charles Louis Napolean Bonaparte** (1808–1873), emperor of the French (1852–1870), nephew of Napoleon I and son of Louis Bonaparte, king of Holland. After Napoleon's only son died in 1832, Louis Napoleon, as he was called, regarded himself as the rightful heir to the throne. In 1836 he tried to stir up a revolution in Strasbourg, and was deported. After a second attempt (1840) to displace Louis Philippe and restore the Bonapartes, he was sentenced to life imprisonment.

Six years later he escaped to England. The revolution of 1848 and abdication of Louis Philippe gave him his opportunity. In June, 1848, Louis Napoleon was elected to the National Assembly and in the following December was chosen president of the new republic. By the *coup d'état* of 1851, he secured his office for the next 10 years. He dissolved the constitution in the following year and became emperor.

His foreign policy was unsuccessful. The Franco-Prussian War, into which he was drawn by Bismarck, resulted in the total defeat of the French and the collapse of the empire. Napoleon fled to England, where he died. His son Napoleon was killed in 1879 while fighting in Africa against the Zulus.

Nash, Ogden (1902–   ), American poet and humorist, noted for his short, doggerel verse. Born in Rye, N.Y., he began contributing light verse to magazines at an early age. Most of his poems were published in *The New Yorker* and other magazines, and collected in such volumes as *Hard Lines* (1931), *I'm a Stranger Here Myself* (1938), and *Good Intentions* (1942). Nash has also collaborated on the books for several musical comedies.

Nashe or **Nash, Thomas** (1567–1601), English writer, notable chiefly as the author of *The Unfortunate Traveller, Or the Life of Jack Wilton* (1594), an early example of the picaresque novel in English. Nashe was born in Lowestoft and attended St. John's College, Cambridge, where he associated with a group known as the university wits. By 1588 he had settled in London, where he became a literary hack and stormy controversialist. In his first book, *Anatomie of Absurdities* (1589), he attacked contemporary follies and baited a number of writers. In another, *Pierce Pennilesse, His Supplication to the Divell* (1592), he sardonically assails London society. Nashe also wrote a satirical masque, *Summer's Last Will* (1592), and finished Marlowe's play *Dido*. At best his style was vigorous, racy, and often pleasantly erudite.

Nasser, Gamal Abdel (1918–   ), Egyptian soldier and statesman, president of the United Arab Republic since 1958. After graduating from the Cairo Military Academy in 1942, he formed a secret group of officers who plotted to overthrow the corrupt regime of King Farouk. In 1952 he was a leader of the bloodless coup that ousted Farouk, and he became deputy prime minister in the new government headed by Gen. Mohammed Naguib. He succeeded Naguib as premier in 1954 and became president in 1956. In his first year, Nasser gained much prestige throughout the Arab world when he nationalized the Suez Canal and forced the British to withdraw. In 1958 he merged Egypt with Syria to form the United Arab Republic. In domestic affairs, Nasser's greatest achievement has been land reform. Outside Egypt, he has sought to play a central role in Arab affairs, influence the Afro-Asian bloc, and negotiate with both the Soviet Union and the United States for economic aid.

UNITED PRESS INTERNATIONAL

NASSER'S image, woven into a rug, rides above a cheering crowd of his supporters.

Nast, Thomas (1840–1902), American cartoonist, famed for his scathing political cartoons of Tammany Hall politicians. Born in Germany, he was brought to the U.S. as a child. He studied art in New York and by the age of 15 was drawing for prominent magazines. His Civil War cartoons made him famous. In the 1870's he added to his reputation with a series of cartoons in *Harper's Weekly* that did more than anything else to break up the corrupt ring of "Boss" Tweed that was ruling New York City. It was Nast who created the political party symbols of the donkey for the Democrats and the elephant for the Republicans. His fat, jolly, bearded Santa Claus became the standard version of the Christmas figure.

Nathan, George Jean (1882–1958), American drama critic and editor, one of the most influential of his time. Born in Fort Wayne, Ind., he graduated from Cornell University and studied for a year in Bologna, Italy. For some 40 years Nathan dominated American drama criticism with his witty, often harsh, but always entertaining reviews. It has been said that the success of a play often hinged on his opinions. Nathan was equally important as the founder and editor (with H. L. Mencken) of *The Smart Set* (1914–1923) and *The American Mercury* (1924–1941), both lively repositories of distinguished contemporary writing. From 1943 until shortly before his death, Nathan was drama critic for the New York *Journal-American*. A prolific writer, his best-known publications include *The Critic and the Drama* (1922), *The Testament of a Critic* (1931), *Since Ibsen* (1933), and *The World of George Jean Nathan* (edited by Charles Angoff, 1952).

Nation, Carry Amelia Moore (1846–1911), American temperance leader, born in Garrard County, Ky. Unhappily married to an alcoholic, she felt repugnance for drinking and saloons. After moving to Kansas (a prohibition state) in 1889, she began a series of hatchet-wielding raids on saloons that earned her a national reputation. She was also active in the women's suffrage movement. Her autobiography appeared in 1904.

Nebuchadnezzar II, (d.562 B.C.) king of Babylon (605–562 B.C.) who fought many wars against Egypt and the Jews. His father, Nabopolassar, founded the Chaldean dynasty in Babylon. His most famous battle, described in the Old Testament, came in 597, when King Jehoiachin of Judaea rebelled against him. Nebuchadnezzar besieged Jerusalem; when the city fell, he sent the king and 10,000 of his subjects into exile. Zedekiah, who was placed on the vacated throne, also revolted, and in 586 Nebuchadnezzar destroyed the city, blinded the king, and carried about 4,000 Jews into captivity. He captured Tyre after a 12 years' siege and invaded Egypt. Nebuchadnezzar built tne Hanging Gardens in Babylon, one of the Seven Wonders of the Ancient World, to please his wife, who had complained of the flatness of the country.

Nehru, Jawaharlal (1889–1964), Indian statesman who from 1947 until his death was the first prime minister of independent India. Born in Allahabad of prosperous Brahman parents, he was educated at Cambridge, England. After returning to India, he joined his father in support of Mahatma Gandhi and the struggle for Indian independence. A member of Gandhi's civil disobedience movement, he was arrested in 1921 and spent several years in prison. Beginning in 1929 he served three terms as president of the Indian National Congress and took a leading part in the negotiations with the British for Indian independence. In May, 1946, he was chosen head of the first all-India executive council. After becoming prime minister, he set as his chief goal the completion of a series of five-year plans to strengthen India's economy. In international affairs, he advocated a policy of strict neutrality, seeing himself as an intermediary between the East and West.

Nehru, Indira. See *Gandhi, Indira*.

Nelson, Horatio, Viscount (1758–1805), British admiral, the most famous of all British naval heroes. Born in Norfolk, he entered the navy at the age of 12, serving on his uncle's ship. After voyages to the West Indies, the Arctic regions, and the East Indies, he became a lieutenant in 1777, and in 1779 was promoted to captain. He saw continuous service until 1787, when he married and retired. Nelson returned to active duty in 1793 to take part in the war with France. He commanded the *Agamemnon*, one of the squadron under Admiral Samuel Hood. He aided in the capture of Corsica. During the blockade of Calvi he lost his right eye, but he remained on duty in the Mediterranean and as commodore was responsible for the victory off Cape St. Vincent in 1797. Later that year, he suffered his only major defeat in an attack on Teneriffe, in the Canary Islands. Here Nelson lost his right arm.

Napoleon was winning victories on land and threatening to become the conqueror of all Europe, but his plans were hampered by Nelson's telling blows at the French navy. In 1798 he annihilated a French fleet in the Aboukir Bay (the battle of the Nile) and was made a baron. In 1801, having become vice admiral, he defeated the Danish fleet at Copenhagen and was created viscount. When the war with France was renewed in 1803, Nelson took command of the Mediterranean fleet, with the *Victory* as his flagship. For two years the French fleet evaded him, but on October 21, 1805, he met the enemy in a decisive battle off Cape Trafalgar, annihilating the combined French and Spanish fleets but losing his own life at the moment of victory. At the start of the battle he gave his famous signal "England expects every man to do his duty."

Nero, in full **Nero Claudius Caesar Drusus Germanicus** (37–68 A.D.), Roman emperor (54–68), notorious for his depravity and cruelty. Adopted by Emperor Claudius in the year 50, he succeeded him in 54, displacing Claudius' son Britannicus, whom he had poisoned. To please his mistress Poppaea Sabina, he ordered his mother Agrippina put to death. Afterward he divorced and murdered his wife, Octavia, in order to marry Poppaea; he later killed Poppaea in a burst of passion. When Antonia, daughter of Claudius, refused to marry him, he caused her death; then he married another woman after he had her husband killed. He accused the Christians of the burning of Rome and had many put to death; afterward he built a magnificent new city. In 68 his troops revolted in favor of Galba, and Nero fled from Rome, saving himself from execution by committing suicide.

Nerva, Marcus Cocceius (32–98 A.D.), Roman emperor (96–98). A member of a senatorial family, he was consul for two terms and, after the assassination of Emperor Domitian, was elected emperor by the Senate. The army and the people favored this choice, and Nerva fulfilled their hopes by ruling with moderation and justice, although his reign was not inspired. Childless, he was succeeded by his adopted son, Trajan.

Nestorius (died c.451 A.D.), Syrian religious leader who promulgated what came to be known as the Nestorian Heresy. After spending many years as a monk, he became bishop of Constantinople in 428. He taught the controversial doctrine that Mary should be called the Mother of Christ and the Mother of God, because Jesus had two separate natures as Son of God and Son of Mary. At the Council of Ephesus (431), his teachings were condemned and he was banished. Nestorius still has followers in Turkey and Persia.

Neville, Richard, Earl of **Warwick** and **Salisbury** (1428–1471), English soldier and statesman whose military and political power made him known as "the Kingmaker." The son of the earl of Salisbury, he married Anne, the earl of Warwick's daughter, and supported the House of York in the War of the Roses. In 1460, after the duke of York had been slain in battle, Neville threw his support to the duke's son, Edward. In the next year, after the decisive defeat of the Lancastrians, Neville proclaimed Edward king of England as Edward IV. As duke of Warwick, Neville became the virtual ruler of England for the next few years, but eventually he and Edward quarreled, and Neville was forced to flee to Holland. In 1470 he switched his support to the House of Lancaster, joined Queen Margaret in invading England, and placed the Lancastrian Henry VI on the throne. In 1471, however, Edward IV returned to England at the head of an army and was victorious at the battle of Tewkesbury, where Neville was killed.

Nevski. See *Alexander Nevski.*

Newcomb, Simon (1835–1909), the leading American astronomer of the nineteenth century. Born in Nova Scotia, he came to the United States in 1853 and graduated from Harvard in 1858. In 1861, as professor of mathematics in the U. S. navy, he supervised the construction of the 26-inch telescope at the Naval Observatory. He was appointed professor of mathematics at Johns Hopkins in 1884, and from 1877 to 1897 directed the *Nautical Almanac,* a book of astronomical data for navigators. He was a brilliant mathematician and astronomer. He collected the accumulated records of 25 centuries on the moon's motion and thus made possible the preparation of accurate tables.

Newman, John Henry (1801–1890), Church of England leader who converted to Roman Catholicism and eventually became a cardinal. Born in London and educated at Oxford, he entered the Anglican Church in 1824. Four years later he became vicar of St. Mary's in Oxford, where he gained a wide reputation for his eloquence and strong character. He then became a leader of the Oxford Tractarian (or High Church) Movement. In 1845, after much soul-searching, Newman resigned from the Church of England and announced his conversion to Roman Catholicism. After being ordained a priest in Rome, he was rector of Catholic University in Dublin (1854–1858). In 1879 Pope Leo XIII created him a cardinal. Newman defended his beliefs in several books, most notably *Apologia pro Vita Sua* (1864) and *The Grammar of Assent* (1870). A skillful poet, he is remembered for the hymn *Lead, Kindly Light* and the poem *The Dream of Gerontius* (1865). His essay *The Idea of a University* (1852), a discourse on education, is still acclaimed for its good sense and exemplary prose style.

Newton, Sir Isaac (1642–1727), English mathematician and scientist, one of the greatest of all time. Born in Lincolnshire, he graduated from Cambridge (1665), where he remained for 30 years as a teacher. Many of his discoveries came from research he did at Cambridge. Between 1665 and 1668 Newton discovered the binomial theorem and the method of tangents; laid down the first rules of differential calculus, which he announced at the same time as Leibniz; explained the influence of the earth's gravity on the moon; and built his first reflecting telescope.

During this time, he is said to have watched an apple falling in his garden, which suggested to him that every particle of matter in the universe attracts every other particle. Many years later he completed the mathematical statement of the law of universal gravitation, thus laying the foundation of modern astronomy. His great work, *Principia Mathematica* (1687), in which he formulated his basic theories, is said to herald the beginning of modern science.

Newton also did much research on optics.

He was the first to show that white light is a combination of the colors seen in the rainbow. In his *Opticks* (1704) he sums up his findings in this field. After 1699 he was master of the mint in London. He became president of the Royal Society in 1703 and was knighted in 1705. He died in London and was buried in Westminster Abbey.

Ney, Michel (1769–1815), French marshal who was the leading commander under Napoleon I. Born in Prussia, the son of a cooper, he entered the French army as a private in 1788 and by 1796 had reached the rank of brigadier general. During the Napoleonic wars, Napoleon himself called Ney "the bravest of the brave." In 1804 he was made a marshal of the empire. As commander of the rear guard during the retreat from Moscow, he saved the remnants of the French army. After Napoleon's exile to Elba, Louis XVIII made Ney a peer of France. Sent to oppose Napoleon, who had returned to France in 1815, Ney rejoined him instead and fought bravely at Waterloo. After Louis XVIII was restored he was tried by the Chamber of Peers and found guilty and condemned for high treason.

Ngo Dinh Diem (1901–1963), president of South Vietnam (1955–1963). He began his career in the civil service and later headed a committee that investigated government corruption. After serving as minister of the interior, he retired in 1933. During the guerrilla warfare that preceeded the division of Vietnam, he was captured by Viet-Minh (now called Vietcong) forces, but later released. Diem then went to Europe in self-imposed exile, but returned to South Vietnam as prime minister and became president in 1955, ruling with his brother, Ngo Dinh Nhu, and his sister-in-law, Mme. Nhu. He was deposed in November, 1963. He and his brother were assassinated, and Mme. Nhu went into exile.

Nicholas I (1796–1855), czar of Russia (1825–1855), son of Paul I. In 1825 he succeeded his brother, Alexander. At the beginning of his reign he relentlessly crushed a rebellion and ruled so sternly that he became known as the Iron Czar. Nicholas extended Russian territory by successful wars with Persia and Turkey, and he made the kingdom of Poland a Russian province. He died during the Crimean War, in which Turkey defeated Russia with the aid of Britain and France.

Nicholas II (1868–1918), last czar of Russia, the son of Alexander III, whom he succeeded in 1894. In 1899 he was responsible for the first meeting of the International Peace Congress at The Hague. At home he refused the people a share in internal affairs and opposed the growth of social democracy. However, as a concession to the strong revolutionary feeling, he set up a representative assembly, the Duma, in 1905, but this body possessed little real power.

After the defeat of Russia in the Russo-Japanese War (1905–1906) conditions grew steadily worse. A revolution was averted only by the outbreak of World War I, which Russia entered as a protector of the small nations. The Russian people revolted early in 1917, and the czar abdicated on March 15. He and his family were later imprisoned at Ekaterinburg by the new Bolshevik powers. In July, 1918, Nicholas, his wife, and five children (four daughters and a son) were executed by the revolutionists.

Nicolle, Charles Jean Henri (1866–1936), French bacteriologist who discovered that the body louse transmits typhus. For this he was awarded the Nobel Prize for medicine in 1928. After studying medicine in Rouen, he practiced in Paris, where he also worked at the Pasteur Institute. In 1903 he went to Tunis, where he studied many types of bacteriological diseases, including typhus. Nicolle made other important contributions to bacteriological research.

Niebuhr, Barthold Georg (1776–1831), German historian, one of the leading exponents of modern historical method. Born in Copenhagen, Denmark, he held several government positions before entering the Prussian civil service. At the opening of the University of Berlin in 1810 he became professor of Roman history. From 1816 to 1823 he was Prussian envoy to Rome. Niebuhr is best known as one of the first to apply scientific methods to the study and writing of history. In his time it was considered revolutionary to urge that history be taught on the basis of facts and figures rather than legend and tradition. His greatest work is the three-volume *Römische Geschichte* (*Roman History,* 1811–1832).

Niebuhr, Reinhold (1892–   ), American Protestant theologian, famed for his ecorts to relate Christian doctrine to modern social and political issues. Born in Wright City, Mo., he graduated from the Yale Di-

vinity School in 1914 and served as a pastor in Detroit from 1915 to 1928. From 1928 to 1960 he was a professor at the Union Theological Seminary in New York. In his many writings, Niebuhr has approached religion from the standpoint of a liberal in politics and social issues. His major works include *The Nature and Destiny of Man* (1943), *The Children of Light and the Children of Darkness* (1945), *The Irony of American History* (1952), and *The Structure of Nations and Empires* (1959). His brother, **Richard Niebuhr** (1894–1962), was also a leading theologian and religious writer.

Nietzsche, Friedrich Wilhelm (1844–1900), German philosopher remembered chiefly for his doctrine of the superman. His unorthodox views on religion and morality made him one of the most controversial of modern philosophers. Educated in Bonn and Leipzig, he was professor of classical philology at the University of Basel from 1869 to 1879, when he retired because of ill health. Nearly all his writings attack the foundations of Christian society. Nietzsche taught that there must be a dual morality, one for supermen or leaders and the other for followers or slaves. Anyone who is unable to assume power is unimportant, fit only to be ruled. His whole philosophy might be summed up as "might is right." His leading works are *The Birth of Tragedy* (1872), *Thus Spake Zarathustra* (1884), and *Beyond Good and Evil* (1886).

Nightingale, Florence (1820–1910), English nurse and hospital reformer, regarded as the founder of modern nursing. Born in Florence, Italy, and educated in England, she became interested in hospitals and nursing and took a training course at the Protestant Deaconess's Institute at Kaiserswerth, Germany. After she had served as superintendent of a hospital in London, she took a staff of 38 women to nurse the wounded during the Crimean War. In four months the death rate in the hospitals was reduced from 42 per cent to 2 per cent. From her habit of visiting the wards at night with a lamp, comforting the sick, she became known as "The Lady of the Lamp." After the war she founded nursing schools. In 1907 she received the Order of Merit.

Nijinsky, Vaslav (1890–1950), Russian ballet dancer regarded as one of the greatest dancers of all time. He had phenomenal technique and such great ability that in his leaps he seemed to suspend himself in midair. Born in Kiev, he studied dancing in St. Petersburg, where he made his debut with the Imperial Ballet in 1907. Two years later he was taken by the impresario Serge Diaghilev to Paris, where he danced the title role in the debut of Igor Stravinsky's ballet *Petrouchka.* In Paris, Nijinsky was acclaimed for his performances in such ballets as *Le Spectre de la rose* and *L'Après-midi d'un faune.* Later he made a triumphant world tour. In 1917, however, a severe mental breakdown forced him to retire from the stage.

Nimitz, Chester William (1885–1966), American naval officer who commanded the U.S. Pacific Fleet during World War II. Born in Fredericksburg, Texas, he graduated from Annapolis in 1905. During World War I, he was chief of staff to the Atlantic Fleet submarine commander. He was made a rear admiral in 1938. From 1941 to 1945 he was commander in chief of the Pacific Fleet and Pacific Ocean area, reorganizing Pacific strategy with brilliant success. He was made a five-star fleet admiral in 1944 and signed the Japanese surrender terms on the battleship *Missouri.* He retired in 1947 but in March, 1949, was recalled to service to act as UN plebiscite administrator for Jammu and Kashmir. In 1951 he served as head of the Commission on Internal Security and Individual Rights.

Nixon, Richard Milhous (1913–   ), vice-president of the United States (1953–1961) and the unsuccessful Republican candidate for the presidency in 1960. Born in Yorba Linda, Calif., he graduated from Whittier College in 1934 and earned a law degree from Duke University in 1937. After serving as a naval lieutenant in World War II, he returned to California, where he practiced law briefly. In 1946 he was elected to Congress. As a member of the House Committee on Un-American Activities, Nixon won national renown during the Alger Hiss perjury trial. He was elected to the Senate in 1950. He became vice-president in 1952 and was reelected in 1956.

Pres. Eisenhower encouraged Nixon to be more than a figurehead. He was the first vice-president to preside over meetings of the Cabinet and the National Security Council. He made official visits to the Soviet Union, Europe, the Far East, and South

America. As Republican nominee for the presidency in 1960, he was defeated by John F. Kennedy in a very close race.

Nkrumah, Kwame (1909–   ), Ghanaian statesman who became prime minister (later president) of Ghana when the former Gold Coast colony gained its independence in 1957. Educated in the United States and England, he returned to the Gold Coast in 1947, where he became active in independence movements. Imprisoned in 1950, he was elected to the Gold Coast parliament while still in jail. Released in 1951, he quickly assumed great power in the government, becoming prime minister in 1952 and retaining that post when Ghana became independent in 1957. In 1960, when Ghana was proclaimed a republic, he was elected its first president. In late February, 1966, Nkrumah was ousted from office while he was on a visit to Peking, the capital of Communist China.

Nobel, Alfred Bernhard (1833–1896), Swedish chemist and inventor of dynamite, who endowed the annual prizes that bear his name. In 1867 he discovered, through the accidental escape of some nitroglycerine from a cask into the siliceous sand of the packing, how to make a safe and manageable explosive—dynamite. He also invented blasting jelly and several kinds of smokeless powder. At his death he left a fortune of some $10,000,000, most of which he ordered to be used to found the five Nobel prizes, which are awarded annually for the most important discoveries and works for the benefit of humanity in chemistry, physiology, medicine, physics, literature, and peace in the world.

Norris, Frank, in full **Benjamin Franklin Norris, Jr.** (1870–1902), American novelist of the naturalistic school. Born in Chicago, he studied art in Paris and attended Harvard and the University of California. After a few years as a newspaper correspondent, he published *McTeague* (1899), which attracted wide attention for its vivid descriptions of San Francisco slums. His greatest work was a projected trilogy, *The Epic of the Wheat.* He lived to complete only the first two novels: *The Octopus* (1901), describing the struggle between wheat growers and the railroads in California, and *The Pit* (1903), dealing with wheat speculation. In these and other novels, Norris followed the French naturalists in picturing life as fatalistic and gloomy.

North, Frederick, 2d Earl of **Guilford,** known as **Lord North** (1732–1792), English prime minister (1770–1782) during the American Revolutionary War. He was a member of the House of Commons from 1754 to 1767, when he became chancellor of the exchequer. He upheld the tea tax, which was so unpopular in America. As prime minister he was much criticized for his halfhearted attempts to prosecute the war. He resigned in 1782, after Cornwallis' surrender at Yorktown.

Norton, Charles Eliot (1827–1908), American scholar, editor, and teacher, born in Cambridge, Mass. He graduated from Harvard in 1846 and entered the publishing business. He was co-editor (with James Russell Lowell) of the *North American Review* from 1864 to 1868, and one of the founders of the *Nation* magazine in 1865. In these capacities, he edited and published many works by Carlyle, Emerson, Ruskin, and Lowell. As professor of art history at Harvard (1873–1897), he was regarded as one of the leading educators in America, beloved by generations of students. He founded the American Dante Society and the Archaeological Institute of America. As a literary scholar of world renown, he is best remembered for his prose translation of Dante's *Divine Comedy* (1891–1892).

Nostradamus, born **Michel de Nostredame,** or **Notredame** (1503–1566), French astrologer, famed for his prophecies. After studying philosophy and medicine, he began making a series of prophecies in the 1540's. In 1555 he published his first book, *Centuries,* a collection of rhymed prophecies that made him famous. Long after his death, his prophecies continued to be discussed, amid much controversy. In 1781 his work was placed on the papal index of prohibited books.

Noyes, Alfred (1880–1958), English poet best remembered for such ballads as *The Highwayman* and *The Barrel-Organ.* Born in Wolverhampton, he attended Oxford, where as a student he published his first book of poems, *The Loom of Years* (1902). In later volumes, such as *Drake: an English Epic* (1906–1908) and *Forty Singing Seamen* (1907), he showed his love for the sea. Noyes' most ambitious work was *The Torch-Bearers,* a trilogy (1922–1930). His autobiography, *Two Worlds for Memory,* was published in 1953.

O

Obregón, Álvaro (1880–1928), president of Mexico (1920–1924). He entered public life in 1912 when he led a group of volunteers in support of Pres. Francesco Madero. In 1913, when Madero was overthrown by Victoriano Huerta, he joined forces against Huerta, and in 1914 his soldiers occupied Mexico City. In the next few years he served in various government posts. Elected president in 1920, he held office until he was succeeded by Plutarco Calles in 1924. In 1928 Obregón was again elected president, but was assassinated by a religious fanatic before he could assume office.

O'Casey, Sean (1880–1964), Irish dramatist, famed for his poetic, controversial plays. Born in Dublin, he grew up in the slums, which formed the background of several of his plays. His finest plays deal with Ireland's internal politics, and for this reason he was much criticized. In 1926, after bitter attacks, he left Ireland to settle permanently in England. His best plays are considered to be *The Shadow of a Gunman* (1923), *Juno and the Paycock* (1924), and *The Plough and the Stars* (1926). His six-volume autobiography, beginning with *I Knock at the Door* (1939) and ending with *Sunset and Evening Star* (1954), is regarded as a masterpiece.

Ochs, Adolph Simon (1858–1935), American newspaper publisher who in 1896 bought the New York *Times* and made it one of the world's great newspapers. Born in Cincinnati, Ohio, of Jewish parents who had emigrated from Germany, he became publisher of the Chattanooga *Times* at the age of 20 and made it a leading Southern newspaper. His direction of the New York *Times* proved equally successful. It was Ochs who invented the *Times* motto, "All the news that's fit to print."

Octavia (d.11 B.C.), sister of Roman emperor Augustus. After the death of her husband, Gaius Claudius Marcellus, in 41 B.C., she married Mark Antony. Her marriage lasted only a short time (32 B.C.) for Antony soon left her for Cleopatra; this brought about the renewed quarrel with Augustus that ended in Antony's defeat and death. Octavia reared Antony's children by his first wife and by Cleopatra, as well as her own.

Odets, Clifford (1906–1963), American dramatist best known for his plays based on social and political themes. Born in Philadelphia, he was an actor in minor roles during the 1920's before turning to playwriting. Among his most successful plays were *Waiting for Lefty* (1935), *Awake and Sing* (1935), *Golden Boy* (1937), and *Rocket to the Moon* (1940). In later years he was a motion-picture writer and director.

Odoacer or **Odovacar** or **Odovakar** (c.435–493), Italy's first barbarian king, who ruled from 476 to 493. Of German descent, he entered the service of Rome as a soldier and after years of intrigue and battles was proclaimed king by his army. He extended his kingdom by conquest, but in 489 he was decisively defeated by Theodoric, king of the Ostrogoths. He spent his later years harassing Theodoric with small wars. Finally, in 493, Theodoric had Odoacer killed after inviting him to reign jointly.

Offenbach, Jacques (1819–1880), German-French composer noted for his light, frothy operettas. Born in Cologne, Germany, he moved to Paris at an early age, where he studied music and became a conductor. Later, as a theater manager, he produced many of his own operettas, notably *Orphée aux enfers* (1858), *La Belle Hélène* (1865), *Barbe Bleue* (1866), *La Grand-duchesse de Gérolstein* (1867), and *Madame Favart* (1878). In all, Offenbach wrote some 100 works for the stage, all of them characterized by elegance, wit, and satire. His only grand opera, *Contes d'Hoffmann (The Tales of Hoffmann),* which was produced after his death, has been one of the most frequently performed French operas.

O'Flaherty, Liam (1896–   ), Irish novelist noted for his realistic works on modern Ireland. During World War I he served in an Irish division of the British army. Later, he traveled widely and took an interest in labor movements. His first novel, *Thy Neighbor's Wife,* appeared in 1924. He published his most famous work, *The Informer,* in 1925. In 1935 this novel was made into a memorable motion picture, which won an Academy Award. He also published several collections of short stories, and the autobiographies *Two Years* (1930) and *Shame the Devil* (1934).

Oglethorpe, James Edward (1696–1785), English general and statesman, founder of the colony of Georgia in America. Born in London, he served in the army before entering Parliament in 1722. While working on prison reform, he conceived the idea of establishing a colony in America for the poor and persecuted. In 1732 he obtained a charter to found the colony, and in the next year he arrived with the first colonists and founded the city of Savannah. Ten years later, he returned to England where he resumed his military career and then returned to serve in Parliament.

O'Hara, John Henry (1905–   ), American writer, acclaimed for his realistic novels and short stories of middle-class America. Born in Pottsville, Pa., he published his first novel, *Appointment in Samarra,* in 1934. The book was highly regarded, as were such later novels as *Butterfield 8* (1935), *Ten North Frederick* (1955), and *From the Terrace* (1958). His collections of short stories include *The Doctor's Son* (1935), *Hellbox* (1947), *Assembly* (1961), and *The Cape Cod Lighter* (1962). In his best work, O'Hara exhibits an uncanny gift for dialogue and a lean, masculine style.

O. Henry. See *Porter, William Sydney.*

Ohm, Georg Simon (1787–1854), German physicist. In 1827 he announced the principle of the relationship between the force of a current, the current strength, and the resistance of a conductor, now known as Ohm's law. He taught physics in Bamberg and Cologne, and was a professor at the University of Munich. The ohm (unit of electrical resistance) was named in his honor.

Oistrakh, David Feodorovitch (1908–   ), Russian violinist, one of the finest in the twentieth century. Born in Odessa, he graduated from the Odessa Musical-Dramatic Institute in 1926. He won first prize in the Ukrainian violin competition of 1930, and three years later made his debut in Moscow. In 1934 he was appointed to the faculty of the Moscow Conservatory, where he has taught ever since. In 1937 he won first prize at the International Competition in Brussels, competing among 68 violinists from 21 countries. He has made several world concert tours, and first appeared in the U.S. in 1955.

O'Keeffe, Georgia (1887–   ), American painter, noted for her stark, sunlit desert landscapes. Born in Sun Prairie, Wis., she studied at various art schools before gaining prominence in 1916, when Alfred Stieglitz included her drawings in his show at "291," his famous New York gallery. Eight years later, she married Stieglitz. In 1939 the New York World's Fair Committee chose her as one of the 12 most outstanding women of the past 50 years. For her numerous murals and landscapes, she has received several honorary doctorates.

SEAN O'CASEY

© ANGUS MCBEAN. THE NATIONAL THEATER

LAURENCE OLIVIER in the role of Othello.

Olaf I, known as **Olaf Tryggvesson** (969–1000), king of Norway (995–1000), whose adventurous life is the subject of many songs and legends. Little is known of his early life except that part of it was spent in exile and slavery. He helped his father-in-law, the Wendish king Burislav, in his wars. He raided the British and French coasts, but when he converted to Christianity he made peace with England, (c.994). The next year he went to Norway, overthrew King Haakon, and took the throne. He tried to convert Norway to Christianity by force as well as by argument. He was defeated when he tried to conquer Sweden and Denmark, and died in a naval battle.

Olivier, Sir Laurence Kerr (1907–   ), English actor, director, and producer noted for his interpretations of Shakespeare. In 1922 he began his career at Stratford-on-Avon and rose to fame through his work with the Old Vic company, of which he became a director in 1944. In addition to his stage performances, Olivier has also filmed, with striking success, four of Shakespeare's plays: *Hamlet, Henry V, Richard III,* and *Othello.* Among his non-Shakespearean productions, *Oedipus* and *Uncle Vanya* are outstanding. Olivier has also appeared in many films on modern themes. Knighted in 1947, he was appointed director of the newly established National Theatre of England in 1962.

Olmstead, Frederick Law (1822–1903), American landscape architect who designed some of the best-known public parks in the United States. Born in New York City, he studied architecture under his father. In the 1850's he won first prize (with Calvert Vaux) in a competition to design New York's Central Park. After directing this project, Olmstead designed parks in Philadelphia and Chicago, and the Capitol grounds in Washington. A leading advocate of national parks, he was the first park commissioner at Yosemite.

Olney, Richard (1835–1917), American statesman. As secretary of state in Grover Cleveland's Cabinet, he announced the so-called "Olney corollary" to the Monroe Doctrine. Born in Oxford, Mass., he graduated from Brown University in 1856 and from Harvard Law School in 1858. After practicing law for many years, he became Pres. Grover Cleveland's attorney general in 1893. Two years later he became secretary of state when his predecessor died in office. The "Olney corollary," directed against Britain in her dispute with Venezuela in 1895, stated that the U.S. would intervene in any dispute that involved the Monroe Doctrine. For many years, this was an important part of American foreign policy.

Olympias (d.316 B.C.), wife of Philip II of Macedon and mother of Alexander the Great. During Alexander's reign (337–323 B.C.) she had much influence, and after his death attempted to seize Macedonia from King Cassander. In 317 she began a series of battles against Cassander, and in the following year was defeated, captured, and executed. In literature, Olympias is pictured as the archetype of a scheming, ruthless woman.

Omar I, Arabic name **'Umar ibn-al-Khattâb** (c.581–644), second Muslim caliph (634–644). At first he opposed Mohammed, but was later converted and became one of

Mohammed's most trusted advisors. After Mohammed's death he was influential in having abu-Bakr proclaimed caliph. When abu-Bakr died in 634, Omar succeeded him. As caliph, he led the Mohammedans to victories over Palestine, Syria, and Egypt. During his reign, Islam changed from a provincial state to a world power. In 644 he was slain by a Persian slave.

Omar Khayyám (c.1050–1123), Persian astronomer and poet whose *Rubáiyát,* a collection of four-line poems, is one of the masterpieces of world literature. During his lifetime he served as philosopher, mathematician, and astronomer to the sultan, Malik Shah. Today his fame, especially in the Western world, rests upon the quatrains that he wrote in celebration of life and love. Translated into English by Edward Fitz-Gerald in 1859, the poems are memorable for their hedonistic outlook.

O'Neill, Eugene Gladstone (1888–1953), American playwright, acknowledged as one of the greatest of the twentieth century. Born in New York City, the son of the actor James O'Neill, he attended Princeton and Harvard briefly, then quit school to join the merchant marine. In 1913, while recovering from a mild case of tuberculosis, he began writing plays. He spent the summer of 1916 at Provincetown, Mass., where he met the Provincetown Players, a theatrical group who produced his first play, the one-act *Bound East for Cardiff.* His first full-length play, *Beyond the Horizon,* won the Pulitzer Prize in 1920. Over the next 30 years O'Neill produced many brilliant plays, almost single-handedly changing the tone of America drama from romantic sentimentality to harsh, uncompromising realism. Among his greatest dramas are *The Emperor Jones* (1921), *Anna Christie* (1922, awarded a Pulitzer Prize), *Desire Under the Elms* (1925), *The Great God Brown* (1926), *Strange Interlude* (1928 Pulitzer Prize winner), *Mourning Becomes Electra* (1931), *The Iceman Cometh* (1946), and the autobiographical *Long Day's Journey Into Night* (1956). His play *Ah, Wilderness!* (1933), representing his only comedy of importance, is a perennial favorite. O'Neill's main themes are man's frustrated dreams, sense of guilt, and thwarted love. In 1936 O'Neill received the Nobel Prize for literature.

Oppenheimer, Robert (1904–   ), American theoretical physicist who, during World War II, directed the laboratory that built the first atomic bomb. Born in New York City, he studied at Harvard and Cambridge (England), and in 1927 received his doctorate from the University of Göttingen (Germany). During the next decade he taught at several schools, most notably at the California Institute of Technology, where he built up the largest graduate program in theoretical physics in the U.S. After playing a leading part in the development of the atomic bomb, he was appointed (1947) director of the Institute for Advanced Study at Princeton, N.J., serving until 1966. Continuing his work in atomic physics, he served as chairman of the Atomic Energy Commission's general advisory committee until 1954, when he was declared a security risk because of alleged leftist activities. Many years later, he was declared innocent of the charges. In 1963 he received the Fermi Award given by the Atomic Energy Commission.

Optic, Oliver pen name of **William Taylor Adams** (1822–1897), American editor and author, born in Bellingham, Mass. He was a teacher in the Boston public schools from 1845 to 1865. His books, numbering over 100, are mainly adventure and travel stories written for the young reader. He founded and edited *Oliver Optic's Magazine.* His series of books include *Young America Abroad,* and *Boat Club.*

Origen, Latin name **Origenes Adamantius** (c.185–c.254 A.D.), Greek writer, teacher, and church father who was an important influence on the formulation of Christian doctrine. His writings were said to have numbered more than 6,000 titles. In his works, Origen defended Christianity against pagan attack and also interpreted the Bible for his fellow men. He was head of the catechetical school at Alexandria (c.203–c.232), then established one at Caesarea.

Ormandy, Eugene (1899–   ), American conductor noted for his interpretations of nineteenth century Romantic music. Born in Budapest, Hungary, where he studied music, he came to the United States in 1921, and was naturalized six years later. After years of guest conducting, he became conductor of the Minneapolis Symphony Orchestra in 1931. He was appointed associate conductor of the Philadelphia Orchestra in 1936, and its chief conductor in 1938. Under his leadership, that orchestra

ROBERT OPPENHEIMER, nuclear physicist.

has become one of the most prominent in the world.

Orozco, José Clemente (1883–1949), Mexican painter of social and political themes. With Diego Rivera he led the renaissance in Mexican art during the 1920's. In this period, he painted some of his most outstanding murals in government buildings in Mexico City. His well-known *Zapatistas,* in the Musum of Modern Art, New York, is typical of his strong, simple style.

Ortega y Gasset, José (1883–1955), Spanish philosopher whose writings have profoundly influenced modern Spanish thought. He was a professor of philosophy at the University of Madrid, and active in politics. During the Spanish Civil War, he taught in Argentina, Peru, and Portugal, returning to Spain in 1949. In his writings, he examined the basic structure of political and social institutions, relating them to contemporary literature and art. He regarded himself as a humanist and rejected absolutes in considerations of reality, truth, and justice. Among his many works, *The Modern Theme* (1923) and *The Revolt of the Masses* (1930) best illustrate his thinking.

Osborn, Henry Fairfield (1857–1935), American paleontologist who made the American Museum of Natural History in New York one of the world's great centers of its kind. Born in Fairfield, Conn., and educated at Princeton, he taught anatomy, biology, and zoology for several years. In 1891 he was appointed curator of vertebrate paleontology at the Museum of Natural History. As president of the museum (after 1908), he extended its educational work and introduced new methods of mounting the collections. Osborn published many important works on fossil vertebrates and books on natural history and naturalists.

Osborne, John (1929–   ), British dramatist, who in the 1950's was a leading figure in the "angry young men" group of writers who revolutionized British literature and theater. He began his career as an actor and playwright in provincial theaters. His first play, *Look Back in Anger* (1956), was an immediate success, followed by *The Entertainer* (1957) and *Epitaph for George Dillon* (1958). In these plays, Osborne portrayed the hopes and frustrations of the British working classes, departing from the traditional English preoccupation with the middle and upper classes. His historical drama, *Luther,* was produced in 1961.

Osceola (c.1800–1838), Seminole Indian leader who led his tribe to war against the United States. Born in Georgia, he settled in Florida territory. When in 1835 the government attempted to move the Seminoles into Indian territory west of the Mississippi, he and his forces declared war. After two years, Osceola accepted a truce to discuss peace terms, but at the parley he was seized and sent to prison, where he died.

Osler, Sir William (1849–1919), Canadian physician who made many contributions to knowledge of heart and blood diseases. Born in Ontario and educated at McGill University in Montreal, he taught at McGill, the University of Pennsylvania, and Johns Hopkins. In 1905 he became professor of medicine at Oxford University, England. He did much research work on spleen and blood diseases, heart infections, and malaria.

Oswald, Lee Harvey (1939–1963), presumed assassin of Pres. John F. Kennedy on November 22, 1963. Born in New Orleans, La., he spent most of his boyhood in Fort Worth, Tex., leaving in 1956 to join the Marine Corps. He was dishonorably discharged in 1959, and went to the Soviet Union, returning in 1962 with his Russian wife and small daughter. In Dallas, Tex., he worked at the Texas State School Book Depository; it was from this building that the shots that killed Pres. Kennedy were thought to have been fired. Following the assassination, Oswald was captured after shooting a police officer. On November 24, 1963, in full view of the television audience, he was shot and killed, while in police custody, by Jack Ruby. The *Warren Report* (1965), a record of the hearings of the investigative committee appointed by Pres. Johnson, concluded that Oswald alone was guilty. These findings have been strongly criticized.

Otis, Elisha Graves (1811–1861), American inventor of the safety elevator, born in Halifax, Vt. In 1852 he invented a safety device to prevent an elevator from falling, even though its cables broke. Two years later, he demonstrated his new elevator in New York City. Otis' safety elevator made practical the erection of tall buildings.

Otis, James (1725–1783), American patriot whose oratory and writings helped strengthen the cause of American colonists against the British. Born in West Barnstable, Mass., he studied law, became a leader of the Boston bar, and in 1760 was appointed advocate general by British authority. When the British demanded warrants for the arrest of smugglers among the colonists, he refused to issue them and resigned his post. Thereafter, he was prominent in resisting the revenue acts. A head wound received during a brawl with revenue officers in 1769 left him mentally incapacitated. His fame rests chiefly on *The Rights of the British Colonies Asserted and Proved*, published in 1764.

Otto I, called **Otto the Great** (912–973), Holy Roman emperor (962–973). The son of Henry I, he was crowned king of Germany in 936 and spent some years subduing his dissatisfied nobles—the Bohemians, Danes, and Wends. In 955 he defeated the Magyars. While in Italy to quell disturbances, he was crowned Holy Roman emperor by Pope John XII. Later Otto asserted the superiority of the civil over the papal authority by deposing John XII and installing Leo VIII in the papal chair.

Otto II (955–983), Holy Roman emperor (973–983), son of Otto I. His reign began peacefully, but he was soon embroiled in wars with nearby rulers of Bavaria, Lorraine, and Bohemia, whom he defeated. He consolidated his power in Italy but met defeat at the hands of the Greeks.

Otto III (980–1002), Holy Roman emperor (996–1002), son of Otto II. He was crowned king of Germany at the age of three and ruled during his minority through his maternal relatives. After becoming emperor in his own right he conquered rebellious portions of Italy and supplanted Pope Gregory V with Sylvester II. His ambition was to make Rome his great capital, but the Romans rose against him and he fled to Ravenna, where he died.

Ovid, Latin name **Publius Ovidius Naso** (43 B.C.–c.17 A.D.), one of the finest and most influential of the Roman poets. As a member of a noble family, he was educated to serve in the Roman government, but soon left public life to devote himself to poetry. He became a favorite of Emperor Augustus, but in 8 A.D. he was banished, for unknown reasons, to Tomis on the Black Sea, where he spent the rest of his life. His masterpiece, *Metamorphoses*, a long poem of almost 12,000 lines, describes all the changes that people and things had undergone from the beginning of the world until the time of Julius Caesar. Ovid is also at his best in *The Art of Love*, a poem in three books exploring amatory relations.

Owen, Robert (1771–1858), British social reformer and founder of socialist communities. Born in Wales, he started to work when he was 10; at 19 he was manager of a cotton mill and at 28 was part owner. He set up a paternal rule over his employees, something unheard of in the British factory system, demanding that his workmen live temperate and orderly lives. He came to the U.S. in 1824 and tried to found a socialist society at New Harmony, Ind., but the scheme failed. In 1828 Owen returned to England, where he again tried to run experimental communities on cooperative lines. He lost his wealth and devoted the rest of his life to socialist, spiritualist, and secularist affairs.

P

Paderewski, Ignace Jan (1860–1941), Polish pianist, composer, and statesman. He studied music in Warsaw, Berlin, and Vienna, where he made his debut in 1887. He soon became a virtuoso, world-famous for his highly personal interpretations. During World War I he organized a relief fund for Polish sufferers and formed a corps of Polish volunteers. He helped to establish the Polish Republic (1918–19), and became its first premier and foreign minister in 1919. He was Poland's representative to the League of Nations (1920). In 1922 he abandoned politics and returned to the concert stage. In 1937, from his retirement in Switzerland he sent a message to Poland decrying dictators and preaching democracy. In 1936 he starred in a British film, *The Moonlight Sonata*.

Paganini, Niccolò (1782–1840), Italian violinist and composer who revolutionized the technique of playing the violin. He first performed in public at the age of 11 and thereafter gave recitals in all the principal cities of Europe. His performances were so successful that he amassed a fortune before he retired in 1835. A romantic, flamboyant figure on the concert stage, he specialized in playing 24 caprices, which he had composed. Extremely difficult to play, these pieces demanded a new approach to the violin and had a considerable influence on later violinists.

Page, Thomas Nelson (1853–1922), American writer and diplomat, noted for his stories of the South before the Civil War. Born in Hanover County, Va., he was educated at the University of Virginia and practiced law in Richmond. In 1884 he published his first story, *Marse Chan*, in Negro dialect, and then devoted himself chiefly to literature. In the story collections *In Ole Virginia* (1887) and *Bred in the Bone* (1904), Page presents a detailed, though idealized, picture of Southern life. Much in the same vein are the essays and sketches in *The Old South* (1892) and *Social Life in Old Virginia* (1897). Page also wrote children's stories, poems in dialect, and a biography of Robert E. Lee. He was Pres. Woodrow Wilson's ambassador to Italy (1913–1919).

Pagnol, Marcel (1895–), French film writer, director, and producer. He gained early prominence as a playwright with *The Merchants of Glory* (1925), *Jazz* (1926), and *Topaz* (1928), all satirizing contemporary French society. He later turned to motion pictures and, as a writer and director, scored hits with *The Baker's Wife* (1938) and *The Well-Digger's Daughter* (1940). In 1946 he was elected to the French Academy, the first film personality to be so honored. Returning to the theater, Pagnol wrote and produced *Judas* (1955) and *Fabien* (1956), and several other popular plays.

Paine, Thomas (1737–1809), American patriot and writer who had a profound influence on public thinking before and during the Revolutionary War. Born in Thetford, England, he came to America in 1774 and joined the staff of the *Pennsylvania Magazine* in Philadelphia. He took up the colonists' cause and published a pamphlet, *Common Sense* (1776), which was widely acclaimed and gave impetus to the drive for independence. For his series of treatises called *The Crisis* (1777–1783), Congress voted him $3,000, and the State of New York gave him 300 acres of land. He went to England and France, where his literary efforts were less successful. On the appearance of Edmund Burke's *Reflections on the French Revolution*, Paine wrote a fierce vindication of the Revolution, *The Rights of Man* (1791–1792). His radical opinions forced him to flee England in 1792. He went to France and became a member of the National Convention, but refused to support the excessive radicalism of the Jacobin party and was imprisoned. The attack on the Bible in his *Age of Reason* (three parts, 1794–1807) practically caused him to be ostracized on his return to the United States in 1802.

LIBRARY OF CONGRESS

TOM PAINE, Revolutionary pamphleteer.

Palestrina, Giovanni Pierluigi da (1526–1594), Italian composer whose church music, composed in medieval modes, represents the highest achievement of its kind. He first came to Rome in 1536, where he studied music and became a protégé of Pope Julius III. Afterwards he held several church posts as composer and music master. His numerous works include more than 250 motets, 15 books of masses, and many hymns, lamentations, and madrigals.

Palgrave, Francis Turner (1824–1897), English poet and critic whose anthology, *Golden Treasury of the Best Songs and Lyrical Poems in the English Language* (1861; second series 1897), has been a popular favorite. After graduating from Oxford, where he was later (1885–1895) professor of poetry, he held various posts in the government education office, at the same time writing poetry and literary criticism. But his best-remembered work is the *Golden Treasury*, a discriminating selection of English poems, which has gone through numerous editions.

Palma, Jacopo, called **Palma Vecchio** or **Il Vecchio** (the Elder) (c.1480–1528), Venetian painter. Working in the tradition of Giovanni Bellini and Giorgione, he specialized in groups of religious figures in idyllic settings. His paintings, while overshadowed by those of his contemporary Titian, are noted for their brilliant coloring and lighting.

Palmerston, 3d Viscount, born **Henry John Temple** (1784–1865), English statesman who was prime minister for most of the period from 1855 to 1865. He entered Parliament in 1807 and at once became junior lord of the admiralty. For 20 years after 1811 he represented Cambridge University in Parliament. He began a long career as foreign secretary in 1830 and was widely influential in European political affairs. At various times he was extremely unpopular, even in his own country, and was dismissed in 1851 because of his unofficial approval of the coup d'état that put Napoleon III on the French throne. He became home secretary in 1852 and prime minister in 1855; during his term he carried on the Crimean War. His administration fell in 1858, but he was returned to office in 1859, and remained in power until his death.

Pandit, Madame **Vijaya Lakshmi** (1900–), sister of Jawaharlal Nehru who, before and after Indian independence, held a number of important posts. In 1937 she became India's first woman minister in its Congress Cabinet of the United Provinces. When India won its independence in 1947, Madame Pandit was appointed ambassador to Moscow, and from 1949 to 1951 she was ambassador to the U.S. and Mexico. She was a member of the Indian Parliament (1952–1954) and was president of the United Nations General Assembly in 1953 and 1954, the first woman to hold this office. After serving in diplomatic posts in England, Ireland, and Spain, she returned to the UN as head of India's delegation to the General Assembly.

Paolo Veronese. See *Veronese, Paolo*.

Papini, Giovanni (1881–1956), Italian author whose *Storia di Cristo* (*Life of Christ*, 1921) achieved immense popularity. A professional journalist, he was an influential literary critic and historian, noted for his studies of Italian culture. At first he was an atheist, but in 1920 was converted to Roman Catholicism. Two years later his best-known work appeared.

Paracelsus, Philippus Aureolus, real name **Theophrastus Bombastus von Hohenheim** (c.1493–1541), Swiss alchemist and physician whose theories attracted wide attention in his time. At 16 he entered

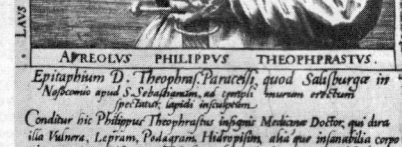

NEW YORK PUBLIC LIBRARY

TWO DOCTORS of the sixteenth century: Ambroise Paré (*left*) and Paracelsus (*right*).

Basel University, where he studied alchemy and chemistry, and learned the properties of metals and minerals at the mines in the Tirol. He became a famous doctor and lectured on medicine at Basel. Paracelsus disproved many accepted medical theories, taught the use of specific remedies instead of indiscriminate bleeding and purging, and introduced many new medicines. However, much of his work was colored by his beliefs in magic and alchemy. Not more than a tenth of the 250 works attributed to him are genuinely his, according to critics. The others are supposed to have been written by his followers, known as the Paracelsists.

Paré, Ambroise (c.1517–1590), French surgeon, noted for his contributions to general surgery. In 1529 he went to Paris, became a hospital attendant, and later served as army surgeon in several wars. He was the first to use a ligature of the arteries instead of cauterization in amputations and led surgeons away from treating wounds with boiling oil. He was surgeon to Henry II, Francis II, Charles IX, and Henry III.

Paris, Comte de, Louis Philippe Albert d' Orléans (1838–1894), grandson of King Louis Philippe who became a claimant to the French throne. He was born in Paris and educated in England. During the American Civil War, he and his brother were attached to the staff of Gen. George B. McClellan and fought in several battles. They returned to France when relations between the United States and France became strained over Mexico. As a claimant to the French crown, he was expelled from France in 1886 and went to England, where he published an eight-volume history of the American Civil War (1874–1889).

Parker, Dorothy Rothschild (1893–1967), American writer, famed for her satirical verse and witty, sophisticated short stories. Born in West End, N.J., she was drama critic for *Vanity Fair* and book reviewer for *The New Yorker*. Many of her poems and stories were first published in *The New Yorker*. Among her collected poems are *Enough Rope* (1926), *Sunset Gun* (1928), *Death and Taxes* (1931), and *Not So Deep as a Well* (1936). Her collected short stories include *Laments for the Living* (1930), *After Such Pleasures* (1933), and *Here Lies* (1939). She died June 7, 1967 in New York City.

Parkinson, James (1755–1824), English surgeon and paleontologist who first described the disease that bears his name. In 1812 he published the first article on appendicitis. He was also the first to discover that perforation is the cause of death in appendicitis. In 1813 he described what is now known as Parkinson's disease (*paralysis agitans*), a chronic disorder of the central nervous system. In addition to several medical works, he also wrote *Organic Remains of a Former World* (3 vols., 1804–1811).

Parkman, Francis (1823–1893), American historian, famed for his writings on pre-Revolutionary America. Born in Boston, he graduated from Harvard (1844), and studied law briefly before devoting himself to historical literature. Fascinated by the wilderness, he lived for some time among the Indians of the Rocky Mountains, gaining first-hand experience for such works as *The Conspiracy of Pontiac* (2 vols., 1851) and *The California and Oregon Trail* (later called *The Oregon Trail*, 1849). Parkman's masterwork was the seven-volume history *France and England in the New World*, published between 1865 and 1892.

Parmenides (c.5th century B.C.), Greek philosopher, born in Elea, Italy, who was the leader of the Eleatic school of philosophy. Parmenides is often considered the first metaphysical philosopher, since those who preceded him had been concerned chiefly with physical processes. In his poem *Nature*, Parmenides emphasized abstract thought as the best approach to truth and reality. Only fragments of his work are extant.

Parnell, Charles Stewart (1846–1891), Irish political leader who led in the struggle for Irish self-government. Educated at Cambridge, he returned to Ireland and became a leader in the Home Rule party. He was elected to the House of Commons in 1875, where he and his party gained influence by obstructing parliamentary business. In 1887 the London *Times* accused Parnell and his followers of certain crimes committed in Ireland. A special commission was appointed to examine the charges; Parnell was acquitted and sued the *Times* for libel. He was given about $25,000 in damages. Entanglement in a divorce case led to his withdrawal into private life and to a split in the Irish party.

Parry, Sir William Edward (1790–1855), English explorer who attempted to find a Northwest Passage in the Arctic. He joined the navy at 13, and made his first trip to the Arctic when he was 20. In 1819 and again in 1821 and 1824, he tried to find a Northwest Passage. In 1827 he made an unsuccessful attempt to reach the North Pole by going north of Spitsbergen and reached an unprecedented latitude of 82°45'. In 1829 he was knighted for his achievements. In 1852 he retired from the navy with the rank of rear admiral.

Parsons, William Barclay (1859–1932), American civil engineer who designed and supervised the construction of New York City's subway system. Born in New York and educated at Columbia University, he first won recognition in China by surveying for a railroad line that went 1,000 miles inland from Canton. Returning to New York, from 1894 to 1904 he designed and constructed the East River tunnels and the first units of the subway system. Later, Pres. Theodore Roosevelt appointed him a member of the commission that planned the construction of the Panama Canal. He wrote *Robert Fulton and the Submarine* (1922).

Pascal, Blaise (1623–1662), French scientist and religious philosopher. He was an extraordinary mathematician; before he was 17, he had written a work on conic sections. At 18 he invented a calculating machine. Pascal contributed a number of theories and methods to mathematics and aided in the development of differential calculus. He worked out the physical principle known as *Pascal's Law*, which covers the transmission of pressure by an enclosed liquid. It is the basic principle of most hydraulic machinery, such as presses and elevators.

He took great interest in the religious doctrines of the Jansenists, became identified with them and came to their defense in his famous *Les Provinciales* (1656–1657). Pascal's *Pensées*, a collection of thoughts on philosophical, religious, and social themes, has been regarded as a masterpiece.

Passos, John Dos. See *Dos Passos, John*.

Pasternak, Boris Leonidovich (1890–1960), Russian poet and novelist who won the Nobel Prize for literature in 1958. Born in Moscow, he joined the Soviet civil service after the 1918 revolution. After achieving renown as a poet, he added to his reputation as a translator of Keats, Shelley, Shakespeare, and Goethe. His novel *Doctor Zhivago*, turned down by Soviet authorities in 1956 but published in Italian in 1957 and in English in 1958, was instrumental in his being awarded the Nobel Prize. At first he accepted the prize, but later declined under pressure from Soviet's political circles. The book contains Pasternak's most eloquent plea for freedom of the human spirit.

Pasteur, Louis (1822–1895), French chemist who is regarded as the founder of the modern science of bacteriology. Born in Dôle, he was educated at the École Normale in Paris, and taught physics and chemistry at Dijon, Strasbourg, and Lille. At Lille he made his famous discovery that souring of wine was caused by living microorganisms, and went on to study the whole subject of fermentation. He then taught and carried on his research in Paris. In the years that followed he studied and successfully combated fowl cholera, anthrax, and the contagious silkworm disease. He learned to treat many diseases by the use of vaccines. He made an extensive study of hydrophobia; the Pasteur Institute was founded in 1888 to put into practice Pasteur's method of vaccination against that disease. Thanks to his experiments, prophylactic treatment of diphtheria, tubercular disease, yellow fever, cholera, and plague has been made possible. The principle of milk pasteurization, named for him, is based upon his discoveries.

Patanjali (c.2d century B.C.), ancient Indian scholar and grammarian. Hindu scholars generally identify him as the founder of Yoga and claim that he was the first writer to explain Yoga doctrines, although some scholars contend that the philosopher of Yoga was someone else who lived in the fourth century A.D. Among the works attributed to him are treatises on medicine, grammar, music, and metrics, as well as philosophy.

Pater, Walter Horatio (1839–1894), English essayist noted for his works on classical and Renaissance art and civilization. Born near London and educated at Oxford, he began his literary career with a series of articles contributed to various journals. His *Studies in the History of the Renaissance* (1873) reveals the work of a penetrating critic with a highly polished prose style. His other writings include *Marius the Epicurean* (1885), *Imaginary Portraits* (1887), and *Plato and Platonism* (1893).

Patrick, Saint, original name Sucat (c.389–c.461), patron saint of Ireland. Born in England, he was the son of a deacon. When Patrick was 16 years old, he was captured by Irish raiders, and after being enslaved for six years he escaped to the Continent and studied at Tours, France. He declared that a vision urged him to return to Ireland as a missionary, which he did in the year 432. Then for more than 60 years he worked for the physical and spiritual welfare of the islanders. Pope Celestine I consecrated him bishop, entrusting him with Ireland's conversion. He established missionary settlements in Armagh and Down. Downpatrick remains the great shrine of St. Patrick. His feast day is March 17, an Irish holiday the world over.

Patton, George Smith, Jr. (1885–1945), American general famed for his armored tank attacks during World War II. Born in San Gabriel, Calif., he graduated from West Point in 1909. During World War I he was the first man to command the newly-formed tank corps of the U.S. army. In World War II Patton commanded American forces in Morocco, and in 1943 at El Guettar, he won the first major American victory over the Nazis. After this, he led successful campaigns through northern Africa and Sicily. Patton won further fame as the leader of the Third Army in Europe. His memoirs, *War As I Knew It*, were published in 1947.

Pauker, Ana (1890–1960), Rumanian Communist leader who was the most powerful figure in her country after World War II. Born in Moldavia, she studied medicine but later entered politics. In 1921 she joined the Communist party and fled to Switzerland to avoid arrest. She was imprisoned from 1936 to 1944, however. In 1944 she helped organize the Communist-sponsored National Democratic Front, and in 1947, the Cominform (Communist Information Bureau). Pauker was Romania's minister of foreign affairs from 1947 to 1952, when she was removed from office in a purge.

Paul I (1754–1801), emperor of Russia (1796–1801), the son of Peter III and Catherine the Great. He was half insane, and his condition grew worse as he became older. Nevertheless, he was crowned in 1796, and proved to be extremely cruel and autocratic. His foreign policies were unpredictable: after joining a coalition against Napoleon, he then joined Napoleon in war against England. His conduct finally became unbearable; members of the court demanded his abdication and killed him when he refused.

Paul I (1901–1964), king of Greece (1947–1964). His father was Constantine I, who was forced twice to abdicate by powerful republican forces (1917, 1922). Born in Athens and educated at the Greek Naval Academy, Paul spent most of his early life abroad. He returned to Greece in 1935 when his brother George II was restored to the throne after a 12-year abdication. Paul was made a crown prince and in 1938 married Princess Frederika of Germany. The royal family was in exile during World War II and returned after the liberation of Greece. When George died in 1947, Paul succeeded him under a new constitutional government. He was regarded as an able monarch who aided Greece's postwar development by establishing good relations with the West, securing American financial and technical aid, and suppressing communism at home.

Paul III, born **Alessandro Farnese** (1468–1549), Roman Catholic pope (1534–1549). In the 15-year period preceding Paul's pontificate, the Protestant Reformation had spread throughout northern Europe and threatened to destroy Catholicism. With Pope Paul began the Catholic Counter Reformation, a movement designed to reform the Church from within and to check the spread of heresy. He convened the Council of Trent and approved the formation of the Society of Jesus (Jesuits) by Ignatius Loyola. A great patron of the arts, he commissioned Michelangelo to direct work on the Vatican.

Paul VI, born **Giovanni Battista Montini** (1897–), Roman Catholic cardinal who succeeded John XXIII as pope in 1963. Born in northern Italy, he became a Vatican diplomat early in his career. After serving in a number of important posts, he was created a cardinal in 1958. Elevated to the pontificate on June 21, 1963, he quickly showed his interest in international affairs by traveling to India and the Holy Land. In 1965 he came to New York to address the United Nations in a plea for world peace, thus becoming the first pope ever to set foot on American soil. Pope Paul led the 21st Ecumenical council, opened by Pope John in 1962, to a number of resolutions concerning interfaith relations.

CULVER

LOUIS PASTEUR, French bacteriologist.

Pauling, Linus Carl (1901–), American chemist and pacifist leader. One of the world's leading chemists, he was among the first to apply the laws of quantum mechanics to chemistry. An expert on molecular structure, he was awarded the Nobel Prize (1954) for demonstrating how proteins are linked with other molecules. This work also contributed importantly to the understanding of the molecular structure of the genes that determine heredity.

For many years, Pauling led a worldwide movement to ban nuclear testing in the atmosphere, on the ground that increased radiation would have harmful genetic effects. For this and his efforts on behalf of world peace, he was awarded the Nobel Peace Prize (1962).

Born in Portland, Ore., Pauling graduated from Oregon State College and did advanced study at the California Institute of Technology, where (since 1927) he has been a professor of chemistry.

Pausanias (2d century A.D.), Greek traveler and geographer. Thought to be a native of Lydia (in Asia Minor), he traveled widely through the known world before coming to Greece. His *Description of Greece* is one of the most valuable sources of information on the art, history, legends, religion, and topography of ancient Greece.

Pavlov, Ivan Petrovich (1849–1936), Russian physiologist, famous for his researches on conditioned reflexes and glandular functions. He studied and practiced medicine, and then became director of the Institute for Experimental Medicine at St. Petersburg (Leningrad). He is best known for his study of the digestive organs, for which he received the Nobel Prize for medicine in 1904, and for his research in blood circulation and in conditioned reflexes.

Pavlova, Anna (1881–1931), Russian ballerina, the most celebrated dancer of her time. At 10 she entered the Imperial Ballet School in St. Petersburg, and eventually was named prima ballerina. In 1910 she visited London and New York, where she scored sensational triumphs. Later she formed her own ballet company and toured the world for many years until her death. Pavlova's repertory consisted mainly of classical ballets. Her most famous dance was *The Dying Swan*, set to the music of Saint-Saëns.

Peabody, Elizabeth Palmer (1804–1894), American educator who opened the first kindergarten in the U.S. Born in Billerica, Mass., she was educated at a private school and began teaching at the age of 16. In 1860 she opened her first kindergarten school in Boston, and set up a training school for kindergarten teachers. She was also prominent in the Transcendentalist movement, and publisher of its organ, the *Dial*. She was the sister-in-law of Nathaniel Hawthorne and Horace Mann.

Peabody, George (1795–1869), American merchant who was one of the first great philanthropists in the U.S. Born in South Danvers, Mass., he made a fortune in dry goods and as a banker and broker. Among the institutions he founded and endowed are the Peabody Institute in Baltimore and the Peabody Museum at Yale.

Peale, Norman Vincent (1898–), American Methodist Episcopal clergyman, widely known for his best-selling inspirational book, *The Power of Positive Thinking* (1952), which sets forth a message of personal fulfillment through self-confidence, initiative, and optimism. Born in Bowersville, Ohio, Dr. Peale graduated from Ohio Wesleyan University (1920), received divinity degrees from Boston and Syracuse universities, and was ordained a minister in 1922. He held pastorates in Berkeley, R.I., Brooklyn, N.Y., and Syracuse, and since 1932 has been pastor of Marble Collegiate Reformed Church in New York. An energetic, forthright speaker and writer, Dr. Peale has been known to millions of Americans via radio, television, and newspaper columns. His other writings include *Stay Alive All Your Life* (1957) and *Sin, Sex, and Self-Control* (1965).

Pearson, Lester Bowles (1897–), Canadian statesman who won the Nobel Peace Prize in 1957 and was elected prime minister of Canada in 1963. He was born in Toronto and educated there and at Oxford. In 1928 he was appointed undersecretary of state for external affairs, and held several other diplomatic posts. He served as ambassador to the U.S. in 1945–1946, and served another two years as undersecretary of state for external affairs. In 1948 he entered the House of Commons as a Liberal and served as secretary of state for external affairs until 1957. In that year he received the Nobel Peace Prize for his work in helping to resolve the Suez Canal crisis of 1956. As the Liberal candidate for prime minister, he won the election of April, 1963.

Peary, Robert Edwin (1856–1920), American explorer who discovered the North Pole on April 7, 1909. Born in Cresson, Pa., he graduated from Bowdoin College and in 1881 entered the Navy as a civil engineer. A few years later he began a series of Arctic explorations that culminated, on the eighth expedition, in his reaching the North Pole. He wrote several books about his expeditions, notably *Northward Over the Great Ice, Nearest the Pole*, and *The North Pole*.

Pedro I, Dom, in full Dom **Antonio Pedro de Alcántara Bourbon** (1798–1834), first emperor of Brazil, son of John VI of Portugal. As a boy he went with his parents to Brazil. When his father returned to Portugal, Pedro remained as regent in Brazil. The Portuguese legislature tried to transform the country into a Portuguese colony, but the Brazilians sought independence, and Pedro was declared emperor in 1822. He became unpopular and in 1831 was forced to abdicate in favor of his son Pedro II.

Pedro II Dom, in full Dom **Pedro de Alcántara** (1825–1891), second emperor of Brazil, son of Pedro I. Pedro was proclaimed emperor in 1831 at the age of six when his father abdicated. However, he was not crowned until he was 16. For about 30 years he had to contend with rebellions. In 1838 slavery was abolished, largely through his efforts. He then left Brazil on a visit to Europe and the United States and on his return faced a revolution that overturned the empire. Pedro received a grant of money from the revolutionary government and spent the rest of his life in Portugal.

Peel, Sir **Robert** (1788–1850), British statesman who was three times prime minister of England. He entered Parliament at the age of 21 and held office as secretary for Ireland when he was 24. In 1822 he became home secretary and in this capacity formed a new police force in England, known to this day as *Bobbies* and as *Peelers*. In 1833 he became leader of the Conservative opposition in Parliament and was elected prime minister in 1834 and again in 1839. Elected a third time in 1841, he held office for five years.

Peel introduced and passed the Bank Charter Act, which still regulates England's currency; repealed the penal laws against Roman Catholics (1829); and repealed the Corn Laws (1846) in spite of opposition.

Penn, William (1644–1718), English Quaker who founded Pennsylvania. As a youth, he was frequently imprisoned for his Quaker beliefs. In 1670 his father died, and some years later Penn settled his father's claim against the government by accepting a large tract of land in America, west of the Delaware River and north of Maryland. It was called "Pennsylvania" in the royal patent Penn resolved to form this territory into a commonwealth based upon religious tolerance. He arrived in Delaware Bay in 1682 and signed a treaty with the Indians. In the next year he founded Philadelphia, intending it to be what the name denotes, a "City of Brotherly Love." In 1684 he returned to England, where he was again persecuted for his religious views. Penn went to debtor's prison rather than pay the claims of a dishonest steward. After his death his son **Thomas Penn** (1702–1775) represented him in Philadelphia. Many of William Penn's books, notably *The Cause of Liberty of Conscience*, were written in prison.

Pepys, Samuel (1633–1703), English public official and diarist. His diaries, published after his death, provide a valuable record of seventeenth-century England. Born in London and educated at Cambridge, he held several important government posts and sat in Parliament as secretary of the admiralty. In 1684 he became president of the Royal Society. From 1659 to 1669 he kept his famous *Diary*. His detailed description of his own daily life and of important events of the day make interesting reading and are highly important as history. The *Diary* (1825) was written in shorthand. John Smith began translating it in 1819.

Percy, Sir **Henry,** called **Hotspur** (1364–1403), eldest son of the 1st earl of Northumberland. With his father, he placed Henry IV on the throne in 1399 and helped suppress the Scots in the north, capturing the earl of Douglas in 1402. When Henry IV asked that Douglas be turned over to him, Percy countered with a proposal to ransom his brother-in-law, Sir Edmund de Mortimer, which the king refused. After this quarrel, Percy and his father led a revolt against the king, which ended when Percy was killed at the battle of Shrewsbury. Shakespeare portrayed Percy as a hot-tempered soldier in his play *Henry IV* (Part I).

Perelman, Sidney Joseph, known as **S. J. Perelman** (1904–), American writer, a leading humorist in contemporary literature. Born in Brooklyn, N.Y., he graduated from Brown University in 1925, and began writing for humor magazines. His first book, *Dawn Ginsbergh's Revenge* (1929), was a howling success. His humorous sketches in the *New Yorker* magazine have delighted readers since 1934. Perelman's style, unique among humorists, depends for its effects on a whimsical combination of erudite diction, puns, clichés, and unexpected turns, by which he examines matters of current interest and indicates their absurdities. Notable among his books are *Strictly from Hunger* (1937), *Acres and Pains* (1947), *Westward Ha!* (1948), *The Swiss Family Perelman* (1950), *The Ill-Tempered Clavichord* (1952), and *The Road to Miltown* (1957). With Ogden Nash, he wrote the lyrics for the musical *One Touch of Venus* (1943). In 1956 he won an Academy Award for his script for the film *Around the World in Eighty Days.*

Pergolesi, Giovanni Battista (1710–1736), Italian composer, noted for his comic operas. In his short life he composed several serious and comic operas, as well as sacred vocal pieces and chamber music. His master work was the comic opera *La Serva Padrona* (1733), which became the model for future comic operas. He is also remembered for his *Stabat Mater* for voices and strings.

Periander (d.585 B.C.), ruler of ancient Corinth (625–585 B.C.). Under his reign, Corinth reached its height of power and prosperity. He fostered the development of commerce and industry, and established several colonies in other parts of Greece. A patron of the arts, Periander was considered one of the seven sages of Greece.

Pericles (c.495–429 B.C.), Greek statesman who guided Athens to its highest development in arts and science, his time being known as the Age of Pericles. As a young man, he took an active part in public affairs, usually siding with the majority against the aristocracy. About 460, he became prominent in Athens, and for the remainder of his life worked to make Athens a great state famous for its culture and beauty. His friend Phidias, the great sculptor, was commissioned to adorn Athens. As rapidly as the city could afford them, Pericles ordered the building of the Parthenon, the Propylaea, and other famous structures. He distinguished himself as a general and a statesman, notably in his recovery of the rebellious island of Euboea and by subduing Samos. In the Peloponnesian War with Sparta most of his work was undone, and he lost much of his standing in Athens, although he was still in power when he died.

Perkins, Frances (1882–1965), American public official who, as secretary of labor (1933–1945), was the first woman member of a president's cabinet. Born in Boston, Mass., she was educated at Mount Holyoke College and Columbia University, taught in a girls' school near Chicago, and studied social work under Jane Addams. In 1917 she became executive director of the New York Council of Organizations for War Service. In 1923 Gov. Alfred E. Smith appointed her to the N.Y. State Industrial Commission, and she served as its chairman from 1926 to 1929, when she was named labor commissioner of New York State by Gov. Franklin D. Roosevelt. When Roosevelt was elected president, he appointed her secretary of labor. She later served as a member of the U.S. Civil Service Commission. She wrote *The Roosevelt I Knew.*

Perón, Juan Domingo (1896–), president and virtual dictator of Argentina from 1946 to 1955. He entered military service in 1913, and spent 30 years in the army, rising to the rank of colonel. He was one of the leaders of the revolution of 1943 that overthrew the Argentine government. After a brief term as vice-president in the new government, he was elected president and assumed office in 1946. A new constitution was adopted that year, giving Perón the right to succeed himself in 1952 for another six-year period. Perón exercised dictatorial powers, and though he did much to improve conditions for the working classes, his suppression of constitutional liberties and other excesses led to a military coup in 1955. He was deposed and forced into exile.

Perry, Matthew Calbraith (1794–1858), American naval officer who in 1854 negotiated the first commercial treaty between Japan and the U.S. Born in Newport, R.I., he entered the navy at 15. From 1833 to 1843 he was construction superintendent of steam-driven naval vessels. After service in the Mexican War, he was put in command of an expedition to Japan (1852), where his show of naval force impressed the Japanese government. Two years later, he successfully negotiated the treaty he sought. An authority on the Far East, Perry urged the U.S. to play a more active role in the Orient.

Perry, Oliver Hazard (1785–1819), American naval officer who defeated the British in the battle of Lake Erie in the War of 1812. Born in South Kingston, R.I., he entered the navy at 14 as a midshipman. During the War of 1812, as commander of naval forces on Lake Erie, he routed the British, and dispatched the now-famous report, "We have met the enemy and they are ours." In 1819 Perry commanded an expedition to Colombia. While sailing up the Orinoco River in Venezuela, he contracted yellow fever and died.

Pershing, John Joseph (1860–1948), American army commander of the American Expeditionary Force during World War I. Born in Linn County, Mo., and a graduate of West Point, he fought against the Apaches and the Sioux during the 1880's and 1890's. He also served in the Spanish-American War, and in 1902 he commanded an expedition against the Moros in the Philippines. In 1914 he was placed in command of American troops on the Mexican border. When the U.S. entered World War I, he was appointed commander in chief of American forces and made a general (the fourth person since Washington to hold this rank). As army chief of staff (1921–1925), he built the framework for the modern army. In recognition of his achievements, Congress created for him the rank of general of the armies, making him the highest ranking officer in American history up to that time.

Perugino, Il, born **Pietro Vannucci** (1450–1523), Italian painter who was a leader of the Umbrian school. Born near Perugia (whence his name), he became a favorite of Pope Sixtus IV, who commissioned him to decorate parts of the Sistine Chapel. During his career, Perugino painted many frescos in Rome, Florence, and Perugia, and taught many young artists his techniques. Raphael was one of his students.

Peruzzi, Baldassare (1481–1536), Italian architect and painter. In 1520 he was appointed by Pope Leo X to succeed Raphael as architect of St. Peter's. After the sack of Rome in 1527, he became chief architect of Siena. He later returned to Rome, where he designed his best-known building, the Palazzo Massimi alle Colonne. Notable among his other major buildings are the Villa Farnesina and the Palazzo Ossoli.

Pestalozzi, Johann Heinrich (1746–1827), Swiss educator whose teaching methods have been widely used in the training of children. Born in Zurich, he became a champion of social reform, and in 1774 he established on his estate a school for waifs and strays. Governing his educational system was the idea that studies should be related to actual experience and concrete objects. Hence, he pioneered such teaching aids as field trips, the making of models, and the collection of specimens. In 1805 he founded his famous boarding school at Yverdon. Almost all of his methods have been adopted by European and American schools. Pestalozzi is often considered the father of modern elementary education.

Pétain, Henri Philippe (1856–1951), French general, a hero of World War I, who was chief of state of France during the German occupation in World War II. A colonel at the outbreak of World War I, he was given command of an army corps in 1914. Two years later, he became famous as the man who stopped the Germans at Verdun. In 1917 he became chief of the general staff and later was made commander in chief of the French armies under Gen. Ferdinand Foch, the Allied commander. In 1918 he was created marshal of France and served in several important posts between world wars. After the Germans defeated France in 1940, he became chief of state of the Vichy government, a post he held until France was liberated. After the war, he was tried for treason by the French government and sentenced to death, but his sentence was commuted to life imprisonment.

Peter I, Russian name **Pëtr Alekseevich,** called **Peter the Great** (1672–1725), czar of Russia (1682–1725). Under his rule, Russia became a European nation. In 1682 he succeeded Ivan, his feeble-minded half brother. Peter's mother, widow of the former Czar Alexius, served as regent for him. His half sister Sophia was full sister of Ivan and another brother, Feodor; she wanted Feodor to be co-ruler with Peter. Feodor died in 1682, and Ivan in turn claimed equal rights with Peter. Both brothers were crowned, but in 1689 Peter forced Sophia into a convent. After that he was virtually sole ruler, though outwardly the dual reign of Peter and Ivan was recognized until Ivan's death in 1696.

Peter was determined to raise his country out of barbarism and place it in the ranks of civilized nations. He traveled in Holland and England (1796–1798), worked in shipyards and wherever he might learn anything he could turn to his advantage. He used that information when he returned to Russia. Young Russian nobles were obliged to travel for study and observation; schools of navigation were founded; agriculture was improved. Peter established factories, distributed metallurgists through the mining districts of Russia and built roads and canals.

Peter created a navy and gave Russia a seaboard. In 1696 he won a war against Turkey, but three years later he was defeated at Narva by Charles XII of Sweden. He married Catherine, the wife of a Swedish soldier.

In 1703 he laid the foundation of St. Petersburg, made it the capital and established an academy of sciences. He abolished or altered laws and institutions that in any way interfered with his projects. He repudiated Catherine on the ground that she conspired against him in favor of his son Alexis, who opposed Peter's reorganization of the Russian Church. Peter then forced Alexis to renounce his right to succession and condemned him to death. Alexis died suddenly before sentence could be carried out. After Peter's death, Catherine was crowned empress of Russia.

Peter II (1923–), last king of Yugoslavia (1934–1945) before it became a republic. He succeeded his father, Peter I, who was assassinated at Marseilles, and ruled under the regency of his uncle, Prince Paul. Peter assumed full sovereignty after Prince Paul was overthrown in 1941 for signing a pact with the Axis powers. When the Germans invaded Yugoslavia, he fled to England, where he ruled in exile. Yugoslavia became a republic in November, 1945, and since that time Peter has been in exile.

Peter the Hermit (c.1050–1115), medieval preacher whose oratory persuaded pilgrims to join the first Crusade. Born in France, he allegedly made a pilgrimage to the Holy Land about 1093 and saw there the cruelties inflicted upon Christians by the Muslims. It has been said that upon his return he reported to Pope Urban II, who authorized him to preach for a crusade that would recover Jerusalem from the Turks. His efforts met with great success, but he played a subordinate role in the actual crusade. He spent his later years in obscurity at a monastery that he had founded in France.

Petrarch, Italian name **Francesco Petrarca** (1304–1374), Italian poet who has been called the first of the Humanists. Born in Tuscany, he later settled at Avignon, France, where he fell in love with the beautiful Laura, in whose honor he wrote the sonnets and odes that made him famous. Esteemed as a scholar, he was invited to lecture in many European cities. In 1341, he was crowned poet laureate in Rome. Petrarch wrote both in prose and in verse, but he is remembered principally for his lyrics and for the sonnets still called Petrarchan. He was one of the first Humanists, the group that renounced much of medieval culture in favor of the classics of Greek and Roman antiquity.

Phaedo or **Phaedon** (early 4th century B.C.), Greek philosopher of Elis, founder of the Elian school of philosophy. A pupil of Socrates, he also knew Plato, who named one of his dialogues after Phaedo. In the dialogue, which purports to be the imprisoned Socrates' last conversation, Phaedo debates with Socrates on the immortality of the soul. Phaedo's works are not extant.

Phidias (c.500–432 B.C.), Athenian sculptor, regarded as the greatest in ancient Greece. He became famous about 460 with his bronze group at Delphi and other statues. When Pericles came to power in Athens, he commissioned Phidias to beautify the city. Phidias supervised the building of the Parthenon and made the statue of Athena for that temple. From about 437 to 433, he worked on the statue of Zeus for the temple at Olympia, one of the Seven Wonders of the ancient world.

The chief characteristics of his work were largeness, dignity, and magnificence. All his work was marked by a certain repose; he believed that violent action cannot be represented in sculpture. His principal works contained an inner core of wood or stone; this was covered with plates of polished ivory for the parts representing flesh, and gold was used for the drapery. He was equally skilled with ivory, bronze, marble, gold, and ebony. Emperor Theodosius I took the statue of Zeus to Constantinople about 390 A.D., where it was destroyed in a fire in 475. A little remains of the outside sculptures of the Parthenon, especially the frieze (of which the Elgin marbles are a part), but it is not certain that they were all actually his own work.

Philip, called **King Philip,** born **Metacomet** (d.1676), American Indian chief who in 1670 declared war on the New England colonists. He was the second son of Massasoit, and became chief of his tribe in 1662. For several years he remained outwardly friendly toward the white settlers, but their gradual encroachments angered him. He organized an alliance of several tribes and in 1670 began "King Philip's War," in which hundreds of colonists were massacred during the next six years. Philip was finally caught and killed in Rhode Island.

Philip II (382–336 B.C), king of Macedonia (359–336 B.C.) who conquered all of Greece during his reign. Upon assuming the throne he at once set out to pacify and consolidate his kingdom and to bring all Greece under his dominion. The Amphictyonic Council, a union of Grecian states to which Athens did not belong, appointed Philip commander of their forces against the Athenians. Athens was alarmed for its safety; Demosthenes spoke his "Philippics" against the coming invader, and the city prepared to defend itself. It formed an alliance with Thebes, but Philip defeated the united force and became master of all Greece after the battle of Chaeronea (338). He ruled only two years before he was assassinated. His son succeeded him as Alexander the Great.

Philip II, known as **Philip Augustus** (1165–1223), king of France (1179–1223), remembered for his role in the Crusades and for his battles with England. In 1179 he was crowned co-ruler with his father, Louis VII, and became ruler himself after Louis' death in 1180. In 1181 he had to fight against a coalition of Flanders, Burgundy, and Champagne. By 1186 he had won out and regained control over much territory. In 1187 he attacked the English possessions in France and with the help of Richard, son of Henry II of England, won a little territory by 1189. In 1190 Philip and Richard, who had succeeded to the throne after Henry's death, set out on the Third Crusade, but they soon quarreled, and Philip returned to France in 1191.

He made war against Richard and by 1199 had lost most of the territory he had gained. After John came to the English throne, Philip opposed him, too, but with better success, for he forced John to give up Normandy, Brittany, Anjou, Maine, and Touraine. In 1214 Philip defeated an alliance between John and the Holy Roman Emperor Otto IV and thereby made France a leading power. By the end of his reign Philip had strengthened royal power at the expense of that of the nobles and had made many changes in the administration of justice and finance.

Philip II (1527–1598), king of Spain (1556–1598) at the height of its power. The son of Charles V and Isabella of Portugal, he succeeded his father in 1556 as ruler of a vast empire that included Sicily, Milan, the Netherlands, Mexico, Peru, and part of France. He regarded himself as the champion of Catholicism against Protestantism, a stance which continually subjected Spain to external pressures. In 1588 he sent the Spanish Armada to crush England. Its rout by the English navy finally broke the power of Spain.

Philip V (1683–1746), king of Spain (1700–1724; 1724–1746) who founded the Bourbon dynasty. Born at Versailles, the grandson of Louis XIV, he was titular duke of Anjou. He succeeded Charles II to the throne. During his reign, he worked chiefly to secure his rights to succeed to the French throne. It was while he was in power that Spain lost Gibraltar to the English (1704).

Phillips, Wendell (1811–1884), American orator and reformer, regarded as one of the finest speakers of his time. Born in Boston and educated at Harvard, he gave up his law practice to fight for the abolition of slavery. After the slaves were freed, he interested himself in such movements as suffrage for women, prison reform, and prohibition.

Philo, or **Philo Judaeus,** also known as **Philo of Alexandrial** (c.30 B.C.–c.40 A.D.), Jewish philosopher, noted for his application of Greek philosophy to Judaism. He spent most of his life in Alexandria where, known as the "Jewish Plato," he wrote many works seeking to reconcile the teachings of the Pentateuch with the philosophies of Plato and Aristotle.

Phocion (c.402–317 B.C.), Athenian general and statesman who rose to power during the domination of Greece by Macedonia. Recognizing Athen's weakness and Macedonia's strength, he opposed the anti-Macedonian faction in Athens. He soon became virtual ruler of Athens. When democracy

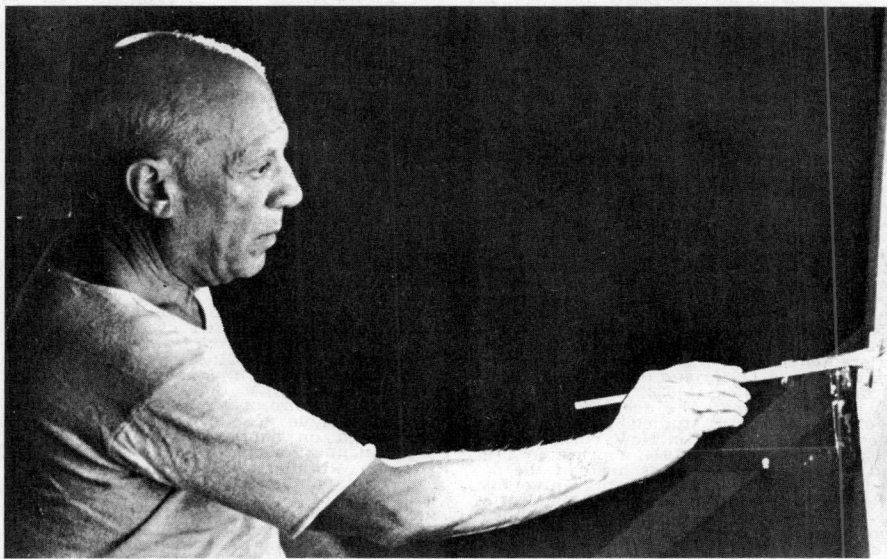

FRENCH EMBASSY PRESS AND INFORMATION

PABLO PICASSO, one of today's foremost artists, is considered the father of modern art.

was restored in 318, Phocion was forced to flee. Captured and condemned without a trial, he was forced to drink poison.

Phyfe, Duncan (c.1768–1854), American cabinetmaker whose delicate pieces of furniture are highly prized by collectors. Born in Scotland, he came to Albany, N.Y., in 1783 and became an apprentice cabinetmaker. About 1790 he moved to New York City, where he set up a furniture shop. His designs in furniture had great influence in his day and are still copied. His earlier work, before 1820, is best; he then adapted his work from that of Adam and Sheraton. Later his designs followed the Empire style and became heavy and over-ornamented. His best work has graceful curves and parallel rows of reeding, with well-placed and simple ornaments, usually a lyre, acanthus, or oak leaf.

Piatigorsky, Gregor (1903–   ), Ukrainian-American cellist. He studied at the Moscow Conservatory and became first cellist of the Berlin Philharmonic in 1924. He came to the United States in 1929 and became an American citizen in 1942. He has been acclaimed a leading cellist, and several composers, including Paul Hindemith and Sergei Prokofiev, have written concertos for him.

Picasso, Pablo Ruiz y a (1881–   ), Spanish painter and sculptor, regarded as one of the greatest artists of the twentieth century. Born in Málaga, he settled in Paris (1903); there he began painting in what has been called his "blue" and "rose" periods, taking as his subjects scenes from circus and city life. A few years later he developed cubism, and his painting changed radically. After World War I he returned to more traditional painting, but since then his works have always been highly original and individualistic. In addition to his oils, Picasso has worked extensively in sculpture and has done many lithographs, etchings, and ceramics. Among his most famous paintings are *Demoiselles d' Avignon, The Guitarist, Portrait of Gertrude Stein, Harlequin, Three Musicians,* and *Guernica.*

Piccard, Auguste (1884–1962), Swiss physicist, famed for his balloon ascents into the stratosphere and his descents into the ocean. Educated in Switzerland, he taught physics in Belgium. He achieved worldwide renown in 1931, when he and a co-worker ascended to almost 52,000 feet in a balloon with a pressurized cabin. The following year he bettered this record, obtaining valuable data on cosmic rays in the stratosphere. Piccard developed a device for underwater exploration, known as the bathyscaphe, in which he once descended to a depth of more than 10,000 feet.

Pickering, Edward Charles (1846–1919), American astronomer and physicist, noted for his pioneer work in measuring the light intensity of stars. Born in Boston, he graduated from Harvard, and was a professor of physics at the Massachusetts Institute of Technology. In 1876 he was named professor of astronomy at Harvard. As director of the Harvard Observatory he introduced photometry and photography into astro-

nomical observation and collected the "photographic library of the sky"—more than a quarter of a million photographic plates. Pickering directed the building of the observatory at Arequipa, Peru.

Pickering, Timothy (1745–1829), American soldier and statesman. Born in Salem, Mass., and educated at Harvard, he fought in the Revolutionary War, rising to the post of adjutant general. He was postmaster general under Pres. George Washington from 1791 to 1795, when he became secretary of war and secretary of state. He was dismissed by Pres. John Adams for his part in Alexander Hamilton's plot to involve America in a war with France.

Pickett, George Edward (1825–1875), American Confederate general, remembered for leading a charge at the battle of Gettysburg. Born in Richmond, Va., and a graduate of West Point, he served in the Mexican War and against the Indians on the frontier, rising to the rank of captain. When Virginia seceded from the Union, he joined the Confederate army as a colonel and rose to the rank of major general. At the battle of Gettysburg (1863) "Pickett's charge" on Cemetery Ridge made him famous. He and his men faced heavy rifle fire and took the first Union line. He also won distinction in the battles of Fredericksburg, Petersburg, Five Forks, and Dinwiddie Court House.

Pickford, Mary, born **Gladys Smith** (1892–   ), American motion-picture actress, born in Toronto, Canada. She began her screen career under D. W. Griffith, and soon became known as "America's Sweetheart." Among her films were *Rebecca of Sunnybrook Farm, Poor Little Rich Girl, Daddy Long Legs, Pollyanna, Sparrows* and *Secrets.* Her marriages to Owen Moore and Douglas Fairbanks ended in divorce, and in 1937 she married Charles "Buddy" Rogers. She is the author of *Why Not Try God?* (1934) and *My Rendezvous with Life* (1935).

Pico della Mirandola, Count **Giovanni** (1463–1494), Italian Humanist who has been regarded as the model Renaissance man of learning. In 1484 he went to Florence as a protégé of Lorenzo de' Medici. His studies in Hebrew and Arabic led to the composition of his celebrated 900 theses on the reconciliation of Christianity and Platonism. In 1487 he was branded a heretic by Pope Innocent VIII and forced to recant 13 of the theses. He fled to France, and a few years later returned to Florence, where he was poisoned by his secretary.

Pierce, Franklin (1804–1869), fourteenth president of the United States (1853–1857). Born in Hillsboro, N.H., he graduated from Bowdoin College in 1824. He was admitted to the bar in 1827 and two years later began his political career as a Democratic member of the state legislature. He was speaker in 1831 and 1832. In 1833 he entered Congress, first as a representative and later as the youngest member in the Senate (1837). He resigned in 1842 to resume his law practice.

Pierce joined the army at the outbreak of the Mexican War (1846), and was rapidly promoted; he was brigadier general when he entered Vera Cruz with Gen. Winfield Scott in 1847.

The Democratic convention of 1852 was split into many hostile factions, and to break the deadlock Pierce was nominated as a compromise candidate for the presidency against Scott, the Whig nominee. He received the votes of all but four states. During his administration the Missouri Compromise was repealed, the Gadsden Purchase was made, a treaty with Japan was negotiated, and the U. S. court of claims was created.

Pike, James Albert (1913–), American Episcopal clergyman who is noted for his liberal views on the role of religion and the church in contemporary society. From 1958–1966 Dr. Pike was his church's bishop of California. Born in Oklahoma City, Okla., he graduated from the University of Southern California (1934) and earned a doctorate in law from Yale in 1938. After practicing law for a few years, he decided to become a clergyman, and studied at the Union Theological Seminary in New York. He was ordained a deacon in 1944, a priest in 1946, and from 1949 to 1952 was head of the department of religion at Columbia University. After six years as dean of the Cathedral of St. John the Divine in New York, he was appointed bishop of California. Bishop Pike's writings include *Beyond Anxiety* (1953), *If You Marry Outside Your Faith* (1954), *Doing the Truth* (1955), and *Beyond the Law* (1963).

Pike, Zebulon Montgomery (1779–1813), American soldier and explorer who discovered Pikes Peak in Colorado. Born in Lamberton (Trenton), N.J., he joined the army at 15 and became a lieutenant at 20. In 1805 he commanded an expedition to find the source of the Mississippi, which he mistakenly reported to be Cass Lake, but gathered much valuable information. He was then sent to find the source of the Red River. He explored westward along the Missouri River, followed the Arkansas River to the Royal Gorge, then traveled westward to the site of Pueblo, Colo. On a side trip to the north, he discovered the peak which is named for him. Pike rose to the rank of colonel and took part in the opening phases of the War of 1812. He was killed in an attack on York, Canada.

Pilate, Pontius, Roman governor of Judaea (26–36 A.D.) who presided over the trial of Jesus Christ. Little is known of Pilate's early life. During his rule he kept peace in his region, but was considered somewhat ruthless. The circumstances surrounding Jesus' trial are hazy. To many students Pilate was forced to condemn Jesus in order to placate the high priests of Judaea. The story that he took his life after returning to Rome in 37 A.D. may well be legendary.

Pinckney, Charles Cotesworth (1746–1825), American statesman who was minister to France at a crucial time in French-American relations. Born in Charleston, S.C., and educated in England and France, he practiced law in England but returned home in 1769. He fought in the Revolutionary War and was a member of the Constitutional Convention. When difficulties arose with France in 1796, Pinckney was made minister to that country, and with John Marshall and Elbridge Gerry he discussed with Talleyrand future relations between the two countries. When Talleyrand hinted that a money payment might smooth diplomatic relations, Pinckney is said to have replied, "We have millions for defense, but not one cent for tribute." In 1804 and 1808 Pinckney was an unsuccessful Federalist candidate for president.

Pindar (c.522–438 B.C.), Greek poet of Thebes, considered the greatest writer of choral lyrics. He began writing verse at an early age, and soon his poetry was in demand throughout Greece for occasions of all kinds. His greatest works were odes, the best of which were known as *Epinicia*, songs in honor of the victors at the Olympian, Pythian, Nemean, and Isthmian games. He also wrote many sentimental poems, hymns, and dirges.

Pinkerton, Allan (1819–1884), American detective who founded the private detective agency that bears his name. Born in Glasgow, Scotland, he emigrated to America in 1842 and settled in Chicago, where he won distinction by capturing a gang of counterfeiters. He served a term as deputy sheriff, and in 1850 he opened a detective agency in Chicago. During the Civil War, Pinkerton operated a secret service organization for the Union army. After the war his detective agency became famous by breaking up the "Molly Maguires," an Irish terrorist organization in Pennsylvania. Pinkerton's agency was notorious for its strikebreaking and other antilabor activities.

Pinter, Harold (1930–), British playwright, noted for his bleak, uncompromising portrayals of alienated persons. From 1949 to 1958 he acted in English and Irish provincial theaters. In 1957 he wrote his first plays, *The Room, The Dumb Waiter,* and *The Birthday Party. The Caretaker* (1960) and *A Slight Ache* (1961) are among his works.

Pirandello, Luigi (1867–1936), Italian dramatist and fiction writer who won the Nobel Prize for literature in 1934. Born in Sicily, he was educated in Rome and in Bonn, Germany. He taught Italian literature in Rome from 1897 to 1921. His first works were short stories and novels, which were acclaimed only after he made his reputation as a dramatist. His first successful play was *Six Characters in Search of an Author*, produced in Rome in 1921. He also wrote *Right You Are If You Think You Are, Each in His Own Way, As You Desire Me,* and *Tonight We Improvise*. His characters are usually humble people, but his plays often are based on subtle and abstract philosophical questions.

Piranesi, Giambattista (1720–1778), Italian architect, painter, and engraver noted for his prints of buildings in Rome. He spent most of his life in Rome, making engravings of the city's ancient and modern architecture. His copperplate engravings provide an invaluable record of the various architectural styles of his and earlier times. During his career Piranesi produced more than 1,000 engravings, noted for their dramatic presentation of architectural features.

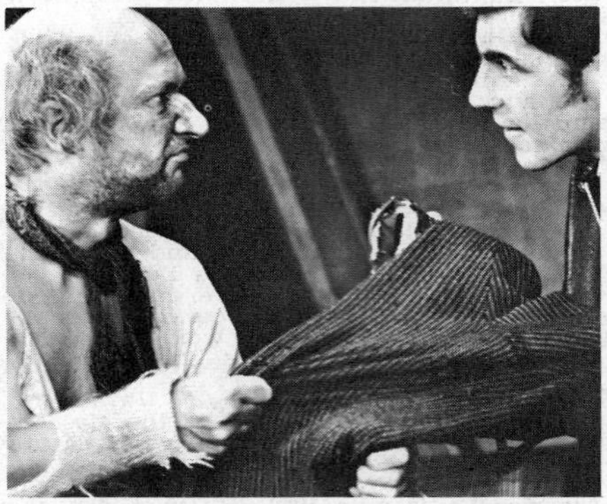

SAM SIEGEL

HAROLD PINTER'S *The Caretaker*, on stage.

Pisano, Andrea, also called **Andrea da Pontedera** (c.1290–1348), Italian sculptor and goldsmith whose master work is the earliest bronze door on the baptistery of the cathedral in Florence. Little is known of his activity until 1330, when he began work on the bronze door. In 1336 he succeeded Giotto as chief artist for the Duomo (cathedral) in Florence. A few years later, he became the chief artist for the Cathedral of Orvieto, and spent his last year directing work on the façade of that church.

Pisano or **da Pisa, Nicola** or **Niccoló** (1220–1284), Italian sculptor whose work represents a transition from Gothic to Renaissance art. He spent most of his life in Pisa, where his greatest work was the hexagonal marble pulpit in the baptistery depicting scenes from the life of Christ. In this and other sculpture, Pisano reveals a marked Greek and Roman influence, although he freely substituted Christian figures for the classical figures that inspired him.

Pisistratus, or **Peisistratus** (c.605–527 B.C.), Greek statesman and early ruler of Athens. He was the son of Hippocrates, who left him a large fortune. In 560 he usurped the throne and, although later expelled twice, regained it and ruled with clemency and justice. He enforced the laws of his friend Solon, founded the first public library in Athens, and collected and arranged the poems of Homer.

Pissarro, Camile (1830–1903), French painter who was a leader of the Impressionist school. Born in the Virgin Islands, he studied in Paris and later returned there to live. He was a pupil of Camille Corot and was influenced by Gustave Courbet and Édouard Manet. Later he joined Cézanne, Monet, Renoir, and others to form the Impressionist group, and exhibited in all the group's shows in the 1870's and 1880's. Many of his best paintings were landscapes, noted for their bright, spontaneous atmosphere. He also painted portraits and still lifes.

Pitcher, Molly. See *McCauley, Mary*.

Pitman, Sir **Isaac** (1813–1897), English inventor of a system of shorthand. His textbook *Stenographic Sound Hand* was published in 1837, and his *Phonetic Journal*, in 1843. Shorthand became very popular in Britain. **Benn Pitman** (1822–1910), a brother of Isaac, introduced a system of shorthand into the United States, founded the Phonographic Institute in Cincinnati, and invented a process of relief engraving.

Pitt, William, 1st earl of **Chatham** (1708–1778), English statesman, known as "the Elder Pitt" and "the Great Commoner." He is noted for his efforts to hold the British Empire together prior to the American Revolution. Born in London and educated at Oxford, he entered Parliament in 1735 and became a member of the privy council. He was called upon to form a new cabinet in 1756, of which the duke of Devonshire was prime minister. He resigned in 1761 but in 1766 was called upon to form another cabinet. He then was made Viscount Pitt and earl of Chatham. Ill health forced his retirement in 1768, but he kept up an active interest in public affairs in the House of Lords. He opposed Lord North's policy of taxing the colonies and, upon the alliance of the colonies and France, protested in a last great effort against the proposal to make peace. He advocated just treatment of the colonies but opposed independence, as this would weaken the British Empire. At the close of a speech he collapsed, and died days later.

Pitt, William, 1st earl of **Chatham** (1708–man, known as "the Younger Pitt." He was prime minister during much of the Napolenonic wars, and led England through a troubled period. The son of William Pitt, 1st earl of Chatham, he entered Parliament in 1781. At the age of 23 he became chancellor of the exchequer and at 25 was regarded as one of England's most powerful ministers. He held the position until 1801, during one of the most stormy periods of British history. In 1784 he established a new constitution for the East India Company.

In 1799 he brought about union with Ireland. He had intended to free the Roman Catholic laity from all restrictions and to grant a public maintenance to their clergy, but he was blocked by King George IV. Chagrined by this failure, Pitt resigned in 1801. He returned in 1804 when fear of a Napoleonic invasion brought him support from all parties, for he was known as a great war minister. As head of the government he formed a new coalition with Austria and Russia against France. When he heard the news of Napoleon's success at Austerlitz, Pitt, then in poor health, returned from Bath to London where he died.

Pius IX, born **Giovanni Maria Mastai-Ferretti** (1792–1878), Roman Catholic pope (1846–1878). His reign, the longest in history, covered one of the most eventful periods of the papacy. After the insurrection of Rome (1848) he fled to Gaeta but was restored by French aid in 1850. In the same year, he established a Catholic hierarchy in England. In 1854 he defined the dogma of the Immaculate Conception and in 1870 he decreed the dogma of papal infallibility. After the French left Rome in 1870, it was declared the capital of Italy and was occupied by the troops of Victor Emmanuel. The pope was held a virtual prisoner in the Vatican until his death.

Pius X, born **Giuseppe Melchiorre Sarto** (1835–1914), Roman Catholic pope (1903–1914). He was ordained a priest in 1858 and in 1884 was appointed bishop of Mantua; Leo XIII made him a cardinal and patriarch of Venice in 1893. His charity and tact made him popular, and more than once he settled serious strikes and labor disputes. On the death of Leo XIII (1903), the conclave met and elected him pope. His life was spent in the pastoral and episcopal service of the Church rather than in diplomatic and official affairs. He was interested in the reform of church music and in other matters of ecclesiastical discipline. In 1907 he issued a degree entrusting the revision of the Vulgate Bible to the Benedictine Order and later issued an encyclical against the modernist movement in the Church.

Pius XI, born **Achille Ambrogio Damiano Ratti** (1857–1939), Roman Catholic pope (1922–1939). He was ordained a priest in 1879 and taught in the seminary at Milan from 1882 to 1888, when he joined the Ambrosian Library of which he became chief librarian in 1907. He was assigned to the Vatican Library in Rome in 1910, and became its prefect in 1914.

During the last days of World War I he was papal nuncio to Poland, where he endeared himself to all classes while the new republic was in the making. For his success there he was raised to the rank of archbishop of Milan in 1921 that same year. Pope Benedict XV created him a cardinal. on February 6, 1922, after 8 months in that office, he was elected pope to succeed Benedict. The outstanding event of his reign was the understanding reached with the government of Italy whereby Vatican City was established as an independent state (1929), thus reestablishing the temporal power of the papacy.

Pius XII, born **Eugenio Pacelli** (1876–1958), Italian pope (1939–1958). From boyhood he was trained for the papal diplomatic service. When first ordained a priest (1899), he was assigned to a minor position in the office of the papal secretary of state. In 1912 he was promoted to undersecretary of state. Soon after his appointment, World War I began, and the Vatican entered upon its most trying times. For the next five years Pacelli kept at his desk constantly. When Pope Pius X died in 1914, Pope Benedict succeeded him, and soon noticed that it was young Pacelli who was doing most of the work. In 1917 Pope Benedict made Pacelli the papal nuncio in Munich, where he made a brilliant effort to carry out Pope Benedict's plan for an end to the war. Pacelli next became papal nuncio to the new German republic. He worked out with Prussia, then a stronghold of Lutheranism, a treaty so favorable to the Vatican that he was elevated to cardinal.

When Cardinal Gasparri resigned, Pacelli was named papal secretary of state (1930–1939). It was in this position that he gained world-wide popularity, for he covered both hemispheres in his travels. In 1934 he attended the Eucharistic congress in Buenos Aires. In 1936 he toured the United States by airplane, the first such tour by a papal dignitary. He had a good radio voice, and made many good-will broadcasts.

He was elected pope in 1939, after one of the shortest conclaves in history. His diplomatic training made him familiar with modern ideas, and his ability to read and speak seven modern languages enabled him to surmount national barriers.

Pizarro, Francisco (c.1470–1541), Spanish explorer who discovered and conquered Peru. In 1509 he made a voyage of exploration to America with Alonso de Ojeda and was with Vasco Núñez de Balboa when the Pacific Ocean was discovered (1513). In 1526 he joined Diego de Almagro and others in exploring the west coast of South America. Pizarro and a small party landed on a Peruvian island, and, after overcoming native hostility, they explored the mainland. Pizarro, had too few men to attempt a settlement; it was not until six years later that Pizarro, Almagro, and 183 men landed at Tambez. He found the country weakened by warfare between two native princes, Atahualpa and Huáscar. By treachery he captured and executed Atahualpa and set up Manco Capac as ruler. Cuzco was taken in 1533, and on January 6, 1535, Pizarro founded the city of Lima as the new capital.

The Spanish king made Pizarro a marquis and gave Almagro a vast tract of land. Almagro then seized control of Cuzco, but was later captured and put to death by Pizarro's men. This act incensed Almagro's followers; they announced their support of their dead leader's son as his successor, intending to dispossess Pizarro. The matter was soon settled, for in a quarrel at Lima the Almagro clan in a surprise attack mortally wounded Pizarro.

Planck, Max Karl Ernst Ludwig (1858–1947), German physicist whose quantum theory earned him the Nobel Prize for physics in 1918. Born in Kiel, he studied in Munich and Berlin. He was professor of physics at Berlin (1889–1928). Planck introduced his quantum theory in 1900; in general, the theory states that light and other forms of energy are emitted as discrete quanta or particles of energy. From this theory have come many major advances in modern science. During World War II Planck remained in Germany, where he openly opposed many of Adolf Hitler's policies.

Plato, originally **Aristocles** (c.427–347 B.C.), Greek philosopher of Athens, regarded as one of the greatest thinkers of Western civilization. When he was 20, the tragic death of his mentor, Socrates, forced him to leave Athens for a time, and he lived at Megara with Euclid. During two visits to Syracuse (367, 361), he became closely connected with Archytas and the Pythagorean philosophers. When he returned to Athens (387), he began to teach philosophy publicly, which led to the establishment of the Academy, the first known university in history. He soon attracted a large school of distinguished followers, who carried on his work after his death until 529 A.D. He never married or held any public office, but devoted his life to teaching and writing.

After the death of Socrates, Plato wrote dramatic dialogues, some of them concerning the trial and conviction of his former teacher. The dialogues not only pay tribute to Socrates by dramatizing his tragedy, but are an effective vehicle for the presentation of Plato's philosophy. As chief speaker in most of the dialogues, Socrates is the spokesman of Plato's ideas. He employed the dialectic form believing that knowledge is acquired mainly through discussion and inquiry. In fact, the dialogues fall into three parts that conform to the same stages of the Platonic method of learning: inquiry, speculation, and criticism and application. To Plato, wisdom is the greatest good; the philosopher who employs his intellect and not his senses is capable of reaching the highest level of reality, and is therefore the best candidate to lead the state. In his *Republic* he describes the ideal state, in which each person is grouped according to his greatest virtue. The lowest form of reality to Plato is the world of the senses, thus Platonic love, as discussed in his *Symposium,* is not a physical union but a spiritual one. Throughout the dialogues Plato presents his theory of forms, or idealism, while negating the rival philosophy schools of the humanists and realists. These dialogues include, among others, *Phaedrus, Timaeus, Apology, Phaedo, Criticas, Crito, Hysis, Meno,* and *Protagoras.*

Plautus, Titus Maccius (c.254–184 B.C.), the leading comic dramatist of ancient Rome. Little is known of his life, except that he possibly first entered the theater as an actor. Of 150 comedies ascribed to him only 21 are considered genuinely his; of these, 20 exist in entirety, and the 21 is fragmentary. They are adaptations from Greek originals; the action is rapid, the humor keen and shrewd, and the characters lifelike. Many plays by Dryden, Molière, Jonson, and Shakespeare are based on comedies by Plautus. Some of his plays are *Amphitruo, Aulularia, Bacchides, Captivi, Casinoa,* and *Menaechmi.*

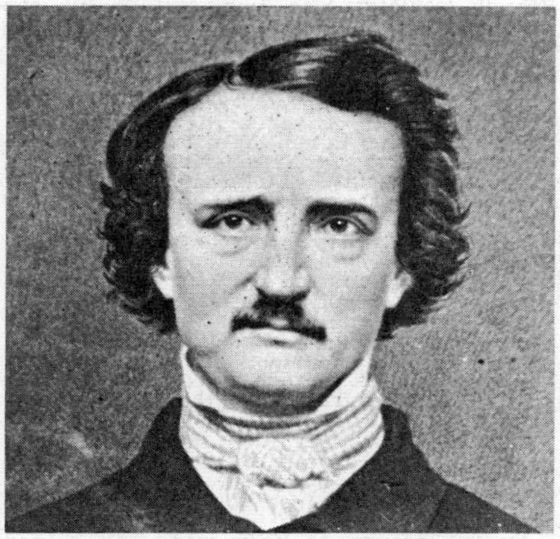

WIDE WORLD

EDGAR ALLAN POE, author and critic.

Pliny the Elder, born **Gaius Plinium Secundus** (23–79 A.D.), Roman scholar and naturalist whose only surviving work is the celebrated *Historia Naturalis* (*Natural History,* 77 A.D.). Representing vast scholarship, the work consists of 37 books and covers about 20,000 topics. Pliny not only recorded data from his own researches, but also included the best information from at least 2,000 volumes written by others. As science, the book contains little of value for today, but it has great historical interest to students of ancient civilization. Pliny was appointed commander of the fleet at Misenum by Vespasian. He died when the eruption of Vesuvius destroyed Pompeii.

Pliny the Younger, born **Gaius Plinius Caecilius Secundus** (62–113 A.D.), Roman orator and statesman, the nephew and adopted son of Pliny the Elder. At the age of 20 he was considered one of the most brilliant Romans. He is especially known for a series of *Letters.* Noted for their precise, yet charming style, the *Letters* throw a great deal of light on the history of his period, including treatment of early Christians. Pliny was, in turn, military tribune, quaestor, praetor, and consul.

Plotinus (c.205–270 A.D.), Roman philosopher who founded the Neoplatonic school that deeply influenced later thinkers such as Saint Augustine. He was probably born in Egypt, for it is known that he studied in Alexandria. In 242 he joined the expedition of Emperor Gordian III to the East. When Gordian was murdered in Mesopotamia, Plotinus escaped and went to Rome. There he taught and began to write, and won many followers with his revival of Plato's doctrines, which he translated into a kind of religious mysticism. After his death, his writings were collected by a disciple, Porphyry, and published in an edition called the *Enneads.*

Plutarch (c.46–c.120 A.D.), Greek writer, famed for his biographies of ancient Greeks and Romans. Born in Boeotia, he studied philosophy in Athens and later lectured in Rome. He returned to his native town, where he held various magistracies and was appointed priest of Apollo. He was still living in 120, but the exact time of his death is not known.

His great work is entitled *Parallel Lives,* biographies of 46 eminent Greeks and Romans, arranged in pairs, each pair accompanied by a comparison of characters. They are written with a moral purpose and present not orderly narratives of events but portraitures of men, drawn with graphic power, good sense, honesty, and sympathy. Few books of ancient or modern times have been so widely read and so generally admired as these *Lives.* Plutach's other writings entitled *Moralia* (*Morals*), are devoted to ethics and other subjects.

Pocahontas, Indian name **Matoaka** (c.1595–1617), American Indian girl who was the daughter of Powhatan, chief of the Algonquian tribes of Virginia. According to legend, her father captured Capt. John Smith from the Jamestown colony and was about to kill him, when she begged her father to spare his life. The incident supposedly occurred in 1608. In 1612 the colonists held her as a hostage for the safe return of colonists who had been captured by the Indians. During her captivity she became a Christian and in 1614 married John Rolfe, a settler. She went with her husband to England, where she was welcomed as a princess. While in England, she died of smallpox.

Poe, Edgar Allan (1809–1849), American poet, story writer, and literary critic. Born in Boston, he was orphaned at an early age, and reared by his godfather, John Allan of Richmond, Va. He was educated in Scotland and England (1815–1820), then returned to Richmond, where he began to write poetry. After short periods at the University of Virginia and at West Point, he ended his formal education. He had already published his first two volumes of poetry, *Tamerlane and Other Poems* (1827) and *Al Aaraaf* (1829).

In New York Poe produced a third volume of verse, *Poems,* in 1831. Some time later he went to Baltimore, where he began to write short stories. For the remainder of his life he was an editor on various magazines, where his brilliant work was offset by a growing tendency to alcoholism.

During his relatively short life, Poe produced some of the masterpieces of American literature. His poems *The Raven, Lenore, To Helen, Ulalume,* and *The Bells* are among the best-known poems in modern literature. Tales of the grotesque like *The Fall of the House of Usher, The Pit and the Pendulum,* and *The Cask of Amontillado* made him a master of this story form. With such tales as *The Gold Bug* and *The Murders in the Rue Morgue,* classics of their kind, Poe is often regarded as the inventor of the modern detective story. Poe was also highly esteemed as a literary critic. He was the first American critic to formulate a theory of short-story and poetic composition based entirely on artistic standards.

Poincaré, Raymond (1860–1934), president of France (1913–1920). Born in Bar-le-Duc, he was a highly successful lawyer in Paris before entering politics. He was elected to the Chamber of Deputies (1887), became finance minister (1894, again in 1906), and premier and foreign minister (1912). He was elected president on January 17, 1913, the ninth president of the Republic. He improved France's relations with Britain and Russia, fostered French nationalism, and inspired the nation to great effort in World War I. During the remainder of his career, he served as a senator and was twice premier (1922–1924, 1928–1929).

Politian, born **Angelo Ambrogini** (1454–1494), Italian Renaissance poet and Humanist, born in Montepulciano, Tuscany. Well-versed in Greek, Latin, Hebrew, and philosophy, he became a protége of Lorenzo de' Medici. After a period as tutor to Lorenzo's children, he taught at the University of Florence, where he won great renown for his lectures on the classics. In addition to writing poetry in Greek and Latin, Politian was also noted for his translations of such classical authors as Vergil, Plato, and Homer. His verse and drama in the Tuscan dialect were also considered to be models of their kind.

Polk, James Knox (1795–1849), eleventh president of the United States (1845–1949). Born in Mecklenburg County, N.C., he moved with his family to Tennessee at the age of 11. He graduated from the University of North Carolina in 1818, and was admitted to the Tennessee bar in 1820. He practiced law for nearly 20 years and held several political offices. A Jacksonian Democrat, he was elected to Congress in 1825 and became speaker of the House in 1835. He was elected governor of Tennessee in 1839 and served one term. In the national convention of 1844 Lewis Cass, Martin Van Buren, and James Buchanan fought for the presidential nomination. The deadlock was broken by nominating Polk, who had been a candidate for the vice presidency. He defeated Henry Clay in an exciting campaign in which the Texas and Oregon boundary disputes were prominent. During his administration the Oregon question was settled by compromise with Great Britain.

The Texas boundary disagreement led to the Mexican War in 1846. The Rio Grande had been considered the southeast boundary of Texas, and in 1845 the Texas Republic was admitted to the Union, with the boundary so fixed. Mexico claimed the boundary was at the Neuces. Polk ordered Gen. Zachary Taylor to occupy the area in dispute. The Mexican army advanced and engaged Taylor at Palo Alto. Polk then asked for a declaration of war, and Congress complied. As a result, the vast territory was added to the national domain. During Polk's term an independent treasury system was adopted, and the tariff was reduced. At the close of his term, Polk retired to Tennessee, where he died three months later.

Pollaiuolo, Antonio (1429–1498), Italian painter, goldsmith, sculptor, and engraver. Supported by the Medici and other Florentine families, he became head of one of the leading studios in Florence. He is considered the first artist to have studied anatomy by dissection. At the request of Pope Innocent VIII he came to Rome, where he executed two monuments for St. Peter's Basilica. Perhaps his most famous work is the bronze statue *Hercules Strangling Antaeus.*

Pollock, Jackson (1912–1956), American painter who was a leader of the artistic movement called abstract expressionism. Born in Cody, Wyo., he studied (1929–1931) under Thomas Hart Benton at the Art Students League of New York. In the 1930's his paintings were fairly conventional, but in the 1940's he developed a highly abstract art, culminating in his famous "drip" technique of literally dripping paint upon enormous canvases to produce highly abstract forms. Pollock was killed in an automobile accident.

Polo, Marco (1254–1324), Italian traveler who was the first European to traverse all of Asia. His father was a wealthy Venetian merchant, and in 1271 Marco accompanied him on a journey to the court of Kublai Khan. Marco was given a governorship by the khan (emperor) and sent on missions to India and China. Eventually the Europeans wanted to return home. The emperor wanted them to stay, but arranged for them to join a westbound caravan, which started for Persia in 1292. The journey was long and arduous, and in 1295 they reached Venice after an absence of 24 years. In a war against Genoa (1298), Marco was captured by the enemy and imprisoned. While in prison, he dictated to a fellow prisoner the story of his experiences in China, and it was published as *The Book of Marco Polo.* The narrative created a great sensation throughout Europe. Many believed the tale to be imaginary, but other explorers came back to verify the facts that had been written. Marco became a member of the Grand Council of Venice.

Polybius (c.205–c.25 B.C.). Greek historian, noted for his history of Rome covering the fifty-year period beginning in 220 B.C. During this period Rome has conquered most of the known world. After the Roman conquest of (Greece (168), Polybius and a thousand other prominent Greeks were taken to Rome as hostages. Polybius remained there for 17 years, and made friends with influential Romans. One of them was Scipio Aemilius, whom Polybius accompanied to Africa during the Third Punic War. Polybius returned to Greece, which was again defeated by Rome. However, Polybius was able to arrange good peace terms through his Roman friends. In his 40-volume *Universal History,* he gave an account of Rome and neighboring countries. Only five have been preserved, but fragments of others still exist.

Polycarp, Saint (c.69–155 A.D.), Greek bishop who was an important link between the Apostles of Jesus and the early Christian church. Born in Smyrna (now Izmir), Turkey, he became a Christian and, in the organization of the new religion, was appointed bishop of his native city. He was on intimate terms with Saint John. After Polycarp's return from a conference in Rome concerning the proper date for the celebration of Easter, he was arrested by Roman officials on the charge of being a Christian, and was executed. Of several episcopal letters that he wrote, only one has been preserved, the *Epistle of St. Polycarp to the Philippians.*

Polyclitus, or **Polycleitus** (5th century B.C.), Greek sculptor, whose statues were noted for their perfection of form. His most famous statue, the *Doryphorus* (spear bearer), embodied his ideal of physical perfection and correct proportion. Working chiefly in bronze, he established standards for proportion and symmetry that greatly influenced later Greek sculptors. He was a contemporary of Phidias, with whom he contended for recognition as the greatest sculptor of their time.

Pompadour Marquise **de,** born **Jeanne Antoinette Poisson** (1721–1764), mistress of Louis XV of France. Her supposed parents were poor, but a rich man, though to be her real father, provided lavishly for her and prepared her for the most exclusive French society. She had suitors by the score but became the wife of her benefactor's nephew, Lenormand, Louis XV saw her at a masked ball and persuaded her to take up residence at Versailles as his mistress. She had great influence over the king and brought about the alliance with Austria in the Seven Year's War because of her dislike for Frederick the Great. Ministers of state sought her support in carrying out their policies, and prominent literary men, her patronage.

Pompey the Great, born **Gnaeus Pompeius Magnus** (106–48 B.C.), Roman general and statesman, celebrated for his victories in Spain, Africa, and Asia. He was one of Julius Caesar's chief rivals for power. As a young man he allied himself with Sulla and helped to crush Marius. He was granted a triumph for his victories over the Marians in Sicily and Africa, and the title *Magnus* (the Great) was conferred upon him by Sulla in 81. After the death of Sulla, Pompey helped to put down the uprising of Lepidus (77), and for several years conducted a war against the rebellious Sertorius in Spain.

On his return to Italy in 71, he gained additional reputation by stamping out the remnants of the slave insurrection of Spartacus. He formed a political alliance with the great capitalist Marcus Licinius Crassus and thus secured the consulship for the year 70, although he was several years younger than the legal age. In 67 he received extraordinary military powers to deal with the Cilician pirates who were terrorizing the Mediterranean. In the following year his powers were extended. He swept the pirates from the Mediterranean in 40 days, defeated Mithradates and added his province of Pontus to Rome, defeated the Armenian king, annexed Syria, conquered Jerusalem and made its territory a tributary province.

Pompey's political ties with Caesar were strengthened when he, Caesar, and Crassus formed their powerful triumvirate (60). The following year he married Caesar's daughter, Julia. As Caesar's influence increased, Pompey's declined. When the inevitable civil war broke out, Pompey was decisively defeated at Pharsalus (48). He fled to Egypt, where he was assassinated.

Ponce de León, Juan (c.1460–1521), Spanish explorer who discovered Florida. He is thought to have been a member of Columbus' second voyage to the New World (1493). In 1508 he explored and colonized Puerto Rico, and two years later served as its first governor. He had heard a fable about a fountain on an island called Bimini with water that contained curative properties—a "fountain of eternal youth." He went in search of it and on Easter Sunday, 1513, found a new land, the Florida peninsula. He gave the territory its present name. In 1521, while attempting to colonize the land, he was killed by an Indian arrow.

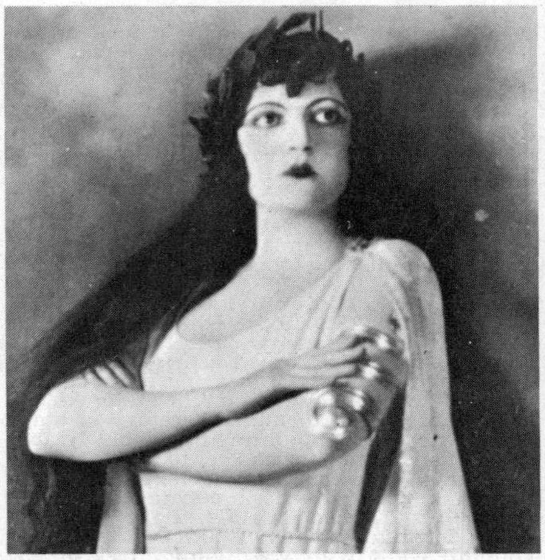

METROPOLITAN OPERA

ROSA PONSELLE in the role of "Norma."

Pons, Lily (1904–), French operatic soprano, famed for her interpretations of difficult coloratura roles. Born in Cannes, she made her debut in *Lakmé* at Mulhouse, France, in 1925. In 1931 she joined the Metropolitan Opera in New York, where she performed regularly for more than 25 seasons, During her lengthy career she sang the lead in *Rigoletto, La Traviata, Lucia di Lammermoor,* and *La fille du régiment.*

Ponselle, Rosa Melba, born **Rosa Ponzillo** –1897, American operatic soprano, born in Meriden, Conn. She was a vaudeville singer as a young girl. In 1918 she made a sensational debut in the role of Leonora in Verdi's *La Forza del Destino.* During the next two decades, she was the most famous American dramatic soprano, scoring successes in *Norma, La Vestale, Aïda,,* and *Carmen.* In 1937, she retired to Baltimore, where she has been a voice teacher and sponsor of operatic productions.

Pontiac (c.1720–1769), chief of the Ottawa Indians. From his youth he favored the French cause in America. In 1763 he formed a confederacy of Indian tribes and launched attacks on 12 British settlements. This campaign, known as the "Conspiracy of Pontiac," was at first successful, but he was finally forced to surrender in 1765. Pontiac was an outstanding organizer, military leader, and statesmen. In 1769 he was killed by an Illinois Indian.

Pope, Alexander (1688–1744), English poet, famous for his witty satires on the foibles of man. Born in London, he showed an early talent for poetry, and published his first verse at the age of 12. With his *Essay on Criticism* (1711), he became one of London's most talked-about writers. His translations of Homer's *Iliad* (1715–1720) and *Odyssey* (1725–1726) occupied much of his time until about 1726.

Pope achieved his greatest renown with *The Dunciad* (1728, revised 1743) a satire directed against his critics and adversaries. His other important works include *The Rape of the Lock* (1712), *An Essay on Man* (1733–1734), and a series called *Moral Essays,* which first appeared in 1731. Pope was a master of the heroic couplet. One of the most quotable of poets, he contributed such lines as "Hope springs eternal in the human breast," "The proper study of mankind is man," and "An honest man's the noblest work of God."

Porter, Cole (1893–1964), American composer of popular songs. Born in Peru, Ind., and educated at Yale, he studied music theory for a time, and then began writing for the Broadway theater. During his highly successful career, he produced the scores for such musicals as *Anything Goes* (1934), *Dubarry Was A Lady* (1939), *Panama Hattie* (1940), and *Kiss Me Kate* (1948), based on Shakespeare's *The Taming of the Shrew.* Among his many songs are such popular favorites as *Night and Day, Begin the Beguine, In the Still of the Night,* and *So in Love.*

Porter, David (1780–1843), American naval officer who carried out devastating raids on British vessels during the War of 1812. Born in Boston, Mass., he served on merchant vessels as a boy, then joined the U.S. navy to fight in the war with Tripoli. When the War of 1812 began, he was put in command of the *Essex* with a roving commission to harass the enemy. He sailed around Cape Horn and captured several British vessels. On his return to home waters he was acclaimed a hero. Trouble with the Spanish authorities in Puerto Rico forced him to resign in 1826. He was charged with exceeding his authority in compelling an apology from the Spanish authorities for arresting one of his officers. Porter then served as an admiral in the Mexican navy for three years. After his return to the U.S. he was appointed consul general to Algiers. He later served in the diplomatic service at Constantinople, where he died.

Porter, David Dixon (1813–1891), American naval commander who was a leading officer in the Union navy during the Civil War. He was born in Chester, Pa., the son of David Porter. At 13 he accompanied his father on a cruise to the West Indies in search of pirates. He entered the Mexican navy with his father but returned to the U.S. in 1829. As a naval lieutenant he commanded an American gunboat in the Mexican War and rendered distinguished service. When the Civil War began he was promoted to the rank of commander. He could have been chief officer in charge of the campaign to blockade the Mississippi, but he asked that David G. Farragut be given the task. For his work as second in command he was promoted to rear admiral. He supported Grant at the siege of Vicksburg (1863), was transferred to the Atlantic squadron, and took Fort Fisher (1865). He was superintendent of the U.S. Naval Academy at Annapolis (1865–1869). He became a vice admiral in 1866. When Farragut, the first American admiral, died in 1870, Porter was raised to that rank.

Porter, Katherine Anne (1890–), American author, noted for her short stories. Born in Indian Creek, Texas, she was educated at convent schools in the South. During most of her formative years, she lived in Europe and in Mexico, which are the settings of many of her best stories. Her first collection of stories, *Flowering Judas* (1930), won immediate critical acclaim. Later collections include *Hacienda* (1934), *Pale Horse, Pale Rider* (1939), and *The Leaning Tower* (1944). Her only novel, *Ship of Fools*, was published in 1962 and made into a successful motion picture in 1965.

Porter, William Sydney, real name of **O. Henry** (1862–1910), American writer, noted for his short stories with unexpected endings. Born in Greensboro, N.C., he settled in Austin, Texas, where he edited a humorous paper for a time, and then became a bank teller. Convicted of embezzlement, he spent over three years in prison, where he began writing stories. He continued his story writing when, in 1902, he moved to New York. Adopting the pen name O. Henry, he wrote more than 200 stories, published in such collections as *The Four Million* (1906), *The Voice of the City* (1908), and *Options* (1909). As a writer he had a remarkable gift for delineating character and the little ironies in the lives of ordinary people. Most of his stories are brief and depend on understatement for their subtlety.

Post, Emily Price (1873–1960), American writer and authority on etiquette. Born in Baltimore, Md., she wrote several novels before turning to the study of manners and etiquette. Among her best-selling books are *Etiquette* (1st ed. 1922), *How to Behave Though a Debutante* (1928), *Children are People* (1940), and *The Personality of a House* (1948).

Post, Wiley (1898–1935), American aviator, regarded as one of the greatest in the early days of flying. Born in Grand Saline, Texas, he studied automobile mechanics in Kansas City, worked as an oil driller, then became a parachute jumper at fairs and exhibitions. He learned to fly in 1925 and toured the West with exhibition flights and parachute jumps. He lost the sight of one eye in an oilfield accident, but this did not interfere with his flying, and he became an airmail pilot and a racer. In 1931 he joined Harold Gatty in an around-the-world flight. They covered 15,474 miles in 8 days, 15 hours, 51 minutes. In 1933 Post made a solo flight around the world and broke the previous record by more than a day. He was killed with Will Rogers in a plane crash near Point Barrow, Alaska, on August 17, 1935.

Potemkin, Grigori Aleksandrovich (1739–1791), Russian statesman, remembered for his attempts to colonize and fortify southern Russia. In 1762, his part in the conspiracy against Peter III brought him to the attention of the new empress, Catherine II. After he had distinguished himself in a war with Turkey (1769), he became Catherine's lover, and received many honors. Among his accomplishments were the construction of the Black Sea fleet and the plans for colonizing the south Russian steppes. In 1783 he played a key role in the annexation of the Crimea, where he built the harbor of Sebastopol. He was made a field marshal in 1784 and was named Prince of Tauris in 1787. At the time of his death he was commander in chief of Russian forces fighting Turkey.

Poulenc, Francis (1899–1963), French composer of the post-Ravel school, noted for his witty, sophisticated songs and orchestral works. His early compositions were predominantly songs, piano pieces, and works for chamber orchestra. Turning later to larger pieces, he wrote ballets, religious compositions, and operas. His most ambitious work, the opera *Les Dialogues des Carmélites* (1957), has been performed in the leading opera houses of Europe and the United States. Poulenc was a member of the group called *Les Six*, which exercised considerable influence on music in the 1920's and 1930's.

Pound, Ezra Loomis (1885–), American poet and critic, regarded as one of the foremost influences on modern poetry. Born in Hailey, Idaho, he was educated at Hamilton College and the University of Pennsylvania. He lived most of his life in Europe, where as editor and critic he promoted such writers as T. S. Eliot, W. B. Yeats, and James Joyce. At the same time, Pound was writing his own revolutionary poetry, producing works like *Hugh Selwyn Mauberley* (1920) that were to influence a whole generation of poets. In the early 1920's he began publishing a series of *Cantos* that were to occupy his attention for the next three decades. An admirer of fascism, he made pro-Mussolini broadcasts from Italy during World War II. After the war, the United States government indicted him for treason, but he was judged too sick to stand trial, and he spent several years in a mental institution. Released in 1958, he returned to Italy.

Poussin, Nicolas (1594–1665), French painter, generally considered the master of his period. After working in the Paris studios of several painters and sculptors, he settled in Rome (1624), where he developed the classical style that was to mark his mature painting. Poussin's reputation today rests on his success with landscape and historical paintings strongly influenced by ancient sculpture and Renaissance paintings. About 40 of his paintings are in the Louvre in Paris. His work had a notable influence on several generations of later French artists.

Powhatan, Indian name **Wahunsonacook** (c.1550–1618), American Indian chief who was the father of Pocahontas. He was head of an Algonquian confederacy that at one time included about 30 tribes. His domain in Virginia extended about 200 miles inland from the sea, and its length from north to south was still greater. He is remembered chiefly for the incident in which his daughter, Pocohontas, saved the life of Capt. John Smith. In 1609, when the settlers' supplies were low, Smith created Powhatan "Emperor of the Indies," hoping that the honor would lead the natives to provide food. In 1612, three years after Smith left the colony, Pocahontas was taken captive by the English and held as hostage. Powhatan accepted the situation and thereafter remained friendly with the English.

Prajadhipok or **Rama VII** (1893–1941) king of Siam (1925–1935). He and Queen Rambaibarni traveled widely and introduced modern institutions into Siam, built railroads, and encouraged education. After a bloodless revolution in 1932 he signed a constitution that limited his powers, set up an elected parliament, and gave full franchise to the people. His efforts to liberalize the government were opposed by the aristocracy, and he abdicated. He was succeeded by his young nephew, Ananda Mahidol.

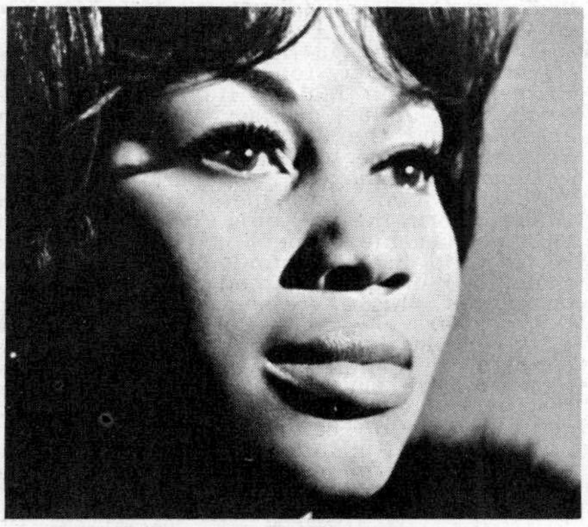

LEONTYNE PRICE, American operatic soprano, appeared in Barber's new opera.

Praxiteles (4th century B.C.), Greek sculptor, considered one of the finest of all time. He lived in Athens, where he was probably born. His only surviving major work is a marble statue of Hermes carrying the infant Dionysus, but numerous Roman copies of other works exist, including statues of Aphrodite, Eros, and Apollo. Although he worked in several media, Praxiteles' most distinguished works were in marble, and have been acclaimed for their gracefulness and sensuousness.

Prendergast, Mauricce Brazil (1861–1924), American painter, famous for his genre paintings. Born in Roxbury, Mass., he studied art in Paris. From 1914 to 1924 he had a studio in New York, where he belonged to a group of artists called *The Eight*. His watercolors and oils are rich in color and resemble mosaics. He was one of the artists represented in the controversial Armory Show of 1913, after which his reputation grew steadily.

Prescott, William Hickling (1796–1859), American historian, noted for his studies of Spanish rule in Europe and America. Born in Salem, Mass., he was educated at Harvard, where he lost the sight of one eye in an accident. His studies so affected the other eye that he became nearly blind. As a result he gave up the study of law, went to Europe for medical treatment, and took up writing when he returned home. His first important work, *The History of the Reign of Ferdinand and Isabella the Catholic* (3 vols.) appeared in 1838. He next devoted four years to the *History of the Conquest of Mexico* (3 vols., 1843) and four years to the *Conquest of Peru* (2 vols., 1847). These two histories have ranked as classics ever since. Between 1855 and 1858 he published three volumes of the *History of the Reign of Philip the Second*, which was left unfinished.

Pretorius, Andries Wilhelmus Jacobus (1799–1853), South African Dutch colonizer and one of the leaders of the Great Boer Trek. In 1838 he was made commandant general of the Boers of Natal and defeated a force of 10,000 Zulus, making possible the organization of a Boer republic of Natalia. Pretorius then led the Boers in their fight for independence from Britain. In 1852, after numerous battles, the British acknowledged the sovereignty of the South African Republic (the Transvaal). In 1853 his eldest son, Marthinus Wessels Pretorius, succeeded him as commandant general. The city of Pretoria was named in his honor.

Prévost d'Exiles, Antoine François, known as **Abbé Prévost** (1799–1853), French novelist and cleric, remembered as the author of *Manon Lescaut*. A dissolute youth, he entered the Benedictine order in 1721, but in 1729 wearied of the discipline and fled to England. After leading an adventurous life, he later returned to the order and in 1754 was made head of a priory. From 1728 to 1732 he wrote a seven-volume series of novels called *Mémoires d'un homme de qualité*. Of these, only the last volume, *Manon Lescaut* (1731), was well received.

Price, Leontyne (1927–), American soprano who was the first Negro singer to appear in the world's major opera houses. Born in Laurel, Miss., she graduated from the Juilliard School of Music in New York (1952). For the next two years she sang the part of Bess in George Gershwin's *Porgy and Bess*, in a company that toured Europe. Among her early opera roles, perhaps the most significant was the title role of *Tosca* on television in 1955. She later sang with the San Francisco Opera (1957), the Chicago Lyric Opera (1959), and the Metropolitan Opera in New York (1961), and performed regularly with leading opera companies in Austria, England, and Italy. A prima donna of the Metropolitan Opera Company, she was honored with the leading role in Samuel Barber's new opera *Antony and Cleopatra*, at the opening of the company's new house in 1966.

Priestley, Joseph (1733–1804), English chemist who discovered oxygen. Born in Yorkshire, he studied for the ministry and was a Presbyterian clergyman for several years. He then devoted himself to science and in 1767 published his *History of Electricity*. His fame rests chiefly on his discovery of oxygen in 1774. Priestley became a Unitarian and expressed his approval of the French Revolution. This enraged many people, who burned his house, library, manuscripts, and apparatus. He found safety in the U.S. and settled in Northumberland, Pa., where he died.

SOVFOTO

SERGEI S. PROKOFIEV, Russian composer.

Priestley wrote more than 70 books on a wide variety of subjects. Among his other discoveries were the properties of nitrous oxide, ammonia, carbon monoxide, and sulfur dioxide. His work on gases led to Dalton's atomic theory. He was the first to use carbon dioxide in the preparation of "mineral" waters.

Prokofiev, Sergei Sergevich (1891–1953), Russian composer, noted for his bold originality in harmony and rhythm. He studied privately under Reinhold Glière and then attended the St. Petersburg Conservatory, where one of his teachers was Rimsky-Korsakov. In 1910 he won the Rubinstein Prize for a piano concerto. He lived in Paris from 1923 to 1931 and returned to Russia to stay in 1932. Prokofiev is one of the most frequently performed of modern composers. Among his many works are six symphonies, the familiar *Peter and the Wolf* suite for children, the operas *War and Peace* and *The Love for Three Oranges*, and motion picture scores for *Lieutenant Kije* and *Alexander Nevsky*.

Protagoras (c.481–411 B.C.), Greek Sophist in Athens, who was one of the first professional teachers of philosophy and literature. He was an agnostic and taught that truth and right are relative, not absolute. His favorite saying was that "Man is the measure of all things." His works survive only in fragments. He is the principal subject of Plato's dialogue *Protagoras*.

Protogenes (late 4th century B.C.), Greek painter who was one of the leading artists of his time. Born in Asia Minor, he spent most of his mature years at Rhodes. Known chiefly as a decorator of ships, his artistic talent was first discovered in his fiftieth year by the painter Apelles. His most famous work, the *Ialysus*, was removed by Vespasian to Rome, where it was later destroyed by fire. Protogenes was famous for the minute detail and finish of his paintings.

Proudhon, Pierre Joseph (1809–1865), French Socialist and political theorist who was a leading proponent of social and economic reform. In 1840 he published *Qu'est-ce que la propriété?* (*What is Property?*) to which his answer was "Property is theft." During the revolution of 1848 he was active in the Socialist movement, publishing several radical journals. In this and other writings, Proudhon advocated cooperatives for small-business men, a monetary system based on productivity rather than on gold reserves, the dissolution of giant capitalistic concerns, and the final abandonment of all government.

Proust, Marcel (1871–1922), French novelist whose seven-part *À la recherche du temps perdu* (*Remembrance of Things Past*, 1913–1927), is considered a monument of modern French literature. Born in Paris, he was prominent in Paris society until 1905, when the death of his mother and failing health led him to retire to the seclusion of a soundproofed apartment. There he began writing the series of novels, based on the social life he had observed, that represent his major achievement. The first of the series was *Swann's Way* (1913); three other parts appeared during his lifetime, and the remaining three were published posthumously. In these works (13 to 16 vols. depending on the edition). Proust probes deeply into contemporary society and subtly lays bare the private feelings and thoughts of his characters, many of whom lead shallow lives occupied with trivia and self-

conscious concern for status in the world of French society before the first world war.

Ptolemy, Latin name **Claudius Ptolemaeus** (2d century A.D.), Alexandrian astronomer, geographer, and mathematician. From 127 to 151 A.D. he lived in Alexandria, where he conducted his astronomical observations. In a 13-volume series known as the *Almagest,* Ptolemy developed his view of the universe: the earth is described as the fixed center of the universe, with the sun, moon, planets, and stars revolving around it in separate zones from east to west. The Ptolemaic theory was accepted until the Copernican system supplanted it in the sixteenth and seventeenth centuries.

Ptolemy I, surnamed **Soter** (c.367–285 B.C.), first king (323–285 B.C.) of the Macedonian dynasty of Egypt. He was one of the 'favorite generals of Alexander the Great. When Alexander died, his vast empire was divided, and Ptolemy chose Egypt 'for his share (323 B.C.). The Egyptians disputed his claim to rule, but he won their respect by a series of military victories and domestic improvements. He made Alexandria his capital, built its library and museum, and was a patron of literature and science. Under his rule Egypt became a leading commercial nation. Two years before his death he abdicated in favor of his son.

Ptolemy II, surnamed **Philadelphus** (c.309–274 B.C.), king of Egypt (285–246 B.C.), son of Ptolemy I. He built a canal from the Red Sea to the Nile River to help Egyptian commerce. The famous lighthouse on Pharos, considered one of the Seven Wonders of the ancient world, was erected during his reign. He patronized the arts and engaged Manetho to write a history of the Egyptians and was instrumental in causing Bible translation known as the septuagint.

Ptolemy III, surnamed **Euergetes** (c.282–222 B.C.), king of Egypt (246–221 B.C.), son of Ptolemy II. He fought wars in western Asia and brought home many images of the Egyptian gods that had been taken away when Cambyses despoiled Egypt. The return of these sacred treasures gave him the name Euergetes (benefactor). He controlled the country as far east as Damascus and Antioch. A patron of learning, he extended the Alexandrian library. During his reign Egypt reached its peak in wealth and power.

Puccini, Giacomo (1858–1924), Italian operatic composer whose operas are highly popular because of their melodic arias and dramatic intensity. He was born in Lucca of a family of professional musicians, and studied at the Milan Conservatory. After composing several operas, he scored his first success with *Manon Lescaut* in 1893. This was followed by three works familiar to every music lover: *La Bohème* (1896), *La Tosca* (1900), and *Madame Butterfly* (1904). Puccini's other operas include *The Girl of the Golden West* (1910) and the one-act opera *Gianni Schicchi* (1918).

Pulaski, Casimir, Polish name **Kazimierz Pulaski** (1748–1779), Polish nobleman who fought in the American Revolution. He was forced into exile in 1772 for conspiring to capture the king of Poland. He met Benjamin Franklin in France and offered his services to the American army, which he joined in 1777. For his distinguished service at the battle of Brandywine he was made a brigadier general of cavalry. He held this command until March 1778, when he chose to resign rather than serve under Gen. Anthony Wayne. He then organized an independent cavalry unit, the Pulaski Legion, and was defeated at Egg Harbor, N.J., and in South Carolina. He was mortally wounded while leading a cavalry charge.

Pulitzer, Joseph (1847–1911), American editor and publisher, founder of the Pulitzer Prizes. Born in Makó, Hungary, he came to the U.S. in 1864 and served in the Union army during the Civil War. He moved to St. Louis, where he became a reporter for a German-language newspaper. In 1878 he purchased two newspapers and combined them to form the St. Louis *Post-Dispatch.* In 1883 he became owner of the New York *World,* and in 1887 founded the New York *Evening World;* he gained national prominence with his aggressive editorial policy. Pulitzer was elected to Congress from New York in 1885, but dislike for public life coupled with failing eyesight led him to resign before the end of his term. Within two years he became totally blind, but he continued to direct his newspapers almost to the day of his death. He endowed the School of Journalism at Columbia University and provided a fund for annual awards in American journalism, letters, drama, and music, known as the Pulitzer Prizes. These awards vary from $500 to $1,000 and are given yearly for the best play; the best books in the fields of the novel, poetry,

CHARLES PHELPS CUSHING

ALEKSANDER S. PUSHKIN, Russian writer.

American history, and American biography; the best work done in eight different phases of journalism; and the best musical composition.

Pullman, George Mortimer (1831–1897), American industrialist who invented the railway sleeping car that bears his name. Born in Brocton, N.Y., he worked at various construction jobs before settling in Chicago as a builder. In 1863 he built the first Pullman sleeping car, after which he designed the corridor train and the modern restaurant car. In 1880 he founded the town of Pullman, near Chicago, for his plant and employees. It later became a part of the city of Chicago.

Pupin, Michael Idvorsky (1858–1935), American physicist, noted for his electrical inventions. Born in Yugoslavia, he came to the U.S. in 1874. He was educated at Columbia University and took a doctor's degree at the University of Berlin. He taught physics at Columbia from 1892 to 1931. Among his numerous inventions were several improvements in telephone communication and X-ray technology. His autobiography, *From Immigrant to Inventor* (1923), won the Pulitzer Prize in 1924.

Purcell, Henry (1659–1695), English composer, born in London. During his career, he rose from an obscure church post to that of composer-in-ordinary to the king. Among his many works, the operas *Dido and Aeneas* (1680) and *The Fairy Queen* (1693), and *Te Deum and Jubilate,* created for Saint Cecilia's Day (1694), are considered his outstanding achievements. Purcell also wrote many sonatas, anthems, and incidental music for plays. Not until the twentieth century was his greatness fully realized.

Pushkin, Aleksander Sergeevich (1799–1837), Russian poet, regarded as one of the outstanding writers of Russian literature. Born in Moscow, he was exiled in 1820 for writing revolutionary poetry. When Nicholas I became czar, he made Pushkin a court official, affording him time for writing. Among Pushkin's major works are the long poems *Ruslan and Lyudmila* (1820) and *Eugene Onegin* (1832); the tragedy *Boris Godunov* (1831); the novel *The Captain's Daughter* (1836); and the short story *The Queen of Spades* (1834). Almost all of these works have been adapted for opera by various Russian composers. In addition, Pushkin wrote some of the finest lyric poems in the Russian language. He was killed in a duel.

Putnam, Israel (1718–1790), American general in the Revolutionary War. Born in Danvers, Mass., he was a captain in the French and Indian War and was later active in movements that led to the Revolutionary War. Putnam commanded the American troops in the battle of Long Island (1776) and was prominent at Brooklyn Heights, where he was defeated by Gen. William Howe. He campaigned in Connecticut, the Hudson Highlands, and at West Point. He became paralyzed before the war ended and never recovered.

Pu-yi, Henry. See *Hsüan T'ung.*

Pynchon, William (1590–1662), American colonist who founded Springfield, Mass. Born in Springfield, England, he came to America in 1630, settling at Dorchester in the Massachusetts Bay colony. He was treasurer of the colony from 1632 to 1634. In 1636 he was commissioned to settle and govern a plantation at the junction of the

Connecticut and Agawam rivers. He called the settlement Agawam, but it was renamed Springfield in 1641. In 1650 Pynchon published *The Meritorious Price of Our Redemption*, a tract that attacked traditional Puritan theology and infuriated the colonists. Denounced as a heretic, he returned to England in 1652.

Pyrrhus (c.318–272 B.C.), Greek military leader. As a young boy he succeeded his father as king of Epirus (306 B.C.). He was soon forced out and took refuge in Egypt; there he married the daughter of Ptolemy I, who helped him to recover his throne (295 B.C.). He conquered Macedonia and defeated the Romans in two famous battles: near Heraclea in 280 B.C. and at Asculum in 279 B.C. These victories were won at great cost of life, after which Pyrrhus is said to have remarked: "Another such victory, and Pyrrhus will be ruined." Thus, the expression "Pyrrhic victory" has come to mean any victory or gain at a ruinous cost.

Pythagoras (6th century B.C.), Greek philosopher and mathematician who developed some of the fundamental principles of geometry. As a young man in search of learning, he is said to have roamed from Persia to Gaul and from India to Egypt. On his return, he became a teacher of mathematics. He later (c.539) established a school of philosophy at Crotona, Italy, numbering several hundred students. There, he proved one of the fundamentals of geometry, which came to be called the *Pythagorean theorem*. Mathematicians refer to it as the 47th Proposition in Euclid: "The square of the hypotenuse of a right-angled triangle is equal to the sum of the squares of the other two sides." This proposition required proof from the simplest admitted fact to the ultimate conclusion, and its demonstration showed Pythagoras to be a mathematical genius.

The central idea of his philosophy was that number was the first principle of the universe and that on it depended the harmonies that keep the universe in ordered motion and create music and art. He left no writings; the *Golden Sentences* extant under his name were compiled by later philosophers.

Pytheas (4th century B.C.), Greek navigator and geographer, born in Massilia (modern Marseilles, France). He was the first to describe the relationship between the moon and the periodic fluctuation of the tides. None of his writings survives, but he had a considerable influence on later geographers. In his travels, he sailed as far north as the British Isles.

Q

Queensberry, Marquis of, See *Douglas, John Sholto*.

Quercia, Jacopo della (c.1378–1438), Italian sculptor of Siena. His works include the tomb of Ilaria del Caretto in the cathedral at Lucca; *Zacharias in the Temple*, a bronze relief in the baptistery at Siena; and *Fonte Gaia* in the public square of Siena.

Quincy, Josiah (1772–1864), American educator and statesman. Born in Boston and educated at Harvard, he became a lawyer and served four terms in the U.S. Congress (1805–1813). In 1813 he was elected to the Massachusetts Senate. Quincy was one of the first to protest against slavery, in a speech against the admission of Louisiana to the Union in 1811. He was mayor of Boston (1823–1829) and then left public life to become president of Harvard College (1829–1845). His writings include a *History of Harvard University* (2 vols., 1840), *The Municipal History of the Town and City of Boston During Two Centuries* (1852), and *The Life of John Quincy Adams* (1853).

Quintana, Manuel José (1772–1857), Spanish poet, born in Madrid. He wrote many tragedies and odes, and his *Vidas de Españoles Célebres* (3 vols., 1807–1834) is regarded as a Spanish prose classic. Associated with a group of Liberals against Louis Napoleon, he was imprisoned from 1814 to 1820. He later regained political favor and became tutor to Queen Isabella in 1833 and a senator in 1835.

Quintilian, in full **Marcus Fabius Quintilianus** (c.35–c.100 A.D.), Roman teacher and rhetorician, born in Spain. He went to Rome and organized a school of oratory. His pupils included Pliny the Younger. Quintilian prepared a series of 12 books called *Institutio Oratoria* (*Institutes of Oratory*), a collection of what he considered the finest available methods in education and rhetoric.

R

Rabelais, François, pseudonym **Alcofribas Nasier** (c.1494–1553), French humorist and satirist, born in Chinon. He was successively a Franciscan, a Benedictine monk, a physician, and a priest at Meudon. He went to Rome several times to be with his close friend Jean du Bellay, bishop of Paris and later a cardinal. Rabelais invented the giants Gargantua and Pantagruel and described with ribald wit their amusing adventures in five books, written between 1532 and 1564.

Rachmaninoff, Sergei Wassilievich (1873–1943), Russian composer, pianist, and conductor. Born in the province of Novgorod, he studied music at St. Petersburg (Leningrad) and Moscow. He made several concert tours and was conductor for the Moscow Imperial Theater (1904–1906). After the Russian Revolution he settled in the United States. He wrote operas, symphonies, piano concertos, and smaller piano works, notably the *Prelude in C Sharp Minor*.

Racine, Jean Baptiste (1639–1699), French dramatist, born in La Ferté-Milon, and educated at Beauvais and Port Royal. He went to Paris in 1663 and was closely associated with La Fontaine, Boileau, and Molière. Racine's first plays, *La Thébaïde* (1664) and *Alexandre le Grand* (1665) were produced at the Palais Royale by Molière's group. Successive plays were produced at the Hôtel de Bourgogne. Racine's great tragedies include *Andromaque* (1667), *Britannicus* (1669), *Bérénice* (1670), *Bajazet* (1672), *Iphigénie* (1674), and *Phèdre* (1677). After a period of intense rivalry between Racine and Jacques Pradon and his followers, Racine produced no new plays until *Esther* (1689) and *Athalie* (1691).

Radek, Karl Bernardovich (1885–   ), Russian Communist leader, born in Lvov, and educated at Cracow and Bern. He joined the Social Democrats in 1904 and published Communist propaganda in Switzerland during World War I. Radek returned to Russia after the revolution of 1917, attended the peace negotiations between Russia and Germany at Brest-Litovsk, and worked with the German Communists (1918–1919). After his return to Russia, Radek became an important figure in the Communist International, but he lost favor through his association with Leon Trotsky and was expelled from the party in 1925. He was readmitted in 1930 but was convicted of treason in 1937 and sentenced to a ten-year prison term.

Raeburn, Sir Henry (1756–1823), Scottish portrait painter, born at Edinburgh. At 22 he painted the Countess Leslie whom he married; together they visited Rome, where he studied for two years. He then settled in Edinburgh and soon attained preeminence among Scottish artists. He was elected to the Royal Academy in 1815, was knighted in 1822, and was appointed king's painter for Scotland a few days before his death. His style resembled that of Sir Joshua Reynolds. He excelled at portraits of famous men, notably Sir Walter Scott, David Hume, and James Boswell.

Rafael, Raffaelo. See *Raphael*.

Raleigh or **Ralegh, Sir Walter** (c.1552–1618), British explorer and writer, born in Devonshire and educated at Oxford. He went on an expedition to America with his half brother Sir Humphrey Gilbert, later fought in Irish wars and in 1582 attracted the attention of Queen Elizabeth, with whom he rose high in favor. In 1584 he fitted out two ships at his own expense, sailed to America, and claimed for England the territory known as Virginia. Later he sponsored several unsuccessful colonization projects there. He introduced the potato and tobacco into England at this time. In 1595 he sailed to South America in search of gold but failed to find any. He wrote *Discovery of Guiana* about the journey. Later he fought in several wars and for a time was governor of Jersey. Elizabeth died in 1603. Her successor, James, regarded Raleigh with suspicion. Raleigh was accused of plotting against the king and was sentenced to death, but James did not dare execute him, and kept him prisoner in the Tower of London for 13 years. During his imprisonment he wrote his *History of the World*. He was released in 1616 so that he might make another voyage to Guiana in search of gold. On his return he was beheaded under his original (1603) sentence.

Rambaud, Alfred Nicolas (1842–1905), French historian, born at Besançon. He was a member of the French Cabinet from 1879 to 1880 and in 1896 became minister of public instruction. He was appointed professor of history at the University of Paris in 1883. He wrote a number of great works on Byzantine, Russian, and French history and was editor of a general history covering the period from the fourth to the twentieth century, *Histoire général du IV. siècle jusqu'à nos jours* (1893–1901).

Ramée, Marie Louise de la, pen name **Ouida** (1839–1908), British novelist, born in Bury St. Edmunds. She is best known for romantic adventure stories, featuring upperclass characters, notably *Under Two Flags* (1867) and *Street Dust* (1901). She also wrote several books on Italian peasant life, such as *A Village Commune* (1881), based on her experiences in Florence, and many animal and children's stories.

Ramsay, Sir William (1852–1916), British chemist, born in Glasgow, Scotland. He studied at Glasgow and at German universities, and was appointed professor of chemistry at University College, London. He is especially known for his discovery of the five inert atmospheric gases: helium, argon, krypton, neon, and xenon. He was assisted in some of the work by Lord Rayleigh and Morris William Travers. He won the Nobel Prize in chemistry in 1904 and was knighted in 1906. His writings include many scientific papers and books, notably *Gases of the Atmosphere* (1896) and *Elements and Electrons* (1912).

Ramses or **Rameses,** the name of several Egyptian kings.

Ramses I (d.1314 B.C.), second king of the XIXth dynasty, reigned only 2 years. He planned and began construction of the great hall at Karnak.

Ramses II (reigned 1292–1225 B.C.), fourth king of the XIXth dynasty. He carried on a 16-year war with the Hittites and finally made peace with them and married the Hittite king's daughter. He built temples at Abydos, Thebes, and Abu-Simbel and added to the great temple at Karnak. He is believed to have been the pharaoh who oppressed the Israelites (*Genesis* and *Exodus*).

Ramses III (reigned 1198–1167 B.C.), second king of the XXth dynasty. He carried on wars in Libya and Syria. He constructed many public buildings and endowed numerous temples.

Randolph, Edmund Jennings (1753–1813), American statesman, born in Williamsburg, Va., He graduated from William and Mary College, studied law with his father, and practiced in Williamsburg. During the Revolutionary War he was an aide to Gen. George Washington. In 1776 he helped to draw up the Virginia constitution and became attorney general of Virginia. He served in the Continental Congress (1779–1782) and was elected governor of his state (1786–1788). He was prominent in the Constitutional Convention; it was he who presented the Virginia Plan, and he opposed the Constitution as it was finally drawn up. He became attorney general in Washington's first cabinet and later was secretary of state. In 1795 he resigned public office and again took up the practice of law in Virginia. He defended Aaron Burr against charges of treason.

Randolph, John (1773–1833), American statesman, known as John Randolph of Roanoke.

METROPOLITAN MUSEUM OF ART

SIR WALTER RALEIGH, Elizabethan explorer.

He was born in Prince George County, Va. A superb orator with a sharp wit, Randolph was a member of the U.S. House of Representatives (1799–1813, 1815–1817, 1819–1825, and 1827–1829), and was a member of the Senate (1825–1827). In 1830 he was U.S. minister to Russia. Randolph was firmly opposed to the War of 1812 and to the Missouri Compromise. To supporters of the compromise he attached the epithet "Doughfaces." His eccentricities developed into insanity in the latter years of his life.

Ranke, Leopold von (1795–1886), German historian, born in Wiehe, Thuringia. He studied at Halle and Leipzig, and was professor of history at the University of Berlin (1825–1871). He developed a new school of historians who based their accounts on primary sources and read and synthesized with as much objectivity as possible. Ranke himself wrote *History of the Roman and German Peoples from 1494 to 1535* (1824), *History of the Popes* (3 vols., 1834–1839), *German History in the Time of the Reformation* (6 vols., 1839–1847), and *World History* (9 parts, 1881–1888), completed by his assistants.

Rankin, Jeannette (1880–), American suffragist and legislator, born near Missoula, Mont., and educated at the University of Montana. In 1916 she was elected to Congress as Republican representative-at-large from Montana. She was the first Congresswoman. She served a second term from 1941 to 1943. In December, 1941, she was the sole member of Congress to vote against the declaration of war.

Raphael, in full **Raffaello Santi** or **Sanzio** (1483–1520), Italian painter, born in Urbino. He studied under his father, Giovanni Santi, and Timoteo Viti, and served as assistant to Il Perugino. He went to Florence in 1504 and to Rome in 1508, where Pope Leo X became his patron and appointed him chief architect of St. Peter's to succeed Donato Bramante. Constantly enriching his style by learning from his contemporaries, including Il Perugino, Michelangelo, Pintoricchio, Leonardo da Vinci, Fra Bartolommeo, and Sebastiano del Piombo, Raphael became one of the most famous painters of the Renaissance. His works include several frescoes in the Vatican, notably *Theology, Poetry, Justice, Disputa,* and *Philosophy; St. George and the Dragon; Coronation of the Virgin; La belle jardinière; Holy Family; Adoration of the Trinity; Assumption of the Virgin; Crucifixion; the Maddalena Doni; Galatea;* and his portrait of Leo X.

Rashīd al-Dīn (c.1250–1380), Arab historian, born in Hamadan. He served as physician to the Mongol leaders of Iran and was a vizier in their empire. He wrote *History of the Mongols of Persia.*

Rasmussen, Knud Johan Victor (1879–1933), Danish explorer, born in Greenland of an Eskimo mother. In 1902 he began 30 years of exploration in the Arctic. He tried to prove that the ancestors of the Eskimos migrated to northern America from Asia. In 1910 he set up the Thule base camp, Cape York, and from this station carried on seven expeditions. He was one of the greatest authorities on the Eskimos. His books include *Lapland* (1907) and *Across Arctic America* (1927).

Rasputin, Grigori Efimovich (c.1871–1916), Russian religious mystic, born in Siberia. He became a monk and gained the reputation of being a holy man. He lived in St. Petersburg and became a major influence over the czar and czarina of Russia. Corrupt and licentious, his power over the absolutist ruler was a threat to the nation. He was assassinated by a group of nobles in order to rid Russia of his influence.

Rauch, Christian Daniel (1777–1857), German sculptor, born in Arolsen. His works include the monument to Frederick the Great, dedicated in 1851 in Berlin; a reclining marble figure for the sarcophagus of Queen Louise of Prussia, in Charlottenburg; and statues of many famous Europeans including Dürer, Goethe, Kant, Luther, Schiller, and others.

Ravel, Maurice Joseph (1875–1937), French composer, born in Ciboure. He studied music at the Paris Conservatoire. His works include the ballets *Daphnis et Chloë* (1912) and *Boléro* (1928); the cantata *Myrrha;* the songs *Shéhérazade* (1903); *La valse, Rhapsodie espagnole,* and *Tzigane* (1915), and a concerto for piano and orchestra (1932). Ravel's *Boléro,* originally composed for ballet, has been a popular concert piece in the twentieth century.

Rawlinson, Sir Henry Creswicke (1810–1895), English Orientalist, born in Chadlington. He was in the military service of the East India Company from 1827 until 1833, when he was assigned to reorganize the troops of the shah of Persia. He became interested in Persian lore and studied Persian history for many years. Rawlinson became an authority on cuneiform inscriptions and translated the famous Behistun inscriptions of King Darius I. In 1851 he continued the excavations in Assyria and Babylonia begun by the French. He was British ambassador to Persia (1859–1860) and served on the Council of India (1858, 1868–1895).

George Rawlinson (1812–1902), his brother, was also an Orientalist. A graduate of Oxford, he was a professor of history (1861–1889). He took holy orders and became canon of Canterbury Cathedral in 1872. His writings include *The History of Herodotus,* edited with his brother (1858–1860); *The Five Great Monarchies of the Ancient Eastern World* (1862–1867); *The Sixth Great Oriental Monarchy—Parthia* (1873); and *The Seventh Great Oriental Monarchy—the Sassanian or New Persian Empire* (1876).

Ray, John, until 1670 **Wray** (c.1627–1705), English naturalist, born in Black Notley, Essex. With Francis Willughby, he toured the United Kingdom and Europe, collecting specimens of plant and animal life for classification. He provided a workable definition for the term *species,* and used anatomy as the basis of classifying plants. He was the first to divide flowering plants into the classifications of dicotyledons and monocotyledons. In zoology, he worked out the classifications of Metabola and Ametabola. His works include *Methodus plantarum nova* (1682) and *Historia generalis plantarum* (1686, 1688, and 1704), as well as several theological works.

Ray, Man (1890–), American painter and photographer. A surrealist, he created the films *Emak Bakia* (1926) and *L'Étoile de Mer* (1928).

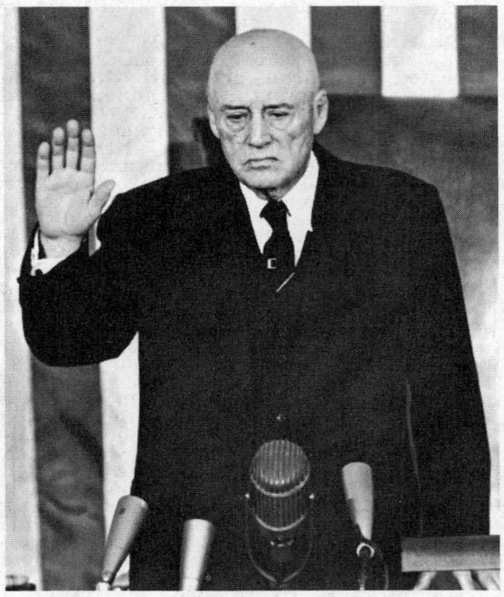

ASSOCIATED PRESS

SAM RAYBURN as Speaker of the House.

Rayburn, Samuel Taliaferro (1882–1961), American statesman. Born in Roane County, Tenn., he was educated at East Texas Normal College (B.S., 1903) and the University of Texas' Law School. Prior to passing the Texas bar, he was elected to the state legislature (1906); in 1911, at age 29 he became its youngest speaker. In 1912 he was elected to the national House of Representatives, where he subsequently composed the War Risk Insurance Act and considerable holding company legislation, and sponsored the legislation that established the Federal Communications Commission. In 1941 he brought about House passage of the Selective Service Act. He set records for length of service in the house (48 years, 258 days, consecutively) and as its speaker (1940–1946, 1949–1953, 1955–1961).

Rayleigh, John William Strutt, 3d Baron (1842–1919), English physicist, born in Witham, Essex, and educated at Cambridge. He became professor of experimental physics at Cambridge in 1879 and later taught at the Royal Institute (1897–1905). He carried on much research in light and sound and did valuable work in electricity. With Sir William Ramsay he discovered the element argon. He received the Nobel Prize for physics in 1904.

Raynal, Guillaume Thomas Francois (1713–1796), French historian and reformer. Educated for the priesthood, he became a writer and freethinker. As coauthor of *Histoire philosophique et politique des établissements et du commerce des Européens dans les deux Indes* (1770), he attacked European treatment of the natives in the Indies. In 1781 the government ordered the book burned and its author exiled.

Read, Thomas Buchanan (1822–1872), American painter and poet, born in Chester County, Pa. He studied painting in Cincinnati, Boston, and Philadelphia, before going to Florence, Italy, where he spent most of the rest of his life. He was a successful portrait painter; among his subjects were George Peabody, Mrs. Elizabeth Barrett Browning, and Henry W. Longfellow. However he is best known today for his poem *Sheridan's Ride,* commemorating an incident of the Civil War. His collected poems include *Lays and Ballads* (1849), *The New Pastoral* (1855), and *The House by the Sea* (1856). He also edited *Female Poets of America* (1848), which he illustrated.

Reade, Charles (1814–1884), English novelist and dramatist, born in Ipsden, educated at Oxford. His works include the play *Masks and Faces* (with Tom Taylor, 1852), which he revised as the novel *Peg Woffington* (1852); the novel *It Is Never Too Late to Mend* (1856), an exposé of cruelty in the British prisons. His greatest novel, *The Cloister and the Hearth* (1861), deals with the father of Erasmus. In *Hard Cash* (1863), he exposed abuses in private mental institutions, and in *Put Yourself in His Place* (1870), he attacked the violent practices of labor unions. Another novel, *A Terrible Temptation* (1871), is autobiographical.

Reading, Rufus Daniel Isaacs, 1st Marquis (1860–1935), English statesman, born in London. He studied at University College, London, and in Brussels and Hanover. He became a prominent lawyer and entered Parliament (1904). His rise was rapid. He was attorney general (1910–1913), and lord chief justice of England (1913–1921). He received a peerage, and as Viscount Reading he visited the United States in 1918 as special envoy. From 1921 to 1926 Lord Reading was viceroy of India. When he returned to England in 1926, he was raised in rank to marquis.

Réaumur, René Antoine Ferchault de (1683–1757), French physicist and biologist. Born in La Rochelle, he was educated at Poitiers, Bourges, and Paris. At the age of 25 he was elected to the French Academy of Sciences. He devised the thermometer scale named for him, in which the freezing point of water is 0° and the boiling point 80°. He discovered the method of tinning iron. He wrote several works on biology, of which his *Memoirs pour servir à l'histoire naturelle des insectes* (1732–1742) is noteworthy.

Redfield, William Charles (1789–1857), American meteorologist, born in Middletown, Conn. His studies of gales and hurricanes contributed much to meteorology, especially as a result of his theory that storms were rotary in nature. He also did much research on railroads and proposed several new routes. Redfield was president of the American Association for the Advancement of Science in 1848.

Redon, Odilon (1840–1916), French painter and engraver, born in Bordeaux. A Post-impressionist, he is best known for his floral paintings. His work is suffused with symbol and has a dream-like, mystical quality.

Red Wing (c.1750–c.1825), American Indian chief, born near the present site of Red Wing, Minnesota. A Sioux, he was helpful to the British in the War of 1812, but later maintained peaceful relations with the Americans.

Reed, John (1887–1920), American journalist and poet, born in Portland, Ore., and educated at Harvard. He was a war correspondent in Mexico (1914) and in eastern Europe (1914–1916). A witness to the Russian revolution of 1917, he returned to the U.S. to found the Communist Labor party. He was indicted for sedition and fled to Russia. On his death, he was buried in the Kremlin. His best-known work is *Ten Days that Shook the World* (1919), a first-hand account of the 1919 Bolshevik revolution.

Reed, Walter (1851–1902), American surgeon, born in Belroi, Va. He joined the U.S. Army Medical Corps in 1875 and was appointed professor at the Army Medical College, Washington, D.C., in 1893. In 1900 he studied yellow fever and showed that the disease is transmitted by a certain mosquito.

Regulus, Marcus Atilius (died c.250 B.C.), Roman general. He took Brundisium while he was consul in 267 B.C. In 256 B.C. he was again made consul, and with Manlius he defeated the Carthaginian fleet, landed at Clypea and ravaged the enemy's territory. The Carthaginians at last defeated him and took him prisoner. After five years' captivity he was sent to Rome as a hostage on parole to sue for peace between Rome and Carthage. Although he could have been a free man had he advocated peace, he refused to take such a step. Instead he urged before the Senate that Rome give Carthage no quarter and that the war against Carthage be relentlessly pursued. He voluntarily returned to Carthage where the angry rulers put him to death.

Reiner, Fritz (1888–1963), American conductor, born in Budapest, Hungary. He studied at the Royal Academy of Music in Budapest and conducted the Dresden Royal Opera (1914–1922). After coming to the U.S., he conducted the Cincinnati Symphony Orchestra (1922–1931), and was director of the Pittsburgh Symphony Orchestra (1938–1948). He was a conductor of the Metropolitan Opera Company (1948–1953) and musical director of the Chicago Symphony Orchestra from 1953 to 1960.

Reinhardt, Max, original surname **Goldman** (1873–1943), Austrian theatrical manager and producer, born near Vienna. He owned several cabaret theaters and was director at important German theaters. He became world-famous for his productions, among which were *Faust, Oedipus Rex, Salome, Everyman, The Miracle,* and *The Eternal Road.*

Remarque, Erich Maria (1898–   ), German-American novelist, born in Osnabrück, Westphalia. He served in the German Army in World War I, and lived in Switzerland (1929–1939). He came to the U.S. in 1939 and became an American citizen. An antimilitarist, his novels include *All Quiet on the Western Front* (1929), *The Road Back* (1931), *Three Comrades* (1937), *Arch of Triumph* (1946), and *A Time to Love and a Time to Die* (1954).

Rembrandt, in full **Rembrandt Harmensz van Rijn** or **Ryn** (1606–1669), Dutch painter and etcher, born in Leiden. He moved to Amsterdam in 1631 and married Saskia van Uijlenburgh in 1634. Although he enjoyed early success, Rembrandt went bankrupt in 1656, 14 years after the death of his wife, and began painting for a shop run by his son, Titus, and his housekeeper, Hendrickje Stoffels. He died in poverty. Rembrandt's works include genre scenes, portraits, landscapes, still lifes, and biblical and mythical scenes. Among them are *The Anatomy Lesson of Dr. Tulp, The Sortie of the Banning Cocq Company* (the so-called *Night Watch*), *Simeon in the Temple,* and *Danaë;* several portraits of himself, his wife, and his son; and the etchings *Descent from the Cross, Christ Healing the Sick,* and *Christ Preaching.* In 1961, Rembrandt's painting *Aristotle Contemplating the Bust of Homer* was purchased by the New York Metropolitan Museum of Art for $2.3 million.

Remington, Frederic (1861–1909), American artist, born in Canton, N.Y. He studied art at Yale and at the Art Students League in New York before ill health drove him to the western plains, where he lived as a rancher and cowboy and fought against the Indians. He became a painter of western scenes of action and everyday life. Among

ST. LAWRENCE UNIVERSITY

FREDERIC REMINGTON'S Broncho Buster.

his paintings are *The Last Stand* (an Indian battle scene), *A Dash for the Timber, Conjuring the Buffalo Back, The Emigrants,* and *Past All Surgery.* Two of his finest sculptures are *Broncho Buster* and *Wounded Bunkie.* He also wrote and illustrated *Crooked Trails* (1898), *Pony Tracks* (1895), and *The Way of an Indian* (1906).

Reni, Guido (1575–1642), Italian painter, born near Bologna. A member of the Eclectic school, he painted *Crucifixion of St. Peter, Aurora, Massacre of the Innocents, St. Sebastian,* and *Ecce Homo.*

Renoir, Pierre Auguste (1841–1919), French painter, a founder of the Impressionist school and one of the foremost masters of European art. He was born in Limoges and studied painting at the École des Beaux-Arts in Paris, where he formed a close friendship with Claude Monet. His landscapes, portraits, and flower pictures include *Madame Charpentier et ses Enfants, Baigneuses, La Balançoire,* and *Le Moulin de la Galette.*

Respighi, Ottorino (1879–1936), Italian composer, born in Bologna. He studied with Rimski-Korsakov in St. Petersburg and with Max Bruch in Berlin. His works include the symphonic poems *Pini di Roma* and *Fontane di Roma,* the operas *Re Enzo* and *La Fiamma,* and *Sinfonia Drammatica.*

Reuther, Walter Philip (1907–   ), American labor leader, born in Wheeling, W. Va. He studied at Wayne State University then became an apprentice tool-and-die maker for Wheeling Steel Corporation in 1924. Later he was employed by Briggs Manufacturing Company, General Motors, and Ford Motor Company. In 1932 he went abroad, traveling by bicycle through Europe and the Orient to observe auto plants and machine shops. Reuther returned to the U.S. in 1935 to organize the auto workers. In 1945–1946 he led the 113-day strike by General Motors workers. He became president of the Congress of Industrial Organization in 1952, and vice-president of the combined unions AFL and CIO in 1955.

Revere, Paul (1735–1818), American patriot, born in Boston, Mass. An engraver by trade, he was among the finest of America's silversmiths. He is most famous, however, for the ride he made the night of April 18, 1775, from Charlestown (Boston) to Lexington to warn of the coming of the British. This inspired Longfellow to write his well-known poem *The Midnight Ride of Paul Revere.* Later, Revere designed and printed the first issue of Continental money. He prospered in business after the Revolutionary War. He operated a copper foundry and discovered a way to roll sheet copper.

Reynolds, Sir Joshua (1723–1792), English painter, born in Plympton, Devonshire. He began his career as a portrait painter at Devonport but soon moved to London, where he lived and worked throughout a busy life, except for three years in Italy. He was elected the first president of the Royal Academy in 1768 and in 1784 was appointed painter to George III. He founded the Literary Club that included Dr. Johnson, Garrick, Goldsmith, Boswell, Burke, and Sheridan. He was especially famous for his portraits, of which he executed fully 2,000, including the celebrated *Mrs. Siddons as the Tragic Muse, The Strawberry Girl,* and *The Age of Innocence.*

Rhee, Syngman (1875–1965), Korean politician and first president, born in Whanghai province, Korea. He learned English in a mission school and then came to the United States for study. He returned to Korea, worked for Korean independence, was imprisoned; and after his release returned to the United States to study at Princeton University. He again returned to Korea in 1910 and in 1919 was elected president of the Korean provisional government-in-exile (in China) returning to Korea in 1945 after the defeat of the Japanese. He established the provisional government in the American occupied southern half of Korea and on July 20, 1948, was elected the first president of the Korean republic. He resigned in 1960, after severe rioting and the resignation of his cabinet.

Rhodes, Cecil John (1853–1902), English statesman, born in Hertfordshire. He went to Natal, South Africa, for the sake of his health. He reaped a fortune from the diamond fields around Kimberley, then went home to complete his education and graduated from Oriel College, Oxford, in 1881. He then returned to South Africa to try to extend British possessions, Rhodes entered the Cape Colony house of assembly, was made a member of the cabinet and from 1890 to 1896 was prime minister. He made Bechuanaland a British protectorate and in 1889 formed the British South Africa Company. The company was given control over what was later known as Rhodesia.

METROPOLITAN MUSEUM OF ART

REMBRANDT, a detail of a self-portrait.

He planned the Cape-to-Cairo railroad connecting British interests in Africa. Rhodes approved the Jameson Raid into the Boer Republic of the Transvaal, and as a result had to withdraw as prime minister. For the rest of his life he worked for the development of Rhodesia. In his will he left about six million pounds to various philanthropies, including the famous Rhodes Scholarships at Oxford University, England.

Ribbentrop, Joachim von (1893–1946), German diplomat, born in Wesel. A wine merchant after World War I, he joined the National Socialist party in 1932. He was instrumental in setting up the first Nazi government in 1933, became ambassador at large in 1935, and served as ambassador to Great Britain (1936–1938). As minister of foreign affairs (1938–1945), he negotiated the Anglo-German naval agreement, the German-Japanese anti-Comintern agreement, and a nonaggression pact with Russia. He was condemned to death in the war trials at Nürnberg and executed.

Ribera José or **Jusepe,** called **Lo Spagnoletto** (1588–1652), Spanish painter and etcher, leader of the Neopolitan school. He was born in Jativa and lived mostly in Naples, Italy. His paintings include the *Martyrdom of St. Bartholomew* and *Descent from the Cross.*

Rice, Elmer L., original surname **Reizenstein** (1892–1967), American playwright, born in New York City; graduated *cum laude* from New York Law School. His first play, *On Trial,* produced in 1914, was an immediate success. His *Street Scene* (1929) won a Pulitzer Prize and was later made into a musical by Kurt Weill and Langston Hughes. Other successes included *We the People, Counsellor-at-Law,* and *Dream Girl.* He died May 8, 1967 in Southampton, Eng.

Richard I, known as **Richard Coeur de Lion** or **Richard the Lionhearted** (1157–1199), king of England (1189–1199), third son of Henry II and Eleanor of Aquitaine. He succeeded Henry as king and reigned for ten years, but passed only a few months in England. Soon after his coronation he joined Philip II of France in the third Crusade. Richard nearly impoverished his kingdom by borrowing money to finance the enterprise, but he won a great reputation as a warrior. On the return home in 1192 Richard was held for ransom in Austria until 1194, when a large sum was paid for his release. He was killed in battle.

Richard II (1367–1400), king of England (1377–1399), born in Bordeaux, France, the son of Edward the Black Prince and grandson of Edward III, whom he succeeded. He became king under a regency at the age of 11, submitting to the counsels of the dukes of Lancaster and of Gloucester. In 1389 he became sole ruler. During his reign the peasants of the Wat Tyler rebellion of 1381 tried to bring about recognition of their demands to alleviate the economic distress of the period. Richard was defeated by Henry Bolingbroke, duke of Hereford, whom he had banished. After his arrest and probable execution in prison, he was succeeded by Bolingbroke, who became Henry IV.

Richard III (1452–1485), king of England (1483–1485), brother of Edward IV. Throughout Edward's reign Richard supported him loyally and was rewarded with many high offices. However, when Edward died he usurped the crown from his nephew, Edward V. Richard's young heir and his younger brother, the duke of York, were killed in the Tower of London; Richard is believed to have ordered their death. In 1485 Henry, earl of Richmond, landed at Milford Haven with his forces and defeated the king in the battle of Bosworth Field, in Leicestershire. Richard was killed in this battle. The House of York and the Plantagenet line of kings ended with his death. He was succeeded by Henry VII, the former earl of Richmond, the first of the Tudor line.

Richards, Ivor Armstrong, known as **I. A. Richards** (1893–), British literary critic. With C. K. Ogden and James Wood he wrote *Foundations of Aesthetics* (1921), and with Ogden *The Meaning of Meaning* (1923). He also wrote the highly influential *Principles of Literary Criticism* (1924), in addition to *Practical Criticism* (1929), *Coleridge on Imagination* (1934), and *How to Read a Page* (1942). A leading proponent of Basic English, he wrote *Basic English and Its Uses* (1943).

Richards, Theodore William (1868–1928), American chemist, born in Germantown, Pa. He studied at Haverford College and in Germany. He taught at Harvard and later was associated with the Carnegie Institute. Much of his work was with isotopes and in several fields of physical chemistry. He won the Nobel Prize for chemistry in 1914 for his determination of atomic weights.

Richardson, Sir **Owen Willans** (1879–1959), British physicist, born in Yorkshire, and educated at Cambridge. He taught physics at Princeton (1906–1914), then returned home to teach at King's College. His best-known experimental work was with the emission of electrons from hot bodies. He won the Nobel Prize for physics in 1928.

Richardson, Samuel (1689–1761), English novelist, often called the father of the English domestic novel. He was born in Derbyshire, established a printing business in London, and became official printer to the House of Commons and a printer to the king. His first novel, *Pamela: or Virtue Rewarded* (1740) was followed by *Clarissa; or the History of a Young Lady* (7 vols., 1747–1748), and *The History of Sir Charles Grandison* (7 vols., 1753).

Richelieu, Armand Jean du Plessis, Duc de, called **Éminence Rouge** (1585–1642), French cardinal and minister of Louis XIII. He received an education along two distinct lines—military and ecclesiastical. He chose the Church and in 1606 was made a bishop. He was selected as a Church representative in the States-General in 1614, where he came to the notice of Marie de Médicis, mother of King Louis XIII. She kept him at court, and in 1616 he became secretary for foreign affairs. In 1622 he was made a cardinal and within two years was the dominant power in France. In order to bring about an alliance with England he arranged a marriage between the prince of Wales and Henrietta Maria, sister of Louis XIII.

His policy throughout had three great aims: to suppress the political power of the Huguenots; to strengthen the royal authority; and to make France secure against the threatened domination of the Hapsburgs. He pursued these goals until his death. Heavy taxes levied to cover the enormous amounts he spent in the Thirty Years' War led to widespread revolts and dislike of Richelieu. During his ascendancy he founded the French Academy in 1635.

Richter, Jean Paul Friedrich, pseudonym **Jean Paul** (1763–1825), German novelist, born in Bavaria. He studied at Leipzig and began his literary career in 1783 with the publication of *The Greenland Lawsuits*. In 1789 he published *Selections from the Papers of the Devil* and in 1793 *The Invisible Lodge*. This was followed by *Hesperus* (1794), the work by which he is best known outside of Germany.

Rickenbacker, Edward Vernon (1890–), American aviator, born in Columbus, Ohio. He went to France with the American Expeditionary Force as a mechanical expert in the automotive division, but soon transferred to aviation. He rose to the command of the 94th Aero Pursuit squadron and personally accounted for 26 of the 69 enemy planes destroyed by his unit. He received the Congressional Medal of Honor. Rickenbacker became president and general manager of Eastern Airlines.

Ridgway, Matthew Bunker (1895–), American general, born in Fort Monroe, Va., and a graduate of West Point (1917). During World War II Gen. Ridgway commanded the first air-borne operation in American history in the attack on Sicily. He also participated in the invasion of France. While commander of the 8th U.S. army in Korea, he was appointed in 1951 to replace Douglas MacArthur in his commands in the Far East. In 1952 Gen. Ridgeway was selected to succeed Dwight D. Eisenhower as supreme commander of the allied forces in Europe; he became commander in chief of the U.S. European command and served as army chief of staff (1953–1955).

Ridpath, John Clark (1840–1900), American historian, born in Putnam County, Ind., and educated at Asbury University (now DePauw). He was professor of history at Baker University in Baldwin, Kan., and later taught history and English literature at his alma mater. His writings include *A Popular History of the United States of America* (1876), and *The Great Races of Mankind* (4 vols., 1884–1894).

Riel, Louis (c.1844–1885), Canadian revolutionary leader, born in Manitoba of French and Indian ancestry. In 1869–1870 he led the French half-breeds of the Northwest in a rebellion against the Dominion government. They resented the fact that the government was about to take over their territory, hitherto controlled by the Hudson's Bay Company. The revolt, known as the Red River Rebellion, failed, and Riel fled to the United States. He was elected to the Dominion Parliament, and on his return attempted to take his seat, but he was expelled and declared an outlaw in 1875. He started another rebellion in 1885, was arrested on a charge of high treason, for which he was found guilty and hanged.

Rienzi or **Rienzo, Cola di,** real name **Niccolò Gabrini** (1313-1354), Roman patriot. Born in Rome, the son of an innkeeper. His aim was to restore the former glory of Rome by putting an end to the disorders that prevailed in and around the city. In 1347 he led an attack against the nobles and took the title of tribune with dictatorial powers. He proved an excellent leader at first but soon became blinded by success, and took to extravagant living. The people tired of him and his vanity, and he was forced to escape from the city. Attempting to regain power in 1354, he was assassinated.

Riis, Jacob August (1849–1914), American journalist and social reformer born in Ribe, Denmark. He came to the U.S. in 1870 and became a police reporter on the New York *Sun* and *Tribune*. His investigations of slum conditions led to housing and other social reforms. Among his publications are *How the Other Half Lives* (1890), *The Children of the Poor* (1892), *The Battle With the Slum* (1902), and *Children of the Tenements* (1903). His autobiography, *The Making of an American* (1961), been widely read for generations.

Riley, James Whitcomb (1849–1916), American poet, born in Greenfield, Ind., known as "the Hoosier poet." In 1877 he began to contribute poems to the Indianapolis *Journal*. Often written in local dialect, these poems brought him national popularity. Among his best known poems are *The Old Swimmin' Hole, Afterwhiles, Old Fashioned Roses, When the Frost is on the Pumpkin*, and *The Little Orfant Annie Book*.

Rilke, Rainer Maria (1875–1926), German poet and writer, born in Prague. Originally a student of art history, he served as secretary to the sculptor Auguste Rodin for several years. His lyric poems and tales, which established him as a leading German writer, include *Die Weise von Liebe und Tod des Cornets Christoph Rilke* (1906; *Tale of Love and Death of Coronet Christoph Rilke*, 1932), and *Die Aufzeichnungen des Malte Laurids Brigge* (2 vols., 1910; *The Notebook of Malte Laurids Brigge*, 1930).

Rimbaud, Arthur, full name **Jean Nicolas Arthur Rimbaud** (1854–1891), French poet, born in Charleville, in the Ardennes. A symbolist, he was a close friend of Paul Verlaine for a few years. His volumes of poetry, published mainly before the age of 20, include *Le Dormeur du val, Le Bateau ivre, Une Saison en enfer*, and *Les Illuminations*, published by Verlaine after Rimbaud had abandoned poetry. After this period of writing he traveled in Europe, the Middle East, and finally in North Africa, where he became a merchant and trader.

Rimski-Korsakov, Nikolai Andreyevich (1844–1908), Russian composer, born in Tikhvin, Novgorod. He studied at a naval academy and served in the Russian navy. He soon turned to music, however, and became acquainted with Balakirev, Moussorgsky, and Borodin. In 1871 he became a professor at the St. Petersburg Conservatory of Music. His works include the operas *The Maid of Pskov, The Snow Maiden*, and *Le coq d'or;* the symphonic poem *Scheherazade;* and several symphonies.

Rinehart, William Henry (1825–1874), American sculptor, born near Union Bridge, Md. For a time he worked as a stonecutter in Baltimore, then studied sculpture in Rome (1855–1857). He completed Thomas Crawford's bronze doors for the Capitol in Washington. His other works include *Rebecca, Hero, Day, Night*, and *Strewing Flowers*, and *Love Reconciled with Death*.

Ringling, family name of five brothers, **Albert C.** (1852–1916), **Otto** (1858–1911), **Alfred T.** (1861–1919), **Charles** (1863–1926), and **John** (1866–1936). In 1884 they organized a circus, which they continually expanded. They bought the Forepaugh-Sells Circus in 1906 and Barnum and Bailey Circus in 1907.

Rittenhouse, David (1732–1796), American astronomer, born near Germantown, Pa. He built two orreries, an observatory, and a transit telescope, and invented the collimating telescope in 1785. He was the first director of the U.S. mint and succeeded Benjamin Franklin as president of the American Philosophical Society (1791–1796).

Rivera, Diego (1886–1957), Mexican mural painter, born in Guanajuato. He studied in Spain, Paris, and London. A Socialist, he revealed his proletarian sympathies in his murals, which often combined folk art with political propaganda. His mural for Rockefeller Center in New York City was removed because of its implicit Communist sympathies. His other works include murals in the Detroit Institute of Arts, in the New School for Social Research (New York), and in the Ministry of Education building in Mexico City.

Rivera y Orbaneja, Miguel Primo de, Marqués **de Estella** (1870–1930), Spanish general and dictator. He received a military education and served in the Spanish-American War. In 1923, when anarchy threatened Spain, he became dictator with the approval of King Alfonso XIII and popular support from the people. After restoring order in Spain and subduing the Riff rebels in Morocco with the aid of the French, he gave up his formal dictatorship in 1925 and became premier in a constitutional government, while retaining almost all of his previous powers. In the next few years his enemies increased. He was dismissed by the king and went to Paris.

Rizzio or **Riccio, David** (c.1533–1566), Italian musician, the favorite of Mary, Queen of Scots. Born in Piedmont, he went to Scotland (1561) as secretary of the Piedmontese ambassador. He came to Mary's attention as a singer and musician, and soon he became her foreign secretary and chief adviser. He arranged her marriage with Lord Darnley. His haughty manner made him unpopular and the nobles disliked his influence over the queen. Darnley organized a conspiracy of Protestant lords who murdered him.

Robbia, Luca della (c.1400–1482), Florentine sculptor. Trained as a goldsmith, he turned to sculpture and produced works in terra cotta, bronze, and marble. One of his best-known works is the series of *Singing Galleries* in Florence, 10 panels in high relief representing children singing.

Robert VIII, called **the Bruce.** See *Bruce, Robert*.

Roberts, Elizabeth Madox (1886–1941), American poet and novelist, born in Springfield, Ky. Her novels, written in the Kentucky mountain dialect, concern themselves with the strivings of poor whites to improve themselves. The best of these include *The Time of Man* (1926), *Jingling in the Wind* (1928), *The Great Meadow*, (1930), and *He Sent Forth a Raven* (1935). *Under the Tree* (1922) is an anthology of poems for children.

Roberts, Frederick Sleigh, 1st Earl **Roberts of Kandahar, Pretoria and Waterford** (1832–1914), British soldier, born at Cawnpore, India, where his parents were stationed with an army garrison. He was educated at Eton College and Sandhurst (military school), England. In 1851 he went back to India with an army commission. He served through the Sepoy Mutiny and made his famous march (1880) through Afghanistan to the relief of Kandahar. From 1885 to 1893 he was commander in chief in India. In 1895 he was made field marshal and commander in chief of the forces in Ireland. He was put in command of the British army in South Africa, which brought about the annexation of the Orange Free State and the Transvaal and the occupation of Pretoria in 1899. Roberts then turned over the command to Lord Kitchener and returned to England to receive an earldom. Several years later he died while reviewing the British army in France.

Roberval, Gilles Personne de or **Personier de** (1602–1675), French mathematician, born near Beauvais. He studied in Paris (1627-

1631), became professor of philosophy at Gervais College, Paris, and from 1633 until his death was professor of mathematics at the Royal College of France. He discovered a way to construct and determine the area of a cycloid and a method of determining tangents. Outside the field of pure mathematics he devoted considerable study to the system of the universe, and he invented the Robervallian balance.

Robeson, Paul (1898–), American Negro singer and actor, born in Princeton, N.J. He graduated from Rutgers, where he was an All-American in football (1918) and earned a law degree at Columbia. He made his concert singing debut in New York City in 1925, then went on to tour Europe, America, and Russia. His rich bass-baritone voice won him universal acclaim. He is especially remembered for the interpretation of the song *Ol' Man River*, from the operetta *Show Boat*. As an actor he is famous for his roles in the plays *Emperor Jones, Porgy, Black Boy*, and *Othello*.

Robespierre, Maximilien François Marie Isidore de (1758–1794), French lawyer and revolutionary leader, born in Arras. He became a deputy to the States-General in 1789 and rose rapidly to power. As deputy to the National Convention he became leader of the Montagnards. He became a leader of the Committee of Public Safety and was largely responsible for the Reign of Terror, which began in 1793. Among the many guillotined were former close associates such as Georges Danton and Jacques Hébert. After the Revolution of the 9th Thermidor (July 27, 1794) he was arrested and guillotined.

Robinson, Edwin Arlington (1869–1935), American poet, born in Head Tide, Me. He was educated at Harvard and became a member of the National Institute of Arts and Letters. His work became widely recognized with the publication in 1916 of *The Man Against the Sky*. It was followed by *Merlin* (1917), *Lancelot* (1920), *The Three Taverns* (1920), *and Avon's Harvest* (1921). He won the Pulitzer Prize for poetry three times: in 1921 for *Collected Poems;* in 1925 for *The Man Who Died Twice;* and in 1927 for *Tristram*. Later works include *The Glory of the Nightingales* (1930), *Matthias at the Door* (1931), and *Nicodemus* (1932).

Robinson, James Harvey (1863–1936), American historian and educator, born in Bloomington, Ill. He was educated at Harvard and in Germany, and was professor of history at Columbia (1892–1919). In 1919 he was one of the founders of the New School for Social Research, New York City. In his teaching and writing, he stressed the importance of the social, intellectual, and scientific aspects of history to enrich the traditional political and diplomatic studies. His works include *The Mind in the Making* (1921), *Introduction to the History of Western Europe* (1903), and *The Ordeal of Civilization* (1926).

Robinson, Joseph Taylor (1872–1937), American lawyer and legislature, born near Lonoke, Ark. In 1903 he was elected to the U.S. House of Representatives and in 1913 to the U.S. Senate. He was Democratic leader in the Senate (1923–1937). He was a cosponsor of the Robinson-Patman Act (1936), known as the Fair-Trade Agreement.

Rob Roy. See *MacGregor, Robert*.

Rochambeau, Comte de, title of **Jean Baptiste Donatien de Vimeur** (1725–1807), French soldier, born in Vendôme. He served in the War of the Austrian Succession and in the Seven Years' War. He commanded 6,000 French soldiers sent to help the Americans during the Revolutionary War. He was created a marshal of France in 1791.

Roche, Josephine Aspinwall (1886–), American public official, born in Neligh, Neb. She was educated at Vassar and Columbia and was a probation officer with the Family Court of Denver, Colo. She also served with the Children's Bureau in Washington and later returned to the Denver Court as referee. She inherited a mining company and immediately set up a new standard of relations between employer and employee. In 1933 she was made an executive in the WPA and in 1934 became assistant secretary of the treasury. In 1938 she was chairman of the National Health Conference.

Rochefoucauld, La. See *La Rochefoucauld*.

Rockefeller, John Davison (1839–1937), American oil magnate and philanthropist, born in Richford, N.Y., and educated in the public schools. At the age of 19, he formed a produce commission firm—Clark and Rockefeller—with a partner; by 1867, it operated the largest oil refinery in Ohio. A merger in 1870 of this company and others created the Standard Oil Company of Ohio. Rockefeller ultimately controlled

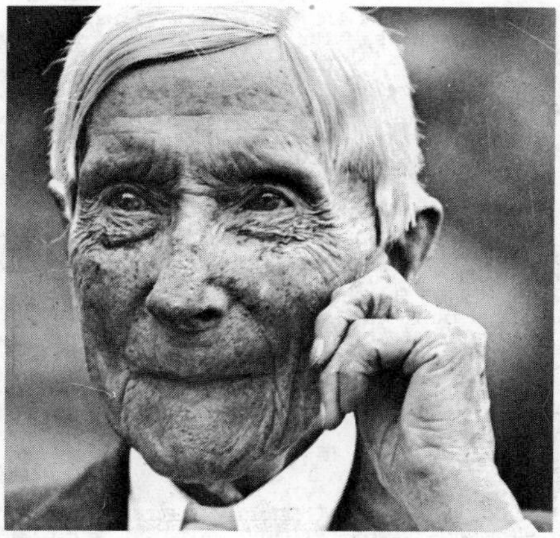

INTERNATIONAL NEWS

JOHN D. ROCKEFELLER

about 90 per cent of all American refineries. The Standard Oil Trust was dissolved in 1892, when the U.S. government attacked it under the antitrust laws. Rockefeller continued as president of Standard Oil Company of New Jersey until 1911, when he retired, the richest man in the world. As a philanthropist, he gave over $600 million, establishing the Rockefeller Foundation (1913), the General Education Board (1902), the Laura Spelman Rockefeller Memorial Foundation (1918), and the Rockefeller Institute for Medical Research (1901).

Rockefeller, Nelson Aldrich (1908–), American business executive and government administrator, born in Bar Harbor, Me., grandson of John D. Rockefeller. Rockefeller was appointed U.S. coordinator of inter-American affairs (1940) and assistant secretary of state (1944–1945). He was elected governor of New York and reelected in 1962. Rockefeller was a leading contender for the 1964 Republican presidential nomination but was defeated at the convention by Sen. Barry Goldwater.

Rockne, Knute Kenneth (1888–1931), American football coach, born in Voss, Norway. He came to the U.S. in 1891 and in 1914 graduated from Notre Dame. After graduation Rockne remained at Notre Dame as a chemistry instructor and football coach, becoming head coach in 1918. Rockne has been called the greatest college football coach of all time, and in his use of the forward pass and attention to basic football skills helped, more than any other coach, to perfect this sport.

Rodin, François Auguste René (1840–1917), French sculptor, born in Paris. His first exhibition in the Paris salon was *The Age of Bronze* (1877). This was followed by *The Kiss, The Bather, Adam, Eve, La Guerre, The Hand of God*, and *The Thinker*. He executed a great monument of Victor Hugo, as well as busts of George Bernard Shaw, Clemenceau, and Balzac. His famous bronze doors, *The Gates of Hell*, was the product of 30 year's work.

Rodney, George Brydges, 1st Baron (1719–1792), British admiral, born at Walton-on-Thames. He joined the navy in 1732 and ten years later had his own ship. He was governor of Newfoundland (1748–1752). In 1762 he seized Martinique and a few other French islands and was made a vice admiral in 1763. He became commander in chief of Jamaica and then of the Leeward Islands, and in 1778 was made an admiral. In 1781 he captured territory in the Dutch West Indies and in 1782 defeated and captured the French admiral François de Grasse off the coast of Dominica. He was then created a baron and spent the rest of his life in retirement.

Roebling, John Augustus (1806–1869), American civil engineer, born in Mühlhausen, Germany. After coming to the U.S. in 1831, he began to manufacture steel cable and became a pioneer builder of suspension bridges. He built suspension bridges over the Ohio River at Cincinnati, at Niagara Falls, and designed and began construction of the Brooklyn Bridge across the East River in New York City. Construction was completed under the direction of his son. **Washington Augustus Roebling** (1837–1926), also a civil engineer.

Roentgen or **Röntgen, Wilhelm Conrad** (1845–1923), German physicist, born in Lennep, Prussia. He was educated at Zurich and taught physics at Strasbourg, Giessen, Würzburg, and Munich. In 1895 he discovered X rays, also known as Roentgen rays. In 1901 he won the Nobel Prize in physics.

Rogers, Will, in full **William Penn Adair Rogers** (1879–1935), American humorist, and actor, born in Oologah, Okla. His public career began in 1905, when he appeared on the vaudeville stage in an act that combined monologue with rope tricks. This was followed by several engagements in the Ziegfeld Follies. He became a popular motion-picture actor as well as a writer, lecturer, and newspaper columnist. He died with Wiley Post in an airplane crash. His books include *The Cowboy Philosopher on Prohibition* (1919), *What We Laugh At* (1920), *Illiterate Digest* (1924), and *Letters of a Self-Made Diplomat to His President* (1927).

Rogier van der Weyden. See *Weyden*.

Roland de La Platière, Jean Marie (1734–1793), French revolutionary leader, born in Thizy. After an early career as an industrial inspector, he turned to politics and became leader of the Girondists in 1791. He was minister of the interior in 1792 and 1793. When Robespierre came to power he opposed the leader's plans to execute Louis XVI and was forced to flee Paris. He committed suicide when news reached him of the execution of his wife, **Jeanne Manon Phlipon** (1754–1793). Her home had been a meeting place for Republicans and Girondists. As she awaited execution she is reported to have said "O Liberty, what crimes are committed in thy name."

Rolfe, John (1585–1622), English colonist in America. He reached Virginia in 1610. Rolfe was the first colonist to cure tobacco, and make it an exportable and profitable commodity. In 1614 he married Pocahontas, daughter of the Indian chief Powhatan. The couple visited England, where Pocahontas died. Rolfe returned to Virginia where he is thought to have been killed in an Indian raid.

Rolland, Romain (1866–1944), French writer and scholar, born in Clamecy. He was professor of music history at the Sorbonne and at the École Normale. He wrote several plays, notably *Danton* (1900), *Le Quatorze Le 14 julliet* (1902), and *Robespierre* (1938). In *Le Théâtre du peuple* (1903), he urged the creation of a popular theater. He also wrote biographies of Beethoven, Michelangelo, Tolstoy, and Mahatma Gandhi. His masterpiece, *Jean Christophe* (1906–1912), is a ten-volume novel about a musical genius. Rolland was awarded the Nobel Prize for literature in 1915.

Romains, Jules, real name **Louis Farigoule** 1885–), French author, born in Saint-Julien-Chapteuil. Much of his writing is based on the philosophy known as unanism, which considers the study of man in groups more meaningful than studies of individuals. He came to the U.S. during World War I and in 1946, after his return to France, was elected to the French Academy. His novels include *Mort de quelqu'un* (*Death of a Nobody*, 1911), *Les copains* (*The Boys in the Back Room*, 1913), and a series entitled *Les Hommes de bonne volonté* (*Men of Good Will*, 1932–1947). He also wrote plays, such as *Dr. Knock* (1923) and *Volpone* (1928). His collections of verse include *L'ame des hommes* (*Men's Souls*, 1904) and *Odes et prières* (*Odes and Prayers*, 1913).

Romanes, George John (1848–1894), British biologist, born in Kingston, Canada. A friend of Charles Darwin, he supported Darwin's theory of evolution by studies relating the mental faculties of animals and men. His writings include *Animal Intelligence* (1881), *Mental Evolution in Animals* (1883), and *Mental Evolution in Man* (1888). Originally a skeptic, he became a Christian in later life.

Romano, Giulio, real name **Giulio Pippi de' Gianuzzi** (1499–1546), Italian painter and architect, born in Rome. A student of Raphael, he was appointed chief artist to Duke Federigo Gonzaga in Mantua in 1524. His paintings include *Madonna*, frescoes in the Vatican loggia, a fresco of the *Fall of the Titans, Holy Family*, and *Martyrdom of St. Stephen*. As an architect, he designed the ducal palace at Mantua, the Palazzo del Tè at Mantua, and the nearby church of San Benedetto.

Romberg, Sigmund (1887–1951), American composer, born in Szeged, Hungary. He studied in Vienna, graduated from the University of Bucharest, and came to the U.S. in 1910. He wrote many popular operettas, including *Maytime* (1917), *The Student Prince* (1924), *Blossom Time* (1926), *The Desert Song* (1926), *The New Moon* (1927), *The Night is Young* (1935), *May Wine* (1935), *Sunny River* (1941), and *Up in Central Park* (1945).

Rommel, Erwin (1891–1944), German general, born in Heidenheim. As a lieutenant in World War I, he received the Iron Cross for his actions. In World War II he commanded the capture of Prague in 1939, then led a Panzer division in the invasion of France in 1940. As commander in North Africa, he was known as the "Desert Fox." After he recaptured Tobruk, he was promoted to general field marshal. After several victories, he was defeated by the British at El Alamein. He was recalled and sent to southern Europe, then to western Europe when the Allies invaded Normandy. He was implicated in a plot in July 1944 to assassinate Hitler, and committed suicide.

Röntgen, Wilhelm Konrad. See *Roentgen*.

Roosevelt, Franklin Delano (1882–1945), thirty-second president of the United States (1933–1945), fifth cousin of Theodore Roosevelt, son of James and Sara Delano Roosevelt. He was born at the family estate, Hyde Park, N.Y. He graduated from Harvard in 1904 and received a law degree from Columbia in 1907. After he was admitted to the bar he began to practice with a firm of lawyers in New York City. He was elected as a Democrat to the New York Senate in 1910 and resigned in 1913 to become assistant secretary of the Navy in Woodrow Wilson's administration. In 1920 he was nominated as vice-president on the ticket with James M. Cox, but was defeated.

In 1921 his political career was temporarily halted by an attack of infantile paralysis. In 1924, seated in a wheel chair on the platform of the Democratic national convention, he nominated Alfred E. Smith for the presidency. As governor of New York (1929–1931), he promoted social legislation, regulation of public utilities, and state development and operation of water power. In 1932 he was the Democratic nominee for president. He won 472 of the 531 electoral votes to defeat Herbert Hoover, the Republican incumbent. In February 1933, an attempt to assassinate Roosevelt in Florida failed. He was inaugurated on March 4, 1933, at a time of national financial crisis, and he began to set in operation forces for national recovery. Almost at once he closed all the banks in the country, declaring a "bank holiday" for a brief period. This he followed with his "New Deal" program, which he broadcast to the public, the first president to make use of the radio in this manner.

Roosevelt quickly acquired enormous powers. Appropriations amounting to seven billion dollars were placed at his disposal to restore buying power among the people and to put millions of idle men and women to work. Thus he established the National Recovery Administration (NRA), the Home Owners Loan Corporation, the Federal Emergency Relief Administration (replaced by the Works Progress Administration in 1935), and the Federal Deposit Insurance Corporation, and instituted Social Security. The president was supported by a strong Democratic Congress; a huge public-works program was put through, and an elaborate plan of farm relief was instituted. The eighteenth amendment was repealed in 1933. The NRA and the AAA (Agricultural Adjustment Act) were later declared unconstitional by the U. S. Supreme Court, as

were other New Deal programs. This led to the president's later effort to reform the Supreme Court.

The dollar was devalued to 59 cents, and the government impounded all the nation's monetary gold. A widespread conservation program was set up. The Civilian Conservation Corps, made up of young men, began to improve forests and plant trees and to build antierosion projects. Rivers were dammed for power, flood control, and irrigation. The Tennessee Valley power and flood-control project was set up in order to make the valley a new industrial center.

In 1936 Roosevelt was reelected over Alfred Landon, the Republican candidate, by the greatest plurality any candidate had received. This verdict Roosevelt interpreted as a mandate to continue in some form the features of the NRA. Roosevelt was the first U.S. president to be elected for a third term in 1940 over Wendell Wilkie, and for a fourth term, in 1944 over Thomas A. Dewey. He was a vigorous war leader throughout World War II, but died just a few days before Germany surrendered in 1945. Roosevelt's writings include *Whither Bound?* (1926), *The Happy Warrior—Alfred E. Smith* (1928), *Looking Forward* (1933), *On Our Way* (1934), and *The Public Papers and Addresses of Franklin D. Roosevelt* (1928–1936).

His wife, **Anna Eleanor Roosevelt** (1884–1964), a niece of Theodore Roosevelt, was active as a writer, lecturer, and public servant. She was assistant director of the Office of Civilian Defense in 1941; a delegate to the United Nations Assembly in 1946; chairman of the American UN Association; chairman of the UN Human Rights Commission (1947–1951); and U.S. representative at the UN General Assembly (1946–1952). She wrote *It's Up to the Women* (1933), *My Days* (1938), *The Moral Basis of Democracy* (1940), *This I Remember* (1949), and *On My Own* (1959).

Roosevelt, Theodore (1858–1919), twenty-sixth president of the United States (1901–1909), born in New York City, son of Theodore and Martha Bullock Roosevelt. His father was of Dutch descent and his mother, Scottish-Irish-Huguenot. He graduated from Harvard in 1880 and served in the New York legislature (1882–1884). He was a delegate to the Republican national convention (1884), and spent the next two years as a cattle rancher in North Dakota. In 1886 he was an unsuccessful candidate for mayor of the city of New York. He was appointed a member of the United States Civil Service Commission in 1889 and served until 1895, when he resigned to become president of the police commissioner's board of New York City in a reform administration.

In 1897 he was appointed assistant secretary of the navy in Pres. William McKinley's administration. Upon the outbreak of the Spanish-American War in 1898 he resigned to help organize the first U. S. volunteer cavalry—the "Rough Riders." Shortly after the war he was nominated for governor of New York and was elected in November, 1898. Two years later he was unanimously nominated for vice-president of the United States by the Republican national convention at Philadelphia and was elected. He succeeded to the presidency on September 14, 1901, when Pres. McKinley

was assassinated, and at the close of the term he was reelected. He had long been an advocate of administrative, political, and social reform.

One of the high points in his administration was his "trust-busting" campaign, an attempt to break up or at least to bring under control the huge industrial combinations. He made the Interstate Commerce Commission an active and powerful body, supported the growing demand for meat inspection and pure-food laws, and began the building of the Panama Canal.

His efforts to bring about peace between Japan and Russia in 1905 were important and effective; in 1906 he was awarded the Nobel Peace Prize. He was an enthusiastic hunter of big game, and after the close of his term, March 4, 1909, he led a scientific expedition to East Africa to collect specimens for the Smithsonian and National museums at Washington. When he returned, he again entered politics. There had been a strong sentiment in favor of his candidacy for a third term, but President William H. Taft was nominated by the Republicans. A long friendship between the two men was broken off; Roosevelt withdrew from the party and entered the race as head of the Progressive party call the Bull Moose. This so split the Republican vote that the Democratic candidate Woodrow Wilson was elected president in 1912.

Roosevelt then went on another exploring trip, this time into the jungles of the Amazon in Brazil. He returned and became a bitter critic of Wilson's administration. He wanted to raise a volunteer force to serve in World War I, but the War Department would not allow this.

A prolific writer, his books include *The Naval War of 1812* (1882), *The Winning of the West* (4 vols., 1889–1896), *The Rough Riders*, (1899), *Life of Oliver Cromwell* (1900), and *The Strenuous Life*.

Roosevelt, Theodore, Jr. (1887–1944), American statesman, born in Oyster Bay, N. Y., son of Theodore Roosevelt. He graduated from Harvard in 1908. He was an executive in several industries and distinguished himself as a soldier during World War I. He was assistant secretary of the navy from 1921 to 1924, when he resigned to run for the governorship of New York; he was defeated by Alfred E. Smith. Roosevelt was governor of Puerto Rico (1929–1932) and governor general of the Philippine Islands from 1932 to 1933.

Root, Elihu (1845–1937), American statesman and lawyer, born in Clinton, N.Y. He studied at Hamilton College and at the law school of New York University. He was U.S. attorney for the southern district of New York (1883–85), secretary of war (1899–1904), and secretary of state (1905–1909). Turning to the cause of international peace, he was president of the Carnegie Endowment for International Peace in 1910. He won the Nobel Peace Prize in 1912.

Root was U.S. senator from New York (1909–1915). He headed a diplomatic mission to Russia in 1917 and represented his country at the Washington Disarmament Conference in 1921. As one of the founders of the World Court (1920) he suggested in 1929 that the United States enter the Court as a member with reservations.

Rosa, Salvator, also called **Salvatoriello** (1615–1673), Italian painter of the Neapolitan school, born in Arenella near Naples. His talents as a musician, actor, and poet—and his princely generosity—made him a great favorite at Rome. But he also made powerful enemies by his satires and had to retire to Florence for nine years. He owes his reputation mainly to his landscapes and battle scenes.

Roscius, Quintus (c.126–62 B.C.), Roman actor, born a slave at Solonium. He taught oratory to many prominent Romans, including Cicero. Sulla befriended him and raised him to higher rank. Roscius was the greatest actor of his time. Cicero defended him in a lawsuit.

Rosecrans, William Starke (1819–1898), American soldier, born in Kingston, Ohio. He graduated from West Point and was an engineer when the Civil War broke out. He joined the Federal army in 1861 and distinguished himself during the campaigns of 1862 and 1863. After the war, he was minister to Mexico, a member of Congress, and register of the treasury (1885–1893).

Rosenwald, Julius (1862–1932), American merchant and philanthropist, born in Springfield, Ill. He was a clothing manufacturer from 1885 to 1906, and in 1910 was elected president of Sears, Roebuck and Company. He gave generously to Jewish and Negro philanthropic causes. In his will he left $30 million to be used for "the well-being of mankind." In 1929 he established the Museum of Science and Industry for Chicago.

INTERNATIONAL NEWS

FRANKLIN D. ROOSEVELT (*center*) and family: his wife, Eleanor; his mother; his grand-daughter Anna Dall and a friend; his son James; his daughter Anna; and his son Franklin.

Ross, Betsy Griscom (1752–1836), American seamstress who is reputed to be the maker of the first American flag. She was born in Philadelphia, Pa. On June 14, 1777, the Continental Congress resolved that the stars-and-stripes flag would be the national emblem. At the request of George Washington, Robert Morris, and George Ross, she made the first flag.

Ross, Sir James Clark (1800–1862), British explorer, born in London. He made five voyages to the Arctic regions. On the last of these expeditions (1831) he determined the position of the north magnetic pole. He commanded a famous Antarctic expedition in the ships *Erebus* and *Terror* and reached the farthest point south that had ever been attained, 78° 10'. During this trip he discovered and named Victoria Land, in honor of his queen, and located Mt. Erebus. He commanded an expedition in search of Sir John Franklin in 1848.

Ross, Nellie Tayloe (1880–   ), American public official, born in St. Joseph, Mo. In 1902 she married William Bradford Ross, who was elected governor of Wyoming in 1922 and died in 1924. She succeeded him and became the first woman governor. She served until 1927. In 1933 she became the first woman director of the U.S. Mint.

Ross, Sir Ronald (1857–1932), English physician, born in India, and educated in London. He entered the Indian Medical Service in 1881 and began a special study of malaria. He discovered much about transmission of the disease by mosquitoes and about tropical diseases in general. Ross received the Nobel Prize in physiology and medicine in 1902. In 1926 he was honored with the founding of the Ross Institute and Hospital for Tropical Diseases.

Rossetti, Dante Gabriel (1828–1882), British poet and painter, born in London of Italian descent. He was educated at King's College and several London art academies. In 1848 with John Everett Millais, Holman Hunt, and other artists, he formed the Pre-Raphaelite Brotherhood. The interest of the group in the romance, symbolism, and mysticism of the Middle Ages is seen in most of Rossetti's works. These include such paintings as the *Beata Beatrix, The Annunciation, Pandora, Proserpina in Hades,* and *Dante's Dream.* His poems include *The Blessed Damozel* and *Ballads and Sonnets* (1881). He also translated early Italian poetry; the first volume appeared in 1861, and was later reprinted as *Dante and his Circle* (1874). Some of his poems he buried with his wife when she died in 1862, two years after their marriage, but they were exhumed and published in 1870.

Christina Georgina Rossetti (1830–1894), his sister, was also a poet. Like her brother, she contributed poems to *The Germ,* the organ of the Pre-Raphaelite Brotherhood, and she also served as model to her brother, Hunt, Millais, and others. Her books of poetry include *Sing Song* (children's poems, 1872), *Time Flies* (1885), *The Prince's Progress* (1866), *A Pageant* (1881), and *New Poems* (1896).

William Michael Rossetti, brother of Dante and Christina, (1829–1919), was an art critic and editor of *The Germ.* A contributor to *The Spectator,* he edited books of poetry of his brother and sister, of Coleridge, Blake, Milton, Whitman, and others. He wrote biographies of Shelley and Keats.

Rossini, Gioacchino Antonio (1792–1868), Italian operatic composer, born in Pesaro. The son of a strolling musician, Rossini was sent at the age of 14 to Bologna to study music. When he was only 21, he produced the opera *Tancredi,* which made him famous. This was followed by *The Barber of Seville* (1816), *Otello* (1816), and *William Tell* (1829). His *Stabat Mater* was published in 1842.

Rostand, Edmond (1868–1918), French dramatist, born in Marseilles. His first three plays, *Les Romanesques* (1894), *La Princesse Lointaine* (1895), and *La Samaritaine* (1897), were produced with fair success. His masterpiece, *Cyrano de Bergerac* (1898), was an immediate sensation and has been a favorite ever since. His other plays include *L'Aiglon* (1900), a play about Napoleon's son, the duke of Reichstadt, and *Chantecler* (1910), a dramatization of the animal fable. Rostand was elected to the French Academy in 1901.

Rothschild, family of financiers. **Meyer Amschel Rothschild** (1743–1812), founder of the family, was born in Frankfort, Germany. He became a moneylender and was later financial adviser to the landgrave of Hesse-Cassel. He died in 1812, leaving five sons well trained in the banking business. **Meyer Amschel Rothschild** (1773–1855), headed the family business in Frankfort. Branches were opened in Vienna by **Salomon Rothschild** (1774–1855); in London by

BETTMANN ARCHIVE
CHRISTINA ROSSETTI, drawn by her brother.

Nathan Rothschild (1777–1836), the most brilliant of the brothers; in Naples by **Karl Rothschild** (1788–1855); and in Paris by **James Rothschild** (1792–1868). All were made barons by the Austrian government. The Rothschilds financed wars, philanthropic measures, and industrial growth, and had major European political influence. The importance of the Rothschilds in Vienna, Frankfurt, and Naples gradually declined, but the London and Paris families have remained major figures in the world of finance.

Rouault, Georges (1871–1958), French painter, born in Paris. He studied under Gustave Moreau, and in 1905 exhibited with the Fauvists His canvases, ranging from religious scenes to his many paintings of clowns are marked by rich, vibrant colors heavily outlined in black lines.

Rouget de Lisle, Claude Joseph (1760–1836), French poet, born in Lons-le-Saulnier. He is best known as the author of *La Marseillaise,* the French national anthem. The song was originally named the *Chant de l'Armée du Rhin* (Song of the Army of the Rhine), for he was stationed with French troops at Strasbourg at the time he composed it (April 24, 1792). It was first heard in Paris when a detachment of soldiers from Marseilles returning from the Rhine sang it in 1796, and it was named for their city. In 1876 it was adopted as the national anthem.

Rousseau, Henri (1844–1910), French painter, born in Laval. He was known as *Le Douanier* (customs officer) for his service in the customs department (1871–1884). He has been classified as a "primitive," because of the flatness and simple colors of his canvases. His most representative work includes *The Snake Charmer, The Sleeping Gypsy,* and *The Dream.*

Rousseau, Jean Jacques (1712–1778), French philosopher and writer, born in Geneva, Switzerland. After 1741 he lived mainly in Paris, where he was associated with Denis Diderot and wrote articles for the *Encyclopédie.* In 1750 he won a prize at the academy of Dijon for his *Discours sur les arts et les sciences,* which extolled living in a primitive state, uncorrupted by the vices of civilization. From 1756–1757 he lived at *The Hermitage,* a cottage near Montmorency, owned by Mme. d'Épinay, where he wrote *Julie, ou la Nouvelle Heloïse* (1761), an epistolary novel. After quarrels with Mme. d'Épinay, Diderot, and Voltaire, he wrote *le Contrat Social* and *Émile* (1762), the first a discussion of the ideal political primacy of the general will, the second a major dissertation on the education of children. *Émile* was condemned by the Parlement of Paris for its antiroyalist views and Rousseau went to Switzerland and England, returning to France in 1767. In the last years of his life he wrote *Confessions* (1781 and 1788), *Dialogues,* and *Rêveries du Promeneur Solitaire* (1782).

Royce, Josiah (1855–1916), American philosopher and educator, born in Grass Valley, Calif. He studied at the University of California, Johns Hopkins, and in Germany. He returned to the University of California to teach English literature and after 1882 taught philosophy at Harvard. In his philosophy he taught the importance of personality and will; he held that ethics and morality were to be explained in terms of loyalty. Among his books are *The Religious Aspect of Philosophy* (1885), *The World and the Individual* (1900), and *The Problem of Christianity* (1913).

Rubens, Peter Paul (1577–1640), Flemish painter, born in Siegen, Westphalia. He studied at the Jesuit College at Antwerp, and in 1600 he went to Italy. There he was befriended by the duke of Mantua, who sent him to the court of Spain, where he painted several court portraits. He also spent much time in Venice and Rome. In 1621 he was commissioned by Marie de Médicis to paint illustrations of her life to decorate the Luxembourg palace in Paris. He was sent (1628) by the Infanta Isabella on a mission to Philip IV of Spain, and in the following year on a similar mission to Charles I of England, who knighted him. Among Rubens' famous paintings are *The Descent from the Cross, The Rape of the Sabines, Adoration of the Magi, The Assumption of the Virgin,* and *St. George.*

Rubinstein, Anton (1829–1894), Russian musician and composer, born in Bessarabia. He made his debut as a pianist at the age of eight. His best-known works include *Ocean Symphony, Paradise Lost,* and the opera *Nero.* He founded (1862) and was the first director of the St. Petersburg Conservatory of Music (until 1867).

Rubinstein, Artur (1886–   ), American pianist, born in Lódz, Poland. He made his debut in Berlin at the age of 12. His first U.S. tour was in 1906; he has since toured much of the world. In addition to performing he has composed piano pieces and chamber music.

Rucellai, Giovanni (1475–1525), Italian poet and dramatist, cousin of Pope Leo X. His works include the blank-verse poem *Le Api* (1524) and the plays *Rosmunda* (1515) and *Creste* (1525), both classic tragedies. His father **Bernardo Rucellai** (1449–1514). Italian humanist, brother-in-law of Lorenzo the Magnificent, was head of the Platonic Academy.

Rudolf I (1218–1291), German king, Holy Roman emperor, and founder of the Hapsburg dynasty. As count of Hapsburg, Rudolf was chosen German king in 1273. He increased his possessions through marriage, conquest, and inheritance, gaining control over Austria and Styria by the time of his death.

BETTMANN ARCHIVE
ROTHSCHILD chateau near Paris housed the French branch of the family of financiers.

LOOK MAGAZINE

DEAN RUSK, Secretary of State since 1961.

Rufus of Ephesus (2nd century A.D.), Greek physician and anatomist. He is the author of a treatise on anatomy and another describing known diseases, including the earliest record of bubonic plague.

Ruisdael or **Ruysdael, Jacob van** (c.1628–1682), Dutch painter and etcher, born in Haarlem. Little is known of his life, except that it was full of illness, disappointment, and privation. He died in an almshouse. His work was not appreciated in his lifetime. His pictures are chiefly of rural scenes, including *Storm at Sea* (Louvre, Paris), *Cottage Under Trees, Wheatfields* and *Forest Stream* (Metropolitan Museum, New York), *View of Haarlem* and *Agitated Sea* (British Museum), *Jewish Cemetery* (Dresden Gallery), and *Landscape with Ruins* (National Gallery, London).

His uncle, **Salomon van Ruisdael** (c. 1600–1670), was also a landscape painter.

Rumford, Count. See *Thompson, Benjamin.*

Rush, Benjamin (1746–1813), American physician, and politician, born near Philadelphia, Pa. Educated at the College of New Jersey (Princeton) and the University of Pennsylvania, he was professor of chemistry at the College of Philadelphia and later at Pennsylvania. In 1786 he established in Philadelphia the first free dispensary in the U.S. Rush was a member of the Continental Congress, signed the Declaration of Independence, was surgeon general of the Continental army, and served as treasurer of the U.S. Mint (1797–1813).

Rusk, Dean (1909–   ), American statesman born in Cherokee County, Ga. He graduated from Davidson College (N.C.) and attended St. John's College, Oxford, as a Rhodes scholar. Rusk was associate professor of government and dean of the faculty at Mills College (1934–1940). He was deputy undersecretary of state (1949–1950), assistant secretary of state for Far Eastern affairs (1950–1951), and president of the Rockefeller Foundation (1952–1960). In 1961 he was appointed secretary of state by Pres. John F. Kennedy, and he continued in that post under Pres. Lyndon B. Johnson.

Ruskin, John (1819–1900), British art critic and writer, born in London and educated at Oxford. His first work, *Modern Painters* (1843), was a highly influential treatise on the principles of art. In *The Seven Lamps of Architecture* (1849) and *The Stones of Venice* (1851–1853), he advocated the natural and spiritual bases of architecture, and helped to stimulate the Gothic revival. In *Unto this Last* (1860), *Munera Pulveris* (1862) and *Sesame and Lilies* (1865), he urged social reform and the application of wealth to the benefit of all. His autobiography, *Praeterita* (1864), is a detailed record of his early life.

Russell, Bertrand Arthur William, 3d Earl (1872–   ), English philosopher and mathematician, born in Trelleck, Wales. He was a grandson of Lord John Russell, who was prime minister from 1846 to 1852. He was educated at Cambridge and taught there for many years. He campaigned actively against World War I, and was imprisoned for his antiwar publications. He has lectured in the United States and China at several universities.

In his writings he brings mathematics and philosophy together and expresses logic in terms of mathematical symbols. His books include *Principia Mathematica* (with A.N. Whitehead; 3 vols., 1910–1913), *Introduction to Mathematical Philosophy* (1919), *Marriage and Morals* (1929), *Freedom versus Organization, 1814–1914* (1934), *History of Western Philosophy* (1945), *Human Knowledge* (1948), *Authority and the Individual* (1949), and *New Hopes for a Changing World* (1952). He won the Nobel Prize for literature in 1950.

Russell, Lord John, 1st Earl of **Kingston Russell** (1792–1878), British statesman, born in London. He was elected to Parliament at the age of 21 and became a leader in the parliamentary reform movement. He supported the Catholic Emancipation Bill (1829) and became popular as a champion of the Reform Bill (1832), which greatly extended the franchise. Later he served as home secretary (1835), colonial secretary (1839), and prime minister and first lord of the treasury (1846–1852). In that office, he subdued agitation in Ireland and urged the adoption of free trade. In 1852 he was ousted from office through the efforts of Lord Palmerston, whom Russell had dismissed from the Foreign Office in 1851 for recognizing the coup d'état of Napoleon. Russell was foreign secretary (1852–1853) and was given an earldom in 1861. He became prime minister upon the death of Palmerston in 1865, and after his new reform bill was defeated, retired in 1866.

Russell, Lillian, real name **Helen Louise Leonard** (1861–1922), American actress, born in Clinton, Iowa. She made her stage debut in 1879 in the chorus of a production of *Pinafore*, and soon became one of the most popular actresses in vaudeville, operettas, and musicals. In 1899 she joined the Weber and Fields burlesque company.

Ruth, George Herman, known as **Babe Ruth** (1895–1948), American baseball player, born in Baltimore, Md. He began his major league career with the Boston Red Sox in 1914, and immediately distinguished himself as a pitcher and slugger. He was traded to the New York Yankees in 1920, and in 1927 he set a record of 60 home runs in a single season. In his career, he batted .342 and hit 714 home runs. He retired in 1934, played one season with the Boston Braves (1935) and coached the Brooklyn Dodgers in 1938. Ruth was an original member of the Baseball Hall of Fame.

Rutherford, Ernest, 1st Baron **Rutherford of Nelson** (1871–1937), British physicist, born in New Zealand. He was educated at Canterbury College, the University of New Zealand, and Trinity College, Cambridge. He was professor of physics and director of physics research at Manchester (1907–1919), and later at Cambridge (1919–1937). He is best known for his work in radioactivity and was a pioneer in changing one element to another by bombarding its atoms. He won the Nobel Prize in chemistry in 1908.

Rutledge, John (1739–1800), American jurist, born in Charleston, S.C. He was a member of the Continental Congress (1774–1776, 1782–1783), and was governor of South Carolina (1779–1782). In 1789 he was appointed an associate justice of the U.S. Supreme Court and in 1795 became chief justice, though he was never confirmed and served only one term.

Ruysdael. See *Ruisdael.*

Ryder, Albert Pinkham (1847–1917), American painter, born in New Bedford, Mass. He studied art in New York City and lived most of his life as a recluse. His paintings subordinate detail to design, and are characteristically dark; his canvases are thickly built up of numerous layers of paint. The best of his paintings include *Toilers of the Sea, The Bridge,* and *Moonlight at Sea.*

LOOK MAGAZINE

BERTRAND RUSSELL, English philosopher.

S

Saadi or **Sadi,** real name **Muslih-ud-Din** (c.1184–1291), Persian poet, born in Shiraz, and educated at Baghdad. His works in both Arabic and Persian, contain twenty-two different forms of writing in prose and poetry. Especially famous are his *Būstān* (*Fruit Garden,* 1257), *Gulistān* (*Rose Garden,* 1258), and *Diwān* (*Many Leaves*), a collection of lyrics.

Saarinen, Gottlieb Eliel (1873–1950), Finnish architect, born in Helsinki. He came to the United States in 1907. He built the Cranbrook School at Bloomfield Hills, Michigan, and served as architectural director of the Cranbrook Foundation in Detroit. A specialist in urban planning, Saarinen wrote *The City: Its Growth, Its Decay, Its Future* (1943).

Saarinen, Eero (1910–1961), American architect, son of Gottlieb Eliel Saarinen. He designed the Yale Hockey Rink, several buildings for the Massachusetts Institute of Technology, and the Dulles International Airport. He was also a furniture designer.

Sabatini, Rafael (1875–1950), English novelist, born in Jesi, Italy, and educated in Switzerland and Portugal. He wrote scores of romantic, historical novels, notably *The Sea Hawk* (1915), *Sacramouche* (1921) *Captain Blood* (1922), *The Carolinian* (1925), *Columbus* (1942), and *The Gamester* (1949). Most of these were best sellers and several were made into motion pictures.

Sacco, Nicola (1891–1927) and **Bartolomeo Vanzetti** (1888–1927), Italian immigrants to the United States in 1908. Both were arrested in 1920 for the robbery and murder of a paymaster and guard of a shoe factory in South Braintree, Mass. Both were anarchists, pacifists, and labor agitators. In spite of conflicting and circumstantial evidence, and the confession of another man, a worldwide outcry in their behalf was not heeded and they were executed in 1927.

Sachs, Hans (1494–1576), German poet and playwright, born in Nuremberg. He wandered through Germany as a traveling shoemaker but devoted all his spare time to writing. In all he wrote about 6,000 songs and poems and more than 200 comedies and tragedies. Wagner made him a central figure in his opera *Die Meistersinger von Nürnberg* (1868).

Sackville-West, Victoria Mary (1892–1962), English poet and novelist, daughter of the 3rd Baron Sackville of Knole. Among her historical studies is *Knole and the Sackvilles* (1923), *The Edwardians* (1930), and *Saint Joan of Arc* (1936).

Sade, Comte Donatien Alphonse François de, known as **Marquise de Sade** (1740–1814), French writer, born in Paris. He spent much of his life in prisons and died in an insane asylum. Condemned to death in 1772 for his cruel sex vices, he escaped but was later confined to the Bastile. In prison, he wrote the scandalous novel *Justine* (1791), *La Philosophie dans le Boudoir* (1793), and *Les Crimes de L'Amour* (1800). The term "sadism," gratification through afflicting pain on one's love object, is derived from his name.

Sagan, Françoise, real name **Françoise Quoirez** (1936–   ), French novelist, born in Paris, and educated at a convent and in private schools. She won international fame at the age of 18 with *Bonjour Tristesse* (1954). She also wrote *Un Certain Sourire* (1957) and *Aimez-vous Brahms?* (1959).

Sage, Margaret Olivia Slocum (1828–1918), American philanthropist, born in Syracuse, New York. She inherited a $70 million fortune from her husband, Russel Sage, which she used to establish the Russell Sage Foundation and to support other philanthropic causes in the United States.

Sage, Russell (1816–1906), American financier, born in Oneida County, N.Y. He was educated in the public schools, became a grocer's clerk, and established himself as a wholesale grocer in Troy, N.Y. in 1839. He was a member of Congress (1852–1856), He moved to New York (1863) and purchased a seat on the Stock Exchange. In New York, he became associated with Jay Gould in extensive railway operations, and by close bargaining and successful speculation amassed a fortune.

Sagittarius. See *Schütz, Heinrich.*

St. Clair, Arthur (c.1736–1818), American general, born in Thurso, Scotland. During the French and Indian War he sailed to the American colonies and later joined the Continental Army under Washington. He served in the battles of Trenton and Princeton, commanding the New Jersey troops.

LOOK MAGAZINE

EERO SAARINEN, architect and designer.

After the war he became a member of the Continental Congress; for two years he was its presiding officer. In 1780 he became the first governor of the newly organized Northwest Territory.

Sainte-Beuve, Charles Augustin (1804–1869), French writer, born in Boulogne. He studied medicine in Paris but gave it up for writing. Sainte-Beuve is best known for his volumes of literary criticism, especially the *Causeries du lundi* ("Monday Chats," 15 vols., 1849–1861), made from his newspaper articles. For his breadth of scholarship, attention to details, and objective method of evaluating literary works, he has been regarded as the founder of modern literary criticism.

Saint-Exupéry, Antoine de (1900–1944), French aviator and author, born in Lyon. His books, noted for their evocative poetic style, include *Vol de nuit* (*Night Flight*, 1932), *Terre des hommes* (*Wind, Sand, and Stars*, 1939), *Pilote de guerre* (*Flight to Arras*, 1942), and *Le Petit Prince* (*The Little Prince*, 1943). He was reported missing after a Mediterranean reconnaissance flight in World War II.

Saint-Gaudens, Augustus (1848–1907), American sculptor, born in Dublin, Ireland, of French and Irish parentage. He studied art in New York and at the École des Beaux-Arts in Paris, and soon became the leading American sculptor. His well-known portrait sculptures include those of Robert Louis Stevenson (in Edinburgh), Adm. David Farragut, Gen. William T. Sherman, and Peter Cooper (in New York).

St. Laurent, Louis Stephen (1882–), Canadian statesman and lawyer, born in Compton, Quebec, of French and Irish descent. He was educated at St. Charles College and Laval University. St. Laurent was active in Canada's external affairs for several years. From 1948–1957, as leader of the Liberal party, he was prime minister.

Saint-Pierre. See *Bernardin de Saint-Pierre, Jacques Henri.*

Saint-Saëns, Charles Camille (1835–1921), French composer, pianist, and organist. He was educated at the Paris Conservatoire. In 1853 he was appointed organist of the Church of Saint Merri in Paris and in 1858 of the Church of the Madeleine. He retired from that position in 1877 and gave recitals in Europe and America. His best-known compositions include the opera *Samson et Dalila* (1877), the symphonic poem *Danse macabre* (1847), and the suite *Le carnaval des animaux* (1886).

Saintsbury, George Edward Bateman (1845–1933), English literary critic, journalist, and educator. He was born in Southampton and educated at Merton College, Oxford. After serving as a schoolmaster at Manchester, Guernsey, and Elgin (1868–1876), he established himself as one of the most active critics of the day and was appointed professor of English literature at Edinburgh University. Among his many books are *Short History of French Literature* (1882), *History of Nineteenth-Century Literature* (1896), and *A History of the French Novel* (2 vols., 1917, 1919).

Saladin, in full **Salāh-al-Dīn Yūsuf ibn-Ayyūb** (1138–1193), sultan of Egypt and Syria, born in Tikrit, Mesopotamia. Saladin won renown in Egypt fighting for the Caliph Nureddin against the Christians, and in 1170 became vizier of the country. He came to the throne in 1171, when Nureddin died. He was soon Sultan of Egypt and Syria and further extended his authority by conquering Mesopotamia and most of Asia Minor. Saladin is best known for his campaigns against the Latin kingdom of Jerusalem in the third Crusade, which began in 1187. In spite of the efforts of the Crusaders he captured Jerusalem, but he was checked by Richard I of England and Philip II of France, who arrived with a fresh army. A truce was made in 1192, and a few months later Saladin died.

Salazar, Antonio de Oliveira (1889–), Portuguese dictator, born near Coimbra. He was professor of economics at Coimbra, and in 1928 was appointed minister of finance. In 1932 he was elected prime minister, and since 1936 he has also served as minister of war and foreign affairs, making him the virtual dictator of Portugal.

Salinger, J. D., in full **Jerome David Salinger** (1919–), American author, born in New York City. He studied at New York and Columbia universities. His books include *Catcher in the Rye* (1953), *Nine Stories* (1953), *Franny and Zooey* (1962), and *Raise High the Roof Beam, Carpenters and Seymour—an Introduction* (1963). He has earned a reputation for invoking the rebellious spirit of adolescents.

Salk, Jonas Edward (1914–), American physician and virologist, born in New York City. He graduated from the College of the City of New York (1934) and received his medical degree from New York University College of Medicine (1939). As head of the research laboratory at the University of

DR. JONAS SALK, polio vaccine discoverer.

Pittsburgh (1947–1949), he conducted research on influenza and other virus diseases. There, in 1953–1954, he developed a vaccine (known as the "Salk Vaccine"), which has been successful in immunization against poliomyelitis. He has since devoted himself to cancer research.

Sallust, full name **Gaius Sallustius Crispus** (86–34 B.C.), Roman historian, born in the Sabine region. He was made tribune in 52 B.C. After serving in Africa, he became governor of Numidia, where he amassed great wealth by oppressing the people. He returned to Rome and built a magnificent palace; the spot where it stood is now called *Sallust's Garden.* He then devoted himself to historical writing. Only fragments exist of his *History of the Roman Republic* for the years 78 to 67 B.C. *The Conspiracy of Catiline* and *History of the Jugurthine War* are preserved intact.

Sand, George, pen name of **Amandine Aurore Lucie Dupin** (1804–1876), French novelist, born in Paris and educated in convents. She married Casimir Dudevant (1822), with whom she passed an unhappy time until she left him in 1831. She became a journalist in Paris, where she lived openly with Jules Sandeau, and the two collaborated in writing several books under the name *Jules Sand.* She took for her pen name *George Sand,* and in her first book *Indiana* (1832) she wrote about marriage problems. She formed a liaison with the poet Alfred de Musset and later with Frédéric Chopin, the composer. The latter half of her life was spent mostly in the country at Nohant. She wrote more than 80 novels. Her earlier books, including *Lélia* (1833) and *Jacques* (1834), show a spirit of revolt, but her best work is in the later pastoral novels, such as *Jeanne* (1844) and *La Mare au Diable* (1846). She is the heroine in one series of novels, but in the next phase her books show an interest in socialism and kindred political subjects. It is said that in *Lucrezia Floriani* she portrayed herself and Chopin as the leading characters.

Sandburg, Carl (1878–1967), American poet, born in Galesburg, Ill. His early years were spent in a great variety of service and laboring jobs. He later became a journalist and started to publish poetry. The subjects of his poems are often industrial American scenes. His first volume of verse appeared in 1904, but he was unknown to the literary world until 1914, when one of his poems, *Chicago,* was awarded the Levinson Prize. A lifelong student of Abraham Lincoln, he won the 1940 Pulitzer Prize for history with his *Abraham Lincoln: the War Years.* For his *Complete Poems,* he received the Pulitzer Prize in 1950. His *Rootabaga Stories* (1922) for children have become a classic. Other works include *The American Song Bag* (1927), *Abraham Lincoln—The Prairie Years* (4 vols., 1926), and *Storm Over the Land* (1942). An autobiographical book, *Always the Young Strangers,* appeared in 1953. He died June 23, 1967 in Flat Rock, N.C.

Sanger, Margaret (1883–1966), American leader in the birth-control movement. She was born in Corning, N.Y. and educated as a nurse. Believing that families with low incomes should not have many children, she founded the American Birth Control League in 1917 and set up clinics in which she taught birth-control methods. As a result she was often in trouble with the police, but a series of court actions led to the legal decision that physicians can give birth-control information for the sake of health. Later she traveled all over the world, lecturing and opening clinics. She founded and edited the *Birth Control Review.* Among her books are *The Case for Birth Control* (1917), *Woman and the New Race* (1920), *My Fight for Birth Control* (1931), and *Margaret Sanger: An Autobiography* (1938).

San Martín, José de (1778–1850), South American revolutionist, born in Yapeyú, now in Argentina. He served with the Spanish army in Europe but returned home in 1812 to take part in a revolution in his country. He led the army of liberation against Upper Peru and decided that the best way to the royalist stronghold in Peru would be through Chile. He led his army across the Andes and defeated the Spanish at Chacabuco in 1817 and at Maipú in 1818. He thus freed Chile from Spanish rule. San Martín refused dictatorship over Chile; instead he set out to conquer Peru. He had partially succeeded when he met Simón Bolívar (1822) and he turned over the rest of the work to him. San Martín spent the last part of his life in Europe.

Santa Anna or **Santa Ana, Antonio López de** (c.1795–1876), Mexican politician and soldier, born in Jalapa, Vera Cruz. He enlisted in the army at 15 and by 1821 had joined Augustín de Iturbide in opposing Spanish occupation. He became a revolutionist, and when he was elected president of Mexico in 1833 he became a virtual dic-

CARL SANDBURG, twentieth-century poet.

tator. After Texas declared its freedom from Mexico, Santa Anna and his Mexican forces were victorious at the Alamo, but he was defeated and made prisoner at San Jacinto. He was deposed but resumed his dictatorship as president in 1841. In 1845 he was banished for 10 years but in 1846 was recalled. As commander of the Mexican army in the war with the United States he was largely unsuccessful and was again deposed in 1848. Santa Anna left Mexico and traveled in South America, only to be recalled in 1853. Two years later he was banished but returned to serve under Maximilian. Again ordered out of the country, he was an exile for a while but returned in 1874 and died in Mexico City.

Santayana, George (1863–1952), Spanish poet and philosopher, born in Madrid, Spain. He came to the United States in 1872, settled with his family in Boston, and was educated at Harvard. After graduate study in Germany, he joined the Harvard faculty in 1889 and taught there for 20 years. His first book was *Sonnets and Poems* (1894), followed by the *The Sense of Beauty* (1896), a philosophical work. After this book was published, he studied at Cambridge University and lectured at the Sorbonne, Paris. His other works include *The Life of Reason* (5 vols., 1905–1906), *Scepticism and Animal Faith* (1923), *Platonism and the Spiritual Life* (1927), *The Realm of Matter* (1930), *The Genteel Tradition at Bay* (1931), *Philosophical Opinion in America*, and *Character and Opinion in the United States.* His first novel, *The Last Puritan* (1936), was a popular and critical success.

Santi, Raffaello. See *Raphael.*

Santos-Dumont, Alberto (1873–1932), Brazilian aviator and inventor, born in São Paulo, and educated in France. He made his first ascent in a balloon in 1897. Later he attached a gasoline motor and a screw propeller to a dirigible balloon and, after several failures, flew for some minutes over Paris. In 1901 he won a prize offered for a roundtrip flight from St. Cloud, circling the Eiffel Tower. He later experimented with airplanes and in 1909 built a forerunner of the modern light aircraft.

Sanzio, Raffaello. See *Raphael.*

Sappho (7th century B.C.), Greek lyric poet, probably a native of Mytilene, in Lesbos. She was a contemporary and friend of Alcaeus. Except for some fragments, only two of her compositions have come down to us anywhere near complete—one of 27 lines and one of 16. Her famous plunge into the sea from the Leucadian rock, because of unrequited love for Phaon, is legendary.

Sardou, Victorien (1831–1908), French dramatist, born in Paris. He gave up the study of medicine for literature and wrote more than 70 plays. Among his best-known plays are *Les pattes de mouche* (1860), *Divorçons* (1880), *Cléopâtre* (1890, with Émile Moreau), *La Tosca* (1887), *Madame Sans-Gêne* (1893, with Émile Moreau), and *Robespierre* (1899).

Sargent, John Singer (1856–1925), American painter, born in Florence, Italy. He was educated in Europe and spent most of his life in England. He is probably best known for his portraits and his murals in the Boston Public Library. His portraits include those of Ellen Terry, *Madame Gatreau* (*Madame X*), Edwin Booth, Joseph Jefferson, and Woodrow Wilson. Sargent won the Grand Prize at the Paris Expositions of 1889 and 1900, the Grand Prize at the St. Louis Exposition of 1904, and the gold medal of the National Institute of Arts and Letters (American) in 1914.

Saroyan, William (1908–   ), American author and dramatist, born in Fresno, Calif. The son of Armenian parents, he was educated in the public schools of Fresno. His short story collection, *The Daring Young Man on the Flying Trapeze*, appeared in 1934. One of his plays, *The Time of Your Life*, won the Drama Critics Circle Award and the Pulitzer Prize in 1940. He also wrote *My Name Is Aram* (1940), *The Human Comedy* (1943), and television plays.

Sarto, Andrea del, real name **Andrea Domenico d'Agnolo di Francesco** (1486–1531), Italian painter, born in Florence. He painted two series of frescoes in Florence, the most significant being *Birth of the Virgin* and *Journey of the Three Kings*. The most celebrated of his single pictures are the *Last Supper*, the *Madonna of the Harpies*, and *Fathers of the Church Disputing*. *The Holy Family* is in the New York Metropolitan Museum. He is known as a colorist and a master of chiaroscuro (painting with dark and light contrasts for dramatic effect).

Sartre, Jean-Paul (1905–   ), French philosopher, novelist, critic, and dramatist, born in Paris. Following World War II, he emerged as the leader of the existentialist philosophical and literary movement. This philosophy states that man rules his own destiny with the choices he makes. Since there is no God, man is condemned to be free, relying only on his will and moral insight. These doctrines are explained in *L'être et le néant* (1943; *Being and Nothingness*, 1956) and *L'Existentialisme est un humanisme* (1946; *Existentialism and Humanism*, 1948). The leader of postwar Parisian intellectuals, he took an active role in French left-wing politics but later broke with the Communists. Other works include *La nausée* (1938; *Nausea*, 1949), *Le mur* (1939; *The Wall*, 1938), and the plays *Les mouches* (1943; *The Flies*, 1946), and *Les séquestrés d'Altona* (1959; *The Condemned of Altona*, 1959). In 1964 Sartre was offered but declined the Nobel Prize for literature.

Satie, Erik, full name **Alfred Erikit Leslie-Satie** (1866–1925), French composer, born in Honfleur. He led the early twentieth-century revolt against the impressionistic style of Debussy and Ravel. He inspired "Les Six" (including Milhaud and Honegger), who honored him as their leader. Satie's compositions were as influential in France as those of Arnold Schönberg in Germany.

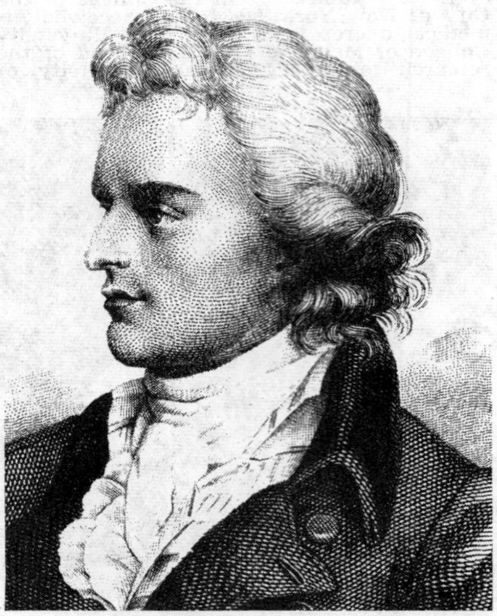

FRIEDRICH VON SCHILLER

Saud, or **ibn-Saud, Abdul-Aziz** (1880–1953), king of Saudi Arabia (1932–1953), born in Riyadh, Nejd. He succeeded his father on the throne and extended the holdings of Nejd and brought able administration in the lands, abetting nationalism. He conquered the Hejaz (1924–1925) and proclaimed himself king in 1926. He declared Saudi Arabia the official name of Hejaz and Nejd in 1932 by decree and generally stabilized the country. Oil was discovered there in 1936 and he granted extensive concessions to Standard Oil of California. In World War II he was neutral but friendly to the Allies.

Savonarola, Girolamo (1452–1498), Italian religious and political reformer, born in Ferrara. He joined the Dominican Order in 1475 and preached on the sinfulness and corrupting influence of power. After the death of Lorenzo the Magnificent in 1492, he led his party in the new republic and ruled Florence as a Christian commonwealth, sternly putting down all luxury and frivolity. He was accused of heresy by Rome and excommunicated. The new system in Florence failed, and the people turned against him. In 1498 he was strangled and burned at the stake. He is the subject of George Eliot's *Romola.*

Scarlatti, Alessandro (1659–1725), Italian composer, born in Palermo, Sicily. *Tigrane* (1715) is the best known of his 114 operas. He also composed 200 masses, 10 oratorios, and 500 cantatas.

Scarlatti, Domenico (1683–1757), Italian composer and performer, son of Alessandro Scarlatti, born in Naples. He is remembered particularly for his more than 550 harpsichord sonatas. He also was choirmaster of St. Peter's Rome (1714–1719) and wrote much church music.

Scarron, Paul (1610–1660), French writer, born in Paris. Although crippled by illness at the age of 30, he began to write burlesque plays and poems, for which he became famous. His *Roman comique* (1651–1657) is a novel of the strolling players of the time. In 1652 he married Françoise d'Aubigné, who later became Madame de Maintenon.

Scheele, Karl Wilhelm (1742–1786), Swedish chemist, born in Stralsund. By profession an apothecary and to a large extent self-taught, he made many important chemical discoveries. He discovered oxygen gas as early as 1771, independently of Joseph Priestley. Among his other discoveries are the element chlorine (1774), tartaric acid, and glycerin. The substance known as *Scheele's green* is the arsenite of copper identified by him.

Schelling, Friedrich Wilhelm Joseph von (1775–1854), German philosopher, born in Württemberg. He lectured on philosophy at Jena (1798), at Würzburg (1803–1808), and then served as secretary of the Royal Academy of Arts at Munich until 1820. He was a professor at Erlangen (1820–1827) and after 1841 he taught at Berlin. His works may be grouped in three sections: the first (1797–1800) includes *Philosophy of Nature* (1799); the second (1801–1803) emphasizes the philosophy of "identity," influenced by Spinoza and Boehme; the third is characterized by the growth of his positive philosophy.

Schick, Béla, (1877–1967), American pediatrician. Born in Boglar, Hungary; came to the U.S. in 1923 as chief pediatrician at Mt. Sinai Hospital, New York. He developed the Schick test (1913) for susceptibility to diphtheria. He wrote on scarlet fever, tuberculosis, and child nutrition. He died Nov. 27, 1967 in New York City.

Schiller, Johann Christoph Friedrich von (1759–1805), German poet and dramatist, born in Marbach, Württemberg. He was educated at a military school under the patronage of the duke of Württemberg and was trained to become a military surgeon. His first play, *Die Räuber* (*The Robbers*), appeared in 1782 and created a tremendous sensation by its revolutionary sentiments. Schiller, after neglecting his medical duties to attend the opening of the play, was forbidden to write anything but medical books. He fled to Franconia where he completed his *Fiesco* and *Kabale und Liebe* (*Intrigue and Love*) and where he also outlined *Don Carlos.*

In 1783 he went to Mannheim, where he was closely connected with the theater for some time. Several of his lesser poems were written during this period. *Kable und Liebe* marked the end of his first poetic period, known as the *Sturm und Drang* period. In 1785 he was invited to Leipzig, where he wrote the *Lied an die Freude* later extolled in Beethoven's choral symphony. Later, in Dresden, he wrote *Der Geisterseher* (*The Visionary*) and completed his first nature drama, *Don Carlos* (1797).

In 1787 he was invited to Weimar, where he and Goethe became close friends. He began his history of the Netherlands' revolt, and published his *History of the Thirty Years' War* in 1792. Upon his marriage to Charlotte von Lengefeld (1788), the duke of Meiningen made him a privy councilor. In 1802 the emperor raised him to the rank of a noble.

During a year's stay with relatives in Württemberg, he wrote his letters on esthetic education (1795) and the famous *Über naive und sentimentalische Dichtung* (*On Naive and Sentimental Poetry*, 1795–1796), in which he contrasts ancient and modern poetry in approaches to nature.

After 1795 he wrote some of the finest lyrics in German poetry, notably *Der Spaziergang* (*The Walk*) and the *Lied von der Glocke* (*Song of the Bell*). In this period, also, he wrote such plays as *Wallenstein* trilogy, *Maria Stuart*, *Die Jungfrau von Orleans* (*The Maid of Orleans*), *Die Braut von Messina* (*The Bride of Messina*), and *Wilhelm Tell.* In the history of German literature, Schiller ranks as the foremost dramatist. In German poetry, he is second only to Goethe.

Schlegel, August Wilhelm von (1767–1845), German historian and critic, born in Hannover. He first received public notice for his literary work while a lecturer at Jena. He published his first volume of poems in 1800, and in 1801 *Charakteristiken und Kritiken* appeared. His influential book, *Über dramatische Kunst und Literatur* (*Lectures on Dramatic Art and Literature*), was based on lectures delivered at Vienna in 1808 and has been widely translated. From 1805 to 1819 he was closely associated with Madame de Staël. In 1818 Schlegel was raised to the nobility and became professor of history at the University of Bonn.

Schlegel is famous for his translations of Shakespeare, Dante, and Cervantes. As one of the first students of Sanskrit, he edited the *Bhagavad-Gita* (1823). He was a leading figure in the German Romantic movement and severely criticized Schiller and Christoph Wieland. Although his poetry has been forgotten, his lectures, essays, and history of the fine arts are still valued.

Schleiermacher, Friedrich Ernst Daniel (1768–1834), German philosopher, born in Breslau. He was celebrated for his defense of religion against the attacks of skeptics and materialists. As a professor at the University of Halle and dean of theology at the University of Berlin (1810–1834), Schleiermacher's powerful personality influenced thousands of students. He drew his main philosophical inspiration from Plato and Kant. While he rejected the crude supernaturalism of dogmatic theology, he was tireless in insisting on the religious experience as the only way to the good life and on an attitude of reverence for the performance of any constructive work. He saw no conflict between religion, philosophy, and science. He was closely allied with the devotees of romanticism, including Schlegel.

Schleiermacher's principal works were *Reden über die Religion* (1799) and *Monologen* (1800). His *Letters* (first published in 1860) document the German philosophical revolution of his time.

Schlesinger, Arthur Meier (1888–1966), American historian, born Xenia, Ohio. Professor at Harvard from 1925 until his death, he authored many books, including *Political and Social History of the United States, 1829–1925*.

Schley, Winfield Scott (1839–1911), American naval officer, born in Frederick County, Md. In 1884, after two previous relief expeditions to the Arctic had failed, Schley rescued Adolphus Greely and six survivors. In 1898, while in temporary command of the American fleet at Santiago, he defeated the Spanish fleet under Adm. Pascual Cervera. He became involved in a dispute with his superior, Adm. William T. Sampson, over who should receive credit for the victory. Schley was censured, but made a rear admiral in 1899.

Schnabel, Artur (1882–1951), Austrian-American pianist and composer, born in Lipnik. A child prodigy, Schnabel concertized throughout Europe and America. He went to Switzerland with the advent of Nazism, came to the U.S. in 1939, and became a citizen in 1945. As a performer, Schnabel was noted for his authoritative interpretations of Beethoven (whose works he edited), Mozart, and Schubert.

Schnitzler, Arthur (1862–1931), Austrian novelist and playwright, born in Vienna. He gave up his medical practice for literature. His short plays and novels, written with great skill, often emphasize psychological and social problems. Among his plays are *Anatol* (1893) and *Reigen* (1900). Other works include *Liebelei* (1895), *Der grüne Kakadu* (1899), and *Professor Bernhardi* (1912), a book on anti-Semitism.

Schofield, John McAllister (1831–1906), American general, born in Gerry, N.Y. A West Point graduate (1853), Schofield entered the Civil War as a major and fought under Gen. William T. Sherman in the southern campaign and the taking of Atlanta. In 1868 he became a major general in the regular army. At the death of Gen. Philip H. Sheridan (1888), Schofield was appointed commander of the U.S. army.

Schönberg, Arnold (1874–1951), Austrian-American composer, born in Vienna. Except for lessons in counterpoint, Schönberg was entirely self-taught. While earning a living orchestrating operettas he composed such works as the string sextet *Verklärte Nacht* (*Transfigured Night*, 1899), and the *Gurrelieder* (*Songs of the Dove*, 1901–1913). His search for a personal style is seen first in the *Chamber Symphony* (1906–1913), which caused a riot at its first performance because it abandoned the traditional concept of tonality. From Schönberg's atonal style evolved the basis of modern twelve-tone or serial music. Exiled by thhe Nazis in 1933, he settled in America and was recognized as an outstanding teacher. His works include the symphonic poem *Pelleas und Melisande* (1905), the *Pierrot Lunaire* cycle (1912), dramatic works, pieces for chorus, chamber music, orchestral and piano works.

Schongauer, Martin, also known as **Martin Schön** and **Hipsch** or **Hübsch Martin** (c.1445–1491). German engraver and painter, born in Colmar. He established a school of painting in Colmar that became an important center of late Gothic art. Famous for his *Madonna of the Rose Garden*, he was reputed to be the greatest engraver of the 15th century.

Schoolcraft, Henry Rowe (1793–1864), American ethnologist, born in Albany County, N.Y. He made a geological survey of Missouri and accompanied Gen. Lewis Cass on a geological expedition to Lake Superior in 1820. In 1822 he became the Indian agent for the tribes around the lake, and during his service negotiated treaties whereby the U.S. acquired 16 million acres of land from the Indians (1836). In 1832 he headed an expedition which discovered the sources of the Mississippi. His writings include narratives of his travels and a 6-volume history of American Indian tribes.

Schopenhauer, Arthur (1788–1860), German philosopher, born in Danzig. He studied first at Weimar and Göttingen, then at Berlin and Jena. At Dresden he published *Sight and Color* (1816), and his major work, *The World as Will and Idea* (1819) After lecturing with little success at the University of Berlin (1820–1821), he retired to Frankfurt am Main where he lived in friendless solitude. His disposition was generally regarded as mistrustful, severe, and violent

Schopenhauer presents his ideas with such skill that he ranks with the greatest of philosophical writers. His basic philosophy asserts that every living thing has in it a

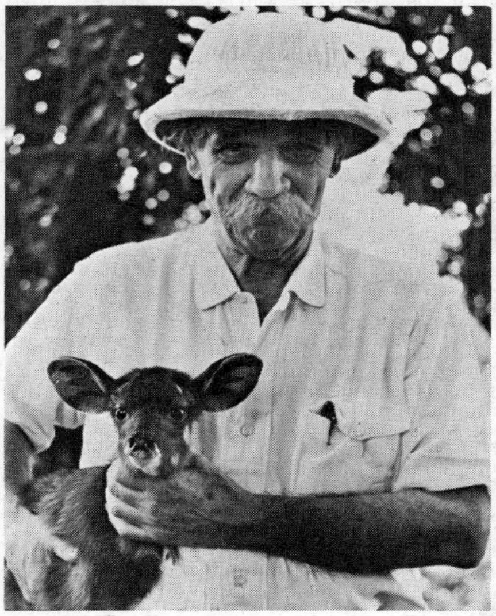

UNITED PRESS INTERNATIONAL

ALBERT SCHWEITZER

blind "will-to-live," but in trying to express itself is continually resisted by all other beings and objects in the world. Life, therefore, is an endless struggle. To will and not to find satisfaction is pain; pleasure is only the temporary absence of pain. If all desire were to be realized, however, there would be only boredom left. Therefore, we should give up all desires and wants, finding some relief from sorrow and struggle in science and the arts.

This doctrine of the will is reflected in the thought of Friedrich Nietzsche, Henri Bergson, William James, and John Dewey, as well as in the works of Thomas Mann.

Schubert, Franz Peter (1797–1828), Austrian composer, born in Vienna. His rich melodic vocabulary gave him popular acclaim, yet only recently has his compositional genius been justly acknowledged. He composed his first symphony in 1813, and two masterpieces in 1814, the songs *Gretchen am Spinnrade* and *Erlkönig*. Schubert's famed "Trout" piano quintet was written in 1819. His other works include the *Unfinished Symphony* (1822), the *Die schöne Müllerin* song cycle, String Quartets in A minor and D minor (1824), the *Winterreise* song cycle (1826), the String Quartet in G major and the songs *Who is Sylvia?* and *Hark, Hark the Lark*. In 1827, the year before his death, he wrote the great C Major Symphony (No. 9) and the posthumously published *Schwanengesang* (*Swan Song*). He is famed as the originator and greatest exponent of German *lieder*. Before his death from typhus in 1828, he had composed over 600 songs and many chamber and orchestral works.

Schuman, William (1910–), American composer, born in New York City. He won the first Pulitzer Prize awarded a composer in 1943, for his *Secular Cantata No. 2, A Free Song*. In 1945 he became president of the Juilliard School of Music in New York. He has composed symphonies, string quartets, orchestral, vocal, and choral music, including the *American Festival Overture, The Mighty Casey* (opera), and *This Is Our Time* (cantata).

Schumann, Robert (1810–1856), German composer, born in Zwickau. He gave up the study of law for music, and studied piano with Friedrich Wieck, his future father-in-law. Schumann founded and edited the musical journal *Die Neue Zeitschrift für Musik* (1834–1844), in which he championed romanticism. In 1847 he was appointed professor to the new Leipzig Conservatory, and he completed the Symphony in C in Dresden in the same year. The Schumanns fled Dresden at the outbreak of revolution and settled in Düsseldorf, where Schumann was made musical director. Mental illness set in and the composer was committed to an asylum in 1854.

Schumann was a prolific composer and one of Schubert's greatest successors in the art of song writing. His works include a piano quintet, the overture to *Manfred*, and many songs and piano pieces. His wife, Clara, a pianist renowned for her interpretations of both Chopin's and her husband's works, edited Schumann's complete works after his death.

Schumann-Heink, Ernestine (1861–1936), American contralto, born in Lieben, near Prague. She made her operatic debut in Dresden in 1878. She came to the U.S. in 1898, and made her debut in Chicago in *Lohengrin*. Her deep, rich voice was well-suited for Wagnerian roles as well as for concert recitals. She sang at the Metropolitan Opera House, New York (1899–1904), and also appeared there in 1926 in *Das Rheingold*. She also gave radio concerts.

Schurz, Carl (1829–1906), German-American statesman and journalist, born in Liblar, near Cologne. For his part in the revolutionary movement of 1849, he was forced to flee Germany. After coming to the U.S. in 1852, he was a politician, lecturer, lawyer, and a major-general in the Civil War. After the war, he was a journalist in St. Louis, a U.S. senator (1869–1875), and secretary of the interior (1877–1881). He wrote *Life of Henry Clay* (2 vols., 1887).

Schütz, Heinrich, also known as **Sagittarius** (1595–1672), German composer, born near Gera. He studied music in Venice under Giovanni Gabrieli and in 1611 published a book of madrigals. He introduced Italian music and styles of performance to Germany, and for this he is considered the founder of the German baroque style of music. His compositional style lies between the polyphony of Palestrina and the more lavish orchestrations of Bach and Handel. His *Daphne* is considered the first German opera. He also composed much church music for voice.

Schuyler, Philip John (1733–1804), American statesman, born in Albany, N.Y. He served in the French and Indian War (1755–1760), was a delegate to the Continental Congress (1775), and was one of the four generals of the Continental army, in command of northern troops. Disagreements with his superiors forced him to resign in 1779. He negotiated treaties with the six Indian nations, and served as U.S. senator from New York. With Alexander Hamilton (his son-in-law) and John Jay, he led New York's Federal party.

Schwab, Charles Michael (1862–1939), American industrialist, born in Williamsburg, Pa. Beginning as an engineering stake driver, he rose to become president of the Carnegie Steel Company (1897–1901). He served as president of U.S. Steel (1901–1903) and Bethlehem Steel (1903–1913), and he was chairman of the board at Bethlehem from 1913 until his death.

Schweitzer, Albert (1875–1965), Alsatian medical missionary, physician, Protestant theologian, organist, musicologist, and author, born in Kaysersberg, Alsace. He studied theology at Strasbourg. Later, he studied organ with the French composer Charles Widor and became an authority on the works of J. S. Bach. He had vowed as a boy to serve humanity after reaching the age 30. To this end, in 1905, he began to study medicine and resigned as principal of the Strasbourg Theological College. In 1913 he founded a hospital at Lambaréné in French Equatorial Africa, where he served as director and missionary surgeon for the rest of his life. In 1952 he received the Nobel Peace Prize. Notable examples of his writings include: *Johann Sebastian Bach, the Musician Poet* (1905); *The Quest of the Historical Jesus* (1906), marking a revolution in New Testament criticism; *The Forest Primeval in Equatorial Africa* (1921); and *Out of My Life and Thought* (1931).

Scipio the Younger, in full **Publius Cornelius Scipio Aemilianus Africanus Numantinus** (c.185–129 B.C.), Roman soldier, the adopted grandson of Scipio the Elder. After distinguishing himself in Spain, he took part in the third Punic War. In Africa, he laid siege to Carthage, took it by storm, and leveled it to the ground (146 B.C.). He was then sent to Spain, where he captured Numantia in spite of stubborn resistance. Upon his return to Rome, he entered politics as a leader of the aristocratic party. It is thought that he was killed by his political enemies.

Scipio the Elder, in full **Publius Cornelius Scipio Africanus** (c.237–183 B.C.), Roman general. He was elected aedile (212) and proconsul (211), with command of the Roman forces in Spain. He defeated the Carthaginians in Ilipa in 206. On his return to Rome (205), he was elected consul. In 206 he sailed from Sicily, at the head of a large army, for the invasion of Africa. His success compelled the Carthaginian Senate to recall Hannibal from Italy. When peace was concluded in 205, Scipio returned to Rome and enjoyed a triumph. His laurels, however, did not protect him from the intrigues of his enemies in Rome. Various charges were brought against him, and at length he retired in disgust to his country estate at Liternum. He is commonly regarded as the greatest Roman general before Julius Caesar.

Scot or **Scott, Michael** (c.1175–c.1234), Scottish translator and astrologer who attained posthumous fame as a magician. He studied at Oxford, learned Arabic at Toledo, and at the court of Frederick II helped translate Aristotle's works into Latin from the Arabic. Because of his original works in the occult sciences, he became known as "the wondrous wizard."

Scott, Dred (c.1795–1858), American Negro, born of slave parents in Virginia. While residing in Illinois, he instigated the famous Dred Scott case when he claimed that, because he lived with his master in a free state, he could not be sold back into slavery upon his master's death. The U.S. Supreme Court held (1857) that he was not a citizen and thereby had no rights in the courts. It further declared that no citizen of any state could be hampered from bringing his slave property into any territory. After the decision, Scott was transferred to a new master and freed soon after.

Scott, Sir George Gilbert (1811–1878), English architect, born in Gawcott. He became a leading exponent of the Gothic revival style and was sought after for many public commissions. His work includes government domestic offices in London (1858), the Albert Memorial in Hyde Park, London (1862–1863), and a cathedral in Edinburgh.

Scott, Robert Falcon (1868–1912), English Antarctic explorer, born near Devonport. In command of the *Discovery* exploring the Antarctic regions (1901–1904), he discovered King Edward VII Land and was rewarded with a captaincy. He began his second Antarctic journey in 1910. Together with four companions, he reached the South Pole, only to find that Roald Amundsen had discovered it a month and four days earlier. The entire party perished while on their journey. Scott's diary of the expedition, found by searchers the next spring, tells of his heroic efforts.

Scott, Sir Walter (1771–1832), Scottish novelist, poet, historian, and biographer, born in Edinburgh. As a youth, Scott was an insatiable reader of ballads and romances. While studying law at Edinburgh, he explored the Scottish countryside, collecting old songs and stories. He practiced law with fair success, but in 1799 he received a political appointment that allowed him more time for writing. He translated several books from the German, and published his song collection, *Minstrelsy of the Scottish Border* (1802–1803). This and *The Lay of the Last Minstrel* (1805) earned him wide popularity. He bought a partnership in a publishing firm and in a theater and began to accumulate a large fortune. During this period he wrote romances, notably *The Lady of the Lake* (1810). In 1814, *Waverly*, the first of a series of novels, was published anonymously and was instantly successful. Many novels followed: *Guy Mannering* (1815) *Rob Roy* (1817), *Ivanhoe* (1819), and others. In 1826 he was ruined financially through the failure of his publishing house, and to repay his indebtedness, drove himself to write *Tales of a Grandfather, The Fair Maid of Perth, Castle Dangerous,* and other books before his death.

Scott, Walter Dill (1869–1955), American psychologist and educator, born in Cooksville, Ill. He graduated from Northwestern University and earned his doctorate at the University of Leipzig, Germany. After several years as professor of psychology at Northwestern, he became president of the university. He wrote on business psychology, personnel and advertising.

Scott, Winfield (1786–1866), American general, born near Petersburg, Va. He was educated at William and Mary College, practiced law for a year, and entered the army (1808). During the War of 1812, he served in the Canadian front, where he was wounded and decorated for heroism, and was made a major general. In 1847 he commanded American forces in the Mexican War, and for his leadership was brevetted lieutenant general. Scott was the Whig candidate for president in 1852, but was defeated by Franklin Pierce. When the Civil War broke out, he remained in the U.S. army, but retired in November, 1861.

Scriabin, Alexander, in Russian **Aleksandr Nikolaevich Skryabin** (1872–1915), Russian composer and pianist, born in Moscow. He studied at the Moscow Conservatory and was professor there from 1898 to 1904. Among his orchestral works are three symphonies, the tone poems *The Divine Poem, Poem of Ecstasy,* and *The Poem of Fire (Prometheus).* His piano works include sonatas, etudes, preludes, and dances.

Scribe, Augustin Eugène (1791–1861), French dramatist born in Paris. The best known of his many plays include: *Le verre d'eau* (1840) and *Adrienne Lecouvreur* (1849). Scribe wrote the librettos for *Fra diavolo* (1830) and *Les huguenots* 1836. He was elected to the French Academy in 1834.

Scripps, Edward Wyllis (1854–1926), American newspaper publisher, born near Rushville, Ill. He established more than 30 newspapers and was a founder of the Scripps-McRae Press Association (1897), which later developed into the United Press. His political views were liberal. Scripps also organized the first modern syndicated press service.

See, Thomas Jefferson Jackson (1866–1962), American astronomer and mathematician, born near Montgomery City, Mo. He was an astronomer at the University of Chicago (1893–1896) and at Lowell Observatory in Arizona (1896–1898), and was in charge of the U.S. Naval Observatory (1899–1902). He is particularly famous for his investigations of double stars, the ether, the cause of universal gravitation, magnetic earthquakes, and cosmic magnetism. He discovered the precession of the earth's magnetic poles and established the wave theory of solid bodies and of the cosmic ray.

Seeger, Alan (1886–1916), American poet, born in New York City. He graduated from Harvard (1910), and in 1912 he went to Paris, where he published a number of poems entitled *Juvenilia.* He enlisted in the French Foreign Legion and was killed in 1916. His best-known poem is *I Have a Rendezvous with Death.*

Seleucus I, surnamed **Nicator,** *the Conqueror* (c.358–280 B.C.), founder of the Seleucid dynasty. At its height, the dynasty controlled Bactria, Persia, Babylonia, Syria, and part of Asia Minor. Seleucus founded Greek and Macedonian colonies and also built Antioch as his capital. He ruled the empire from 306 B.C. until he was assassinated by Ptolemy Keraunos. He was succeeded by his son, Antiochus I Soter.

Selkirk, or **Selcraig, Alexander** (1676–1721), Scottish sailor whose experience on a lonely island was the basis of Defoe's *Robinson Crusoe.* Following a violent quarrel with the captain of his ship, Selkirk asked to be put ashore at Juan Fernandez island, 400 miles off Chile. He was rescued four years later and published his experiences, which Defoe used in his novel.

Semmelweis, Ignaz Philipp (1818–1865), Hungarian obstetrician, born in Ofen. He studied medicine in Budapest and Vienna, and taught obstetrics in these cities. He proved that puerperal fever is contagious and is controllable by use of antiseptics.

Semmes, Raphael (1809–1877), American naval officer, born in Charles County, Md. He was a commander in the Mexican War. When the Civil War broke out, he joined the Confederate navy and was given command of the *Sumter* and the *Alabama,* winning many victories. Semmes lost the *Alabama* in a fight with the *Kearsarge* off Cherbourg, France, in 1864. and was rescued by a British vessel. After the war he practiced law in Mobile, Ala.

Seneca, Lucius Annaeus (c.4 B.C.–65 A.D.), Roman philosopher of the Stoic school born in Cordoba, Spain. He was banished by Claudius to the island of Corsia. When Claudius married Agrippina, Seneca was recalled and appointed tutor to her son Domitius, afterward Emperor Nero. Five years later his pupil ascended the throne, and Seneca became one of Nero's chief advisers. After Nero murdered Agrippina, Seneca asked permission to retire from court, hoping to devote himself to his philosophical studies. But the emperor both disliked and feared him; after the conspiracy of Piso (65 A.D.), Seneca was accused by the conspirators of aiding the plot, and without further proof was ordered to put himself to death. The most significant of Seneca's works are his philosophical essays, including *Ad Marciam de consolatione, De ira* and *Ad Helviam de consolatione.* Seneca was also a popular dramatist whose melodramatic tragedies of violence and revenge were much admired and imitated by Elizabethan playwrights.

Serkin, Rudolf (1903–), American pianist, born in Cheb, Bohemia. His European concert tours began in 1920, and he made his American debut in 1933. In 1939 he was appointed to the Curtis Institute of Music, Philadelphia, and he now heads the Marlboro Music School in Vermont.

Serra, Junípero original name **Miguel José Serra** (1713–1784), Spanish Franciscan missionary, born on Majorca. He was educated in theology and philosophy, and became a missionary to Mexico (1749). In 1767 he led a company of monks to California to found missions there. Mission San Diego (1769) was the first white settlement in Upper California. He established 21 missions in California, and spent the rest of his life developing the missions.

Seti I (died c.1292 B.C.), king of Egypt (1313–1292 B.C.). He sent his armies eastward into Syria with considerable success, though the Hittites could not be conquered. He completed the remarkable Hall of Columns at Karnak, started by his father, Ramses I. The mummy of Seti was discovered during British excavations in 1881, as was also that of Ramses II, his illustrious son.

Seton, Ernest Thompson (1860–1946), American naturalist, writer, and illustrator, born in South Shields, England. He lived in the backwoods of Canada (1866–1870) and on the Western plains (1882–1887), where he observed Indian life and wildlife. His books, many illustrated by himself, include *Wild Animals I Have Known* (1898), *Biography of a Grizzly* (1900), and *Biography of an Arctic Fox* (1937). One of the founders of the Boy Scouts of America, he was chief scout from 1910 to 1915.

Seurat, Georges Pierre (1859–1891), French painter, born in Paris. Seurat's style is recognized by his breakup of color into dots (termed *pointillism*) that merge together when viewed from a short distance. His color theories helped make him an influential Postimpressionist artist.

Seward, William Henry (1801–1872), American statesman, born in Orange County, N.Y. A lawyer with a large practice, he entered New York state politics in 1830, serving in the state senate and later as governor (1839–1843). In 1849 he was elected U.S. senator from New York and constantly fought against slavery. He became Pres. Abraham Lincoln's secretary of state (1861) and served until 1869. He showed remarkable ability in handling the delicate diplomatic relations with foreign powers, especially in the troublesome Trent Affair and the *Alabama* Claims. The assassins who killed Lincoln also shot Seward on the same night, but he recovered and served as Pres. Andrew Johnson's secretary of state. In this post, he arranged for the purchase of Alaska from Russia (1867).

Seymour, Horatio (1810–1886), American politician, born in Pompey Hill, N.Y. He was educated at military school, studied law at Utica, and was admitted to the bar (1832). He was elected governor of New York in 1852, and again in 1862, and was prominent as one of the North's "war governors." He was Democratic candidate for president against U. S. Grant in 1868.

Sforza, Count Carlo (1873–1952), Italian statesman, born in Lunigiana. He was minister of foreign affairs (1920–1921), and negotiated the Treaty of Rapallo with Yugoslavia. A senator (1919–1926) he was the leader of the anti-Fascist opposition. After 1922 he lived outside Italy, and he moved to the United States in 1940. He wrote many books, including *European Dictatorships* (1931) and *The Real Italians* (1942).

Sforza, Lodovico, called **Il Moro,** *the Moor* (1451–1508), Italian ruler, member of the celebrated Milanese family. As duke of Milan (1481–1499) he was a sound administrator. He is best remembered as the patron of Leonardo da Vinci. He was defeated by Louis XII (1499), and died a prisoner in France.

Shackleton, Sir Ernest Henry (1874–1922), British explorer, born in Kilkee, Ireland. He sailed on merchant ships and later accompanied Capt. Robert F. Scott in the Antarctic expedition of 1901–1904. In 1908 he sailed from New Zealand on the *Nimrod,* in command of an expedition that reached a point about 99 miles from the South Pole (1899). In 1914–1916 the second expedition of which he was commanding officer made an unsuccessful attempt to cross the Antarctic continent. In 1921 he again set out in the *Quest*, but he died of heart disease on board his ship near South Georgia Island. His writings include *Heart of the Antarctic* (1909) and *South* (1919).

Shaftesbury, Anthony Ashley Cooper, 1st Baron Ashley and 1st Earl of Shaftesbury (1621–1683), English statesman, born in Wimborne St. Giles. He was educated at Exeter College, Oxford, and studied law at Lincoln's Inn. He entered the Short Parliament in 1640 and in 1654 supported the Cromwellian party. Later he rejoined the Royalists, and Charles II made him chancellor of the exchequer in 1661. In the same year he was created 1st Baron Ashley. In 1672 he was created an earl and appointed lord chancellor. His judgment was able and impartial, but he lost his office and at once became one of the most powerful leaders of the opposition. In 1679 he became president of the Privy Council and was instrumental in passing the Habeas Corpus Act (1679). He entered into the plots of the Monmouth Rebellion and fled to Holland, where he spent his remaining years.

Shah Jahan (c.1592–1666), Mogul Emperor of Delhi, succeeding his father in 1627. He was an able administrator, and he greatly increased his own power and dazzled his subjects with architectural wonders. He founded the modern city of Delhi (1639–1648) and built the beautiful Taj Mahal at Agra (1632–1645), a mausoleum for his favorite wife, known as Mumtz Mahall (the distinguished one of the palace). In the new imperial palace he built the Peacock Throne (1628–1635).

Shakespeare, William (1564–1616), English poet and dramatist, one of the greatest writers in the English language. He was born in Stratford upon Avon. His father, John Shakespeare, was a glover and produce merchant. His mother, Mary Arden, came of an old Warwickshire family. William was the third of seven children. He received all of his education at the free grammar school in Stratford. At the age of 18 he married Anne Hathaway, who was eight years his senior. Of their three children, Hamnet, the son, died in childhood (1596), and Susanne and Judith, the two daughters, survived their parents.

At the age of 22 Shakespeare went to London. By 1592 he was an experienced actor, and his skill as a playwright made him a considerable rival of the university wits. One of these, Robert Greene, referred to him as "an upstart crow, beautified with our feathers." In 1593 and 1594, when the theaters were closed due to plague, he wrote *Venus and Adonis* and *The Rape of Lucrece*, dedicating both long poems to his patron, the earl of Southampton. He was a member of the Chamberlain's Players (formed in 1594), which became the King's Players in 1603.

His first play, the three parts of *King Henry VI*, seems to have been produced in 1590, and from then until 1613 he produced at least one play every year. Both his reputation and his prosperity increased, and he was soon a favorite with the common people and the nobility. He had the ap-

proval of both Queen Elizabeth and James, her successor. In 1597 he purchased New Place, the largest house in Stratford, and began spending more time there; in 1610 he settled there, although he continued to write for three more years. He seems to have accumulated a comfortable fortune at that time. He died on his 53d birthday and was buried in Stratford churchyard.

His collected works, as published today, contain 37 plays, 2 long poems, and 154 sonnets, as well as other verse. The plays have been divided into 17 comedies, 10 histories, and 10 tragedies. The following are his best known (many of the dates are conjectural): *Henry VI* (1590), *Comedy of Errors* (1591–1592), *Two Gentlemen of Verona* (1592), *Richard III* (1592–1593), *Titus Andronicus* (1593), *Love's Labour's Lost* (1594), *King John* (1594), *Romeo and Juliet* (1594–1595), *Richard II* (1595), *A Midsummer Night's Dream* (1595), *Taming of the Shrew* (in collab.; 1596), *Merchant of Venice* (1596), *Henry IV*, 1 and 2 (1597–1598), *Much Ado About Nothing* (1598–1599), *Henry V* (1599), *Julius Caesar* (1599–1600), *As You Like It* (1599–1600), *Merry Wives of Windsor* (1599–1600), *Hamlet* (1600–1601), *Twelfth Night* (1601), *Troilus and Cressida* (1602), *All's Well That Ends Well* (1602), *Measure For Measure* (1604), *Othello* (1604), *King Lear* (1605–1606), *Macbeth* (1605–1606), *Antony and Cleopatra* (1607), *Timon of Athens* (1607–1608), *Pericles* (in collab.; 1608), *Coriolanus* (1608–1609), *Cymbeline* (1610), *A Winter's Tale* (1611), *The Tempest* (1611), *Henry VIII* (in collab.; 1612–1613), and *The Two Noble Kinsmen* (in collab.; 1612–1613). His poems include: *Venus and Adonis* (pub. 1593), *The Rape of Lucrece* (pub. 1594), and *Sonnets* (pub. 1609).

Shankaracharya, also **Shankara** or **Sankara** (c.788–c.820), Hindu philosopher, one of the most famous Indian theologians. His commentaries on Vedanta philosophy are respected and revered in India today.

Shastri, Lal Bahadur (1904–1966), prime minister of India and leader of the ruling National Congress party. Upon the death of Nehru (1964), Shastri became the prime minister. He died while attending a peace conference with Pakistan in Tashkent, Soviet Central Asia.

Shaw, Anna Howard (1847–1919), American woman suffrage leader, born in Newcastle-on-Tyne, England. She was brought to the United States in early childhood. She was ordained a minister of the Methodist Protestant church and received her M.D. from Boston University Medical School (1886). She preached in several churches in Massachusetts and became the chief lecturer and later president of the National American Woman Suffrage Association (1904–1915).

Shaw, George Bernard (1856–1950), British playwright, born in Dublin, Ireland. At the age of 20 he went to London to become a writer. He published a few novels, wrote music criticism for newspapers, and began work as a dramatic critic for the *Saturday Review* in 1895. In 1882 he had become a socialist and was active as a propagandist for the Fabian Society. He gained recognition as a brilliant debater before he became known as an author.

Shaw began to write for the stage about 1890. One of his plays, *Mrs. Warren's Profession*, written in 1893, was banned until 1902. His *Candida* (1894) won success only

in Germany. His first stage success in England was *Man and Superman* (1903). This was followed by *Major Barbara* (1905), *The Doctor's Dilemma* (1906), *Getting Married* (1908), *Androcles and the Lion* (1912), *Pygmalion* (1912), *Arms and the Man* (1894), and others. Three of his greatest plays, *Heartbreak House* (1917), *Back to Methuselah* (1921), and *Saint Joan of Arc* (1923), were written after he was 60. *The Apple Cart* was produced in 1929 and *Too True to be Good* in 1932. Other late works, not plays, were *The Intelligent Woman's Guide to Socialism and Capitalism* (1928) and *The Black Girl in Search of God* (1932). The plays have qualities that have come to be known as Shavian—wit, epigram, and exaggeration for effect. Shaw received the Nobel Prize for literature in 1925.

Shaw, Thomas Edward. See *Lawrence, T. E.*

Shays, Daniel (c.1747–1825), American soldier and rebel, born probably in Hopkinton, Mass. He attained the rank of captain (1777) in the Continental army. The financial depression after the Revolution caused much discontent among farmers of western Massachusetts, and Shays and his followers protested. Shays' Rebellion started in 1786 when he led 600 men in a demonstration before the state Supreme Court at Springfield. In 1787 he headed 2,000 men and tried to take several arsenals. Shays escaped to Vermont after the insurrection and was condemned to death, but was pardoned in 1788.

Shelley, Mary Wollstonecraft Godwin (1797–1851), English novelist, born in London. She was the daughter of the English philosophical writer, William Godwin. She accompanied Percy Shelley to the Continent (1814) and married him in 1816. She is the author of *Frankenstein* (1818) and the autobiographical *Lodore* (1835), among other novels.

Shelley, Percy Bysshe (1792–1822), English poet, born in Sussex. He studied at Eton and in 1808 he left school for two years. He then went to Oxford, where, in his sophomore year, he was expelled for his pamphlet *The Necessity of Atheism* (1811). That year he married Harriet Westbrook, but they were separated in 1814. Shelley later moved to the Continent, and following his wife's suicide he married Mary Wollstonecraft Godwin in 1816. He left England permanently in 1818 and spent much time in Italy in the company of Byron, Edward Trelawny, and Edward Williams. He visited Leigh Hunt at Pisa and was lost in a storm while sailing back. His works include the antireligious poem *Queen Mab* (privately published, 1813), the lyric drama *Prometheus Unbound* (1818), the tragedy *The Cenci* (1818), *Ode to the West Wind* (1819), *The Skylark* (1820), and the elegy *Adonais* (1821), on the death of Keats.

Sheridan, Philip Henry (1831–1888), American general, born in Albany, N. Y., and a graduate of West Point (1853). At the outbreak of the Civil War he was made quartermaster of the Department of Missouri. Before the end of 1863 he had distinguished himself in many battles. Sheridan's hurried dash from Winchester to Cedar Creek (1864), where he arrived in time to rally his disorganized force and pull victory out of almost certain defeat, won him a major generalship and the special thanks of Congress. Sheridan was appointed commander in chief of the U.S. army in 1884, and in 1888 he became a general.

Sheridan, Richard Brinsley (1751–1816), British dramatist and politician, born in Dublin, Ireland. He was educated at Harrow and studied law at the Middle Temple, London. In 1775 he produced *The Rivals*, the first of his successful comedies of manners. In 1777 he became part proprietor of Drury Lane Theatre, London, which produced his *The School for Scandal* (1777). Sheridan then turned to politics. He was elected to Parliament in 1780 and became foreign secretary in 1782. His part in the impeachment of Warren Hastings made his political reputation. His theatrical affairs met with disaster, and he died in poverty. He was buried in Westminster Abbey.

Sherman, John (1823–1900), American statesman, born in Lancaster, Ohio, a brother of William T. Sherman. He was admitted to the bar in 1844, entering into law practice with his brother. He became an antislavery Whig, entered Congress in 1855, and continued in the House until 1861, the recognized leader of the Republican party. He was elected U.S. senator and held that post from 1861 to 1897, with the exception of the years 1877 to 1881, when he was secretary of the treasury, and the years 1897–1898, when he served as secretary of state. The many important financial measures that he fostered include the Sherman Antitrust Act (1890) and the Sherman Silver Law (1890).

CHARLES PHELPS CUSHING

GREAT PLAYWRIGHTS of two eras: Shakespeare (*right*) and George Bernard Shaw (*left*).

Sherman, Roger (1721–1793), American political leader and signer of the Declaration of Independence, born in Newton, Mass. He was an important figure in the Continental Congress from 1774 to 1784 and in the Constitutional Convention in 1787, when he and his Connecticut colleagues helped compromise disagreements between the large states and the small states. He helped to draft the Declaration of Independence and the Articles of Confederation. In 1789 he entered Congress and in 1791 became a senator.

Sherman, William Tecumseh (1820–1891), American general, born in Lancaster, Ohio, brother of John Sherman. A graduate of West Point (1840), he was a captain during the Mexican War, although he saw no service. He resigned from the army in 1853 and was a banker for several years, ending in bankruptcy. When the Civil War broke out, he reentered the army as a colonel and distinguished himself at the battle of Shiloh and in the siege of Vicksburg. He marched across Mississippi, captured Savannah, Ga., and Charleston, S.C., and then moved north, compelling the evacuation of Richmond and the surrender of Lee to Grant on April 9, 1865. He was appointed lieutenant general in 1866 and in 1869 became general and commander of the army. He retired in 1884.

Sholokhov, Mikhail Aleksandrovich (1905–), Russian novelist. At the age of 12, Sholokhov became a revolutionist when civil war broke out in his native Don region. Not until 1923 did he leave, reluctantly, to continue his education and begin his literary career in Moscow. He began by submitting short stories and sketches to various Komsomol publications; by 1925 he had married, published his first book, the *Don Tales,* and returned to the Don. The *Don Tales* engendered his later four-volume masterpiece, *The Quiet Don* (two volumes in English translation: *And Quiet Flows the Don,* 1934, and *The Don Flows Home to the Sea,* 1940). The novel, which relates the Don Cossacks' involvement in World War I, the Russian Revolution, and the subsequent civil strife, was widely translated, and then retold in an opera by Ivan Dzerzhinsky, in films, and in a play. Sholokhov also wrote: *Virgin Soil Upturned* (1932) and *They Fought For their Fatherland* (1943–1944 and 1949–1954), and has received the first Stalin prize in literature (1941), the Order of the Fatherland (1945), the Order of Lenin (1955), and the Nobel Prize for literature (1965). He is a member of the Academy of Sciences and of the Presidium of the Union of Soviet Writers.

Shostakovich, Dmitri Dimitriyevich (1906–), Russian composer, born in St. Petersburg (Leningrad). He studied at Leningrad Conservatory (1919–1925). His most notable works include his Fifth Symphony (1937), commemorating the twentieth anniversary of the Russian Revolution; the Seventh Symphony (1942), depicting the battle of Leningrad; and the opera *Lady Macbeth of Mtsensk* (1934).

Sibelius, Jean (1865–1957), Finnish composer, born in Tavastehus. He studied music in Helsingfors, Berlin, and Vienna. He wrote a number of symphonies, symphonic poems, operas, and concertos. His best-known compositions are full of the spirit of his own country, notably *Finlandia* (1899), *Valse Triste* (1903), *Oceanides* (1914), and *Swan of Tuonela* (1893).

Sidney, Sir Philip (1554–1586), English poet and statesman, born in Kent, and educated at Oxford. He traveled in Europe on diplomatic missions, and upon his return home he became for a time a favorite at the court of Elizabeth. He was ordered to go to the support of the Netherlands in their struggle against Spain and was killed at the battle of Zutphen. His literary contributions include *Arcadia* (1580–1581), written for his sister's amusement; the passionate love sonnets *Astrophel and Stella* (1580–1584); and *Apologie for Poetrie* (later *Defence of Poesie,* 1595).

Sienkiewicz, Henryk (1846–1916), Polish novelist, born in Lithuania, and educated at the University of Warsaw. He visited the U.S. in 1876, but later returned to Poland where he wrote the famous *Quo Vadis?* (1896), a tale of the time of Nero, and *The Crusaders* (4 vols., 1900).

Signac, Paul (1863–1935), French painter, born in Paris. In 1884 he exhibited with the Impressionists and later was associated with Georges Seurat in the Postimpressionist movement. In his style, Signac used mosaic-like patches of pure color (similar to Seurat's pointillist dots). His subjects were often seascapes.

Sigsbee, Charles Dwight (1845–1923), American naval officer, born in Albany, N.Y., and a graduate of Annapolis. He was in command of the battleship *Maine* when it was blown up by a torpedo in Havana harbor in February, 1898. He commanded the battleship *St. Paul* in the Spanish-American War. In 1903 he received the rank of rear admiral. He wrote *The Maine: an Account of Her Destruction in Havana Harbor* (1899). He retired in 1907.

Sikorsky, Igor Ivan (1889–), American aeronautical engineer, born in Kiev, Russia. A graduate of the Naval College at St. Petersburg in 1906, he started designing and building flying machines in 1908. In 1913 he built and flew the first multi-motored airplane. During World War I he designed bombers for the Russian army. Sikorsky came to the U.S. in 1919 and was naturalized in 1928. He has pioneered in many fields of aviation. He developed the first long-range passenger plane that initiated transoceanic air service. In 1928 he organized the Sikorsky Aviation Corporation and in 1939 was the first to develop a workable helicopter.

Silhouette, Étienne de (1709–1767), French minister of finance (1759) under Louis XV. His reforms evoked hostility and ridicule. The nobility mocked him, applying his name to profile shadow drawings for their suggestion of stinginess.

Silone, Ignazio (1900–), real name **Secondo Tranquilli,** Italian writer. He was exiled to Zurich for actively opposing the Fascists during the 1920's. An executive of the Socialist party and editor of the Socialist newspaper *Avanti* since the early forties, he is also the author of many novels including *Fontamara* (1930), *Bread and Wine* (1937), and *The Fox and the Camellias* (1961).

Simpson, Sir James Young (1811–1870), Scottish physician, born in Bathgate. He received his medical degree from the University of Edinburgh (1832) and in 1840 began to teach obstetrics there. In 1847 he discovered the anesthetic property of chloroform and introduced it into his practice. In this field he was the first to use anesthesia by ether in childbirth. He was made a baronet in 1866.

Sinclair, Upton Beall (1878–), American writer and politician, born in Baltimore, Md. He was educated at the College of the City of New York and Columbia University. He became prominent in Socialist affairs and from time to time was active in experimental communities, such as the Helicon Home Colony (1906) at Englewood, N.J. He ran for Congress twice on the Socialist ticket—in New Jersey in 1906 and in California in 1920. He also sought election to the United States Senate in 1922. His book *The Jungle* (1906) exposed conditions in the stockyards. *The Brass Check* (1919) attacked the evils of journalism. Other novels include *King Coal* (1917), *Oil* (1927), *World's End* (1940), *Dragon's Teeth* (1942), (for which he received the Pulitzer Prize in 1943), *Presidential Mission* (1947), and *O Shepherd Speak* (1949).

Singer, Isaac Merrit (1811–1875), American inventor and manufacturer of sewing machines, born in Pittstown, N.Y. He patented the sewing machine in 1851 and formed the I. M. Singer Company to manufacture it.

Siqueiros, David Alfaro (1898–), Mexican painter, born in Chihuahua. For his part in the revolutionary movement among Mexican workers he was imprisoned (1930). He was expelled from the U.S. for incorporating his political views in his frescoes in public buildings. He is considered one of the foremost revivers of true fresco painting in America.

Sitting Bull (c.1837–1890), American Indian leader, born in what is now North Dakota. He succeeded his father as chief of the Sioux, after distinguishing himself in plains warfare. He first came to the attention of white settlers when he raided Fort Buford in 1866. For ten years he was a menace to westward migration. In 1876 Gen. William T. Sheridan headed an expedition against him; in the campaign Sitting Bull massacred Gen. George A. Custer and his men. He escaped to Canada but returned to surrender in 1881. He still urged opposition to white invasion. Captured again, he was killed attempting to escape.

Sitwell, Dame Edith (1887–1965), English poet, born in Scarborough. She was the sister of Sir Osbert Sitwell and Sacheverell Sitwell, both writers and critics. A book of poems, *Façade* (1922), accompanied by William Walton's music, is representative of her earlier avant-garde romantic style. Her other collected poems include *Elegy for Dead Fashion* (1926), *Gold Cost Customs* (1929), and *Canticle of the Rose* (1949). A famous eccentric herself, she included a prose work, *The English Eccentrics* (1933), among her many books.

Skeat, Walter William (1835–1912), English philologist, born in London. He graduated from Christ's College, Cambridge (1858) and in 1878 was appointed professor of Anglo-Saxon there. He was the first director of the English Dialect Society, established in 1873, which later published the *English Dialect Dictionary.* Skeat contributed extensively to studies of old and middle English philology. His *Etymological English Dictionary* (1879–1882) is still a standard work.

Skelton, John (c.1460–1529), English satirical poet, born probably in Norfolk, and educated at Oxford and Cambridge. His work is characterized by original satire, complete with slang and unrestrained humor, that attacked the abuses of the clergy, the church, and the state. His writings include *The Bowge of Courte; Why come ye not to Courte;* and the anticlerical *Speke, Parrot.*

Skinner, Cornelia Otis (1901–), American actress and author, born in Chicago, Ill., the daughter of actor Otis Skinner. Her writings include the play *Captain Fury* (1925), the essay *Excuse It, Please* (1936), and the novel *Our Hearts Were Young and Gay* (with Emily Kimbrough, 1942).

Slater, Samuel (1768–1835), industrialist, born in Derbyshire, England. He is regarded as the founder of the American cotton industry. He worked for Richard Arkwright, the inventor of cotton-spinning machinery (1783), in England, and then brought the plans to America. He reproduced the machinery from memory in 1790 for a mill in Providence, R.I.

Slidell, John (1793–1871), American statesman, born in New York City. He graduated from Columbia College, became a successful lawyer in New Orleans, and was elected to the U.S. House of Representatives in 1843. He entered the U.S. Senate in 1853 but resigned in 1861. He represented the South in France during the Civil War. He and James M. Mason, the Confederate minister to England, sailed for Europe on the British ship *Trent.* They were captured on the high seas by a Union ship and both were carried as prisoners to the U.S. where they were confined in Fort Warren. On the demand of England they were released, with apologies, and proceeded on their missions. After the war Slidell lived in England.

Smetana, Bedřich (1824–1884), Czech pianist and composer, born in Litomsyl, Bohemia. He began to make public appearances as a pianist at the age of six. In 1856 he became Philharmonic conductor in Göteborg, Sweden, and was conductor of the National Bohemian Theatre from 1866 until deafness caused his retirement. His compositions were full of the spirit of his native country. His opera *The Bartered Bride* (1866), typifying Bohemian life, has been popular.

Smith, Adam (1723–1790), Scottish economist, born in Kirkcaldy and educated in the universities of Glasgow and Oxford. He became professor of logic and moral philosophy at Glasgow in 1751 and published his *Theory of the Moral Sentiments* in 1759. His *Inquiry into the Nature and Causes of the Wealth of Nations* (1776), the first scientific exposition of the principles of political economy, had a wide influence and has been translated into many languages. It recommended freedom of trade and circulation of gold as the bases of national prosperity, and influenced England in making commercial treaties.

Smith, Alfred Emanuel (1873–1944), American political leader, born in New York City of Irish parentage, educated at a parochial school. In 1903 he was elected to the New York Assembly as a Democrat and became speaker in 1913. In 1918 he was elected governor of the state and again in 1922, 1924, and 1926. He was nominated for president in 1928, and in 1932. Smith continued to be an important figure in national politics and in Tammany Hall after his defeats.

Smith, Goldwin (1823–1910), English author and educator, born in Reading. He graduated from Magdalen College, Oxford, was admitted to the English bar in 1847, and later taught history at Oxford. He came to the United States in 1864, anxious to support the cause of the Union in the Civil War. After teaching English and history at Cornell, he lived in Canada, where he founded and edited two magazines, from 1871 until his death. He wrote numerous works on history and politics.

Smith, John (1580–1631), English adventurer and colonist, founder of Virginia, born in Lincolnshire, England. He had many adventures as a soldier of fortune in Europe, Asia, and Africa. In 1606 he joined an expedition which sailed from England to found a colony in Virginia. He was captured by Powhatan's Indians on one of his journeys into the country for corn. According to his story, his life was saved by the chief's daughter Pocahontas. On his return to

Jamestown he found the colony reduced to about 40 men, who were anxious to return to England but were induced by Smith to remain until others arrived. He then explored the coasts of Chesapeake Bay in two voyages and made a map of the country. In 1614 he explored the coast of New England and undertook the founding of a colony in New England in 1615, but his vessel was captured by a French warship, and he was carried to La Rochelle.

Smith, Joseph (1805–1844), American religious leader, born in Sharon, Vt. He was the founder of the Mormon sect or the Church of Jesus Christ of Latter-day Saints. During a religious revival he declared that he had seen a vision in which he was ordered not to join any church but to await further guidance. According to his account, he was led to discover hidden gold plates on which were inscribed the tenets of a new religion. He translated the inscriptions and announced them as *The Book of Mormon* (1830). He became leader of the Church of Jesus Christ of Latter-day Saints, or the Mormons, in 1830 at Fayette, N.Y. Missionaries were sent out; one of the early converts was Sidney Rigdon of Mentor, Ohio. With Smith he greatly enlarged the new faith and built a Mormon community at Kirtland, Ohio. The sect spread to Nauvoo, Ill., where the legislature granted Smith almost unlimited power. The town was Mormon governed, and a temple was designed. By this time Brigham Young had become one of Smith's ablest leaders. A rumor was circulated to the effect that Mormonism was about to declare in behalf of polygamy. The anti-Mormons in the community rose in arms. Smith and his brother Hyrum and other leaders were arrested (June 27, 1844) and taken to Carthage for safety. Two days later a mob stormed the jail and shot Smith and his brother. Brigham Young then became leader.

Smith, Sydney (1771–1845), English journalist and clergyman, born in Essex, and educated at Oxford. He entered the ministry (1794) of the Church of England and from 1831 was a canon in St. Paul's Cathedral, London. He was one of three who in 1802 founded the *Edinburgh Review* and was one of its most influential contributors. Author of many works, he was noted for his wit and his humanity. He vigorously championed the removal of the civil disabilities of Catholics at a time when such advocacy of an unpopular cause was injurious to his clerical career.

Smithson, James Macie (1765–1829), British chemist and minerologist, born in France, and educated at Oxford. He was elected a fellow of the Royal Society in 1790 in recognition of his discovery of an ore of zinc (calamine), which was named smithsonite. The Smithsonian Institution in Washington, D.C., was founded under the provisions of his will and established by Congress (1846).

Smollett, Tobias George (1721–1771), British novelist, born in Dumbartonshire, Scotland, and educated at the University of Glasgow. He became a surgeon but gave up medicine for a literary career. His writings were many and varied. In 1748 he published *The Adventures of Roderick Random*, about his adventures as a ship's surgeon. Then followed *Peregrine Pickle* (1751), *History of England* (1756–1757), *Travels through France and Italy* (1766), and *The Expedition of Humphry Clinker* (1770).

Smuts, Jan Christiaan (1870–1950), South African statesman, born in Cape Town and educated at Cambridge. As a lawyer, practicing first at Cape Town and later at Johannesburg, he became state attorney under Pres. Stephanus Kruger in the Transvaal republic. In the South African War (1899–1902) he filled important positions in the Boer army and took part in the peace negotiations. He helped organize the Union of South Africa, took part in World War I, and helped draft the covenant of the League of Nations. He was prime minister of the Union of South Africa, 1919–1924 and 1939–1948. Smuts served in World War II and as a delegate to the United Nations General Assembly. He was leader of the opposition in the South African parliament (1948–1950).

Snorri Sturluson (1178–1241), Icelandic poet and historian, born in Hvamm. He made a collection of Norse sagas called the *Heimskringla* (Ring of the World). Snorri became chief judge of Iceland, but his ambitious and intriguing character led to his assassination. He is honored as the composer of the *Younger, or Prose, Edda.*

Snowden, Philip, 1st Viscount Snowden of Ickornshaw (1864–1937), English politician, born in Yorkshire. He joined the Independent Labour party in 1893 and was its chairman (1903–1906; 1917–1920). From 1906 to 1932 he was a Labour member of Parliament. He was chancellor of the exchequer under Ramsay MacDonald in 1924 and in 1929. He wrote *Socialism and the Drink Question, Socialism and Syndicalism, The Living Wage, Labour and Finance,* and *Labour and the New World.*

Socrates (c.470–399 B.C.), Greek philosopher, born in Athens. His father, Sophroniscus, was a sculptor, and he followed the same profession in the early part of his life.

He had the education of an Athenian citizen, which included readings in the Greek poets and the elements of arithmetic and geometry, and astronomy, as then known. Little is known of his life except in connection with his philosophical studies. He served as a foot soldier, but about the middle period of his life he gave himself up to philosophy. He developed an original method of teaching (still known as the Socratic method), consisting of a series of questionings, the object of which is to draw out implicitly understood ideas. He gathered around him a number of pupils, the most famous being Xenophon, Alcibiades, and Plato. He taught that self-knowledge is more important than speculation about the universe, that truth and virtue are inseparable, and that vice arises from ignorance. His doctrines have profoundly influenced philosophical thought through succeeding centuries. His contempt for conventional ways and ideas brought him many enemies. He was accused of corrupting the youth of Athens and was condemned to death by drinking hemlock. His defense is preserved by Plato, under the title of the *Apology of Socrates.* Socrates was not a writer, and what we know of his teaching was recorded by Xenophon in his *Memorabilia* and Plato in his *Dialogues,* in most of which Socrates is the chief speaker. He was grotesquely ugly and was henpecked by his shrewish wife, Xanthippe.

Solon (c.638–c.559 B.C.), Athenian lawgiver, born in Salamis of a family of ancient royal lineage. He first gained fame by winning Salamis from the Megarians and more than once exercised unusual administrative powers. Solon was made chief magistrate and was entrusted with the writing of a new constitution and the compilation of a legal code. He divided the population into four classes according to their means, each class having definite duties. If fragmentary history can be relied upon, he then left Athens for ten years to see how the constitution would work. At the end of that time he returned to find the government in the hands of the tyrant Pisistratus. Solon left again and lived in Cyprus until his death.

Solyman. See *Suleiman.*

Sophocles (c.496–406 B.C.), Greek tragic playwright, born in Colonos, near Athens. His first appearance as a dramatist was in 468 B.C. when he defeated Aeschylus for the prize for tragedy. Of the next 28 years of his life nothing is recorded; but it is known that he made poetry his vocation, and that he composed a great many plays, winning altogether 18 or 20 prizes.

Antigone, the earliest of his extant tragedies, appeared in 440 B.C. The number of plays attributed to him was 113. Seven are extant: *Antigone, Electra, Trachinian Women, King Oedipus, Ajax, Philoctetes,* and *Oedipus at Colonus.* He carried Greek drama to its highest level and greatly changed the accepted forms in which drama was presented.

Sordello (c.1200–1270), Italian troubador who lived chiefly in Provence. His works are known mainly through Dante's account in *Purgatorio VI* and *VII.* Several of his poems survive.

Sousa, John Philip (1854–1932), American bandmaster and composer, born in Washington, D.C., known as "the March King." When he was 26 he was bandmaster of the U.S. Marine Corps. He left this post in 1892 to organize his own band, which he led on tours through the U.S. and most of Europe. His most popular marches are *Stars and Stripes Forever, Washington Post March, El Capitan,* and *Semper Fidelis.*

Southey, Robert (1774–1843), English writer, born in Bristol and educated at Oxford. He was intimately associated with Coleridge and Wordsworth. In 1795 Southey traveled in Spain and Portugal and returned to England to settle permanently in the Lake District. He became poet laureate in 1813. Today he is better appreciated for his prose, notably his *Life of Nelson* (1813), *History of Brazil* (1810–1819), and *History of the Peninsular War* (1823–1832). He also wrote *Goldilocks and the Three Bears,* a classic children's story.

Spaak, Paul Henri (1899–   ), Belgian statesman, born in Brussels. A practicing lawyer after 1922, he has been minister of foreign affairs almost continuously from 1936. In 1946 he was elected the first president of the General Assembly of the United Nations. He also served as secretary-general of the North Atlantic Treaty Organization (NATO) from 1957 to 1961.

Sparks, Jared (1789–1866), American historian, born in Willington, Conn., and educated at Harvard. In 1832 he bought and became editor of the *North American Review.* He was professor of history (1839–1849) at Harvard, and president from 1849 to 1853. He published *The Diplomatic Correspondence of the American Revolution* (12 vols., 1829–1830), *The Life of Gouverneur Morris* (3 vols., 1832), *The Writings of George Washington* (12 vols., 1834–1837), and *The Works of Benjamin Franklin* (10 vols., 1836–1840).

Spartacus (d. 71 B.C.), leader of an uprising of Roman slaves. Born in Thrace, he became a shepherd. Later he was taken by the Romans and trained as a gladiator, but he escaped from Capua and joined a band of slaves. He soon became their leader; under his direction they started on a career of plunder, in which much of Italy was devastated. Several Roman armies were sent against them, but the Spartacists maintained themselves for two years (73–71 B.C.). Spartacus was finally killed in the battle in Calabria, near Strongoli, and 6,000 of his followers captured by the Roman generals Crassus and Pompey were crucified.

Speaker, Tristram E. known as Tris (1888–1958), American baseball player, born at Hubbard City, Tex. He was a brilliant, hard-hitting outfielder in the American League, with a lifetime batting average of .345 for his 2,789 games. He was manager of the Cleveland Indians (1919–1927), and was named an original member of the Baseball Hall of Fame.

Spellman, Francis Joseph, Cardinal (1889–1967), American Roman Catholic clergyman. Born in Whitman, Mass.; educated at Fordham and Urban universities. Ordained in 1916, he was consecrated bishop in 1932. After seven years in Rome as an attaché to the Vatican secretariat of state, he was named archbishop of New York in 1939. In 1946 he was created cardinal. Active in Church press and radio, Cardinal Spellman also wrote many books, including *No Greater Love* (1945), *The Foundling* (1951), and *What America Means to Me* (1953). He died Dec. 2, 1967 in New York City.

Spemann, Hans (1869–1941), German zoologist, born in Stuttgart and educated at Heidelberg. He was professor of zoology at the University of Freiburg (1919–1935). In embryonic research, he discovered the directive function (organizer effect) of certain tissues. In 1935 he received the Nobel Prize for physiology and medicine.

Spencer, Herbert (1820–1903), English philosopher, born in Derby, educated at home by his father. In 1848 he became subeditor of *The Economist.* His first important book, *Social Statics,* appeared in 1851. Spencer's philosophy applied a form of evolutionary process to all phases of life. Every structure in nature, he said, divides itself by entering into relationships with other structures, but all the divisions come together again in new and better form. Therefore man's ideas, as well as man's body, have been continuously adapting themselves to surroundings, and only the best survive in the long run. His first work showing this broader application of evolutionary theories was *Principles of Psychology* (1855). With T. H. Huxley he helped to bring about popular acceptance of Darwin's theory of evolution. His *System of Synthetic Philosophy* (announced in 1860) appeared in sections: *First Principles* (1862), *Principles of Biology* (2 vols., 1864, 1867), *Principles of Sociology* (3 vols., 1876, 1882, 1896), *Data of Ethics* (1879), *Principles of Ethics* (2 vols., 1892, 1893).

Spender, Stephen (1909–   ), English poet and critic, born in London, and educated at University College, Oxford. He was one of the Thirties' modern poets, left-wing in outlook and giving poetry a new style and vitality. He is author of *Poems* (1933), *Burning Cactus* (1936), *Poems for Spain* (1939), *Ruins and Visions* (1941). His *Collected Poems, 1928–1953,* appeared in 1955.

Spengler, Oswald (1880–1936), German philosopher and historian, born in Blankenburg. Spengler held that every civilization or culture passes through a cycle from youth through maturity and finally to death. His belief that western civilization is approaching its end is set forth in *The Decline of the West* (2 vols., 1918–1922). Among his other works are *Man and Technics* (1931) and *The Hour of Decision* (1933), which lauds the old German militaristic ideas.

Spenser, Edmund (c.1552–1599), English poet, born in London of humble parents. He spent seven years at Cambridge on a grant. The earl of Leicester and Sir Philip Sidney became his patrons. In 1579 Spenser published *The Shepheardes Calender* (dedicated to Sidney), which was widely hailed as an important contribution to literature.

He is best remembered for his *Faërie Queene* (three books appeared in 1590). He intended it to be a narrative poem in 12 books, in which 12 knights were to embody as many great moral qualities; however, only 6 books were completed. In these books, he introduced a new form of verse, known as the Spenserian stanza (ababbcbcc). Among his other works are *Astrophel* (1586) and *View of the Present State of Ireland* (1596). He was buried in Westminster Abbey.

Spinoza, Baruch, or **Benedict** (1632–1677), Dutch philosopher, born in Amsterdam of Portuguese-Jewish parentage. His first serious studies were of the Bible and the Talmud, but he could not accept their teachings fully. He was excommunicated from the Jewish synagogue (1656) and, driven from Amsterdam, lived for a time near Leiden and afterward at The Hague. He devoted himself wholly to philosophy, earning a living by grinding lenses.

His aim was to build, with the knowledge of God as a foundation, a system of morals by a rigorously mathematical method. Everything in the universe, he said, works by the interaction of one part on another: human lives and actions are entirely directed by the influences of other humans and things, therefore there is no free will and no such thing as choice or chance. Today he is regarded as the outstanding exponent of pantheism. His works include *Tractatus Theologico-Politicus* (1670) and his masterpiece *Ethica*, completed in 1674, but published posthumously.

Spreckels, Claus (1828–1908), U.S. sugar manufacturer, known as the "Sugar King." He was born in Lamstedt, Germany, and came to the U.S. in 1846. He set up as a sugar refiner in 1856 in San Francisco, where he gradually acquired a virtual monopoly on the manufacture and sale of sugar on the West Coast.

Staël, Madame **de,** in full **Anne Louise Germaine Necker,** Baronne **de Staël-Holstein** (1766–1817), French writer, born in Paris, the daughter of Jacques Necker, who was Louis XVI's finance minister. She married Baron de Staël-Holstein in 1788. Her first published work was *Lettres sur le caractère et les écrits de J. J. Rousseau* (1788). She was compelled to leave France during the Revolution and wrote a defense of Marie Antoinette, She gathered the materials for the novel *Corinne* (1807) in Italy. Her *De l'Allemagne*, a description of the habits, literature and political tendencies of the German people, was printed in Paris in 1810, but by the order of Napoleon Bonaparte was immediately suppressed. Soon afterward she visited England, where she wrote *Dix années d'exil* (1821), a denunciation of Bonaparte and his arbitrary rule. Other writings include *Delphine* (1803) and *De l'influence des passions sur le bonheur des individus et das nations* (1796).

Stalin, Joseph, real name **Iosif Vissarionovich Dzhugashvili** (1879–1953), Russian political leader, born in Gori, Georgia, the son of a poor cobbler. He was expelled from the Theological Seminary at Tiflis for his radical political views. He joined the Social Democrats (1896) in Russia and started a revolutionary agitation in Georgia. For ten years he wandered over Russia spreading propaganda and organizing strikes. This led to frequent imprisonments in Siberia, from which he managed to escape. He directed the Bolshevik campaign of 1913 in the Duma, though he was not himself a member. During the Revolution (1917) he became general secretary of the Central Committee of the Russian Communist party and on Lenin's death (1924) succeeded him as dictator. When opposed by Trotzky, he maneuvered Trotzky into exile to Siberia (1929). Stalin speeded up the modernization of Russia with his 5-year plans (1st, 1928; 2d, 1934; 3d, 1937). To consolidate his power, Stalin "purged" the Communist party (1936–1937) and the Russian army (1937) of opposition. In 1939 he annexed eastern Poland after the German invasion, and in 1940, Latvia, Estonia, Lithuania, and Bessarabia. In June, 1941, after Germany's invasion, Stalin became commissar of defense and chairman of the Council of People's Commissars, giving himself complete military control of the country. As the war concluded, Stalin pressed his army westward into half of Germany, and then, consolidating his gains, dropped an Iron Curtain dividing the new "satellites" from western Europe. Having relinquished control of the army in 1947 and retaining only his premiership, Stalin stayed in the background until 1953, when he is reported to have died of a cerebral hemorrhage.

Stallings, Laurence (1894–1968), American author, born in Macon, Ga. With Maxwell Anderson he wrote the play *What Price Glory?* (1924). He also wrote a novel, *Plumes* (1924), and movie scripts. Died Feb. 28, 1968 in Pacific Palisades, Cal.

Standish, Myles (c.1584–1656), English colonist in America, born in Lancashire. He joined the army and distinguished himself in a war in Holland. He joined the Pilgrims and came to America in the *Mayflower* in 1620. He was one of the founders of the colony of Massachusetts. Chosen military leader of the settlers, he led them in several fights with the Indians. He was sent to England on a mission for the colony and on his return, with John Alden, founded Duxbury, Mass. (1631), where he was made a magistrate and held the post for the rest of his life.

Stanford, Leland (1824–1893), American businessman and politician, born in Watervliet, N.Y. In 1852 he went to California and became a merchant in San Francisco. He served as governor of California (1861–1863) and was one of the builders and presidents of the Central Pacific Railroad. From 1885 to 1893 he was in the U.S. Senate. He gave a large sum for the founding of Stanford University, as a memorial to his son.

Stanhope, Lady **Hester Lucy** (1776–1839), English traveler, born in London. She was private secretary to her uncle, William Pitt. After his death she left society and in 1810 she went to live on Mt. Lebanon. She be-

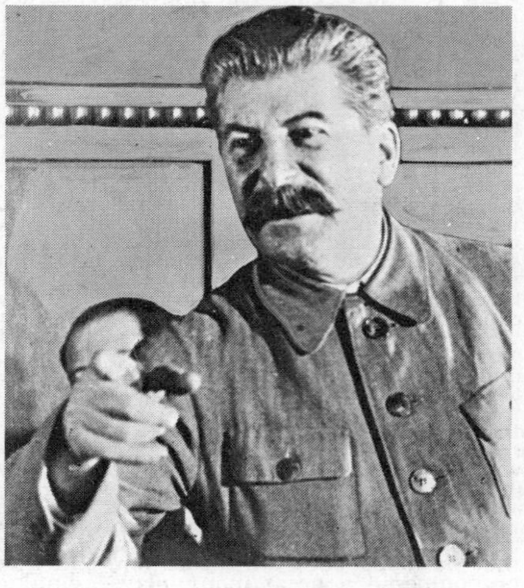

JOSEPH STALIN as Soviet chief of state.

came a powerful figure among the Arabs, who regarded her as a prophetess.

Stanley, Sir **Henry Morton,** original name **John Rowlands** (1841–1904), British explorer, born near Denbigh, Wales. He came to the United States in 1859 to work for a New Orleans merchant named Stanley, whose name he took. He fought in the Confederate army and after the war became a newspaper correspondent. In 1869, the New York *Herald* sent him to find the English explorer, David Livingstone, lost in Central Africa. He reached Zanzibar early in 1871, organized a large expedition, and found Livingstone on November 10, 1871, greeting him with the famous, "Dr. Livingstone, I presume?" In 1874 he set out on a second African expedition for the New York *Herald* and the London *Daily Telegraph*. He reached Victoria Nyanza in February, 1875, and was the first to circumnavigate the lake. He also discovered the Mountains of the Moon and Lake Edward. In 1879–1884 he helped develop the Congo Free State. Near the close of 1886 Stanley, under the auspices of the Egyptian government and of English societies and individuals, undertook an expedition for the rescue of Emin Pasha. He wrote *How I Found Livingstone* (1872), *Through the Dark Continent* (1878), *The Congo and the Founding of Its Free State* (2 vols., 1885), and *In Darkest Africa* (2 vols., 1890). He was a member of Parliament (1895–1900) and was knighted in 1899.

Stanton, Edwin McMasters (1814–1869), American politician, born in Steubenville, Ohio. He served as attorney general under Pres. James Buchanan (1860–1861) and was Pres. Lincoln's secretary of war. During the Civil War he ably discharged his duties, although his strong individualism often brought him into conflict with others. After Lincoln's assassination he continued in office and clashed with Pres. Andrew Johnson. When Stanton refused to resign he was suspended (1868); this led to Johnson's impeachment. Congress reinstated Stanton, but, when Johnson was acquitted, Stanton resigned (May, 1868).

Stanton, Elizabeth Cady (1815–1902), American suffragist and reformer, born in Johnstown, N.Y. She organized the first woman's rights convention, held at Seneca Falls, N.Y., and was the first president of the National Woman Suffrage Association (1869–1890). With Susan B. Anthony, she wrote *History of Woman Suffrage* (1881–1886).

Stark, John (1728–1822), American soldier, born in Londonderry, N.H. In the Revolutionary War, he distinguished himself at Bunker Hill, and in 1777 he won the battle of Bennington, which brought him the rank of major general. He cut off British Gen. John Burgoyne's retreat at Saratoga, and, in 1781, commanded the northern department.

Steele, Sir **Richard** (1672–1729), British playwright and essayist, born in Dublin and educated at Oxford. His early writings include *The Funeral, or Grief a la Mode* (1701), *The Lying Lover* (1703), and *The Tender Husband* (1705). In 1709, with Joseph Addison, he founded the famous journal *Tatler*, for which he wrote essays on manners and morality under the name of Isaac Bickerstaff. It was followed by the *Guardian* (1713) and the *Plebian* (1718), Addison cooperating in all. Steele was elected to Parliament in 1714 but soon was expelled for libelous utterances in a pamphlet called *The Crisis*. His last play was *The Conscious Lovers* (1722).

Steen, Jan (1626–1679), Dutch painter, born and educated in Leiden. He brought sympathy and a sense of humor into his canvases, showing family scenes of everyday life (*genre* painting). His best-known works are *The Rustic Wedding, Saint Nicholas Day, The Marriage Contract, The Painter's Family, The Oyster Party, Twelfth Night, A Merry Company*, and *Bad Company*.

Stefansson, Vilhjalmur (1879–1962), American Arctic explorer, born in Arnes, Canada, of Icelandic parentage. He graduated from the University of Iowa, then studied anthropology and theology at Harvard. He began his explorations in 1904 with an archeological trip to Iceland, and made another for Harvard in 1905. On one Arctic expedition (1908–1912) he discovered a tribe of blonde Eskimos that had never seen a white man. He commanded a Canadian expedition to the Arctic (1913–1918), and in 1924 he penetrated the northern territory of Australia. Stefansson Strait, named in his honor, separates the Antarctic Archipelago from Hearst Land in Antarctica. His books include *The Friendly Arctic* (1921), *Unsolved Mysteries of the Arctic* (1931), and *Northwest to Fortune* (1957).

Steffens, Lincoln, in full **Joseph Lincoln Steffens** (1866–1936), American editor and author, born in San Francisco, Calif. He was educated at the University of California and in Germany and France. He returned to enter newspaper work in New York and was later an editor on several magazines. He traveled about the country investigating municipal corruption and reporting his findings in magazines and books. Among his books are *The Shame of the Cities* (1904), *The Least of These* (1910), and an autobiography (1931).

Stein, Gertrude (1872–1946), American author, born in Allegheny, Pa., and educated at Radcliffe. After 1903 she spent most of her time in Paris, where she associated with authors, composers, and painters. She owned one of the finest collections of contemporary art. Her writing, which at one time had a reputation for repetition and obscurity, includes *The Making of Americans* (1925), *Matisse, Picasso and Gertrude Stein* (1932), *The Autobiography of Alice B. Toklas* (1933), the play *Four Saints in Three Acts* (1934), *Everybody's Autobiography* (1937), and *Ida* (1941).

Steinbeck, John Ernst (1902–), American journalist, novelist, and short-story writer, born in Salinas, Calif., and educated at Stanford. Steinbeck was a correspondent for the New York *Herald Tribune* during World War II and afterward in Russia (1948). His many works include *Cup of Gold* (1929), *Pastures of Heaven* (1932), *To a God Unknown* (1933), *Tortilla Flat* (1935), *In Dubious Battle* (1936), *Of Mice and Men* (1937), *The Grapes of Wrath* (1939; awarded the Pulitzer Prize), *The Moon is Down* (1942), *Cannery Row* (1944), *The Wayward Bus* (1947), *East of Eden* (1952), and *Travels with Charley* (1961). He won the Nobel Prize for literature in 1962.

Steiner, Rudolf (1861–1925), Austrian social philosopher and founder of the spiritualistic doctrine known as anthroposophy. In 1912 he established Der Anthroposophische Bund and the first of several teaching institutions, the Goetheanum at Dornach, Switzerland.

Steinmetz, Charles Proteus (1865–1923), American electrical engineer, born in Breslau, Germany. He studied at Breslau, Zurich, and Berlin, became involved in political troubles, and came to the U.S. in 1889. From 1893 he was a consulting engineer with the General Electric Company. His many contributions to the field of electricity include a metallic electrode arc lamp and an induction regulator. He patented over 100 inventions. In the hope of developing a lightning arrester, he produced a bolt of artificial lightning of one million horsepower. He was professor of electrical engineering and electrophysics at Union College, Schenectady, from 1902 to 1923.

Stendhal, pen name of **Marie Henri Beyle** (1783–1842), French novelist and biographer, born in Grenoble. He admired Napoleon greatly and served under him in several campaigns. Later he was involved with Italian revolutionary movements and was banished from Italy. He is best known today for two novels *Le Rouge et le noir* (*The Red and the Black,* 1831) and *La Chartreuse de Parme* (*The Charter House of Parma,* 1939). He also wrote the biographies *Haydn* (1814), *Rossini* (1824), and *Napoléon* (pub. 1876).

Stephen, Sir **Leslie** (1832–1904), English philosopher, critic, and biographer. He was born in London and educated at Cambridge. He abandoned orthodox religious views and defined his agnostic position in *Essays on Free Thinking and Plain Speaking* (1873). He twice visited the U.S. where he established close relations with J. R. Lowell, Emerson, and Holmes and contributed to several literary journals. His chief work is *History of English Thought in the Eighteenth Century* (1876). Among his readable, authoritative biographies are *Samuel Johnson* (1878), *Alexander Pope* (1880), *Jonathan Swift* (1882), and *George Eliot* (1902). Stephen was editor (1882–1891) of the *Dictionary of National Biography.*

Stephens, Alexander Hamilton (1812–1883), American politician, born near Crawfordsville, Ga. He was a member of the House of Representatives (1843–1859) where he yielded to the majority who favored Georgia's secession. He was vice-president of the Confederate states (1861–1865) but he opposed Pres. Jefferson Davis' policies. He was again in the House of Representatives (1873–1882) and governor of Georgia from 1882 until his death.

Stephens, James (1882–1950), Irish poet and novelist, born in Dublin. He is best known for the novels *The Crock of Gold* (1912) and *Deirdre* (1923), and the collected poems *Strict Joy* (1931).

Stephenson, George (1781–1848), English inventor and founder of railways, born in Wylam, near Newcastle. In 1915 he devised a miner's safety lamp, independently of Sir Humphry Davy. In 1814 he built the first successful locomotive and in the next year equipped it with a steam blast, making it quite successful. He continued to improve the engines and went on to found several railroads, including one at the Hetton Colliery (opened 1822) and the works at Newcastle (1823). Under his supervision the Liverpool and Manchester Railway opened in 1830 with his locomotive, *Rocket.*

Stern, Isaac (1920–   ), American violinist, born in Kreminiecz, Russia. He came to the U.S. in 1921 and studied at the San Francisco Conservatory from 1930 to 1937. Stern made his debut with the San Francisco Symphony Orchestra as a guest artist in 1931 and then appeared in concerts in many Pacific Coast cities. He first came to New York in 1937 and has since given concerts throughout the U.S. and the world. He has introduced many new violin pieces including Bartók's *Rhapsodie No. 2.*

Sterne, Laurence (1713–1768), British novelist, born in Clonmel, Ireland. He was ordained in 1738 after studying at Jesus College, Cambridge, and was made prebendary of York (1741). He created a sensation with the first two volumes of *The Life and Opinions of Tristram Shandy* (1760), partly for their eccentric humor and also for their lack of decorum; the ninth volume appeared in 1767. Other writings include *Sermons of Mr. Yorick* (1760) and *A Sentimental Journey through France and Italy* (1768).

Steuben, Baron **Friedrich Wilhelm Ludolf Gerhard Augustin von** (1730–1794), Prussian-American general, born in Magdeburg, Prussia, a descendant of a noble family. He served with distinction in the Seven Years' War and at its close became grand marshal in a princely German house. He came to America in 1777 and the next year joined the Continental army and directed the training of the troops. He was commissioned a major general and was honorably discharged in 1784.

Stevens, John (1749–1838), American inventor, born in New York City. In 1790 he helped establish the first patent laws in the U.S., and in 1791 he secured a patent for a vertical steam boiler. He built the *Phoenix* in 1808, the first seagoing steamboat in the world. In 1823 he organized the Pennsylvania Rail Road.

Stevens, Wallace (1879–1955), American poet, born in Reading, Pa., and educated at Harvard. He practiced journalism and law, then joined a Hartford insurance company, serving as its vice president for many years. His first verse, *Harmonium,* was published in 1923. This was followed by *Ideas of Order* (1935), *Owl's Clover* (1936), *The Man With the Blue Guitar* (1937), *Parts of a World* (1942), *Transport to Summer* (1947), and *The Auroras of Autumn* (1950). For his *Collected Poems* (1954) he received the National Book Award and in 1955 the Pulitzer Prize for poetry.

Stevenson, Adlai Ewing (1835–1914), twenty-third vice-president of the United States (1893–1897), born in Christian County, Ky., and educated at Center College, Danville. He was admitted to the bar in Illinois in 1859, was elected to Congress in 1875 and again in 1879.

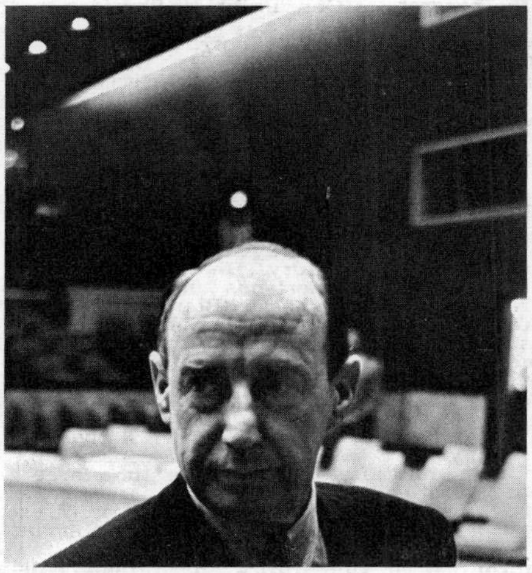

LOOK MAGAZINE

ADLAI STEVENSON at the United Nations.

Stevenson, Adlai Ewing (1900–1965), American statesman, born in Los Angeles, Calif., and educated at Princeton and Northwestern Law School. He was U.S. Representative to the United Nations (1961–1965). He practiced law in Chicago (1927–1933) and elsewhere until 1941. During World War II, he served on several economic and war department missions to Europe (1941–1944), and he was in the U.S. delegation to the General Assembly of the United Nations (1946). He was governor of Illinois (1949–1953). He was Democratic candidate for president in 1952 and in 1956, but was defeated both times by Dwight D. Eisenhower. In 1961 Pres. John F. Kennedy appointed him U.S. ambassador to the UN; he served in this post until his death.

Stevenson, Robert Louis Balfour (1850–1894), Scottish essayist, novelist, and poet, born and educated in Edinburgh. In 1875 he was admitted to the bar but soon abandoned law for writing. His first book, *An Inland Voyage,* appeared in 1878, followed by *Travels with a Donkey in the Cévennes* (1879). Later that year he traveled by steerage and immigrant train to San Francisco to join a divorcée, Mrs. Fanny Osbourne, and they were married in 1880. They returned to Scotland where *New Arabian Nights* (1882), *Treasure Island* (1883), *A Child's Garden of Verses* (1885), and *Dr. Jekyll and Mr. Hyde* (1886) appeared. As a writer of adventure and romance he established himself permanently with *Kidnapped* in 1886, followed by *The Merry Men* (1887) and *The Black Arrow* (1888). He and his family left for America in 1887 and in 1888 sailed to the South Seas where he settled in Samoa a Vailima. His last writings include *Island Nights' Entertainments* (1893) and *Weir of Hermiston* (unfinished).

Stewart, Charles Edward. See *Stuart, Charles Edward Louis Philip Casimir.*

Stimson, Henry Lewis (1867–1950), American statesman, born in New York City, educated at Yale and Harvard. He was secretary of war in Pres. William H. Taft's cabinet (1911–1913). He was governor general of the Philippine Islands (1927–1929) and was secretary of state under Pres. Herbert Hoover (1929–1933). In Pres. Franklin D. Roosevelt's cabinet, he served as secretary of war from 1940 to 1945.

Stoddard, Richard Henry (1825–1903), American writer, born in Hingham, Mass. He is best known for two anthologies, *Poets and Poetry of America* and *Female Poets of America.* Among his volumes of poetry are *Songs of Summer* (1857), *Under the Evening Lamp* (1893), and *The Lion's Cub; with Other Verse* (1890).

Stokowski, Leopold Antoni Stanislaw (1887–   ), American conductor, born in London of Polish parentage. He studied in Paris and London and conducted opera and orchestras abroad before he came to the United States in 1905. He conducted the Cincinnati Symphony, 1909–1912, the Philadelphia Orchestra, 1912–1936, the N.Y. City Symphony, 1944–1945, and the N.Y. Philharmonic, 1947–1950. In 1962 Stokowski founded the American Symphony Orchestra. He is the author of *Music for All of Us* (1943).

Stone, Harlan Fiske (1872–1946), American jurist, born in Chesterfield, N.H., and educated at Amherst and Columbia Law School. He was professor of law and dean of Columbia Law School (1910–1923). He was attorney general (1924), associate justice of the U.S. Supreme Court (1925), and in 1941 he was made chief justice.

Stone, Irving (1903–   ), American writer, born in San Francisco, Calif. His popular novels include *Lust for Life* (biography of Vincent van Gogh; 1934), *Sailor on Horseback* (biography of Jack London; 1938), *They Also Ran* (1943), and *The Agony and the Ecstasy* (biography of Michelangelo; 1961).

Stone, Lucy (1818–1893), American woman suffragist, born near West Brookfield, Mass. She helped organize the first national woman's rights convention at Worcester, Mass. (1850). In protest against taxation without representation, she attracted attention to the suffrage movement by selling her belongings for taxes (1858). After her marriage (1855) to Henry Brown Blackwell, she retained her maiden name. The Lucy Stone League was formed of married suffragettes who used their maiden names.

Story, Joseph (1779–1845), American jurist, born in Marblehead, Mass., and educated at Harvard. After serving as a member of Congress (1808–1809), he was an associate justice of the Supreme Court (1811–1845). He was professor of law at Harvard from 1829–1845. His standard books on law and government include *Commentaries on the Constitution of the United States* (3 vols., 1833) and *The Conflict of Laws* (1834).

Stowe, Harriet Elizabeth Beecher (1811–1896), American author, born in Litchfield, Conn., the sister of Henry Ward Beecher. From 1833 she was an ardent abolitionist, and encouraged by her family, she wrote *Uncle Tom's Cabin, or Life Among the Lowly,* published first as a serial (1851–1852) in an antislavery paper in Washington, D.C. and then as a book in 1852. The book was very influential in solidifying the northern sentiment against slavery. Mrs. Stowe also wrote *Dred, A Tale of the Great Dismal Swamp* (1856), *The Minister's Wooing* (1859), and *Oldtown Folks* (1869).

Strabo (c.63 B.C.–c.24 A.D.). Greek geographer, born at Amasia in Pontus. He spent many years in travel and wrote a geography in 17 parts, in which he describes Europe, Asia, Libya, and Egypt. It is considered to be one of the most important geographies of ancient times. He wrote a history of Rome down to the year 27 B.C. (now lost).

Strachey, Giles Lytton (1880–1932), English writer, born in London and educated at Cambridge. Among his books are *Landmarks in French Literature* (1912), *Eminent Victorians* (1918), *Queen Victoria* (1921), and *Elizabeth and Essex* (1928).

Stradivari, Antonio, Latin name **Antonius Stradivarius** (1644–1737), Italian violinmaker, born in Cremona. He was apprenticed to Nicolò Amati, one of a great family of violinmakers, and improved on his master's work. It is believed that Stradivarius made 2,000 violins during his lifetime; today more than 500 are known to exist, as well as about a dozen violas and more than 50 cellos.

Strafford, Thomas Wentworth, 1st Earl (1593–1641), English statesman, born in London and educated at Cambridge. He was a member of four Parliaments—three under James I and one under Charles I. His political career was erratic. In 1629 he first opposed Charles and then sided with him and strove to put down all opposition to the royal authority. He went to Ireland in 1632 as lord lieutenant and changed the country from anarchy to order and prosperity. Accused of high treason during the Scottish Rebellion, he was beheaded on Tower Hill.

Strauss, David Friedrich (1808–1874), German theologian and critic, born in Württemberg. He was educated at Tübingen, where he was influenced by Ferdinand Christian Baur, the most radical theological thinker and biblical critic of the time. He later studied at Berlin under Hegel and Schleiermacher. In 1835 he startled conservative Europe by his *Das Leben Jesu* (*Life of Jesus*), which treated the gospel narratives as myths, to be judged by the standards of ancient secular writings.

Strauss, Johann (1804–1849), Austrian composer and conductor, born in Vienna. He gained great popularity in his day with his dance music that included over 150 waltzes and polkas, galops, quadrilles, and marches. He toured Europe with his band of 200 performers.

Strauss, Johann (1825–1899), Austrian composer, born in Vienna, and known as "the Waltz King." The son of Johann Strauss, he took over his father's orchestra and also toured successfully. After 1863 he devoted himself to composition. He wrote over 400 waltzes, including *The Blue Danube* and the *Artist's Life* (both 1867), *Voices of Spring* (1882), and *The Emperor* (1888). Among his operettas were *Die Fledermaus* (1874), and *Eine Nacht in Venedig* (1883).

Strauss, Richard (1864–1949), German composer and conductor, born in Munich. He began his professional career as conductor at Meiningen in 1885, and in 1889 went to Weimar as Kapellmeister. In 1894, he was appointed conductor at the Munich Opera House, and in 1898 at Berlin (to 1919). As a composer, he is regarded as a leader of the New Romantic school. His works include the operas *Salome* (1905), *Elektra* (1909), *Der Rosenkavalier* (1911), *Ariadne auf Naxos* (1912), and *Arabella* (1933); his tone poems include *Tod und Verklärung* (1891), *Till Eulenspiegels lustige Streiche* (1895), *Also sprach Zarathustra* (1896). *Don Quichote* (1898), and *Ein Heldenleben* (1899); as well as choral, symphonic, and chamber music.

Stravinsky, Igor Fëdorovich (1882–), Russian-American composer, born in Oranienbaum, Russia. He studied under Rimski-Korsakov in 1902. He moved to the U.S., but earlier lived in Paris where he first became famous for his compositions for the Diaghilev Ballet. These include his first ballet *L'Oiseau de Feu* (*The Firebird;* 1910), and then *Petrouchka* (1911) *Les Noces*, and *Le Sacre du Printemps* (*The Rite of Spring;* 1913) whose multi-rhythms and key superimpositions induced a riot at its first performance. Other important works include *L'Histoire du Soldat* (1918), *Oedipus Rex* (an opera oratorio; 1927), the choral *Symphony of Psalms* (1930), *Symphony in C major* (1940), the opera *The Rake's Progress* (1951), *In Memoriam Dylan Thomas* (1954), and the ballet *Agon* (1957).

Stresemann, Gustav (1878–1929), German statesman, born in Berlin and educated at the universities of Berlin and Leipzig. He was a member of the Reichstag from 1907 and minister of foreign affairs from 1923. He pursued a postwar conciliatory policy; he negotiated the Locarno Pact, Germany's admission to the League of Nations, and her adoption of the Dawes (1923) and Young plans (1929). He shared the Nobel Peace Prize with Aristide Briand in 1926.

Strindberg, Johan August (1849–1912), Swedish author and dramatist, born in Stockholm. His first great drama, *Master Olof*, appeared in 1874. Three tragic marriages did not tend to give him a cheerful outlook, and he was known for his abhorrence of women's freedom. His works include many plays and stories, and treatises on history, the theater, philosophy, and other subjects. Among his plays are *The Father* (1887), *Lady Julia* (1888), *Crimes and Crimes* (1899), and *A Dream Play* (1902).

Stuart, Charles Edward Louis Philip Casimir, often called **Charles Edward** (1720–1788), English prince, known as "the Young Pretender" (to the throne) and "Bonnie Prince Charlie." Born in Rome, at the age of 14 he served with Berwick in the siege of Gaeta, an attempt to restore Don Carlos. Urged by the English and Scottish Jacobites to try to regain the English throne for the Stuarts, Charles landed in Scotland with an army in 1745. The Highland clans flocked to his support and he had early successes against the English army that came north to meet him. But he did not receive much support from the Jacobites of England and his army was defeated with much loss of life at Culloden Moor in April 1746. He went into hiding in Brittany but was expelled from France (1748) and traveled incognito under the name of the count of Albany. He alienated supporters by his dissolute life and vicious temper. He was never able to return to England, and he died in Rome.

Stuart, Gilbert Charles (1755–1828), American painter, born in Narragansett, R.I. In 1776 he went to London, where he studied under Benjamin West. He gained a reputation there and ranked with Gainsborough and Reynolds. Stuart returned to America in 1792 where he had studios in New York, Washington, D.C., and Boston. He is best known for his portraits of George Washington. He also painted John Adams, John Quincy Adams, Jefferson, Madison and, while in England, George II, George IV, and Sir Joshua Reynolds.

Stuart, James Ewell Brown, known as **Jeb** (1833–1864), Confederate general, born in Patrick County Va. He graduated from West Point in 1854. When the Civil War broke out he was a captain in the Union army but resigned (1861) to enter the Confederate service. He was one of the outstanding cavalrymen of the Civil War, a dashing and romantic figure as well as a clever and daring officer. He was mortally wounded at Ashland in an attempt to halt the progress of Gen. Philip H. Sheridan and died at Richmond, Va.

Sturluson, Snorri. See *Snorri Sturluson.*

Stuyvesant, Peter (1592–1672), Dutch colonial governor, born in West Friesland, the Netherlands. Military service for the West India Company took him to Curaçao (1643), where he was governor. He was sent to New Amsterdam (later New York City) to direct colonial affairs for the company and arrived in 1647. He expanded the territory but his dictatorial methods made him very unpopular. When English ships sailed into the harbor in 1664, Stuyvesant was forced to surrender his territory. He defended his actions in the Netherlands and returned to New York to live on his "Bouwerij" (Dutch for farm), from which the present-day street called the Bowery was named.

Sue, Eugène, real name **Marie Joseph Sue** (1804–1857), French novelist, born in Paris. After completing a course in medicine he became a surgeon in the army. In 1850 he was elected to the Legislative Assembly, but he inherited a considerable fortune and after that gave his time largely to literature. His reputation as a writer rests mainly on *Le Mystères de Paris* (*Mysteries of Paris*, 1842–1843) and *Le Juif errant* (*The Wandering Jew*, 1844–1845).

Suetonius, in full **Gaius Suetonius Tranquillus** (2d century A.D.), Roman biographer and historian. Little is known of his life except that he was Hadrian's private secretary (c.119–121 A.D.). His only remaining work is *Lives of the Caesars* from Julius to Domitian. He dealt mostly with the private lives of the Caesars, but the book is valuable historically. He wrote biographies of other important men of his time, but only fragments remain.

Suger (c.1081–1151), French churchman and statesman. He became abbé of Saint-Denis in 1122. From 1124 he was adviser to Louis VI and official minister (1130–1137). Under Louis VII, Suger was minister and during the king's journey with the second Crusade, he served as regent (1147–1149). He wrote a life of Louis VI and other historical works.

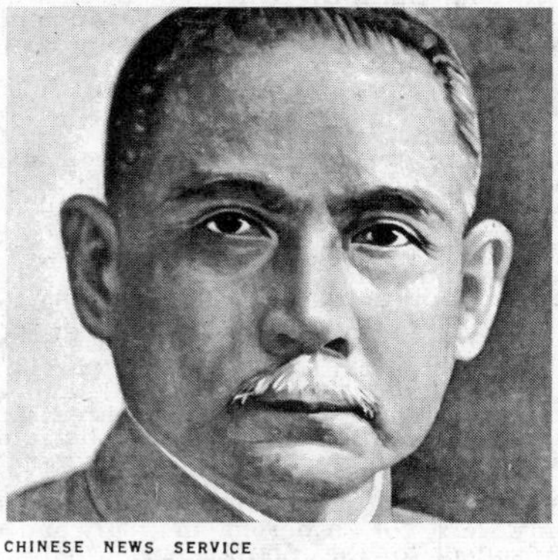

CHINESE NEWS SERVICE

SUN YAT-SEN

Suleiman I, known as **the Magnificent** (c. 1496–1566), Turkish sultan (from 1520), son of Sultan Selim I. He added to his dominions through his conquest of Belgrade, Budapest, Rhodes, Tabriz, Baghdad, Aden, and Algiers. He reformed and improved the administration of his country and was a great patron of the arts.

Sulla, Lucius Cornelius surnamed **Felix,** (138–78 B.C.), Roman commander and dictator. He became quaestor in 107 B.C. under Marius in Africa and brought about the surrender of Jugurtha. After distinguishing himself in the Teutonic Wars, he became propraetor in Cilicia, returning to Rome in 91 B.C. Coming into political conflict with Marius, he was driven from Rome but returned and drove Marius from the city. Sulla conducted the Mithridatic War from 87 to 83 B.C. In 82 B.C. he returned from the East at the head of a victorious army and made himself dictator. He put down opposition with ruthless energy, proscribing many political enemies. He remodeled the constitution in the interest of the senatorial oligarchy, but he abdicated in 79 B.C. at the height of his power.

Sullivan, Sir **Arthur Seymour** (1842–1900), English composer, born in London. The composer of many serious choral and orchestral works, he is best remembered, however, for his collaboration with Sir W. S. Gilbert in the composition of light operas that include *The Mikado, Pirates of Penzance, The Yeomen of the Guard, H. M. S. Pinafore*, and *The Gondoliers*. He also wrote the hymn *Onward Christian Soldiers* and many songs, including The *Lost Chord*.

Sullivan, John Lawrence (1858–1918), American heavyweight prizefighter, born in Boston, Mass. He defeated Paddy Ryan for the heavyweight championship in 1882 and lost it to James J. Corbett in 1892. While he held the title the Marquis of Queensberry rules came into use. Sullivan won the championship under bare-knuckle rules and lost it under modern rules.

Sullivan, Louis Henri (1856–1924), American architect, born in Boston, Mass. His buildings were original and experimental; his skyscrapers and office towers adapted good design to modern needs. He is known as "the father of modernism," and, among others, influenced Frank Lloyd Wright. His buildings include the Wainwright Building and the Union Trust Building (both in St. Louis); the Shiller Theater, the Auditorium Buildings, and the Gage Building in Chicago; and the Bayard Building in New York.

Sully, Thomas (1783–1872), American painter, born in Lincolnshire, England. He was best known for his portraits and is remembered today particularly for *Washington Crossing the Delaware*.

Sully Prudhomme, René Francois Armand (1839–1907), French poet, born in Paris. He was associated with a group called Les parnassiens. *La justice* (1878) and *Le bonheur* (1888) are his best-known philosophical poems. He won the first Nobel Prize for literature, in 1901.

Sulzberger, Arthur Hays (1891–1965), American journalist and publisher, son of Cyrus Lindauer Sulzberger, American merchant and philanthropist. He was president and director of the New York Times Company (1935–1957) and publisher of The New York *Times* (1935–1961).

Sumner, Charles (1811–1874), American statesman, born in Boston, Mass., and educated at Harvard. He studied law and was admitted to the bar in 1834. He entered the U.S. Senate in 1851, retaining his seat until his death. He was prominent in debate, especially on the repeal of the Missouri Compromise and on the contest in Kansas. His speech "The Crime Against Kansas" incensed pro-slavery Preston S. Brooks of South Carolina, who assaulted Sumner and crippled him. He wrote *White Slavery in the Barbary States* (1860) and collected and edited his *Works* (1870–1883).

Sun Yat-sen, also known as **Sun Wen** and **Chung Shan** (1866–1925), Chinese reformer, born near Macao. He was educated to be a physician in the Hong Kong School of Medicine and practiced for a year in Macao. He organized a revolutionary party in 1893 and after many desperate attempts against the government he returned in 1911 from years in exile to overthrow the Manchu dynasty that had ruled China for nearly 300 years. He was elected provisional president of the new Chinese Republic, but in 1912 he gave the leadership to the northern general Yüan Shih-k'ai. In 1912 Sun founded the Kuomintang, a political party that stood for the principles of nationalism, democracy, and people's livelihood. Sun disagreed with the new president, who had become despotic, and was again forced into exile. In 1923 he secured the support of the southern republic and he declared war against Gen. Ts'ao K'un. He gained in influence and attended a conciliatory conference of Chinese leaders in Peking, where he died of cancer. Sun was influenced by communist doctrines but he did not fully accept them. A great mausoleum was erected for him at Nanking in 1928.

Sutter, John Augustus (1803–1880), American frontiersman, born in South Baden, Germany. He arrived in America in 1834 and in 1839 reached California, where in the Sacramento Valley he established a colony he called New Helvetia. In 1848 the first gold was discovered on his property, but Sutter was unable to remove the squatters or uphold his land claims in the courts, and he went bankrupt in 1852.

Swan, Sir Joseph Wilson (1828–1914), English chemist and physicist, born in Sunderland. As a manufacturing chemist he patented the carbon process for photographic printing in 1864, invented the dry plate in 1871, and bromide paper in 1879. He anticipated Edison's invention with his electric lamp in 1860. He also was the first to produce practical artificial silk.

Swedenborg, Emanuel (1688–1772), Swedish scientist, philosopher, and mystic, born in Stockholm. He was a well-known engineer and studied in almost every field of science. In 1743 he claimed a divine commission to interpret the true inner doctrines of Scripture. He told of seeing visions and conversing with spirits. Of these he treats in many theological writings, including *Arcana Coelestis* (1756) and *Vera Christiana religio* (1771). He lived in Stockholm, London, and Amsterdam, spreading his beliefs but not trying to establish a new sect. His followers, called Swedenborgians, developed a religious organization, known as the New Jerusalem Church, or the New Church.

Swift, Jonathan (1667–1745), British author, born in Dublin of English parents, and educated at Trinity College, Dublin. He moved to London, where he became secretary to Sir William Temple. In Sir William's house he met "Stella" (Esther Johnson) and wrote *The Tale of a Tub* (pub. 1704), a brilliant satire on abuses in religion and learning. He studied for the Church, was ordained in 1694, and held benefices in Ireland. He divided his time between Dublin and London, where his gifts as a satirist made him a valuable ally to the Tory party. In 1713 he was made dean of St. Patrick's Cathedral, Dublin, and from there he wrote the famous *Drapier Letters* (1724) that compelled the government to abandon a scheme for supplying Ireland with copper coinage. The triumphant author made his last visit to England in 1726. In that year *Gulliver's Travels* was published, the most popular of all his works. It is now a children's classic, although it was originally intended to express Swift's savage misanthropy, his view of mankind as "the most pernicious race of little odious vermin that nature ever suffered to crawl upon the surface of the earth." His *Journal to Stella* is a collection of letters written to her. It is not definitely known whether she was his wife.

Swinburne, Algernon Charles (1837–1909), English poet and critic, born in London and educated at Oxford. His first productions were comedy dramas but they were only moderately successful. In 1865 he wrote the lyric tragedy *Atalanta in Calydon*, considered to be his finest work. His other volumes of poetry include *Songs before Sunrise* (1871), *A Song of Italy* (1867), and *Tristram of Lyonesse* (1882).

Sylla. See *Sulla*.

Symington, William (1763–1831), Scottish engineer and inventor. In 1786, with his brother, he built a working model of a steam road carriage, and in the next year he patented a steam engine with rotary motion. He experimented on boats, and in 1801 made the first workable steam engine; it was used to propel the tugboat *Charlotte Dundas*.

Synge, John Millington (1871–1909), Irish poet and dramatist, born in Dublin and educated at Trinity College. He lived in Paris (1895-1902) working at literary criticism, but he was persuaded by his compatriot W. B. Yeats to return to Ireland and lead in the movement to revive Irish folklore and the Irish drama. Synge had an unusually deep insight into the character of the peasantry and wrote a series of plays illustrative of their life and their feelings. *The Playboy of the Western World* (1907) is considered by many to be the greatest of these plays. His other plays include *The Shadow of the Glen* (1903), *Deirdre of the Sorrows* (produced 1910), and *Riders to the Sea* (1909). From 1904, he wrote for the Abbey Theatre, Dublin, with Lady Gregory and W. B. Yeats.

T

Tacitus, Cornelius (c.55–c.117 A.D.), Roman historian, politician, and orator. One of the greatest Roman lawyers of his day, he held several political positions, including quaestor, praetor, consul, and governor of the province of Asia. His wife was the daughter of Julius Agricola, conqueror and governor of Britain. Tacitus' works include *Dialogus de Oratoribus*, a critical study of oratory since the time of Cicero; a biography of Agricola, his father-in-law; *Germania*, a history of the people and customs of Germany; and the *Annals* and *Histories*, which together cover the history of the Roman Empire from 14 to 96 A.D.

Taft, Robert Alphonso (1889–1953), American political leader, son of Pres. William H. Taft. Born in Cincinnati, Ohio, he graduated from Yale (1910), took a law degree at Harvard (1913), and practiced law in Ohio. Rejected for military service in World War I because of poor eyesight, he worked for the American food and relief administrations in Europe (1917–1921). A member of the Ohio legislature (1921–1926, 1931–1933), he was elected U.S. senator in 1938 and reelected in 1944 and 1950. He was an unsuccessful candidate for the Republican presidential nomination in 1940, 1944, 1948, and 1952. Taft was joint author of the Taft-Hartley Labor Act in 1947 and leader of the Republican party in the U.S. Senate.

Taft, William Howard (1857–1930), twenty-seventh president of the United States (1909–1913), born in Cincinnati, Ohio. He graduated from Yale (1878), studied law in Cincinnati, and was a practicing member of the Ohio bar for several years. He was a judge in the Ohio Superior Court from 1887 to 1890, when he was appointed solicitor general by Pres. William H. Harrison. He was a federal circuit judge from 1892 to 1900. Taft was prominent in the establishment of civil government in the Philippines and was civil governor of the islands (1901–1904). In 1904 he became secretary of war in Pres. Theodore Roosevelt's cabinet. When the war department intervened in a Cuban crisis in 1906, Taft went to the island as provisional governor. While in the cabinet, he was sent as one of Roosevelt's most trusted advisors to Panama, Cuba, Puerto Rico, the Philippine Islands, Japan, and Russia.

In 1908 Taft, Roosevelt's choice as his successor, was elected president on the Republican ticket, defeating William Jennings Bryan. During his administration the sixteenth and seventeenth amendments, establishing a direct federal income tax and providing for the direct election of senators, were passed; the cabinet post of secretary of labor was established; and Roosevelt's antitrust policies continued, notably by dissolving the Standard Oil and American Tobacco Company trusts. Taft also continued Roosevelt's conservation policies.

Progressive Republican support for Taft diminished after Taft's defense of the Payne-Aldrich Act of 1909, which maintained tariff protection, and also because of his dismissal from the forestry service of Gifford Pinchot, who was a conservation supporter and friend of Roosevelt and a severe critic of several policies of Secretary of the Interior Richard Ballinger. After the nomination of Taft as the Republican candidate for president in 1912, Theodore Roosevelt and his followers left the party and formed the Progressive party, nominating Roosevelt for president. Woodrow Wilson, the Democratic candidate, defeated the two candidates of the divided Republicans.

From 1913 to 1921 Taft was professor of law at Yale. During World War I, he served as joint chairman of the War Labor Board, and following the war he lectured in support of the League of Nations. In 1921 he became chief justice of the Supreme Court. He retired shortly before his death.

Tagore, Sir Rabindranath (1861–1941), Indian poet and philosopher, born in Calcutta. He was educated in India and traveled widely. In 1901 he founded at Bolpur, near Calcutta, a school called Santini Ketan (renamed Visvabharati), for the study of Eastern civilizations. In 1913 he won the Nobel Prize for literature and in 1915 was knighted by King George V. Tagore's 30 volumes of poetry and his numerous novels, dramas, essays, and sermons reveal a deep understanding of ancient Indian culture and a desire to interpret it to the modern Western world. He himself translated many of his writings from Bengali into English.

Taillefere, Germaine (1892–), French composer, born near Paris. She was an original member of "Les Six," a group of avant-garde composers living in Paris in the 1920's.

Taine, Hippolyte Adolphe (1828–1893), French historian, literary critic, and philosopher, born in Vouziers. He was professor of aesthetics and art history at the École des Beaux-Arts in Paris (1864–1884). Taine interpreted literature and art in a materialistic, positivistic way, asserting that all creative efforts are to be understood according to the criteria of time, race (or people), and milieu (or environment). His chief writings include *Essai sur les Fables de La Fontaine* (1853), *Voyage aux Pyrénées* (1855), *Histoire de la littérature anglaise* (1863), *Philosophie de l'art* (1865), *De l'idéal dans l'art* (1867), and *Origines de la France contemporaine* (1871–1894).

Talbot, William Henry Fox (1800–1877), English pioneer in photography, born in Wiltshire. In 1839 he invented a process he called *photogenic drawing*, later known as calotype or Talbotype. He also was a scholar of Assyriology and was one of the first to decipher the cuneiform inscriptions of Nineveh. His book *Pencil of Nature* (1884) was the first to be illustrated with photographs.

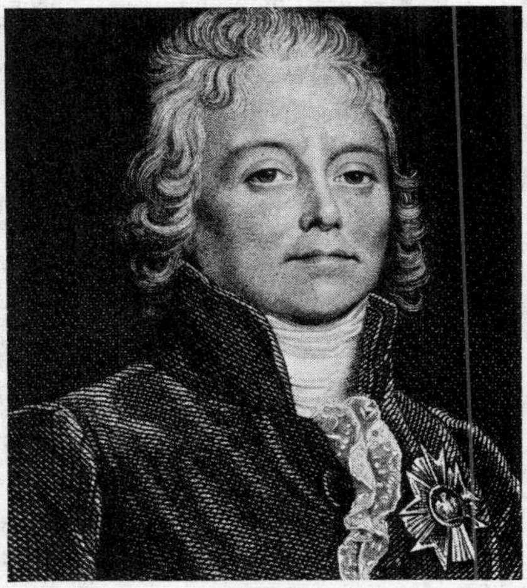

CHARLES DE TALLEYRAND

Talleyrand-Périgord, Charles Maurice de, Prince de Bénévent (1754–1838), French statesman, born in Paris. He was ordained a priest in 1775. As bishop of Autun he was a member of the States-General, which was convened in 1789. With the outbreak of the French Revolution, Talleyrand was elected to the constitutional committee of the National Assembly and was influential in the drafting of the Declaration of the Rights of Man. His proposal that Church lands be administered by the state was accepted by the Assembly. In 1790 he was elected president of the Constituent Assembly. As the revolutionary government adopted increasingly radical policies, Talleyrand, a constitutional monarchist, was forced into exile, first to England and later to America. After the fall of Robespierre he returned to Paris and was appointed foreign minister. He continued in this office under the consulate of Napoleon, but resigned in 1807 in opposition to Napoleon's war plans. After the defeat of Napoleon, he served as a minister under Louis XVIII. His skillful diplomacy at the Congress of Vienna (1815) helped save France from heavy territorial losses and excessive financial indemnities. At the Congress he supported royal legitimacy and the restoration of the balance of power. In 1830 he helped make possible the independence of Belgium, and as ambassador to England, negotiated the Quadruple Alliance, involving England, France, Spain, and Portugal.

Tallis, Tallys, or Talys, Thomas (c.1510-1585), British composer and organist. He was organist of the royal chapel under Edward VI, Mary, and Elizabeth I, and is regarded as one of the first composers of Anglican Church music.

Tamayo, Rufino (1899–), Mexican artist, born in Oaxaca. Some of his frescoes, combining ancient Mexican and modern European styles, are in the National Conservatory of Music and the National Museum in Mexico City.

Tamerlane, Tamburlaine, or **Timur** (c.1336–1405), Mongol conqueror, born near Samarkand. He was a direct descendant of Genghis Khan. In 1361 he became leader of part of the Samarkand region and in 1369 of the territory from Balkh to Samarkand. His military campaigns extended his domain into Iran, into Armenia and Georgia (1392), into India (1389–1399), and into Turkey and Syria (1400–1402). In the latter campaign he captured Aleppo and Damascus and at Angora seized the Turkish sultan, Bayezid I, as prisoner. His exploits are celebrated in Christopher Marlowe's drama *Tamburlaine the Great* (1590).

Taney, Roger Brooke (1777–1864), American jurist, born in Calvert County, Md. A graduate of Dickinson College, he studied law and was admitted to the bar. He entered politics as a Federalist and then a Democrat, and served as U.S. attorney general (1831–1833). Taney was appointed (1834) secretary of the treasury by Pres. Andrew Jackson, but his support of Jackson's plan to remove government deposits from the Bank of the United States was very unpopular, and the Senate refused to confirm his appointment. In 1836 Taney succeeded John Marshall as chief justice of the Supreme Court, where he became a champion of states' rights. In his most famous decision on the Dred Scott Case, he ruled that the Missouri Compromise was unconstitutional—since according to the Constisution slaves were property, Congress was bound to maintain slavery in the territories.

Tanguy, Ives (1900–1955), French-American painter, born in Paris. A surrealist, he is noted for highly imaginative landscapes, featuring rock formations and weird play of light and space. He came to the U.S. in 1939 and became a citizen in 1948.

Tarbell, Ida Minerva (1857–1944), American journalist and biographer, born in Erie County, Pa. She was associate editor of *The Chautauguan* magazine (1883–1891), of *McClure's Magazine* (1894–1906), and of the *American Magazine* (1906–1915). She was a crusader against business abuses. Her most famous book is *History of the Standard Oil Company* (1904), in which she attacked this and other companies as monopolies. Her other works include *New Ideals in Business* (1916), *Owen D. Young—A New Type of Industrial Leader* (1932), and biographies of Abraham Lincoln and Napoleon Bonaparte. Her autobiography, *All in the Day's Work*, was published in 1939.

Tarkington, Booth, in full **Newton Booth Tarkington** (1869–1946), American novelist, born in Indianapolis, Ind. A popular novelist of the twentieth century, he twice won the Pulitzer Prize: in 1919 for *The Magnificent Ambersons* and in 1922 for *Alice Adams*. Among his other novels, all best sellers, are *The Gentleman from Indiana* (1899), *Monsieur Beaucaire* (1900), *The Conquest of Canaan* (1905), *Penrod* (1914), *Penrod and Sam* (1916), *Seventeen* (1916), *Clare Amber* (1928), *The Fighting Littles* (1941), and *Kate Fennigate* (1943).

Tartini, Giuseppe (1692–1770), Italian violinist and composer, born in Pirano. He was concertmaster at Padua (after 1721), where he composed many violin concertos and sonatas. One of his best-known works is *Il trillo del diavolo* (*The Devil's Trill*). Tartini also made many structural improvements of the violin and is given credit for discovering the so-called "third tones."

Tasso, Torquato (1544–1595), Italian poet of the late Renaissance, born in Sorrento, son of **Bernardo Tasso** (1493–1569), scholar and poet. His masterpiece, the epic poem *Gerusalemme liberata* (*Jerusalem Delivered*), was completed in 1575. Within a few years he became extremely sensitive to criticism and suffered from an acute sense of persecution. From 1579 to 1586 he was confined in an insane asylum. His other works, written before and after this period, include the romantic narrative poem *Rinaldo* (1562), the pastoral drama *Aminta* (1573), a tragedy, *Il Re Torrismondo* (1590), and treatises on the art of poetry.

Taylor, Deems in full **Joseph Deems Taylor** (1885–1966), American composer and music critic, born in New York City. He was educated at New York University and served as a newspaper correspondent during World War I. He was music critic of the New York *World* (1921–1925), and the New York *American* (1931–1932), editor of *Musical America* (1927–1929), and music consultant for the Columbia Broadcasting System (1936–1943). His most famous works are the operas *The King's Henchmen* (1927, libretto by Edna St. Vincent Millay) and *Peter Ibbetson* (1931, libretto by Constance Collier). He also wrote *Through the Looking Glass* (1918), a suite for chamber music ensemble, and *Elegy* (1944), for orchestra. His books include *Of Men and Music* (1937), *The Well-Tempered Listener* (1940), and *Some Enchanted Evenings* (1953).

Taylor, Jeremy (1613–1667), English clergyman and writer, born in Cambridge. He served as chaplain to Archbishop Laud and King Charles I, and was awarded in 1642 the degree of doctor of divinity from Oxford. During the English Civil War and before the Restoration, he lived in Wales and then in Ireland, where he became bishop of Down and Connor after the Restoration. His theological works, noted for their lucid style, include *The Liberty of Prophesying* (1646), *The Rule and Exercises of Holy Living* (1650), *The Rule and Exercises of Holy Dying* (1651), *The Golden Grove* (1965), and *Dissuasive from Popery* (1664).

Taylor, Zachary (1784–1850), twelfth president of the United States (1849–1850), born in Orange County, Va. He entered the army in 1808 as a lieutenant, became a major in the War of 1812 and a colonel during the Black Hawk War (1832). After serving against the Seminoles in Florida, he was sent to the Southwest, and in 1845 was ordered to Texas to defend the new state from possible Mexican invasions. During the Mexican War (1846–1848), Taylor was victorious at the battles of Palo Alto and Resaca de la Palma. He also won the battle of Buena Vista, although the Mexicans, led by Gen. Santa Anna, outnumbered his men four to one. A national hero, popularly known as "Old Rough-and-Ready," he was nominated by the Whigs for the presidency in the election of 1848. Taylor defeated Lewis Cass, the Democratic candidate, and Martin Van Buren, candidate of the Free Soil Party. In his brief term, he recommended that the territories of California and New Mexico seek statehood, and he tried to limit the territorial ambitions of Texas. He died before the passage of the Compromise of 1850, which temporarily settled the most crucial issues of the extension of territory and of slavery.

Tchaikovsky or **Chaikovski, Pëtr Ilich** (1840–1893), Russian composer, born in Kamsko-Vatkinsk. He studied law in St. Petersburg but gave it up for a musical career. At the conservatory, he studied harmony and orchestration under Nikolay Zaremba and Anton Rubinstein. He was professor of harmony at the Moscow Conservatory (1866–1878), composing in his free time. With the patronage of a wealthy window, Madame von Meck, he was able to devote himself entirely to composing. Despite an unhappy personal life—he once attempted suicide—he was extraordinarily prolific in his musical compositions. Of his six symphonies, the last three, especially the *Sixth Symphony* or the *Symphonie Pathétique*, are the best known. He also wrote overtures to *Hamlet* and *Romeo and Juliet* and the *1812* Overture, written for the Moscow Exhibition in 1881. His other productions include the operas *Eugene Onegin, The Queen of Spades*, and *Iolanthe*; the symphonic poem *Francesca da Rimini; March Slav* and *Italian Capriccio;* and the ballets *Swan Lake, The Nutcracker*, and *The Sleeping Beauty*.

Teasdale, Sara (1884–1933), American poet, born in St. Louis, Mo. Esteemed for her polished subtle lyrics, she acknowledged the influence of Christina Rossetti. Her works include *Sonnets to Duse* (1907), *Helen of Troy* (1911), *Rivers to the Sea* (1915), *Love Songs* (1917, awarded a special Pulitzer Prize), *Flame and Shadow* (1920), *Dark of the Moon* (1926), and *Strange Victory* (1933). Her *Collected Poems* was published in 1937.

Tecumseh, Tecumtha, or **Tikamthi** (1768–1813), American Indian chief of the Shawnee tribe, born near what is now Springfield, Ohio. With his brother, Tenskwatawa (known as the Prophet), he tried to organize an Indian confederation against the white settlers. While Tecumseh was away, his brother was defeated by U.S. troops led by William Henry Harrison at the battle of Tippecanoe (November 7, 1811). During the War of 1812, Tecumseh entered the service of the British. He was killed at the battle of the Thames (October 5, 1813).

Telemann, Georg Philipp (1681–1767), German composer, born in Magdeburg. He wrote church music, passions, operas, cantatas, oratorios, and chamber music, which were very popular in his day. His works fell into obscurity after his death but revival of interest in his works occurred during the early 1960's.

Teller, Edward (1908–), American physicist, born in Budapest, Hungary. He studied and taught in Budapest, Karlsruhe, Leipzig, Göttingen, London, and Denmark before coming to the U.S. in 1935. From 1941 to 1946 Teller worked on the atomic bomb project at Los Alamos, New Mexico. After several disagreements with the wartime director of the Los Alamos laboratories, J. Robert Oppenheimer, he left to accept a professorship at the University of Chicago. In the 1950's Teller headed a program to develop a hydrogen bomb, and has been called the "father of the hydrogen bomb." He was head of the Radiation Laboratory of the University of California at Livermore (1952–1960), and has since been a professor-at-large at the university.

Temple, Sir **William** (1628–1699), British diplomat and essayist, born in London. As envoy to Brussels, he negotiated the Triple Alliance in 1668 between England, Sweden, and the Netherlands against France. He was English ambassador to The Hague (1668–1670, 1674–1679). He arranged the marriage between William of Orange and Princess Mary. Unsuccessful in his efforts to reform the Privy Council, he belonged for a time to an inner council of four with Halifax, Essex, and Sunderland. His many and varied writings include *Essay upon the Present State of Ireland* (1668), *Essay on the Origin and Nature of Government* (1672), and *Of Ancient and Modern Learning* (1692), which precipitated a literary quarrel between Richard Bentley and Temple, in which Temple was aided by his young secretary, Jonathan Swift. Most of his works were published in *Miscellanea* (3 vols., 1680, 1692, and 1701).

Teniers, the family name of two Flemish painters: **David Teniers,** known as **the Elder** (1582–1649), born in Antwerp. He is noted for his genre, landscape, and historical paintings, including *The Temptation of St. Anthony* and *Dutch Kitchen*. His son and student, **David Teniers,** known as **the Younger** (1610–1690), is noted for genre and landscape paintings and for portraits. His works include *The Denial of St. Peter, The Prodigal Son, Cow Stable, A Merry Repast, The Barber Shop, Backgammon Players, Guard Room, Flemish Tap-Room, Judith, Archers of Antwerp*, and *Village Festival*.

Tenniel, Sir **John** (1820–1914), English cartoonist and illustrator, born in London. He was famous for his cartoons in *Punch*, with which he was associated from 1850 to 1901. He is also known for his illustration of Lewis Carroll's *Alice's Adventures in Wonderland* (1865) and *Through the Looking Glass* (1872). He was knighted in 1893.

Tennyson, Alfred, known as **Alfred,** Lord **Tennyson,** 1st Baron (1809–1892), English poet, born in Somersby and educated at Trinity College, Cambridge. As a student he won the chancellor's medal for his blank-verse poem *Timbuctoo* (1829). In 1830 his *Poems, Chiefly Lyrical* appeared. Tennyson left Cambridge before completing his degree. In 1832 his *Poems* was published, and with the appearance in 1842 of two more volumes of *Poems*, his reputation was established. In 1847 *The Princess, A Medley* appeared, followed in 1850 by the great volume *In Memoriam*, dedicated to his friend Arthur Hallam. In 1850 Tennyson succeeded William Wordsworth as poet laureate. In 1855 *Maud* was published, and in 1859 the first part of *Idylls of the King* (other parts in 1869, 1872, and 1885). His narrative poems include *Enoch Arden* and *Aylmer's Field* (both 1864). Of his plays, *Becket* (1884) became one of the most popular. Among his other volumes of poems was *Demeter and Other Poems* (1889), containing the famous *Crossing the Bar*. In 1884 he was created a hereditary peer, Baron Tennyson of Freshwater and Aldworth.

Terence, Latin name **Publius Terentius Afer** (c.185–159 B.C.), Roman playwright, born in Carthage. Taken to Rome as a slave, he was later freed and educated by his master, a Roman senator. His main patrons were Scipio the Younger and Laelius. All his plays were sentimental comedies of manners: *Andria* (*The Girl from Andros*, 166 B.C.); *Hecyra* (*The Mother-In-Law*, 165); *Heautontimoroumenos* (*The Self-Punisher*, 163); *Eunuchus* (*The Eunuch*, 161); *Phormio* (161); and *Adelphi* (*The Brothers*, 160).

Teresa, Saint. See *Theresa, Saint.*

Terhune, Albert Payson (1872–1942), American writer, born in Newark, N.J., and educated at Columbia. Terhune was on the staff of the New York *Evening World* from 1894 to 1916. He is best known for his stories about dogs, notably *Lad: A Dog* (1919) and *Way of a Dog* (1934).

Terry, Dame **Ellen Alicia** or **Alice** (1847–1928), English actress, born in Coventry. In 1878 she began her long association with Henry Irving and the London Lyceum Theatre. She was well known for her Shakespearean roles, especially those of Juliet and Portia. In 1925 she was created Dame of the British Empire by George V. She was a

UNITED PRESS INTERNATIONAL

U THANT as secretary-general of the U.N.

friend of George Bernard Shaw, with whom she carried on a long correspondence. Their letters to each other were published in 1932.

Tertullian, in full **Quintus Septimius Florens Tertullianus** (c.160–c.230 A.D.), Latin theologian and influential Church father, born in Carthage. One of the foremost scholars of his time, he was converted to Christianity about 190 A.D. He became a leader of the Montanist sect about 203 A.D., in opposition to what he considered excessive participation of the Church in worldly affairs. Among his works are *Apologeticus,* a defense of Christianity; *Ad martyres; De poenitentia; De monogamia;* and *De baptismo.* Several of his sayings have become proverbial; for example: "The blood of the martyrs is the seed of the Church"; "The unity of heretics is schism." On the question of faith, he declared: "I believe because it is absurd."

Tesla, Nikola (1857–1943), American inventor and electrical engineer, born in Smiljan, Croatia. He was educated at the Graz Polytechnic Institute and at the University of Prague. He came to the U.S. in 1884 and was employed by the Edison Company for several years. He invented the alternating-current induction motor, the Tesla coil or transformer, a system of arc lighting, generators for high-frequency currents, a wireless system of communication, and a high-potential magnifying transmitter.

Tetrazzini, Luisa (1874–1940), Italian coloratura soprano, born in Florence. She made her operatic debut in Florence in 1895, first appeared in London at Covent Garden in 1907 and in New York at the Metropolitan Opera House in 1908. From 1910 to 1913 she toured the U.S. and sang with the Chicago Opera Company (1913–1914). Her favorite roles were in *Rigoletto, Lucia di Lammermoor, Les Huguenots* and *La Traviata.*

Thackeray, William Makepeace (1811–1863), English novelist, born in Calcutta, India, and educated at Cambridge. From 1842 to 1854 he contributed to *Punch* as a writer and artist. The serialization of *Vanity Fair* in 1847–1848 established Thackeray's reputation as a major English novelist. This was followed by *Pendennis* (1848–1850), *Henry Esmond* (1852), and *The Newcomes* (1853–1855). He delivered and published lectures on *English Humorists of the Eighteenth Century* (1851) and the *Four Georges* (1855). Many of these had been heard in his lecture tours in the U.S. between 1852 and 1855. In 1858 he published *The Virginians,* a sequel to *Henry Esmond.* Thackeray's novels are an interesting guide to English society of the eary nineteenth century. He especially satirized the upper classes.

Thales (c.640–546 B.C.), Greek philosopher, mathematician, and astronomer, born in Miletus, Asia Minor. He believed that water was the first element of the universe, from which everything else was created. As the first to study the geometry of lines, he is often called the founder of abstract geometry. He gained great fame in his time by accurately predicting an eclipse of the sun in 585 B.C. Thales was the first of the Seven Sages of Greece.

Thant, U (1909–   ), Burmese diplomat, born in Pantanaw, Burma, and educated at the University of Rangoon. He was first active in education and then in various Burmese government public information posts. He was secretary to Burma's prime minister from 1953 to 1957, when he was appointed Burma's ambassador to the United Nations. On November 3, 1961, he was elected as an East-West compromise candidate to succeed the late Dag Hammarskjöld as UN secretary-general.

Themistocles (c.527–c.460 B.C.), Athenian general and statesman. He became the political leader in Athens after Aristides was exiled (482), and induced the Athenians to build a navy and fortify the harbor at Piraeus. In 480 B.C. Xerxes attacked Athens with a huge fleet, and Themistocles defeated him near the isle of Salamis. This victory and others over the Persians made Athens the foremost maritime power of the period. Themistocles, however, lost the confidence of the people. He was exiled in 471 B.C. and settled at Magnesia, where he died.

Theocritus (fl. 3d century B.C.), Greek pastoral poet, born in Syracuse, Sicily. Little is known of his life. He is usually considered the last of the great Greek poets and the creator of the pastoral tradition in poetry. Of his works, 30 idyls and over 20 epigrams are extant. He was imitated by Vergil in his *Eclogues* and in modern times by many poets, including Spenser, Milton, Tennyson, and Swinburne.

Theodora (c.508–548 A.D.), Byzantine empress, the wife of Justinian I. Born in Constantinople, she was an actress for several years before marrying Justinian in 523. She strongly influenced her husband's policies as emperor from his accession in 527 until her death. In 532 she induced him to stay in Constantinople and suppress the Nika rebellion rather than flee the city and thus forfeit his power.

Theodoric, often called **Theodoric the Great** (c.454–526 A.D.), Ostrogoth king succeeding his father, Theodemer, in 474. By conquest he greatly extended his kingdom, which eventually included Sicily, Italy, Dalmatia, and parts of Germany. A strong ruler, Theodoric brought relative peace and security to his kingdom.

Theodosius I, in full **Flavius Theodosius,** often called **Theodosius the Great** (c.346–395 A.D.), Roman emperor, born in Spain. In 378 he was selected by Gratian, emperor of the West, as the successor to Valens, emperor of the East, who had been killed in the battle of Adrianople against the Visigoths. Theodosius continued the war against the Visigoths with success and removed the usurper Maximus, who had seized the imperial throne in the West and murdered Gratian. After the suppression of a revolt in Thessalonica, where he had 7,000 people executed, Theodosius did public penance before Saint Ambrose, who was then bishop of Milan.

Theotokopoulos, Kyriakos. See *Greco, El.*

Theresa or **Teresa,** Saint (1515–1582), Spanish Carmelite nun and reformer, born in Avila. Her mystical visions inspired her work and her writings, which include *El Camino de la Perfección (The Road of Perfection,* 1563) and *El Castillo Interior (The Interior Castle,* 1577). She was canonized in 1622. Her feast day is October 15.

Thibault, Jacques Anatole François. See *France, Anatole.*

Thiers, Louis Adolphe (1797–1877), French statesman and historian, born in Marseilles. He studied law at Aix-en-Provence and went to Paris in 1821. After the accession of Louis Philippe (1830), he held several cabinet posts and was twice minister of foreign affairs (1836, 1840). After the coup d'état of 1851, he was banished from France, but was allowed to return the next year. He spent the next 12 years studying and writing, and reentered politics in 1863 as a vigorous critic of Napoleon III's foreign policy. After the fall of the Empire in 1870, he negotiated the peace treaty between France and Germany. Thiers became the first president of the Third Republic in 1871, remaining in office until his defeat in 1873, when he retired from public life. As a historian, he is noted for his *Histoire de la révolution française* (10 vols., 1823–1827), and *Histoire du consulat et de l'empire* (20 vols., 1845–1863).

Thomas, Dylan (1914–1953), Welsh poet, born in South Wales. His sensitive vision of nature and men was matched by his great zest for life. He brought to modern poetry a refreshing awareness of the melodies and subtleties inherent in English speech; and with his deep, rich voice he impressed this upon millions who heard his radio and lecture-platform recitals. His published poems include *The Map of Love* (1939), *The World I Breathe* (1939), *In Country Sleep* (1952), *Collected Poems* (1953), *Under Milk Wood* (1954), and *A Child's Christmas in Wales* (1954). His *Portrait of the Artist as a Young Dog* (1940) is an amusing collection of sketches and anecdotes.

Thomas, Lowell Jackson (1892–   ), American news commentator, author, and motion picture producer. Born in Woodington, Ohio, and educated at the universities of Northern Indiana and Denver and Princeton. Thomas began his news career as a reporter for the Chicago *Journal* in 1914. After several years of teaching oratory and English in Chicago and at Princeton, he served as an overseas correspondent during World War I. After the war, Pres. Wilson appointed him chief of the civilian commission that compiled a historical account of the war years. In 1930 Thomas began a radio program of news commentary that is still broadcast. In 1935 he began to narrate movie, and later television, travelogues, and since 1952 he has appeared as the narrator of three Cinerama motion pictures he produced. Thomas is perhaps best known as an adventurer and globetrotter, writing on and reporting from remote corners of the world. His books include *With Lawrence in Arabia* (1924), which brought world fame to T. E. Lawrence; *The First World Flight* (1925); *Count Luckner—the Sea Devil* (1927); and *Book of the High Mountains* (1964).

Thomas, Norman Mattoon (1884–   ), American Socialist leader, born in Marion, Ohio. He graduated from Princeton (1905) and Union Theological Seminary (1911). He

BUNNY ADLER-PIX

DYLAN THOMAS

WIDE WORLD

NORMAN THOMAS

served as a minister in New York churches until 1918, when he founded a paper called *The World Tomorrow* and began to lecture on political and economic subjects. He became an editor of *The Nation* and was active in a number of associations holding advanced political and economic views. He ran unsuccessfully on the Socialist ticket for governor of New York (1924), mayor of New York City (1925, 1929), and representative to Congress (1930). He was a presidential candidate in 1928, 1932, 1936, 1940, and 1948. Throughout his political career he has lectured, debated, and written on politics, pacifism, and reform. Among his books are *America's Way Out* (1930), *What is our Destiny?* (1944), *The Test of Freedom* (1954), and *The Great Dissenter* (1961).

Thomas, Theodore, in full **Christian Friedrich Theodore Thomas** (1835–1905), American orchestra conductor, born in Essen, Germany. He studied violin under his father and came to the U.S. in 1845. After playing with several orchestras he organized his own concert company in New York in 1862. He gave concerts in New York and on tours until 1890, when he helped found the Chicago Symphony Orchestra, which he conducted from 1891.

Thomas à Becket. See *Becket, Thomas à.*

Thomas a Kempis, also called **Thomas Hamerken** or **Hämmerlein** (1380–1471), German Roman Catholic religious writer, born in Kempen, Prussia. In 1407 he entered the Augustinian monastery of Mount St. Agnes, near Zwolle, and was ordained in 1413. He is best known as the reputed author of the great religious classic *Imitation of Christ.*

Thomas Aquinas. See *Aquinas, Thomas.*

Thomashefsky, Boris (1864–1939), American Yiddish actor and producer, born in Kiev, came to the U.S. in 1877. He introduced and developed the American Yiddish theater and translated many of Shakespeare's plays into Yiddish. He established the National Theater in New York and wrote many operettas and short plays.

Thompson, Benjamin, Count **Rumford** (1753–1814), American physicist, born in North Woburn, Mass. A Loyalist during the American Revolution, he was sent to England (1776) with dispatches. He was then given a position in the Foreign Office, and by 1780 was undersecretary of state. In the service of the elector of Bavaria (1784–1795) Thompson introduced important reforms. Returning to England (1795) he applied himself to experiments in light and heat. From 1802 he resided in France.

Thompson, Francis (1859–1907), English poet, born in Preston, Lancashire. After abandoning his training for the priesthood, he went to London (1885) to become a writer. After three years of poverty and opium addiction, he was discovered by Wilfrid and Alice Meynell, editors of the magazine *Merry England.* They cared for him and helped him publish several volumes of his poetry. Among his works are *Poems* (1893 including the celebrated poem *The Hound of Heaven*); *Sister Songs* (1895); *New Poems* (1897); essays in literary criticism; biographies of St. Ignatius Loyola and John the Baptist; and *Essay on Shelley* (1909).

Thomson, Elihu (1853–1937), American inventor and electrician, born in Manchester, England, and raised in Philadelphia, Pa. With Edwin J. Houston he invented an electric dynamo and founded (1880) the Thomson-Houston Electric Company, which merged with the Edison Company to form the General Electric Company. He invented the electric welding process that bears his name, the standard 3-phase alternating-current generator, the watt meter, and the street arc lamp.

Thomson, James (1700–1748), Scottish poet, born in Ednam and educated at the University of Edinburgh. He went to London in 1725, where he wrote his famous poem *The Seasons.* Written in blank verse, it consists of four parts: *Winter* (1726), *Summer* (1727), *Spring* (1728), and *Autumn* (1730). This was followed by *The Castle of Indolence* (1748), a romantic fantasy in rhymed verse.

Thomson, Sir **Joseph John** (1856–1940), English physicist, born near Manchester and educated at Cambridge. He was professor of experimental physics at Trinity College, Cambridge (1884–1918). Thomson is famous for his discovery of the electron and for his work in radioactivity and the study of the passage of electricity through gases. He won the Nobel Prize in physics for 1906 and was knighted in 1908. His writings include *Conduction of Electricity Through Gases* (1903), *Corpuscular Theory of Matter* (1907), *The Electron in Chemistry* (1923), and *Recollections and Reflections* (1936).

Thomson, Virgil (1896–   ), American composer and music critic, born in Kansas City, Mo., and educated at Harvard, École Normale Supérieure in Paris, and Juilliard School of Music. Between 1920 and 1925 he taught music at Harvard while serving as music critic on the Boston *Transcript.* In 1925 he moved to Paris, where he came under the influence of Erik Satie and his avant-garde music. Returning to the U.S. in 1940, Thomson became chief music critic of the New York *Herald Tribune* and for five years filled his column with what were considered unorthodox views of compositions and performances. Since 1945, although he has appeared as guest conductor with orchestras in Paris, London, Chicago and New York, he has devoted most of his time to composing. Thomson's philosophy of music is that its primary purpose is to entertain, and his compositions are simple, melodious, and up-to-date. Although he is at his best when composing vocal music, many of Thomson's works have been instrumental pieces, including two symphonies, two piano sonatas, chamber music, and a number of concertos, as well as incidental music for plays and motion pictures. He has also written, however, a Requiem Mass and two operas, *Four Saints in Three Acts* (1934, with a libretto by Gertrude Stein), and *Mother of Us All* (1947).

Thomson, William. See *Kelvin, 1st Baron.*

Thoreau, Henry David (1817–1862), American naturalist, essayist, and poet, born in Concord, Mass. After he graduated from Harvard (1837), he taught school for a time and held odd jobs, from pencil making to surveying. A lifelong friend of Ralph Waldo Emerson, he was much influenced by Emerson's transcendental philosophy, but he developed his own radical version based on absolute simplicity and purity. He lived alone in a cabin at the edge of Walden Pond near Concord, where he studied nature and wrote. In 1849 he returned to his father's home, where he lived until his death. His works include *A Week on the Concord and Merrimack Rivers* (1849), *Walden* (1854), the posthumous *The Main Woods* (1864), and *Cape Cod* (1865). His journals, letters, and manuscripts were collected and published in 1906. Two essays, *Civil Disobedience* (1849) and *Life Without Principle* (pub. 1863), are acclaimed as masterpieces of idealistic philosophy.

Thorndike, Ashley Horace (1871–1933), American literary scholar, born in Houlton, Me., and educated at Wesleyan and Harvard. He taught English at a number of universities and was professor of English at Columbia from 1906 until his death. He was an authority on the drama, especially on Shakespeare. Among his books are *Tragedy* (1908), *Shakespeare's Theatre* (1916), and *English Comedy* (1929). He also edited a number of textbooks and anthologies.

Thorndike, Edward Lee (1874–1949), American psychologist and lexicographer, born in Williamsburg, Mass., and educated at Wesleyan, Harvard, and Columbia. He taught at Western Reserve University before beginning his long service at Columbia in 1899. There he helped develop Teachers College and taught several courses in educational methods and psychology. He wrote *Educational Psychology* (1903), *The Measurement of Intelligence* (1926), and *Fundamentals of Learning* (1933). He also planned and edited *The Thorndike-Century Junior* (1935) and *Senior* (1941) dictionaries, highly regarded works in lexicography.

Thorndike, Lynn (1882–1965), American historian, born in Lynn, Mass. He was professor of medieval history at Columbia from 1924. Thorndike wrote *The History of Medieval Europe* (1917), *A Short History of Civilization* (1926), and other histories.

Thorpe, Jim, in full **James Francis Thorpe** (1888–1953), American athlete, born near Prague, Okla., of Indian parentage. He first distinguished himself as an athlete at the Carlisle (Pa.) Indian School, where he excelled in football, baseball, and track. He twice was chosen to the All-American football team (1911, 1912), and at the Olympic Games of 1912 he became the first person to win both the decathlon and pentathlon. He had to return his Olympic medals, however, for having previously played professional baseball. After a career as a professional football and baseball player, he retired in 1929 to devote himself to service to his Indian tribe in Oklahoma.

Thorvaldsen or **Thorwaldsen, Bertel** (1768–1844), Danish sculptor, born in Copenhagen. He studied art in Copenhagen and Rome, and became the leading neoclassic sculptor of his time. Among his famous works are *Triumphal Entry of Alexander into Babylon, Cupid and Psyche, The Dying Lion,* and *Christ and the Twelve Apostles.*

Thucydides (c.471–400 B.C.), Greek historian, born in Athens. He commanded an expedition (424 B.C.) of the Athenian navy against the Spartans at Amphipolis. For failing to prevent the surrender of Amphipolis, he was exiled for 20 years. During this period he wrote the *History of the Peloponnesian War,* universally acclaimed for its painstaking accuracy, critical insight, and artistic sensitivity. Of his great work, he hoped it would be "not . . . an essay which is to win the applause of the moment, but . . . a possession for all time."

Thurber, James Grover (1894–1961), American humorist and cartoonist, born in Columbus, Ohio. Blind in one eye since childhood, he suffered from imperfect vision and total blindness in his last years. After several years as a newspaperman, he became (1926) a contributor of both drawings and essays to *The New Yorker.* His many humorous works, published with his own drawings, include *The Owl in the Attic* (1931), *The Seal in the Bedroom* (1932), *My Life and Hard Times* (1934), *The Middle-aged Man on the Flying Trapeze* (1935), *Let Your Mind Alone* (1937), *The Last Flower* (1939), *Fables for Our Time* (1940), *The Thurber Carnival* (1945), and *The Thirteen Clocks* (1950). With Elliott Nugent he wrote the successful play *The Male Animal* (1940).

Thutmose III or **Thothmes** (c.1490–1436 B.C.), Egyptian pharaoh of the 18th dynasty. He ruled jointly (c.1501–1496, 1493–1481) with his half sister and wife, Hatshepsut, most of his reign. Thutmose extended his kingdom by conquest into Syria, Palestine, and Phoenicia. He enlarged the great temple of Amon at Karnak and erected many obelisks, two of which, known as Cleopatra's Needles, are now in London and New York.

Tibaldi, Pellegrino (1527–1596), Italian painter and architect, born in Bologna. His architectural achievements include the Milan cathedral, the churches of San Fidelis and San Sebastiano at Milan, and the church of San Gaudenzia at Novara. His paintings include frescoes in the Escorial at Madrid, *Adoration of the Shepherds,* and *St. Jerome.*

Tibbett, Lawrence Mervil (1896–1960), American baritone, born in Bakersfield, Calif. He made his operatic debut (1923) as Amonasro in *Aïda,* at the Hollywood Bowl. Later in the same year he appeared at the Metropolitan Opera House, New York, as Valentine in *Faust.* He sang with the Metropolitan Opera Company from 1925 until his death. He also appeared in several movies.

Tiberius, in full, **Tiberius Claudius Nero Caesar** (42 B.C.–37 A.D.), second Roman emperor, son of Tiberius Claudius Nero and Livia Drusilla. He won early recognition in campaigns in Armenia and, with his brother, Drusus, on the Rhine and Danube. He was consul (13 B.C., 7 B.C.) under the rule of the Emperor Augustus, whom his mother had married in 38 B.C. Augustus forced Tiberius (11 B.C.) to divorce his wife, Vipsania Agrippina, and marry Augustus' daughter Julia. After a period of retirement in Rhodes (6 B.C.–2 A.D.), Tiberius returned and was named the heir of Augustus.

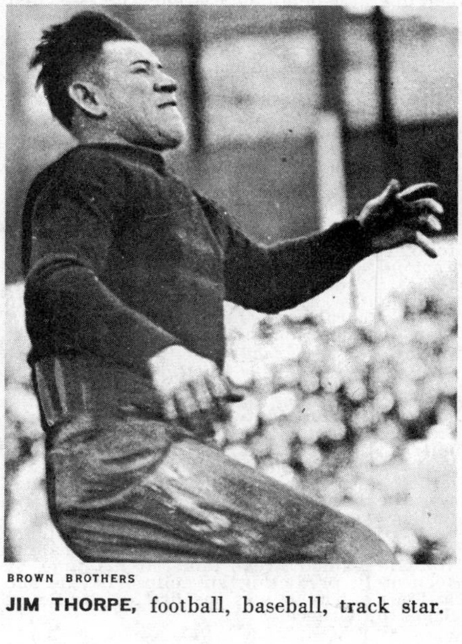

BROWN BROTHERS

JIM THORPE, football, baseball, track star.

INTERNATIONAL NEWS

JAMES THURBER

After several more campaigns, he became emperor in 14 A.D. A capable leader at first, he came increasingly under the influence of the cruel Sejanus, captain of the Praetorian Guard. After his son, Drusus, and his nephew, Germanicus Caesar, were killed, Tiberius had Sejanus put to death. During his rule, the execution of Jesus took place.

Tieck, Ludwig (1773–1853), German writer, born in Berlin and educated at the universities of Halle, Göttingen, and Erlangen. He wrote novels, short stories, dramas, and books of literary criticism. His works include the comedies *Blaubart* (*Bluebeard*) and *Der gestiefelte Kater* (*Puss in Boots*).

Tiepolo, Giovanni Battista (1696–1770), Italian painter, born in Venice. Through his frescoes, easel paintings, and etchings, characterized by movement and rich colors, he became one of the greatest as well as the last of the Venetian school of painters. His works include *The Last Supper, Adoration of the Kings, Anthony and Cleopatra,* and *Neptune and Venus.*

Tiffany, Louis Comfort (1848–1933), American painter and stained-glass artist, born in New York City. He was the son of Charles Lewis Tiffany, founder of Tiffany and Company, jewelers. He developed the Tiffany favrile glass, which was worked into the popular "Tiffany lamps" and elaborate colored-glass ornaments He organized and endowed the Louis Comfort Tiffany Foundation at Oyster Bay, New York, for art students.

Tilden, Samuel Jones (1814–1886), American statesman, born in New Lebanon, N. Y. He was educated at Yale and New York universities and was admitted to the bar in 1841. Elected as a Democrat in 1845 to the New York state assembly, he was associated with the faction known as the Barnburners and with the Free Soil movement. He led the attack on the "Tweed Ring" of New York City, a group of corrupt politicians headed by William Tweed. In 1874 he was elected governor of New York and in 1876 was the Democratic candidate for president. Although Tilden appeared to have received more popular votes than his Republican opponent, Rutherford B. Hayes, the electoral vote was contested and an electoral commission was selected by Congress to determine the winner. Hayes, according to the Commission's conclusions, had won by one electoral vote. At his death, Tilden left an endowment to found a public library in New York City.

Tilden, William Tatem, Jr. (1893–1953), American tennis player, born in Germantown, Pa. He won the U.S. singles championship seven times (1920–1925, 1929) and the Wimbledon (England) championship three times (1920, 1921, 1930). He led the U.S. Davis Cup team from 1920 to 1930. In 1931 he became a professional tennis player.

Tillich, Paul Johannes (1886–1965), German-American Protestant theologian and philosopher, born in Starzeddel, Germany. He was a professor at German universities from 1919 to 1933. When Hitler came to power, Tillich left for the U.S. He taught at the Union Theological Seminary, New York, from 1934 to 1955, when he was appointed to the divinity school at Harvard. Tillich's approach to religion sought to define Christianity in terms of modern needs, and utilized much of modern science, psychology, and sociology. His works include *The Courage to Be* (1952), *Dynamics of Faith* (1957), *Theology of Culture* (1959), and *The Eternal Now* (1963).

Tilly, Johan Tserclaes, Count of (1559–1632), Flemish soldier, born in Brabant. He commanded the field forces of the Catholic League in the Thirty Years' War, replacing Wallenstein as head of the Imperial forces in 1630. He commanded the storming of Magdebug (1631), where thousands were slaughtered. In the same year he and his forces were in turn defeated at Breitenfeld by Gustavus Adolphus of Sweden. In 1632 he was again defeated by the Swedes at the battle of Lech, where he was killed.

Timrod, Henry (1828–1867), American poet, born in Charleston, S.C. He was known as the "laureate of the Confederacy." His most representative poems include *Ode to the Confederate Dead, Carolina, A Cry to Arms,* and *Katie.*

Tintoretto, Il, real name **Jacopo Robusti** (1518–1594), Italian painter, born in Venice. He was the son of a dyer (*tintore*), hence, his nickname Tintoretto (little dyer). Influenced greatly by Titian's use of color and Michelangelo's representations of the human figure, Tintoretto created such masterpieces as *Crucifixion, Presentation of the Virgin, The Discovery of the Body of St. Mark, The Last Supper,* and *Last Judgment.*

Tirpitz, Alfred von (1849–1930), German naval commander, born in Küstrin. A career officer, he entered the German navy in 1865, became an admiral in 1903, and admiral of the fleet in 1911. As secretary of state for the navy (1898–1916), he made Germany a great naval power. During World War I he supported the policies of submarine blockade and unrestricted submarine warfare. He fled to Switzerland after Germany's defeat but returned and served in the Reichstag from 1924 to 1928.

Titian, real name **Tiziano Vecelli** (1477–1576), Italian painter, born in Pieve di Cadore. A student of Giovanni Bellini, he also worked with and was influenced by Giorgione. His great works, which made him the most recognized Venetian painter of his times, include *Assumption of the Virgin, Bacchanal, Bacchus and Ariadne, Man with a Glove, Ecce Homo, Christ Crowned With Thorns, Rape of Europa, Venus and Adonis,* and *Allegory.*

Tito, Marshal, real name **Josip Broz** or **Brozovich** (1892–   ), Yugoslav political leader, born in Zagorye, Croatia. He served in the Austro-Hungarian army in World War I and was captured by Russian Czarist troops. After the Bolshevik revolution, he returned to Yugoslavia (1924) and was a metal worker and union organizer. From 1929–1934 he was imprisoned as a conspirator for his activity in the Communist party. During World War II he organized guerrilla partisans to fight the Italians and Germans. In 1943 Tito became head of the Yugoslav Federal People's Republic, serving as marshal of the People's army and president of the National Liberation Council; he was prime minister (1945–1953) and president from 1953. Tito severed relations with the Soviet Union in 1948, and although they were reconciled in 1953, Tito has remained independent of Moscow.

Titus, in full **Titus Flavius Sabinus Vespasianus** (c.40–81 A.D.), Roman emperor, eldest son of Emperor Vespasian. He led the siege and capture of Jerusalem (70 A.D.), which was commemorated by the Arch of Titus, erected (81 A.D.) in Rome. He became joint emperor with his father (71 A.D.) and sole emperor on his father's death in 79 A.D. He was regarded as a just and liberal ruler.

Tocqueville, Alexis Charles Henri Maurice Clérel de (1805–1859), French statesman and writer, born in Verneuil. A magistrate in Versailles, he was sent (1831) to study American prisons. His observations of the United States served as a basis for his *Democracy in America* (2 vols., 1835, 1840), a work hailed as a classic analysis of political, social, and cultural institutions. He served in the French Constituent Assembly (1848) and Legislative Assembly (1840) and was minister of foreign affairs (1849). Briefly imprisoned for opposing Napoleon III, he retired from political life.

Todd, Mary. See *Lincoln, Mary Todd.*

Togo, Count Heihachiro (1847–1934), Japanese admiral. He received his naval training in England and returned to Japan to build a modern Japanese navy. He commanded the Japanese fleet in the Russo-Japanese War (1904–1905). Togo's great victory was in the Sea of Japan, where he destroyed the Russian fleet. For his distinguished service he was made a count in 1907.

Tolstoi or **Tolstoy, Count Lev** or **Leo, Nikolaevich** (1820–1910), Russian writer and social reformer, born in Yasnaya Polyana, his family's estate in Tula. He studied at the University of Kazan, joined the army, and served in the Crimean War. After the war he devoted himself to literature and philosophy. His most famous novels were written soon after: *War and Peace* (1866) and *Anna Karenina* (1875–1877). Other important works include *What is Art?* (1896), *Resurrection* (1899–1900), and *The Kreutzer Sonata* (1899). About 1876 Tolstoi renounced orthodox Christianity and began to develop his own religious creed. He became greatly preoccupied with his religious search, with the preaching of the creed he had envolved, and with his concern for the welfare of the peasantry. Following the teachings of Christ, Tolstoi divided his property among his wife and children and renounced all his personal possessions.

Tonti or **Tonty, Henry de** (1650–1704), Italian explorer. In 1678 he sailed to Canada with La Salle, with whom he established Fort Crevecoeur (now Peoria, Illinois). Also with La Salle, he explored the Mississippi River to its mouth, and claimed the territory for France. Tonti often led the Illinois Indians, his allies, in wars against hostile tribes.

Toombs, Robert Augustus (1810–1885), American statesman, born in Wilkes County, Ga. He was a member of the U.S. Senate from 1853 to 1861, when he resigned to become secretary of state of the Confederacy. He gave up that post to become brigadier general in the Confederate army. After the war he lived in France, England, and Cuba, and on his return to the South he refused to take the oath of allegiance to the United States. He practiced law until his death.

Torquemada, Tomás de (c.1420–1498), Spanish religious leader and inquisitor, born in Valladolid. He became prior in the monastery of Santa Cruz and confessor to Ferdinand and Isabella of Spain. In 1483 he became the first inquisitor general for all Spanish possessions and in 1487 grand inquisitor, one of the most ruthless to ever hold the position. During the 18 years in which he remained inquisitor general he caused 2,000 heretics to be put to death at the stake. The pope rebuked him, but Torquemada replied by sending embassies to Rome to defend his actions. He drove the Moors and (in 1492) about 800,000 Jews from Spain; their loss to the business of Spain was inestimable. He was so intensely disliked that he never dared appear in public without a strong guard. Near the close of his career he retired to a monastery.

Torricelli, Evangelista (1608–1647), Italian physicist and mathematician, born in Faenza. He was an admirer of Galileo, whom he succeeded as professor at the University of Florence. He is credited as the inventor of the barometer (1643). He also made improvements on Galileo's telescope and constructed a simple microscope.

Toscanini, Arturo (1867–1957), Italian conductor, born in Parma. He graduated from the Parma Conservatory in 1885, and after conducting concerts and operas for several

NATIONAL BROADCASTING COMPANY

TOSCANINI conducting the NBC Orchestra.

years, he was appointed conductor of the La Scala Opera Company in Milan in 1898. He became chief conductor of the Metropolitan Opera House in New York in 1908, and from 1928 to 1935 he was conductor of the New York Philharmonic Orchestra. From 1937 until his retirement to Italy in 1954 he conducted the N.B.C. Symphony Orchestra. In all these endeavors he exhibited extraordinary skill and communicated great enthusiam to his musicians, marking him as one of the world's greatest conductors.

Toulouse-Lautrec, Henri in full **Count Henri Marie Raymond de Toulouse-Lautrec Monfa** (1864–1901), French painter, born in Albi. Malformed as a result of a childhood accident, he led a dissipated life and was frequently depressed. His famous paintings, posters, illustrations, and lithographs of the Parisian entertainment world are masterpieces of characterization.

Toussaint L'Ouverture, Pierre Dominique (1743–1803), Haitian Negro general and liberator, born near Cap-Haïtien. A slave until he was nearly 50, he led a slave rebellion in 1791 against the French. After the abolition of slavery by the French National Convention, he helped the French fight the Spaniards. During a civil war in 1799 between Negroes and mulattoes, Toussaint, as leader of the island's Negroes, defeated the mulattoes and became head of the government. When Napoleon I tried to reestablish slavery in 1801, Toussaint rebelled and was finally captured and taken to France, where he died in prison.

Toynbee, Arnold Joseph (1889–   ), English historian, born in London and educated at Balliol College, Oxford. He also studied Greek language and culture at the British Archaeological School at Athens, Greece. He was an intelligence officer during World War I, and was professor of Greek civilization and international history at London University from 1921 to 1955. The author of many histories, Toynbee is best known for his *A Study of History* (10 vols., 1934–1954); in this work, he divides world history into 26 civilizations and traces the rise, decline, and fall of each. Seeing present western Christian civilization in a state of decline, he expresses the hope that a rebirth of Christianity will reverse this trend.

Trajan, in full **Marcus Ulpius Trajanus** (c.53–117 A.D.), Roman emperor, born in Italica, Spain. After serving as praetor and consul, he was adopted by the Emperor Nerva as his successor in 97. Under his rule, Dacia, Mesopotamia, Armenia, and Assyria became Roman provinces. He improved and built many roads, bridges, and buildings in the empire. The famed Trajan's Column was erected in 114.

Tree, Sir Herbert Beerbohm (1853–1917), British actor and manager, born in London. He made his stage debut in 1878. His first great success was as the curate in *The Private Secretary* in 1884. As the manager of several theaters, he was noted for his productions of Shakespearean and classical plays. He was knighted in 1909.

LOOK MAGAZINE

ARNOLD TOYNBEE, English historian.

Treitschke, Heinrich von (1834–1896), German historian, born in Dresden. He taught history at universities in Freiburg, Kiel, Heidelberg, and Berlin. A militant nationalist, he stressed the superiority of the so-called Aryan race, and was strongly antidemocratic, anti-Socialist, anti-Catholic, and anti-Semitic. His major works is the *History of Germany in the Nineteenth Century* (5 vols., 1878–1894).

TOULOUSE-LAUTREC, French painter.

Trent, William Peterfield (1862–1939), American literary scholar, born in Richmond, Va. He taught at the University of the South (1888–1900) and at Columbia (1900–1929), and was one of the founders (1892) of the *Sewanee Review.* His *Life of Defoe* (1916) is considered one of the most authoritative. His other works include *War and Civilization* (1901), *Greatness in Literature* (1905), and *Great American Writers* (1912).

Trevelyan, George Macaulay (1876–1962), English historian, born near Stratford-on-Avon. He was educated at Cambridge, where he later was professor of modern history (1927–1951). His works include *British History in the Nineteenth Century,* 1782–1901 (1922), *History of England* (1926), *England under Queen Anne* (3 vols., 1930–1934), *The English Revolution, 1688* (1938), and *English Social History* (1942). He also wrote *biography,* published posthumously (1883),

Trollope, Anthony (1815–1882), English novelist, born in London. As a post office surveyor, he travelled to Ireland, the West Indies, Egypt, the United States, Africa, and Australia. From these journeys he obtained material for many of his books. He wrote some 50 novels, including *The Warden* (1855), *Barchester Towers* (1857), *The Claverings* (1867), and *Phineas Finn* (1869). His *Autobiography,* published posthumously (1883), describes his method of writing.

Trotsky or **Trotski, Leon,** real name **Leib** or **Lev Davydovich Bronstein** (1877–1940), Russian revolutionary and Communist leader, born of Jewish parents at Elisavetgrad. He was twice deported to Siberia (1898, 1905) for revolutionary activities. Each time he escaped and continued to spread Communist doctrine in Germany, France, Switzerland, and the United States. In 1917, after the fall of the czarist regime, he returned to Russia and helped Lenin organize the Bolshevik seizure of power. He became commissar for foreign affairs in the new Soviet government, and after the treaty of Brest-Litovsk (1918) between Russia and Germany he became commissar for war. During the bitter contest for leadership of the Communist party following Lenin's death, he was defeated by Stalin. Expelled from the party in 1927 and then exiled from Russia, he was assassinated in Mexico

in 1940. Among his books are *Defense of Terrorism* (1920), *Lenin* (1924), *History of the Russian Revolution* (3 vols., 1932), and *Stalin* (1941). His autobiography, *My Life,* appeared in 1930.

Trujillo Molina, Rafael Leonidas (1891–1961), Dominican political leader, born in San Cristóbal. He entered the army as a cadet (1918) and by 1927 was commander in chief. As president (1930–1938, 1942–1952) he was a virtual dictator. He was assassinated in 1961.

Truman, Harry S (1884–   ), thirty-third president of the United States (1945–1952), born in Lamar, Mo. Not accepted at West Point because of poor eyesight, he nevertheless distinguished himself in World War I as a captain in the field artillery. He married Bess Wallace in 1919 and opened a haberdashery in Kansas City. When his business failed, he spent ten years paying off his debts. He entered politics and was elected county judge for Jackson County. While serving as judge, he studied law in Kansas City (1923–1924) and was elected presiding judge for the county court (1926). In 1934 he was elected U.S. senator from Missouri and became famous as chairman of a Senate committee to investigate the national defense program. The so-called Truman Committee discovered waste of food, money, and labor, and faulty defense materials. In 1944 Truman became vice-president on the Democratic ticket with the reelection of Pres. Franklin D. Roosevelt for a third term. When Roosevelt died on April 12, 1945, Truman succeeded him as president.

During his first months in office, he led the nation to victory in World War II, aided by the use of the first atomic bombs. After the war he established the Truman Doctrine, assuring American resistance to any international aggression, and the Marshall Plan, promising aid for the economic recovery of Europe. Reelected in 1948 in a surprise victory over Thomas E. Dewey, he developed a new program of civil rights, economic reform, and national health insurance, known as the Fair Deal. When South Korea was attacked in 1950, Truman immediately came to its aid, and gained the support of the United Nations.

Trumbull, John (1756–1843), American painter, son of Jonathan Trumbull, born in Lebanon, Conn. He graduated from Harvard and served in the Revolutionary War. In 1780 he went to London to study art under Benjamin West. His works include the historical paintings *Battle of Bunker's Hill, Death of Montgomery in the Attack of Quebec, Declaration of Independence, Surrender of Lord Cornwallis at Yorktown,* and *Resignation of Washington.* He also did portraits of George Washington, Alexander Hamilton, and John Jay.

Trumbull, Jonathan (1710–1785), American colonial governor, born in Lebanon, Conn. He was deputy governor of Connecticut (1766–1769) and governor (1769–1784). A strong supporter of the colonial cause during the Revolutionary War, he was reputedly referred to by Washington as "Brother Jonathan," a name which came to denote any typical American.

Trumbull, Lyman (1813–1896), American jurist and legislator, born in Colchester, Conn. He was a justice in the Illinois supreme court (1848–1854) and a U.S. senator (1855–1873). In 1864 he proposed in Congress the bill that led to the adoption of the 13th Amendment to the U.S. Constitution.

Tschaikovsky. See *Tchaikovsky.*

Tupper, Sir Charles (1821–1915), Canadian statesman, born in Amherst, Nova Scotia. An advocate of Canadian federation, he was premier of Nova Scotia (1864–1867) and held several offices in the ministries of Sir John A. Macdonald (1872–1888). He promoted the extension of the Canadian Pacific Railway. He was Canadian high commissioner in London from 1884 to 1896, when he was elected prime minister of Canada. After a few months, his party was defeated, and he remained as leader of the opposition until his retirement in 1900.

Turenne, Vicomte de, Henri de La Tour d'Auvergne (1611–1675), French marshal, born in Sedan. He commanded French troops during the Thirty Years' War, frequently with Louis II, prince de Condé. However, in the French civil wars of the Fronde, he fought against Condé, finally defeating him in 1658. Under Louis XIV, Turenne led French armies in the conquest of Holland, Alsace, and the Palatinate. He was killed near Sasbach, Baden.

Turgenev, Ivan Sergeevich (1818–1883), Russian author, born in Orel and educated in St. Petersburg, Moscow, and Berlin. His first successful work was *A Sportsman's Sketches* (1852), on peasant life. Some of

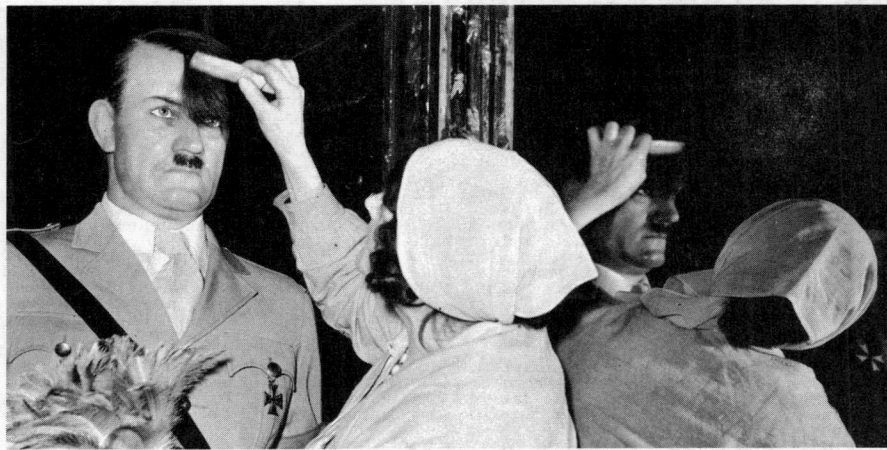

TUSSAUD wax museum worker dusts off and tidies up the wax statue of Adolph Hitler.

his works, in addition to the well-known *Fathers and Sons* (1862), are *Smoke* (1867), *Rudin* (1855), *On the Eve* (1860), *Virgin Soil* (1867), and *Clara Milich* (1882).

Turgot, Anne Robert Jacques, Baron de l'Aulne (1727–1781), French statesman and economist, born in Paris. As intendant of Limoges (1761–1774), he tried to remove oppressive taxes, promote the development of industries, and build roads and bridges. Under Louis XVI he was comptroller general of finance (1774–1776). He warned the court that widespread economic reforms were necessary, notably a carefully controlled economy and the elimination of many feudal privileges, but his ideas were disliked and he was dismissed from office. Associated with the physiocrats, a group of economic theorists, he wrote *Reflections upon the Formation and Distribution of Riches* (1766) and *Usury* (1769).

Turner, Frederick Jackson (1861–1932), American historian, born in Portage, Wis. He was educated at the University of Wisconsin and Johns Hopkins and was professor of history at Harvard (1910–1924). His best known work, *The Frontier in American History* (1920), stressed the importance of the frontier on the development of the American nationality, and became a major influence on interpretations of American history. His *The Significance of Sections in American History* (1932) was awarded the Pulitzer Prize in 1933.

Turner, Joseph Mallord William (1775–1851), English landscape painter, born in London. His works were first exhibited at the Royal Academy when he was 19. His early paintings, influenced by Claude Lorrain and Nicolas Poussin, were less dramatic and colorful than his later ones. Turner excelled in the art of watercolor, but after achieving recognition in that medium he gradually turned to oils, capturing the same effect of splendid color and brilliant light that he mastered as a watercolorist. The works of his middle and later periods, with the subject absorbed into a vision of pure light and color, transcend the Romantic period in art and anticipate modern abstract painting. A prolific painter, among his finest works are *Ulysses Deriding Polyphemus* (1829), the watercolors of the burning of the Houses of Parliament (1834), *The Golden Bough* (1834), *The Fighting Téméraire Tugged to Her Last Berth* (1839), and *Rain, Steam, and Speed* (1844).

Tussaud, Marie Gresholtz, known as **Madame Tussaud** (1760–1850), Swiss modeler in wax, born in Berne. In 1802 in London she founded Madame Tussaud's Exhibition. This exhibition of wax figures of prominent and notorious persons has been continually expanded by her descendants.

Tutankhamen, known as **King Tut** (fl. about 1358 B.C.), Egyptian king of the 18th dynasty. Little is known of his life, except that he restored the old religion of Amen after the death of his father-in-law, Ikhnaton, and moved the Egyptian capital from Akhetaton (modern Tell el-Amarna) back to Thebes. He was buried in the Valley of the Kings, near Luxor. In 1922 his tomb was discovered by Lord Carnarvon and Howard Carter with his possessions, originally buried with him, intact.

Twain, Mark. See *Clemens, Samuel Langhorne.*

Tweed, William Marcy (1823–1878), American politician, born in New York City. In his long political career he was a U.S. congressman (1853–1855) and a New York State senator (1867–1871). Appointed commissioner of public works of New York City (1870), he became head of the notorious "Tweed Ring," a group of politicians who plundered millions of dollars from the public treasury. He was exposed, arrested, convicted, and imprisoned for two years. Arrested once again after his release, he escaped to Spain. He was returned to the U.S. in 1876 and placed in a New York prison, where he died after two years.

Tyler, John (1790–1862), tenth president of the United States, born in Charles City County, Va. He graduated from William and Mary (1807), studied law, and was admitted to the bar. In 1825 he was elected governor of Virginia and a U.S. senator in 1827. In 1840 he was elected vice-president on the ticket with William Henry Harrison. Tyler became president when Harrison died a month after his inauguration. His term of office was marked by almost continual controversy with Congress, which brought impeachment proceedings against him but did not convict him; and with his cabinet, which except for Daniel Webster, his secretary of state, resigned in 1841. During his administration Texas was annexed (1845) and the Webster-Ashburton Treaty was drawn up, settling the northeast boundary dispute with England. In 1861 Tyler came out of retirement to preside at the Peace Convention in Washington D.C. After its failure, he was elected to the Confederate Congress, but he died before it convened.

Tyler, Wat or **Walter** (d.1381), English rebel. He led the Peasants' Revolt of 1381, a rebellion that began in the area of Essex and Kent. The rebels were protesting against the Statute of Labourers (1351), which fixed prices and wages. They also demanded the removal of the poll tax and feudal duties. Although Richard II initially promised to grant the peasants their wishes, the combined military might of the aristocracy put down the rebellion. Tyler and many others were killed, and the demands were forgotten.

Tyndale, Tindale, or **Tindal, William** (c.1492–1536), English religious reformer and translator of the Bible, born in Gloucestershire and educated at Oxford. Unable to publish his translation of the New Testament in England, he went to Germany, visited Martin Luther, and in 1525 began to print the translation in Cologne. He remained in Europe and in 1530 published a translation of the Pentateuch (the first five books of the Old Testament). An advocate of the English reformation, he was disliked by Henry VIII because he had criticized the King's divorce. He was arrested in Flanders and finally burned at the stake. His translation became the basis of the King James Version of the Bible (1611).

Tyndall, John (1820–1893), British scientist, born in County Carlow, Ireland. He was professor of physics at the Royal Institution, London (1853-1887) and director (after 1867), succeeding Michael Faraday. He lectured in England and the United States and studied Alpine glaciers in Switzerland. His studies contributed to knowledge of heat, sound, and light.

U

Ucello, Paolo, real name **Paolo di Dono** (1397–1475), Italian painter, born in Florence. He was among the first painters to experiment with foreshortening and linear perspective. His best-known works include a mosaic for St. Mark's in Venice; an equestrian portrait of Sir John de Hawkwood in the cathedral at Florence; the *Battle of San Romano;* and the series of frescoes of Noah's Ark in Santa Maria Novella in Florence.

Udall or **Uvedale, Nicholas** (1505–1556), English playwright and scholar, born in Hampshire. He was educated at Oxford, and was headmaster of Eton (1534–1541) and of Westminster (1554–1556). He translated Eramus' *Apothegms* and parts of the Bible. His play *Ralph Roister Doister,* written about 1553, is the earliest extant English comedy.

Ulanova, Galina (1910–   ), Russian ballerina, born in St. Petersburg (now Leningrad). Her debut (1928) was at the Kirov Theater, Leningrad, in *Les Sylphides.* She created the part of Juliet in the ballet *Romeo and Juliet* by Sergei Prokofiev in 1940. One of the Soviet Union's leading ballerinas, she was awarded the Stalin prize four times and the Lenin prize in 1957. In 1961 she retired from the Bolshoi Theatre Ballet, of which she had been prima ballerina since 1944, becoming ballet-mistress of the company in 1963.

Uncle Sam, See *Wilson, Samuel.*

Underwood, Oscar Wilder (1862–1929), American legislator, born in Louisville, Ky. He was a member of Congress (1895–1896, 1897–1915) and a U.S. senator (1915–1927). With Sen. F. M. Simmons he sponsored the Underwood-Simmons Tariff Act of 1913.

Undset, Sigrid (1882–1949), Norwegian novelist, born in Kalundborg, Denmark. She made a thorough study of medieval life, which formed the basis of her highly acclaimed novel *Kristin Lavransdatter* (1920–1922). Her other novels include *Jenny* (1911), about art students in Rome, *Olav Audunsson* (4 vols., 1925–1927; English title *The Master of Hestviken*), *Ida Elizabeth* (1932), and *Saga of Saints* (1934). She won the Nobel Prize for literature in 1928.

Untermeyer, Louis (1885–   ), American poet and editor, born in New York City. He left his father's jewelry business after 21 years (1923) to study and write. He was poetry editor of *The American Mercury* (1934–1937), to which he contributed several of his poems. Among his many books are collections of his own poems, such as *Roast Leviathan* (1923) and *Burning Bush* (1928); anthologies including *Modern American Poetry, This Singing World,* and *Modern British Poetry;* an autobiography, *From Another World* (1939); and *Heinrich Heine —Paradox and Poet* (1937).

WIDE WORLD

GALINA ULANOVA, Soviet ballerina.

WIDE WORLD

UREY, chemist on atom bomb project.

Untermyer, Samuel (1858–1940), American lawyer, born in Lynchburg, Va. He was educated in New York and studied law at Columbia. He was a legal adviser to some of America's largest corporations and U.S. counsel in the Pujo money-trust investigation. He helped frame the income tax laws during World War I.

Updike, John Hoyer (1932–), American novelist and short-story writer, born in Shillington, Pa. After obtaining his A.B. at Harvard (1954), he attended the Ruskin School of Drawing and Fine Art in England. Upon returning from abroad he was employed as a journalist for the *New Yorker* magazine (1955–1957). His novels include *The Poorhouse Fair* (1959), *Rabbit, Run* (1960), and *The Centaur* (1963). He is the author of short-story anthologies: *The Same Door* (1959) and *Pigeon Feathers* (1962).

Urban VIII, original name **Maffeo Barberini** (1568–1644), Roman Catholic pope (1623–1644), born in Florence. He founded the College of Propaganda (1627) and built the Barberini Palace and other buildings in Rome. He also censured Galileo for supposed impiety. In the Thirty Years' War he joined France against Spain and the Holy Roman emperor.

Urey, Harold Clayton (1893–), American chemist, born in Walkerton, Ind. He was educated at the universities of Montana and California, and studied atomic physics under Niels Bohr in Denmark. He was an industrial chemist for a time and taught chemistry at several universities. He investigated isotopes and received the Nobel Prize for chemistry in 1934 for his discovery of heavy hydrogen. He also directed research on the production of heavy water and U-235 for the atom bomb.

Utrillo, Maurice (1883–1955), French painter, born in Paris. His best-known paintings are of Paris street scenes, especially of Montmartre, as well as of cathedrals and villages. His early works were influenced by the impressionists, but he is more noted for his "white period" paintings (1909–1914), for example his *Rue de Mont Cenis, Panorama of Paris,* and *Reims Cathedral.*

UNIVERSITY OF IOWA

JAMES VAN ALLEN

V

Vaihinger, Hans (1852–1933), German philosopher, founder of the "as if" philosophy. He was born in Nehren, Württemberg, and studied at Tübingen, Leipzig, and Berlin. He was professor of philosophy at Halle from 1884 until his death. His earlier philosophical work was a careful criticism and exposition of the work of Kant. He later developed his own system. Vaihinger's leading idea was that the ultimate nature of reality must always be unknown, but that man develops fictions of theories as a basis for action and then proceeds "as if" the theories were true. The philosophy of "as if" thus has much in common with the philosophy of pragmatism espoused by William James and John Dewey.

Valentinus (2d century A.D.), Gnostic philosopher and teacher, probably born in Egypt, educated in Alexandria. He taught in Rome from about 135 to 160 A.D. His doctrines, followed by such men as Clement of Alexandria, Origen, and Heracleon, were known as Valentinianism or Valentinian Gnosticism.

Valera, Eamon de. See De Valera, Eamon.

Valéry, Paul Ambroise (1871–1945), French poet and essayist, born in Sète. He began his literary career under the influence of the symbolist movement. He wrote a critical study, *Introduction à la méthod de Léonardo da Vinci* (1894), but shortly after withdrew from an active career and lived as a student and recluse for nearly 20 years. He began publishing poetry again in 1917. He was elected to the French Academy in 1925 upon the death of Anatole France. His works include *La Jeune Parque* (*The Young Fate,* 1917), *Le Cimitière marin* (*The Graveyard by the Sea,* 1920), and *Eupalinos* (*The Architect,* 1924).

Vallandigham, Clement Laird (1820–1871), American politician, born in Lisbon, Ohio. After serving in the Ohio legislature, he was a member of the U.S. Congress (1858–1963). He vigorously opposed the government policies that preceded the Civil War. As head of the Copperheads, or Peace Democrats, he opposed Union conscription. For his attacks on the government, he was court-martialed and sentenced to prison, but Pres. Abraham Lincoln commuted the sentence to banishment to the Confederacy. He escaped to Canada and returned in 1864 to Ohio, where he accidentally shot himself at a murder trial.

Van Allen, James Alfred (1914–), American physicist whose work led to the discovery of radiation belts around the earth. Born in Mount Pleasant, Iowa, he was educated at Iowa Wesleyan College and the State University of Iowa. During World War II he helped to develop the proximity fuse, which detonates if it passes near a target; but he later specialized in rocketry and cosmic-ray research, directing the basic design of the first American satellites, the *Explorer* series. He also developed the cosmic-ray recording devices for the *Explorer* and *Pioneer* rockets, which, in 1958, revealed the existence of the two radiation belts that surround the earth. These were named after Van Allen.

Van Buren, Martin (1782–1862), eighth president of the United States (1837–1841), born in Kinderhook, N.Y. Admitted to the bar in 1803, he became a state senator in 1812 and state attorney general in 1816. In 1821 he entered the U.S. Senate. He resigned from the Senate to become governor of New York in 1828, leaving that office when he was appointed secretary of state by Pres. Andrew Jackson. He was made ambassador to Great Britain in 1831, but the Senate rejected his appointment in 1832. That same year he was elected vice-president on the ticket with Andrew Jackson and in 1836 he was elected president. As president, he opposed the deposit of state funds in a national bank and the extension of slavery. He was unable to alleviate the severe business depression that began in 1837. He ran unsuccessfully for the presidency as a Democrat in 1840 and as a member of the Free Soil party in 1848.

Van Cliburn. See Cliburn, Van.

Vancouver, George (1758–1798), English navigator and explorer. He was a member of Capt. James Cook's second and third expeditions (1772–1780). In command of the ship *Discovery,* he led an exploration (1791–1792) around the Cape of Good Hope to Australia, New Zealand, and the Sandwich Islands (Hawaii), and later sailed up the Pacific coast and around Vancouver Island, named in his honor.

Vandenberg, Arthur Hendrick (1884–1951), American political leader, born in Grand Rapids, Mich. He was educated at the University of Michigan and was editor of the Grand Rapids *Herald* (1906–1923). Elected to the U.S. Senate in 1928, he became a leading Republican spokesman on international affairs. At first opposed to lend-lease aid to Britain, he changed his attitude after the entry of the U.S. into World War II. He was the U.S. delegate to the United Nations Conference in San Francisco (1945), U.S. representative at the Council of Foreign Ministers in Paris (1946), chairman of the Senate Committee on Foreign Affairs (1947–1949), and a leading advocate of the adoption of the Marshall Plan and the establishment of NATO.

Vanderbilt, Cornelius (1794–1877), American financier, born in Staten Island, N.Y. Known as "Commodore," he began his business career ferrying passengers and freight between Staten Island and Manhattan, New York. His enterprise expanded continually, and a line to California was established in 1850. Turning from shipping, he gained control of several railroads, which he consolidated as the New York Central Railroad.

Van Doren, Carl (1885–1950), American scholar and critic, born in Hope, Ill., the brother of Mark Van Doren. A graduate of the University of Illinois, he was professor at Columbia University from 1911 to 1934. He was literary editor of *The Nation* (1919–1922) and *Century Magazine* (1922–1925), and managing editor of *The Cambridge History of American Literature* (1917–1921). His works include *The American Novel* (1921), *Contemporary American Novelists* (1922), and studies of Jonathan Swift, Sinclair Lewis, and James Branch Cabell. For his biography *Benjamin Franklin* (1938), he received the Pulitzer Prize in 1939. His autobiography, *Three Worlds,* appeared in 1936.

Van Doren, Mark (1894–), American poet and critic, born in Hope, Ill. and educated at the University of Illinois and Columbia. He taught English at Columbia for over 40 years. He was literary editor of *The Nation* (1924–1928). His *Collected Poems* (1939) was awarded the Pulitzer Prize in 1940. His critical studies of Thoreau, Hawthorne, Dryden, and Shakespeare have been highly regarded.

Vandyck or **Van Dyck, Sir Anthony** (1599–1641), Flemish painter, born in Antwerp, a pupil of Rubens. Although he painted several religious works, including *Crucifixion* and *Elevation of the Cross,* he is best known for his many portraits of the English royalty and nobility. He was court painter to Charles I (1627–1641).

Vane, Sir Henry or **Harry** (1613–1662), English statesman, called **the Younger** to distinguish him from his father, Sir **Henry Vane, the Elder** (1589–1654), one of Charles I's advisers. Sir Henry emigrated to New England in 1635 and served as governor of Massachusetts (1636–1637). Attempting to prevent the banishment of Anne Hutchinson for preaching salvation outside the specific doctrines of the church, he lost popularity and was not reelected governor; he then returned to England. He was a member of the Long Parliament as a supporter of the anti-episcopal party. In 1643 he helped negotiate the Solemn League and Convenant with the Scots. Although he opposed the execution of Charles I in 1649, he remained a member of the council of state. After the dissolution of the Rump Parliament he opposed Cromwell. Upon Cromwell's death Vane returned to politics, but when Charles II was restored Vane was arrested, charged with high treason, and executed.

Van Gogh. See Gogh, Vincent van.

Van Loon, Hendrik Willem (1882–1944), American writer, born in Rotterdam, Holland, and educated at Cornell, Harvard, and Munich. He was a newspaper correspondent in Washington, D.C., and Europe during World War I, after which he lectured on modern history and the history of art. Among his best-known books are *The Story of Mankind* (1921), *Short History of Discovery* (1918), *Ancient Man* (1920), *America* (1927), *Life and Times of Rembrandt van Rijn* (1931), *The Arts* (1937), and *Van Loon's Lives* (1942).

Vanzetti, Bartolomeo. See Sacco, Nicola.

Varro, Marcus Terentius, surnamed **Atacinus** (116–27 B.C.), Roman scholar, born in Reate. He was a prolific writer and well versed in many subjects, although few of his works are extant. His chief work was a lengthy scholarly study of Roman political and religious institutions. Quintilian regarded him as the most learned of the Romans.

Varus, Publius Quintilius (d.9 A.D.), Roman soldier and statesman. He was consul at Rome (13 B.C.) and governor of Syria (6-4 B.C.). In 9 A.D. he was appointed governor in Germany by Emperor Augustus. His army was defeated and he committed suicide in a battle in the Teutoburger Forest.

Vasari, Giorgio (1511-1574), Italian painter, architect, and writer, born in Arezzo. He studied painting in Florence under Andrea del Sarto and Michelangelo. In 1550 his *Lives of the Greatest Italian Architects, Painters and Sculptors* appeared. Vasari's artistic works include several Vatican murals, frescoes in the Duomo at Florence, and ceiling paintings in the Palazzo Vecchio at Florence.

Vasco da Gama. See *Gama, Vasco da.*

Vaughan, Henry (1622-1695), English mystic poet, called "the Silurist" (he was born in South Wales, where the ancient Silures lived). His poems include *Silex Scintillans* (*Sparks from the Flint;* 1650, 1655), *Olor Iscanus* (*Swan of Usk,* 1651), and *Thalia Rediviva* (1678). All are characterized by religious mysticism. His most famous single poem is *They Are All Gone into the World of Light.*

Vaughan Williams, Ralph (1872-1958), English composer, born in Down Ampney, Gloucestershire. He was educated at the Royal College of Music and Trinity College, Cambridge. The influence of folk music is strong in many of his compositions. His works include *London Symphony, Pastoral Symphony, Symphony in F Minor,* and *Sea Symphony.* He also composed in a wide variety of other forms.

became court painter to Philip IV. His works include portraits of Philip IV, the Infanta Maria, court jesters, beggars, and dwarfs; religious paintings such as the *Adoration of the Magi* and *Crucifixion;* mythological works such as *Mars, Mercury and Argus* and *Venus with a Mirror;* genre paintings of *Water Carrier of Seville* and *Boar Hunt;* and the historical *Surrender of Breda* (also called *Las Lanzas*).

Vendôme, Louis Joseph, Duc de, also known as duc de Penthièvre (1654-1712), French general, born in Paris. He commanded French forces at Catalonia and became a marshal of France. In 1697 he led the capture of Barcelona. He fought at Luzzara against Prince Eugene of Savoy in 1702, where neither army was able to defeat the other. Defeated in 1708 at Oudenarde, he was victorious at Brihuega against the British and at Villaviciosa in 1710 against the Austrians.

Venizelos, Eleutherios (1864-1936), Greek statesman, born near Canea in Crete. He was educated at the University of Athens, practiced law, and became president of the Cretan assembly. He participated in the Cretan insurrectionary movements of 1896 and 1904. In 1909 he settled in Athens and became premier of Greece in 1910. He was sympathetic to the Allies during the early part of World War I, but he was not supported by King Constantine, and resigned in 1915. After Constantine was dethroned in 1917, Venizelos was again elected premier and served until 1920. He held the office briefly in 1924 and again from 1928 to 1933, when he retired to Crete.

Bucolics, a series of pastoral poems; the *Georgics,* poems about peasant life; and the *Aeneid, the* epic tale of Aeneas' wanderings after the fall of Troy and his life in Latium.

Verlaine, Paul (1844-1896), French poet, born in Metz. He is associated with the French symbolist movement but more particularly with the literary group known as the Decadents. His poetic works include *Sagesse* (1881), *Jadis et naguère* (1884), and *Mort* (1895). In his influential critical work *Arts poétique* (pub. 1884), he expressed the basic theories of symbolism in poetry.

Vermeer, Jan, also known as **Jan van der Meer van Delft** (1632-1675), Dutch painter, born in Delft. His genre paintings and portraits are brilliant studies of forms in light and shadow. They include *Diana at her Toilet, The Coquette, Young Woman with a Water Jug, The Lace Maker,* and *Lady with a Lute.*

Verne, Jules (1828-1905), French writer, born in Nantes. In Paris he became a well-known writer of librettos and comedies. The travel stories of his friends and his own interest in science led him to write the tales for which he is famous. He anticipated the submarine in *Vingt mille lieues sous les mers* (*Twenty Thousand Leagues under the Sea,* 1870) and pictured the flying machine and fast steamships in *Le tour du monde en quatre-vingt jours* (*Around the World in Eighty Days,* 1873). His other imaginative stories include *Cinq semaines en balloon* (*Five Weeks in a Balloon,* 1863), *Voyage au centre de la terre* (*Voyage to the Center of the Earth,* 1864), and *Michel Strogoff,* 1876.

Veronese, Paolo, real name **Paolo Cagliari** or **Caliari** (1528-1588), Italian painter, born in Verona. His works, frequently of religious or mythological pageants, include *Mars and Venus, Marriage at Cana, Feast of the Levite, Feast of Simon, Family of Darius Before Alexander,* and *The Adoration of the Magi.*

Verrazano, Giovanni da (c.1485-c.1528), Italian navigator, born near Florence. In 1524 he explored the North American coast, probably in the service of Francis I. He discovered Manhattan, the Hudson River, and Narragansett Bay. The Verrazano-Narrows Bridge across New York Bay is named in his honor.

Verrocchio, Andrea del, real name **Andrea di Michele di Francesco Cione** (1435-1488), Italian painter and sculptor, born in Florence. His works include the paintings *Baptism of Christ* and *Madonna and Child,* a bronze statue of David, an equestrian statue of Gen. Bartolommeo Colleoni, and the sarcophagus of Cosimo de Medici. He was a leading sculptor of the Tuscan School.

Vesalius, Andreas (1514-1564), Flemish anatomist and physician born in Brussels. His principal work *De humani corporis fabrica* (*On the Structure of the Human Body,* 1543) was the first substantial contribution to anatomy since the days of Galen. Vesalius turned from slavish study of the ancient writers to actual dissection and observation. He is thus an important figure of the Renaissance revolt against authority in favor of observation and induction that ushered in the modern scientific era. Vesalius was also considered as one of the boldest and most skillful of the early urgeonss.

Vespasian, in full **Titus Flavius Sabinus Vespasianus** (9-79 A.D.), Roman emperor, born near Reate in Latium. In 43 A.D. he headed an expedition to Britain and conquered the Isle of Wight. He was consul (51) and proconsul (63) of Rome's African provinces. In 66 he waged war in Judaea. In 69 he was declared emperor and seized Rome from Vitellius and Otho. He began the construction of the Colosseum (completed by his son Titus) and sent Agricola to Britain, where North Wales and Anglesea were added to the empire.

Vespucci, Amerigo (1451-1512), Italian navigator, geographer, and explorer, born in Florence. After working as a provision contractor, furnishing supples for sea voyages, he made several voyages to the New World (1497, 1499, 1501, 1503, 1505, and 1507). On the first, the mainland of North America was discovered. The continents of North and South America were named for him.

Victor Emmanuel II (1820-1878), last king of Sardinia (1849-1861) and first king of Italy (1861-1878). He was born in Turin and succeeded his father, Charles Albert. Through the diplomacy of his prime minister, Camillo di Cavour, Italy was united under Sardinia. After defeating Austria in a short war (1859-1861), Sardinia annexed Lombardy, Tuscany, Modena, Parma, and Romagna. With Garibaldi's victory in the

COLUMBIA UNIVERSITY
MARK VAN DOREN

CULVER
THORSTEIN VEBLEN

Veblen, Thorstein Bunde (1857-1929), American economist and social scientist, born in Cato, Wis., and educated at Carleton College, Johns Hopkins, and Yale. A severe and incisive critic of modern social and economic institutions, he wrote *The Theory of the Leisure Class* (1899); *The Theory of Business Enterprise* (1904); *The Higher Learning in America* (1918); and *The Vested Interests and the State of the Industrial Arts* (1919). He originated the phrase "conspicuous consumption" in describing the economic waste of the wealthy.

Vecchio, Palma. See *Palma, Jacopo.*

Vega, Lope de, in full **Lope Félix de Vega Carpio,** called **El Fénix de España** (1562-1635), Spanish playwright, born in Madrid. He is said to have written 1,000 plays and more than 400 other works, including novels, epics, and poems. He founded the Spanish national theater. His works include the poem *La Hermosura de Angélica;* the short *Rimas; El Peregrino en su patria,* a romance; *Jerusalén conquistada,* an epic patterned after that of the Italian poet Tasso; *Gatomaquia,* a mock heroic poem; and *Dorotea,* a prose drama. Some of his famous plays are *El Castigo sin venganza, Porfiar hasta morir, La Estrella de Sevilla, Azero de Madrid, El principe perfecto, La Fuente ovejuna,* and *El mejor alcalde el rey.*

Velázquez or **Velásquez, Diego Rodríguez de Silva y** (1599-1660), Spanish painter, born in Seville. He studied under Francisco de Herrera and Francisco Pacheco. In 1623 he

He led a futile revolt in 1935 to prevent the recall of George II (Constantine's son) to the throne. He then fled to France, where he died.

Vercingetorix (d.46 B.C.), Gallic leader, chief of the Averni. He led a revolt against Julius Caesar, which began the Gallic wars, and won several battles against the Roman armies. He was defeated at Alesia · in 52 B.C., taken to Rome as a prisoner, and exhibited in public ceremonies lauding Caesar's triumph. After some years, he was executed.

Verdi, Giuseppe (1813-1901), Italian operatic composer, born in Le Roncole, near Busseto. He received his early musical training from the organist of Busseto Cathedral, Antonio Barezzi. After being refused admission to the Milan Conservatory in 1832, he studied in Milan at La Scala with Vincenzo Lavigna. Verdi achieved his first success with his opera *Nabucodonoser,* or *Nabucco* (1842) and from then on he rapidly achieved world renown. Among his 26 operas are *Ernani* (1844), *Rigoletto* (1851), Il *Trovatore* (1852), *La Traviata* (1853), *La Forza del Destino* (1862), *Don Carlos* (1867), *Aïda* (1871), *Otello* (1887), and *Falstaff* (1893).

Vergil or **Virgil,** in full **Publius Vergilius Maro** (70-19 B.C.), Roman poet, born near Mantua in Cisalpine Gaul. He studied in Cremona, Milan, Naples, and Rome. He returned to Rome (c.41-40 B.C.), where Augustus, Maecenas, and Asinius Pollio became his patrons, and Horace his intimate friend. His works include the *Eclogues* or

CAMERA PRESS-PIX

ROYALTY: King Victor Emmanuel II of Italy (*left*) and Queen Victoria of England (*right*).

South overthrowing the rulers of the Kingdom of the Two Sicilies, and Cavour's success in linking Garibaldi's territory to that controlled by the government in Sardinia, the Kingdom of Italy was established in 1861 with Victor Emmanuel II as constitutional monarch. Only Venetia and Rome were not included in the initial kingdom, but they were annexed in 1866 and 1870 respectively.

Victor Emmanuel III (1869–1947), king of Italy, born in Naples, son of King Humbert I and grandson of Victor Emmanuel II. Under his rule Italy participated in World War I and increased her territory during and after the Treaty of Versailles to include Zara and the Adriatic Islands and Fiume. He assumed the titles of Emperor of Ethiopia in 1936 and King of Albania in 1939. He surrendered to the rise of Fascism after 1922, the year of Benito Mussolini's successful march on Rome. In 1946 he abdicated and his son, Humbert II, became king.

Victoria, in full **Alexandrina Victoria** (1819–1901), queen of the United Kingdom of Great Britain and Ireland and empress of India. She was born in the royal palace at Kensington, London, the only child of Edward, duke of Kent (fourth son of George III). Her mother was Victoria Maria Louisa, a daughter of the duke of Saxe-Coburg-Gotha. Only William IV, the reigning king, stood between her and the English throne after she was 10 years old. However, until she was 12 she was not told that she was destined to be the future queen of millions of subjects. When informed of her future power and dignity, she is reported to have said simply, "I will be good." She succeeded William IV on his death (June 20, 1837) and married her cousin, Prince Albert of Saxe-Coburg-Gotha in 1840. Victoria became the mother of four sons and five daughters.

Victoria made her influence felt in the political affairs of the empire, although as a constitutional monarch she followed the policy of her prime ministers. Among these were Melbourne, Peel, Palmerston, Disraeli, Gladstone, and Salisbury. During her long reign, major political, social, economic, and scientific changes occurred in the British Empire. The British Empire was considerably enlarged; Canada, New Zealand, and Australia were granted self-government; successive reform bills extended the franchise; free trade was adopted; wars were waged in China and Afghanistan; and the Indian Mutiny of 1857 was suppressed. In Africa there were Zulu wars, the Boer War, and the South African War. In Europe, England took part in the Crimean War. Prince Albert, Victoria's husband, died in 1861. Under her rule the court obeyed strict rules of propriety. Her influence was reflected in social life throughout the empire.

Viète or **Vieta, François,** Seigneur de la **Bigotière** (1540–1603), French mathematician, born in Fontenay-le-Comte. While in the service of Henry IV of France, he discovered the key to the code in which Spain sent secret messages to the Netherlands. He is regarded as the father of modern algebra.

Vignola, Giacomo da, real name **Giacomo Barocchio** or **Barozzi** (1507–1573), Italian architect, born in Vignola, near Modena. In 1564 he succeeded Michelangelo as chief architect for St. Peter's. His greatest work was designing the Church, Il Gesù, and the Villa di Papa Giulio for Pope Julius III. He wrote books on the five orders of architecture and on principles of perspective.

Vigny, Comte Alfred Victor de (1797–1863), French poet and novelist, born in Loches. He was an admirer of Victor Hugo and associated with the French Romantics of his own generation. Vigny wrote many volumes of poetry, plays, and novels, including *Poèmes* (1822), *Éloa, ou la Soeur des anges* (1824), *Poèmes antiques et modernes* (1826), the historical novel *Cinq-Mars* (1826), and the romatic play *Chatterton* (1835).

Villa, Francisco, real name **Doroteo Arango,** known as **Pancho Villa** (1877–1923), Mexican revolutionary, born in Río Grande, Durango, Mexico. He began his career as a bandit and cattle thief and developed a reputation as a modern Robin Hood. He supported Francisco Madero as provisional president of Mexico (1910), and later Pres. Victoriano Huerta. He then supported Venustiano Carranzo, who was attempting to overthrow Huerta, but later turned against Carranzo when the latter forced Huerta out of office and was recognized by the U.S. as de facto president. When Villa and his forces raided Columbus, New Mexico, in 1916 in protest against American recognition of Carranzo, Col. John J. Pershing was sent into Mexico with an army to capture him, but Villa escaped. In 1920 Villa made peace with the government that succeeded Carranza's. He was killed by his own men three years later.

Villard, Henry, originally **Ferdinand Heinrich Gustav Hilgard** (1835–1900), American publisher and financier, born in Speyer, Bavaria. He came to the U.S. in 1853 and was a newspaper correspondent during the Civil War. He organized the Northern Pacific Railroad in 1881, founded the Edison General Electric Company in 1889, and became owner of the New York *Evening Post* in 1881.

Villiers de L'Isle-Adam, Comte Philippe Auguste Mathias de (1838–1889), French writer, born in St. Brieuc, Brittany. He became one of the first members of the French symbolist movement. Contemptuous of democracy and materialism, he was influenced greatly by Vigny, Poe, Wagner, and Baudelaire. His works include *Premières Poésies* (1856–1858), the symbolic novel *Isis* (1862), the poetic drama *Axël* (pub. 1890), regarded as his masterpiece, the short stories *Contes cruels* (1883) and the plays *Élan* and *Morgane* (1862).

Villon, François (1431–c.1463), French poet born in Paris. A vagabond and in frequent trouble with the police, Villon was condemned to death in 1463. The sentence was commuted to exile from Paris, but it is thought that he died soon thereafter. Villon was one of the greatest lyric poets of his time. His works are gay and tender but show a preoccupation with death. Most of his works are collected in *Petit testament* (1456) and *Grand testament* (1461); each is in the form of a burlesque will. Among the best-known individual poems are *Prayer for our Lady* and the *Ballad of Dead Ladies,* with the refrain "Where are the snows of Yesteryear?"

Vincent, Jean Hyacinthe (1862–1950), French physician, born in Bordeaux. He discovered the bacteria causing Vincent's angina or Vincent's infection (known as trench mouth). He also produced a serum to treat gas gangrene and a vaccine for typhoid.

Vincent de Paul, Saint (c.1581–1660), French Roman Catholic priest, born in Pouy, Gascony. He was ordained a priest in 1600. In 1625 he founded the Congregation of the Priests of the Mission, often called *Lazarists* or *Vincentians,* and in 1632 the Mission of Sisters of Charity. He was canonized by Pope Clement XII in 1737. His feast day is July 19.

Vincent of Beauvais (c.1190–c.1264), French Dominican and scholar. He compiled the *Speculum Majus,* an encyclopedia in all branches of knowledge known in his time.

Vinci, Leonardo da (1452–1519), Italian painter, sculptor, architect, scientist, and engineer, born in Vinci, near Florence. A man of astonishing versatility and genius, Leonardo achieved as great a fame in science as in the arts. His paintings include the *Last Supper, Mona Lisa, The Virgin of the Rocks,* and *The Virgin and Child with St. Anne.* He was one of the architects who built the Milan cathedral. In addition, he constructed the Martesana Canal, designed and invented machinery, made plans for tunneling and swamp draining projects, and made several experiments in the effort to develop a method of mechanical flight. He is the author of *Notes for a Treatise on Painting.*

Vinson, Frederick Moore (1890–1953), American legislator, government official, and twelfth chief justice of the United States. He was born in Louisa, Ky., educated at Centre College and Kentucky Normal College, and he began the practice of law in 1911. He represented Kentucky in Congress (1923–1929, 1931–1931) and was an active supporter of Pres. Franklin D. Roosevelt's New Deal programs. He then served as associate justice in the U.S. Court of Appeals for the District of Columbia (1939–1943). He was director of the Office of Economic Stabilization (1943–1945), director of the Office of War Mobilization and Reconstruction, and was then appointed secretary of the treasury by Pres. Harry S Truman. He served until 1946, when he was chosen chief justice of the Supreme Court.

Viollet-le-Duc, Eugène Emmanuel (1814–1879), French architect, born in Paris. An expert on Gothic architecture, he helped restore many medieval buildings, notably the cathedral of Notre Dame in Paris and the Château de Pierrefonds. He also compiled two architectural dictionaries.

Virgil. See *Vergil.*

Vishinsky. See *Vyshinsky.*

Vitruvius Pollio, Marcus (1st century B.C.), Roman architect and engineer. He was military engineer to Emperor Augustus, and served in Africa. His major work, *De architectura,* greatly influenced the development of Renaissance architecture.

Vivaldi, Antonio (c.1675–1741), Italian composer, born in Venice. A prolific composer, he produced more than 40 operas, 48 sonatas, 400 concertos, and 50 sacred works. His best-known work today is the suite *The Four Seasons* (1725).

Vlaminck, Maurice de (1876–1958), French painter, born in Paris. With Henri Matisse and others, he founded the Fauvist school of art. He is noted for his water-colors and oils of landscapes and still life.

Volney, Constantin François de Chasseboeuf, Comte de (1757–1820), French scholar, born in Craon. He was a member of the States-General in 1789 and of the National Assembly. Under Louis XVIII he was made a peer. In his major work, *Ruines, ou méditations sur les révolutions des empires* (1791), he set forth his theories on the equality of man and the importance of natural religion.

Volstead, Andrew Joseph (1860–1947), American legislator, born in Goodhue County, Minn. A member of the U.S. Congress (1903–1923), he was the author of the Volstead Act (passed over the veto of Pres. Woodrow Wilson in October, 1919), which defined an intoxicating beverage as one containing more than 0.5 per cent alcohol. This made possible the enforcement of prohibition under the eighteenth amendment.

Volta, Count **Allessandro** (1745–1827), Italian physicist, born in Como. He was professor of physics at Como (1774–1779) and at Pavia (1779-1804). He discovered constant-current electricity and invented the voltaic pile, the first primary battery; an electric condenser; and the electrophorus. The volt was named in his honor.

Voltaire, assumed name of **Francois Marie Arouet** (1694–1778), French writer, born in Paris. He was educated at the Jesuit Collège Louis le Grand in Paris. Frequently in trouble for his social and political satires, he was imprisoned in the Bastille in 1717 and again in 1726. He lived in England (1726-1729), at the Château de Cirey in Lorraine with Madame du Châtelet (1734-1749), at the court of Frederick the Great of Prussia (1750–1753), and at Ferney, France, near Geneva (1758–1778) with his niece, Madame Denis. Among his works are *Lettres philosophiques* (1734), in praise of English institutions; the historical works *Le Siècle de Louis XIV* (1751), *Charles XII* (1730), and *Essai sur les moeurs* (1756); the satirical novel *Candide* (1759); the philosophical poems *Discours sur l'Homme* (1738), and *Poème sur le désastre de Lisbonne* (1756); and a dictionary of philosophy, *Dictionnaire Philosophique* (1764).

VOLTAIRE, eighteenth-century French satirist.

Vondel, Joost van den (1587–1679), Dutch poet and dramatist, born in Cologne, Germany. Author of several satirical poems concerning the religious disputes of his times, he also wrote Biblical and historical dramas; lyric, historical, and religious poems; and translations of the Greek and Latin classics. His works include *Jephtha* (1659) and *Lucifer*, a religious drama (1654).

Vorländer, Karl (1860–1928), German philosopher who tried to synthesize the theories of Kant and those of Marxian socialism. He edited the works of Kant (9 vols., 1901–1924), and was the author of *Kant and Socialism* (1900), *Kant and Marx* (1911), and *Marx, Engels, and Lasalle as Philosophers* (1920).

Vuillard, Jean Édouard (1868–1940), French painter, born in Cuiseaux. Influenced by Pierre Bonnard, with whom he shared a studio at one time, and by Gaugin and Japanese painters, he specialized in floral still lifes and interior scenes.

Vyshinsky, Andrei Yanuaryevich (1883–1954), Soviet government official, born in Odessa. He received a law degree at the University of Kiev in 1913. An active Bolshevist supporter during the Russian revolution of 1917, he joined the Communist party in 1920. In 1925 he became rector of Moscow University and in 1935 was appointed procurator (attorney general) of the Soviet Union, serving as public prosecutor during the purge trials (1936–1939). In 1939 he became a member of the central committee of the Communist party, and in 1940 he was appointed deputy commissar for foreign affairs; in this office he helped to establish Communist governments in Latvia (1940) and in Romania (1945). He was present at the Potsdam Conference and frequently headed the Soviet delegation to the United Nations. He was Soviet minister of foreign affairs (1949–1953) and first deputy foreign minister from 1953 to 1954.

W

Waddington, William Henry (1826–1894), French statesman and archaeologist, born in Paris of English parents. He was premier of France (1879) and French ambassador to Great Britain (1883–1893). On the basis of travels in Greece, Syria, and Asia Minor he wrote *Voyage archéologique en Grèce et Asie Mineure* (1866–1877).

Wade, Benjamin Franklin (1800–1878), American politician and lawyer, born near Springfield, Mass. As a U.S. senator from Ohio (1851–1869), he was intransigent and uncompromising in his opposition to slavery and his support of radical Reconstruction policies after the Civil War. He helped write the Wade-Davis Manifesto of 1864 (vetoed by Pres. Abraham Lincoln), which would have asserted congressional supremacy over the executive branch of government in carrying out Reconstruction. Wade was a firm opponent of Pres. Andrew Johnson and voted to convict Johnson during his impeachment trial.

Wagner, Richard, in full **Wilhelm Richard Wagner** (1813–1883), outstanding German operatic composer, born in Leipzig. As a boy he developed a great interest in the music of Beethoven, and he studied under several composers as well as at the University of Leipzig. He was a musical director in Magdeburg, Riga, and Königsberg (1834–1839), and spent the next few years in Paris, where he composed *Eine Faust-ouvertüre* (1840) and the operas *Rienzi* (1840) and *Der Fliegende Holländer* (1841). From Paris he went to Dresden, where he was appointed court Kapellmeister in 1843. After participating in the insurrection of 1848–1849 he fled to Switzerland. *Tannhäuser* had appeared in 1845 and *Lohengrin* in 1848. In 1872 he moved to Bayreuth. At the new theater there his famous tetralogy *Der Ring des Nibelungen,* consisting of *Das Rheingold, Die Walküre, Siegfried,* and *Götterdämmerung,* was performed in 1876. Then followed *Tristan und Isolde* (1859), *Die Meistersinger von Nürnberg* (1867), and *Parsifal* (1882). Frequently selecting his subjects from old German heroic legends, Wagner tried in his works to weave poetry, music, and drama into a balanced whole.

Waite, Morrison Remick (1816–1888), American jurist, born in Lyme, Conn. He graduated from Yale in 1837, joined an Ohio law office and was admitted to the bar in 1839. He rose to distinction and in 1871 was one of the tribunal to negotiate the *Alabama* claims. In 1874 Pres. Ulysses S. Grant named him as chief justice of the United States Supreme Court.

Wald, Lillian D. (1867–1940), American social worker, born in Cincinnati, Ohio. She founded (1893) the Henry Street Settlement in New York City. In 1902 she organized the first city school nursing service in the world. She was also instrumental in the establishment of the Federal Children's Bureau (1908) and the town and country nursing service of the Red Cross.

Walker, William (1824–1860), American adventurer, born in Nashville, Tenn. A graduate of the University of Nashville (1838), he earned a medical degree at the University of Pennsylvania (1843). After a brief career as a newspaper publisher in New Orleans, he went to California in 1850 to look for gold. In 1853 he tried to conquer the Mexican state of Sonora with a group of followers. Thwarted, he fled across the border and surrendered to U.S. authorities. He was tried for violating neutrality laws, but was acquitted. In 1855 he invaded Nicaragua and proclaimed himself president of that country and of Costa Rica. Forced out of Nicaragua after a year, he tried in 1860 to capture Honduras. He was seized by Honduras authorities, court-martialed, convicted, and executed.

Wallace, Alfred Russel (1823–1913), English naturalist, born in Usk. He developed a theory of evolution through natural selection at the same time as Charles Darwin. An extensive traveler, influential naturalist and social philosopher, he wrote *Travels on the Amazon and Rio Negro* (1853), *The Malay Archipelago* (1869), *Darwinism* (1889), *Man's Place in the Universe* (1903), and *Social Environment and Moral Progress* (1912).

Wallace, Henry Agard (1888–1965), American public official, born in Adair County, Iowa. Educated at Iowa State College, he took over the magazine *Wallace's Farmer* from his father. Wallace was secretary of agriculture (1933–1940) and vice-president (1941–1945). Appointed secretary of commerce in 1945, he became critical of administration policies toward Russia, and resigned in 1946 at the request of Pres. Harry S. Truman. He was editor of the *New Republic* (1946–1947) and the unsuccessful Progressive party candidate for the presidency in 1948.

Wallace, Lewis, known as **Lew Wallace** (1827–1905), American writer and soldier, born in Brookville, Ind. He was a lieutenant in the Mexican War and then entered law practice. A colonel and then major general during the Civil War, he became governor of the territory of New Mexico in 1878 and was minister to Turkey (1881–1885). He is the author of *Ben Hur* (1880), one of the best sellers of all time. His other works include *The Fair God* (1873) and *The Prince of India* (1893).

Wallace, Sir William (c.1272–1305), Scottish national hero, believed to have been born in Elderslie. He and his followers drove the English out of much of Scotland, and Wallace then proclaimed himself warden of the country. He was defeated by Edward I at Falkirk. He again tried to remove the English from Scotland but was seized in Glasgow in 1305, taken to London, and executed.

Wallach, Otto (1847–1931), German chemist, born in Königsberg, Prussia. He was director of the Chemical Institute of Göttingen (1889–1915). He carried out valuable research in the composition of essential oils and terpenes and received the Nobel Prize for chemistry in 1910.

Wallenstein, Albrecht Wenzel Eusebius von, Duke of **Friedland** and **Mecklenburg,** Prince of **Sagan** (1583–1634), Austrian gen-

GERMAN TOURIST INFORMATION OFFICE

RICHARD WAGNER'S opera *Lohengrin* as it was staged by the Bayreuth Wagner Festival.

eral, born in Hermanice, Bohemia. He gained fame as commander of the Imperial armies during much of the Thirty Years' War. He was defeated by Gustavus Adolphus of Sweden at the Battle of Lützen (1632), in which Gustavus was killed. Jealous of Wallenstein's ambition and success, many of the German princes persuaded Emperor Ferdinand II to remove him from power. He was assassinated in Eger, Bohemia.

Wallis, John (1616–1703), English mathematician born in Ashford, Kent. In his book *Arithmetica infinitorum* (1655), he expressed his conception of limit, which became the basis for the development of differential and integral calculus and the binomial theorem. He introduced the symbol for infinity.

Walpole, Horace, 4th Earl of **Orford** (1717–1797), English writer, born in London and educated at Cambridge. In 1757 he purchased his famous estate, Strawberry Hill, Twickenham, where he collected works of art and curios. He installed a private printing shop and published his own works and those of his friends. Among his works are *Anecdotes of Painting in England* (1762–1771) and *The Castle of Otranto* (1764), one of the first Gothic romances. His fame as a writer rests, however, on his witty and charming letters, many of which have been collected and published.

Walpole, Sir Hugh Seymour (1884–1941), English novelist, born in Auckland, New Zealand. He taught for a time, then served with the Russian Red Cross in World War I. Among his novels are *Fortitude* (1913), *Dark Forest* (1916), *Jeremy* (1919), *The Cathedral* (1922), *Harmer John* (1926), *Judith Paris* (1931), *The Fortress* (1932), and *Vanessa* (1933).

Walpole, Sir Robert, 1st Earl of **Orford** (1676–1745), English statesman, born in Norfolk and educated at Cambridge. He began his 40-year career in Parliament in 1701. He was secretary of war (1708–1710); treasurer of the navy (1710–1711); chancellor of the exchequer (1715–1717); and prime minister (1715–1717, 1721–1742). A strong leader, Walpole was the first to establish the principle of unity between cabinet and prime minister, owing responsibility to the House of Commons. He urged the establishment of a sinking fund for reducing the national debt, attempted to establish a sound economy, and opposed war. On his retirement in 1742 he was created earl of Orford.

Walsh, Thomas James (1859–1933), American legislator, born in Two Rivers, Wis., and educated at the University of Wisconsin. In 1890 he moved to Helena, Mont., where he practiced law and entered politics. He was elected to the U.S. Senate in 1912 and remained in office until his death. Walsh received nation-wide attention in 1923 when he directed the investigation of the leasing of naval oil reserves in the Teapot Dome inquiry.

Walter, Bruno, real name **Bruno Schlesinger** (1876–1962), German conductor, born in Berlin and educated at the Stern Conservatory there. An opera and symphony conductor in Austria and Germany (1901–1938), he came to the U.S., in 1939. After conducting several orchestras, he was conductor of the New York Philharmonic from 1947 until his retirement in 1957.

Walter, Thomas Ustick (1804–1887), American architect, born in Philadelphia, Pa. He designed Girard College in Philadelphia in 1833. In 1848 his design for the wings and dome of the Capitol in Washington, D.C., was adopted. In Washington, also, he designed the extensions of the patent office, treasury, and post office buildings.

Walther von der Vogelweide (c.1170–c.1230), German poet, believed to have been born in the Austrian Tirol. One of the greatest lyric poets of the Middle Ages, he wandered from court to court singing his songs, which were frequently critical on political and religious subjects. He is also known for his love songs, one of the most famous being *Unter der Linden.* Among his religious songs is *Kreuzlied.*

Walton, Izaak (1593–1683), English writer, born in Stafford. He was an ironmonger in London until 1644, when he retired from business and became a writer. Fishing was his delight and in 1653 he published *The Compleat Angler, or the Contemplative Man's Recreation,* a book noted for its gracious prose style and charming glimpses of rural scenes and pastimes. Walton also wrote biographies of John Donne, Richard Hooker, and George Herbert.

Warbeck, Perkin (1479–1499), Flemish pretender to the English throne during the reign of Henry VII. Born in Tournai, Flanders, he claimed to be one of the two young sons of King Edward IV who were killed in the Tower of London by their uncle, Richard III. Among his supporters were the Emperor Maximilian and Charles VIII of France. Warbeck went to England in 1495, then to Scotland, where James IV married him to Lady Catherine Gordon. He went to Cornwall in 1499 and raised a rebel army but surrendered when the royal forces attacked. He was imprisoned in the Tower of London and executed while attempting to escape.

Warburg, Otto Heinrich (1883–), German physiologist, born in Freiburg. He was acclaimed for his research on the composition and respiration of living cells and enzymes, for which he was awarded the Nobel Prize in 1931.

Ward, John Quincy Adams (1830–1910), American sculptor, born in Urbana, Ohio. His many statues, which were commissioned for public monuments, include the *Indian Hunter and Pilgrim* in Central Park, New York; *Washington* in Wall Street, New York; *Horace Greeley* in Greeley Square, New York; and *Henry Ward Beecher* in Brooklyn, New York. He also did statues of Gen. Philip H. Sheridan and Gen. George Thomas in Washington, D.C., and of John Hancock in Philadelphia.

Ward, Mary Augusta Arnold, known as **Mrs. Humphrey Ward** (1851–1920), English novelist, born in Hobart, Tasmania, Australia. She was the granddaughter of Thomas Arnold, the famed master of Rugby. In 1872 she married Thomas Humphry Ward, a teacher, writer, and critic, and settled with him in London. Her novels include *Robert Elsmere* (1888), *David Grieve* (1892), and *The Marriage of William Ashe* (1905).

Warner, Seth (1743–1784), American Revolutionary War hero, born in Roxbury, Conn. He was a leader with Ethan Allen in resisting the claim of New York to the territory that is now Vermont, and as a result was outlawed by New York authorities in 1771. When the Revolutionary War began, he was a leader of the Green Mountain Boys, and he captured Crown Point from the British. Later he took part in the invasion of Canada and in other campaigns.

Warren, Earl (1891–), chief justice of the U.S. Supreme Court, born in Los Angeles, Calif. After graduating from the University of California in 1912, he practiced law in San Francisco and Oakland. He was an infantry lieutenant in World War I (1917–1918). Warren became interested in politics, holding the office of attorney general of California (1939–1942). In 1942 he was elected governor of California, and was reelected for two additional terms. In 1953 he was appointed chief justice. He was an unsuccessful Republican candidate for vice-president in 1948.

Warren, Joseph (1741–1775), American Revolutionary leader, born in Roxbury, Mass., and educated at Harvard. He became a leading physician in Boston. He was prominent in the opposition to the Stamp Act and supported forcible resistance against England. Warren was a member of the original Committee of Correspondence in Boston, and it was he who sent Paul Revere on his famous ride. He was killed at Bunker Hill.

Warren, Robert Penn (1905–), American author, poet, and critic, born in Guthrie, Ky. He graduated from Vanderbilt University, studied at the Universities of California and Yale, and was a Rhodes scholar at Oxford. Among his novels are *Night Rider* (1939), *At Heaven's Gate* (1943), *All the King's Men* (1946, awarded Pulitzer Prize in 1947), *World Enough and Time* (1950), *Band of Angels* (1955), *The Cave* (1959), and *Wilderness* (1961). For his *Promises: Poems 1954–1956* (pub. 1957), he was awarded the Pulitzer Prize in 1958. He has written critical works on poetry, fiction, and literary theory.

Warwick, Earl of. See *Neville, Richard.*

Washington, Booker Taliaferro (1856–1915), American Negro educator, born a slave in Franklin County, Va. He was educated at the Hampton Institute, supporting himself by working as a janitor. In 1879 he became a teacher at Hampton and in 1881 was chosen by the state authorities to organize and lead Tuskegee Institute for the vocational and professional training of Negroes. His autobiography, *Up from Slavery,* was published in 1901.

Washington, George (1732–1799), first president of the United States (1789–1797), born in Westmoreland County, Va. He was the great-grandson of John Washington, an Englishman who had emigrated in 1657, and the son of Augustine Washington, a wealthy planter. He received his education at home, and worked briefly as a surveyor. His military career began at the age of 20, when he was appointed district adjutant of the Virginia militia. He served in the French and Indian War and in 1755 was with the expedition under Gen. Edward Braddock that was routed at the Monongahela River, near Fort Duquesne. In 1758 he was an important member of the expedition that captured Fort Duquesne.

When he returned to his home, Mount Vernon, it was as its master. He had inherited it upon the death of his elder half brother, Lawrence, in 1752. In 1759 he married Mrs. Martha Custis, a wealthy widow. He was a member of the Virginia House of Burgesses (1759–1774) and a member of the first and second Continental Congresses. Shortly after the outbreak of the American Revolution, Washington was appointed commander in chief of the American forces. Guiding American troops until the independence of the 13 colonies was finally achieved, he then retired from the army.

In 1787 he presided at the Constitutional Convention in Philadelphia. He was chosen as the first president of the newly formed United States and was inaugurated in New York on April 30, 1789. He was reluctantly persuaded to serve a second term in office. In 1796 he declined reelection and returned in the following year to Mount Vernon. In 1798, when war threatened with France, he again took command of the army.

Wassermann, August von (1866–1925), German bacteriologist, born in Bamberg. He was director of research at the Koch Institute for Infectious Diseases in Berlin and later at the Kaiser Wilhelm Institute in Berlin-Dahlem. He is best known for devising the Wassermann test for syphilis.

Watson, John Broadus (1878–1958), American psychologist, born in Greenville, S.C. He studied at Furman University and the

WIDE WORLD
EARL WARREN

LOOK MAGAZINE
ROBERT PENN WARREN

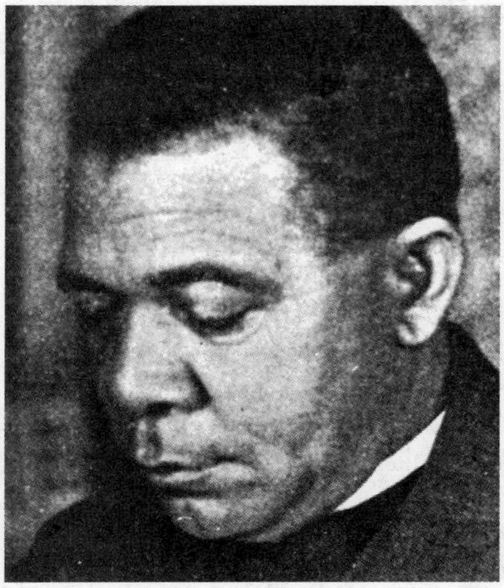

NEW YORK PUBLIC LIBRARY

BOOKER T. WASHINGTON

University of Chicago. He taught at Chicago and Johns Hopkins universities and in 1920 entered the advertising business in New York City. He is known chiefly as the originator of the Behaviorist school of psychology, which explains all human behavior as conditioned responses to external stimuli. He was editor of the *Psychological Review* (1908–1915) and of the *Journal of Experimental Psychology* (1915–1927). His books include *Behavior* (1914), *Behaviorism* (1925), and *Ways of Behaviorism* (1928).

Watt, James (1736–1819), Scottish engineer and inventor, born in Greenock. At the University of Glasgow he was mathematical instrument maker from 1757 to 1763. He improved the steam engine of Thomas Newcomen by creating a separate condenser. In later years he continually improved steam engine designs, inventing a double-acting engine in 1782. He invented a sun-and-planet wheel, a governor, and copying ink. He also conducted significant research on the composition of water. Watt was the first to use the term *horsepower*. The watt (unit of electrical power) is named for him.

Watteau, Jean Antoine (1684–1721), French painter, born in Valenciennes. He studied painting in Paris. His festive pastoral scenes, filled with elegantly costumed figures, show an expert handling of design and color. Watteau is regarded as the master of the rococo style. His paintings include *Embarquement pour Cythere, L'assemblée dans un parc, Les amusements champêtres,* and *La gamme d'amour*.

Watterson, Henry, known as **Marse Henry** (1840–1921), American journalist, born in Washington, D.C. He served with distinction in the Confederate army and later settled at Louisville, Ky., where he founded the *Courier-Journal*, and became known as one of the foremost American editors. After the Civil War he campaigned for civil rights for Negroes and reconciliation between the North and South. He served in the U.S. Congress (1876–1877). His paper gave editorial support to the entrance of the U.S. into World War I, for which he was awarded the Pulitzer Prize for journalism in 1917. He wrote *The Compromises of Life* (1903) and *"Marse Henry": An Autobiography* (1919). His editorials were published in 1923.

Watts, George Frederic (1817–1904), English painter and sculptor, born in London. His paintings include *Caractacus, Life's Illusions, Sir Galahad, Love and Death,* and *Paolo and Francesca*. He painted portraits of Browning, Tennyson, Gladstone, Carlyle, and other prominent men. His best-known sculpture is *Physical Energy*, a bronze memorial to Cecil Rhodes.

Waugh, Evelyn Arthur St. John (1903–1966), English novelist, born in London, the son of Arthur Waugh, a literary critic. He attended Hertford College, Oxford. His novels, frequently bitter satires of contemporary society, include *Decline and Fall* (1929), *Vile Bodies* (1930), *A Handful of Dust* (1934), *Put Out More Flags* (1942), *Brideshead Revisited* (1945), *The Loved One* (1948), *Helena* (1950), and *Men at Arms* (1952).

Wayne, Anthony (1745–1796), American general, born in Chester County, Pa. A colonel at the beginning of the Revolutionary War, he led an expedition into Canada, and showed a great sense of strategy in covering the retreat of his troops. He commanded Fort Ticonderoga until 1777, when he was made brigadier general. His most brilliant victory was at Stony Point in 1779 over the British. Known as "Mad Anthony" for his daring, he became a major general and in later years was sent to subdue the Indians in the Northwest. He represented Georgia in the U.S. Congress (1791–1792).

Webb, Sidney James, 1st Baron **Passfield** (1859–1947), English economist, statesman, and social reformer, born in London. A founding member of the Fabian Society, he taught economics at the University of London (1912–1927), was a member of the London County Council (1892–1910), and of the royal poor law commission (1905–1909). He was a founder (1913) of the *New Statesman* and a dedicated supporter of the London School of Economics and Political Science. He was a member of Parliament (1922–1929), president of the Board of Trade (1924), secretary of state for the colonies (1929–1931), and for the dominions (1929–1930). In much of his work, he was aided by his wife, **Beatrice Webb** (1858–1943), with whom he wrote *History of Trade Unionism* (1894), *Consumers' Co-operative Movement* (1921), *Soviet Communism: A New Civilization?* (2 vols., 1935), and *The Truth about Soviet Russia* (1942). Alone he wrote *Socialism in England* (1890), *The Co-operative Movement in Great Britain* (1891), and *My Apprenticeship* (1926).

Weber, Baron **Karl Maria Fredrich Ernst von** (1786–1826), German composer and operatic conductor, born in Eutin. He was a conductor in Breslau (1804–1806), in Prague (1813–1817), and in Dresden in 1817. His operas include *Das Waldmädchen* (1800), *Peter Schmoll und seine Nachbarn* (1803), *Rübezahl* (unfinished), *Abu Hassan* (1811), *Der Freischütz* (1821), *Euryanthe* (1823), and *Oberon* (1826). He also composed sonatas, chamber music, overtures, chorals, cantatas, songs, mixed quartets, and two masses.

Weber, Max (1864–1920), German sociologist and political economist, noted for his study of Protestant ethics as the motivating force behind capitalism. He was born in Erfurt and studied law. He taught at Berlin (1893), Freiburg (1894), Heidelberg (1897), and Munich (1919). Among his most important works are *The Protestant Ethic and The Spirit of Capitalism* and *The Theory of Social and Economic Organization*.

Webster, Daniel (1782–1852), American statesman and orator, born in Salisbury, N.H. He graduated from Dartmouth College in 1801, studied law at Boston, and in 1805 was admitted to the bar. He practiced law at Boscawen and later at Portsmouth, N.H. Webster entered politics as a member of the Federalist party and was elected to Congress. He took his seat in the special session of May, 1813, during the War of 1812. On June 10, 1813, he delivered his first speech, on the repeal of the Berlin and Milan decrees; his oratory and his knowledge of currency and finance won him great prestige. At the close of the session Webster moved to Boston, where he practiced law for seven years. He refused political office and became the acknowledged leader of the New England bar.

In 1822 he became a member of the Massachusetts constitutional convention and later in the same year was elected to Congress from Boston, taking his seat after an absence of seven years. He quickly gained a dominant place in the House by his oratory and his efforts to revise the criminal laws of the United States. He was elected U.S. senator from Massachusetts in 1826 and rose to great heights in debates with R. Y. Hayne and John C. Calhoun on states' rights and nullification.

Webster was secretary of state under Pres. John Tyler (1841–1843). He kept the post long enough to complete his work on the Webster-Ashburton Treaty, which settled the Northeastern boundary dispute with Great Britain. He returned to the Senate (1845–1850) and took part in the slavery disputes, but his moderate stand won favor with neither side. He served again as secretary of state under Pres. Millard Fillmore (1850–1852).

Webster was as prominent in private practice as in national affairs. He took part in many important court cases, including the Dartmouth College Case, the Rhode Island Case, and the Girard Will Case.

Webster, Noah (1758–1843), American lexicographer, born in Hartford, Conn., and educated at Yale College. He served in the Revolutionary War, practiced law in Hartford, Conn., and worked for New York newspapers. Webster served in the Massachusetts legislature and was on the board of trustees of Amherst Academy (1816–1820), serving as president (1820–1821). He helped found Amherst College (1819–1821). He was an active member of the Federalist party and edited a Federalist newspaper in New York from 1793 to 1798.

In 1783 his *Elementary Spelling Book* (often called the *Blue-Back Speller*) was published. Millions of copies were sold before his death, and it was a standard school textbook for a century. His *Philosophical and Practical Grammar of the English Language* was published in 1807. His *Compendious Dictionary* appeared in 1806, and his major work, *The American Dictionary of the English Language*, appeared in 1828. Webster had spent ten years in study before he began the seven years of actual preparation of the dictionary. He had 10,000 more words and 30,000 more definitions than had been published in any previous dictionary. He was responsible for the American method of simplified spelling—*honor* instead of the British *honour*, for example.

Wedgwood, Josiah (1730–1795), English pottery maker, born in Burslem, Staffordshire. His family had been makers of pottery for generations. In 1769 he established his own factory, called Etruria. He was impressed by discoveries of ancient Greek and Roman vases, and began to make classic shapes with small white cameo figures in relief on them. Wedgwood pottery is still being produced.

Weill, Kurt (1900–1950), German-American composer, born in Dessau, Germany. He composed the music for a number of highly popular musical plays, the most famous being *The Threepenny Opera* (1928, with libretto by Bertolt Brecht), based on John Gay's eighteenth-century work, *The Beggar's Opera*. His popular musical comedies include *Knickerbocker Holiday* (1938); *Lady in the Dark* (1941); *One Touch of Venus* (1943); *Street Scene* (1947); and *Lost in the Stars* (1949), Maxwell Anderson's stage version of *Cry, the Beloved Country*.

Weingartner, Felix von (1863–1942), Austrian composer and conductor, born in Zara. He was a conductor in Berlin, Munich, Vienna, and Basel. He composed several operas, including *Genesius* (1892), *Kain und Abel* (1914), *Dame Kobold* (1916), and *Meister Andrea* (1920), in addition to symphonies, songs, and chamber music.

Weizmann, Chaim (1874–1952), British Zionist leader and first president of Israel. He was born near Pinsk, Russia, studied chemistry in Germany, and taught at Geneva and Manchester. He became a British subject in 1916 and served as chief of the British Admiralty Laboratories in London (1916–1919). He became a leader in the Zionist movement and urged the acceptance of the Balfour Declaration of 1917, which proclaimed Palestine a Jewish homeland. Weizmann was president of the World Zionist Organization (1920–1931) and of the Jewish Agency (1929–1931, 1935–1946). After a year as head of the provisional government of Israel, he was elected its first president in 1949.

Welles, Orson, in full **George Orson Welles** (1915–), American actor, director, writer, and producer. He was born in Kenosha, Wis., and began his acting career in 1931. He became associated with radio and for several years his *Mercury Theater* provided the finest dramatic entertainment in the U.S. His famous radio production in 1938 of H. G. Wells' *War of the Worlds* was so realistic that thousands of listeners really believed that the U.S. was being invaded by Mars. Among his film successes are *Citizen Kane* (1940), *The Magnificent Ambersons* (1941), and *The Trial* (1963).

Wellington, 1st Duke of, **Arthur Wellesley** (1769–1852), British soldier and statesman, born in Dublin. He was educated at Eton College and at a military school in France. By 1797 he had reached the rank of colonel in the British army through service in Flanders and in India. He was a major general before he was 35. His military career was interrupted by his election to Parliament in 1805. He became secretary of state for Ireland two years later. In 1808 he was made a lieutenant general and sent to command the English army in the Peninsular War, which he won in a series of brilliant campaigns. He was made duke of Wellington and ambassador to Paris in 1814, and in 1815 was given command of the allied armies and defeated Napoleon at Waterloo. He was elected prime minister in 1828, but after he refused to support parliamentary reform he was defeated in 1830. He was foreign secretary under Sir Robert Peel (1834–1835) and a member of the Cabinet (1841–1846), during which time he supported Peel's repeal of the Corn Laws. From 1842 to 1846 he was commander in chief of the army.

Wells, Herbert George, known as **H. G. Wells** (1866–1946), English writer, born in Bromley, Kent, and educated at the Royal College of Science and London University. He taught in private schools for five years. In 1895 his first novel, *The Time Machine,* was published. This was the first of a long series of books on scientific subjects, written as fiction and incorporating Wells' social philosophy. It includes *The Invisible Man* (1897), *The Food of the Gods* (1904), and *The War of the Worlds* (1898). The social philosophy is more dominant in *Tono-Bungay* (1909), *Mr. Britling Sees It Through* (1916), and *The World of William Clissold* (1926). As a part of his plan of social betterment by more accurate information, he wrote *Outline of History* (1920) and *The Work, Wealth, and Happiness of Mankind* (1932). With his son, George Philip Wells, and Julian Huxley he wrote *The Science of Life* (1929).

Welsbach, Baron **Carl Auer von** (1858–1929), Austrian chemist, born in Vienna, studied at the universities of Berlin and Heidelberg. He invented the Welsbach gas mantle and burner (1885) which greatly improved gas lighting for homes. Welsbach discovered and isolated two chemical elements: neodymium and praseodymium, both rare-earth elements.

Wentworth, William Charles (1793–1872), Australian statesman, born in New South Wales. He studied at Cambridge and was admitted to the bar in 1822. Known as "the Australian patriot," he was one of the most important advocates of Australian self-government. He was a founder of the newspaper, *The Australian* (1824), and of the University of Sydney (1852).

Werfel, Franz (1890–1945), German-Czech novelist, born in Prague. His first publication *Einander* (1915), was a book of poems. Later he turned to prose, in which he was influenced by the revolutionary viewpoints he had acquired during World War I. Although he wrote several plays, he is best known for his novels, including *Verdi* (1924), *The Pure in Heart* (1929), *The Forty Days of Musa Dagh* (1933), *The Song of Bernadette* (1941), and *Jacobowsky and the Colonel* (1944). He came to the U.S. in 1940.

Werner, Alfred (1866–1919), Swiss chemist, born in Mulhouse, France. He was professor of chemistry at Zurich (1893–1919) and did valuable research on isomerism. He received the Nobel Prize in 1913.

Wesley, John (1703–1791), English religious leader, born in Epworth, Lincolnshire. While at Oxford, he and his brother Charles and a few other students formed a religious society (1729–1734). They became known as Methodists because they acted according to a strict set of self-imposed rules. Wesley and his brother went to Georgia in 1735, where they were influenced by a group of Moravians. Sent as a missionary to the colonists and Indians, John Wesley was disliked for the strict discipline he tried to introduce. After less than two years in America he returned to England, where he began preaching at open-air meetings and gathered many followers. For a time he was associated with George Whitefield, but their theological doctrines were different and they separated. Wesley's followers grew continuously in number as a movement within the Anglican Church, although they opposed its rigidly hierarchical organization.

West, Benjamin (1738–1820), American artist, born in Springfield, Pa. As a boy he taught himself to paint with homemade materials. He had studios in Philadelphia and New York, and went to Italy in 1860. From 1763 until his death he lived in London, where he was a close friend of Sir Joshua Reynolds, succeeding him as president of the Royal Academy in 1792. King George III, who had appointed him a charter member of the Academy, commissioned him for many historical paintings and royal family portraits. Among his famous works are *The Death of General Wolfe, Penn's Treaty with the Indians,* and *The Battle of La Hogue.*

West, Dame **Rebecca,** pen name of **Cicily Isabel Fairfield Andrews** (1892–), English novelist, essayist, and critic, born in Kerry, Ireland. Among her novels are *The Return of the Soldier* (1918), *The Judge* (1922), *The Thinking Reed* (1936), and *Black Lamb and Grey Falcon* (1942). Her

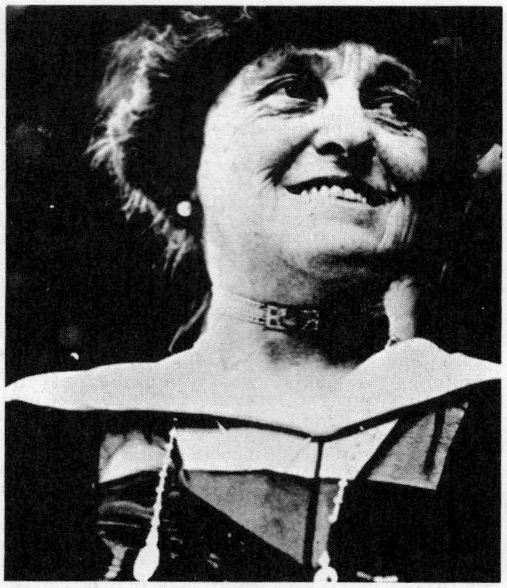

WIDE WORLD

NOVELIST of American life, Edith Wharton.

critical works include *Henry James* (1916) and *D. H. Lawrence* (1928). She also wrote *The Meaning of Treason* (1949), *The Fountain Overflows* (1957), and *The New Meaning of Treason* (1966).

Westinghouse, George (1846–1914), American inventor and manufacturer, born in Central Bridge, N.Y. He studied engineering at Union College, Schenectady. Westinghouse invented the air brake for trains, improved railway signaling devices, and attempted to increase the use of the alternating-current single phase system for transmitting electricity in the United States. In 1886 he organized the Westinghouse Electric Company.

Weyden, Rogier van der (c.1399–1464), Flemish painter, born in Tournai, Belgium. His paintings include *Descent from the Cross, St. Luke Painting the Virgin, Young Lady in a White Headdress,* and *The Last Judgement.*

Wharton, Edith Newbold Jones (1862–1937), American novelist, born in New York City and privately educated. In 1885 she married Edward Wharton, a Boston banker, and spent much of her life in France and Italy. Among her best-known books are *The House of Mirth* (1905), *Ethan Frome* (1911), *The Old Maid* (1924), and *Hudson River Bracketed* (1929). Mrs. Wharton won the Pulitzer Prize in 1920 for *The Age of Innocence.* Her autobiography, *A Backward Glance,* appeared in 1934.

Wheatstone, Sir **Charles** (1802–1875), English physicist, born in Gloucester. As professor of experimental philosophy at King's College, London, he carried out research in sound, light, and electricity. With W. J. Cooke, he invented (1837) a system for transmitting messages by means of electric currents. In 1938 he suggested the stereoscope. The Wheatstone bridge, used to measure resistance, is named for him. He was knighted in 1868.

Wheeler, Joseph (1836–1906), Confederate general, born near Augusta, Ga. He graduated from West Point (1859) and was an officer in the U.S. army. At the outbreak of the Civil War, he joined the Confederate forces. After the war he became a planter and lawyer and served in the U.S. Congress (1881–1882; 1883; 1885–1900), where he advocated reconciliation between the North and the South. He was a major general in the Spanish-American War. At his retirement he was a brigadier general.

Wheeler, Wayne Bidwell (1869–1927), American reformer, born in Brookfield, Ohio. He became superintendent of the Ohio Anti-Saloon League and was later attorney for the national society and helped draft the Volstead Act.

Wheeler, William Almon (1819–1887), vice-president of the United States, born in Malone, N.Y. He studied at the University of Vermont and became a lawyer in 1845. In Congress, as a Republican from New York (1861–1863, 1869–1877), he wrote the compromise (Wheeler Compromise) that settled the Louisiana election dispute in 1874. In 1876 he was elected vice-president on the ticket with Rutherford B. Hayes.

Whistler, James Abbott McNeill (1834–1903), American artist, born in Lowell, Mass. He traveled with his father to Moscow, where he studied at the Imperial Art Academy. He returned to the U.S. in 1849 and studied at West Point for three years. He went to Paris in 1855 and never returned to the U.S. His paintings include *Portrait of My Mother, Portrait of Carlyle, The White Girl, The Peacock Room, Blue Wave—Biarritz,* and *Trafalgar Square.* Among his etchings are the *Thames Series* and the *Venice Series.*

White, Elwyn Brooks, known as **E. B. White** (1899–), American writer noted for his essays and children's stories. He was born in Mt. Vernon, N.Y., and educated at Cornell. White started his career as a reporter and a freelance writer and later became contributing editor of the *New Yorker* magazine. It was during his long association with the "Talk of the Town" column that he acquired his reputation as the spokesman of the contemporary urban generation. He is best known for his books *Stuart Little* (1945) and *Charlotte's Web* (1952), considered to be classics of children's literature. His other works include *Is Sex Necessary?* (1929, in collaboration with James Thurber); *The Lady is Cold* (1929), a collection of his poetry; and a revised edition of William Strunk, Jr.'s *The Elements of Style* (1959).

White, Henry (1850–1927), American diplomat, born in Baltimore, Md. He entered the diplomatic service and served as secretary of the legation at Vienna and at London. Pres. William McKinley appointed him ambassador to Italy (1905–1907) and later to France (1907–1909). He helped to prevent a break between France and Germany at the Algeciras Conference. He was sent to Chile on a special mission in 1910 and took part in the Paris Peace Conference in 1919. White was the first American career diplomat—the first to rise from the ranks to became an ambassador.

White, Margaret Bourke. See *Caldwell, Erskine.*

White, Peregrine (1620–1704), American pioneer. He was born on the *Mayflower* in Cape Cod Bay, November 20, 1620, and so was the first child of English parents born in New England. He settled in Marshfield, Mass., where he became a minor official.

White, Stanford (1853–1906), American architect, born in New York City. He learned architecture by practical experience with architectural firms, and formed a corporation with Charles F. McKim and William R. Mead. He designed the old Madison Square Garden, Madison Square Presbyterian Church, the Century Club, the Metropolitan Club (all in New York), and several buildings for the University of Virginia. His buildings are usually neo-Renaissance in style.

White, William Allen (1868–1944), American journalist, born in Emporia, Kan., and educated at the University of Kansas. He began his journalistic career on the El Dorado *Republican,* then worked on several Kansas papers until he bought the Emporia *Gazette* in 1895. In 1896 he wrote the famous editorial *What's the Matter with Kansas?* Soon his editorials drew comment from all over the country. His published books include *A Certain Rich Man* (1909), *In the Heart of a Fool* (1918), and *The Changing West* (1939). His autobiography (pub. 1946) has been regarded as a classic American memoir.

Whitefield, George (1714–1770), English preacher, born in Gloucester and educated at Oxford. He was one of the original Methodist group formed at Oxford by John and Charles Wesley. He was a missionary in Georgia briefly in 1738, and later made other trips to the United States. On his return to England he began preaching in the open, attracting increasingly large crowds. In 1741 he broke away from the Wesleys and became the leader of the Calvinist Methodists.

Whitehead, Alfred North (1861–1947), English mathematician and philosopher, born in Ramsgate and educated at Trinity College, Cambridge. He was a professor at the University of London and taught at Harvard (1924–1937). He is the author of *Principia Mathematica* (1910, with Bertrand Russell), *The Principles of Natural Knowledge* (1919), *Science and the Modern World* (1925), *The Aims of Education* (1928), and *Adventures of Ideas* (1933).

Whitman, Marcus (1802–1847), American pioneer and missionary, born in Rushville, N.Y. He studied medicine at Pittsfield, Mass., and practiced for four years in Canada. He offered to do medical missionary work among the Indians of the West and in 1836 went to Oregon in a covered wagon. Whitman was largely responsible for the early interest in the Pacific Northwest. Back in the East (1842–1843), he wrote pamphlets and newspaper articles about the fertility and resources of the new territory. When he returned to Oregon, he led a group of new settlers.

Whitman, Sarah Helen Power (1803–1878), American poet, born in Providence, R.I. She was the fiancée of Edgar Allen Poe in 1848, a year before his death, and was the inspiration for his poem *To Helen*. In addition to her poems, which are much like Poe's in style, she wrote *Edgar Poe and his Critics* (1860). *The Last Letters of Edgar Allan Poe to Sarah Helen Whitman* was published in 1909.

Whitman, Walt, in full **Walter Whitman** (1819–1892), American poet, born in West Hills, Long Island, N.Y. As a young man he was employed in a variety of occupations—typesetter, carpenter, drayman, ferryman, and schoolteacher. He was also editor of the Brooklyn *Eagle* (1846–1848). In the course of several years he wrote nearly 400 poems, which he published as *Leaves of Grass* in 1855. Dominant themes in these poems are his love of freedom and his faith in democracy. Although Emerson and other writers acclaimed the book, it was poorly received in America. European literary critics, however, hailed the work as revolutionary and uniquely American. Whitman's prose works include *Specimen Days and Collect* (1883) and *Democratic Vistas* (1871). Among his best known individual poems are *O Captain! My Captain!*, *Song of the Open Road*, and *When Lilacs Last in the Dooryard Bloom'd*.

in Württemberg. He lived mainly in Weimer and was a friend of Goethe, Schiller, and Herder. His dramas, verse narratives, epics, and novels include *Lady Johanna Gray* (1758), *Don Sylvio von Rosalva* (1764), *Musarion* (1768), *Oberon* (1780), and *Aristipp* (4 vols., 1800–1801). He translated Shakespeare's plays and the works of Horace, Cicero, and Lucian into German.

Wiener, Norbert (1894–1964), American mathematical logician, founder of cybernetics. He was born in Colombia and educated at Tufts College, Harvard, and Cornell. He also studied under Bertrand Russell at Cambridge, and at Göttingen. In 1932 he was made a professor of mathematics at M.I.T. It was during World War II, while working on predicators and guided missiles, that he made his famous study of the handling of information by electronic devices that led to the comparison of these with the automatic control system formed by the nervous system and brain. The results of Wiener's work are recorded in *Cybernetics* (1948). He is also the author of several detective stories published under the pseudonym of W. Norbert.

Wiggin, Kate Douglas Smith (1856–1923), American novelist, born in Philadelphia, Pa. She was educated at Abbott Academy, Andover, Mass. She founded in San Francisco the first free kindergarten on the West Coast. The most famous of her novels is *Rebecca of Sunnybrook Farm* (1903). She wrote many others, including *The Birds' Christmas Carol* (1887), *Timothy's Quest* (1890), and *Penelope's Progress* (1898).

The Importance of Being Earnest (1895), and *Salomé* (1894). His other books include *The Ballad of Reading Gaol* (1898), written after he served a prison sentence for immorality, and *De Profundis* (pub. 1905), an explanation of his aesthetic and social beliefs, written while in prison.

Wilder, Thornton Niven (1897–), American playwright and novelist, born in Madison, Wis. He was raised in China, where his father was a member of various U.S. consuls, and was educated at Oberlin College and Yale. He taught literature and writing for several years at the University of Chicago. His first successful novel was *The Bridge of San Luis Rey*, for which he received the Pulitzer Prize in 1927. This was followed by several other novels, including *The Ides of March* (1948). His plays include *Our Town* (which won him the Pulitzer Prize in 1938) and *The Skin of our Teeth* (1942, also awarded the Pulitzer Prize). His play *The Matchmaker* (1954) was a revision of an older play, *The Merchant of Yonkers*, and in turn was the basis of the successful musical *Hello, Dolly!*

Wilhelmina, in full **Wilhelmina Helena Pauline Maria** (1880–1962), queen of the Netherlands, born in The Hague. She was the only child of William III, whom she succeeded in 1890 under the regency of her mother, Queen Emma. Wilhelmina was crowned when she was 18. In 1901 Queen Wilhelmina married Henry Wladimir Albert Ernst, Duke of Mecklenburg-Schwerin, who died in 1934. When the Germans entered Holland in 1940, Queen Wilhelmina transferred the government to London. Back in Holland in September, 1948, the queen abdicated in favor of her daughter, Juliana, and went into retirement.

Wilkes, Charles (1798–1877), American naval officer and explorer, born in New York City. As a lieutenant he commanded a small vessel in South Atlantic waters on a government expedition, and charted the coast of Antartica. One spot in that continent, 3,000 miles south of Australia, has been named Wilkes Land. During the Civil War he stopped the British mail steamer *Trent* on the high seas and seized James M. Mason and John Slidell, high commissioners of the Confederate government, who were on their way to Europe to obtain aid and recognition for the Confederacy. This act violated international law; Mason and Slidell were set free and an apology was sent to the British government to avoid serious complications.

Wilkes, John (1727–1797), English political leader, born in London. He became a member of Parliament in 1757. He was a founder (1762) of the newspaper *North Briton*, in which he wrote articles sharply critical of the prime minister, Lord Bute, who was soon ousted from office. In 1764 he was expelled from the House of Commons for a libelous article against King George III and the obscene and blasphemous poem *Essay on Women*. He fled to France and was outlawed for failing to return to England for his trial. On his return in 1768 he was elected to Parliament from Middlesex and submitted to trial. When found guilty and sentenced, he declared the trial illegal and was again expelled from the Commons (1769). Three times again elected from Middlesex and each time refused by the Commons, he organized a parliamentary reform party and was elected to the House of Commons in 1774. He had also been elected lord mayor of London. He supported the cause of the American colonists during the Revolutionary War, but his suppression of the Gordon Riots (1780) lost him much popularity among the lower classes.

Wilkins, Sir George Hubert (1888–1958), Australian explorer, born in Mount Bryan East. He studied engineering at the Adelaide School of Mines, then became an aeronautical photographer. As a photographer and newspaper correspondent, he reported much of the action in the Balkan Wars (1912–1913). He was with the Arctic expedition of Vilhjalmur Stefansson from 1913 to 1917, then enlisted in the Australian Flying Corps and became head of the Australian photographic section in France. He was a member of expeditions to the Arctic (1920–1922, 1926, 1927), which contributed much to knowledge of the region's geography. In 1928 and 1929 he explored some of the Antartic continent by air. In 1931 he unsuccessfully attempted to explore the Arctic by submarine.

Wilkins, Roy (1901–), American Negro social welfare executive, born in St. Louis, Mo., and educated at the University of Minnesota. A leader in the N.A.A.C.P., he has held various offices in the organization,

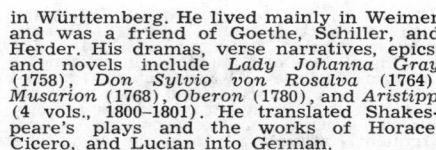

FREDERIC LEWIS

POETS of the nineteenth century: Irishman Oscar Wilde (*left*), author of *The Ballad of Reading Gaol*, and American Walt Whitman (*right*), author of *Leaves of Grass*.

Whitney, Eli (1765–1825), American inventor, born in Westboro, Mass., and educated at Yale. After visiting the Georgia plantation of Mrs. Nathaniel Greene, wife of the Revolutionary War general, he invented the cotton gin, which speeded the slow process of separating cotton fibers from the seeds. He was constantly involved in legal battles with those who copied the plans of his patented machine. He later began manufacturing firearms. In his factory he introduced the concept of interchangeable parts and the system of production based on division of labor.

Whittier, John Greenleaf (1807–1892), American poet, born near Haverhill, Mass. As a young man he worked as a cobbler and teacher. From 1828 to 1832 he was an editor and contributor to newspapers in Haverhill, Boston, and Hartford, and active as an abolitionist. His narrative poems, describing many aspects of American life and frequently reflecting his Quaker background, include *Skipper Ireson's Ride*, *Barbara Frietchie*, *Maud Muller*, *The Barefoot Boy*, and the memorable *Snow-Bound*. Among his books are *Legends of New England in Prose and Verse* (1831), *Moll Pitcher* (1832), *Lays of My Home and Other Poems* (1843), *The Voices of Freedom* (1846), *Snow-Bound* (1866), and *At Sundown* (1890).

Wiclif or **Wickliffe, John.** See *Wycliffe*.

Wieland, Christoph Martin (1733–1813), German poet, translator, and novelist, born

Wilberforce, William (1759–1833), English philanthropist and abolitionist, born in Hull and educated at Cambridge. He entered Parliament in 1780 where he waged a lifelong campaign for the abolition of slavery, which was legislated after his death. A leader of the "Clapham Sect" of evangelical Christians, he founded the Anti-Slavery Society in 1823. He was also a supporter of Catholic emancipation.

Wilcox, Ella Wheeler (1850–1919), American poet, born near Madison, Wis., and educated at the University of Wisconsin. Her writings include *Drops of Water* (1872), *Poems of Passion* (1833), *Sweet Danger* (1902), and *The Art of Being Alive* (1914). Most memorable from her poems are the lines: "Laugh and the world laughs with you; weep and you weep alone."

Wilde, Oscar Fingal O'Flahertie Wills (1854–1900), Irish playwright, novelist, and poet, born in Dublin. He was educated at Trinity College, Dublin, and at Oxford. While in college he became known as an aesthete and wit, a reputation he carried throughout his life. His early poems were successfully received, and in 1882 he toured the United States giving lectures designed chiefly to shock provincial Americans. Most of his works were immediately popular, notably *The Happy Prince and Other Tales* (1888) and *The Picture of Dorian Gray* (1891); and the plays *Lady Windermere's Fan* (1892), *A Woman of No Importance* (1893), *An Ideal Husband* (1895),

including editor of *Crisis*, the official N.A.A.C.P. organ (1934–1949), and has been executive secretary since 1955.

Wilkinson, James (1757–1825), American soldier and adventurer, born in Calvert County, Md. A brigadier general in the Revolutionary Army, he was later in the pay of the Spanish authorities in Louisiana, with whom he intrigued against the United States. In 1805, as governor of the upper part of Louisiana Territory, he was implicated in Aaron Burr's plot to conquer the Southwest and set up an independent empire. He was court-martialed but acquitted, and later served as a major general in the War of 1812.

Willard, Emma Hart (1787–1870), American educator, born in Berlin, Conn. Convinced of the need for better education for women, she opened a small boarding school in her home in Middlebury, Vt., in 1814. She moved her school to Waterford, N.Y., in 1819, and in 1821 she moved it to Troy, N.Y., where it became known as the Emma Willard School. She also helped found a school for training women teachers in Athens, Greece, in 1832. The title poem of her book *Rocked in the Cradle of the Deep* (1831) was a favorite.

William I, known as **William the Conqueror** (1027–1087), king of England (1066–1087). Born in Normandy, he was the illegitimate son of Robert, duke of Normandy. By his marriage with Matilda of Flanders, that area was joined to his domain of Normandy, and the County of Maine was added by conquest. On the death of his cousin Edward the Confessor, king of England, William went to claim the throne he considered legitimately his by succession and which Edward's brother-in-law, Harold, earl of Wessex, had claimed for himself. In 1066 William landed in Sussex, defeated Harold at the battle of Hastings, and was crowned king of England on Christmas Day. William established a relatively well-ordered kingdom, run by the system of Norman feudalism that he had developed so successfully in his earlier domains. He carried out a complete survey of the English realm, known as the *Domesday Book*, and established church reforms.

William II, called **Rufus** (1056–1100), king of England (1087–1100), son of William the Conqueror. After becoming king in 1087, he was faced with a revolt of the barons, headed by Bishop Odo of Bayeux, his uncle. After suppressing the rebellion, he tried to gain control of Normandy. Failing in three invasions, he finally received a mortgage on it when his brother Robert, duke of Normandy, joined the Crusades and needed finances. He recovered Maine but failed to recover Vexin. William's main domestic problem was with Anselm, archbishop of Canterbury, who tried to maintain Church liberties against encroachment by the monarchy.

William IV (1765–1837), king of Great Britain and Ireland and of Hanover (1830–1837), born in London. He was the third son of George III, and as Prince William Henry held the titles duke of Clarence and St. Andrews and earl of Munster. For his service in the navy (1779–1818) he was often called "the sailor king." For many years he lived with Mrs. Dorothea Jordan, an actress, by whom he had several illegitimate children. In 1818 he married Princess Adelaide of Saxe-Meiningen; both daughters of the marriage died in infancy. He was made lord high admiral in 1831, and crowned king in 1830 on the death of his brother, George IV. During his reign the Reform Bill of 1832 was passed. He was succeeded by his niece, Victoria.

William I, in full **Wilhelm Friedrich Ludwig** (1797–1888), king of Prussia (1861–1888) and emperor of Germany (1871–1888). Born in Berlin, he was the second son of Frederick William III of Prussia and Louise of Mecklenburg-Strelitz. As prince of Prussia, he was unpopular because of his absolutist ideas and he fled to England during the revolutions of 1848. He was made regent for his brother in 1858 when the king became insane, and succeeded him on his death in 1861. His reign was dominated by his minister, Otto von Bismarck. During the war with Austria in 1866 he commanded at the battle of Sadowa. In 1867 he became head of the newly-formed North German Confederation. During the Franco-Prussian War (1870–1871) he commanded at Gravelotte and Sedan. In 1871 he became emperor of Germany. He supported Bismarck's policies against the Catholics (1872–1887), known as the *Kulturkampf*) and the Socialists, and his other efforts to strengthen Prussian domination of Germany.

William II, in full **Friedrich Wilhelm Viktor Albert** (1859–1941), king of Prussia and emperor of Germany (1888–1918). He was born in Potsdam, the eldest son of Emperor Frederick III and Victoria (daughter of Queen Victoria). Two years after his accession in 1888, he dismissed his father's chancellor, Otto von Bismarck, from office. Frequently anti-British in foreign policy, he congratulated Pres. Stephanus Kruger of the Transvaal by telegram for having successfully repulsed the Jameson Raid. Under his rule, two Moroccan crises put further strains on Franco-German and Anglo-German relations. William supported the expansion of the German navy. He favored Austria-Hungary in her dispute with Serbia. During World War I Germany was increasingly ruled by her top army generals. In 1918 William abdicated and fled to the Netherlands, where he lived until his death.

William I, known as **William the Silent** (1533–1584), founder of the Dutch Republic and its first stadholder. In 1555 Emperor Charles V appointed him commander of the Imperial army and governor of the northern provinces of Holland. In 1568 he led the revolt against Spanish rule. Under his leadership the seven northern provinces were able to free themselves from Spanish rule. William was chosen the first stadholder in 1579, an office which was made hereditary two years later. He was assassinated by Balthasar Girard in Delft.

LOOK MAGAZINE

TENNESSEE WILLIAMS

William III (1650–1702), stadholder of Holland (1672–1702) and king of England (1689–1702). He was the posthumous son of William II, prince of Orange, and Mary, daughter of Charles I. He carried on the struggle of the Dutch against Louis XIV. In 1677 he married Mary, daughter of James II of Britain. In 1689, after James II lost the throne, he and Mary were invited to become the joint sovereigns of England. As king he accepted the Declaration of Rights and the passage of the Act of Toleration. He participated in the war of the Grand Alliance against France (1689–1697) and helped form a second Grand Alliance in 1701. In 1701 he also accepted the Act of Settlement.

Williams, Roger (c.1603–1683), American religious leader and founder of the Rhode Island colony. He was born in London and educated at Cambridge. He came to America in 1631 and was pastor of the Puritan Church at Salem. His tolerant religious views brought conflicts with the civil authorities, and he was banished from Massachusetts. In 1636 he went to the present site of Providence, Rhode Island, and founded the first settlement based on religious toleration. In 1643 he journeyed to England and secured from the king a charter for "The Providence Plantations in the Narragansett Bay." He was president of the colony from 1654 to 1657.

Williams, Tennessee, real name **Thomas Lanier Williams** (1914–), American playwright. He was born in Columbus, Miss., and educated at the universities of Missouri and Iowa and Washington University (St. Louis). He has been the recipient of many awards and is considered one of America's finest playwrights. In 1959 a group of four one-act plays called *American Blues* won a Group Theater Prize. In 1945 *The Glass Menagerie* won both the New York Drama Critics' Circle Award and the Sidney Howard Memorial Award. Other works by Williams include *You Touched Me* (1946), *A Streetcar Named Desire* (1947; Pulitzer Prize, New York Drama Critics' Circle Award), *The Rose Tattoo* (1950), *Cat on a Hot Tin Roof* (1954; New York Drama Critics' Circle Award, Pulitzer Prize), *Sweet Bird of Youth* (1959), and *The Night of the Iguana* (1961).

Williams, William Carlos (1883–1963), American writer and physician, noted for the colloquial style of his poetry. He was born in Rutherford, N.J., and later practiced medicine there. While attending the University of Pennsylvania, Williams became a good friend of Ezra Pound, who encouraged and influenced his poetry. In 1926 he received the Dial Prize for his services to American literature, and in 1950 the National Book Award for poetry. *Paterson* (1946–1951), his major poetic work, is characterized by Williams' concentration on the specific and his ability to bring details alive. His other works include *The Complete Collected Poems of William Carlos Williams* (1906–1938), the novels *White Mule* (1937) and *In the Money* (1940), *Selected Essays* (1954), and *Selected Letters* (1957).

Willkie, Wendell Lewis (1892–1944), American lawyer, business executive, and political leader, born in Elwood, Ind. Originally a public utilities executive and a Democrat, he became critical of New Deal policies and became a Republican. As the Republican nominee for president in 1940, he was defeated by Pres. Franklin D. Roosevelt. He later served as Roosevelt's unofficial ambassador to Egypt, the Middle East, Russia, and China (1941–1942), on a tour to encourage international cooperation. He wrote *One World* (1943), which describes this trip and explains his internationalist point of view.

Wilson, Charles Erwin (1890–1961), American business executive and government official, born in Minerva, Ohio, and educated at the Carnegie Institute of Technology. He became vice-president of General Motors Corporation in 1929 and president in 1941. He served as secretary of defense (1953–1957) in the cabinet of Pres. Dwight D. Eisenhower.

Wilson, Edmund (1895–), American writer, noted for his vigorous literary and social criticism. He was born in Red Bank, N.J., and educated at Princeton. Starting as a reporter for the New York *Evening Sun* (1916–1917), he later became associate editor of the *New Republic* (1926–1931) and a book reviewer for the *New Yorker* magazine (1944–1948). In 1946 his book *Memoirs of Hecate County*, a collection of his short stories, was banned for obscenity by the Court of Special Sessions. Wilson's works include literary criticism: *Axel's Castle* (1931), *The Wound and the Bow* (1941), and *Patriotic Gore* (1962); social criticism: *The American Jitters* (1932) and *The American Earthquake* (1958); and a number of plays. He also wrote several books about his travel experiences.

Wilson, Harold (1916–), British statesman, born in Linthwaite, Yorkshire, and educated at Oxford. In 1964 he was elected prime minister of Britain on the Labour party ticket. He entered Parliament in 1945 and headed the Board of Trade from 1947 to 1951. He wrote *New Deal for Coal* (1945), *In Place of Dollars* (1952), and *The War on World Poverty* (1953).

Wilson, James (1742–1798), American legislator and jurist, born in St. Andrews, Scotland. He came to America in 1765, was admitted to the bar in 1767, and was a member of the Continental Congress and a signer of the Declaration of Independence. In 1789 he was appointed associate justice of the first U.S. Supreme Court and served until his death. He was the first professor of law at the University of Pennsylvania (1790).

Wilson, Samuel (1766–1854), American patriot and merchant, born in Arlington, Mass. As a meatpacker in Troy, N.Y., where he was known as "Uncle Sam," he inspected meat for a government contractor. The initials U.S. (standing for the United States), with which he stamped the barrels of meat, were mistakenly thought to stand for his nickname, thus "Uncle Sam" came to be the personification of the U.S. government.

Wilson, Woodrow, in full **Thomas Woodrow Wilson** (1856–1924), twenty-eighth president of the United States, born in Staunton, Va., and educated at Princeton and Johns Hopkins universities. He was president of Princeton from 1902 until 1910, when he resigned to run for governor of New Jersey. Elected as a reform governor in 1911, he secured the passage of a direct primaries law, a corrupt practices act, and an employers' liability act, and promoted the organization of a public utilities commission. Nominated Democratic candidate for president in 1912, he defeated William H. Taft and Theodore Roosevelt. In his administration, tariffs were reduced by the Underwood Tariff Act, currency policies were reformed by the Federal Reserve Act, and the Federal Trade Commission Act and Clayton Antitrust Act were passed.

In the area of foreign policy, the difficult problems in South America that troubled his first term were soon overshadowed by the outbreak of World War I, which followed his reelection in 1914 over Charles Evans Hughes. After three years of neutrality, the U.S., at the recommendation of Wilson, joined the Allies in the war in 1917. In 1918 Wilson proposed a program known as the Fourteen Points, on which a peace treaty could be based. The Germans accepted an armistice on the basis of these propositions in 1918. Wilson himself represented the U.S. at the Peace Conference at Paris, where he insisted on the establishment of a League of Nations as a basic provision of the treaty. When he returned to the U.S., opposition to the treaty and to the League of Nations was increasing and the Senate refused to ratify the treaty. Already broken in health, Wilson had a stroke of paralysis in October 1919 and thereafter remained an invalid. He retired when his term of office expired. In 1920 he received the Nobel Peace Prize. His works include *A History of the American People* (5 vols., 1902) and *Constitutional Government in the United States* (1908).

Winckelmann, Johann Joachim (1717–1768), German archaelogist and art critic, born in Stendal, Prussia. A classical art scholar, he was the first scientific archaeologist. In 1763 he was appointed prefect of antiquities and scriptor of the Vatican. Of his many writings, the best and most influential is *Geschichte der Kunst des Alterthums* (1764; Eng. tr. *History of Ancient Art*, 1849–1873).

Windaus, Adolf (1876–1959), German chemist, born in Berlin. In 1915 he was appointed head of the chemical research institute at Göttingen. For his studies of the composition of sterols and their relation to vitamins, he was awarded the Nobel Prize in chemistry in 1928.

Winkelried, Arnold von (died 1386), Swiss hero. According to legend, his actions turned the tide in favor of the Swiss during a war with the Austrians. He is supposed to have rushed against the enemy ranks single-handed, gathered all the enemy spears within reach to his breast, and thus formed an opening through which his comrades attacked.

Winslow, Edward (1595–1655), American colonist, and a leading founder of Plymouth Colony, Massachusetts. Born in Droitwich, England, he came to America on the *Mayflower* and was governor of the Plymouth colony in 1633, 1636, and 1644. He went back to England in 1646. Later he was sent by Cromwell to the Spanish West Indies on an expedition and died on his return voyage. He wrote several accounts of early settlement days in New England.

Winthrop, John (1588–1649), American colonial governor, born in Suffolk, England, and educated at Cambridge. Appointed governor of the Massachusetts Bay Company, he sailed with other colonists and landed in Salem, Mass., in 1630. Winthrop was reelected six times as governor. He left a voluminous journal, which is one of the most valuable sources of New England colonial history.

Wise, Stephen Samuel (1874–1949), American rabbi, born in Budapest, Hungary, and educated at Columbia University. In 1907 he founded the New York Free Synagogue and served as its rabbi until his death. He was one of the founders and president (1936–1938) of the Zionist Organization of America. He was also a founder and president (1925–1929, 1935–1949) of the American Jewish Congress.

Wister, Owen (1860–1938), American writer, born in Philadelphia, Pa. He was educated at Harvard and after a brief career as a composer, became a lawyer and practiced in Philadelphia. He became interested in western frontier life about 1890 and began to write stories. His best-known novel, *The Virginian* (1902), is a classic of its kind. A friend of Theodore Roosevelt, he wrote his biography, *Roosevelt—The Story of a Friendship* (1930).

Witte, Count Sergei Yulievich (1849–1949), Russian statesman, born in Tiflis and educated at Odessa. As minister of finance (1893–1903), he instituted a program for improving and modernizing the Russian economy. He put Russia on the gold standard, gave government subsidies to industry, and encouraged foreign investment in Russia. In 1905 he negotiated the Treaty of Portsmouth (New Hampshire), ending the Russo-Japanese War.

Wodehouse, Pelham Grenville (1881–   ), English humorist, born in Guildford. Most of his works portray characters in amusing, often hilarious, situations. Notable among his comic figures are Psmith, Jeeves, and Bertie Wooster, who are frequently the title characters of many of his stories and novels. Among his many publications are *Leave it to Psmith* (1923), *The Inevitable Jeeves* (1924), *Blandings Castle* (1935), *Mating Season* (1949), *French Leave* (1956), *Carry on Jeeves* (1960), and *Author, Author* (1962).

Wolcott, Oliver (1726–1797), American political leader, born in Windsor, Conn., the son of **Roger Wolcott** (1679–1767), governor of Connecticut (1750–1754). He was a delegate to the Continental Congress and one of the signers of the Declaration of Independence. After serving in the Revolutionary War, he was elected governor of Connecticut in 1796. His son, **Oliver Wolcott** (1760–1833), was secretary of the treasury from 1795 until 1800.

Wolf, Friedrich August (1759–1824), German classical philologist, born near Nordhausen and educated at Göttingen. In his *Prolegomena ad Homerum* (1795) he stated that the *Iliad* and *Odyssey* were written by more than one author. In his scholarly and critical writings he stressed the importance of studying classical antiquity. Wolf is regarded by many as the founder of modern philology.

Wolf, Hugo (1860–1903), Austrian composer, born in Windischgraz (now in Yugoslavia). Strongly influenced by the music of Richard Wagner, Wolf composed over 200 songs, many of which were musical settings for famous German poems. His other works include a symphonic poem, *Penthesilea* (1883), and *Italian Serenade* (1894).

Wolfe, James (1727–1759), English general, born in Westerham, Kent. He served in Flanders and Germany (1742–1747) and distinguished himself at the siege of Louisburg under Lord Jeffrey Amherst (1748). In command of the expedition to capture Quebec in 1759, he was killed in action.

Wolfe, Thomas (1900–1938), American novelist, born in Asheville, N.C., educated at the University of North Carolina. His works include *Look Homeward, Angel* (1929), *Of Time and the River* (1935), *The Web and the Rock* (pub. 1939), *You Can't Go Home Again* (pub. 1940), *The Hills Beyond* (pub. 1941), and *Letters to his Mother* (1943).

Wollstonecraft, Mary. See *Godwin, Mary Wollstonecraft.*

Wolsey, Thomas (c.1475–1530), English cardinal and statesman, born in Ipswich and educated at Oxford. In 1503 he became chaplain to Henry VII. Under Henry VIII he became archbishop of York (1514) and lord chancellor (1515). In 1515 he was made a cardinal by Pope Leo X, who also made him a papal legate in 1518. As Henry's chief minister, he helped strengthen royal power and allied England with Charles V against France. In his attempts to finance campaigns against France he gained great unpopularity. His downfall came after his failure to get papal sanction for a divorce for Henry VIII from Catherine of Aragon. He was arrested in 1530 and taken to London. He died en route.

Wood, Grant (1892–1942), American painter, born near Anamosa, Iowa. His paintings are characterized by stark realism and portray, often with a suggestion of irony, the rural American life. The best known of these are *John B. Turner, Pioneer* (1929), *American Gothic* (1930), and *Daughters of the American Revolution* (1932).

Wood, Leonard (1860–1927), American soldier and administrator, born in Winchester, N.H. He graduated from Harvard Medical School (1884) and served with the U.S. army (1885–1886) against the Apaches in the West, for which he received the Congressional Medal of Honor. In 1897–1898, he helped Theodore Roosevelt organize the Rough Riders, with whom he fought in Cuba in the Spanish-American War. He was military governor of Cuba (1899–1902) and then of Moro Province in the Philippines (1903–1906). After serving as commander of the army in the Philippines (1906–1908), he returned home in 1910 to become chief of staff of the army. An unsuccessful candidate for the Republican presidential nomination (1920), he was governor general of the Philippines from 1921 until his death.

Woollcott, Alexander (1887–1943), American journalist and writer who has been called one of the best "yarn spinners" of our time, born in Phalanx, N.J. He started his career as a drama critic for the New York *Times* (1914–1922) and later worked for the New York *Herald* (1922) and the New York *World* (1925–1928). In 1929 he became a radio broadcaster and achieved repute as radio's "Town Crier." He also wrote the "Shouts and Murmurs" column for the *New Yorker*. He is the author of *The Command is Forward* (1919), *The Story of Irving Berlin* (1925), *While Rome Burns* (1934) and the editor of several anthologies, including *The Woollcott Reader* (1935). Woollcott played Sheridan Whiteside in Kaufman and Hart's *The Man Who Came to Dinner;* the character was modeled after Woollcott.

Woolf, Virginia (1882–1941), English novelist, essayist, and critic, born in London. She was the daughter of Sir Leslie Stephen. With her husband, Leonard Woolf, she founded the Hogarth Press (1917). In her novels she used the stream of consciousness technique to effect a subtle self-revelation of character. Her works include *The Voyage Out* (1915), *Jacob's Room* (1922), *Mrs. Dalloway* (1925), *To the Lighthouse* (1927), *Orlando* (1928), *A Room of One's Own* (1930), and *The Common Reader* (1925, 2nd series 1932).

Woolworth, Frank Winfield (1852–1919), American merchant, born near Rodman, N.Y. He began his business career in 1879 with a 5-cent store at Utica, N.Y. He found that the articles he sold lasted for a long time and that there was no immediate demand for new purchases. In 1879 he moved to Lancaster, Pa., and opened a 5-and-10-cent store; this time he selected goods for which there was a more constant demand. From this start, the Woolworth chain of stores grew until they numbered thousands and were internationally located. The Woolworth Building in New York City, erected in 1911, was then the highest commercial building in the world.

Wordsworth, William (1770–1850), English poet, born in Cockermouth, Cumberland, and educated at St. John's College, Cambridge. Upon graduating (1791) he made a walking tour of France and Switzerland. After a brief stay in London he returned to France in the same year, where he observed with sympathy the actions of the French revolutionists. Repulsed by their extremist actions, he became a staunch political conservative. On his return to England in 1792 he published *An Evening Walk* and *Descriptive Sketches*. In 1779 Wordsworth became a close associate of Samuel Taylor Coleridge, with whom he published *Lyrical Ballads* (1798). The volume included *Tintern Abbey* by Wordsworth and *The Ancient Mariner* by Coleridge. In 1799 Wordsworth and his sister Dorothy, with whom he lived, moved to Grasmere, Westmorland, in the Lake District of England. In 1801 Wordsworth himself published another volume of *Lyrical Ballads*, which included four of the *Lucy* poems. Soon afterward he wrote his great ode *Intimations of Immortality* and *Solitary Reaper*. In 1813, with his wife Mary (whom he married in 1802) and his sister, Wordsworth moved to Rydal Mount, where he lived for the rest of his life. In 1839 he finished revising his autobiographical poem, *The Prelude*. Wordsworth's later published works include *Poems in Two Volumes* (1807), which contains *Ode to Duty; The Excursion* (1814); *Miscellaneous Poems* (2 vols., 1815); *The Waggoner* (1819); and *Poems, Chiefly of Early and Late Years* (1842). In 1843 he was named poet laureate, succeeding Robert Southey.

Wouk, Herman (1915–   ), American novelist, born in New York City. He was educated at Columbia University and began his career writing radio programs for comedians, including Fred Allen. He served with the U.S. navy during World War II. His novels include *Aurora Dawn* (1947), *The Caine Mutiny* (1951; winner of the Pulitzer Prize in 1952), and *Marjorie Morningstar* (1955). He has also written film scripts for Hollywood.

Wrangel or Wrangell, Baron Ferdinand Petrovich von (1794–1870), Russian explorer, born in St. Petersburg (now Leningrad). In 1820 he commanded an expedition that explored the Arctic. He tried unsuccessfully to reach a large land area north of Siberia, now called Wrangel Land in his honor. He was governor of Alaska (1829–1834), and opposed the sale of Alaska to the United States.

Wren, Sir Christopher (1632–1723), English architect, born in Wiltshire. He was educated at Oxford, where he became a professor of astronomy. He had little actual training in architecture. The Great Fire of 1666 in London gave Wren his opportunity, and he prepared a plan for rebuilding the city. Though his scheme was not followed, he designed several new buildings, including St. Paul's Cathedral, his greatest work. For many years thereafter he designed important buildings in London and furnished plans for 53 churches. He was knighted in 1672. During his lifetime he was famous also as a mathematician.

Wright, Sir Almroth Edward (1861–1947), English physician and bacteriologist, born in Yorkshire, and educated at Dublin, Leipzig, Strasbourg, and Marburg. He developed an antityphoid inoculation and made extensive studies of other toxins. He was knighted in 1906.

Wright, Frances or **Fanny** (1795–1852), American social reformer, born in Dundee, Scotland. Based on a visit to the United States in 1818, she published *Views of Society and Manners in America*. She returned to the U.S. in 1824, and founded a

devices for use on bicycles. Their interest in aviation began in 1896, when they read of the death of Otto Lilienthal, the German experimenter, in a glider accident. In 1900 they built their first glider and took it to Kitty Hawk, N.C., for trial. That spot was chosen for its favorable flying weather. They experimented for two years and made many glider flights.

Then they designed and built their own gasoline engine, installed it in a plane, and on December 17, 1903, made the first successful man-carrying flight. They continued their work but received little notice for several years. In 1908 they started an airplane factory. They made flights in the U.S. and abroad, and in 1909 the U.S. government accepted their plane for army use.

Wundt, Wilhelm (1832–1920), German physiologist and psychologist, born in Neckerau, and educated at Tübingen, Heidelberg, and Berlin. In 1879 Wundt established the first laboratory for experimental psychology. Basing psychology on experience, he tried to develop it as a science by correlating its various aspects—mathematical, physiological, and psychophysical.

Wyant, Alexander Helwig (1836–1892), American artist, born in Evans Creek, Ohio. A member of the Hudson River school, he is known primarily for his scenes of woods and valleys.

Wyatt, James (1746–1813), English architect,

anyone who had been living in a sinful way. He was declared a heretic by a papal bull (1377) and was subsequently refused the right to carry on his priestly functions. Nevertheless, he found sympathy in many prominent social and political circles. He later denied the doctrine of transubstantiation. With John Purvey, he was the first to translate the Bible into English. He was posthumously condemned at the Council of Constance (1415).

Wyeth, Andrew (1917–   ), American painter noted for his unique watercolors and temperas. He was born in Chadds Ford Pa., and educated by private tutors. Although he is usually classified as a realist, Wyeth claims that his work is abstract and that he uses a highly factual technique only as a means of bringing out the poetic and fanciful qualities inherent in his subjects. Wyeth is the recipient of many awards, including the Obrig Prize of the American Watercolor Society (1945) and a Gold Medal from the National Institute of Arts and Letters (1964). Among his best known works are *Blackberry Picker* (1943), *The Skaters* (1945), *Winter* (1946), and *Christina's World* (1948).

Wylie, Philip (1902–   ), American author and journalist. He was born in Beverly, Mass., and educated at Princeton University (1920–1923). Wylie began his literary career on the staff of the *New Yorker* magazine (1925–1927). Later he worked for Paramount Pictures (1931–1933) and Metro-Goldwyn-Mayer (1936–1937). A prolific writer, Wylie often contributes to *Look* magazine, *Readers' Digest*, the *Saturday Evening Post*, and *Redbook*. His many books include *When Worlds Collide* (1933), *The Big Ones Get Away* (1940), *Generation of Vipers* (1942), *The Innocent Ambassadors* (1957), and *They Both Were Naked* (1965).

Wyss, Johann Rudolf (1781–1830), Swiss writer, born in Bern, where he spent his life as professor of philosophy at the university. He is best known as the author of *The Swiss Family Robinson* (1813), an adventure narrative. Some authorities claim that the story was written by his father, Johann David Wyss, and merely edited and published by the son. He also composed the Swiss national anthem and collected Swiss folktales and legends.

X

Xavier, Saint Francis (1506–1552), Spanish missionary, born in Navarre. He was a disciple of Saint Ignatius Loyola, whom he assisted in missionary work in Italy. He was ordained a priest in 1537 and was one of the founding members of the Society of Jesus, founded by Loyola in 1534. He did missionary work in Malacca, the Molucca Islands, the Banda Islands, India, Ceylon, and Japan. Xavier's great success in his work in this part of the world gave him the title "Apostle of the Indies." The mission he founded in Japan existed for 100 years. Xavier died while he was making preparations to go to China to establish a Jesuit center. He was canonized in 1622. His feast day is December 3.

Xenophon (c.434–c.355 B.C.), Greek historian and soldier, born in Athens, a pupil of Socrates. When Cyrus the Younger of Persia organized a military expedition against Artaxerxes, a Greek group of 10,000 mercenary soldiers joined it, and Xenophon went with that group. The event became one of the great episodes in Xenophon's life. The Persians quarreled with the Greek contingent and killed all their chief officers. The story of the entire expedition and an account of the perilous march back under Xenophon's leadership is given in the *Anabasis*. Xenophon also wrote the *Memorabilia*, a record of the life and teachings of his friend Socrates; the *Hellenica*, a history of Greece from the year 411; and the *Cyropaedia*, a romance having Cyrus the Elder as its central figure.

Xerxes I, called the Great (c.519–465 B.C.), king of Persia, son of Darius I, whom he succeeded in 486. Like his father, he tried to subdue the Greeks. He advanced as far as Thermopylae where he was checked by the Spartan forces under Leonidas. He then came to a deserted Athens, which he burned, but his fleet was defeated at Salamis. Xerxes fled to Asia Minor and his remaining army was defeated at Plataea in 479. He was assassinated by Artabanus, captain of the guards.

CULVER

THE WRIGHT BROTHERS

LOOK MAGAZINE

FRANK LLOYD WRIGHT

colony of emancipated slaves in Nashoba, Tenn., in 1825. She lectured throughout the country against slavery, ecclesiastical influence in politics, and discrimination against women. She advocated free public education and held that marriage should be a moral not a legal contract. She was associated with Robert Owen as coeditor of the *New Harmony Gazette* in 1828.

Wright, Frank Lloyd (1869–1959), American architect, born in Richland Center, Wis. He studied civil engineering at the University of Wisconsin and worked seven years under Louis Sullivan in Chicago. He set up his own firm in 1899. Wright's designs for public and private buildings and city planning schemes, at first considered daring and unconventional, had a major influence on American and European architecture. In private residences, Wright tried to harmonize the architecture with the natural site. He frequently used patterned concrete blocks and cantilevered concrete construction. His famous buildings include the Imperial Hotel, Tokyo; Fallingwater, a home in Bear Run, Pennsylvania, built over a waterfall; and the Guggenheim Museum in New York City.

Wright, American brothers, pioneers in aviation and aeronautics. **Orville Wright** (1871–1948), was born in Dayton, Ohio, and **Wilber Wright** (1867–1912) near Millville, Ind. They graduated from high school in Dayton, Ohio, then established a weekly newspaper which they gave up to enter the bicycle business. Both were mechanics and they invented and made

born in Staffordshire. He restored several cathedrals and was an expert on Gothic architecture. In 1796 he was appointed surveyor to the Board of Works. His works include Fonthill Abbey (1795) and the Royal Military Academy, Woolwich (1796).

Wyatt, Sir Thomas (1503–1542), English poet and diplomat, courtier in the favor of Henry VIII, and reputed lover of Anne Boleyn. He was born in Allington Castle, Kent, and educated at St. John's College, Cambridge. Wyatt is renowned as the pioneer of the sonnet form in England. In addition to writing his own sonnets, he was one of the first to translate the Petrarchan sonnets into English. Much of his poetry is collected in *Tottel's Miscellany* (1557). Wyatt was knighted in 1536.

Wycherley, William (c.1640–1716), English dramatist, born near Shrewsbury and educated at Oxford and in France. His plays, all comedies of manners, portray upper-class social life during the Restoration, and are marked by witty dialogue, burlesque, and licentious, though highly amusing, situations. His plays include *Love in a Wood* (1671), *The Gentleman Dancing Master* (1672), *The Country Wife* (1675), and *The Plain Dealer* (1676).

Wycliffe or **Wiclife, John** (c.1320–1384), English religious reformer, born in Yorkshire and educated at Oxford. A rector at several churches, he supported John of Gaunt's attacks on excessive Church control of secular affairs. He further attacked the hierarchy by denying the validity of ecclesiastical authority when exercised by

Y

Yale, Elihu (1649–1721), English philanthropist, born in Boston, Mass. In 1652 his family went to England, where he was educated. He joined the East India Company and in 1672 went to Madras, where he was appointed governor of the company in 1678. He amassed a fortune through trading and speculation, and returned to England in 1699. He donated money and supplies to the Collegiate School at Branford, Conn. When the school was moved to New Haven, it was renamed in his honor.

Yeats, William Butler (1865–1939), Irish poet and dramatist, born in Dublin and educated in London and in Dublin. At 21 he turned from painting to the study of ancient Irish life and became the chief writer of a new school of Irish poetry. He was one of the founders of the Abbey Theatre in Dublin (1904). His works include *The Countess Kathleen* (1892), *The Pot of Broth* (1902), *The King's Threshold* (1904), *Deirdre* (1907), *Reveries over Childhood* (1915), *The Vision* (1926), and *The Tower* (1927). *The Cutting of Agate* (1912) and *The Trembling of the Veil* (1922) are among his best critical and reminiscent works. He also wrote volumes of short stories and collected Irish folk and fairy tales. In 1922 he was appointed a senator of the Irish Free State. He received the Nobel Prize for literature in 1923.

Yerkes, Charles Tyson (1837–1905), American financier, born in Philadelphia, Pa. He built up a fortune in the stock market and later controlled the street-railway systems in Philadelphia and Chicago and then the London underground railway. He endowed the Yerkes Observatory of the University of Chicago, in Williams Bay, Wis. His career was the basis for Theodore Dreiser's novels *The Financier* (1912), *The Titan* (1914), and *The Stoic* (1947).

Yevtushenko or **Evtushenko, Yevgeni** (1933–), Russian poet, leader of the new wave Soviet writers. He was born in Zima and studied at the Moscow Literary Institute. Yevtushenko first received attention in the West with the publication of his *A Precocious Autobiography* (1963). This book is one of the few which has managed to be published abroad without careful screening by the Soviet censorship. However, as a result of its implications that some present Soviet leaders are tainted by the crimes of the Stalin era, its author became the target of the Soviet pressure on young intellectuals. Yevtushenko was instructed to learn to write "properly" and was banished from the literary scene until he could meet Soviet standards. His latest verse has proved more acceptable to the authorities, but less palatable to his former followers, who now feel that he has betrayed them. Yevtushenko's works include *Third Snow* (1955); *Longbow and Lyre* (1959); *Babi Yar* (1962), his attack on anti-Semitism; and *Back Again at Zima Junction* (1963).

SOVFOTO

POETS William B. Yeats (*left*) of Ireland and Yevgeny Yevtushenko (*right*) of U.S.S.R.

York, Alvin Cullum (1887–1964), American soldier, born in Pall Mall, Tenn. During World War I he enlisted in the U.S. army (1917) and went to France with the American Expeditionary Force (1918). On October 8, 1918, armed with an automatic revolver and a Springfield rifle, he advanced alone against the enemy, captured Hill 223, killed 20 Germans, compelled the surrender of 132 others—including a major and three lieutenants—and captured 35 machine guns. For this he received the French Croix de Guerre and the Congressional Medal of Honor. In Tennessee he was given a farm, purchased by popular subscription. He established the York Foundation for the education of mountain children and became president of the Alvin York Agricultural Institute.

Yoshihito, Harunomiya, regnal name **Taisho** (1879–1926), Japanese emperor, born in Tokyo. He succeeded his father, Mutsuhito, in 1912. Under his reign, Japan joined the Allies in World War I. Mentally unstable, he was succeeded by his eldest son, Hirohito, who had acted as regent during the last five years of his father's life.

Young, Brigham (1801–1877), American Mormon leader, born in Whitingham, Vt. In 1832 he joined the Mormon community at Kirtland, Ohio, began to preach, and was later chosen as one of the 12 apostles of the Mormon church. In 1847 he succeeded Joseph Smith as the leader of the sect. He led a group of Mormons from Nauvoo, Illinois, to Utah where they founded Salt Lake City. Young was the first governor of the Territory of Utah (1849–1857), and served as the leader of the Mormons until his death.

Young, Charles Augustus (1834–1908), American astronomer, born in Hanover, N.H., and educated at Dartmouth College. He was the first to study the spectrum of the solar corona using a type of spectroscope. His works include *The Sun* (1881) and *Manual of Astronomy* (1902).

Young, Edward (1638–1765), English poet, born in Upham and educated at Oxford. His most famous work is *The Complaint; or, Night-Thoughts on Life, Death and Immortality* (1742–1745), a series of melancholy poems. He took holy orders in 1724 and became rector of Welwym in 1730.

Young, Francis Brett (1884–1954), English novelist, born in Halesowen. He studied medicine and served in a medical corps in Africa during World War I. His *Portrait of Clare* (1927) won the James Tait Black Memorial Prize. His other books include *Dark Tower* (1914), *My Brother Jonathan* (1928), *A Man About the House* (1942), and *Portrait of a Village* (1951).

Young, Mahonri Mackintosh (1877–1957), American sculptor, painter, and etcher, born in Salt Lake City, Utah. He is best known for his simple, realistic figures of laborers, cowboys, and prizefighters. Among his works are *Man with Pick*, *A Laborer*, *Rolling His Own*, *Stevedore*, and the *Sea Gull Monument* (in Salt Lake City).

Young, Owen D. (1874–1962), American lawyer and financier, born in Van Hornesville, N.Y. He studied law and practiced in Boston from 1896 to 1913. Appointed counsel of the General Electric Company in 1913, he was later chairman of the board (1922–1939, 1942–1944). Young and Charles G. Dawes represented the United States at the conference on German reparations in 1924 and administered the Dawes Plan while it was in effect. Young headed the London Reparations Conference of 1929; his Young Plan, adopted at the conference, decreased the reparations payments Germany was to pay the Allies.

Younghusband, Sir Francis Edward (1863–1942), British explorer and author, born in Murree, India. He explored Manchuria in 1886 and went on a special mission to Tibet in 1902. He was a resident of Kashmir (1906–1909). Among his writings are *Heart of a Continent* (1898), *India and Tibet; Within* (1912), *A Venture of Faith* (1937), and *The Sum of Things* (1939).

Ysaÿe, Eugène (1858–1931), Belgian violinist, born in Liège. He studied in Liège, Brussels, and Paris, and was professor of violin at the Brussels Conservatory (1886–1898). He made concert tours throughout Europe and America and composed several pieces for the violin.

Yüan Shih-k'ai (1859–1916), Chinese statesman, born in Honan Province. His diplomatic career began with army service in Korea. In 1900 he became governor of Shantung and was viceroy of Pechili (1901–1907). After the overthrow of the Manchu dynasty, he became president of the Chinese Republic in 1912. In 1915 he tried to restore the monarchy but he was unsuccessful.

BETTMANN ARCHIVE

SAINT FRANCIS XAVIER

MORMON memorial of rescue by sea gulls.

GRAF ZEPPELIN, one of the airships designed and built by Count Ferdinand von Zeppelin.

Z

Zangwill, Israel (1864–1926), English writer, born in London and educated at London University. He is best known for his novels and stories about the lives of poor Jews in cities and villages. Notable among these are *The Children of the Ghetto* (1892), *The King of Schnorrers* (1894), and *Ghetto Comedies* (1907). His play *The Melting Pot* (1908) was a great American success.

Zapata, Emiliano (c.1877–1919), Mexican revolutionist, born in Morelos State. He was the leader of an agrarian movement from 1911 to 1916.

Zarathustra. See *Zoroaster*.

Zeeman, Pieter (1865–1943), Dutch physicist, born in Zonnemaire, Zeeland, and educated at the University of Leiden. He became professor of physics at the University of Amsterdam in 1900 and director of the Physical Institute at Amsterdam in 1908. His greatest work was in splitting up the spectral lines in a magnetic field, known as the *Zeeman effect.* He received the Nobel Prize for physics in 1902.

Zeiss, Carl (1816–1888), German manufacturer of optical instruments, born in Weimar. In 1846 he founded the Carl Zeiss factory at Jena, noted for microscopes, telescopes, and cameras.

Zenobia (3d century A.D.), queen of Palmyra. When her husband, Odenathus, was assassinated she served as regent for her son. Her armies were defeated by the Roman emperor Aurelian and she herself was captured and taken to Rome. Aurelian pardoned her, however, and gave her an estate near Tivoli.

Zeno of Citium (c.335–c.263 B.C.), Greek philosopher, born in Citium, Cyprus. He studied at Athens with the Cynic philosophers, then opened his own school, called *Stoa Poikile* (Painted Porch), from which the name *Stoic* was derived. The Stoics believed that man must control his emotions and accept the laws of the universe.

Zeno of Elea (5th century B.C.), Greek philosopher, born in Elea, Italy. A disciple of Parmenides, he went with him to Athens, where they founded the Eleatic school. Zeno opposed Pythagorean pluralism, notably in his four arguments that used its precepts to prove that motion is impossible. In the argument of Achilles and the Tortoise, for example, Achilles can never reach the starting location of the tortoise since he cannot cover the infinite number of points between them. Aristotle called Zeno "the father of dialectic."

Zeppelin, Count Ferdinand von (1838–1917), German inventor and aeronautical engineer, born in Constance, Baden. He fought with the Union army in the American Civil War and with the German army in the Austro-Prussian and Franco-Prussian wars. He retired from the army in 1891 as a lieutenant general and began experimenting with dirigible balloons. In 1900 he began manufacturing airships with rigid metal frameworks, including the *Graf*

Zeppelin and the *Hindenburg*, in his factory at Friedrichshafen.

Zeuxis (5th century B.C.), Greek painter, born in Heraclea, Italy. He was noted for his skill in expression and coloring. Among his great paintings were *Pan, Alcmena, Helena at Croton,* and *Penelope.* He is said to have painted a bunch of grapes so realistically, birds tried to eat them.

Zhukov, Georgi Konstantinovich (1894–), Russian general, born in Kaluga Province. He joined the Red army in 1918 and headed the defense of Moscow against the Germans in World War I. He became chief of staff in 1941 and in World War II helped break the German sieges of Leningrad and Stalingrad (1942–1943). He led the Russian offensive against Berlin (1944–1945) and commanded the Soviet occupation of Germany (1945–1946). After a period of disfavor, Zhukov became minister of defense in 1955.

Ziegfeld, Florenz (1867–1932), American theatrical producer, born in Chicago, Ill. He originated the American revue with *The Follies of 1907,* which was followed each year by successive shows known as *The Ziegfeld Follies.* He also produced *Rio Rita* (1927), *Show Boat* (1927), and *Bitter Sweet* (1929).

Zinoviev, Grigori Evseevich original name **Hirsch Apfelbaum** (1833–1936), Russian Communist leader, born in Elisavetgrad, Ukraine. With Lenin he founded the Social Democratic party in 1903, and in 1908 he was exiled from Russia. He returned after the Revolution of 1917 and became president of the Petrograd (now Leningrad) Soviet and a member of the Politburo in 1918. In 1919 he served as president of the Third International. With Stalin and Lev B. Kamenev he formed a triumvirate that ruled after Lenin's death in 1924. He and Kamenev soon became opponents of Stalin, and Zinoviev lost his government and party offices (1926–1927). Although he was readmitted to the party (1928), he was unable to regain power. In 1936 he was accused of, and confessed to, involvement in the murder of Sergei Kirov, and was executed.

Zinzendorf, Count Nikolaus Ludwig von (1700–1760), German religious leader, born in Dresden. Sympathetic with the Bohemian Brethren, Zinzendorf invited them to settle on his estate at Herrnhut. In 1737 he was expelled from Saxony after reorganizing the sect as the Moravian Brethren and serving as its bishop. He traveled extensively and set up several Moravian communities in Pennsylvania. He was allowed to return to Saxony in 1748, and he remained there until his death.

Zog I or **Zogu I,** also known as **Scanderbeg III,** original name **Ahmed Bey Zogu** (1896–1961), king of Albania. He fought for Austria during World War I. After the war he was minister of the interior (1920, 1921–1922) and minister of war (1921). From 1922 to 1924 he was premier of Albania and in 1925 became president of the Albanian republic. In 1928 he proclaimed himself king. He fled when Albania was invaded by Italy in 1939. He was deposed in 1946.

Zola, Émile (1840–1902), French novelist, born in Paris. With Gustave Flaubert, Alphonse Daudet, and the Goncourt brothers he was a leader of the naturalist school of fiction. In a series of 20 novels called *Les Rougon-Mocquart* (1871–1893), Zola tried to show the effects of heredity and environment on the members of a single family. In 1898 he defended the case of Capt. Alfred Dreyfus in his pamphlet *J'accuse,* a denunciation of Dreyfus' prosecutors. He was tried for libel and sentenced to imprisonment; however, he went to England and lived in exile until permitted to return to France. His other works include *La confession de Claude* (1865), *Le voeu d'une morte* (1866) and *Thérèse Raquin* (1867). *Germinal* (1885) is considered one of his best works. Among his works of criticism are *Mes Haines* (1886), *Le naturalisme au théâtre* (1881), and *Les romanciers naturalistes* (1881).

Zorach, William (1887–1966), American sculptor, born in Lithuania. Sculptor for the U.S. Post Office Building, Washington, D.C. He died Nov. 15, 1966, in Bath, Maine.

Zorn, Anders Leonhard (1860–1920), Swedish painter, etcher, and sculptor, born in Mora, where he remained much of his life. He painted the portraits of Anatole France, Paul Verlaine, Marcel Proust, Auguste Rodin, and others. His sculptures include a bronze statue of Gustavus Vasa, in Mora. Many of his paintings portray Swedish country life.

Zoroaster or **Zarathustra** (c.6th century B.C.), founder of the religion Zoroastrianism of the ancient Persians, which saw life as a struggle between the spirit of good (Ahura Mazda) and that of evil (Ahriman), who would be defeated eventually. Their sacred book is the Zend-Avesta.

Zsigmondy, Richard (1865–1929), German chemist, born in Vienna, Austria, and educated at Vienna and Munich. From 1907 to 1929 he was director of the Institute for Inorganic Chemistry at Göttingen. He contributed much to knowledge of colloidal chemistry and invented the ultramicroscope. He won the Nobel Prize for chemistry in 1925.

Zwingli, Huldreich or **Ulrich** (1484–1531), Swiss religious reformer, born in Wildhaus and educated at Bern, Vienna, and Basel. He became pastor at Glarus in 1506 and a rector and teacher in Zurich in 1519. Zurich accepted Zwingli's 67 theses in 1523; these firmly established the Reformation in Switzerland. Zwingli opposed the sale of indulgences and denied the sacrament of transubstantiation. He was killed when the forces of the Forest Cantons, in alliance with the Archduke Ferdinand of Austria, marched against Zurich at the battle of Kappel. Zwingli had met with other reformers, including Luther, at Marburg in 1529, but he was not in complete doctrinal accord with them.

BIBLIOGRAPHY

Biography Index (7 vols., with supplements). The H. W. Wilson Company, 1946–1965.

Chamber's Biographical Dictionary, J. O. THORNE (ed.). St. Martin's Press, 1962.

Current Biography, CHARLES MORITZ (ed.). The H. W. Wilson Company, 1962.

Dictionary of American Biography, ALLEN JOHNSON and DUMAS MALONE (eds.). Charles Scribner's Sons, 1930.

The International Who's Who. Europa Publications, Ltd., 28th edition, 1964.

The New Century Cyclopedia of Names (3 vols.), CLARENCE L. BARNHART and WILLIAM D. HALSEY (eds.). Appleton-Century-Crofts, Inc., 1954.

Webster's Biographical Dictionary, WILLIAM ALLEN NEILSON (ed.). G. & C. Merriam Company, 1964.

Who's Who. St. Martin's Press, 1966.

Who's Who in America, JACKSON MARTINDELLI (ed.). A. N. Marquis Company, 1966.

Who Was Who. St. Martin's Press, 1960.

VOLUME FOUR

CAREERS

Choosing a career   371

Occupations   373

Bibliography   394

NYU

VOLUME 4

Careers

Choosing a career is more difficult today than ever before. In the past, children followed in their parents' occupational footsteps. Farmers' sons became farmers, and the sons of business and professional men chose similar vocations. Today, however, universal education and a wider variety of occupational choices open literally thousands of different careers to young men and women. What is more, these choices are constantly shifting. The harness maker and blacksmith were once essential members of every medium-sized community. As horses were replaced by automobiles, these once important vocations disappeared almost entirely. The space age and automation, however, have created new crafts in recently developed fields, such as transistorized circuitry, inertial guidance, and gyrodynamics. Finally, the general level of skills needed for the most rewarding occupations is rising. Shoeshine boys in Horatio Alger's novels could become heads of great enterprises solely through hard work, good judgment, and sheer pluck. Today, however, our society is fast becoming one of highly educated and skilled persons. A man's vocational status is strongly influenced by his educational background.

Factors in Occupational Choice.—Your future life will be strongly affected by your occupational choice. This choice may determine whether you will work or be unemployed; in some

callings employment is quite stable, and in others workers are frequently out of jobs. Your choice will also affect your chances of success or failure: a good selection will help you draw on your best talents. By the same token, a poor selection may emphasize your weaknesses. By satisfying your emotional needs, a good choice may lead to happiness. Success in an occupation that does not provide an acceptable emotional outlet may well lead to frustration. Your career will also help determine what friends you make. A woman will find it affects her chances of marriage. And a career will help determine the circumstances under which you retire.

EMOTIONAL MATURITY.—An intelligent choice of occupation demands a certain amount of emotional maturity. The young child is remote from the world of work, and he often indulges in fantasy. That is why he may dream of a "glamour" job, like frontier scout, Hollywood star, or big-league ball player. Gradually he settles down to a more realistic appraisal of his vocational opportunities. In his early adult years he begins to limit his choices to callings in which he stands a reasonable chance of success.

CAREER GOAL.—Whether you are a student who is thinking ahead or a person who is considering shifting occupations, it is important for you to select a career goal. If not, you are likely to shift from one unrewarding job to another. At the start you need not focus on a single job. Selecting a

broad vocational area, however, will enable you to plan your future education and training in the light of your occupational goal.

SELF-ANALYSIS.—Your choice of work should be influenced by your own interests and abilities as well as your knowledge of available jobs. You can best make an intelligent career decision if you analyze your aptitudes, capabilities, and personality before you make an appraisal of the occupational world. Finally, you should find the careers that require the things you have to offer. This strategy does not guarantee success, but it greatly improves your chances.

As indicated above, no career planning can be complete without self-analysis. Physical status can be important. Color-blind men, for example, are not hired as locomotive engineers. Some jobs require strong backgrounds in certain subjects. An interpreter, for example, must be fluent in at least two languages, and prospective engineers should have good school records in mathematics and science. Since self-analysis is difficult, it will be helpful to talk things over with a school counselor or a vocational counselor. Most city schools have counselors, and every large community has a state employment office, staffed with vocational counselors. They may be able to offer career and aptitude tests without charge. In some instances applicants for apprenticeships or jobs are required to take these tests.

JOB OPPORTUNITIES.—The next step is to familiarize yourself with the world of work. The survey of occupations and professions that follows will give you a start in exploring this world, but you should not be satisfied with a single source. The public libraries, school libraries, and school guidance offices usually have a wealth of occupational information. Public employment offices are good sources of up-to-date literature.

After you have thoughtfully surveyed the job outlook, you may be ready to match your opportunities with your capabilities. If you are a good "mixer," for example, you might be happy in a sales position. If you have an analytical mind and prefer to work alone, you may have the temperament of a researcher. It is important that you relate your choice to your abilities and interests.

EDUCATION.—Education and training are more important today than ever before. A high school or college education does not automatically assure you of success in a career. However, men and women with such educations tend to get better jobs, and generally

COLUMBIA BROADCASTING SYSTEM

LOUISVILLE COURIER-JOURNAL

CAREER CHOICE is guided by one's talents, education, and job opportunities. On the left is the noted orchestra conductor, Leonard Bernstein; on the right, a professional sky diver.

LOOK MAGAZINE

POLICE ATHLETIC LEAGUE

CAREERS. Bakers (*above left*), television performers and technicians (*above right*), and a worker in the aluminum industry (*below*).

ARKANSAS PUBLICITY AND PARKS COMMISSION

experience less unemployment than those with less education. Government studies show that adults who graduate from high school earn an average of $1,000 in yearly income more than their classmates who drop out. Over a lifetime, the average college graduate earns $100,000 more than a high school graduate. A Ph.D. in science is worth another $100,000. The poorly educated, on the other hand, form the hard core of the unemployed; disproportionately high numbers are on relief.

These differences are growing more marked because employment opportunities have been shifting from jobs requiring arduous work toward those that demand more training, skill, and education. Among the "blue collar," or manual, workers, for example, the number of unskilled jobs is shrinking. There is less need for workers in jobs that require unloading, digging, or hauling because mechanical equipment is replacing manual labor. Power-driven equipment, such as fork-lift trucks, derricks, and cranes, is taking the place of human muscle power. On the other hand, more skilled workers, such as mechanics and repairmen, are needed to install, maintain, and repair the ever increasing amount of complex equipment used in industry. Automation reduces the demand for unskilled laborers, but it calls for brand-new skills among workers who build and service automatic machines.

Farmers and farm managers will probably decrease in number in the years ahead, but business managers, government and corporate officials, and independent proprietors will increase rapidly. Sales, service, and clerical workers will be needed even more urgently. The most marked rise will take place among professional, technical, and similar occupations. Scientists and technicians, engineers, mathematicians, and teachers are but a few of the occupational groups included in these areas.

The reasons for this growth in "white collar" jobs are the increasing demand for persons who can do research and apply scientific findings to industry, the growing need for educational and health services, and the continuing rise of paperwork in business and industry. Relatively few new entrants can get "white collar" jobs without a high school education. Many positions require a college degree or graduate training. In short, workers who lack education and training are likely to be condemned to low-paying service industries or the ranks of the unemployed.

The panorama of job opportunities in the next few pages provides an overview of the world of work. It may help you to choose a general area of work, or it may suggest areas that you would like to study further. It is based on conditions in the country as a whole. Opportunities in your community may not be typical. One way to find out what local opportunities exist is to get a first-hand glimpse by trying part-time and temporary employment. Visits to your local chamber of commerce, labor unions, and professional and trade

associations may also prove rewarding. Among the best sources of information are the employers and workers in the fields in which you are interested.

If you find it difficult to make a suitable occupational choice, you are in good company. Millions of men and women share this problem. Solving it well, however, can provide one of life's great satisfactions. "Blessed is he who has found his work," declared the writer Thomas Carlyle. "Let him ask no other blessedness."

OCCUPATIONS

Architecture.—Architecture is as old as civilization itself. History records the names of a young architect, Imhotep, who built the Pyramid of Sakhara in Egypt 6,000 years ago, and of Ictinus, who planned the Parthenon in Athens more than 4,000 years later.

Architects plan buildings and supervise their construction. A successful architect may have many different kinds of commissions. A call to plan a small house may be followed by a request to design a bank with burglarproof vaults. The next assignment may be a shopping center. The architect's task is not merely to draw pictures of handsome buildings. He arranges the interior space efficiently; plans for corridors, stairs, elevators, and parking space; works out details for ventilation, heating, wiring, plumbing, and air conditioning.

The successful architect has an unusual combination of abilities—business acumen, a grasp of engineering and technical subjects, and an artistic flair. All states require an architect to have a license to practice the profession; in some states the only required formal education is high school graduation, and a budding architect may qualify to take the examination by working for twelve years in the

office of a registered architect. In practice, most successful architects receive professional training in architectural schools and liberal arts colleges.

Opportunities for qualified men are good, and they will grow in the 1960's and 1970's. The outlook for women is less favorable, unless they remain draftsmen. Architects who work for established firms get beginning salaries of $80 to $100 a week, and their earnings may reach five figures. Private practice usually yields small returns at the beginning, but well established architects may earn $500 a week.

■**DRAFTSMEN.**—Before a new house, ship, television set, or electric iron can be built, detailed plans must be made. The draftsman translates the ideas of the architect or engineer into detailed working plans. Most draftsmen are specialists, working in such areas as architecture, electronics, naval architecture, or structural drafting. A draftsman should have an interest in drawing mechanical objects and should possess numerical ability, motor coordination, and good form perception. The minimum educational requirement is graduation from a high school specializing in technical subjects (drafting, mathematics, and science). Opportunities will be favorable during the 1960's and 1970's. Some employers require two years of pre-engineering college training. Junior draftsmen begin at $75 to $90 a week, and a leader may make as much as $160 a week. Many architects begin as junior draftsmen in architectural firms.

The Arts.—This field embraces a variety of callings that fall into several groups—the performing arts, artistic drawing, and artistic arranging.

■**THE PERFORMING ARTS.**—Millions of people derive daily pleasure from listening to music or watching dra-

FORD MOTOR COMPANY

WESTERN ELECTRIC

MODERN METHODS of production require a high degree of technical ability and specialization, as in efficient agriculture (*left*) and in the development of missiles (*right*).

FRIEDMAN-ABELES

ACTING, often thought of as a glamorous career, is a demanding, competitive profession.

matic or dancing performances on radio, television, the movies, the theater, concerts, or ballet. The rewards are great for famous stars, but relatively few among the many thousands who seek a living as performers succeed in finding full-time employment. Fewer still find outstanding success.

Actors and actresses are in a "glamour" profession that fascinates many by presenting the prospect of making a stage character live for an audience. Not all aspirants, however, realize that it requires special talent and hard work to "make good." Among the 20,000 performers in the United States, only a few can become "stars." A larger group is employed regularly in supporting roles, and the great majority struggle to find small parts.

The prospective actor should have definite talent. Such talent includes a pleasant voice, good diction, and an attractive personality. An understanding of people is most helpful, and courage and perseverance are almost indispensable. Most important is the ability to be believable in a role.

The best way to learn how to act is to act, that is, to get experience as an amateur. Many do this in high school or college plays, or work in "little theater" groups in their home towns. Formal training for stage, screen, radio, and television is not altogether necessary, but it can be helpful. This training may be obtained at special schools for the dramatic arts and in some colleges and universities.

The financial rewards vary tremendously. Actors in the legitimate theater, movies, television, or radio enjoy a minimum wage and hours of work negotiated by labor unions. In a recent year, for example, the minimum weekly salary for actors in Broadway shows was $110. Well-known performers, of course, sign individual contracts at rates far above the minimums. Unfortunately, periods of unemployment are frequent, bringing annual earnings for all but a few outstanding actors very low. This figure has been below $2,000 for actors in the legitimate theater.

Dancers have performed since the beginning of civilization, and the dance is usually regarded as a theater art. Many dancers perform in musical shows and classical ballet, while others work part time in schools of the ballet or in colleges and universities. Still others become dance directors, heads of dance studios, or choreographers, creating new dance routines. This profession requires unusual talent as well as good health and vitality.

Professional dancers usually begin serious preparation no later than age twelve. The choice of a school is important, for a good one can appraise a pupil's ability, prescribe the right kind of training, and even help him to obtain employment. Top-notch dancers also master a broad liberal arts program to enable them properly to interpret dramatic scenes. Many colleges and graduate schools offer courses in the dance.

Like actors, professional dancers face heavy competition for a limited number of jobs; few dancers can boast steady employment. The outlook for qualified teachers of dancing, however, is much more favorable.

Musicians play in dance bands, symphony orchestras, theater orchestras, operas, and concerts. Many give private performances for small groups or play the organ in churches. Most work in large cities.

A top-notch performer must have talent, but this talent should be sparked by ambition, imagination, enthusiasm, and perseverance.

Professional musicians usually begin studying their instruments early in life. Many train under the direction of accomplished performers or in conservatories or universities with strong music departments. The latter offer broad backgrounds in musical history and theory as well as training in a particular instrument.

Singers of classical music occasionally become opera or concert stars. More frequently they are employed in the choruses of operas and musical comedies, and the majority are soloists in churches and religious institutions. Another group of singers specializes in popular music, working in musical shows on stage and screen, radio and television, and night clubs. The most popular make recordings.

Vocal talent is important in this field, but talent alone is no guarantee of success. It requires an engaging personality, good appearance, and excellent contacts. No one should consider this calling unless he has been auditioned by a qualified voice teacher to determine whether he has a chance of succeeding.

Singers of classical music usually take private lessons or obtain their training in music conservatories or departments of music in colleges and universities. Voice training is only one part of their education. It is supplemented by background studies in musical theory and history, as well as foreign languages for classical singers. Less rigorous training is required of popular singers.

Like the other performing arts, singing is a highly competitive vocation, and little growth is expected in this area. The demand for music teachers, however, will continue to grow, along with the expansion of schools and colleges. Financial rewards are high for a few outstanding singers, but the great majority will have to supplement their income with employment in other fields. Most musicians work irregularly; consequently, income is often low. Many musicians earn $2,000 to $4,000 yearly.

■**ARTISTIC AND RELATED WORK.**—Artistic drawing may be as old as man himself. We have learned about primitive man largely through his drawings in caves, made thousands of years ago. More recently, painting was a "fine" art, produced by an artist who was supported by a powerful patron. Today "commercial" art gives creative men and women greater scope for earning a livelihood by using their talents.

The most obvious and most important requirement for work in these fields is artistic ability. This talent should be developed by specific training, not only in commercial and applied art, but also in the fine arts (painting, sculpture, and architecture) and general academic studies. Training of this kind is available in art schools or post-high school institutes specializing in commercial and applied arts. Many art schools which are connected with universities offer bachelor's degrees in fine arts. After graduation, the budding artist should have on-the-job training.

Commercial artists comprise the bulk of illustrators, paint magazine covers, and illustrate advertisements in newspapers and magazines. They also prepare television and movie cartoons, greeting card illustrations, and package and wallpaper designs.

Commercial artists may do freelance work, selling their products to advertising agencies, commercial art studios, painting and publishing firms, television and motion picture studios, and department stores. They may also be employed on a regular salary basis as staff artists by sign shops, mail-order houses, greeting card companies, and other business firms. These artists work at different levels of skill. Some cut and paste up the basic parts of artwork. Others work at the drawing board, sketching, lettering, retouching photographs, or cartooning. Still others do lettering work. There are many specialities in this area. Several are briefly described:

Advertising artists and layout men work with advertising managers to plan advertising and to help arrange eye-catching advertisements.

Art directors develop ideas and designs, assign specialists to particular phases of a job, and buy artwork to use in their programs.

Cartoonists may work for newspapers, drawing their reactions to important current events. Others have become celebrities through their daily "comic strips," many of which are syndicated on a nationwide basis. In recent years cartoons have come into wide use in advertising.

Fashion illustrators sketch for fashion bulletins, catalogs, and newspaper and magazine advertisements. They work for fashion magazines, newspapers, garment firms, advertising agencies, and department stores.

Medical and scientific illustrators work for hospitals, clinics, and medical schools. They may make sketches of operations, prepare clinical photographs or models, or set up exhibits of posters or graphs.

■**ARTISTIC ARRANGING.**—No hard and fast boundaries can be set between artistic drawing, and designing and photography. There is ample opportunity for workers with talents in both areas to use them accordingly. In the latter area, however, the greater emphasis is on harmonious arrangement rather than on actual sketchwork.

Fashion designers are employed by large garment manufacturers, fabric companies, pattern houses, and theatrical companies. They create original designs or adapt existing designs for all types of apparel, with the emphasis on that for women and children. Creative designers are in constant demand in such areas as New York, Chicago, St. Louis, San Francisco, Los Angeles, and Miami.

A fashion designer should have a good sense of style, good taste, imagination, and a knowledge of color, design, and fabrics. A high proportion of the workers in this field are women. An experienced designer can earn $100 a week and higher. The top salaries run as high as $15,000 to $30,000 a year. An independent designer whose name is known will earn more.

Display workers usually arrange merchandise in show windows or showcases in department and chain stores, buying offices, and furniture and fabric showrooms. He may follow a plan prepared for him, or he may develop his own arrangements. Display work requires a combination of knowledge of merchandising, artistic talent, and skill in using such tools as spray guns and air brushes. Workers in the field are usually trained in high schools, vocational schools, or art schools. Those who advance to the top usually have college training. Courses in literature, the fine arts, and the theater provide a good background for developing imagination and creativity.

Industrial designers devise plans for a great variety of products, from ash trays to autos. The industrial designer may give furniture, accessories, lamps, utensils, or railroad trains new form and character. This requires a combination of artistic talent, merchandising know-how and knowledge of engineering. The industrial designer should have a four- or five-year post-high school course in industrial design. Beginners earn $4,000 to $5,000 a year; experienced workers, $10,000 and over.

Interior designers and decorators are employed by department stores, shops, hotels, steamship lines, and private home owners and apartment owners to plan and furnish interiors. They select and arrange furniture, draperies, floor coverings, and other decorations to achieve the maximum artistic effect and greatest comfort. Entrants into the field should have artistic talent, creative imagination, and a good business sense. The minimum course accepted by employers is usually a three-year course in a recognized art school or four years of college, with a major in interior decorating, followed by an apprenticeship of one to three years. Experienced workers draw as much as $150 a week. Top decorators earn salaries like those in other professions.

Photographers may be employed by newspapers, magazines, advertising agencies, printing or mail-order firms, hospitals, and colleges. Some freelancers sell their products; others own their own studios. It is an occupation that combines the artistic with the technical: ability to foresee pictorial possibilities with knowledge of light, filters, and other equipment. The minimum education is apprenticeship or training in a school of photography. The talented and well trained photographer has many opportunities for employment. The field is crowded, however, by part-time photographers. Such competition makes it difficult for

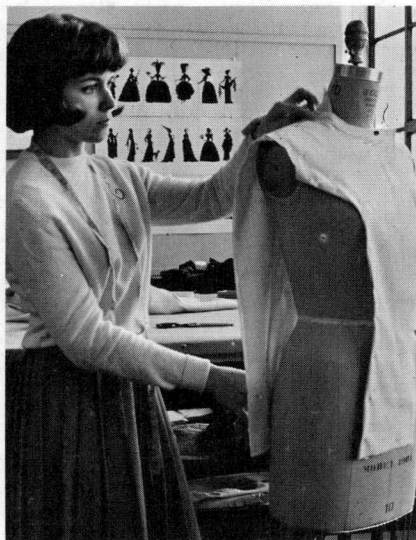

TRAPHAGEN SCHOOL OF FASHION
FASHION DESIGN: creativity in clothing.

aspiring photographers with less ability and training to find good positions.

Banking.—Many people keep bank accounts to safeguard their money, to earn interest, and to pay bills conveniently by check. Banks also issue cashier's checks and money orders, rent safe-deposit boxes, and handle estates in trust. The principal job of banks, however, is to provide funds for business enterprise. Indeed, bank credit has been called the "lifeblood of business."

Most cities and towns have one or more banks. These banks employ close to 750,000 people a year. Thousands of workers with similar occupational skills hold jobs in other financial institutions, such as savings and loan associations, personal finance companies, and government-sponsored organizations like the Federal Reserve System. The principal types of bank jobs are discussed in the paragraphs that follow.

Bank officers consist of the president, who supervises overall operations; one or more vice-presidents, who act as general managers or direct particular departments; a cashier; and an executive officer responsible for bank funds.

These men are responsible for making important decisions. A loan officer, for example, decides whether credit should be granted to or withheld from applicants. These applicants may be individuals who seek personal loans or businessmen who need credit for their enterprises. Banks may lend money for dental bridges or drawbridges, for carports or airports, for kitchen ranges or cattle ranges. The banker channels funds into businesses that are well run and have intelligent programs.

College training is not an absolute prerequisite for a position as a bank officer, for some banks tap potential leaders among their rank-and-file employees. Many banks, however, prefer college graduates, particularly those who have specialized in business administration, finance, or economics. The employment outlook for bank officers is most favorable, for banking operations are expected to expand. Officers in country banks and small city banks may start at about $9,000 a year. In the largest financial institutions their annual salaries may eventually reach six figures.

Bank tellers receive and pay out customers' money. Most tellers handle deposits and withdrawals, cash checks, and keep records of these transactions. Others have specialized jobs, such as taking care of Christmas Club accounts, computing interest on promissory notes, or handling payments on loans. Teller positions are usually filled by promotions from within the bank. A teller may be promoted to head teller or even to a bank officer position, particularly if he has college training.

Bank clerks handle the tremendous amount of paperwork required by banking. Every day, for example, about 30 million checks are written in this country. Most bank clerks are employed in sorting, recording, filing, and mailing these checks. Banks also hire thousands of bookkeepers, secretaries, stenographers, and typists. In many cases their tasks are much the same as those of office workers in other types of business.

Bank clerks should be able to handle figures quickly and accurately and should have office skills. High school graduation is usually required. Courses in bookkeeping, shorthand, typing, and business arithmetic are often helpful. The banking business is expected to expand, which will mean more clerical positions. Pay ranges from $45 a week for routine positions to $90 a week for secretaries.

Building Trades.—The nation's largest group of skilled workers, three million in all, are employed in the building trades. Good craftsmen can find jobs in all sections of the country, and their wages are higher than those paid to most manual workers. They also have opportunities to strike out for themselves as independent businessmen who contract to do specific jobs. These advantages are partly balanced by the seasonal nature of the work, sharp employment fluctuations that follow general business conditions, and the loss of time during bad weather.

Workers in the building trades are employed in two major types of industry, heavy engineering construction and building construction. Heavy engineering construction is the building of dams, canals, roads, mines, and the like. Such operations are often conducted in remote places, far from big cities. Building construction is the erection of homes, hospitals, commercial structures, and schools. It usually proceeds in or near large cities. In addition, building-trades craftsmen are employed to maintain and repair factories, stores, mines, hotels, and almost every other large business establishment. The principal workers are highly skilled journeymen, who are often assisted by apprentices, tenders, and laborers.

A college degree is not essential in the building trades, but a high school education, followed by training in a technical school, is desirable. The usual method of learning specific skills is through apprenticeship, a period of on-the-job training supplemented by classroom instruction. During this period the novice becomes thoroughly conversant with the trade's materials, tools, and methods.

Journeymen had a minimum average hourly rate of just under $4.00 in a recent year. This rate, however, was not identical for all trades. It ranged from a high of $4.20 for bricklayers to a low of $3.50 for paperhangers. Contractors averaged $6,000 to $10,000 yearly, depending on the size of their projects.

A building-trades craftsman may advance by becoming a foreman in charge of a small crew, an estimator of material requirements and labor costs for a contractor, a superintendent of a large project, an instructor in a trade, or an independent contractor.

The building trades have expanded tremendously in recent decades. Population growth and higher living standards are expected to continue this growth. Thus, workers in most building trades will be in demand.

In the paragraphs that follow, the work of the principal building trades will be briefly explored. This account will not include such trades as marble setter, asbestos and insulating worker, or stonemason, which employ only a few thousand men each. Each craft included in the text has at least 100,000 workers. Carpenters alone number more than a million, and over 400,000 painters are working in the building trades.

Carpenters work in almost all construction industries. They are often categorized in two ways—"rough" carpenters, who construct rough frameworks, subflooring, partitions, and rafters; and "finish" carpenters, who build stairs, lay floors, and install window sashes, doors, and hardware. Carpenters tend to work in a single area of construction, such as home, bridge, or highway construction. Some are employed in maintenance.

Carpenters should have good eyesight, mechanical aptitude, and a liking for outdoor work. The normal preparation is high school or trade school plus four years of apprenticeship training.

Painters and paperhangers work in different trades, although some craftsmen can do both kinds of work. Painters apply paint, varnish, and other such materials to the interior or exterior surfaces of buildings, while paperhangers cover room interiors with wallpaper, fabric, or plastic materials. Most painters and paperhangers work in new-building construction or do alteration work. Many are employed to maintain hotels, office buildings, manufacturing firms, schools, or other large structures.

Craftsmen in these trades should have good color perception, willingness to work at a height, neatness, and manual dexterity. High school and a three-year apprenticeship is the usual preparation.

Plumbers and pipefitters install pipes that carry water, steam, or other substances for sanitation, industrial production, or other uses in residences, industrial plants, and schools. Some other structures are installed by plumbers. Most are employed in constructing new buildings, although substantial numbers do repairs or alterations. Many plumbers are self-employed.

These craftsmen should have a high degree of mechanical aptitude, accuracy, and a sense of responsibility. In some areas they are licensed after passing an examination. High school or vocational school training is recommended as the best preparation, but some plumbers qualify through on-the-job training plus trade school or correspondence school courses.

Bricklayers have traditionally built walls, chimneys, and fireplaces of brick. Today they use many other materials, such as concrete, gypsum block, or structural tile. Bricklayers are largely employed in new construction of buildings and sewers, but some do alteration, modernization, and repair work. Most bricklaying jobs are found in big cities and industrial areas.

This craft requires an eye for straight lines and proportions, good health, and manual dexterity. Journeymen should have a high school education and an apprenticeship of three to four years. Some learn informally by working as helpers or hod carriers and observing or getting instruction from bricklayers.

Operating engineers are operators of power-driven construction machinery, such as power shovels, pile drivers, concrete mixers, and trench excavators. They work chiefly in construction of highways, dams, airports, and buildings, or operate machinery in factories and mines. Mechanical aptitude, physical endurance, and a good knowledge of machinery are required. Some craftsmen enter the trade after a formal apprenticeship, but many begin as assistants to operating engineers and obtain instruction from their supervisors.

Electricians lay out, assemble, and install electrical apparatus and wiring. Most construction electricians are employed by electrical contractors, government agencies, or businesses that do their own construction electrical work. Large numbers, however, are self-employed. Incidentally, their work is similar to the tasks performed by maintenance electricians, who outnumber them 150,000 to 125,000.

The work demands manual dexterity and the ability to do accurate, detailed work. High school training and an apprenticeship of four to five years are recommended, but some electricians' helpers gain a working knowledge of the trade by observation and trade school training. Journeymen electricians often set up their own businesses. Some later become electrical contractors, hiring their own workers.

Business Administration.—The owner of a small television repair shop runs his business himself. He buys electronic parts, hires and fires employees, places advertisements in local newspapers to attract new customers, and often keeps his own accounts; management officials do the same things for larger businesses. Their work, however, is more specialized and is conducted on a much larger scale. Often the quality of its management determines whether an enterprise will succeed or fail.

The top positions are held by corporation presidents, vice-presidents, and other company officials. They set company goals, make major decisions, and coordinate company activities. Management workers at the next level direct the work of such departments as sales, accounting, and personnel.

Management workers are an extremely large and important group. They number three million, excluding thousands of supervisors, engineers, and other professional specialists with managerial responsibilities, and many thousands in government service who have comparable positions. This is one of the fastest-growing groups of workers in the United States. It is estimated that 150,000 men and women will be needed each year to fill new positions of this type and to replace those who drop out. The paragraphs that follow will describe the work of the principal categories of business administrators.

■ACCOUNTING.—The principal types of accountants are public, private, and governmental. *Public accountants*, known as "certified public accountants," are private practitioners who serve their clients on a fee basis, like architects or lawyers. They help clients install accounting systems for record-keeping and later audit these accounts periodically to ascertain whether the company is operating profitably, to calculate taxes, and to forecast trends. *Private accountants* are employed as officials of business enterprises, with such titles as controller, chief accountant, or internal auditor. Their work is much the same as the public accountants', but they work for individual organizations. *Government accountants* work on the financial records of government agencies or private firms subject to government regulation.

Accountants may specialize in a number of areas. *Budget accountants* analyze the expenses of various departments to ensure their remaining within their allotted budgets. *Tax accountants* prepare tax returns for individuals or businesses. *Auditors* examine and vouch for the accuracy of a firm's bookkeeping records. *Cost accountants* install systems for determining a business organization's cost of production.

Few professions include more men than accounting. In a recent year 400,000 men worked in this area. Future employment opportunities are excellent, and highly trained accountants will be in great demand.

Accounting work requires facility with numbers, aptitude for detailed work, and accuracy. College training in accounting or a related field, such as business administration, is necessary; graduate work is desirable. In every state a certified public accountant may obtain his certificate only after passing a state examination. Almost all certificate candidates are required to have at least two years of public accounting experience.

■ADVERTISING.—Big business is based on mass production, which demands mass consumption. Advertising is the key to mass consumption, for it tells the public what goods are available, stresses their advantages, and encourages people to buy them. That is why "ads" are found in newspapers and magazines, on radio and television, on buses and subways, in window displays, and even written in smoke in the sky. We spend about ten billion dollars a year for advertising, and about 125,000 people work in the field. Some are employed directly by the firms that do the advertising. Even larger numbers work for advertising agencies. Others are on the staffs of advertising media, such as those mentioned above. Advertising workers include executives who plan the advertising and supervise the execution of these plans; copywriters who prepare the headlines, slogans, and text; media directors who determine

where to place the ads; research directors and their staffs who solicit the information needed for effective advertising; and artists and layout men who prepare eye-catching illustrations. Statisticians, sales experts, printing production men, and account executives (men who come into contact with advertisers) are also needed.

An advertising worker should have a flair for language, initiative, imagination, and definite ability to get along with people. A college education is not absolutely required, but most employers prefer to hire college graduates, particularly those with backgrounds in English, literature, and history. Competition for jobs is keen, but opportunities are abundant. Beginners can expect to make only $60 to $75 a week, but top salaries reach $25,000 a year.

■PUBLIC RELATIONS.—Advertising workers strive to sell a company's products; public relations workers try to "sell" the company itself. More specifically, their task is to promote a good public image for the individuals or organizations that use their services. They may prepare material for news releases, magazines, company publications, booklets, or brochures. They may use radio, television, or the public platform, speaking themselves or through others to whom they have given materials. They may use films, displays, posters, or signs. They may also advise their employers on what and when to communicate to the public, or whether to communicate at all.

The same personal assets and educational background that are essential to advertising workers are needed by public relations workers. It is a relatively new and fast-growing area, and opportunities for top-notch people are good. Salaries are comparable to those in advertising.

■PERSONNEL.—Personnel workers help their employers recruit good workers, train them, place them in the proper jobs, maintain records on them, and discharge them, if necessary. They may suggest employee policies to the organizations they serve, which may be business firms or government agencies. Some personnel workers, particularly management consultants

METROPOLITAN LIFE INSURANCE COMPANY

WORKING WITH PEOPLE is an essential part of both public relations and personnel work.

and labor relations experts, are self-employed. The personnel specialist may be responsible for a limited area, such as labor relations, employee training, safety, or job classification.

Personnel workers should have skill in handling people, leadership ability, and a knack for expressing themselves well. At least a bachelor's degree is necessary in this calling, and graduate work is helpful.

■PURCHASING.—An intelligent businessman once declared, "The biggest challenge in selling is smart buying." What he meant was that far-sighted purchasing can make the difference between profit and loss. That is why business enterprises and nonprofit community services employ 100,000 purchasing agents and similar buyers. In a large firm such a worker may be called "director of purchasing" or "purchasing officer"; in a retail store, "buyer." In any event, he is responsible for buying the raw materials, supplies, and machinery required by his employer.

A purchasing agent should have a good knowledge of the business that employs him and of the goods it needs. He should be at least a high school graduate, but college training is recommended. The outlook for entry and advancement for qualified persons in this calling is favorable.

There are other occupations in business administration. *Marketing research* helps company officials get a better idea of the kinds of products the people want and where new customers can be found by ascertaining the public's needs and preferences. *Industrial traffic management* involves direction of the movement of raw materials and finished products to and from business firms.

Communications Industries.—The post office, telephone service, and radio and television broadcasting are included in the communications industries. About 1,250,000 people are employed in occupations related to these industries, chiefly in the post office.

■POST OFFICE OCCUPATIONS.—Over 200 million pieces of mail are sent through the post office every day. Post offices also provide registration and insurance, sell money orders, and receive deposits in postal savings.

The great majority of the post office's 550,000 employees are postal clerks and mail carriers.

Postal clerks work behind the scenes and are rarely noticed by the public, except when they sell stamps or money orders, or provide other services directly to the public. They sort mail, cancel stamps on outgoing mail, and arrange for transportation of mail. Many of the operations that postal clerks once performed by hand are now automated. Electronic devices receive, process, and dispatch mail, at a saving in human labor.

Mail carriers, or "mailmen," as they are usually called, deliver and collect letters on given routes, usually traveling on foot in cities and in motor vehicles in rural areas. Carriers who deliver and pick up parcel post use trucks.

Other post office positions include *postmasters* and *postal supervisors,* who direct the work of postal clerks and mail carriers; *custodial service employees,* who maintain and service post office buildings; *motor vehicle operators,* who drive trucks carrying bulk mail. Despite the introduction of automated machinery, population growth and business expansion will increase the number of post office employees in the future. About 100,000 will be hired each year.

■**TELEPHONE OCCUPATIONS.**—Most workers in communications industries work for telephone companies. About two-thirds are telephone operators and telephone craftsmen. These callings, along with others in the telephone industry, will be described in the paragraphs that follow.

Employment in the telephone industry is expected to grow, but at a relatively slow rate. Most new workers will be replacements for some of the 700,000 currently employed.

Telephone operators help customers make special types of calls. A generation ago all calls were made by contacting the operator. Today most calls are dialed directly by the customer, but *information operators* are still needed to handle customers' requests for telephone numbers, while *long distance operators* help customers make person-to-person calls, collect calls, and calls they cannot dial.

A telephone call brings a vast amount of communications equipment into operation. Almost 200,000 craftsmen are required to install, repair, and maintain the telephone wires and equipment that handle the 325 million calls made in the United States every day. The principal occupations in this area are described below.

Telephone installers and repairmen place telephone receivers and complex switchboards into operation and service them. The latter involves locating trouble, making repairs, and restoring service.

Central office craftsmen check customers' lines to prevent breakdowns in service, maintain, and repair automatic equipment in central offices.

Linemen and cable splicers keep the network of wires connecting central offices to customers' telephones in good operating condition.

■**RADIO AND TELEVISION.**—Virtually every American home has a radio or television receiver. Programs reach Americans over these sets every moment of the day, which gives the impression that broadcasting is a huge business. Actually, only about 100,000 people are employed in it. This number includes free-lance workers, such as actors, singers, dancers, and comedians, called in for special assignments, as well as workers in allied occupations, such as the preparation of filmed programs and commercials. Broadcasting work falls into four general categories—programing, engineering, sales, and general business. Each will be considered in turn.

Programing workers plan, prepare, and produce radio and television programs. The work is supervised by a *program director,* who determines policy and makes arrangements for programs. A *traffic manager* prepares daily program schedules and determines the time available for advertisers. Individual programs or series are planned and supervised by *producer-directors.* At larger stations a *producer* assumes overall responsibility, including supervision of the program director. The latter may have aides, called *program assistants,* who assemble and coordinate items needed in a show, such as props, artwork, and slides. *Announcers* introduce programs, guests, and musical selections, and deliver commercial messages. Other important staff employees are *studio supervisors,* who are in charge of studio and stage equipment; *stage managers,* who direct actors' positions and movements; and *news directors,* who supervise the coverage of news and special events.

The engineering department of a broadcasting station operates the equipment that translates picture and

WESTERN ELECTRIC

TELEPHONE CABLE repairs are promptly made to restore vital communications.

sound into electric impulses that can be picked up by radio or television receivers. At larger stations this work is supervised by a *chief engineer.* All stations, whatever their size, employ *broadcast technicians,* who set up and operate the equipment needed to transmit pictures and sound.

Commercial broadcasters are supported largely by the sale of air time to advertisers. This is usually done by *time salesmen.* Large stations may have this work supervised by a *sales manager.* He may be briefed by *research personnel,* who analyze and report market information.

Finally, the business management of the station is under the control of *executive purchasing agents, personnel workers,* and other specialists in business administration. In general, this group performs the same kind of work as administrators in other lines of business.

In the near future, broadcasting will grow slowly, hiring about 3,000 new employees each year. Competition for this small number of jobs will be keen because many young people consider radio and television "glamour" industries. The best opportunities to enter the field will be in small population centers.

Community and Social Services.—A common thread runs through these occupations—all who follow them instruct, guide, and counsel their charges. Some, such as social and welfare workers, concentrate on social betterment of the underprivileged. Others, such as clergymen and teachers, serve all groups—the prosperous, the gifted, and the well-adjusted as well as the poor, the handicapped, and those who need guidance.

■**TEACHERS.**—Teachers comprise the largest group in this category. Full-time teachers outnumber all the others combined by more than two to one. Elementary school teaching alone employs more than a million persons; more women enter teaching than any other profession. Teachers are usually grouped as *kindergarten and elementary school teachers,* who provide programs for younger children; *secondary school teachers,* employed in junior and senior high schools; and *college and university teachers,* who instruct undergraduate and graduate students.

A good teacher must be thoroughly familiar with the subject areas in which he offers instruction, particularly in secondary schools and colleges. He should be interested in other people, especially the age group he teaches, and should have good health and nerves, for teaching is a complicated, demanding profession. At least a bachelor's degree (including professional courses required for certification) is required, and graduate work is recommended. Salaries vary throughout the country; usually they are lower in towns and small cities than in larger school systems. Classroom teachers' salary scales have risen to more than $10,000 in the biggest cities. In recent years high birth rates have led to a great demand for new teachers. In the near future about 250,000 will be required each year. The greatest demand will be in science, mathematics, and industrial arts.

■ **CLERGYMEN.**—Most young people choose the ministry, priesthood, or rabbinate as their life's work because they feel a call to follow their religious faith. Today, however, the typical clergyman is not merely a minister of his religion. He has civic, social, and recreational duties. He must be "all things to all men": preacher, teacher, pastor, counselor, administrator, architect, and financier. He serves his congregation on a close personal basis, and works in local projects and civic organizations.

The prospective clergyman should have deep religious convictions, a sense of dedication, a genuine concern for people, and high moral standards. Graduation from college is only the beginning. All major denominations require at least three years of seminary training, and some ask for twelve. There is an acute shortage of clergymen. The growth of population and increased church membership and attendance have created a tremendous need for men in this profession.

■ **SOCIAL AND WELFARE WORKERS.**—Welfare and social workers help others with difficulties that interfere with healthful and useful living. Social workers should be well-adjusted, interested in people and their problems, and able to encourage social adjustment in others. Professional status demands college graduation and the completion of two years of graduate study in a recognized school of social work. To be certified, a person must have an additional two years of paid employment in social work. There is an acute shortage of trained social workers, and fully qualified persons have excellent employment opportunities. This profession has a number of specialties.

Social caseworkers directly contact individuals and families, in an effort to help them overcome such problems as poverty, illness, and difficult family relationships. *Public assistance workers* are employed by state and local governments to screen candidates for public welfare and to appraise their needs. *Child welfare workers* deal with children whose parents are unable to care for them, or have neglected or maltreated them, and with children who have become delinquents. *Psychiatric social workers* work with psychiatrists and psychologists to help mental patients return to community life. *Probation and parole officers* work for national, state, and local governments, helping probationers and parolees readjust to society. *Social group workers* are employed by such agencies as settlements and community centers, public housing developments, and day centers for children or elderly people to develop group experiences in educational, recreational, or other social activities. *Community organization workers* are hired by such organizations as community chests, welfare councils, and religious federations to plan health and welfare services, assist in fund raising, and distribute the funds collected.

■ **HOME ECONOMISTS.**—Home economists were once employed only in teaching. The largest group of home economists is still comprised of teachers, but women who have been trained in the area may also find jobs in business, research, social welfare programs, and rehabilitation. Another point of difference is that home economics was once confined largely to cooking and sewing. Today, while still including those categories, it embraces such additional areas as use of home equipment, home management, and child care.

Home economists in business are specialists who help private firms promote the development of home products by testing food in kitchens or offering advice on kitchen planning and laundry problems on behalf of gas or electric utility companies. Some conduct programs for radio or television stations. Others perform research in food, clothing, or household equipment for the federal government, states, or universities. Still others serve as consultants who develop budgetary standards for social welfare programs. Finally, home economists help handicapped homemakers cope with problems.

Women aspiring to enter this profession should be well groomed, able to gain cooperation, and capable of working with many different types of people. At least four years of college training are required. There is a critical shortage of home economists in both the teaching field and the other areas.

■ **LIBRARIANS.**—Librarians are no longer mere custodians of books. Although they still guide the reader to the world of literary thought, they do much more as well. A librarian may conduct a story hour for small children, help a commercial artist find special prints, look up census data for a businessman, help a scientist check facts, or unearth historical information for a novelist. *Public librarians* serve all types of readers. *School librarians* work in school libraries with students and teachers. *College and university librarians* serve the needs of students, faculty members, and research workers. *Special librarians* work for trade and service establishments, industrial firms, research laboratories, hospitals, labor unions, and other groups, providing the specialized kinds of information and materials required.

The librarian should have above-average intelligence, an enthusiastic interest in scholarship and books, and an interest in people. Training usually includes a college degree and a fifth year of study in library science. There is a nationwide shortage of trained librarians, and this shortage is expected to worsen. Thus there are excellent opportunities.

Engineering.—Engineers belong to the largest men's profession in the United States. They have made impressive contributions in the design and construction of machines, equipment, and buildings; and they have developed many new products and processes, such as electronic computers, guided missiles, and color television sets.

Their chief jobs are to devise efficient ways of transforming raw materials into usable products and of producing and exploiting water power, nuclear energy, and other power sources.

All engineers must be interested in mathematics and science and have a strong aptitude for these subjects. They should also have good judgment and be accurate, systematic workers. A four-year college course in engineering is essential. Indeed, some colleges prescribe five years for an engineering degree. Every state provides for the licensing or registration of its engineers.

Engineering has been one of the fastest-growing professions in the United States, and rapid expansion will probably continue in the near future. Not all branches of engineering, however, will offer equally favorable opportunities. Specialties such as chemical engineering and electrical engineering are expected to grow quite rapidly, but relatively few new mining engineers will be needed.

Most engineers specialize in a single branch of the profession.

Aeronautical engineers develop and test aircraft and design aircraft parts. Some specialize, working on military planes, seaplanes, rockets, or guided missiles.

Agricultural engineers develop equipment and methods that make farming more productive and economical. Their efforts are directed toward designing tractors and other farm machinery, helping farmers make better use of electricity, and processing agricultural products.

Air-conditioning and refrigeration engineers work on the design and manufacture of heating, ventilation, refrigeration, and air-conditioning equipment.

Ceramic engineers design the plants and equipment used for manufacturing porcelain and chinaware, bricks and tiles, dentures, and coatings for rocket nose cones.

Chemical engineers design and operate plants and equipment that produce chemicals in large quantities. Many specialize in the products of a single industry, such as petroleum, plastics, rubber, or food.

Civil engineers design and supervise the construction of roads, harbors, airfields, dams, buildings, and many other structures. This is one of the oldest and largest branches of the profession. Civil engineers may have such specialties as structural, highway, hydraulic, railroad, and sanitary engineering.

Electrical engineers design and develop electrical and electronic equipment, communications equipment, and such electronic apparatus as television, radar, computers, and missile guidance systems.

Industrial engineers are specialists in the efficient use of machines, materials, and manpower. They often design plant layouts to ensure an efficient flow of work or install automated manufacturing processes.

Mechanical engineers design machines, such as jet and rocket engines and nuclear reactors, that produce power. They also develop power ma-

WESTERN ELECTRIC

ELECTRONICS TECHNICIANS using radar and telephone to route and guide air traffic.

chines, such as printing presses, elevators, and steel rolling mills.

Metallurgical and mining engineers are responsible for the extraction of minerals from the earth, the processing of metals, and their conversion into useful products.

Technology.—Technicians in engineering and related fields, such as science, are neither engineers nor scientists, but act as "right hands" to these professionals. Some technicians do work of a highly complex nature, as assistants to engineers and scientists. They cooperate in research, development, or design. Many conduct tests or experiments, operate instruments, and make calculations.

Positions in science technology require mechanical aptitude, mathematical ability, and manual dexterity. A high school education is the minimum prerequisite. A few technical high schools, particularly in large cities, train their graduates for initial entry. Other aspirants may take correspondence courses. Some large corporations conduct training programs, including formal class instruction and on-the-job training. Technical institutes and junior colleges (called community colleges in some areas) frequently offer courses of training, usually lasting two years, that may lead to associate degrees. These institutions often include engineering and science in their courses, which may help their graduates qualify as engineering technicians. Starting salaries range from $3,600 to $5,400 a year. Technicians with five years of experience usually have annual earnings of $6,000 to $8,000.

Aeronautical technology involves work in aircraft design and production. Technicians prepare layouts of aircraft structures and help in experimental studies of stress, flight tests, weight control, and the like.

Air-conditioning, heating, and refrigeration technology means work in research and testing equipment and analyzing production methods in these areas.

Chemical technology brings workers into contact with chemists and chemical engineers in the develop-

ment, production, and utilization of chemical products and equipment.

Civil engineering technology deals with the planning and construction of highways, railroads, bridges, viaducts, dams, and other structures. Technicians help engineers by preparing specifications for materials, estimating costs, drafting, designing, or surveying before actual work begins. Men trained in this area often become draftsmen, surveyors, or highway inspectors, or get jobs related to their training and experience.

■ **ELECTRONICS.**—Electronics technicians are concerned with radio, radar, television, navigational equipment, missile and space guidance, electronic computers, and other types of equipment that require vacuum tubes and semiconductor circuits. Technicians in this field generally become specialists in such aspects of electronics as induction heating, automation controls, or ultrasonics.

■ **INDUSTRIAL ENGINEERING.**—Industrial technicians, or production technicians, help engineers resolve problems relating to the use of men, materials, and machines in mass production. Some technicians make time-and-motion studies, analyzing workers' movements to bring about the most efficient use of tools and equipment. Others prepare layouts of machinery and equipment, plan the flow of work, or prepare statistical analyses of production costs to eliminate unnecessary expenses. These operations may help them advance into other fields, such as industrial safety and job classification and description in personnel. (See *Personnel* under BUSINESS ADMINISTRATION.)

■ **INSTRUMENTATION.**—A relatively new job that has arisen from the development of automatic controls and precision measurements in manufacturing is that of instrumentation technician. These technicians are trained in instrumentation, or in electronics, mechanics, or hydraulics. They help engineers or scientists to develop instruments for recording data, for regulating the operation of machinery, or for measuring the flow, strain, or pressure of moving parts or mixtures.

■ **MECHANICAL ENGINEERING.**—Such specialized categories as automotive technology, diesel technology, tool design, and machine design are handled by mechanical engineering technicians. They help engineers engaged in design and development by making sketches and layouts of machinery, equipment, and parts. Others test experimental engines and equipment. Still others help engineers in manufacturing departments of business concerns to eliminate production problems.

■ **METALLURGY.**—The processing of metals and their conversion into finished products are the responsibilities of metallurgical technicians. They may test metals and alloys to determine their physical properties and help metallurgists develop new ways of using metals and alloys.

■ **SAFETY.**—Recognition of the need for a more systematic approach to the reduction of industrial hazards has led to the job of the safety technician. In the area of atomic energy, for example, safety technicians help scientists cope with the problems of radiation safety, inspection, and decontamination.

Farming.—Farming is a way of life that attracts many families. The farmer has greater freedom of thought and action than most people, and he usually chooses his own hours. Most of the drudgery of farm work is now performed by farm equipment. The farmer's wife usually has as much automatic equipment (washer, dryer, ironer, dishwasher, freezer) as her city sisters. Children are given work responsibilities at an early age. These responsibilities instill a feeling of self-confidence that city life rarely can match.

Many years ago most farmers worked on general, or subsistence, farms. They raised what their families needed, with a little surplus to sell in town. Today almost all farms specialize in one product or a few. Indeed, specialized farming is increasing because efficient production requires specialized equipment. Three out of four American farmers own their land. Most of those who do not are tenant farmers, who rent the land they work. Usually the tenant owns his livestock and equipment. In some areas, particularly in the South, the landowner furnishes a cabin, tools, seeds, and work animals. In return, he obtains a share of the proceeds, after the crop is sold. Many sharecroppers, as these tenant farmers are called, have been displaced in recent years by the machinery used in cotton cultivation.

Many farm workers are hired. Their ranks fluctuate seasonally, reaching a peak of three million at harvest time. Many of these temporary farmhands are migrant workers who travel from one section of the country to another, "following the crops." These workers, whose plight was described in John Steinbeck's *The Grapes of Wrath*, are at the bottom rung in the agricultural and economic ladder.

Farmers should have physical stamina and coordination, a liking for outdoor life, and mechanical aptitude. College training is not absolutely necessary, but the more education a farmer has, the better his chances of success. The farmer today is more of a scientist than a laborer. He should know enough chemistry to handle soil and fertilizers properly, enough entomology to fight insects, enough plant and animal physiology to produce good stock and crops, and enough economics to market his produce profitably.

The number of farm workers has decreased sharply as agricultural productivity has risen. In 1860 a farmer could produce food and fiber for his family and four others. Today the figure includes 25 others. This helps to explain why only 9 per cent of the American labor force today consists of farmers. In 1860 the corresponding figure was 65 per cent. Farming still employs about six million persons, but the employment outlook is not rosy. Good opportunities may arise in particular areas of farming, but the general employment situation in agriculture is unfavorable. By 1975 fewer than five million persons are expected to work in this area.

A number of different types of farms are briefly described below.

■DAIRY FARMS.—"Milk factories," which produce milk and milk products, are found in most parts of the country, particularly near big cities. Many produce their own feed for livestock as well.

■LIVESTOCK FARMS AND RANCHES.— Hogs, beef, and sheep are produced on livestock farms and ranches. Methods of production are quite different in various parts of the country. In areas of low rainfall, few feed crops are harvested; many ranchers buy the rights to graze their livestock on public land. These ranchers spend much of their time in the saddle, truck, or Jeep, managing the herds, because many acres of pasture are needed to feed their stock. Many range cattle are sent to the Middle West, where farmers "finish" them by adding 200 to 500 pounds of beef through careful feeding. Hog producers usually breed their own stock and take care of fattening the animals for market.

■POULTRY FARMS.—Only a small percentage of all farms in the United States are poultry farms, but they are important in both domestic and foreign markets. Indeed, they caused considerable comment in international circles when the President of the United States, in 1964, attempted to persuade the Common Market countries in Europe to lower tariff barriers for American chickens. Many poultry farms concentrate on egg production. Others specialize in turkeys or ducks.

■CORN AND WHEAT FARMS.—Concentrated in the West and Middle West, corn and wheat farms offer certain advantages. Unlike farmers who tend livestock, grain farmers work long hours during the growing season, then take things easy when it has passed. Because corn and wheat are "cash" crops—they are sold on the market rather than consumed by the farmer —their production involves certain

risks. High prices mean prosperity for the farmer, but a drop in market price may cut his profits or lead to a loss for the year.

■FRUIT AND BERRY FARMING.—Fruit and berry farms need less acreage than most other farms. Such farms are located in sections where soil and climate are favorable. This is particularly true of citrus fruits, which require year-round warmth.

■TRUCK FARMS.—Vegetables, usually for large population centers, are produced on truck farms. At one time they were concentrated near big cities, but refrigerated trucks now make it possible to transport vegetables to market over long distances.

■COTTON, TOBACCO, AND PEANUT FARMS. —A substantial proportion of farms in the southern states grow cotton, tobacco, and peanuts. Competition from irrigated areas in the Southwest, however, has eliminated many cotton farms in the South.

■CROP SPECIALTY FARMS.—Crop specialty farms produce single crops, such as potatoes, sugarcane, or melons, or a combination of specific crops. They require experience, skill, and special equipment and machinery. This is even more true of such farms as fur farms, hop farms, and cranberry farms.

Occupations Related to Agriculture.— While the number of farm workers has greatly decreased, the number holding jobs closely related to agriculture has greatly increased. Such activities are often dubbed "Agri-Business." They include workers in feed mills, fertilizer plants, farm machinery industries, farm supply stores, and businesses that process, distribute, or transport farm products or supplies. Other related callings are professional or technical in nature and demand college training. The number of trained persons in these areas is constantly rising, and opportunities are very favorable. Some of these professional vocations, for which a farm background is helpful but not absolutely essential, are described below.

AGRICULTURAL EXTENSION SERVICES.— State land-grant colleges and the United States Department of Agriculture hire county agricultural agents to train farmers in the latest agricultural technology. *County home demonstration agents* help train farmers' wives in the latest homemaking techniques. Largely educational in nature, agricultural extension service is conducted chiefly through meetings, tours, and demonstrations.

■SOIL SCIENCE.—Soil scientists help farmers to understand and realize the possibilities of cultivated crops, grasses, and trees on their land under given management practices. This is done by analyzing soils in the field in terms of their physical, chemical, and biological characteristics.

■SOIL CONSERVATION.—Soil conservationists help farmers protect land against soil deterioration, rebuild eroded soil, conserve water, and reduce flood damage by providing technical information on proper land use.

■BIOLOGICAL SCIENCES.—*Plant and animal pathologists* do research on the

causes and control of diseases attacking farm animals and plants. *Geneticists* develop the strains and breeds of animals and plants that are best suited to the production of food and fiber.

■AGRICULTURAL ECONOMISTS.—These economists analyze the production, financing, and marketing of farm products. Their fact-finding, analysis, and evaluation help farmers in the economic aspects of their work.

■AGRICULTURAL COMMUNICATIONS.—This is an area that includes *crop reporters,* who gather information on crop production during the growing season, and *market news reporters,* who collect information on the trends of agricultural prices. *Agricultural reporters* and *agricultural editors* compile farm news and data for farm journals, farm bulletins, and farm broadcasts.

Health Service Occupations.—Recent impressive advances in preventive medicine, diagnosis, and surgery, as well as the development of "miracle" drugs, have enabled the medical profession to make significant progress. Higher educational levels and a rising standard of living have given the American public an appreciation of better medical care and the means to pay for it. Better medical attention has also become readily available to millions through the development of new forms of medical insurance. These influences have led to an appreciable expansion of employment in the health field. This growth will probably continue in the foreseeable future.

Everyone is familiar with some of the professional services rendered by doctors, dentists, and pharmacists. The work of psychologists, occupational therapists, dental laboratory technicians, and others who meet only a small proportion of the general public is less well known. In the paragraphs that follow, the work of the principal occupations in this field will be briefly outlined. The first group will be professional occupations; the second, semiprofessional.

■CHIROPRACTORS.—Chiropractors treat their patients without the use of drugs or surgery. Their system of treatment consists of "adjustments" of parts of the body, especially the spinal column.

Most states license chiropractors who fulfill certain educational requirements and pass state examinations. Most states require four years of training in a chiropractic school after graduation. Opportunities in this field vary according to the locality's acceptance of the profession. In a recent year the typical chiropractor earned about $10,000.

■DENTISTS.—Once limited to pulling diseased teeth, dentists today stress fundamental mouth health and the prevention of mouth deterioration. When teeth become diseased, dentists attempt to repair and treat them before resorting to extraction. Dentists now write prescriptions and advise on diet, oral infections, and disorders that may affect the general health of the patient.

A dentist should have a high level

of intelligence, manual skills, and scientific ability. A license to practice dentistry is required in all states. All aspirants must have four years of professional training in dental schools following at least two years of college training. The average dentist earns $13,000 a year, although some specialists make as much as $30,000. Population growth is outrunning the output of dental schools, and the need for dentists will probably increase in the near future.

■OCCUPATIONAL THERAPISTS.—Occupational therapists work with doctors, nurses, social workers, and other specialists to help mentally or physically disabled patients return to health. The occupational therapist selects recreational, educational, and vocational activities that will lead to the rehabilitation of patients.

Work in this area requires emotional stability, an interest in medical work, and a sympathetic but objective interest in people. The minimum education is four years of college training, followed by nine to ten months of supervised practice. There is no competition for jobs in this field. Indeed, an acute shortage exists. The shortage will continue, especially in cities and large towns.

■OPTOMETRISTS.—Optometrists examine patients' eyes with special instruments, diagnose visual defects, prescribe glasses or contact lenses, and recommend exercises or treatments that do not require drugs or surgery. Some optometrists specialize in such work as fitting glasses for persons who are almost blind, analyzing the role of vision in highway safety, or studying lighting conditions as they affect workers' efficiency.

Future optometrists should have mathematical and scientific aptitude, an ability to use delicate instruments, and good vision. At least two years of college and three years of training in a school of optometry are required to qualify for a license. Such licenses are required by all states. The average income of self-employed optometrists is about $10,000 a year. Some earn as much as $20,000. There is a tremendous demand for optometrists, and the supply of graduates from schools of optometry is unlikely to match the need in the near future.

■OSTEOPATHIC PHYSICIANS.—Osteopathic physicians usually develop a private practice, although a few treat patients in osteopathic clinics and hospitals, and a few are writers or editors for scientific books or journals. These doctors emphasize manual manipulation in their treatment of physical disorders.

Aspirants should have an interest in and aptitude for science, good manual dexterity, and good health. All states require a license to practice. A prerequisite is graduation from a recognized school of osteopathy, preceded by at least three years of college work. Most osteopathic physicians earn $9,000 to $15,000 a year. Specialists average $23,000.

Employment opportunities are growing for osteopathic medicine. Growing acceptance of osteopathy and the establishment of osteopathic

hospitals will continue to create highly favorable opportunities for osteopathic physicians.

■PHARMACISTS.—The pharmacist translates the physician's prescription into an effective and usable medication. At one time the mixing of ingredients into powders, pills, capsules, and ointments was his principal job; today he also offers many prepared drugs. Americans make tremendous demands on their drug stores, visiting them billions of times annually. The 55,000 drug stores in the United States dispensed 750 million prescriptions in a recent year. Besides filling prescriptions, drug stores also offer such items as ice cream, cosmetics, and books.

Pharmacists also fill prescriptions in hospitals and dispensaries, advise hospital staffs on the selection of new drugs, and teach in schools of nursing. Some are employed by drug manufacturers to inform physicians about new drugs and to sell medicines to retail pharmacists.

A pharmacist must be orderly, meticulous, and studious. He should have an aptitude for science and should enjoy dealing with people. All states require a license to practice. Post-high school studies, including undergraduate college instruction and pharmacy college, should take at least five or six years. Beginning pharmacists make $125 to $150 a week. Managers of chain drug stores earn about $8,000 a year, and proprietors of their own stores have incomes ranging from $10,000 to $40,000 a year. There is little competition for jobs in this area. Indeed, the annual crop of graduates has not been big enough to fill the demand.

■PHYSICIANS.—Physicians treat people who are ill or in poor health, help prevent disease, and direct the rehabilitation of those who are recovering from injury or illness. Treatment usually takes place in the doctor's office or in a hospital. When necessary, however, doctors visit patients in their homes.

Almost everyone is familiar with the general practitioner, or "family doctor." This group comprises half the physicians in private practice. In recent years the number of medical specialists has rapidly increased. Their specialties include:

Gynecology, women's functions and diseases.

Obstetrics, medical care before, during, and after childbirth.

Ophthalmology, the eye and its functions and diseases.

Otolaryngology, diseases of the ear, nose, and throat.

Pathology, laboratory diagnosis of origin, nature, and cause of diseases.

Pediatrics, the medical care of children.

Radiology, the use of X rays, radium, and other radioactive materials for healing purposes.

Psychiatry (to be discussed later), the treatment of mental illness.

Physicians must have above-average intelligence, an interest in science, an ability to make decisions in emergencies, and a good deal of emotional stability. All states require a license to practice. A prerequisite is

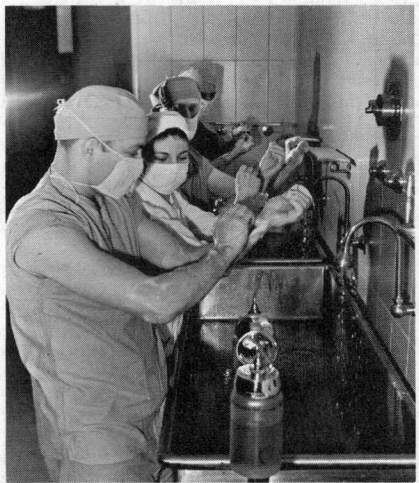

SURGERY requires antiseptic conditions.

graduation from an approved medical school. Most medical schools require three years of college work in exceptional cases and four years in most cases. Almost all states also require a hospital internship of at least one year. Most physicians earn between $10,000 and $20,000 a year. Some specialists make several times this sum. Physicians are needed everywhere in the United States, and future demands are expected to exceed the supply of medical school graduates.

■REGISTERED NURSES.—People "in trouble, sorrow, need, sickness, or any other adversity" are served by registered nurses. The need for nursing is as old as humanity itself; but nursing made its first step toward professional status in 1873, when the first schools for nursing were opened in this country. Since then, nursing has become a profession, and the registered professional nurse adds the letters *R.N.* after her name. The nurse is now a highly skilled expert who assists and collaborates with the doctor to "help people to live."

A prospective nurse should be reliable, a good student, and physically and mentally healthy. Above all, she must have a genuine desire to help the sick and injured. To qualify as an *R.N.,* a girl may pursue a three-year program in a hospital school, obtain a degree in nursing at a college or university, or complete an associate degree program in a community or junior college. General duty nurses earn $60 to $75 a week. The top pay for supervisors in industry and some school systems is $12,000 a year.

Professional nurses, more than 500,000 strong, comprise the largest group of health workers. The following are the principal specialties:

Hospital nurses, the largest group, are general-duty nurses who perform the more skilled bedside services. Sometimes they supervise auxiliary nurses, who have had less training.

Private-duty nurses are employed by patients or their families to provide individual nursing care in the hospital or the patient's home.

Office nurses work for physicians

or dentists in private practice or for clinics.

Public health nurses are employed in public and private health agencies, such as city and county health departments, schools, or the World Health Organization, a U.N. agency.

Occupational health nurses, or *industrial nurses,* provide care for employees of large business concerns.

Nurse educators teach in hospital nursing schools, colleges and universities, high schools, and schools of practical nursing.

■**PSYCHIATRISTS.**—Psychiatrists are physicians who are specially trained for diagnosing and treating mental illness. After studying their patients' problems, they plan systematic treatment, employing psychotherapy, psychoanalysis, or other methods. Many psychiatrists are in private practice; others are employed in hospitals, clinics, social welfare agencies, or counseling services.

A psychiatrist should be intelligent and should possess an analytical mind as well as emotional stability. He should have a good understanding of people and should be able to win their confidence. Long training is required before a physician can be certified as a psychiatrist. In addition to the formal training other doctors undergo, he must have three years as resident physician in a mental hospital or the psychiatric department of a general hospital and two years of approved experience. Psychiatrists in salaried positions receive $7,000 to $15,000 a year. Those in private practice generally earn $10,000 to $20,000 a year, but higher incomes are not unusual. There is little or no competition for positions in this field, since the need for treating the mentally ill cannot be met by the number of psychiatrists now practicing.

■**PSYCHOLOGISTS.**—Psychologists study human behavior through interviews, tests, rating scales, and personal case histories. Some analyze group opinions by conducting oral surveys or by using written questionnaires. Some teach in colleges and universities. Others counsel individuals or conduct training programs for workers. Still others administer psychology programs in hospitals, clinics, or schools.

A psychologist should have patience, dependability, and an understanding of people. The professional psychologist should have at least a master's degree in psychology, but the Ph.D. is becoming more and more important for advancement. Many states have certification or licensing requirements for private practice. Beginning salaries for psychologists with a master's degree are usually $5,000 to $6,000 a year; for those with a doctorate, $7,000 to $8,000. Experienced psychologists of course earn much more. In recent years the number of vacancies has exceeded the number of available psychologists in mental hospitals, mental hygiene clinics, schools, and counseling jobs.

A psychologist usually specializes in one of the following branches:

Clinical psychology, the most common specialty is concerned with maladjusted or disturbed people, usually in mental hospitals or clinics.

Child psychology concerns the problems of children from the very early years through adolescence.

Social psychology is the study of the social forces that influence individuals and groups.

Physiological psychology is the analysis of the relationship of behavior to the body's processes.

Counseling psychology helps people to make personal, emotional, or social adjustments.

Educational psychology is concerned with learning processes.

Industrial psychology involves the development of methods of training workers and of improving morale.

■**REHABILITATION WORKERS.**—Rehabilitation workers have helped victims of polio, arthritis, cerebral palsy, accidents, and war overcome despair and lead useful lives. At the end of World War II, for example, thousands of paraplegic American soldiers were confined to hospitals. Today about 70 per cent of these men are living in their own homes and driving their own cars. Most are earning their own living.

Rehabilitation is the restoration of a disabled person to his maximum physical, social, and vocational capacity, retraining him to live and work within the limits of his disability. Conducted under the supervision of a physician, rehabilitation has various aspects.

Physical therapists, in hospitals, rehabilitation centers, or schools for handicapped children, show patients how to use braces, crutches, or other prosthetic devices. Using special lamps and machines, whirlpool baths, or scientific massage, they retrain the patient to carry on normal activities.

Occupational therapists study the patient's abilities, ambitions, and interests, and provide appropriate activities that will shorten his convalescence, strengthen his muscles, and teach him new job skills. Occupational therapists work in the same kinds of institutions as physical therapists.

If the victim of a stroke, cerebral palsy, or a neurological disability cannot speak or hear well, a *speech therapist* or *hearing therapist* may enter the picture. He may also work with children who have cleft lips or palates, or persons who lisp and stutter. Such services were once offered almost exclusively in school and college clinics, but today they are available in hospitals and rehabilitation centers as well.

The *rehabilitation counselor* interviews the disabled person, administers aptitude tests, and helps him decide on his job field in the light of his disability and his talents. Thus he helps the patient enter the most suitable vocation. Like other members of the rehabilitation team, rehabilitation counselors are found in hospitals and rehabilitation centers. Others work for voluntary agencies or state and federal governments.

Success in this area demands an interest in people, an ability to get along well with others, patience, and emotional maturity. All workers in this area should have at least a college degree; speech and hearing ther-

apists should have a master's degree as well. Beginning physical therapists make $4,000 to $5,000. Rehabilitation counselors make $4,000 to $6,500 at the start. Supervisors and administrators can earn $8,000 to $9,000 annually, while the earnings of speech pathologists and audiologists with doctoral degrees may reach $12,000 a year. There is no competition for jobs; almost all institutions with rehabilitation services are understaffed.

■**VETERINARIANS.**—Veterinarians may be credited with great accomplishments in man's struggle against livestock diseases. They have destroyed pleuropneumonia, which almost wiped out the American cattle industry. They have almost eradicated bovine tuberculosis, which made hunchbacks of so many people in the past. They have learned how to control hog cholera, which once threatened the entire U.S. hog industry.

Veterinarians must have a love for animals and an interest in their welfare. They should have good powers of observation, for animals cannot talk. Finally, they must be strong enough to handle difficult animals. All practitioners are licensed in the states in which they practice. This license universally requires four years of study in a school of veterinary medicine, preceded by two or three years of preveterinary college work. Some states also require practical work under the direction of a veterinarian. No qualified veterinarian need fear unemployment, for the demand has far outrun the supply of graduates of veterinary colleges.

In government service, veterinarians protect U.S. livestock and poultry from foreign animal diseases by inspecting animals brought in from abroad. Within U.S. borders, they safeguard public health by inspecting meat, poultry, eggs, and butter.

Veterinarians in research laboratories are developing serums, vaccines, and medicines that will save millions of human and animal lives. Today their knowledge is exploited in space and nuclear experiments.

In industry, veterinarians serve pharmaceutical manufacturers in the development, production, and sale of biological products. They also serve feed and meat-packing companies.

Veterinarians in military service protect military personnel against animal-communicated diseases and help care for the animals used by the armed forces.

Many veterinarians are members of university faculties.

The largest number of veterinarians have private practices. Some specialize in livestock, poultry, or horses; others have hospitals to board pets—cats and dogs.

Semiprofessionals in Health Service.—Semiprofessional positions in health service combine some of the responsibilities and duties of the doctor, nurse, and scientist, but do not require the intense preparation needed to enter those areas of work.

■**DENTAL HYGIENISTS.**—Busy dentists employ dental hygienists to clean and polish patients' teeth (a process called oral prophylaxis), to chart mouth conditions, and to show patients proper mouth care. They may also act as chairside assistants to dentists, take X rays, and maintain instruments and supplies. Most work in private dentists' offices, but some are employed by public health agencies, schools, or the armed forces.

Dental hygienists are licensed by the states in which they practice. Successful completion of the examination entitles a candidate to assume the title Registered Dental Hygienist (*R.D.H.*). Preparation for the occupation includes completion of a two-year dental hygiene certification course or a four-year course leading to a college degree. Incomes of dental hygienists range from $2,000 to $8,000, the average being close to $4,500 a year. Since an acute shortage of dental hygienists exists, employment opportunities for qualified women are excellent.

■DENTAL LABORATORY TECHNICIANS.—Work that was once performed by dentists—the making of artificial dentures and dental appliances—is now done by dental laboratory technicians. Every job is a custom job, for no two patients have precisely the same problem. Some technicians do all types of laboratory work; others specialize in making crowns and bridges, arranging artificial teeth on dental appliances to make them look natural, or making castings of gold or alloys. Most work in commercial laboratories, but some work for individual dentists or for the federal government.

Experienced dental technicians usually make $80 to $125 a week. Most of them learn on the job. In the future the National Association of Dental Laboratories and the American Dental Association will jointly sponsor technicians who have completed a two-year training program at an accredited school and who have also had three years of experience in a dental office or a commercial laboratory. The job outlook in this area is good because the need for dental laboratory technicians is growing.

■DIETITIANS.—Dietitians work in hospitals, commercial eating places, industrial establishments, and such institutions as homes for the aged. In the 1960's, salaries for most dietitians ranged between $5,000 and $10,000. Top administrators may command $15,000 a year. The usual training is college graduation, followed by a year as a dietetic intern. A dietitian must also pass the certifying examination of the American Dietetics Association (ADA). There is a shortage of dietitians, and employment opportunities in this field will be excellent for years to come. They usually specialize in one of the four areas that are described below.

Administrative dietitians are really food service managers. They supervise the purchase and preparation of nutritious, well-balanced, and appetizing meals in hospitals, schools and colleges, company-owned cafeterias, airlines, steamships, and railroads.

Therapeutic dietitians, who usually work in hospitals and clinics, plan special diets for patients suffering from such disorders as diabetes, tu-

berculosis, hepatitis, and ulcers.

Teaching dietitians instruct classes in dietetics, food, and nutrition in nursing schools, colleges, and universities.

Research dietitians conduct investigations to learn how food can help people to maintain good health or combat disease. Space-travel nutrition has been their province in the recent past. Research nutritionists developed the tube-packed, semisolid foods consumed by the American astronauts as they orbit the earth.

■MEDICAL TECHNICIANS.—Like dental technicians, medical technicians work in an area that developed because fully qualified medical men, too busy to do their own technical work, began to delegate it to their assistants. Doctors who maintained their own laboratories and pathologists, who diagnose diseases in laboratories, were swamped with work. As a result they began to train assistants to take over some of their laboratory duties. Medical technology as a full-time profession was the result.

Medical technicians perform a great variety of chemical, microscopic, and bacteriological tests to aid in the detection and treatment of disease. They type and match blood for transfusions; make blood counts to diagnose anemia and other blood conditions; and perform diagnostic tests for other diseases, as hepatitis and cancer. Medical technicians also assist scientists who are conducting important experiments. Some are employed by pharmaceutical manufacturers to test medications. When the nation's children were inoculated against polio, hundreds of medical technicians were required to produce Salk vaccine.

Salaries of medical technicians usually range from $70 to $110 a week. Persons qualified to do this type of work may use the professional designation *M.T. (ASCP)* after their names. This means that they have been recognized by the Registry of Medical Technologists of the American Society of Clinical Pathol-

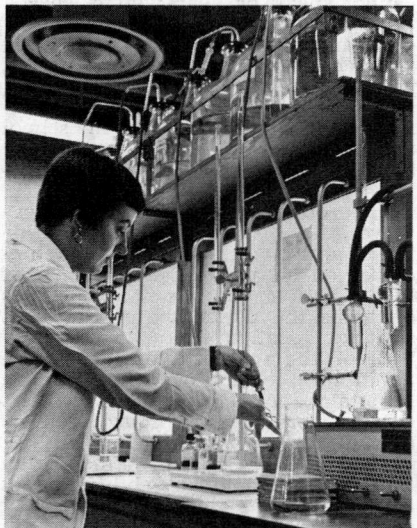

UNITED STATES RUBBER COMPANY

MEDICAL TECHNOLOGY, laboratory testing.

ogists. To qualify for this designation, a candidate must complete at least three years of college and one year in a school of medical technology approved by the Council on Medical Education and Hospitals of the American Medical Association (AMA). He must also pass an examination given by ASCP's Registry of Medical Technologists. At the present time there is an acute shortage of qualified workers in this field, and the demand for them is constantly growing. This means the employment outlook will be bright for many years.

Medical X-ray technicians work in hospitals, medical and research laboratories, public health services, doctors' offices, and business establishments. They work as part of a diagnostic or therapeutic team. In diagnostic work they help to take pictures of the body's internal organs to detect the presence of foreign matter, injuries, or malfunctions. In therapeutic work they operate X-ray equipment to treat cancer and tissue infections. A new and growing field is atomic medicine. In this area, radioisotope technicians help employ radioactive isotopes to diagnose and treat certain diseases.

Salaries for most medical X-ray technicians were about $4,500 to $5,500 in the mid-1960's. Top technicians earn $10,000 annually. High school graduates may enroll for a two-year program of studies in a hospital school or a medical school affiliated with a hospital. Fully qualified technicians who have passed the examination of the American Registry of X-Ray Technicians and have been certified by it may write *R.T. (ARXT)* after their names. Well-trained X-ray technicians will find very little competition for jobs. Indeed, the demand has outrun the supply for a number of years. This condition is expected to continue.

Lawyers.—Lawyers have played a prominent role in American history. Twenty-four signers of the Declaration of Independence were lawyers, and 21 presidents of the United States—three-fifths the total number —have been members of the profession. So are most congressmen and members of state legislatures.

A famous statesman, Joseph H. Choate, once idealized the aims of the legal profession in the following terms: "to establish justice, to maintain the rights of man, to defend the helpless and oppressed, to succor innocence and to punish guilt, to aid in the solution of those great questions, legal and constitutional, which are constantly being evolved from the ever-varying affairs and business of men, duties that may well challenge the best powers of men's intellect and the noblest qualities of the human heart."

Success in law requires an ability to think clearly and logically and to express oneself well in speech and writing, trustworthiness, and the knack of winning people's confidence. Before a lawyer can be admitted to practice, he must "pass the bar"— pass a state-administered written examination. At one time an aspirant was allowed to take this examination after serving an apprenticeship with an established lawyer. Technically, this method of qualifying for the bar examinations is still possible, provided it is combined with some study in a law school, but few candidates take advantage of it. Two states, nevertheless, still require a clerkship in a law office after the budding lawyer has completed his legal studies. These studies entail six years of full-time study after high school, three or four of them in law school.

Lawyers' incomes vary greatly, particularly among those who practice privately. Beginners who work for large concerns have an average annual salary of $6,000. At the other end of the scale, a small minority earn more than $25,000 a year. The need for lawyers will gradually increase, particularly in the areas of corporation, patent, and labor law. Competition for jobs, nevertheless, is keen. Graduates of well-recognized law schools and those who place in the upper 10 per cent of their classes are sought out for employment. The remainder have a more difficult time finding salaried positions or establishing their own practices.

Most lawyers are *general practitioners,* who handle a wide variety of legal activities for their clients. Others are *advocates,* or trial lawyers, who represent their clients in court. Others still are *advisers,* who show their clients how to stay out of court. They inform them of their rights and duties in the conduct of their affairs.

Lawyers also specialize in particular areas, such as corporation law, criminal law, labor law, patent law, real estate law, tax law, and international law.

Many persons with legal training do not practice law, but enter occupations that enable them to use their knowledge of law. They may become FBI agents, insurance adjusters, tax collectors, or probation officers.

The vast majority of lawyers are engaged in private practice. Among the salaried attorneys, most hold positions in government agencies. Some are judges. Most of the remainder are employed by private corporations, such as large manufacturing firms, banks, and insurance companies.

Mathematics.—Mathematics is both a field of study and a vocation. Contrary to popular opinion, it is not an area that has been thoroughly explored. New, vital fields are constantly opening. Albert Einstein's theory of relativity, for example, unlocked the atomic age. In the more recent past, mathematicians have helped give the world radar, supersonic flight, and nuclear power for industrial use.

The professions described below are not the only ones that employ mathematics extensively. Engineers, chemists, physicists, astronomers, and other scientists make constant use of it. What distinguishes the professions outlined in the section that follows from other professions is that their work is concentrated most closely about mathematics.

WESTERN ELECTRIC

MATHEMATICS, a field for the qualified.

■**MATHEMATICIANS.**—There are two general categories of mathematicians, those who perform research in "pure," or theoretical, mathematics and those engaged in applied mathematics.

Theoretical mathematicians are interested in basic truths, regardless of their future applications. Nevertheless, some of their findings have had important practical applications. It was the theory of electromagnetic waves, expounded by James Clerk Maxwell in 1873, that led to television broadcasting. His explanation of the nature of radio waves made this industry possible. Theoretical mathematicians often conduct their activities at universities where they teach mathematics.

Applied mathematicians are more likely to see the results of their efforts, which are usually concerned with specific scientific or industrial problems. In developing Nike, the American Army's anti-aircraft missile, for example, mathematicians first explored the paths taken by aerodynamic, radar, and military experts. Today many mathematicians are exploiting electric computers, machines that can perform 60,000 different computations each second.

Mathematicians must have keen, logical minds and a desire to solve new and difficult problems. Beginning mathematicians with bachelor's degrees can earn about $6,000 a year in industry. New graduates with doctorates average $11,000 a year. A college degree, with a strong major in mathematics, is a minimum essential. There is a great shortage of well-trained mathematicians, and employers compete to secure their services. In short, qualified persons can enter the field with little or no difficulty. This situation will probably continue for years.

■**STATISTICIANS.**—Statisticians collect, analyze, and interpret data that are used for forecasting the population growth, estimating the size of farm crops, the effects of new marketing programs, the effectiveness of a vaccine in preventing polio, and many other purposes. Some statisticians specialize in mathematical statistics. They attempt to improve statistical methods used in any subject area. Applied statisticians collect and analyze data in a particular field, such as economics, psychology, public health, finance, or engineering.

Like mathematicians, statisticians are required to have bachelor's degrees. A doctorate is a definite asset for those seeking advancement. Beginning salaries for statisticians with bachelor's degrees, for example, are usually $5,500 to $6,500; for those with doctorates, $7,500 to $9,000. The employment trend in this area is quite favorable: the growing use of computers will increase the demand. There is little competition for jobs, except in high-level positions.

■**ACTUARIES.**—Actuaries have been called the "mathematical pilots" of life insurance companies." They prepare tables of death rates and calculate premiums on the basis of the data in these tables. They suggest the benefits that a policy should pay. When premiums paid by insured persons greatly exceed actual payouts, actuaries determine the dividends that policyholders should receive.

Actuaries are not confined to insurance companies. They may act as consultants to welfare and pension funds for private companies, unions, or government agencies. Actuaries are indispensable in the management of the Social Security System.

The minimum education required for actuarial work is a bachelor's degree. Novices draw $6,000 a year. Some rise to the position of chief actuary, which may pay $35,000. There is an enormous unfilled demand for actuaries, and some companies award scholarships to promising students. A top-notch person in this area will have no difficulty in finding a position.

Mechanics and Repairmen.—The general public has long patronized craftsmen who specialize in the repair of particular items, such as jewelry, watches, and shoes. With the increased use of automobiles and home appliances, the need for repair services has vastly increased. Almost every home has a gas or electric refrigerator, dishwasher, washing machine, range, vacuum cleaner, or electric pad; some have as many as twenty of these appliances. As automation becomes more widespread, the need for repairmen in industry will also expand.

The paragraphs that follow describe the work of these craftsmen. Earnings in these occupations usually range from $4,000 to $8,000 a year, depending on experience and training, number of hours of work, and wage rates. A few "aristocrats," like fender or body repairmen among the automotive mechanics, or servicers of electronic computers among the business machine repairmen, draw $10,000 a year.

In each of these callings the repairman should have mechanical aptitude, manual dexterity, and accuracy.

BOEING AIRCRAFT COMPANY

AIRPLANE MECHANICS, highly specialized technicians, assure the safety of air travelers.

Advanced education is not necessary for any of these trades, but employers almost universally prefer graduates of high schools or trade schools. In most instances the craft is learned through apprenticeship or on-the-job training. However, some employers of business machine repairmen, diesel mechanics, industrial machinery repairmen, and instrument repairmen supplement work experience with formal classroom instruction. Specific school training is required by television and radio servicemen, and trade courses have been established for watch repairmen in private schools.

A thoroughly trained worker should have little or no trouble in finding a job in any of these industries. Indeed, there are shortages of aircraft mechanics, business machine repairmen, and radio and television repairmen. The older trades, like jewelry repair and watch repair, however, are not expanding as rapidly as the newer crafts that deal with machines widely used only within the last one or two generations.

Air-conditioning and refrigeration mechanics install and repair equipment of this kind in homes, factories, office buildings, and other establishments. They are employed by shops that specialize in this type of repair and installation work (construction companies, air-conditioning or refrigeration equipment manufacturers, and dealers).

Airplane mechanics overhaul, service, and repair airplane parts or certify a plane's airworthiness after inspecting it. They work in airlines' maintenance shops, manufacturing firms, and the armed forces.

Appliance servicemen repair washing machines, refrigerators, toasters, and dozens of other appliances found in the home. Most appliance servicemen are hired by stores. Some work for independent repair shops, which they sometimes own. Others are employed by gas and electric companies or appliance manufacturers who operate service centers for their machines.

Automotive mechanics keep buses, trucks, and other motor vehicles in running order. About a third may be found in the service departments of car dealers and another third in repair shops. The remainder are employed by service stations, business firms that maintain their own fleets of motor vehicles, and manufacturers of motor vehicles. Mechanics employed by the latter make minor adjustments and repairs on assembly line automobiles.

Business machine servicemen adjust and repair office machines, such as typewriters, adding machines, calculators, cash registers, and accounting machines. They find employment chiefly in the service offices of business machine manufacturers. Some work in small, independent service and repair shops; and a few are on the federal government payroll.

Diesel mechanics keep farm machines, highway equipment, and industrial equipment like bulldozers, tractors, and other diesel-powered machinery in good operating condition. They work for the service departments of machine distributors and dealers or for government agencies and private firms that maintain their own fleets.

Instrument repairmen service automatic pilots on airplanes, voltmeters that measure electricity, and a host of other parts. They are found wherever many instruments are used—in gas and electric utility companies, chemical plants, and manufacturers of missiles, automobiles, metals, and many other products.

Jewelry repairmen refashion old jewelry, reset stones, and repair damaged pins, bracelets, and other types of jewelry. Most are owners or employees of small stores, but a few work in department stores.

Television and radio servicemen install and repair television sets, ra-

dios, phonographs, high-fidelity sound equipment, tape recorders, and public address systems. Many own their own shops. Local service shops, factories, and service branches of equipment manufacturers employ the rest.

Watch repairmen, or "watchmakers," repair and adjust watches, clocks, and other timepieces. They may own watch repair shops or work for the proprietors of such shops, or mail order houses.

Clerical Occupations.—Until the 1950's, "blue collar" (manual) workers outnumbered "white collar" (clerical) employees. Since that time the situation has been reversed; the nation's working force has become predominantly "white collar." The largest group of "white collar" workers is clerical. They perform record-keeping and other routine work required by business firms and government agencies. Among the approximately ten million people in the group are one third of all employed women.

The largest group of clerical workers includes stenographers, typists, and secretaries. Bookkeepers, office machine workers, and electronic computer operators comprise another big group. Other clerical workers are census takers, notary publics, and file clerks.

■**SECRETARIAL.**—Secretaries, stenographers, and typists are employed in almost every kind of office—government agencies, industrial corporations, medical offices, and many more. While all do some typing, those hired specifically as *typists* spend the major portion of their time at the typewriter. They may also proofread typewritten copy, sort mail, operate office machines, or perform other duties required by their respective offices. *Stenographers,* in addition to all these tasks, take dictation. *Secretaries'* duties range most broadly. Doing stenographic work is only a small part of their function. Indeed, they are invaluable members of the business "team." They often handle confidential matters, screen visitors for their employers, and handle situations that require intelligence, tact, and loyalty. Many work closely with the key executives in large firms.

These jobs require good manual and finger dexterity, neatness, and dependability. For positions demanding greater responsibilities, discretion and good judgment are essential. High school graduation is mandatory for new workers, and many obtain further training in business schools and junior colleges. There are many colleges now offering courses in secretarial studies. The pay ranges from $45 per week for junior typists to $110 for secretaries. Opportunities are excellent, partly because this area of work is expanding, and partly because there is a 25 per cent annual turnover.

■**BOOKKEEPING.**—Bookkeeping workers keep systematic financial records for business enterprises that show receipts and disbursements of funds, sums of money owed to the firm, and amounts it owes, as well as profit and loss. In a small establishment all the work may be handled by a general bookkeeper who also answers the telephone and acts as a general assistant. Larger firms have a more specific division of labor. Most workers in their bookkeeping departments are *bookkeeping and accounting clerks,* who perform routine tasks. Others, called *bookkeeping machine operators,* use machines to do similar work. These employees often work under a *head bookkeeper.*

These workers should be able to perform arithmetic computations rapidly and accurately. Those who operate machines should have good finger dexterity and good coordination of hand and eye movements. High school training is the minimum requirement, and some employers prefer workers who have completed junior college. Many companies offer on-the-job training. Earnings range from $55 to $90 per week. Opportunities in this area are good, but they may diminish as electronic computers and other machines come into more general use.

Office machine operators work in a growing field, for business offices, particularly large ones, are becoming more mechanized. Some of the simplest machines are operated by general clerical employees or statistical workers. The personal qualifications and training for office machine operators are much the same as for bookkeeping machine operators. So is the pay, except that the highest salaries of office machine operators are a little higher. The expansion of this field of work may be slowed by automation of offices, but the number of job openings is expected to increase in the years ahead.

The following kinds of workers are hired specifically for office machine work:

Billing machine operators prepare statements that detail customers' purchases.

Adding machine and calculating machine operators use electrically and manually operated machines to perform a variety of statistical calculations.

Mail-preparing and mail-handling machine operators are responsible for automatic equipment that handles mail entering or leaving the office.

Operators of tabulating machines and related equipment help sort and count large quantities of accounting and statistical information by transferring the data to punched cards and by running the cards through machines that record the information stored on the cards.

Electronic computer operating personnel work in a very rapidly growing area because in recent years the need for record-keeping for accounting, tax, and research purposes has soared. Electronic computers are being installed in many offices to save business and government from being drowned in a rising ocean of paper. These machines sort millions of facts and figures and process these data extremely rapidly. Calculations that once required months are now done in hours. Those that took days are now completed in a few seconds. Data-processing machines can operate with remarkable speed and accuracy, calculating and writing payroll checks, handling credit cards, and controlling inventories. These are but a few of the many operations they perform. This transformation from hand computations to complex electronic machines has been called an "information revolution."

Computer operators should have good eye-hand coordination, the ability to concentrate, and the power to reason logically. A high school education is an absolute minimum, and college training is often required for console operators. Salaries for peripheral equipment operators start at $3,700 per year. Console operators may earn $8,000 per year. A rapid increase in the use of electronic computer machines is expected, with a corresponding growth of opportunities for workers in this area.

Computers vary considerably, but most require the following workers:

Key-punch operators prepare data for "input" into computers by operating machines that record facts and figures by punching holes into cards. In some cases the data are recorded on paper tapes.

Peripheral equipment operators work for the fastest machines, computers that get information from magnetic tapes. The peripheral equipment operator transfers the information to be fed into the computer from punch cards or paper tapes onto magnetic tapes.

Console operators run the facts and figures that have been recorded on cards, paper tapes, or magnetic tapes through machines that perform computations. This is a key job, and sometimes console operators supervise other electronic computer workers as well. The output of these machines must be translated into words or numbers that people can understand. This is often done by peripheral equipment operators using "printers."

Tape librarians store tapes or cards that are used repeatedly.

Proprietors.—Some believe proprietors are a dying breed. After all, every one of the nation's 100 largest manufacturing concerns is a corporation, and these 100 corporations employ five million people and own assets amounting to 70 billion dollars. The fact of the matter is that small businessmen are flourishing as never before. In 1900 there were 21 business firms for every 1,000 people. In 1965, there were 26 per 1,000 population. These figures prove that small, privately owned business is not disappearing.

Many farms are owned by the men who till them. Four out of five service establishments, such as beauty shops and barber shops, laundries, repair shops, and amusement places, are operated as single proprietorships. Retail trade is also an area where there are many thriving small businesses that need only a small investment of capital and must be located conveniently near the customer. Businesses that depend on individual craftsmanship are also frequently privately owned. Custom tailors, photographers, and jewelers, for example, often run their own thriving businesses. About 3½ million people are in business for themselves, and this figure does not include farmers.

The great attraction of being self-employed is that the owner of the business knows his economic future is in his own hands. He uses his own ideas and makes his own decisions. Whatever he builds, he keeps.

The business proprietor should have initiative, a friendly, positive attitude toward others, organizational ability, and a willingness to work long hours. No specific education is required, but private business is a skilled occupation. A government survey showed that those who run their own business have better educational backgrounds than any other group of workers except professionals and clerical employees. Thousands of op-

WESTERN ELECTRIC

TELETYPE OPERATORS use machines capable of receiving and sending 100 words per minute.

U.S. ARMY

MILITARY DEFENSE of the nation is only one aspect of a career in the armed forces.

portunities are available to men and women with intelligence and initiative—4,000 new businesses are established every week. The turnover, however, is high. One out of every two new businesses fails within two years, two out of three in the first five years.

Publishing and Writing

■NEWSPAPERS.—More than 25,000 periodicals, including 10,000 daily or weekly newspapers, are published in the United States. About 125,000 workers are employed by these publications, half of them as reporters and editors.

Newspaper reporters gather information and write stories for publication. Some have specific "beats," such as police stations or courts. Others specialize in particular areas, such as sports, politics, and religion. On smaller newspapers, reporters may handle every kind of assignment as well as perform some of the technical "inside" work in newspaper offices.

Editors in newspaper work, as in other areas of publishing, make important decisions that affect the planning, selection, and approval of written materials. They often prepare leading articles or editorials that express the paper's point of view. Sometimes they assign reporters to cover specific stories or subjects.

Copy editors analyze typewritten copy to insure its technical accuracy and readability. The *editor-in-chief* has the responsibility for determining what will be published, in the light of its appropriateness and timeliness.

Newspaper work is more than a calling—it is a way of life. Outsiders often regard it as a glamorous occupation; but veteran reporters know it is really a demanding job, for successful reporters work hard to beat deadlines. Newspapermen nevertheless often turn down tempting offers of other jobs; there is always a chance of achieving immortality. Richard Harding Davis, Lincoln Steffens, Walter Lippman, and Ernie

Pyle are but a few among the legion of newspapermen who have achieved lasting fame.

■MAGAZINE WORK.—Like newspaper work, magazine work seems glamourous to would-be writers. That is why there is keen competition for a limited number of job openings in this field.

Free-lance writers are self-employed persons who contribute pieces to one or more magazines. They range from writers of "fillers"—small pieces that fill space between the magazine's main articles—to Pulitzer Prize winners. The range of payment, of course, is tremendous.

Technical writers are employed by specialized magazines, such as medical and scientific journals, to write pieces that require a thorough knowledge of the area involved. They must be both well informed in their fields, and capable writers.

Editors perform much the same kind of work for books and magazines that they do for newspapers: they procure stories or articles and transform them into the kind of reading matter that will prove interesting and understandable to the magazine's audience. An editor is usually responsible for one of the magazine's departments—fiction, books, art, music, public affairs, home furnishings, and so on.

Literary agents are not employed by publishers. They receive commissions from the sales of works by the authors whom they represent. They appraise manuscripts in the light of their potential salability and offer publishers the "cream of the crop." They serve as a marketing link between writers and readers.

Public Service.

—There are five principal kinds of jobs in public service: elective office, which requires that an officeholder receive a mandate from the people; appointive office, which usually depends on the will of the official who appoints the officeholder and on that official's victory at the polls; the armed forces; jobs in the

federal, state, or local government, usually in Civil Service; and protective service occupations.

■THE ARMED FORCES.—Our history is replete with military heroes—John Paul Jones, Admiral Farragut, Sergeant York, and scores of other men who showed their mettle in battle. Every schoolboy knows their stories. Less well known is the fact that the United States armed forces serve their country in peace as well as war. It was an Army engineer, Col. George W. Goethals, who built the Panama Canal; and an Army physician, Dr. William C. Gorgas, stamped out yellow fever and malaria in the Canal Zone. Our largest dams and flood-control systems were built by Army engineers. Physicians in our armed forces were among the first to use penicillin, sulfa drugs, and blood plasma. Some of our principal aids to navigation, such as radar, were developed by Navy scientists. Today our armed forces are active in exploring outer space.

There is more to the armed forces than combat. Many Army men and Navy "tars" are trained as riflemen and gunners; many others learn skills that they can later use in civilian life. A G.I. can learn such skills as radio and television repair, surveying, automotive maintenance, and drafting in the Army's 55 schools. The Navy teaches its "bluejackets" 60 skills in such fields as aviation, electronics, engineering, and photography. Girls in the Army WACS, the Navy WAVES, and Air Force WAFS can obtain training in such areas as hospital work, machine accounting, dental work, and aviation flight control. Many of the occupations found in civilian life are matched among the 2,600,000 men and women in our armed forces.

■PROTECTIVE SERVICE OCCUPATIONS.—Protective service occupations involve the enforcement of laws and the preservation of life, safety, and property. These jobs are found at all levels of government—federal, state, and local.

The United States has 315,000 *law enforcement officers*, such as FBI agents and federal, state, and local policemen—this number is not large enough to do the job. Each minute of the day and night, four serious crimes are committed—a burglary every 39 seconds, an auto theft every 2 minutes, and a serious assault every 4 minutes. The nation's crime bill is estimated to be the staggering sum of $25 billion each year!

Years ago the merchants of a medium-sized city would have a single night watchman to guard their property. Today the police department of a city of respectable size will include foot patrolmen, motorcycle squads, a detective bureau, an identification division, and special agencies to deal with juveniles and women. A large proportion of the uniformed force patrols the city in cars rather than on foot. Two-way radios keep these cars in touch with headquarters.

Scientific crime laboratories aid in crime detection. The kidnaping of the infant son of Col. Charles A. Lindbergh in 1932 was solved partly by a microscopic study of the wood in a ladder left at the scene of the crime. This analysis helped trace the criminal to his home. Footprints, forgeries, wood chips, and paint help pin crimes on their perpetrators.

Fighting crime is not the policemen's sole assignment. In every city they must unsnarl traffic jams, speed the flow of automobiles, and safeguard pedestrians. When the automobile was the "horseless carriage," the typical city stationed a few policemen at busy crossings to work hand-operated signs. Today's traffic systems are infinitely more complex. They include not only policemen personally directing motor vehicles, but also electronic traffic-light systems that adjust automatically to the flow and ebb of traffic.

Firemen have the job of protecting life and property against fire. Everyone has seen them draw up to a spectacular blaze with fire trucks and hoses, to direct streams of water at the fire. More important, however, is the quiet fire prevention work they conduct—inspecting factories, theaters, and other public buildings for hazards, checking the enforcement of local fire regulations, and educating the public.

Guards and watchmen are hired in many public institutions, such as jails, to protect property and to enforce rules and regulations. Others work for private enterprises.

■OTHER CIVILIAN OCCUPATIONS.—The federal government's *Foreign Service* has been called "not only our first line of defense in peacetime, but also our first line against war itself." The Foreign Service protects American interests abroad and improves the relations of the United States with other countries. "Today, as never before, is the golden period of the Foreign Service," declared the late President Kennedy, "and it will be so through this decade, and perhaps even more in the years to come."

At the urban and metropolitan level, *city and regional planners* are relatively few in number, but they are gaining ever wider recognition. A number of reasons contribute to this. In the first place, the United States is becoming more citified. In 1900 only two out of five Americans lived in cities; by 1980 the figure will be four out of five. Second, it is realized that the urban unit of the future will not be limited to a single city, but will encompass a whole metropolitan area. Air pollution, flood hazards, and sewage do not observe city limits. Nor do people. Commuters who live in the suburbs and work in a central city create vast regional transportation problems. Over three million people, for example, pour into New York City from three states every working day. Such problems cannot be solved locally. They call for area-wide solutions. City and regional planners are the most qualified persons to develop answers to these knotty problems.

The callings given above, like *postal clerks*, are not found outside government employment. This is not true, however, of most of the eight million positions in public service. (This number, which includes about 12 per cent of the workers in the United States, excludes the armed forces.) On the contrary, most of the occupational areas in public employment are also found in private industry. Accounting, engineering, medicine, law, stenography, and mechanical trades are but a few. About one-third of all government workers provide educational services, the great majority in elementary or secondary schools. The next largest civilian group, about a million, is engaged in defense activities or employed by the armed forces or such defense-related agencies as the Atomic Energy Commission. Then come several groups, each with more than a half-million workers. In descending order, they include health and hospital workers, general administrators (like enforcement authorities), postal service employees, and highway department employees.

What are the advantages of working for the government? There is a wide variety of jobs from which to choose. Many Civil Service employees, particularly those who have earned their jobs through competitive examinations, have tenure, or job security. Advancement may be attained by those willing to work for it, since there is usually a strong trend toward promotions from within. Salaries in the lower and middle brackets are generous, as are sick leave, pensions, and vacations with pay. In many instances public employees combine professional work with a strong dash of idealism. Many genuinely feel their efforts are helping their country or aiding mankind.

Sales and Merchandising.—In some places, people can buy farm products at roadside stands, sold by the very man who raised them. Direct sale from producer to customer, however, is the exception rather than the rule; salespersons usually provide the link between producers and consumers. About 4½ million persons are engaged in occupations of this kind. Most are retailers who sell directly to the public. The next largest contact is employed by wholesale or manufacturing firms who sell to retailers. Another sizable group consists of real estate and insurance agents and brokers. Relatively few people are engaged in miscellaneous sales occupations, such as newsboys, advertising salesmen, hucksters and peddlers, and securities salesmen. Finally, there are demonstrators and personal shoppers, whose jobs are closely allied to sales occupations. The following paragraphs are devoted to the principal callings in sales and merchandising.

Retail salesmen promote the sales on which the success of a retail business depends. These enterprises range from small retail shops, hiring a single part-time worker, to giant department stores, employing thousands of salespersons. All told, over 2½ million persons work in sales jobs. Every salesman must know his merchandise; some positions require special skills as well. A salesperson in the music department of a store, for example, may be required to play an instrument; and an automobile salesman should know how to drive and demonstrate the use of various auto accessories. In a self-service store, however, the salesperson has little more to do than ring up sales and pack the merchandise.

Wholesale salesmen work for business firms that buy goods for resale to other concerns, usually to retailing establishments. A wholesaler in automotive parts, for example, will stock the many kinds of automobile parts and appliances that are sold by garages, service stations, and retail stores. The wholesale salesmen calls on retail firms and attempts to convince their owners or purchasing agents to buy, using pictures, catalogs, or actual samples. Wholesale salesmen usually have regular routes, and visit their customers regularly.

Manufacturers' salesmen operate very much like salesmen in the wholesale trade. A food salesman, working out of his firm's home or branch office, makes the rounds of retail establishments that regularly buy his products. Salesmen of technical products, like air-conditioning systems or power plants, are sometimes called sales engineers or *industrial salesmen*. They spend long periods of time in the potential customer's plant, discussing technical details. After the equipment is sold, the sales engineer may train his customer's personnel to operate and maintain it.

Insurance agents sell life insurance, which pays a man's survivors in the event that he dies; they also sell property and casualty insurance, which give financial help to individuals or companies that have suffered losses through fire, burglary, accidents, hurricanes, and other emergencies. The latter agents are sometimes called property and casualty underwriters. Auto insurance and liability insurance are also sold by agents. An *insurance agent* usually works under contract to one or more insurance companies. An *insurance broker* is in business for himself or is employed by another broker to contact insurance firms that will best serve his customers' interests.

Real estate salesmen and brokers find renters or buyers and those who have homes or other property to lease or sell. *Brokers* are independent businessmen who not only sell and rent real estate but also often manage properties, arrange for property loans, and plan new building projects. *Salesmen* work for brokers. Their work consists chiefly of selling and renting real estate. Brokers and salesmen usually specialize—in private homes, hotels, office buildings, or other types of property.

Natural Sciences.—This era has been called the "golden age of pure research." Man has made great breakthroughs in knowledge of the atom, the chemical structure of matter, the biological laws of inheritance, and the stars in the universe. The most spectacular advances have been in the applied sciences. They have literally transformed the world, giving man supersonic airplanes, rockets that can travel 18,000 miles an hour and lift satellites into space, and instant worldwide communication. In the United States, the problem of major infectious disease is largely solved; and in coming years there should be great progress in fighting cancer and heart disease. Nuclear energy should bring about the tapping of the atom for power long before coal and oil supplies give out, thus bringing electricity to remote parts of the planet.

Numerically, scientists comprise a relatively small group, about 330,000 in all. Billions of dollars, however, are spent each year on the research projects they supervise, for they are indispensable to the nation's defense and welfare. Scientists are usually grouped into several distinct categories—physical scientists, like chemists and physicists; earth scientists, like geologists and meteorologists; and life scientists, like botanists and zoologists. The principal types of scientists will be discussed in the paragraphs that follow.

■PHYSICAL SCIENCES.—"Science moves, but slowly, creeping on from point to point," declared Alfred, Lord Tennyson. In recent years the pace of change in science has quickened, and the number of scientists has risen.

Chemists are usually found in laboratories. Some are employed in research or development to create new products or to find new uses for existing ones. Rocket fuels, synthetic fibers, and antibiotics are but a few of the many products they have helped to create. Other chemists analyze or test substances for quality, purity, and other characteristics. Chemistry is easily the largest field of employment for scientists. About 120,000 are now employed in this area, most of them in private industry. Others work for colleges and universities, the federal government, research institutes and foundations, and small commercial laboratories.

Physicists work in one of the fastest-growing sciences. A physicist may calculate the path a satellite will follow around the earth, develop a stronger textile fiber, or work a microwave amplifier to test a new theory. Physicists are in the forefront in developing electronic computers, readying astronauts for orbiting into space, studying the fusion of hydrogen atoms to tap the oceans' supply of energy, and many other pioneering enterprises. Whatever his immediate duties, the physicist tries to discover the fundamental laws of nature. He explores the nature and behavior of space, time, matter, and energy.

Astronomers study the universe and all its bodies, such as the sun, the planets, and the stars. Their observations form the basis of sea and air navigation, the calendar, and measurement of time. A few astronomers work for private firms, chiefly in the aircraft and missile industry. Many more are employed by colleges and universities. Only a small fraction of all scientists are astronomers, but they will be needed in growing numbers as more attention is devoted to rockets, man-made earth satellites, and space travel.

■EARTH SCIENCES.—Earth scientists are concerned with the earth and the atmosphere that encases it.

Geologists study the rocks, soils, and minerals of the earth to develop new mineral resources, among them deposits of oil and gas, and reconstruct the geological development on earth. They are employed by colleges, universities, and government agencies, as well as by oil, natural gas, and mining companies.

Geophysicists investigate magnetic, electrical, gravitational, and radioactive forces within the earth. *Exploration geophysicists* search for oil and mineral deposits. *Hydrologists*, who study the earth's waters, work on such projects as water supply for cities, irrigation, and flood control. *Oceanographers* study seashores, sea bottoms, and the oceans themselves. *Seismologists* analyze the vibrations

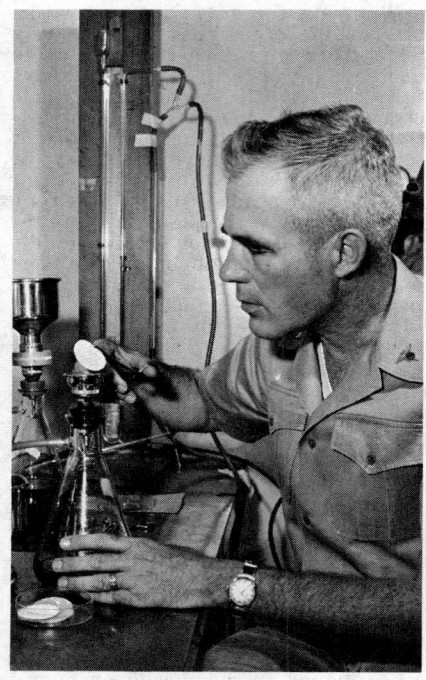

U.S. ARMY

BACTERIOLOGISTS study the structures, the functions, and the effects of bacteria.

in the earth resulting from earthquakes or blasts of atomic bombs. *Volcanologists* analyze volcanoes, hot springs, and the earth's heat processes. Most geophysicists work for private industry, chiefly the petroleum industry.

Meteorologists promote a better understanding of the forces that produce weather changes. The best-known meteorologists are the "weathermen," or *synoptic meteorologists*, who make daily weather forecasts. *Climatologists* work on long-range weather forecasts, while *industrial meteorologists* are concerned with practical applications of their science. Some of them seed clouds to induce rain or snow, and others are involved in control of smoke and air pollution. Most meteorologists are employed by the armed forces, the

Weather Bureau, or airlines.

■BIOLOGICAL SCIENCES.—Biological scientists deal with the basic processes of animal and plant life. *Botanists* study all aspects of plant organisms; *zoologists* are concerned with animals. *Microbiologists* analyze bacteria, viruses, and other organisms of microscopic size. *Anatomists* specialize in the form and structure of organisms and their organs. *Entomologists* are interested in the nature and behavior of insect life. The transmission of biological characteristics from one generation to another is the special concern of *geneticists*. *Nutritionists* work on the composition of foods and the processes by which living beings utilize food. *Pharmacologists* observe how drugs affect life processes; some discover new drugs or find new uses for known drugs.

Service Workers.—Service workers comprise a large and growing group. Most countries in the United Nations have populations smaller in number than the 7½ million men and women employed in this category in the United States.

What these workers have in common is that they all perform services for the public, instead of producing actual goods. The service station attendant, for example, supplies cars and trucks with gasoline, oil, and water. He also changes the oil, tires, and batteries. A restaurant hostess greets customers, escorts them to their tables, distributes menus, and makes certain that a waitress is available to serve them.

Service occupations include a broad variety of jobs requiring different background, training, and personal traits. Barbers, beauty operators, and restaurant chefs, for example, must be specially trained for their jobs; but kitchen helpers, maids, and janitors require little or no formal training. Physical strength is needed by porters, lifeguards, and men in many other occupations. A hat-check girl or a theater usher should have good manners and a pleasant appearance. A practical nurse or a travel guide should know how to deal with people.

Social Sciences.—The poet Alexander Pope wrote: "Presume not God to scan; the proper study of mankind is man." Social scientists are engaged in the study of man. *Anthropologists*, for example, concentrate on primitive tribes. *Archeologists* uncover buried civilizations and reconstruct the lives of ancient people. *Ethnologists* live among primitive tribes, learning about their ways of life. *Economists* concentrate on the ways man makes a living; they deal with international trade, taxation, money, banking, and other forms of business. *Historians* concentrate on man's past —his institutions and ideas, all peoples and nations. *Political scientists* study government and administration on the international, national, and local levels.

Most social scientists are employed by colleges and universities, but some are in the employ of the government.

—Daisy K. Shaw and Frederick Shaw

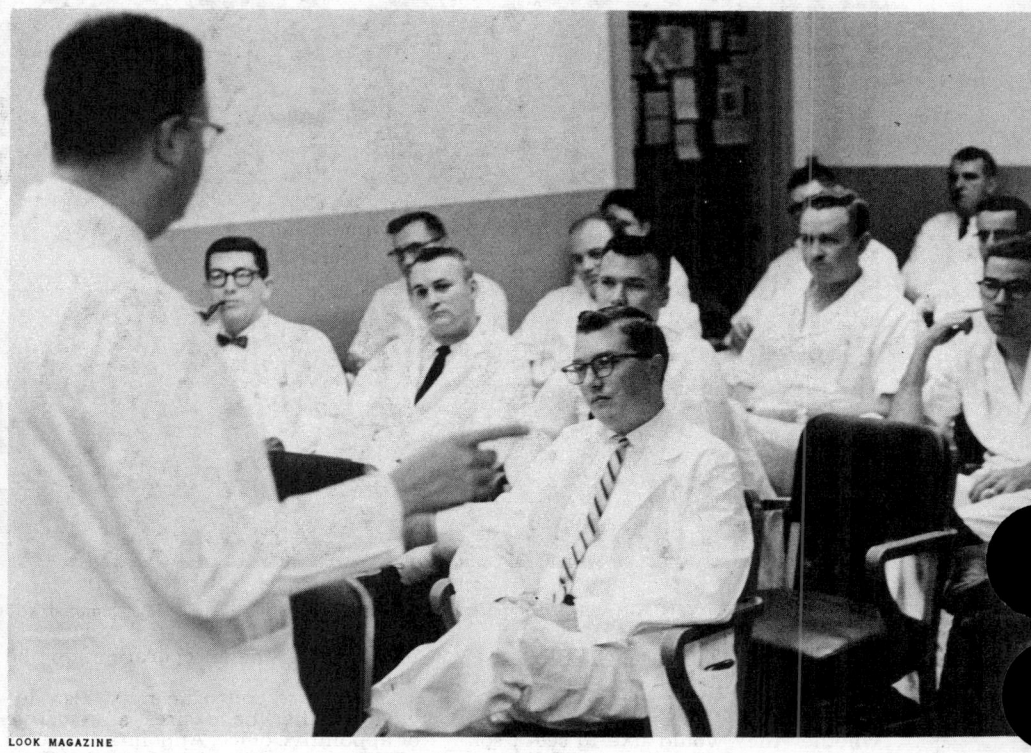

LOOK MAGAZINE

SERVICE CAREERS. A desire to help people can have an important influence upon the choice of a career. Opportunities for service are available in many fields, including religion (*above left*), medicine (*above right*), and youth work (*below*).

CHASE MANHATTAN BANK

LOOK MAGAZINE

THE NATIONAL CONVENTION selects the party's presidential candidate. Above is a demonstration for Johnson at the 1964 Democratic Convention.

A POLITICAL CAREER

Years ago, in a national public opinion poll, parents were asked whether they would like to see a son or daughter pursue a political career. The answer was a resounding, unanimous "no." Politics, they felt, was a dishonest and immoral field of endeavor that could only corrupt those who entered it.

This is a strange but understandable attitude. It is understandable because mass media inevitably bring the evils of politics and the misdeeds of politicians to the public's attention. On the other hand, it is a strange attitude because politics, as the profession dealing with the management of public affairs, conditions the climate of all human activity.

Today, the farmer, the laborer, the businessman, the industrialist, and the educator are directly affected by governmental action. One can name no field of activity that is not touched by public law; hence the art of government becomes increasingly important. Moreover, every year there is a deeper involvement of government in the affairs of people; and this involvement is acted out by those who carry on the work of government.

Is the political field a worthwhile endeavor? The honest answer is that it is frustrating, disappointing, and disillusioning. However, the opportunities are many; the life is exciting and brings the singular satisfaction derived from serving the community, the state, and the nation.

The first determination to be made is whether the individual's interest lies in the field of local, state, or national politics. To this should be added the field of party politics, aside from public office. Whatever the interest—whether the goal be the city council, the mayoralty, the governorship, the Congress, or the presidency—the objective determines the course to be pursued, the specialization of effort, and the preparation to be undertaken.

The future politician must also decide whether he desires an elective or appointive office. Appointive officers at the national level include the Cabinet and the heads of the many federal agencies and bureaus. At the state and local levels, they include the same general group, from department heads on down.

There are approximately 2,500,000 persons on the federal civilian payroll and 7,000,000 on state and local rolls. Although these estimates include both blue-collar and white-collar workers, they are still impressive indications of the steady growth of governmental activity.

To anyone interested in the administrative field, one can give only a general hint of the preparation to be made. Today there are thousands of lawyers in government, so that a basic legal education will suffice, leaving specialization for later. The Department of Agriculture has a veritable army of employees, but obviously the top career positions are occupied by those who have become specialists in some field of agriculture. The same pattern of opportunity is found in the field of space and

UNITED PRESS INTERNATIONAL

SENATOR EVERETT M. DIRKSEN of Illinois.

space technology. In any event, the goal is important, for it will automatically dictate the type of preparation that must be made.

The elective field offers a more precarious career than the appointive because the sufferance of the voters determines whether or not one can make it a lifetime work.

It has often been observed that a young man or woman preparing for a venture into politics should begin at the very bottom of the political structure. However, one can point to many governors, senators, congressmen, and mayors who have had very little contact with party organizations. They have been elected because they are well-known in some other line of endeavor, such as law, business, or industry.

Generally speaking, however, it is a good rule to take an elementary approach to politics. Nomination and election to a public office—whether local, state, or national—is essentially a party matter. The major political parties—Republican and Democratic—function through a vertical organization that runs from the precinct committeemen and county chairmen, through the state organizations, on up to the national committees and the national chairmen. Through party service, one can be put in line for a party call to fill a place on the ballot. Hence, the precinct—the very keystone of the party structure—is the ideal place to begin.

No better experience can be had than that which comes from doing volunteer work in the precinct and in party headquarters during a campaign. Here, as at no other level, one can learn about voter reactions, the nature of the appeal to be made by the candidates, the quality of party literature, candidates' personalities, how votes can be influenced, the importance of personal qualities in securing the confidence of the voters, and a score of other elements that

Typical Political Party Organization

Level	Conventions: Attendance and Business	Committees: Composition and Function
National	Delegates and alternates elected at state or district convention • Nominate candidates for the presidency and the vice-presidency of the United States, elect a national committee, and adopt a national platform	National party officers and representatives of each state • Direct national election campaign and act as liaison between state and national committees
State	State executive committee and delegates elected at county or other local conventions • Endorse candidates for state offices, adopt state platform, elect delegates to national convention, and elect presidential electors	County and/or congressional district chairmen and chairwomen and state executive committee • Direct party apparatus in congressional districts and counties, elect state party officers, and nominate national committeeman and committeewoman
Congressional District	Delegates elected at county convention • Endorse a congressional candidate, adopt resolutions for consideration by state convention, and elect district officers, representatives to state executive committee, and delegates to national convention	District officers and county chairmen and chairwomen • Conduct the congressional campaign, manage party affairs in district, act as liaison between county and state party officers, and plan district convention
County	Delegates elected by precincts • Endorse candidates for state legislature, elect county officers and delegates to state and district conventions, and adopt resolutions on issues	County officers and precinct representatives • Carry out party business in county, recruit and train precinct leaders, and organize precinct caucuses and county convention
Precinct	Any registered party member • Elect precinct or ward officers and delegates to the county convention and adopt resolutions on issues and candidates	Precinct officers elected at precinct caucus • Elect party candidates to office, get out the local party vote, and manage party affairs in precinct

enter into a campaign. This basic knowledge obviously leads to advancement in the party councils, and readies the individual for the day when his own name will appear on the ballot.

What basic academic or professional preparation does one make for all this? All basic knowledge is useful, whether it be the study of the classics, history, economics, or science. Several specific items, however, merit emphasis. The first is logical thought in presenting a case, whether for one's party or for oneself. The second is the capacity to present the case clearly, in terms that the public will readily understand. The third is the type of poise that begets confidence. The fourth is the development of a manner that wins friends; the whole political art is an intensely human business. The fifth is facility in using the mass media, on which a candidate must rely to reach the vast electorate.

How, then, shall a young man or a young woman start a political career? Perhaps, when all is said and done, there is only one worthwhile and very succinct piece of advice: Make a start.

—Everett McKinley Dirksen

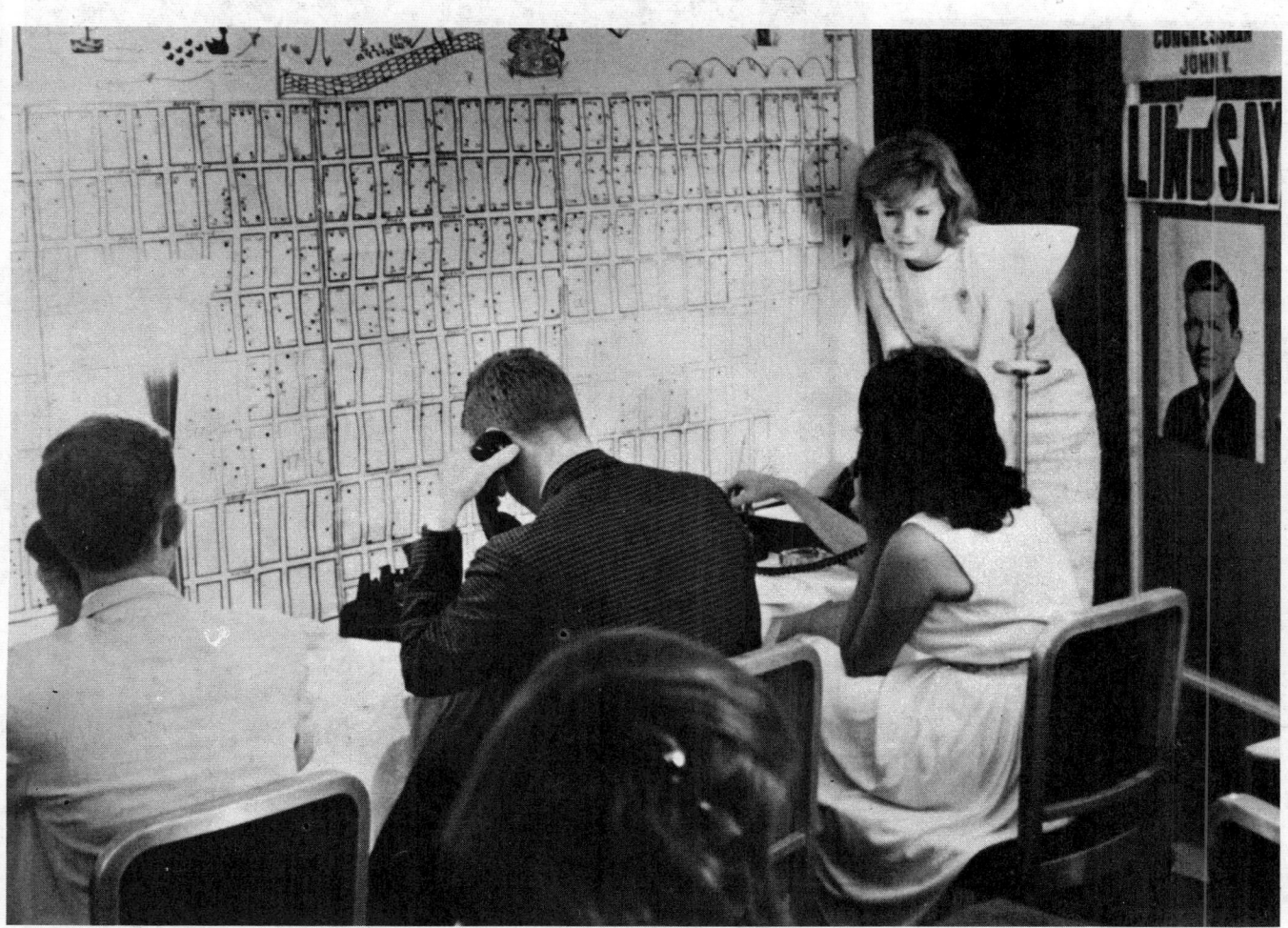

JOHN V. LINDSAY HEADQUARTERS

VOLUNTEERS perform an important role in a politician's campaign for elective office, as they constitute the major portion of workers.

PEACE CORPS

PEACE CORPS VOLUNTEERS spend much time with people. One volunteer treats a sore foot while another teaches baseball.

THE PEACE CORPS

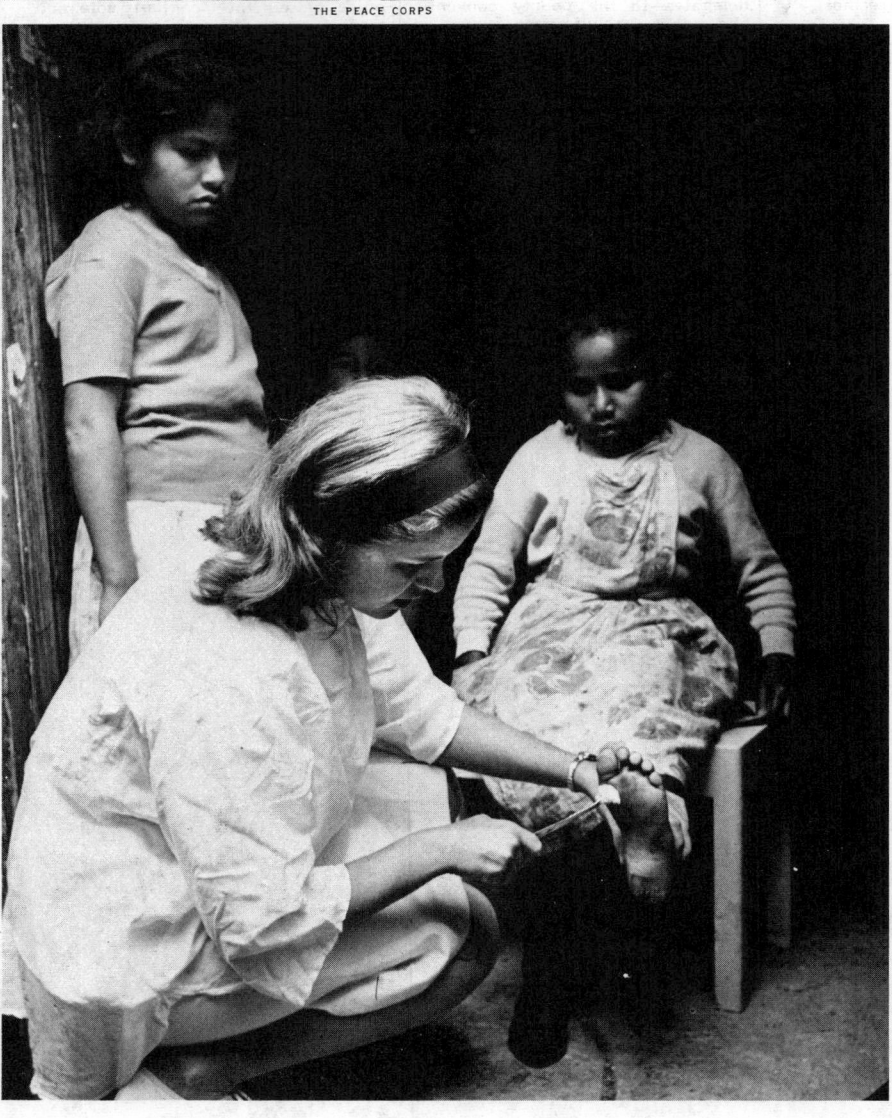

BIBLIOGRAPHY

CUNNINGHAM, ED and REED, L. *Guide to Earning a Living.* Simon & Schuster, Inc, 1955.

DAVEY, MILDRED A. and others. *Everyday Occupations.* D. C. Heath & Co., 1950.

How to Create Your Career. National Vocational Guidance Association, 1956.

KING, ALICE GORE. *Career Opportunities for Women in Business.* E. P. Dutton & Co., Inc., 1963.

KITSON, HARRY D. *I Find My Vocation.* McGraw-Hill, Inc., 1954.

MAULE, FRANCES. *Executive Careers for Women.* Harper & Bros., 1961.

McLEAN, BETH BAILEY and PARIS, JEANNE. *The Young Woman in Business* (rev. 2nd ed.). Iowa State University Press, 1961.

MYERS, G. E., and others. *Planning Your Future.* McGraw-Hill, Inc., 1953.

Occupational Outlook Handbook: Employment Information on Major Occupations for Use in Guidance. U.S. Bureau of Labor Statistics, Department of Labor, 1959.

SEEMING, JOSEPH. *Jobs That Take You Places.* David McKay Co., Inc., 1950.

SMITH, LEONARD J. *Career Planning.* Harper & Bros., 1959.

U.S. DEPT. OF LABOR. *Occupational Outlook Handbook.* Superintendent of Documents, U.S. Government Printing Office, 1963.

Vocational Guidance Manuals (a series of 50 paperback books on specific occupations). Universal Publishing and Distributing Corp.

Vocational and Professional Monographs (a series of 59 paperback books on numerous occupations and professions). Bellman Publishing Co.

Kindergarten methods 397
Educational playthings 406
Mother goose rhymes 408
Favorite poems 412
Songs and singing games 418
Stories 424
Fables 442
Bibliography 444

VOLUME FIVE

CHILD DEVELOPMENT

ARTHUR FREED

Child Development

KINDERGARTEN METHODS

THE MODERN kindergarten is an active, busy place. It is a small community planned for children, and in this community the children learn to live happily and constructively together. Parents often ask, "Is it essential that I send my four- or five-year-old child to kindergarten? What does he learn in kindergarten? Wouldn't it be just as well to wait another year or two and send him to first grade? How shall I tell a good kindergarten from a poor one?"

A DAY IN A KINDERGARTEN

Equipment of a Kindergarten.—The answer to all these questions lies in a visit to a well-planned, well-organized, progressive kindergarten. One day spent in such a situation will show most clearly some of the things that children learn and what kindergarten experience may do for them. As we watch the children at play, it is well to keep one outstanding thought in mind: Society today is organized in a way that makes it absolutely essential that people should live and work together. All the activities of the kindergarten are planned with this in mind. Four- or five-year-old children are individual rather than social, and we must give them an opportunity to be individuals; but they must also begin to learn their relationship to other people. In the home the child does not have as many opportunities for this as he does when he is playing with a group of children of his own age. The kindergarten teacher is trained in child psychology, and knows how to direct children's activities so that they will be educational and worth while.

We enter the kindergarten room before the children arrive. It does, indeed, seem to be a place planned for children. It is bright, sunny, attractive. There are small tables and chairs, a large sandbox, a piano. There are various arrangements of climbing bars and ladders, much provision for activity, for five-year-old children must be active. There is a workbench with tools; there are cupboards with materials; there are shelves filled with large wooden blocks. One corner is arranged as a play corner with doll furniture, a doll carriage and dolls. A bookcase is well filled with attractive picture books and storybooks.

The Day Begins.—Now the children are coming in. They have taken off their wraps in an adjoining cloakroom. Not all the children arrive at once. The first comer remarks joyfully, "I got here first!" He goes over and begins to climb on the "jungle gym." This little boy lives in an apartment where he cannot have a great deal of physical activity, and climbing and hanging on the bars of the jungle gym gives him much-needed exercise. More children are coming in. They all find something to do, for this first period is one in which every child is free to choose his own activity. Some begin to play with blocks; others go to the workbench with an air of great purpose; some use materials at the tables; a group is playing in the play corner. After they are well established, let us see what is happening.

A group of boys is playing with blocks. They are making a railroad station and tracks. A toy train runs on the tracks. Their talk is very interesting. It shows that they are doing good clear thinking as they work.

"The station must have a platform."

"I'm going to make a signal."

"Let's have a switch here."

"I'll build a tunnel."

The teacher comes over to see what they are doing. She talks with them, perhaps giving a suggestion or getting suggestions from them to make the play more valuable.

Over in the play corner, there seems to be a good deal of trouble. The children have organized a "family." They are cooking imaginary meals on the toy stove, serving them at the little table. The trouble is made by one member of the family whose behavior at table does not meet with the approval of the others. The teacher watches for a while to see if the children can settle it themselves. The dispute continues, so she gives a suggestion which helps the play to continue in a more organized way.

In another part of the room several children are playing "airport." They have made small wooden airplanes and have outlined a landing field on the floor with blocks, building several hangars. Now they "fly" around the room with the airplanes held high above their heads. They go very close to the group who are playing house. Soon the members of the "family" in the house complain that the airplanes are flying too close to them, and making too much noise. The teacher calls the airport group together and discusses with them the fact that airplanes are not allowed to fly low over houses and annoy the people who live in them. The children are very much interested, and when they go back to their play there are no more complaints from the "family." Two airplanes, however, try to land in the same space on the landing field and there is some confusion. This leads to a discussion of the care that aviators must take to avoid collisions, and of the way that airplanes land. Again the play is improved.

At the workbench, a number of children are carrying out some very interesting plans of their own. They saw and hammer most efficiently, occasionally needing help from the teacher, but on the whole working very independently. John is making a bridge. Peter is making a garage for his toy cars. Jean is making a doll's bed. Philip has a plan all his own: he is making a curious square object on legs—he says it is a camera. Some of the children who have finished their work at the bench have gone to another table to paint their wooden products.

In all parts of the room there is activity. The quietest place of all is at the table, where several children sit looking at picture books. At another table Mary is modeling with clay, and Hazel and Joan are drawing. They are talking to one another. We hear them making plans:

"I'm going to work with wood tomorrow," says Hazel. "I'm going to make a box for my mother."

"I'm going to make a dress for my doll."

A Formal Session.—After about an hour the teacher tells the children that it is time to put their work away. Unfinished work is put in each child's own locker or in another place provided for it. The children are most efficient in cleaning up. Some of them sweep up the sawdust around the workbench and hang up the tools. Others wash the tables that have been used for clay work. The dolls are left in good condition. Of course the teacher helps with all this, but the children are astonishingly efficient.

Now it is time for a story. The children bring chairs and sit in groups with the teacher. For a little while they talk over some of the work they have been doing. They are eager, however, to get to the story. Sometimes the teacher tells a story, but today she is going to use a picture book. It is a picture book showing life on the farm during four seasons. The children discuss it eagerly and ask many questions, some of which are answered by the teacher and some by other children.

"How does the farmer milk the cow?"

"What is a churn?"

"Why does he put corn in the silo?"

"Why do they spray the trees?"

A number of children have had interesting experiences on farms and tell about them. One little boy constantly breaks into the conversation. The teacher has to help him to wait his turn to talk.

After the story the children go to

the toilet, wash their hands, and set the table for lunch. It is a very simple lunch of orange juice or milk, with—in some cases—a cracker. It is a time that gives a great deal of opportunity for learning how to behave at the table and how to have pleasant, constructive conversation. Again one child tries to monopolize the conversation and has to be helped to see that he is only one of a group. He is an only child, and at home everyone is willing to listen to him all the time.

With young children who are so active, periods of rest are essential. Some kindergartens are fortunate in having folding cots on which children may relax. In others each child has a washable rug which he places on the floor and lies on for a period of from ten to twenty minutes. The children do not lie absolutely still, but they relax and lie there quietly.

After rest the children gather around the piano for music. They ask for favorite songs. Barbara says, "I've made up a song," and sings an original one. This is a period for singing, for listening to music, for rhythmic activity. The children skip, march, gallop, play that they are rabbits, horses, elephants. Muscles that have not previously come into play are being used as they play animals on all fours. There are many suggestions as to activities that might be tried. It is a time for free, joyous activity and for exchange of ideas.

The rest of the morning may be spent out of doors, or the children may draw, dramatize or go on an excursion. On this particular day the children are going with the teacher on a short excursion. So many of them are interested in trains that they are walking over to a place where they can see the railroad track. A freight train comes by. The children and teacher discuss it. Again one is amazed at the variety of their knowledge, the intelligence of their questions. There are other things besides information that one gains on an excursion: one has to learn how to conduct oneself in public places, observe rules for crossing the street and so forth. Now back to the kindergarten again and home for lunch.

Lessons for Life.—This, of course, is only a sample morning, and there are many things we have not seen. We have, however, seen the children learning to adjust themselves to one another, to share and take turns, to do their own planning and working out of problems, to take certain responsibilities and to recognize organization. We have seen them gaining actual information and having rich opportunities for creative work. Now it is worth while to consider in detail some of the activities that make up the kindergarten curriculum. In communities where no kindergarten is available, many of these activities may be carried on in the home.

One thing to be kept in mind is that the organization we have just been watching is one in which the children have spent several months in kindergarten. It has been built up slowly but surely under the guidance of a skilful teacher. If we were to visit on a first day, we would see a very differ-

ent picture. A few children might be crying, because this first break with the home is a difficult one for them. These are the children who especially need to learn independence. These are children who have never shared playthings, so there is a good deal of quarreling and snatching. All of them have to learn to respond to organization, to follow group directions.

One thing to be kept in mind is that this is only the organization of *one* kindergarten. The essential features of the organization, however, should be that they give the child plenty of opportunity for free bodily activity, plenty of opportunity for doing his own planning and thinking. Some kindergartens of the old, formal type do not give the child enough freedom, and in these kindergartens the teacher does most of the planning.

What Constitutes a Good Kindergarten.—To summarize the essentials of a good kindergarten:

1. It must give opportunity for children to move around freely. Young children cannot sit still for long periods of time.

2. It must provide materials which will exercise the large muscles. There should be no materials that require the use of the child's smaller muscles (such as those of the fingers), as they are not sufficiently developed. Close work also causes eye strain.

3. There should be plenty of material with which the child can do creative thinking, can carry out his own ideas—material that he *enjoys* using.

4. There should be many rich experiences which will broaden the child's outlook, enrich his thinking.

The actual curriculum of the kindergarten can best be explained through a series of questions:

Does the kindergarten have a real curriculum such as is found in the rest of the school?—Decidedly. The kindergarten curriculum is informal, but it is carefully planned, and the beginnings of all the school subjects are found in it.

What is the most important part of the kindergarten curriculum?—This is difficult to determine. The most important part is perhaps all those experiences which help children to live constructively with other children. These experiences may be termed Social Study.

What does Social Study include?—It includes all the child's relationships with other children, the beginnings of civics. It also includes information about the world in which the child lives, for we cannot live constructively in a world of which we are ignorant.

From the first the child is learning to respond to organization and to help to make his own rules for organization. If children playing around the sandbox spill sand on the floor, the teacher calls a group meeting and discusses with the children what can be done about it. Instead of making a rule herself, she helps them to see why some rule is needed and gets from them suggestions as to what is to be done about the matter.

Sometimes it is a larger social problem that is approached in this way. The situation of a group of children

playing "gangster" or "war" calls for serious group discussion. The teacher discusses with the children the undesirability of even playing at shooting, and tells what serious consequences have sometimes followed when children have formed the habit of playing with guns. The question of war also comes up for frank and free discussion.

The many interests of children give a great deal of opportunity for the kindergarten group to acquire valuable information. Children interested in airplanes may perhaps make an airplane of blocks or boxes; they may play airplane after their own fashion, talk with one another and with the teacher about airplanes, look at pictures of various types of aircraft, go on an excursion to see an airplane. All the things that children are most interested in appear in their play—train, boat, store, house. All of these are opportunities for rich educational experience. Social study is not to be thought of as an isolated part of the curriculum. It is a part of every activity. In the children's interests, we see the beginnings of history and geography; toy boats go "up the river to Albany"; the children compare present-day trains with "old-fashioned trains." All this is laying a sure foundation for later work.

Children seem to spend a good deal of time in kindergarten playing house, boat, train, fire engine and many other things of this sort. Is this play valuable? Is it a part of the curriculum?—It is a very valuable part of the curriculum. A great deal of the child's play is dramatic. He is constantly playing that he is someone or something else. Aside from the enjoyment that the child gets from dramatic play, the play has a distinct educational value. It is the child's way of "trying out" life. When he sees someone engaged in an activity that interests him, he imitates that activity and tries the experience on himself. It is his way of understanding a new experience, of getting to know how it *feels*. Much of the value of dramatic play lies in the fact that children not only play alone but play *together*. There must be a constant give and take, a willingness to share materials and not always to take the leading part.

We find children of this age playing house, store, post office, fireman, hospital—all kinds of community activities. Some of the materials that aid children's dramatic play are the following:

a. Dolls and materials for doll play.—Both boys and girls should play with dolls, and boys should not be made self-conscious about this. Both boys and girls enjoy sweeping, washing and housekeeping play.

b. Blocks.—There should be a good durable set of large wooden blocks. Project Play Blocks are an excellent set. The Hill Floor Blocks make good houses for children actually to get inside of. If there are no blocks, packing boxes make satisfactory houses, trains and boats.

c. Toys.—Wooden toys, such as a train, boats, airplane, wooden people, wooden animals, suggest things to play. Wooden toys may be used to present the episodes in Alice Dalgliesh's story, "The Little Wooden Farmer," and various other stories.

d. *Materials for "dressing up."*— Home and kindergarten should provide a variety of materials for dressing up —squares of colored cloth, small aprons and odds and ends of brightly colored material.

Sometimes the children dramatize a story that they have heard. They enjoy dramatizing stories, but these should be carried through in the simplest way without any thought of playing to an audience. Occasionally the children suggest "giving a show" or "playing theater," and some of the children act as audience. Elaborate performances for an adult audience are not desirable, as they require too much rehearsing and tend to make the children self-conscious. Among the stories which are great favorites of children and are simple enough for them to dramatize are the following:

"The Little Red Hen."
"Little Black Sambo."
"Peter Rabbit" (more difficult; sometimes the children play only part of this).
"Pelle's New Suit."
"The Three Bears" (also more difficult, and perhaps played only in part).
"The Gingerbread Boy."
"The Three Little Pigs."

These stories will all be found in the group of stories for children printed later in this section.

Children of this age are more interested in the *action* of stories than they are in the words, so their dramatization is sometimes entirely carried through in action or with a very little conversation.

Does the kindergarten give opportunity for language development?— Almost every activity of the day provides opportunity for this. The children are constantly adding new words to their vocabularies and having rich meaningful experiences which give them something to talk about. Conversations around the luncheon table are most interesting and stimulating. The children learn to take turns, for at first they all tend to talk at once. Shy children who do not talk very much are encouraged to do so. Emphasis is placed on having something of real interest to talk about and telling it so that other children can understand and enjoy it. The children also make up stories and tell them to a small group. Dramatic play gives much opportunity for language and vocabulary development.

The beginnings of written language are seen when the children dictate to the teacher a letter to a child who is absent. This gives fine opportunity for discrimination as to things that would be of interest to the child who is to receive the letter. Then, too, the children often dictate stories that they originate or ask to have a story written about a picture they have drawn.

This activity should be spontaneous, not forced by the teacher.

What form of art experience do children have in kindergarten?—In the first place the kindergarten room itself should be colorful and well arranged. Good pictures, flowers, plants, colorful materials, all help to make the room attractive. Fine picture books give art experiences. Then the child himself has many opportunities to experiment with and express himself through art materials. A good-sized easel with large sheets of unprinted newspaper, large brushes and jars of poster paint in the primary colors are the most desirable materials for painting. If no easel is available, sheets of paper thumb-tacked to a large sheet of heavy cardboard or compo board will answer the purposes.

The kindergarten teacher does not give the child lessons in painting or try to give him much technique. She shows him how to hold his brush, how to wipe the paint off on the edge of the jar so that it will not drip, how to keep colors from running into each other. She is interested in his painting and talks to him about it, carefully avoiding saying, "What *is* that?" and letting the child *tell her* what he is painting. Painting and drawing are a form of language, a way of telling about the things a child sees. He may not even be painting anything in particular, simply experimenting with color. He has little idea of rela-

LOOK MAGAZINE

GEOGRAPHY is taught in kindergarten. To a young child the earth is only a flat surface, like a map or a round ball. Although the small child has no concept of distance, being able to locate a place is fun. Along with this goes learning about the people in the distant place: their appearance, dress, and life. Thus, geography encompasses reading, spelling, and history.

tive size, and flowers growing beside a house are likely to be as large as the house. He has no idea of perspective and is not ready for training in this.

A good box of crayons and sheets of 6″ × 9″ manila paper give the child opportunity to express himself through drawing. Little children go through a scribble stage in which their scribbles represent different objects to them, though looking like nothing at all to the grown-up. By the time a child is five, he usually can draw some recognizable objects. He knows what his pictures represent, and sometimes he tells interesting stories about them.

Clay is still another art medium. Most kindergarten supply houses now carry a good quality of clay mixed ready for use. At first the children like to experiment with clay by rolling, patting and pounding it. They soon begin to make simple objects such as cakes, pies, balls and, later, more interesting things. Here again they should not be given technique ahead of their ability. The teacher shows them how to smooth the clay, how to join pieces together so the object will not fall apart when dry. When the clay is dry, it may be painted with the same poster paints used at the easel or with water colors.

Are there any science experiences suitable for a child of kindergarten age?—The kindergarten child asks innumerable questions, and he is intensely interested in natural phenomena. He wants to know where rain comes from, what ice is, why the sun dries up water, how fish breathe under water and many other things.

The kindergarten provides for experience with plants and animals. Many plants may be grown indoors, in water or in window boxes or in a tray arranged as an indoor garden. Some kindergartens are fortunate in having an outdoor garden, where children may plant quick-germinating seeds and watch their growth. Certain pets may be permanent in the room—goldfish, small turtles, a canary; others, such as rabbits, guinea pigs; mice and frogs, may be kept for a shorter period. No pets should be kept in a room unless adequate provision is made for their care. Excursions to the zoo to see wild animals, to parks or woods to see spring birds, enrich the children's experience. These actual experiences are supplemented by pictures of flowers, birds, animals and stories about them.

All the literature used in connection with science experiences should be true to fact. Children do not need fanciful nature stories, and these are confusing to them. Through contact with animals and plants, children not only develop a friendly feeling toward them and an interest in them but at the same time learn in a very natural way something of the facts of the development of life. A pair of mice or rats may be kept long enough to produce a family, and the children's questions about the baby animals should be answered frankly and intelligently.

Children of this age are not too young for simple scientific experiences, such as: noticing the rise and fall of the mercury in a thermometer; seeing how a magnet picks up nails; putting a pan of water out to freeze, a pan of water to evaporate; melting ice. A number of simple science experiences suitable for young children are given in *We Look About Us*, by Agnes Burke and Gerald Craig (Ginn & Company), the first book of a series of science readers.

Does the kindergarten teach the 3 Rs?—There is no formal work in reading, writing and arithmetic, but there is a great deal of informal work which prepares the child for further work in first grade.

Contacts with attractive picture- and storybooks develop in the children the *desire* to read that is so important as a forerunner of beginning reading. Sometimes the children "read" stories to one another that they have memorized or make up stories to go with the pictures in favorite books. While reading is not emphasized, everything is done to give children experiences that will develop a readiness for reading. Names are printed clearly on the children's lockers and on all their belongings. There are animal-stamping outfits and a hand printing set with large letters for those children who are interested. Sometimes the children need in their play signs such as "Grocery Store," "No Parking." These are printed for them to copy, or they are helped to make them with the printing set. Reading and writing go very closely together, and children are always interested in learning to print their own names and sometimes other words. Most important of all in kindergarten is the background of experience that the children are gaining. This makes reading more meaningful later on.

There is no formal arithmetic, but many informal opportunities present themselves for using numbers and for counting. The children learn number terminology through actual experience. "This piece of wood is twice as long as that one." "This block is taller than that one." A project such as the grocery store gives a great deal of experience in using numbers, though at kindergarten age children have vague ideas of relative prices and of the value of money.

Counting is an activity that children enjoy. They like to count the number of children sitting at a table, the number of times they have done a certain thing, and they also enjoy counting as a rhythmic activity. There is the beginning of the desire to tell time. Some children learn this while they are in kindergarten. Most of the children learn the large divisions of time, such as nine o'clock, twelve o'clock, if there is a clock in the room.

How does the kindergarten introduce the child to literature?—Most children come to kindergarten with some knowledge of books and stories, and they are eager for more experience of this sort. There should be a bookcase and a reading table to encourage the children to look at books by themselves, as well as a time for listening to stories read or told by the teacher.

Books and stories used in kindergarten are very simple and deal chiefly with everyday experiences. Some fanciful stories are used, but these are of the simpler type, and the traditional fairy tale is better kept for a later age. It is desirable to have a number of books with fine illustrations by outstanding artists. There should also be a number of books of the informative type, to which the children can go for suggestions to aid in their work or play. Sometimes one sees a child at the workbench making a wooden airplane, with the airplane book spread open beside him; the children who are building a farm with the blocks consult the farm book for suggestions.

Poetry is important, and many poems should be used with the children in a free and natural way, but there should be no forced memorizing. A child loses all his joy in poetry if he is forced to memorize poems and recite them for the entertainment of adults. The best time to use poems is when they fit in with some experience the children are having—a rain poem on a rainy day, a swing poem when the children are swinging.

Stories which are the greatest favorites of children are included later in this section. Other suggestions for the kindergarten library are:

Short, simple stories for children from 4 to 6 are:

Little - or - Nothing from Nottingham, by Marguerite Henry (Whittlesey House) $2.00.

Kiki Dances, by Charlotte Steiner (Doubleday) $1.25.

Bartholomew and the Oobleck, by Dr. Seuss (Random House) $2.00.

The Flying Postman, by V. H. Drummond (Penguin).

Foxie, by I. M. d'Aulaire (Doubleday) $2.00.

Cocolo, by Bettina (Harper and Bros.) $2.50.

Cocolo Comes to America, by Bettina (Harper and Bros.) $2.50.

The Box With Red Wheels, by Maud and Miska Petersham (Macmillan Co.) $1.50.

Two Little Trains, by Margaret Wise Brown (William R. Scott) $1.50.

The Happy Day, by Ruth Krauss (Harper and Bros.) $1.50.

Little Bruin, by Haaken Christensen. Translated from the Norwegian by Gudrun Thorne-Thomsen (Abingdon - Cokesbury Press) $1.00.

Cable Car Joey, by Naomi and Lorin McCabe (Stanford University Press) $1.95.

Somewhat more advanced picture stories are:

Miss Flora McFlimsey's Christmas Eve, by Mariana (Lathrop) $1.00.

Big Book of Real Trains, by George J. Zoffo (Grosset & Dunlop) $1.00.

Angus and the Ducks, by Marjorie Flack (Doubleday).

Snipp Snapp Snurr and the Red Shoes, by Maj. Lindman (Laidlaw).

Little Black Sambo, by Helen Bannerman (Stokes).

Peter Rabbit, by Beatrix Potter (Warne).

It Looks Like This, by I. E. S. Webber (W. R. Scott) $1.00.

Licorice, by Barbara Briggs (Aladdin) $2.00.

The Tale of Tubby the Tuba, by Paul Tripp (Vanguard) $2.00.

Collections of stories and poems:

Told Under the Blue Umbrella (Macmillan).

Sugar and Spice, poems by Maru Tileston (Little, Brown & Co.).

When We Were Very Young, by A. A. Milne (Dutton).

Ring-O-Roses, Mother Goose, by L. Leslie Brooke (Warne).

Read Me Another Story, by Child Study Assoc. of America (Croll) $2.00.

Once Upon A Time, stories by Rose Dobbs (Random House) $2.00.

The Little Whistler, poems by Frances Frost (Whittlesey House) $2.00.

Rainbow In the Sky, poems by Louis Untermeyer (Harcourt Brace) $3.75.

Kindergarten children also enjoy the old folk tales, such as "The Three Bears," "Three Little Pigs," "Three Billy Goats Gruff." They like to listen to stories about their own experiences, especially stories in which their own names are included.[1]

How does the kindergarten provide for musical experience?—Children of this age are naturally active and rhythmic, so the approach to music is through rhythmic activity. The teacher watches the children's natural activities, then provides music which fits these. Several children, for instance, may be jumping up and down; the teacher encourages these movements and supplies appropriate music. Other children may be skipping, running, hopping. These activities also may be used in a rhythmic way. The children suggest many things to play: "Let's play bunny," "Let's play we are horses," "I saw an elephant in the circus"; all these are leads which the teacher is quick to follow. Rhythmic work may have a close connection with the child's dramatic play.

While it is desirable to have a piano or phonograph for rhythmic work, it is possible to use a drum or, preferably, a tom-tom, for many rhythmic activities. A tom-tom is excellent to use *before* playing the piano, at the beginning of the children's rhythmic experience.

Songs that kindergarten children sing should be very simple and within range of the child's voice or should have an easily carried melody such as that of old folk songs, for example, "Lavender's Blue."[2] The content of the song should be simple, easily understood by the children and interesting to them. There are several beautifully illustrated songbooks. These add interest to musical experience. Children who have difficulty with singing may be helped by tone play, such as matching tones, or the child's imitation of a boat whistle.

Musical experiences need not be limited to singing or rhythmic activity. There should be ample opportunity for listening to good music and for experimenting with different types of mu-

[1] *First Experiences with Literature*, by Alice Dalgliesh (Scribner), discusses fully the use of literature in kindergarten.

[2] This and other famous old folk songs will be found in the group of songs in this section.

LOOK MAGAZINE

KINDERGARTEN TEACHES ABOUT LIFE, whether it is human or animal. These children are fascinated by a little chick, for many, their first experience with this fuzzy creature.

sical instruments. Among the instruments suitable for musical experience are Swiss bells, on which easy melodies may be played, and a *good* xylophone, used for the same purpose. Cheap musical instruments or those with inaccurate pitch are to be avoided. Then, too, there are instruments which the child can use in a very simple rhythmic way. These include wrist bells (several bells sewed on a piece of webbing which fits the wrist), tambourines and triangles. The beginnings of a simple "orchestra" may come through use of several of these instruments, but work of this kind should not be too formalized. All too often the "kindergarten band" is a formally organized activity used for showing off the children's supposed musical progress. As in other phases of kindergarten work, the child's own development is the first consideration.

Collections containing songs suitable for kindergarten use are these:

Singing Time, by Satis N. Coleman and Alice Thorn.

Songs to Sing, by Edna Shaw.

First Year Music, by Hollis Dann.

Our Old Nursery Rhymes, illustrated by W. L. LeMair.

Little Songs of Long Ago, illustrated by W. L. LeMair.

This Way and That, illustrated by Edna Potter (a book of singing games).

Books containing music for rhythmic play and listening include:

Rhythms of Childhood, by Crawford and Fogg.

First Year Music, by Hollis Dann.

Rhythms for Children, by Jean Taylor.

What other materials do the children use in their creative work?—A great variety of materials, including wood, cloth, paper, scissors, paste. These are used by the children to

LOOK MAGAZINE

SURPRISES always bring joy in kindergartens even if they are a little scary, like this paper snake that pops from its container.

carry out their own ideas. Some children are naturally more creative with materials than are others; these will find many original uses for material. Some follow the suggestions originated by others or will need stimulation from the teacher. At the beginning of the year when the children are interested in trying out their new surroundings and are likely to flit from one activity to another, very few materials should be provided. Gradually materials such as clay and wood may be added. With woodwork the children should be shown how to use tools with safety to themselves and others; with clay they should be allowed much opportunity to experiment but should be shown how to smooth the clay and how to join pieces together.

Children who have not had much experience with materials are likely to go through a stage where they manipulate and experiment with materials. Clay is rolled and patted and pounded; the first objects made are likely to be "snakes" and "pies" and "balls." Wood will be sawed for the pleasure in the activity; nails will be pounded into boards for the same reason. The first objects made of wood are likely to be suggested by the shapes of pieces of wood found in the wood box, so it is a good plan to start with a wood box filled with miscellaneous pieces of wood in many sizes and shapes.

Adults must not be impatient with this first experimental stage nor expect very definite results. Before long most children will begin work with some definite idea in mind. Later, as they become interested in group activi-

ties, many materials will be used to carry out these activities. The fruits and vegetables for the grocery store call for paper or clay; the playhouse needs curtains and furniture.

Sewing is an imitative activity. Children usually want to sew because they see grown-ups sewing. It is not an activity on which small children should spend long periods of time, for it is close work and may involve eye or muscle strain. Sometimes the children may want to make costumes for themselves. They should have large-eyed needles and coarse thread, and the needles should be threaded for them. Stitches should not be too small, and in general the sewing process should be made as easy as possible.

Colored paper is another medium for experimentation. Children love to cut paper. Where wood is not available, paper and cardboard boxes have a variety of uses, though they are never quite as satisfactory for construction work as the more durable wood. Excellent trains and wagons may, however, be constructed from cardboard boxes and milk-bottle tops. Paper lends itself to many decorative uses: costumes may be decorated with cut paper; parts of costumes may be made from crepe paper. Christmas-tree decorations made from colored paper are more satisfactory than the traditional glass balls. Christmas cards, valentines, birthday cards—all these are uses for paper. Children also enjoy making small scrapbooks.

There are other kindergarten materials with which the child does manipulative, rather than creative, work, though these materials do give some

opportunity for experimentation in design. There are color pegs to be placed in holes in a peg board, large colored wooden beads to be strung, small colored blocks to be used in making designs. These are good materials for the beginning of the year when the children like to manipulate material, but they have not very extended educational possibilities.[1]

What provision is made for the teaching of health and hygiene?— While children of this age should not be made overconscious of their own health, there are certain hygienic habits which it is important to emphasize, and a good deal of health information which may be given incidentally. The children should understand the real reason for precautions to be taken with regard to colds and contagious diseases and the reason for keeping fingers and other objects out of their mouths, using individual towels and drinking cups, washing their hands before eating and after going to the toilet. They may have the very simplest explanation of the fact that germs are carried when hygienic precautions are not taken.

Food difficulties may often be overcome by conversations about the types of food needed for good health. Too often parents do not give straightforward information of this kind. A little boy who refused cod-liver oil had never been told that cod-liver oil takes the place of the warmth of sunshine in the winter. A simple explanation of this entirely overcame the difficulty. Some-

[1]Places where these materials may be obtained are mentioned in *Permanent Play Materials*, by Charlotte Garrison, author of our article, "Educational Playthings."

times cooking carrots, spinach or other vegetables at school and eating them with satisfaction overcomes a special food dislike.

Are there any formal games suitable for use in kindergarten?—There are a few formal games that are simple enough for little children to enjoy, but children of this age should not be required to play together in a large group for any length of time. After they have had a good deal of experience in playing together informally, games such as the following may be enjoyed:

Ring-around-a-rosy
Drop the Handkerchief
London Bridge
Here We Go Round the Mulberry Bush
The Farmer in the Dell
Looby Loo
Little Sally Waters[1]

It is often better to use with young children a simplified form of a game. "London Bridge" may be played without the competitive element. A still simpler form of this is—

Open the gates as high as the sky
And let the king and his men go by.

Two children form an arch; the others go through it. One child is occasionally caught by the "gates," but there is no more organization than this.

The work of the primary grades usually centers around some large group interest. Do such group interests exist in the kindergarten?—Decidedly so, though the interests are not as centralized as they are in the grades, for kindergarten children are individual, and they like to play in small groups. Four-year-old children seldom develop a large group interest, while, in the latter part of the year, five-year-old children have many such interests.

A group of kindergarten children built a grocery store, using the Hill Floor Blocks. (If these blocks had not been available, packing boxes would have answered the purpose.) They named the grocery the "Snow White Grocery Store," and one child painted a sign for it. The children made paper fruit and vegetables to sell in the store, and there was a great deal of discussion about buying and selling. A visit to a grocery store helped to make their ideas clearer and supplied suggestions for more things to do. The social science reader, "Mr. Brown's Grocery Store," also added to the children's experience. Almost all the children in the room were interested in the grocery store, and they participated in the activity of buying and selling. Naturally certain social problems arose, as everyone wanted to sell, and there were times when many children tried to crowd into the grocery at once. Whenever such difficulties arose, a group meeting was called to formulate suggestions for better play.

Another group of children made an ocean liner of the large blocks. (Here again packing boxes would answer the purpose.) As they built the liner, they felt more and more the necessity for accurate information about liners, and books and pictures had to be consulted. How many funnels do liners have?

[1]The music and words for many of these games and several others will be found in the group of songs in this section.

How are the funnels painted? Where does a ship keep its anchor? What are portholes? What flags does a ship fly? These are only a few of the questions that arose. When the liner was ready to "sail," a great many more problems presented themselves, and interest extended to the countries to which the liner was going.

One very interesting and worthwhile group activity which took place in a five-year-old kindergarten group was the making and selling of newspapers. Bobby and Billy decided to have a newspaper stand. They made a crude one from wood, painting a sign which said, "Bobby and Billy's Newspaper Stand." All the children in the group became interested and joined in the activity. The children painted the newspaper heading and the pictures for the papers, dictating the "news" to the teacher. This led to an interest in newspapers, the things we find in them and keen enjoyment of news pictures from the Sunday picture supplement. When the newspapers were made, Bobby and Billy set up their stand and sold papers to adults and other children. The twenty cents they made was given by common consent to the unemployed.

In these group interests we see all phases of subject matter. They are an excellent preparation for the group work which the children will be doing in first grade. Small group interests, however, in which three or four children play together, are equally as valuable as the large ones—sometimes more so. Group activities should not extend over a long period of time. A week or two weeks is sufficient. Children lose interest and have to be stimulated by the teacher if the interest extends over too long a period.

What tangible results should be expected at the end of the kindergarten year?—By the end of the year, the children should show physical, mental, social and emotional growth. The records that the teacher has kept of each child's development will show how he has progressed. Great changes often occur in children. The following brief summaries show some of the changes that took place in children during a year in kindergarten:

Joan was a very shy child. When she came to kindergarten, she did not join in any activities or play with any other children. She stood at one side, or wandered about the room, scowling if anyone looked at her. Gradually the teacher interested her in materials, helped her to feel her ability to do things, encouraged the children to ask her to join in their play. By the end of the year, Joan was a normal, happy little girl, participating in everything, with much of her self-consciousness overcome.

John was an active little boy who had practically no feeling for the rights of others. If he played in a group, there was always trouble, for John took the best materials or toys for himself and used every method to gain his own ends—pushing, slapping, fighting. The teacher talked with him about this, showing him that other children soon would not want to play with him. This did not, however, make much impression, but soon the other

children began to ostracize him. The teacher also adopted the method of removing him temporarily from the group whenever he hurt another child. John's mother co-operated by following the same method at home. By the end of the year John was able to play with a group of children with only occasional difficulty.

Jim was a timid little boy who was afraid of almost any physical activity. He would not go downstairs without holding someone's hand, would not jump even from a small height. The teacher worked with him slowly but constantly, encouraging him first to try the lower bars of the climbing ladders, to jump off one step, to walk across the walking beam, holding her hand. Gradually, she withdrew her support and Jim became more independent. By the end of the year, he could go down steps alone, could climb to the top of the jungle gym and showed great pride in his accomplishments.

Each child is considered as an individual. The resourceful child is given much opportunity to work out his creative ideas; the child with little originality is encouraged to do more original thinking; the shy child is helped to gain confidence in himself; the overconfident child is helped to take his place in relation to other children. By the time the children are ready for first grade, many physical and emotional difficulties should at least be partly overcome, if not entirely so.

There are other aspects of kindergarten work which are not included in the actual plan for work with the children but which have a very close connection with the work.

Records.—In order to know what the children are doing and how they are growing, the teacher must keep some form of record of their progress. These records are talked over with the parents. They show how the child is growing in his ability to be a good member of a group, to contribute to discussion, to plan his work and so forth. The teacher also keeps a record of the activities that have gone on in the kindergarten, so that she may see which are valuable and enable her to plan new directions for her work.

Parent-teacher Relationships.—It is essential that parents and teachers should work closely together, so that the child's whole day will be organized in somewhat the same way. Conferences between parent and teacher are helpful to both. The teacher needs much information about the child that she can gain from the parent; the parent can get many helpful suggestions from the teacher. If kindergarten work is to be of real benefit to a child, some consistent plan must be followed throughout the day, not one course of procedure for home and one for kindergarten. If Mary has tantrums and they are wisely handled both at home and at school, she will soon outgrow them. Inconsistent treatment will mean that she will develop different ways of acting in various situations.

In most kindergartens, regular times are set aside not only for individual conferences between parent and teacher but for group meetings. At these meetings the parents and teachers of the whole kindergarten group discuss the things that children are learning at home and at school and problems concerning them. There may be an outside speaker on some topic, such as health, nutrition, clothing, discipline, art or the literary or musical experiences of children.

Health.—When children come together in a group, it is most essential that their health be watched carefully and contagious diseases guarded against. Most good schools provide medical supervision, a school doctor and nurse who give physical examinations and to whom the children go for first aid or to be readmitted after illness. As the common cold is so contagious and also may be the forerunner of several of the contagious diseases of childhood, it is most important that children with any sign of a cold should be excluded from school. If the right attitude is built up in parents with regard to this, and they are urged to be responsible for keeping children with colds at home, the group will have a much better health record than a group in which such precautions are not observed.

It is also important for children of kindergarten age to spend as much time out of doors as possible, and a kindergarten with facilities for outdoor play should use them at all convenient periods. In fine weather, it is possible to have almost all activities out of doors. The outdoor playground should be well equipped, so that the children will have plenty of constructive activity. When there is no kindergarten, parents should consider the possibilities of any backyard or outdoor play space. It does not take expensive equipment to make a backyard an ideal place in which to play.

THE HOME KINDERGARTEN

Mothers who cannot send their young children to kindergarten, but who wish them to have valuable educational experiences, may organize a small kindergarten or play group in the home. The description of the kindergarten curriculum which precedes this discussion offers many suggestions for worth-while experiences. These may be adapted to the home kindergarten.

The equipment of a home kindergarten need not be expensive. It can be very simple. There should be low tables and chairs. As the children will spend a good deal of time sitting in the chairs, it is best to get chairs of a recognized make, planned expressly for good posture. The chairs should be the right height, so that the children can sit in them comfortably, with feet resting on the floor.

A low cupboard or set of shelves is essential for keeping the materials with which the children are to work. On one shelf there should be pieces of newspaper cut to a convenient size for protecting the table when children are painting, and clay boards or squares of oilcloth for clay work. A part of the cupboard should be set aside as a place to keep their smocks or work aprons and their unfinished work. If this space can be divided

into individual lockers, so much the better. In a small group of children, or with a family of children, it is possible for each child to have his own work tray, which he can get out and use without asking help from an adult. This tray may contain scissors with blunt ends, a jar of paste, a paste brush, a box of crayons and perhaps a paint box and brushes.

Cleaning up after work is an important habit to form, and the right facilities for this must be provided. On a set of low hooks (in the cupboard or beside it), there should be a small broom, a long-handled dustpan, a small mop and a cloth which can be dampened and used for wiping tables. Paper towels should be available for wiping up water or paint that may be spilled.

A piano or phonograph is almost a necessity, though a good deal of rhythmic work may be done with a drum or tom-tom. There are a good many phonograph records which are made especially for children. Other musical instruments, such as bells and tambourines, are desirable.

One corner of the room should be arranged for doll play. A low screen will form the walls of a good playhouse. This may be made of a clothes horse covered with burlap. Doll furniture should be simple and strong. This may be made by the children. The very simplest form of construction should be used in making doll furniture: a chair, for example, being made with a seat, a back and four legs; a bed in the same way; a table with a top and legs.

Blocks are among the most important pieces of equipment, and a good set of blocks should be provided. These should be unpainted blocks of white wood, large enough for satisfactory building. Shelves for the blocks, or a box on casters, also must be provided, so that they may be kept in an orderly way. Smaller colored blocks also are popular with children.

A satisfactory bookcase, with books, and a library table and chairs are conducive to good beginning "reading" habits.

Provision for physical activity must be made. If the children can go out of doors to play, this is not so essential, but in the city it is most desirable. If the space is small, a "doorway gymnasium" with swing, rugs, trapeze and horizontal bar is most satisfactory. Attractive plants and pictures add to the appearance of the room.

A Day's Program.—Here is a suggestion for a time schedule. It is only tentative and should be rearranged to fit the individual situation. The group may be organized for an hour or for two hours only. Below is a three-hour schedule:

9:00–9:45 A.M.—The children arrive, remove their wraps and hang them up (low hooks necessary). During this first period they select the materials they wish to use and use them in any way that appeals to them. The adult in charge takes an interest in all their activities, answers questions and gives suggestions and help when necessary.

9:45–10:10 A.M.—The children put away their materials, then bring their

chairs together in a group for story or discussion.

10:10–10:40 A.M.—The children go to the toilet and wash their hands, then set the table for lunch. A good midmorning lunch is orange juice, with perhaps a cracker. Milk may be taken by those children who seem especially to need it. Often, a child who does not care for milk will drink it in company with other children. Lunch time may be one of the most educational periods of the day, for it gives opportunity for interesting conversation on many topics. There is opportunity for learning courtesy and table manners, but all of this should be incidental, and a meal period should never be a time for direct criticism.

10:45–11:00 A.M.—A fifteen-minute rest is desirable. If cots are not obtainable, the children may rest on bath mats or rag rugs spread on the floor. The room should first be aired; then the windows closed, to avoid draughts. Rugs should be marked with a name tag at the top, so that the children will always put their heads at the same end and always put the same side of the rug on the floor.

11:00–11:25 A. M.—The children sit around the piano or phonograph. During this period they listen to music, take part in rhythmic activity and sing. It is also a good time for interesting conversation and discussion.

11:25 A.M.–12:00 M.—This is a period which may be used in a variety of ways. These are suggestions:

1. Outdoor play: The children should be out of doors as much as possible in fine weather.
2. Using materials, such as those for drawing or painting, at the tables.
3. Dramatic play.
4. Simple games (outdoors, if possible).
5. Excursions to places of interest in the neighborhood. All the possibilities for interesting excursions should be considered.

12:00 M.—The children get their wraps and put them on with as little assistance as possible. In all their work, whether it is with an individual child or with a group, it is important to see that the child is forming good habits of thinking, of workmanship, and of social living.

A few books that will give an understanding of young children and that help in the organization of a home kindergarten are:

Happy Childhood, John E. Anderson, Ph.D. (Appleton-Century).

Healthy Childhood, Harold C. Stuart (Appleton-Century).

Busy Childhood, Josephine C. Foster (Appleton-Century).

A Conduct Curriculum, Agnes Burke and others (Scribner).

MATERIALS FOR THE HOME KINDERGARTEN

Furniture and other permanent equipment.—
Tables, chairs and blackboard.
A piece of apparatus for physical activity—jungle gym, hi-low gym or tower gym.

Closet or shelves for keeping materials

Bookcase

Sandbox, with toys for use in the sand

Piano or victrola

Block box or shelves for blocks

Workbench and tools. Tools should include substantial hammers, good quality saws, ruler, brace and bit, screwdriver, nails.

Materials which encourage dramatic and constructive play.—

Dolls (Durable washable dolls are best)

Doll furniture (including stove)

Doll carriage

Dishes

Laundry set

Screen for playhouse

Blocks—large wooden blocks

Wooden train, truck, auto, boat

Wooden animals and people

Sand toys (molds, containers, spoons, trees, houses, people, animals)

Housekeeping materials.—

Small broom

Dustpan with long handle

Small mop

Cloths for wiping tables—dishcloths are good for this

Small electric iron

Dishpan

Mop

Soap saver

Small dish towels

(A small carpet sweeper also is enjoyed by children.)

Materials for nature-study and science.—

Ruler

Scales

Thermometer (large, so children can easily see changes)

Weather house (small house barometer in which little man or woman comes out to indicate weather)

Calendar (large, hung where children can easily see it)

Magnet

Magnifying glass

Prism (this hung in a sunny window makes a rainbow on floor.)

Fish globe

Japanese garden

Garden tools (for outdoors)

Materials for manipulative play.—

Peg board (a board with holes and colored pegs to fit into the holes)

Wooden beads (large wooden kindergarten beads for stringing)

Stone tiles (these are for making designs and may be obtained from floor tiling companies)

Picture puzzles (simple ones, not too many pieces)

Printing set (sets of rubber stamp animals for printing; also alphabet)

Musical instruments (drum, xylophone, bells, tambourines, etc.)

Materials for construction and creative work.—

For Clay Modeling:

Clay, good quality, ready-mixed

Clay boards

Stone crock in which to keep clay

For Woodwork:

Soft pine boards cut in convenient lengths—36x1x1", 36x1x1½", 36x 2½", 36x4x½", 36x6x½"; also

cylinders of soft wood with diameters of 2", 1", ½". These are used for smoke stacks and chimneys. Button molds make excellent wheels.

Hammers, adze eye (No. 3)

Saws, Disston cross-cut, short blade

Brace and bit

Screwdriver

Nails, flat-head wire nails, in assorted sizes

For Sewing:

Sewing box containing large-eyed embroidery needles, coarse thread, pincushion, pins, scissors

LOOK MAGAZINE

PAINTING is good for self-expression, and admiration for talent can be found everywhere.

Colored cloth (cambric)—scraps of colored material, unbleached muslin

For Painting:

Large easel with jars for paint

Japanese paint brushes

Unprinted newspaper

Jars of poster paint in primary colors

For Drawing:

Manila paper

Crayons

For Cutting and Pasting:

Blunt scissors

Jars of paste with small brushes or sticks for pasting

Colored paper (obtainable in packages)

Silver and gold paper

Many of these materials are now obtainable in five-and-ten-cent stores. All of them are carried by kindergarten supply houses.

THE OUTDOOR PLAY GROUP

A backyard or any outdoor play space may be made a place for educational play experiences. A group of mothers may arrange the supervision of this among themselves. The play of small children should always be supervised by an adult. If children

are simply turned loose out of doors, they are likely to be physically active all the time and to come in from play tired and cross. Children need exercise, but they also need periods of rest, for they very quickly burn up their energy. This means that when they are playing out of doors for a long period there should be materials and toys which suggest quieter play, as well as those which suggest physical activity. On a cool day, if the children are spending all their time in too-quiet activities, the adult may need to suggest that they play a game or have a scooter race. On a hot day, if the children are too active, the suggestion may be that they blow bubbles or play house.

A backyard does not need expensive equipment to make it a good place to play. Children like to climb, so if there are no trees, provide a ladder or other climbing equipment. Packing boxes of various sizes and a sawhorse are inexpensive materials in which children find endless play possibilities.

Materials for active play.—

Toys, such as a scooter, express wagon, hoop, ball.

A swing (an old automobile tire makes a good swing.)

Something to climb. (A low horizontal ladder is good.)

Long substantial wooden boards. (The children will use these in a variety of ways. They will stand them against the fence and run or slide down them.)

A seesaw. (The kind with an immovable board is best, as there will not be pinched fingers. Children, however, will improvise their own seesaw if boards are provided.)

A slide. (A slide is a desirable, but somewhat more expensive, piece of material. Children often improvise a slide with boards. The boards should be smooth or there is danger from splinters.)

Materials for less active play.—

Packing boxes, large and small. (The children will use these for houses, boats, wagons.)

A sandbox. (There is perhaps nothing out of which children get so much enjoyment.)

The outdoor sandbox should be low and large enough so that the children can get inside; not under cover, as it needs the germ-destroying rays of the sun. On a very hot day it may be possible to put up temporary shade, such as a large garden umbrella. We do realize, however, the importance of sunlight for little children. They should spend some time playing in the direct sunshine with as little clothing as possible, but with their heads covered. There should be a tarpaulin cover for the sandbox at night and in wet weather. Sand play will be much more valuable if there are many sand toys, such as spoons

and spades for digging, and containers for sand, a rolling pin, molds for "pies." Other materials are a village with little wooden houses and trees and animals.

These materials should not all be given to the children at once. At first they should have the simpler materials for digging; the others may be added gradually. In this way interest in the sandbox may be kept alive, and sand play will be a growing interest throughout the year.

*Facilities for water play.—*Children do not have enough opportunity to play with water. If there is a brook nearby, they should have many opportunities to play in it, wearing rubber boots if it seems unwise for them to wade with bare feet. A small concrete pool in which the children may "fish," sail boats and build docks would be a fine addition to any backyard. There are attractive, inexpensive water tanks which may be purchased. A zinc-lined sand table may be filled with water, but even a large pan of water has play possibilities. If

children are suitably dressed, play in water will not hurt them or their clothes. Rubber aprons will protect dresses and suits. The backyard is a fine place to blow bubbles, for there is space to chase them.

*Other materials.—*On warm days, children may have a table in a shady place at which they can draw, model or paint or use wood and tools. In fact most of the indoor occupations may be transferred outdoors in hot weather. Dolls and doll furniture may move into the backyard; so may blocks and toy animals. Cooking on the doll's stove is favorite outdoor play. Making a garden of their own is a delightful and educational experience for children.

In winter, the backyard has other possibilities. The sandbox and playhouse must be put aside, but sleds and a snow shovel take their place. Children should be warmly and suitably dressed, so that they may have the experience of coasting, of shoveling snow and of making snowballs and snow men.

EDUCATIONAL PLAYTHINGS

For little children, play is the business of life, as work is for adults; and good toys are as necessary for children's play as good tools, good materials, good equipment are for adult work. Good toys make play full of rich, vital and joyful experiences.

Selection of Toys.—An environment and materials which encourage wholesome and creative play aid the child in finding ways to interpret the physical and social life surrounding him; it is through constructive play that the child has opportunities for proper physical, intellectual and social development and thus day by day be-

comes a more and more useful member of society even while he is a child.

In selecting playthings for children, certain fundamental qualities and characteristics must be sought. All toys, if they are to hold the interest of the child, must have a "do with" quality—the toy must be one with which the child can experiment and through this experimentation produce creative results.

Value of Simple Playthings.—Children want to understand their playthings, and a toy that is simple, easily used, easily taken apart and put together is more satisfactory in every way to a

child than the elaborate mechanical toy of which he cannot understand the workings, and which will be broken and useless if he does more than wind the key and watch it go.

The elaborate toy, such as the fully furnished doll house, the doll supplied with a trunk full of fussy, flimsy, unpractical clothes and toilet articles, the grocery store with every detail perfect, may be rather overwhelming and interesting to the child only for a short time. Then they are pushed aside and forgotten; whereas if the little girl is given materials and encouraged and helped to make her own doll house and simple furniture, or the boy his own grocery store, the pleasure and profit will be far greater, and the child's interest in using them more lasting.

Characteristics of Good Toys.—Toys must be well made, very strong and of some nonbreakable material if they are to withstand the constant vigorous and inexpert handling which they are sure to get if they are worth while and embody the qualities which make them interesting to children. As far as possible, toys should be of such material, finish and workmanship as will allow thorough washing and sterilization—especially those playthings designed particularly for the use of very little children.

Toys should be gay and attractive in appearance as well as durable. Good line, proportion, material and workmanship all help to make the plaything artistic, while bright-colored paint adds to the interest and effectiveness of many toys, although certain wooden toys are more suggestive and attractive when left unpainted. Only nonpoisonous paints and dyes should be used on children's toys.

Toys should be realistic, representing as faithfully and simply as possible the things children see and use

LOOK MAGAZINE

SMALL CHILDREN require very little to play with in order to enjoy themselves.

FREE EXPRESSION is given vent in this modern dance group. Held together by a free-flowing net, these barefoot children are allowed moments of individual creativeness. They each have a chance to be whatever they want and act it out in any manner in time with the music.

in the world around them; thus toy animals should resemble real animals and not be grotesque caricatures of them; dolls should be pretty, childlike in feature, natural, and simply and attractively dressed—not oddities or overly sophisticated.

Toys which embody humorous characteristics and possibilities without being grotesque are great favorites. These toys are hard to find, but there are some constructive materials which can be put together in all sorts of fantastic and funny combinations without being ugly or gruesome, and there are some good picture puzzles with funny pictures.

There should be some toys or playthings which satisfy the child's dramatic interest and can be used as properties in his dramatization of social situations in the life around him. Dolls, housekeeping playthings, toy animals, trains, boats, automobiles, the sandbox, and simple materials for "dressing up" and fanciful play are all valuable in his life.

Blocks.—Probably blocks are the playthings which stimulate the best form of dramatic play, and they offer the best early opportunity for experiments in construction. Perhaps nowhere in the toy world has there been such a change and development for the better as there has been with blocks. Instead of sitting at tables handling a few small blocks which hold very limited possibilities of play, children nowadays build on the floor, exercising their whole bodies in lifting, carrying and placing big blocks—blocks large enough to make real things of such size, form and combinations of construction as they need in their play.

There are available some sets of blocks with which children can build structures big enough and strong enough to get into and use in their dramatic play.

Think of the satisfaction in this type of block building, of the possibilities for valuable social contacts and adjustments, for physical exercise, for planning and construction! Above all, consider the possibilities of children making their own usable playthings and of being able to change, reconstruct and build over again.

Opportunity for Physical Activity.—Very definite care should be taken to provide playthings and apparatus especially designed for physical activity—a few well-chosen pieces of apparatus which will give opportunity for all-round exercise. It is wise to keep a balance in this selection and provide equipment for climbing, swinging, hanging, pulling, balancing and similar play. This type of play material is particularly necessary for the city child whose opportunity for vigorous exercise is likely to be more limited than that of the country child, both in the house and out of doors.

Many large pieces of apparatus are available now for schools and playgrounds and for those who have large nurseries, such as the jungle gym, the tower gym, the high-low gym, low parallel bars, climbing rope, seesaw, rocking boats and slide. For those who have only limited space there are excellent compact combinations of swing, swinging bars and rings.

Place for Keeping Toys.—A convenient place for keeping playthings is necessary. A set of low, open shelves is suggested—these shelves made wide enough to hold the large toys and close enough together to provide ample space for everything without having to pile one plaything on another. If children have a convenient place for their toys, they can soon be taught to keep them in order.

Playthings for Later Years.—Children who, when young, have used and experimented with the kind of toys and play materials which we have been discussing, will continue as they grow older to want playthings which enable them to pursue constructive, experimental, scientific and artistic activities. They will continue their interest in construction, but soon, instead of using blocks, they will use materials which offer more exact and elaborate possibilities.

For the Very Youngest

Pat-a-cake, pat-a-cake, baker's man;
Make me a cake as fast as you can:
Pat it and prick it and mark it with B,
Put it in the oven for Baby and me.

* * *

This little pig went to market;
This little pig stayed home;
This little pig had roast beef;
This little pig had none;
This little pig said, "Wee, wee, wee,"
All the way home.

* * *

Dickory, dickory, dock;
The mouse ran up the clock;
The clock struck One,
The mouse ran down,
Dickory, dickory, dock.

Ride a cock-horse to Banbury Cross,
To see a fine lady upon a white horse;
With rings on her fingers and bells on
her toes,
She shall have music wherever she goes.

* * *

Pease porridge hot,
Pease porridge cold,
Pease porridge in the pot,
Nine days old.

Some like it hot,
Some like it cold,
Some like it in the pot,
Nine days old.

* * *

Rain, rain,
Go away,
Come again
Another day.
Little Johnny
Wants to play.

To market, to market, to buy a fat pig,
Home again, home again, dancing a jig;
Ride to the market to buy a fat hog,
Home again, home again, jiggety-jog.

* * *

Hippity hop to the barber shop,
To buy a stick of candy,
One for you and one for me,
And one for sister Annie.

* * *

I love little pussy, her coat is so warm,
And if I don't hurt her, she'll do me no
harm;
So I'll not pull her tail, nor drive her
away,
But pussy and I together will play.

* * *

Little Jack Horner
Sat in a corner,
Eating his Christmas pie
He put in his thumb
And he took out a plum,
And said, "What a good boy am I!"

* * *

Bye, baby bunting,
Daddy's gone a-hunting,
To get a little rabbit skin
To wrap the baby bunting in.

* * *

Hickety, pickety, my black hen,
She lays eggs for gentlemen:
Sometimes nine,
Sometimes ten.
Gentlemen come every day,
To see what my black hen doth lay.

* * *

Ring-a-ring of roses,
A pocketful of posies,
Tisha! Tisha!
We all fall down.

* * *

For Kindergarten and Later

Baa, baa, black sheep,
Have you any wool?
Yes, sir, yes, sir,
Three bags full:
One for my master,
And one for my dame,
And one for the little boy
Who lives in the lane.

* * *

Tom Tom, the piper's son,
Learned to play when he was young;
But the only tune that he could play,
Was "Over the hills and far away."

* * *

Curly locks! Curly locks! Wilt thou be
mine?
Thou shalt not wash dishes nor yet feed
the swine;
But sit on a cushion and sew a fine seam
And feast upon strawberries, sugar and
cream.

Little Miss Muffet
  Sat on a tuffet,
  Eating her curds and whey.
Along came a spider
  And sat down beside her,
  And frightened Miss Muffet away.

* * *

Little Boy Blue, come blow your horn,
The sheep's in the meadow, the cow's
  in the corn.
Where's the little boy that tends the
  sheep?
He's under the haystack, fast asleep.

* * *

Little Bo-peep has lost her sheep,
  And can't tell where to find them.
"Leave them alone, and they'll come
  home,
  And bring their tails behind them!"

Little Bo-peep fell fast asleep
  And dreamt she heard them bleating.
But when she awoke, she found it a
  joke,
  For they were still a-fleeting.

Then up she took her little crook,
  Determin'd for to find them;
She found them indeed, but it made her
  heart bleed,
  For they'd left their tails behind them.

* * *

Jack and Jill went up the hill
  To fetch a pail of water;
Jack fell down and broke his crown,
  And Jill came tumbling after.

* * *

Mary had a little lamb,
  Its fleece was white as snow;
And everywhere that Mary went
  The lamb was sure to go.

* * *

Jack be nimble,
Jack be quick,
Jack jump over the candlestick.

* * *

See, saw, Margery Daw,
Johnny shall have a new master:
He shall have but a penny a day,
Because he can't work any faster.

* * *

Tom, Tom, the piper's son,
Stole a pig and away he run!
The pig was eat, and Tom was beat,
And Tom went howling down the street.

* * *

"Willy boy, Willy boy, where are you
  going?
  I will go with you, if I may."
"I am going to the meadows to see them
  mowing,
  I am going to see them make the
  hay."

* * *

Bobby Shaftoe's gone to sea,
  Silver buckles on his knee;
He'll come back and marry me,
  Pretty Bobby Shaftoe.

Polly put the kettle on,
Polly put the kettle on,
Polly put the kettle on,
And let's drink tea.

Sukey, take it off again,
Sukey, take it off again,
Sukey, take it off again,
They've all gone away.

* * *

There was an old woman who lived in a
  shoe,
She had so many children she didn't
  know what to do.
She gave them some broth without any
  bread.
She whipped them all soundly and sent
  them to bed.

* * *

There was a little girl
Who had a little curl
  Right in the middle of her forehead.
When she was good,
She was very, very good,
  But when she was bad—
    She was horrid.

* * *

Georgie Porgie, pudding and pie,
Kissed the girls and made them cry.
When the boys came out to play,
Georgie Porgie ran away.

Little Tommy Tucker,
Sing for your supper;
What shall he sing for?
White bread and butter.
How can he cut it
Without any knife?
How can he marry
Without any wife?

* * *

Wee Willie Winkie runs through the
  town,
Upstairs and downstairs in his night-
  gown,
Rapping at the window, crying through
  the lock,
"Are the children in their beds, for it's
  now eight o'clock?"

* * *

Girls and boys, come out to play,
The moon doth shine as bright as day.
Come with a whoop, come with a call,
Come with a good-will or not at all.
Up the ladder and down the wall,
A halfpenny roll will serve us all.
You find milk, and I'll find flour,
And we'll have a pudding in half an
  hour.

* * *

Sing a song of sixpence,
  A pocket full of rye;
Four and twenty blackbirds
  Baked in a pie;

When the pie was open'd
  The birds began to sing;
Was not that a dainty dish,
  To set before the king?

"Jack Spratt could eat no fat,
  His wife could eat no lean,
And so betwixt them both,
  They licked the platter clean."

* * *

Pussy-cat, Pussy-cat, where have you
  been?
I've been to London to look at the
  Queen.
Pussy-cat, Pussy-cat, what did you
  there?
I frighten'd a little mouse under the
  chair.

* * *

Mistress Mary, quite contrary,
How does your garden grow?
With silver bells and cockle-shells,
And pretty maids all in a row.

* * *

Simple Simon met a pieman
  Going to the fair.
Says Simple Simon to the pieman,
  "Let me taste your ware."

Says the pieman to Simple Simon,
  "Shew me first your penny."
Says Simple Simon to the pieman,
  "Indeed I have not any."

Simple Simon went a fishing
  For to catch a whale.
All the water he had got
  Was in his mother's pail.

Simple Simon went to look
  If plums grew on a thistle.
He prick'd his fingers very much,
  Which made poor Simon whistle.

* * *

Peter, Peter, pumpkin-eater,
Had a wife and couldn't keep her.
He put her in a pumpkin-shell,
And there he kept her very well.

* * *

Little drops of water,
  Little grains of sand,
Make the mighty ocean
  And the pleasant land.

Old Mother Hubbard
Went to the cupboard
  To get her poor dog a bone;
But when she came there,
The cupboard was bare,
  And so the poor dog had none.

* * *

Old Mother Goose, when
She wanted to wander,
Would ride through the air
On a very fine gander.

* * *

Humpty Dumpty sat on a wall,
Humpty Dumpty had a great fall.
All the King's horses and all the King's
  men
Couldn't put Humpty back again.

* * *

Hey! diddle, diddle,
The cat and the fiddle,
  The cow jumped over the moon.
The little dog laughed
To see such sport,
  And the dish ran away with the spoon.

* * *

There was a crooked man, and he went
  a crooked mile,
He found a crooked sixpence against a
  crooked stile;
He bought a crooked cat, which caught
  a crooked mouse,
And they all lived together in a little
  crooked house.

* * *

All around the cobbler's bench
  The monkey chased the weasel;
The monkey thought 'twas all in fun
  Pop! goes the weasel!

* * *

Lady bird, lady bird, fly away home,
Your house is on fire, your children are
  gone;
All but one, and her name is Ann,
And she crept under the pudding pan.

* * *

One little, two little, three little Indians,
Four little, five little, six little Indians,
Seven little, eight little, nine little Indians,
    Ten little Indian boys.

Ten little, nine little, eight little Indians,
Seven little, six little, five little Indians,
Four little, three little, two little Indians,
    One little Indian boy.

* * *

Three little kittens
Lost their mittens,
  And they began to cry:
"Oh, mother dear,
We very much fear
  That we have lost our mittens!"
"Lost your mittens,
You naughty kittens!
Then you shall have no pie."
"Mee-ow, mee-ow, mee-ow,
And we can have no pie!
Mee-ow, mee-ow, mee-ow!"

A diller, a dollar,
A ten o'clock scholar,
What makes you come so soon?
You used to come at ten o'clock,
But now you come at noon.

* * *

Rub a dub dub,
Three men in a tub;
The butcher, the baker,
The candlestick-maker;
And they all jumped over a hot potato.

* * *

Eena, meena, mina, mo,
Catch a piggy by his toe,
If he hollers, let him go,
Eena, meena, mina, mo.
O—U—T spells out!

* * *

One, two,
Buckle my shoe.
Three, four,
Shut the door.
Five, six,
Pick up sticks.
Seven, eight,
Lay them straight.
Nine, ten,
A good fat hen.
Eleven, twelve,
Dig and delve.
Thirteen, fourteen,
Maids a-courting.
Fifteen, sixteen,
Maids a-kissing.
Seventeen, eighteen,
Maids a-waiting.
Nineteen, twenty,
My platter's empty.

* * *

When the wind is in the east,
'Tis neither good for man nor beast.
When the wind is in the north,
The skillful fisher goes not forth.
When the wind is in the south,
It blows the bait in the fishes' mouth.
When the wind is in the west,
Then 'tis at the very best.

* * *

Monday's child is fair of face.
Tuesday's child is full of grace.
Wednesday's child is full of woe.
Thursday's child has far to go.
Friday's child is loving and giving.
Saturday's child works for its living.
But the child that is born on the Sab-
   bath day
Is bonny and bright and good and gay.

* * *

Thirty days hath September,
April, June and November:
February has twenty-eight alone;
All the rest have thirty-one,
Excepting leap-year, that's the time
When February's days are twenty-nine.

* * *

Three wise men of Gotham,
Went to sea in a bowl,
If the bowl had been stronger,
My song had been longer.

A FROG HE WOULD A-WOOING GO

A frog he would a-wooing go,
   Heigho, says Rowley,
Whether his mother would let him or
   no,
      With a rowley, powley, gammon
      and spinach.
      Heigho, says Anthony Rowley.

So off he set with his opera hat,
   Heigho, says Rowley,
And on the road he met with a rat,
      With a rowley, powley, etc.

When they came to the door of
   Mousey's hall,
      Heigho, says Rowley,
They gave a loud knock, and they gave
   a loud call.
      With a rowley, powley, etc.

"Pray, Mrs. Mouse, are you within?"
      Heigho, says Rowley,
"Oh, yes, kind sirs, I'm sitting to spin."
      With a rowley, powley, etc.

"Pray, Mrs. Mouse, will you give us
   some beer?"
      Heigho, says Rowley,
"For Froggy and I are fond of good
   cheer."
      With a rowley, powley, etc.

But while they were all a-merrymaking,
      Heigho, says Rowley,
A Cat and her kittens came tumbling
   in.
      With a rowley, powley, etc.

The Cat she seized the Rat by the
   crown,
      Heigho, says Rowley,
The kittens they pulled the little Mouse
   down.
      With a rowley, powley, etc.

This put Mr. Frog in a terrible fright;
      Heigho, says Rowley,
He took up his hat, and he wished them
   good night.
      With a rowley, powley, etc.

As Froggy was crossing it over a brook,
      Heigho, says Rowley,
A lily-white Duck came and gobbled
   him up.
      With a rowley, powley, etc.

So here is an end of one, two, three—
      Heigho, says Rowley,
The Rat, the Mouse and little Froggy.
      With a rowley, powley, etc.

Peter Piper picked a peck of pickled
  peppers;
A peck of pickled peppers Peter Piper
  picked;
If Peter Piper picked a peck of
  pickled peppers,
Where's the peck of pickled peppers
  Peter Piper picked?

* * *

Old King Cole
Was a merry old soul,
And a merry old soul was he;

He called for his pipe,
And he called for his bowl,
And he called for his fiddlers three.

Every fiddler, he had a fiddle,
And a very fine fiddle had he;
Twee tweedle dee, tweedle dee, went
  the fiddlers.

FOR OLDER CHILDREN

THE HOUSE THAT JACK BUILT

This is the house that Jack built.
This is the malt
  That lay in the house that Jack built.
This is the rat
  That ate the malt that lay in the
  house that Jack built.
This is the cat
  That killed the rat that ate the malt
  that lay in the house that Jack built.
This is the dog
  That worried the cat that killed the
  rat that ate the malt that lay in the
  house that Jack built.
This is the cow with the crumpled horn
  That tossed the dog that worried the
  cat that killed the rat that ate the
  malt that lay in the house that Jack
  built.
This is the maiden all forlorn
  That milked the cow with the
  crumpled horn that tossed the dog
  that worried the cat that killed the
  rat that ate the malt that lay in the
  house that Jack built.
This is the man all tattered and torn
  That kissed the maiden all forlorn
  that milked the cow with the
  crumpled horn that tossed the dog
  that worried the cat that killed the
  rat that ate the malt that lay in the
  house that Jack built.
This is the priest all shaven and shorn
  That married the man all tattered
  and torn that kissed the maiden all
  forlorn that milked the cow with the
  crumpled horn that tossed the dog
  that worried the cat that killed the
  rat that ate the malt that lay in the
  house that Jack built.
This is the cock that crowed in the morn
  That waked the priest all shaven and
  shorn that married the man all tattered and torn that kissed the maiden
  all forlorn that milked the cow with
  the crumpled horn that tossed the
  dog that worried the cat that killed
  the rat that ate the malt that lay in
  the house that Jack built.
This is the farmer sowing his corn
  That kept the cock that crowed in the
  morn that waked the priest all shaven
  and shorn that married the man all
  tattered and torn that kissed the

maiden all forlorn that milked the
cow with the crumpled horn that
tossed the dog that worried the cat
that killed the rat that ate the malt
that lay in the house that Jack built.

* * * * * *

THE QUEEN OF HEARTS

The Queen of Hearts,
She made some tarts,
All on a summer's day.
The Knave of Hearts,
He stole the tarts
  And took them clean away.

The King of Hearts
Call'd for the tarts
  And beat the knave full sore.
The Knave of Hearts
Brought back the tarts
And vow'd he'd steal no more.

* * *

Twinkle, twinkle, little star—
How I wonder what you are!
Up above the world so high,
Like a diamond in the sky.

When the blazing sun is gone,
When he nothing shines upon,
Then you show your little light,
Twinkle, twinkle, all the night.

Then the traveler in the dark
Thanks you for your tiny spark;
He could not see which way to go,
If you did not twinkle so.

As your bright and tiny spark
Lights the traveler in the dark:
Though I know not what you are,
Twinkle, twinkle, little star.

* * *

DAME WIGGINS OF LEE
AND
HER SEVEN WONDERFUL CATS

Dame Wiggins of Lee
  Was a worthy old soul
As e'er threaded a needle
  Or washed in a bowl.

She held mice and rats
  In such antipathee,
That seven fine cats
  Kept Dame Wiggins of Lee.

The rats and mice scared
  By this fierce-whiskered crew,
The seven poor cats
  Soon had nothing to do;

So, as anyone idle
  She ne'er loved to see,
She sent them to school,
  Did Dame Wiggins of Lee.

The master soon wrote
  That they all of them knew
How to read the word "milk"
  And to spell the word "mew,"

And they all washed their faces
  Before they took tea.
"Were there ever such dears?"
  Said Dame Wiggins of Lee.

He had also thought well
  To comply with their wish
To spend all their play time
  In learning to fish—

For titlings; they sent her
  A present of three,
Which fried were a feast
  For Dame Wiggins of Lee.

But the Dame soon grew tired
  Of living alone;
So she sent for her cats
  From school to come home.

Each rowing a wherry,
  Returning you see:
The frolic made merry
  Dame Wiggins of Lee.

The Dame was quite pleas'd,
  And ran out to market;
When she came back
  They were mending the carpet.

The needle each handled
  As brisk as a bee.
"Well done, my good cats!"
  Said Dame Wiggins of Lee.

To give them a treat,
  She ran out for some rice;
When she came back,
  They were skating on ice.

"I shall soon see one down,
  Aye, perhaps, two or three,
I'll bet half a crown,"
  Said Dame Wiggins of Lee.

When springtime came back,
  They had breakfast of curds
And were greatly afraid
  Of disturbing the birds.

"If you sit like good cats,
  All the seven in a tree,
They will teach you to sing,"
  Said Dame Wiggins of Lee.

So they sat in a tree
  And said "Beautiful! Hark!"
And they listened and looked
  In the clouds for a lark.

Then sang by the fireside
  Sym-pho-ni-ous-ly
A song without words
  To Dame Wiggins of Lee.

They called the next day
  On the tomtit and sparrow
And wheeled a poor sick lamb
  Home in a barrow.

"You shall all have some sprats
  For your humanitee,
My seven good cats,"
  Said Dame Wiggins of Lee.

While she ran to the field
  To look for its dam,
They were warming the bed
  For the poor sick lamb:

They turned up the clothes
  All as neat as could be.
"I shall ne'er want a nurse,"
  Said Dame Wiggins of Lee.

She wished them good-night
  And went up to bed:
When, lo! in the morning,
  The cats were all fled.

But soon—what a fuss!
  "Where can they all be?
Here, pussy, puss, puss!"
  Cried Dame Wiggins of Lee.

CAMERON WRIGHT

The Dame's heart was nigh broke,
 So she sat down to weep,
When she saw them come back
 Each riding a sheep:

She fondled and patted
 Each purring Tommee:
"Ah! welcome, my dears,"
 Said Dame Wiggins of Lee.

The Dame was unable
 Her pleasure to smother
To see the sick lamb
 Jump up to its mother.

In spite of the gout
 And the pain in her knee,
She went dancing about,
 Did Dame Wiggins of Lee.

The farmer soon heard
 Where his sheep went astray
And arrived at Dame's door
 With his faithful dog Tray.

He knocked with his crook,
 And the stranger to see,
Out of window did look
 Dame Wiggins of Lee.

For their kindness he had them
 All drawn by the team,
And gave them some field-mice
 And raspberry cream.

Said he, "All my stock
 You shall presently see,
For I *know* the cats
 Of Dame Wiggins of Lee."

He sent his maid out
 For some muffins and crumpets;
And when he turned round
 They were blowing of trumpets.

Said he, "I suppose
 She's as deaf as can be,
Or this ne'er could be borne
 By Dame Wiggins of Lee."

To show them his poultry,
 He turned them all loose,
When each nimbly leap'd
 On the back of a goose,

Which frighten'd them so
 That they ran to the sea
And half-drown'd the poor cats
 Of Dame Wiggins of Lee.

For the care of his lamb
 And their comical pranks
He gave them a ham
 And abundance of thanks.

"I wish you good-day,
 My fine fellows," said he.
"My compliments, pray,
 To Dame Wiggins of Lee."

You see them arrived
 At their Dame's welcome door;
They show her their presents
 And all their good store.

"Now come in to supper
 And sit down with me,
All welcome once more,"
 Cried Dame Wiggins of Lee.

* * * * * *

THE OWL AND THE PUSSY-CAT
By Edward Lear

The Owl and the Pussy-Cat went to sea
 In a beautiful pea-green boat,
They took some honey, and plenty of
 money,
Wrapped up in a five-pound note.
The owl looked up at the stars above
 And sang to a small guitar,
"O lovely Pussy! O Pussy, my love,
 What a beautiful Pussy you are,
 You are!
What a beautiful Pussy you are!"

Pussy said to the Owl, "You elegant
 fowl!
How charmingly sweet you sing!
O let us be married! Too long we have
 tarried.
 But what shall we do for a ring?"
They sailed away for a year and a day,
 To the land where the Bong-tree
 grows,
And there in a wood a Piggy-wig stood,
 With a ring at the end of his nose,
 His nose,
With a ring at the end of his nose.

"Dear Pig, are you willing to sell for
 one shilling
 Your ring?" Said the Piggy, "I will."
So they took it away and were married
 next day
By the Turkey who lives on the hill.
They dined on mince and slices of
 quince,
 Which they ate with a runcible spoon;
And hand in hand, on the edge of the
 sand,
 They danced by the light of the moon,
 The moon,
They danced by the light of the moon.

* * * * *

From
UNDER THE WINDOW [1]
By
Kate Greenaway

In go-cart so tiny
 My sister I drew;
And I've promised to draw her
 The wide world through.
We have not yet started—
 I own it with sorrow—
Because our trip's always
 Put off till tomorrow.

* * *

Little wind, blow on the hill-top,
 Little wind, blow down the plain:
Little wind, blow up the sunshine,
 Little wind, blow off the rain.

[1] By arrangement with Frederick Warne &
Co., Inc.

From
A CHILD'S GARDEN OF VERSES
By Robert Louis Stevenson

THE LITTLE LAND

I have just to shut my eyes
To go sailing through the skies—
Tc go sailing far away
To the pleasant Land of Play.

* * *

THE SWING

How do you like to go up in a swing,
  Up in the air so blue?
"Oh, I do think it the pleasantest thing
  Ever a child can do!"

"Up in the air and over the wall,
  Till I can see so wide,
Rivers and trees and cattle and all
  Over the countryside—

"Till I look down on the garden green
  Down on the roof so brown—
Up in the air I go flying again,
  Up in the air and down!"

* * * * * *

BED IN SUMMER

In winter I get up at night
And dress by yellow candle-light.
In summer, quite the other way,
I have to go to bed by day.

I have to go to bed and see
The birds still hopping on the tree,
Or hear the grown-up people's feet
Still going past me in the street.

And does it not seem hard to you,
When all the sky is clear and blue,
And I should like so much to play,
To have to go to bed by day?

* * *

THE WIND

I saw you toss the kites on high
And blow the birds about the sky;
And all around I heard you pass,
Like ladies' skirts across the grass—
  O wind, a-blowing all day long,
  O wind, that sings so loud a song!

I saw the different things you did,
But always you yourself you hid.
I felt you push, I heard you call,
I could not see yourself at all—
  O wind, a-blowing all day long,
  O wind, that sings so loud a song!

O you that are so strong and cold,
O blower, are you young or old?
Are you a beast of field and tree,
Or just a stronger child than me?
  O wind, a-blowing all day long,
  O wind, that sings so loud a song!

* * *

FOREIGN CHILDREN

Little Indian, Sioux or Crow,
Little frosty Eskimo,
Little Turk or Japanee,
O! don't you wish that you were me?

You have seen the scarlet trees
And the lions over seas.
You have eaten ostrich eggs
And turned the turtles off their legs.

Such a life is very fine,
But it's not so nice as mine.
You must often, as you trod,
Have wearied *not* to be abroad.

You have curious things to eat,
I am fed on proper meat;
You must dwell beyond the foam,
But I am safe and live at home.

Little Indian, Sioux or Crow,
Little frosty Eskimo,
Little Turk or Japanee,
O! don't you wish that you were me?

* * *

MY BED IS A BOAT

My bed is like a little boat;
  Nurse helps me in when I embark;
She girds me in my sailor's coat
  And starts me in the dark.

At night, I go on board and say
  Good night to all my friends on shore;
I shut my eyes and sail away
  And see and hear no more.

And sometimes things to bed I take,
  As prudent sailors have to do;
Perhaps a slice of wedding cake,
  Perhaps a toy or two.

All night across the dark we steer;
  But when the day returns at last,
Safe in my room, beside the pier,
  I find my vessel fast.

* * *

BLOCK CITY

What are you able to build with your
  blocks?
Castles and palaces, temples and docks.
Rain may keep raining, and others go
  roam,
But I can be happy and building at
  home.

Let the sofa be mountains, the carpet be
  sea,
There I'll establish a city for me:
A kirk and a mill and a palace beside,
And a harbor as well where my vessels
  may ride.

Great is the palace with pillar and wall,
A sort of a tower on the top of it all,
And steps coming down in an orderly
  way
To where my toy vessels lie safe in the
  bay.

This one is sailing and that one is
  moored:
Hark to the song of the sailors on board!
And see on the steps of my palace, the
  kings
Coming and going with presents and
  things!

Now I have done with it, down let it go!
All in a moment the town is laid low.
Block upon block lying scattered and
  free,
What is there left of my town by the
  sea?

Yet, as I saw it, I see it again,
The kirk and the palace, the ships and
  the men,
And as long as I live and where'er I may
  be,
I'll always remember my town by the
  sea.

RAIN

The rain is raining all around,
  It falls on field and tree,
It rains on the umbrellas here
  And on the ships at sea.

* * *

HAPPY THOUGHT

The world is so full of a number of
  things,
I'm sure we should all be as happy as
  kings.

* * *

TIME TO RISE

A birdie with a yellow bill
Hopped upon the window-sill,
Cocked his shining eye and said:
"Ain't you 'shamed, you sleepy head!"

* * *

MY SHADOW

I have a little shadow that goes in and
  out with me,
And what can be the use of him is more
  than I can see.
He is very, very like me from the heels
  up to the head;
And I see him jump before me, when I
  jump into my bed.

The funniest thing about him is the way
  he likes to grow—
Not at all like proper children, which is
  always very slow;
For he sometimes shoots up taller like
  an india-rubber ball,
And he sometimes gets so little that
  there's none of him at all.

He hasn't got a notion of how children
  ought to play,
And can only make a fool of me in
  every sort of way.
He stays so close beside me, he's a
  coward you can see;
I'd think shame to stick to nursie as
  that shadow sticks to me!

One morning, very early, before the sun
  was up,
I rose and found the shining dew on
  every buttercup;
But my lazy little shadow, like an ar-
  rant sleepy-head,
Had stayed at home behind me and was
  fast asleep in bed.

* * *

WHERE GO THE BOATS?

Dark brown is the river,
  Golden is the sand,
It flows along for ever,
  With trees on either hand.

Green leaves a-floating,
  Castles of the foam,
Boats of mine a-boating—
  Where will all come home?

On goes the river
  And out past the mill,
Away down the valley,
  Away down the hill.

In a golden crown,
And a scant green gown
    While the spring blows chilly,
Lady Daffadown,
    Sweet Daffadowndilly.

* * *

Love me,—I love you,
    Love me, my baby;
Sing it high, sing it low,
    Sing it as may be.

Mother's arms under you,
    Her eyes above you;
Sing it high, sing it low,
    Love me—I love you.

* * *

Is the moon tired? she looks so pale
Within her misty veil:
She scales the sky from east to west,
And takes no rest.

Before the coming of the night
The moon shows papery white;
Before the dawning of the day
She fades away.

* * *

Lullaby, oh lullaby!
Flowers are closed and lambs are
    sleeping;
Lullaby, oh lullaby!
Stars are up, the moon is peeping;
Lullaby, oh lullaby!
While the birds are silence keeping,
    (Lullaby, oh lullaby!)
Sleep, my baby, fall a-sleeping,
    Lullaby, oh lullaby!

* * * * *

THE ROCK-A-BY LADY FROM HUSHABY STREET
By Eugene Field

The Rock-a-By Lady from Hushaby
    Street
    Comes stealing; comes creeping;
The poppies, they hang from her head
    to her feet,
And each hath a dream that is tiny and
    fleet—
She bringeth her poppies to you, my
    sweet,
    When she findeth you sleeping!

There is one little dream of a beautiful
    drum—
    "Rub-a-dub!" it goeth;
There is one little dream of a big sugar
    plum,
And lo! thick and fast the other dreams
    come
Of popguns that bang, and tin-tops that
    hum,
    And a trumpet that bloweth!

And dollies peep out of those wee little
    dreams
    With laughter and singing;
And boats go a-floating on silvery
    streams,
And the stars peek-a-boo with their own
    misty gleams,
And up, up, and up, where the Mother
    Moon beams,
    The fairies go winging!

Would you dream all these dreams that
    are tiny and fleet?

Away down the river,
    A hundred miles or more,
Other little children
    Shall bring my boats ashore.

* * *

From
SING-SONG[1]
By Christina Rossetti

Who has seen the wind?
    Neither I nor you:
But when the leaves hang trembling
    The wind is passing thro'.

Who has seen the wind?
    Neither you nor I:
But when the trees bow down their
        heads
    The wind is passing by.

[1] The seven poems from "Sing-Song" by
Christina Rossetti are reprinted by permission of The Macmillan Company, publishers.

A frisky lamb
And a frisky child
Playing their pranks
    In a cowslip meadow:

The sky all blue
And the air all mild
And the fields all sun
    And the lanes half shadow.

* * *

On the grassy banks
Lambkins at their pranks;
Woolly sisters, woolly brothers,
    Jumping off their feet,
While their woolly mothers
Watch by them and bleat.

* * *

Growing in the vale
    By the uplands hilly,
Growing straight and frail,
    Lady Daffadowndilly.

They'll come to you sleeping;
So shut the two eyes that are weary,
    my sweet,
For the Rock-a-By Lady from Hushaby
    Street,
With poppies that hang from her head
    to her feet,
    Comes stealing; comes creeping.

* * * * * *

WYNKEN, BLYNKEN AND NOD
By Eugene Field

Wynken, Blynken and Nod one night
    Sailed off in a wooden shoe—
Sailed on a river of crystal light
    Into a sea of dew.
"Where are you going, and what do you
    wish?"
    The old moon asked the three.
"We have come to fish for the herring
    fish
That live in this beautiful sea;
Nets of silver and gold have we,"
        Said Wynken,
        Blynken
        And Nod.

The old moon laughed and sang a song,
    As they rocked in the wooden shoe;
And the wind that sped them all night
    long

Ruffled the waves of dew;
The little stars were the herring fish
    That lived in the beautiful sea.
"Now cast your nets wherever you
    wish—
    Never afeard are we!"
So cried the stars to the fishermen
    three,
        Wynken,
        Blynken
        And Nod.

All night long their nets they threw
    To the stars in the twinkling foam—
Then down from the skies came the
    wooden shoe,
    Bringing the fishermen home;
'Twas all so pretty a sail, it seemed
    As if it could not be;
And some folk thought 'twas a dream
    they'd dreamed
    Of sailing that beautiful sea.
But I shall name you the fishermen
    three:
        Wynken,
        Blynken
        And Nod.

Wynken and Blynken are two little
    eyes,
    And Nod is a little head,
And the wooden shoe that sailed the
    skies
    Is a wee one's trundle-bed;

So shut your eyes while mother sings
    Of wonderful sights that be,
And you shall see the beautiful things
    As you rock on the misty sea
    Where the old shoe rocked the fisher-
    men three—
        Wynken,
        Blynken
        And Nod.

* * * * *

THE YEAR'S AT THE SPRING
By Robert Browning

The year's at the spring,
And day's at the morn;
Morning's at seven;
The hill-side's dew-pearl'd;
The lark's on the wing;
The snail's on the thorn;
God's in His heaven—
All's right with the world.

* * * * *

THE PIPER
By William Blake

Piping down the valleys wild,
    Piping songs of pleasant glee,
On a cloud I saw a child,
    And he laughing said to me:

"Pipe a song about a lamb!"
    So I piped with merry cheer.
"Piper, pipe that song again;"
    So I piped: he wept to hear.

"Drop thy pipe, thy happy pipe;
    Sing thy songs of happy cheer!"
So I sang the same again,
    While he wept with joy to hear.

"Piper, sit thee down and write
    In a book that all may read."
So he vanished from my sight;
    And I plucked a hollow reed,

And I made a rural pen,
    And I stained the water clear,
And I wrote my happy songs
    Every child may joy to hear.

* * *

THE NIGHT BEFORE CHRISTMAS
By Clement Moore

'Twas the night before Christmas,
When all through the house
    Not a creature was stirring,
Not even a mouse.

The stockings were hung
By the chimney with care,
    In hopes that St. Nicholas
Soon would be there.

The children were nestled
All snug in their beds,
    While visions of sugar-plums
Danced through their heads.

Mamma in her kerchief
And I in my cap
    Had just settled our brains
For a long winter's nap.

When out on the lawn
There arose such a clatter
    I sprang from my bed
To see what was the matter.

Away to the window
I flew like a flash,
  Tore open the shutters
And threw up the sash.

The moon on the breast
Of the new fallen snow
  Gave a lustre of mid-day
To objects below,

When what to my wondering eyes
  Should appear—
But a miniature sleigh
  And eight tiny reindeer!

With a little old driver,
  So lively and quick,
I knew in a moment
  It must be St. Nick.

More rapid than eagles,
His coursers they came,
  And he whistled and shouted
And called each by name:
  "Now, Dasher, now, Dancer,
Now, Prancer, now, Vixen!
  On, Comet! On, Cupid!
On, Donner and Blitzen!

To the top of the porch,
To the top of the wall,
  Now, dash away, dash away,
Dash away, all!"

As dry leaves before the wild hurri-
  cane fly,
When they meet with an obstacle,
  mount to the sky:
So up to the house-top the coursers
  they flew,
With the sleigh full of toys, and St.
  Nicholas, too.

And then, in a twinkling,
I heard on the roof
  The prancing and pawing
Of each little hoof.

As I drew in my head,
And was turning around,
  Down the chimney St. Nicholas came
    With a bound!

He was dressed all in fur
From his head to his foot,
  And his clothes were all tarnished
With ashes and soot;

A bundle of toys
He had flung on his back,
  And he looked like a peddler
Just opening his pack.

His eyes, how they twinkled!
His dimples, how merry!
  His cheeks were like roses,
His nose like a cherry.

His droll little mouth
Was drawn up like a bow,
  And the beard on his chin
Was as white as the snow.

The stump of a pipe
He held tight in his teeth,
  And the smoke, it encircled
His head like a wreath.

He had a broad face,
And a little round belly
  That shook when he laughed
Like a bowlful of jelly.

He was chubby and plump—
A right jolly old elf,

CAMERON WRIGHT

And I laughed when I saw him
In spite of myself.

A wink of his eye
And a twist of his head
  Soon gave me to know
I had nothing to dread.

He spoke not a word
But went straight to his work
  And filled all the stockings,
Then turned with a jerk—

And, laying his finger
Aside of his nose
  And giving a nod,
Up the chimney he rose.

He sprang to his sleigh,
To his team gave a whistle,
  And away they all flew
Like the down on a thistle.

And I heard him exclaim
Ere he drove out of sight:
  "MERRY CHRISTMAS TO ALL
AND TO ALL A GOOD NIGHT!"

* * * * *

SWEET AND LOW
By Alfred Tennyson

Sweet and low, sweet and low,
Wind of the western sea;
Low, low, breathe and blow,

Wind of the western sea!
  Over the rolling waters go,
  Come from the dying moon and blow,
Blow him again to me,
  While my little one,
  While my pretty one
    Sleeps.

Sleep and rest, sleep and rest,
Father will come to thee soon;
Rest, rest, on mother's breast,
Father will come to thee soon.
  Father will come to his babe in the
    nest,
  Silver sails all out of the west,
Under the silver moon.
  Sleep, my little one,
  Sleep, my pretty one,
    Sleep!

* * *

THE PUZZLED CENTIPEDE

A centipede was happy quite,
  Until a frog in fun
Said, "Pray, which leg comes after
    which?"
  This roused her mind to such a
    pitch,
She lay distracted in the ditch
  Considering how to run.

* * *

As Tommy Snooks and Bessy Brooks
  Were walking out one Sunday,
Says Tommy Snooks to Bessy Brooks,
  "Tomorrow will be Monday."

DECK THE HALLS

Old Welsh Air

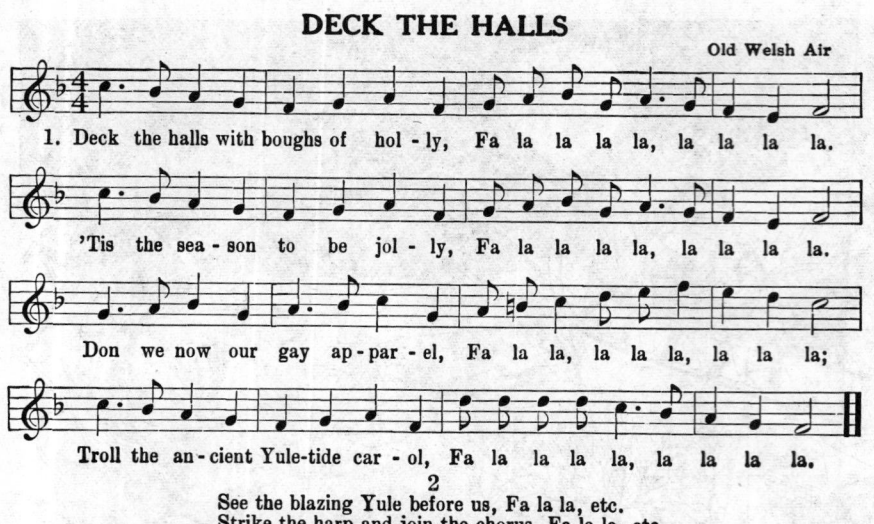

1. Deck the halls with boughs of hol-ly, Fa la la la la, la la la la.

'Tis the sea-son to be jol-ly, Fa la la la la, la la la la.

Don we now our gay ap-par-el, Fa la la, la la la, la la la;

Troll the an-cient Yule-tide car-ol, Fa la la la la, la la la la.

2
See the blazing Yule before us, Fa la la, etc.
Strike the harp and join the chorus, Fa la la, etc.
Follow me in merry measure, Fa la la, etc.
While I tell of Yuletide treasure, Fa la la, etc.

3
Fast away the old year passes, Fa la la, etc.
Hail the new, ye lads and lassies, Fa la la, etc.
Sing we joyous, all together, Fa la la, etc.
Heedless of the wind and weather, Fa la la, etc.

JINGLE BELLS

J. PIERPONT

Jin-gle bells, Jin-gle bells, Jin-gle all the way!

Oh, what fun it is to ride In a one-horse o-pen sleigh!......

Jin-gle bells, Jin-gle bells, Jin-gle all the way!

Oh, what fun it is to ride In a one-horse o-pen sleigh!

COME, LASSES AND LADS

English

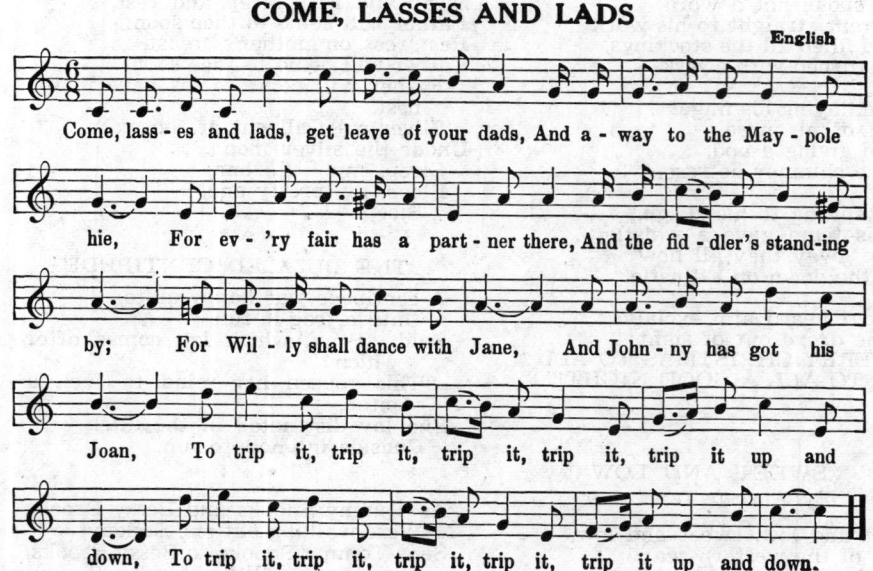

Come, lass-es and lads, get leave of your dads, And a-way to the May-pole

hie, For ev-'ry fair has a part-ner there, And the fid-dler's stand-ing

by; For Wil-ly shall dance with Jane, And John-ny has got his

Joan, To trip it, trip it, trip it, trip it, trip it up and

down, To trip it, trip it, trip it, trip it, trip it up and down.

SONGS AND SINGING GAMES

INTRODUCTION

The following songs have been carefully selected for this volume as typical examples of songs that have stood the test of time and are still universally popular. They are suited to children of almost any age, and no child should pass the age of eight or ten without having sung and learned every song in this collection. It has been the aim of the editors to include various kinds of songs in order that music for different interests and activities of children might be made available to them.   There are:

1.   Five Seasonal Songs: *Deck the Halls* and *Jingle Bells* for winter; *Come Lasses and Lads* for springtime singing; *Harvest Home*, a characteristic autumn song; and *Row, Row, Row Your Boat* (a round), which is very popular in summer.

2.   Two modern songs for very young children which represent the everyday interests of the present time: *The Postman* and *Down by the Station.*

3.   Six Game Songs, with directions for playing the games: *The Farmer in the Dell; Here We Go Round the Mulberry Bush; London Bridge; Oats, Peas, Beans and Barley Grow; Round and Round the Village* and *The King of France.*

4.   Five traditional English songs: *Lavender's Blue, Oh! Dear! What can the Matter be? Where are You Going To? Old King Cole* and *Rock-a-bye Baby.* All these furnish not only good song material but good dance music as well.

5.   Four sense games: *Sight, Smell, Taste* and *Touch.*

Five Seasonal Songs
DECK THE HALLS

Although this old song is of Welsh origin, it is an especial favorite of American children, and our Christmas festivities do not seem complete without it.

JINGLE BELLS

Everywhere in America this old sleighing song is sung in the wintertime, even in the balmy South where the snow seldom falls.

COME, LASSES AND LADS

This merry old English song furnishes a jolly dance for groups of any age. It is very effective when played on the violin out of doors—with singing also—while children dance on the grass, as they did in the days of Merrie England.

HARVEST HOME

The music of *Harvest Home* was written in the late 17th century by England's greatest composer, Henry Purcell. For more than two hundred years this has been one of the standard autumn songs.

ROW, ROW, ROW YOUR BOAT

This is a four-part *round*, and the singers should be divided into four groups.

The first group starts the song, and when they have reached the word *gently*, the second group starts at the beginning of the song. When the second group reaches the word *gently*, the third group begins at the beginning; and when the third group reaches the word *gently*, the fourth group begins. Sing through the song at least twice. The first group will finish first, and the fourth group will have to sing the last phrase alone after all the others have finished. If every one keeps on the tune and starts at exactly the right time, the result will be very pleasing harmonies.

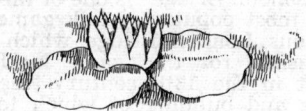

THE POSTMAN

The Postman is suited to children from three to five years of age. Most children will enjoy acting it out as they sing.

DOWN BY THE STATION

Down by the Station may be sung and dramatized by children of nursery school and kindergarten age by using a row of chairs to represent the train.

HARVEST HOME

Words by JOHN DRYDEN   Music by HENRY PURCELL

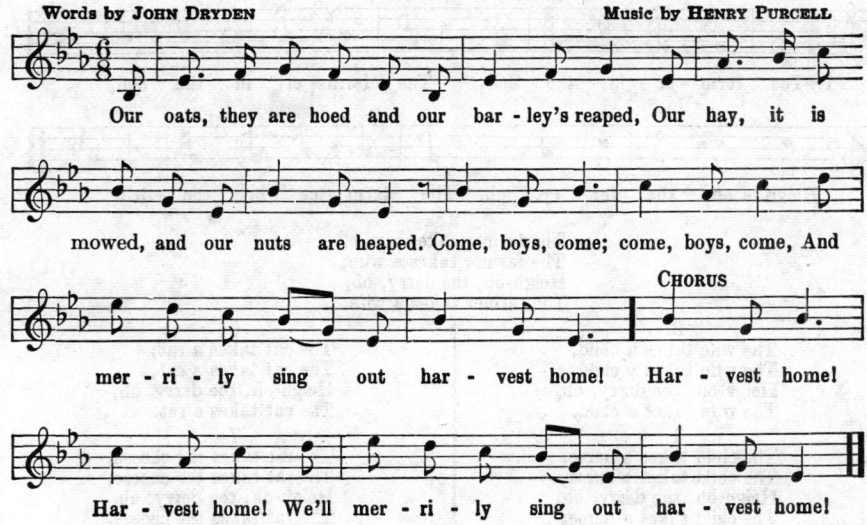

Our oats, they are hoed and our bar-ley's reaped, Our hay, it is mowed, and our nuts are heaped. Come, boys, come; come, boys, come, And

CHORUS

mer-ri-ly sing out har-vest home! Har-vest home!

Har-vest home! We'll mer-ri-ly sing out har-vest home!

ROW, ROW, ROW YOUR BOAT

A Round

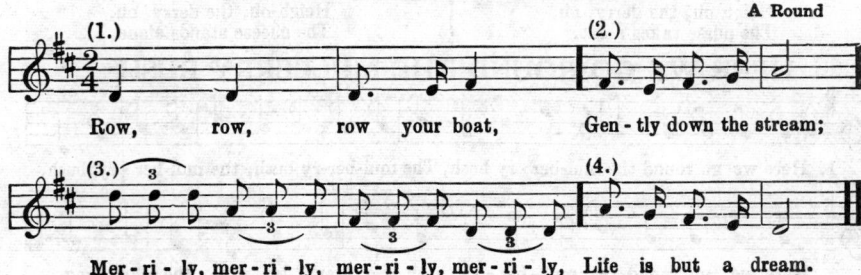

(1.) Row, row, row your boat, (2.) Gen-tly down the stream;

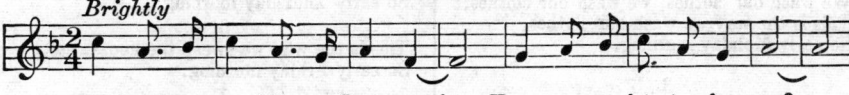

(3.) Mer-ri-ly, mer-ri-ly, mer-ri-ly, mer-ri-ly, (4.) Life is but a dream.

THE POSTMAN[1]

Brightly

Ho, there you are, Mis-ter Post-man! Have you a let-ter for me?

O-pen your bag, Mis-ter Post-man. Have you a let-ter for me?

DOWN BY THE STATION[1]

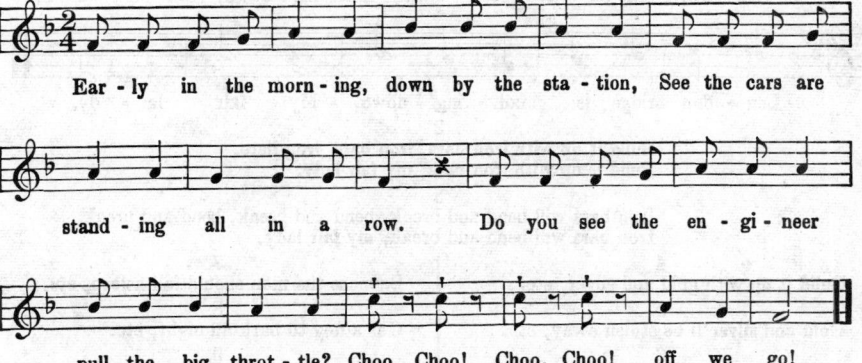

Ear-ly in the morn-ing, down by the sta-tion, See the cars are stand-ing all in a row. Do you see the en-gi-neer

pull the big throt-tle? Choo, Choo! Choo, Choo! off we go!

[1] Reprinted from "Singing Time" (by Satis N. Coleman and Alice G. Thorn), by permission of the authors and the John Day Company, Inc.

THE FARMER IN THE DELL

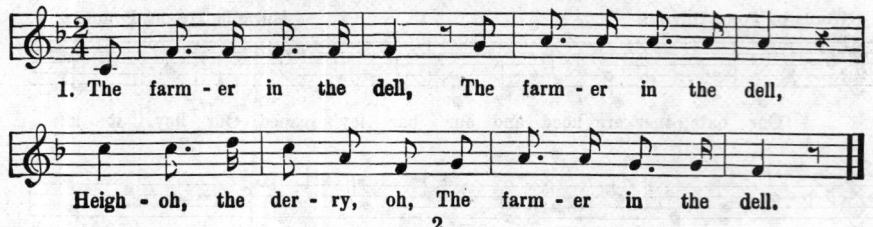

1. The farm-er in the dell, The farm-er in the dell,

Heigh-oh, the der-ry, oh, The farm-er in the dell.

2
The farmer takes a wife,
The farmer takes a wife,
Heigh-oh, the derry, oh,
The farmer takes a wife.

3
The wife takes a child,
The wife takes a child,
Heigh-oh, the derry, oh,
The wife takes a child.

4
The child takes a nurse,
The child takes a nurse,
Heigh-oh, the derry, oh,
The child takes a nurse.

5
The nurse takes a cat,
The nurse takes a cat,
Heigh-oh, the derry, oh,
The nurse takes a cat.

6
The cat takes a rat,
The cat takes a rat,
Heigh-oh, the derry, oh,
The cat takes a rat.

7
The rat takes the cheese,
The rat takes the cheese,
Heigh-oh, the derry, oh,
The rat takes the cheese.

8
The cheese stands alone,
The cheese stands alone,
Heigh-oh, the derry, oh,
The cheese stands alone.

HERE WE GO ROUND THE MULBERRY BUSH

1. Here we go round the mul-ber-ry bush, The mul-ber-ry bush, the mul-ber-ry bush,

Here we go round the mul-ber-ry bush, So ear-ly in the morn-ing.

(Repeat first verse after each stanza)

2
This is the way we wash our clothes,
We wash our clothes, we wash our clothes;
This is the way we wash our clothes,
So early Monday morning.

3
This is the way we iron our clothes, etc.,
So early Tuesday morning.

4
This is the way we scrub the floor, etc.,
So early Wednesday morning.

5
This is the way we mend our clothes, etc.,
So early Thursday morning.

6
This is the way we sweep the house, etc.,
So early Friday morning.

7
This is the way we bake our bread, etc.,
So early Saturday morning.

8
This is the way we go to church, etc.,
So early Sunday morning.

LONDON BRIDGE

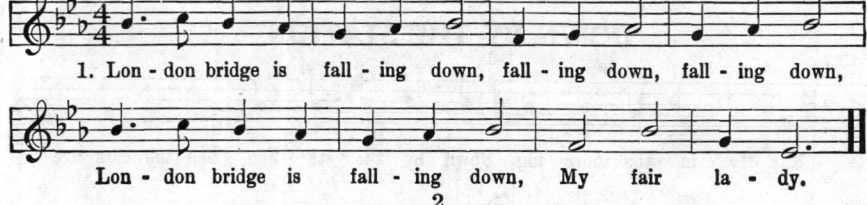

1. Lon-don bridge is fall-ing down, fall-ing down, fall-ing down,

Lon-don bridge is fall-ing down, My fair la-dy.

2
Build it up with iron bars, iron bars, iron bars,
Build it up with iron bars, my fair lady.

3
Iron bars will bend and break, bend and break, bend and break,
Iron bars will bend and break, my fair lady.

4
Build it up with gold and silver, etc.

5
Gold and silver'll be stolen away, etc.

6
Get a man to watch all night, etc.

7
Suppose the man should fall asleep, etc.

8
Get a dog to bark all night, etc.

9
Suppose the dog should meet a bone, etc.

10
Get a cock to crow all night, etc.

Six Singing Games

THE FARMER IN THE DELL

One child is chosen to stand inside the circle to represent the farmer in the dell, while the circle moves around him, singing. In the second verse where the farmer "takes a wife," he touches or beckons to another child who joins him inside the circle. In each verse, the newcomer chooses the next one. In the last verse, every one except the "cheese" returns to the circle, they all clap hands, and the game is repeated.

In one variant of the game, the children of the circle stand still, and those on the inside march around, the last one chosen marching at the front.

HERE WE GO ROUND THE MULBERRY BUSH

This is a game for children of all ages, from the time they can walk steadily and move around in a circle. During the singing of the first verse, all take hands and circle around as they sing, stepping quietly and slowing gradually. During the phrase, "So early in the morning," the circle stops, hands are loosened, and each child spins around rapidly in place.

Each verse following is acted out according to the words, each child making the motions he thinks best suited to the lines, but keeping the motions in rhythm with the swing of the song. After each verse, the first verse is sung again, and the children move around in a circle and spin at the end.

At Christmas time, the words may be sung: "Here we go round the Christmas tree"; or if played out in the garden, "Here we go round the apple tree," etc.

LONDON BRIDGE

"London Bridge" is one of the oldest and most popular of folk games. The famous London Bridge which is responsible for this game is the one built in the 13th century, the planning and building of which took almost a hundred years.

Two players represent the bridge by standing face to face with hands clasped and held high. The others form a line, holding each other by the hand or by the dress, and pass under the "bridge." Before the game starts, the two persons forming the bridge decide on two metals which they will represent, usually silver and gold, but those in the line do not know which is silver and which is gold. The children representing the bridge sing the first verse while the others march under. As the last one passes under, their arms come down and he is caught. He is then asked to choose silver or gold, and he belongs to the side he chooses. The line of marchers sing the second verse, and again the last one is caught and joins a side. The two groups alternate singing the verses, and the song is repeated until all the children in the line have been caught and have lined up behind their leaders (the makers of the bridge). Each child holds the one in front of him by the waist, and a tug of war takes place between the two lines. The side which pulls the others across a given line is the winning side.

OATS, PEAS, BEANS AND BARLEY GROW

This is a game that is played in every civilized country on the globe, and it has been traced back for more than 500 years. In playing it, one member is chosen to represent the farmer, who stands in the center, and the others clasp hands and circle about him as they all sing the first verse. During the singing of the second verse, they all stand still, and each one goes through the motions suggested by the words: sowing the seed with a broad sweep of the arm; standing erect with folded arms; stamping the foot; clapping the hands; and turning around at the end of the verse.

For the second verse, clasp hands and circle around while singing the first two lines, and stand still for the last two while a partner is chosen.

While singing the third verse, the members of the circle shake warning fingers to the two inside the circle. The last one chosen remains in the center while the game is repeated.

ROUND AND ROUND THE VILLAGE

The children form a circle, clasping hands, with one child outside the circle. The children in the circle stand still and represent the houses of the village. While the children of the circle sing the first verse, the outside child skips around the circle as many times as it may require for the completion of the verse. During the second verse, the clasped hands are raised high to represent windows of the houses, and the outside child winds in and out trying to complete the circle by the end of the verse.

During the singing of the third verse, the child remains inside the circle and selects a partner, and they bow to each other at the fourth line of the song. At the beginning of the fourth verse, the first child dashes outside the circle, and the partner chases him around the circle. At the end of the verse, they stop and bow to each other. The chosen partner now remains outside the circle to run around the village in a new game.

In a large group of children, two or three may be chosen to go round the village, choose partners, etc., at the same time.

THE KING OF FRANCE

The players stand in two rows, facing each other. The leader of each row stands in the middle as king.

The first verse is sung alone by one of the kings who marches out toward the line opposite him and marches back to his place, singing as he goes. Then the two lines sing and march forward toward each other and back again, imitating what the king has done. In the second verse, the other king marches out singing, gives salute and marches back again. Then both lines sing and imitate him. The two kings take turns as leader, throughout all the verses, both lines always imitating, as nearly as possible, the song and motions of the king. When played by older children, interest is added to the game if the kings put in motions that are difficult to imitate. Other verses may be added.

OATS, PEAS, BEANS AND BARLEY GROW

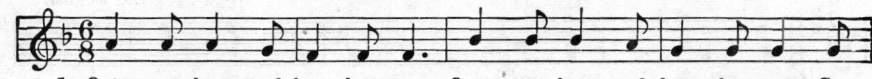

1. Oats, peas, beans and bar - ley grow, Oats, peas, beans and bar - ley grow, Can

you or I or an - y - one know How oats, peas, beans and bar - ley grow?

2
Thus the farmer sows his seed,
Thus he stands and takes his ease,
Stamps his foot and claps his hands,
And turns around to view his lands.

3
Waiting for a partner,
Waiting for a partner,
So open the ring and choose one in,
Make haste and choose your partner.

4
Now you're married you must obey,
You must be true to all you say.
You must be kind, you must be good,
And keep your wife in kindling wood.

ROUND AND ROUND THE VILLAGE

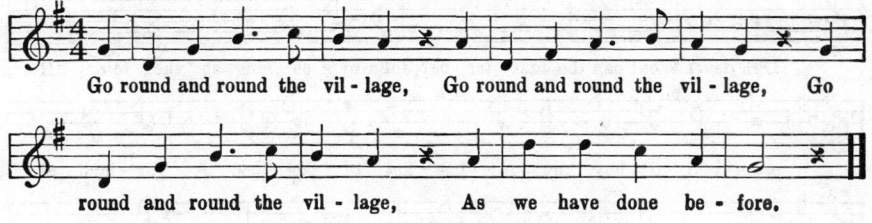

Go round and round the vil - lage, Go round and round the vil - lage, Go round and round the vil - lage, As we have done be - fore.

2
Go in and out the windows,
Go in and out the windows,
Go in and out the windows,
As we have done before.

3
Now stand and face your partner,
Now stand and face your partner,
Now stand and face your partner,
And bow before you go.

4
Now follow me to London,
Now follow me to London,
Now follow me to London,
As we have done before.

THE KING OF FRANCE

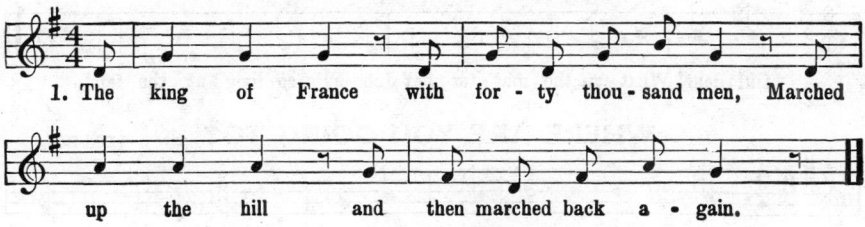

1. The king of France with for - ty thou - sand men, Marched up the hill and then marched back a - gain.

2
The King of France with forty thousand men
Gave salute, and then marched back again.

3
The King of France with forty thousand men
Beat their drums, and then marched back again.

4
The King of France with forty thousand men
Blew their horns, and then marched back again.

5
The King of France with forty thousand men
Waved their flags, and then marched back again.

6
The King of France with forty thousand men
Drew their swords, and then marched back again.

7
The King of France with forty thousand men
Shouldered arms, and then marched back again.

8
The King of France with forty thousand men
Pranced on their horses, and then marched back again.

LAVENDER'S BLUE

Old English

1. Lav-en-der's blue, dil-ly, dil-ly, Lav-en-der's green,

When I am King, dil-ly, dil-ly, You shall be Queen.

2
Call out your men, dil-ly, dil-ly,
Set them to work,
Some to the plow, dil-ly, dil-ly,
Some to the cart.

3
Some to make hay, dil-ly, dil-ly,
Some to cut corn,
While you and I, dil-ly, dil-ly,
Keep ourselves warm.

OH! DEAR! WHAT CAN THE MATTER BE?

English

Oh! dear! What can the mat-ter be? Dear! dear! what can the mat-ter be?

Oh! dear! What can the mat-ter be? John-ny's so long at the fair. He

prom-ised to buy me a bas-ket of pos-ies, A gar-land of

lil-ies, a gar-land of ros-es, He prom-ised to bring me a

bow of blue rib-bon To tie up my bon-ny brown hair. And it's

Oh! dear! What can the mat-ter be? Dear! dear! What can the mat-ter be?

Oh! dear! What can the mat-ter be? John-ny's so long at the fair!

WHERE ARE YOU GOING TO?

Old Song

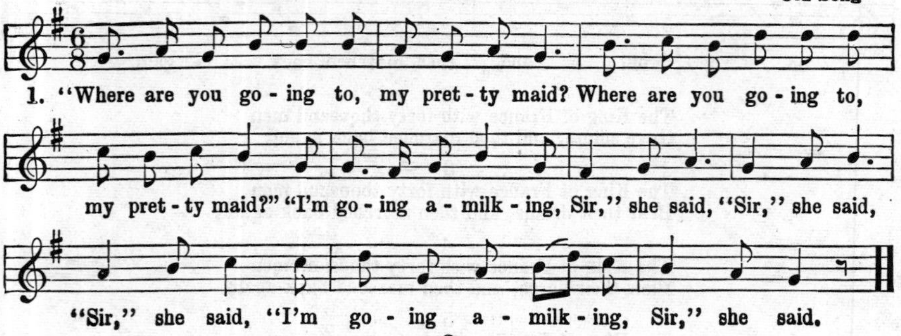

1. "Where are you go-ing to, my pret-ty maid? Where are you go-ing to,

my pret-ty maid?" "I'm go-ing a-milk-ing, Sir," she said, "Sir," she said,

"Sir," she said, "I'm go-ing a-milk-ing, Sir," she said.

2
"May I go with you, my pretty maid?
May I go with you, my pretty maid?"
"Yes, if you please, kind Sir," she said,
"Sir," she said, "Sir," she said,
"Yes, if you please, kind Sir," she said.

3
"What is your fortune, my pretty maid?" etc.
"My face is my fortune, Sir," she said, etc.

4
"Then I can't marry you, my pretty maid," etc.
"Nobody asked you, Sir," she said, etc.

Five Folk Songs
LAVENDER'S BLUE

This is an old song that is sung and loved by children of all English-speaking peoples. The tune may be played as a slow waltz, or, if played rapidly, it furnishes good music for skipping.

OH! DEAR! WHAT CAN THE MATTER BE?

When played briskly, this tune is a good dance for almost any form of hopping or skipping steps. Play it in various ways and let the children respond to it in any kind of bodily movement they wish. The dances that children improvise are far better for them than trying to follow adult directions in their movements.

WHERE ARE YOU GOING TO?

This makes excellent music for skipping, if played rapidly with two strong accents in each measure. If it is acted out, the milkmaid may skip for a while before the song begins; and after the song is finished, both the maid and the "Sir" may skip in opposite directions. Half the group may take the part of the maid, and the other half sing and act the part of the man.

A slow, walking step (two steps to each measure) is also suitable for this music if the children prefer it to skipping. Let the children make their own plans for acting the song.

OLD KING COLE

In dramatizing this song, one child may be selected for the king, to sit in a large chair, with a crown upon his head; one child to bring the pipe; another to bring the bowl; and three fiddlers who pretend to play fiddles. The rest of the children sing while the actors play the pantomime.

At the end of the song the children, actors and all, may dance to the tune played either on the piano or the fiddle. It may be played slowly for a dignified, paradelike dance; or if played rapidly, a skipping step would suit very well.

ROCK-A-BYE BABY

For generations babies have been rocked to sleep with this old song. Its swinging rhythm brings very naturally a rocking rhythm of the arms and body. Some children will wish to swing their entire bodies to and fro to this music; others will swing from the waist up; but probably most of them will wish to hold an imaginary baby in the arms and move the arms back and forth in a gentle, rocking motion. It should be played very smoothly and languidly. The children may sing and sway at the same time and continue swaying to the music after the song is finished.

Sense Games

SIGHT

Place a number of objects in front of the children, who are standing in a row or circle with their eyes closed, and cover the objects with a cloth. When all is ready, have them open their eyes and sing, lifting the cloth only during the last measure. When the cloth is on again, let each one tell what he saw.

OLD KING COLE

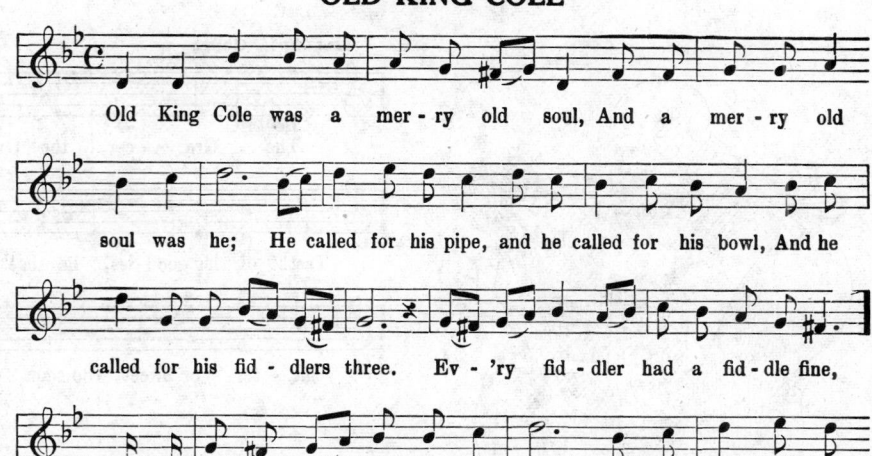

Old King Cole was a mer-ry old soul, And a mer-ry old soul was he; He called for his pipe, and he called for his bowl, And he called for his fid-dlers three. Ev-'ry fid-dler had a fid-dle fine, And a ver-y fine fid-dle had he. "Twee-dle dum, twee-dle dee," went the fid-dlers three, "Twee-dle dum dee, dum dee, did-dle dee!"

ROCK-A-BYE BABY

An Old Cradle Song

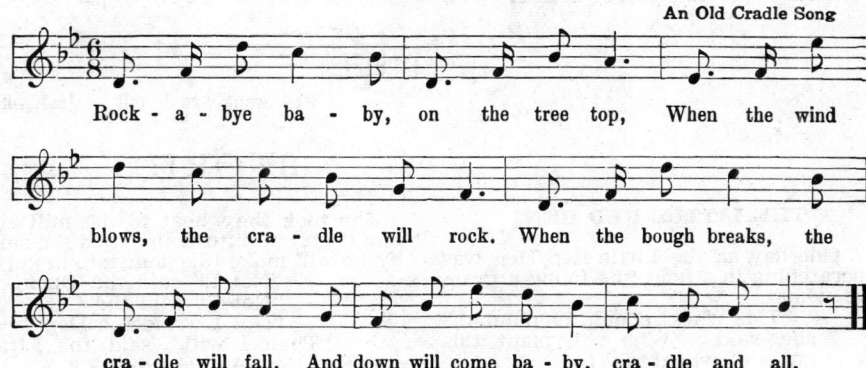

Rock-a-bye ba-by, on the tree top, When the wind blows, the cra-dle will rock. When the bough breaks, the cra-dle will fall, And down will come ba-by, cra-dle and all.

SIGHT

LILLIAN M. GOETZ

Lit-tle fai-ry, rub our eyes, And make them bright to see How man-y things you have for us While we count one, two, three.

SMELL

LILLIAN M. GOETZ   MRS. JOHN D. KAY

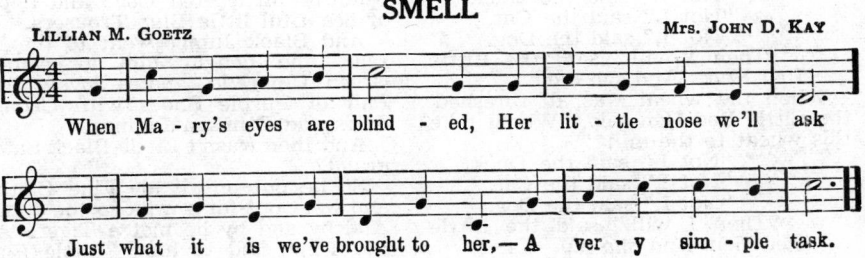

When Ma-ry's eyes are blind-ed, Her lit-tle nose we'll ask Just what it is we've brought to her,—A ver-y sim-ple task.

TASTE

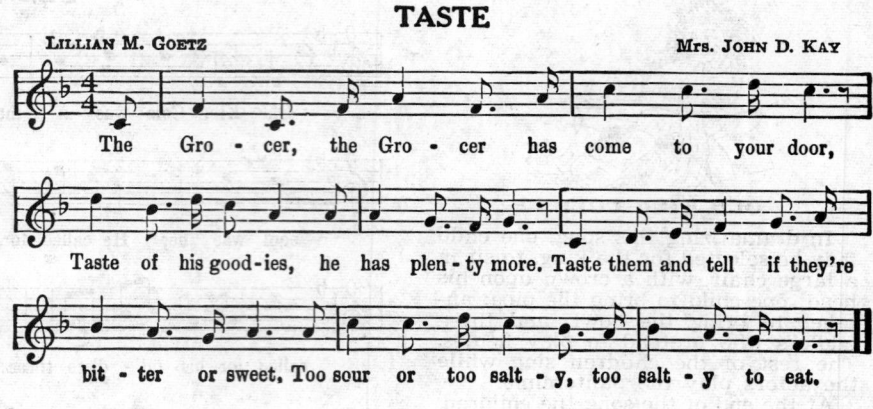

LILLIAN M. GOETZ · Mrs. JOHN D. KAY

The Gro-cer, the Gro-cer has come to your door,
Taste of his good-ies, he has plen-ty more. Taste them and tell if they're
bit-ter or sweet. Too sour or too salt-y, too salt-y to eat.

TOUCH

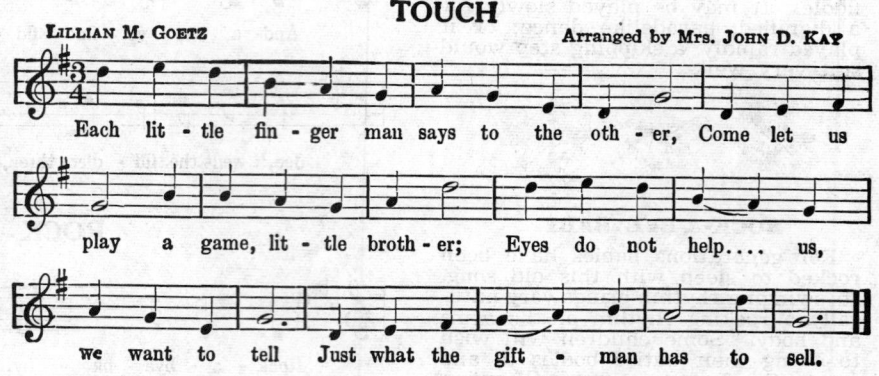

LILLIAN M. GOETZ · Arranged by Mrs. JOHN D. KAY

Each lit-tle fin-ger man says to the oth-er, Come let us
play a game, lit-tle broth-er; Eyes do not help.... us,
we want to tell Just what the gift-man has to sell.

TOUCH

The children stand with their hands behind them, while the gift-man walks up and down with his bag singing and placing some object in each pair of hands. When the children all have something, they feel of the object and tell its name or what it is like.

STORIES

THE LITTLE RED HEN

One day as the Little Red Hen was scratching in a field, she found a grain of wheat.

"This wheat should be planted," she said. "Who will plant this grain of wheat?"

"Not I," said the Duck.
"Not I," said the Cat.
"Not I," said the Dog.
"Then I will," said the Little Red Hen. And she did.

Soon the wheat grew to be tall and yellow.

"The wheat is ripe," said the Little Red Hen. "Who will cut the wheat?"

"Not I," said the Duck.
"Not I," said the Cat.
"Not I," said the Dog.
"Then I will," said the Little Red Hen. And she did.

When the wheat was cut, the Little Red Hen said, "Who will thresh this wheat?"

"Not I," said the Duck.
"Not I," said the Cat.
"Not I," said the Dog.
"Then I will," said the Little Red Hen. And she did.

When the wheat was all threshed, the Little Red Hen said, "Who'll take this wheat to the mill?"

"Not I," said the Duck.
"Not I," said the Cat.
"Not I," said the Dog.
"Then I will," said the Little Red Hen. And she did.

She took the wheat to the mill and had it ground into flour. Then she said, "Who will make this flour into bread?"

"Not I," said the Duck.
"Not I," said the Cat.
"Not I," said the Dog.
"Then I will," said the Little Red Hen. And she did.

She made and baked the bread. Then she said, "Who will eat this bread?"

"Oh! I will," said the Duck.
"And I will," said the Cat.
"And I will," said the Dog.
"No, no!" said the Little Red Hen. "I will do that." And she did.

THE STORY OF LITTLE BLACK SAMBO

Once upon a time there was a little black boy, and his name was Little Black Sambo.

And his Mother was called Black Mumbo.

And his Father was called Black Jumbo.

And Black Mumbo made him a beautiful little Red Coat and a pair of beautiful little Blue Trousers.

And Black Jumbo went to the Ba-zaar, and bought him a beautiful Green Umbrella, and a lovely little Pair of Purple Shoes with Crimson Soles and Crimson Linings.

And then wasn't Little Black Sambo grand?

So he put on all his Fine Clothes, and went out for a walk in the Jungle. And by and by he met a Tiger. And the Tiger said to him, "Little Black Sambo, I'm going to eat you up!" And Little Black Sambo said, "Oh! Please Mr. Tiger, don't eat me up, and I'll give you my beautiful little Red Coat." So the Tiger said, "Very well, I won't eat you this time, but you must give me your beautiful little Red Coat." So the Tiger got poor Little Black Sambo's beautiful little Red Coat, and went away saying, "Now I'm the grandest Tiger in the Jungle."

And Little Black Sambo went on, and by and by he met another Tiger, and it said to him, "Little Black Sambo, I'm going to eat you up!" And Little Black Sambo said, "Oh! Please Mr. Tiger, don't eat me up, and I'll give you my beautiful little Blue Trousers." So the Tiger said, "Very well, I won't eat you this time, but you must give me your beautiful little Blue Trousers." So the Tiger got poor Little Black Sambo's beautiful little Blue Trousers, and went away saying, "Now I'm the grandest Tiger in the Jungle."

And Little Black Sambo went on and by and by he met another Tiger, and it said to him, "Little Black Sambo, I'm going to eat you up!" And Little Black Sambo said, "Oh! Please Mr. Tiger, don't eat me up, and I'll give you my beautiful little Purple Shoes with Crimson Soles and Crimson Linings."

But the Tiger said, "What use would your shoes be to me? I've got four feet, and you've got only two; you haven't got enough shoes for me."

ELLEN GILBERT

LITTLE BLACK SAMBO

But Little Black Sambo said, "You could wear them on your ears."

"So I could," said the Tiger: "that's a very good idea. Give them to me, and I won't eat you this time."

So the Tiger got poor Little Black Sambo's beautiful little Purple Shoes with Crimson Soles and Crimson Linings, and went away saying, "Now *I'm* the grandest Tiger in the Jungle."

And by and by Little Black Sambo met another Tiger, and it said to him, "Little Black Sambo, I'm going to eat you up!" And Little Black Sambo said, "Oh! Please Mr. Tiger, don't eat me up, and I'll give you my beautiful Green Umbrella." But the Tiger said, "How can I carry an umbrella, when I need all my paws for walking with?"

"You could tie a knot on your tail and carry it that way," said Little Black Sambo. "So I could," said the Tiger. "Give it to me, and I won't eat you this time." So he got poor Little Black Sambo's beautiful Green Umbrella, and went away saying, "Now *I'm* the grandest Tiger in the Jungle."

And poor Little Black Sambo went away crying, because the cruel Tigers had taken all his fine clothes.

Presently he heard a horrible noise that sounded like "Gr-r-r-r-rrrrrr," and it got louder and louder. "Oh! dear!" said Little Black Sambo, "there are all the Tigers coming back to eat me up! What shall I do?" So he ran quickly to a palm-tree, and peeped round it to see what the matter was.

And there he saw all the Tigers fighting, and disputing which of them was the grandest. And at last they all got so angry that they jumped up and took off all the fine clothes, and began to tear each other with their claws, and bite each other with their great big white teeth.

And they came, rolling and tumbling right to the foot of the very tree where Little Black Sambo was hiding, but he jumped quickly in behind the umbrella. And the Tigers all caught hold of each other's tails, as they wrangled and scrambled, and so

they found themselves in a ring round the tree.

Then when the Tigers were very wee and very far away, Little Black Sambo jumped up, and called out, "Oh! Tigers! why have you taken off all your nice clothes? Don't you want them any more?" But the Tigers only answered, "Gr-r-rrrrr!"

Then Little Black Sambo said, "If you want them, say so, or I'll take them away." But the Tigers would not let go of each other's tails, and so they couldn't say anything but "Gr-r-rrrrr!"

So Little Black Sambo put on all his fine clothes again and walked off.

And the Tigers were very, very angry, but still they would not let go of each other's tails. And they were so angry, that they ran round the tree, trying to eat each other up, and they ran faster and faster, till they were whirling round so fast that you couldn't see their legs at all.

And they still ran faster and faster and faster, till they all just melted away, and there was nothing left but a great pool of melted butter (or *ghi,* as it is called in India) round the foot of the tree.

Now Black Jumbo was just coming home from his work, with a great big brass pot in his arms, and when he saw what was left of all the Tigers he said, "Oh! what lovely melted butter! I'll take that home to Black Mumbo for her to cook with."

So he put it all into the great big brass pot, and took it home to Black Mumbo to cook with.

When Black Mumbo saw the melted butter, wasn't she pleased! "Now," said she, "we'll all have pancakes for supper!"

So she got flour and eggs and milk and sugar and butter, and she made a huge big plate of most lovely pancakes. And she fried them in the melted butter which the Tigers had made, and they were just as yellow and brown as little Tigers.

And then they all sat down to supper. And Black Mumbo ate Twenty-seven pancakes, and Black Jumbo ate Fifty-five, but Little Black Sambo ate a Hundred and Sixty-nine, because he was so hungry.

—*Helen Bannerman*[1]

THE LITTLE PINE TREE

In the woods there grew a little pine tree, and its leaves were long, slender, green needles. It was very little, indeed, and although there were many other trees around it, it felt quite alone as there were no other pine trees near by.

The little pine tree was proud of its fine, green needles when the other trees in the forest were bare, and the snow was white on the ground. But in summer time, when the other trees had beautiful, large, green leaves, the pine tree thought that it would be nice if it could have large leaves also.

"I wish that I could have beautiful large leaves, but leaves which are more beautiful than those of any of

[1]*The Story of Little Black Sambo,* by Helen Bannerman, is included by arrangement with Frederick A. Stokes Company, publishers of the authorized American edition.

ELLEN GILBERT

TIGER who took Sambo's clothes.

the other trees," it thought. "If I could have my wish, I would have leaves of shining gold."

The little pine tree slept through the night, and in the morning when it awoke it had leaves of shining gold.

"How very beautiful I am," it thought. "How my leaves glisten in the sun! Now I shall always be happy."

In the afternoon a man came through the woods along a path which passed by the little pine tree. When he came to the little tree and saw the beautiful golden leaves, he stopped and picked them all and put them into the bag which he was carrying and took them home with him. Then the poor little tree had no leaves.

"What shall I do?" it cried. "I will not wish for gold leaves again. If I could have another wish, I would have leaves of glass. They would sparkle in the sun, and no one would take them away."

Again the little pine tree slept through the night, and when it awoke the next morning it had leaves of sparkling glass.

"How beautiful I am now," it thought, "my leaves are of clear crystal and they tinkle as the wind passes through them."

All through the morning, the little tree was very happy. But, in the afternoon, black clouds hid the sun, and the rain came down, and the wind turned cold and harsh. The little tree shivered. It shook and shook, and when the storm was over, all of the glass leaves had been broken and had fallen to the ground. Again the poor little tree had no leaves.

"What can I do now?" it cried. "A man took my leaves of gold, and the storm broke my leaves of glass. If I could have still another wish, I would have large green leaves like the other trees in the forest."

Once more the little pine tree slept through the night and when it awoke the next morning it had beautiful, large, green leaves.

"Now I am like the other trees and as beautiful as they are," it thought.

The little tree was happy once more. But soon a goat came along the path looking for something to eat. The little tree was so small that the goat could easily reach the leaves, and they looked so good and juicy that he nibbled at each of the branches and ate up all the leaves.

"Alas!" cried the little tree, "a man took my leaves of gold; the storm broke my leaves of glass; a goat ate my large green leaves! If I could have just one more wish, I would have my long green needles again."

Toward evening, the little tree fell asleep and again slept through the night. And when it awoke in the morning it had its long slender green needles again. The birds flew to the little pine tree, and they were as happy as it was that it was covered again with long green pine needles.

"Gold leaves, glass leaves, and large, green leaves are very fine;" thought the little tree, "but there is nothing so good for a little pine tree as its own long needles."
—*An Old German Legend.*

THE THREE LITTLE PIGS

Once upon a time there was an old sow who had three little pigs, and as she had not enough for them to eat, she had to send them out to seek their fortunes.

The first little pig had not gone very far when he met a man with a bundle of straw, and he said to the man:

"Please, man, give me that straw to build me a house."

The man gave the straw to the little pig, and the little pig built a house of straw, and lived in it.

By and by an old wolf came along and knocked at the door of the little straw house, and called:

"Little pig, little pig, let me come in!"

"No, no, by the hair of my chinny chin chin, I'll not let you in," answered the little pig.

"Then I'll huff and I'll puff and I'll blow your house in," said the wolf.

So he huffed and he puffed, and he blew the house in, and he ate up the little pig.

The second little pig had not gone very far when he met a man with a bundle of sticks, and he said to the man:

"Please, man, give me those sticks to build me a house."

The man gave the sticks to the little pig, and the little pig built a house of sticks, and lived in it.

By and by the old wolf came along, and knocked at the door of the little house of sticks, and called:

"Little pig, little pig, let me come in!"

"No, no, by the hair of my chinny chin chin, I'll not let you in," answered the little pig.

"Then I'll huff and I'll puff and I'll blow your house in," said the wolf.

So he huffed and he puffed, and he blew the house in, and ate up the second little pig.

The third little pig had not gone

CAMERON WRIGHT

very far when he met a man with a load of bricks.

"Please, man, give those bricks to build me a house."

The man gave the bricks to the little pig, and the little pig built a house of bricks, and lived in it.

By and by the old wolf came along and knocked at the door of the little brick house, and called:

"Little pig, little pig, let me come in!"

"No, no, by the hair of my chinny chin chin, I'll not let you in," answered the little pig.

"Then I'll huff and I'll puff and I'll blow your house in," said the wolf.

So he huffed and he puffed, and he puffed and he huffed, but he could not blow the little brick house in.

When the old wolf found that with all his huffing and puffing he could not blow the brick house down, he called:

"Little pig, I know where there is a nice field of turnips."

"Where?" asked the little pig.

"In Farmer Smith's field," said the wolf. "If you will be ready tomorrow morning at six o'clock, I will call for you and we will go together and get some turnips for dinner."

"Very well," said the little pig, "I will be ready."

Now the little pig got up at five

o'clock, and went to Farmer Smith's field for the turnips and was back before six.

When the wolf came, he called, "Little pig, little pig, are you ready?"

"Ready!" said the little pig, "I have been and come back again, and I have a nice potful of turnips for dinner."

The old wolf was very angry at this, but he said, "Little pig, I know where there is a nice apple tree."

"Where?" asked the little pig.

"Down in Merry Garden," answered the wolf. "If you will be ready at five o'clock tomorrow morning, I will call for you at your house and we will go together and get some apples."

"Very well," said the little pig, "I'll surely be ready."

The next morning the little pig got up at four o'clock and hustled off for the apples, hoping to get back before the wolf came, but he had a long way to go and when he was coming back whom should he see in the road just ahead of him but the old wolf.

"Little pig, did you get there first?" called the wolf. "Are the apples nice?"

"Yes," said the little pig, "I will throw you one." And he threw it so far from the road that while the wolf was running to get it, the little pig passed him and reached home safely.

The old wolf was furiously angry, but he went away.

The next day he came again and said to the little pig, "Little pig, will you go with me to the Fair at Shanklin this afternoon?"

"Yes," said the little pig, "what time will you be ready?"

"At three o'clock," said the wolf.

Well, the little pig went off to Shanklin before noon, and bought a butter churn which he needed very much. He was almost home again when he saw the old wolf coming. The little pig was frightened and did not know what to do. He got into the big butter churn to hide and as he pulled the lid over him, the churn fell over and began rolling, rolling down hill and went rolling, rolling, with the little pig inside. The rolling churn frightened the wolf so much that he ran home without going to the Fair. When the churn stopped rolling, the little pig peeped out and saw that he was near his house and the wolf was gone, so he got out, picked up the churn and again got home safely.

A little later, the old wolf came to the house again, and called through the door, telling the little pig how sorry he was that he could not keep his promise to go to the Fair, and told how he had seen a frightful wooden thing rolling down the hill making a terrible noise.

"Hah!" said the little pig, "I frightened you then! I had been to the Fair and bought a butter churn, and when I saw you I got into it and rolled down the hill."

Then the wolf was terrifically angry, angrier than ever before, and he called out that he would eat up the little pig and that he would come down the chimney to get him.

As soon as the little pig heard him say this, he made a blazing fire in the fireplace; and when the wolf began to climb up to the chimney, he put a big potful of water over the fire to boil. And just as the wolf climbed into the chimney, the little pig took the lid off the pot and the wolf fell into the scalding water. Then the little pig quickly put the lid on again, and that was the end of the old wolf, for the little pig had him for supper, and lived happily ever afterwards.

THE GINGERBREAD BOY

A little old woman and a little old man once lived all alone in a little old house in the country. One morning the little old woman decided to make a gingerbread boy.

When the little old woman opened the oven to see whether the gingerbread boy was done, out jumped the little gingerbread boy, looking all brown and good to eat. He saw that the door of the house was open, and he ran away as fast as his legs would carry him.

The little old woman and the little old man ran after him as fast as they could.

The little gingerbread boy laughed, and called to them:

"I am a gingerbread boy, I am.
I can run away from you, I can."

And the little old woman and the little old man could not catch him.

The little gingerbread boy ran on and on, until he came to a cow by the roadside.

"Stop, little gingerbread boy," said the cow; "you look good to eat."

The little gingerbread boy laughed and called to the cow:

"I am a gingerbread boy, I am.
I've run away from a little old woman and a little old man.
I can run away from you, I can."

And the cow ran after the gingerbread boy, but couldn't catch him.

The little gingerbread boy ran on, and on, until he came to a horse in a pasture.

"Please stop, little gingerbread boy," said the horse, "you look very good to eat." But the little gingerbread boy laughed out loud, and called to the horse:

"I am a gingerbread boy, I am.
I've run away from a little old woman and a little old man, and a cow.
I can run away from you, I can."

And the horse ran after the gingerbread boy, but couldn't catch him.

By and by, the little gingerbread boy came to a barn full of threshers.

"Don't run so fast, little gingerbread boy," cried the threshers, "you look very good to eat." But the little gingerbread boy laughed louder than ever, and as he ran he called to the threshers:

"I am a gingerbread boy, I am.
I've run away from a little old woman and a little old man, and a cow, and a horse.
I can run away from you, I can."

And the threshers ran after the gingerbread boy, but couldn't catch him.

Then the little gingerbread boy hurried on until he came to a field full of mowers.

"Wait a bit! wait a bit, little gingerbread boy," called the mowers, "you look very good to eat." But the little gingerbread boy ran faster than ever and called to the mowers:

"I am a gingerbread boy, I am.
I've run away from a little old woman and a little old man, and a cow, and a horse, and a barn full of threshers.
I can run away from you, I can."

And the mowers ran after the gingerbread boy, but couldn't catch him.

Soon the little gingerbread boy saw a fox lying quietly near a fence.

"Where are you going?" asked the fox, without getting up. But the little gingerbread boy didn't answer him. He ran on, and called:

"I am a gingerbread boy, I am.
I've run away from a little old woman and a little old man, and a cow, and a horse, and a barn full of threshers, and a field full of mowers.

I can run away from you, I can."

"I would not catch you if I could," said the fox. But the fox ran after him.

On and on ran the little gingerbread boy until he came to a river, and the fox was close behind. The gingerbread boy could not swim. "Jump on my tail, and I'll take you across," said the sly old fox.

So the little gingerbread boy jumped on the fox's tail, and the fox began swimming across the river. But the fox had gone only a few strokes when he turned his head and said: "You are heavy on my tail, and you may fall off. Jump on my back."

So the little gingerbread boy jumped on the fox's back. After swimming a little farther, the fox said: "I'm afraid you will get wet on my back. Jump on my shoulder."

So the little gingerbread boy jumped on the fox's shoulder. When they were near the other side of the river, the fox said: "My shoulder is tired. Jump on my nose."

So the little gingerbread boy jumped on the fox's nose. But just then they reached the other bank. The sly old fox opened his mouth wide, and in went the little gingerbread boy!

"Dear me!" said the gingerbread boy, "I am one-quarter gone." And then he said: "Now, I'm half gone!" And then, "I'm three-quarters gone!" And then he said: "Oh, dear; I'm all gone!"

And the little gingerbread boy was all gone.

THE THREE BEARS

In a far-off country there was once a little girl who was called Goldilocks, because her hair was curly and shone like gold. She liked to roam in the open, and one day she started off into the woods to gather wild flowers and into the fields to chase butterflies. She wandered on and on taking little heed of the way until she found herself in a lonely spot, where she saw a snug little house. It was the house in which three bears lived, but they were not at home.

First, Goldilocks looked in at the window and then she peeped in at the keyhole, and seeing nobody inside, she lifted the latch. The door was not fastened, so little Goldilocks got in easily and looked about, wondering what sort of people lived there.

Now the three bears had gone out for a walk in the woods a little before this, leaving their breakfast porridge cooling. They were the great big father bear, and the middle-sized mother bear, and the little wee bear.

Goldilocks went into the kitchen, and on the table she saw three bowls of porridge, and she was well pleased. First she tasted the porridge in the great big bowl, which belonged to the Great Big Bear, and found it too hot for her. Then she tasted the porridge in the middle-sized bowl, which belonged to the Middle-sized Bear, and found it too cold. And then she tasted the porridge in the little wee bowl, which belonged to the Little Wee Bear, and it was just right, and she ate it all up.

Goldilocks went into the parlor, and there were three chairs. First, she sat down in the great big chair, which belonged to the Great Big Bear, and found it too hard for her. Then, she sat down in the middle-sized chair, which belonged to the Middle-sized Bear, and found it too soft. And then, she sat down in the little wee chair, which belonged to the Little Wee Bear, and it was just right, but she sat down in it with such force that she broke it and down she fell—plump—upon the floor.

By this time, Goldilocks was tired, and she went upstairs into the bed-chamber in which the Three Bears slept. First, she lay down upon the great big bed, which belonged to the Great Big Bear, and found it too high for her. Then she lay down upon the middle-sized bed, which belonged to the Middle-sized Bear, and found it too broad. And then she lay down upon the little wee bed, which belonged to the Little Wee Bear, and it was just right, so she covered herself up comfortably and fell fast asleep.

By this time, the Three Bears thought their porridge would be cool enough; so they came home to breakfast.

When the Great Big Bear went to his porridge, he said in his great big voice:

"SOMEBODY HAS BEEN TASTING MY PORRIDGE!"

Then the Middle-sized Bear looked at her bowl, and said in her middle-sized voice:

"SOMEBODY HAS BEEN TASTING MY PORRIDGE!"

Then the Little Wee Bear looked at his bowl, which was quite empty, and he said, in his little wee voice:

"Somebody has been tasting my porridge and has eaten it all up!"

Then the Three Bears, knowing that someone had been in their house, began to look about. They went into the parlor, and the Great Big Bear

seeing that his hard cushion was not straight, said in his great big voice:

"SOMEBODY HAS BEEN SITTING IN MY CHAIR!"

And the Middle-sized Bear seeing that her soft cushion had been flattened out, said in her middle-sized voice:

"SOMEBODY HAS BEEN SITTING IN MY CHAIR!"

The Little Wee Bear went over to his chair and cried out in his little wee voice:

"Somebody has been sitting in my chair, and has broken it all to pieces!"

Then the Three Bears went upstairs to their bed-chamber. And the Great Big Bear seeing that his pillow was all rumpled, said in his great big voice:

"SOMEBODY HAS BEEN LYING IN MY BED!"

And the Middle-sized Bear, seeing that the covers of her bed were out of place, said in her middle-sized voice:

"SOMEBODY HAS BEEN LYING IN MY BED!"

Then the Little Wee Bear went to his bed, and cried out in his little wee voice:

"Somebody has been lying in my bed, and here she is!"

At that moment, Goldilocks woke up. When she saw the Three Bears standing there looking at her, she jumped out of the bed and ran to the window; and seeing that it opened right onto the ground, she quickly climbed out, and ran away as fast as her legs could carry her. And the Three Bears never saw anything more of her.

THE UGLY DUCKLING

It was so glorious out in the country; it was summer; the cornfields were yellow, the oats were green, the hay had been put up in stacks in the green meadows, and the stork

went about on his long, red legs, and chattered Egyptian, for this was the language he had learned from his good mother. All around the fields and meadows were great forests, and in the midst of these forests lay deep lakes. Yes, it was really lovely out in the country.

In the midst of the sunshine, there lay an old farm, with deep canals about it, and from the wall down to the water great burdocks, so high that little children could stand upright under the loftiest of them. It was just as wild there as in the deepest wood, and there sat a Duck upon her nest; she had to hatch her ducklings; but she was almost tired out before the little ones came; and then she so seldom had visitors. The other ducks liked better to swim about in the canals than to run up to sit down under a burdock, and cackle with her.

At last one egg-shell after another burst open. "Piep! Piep!" it cried, and in all the eggs there were little creatures that stuck out their heads.

"Quack! quack!" they said; and they all came quacking out as fast as they could, looking all round them under the green leaves; and the mother let them look as much as they chose, for green is good for the eyes.

"How wide the world is!" said all the young ones, for they certainly had much more room now than when they were in the eggs.

"Do you think this is all the world?" asked the mother. "That stretches far across the other side of the garden, quite into the parson's field; but I have never been there. I hope you are all together," and she stood up. "No, I have not all. The largest egg still lies there. How long is that to last? I am really tired of it." And she sat down again.

"Well, how goes it?" asked an old Duck who had come to pay her a visit.

"It takes a long time with that one egg," said the Duck who sat there. "It will not burst. Now, only look at the others; are they not the prettiest little ducks one could possibly see? They are all like their father; the rogue, he never comes to see me."

"Let me see the egg which will not burst," said the old visitor. "You may be sure it is a turkey's egg. I was once cheated in that way, and had much anxiety and trouble with the young ones, for they are afraid of the water. Must I say it to you? I could not get them to venture in. I quacked and I clacked, but it was no use. Let me see the egg. Yes, that's a turkey's egg. Let it lie there, and teach the other children to swim."

"I think I will sit on it a little longer," said the Duck. "I've sat so long now that I can sit a few days more."

"Just as you please," said the old Duck; and she went away.

At last the great egg burst. "Piep! piep!" said the little one, and crept forth. It was very large and very ugly. The Duck looked at it.

"It's a very large duckling," said she; "none of the others look like that. Can it really be a turkey chick? Well, we shall soon find out. It must go into the water, even if I have to thrust it in myself."

The next day, it was bright, beautiful weather; the sun shone on all the green trees. The Mother Duck went down to the canal with all her family. Splash! she jumped into the water. "Quack! Quack!" she said, and one duckling after another plunged in. The water closed over their heads, but they came up in an instant, and swam beautifully, and they were all in the water, for the ugly gray Duckling swam with them.

"No, it's not a turkey," said the Mother Duck; "look how well it can use its legs, and how straight it holds itself. It is my own child! On the whole it's quite pretty, if one looks at it rightly. Quack! quack! come with me, and I'll lead you out into the great world and present you in the duck yard; but keep close to me, so that no one may tread on you, and take care to keep away from the cats!"

And so they came into the duck yard. A terrible riot was going on there, for two families were quarreling about an eel's head, and the cat got it after all.

"See, that's how it goes in the world!" said the Mother Duck; and she whetted her beak, for she, too, wanted the eel's head. "Only use your legs," she said. "See that you bustle about, and bow your heads before the old Duck yonder. She's the grandest of all here; she's of Spanish blood—that's why she's so fat. And do you see that she has a red rag round her leg? That's something particularly fine, and the greatest distinction a duck can enjoy: it signifies that people do not want to lose her, and that she's to be known by animals and by men too. Shake yourselves—don't turn in your toes; a well-brought-up duck turns its toes quite out, just like father and mother —so! Now bend your necks and say 'Quack!'"

And they did so; but the other ducks round about looked at them, and said quite boldly:

"Look there! Now we're to have these hanging on, as if there were not enough of us already! And fie! How that Duckling yonder looks; we won't stand that!" And one duck flew up at it, and bit it in the neck.

"Let it alone," said the mother; "it does no harm to anyone."

"Yes, but it's too large and peculiar," said the Duck who had bitten it; "and, therefore, it must be shown its proper place."

"Those are pretty children that the mother has there," said the old Duck with the rag round her leg. "They're all pretty but that one; that was rather unlucky. I wish she could make it over again."

"That cannot be done, my lady," replied the Mother Duck. "It is not pretty, but it has a really good disposition, and swims as well as any other; yes, I may even say it swims better. I think it will grow up to be pretty, and become smaller in time; it has lain too long in the egg, and therefore is not properly shaped." And then she pinched it in the neck, and smoothed its feathers. "More-

over, it is a drake," she said, "and, therefore, it is not of so much consequence. I think he will be very strong; he makes his way already."

"The other ducklings are graceful enough," said the old Duck. "Make yourself at home; and if you find an eel's head, you may bring it to me."

And now they were at home. But the poor Duckling which had been the last to creep out of the shell and looked so ugly, was bitten and pushed and jeered, as much by the ducks as by the chickens.

"It is too big!" they all said. And the turkey cock, who had been born with spurs, and therefore thought himself an emperor, blew himself up like a ship in full sail, and bore straight down upon it; then, he gobbled and grew quite red in the face. The poor Duckling did not know where it should stand or walk; it was quite melancholy because it looked ugly and because the whole yard made fun of it.

So it went on the first day, and afterwards it became worse and worse. The poor Duckling was chased by every one; even its brothers and sisters were quite angry with it, and said, "If the cat would only catch you, you ugly creature!" And the mother said, "If you were only far away!" And the ducks bit it, and the chickens beat it, and the girl who had to feed the poultry kicked at it with her foot.

Then it ran and flew over the fence, and the little birds in the bushes flew away in fear.

"That is because I am so ugly!" thought the Duckling; and it shut its eyes, but flew on further; and so it came out into the great moor, where the wild ducks lived. Here it lay the whole night long; and it was tired and sad.

Toward morning, the wild ducks flew up and looked at their new companion.

"What are you?" they asked; and the Ugly Duckling turned in every direction, and bowed as well as it could. "You are remarkably ugly!" said the Wild Ducks. "But that is nothing to us, so long as you do not marry into our family."

Poor thing! it certainly did not think of marrying, and only hoped to obtain leave to lie among the reeds and drink some of the swamp water. Thus it lay two whole days; then there came two wild geese, or, properly speaking, two wild ganders. It was not long since each had crept out of a shell, and that's why they were so saucy.

"Listen, comrade," said one of them. "You're so ugly that I like you. Will you go with us, and become a bird of passage? Near here, in another moor, there are a few sweet, lovely wild geese, all unmarried, and all able to say 'Quack!' You've a chance of making your fortune, ugly as you are."

"Piff! paff!" resounded through the air; and the two ganders fell dead in the swamp. "Piff! paff!" it sounded again, and the whole flock of wild geese rose up from the reeds. And then there was another report. A great hunt was going on. The sportsmen were lying in wait all round the

moor, and some were even sitting up in the branches of the trees, which spread far over the reeds. The blue smoke rose up like clouds among the dark trees, and was wafted far away across the water; and the hunting dogs came—splash! splash!—into the swamp, and the rushes and the reeds bent down on every side. That was a fright for the poor Duckling! It turned its head, and put it under its wing; but at that moment a frightful, great dog stood close by the Duckling, and thrust out his nose close against the Duckling, showed his sharp teeth, and then—splash! splash!—on he went without seizing it.

"O, Heaven be thanked!" sighed the Duckling. "I am so ugly, that even the dog does not want to bite me!"

And so it lay quite quiet, while the shots rattled through the reeds and gun after gun was fired At last, late in the day, all was still; but the poor Duckling did not dare to rise; it waited several hours before it looked round, and then hastened away out of the moor as fast as it could. It ran on over field and meadow; such a storm was raging that it was difficult to get from one place to another.

Toward evening, the Ugly Duckling came to a miserable little peasant's hut, so dilapidated that it did not itself know on which side it should fall; and that's why it remained standing. The storm whistled round the Duckling in such a way that the poor creature was obliged to sit down to keep from falling; and the wind blew worse and worse. Then the Ugly Duckling noticed that one of the hinges of the door had given way, and the door hung so slantingly that the Duckling could slip through the crack into the room; and that is what it did.

Here lived a woman, with her Cat and her Hen. And the Cat, which she called Sonnie, could arch his back and purr; he could even give out sparks; but for that, one had to stroke his fur the wrong way. The Hen had quite little, short legs, and, therefore, she was called Chickabiddy Shortshanks; she laid good eggs, and the woman loved her as her own child.

In the morning, the strange Duckling was at once noticed, and the Cat began to purr and the Hen to cluck.

"What's this?" asked the woman, and looked all round; but she could not see well, and, therefore, she thought the Ugly Duckling was a fat duck that had strayed. "This is a rare prize!" she said. "Now I shall have duck's eggs. I hope it is not a drake. We must wait to see."

And so the Ugly Duckling was admitted on trial for three weeks; but no eggs came. And the Cat was master of the house and the Hen was the lady, and always said, "We and the world!" for she thought they were half the world, and by far the better half. The Ugly Duckling thought one might have a different opinion, but the Hen would not allow it.

"Can you lay eggs?" she asked.
"No."

CAMERON WRIGHT

"Then will you hold your tongue!"

And the Cat said, "Can you curve your back, and purr, and give out sparks?"

"No."

"Then you will please have no opinion of your own when sensible folks are speaking."

And the Ugly Duckling sat in a corner and was sad, then the fresh air and the sunshine streamed in; and it was seized with such a strange longing to swim on the water that it could not help telling the Hen of it.

"What are you thinking of?" cried the Hen. "You have nothing to do, that's why you have these strange fancies. Lay eggs, or purr, and they will go away."

"But it is so charming to swim on the water!" said the Ugly Duckling, "so refreshing to let it close above one's head, and to dive to the bottom."

"Yes, that must be a mighty pleasure, truly," said the Hen. "I fancy you must be crazy. Ask the Cat about it; he's the cleverest animal I know; ask him if he likes to swim on the water, or to dive. I won't speak about myself. Ask our mistress, the old woman; no one in the world is cleverer than she. Do you think she has any desire to swim, and to let the water close above her head?"

"You don't understand me," said the Ugly Duckling.

"We don't understand you? Then pray who is to understand you? You surely don't pretend to be cleverer than the Cat and the woman. I won't say anything of myself. Don't be conceited, child, and thank your Maker for all the kindness you have received. Did you not get into a warm room, and have you not fallen into company from which you may learn something? But you are a chatterer, and it is not pleasant to associate with you. You may believe me, I speak for your own good. I tell you disagreeable things; and, by that, one may always know one's true friends! Only take care that you learn to lay eggs, or to purr and give out sparks!"

"I think I will go out into the wide world," said the Ugly Duckling.

"Yes, do go," replied the Hen.

And so the Ugly Duckling went away. It swam on the water, and dived, but it was slighted by every one because of its ugliness.

Now came the autumn. The leaves in the forest turned yellow and brown; the wind caught them so that they danced about and up in the air; it was very cold. The clouds hung low, heavy with hail and snowflakes, and on the fence stood the raven, crying, "Croak! croak!" for mere cold; yes, it was enough to make one feel cold to think of this. The poor little Duckling certainly did not have a good time. One evening, the sun was just setting in his beauty when a whole flock of great, handsome birds came out of the bushes; they were dazzlingly white, with long, flexible necks; they were swans. They uttered a very peculiar cry, spread forth their glorious great wings, and flew away from that cold region to warmer lands, to fair open lakes. They mounted so high, so high! and the Ugly Duckling felt quite strangely as it watched them. It turned round and round in the water like a wheel, stretched out its neck toward them, and uttered such a strange, loud cry that it frightened itself. O! it could not forget those beautiful, happy birds; and as soon as it could see them no longer, it dived to the very bottom, and when it came up again, was quite beside itself. It knew not the name of those birds, and knew not whither they were flying; but it loved them more than it had ever loved anyone. It was not at all envious of them. How could it think of wishing to possess such loveliness as they had? It would have been glad if only the ducks would have endured its company. The poor, ugly creature!

And the winter grew cold, very cold! The Ugly Duckling was forced to swim about in the water, to prevent the surface from freezing entirely; but every night the hole in which it swam about became smaller and smaller. It froze so hard that the ice cracked, and the Ugly Duckling was obliged to use its legs continually to prevent the hole from freezing up. At last it became exhausted, and lay quite still, and thus froze fast into the ice.

Early in the morning a peasant came by, and when he saw what had happened, he took his wooden shoe, broke the ice crust to pieces, and carried the Duckling home to his wife. Then, it came to itself again. The children wanted to play with it; but the Duckling thought they wanted to hurt it, and in its terror fluttered up into the milk pan, so that the milk spurted down into the room. The woman clasped her hands, at which the Ugly Duckling flew down into the butter tub, and then into the meal barrel and out again. How it looked then! The woman screamed, and struck at it with the fire tongs; the children tumbled over one another in their efforts to catch the Ugly Duckling; and they laughed and they screamed! It was well that the door stood open, and the poor creature was able to slip out between the shrubs into the newly fallen snow, and there it lay quite exhausted.

But it would be too sad if I were to tell all the misery and care which the

Ugly Duckling had to endure in the hard winter. When the sun began to shine again and the larks to sing, it lay out on the moor among the reeds. It was a beautiful spring. The Ugly Duckling forgot its troubles for a time. It tried to sing, but could make only a harsh croaking sound. It swam, dived and ruffled its feathers in the warm sunshine.

Then, all at once, the Duckling could flap its wings; they beat the air more strongly than before, and bore it strongly away; and before it well knew how all this happened, it found itself in a great garden, where the elder trees smelt sweet, and bent their long green branches down to the canal that wound through the region. O! here it was so beautiful, such a gladness of spring! and from the thicket came three glorious white swans; they rustled their wings, and swam lightly on the water. The Ugly Duckling recognized the splendid creatures, and felt a strange sadness.

"I will fly away to them, to the royal birds! and they will beat me, because I, that am so ugly, dare to come near them. But it is all the same. Better to be killed by *them* than to be pursued by ducks, and beaten by fowls, and pushed about by the girl who takes care of the poultry yard, and to suffer hunger in winter!" And it flew out into the water, and swam toward the beautiful swans. These looked at it, and came sailing down upon it with outspread wings. "Kill me!" said the poor creature, and bent its head down upon the water, expecting nothing but death. But what was this that it saw in the clear water? It beheld its own image; and, lo! it was no longer a clumsy, dark-grey bird, ugly and hateful to look at, but a—swan!

It matters not if one is born in a duck yard, if one has only lain in a swan's egg.

It felt quite glad at the thought of all the want and misfortune it had suffered, now that it realized its happiness in all the splendor that surrounded it. And the great swans swam around it, and stroked it with their beaks.

Into the garden came little children, who threw bread and corn into the water; and the youngest cried, "There is a new one!" and the other children shouted joyously, "Yes, a new one has arrived!" And they clapped their hands and danced about, and ran to their father and mother; and bread and cake were thrown into the water; and they all said, "The new one is the most beautiful of all! so young and handsome!" and the old swans bowed their heads before him.

Then he felt quite ashamed, and hid his head under his wings, for he did not know what to do; he was so happy, and yet not at all proud. He thought how he had been persecuted and despised; and now he heard them saying that he was the most beautiful of all birds. Even the elder tree bent its branches straight down into the water before him, and the sun shown warm and mild. Then, his wings rustled, he lifted his slender neck, and cried rejoicingly from the depths of his heart: "I never dreamed of so much happiness when I was the Ugly Duckling!" —*Hans Christian Andersen.*

HANSEL AND GRETEL

Near a great forest there lived a poor woodcutter and his wife, and his two children; the boy's name was Hansel and the girl's, Gretel. They had very little to eat, and once, when there was a great famine in the land, the woodcutter could hardly earn the daily bread. As he lay in bed one night thinking of this, and turning and tossing, he sighed heavily, and said to his wife:

"What will become of us? we cannot even feed our children; there is nothing left for ourselves."

"I will tell you what, husband," answered the wife; "we will take the children early in the morning into the thickest part of the forest; we will make them a fire, and we will give each of them a piece of bread, then we will go to our work and leave them alone; they will never find the way home again, and we shall be rid of them."

"No, wife," said the man, "I cannot do that; I cannot find it in my heart to take my children into the forest and to leave them there alone; the wild animals would soon come and devour them."

"O you fool," said she, "then we will all four starve"; and she gave him no peace until he consented.

"But I pity the poor children," said the man.

Hansel and Gretel had not been able to sleep for hunger, and had heard what their stepmother had said to their father. Gretel wept bitterly, and said to Hansel,

"It is all over with us."

"Do be quiet, Gretel," said Hansel, "and do not fret; I will find some way to help us." And when the parents had gone to sleep, he got up, put on his little coat, opened the back door, and slipped out. The moon was shining brightly, and the white pebbles that lay in front of the house glistened like pieces of silver. Hansel stooped and filled the little pocket of his coat as full as it would hold. Then he went back again, and said to Gretel,

"Be at ease, dear little sister, and go to sleep quietly; God will not forsake us," and he laid himself down again in his bed.

When the day was breaking, and before the sun had risen, the wife came and awakened the two children, saying:

"Get up, you lazybones; we are going into the forest to cut wood."

Then she gave each of them a piece of bread, and said:

"That is for dinner, and you must not eat it before then, for you get no more."

Gretel carried the bread under her apron, for Hansel had his pockets full of the pebbles. Then they all set off together on their way to the forest. When they had gone a little way, Hansel stood still and looked back toward the house, and this he did again and again, till his father said to him,

"Hansel, what are you looking at? Take care not to lose your footing."

"Oh, father," said Hansel, "I see my little white kitten, sitting on the roof and bidding me good-by."

"You young fool," said the woman, "that is not your kitten, but the morning sun shining on the chimney."

Of course, Hansel had not seen his kitten, but he had taken a pebble from his pocket every now and then and had dropped it on the road.

When they reached the middle of the forest, the father told the children to collect wood to make a fire to keep them warm; and Hansel and Gretel gathered brushwood enough for a little mountain. Then they set it on fire, and when the flame was burning quite high, the wife said:

"Now lie down by the fire and rest yourselves, children, and we will go and cut wood; and when we are ready we will come and fetch you."

So Hansel and Gretel sat by the fire, and at noon they ate their pieces of bread. They thought their father was in the wood all the time, as they seemed to hear the strokes of the axe; but it was only a dry branch hanging on a withered tree that the wind moved to and fro. After they had stayed there a long time, their eyelids closed with weariness, and they fell fast asleep. When at last they awoke, it was night, and Gretel began to cry, and said:

"How shall we ever get out of this wood?" But Hansel comforted her, saying:

"Wait a little while longer, until the moon rises, and then we can easily find the way home."

And when the full moon rose, Hansel took his little sister by the hand, and followed the track of the pepples which shone like silver, and showed them the road. They walked on, the whole night through, and at the break of day they came to their father's house. They knocked at the door, and when the wife opened it and saw that it was Hansel and Gretel she said:

"You naughty children, why did you sleep so long in the wood? We thought you were never coming home!"

But the father was glad, for he had been sorry to leave them in the woods alone.

Not long after this, there was a great famine in the country again, and the children heard their mother say at night to their father:

"Everything is gone once more; we have only half a loaf left, and after that, the tale comes to an end. The children must be off; we will take them farther into the wood this time, so that they cannot find the way back again; that is our only hope; there is no other way to manage."

The man felt sad at heart, and he thought:

"It would be better to share one's last morsel with one's children."

But the wife would not listen to him, and only scolded and reproached him.

Again the children were awake, and heard all that was said. When the parents were asleep, Hansel got up to go out and get more pebbles, as he did before, but the wife had locked the door, and Hansel could not get out. However, he comforted his little sister, and said:

"Don't cry, Gretel, and go to sleep quietly, and God will help us."

Early the next morning the wife

came and pulled the children out of bed. She gave them each a little piece of bread—less than before; and on the way to the wood Hansel crumbled the bread in his pocket, and often stopped to throw a crumb on the ground.

"Hansel, what are you stopping for?" asked the father.

"I am looking at my little pigeon sitting on the roof, to say good-by to me," answered Hansel.

"Silly boy," said the wife, "that is no pigeon, but the morning sun shining on the chimney."

Hansel went on as before, and strewed breadcrumbs all along the road.

The woman led the children far into the wood, where they had never been before in all their lives. And again there was a large fire made, and the mother said:

"Sit still there, you children, and when you are tired go to sleep; we are going into the forest to cut wood, and in the evening, when we are ready to go home we will come back here and fetch you."

So when noon came Gretel shared her bread with Hansel, who had strewn his along the road. Then they went to sleep, and the evening passed, and no one came for the poor children. When they awoke, it was dark night, and Hansel comforted his little sister, and said:

"Wait a little, Gretel, until the moon comes up, then we shall be able to see our way home by the crumbs of bread that I have scattered along the path."

So when the moon rose they got up, but they could find no crumbs of bread, for the birds of the woods and of the fields had come and picked them up. Hansel thought they might still find the way, but they could not. They went on all that night, and the next day from morning until evening, but they could not find the path out of the wood, and they were very hungry, for they had nothing to eat but a few berries which they had picked. And when they were so tired that they could no longer drag themselves along, they lay down under a tree and fell asleep.

It was now the third morning since they had left their father's house. They were always trying to get back to it; but instead, they only found themselves farther in the wood. About noon, they saw a pretty snow-white bird sitting on a bough, and he was singing so sweetly that they stopped to listen. And when he had finished, the bird spread his wings and flew before them, and they followed after him until they came to a little house. The bird perched on the roof, and when they came nearer they saw that the house was built of bread, and roofed with cakes; and the window was of transparent sugar.

"We will have some of this," said Hansel, "and make a fine meal. I will eat a piece of the roof, Gretel, and you can have some of the window—that will taste sweet."

So Hansel reached up and broke off a bit of the roof, just to see how it tasted, and Gretel stood by the window and bit at it. Then they heard a thin voice call out from inside:

"Nibble, nibble, like a mouse, Who is nibbling at my house?" And the children answered: "Never mind, It is the wind."

And then they went on eating, without troubling themselves further. Hansel, who found that the roof tasted very nice, took down a great piece of it, and Gretel pulled out a large round windowpane, and sat down and began to eat it. Then the door opened, and an aged woman came out, leaning upon a crutch. Hansel and Gretel were very frightened, and let fall what they had in their hands. The old woman, however, nodded her head, and said:

"Ah, my dear children, how came you here? You must come indoors and stay with me. No harm will come to you."

So she took them each by the hand, and led them into her little house. And there they found a good meal laid out, of milk and pancakes, with sugar, apples, and nuts. After that she showed them two little white beds, and Hansel and Gretel lay down on them, and thought they were in heaven.

The old woman, although her behavior was so friendly, was a wicked witch, who lay in wait for children, and who had built the little house on purpose to entice them. When they were once inside, she used to kill them, cook them, and eat them, and then it was a feast day for her! When she knew that Hansel and Gretel were coming, she gave a spiteful laugh, and said triumphantly:

"I have them, and they shall not escape me!"

Early in the morning, before the children were awake, she got up to look at them, and as they lay sleeping so peacefully with round, rosy cheeks, she said to herself:

"What a fine feast I shall have!"

Then she grasped Hansel with her withered hand, and led him into a little stable, and shut him up behind a grating; and though he fought and screamed, he could not get out. Then she went back to Gretel and shook her, crying:

"Get up, lazybones; fetch water, and cook something nice for your brother; he is outside in the stable, and must be fattened up. And when he is fat enough I will eat him."

Gretel began to weep bitterly, but it was of no use; she had to do what the wicked witch bade her.

And so the best food was cooked for poor Hansel, while Gretel got nothing but crab shells. Each morning the old witch visited the little stable, and cried:

"Hansel, stretch out your finger, that I may tell if you will soon be fat enough."

Hansel, however, used to hold out a little bone, and the old witch, who could not see very well thought it was Hansel's finger, and wondered very much why it did not get fatter. When four weeks had passed and Hansel remained so thin, she lost patience and could wait no longer.

"Now then, Gretel," she cried to the little girl, "be quick and draw water; be Hansel fat or be he lean, tomorrow I must kill and cook him."

Oh how the tears flowed down over Gretel's cheeks as she went to fetch the water.

"Dear God, pray help us!" she cried; "if we had been devoured by wild beasts in the wood, at least we should have died together."

"Stop your complaining," said the old witch; "it is of no avail."

Early next morning Gretel had to get up, make the fire, and fill the kettle.

"First we will do the baking," said the old witch; "I have heated the oven already, and kneaded the dough."

She pushed poor Gretel toward the oven, out of which flames were already shining.

"Creep in," said the witch, "and see if it is properly hot so that the bread may be baked."

As soon as Gretel was inside, she meant to shut the door upon her and let her be baked, and then she would have eaten her. But Gretel saw what she was going to do and said:

"I don't know how to do it; how shall I get in?"

"Stupid goose," said the old witch, "the opening is big enough, do you see? I could get in myself!" and she stooped down and put her head in the oven's mouth. Then Gretel gave her a push, so that she went in farther, and she shut the iron door upon her, and put up the bar. Then Gretel ran away, and went straight to Hansel, opened the stable door and cried:

"Hansel, we are free! the old witch is dead!"

Then out flew Hansel as soon as the door was opened. How happy they both were! how they danced about, and kissed each other and laughed for joy. And as they had nothing more to fear they went over the old witch's house, and in every corner there stood chests of pearls and precious stones.

"These are better than pebbles," said Hansel, filling his pockets, and Gretel, thinking she also would like to carry something home with her, filled her apron full.

"Now, away we go," said Hansel, "if we can only get out of the witch's wood."

When they had walked an hour or two, they came to a great lake.

"We can never get across," said Hansel, "I see no stepping-stones and no bridge."

"And there is no boat either," said Gretel; "but here comes a white duck; if I ask her she will help us over." So she cried:

"Duck, duck, here we stand, Hansel and Gretel, on the land, Stepping-stones and bridge we lack, Carry us over on your nice white back."

And the duck came accordingly, and Hansel jumped on her back and told his sister to come too.

"No," answered Gretel, "that would be too heavy for the duck; we can go separately, one after the other."

And that is what they did. Afterwards, they went on happily, until the wood grew more and more familiar, and at last they saw in the distance their father's house. Then they ran till they came up to it, rushed in at the door, and fell on their father's neck. The man had not spent one happy moment since he left his children in the wood; but his cruel wife had gone away and not come back.

When Gretel opened her apron, the pearls and precious stones were scattered all over the room, and Hansel took one handful after another out of his pocket. Thus all their troubles were ended, and they lived in great joy together.

—From Grimm's Household Stories.

THE TALE OF PETER RABBIT

Once upon a time there were four little Rabbits, and their names were: Flopsy, Mopsy, Cotton-tail, and Peter. They lived with their mother in a sandbank, underneath the root of a very big fir tree.

"Now, my dears," said old Mrs. Rabbit one morning, "you may go into the fields or down the lane, but don't go into Mr. McGregor's garden; your father had an accident there—he was put in a pie by Mrs. McGregor."

Then old Mrs. Rabbit took a basket and her umbrella, and went through the wood to the baker's. She bought a loaf of brown bread and five currant buns.

Flopsy, Mopsy, and Cotton-tail, who were good little bunnies, went down the lane to gather blackberries; but Peter, who was very naughty, ran straight away to Mr. McGregor's garden, and squeezed under the gate!

First he ate some lettuces and some French beans; and then he ate some radishes; and then, feeling rather sick, he went to look for some parsley.

But round the end of a cucumber frame, whom should he meet but Mr. McGregor! Mr. McGregor was on his hands and knees planting out young cabbages, but he jumped up and ran after Peter, waving a rake and calling out, "Stop thief!"

Peter was most dreadfully frightened; he rushed all over the garden, for he had forgotten the way back to the gate. He lost one of his shoes among the cabbages and the other shoe amongst the potatoes.

After losing them he ran on four legs and went faster, so that I think he might have got away altogether if he had not unfortunately run into a gooseberry net, and got caught by the large buttons on his jacket. It was a blue jacket with brass buttons, quite new.

Peter gave himself up for lost, and shed big tears; but his sobs were overheard by some friendly sparrows who flew to him in great excitement and implored him to exert himself. Mr. McGregor came up with a sieve which he intended to pop upon the top of Peter; but Peter wriggled out just in time, leaving his jacket behind him, and rushed into the tool-shed, and jumped into a can. It would have been a beautiful thing to hide in, if it had not had so much water in it.

Mr. McGregor was quite sure that Peter was somewhere in the tool-shed, perhaps hidden underneath a flower pot. He began to turn them over carefully, looking under each.

Presently Peter sneezed—"Kertyschoo!" Mr. McGregor was after him in no time, and tried to put his foot upon Peter who jumped out of a window, upsetting three plants. The win-

From Beatrix Potter: The Tale of Peter Rabbit (Frederick Warne & Co.)

"Now, my dears," said Mrs. Rabbit one morning, "you may go into the fields or down the lane, but don't go into Mr. McGregor's garden: your father had an accident there; he was put in a pie by Mrs. McGregor."

dow was too small for Mr. McGregor, and he was tired of running after Peter. He went back to his work.

Peter sat down to rest; he was out of breath and trembling with fright, and he had not the least idea which way to go. Also he was very damp with sitting in that can. After a time he began to wander about, going lippity-lippity—not very fast, and looking all around.

He found a door in a wall; but it was locked, and there was no room for a fat little rabbit to squeeze underneath.

An old mouse was running in and out over the stone doorstep, carrying peas and beans to her family in the wood. Peter asked her the way to the gate, but she had such a large pea in her mouth that she could not answer. She only shook her head at him. Peter began to cry.

Then he tried to find his way straight across the garden, but he became more and more puzzled. Presently he came to a pond where Mr. McGregor filled his watering cans. A white cat was staring at some goldfish; she sat very, very still, but now and then the tip of her tail twitched as if it were alive. Peter thought it

best to go away without speaking to her; he had heard about the ways of cats from his older cousin, little Benjamin Bunny.

He went back toward the tool-shed, but suddenly, quite close to him, he heard the noise of a hoe—scr-r-ritch, scratch, scratch, scratch. Peter scuttered underneath the bushes. But presently, as nothing happened, he came out, and climbed upon a wheelbarrow, and peeped over. The first thing he saw was Mr. McGregor hoeing onions. His back was turned toward Peter, and beyond him was the gate!

Peter got down very quietly off the wheel-barrow, and started running as fast as he could go, along a straight walk behind some black-currant bushes. Mr. McGregor caught sight of him at the corner, but Peter did not care. He slipped underneath the gate and was safe at last in the wood outside the garden.

Mr. McGregor hung up the little jacket and the shoes for a scare-crow to frighten the blackbirds.

Peter never stopped running or looked behind him till he got home to the big fir tree. He was so tired that he flopped down upon the nice soft

From Beatrix Potter: The Tale of Peter Rabbit (Frederick Warne & Co.)
But Flopsy, Mopsy and Cotton-tail had bread and milk and blackberries for supper.

sand on the floor of the rabbit-hole, and shut his eyes.

His mother was busy cooking; she wondered what he had done with his clothes. It was the second little jacket and pair of shoes that Peter had lost in a fortnight!

I am sorry to say that Peter was not very well during the evening. His mother put him to bed, and made some camomile tea, and she gave a dose of it to Peter, who made a face when he tasted it. "One tablespoonful taken at bed-time!" But Flopsy, Mopsy, and Cotton-tail had bread and milk and blackberries for supper.
—Beatrix Potter[1]

LITTLE GOLDEN HOOD

You know the tale of poor Little Red Riding Hood, that the wolf deceived and devoured, with her cake, her little butter can, and her grandmother; well, the true story happened quite differently, as we know now. And first of all, the little girl was called and is still called Little Golden Hood; secondly, it was not she, nor the good granddame, but the wicked

[1]*The Tale of Peter Rabbit*, by Beatrix Potter, is included by arrangement with Frederick Warne & Co., Inc., publishers of the authorized American edition.

wolf who was, in the end, caught and devoured.

The story begins something like the tale.

There was once a little peasant girl, pretty and nice as a star in its season. Her real name was Blanchette, but she was more often called Little Golden Hood, on account of a wonderful little cloak with a hood, gold and fire colored, which she always had on. This little hood was given her by her grandmother, who was so old that she did not know her age; it ought to bring her good luck, for it was made of a ray of sunshine, she said. And as the good old woman was considered something of a witch, everyone thought the little hood rather bewitched too.

And so it was, as you will see.

One day the mother said to the child: "Let us see, my little Golden Hood, if you know how to find your way by yourself. You shall take this good piece of cake to your grandmother for a Sunday treat tomorrow. You will ask her how she is, and come back at once, without stopping to chatter on the way with people you don't know. Do you quite understand?"

"Yes, mother," replied Blanchette gayly. And off she went with the cake. But the grandmother lived in an-

other village and there was a big wood to cross before getting there. At a turn of the road under the trees, suddenly "Who goes there?"

"Friend Wolf."

He had seen the child start alone, and the villain was waiting to devour her, when at the same moment he saw some woodcutters who might observe him, and he changed his mind. Instead of falling upon Blanchette he came frisking up to her like a good dog.

" 'T is you! my nice Little Golden Hood," said he. So the little girl stops to talk with the wolf, who, for all that, she did not know in the least.

"You know me, then!" said she; "What is your name?"

"My name is Friend Wolf. And where are you going thus, my pretty one, with your little basket on your arm?"

"I am going to my grandmother, to take her a good piece of cake for her Sunday treat tomorrow."

"And where does she live, your grandmother?"

"She lives at the other side of the wood, in the first house in the village, near the windmill with the red sails, you know."

"Ah! yes! I know now," said the wolf. "Well, that's just where I'm going; I shall get there before you, no doubt, with your little bits of legs, and I'll tell her you're coming to see her; then she'll wait for you."

Thereupon the wolf cuts across the wood, and in five minutes arrives at the grandmother's house.

He knocked at the door: toc, toc.

No answer.

He knocks louder.

Nobody answers.

Then he stands upon end, puts his two fore paws on the latch, and the door opens.

Not a soul in the house.

The old woman had risen early to sell herbs in the town, and she had gone off in such haste that she had left her bed unmade, with her great nightcap on the pillow.

"Good!" says the wolf to himself, "I know what I'll do."

He shuts the door, pulls on the grandmother's nightcap down to his eyes, then he lies down all his length in the bed and draws the curtains.

In the meantime the good Blanchette went quietly on her way, as little girls do, amusing herself here and there by picking Easter daisies, watching the little birds making their nests, and running after the butterflies which fluttered in the sunshine.

At last she arrives at the door.

Knock, knock.

"Who is there?" says the wolf, softening his rough voice as best he can.

"It's me, granny, your Little Golden Hood. I'm bringing you a big piece of cake for your Sunday treat tomorrow."

"Press your finger on the latch, then push and the door opens."

"Why, you've got a cold, granny," said she, coming in.

"Ahem! a little, my dear, a little," replied the wolf, pretending to cough. "Shut the door well, my little lamb. Put your basket on the table, and then take off your frock and come and lie down by me; you shall rest a little."

The good child undresses, but observe this: She kept her little hood upon her head. When she saw what a strange figure her granny cut in bed, the poor little thing was very much surprised.

"Oh!" cried she, "how like you are to Friend Wolf, grandmother!"

"That's on account of my nightcap, child," replies the wolf.

"Oh! what hairy arms you've got, grandmother!"

"All the better to hug you, my child."

"Oh! what a big tongue you've got, grandmother!"

"All the better for answering, child."

"Oh! what a mouthful of great white teeth you have, grandmother!"

"That's for crunching little children with!" And the wolf opened his jaws wide to swallow Blanchette.

But she put down her head, crying:

"Mamma! mamma!" and the wolf only caught her little hood.

Thereupon, oh, dear! oh, dear! he draws back, crying and shaking his jaw as if he had swallowed red-hot coals.

It was the little fire-colored hood that had burnt his tongue right down his throat.

The little hood, you see, was one of those magic caps that they used to have in former times, in the stories, for making oneself invisible or invulnerable.

So there was the wolf with his throat burned, jumping off the bed and trying to find the door, howling and howling as if all the dogs in the country were at his heels.

Just at this moment the grandmother arrives, returning from the town with her long sack empty on her shoulder.

"Ah, brigand!" she cries, "wait a bit!" Quickly she opens her sack wide across the door, and the maddened wolf, with his eyes shut tight, springs in head downward.

It is he now that is caught, swallowed like a letter in the post.

For the brave old dame shuts her sack, so; and she runs and empties it in the well, where the vagabond, still howling, tumbles into the water and is drowned.

"Ah, scoundrel! you thought you would crunch my little grandchild! Well, tomorrow we will make her a muff of your skin, and you yourself shall be crunched, for we will give your carcass to the dogs."

Thereupon the grandmother hastened to dress poor Blanchette, who was still trembling with fear in the bed.

"Well," she said to her, "without my little hood where would you be now, darling?" And, to restore heart and legs to the child, she made her eat a good piece of her cake, and drink a good draught of wine, after which she took her by the hand and led her back to the house.

And then, who was it scolded her when she knew all that had happened?

It was the mother.

But Blanchette promised over and over again that she would never more stop to listen to a wolf, so that at last the mother forgave her.

And Blanchette, the Little Golden Hood, kept her word. And in fine weather she may still be seen in the fields with her pretty little hood, the color of the sun.

But to see her you *must rise* early.

THE STRAW, THE COAL, AND THE BEAN

In a village dwelt a poor old woman, who had gathered together a dish of beans and wanted to cook them. So she made a fire on her hearth, and that it might burn the quicker, she lighted it with a handful of straw. When she was emptying the beans into the pan, one dropped without her observing it, and lay on the ground beside a straw, and soon afterward a burning coal from the fire leaped down to the two.

Then the straw began and said, "Dear friends, from whence do you come here?"

The coal replied, "I fortunately sprang out of the fire, and if I had not escaped by main force, my death would have been certain—I should have been burned to ashes."

The bean said, "I too have escaped with a whole skin, but if the old woman had got me into the pan I should have been made into broth without any mercy, like my comrades."

"And would a better fate have fallen to my lot?" said the straw. "The old woman has destroyed all my brethren in fire and smoke; she seized sixty of them at once, and took their lives. I luckily slipped through her fingers."

"But what are we to do now?" said the coal.

"I think," answered the bean, "that as we have so fortunately escaped death, we should keep together like good companions, and lest a new mischance should overtake us here, we should go away together, and repair to a foreign country."

The proposition pleased the two others, and they set out on their way in company. Soon, however, they came to a little brook, and as there was no bridge or foot-plank they did not know how they were to get over it.

The straw hit on a good idea, and said, "I will lay myself straight across, and then you can walk over me as on a bridge."

The straw thereupon stretched itself from one bank to the other, and the coal, who was very impetuous, tripped quite boldly on to the newly built bridge. But when she had reached the middle, and heard the water rushing beneath her, she was afraid, and stood still and ventured no further. The straw, however, began to burn, broke in two pieces, and fell into the stream. The coal slipped after her, hissed when she got into the water, and breathed her last.

The bean, who had prudently stayed behind on the shore, could not help laughing at the event, and laughed so heartily that she burst. It would have been all over with her, likewise, had not a tailor, who was traveling in search of work, sat down by the brook to rest. As he had a compassionate heart he pulled out his needle and thread, and sewed her together. The bean thanked him most prettily, but as the tailor used black thread, all beans since then have had a black seam.

HANS IN LUCK

Hans had served his master seven years, and at last said to him: "Master, my time is up; I should like to go home and see my mother; so give me my wages." And the master said: "You have been a faithful and good servant, so your pay shall be handsome." Then he gave him a piece of silver that was as big as his head.

Hans took out his pocket handkerchief, put the piece of silver into it, threw it over his shoulder, and jogged off homeward. As he went lazily on, dragging one foot after the other, a man came in sight, trotting along gayly on a capital horse. "Ah!" cried Hans aloud, "what a fine thing it is to ride on horseback! He trips against no stones, spares his shoes, and yet gets on he hardly knows how." The horseman heard this, and said: "Well, Hans, why do you go on foot, then?" "Ah," said he, "I have this heavy load to carry; to be sure it is silver, but it is so heavy that I can't hold up my head, and it hurts my shoulders sadly." "What do you say to changing?" said the horseman: "I will give you my horse, and you shall give me the silver." "With all my heart," said Hans; "but I tell you one thing—you'll have a weary task to drag it along." The horseman got off, took the silver, helped Hans up, gave him the bridle into his hands, and said: "When you want to go very fast, you must smack your lips loud, and cry 'Jip.'"

Hans was delighted as he sat on the horse and rode merrily on. After a time he thought he should like to go a little faster, so he smacked his lips and cried "Jip." Away went the horse full gallop; and before Hans knew what he was about he was thrown off, and lay in a ditch by the roadside; and his horse would have run off if a shepherd who was coming by, driving a cow, had not stopped it. Hans soon came to himself, and got up on his legs again. He was sadly vexed and said to the shepherd: "This riding is no joke when a man gets on a beast like this, that stumbles and flings him off as if he would break his neck. However, I am off now once for all: I like your cow a great deal better; one can walk along at one's leisure behind her, and have milk, butter, and cheese every day into the bargain. What would I give to have such a cow!" "Well," said the shepherd, "if you are so fond of her, I will exchange my cow for your horse." "Done!" said Hans merrily. The shepherd jumped upon the horse, and away he rode.

Hans drove off his cow quietly and thought his bargain a very lucky one. "If I have only a piece of bread, I can, whenever I like, eat my butter and cheese with it; and when I am thirsty, I can milk my cow and drink the milk: what can I wish for more?" When he came to an inn, he halted, ate up all his bread, and gave his last penny for a glass of beer: then he drove his cow towards his mother's village: and the heat grew greater as noon came on, till he began to be so hot and parched that his tongue clave to the roof of his mouth. "I can find a cure for this," thought he, "now will I milk my cow and quench my thirst;" so he tied her to the stump of a tree, and held his leathern cap to milk into; but not a drop was to be had.

While he was trying his luck and managing the matter very clumsily, the uneasy beast gave him a kick on the head that knocked him down, and there he lay a long while senseless. Luckily a butcher soon came by, wheeling a pig in a wheelbarrow. "What is the matter with you?" said the butcher, as he helped him up. Hans told him what had happened, and the butcher gave him a flask, saying: "There, drink and refresh yourself; your cow will give you no milk, she is an old beast good for nothing but the slaughterhouse." "Alas, alas!" said Hans, "who would have thought it? If I kill her, what would she be good for? I hate cow beef, it is not tender enough for me. If it were a pig, now, one could do something with it; it would, at any rate, make some sausages."

"Well," said the butcher, "to please you I'll change, and give you the pig for the cow." "Heaven reward you for your kindness!" said Hans, as he gave the butcher the cow, and took the pig off the wheelbarrow, and drove it off, holding it by the string that was tied to its leg.

So on he jogged, and all seemed now to go right with him. The next person he met was a countryman, carrying a fine white goose under his arm. The countryman stopped to ask what o'clock it was; and Hans told him all his luck, and how he had made so many bargains. The countryman said he was going to take the goose to a christening. "Feel," said he, "how heavy it is, and yet it is only eight weeks old. Whoever roasts and eats it, may cut plenty of fat off it, it has lived so well!" "You're right," said Hans, as he felt it in his hand; "but my pig is heavy, too." Meantime the countryman began to look grave, and shook his head. "Listen, my friend," said he, "your pig may get you into trouble; in the village I have just come from, the squire has had a pig stolen from his sty. I was very much afraid, when I saw you, that you had the squire's pig; it will be hard for you if you are caught, because you will be thrown into the horsepond."

Poor Hans was badly frightened. "Good man," cried he, "help me out of this scrape; you know this country better than I; take my pig and give me the goose." 'I ought to have something into the bargain," said the countryman; "however, I will not be hard upon you, as you are in trouble." Then he took the string in his hand, and drove off the pig by a side path, and Hans went on his way homewards, free from care.

As he came to the last village, he saw a scissors-grinder, working away at his grinding, and singing. Hans watched him for a while, and then said, "You must be well off, master-grinder, you seem to be so happy." "Yes," said the other, "mine is a fine trade; a good grinder always has money in his pocket. But where did you get that splendid goose?" 'I did not buy it, but exchanged a pig for it." "And where did you get the pig?" 'I gave a cow for it." "And the cow?" "I gave a horse for it." "And the

horse?" "I gave a piece of silver as big as my head for that." "And the silver?" "Oh! I worked hard for that seven long years." "You have done well in the world hitherto," said the grinder; "now if you could find money in your pocket whenever you put your hand into it, your fortune would be made." "That is true; but how is that to be done?" "You must turn grinder like me," said the other, "all you want is a grindstone; the rest will come of itself. This one is a little the worse for wear: I would not ask more than the value of your goose for it; will you buy?" "How can you ask me such a question?" said Hans; "I should be the happiest man in the world if I could always have money in my pocket; what more could I wish for? Take the goose!" "Now," said the grinder, as he gave him a rough stone that lay by his side, "this is an excellent stone; manage it properly, and you can make a rusty nail cut with it."

Hans took the stone and went off with a light heart, and he said to himself: "I must have been born under a lucky star, for everything that I wish for comes to me of itself."

Meantime he began to feel tired, for he had traveled ever since daybreak; he was hungry, too, for he had given away his last penny in his joy at getting the cow. At last he could go no further, and the stone tired him very much; so he dragged himself to the edge of a pond, that he might drink and rest; so he laid the stone carefully by his side on the bank: but as he stooped down to drink, he forgot it, pushed it a little and down it went into the pond. For a while he watched it sinking in the deep clear water, then sprang up for joy, and again fell upon his knees, and thanked heaven for taking away his only plague, the heavy stone. "How happy am I," cried he: "no one was ever so lucky as I am." Then he got up with a light and merry heart, and went on free from all his troubles, till he reached his mother's house.

GULLIVER AND THE LILIPUTIANS

Once there lived a lad in England who was very fond of the sea. He would watch the ships come in and out of the harbor, and at last he hired himself out to be a sailor on one of the ships. In those times they had not steamships with choo-choo engines, and smokestacks, oh no! but only vessels that were driven by the wind blowing against their sails; and they were so much smaller than the big steamers you know that the winds often played with them and drove them hither and thither, and sometimes threw them on the rocks and smashed them all to pieces.

Well, this young man, Gulliver was his name, was on one of these little sailships when a big storm came and hurled the ship hither and thither, and at last broke it up against the rocks of a strange land. All on board, the captain, and the sailors, and the boys, perished in the sea. Only Gulliver escaped. A big wave threw him upon the land, and the shock was so great that he knew nothing of himself. He lay on the shore like one dead. Yes, he did.

At last he awoke. But what was his wonder and fright when he saw the sun shining in his eyes, and he knew he was alive, and wanted to rise up, to find that he could not move. No, not even his hand, or his little finger. He could not turn his head from side to side. He just had to lie quite still. Then he heard a strange whispering all about him, and at last he felt something crawling up his side. And then, would you believe it: he saw something, or somebody, he did not know what it was, standing on his chin, looking straight into his eyes—and he did not know whether he, or the little man he saw there, must have looked more frightened. The little man was not more than six inches tall, about as long as daddy's hand, from the wrist to the tip of his long man finger. But the little man had a real head and real eyes, and was dressed like a fine gentleman, only his coat, and his trousers, and his hat, were, oh, so tiny and small. And he spoke to Gulliver in a strange language which Gulliver did not understand, and his voice was so faint that he could hardly hear him anyway.

When Gulliver tried to say that he did not understand, and to ask what it all was about, and why he could not move, the little man looked so scared, oh, so scared, and held his tiny hands to his tiny ears—yes, he even fell back and nearly broke his little neck in his fall from Gulliver's chin. For you see, Gulliver's voice must have sounded like thunder to the little man, and the breath from Gulliver's mouth like a strong wind. And so Gulliver lay there, unable to move, and did not know what to make of it. He certainly had never seen such little people before.

Then, he heard a rip-rip-rip—and he felt that he could move his left arm. Then more of rip-rip-rip, and he could move his right arm. Then more and more of rip-rip-rip, and rip-rip-rip; and at last he could move his head, and raise his shoulders, and then his body, and finally he could rise up in his whole bigness. The little people had thought they might find out what had come to them, in another way.

When Gulliver had stood up, he looked about him, but he could not see anybody or anything. Just the blue sky above him. Then he looked down on the ground; he saw bushes which looked like little trees, quite perfect, but oh, so much smaller than the trees he used to know. Of course, he could not see, at first, any of the little people one of whom had been scared off his chin by his words, for they had all hidden away when they saw that big giant of a man rise up like a huge mountain. In a little while, however, when they saw that Gulliver did not do anything wicked, or violent, but just stood there, they peeped out from behind the trees, and he could see little faces and little bodies which looked too funny for anything, just like little doll babies.

When he spied them, he sat down on the ground to see them better, and talked to them in the softest tone of his voice, and smiled at them. Of course, they did not understand what he said, but they thought he looked

NEW YORK PUBLIC LIBRARY

LEMUEL GULLIVER, world traveler, salutes the giant citizens of Brobdingnag, who find his diminutive size a source of amusement.

NEW YORK PUBLIC LIBRARY

KING OF BROBDINGNAG (*left*), 60 feet tall, holds Gulliver in hand; in Lilliput (*right*), the hero towers over the 6-inch-high people.

friendly and would do them no harm. So they ventured out and at last he saw so many of them, he could hardly count them: soldiers in gay uniforms, many on horseback, and fine ladies and gentlemen all dressed up in silks and gold, and women and children—oh, you ought to have seen those children! They were so very, very tiny, not larger, some of them, than your own little finger, and even smaller—those that had been brought there in their little gocarts. Gulliver wondered at them prodigiously, yes, prodigiously. For think of it, what tiny little heads they had, and such tiny little eyes, and such tiny little noses, and such tiny little mouths and lips, and such tiny little tongues, and such tiny, tiny, tiny little teeth! And their tiny little hands and tiny little fingers, and tiny little feet. And their clothes, such tiny little coats, and trousers, and skirts, and stockings and shoes!

And you ought to have seen the horsemen on their fiery steeds! Well, they were so small and tiny that it was quite a jump when one of them vaulted across Gulliver's left foot which he had moved too far over! A whole regiment of cavalry marched through from between Gulliver's legs—as through a big, tall arch.

Then Gulliver saw what had bound him tight: millions and millions of little, fine threads, like silk, had been woven about him, and there was a little ladder on which the little man had climbed up to his chin, lying on the ground. And he saw that all the people of the land near by had come to see the big monster that had come to them from out of the sea, and he understood that they had been afraid, and had tied him while he did not know anything of himself, and was asleep, so that he might not hurt them. And he was thankful to them that they now trusted him for he knew he must look to them like a big, *big,* BIG giant. Well, he could pick up several of them in one hand, and put them into his pocket without feeling any weight, and if he was not careful he could walk over them with his big feet and crush a dozen of them at a time. Of course, they were afraid. But he was so careful that they soon knew he would not hurt them, and they showed him all around.

And what he saw was very wonderful. He saw their little houses, with the tiny little doors and windows; and their tiny little rooms smaller than those in your own doll's house, with tiny little beds, and tables and chairs, oh, so small! And think of the tiny little plates and cups and spoons and knives and forks. Well, the carpet in one of their biggest rooms was not any bigger than your little handkerchief!

And he saw their city which looked just like one made up of the toy houses you buy in the store. Their highest steeple was not any taller than the post of mamma's bed.

And there the tiny little cows they had! When the little milkmaid had milked one there was just enough milk to fill a fair-sized thimble. Now think, how many cows they had to milk to give Gulliver just one good glassful! And their tiny little dogs and cats!

From Elsa Beskow: Pelle's New Suit (Harper & Brothers)

Then Pelle went to his grandmother and said: "Grandmother dear, please spin this wool into yarn for me!" "That I will do gladly, my dear," said his grandmother. "If while I am spinning it you will tend my cows for me."

And the tiny little hens—oh! you will hardly believe how tiny their little eggs were. How big do you think they were? Well, just about like peas, and you may imagine how many Gulliver could eat for his breakfast.

Yes, they had a hard time, these little people, to feed their big giant guest, but they did their best. And they built him a house. Ten thousand workmen had to work at it for oh, so many days; and they had to cut down a hundred big forests with a thousand trees in each one of them, to make the walls and the roof. And then the house was small for Gulliver. But he made the best of it.

And they thought that Gulliver might help them in their trouble. For by this time he had learned enough of their language to understand what they said to him. And they told him of their enemies, on an island across the sea, who were coming to attack them with their big fleet of ships. Gulliver laughed when he saw the great fear of these people who had told him that they were the Liliputians.

He made them describe to him where the enemy lived, that there was a big stretch of deep sea between their own land of Liliputia and the land of the enemy. Of course, the sea looked big and deep to them, but it was not much more than a pond to Gulliver.

So he asked them for a hundred pieces of their strongest rope. Their rope, indeed, was so thin that it looked more to Gulliver like cotton thread, such as mamma uses in sewing. But he twisted every two of the pieces together so that they made a stronger thread, and then started out.

He rolled up his trousers and waded into the sea. By the shore were collected all the men, women and chil-dren of Liliputia, watching their big friend on his trip across the deep sea. They were trembling after all for they had never seen anything like it, and they did not know whether the enemy would kill him.

At first, the water only wetted his feet, then it came up to his knees, and finally it reached his waist. But it was not any deeper than that. After he had passed the deep stretch, and was out of sight of the Liliputians, he began to rise again out of the water, as it became more shallow towards the other shore. And so, his legs began to show above the water down to the knees, then his feet only were covered, and then he came quite close to the land on the other side.

And there he saw another crowd of little people assembled on the shore, shouting and screaming in terror. For they did not know what was happening to them, seeing such a big man mountain rising from the sea. And in the harbor of their city there lay fifty warships at anchor—big ships for them, but just like the toy boats you swim in the lake, to Gulliver. And everywhere were soldiers with bows and arrows and spears. And when they saw Gulliver they shot their arrows at him and threw their spears at him. But their arrows were only as big as pins, and their spears as long as darning needles; and neither their arms nor their bows were strong enough to harm Gulliver. Whatever of their spears and arrows reached him felt only like little pin pricks, and he did not mind them.

Then he took out of his pocket the fifty pieces of twisted string and tied one end of each to one of the enemy's warships, holding the other end in his left hand. And when he had tied them all to the fifty pieces of string he started back again, dragging the fifty

From Elsa Beskow: Pelle's New Suit (Harper & Brothers)
And on Sunday morning Pelle put on his new suit and went to his lamb and said: "Thank you very much for my new suit, little lamb." "Ba-a-ah," said the lamb, and it sounded almost as if the lamb were laughing.

warships of the enemy with him. Now you ought to have seen the startled faces of the distressed enemy; and their cries and shouts and screams when they saw their big fleet of fine warships pulled away, and the soldiers with all their bows and spears could not stop Gulliver. But it served them right, for the Liliputians had done no harm to them, and the enemy just wanted to sail over and take all their goods away from them. The Liliputians only wanted to live in peace.

And so Gulliver, with the enemy's fleet in tow, waded back to Liliputia. First the water reached to his knees, then up to his waist, and then, coming up on the other side, he saw the Liliputians waiting for him on the other shore, on roofs of buildings, on the docks, and everywhere. And when they perceived Gulliver coming home to them with the mighty fleet of the enemy dragging behind him they gave a big shout of joy and welcomed him gratefully. They came to meet him, and took the arms away from the enemy soldiers, and fastened their ships to their own docks, and were happy that they could now be without fear.

They never forgot Gulliver's help but made him live in comfort while he stayed with them, and did all they could to show him how much they thought of the great help he had given them.

PELLE'S NEW SUIT

There was once a little Swedish boy whose name was Pelle.

Now, Pelle had a lamb which was all his own and which he took care of all by himself.

The lamb grew and Pelle grew. And the lamb's wool grew longer and longer, but Pelle's coat only grew shorter!

One day Pelle took a pair of shears and sheared off all the lamb's wool.

Then he took the wool to his grandmother and said:

"Granny dear, please card this wool for me!"

"That I will, my dear," said his grandmother, "if you will pull the weeds in my carrot patch for me."

So Pelle pulled the weeds in Granny's carrot patch and Granny carded Pelle's wool.

Then Pelle went to his other grandmother and said:

"Grandmother dear, please spin this wool into yarn for me!"

"That I will gladly do, my dear," said his grandmother, "if while I am spinning it you will tend my cows for me."

And so Pelle tended Grandmother's cows and Grandmother spun Pelle's yarn.

Then Pelle went to a neighbor who was a painter and asked him for some paint with which to color his yarn.

"What a silly little boy you are!" laughed the painter. "My paint is not what you want to color your wool. But if you will row over to the store to get a bottle of turpentine for me you may buy yourself some dye out of the change from the shilling."

So Pelle rowed over to the store and bought a bottle of turpentine for the painter, and bought for himself a large sack of blue dye out of the change from the shilling.

Then he dyed his wool himself until it was all, all blue.

And then Pelle went to his mother and said:

"Mother dear, please weave this yarn into cloth for me."

"That will I gladly do," said his mother, "if you will take care of your little sister for me."

So Pelle took good care of his little sister, and his mother wove the wool into cloth.

Then Pelle went to the tailor:

"Dear Mr. Tailor, please make a suit for me out of this cloth."

"Is that what you want, you little rascal?" said the tailor. "Indeed I will, if you will rake my hay and bring in my wood and feed my pigs for me."

So Pelle raked the tailor's hay and fed his pigs. And then he carried in all the wood.

And the tailor had Pelle's suit ready that very Saturday evening.

And on Sunday morning Pelle put on his new suit and went to his lamb and said:

"Thank you very much for my new suit, little lamb."

"Ba-a-ah," said the lamb, and it sounded almost as if the lamb were laughing.

—*Elsa Beskow*[1]

THE NOSE

Did you ever hear the story of the three poor soldiers, who, after having fought hard in the wars, set out on their road home, begging their way as they went?

They had journeyed on a long way, sick at heart with their bad luck at thus being turned loose on the world in their old age, when one evening they reached a deep gloomy wood through which they must pass; night came fast upon them, and they found that they must, however unwillingly, sleep in the woods; so to make all as safe as they could, it was agreed that two should lie down and sleep, while a third sat up and watched lest wild beasts should break in and tear them to pieces; when he was tired, he was to wake one of the others and sleep in his turn, and so on with the third, so as to share the work fairly among them.

The two who were to rest first soon lay down and fell fast asleep, and the other made himself a good fire under the trees and sat down by the side to keep watch. He had not sat long before suddenly up came a little man in a red jacket. "Who's there?" said he. "A friend," said the soldier. "What sort of a friend?"

"An old broken soldier," said the other, "with his two comrades who have nothing left to live on; come, sit down and warm yourself." "Well, my worthy fellow," said the little man, "I will do what I can for you; take this and show it to your comrades in the morning." So he took out an old cloak and gave it to the soldier, telling him that whenever he put it over his shoulders anything that he wished would be fulfilled; then the little man made him a bow and walked away.

The second soldier's turn to watch soon came, and the first laid himself down to sleep; but the second man had not sat by himself long before up came the little man in the red jacket again. The soldier treated him in a friendly way as his comrade had done, and the little man gave him a purse, which he told him was always full of gold, let him draw as much as he would.

Then the third soldier's turn to

[1]*Pelle's New Suit*, by Elsa Beskow (written in Swedish), is included by permission of Harper & Brothers.

watch came, and he also had the little man for his guest, who gave him a wonderful horn that drew crowds around it whenever it was played; and made everyone forget his business to come and dance to its beautiful music.

In the morning each told his story and showed his treasure; and as they all liked each other very much and were old friends, they agreed to travel together to see the world, and for a while only to make use of the purse. And thus they spent their time very joyously, till at last they began to be tired of this roving life, and thought they should like to have a home of their own. So the first soldier put his cloak on, and wished for a fine castle. In a moment it stood before their eyes; fine gardens and green lawns spread around it, and flocks of sheep and goats and herds of oxen were grazing about, and out of the gate came a fine coach with three dapple-gray horses to meet them and bring them home.

All this was very well for a time; but it would not do to stay at home always, so they got together all their rich clothes and servants, and ordered their coach with three horses, and set out on a journey to see a neighboring king.

Now this king had an only daughter, and as he took the three soldiers for princes, he gave them a kind welcome. One day as the second soldier was walking with the princess, she saw him with the wonderful purse in his hand. When she asked him what it was he was foolish enough to tell her; —though indeed it did not much signify, for she was a witch and knew all the wonderful things that the three soldiers brought. Now this princess was very cunning and artful; so she set to work and made a purse so like the soldier's that no one would know one from the other, and then asked him to come and see her, and made him drink some wine that she had got ready for him, till he fell fast asleep. Then she felt in his pocket, and took away the wonderful purse and left the one she had made in its place.

The next morning, the soldiers set out home, and soon after they reached their castle, happening to want some money, they went to their purse for it, and found something indeed in it, but to their great sorrow when they had emptied it, none came in place of what they took. Then the cheat was soon found out; for the second soldier knew where he had been, and how he had told the story to the princess, and he guessed that she had betrayed him. "Alas!" cried he, "poor wretches that we are, what shall we do?" "Oh!" said the first soldier, "let no gray hairs grow for this mishap; I will soon get the purse back."

So he threw his cloak across his shoulders and wished himself in the princess's chamber. There he found her sitting alone, counting the gold that fell around her in a shower from the purse. But the soldier stood looking at her too long, for the moment she saw him she started up and cried out with all her voice: "Thieves! Thieves!" so that the whole court came running in, and tried to seize

him. The poor soldier now began to be dreadfully frightened in his turn, and thought it was high time to make the best of his way off; so without thinking of the ready way of traveling that his cloak gave him, he ran to the window, opened it, and jumped out; and unluckily in his haste his cloak caught and was left hanging, to the great joy of the princess, who knew its worth.

The poor soldier made the best of his way home to his comrades on foot and in a very downcast mood; but the third soldier told him to keep up his heart, and took his horn and blew a merry tune. At the first blast, a countless troop of foot and horse came rushing to their aid, and they set out to make war against their enemy. Then the king's palace was besieged, and he was told that he must give up the purse and cloak, or not one stone would be left upon another. And the king went into his daughter's chamber and talked with her; but she said: "Let me try first if I cannot beat them some other way." So she thought of a cunning scheme to overreach them, and dressed herself as a poor girl with a basket on her arm; and set out by night with her maid, and went into the enemy's camp to sell trinkets.

In the morning, she began to wander about, singing so beautifully that all the tents were emptied, and the soldiers ran round in crowds and thought of nothing but hearing her sing. Amongst the rest, came the soldier to whom the horn belonged, and as soon as she saw him she winked to her maid, who slipped quietly through the crowd and went into his tent, where it hung, and stole it away. This done, they both returned safely to the palace; the besieging army went away, the three wonderful gifts were left in the hands of the princess, and the three soldiers were as penniless and forlorn as when the little man with the red jacket found them in the wood.

Poor fellows! They began to wonder what they could do now. "Comrades," at last said the second soldier, who had had the purse, "we had better part; we cannot live together, let each seek his bread as best he can." So he turned to the right and the other two to the left; for they preferred to travel together. Then on he went till he came to the wood where they had met with such good luck before. He walked on a long time, till evening began to fall, when he sat down beneath a tree and soon fell asleep.

In the morning, when he awoke, he was delighted to see that the tree was laden with beautiful apples. He was hungry enough, so he soon plucked and ate first one, then a second, then a third. A strange feeling came over his nose; when he put the apple to his mouth something was in the way. He felt it, and found that it was his nose, which had grown till it hung down on his breast. It did not stop there, but grew and grew. "Heavens!" thought he, "when will it have done growing?" And well might he ask, for by this time it had reached the ground as he sat on the grass, and it kept on growing till he could not bear its weight, or raise himself up;

and it seemed as though it would never end, for already it stretched its great length all through the wood.

Meantime his comrades were journeying on, till suddenly one of them stumbled against something. "What can that be?" asked the other. They looked, and could think of nothing that it looked like but a nose. "We will follow it and find the owner," said they; so they traced it till at last they found their poor comrade lying stretched out beneath the apple tree. What could they do? They tried in vain to carry him. They caught a horse that was passing by, and raised him upon its back; but it soon tired of carrying such a load. They sat down in despair, when up came the little man in the red jacket. "Why, how now, friend?" said he, laughing; "well, I must find a cure for you, I see." So he told them to gather a pear from a tree that grew close by, and the nose would come all right again. No time was lost, and the nose was soon brought to its proper size, to the poor soldier's great joy.

"I will do still more for you," said the little man; "take some of those pears and apples with you; whoever eats one of the apples will have his nose grow just as yours did; but if you give him a pear, it will become natural again. Go to the princess and get her to eat some of your apples; her nose will grow twenty times as long as yours did, and you will get what you want of her."

They thanked their old friend heartily for all his kindness, and it was agreed that the poor soldier who had already tried the power of the apple should undertake the task. So he dressed himself as a gardener, and went to the king's palace, and said he had some remarkable apples to sell. Everyone that saw them was delighted and wanted to taste them, but he said they were for the princess only; and she soon sent her maid to buy his stock. They were so fine that she soon began eating them, and had already eaten three when she too began to wonder what ailed her nose, for it grew and grew, down to the ground, out of the window, and over the garden, nobody knows where.

Then the king issued a proclamation that whoever would heal this dreadful disease should be richly rewarded. Many tried, but the princess got no relief. And now the old soldier dressed himself very sprucely as a doctor, and said he could cure her; so he chopped up some of the apple, and to punish her a little more gave her a dose, saying he would call to-morrow and see her again. The morrow came, and as, of course, the nose had been growing fast all night, the poor princess was in a dreadful plight. So the doctor chopped up a very little of the pear and gave it to her, and said he was sure that would do her good, and that he would call again the next day. Next day came, and although the nose was a little smaller, yet it was still bigger than when the doctor first attended her.

Then he thought to himself, "I must frighten this cunning princess a little more before I shall get what I want of her;" so he gave her a little more

LOOK MAGAZINE

SLUM CLEARANCE programs have led to the rehabilitation of substandard housing in the major cities of the United States. Apartments infested with disease and vermin are being razed (*right*) to make way for new homes, schools, and playgrounds (*below*). Communities have been rebuilt and families resettled. As a result of multi-million-dollar housing programs sponsored by federal, state, and local governments, the incidence of crime has been reduced, disease is being brought under control, and children are given the opportunity to grow up in a healthy environment. People who once lived in squalor can now take pride in their homes and their new communit

MONKMEYER

of the chopped apple, and said he would call on the morrow. The next day the nose was much bigger than before, and the doctor said: "Something is working against my medicine, and is too strong for it; but I know through my art what it is; you have stolen goods about you, and if you do not return them, there is no hope for you." But the princess very stoutly denied this, so the doctor said: "Very well, you may please yourself, but I am sure I am right, and if you do not do as I say, you will die." Then he went to the king and told him how it was. "Daughter," said the king, "send back the cloak, the purse, and the horn that you stole."

So she ordered her maid to fetch all three, and gave them to the doctor, and begged him to give them back to the soldiers. As soon as he had them safe, he gave her a whole pear to eat, and the nose returned to its proper shape. Then the doctor put on the cloak, wished the king and all his court a good day, and was soon with his two brothers, who lived from that time happily at home in their palace, except when they went out in their coach with the three dapple-gray horses.

FABLES

The Fox, the Cock and the Dog—One moonlight night a Fox was prowling about a farmer's hencoop, and saw a Cock roosting high up beyond his reach. "Good news, good news!" he cried.

"Why, what is that?" said the Cock.

"King Lion has declared a universal truce. No beast may hurt a bird henceforth, but all shall dwell together in brotherly friendship."

"Why, that is good news," said the Cock; "and there I see some one coming, with whom we can share the good tidings." And so saying he craned his neck forward and looked afar off.

"What is it you see?" said the Fox.

"It is only my master's Dog that is coming towards us. What, going so soon?" he continued, as the Fox began to turn away as soon as he had heard that news. "Will you not stop and congratulate the Dog on the reign of universal peace?"

"I would gladly do so," said the Fox, "but I fear he may not have heard of King Lion's decree."

Cunning often outwits itself.

The Wind and the Sun.—The Wind and the Sun were disputing which was the stronger. Suddenly they saw a traveler coming down the road, and the Sun said: "I see a way to decide our dispute. Whichever of us can cause that traveler to take off his cloak shall be regarded as the stronger. You begin." So the Sun retired behind a cloud, and the Wind began to blow as hard as he could upon the traveler. But the harder he blew the more closely did the traveler wrap his cloak round him, till at last the Wind had to give up in despair. Then the Sun came out and shone in all his glory upon the traveler, who soon found it too hot to walk with his cloak on.

Kindness effects more than severity.

The Fox and the Lion.—When first the Fox saw the Lion, he was terribly frightened and ran away and hid himself in the wood. Next time however, he came near the King of Beasts; he stopped at a safe distance and watched him pass by. The third time they came near each other the Fox went straight up to the Lion and passed the time of day with him, asking him how his family were, and when he should have the pleasure of seeing him again; then turning his tail, he parted from the Lion without much ceremony.

Familiarity breeds contempt.

The Fox and the Crow.—A Fox once saw a Crow fly off with a piece of cheese in its beak and settle on a branch of a tree. "That's for me, as I am a Fox," said Master Reynard, and he walked up to the foot of the tree. "Good day, Mistress Crow," he cried. "How well you are looking today: how glossy your feathers; how bright your eyes. I feel sure your voice must surpass that of other birds, just as your figure does; let me hear but one song from you that I may greet you as the Queen of Birds." The Crow lifted up her head and began to caw her best; but the moment she opened her mouth the piece of cheese fell to the ground, only to be snapped up by Master Fox. "That will do," said he. "That was all I wanted. In exchange for your cheese I will give you a piece of advice for the future:

"Do not trust flatterers."

The Fox and the Cat.—A Fox was boasting to a Cat of its clever devices for escaping its enemies. "I have a whole bag of tricks," he said, "which contains a hundred ways of escaping my enemies."

"I have only one," said the Cat; "but I can generally manage with that." Just at that moment they heard the cry of a pack of hounds coming toward them, and the Cat immediately scampered up a tree and hid herself in the boughs. "This is my plan," said the Cat. "What are you going to do?" The Fox thought first of one way, then of another, and while he was debating the hounds came nearer and nearer, and at last the Fox in his confusion was caught up by the hounds and soon killed by the huntsmen. Miss Puss, who had been looking on, said:

"Better one safe way than a hundred on which you cannot reckon."

The Fox and the Stork.—At one time the Fox and the Stork were on visiting terms and seemed very good friends. So the Fox invited the Stork to dinner and for a joke put nothing before her but some soup in a very shallow dish. This the Fox could easily lap up, but the Stork could only wet the end of her long bill in it and left the meal as hungry as when she began. "I am sorry," said the Fox, "the soup is not to your liking."

"Pray do not apologise," said the Stork. "I hope you will return this visit and come and dine with me soon." So a day was appointed when the Fox should visit the Stork; but when they were seated at table, all that was for their dinner was contained in a very long-necked jar with a narrow mouth, in which the Fox could not insert his snout, so all he could manage to do was to lick the outside of the jar.

"I will not apologise for the dinner," said the stork.

"One bad turn deserves another."

The Fox and the Grapes.—One hot summer's day a Fox was strolling through an orchard till he came to a bunch of grapes just ripening on a vine that had been trained over a lofty branch. "Just the thing to quench my thirst," quoth he. Drawing back a few paces, he took a run and a jump, and just missed the bunch. Once again he jumped up, but with no greater success. Again and again he tried after the tempting morsel but at last had to give it up and walked away with his nose in the air, saying: "I am sure they are sour."

It is easy to despise what you cannot get.

The Wolf in Sheep's Clothing.—A Wolf found great difficulty in getting at the sheep owing to the vigilance of the shepherd and his dogs. But one day it found the skin of a sheep that had been flayed and thrown aside, so it put it on over its own pelt and strolled down among the sheep. The Lamb that belonged to the sheep, whose skin the Wolf was wearing, began to follow the Wolf in the Sheep's clothing; so, leading the Lamb a little apart, he soon made a meal of her and for some time he succeeded in deceiving the sheep and enjoying hearty meals.

Appearances are deceptive.

The Ant and the Grasshopper.—In a field one summer's day a Grasshopper was hopping about, chirping and singing to its heart's content. An Ant passed by, bearing a grain of corn he was taking to the nest.

"Why not come and chat with me," said the Grasshopper, "instead of toiling and moiling in that way?"

"I am helping to lay up food for the winter," said the Ant, "and recommend you to do the same."

"Why bother about winter?" said the Grasshopper; "we have got plenty of food at present." But the Ant went on its way and continued its toil. When winter came the Grasshopper had no food and found itself dying of hunger while it saw the ants distributing every day corn and grain from stores they had collected in the summer. Then the Grasshopper knew:

It is best to prepare for the days of necessity.

The Dog and the Shadow.—It happened that a Dog had got a piece of meat and was carrying it home in his mouth to eat it in peace. Now on his way home he had to cross a plank lying across a running brook. As he crossed, he looked down and saw his own shadow reflected in the water beneath. Thinking it was another dog with another piece of meat, he made up his mind to have that also. So he made a snap at the shadow in the water, but as he opened his mouth, the piece of meat fell out, dropped into the water and was never seen more.

Beware lest you lose the substance by grasping at the shadow.

The Hare and the Tortoise.—The Hare was once boasting of his speed before the other animals. "I have never yet been beaten," said he, "when I put forth my full speed. I challenge anyone here to race with me."

The Tortoise said quietly: "I accept your challenge."

"That is a good joke," said the Hare; "I could dance around you all the way."

"Keep your boasting till you've beaten," answered the Tortoise. "Shall we race?"

So a course was fixed and a start was made. The Hare darted almost out of sight at once but soon stopped and, to show his contempt for the Tortoise, lay down to have a nap. The Tortoise plodded on and plodded on, and when the Hare awoke from his nap, he saw the Tortoise just near the winning post and could not run up in time to save the race. Then said the Tortoise:

"Plodding wins the race."

The Hares and the Frogs.—The Hares were so persecuted by the other beasts they did not know where to go. As soon as they saw a single animal approach them, off they used to run. One day they saw a troop of wild Horses stampeding about and in quite a panic all the Hares scuttled off to a lake hard by, determined to drown themselves rather than live in such a continual state of fear. But just as they got near the bank of the lake, a troop of Frogs, frightened in their turn by the approach of the Hares, scuttled off, and jumped into the water. "Truly," said one of the Hares, "things are not so bad as they seem."

There is always some one worse off than yourself.

The Dog in the Manger.—A Dog looking out for its afternoon nap jumped into the Manger of an Ox and lay there cosily upon the straw. But soon the Ox, returning from its afternoon's work, came up to the Manger and wanted to eat some of the straw. The Dog in a rage, being awakened from its slumber, stood up and barked at the Ox and whenever it came near, attempted to bite it. At last the Ox had to give up the hope of getting at the straw and went away muttering:

"Ah, people often grudge others what they cannot enjoy themselves."

The Town Mouse and the Country Mouse.—Now you must know that a Town Mouse once upon a time went on a visit to his cousin in the country. He was rough and ready, this cousin, but he loved his town friend and made him heartily welcome. Beans and bacon, cheese and bread were all he had to offer, but he offered them freely. The Town Mouse rather turned up his long nose at this country fare and said: "I cannot understand, Cousin, how you can put up with such poor food as this, but of course you cannot expect anything better in the country. Come you with me and I will show you how to live. When you have been in town a week, you will wonder how you could ever have stood a country life."

No sooner said than done: the two mice set off for the town and arrived at the Town Mouse's residence late at night. "You will want some refreshment after our long journey," said the polite Town Mouse and took his friend into the grand dining room. There they found the remains of a

fine feast, and soon the two mice were eating up jellies and cakes and all that was nice. Suddenly they heard growling and barking. "What is that?" said the Country Mouse. "It is only the dogs of the house," answered the other. "Only!" said the Country Mouse. "I do not like that music at my dinner."

Just at that moment the door flew open, in came two huge mastiffs, and the two mice had to scamper down and run off. "Goodbye, Cousin," said the Country Mouse. "What! going so soon?" said the other. "Yes," he replied:

"Better beans and bacon in peace than cakes and ale in fear."

The Lion and the Mouse.—Once when a Lion was asleep, a little Mouse began running up and down upon him. This soon wakened the Lion, who placed his huge paw upon him and opened his big jaws to swallow him. "Pardon, O King," cried the little Mouse; "forgive me this time, I shall never forget it. Who knows but that I may be able to do you a turn some of these days?" The Lion was so tickled at the idea of the Mouse being able to help him that he lifted his paw and let him go. Some time after the Lion

was caught in a trap, and the hunters, who desired to carry him alive to the King, tied him to a tree while they went in search of a wagon to carry him on. Just then the little Mouse happened to pass by and seeing the sad plight the Lion was in, went up to him and soon gnawed away the rope that bound the King of the Beasts. "Was I not right?" said the little Mouse.

Little friends may prove great friends.

The Four Oxen and the Lion.—A Lion used to prowl about a field in which Four Oxen used to dwell. Many a time he tried to attack them; but whenever he came near, they turned their tails to one another, so that whichever way he approached them he was met by the horns of one of them. At last, however, they fell a-quarreling among themselves, and each went off to pasture alone in a separate corner of the field. Then the Lion attacked them one by one and soon made an end of all four.

United we stand, divided we fall.

The Frog and the Ox.—"Oh father," said a little Frog to the big one sitting by the side of a pool, "I have seen such a terrible monster! It was as big as a mountain with horns on its head and a long tail, and it had hoofs divided in two."

"Tush, child, tush," said the old Frog, "that was only Farmer White's Ox. It isn't so big either; he may be a little bit taller than I, but I could easily make myself quite as broad; just you see." So he blew himself out and blew himself out and blew himself out. "Was he as big as that?" asked he.

"Oh, much bigger than that," said the young Frog.

Again the old one blew himself out and asked the young one if the Ox was as big as that.

"Bigger, father, bigger," was the reply.

So the Frog took a deep breath and blew and blew and blew and swelled and swelled and swelled. Then he said: "I'm sure the Ox is not as big as. . . ." But at this moment he burst.

Self-conceit may lead to self-destruction.

The Ass in the Lion's Skin.—An Ass once found a Lion's skin that the hunters had left in the sun to dry. He put it on and went toward his native village. All fled at his approach, both men and animals, and he was a proud Ass that day. In his delight he lifted up his voice and brayed, but then everyone knew him, and his owner came up and gave him a sound cudgeling for the fright he had caused. And shortly afterward a Fox came up to him and said: "Ah, I knew you by your voice."

Fine clothes may disguise, but silly words will disclose a fool.

The Lion's Share.—The Lion went once a-hunting along with the Fox, the Jackal and the Wolf. They hunted and they hunted till at last they surprised a Stag and soon took its life. Then came the question how the spoil should be divided. "Quarter me this Stag," roared the Lion. So the other animals skinned it and cut it into four parts. Then the Lion took his stand in front of the carcass and pronounced judgment: "The first quarter is for me in my capacity as King of Beasts; the second is mine as arbiter; another share comes to me for my part in the chase; and as for the fourth quarter, well, as for that, I should like to see which of you will dare to lay a paw upon it."

"Humph," grumbled the Fox as he walked away with his tail between his legs; but he spoke in a low growl:

"You may share the labors of the great but you will not share the spoil."

The Goose with the Golden Eggs.—One day a countryman going to the nest of his Goose found there an egg all yellow and glittering. When he took it up, it was as heavy as lead, and he was going to throw it away because he thought a trick had been played upon him. But he took it home on second thoughts and soon found to his delight that it was an egg of pure gold. Every morning the same thing occurred, and he soon became rich by selling his eggs. As he grew rich he grew greedy; and thinking to get at once all the gold the Goose could give, he killed it and opened it only to find—nothing.

Greed oft o'erreaches itself.

The Tree and the Reed.—"Well, little one," said a Tree to a Reed that was growing at its foot, "why do you not plant your feet deeply in the ground and raise your head boldly in the air as I do?"

"I am contented with my lot," said the Reed. "I may not be so grand, but I think I am safer."

"Safe!" sneered the Tree. "Who shall pluck me up by the roots or bow my head to the ground?" But it soon had to repent of its boasting, for a hurricane arose which tore it up from its roots and cast it a useless log on the ground, while the little Reed, bending to the force of the wind, soon stood upright again when the storm had passed.

Obscurity often brings safety.

The Bat, the Birds and the Beasts.—A great conflict was about to come off between the Birds and the Beasts. When the two armies were collected together, the Bat hesitated which to join. The Birds that passed his perch said, "Come with us"; but he said: "I am a Beast."

Later on, some Beasts who were passing underneath him looked up and said: "Come with us"; but he said "I am a Bird." Luckily at the last moment peace was made, and no battle took place, so the Bat came to the Birds and wished to join in the rejoicings, but they all turned against him and he had to fly away.

He then went to the Beasts, but had soon to retreat, or they would have torn him to pieces. "Ah," said the Bat, "I see now:

He that is neither one thing nor the other has no friends."

The Jay and the Peacock.—A Jay venturing into a yard where Peacocks used to walk, found there a number of feathers which had fallen from the Peacocks when they were molting. He tied them all to his tail and strutted down toward the Peacocks. When he came near them they soon discovered the cheat and striding up to him pecked at him and plucked away his borrowed plumes.

So the Jay could do no better than go back to the other Jays, who had watched his behaviour from a distance; but they were equally annoyed with him and told him:

"It is not only fine feathers that make fine birds."

The Shepherd Boy.—There was once a young Shepherd Boy who tended his sheep at the foot of a mountain near a dark forest. It was rather lonely for him all day, so he thought of a plan by which he could get a little company and some excitement. He rushed down toward the village calling out "Wolf! Wolf!" and the villagers came out to meet him, and some of them stopped with him for a considerable time.

This pleased the boy so much that a few days afterward he tried the same trick, and again the villagers came to his help.

Shortly after this a Wolf actually did come out from the forest and began to worry the sheep, and the boy of course cried out "Wolf! Wolf!" still louder than before.

But this time the villagers, who had been fooled twice before, thought the boy was again deceiving them, and nobody stirred to come to his help. So the Wolf made a good meal off the boy's flock, and when the boy complained, the wise man of the village said:

"A liar will not be believed even when he speaks the truth."

Androcles.—A slave named Androcles once escaped from his master and fled to the forest. As he was wandering about there, he came upon a Lion lying down moaning and groaning. At first he turned to flee but finding that the Lion did not pursue him, he turned back and went up to him.

As he came near, the Lion put out his paw, which was all swollen and bleeding, and Androcles found that a huge thorn had got into it and was causing all the pain. He pulled out the thorn and bound up the paw of the Lion, who was soon able to rise and lick the hand of Androcles like a dog.

Then the Lion took Androcles to his cave and every day used to bring him meat from which to live; but shortly afterward both Androcles and the Lion were captured, and the slave was sentenced to be thrown to the Lion, after the latter had been kept without food for several days.

The Emperor and all his Court came to see the spectacle, and Androcles was led out into the middle of the arena. Soon the Lion was let loose from his den and rushed bounding and roaring toward his victim. But as soon as he came near to Androcles, he recognized his friend and fawned upon him and licked his hands like a friendly dog.

The Emperor, surprised at this, summoned Androcles to him, who told him the whole story. Whereupon the slave was pardoned and freed, and the Lion let loose to his native forest.

Gratitude is the sign of noble souls.

BIBLIOGRAPHY

COLEMAN, SATIS NARRONA. *Another Dancing Time.* The John Day Co., Inc., 1954.

FOREST, ILSE. *Child Development.* McGraw-Hill, Inc., 1954.

GRUENBERG, SIDONIE MATSNER (ed.). *The Encyclopedia of Child Care and Guidance* (rev. ed.). Doubleday & Co., Inc., 1963.

LAMBERT, HAZEL M. *Teaching the Kindergarten Child.* Harcourt, Brace & World, Inc., 1958.

OPIE, IONA and PETER (eds.). *The Oxford Dictionary of Nursery Rhymes,* Oxford University Press, Inc., 1951.

RUDOLPH, MARGUERITA. *Living and Learning in Nursery School.* Harper & Bros., 1954.

B'RER FOX, by Joel Chandler Harris.

Geology 447

Oceanography 461

Meteorology 468

Dictionary of earth

sciences 479

VOLUME SIX

EARTH SCIENCE

THE AMERICAN MUSEUM OF NATURAL HISTORY

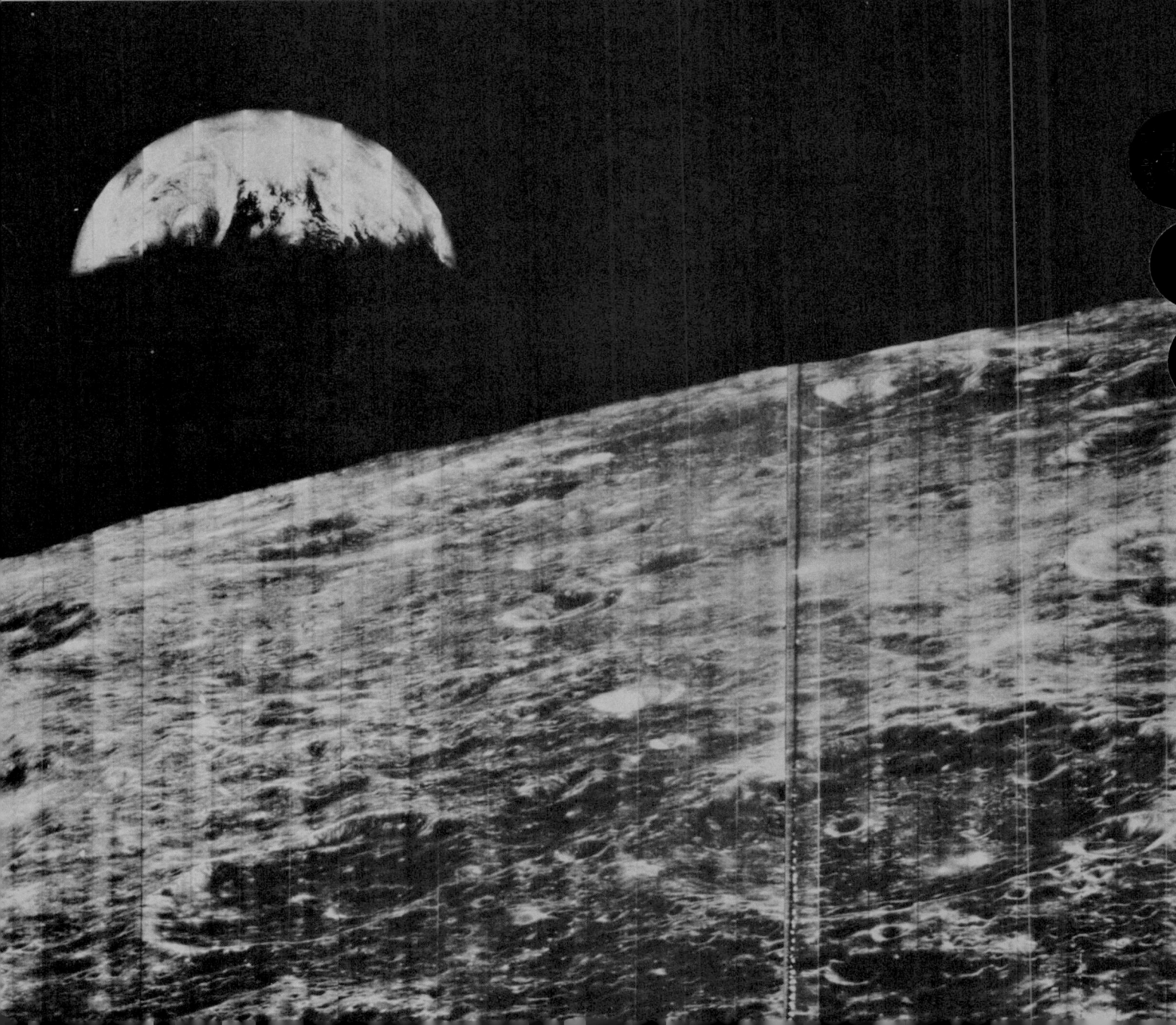

Earth Sciences

Earth Science, often called Geology, is the branch of physical science that deals with the origin, development, and history of the rocky crust of the earth. It draws on other branches of science, both physical and biological, and also contributes to them. The geologist uses chemistry to determine the composition of minerals and rocks, and biology to classify the fossils found in rocks.

GEOLOGY

Geology is divided into a number of somewhat separate branches of study. *Paleontology* is the study of ancient life—the evolution of animals and plants, their various adaptations and extinctions, and their environments. The need for metals and for fuels other than wood has led to *economic geology,* the study of commercially usable fuel and mineral deposits in the earth's crust. *Mineralogy* explains the origin of ores and minerals, the building blocks of rocks. The search for minerals and petroleum has led to *structural geology,* the study of rock structures and how they are formed. The study of rocks themselves is called *petrology.* The application of physical investigations to geology is known as *geophysics.*

The two general divisions of geology that include the branches mentioned above are physical geology and historical geology. *Physical geology* is the study of the earth as we see it around us; of the physical development of the face of the earth and its associated rocks. *Historical geology* is the study of the development of our planet and its life.

Physical Geology.—To understand the earth's surface we must know what it is made of, how it changes, and the processes that cause it to change. A number of processes can operate at the same time. There are some that operate quite abruptly with spectacular effect, but these are only occasional. Most act slowly but continuously, and have done so for billions of years.

■WEATHERING.—*Weathering,* or mass wasting, is one of the slow, continuous processes. The crust of the earth is made up of many kinds of rock, each with a different chemical composition. The elements in rock may be attacked by elements in the atmosphere, with a resulting change in composition that may also alter the durability or size of the particles. On the other hand, physical forces may break up rocks, with little or no chemical change. The first process is called chemical weathering; the second, mechanical weathering.

In *chemical weathering,* or decomposition, certain minerals in rocks are affected by the carbon dioxide, oxygen, or water vapor in the atmosphere. For example, when feldspar—a hard, glassy mineral common in granitic rocks—is attacked by carbon dioxide, it changes to a claylike material. Oxygen and water vapor may attack the iron in rocks, causing a change in the size and composition of the particles. Such reactions can occur only as far below the earth's surface as air and water vapor penetrate; they do not take place below the water table (the level of standing groundwater). In humid, hot climates they occur much deeper than they do in dry, cool climates. In some places in the Arctic and Antarctic, unweathered rock is exposed at the surface; but toward the equator there is a thickness of overlying weathered rock. Weathering may extend several hundred feet below the surface in parts of the wet tropics. These changes soften and break the rock, and it is more easily eroded.

Mechanical weathering, or disintegration, does not change the chemical composition of rocks or minerals, but breaks them into smaller particles. If water seeps into a crack in a rock, then freezes and expands, it may break the rock. This is especially common where freezing and thawing alternate rapidly. In areas where the nights are cool and the days are hot, such as in some deserts, the outer layer of rock expands and contracts faster than the inner part, making flakes splinter off. The roots of plants may push into cracks in a rock and grow, slowly forcing the sides of the cracks apart. Burrowing animals often expose rocks to the attack of mechanical weathering.

Where the earth's surface is relatively level, the layer of weathered rock gradually becomes thicker. The weathering processes become slower with depth, however, until they almost stop. If the surface is relatively vertical, the weathered fragments continually fall off and expose a fresh surface to the effects of weathering, the process continuing until the slope almost disappears. The weathered material and fragments usually accumulate at the bottom of the slope, forming *talus,* or *scree.*

Weathering softens and loosens rocky material but does not move it, unless mudflows or landslides develop. *Mudflows* are usually narrow tongues of mud that flow downhill a short distance, lose their water, and stop. *Landslides* are composed of large chunks of rock, soil, trees, and other debris. A landslide may travel downhill for thousands of feet and, if there is enough momentum, push part of the way up the next hill. In both mudflows and landslides, a slope of loose material is overloaded and lubricated by excessive water.

■EROSION.—The process of wearing away and transporting of weathered particles by wind, water, or glacial ice is sorted according to particle size and density, and dropped in a new area. Glaciers carry unsorted debris; this settles wherever the ice melts.

Wind erosion can occur only if the surface of the ground is composed of loose particles that are small enough to be moved. These conditions exist in deserts, along lake shores and seashores, and, less commonly, in fields where plant cover is scarce or absent. Fine dust blows entirely out of such areas, leaving only the heavier and coarser sand grains behind. The dust may accumulate elsewhere in a thick deposit called *loess,* which is usually very fertile. As it compacts, the loess develops a vertical, columnar structure, and water can pass downward through it easily. Therefore it does not erode readily, but tends to stand in high banks if cut into by a river or man-made excavation. Loess deposits, thought to have blown out of the Gobi Desert, are common in parts of China. In Europe there are deposits of loess that probably came partly from the Sahara Desert and partly from glacial debris deposited during the Ice Ages. Other loess deposits probably of Ice Age origin, occur in the upper Mississippi valley in the United States.

As desert sand is blown along the ground by the wind, the grains cut and shape the surfaces they move over. This action sometimes carves weird shapes in rocks by wearing away the soft material while leaving the harder rock standing out in relief. Where sand has been blown off the desert floor, there is *desert pavement,* usually covered with sand-blasted stones and bare rock. Elsewhere the sand accumulates in wind-deposited *dunes,* shaped much like snowdrifts. A dune is formed when the velocity of the wind is lessened by some obstacle, and the wind-borne sand is dropped. Oncoming sand is rolled up the windward side of the dune, and the grains drop down the lee side through the force of gravity. In general, the side toward the wind is less steep. Dunes are slowly moved before the wind; this movement often exposes objects previously buried.

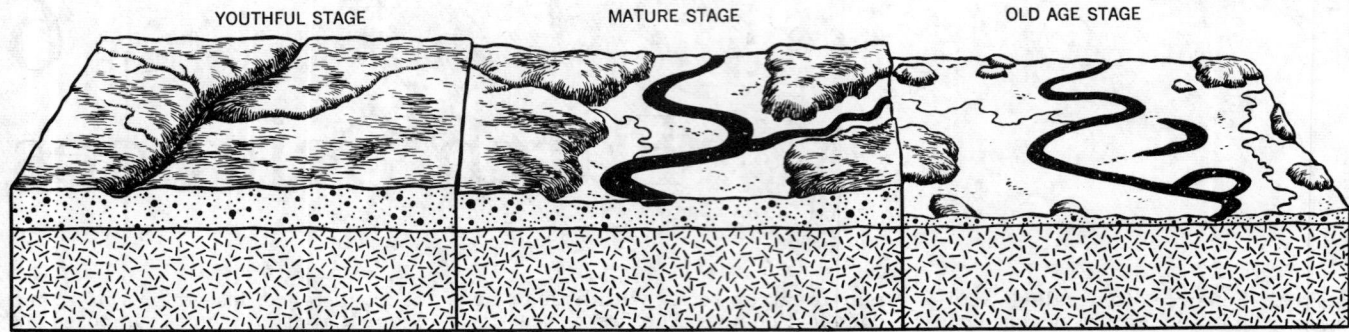

YOUTHFUL STAGE   MATURE STAGE   OLD AGE STAGE

THE FLUVIAL CYCLE is the process by which landmasses are eroded by rivers and streams. The complete cycle may take millions of years.

Where there is little shift in the wind's direction, the dunes tend to be *crescentic* as seen from above; but most dunes have an irregular outline.

Stream erosion is among the most active agents in lowering the elevation of the land. Clear water is a poor cutting agent; but armed with fragments of weathered rock, it can cut even the solid rock of a stream bed. Very fine material, like mud, is carried in suspension; coarse material is pushed along the stream floor; and the intermediate sizes are rolled and bounced over the bottom. All of this material is the stream's *load*. Sediment in suspension may travel the river's entire course without being dropped; the largest fragments move only during floods, when the current is exceptionally strong.

River valleys go through a three-stage cycle of erosion: *youth, maturity,* and *old age.* A typical old-age valley is that of the Mississippi River in Louisiana. It is wide and relatively flat, with the broad river winding across it in great *meanders,* or loops. The river flows across a *floodplain,* or surface of unconsolidated, relatively fine-grained sediment deposited in times of flood. Such material is dropped when floodwaters spread out, slow down, and lose their load-carrying ability. In many places natural *levees* have been built up along the main channel, where the initial decrease in velocity occurs when the river overflows its banks. Man has enlarged the levees along the Mississippi to contain the river, but it still overflows the floodplain.

An example of a youthful river valley is the Grand Canyon of the Colorado River in Arizona. The valley is narrow, with high, steep walls, and the divides are far above sea level. The river actively cuts downward, with many rapids, and it passes through a semiarid region where there is very little side wash and wastage to widen its valley. Its *gradient,* or longitudinal slope, is much steeper than that of an old river, such as the lower Mississippi.

Between the extremes of youth and old age are the mature valleys, such as that of the upper reaches of the Mississippi River. A mature valley is wider and has a gentler gradient than a young valley, but it is less flat than an old-age valley.

Stream erosion slowly reduces the land almost to sea level unless the cycle of erosion is interrupted by uplift of the earth's crust. An almost sea-level plain, called a *peneplain,* represents the ultimate downward cutting of stream erosion. No intact peneplains are known today, but geologists have recognized the remains of several ancient ones that have been uplifted. A noted example is the surface from which the Appalachian Mountains were carved millions of years ago. The tops of the ridges (especially in Pennsylvania) all have about the same elevation, and the rivers wind between them in narrow, steep-sided valleys. This shows that the area was once almost flat, with meandering, old-age streams, and that uplift later caused *rejuvenation,* the beginning of a new cycle of erosion.

Groundwater.—Almost everywhere from a few feet to several thousand feet below the surface, water is present in the cracks and pore spaces of rocks and unconsolidated sediments. Called *groundwater,* it is the source of all well water. In some places the consumption of groundwater has been so great that the *water table,* or upper surface of the groundwater, has been lowered several hundred feet. In coastal areas this lowering has brought sea water into many wells. Inland, however, the salt water that is sometimes pumped from deep oil wells is usually water that was trapped at the time when the rocks were deposited in ancient seas.

Easily soluble rocks, such as limestone, is sometimes dissolved by circulating groundwater to form caves below the ground and *sinkholes,* or *swallow holes,* on the surface. In such areas, the drainage may be entirely underground, with no surface streams in evidence. The subterranean water may come to the surface elsewhere in large springs, like some of those in Florida. Where the rock is less soluble, instead of solution there may be commercial mineral deposits enriched by groundwater.

Oceans and Lakes.—On the shores of oceans, seas, and large lakes, waves constantly attack the land. When a wave recedes, the drag of the undertow becomes evident. This continual bombardment by waves gradually erodes the shore. In areas where there are high tides, a wider vertical range of wave action is possible. Incoming waves sometimes force air into cracks in a rock and, in so doing, burst the rock apart. Waves may also carry rocks and pebbles that shatter the loose shoreline material and thereby cause erosion. The retreating waves then drag the finer debris into deep water and return the coarser material for another attack. This wave action gradually cuts back the shoreline, eventually forming a wavecut platform bordered on the land side by a cliff. The platform may become so wide that the waves hit the cliff only during storms. In general, this kind of erosion is more advanced along the coasts of oceans and seas than on lake shores.

Geologically speaking, lakes are temporary inland bodies of standing water. They may contain either fresh or salt water, depending on the presence or absence of outlets. A lake with no outlet eventually grows salty because the water that drains into it tends to evaporate, leaving behind an ever-growing concentration of dissolved minerals. Streams that empty into a lake bring sediment with them, and in the quiet water this sediment settles. This explains why water flowing out of a lake is usually clear. Lakes gradually fill with this sediment and turn first into swamps, then into level plains with streams wandering over them. Most lake deposits are thin-bedded clays and silts, which may contain remains of land-dwelling or fresh-water plants and animals. The world's coal deposits are the remains of lush vegetation that once grew in swamps that were cool enough so that the plant material did not rot, but was preserved in the form of carbon.

Oceans and seas are large, relatively permanent bodies of water. They are always saline, but the salinity varies. For example, the Baltic Sea is only slightly salty, whereas parts of the Indian Ocean, where the rate of evaporation is extremely high, are very salty. The shores of seas and oceans show considerably more evidence of wave action than do lake shores. This is strongly emphasized where the shoreline has moved up or down with regard to sea level. In theory, one cycle of the erosion is possible for an uplifted shore, and another for a submerged shore; but usually a cycle is not completed before a shift of sea level starts a new one.

The ideal cycle of a *submerged shoreline* is illustrated by that of Chesapeake Bay, which is bordered by headlands, drowned valleys, and marshes. Along the shore are sedimentary deposits, called *bars*, *spits*, and *hooks*, that extend from the headlands. These deposits are usually built up by currents flowing roughly parallel to the shore. As the cycle progresses, the headlands are cut back, forming cliffs, and the shoreline becomes straighter. On the seaward side the cliffs are bordered by wave-cut and wave-built *terraces*. Wave-cut terraces are carved by wave action at the base of the cliffs; wave-built terraces are composed of eroded material that has been carried seaward by the undertow.

An ideal *emergent shoreline* has a low, even beach. The waves break some distance from the beach and gradually build up an *offshore bar*, which finally rises above sea level. This forms a *lagoon* on the landward side of the bar. Next, the bar is slowly moved shoreward, becoming a *longshore bar*, and the lagoon is filled in. Eventually the waves attack along the line of the original beach again. In some areas there are features of both submerged and emergent coasts combined in a *compound shore development*, which may have both drowned valleys and longshore bars. The best harbors are commonly found along submerged shores, whereas along emergent shores there are few good harbors.

River water entering the sea is slowed down, and its sediment is deposited to form a large, low, flat, swampy area called a *delta*. A delta is roughly triangular, with the apex of the triangle pointing upstream, thereby splitting the river into a number of channels called *distributaries*. As the water slows down, the heaviest and coarsest sediment is dropped first; the finest, last. This forms a series of inclined layers of sediment, called *fore-set beds*, on the slope of the land margin. Beyond the fore-set beds are roughly horizontal layers of fine material called *bottom-set beds*. On top of the fore-set beds near the land margin are the finest sediments, the *top-set beds*. Deltas are fertile because of the constant addition of fresh soil.

Glaciation.—In Antarctica and Greenland, and on the upper slopes of high mountains elsewhere, there are *glaciers*—accumulations of snow and ice that move slowly over the ground. Some 10,000 to 20,000 years ago, during the Ice Age, the northern parts of North America, Europe, Asia, and much of southern South America were covered with ice just as Greenland and Antarctica are today. Such conditions result from a climate so cold that the winter's snows never melt entirely. The snow accumulates, and the lower layers gradually turn into ice under the increased weight.

Glaciers are generally divided into two types: *mountain*, or *alpine*, *glaciers* and *continental glaciers*, or *ice sheets*. Alpine glaciers have been compared to rivers of ice, but they are more like bulldozers that slowly plow down a valley, straightening it out and deepening it. When an alpine glacier eventually disappears, it leaves

a U-shaped valley with steep sides and a *cirque*, or amphitheater-like depression, in the mountainside at its head; the cirque often contains a lake. Alpine glaciers produced the rugged landscapes of the Alps and Himalayas.

Continental glaciers, on the other hand, tend to smooth out the surface over which they move. At the margin of the ice, a continental glacier pushes up a mass of irregular, unsorted rock debris called an *end moraine*. On the side of the moraine away from the ice is a relatively level area, called an *outwash plain*, composed of fine material washed away from the end moraine by meltwater from the glacier. There are irregular *kettle holes* in both the end moraine and the outwash plain, caused by the melting of buried blocks of ice. Behind the end moraine is the *till plain*, or *ground moraine*, a wide, gently undulating area of unsorted debris called *till*, which was carried in and under the ice and was dropped when the glacier receded. Continental glaciers also form *eskers*, or winding ridges of sorted till, and *drumlins*, or long, narrow hills of sorted till. When it melts back, the ice also deposits *erratics*, or single boulders composed of rock foreign to the area. There may be many

lakes in end moraines, but few in ground moraines or outwash plains.

Rocks.—The crust of the earth is made up of three main kinds of rock: igneous, sedimentary, and metamorphic. *Igneous rock* has crystallized and hardened from a hot, liquid mass. *Sedimentary rock* is derived from fragmental material carried as sediment, or in solution by water. *Metamorphic rock* is formed by the alteration of other kinds of rock by pressure or heat. Igneous rock makes up the greatest volume of the crust, but is often hidden under layers of sedimentary or metamorphic rock. Compared with the bulk of the crust, the sedimentary rocks are relatively insignificant, but spread over a greater area. Metamorphic rocks are common in areas of mountain-building.

■**SEDIMENTARY ROCKS.**—There are three groupings of sedimentary rock, based on origin. Those that were carried in suspension are *clastic sediments*; those that were deposited from solutions are *chemical*, or *precipitated*, *sediments*; those that form such deposits as coal beds and coral reefs are *organic rocks*—that is, they are composed of the remains of either plant or animal organisms.

Clastic sedimentary rocks are classified largely according to the size of

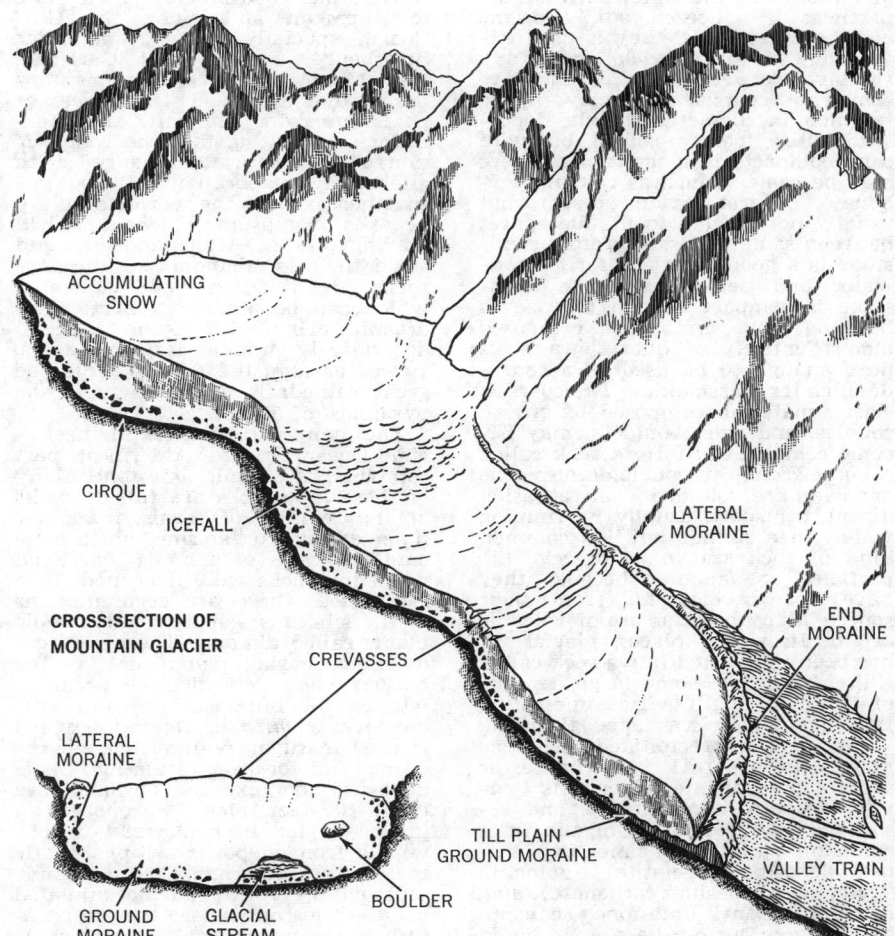

ACCUMULATING SNOW

CIRQUE

ICEFALL

LATERAL MORAINE

END MORAINE

CROSS-SECTION OF MOUNTAIN GLACIER

CREVASSES

LATERAL MORAINE

GROUND MORAINE

GLACIAL STREAM

BOULDER

TILL PLAIN GROUND MORAINE

VALLEY TRAIN

MOUNTAIN GLACIERS flow from high snowfields through mountain valleys, gouging boulders from mountain valleys and walls and changing the configuration of the terrain as they pass.

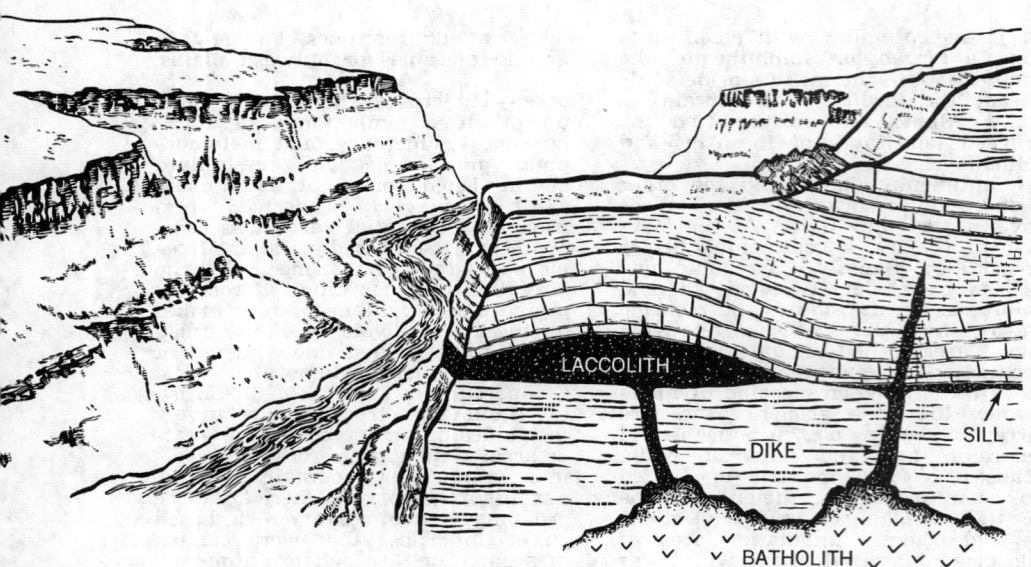

VOLCANIC INTRUSIONS such as the batholith extend deep beneath the earth's crust. From the igneous batholiths emerge lens-shaped laccoliths, vertical dikes, and horizontal sills.

the fragments of which they are composed. The finest sediments are deposited as *clay*—a soft, slippery, plastic, mudlike material that varies greatly in color. As clay becomes more compact, the water between the particles is squeezed out, and the clay becomes *shale*. Clay is used extensively to make brick, china, and similar products. *Sand grains* are somewhat coarser than clay—up to $\frac{1}{16}$ inch in diameter. Newly deposited sand is loosely packed, but with time compacts into *sandstone*. There may be *cement,* such as calcium carbonate, or iron oxide present, but usually not enough to fill the spaces between sand grains. Therefore sandstone is a good reservoir for groundwater and petroleum. Some sandstone is compact enough for use as building stone and some, composed almost entirely of quartz grains, is pure enough to be used as a source of silica for glassmaking. The coarsest clastic material, composed of gravel, cobbles, and even boulders, may become cemented to form a rock called *conglomerate.* In conglomerates, the particles are rounded from abrasion during transport, usually by running water. In a similar but less common kind of rock known as *breccia,* the particles are angular because they have not traveled far from their source. Many breccias are of volcanic origin. In a few places, glacial till has been compacted into a rock called *tillite.* There are some large deposits of tillite in South Africa, indicating that this region was once glaciated.

Among the precipitated sedimentary rocks are rock salt (halite, or sodium chloride), fertilizer salts (sylvite, or potassium chloride, and associated chlorides), gypsum, anhydrite (calcium sulfate), sedimentary iron ore deposits (hematite), dolomite (calcium magnesium carbonate), and, most abundant, limestone (calcium carbonate). During the past in many parts of the world there have been times when great quantities of so-

dium chloride were precipitated as rock salt, or halite, in beds hundreds of feet thick. Halite, which has only to be crushed to be used as table salt, is mined in great quantities in North America from New York State to Michigan and along the Gulf Coast, especially in Louisiana. Near Strasbourg, France, and Carlsbad, New Mexico, there are sedimentary basins that are the chief sources of potassium salts. The salts are interbedded, indicating that the composition of the sea water changed with alternating evaporation and flooding. In other parts of the world there are deposits of gypsum, which is used in making plaster. After sandstone and shale, the most abundant sedimentary rocks are limestone and dolomite, which can be of either chemical or organic origin. Limestone is used decoratively on many large buildings. It was used in the past to build the great cathedrals of Europe and the pyramids of Egypt.

The many coral islands in the Pacific Ocean are for the most part composed of organic limestone. Many of these limestones are full of shells or the remains of corals and other lime-secreting organisms, which indicate the kinds of animals that lived when the rocks were deposited. In a few places there are accumulations of the siliceous shells of microscopic plants called diatoms. These surface-dwelling marine plants sink to the bottom when they die, and accumulate by the billions. They form *diatomaceous earth,* or *diatomite,* which is used in sugar refining and oil refining, and for heat insulation. Some deposits, now exposed on land, are up to 100 feet thick. *Phosphorus,* an important fertilizer material, is obtained from deposits of *phosphatic rock* of organic origin. *Coal* is organic sedimentary rock that accumulated in large swamps where the temperature of the water was low enough to keep the material from decaying completely. Coal seams range in

thickness from a fraction of an inch to over 400 feet. A few seams as thin as one foot have been mined, but those less than two feet thick are not usually worked by underground mining. If they are not too deep, however, they can be worked by *strip mining,* or surface mining. Other organic materials that originate in sedimentary rocks are *petroleum* and *natural gas* which, together with coal, are known as *fossil fuels.*

■**IGNEOUS ROCKS.**—By far the most abundant rocks are the igneous rocks that crystallized from hot liquids, such as *lava,* which flows from erupting volcanoes, cools, and hardens to form such rocks as *basalt* and *felsite.* Lava can be any color, and some types contain gas bubbles. The amount of bubbles in lava and its color and fluidity depend on its formation temperature and its composition. Lava that is viscous, dark, and full of large bubbles forms *scoria;* whereas lava that is light gray, relatively fluid, and full of small bubbles forms *pumice.* Scoria and pumice are types of volcanic glass that cooled so rapidly crystals could not form. Pumice is so lightweight that it will float on water. Volcanic glass that does not contain bubbles is called *obsidian.* Other volcanic rocks are crystalline, even though the crystals may be microscopic. These rocks are either *acidic* or *basic,* depending on their composition. The acidic rocks are usually white to gray or pink; and the basic ones are dark green to black. Acidic rocks are often called *felsites;* and the basic rocks, *basalt.* Basalt is a fairly common rock, underlying such large areas as the Columbia Plateau in the northwestern United States and the Deccan Plateau in India. Basaltic rocks also underlie most ocean basins.

Underlying the lava flows and sediments on the continents are large quantities of igneous rock with easily visible crystals. If this coarse-grained rock is light-colored, like felsite, it is called *granite.* Granite is widely used as building stone and for curbstones and cobblestones. It is strong and durable. The corresponding basic rock is *gabbro,* a coarse, black rock that differs little from basalt in composition. *Porphyry,* an igneous rock that contains relatively large crystals in a fine-grained matrix, may be either acidic or basic.

Igneous rocks do not occur in beds like sedimentary rocks, since they are intruded, or injected, from below into preexisting rocks, or flow on the surface as lava. Tabular, relatively horizontal intrusions are called *sills.* Tabular intrusions that are more or less vertical are called *dikes.* Sills that have arched up the overlying rocks are known as *laccoliths.* The largest igneous intrusions are *batholiths,* which have no recognized floor and may have incorporated some of the overlying rock. These bodies underlie many mountain ranges.

■**METAMORPHIC ROCKS.**—Alteration, or *metamorphism,* is caused by heat or pressure. *Gneiss* is one of the most easily recognized metamorphic rocks. It is altered granite, with the mineral grains so oriented that the rock is banded. *Slate* is altered shale, a fine-grained metamorphic rock that can be split into thin layers. This again is caused by orientation of the mineral grains. Slate is used for roofing and blackboards. *Schist* is an altered basic igneous rock. It contains tabular mineral grains that are easily visible, and shows *foliation.* Sandstone becomes *quartzite* when it is metamorphosed. The *carbonate rocks* are altered to *marble,* which may be fine-grained or coarse-grained. Very fine-grained marble is used in sculpture, and coarse-grained marble is often used as building stone. In marble, the original fragments have recrystallized, destroying any fossils. Partly recrystallized marble, which is sometimes used for interior decoration, usually contains some fossil remains.

At the boundary between many igneous intrusions and the surrounding rock there is a zone of contact metamorphism, where the surrounding rock has been baked or burned. There may also be a zone of chemical alteration caused by the movement of solutions from the igneous mass into the surrounding rock or by the dissolving of some of the preexisting rock by the molten intrusion. Valuable mineral deposits are formed in this manner.

Diastrophism.—The deformation of the earth's crust is called *diastrophism.* Beds of rock are sometimes bent, and rock materials sometimes abruptly change. These changes are caused by the *folding* or *faulting* (breaking) of the rocks in the crust by natural phenomena, such as internal pressure and strain. Uparched folds are called *anticlines,* downfolds are called *synclines,* and simple folds from one level to another are called *mono-clines.* When layers of rock are faulted, beds that were once continuous are offset laterally or vertically. Sometimes younger beds are found under older ones without evidence of overturning, indicating that the older deposits have been thrust over the younger ones. In all cases the opposite sides of the fault zone have been moved in different directions. More or less vertical faults often have displacements of up to a few thousand feet, whereas relatively horizontal faults may have displacements measured in miles. Where a fault intersects the surface there may be a definite *scarp,* but this, like all surface features, will eventually disappear through erosion. Some faults continue to be active, but a great many are stationary. Old fault zones may be filled with mineral veins of economic value because they often form channels for mineralizing solutions. The study of faults and folds is important because of the relation of geologic structures to the production of oil, gas, and various minerals. Other aspects of diastrophism are *volcanoes* and *earthquakes.*

■**VOLCANOES.**—Active volcanoes occur mainly in two belts. One follows the shores of the Pacific Ocean; the other extends around the earth from east to west, crossing the Pacific belt in Indonesia and Central America. However, traces of ancient volcanism can be found in many other parts of the world. Volcanoes are relatively quiet most of the time, but now and again they explode violently, ejecting thousands of tons of liquid rock and fragmental material, along with large quantities of water vapor and other gases. Many volcanoes form large, cone-shaped mountains, like Mt. Hood in Oregon. Some build cones of lava that have low, gently sloping sides, like volcanoes in the Hawaiian Islands. Others are combinations of lava and cinders and form steep cones, like Mt. Vesuvius in Italy. Some volcanic cones cave in or blow up to form *calderas,* like Crater Lake in Oregon. If a volcano becomes dormant, the cone starts to wear away, leaving a core standing alone or with dikes radiating from it. Ship Rock in New Mexico had such an origin. The estimate of active volcanoes in the world is 400 to 500.

■**EARTHQUAKES.**—*Earthquakes* are the result of a sudden release of strains in the earth's crust. If a strain is released slowly, there is little noticeable effect; but if the release is sudden, the rocks in the crust move against one another and set up vibrations. When these vibrations reach the surface, loose soil and surface objects are shaken, sometimes violently. The violent earthquake belts of the world are roughly the same as the volcanic belts, but no region is immune to earthquake shocks.

Conclusion.—The information quite literally dug out of the earth by geologists is used in many fields, from exploration for fuels and building materials to the location of power and water-storage dams. Even the disposal of atomic wastes involves geology, because it is essential that these wastes not leak through porous rocks or fault zones and cause harm to life. The earth's geological processes, such as erosion and diastrophism, are slow and continuous. Spectacular events, such as earthquakes and volcanic eruptions, are relatively infrequent, and they constitute only minor aspects of the continuing changes that affect the earth.

—E. Willard Berry

MINERALOGY

History.—Mineralogy, a branch of geology, is a systematic, integrated science intimately related to chemistry and physics. Historically, it is one of the oldest sciences practiced by man. Minerals were known to, and used by, early man throughout the Stone Age, the Bronze Age, and the Iron Age. As far back as 3400 B.C. the inhabitants of the valleys of the Tigris and Euphrates and surrounding areas were searching for, mining, and polishing many-colored gem stones. They were familiar with amethyst, carnelian, agate, beryl, turquoise, lapis lazuli, malachite, jasper, chalcedony, and garnet. In the societies of those days, gems were as much of a status symbol as they are today. They were of special importance to the Egyptians, who used them to adorn the bodies of their dead, which they considered sacred. These gem stones were also buried in ancestral tombs, to be taken along by the deceased and enjoyed in the afterlife. It was from such religious and social practices that mineralogy was born.

The first mineralogy textbook was the *Book of Stones,* written by Theophrastus (c. 372–c. 287 B.C.), a stu-

MONOCLINE

ANTICLINE

SYNCLINE

FAULT

FOLDING AND FAULTING of the rocks in the earth's crust are part of the diastrophic process.

dent of Aristotle. In this book he classified 16 minerals under three groupings: metals, stones, and earths. Pliny the Elder (23–79) described minerals and mineral deposits in his books on natural history, and Georg Bauer (1494–1555), better known as Agricola, published an outstanding treatise on economic mineralogy over 400 years ago. Through the years, mineralogy has prospered, and its scope has enlarged to encompass many new areas.

Today mineralogy is divided into a number of branches, including chemical mineralogy, crystallography, descriptive mineralogy, determinative mineralogy, and physical mineralogy. The mineralogist employs geological methods to map rock formations, mineral deposits, and structures of the earth's crust. He collects mineral specimens, tests them by sight, touch, taste, and weight—and then examines them further in the laboratory, using the techniques of the chemist and the physicist.

Minerals.—A *mineral* is defined as a solid, homogeneous, natural substance with definite physical properties and a chemical composition that is fixed within narrow limits—its composition must be such that it can be expressed with a chemical formula.

In order to be classified as a mineral, a substance must be formed by inorganic processes. Thus coal, oil, amber, and pearls are not minerals, for they are produced from plant and animal substances. Also, materials such as the man-made sapphire are not minerals, even though they may be chemically, structurally, and physically identical with the natural substance.

Minerals are the building blocks of the earth's crust. Yet of all the known minerals, only about 50 are rock-making, and only about 20 of the 50 could be said to be essential constituents of rock.

Crystal Structure.—Minerals are crystalline; that is, their atoms or groups of atoms are arranged in a symmetrical, three-dimensional, geometric pattern called a *crystal lattice.*

There are a few minerals, known as *mineraloids,* that have a haphazard internal structure. These are said to be *amorphous.*

When minerals are free and uncrowded, they develop as *crystals*—solid bodies having smooth plane surfaces, or *faces.* Crystals give minerals characteristic outward shapes that reflect the internal crystalline arrangement. The angle between corresponding faces of any given mineral is always the same, no matter what the size of the specimen or its origin. An important part of mineralogy consists of measuring these angles. This is done with an instrument called a *goniometer.*

All similar faces on a crystal constitute a *form.* The most common forms are cubes, prisms, and pyramids. Crystal faces on the minerals contained in rocks are seldom distinguishable because they are so closely packed.

■**CRYSTAL FORMS.**—The symmetry in the geometrical form of a crystal is due to regularities in the positions of the corresponding similar faces and edges. Because of this regularity, crystals have planes and axes of symmetry. A *plane of symmetry* divides the crystal into two similar halves, one the mirror image of the other. Crystal forms are divided into six systems: cubic, tetragonal, orthorhombic, monoclinic, triclinic, and hexagonal. The systems are identified by the relative lengths of the axes of symmetry and the angles that the axes make with one another. In *cubic* crystals, the axes are all of the same length and are perpendicular to one another. In *tetragonal* crystals, two axes are of the same length and different from the third; all three axes are perpendicular to one another. In *orthorhombic* crystals, the three axes are of different lengths and perpendicular to one another. In *monoclinic* crystals, the three axes are of different lengths; two of the axes are perpendicular to one another but the third is not perpendicular to either. In *triclinic* crystals, the three axes are of different lengths and none is perpendicular to either of the other two. In *hexag-*

onal crystals, there are four axes—three of them are of identical lengths and at angles of 60° to one another in one plane; the fourth is of a different length and perpendicular to the plane of the other three.

■**HABIT.**—The crystal form that a mineral characteristically takes in response to rate of growth, heat, and pressure is called its *habit.* In the case of a mineral made up of single and distinct crystals, its habit may be *acicular* (needlelike), *capillary* and *filiform* (hairlike and threadlike), or *bladed* (elongated and flattened).

If the mineral is made up of a group of distinct crystals, its habit may be *dendritic* (branchlike), *reticulated* (latticelike), *divergent* (or *radiated*), or *drusy* (covered with a layer of small crystals).

When a mineral is made up of parallel or radiating groups of single crystals, its habits may be *columnar, bladed, fibrous, stellated* (starlike), *globular, botryoidal* (grapelike), *reniform* (kidney-shaped), or *mammillary* (breastlike). A material consisting of scales could have a habit that is *foliated, micaceous* (capable of being split into very fine sheets), *tabular,* or *plumose* (featherlike). A mineral habit can also be *granular, stalactitic* (with pendant cylinders or cones), *oölitic* (like fish roe), or *pisolitic* (rounded and pea-sized).

Mineral Identification.—When the hand specimen of a mineral is examined, the first thing seen is its outward appearance. It can be granular, compact, or earthy. Other physical aids in identification are the color, luster, hardness, cleavage, tenacity, specific gravity, and magnetism.

■**COLOR.**—Among the rock-forming minerals, the color depends largely upon the presence of iron. Minerals that contain this element are dark: black, brown, deep red, rust, or green. Minerals without iron are usually light-colored or white and are lighter in weight than the dark ones. Some dark minerals can be powdered by rubbing them against a hard, rough surface. In the testing laboratory, a streak plate made of unglazed porcelain is used for this purpose. The

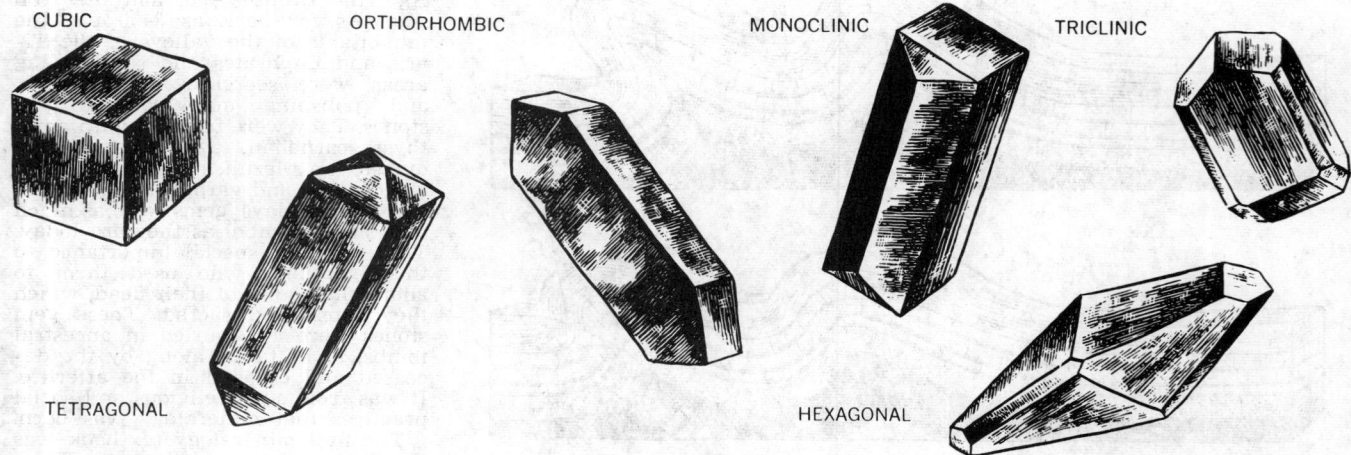

CUBIC   ORTHORHOMBIC   MONOCLINIC   TRICLINIC

TETRAGONAL   HEXAGONAL

CRYSTAL STRUCTURE of a mineral is helpful in identification. Most of the minerals have their own characteristic crystalline configuration.

color of the streak is, in most cases, characteristic of the mineral.

■**LUSTER.**—Luster is the quality and intensity of the light that a mineral reflects. Luster can be metallic (resembling iron or brass) or nonmetallic—pearly, greasy, silky, resinous, vitreous (glasslike), or adamantine (diamondlike). Some minerals will show a play of colors, or an iridescent effect.

■**HARDNESS.**—The hardness of a mineral is tested by attempting to scratch it with a series of minerals that have been chosen as a standard scale. This scale, called *Mohs' scale,* was proposed by the German mineralogist Friedrich Mohs in 1820. Mohs designated the softest known mineral, talc, as having a hardness of 1; and the hardest, diamond, 10. The ten minerals of the scale, arranged in order of increasing hardness (with their numerical designation on Mohs' scale in parentheses) are: talc (1), gypsum (2), calcite (3), fluorite (4), apatite (5), orthoclase (6), quartz (7), topaz (8), corundum (9), and diamond (10). Each of these minerals will be scratched only by minerals with a higher number on the scale and will scratch only those with a lower number; hence talc will be scratched by all (and will scratch none) and diamond will scratch all (and be scratched by none). Quick approximations of the hardness of minerals may be made by using handy substances to scratch them. These substances, with their numerical designation on the Mohs' scale, are: a fingernail (2½), a copper penny (3), the blade of a penknife or a piece of window glass (5½), and a steel file (6½).

■**CLEAVAGE.**—Many minerals have the tendency to split evenly or break in definite directions along the planes of weakness in their crystal lattice. This is called *cleavage.* The number and arrangement of cleavage planes provide a reliable clue to the identification of minerals. Mica, for instance, has only one direction of cleavage; orthoclase has two, at right angles; calcite has three, mutually oblique. Minerals that break irregularly are said to *fracture.* Fractures can be *conchoidal* (shell-like), as in glass; *hackly* (jagged-edged); *even,* if the break is smooth; *uneven,* if it is irregular; *fibrous* or *splintery,* if like wood; or *earthy.*

■**TENACITY.**—*Tenacity* is the resistance of a mineral to breaking, crushing, bending, or tearing. Some minerals are *sectile* (cutable), *malleable* (capable of being hammered into thin plates), *ductile* (can be drawn into wires), *flexible,* or *elastic.*

■**SPECIFIC GRAVITY.**—The *specific gravity* refers to a mineral's weight, expressed in a number that shows how many times heavier a given volume of that mineral is than an equal volume of water. The specific gravities of minerals range from 1.5 to 20.0, but most fall in the range between 2.0 and 4.0.

■**MAGNETISM.**—A few minerals, such as magnetite, an oxide of iron, will respond to an ordinary pocket magnet and can be identified by this property.

Common Rock-Forming Minerals.—A rock is an aggregate of minerals of different kinds in varying proportions. The following are some of the minerals more commonly found in rocks.

Quartz, whose chemical composition is silicon dioxide, is one of the most widely occurring minerals. It is the most common vein mineral, and makes up the largest part of most sands. Quartz is usually colorless or white; but it can be any color, depending upon its impurities. The colored varieties—amethyst, rose quartz, smoky quartz, citrine, chalcedony, and agate—are used in the manufacture of jewelry. Quartz is also used as an abrasive, in the manufacture of glass and porcelain, in paints, and in scouring soaps. As sand it is used in mortars and cements. Quartzite and sandstone—rocks made up largely of quartz—are used in the building trades.

Orthoclase feldspar, whose chemical composition is sodium-calcium-aluminum silicate, is usually found in various shades of gray, and sometimes white, although the latter is less common. It is a feldspar with a pearly to vitreous luster. Two distinctive subspecies are white *albite* and the dark *labradorite,* which often shows a play of colors when rotated in a good light. These subspecies occur in the same way as orthoclase.

Pyroxene is a silicate of calcium and magnesium, and also contains varying amounts of aluminum, iron, and sodium. It is the name of a group of minerals comprising many varieties that differ slightly in chemical composition. It is light green to dark green or black in color and commonly opaque. The most frequent member of this group is *augite,* which occurs in stubby, irregular crystals. It is a very abundant rock-making mineral that occurs chiefly in dark-colored igneous rocks. It is rarely found in rocks that contain quartz.

Amphibole, like pyroxene the name of a group of slightly differing minerals, is a silicate of calcium and magnesium, with varying amounts of aluminum, iron, and sodium. It is similar to pyroxene in composition, but differs in that it also contains water of constitution. Amphibole has a brighter luster and longer crystals than pyroxene. This mineral is usually opaque. The most familiar member of this group is *hornblende,* which has a luster of silky to dull and a color of black, dark brown, or dark green. It is a common rock-forming mineral that occurs in both igneous and metamorphic rocks.

Mica consists of characteristically shiny, flexible, elastic flakes that are stronger than steel. *Muscovite* (white mica) is a complex silicate containing potassium and aluminum. It occurs in granite, together with quartz and feldspar. Muscovite is typical of mica *schists*—rocks that split in flakes and slabs parallel to the cleavage of mica. It is used in insulation materials and in the manufacture of electrical equipment. *Biotite* (black mica) is a complex silicate containing potassium, magnesium,

iron, and aluminum. It is generally dark green, brown, or black. Thin sheets of biotite have a smoky color, which distinguishes it from muscovite. This common rock-making mineral is found in *gneisses*—laminated or foliated rocks—and schists.

Hematite is the most abundant ore of iron. Some specimens are metallic, others earthy and red. More than 90 per cent of iron in the United States comes from ores containing this mineral. Michigan, Wisconsin, and Minnesota are important hematite mining areas.

Limonite is the general name for all hydrous oxides of iron. It is an earthy material, reddish brown, yellow, or orange, that often forms crusts. Limonite, also a valuable source of iron, is formed by the oxidation and hydration of iron in previously existing minerals.

Pyrite, or iron sulfide, is also known as "fool's gold." It is metallic, brassy, and generally granular. It is the most common sulfide ore and an important vein mineral. Pyrite is often a carrier of gold or copper, thus becoming an ore for both of these metals. It is an important source of sulfur in the manufacture of sulfuric acid.

Chalcopyrite is a copper-iron sulfide. It is a golden yellow mineral, although it is generally seen tarnished to iridescent or bronze. It is the most important ore of copper, and is often an ore of gold or silver.

Sphalerite, the most important source of zinc, is a zinc sulfide. It is yellow-brown to dark brown, and has a resinous to submetallic luster. It is widely distributed, generally in veins or irregular bodies in limestone.

Galena, a lead sulfide, is the chief source of lead. Its color is lead-gray, and it has a bright metallic luster. Galena sometimes contains silver; therefore it is also an ore of this metal.

Cassiterite, a tin dioxide, is almost the sole source of tin. It usually occurs in pyramid crystals or rounded pebbles. It is brown to black, with a diamond to metallic luster. Cassiterite is mined on a commercial scale in Malaysia, Bolivia, Indonesia, the Congo republics, and Nigeria.

Bauxite, a mixture of hydrous aluminum oxides of indefinite composition, is the only commercial source of aluminum. Its color varies from white to gray, yellow, or red. Bauxite is translucent, with a dull to earthy luster. The chief deposits of bauxite in the United States are in Georgia, Alabama, Mississippi, and Arkansas. The principal world producers are Jamaica and Surinam.

Uraninite, or *pitchblende,* a uranium dioxide, is usually massive and grapelike in crystal structure. It is black, with a submetallic to pitchlike, dull luster. It is the most valuable source of uranium. The Congo republics and Canada are the most important producers.

Other important rock-forming minerals are *garnet* (a ferromagnesium silicate), used as a gem stone; *calcite* (a calcium carbonate), the chief constituent of marbles and limestones;

and *chlorite,* a complex hydrous magnesium-iron-aluminum silicate with micaceous cleavage. Chlorite is a common rock-forming mineral that gives a green color to many rocks. It is typical of schists and green roofing slates. *Serpentine,* a hydrous magnesium silicate, usually is the altered product of *olivine,* and is the chief constituent of the rock of the same name. *Gypsum,* a hydrous calcium sulfate, is used in the production of plaster of Paris. *Halite,* chemically sodium chloride, is common table salt and is used for seasoning food, as a preservative, and in the chemical industry. *Kaolinite,* chemically hydrous aluminum disilicate, is common clay. It occurs widely and is used in making pottery and brick.

—Doris D. Grandelis

HISTORICAL GEOLOGY

Origin of the Earth.—Man's desire to explain the means by which the earth was formed extends to prehistoric times. From the early legends of mythology to the modern theories of cosmogony, numerous explanations of the earth's formation have been offered. Today almost all scientists agree on one point—that the earth and its sister planets are related in their origin. However, no theory yet presented has been generally accepted, for each has left many important questions unanswered.

■**TWO-STAR HYPOTHESIS.**—Probably the most popular theory prior to World War II was that proposed by the American geologist-astronomer team of Thomas Chrowder Chamberlin (1843–1928) and Forest Ray Moulton (1872–1952), called the *two-star,* or *collision, hypothesis.* Chamberlin and Moulton proposed that the planets were born when the sun and a larger star passed so closely that they almost collided. Great bolts of gaseous material were pulled from the sun by the larger star's gravitational attraction. This gaseous material assumed an elliptical orbit around the sun and then condensed to form the planets and their satellites.

■**ONE-STAR HYPOTHESIS.**—In recent years a number of new theories have been suggested. The general trend today is toward the acceptance of a modification of the oldest truly scientific hypothesis ever proposed, the *one-star,* or *nebular, hypothesis.* It was presented in 1755 by the German metaphysician Immanuel Kant (1724–1804), who based his theory on the work of Nikolaus Copernicus (1473–1543), Johannes Kepler (1571–1630), and Sir Isaac Newton (1642–1727). This theory was further refined some 40 years later by Pierre Simon de Laplace (1749–1827), a French mathematician and astronomer. The one-star hypothesis assumes that a hot gaseous *nebula,* or cloud, automatically developed into a solar system as it cooled, without interference by an outside star or other body. This theory was widely accepted during the nineteenth century, then fell into disfavor until it was reconsidered in recent years.

The one-star theory can be summed up in the following way: Eons ago a greatly diffused, spherical gas cloud, or nebula, existed, the radius of which was at least as great as the distance of Pluto, the outermost planet, from the sun today. The cloud rotated slowly, and as it cooled—and therefore contracted—its velocity increased in the same way that a dancer will whirl faster and faster as he draws his arms closer to the body. The gaseous mass developed a disk, or equatorial bulge, around it; indeed, the present appearance of the planet Saturn, with its equatorial rings, resembles this, although on an infinitely smaller scale. At critical points during its rotation, rings of fiery gas are assumed to have been thrown off from the whirling disk by centrifugal force. Each ring then broke up into fragments, which gathered into a sphere. In this way a planet, which began to revolve in the same orbit as the ring from which it had been formed, was produced. A comparable process accounts for the formation of satellites, such as the moon. The planet liquefied as it cooled, and with further cooling acquired a solid crust. The main body of the gas meanwhile condensed and became the sun.

In 1943 a German physicist, Carl von Weizacker, was able to answer the greatest objection to the Kant-Laplace one-star hypothesis. According to mathematical analysis, the forces operating to cause the dispersion of the gaseous nebula revolving around the sun should have been just as strong as those forces acting toward the nebula's formation into planets. Weizacker's addition to the one-star hypothesis was that the materials that went into the formation of a planet such as the earth would have constituted no more than 1 per cent of the entire revolving gaseous mass—which would have been composed mostly of hydrogen and helium. In this milieu, tiny particles of dense material, revolving with the greater part of the gaseous nebula, could have collided. The smaller particles would have been absorbed into the mass of the larger, resulting in the eventual depletion of the supply of particles and the formation of the giant aggregates we know as planets.

Age of the Earth.—Until recently most geologists, astronomers, and cosmogonists (specialists dealing with the origin of the universe), believed the earth to be about two billion years old. But new data seem to indicate that the earth and the solar system are at least four, and perhaps as much as five, billion years old.

■**DATING METHODS.**—One of the most valuable tools available to scientists today for dating the earth is *radioactive decay,* or *disintegration.* Certain radioactive elements, such as uranium, found in minerals and rocks are very unstable. Uranium breaks down into lead at a constant and measurable rate that apparently is unaffected by heat, pressure, or other conditions. If the amount of lead and the amount of uranium are known, the age of the rock can be determined. The ratio is 1/7,600,000,000. This means that the presence in a sample of one gram of lead to 76 grams of uranium indicates that the parent rock is 100 million years old. This method is good exclusively for igneous rocks, since uranium is not likely to be found in either metamorphic or sedimentary rock.

Scientists are experimenting with other ratios, too, such as the ratio between several different isotopes of lead (the isotopes of an element are distinguished by differences in their atomic weights). Scientists are also experimenting with the decay of potassium to argon, and of rubidium to strontium.

■**GEOLOGIC PROCESSES.**—The present is the key to the past—all changes in the earth's crust that occurred billions and billions of years ago are the result of the same physical laws that are in operation today. Thus, mountains have loomed, then have been leveled to nothing by erosion; and arid lands have been flooded by invading seas that later retreated, leaving behind traces of the marine life that inhabited them.

All of the methods of radioactive dating, however, have one disadvantage—they cannot be used to date "recent" events in geologic history; that is, events that occurred less than two million years ago. Only one technique, which uses the radioactive isotope carbon-14, has proved to be an accurate time gauge within this period. And even this technique, known as *radiocarbon dating,* has its limitations, for it can be used to date only organic material that is less than 40,000 years old. The principle of radiocarbon dating is as follows: When cosmic rays bombard nitrogen in the outer atmosphere, the nitrogen may be converted into carbon-14. This carbon-14 combines with oxygen to form a special carbon dioxide. The carbon dioxide circulates through the atmosphere, reaches the earth's surface, and is absorbed by living, or organic, matter. The distribution of this special carbon dioxide has been found to be constant throughout the world. Therefore, there is an identical—although very small—amount of carbon-14 in all living organisms. When death comes to an organism—whether it is an animal or a plant—it ceases to absorb carbon-14. Instead, the carbon-14 present in the organism begins to be converted back to nitrogen at a constant rate. Thus, the longer the organism has been dead, the smaller the amount of carbon-14 that will remain within it. By comparing the amount of carbon-14 present in a no-longer-living organism with the uniform amount of carbon-14 present in all living organisms, the amount of time that has elapsed since death can be calculated.

Geologic Time.—Geologic time is generally taken as the period extending from the end of the earth's formative period to the beginning of the historical period. Thus, geologic time did not begin when the earth was born, but much, much later. The hot gaseous jets thrown off by the sun had to cool into a liquid and then into a solid crust. There was upheaval beneath the earth's crust; the crust broke, and the fragments sank into the thick, molten rock underneath; then the crust solidified once more. Gradually, the earth cooled enough to allow the water vapor in the envelope of gas surrounding it to condense into rain, and the earth's surface was sufficiently cooled so that the rain could remain as water. It is with erosion that geologic processes, and consequently geologic time, started.

The geologic processes that have left their mark on the face of the earth during the period of geologic time fall into three categories: gradation, volcanism, and diastrophism. The process of *gradation* consists of *erosion,* which is the weathering (wearing away) of rocks and soil by the action of water, ice, and wind, and *deposition,* which is the building up of rock layers through the accumulation of sediments laid down by the action of water, ice, and wind; thus deposition is the converse of erosion. *Volcanism* includes all movements of molten rock, or *magma*—which is assumed to be the earth's inner core—and the formation of solid rock from the molten state, both within the solid crust and on the surface. *Diastrophism* is the process by which the earth's crust is deformed to produce continents, mountains, ocean basins, and plateaus; it therefore includes the processes of *epeirogenesis,* or continent building, and *orogenesis,* or mountain building.

■**GEOLOGIC TIME DIVISIONS.**—A logical way had to be found to divide the vast periods of geologic time. This was done by using the most obvious physical breaks in the biological record. Because the progress of life has been greatly affected by physical disruptions on the earth, a correspondence can be found between the radical changes that occurred on the earth and those that occurred in the development of plants and animals.

During periods of radical change or great diastrophism, tremendous upheavals of the earth's crust occurred, and the forces within the crust caused the rocks to fold like layers of soft modeling clay. The molten interior of the earth pushed into the overlying older rocks of the crust in the form of great *batholiths*—masses of intruded igneous rock—mountains were formed, and parts of the continents were lifted high above sea level. Then shorelines emerged, streams were rejuvenated, and a great amount of erosion took place.

This uplift of the continents caused a change in the climate, which became cold as the lands were removed from the tempering effects of the ocean. *Glaciation,* the formation of large bodies of ice over the land, occurred when the uplift was great enough; and life changed accordingly. Some of the forms of life adapted themselves to colder climates; some died out or migrated to warmer areas. The climate at times destroyed vegetation; and as a result, the animals feeding on it died out. Each new cycle—the uplift of the land, the retreating of the seas, the downwarp of the continents, and the encroaching seas—meant a new phase with new life.

The largest portions of geologic time are called *eras,* and are separated by periods of revolution. These revolutions were most likely worldwide in scope and profoundly affected plant and animal life. The rocks deposited during an era are called a *group.* Eras are divided into *periods,* which are separated by such minor diastrophism as folding, the advance or retreat of the sea, or simply a change in life. A *system* of rocks is deposited during one period. Periods are further subdivided into *epochs,* which are often separated by retreats of the sea on a local scale. A *series* of rocks is deposited during one epoch. Epochs are divided into *stages;* and the rocks deposited then constitute a *stage,* which can be broken down into *substages* and still further into *zones,* named according to the fossils they contain. Basic rock units are called *formations* and are made up of a single layer or several layers in which all sediments have been deposited continuously and under the same conditions.

■**GEOLOGIC COLUMN AND TIME CHART.**—The seas have flooded the land many times since the world began. This has occurred either because the sea level has risen generally or because the continent has warped downward. Consequently, the profile of the land and sea has been vastly different from age to age. All these movements of the continents and the seas have left their telltale marks in the rocks.

To trace the earth's history, records of local regions all over the world have to be painstakingly pieced together, like a jigsaw puzzle, in the proper chronological order. This way, geologists can construct a composite for the world—by superposing the major rock units from different parts of the world in the form of a *geologic column,* representing formations as they would appear in a well core, with the oldest bed at the bottom and the youngest layer on top. The counterpart of the geologic column is the *geologic time chart,* where major units of geologic time are arranged to correspond with the geologic column. Within this framework, geologists are reconstructing the history of the earth.

A complete record of all geologic time cannot be found in any single area. Because of the irregular warping of the earth's surface, the areas of deposition have shifted. However, deposition has always been going on in one place or another. Therefore, while no area contains a complete record, it is only necessary to discover and correlate enough of the scattered fragments to piece together a composite record of all geologic time. Geologists and allied scientists the world over have pooled their knowledge and skill in tagging and timing the earth's rocks. More than 500,000 feet of rock are classified.

Two laws of historic geology form the basis for the construction of the geologic column and time chart. These are the law of superposition and the law of faunal and floral (animal and plant life) succession.

The *law of superposition* assumes that layers of sediments are deposited one at a time, one on top of the other. Therefore, in any normal section—one that has not been deformed—the oldest bed is on the bottom and each bed in turn is younger than the one on which it rests.

The *law of faunal and floral succession* assumes that any grouping of remains of animal and plant life is a collection of organisms that existed together at one time and in one place. In addition, fossil floras and faunas succeed one another in a definite and determinable order.

Fossils.—Fossils are any recognizable organic structures or impressions of organisms preserved from prehistoric time. Referred to in former times as "devices of the Devil placed in rocks to delude men" and "relics of the accursed race that perished with the Flood," fossils were not universally recognized until 1800 A.D., as representatives of life in the geologic past. There were great controversies concerning fossils during the Dark Ages because men took their Scripture so literally. These men, who believed in a special creation, could not accept relics of a life older than 6,000 years. But there have been men through the ages who have recognized the significance of fossils. Herodotus, around 450 B.C., was one of the first to identify fossils. He found fossil seashells in Egypt and the Libyan desert during his African travels, and he came to the accurate conclusion that the Mediterranean Sea must have extended much farther to the south at some past time than in his day.

Fossils can be found in the state of original preservation, such as the woolly mammoth embalmed intact in the Arctic ice. They can also exist as molds, casts, and imprints, as well as footprints and trails. *Coprolites*—prehistoric excrement—are also considered a class of fossils. Although coal and petroleum are referred to as fossil fuels, they are not true fossils despite their age and organic beginnings because they have no recognizable structure. Remains of animals or plants recently dead are not considered fossils even though the species may be extinct because the word "fossil" necessarily implies antiquity. Fossils occur only when and where the environment was favorable for their existence and preservation, and two special conditions are of the utmost importance: the fossils must possess such internal or external hard parts as bones, teeth, scales, shells, or wood, which are left behind when the animal or plant decomposes; and the remains must be buried quickly to protect them against weathering, bacteria, and scavengers. Molds, casts, and imprints also must have quick burial if they are to be preserved. The sea bottom is by far the most important and favorable environment for the preservation of fossils because marine life is particularly prolific; and the shells are quickly, sometimes instantaneously, buried with mud and sand during storms. The beds of prehistoric lakes, bogs, the frozen tundra, asphalt or tar pits, volcanic ash, lava flows, and windblown sediment, such as loess,

CRYPTOZOIC — "Time Of Hidden Life"		PHANEROZOIC—					
PRE-CAMBRIAN		PALEOZOIC "Era Of Old Life"					
KEWEENAWAN, HURONIAN, TIMISKAMING & KEEWATIN	CAMBRIAN	ORDOVICIAN	SILURIAN	DEVONIAN	MISSISSIPPIAN	PENNSYLVANIAN "Age Of Cockroaches"	PERMIAN
?	100	70	15	43	40	45	40
4 ? BILLION	550	450	380	355	310	270	225

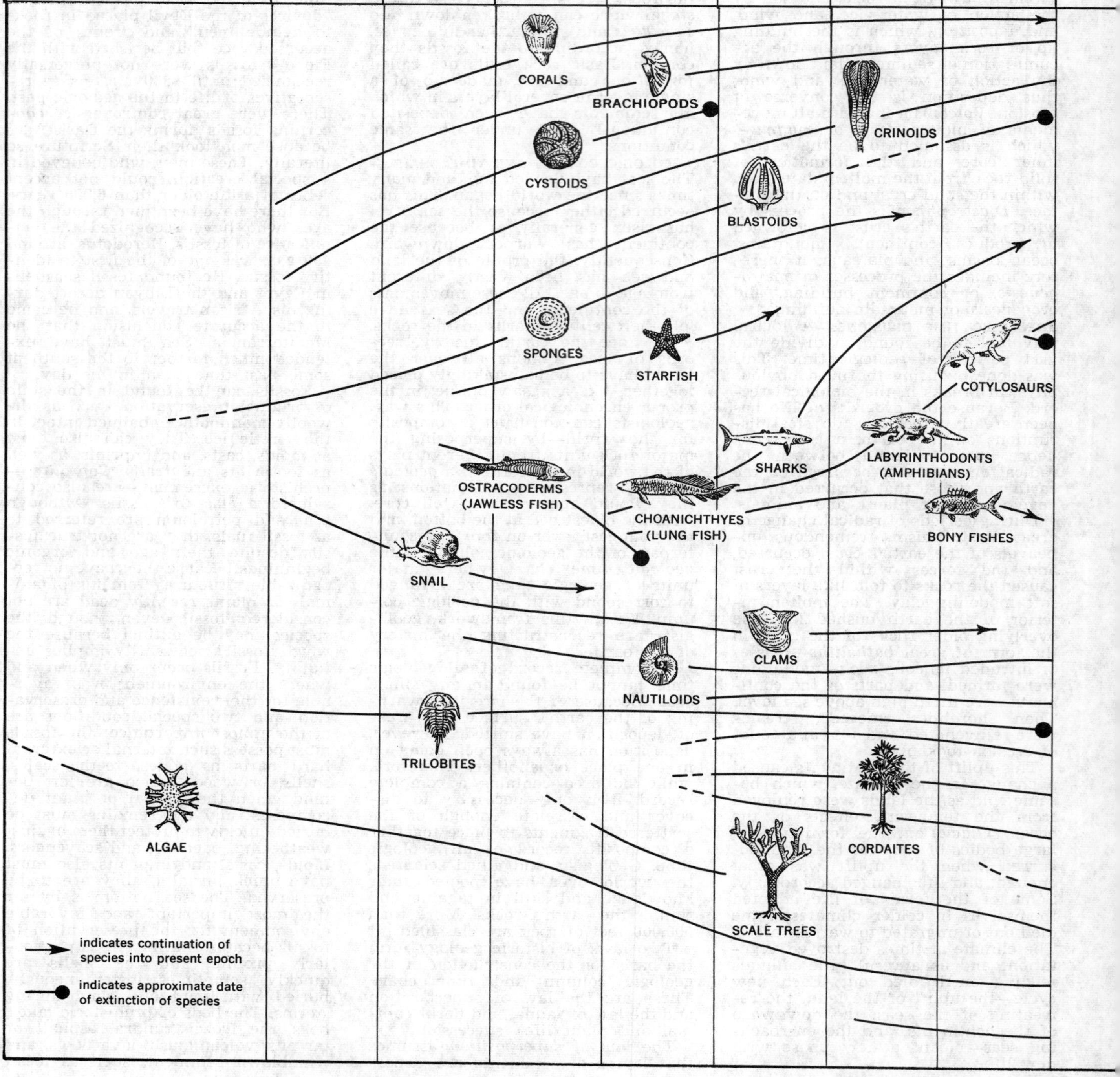

CORALS

BRACHIOPODS

CRINOIDS

CYSTOIDS

BLASTOIDS

SPONGES

STARFISH

COTYLOSAURS

SHARKS

LABYRINTHODONTS (AMPHIBIANS)

OSTRACODERMS (JAWLESS FISH)

CHOANICHTHYES (LUNG FISH)

BONY FISHES

SNAIL

CLAMS

NAUTILOIDS

TRILOBITES

CORDAITES

ALGAE

SCALE TREES

→ indicates continuation of species into present epoch

● indicates approximate date of extinction of species

"Time Of Visible Animal Life"										EON
MESOZOIC "Era Of Middle Life"			CENOZOIC "Era Of Recent Life"							ERA
TRIASSIC	JURASSIC	CRETACEOUS "Time Of Great Dying"	TERTIARY					QUATERNARY		PERIOD
			PALEOCENE	EOCENE	OLIGOCENE	MIOCENE "Golden Age Of Mammals"	PLIOCENE	PLEISTOCENE "The Ice Age"	RECENT	EPOCH
27	33	65	10	10	10	15	14	1	LATE ARCHEOLOGIC AND HISTORIC TIME	DURATION (Millions of Years)
185	158	125	60	50	40	30	15	1		BEGAN Millions of Years Ago

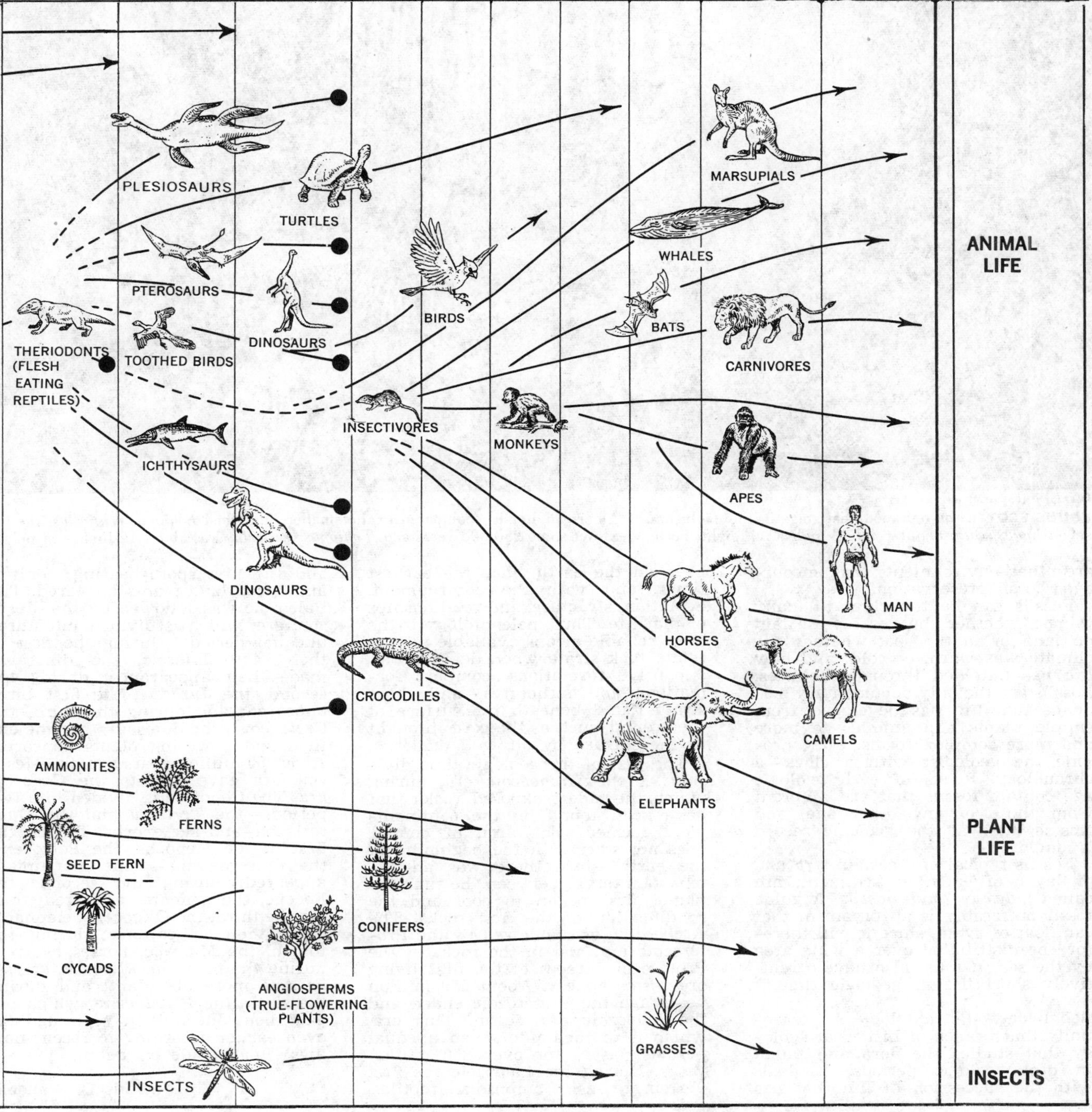

PLESIOSAURS

TURTLES

PTEROSAURS

DINOSAURS

THERIODONTS (FLESH EATING REPTILES)

TOOTHED BIRDS

BIRDS

MARSUPIALS

WHALES

BATS

CARNIVORES

INSECTIVORES

MONKEYS

APES

ICHTHYSAURS

DINOSAURS

HORSES

MAN

CROCODILES

CAMELS

AMMONITES

ELEPHANTS

FERNS

SEED FERN

CONIFERS

CYCADS

ANGIOSPERMS (TRUE-FLOWERING PLANTS)

GRASSES

INSECTS

ANIMAL LIFE

PLANT LIFE

INSECTS

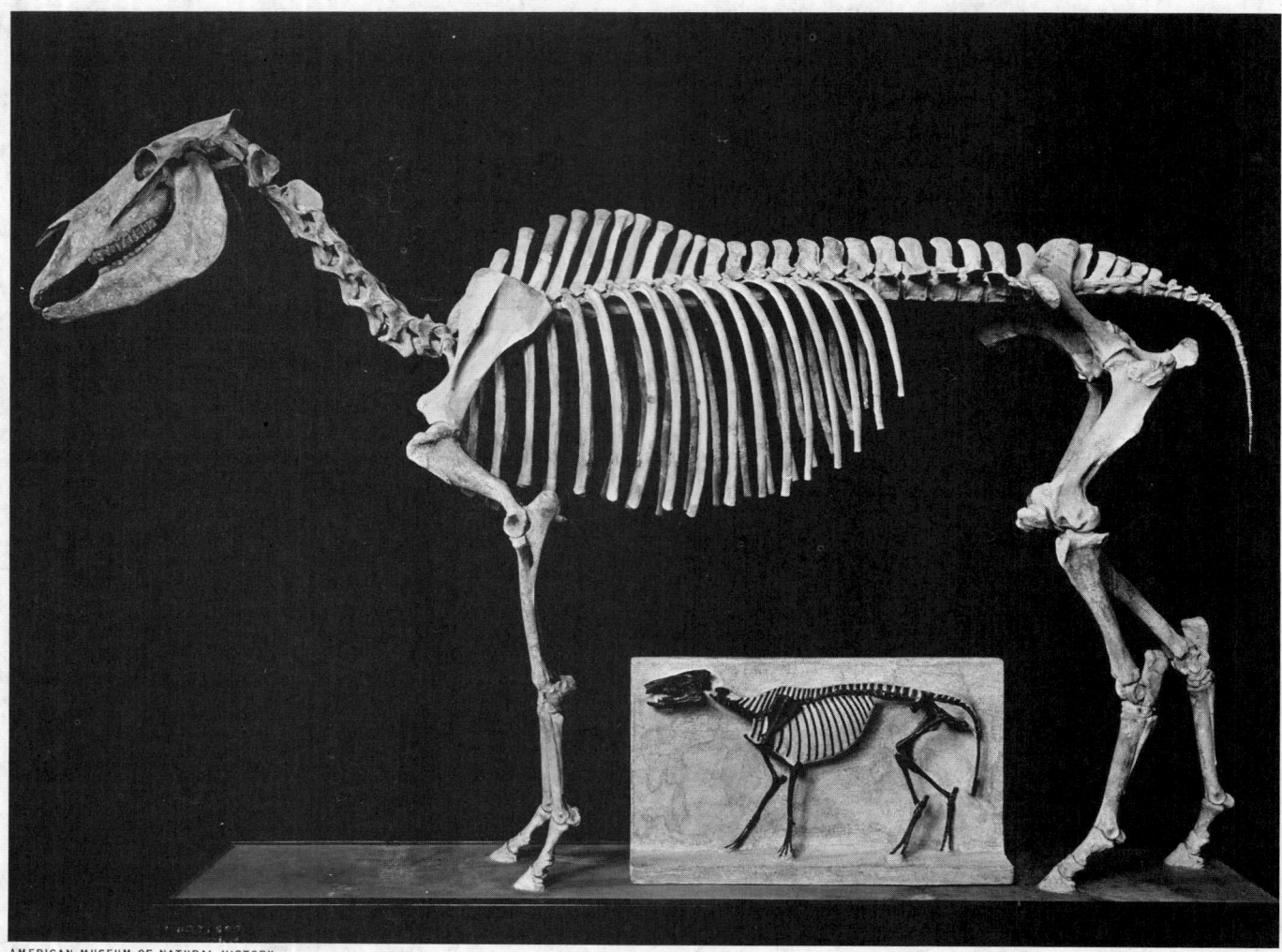

AMERICAN MUSEUM OF NATURAL HISTORY

EQUUS SCOTTI, the one-toed, last stage in the evolution of American horses, compared to the smaller, four-toed *Eohippus venticolus*, the first stage. *Equus scotti,* about 3 feet 9 inches in height, became extinct some 250,000 years ago. *Eohippus venticolus* was about 12 inches in height.

are other environments that encouraged fossil preservation.

Fossils can be the clues to many things: whether the rocks were laid on land or in the sea; whether the climate was warm or cold; and how life has unfolded through the ages. Fossils are the only documentary evidence that life has developed from simple plants and animals to more and more complex forms. They provide the geologist with a clock—a chronology. Rocks of each geologic age contain fossils that are different from those of any other age, and this is the way the geologic record is dated.

Fossils typical of a certain *stratum,* or layer of earth or sediment, are called *index* or *guide fossils.* A guide fossil preferably is an organism that can float or swim, since it will therefore be distributed over a wide area by the sea. It must also have a relatively short life in geologic time.

Paleontology.—*Paleontology* is essentially that branch of historical geology that studies the flora and fauna in past geologic periods. It deals with the succession of life that has

been on the earth since the earliest times, and with the environment, evolution, structure, and relationships of that life. Thus, paleontology is the most reliable means available to correlate rock strata when dealing with expansive formations, complex formations and structures, and those strata found beneath the surface of the ground, such as the cores brought to the surface by oil well drillers.

The first of the geologic time divisions is the *Archeozoic era,* during which the oldest exposed rocks that have been found on the continents were formed. This era, of course, does not start with the beginning of the earth, since there was an extensive interval between the time the planet first began to cool and the solidification of the first rocks. The Archeozoic was followed by the *Proterozoic era,* and in the rocks of the Proterozoic, traces of the first living organisms appear. About 550 million years ago the Proterozoic ended and the *Paleozoic era* began. This era, which is divided into seven unequal periods, lasted for over 350 million years. During the Paleozoic the first vertebrate fish, amphibia, reptiles,

and the first spore-bearing, conifer, and cycad land plants appeared. The Paleozoic was followed by the *Mesozoic era,* which is divided into three unequal periods. During the first of these, the *Triassic,* the dinosaurs made their appearance; during the second, the *Jurassic,* the first birds appeared; and during the third, the *Cretaceous,* the dinosaurs became extinct and flowering plants appeared. About 60 million years ago, the Mesozoic era gave way to the *Cenozoic era.* The Cenozoic is divided into two periods—the *Tertiary* and the *Quaternary*—and six epochs. During the first of these epochs, the *Paleocene,* the first mammals, the marsupials, appeared; during the second, the *Eocene,* the primates appeared; during the third, the *Oligocene,* elephants made their appearance; during the fourth, the *Miocene,* horses evolved; during the fifth, the *Pliocene,* grasses became more abundant; and during the sixth, the *Pleistocene,* which began about one million years ago (or even earlier according to recent datings), man made his debut.

—Doris D. Grandelis

ARABIAN AMERICAN OIL COMPANY

SCIENTIFIC OIL EXPLORATION in Saudi Arabia. A portable corer drills shallow holes in the desert floor and flushes rock fragments to the surface. Petroleum geologists study the rock fragments to learn whether, farther below, there is the type of strata that may contain oil.

ECONOMIC GEOLOGY

Scope.—The economic geologist is concerned with the mineral substances in the earth's crust that are necessary to man's survival and comfort. Only about 200 of the nearly 2,000 minerals that have been identified are of economic interest. The most important of these in today's economy are the mineral or fossil fuels, such as petroleum and coal. (Technically, these fuels are neither true minerals, since their composition cannot be expressed by a chemical formula, nor fossils, since they have no identifiable structure.) Economic geology deals not only with ores and mineral deposits, but also with the rocks that contain them—how the rocks were formed, their nature and structure, and the geological formations developed on them. An economic geologist uses all the principles and techniques of physical and historical geology.

Historical Development.—The early history of economic geology closely parallels that of mineralogy, since both sciences evolved from man's desire for ornamentation. One might say that economic geology, however, began when the first man used a rock to help him survive. The first known economic geologist was probably Haroeris—an Egyptian captain who led an expedition to the Sinai Peninsula around 2000 B.C. After prospecting for several months, Haroeris found and extracted large amounts of the semiprecious stone turquoise. The early Egyptians, the Greeks, and their various neighbors prized gems, gold, and silver highly for the ornamentation of their bodies, their homes, and their dead.

Mining as an industry began with the search for gems and decorative stones during the time when the Egyptian pharaohs were most powerful. Gems and ornaments were so much a part of religious belief in those days that they were considered a necessity of life. However, the gem minerals that were economically important at that time play only a minor role in our life today—they are our luxuries. At the conclusion of the Dark Ages, the chief mineral substances in use were iron, copper, lead, tin, gold, silver, mercury, precious stones, clay, and building stones—compared with more than 75 minerals traded internationally today. The chief minerals now are oil and gas, coal, iron ores, iron-alloy metals (chromium, manganese, molybdenum, nickel, tungsten, vanadium), nonferrous metals (copper, lead, zinc, tin, aluminum), the minor metals, metallurgical minerals, chemical minerals, ceramic materials, and abrasives. Gold is not considered as an industrial mineral because of its monetary value, but it plays an important part in affording means of purchasing needed mineral supplies.

Locating Minerals.—All the easy-to-find mineral deposits have already been exploited, and the search for new deposits has taken scientists to strange and hard-to-reach places, such as deep into the earth and far out over the oceans. One of the main jobs of the economic geologist is to use the principles of geology in searching for and helping to develop valuable mineral deposits. He also works with other scientists and technicians in finding new methods and developing new instruments that will aid in this search and lower production costs. In the future, such new techniques will help develop deposits that are considered too costly to exploit today.

The economic geologist has such powerful prospecting aids as the *seismograph,* a device for recording shock waves that travel through the earth, the airborne *magnetometer,* a device for measuring the strength and direction of magnetic forces, and the *gravity meter,* a device for detecting differences in gravitational attraction. He takes readings from these instruments, interprets them according to his knowledge of the geology of the area, and evaluates the results. From this information, he constructs a map of the geologic structures below the surface of the ground. Thus a geologist can select spots where economically exploitable mineral deposits are most likely to be found.

Mineral Products.—The principal mineral products in the United States, in order of value, are crude petroleum, coal, and natural gas—with petroleum contributing more than half of all the revenue received from the total mineral production. In 1963 about 3 billion barrels of crude oil were produced; at the wells, this quantity of oil was valued at $8.5 billion. In the same year, 19 million tons of anthracite (hard coal) were produced, with a value of $173 million, and 452 million tons of bituminous (soft coal) with a value of $2 billion. A ready yardstick to indicate the order of importance of mineral fuels in the American economy is the fact that three-fourths of the geologists in the United States are petroleum geologists, employed by oil companies in the search for oil and natural gas. The nation produces about half of the world's oil, and consumes some two-thirds of it. The greatest oil deposits are found in the Middle East. However, significant new discoveries of deposits in North Africa in recent years indicate that this, too, may become a major production region. Besides petroleum and coal, the nonmetallic minerals of economic value include cement materials, ceramic products, building stones, gems, and sulfur. The total value of these nonmetals (excluding fuels) in the United States in 1960 was $3.7 billion.

Metallic minerals include the industrial and precious metals—gold, copper, tin, lead, zinc, uranium, and a host of others. They produced a revenue of over $2 billion in the United States during 1960.

■**PETROLEUM.**—Petroleum is a complex mixture of gaseous, liquid, and solid hydrocarbons (compounds containing hydrogen and carbon). The consensus among geologists is that petroleum originated from marine plant and animal life that died and fell to the bottom of the shallow prehistoric seas. Here it decomposed as the result of bacterial action, yielding carbon and hydrogen. The residue was buried by sediments and subjected to further chemical change. Finally, the weight of the sediments squeezed the oil and gas into porous rocks, from which they eventually migrated to suitable reservoirs.

Four conditions are necessary for the formation of an oil deposit. First, a *source rock,* which contains the carbonaceous matter from which oil can be formed, must be present. The most common source rocks are marine bituminous shales. Next, there must be a *reservoir rock* in which the oil can collect. Sandstones are the most common reservoir rocks because they are porous and permeable—that is, they have connected pore spaces large enough to permit the oil to move through the rock. Limestones and dolomites are also important reservoir rocks. The third condition is a *structural* or *stratigraphic trap*—the rock strata must be arranged or deposited in such a way that there is a place where oil can collect in quantity. The simplest structure is an *anticline,* where the rock strata have been folded into the shape of an inverted soup bowl. This was the first type of trap recognized, but today more than a score of different traps are known. Finally, there must be an impervious layer called *cap rock*—generally shale or clay—that overlies the reservoir rock and seals in the oil.

■**COAL.**—Coal, another vitally important mineral fuel, is a compact mass of carbonized plant debris. It occurs in beds, which are usually sandwiched between layers of sandstone and shale. The great coal-making eras of geological history were the Mississippian and the Pennsylvanian periods, over 230 million years ago. During these periods, tropical climates and lush swamp vegetation encouraged great accumulations of vegetable matter, from which coal was later formed. Coal beds range in thickness from hardly more than a film to hundreds of feet. The grades of coal depend on the concentration of carbon, or how much of the volatile constituents of the carbonaceous mass have been driven off. The stages in coal formation are *peat, lignite* (brown coal), *bituminous* (soft coal), *anthracite* (hard coal), and under favorable conditions, *graphite.*

■**ORE DEPOSITS.**—Most ores (metal-bearing mineral deposits) are concentrations of metals brought about by igneous activity. *Magma,* the molten material underneath the surface of the earth from which the igneous rocks were formed, supplied the metals in the ore deposits. The metals were released from the magma at the time it solidified. Most deposits of metallic minerals are situated either in border zones of granite *batholiths* or *stocks,* or in the rocks immediately surrounding such intrusive masses.

However, other methods of concentration were also important. Iron ore deposits—iron is by far the most useful and abundant metal—were formed in more ways than deposits of any other metal. But the most important method was *sedimentation,* a process that has produced far larger accumulations of ore than any other process of concentration.

—Doris D. Grandelis

BIBLIOGRAPHY

AMERICAN GEOLOGICAL INSTITUTE. *Dictionary of Geological Terms.* Doubleday & Co., Inc., 1960.
COMPTON, ROBERT ROSS. *Manual of Field Geology.* John Wiley & Sons, Inc., 1962.
DUNBAR, CARL OWEN. *Historical Geology.* John Wiley & Sons, Inc., 1960.
LEET, LEWIS DON and F. J. (eds.). *World of Geology.* McGraw-Hill, Inc., 1961.
LONGWELL, CHESTER R. and FLINT, R. F. *Introduction to Physical Geology.* John Wiley & Sons, Inc., 1962.
MOORE, RUTH. *The Earth We Live On.* Alfred A. Knopf, Inc., 1956.
THOMPSON, HENRY DEWEY. *Fundamentals of Earth Science.* Appleton-Century-Crofts, 1960.

OCEANOGRAPHY

Scope.—The ocean is the most striking physical feature of our planet, covering over two-thirds of the globe's surface. Without the waters of the seas, there could be no life. Since earliest time, man has used the ocean as a highway, as a great moat to protect him from enemies, as a source of food, and as a final resting place. Only recently, however, has man begun to delve deeply into the sea to learn its secrets.

Oceanography is an environmental science encompassing the study of all processes in the ocean and its boundaries. It includes the study of plant and animal life at all depths (*biological oceanography,* or *marine biology*); the study of the origin of the ocean, its structure, and its bottom sediments (*geological oceanography,* or *marine geology*); the study of sea water and its composition (*chemical oceanography*); the study of currents, tides, waves, temperature, salinity, density, and the general circulation of the sea (*physical oceanography*); the study of the food, mineral, and energy sources of the sea and the uses of the ocean for recreation, navigation, communication, and war (*marine technology*).

The Oceans.—Billions of years ago the earth was a lifeless planet plummeting through the darkness of space. As the mass of gases and molten metals cooled, water was squeezed from its interior. The planet became a world unique, as far as we know, in the entire solar system: it was covered with an ocean.

■**ORIGIN OF LIFE.**—For millions of years the sterile waves lapped against the cold, dead shores. Then, through a series of processes whose nature is still unknown, matter developed and finally became organized into a living cell capable of reproducing itself.

There is no way of knowing what this first life was like, or what the conditions were that produced it. Chances are that some of the earliest organisms were similar to the single-celled plants still found in the surface layers of the ocean. These contain chlorophyll, the substance that enables plants to utilize the energy of sunlight to produce organic material from water and carbon dioxide. Through this process, known as *photosynthesis,* the oxygen of the earth's atmosphere was created from the water in the ocean.

Over the countless generations, spanning millions of years, differences developed among the single-celled organisms. Some preyed on others, so organisms evolved different methods of finding food and of escaping from being eaten; in response to changing conditions they developed different tolerances and sensitivities to light and to chemical variations. Eventually, life in the sea made the jump from simple individual cells to complicated, highly specialized plants and animals.

■**CURRENTS.**—Only recently has man known anything of the internal movements of the sea. The movement of

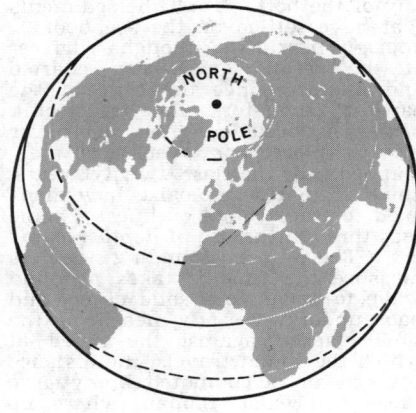
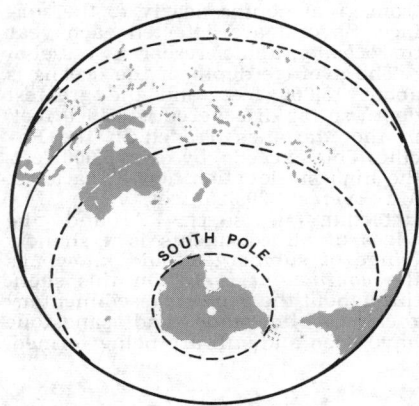

OCEANS, covering two-thirds of the earth, are our most striking physical feature.

water on the surface has been charted, but not the currents that flow beneath the surface. Now, however, through new techniques of measuring natural radioactivity, heat flow, and salt content, and by taking direct measurements of deep currents, a new picture of the ocean's circulation is being revealed.

Along with the horizontal currents in the ocean, there is a constant vertical motion. Practically nothing is known of this vertical movement, but it is vital to life in the sea, since it is the chief process by which the surface waters are constantly supplied with the nutrients required by the *phytoplankton,* the microscopic plants and animals without which no life could exist in the ocean.

Origin of Oceanography. — When man first ventured onto the sea to travel from one place to another, he began to navigate. He found that waves and currents would either help or hinder him in reaching his destination. He noticed that the tidal movements were greatest at certain times of the month, and he saw a correlation between the tidal movements and the moon phases. Going to the sea in search of food, he learned that certain types of bottoms were apt to harbor certain kinds of fishes, mollusks, or

crustaceans. As he became conscious of these things and began to search into their causes and relationships, he became, in essence if not in name, a student of oceanography.

The study of oceanography is as important today to navigation and shipping as it was to primitive seagoing man. Today oceanographic knowledge is vital not only to ships traveling on the surface of the sea, but also to craft that travel under the sea and in the air above. Information about currents, tides, and temperatures is necessary in both peacetime and wartime navigation and shipping, as are further studies of the strange behavior of sound and light under water. And today, more than ever before, knowledge of the ocean's circulation is of prime importance—for the sea may be the only place on earth where man can safely store nuclear waste products.

History of Oceanography.—Oceanography as a science began fairly recently. In 1750 the first scientific dredge was invented by Marsigli and Donati; a few years later, in 1769, Benjamin Franklin published the first chart of the Gulf Stream. During the following decade Captain James Cook, in his explorations of the Pacific, took a naturalist along to make observations and to record data. During Cook's second voyage, the first subsurface water temperatures were taken and were found to differ markedly from temperatures on the surface. On this voyage, too, some deep-water soundings were made, and a sample of blue mud was brought up from a depth of 683 fathoms.

■**DARWIN.**—It later became customary to take a trained naturalist on long survey or exploratory voyages. Charles Darwin's around-the-world voyage on the H.M.S. *Beagle* from 1831 to 1836 was one of the first purely scientific voyages. On this trip Darwin's two great theories were developed: the theory of natural selection and the less revolutionary but oceanographically more important theory of the origin of coral reefs.

■**MAURY.**—The first textbook on the subject of oceanography, entitled *The Physical Geography of the Sea,* appeared in 1855. The author, Matthew Fontaine Maury (1806–1873), was an American naval officer who was forced by an accident to retire from sea duty. He compiled and analyzed material from ships' logs; and the wind and current charts he drew from them soon became well-known throughout the world and greatly shortened sailing times between the continents. With the aid of a new sounding apparatus that employed a detachable weight, data were obtained from which Maury prepared the first bathymetric chart of the region of the North Atlantic.

■**THOMPSON** —Until a century ago, most marine scientists believed the depths of the ocean to be utterly devoid of life. The absolute limit of life was thought to be about 300 fathoms. In 1860, however, the transatlantic cable, laid only two years before, was broken. Upon being brought up from a depth of 1,000 fathoms, it was found to be encrusted with living organisms, including a deep-sea coral. Subsequently Wyville Thompson made a series of deep hauls in North Atlantic waters—to a maximum depth of 2,435 fathoms—and in every case the dredge brought up living organisms.

The stage was now set for the first world-wide scientific investigation of the oceans. In 1872 Thompson's book, *The Depths of the Sea,* was published, and it stimulated the scientific world to renewed interest in the deep sea. In the same year the 2,000-ton British corvette H.M.S. *Challenger* embarked on a 70,000-mile voyage through the Atlantic, Pacific, and Indian oceans for the purpose of learning "everything about the sea." During the next three and a half years the *Challenger* scientists, under the direction of Wyville Thompson, and his assistant John Murray, collected animals at great depths, settling for all time the dispute over whether or not the depths are inhabited. Altogether they described a total of 4,417 new species of plants and animals. The *Challenger* expedition occupied 362 oceanographic stations and collected 77 water samples for total chemical analysis. Papers and reports of the voyage filled 50 volumes and required 20 years to complete. This mass of data, and the wide range of the samples collected, were vitally important to the development of modern oceanographic theory.

Geological Oceanography.—The marine geologist is interested in the structure of the ocean basins, the topography of the bottom, and the sediments that have settled on the sea floor.

■**OCEAN DEPTHS.**—Although surfaces of the oceans have been charted and mapped since the time of the earliest navigators, the great bulk of the vast oceanic depths have never been explored or even accurately mapped. In the last twenty years, however, marine geologists have managed to trace rough outlines of some seas through the use of *depth recorders.* These echo-sounding devices measure the time it takes a sound wave to travel to a solid object and back under water. By measuring the time elapsed against the speed at which the sound travels, the distance covered can be computed. Many large areas still exist, though, where no soundings have been made, and precipitous peaks still unknown may rise from great depths nearly to the surface. Several are detected each year by oceanographic research vessels.

The average depth of the oceans is about 13,000 feet, and the greatest depth so far discovered is 35,640 feet, in the Marianas Trench in the Pacific. This exceeds, by over 6,000 feet, the highest elevation above sea level, Mt. Everest, 29,025 feet.

■**CONTINENTAL SHELF.** — Around the edges of all continents is a shallow fringe of submerged land known as the *continental shelf.* On this shelf, throughout the ages, such sedimentary rocks as limestone and sandstone have been and still are being formed.

The continental shelf averages about 30 miles in width along most continents, although in some parts of Siberia it extends to 800 miles and along mountainous coasts it diminishes to almost nothing. The shelf is not a smooth, flat surface but is broken up into terraces, ridges, and hills. Beyond the shelf, at a depth of about 600 feet, a more precipitous drop occurs. This is known as the *continental slope,* and it continues downward to the bottom of the sea—two or three miles, on the average. The deepest spots in the ocean, the ocean *trenches,* are found at the bottoms of the continental slopes.

It is not known why all continents should rise so sharply from the sea floor. Some scientists feel that such straight slopes indicate a geological event of great violence, such as a wrenching apart of the continents. Most authorities, however, believe that the continental slopes are a result of some slow evolutionary process of the earth itself. Within the continental shelf and slopes are found great canyons similar to deep-cut river valleys, some as large as the Grand Canyon.

■**OCEAN FLOOR.**—The floor of the sea is quite different from the surface of the land. One reason is that the lack of erosion caused by wind, rain, and ice has preserved the submerged peaks, valleys, and canyons nearly in their original crisp outlines—just as the face of the moon has not been changed by weathering.

■**SEAMOUNTS.**—All ocean basins have a mid-ocean rise and a range of moun-

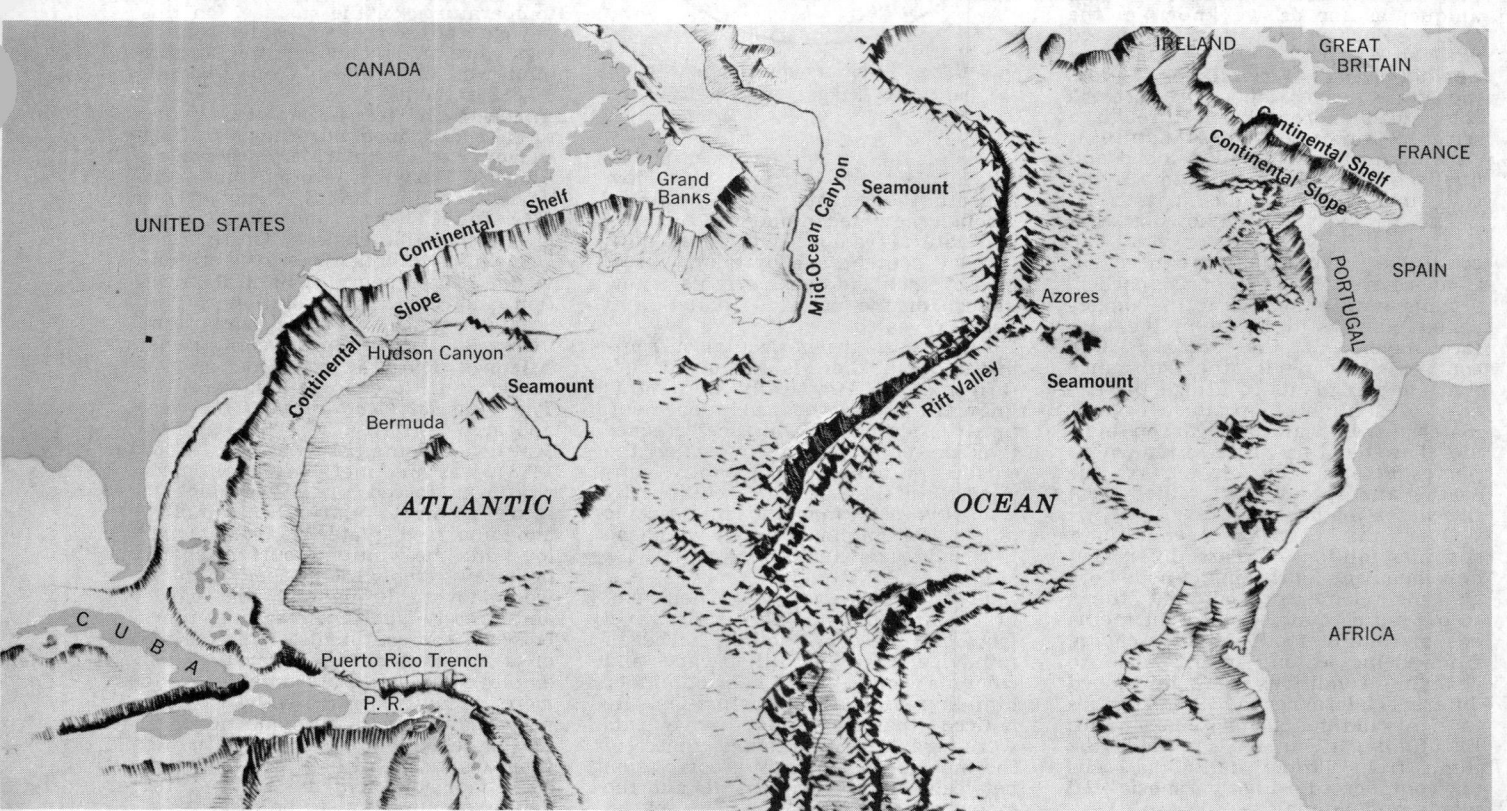

RELIEF OF THE OCEAN FLOOR. The floors of the oceans have their own valleys, mountains, and plains. Until recently, these regions could not be mapped. Today, scientists are discovering new regions at the ocean's bottom. Notice the 10,000-mile-long Mid-Atlantic Ridge.

tains down the middle. Thousands of volcanic peaks called *seamounts* dot the ocean floor. A comparative few of these peaks reach the surface to form islands, such as the Hawaiian chain in the Pacific or the Azores in the Atlantic. Many of the drowned peaks are the foundations of coral atolls, with the dead remains of reef-building corals and calcareous algae extending sometimes thousands of feet downward to the submerged peak. Since reef corals grow only in well-lighted waters (to a maximum depth of about 180 feet), a dead coral cap several thousand feet thick suggests that the atoll's base sank slowly over many thousands of years or, alternatively, that the waters rose slowly while the growth of corals kept pace with the rising water.

Many seamounts are flat on top, their peaks cut off at depths of 2,000 to 6,000 feet below the ocean's surface. These flattened seamounts are called *tablemounts* or *guyots*. Evidently they were flattened by erosion at some period in the past when they were islands. Since the tops of these tablemounts are found at various levels, it is unlikely that they were decapitated by a succession of great rises and falls of sea level. A more likely explanation is that they sank with the collapse of the earth's crust under their tremendous weight.

■SEDIMENT.—Much of the ocean floor is covered with a layer of sediment that has, in undisturbed regions, been accumulating for hundreds of millions of years. This sediment contains a record of the earth's early history. Layers of volcanic ash are there, telling of great eruptions; ice-scarred stones from glaciers; and the remains of multitudinous planktonic plants and animals. Hollow tubes, or *corers*, are pushed into the sea floor to withdraw cross sections of the sedimentary carpet. An examination of the types of shells and other materials in these cores reveals the climatic variations of the past, and, by deduction, much information about the early evolution of life. Since some species of ancient marine life lived only in cold waters and others flourished in temperate or tropical waters, the sequence of fossils tells a great deal about sea temperatures and productivity millions of years ago.

Of primary importance in geological research into sediment components is the determination of their specific origin. All sediments can be divided into three different groups according to their mode and place of origin. The first group is composed of material having its origin on land, such as soil, clay, and unweathered rock fragments. The second is made up of material formed in the ocean by inorganic precipitation. To this group belong some clays, manganese nodules, and other components of crystalline and gel consistency. The third group consists of organic material formed in the ocean, such as skeletons and other remains of animal and plant life. In addition to these sources, which account for most of the material, outer space contributes very tiny spherules of nickel-iron, remnants of meteorites.

By a careful study of the composition of the sediments, the relationship of the different components to one another, the shape of the particles, their chemical composition, their grain, their size, and their color, oceanographers can trace their origin and mode of transport before they were buried in the scientist's great treasure trove—the ocean floor.

There are several means by which sediments are transported to the ocean. The finest dust can be blown long distances from the land; thus desert sand is found 2,000 miles from Africa in the Atlantic Ocean. Soil particles transported from North Africa across the Mediterranean may settle in rain on Germany, causing the landscape to be colored red. In many places on the ocean floor, the inorganic material consists nearly entirely of wind-transported matter.

The ocean currents also play a part. Their speed is much slower than the wind speed; on the other hand, the particles settle much more slowly in water than in air. Consequently, they may be carried across the ocean before they settle to the bottom. The greatest quantity of sediment, however, settles on the continental shelf. There is evidence that on occasion large quantities of this unconsolidated material slide off the shelf and down the continental slope to the sea floor, spreading over large areas. Such large-scale movements, known as *turbidity currents*, may have played a part in forming the great canyons found in the continental slopes.

Chemical Oceanography. — The water that makes up the ocean probably had two sources. Some came as rain from the gases surrounding the earth; some from the earth's interior, forced from the rocks as they recrystallized to form the crust. Water is still being released from the interior of the earth through volcanic eruptions.

■SEA WATER.—Analyses of 77 water samples taken on the around-the-world cruise of H.M.S. *Challenger* established two vitally important properties of sea water: the *salinity*, or total content of salts, in sea water varies only slightly throughout the world; and, even where variations do exist, the relative quantity of the major dissolved salts remains constant. This property, known as the *constancy of relative proportions*, helps determine the salinity of water.

The major constituents of sea-water salts are sodium, chlorine, magnesium, sulfur, calcium, and potassium. In addition, sea water contains traces of all natural elements. Unlike the major constituents, these trace elements are found in widely differing proportions in different places and at different times. Studies of the concentrations of trace elements aid in understanding life processes in the ocean. Perhaps the appearance or

SEDIMENTS found on the ocean's floor are composed of many organic materials. When more than 30 per cent is composed of dead plant and animal life, it is called an *ooze*. Globigerina ooze covers more than 45 per cent of the ocean's floor.

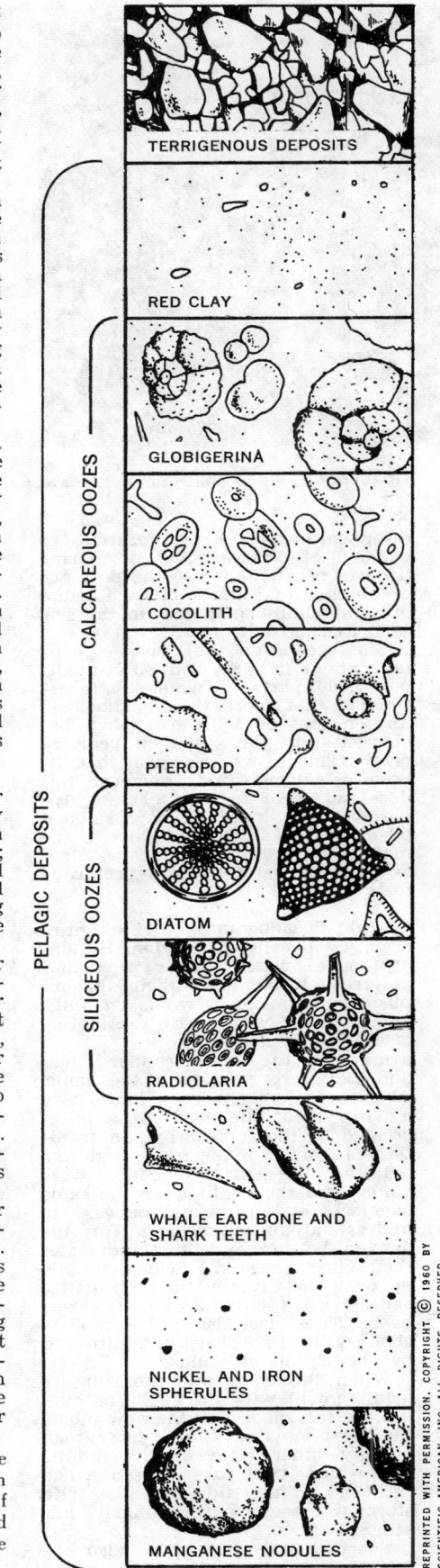

TERRIGENOUS DEPOSITS

RED CLAY

GLOBIGERINA

COCOLITH

PTEROPOD

CALCAREOUS OOZES

DIATOM

RADIOLARIA

SILICEOUS OOZES

PELAGIC DEPOSITS

WHALE EAR BONE AND SHARK TEETH

NICKEL AND IRON SPHERULES

MANGANESE NODULES

REPRINTED WITH PERMISSION. COPYRIGHT © 1960 BY SCIENTIFIC AMERICAN, INC. ALL RIGHTS RESERVED.

CANADIAN NATIONAL RAILWAYS

TIDAL BORE sweeps upstream as a wave.

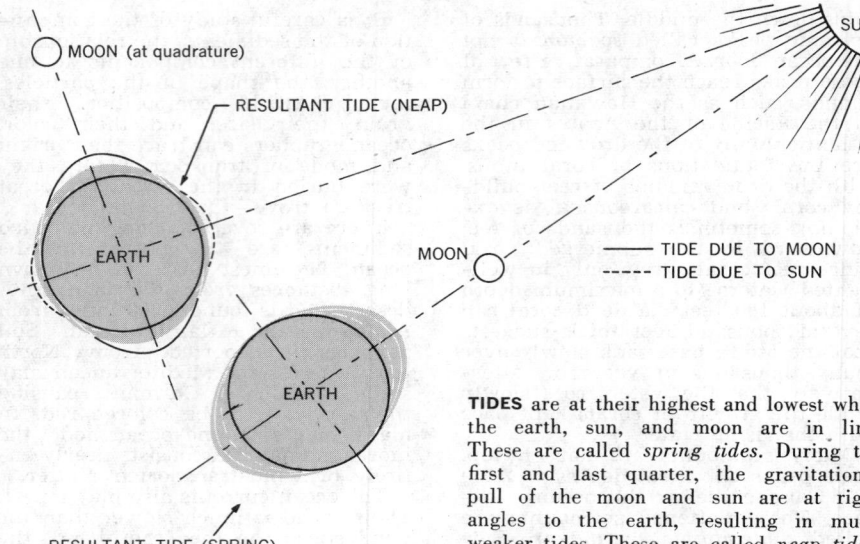

MOON (at quadrature)

RESULTANT TIDE (NEAP)

EARTH

MOON

SUN

TIDE DUE TO MOON
TIDE DUE TO SUN

EARTH

RESULTANT TIDE (SPRING)

TIDES are at their highest and lowest when the earth, sun, and moon are in line. These are called *spring tides*. During the first and last quarter, the gravitational pull of the moon and sun are at right angles to the earth, resulting in much weaker tides. These are called *neap tides*.

disappearance—the proliferation or decline—of certain kinds of marine life can be attributed to the presence or absence of some substance found only in minute quantities in the sea, such as iron or copper.

The ocean, on the average, contains about 35 parts of dissolved salts per 1,000 parts of water. It is estimated that more than a thousand million tons of salts are being discharged into the sea each year by rivers. Thus, it would appear that the ocean is getting saltier; however, this does not seem to be the case. Apparently the input of new salts is offset by the amount of salts in the materials deposited on the sea floor as sediments and by spray returned to the land.

Physical Oceanography. — The entire ocean is in constant motion. Billions of tons of water course in various patterns throughout their basins, pushed and pulled by winds, currents, and tides, as well as by the motion of the earth itself.
■TIDES.—To the oceanographer waves and tides are physically the same. A tide is merely a very long wave moving about the earth as a bulge created on the surface by the gravitational forces of the moon and sun.

If all the earth's surface were water, and the depth were the same everywhere, tides would be easy to understand and to predict. But the uneven bottom and the landmasses themselves cause the waves to pile up or to be diverted in their paths, setting up oscillations in enclosed bays. Tides are also influenced by changes in atmospheric pressure and by the action of winds.

When the moon and the sun are in alignment with the earth, as during the full moon and the new moon, the tidal movement is greater than at any other time of the month. Extra-high tides are caused when the time of high tide coincides with storm winds and extraordinarily low atmospheric pressure.

Spectacular tides can also be caused when a large standing wave

arrives at the same time as a high tide. When the tide in some areas rises high enough to move against a river, it may sweep upstream as a thundering wave called a *tidal bore*. Tidal bores occur at certain rivers in Europe, North America, South America, and Asia. One of the best known is that which occurs in the Petitcodiac River in the Bay of Fundy.
■WAVES.—There are two basic kinds of waves: standing waves and progressive waves. A *standing wave* moves back and forth in a confined space, its speed and size determined by the size and depth of the bay or estuary where it moves. A *progressive wave*, on the other hand, moves across an open area. In neither case do the particles of water themselves move very much. They may move in the arc of a pendulum, or they may travel in a circular motion, but they move very little horizontally.

This motion is the same in all waves, from the smallest ripple to the greatest ocean roller. The highest point in a wave is the *crest,* and the

lowest is the *trough;* the *height* is measured by the distance between these two points. The *length* is the distance from one crest to that of the following wave, while the *period* of a wave is the time it takes to pass a given point. In the open ocean, waves higher than 25 feet are rare, although waves of 60 and perhaps even 100 feet have been reported in the great unbroken expanses of the Pacific and Antarctic oceans.

The great waves commonly known as *tidal waves,* but more accurately called *tsunamis,* are of seismic, not tidal, origin. Caused by geological disturbances on the sea floor, a tsunami wave is hardly noticeable at sea, but it may pile up to form tremendous crests on striking shore. Hawaii and Japan have suffered many devastating tsunamis. The speed of a tsunami wave is very great and is determined by the ocean depth.

Not all ocean waves are on the surface; the sea has internal waves as well. These waves develop on the interfaces between layers of dif-

EWING GALLOWAY

TIDAL WAVES are caused by earthquakes, not by tides. They are most common in the Pacific.

ferent density and are usually larger than surface waves, although they move more slowly. The existence of these waves has only recently been determined, largely because of their effect on submarines; and much more is still to be learned about their formation and movements.

■CURRENTS.—Surface currents of water are driven mainly by winds. Each hemisphere has three similar wind zones. Along the equator and extending north and south for some 30 degrees of latitude, the wind blows from the east. For the next 30 degrees, the wind is primarily from the west. Nearer the poles, the wind comes from the east again. The prevailing winds—equatorial easterlies and middle latitude westerlies—impart a clockwise circulation to the surface waters of the North Pacific and North Atlantic and counterclockwise circulation of waters of the South Pacific and South Atlantic.

Where the wind blows steadily in the same direction the water mass, on the average, tends to move away at an angle 90 degrees to the right of the wind direction in the Northern Hemisphere and 90 degrees to the left in the Southern Hemisphere. The surface moves at 45 degrees. This angle of difference increases with depth. This effect, known as the *Ekman transport*, can produce upwellings when winds blow parallel to coastlines. As warm surface water is pushed away from a coast, colder water from underneath takes its place. The Ekman transport also creates *eddies*, or circular movements of water, such as the Sargasso Sea.

The direction of the ocean currents, as well as the great vertical movements in the sea, are determined as well by the differences in the temperature of the water. All parts of the ocean are layered, with the warmer water at the surface. Deep water is always close to the freezing point, even at the equator. In tropical and temperate regions, the upper warmer layers tend to stay on top because they are lighter than the cold, deeper water. Near the poles, however, the surface layers are cooled by the frigid air, become heavy, and tend to sink underneath warmer layers. They then move in the direction of the equator.

Water flows toward areas of lower pressure. Cold water weighs more than warm water, and the higher the salinity, the greater the weight. A horizontal movement of water results as the water flows down a horizontal pressure gradient. As water flows from a high-pressure area to a low-pressure area, it follows a curved path. This curving path is caused by the rotation of the earth and is known as the *Coriolis force*. This phenomenon causes the paths of objects moving in the Northern Hemisphere to turn to the right, and those in the Southern Hemisphere to turn to the left.

Biological Oceanography.—It is almost certain that life began in the sea, for all animal phyla on earth have members living in the marine environment. Furthermore, the body

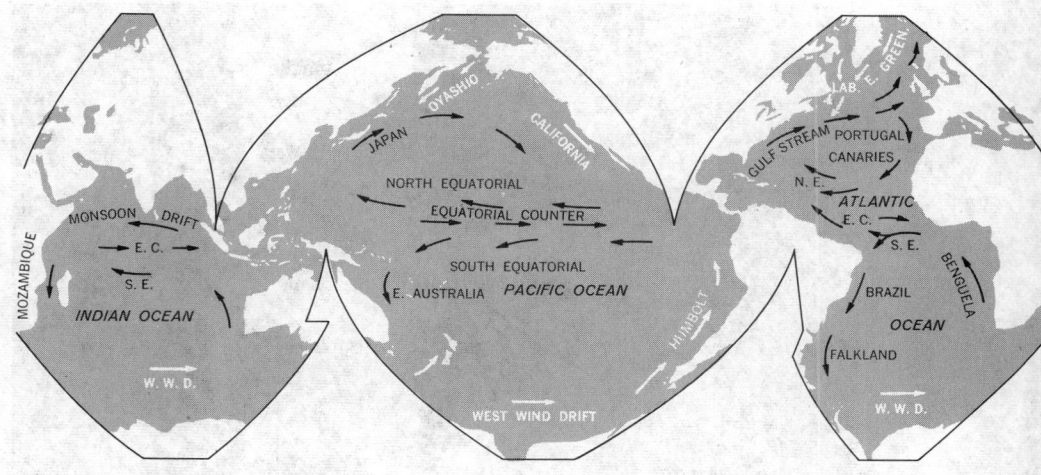

SURFACE CIRCULATION of the world's oceans is controlled mainly by winds. The flow is in a clockwise direction in the Northern Hemisphere and a counterclockwise direction in the Southern Hemisphere. The cooler surface currents are indicated with white arrows.

fluids of even the land animals are similar to the salty liquid known as sea water. Human blood, for example, is a saline solution that has many of the properties of sea water.

■PLANKTON.—All living organisms are either plants or animals. The tiny plants that drift free in the ocean are known as *phytoplankton*. "Phyto" means 'plants,' and "plankton" is from the Greek *planktos*, meaning 'wandering.' Since all plant life depends on sunlight, and sunlight penetrates only to about 600 feet, all chains of life in the sea are linked to the tiny organisms of the upper layers.

Plankton can be defined as those animals and plants that are carried by currents. Since they either drift without independent movement or swim weakly, they cannot move against the current.

The *diatoms* are among the most important forms of life in the sea. These single-celled plants are composed of two shells of silica that fit together like a box with a lid. Other forms of phytoplankton are the *dinoflagellates*, microscopic plants that swim about by beating appendages called flagella.

Mixed with the plants in the upper layers are the planktonic animals that are known collectively as *zooplankton*. Smallest and simplest of these are the *protozoa,* single-celled creatures of a wide diversity of form that feed on the single-celled plants and are themselves eaten by larger and more complex planktonic animals, for instance, the copepods, worms, jellyfish, crabs, mollusks, and the larval forms of fishes.

The surface waters of the colder seas hold prodigious quantities of plankton, which furnish food for the great schools of mackerel and herring, the sea birds, and even the herds of baleen whales that subsist on planktonic crustaceans known as krill. This abundance of plant and animal life is made possible by the mineral richness of the colder waters rising from deeper layers.

But while it is evident that the cool waters support more food, the

warmer seas show a much greater diversity of forms. While an area like the Grand Banks of Newfoundland might hold schools of millions of cod and haddock and support a great fishery, a coral atoll might hold thousands of species of marine animals but relatively few of any one species. The reason for this is that life cycles are speeded up in tropical waters; hence a greater number of genetic differences show up.

■NEKTON.—The term *nekton* covers the free-swimming creatures that are largely independent of tides, currents, and waves. This group includes most marine fishes, from the tiny sardines to the great whale sharks, which may exceed 50 feet in length. Also among nektonic creatures are the animals of the middle depths, those perpetually black regions thousands of feet down, inhabited by bizarre lantern fish and other grotesque creatures with luminous organs, cavernous mouths, and rapierlike teeth. Here there is no light, and no plants grow. All life must subsist on other living creatures or on the remains of dead animals and plants sifting down from the surface. Most creatures in the middle regions are small, but here are also found the giant squid and the massive sperm whale that pursues the squid in prodigious breath-holding dives of 2,000 feet or more.

■BENTHOS.—The *benthic* animals, the dwellers of the sea floor, are, in many cases, almost identical to bottom forms found in shallow water. There are brittle stars, sea cucumbers, sea spiders, crustaceans, flounderlike fishes, and others that would not look greatly out of place on any tidal flat. On the floor of the ocean, the pressure is thousands of pounds per cubic inch, but it is so evenly distributed throughout the bodies of these creatures that they feel no pressure at all. Except for certain animals with air spaces in their bodies (such as many fishes that have air bladders), the deep-water creatures can be raised from the greatest depths to the surface without injury due to changes in pressure.

AUSTRALIAN NEWS AND INFORMATION BUREAU

MARINE LIFE occurs in many forms, from the smallest one-celled animal to the largest living earth creature, the whale. Very common are the many varieties of coral (*above*) that abound in all oceans. A more familiar sea mammal, the porpoise (*above right*), leaps high above the water. Some sea creatures are as deadly as they are beautiful. The Portuguese man-of-war (*below left*) is also known as the "cobra of the sea" because of its poisonous sting. Fish, such as these mullet (*below center*), are a food source for many people. The tiny rotifers (*below right*) are consumed by the larger sea animals.

MARINE LABORATORY, UNIVERSITY OF MIAMI

AMERICAN MUSEUM OF NATURAL HISTORY

GENERAL ELECTRIC RESEARCH LABORATORY

ARTIFICIAL GILL extracts air from the water but prevents the passage of the liquid.

■**TAXONOMY.**—Biological oceanography takes many forms. Most early students were primarily taxonomists who collected, pickled, classified, and described organisms. Many an outstanding authority on a certain group never saw a living member of that group. Now that the kinds of organisms found in the sea have become better known, biologists have begun to study these animals and plants as living organisms, not as museum specimens. Today studies are made in the undisturbed natural habitats of organisms, wherever possible.

Such environmental studies have been given great impetus by the development of undersea research vehicles and by SCUBA (Self-Contained Underwater Breathing Apparatus). With SCUBA, almost any scientist can become a diver and observe marine life in its own habitat. Many shallow-water studies, in fact, are being made with no more than a diving mask and a pair of flippers.

■**MARINE ECOLOGY.**—With this new ease of penetration into the sea—or at least into the upper sunlit layers—the scientific discipline known as *marine ecology* is coming into its own.

Ecology, or environmental biology, can be defined as a study of organisms in relation to their environment; it is the study of the interrelationships of individuals and groups. There are many different approaches to ecology, of course. One biologist may be interested in the ecology of a particular taxonomic group—for example, fishes, crustaceans, worms—or even a single species of one of these. Others may be interested in pelagic, benthic, littoral, or coral reef ecology, and yet others in communities or populations. One kind of ecologist may be interested in *function,* the things that animals and plants do. The study of animal *behavior* is still in its infancy, especially as applied to marine animals, but several long-range projects are now under way.

Marine Technology.—Marine scientists and technicians are using the tools and techniques of the oceanographer to harvest many of the resources of the sea. Offshore drilling rigs in the Gulf of Mexico tap reservoirs of oil beneath the sea floor, while prospectors with aqualungs and dredges are bringing up diamonds from the continental shelf off Africa. The use of recorded mating sounds to attract food fishes to nets is under experiment by some fishing fleets. Another technological invention transferred from land is undersea television, which is in use as an important oceanographic research aid and also as a tool of the fishing and communications industries. Even the water of the sea and the·invisible plankton that inhabit it are being put to man's service. Modern plants now extract magnesium from sea water, and new and cheaper methods are being developed for producing fresh water from the sea. Eventually we will find a way to utilize directly the vast supply of protein-rich plankton.

Researchers are working on ways to reduce the devastation of hurricanes and the perennial damage caused by beach erosion and by shipworms, barnacles, and other ocean pests. Investigators seek safe, clean methods of disposing of industrial, human, and atomic wastes and of coping with increased oil pollution.

From a military standpoint, our greatest problem of national defense is an oceanographic one. More effective methods of communication under water must be found—from submarine to submarine and from submarine to surface craft and airplanes—and of detecting and destroying enemy submarines in time of war. Radar and radio cannot be used under water, so all detection and communications systems in the sea involve the use of sound.

The unknown regions and untapped resources of the sea present one of the greatest challenges to man's ingenuity and daring. As new methods of oceanic exploration are devised and made safer, and more maneuverable craft descend for longer periods into the ocean depths, men will finally return to the seas from which they came, to explore, to work, and perhaps even to live in the last mysterious frontier regions of the earth.

—Friedrich Frans Koczy

BIBLIOGRAPHY

BASCOM, WILLARD. *Waves and Beaches.* Anchor Books, 1964.
CARRINGTON, RICHARD. *Biography of the Sea.* Basic Books, Inc., 1960.
COWEN, ROBERT C. *Frontiers of the Sea.* Doubleday & Co., Inc., 1960.
KING, CUCHLAINE AUDREY MURIEL. *Introduction to Oceanography.* McGraw-Hill, Inc., 1963.
MAURY, MATTHEW FONTAINE. *The Physical Geography of the Sea.* Edited by John Leighly. Harvard University Press, 1963.
WALFORD, LIONEL ALBERT. *Living Resources of the Sea.* The Ronald Press Co., 1958.

STANDARD OIL COMPANY, NEW JERSEY

WEALTH FROM THE SEA. The vast mineral reserves stored beneath the ocean's floor are only now being tapped. Here, an oil derrick is being set up in the Gulf of Mexico.

METEOROLOGY

Meteorology is the science of the atmosphere. The *meteorologist* deals with atmospheric processes. Although the meteorologist is often thought of as one who forecasts weather conditions, there is much more to meteorology than weather forecasting. Some meteorologists, for instance, are concerned only with the effects of the atmosphere on the flight of missiles and satellites. Some deal with atmospheric processes as they affect the health and behavior of plants, animals, and human beings. Other meteorologists work with weather conditions as they influence the operations of specific businesses and industries, and still others concern themselves entirely with seeking ways to modify and control the weather. These are only a few of the studies that make up the science of meteorology. In essence, the goal of the meteorologist is to be able to describe and predict the atmosphere's behavior. The first step is to learn everything possible about the properties of the air in which we live.

Historical Background.—The early attempts at weather forecasting related the condition of the surroundings, or the appearance of certain objects, to particular types of future weather. This type of weather prediction dates back to at least 700 B.C., when the Assyrians used the ring around the sun or moon as a sign of coming weather—a sign that is still used. The first book on meteorology was written by Aristotle in about 350 B.C., but no real progress was made in the development of meteorology as a science until the invention of the thermometer by Galileo Galilei in 1640 and of the barometer by Evangelista Torricelli in 1643. The use of these instruments led to recognition of the fact that high-pressure and low-pressure areas can be associated with certain types of weather. In 1743 Benjamin Franklin presented evidence that high-pressure and low-pressure systems move across the earth and carry the weather with them.

Composition of the Atmosphere.—We live at the bottom of a mixture of gases that envelops the earth. This mixture of gases is called *air*. *Pure, dry air* is made up of 78 per cent nitrogen, 21 per cent oxygen, less than 1 per cent argon, and very small amounts of carbon dioxide, hydrogen, neon, helium, krypton, and xenon. *Ordinary air* contains many other substances, the most important of which is water vapor. Depending upon prevailing conditions, the water vapor can be either liquid or solid, producing fog, clouds, rain, sleet, snow, or hail. Very small sea-salt and dust particles in the air provide nuclei around which rain drops form. Impurities in the air such as smoke and dust sometimes become great enough to cause the condition known as *smog*.

■**TROPOSPHERE.**—Although the atmosphere extends to great heights, most of it is contained in a six- to ten-

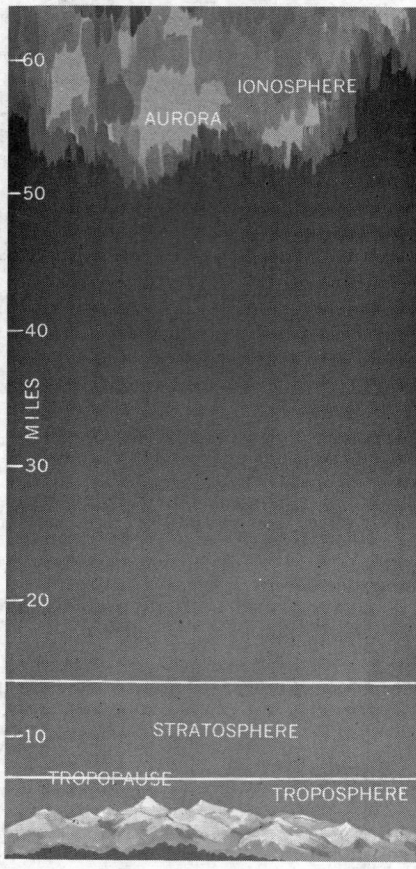

ATMOSPHERE is divided into four regions.

mile-high layer that is highest over the equator and lowest over the poles. Since almost all water vapor is distributed throughout this layer, most ordinary weather conditions occur within it. This region of the atmosphere is called the *troposphere*. The troposphere is characterized by a decrease in temperature with each increase in altitude—the greater the height, the lower the temperature. On the average the temperature in the troposphere drops slightly more than 1° F. with each 300-foot increase in elevation.

■**TROPOPAUSE AND STRATOSPHERE.**—The layer separating the troposphere and *stratosphere* is known as the *tropopause*. Within the stratosphere the atmosphere thins with each increase in altitude until, at a height of 60 miles, all but one-millionth of the atmosphere is below.

■**IONOSPHERE.**—The region above the stratosphere is called the *ionosphere* because it contains several layers of electrically charged particles known as *ions*. These particles reflect radio waves, thereby making world-wide radio communication possible. The colorful *aurora borealis,* or northern lights, produced by charged particles from the sun, also occurs in the ionosphere.

■**TEMPERATURE.**—The temperature of the atmosphere decreases through

the troposphere, becoming as low as —80° F. at the tropopause. It remains constant through the lower stratosphere until, at an elevation of from 12 to 15 miles, it begins to rise again. Above 30 miles the very thin air may become as warm as 70° F. This rise in temperature is due to absorption of ultraviolet rays from the sun by the *ozone,* a form of oxygen found in this region. Above this warm layer the temperature again decreases steadily until, at a height of 45 to 50 miles, it has fallen to as low as —90° F. There are indications that the temperature again begins to rise above the 50-mile level, but the atmosphere is so thin at this height that it is difficult to measure temperature in the usual manner.

Elements of Weather

■**ATMOSPHERIC PRESSURE.**—The expression "light as air" and the fact that air is invisible to the eye imply that, in a physical sense, there is nothing to the atmosphere. Air is quite heavy, especially near the surface of the earth. The weight of air over a unit area is called *air pressure.*

On the average the weight of the atmosphere over every square inch of the earth's surface at sea level is 14.7 pounds, or *one atmosphere.* Thus the total weight of air on a 100-foot square plot of ground is more than 10,000 tons. Buildings and other objects are not crushed by this weight because the same pressure inside them equalizes the outside pressure and makes the resultant force zero.

Air pressure is an important element of weather because, generally speaking, high pressure can be associated with fair weather and low pressure can be associated with clouds and precipitation. Pressure patterns and pressure changes are important, therefore, as indicators of future weather. In addition, it is the difference between pressure in one area and another that causes the air to move, thereby creating winds.

■**PRESSURE MEASUREMENT.**—An instrument used to measure air pressure is a *barometer.* The most direct method of measuring the pressure or weight per unit area of air is to balance it against the weight of some other substance. Mercury is usually used for this purpose because it is the heaviest of liquids.

A simple *mercury-in-glass barometer* consists of a glass tube about three feet long that is open at one end and closed at the other. The tube, filled with mercury, stands vertically in a dish of mercury, its open end submerged. Since the weight of the air pressing down on the surface of the mercury in the container will support a column of mercury of equal weight in the glass tube, air pressure is often spoken of in terms of the equivalent height of a mercury column. When barometric pressure is stated as 30.00 inches, it means simply that the weight per unit area of the air is equal to the weight per unit area of a column of mercury 30 inches high. This type of barometer is very accurate, but has numerous disadvantages. It is difficult to transport; the glass tube is easily broken; mercury can be harmful under certain circumstances and is subject to expansion and contraction with temperature variations.

The *aneroid barometer* is portable, liquidless, and automatically corrected for temperature contraction and expansion. Most aneroid barometers have a dial face with the descriptive words "stormy," "rain," "fair," and "dry" printed on it. Mechanically, it consists of a "dry" pressure-sensing element linked by a system of levers and gears to a pointer moving across the dial face.

The barometer is probably the most useful instrument in making a weather forecast, but should not itself be considered as a forecaster of weather. Although it frequently proves true that high pressure means "fair" weather and low pressure means "bad" weather, there are some exceptions. It is, therefore, important to realize that the function of the barometer is to read air pressure; the change in pressure is more important than the actual reading. A pressure change indicates that a change in the weather is imminent; the more rapid the change in pressure, the sooner the change in prevailing weather conditions will occur.

■ **TEMPERATURE.**—The earth's atmosphere behaves much like a heat engine operating on energy supplied by the sun. *Temperature* is the measure of the intensity of heat energy supplied. Although as a concept temperature is technically more difficult to define than pressure, it is more easily understood because of the human body's temperature sense. The body can feel temperature differences (that some things are warmer than others), but it cannot ordinarily feel differences in atmospheric pres-

sure. The body sensations of hot and cold are very crude measurements, but accurate values of temperature can be established with instruments.

■ **TEMPERATURE MEASUREMENT.** — Most objects change in size as the temperature changes, expanding as the temperature increases and contracting as the temperature decreases. This relationship is used to assign a definite numerical value to a temperature.

In 1724 Gabriel Daniel Fahrenheit, a German physicist, produced a *thermometer* similar to the instrument in use today, consisting of a thin glass tube with a bulb or "bulge" at one end. The bulb is filled with mercury; as the temperature rises, the mercury expands and is forced up into the tube. The level of the mercury in the tube, gauged on a calibrated scale, indicates the temperature—the higher the mercury rises in the tube, the higher the temperature.

Alcohol is frequently used in place of mercury because it has two advantages. Alcohol has a much lower freezing point and can therefore be used to measure air temperatures at which mercury would freeze; and it can be colored, making it readable.

There are many other types of thermometers used for special purposes. The *bimetallic thermometer* consists of two strips of different metals with different expansion characteristics—one expands more than the other as the temperature rises. When the two metals are fastened together, the resulting compound strip bends as the temperature changes because of the difference in rates of the metals' expansion. One end of the compound strip is fixed, and a pointer attached to the free end moves across a temperature scale as the strip changes shape. A pen is sometimes attached to the free end of the bimetal strip instead of a

pointer. The pen is positioned so that it touches a piece of graph paper wrapped around a slowly rotating cylinder. Such an instrument, called a *thermograph,* keeps a continuous record of temperature. Thermometers designed to read the highest and lowest temperatures over a given period of time are called *maximum thermometers* and *minimum thermometers,* respectively.

■ **HUMIDITY.**—The amount of water in the air in vapor or gaseous form is referred to as *humidity.* Compared to the amount of oxygen and nitrogen in the atmosphere, the amount of water vapor is very small—usually only 1 to 2 per cent. The total volume of water vapor in the atmosphere, however, is substantial. The amount of water, for instance, carried in the atmosphere over the continent of North America is about six times the amount flowing in all the rivers on the continent.

Water vapor in the atmosphere sometimes condenses to form clouds, fog, or rain; sometimes it solidifies to form snow, sleet, or hail. Water vapor is, therefore, responsible for most of the conditions we commonly call "weather." Water vapor also affects the distribution of heat in the atmosphere by absorbing and reflecting solar radiation and by releasing heat during the process of condensation. The amount of water vapor in the air also governs, to a large extent, the degree of human comfort, especially in hot weather.

■ **HUMIDITY MEASUREMENT.**—A *hygrometer* measures water vapor (humidity) in the atmosphere through the use of substances that vary in size with humidity. Hair, for instance, expands when the humidity increases and contracts when it decreases. Human hair is especially sensitive to such changes, and is used in an instrument called a *hair hygrometer.*

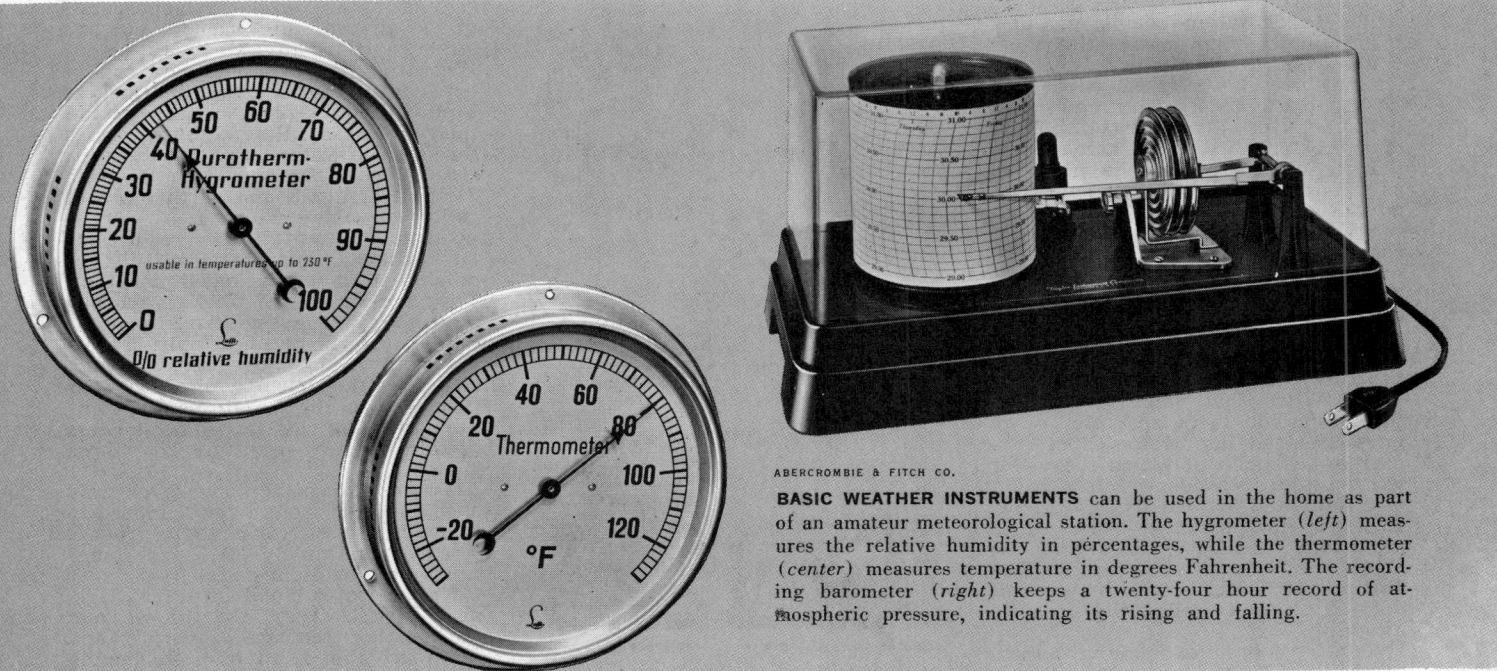

ABERCROMBIE & FITCH CO.

BASIC WEATHER INSTRUMENTS can be used in the home as part of an amateur meteorological station. The hygrometer (*left*) measures the relative humidity in percentages, while the thermometer (*center*) measures temperature in degrees Fahrenheit. The recording barometer (*right*) keeps a twenty-four hour record of atmospheric pressure, indicating its rising and falling.

One end of a bundle of hairs is fixed, and the other end is attached to a pointer that moves across a humidity scale as the hair length changes. An instrument of this type making a constant record of humidity changes, in the same manner that a thermograph records temperature changes, is called a *hygrograph*.

An instrument that measures humidity through the principle of evaporation is called a *psychrometer*. *Evaporation,* the process of changing a liquid into a gas, is a cooling process. As such it is used to measure atmospheric humidity. The psychrometer consists of two liquid-in-glass thermometers. The bulb of one of these, called the *wet-bulb thermometer,* is covered with a tight-fitting piece of cloth that has been dipped in water. As the water evaporates, the bulb is cooled, thus lowering the wet-bulb thermometer's temperature reading. The other thermometer records the ordinary air temperature, known in this instance as the *dry-bulb temperature.* Due to the evaporative cooling, the temperature of the wet-bulb thermometer is normally lower than that of the dry-bulb thermometer—the lower the relative humidity, the greater the difference between wet-bulb and dry-bulb temperatures. Using these readings, the relative humidity is then determined by reference to *psychrometric tables.*

An instrument that utilizes condensation in measuring the water vapor content of the atmosphere is called a *dew-point hygrometer.* Just as liquid water can be evaporated into the air, water vapor can also be drawn from the air in the form of a liquid. This process is called *condensation.* As air is cooled, a temperature is reached at which condensation occurs. This is known as the *dew-point temperature.* For every value of water vapor content (humidity) there exists a corresponding dew point. The point at which condensation begins and dew forms is the *dew point*—the more water vapor in the air, the higher the temperature at which the vapor will begin to condense. The dew-point hygrometer usually consists of a piece of highly polished metal arranged so that its temperature can be measured as it is cooled to the dew point. An advanced type of this instrument consists of an electronically cooled mirror that is automatically monitored by a photoelectric cell, which signals the point at which condensation occurs.

■**HUMIDITY UNITS.**—The amount of water vapor in the air at a given temperature has a certain maximum value. When that value is reached, the air is said to be *saturated* or to have reached its water-vapor capacity—the point at which the water vapor begins to condense into a liquid or a solid, and fog, clouds, rain, snow, frost, or dew begin to form. It is important, therefore, to know just how close the air is to saturation. The amount of water vapor in a unit volume of air is called the *absolute humidity.*

Relative humidity defines the ratio of absolute humidity to capacity—a measure of how close the air is to saturation at a given temperature.

$$\text{relative humidity (per cent)} = \frac{\text{absolute humidity}}{\text{capacity}} \times 100$$

Since capacity depends upon temperature, relative humidity also depends upon temperature. Thus, even if the absolute humidity remains the same, the relative humidity will change; it will be higher at lower temperatures. In other words, although the actual amount of water vapor in the air remains the same, the relative humidity will fall during the day as the temperature rises and increase at night as the air cools. Atmospheric pressure is another factor to be considered because as the pressure changes, the volume of air will also change, thus affecting both absolute and relative humidity.

A humidity unit that remains constant although pressure or temperature varies is defined as *specific humidity,* the amount of water vapor per unit *mass* of air. Specific humidity is usually expressed as grams of vapor per kilogram of air. One kilogram of air containing 15 grams of water vapor at a given temperature and pressure has a specific humidity of 15 grams per kilogram. If the water vapor content remains the same, this value will likewise remain the same for all temperatures and pressures because the mass of air is not affected by temperature and pressure changes.

Clouds.—Weather conditions on the earth's surface are often governed by conditions at higher altitudes. In the past, cloud observations were the only available means of determining conditions in the upper atmosphere. They are still useful indicators of weather changes.

U.S. DEPARTMENT OF COMMERCE, WEATHER BUREAU
RADIOSONDE is carried aloft by a balloon.

■**CLOUD TYPES.**—The highest clouds are *cirrus clouds.* "Cirrus," which means "curl" in Latin, describes the characteristic hooks or curls these clouds have at their borders (sometimes called "mares' tails"). Cirrus clouds are feathery and white, and range to heights at which temperatures are well below freezing. These clouds are therefore usually composed of ice crystals. When the cirrus clouds remain feathery or slowly disappear, fair weather is indicated. When they grow thicker and blanket the sky, it is likely that lower clouds will form, followed by rain or snow.

Cirrostratus clouds take the form of a continuous white sheet and often give the sky a milky appearance. Enough sunlight penetrates this sheet to cast shadows on the ground. Like cirrus clouds, the cirrostratus are made up of ice crystals, and generally produce a halo or ring around the sun or moon; only clouds composed of ice crystals produce such a ring. When cirrostratus clouds increase and thicken, rain or snow can be expected within 24 hours.

Cirrocumulus clouds appear at high levels as small, white patches. When arranged in rows or waves, they produce what is sometimes called a "mackerel sky." Cirrocumulus, cirrus, and cirrostratus clouds are usually classed together. They all form at altitudes exceeding 20,000 feet, and are sometimes called *high clouds.*

Altostratus clouds form a heavy, gray sheet across the sky. The sun is usually visible as a bright spot, but is not bright enough to cast shadows on the ground. These clouds are composed of water droplets, even at temperatures below freezing, and therefore do not form halos. The appearance of altostratus clouds usually means that rain or snow will follow shortly.

Altocumulus clouds appear in closely spaced patches and are white or gray. They are similar in appearance to the cirrocumulus variety, but are larger and usually at lower levels. When they are in the proper position between the sun and the earth below, beautiful colors often appear around their edges as the sunlight passes through the water droplets. Alto-type clouds usually range from 6,500 to 20,000 feet above the earth and are called the *middle clouds.*

Stratocumulus clouds are irregularly shaped, appearing in rolls or patches that often blend together. They are larger and thicker, and appear at lower levels than altocumulus clouds. Sometimes only a few thousand feet above the ground, stratocumulus clouds often appear just after a storm, but before complete clearing sets in. Light showers of rain or snow may fall from these clouds.

Stratus clouds are low-level gray sheets located from a few hundred to a few thousand feet above the ground. They are relatively thin, and sometimes produce light drizzle.

Nimbostratus clouds are low, dark, gray clouds. They are thicker and darker than the stratus variety and often are the result of a thickening and lowering of altostratus clouds.

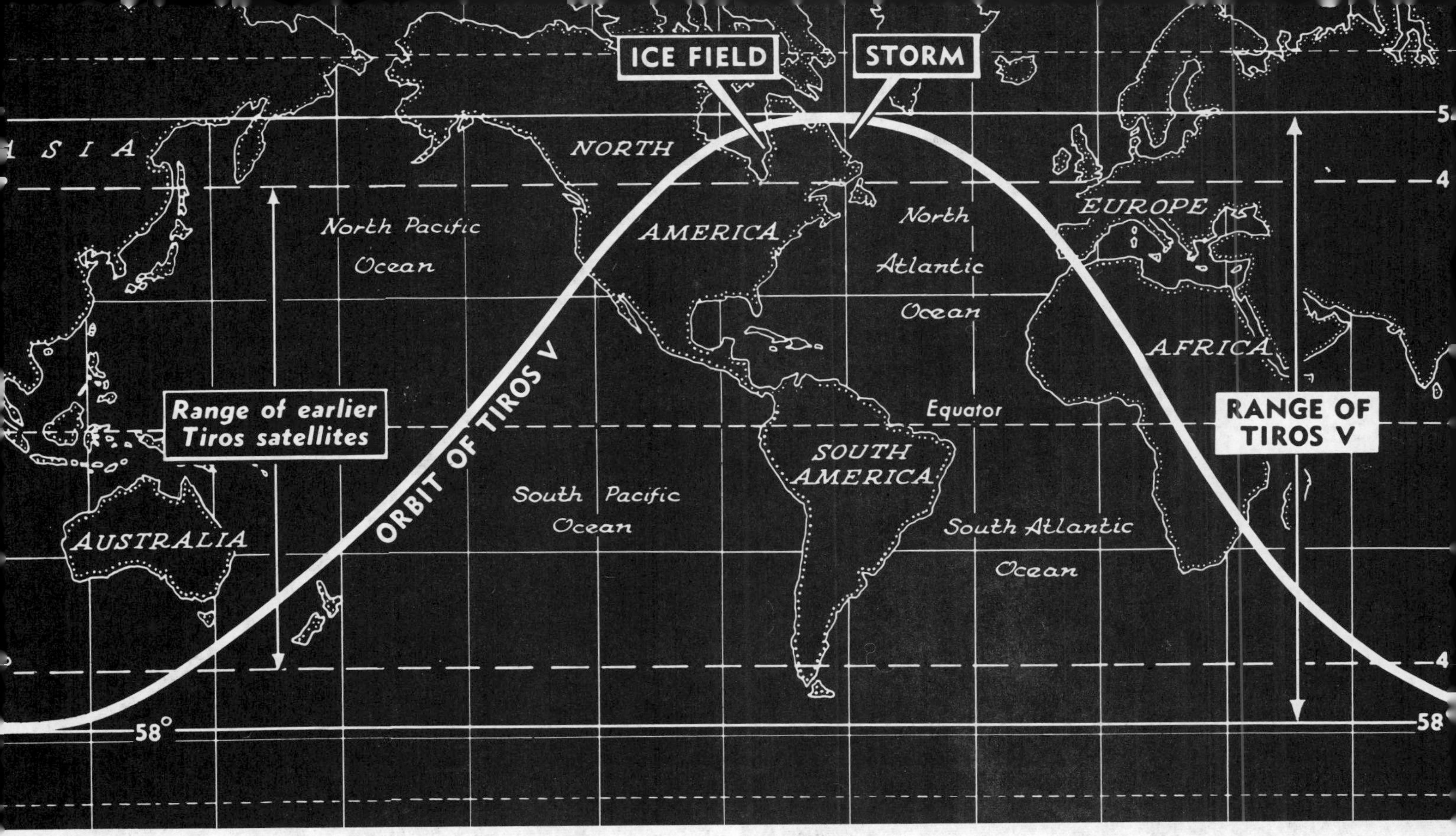

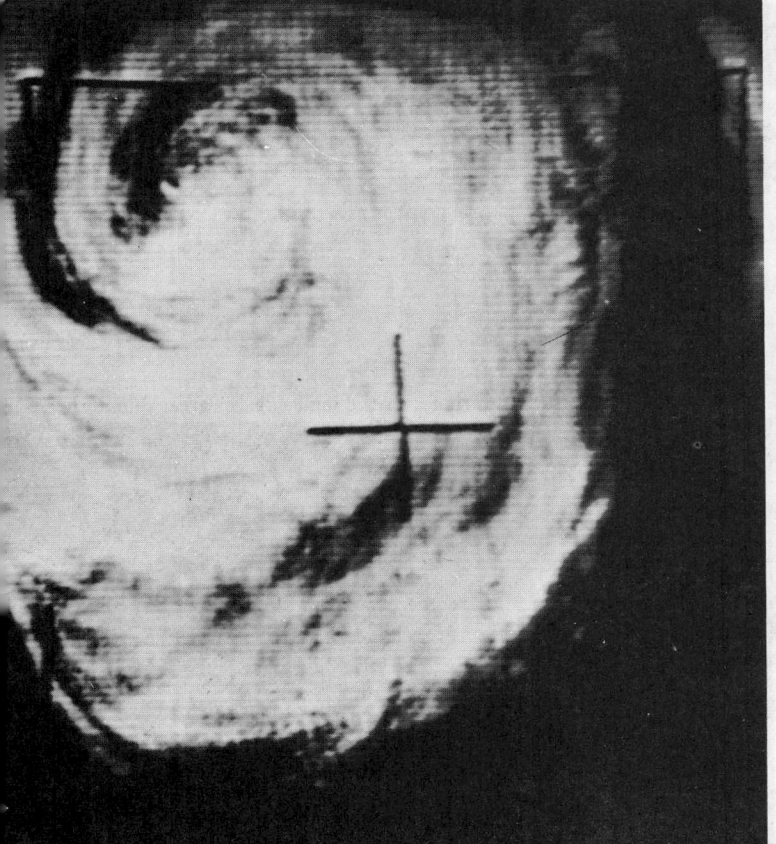

ICE FIELD   STORM

ASIA   NORTH   EUROPE
North Pacific   AMERICA   *North*   AFRICA
Ocean   *Atlantic*
Ocean

**Range of earlier
Tiros satellites**   **RANGE OF
TIROS V**

Equator

AUSTRALIA   SOUTH   *South Atlantic*
AMERICA   *Ocean*
South Pacific
Ocean

ORBIT OF TIROS V

58°   58°

THE NEW YORK TIMES

NASA

Weather eyes on the world
watch, predict and warn

FROM 400 MILES above the earth, artificial satellites like Tiros V, whose orbital path is shown above, look down on the globe through the eyes of their television cameras. The pictures they transmit enable meteorologists to keep constant track of weather all over the world. Left, a glimpse into the vortex of an Atlantic storm sheds light on the origin, development and movement of storms, to warn against their approach and perhaps, eventually, to tame them. Right, photograph of an ice field in Hudson Bay helps predict future icebergs which menace shipping lanes.

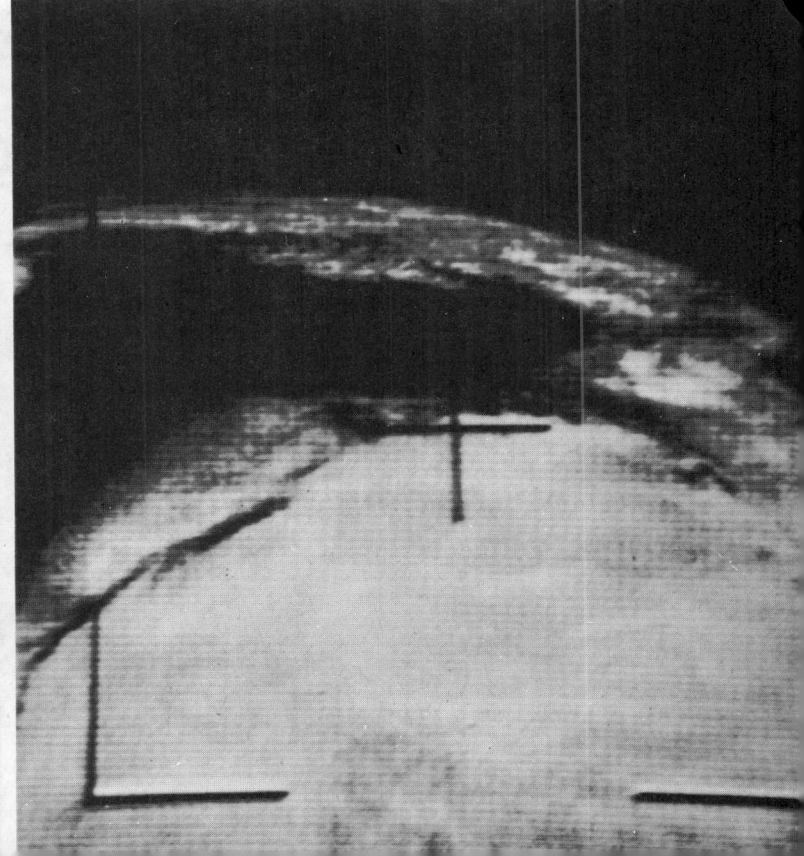

TUFTED PATCHES of Alto-Cumuli
water clouds spread across the sky

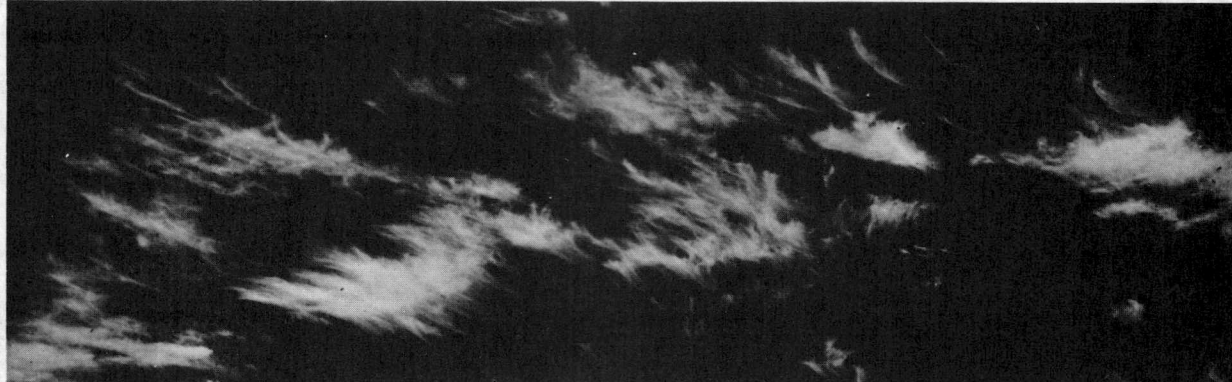

CIRRUS, high ice clouds,
may portend rain or snow

CUMULUS, usually seen on sunny days, can develop into rain-clouds

CIRROCUMULUS, merging with Cirrostratus, are harbingers of rain

CUMULONIMBUS, towering over the landscape in great thunderheads

ALTOCUMULUS LENTICULARIS, named for their strange lens-like shape

E. FONTSERÉ

COURTESY OF U.S. DEPT. OF COMMERCE, WEATHER BUREAU

When nimbostratus clouds appear, heavy rain or snow usually follows immediately.

Cumulus clouds are probably the most familiar. They are fluffy, white, flat-based, puff-sided, and round-topped, and usually result from surface heating of the earth. Over land they form most frequently in the late morning and early afternoon. They are essentially fair-weather clouds. If they slowly disappear as the sun begins to set, the weather will probably remain fair throughout the night. The air inside cumulus clouds is in a continuous state of up-and-down motion; so much so, in fact, that airplanes flying through them often experience a bumpy ride. Cumulus clouds change size and shape very rapidly.

Cumulonimbus clouds are the largest clouds in the sky. They are actually overgrown cumulus clouds, often extending to more than five miles above the earth. At the top of these clouds the rounded edges break into a flattened, anvil-shaped layer. Cumulonimbus clouds are the familiar thunderclouds that produce heavy showers, lightning, thunder, and often hail and high winds. As cumulus clouds grow in the process of becoming cumulonimbus clouds, but before the anvil-shaped top appears, they are known as *cumulus congestus*.

The accompanying illustration shows the forms and relative heights of the main cloud types. There are two main divisions based on shape. Cumulus-type clouds have a heaped-up, or bulging, appearance. Stratus-type clouds are spread out in a layer. There are four main divisions based on height. Cirrus-type clouds appear at the greatest heights; alto-type clouds appear at middle levels; stratus and stratocumulus are at low levels; and nimbostratus, cumulus, and cumulonimbus occur in more than one level. The nimbus-type clouds usually produce large amounts of rain.

Condensation and Precipitation

■**CONDENSATION.**—When the air becomes *saturated* (relative humidity reaches 100 per cent), the water vapor in it usually condenses into a liquid. The drops form upon small airborne particles of sea salt, dust, and other matter, known in this instance as *condensation nuclei.* Air may become saturated by the addition of water vapor or through cooling. Condensation in the atmosphere is most often due to cooling, which may take place in a number of ways.

Radiative cooling occurs when, on a clear night, heat from the earth's surface is radiated into space; air near the ground is cooled by contact with the earth. Air may also be cooled by *expansion.* Since atmospheric pressure decreases with each increase in altitude, air rising from a lower level expands. In so doing, its temperature decreases.

An upward air movement can result from the heating of the earth's surface by the sun. Air may also be forced upward by hills or mountains over which it flows, or may be displaced by a heavier mass of air.

SNOWFLAKES are symmetrical hexagons.

Condensation sometimes results in the formation of small drops of water near the ground, called *fog.* These drops are so tiny it would take billions to fill a teaspoon. If the drops formed by this near ground-level condensation grow large enough to fall to the ground, they produce *drizzle* or *mist,* although drizzle most often falls from low clouds. If condensation forms directly on the ground or on some other surface, it is called *dew.* Dew that forms on a surface whose temperature is below freezing will become small ice needles called *frost.* Condensation that is produced by the expansion of rising air and takes place above ground level will result in the formation of *clouds.*

■**PRECIPITATION.**—When cloud drops grow big enough to fall from a cloud and reach the ground, the condition produced is known as *precipitation.* Very few clouds produce precipitation unless the interior temperature first falls below freezing, and ice crystals form. Thus, most precipitation begins as ice. The small cloud drops begin to condense on the ice crystals, forming larger drops. As the drops grow in size, they begin to fall through the cloud, collecting still more cloud drops. The average rain drop equals about one million cloud drops.

■**TYPES OF PRECIPITATION.**—Precipitation that reaches the ground in liquid form is called *rain* or *drizzle.* If the liquid freezes on coming in contact with the ground, it is known as *freezing rain* or *freezing drizzle.* Precipitation that falls through the air as ice is called *sleet.* These ice crystals sometimes have very complex and beautiful shapes and are known as *snow.* Snow crystals are always hexagonal in shape, but no two are alike. *Hail* is formed from raindrops that freeze. Often hail is carried up and down by air currents within a cloud, collecting liquid water drops as it falls and is again carried aloft. This

process is sometimes repeated many times, the *hailstones* growing larger with each passage. Hail is almost always associated with thunderstorms.

■**PRECIPITATION MEASUREMENT.**—All that is needed to measure rainfall is a large, open can to catch the rain-water and a ruler to measure the depth of the water collected. A rainfall measurement, therefore, represents the height to which rainwater accumulates on a level surface. The *standard rain gauge* used by the U.S. Weather Bureau is a cylindrical can 24 inches high and 8 inches across. A funnel channels the rain water into a measuring tube with cross-sectional area exactly one-tenth that of the catching can. The depth of rain water measured is, therefore, ten times its actual depth. In other words, one inch of rain in the catching can is measured as ten inches in the tube. The height of rainwater in the measuring tube is divided by ten to find the actual reading. This allows for more accurate measurement—to 1/100 of an inch. The funnel minimizes evaporation because it covers the collected water, except a very small opening.

Snowfall is measured in terms of both depth and weight. The depth is determined by choosing a level area where there has been no drifting and inserting a ruler into the snow until it reaches the ground. Several depth measurements are taken at different points in the area, and the average of these is used. Weight is determined by melting a volume of snow and then measuring the depth of the resultant water. This is known as the *water equivalent* of snow. A standard rain gauge, with the measuring tube and funnel removed, is used to catch the snow. The snow collected in the can is then melted, and the water depth is measured. On the average, ten inches of snow will melt down to approximately one inch of water, but the water equivalent (weight) of snow varies widely.

Wind

■**PRESSURE GRADIENTS.**—*Wind,* which is air in motion, sharply influences the weather by transporting heat and moisture. If the temperature of the atmosphere were the same all over the world, atmospheric pressure would also be the same and air would not move—there would be no wind. Heat from the sun, however, is distributed unevenly over the earth. The variations in temperature produce the differences in atmospheric pressure that, in turn, produce air movement. (The greater the difference in pressure, the faster the air will move.) The force producing this air movement is known as the *pressure-gradient force.* If this were the only force acting on the atmosphere, winds would always blow directly from areas of high pressure to areas of low pressure.

■**CORIOLIS EFFECT.**—The rotation of the earth deflects the wind; instead of flowing in a straight line from high to low, winds flow *around* pressure centers. This *Coriolis force* turns the wind to the right (clockwise) in the Northern Hemisphere and to the left (counterclockwise) in the Southern

Hemisphere. If a person stands with his back to the wind in the Northern Hemisphere high pressure will be on the right; low pressure on the left. In the Southern Hemisphere, it would be just the opposite; low pressure on the right, high on the left. Thus, in the Northern Hemisphere, winds blow counterclockwise around a low-pressure center and clockwise around a high-pressure center (*anticyclone*). In the Southern Hemisphere, winds blow clockwise around a low-pressure center; counterclockwise around a high-pressure center. Friction with the earth's surface also affects the wind, making it spiral *in* toward the center of a low-pressure area, *out* from a high-pressure area.

■**WIND SYSTEMS.**—The distribution of heat over the surface of the earth results in world-wide pressure patterns and relatively steady wind systems. These *prevailing winds* are known as *polar easterlies* in polar latitudes, *prevailing westerlies* in middle latitudes, and *trade winds* in tropical regions. Smaller cyclones and anticyclones migrate within these large-scale wind systems.

■**MONSOONS.** — Localized temperature variations sometimes create small-scale wind systems. The *sea breeze* is one example. During the day the air over the land becomes hot and rises, reducing the air pressure near the ground. The cooler (higher-pressure) air over the water flows toward the land. A wind system produced in this manner is called a *monsoon*. The most famous monsoon circulation occurs over India.

■**JET STREAM.**—A special, high-altitude wind system, generally found from 30,000 to 35,000 feet above the earth, just below the tropopause, is known as the *jet stream*. Winds in the jet stream average 175 miles per hour, but speeds as high as 400 miles per hour have been recorded.

■**WIND MEASUREMENT.**—In some localities, the direction from which the wind blows can be associated with a particular kind of weather. For example, in many sections of the United States a south wind signals the approach of warmer weather, while a north wind indicates the opposite. A wind from the west will most often bring fair weather; an easterly wind, rain or snow. A change in wind direction can therefore serve as a useful indicator of a change in the weather. *Wind speed* is expressed in either knots or miles per hour and can be estimated on the basis of constant observations. The first wind scale was devised in 1805 by the British admiral, Sir Francis Beaufort. The *Beaufort Scale* is still used in a modified form.

An instrument that shows wind direction is called a *wind vane*. The most common wind vane is an arrow with a large tail. This arrow rotates freely on a fixed base and points *into* the wind—in the direction from which the wind blows.

The instrument used to measure wind speed is called an *anemometer*. The *cup anemometer* is made up of three or four hollow, hemispherical cups attached to horizontal arms extending from a vertical axis. The force of the wind on the cups causes the apparatus to turn on the axis—the higher the wind speed, the faster the cups turn. The spinning apparatus is linked mechanically to a pointer that moves over a scale and indicates speed in knots or miles per hour.

There are some instruments designed to measure wind direction and wind speed simultaneously. One of these looks like a wind vane, but has a hollow tube in the head of the arrow. The wind speed is measured in terms of the pressure of the air blowing into the tube. Another instrument that measures wind speed and direction simultaneously is the *aerovane*, which looks like a miniature airplane without wings. A tail fin keeps the instrument facing into the wind, and the wind speed is determined by a spinning propeller.

■**WIND VELOCITY.**—*Wind velocity* encompasses both wind speed and wind direction. It should never be used to indicate wind speed alone. *Wind direction* is specified in compass degree points and indicates the direction *from* which the wind is blowing. An east (90°) wind blows from east to west; a south (180°) wind blows from south to north.

Weather Control.—Since all of us participate in outdoor activities of some sort, we must at times be concerned about the weather. Man has therefore always thought about the possibility of exercising some control over it. The *smudge pots* (pots of burning oil) used by citrus growers to prevent their crops from freezing are one example of small-scale weather control. Weather, of course, also affects indoor environment.

■**RAINMAKING.**—In most cases, precipitation is the kind of weather we want to regulate. In the past, ritual ceremonies were performed to conjure up, or to stop, rainfall. The most famous of these is the *rain dance* of the North American Hopi Indians.

The modern era of rainmaking began in 1946, when it was discovered that dropping small particles of dry ice into a cloud could initiate precipitation by converting some of the small water drops in the cloud to ice crystals. (Natural precipitation usually begins with the formation of ice

U.S. DEPARTMENT OF COMMERCE, WEATHER BUREAU   U.S. NAVY

HURRICANES periodically lash the Florida coast with high winds and heavy rain (*left*). As part of the hurricane-surveillance program, a photographic plane flies above a hurricane (*right*); the clouds circle into the storm's eye, visible above the tail of the aircraft.

crystals.) This process became known as *cloud seeding.* Later it was discovered that if large amounts of dry ice were dropped into thin clouds, the resulting rain drops would be so small they would evaporate before reaching the ground. A hole could thus be cut in a cloud without causing precipitation. Even later it was found that crystals of silver iodide could produce the same effect as the dry ice. This was important because it enabled scientists to "seed" clouds from the ground by burning a solution containing silver iodide and allowing the crystals to float up into the clouds—a much less expensive method than flying above a cloud to drop dry ice into it.

Clouds must be present before rainmaking activities can begin. No one has yet devised a way to form clouds in clear, dry air. Thus, it is very difficult to determine whether cloud seeding really produces rainfall, over and above that which would have occurred naturally. This question will be answered only after years of experiment and observation.

■STORM CONTROL.—Experiments have been performed to determine whether seeding special types of clouds can prevent damaging storms. The idea is that seeding thunderstorm clouds before they develop fully may start premature precipitation and eliminate the clouds before they reach the thunder, lightning, and hail stage. It is believed that such early seeding may prevent tornadoes and that seeding hurricanes early in their development may stop them from maturing.

■REGULATING SOLAR ENERGY.—Future efforts to control the weather will most likely be concerned with discovering a way to influence and control the distribution of solar energy. This will really be going to the heart of the matter because it is the sun's energy that conditions the earth's atmosphere, producing most of the conditions we call "weather." A number of devices have already been suggested to capture or reject the sun's energy, thereby producing very extensive weather modification. If more solar energy, for instance, could be concentrated on the polar regions, it would increase the rate at which the ice and snow in these regions melt. This would result in a rise in the level of all the oceans. Winters would become much milder, and precipitation in the middle latitudes might be drastically reduced.

Special Storms

.■HURRICANES.—High-speed winds sometimes occur near the surface of the earth in conjunction with some types of cyclones. One of these is the most destructive of all weather systems, the *hurricane.* Hurricanes are seasonal storms (most prevalent in August and September) that originate over the tropical regions of the Atlantic Ocean. Sometimes more than 300 miles in diameter, these storms move at 10 to 20 miles per hour and have winds of over 75 miles per hour. (A hurricane generates more energy in one hour than all the electric power generated in the United States in one year.) At the center, or *eye,*

of a hurricane is an area about five miles wide where the winds are usually calm and the sky above is sometimes clear. Hurricanes usually last from 5 to 10 days. They lose force rapidly when they move over land. On the average, two hurricanes strike the United States each year. No hurricane has ever been observed south of the equator.

The most destructive element of a hurricane is the extraordinarily high tides it drives before it. The hurricane of 1938 caused 500 deaths in New England, most of them drownings. The tragic Galveston hurricane of 1900 swept a 15-foot wall of water out of the Gulf of Mexico and across the city, killing over 5,000 people.

■TYPHOONS.—A *typhoon* is the Pacific version of a hurricane. It occurs mainly during February and March.

■TORNADOES.—Although limited in size and duration, *tornadoes* are the most violent and deadly of all storms. Ranging from 100 to 500 feet wide, they move at from 25 to 40 miles per hour for up to 50 miles. Tornadoes are characterized by a dark funnel shape descending from a low cloud.

A tornado presents a double hazard—high-speed winds and low pressure. Wind speeds have been estimated to be as high as 500 miles per hour. The air pressure at the center of a tornado is very low—perhaps two-thirds that of the surroundings. Thus, closed houses over which a tornado passes usually explode—the pressure within the house pushes against the abnormally low pressure outside. Tornadoes have played many curious tricks, such as driving boards through utility poles and carrying children and animals through the air for miles without harming them. A tornado occurring over water is a *waterspout.*

Most tornadoes occur in Australia and in the southern and the western sections of the United States. More than 100 tornadoes, killing more than 200 people, are recorded every year in the United States.

■THUNDERSTORMS.—One of the most common and spectacular storms is the *thunderstorm,* a composite of high winds, heavy rain, loud noises, and flashing light. *Thunder* is the result of a weather phenomenon called lightning. *Lightning* is untamed electricity that shoots across the sky, causing intense heating along its path. This heating causes the air to expand suddenly. When the air surfaces separated by the expansion come together again, a series of vibrations causes the violent crash known as thunder. Thunder in itself is not dangerous. Many thunderstorms sometimes travel together, forming what is known as a *squall line.*

Sound waves travel about one mile in five seconds, while light travels at more than 186,000 miles per second. Lightning is therefore seen practically at the instant it occurs, while the thunder is heard somewhat after the flash of light appears in the sky. Hence, the distance of a thunderstorm can be calculated by counting the seconds between the time the lightning flash is seen and the time the thunder is heard, allowing five seconds per mile.

U.S. DEPARTMENT OF COMMERCE, WEATHER BUREAU

THUNDERSTORMS, caused by electrical discharges in the atmosphere, are characterized by streaks of lightning and thunder.

More than 1,800 thunderstorms occur in the atmosphere every hour. Every year about 400 people in the United States are killed by lightning. While the chances of being struck by lightning are very small, the following precautions should be taken. Indoors, the center of a room is the safest spot, provided it is not under a light fixture. Radiators and corners near outside rainspouts should be avoided. Outdoors, isolated trees, tops of hills, and metal fences should be avoided. The inside of an automobile is one of the safest places to be during a thunderstorm. If you are caught on open water in a small boat, or on a wide expanse of flat land, the best precaution is to lie down.

Air Masses.—Weather in any area depends greatly upon the characteristics of the air mass over the area. An *air mass* is a large portion of the atmosphere with relatively uniform properties throughout. An air mass develops when a large section of the atmosphere remains relatively stationary over a surface area with

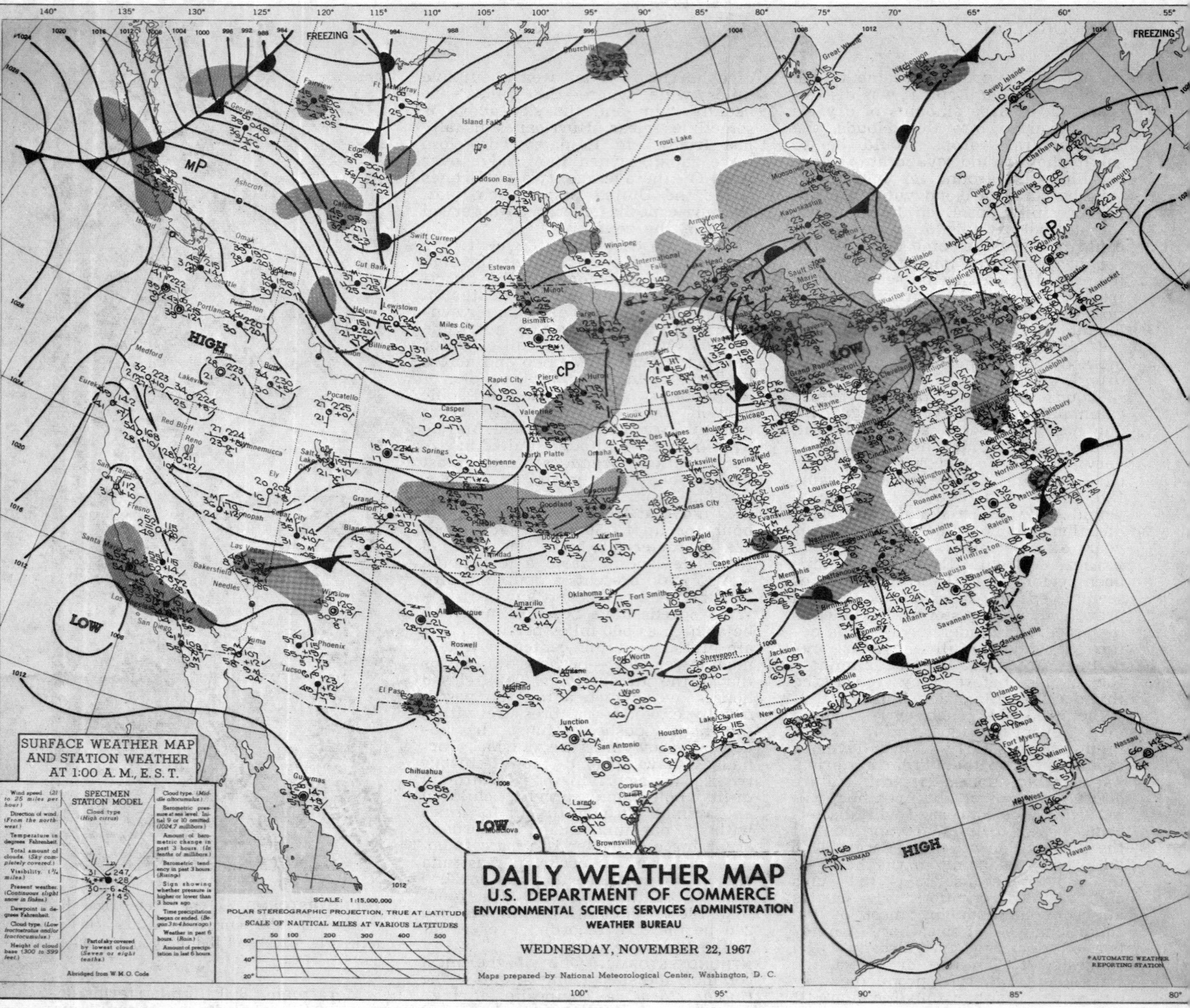

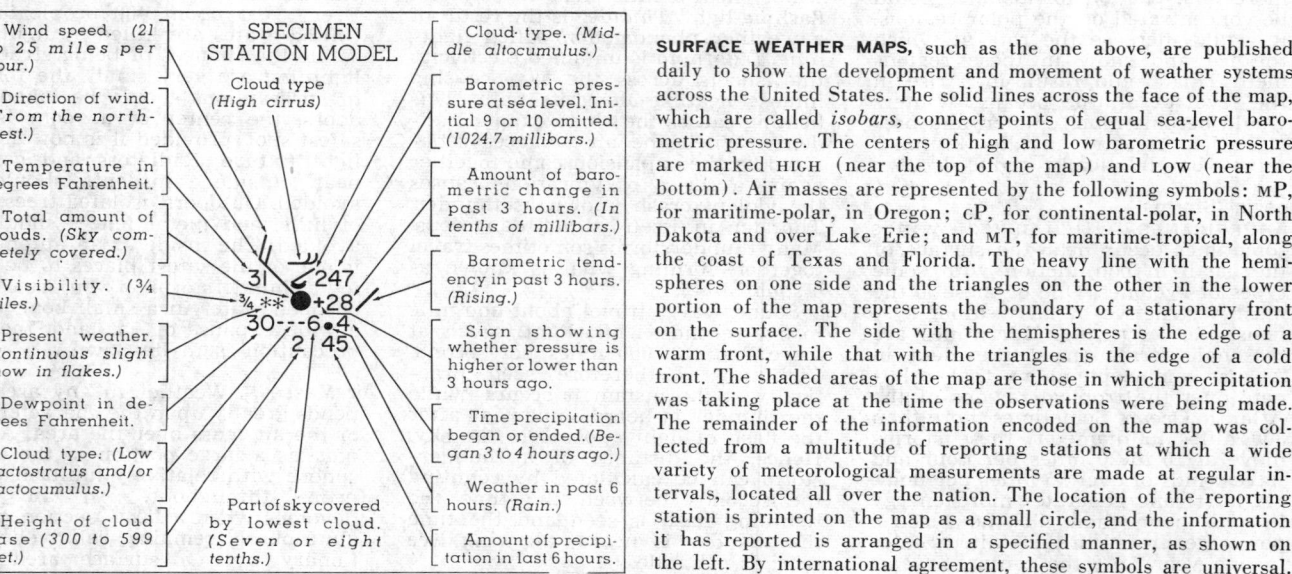

SURFACE WEATHER MAP
AND STATION WEATHER
AT 1:00 A. M., E.S.T.
DAILY WEATHER MAP
U.S. DEPARTMENT OF COMMERCE
ENVIRONMENTAL SCIENCE SERVICES ADMINISTRATION
WEATHER BUREAU
WEDNESDAY, NOVEMBER 22, 1967
Maps prepared by National Meteorological Center, Washington, D. C.
SCALE: 1:15,000,000
POLAR STEREOGRAPHIC PROJECTION, TRUE AT LATITUDE
SCALE OF NAUTICAL MILES AT VARIOUS LATITUDES
SPECIMEN STATION MODEL
Abridged from W.M.O. Code
FREEZING
HIGH
LOW
mP
cP
*AUTOMATIC WEATHER REPORTING STATION

SPECIMEN
STATION MODEL
Wind speed. (21 to 25 miles per hour.)
Direction of wind. (From the northwest.)
Temperature in degrees Fahrenheit.
Total amount of clouds. (Sky completely covered.)
Visibility. (3/4 miles.)
Present weather. (Continuous slight snow in flakes.)
Dewpoint in degrees Fahrenheit.
Cloud type. (Low fractostratus and/or fractocumulus.)
Height of cloud base (300 to 599 feet.)
Cloud type (High cirrus)
Part of sky covered by lowest cloud. (Seven or eight tenths.)
Cloud type. (Middle altocumulus.)
Barometric pressure at sea level. Initial 9 or 10 omitted. (1024.7 millibars.)
Amount of barometric change in past 3 hours. (In tenths of millibars.)
Barometric tendency in past 3 hours. (Rising.)
Sign showing whether pressure is higher or lower than 3 hours ago.
Time precipitation began or ended. (Began 3 to 4 hours ago.)
Weather in past 6 hours. (Rain.)
Amount of precipitation in last 6 hours.
31
247
3/4
+28
30
6
4
2
45

SURFACE WEATHER MAPS, such as the one above, are published daily to show the development and movement of weather systems across the United States. The solid lines across the face of the map, which are called *isobars,* connect points of equal sea-level barometric pressure. The centers of high and low barometric pressure are marked HIGH (near the top of the map) and LOW (near the bottom). Air masses are represented by the following symbols: MP, for maritime-polar, in Oregon; cP, for continental-polar, in North Dakota and over Lake Erie; and MT, for maritime-tropical, along the coast of Texas and Florida. The heavy line with the hemispheres on one side and the triangles on the other in the lower portion of the map represents the boundary of a stationary front on the surface. The side with the hemispheres is the edge of a warm front, while that with the triangles is the edge of a cold front. The shaded areas of the map are those in which precipitation was taking place at the time the observations were being made. The remainder of the information encoded on the map was collected from a multitude of reporting stations at which a wide variety of meteorological measurements are made at regular intervals, located all over the nation. The location of the reporting station is printed on the map as a small circle, and the information it has reported is arranged in a specified manner, as shown on the left. By international agreement, these symbols are universal.

uniform properties. Such a surface area is known as a *source region*.

Movements and interactions among different air masses also affect the weather.

Air masses are classified primarily by source region or place of origin. The principal air-mass source regions are those areas where high pressure centers tend to develop—over the land in high latitudes and over the ocean in low latitudes. The principal air masses are classified as *polar* and *tropical*, identified P and T on a weather map. Classifications *arctic* (A) and *equatorial* (E) are also used.

A secondary classification distinguishes whether the air mass formed over land or over water, designated *continental* (c) and *maritime* (M) respectively. In general, maritime-tropical air (MT) is warm and humid, continental-tropical (cT) warm and dry, maritime-polar (MP) cold and moist, and continental-polar (cP) cold and dry.

■**FRONTS.**—Major weather changes occur at the boundaries separating air masses, called *fronts*. When cold air is advancing at the boundary, the boundary line is called a *cold front*. Cold fronts are usually accompanied by heavy showers and followed by lower temperatures. When warm air is advancing at the boundary, the boundary line is called a *warm front*. Gentle rains usually precede a warm front, followed by higher temperatures. A boundary line that is not moving is called a *stationary front*.

Frontal boundaries are shown as lines on a weather map, but they really extend upward from the ground. Since cold air is heavier than warm air, the surface slopes; and the cold air forms a wedge underneath the warm air. When cold and warm fronts meet, one of the air masses is lifted from the ground, thus forming an *occluded front*.

Climate.—The condition of the weather at a given time and place is the sum total of temperature, air pressure, relative humidity, wind velocity, precipitation, and cloudiness. Although changes in the weather in one particular area are many and varied, it is possible to arrive at a composite picture of the weather by averaging these variations. Such a generalization is called the *climate* of an area.

The climate of an area, however, is not determined solely by the long-term annual averages of the meteorological elements. Edinburgh, Scotland, and Boston, Massachusetts, for example, have nearly the same annual average temperature (48° F.), but the temperature extremes to which they are subjected during the year are markedly different. At Edinburgh average temperatures range from 38° F. to 58° F., and at Boston, from 27° F. to 70° F. Thus, to characterize climate it is first necessary to consider the regular variations the meteorological elements are subjected to, particularly seasonal changes. But temperature is not the only element to be considered. Cairo, United Arab Republic, and New Orleans, Louisiana, have about the same mean temperature (68° F.) and similar temperature variations, but the annual 1.3-inch rainfall at Cairo and the 56.5-inch rainfall at New Orleans make their climates quite different. Climate thus can be defined as the mean state of the atmosphere at a given place and the variations to which that mean state is subjected.

In general, climates are classified according to the effect they have on animal and plant life. Temperature and precipitation are the two principal elements in most classifications because heat and water are the two factors most profoundly affecting living organisms. They are also the two variables most regularly and generally observed. Evaporation, ground temperature, radiation, and winds are also important, but the distribution of these elements is reflected in temperature and precipitation.

Climate is governed by a number of geographic factors. The most important are latitude, altitude, topography, and proximity to an ocean. Latitude influences average temperatures. Warm climates are generally nearer the equator than cold climates, and vice versa. Altitude and topography influence average temperatures and precipitation—the higher the altitude, the colder the climate. The average midsummer temperature on Pike's Peak in Colorado is more than 30° lower than at Denver, which is 9,000 feet lower. The topographical location of an area in relation to mountains is also important. Air flowing up the windward side of a mountain is cooled, and the water vapor condenses to form clouds and rain. The air flowing down the leeward side of the mountain is heated as it descends and thus is dry. The climate therefore is often cool and wet on the windward side of a mountain range, warm and dry on the lee side. Mountains can also block the flow of air. The Rocky Mountains in the United States, for instance, act as a barrier preventing cold winter air masses from reaching the Pacific Coast.

Finally, oceans are relatively cool in the summer and relatively warm in the winter. Thus they tend to stabilize the climates of nearby land areas, particularly if the prevailing winds are from the ocean to the land. Such climates (*maritime*), on the average, change very little in temperature from season to season. Amid large land masses, temperature variations are usually more pronounced; winters are frequently very cold and summers very hot. This type of climate is called a *continental climate*.

—Francis K. Davis, Jr.

THE WEATHER BUREAU

The *Weather Bureau,* operated by the U.S. Department of Commerce, provides daily weather bulletins, forecasts, and storm warnings for use by public, agricultural, aviation, commercial, industrial, and other interests. It maintains approximately 300 offices inside and outside the continental United States.

History.—The *National Weather Service,* first organized in 1870, was operated by the U.S. Army Signal Corps. In 1891 it was transferred to the newly formed Weather Bureau, an agency put under the jurisdiction of the Department of Commerce in 1940.

Operations.—Today, weather observations are made at stations located in cities, at airports, in the Antarctic and the Arctic, and at fixed points in the Atlantic and Pacific oceans. These observations are supplemented by reports from military land and sea stations, other federal agencies, avia-

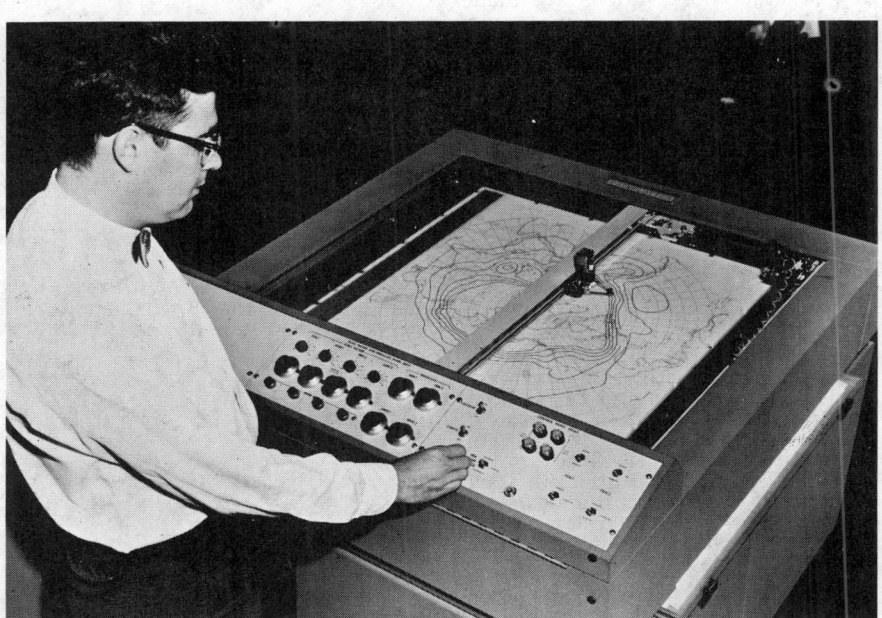

U.S. DEPARTMENT OF COMMERCE, WEATHER BUREAU

ELECTRONIC COMPUTER-PLOTTER automatically draws contours of the pressure surface of the atmosphere at specified altitudes above the Northern Hemisphere in under three minutes.

tion interests, merchant vessels of all nationalities, and from foreign countries under international agreement. In addition, there are almost 13,000 private citizens in the United States who assist the Bureau by making daily weather observations.

Weather information collected by this vast network is transmitted to the Weather Bureau's *National Meteorological Center* near Washington, D.C. Meteorologists there use the collected data to analyze the current weather situation and in turn issue comprehensive forecasts covering areas as large as the entire Northern Hemisphere. Much of this work is done with the help of electronic computers and other automatic equipment. One such machine is capable of drawing weather maps automatically. The completed forecasts and maps are then transmitted to area Weather Bureau offices and military field stations.

Using the guidance material provided by the National Meteorological Center, the Weather Bureau's *Area Forecast Centers* issue forecasts and storm warnings covering their specific areas of responsibility. Each local station in turn adapts the forecasts prepared by the Area Forecast Centers to its particular locality. Local weather information is then distributed by the press, radio and television stations, and automatic telephone answering devices.

Modern Observational Instruments

■SATELLITES.—Since 1960, eight *Tiros* weather satellites have been launched by the *National Aeronautics and Space Administration*. The cloud pictures taken by cameras in these satellites are used by the Weather Bureau to supplement other reports. The satellites have been of great value to forecasters by providing information about vast areas of the earth where few weather observations are made. Satellite photographs also provide early storm warnings. Since their inception the Tiros satellites have demonstrated their effectiveness by identifying and tracking storms. When significant weather developments, such as hurricane and typhoon formations, are detected by the satellites, the Weather Bureau issues special international bulletins to the nations that may be affected. Several Tiros satellites have carried sensors that measure the radiation balance of the earth and its atmosphere, thereby yielding valuable information that will aid in understanding the atmosphere and predicting its behavior.

■RADAR.—The Weather Bureau maintains 32 long-range, and 64 medium-range, radar installations at strategic points in the United States. This equipment is used to track severe storms. The eye of hurricane Carla (1961), for example, first appeared on the scope of the Galveston, Texas, radar when the storm was 220 nautical miles south, over the Gulf of Mexico. This particular hurricane was tracked continuously by the Galveston station for 46 hours.

■AUTOMATIC STATIONS.—In addition to manned installations, the Weather Bureau also maintains automatic sta-tions to provide weather information from remote, inaccessible locations. These automatic stations observe cloud height, runway visual range for pilots, air pressure, and other weather conditions, transmitting these observations over teletype circuits. A marine automatic meteorological observation station is being tested in the Gulf of Mexico. For extremely remote locations, an atomic-powered weather station was developed through the efforts of the Atomic Energy Commission and the Weather Bureau. One such station was installed in the Canadian Arctic during the summer of 1961, and has been operating satisfactorily ever since.

■COMPUTERS.—To aid the weatherman in assembling and analyzing the wealth of weather data received, high-speed electronic computers have been installed at the *National Meteorological Center*, the *National Weather Satellite Center*, the *National Weather Records Center* at Asheville, North Carolina, and at various other research and forecast centers.

Weather Research.—Much of the progress made in hurricane forecasting is the result of intensive studies made by the Weather Bureau's *National Hurrican Research Project*. Basic information for this research is gathered by a fleet of flying laboratories and networks of upper-air observational stations. In 1961, under the joint sponsorship of the Weather Bureau, the Navy, and the *National Science Foundation*, a series of experiments began to explore the possibilities of modifying hurricanes by releasing silver iodide into the cloud tops near the area of maximum hurricane winds.

The Weather Bureau also initiated the *National Severe Storms Project* in 1961. This project is designed to collect detailed and comprehensive information on the behavior of tornadoes and severe local storms, using aircraft, radar, and observational networks in Oklahoma, Texas, and Kansas—the heart of the tornado belt. The program has received the active cooperation of many government agencies, including the Air Force, the Navy, the *Federal Aviation Agency*, and the National Aeronautics and Space Administration. Many universities and private agencies have also cooperated in the project.

Weather Bureau Publications.—The Weather Bureau publishes the *Daily Weather Map*, the *Weekly Weather and Crop Bulletin*, *Climatological Data*, the *Mariners Weather Log*, the *Average Monthly Weather Resumé and Outlook*, and the *Monthly Weather Review*. Its research findings are published in the *Research Paper Series*, the *Monthly Weather Review*, and various scientific journals.

—Robert M. White

BIBLIOGRAPHY

BLUMENSTOCK, DAVID IRVING. *Ocean of Air*. Rutgers University Press, 1959.

GIEGER, RUDOLPH. *The Climate near the Ground*. Harvard University Press, 1957.

KOEPPE, CLARENCE EUGENE, and DE-LONG, GEORGE CASS. *Weather and Climate*. McGraw-Hill, Inc., 1958.

LONGSTRETH, THOMAS MORRIS. *Understanding the Weather*. Collier Books, Inc., 1962.

MASON, BASIL JOHN. *Clouds, Rain, and Rainmaking*. Cambridge University Press, 1962.

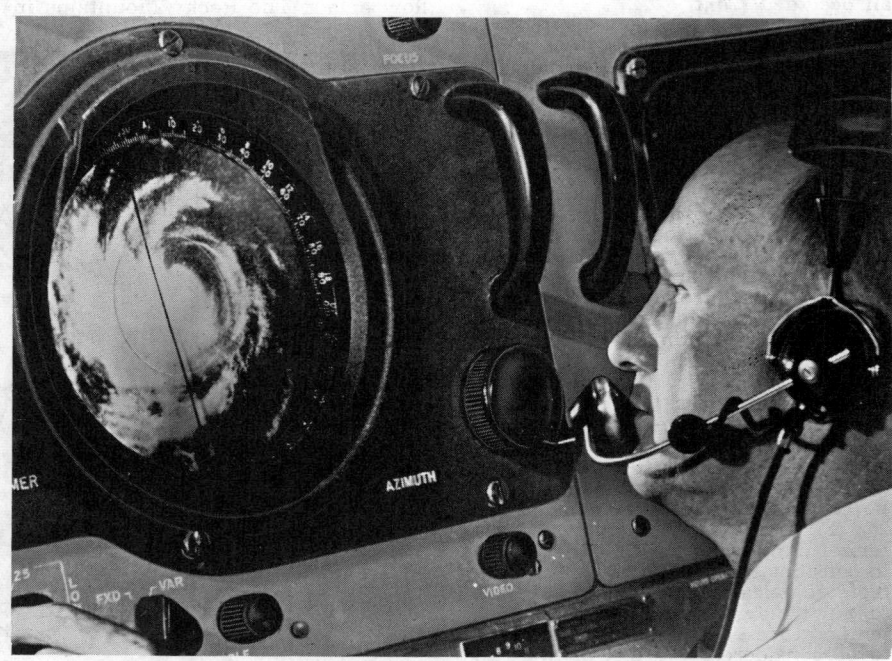

U.S. DEPARTMENT OF COMMERCE, WEATHER BUREAU

RADAR has become a valuable tool to meteorologists for the tracking of storms. The storm vortex, presented on this radarscope, can be tracked at distances of up to 250 miles.

DICTIONARY OF EARTH SCIENCES

AA. Hawaiian term for a lava flow whose surface has broken into rough, jagged blocks bristling with sharp points. Also called block lava.

ABLATION. Reduction of the surface of a glacier or snow field through evaporation and melting.

ABNEY LEVEL. An instrument with a tube containing a movable bubble; used to measure the steepness of a slope or a vertical angle. It resembles a carpenter's level.

ABRASION. The wearing down of land surfaces by the frictional action of solid particles moved by ice, wind, water, or gravity.

ABSOLUTE ATMOSPHERE. A unit of pressure equaling 1 million times the pressure produced on a square centimeter by a force of one dyne.

ABSOLUTE TIME. Measurement of a sequence of events in geological time in years rather than in chronological sequence, which indicates only relative time.

ABYSSAL. Referring to the deepest parts of the oceans, generally below 2,000 fathoms (12,000 feet). See *Ocean depth zones.*

ABYSSAL DEPOSITS. Solid material covering the floor of ocean basins lying at a depth of more than 2,000 fathoms (12,000 feet).

ACCRETION. The process by which inorganic masses become larger through the addition of new matter to the outside. *Natural accretion* is the gradual buildup of land over time by the deposit of material carried by water or air. *Artificial accretion* is the same buildup caused by human action.

ACIDIC. A term describing igneous rocks containing a large proportion of silica, usually more than 66 percent.

ADIABATIC RATE. The change in temperature of a rising or falling body of air due to its expansion or compression. Rising, expanding air loses about 1.6°F per 300 feet, and the temperature of falling bodies of air increases at the same rate.

ADOBE. Heavy clay and silt surface soils found in desert and dry areas, as in the U.S. southwest. Also, the sun-dried bricks made from the clay and silt.

ADVECTION. Horizontal movement of parcels of air, such as sea fog, and the flow of sea water, as a current.

AERATION ZONE. See *Zone of aeration.*

AEROLOGY. The scientific study of the atmosphere.

AFFLUENT. A stream or river flowing into a larger river or other body of water; a tributary.

AFTERGLOW. Radiance seen in the sky when the sun is below the horizon.

AFTERSHOCK. An earthquake following a larger earthquake. Major earthquakes are usually followed by several aftershocks.

AGATE. A varied-colored waxy quartz, or silica, with bands of chalcedony; commonly found embedded in limestone or in rock cavities.

AGGLOMERATE. A mass of coarse, volcanic rock fragments. The fragments are usually slightly rounded in shape and larger than volcanic ash.

AGGLUTINATE. A volcanic deposit consisting of fragments fused at their point of contact. It is distinguished from agglomerate by the presence of glassy cement and bits of scoria or cinders between the blocks, and the absence of ash.

AGGRADATION. The building up of a land surface by the deposit of loose materials as by a stream or river.

AGGREGATE. A grouping or mixture of particles of earth material, as a rock, which may be separated into its components by mechanical means.

AGONIC. No magnetic declination. An agonic line connects points on the earth's surface at which the needle of a magnetic compass points to true north and magnetic north simultaneously.

A HORIZON. See *Soil profile.*

AIR MASS. A large body of air generally homogeneous with respect to temperature and moisture, vertical variations being about the same throughout its horizontal extent.

AMERICAN MUSEUM OF NATURAL HISTORY

ALLUVIAL FAN, land counterpart of a delta, is formed of debris from the cliff face.

ALBEDO. The ratio between the amount of light falling on a surface and the amount reflected. The albedo of earth is about 0.4, which means that 4/10 of the sun's radiation is reflected by the earth's surface.

ALEUTIAN LOW. A semipermanent center of low pressure that develops during the winter in the North Pacific Ocean in the vicinity of the Aleutian Islands.

ALIDADE. A straight-edge ruler mounted with a sighting device, such as a telescope; used to measure horizontal angular distances.

ALKALI FLAT. A broad, barren, flat plain into which desert streams drain. As accumulated water evaporates, it deposits fine sediment and dissolved minerals, thus forming a salt surface.

ALLOTROPIC. Substance which may exist in two or more structural forms, such as carbon as graphite and as diamond.

ALLUVIAL FAN. A fan-shaped, or cone-shaped, mass of soil deposited by a stream.

ALLUVIUM. Loose stream or river-borne deposits of sand, silt, and gravel.

ALPIDES. A great structural belt extending eastward from the Alps in Europe to the Himalayas and related mountains in Asia; formed in the Tertiary period, between 60 million and 1 million years ago.

ALPINE. Referring to a mountain region above the timberline but below the snowline.

ALTIMETER. An instrument used to measure height above ground level or sea level.

ALTITUDE. The vertical distance above sea level or the angular distance above the horizon plane.

AMORPHOUS. Without a distinctive form. The absence of a definite crystalline structure in rocks or minerals.

AMPHIBOLE. A group of common rock-forming minerals. The most important is hornblende.

AMYGDALE. A vesicle, or gas cavity, in igneous rock which has been filled with some mineral such as calcite, chalcedony, or quartz.

ANABATIC. A local, upward-flowing wind found in mountainous areas. It is caused by the convectional rise of air that has been heated.

ANCHOR ICE. Ice formed on the bottom of a stream or river which is not frozen solid.

ANDESITE. A fine-grained volcanic rock composed largely of plagioclase feldspars.

U.S. DEPARTMENT OF THE INTERIOR NATIONAL PARK SERVICE

ANTECEDENT RIVER. The Colorado cuts through the rocks to form the Grand Canyon.

ANALEMMA. A chart giving the declination of the sun, on the vertical scale, and the equation of time, on the horizontal, for every day of the year. It forms a figure "8" on the globe.

ANEMOGRAPH. A self-recording instrument that traces a curved line showing the speed or force of the wind.

ANEMOMETER. An instrument measuring the speed of wind.

ANEROID. See *Barometer*.

ANGLE OF REPOSE. The maximum angle at which material such as sand, soil, or loose rock can remain stable. If the angle is exceeded, the material will slide.

ANGULAR UNCONFORMITY. An unconformity in which older, lower, beds of rock tilt at a different angle than the later, upper layers.

ANHYDROUS. Essentially without water, as opposed to hydrous.

ANIMATE ENERGY. Energy or work created by living organisms such as a man or a horse. The opposite of inanimate energy.

ANISOTROPIC. Having different physical properties when tested in different directions, as opposed to isotropic. Characteristic of most crystalline structures.

ANNULAR DRAINAGE PATTERN. A circular pattern of stream paths developed on the weaker sedimentary rocks of dome or basin structures.

ANOMALY. An area which differs from its surroundings, often associated with valuable mineral deposits such as petroleum.

ANORTHITE. See *Feldspar*.

ANTARCTIC CIRCLE. The parallel of latitude 66½° South.

ANTECEDENT RIVER. A river, or stream, that has maintained its original course by cutting through land that rose in its path.

ANTHRACITE. Hard, black, highly metamorphosed lustrous coal containing a high percentage of carbon and a low percentage of volatile matter. It burns with little smoke and gives great heat.

ANTHROPOGEOGRAPHY. The study of the distribution of human societies on the earth in relation to their environment.

ANTICLINAL THEORY. The theory that water, petroleum, and natural gas accumulate in up-bowed strata in the order named (water lowest), provided that the structure contains reservoir rocks in proper relation to source beds and is capped by an impervious barrier.

ANTICLINE. A fold of stratified rocks that was arched upward. It is the reverse of a syncline.

ANTICLINORIUM. A series of anticlines and synclines forming a general anticline covering an extensive area.

ANTICYCLONE. A high-pressure air mass, generally circular in shape, around which winds spiral outward in a clockwise direction in the northern hemisphere and counterclockwise in the southern hemisphere. It is often called a "high" and is characterized by clear or clearing skies.

ANTIPODES. Two points on diametrically opposite sides of the earth's surface. A line drawn between them passes through the center of the earth.

ANTITRADES. Upper air winds moving in a direction opposite that of surface trade winds.

APHANITIC. Referring to a fine-grained igneous rock, such as basalt, in which the crystals are too small to be seen with the unaided eye. The material cooled too rapidly to form large mineral crystals.

APHELION. The position of a planet in its orbit when it is farthest from the sun.

APOGEE. The position of a celestial body or satellite in its orbit when it is at its greatest distance from the body around which it is revolving.

APPARENT TIME. Solar time, or time based on the apparent motion of the sun as seen by an observer on the earth.

AQUEOUS. Pertaining to water and the sediment it deposits. Used to describe ripple marks made by waves and water currents, as opposed to eolian, or those made by the wind.

AQUICLUDE. A porous sedimentary rock that does not readily transmit water.

AQUIFER. A porous layer of sedimentary rock that freely transmits water.

AQUIFUGE. A nonporous rock that neither absorbs nor transmits water.

ARCHIPELAGO. A cluster of related islands; often tops of submerged mountains.

ARCTIC AIR MASS. An air mass originating over northern Canada.

ARCTIC CIRCLE. The parallel of latitude 66½° North.

ARCTIC PACK. The drifting ice floes of the Arctic Ocean. Also, nearly salt-free sea ice more than two years old.

ARENACEOUS. Referring to rocks derived from or composed largely of sand or other small particles.

ARÊTE. A sharp mountain ridge carved by a glacier. It can be the crest of a mountain range, a subsidiary ridge between two mountains, or a spur between two rock basins.

ARGILLACEOUS. Rocks composed primarily of clay.

ARID. Deficient in moisture. A territory where rainfall is insufficient to support vegetation (less than 10 inches of rain a year) or where it is subject to great evaporation.

ARKOSE. Sandstone containing a large proportion of quartz and feldspar.

ARROYO. A stream bed, usually dry for all or most of the year; found in semi-arid and arid regions.

ARTESIAN WATER. Ground water confined in an aquifer between two impermeable layers and under sufficient pressure to rise above the level at which it is first encountered. It does not necessarily rise to the surface.

ASBESTOS. Also called "rock wool." Fibrous form of various minerals. It is fire resistant and is a poor conductor of heat. Some types of asbestos have fibers long enough to be woven.

ASH. Inorganic residue left after combustion. Also, the small particles of matter, or dust, thrown up during a volcanic eruption.

ASPHALT. A brown to black solid or semisolid bituminous substance. A combination of hydrocarbon compounds, it occurs in nature and is also obtained by distillation in the refining of certain petroleums, when it is known as artificial asphalt.

ASSAY. Analysis of ores to determine the proportion of metals they contain.

ASSIMILATION. The incorporation into a pool of molten rock of material originally present in the surrounding wall rock, resulting in "hybrid" rock.

ASTEROID. A minor planet, or planetoid, of the solar system, revolving between the orbits of Mars and Jupiter.

ATMOSPHERE. The gaseous envelope surrounding a heavenly body and bound to it by gravitational attraction. Earth's atmosphere, which is also called air, consists chiefly of nitrogen (about 76 percent) and oxygen (about 23 percent), with small amounts of carbon dioxide, argon, hydrogen, helium, neon, krypton, xenon, ozone, water vapor, dust, and gaseous impurities.

At the earth's surface the atmosphere has a density of about 1/800 that of water and exerts a pressure of 14.7 pounds per square inch at sea level. Earth's atmosphere may extend more than 1,000 miles above the land and water surface, but one-half its mass lies below 3.46 miles. There are three major divisions: the *troposphere, stratosphere,* and *ionosphere.*

The *troposphere,* or lowest layer, extends from the earth's surface to about 5 miles at the poles and about 11 miles at the equator, and contains the eddies and convection currents (caused by uneven heating and cooling) that create most of the earth's weather.

The *stratosphere,* the next higher region, is approximately 50 miles deep and has relatively uniform temperatures and wind, although jet streams appear at high midlatitudes. It contains a layer of ozone which absorbs most of the sun's ultraviolet rays.

The *ionosphere,* or highest layer, has a lower limit of about 35 miles during the day and about 60 miles at night. It consists of a series of constantly changing layers of highly ionized molecules, which reflect radiowaves back to earth, thereby making possible radio transmission around the earth's curvature.

In polar regions, the ionosphere contains the edges of the Van Allen belt, which, when it dips to an altitude of about 50 miles above the earth in subpolar latitudes, may cause aurora borealis (northern lights) in the northern hemisphere and aurora australis (southern lights) in the southern hemisphere.

ATOLL. A circular coral reef enclosing a lagoon.

AUGEN. Large, lenslike mineral grains or aggregates of minerals, usually occurring in metamorphic rocks.

AUREOLE. A zone surrounding an igneous intrusion in which contact metamorphism has taken place.

AURORA. Light, in streaks or arcs, seen in the atmosphere in the northern and southern hemispheres most frequently in spring and autumn, when the sun reaches both the Arctic and Antarctic circles. Auroras are believed to occur when negative electrons from the sun are trapped in the magnetic field of the earth and ionize the atoms of such gases as oxygen, nitrogen, helium, neon, ozone, hydrogen and krypton. They may range from 50 to 600 miles in height.

The aurora borealis, or northern lights, is visible in North America between the 40th and 60th parallels and in Europe and Asia between the 50th and 70th parallels. The aurora australis, or southern lights, is visible only between the 40th and 55th parallels in South America.

AVALANCHE. A large mass of snow, ice, or loose earth material sliding rapidly down a mountain slope. It can also be called a landslide when primarily composed of earth and loose rock.

AXIS. A straight line, real or imaginary, passing through a body or system, around which the parts are symmetrically arranged. The polar diameter of the earth around which the earth rotates. The place of sharpest folding of an anticline or syncline.

AZONAL SOILS. A group of young soils without well-developed profile characteristics. See also *Soil.*

BACKING. The counterclockwise change of direction of a wind (e.g., the wind goes from east through northeast to north). The opposite of veering.

BACKSET BEDS. Layers of sand developed on the gentler, windward slope of a dune.

BACKSET EDDY. Small current revolving in a direction opposite that of the great eddies of the ocean.

BADLANDS. A region of soft rock and dry soil where erosion has cut an intricate maze of narrow ravines and sharp crests. The name refers to the difficulty of travel across such areas, as the South Dakota Badlands.

U.S. DEPARTMENT OF THE INTERIOR NATIONAL PARK SERVICE

BADLANDS, a barren region of South Dakota and Nebraska, has an eroded land surface.

AUSTRALIAN NEWS AND INFORMATION BUREAU

BARRIER REEF, a coral reef separated from the mainland by a lagoon. Heron Island, a coral cay, is part of Australia's Great Barrier Reef.

BAJADA. A sloping fringe of coarse material, such as gravel, surrounding a desert basin.

BAND. A layer of rock or soil differing in color from adjacent layers.

BANK. The sloping land border of a stream, designated as right or left as it would appear facing downstream. Also, a raised but underwater portion of a sea or ocean bed.

BAR. A unit of atmospheric pressure, commonly expressed in millibars (1/1000 of a bar) and equal to the mean atmospheric pressure at about 100 meters, or some 328 feet, above mean sea level. Standard atmospheric pressure is 1,013.3 millibars. Also, a ridge of sand, gravel, or mud deposited by streams, currents, or waves.

BARCHAN, or barkhan, a crescent-shaped sand dune whose horns point downwind. Barchans are sometimes migrating, or moving. The convex, or windward, side of the dune is the gentler slope.

BAROMETER. An instrument for measuring the pressure of the atmosphere. The *mercury barometer* is a calibrated glass tube, closed at one end, the other resting in a cup of mercury. The *aneroid barometer* is a corrugated vacuum box sensitive to external pressure; its expansion or contraction is indicated on a graduated dial by mechanical devices. When it is self-recording it is called a barograph.

BARRAGE. An artificial barrier placed across a stream to increase the depth of the water.

BARRANCA. A deep gully made by heavy rain.

BARRANCO. An amphitheater-shaped valley on the side of a volcano in which streams converge to pass through a narrow exit.

BARRIER REEF. A coral reef generally parallel to the coast and separated from the landmass by a lagoon, too deep for coral growth, that is open to the sea through passes in the reef.

BARYSPHERE. See *Earth structure.*

BASAL CONGLOMERATE. A coarse, usually homogeneous rock deposit above an eroded surface or unconformity, formed by a rising sea level.

BASALT. A dark-colored, finely-grained extrusive igneous rock composed primarily of plagioclase feldspars.

BASE LEVEL. The lowest level to which a land surface can be reduced by running water. For a region, the base level is a plane extending inland from the sea and sloping upward from sea level. For a stream, the base level is usually sea level, athough there may be "temporary base levels," such as lakes or resistant rock layers, along its course.

BASE LINE. An accurately surveyed line on the earth's surface used as a base for further surveys.

BASEMENT COMPLEX. A mass of igneous or metamorphic rocks, generally with complex structure, underlying the oldest identifiable rocks in any region.

BASIC. A term describing a rock low in silica and high in ferromagnesians.

BASIN. A depression in the earth's surface formed by faulting, folding (in which case a circular or eleptical syncline tilts the beds inward to a central

low point), erosion by water or a glacier, or by volcanic flows or landslides that dam valleys. The opposite of dome. Also used to describe the area drained by a river.

BASIN FLOODING. A method of irrigation in which a stream is permitted to overflow its banks during flood stage and is controlled to inundate large areas with its floodwaters.

BATHOLITH. A large, coarse-textured, irregularly dome-shaped mass of igneous rock which, when molten, penetrated older formations. It may be "concordant" (having pushed up overlying beds and being composed of granite gneiss) or "discordant" (having cut through overlying beds and being composed of granite). It may form the backbone of a mountain range.

BATHYAL. See *Ocean depth zones.*

BATHYSPHERE. A vehicle for investigating the deeper portions of the ocean basin.

BAUXITE. A hydrated aluminum oxide, the chief ore of aluminum.

BAY. An indentation in the shore line or an inlet of a sea or lake between two headlands. A bay is smaller than a gulf and larger than a cove.

BAYMOUTH BAR. A sandbar extending partially or fully across the mouth of a bay.

BAYOU. A sluggish stream or creek in a swamp or river delta.

BEACH. The gently sloping, narrow strip of land bordering a lake or sea, formed by wave or tidal action. Beaches consist of silt, sand, gravel, or rocks.

Because of the water's constant action the structure of a beach changes continuously.

BEADED DRAINAGE. The pattern of small pools connected by short streams characteristic of an area underlain by permafrost.

BEAUFORT WIND SCALE. A series of numbers used to designate wind velocities.

No.	Description	Mph	Knots
0	Calm	1	1
1	Light air	1- 3	1- 3
2	Light breeze	4- 7	4- 6
3	Gentle breeze	8- 12	7- 10
4	Moderate breeze	13- 18	11- 16
5	Fresh breeze	19- 24	17- 21
6	Strong breeze	25- 31	22- 27
7	Moderate gale	32- 38	28- 33
8	Fresh gale	39- 46	34- 40
9	Strong gale	47- 54	41- 47
10	Whole gale	55- 61	48- 55
11	Storm	62- 72	56- 63
12	Hurricane	73- 80	64- 71
13		81- 91	72- 80
14		92-101	81- 89
15		102-112	90- 99
16		113-124	100-109
17		125-134	110-118

BED. The smallest division of a series of rock layers, clearly separated from the older rock layers below and the younger rock layers above. It lies parallel to the stratification. Also, the bottom or floor of a body of water, such as a river, lake, or sea.

BEDDING PLANE. The surface on which material forming sedimentary rock was originally deposited.

BED LOAD. The loose material moved by a stream along its channel floor, as compared to silt load, which is material carried in suspension.

BEDROCK. Solid rock exposed at the earth's surface or covered by soil or unconsolidated weathered material, or regolith. Also, the parent material in the soil profile.

BEHEADED STREAM. A stream, or river, from which the upper portion of its watercourse has been captured by a stronger stream. See also *Stream capture.*

BEN. In Scottish, a peak or mountain. The term is often used as a prefix in names of mountains, such as Ben More-Mt. More.

BENCH MARK. A special mark indicating a point on the earth's surface whose elevation and location have been accurately found by surveying.

BENTHIC. See *Ocean depth zones.*

BERGSCHRUND. A crevasse or series of open fissures at the head of a mountain glacier, between the moving glacial ice and snow and the immobile ice and snow on the headwall of the valley, or cirque.

BERG WIND. A warm dry wind of the foehn type that occurs in South Africa.

BERM. A terrace formed when an erosion cycle is interrupted with the rejuvenation of a stream in its mature stage, leaving remnants of the earlier valley floor above flood level. Also, a storm-built beach terrace whose seaward edges are low ridges built by waves.

BEVELING. The wearing down or planing by erosion of outcropping edges or tops of ridges or hills.

B HORIZON. See *Soil profile.*

BIGHT. A bend in a shore line between comparatively distant headlands, forming a shallow opening toward the sea.

BIOCLIMATOLOGY. The study of climate in relation to living organisms and their distribution.

BIOGEOGRAPHY. The study of the geographical distribution of plants and animals on the earth.

BIOSPHERE. All living organisms on the earth's surface, as distinguished from those living only in the atmosphere, hydrosphere, or lithosphere.

BIOSTRATIGRAPHY. Differentiation of rocks on the basis of the fossils they contain.

BIOTA. The collective plant and animal life of a region.

BIOTITE. See *Micas.*

BISE. A cold, dry wind from the north, northeast, or northwest occurring in southern France, Switzerland, and northern Italy. It is accompanied by heavy clouds.

BITUMINOUS. A type of soft coal with a blocky structure that has experienced intermediate metamorphosis.

BLACKBODY. An ideal body whose surface completely absorbs all radiation that falls upon it.

BLACK EARTH. Dark-colored soils high in humus. See *Soil.*

BLIND VALLEY. A feature in limestone areas where a stream disappears underground at the closed end of a valley.

BLIZZARD. A heavy, blinding snowstorm, usually accompanied by a freezing wind. Blizzards result from the action of a high wind on dry, powdery snow.

BLOCK DIAGRAM. A technique for showing the topography of a region by sketching the surface features on a perspective block to give a three-dimensional effect.

BLOCK LAVA. See *Aa.*

BLOCK MOUNTAINS. Mountains formed by uplifted and tilted earth-blocks and bounded by fault scarps or cliffs.

BLOWOUT. A hollow made by wind in sandy soil or in a dune. Its size may vary from a few feet to several miles in diameter.

BLUE MUD. A deposit on the ocean floor having a blue-gray color. The color is the result of incomplete oxidation because of rapid deposition.

BLUFF. A headland or high, steep cliff with an almost perpendicular front.

BODY WAVE. A seismic wave that travels through the interior of a medium, as distinguished from a surface wave. See *Earthquake.*

BOG. A poorly drained, spongy land composed of decaying vegetation, or peat.

BOGAZ. Narrow, deep chasms in a limestone area caused by water penetrating a fault, bedding plain, or joint.

BOHOROK. A warm, dry wind occurring in Southeast Asia during the winter (the northeast monsoon season) caused by the descent of air on the lee side of mountains.

BOLSON. A basin, depression, or wide mountain valley drained by a stream flowing through canyons at either end; found in arid or semiarid regions.

BOMB, VOLCANIC. Lava thrown up during a volcanic eruption and solidifying before reaching the ground. The round rock masses formed range up to several feet in diameter.

BORA. A cold, dry northeasterly wind that blows across the Yugoslav Adriatic coast and northern Italy, mainly during the winter season.

BORE. A huge wave moving upstream (in opposition to the current) in funnel-shaped bays or narrow estuaries.

BOREAL FOREST. A regional plant cover consisting of coniferous trees found in the subarctic climate zone.

BOSS. A knob-like or dome-shaped mass of rock, circular in shape and often about 40 square miles in area.

BOTTOM LAND. See *Floodplain.*

BOTTOMSET BEDS. The layers of fine sediment deposited on the bottom of a sea or lake beyond the advancing edge of a growing delta. As the delta advances they are covered by thick foreset beds. Above this, where erosion and deposition alternate with the fluctuation of the stream current, thin topset beds are deposited.

BOULDER CLAY. A mass of silty and clayey materials containing matter ranging in size from rock flour to boulders; formed by glacial action. The material is dragged along the foot of a glacier and left behind when the ice melts.

BOWEN'S REACTION SERIES. Two orders of crystallization of silicate minerals in which any early-formed phase tends to react with the melt that remains, yielding a new mineral further along in the series.
In the continuous feldspar series, comprising the plagioclase minerals, early-formed crystals react with the

U.S. DEPARTMENT OF THE INTERIOR NATIONAL PARK SERVICE
A CAPE is a pointed headland extending into the sea or a lake. Cape Cod extends from Massachusetts into the Atlantic Ocean.

remaining liquid without abrupt changes. In the discontinuous ferro-magnesian series, including the minerals olivine, augite, hornblende, and biotite, each change represents a different crystalline structure and composition.

Fractionation is an interruption in the series, occurring when crystals settle out of the melt and do not enter into further reactions.

BOX CANYON. A steep-sided, flat-floored valley with a zigzag course; formed in dry regions. It appears to have four almost vertical walls.

BRACKISH. Referring to water with a salt content between that of freshwater and seawater.

BRAIDED STREAM. A stream flowing in several separating and reuniting channels divided by sediment the stream has deposited.

BRASH ICE. Fragment of sea or river ice less than 6.6 feet in diameter.

BREAKER. A wave that breaks into foam as it moves toward the shore, or a wave that breaks against a rock or other obstacle.

BREAKWATER. See *Jetty.*

BRECCIA. Rock composed of cemented angular fragments and thereby distinguished from conglomerates, which contain waterworn fragments.

BRODEL. A bulbous mass of silt, without horizontal continuity and enclosed by clay except at "necks," which connect with overlying silt beds.

BROOK. A small stream, one of the smallest branches of a drainage system. In the northeastern United States it is considered smaller than a creek.

BROWN COAL. See *Lignite.*

BULK MODULOUS. Volume elasticity of a body or number of pounds per square inch required to cause a specific change in volume. A body under increasing force per unit area will decrease in size but increase in density.

BUSH. A type of vegetation region having a dense undergrowth, with or without trees.

BUTTE. A small, flat-topped, steep-sided mountain standing above an adjacent plain.

BUYS BALLOT'S LAW. A general law of storms. It states that when standing with one's back to the wind in the northern hemisphere, the low pressure center will be on the left; in the southern hemisphere, the low pressure center will be on the right. Therefore, winds move counterclockwise around low pressure centers in the northern hemisphere and clockwise in the southern hemisphere. See also *Cyclone.*

CAATINGA. A type of vegetation region composed of thorny scrub and stunted, sparse forest in an area of slight rainfall. It is found in parts of northeastern Brazil.

CADASTRAL SURVEY. A large-scale survey of land to show accurately the property lines of every plot.

CALCAREOUS. Containing calcium carbonate ($CaCO_3$).

CALCITE. One of the commonest minerals and the principal constituent of limestone. It is composed of calcium carbonate ($CaCO_3$) and effervesces freely upon the application of acid.

CALDERA. A great, basin-shaped depression with a diameter at least three times its depth, as contrasted with a crater. It is formed by explosion or, more often, by the collapse of the peak of a volcano.

CALICHE. Gravel, sand, or desert debris cemented by calcium carbonate. It is found in dry regions. Also, the hardpan deposit of calcium carbonate found close to the surface.

CALVING. The formation of icebergs by the breaking off of a large block of ice from a glacier where it reaches into the sea. A piece of ice which rises to the surface after breaking away from the submerged portion of its parent body is called a calf.

CAMBRIAN PERIOD. The earliest period of the Paleozoic era in geological time. It began approximately 550 million years ago and ended approximately 450 million years ago.

CAMPOS. The tropical grasslands, or savanna, of interior Brazil.

CANAL. An artificial watercourse cut through a narrow stretch of land separating two bodies of water.

CANYON. A steep-walled, relatively narrow gorge, chasm, or ravine formed by the down cutting of a river.

CAPE. A headland, generally pointed, jutting out beyond the ordinary coastline into the sea or a lake. It differs from a peninsula in that it narrows as it projects into the water. It is usually larger than a point.

CAPILLARY FRINGE. A soil belt above the zone of saturation and composed of pores filled with water, held there by capillarity, or the ability to hold water by molecular attraction.

CAP ROCK. A layer of resistant rock overlying a layer of less resistant material.

CARBONATION. A chemical weathering process in which air or rain-borne carbon dioxide reacts with rock constituents to form carbonates.

CARBON 14. A radioactive isotope of carbon with a half life (time required for half the radioactive particles present to disintegrate into stable atoms) of about 5,700 years. It is used to date carbonaceous material younger than 50,000 years.

CARBONIFEROUS PERIOD. See *Mississippian period* and *Pennsylvanian period.*

CARDINAL POINTS. The four main directions of the compass: north, south, east, west.

CARTOGRAPHY. The art and science of representing in charts and maps the visible physical features—both natural and man-made—of the earth's surface.

CASCADE. A small waterfall, or a series of falls.

CATACLASTIC. A texture in metamorphic rocks in which brittle minerals have been broken and flattened in a direction at a right angle to the pressure stress.

CATARACT. A large waterfall. Also, a series of steep falls or rapids in a river.

CATASTROPHISM. The theory that certain geologic events were caused by sudden and violent disturbances of nature.

CATAZONE. The deepest zone of rock metamorphism. It is marked by very high pressures and high temperatures.

CATCHMENT BASIN. Drainage basin or area from which a stream draws its water.

CATS–PAW. An occasional feeble wind in the doldrums.

CAVE. A natural opening or underground cavity formed by the dissolution of limestone or gypsum by ground water, wave action against a cliff, faulting, or earthquakes.

CAVERN. A large cave or group of connected caves.

CAVITATION. Local reduction of a stream's pressure (by contraction or curvature) to a point at which partial vacuums are formed. As these vacuums collapse, the solid surfaces they contact are worn away in the process called cavitation erosion.

CAY. A low, flat island slightly above high tide level.

CELESTIAL SPHERE. A sphere whose center lies at some point within the solar system, most commonly the center of the earth. All members of the solar system may be projected onto this imaginary sphere.

CEMENTATION. The precipitation of a binding mineral matter, commonly calcite, silica, and iron oxide, in the spaces between the individual particles of an unconsolidated deposit.

CENOZOIC ERA. The "Era of Recent Life," the Cenozoic, or Caenozoic, is the latest of the three main eras of geological time. It began approximately 60 million years ago and continues into the present. Also called the Age of Mammals.

CENTRIFUGAL FORCE. The force which pulls a moving body out from its center of rotation. It is the opposite of gravitation, with which it combines to form gravity.

CENTROSPHERE. See *Earth structure.*

CHAIN. In the United States, the legal unit of length (66 feet) for the survey of public lands; ten square chains equal one acre. Also, a series of related or connected natural features such as mountains or lakes.

CHALCEDONY. An extremely fine-grained (cryptocrystalline) quartz, often deposited by aqueous solutions in a rock cavity, such as a geode, and having a hardness of 7.

CHALK. A soft, fine-grained variety of weakly cemented limestone. It is white, yellowish, or gray in color.

CHANNEL. The deepest part of a body of water (stream, bay, or strait) through which the main volume or current flows. Also, a narrow sea lane between two landmasses and connecting two larger bodies of water. The navigable part of a river or harbor.

CHAPARRAL. A dense thicket of stiff or thorny shrubs or dwarf trees, found in an area of Mediterranean climate—dry, sunny summers and moist winters.

CHASM. A deep cleft in the earth, often made by an earthquake.

CHEMICAL WEATHERING, or Chemical erosion. The decomposition of rock materials by oxidation, carbonation, hydrolysis, and chemicals in solution which transform the original material into new chemical combinations.

CHEMOSPHERE. The zone of the atmosphere from 40 to 160 miles above the surface of the earth containing a concentration of ozone.

CHERNOZEM. A zonal great soil group classified in the United States under the order *Mollisols.* It is a very dark, or black, soil, rich in humus and high in calcium, formed under cool subhumid grassland climatic conditions, as in the East European region between the Ural and Carpathian mountains.

CHERT. Cryptocrystalline varieties of silica often occurring in limestone as compact massive rock or as nodules. Flint is a darker, less brittle, and finer-grained variety of chert.

CHESTNUT SOIL. A zonal great soil group classified in the United States under the order *Mollisols.* It has a moderately thick top layer, high in organic matter, above a zone of calcium carbonate. It develops in the semiarid grasslands of the middle latitudes.

CHINOOK. A warm, dry wind, or foehn, blowing down the eastern side of the Rocky Mountains in the winter and early spring.

CHLORITE. A group of green minerals, the hydrous silicates of aluminum, magnesium, and ferrous iron, related to the micas.

C HORIZON. See *Soil profile.*

CHUTE. A narrow waterway between the mainland and an island. For a stream, a quick drop.

CIENAGA. An area where the water table is at or near the surface. It is covered with grass or heavy vegetation and sometimes short springs flow from it. In the southwestern United States, an elevated marsh with springs.

CINDER CONE. A cone of volcanic ash and small fragments formed around the mouth, or vent, of a volcano.

CIRQUE. A saucer-shaped, steep-walled hollow formed in rock by a mountain glacier and the alternate melting and freezing of the ice, or nivation. When glacier ice has melted from a cirque and the basin is filled with water, the lake formed is called a tarn. When two or more cirques gnaw into a ridge from opposite sides, an arête, or sharp, jagged ridge is formed.

CLASTIC ROCK. A class of sedimentary rocks, such as sandstone and shale, composed of particles produced by the disintegration of previous rocks by weathering processes.

THE AMERICAN MUSEUM OF NATURAL HISTORY

CLAY, a fine-textured earth material, goes into the composition of shale.

CLAY. A fine-textured earth material, one of the commonest materials in the mantle. It goes into the composition of shale, the most abundant type of sedimentary rock. See also *Wentworth grade scale.*

CLEAVAGE. In minerals, the characteristic of breaking in certain directions along smooth plane surfaces, being governed by the atomic structure of the material.

In rocks, the property of breaking along parallel planes or surfaces. There are four degrees of rock cleavage: *slaty,* the planes are separated by microscopic distances; *phyllitic,* the distance is barely visible; *schistose,* the distances are clearly visible; and *gneissic,* the distance is as great as ½ inch.

CLIFF. A high, steep rock face caused by weathering or wave action.

CLIMATE. The average weather conditions of an area as characterized by temperature, humidity, wind, and atmospheric pressure, and controlled by latitude, altitude, topography, distribution of land and sea, ocean currents, and prevailing winds.

CLIMATIC ZONE. An area having a distinctive climate. See *Frigid zone, Temperate zone, Torrid zone.*

CLIMATOLOGY. The study of the formation, distribution, and characteristics of earth climates.

CLIMAX. The plant cover believed to be in equilibrium with its environment. It is stable for the site.

CLIMOGRAPH. A graphic representation of the relation of two climatic elements in a region, such as temperature and rainfall, plotted at monthly intervals throughout the year.

CLINOMETER. An instrument for determining vertical angles, particularly dips, in a surface. It is essentially a pendulum swinging through a graduated arc.

CLOUD. A mass of visible vapor or collection of water or ice particles formed in the atmosphere by the condensation of water vapor at various elevations. Clouds are found in a variety of forms.

CLOUDBURST. A very heavy downpour of rain, averaging 3.94 inches per hour, usually of short duration and accompanied by thunder.

CLOUDINESS. An estimate of the amount of sky covered by clouds and expressed in tenths of sky covered. When the sky is up to 3/10 clouds, weather is considered clear; 3/10 to 7/10, partly cloudy; 7/10 to 9/10, cloudy; 9/10 or more, overcast.

COAL. A series of sedimentary rocks in which vegetable matter has been disintegrated, decomposed, and compacted, increasing in carbon content and, thus, increasing in effectiveness as fuel.

There are four types of coal, classified according to composition, degree of change, and hardness: peat, the softest, with about 60 percent carbon; lignite; bituminous; and anthracite, the hardest, with 92 to 98 percent carbon.

COAL MEASURES. The series of strata containing coal seams or minable deposits of coal and other sedimentary rocks, such as shale.

COAST. The edge of land bordering the sea, extending from the shoreline inland to the first major change in surface features.

COASTAL PLAIN. A low-lying level region or plain composed of sand, gravel, silt, and clay bordering the seacoast and extending inland to the first elevated land surface. Coastal plains represent a falling sea level or emerging sea bottom.

COASTLINE. The outline of a landmass where it meets the sea.

COBBLE. See *Wentworth grade scale.*

COKE. A hard, porous residue produced by the baking of bituminous coal. The heat drives off volatile constituents leaving a fuel useful in blast furnaces.

COL. A gap across a ridge or between two peaks; a high pass through a mountain range.

COLD POLE. The point on the earth's surface where the lowest winter temperatures are recorded. It is in the vicinity of Verkhoyansk, in the Siberian region of the Soviet Union.

COLD WAVE. A burst of cold polar air that causes a sudden drop in temperature.

COLLOID. A substance resulting from submicroscopic, yet larger than molecular, subdivision of one substance in another. When apparently dissolved in a liquid, it diffuses through a membrane very slowly or not at all, as contrasted with a crystalloid.

COLLUVIUM. A mixture of loose and incoherent material moved down a slope by gravity and usually found at the foot of a slope or cliff.

COLUMNAR JOINTING. A pattern of cracking breaking igneous rocks into columns. It is caused by contraction during cooling.

COMPACTION. A decrease in the volume of sediments by the reduction of the space between individual grains. It is the result of the evaporation or pressure of later deposits above or from earth movements.

COMPASS. An instrument indicating direction, usually by the pointing of a magnetized needle free to rotate in a horizontal plane. The needle responds to variations in the earth's magnetic field. Also, an instrument used for drawing circles and transferring measurements.

COMPETENCE. The maximum size of particles of given specific gravity that can be moved by a transporting agency such as a stream, glacier, or wind moving at a given velocity.

COMPLEX. A complicated assemblage of rocks of any age or origin.

COMPOSITE CONE, or stratovolcano. A volcanic cone, usually large with steep sides, built up over time by a number of eruptions.

CONCORDANT PLUTON. An igneous body lying parallel to the layering of the rocks into which it was intruded, as opposed to a discordant pluton.

CONCRETION. A rounded mass, or nodule, of material harder than the rock in which it is found. It is formed within sedimentary rocks by the concentration of cementing material around a nucleus such as a fossil or grain of sand.

CONDENSATION. The change of a substance from a gaseous state into a liquid or solid state. Condensation is the opposite of evaporation.

CONDUCTION. The transmission of energy through matter (the conductor) away from the source of energy.

CONE OF DEPRESSION. A dimple, or drop, in the water table surface produced by pumping or artesian outflow greater than the replacement of water.

CONE SHEET. A concentric set of dikes forming a funnel-shaped zone around an igneous intrusion.

CONFLUENCE. The point at which two streams meet.

CONFORMABLE. Referring to conformity—the parallel order of strata lying one above the other in unbroken geologic sequence.

CONGLOMERATE. A sedimentary rock composed of pebble-sized, waterworn rocks (generally of some durable material such as quartz) mixed with sand and cemented together with a mineral such as calcium carbonate. Conglomerate is distinguished from breccia, which is composed of angular rock fragments.

CONNATE WATER. Water trapped in the pores or interstices of sedimentary or extrusive igneous rock at the time the rock material was deposited, and therefore not participating in the hydrologic cycle.

CONSEQUENT STREAM. A stream whose course is a direct consequence of the original slope of the surface on which it developed.

CONTACT METAMORPHISM. Metamorphism at or near the point of contact between an intrusive igneous body and the surrounding rocks. Contact metamorphism occurs in relatively narrow zones called aureoles, in contrast to regional metamorphism.

CONTEMPORANEOUS DEFORMATION. Deformation, especially folding and faulting, that takes place during the time sedimentary rocks are being deposited.

CONTINENT. A large, unbroken landmass rising abruptly above the deep ocean floor. The earth's six major landmasses (Eurasia, Africa, North America, South America, Australia, and Antarctica), with islands, make up about 30 percent of the earth's surface, or an area of some 55 million square miles.

CONTINENTAL AIR MASS. A large, dry panel of air originating over a land surface. The air mass may be either hot or cold.

CONTINENTAL CLIMATE. A type of climate found in the interior of large landmasses. It is characterized by a wide range of temperature difference between winter and summer.

CONTINENTAL DRIFT. The idea that continents can shift, or drift. Proponents of the concept cite as an example the matching continental margins of western Africa and eastern South America.

CONTINENTAL GLACIER. An ice sheet covering a large part of a continent, obscuring mountains and plains, such as the glaciers on Greenland and in Antarctica.

CONTINENTAL SHELF. The gently sloping extension of a continent beneath its bordering seas. The shelf extends from the low-water mark to the point where there the continental slope begins its drop to the ocean floor. It may range in width from less than 10 to more than 200 miles.

CONTINENTAL SLOPE. The sharply sloping portion of the continental margin extending from the continental shelf to the ocean floor.

CONTINUOUS FELDSPAR SERIES. See *Bowen's reaction series.*

CONVECTION. The transmission of heat in a gas or liquid by the movements of the particles themselves. A temperature rise in one area of air, for example, will decrease its density and, therefore, its pressure. The denser portion surrounding that area moves into the low-pressure area, thus producing a convection current. A pair of such convection currents is known as a convection cell.

COPROLITE. Petrified excrement, or fecal pellets, found in Paleozoic, Mesozoic, and Tertiary strata.

COQUINA. A soft, coarse-grained porous limestone composed of cemented shell fragments.

CORAL. Various sessile (lacking voluntary mobility) marine animals that excrete an external skeleton of calcium carbonate, which they extract from sea water. They are usually found in colonies. Most corals require warm water and although they may grow as far below the ocean surface as sunlight penetrates, they are usually found where the water is 200 feet deep or less.

CORAL REEF. An accumulation of coral skeletons in three types of shore lines: *fringing reef,* which grows directly out from a landmass; *barrier reef,* which is separated from the landmass by a lagoon; and *atoll,* which is a ring of low coral islands around a central lagoon.

The term "coral" island for many tropical islands is often incorrect. In many cases they are made up largely of calcareous algae.

CORDED LAVA. See *Pahoehoe.*

CORDILLERA. A unified belt or series of mountain systems extending over considerable distances and including such intermontane features as valleys, plains, rivers, and lakes.

CORE. The innermost zone of the earth. See *Earth structure.*

CORIOLIS FORCE. The force exerted on freely moving bodies by the earth's rotation. It deflects a moving body, or currents of air or water, to the right in the northern hemisphere and to the left in the southern hemisphere.

CORN BELT CLIMATE. The type of climate found in the corn belt region of the United States and other similar areas in Europe and Asia. It is a type of humid continental climate with a long summer.

CORONA. Concentric luminous circles around the sun or moon. Also, a zone of minerals around another mineral or at the point of contact between two minerals.

CORRASION. The mechanical erosion, or wearing away, of the bed or bank of a stream by the abrasive action of loose material carried in suspension.

CORRELATION. The process of establishing the equivalence in geologic age and stratigraphic position of rocks or events in one area with rocks or events in another area.

CORRIE. See *Cirque.*

CORROSION. The erosion, or wearing away, of rocks by chemical action. It is an oxidizing process.

COSMIC RAYS. Streams of subatomic particles with enormous energy surrounding the earth. Although their activity increases with the altitude above the earth, their effects are measurable not only at the earth's surface, but well below the surface of bodies of water.

COSMOGONY. The science of the origin and development of the universe and its components.

THE AMERICAN MUSEUM OF NATURAL HISTORY

A CORAL COLONY consists of marine animals and the calcium carbonate skeletons they excrete. The shells may be white, pink, or red.

COSMOLOGY. The study of the universe, its origin, structure, and space-time relationships.

COTTON BELT CLIMATE. A type of climate found in the cotton belt area of the United States and other similar areas in Asia, Africa, Australia, and South America, It is a humid, subtropical climate.

COULEE. A steep-sided gulch. Also, a congealed lava flow.

COUNTER–TRADE WINDS. See *Antitrades*.

COUNTRY ROCK. A general term for rock penetrated by mineral veins or invaded by an igneous intrusion.

COVE. A small, baylike recess or hollow along a shore or in a mountain.

CRAG, A rough, steep, rock outcrop or broken cliff.

CRATER. A bowl-shaped, steep-sided basin such as in the top or side of a volcano or a depression in the earth caused by the impact of a meteor.

CREEK. A small stream tributary, larger than a brook but smaller than a river. Also, a small, narrow bay longer than it is wide.

CREEP. A slow but continuous downward and outward movement of slope-forming soil or rock carrying its plant cover with it unbroken.

CRETACEOUS PERIOD. The third and latest period of the Mesozoic era in geologic time. It began about 125 million years ago and lasted some 65 million years.

CREVASSE. A deep, vertical crack, or fissure, in a glacier.

CROSS–LAMINATION. Layers of deposits tranverse or oblique to the general plane of stratification of the rocks above and below. It is found in granular sedimentary rocks. Also called bedding.

CRUDE OIL. Oil as it comes from a pool in the earth before refining and treatment.

CRUST. The outermost layer of the earth. See *Earth structure*.

CRYPTOCRYSTALLINE. Having a structure so fine that although crystalline, it cannot be seen with an ordinary microscope.

CRYPTOZOIC EON. The eon of "hidden life" which preceded the Phanerozoic eon and includes perhaps as much as 9/10 of the history of earth. Its rocks range in age from less than 600 million years to almost 3 billion years. It lacks fossils to aid correlation and is not divisible into units of more than local application.

During the Cryptozoic, magma was intruded in great areas which stabilized by the beginning of the Phanerozoic eon. These areas are gently arched interior plains, called shields, and they are found in each of the continents. There is a fossil record only of calcareous algae, fungi, and the trails of wormlike creatures.

CRYSTAL. A solid (e.g., most minerals) with a definite, orderly internal arrangement of atoms.

CRYSTALLINE ROCK. Rock containing minerals of crystalline form. Applied to igneous and metamorphic rocks but not to sedimentary rocks.

CRYSTALLIZATION. The formation of crystals from solution, a fluid that is evaporated or cooled; fusion, a viscous substance that is cooled; or sublimation, a gas that is condensed as a solid without passing through the liquid state.

CRYSTALLOBLASTIC. A crystalline texture in which the essential constituents are included in all the others. The result is simultaneous crystallization. See also *Metamorphic facies*.

CRYSTALLOID. A substance that forms a true solution in which it diffuses readily through a membrane and is capable of being crystallized.

CUESTA. An asymmetrical ridge with one steep slope, or scarp, and one long, gentle slope generally parallel to the dip of the resistant sedimentary rock beds that form it.

CURRENT. The vertical motion of the air, wind being the horizontal movement. Also the horizontal movement of water. See also *Ocean current*.

CURRENT METER. An instrument used to determine the velocity of streams.

CYCLE OF EROSION. See *Geographical cycle*.

CYCLONE. A low-pressure air mass, nearly circular, around which winds spiral inward, turning counterclockwise in the northern hemisphere, clockwise in the southern. It is commonly referred to as a low. It tends to produce cloudiness and precipitation, sometimes severe storms, such as a hurricane, tornado, or typhoon.

DACITE. A group of dense volcanic rocks, the extrusive equivalent of quartz diorite, consisting of plagioclase, quartz, pyroxene, or hornblende, with some biotite and sanidine. Structurally they are either glassy or crystalline.

DALLES. The nearly vertical walls of a canyon or gorge, usually containing a rapid. Also, the plural of dell.

DAM. A natural or man-made obstruction across a stream raising the level of water in the stream channel.

DARCY'S LAW. An equation expressing the rate of flow of water through permeable rock. In a rock of constant permeability (P), the velocity (V) of water will increase as the hydraulic gradient $(\frac{h}{l})$, or slope of the water table, increases: $V = P\frac{l}{h}$.

DATUM LEVEL. The base level against which the altitudes of land surfaces are measured, usually mean sea level.

DAUGHTER ELEMENT. An element formed from another element through radioactive decay.

DEBRIS. Loose, or unconsolidated, surface material containing larger rock fragments than detritus, or pulverized rock.

DECLINATION. The declination of the sun is the angular distance, covering a range of 47° (from 23½° north of the equator to 23½° south of the equator), in which the sun attains a zenith position. See also *Magnetic declination*.

DEEP. A narrow, troughlike depression found along some margins of the ocean basins, generally more than 3,000 fathoms (18,000 feet) deep. Also called the hadal zone. See *Ocean depth zones*.

DEFLATION. An erosive process in which material is removed from a land surface by wind action.

DEFORMATION OF THE EARTH'S CRUST. See *Diastrophism*.

DEFORMATION OF ROCKS. Changes in the volume and shape of rocks. There are three types of deformation—*elastic, plastic,* and *rupture*.

In *elastic* deformation, a rock changed by stress will return to its original shape or volume when the stress is removed (see also *Hooke's law*). In *plastic* deformation, a rock will flow at a certain intensity of stress and accompanying heat and will not recover its original shape or volume. In *rupture*, the rock is actually cracked or broken.

DEGRADATION. The process of wearing down the land and transporting the material elsewhere, usually by a river.

DEGREE–DAY. The number of degrees Fahrenheit the mean temperature drops below 65°F in one day. It is used to estimate heating fuel needs.

DELL. A small wooded valley or hollow.

DELTA. A plain or extension of land at the mouth of a river, often roughly triangular in shape, resembling the Greek letter delta (△). Deltas result from the deposit of material carried in suspension by a stream whose velocity is suddenly reduced upon entering more quiet waters. See also *Bottomset beds*.

DENDRITIC DRAINAGE PATTERN. A system of streams in which tributaries join the mainstream at all angles, thus resembling the branching of a tree when shown on a map.

DENDROCHRONOLOGY. The study of tree rings to determine the past climatic history of an area and to date events in the past.

DENSITY. The ratio of mass to volume, showing the quantity of a substance in grams per cubic centimeter or pounds per cubic foot. The ratio between the density of a substance and that of water at 39.2°F is specific gravity.

DENSITY CURRENT. A current which may be colder, more salty, or muddier, and therefore more dense, than the water through, over, or under which it flows. It does not mix with the surrounding water. A muddy density current is called a turbidity current.

DENUDATION. The wearing away of a land surface by natural agencies such as streams, glaciers, frost, wind, rain, and the sea.

DEPOSITION. The laying down of solid material transported from one part of the earth's surface to another by a natural agency, such as wind (eolian deposits), ice, rainfall, and earth movements. Also, the precipitation of mineral matter from solution.

DEPRESSION. An area of lower elevation than the surrounding land surface with no natural outlet for surface drainage. Also, a region where the atmospheric pressure is lower than that of the surrounding area.

DESALINIZATION, or desalination. The removal of salt from water or soil, or the reduction of salt content.

DESERT. A region in which vegetation is too sparse to support any but specialized animals. A *cold desert,* such as the wastes of Antarctica, is caused by perpetual snow and temperatures too low to permit plant growth. A *hot* or *tropical desert,* such as the Sahara, is caused by low rainfall and tempera-

tures and winds so high that evaporation exceeds precipitation.

A "topographic" desert, such as the Takla Makan in Asia, is caused by a rainfall deficiency either because it is located far from the oceans in the center of a continent, or because it is ringed by high mountains that deprive it of rain-bearing winds.

DESERT PAVEMENT. The layer of stone or pebbles fitted closely together in desert regions after wind action has removed the fine dust and sand.

DESICCATION. The loss of water from pore spaces of sediments by evaporation or compaction. Also, the drying up, or increasing aridity, of an area of the earth as a result of long-term changes in climate.

DETRITUS. Loose, pulverized pieces of earth material; the product of mechanical weathering.

DEVONIAN PERIOD. The fourth period of the Paleozoic era in geological time. It began 355 million years ago and lasted 43 million years. During that time trees grew in swamps, amphibians developed, and fish became common in the sea and in freshwater. Also called the Age of Fishes.

DEW. Moisture condensed onto objects on or near the earth's surface. It is caused by the objects having cooled below the dew point of the adjacent air through radiational cooling during the night.

DEW POINT. The temperature at which air becomes saturated with water

vapor. Condensation will occur when the air temperature falls below the dew point.

DIALYSIS. A method of separating mixed substances — crystalloids from colloids — in solution by diffusion through a membrance. The crystalloid particles will pass through the membrane, but the colloid particles are too large and are retained.

DIAMOND. A form of carbon. It is the hardest substance known (10 on Moh's Hardness Scale). It is insoluble, inert at ordinary temperatures, and has perfect cleavage. Its specific gravity is 3.52.

DIASTROPHISM. The process by which the earth's crust is bent, folded, broken, or warped, producing continents, ocean basins, plateaus, and mountains.

DIATOMACEOUS OOZE. A soft siliceous deposit, chiefly composed of the frustules, or shells, which diatoms, or one-celled marine algae, have built by extracting mineral matter from seawater. It is found on the deep-sea floors. See also *Ooze.*

DIFFERENTIAL WEATHERING. The process in which different sections of a rock mass weather at different rates. It is caused by variations in the composition of the rock itself and differences in the intensity of weathering from one section to another in the same rock.

DIKE. A mass of igneous rock. Also, a bank of earth materials used to protect lowlying areas from flooding by the sea or a river.

GEORGE HUNTER/OTTAWA
DELTA on the Mackenzie River in northwestern Canada. Slowed crossing the delta, the river meandered and formed a series of oxbow lakes.

DINOSAURS

Reptilia—cold-blooded, scaly-skinned, egg-laying animals.

  Archosauria—distinguishing bony arch in skull.

    Thecodontia—teeth in sockets in the jaw.

      Pterosauria—flying reptiles.

      Phytosauria—primitive crocodiles.

      Pseudosuchia (false crocodiles)—fast-running, bipedal reptiles.

        Dinosauria (terrible lizards)—originally bipedal and rarely more than 15 feet long.

Saurischia (lizard-hipped)—originally carnivorous bipeds; late in the Triassic diverged into two sub-orders.

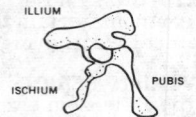

TYRANNOSAURUS

Theropoda (beast-footed)—earliest dinosaurs; carnivorous bipeds; provided the stock from which Sauropoda arose; late in the Cretaceous culminated in Tyrannosaurus, the 50-foot-long "King of Dinosaurs."

BRONTOSAURUS

Sauropoda (reptile-footed)—giants among terrestrial reptiles; became herbivorous quadrupeds in the Jurassic; had long necks and tails; probably spent most of their time in shallow water for protection from enemies and support for their enormous weight; culminated in Brontosaurus, often more than 80 feet long.

Ornithischia (bird-hipped)—dominant terrestrial reptiles of the late Cretaceous; herbivorous; in general, more advanced than Saurischia, with many specializations.

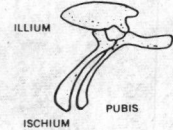

TRACHYDON

Ornithopoda · (bird-footed)—bipedal, but could assume quadrupedal stance; some had webbed feet; culminated in the duck-billed Trachydon.

STEGOSAURUS

Stegosauria—plated dinosaurs; herbivorous quadrupeds; one member, Stegosaurus, was over 20 feet long with alternating bony plates on either side of the backbone, a walnut-size brain and a nerve center near its hip 20 times as large as the brain.

SYRMOSAURUS

Ankylosauria—armored dinosaurs; herbivorous quadrupeds; best-known member is the Syrmosaurus, which resembled a large horned toad.

TRICERATOPS

Ceratopsia—horned dinosaurs having a bony frill extending from the back of the skull; herbivorous quadrupeds; best-known member, Triceratops, was 20 feet long, with a horn over each eye and on the snout.

DINOSAUR. Any of the large, extinct reptiles that dominated the earth for more than 100 million years, during the Mesozoic era. They ranged in size from less than 10 pounds to over 85 tons. They were herbivorous and carnivorous and could be found on land and in the water. They are classified as shown in the chart at left.

DIORITE. A coarse-grained, equigranular igneous rock composed of about 75 percent plagioclase feldspars and the balance ferromagnesian silicates.

DIP. The maximum slope of an inclined rock layer, or fault surface, measured from the horizontal and stated in terms of angle and direction (e.g., 15° west). Also, the angle between the direction of the earth's magnetic field and the horizontal plane at any point on the surface of the earth as shown by a compass needle.

DISCHARGE. The volume of water or ice flowing through a river, fjord, or harbor during a unit of time. It is usually expressed in terms of cubic feet per second.

DISCONFORMITY. An unconformity in which the older and newer beds of rock are parallel, as opposed to angular unconformity; indicates that the older beds were uniformly uplifted and eroded before deposit of the newer beds.

DISCONTINUITY (in the earth's interior). Sudden or rapid changes with depth in the physical properties of the material constituting the earth, as shown by seismic data. See *Earth structure.*

DISCORDANT PLUTON. An intrusive igneous body cutting across the layers of the rocks into which it was intruded, as contrasted with a concordant pluton.

DISINTEGRATION. See *Mechanical weathering.*

DISSECTION. The erosion of a land surface into ravines and valleys by the action of streams.

DISTRIBUTARY. A branch of a river that does not rejoin the mainstream, as in a delta.

DIURNAL RANGE. The range, or difference, between the maximum and minimum value of any property, such as temperature or humidity, during a 24-hour period.

DIVIDE. A ridge separating two drainage basins.

DOLDRUMS. The equatorial belt of calm or light, fitful winds where the northeast and southeast trade winds converge. In addition to the absence of sustained wind, the area is subject to heavy downpours, thunderstorms, and squalls. Temperature and humidity are high.

DOLINEN. Closed, rounded depressions found in limestone regions. They vary from 30 feet to 3,000 feet in diameter and from 6 feet to over 300 feet in depth, and may be dish, funnel, or well shaped. Dolinen contain sinkholes into which runoff surface water disappears.

DOLOMITE. A common rock-forming mineral, the carbonate of calcium and magnesium.

DOME. An anticlinal fold in rock layers in which the beds dip in all directions from a central area. The opposite of basin.

DOWN. An undulating, grassy, and generally treeless upland with sparse soil.

DRAG. Minor folding of rock layers near a fault surface. It indicates the direction of faulting.

DRAINAGE BASIN. An area within which all precipitation flows toward one collection point.

DREDGING. The process of excavation in shallow water or swamps to recover mineral deposits or to create or maintain a channel.

DRIFT. The loose material transported and deposited by glaciers. Also, the motion of sea, ice, or vessels as a result of ocean currents and wind. See also *Continental drift.*

DRIFT–ICE. Detached portions of icebergs carried by currents into the open sea.

DRIPSTONE. Calcite precipitated by subsurface water. An inclusive term for stalagtite and stalagmite.

DROUGHT. Long period of dry weather.

DROWN. To submerge land, whether by a rise in the water level or by a sinking of the land.

DRUMLIN. An elongated, oval-shaped hill deposited by glaciers. A drumlin may be up to 300 feet high. It resembles an inverted teaspoon bowl. The axis of a drumlin is parallel to the direction in which the ice sheet moved and may be more than a mile long. Drumlins are composed of unstratified clayey till.

DRY. A state of ground in which pore spaces to the depth of 3 inches or more are essentially free of water.

DRY FARMING. A method of agriculture in areas of low rainfall without irrigation. A system of crop fallowing and other moisture-conserving practices are followed.

DRY HOLE. A drill hole that has failed to produce oil or gas in commercial quantity.

DRY SNOW. Snow at a temperature below the freezing point.

DRY VALLEY. A valley in an area high in chalk and limestone without a permanent stream.

DUN. See *Downs.*

DUNE. A low ridge or hill of shifting, loose sand transported and formed by wind. See also *Barchan, Longitudinal dune,* and *Parabolic dune.*

DUST. Finely divided organic and inorganic matter easily carried by wind.

DUST BOWL. A dry area in which the wind removes the surface soil.

DUST DEVIL. A whirling pillar of sand or a sand spout which moves across the country at up to 30 miles an hour. Occurring during the heat of the day, it is caused by strong convection in hot, dusty regions.

Although only a few yards in diameter, it may extend upward to 3,000 feet.

DUST STORM. A storm in which the wind carries a large volume of dust or silt.

DYNE. A force which produces on a one-gram mass an acceleration of one centimeter per second per second.

U.S. DEPT. OF THE INTERIOR NATIONAL PARK SERVICE

DOME STRUCTURE exposed by erosion, showing beds dipping outward from the center. An example of the effects of differential weathering.

EARTH. The third planet in order of distance from the sun and the fifth in size in our solar system. A flattened sphere, or oblate spheroid, it is somewhat flattened at the poles and bulges slightly at the equator. The equatorial diameter is 7,926.68 miles and the polar diameter is 7,899.99 miles.

The earth rotates on its axis, at a velocity of 1,037 miles per hour (mph) at the equator, once every 23 hours, 56 minutes, 4.09 seconds, or one sidereal day. It completes one elliptical orbit, or revolution, around the sun, at a speed of 66,000 mph, every 365 days, 6 hours, 9 minutes, 9.54 seconds, or one sidereal year, at a mean distance of 92.9 million miles which, because of the elliptical orbit, varies 3 million miles in the course of a year.

The earth is tilted on its axis 23 degrees, 26 minutes, 40.15 seconds. This causes the seasons. The sun's rays are perpendicular to the tropic of Cancer (23½°N) on about June 21 and to the tropic of Capricorn (23½°S) on about December 21. When perpendicular to the tropic of Capricorn, the sun's rays make an obtuse angle with the northern hemisphere, providing less heat.

The precession, or gyration, of the earth's axis around the (imaginary) perpendicular to its orbit, is caused by the gravitational pull of the sun and moon on the earth's equatorial bulge. It completes one cycle every 25,800 years, and 12,000 years from now Vega will be the North Star.

While the earth is rotating, revolving, and precessing, the entire solar system is traveling toward Vega at a velocity of nearly 40,000 mph. Thus, in one year the earth ascends approximately 400 million miles along a spiral in the general direction of Vega.

The earth is generally believed to be 5 billion years old. It is composed of a series of concentric shells—crust, mantle, and core. See *Earth structure.*

EARTHFLOW. The gravitational movement down a slope of a mass of water-saturated soil, mantle, or weak bedrock. It is common in humid regions.

EARTHQUAKE. A sudden movement or tremor in the earth's crust resulting from the creation and transmission of waves in the earth caused by the faulting of rocks or by volcanic activity. The focus, or source, of a given set of earthquake waves may be near the surface or more than 400 miles down (1/10 of earth's radius). The epicenter is on the surface directly above the focus.

Earthquakes occur most often in regions of weak rocks where volcanic activity is most pronounced and where high mountains and ocean deeps are close together. Almost 80 percent of all earthquakes occur around the edge of the Pacific Ocean. Another belt of earthquakes runs along the north shore of the Mediterranean Sea, extending into Central Asia.

An earthquake begins with minor tremors, or body waves, which are generated simultaneously and travel through the earth. P waves are longitudinal, or push-pull, waves which travel several miles a second, pushing particles along the line of their travel.

S waves are transverse, or shake, waves which travel at about half the speed of P waves, moving particles across the line of their travel.

The interval between the arrival of P and S waves at a seismograph is proportional to the distance traversed, which is the radius of a circle. Comparable information from seismographs in three different locations describes three different circles, their intersection being the epicenter of the earthquake. See also *Seismology.*

At the epicenter, body waves generate long surface, or L, waves which travel along the earth's surface, causing at least one major, violent shock. This is followed by aftershocks or vibrations of decreasing intensity which eventually fade out.

The total energy of an earthquake at its source is indicated by the Richter Magnitude Scale. A magnitude of 2.5 is just large enough to be felt nearby; a magnitude of 4.5 causes slight local damage; 6 is moderately destructive; and 8.6 is the largest earthquake known.

EARTH STRUCTURE. The earth is composed of concentric shells. The outermost shell is the crust, or lithosphere, beneath the crust is the mantle, or asthenosphere, and at the center is the core, or centrosphere.

The crust varies in depth from more than 20 miles under the continents to as little as 3 or 4 miles under the oceans. It consists of two layers of approximately equal thickness—a sialic (silica and aluminum), or granitic, layer and a simatic (silica and magnesium), or basaltic, layer. The sialic layer is thinner under the oceans, disappearing completely in areas under the Pacific Ocean. The surface separating the crust from the mantle is called the Mohorovičić discontinuity.

The mantle, about 1,800 miles in depth, is a relatively solid region that probably consists of ferromagnesian minerals, or sima, and may be glassy in its upper portion.

The earth's core, or centrosphere, is also called the barysphere. It is approximately 2,100 miles from the lower edge of the mantle to the center of the core. It has two parts—an outer zone 1,300 miles thick, probably in a plastic

or liquid state, and an inner core with a radius of 800 miles, probably composed of solid iron mixed with about 8 percent nickel and some cobalt.

EBB CURRENT. The tidal current generally flowing seaward after high tide and before low tide.

ECOLOGY. The study of the interrelationships of organisms, both plants and animals, and their environment.

EDAPHOLOGY. The study of the influence of soil properties on organisms.

EFFLUENT. Outflow, such as lava through fissures in a volcano or water in a stream forming the outlet of a lake. Also, liquid discharged as waste.

EJECTA. Material thrown out by a volcano, such as cinders and other pyroclastic rocks.

ELEMENT. A substance whose atoms have the same atomic number and which cannot be broken down by ordinary chemical methods.

ELEVATION. The altitude or angular height of a body or object above a general level. In the U.S. it generally refers to the vertical distance in feet above mean sea level.

ELUVIATION. The removal of material in solution or suspension from a layer of soil by percolating water through earth material. Soil horizons that have lost material through eluviation are termed eluvial; those that have gained material are termed illuvial (see *Illuviation*). Distinguished from leaching, which refers to the complete removal of material in solution.

ELUVIUM. Deposits of sand, silt, and gravel accumulated in a place or shifted by wind, as contrasted with alluvium.

EMERGENCE. A term implying that a portion of the ocean floor has become dry land. It does not distinguish between a lowered water level and a raised land level.

ENDOGENETIC. Refers to a rock formed by solidification from fusion, the separation of minerals from a solution (*precipitation*) or from a vapor (*sublimation*), as contrasted with *exogenetic*.

ENTRENCHED MEANDER. A mature stream that has cut deeply into underlying bedrock.

EOCENE EPOCH. The second epoch of the Tertiary period of the Cenozoic era. It began about 50 million years ago and lasted some 10 million years. During this time, mammals became prominent on the earth.

EOLIAN. Relating to or caused by the action of wind, as eolian erosion or deposition. Subaerial was often used in much the same sense.

EON. One of the grand divisions in geological time, such as the Phanerozoic eon, which includes the Paleozoic, Mesozoic, and Cenozoic eras.

CRUST
MANTLE
MOHOROVICIC DISCONTINUITY
GUTENBERG DISCONTINUITY
CORE
OUTER
INNER
3 to over 20 miles
2,100 miles
1,800 miles
800 miles
1,300 miles
CENTROSPHERE (Barysphere)
ASTHENOSPHERE
LITHOSPHERE

EARTH STRUCTURE shown in cross section.

THE STRATOSPHERE

Top of Troposphere and Base of Stratosphere approximately 37,300 feet above sea level.

The Troposphere – (region of dust and clouds)

Ground Horizon

Devils Tower

Bear Butte
Belle Fourche River
Will...
Belle Fourche R
Deadwood
Lead
Fort Meade
Alkali Cr.
Elk Cr.
Box Elder Cr.
Inyan Kara Mt.
Mt. Rushmore
Rapid City
Stratosphere Bowl
Harney Peak
Rapid Cr.
Spring Cr.
B L A C K H I L L S
S O U T H D A K O T A
Scenic

Jewel Cave Nat. Mon.
Mt. Coolidge
Buffalo Gap
French Cr.
Wind Cave Nat. Park
Cottonwood Cr.
Hot Springs
South Fork of Cheyenne River

Fossil Cycad Nat. Mon.
White River
Wounded Knee Cr.
Porcupine Cr.
Bear in the Lodge Cr.
Potato Cr.

Ground Horizon

South Fork of Cheyenne River
White Cl...

© National Geographic Magazine. Reproduced from the National Geographic Magazine by special permission.

The First Photograph Ever Made Showing the Actual Curvature of the Earth

EPEIRIC SEAS. Almost landlocked seas less than 250 meters (820 feet) deep.

EPEIROGENY. Large-scale movements of uplift and subsidence which affect vast areas of the earth's crust.

EPHEMERAL STREAM. A stream that flows only during and shortly after precipitation in the immediate locality. Its channel is always above the water table. See also *Intermittent stream.*

EPICENTER. The point on the surface of the earth directly above the focus, or origin point, of an earthquake.

EPICONTINENTAL. Located on or overlying a continent or continental shelf.

EPICONTINENTAL SEA. A shallow sea or portion of the sea on the continental shelf.

EPIDOTE. A common mineral in metamorphic rocks. It is a silicate of aluminum, calcium, and iron and is characteristic of low-grade metamorphism.

EPIGENE. Geological processes occurring at or near the surface of the earth, as opposed to hypogene.

EPOCH. A small division of time in geological time, a subdivision of a period. A time unit corresponding to a series in time-stratigraphic units.

EQUATOR. The imaginary parallel lying midway between the poles of rotation of a celestial body, determining northern and southern latitudes (its own latitude being everywhere 0°).

ERA. In geological time, one of the major divisions of an eon. A time unit corresponding to a group in time-stratigraphic units.

ERG. A vast desert sand region. Also, a unit of energy equal to that expended when a force of one dyne acts through a distance of one centimeter in the direction of the force.

EROSION. The wearing away of the land surface by natural agencies such as water and the acids it may contain, wind, waves, frost, and glaciers. Erosion includes the processes of weathering, solution, corrasion, and transportation. If man-induced, the wearing away process is termed accelerated erosion.

ERRATIC. A large rock or rock fragment transported by a glacier from its place of origin to rest on or near bedrock of different composition.

ERUPTION. The discharge of solid, liquid, or gaseous material from the interior of the earth onto the earth's surface.

ESCARPMENT. A cliff or steep slope.

ESKER. A type of glacial drift. It is a long, narrow, sinuous ridge of stratified gravel and sand deposited by the action of glacial streams. It may range from 10 feet to 100 feet in height and from a fraction of a mile to more than 100 miles in length.

ESTUARY. A tidal bay formed by the sinking or drowning of a river mouth by the sea. Because of the effect of river and tidal currents, estuaries may be quite deep and provide good harbors.

EUSTASY. Simultaneous, worldwide changes in sea level.

EVAPORATION. The change of a substance from a liquid to a gaseous state.

EVAPORITE. A sedimentary rock precipitated or separated from a solution as a result of the evaporation of a watery solution, such as rock salt or gypsum.

EVAPOTRANSPIRATION. The loss of water from a body both by evaporation and by transpiration of plants.

EVERGLADE. A tract of swampy land with tall grass and some trees. In peninsular Florida, the Everglades refers specifically to the oblong basin of approximately 4,000 square miles which is the largest saw-grass marsh in the world.

EXFOLIATION. A weathering process in which thin surface layers of a rock peel.

EXOGENETIC. Refers to a rock composed of fragments of older rocks and owing its origin to erosion or metamorphism through contact with an adjacent igneous intrusion, as contrasted with endogenetic. An exogenetic sedimentary rock may also be called a clastic rock.

EXOTIC RIVER. A river flowing through an arid region whose headwaters are in a humid area.

EXPLOSION CRATER. A volcanic crater formed by violent explosion on the flanks or at the summit of a large volcano. There is no lava outflow.

EXTRATROPICAL CYCLONE. An atmospheric low-pressure center that develops outside the tropics.

THE AMERICAN MUSEUM OF NATURAL HISTORY

FELDSPAR, a group of common minerals that decompose into clay with weathering.

EXTRUSIVE ROCK. An igneous rock formed from the cooling of magma at the earth's surface.

FABRIC. The characteristic pattern of a rock produced by the shape of mineral grains and their orientation to each other. A factor of rock texture.

FACIES. The mineral, rock, or fossil features which reflect the specific environment in which a rock was formed. A sedimentary rock may grade from a sandstone facies into a shale facies. Although the two facies were deposited at the same time, they reflect an environment of quiet water where the shale was formed and water of some velocity where the sandstone was formed.

A particular fossil found in one area of a rock and not in another reflects favorable conditions for that animal in that area and a change of those conditions in the rest of the rock. A metamorphic rock may have one to four facies, according to the temperature-pressure conditions under which it was formed. See *Metamorphic facies.*

FALL LINE. An imaginary line connecting a number of streams where they make a sudden descent, as at the edge of a highland. Also, the natural downward course between two points on a slope.

FAST ICE. Sea ice that remains where it was originally formed, whether attached to the shore or over shoals where it is held by islands or grounded icebergs.

FATHOM. A unit of measurement equal to 6 feet (1.83 meters) used mainly to measure the depth of water.

FAULT. A fracture in rock along which there has been differential movement, as opposed to a joint. The surface may be vertical, horizontal, or inclined. The line formed at the intersection of the fault and a horizontal plane is the strike; the angle between the fault surface and the horizontal plane is the dip. Near the fault surface friction causes drag, or bending, of the rock layers which serves as a clue to the direction of movement.

Faults are generally caused by excessive deformation, which results in the rupture of rocks. In igneous rocks, faults may also occur during the cooling process.

FAULT BLOCK. A body of rock bounded on at least two opposite sides by faults.

FAULT SCARP. The steep face of a rock on the uplift side of a fault.

FAUNA. All animal life of a region in a geologic time period.

FELDSPAR. A group of common non-ferromagnesian rock-forming minerals, generally light-colored, composed of silicates of aluminum and potassium, calcium, and sodium.

Feldspars comprise about 60 percent of igneous rocks, are the dominant minerals in a large group of metamorphic rocks (gneisses), and are impor-

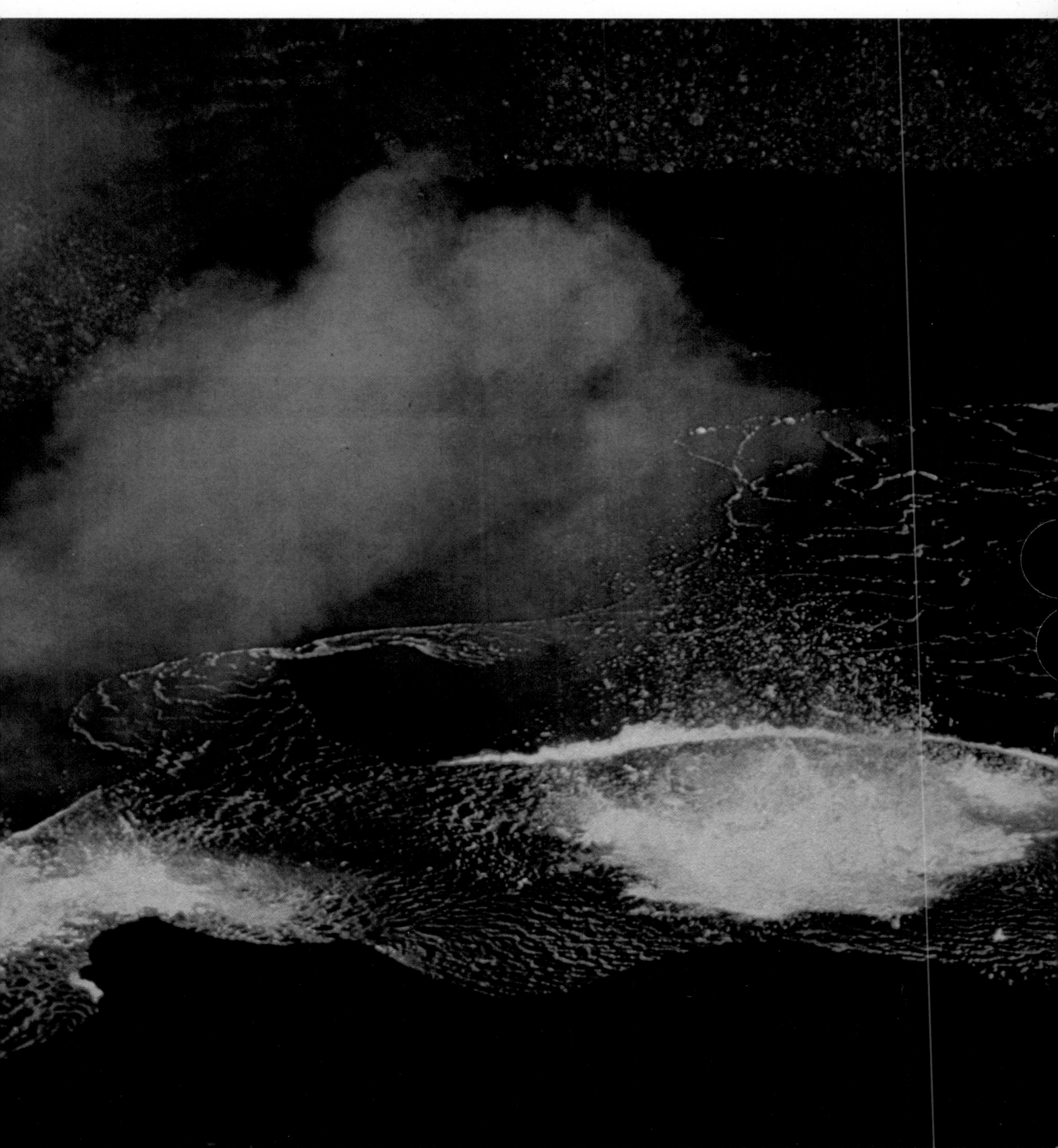

© WALT DISNEY PRODUCTIONS

HAWAIIAN VOLCANO ERUPTING

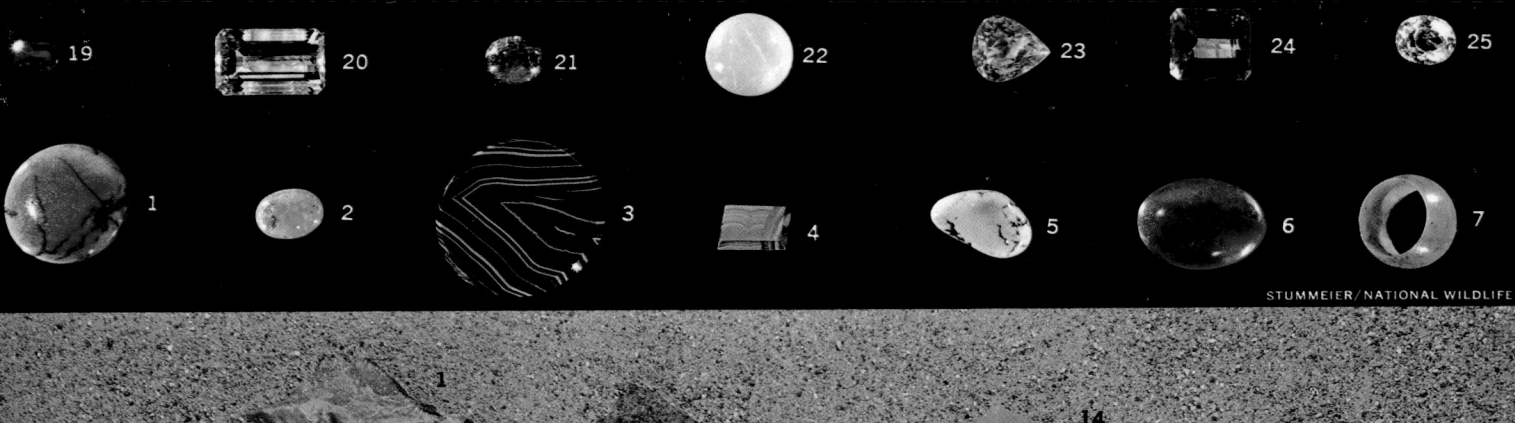

STUMMEIER/NATIONAL WILDLIFE

1. RHODENITE with cabochon.

2. TURQUOISE with cabochon.

3. FORTIFICATION AGATE with flat cabochon.

4. MALACHITE with square cabochon.

5. VARISCITE with tumbled specimen, also called Utahite.

6. JASPER with oval cabochon; usually red, also brown and green, sometimes banded.

7. JADE with carved ring.

8. EPIDOTE.

9. PETRIFIED WOOD; minerals are opal, agate, and jasper.

10. CHRYSOCOLLA; soft, but gem value if evenly colored.

11. BERYL EMERALD when dark green and clear.

12. AMAZONITE, also Amazon stone.

13. SULPHUR CRYSTALS; too soft to cut, but sought as beautiful specimens.

14. SMITHSONITE; most valuable in sea green.

15. SODALITE; bright, deep blue most valuable.

16. OBSIDIAN, a volcanic glass, here with white "snowflakes."

17. UNIKITE, a form of epidote with feldspar blotches.

18. MOSS AGATE, another popular agate type; note "madonna" pattern in this piece.

19. GARNET with faceted stone.

20. AQUAMARINE with faceted stone; a popular light green beryl.

21. TOURMALINE with faceted rubellite.

22. ROSE QUARTZ with deep cabochon; popular pinkrose quartz.

23. CITRINE with faceted stone; another popular quartz variety.

24. AMETHYST with faceted stone; another quartz.

25. CLEAR QUARTZ with faceted stone, called rock crystal.

tant constituents of sedimentary rocks. In weathering they decompose into clay. They have a hardness of 6.

There are two kinds of feldspar—orthoclase and plagioclase. Orthoclase feldspars are potassium aluminum silicates and are white, gray, or pink. Plagioclase feldspars are aluminum silicates. They may be white or gray, or transparent or opalescent.

FELSENMEER. A surface littered with angular blocks that accumulate at the foot of a large outcrop of rock as a result of separation and shattering. Characteristic of high mountain slopes where there is rapid disintegration.

FELSITE. An igneous rock with cryptocrystalline groundmass consisting of feldspar, quartz, and interstitial volcanic glass. It is red in color.

FEN. A low-lying, marshy area.

FERREL'S LAW. The first complete explanation of the effects of the Coriolis force.

FERROMAGNESIAN. A group of dark-colored minerals containing iron and magnesium, especially amphibole, pyroxene, biotite, olivine, and magnetite.

FERTILIZER. Any material, organic or inorganic, that is applied to the soil to increase its fertility. Generally, it furnishes one or more of the elements nitrogen, which promotes vegetative growth; phosphorus, which promotes root growth and speeds maturity; and potassium, which increases plant resistance to disease and weather.

FETCH. The distance traveled by sea waves before reaching a shore line. Also, the distance wind travels over open water or land.

FIARD. A sea-drowned valley formed by glacial action in a lowland area. It is shorter and shallower than a fiord.

FIELD CAPACITY. The amount of water a soil is able to hold by capillary attraction against gravity. It is expressed as a percentage of the dry weight of the soil.

FILL. Material deposited in the outer side of a curve where a river current has lost velocity.

FIRN SNOW, or névé. Granular snow which has become coarse and partially compacted through temperature changes, forming the transition stage to glacier ice.

FIRTH. A long, narrow arm of the sea. Also, the opening of a river into the sea.

FISSILITY. The ability to split readily along the grain or closely spaced parallel planes. A characteristic of shale.

FISSURE. In rocks, an extensive crack or fracture whose walls are distinctly separated but not otherwise dislocated.

FJORD, or fiord. A long, narrow inlet of the sea formed by rivers and glaciation. Fjords are shallow near the mouth but very deep inland, and are characterized by steep surrounding cliffs extending below the surface of the water.

FLATIRON. A triangular landform composed of sedimentary rocks adhering to the crystalline core of an eroded dome mountain. Flatirons often appear in a series on the flank of a mountain.

FLINT. Granular cryptocrystalline siliceous rock, usually dull, dark, and nodular, occurring in calcareous beds and having conchoidal fracture. It is a purer and less brittle chert.

FLOCCULATE. To collect in small lumps or loose clusters. It often applies to soils and colloids.

FLOE. A large sheet of floating ice.

FLOODPLAIN. A level area, or plain, in a river valley, built up by sediment from the river overflow. It may be submerged in time of flood.

FLOOD CURRENT. The current associated with a rising tide.

FLORA. All plant life of a given region in a geological time period.

FLOTATION. A method of ore concentration in which gas bubbles selectively attach themselves to particles of a particular mineral suspended in water, holding them at the surface while other particles sink.

FLOW. The movement of air, water, or lava. Of rocks, see Deformation.

FLUME. A deep, narrow ravine through which a stream flows forming a series of cascades.

FLUVIAL CYCLE. The geographical cycle (upheaval through reduction to base level of a region) controlled by steams and mass-wasting.

FOCUS. The point of generation of an earthquake. Earthquakes are classified by their energy and depth to focus. Shallow focus earthquakes originate within 40 miles of the earth's surface; intermediate, from 40 to 185 miles; deep, from 185 to 435 miles.

FOEHN. A warm, dry wind that blows down the leeward side of a mountain. As the air moves up the windward side of the mountain, moisture is removed by cooling and the resultant condensation. Then the air is warmed by compression as it descends the leeward slope.

FOG. A dense mass of small water droplets (much smaller than the droplets in rain-bearing clouds) forming in the lowest layers of the atmosphere. Fog is caused by condensation produced by a sudden cooling of the air, usually when a warmer air current meets a colder air current. Fog, by international definition, reduces visibility below 0.62 miles.

Ground fog, or radiation fog, is a shallow layer formed over low ground on calm, clear nights by cool air which suddenly lowers the temperature of the ground.

Advection fog results when clouds formed in moist air are blown from warm regions over cold water and ground.

Warm-front fog is caused by the saturation of the air by rain falling through it from a cloud system associated with cyclonic disturbances.

Steam fog, rare and transitory, is produced by the evaporation of relatively warm water into cold air.

FOLD. A bend in rock strata, caused by crustal movement, which may form a series of arches, upfolds or anticlines, and troughs, downfolds or synclines. When the axis of a fold is not horizontal, it is termed a *plunging fold,* the angle between the axis and the horizontal plane being the plunge. In an *isoclinal fold* the strata are so compressed that the limbs are parallel and thus have the same dip. A *monocline* is a one-limb fold; the strata on either side are horizontal.

A series of folds (anticlines and synclines) forming an arch is an *anticlinorium;* if a trough is formed, it is a *synclinorium. Geosynclines* and *geanticlines* are large-scale synclines and anticlines, respectively, and are formed by very gentle folding.

FOLIATION. The tendency of certain rocks to break in thin layers along almost parallel planes. It is caused by the parallel alignment of minerals resulting from pressure and higher than normal temperatures during regional metamorphism. Such rocks are commonly called *schists* (well-defined foliation) and *gneisses* (poorly defined foliation).

FOOTHILLS. A series of hills at the foot of a mountain or mountain range lying between the mountains and a plain.

FORAMINIFERAL OOZE. A deposit on the ocean floor containing a large percentage of calcium carbonate, being the shells of foraminifera, a single-celled, minute animal.

FORD. A shallow part of a stream or other body of water which may be crossed by wading.

FORESHOCK. An earthquake which precedes a larger earthquake, announcing that the stress has become critical. It originates at or near the focus of the larger earthquake.

FORESHORE. The part of the shoreline lying between high and low water levels.

FOSSE. A depression between a glacier and a moraine or rock wall.

FOSSIL. Animal or plant remains or impressions from the geologic past preserved in the earth's crust.

FOSSIL FUELS. Commercial sources of inanimate energy derived from the alteration of the remains of organic matter, such as coal, oil, and natural gas.

FOUCAULT PENDULUM. A pendulum demonstrating the earth's rotation on its axis, made public by J. B. L. Foucault in 1851. Each swing of the pendulum describes a plane of vibration which appears to move clockwise (counterclockwise in the southern hemisphere) around a circle drawn on the surface of the earth. Actually, the plane is constant—the circle rotates.

Because of the earth's curvature, the northern edge of the circle describes a smaller circle (or shorter line of latitude) around the earth than the southern edge.

The time required for a complete rotation varies with the degree of latitude, ranging from 5 days, 18 hours, 13 minutes at 10° latitude to one day at 90° latitude. At the equator there is no apparent movement of the plane of vibration because the north and south edges of the circle are equidistant from the earth's axis.

FRACTURE. The manner of breaking of a mineral that does not exhibit cleavage. A *conchoidal fracture* has a smooth, curved surface similar to that of a seashell. An *uneven fracture* is rough and irregular. A *fibrous* or *splintery fracture* is similar to that of wood. A *hackly fracture* has a jagged surface with sharp edges. Also, a joint, fault, or fissure.

FREE WATER. Groundwater moved by the force of gravity through the pore spaces of soil and not held by capillary attraction.

FRESHET. An area of comparatively fresh water at the mouth of a stream flowing into the sea. Also, a sudden rise in the level of a stream caused by heavy rains or melting snow.

FRESH WATER. Water containing no significant amount of salt, usually having less than 0.2 percent salinity.

FRIABLE. Referring to easily pulverized rock or easily crumbled soils.

FRIGID CLIMATE. The climate in a region of permafrost or in a region with a permanent cover of ice and snow.

FRIGID ZONE. The area north of the Arctic Circle and south of the Antarctic Circle.

FRINGING REEF. A reef attached to the shore. The outer edge of the reef is submerged.

FRONT. The boundary or zone of transition between two air masses of different density.

FROST. Small particles of frozen moisture formed by the condensation of water vapor or dew on objects having temperatures below freezing.

FROST HEAVING. The upthrusting of a surface by the internal action of frost. It generally occurs after a thaw has released water droplets into the soil, and a sudden drop in temperature to below freezing changes the water droplets into ice crystals. As freezing expands the volume of water, there is an upward and outward movement of the soil.

FROST LINE. The maximum depth to which soil can freeze.

THE AMERICAN MUSEUM OF NATURAL HISTORY
GEODES AND CRYSTALS. Geodes are hollow bodies lined with mineral crystals.

FULLER'S EARTH. Fine, claylike earth with a high percentage of water. It does not retain a form when molded.

FUMAROLE. A vent in the earth's crust emitting steam and other gases; common in volcanic regions.

FUNNEL CLOUD. See *Tornado; Water spout.*

GABBRO. A dark, coarse-grained plutonic or intrusive igneous rock, composed of plagioclase feldspars and dark, ferromagnesian minerals such as hornblende, pyroxene, or olivine.

GAL. A unit expressing acceleration equal to one centimeter per second per second (1 cm./sec.^{2}). The term gal honors Galileo and is not an abbreviation.

GALE. A wind with a velocity between 32 and 61 miles per hour, designated 7-10 on the Beaufort scale.

GALENA. Lead sulfide, the principal source of lead. It has a bright metallic luster, a hardness of 2.5, a specific gravity of about 7.5, and perfect cleavage in three planes at right angles to each other, forming cubes.

GANGUE. Earth material of small value enclosing valuable mineral matter.

GAP. A cut or break through a ridge, either complete, as in a water gap, or through the upper part, as in a wind gap.

GARNET. A group of silicates (iron, magnesium, aluminum, calcium, manganese, chromium, and titanium) with a vitreous to resinous luster, a hardness of 6.5 to 7.5, a specific gravity of 3.4 to 4.3, and uneven fracture. It usually has 12-sided or 24-sided fully-developed crystals. Characteristic of metamorphic rocks, it is used to define one of the zones of middle-grade metamorphism.

GAT. A natural opening through cliffs leading inland from the sea. Also, a passageway extending inland through shoals or steep banks.

GEANTICLINE. A broad uplift, formed slowly by gentle pressure and covering hundreds of miles. See *Fold.*

GEM. A general term for any cut and polished precious or semiprecious stone.

GEO. A prefix meaning earth. Also, in Icelandic, a deep, narrow coastal inlet walled by steep cliffs.

GEOCHEMICAL CYCLE. The sequence of rock change in which magma, or molten matter, is cooled and solidified or crystallized into igneous rocks, which are weathered to sediments. The sediments are compacted and hardened into sedimentary rocks, which are metamorphosed by pressure, heat, and chemicals into metamorphic rocks. They, in turn, undergo further metamorphism and are melted into magma.

GEODE. A hollow, globular body that may be an inch, or more than a foot, in diameter, lined with mineral crystals. It is formed in sedimentary deposits where a piece of organic matter is buried, decays, and leaves a water-filled pocket.

As the deposit begins to consolidate into rock, a wall of silica forms around the water and isolates it. The silica wall dries, crystallizes into chalcedony, contracts, and cracks. Later, mineral-bearing water may seep through the cracks and precipitate minerals just inside the geode wall where the crystals begin to grow toward the center. Geodes are characteristic of certain limestone beds.

GEODESY. The study of the shape, size, and gravity field of the earth.

GEOGRAPHICAL CYCLE. The relatively systematic series of changes through which a landform passes—from youth, when constructional processes define its form, through maturity, when erosion carves and molds it, to old age, when the landform is reduced to base level.

GEOGRAPHY. The study of the earth's surface and the relationship between man and his environment, with particular emphasis on the location of physical, economic, and cultural conditions.

GEOID. The figure of the earth considered as a mean sea level surface extended continuously through the continents. It is an equipotential surface in that the direction in which gravitational force acts is perpendicular to any point on the surface.

GEOLOGIC TIME. The measurement of earth's physical history through fossil evidence, the interrelationship of rock strata, and radioactive dating. Geologic time has been divided into eons, eras, periods, epochs, and sometimes ages. These intervals correspond to time-stratigraphic units in the geologic column: group (era), system (period), series (epoch), stage (age). See chart, CHRONOLOGICAL HISTORY OF GEOLOGIC TIME.

GEOLOGIC EROSION. The wearing down of land surfaces at natural rates. See *Erosion.*

GEOLOGY. The study of the composition, structure, processes, and history of the earth.

GEOMORPHIC CYCLE. The cycle of upheaval through reduction to base level of the earth's surface.

GEOMORPHOLOGY. The study of the form of the earth, the general configuration of its surface, and the changes that take place in the evolution of land-forms.

GEOPHYSICS. The physics or nature of the earth. The study of the composition and the physical processes operating on and within the earth. It makes use of meteorology, oceanography, seismology, and related sciences.

GEOSPHERE. The solid portions of the earth.

GEOSTROPHIC. Pertaining to the deflective force caused by the rotation of earth.

GEOSYNCLINE. A large syncline, or a great trough or basin of accumulated sediments which slowly downwarps.

GEOTHERMAL GRADIENT. The increase in temperature of the earth with depth.

GEYSER. A hot spring which throws hot water and steam into the air at intervals. The vent to the surface must be narrow or winding, or a boiling spring would result. Geysers are found in Yellowstone National Park, in Iceland, and in New Zealand.

GLACIAL. Referring to the existence, size, composition, and actions of glaciers (large masses of land ice).

GLACIAL MILK. Glacial meltwater carrying light-colored rock flour or rock particles of the size of silt or clay.

GLACIAL PERIOD. Generally applied to the time during the Pleistocene epoch when continental ice sheets and valley glaciers covered large areas of the continents. Other glacial periods are not so abundantly recorded, although there is evidence of extensive glaciation in the late Precambrian and Permian periods.

GLACIER. A mass of land ice moving slowly over the surface of the earth. A glacier is classified according to the way it occurs. There are three basic types, which grade into each other: *valley glaciers, piedmont glaciers,* and *ice sheets.*
Valley glaciers are the most common type. They are formed on mountain sides along well-defined valleys. They carve precipitous walls (cirque) at their upper limit and are melting at their lower limit. They tend to be long and narrow, following valleys

cut by streams and sculpting them into U-shaped profiles.
Piedmont glaciers occur where valley glaciers emerge from the mountains to spread out onto plains. They coalesce to form a continuous thick sheet of ice.
Ice sheets are formed on plateau areas by the accumulation of snow and the amalgamation of valley glaciers and ice caps flowing from higher places.

GLADE. A natural or man-made open area or passage in a forest.

GLASS. An amorphous solid, generally treated as a rock, which results when molten rock, or magma, is rapidly cooled. The ions are disorganized, as in a liquid, but are frozen in place by the quick change of temperature.
Also, one of the first-made compound materials in which sand or another form of silica and a fluxing alkali, such as soda or potash, are combined and heated to about 2800° F, then gradually cooled.

GLEI. A blue-gray soil with mottled discolorations. It is somewhat sticky, often structureless, and indicates poor drainage.

GLEN. A long, narrow, steep-sided valley.

GLOBIGERINA OOZE. A chalky, or calcareous, marine deposit consisting of the shells of surface-dwelling forms of Foraminifera that reach the sea floor after death. It is found in deep water, to 12,000 feet, in the Atlantic, Pacific, and Indian oceans.

GNEISS. A metamorphic rock with alternating bands of granular and schistose minerals; commonly formed by the metamorphism of granite.

GORGE. A deep, narrow valley with steep sides and enclosed among mountains, as contrasted with a ravine, which is not necessarily enclosed.

GRABEN. A narrow depression, or structural valley, long in comparison to its width and bounded on at least two sides by faults. The opposite of a horst.

GRADATION. The reducing of elevations and the filling of depressions to make a land surface level.

GRADED BEDDING. Sedimentary deposits with a gradation in grain size from coarse at the bottom to fine at the top. It is also called diadactic structure.

GRADED SHORE LINE. A shore line straightened by the building of bars across indentations and the cutting back of headlands.

GRADED STREAM. A stream that has eliminated irregularities, such as falls, and adjusted its gradient, or slope, so that its velocity is sufficient to transport the load from its drainage basin.

GRADE SCALE. See *Wentworth grade scale.*

GRANITE. A coarse-grained plutonic, or intrusive, igneous rock composed largely of feldspar, quartz, and some common mica (biotite or muscovite). It is the most abundant rock in the earth's crust.

GRANULE. Rounded rock fragment larger than ä coarse sand grain and smaller than ä pebble. See *Wentworth grade scale.*

GRAPHITE. A soft form of carbon, having a hardness of 1. It is black or gray, and has a metallic luster and a specific gravity of 2.25.

GRAPTOLITE. An extinct colonial organism whose remaining shell and supporting structures are important in dating Ordovician and Silurian rocks.

GRASSLANDS. Regions of the world where the natural plant cover consists of grass. In the tropics they are called savannas and steppes, and in the middle latitudes, prairies and steppes.

GRAVEL. A loose mixture of rounded stones, composed of granules, pebbles, cobbles, and boulders. See *Wentworth grade scale.*

GRAVITATION. The mutual attraction between bodies or masses of matter, directly proportional to the product of their masses and inversely proportional to the square of the distance between them. It is the opposite of centrifugal force and a component of gravity.

GRAVITATIONAL THEORY. The theory that, because of buoyancy, or lower specific gravities, oil will rise to the top of water and gas will rise to the top of oil. See also *Anticlinal theory.*

GRAVITY. The attraction of earth's mass for other bodies at or near earth's surface (gravitation), as modified by earth's rotation (centrifugal force).

GRAYWACKE. A hard, dark sandstone marked by large angular fragments of quartz and feldspar and small rock fragments (chert, quartzite, slate, and phyllite).

GREENHOUSE EFFECT. The heat resulting from the fact that incoming short-wave solar radiation freely penetrates the atmosphere to be absorbed at the earth's surface, while outgoing long-wave terrestrial radiation passes upward with difficulty, thus heating the area in which it is contained.

GREENWICH MEAN TIME (GMT). A system of international time based on the local mean time at the meridian that passes through Greenwich, England (the prime or zero meridian).

GROIN. A low wall built out into the sea, roughly perpendicular to the coastline, for a particular purpose, such as to change a current or protect a coast.

GROOVES. Scour marks, or large striations, cut into hard rocks by the movement of glacial ice over their surface.

GROTTO. A small cave often found in a limestone region. Also, a small cave eroded in the wall of a larger cave.

GROUNDWATER. Water passing through or standing in the soil and the subsoil layers.

GROUP. A time-stratigraphic unit corresponding to an era in geological time.

GROVE. A small group of trees in an open area.

GROWING SEASON. The interval of time between the last spring frost and the first fall frost in any given area.

GRUS. An accumulation of fragments derived from the weathering of granite.

GUANO. A deposit of partially decomposed excrement of fish-eating creatures. It is rich in nitrogen and phosphorous and is used as fertilizer.

GULCH. A narrow, steep-sided ravine.

GULF. A large, deep inlet of the sea. The entrance generally is wider than a bay and smaller than a sea.

GULF STREAM. A major ocean current originating in the Gulf of Mexico, where the Florida and Antilles currents meet. It is a warm, swift (3 to 4 miles per hour), and relatively narrow current. It flows out of the gulf between Florida and Cuba, turns north to join the North Equatorial Current, and then flows generally parallel to the U.S. coast, bending northeast off Norfolk, Virginia.

Southeast of Newfoundland it separates into two main streams. One stream flows northeast to the Grand Banks, where it joins with the cold Labrador Current to form the North Atlantic Current, which flows north to Sweden and the Soviet Union. There its force and warmth are dissipated.

The other branch flows eastward to Europe and bends south. Off the coasts of Portugal and northwestern Africa it merges with the Canary Current, which eventually joins the North Equatorial Current.

GULLY. A relatively small, narrow channel, or a miniature valley, carved out of the earth's surface by intermittent running water, usually during and following a heavy rain.

GUMBO. A term used in the southern and western United States for fine-grained, silty soils which yield a sticky mud when wet.

GUMBOTIL. A dark, thoroughly leached, unlayered deposit resulting from the complete chemical decomposition of clay-rich glacial till. It is very hard when dry, sticky when wet.

GUT. A narrow channel or strait.

GUYOT. A flat-topped mountain beneath the sea. The preferred term is tablemount.

AMERICAN MUSEUM OF NATURAL HISTORY

HEMATITE, an oxide of iron, in botryoidal (grape) form is commonly known as *kidney ore.*

GYPSUM. A common mineral in sedimentary rocks, composed of calcium sulfate and hydrated water molecules. It is usually white or colorless and has a hardness of 2. It is one of the first minerals to crystallize with the evaporation of seawater.

GYRE. A closed circulatory system in major ocean basins, larger than an eddy or whirlpool.

HAAR. A cold, wet sea fog which sometimes invades eastern Scotland and parts of eastern England, especially during summer.

HABITAT. The natural characteristics of a region; the environment.

HACKLY. A fracture having a jagged, irregular surface with sharp edges.

HADAL ZONE. Referring to the greatest depths of the oceans. See *Ocean depth zones.*

HALF–LIFE. The average time required for one-half the atoms of a sample of a radioactive substance to decay.

HALITE. A mineral, sodium chloride (common salt), which has cubic cleavage, a hardness of 2.5, and occurs in thick beds with layers of sedimentary rock. It is also called rock salt.

HALMYROLYSIS. The chemical rearrangement, replacement, and weathering of sedimentary rocks on the sea floor.

HALO. A ring of light which surrounds the moon, sun, or other heavenly bodies when their light is refracted by ice crystals in the atmosphere, usually in the form of a thin veil of cirrostratus clouds.

HALOGENS. Any of four elements—chlorine, bromine, iodine, and fluorine—found as ions in seawater.

HALOMORPHIC. A soil with a high content of salts.

HAMMADA. A plateau or rocky upland in a desert whose surface has been swept clear of sand by the wind.

HANGING GLACIER. A small glacier protruding from a high mountain slope and from which pieces continually break off.

HANGING VALLEY. A tributary valley whose floor is higher than the valley into which it leads.

HARDNESS SCALE. A means of determining the relative hardness of a mineral by comparing it with Mohs' scale, in which each mineral is harder than those that precede it: (1) talc; (2) gypsum; (3) calcite; (4) fluorite; (5) apatite; (6) orthoclase; (7) quartz; (8) topaz; (9) corundum; (10) diamond.

HARDPAN. A hardened soil layer caused by the cementation of soil particles with relatively insoluble materials which will not become plastic when mixed with water.

HARD WATER. Water with dissolved calcium and magnesium compounds.

HARMATTAN. A strong, dry wind blowing from the Sahara in the direction of the western coast of Africa.

HAWAIIAN PHASE. See *Volcano.*

HAZE. An accumulation of fine dust or salt particles in the atmosphere sufficient to reduce visibility.

HEADLAND. A high, steep projection of the shoreline into a body of water. Usually called "head" when coupled with a specific name.

HEADWALL. A steep cliff at the back of a cirque.

HEADWARD EROSION. The action of a stream in lengthening its valley by cutting back into its source area or upper end. Also, the action of a glacier in gnawing into the mountain above and beside it by frost heaving, creating a cirque.

HEADWATER. The upper reaches of a stream; also the water area at or near the source of a stream.

HEAT GRADIENT. See *Geothermal gradient.*

HEATH. An open tract of level, uncultivated ground covered with small shrubs.

HEMATITE. An oxide of iron (Fe_2O_3), the principal source of iron ore.

HIGH. A high-pressure air mass. See *Anticyclone*.

HIGH WATER. The highest level reached by rising tide.

HILL. A prominence on the earth's surface rising less than 1,000 feet above the surrounding country, as contrasted with a mountain.

HILLOCK. A small hill or mound.

HINGE FAULT. A fault whose displacement dies out gradually.

HINTERLAND. Literally, the land behind. The area inland from a coastline to a distance of about five miles, or the land beyond a mountain range which is relatively undisturbed by folding.

HOGBACK. A sharp ridge of rock with steeply sloping sides.

HOMEOBLASTIC. In metamorphic rocks, an equigranular texture caused by recrystallization.

HOMOCLINE. Rock strata sloping in the same direction over a large area.

HOMOPYCNAL INFLOW. Literally, equally dense inflow. Refers to a sediment-laden stream entering a body of water of comparable density.

HOMOSEISMAL LINE. A line drawn on a map through points affected by an earthquake at the same time; used to locate the epicenter of the quake.

HOOK. A spit or narrow cape of sand or gravel whose end turns sharply landward.

HOOKE'S LAW. Within the limits of elastic deformation, a solid whose physical properties are the same in all directions is subject to deformation (strain) in proportion to the force per unit area acting on it (stress).

HORIZON. The physical limit to vision imposed by the curvature of the earth's surface. It is a circle bounding the portion of the earth's surface visible from a given point. Also, a layer in the soil profile.

HORN. A high pyramid peak with steep sides formed by the headward erosion of a ring of cirques around a single high mountain.

HORNBLENDE. A rock-forming mineral, a variety of black or greenish black aluminous amphibole containing a considerable amount of iron.

HORNFELS. A fine-grained silicate resulting from contact metamorphism.

HORSE LATITUDES. A belt of high pressure and variable light winds and calms formed by descending air near 30°-35° N and 30°-35° S latitudes (between trade winds and prevailing westerlies). It moves north and south south by about 5° following the sun.

HORST. A rock body, long in comparison to its width and bounded on at least two sides by faults, elevated relative to the adjacent rock bodies. The opposite of graben.

HOT SPRINGS. The discharge of water hotter than 98°F from the ground. Found commonly, although not exclusively, in volcanic regions.

HUMIDITY. The amount of water in the atmosphere in vapor or gaseous form.

HUMMOCK. A small elevation or mound.

HUMUS. Partly decomposed organic matter found in the soil or in sediment under water.

HURRICANE. A severe cyclonic storm. See *Meteorology*.

HUYGENS' PRINCIPLE. A principle applying to wave motion which states that every point on an advancing wave front at a given time may be regarded as a source of secondary wavelets. A moment later, the position of the front is as an envelope for all the secondary wavelets.

HYDRAULIC GRADIENT. The slope of the water table, found by dividing the head, or vertical, distance between intake and discharge by the length of the flow between those two points.

HYDROGRAPH. A chart showing the level, flow, velocity, or other property of water through time.

HYDROGRAPHY. The description and mapping of the distribution of the waters of the earth's surface.

HYDROLOGIC CYCLE. The cycle through which water passes—atmospheric water vapor passing into liquid and solid form as precipitation, then to the surface of the earth, where evaporation and transpiration through plants return it to the atmosphere as water vapor.

HYDROLOGY. The study of the properties, distribution, and circulation of the waters of the earth and how they are affected by precipitation and evaporation.

HYDROLYSIS. A chemical process whereby a substance is decomposed by water.

HYDROSPHERE. The water portion of the earth, as distinguished from the solid portion, or lithosphere, and the gaseous envelope, or atmosphere. It includes liquid and solid water (ice) in the oceans, seas, lakes, and streams groundwater, and water vapor in the atmosphere. It comprises 139.5 million square miles of the earth's surface, as compared with the lithosphere, which comprises 57.5 million square miles.

HYDROTHERMAL. Relating to the action of heated water in the earth's crust.

HYGROMETER. An instrument used to measure the relative humidity of the atmosphere.

HYGROSCOPIC WATER. Water held so tightly by the attraction of soil particles that it cannot be removed except as a gas, by raising the water temperature above the boiling point. Such water is unavailable to plants.

HYPABYSSAL. Refers to fine-grained igneous rocks formed in minor intrusions, such as sills and dikes. These rocks are crystallized under conditions intermediate between plutonic (slow cooling) and extrusive (rapid cooling) and are distinguished from them by texture or mode of occurrence.

HYPERPYCNAL INFLOW. An inflow so dense that the sediment-laden fluid flows down the side of the basin and then along the bottom as a turbidity current. Vertical mixing is inhibited by the tendency of the dense fluid to stay at the lowest possible level. It forms deltas at the mouth of submarine canyons. It is the opposite of hypopycnal inflow.

HYPOGENE. Originating or lying below the earth's surface, as opposed to epigene.

HYPOPYCNAL INFLOW. Inflow less dense than the fluid filling a basin and therefore flowing out over the surface of the basin. If the discharge is small, a crescent-shaped bar will form off the point of inflow. If it is moderate to large, a birdfoot delta, such as the Mississippi delta, will form. It is the opposite of hyperpycnal inflow.

HYSTERESIS. A lag in a body's return to its original shape after elastic deformation.

ICE. The solid form of water. Ice is formed at 0°C (32°F) by the freezing of water, by the compaction of snow, and by condensation of atmospheric water vapor directly into ice. Ice has a density of 0.917, whereas water has a density of 1.0 and therefore ice floats. But ice is only slightly less dense and as much as 9/10 of its bulk may be below the surface of the water.

ICE AGE. See *Glacial period*.

ICEBERG. A mass of ice that has broken off the seaward edge of a glacier and floats in the sea.

ICE CAP. A large mass of permanent ice and snow covering an extensive land area.

ICE CAP CLIMATE. The type of climate found over large ice sheets, such as in Greenland and Antarctica, where the mean annual temperature is estimated to be below 0°F.

ICE FLOE. An extensive, generally flat mass of free-floating ice.

ICELANDIC LOW. A low-pressure area that develops in the vicinity of Iceland during the winter season.

ICE SHEET. A vast extent of ice and snow covering a large area. Ice sheets are very thick. When resting on rock, they are called *inland ice sheets*. A floating ice sheet is called an *ice shelf*.

IGNEOUS ROCK

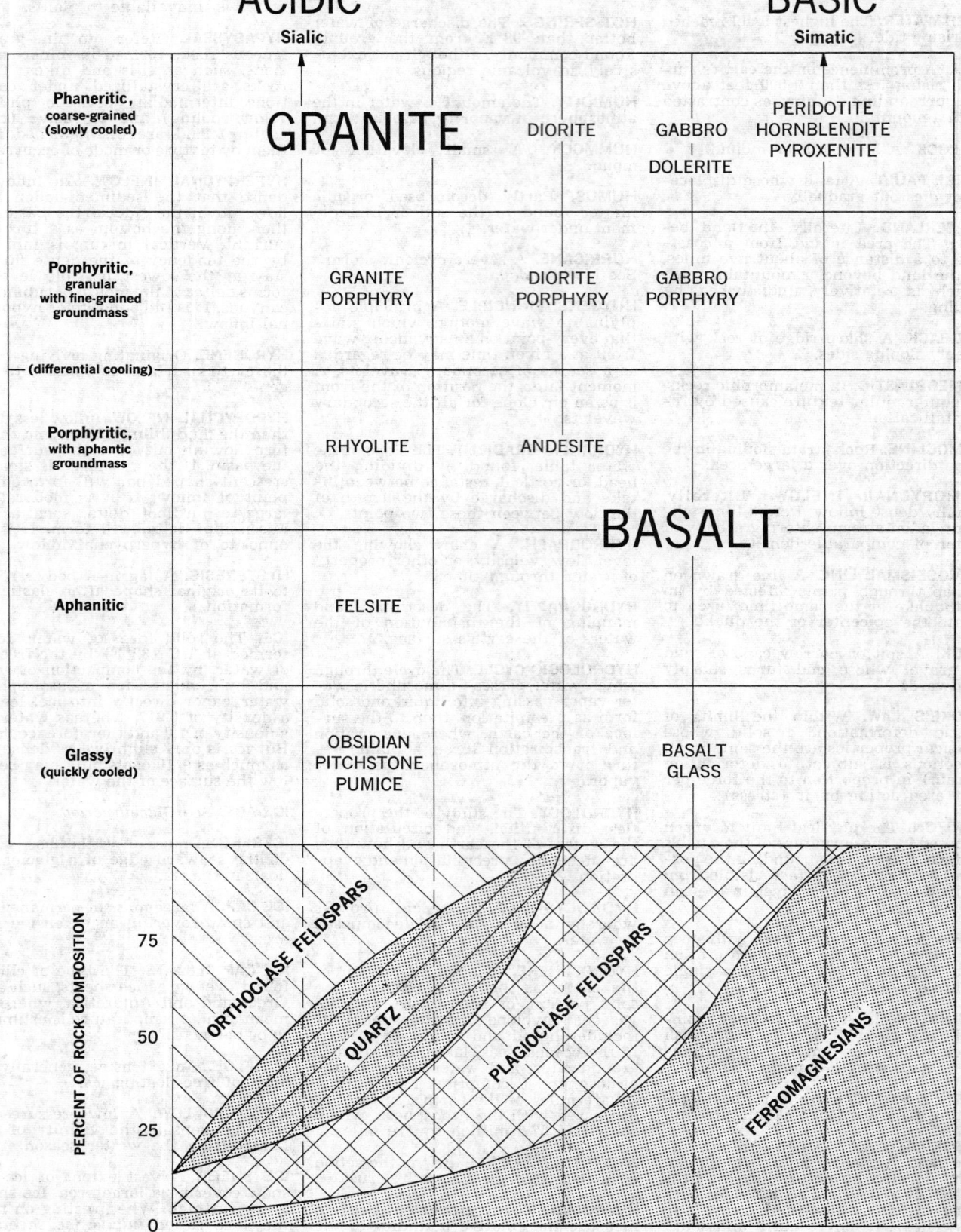

	ACIDIC Sialic		BASIC Simatic
Phaneritic, coarse-grained (slowly cooled)	GRANITE	DIORITE	GABBRO PERIDOTITE HORNBLENDITE DOLERITE PYROXENITE
Porphyritic, granular with fine-grained groundmass	GRANITE PORPHYRY	DIORITE PORPHYRY	GABBRO PORPHYRY
(differential cooling)			
Porphyritic, with aphanic groundmass	RHYOLITE	ANDESITE	BASALT
Aphanitic	FELSITE		
Glassy (quickly cooled)	OBSIDIAN PITCHSTONE PUMICE		BASALT GLASS

PERCENT OF ROCK COMPOSITION

75

50

25

0

ORTHOCLASE FELDSPARS

QUARTZ

PLAGIOCLASE FELDSPARS

FERROMAGNESIANS

IGNEOUS ROCK. One of the three principal groups of rock, the others being sedimentary and metamorphic rock. Igneous rock is formed by the solidification or crystallization of molten material, or magma. An igneous rock is classified by texture, the minerals present and their proportions, and feldspar content.

ILLITE. A family of hydrous aluminous silicates. Illite is the most common clay mineral in clayey rocks, marine sediments, and many soils.

ILLUVIATION. The deposition in a soil horizon of material in solution or suspension which has been leached out of an overlying horizon by percolating water. The opposite of eluviation.

ILMENITE. A mineral ($FeTiO_3$), the principal ore of titanium.

IMPERMEABLE ROCK. Rock that does not permit the free passage through it of water, petroleum, or natural gas.

INANIMATE ENERGY. Energy derived from nonliving materials, such as water power, nuclear fuels, coal, or oil. The opposite of animate energy.

INCISED MEANDER. See *Entrenched meander.*

INDIAN SUMMER. A spell of mild weather occurring in late autumn, especially after a frost. It is characterized by a cloudless sky and a haze on the horizon.

INDURATED. Refers to rocks hardened by heat, pressure, and cementation.

INFILTRATION RATE. The maximum rate at which loose earth material such as soil can absorb surface water. It is measured in inches per hour. Infiltration refers to flow into soil; percolation refers to flow through soil.

INFLUENT STREAM. A stream whose channel lies above the water table and therefore loses much of its water to the zone of saturation.

INLET. A small opening into the coastline which may connect a bay or lagoon with the sea.

INLIER. A mass of old rock surrounded by younger rocks; often the crest of an anticline which has been exposed by erosion. The opposite of outlier.

INSEQUENT STREAM. A minor stream whose course is determined by minor surface irregularities of rock resistance and not by the slope of the surface.

IN SITU. Latin for "in place." Refers to a rock, soil, or fossil found in the situation in which it was originally formed or deposited.

INSOLATION. Contraction of "incoming solar radiation." It refers to radiation from the sun received at the earth's surface.

INSULATED STREAM. A stream separated from the zone of saturation by impermeable rock. It therefore does not contribute to or receive water from the water table.

INTERFLUVE. The area between adjacent streams.

INTERGLACIAL PERIOD. The time between two glacial periods when climates grew warm and the ice retreated.

INTERIOR. The country extending indefinitely inland of the hinterland.

INTERMITTENT STREAM. A stream that flows only at certain times, such as after a rainstorm or during a spring thaw.

INTERMONTANE. Lying between mountains.

INTERNATIONAL DATE LINE. The line roughly approximating the 180th meridian of longitude (exactly opposite the prime meridian) used to adjust for the necessary difference of one day in traveling the full circumference (360°) of the world. It is made necessary by the hour change with each 15° of longitude covered. Crossing the date line from east to west adds one day; crossing it west to east subtracts one day.

INTERRUPTED STREAM. A stream that flows only at certain places and not at others, either because portions of it are ephemeral, or intermittent, or because it drains into an underground channel. See also *Lost river.*

INTERSTICE. A pore in soil or rock.

INTERSTITIAL WATER. Water contained in the pore spaces between the grains in rock and sediments.

INTRAMONTANE. Situated or acting within a mountain.

INTRATELLURIC. Refers to the crystallization of molten matter, or magma, before its outflow as lava. It is represented in volcanic rocks by large crystals, or phenocrysts, which form under comparatively deep conditions.

INTRAZONAL SOIL. One of the three orders in soil classification. A group of soils whose formation is influenced strongly by local factors, such as the nature of the parent material or age, which prevail over such normal soil-forming factors as climate and vegetation. See also *Soil.*

INTRUSIVE ROCK. An igneous rock which, while molten, invaded other rocks and solidified below the surface. It is also called plutonic rock.

INVERSION. Reversal of the normal order of succession, whether referring to the folding back of rock layers on themselves, as in an overturned fold, or an increase of temperature with elevation above the earth's surface.

IONOSPHERE. See *Atmosphere.*

ISLAND. A landmass, smaller than a continent, surrounded by water.

ISOBAR. A line on a map or chart joining places on the earth that have the same atmospheric pressure.

ISOGONIC LINE. A line on a map or chart joining places having an equal magnetic declination.

ISOSEISMIC LINE. A line on a map joining points on the earth's surface where an earthquake shock is of the same intensity.

ISOSTASY. The theory that the crust of the earth is in a state of equilibrium because the lighter, less-dense continental masses float on heavier, denser material. The continental masses consist primarily of silica and alumina, or sial, which has a specific gravity of about 2.7. Under this is a layer consisting of silica and magnesium, or sima, which has a specific gravity that may be as high as 3.3.

ISOSTATIC COMPENSATION. The process in which mountains are eroded and the material deposited on the ocean floor, which sinks under the weight. In sinking, the floor pushes down on the sima under it. The sima compensates by pushing up under the portion of sial where the mountain stood.

ISOTROPIC. Having the same physical properties in all directions. Isotropism is characteristic of amorphous substances.

ISTHMUS. A narrow strip of land joining two larger landmasses.

JAPAN CURRENT. See *Kuroshio.*

JET STREAM. A narrow band of very fast westward moving winds, or westerlies, that develops in the upper troposphere. The winds average 75 miles per hour (mph) in winter and 35 mph in summer, although they have been known to exceed 200 mph.

JETTY. A structure, such as a wharf, pier, or low wall, so located as to influence water current or to protect the entrance to a harbor or river. A jetty extending into the sea to protect the coast from erosion is called a *groin.* A jetty which breaks the force of the sea at any place is called a *breakwater.* A jetty built to direct or confine the flow of a river or tidal current is called a *training wall.*
A jetty or a wall along a waterfront to resist the encroachment of the sea is called a *sea wall.*

JOINT. Cracks in a rock mass which form along planes of weakness. There is no relative movement of the rock around the cracks.

JUNGLE. Uncultivated land with a dense undergrowth, usually applied to the tropical rain forest.

JURASSIC PERIOD. The second, or middle, period of the Mesozoic era in geologic time. It began 158 million years ago and lasted 33 million years. During this period the first birds appeared in Europe and dinosaurs flourished.

BUREAU OF RECLAMATION—DEPARTMENT OF THE INTERIOR

CRATER LAKE, formed by water accumulated in an almost perfect example of a caldera. Volcanic activity built the small cone, Wizard Island.

JUVENILE WATER. Water from molten material, or magma, either brought to the surface by an eruption or added to underground water after magma crystallizes. This water was not previously part of the hydrologic cycle.

KAME. A steep, irregular ridge or hill of stratified glacial drift.

KAME TERRACE. A body of stratified glacial drift deposited between a wasting glacier and an adjacent valley wall. It stands as a terrace along the valley wall after the ice melts.

KANAT. See *Qanat.*

KAOLINITE. A common clay mineral, hydrous aluminous silicate, that develops from the weathering of plagioclase feldspars.

KARST TOPOGRAPHY. A type of landscape with numerous surface depressions, unsystematic drainage patterns, caverns, and disappearing streams. It occurs in an area underlain by limestone which has been dissolved by rain or rivers. Named for a limestone plateau area in Yugoslavia.

KATABATIC WIND. A cool wind blowing downhill. Also, the flow of cold air off ice caps.

KETTLE. A depression, frequently containing a pond, formed in glacial deposits by an isolated mass of glacier ice that later melted.

KEY. A low island chain formed by a sandbank or reef.

KLIPPE. A block of rocks, generally older than the underlying rocks and separated from them by a fault with a gentle dip. It may be the remnant of an overthrust layer of rock.

KNOB. A rounded hill or mountain, especially an isolated one.

KNOLL. A small, rounded hill. Also, an undersea hill less than 1,000 meters (about 3,280 feet) above the sea floor and of limited extent across its summit. It is smaller than a seamount.

KNOT. A unit of speed equal to one nautical mile (6,076.12 feet) per hour.

KUROSHIO. A warm, fast (2 to 4 knots) ocean current, the Pacific counterpart of the Atlantic Gulf Stream. It is also called the Japan Current. It originates in the Pacific North Equatorial Current, which divides east of the Philippines. It flows northeastward from Taiwan, close to Japan, ultimately joining with the Oyashio to form the North Pacific Current.

KYMATOLOGY. The science of waves and wave motion.

LABRADOR CURRENT. A cold ocean current flowing southward from Baffin Bay and southeastward along the coasts of Labrador and Newfoundland. East of Newfoundland it meets the Gulf Stream, and the two flow eastward as the North Atlantic Current.

LACCOLITH. A landform caused by the intrusion of a mass of molten material, or magma, into the crust of the earth to produce a dome-shaped surface of overlying rock.

LACUSTRINE. Referring to a lake.

LADU. An avalanche of glowing volcanic debris.

LAGOON. A shallow body of water partly or completely separated from the sea by a narrow strip of land, such as a reef or bar.

LAKE. A standing body of inland water formed when a substantial amount of water collects in a depression in the earth's surface. It may be fed by surface and groundwater.

LAMINAR FLOW. A smooth and relatively slow movement, or flow, of a liquid in which the fluid moves in straight-line paths parallel to the channel.

LAND BREEZE. A light wind blowing from the land to the sea. It is caused by unequal cooling of land and sea at night. The cooler, denser air over the land moves into an area of warm, less dense air.

LANDLOCKED. A body of water enclosed, or nearly enclosed, by land.

LANDSCAPE. A portion of the earth's surface having a complex of natural and cultural features which gives it a distinctive character.

LANDSLIDE. The downward movement of a large mass of loose earth material containing varying amounts of water.

A *debris slide* is the rapid movement of rock fragments, such as gravel. It produces a surface of low rounded hills. A *rockslide* is the sliding of sheets of bedrock along planes of weakness and the tumbling of rocks and boulders down a slope. It produces a dam-like structure in the valley below. A *slump,* or slope failure, is the downward and outward movement of rock or unconsolidated material. It produces a scarp, or cliff, above it.

Other relatively slower movements are creep, earthflow, mudflow, and solifluction.

LAPIES. Furrows and sharp crests on a limestone surface. The furrows can be more than 40 feet deep.

LAPILLI. Small cinder fragments ejected from a volcano.

LAPSE RATE. The rate of decrease in the temperature of the atmosphere with increase in height.

LATERITE. A red-colored soil high in iron and aluminum found in tropical regions.

LAVA. Molten material reaching the surface from a pool of magma, or molten rock, in the interior of the earth. Also, the same material when cooled and solidified. It may be called pumice if light in color and weight, or scoria if dark and heavy.

LAVA FLOW. A stream of lava. A basic lava flow usually erupts gently, is relatively fluid, and may flow for miles. A silicic lava flow usually erupts explosively and is more viscous or gluey. A silicic lava flow usually piles up around the volcano.

LAW OF CROSS–CUTTING RELATIONSHIPS. Any rock is younger than any rock it cuts across.

LAW OF SUPERPOSITION. The basis of geologic chronology in that if a series of sedimentary rock has not been overturned, the underlying strata must be older than the overlying strata.

LEACHING. The removal or washing away of soluble material by water percolating through layers of soil or shattered bedrock.

LEAD. A soft, heavy metallic element (Pb) with a boiling point of 1,750°C and a specific gravity of 11.34.

LEAD–URANIUM RATIO. As the radioactive element uranium disintegrates, lead is formed. On the basis of the relative amounts of these two elements in a rock or mineral the geologic age can be computed. See also *Radioactive decay*.

LEAN ORE. A mineral deposit in which the ore content is low.

LEE. The sheltered side of an object, as a mountain.

LEEWARD. The direction toward which the wind is blowing, as opposed to windward.

LENTICULAR. A body of ore or rock thick in the middle and thinning toward the edges, thus resembling a double convex lens.

LEVEE. A natural or man-made river bank higher in elevation than the land running parallel to the stream.

LEVEL, or spirit level. An instrument for establishing a true horizontal. It consists of a hermetically sealed small glass tube nearly filled with a nonfreezing liquid, but with enough space left for the formation of an air bubble. The tube is mounted horizontally in a form with a straight edge, which provides a reference to the surface being tested. The bubble will always find the top of the tube.

LIGHT YEAR. The distance light can travel in one year, about 6,000 billion miles.

LIGNITE. An intermediate form of coal.

LIMB. The side of a fold.

LIME. Calcium Oxide, CaO.

LIMESTONE. A sedimentary rock formed from calcareous remains of plants and animals or precipitated from solution. It is natural calcium carbonate ($CaCO_3$) and will yield lime when heated.

LIMNOLOGY. The study of freshwater lakes and ponds.

LIMONITE. A brown hydrous iron oxide derived from the weathering of dark-colored minerals.

LITHIFICATION. The processes of cementation, compaction by pressure, and crystallization which convert magma, or molten material, and sediments into rock.

LITHOLOGY. The study and description of rocks.

LITHOSOLS. A great soil group of azonal soils consisting of partially weathered rock fragments. They are largely confined to steep hillsides.

LITHOSPHERE. The solid crust of the earth. See also *Earth structure*.

LITTORAL. Refers to a narrow strip of land along the coast between high and low water marks. See also *Ocean depth zones*.

LLANO. An extensive tropical grassland plain. The term is generally applied to vast savanna regions of South America.

LOAD. The solid material carried by a stream in suspension or rolled along the bed. The quantity of material depends upon the discharge and velocity of the stream and the particle size.

LOAM. A soil in which there is 28 to 55 percent silt, 7 to 27 percent clay, and less than 52 percent sand.

LOCH. A lake or an arm of the sea, especially when narrow or nearly landlocked.

LODE. A deposit of economically valuable mineral lying within definite boundaries, as in a fissure in country rock. The term may also refer to a system of closely spaced veins.

LOESS. An unconsolidated, unstratified deposit of silt and fine sand or clay, probably carried by the wind.

LONGITUDINAL DUNES. Long ridges of sand running in the general direction of wind movement. Longitudinal dunes are formed by two alternating wind directions or by the funnel-effect of valleys as wind sweeps sand through them. In the Libyan Desert they may be 60 miles long and are called seif (sword) dunes.

LONGITUDINAL VALLEY. A mountain valley parallel to the main trend of the range.

LONGSHORE CURRENT. A current moving roughly parallel to the shore. It is usually generated by waves breaking at an angle to the shoreline.

LOST RIVER. A surface stream that has lost its trunk and tributaries either because of increased aridity, in which evaporation exceeds precipitation, or because it drains into an underground channel, as may occur in a region of karst topography.

LOW. A parcel of air of lesser atmospheric pressure than the surrounding air.

LOW WATER. The lowest level reached by a falling tide.

LUNAR DAY. The interval of time between two successive passes of the moon across the same meridian. It is equal to approximately 24 hours, 50 minutes. Also called *tidal day*.

LUNAR MONTH. The period of time in which the moon makes one complete revolution around the earth, or from new moon to new moon. It is approximately equal to 29½ days.

LUSTER. A means of identifying a mineral according to its appearance in reflected light. There are several kinds of luster: *metallic*, having the luster of a metal (selective surface absorption with strong reflection); *vitreous*, having the luster of glass; *resinous*, having the luster of yellow resin; *pearly*, having the iridescence of a pearl; *greasy*, appearing to be covered with a thin layer of oil; *silky*, appearing like silk, with a finely fibrous structure; *adamantine*, having the brilliance of a diamond.

LYSIMETER. An instrument for measuring the percolation of water through soil and for determining the materials removed in solution by the drainage.

MAAR. A relatively shallow, flat-floored crater at a volcanic vent which is coneless or nearly so. It is formed by a violent explosion not accompanied by lava or ash. If it intersects the water table, the maar will be occupied by a lake.

MACCHIA. See *Maquis*.

MAGMA. Molten rock material (primarily silicates) existing deep within the earth. It cools and crystallizes to form igneous rock. When extruded it is called lava. It may be forced to the surface either by gases imprisoned within the magma or by the gross weight of the overlying solid rock on the basaltic layer below the crust.

MAGMATIC DIFFERENTIATION. The process by which initially homogeneous magma results in rocks of various textures and compositions. As magma cools, certain minerals crystallize more readily than others. Some of these crystals settle out of the magma, the rest react with the remaining melt (see *Bowen's reaction series*).

The rate of cooling affects the texture of the resultant rock. If rapidly cooled, it will have an extremely fine or glassy texture. If it cools slowly, it will have a coarse-grained texture.

MAGNETIC DECLINATION. The angle between geographic, or true, north and magnetic north.

MAGNETIC POLE. One of the two ends of the bipolar magnet at which magnetic properties appear to be concentrated, thus establishing the earth's magnetic field. These poles do not coincide with the geographic poles, as the axis connecting them passes approximately 750 miles from the earth's center.

MAGNETIC STORM. A large, temporary, often sudden variation in the earth's magnetic field. It is frequently associated with sunspots.

MAGNETITE. Iron oxide (Fe_3O_4), an important ore of iron. It is black and strongly magnetic.

MAGNETOMETER. An instrument for measuring the intensity and direction of the earth's magnetic field.

MALLEE. A shrubby vegetative cover consisting mostly of low eucalyptus bushes. It is found in Australia's dry regions.

AMERICAN MUSEUM OF NATURAL HISTORY

MAGNETITE, an iron oxide, is black, strongly magnetic, and an important ore of iron.

MANGROVE SWAMP. A salty, or brackish, marsh found in the coastal regions of tropical and subtropical climates in which mangrove trees develop aerial roots, forming an almost impenetrable tangle.

MANTLE. The interior portion of the earth lying between the core and the crust. See *Earth structure*.

MAQUIS. A low, thick, shrubby vegetation consisting of drought-resistant trees found along the shores of the Mediterranean Sea. Maquis is the French term, macchia the Italian.

MARBLE. The metamorphic equivalent of limestone or dolomite with grains large enough to be seen by the unaided eye. Commercially, any limestone that can take a polish.

MARINE. Of, or relating to, the sea.

MARINE CLIMATE. A climate under the predominant influence of the sea. It is characterized by small daily and annual temperature ranges and high relative humidity. It is found where the prevailing winds blow onshore, such as ocean islands and continental shores.

MARITIME. On, or near, the sea.

MARITIME CLIMATE. See *Marine climate*.

MARL. A calcareous clay. A sedimentary deposit of silt or clay and calcium carbonate, of marine or freshwater origin.

MARSH. An area of soft, wet, and poorly drained land, usually covered with grasses.

MARSH GAS. Methane (CH_4), the chief constituent of natural gas. It also results from the partial decay of plants in swamps.

MASSIF. A mountainous mass or group of uplands with relatively uniform characteristics. It may break up into peaks near the summit.

MASS—WASTING. The wearing down of the land surface by the downward movement of large masses of earth material directly controlled by gravity. It includes such gradual movements as creep and solifluction and such rapid movement as landslides.

MATTERHORN. A sharply pointed mountain peak resembling the Swiss peak of that name. See *Horn*.

MEADOW. A level grassland that is used generally for hay.

MEANDER. A loop, or curve, in a mature stream. It is formed when the current is turned against one bank by an obstruction and then is deflected against the other. A meander grows and migrates downstream by erosion on the outside of the bend and deposition on the inside. If the base level is lowered the stream will resume downward cutting and form an entrenched meander.

MEAN SEA LEVEL. The mean surface water level determined by averaging heights at all stages of the tide over a 19-year period.

MECHANICAL WEATHERING. The disintegration of rock material by expansion and contraction during temperature change, frost heaving, exfoliation, and the action of plant roots, streams, wind, glaciers, and ocean waves. There is no chemical change involved. See *Geology*.

MEDITERRANEAN CLIMATE. A type of climate characterized by hot, dry summers and cool, moist winters.

MELT. A liquid solution of ions at high temperature. A naturally occurring silicate melt is called magma.

MELTWATER. Water derived from the melting of snow or glacial ice.

MERCALLI INTENSITY SCALE. A system of registering the intensity of an earthquake on a scale ranging from 1, only barely detectable, to 12, force great enough to demolish large buildings. It has been replaced by the Richter magnitude scale.

MESA. A tablelike, flat-topped mountain with steep sides.

MESOTHERMAL. Referring to warm temperature.

MESOZOIC ERA. The "Era of Middle Life," the second of the three eras into which the Phanerozoic eon is divided. It began 185 million years ago and lasted 125 million years.

METAMORPHIC FACIES. A group of rocks characterized by particular mineral associations that indicate an origin under specific temperature-pressure conditions.

Four metamorphic facies have been identified: *hornfels* facies, formed at temperatures greater than 700°C (1,300°F); *amphibolite* facies, formed at temperatures from 450°C (850°F) to 700°C; *epidote-amphibolite* facies, formed at temperatures from 250°C (500°F) to 450°C; *greenschist* facies, formed at temperatures from 150°C (300°F) to 250°C. The hornfels facies are formed by contact metamorphism, the other facies by regional metamorphism.

METAMORPHIC ROCK. One of the three principal groups of rock, the others being sedimentary and igneous rock. Metamorphic rock is formed when solid rock is physically or chemically changed by deforming pressures, heat, and chemically active fluids. See also *Geochemical cycle*.

METASOMATISM. The changes in the composition of rock as a result of the replacement of one mineral by another. It is a process of almost simultaneous solution and deposition by which a mineral of differing chemical composition may grow within another mineral or mineral aggregate.

METASTASIS. Lateral shifting of the earth's crust, such as continental drift.

METEOR. A small body of matter traveling through space and which may enter the atmosphere. In the atmosphere it is heated by friction and is either wholly or partially consumed. If only partially consumed, it reaches the earth's surface as a meteorite.

METEORIC WATER. Water derived from the earth's atmosphere.

METEORITE. See *Meteor*.

METEOROLOGY. The scientific study of the atmosphere and its phenomena.

METHANE. The simplest paraffin hydrocarbon (CH_4) and the principal constituent of natural gas. Also called marsh gas.

MICA. A group of minerals with flat or perfect sheetlike structures composed of aluminum silicate with iron, calcium, magnesium, potassium, sodium, or lithium. The two most common types are biotite, or ferromagnesian black mica, and muscovite, or potassic white mica.

MICROSEISM. A disturbance of the earth's crust of very low intensity and short duration that may be produced by such factors as atmospheric storms or the activities of man.

MIDNIGHT SUN. A phenomenon seen in the high latitudes, above 63½°, during the summer season, when the sun does not fall below the horizon plane and is visible for 24 hours.

MIDOCEAN RIDGE. A great median arch or sea bottom swell extending the length of an ocean basin roughly parallel to the continental margins.

MIGMATITE. A mixed rock produced by the injection of granitic magma between the layers of a rock.

MILE. A unit of linear measurement. A *geographic* mile is 1/60 of a degree measured along the equator, or 6,087 feet. A *nautical* mile is equal to 1/60 of a degree of a great circle on a sphere whose surface is equal to that of earth. One international nautical mile equals approximately 6,076 feet. A *statute* mile is equal to 5,280 feet.

MILLIBAR. A unit of atmospheric pressure equal to 1/1000 of a bar. In meteorology, it is equal to a force of 1,000 dynes per square centimeter.

MINERAL. A naturally occurring inorganic substance with distinctive physical and chemical properties and a tendency to assume a crystal form. A mineral is classified according to its structure, cleavage, and fracture; its luster, hardness, and specific gravity; and its color and the color of the streak it makes on unglazed porcelain.

MINERALOGY. The study of the origin, chemical composition, and physical characteristics of minerals.

MINUTE. A unit of time equal to 1/60 of an hour. Also, a unit of angular measurement equal to 1/60 of a degree.

MIOCENE EPOCH. The fourth epoch of the Tertiary period of the Cenozoic era. It began 30 million years ago and lasted 15 million years. During this time such major mountain ranges as the Alps, the Andes, and the Himalayas were raised and certain ruminating animals, such as cows, developed. Also, there arose the Hominidae (which later gave rise to the Homo sapiens).

MIRAGE. An optical illusion seen on deserts, at sea, and in polar regions. It is caused by layers of air that have been unequally heated, and therefore, have differing densities. If the difference in density between two layers is great enough, the common surface will act as a mirror. In this way distant objects may appear magnified, distorted, and often inverted. Because the surface is not smooth there is continual shimmering.

MISSISSIPPIAN PERIOD. The fifth period of the Paleozoic era in geologic time. It began 310 million years ago and lasted 40 million years. During this time, coal beds were formed and reptiles and amphibians developed. Formerly, the Mississippian with the Pennsylvanian composed the Carboniferous period. This grouping is now considered obsolete in the United States, and the Mississippian and Pennsylvanian are each ranked as periods.

MIST. A parcel of air containing dispersed water droplets that reduce visibility. It is less severe than a fog.

MISTRAL. A cold, dry, and gusty north or northwest wind that blows from a high pressure area in snow-covered mountains to the low pressure area extending along the Mediterranean coast of France.

MOHO, or Mohorovičić discontinuity. See *Earth structure*.

MOHOLE. a U.S. scientific project to dig a deep borehole to penetrate the earth's crust and on into the mantle below the Mohorovičić discontinuity. The site chosen was in the ocean, 100 miles northeast of Maui, Hawaii, where the crust is thinner. By analyzing the material brought up from the hole and then lowering instruments to record temperature, magnetism, and other factors, scientists hoped to answer some questions about the structure of the inner earth. The project was abandoned.

MOHS' SCALE. See *Hardness scale*.

MONADNOCK. An isolated residual mass of resistant rock that stands above the surrounding land.

MONOCLINE. See *Fold*.

MONSOON. A wind system characterized by a complete reversal of direction from winter to summer. In winter it is a dry, offshore wind formed in high pressure areas over cold continents. In summer, it is a damp onshore wind blowing toward the heated interior of the continents.

NORWEGIAN INFORMATION SERVICE
MIDNIGHT SUN at North Cape on Magery Island, Norway, during the summer.

MOON. The only natural satellite of the earth, traveling at a mean distance of 238,866 miles from the earth at an average speed of almost 2,300 miles per hour. The moon makes a complete revolution around the earth every 27 days, 7 hours, 43 minutes, 11.47 seconds—one sidereal month. It moves into the same relationship with the earth and sun every 29 days, 12 hours, 44 minutes, 2.8 seconds—one synodic month.

The moon's diameter is 2,160 miles or slightly more than ¼ that of the earth; its mass is 1/81 that of the earth. The moon's temperature ranges from over 200°F in the sun to below −250°F in complete shadow. The moon has no atmosphere.

Because the moon completes one rotation about its axis in the same time it takes to complete one revolution around the earth, the same side of the moon always faces the earth. The phases of the moon are new moon (invisible from the earth), first quarter, full moon, and last quarter.

MOOR. An extensive area of open rolling land covered with heather or wild grasses, with or without marshy patches.

MORAINE. Unconsolidated, disordered rock material, or debris, deposited by a glacier. *Lateral moraines* are built along the lateral, or side, margins of a glacier. These merge to form a *medial moraine* at the meeting of two valley glaciers. *Terminal,* or *end, moraines* are formed at the farthest advance of a glacier.

Recessional moraines are formed at temporary positions during the retreat of a glacier. *Ground moraines* are formed as the main body of a glacier melts, creating gently rolling plains across a valley floor. *Superficial moraines* are formed on a glacier as the ice melts and the drift it had contained accumulates on the surface.

MOTE. A large dust particle visible in a beam of light.

CANADIAN INFORMATION OFFICE

MOUNTAINS are elevations in the earth's surface caused by a variety of geological factors.

MOUNTAIN. A natural elevation, usually of at least 2,000 feet, formed as a fold, fault, volcano, or as the remnant of erosion. A single mountain is a peak; connected peaks, a ridge; an elongated ridge, a chain or range; a series of ranges, often parallel, a system; a number of systems, including intervening valleys, rivers, and plains, a cordillera.

MOUNTAIN BUILDING. See *Orogeny*.

MOUNTAIN CLIMATE. A type of climate whose properties are mostly determined by relief and altitude rather than latitude and proximity to the ocean.

MOUTH. The place of discharge of a stream into a larger body of water.

MUCK. A dark-colored soil high in organic matter, usually formed in wet places.

MUD CRACKS. Irregular polygonal cracks formed by shrinkage as a mud deposit dries. On further exposure they bake and harden so that the polygonal form is preserved through repeated flooding.

MUDFLOW. A downward moving, thick mixture of rock fragments, soil, and water. It produces a widening tongue of rock when dried and solidified. It occurs in the canyons of desert regions after a rainstorm or on the slopes of a volcano.

MUDSTONE. A fine-grained sedimentary rock consisting of an indefinite mixture of clay, silt, and sand particles. The term also refers to a clay rock, or shale, without fissility (ready breaking along closely spaced parallel planes).

MUSCOVITE. See *Mica*.

MUSKEG. A moss-covered swamp in northern North America.

NAPPE. A faulted, overturned fold thrust over other rocks.

NATURAL BRIDGE. An arch of rock or earth spanning a gorge or other depression. It is formed by erosion.

NATURAL GAS. A mixture of gaseous hydrocarbons that occurs in nature.

NAUTICAL MILE. See *Mile*.

NEAP TIDE. The tide with the smallest range between high water and low water. Neap tides occur about every two weeks when the moon is in the first or third quarter, the sun and moon being at right angles to each other with respect to a place on the earth (quadrature).

NECK. A mass of hardened lava which has filled the conduit or vent of a volcano and which has been exposed by erosion of the surrounding material. Also, a narrow strip of land connecting a peninsula with the mainland or a narrow channel connecting two larger bodies of water.

NECK CUTOFF. A channel cut by a stream across the neck of land between two meanders. The abandoned loop is called an oxbow.

NERITIC. See *Ocean depth zones*.

NÉVÉ. Granular snow, the intermediate stage between snow and ice in a glacier. It is also called firn.

NITRATES. A group of nitrogen fertilizers in which the nitrogen is available as a salt of nitric acid—a compound containing the radical of nitrogen and oxygen (NO_3).

NIVATION. Frost heaving and erosion beneath and around a snowbank.

NODULE. An irregular, knobby-surfaced body of mineral matter whose composition differs from the sedimentary rock in which it was formed. Silica, in the form of chert or flint, is the major component of a nodule.

NONCONFORMITY. An unconformity in which igneous rocks were partially eroded and then covered by sedimentary rocks.

NORTHERN LIGHTS. See *Aurora*.

NORTH POLE. See *Poles*.

NOTCH. A deep cut, or notch, in the base of a sea cliff made by breaking waves. Also, a narrow pass between two hills or mountains.

NUÉE ARDENTE. A cloud of hot gas and ash ejected horizontally from beneath a lava plug in a volcano. The cloud travels swiftly down the side of the volcano.

NUNATAK. An isolated mountain peak projecting through the surface of a glacier.

OASIS. An area in a desert where water is permanently available. Oases range in size from a small patch with a few palm trees to an area of several hundred square miles.

OBLATE. Flattened at the poles. For example, the earth is an oblate spheroid.

OBSEQUENT STREAM. A stream flowing in a direction opposite to that of the dip of the strata or the tilt of the surface. It occurs in rock beds of differing resistance. Also called a reversed stream. It is the opposite of a consequent stream.

OBSIDIAN. Volcanic glass. An extrusive igneous rock containing a large proportion of silica.

OCEAN. The great body of salt water that occupies the depressions in the earth's surface.

OCEAN CURRENT. A large stream moving continuously through the ocean in approximately the same path, distinguished chiefly by temperature and salinity from the water through which it flows.

OCEAN DEPTH ZONES. The primary divisions of ocean depths are the *pelagic*, the entire mass of water, and the *benthic*, the ocean floor.

The *pelagic* division is composed of the neritic province, which extends from the low water point to a depth of 100 fathoms (600 feet), and the oceanic province, which includes water deeper than 100 fathoms. The upper 50 fathoms of the pelagic division comprise the photic zone, where there is ample sunlight for plants to carry on photosynthesis. Below that is the aphotic zone.

The *benthic* division includes the supralittoral zone, or land just above the high water level kept moist by waves and spray; the littoral zone, between high water and low water levels; the sublittoral zone, from the low water level to 100 fathoms (underlying the neritic province); the bathyal

MAGNUM: GEORGE RODGER

OASIS, in the Sahara, consists of a group of date palms watered by underground springs.

zone, between 100 and 2,000 fathoms; and the abyssal zone, below 2,000 fathoms. The hadal zone comprises the greatest depths, over 3,000 fathoms.

OCEANOGRAPHY. The study of the ocean, including its physical boundaries, the chemistry and physics of the sea, and marine biology.

OFFSHORE WIND. A wind blowing from the land toward the sea, a land breeze, as contrasted with an onshore wind, or sea breeze.

OIL. See *Petroleum.*

OLIGOCENE EPOCH. The third epoch of the Tertiary period of the Cenozoic era. It began 40 million years ago and lasted 10 million years.

OLIVINE. A dark green mineral consisting of silicates of magnesium and iron which crystallizes early from magma, or molten material, and weathers readily at the earth's surface.

ONSHORE WIND. A wind blowing from the sea toward the land, a sea breeze, as contrasted with an offshore wind, or land breeze.

OÖLITE. A rock made up of spherical, sand-sized grains, usually composed of calcium carbonate.

OOZE. Wet mud or slime. Also a fine-grained deep-sea deposit, 30 percent or more of which is composed of the hard parts of small organisms.

ORDOVICIAN PERIOD. The second period of the Paleozoic era in geologic time. It began 450 million years ago and lasted 70 million years.

ORE. A mineral deposit of economic value.

OROGENY. The process of forming mountains by folding, faulting, and thrusting.

OROGRAPHIC RAIN. Rainfall produced when a mountain deflects moist air upward. The moist air cools at the higher elevation and the moisture falls as rain.

OROGRAPHY. The branch of physical geography concerned with the study of mountains and mountain systems.

OUTCROP. A naturally protruding portion of a rock formation, most of which is covered by overlying material.

OUTLIER. A mass of younger rocks separated by erosion from the main mass and surrounded by older rocks. The opposite of inlier.

OUTWASH PLAIN. A plain formed of material deposited by streams flowing from a melting glacier.

OVERBURDEN. The loose earth material lying over other material, such as an ore deposit.

OXBOW. A crescent-shaped lake formed in a meander cut off from the main stream.

OXYSPHERE. A proposed synonym for lithosphere on the basis that 60 percent of the atoms in the earth's crust are oxygen and these atoms occupy more than 90 percent of the volume of the familiar rocks.

OYASHIO. A cold ocean current flowing south along the Kuril Islands. It meets the Kuroshio and with it forms the North Pacific Current.

PACK ICE. Any area of sea ice other than fast ice. Specifically, an area of floating ice which has been driven together. It is often referred to as drift ice.

PAHOEHOE. Hawaiian term for a lava flow whose surface is smooth, billowy, or ropy. Also called corded lava. The opposite of aa.

PALEOCENE EPOCH. The first epoch of the Tertiary period of the Cenozoic era. It began 60 million years ago and lasted 10 million years.

PALEOGEOGRAPHY. The study of the distribution of land and water masses during earlier periods of geologic time.

PALEONTOLOGY. The study of extinct plant and animal organisms based on their fossil remains.

PALEOZOIC ERA. The "Era of Old Life," the earliest era of the Phanerozoic eon. It began approximately 550 million years ago and lasted approximately 350 million years.

PALISADE. An extended rock cliff rising abruptly from the margin of a stream or lake.

PALUDAL. Referring to swamps or marshes and to material deposited in a swamp.

PALUSTRINE. Pertaining to material deposited in a swamp or marsh.

PAMPA. A treeless grassland plain. Specifically, the extensive grassland area around the River Plate (Río de la Plata) in South America.

PAMPERO. A strong, cold, west or southwest wind which sweeps over the pampas of South America.

PARABOLIC DUNE. A U-shaped sand dune whose tips point upwind and whose concave, or windward, side is the gentler slope. It is formed in sandy areas along coasts and is often covered with sparse vegetation which limits its advance.

PARAMO. A high, bleak plateau with scattered, stunted vegetation, as in the Andes of South America.

PASS. A narrow gap or low break in a mountain barrier.

PATER NOSTER LAKES. A chain of small lakes along a glaciated valley where ice-plucking and gouging have scooped out a series of basins.

PEAK. The summit of a mountain.

PEAT. The semisolid remains of decayed marsh plants. It is the first stage in the formation of coal.

PEBBLES. See *Wentworth grade scale.*

PEDALFER. A soil type characterized by the accumulation of iron and aluminum salts. Such soluble materials as calcium carbonate or magnesium carbonate generally do not occur in a pedalfer. It is found in humid climates, beneath forest vegetation.

PEDIMENT. A gently sloping rock surface at the base of a highland in arid and semiarid regions.

PEDOCAL. A soil type characterized by the accumulation of calcium carbonate. It is commonly found in temperate climates with low rainfall, below brush or grass growth.

PEDOLOGY. The study of the origin, character, and use of soils.

PEGMATITE. A small pluton or dike of very coarse texture with crystals up to 40 feet long, usually associated with a batholith of finer texture.

PELAGIC. See *Ocean depth zones.*

PENEPLAIN. An extensive level land surface close to base level formed by a long period of erosion.

PENINSULA. A body of land nearly surrounded by water and connected to a larger body of land by a neck.

PENNSYLVANIAN PERIOD. The sixth period of the Paleozoic era in geological time. It began 270 million years ago and lasted 45 million years. During this time large insects developed. Cockroaches achieved a length of 3 or 4 inches, and the period is also called the "Age of Cockroaches." Formerly, with the Mississippian, it comprised the Carboniferous period.

PERCHED WATER TABLE. A body of groundwater held above the main water table by a layer of impermeable rock.

PERCOLATION. The downward passage of water moved by its own weight through the crevices or pores of rock or soil.

PERIDOTITE. A group of coarse-grained intrusive igneous rocks, such as granite, containing ferromagnesian silicates and little or no feldspar.

PERIOD. In geologic time, a subdivision of an era; a time unit corresponding to a system in time-stratigraphic units.

PERMAFROST. Permanently frozen subsoil.

PERMEABILITY. The ability of earth material to transmit liquids.

PERMIAN PERIOD. The seventh and last period of the Paleozoic era in geologic time. It began some 225 million years ago and lasted for approximately 40 million years.

PETROGRAPHY. See *Lithology.*

PETROLOGY. The study of the origin, present conditions, and alterations of rocks, including ore and mineral deposits.

pH. A means of expressing the relative acidity and alkalinity of a soil in terms of a scale in which complete acidity is 0 and alkalinity is 14 (7 is neutral).

PHANERITIC. Refers to equigranular, coarse-grained (hence visible), and therefore slowly cooled rock.

PHANEROZOIC EON. The "Time of Visible Life." It began 550 million years ago with the Cambrian period of the Paleozoic era and continues into the present.

PHENOCRYST. A large, conspicuous crystal in an aphanitic, or fine-grained, groundmass.

PHENOLOGY. The study of the relationship between seasonal climate change and animal and plant life.

PHOROGENESIS. The slipping of the earth's crust over the mantle.

PHOSPHATES. Salts of phosphoric acid used as fertilizers to supply phosphorous compounds to the soil. A compound containing the chemical radical of phosphorus and oxygen, such as PO_4.

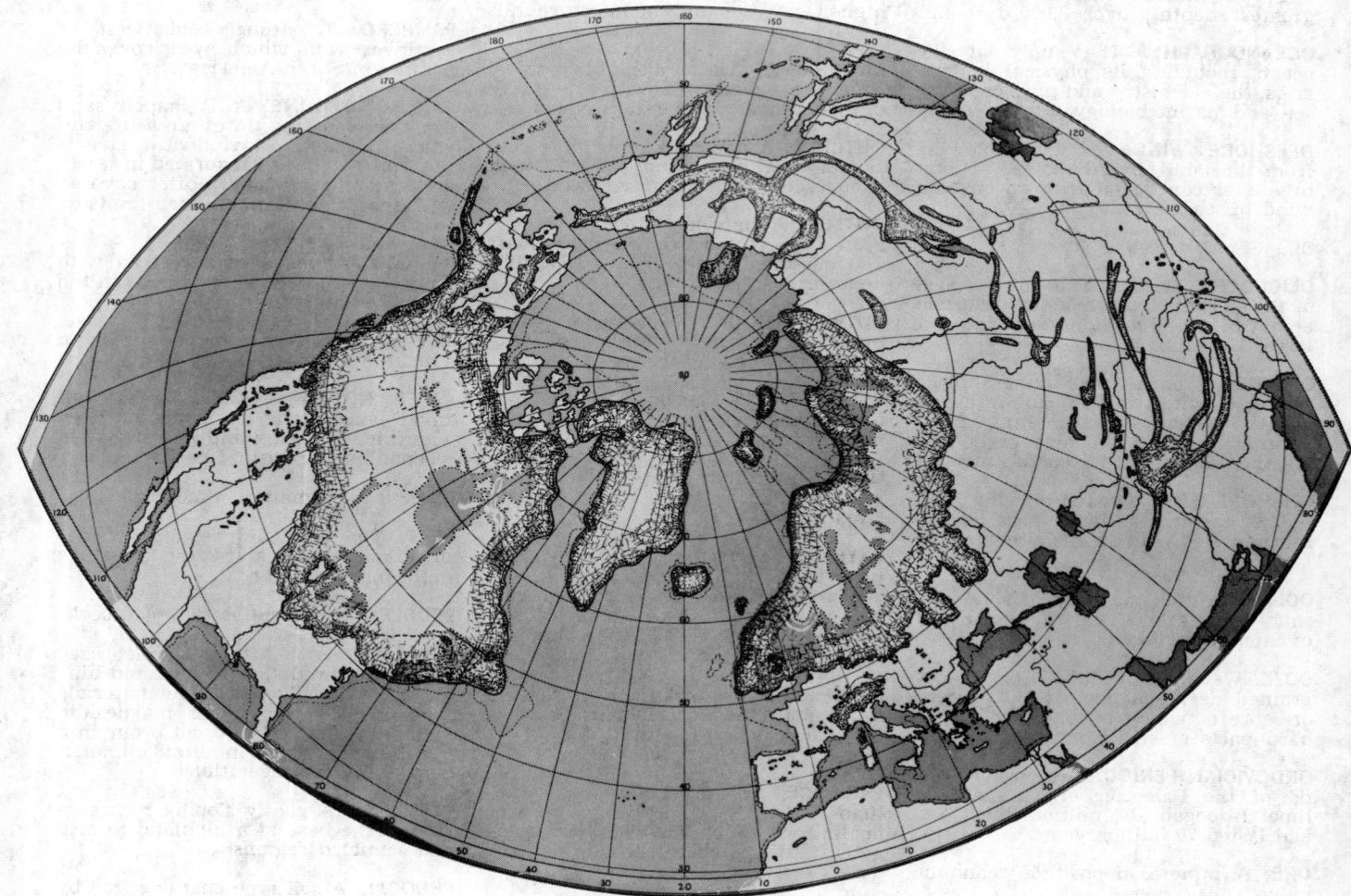

AMERICAN MUSEUM OF NATURAL HISTORY
PLEISTOCENE GLACIATION at its maximum extent covered northern Europe, the British Isles, and North America as far south as the Ohio River.

PHREATIC. Pertaining to groundwater.

PHYLLITE. A clayey metamorphic rock with cleavage coarser than slate and finer than schist.

PHYSIOGRAPHY. The study of the physical features of the earth.

PICACHO. A large, pointed mountain or hill with steep sides.

PIEDMONT. Refers to any feature lying or formed at the base of a mountain.

PIEZOMETRIC SURFACE. The imaginary surface corresponding to the level to which groundwater will rise under hydrostatic pressure in wells or springs.

PILLOW LAVAS. Rounded masses of lava occurring in basic lava, such as basalt.

PIRACY. See *Stream capture*.

PITCH. See *Rake*.

PITCHSTONE. A dull, pitch-lustered variety of volcanic glass containing more water than other glassy rocks.

PLACER DEPOSIT. A mass of gravel or similar material containing particles of valuable minerals, such as gold or platinum.

PLAIN. A large area of level or gently undulating land not broken by any great elevations or depressions.

PLANETARY WINDS. The major winds of the earth—the polar easterlies, trade winds, westerlies.

PLANOSOL. A great soil group of intrazonal soils consisting of eluviated surface horizons, overlying compacted B horizons.

PLATEAU. An extensive, comparatively flat surface rising sharply above adjacent land on at least one side and often dissected by canyons.

PLATEAU BASALT. A vast horizontal lava flow.

PLAYA. A shallow central portion of a basin floor where water gathers after a rain and is evaporated, leaving an alkali flat.

PLAYA LAKE. A temporary lake in a playa.

PLEISTOCENE EPOCH. The first epoch in the Quaternary period of the Cenozoic era in geologic time. It began 1 million years ago and, according to some authorities, ended with the beginning of history, 10,000 to 25,000 years ago. During this epoch, glaciers made several advances and retreats, at times covering almost one third of the earth's land surface. It is thus also called the Ice Age.

PLIOCENE EPOCH. The fifth and latest epoch in the Tertiary period of the Cenozoic era in geologic time. It began 15 million years ago and lasted 14 million years.

PLUCKING. The chief process in glacial erosion by which meltwater freezes around pieces of rock, incorporates them into the glacier, and, by the pressure of the thick moving glacier, breaks off or quarries blocks of bedrock.

PLUTONIC ROCK. Igneous rock that has solidified below the surface of the earth and therefore cooled slowly.

PLUVIAL. Pertaining to rain.

PODZOL. A great soil group consisting of soils formed in temperate, humid climates under coniferous or mixed coniferous and deciduous forests. It is characterized by an ashy-gray, highly leached layer.

POINT. The extreme end of a cape.

POLAR FRONT. The boundary, or front, between cold, polar air and the warm air of temperate or tropical regions. The majority of atmospheric depressions of temperate latitudes develop there.

POLAR WIND. An extremely cold wind blowing out of the high-pressure zone around the poles.

POLDER. An area of flat land at or below sea level, or the level of the nearest river, which has been drained.

POLES. The intersections of the extremities of the earth's axis with the earth's surface, located at 90°N and 90°S latitudes.

POLJE, or polye. An extensive depression with a flat floor and steep walls in a region of karst topography.

POLYGONAL GROUND. See *Mud cracks*.

POND. A small, rather deep body of water, usually fresh. Also, an underground accumulation of oil or gas in a natural reservoir composed of such porous rock as sandstone or limestone and bounded by impermeable strata of rock.

PORE. An interstice or void in rock or soil.

POROSITY. The ratio between the volume occupied by pores in a material to its total volume.

PORPHYRY. An igneous rock containing conspicuous crystals, or phenocrysts, in a fine-grained, or aphanitic, groundmass.

POTASH. Potassium salts, used as a source of potassium fertilizer.

POTHOLE. A hole in rock, generally deeper than it is wide, caused by the abrasive action of rock fragments. Potholes are commonly found in the bed of a stream or at the base of a waterfall.

PRAIRIE. An extensive, undulating to flat, grassland area. Also, a zonal great soil group composed of soils formed under grass cover in cool to temperate, humid regions.

PRECAMBRIAN. Refers to the Cryptozoic eon, preceding the Cambrian period of the Palezoic era in geologic time.

PRECIPICE. A very steep cliff, particularly one that is almost perpendicular or overhanging.

PRECIPITATION. The deposit of water on the earth from the atmosphere. It occurs when water vapor particles grow large enough to fall to the earth and the moisture content of the air exceeds the saturation point. Precipitation may be in the form of rain, snow, sleet, hail, dew, frost, or fog. Also, the separation of minerals from a solution by evaporation, centrifugal force, or fractionation.

PRESSURE GRADIENT. See *Hydraulic gradient*.

PREVAILING WIND. The wind direction at a given place with the greatest frequency of occurrence.

PROFILE. A cross section or outline. A longitudinal section of a stream showing its change in elevation. A soil profile is a vertical section through the soil showing the nature and sequence of the different layers.

PROMONTORY. A headland or high cape projecting into a body of water.

PSYCHROMETER. An instrument which measures the humidity of the atmosphere.

PUMICE. A light, porous volcanic glass filled with gas-bubble holes.

PUNA. A treeless, windswept tableland in the higher Andes mountain system of South America.

P WAVE. See *Earthquake*.

PYRITE. Iron sulfide (FeS_2). An important ore of sulfur. Because of its brassy color, it is often called "fool's gold."

PYROCLASTIC ROCK. Fragmental extrusive volcanic rock, including bombs (rounded fragments), blocks (angular), cinders (coarse, slaglike), ash (dust-sized), tuff (consolidated ash), and pumice (bombs or blocks with gas-bubble holes).

PYROMETER. An instrument for measuring temperatures beyond the range of mercurial thermometers by means of the change of electric resistance, the production of thermoelectric current, the expansion of gases, the specific heat of solids, or the intensity of heat or light radiated.

PYROXENE. A group of common rock-forming minerals, calcium and magnesium silicates with varying amounts of aluminum, iron, and sodium.

PYRRHOTITE. Iron sulfide. An important nickel ore.

QANAT. An underground channel, or tunnel, used to divert water for irrigation.

QUADRATURE. The position of the moon at a 90° angle from the sun in respect to a point on earth. It causes neap tides.

QUAGMIRE. An area of soft, wet land that gives way under foot. A bog or marsh.

QUARRY. An open cut into the earth for the extraction of stone.

QUARRYING. The removal of earth and rock by a glacier or a stream. See also *Plucking.*

QUARTZ. A common mineral, silicon dioxide (SiO_2), usually colorless or white, although it may be colored by impurities. It has a vitreous luster, conchoidal fracture, and a hardness of 7. There are several varieties of quartz, including rock crystal, amethyst, chalcedony, and agate.

QUARTZITE. A rock formed by the metamorphism of sandstone. Quartzite has no cleavage, breaking through grains instead of around them as in sandstone.

QUATERNARY PERIOD. The second period in the Cenozoic era and the most recent in geologic time. It began 1 million years ago and continues into the present.

QUICKSAND. A mass of loose, wet, unstable sand that readily yields to pressure, thus engulfing any heavy object resting on its surface.

RACE. A very fast current flowing through a relatively narrow channel.

RADIAL DRAINAGE PATTERN. A system of streams flowing outward from a central area.

RADIATION. The process by which a body emits energy in the form of waves.

RADIOACTIVE AGE DETERMINATION. The establishment of the age of a rock or sediment by measuring the proportion of the radioisotope Carbon 14 in the organic material it contains.

RADIOACTIVE DECAY. The disintegration of the nucleus of an unstable atom by the spontaneous emission of charged particles, the original element thus becoming a new element. For example, Uranium 238 (an isotope of uranium) disintegrates into helium and lead; its half-life is 4.56 billion years. Therefore, it can be used to date very old igneous and metamorphic rocks and some sedimentary rocks.

RADIOACTIVITY. The spontaneous and continuous breakdown of the nucleus in such elements as uranium, thorium, and radium by the emission of alpha, beta, and gamma rays.

RADIOLARIAN OOZE. A siliceous ooze composed of the hard parts of minute marine protozoa called Radiolaria. The greatest concentration of this siliceous mud occurs in a long east-west belt in the Pacific Ocean just north of the equator.

RADIOSONDE. A miniature radio transmitter with recording instruments carried aloft, usually by a balloon. Every few seconds it broadcasts signals giving temperature, humidity, and pressure.

RAIN. See *Precipitation.*

RAINBOW. An arc with bands of the various colors of the spectrum formed by the refraction and reflection of sunlight by water drops.

RAIN SHADOW. An area of low rainfall on the lee side of a mountain or mountain range.

RAISED BEACH. A beach elevated above the present shoreline resulting from uplift or change in sea level.

RAKE. The angle between a line in a plane and a horizontal line in that plane. Preferred over pitch in structural geology.

RAMP. A normal, or gravity, fault at the surface, curving or dipping at depth in the opposite direction. Also, an accumulation of snow forming an inclined plane between land or land ice and sea ice.

RAND. A low, marshy border around a lake or lagoon.

RANGE. An elongated ridge or chain of mountains. An open region over which livestock graze. Also, a unit of measurement, used in surveying, equal to 6 miles along a parallel.

RAPID. A turbulent portion of a stream where velocity is increased by a slope of more than one foot every 200 feet or where the current is diverted by successive outcrops of resistant rock.

RAVINE. A small, narrow, steep-sided depression in the earth, larger than a gully and smaller than a canyon.

REACTION SERIES. See *Bowen's reaction series.*

RECENT. The latest, or most recent, epoch in geological time, beginning 10,000 to 25,000 years ago and continuing to the present.

RECTANGULAR DRAINAGE PATTERN. A system of streams in which tributaries join the mainstream at 90° angles because of the right-angled faulting of rocks.

RECURVED SPIT. A hook developed as the end of a spit is turned toward the shore by the current or by the opposing action of two or more currents.

RED AND YELLOW SOILS. A combination of Red Podzolic and Yellow Podzolic zonal great soil groups formed in humid climates under forest cover.

RED CLAY. A widespread fine-grained deposit, or ooze, on the ocean floor at depths exceeding 13,000 feet, especially in the Pacific Ocean. Its red color probably results from oxidation during its slow rate of accumulation, one inch in 3,000 years.

REEF. A ridge of rocks at or near the surface of the sea, narrower than a shoal.

REFRACTORY. Refers to a mineral or compound that resists the action of heat and chemicals.

REG. A desert surface covered with tightly-packed gravel.

REGELATION. The process by which ice is melted under pressure and the meltwater is refrozen on the release of that pressure. It is believed to play a role in the movement of a glacier.

REGIMEN. In glaciers, the balance between accumulation and wastage. In streams, the stability of a stream and its channel, including seasonal fluctuations.

REGIONAL METAMORPHISM. Metamorphism on a large scale, usually unrelated to obvious igneous bodies.

REGOLITH. The layer of loose rock material resting on bedrock. It forms the surface of the earth nearly everywhere.

REGOSOLS. An azonal soil consisting primarily of soft and imperfectly consolidated material, such as sand or recent volcanic ash.

REGUR. A group of dark soils high in clay formed mainly from rocks with low quartz content. It is found extensively on the Deccan Plateau of India.

REJUVENATION. The renewal of the erosion of a land surface. It usually is caused by uplift or an increase in the discharge of a stream following an increase in precipitation.

RELATIVE TIME. Measurement of a sequence of events in geological time in terms of position in a chronological order of occurrence.

RELIEF. The difference in elevation between the highest and lowest points in a given area.

RESIDUAL SOIL. A soil formed by the disintegration and decomposition of the rocks on which it rests.

REVERSED STREAM. See *Obsequent stream.*

REVOLUTION. A time of major crustal deformation, or orogeny.

RHYOLITE. The extrusive equivalent of granite. It has a fine-grained, or aphanitic, texture.

RIA COAST. An irregular coastline with many short, funnel-shaped bays which broaden and deepen seaward, although not reaching the depth of fiords.

RICHTER MAGNITUDE SCALE. See *Earthquake.*

RIDGE. A long, narrow elevation. An elongated crest.

RIFT. A large strike-slip fault parallel to the regional structure, such as the San Andreas rift in California.

RIFT VALLEY. See *Graben.*

RILL. A very small, shallow, often temporary stream.

RIPARIAN. Pertaining to the banks of a stream.

RIP CURRENT. A strong, narrow surface current which returns to the sea the water piled up on shore by incoming waves and wind.

RIPPLE MARK. A system of small waves produced on unconsolidated material, such as sand, by wind, water current, or wave action.

RISE. A long, broad elevation rising gently and smoothly from the sea floor.

RIVER. A large stream flowing to progressively lower levels in a natural channel.

ROARING FORTIES. A belt of strong, often stormy, prevailing westerly winds which blow throughout the year in the oceans of the southern hemisphere between 40° and 60° South latitude.

ROCHE MOUTONNÉE. An exposed knob of bedrock that has been smoothed and striated by a glacier on the upstream side and left with a rugged, steeper slope on the downstream side.

ROCK. A consolidated, relatively hard, naturally formed mass of mineral matter.

ROCK FLOUR. Finely ground rock material resulting from the abrasive action of a glacier.

ROCK GLACIER. A glacierlike tongue of angular boulders usually found in cirques. In many cases a rock glacier grades into a true glacier.

ROCK MANTLE. See *Regolith.*

ROCK SALT. See *Halite.*

ROCKSLIDE. See *Landslide.*

ROCK–STRATIGRAPHIC UNIT. A group of sedimentary rocks identified by structural features without regard to fossils or time boundaries.

ROCK WOOL. See *Asbestos.*

ROPAK. A slab of sea ice standing vertically on edge.

ROPY LAVA. Corded pahoehoe.

ROSSI–FOREL INTENSITY SCALE. A scale for rating earthquake intensity replaced in 1931 by the Modified Mercalli intensity scale, which in turn was generally replaced by the Richter magnitude scale.

ROTARY FAULT. A fault which has rotated or pivoted one side of the fault away from the other.

RUNOFF. The portion of precipitation falling on a surface that runs downslope to join streams, neither evaporating nor sinking into the ground.

SADDLE. A mountain pass or low point on a ridge.

ST. ELMO'S FIRE. A luminous electrical discharge with the appearance of a brush of red or blue fire which may occur during storms at the extremities of tall objects, such as the tops of trees or steeples, or at prominent points on an airplane or ship.

SALINITY. The measure of the quantity of dissolved salts in a substance.

SALT. Halite, sodium chloride (NaCl). Also, a substance obtained when the hydrogen of an acid is displaced by a metal. Also, a compound formed from an acid and a base.

SALTATION. The bouncing movement of sand particles. In deserts, wind pushes particles of sand along the surface. When one grain collides with another the impact lifts it into the air where wind and gravitation combine to push it forward through the air and pull it back to the ground in a parabolic path from its former position. Saltation also occurs in streams; however, instead of wind, the activating force is a current of turbulent water.

SALT DOME. A mass of rock salt which has been forced to flow plastically and intruded into overlying sedimentary rock. It tends to be cylindrical and have a top diameter of about a mile.

SALT GLACIER. Generally, an exposed salt dome. It is found only in extremely arid regions.

SALT LAKE. A lake containing a predominant amount of sodium chloride and other salts. It occurs in arid regions where evaporation exceeds precipitation and runoff.

SALT MARSH. A flat, poorly drained coastal swamp often covered at high tide.

SALT PAN. A shallow basin lined with salt and often containing a salt lake.

SALT PLUG. See *Salt dome.*

SAND. Earth material (often pure silica) finer than gravel and coarser than silt. See *Wentworth grade scale.*

SANDBAR. See *Bar.*

SAND DUNE. See *Dune.*

SAND SPOUT. See *Dust devil.*

SANDSTONE. A porous sedimentary rock composed of cemented sand-sized grains, predominantly quartz.

SANDSTORM. A strong wind carrying relatively coarse sand. It rarely extends to more than 100 feet above the ground.

SAPROLITE. Residual clay, silt, or other substance from rock decomposed in situ. It is commonly red or brown and found in warm, humid climates.

SAPROPEL. An ooze, or sludge, that accumulates in swampy areas. It is rich in organic (carbonaceous or bituminous) matter.

SASTRUGI. Irregularities or wave formations caused by persistent winds on a snow surface.

SAVANNA. A plain covered with tall grasses and scattered low trees. It is found in tropical regions of alternate rainfall and drought.

SCHIST. A foliated metamorphic rock dominated by fibrous or platy minerals, such as mica. See also *Foliation.*

SCORIA. Pieces of dark, heavy, partly glassy basaltic lava with many large, irregular cavities. A pyroclastic rock.

SCOUR AND FILL. A stream in flood scours out its channel (degradation) and, as it subsides, refills its channel (aggradation).

SCREE. A heap of debris at the base of a cliff or a sheet of debris covering a mountain slope. It is distinguished from talus, which occurs only at the base of a cliff.

SCRUB. A thick vegetation consisting of stunted trees and shrubs. It grows in poor soil or in sand.

SEA. A body of salt water secondary in size to an ocean. It may be partially or completely surrounded by land. Also, waves generated or sustained by

ARABIAN AMERICAN OIL COMPANY

SAND. Blown by the wind, particles of sand are constantly forming new surface patterns.

winds within their fetch, or generating area, as opposed to swell, which refers to more regular, longer waves that have traveled out of their generating area.

SEA BREEZE. A light wind blowing from the sea to the land. It is caused by unequal heating of land and sea during the day. The cooler, denser air over the water moves into an area of warm, less dense air.

SEA LEVEL. See *Mean sea level*.

SEA MILE. A nautical mile. See *Mile*.

SEAMOUNT. An elevation rising 500 fathoms (3,000 feet) or more from the sea floor and of limited extent across its summit.

SEDIMENTARY ROCK. One of the three principal groups of rock, the others being igneous and metamorphic. Sedimentary rock is formed by the compaction of such sediments as rock fragments, the remains of plants or animals, or the products of chemical action or evaporation which water, ice, or wind have deposited. See also *Geochemical cycle*.

SEICHE. A variation in the surface of a body of water occurring every few minutes or hours. It is believed to be caused by variations in atmospheric pressure, by earth movements, or by wave action, and aided by winds and tidal currents. Tides are considered seiches caused primarily by the gravitational pull of the sun and moon.

SEISMICITY. Seismic activity, the phenomenon of earth movements.

SEISMIC SEA WAVE. See *Tsunami*.

SEISMOGRAPH. An instrument for measuring and recording earthquake vibrations and other earth tremors.

SEISMOLOGY. The study of earthquakes, their force, duration, direction, frequency, and other characteristics.

SEMIARID. Having 10 to 20 inches of precipitation a year. A semiarid region is characterized by the growth of short grasses.

SERACS. Jagged ice pinnacles on the surface of a glacier formed by the intersection of two or more sets of crevasses.

SERIES. The time-stratigraphic unit corresponding to an epoch in geologic time.

SHALE. A fine-grained sedimentary rock composed of cemented silt and clay-sized particles. Metamorphosed shale is slate.

SHEET EROSION. The erosion of the earth's surface by the slow removal of thin layers of material from an extensive area.

SHEETING. A series of closely spaced joints essentially parallel to the surface. They grow farther apart with depth.

SHIELD. A stable, continental block of the earth's crust primarily composed of Precambrian rocks, which may have undergone gentle warping in contrast to the strong folding of the geosynclines at its borders.

SHINGLE. A mass of rounded, often flat waterworn rocks.

SHOAL. A submerged ridge, bank, or bar covered with mud, sand, or gravel. It is near enough to the water surface, at 10 fathoms (60 feet) or less, to be a danger to navigation.

SHORE. The narrow strip of land in immediate contact with the sea, including the zone between high and low water.

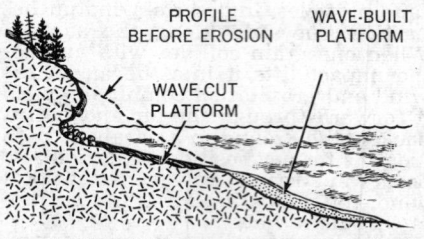

SHORE PROFILE shows how the constant action of water will erode a shoreline.

SHORELINE. The line of intersection of the sea at mean high water and the land. The region landward of the shoreline is the coast, that seaward is the shore.

SHOTT. A shallow salt lake in a desert region.

SIAL. The layer of rocks high in silica and aluminum underlying all continents. It ranges from granitic at the top to gabbroic at the bottom, where it grades into sima. It may be approximately 20 miles thick but thins out under the Pacific Ocean. It has a specific gravity of 2.7.

SIDEREAL DAY. See *Earth*.

SIERRA. A chain of jagged mountain peaks whose outline resembles the teeth of a saw.

SIKUSSAK. Very old (at least 25 years) sea ice.

SILICA. Silicon dioxide (SiO_2). It commonly comprises 40 to 80 percent of igneous rocks. It is an acid-forming oxide.

SILICEOUS. Pertaining to or containing or having the character of silica.

SILICON. The second most abundant element in the earth's crust. It occurs in all ordinary rocks except limestone.

SILL. An intrusive sheet of igneous rock lying parallel to the surrounding rock layers. It is formed when magma, or molten matter, forces its way between two layers of sedimentary rock. Also, a ridge at a relatively shallow depth separating two ocean basins.

SILT. See *Wentworth grade scale*.

SILT LOAD. The loose material carried in suspension by a stream, as opposed to bed load.

SILTSTONE. A fine-grained, consolidated clastic rock composed predominantly of silt-size particles.

SILURIAN PERIOD. The third period of the Paleozoic era in geologic time. It began 380 million years ago and lasted 15 million years.

SIMA. The basic outer shell of the earth, primarily composed of silica and magnesium. Sima underlies the sial of continents but directly underlies the water of the Pacific Ocean. It has a specific gravity of 3.3.

SIMOOM. A hot, dry, violent wind laden with hot sand and dust. It occurs during spring and summer in Asian and African deserts.

SINKHOLE. A funnel-shaped depression through which surface water drains, found within dolinen in limestone regions.

SINTER. A mineral substance deposited by hot or cold springs. Siliceous sinter is also called geyserite and fiorite. Calcareous sinter is also called tufa, travertine, and onyx marble.

SIROCCO. A hot, dust-laden wind, similar to a simoom, which blows on the northern Mediterranean coast. Blowing over the sea it becomes moist and enervating; blowing over land it becomes dry, dusty, and irritating.

SKARN. Lime-bearing silicates with large amounts of silicon, aluminum, iron, and magnesium.

SLACK WATER. Refers to the period of reversal between ebb and flood currents when the velocity of the current is very weak or zero.

SLAKING. The breaking up of dried clay when saturated with water.

SLATE. A fine-grained metamorphic rock formed from shale by regional metamorphism. It is harder, more lustrous than shale and when split yields approximately plane surfaces.

SLEET. Precipitation in the form of hail or snow mingled with rain. It is produced at the same time as hail but is partially melted in an upper layer of air, refreezing as it falls.

SLICKENSIDE. A fault surface smoothed and striated or scratched by friction from the pressure and motion of fault blocks.

SLOUGH. An area of deep mud or mire.

SMOG. A contraction of smoke and fog. A condition in the atmosphere when a high concentration of smoke particles and water droplets reduces visibility.

SNOW. Precipitation consisting of six-sided ice crystals formed directly from water vapor.

NEW YORK JOURNAL-AMERICAN

SMOG, particularly serious in midtown Manhattan, almost obscures the Empire State Building.

SNOWDRIFT. Snow that has been driven by the wind to form a bank.

SNOWFIELD. An area with a permanent snow cover.

SNOWLINE. The lower limit of a snowfield, rising from near sea level in polar regions to more than 20,000 feet in the Andes and Tibet.

SOAPSTONE. An impure variety of talc.

SOFT COAL. Bituminous coal.

SOFT WATER. Water with virtually no dissolved calcium or magnesium salts.

SOIL. The unconsolidated, or loose, material at the earth's surface that can support rooted plants. It is formed from rocks and plants by physical, chemical, and biological processes. Climate, vegetation, bedrock, relief of the land surface, and time combine to develop three soil orders—zonal, intrazonal, and azonal soils. The orders are divided into suborders.

There are six suborders of zonal soils—(1) soils of the cold zone; (2) light-colored soils of any region; (3) dark colored soils of semiarid, subhumid, and humid grasslands; (4) soils of the forest-grassland transition; (5) light-colored podzolized soils of the timbered regions; and (6) lateritic soils of forested warm-temperate and tropical regions.

The intrazonal order includes three suborders—(1) halomorphic soils of imperfectly drained arid regions and littoral deposits; (2) hydromorphic soils of marshes, swamps, seep areas and flats; and (3) calcemorphic soils. There are no suborders of azonal soils.

SOIL PROFILE. A vertical section through layers, or horizons, of soil from the surface to the limit of plant roots or bedrock.

The A horizon forms at or near the surface. It is the zone of eluviation or leaching. Soluble salts and colloids are washed from it and organic matter accumulates in it, grading downward from fresh or partially decomposed organic matter (O horizon), undecomposed vegetable litter (O1, or Aoo, horizon) to pure humus (O2, or Ao, horizon).

The B horizon is the zone of accumulation, containing clayey material and soluble minerals deposited by water percolating down from the A horizon and water evaporating from the C horizon.

The C horizon is the zone of unconsolidated material, little influenced by organisms. It consists of partially decomposed parent material or bedrock and grades down to unweathered bedrock, the R horizon.

SOLAR CONSTANT. The rate at which solar radiation is received normally at the outer layer of the earth's atmosphere at the earth's mean distance from the sun.

SOLIFLUCTION. The downslope flowage of loose earth material under saturated conditions in high latitudes where soil is affected by alternate freezing and thawing. It occurs during periods of thaw when the water released from the surface cannot percolate into the still frozen soil and rock beneath.

SOLUM. "True soil," the A and B horizons in the soil profile.

SOUND. An arm of the sea connecting two larger bodies of water, wider and more extensive than a strait.

SOUNDING. The determination of the depth of a body of water, either by a pressure-sensing device or by measuring the time required for sound waves to reflect from the bottom.

SPALLING. The disintegration of rock by the successive peeling of shells from the surface. See *Exfoliation.*

SPAR. A transparent or translucent, readily cleavable, crystalline mineral with a vitreous luster.

SPATHIC. Resembling spar in having good cleavage.

SPECIFIC GRAVITY. The ratio of the density of a substance to that of water at 4°C (39.2°F).

SPELEOLOGY. The study or exploration of caverns and related features.

SPHALERITE. The principal ore of zinc. It is composed primarily of zinc sulfide, but it often contains iron, manganese, or other elements. It is commonly yellow to dark brown and has a resinous to almost metallic luster, a hardness of 3.5 to 4, and a specific gravity of 3.9 to 4.1. It is also called false galena.

SPHEROID. An ellipsoid of revolution—a figure formed by rotating an ellipse around one of its axes. The earth is called an oblate, or flattened, spheroid because it bulges at the equator and is flattened at the poles.

SPILLWAY. A channel or passageway for surplus water to flow over or around a dam.

SPIT. A long, narrow deposit of sand or gravel projecting into a body of water from the land.

SPLASH EROSION. Erosion caused by the downslope movement of loose surface material resulting from the beating effect of falling raindrops.

SPRING. A continuous or intermittent natural flow of water from the ground. It occurs where a water table intersects the earth's surface.

SPRING TIDE. A tide which rises highest and falls lowest from its mean level about every two weeks at the new moon, when the moon is directly between the sun and the earth (conjunction), and at the full moon, when the moon and the sun are directly in line with, but on opposite sides of the earth (opposition).

SPUR. A subordinate elevation, ridge, or rise projecting outward from a larger feature.

SQUALL. A sudden violent wind of brief duration. It may be accompanied by thunder, lightning, and precipitation.

STACK. A rock mass cut off from the mainland by wave erosion. It first becomes a sea cave, then a sea arch, and finally an isolated stack.

STALACTITE. A deposit of minerals, usually calcite, precipitated by water on the ceiling of a cavern. In appearance, it resembles an icicle. A type of dripstone.

STALAGMITE. A deposit of minerals, usually calcite, precipitated by water on the floor of a cavern. In appearance it resembles an inverted, broad-based stalactite. A type of dripstone. Where a stalactite meets a stalagmite a column is formed.

STATUTE MILE. See *Mile.*

STEPPE. An extensive treeless, grassy plain found in semiarid regions.

STOPING. The process by which magma, or molten matter, detaches and engulfs blocks of the overlying country rock, thus working its way upward toward the surface.

STORM. A disturbance of the ordinary conditions of the atmosphere. It includes meteorological disturbances, such as wind, rain, snow, hail, and thunder. Also, a wind force of 11 on the Beaufort scale.

STOSS. Facing the direction from which a glacier moved.

STRAIN. Deformation of matter in response to force per unit area, or stress. Within elastic limits, strain is proportional to stress.

STRAIT. A narrow waterway connecting two larger bodies of water or separating two landmasses.

STRAND. A beach.

STRATH. A broad river valley.

STRATIFIED. Having layers.

STRATIFIED DRIFT. Drift deposited in layers.

STRATIGRAPHIC TIME. See *Time-stratigraphic unit.*

STRATIGRAPHIC TRAP. A natural reservoir that traps petroleum or natural gas because of variation in the permeability of the rock. The termination of an inclined reservoir on the higher side.

STRATIGRAPHY. The study of rock strata, including their origin, composition, order of sequence, and distribution.

STRATOSPHERE. See *Atmosphere.*

STRATUM. A single sedimentary layer of generally homogeneous rock, regardless of its thickness.

STREAK. A means of identifying a mineral by the color of the powder obtained by rubbing the mineral on an unglazed porcelain surface, such as a dish. The color of the streak may be similar to the color of the mineral or quite different.

STREAM. Any body of flowing water, from a rill to a river.

STALACTITES are deposits of calcium carbonate that grow downward from cave ceilings.

STREAM CAPTURE (or piracy). The diversion of the upper part of a stream by headward erosion of another stream.

STRENGTH. The amount of stress a solid can withstand without rupturing or flowing.

STRESS. Force per unit area required for the deformation of rocks.

STRESS–STRAIN LAW. See *Hooke's law.*

STRIAE (or striations). Minute parallel grooves and scratches on a rock, produced by rocks trapped in a glacier grinding against other rocks.

STRIKE. The direction of a line formed at the intersection of the horizontal plane with a tilted bedding plane or a fault surface. The strike is always perpendicular to the dip.

STROMBOLIAN PHASE. See *Volcano.*

STRUCTURAL GEOLOGY. The branch of geology concerned with the form, arrangement, and internal structure of rocks.

STRUCTURE. The attitude and relative position of a rock mass. In soils, the combination of primary particles into units forming a distinctive pattern that is classified on the basis of such factors as size and shape.

SUBAERIAL. Formed, existing, or taking place on the land surface.

SUBAQUEOUS. Formed, existing, or taking place beneath a body of water, as on the ocean floor.

SUBARCTIC. Referring to a climate similar to that immediately south of the Arctic Circle, where the mean temperature is less than 50°F in the warmest month and 32°F in the coldest month.

SUBHUMID. Referring to a climate too dry for natural forest growth, such as a prairie or pampa region. It is characterized by the growth of tall grasses.

SUBLIMATION. The direct transition of a substance from a solid state into a gaseous state, or the reverse, without an intervening liquid stage.

SUBLITTORAL. See *Ocean depth zones.*

SUBMARINE CANYON. A steep underwater depression, or trench, crossing the continental shelf. It may be as much as 10 miles wide and more than 6,000 feet deep. Some submarine canyons appear to be extensions of valleys on the land.

SUBSEQUENT STREAM. A tributary stream developed along a belt of weak rock after a consequent stream has removed the overlying resistant rock.

SUBSIDENCE. The sinking of a large part of the earth's crust.

SUBSOIL. The B and C horizons of the soil profile.

SUBSURFACE WATER. Water below the surface of the earth. If it is between the surface and the water table it is vadose water. If it is below the water table it is groundwater.

SUBTROPICAL. Referring to the regions between the tropic of Cancer and 40°N latitude and the tropic of Capricorn and about 40°S latitude, including their climate and vegetation.

SUPERIMPOSED STREAM. A stream that has eroded, or cut through a younger rock formation to its present level, where its course has no direct relation to the rock structure.

SUPERPOSITION. See *Law of Superposition.*

SUPRALITTORAL. See *Ocean depth zones.*

SURF. The foam, splash, and sound of waves breaking into turbulent water between the shoreline and the outermost limit of breakers.

SURFACE WAVE. A wave that travels on the surface, as distinguished from a body wave. See *Earthquake.*

SWALE. A marshy depression in level land. Also, a depression in a glacial ground moraine.

SWAMP. Low, spongy land, generally saturated or even covered with water.

S WAVE. See *Earthquake.*

SWELL. Regular, long waves which have traveled out of their generating area, or fetch.

SYENITE. An intrusive igneous rock with a composition similar to granite but containing little or no quartz.

SYMMETRICAL FOLD. A fold whose axial plane is vertical, the limbs dipping at similar angles.

SYNCLINE. A fold of stratified rocks in the form of a trough. The reverse of anticline.

SYNCLINORIUM. A series of anticlines and synclines so arranged structurally that together they form a general trough, or syncline, covering an extensive area.

SYNOPTIC. Relating to atmospheric conditions as they exist simultaneously over an extended region.

SYNTHETIC FAULTS. Subsidiary faults parallel to the master fault.

SYSTEM. A time-stratigraphic unit corresponding to a period in geological time.

SYZYGY. Two points in the moon's orbit where it is aligned with the sun and earth, in conjunction (between the sun and earth) and in opposition (on the opposite side of the earth from the sun).

TABLELAND. A comparatively level tract of upland bounded by relatively steep sides.

TABLEMOUNT. A type of seamount having a comparatively smooth, flat top.

TABULAR PLUTON. A pluton that is thin in comparison to its other dimensions. A tabular concordant pluton is a sill; a tabular discordant pluton is a dike.

TAIGA. A cold, humid vegetation zone with a coniferous forest cover. It lies in the northern hemisphere south of the tundra.

TALC. A mineral, hydrous magnesium silicate. It occurs in foliated, granular, or fibrous masses. It has a greasy feel, a hardness of 1, a pearly luster, a specific gravity of 2.6 to 2.9, and is usually gray, green, or white. An impure variety is called soapstone.

TALUS. A mass of rock fragments accumulated at the foot of a cliff.

TARN. A small lake in the bottom of a cirque. It is formed after the glacier has disappeared.

TECTONIC. Relating to the deformation of the earth's crust, the forces producing it, and the resultant structure.

TECTONO–PHYSICS. The study of stress and strain in relation to earth structure.

TEKTITE. Small, rounded, black or green glassy objects with a composition similar to that of clay, found in the earth's surface.

TELLURIC CURRENT. An earth current or natural electric current flowing on or near the earth's surface in a large sheet. By means of these currents the resistance, and therefore the composition, of various portions of the earth may be surveyed.

TEMPERATE ZONE. A general term for the middle latitude climatic zone lying between the tropical and cold zones.

TEMPERATURE GRADIENT. The rate of change of temperature with distance in a specified direction. If the direction is into the earth's crust, it increases with depth and is called geothermal gradient; if it is into the atmosphere, it decreases with height and is called lapse rate.

TEPHRA. A collective term for all materials ejected from a volcano during an eruption. It includes dust, ash, cinders, lapilli, scoria, pumice, bombs, and blocks.

TERRACE. A level band of land cut into a sloping surface either by natural forces, as in the case of a stream terrace, or by man, as in the case of a rice terrace.

TERRA ROSSA. A shallow, red, clayey soil developed from limestone in warm-temperate climates.

TERRIGENOUS. Derived from the earth. Specifically, it refers to material from above sea level, such as volcanic ash, which has been deposited on the ocean floor.

TERRITORIAL WATERS. A portion of the sea adjoining the coast considered to be under the jurisdiction of the country occupying that coast. It is measured outward from the mean low water-mark on the shore.

TERTIARY PERIOD. The first period in the Cenozoic era of geologic time. It began 60 million years ago and lasted 59 million years.

TETHYS. The elongated east-west trough separating Europe and Africa and extending across southern Asia in pre-Tertiary time.

TETON. A rugged, rocky mountain crest.

TEXTURE. The general physical appearance of a rock as determined in the size, shape, and arrangement of the particles that compose it. If the grains can be seen by the unaided eye, the rock is phaneritic; if they cannot be seen by the unaided eye, the rock is aphanitic.

The shape of mineral grains and their arrangement with respect to one another produce a characteristic pattern or fabric. In igneous rocks texture is influenced by the gas content of the magma and the rate of cooling.

Also, the dissection of a land surface by streams and runoff from rainfall.

THAW LAKE. A lake or pond in a permafrost area whose basin is formed by the melting, or thawing, of ground ice.

THEODOLITE. A surveyor's instrument for measuring horizontal and vertical angles. It consists of a telescope mounted to swivel vertically and secured to a table that revolves.

THERMAL EQUATOR. A line drawn around the earth connecting places with the highest mean temperature for any particular period. The position of the thermal equator varies with the seasons.

THERMAL GRADIENT. See *Geothermal gradient*.

THERMAL SPRINGS. See *Hot springs*.

THERMAL STRATIFICATION. The division into three layers of the water of deep lakes on the basis of temperature. The upper layer, or epilimnion, has an almost uniform temperature because it is stirred by wind and convection currents. The middle layer, or thermocline, has a rapid decrease in temperature with depth. The bottom layer, or hypolimnion, is relatively stagnant, low in oxygen, and has a uniform but lower temperature than the upper layers.

THERMOGRAPH. A self-recording thermometer.

THICKET. A dense growth of shrubs and trees.

THORN FOREST. A dense growth of small, thorny trees found in hot, relatively dry areas.

THROW. The vertical displacement caused by a fault.

TIDAL CURRENT. The alternating horizontal movement of water caused by the attraction of the sun and moon. It is associated with the vertical movement, or tide.

TIDAL DAY. See *Lunar day*.

TIDAL FLAT. A marshy coastal area covered by the tide at high water and uncovered at low water.

TIDAL MARSH. A tidal flat.

TIDAL RANGE. The difference between the level of water at high water and low water.

TIDAL WAVE. The wave motion of the tides. Often used for a very high tide.

TIDE. The periodic rising and falling of the earth's oceans and atmosphere caused by the gravitational attraction of the sun and moon.

TIERRA CALIENTE. The lowest and hottest of three vertical climate zones in the tropics. It is found at elevations of less than 3,000 feet.

TIERRA FRIA. The highest and coolest of three vertical climate zones in the tropics. It lies at elevations above about 7,000 feet.

TIERRA TEMPLADA. The middle of three vertical climate zones in the tropics. It lies between 3,000 and 7,000 feet.

TIGHT FOLD. A fold whose limbs are virtually parallel.

TILL. A glacial deposit of loose, unsorted earth material.

TILLITE. A sedimentary rock composed of cemented till.

TIMBERLINE. The upper limit of tree growth. It varies with latitude and climate.

TIME—STRATIGRAPHIC UNIT. Describes sedimentary rocks deposited during a specific interval of geologic time, regardless of their composition or conditions of origin. The units, in descending order, are: group (era), system (period), series (epoch), stage (age).

TOMBOLO. A bar or spit connecting an island to the mainland or to another island.

TOPOGRAPHY. The study and description of physical features, such as heights, depressions, slopes, and other surface forms, on the surface of the earth.

TOR. An isolated mass of rock standing above the surrounding land and usually weathered into an odd shape.

TOREVA—BLOCK SLIDE. A large-scale, slump-type landslide found in arid and semiarid regions. It consists of an undisturbed mass of material which has rotated backward toward the parent cliff during its descent.

TORNADO. A relatively short-lived violent cyclonic storm (see *Cyclone*) with winds as high as 500 miles an hour. It is common in the central Mississippi Valley. It is associated with a fall in atmospheric pressure so rapid that structures may be lifted and burst by the air within them.

TORRENT. A stream of water or lava flowing with great velocity or turbulence.

TORRID ZONE. A general term for the high temperature region of the earth found in the equatorial belt.

TRADE WINDS. The almost constant, mild (10 to 15 miles per hour) winds which blow toward the equator from the northeast in the northern hemisphere and from the southeast in the southern hemisphere. Their point of convergence is called the doldrums.

TRANSPIRATION. The passage of water through a plant to be emitted as vapor from the leaves.

TRANSVERSE DUNE. A dune crossing the path of the wind. The leeward slope is at or near the angle of repose; the windward slope is comparatively gentle.

AUSTRALIAN NEWS AND INFORMATION BUREAU

VALLEYS are depressions in the earth's surface, often separating high elevations. A stream usually flows through and deepens a valley.

TRANSVERSE VALLEY. A valley which cuts across a mountain range.

TRAVERTINE. A light-colored, compact form of calcium carbonate ($CaCO_3$) deposited from solution in water. It forms the stalactites and stalagmites in limestone caves or the incrustations around the mounts of calcareous springs. Also called dripstone, tufa, or calcareous sinter.

TRELLIS DRAINAGE PATTERN. A stream system in which tributary streams flow at almost right angles into the main-streams.

TREMOR. An earthquake of low intensity.

TRENCH. A long, narrow, and deep depression in the sea floor with relatively steep sides. A trench is narrower and deeper than a trough.

TRIASSIC PERIOD. The first, or earliest, period of the Mesozoic era in geologic time. It began 185 million years ago and lasted for about 27 million years.

TRIBUTARY. A stream which contributes its water to a larger stream or to a lake.

TROPICAL CYCLONE. A hurricane or cyclonic storm of great intensity which forms over tropical oceans. It is called a hurricane in the West Indies, a typhoon in the West Pacific, and a willy-willy in the area west of Australia.

TROPICAL ZONE. The region of the earth lying between the tropic of Cancer and the tropic of Capricorn.

TROPIC OF CANCER. The parallel of latitude at 23½° north of the equator. It marks the northernmost point at which the noon sun can be directly overhead.

TROPIC OF CAPRICORN. The parallel of latitude at 23½° south of the equator. It marks the southernmost point at which the noon sun can be directly overhead.

TROPOSPHERE. See *Atmosphere*.

TROUGH. A long depression of the sea floor, wider and shallower than a trench.

TSUNAMI. A great sea wave produced by a submarine earthquake, landslide, or volcanic eruption. A tsunami may go unnoticed for thousands of miles across the ocean building up to great heights over shallow water and causing widespread destruction on shore. Tsunami are also called seismic sea waves.

TUFA. See *Travertine*.

TUFF. A rock composed of cemented or compacted volcanic ash.

TUNDRA. The undulating treeless plain characteristic of the arctic region. It has permanently frozen subsoil, and its vegetation consists primarily of mosses, lichens, some grasses, and dwarf shrubs.

TURBIDITY CURRENT. A density current carrying large quantities of clay, silt, and sand down an underwater slope through less dense water.

TURBULENT FLOW. An irregular movement of a liquid in which the velocity at any given point varies in magnitude and direction with time. It is characteristic of most stream flow.

TWILIGHT. The faint light between sunset and full night and between full night and sunrise. It is caused by the diffusion of sunlight through the dust in the atmosphere.

TYPHOON. A severe tropical cyclone which occurs in the western Pacific Ocean region.

ULTIMATE BASE LEVEL. The level, sea level or below, beyond which land cannot be eroded.

UNCONFORMITY. An erosion surface separating two rock masses. See *Angular unconformity, Disconformity, Nonconformity*.

UNDERTOW. A seaward flow near the bottom of a sloping beach. Also, the undersurface return of the water carried up on shore by waves or breakers.

UNIFORMITARIANISM. The theory that all changes in the earth's crust in the past were caused by processes that are observable today, such as erosion and volcanic activity.

UNPAIRED TERRACES. Terraces formed on one side of a stream but not on the other. They are formed by differential erosion caused by resistant rock.

UVALA. A large, broad depression in a limestone, or karst, region formed by the breaking down of the walls between a series of dolinen. It is considered intermediate between a dolina and a polje in that it is larger than a dolina and its floor is more uneven than that of a polje.

VADOSE WATER. Subsurface water above the water table.

VALE. A broad, level valley.

VALLEY. A long depression in the earth's surface, usually containing a stream. A structural valley is formed by folding or the subsidence of an area with subterranean drainage or with volcanic activity. An erosional valley is formed by the removal of material by a stream.

VALLEY TRAIN. A long, narrow outwash plain or deposit of material carried by a stream from a glacier.

VARVE. A sedimentary deposit, or bed, representing a year's deposition in lakes fringing a glacier. The winter deposit is a dark-colored clay layer. The summer deposit is a light-colored silt layer.

VEERING. A clockwise change of direction of a wind (for example, east to southeast to south). The opposite of backing.

VEIN. A long, thin body of ore with a sharp difference from the rock enclosing it. A fissure vein is formed by deposition from solution by underground water in a rock fissure or crack. A vein may also be formed by chemical replacement, ore-forming solutions changing rocks into ore. Several veins spaced closely enough to be mined as a unit may be called a lode.

VELD. An upland, relatively level area covered with scattered shrubs or trees.

VELOCITY. The distance traveled in a specific direction per unit of time. It differs from speed in that it includes direction.

VENT. The opening through which gases and molten lava leave a volcano enter its crater from a body of magma.

VENTIFACT. Any stone shaped by the abrasive action of wind-driven sand.

VESICLE. A small, round cavity in an aphanitic, or glassy, igneous rock formed by the expansion of a gas bubble during the solidification of the rock. If the vesicle becomes filled with some mineral, the filling is called an amygdale.

VITREOUS. See *Luster*.

VLEI. A temporary lake or marshy depression formed where water collects during the rainy season.

VOLCANO. A vent in the earth's crust through which gas, ash, rock, and molten lava reach the earth's surface from a body of magma, or molten matter, 20 to 60 miles below. Also, the cone-shaped mound formed of material discharged through a vent.

One means of classifying volcanoes is by form. A *shield volcano* is a gently sloping dome built up by a series of lava flows. It may have several vents in addition to the central vent. A *composite volcano*, or stratovolcano, is a steep, conical structure built up over time by successive eruptions. It is formed from rock fragments interspersed with lava flows. A *compound volcano* has two or more cones or an associated dome. *Pyroclastic cones*, consisting of ash, cinders, bombs, and blocks, have no strength and are fissured by explosions and the pressure of the lava during successive eruptions.

The stage or phase of a volcano is determined by the proportion of gas, molten lava, and solid fragments it ejects. During the mildest or *Hawaiian phase*, hot, fluid lava is discharged, unaccompanied by the explosive escape of gases or the ejection of rock fragments. During the *Strombolian phase*, clots of incandescent lava are ejected and the magma in the crater does not crust over between explosions. During the *Vulcanian phase*, fragments of old rock along with a cloud of ash and gas are ejected. Lava in this phase is extremely viscous and consolidates in the crater.

During the *Peléan* phase, the most violently explosive stage, great clouds called *nuées ardentes* are ejected horizontally from beneath the lava plug in the summit. These peléan clouds are extremely hot, travel at great speeds, and carry a great quantity of gas-charged lava fragments, often many yards in diameter.

Volcanic activity is found in the same areas as earthquake activity, around the Pacific basin, in the mid-Atlantic, and the Mediterranean.

VUG. A cavity of any size in a rock, usually lined with a crystalline incrustation of minerals which differ in composition from the surrounding rock.

WADI. A ravine in an arid region, dry except in the rainy season.

WARPING. The gentle bending of the earth's crust without forming pronounced folds or dislocations.

WATER. An odorless, colorless, tasteless liquid compound (H_2O) whose specific gravity of 1 is the standard for comparison of all liquids and solids.

WATER CYCLE. See *Hydrologic cycle.*

WATERFALL. A steep fall in the course of a stream where the water descends perpendicularly, or nearly so.

WATER GAP. A gap, or notch, in a mountain ridge through which a stream flows.

WATERSHED. See *Divide.*

WATERSPOUT. A tornado or cyclone occurring at sea, comparable to a dust devil over land, common over tropical and subtropical waters.

WATER TABLE. The upper surface of the zone of saturation. Its slope or shape is determined by the quantity of groundwater and the permeability of the earth materials. Generally, it is higher under hills and lower under valleys. A prolonged drought will lower the water table.

WEATHER. The condition of the atmosphere at a given time defined by the measurement of air temperature, barometric pressure, wind direction and speed, humidity, clouds, and precipitation.

WEATHERING. The disintegration of rock material through chemical means, such as rainwater or plants and bacteria, and mechanical means, such as

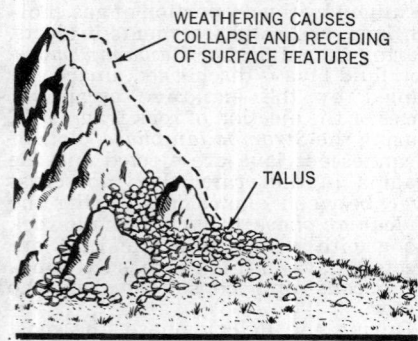

WEATHERING CAUSES COLLAPSE AND RECEDING OF SURFACE FEATURES

TALUS

WEATHERING is one natural process of changing the earth's structural features.

abrasion and temperature variation, which change its color, texture, composition, and form.

WELDING. Consolidation by pressure caused by the weight of overlying material or earth movement.

WELL. A hole drilled into the earth to obtain water, gas, or oil.

WELT. A sharp, narrow uplift.

WENTWORTH GRADE SCALE. A scale for the classification of sediment particles:

Size limit	fragment		Consolidated equivalent
	boulders	⎫	
256 mm.	cobbles	⎪	
64 mm.	pebbles	gravel	conglomerate
4 mm.	granules	⎭	breccia
2 mm.	sand		sandstone
0.0625 mm.	silt		siltstone
0.0039 mm.	clay		shale
0.00024 mm.	colloids		

WESTERLIES. The prevailing winds in the temperate zones, between the polar easterlies and the trade winds, or between 30° and 60° latitude.

WET. The state of ground in which the pore spaces to a depth of 3 or more inches are largely or completely filled with water.

WHIRLPOOL. A circular eddy in the sea or in a stream caused by the shape of the channel or the meeting of two currents. It has a depression in the center into which floating objects may be drawn.

WHIRLWIND. A small rotating windstorm marked by an inward and upward spiral motion in the lower air followed by an outward and upward spiral motion.

WILLIWAW. A sudden violent gust of cold land wind, common along mountainous coasts in high latitudes.

WILLY—WILLY. A tropical cyclone originating west of Australia.

WILTING POINT. The point at which soil moisture becomes unavailable to plants and permanent wilting ensues. It is caused by the lowering of the water table, as may happen during a prolonged drought.

WIND. The horizontal component of air motion. Current is the vertical component. Planetary winds form the generalized surface wind pattern of the earth. They are polar easterlies, westerlies, and trade winds.

Monsoon winds are characterized by a complete reversal of direction from winter to summer. Foehn winds are warm, dry winds warmed by compression in flowing down the lee side of a mountain. Foehn-type winds include the bohorok and the chinook as well as the Swiss foehn.

Bora winds are cold, katabatic winds, flowing from a continental interior toward warm seashores. The mistral and the williwaw are two examples of this type.

There are also winds produced by outbreaks from an atmospheric source region. If the region is hot, a sirocco may develop, if cold, a pampero.

WIND CHILL GAP. The part of the total cooling of a body caused by air motion.

WIND GAP. A notch, or gorge, cutting through the upper part of a ridge.

WIND ROSE. A diagram showing the proportionate distribution of winds by direction and speed at a given place.

WIND SPEED. See *Beaufort scale.*

WIND SHADOW. A portion of a scarp or slope protected from the direct action of the wind blowing over it.

WINDWARD. The direction from which the wind is blowing, as opposed to leeward. The side of an object facing the wind.

WRENCH FAULT. An almost vertical strike-slip fault.

XENOLITH. A rock fragment included in a body of igneous rock.

YARDANG. A sharp-crested ridge between round-bottomed troughs. It is formed by wind erosion from a soft deposit, such as clayey sand.

YAZOO STREAM. A tributary stream on a flood plain flowing parallel to the mainstream.

YIELD POINT. The point at which stress exceeds the plastic limit, causing a solid to flow or rupture. See *Deformation.*

ZEOLITE. A group of hydrous aluminosilicates of sodium, calcium, barium, strontium, and potassium, characterized by their easy and reversible loss of water and tendency to swell when heated. They have a hardness between 3.5 and 5.5 and a specific gravity between 2.0 and 2.4.

ZONE. A region set off from the surrounding area by climate, landforms, time, or other distinctions.

ZONE OF AERATION. The zone in which the pores of permeable rocks are not filled, except temporarily, with water. The water is under pressure less than that applied by the atmosphere on the earth's surface.

ZONE OF ELUVIATION. The A horizon in the soil profile.

ZONE OF OXIDATION. The area above the water table where water provides a good supply of oxygen.

ZONE OF SATURATION. The zone in which permeable rocks are saturated with water. Its upper surface is the water table. The water is under pressure equal to or greater than atmosperic pressure.

Introduction	523
Economics	528
Finance	541
Scientific decision-making tools	547
Research and development	550
Purchasing	553
Manufacturing and production	555
Marketing	560
International operations	565
Business and the computer	569
Administrative Services	576
Personnel and human relations	578
Economics and business glossary	582

VOLUME SEVEN

ECONOMICS

Economics and Business

INTRODUCTION

History and Growth.—Business has been the dominant influence in the development of the American economy and in many ways has shaped the character of American society. This system of allocating economic resources by private, decentralized decision-making, conducted in a search for profit, speeded settlement of the continent, developed its resources, guided the growth of an intricate transportation and communications network, and produced an industrial civilization unparalleled in human experience.

When pursuit of private gain and promotion of the public welfare did not coincide, the unique capacity for pragmatic, workable solutions that has characterized Americans generally, and businessmen in particular, resulted in a sharing of governmental and business responsibilities for the economy. Despite the growth of the public sector in this century, especially since the 1930's, the United States still depends primarily on businessmen to generate wealth and develop new ideas for the goods and services that underpin our position as the leading industrial nation in the world. American business and businessmen have also been in the forefront of both public and private endeavors to promote and maintain world peace and to improve the standards of living not only here but in other countries.

The Ideological Framework.—The national reliance on business goes back to colonial days. It is widely known that religious motives contributed significantly to the early settlement of this country, but it is less widely recognized that the earliest settlements were organized by private companies and were financed by those who sought profit in a new land. For example, Jamestown, Virginia, the first permanent English settlement on these shores, was a privately financed venture. It proved disappointing to investors but established a firm English foothold on this continent and contributed economic and political institutions of enduring significance to America. The religious element was stronger in the Plymouth and Massachusetts Bay settlements, but initially they too relied for support on English investors, operating through a corporate form of business organization that also provided an early framework for colonial civil government.

The American climate of challenge and opportunity, combined with freedom from the social rigidities of the Old World, encouraged individual initiative and acceptance of the social value of hard work, thrift, and dedication to one's calling. These personal attributes were consistent with a religious ethic that called for similar qualities and admitted material success as proof of virtue. Originally associated with Calvinism, this theme has varied from time to time, but it has remained a distinguishing and increasingly secular characteristic of American attitudes toward private business activity.

The admonitions to hard work, thrift, and diligence as individual virtues were reinforced by the realities of developing a raw but rich country. It is clearly not accidental that surveys of leading citizens in Boston and Philadelphia on the eve of the Revolution revealed that a majority were merchants, and that many of them were truly self-made men.

■**FREE ENTERPRISE.**—An economic rationale for private decision-making in the economy appeared in 1776, the same year that the colonies declared their independence from Great Britain. In that country, Adam Smith's *The Wealth of Nations* (1776), the first systematic economic treatise of modern times, attacked the restrictive British mercantilist system that had contributed to the American colonies' decision to shed their imperial ties. Smith argued that individual businessmen free to compete in the marketplace would produce far better economic results than could a system of restraints and imposed monopolies conferred by governments. Goaded by profit and restrained by competition, Smith suggested, individuals could confer public benefit in their pursuit of private gain. Acceptance of this idea, consistent with the American inheritance and the American environment, helped to give business its central place in American life. Although probably few American businessmen of Smith's era were familiar with his work, they were guided by their experience and their opportunities to think along the lines he advocated.

Men of property had a substantial stake in a stable government. When the United States Constitution was written, it contained numerous provisions that were conducive to business development.

The first Congress adopted tariff protection and other semi-mercantilist measures that encouraged private economic activity. These policies changed little over the next century. Government—state and federal—was generally either a neutral force as far as business was concerned, or it provided encouragement and support—financial and otherwise—for private investment and protection of the fruits of such investment.

Freed by distance from the turmoil of European wars, the American businessman of the nineteenth century had unparalleled opportunities and an unprecedentedly favorable political, social, and economic environment to make the most of them. Although business success was far from automatic and failure rates were high, business failure was no disgrace and fresh opportunities were constantly renewed in an expanding country.

As the frontier moved westward and began to vanish, new challenges were presented to apply technology for the benefit of a growing population. Capital and manpower flowed into the country from abroad and westward from the Atlantic seaboard. The supply of entrepreneurial talent was more than adequate to apply these resources. In fact, many mercantile skills and the capital that they had created were carried over into fruitful employment in the new industrial era.

Technology and Business: Nineteenth Century.—Much of the early technology that transformed America, with the businessman as the primary agent of change, was imported. The industrial revolution in this country first appeared in the textile industry and then became inextricably bound to the steam engine, as a source of both stationary and mobile power. In each instance the pioneering inventions came from England, but they were quickly adapted for use in this country and rapidly improved in the process.

After visiting in England and Scotland in 1811, Francis Cabot Lowell, a member of a distinguished Massachusetts merchant family, brought knowledge of the power loom to this country and revolutionized the textile industry. Earlier, a British immigrant, Samuel Slater, had violated his country's ban on the export of technical knowledge and with the aid of Providence merchants had established a cotton textile operation in Rhode Island. However, his operations were on a small scale, and weaving was done outside the factory. In 1814 Lowell and his colleagues, known as the Boston Associates, brought all cotton-manufacturing operations together under one roof at Waltham, Massachusetts, employing water power to operate their looms. This pioneering step was so successful that it soon gave rise to a major textile-manufacturing complex at nearby Lowell and Lawrence, Massachusetts, which long remained leading centers of the American textile industry.

The specialization of tasks and the employment of powered machinery characteristic of these textile operations were followed in other consumers' goods industries, whose demands in turn spurred the development of producers' goods industries. When interchangeable parts were introduced, accompanied by the development of high-precision machine tools, as exemplified in arms and clock manufacture, all but one of the key ingredients of widespread industrial progress had been assembled.

■NEW POWER SOURCE.—The one element needed to tie these others together was a cheap, reliable source of power that could be used in any location. The steam engine provided this link and freed American factories from their dependence on waterpower.

With the steam engine as a source of motive power, a transportation network was developed to bring raw materials to the factory and finished goods to the consumer. Beginning in the East in the 1830's, railroads tied coastal centers together and then linked them to a westward-moving frontier of economic resources.

Although often aided, and in some cases sponsored, by local or state governments, railroads were generally the result of private risk-taking and promotion. Even a small railroad involved heavy capital investment and presented difficult problems of management. In this respect, many of the managerial problems associated with big business were first faced by railroads: the raising of large amounts of capital, the organization and management of a large work force, and the continuous and precise operation of complex systems.

■RAILROAD LEADERS.—Many of the great names of nineteenth-century American business are associated with railroading. Cornelius Vanderbilt, who made the New York Central into a major system; James J. Hill, who created the Great Northern; Jay Gould, whose railroad interests in the West ranging from the Missouri Pacific to the Union Pacific brought him into conflict with many railroad leaders, are textbook staples. So too are such figures as Jim Fisk, whose manipulations of Erie stock won him an enduring, if somewhat tainted, place in American history; and J. P. Morgan, the investment banker who reorganized many of the overbuilt, overcapitalized, and hard-hit railroad companies in the 1880's and 1890's.

The existence of an extensive and intricate railroad network promoted regional specialization, speeded urbanization, and above all created a truly national market. The evolution of the modern meatpacking industry after the Civil War typifies the business significance of these three developments.

Gustavus Swift, a beef packer, introduced the refrigerator car in the late 1870's and with it a new era in meat distribution. It was then possible to centralize slaughtering and meat processing activities at major interior points, such as Omaha, Kansas City, and Chicago, and to ship fresh meat all over the country in competition with local butchers. Philip D. Armour, a pork packer, also recognized these possibilities and developed a private-car line and a branch-house system of distribution that quickly outstripped Swift's. Since profits depended on volume operations and efficient utilization of every edible part of an animal, the big packers also developed extensive lines of by-products.

Comparable developments in the efficient use of resources took place in one new industry after another as business men responded to the national market made possible by reliable mass transportation. Railroads played an especially important role in the early history of extractive industries and in none more notably than the petroleum industry.

■RISE OF PETROLEUM.—The American petroleum industry was born in 1859 in western Pennsylvania, where a high-quality crude oil suitable for an illuminant was discovered. The problem was to make the refined product available in major consuming and export centers. The answer initially hinged on the railroads.

John D. Rockefeller and his associates in The Standard Oil Company (Ohio) and affiliated concerns discovered that they could lower their transportation costs by guaranteeing shipment of full trainloads of oil. This ability to make volume shipments gave them an advantage over competitors which, coupled with efficient management and occasionally tough competitive tactics, soon assured Standard Oil's commanding position in the industry. When this position was threatened by the introduction of the oil pipeline as a competitor of long-distance railroad transport, Standard Oil entered the pipeline business on a large scale and confirmed its place as the leading firm in the oil industry.

Although transportation was a prime consideration in Standard Oil's strategy, success was due to many factors, not the least of which were administrative and organizational innovations. In 1882 the formation of the Standard Oil Trust, which centralized control of diverse companies and activities in a small group of trustees, set an example that was widely followed in many industries. The committee system, which became a hallmark of Standard's management, embraced all facets of policy formulation and administrative implementation. It too came to be widely adopted in American business.

■IRON AND STEEL.—Some firms grew large without resorting to corporate structures like that of Standard Oil. Outstanding among them were companies controlled by Andrew Carnegie, the leader in the new iron-and-steel industry. Beginning as a penniless Scottish immigrant, Carnegie first made his mark in railroading. However, he soon became aware of how heavily the railroads depended on iron. After the Civil War he began building railroad bridges and producing rails. By one astute move after another, he established himself as a leading manufacturer of iron and steel. Eventually, with the aid of men like Henry Clay Frick, who brought extensive coke fields as well as business ability into the combination, and Charles Schwab, a shrewd young businessman, Carnegie developed an almost completely integrated steel business. When J. P. Morgan and others proposed to challenge his position at the turn of the century, Carnegie was persuaded to sell out. The resulting United States Steel Corporation, formed in 1901, was the first billion-dollar corporation in the country. Like Standard Oil by that time, it was a giant holding company.

Business Organization.—The simplest form of business organization is the *sole proprietorship*. In this case one person is both owner and manager of an enterprise. While this type of business can be started and operated with a minimum of formalities, its potential is limited by the resources and ability, as well as by the longevity, of the proprietor. For these reasons, the sole proprietorship is typically confined to areas of business involving very small-scale operations and limited capital, or to some specialized skill of the owner.

A *partnership* brings two or more individuals together in the ownership and management of a business. It usually makes each participant fully liable for the acts of his fellows but it is well suited to small-scale operations, especially where trust is an important ingredient of the business, large capital is not required, and profits can be shared according to ascertainable contributions. However, the partnership is also limited by the life span of its participants and ordinarily it cannot tap wide sources of capital.

These limitations of partnerships, especially the latter one, were recognized in England before the era of American colonization. The answer lay in the organization of *joint-stock companies,* chartered by the government, supplied with capital by the sale of shares of ownership, and governed by officials elected by the shareholders. This form of business organization was employed in founding the Jamestown settlement.

■THE CORPORATION.—From the joint-stock company to the corporation was but a short step. Chartered by state authority, the corporation is regarded as a legal person, its existence is perpetual, and ownership can be divided into units small enough to attract capital from even the smallest investor. Because joint-stock companies in England had been associated with the grant of monopoly rights, they were suspect in America. In any case, large-scale mobilization of capital was not generally required in colonial America. Consequently there were few incorporated enterprises in this country until the nineteenth century. When major undertakings like railroads were organized, however, the corporate form found favor.

Corporations did not come fully into their own until the 1890's. Andrew Carnegie, for example, believed

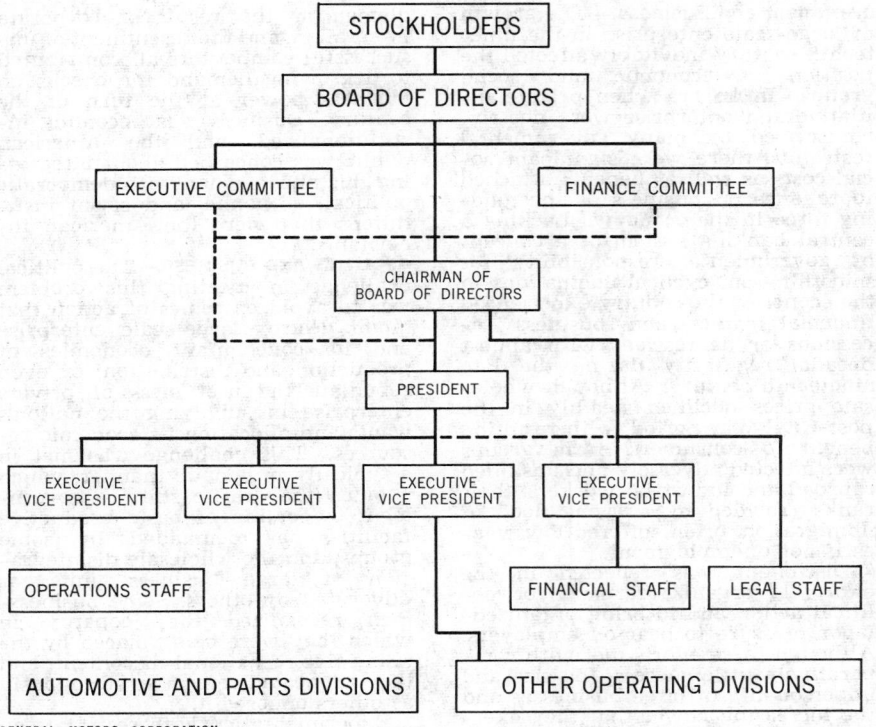

GENERAL MOTORS CORPORATION

ORGANIZATION CHART illustrating the division of controlling interest in a corporation.

that in a partnership his associates would be attached more firmly to the business than they would as corporate officers. Furthermore, as in the case of Armour and Carnegie, the reinvestment of earnings was sufficient to maintain and expand the activities of many growing companies without resorting to capital markets. By the 1890's, however, these conditions were changing and firms such as Procter & Gamble, P. Lorillard, and Westinghouse Electric adopted a corporate form.

Since incorporation was by state rather than federal authority, many problems confronted firms seeking to do business of varied kinds in numerous states. The trust device adopted by Standard Oil had provided one answer, but it proved vulnerable to state antitrust action. After New Jersey in 1889 altered its incorporation law, allowing a corporation to hold stocks in other companies, the holding company supplanted the trust form of organization. The great wave of mergers at the turn of the century, of which United States Steel was the leading example, was facilitated by the availability of the holding company device. Inevitably, under such conditions, ownership and management of large enterprises became increasingly separated.

The Defense of Competition.—Men like Carnegie and Rockefeller created vast business empires by playing the competitive game to its fullest. As a consequence, the conditions of competition were altered to the point that the validity of the system itself began to be questioned. Carnegie became the leading business defender

of the competitive tradition, adapting his arguments from the new Darwinian theory, which explained the evolution of species as the "survival of the fittest." According to social Darwinism, a limited number of businessmen had succeeded in the competitive struggle because they had proved themselves the most fit. Understandably, there were several critics of business, notably Henry Demarest Lloyd (*Wealth Against Commonwealth*, 1894), who argued that survival of this kind was based on ruthlessness, disregard for the public welfare, and absence of any moral standards of conduct.

Technology and Business: Twentieth Century.—If coal and steam were the energy sources that underlay the transformation of business and the economy in the nineteenth century, the internal-combustion engine, electricity, and chemistry dominated developments in the first half of the twentieth century. The automobile transformed American ways of life, with business repercussions that ranged from shifting the major market for petroleum products from illuminating oil to gasoline, to forcing relocation of retailing for the convenience of the suburban motorist. Electricity not only supplanted kerosene as the source of home illumination but provided manufacturing establishments and households with a new and versatile source of light and power. Chemistry created an increasingly varied array of products that served industry, added to the conveniences and comfort of daily life, and brought man-made substitutes for natural resources.

■**NEW TECHNOLOGY.**—These technological advances were the products of pure and applied research, which came to occupy an increasingly important place in the activities of major companies. To such privately financed endeavors was added the stimulus of government's demands for wartime substitute materials and sophisticated military equipment for which the taxpayer footed the bill. The vast expense of developing atomic energy, which will undoubtedly transform the economy in the remaining decades of this century, was borne by government during World War II for military purposes. More recently, with the assistance of private enterprise, atomic energy is being used at an increasingly rapid rate for peaceful applications. The same process has characterized developments in aircraft manufacture and space communications.

The era of technological miracles created new firms and challenged older ones to adapt to the new invironment. In the automotive industry, Henry Ford led the way in mass production but was overtaken by strong competitors—most notably General Motors—in the 1920's. In electricity, General Electric and Westinghouse built on foundations laid before the turn of the century. In chemicals, DuPont expanded from its base as an explosives manufacturer to embrace a wide variety of products based on chemical research. These were perhaps the "biggest names" in their respective fields. In each instance, they obtained positions of ascendancy by meeting competition from other major concerns or from substitute products. Despite their size, they depended heavily on an intricate network of suppliers and distributors of varying size.

The Challenge to Management.—The very scope and complexity of serving national and international markets made effective business organization and systematic management increasingly important ingredients of business success. Here, as much as in the creation and successful promotion of new products, was the test of business leadership.

Most early large-scale enterprises adopted a central-office, departmental type of company organization with management in the hands of functional (that is, production, marketing, and finance) specialists. Gradually, line-and-staff concepts, differentiating between operating and advisory responsibilities, became well defined. Accurate cost and sales statistics played a new role in evaluating managerial performance. As companies expanded their product lines, many decentralized their management by product group and coordinated these various elements from a general office. Marketing assumed a new importance to keep pace with the vast productive capacity of American business.

"Scientific management," which Frederick Taylor popularized as an approach to shop management early in this century, was supplemented by "management science," dealing with more general administrative problems. To these was added a concern for the human factors involved in production and business management. Much of the credit for pioneering work in this field goes to Elton Mayo of Harvard's Graduate School of Business Administration, founded in 1908 and the first of its kind. These developments were paralleled by a growing business interest in long-range forecasting and budgeting to guide strategy and measure company progress.

The computer, which did not come into widespread business use until the 1950's, capped the technological revolution that has been outlined here. It can not only be applied to both routine and complex production tasks but has become an indispensable management tool. Accompanying it has come intensified interest in quantitative approaches to the solution of business problems and to decision-making.

The challenges and opportunities in American business have thus been continually renewed. The way in which they have been met has raised the American standard of living to heights unprecedented in history. But the businessman has not produced this material achievement without the aid of a legion of auxiliary and complementary professional services, provided by such special forms of private enterprise as law and accounting firms. The role of banks, insurance companies, and other financial institutions in amassing and supplying capital for business use should also not be overlooked. And, finally, government has exerted an increasingly important influence on the direction, character, and speed of business development.

Government and Business.—The growth of large-scale enterprise in the nineteenth century inevitably affected the position of economic and social groups. In an era when private initiative and enterprise were not circumscribed by many governmental restraints, there were significant social costs as well as benefits attached to reliance on business as the guiding force in the economy. Lacking a central banking system or a concept of governmental responsibility for smoothing out cyclical fluctuations in the economy, the country experienced financial panics and business recessions or depressions with almost decadal regularity during the late nineteenth century. Although wholesale prices declined steadily in the post-Civil War period, with resulting benefit to consumers, farm groups were affected adversely and unskilled railroad and industrial workers, their ranks crowded by a rising flood of immigration, often suffered low wages if not unemployment.

Discontent was reflected in the efforts to organize farmers for political action and to bring organized-labor pressure to bear on employers. Although these efforts met with comparatively little success, the size and impersonality of large businesses and the increasing power that they exercised over their employees provided grounds for attacks on the results of industrialization and the distribution of its rewards. At the same time, however, most Americans took pride in the material achievements of American business.

The extremes of wealth and poverty, the apparent foreclosure of opportunities for a new generation to achieve success in the competitive tradition, the crowding out of mid-dlemen as the result of corporate integration, and the resentment of unsuccessful competitors all contributed to a growing demand for checks on business power at the turn of the century. Business was becoming institutionalized, and the American public was concerned about integrating this phenomenon with democratic political, economic, and social institutions that were the American inheritance.

■**POLITICS AND BUSINESS.**—The political challenge in meeting this problem was to avoid extremes of action that might destroy large-scale enterprise and its concomitant economies of production and distribution, or even repudiate the usefulness of private enterprise in supplying the nation's wants and allocating its economic resources. This challenge was met in a typically pragmatic manner, which avoided the drastic shift to government ownership of basic productive facilities, as demanded by some groups, and the wholesale disintegration of large business units, as advocated by others. Some businessmen recognized the jeopardy in which they were being placed by the rising tide of national discontent, and they advocated reform as strenuously as others opposed it.

Experimentation with restraints on business often took place at the state level before their adoption as national policy. This process was characteristic of the approach embraced by the federal Interstate Commerce Act of 1887, which sought to regulate interstate railroads, and the Sherman Antitrust Act of 1890, which outlawed combinations and conspiracies in restraint of interstate trade. Initially, however, the courts emptied both acts of much of their potency, while enforcement of the antitrust law which was a responsibility of the executive branch, lacked strong presidential support.

■**LEGISLATIVE RESTRAINTS.**—Government-business relationships began to change when Theodore Roosevelt was unexpectedly catapulted into the presidency following the assassination of President William McKinley in 1901. Politically ambitious and recognizing the benefits of large-scale enterprise, as well as the threat posed by its critics, Theodore Roosevelt sought to give meaning to both railroad regulation and antitrust enforcement. A combination of legislation and selected prosecutions satisfied the public's demand for action. Business fears of the consequences were considerably relieved by the Supreme Court's conservative position, and especially by its announcement in 1911 that it would interpret the antitrust law with a "rule of reason" that recognized a distinction between reasonable and unreasonable restraints of trade.

Both the Interstate Commerce Act and the Sherman Act were supplemented by additional legislation in

BOOM YEARS, 1964–1966, saw retail sales climb $5 billion to 30% over 1960 levels, profits of all industries grow by $20 billion, and expansion spending rise $10 billion.

Business and Industry

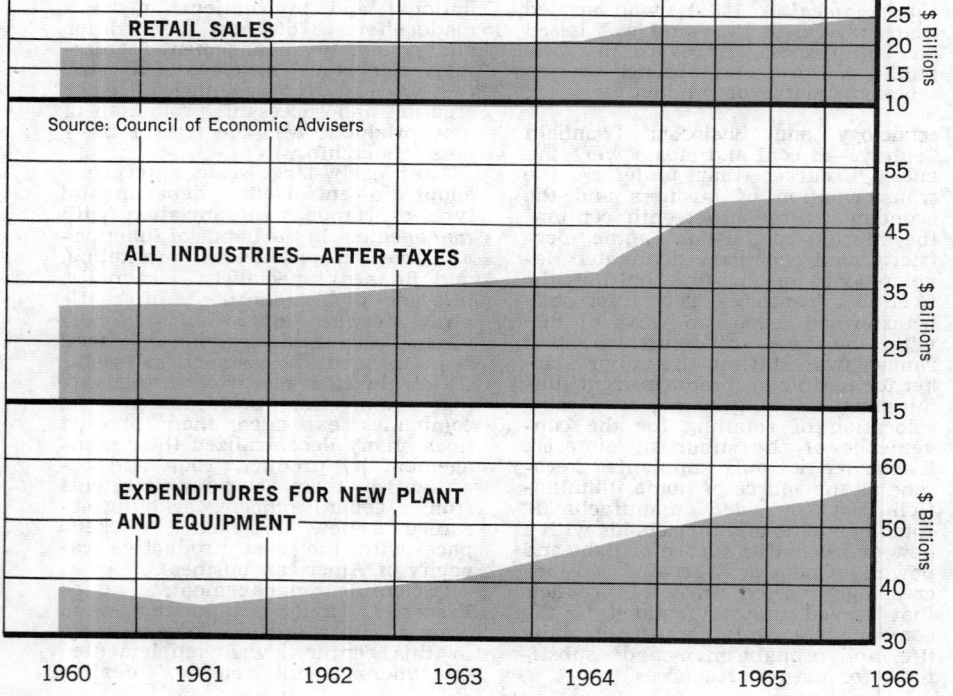

RETAIL SALES

Source: Council of Economic Advisers

ALL INDUSTRIES—AFTER TAXES

EXPENDITURES FOR NEW PLANT AND EQUIPMENT

1960 1961 1962 1963 1964 1965 1966

later years. In each instance there was a gradual shift from emphasis on the punishment of businessmen to positive support of competition, and even of combination when it seemed to be in the national interest. The Transportation Act of 1920, for example, authorized railroad pooling with ICC approval and made promotion of a healthy transportation industry a federal policy. The Sherman Antitrust Act, supplemented by such statutes as the Clayton Act of 1914 and the Robinson-Patman Act of 1938, proved capable of so many interpretations that commentators questioned whether such legislation did more to protect competitors from competition than to strengthen the conditions of competition.

As technology produced new industries and as competitive or other conditions indicated a need for governmental supervision of older ones, the regulatory examples set at the turn of the century were adapted to the new circumstances. Thus, drawing on the example of the Interstate Commerce Commission, the Federal Communications Commission was established to regulate radio and other electronic communications, while the Civil Aeronautics Board was empowered to exercise economic regulation over airline transportation. The issuance of securities became subject to the scrutiny of the Securities and Exchange Commission; the lagging American merchant marine was given federal subsidies, but routes and rates of companies so aided were subject to yet another federal commission. As in the latter instance, some element of government aid or financial assistance generally accompanied extension of regulatory authority, and cooperation between public and business administrators became as characteristic as conflict had been between them formerly.

■FURTHER INTERVENTION.—War and depression accelerated the federal government's intervention in economic and business matters. World War I brought many instances of government-business cooperation, introduced the public to regulation in various segments of the economy, and led to the creation of agencies and boards with emergency powers that were later to provide guidelines for fighting the depression of the 1930's.

The business prosperity of the early 1920's was succeeded by the stock market collapse of 1929 and then a deadening national depression that called for emergency measures. Business leadership, benumbed by the collapse, temporarily surrendered leadership to politicians. Under President Franklin D. Roosevelt, a variety of governmental approaches to national economic recovery was adopted. A number initially fell prey to the Supreme Court, which did not change its opposition to New Deal social and economic experimentation until 1937. Meanwhile, Roosevelt had shifted from his policy of placating business, exemplified by the short-lived National Industrial Recovery Act (1933–1935), to criticize businessmen for reverses in the New Deal's effort to promote economic re-

covery. A searching investigation of the concentration of private economic power was commenced in 1938, accompanied by a revitalized antitrust program under the direction of Assistant Attorney General Thurman Arnold. Although business had made substantial advances since the debacle of the early 1930's, its earlier controlling place in the economy was becoming a conditional one.

Business had borne the primary responsibility for the performance of the economy since colonial days, but in the 1930's the role of government assumed a new importance. The Federal Reserve System, dating from 1913 and combining representatives of both public and private interests in the operation of a central banking system, provided a vehicle for changing monetary policy to affect the conditions of investment and savings. The spread of Keynesian ideas about stimulating economic activity by deficit government spending led to similar experimentation with fiscal policy to promote economic recovery and growth. The adoption of government-administered unemployment, disability, retirement, and death benefits in the mid-1930's gave a new orientation to matters that had traditionally been handled privately by business or individual philanthropy.

■BUSINESS AND LABOR.—Despite the growth of governmental responsibility for social welfare, corporate philanthropy, company pension plans, and other "fringe benefits" also continued to grow. Increasingly, business leaders came—or were forced—to recognize and accept the inevitability of dealing with organized labor. its gains owed much to the National Labor Relations Act of 1935 which made permanent the support to collective bargaining contained in the short-lived National Industrial Recovery Act. In 1947 the Taft-Hartley Act redressed the balance somewhat in the favor of management.

■TRADE ASSOCIATIONS.—Businessmen had already organized to deal with labor, government, and the public. In matters of common interest to an industry or trade group, the trade association provided a broad membership with a common voice. Beginning in the 1920's, these associations, and businessmen generally, accorded a new importance to explaining and interpreting publicly their positions, decisions, and actions. In part, this movement reflected the growing ascendancy of professional management, whose practitioners increasingly were recruited from schools of business administration that stressed the manager's responsibility not only to stockholders but to employees and the public.

■GOVERNMENT-BUSINESS COOPERATION.— Beginning with World War II, business acceptance of the interdependence of business and government gained ground rapidly. Wartime cooperation was essential, and it was extended into the postwar era. Although the Employment Act of 1946 proclaimed the ultimate responsibility of government for full employment, recognition was also accorded the vital role of private enterprise.

The interchange of ideas and personnel between the public and private sectors, in addition to governmental expenditures in many fields to advance technology, to improve economic and educational opportunities at home, and to aid war-devastated and underdeveloped economies abroad, as well as to meet the demands of the "cold war," have aided business as well as other groups.

The new reality of a "mixed" economy has left businessmen free to make decisions within their spheres of interest, but it has also provided a framework of governmental incentives and restraints, often operating indirectly, that have conditioned business decision-making and the overall contours of economic growth. Although the final verdict is yet to be rendered, the pragmatic process of adjusting private and public interests in America has so far produced a viable economic and business system for a complex industrial society.

International Business.—World problems have increasingly occupied governments, and international investment has increasingly attracted American businessmen. The great national corporation of yesterday is the multi-national corporation of today. Progress since World War II encourages the belief that the lessons of American enterprise have an application and an attractiveness that transcend national boundaries and narrow conceptions of national interest. Furthermore, as in the last century, the international flow of technology, capital, and management has been a reciprocal one, advancing now at an accelerating pace in a world where time and distance no longer present major barriers.

—Arthur M. Johnson

BIBLIOGRAPHY

COCHRAN, THOMAS C. *The American Business System: A Historical Perspective, 1900–1955.* Harvard University Press, 1960.

COLE, ARTHUR H. *Business Enterprise in its Social Setting.* Harvard University Press, 1960.

FANCHER, C. AND J. F. GALLAGHER. *Business Fundamentals for Everyone.* Prentice-Hall, 1958.

GENTRY, DWIGHT L. AND CHARLES TAFF. *Elements of Business Enterprise.* Ronald, 1961.

MASON, EDWARD S., ed. *The Corporation in Modern Society.* Harvard University Press, 1959.

OWENS, RICHARD N. *Business Management and Public Policy.* Richard D. Irwin, Inc., 1956.

TONNE, HERBERT A. *Business Principles, Organization and Management.* McGraw-Hill Book Co., 1963.

WALTON, CLARENCE, AND RICHARD EELLS. *Conceptual Foundations of Business: An Outline of the Major Ideas Sustaining Business Enterprise in the Western World.* Richard D. Irwin, Inc., 1961.

WHEELER, BAYARD O. *Business: An Introductory Analysis.* Harper & Row, Publishers, Inc., 1962.

ECONOMICS

Basic Definitions.—Economics is the study of man in the ordinary business of life. *Theoretical economics* seeks to predict how events and policies will affect the economy by drawing out, often with mathematical methods, the consequences of a set of assumptions. *Empirical economics* attempts to find, through economic history and economic statistics, generalizations that explain economic phenomena. *Econometrics* blends economic theory and statistics to develop mathematical models that stand up under rigorous testing. *Applied economics* is the use of the above methods to study problems facing government, business, or consumers.

Economics increasingly has become a positive, predictive science in recent years, particularly under the impact of powerful statistical and mathematical methods. The subject matter of modern economics is best introduced by discussing the criteria with which economists judge how well an economy is functioning.

■**BASIC GOALS.**—Depending on their value judgments, economists vary in the way they state these criteria. However, there is widespread agreement, both among economists and the general public, on the proper goals for economic policy.

1. *Full employment.* Any society that believes its members should have the opportunity to make full use of their creative talents must provide the opportunity for useful, remunerative work to all who seek it. Periods of mass unemployment, like the great depression of the 1930's, are the chief blot on the economic record of the United States and the other advanced industrial countries of the world. After World War II, the U.S. Congress passed The Employment Act of 1946, which states that "maximum employment, production, and purchasing power" is an important target for federal government policy. The United Nations Charter requires similar or stronger legislation of all member countries.

2. *Price Stability.* Because rapidly rising or declining prices affect different social groups in different ways, rapid changes in the overall price level introduce erratic elements to an economy. Old people who live on pensions find that their purchasing power is rapidly reduced during periods of inflation. Farmers, by contrast, suffer drastic declines in income during periods of general deflation. Because there is neither justice nor logic to the income changes that accompany rapid price changes, most economists argue that government policy must seek to promote price stability.

3. *Balance of Payments Equilibrium.* Every country in the world is a member of a community of nations that has a common desire for full employment and price stability. When a country has an adverse balance of payments, that is, when its ordinary receipts from other countries are substantially less than its payments to other countries, its trading

The Circular Flow of Economic Activity

MONEY IN MOTION: the public buys goods produced by business with income paid by business; this consumer spending permits more production and income payments.

partners find it difficult to follow domestic policies that will promote full employment or price stability. Balance of payments equilibrium—approximate equality between ordinary receipts from other countries and ordinary payments to other countries—is a requirement for good international economic relations.

4. *Efficiency.* Because economics developed into a separate discipline in the Anglo-Saxon society of the eighteenth and nineteenth centuries, which abhorred waste, it has always placed great stress on the conditions under which society functions efficiently. Stated in the broadest terms, the social condition for efficiency is that a given quantity of goods or consumer satisfaction be produced at a minimum drain on resources. Alternatively, social efficiency calls for a maximum amount of goods, or consumer satisfaction, to be produced from a given quantity of resources.

5. *Distributive Justice.* Where there is neither charity nor logic in the way a society distributes its supply of worldly goods, social discontent and disorganization are the inevitable consequences. Neither man nor God has found a system of income distribution that seems just to all. Moreover, societies differ widely in the methods used. Yet each must concern itself with the question whether the way in which it distributes income is equitable.

6. *Growth.* A rising standard of living is a goal of all societies. Advanced industrial countries, like the United States, require that individuals are able to fulfill an ever-rising level of aspirations. In the underdeveloped countries, where some 70 per cent of the world's population lives, the principal goal is to overcome starvation and illiteracy.

Types of Economies.—Nations differ markedly in how they seek to achieve the goals of the good economy. Each, however, organizes its economic activity under one of the following three principles.

A *traditional economy* is one in which economic activity arises from ancient customs and traditions. Primitive societies do not decide consciously what to produce or how to produce, or how to distribute income. All these things are done in old, unquestioned ways. Unemployment is not much of a problem in these societies, since each man is assigned a role in economic activity by birth. However, since custom works against innovation, traditional economies are stagnant and the level of productivity is low. Only in the past 5,000 years has mankind succeeded in escaping from the shackles of economic tradition. Indeed, the whole history of civilization could, in a sense, be written as the story of man's success in breaking the fetters of a traditional economy.

A *market economy* is a system of free relations between buyers and sellers, based on the widespread use of money as a medium of exchange and as a standard of value. In the market economy buyers are free to buy what they want at the price they are willing to pay; sellers are free to sell—or not to sell—as they see fit. In a market economy, society makes few decisions, beyond setting ground rules of exchange such as the enforcement of contracts. All economic magnitudes—prices, incomes, level of employment, rate of growth—evolve from the countless decisions made by individuals.

A *command economy* relies on a central authority—a dictator, oligarchy, or political party—to make its basic decisions. These determine the jobs people take, what they produce, their income, and all other economic magnitudes. Usually, the central authority itself makes decisions that spring from an economic plan to bring about specific objectives.

■**COMBINATION TYPES.**—In the modern world, few of these three types of economics exist in a pure form. In the underdeveloped countries of the world, tradition still plays a heavy role, but both the market and central planning are on the rise. In the parts of the world that call themselves Communist, decisions of the central authorities carry the heaviest economic weight, but in recent years market forces have been playing an increasing role in decisions. In America the market makes most decisions. However, at least since the early days of the New Deal administration of President Franklin D. Roosevelt, many of the most important decisions have either been made, or have been heavily influenced, by the federal government.

■**MODERN ECONOMICS.**—The previous discussion of the goals of economic policy affords a convenient way of organizing the content of modern economics. Economists generally agree that the success of a mixed free-enterprise economy in meeting the goals of full employment and price stability depends on governmental monetary and fiscal policy. The study of monetary and fiscal institutions and the way in which they influence economic stability is called *macroeconomics*. Balance of payments equilibrium also depends on monetary and fiscal policy. But it is also importantly influenced by international monetary and trade arrangements, which are the special subject of *international economics*.

Efficiency and distributive justice depend heavily on the actions of particular consumers, particular business firms and particular trade unions. The study of how individual economic units behave and how they mesh to determine prices, incomes, and production is called *microeconomics*.

The study of what determines economic growth is still a relatively new pursuit for economists, and there are still many areas of disagreement. However, in recent years, economists have increasingly come to understand the process of economic growth and *growth economics* has become an established discipline.

Money and Banking.—A dominant characteristic of advanced industrial societies is the use of money in every nook and cranny of economic life. Barter—the direct exchange of one commodity for another—may have been adequate for societies in which specialization and the division of labor were extremely primitive. But modern production is so specialized it requires a generalized means of exchange. It would be extremely inefficient if networks were paid in detergent for commercial television time, or auto executives tried to pay plumbers with cars, or grain farmers tried to buy with wheat itself the thousands of consumer goods that their families need.

Indeed, anthropological studies have established that "money" appears as soon as economic organization becomes the least bit complex. Thus Polynesian islanders used stones called "fei" as money. North American Indians used sea shells called "wampum" as money, and certain African tribes used cattle as money.

Economic history suggests that the commodities used as money characteristically have been both scarce and durable. Gold has served as money throughout most of the history of civilization, but modern industrial societies have moved away from prime reliance on gold for their money supply. In this respect, the United States monetary system is typical. Somewhat surprisingly, there is no consensus among American economists on what should be counted as money. Everyone, however, agrees that the present United States money supply should include coins, paper currency, and checks. Defined this way, the U.S. money supply was $172 billion in December 1965, made up of $37 billion in coins and paper currency and $135 billion in demand deposits. Some economists (including the influential Chicago School of monetary economists headed by Milton Friedman) would also count time deposits, either savings accounts or certificates of deposit in the com-

mercial banks, as part of the money supply. At the end of December 1965, these amounted to $145.3 billion.

In addition to money itself, *near money* also exists in the United States. Near money is any asset that can easily be converted into money itself at par. Such assets include Series E and Series H bonds sold to individuals by the United States Treasury. Indeed, virtually all the assets in the hands of individuals can be ranged along a *liquidity spectrum*, depending on how easily they can be converted into cash at the same price at which they were bought. Such a conversion is relatively easy for short-term government bonds, but may be relatively difficult for admittedly valuable assets such as paintings by Rembrandt or Picasso. An individual or corporation that carries a large proportion of its assets in money or in forms that can easily be converted into money is said to be highly *liquid*.

■**PRIVATE BANKING SYSTEM.**—There are many kinds of banks in the United States. The primary characteristic of the *commercial banks* is that the sums deposited in them are payable on demand and count as part of the money supply. Money deposited in *savings banks* and *savings and loan associations* is ordinarily loaned as first mortgages on residential and commercial buildings. It is not legally payable on demand, but only after a period of time has elapsed, in which the savings institution has a chance to convert the required proportion of its assets into cash. The institutions called *investment banks* are not banks at all in the usual sense of the word, since they do not ordinarily accept deposits from the general public. Instead, they act as intermediaries for business firms to float new issues of stocks or bonds. Government bond dealers do similar work for federal, state, and local governments.

Individuals or groups that wish to found banks are required to have a government charter. The vast majority of the more than 13,000 banks currently in existence received their

The Inverted Pyramid of Credit

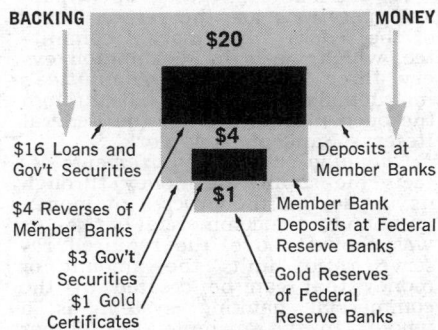

ONE DOLLAR in gold held at Federal Reserve Banks supports $4 of the money that member banks are required to deposit in the Reserve. These deposited reserves, in turn, back $20 deposited with individual member banks. Loans and government securities add the assets needed to provide all bank deposits with 100% backing.

charters from state governments. But most large banks, federally chartered by the office of the comptroller of the currency in the U.S. Treasury, are called *national banks*. Savings and loan associations generally have state charters.

Whether they have federal or state charters, the vast majority of commercial banks and savings banks are members of the *Federal Deposit Insurance Corporation*, which the government set up after the bank failures of the 1930's to insure individual depositors up to a limit of $10,000 for each account. Savings and loan associations have a government deposit-insurance scheme of their own. Because their deposits are payable on demand and count as part of the money supply, commercial banks play a pivotal role in the financial structure of the United States. Moreover, because the United States has developed a *fractional reserve banking system*, the commercial banking system, taken as a whole, has power to actually create money.

Demand deposits are liabilities of the commercial banks. "Fractional reserve banking" means that commercial banks are required to keep only part of their assets in the form of *reserves* against deposits. The rest can be loaned out at interest. In practice, this means that if an individual deposits $1,000 in a commercial bank, and the *required reserve ratio* is, say, 20 per cent, the bank is free to loan $800 to one of its customers, using the promissory note signed by that customer as the asset that backs $800 in deposit liabilities. The customer who received the loan, in turn, is free to spend the $800.

The $800 that is loaned to the original customer is likely to end up in another commercial bank as someone else's deposit. The second commercial bank is then free to repeat the loan process, keeping $160 (20 per cent of $800) in reserve and lending $640 to one of its own customers. This sequence can be continued indefinitely. And if average reserve requirements are, in fact, 20 per cent the original $1,000 will grow to $5,000 in deposits. Mathematically, the sequence of deposit creation is a geometric series whose sum is given by the formula: $D = \dfrac{1}{(r)}$, where D is the original deposit and r is the required reserve ratio. Thus, in the example, $1,000 $\dfrac{1}{(\frac{1}{5})} = \$5,000$.

But where did the first bank get the original deposit of $1,000? If it came from another bank, then the sequence of deposit creation that it initiates is cancelled by a process of deposit destruction initiated by the bank from which the first bank's money came. It is true, of course, that the process of money creation can start if individuals or companies decide to deposit currency or coins in a bank but, in general, the commercial banking system as a whole gets fresh deposits as the result of a deliberate decision by the *Federal Reserve System*, the *central bank* for the United States.

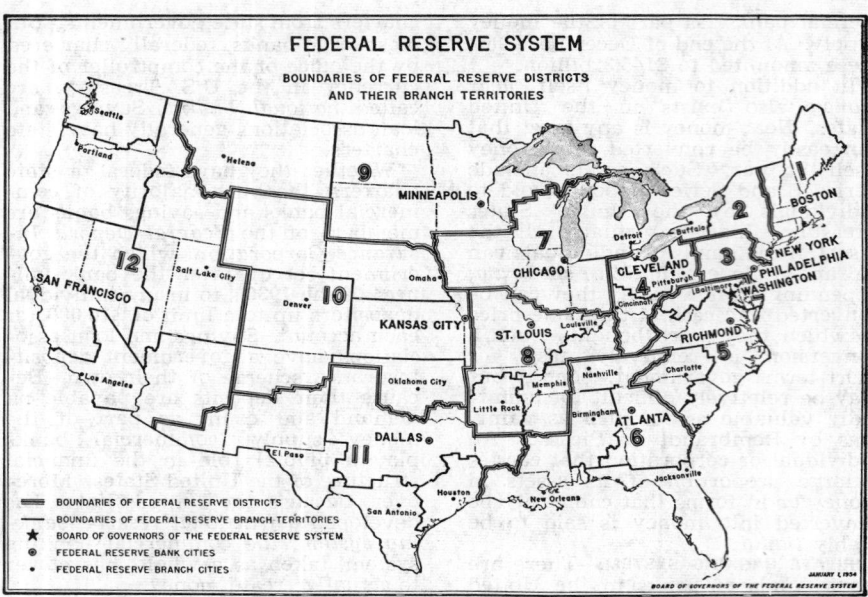

FEDERAL RESERVE SYSTEM

BOUNDARIES OF FEDERAL RESERVE DISTRICTS
AND THEIR BRANCH TERRITORIES

- ▬▬▬ BOUNDARIES OF FEDERAL RESERVE DISTRICTS
- ─── BOUNDARIES OF FEDERAL RESERVE BRANCH TERRITORIES
- ★ BOARD OF GOVERNORS OF THE FEDERAL RESERVE SYSTEM
- ⊙ FEDERAL RESERVE BANK CITIES
- • FEDERAL RESERVE BRANCH CITIES

JANUARY 1, 1954
BOARD OF GOVERNORS OF THE FEDERAL RESERVE SYSTEM

■**FEDERAL RESERVE SYSTEM.**—Because its decisions govern the amount of new money that goes into or is taken out of circulation, the Federal Reserve System has ultimate power to control the supply of money. The system was set up by the Federal Reserve Act of 1913, in the hope that it would end the monetary instability that characterized the economy of the United States throughout the nineteenth century and into the early years of the twentieth century.

Because United States banking institutions have a regional character, the Federal Reserve Act divided the country into 12 Federal Reserve Districts, each with its own Federal Reserve Bank. However, as the Federal Reserve System has evolved in practice, authority is vested in a 7-man board of governors and a 12-man open market committee, with five representatives of the districts (usually presidents of regional banks) as well as the board of governors.

Although the stock of the Federal Reserve System is owned by member commercial banks, it is a public agency that makes decisions on its own judgment of what is in the public interest. Any profits of the system, above a nominal amount, are turned over to the United States Treasury. The governors of the system are appointed by the President of the United States.

■**CONTROLLING THE MONEY SUPPLY.**—The Federal Reserve System has four tools available for controlling the money supply.

Open-market operations are by far the most important and the most frequently used. Every time the Federal Reserve buys something, the creation of new money is the potential result; every time the Federal Reserve sells something, the destruction of money is the potential result. Ordinarily, the Federal Reserve System deals in bonds that have been issued by the United States Treasury, and open market operations have come to mean buying and selling these bonds.

When the Federal Reserve buys bonds, the institution or individual that makes the sale—a private investor, commercial bank, or insurance company, for example—ends up with fresh money that has newly come into the economy. Every time the Federal Reserve sells bonds, individuals or institutions end up with less money. And because most money is held as bank deposits, these transactions affect the reserves of the commercial banks and therefore the potential for monetary expansion. (Commercial banks keep their reserves as deposits at their regional Federal Reserve Bank.)

Open-market operations are an important determinant of interest rates, that is, the price of borrowing money. When the Federal Reserve System is buying bonds, the supply of money grows relative to the demand, and a downward pressure on interest rates is exerted. Similarly, bond sales by the Federal Reserve System exert an upward pressure on interest rates by contracting the supply of money.

As the name suggests, open-market operations are the responsibility of the federal open market committee, which meets in Washington every three weeks. The committee's instructions are carried out through the open market desk of the Federal Reserve Bank of New York.

Changing reserve requirements affects the supply of money through its impact on the process of money creation by the commercial banks. As was shown above, the required reserve ratio limits the amount of money that can be created by the commercial banking system as a whole. In the example, the 20 per cent required reserve ratio meant that each $1,000 in new deposits could lead ultimately to the creation of $5,000 in new money. If the reserve ratio were raised to 25 per cent, the amount of new money would be reduced to $4,000; if it were lowered to 10 per cent, the amount would be increased to $10,000.

Changing the discount rate affects the supply of money, because it influences what commercial banks must pay to borrow from the Federal Reserve System. Although the Federal Reserve does not deal directly with the public, it has the power to make loans to commercial banks. When this rate is raised, it becomes more costly for the commercial banks to borrow, and therefore less profitable for them to lend. Reducing the discount rate has an opposite effect.

Actually, in recent years commercial banks have borrowed relatively little from the Federal Reserve. Thus changes in the discount rate have had mainly a symbolic significance, indicating changes in the intent of Federal Reserve policy.

Moral suasion affects the money supply through its influence on the lending criteria of commercial banks. When Federal Reserve officials suspect that unsound loans are being made, they issue a warning. Federal Reserve officials are particularly concerned about loans that are made to finance the purchase of common stocks on margin. When these loans mount during a speculative phase of the stock market, Federal Reserve officials may express concern to the commercial bankers who are responsible.

Federal Reserve officials deny that they exercise absolute control over the size of the money supply, arguing that the quality of money fluctuates with the demand for loans by business to meet changing conditions. However, recent academic research indicates that the way the total money supply changes bears a definite relation to changes in the amount of currency the public holds and the reserves of the commercial banks, both of which are controlled by the Federal Reserve System.

Monetary Theory.—Analysis of the way in which changes in monetary conditions affect prices, output, and employment is the province of monetary theory. Because some prices fall even in the best of times, and some prices rise even in the worst of times, economists have had to coin special terms to describe movements in the overall price level.

Inflation is the name given to a period when the general level of prices is rising. Although economists differ slightly in their exact definitions they agree that inflation occurs when there is a rise in price indexes that measure the general level of prices. *Deflation* is the name given to a period when general price indexes are falling.

A price index does not show actual prices, but rather compares the prices of a group of items in a particular year with those of a specified base period. Conventionally, the base period is taken as 100. Thus, if the present price index is 120, this means that average prices today are 20 per cent higher than in the base period. In the United States, the Consumer Price Index (CPI) measures changes in the average prices paid by a typical urban family for the goods and services that it buys.

The Wholesale Price Index (WPI) measures the average prices paid by business firms for the commodities they buy. In 1966, both indexes used 1957–1959 as the base period, and the average level of prices prevailing in the period between the beginning of 1957 and the end of 1959 was taken as equal to 100.

■**CHANGES IN PRICE LEVELS.**—In discussing the causes of inflation and deflation, economists find it convenient to distinguish between the *short run* and the *long run*. There is general agreement that long-term changes in the price level are caused by changes in the quantity of money. Ever since the writings of the Scottish philosopher David Hume (1711–1776), economists have noticed that price rises occur when fresh money flows into an economic system. In Europe, for example, rapid price rises during the sixteenth and seventeenth centuries followed the discovery of vast quantities of gold in the New World.

In the United States, inflation has inevitably occurred during and immediately after wars, because financing war has always called for big increases in the money supply. To describe how changes in the money supply lead to changes in prices, the American economist Irving Fisher (1867–1947) devised the *quantity theory of money*. This theory starts off with the *equation of exchange*, which states that in any period *M* (the quantity of money) times *V* (the velocity of circulation, or the average number of times that money turns over) equals *P* (the average price level) times *O* (the quantity of output produced). The quantity theory goes on to state that *O* changes slowly, because output is affected mainly by slow-moving trends in productivity and the size of the labor force. It also argues that *V* changes slowly, because its size is governed by custom, tradition, and the nature of banking institutions. It follows, therefore, that changes in the price level are roughly proportional to changes in the quantity of money. The quantity theory shows, for example, that the main reason prices are now higher than they were before World War II is that the money supply is also much larger.

Inflation

CONSUMPTION AND INVESTMENT
600
500
400
300
200
100
C+I
C
C+I
C
45°
100
200
300
400
500
600
INCOME

INFLATION occurs when consumption and investment spending (C+I) exceeds income and maximum output (400 on chart). Output cannot move above 400, so excess spending only raises prices. At equilibrium (45° line), spending matches income.

■**SHORT-TERM CHANGES.**—There is less agreement among economists over how changes in the supply of money affect the economy in the short-run. This is simply because both velocity and the level of output are variable in the short run, and a change in monetary conditions may affect velocity or output rather than prices.

Nevertheless, one influential group of economists, the Chicago School, holds that monetary conditions are the main determinant of short-run economic stability. While granting that velocity of turnover is not constant, this school argues that controlling the behavior of the money supply will help to control the level of economic activity, simply because changes in velocity will be so small or so predictable that economic activity will move in the same direction as the quantity of money.

But today most economists are skeptical that monetary conditions, in and of themselves, are the key to short-term economic stability, particularly as a method of avoiding recessions. The act of making money more readily available, or lowering interest rates, does guarantee that more money will be spent.

Long- and Short-Term Interest Rates
Weekly

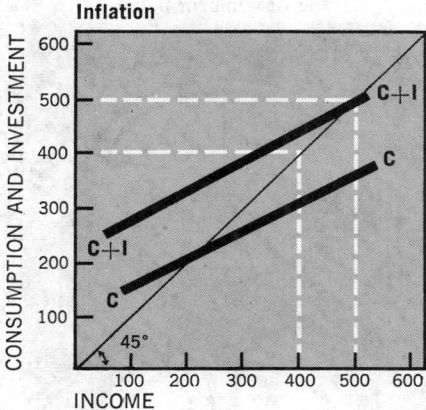

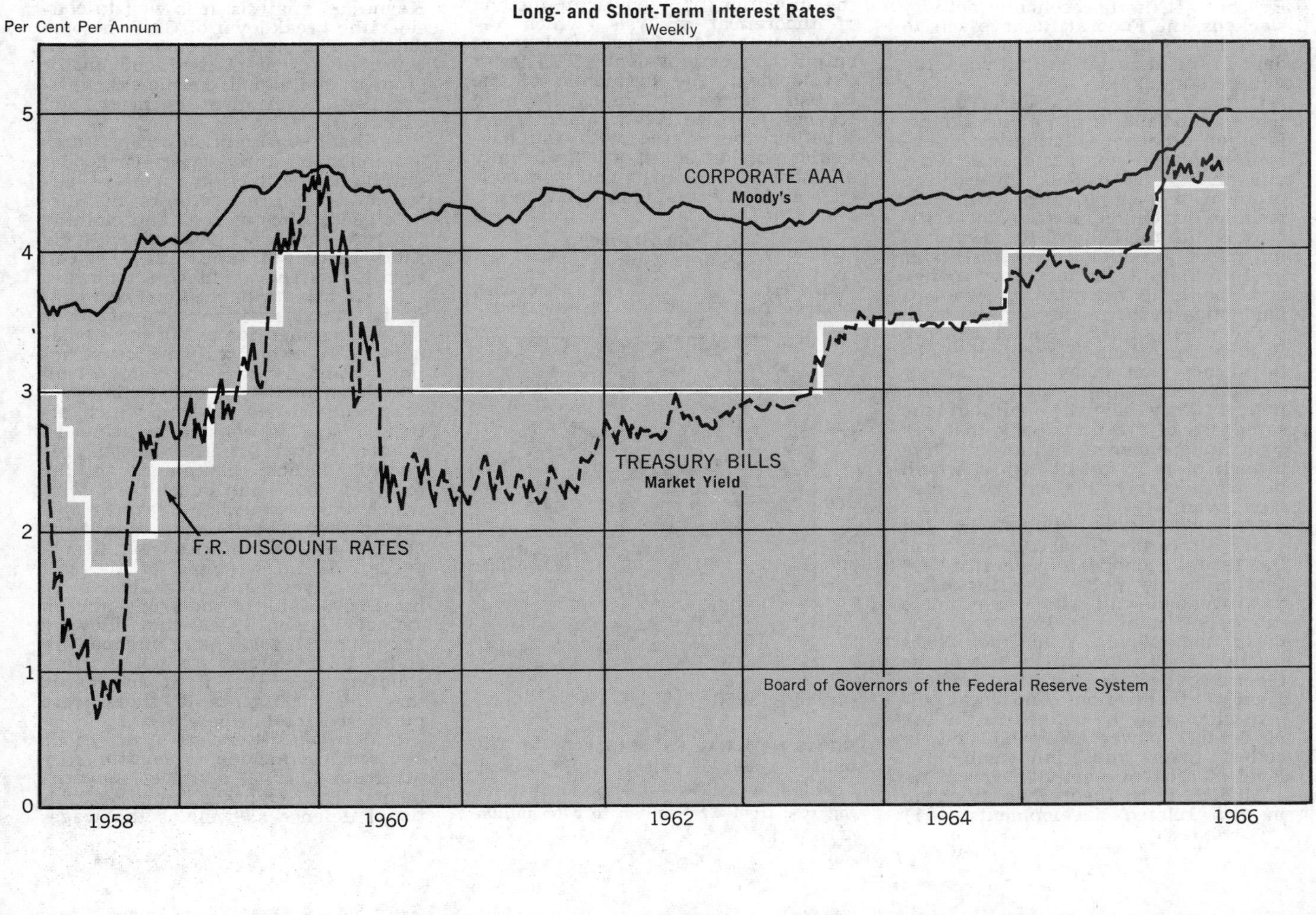

Per Cent Per Annum
5
4
3
2
1
0
CORPORATE AAA
Moody's
TREASURY BILLS
Market Yield
F.R. DISCOUNT RATES
Board of Governors of the Federal Reserve System
1958
1960
1962
1964
1966

532 ECONOMICS

For example, in the early days of the New Deal of President Franklin D. Roosevelt, money was abundant and interest rates were low, but these factors had little effect on business activity.

However, virtually all economists agree on these short-term effects of changes in the quantity of money. A tight-money policy, which denies funds to would-be spenders, is a potent weapon against inflation, although it may bring the risk of a subsequent recession. An easy-money policy, by keeping interest rates low and making credit easily available, helps stimulate spending and therefore helps fight deflation. Monetary conditions have the biggest impact where the proceeds of a loan are invested for a long period of time. In business, for example, changes in interest rates have their greatest impact on the investment plans of public utilities, which expect the new equipment they buy to last perhaps for 50 years. For consumers, the impact is on the demand for housing, where a higher interest rate on a mortgage will affect a family budget for perhaps 30 years.

Monetary Policy.—Federal Reserve officials have often described their policy as one of "leaning against the wind." That is to say, as the economy approaches full employment and prices begin to rise, the Federal Reserve acts to make money scarcer and more expensive. The intention is to slow down the pace of economic activity. By contrast, if the economic activity slackens, the Federal Reserve acts to make money cheaper and more abundant in the expectation that spending will be stimulated.

Critics of the Federal Reserve System contend that it has a bias against inflation, frequently acting too quickly to restrain rising business activity, and that it is callous toward the problem of unemployment. On more technical grounds, a frequent criticism is that the Federal Reserve pays too much attention to interest rates in formulating its monetary policy and too little attention to what is happening to the money supply itself.

Defenders of the Federal Reserve System argue that it is the only public agency that takes price stability seriously as a major goal of public policy. They say that without the safeguard of a central bank that has some independence of the executive branch of government, prices would be considerably higher than they have been.

■THE GOVERNMENT BUDGET.—In the years before the Great Depression of the 1930's, economists generally held that monetary policy was the principal weapon with which to promote economic stability. However, the mass unemployment of the 1930's brought a shift toward the use of the federal budget as an active instrument of stabilization. And fiscal policy, which may be defined as the use of federal power to spend and to collect taxes, thus influencing the level of economic activity, was born.

Modern fiscal theory has its origin in two related developments: (1)

The Government Dollar

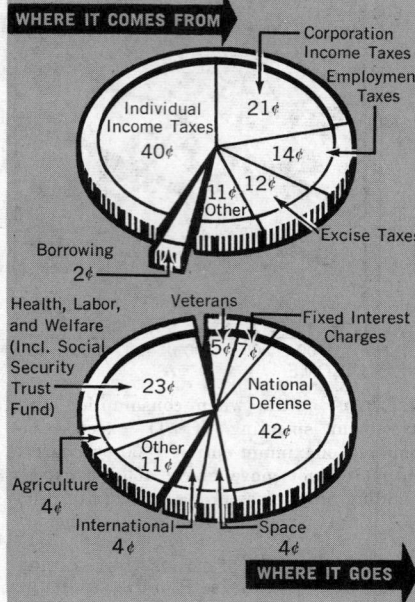

FUNDS received mainly as taxes by the U.S. government in fiscal year 1965 went primarily for public welfare and defense.

the growth of national income accounting, which gave a way to accurately measure the size of a nation's output of goods and services; and (2) the invention of a powerful method of theoretical analysis, which revealed what determines the level of output and employment. This latter development, the brainchild of the British economist John Maynard Keynes, is called Keynesian analysis. Whether they agree with the particular policies he espoused, virtually all modern economists now acknowledge an intellectual debt to Keynes.

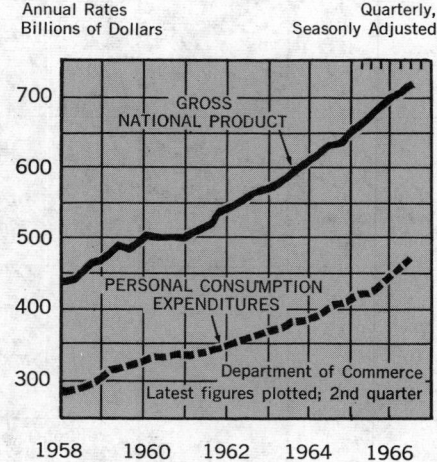

Gross National Product
1966 Dollars

GROSS NATIONAL PRODUCT grew by $270 billion—from $460 billion in 1958 to about $740 billion in 1966—while personal spending rose from $290 billion to $465 billion.

■THE NATIONAL INCOME ACCOUNTS.—The purpose of national income accounting is to measure the flow of goods and services that a nation's economy produces over a particular period of time. This flow has an obvious relation to economic welfare: since the vast majority of the population earns its livelihood by producing goods and services, the level of employment has a close relation to the flow of goods and services. This flow, moreover, determines what is available for consumption and investment, and is therefore the determinant both of a nation's standard of living and of its rate of growth.

■GROSS NATIONAL PRODUCT (GNP).—This is perhaps the most familiar and most widely-used concept in national income accounting. A complicated idea and difficult to describe briefly, the GNP can be roughly defined as the total production of goods for end use —by consumers, business, and government—in a given year. Goods for end use, or *final goods*, are used to eliminate double counting. For example, in one year iron ore is mined and sold to a steel foundry. The foundry makes the ore into steel and, in turn, sells it to a maker of refrigerators. We do not add up the value of the ore, steel, and refrigerators in the GNP, because that would be counting the value of the ore three times. The value of the final product, refrigerators, reflects the value of ore and steel as well.

Since spending for final goods and services plays an important role in Keynesian analysis, it is well to consider the breakdown of GNP in some detail. The total production of a country is bought by four major groups: individual consumers, businessmen, government agencies, and exporters.

Personal consumption expenditures are made on three types of goods: durable goods, such as furniture, automobiles, and refrigerators; nondurable goods, such as food and clothing that are consumed over a relatively short period of time; and services, such as haircuts or tonsillectomies.

Gross private domestic investment is the purchase of investment goods by businessmen for use in their businesses. It comprises new construction, which includes the value of all completed industrial and commercial construction; new houses, which although sold to consumers are considered as part of investment; producers' durable equipment in the form of tools and machinery with which businessmen and farmers operate their businesses; and any change in inventories of unsold goods. As an example of the last type of investment, if a shoe store has 10,000 pairs of shoes on hand on January 1, and 12,000 the following December 31, 2,000 pairs of shoes are added to inventory; for national accounting purposes, it is considered that the 2,000 pairs of shoes were purchased for business use.

Government purchases of goods and services include expenditures by the federal, state, and local governments. They embrace the cost of national defense as well as the wages

ASSOCIATED PRESS

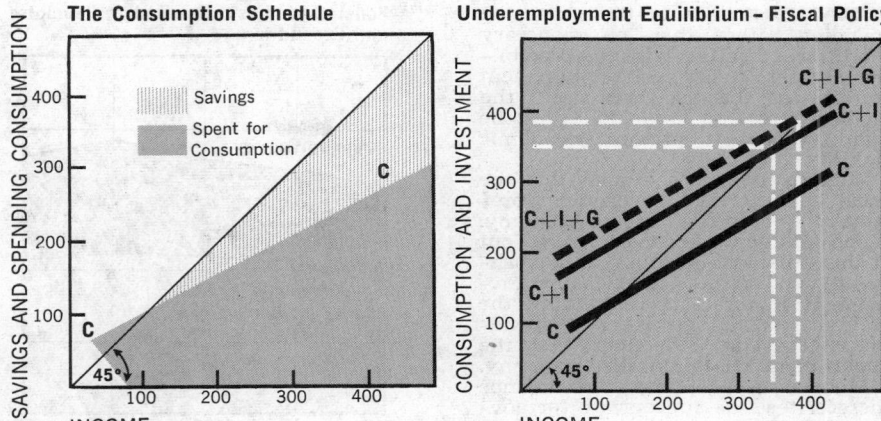

The Consumption Schedule

Savings

Spent for Consumption

Underemployment Equilibrium – Fiscal Policy

KEYNESIAN economic theory, developed by John M. Keynes (*left*), concerns income and expenditure patterns. In Keynesian theory, consumption (C, chart above *left*) and savings vary with income levels. Through affecting income, investment (I, chart above *right*) and government spending (G) ultimately determine the level of consumption (C).

paid to personnel and the cost of all supplies and construction. The money paid out by government agencies in grants, called *transfer payments,* is not included in this category, because GNP counts only the value of final goods and services.

Net exports of goods and services are simply the difference between the value of exports and the value of imports. If exports exceed imports, the nation has sold more to other nations than it has bought, and net exports are positive. A negative net export figure means that the nation bought more from other countries than it sold to them.

■**KEYNESIAN ANALYSIS.**—The concepts of gross national product enter directly into Keynesian economics. This is because Keynes rejected the quantity theory of money, which analyzed changes in income by looking at what was happening to the supply of money and its velocity of circulation. Instead he asked the direct question: what factors determine the income level of each important group in society and the proportion of in-

come that each of these groups spends? For this reason, Keynesian economics is known as the income-expenditures approach to macro-economics.

Keynes started off with a basic equation; stated simply, it says that Y (gross national product) equals C (consumption) plus I (investment) plus G (government spending) plus E-M, or net exports. He then sought to determine the level of spending in each sector of the economy and the way in which they combined to determine the level of GNP.

Keynes argued that changes in investment (I) hold the basic explanation of changes in a society's level of income. This is because business invests in response to long-range opportunities, which may change considerably from year to year, depending on changes in population trends. Moreover, Keynes recognized that the state of business confidence, or expectations about the future, could have an important impact on investment plans. (See above charts.)

In the Keynesian view, consump-

tion is essentially a passive element in the economy, depending on how much after-tax income is available to consumers. The famous Keynesian *consumption function* is simply an equation that relates consumption to income. Government spending in Keynesian economics is regarded as theoretically independent of the level of income, depending as it does on political, rather than economic, considerations.

Keynesian economics readily lends itself to mathematical systems explaining the level of income. The simplest possible system looks something like this. Assume that $I = 40$ and that $G = 60$. Further assume that consumption is a linear function of income, so that $C = 3/4Y + 50$. Remembering that $Y = C + I + G$ (net exports are ignored for the sake of simplicity), and solving the equation, income turns out to be 600.

This is only the simplest possible model. In the years since Keynes, much econometric research has been concerned with formulating elaborate systems of equations that can forecast income accurately. In 1966, for example, the U.S. Department of Commerce released the details of a model with 49 equations to determine income and other important economic magnitudes.

In the years before Keynes, the main body of economic tradition assumed that a free enterprise economy had an automatic tendency toward full employment. It admitted that recessions and unemployment were possible, but it held that the economy would soon come back to full employment if wages were flexible.

Keynes denied that there was any guarantee that private investment and private consumption alone could generate sufficient income to guarantee full employment. He thus admitted the possibility of *underemployment equilibrium.* (Equilibrium is a commonly used term in economics. A system is in equilibrium when disturbances that move it away from a point set in motion forces that return it to the original point.)

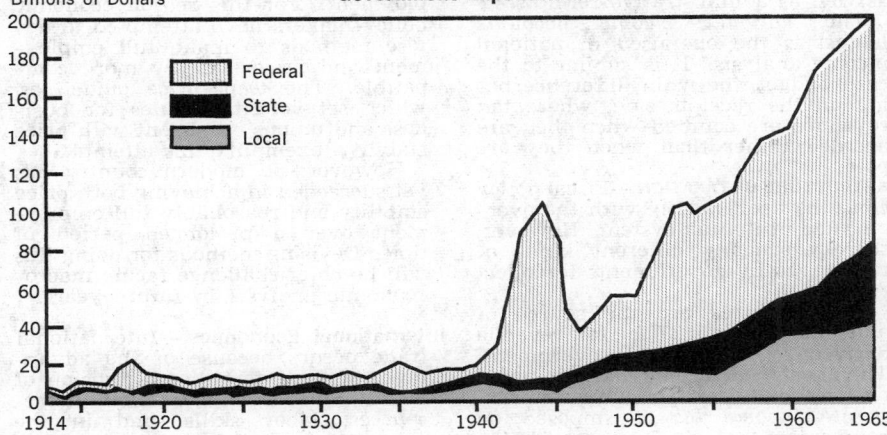
Government Expenditures

Billions of Dollars

Federal
State
Local

PUBLIC SPENDING by local, state, and federal governments has risen from ten billion dollars to two hundred billion dollars annually in the past half century, with federal money providing an increasingly greater proportion of total governmental expenditures.

■**FISCAL POLICY.**—It is the stress on spending rather than on monetary conditions, together with the possibility of persistent underemployment equilibrium, that has given rise to the modern stress on fiscal policy as the main weapon to promote economic stability.

Modern fiscal policy holds that the fiscal operations of government promote the stability of an economy. When taxation takes more money out of the stream of income than government spending puts in, then the government in effect is restraining the economy. When government spending exceeds tax collections, then the government stimulates the economy.

Modern fiscal policy recommends these criteria as appropriate for government fiscal operation:

A *deficit* in the federal budget is appropriate when there is underemployment of resources and prices are weak. When the government budget is in deficit, spending exceeds tax revenues, and the effect is to stimulate economic activity.

A *balanced budget* is appropriate when the economy is close to full employment, and prices are stable. Then government fiscal operations neither add to nor subtract from demand and have an appropriately neutral impact on the economy.

A *surplus* in the federal budget is appropriate when prices are rising and there are more job openings than unemployed workers. Then tax revenues exceed spending, and government exerts needed restraint on the economy.

In recent years, there has been a heavy use of fiscal policy by the governments of the advanced industrial countries of the West, particularly as a weapon against recession. This, perhaps, explains why there have been no major depressions in the years following World War II, either in the United States or in the other industrialized countries of the world.

Special Topics in Macroeconomics.—So far, we have been concerned with the broad outlines of macroeconomics. But certain special subjects have received a great deal of attention from economists in recent years and deserve some comment.

■**THE PUBLIC DEBT.**—Because of past deficits—particularly those incurred during wars—the public debt of the United States exceeded $300 billion at the end of 1966. Does this huge debt mean that the United States is on the verge of bankruptcy? This is not a question that causes economists to lose much sleep. In fact, because no major war has been fought for 20 years, the *burden of debt*—its size as a proportion of gross national product —has generally been declining since 1945. Also, the federal government through its tax powers will always have the revenues needed to meet interest payments.

What effect does the public debt have on the economy? Overwhelmingly, the debt is owned by the citizens of the United States. That means that for every dollar of tax revenues used to pay interest on the federal debt, some American gets

Federal Administrative Budget Receipts and Expenditures

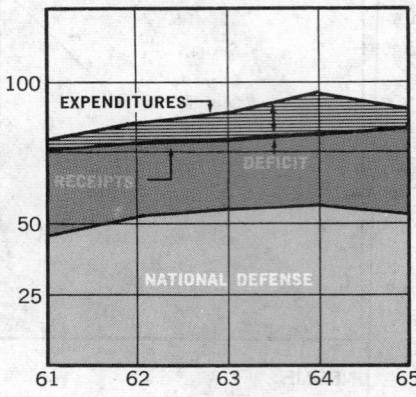

U.S. BUDGET shows a deficit as more money is spent than received, with national defense requiring the major federal expense.

one dollar in interest income. Studies of the holding of public debt indicate that individuals—or institutions that invest their money—own about the same proportion of the public debt as the proportion of their tax money that is used to pay interest.

■**DIFFERING BUDGET CONCEPTS.**—Up to now we have been assuming that the federal budget is measured in only one way. Actually, there are three separate federal budgets. The best known is the *administrative budget.* On the spending side, this budget includes all expenses except those incurred by the federal trust funds. On the receipts side, this budget includes mainly revenues from corporate and individual income taxes and excise taxes.

The cash consolidated budget measures cash actually paid by the federal government to the public in a particular year. In addition to those expenses included in the administrative budget, it also counts the spending of federal trust funds, such as the Social Security trust fund and the highway trust fund. This budget includes trust fund receipts as well as administrative receipts.

The national income accounts budget is the one used in national income analysis. It is similar to the cash budget, the main difference being on the receipts side, where tax revenues are counted when they are accrued rather than when they are paid.

■**STRUCTURE OF TAXATION.**—Fiscal policy concerns itself mainly with the overall yield of the tax system. However, there are many different kinds of taxes used by governments to collect revenue.

Income taxes are the source of almost 90 per cent of the tax revenue derived by the federal government. The *individual income tax* is imposed on individual incomes, while the *corporate income tax* is imposed on companies that do business in the corporate form. *Sales taxes* are imposed on the value of commodities sold, usually at the time of sales. A *general sales tax* is imposed on a

wide range of commodities, usually at a low rate. An *excise tax* is imposed on the value of specific commodities, sometimes, as in the case of liquor, to discourage consumption. Excise taxes may also be *user taxes,* such as the portion of the gasoline tax that goes into the federal highway trust fund, that are designed to collect revenue from the specific individuals who use the government service that is being taxed. A special kind of sales tax, the *value added tax,* has become increasingly popular in Europe in recent years. A tax on business, it is levied on the difference between sales receipts and the cost of commodities and services purchased from other firms. In the United States, sales taxes are the most important source of revenue for state governments, although some states also impose income taxes.

Property taxes are the mainstay of local government. They are imposed on the assessed value of real property, mainly real estate. The federal government and most state governments also impose *estate taxes* on the value of estates that are passed on. Taxes may be *progressive, proportional,* or *regressive.* As an individual's income rises, a progressive tax takes an increasing proportion of that income, a proportional tax an equal proportion, and a regressive tax a declining proportion. The federal income tax is a progressive tax, but because of exceptions, deductions, and exclusions it is not as progressive as the basic tax-rate tables suggest. State sales taxes, because they except savings, which rise as income rises, are generally regressive.

■**CONFLICT BETWEEN GOALS.**—If there were never any conflict between the goals of full employment and price stability, the jobs of economists and public officials would be relatively simple. Unfortunately, in the present world most stabilization problems are complicated, because during a business upswing prices start rising before high employment levels are reached. In the United States, for example, recent economic history suggests that prices start to rise before the economy reaches full employment. For this reason economic policy-makers have attempted to devise methods to make full employment and price stability more compatible. The *wage-price guidelines,* which set voluntary rules for business and unions consistent with price stability, exemplify this attempt.

However, no modern country has yet succeeded in achieving both price stability and reasonably full employment over a prolonged period of time. Devising methods for doing this will be chief challenge facing macroeconomic analysis in future years.

International Economics.—International trade occurs because of the advantages of the international division of labor. Since countries differ in resources, labor skills, and in the amount of capital per capita they possess, it follows that each country will have comparative advantage in the production of some commodities. It is to the advantage of each country

Individual Tax Rate Schedules, 1966

If the amount on line 11d, page 1*, is:	SCHEDULE I Enter on line 12, page 1:	If the amount on line 11d, page 1, is:	SCHEDULE II Enter on line 12, page 1:	If the amount on line 11d, page 1, is:	SCHEDULE III Enter on line 12, page 1:
Not over $500...14% of the amount on line 11d.		Not over $1,000..14% of the amount on line 11d.		Not over $1,000..14% of the amount on line 11d.	

Over—	But not over—	of excess over—	Over—	But not over—	of excess over—	Over—	But not over—	of excess over—
$500	–$1,000	$ 70,+15%–$500	$1,000	–$2,000	$ 140,+15%–$1,000	$1,000	–$2,000	$ 140,+16%–$1,000
$1,000	–$1,500	$ 145,+16%–$1,000	$2,000	–$3,000	$ 290,+16%–$2,000	$2,000	–$4,000	$ 300,+18%–$2,000
$1,500	–$2,000	$ 225,+17%–$1,500	$3,000	–$4,000	$ 450,+17%–$3,000	$4,000	–$6,000	$ 660,+20%–$4,000
$2,000	–$4,000	$ 310,+19%–$2,000	$4,000	–$8,000	$ 620,+19%–$4,000	$6,000	–$8,000	$ 1,060,+22%–$6,000
$4,000	–$6,000	$ 690,+22%–$4,000	$8,000	–$12,000	$ 1,380,+22%–$8,000	$8,000	–$10,000	$ 1,500,+25%–$8,000
$6,000	–$8,000	$ 1,130,+25%–$6,000	$12,000	–$16,000	$ 2,260,+25%–$12,000	$10,000	–$12,000	$ 2,000,+27%–$10,000
$8,000	–$10,000	$ 1,630,+28%–$8,000	$16,000	–$20,000	$ 3,260,+28%–$16,000	$12,000	–$14,000	$ 2,540,+31%–$12,000
$10,000	–$12,000	$ 2,190,+32%–$10,000	$20,000	–$24,000	$ 4,380,+32%–$20,000	$14,000	–$16,000	$ 3,160,+32%–$14,000
$12,000	–$14,000	$ 2,830,+36%–$12,000	$24,000	–$28,000	$ 5,660,+36%–$24,000	$16,000	–$18,000	$ 3,800,+35%–$16,000
$14,000	–$16,000	$ 3,550,+39%–$14,000	$28,000	–$32,000	$ 7,100,+39%–$28,000	$18,000	–$20,000	$ 4,500,+36%–$18,000
$16,000	–$18,000	$ 4,330,+42%–$16,000	$32,000	–$36,000	$ 8,660,+42%–$32,000	$20,000	–$22,000	$ 5,220,+40%–$20,000
$18,000	–$20,000	$ 5,170,+45%–$18,000	$36,000	–$40,000	$ 10,340,+45%–$36,000	$22,000	–$24,000	$ 6,020,+41%–$22,000
$20,000	–$22,000	$ 6,070,+48%–$20,000	$40,000	–$44,000	$ 12,140,+48%–$40,000	$24,000	–$26,000	$ 6,840,+43%–$24,000
$22,000	–$26,000	$ 7,030,+50%–$22,000	$44,000	–$52,000	$ 14,060,+50%–$44,000	$26,000	–$28,000	$ 7,700,+45%–$26,000
$26,000	–$32,000	$ 9,030,+53%–$26,000	$52,000	–$64,000	$ 18,060,+53%–$52,000	$28,000	–$32,000	$ 8,600,+46%–$28,000
$32,000	–$38,000	$ 12,210,+55%–$32,000	$64,000	–$76,000	$ 24,420,+55%–$64,000	$32,000	–$36,000	$ 10,440,+48%–$32,000
$38,000	–$44,000	$ 15,510,+58%–$38,000	$76,000	–$88,000	$ 31,020,+58%–$76,000	$36,000	–$38,000	$ 12,360,+50%–$36,000
$44,000	–$50,000	$ 18,990,+60%–$44,000	$88,000	–$100,000	$ 37,980,+60%–$88,000	$38,000	–$40,000	$ 13,360,+52%–$38,000
$50,000	–$60,000	$ 22,590,+62%–$50,000	$100,000	–$120,000	$ 45,180,+62%–$100,000	$40,000	–$44,000	$ 14,400,+53%–$40,000
$60,000	–$70,000	$ 28,790,+64%–$60,000	$120,000	–$140,000	$ 57,580,+64%–$120,000	$44,000	–$50,000	$ 16,520,+55%–$44,000
$70,000	–$80,000	$ 35,190,+66%–$70,000	$140,000	–$160,000	$ 70,380,+66%–$140,000	$50,000	–$52,000	$ 19,820,+56%–$50,000
$80,000	–$90,000	$ 41,790,+68%–$80,000	$160,000	–$180,000	$ 83,580,+68%–$160,000	$52,000	–$64,000	$ 20,940,+58%–$52,000
$90,000	–$100,000	$ 48,590,+69%–$90,000	$180,000	–$200,000	$ 97,180,+69%–$180,000	$64,000	–$70,000	$ 27,900,+59%–$64,000
$100,000		$ 55,490,+70%–$100,000	$200,000		$110,980,+70%–$200,000	$70,000	–$76,000	$ 31,440,+61%–$70,000
						$76,000	–$80,000	$ 35,100,+62%–$76,000
						$80,000	–$88,000	$ 37,580,+63%–$80,000
						$88,000	–$100,000	$ 42,620,+64%–$88,000
						$100,000	–$120,000	$ 50,300,+65%–$100,000
						$120,000	–$140,000	$ 63,500,+67%–$120,000
						$140,000	–$160,000	$ 76,900,+68%–$140,000
						$160,000	–$180,000	$ 90,500,+69%–$160,000
						$180,000		$104,300,+70%–$180,000

* On U.S. Internal Revenue Form 1040.

Schedule I. SINGLE TAXPAYERS not qualifying for rates in Schedules I and III, and MARRIED PERSONS FILING SEPARATE RETURNS.

Schedule II. MARRIED TAXPAYERS FILING JOINT RETURNS and CERTAIN WIDOWS AND WIDOWERS.

Schedule III. Unmarried (or legally separated) taxpayers who qualify as HEAD OF HOUSEHOLD.

---

to produce those commodities in which it is most efficient, selling them to other countries to acquire those commodities that it cannot produce as efficiently.

Economists generally agree that the international division of labor is determined by resource ratios. Countries that have a high ratio of labor to land (Belgium) will tend to export manufactured goods and import agricultural goods. For agricultural countries (Australia, for example) the opposite is true. Countries rich in capital relative to other resources (the United States, for example) will tend to export commodities whose production requires large amounts of capital (machinery and automobiles) and import commodities whose production requires large quantities of labor (toys).

United States Balance of Payments, 1965

Payments to the U.S. (In billions)		Payments from the U.S. (In billions)	
United States exports:		United States imports:	
Merchandise	$2.05	Merchandise	$2.43
Military sales and grants	.03	Military expenditures	.32
Transportation and travel	.17	Transportation and travel	.21
Services	.12	Services	.02
Income on American investment abroad	.29	Income on foreign investment in America	.10
	$2.66		$3.08[1]
Transactions in government assets	.06	Net unilateral transfers	.03
Transactions in foreign assets in United States	.29	Transactions in United States private assets abroad	.01
	$3.01		$3.12
Errors and omissions and transfers of funds[2]	.11		
	$3.12		

[1] The balance of trade (only goods and services); $3.08 billion minus $2.66 billion equals $420 million which United States owes foreigners.

[2] These "balancing items" are often gold transfers or deposits and investments that foreigners accumulate in the United States with money that is due them.

Source: United States Department of Commerce. Survey of Current Business, June, 1966.

■ **BALANCE OF PAYMENTS.**—A country's *balance of international payments* (or simply balance of payments) is a record of its transactions with the rest of the world. There are various methods of balance-of-payments accounting now in use. The most useful are those that focus on the question whether a country's balance of payments is in *equilibrium* or *disequilibrium*.

Not surprisingly, there is a sense in which a country's balance of payments is always in balance, because spending abroad must be financed or it could not occur. But some kinds of financing indicate balance-of-payment troubles while others do not.

The core of a country's balance of payments is its *current account*. This is a statement of its receipts from merchandise and expenditures and such "invisible" items as transportation, travel expenditure, income from investments, private gifts, and miscellaneous international payments such as insurance and bank charges.

The simple fact that a country has a deficit on current account does not necessarily mean that it is in balance-of-payments trouble. For in addition to goods, capital either in the form of direct investments or purchases of portfolio securities also flows across international boundaries. If a current account deficit is matched by an equivalent surplus provided by a voluntary inflow of capital, then it does not indicate that a country is in balance-of-payments disequilibrium. Canada, for example, has had a current account deficit for many years, but it has never been in severe balance-of-payments disequilibrium.

However, if a country's combined balance on current account and voluntary capital account shows a defect, a true disequilibrium exists, for then the defect must be financed either through the sale of gold, through emergency borrowing (either from other countries or from an international agency), or through private short-term financing. In any case, the country must adopt measures designed to bring its international accounts back into equilibrium.

■THE GOLD STANDARD.—Methods of restoring equilibrium to a country's balance of payments are now varied and complex, and are sharply different from what occurred under the famous international gold standard of the nineteenth century and early twentieth century. Under that standard, each country's currency was tied directly to gold, a fact that brought about automatic adjustment of a balance-of-payments equilibrium. When a country's normal receipts did not match its normal payments, gold flowed to other countries. That automatically meant that the money supply in the deficit country would shrink, bringing down prices and incomes. The effect was to stimulate exports, discourage imports, and restore equilibrium to the country's international accounts.

The trouble with the international gold standard was that it imposed harsh penalties on countries that lived beyond their means. In effect, it asked countries that had balance-of-payments deficits to accept recession, deflation, and unemployment as the only feasible means of restoring payments equilibrium.

The upshot of the great world-wide depression of the 1930's was to end the old gold standard and replace it with *autarkic* trade policies, which attempt to make a country's economy self-sufficient. Countries sought balance-of-payments equilibrium by limiting their imports through raising tariffs and imposing quotas. The use of *exchange controls*, which limited the amount of foreign exchange available to importers, became widespread. The result was a downward spiral of world trade, as countries sought to limit their own unemployment by imposing an artificial barrier on international trade.

■POSTWAR AGREEMENTS.—In the closing days of World War II a great international monetary and trade conference was arranged among the Western allies to seek a new agreement for world trade. The results were the Bretton Woods agreements and the General Agreements on Tariffs and Trade (GATT).

The Bretton Woods agreements established the International Monetary Fund (IMF). Under these agreements, countries with balance-of-payments problems can borrow foreign currencies from the IMF to tide them through emergencies. To get a loan, however, a country has to pledge that it will not impose new exchange restrictions and has to show that it is taking steps to correct

the basic cause of its balance-of-payments problems. In short, that it is doing something to stop inflation.

The 37 signatories of GATT agreed to work toward freer world trade in two ways: to try to end trade discrimination among countries by setting the same tariffs on all imports instead of giving one country more favorable terms on duties and import quotas than another; to work toward a general reduction of tariff levels by negotiating lower tariffs with one another.

The postwar international agreements, which depend on a degree of international cooperation undreamed of in the 1930's, appear on the record to have been successful. The direct evidence is the growth of the sheer volume of world trade from $46.9 billion in 1947 to $164.8 billion in 1965. At the same time, countries seeking to cure a balance-of-payments disequilibrium have managed to avoid cycles of deflation.

The effect of setting up the IMF was to take world currencies off the old gold standard and place them on a new limited international gold exchange standard. Under the new standard, currencies are still tied to gold in the sense that each country's currency unit is based on a fixed ratio to gold. (A U.S. dollar, for example, can still be converted internationally into gold at a rate of $35 an ounce of fine gold.) However, in addition to gold, the so-called *key currencies,* the U.S. dollar and the British pound sterling, can also be held as exchange reserves. Countries facing balance-of-payments disequilibrium may still *devalue* (reduce the gold content of) their currencies. But devaluations must be limited to an amount stipulated by the IMF. Moreover, the IMF seeks to limit the need for drastic measures by granting loans to countries experiencing balance-of-payments difficulties. The loans come out of gold and currencies deposited with the IMF by member countries, according to the quotas established at Bretton Woods.

Although the postwar agreements have greatly improved the atmosphere of world trade, economists agree that the world monetary mechanism still suffers from some defects. And steps have either been taken or proposed to solve them.

■THE "HOT MONEY" PROBLEM.—When money is sent from one country to another, either because of worries over devaluation or because interest rates are higher in the other country, it is called "hot money." As the world monetary mechanism has evolved in the postwar years, the key currencies in particular have become vulnerable to sudden outflows. Both the United States and Britain have suffered substantial balance-of-payments deficits. The result has been that some foreign countries have built up substantial dollar and pound balances, which they can easily convert into gold or other currencies. Thus, under the limited international gold exchange standard, both the dollar and the pound are vulnerable to the speculative outflow of short-term money.

To counter this problem, central bankers in the important countries of the world have begun to cooperate, thus forestalling or countering the effects of hot money when it crosses international boundaries. First, a system of multilateral surveillance has been set up, by which central banks keep themselves informed of international movements of short-term capital and of interest rates. Then, when a currency is in trouble, central banks can take internationally coordinated steps to bail it out. When there was a speculative run on the pound sterling in 1964, for example, world central bankers together with the IMF arranged a massive loan so that the Bank of England could stabilize the pound.

■THE "LIQUIDITY" PROBLEM.—As world trade has grown in the postwar years, there has been an increasing need for exchange reserves, which are required to tide countries over the inevitable swings that occur in their balance-of-payments positions.

The problem arises from two key facts about the postwar world: (1) the ability of the IMF to make emergency loans is limited, because the quotas of the member countries are small relative to the large requirements for reserves that resulted from the rapid growth of world trade; as a result, (2) world trade has expanded in the postwar years, but only because this shortage of reserves has been offset by a persistent deficit in the balance-of-payments of the United States. The effect has been a massive outflow of dollars, which, as will be remembered, are a key currency and therefore may be counted as reserves.

This trend has made the United States dollar, which plays a crucial role in international trade, particularly vulnerable to "hot money" flows. In 1965, for example, the short-term liabilities of the United States, readily convertible into gold, far exceeded the United States gold supply. At the same time, however, because world gold production is small, many economists feel that the growth of world trade, under the system that prevailed in 1965, depends on a continuing United States balance-of-payments deficit, so that a plentiful supply of dollars is available for international trade reserves.

To solve this dilemma, various schemes have been proposed. They have two characteristics in common: (1) to expand the supply of international reserves available to trading nations, and (2) to give the key currency countries the same freedom in international trade policies that other countries possess.

One of the best-known plans for international monetary reform is the *Triffin Plan,* devised by Robert Triffin of Yale University. His proposal is to turn the IMF into an international central bank with the power to create reserves much in the same way, for example, that the Federal Reserve System can create dollars. Another well-known scheme is the *Bernstein Plan,* put forward by Edward M. Bernstein, a government economic consultant. Under this plan, the IMF

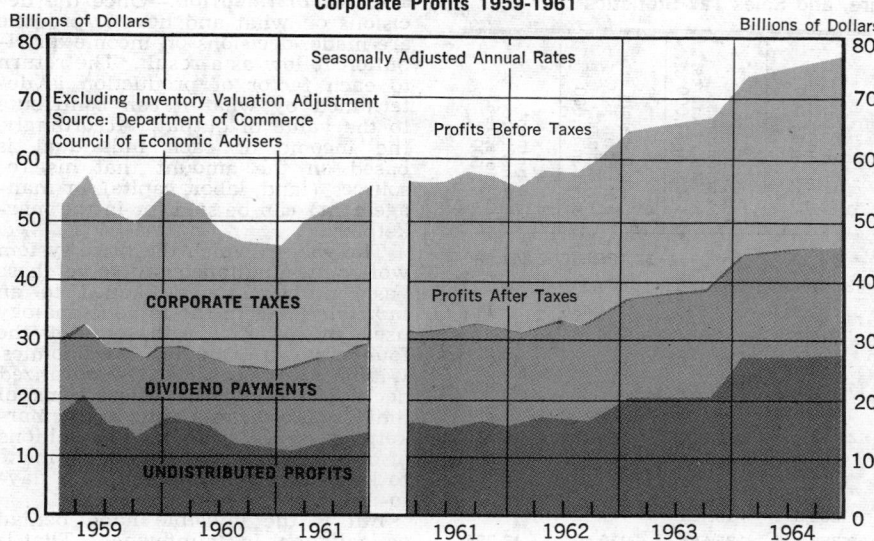

Corporate Profits 1959-1961

Billions of Dollars   Billions of Dollars

Seasonally Adjusted Annual Rates

Excluding Inventory Valuation Adjustment
Source: Department of Commerce
Council of Economic Advisers

Profits Before Taxes

CORPORATE TAXES

Profits After Taxes

DIVIDEND PAYMENTS

UNDISTRIBUTED PROFITS

would retain much of its current status, but quotas would be increased, and reserves would take the form of composite currency based on the underlying currencies of the member countries.

The lesson of postwar monetary relations shows that progress has been made because countries have been willing to substitute cooperation for individual action. Plans for reforming the world payments mechanism obviously depend on further steps in this direction. (See also *International Operations*, page 1769.)

Microeconomics.—Microeconomics is the study of the way in which societies solve their three most basic economic problems: (1) what goods and services shall be produced and in what quantities? (2) how shall these goods and services be produced? (3) how shall the goods and services be distributed among members of society?

As we have seen, three general methods blend when these questions are answered—those of the traditional economy, command economy, and market economy. Since most economic decisions in the United States are made by the market, we shall be concerned mainly with the market economy in this section.

The *market* itself is a system of exchange between buyers and sellers. The price system is central to the market economy's process of exchange. The function of the price system is to give signals that will show individual economic units how to make decisions. With these decisions, planners can simultaneously solve the three basic problems.

In the market economy, individuals and productive enterprises are assumed to act in a way that maximizes their satisfaction. Although economists are well aware that psychological satisfaction and pecuniary income may sometimes diverge, the ordinary assumptions are that consumers seek to get the most for their money, that producers seek to maximize their net returns by keeping

production costs down, and that the suppliers of services seek as much money as the market will bear.

■**LAWS OF SUPPLY AND DEMAND.**—Social decisions on what to produce are made by the forces of supply and demand in markets for products and services. The demand for each commodity or service may be described by a *demand curve* or *demand schedule*. Ordinarily the demand curve for each product obeys the law of demand, which states that the quantity of a commodity demanded (or the quantity that can be sold) increases as the price falls. Demand curves are signals given by consumers as to what they will buy and at what prices.

In a parallel way, *supply schedules* or *curves* are signals given by producers as to what commodities they are willing to produce and at what prices. The "laws of supply" differ in the short run and in the long run.

In the short run, the law of supply

Increased Demand: Its effect on supply and demand and schedules.

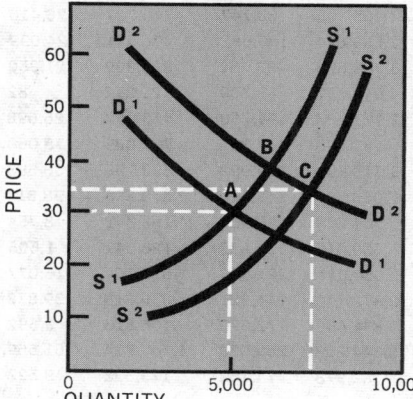

SUPPLY (S¹) equals demand (D¹) at point *A*. By raising price to *B*, increased demand (D²) draws more producers; the resulting price and supply (S²) can be predicted as *C*, where returns decrease to scale.

is analogous to the law of demand: the higher the price, the more producers are willing to supply. The long-run relation between cost and supply is more complex. If the effect of higher production of a commodity in the long run is to reduce the unit cost, the larger supply leads to lower prices and the commodity is said to be produced under conditions of *increasing returns to scale*. If increasing production has no effect on cost in the long run, the commodity is produced under *constant returns to scale*. If the effect of increasing production is to lead to rising long-run costs, then a commodity is subject to *decreasing returns to scale*.

The attempt to classify actual industries in accordance with these categories is treacherous. In the United States, however, most manufacturing industries are thought to enjoy increasing returns to scale, while most agricultural and mining

The Optimum Scale of Enterprise

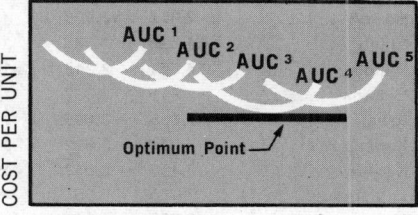

EXPANSION lowers a firm's average unit production costs (AUC) until its optimum size is reached; any further growth increases average unit production costs.

industries are thought to produce under decreasing returns to scale.

Decisions made from the signals given off by demand and supply curves determine the relative prices of all commodities and services. In general, when some change in tastes or other event makes consumers willing to pay more for some commodity, the effect in the short run is to raise the price of that commodity. In the longer run, more resources will be devoted to the production of that commodity and its price may be higher, the same, or lower than the initial price, depending on whether the commodity in question is produced under increasing, decreasing, or constant returns to scale. Thus, price and production are determined by consumer demand, shifting in accordance with changes in what consumers are willing to pay. The consumer, therefore, is sovereign in a market economy.

The price system also gives the signals that underlie decisions on how commodities or services should be produced. For these decisions it is the prices of the factors of production—land, labor, capital, and management—that count. In essence, given the technological alternatives that are available to producers, the decision on what to produce is made by choosing that combination of the factors of production that minimizes total costs.

United States Income, Expenditure, and Sales Tax Statistics

	A. Total Personal Income, 1965 in $1,000,000	B. Per Capita Income, 1965	C. State Sales and Use Taxes 1966, in %	D. Value Added* by Manufactures, 1963, in $1,000	E. Capital Expenditures for Manufactures, 1963, in $1,000	F. Cash Receipts from Farm Marketings, 1965, in $1,000	G. Government Payments to Farmers, 1965 in $1,000
UNITED STATES..	527,890	2,724				39,186,670	2,451,980
Alabama	6,613	1,910	4	2,342,124	152,130	660,640	35,705
Alaska	854	3,375	—	89,311	14,580	4,430	146
Arizona	3,716	2,310	3	617,413	49,154	506,264	7,514
Arkansas	3,490	1,781	3	958,687	72,210	915,507	17,221
California	59,476	3,196	3	17,157,242	955,769	3,709,991	41,258
Colorado	5,328	2,706	3	1,202,958	68,032	728,150	61,291
Connecticut	9,604	3,390	3½	4,477,894	212,905	153,182	688
Delaware	1,684	3,335	—	666,245	65,685	128,253	2,090
District of Columbia	2,942	3,673	3	260,511	13,491	—	—
Florida	14,049	2,420	3	2,326,335	185,666	979,494	17,295
Georgia	9,395	2,156	3	3,238,776	166,673	945,531	49,608
Hawaii	2,017	2,906	4	254,454	16,132	184,572	11,080
Idaho	1,618	2,338	3	365,695	28,140	526,059	29,234
Illinois	34,551	2,245	3½	14,557,060	775,365	2,400,626	139,834
Indiana	13,815	2,827	2	7,687,872	537,900	1,297,978	98,713
Iowa	7,163	2,595	2	2,275,928	126,707	3,009,510	228,800
Kansas	6,014	2,692	3	436,874	86,815	1,210,497	207,251
Kentucky	6,495	2,043	3	2,460,058	226,342	702,767	39,786
Louisiana	7,285	2,061	2	1,917,824	180,313	484,823	22,082
Maine .:.......	2,229	2,245	4	779,260	62,514	282,680	1,996
Maryland	10,612	3,014	3	2,978,013	174,087	328,257	6,197
Massachusetts ...	16,168	3,023	3	6,365,008	273,868	166,737	645
Michigan	24,737	3,009	4	13,003,804	721,073	789,437	53,325
Mississippi	3,636	1,556	3½	1,022,498	62,773	912,498	26,597
Missouri	11,820	2,628	3	4,424,148	208,209	1,241,094	119,357
Montana	1,701	2,409	—	234,783	27,960	420,501	51,057
Nebraska	3,800	2,573	—	743,087	46,063	1,355,289	184,703
Nevada	1,447	3,289	2	111,733	8,760	50,616	1,143
New Hampshire ..	1,719	2,570	—	654,075	28,865	52,960	695
New Jersey	21,965	3,242	3	9,980,065	520,578	265,378	4,741
New Mexico	2,292	2,227	3	170,453	9,491	258,031	22,349
New York	58,595	3,242	2	19,510,191	776,697	938,962	20,256
North Carolina ...	9,968	2,028	3	4,617,912	294,736	1,189,580	43,412
North Dakota	1,502	2,304	2¼	72,484	7,933	664,709	116,317
Ohio	28,857	2,816	3	15,443,018	856,498	1,113,372	76,384
Oklahoma	5,552	2,236	2	965,305	63,747	740,727	76,410
Oregon	5,309	2,794	—	1,569,824	130,582	476,511	24,099
Pennsylvania	31,436	2,728	5	13,968,675	793,752	825,929	21,350
Rhode Island	2,510	2,817	4	949,756	43,300	21,212	82
South Carolina ...	4,673	1,836	3	2,117,387	164,750	418,052	26,698
South Dakota	1,445	2,055	3	142,230	7,351	757,089	78,068
Tennessee	7,663	1,992	3	3,343,790	269,992	622,796	36,693
Texas	24,751	2,346	2	7,053,797	541,410	2,470,304	198,814
Utah	2,317	2,340	3	704,629	29,757	166,847	8,754
Vermont	929	2,340	—	309,416	15,837	128,647	1,606
Virginia	10,657	2,392	2	3,064,019	227,023	513,164	16,077
Washington	8,564	2,864	4.2	2,872,770	144,221	636,818	39,878
West Virginia	3,636	2,007	3	1,834,458	172,870	105,516	3,592
Wisconsin	11,115	2,682	3	5,344,282	280,059	1,249,774	51,569
Wyoming	843	2,479	2½	82,978	14,189	173,632	9,522

*Contribution made to the worth of raw materials or component parts by the manufacturing process; computed by deducting the value of parts and raw materials from the value of the final product.

Sources: Columns A, B, D, and E: U.S. Department of Commerce
Columns F and G: U.S. Department of Agriculture

■INCOME DISTRIBUTION.—Once the decisions on what and how to produce are made, decisions on income distribution follow as a result. The return to each factor of production is determined by what it can contribute to the value of output. Accordingly, the income of each individual is based on the amount that his resources (land, labor, capital, or management) can be sold for in the marketplace.

The way in which the price system works to simultaneously solve these basic problems was likened to an *invisible hand* in the famous analogy used by Adam Smith, one of the founders of modern economics. Without any conscious, centralized decision-making, the interactions of individual economic units in the marketplace serve to make the millions of decisions that a society must make to keep its economy going on a day-to-day basis.

But is the invisible hand benign or malignant in its influence? That is to say, do the prices in a market economy allow production to conform most directly to consumer desires? Are the methods of production those that produce commodities at a minimum drain on resources? Also, what kind of distribution of income will result from the marketplace?

The answers to these questions depend on the conditions of demand and supply in particular markets. Where markets produce optimum economic effects, at least in the short run, they reach what is called a *Paretian optimum,* named for the Italian economist Vilfredo Pareto (1848–1923). When an economy is in a Paretian optimum, *static efficiency* is at a maximum. That is to say, assuming that tastes and technology remain unchanged, there is no way that resources can be transferred from one use to another in a manner that will increase consumer satisfaction. In this happy state, resources are used in a way that most closely conforms with consumer preferences; production takes place under the lowest-cost combination of the factors of production; and income is distributed in such a way that the returns to the factors of production are equal to their actual contribution to production.

Economic analysis has shown that static efficiency is maximized when an economy's markets are perfectly or purely competitive. *Perfect competition* exists where everyone has perfect knowledge, where productive units are small compared to the total size of the market, and where there is complete mobility of the factors of production between different uses.

Perfect competition is an ideal state of affairs. But in the real world economists must also be concerned with *dynamic efficiency.* For in a world in which invention and innovation are the stuff of economic progress, it is not enough to make the best of a given state of technology. Rather, there is the problem of maximizing the rate at which new technology is introduced and other improvements made. And it is a commonplace of everyone's experience that industries in which the leading companies are big relative to the size of the market are often among the most dynamically efficient. The computer, auto, and chemical industries are obvious examples. At the same time, some industries characterized by small producers—apparel makers and coal miners, for example—are often among the most stagnant.

Therefore, social decisions about the kinds of markets that best serve the public interest come down to balancing the requirements of static efficiency against those of dynamic efficiency.

■**KINDS OF MARKETS.**—There are as many ways to classify markets as there are economists who are interested in the problem. However, most people would agree that the market depends on the number of sellers and the relations among them.

Monopoly exists when there is only one seller who is the sole source of supply of some commodity. In the U.S., for example, telephone services and electricity are ordinarily supplied by monopolists in each area. However, the prices charged by these *public utilities* are ordinarily regulated by the state.

Cartels come close to being monopolies. Here there is more than one seller, but the firms in the industry formally agree not to compete with each other. Rather, markets are divided up geographically or on some other basis. Cartels are illegal in the United States.

Oligopoly is a condition in which a few giant firms exist in a particular industry. There is no formal agreement (or collusion) among the companies. But there may be tacit collusion among sellers, which is carried on through price leadership or some other device. When the most technically efficient companies are large relative to the size of the market, oligopoly is an inevitable consequence. Most major manufacturing industries in the United States are oligopolies.

Imperfect or *monopolistic competition* exists where there are a large number of producers, but where the

Kinked Demand Curve: Oligopoly Theory

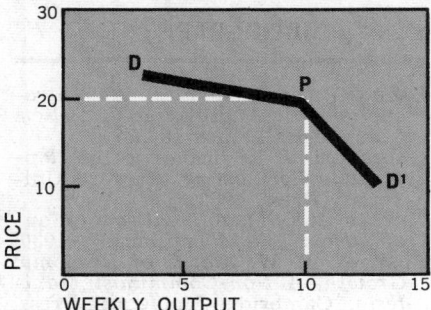

IN AN OLIGOPOLY, an individual firm's demand curve can be kinked: if it raises prices (P), demand (D¹) will decrease disproportionately, as other companies offer equivalent products for less; if it lowers prices, demand (D) may increase only slightly, as other firms will also cut prices.

BETTMANN ARCHIVE

TRUST-BUSTING Theodore Roosevelt inspired these comments on his fight with Big Business.

products sold are *differentiated* rather than *homogeneous*. Competition diverges from the ideal, because each seller (whether through location, advertising, or some other device) succeeds in making his product different from that of his competitor so that he can charge at least some of his customers a somewhat higher price. Gasoline stations, drugstores, and other retailers are examples of this kind of competition.

■**ANTITRUST LAWS.**—The efforts of the United States to make the marketplace serve the public interest are embodied in the history of the antitrust laws.

The basic charter of antitrust activity is the Sherman Antitrust Act of 1890, which was passed by Congress after a vigorous period of trust formation in the 1880's. The act makes it illegal to monopolize trade or conspire in restraint of trade. The Clayton Act (1914) in addition to excluding labor unions from antitrust action tried to define illegal behavior more specifically. The Federal Trade Commission Act (1914) gave the government powers to police competition. The Celler Antimerger Amendment to the Clayton Act (1950) made it illegal for one company to acquire the assets of another company when the effect is to reduce competition substantially.

As interpreted early by the U.S. Supreme Court, antitrust legislation was ordinarily subject to the so-called *rule of reason*: only unreasonable restraints of trade, such as collusion, were defined as coming under the scope of the legislation. In recent years, however, there have been some signs that the courts regard bigness itself as a violation of the antitrust laws, even if specific practices in restraint of trade cannot be moved. In the Alcoa case (1945), the Supreme Court ruled that a company with 90 per cent of the business in its field was violating the Sherman Act, even though unreasonable behavior had not been proved.

Subsequent decisions have tended to blur the precedent set by the Alcoa case. In a case involving cellophane, which was won by DuPont, the court was unable to declare that Du

Pont's production of cellophane (75 per cent of all cellophane produced) in itself constituted a monopoly.

The effects of the antitrust laws on business competition in the United States are difficult to gauge. However, two things are relatively certain: (1) the United States enforces its antitrust legislation more vigorously than any other country, and (2) as a possible consequence, ownership of industry is less concentrated than in other industrial countries. Indeed, in recent years, some European countries have instituted antitrust legislation that is almost a copy of American legislation.

■**WORKABLE COMPETITION.**—Recognizing that the economics of size make bigness inevitable in most basic industries, many United States economists have focused on the concept of *workable competition,* a term invented by John Maurice Clark (1884–1963). Proponents of the idea that workable competition is the appropriate goal of policy argue that perfect competition is neither feasible nor desirable. Instead, they say, the appropriate structure for industry is one that results in a good compromise between static efficiency and dynamic efficiency. In evaluating whether the performance of an industry serves the public interest, proponents of workable competition may ask these questions: Is the industry technologically progressive? Does price bear a reasonable relation to cost? Does the industry adopt collusive practices?

Not all United States economists, however, adhere to the concept of workable competition. Some argue that the companies that dominate most of the nation's basic industries are too big. Breaking the biggest ones up, they say, would clearly serve the goals of both static and dynamic efficiency.

■**SPECIAL TOPICS IN MICROECONOMICS.**—Even if the market operated in such a way as to bring about a Paretian optimum, the results could in certain respects be undesirable.

External Diseconomies. The least expensive method of producing electricity in some areas requires coal and throws a lot of smoke into the

THE AMERICAN ECONOMY: Six Decades of Growth

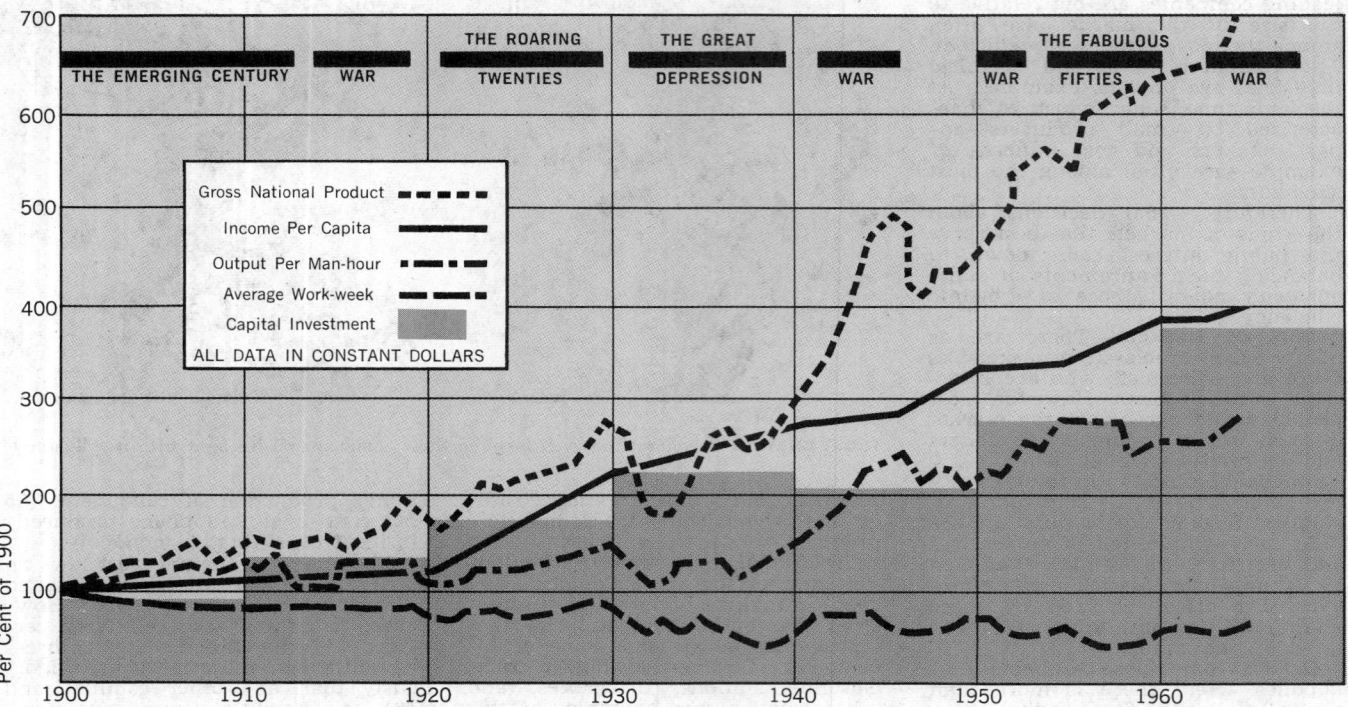

air. The air pollution that results is called an *external diseconomy*. Where maximizing private profit causes social harm, measures to make the market serve the public interest are often the consequence. Laws that control air and water pollution and those that conserve natural resources are well-known examples.

External Economies. Sometimes there is simply no way of marketing the service provided by some kind of investment. When high-level dams are built in the Far West, the electricity can be marketed through the price system, but flood-control benefits cannot be. Nonmarketable benefits that accrue to the public in cases like this are called *external economies,* and their existence explains why some kinds of investments are undertaken by the state.

Income Distribution. If the conditions of the Paretian optimum are met, the income of each factor of production is equal to the value of its contribution to production. But even under these circumstances, the distribution of income that results may be far from ideal.

The problem, of course, is that some members of society, perhaps through no fault of their own, are low-productivity workers who cannot earn enough in the market to provide a decent income. For this reason, society has always provided income supplements for some of its members, either through private charity or public benefits.

In recent years, through the so-called war on poverty, a serious attempt has been made to fight economic deprivation by training low-income individuals in the kinds of skills that the market rewards with an adequate standard of living.

Economic Growth.—The study of economic growth is at the frontier of economic research. If you ask the typical economist what an advanced industrial country should do to achieve full employment, he can give you specific, useful advice. If you ask him what an underdeveloped country should do to increase its growth rate, he may be able to speculate, but if he is realistic he will realize that his advice may be incorrect.

The problem of speeding the rate of economic growth is, obviously, most pressing in the underdeveloped countries of the world. There has been much speculation over the definition of underdevelopment. Practically, it means an average standard of living that is far lower than that of North America, Western Europe, and Australia and New Zealand. In the United States per capita income averaged about $3,000 in 1964. In the same year, only one in ten of the human race averaged more than $800 per year, and for millions annual per capita income was less than $100.

The problems that face the underdeveloped countries of Asia, Africa, and Latin America can be described simply enough by the *bathtub theorem,* which states that Accumulation equals Production minus Consumption. To grow at a decent speed, a society must produce considerably more than it consumes. In the underdeveloped countries, food and the other elementary requirements for subsistence comprise most of what is produced. Little is left for investment.

■**RAISING PRODUCTIVITY.**—The goal of underdeveloped countries, therefore, is to raise the margin of production over consumption. Economists have not yet devised a perfect recipe for doing this. However, analysis suggests that two factors are important.

Capital investment. Since the job of the underdeveloped countries is primarily to raise per-capita productivity, investment for the purpose of increasing productivity is essential. In addition to private capital, development economists stress the need for *social capital,* particularly roads, schools, and hospitals.

Education. The experience of the United States, perhaps, cannot easily be carried over to other countries. However, Robert Solow of the Massachusetts Institute of Technology has estimated that less than half the increase in productivity and real wages can be accounted for by an increase in capital itself. Improvements in methods of production, the education and training of labor, and technology are more important.

—William Wolman

BIBLIOGRAPHY

BACH, G. E. *Economics: An Introduction to Analysis and Policy.* Prentice-Hall, Inc., 1963.

GALBRAITH, J. K. *Economic Development in Perspective.* Harvard University Press, 1962.

KEYNES, JOHN M. *A Treatise on Money.* 2 vols. The Macmillan Co., 1930.

ROSTOW, W. W. *Stages of Economic Growth, A Non-Communist Manifesto.* Cambridge University Press, 1960.

SAMUELSON, PAUL A. *Economics: An Introductory Analysis.* McGraw-Hill, Inc., 1964.

SLOAN, HAROLD S. and ARNOLD J. ZURCHER. *A Dictionary of Economics.* Barnes & Noble, Inc., 1961.

SMITH, ADAM. *The Wealth of Nations.* Random House, Inc., 1964.

FINANCE

The Financial Function.—In any enterprise, the financial function is the management of the cash flow so that the means are always available to achieve the firm's objective as expeditiously as possible. Successful financial administration requires many acts: estimating and planning the flow of cash receipts and expenditures; raising from outside sources the needed funds unavailable from day-to-day operations; controlling operations to ensure a cash flow through the business according to previously adopted plans and handling deviations from the plans immediately so that the continuing financial health of the enterprise is not impaired; and dividing earnings between payments to the owners and investment into the future development of the business.

The basic activities of financial management, regardless of the type of organization, are financial planning; the actual financing of projected operations; financial analysis and control; and the disposition of net earnings. Most of our business operations are carried on by corporations (about 1,400,000 publicly and privately owned corporations file reports with the United States Treasury). This section, therefore, will deal exclusively with *corporate finance*. But a plumbing contractor, in business as a single (sole) proprietorship or a Wall Street brokerage and investment banking firm, organized as a partnership, can fail as quickly as a large corporation if financial operations are neglected or unskillfully conducted. A business can be successful only if it is efficient in the three basic divisions of management: production, marketing, and finance.

For the economy as a whole, the functions of finance are much broader. Many types of governmental and private financial institutions have been developed. They issue financial instruments, formulate policies, and employ procedures that are designed to counteract inflationary and deflationary movements; create an economic and social climate favorable to high levels of employment, a stable currency, a satisfactory economic growth rate, and a rising level of per-capita consumption—without creating an unmanageable balance-of-payments deficit with foreign countries.

In this sense, national financial management must be conducted to provide the following: (1) money that is convenient and efficient to use; (2) a flexible process of credit creation and credit cancellation; (3) an efficient accumulation of savings; (4) lending and investing funds stemming from both credit and savings; (5) financial markets for liquidity; (6) a free flow of information.

Financial Planning.—The departure point for estimating a firm's financial requirements is its projected dollar volume of sales. Sales are the life blood of any business because they furnish the dollars to meet current and long-term obligations and provide, if profitable, a return on the owner's investment and the funds for expansion and future profits.

Management must know what financial requirements a sales increase, say, of 20 per cent will entail. Must inventories be increased? Should new personnel be hired or trained? Will any additions become necessary in the plant (machines, handling devices, buildings)? Is warehousing space adequate? In short, will such a projected sales increase demand greater expenditures for operations and a greater investment in cash resources, accounts receivable, inventory, and fixed assets (plant and equipment), and will these funds come from internal sources or must the money be raised from outside sources? A projected sales decrease raises questions such as these: Did it occur in low- or high-cost items, low- or high-profit items? With projected lower financial requirements, should the amortization of a bond issue or a bank loan be accelerated, or will economic conditions soon change and assure again a higher sales volume? Should employees be laid off, and in what skill categories? Can they easily be rehired, or will a layoff now mean new training expenses later on? What does the company's contract with the labor union have to say about

NEW YORK STOCK EXCHANGE

WALL STREET, U.S. financial center, houses the stock exchange and many major banks.

seniority in this particular situation?

A word of caution is necessary here. Attaining a projected dollar volume of sales does not in itself spell success. A firm will often produce many items or services with varying costs of production and profit margins. A sales goal of $10 million can be reached by more than one route. For example, more lower-priced units could be sold, offsetting reduced sales of units that are higher-priced. But if the latter carry a substantial profit margin and if intense competition for sales in the former category reduces profits to the vanishing point, a serious problem could easily be created for the firm. The reduced earnings could make future financing either very costly or impossible.

When a company fails to meet projected sales, other questions must be raised. Among them: Why are the sales estimates not met? Who was at fault—the salesmen or the estimates themselves? Were the estimates unrealistic, considering foreseeable changes in the economic climate? Or did unforeseen and uncontrollable circumstances develop?

To estimate and plan the flow of cash receipts and expenditures successfully, tools are needed. These we call budgets.

■ **BUDGETS AND BUDGETING.**—Budgets are simply plans in writing that cover the operation of a business over a specified future period of time. Budgeting is applied planning in the broadest sense. In a well-managed business, all types of budgets are drawn up, ranging from sales, production, and research development to personnel budgets. We here are concerned with the cash budget.

The cash budget helps management to (1) anticipate and estimate funds needed over a given future period of time; (2) develop future internal and external sources for these funds; (3) estimate operating results. It is an all-inclusive forecast of cash that comes into the corporation and is thus available for financing operations, paying all maturing liabilities on schedule, and maintaining proper liquidity ratios that stabilize the credit rating of the firm and assure the expansion of activities. From the foregoing, it should be clear that estimating and planning the cash flow are much more than merely assembling estimates of cash requirements from the submitted budgets (plans) of the firm's departments and divisions, then balancing these requirements against money coming in from projected sales. Sales, production, inventory, personnel, pricing, and many other operations and policies must be critically analyzed in the light of the cash budget and changed where necessary to fit the overall objectives of management. The proper execution of the financial function of a business has many ramifications that are not always realized. The better this function is executed, the larger will be a firm's profits and the lower will be the needed investment in assets to reach a given profit objective.

CONSOLIDATED BALANCE SHEETS

XYZ MAGAZINE PUBLISHING CO., INC.

ASSETS		LIABILITIES AND STOCKHOLDERS' EQUITY	
CURRENT ASSETS		**CURRENT LIABILITIES**	
Cash	$ 7,875,000	Trade accounts payable	$13,892,000
Short-term investments and U. S. Government securities at cost	4,845,000	Salaries, commissions and other compensation	1,762,000
Accounts receivable:		Other accrued expenses	1,466,000
Installment accounts arising from subscriptions and sales of publications	26,822,000	Federal income taxes	2,745,000
Advertising and other	12,069,000	Current portion of long-term debt	37,000
Less allowances for newsstand returns, subscription cancellations and collection expenses	(7,310,000)	Total current liabilities	19,902,000
	31,581,000		
Recoverable federal income taxes	1,521,000	LONG-TERM debt less amounts due within one year	15,291,000
Inventories — at cost:			
Magazine paper, including $1,301,000 and $1,367,000 by last-in, first-out method	3,458,000		
Editorial articles and production costs applicable to future issues	1,943,000	UNEARNED SUBSCRIPTION REVENUES, net of related subscription selling expenses	4,270,000
Subscription promotion and other supplies	2,683,000		
	8,084,000		
Prepaid expenses and postage deposits	1,459,000		
Total current assets	55,365,000	RESERVE FOR DEFERRED FEDERAL INCOME TAXES	16,882,000
INVESTMENTS AND OTHER ASSETS			
Subsidiaries not consolidated — capital stocks at cost and advances	1,469,000		
XYZ Research Corporation	1,465,000	**STOCKHOLDERS' EQUITY**	
Cash value of life insurance policies	2,858,000	Preferred Stock, $100 par value, 5% cumulative, voting:	
Sundry investments, receivables and other assets	2,365,000	Authorized and issued — 6,000 shares	—
	8,157,000	Common Stock, $1 par value:	
		Authorized—4,000,000 shares	
PROPERTY, PLANT AND EQUIPMENT		Issued — 2,950,501 shares (less 6,086 shares held in treasury)	2,944,000
Land, buildings, equipment, etc. at cost	14,292,000	Capital surplus	8,826,000
Less accumulated depreciation and amortization	5,417,000	Earned surplus	14,086,000
	8,875,000		25,856,000
EXCESS OF COST OF INVESTMENTS in acquired companies over equity in tangible net assets at dates of acquisition, and other intangible assets	9,804,000		
	$82,201,000		$82,201,000

BALANCE SHEET for fictitious company illustrates method by which assets (cash, accounts payable, investments, property, and equipment) are weighed against liabilities (debts, salaries, and taxes) and stockholders' equity, to provide a summary of the firm's financial status.

Budgets start where the accounting statements leave off. A *balance sheet*, a profile of the business, indicates the condition of the business at a given moment. An *income statement* (a profit and loss statement) tells about the operational results over a given period of time. A statement of the *sources and uses of funds* shows the sources from which funds were made available over this period and what they were used for. A *cash budget*, on the other hand, estimates future cash receipts and disbursements and the projected balance-sheet and income-statement condition at the end of a future period.

A management that borrows money today for expansion, but returns to the capital market or the banker a few months later for additional funds, advertises to the world that it is not "on top of its affairs." It is clear to all concerned that such a management makes snap decisions. The firm's credit rating with lenders and its standing with investors will be quickly tarnished. Once a firm's reputation is lost, it takes a long time to recover it.

■ **FLEXIBLE BUDGETING.**—Budget estimates should not be looked upon as rigid outlines within which a department's operations should be confined and conducted. This would negate the very essence of budgeting, which

aims at the complete freedom of administrative action in order to assure the highest attainable profits. If a sales, production, or any other budget is out of line with actual conditions, say, two months after the formulation of the original budget, then the estimates ought to be revised to comply with the new developments. This is what is known as *flexible* or *variable budgeting*, a system generally in use today.

An erroneous forecast of how much to invest in cash, accounts receivable, or inventory is serious, but not fatal. These items are so-called *current assets*, "current" because they are considered as convertible into cash within one year or less. But suppose the error occurs in improper planning for plant and equipment, or *fixed assets*. The company could then find itself with idle plant capacity, especially if the plant is too large for the smaller, actual sales volume. In other words, the plant was built too large to conform to a sales projection that did not materialize. The result would be higher operating costs and lower profits, for plant and equipment costs are *fixed costs*, which do not change as the volume of output changes. The same plant and equipment costs spread over a smaller sales volume mean higher costs per unit of output. This is in contrast

with so-called *variable costs*, such as labor, fuel and power, and materials. These vary with output, but not necessarily in proportion with output. A larger production volume may mean lower materials costs because larger purchases of materials bring substantial discounts. It could also mean higher labor costs because overtime or a night shift may be involved.

If the sales forecast is too conservative and actual sales and demand run far beyond the estimates, the failure to commit sufficient resources to plant and equipment could mean a loss of leadership or position in the industry. This would weaken a firm's competitive position and consequently reduce its profits.

To be as accurate as possible, a budget forecast should cover a short period. But fixed-asset policy should be a long-term affair. This apparent conflict is reconciled by arranging for a budget period that is a composite of different periods. A year's forecast may serve very well as a basis for anticipating current asset requirements. A much longer projection is needed for the fixed-assets policy. For control purposes both periods are then broken into shorter periods.

Many factors have a bearing on the exact use of budgets: the type and size of the business involved; the stage of the business cycle; the existence of favorable contracts and connections with suppliers; and the experience, skill, and training of management. For example, one financial management might prefer to forecast financial requirements according to the number of days of sales represented by cash, receivables, inventories, and fixed assets, as well as liabilities such as accounts payable and tax and wage accruals. Another may wish to use historical data, recognizing that what happened in the past is likely to happen again.

Internal Sources of Funds.—A corporation has two main sources of funds—*internal* and *external*. A going concern "throws off" cash from day-to-day operations as inventories are used up in the production of goods that are sold. Delivery to the buyer produces either cash or, more usually, an "accounts receivable" item that later on, when paid, turns into cash. But there are other internal sources for the financing of modernization and expansion. They are primarily retained earnings and depletion and depreciation allowances. In addition to these, certain nonrecurring sources provide cash. Among them are sales of assets or plants no longer needed and tax refunds.

■**DEPRECIATION AND DEPLETION.**—The operations of the modern corporation cannot be understood unless one appreciates the significance of depreciation and depletion. Plant and equipment properties wear out and must be replaced. If a $10,000 machine can be expected to last 10 years, a company may "write off" $1,000 a year as depreciation. However, while depreciation is a charge to operations as real as labor or supply costs, it is not an expenditure. This $1,000 stays in the business and becomes immediately available for reinvestment in any asset deemed desirable. Over the 10-year period, the dollars originally invested in the machine will thus be recovered. In industry these charges annually provide huge amounts for reinvestment in fixed or current assets.

A mining or oil company would show, instead of "depreciation," an item called "depletion." As ore or oil in the ground is used up, the company sets up on its books a reserve to compensate for the natural resource that it has withdrawn and sold and which, therefore, the company no longer owns. Just as a manufacturing company must get back the cost of a machine, so an oil company must get back the cost of acquiring and developing a natural resource. On the books of a company we may find the item "properties, plants, and equipment" at cost *"less* accumulated depreciation and depletion." Such accumulated depreciation and depletion could also be shown as a liabilities reserve item. However, in this case it inflates the assets and liabilities of the corporation. To prevent that, the New York Stock Exchange requires that all industrial companies whose securities are traded on its floor show accumulated depreciation as a deduction from plant and equipment.

■**DEPRECIATION METHODS.**—The scrap value is usually deducted from the cost of the asset to be depreciated and the balance is then written off over the *physical* life of the asset. This is *depreciation* as applied to the ordinary wearing out of buildings and equipment. *Obsolescence,* which involves the economic life of an asset, refers to the loss of value caused by a changing technology. These depreciation expenses are important to business not only because they "throw off" cash, but also because they may be deducted before income for tax purposes is determined.

In addition to the *straight-line method,* under which each year of estimated useful life is charged with the same amount, *accelerated methods* of depreciation have come into use. Instead of charging $1,000 a year over a 10-year period to recover $10,000, we may charge 20 per cent on the declining balance. In this case, the first year would show a charge of $2,000 and the second year a charge of $1,600 (20 per cent of the remaining balance of $8,000). The third year the charge would be 20 per cent of $6,400 and so on.

Besides this *double-declining-balance method,* there is the *sum-of-the-year's-digits method.* Under it, the annual depreciation rate is represented by a fraction whose numerator is the number of years of useful life of the asset (in our case 10 years) and the denominator is the sum of the 10 years or 55 ($10 + 9 + 8 + 7 + 6 + 5 + 4 + 3 + 2 + 1$ equals 55). In the first year, 10/55 of $10,000 would be charged off and in the last year 1/55. These accelerated depreciation methods result in heavy charges during the early years and, since they are tax-deductible, cause more cash and hence assets to be retained in the business than is the case under the straight-line method. A deferred-tax liability is set up on the books, for heavier tax payments may come due during the later years of the depreciation period when these tax-deductible expenses decrease. The increased funds and the savings on taxes when reinvested will increase the firm's earning power for both the present and the future. This may be considered an offset to alleged underdepreciation, which results when original cost is used as base for depreciation during periods of rising prices.

Accounting practices have an important effect on reported earnings. When a company switches from a straight-line depreciation to an accelerated method, reported per-share earnings will decline because expenses are now larger.

■**INVENTORY ACCOUNTING.**—The method used for inventory accounting also has important financial implications. When prices are rising, the use of *FIFO* (first-in, first-out) as an inventory costing method will show higher reported earnings than the *LIFO* (last-in, first-out) method because the firm is working off its low-cost inventory, purchased when prices were lower. This will be true as long as prices advance. The situation is reversed when prices turn downward,

for the FIFO company will show inventory losses. Whether these losses will show up in the earnings report will again depend on accounting procedure. They could be charged to an inventory valuation reserve rather than to operating costs. *Weighted-average costs* will lead to still another earnings report.

Three facts must be clear about the use of the foregoing inventory costing methods. (1) Inventory profits are illusory when they are the result of inflationary price rises because a larger amount of funds will now be necessary to maintain the same inventory volume. By the same reasoning, these funds are not available for dividend payments or higher wages or salaries. (2) During periods of rising prices, the FIFO method will show larger assets because it is keeping the recently acquired high-cost inventory on the books. (3) Should prices decline, the LIFO method will put a company in a better competitive position because it has worked off its recently acquired high-cost inventory and can now use, for costing purposes, the lower-priced inventory.

■**LIABILITIES RESERVE ITEMS.**—The accounting treatment of gains or losses on the sale of assets no longer needed in the business, on inventories, or from patent royalties paid or received, has far-reaching effects on reported earnings. Instead of charging an inventory loss, or payments under a damage suit, to current operations, a firm charges it to a liabilities reserve item. A *valuation reserves* item is sometimes set up by transferring funds from the retained earnings account (the accumulation of a number of years of earnings plowed back) to which an inventory loss or a loss on the accounts receivable could be charged. Today, however, such reserves usually are directly deducted from the asset involved. For example, we read on a balance sheet "accounts and notes receivable (less estimated doubtful accounts)." Payments arising out of a lawsuit may be charged to a general *liabilities reserve* account. At other times, a contingency reserve is set up, again by decreasing the amount of retained earnings, or "surplus," as it is called.

These liability reserve items tend to make corporate statements confusing because they obscure the effect of losses and blur the time during which they were incurred. When such losses are not charged against income in the year in which they occur, the earnings for that year will be overstated.

Managements sometimes favor setting up *contingency reserves,* again through a transfer from the retained earnings account. This decreases "surplus" and thus discourages demands for higher dividends or wages that may be made on management when stockholders or employers mistakenly assume that "surplus" represents actual funds which can be paid out. No cash payment can be made out of a liabilities item. The firm has made money in the past, which it has already reinvested and which now appears on the asset side as part of plant, equipment, or inventory or other asset items. Managements like "contingency reserves" for still another reason: they can be used to equalize earnings over good and bad years by transferring excess earnings to such an account or by charging off losses to it. Security analysts and accountants object to such arbitrary procedures. They prefer to see earnings as they actually are. Both the New York Stock Exchange and the Securities and Exchange Commission insist that full disclosure of such liabilities-reserve items must be made to the stockholders.

Each type of these liabilities-reserve items has an effect upon income reported for a given period of operation and also upon the declaration of dividends. If a manager or analyst fails to understand the impact of accounting methods on the measurement of corporate income, he will be prone to errors in analyzing a company's cash flow.

A distinction must also be made between operating income and *nonoperating income,* often found on the income statement as simply "other income." A company may receive dividends and interest from a securities portfolio, or income from investment in a subsidiary or from rental properties, oil and gas leases, patents, or the like. These items should be kept separate from the operating income (the income from operations for which the company primarily exists). *Nonrecurring income* can be considerable at times. A plant or equipment may be sold or a tax refund received. As sources of financing, they tend to be of minor importance. Management must place its main reliance for the financing of operations, modernization, and expansion on the cash internally generated from day-to-day operations and especially on depreciation and depletion allowances and on retained earnings.

External Sources of Financing.—When needed funds cannot be generated from internal sources, management must go to outside sources for accommodation. Two questions must be decided: (1) Shall it be short- or long-term financing? (2) Shall the funds be obtained from creditors or (new) owners? Short- and intermediate-term funds are always obtained as a result of a credit transaction. This always involves a promise to repay a sum of money at some future date. Long-term financing could be obtained either through the sale of long-term promissory notes (bonds) or shares (ownership money or, briefly, equity). When it seeks outside financing, management must make a compromise between assuming the risk inherent in a repayment schedule, whose violation can mean bankruptcy; sharing income with new stockholders, who as owners will share any residual income with the old owners; and possible loss of control if management is voted out.

■ **SHORT-TERM LIABILITIES.**—The right-hand side of the balance sheet will reveal the use of short-term or long-term creditor funds. Under "current liabilities," (that is, any debt that matures within one year or less) we find "accounts payable," "notes payable," and "accruals."

Accounts Payable.—These represent "trade credit." No credit instrument is employed. Goods are sold on open book (say, 2 per cent 10 days, net 60 days); the seller then has an asset item "accounts receivable" and the buyer, a liabilities item "accounts payable." It is a very convenient and informal arrangement, but tends to be expensive. The interest cost per annum to the purchaser of not taking the 2 per cent cash discount by paying within 10 days and paying instead in 60 days is about 14 per cent. Borrowing from a commercial bank is on a more formal basis, but it is decidedly cheaper.

Notes Payable.—When a firm borrows from the bank, the asset item "cash and due from bank" rises and so does "notes payable" on the other side of the ledger. At times, such a designation represents a loan by a finance company, officers, or owners. Past-due accounts are sometimes collected through first obtaining a short-term note from the debtor.

Temporary or seasonal financing needs are usually filled through short-term bank loans. Commercial banks, however, frown on frequent renewals because they tend then to become partners rather than creditors. If the bank in periods of tight money requires a "20 per cent compensatory balance," a deposit of 20 per cent of the borrowed amount, the cost of bank credit rises. Sometimes, a company will sell accounts receivable to a factor "without recourse" rather than show a note payable. At other times, accounts receivable are sold "with recourse" to the seller; should any invoice not be paid within the stipulated period of time the seller is liable; the accounts can also be pledged for a loan. Such "contingent" liabilities should be shown on the balance sheet. Caution must be exercised when comparing the cost of financial accommodation with different types of lenders so that dissimilarities in services are properly accounted for.

Another way to raise short-term funds is to sell *commercial paper* in the money market, in which debt securities with a maturity up to one year are traded. The single-name notes, in convenient denominations, are made payable to the order of the issuer (borrower) and then endorsed by him in blank to make them negotiable. This type of paper is usually sold through a dealer (an investment banking house) or sold directly to an insurance company or pension fund. Like treasury bills, the commercial paper is traded at a discount, bears no interest, and matures at par. The rate tends to be lower than for a bank loan and a borrower can thus keep his line of credit at the bank open. While his credit standing is improved by such sales, the borrower's relationship is strictly impersonal and the notes must be repaid promptly at maturity.

Equipment is often bought under a bank term loan that matures in five or seven or up to ten years. Such loans include specific security provisions, unlike the usual short-term bank loan. An alternative to term borrowing would be the installment (conditional) sales contract. The cost here is higher than under a bank term loan.

Accruals.—These items represent accumulations of indebtedness up to the day the books are closed. They will not be due until a future date; the funds represented by these debts can meanwhile be used in the operation of the business. Accrual items include primarily wages and salaries due, but as yet not paid, and taxes owed to federal, state, and local governments.

■ **LONG-TERM LIABILITIES.**—A company's long-term debt is called its *funded debt;* it is evidenced by the sale of long-term secured or unsecured promissory notes. These notes, usually called bonds, may be secured by (1) first or second mortgages; in the latter case they are usually given as "general" mortgages on plant and equipment; (2) securities of other corporations; (3) equipment alone; (4) all assets not otherwise pledged. The bonds would be classified as (1) first mortgage or general mortgage bonds; (2) collateral trust bonds; (3) equipment trust obligations; (4) debentures.

A company's ability to issue debenture bonds depends upon its general credit rating. If no other type of bond is placed ahead of them, they are the equivalent of first mortgage bonds. At times, they are issued as subordinated debentures, subordinate to one or more other creditors; in that case, they are often made convertible into stock at a given price or ratio. Convertibility, however, can be a feature attached to any bond, in which case the interest rate will be less than on a so-called straight bond. A corporation may achieve the same effect by selling its bonds with warrants that entitle the owners to buy a certain amount of stock at their option for cash at a stipulated price.

All the aforementioned obligations are straight bonds. Failure to pay interest, and of course principal, would be an act of default. *Income bonds,* on the other hand, may miss paying interest without bringing the consequences of default. In this case, interest need only be paid when it is earned by the corporate debtor. Usually the interest is cumulative for three or four years and there is a definite promise to repay the principal when it falls due. For all bonds, a separate debt contract or covenant is signed, called the *indenture;* it spells out the rights and obligations of the debtor, the bondholders, and the trustee, usually a bank whose duty it is to protect the bondholders in seeing that the debtor fulfills his obligations. Such provisions can, at times, severely limit management's freedom of action.

Corporations like to issue bonds for several reasons. (1) As long as the debtor meets the conditions laid down in the indenture, bond holders cannot vote. (2) The interest on bonds is tax-deductible, unlike the dividends paid on preferred or common stock; however, sinking-fund pay-

–1966– High	Low	Stocks	Div.	Sales in 100s	Open	High	Low	Close	Net Chg.
36	23¼	Gen Cable	1	357	26⅞	28	26⅞	28	+1½
33⅜	23	Gen Cig	1.20	13	23	23½	23	23½	....
66½	38½	GenDynam	1	122	44¾	44⅞	43¾	43¾	– ½
120	80	Gen Elec	2.60	237	86¾	88⅛	86½	87¾	+1⅝
83	62¾	Gen Fds	2.20	72	66¾	67½	66½	66¾	+ ⅛
64¾	32⅛	GenInstr	.96t	403	56½	57¼	54	54	–2⅜
63⅞	52	GenMills	1.50	12	57¼	57½	56⅞	57	+ ¾
49⅜	48	G Mills	pf1.75	5	48¾	48¾	48¼	48¼	+ ¼
108¼	70¼	GenMot	3.05e	409	76¼	76⅝	75⅞	76	+ ⅛
111½	92¾	G Mot 5pf	5	13	96	96¾	96	96¾	+ ⅞
85⅛	69	G Mot	pf3.75	5	72½	73	72½	73	+1¼
15¼	10	GenPCem	.80	40	10¼	10⅜	10⅛	10¼	....
64⅞	39	GenPrec	1.20	484	65½	66½	65⅛	65⅛	+ ⅞

THE WALL STREET JOURNAL

DAILY STOCK REPORT. The first two columns show the high and low prices for the current year. "Sales" column shows the number of shares of stock bought and sold on that day. "Open" gives the price at which the first sale of the day was made. The next two columns give the high and low prices. "Close" shows the price at which the last transaction was made. "Net chg." gives the difference between today's last price and yesterday's last price, + if the stock is up; — if the stock is down. Prices are quoted in dollars per share, but sales are made in 100-share lots (except for "odd-lot" buyers).

ments, the annual repayments on debt, are made after income taxes so that a heavy repayment schedule in connection with deferred tax liabilities coming due and a falling off in sales could be embarrassing for a firm. (3) The use of fixed-income senior securities is referred to as *trading on the equity* or *leverage*. The returns available to the owners and stockholders will be increased if the interest paid on the bonds is less than the rate of return earned by the business on its total capital employed. Leverage is a two-edged sword. If the company fails to earn the required bond interest, or if all the earnings are swallowed up by interest payments, the price of common stock quickly declines and closes that avenue of financing to management. This, too, could prove embarrassing. The company cannot keep on selling bonds without increasing its equity, either by plowing back earnings or by selling more equity, because bondholders do not wish to assume an excessive amount of the risk without sharing in the profits.

Bonds can be sold directly to one or more institutional investors, such as life insurance companies, or they can be placed "directly" through an investment banker as agent. In either case, registration with the Securities and Exchange Commission can be avoided and a prospectus need not be furnished to the investor. This saves a considerable amount of money. However, life insurance companies have a reputation for drawing up a very tight and detailed debt covenant and charging a little more than the bonds could be sold for in the market. Offsetting this is the ease with which life insurance companies change the indenture for good cause and a "take-down" privilege, allowing the corporation to take down funds as needed without paying the full interest on the bond issue. They will also often act quickly so that good bond markets are not missed.

Bonds can also be sold to the public through an investment banker, who may obtain the bonds through a sealed bid in a competitive bidding process or through direct negotiation with the issuer. In this case, the bonds must be registered with the SEC and a prospectus must be furnished to the investors. The prospectus is a boiled-down version of the registration statement, containing all the essential facts for the investor.

■**PREFERRED STOCKS.**—Preferred stocks are a cross between a bond and a common stock. If a firm "passes" (misses) four to six quarterly dividends, holders have limited voting rights, such as electing a certain number of individuals to the company's board of directors. They have priority over common stockholders as to income and, usually, also to assets in case of liquidation. The securities are usually cumulative and can be called for redemption, as is true of bonds. At times, they are sold as convertible preferred stock. Except for utilities, little preferred stock is sold today. The individual investor feels it gives him all the disadvantages of a bond and none of the advantages of a common stock. The return is usually limited, but the claim to income and assets is inferior to that of a bond. He cannot share in the prosperity of the company, yet he is subject to the erosion of his capital through inflation as is the bondholder. Corporate investors enjoy an 85 per cent tax exemption on most preferred dividends under the federal income tax laws so that there is today practically no distinction between the yield of bonds and preferred stock. For the corporate issuer, preferred dividends are not tax deductible and no dividends can be paid on the common stock when the preferred stock has been passed by. This makes financing through common stock impossible, depriving the company of financial flexibility. Management, therefore, looks upon preferred dividends as fixed as bond interest payments are, but without the benefit of tax deductibility. Probably another reason for the decline in preferred stock financing has been the ease with which sale and leaseback arrangements can be worked out. A company may sell its plant to an insurance company and then lease it back for its continued use. This type of financing has tax advantages unlike the preferred stock route.

■**COMMON STOCK.**—The remaining items on the liabilities side of the balance sheet are stock outstanding and surplus or retained earnings. They represent the ownership in the corporation. Preferred stock is usually not included, for equity money is permanent capital.

The advantages of common stock financing are (1) reduced dependence on creditors, particularly during bad times; (2) danger of insolvency is greatly reduced because no fixed interest payment or maturity schedule exists; (3) no cash drain because of the absence of interest and amortization (sinking fund) payments; (4) when stock prices are rising, common stock can be sold easily.

But issuing more fully voting stock means more voters who may before long disagree with the old management and owners. It also means a dilution of the equity, spreading earnings over a larger number of shares. Corporations, therefore, like to issue new equity in the form of convertible bonds, more rarely convertible preferred stock, which gives them an opportunity to build up earnings before the total number of outstanding shares is increased. Common-stock dividends are also not a tax-deductible expense under the federal income tax; moreover, common-stock financing costs more. The investment banker through whom the stock is usually distributed will charge more than for a bond issue and the common stock must be sold on a higher yield basis than debt.

When management makes a decision on likely sources for new external financing, it must balance risk, income, and control. Above all, it must retain its financial flexibility. Once the gate is closed to common stock financing, because of passing a preferred dividend or because stock markets are unfavorable to new issues, debt financing will soon also come to an end. Creditors are always looking for a comfortable equity cushion as protection and as shock absorber. If management has properly estimated and planned its cash flow, controls its operations, and is aware of costs, whatever external financing decision it makes will be as sound as human beings can make it.

Controlling Operations.—Control is made up of three divisions: (1) measurement of corporate performance against budgetary objectives; (2) evaluation of the different departments' and subdivisions' performances through comparing the operating results with previously established standards; (3) modifications in policies, budget estimates, and procedures as deviations occur in order to improve operational performance.

Budgets, as pointed out before, are extremely useful in setting up estimates that can serve as measurements for judging actual performance. But one should not overlook the contribution that nonbudgetary devices can make for effective control. In addition to regular reports and analyses in connection with budgets, *special studies* will spot opportunities for cost improvement or more effective use of invested capital. Originally, *internal auditing* was looked upon as solely concerned with accounting methods, procedures, and systematic behavior. Today, internal auditing has become management auditing—to evaluate the quality of corporate management as reflected in policies, procedures, and effectiveness of methods. These devices can help greatly to ensure that budgeting will remain a tool of financial management and not become an end in itself. When conditions change, budgets must be revised to conform to the overall goal of the firm. Too often, a budget becomes a cloak under which inefficient management can hide because the bases by which policies are translated into numerical terms have become too loose and it is now possible to achieve greater output than the budgetary norm had originally indicated. This is why the flexible budget is so widely in use.

■ANALYSIS BY STATIC RATIOS.—Forecasting, budgetary and nonbudgetary procedures go only so far. Management must also review and analyze operations through a study of financial ratios. Its creditors, investors, and security analysts will also make such ratio analyses. Static ratios are balance sheet ratios that indicate a certain condition. The firm may be solvent or insolvent, or it may operate on a desirable financial level or not. The following ratios will reveal that. By calculating ratios between two factors on a balance sheet, then observing how these ratios change from time to time, management can see financial trends.

Working capital is the difference between current assets and current liabilities. An adequate working capital means the company can carry on day-to-day activities without financial pressure and can meet emergencies and losses without trouble. To guard against an excessive investment in inventory, the ratio *inventory: working capital* can be measured. Or the *quick assets* can be calculated: cash, cash equivalent, and accounts receivable are divided by current liabilities. Or the *acid-test ratio* is applied; that is, cash and cash equivalents only are divided by current liabilities. A *current ratio* (current assets: current liabilities) could be 8:1, but if too much money is tied up in inventory (raw materials, goods-in-process-of-production, finished inventory, or supplies) and slow-paying accounts receivables,

and if a large amount of current liabilities should mature soon, a problem could arise. These *liquidity ratios* show the firm's ability to meet its maturing debts on schedule.

Creditors like to measure the degree to which the business is financed by owners, compared with the funds they provide to the owners. They like to see a low *debt: equity* ratio. Management must know how many times all fixed charges (interest, rentals, leases, etc.) have been earned. This is known as the *coverage factor.* Another ratio, *current liabilities: net worth* shows how much the owners have in the business as opposed to funds supplied by short-term creditors. Bonds are difficult to sell if the equity is too thin with respect to current liabilities. Creditors also want to know how much equity has been invested in fixed assets, with their low turnover rates and questionable market value in a recession. These *leverage ratios* are important for two reasons: (1) failure to exploit leverage lowers per share earnings; (2) excessive leverage, with a consequent reduction in the coverage factor, means debt securities cost too much or might be impossible to market, aside from the high risk factor assumed by the owners.

■ANALYSIS BY DYNAMIC RATIOS.—Dynamic ratios indicate the efficiency with which the business operates. *Sales: merchandise* is derived by dividing the net sales by the total inventory. The higher this ratio, the higher the merchandise turnover is likely to be. *Sales: fixed assets* indicates the productivity of the fixed assets in terms of sales and the justification for investing in them, if they are properly valued. *Sales: receivables* reveals total sales and the sales for which payments have not been received. Bad collection of accounts could mean that some of these accounts should be written off or that the credit management is bad. The *sales: net worth* ratio is found by dividing net worth into sales. It indicates the sales activity of the invested capital. An increase in this ratio is favorable to creditors, unless it is the result of a decline in net worth rather than a sales increase.

Gross (or net) operating margins are found by relating gross (or net) operating profit to sales. These ratios show to what degree unit selling prices could decline without inflicting a loss on the firm. Management also wants to know the rate of return on funds invested for the operations of the firm and how productive these resources have been to the owners. In the former case, the ratio of *gross income (after taxes) : total assets* is used; in the latter, the ratio of *net profit (after taxes) : net worth.*

Ratios are like green, amber, and red lights for management. A low total-asset turnover indicates that idle capacity or obsolete equipment exists. A falling coverage factor indicates that the limit of debt financing either has been or is being reached. A declining working capital

in the face of rising sales indicates that working capital is being shifted into fixed assets, which could cause a company to become a candidate for a merger under unfavorable terms, despite a good profit margin. In short, with financial ratios management can judge the progress of the firm, particularly when the ratios are observed over a period of time to reveal trends.

Disposition of Net Earnings.—Once the earnings have been established (a process which, as has been shown, is not too easy), dividend policy determines the division between payment to shareholders and retained earnings. Owners have no "right" to profits until dividends have been declared by the directors. Their judgment is final; they determine whether a dividend shall be paid and in what form, not the stockholders. The courts hesitate to substitute their judgment for that of management, unless judges are convinced that the directors are actuated by a motive other than the best interest of the stockholders. A company's dividend policy will be determined by many factors: the needs of the business as determined by its cash position; maturing debt obligations; the rate of asset expansion; the opportunities for using retained earnings; the effect of a dividend decision on the price of the stock; the ability of selling more stock in the future; the desires of the stockholders; and the stability of earnings.

The disposition of profits is closely associated with the function of financing and financial control. Managers must exercise a high degree of judgment in setting a dividend pattern. They know that investors interested in income are willing to pay more for the stock of companies with a stable and increasing dividend record than for the stock of companies with an erratic payments record. They also know that the dividend policy determines the extent of internal financing.

—Philipp H. Lohman

BIBLIOGRAPHY

CORRIGAN, FRANCIS J. and WARD, HOWARD A. *Financial Management —Policies and Practices.* Houghton Mifflin, 1963.
DAUTEN, CARL A. and WELSHANS, MERLE T. *Principles of Finance— Introduction to Capital Markets.* South-Western Publishing Co., 1964.
GUTHMANN, HARRY G. and DOUGLASS, HERBERT E. *Corporate Financial Policy,* (4th ed.). Prentice-Hall, Inc., 1962.
HELFERT, ERICH A. *Techniques of Financial Analysis.* Richard D. Irwin, Inc., 1963.
HUNT, PEARSON, WILLIAMS, CHARLES M. and DONALDSON, GORDON. *Basic Business Finance.* Richard D. Irwin, Inc. 1966.
MILLER, DONALD E. *The Meaningful Interpretation of Financial Statements. The Cause-and-Effect Ratio Approach.* American Management Association, 1966.

SCIENTIFIC DECISION-MAKING TOOLS

Science of Management.—In the years since World War II, ideas and procedures have been developed, whose general purpose is to aid and improve managerial decision-making in industry, government, and the armed forces. Many of these ideas and techniques fall under the heading "operations research" or "management science," terms which are interchangeable. Although some work that now might be classified as operations research was carried on earlier, the term itself first appeared in connection with the solution of British military operational problems during World War II.

The terms operations research and management science are quite descriptive designations. Workers in this field do research in operations and apply scientific methods to solve managerial problems. The approach is rational and quantitative, and the techniques demand complex tools that require a high level of competence and sophistication to master. The methods derive mainly from statistics, mathematics, economics, and the physical and behavioral sciences. An increasing number of universities offer doctoral programs in this field, and many practitioners feel that this is the level of training required for competent practice.

Operations research may be viewed as both a conceptual approach and a group of procedures whose purpose is to optimize attainment of an objective or group of objectives. The optimal fulfillment of goals may be in terms of maximizing benefits, minimizing costs, or some other measure of the best utilization of resources. In brief, the method consists of identifying alternative courses of action, ascertaining their outcomes, and specifying decisions in terms of the organization's objectives or goals. A "model" is constructed, usually mathematical, which represents the operation or problem under study. A solution is derived from the model; that is, values of the relevant factors are obtained which optimize the attainment of the specified goals. The procedures, therefore, frequently change complex management prob-

lems (which may seem too chaotic or too uncertain to handle, except by intuition) to rational structures that can be analyzed by quantitative, objective methods.

The Decision Problem.—Managerial decision-making has become much more complex as the American economy and the business units within it have grown larger and more intricate. However, regardless of the type of decision—whether it involves long-range or short-range consequences; whether it is primarily in finance, production marketing, or some other area; whether it is at a relatively high or low level of managerial responsibility—certain characteristics of the decision problem are seen to exist:

(1) A need is recognized for a change in the current method of operation or organization.

(2) One or more objectives or goals are to be achieved. Recognizing the need for change implies that there is current dissatisfaction with the existing levels of accomplishment of these objectives.

(3) There are one or more individuals charged with the responsibility for making the decisions.

(4) There are two or more alternative courses of action. The problem is usually viewed as one of choosing the best of these alternatives.

(5) There are a host of environmental factors or conditions which affect the achievement of the objectives. These are generally thought of being outside the control of the decision maker.

(6) The various results, arising from the interplay of the environmental factors, are often referred to as "states of nature," "states of the world," or simply "outcomes." The consequences of the choice of action depend on the action selected and also upon the state of nature that prevails.

(7) There is uncertainty about the states of nature which will exist after the decision is made. The interplay of the action selected and the particular outcomes that occur determine the net benefits of the decision.

The Use of Models.—One outstanding characteristic of the scientific decision-making approach to business problems is the use of mathematical models. A model is simply a representation of some aspect of the real world. In industry, the use of mechanical models is well known. For example, airplane models may be tested in a wind tunnel, or ship models in an experimental water basin. Experimentation is carried out on the models by varying relevant factors and observing the corresponding changes in the performance of the model. Thus, the models may be manipulated and inferences may be drawn about their real-world counterparts. Alternatively, if no models were used and experimentation were carried out after the airplanes or ships were built, the cost and time to acquire the necessary operational information would be vastly increased. As a practical matter, in many instances, the range of experimentation possible with models would simply not be possible with the airplanes or ships themselves.

■ **BUSINESS MODELS.**—Analogously, mathematical models can represent many business operations or business problems. They state, in mathematical terms, the relationships among all the variables. The models may be manipulated by changing the magnitudes of the controllable variables in the system, and responses can be observed that measure such important variables as net profit, production costs, and the like. Predictions can be made from these models of changes that would take place in the real world, and insight can be gained into how sensitive the achievement of overall objectives is to changes in the system's component factors. The overall purpose of such models is to seek out the best combinations of factors under the control of the decision-maker, thus making the organization's goals and objectives more obtainable. By simulating changes in the business system or business problem, researchers can examine and test alternative managerial policies and procedures. If the problem is substantial in size and the mathematical model is therefore complex and detailed, the most efficient way to manipulate the model is with electronic computers. The rich variety of models for business decision-making is discussed in the next section.

Management Science Methods in Business.—There is no clear consensus on which methods are to be classified exclusively as management science or operations research techniques. As indicated earlier, among the distinguishing characteristics of the field is the application of scientific method and quantitative formulation of problems. However, other approaches can similarly claim these char-

SIMULATION by computer of inventory control system shows future trends, allowing the planning of buying policies in advance.

© BURROUGHS CORP. USED WITH PERMISSION.

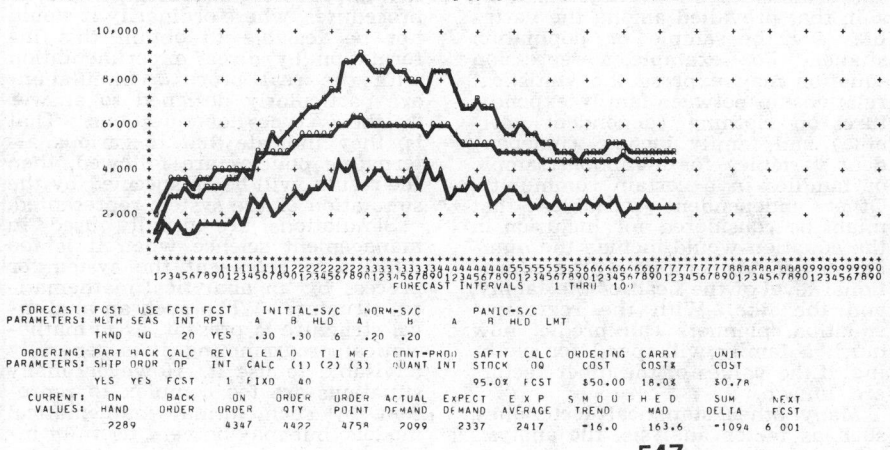

teristics. Furthermore, a classification of techniques alone would not describe adequately the apparatus with which management science practitioners solve business problems. Scientific disciplines such as mathematics, statistics, and economics are employed as well as specific techniques which may or may not fall rather clearly within one or another of these areas. The essence of management science is the use of one or more logical, scientific, or quantitative methods to resolve business problems. Therefore, in the discussion which follows, scientific disciplines as well as specific techniques or tools are included.

Probability and Statistics.—There are two fields of knowledge that have become basic disciplines for many modern management science techniques for decision-making: probability and statistics. The theory of probability is a branch of mathematics that deals with the subject of chance phenomena. It specifies the mathematical laws that govern operations, processes, or experiments that upon repetition yield alternative results. The outcome in any particular trial is not known with certainty, but probability theory develops the mathematical models by which to predict the relative frequency of occurrence of outcomes when many repetitions of the experiment are conducted.

Another view is that probability calculations summarize degrees of belief, or "betting odds," to be placed on these variable outcomes. In this context, statistics may be viewed as a field that is primarily concerned with applying probability theory to draw usable conclusions from the experiments. However, statistics is usually much more broadly conceived to include the design of the experiments from which data are generated, and the collection, analysis, and interpretation of these data. A modern interpretation is that statistics is essentially a theory of experimentation and decision-making for situations where uncertainty is present. Statistical models are particularly useful in management science applications involving complex business situations, where many variables affect possible outcomes.

■**STATISTICAL TECHNIQUES.**—Techniques or subject areas included under the heading of statistics which have been widely employed in industry include sampling, hypothesis testing, statistical estimation, regression analysis, and many others.

Sampling refers to the process by which some elements are drawn from a larger group (known as the "statistical universe" or "population") to test one or more hypotheses concerning the statistical universe or to draw inferences about it. If these samples are drawn in such a way that the probability of inclusion of every population element is known, that is, if "probability" or "random samples" are drawn, statements about the universe can be made with known degrees of precision. Sampling techniques are frequently utilized in quality control, production control,

inventory control, market research, financial problems, and many other business areas.

Hypothesis testing refers to decision-making procedures applied when information has been obtained through random sampling. Decision rules are constructed which select alternative courses of action (hypotheses), with measurable probabilities of making wrong decisions. For example, the alternative hypotheses may concern the proportion of consumers who are in favor of a change in a certain industrial product, the percentage of defective items in an incoming shipment of material, or the average family income in a metropolitan area. In each case, two or more alternative hypotheses are formulated, a random sample is drawn from the appropriate statistical universe, and then choices are made among the alternative hypotheses, based upon preselected criteria concerning risks in making incorrect decisions.

Statistical estimation pertains to the estimation of unknown values of percentages, averages, or other characteristics of a universe or population. For example, an automobile manufacturer may be interested in estimating the average price paid for new automobiles in a certain year by purchasers in New England, or a market researcher may be interested in the percentage of customers who purchase a certain brand of breakfast cereal. If random samples are drawn from the appropriate populations, estimates can be made of the desired values with determinable magnitudes of sampling error. The various television-rating polls, as well as political polls, are typical examples here.

Regression analysis is a technique for studying the relationships between two or more factors or variables. The basic purpose of the analysis is to establish a mathematical equation by which to predict the value of one of these variables (known as the *dependent* variable) from known values of one or more other variables (designated as the *independent* variables). The regression equation is established from statistical data drawn from an appropriate sample or population. The equation represents in mathematical form the best relationship to the data and establishes the average relationship that prevailed among the variables for the sample or population studied. For example, a regression equation may express the statistical relationship between family expenditures on clothing (dependent variable) and family income (independent variable) for a random sample of families in a certain community. Other independent variables that might be considered for inclusion in the equation would include the number of persons per family, the educational level of the head of the family, and the like. With the regression equation, planners can predict how much a family will spend for clothing, if the values of the other factors are known.

Many other statistical techniques, such as factor analysis, the analysis

of variance, discriminant analysis, and time series analysis, are available as aids in planning and decision-making in business. Operations research methods use these probability and statistical principles, as well as other mathematical and logical techniques. A number of the best known and most important operations research techniques will be discussed under the classifications of mathematical programming, simulation, and decision theory models.

Mathematical Programming.—Mathematical programming is a set of mathematical procedures whose purpose is to derive the optimal solution to problems that contain a very great number of possible alternatives. Applied to problems in business, these procedures point out the best way to achieve a specified objective. The objective or goal is expressed as some measure of effectiveness, such as profits, output, or cost. The mathematical programming procedure shows how the greatest amount of profit or output, or the least amount of cost, can be obtained. The problem generally involves allocating resources (men, machines, capital, and materials) among a large number of competing demands. Mathematical programming specifies the best allocation of these resources to achieve the highest profit or other appropriate measure of desired performance. The various types of mathematical programming include linear programming, quadratic programming, dynamic programming, and integer programming. Of these, linear programming has had the greatest number and widest variety of applications to business problems.

Simulation.—Another technique useful for analyzing alternative courses of managerial action is simulation. To simulate, in layman's terms, is to create an entity that has the characteristics of another object. In management science, simulation pertains to the creation and analysis of a model that represents an operational situation or system. Experimentation is carried out by manipulating or experimenting with the model rather than with the real-world situation. The general purpose is to obtain information from the simulation that will improve organization, policies, or procedures, where ordinarily it would not be feasible to obtain this information by direct experimentation with the real process. Simulations are particularly designed to answer "if-then" types of questions. That is, they indicate that if various alternative policies are followed, then the results will be as specified by the simulation of the system represented.

Simulations are usually used in management science when it is too difficult to represent the system or process by an analytical mathematical structure. When such an analytical structure is present, as in mathematical programming, it is generally advisable to use it. However, many situations are too complex to represent by such formal mathematical models, but may be very usefully investigated by simulating the process on paper or in a computer. The most striking applications of simulation have been where the operation of large-scale systems has been reproduced and experimented with in electronic computers.

■TYPES OF SIMULATION.—There are several simulation procedures that have served a number of purposes. Although, as in other management science fields, there is no complete agreement on terminology and classification, the following are generally considered as simulation approaches: Monte Carlo, heuristic programming, and gaming techniques.

Monte Carlo techniques are essentially methods of simulated sampling. They are ways of obtaining data through a sampling process when the data are probabilistic in nature (in other words, subject to chance variation—hence the name "Monte Carlo"). Usually, this sampling takes the form of drawing numbers from a table of random numbers to simulate a sample of real-world data which may represent lengths of time to perform an individual part of an operation, a number of units of demand, the dimension of a produced part, or some other numerical quantity.

Heuristic programming refers to simulation that develops or uses "heuristics" or "rules of thumb" as aids in problem solving or reducing the search required to find a solution. For example, in a simulation of the number and location of warehouses that should exist in a national distribution system, that would involve the least cost of distribution, the following type of heuristic was used: most geographic locations that are likely points for regional warehouses should be close to or in areas where demand is heavily concentrated. Thus, not all possible locations in the country need be examined. This particular heuristic could very well reduce the search for eligible locations to a small part of the United States.

Gaming techniques are usually classified as either "business gaming" or "experimental gaming." Business games are training devices or games that simulate business situations to provide experience in decision making or in management of business control systems. Many persons may play these games at the same time, making decisions concerning pricing policy, advertising expenditures, hiring and firing of personnel, budgets, and other managerial functions. Teams of individuals may function as corporations, thus lending a flavor of realistic strategic competition to the game. The information concerning these decisions is generally fed into a computer that contains a model of the relationships among the factors involved. Usually, the computer is programmed to issue reports on the effect of the decisions on some aspect of corporate structure. In some games, balance sheets and profit-and-loss statements, issued at periodic intervals, show the overall consequences of the simulated operation of the company. Games have also been developed for simulating internal corporate administration on such matters as production scheduling, where the players do not interact with one another competitively. Experimental games have been used primarily for research that usually tests various hypotheses about human behavior. Subjects are presented with simulations of real-world situations and then their reactions to these situations are analyzed.

There have been many applications of simulation in business. A partial list of these areas includes traffic flow, production scheduling and control, distribution systems, operations at air, rail, and bus terminals, inventory control, plant layout design such as continuous industrial plants, corporate financial analysis, marketing managerial decision making, and broad, comprehensive models that depict the interrelationships of all functional areas of a corporation.

Decision Theory Models.—Decision theory or "statistical decision theory" models are formal mathematical-statistical models whose purpose is to rationalize decision making under uncertainty. This may be exemplified by considering a problem in a business setting. A corporation may be thinking about developing and constructing a plant to produce a new product. The size of the plant will depend upon the eventual demand for the product. In this context, the alternative courses of action are the different sizes of plant that may be built. The "states of nature" are the different levels of demand for the product that may eventuate. The particular state of nature (that is, the level of demand which will, in fact, occur) is unknown to the decision maker at the time he must choose his course of action.

The criterion of choice will be the net benefit that will accrue to the decision maker if he adopts the various courses of action considered and then the specified states of nature occur.

Thus, certain net profits (positive or negative) will occur for each of the various sizes of plant considered for construction. This stage of the problem may require estimates based on new information as well as past knowledge. The decision model provides for the assigning of probabilities to the various states of nature or possible outcomes, according to their likelihood of occurrence. These probabilities can be revised as new information is collected, perhaps by a sample survey. Finally, a mathematical procedure determines the best action, based on a criterion such as maximization of net benefits. As in other management science techniques, it is possible to manipulate the data inputs to the problem, such as benefits and probabilities of outcomes, to judge how sensitive the choice of the optimal action is to changes in these ingredients. If the optimal act remains the same despite wide changes in these underlying assumptions, this considerably increases confidence that the best act has been selected from among the alternatives considered.

Decision models are particularly well adapted to handling the problem of uncertainty with the theory of probability. Through the use of a multistage approach, they are also particularly suitable for treating decision problems which are sequential rather than one-time in nature.

■BENEFITS OF MODELS.—Among the advantages cited for these types of decision models is that they assist in structuring the problem and in bringing the application of judgment to it. They provide the framework for creative thinking about the problem. The act of listing alternative strategies and alternative possible outcomes helps to prevent potentially serious omissions.

Decision theory models have been applied in numerous areas, including competitive bidding where a contract is awarded to the lowest bidder, in evaluation of pricing strategies, in new product development, in quality control, in capital budgeting, and in the determination of best levels of promotional expenditures.

■OTHER MODELS.—Many other models are in use for the purpose of assisting and improving managerial decision-making. These include waiting-line models; network models, such as program evaluation and review technique (PERT) and critical path method (CPM); replacement models; and game theory models.

Conclusion.—These formal, logical apparatuses bring an objective, systematic approach to decision-making in business. They specify objectives, define the problem and possible solution, select the best solution, and then specify how the solution is to be maintained, controlled, and modified. Although numerous individual techniques were discussed above, the operating philosophy of management science is the total systems approach, that is, the consideration of solutions for the system as a whole rather than the seeking of "best" solutions for piecemeal portions. Furthermore, these methods are not intended to replace executive intuition and experience with mechanistic decision-making devices. Rather, they attempt to capture this intuition and experience, process them as ingredients of the problem, and thus provide the basic information and alternatives to which managerial judgment may be applied.

—Morris Hamburg

BIBLIOGRAPHY

Bowman, E. H. and Fetter, R. B. *The Analysis of Industrial Operations.* Richard D. Irwin, Inc., 1959.

Churchman, C. W., Ackoff, R. L., and Arnoff, E. L. *Introduction to Operations Research.* John Wiley & Sons, Inc., 1957.

McKean, R. N. *Efficiency in Government Through Systems Analysis.* John Wiley & Sons, Inc., 1958.

Miller, D. W. and Starr, M. K. *Executive Decisions and Operations Research.* Prentice-Hall, Inc., 1960.

Morse, P. M. and Kimball, G. E. *Methods of Operations Research.* John Wiley & Sons, Inc., 1951.

Schuchman, A. (ed.). *Scientific Decision Making in Business.* Holt, Rinehart & Winston, Inc., 1963.

RESEARCH AND DEVELOPMENT

What Is Research and Development?—We and the people of other industrial countries look forward to a life of progress. In the fundamental materials of life—food, shelter, and clothing —as well as in the subtle refinements of art, government, and religion, we expect to see improvements. The adage "what was good enough for my father is good enough for me" is rarely heard today, and we have adopted instead the ideal of progress, a steady change for the better.

To make improvements, we need new knowledge and new ways to apply knowledge. Some new knowledge and new applications are discovered in almost any kind of activity, but within the last century it has become common to organize activities specifically to generate new knowledge and new applications of knowledge. When these are carried out systematically, according to scientific principles, they are called *research and development* (popularly known in industry as R & D).

When the purpose is to increase our knowledge and understanding of nature, it is called *research*. When the purpose is to apply such understanding to human uses, it is called *development*. Most systematic scientific work serves both purposes, and a number of phrases such as basic research, applied research, exploratory development, and final development, have been coined to indicate relative emphasis on the two terms.

The words *research* and *development* are used in this sense only where the work is carried out according to scientific principles, as in mathematics, the physical, biological, and social sciences, engineering, and medicine. In the arts, the nonscientific efforts of artists to create new and improved works and forms are not called research and development.

■**DIFFERENCE IN TERMS.**—The distinction between *research* and *development* varies in different fields of endeavor. For example, in industries based on chemistry and pharmacology, almost all exploratory work is termed *research*, but in industries based on mechanics and electricity, most of it is called *development*.

In the social sciences, the use of these words is less secure. Although Karl Marx's studies in laying out the theoretical foundations of communism might be called research, the application of new knowledge in creating the United Nations or formulating a new decision in the United States Supreme Court is not called development. This probably reflects the fact that systematic scientific study of the social sciences is more recent than that of the physical sciences, and is not so well understood by practicing social scientists.

Not every culture has adopted progress as an ideal. It is quite possible for human society to flourish with a commitment to tradition rather than to change, as in Europe during medieval times or in Japan before Commodore Matthew C. Perry forced a confrontation with western civiliza-

tion. Even today in the United States, groups such as the Amish are committed to tradition, not to progress. Such societies have no place for research and development.

■**BENEFITS OF R & D.**—In the United States, the collaboration of science, industry, and government during the past two decades has produced astonishing results. By investing vast sums in research, the federal government has significantly helped to increase man's knowledge of the physical world. The government has sponsored R & D in a wide range of fields, most notably in the defense industries. The result has been thousands of new or improved products: stronger, lighter metal alloys; ceramics that resist extreme heats; miniature electronic components that are more reliable than their predecessors; high-strength adhesives; supersonic aircraft.

In many instances, industry benefits from government research. Thus a ceramic developed to protect a missile from the heat of re-entry into the earth's atmosphere may become the material from which cooking utensils are made. Or tiny electronic components designed for rockets may end up as parts of television sets.

Today most large corporations maintain staffs that are involved exclusively in basic research and development. Most of today's new plastics, drugs, chemicals, and electronic components have come from intensive R & D. Many corporation executives like to point out that half of their sales today are of products that ten years ago hadn't even been invented.

History of R & D.—During Greek and Roman times philosophers cultivated new knowledge and craftsmen spread new applications, but there was little exchange between them. The prac-

tical application of knowledge was ignored by philosophers, and craftsmen had to make their improvements in ignorance of even the meager scientific knowledge that was available among scholars. Original scholarship never achieved distinction in the Roman Empire, but the crafts were preserved, developed, and spread. After the decline of the Roman Empire, even the crafts declined. During the stable economic and social condition of medieval times, many of the crafts were revived, but this revival owes little to science, philosophy, or scholarship. Most scientific innovations at this time were importations, like gunpowder and the compass, from the East, where intellectual inquiry was more active than in Europe.

The transition from craft secrets to science as the basis of technology is well illustrated by the founding of the Royal Society in England in 1660. Contemporary accounts show that its members were well aware of three factors contributing to this shift. First, the gentlemen of the upper classes, who had the best access to education and the most leisure to devote themselves to it, were becoming interested in technology and science. Second, they generated, often for the first time, systematic and scientific descriptions of the crafts as they were then practiced. Third, they published the results of their activity, and thus spread the word about new science, applications, and inventions instead of confining it to the members of a craft or guild.

By the time of the American and French revolutions at the end of the eighteenth century, all of Europe and the American Colonies had recognized that science, the crafts, and industry were mutually supporting. The participation of men like Thomas

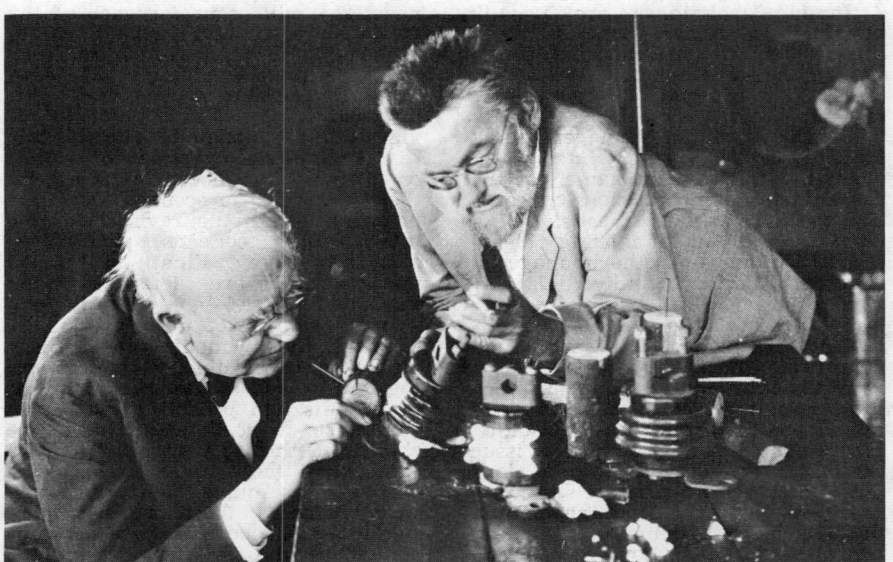

EDISON NATIONAL HISTORICAL SITE

EARLY RESEARCHERS Thomas Edison (*left*) and Alfred Steinmetz (*right*) work on a problem. Edison aided industry greatly by promoting the use of scientific research teams.

GENERAL MOTORS CORPORATION

RESEARCH TODAY is conducted on a large scale: this 330-acre technical center is devoted to research, development, and testing facilities.

Jefferson and Benjamin Franklin in what we would now call research and development is well known. Among those who did not themselves participate, we find George Washington saying, "There is nothing which can better deserve patronage than the promotion of science."

■ R & D IN THE NINETEENTH CENTURY.—Where in the seventeenth and eighteenth centuries gentlemen-amateurs were largely responsible for the synthesis of science and technology, this role was taken over in the nineteenth century by entrepreneurial inventors. It was common for a man to carry out research and development on his own behalf, or with the expectation of founding a business and profiting from ownership. Alexander Graham Bell and Thomas Alva Edison are examples of this tradition

in the United States.

In the meanwhile, responsibility for the study of science—what we would now call basic research—fell on colleges and universities. Cooperation between scholarly scientists in universities and practical inventors and entrepreneurs in industry was not uniformly effective. It was most successful in Germany and in the United States. In England, where higher education was dominated by the classical scholars of Oxford and Cambridge, the support of industry by the universities was inadequate. At the British Exposition of 1875, the backwardness of British technology became obvious, and public alarm led to corrective action in the form of public and private support of scientific work, especially of laboratory work, in the universities.

■ TWENTIETH-CENTURY PATTERNS.—In Charles Proteus Steinmetz (1865–1923) we see the first notable example of a specialist in industrial research and development who was not a man of independent means, a university teacher-scholar, or an owner, but a specialist employee of his sponsors. In the thirty years he worked for the General Electric Company, Steinmetz made great contributions to the understanding of alternating-current circuits, high-voltage electric discharges, and other phenomena, and applied this understanding to problems in the design and use of electrical machinery.

This pattern of activity rapidly became the most common. By 1920 the United States had 240 laboratories organized to carry out research and development, and by 1960 it had 5,420. In 1967, three-quarters of all our research and development was carried out in industrial research laboratories and half of the rest in laboratories operated by the federal government. However, more than one-third of basic research work was undertaken at various colleges and universities.

The United States government began its massive support of scientific research and development during World War I, but this support waned during the depression of the 1930's. When World War II broke out the deficiencies were sorely felt. Federal support of science and technology was expanded with the creation of such institutions as the Office of Scientific Research and Development (1941), the Office of Naval Research (1946), the National Institutes of Health (1946), the Atomic Energy Commission (1946), and the National Science Foundation (1950).

Since World War II the amount of research and development in the United States has grown somewhat faster than that of the rest of the economy. Shortly after the war, it accounted for $2.5 billion, somewhat less than 1.5 per cent of the gross national product. By 1960 it had

FORD MOTOR COMPANY

RESEARCH TEAMS help industry solve current problems. These scientists experiment to develop a new battery to make feasible the use of electrically-powered automobiles.

grown to $21 billion, nearly 3 per cent of the GNP. It appears to be leveling off at under 3 per cent of the GNP, but the total amount continues to grow as the economy expands.

The table below shows the sources of funds that support research and development and the recipients of the funds, that is, the organizations that carried out the work. The period covered is the fiscal year from July 1962 to June 1963 inclusive. Figures for basic research only are shown (in italics) as well as figures for all research and development.

Organizing for R & D.—Theoretical and practical studies have shown that some types of organization inhibit change while others encourage it. Since the purpose of research and development is to produce certain kinds of change, it is important to organize research and development laboratories in a way that encourages change to take place.

The appropriate form of organization is one in which authority is based on knowledge and skill rather than organizational status. This means that critical decision-making is not confined to top management but is diffused throughout the organization, according to each person's ability to contribute wisdom where he has knowledge, experience, or talent. Control comes from having as many individuals as possible refer their decisions and actions to goals and standards. This means that goals must be very well understood throughout the organization, and standards must be sufficiently shared so that decisions made by one will be endorsed by the others. Com-munication is not limited to pre-scribed channels, since who is at the "top" of the decision-making hier-archy depends on the content of the decision. Values and motives must be communicated as well as technical facts, for there is no prescribed chan-nel of authority with a recognized power to give rewards or invoke sanctions.

Advantages of economy and efficien-cy appropriate for a manufacturing plant are sacrificed to encourage indi-vidual initiative everywhere in the organization. The operation of such an organization may seem chaotic to an outside observer, but the im-position of rational order usually de-creases rather than increases its effectiveness.

■**ESSENTIAL REQUIREMENTS.**—Three fac-tors seem to be essential for research and exploratory development. First, the laboratory needs a statement of objectives that people throughout the organization clearly understand. Sec-ond, it must have persons with ex-perience and imagination, who can generate new ideas in response to new stimuli. Third, it must have resources—laboratories, instruments, materials, and people—to undertake exploratory work.

The director has an enormous in-fluence on the productivity of his research laboratory. Although the at-tributes of a good laboratory director have not been fully established, this much is clear: the principal func-tion of a laboratory director is to foster free inquiry, not to give orders or make decisions about scientific and technical matters.

It is now widely accepted that an effective attack upon many technical problems is to form an *ad hoc* team of technical personnel with a wide range of scientific and technical skills. This approach promotes the all-im-portant cross-fertilization and inter-communication that are so vital. Such a project team accomplishes at least four things: it effectively attacks a problem with personnel best able to contribute the needed knowledge; it provides a vital means of com-municating horizontally across the formal laboratory structure; the team members become known throughout the laboratory and can be used more effectively; and it provides an im-portant training mechanism, en-abling project leaders to obtain administrative and fiscal experience in preparation for group leadership.

■**HOW PROJECTS ORIGINATE.**—The most outstanding laboratories, which have the best-qualified and best-informed scientists and engineers, generally practice the least formal and most permissive methods of project selec-tion. These people advise that the selection should be left up to the properly qualified and motivated sci-entist or engineer. The reasoning here is that such a person best under-stands how to proceed in his field and how the project relates to cor-porate objectives and goals.

Most organizations have their over-all objectives approved by top management and communicated throughout the organization and finally to the individual. Research project selection or initiation reverses the process—it starts with the indi-vidual and is communicated upward.

Research in R & D administration is still in its infancy. Admittedly, no two laboratories are exactly alike. Each laboratory is made up of its own particular selection of scientists and engineers, and these people are its most important asset. Outstanding results in research arise from the intellectual quality of the staff rather than from involved administrative procedures. New basic scientific ideas come from individual scientists, not from manpower; the research lab-oratory, therefore, must have the in-dividual scientist clearly in focus. Each laboratory is different in its chosen organizational framework, both in its internal operations and in its relationship with its parent or-ganization and directly interested ex-ternal entities.   —Gordon Raisbeck

BIBLIOGRAPHY

BURNS, T. and STALKER, G. M. *The Management of Innovation.* Quad-rangle Books Inc., 1962.

"Federal Support of Basic Research in Institutions of Higher Learning," National Research Council, 1964.

MEES, C. E. K. and LEERMAKERS, J. A. *The Organization of Industrial Sci-entific Research,* (2nd Ed.) Mc-Graw-Hill Book Co., 1950.

UBBELOHDE, A. R. J. P., "The Begin-nings of the Change from Craft Mystery to Science as a Basis for Technology," *A History of Tech-nology,* vol. IV (ed.: Hall, Holin-gard, Singer, and Williams). Oxford University Press, 1958.

United States Research and Development Funds
by Source and Performer, 1963
(in $1,000,000)

Sources of Funds	Research and Development Performers						Percent Distribu-tion, R & D Sources
	Federal Govern-ment	Industry	Colleges and Universities		Other non-profit Institutions	Total	
			Proper	Federal contract Research centers			
Federal Government	2,400	7,340	775	525	300	11,340	65
			{1,300}				
Basic Research	*908*	*1,240*	*740*	*320*	*230*	*3,438*	*58*
			{1,060}				
Industry	....	5,380	65	....	120	5,565	32
Basic Research		*1,940*	*50*		*90*	*2,080*	*35*
Colleges and Universities	....	....	260	....	....	260	2
Basic Research			*250*			*250*	*4*
Other non-profit Institutions	....	....	75	....	110	185	1
Basic Research			*70*		*105*	*175*	*3*
Total	2,400	12,720	1,175	525	530	17,350	100
			{1,700}				
Basic Research	*908*	*3,180*	*1,110*	*320*	*425*	*5,943*	*100*
			{1,430}				
Percent Distribution, R & D Performance	14	73	7	3	3		100
			{10}				
Basic Research	*15*	*54*	*19*	*5*	*7*		*100*
			{24}				

Source: National Science Foundation.

PURCHASING

Introduction.—To cope with rapid technological advances in recent years, most firms have had to organize their various departments. While changes in engineering, manufacturing, and marketing have been more obvious, perhaps no segment of the average company has undergone greater reorientation and functional change than the purchasing department. Purchasing people today are engaged in such challenging work as systems contracting, value analysis, and the application of electronic data processing to many purchasing functions. Moreover, purchasing personnel are increasingly involved in subcontracts with other firms. Within their own company, these people act as a nerve center for communication and information.

In the past, several divisions of a corporation may have been heavily involved in spending money. Today, purchasing has become essentially the single source for the vast majority of all expenditures. Also, purchasing has a more direct influence upon the achievement of the firm's objectives: to produce a product to established quality standards, on schedule, and at a profit.

Purchasing helps meet these objectives in a number of ways. In a company that produces a product to established quality standards, the purchasing agent knows the range of materials that are on the market and understands their specifications. Moreover, he recognizes market conditions, and with his various analytical tools and experience he can make recommendations that will guide the company in achieving its standards.

To help his company keep "on schedule," the purchasing agent finds suppliers who can provide either the raw materials or the products needed within a reasonable time. This allows his company to produce the final product on schedule. To insure that this objective is achieved, the purchasing agent often serves as an expeditor who speeds delivery of materials needed on the production line.

A central concern of most firms is profit. It is here, perhaps, that the purchasing agent makes his greatest contribution. As markets become increasingly competitive, profit making becomes more difficult. On a given contract or product, profit can be lost in many ways. The purchasing agent contributes to profit by eliminating many of the areas in which it can be lost, thus providing the company with a larger dollar margin upon which to work. He does this through his knowledge of values and "best buys."

Vendor Evaluation and Selection.—This traditionally has been one of the most basic elements of the purchasing agent's job. Today, however, evaluating and selecting vendors is much more complex than it used to be. The purchasing agent is responsible for accumulating information on every material he must buy from vendors. He must also know how his company uses this material, its physical characteristics, its potential usage, and its manufacturing or tooling requirements. To obtain this information, the purchasing agent may turn to a number of sources: trade manuals, buyers' guides, directories, and catalogs. Other sources upon which he can rely for information are sales representatives of vendors, exhibits at trade shows, and contacts he makes with professional organizations.

After the purchasing agent has established his bidders' list from these sources, he must then carefully evaluate the list. At this point he must consider such factors as potential price, technological competition, service and warranty guarantees, geographical location, company size, and available distributors. This evaluation should assure him that the suppliers he selects can deliver material on schedule, at the right quantity and quality standards, and at the most reasonable price. Ideally, he should keep his company's inventory of materials and parts to a minimum. If he orders more than is needed, he ties up too much of the company's cash. At the same time, he should see that stocks do not drop so low that production is held up for want of an item. If he can meet these goals, he will cut costs significantly.

When the purchasing agent evaluates and selects vendors, he must remember that the process must be tailored to the item being bought. Different materials and parts require different kinds of source evaluation and selection. Moreover, the cost of the purchase will also influence the evaluation and selection process. Obviously, the greater the dollar volume, the more care he needs to take before he selects a vendor.

As the purchasing agent considers *quality* he must remember that this means "acceptable" quality and not more than what is required. Often, this is misinterpreted to mean "maximum" quality. This is why the purchasing agent must continually refer to the specifications for his firm's products and come as close as possible to filling them.

■**NEGOTIATING WITH VENDORS.**—This is another function which should be considered as a focal point of the purchasing agent's efforts. In the performance of his job, the agent approaches negotiations with suppliers flexibly. Because the techniques applied depend upon the dollar value and ease or difficulty of procurement, negotiations can range from a simple oral or written communication to complex exchanges involving teams from both the buyer and seller. To negotiate with vendors, the purchasing agent must be careful and objective and take a logical, analytical approach to the problem. If he is to negotiate effectively, he must develop a plan that determines the goals and procedures of negotiation. He then should chair the meetings to see that these goals are met. Here, techniques of cost and price analysis will help make sure that "the price is right."

Success in negotiations not only stems from the purchasing agent's analytical and objective ability but also depends upon his capability as a management man. In becoming involved in negotiations, however, he cannot afford to lose sight of his price objectives. He relies upon his negotiating techniques to help establish more effective price objectives in negotiations with vendors. He may ask the following questions:

1. How much can I afford to pay?
2. How much are others paying?
3. How much can I buy it for elsewhere?
4. How badly does the supplier need the business?
5. What is the future potential business for the item?
6. Considering all of the foregoing, what should the item cost?

■**SYSTEMS CONTRACTS.**—Negotiations with vendors can be very sophisticated if the purchasing agent becomes involved in the systems contract. To understand the complexity of this type of buying, we must define the term *systems.* Essentially, the systems approach is an organized way of dealing with complex problems.

When they classify things to be purchased, companies (particularly those in the aerospace and electronics industries) may establish a "systems" category and another category called "equipment items." The distinction between the two categories is chiefly one of size and complexity. Systems tend to be composed of more complex items, with critical relationships between major components. On the other hand, equipment items are generally less sophisticated, separate units that cost less. A purchasing agent looks at the overall job that the system is supposed to accomplish, then attempts to find the best sources of supply. With advancing technology, there are increasing numbers of electronic, electromechanical, and aerospace systems in industry, and systems contracting is especially related to these complex areas.

Reciprocity.—This essentially refers to the granting of business to those companies who send business to you. However, reciprocity programs usually tend to have management restraints tied to them which may affect price, quality, and service. Where reciprocity does exist, the purchasing agent may be forced to depart somewhat from his customary principles of buying. There are a number of possible drawbacks in reciprocal agreements. For example, during periods of shortage, the customer may take care of other clients first, or he may create fictitious complaints about the supplier's manufactured products to counteract the supplier's criticism of his products. Further, he may make only minimal efforts to improve quality of shipments or to meet time schedules, and he may fail to give full consideration to actual market prices when he bills for his products.

From the buyer's point of view, it is frustrating not to be able to follow normal procurement practices. Moreover, when differences arise with customers, the sales departments and even top management of the two companies may become involved. On occasion, the buyer may have to relax his requirements for inspection and quality assurance.

Value Analysis and Value Engineering.— In any consideration of purchasing activities today, these two functions should not be overlooked. Both techniques have become part of the science of removing unnecessary costs without impairing a product's desired functions. Value engineering eliminates unnecessary costs by considering the functional requirements of the product in the design stage. Value analysis cuts down unnecessary costs by evaluating the product after the design has been completed.

In both techniques, experts examine every component of a product, trying to find the answer to this question: What other material or design would perform the same function at a lower cost? Many companies have made huge savings in recent years by getting the answer to this deceptively simple question.

Compared to value analysis, value engineering tends to be more technical and time-consuming. While value analysis concentrates its attention on attempting to find a more functional product, value engineering probes more deeply and challenges the basic design of the product itself. The very nature of value engineering results in its usually being assigned to design specialists, and many companies have their own value engineering departments. However, purchasing agents may be asked to be members of value engineering teams.

With value analysis it is quite a different matter. Purchasing people are deeply involved in value analysis, which has become an increasingly significant aspect of their jobs.

Both value analysis and value engineering tend to be closely tied to cost improvement programs within the company. The dollar savings reported from these programs are the strongest indications that these approaches are worthwhile. The purchasing agent uses value analysis to assure that he is getting the most value for the money he spends. In determining this, he considers two figures in his analysis of what to pay for an item: the purchase price and the cost for the life of this item.

One of the problems that purchasing people have in dealing with other departments of their firms relates to these two costs, especially when companies have to make financial cutbacks. Company cost-reduction programs usually attack the purchase price of an item. While it is true that reducing the price of purchases is an effective way to reduce expenditures immediately, the purchasing agent knows that the long-range consequences of buying cheaper often may be more costly, because the cheaper items won't last as long. Value analysis concerns itself with total acquisition costs, that is, both the price and the item-life cost.

Buying from Overseas Sources.—Concurrent with the rapid advance in technology, buying and selling between countries have increased sharply. There was a time when the purchasing agent focused his attention only upon local and national markets. Now the international marketplace is prominent in his purchasing deliberations. High-quality materials at reasonable prices are now available from both Asia and Europe. Countries such as Japan, West Germany, and Switzerland compete actively for the American dollar.

There are two major restraints, however, that tend to limit overseas procurements. These are the "Buy American" policies (especially in defense procurement) and the historical short lead-time requirements on material deliveries. More recently, the balance of payments has become a problem for the United States, and companies have been asked to limit foreign purchases. To stem the outflow of gold, some companies are taking the position that purchases from other countries should be limited to emergencies or to materials not available in the United States.

Inventory Control.—Central to the purchasing agent's contribution to profit and meeting schedules is the effectiveness of his inventory control. As noted before, inventory control should be aimed at providing just enough to meet the needs of the firm. Another factor that necessarily influences inventory policy is the buying of large quantities at discounts, but this should be weighed against the higher warehousing costs that follow.

It is of great importance that the purchasing department maintain accurate inventory control records. This is particularly so when items are expensive or require a long time for delivery. One way the purchasing agent deals with low-cost items is the economic order quantity (EOQ) system.

In the EOQ system, complex mathematical formulas are reduced to simple charts that anyone can use. The charts show the purchasing agents two things: (1) *how much* of a given item he should order to get the most economical buy; (2) *when* he should order this quantity. Information needed to assemble the charts is obtained by consulting past records, which show the demand for the item in the past, and production forecasts, which show how much of the item will be needed to meet production schedules.

The first step in developing an EOQ system is to review low-value, simple parts to determine whether there is "over-control," so that the company is spending too much money on parts that aren't worth it. Systematic efforts should be made by the purchasing agent to develop an EOQ for each category of inventory items that are costly enough to warrant it. This should balance the costs of (1) holding inventory, (2) purchases, (3) receipts and inspections, (4) running out of stock, and (5) quantity discounts missed. Such a technique gives the lowest total cost to the corporation.

EDP Applications to Purchasing.—One of the most radical adjustments within purchasing has been brought about by electronic data processing (EDP) equipment. As in other departments within the firm, there has been concern that EDP may replace the purchasing agent himself. Those who fear this, however, do not fully recognize that EDP actually helps the purchasing agent to perform his job more effectively and to concentrate on those aspects of his work in which he can make his greatest contribution to fulfilling his company's objectives.

Here are some of the improvements made possible with EDP:

1. Purchasing is quicker and easier; as a result the company has a shorter wait between ordering and receiving materials.
2. Equipment can quickly retrieve any purchasing data on file.
3. Problem solving is much faster; computers can solve complex problems in minutes that formerly might take days or even weeks.
4. Paperwork (such as purchase orders and the like) is easier and faster. Also, the flow of paperwork from one department to another is speeded up.

Problems with EDP generally crop up when a company fails to understand the potential which the different computer operations afford, and does not plan carefully to fit the system to the company's needs. Perhaps most important, however, the purchasing agent should not fear data processing as a threat to his position. The purpose of EDP is to digest and convert raw data into information, thus enabling the purchasing agent to make better decisions. (See also *Business and the Computer*, page 1773.)
—Reed Powell

BIBLIOGRAPHY

ALJIAN, G. W. *Purchasing Handbook.* McGraw-Hill, Inc., 1958.

AMMER, DEAN S. *Materials Management.* Richard D. Irwin, Inc., 1962.

BERRY, HAROLD A. *Purchasing Management.* Prentice-Hall, Inc., 1964.

EDWARDS, MARSHALL G. (ed.) *Guide to Purchasing.* National Association of Purchasing Agents, New York, 1966.

ENGLAND, WILBUR B. *Procurement.* (4th ed.) Richard D. Irwin, Inc., 1962.

HEINRITZ, S. F. and FARRELL, P. V. *Purchasing: Principles and Applications.* (4th ed.) Prentice-Hall, Inc., 1965.

HODGES, HENRY G. *Procurement: The Modern Science of Purchasing.* Harper & Row Publishers, Inc., 1961.

POOLER, VICTOR H. JR. *The Purchasing Man and His Job.* American Management Association, 1964.

WESTING, J. H., and FINE, I. V. *Industrial Purchasing.* (2nd ed.) John Wiley & Sons, Inc., 1961.

MANUFACTURING AND PRODUCTION

Basic Production Methods.—In the early days of manufacturing the greatest care went into training skilled craftsmen who could produce high-quality precision parts on relatively simple machinery or workbenches. Production volumes were necessarily low because these craftsmen could not produce satisfactory parts in quantity. Where these simple machines were used, a certain amount of bench finishing was invariably necessary, especially when precision parts had to be assembled or fitted together. Once industry recognized the limitations of the hand craftsmen, it began gradually to develop better machines and machine tools which produced parts, within acceptable tolerances, that required a minimum of finishing. At once, production volume increased, and it became obvious that to reduce manufacturing costs and maintain low selling prices high-volume machines which could produce acceptable products with a minimum of after-work had to be developed.

■**AUTOMATED PROCESSES.**—Since about 1940 there has been a tremendous equipment and tooling development throughout industry. Machines have been developed for specialized operations, equipment capabilities have been improved, there have been drastic changes in tooling technology, and many new processing techniques have been developed. And many of these machines have been integrated in automated transfer lines, which perform sequential operations with high precision. (In the transfer line, parts are automatically transferred from one work station to the next; when the automotive industry began installing these units in large numbers during the late 1940's the term *automation* first became popular.) To a large extent, this trend to automated operation has forced manual operation out of manufacturing, where machine operation itself is concerned. Certain intermediate operations, however, must still be carried on by hand, and the machine has still not been able to overcome the advantage of the human being—his ability to think.

It would be an error, however, to state that the automated machine and numerical control (the control of machines by tapes) are completely new developments. The first automatically controlled machinery actually was invented in 1801, when J. M. Jacquard developed his punched-card system for looms that wove complicated fabric parts.

Depending on what is to be manufactured, the automated process can be set up in two ways: a continuous flow of operation, performed by automatic equipment, from raw material to finished product; or a series of automatic operations, interrupted on occasion by manual operation. The steel mill is a good example of continuous operation, where metal poured from the open-hearth furnace is transported as ingots to a series of automatic rolling mills, which eventually form it into the desired

WESTERN ELECTRIC

ASSEMBLY line finishes, packs telephones.

shape. Certain manufacturing processes in the chemical and food industries are also examples of continuous production. Here, raw materials fed into the initial machinery of the plant emerge at the shipping end, with almost no handling of the product as it progresses through the plant.

The semicontinuous operation may best be exemplified by the heavy metal manufacturing industries; automobiles, aircraft, and machine tools are typical products. In these operations, production in automatic machines is interrupted to permit certain nonautomatic operations to take place. These could include loading, unloading, and transfer and inspection of parts. While most of these nonautomatic operations to take by machines, it is frequently considered advisable to deliberately interrupt the automatic transference and machining of items on a production line. Such an operation recognizes that even equipment of the highest precision is sometimes subject to breakdown or a departure from reliability. Anything lower than almost one hundred per cent reliability in a machine component can cause repeated downtime on the production line and consequently lower production. When a plant tries to justify installation of automated lines and equipment, it must carefully consider these factors.

Numerically controlled machines are finding widespread application for producing parts in low quantities or to custom designs. Here, the movement of cutting tools in multiple dimensions can be programmed on the computer and, with the resulting tape, parts of practically any shape, including irregular contours, can be produced without any direct control by an operator. An operator is required, however, to handle exceptional situations, such as tool sharp-

ening, repair, and major machine adjustments, which are still beyond the capacity of the computer.

It is worth noting here that the term *automation* includes both the transfer machine and the tape-controlled machine. But the type of production varies widely. Generally speaking, the transfer machine is designed for mass production of parts. On the other hand, numerically controlled equipment fits best into low-volume production, where only a few parts are produced.

Production Preliminaries.—The decision to manufacture a product comes from a survey of the market, which approximates factors such as sales potential and market price. All other factors, specifications, and cost targets are then determined by management and preliminary designs are begun. It is at this initial engineering stage that the manufacturing engineering group begins its work. The design of the product and the design of the manufacturing process determine the material and labor costs of the product. Because these items represent the major cost, it is important that design and manufacturing work together effectively. Preliminary models for test, analysis, and design evaluation are made, followed by the detailed design and drawings. Testing of the product, performed under actual environmental conditions, assures that the design will meet all the product objectives.

At this point the product engineering (design) and manufacturing engineering groups have developed the product and the manufacturing process to meet the required standards for appearance, quality, and reliability in the most efficient and economical manner.

■**PLANNING PRODUCTION.**—To manufacture the product, the company has selected processes and equipment employing the latest technology to fully utilize materials and labor. All tooling, jigs, fixtures, dies, and inspection equipment have been selected, along with detailed planning and establishment of operator work methods. Effective planning of all manual operations, including estimated time values, enables the plant to schedule production, train operators, accelerate production startup, and establish good working relationships. The foreman is a vital part of this planning and organizing, since he will be responsible for managing his area of responsibility.

Once facilities are completely installed, an initial complement of operators is selected and trained, and pilot or preliminary production starts. Each operation is performed and revisions are made as required.

When production reaches the planned level, all delays and nonstandard practices are studied and corrected. The methods engineer, with the foreman, analyzes all operations to assure that the operators are properly trained and are following the prescribed methods.

Work standards are then established for each operation, providing the basis for budgeting and cost control, manpower planning, cost estimating, planning future improvements, and production scheduling.

Production Scheduling and Control.—
Production scheduling and control of manufacturing operations is an important function to minimize production costs, achieve good utilization of materials, manpower, and facilities and meet the delivery dates specified by the customer. The scheduling function varies with the product and the manufacturing operation. The mass-production or continuous type of manufacturing is relatively simple to schedule since operations are performed in a predetermined sequence on the production line. On the other hand, scheduling of job shop or intermittent production is complex and requires an effective procedure to coordinate the many separate operations. In a job shop, unlike a mass-production shop, scores or hundreds of *different* parts may be produced at any given time.

■**MASTER SCHEDULE.**—After studying customers' orders and projected sales, the plant prepares a master production schedule. Starting with the required shipping date and the production rates established for each operation, the date for delivering subassemblies to the final assembly line can be determined. This, in turn, establishes due dates for starting production of individual components, and for purchasing raw materials and parts that will go into the company's products. Time for in-process movement and storage of materials, machine setup and changeover and other factors relating to a particular plant operation must be allocated in the development of the master schedule. In-process or completed product inventories must also be considered. Cooperation with marketing and sales groups is necessary if schedules are to be accurate and inventories kept to a minimum.

The master schedule is then broken down into production or department schedules, and allocation of work to each machine or work station is carefully planned. This technique of machine loading will assure that target dates are met, provide good utilization of manpower and facilities, and notify management of impending overloads that could affect schedule dates or cause unnecessary overtime. It also permits proper sequencing of similar jobs to a machine to reduce setup and changover labor.

Once orders are released to production, the dispatching groups will assign material, tools, fixtures, specifications, etc., to the workplace to ensure that schedules are met. Close cooperation is maintained with the purchasing department in the procurement and expediting of parts from vendors.

■**CONTROLLING PERFORMANCE.**—Once production begins, a system for measuring progress and warning of delays must be established to assure that schedules will be met. This performance control can vary from daily meetings and use of Gantt charts (which give a visual record of where production stands) to the use of modern electronic data-processing equipment. (See also *Business and the Computer,* page 1773.) The type of control depends on the size, complexity, and needs of the operation. The entire production control system must be flexible and capable of absorbing changes in production plans. Changes in customers' orders, shortages of parts, and equipment breakdowns are but a few contingencies that require changes in schedules. To take care of these changes, expeditors or follow-up people coordinate the production, purchasing, scheduling, and dispatching activities, thus minimizing delays and inefficiency. Whenever schedules are not being met, or delays occur, the expeditor will establish the causes and take the appropriate corrective action.

Equipment Selection and Replacement.
Product design and process design are two important factors to be considered before production equipment can be selected. The design and manufacturing groups must work together to assure the most economical manufacture of the product. This planning will also prevent extra expenditures for production and material handling equipment, keep maintenance costs down, and reduce floor space requirements.

Following the development of the design and manufacturing process, the selection of the most profitable and practical equipment is made. For a given process there are generally many different types of equipment and manufacturers to choose from. The following information must be obtained and evaluated for each machine being considered for a given process.

1. *Quality of the parts produced.* The equipment must be capable of continuously producing parts within the tolerances specified. Scrap and rework costs must be kept to an absolute minimum.

2. *Flexibility.* The equipment should be able to handle increased production volumes. Machines should also be easy to change from manufacture of one part to another with minimum loss of time.

3. *Maintenance.* The equipment must be of high quality, with reliable long-life components, and designed for ease of maintenance.

4. *Cost per piece for direct labor and material.*

5. *Cost per piece for all indirect labor.* This would include inspection, maintenance, material handling, tool changes, changeover, rework, etc.

6. *Cost per piece for operating supplies, power, expense tools, scrap, etc.*

7. *Any other operating cost factors.*

8. *Investment costs for equipment and special tooling.*

9. *Installation cost.* This includes removal of old equipment and providing service facilities.

With these data the practicability and the "investment versus return" for each machine can be established and the selection made.

■**REPLACING EQUIPMENT.**—The above discussion concerned selection of a plant's original equipment, except in this case the proposed equipment must justify itself against the present equipment on the floor. Replacement may be required for one or more of the following factors:

1. The present equipment is worn out and not worthy of repair.

2. It is obsolete. A new and better machine, a new process, or a new design may be available to provide additional savings.

3. It is inadequate from the standpoint of range, size, speed, accuracy or output.

4. It is unsafe to operate.

Age alone is not necessarily an indicator that replacement is required. A twenty-year-old machine may be completely adequate for the job it is required to do.

WESTINGHOUSE

FACTORY PLANNERS decide the most efficient arrangement of equipment for space available in a new plant by laying out scale models of the machines on a floor plan drawn to scale.

A planned replacement program to examine existing equipment against the challenge of new, more efficient machines is necessary. The people concerned with this program must be thoroughly familiar with their own operations and know what new equipment is available on the market. They must have imagination and not settle for newer models of old equipment, but consider new product designs to take advantage of completely new processes. They must recognize the problems that lead to practical and profitable replacement of equipment.

Equipment Maintenance.—Proper maintenance is required to keep machines and equipment in satisfactory condition according to standards established by management. Unfortunately, machines do break down; hence, plants must provide this service to maintain production-system reliability without excessive costs. When a machine breaks down, the following things happen:

1. Production for the downtime period is lost and must be made up with possible extra costs for overtime and premium pay. When the equipment is operating around the clock, makeup time may not be available, resulting in possible loss of sales and dissatisfied customers.

2. Labor is idle.

3. Other processes are delayed.

4. The costs in material and labor to repair the machine can be high.

Consideration of maintenance began when the equipment was originally selected. At this point, components with a high probability of failure were redesigned to make them more reliable. Also considered were accessibility and ease of maintenance to reduce repair time and costs. These goals were achieved by the joint efforts of manufacturing engineer, maintenance engineer, and the manufacturer of the equipment.

Adequate equipment maintenance records are needed to analyze and take the appropriate corrective action to eliminate or reduce breakdowns. Which parts are critical? What are their expected lives? Which parts repeatedly fail? With this information, the maintenance engineering group is in a position to redesign troublesome components. Records are needed to establish sound policies and to adjust practices in the light of more complete data. Records of maintenance costs are important when machine replacement studies are made.

When equipment does break down, an effective answering and dispatch system is mandatory to minimize costs and the losses described.

■ **PREVENTIVE MAINTENANCE.**—Another practice that minimizes breakdowns is preventive maintenance. This is a scheduled inspection that spots conditions leading to production breakdowns, so that components can be replaced before they fail. Preventive maintenance is accomplished at times when the machines are normally idle, such as the second or third shift. Again, maintenance records are the key to establishing long-range master schedules. These must be coordinated with plant production schedules. The

maintenance engineers prepare detailed writeups that include step-by-step descriptions of each inspection or overhaul. The work that each craft will do is prepared so that all activities can be scheduled accurately. The master schedules are then converted into daily and weekly schedules, so that the regular preventive maintenance work becomes a part of the overall maintenance program.

It is not always necessary to check every machine part in a preventive maintenance program. Certainly a simple machine with only a few moving parts is much different from a complex machine with many moving parts and switches, and air, hydraulic, or electronic controls.

The decision of what to include in a preventive maintenance program depends on local conditions and the facts disclosed by good maintenance records. Critical items that could cause costly shutdowns or damage, or harm to an employee, should be included. Also, preventive maintenance should not be so extensive that the cost exceeds the expense of downtime and the repair or replacement of machinery.

Apart from preventive maintenance is the regular oiling and lubrication of equipment. Charts on the machines indicate oiling points, type of lubricant, and frequency of attention.

In summary, a well planned and executed maintenance engineering and preventive maintenance program will have the following rewards: less production downtime and associated cost reduction; less overtime; lower repair and maintenance, labor, and material costs; fewer large-scale repairs and fewer repetitive repairs; and less standby equipment required, thus reducing capital investment.

Plant Layout.—Plant layout is the arrangement of the physical facilities and manpower required to manufacture a product efficiently and at the least cost. The complete scope of the activity encompasses such operations as receiving, production, services, quality, packaging, material handling, storage, and shipping. The ideal layout is one for which the building is specially designed and built. Here there are no restrictions; the layout developed will determine the location of walls and services, ceiling heights, type of structure, etc. Usually, however, the building already exists, and an efficient layout must be developed considering this restriction.

The work of designing a layout starts with an analysis of the product to be manufactured and the overall flow of materials through the various departments. It progresses step by step through the detailed planning of the arrangement of equipment in each area, followed by coordinating each function into a final layout.

The following information is needed for planning before starting the actual layout:

1. Planned volume of production, with projected future requirements.

2. Engineering drawings and specifications.

3. A complete list of all equipment, with process and tool requirements,

sequence of operations, work standards figures, routings, methods, storage requirements, and manpower requirements. This information is developed and available from the manufacturing engineering group.

4. Space available, with floor and structure loading information.

■ **TYPES OF LAYOUT.**—In the analysis of the above information, a flow diagram with symbols for each step in the process will help planners to visualize the entire manufacturing and assembly sequence, as well as the flow of materials. The next step is to decide whether to use a *product* or a *process* layout, or a combination of the two. In a product layout the manufacturing equipment is arranged in the same sequence as the operations performed on the product. The process layout groups the equipment together, so that all machines of a similar type are in the same section of the plant. The advantages and disadvantages of each must be weighed, giving consideration to the type of product and the volumes of production; to the best utilization of space and labor; to a minimum of material handling and inventory; and to the greatest flexibility for future changes in the process or product.

In mass production, the straight-line layout generally works best. Operations are performed in natural sequence—in a straight line; often a U-shaped line layout is employed to fully utilize floor space. Feeder lines, supplying individual components or subassemblies, are introduced at the required point in the process.

The layout is developed with the use of templates, which show the floor space occupied by individual pieces of equipment. They are placed over a floor plan and then rearranged until the most satisfactory layout has been obtained. It may be worthwhile to use three-dimension models instead of templates on large projects, or where many overhead conveyors or facilities are required. As the templates or models are located on the floor plan, the interrelationships between machines, operators, and material handling must be carefully planned and developed. Adequate space must be provided for operators and equipment as well as for storing material at the workplace or machine. Over-generous spacing of equipment and work stations must be avoided, not only to save valuable floor space but to reduce walking or other long moves by operators.

The planning of auxiliary departments, employee facilities, service facilities, aisles, etc., is also introduced at this point. Careful consideration must be made not to overload floors with a concentration of heavy equipment, or roof structures with conveyors carrying loads above the rated roof-loading capacity.

The final or master layout will evolve from the preparation of many preliminary layouts. The review and discussions with operating and service people during the layout development will bring out new points, provide a broader and more objective look, and assist greatly in getting final management approval.

Control of Quality.—Back in the initial product planning stages, management established the level of quality and reliability required to satisfy customers at a competitive market price. The engineer then designed the product and established the specifications for meeting product objectives. Testing was conducted under actual conditions to assure that the product would repeatedly perform as intended.

The system or program that controls quality must be tailored to fit the particular product and needs of the plant. It must be considered a "management tool" to meet the objectives previously described, as well as to assure that operating costs and losses will be minimized.

Special emphasis must be placed on *defect prevention* rather than defect correction. Since a quality product or part comes from the coordinated efforts of all sections of the company, each section and person must be dedicated to this concept. With the unit in actual production, the necessary controls for quality must be established to assure that each component, as well as the final assembled product, can be produced to the standards originally set.

■**COORDINATING CONTROL.**—Consider each of the following important activities and their role in assuring high quality. The purchasing group must select competent vendors to supply parts and materials that meet specifications at a proper price. Selection depends on the purchasing department's knowledge of the vendors' equipment and their ability to repeatedly produce high-quality material. Each vendor must completely understand what is required, and he must use proper inspection procedures and equipment. (See *Purchasing*, page 1757.)

In the receiving department inspection procedures will vary, depending on the type of material and the quality standards specified. Individual components must be dimensionally checked. In some cases the entire lot must be checked, but usually only a sample will be taken to estimate the condition of the entire lot.

The manufacturing engineering group must select or design production equipment, jigs, fixtures, and tools capable of producing parts to the quality specifications. Inspection fixtures and equipment must be designed so that tests or inspections can be made.

The responsibility of manufacturing supervision is to produce the product and the various components at the specified quality standards. This includes training each operator in every aspect of his job and stimulating him to have pride in his work. While employee motivation programs are not new, a recent concept called *zero defects* has been developed to help the worker communicate with management. In this way, he can point out weaknesses or errors in design, tools, materials, etc., and assist management in correcting them. Supervision must also constantly analyze scrap and rework costs, and take the necessary action for improvement

in accuracy and efficiency to reduce errors and waste.

The inspection department is responsible for inspecting or measuring parts against standards, then either accepting or rejecting them. While it is important that inspection be adequate, it is equally important that unnecessary inspection operations be eliminated. Some inspection procedures may require a complete check; in other cases, periodic sampling is adequate.

■**SCIENTIFIC AIDS.**—Mathematical or statistical methods are used to make accurate determinations of quality. Here, the examination of a small group of parts (or samples) will predict accurately the condition of the whole lot. Frequency distributions are made to tabulate the number of times a given quality characteristic occurs within the sample of product being checked. Control charts plot the hour-by-hour quality characteristics, thus giving a picture of what the process is producing. These tools have one common objective—they predict impending trouble and disclose possible causes.

Automatic inspection equipment is feasible where multiple dimensions must be checked simultaneously or where automatic measurements adjust tool or machine settings, thereby assuring the desired quality.

The quality and reliability engineering group is responsible for analyzing all inspection, statistical, and field warranty data. It works with other groups in taking immediate corrective action where problems exist. Also involved are machine and process capability studies on existing facilities and the establishment of adequate tool and gauge design, as well as maintenance programs.

In summary, the quality control system is a united and coordinated effort dealing with every aspect of the organization. Efforts are directed toward the prevention of defects, with special emphasis on taking immediate corrective action wherever problems exist. The benefits of a good quality control system would be to minimize in-plant quality costs and field warranty expenses (product guarantees) and provide the customer a high quality, reliable product.

Material Handling.—Material handling is the moving and handling of materials within the plant. Until the beginning of this century, handling assistance was provided only when loads were too great to be moved by human labor. Over the years industry has become much more aware of the advantages that come from good methods of material handling. Today material handling represents a large portion of a product's cost, and for that reason handling requires special emphasis. Good material handling minimizes labor costs, reduces material damage, and brings the material to the point of use when required.

The material handling techniques adopted must arise from the particular needs of each company's manufacturing processes. Material handling should be integrated into the manufacturing process and flow lay-

out, rather than superimposed as an afterthought. The following are basic principles for planning effective material handling:

1. *Minimize handling and handling effort.* As far as possible, avoid or eliminate handling operations. When these operations cannot be eliminated, they should be mechanized wherever possible.

2. *Coordinate plant handling.* Handling should be considered as a continuity from the supplier through the plant and out to the customer. Plant layout and the materials to be handled must be analyzed and planned together to assure a minimum of handling.

3. *Select the correct equipment.* A complete analysis of conditions and needs should be made to determine the most suitable and economical equipment for performing the operation. As far as possible, the company should select simple standard equipment with known reliability which will serve well with little maintenance. Special-purpose equipment is ordered only when it is essential. Before buying new equipment, the company should check to see if the existing equipment is being effectively used.

4. *Make the most effective use of handling equipment.* Material should be handled in the largest loads practicable. Work containers should be designed so that they can be easily handled, and the transfer of work from one container to another should be avoided. When material is stored, it should be stacked so that maximum use is made of vertical space. Preventive maintenance routines should be developed to minimize equipment breakdowns.

■**TYPES OF EQUIPMENT.**—Of the wide variety of material handling equipment on the market, these are the most common: (1) conveyors; (2) cranes, elevators, and hoists; (3) industrial vehicles; and (4) containers and supports.

A *conveyor* is a horizontal, inclined, or vertical device that moves or transports materials or objects in a predetermined path, with points for loading and unloading. Conveyors transport materials of every kind, shape, or form to and from processing equipment, or they may become an integral part of processing machines. They provide a way to time and pace manufacturing operations which is essential to quantity production and assembly. They also provide out-of-the-way storage for parts and assemblies, and have many other uses. Conveyors take many forms: endless belts; powered or gravity rollers; endless chain, wood or steel slats; vibrating troughs; and monorails.

Cranes, elevators, and hoists are used for both light and heavy jobs that require vertical lifting and moving. Also in this category is automatic or programmed equipment that delivers or retrieves material from a storage area. An operator inserts a punched card or dials instructions. The equipment then travels to a storage location, selects the material, and returns it to the operator or other point of use.

Industrial vehicles, which operate on nonfixed routes in the plant, make the movement of materials very flexible. Fork-lift trucks are the most popular of the industrialized vehicles. At the front of the truck are two tapered forks which are run under the material; these forks can be raised to lift the load, and then tilted back to retain the load in transit. The trucks can lift the materials or pallets (devices, usually made of wood or metal, upon which the material to be moved rests) so that they can be stacked one on top of the other. A variety of attachments can replace the forks to perform other specialized handling.

The storage of materials is an ever-present problem in the plant—thus the need for adequate and efficient *containers and supports.* In this classification are skids, pallets, and pallet boxes for support and easy handling of materials, along with racks and supports designed to support unit loads in storage.

Methods and Work Simplification.—

Methods and work simplification refer to techniques for analyzing and improving the ways of performing the manual elements of an operation. The object is to make the work easier and to reduce costs. The process requires an objective mind, interest in getting the necessary facts, a questioning attitude, and creativeness to develop better ways of doing work. The work simplification concept is "There is always a better way." This can best be illustrated by a case history, in which five people performed the same assembly operation. Each person had materials located at different points; each had his own motion and movement pattern. While all five had the same experience, one person consistently produced more parts with less effort. An analysis revealed that the material and tool locations were close to him, so that he kept the length and number of his movements to a minimum. He had found a better way, thus pointing out the definite need for work simplification or methods improvement, followed by training of each operator on the best way of performing a given task.

Here is the usual procedure for conducting a methods or work simplification study: (1) Select the operation or area to be improved. (2) Study the existing method to obtain all the facts. (3) Analyze and develop alternate methods or plans. (4) Evaluate and arrive at the best plan. (5) Install and then train operators. (6) Follow up to assure the desired results.

An operation with much direct labor is generally a good choice for methods improvement. Other good choices occur where there are production bottlenecks, where specific cost reduction pressures exist, or where it is desirable to reduce operator efforts. The first step in beginning the study is to obtain the basic information relating to the particular operation, such as the scheduled production volumes, present labor hours and cost, equipment requirements, operations delays, etc.

Next comes an on-the-floor analysis of the operation, to obtain all the pertinent facts. Here the observer must record each motion or act performed by each hand, and measure the distance each hand must move for each act or operation. In so doing, the observer is forced to see things he would not normally observe. This analysis should also include a sketch showing all dimensions, location of stock, tools, the operator, etc. The observation should be long enough to assure the inclusion of necessary delays caused by outside factors. Recording the operation on film will enhance the value of the analysis technique.

The next phase is to analyze and develop alternate methods or plans. It is advisable to develop more than one possible solution to the problems and conditions found. To accomplish this, idea development should include manufacturing supervisors and any others closely concerned with the operation. This will also assist in the future selling and implementation of changes.

Evaluation to establish the best method must consider the economy and practicability of the idea. Both of these factors can be evaluated by a mock-up or tryout of each method with stopwatch observations performed to measure improvement. Another effective technique is the use of predetermined-motion-time systems. Here the methods man prepares a detailed breakdown of the new method and assigns a predetermined time value from a prepared table for each motion or movement. In this manner, various methods can be compared and the most economical one chosen.

Following acceptance of the new method by manufacturing supervision, the installation is made, operators are trained, and new work standards established. Frequent followup is required to assure the desired results, and to detect future changes in design, materials, or tools which would necessitate a restudy.

EDP Applications in Production.—*Electronic data processing (EDP)* as applied to production can be defined as the use of electronic computers and data processing machines to assist in the efficient management of the production plant. Its ability to store data and process information at high speeds makes equipment useful to production management. Accurate and usable results depend on the collection of factual and useful data, processed fully on carefully selected equipment. (See *Business and the Computer,* page 1773.)

A wide variety of EDP equipment is available, capable of performing specialized tasks. Production management can adapt a few pieces of equipment or a complete system to meet the needs of a plant. A careful analysis of all factors is required to justify the acquisition of EDP equipment. Justification is made by comparing costs, savings, and benefits of an EDP system with the most efficient manual operation designed for the particular production application.

■**PRODUCTION AIDS.**—The following represent the popular applications of EDP equipment to aid production management:

Inventory Control. A perpetual inventory is maintained in the computer memory system. Orders and changes in stock are introduced into the computer, where corrections are made automatically and a new figure is available for use. The equipment can be programmed to print out complete inventory records or data requiring immediate action, such as shortage items, minimum balances, etc.

Purchased Material Forecasting. Master production schedules are automatically broken down into models, assemblies, individual parts, and finally into purchased material requirements. The computer compares the requirements against the inventory and the equipment automatically prepares purchase requisitions or orders for materials that are insufficient to meet future production needs.

Complete Production Scheduling and Control. The computer compiles all orders and sales forecasts, and then schedules each department. Machine loads are calculated to assure effective use of materials, manpower, and all facilities. When changes in schedules are required or processing shortages or delays occur, the EDP equipment prepares new schedules, changes all production orders, inventory records, purchase requirements, and machine loading data. The speed with which information can be processed makes practical a complete production control system, or individual systems for scheduling, material control, and inventory control.

These examples represent the general applications of EDP equipment in production. Individual plant needs create many specialized applications. The key to successful results lies in the ability to collect good, accurate information, and then process it through carefully selected and programmed equipment.

—Wallace E. Wilson

BIBLIOGRAPHY

Apple, J. M., *Plant Layout and Material Handling,* The Ronald Press Co., 1963.

Barnes, R. M., *Motion and Time Study,* John Wiley & Sons, 1963.

Bolts, H. A., *Materials Handling Handbook,* The Ronald Press Co., 1958.

Bowman, E. H., and R. B. Fetter, *Analysis for Production Management,* R. D. Irwin, Inc., 1957.

Carson, G. B., *Production Handbook,* The Ronald Press Co., 1958.

Eary, D. F. and G. E. Johnson, *Process Engineering for Manufacturing,* Prentice-Hall, Inc., 1962.

Feigenbaum, A. V., *Total Quality Control,* McGraw-Hill, Inc., 1961.

Niebel, B. W., and G. N. Baldwin, *Designing for Production,* Richard D. Irwin, Inc., 1957.

Thuesen, H. G., *Engineering Economy,* Prentice-Hall, Inc., 1950.

Vazsonyi, A., *Scientific Programming in Business and Industry,* John Wiley & Sons, 1958.

The Modern Marketing Concept.—Marketing is concerned with the flow of goods and services from producers to consumers. It began as soon as individuals or small family groups found it worthwhile to exchange goods with others. Sometimes this trade was between communities or kingdoms rather than individuals, but the problems of exchange were there. In 2100 B.C. the Code of Hammurabi helped regulate trade among the highly-developed societies of the Tigris and Euphrates river valleys. Since then, marketing institutions and services have continued to grow, and today an estimated fifty per cent of the American consumer dollar is spent for marketing activities.

While marketing has existed for a long time, a new view of it has evolved in the last few decades. In a world of scarcity, marketing was relatively unimportant. Producers (farmers and manufacturers) concentrated on basic commodities that they could produce or that seemed to be in demand. Frequently there was overproduction of some commodities and real distress in the marketplace. But in the long run, an emphasis on lowering costs of production worked fairly well. It was the job of the marketing people to "get rid of" the product that the production-oriented producers had made available. This meant that wholesale and retail markets, in addition to transportation to more remote markets (including rural areas, other countries, and the colonies) had to be developed. Today, however, most countries can produce their basic necessities. And modern transportation and communication have exposed even the most backward countries to first-quality products. There is much less opportunity to take advantage of consumer ignorance.

■**FOCUSES ON TARGET MARKETS.**—In the modern view of marketing, much more is involved than "getting rid of" products. Businessmen can readily see that it may be more profitable to plan and organize a company's total effort around potential target customers rather than to try merely to make full use of present resources. Instead of regarding marketing as selling, its basic function in earlier times, marketers now view it as the planning and implementing of whole marketing strategies, which direct the flow of goods and services from producers to consumers, thus satisfying customers and accomplishing the firm's objectives. Instead of regarding the firm as a collection of semi-independent departments or activities, the modern marketing concept takes the systems approach; that is, it starts with the assumption that the business is a system and that the whole is greater than the sum of the individual parts.

The modern marketing concept suggests that all the activities of a business should be integrated and planned to satisfy some target customers. The concept does not imply that all the traditional production, accounting, and financial activities are to be changed radically, but rather that they are all to be directed toward accomplishing the firm's objectives. After all, the purpose of business is making sales and profits, not making and offering for sale products that might be sold. It takes coordination of all the activities in a business to make sales at a profit.

■**MARKETING STRATEGY PLANNING.**—Implicit in the wholehearted acceptance of the modern marketing concept is the planning of marketing strategy. This is a two-step process: (1) selecting a target market and (2) developing a marketing mix. While a total market may be quite large, planners who select target markets assume that it probably will be more profitable to focus on particular segments of the total market. This can be visualized with the market grid concept. Here, a total market is represented as a grid, a figure like a checkerboard, on which various customer characteristics are the dimensions. In such a formulation, we would expect to find a particular customer in only one grid box, and the other customers in that box would be expected to have similar characteristics and desires.

The next step in marketing strategy planning is developing a marketing mix for *each* of these target markets. It is axiomatic that each target market will need its own marketing mix. It is quite possible that the marketing mixes may be somewhat similar (for example, the same physical product may be offered to target customers who are in different grid boxes), but each marketing mix will be different because of variations in the promotion (or another marketing variable) that is directed to each of the target markets.

Conceptually, there are an infinite number of marketing mixes when all the various combinations of products and services, promotion, prices, and distribution methods are considered. To simplify the discussion, it is helpful to think of a marketing mix as consisting of four major ingredients, called the four P's: Product, Place, Promotion, and Price. These four P's are considered coequal, and to emphasize this they are shown, in Figure 1, around the target customers (C). In all cases it is necessary to make decisions in all four areas, then come up with a blend that satisfies the particular target market.

■**PRODUCT.**—A product is much more than a tangible object. It includes any services that should be associated with a product, a brand, a package, or perhaps even a whole product line. In the product area we are concerned with developing the right "total product" for the target market. For example, a retailer's total product might include an assortment of goods as well as related services: good parking facilities, giftwrapping, elevators and escalators, charge accounts, and delivery services.

It is useful to classify goods by the way that potential customers typically behave toward them, because the balance of the marketing mix can be organized around these classifications. There are two major categories of products: consumer goods and industrial goods.

Consumer goods fall into four categories: convenience goods, shopping goods, specialty goods, and unsought goods. *Convenience goods* are those that consumers wish to purchase immediately with a minimum of effort. *Shopping goods* are those for which consumers actually shop, for price or quality, or both. *Specialty goods* are those that customers characteristically insist upon, and for which they are willing to make a special shopping effort. *Unsought goods*, on the other hand, are those that potential customers do not yet want or know they can buy. They do not search for these goods and might not buy them even if they saw them. Obviously, planning marketing strategy for unsought goods is especially difficult.

Industrial goods can be placed into six categories: installations, accessory equipment, raw materials, component parts and materials, supplies, and services. *Installations* are large and expensive buildings and equipment that do not become part of the final product and are usually depreciated over several years. *Accessory equipment* is smaller, less expensive equipment that is also depreciated. *Raw materials* do become part of the final product, but they themselves undergo no more processing than is required for convenience, protection, or economy in storage, transportation, or handling. *Component parts and materials,* like raw materials, become a part of the finished product but require more processing than do raw materials. *Supplies*—like raw materials and component parts and materials—are continually used up in a company's operations, but they do not become a part of the final product. *Services* are intangible products which are necessary or desirable to plan, facilitate, or support industrial operations.

Figure 1
The Marketing Mix

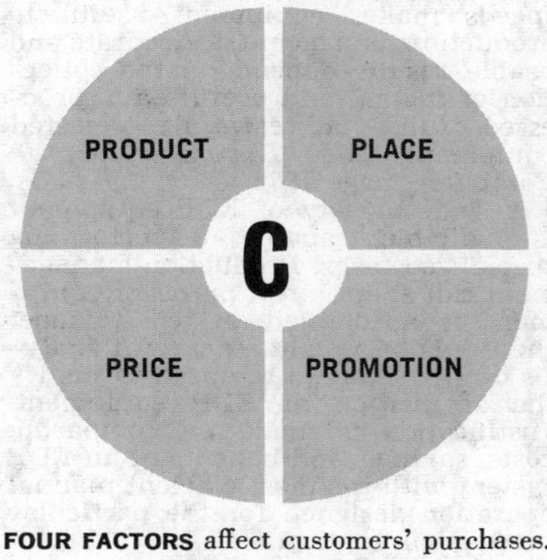

PRODUCT   PLACE

C

PRICE   PROMOTION

FOUR FACTORS affect customers' purchases.

SUPER MARKET PUBLISHING

SUPERMARKET selling requires skillful packaging and distribution to make a product available and attractive to self-service shoppers.

■BRANDING.—Branding a product may have distinct advantages for a company if the customer who makes the decision to buy sees the brand and is impressed by it. Those who make products that are incorporated into others, for example, components for an automobile, have a particularly difficult problem with branding; in fact, spending large sums on branding here might be unwise.

Branding is important to the businessman, because consumers have been observed to demand well-branded items and pay more for them. This consumer loyalty is sometimes called a "consumer franchise." A well-established brand may yield attractive profits for many years. Some of the brands that started in the United States in the 1860's and 1870's are still popular; for example: Doctor Lyon's tooth powder, Borden's Condensed Milk, Quaker Oats, Vaseline, Pillsbury's Best Flour, and Ivory Soap.

It is helpful to recognize three degrees of brand familiarity: recognition, preference, and insistence. Obviously, it would be desirable if a company could achieve the brand-insistence stage for its products.

It is also useful to recognize the difference between family and individual brands. Sometimes, when a number of products are identified under one family brand, the whole line benefits. For example, Heinz "57" would be considered a family brand, and it would be relatively easy to add a new food product under this brand. In other situations, individual brands may be desirable, because one product would not benefit the other. For example, a food product and a glue product manufactured by the same company would probably not benefit each other.

It also is important to recognize the difference between manufacturer (national) and dealer (private) brands. Manufacturers' brands such as Betty Crocker and General Electric are often called national brands because they usually are distributed nationally or at least regionally.

Dealer brands were once considered inferior, but now some dealer brands are distributed nationally and have at least as good a reputation as manufacturer brands. Consider, for example, Ann Page of A & P and the Craftsman, Homart and Kenmore brands of Sears Roebuck.

■PACKAGING.—Packaging is concerned with making the product appear attractive and protecting the product in transit. The former requires artistic talents while the latter increasingly has become a specialty of engineers and packing specialists. Much money time is being devoted to packaging, twice as much, in fact, as for advertising. In the early 1960's, manufacturers spent over $25 billion a year on packaging.

Product Life Cycles.—Products, like people, have life cycles. This is important to recognize because a product's marketing mix should undergo changes during the cycle. We can recognize four major periods: product introduction, market growth, market maturity, and sales decline. Market sales generally increase continuously from the product-introduction stage to the market-maturity stage, but then begin to decline. Significantly, however, the market profit is negative during the product-introduction stage, rises to a peak during the market growth, and then begins to decline. Firms that wish to have a "sure thing," by coming in after the market has been proved, generally come into the more competitive part of a product's life cycle and find total market profits declining. (See Figure 2.)

During the product-introduction stage, the product is not yet sought by customers, so heavy promotion must "pioneer" acceptance. At this time, considerable money may be invested to develop and promote the product. During the market-growth stage, the pioneers begin to enjoy some profits. Competitors are attracted by these profits, however, and

Figure 2   **Life Cycle of a Typical Product**

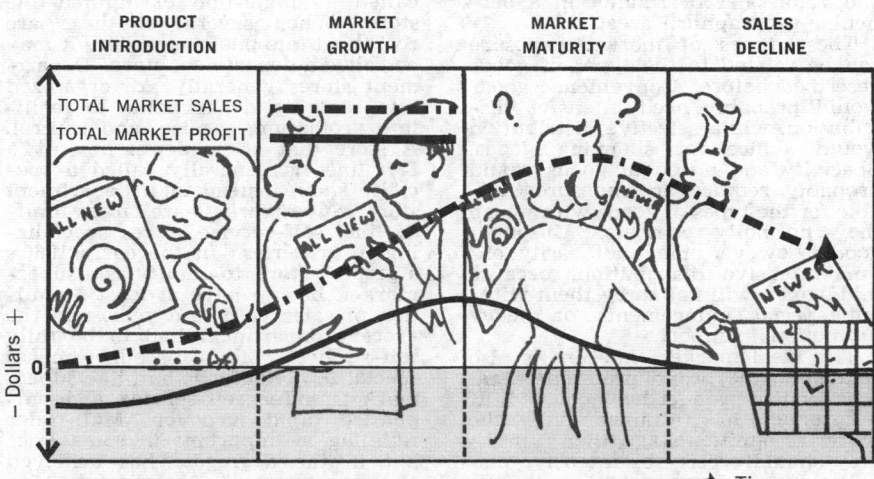

more aggressive competition begins, which emphasizes product quality and variety more than price. During the market-growth stage, total industry profits rise to their highest levels. During the market-maturity stage, competitors may continue to come in, but there is agreement on what products are the most attractive and price competition begins in earnest on these products. Total industry profits begin to decline. Promotion may become more aggressive at this time, helping to account for the declining profits. During the sales-decline stage, those producers who have achieved a "consumer franchise" may continue to enjoy some profits. But price competition may become even more aggressive for the remainder, and competitors will slowly drop out of the market as new products become more attractive to customers.

A great deal of attention and marketing research is devoted to developing new products, but, even so, the results are not impressive. At least four out of every five new products introduced on the market fail. Many more ideas and products are rejected during the development process.

■ **SHORTER LIFE CYCLES.**—Today, product life cycles are becoming shorter, and progressive companies are constantly developing new products, so that they will have a continuous stream of products going into the market-growth stage. During the 1800's and early 1900's it was reasonable to think that products would have twenty-year (or more) life cycles. Now, however, a five-year cycle may be long, in both consumer and industrial goods, because of the billions of dollars that have been going into research and development during the last several years, coupled with the growing acceptance of the modern marketing concept.

Distribution of Products.—A product is not much good to a target customer if it is not available when and where he wants it. The *place* part of the marketing mix is concerned with where, when, and by whom the goods and services are offered for sale. Sometimes, the channels of distribution that connect producers and final customers are very complicated, while in other cases direct contacts between a manufacturer and a final customer are simpler and more satisfactory.

What channels are needed depends on what the product is (discussed above) and what functions are required along the channels.

■ **TYPES OF DISTRIBUTION.**—Two kinds of discrepancies can influence the selection of distribution channels. *Discrepancies of quantity* suggest the addition of middlemen. For example, where there are many small orange growers, it may be economical to assemble their outputs into larger quantities to move them closer to consumers. Further along the channel, however, other middlemen may be needed to break this bulk into smaller quantities again, to satisfy consumers. *Discrepancies in the assortments* produced by some manufacturers and desired by some cus-

tomers may lead to the development of middlemen who assemble more attractive assortments. Retailers, for example, buy a wide assortment of goods from many manufacturers because their customers desire this assortment.

The marketing functions provided along a channel are generally shifted or shared among channel members; in this way, the most efficient channels can be developed. Sometimes, seemingly inefficient channels do very well because they are aiming at different target markets. The marketing concept that a different marketing mix is needed for every target market helps explain why the channels we see in the marketplace are so diverse.

■ **TYPES OF MARKET EXPOSURE.**—There are three types of market exposure. *Intensive distribution* refers to the sale of a product through any responsible wholesaler or retailer who will stock and sell the product. *Selective distribution* refers to the choice of only those wholesalers or retailers who will do a good job with the product. *Exclusive distribution,* which carries selective distribution to the limit, refers to the choice of only one wholesaler or retailer in a particular geographical area.

These types of market exposure can be related to the types of goods described before. Convenience goods would probably need intensive distribution, while selective distribution would suffice for shopping goods. Specialty and unsought goods would probably require an exposure suitable for the types of goods with which they normally compete. Unsought goods, however, may not easily obtain intensive distribution, because middlemen will not carry them without special inducements or heavy promotional support.

The ideal market exposure is also related to the brand preference that a particular product has achieved. If a product has attained only the brand-recognition stage, then it probably should receive as intensive distribution as is consistent with the

goods classification. Potential customers obviously will not expend any effort to locate this product. If the product achieves the brand-preference stage, then perhaps selective distribution will be adequate. Finally, if the brand-insistence stage is reached, selective or even exclusive distribution may be feasible.

■ **TYPES OF WHOLESALERS.**—Two basic types of wholesalers are available for use in channels of distribution: merchant wholesalers and agent middlemen. *Merchant wholesalers* actually take possession and ownership of the goods and provide various other services, such as selling and financing. *Agent middlemen* do not take possession of the goods. Their primary role is selling, but they may also provide financial assistance. The names given wholesalers vary from trade to trade and are not always descriptive of what they do. Therefore, in selecting particular wholesalers, it is critical to determine what functions each one provides and what target markets he serves.

■ **TYPES OF RETAILERS.**—As with wholesalers, there are many types of retailers. The typical small store is called a single-line or limited-line store. When several of these are combined into one larger store it may be called a *department store.* Department stores generally are organized into separate departments to facilitate promotion, service, and control. A store that offers depth in only a few lines is generally called a *specialty shop,* instead of a department store. *Supermarkets* are larger limited-line, self-service stores specializing in groceries. In the early 1960's a grocery store, to qualify as a supermarket, had to have at least $1 million of sales volume a year, and the grocery department had to be fully self-service. Most discount houses specialize in nonfoods but, like supermarkets, offer self-service and emphasize rapid turnover. Mail-order retailing is important in some lines but in the aggregate has achieved about one per cent of total retail sales.

Four Possible (Basic) Channels of Distribution

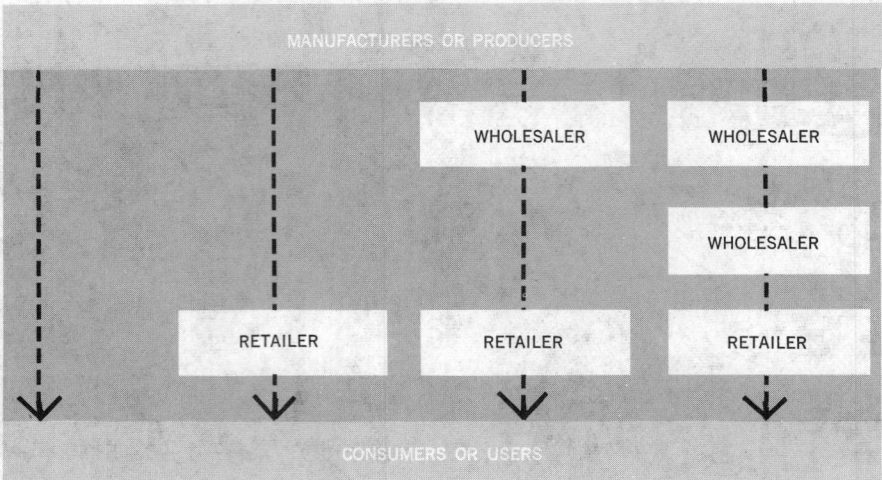

CONSUMERS may receive goods directly or through retailers, whom wholesalers may supply.

■**DISTRIBUTION CENTER CONCEPT.**—The old notion that a middleman is someone who "buys low and sells high," providing storage in the interim, is fast giving way to a new concept. The distribution center concept is concerned with keeping goods moving along the channels of distribution. Wherever some function, such as breaking bulk, assembling, or splitting shipments, must be performed by stopping goods, then there may be a need for a middleman. But, increasingly, middlemen and manufacturers are not stocking goods just to speculate. With better sales forecasting and closer inventory control, they keep goods moving along the channels of distribution.

It is not possible to explain simply all the varieties of distribution channels. In general, each channel reflects the nature of the products that move through the channels (which in turn reflects the attitudes that target customers have toward the product) as well as the adjusting of discrepancies in quantity and assortment that manufacturers and middlemen must do to satisfy the selected target customers. Also important is the size of the manufacturer. A small manufacturer making a single product, for example, may need middlemen, but a larger manufacturer with a wide line will be able to provide the proper assortment and distribute directly to his customers. (See Figure 3.)

Channel selection requires continuous analysis and adaption as target markets shift their needs and preferences and as new competition develops. If a company has used the same channels for more than a few years, it is very likely that some change is in order.

Promotion of Products.—Promotion is concerned with any way of communicating to the target market about the "right" product that will be sold in the "right" place at the "right" price. Specifically, we are concerned with sales promotion, mass selling, and personal selling, which are complementary. *Personal selling* involves direct face-to-face relationships between sellers and potential customers. *Mass selling* seeks to communicate ideas or information to large numbers of customers at the same time. Advertising is the main form of mass selling. It is any paid form of nonpersonal presentation of ideas, goods, or services by an identified sponsor.

Sometimes, a similar result can be accomplished free by publicity. Effective publicity and public relations work can contribute very favorably to a promotional effort, but usually depend on something especially newsworthy or unique, and therefore cannot be depended upon for a sustained promotional effort.

Sales promotion is concerned with nonrecurrent promotional efforts, including the design and distribution of novelties, store signs, catalogues, directories, circulars, and the presentation of displays, sales demonstrations, and trade-show exhibits. Sales promotion men, often concerned with point-of-purchase material and premiums, are generally interested in supplementing the personal and mass selling efforts that are handled by separate company executives.

■**INTEGRATED PROMOTION.**—It is essential that these three promotional ingredients be blended effectively, because the whole may be greater than the sum of these three parts. Advertising may pave the way for the company's salesmen, for example, and sales promotion men may prepare the selling brochures the salesmen will use or the point-of-purchase materials that the salesmen will place in the retail store. Blending these three ingredients may be the job of a marketing manager, who is placed over the sales, advertising, and sales promotion managers.

Promotion is basically concerned with communicating ideas. The behavioral sciences are contributing valuable insights into the communications process and the planning of promotion. Not only the message to be communicated, but also the source of the message and the medium that communicates the message are important in what the receiver finally perceives. The source, message, and medium must be combined in such a way that the receiver hears what the source wishes him to hear. This requires some research on the receiver's values and attitudes. The personal salesman may be able to obtain some immediate feedback from the receiver, so that he can adjust his message to suit the situation. In mass selling and in sales promotion it may be necessary to design research experiments that will give the necessary feedback. (See Figure 4.)

The appropriate promotion blend depends on the size of the promotion budget (a small company may not be able to use the same blend available to a large company), the stage of the product in its life cycle, the target markets (different blends are needed for middlemen and final consumers), and the nature and type of the product itself. Besides the product classification, the complexity of the product and the degree to which the product is different from others (including degree of brand preference) are also important in developing the proper blend.

The Communication Process

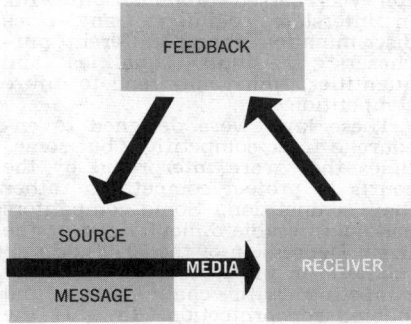

SALES MESSAGES are transmitted from the advertiser by mass media; feedback from receivers influences future advertising.

■**PERSONAL SELLING.**—There is much more to personal selling than just wearing a clean shirt and a new suit. Considerable experience has shown that it is possible to train an alert person to be a good salesman.

It is useful to recognize three different sales tasks: order-getting, order-taking, and supporting activities. Some sales jobs require greater emphasis on one or another of these tasks. *Order-getting* entails aggressively seeking out potential buyers with a well-organized sales presentation that attempts to sell a product, service, or idea. Generally, order-getters are more aggressive and better compensated than *order-takers,* who are more concerned with the routine completion of sales made regularly to the same or similar customers. Order-takers must "wear well." Supporting activities include sales promotion and technical support. Depending on the skills involved, supporting salesmen may be as well compensated as order-takers.

Most sales jobs require some combination of these three sales tasks. It is sales management's or marketing management's job to write job specifications carefully and then select, train, and compensate the men accordingly.

■**ADVERTISING.**—Just as job specifications are needed in personal selling, so advertising objectives should be stated to guide the selling effort.

There are two basic kinds of advertising: product and institutional. *Product* advertising is concerned with informing about and selling a product, while *institutional* advertising focuses on the company or even the industry, and is generally concerned with developing goodwill, with the long-run goal of improving sales and relations with the public.

Product advertising consists of three types: pioneering, competitive, and reminder advertising. *Pioneering* advertising is concerned with selling a product category rather than a specific brand. *Competitive* advertising focuses on a particular brand and would be more appropriate at the market-growth and market-maturity stages. Competitive advertising may be of two types: a direct type, which attempts to get immediate buying action, or an indirect type, which merely attempts to point out features of the product, with the expectation of favorable action when the customer is ready to buy. *Reminder* advertising keeps the company's name before the public when a product has achieved some degree of brand recognition or preference, especially in the market-maturity or sales-decline stages.

Many manufacturers use advertising agencies to handle their advertising. This, in part, is because advertising agencies are specialists in this work and, in part, because of the media discount structure. Generally, national advertisers must pay the full price to advertising media, but their advertising agencies are entitled to a discount if they place the order. In effect, advertising agencies, which serve as sales agents for the advertising media, compete for advertisers' business by offering creative services. This "two-price" system does not apply to local advertisers, and as a result most local retailers create and place their own advertising.

Pricing of Products.—In addition to the other three P's, the marketing manager must decide on the right price, to make his whole marketing mix attractive. He must take into consideration the competition for his target market as well as the practices of competitors and channel members with respect to markups, discounts, and terms of sale.

■**PRICING METHODS.**—There are two basic approaches to setting prices: cost-oriented and demand-oriented. The *cost-oriented* approach attempts to develop good estimates of what it costs to produce or purchase particular items, then adds markups to cover the costs of the functions provided farther along in the channel. This approach may work fairly well, but only by coincidence will it maximize profits, because it ignores demand. Conceivably, the marked-up price would be far too high for potential customers and little or nothing would be sold.

The *demand-oriented* approach attempts to estimate the prices customers will pay for the product (whole marketing mix) and to match this against the costs at different volumes, thus determining the most profitable price and quantity to be sold.

Either pricing approach must take into consideration customary practices in the trade. There may be *quantity discounts* to encourage larger purchases, *seasonal discounts* to encourage purchases at other than the normal period, *cash discounts* to encourage more prompt payment, and *trade discounts* that are given off list price to channel members. Also, there may be special-purpose allowances, such as advertising allowances given to retailers to encourage an unusual amount of promotion.

Specifying who pays the freight, insurance, and other handling charges is part of pricing and is not a minor matter. Sometimes these charges comprise half the delivered cost of the goods. Many sellers traditionally have used "F.O.B. the seller's facility" terms. This means the seller will load the goods onto a truck or railroad car at his own expense, but thereafter the goods belong to the buyer, who assumes complete responsibility, including payment of freight costs.

Sales terms can vary in many ways. Some marketing managers profitably differentiate their firms by adjusting the terms of sale to conform to the preferences of their target customers. For example, some buyers might prefer to pay a delivered price which includes freight and other costs. This relieves them of the responsibility of settling with the transportation agencies in case of damage.

Organizing for Marketing Management. The modern marketing concept often requires a new alignment of management forces. Where the mar-

keting effort might once have been handled by a sales manager with some assistance from an advertising manager, now what is needed is the proper blend of all four P's. Some firms are creating the position of marketing manager or vice-president of marketing to provide this integrating force.

Developing new products is somewhat different from running an ongoing business, and some companies place a manager in charge of new product development. His job may extend beyond the marketing department and involve coordination with the production department or other divisions of the business.

In companies that wholeheartedly adopt the marketing concept, we begin to see a blurring of organizational lines. This is especially true when, with the aid of computers, the functions of sales forecasting, sales analysis, production planning and scheduling, warehousing, inventory control, and shipping are integrated. A number of more progressive companies (for example, General Electric and Westinghouse) have already moved toward the development of "total systems," an extension of the systems approach to marketing.

■**MARKETING MANAGER'S VARIABLES.**— The marketing manager directly controls the four P's. He must also consider and adapt to variables beyond his control, including the following: political and legal environment, economic environment, cultural and social environment, existing competitive situation, and resources and objectives of his own firm. Here we can sketch only the major federal legislation affecting marketing.

■**LEGISLATION AFFECTING MARKETING.**— The Sherman Act (1890) prohibited monopolies or attempts to monopolize. More generally, it banned any contracts, combinations, or conspiracies in restraint of trade. The Clayton Act (1914) went even further, prohibiting price discrimination and exclusive contract arrangements that might substantially lessen competition or tend to create a monopoly in any line of commerce. Also in 1914, the Federal Trade Commission Act was passed to create the Federal Trade Commission and give it control over unfair methods of competition. These laws were not easy to administer, so in 1936 the Robinson-Patman Act was passed to make unlawful, in interstate commerce, any price discrimination among different purchasers of similar qualities and quantities, which may tend to injure competition.

These laws were designed to encourage freer competition, but sometimes they were interpreted by the courts to protect competitors rather than competition. Some competitors had considerable difficulty during the Great Depression of the 1930's. Small retailers, in particular, had difficulty competing with chain stores and lobbied for protection. In 1937 the Miller-Tydings Act (called the Fair Trade law) was passed to permit some price-fixing. This law was strengthened by the McGuire Act of 1952.

In addition to the above laws that affect the general level and nature of competition, the Wheeler-Lea Amendment to the Federal Trade Commission Act was passed in 1938, giving the FTC authority to proceed against unfair or deceptive practices in commerce. This was specifically aimed at unscrupulous advertisers, who could not be reached under the previous legislation because no "injury to competition" was involved.

Modern Marketing Tools.—Computers are now used in product planning, media selection, sales analysis, inventory control, physical distribution planning, pricing, and in the simulation of markets and whole production-marketing systems. With simulation, a firm can experiment with many alternatives without actually trying them in the marketplace. Mathematical and statistical tools are required for such efforts, and increasingly are being applied in marketing. Behavioral science tools—from psychology, sociology, and anthropology—are also being incorporated into marketing research. In fact, marketing researchers are making use of the tools of any disciplines that study human behavior. Further, marketing researchers have gone beyond just studying consumers. They have also adapted tools from operations research, accounting, and statistics to help evaluate alternatives.

Career Opportunities.—Marketing is so all-encompassing that there is opportunity for everyone. From the lowest level order-taker to the most imaginative and competent marketing manager, there is a wide spread of skills and abilities. The opportunities are greater in marketing than in most other business areas, because the marketplace is more dynamic and unpredictable than activities internal to the business. Imaginative young men and women can rise very rapidly by recognizing and exploiting new opportunities. While marketing people may not earn as much to begin with, after five to ten years their salaries match or better those of specialists in other areas. Some businessmen expect that because of the acceptance of the modern marketing concept, the business leaders of the future will come from the marketing area.   —E. Jerome McCarthy

BIBLIOGRAPHY

ALDERSON, W. and SHAPIRO, S. *Marketing and the Computer*. Prentice-Hall, Inc., 1963.

BASS, FRANK. *Mathematical Models and Methods in Marketing*. Richard D. Irwin, Inc., 1961.

BLISS, PERRY. *Marketing and the Behavioral Sciences*. Allyn and Bacon, Inc., 1963.

BOYD, H. and WESTFALL, R. *Marketing Research*. Richard D. Irwin, Inc., 1964.

FREY, ALBERT. *Marketing Handbook*. The Ronald Press Company, 1966.

McCARTHY, E. JEROME. *Basic Marketing—A Managerial Approach* (rev. ed.). Richard D. Irwin, Inc., 1964.

INTERNATIONAL OPERATIONS

Growing Overseas Business.—All but the most shortsighted can clearly see how extensively the United States is involved in international business. Equally as obvious, this involvement is growing steadily, and the time is close at hand when there will be little, if any, distinction between domestic and foreign business for American corporations. Total American direct, private investment abroad exceeds $40 billion, and is increasing by over $6 billion a year. Export sales topped $26 billion in 1965, and this figure is certain to increase.

In fact, in many American companies, international business has become the tail that wags the corporate dog. The worldwide corporation that manufactures worldwide and sells worldwide is a reality. Such a corporation recognizes no geographical boundaries, only regional markets.

Regional Markets and Trade Blocs.—In the drive to create mass markets, countries of the world are joining in trade blocs, which constitute regional markets. One fact stands out: trade blocs are protectionist, regardless of efforts at multilateral, across-the-board tariff reductions. They grant to their member countries better trading conditions than to outsiders. So while it is beneficial to the West for the nations of Europe to band together economically, and perhaps politically, the resulting blocs frustrate rather than promote free trade with the rest of the world.

■**EUROPEAN ECONOMIC COMMUNITY.**—In the forefront of the trade blocs is the European Economic Community (EEC), or *Common Market,* created by the Treaty of Rome, and encompassing Belgium, Luxembourg, France, West Germany, Italy, and the Netherlands. EEC also has several associate members and special economic arrangements with the former French, Belgian, and Italian colonies in Africa. Its purpose is to promote economic integration among its members, and to foster harmonization of labor movement, wages, antitrust laws, patent and trademark provisions, and the like. Despite considerable foot-dragging and a lengthy boycott by France, EEC also is moving toward political integration, although just how much supranational power the six member nations will grant to EEC's governing bodies, and how fast they will grant it, remain a mystery.

EEC is gradually eliminating all internal tariffs and fixing common external tariffs on goods that come in from nonmember countries. In the Kennedy Round of the General Agreement on Tariffs and Trade (GATT), nonmember countries—the U.S. in particular—are negotiating reciprocal tariff cuts with EEC. The president of the United States has the authority to cut tariffs by as much as 50 per cent on broad categories of goods, including agricultural commodities. Negotiations have been held up because EEC members cannot agree on a common policy for agricultural tariffs.

■**EUROPEAN FREE TRADE ASSOCIATION.**—This association was formed by the Treaty of Stockholm as a counter to the European Common Market. Frustrated by France in its attempts to join the EEC, Great Britain led the way in forming EFTA, which includes Norway, Sweden, Denmark, Switzerland, Austria, Portugal, and the United Kingdom, with Finland as an associate. EFTA is a less complicated organization than EEC and has a less ambitious program. Its purpose is to establish a free-trade area in which tariffs and quotas will be gradually eliminated. The seven members, however, will present no common external tariff. Like EEC, EFTA is reducing its internal tariffs in steps, with 1970 as the deadline for complete elimination of all restrictions. Both blocs, however, are ahead of schedule.

■**LATIN AMERICAN FREE TRADE ASSOCIATION.**—In 1960 the Latin American Free Trade Association (LAFTA) was formed by the Montevideo Treaty. Its members—Argentina, Brazil, Chile, Colombia, Ecuador, Mexico, Peru, Paraguay, and Uruguay—are operating on a 12-year schedule to gradually eliminate (a minimum of 8 per cent annually) duties, charges, and restrictions among themselves. The treaty does not call for common tariffs against imports from nonmembers. At best, however, LAFTA is a qualified customs union and its progress has left much to be desired.

■**CENTRAL AMERICAN COMMON MARKET.**—In 1960 the Central American Common Market (CACM) was formed by the Treaty of Economic Integration, signed by Guatemala, Honduras, Nicaragua, and El Salvador. Costa Rica joined in 1962. The plan was to have a common market, which would operate for 20 years, in full swing by 1965. With a few exceptions, all natural and manufactured products of member countries are to move in free trade. A common external tariff is to be applied under a standard Central American customs code. In 1965 certain leading Latin American economists and political leaders lent their support to the formation of a Latin American Common Market that would supersede both LAFTA and CACM. CACM is on record as opposing the union, while most LAFTA officials appear to be in favor.

Methods of Conducting International Business.—The choice among exporting, licensing, or manufacturing abroad seldom is an arbitrary one, and management must be flexible enough to change from one method to another.

■**LICENSING ARRANGEMENTS.**—There are American licensing firms that will assume full responsibility for securing a foreign license and negotiating the contract; if necessary, they will even set up a new manufacturing entity abroad. Such licensing firms usually take an equity position in the new venture instead of, or in addition to, a percentage of the royalty payments from the overseas licensee to the American licensor.

One common drawback to licensing is that the licensor creates a competitor who, once the agreement expires, will go into independent operation on his own. This argument is counterbalanced by the fact that the

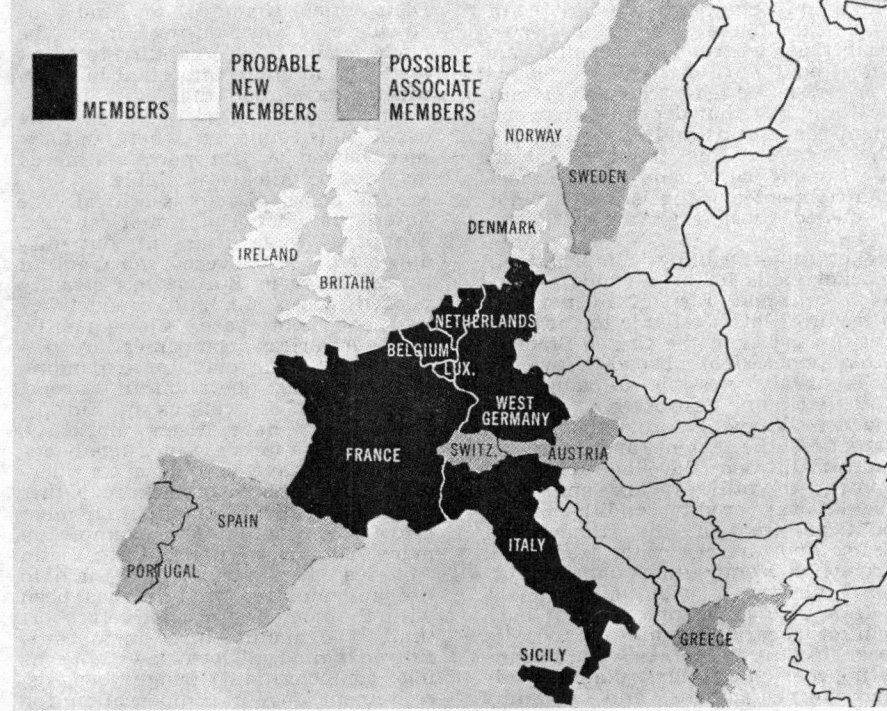

THE COMMON MARKET has a potential trading market of more than 300 million people.

565

licensee often will contribute a reverse flow of technology. Agreements, moreover, can be negotiated for a period long enough to make the original technology obsolete unless new information continually feeds into the manufacturing operation.

■OVERSEAS MANUFACTURING.—Because of currency restrictions, tariffs and other trade restraints, or intense competition (to name but a few reasons), it is no longer feasible to export to many markets. A likely alternative is to set up a manufacturing operation in the country involved. When this happens, the decision must be made to go it alone or take a local partner. Wholly-owned subsidiaries are, all things being equal, the easiest and safest to handle. There is no fear of local interference in the management of the company and no need to distribute profits locally. On the other hand, there may be good reasons for taking in a local partner, who may provide additional capital or facilities, or have access to franchises, licenses, or other special concessions. Often, it is local policy to require that all foreign ventures have a certain percentage of local capital and management participation. (Local control is required in some countries.) And in some politically unstable, or particularly nationalistic, countries it may be wise to take a local partner who can seek and get favors and deal more effectively with labor, government, and the public.

■WHOLLY-OWNED SUBSIDIARIES.—Generally speaking, the wholly-owned subsidiary is best suited for (1) small-scale operations that offer specialized services or import and distribute the parent company's products locally; (2) a new service or manufacturing enterprise where American know-how or capital investment is of overriding importance to the host country; (3) operations in backward countries, where local capital and know-how have not yet developed; (4) extractive industries (oil or mineral mining) that depend on government concessions and export most of the product. The trend is toward local participation, and fewer American companies are insisting on wholly-owned subsidiaries abroad.

Marketing.—Defining international markets calls for an attitude as well as an aptitude. First of all, the kind of refined data available to the market researcher in the United States is often nonexistent abroad. However, it is usually possible to gauge the potential of prospective foreign markets. Some criteria: population statistics; the extent and trend of industrialization; the stage of development of utilities; tax and legal regulations; credit conditions; the political situation; the standard of living and literacy rate; trademark protection; competition, unusual cultural factors, distribution channels.

It is also important to treat each market separately, and to consider local customs and mores when formulating marketing plans, planning advertising campaigns, and designing packaging and promotional materials. For example, a successful trade name in one country can be an objectionable word in another. However, qualified advice is available from local affiliates of American advertising agencies and consultants. Usually, the most severe problems occur when the company attempts to run the overseas marketing operation from the home office in the United States. On-the-scene representation and feedback are essential.

Advertising offers a good illustration of the need to regard each foreign market as an individual challenge, and act accordingly. For example, in countries or areas where illiteracy is high, it is useless to offer lengthy written messages. But radio, electric signs, large billboards with a minimum of copy, and attractive point-of-purchase signs can be effective advertising media. In areas where the lack of electricity makes use of radio and television impossible, sound trucks and billboards have been effective.

Production.—The key to successful production abroad, as in the United States, is maintaining quality control while producing a marketable product at a competitive price. Generally speaking, if the manufacturer carefully selects his plant site and his market, the job is no more difficult abroad than it is in the United States. Of course, there are many problems and conditions to be faced.

Once he decides to manufacture locally, the manufacturer must be sure of all regulations governing his product—local standards and national policy, methods of handling and storage, and safety precautions, to name but a few. These vary from country to country. Accessibility of raw materials, as well as power and transportation, are of course critical. Distribution channels, too, must be adequate. Warehousing must be made available. The ability to think ahead is far more important in manufacturing abroad than it is in domestic production, particularly in the developing countries, where unforeseen power or transportation needs may not be quickly available.

■LABOR COSTS.—Labor is critical. The differential between American and European wages has all but disappeared. A severe shortage of skilled labor in Europe has steadily pushed wages up, and productivity has not kept pace. Consequently, some American companies are re-evaluating their plans of expanding manufacturing operation in Europe.

In Japan, as well as in Europe, labor costs have risen markedly, reflecting the increase in fringe benefits, which have become a considerable part of the wage package. Other vagaries of the labor situation must also be considered. For example, in many countries (particularly Latin America) it is almost impossible to fire an employee once he has been with the company a relatively short time. The manufacturer must carefully examine all local laws governing compensation, fringe benefits, retirement, layoff, compensation for inventions and other contributions, special housing provisions, and the like. Often, local labor conditions prohibit the establishment of a plant, even though other incentives are compelling.

In less-developed areas of industrialized countries (as in southern Italy), and in less-developed countries, however, it is not unusual for the government to make special provisions regarding labor, taxes, and certain legal restrictions in order to attract new industry. These might even include worker education, worker housing, and transportation.

Financing Private Foreign Operations.—An American company, even though it has sufficient funds to finance its overseas operations, may prefer for several reasons to use outside sources. Where nationalism is intense, capital participation by local investors is one means of making a subsidiary more acceptable. Further, local currency loans, repayable in kind, are an excellent hedge against devaluation. A foreign subsidiary, established as a separate entity and capitalized, partly at least, by local financing, is often a better and safer risk than a wholly-owned branch. Local laws often prohibit or restrict the operations of any but locally incorporated structures.

■EDGE ACT CORPORATIONS.—These subsidiaries of American banks, formed under a 1919 amendment to the Federal Reserve Act to promote foreign banking and international investment, are good, but often neglected investment devices. There are more than 30 Edge Act corporations, and others are pending. These corporations function by purchasing equity in foreign companies, including banks. Because there is a greater

AGENCY FOR INTERNATIONAL DEVELOPMENT

FOREIGN factories, like this Kaiser Jeep plant in Taiwan, build for many U.S. firms.

risk in equity investment than in straight loans, Edge Act corporations usually participate in countries where investments are protected by local legislation or United States guarantees, or where the political situation is stable. Often, because of intense local competition from financial institutions, particularly in Europe, Edge Act corporations must buy into local consortiums.

However, Edge Act corporations usually are called upon only when the private enterprise cannot get financing through usual channels and is forced to relinquish an equity share in the business in order to get capital. As a rule, the average Edge Act corporation will hold its equity position from five to seven years until the company is successful, and then sell out at a profit.

■ **U.S. BANKS ABROAD.**—Also meriting consideration are the foreign branches of American banks, of which there are now more than 160. They can give valuable assistance to the American exporter or investor, and often will offer lower interest rates than those charged by foreign subsidiaries or foreign banks.

Finally, many private American investment banking houses are willing to participate in well-conceived foreign ventures. Among these are Deltec Corporation of Panama, American International Investment Corporation of San Francisco, American and Foreign Power Company of New York, and the American Express Company.

Besides these wholly private sources of international financing, more than 125 development banks of various types operate throughout the world under the sponsorship of local governments. They are either privately or publicly owned, or ownership is mixed. They are in business to create local capital markets.

■ **BALANCE OF PAYMENTS.**—The financing of international operations figures strongly in the efforts of the United States government in recent years to correct its unfavorable balance of payments. The government aims to halt the serious outflow of dollars and gold to foreign countries. Stated simply, this means that the United States is paying out more than it is taking in—and has been doing so for several years. This unfavorable balance of payments should not be confused with the very favorable balance of United States trade. The former includes all American international payments—loans, tourist expenditures, payments for imports, expenditures by United States installations (military and civilian) abroad, and all other forms of United States spending overseas. The latter, however, considers only exports relative to imports, and the United States consistently sells more abroad than it buys.

To correct the unfavorable balance of payments and halt the drain on America's dollar and gold reserves, President Johnson requested in February 1965 that business voluntarily limit capital exports. This followed by two years the imposition of the Interest Equalization Tax which pe-

nalized American citizens who purchase foreign securities in the United States. In effect, these two measures have closed the American capital market for international financing.

To continue investing abroad, while at the same time limiting the outflow of dollars, American corporations have had to turn increasingly to Europe for funds. In the nine-month period ending March 1966, some 30 American corporations raised a total of $639 million by floating international bonds in Europe. As a rule, these European dollar bonds are purchased by wealthy individuals whose funds are traditionally administered by banks in Switzerland, Belgium, The Netherlands, and Great Britain. Funds raised in this manner do not adversely affect America's balance of payments, because the bonds are not offered to American residents. The foreign-held dollars being invested in these European dollar bonds are already outside the United States. Some outflow of funds from the United States occurs when foreigners switch funds previously held in American domestic securities, but this is only a bookkeeping transfer and does not harm the balance of payments, unless the dollars involved end up in foreign central banks.

■ **EFFECT OF VOLUNTARY CURBS.**—How well the European capital markets will hold up under their heavy burden remains to be seen. This much is certain: the voluntary curbs on the exportation of American capital have been less than an unqualified success. Although American firms are turning increasingly to foreign capital markets, capital continues to be exported, although at a reduced rate. Critics blame the curbs, in part at least, for the unfavorable shift in America's balance of trade (that is, declining exports); this, they claim, results in a surplus too small to offset part of the investment-associated outflow of dollars. American corporations maintain, and not without factual evidence, that foreign investments generate exports. In any event, the voluntary program of controls on capital exports appears destined to continue for some time to come.

It should be added that attempts to reduce the outflow of dollars and gold tend to tighten the world capital and liquidity situation as a whole. The storing of dollars abroad has given rise to Eurodollars, which are United States dollars deposited in European branches of United States, Canadian, Japanese, and other banks. These dollars draw higher interest rates than can be earned on time deposits in America. They are loaned to high-ranking banks in European and Japanese financial centers, which in turn loan them to corporate borrowers at rates lower than those in the borrowers' home markets.

International Agencies for Financing.—Generally speaking, private American banks do not earmark funds for foreign operations. This is especially true now that banks have been asked to aid the balance-of-payments program by curbing foreign loans. Although commercial banks are a very

valuable source of assistance to exporters, they do not like to allocate funds for foreign operations until they have satisfied domestic demands, and unless they are assured that the loan will be repaid within a short period in an uninflated currency or in currency that can be converted to dollars. Thus, most commercial banks prefer to restrict their export loans to short-term arrangements (no more than 180 days), and are reluctant to grant medium-term foreign credit (180 days to five years). Few private banks ever go beyond four years, and most balk at anything over two years. Long-term loans (beyond five years) are generally out of the question for private banks.

■ **EXIMBANK.**—Fortunately for the American exporter and his overseas customer, the Export-Import Bank of Washington (Eximbank) takes over where the private banks leave off. It is important to remember, however, that Eximbank supplements the private banks' activities; it does not compete with them. Established in 1935 as a corporation and an agency of the United States, Eximbank aids in the financing of exports and imports, underwrites some form of foreign credit insurance, and takes an active part in the exchange of commodities between American overseas territories and foreign countries.

Eximbank, in effect, carries on general banking business by purchasing, discounting, rediscounting, selling, negotiating, and guaranteeing notes, drafts, checks, bills of exchange, acceptances, bankers' acceptances, cable transfers, and other evidences of indebtedness. In practice, Eximbank pays the American manufacturer or seller directly; the buyer abroad then is indebted to Eximbank for the dollars involved. Often Eximbank will work hand in hand with the exporter's commercial bank. For example, the commercial bank will finance its portion of an export sale with recourse to the exporter, and Eximbank will cover the balance of the transaction. This is done by an agreement between the commercial banks and Eximbank, in which the latter guarantees to purchase the debt from the commercial bank if the purchaser defaults on principal or interest.

Eximbank also encourages non-recourse financing of medium-term credit by commercial banks and other private financial institutions. It does so by guaranteeing certain risks that commercial banks otherwise would have to assume.

When export sales are to be financed, the central problem is that of providing dollar credit to overseas purchasers. Eximbank's political-risk guarantees are designed to encourage additional credit from private sources, commercial banks in particular, as an alternative to increased government financing. Briefly, then, the short- and medium-term political risk programs rely on the exporter or a commercial bank to put up the dollars as well as assume the commercial risk (which can be insured through the Foreign Credit Insurance Association) for export credit transactions.

Since a substantial number of capital goods and allied product exports are sold on short-term credit, Eximbank provides short-term political risk guarantees, including transfer risk (that is, inability to transfer local currency into dollars or to the exporter within six months), as well as the usual war risks.

Eximbank covers the same noncommercial risks on medium-term export credit transactions (180 days to five years) that it includes under its short-term political risk guarantee. The main differences between the two are that medium-term guarantees are issued directly by the Bank; the exporter is not required to cover all his export sales involving medium-term credit terms; and Eximbank does not offer to guarantee credit for all countries to which its short-term program applies.

■ FCIA.—Since February 1962, Eximbank, working with a syndicate of more than 65 private insurance firms known as the Foreign Credit Insurance Association, has provided a cover to American exporters for commercial as well as political risks. FCIA, a quasipublic organization, by the middle of 1966, had already insured more than $2 billion of American exports. Under FCIA's short-term comprehensive policy, the average cost is less than $5,000 per $1 million of coverage.

Generally speaking, commercial risks—the ordinary risks of doing business, such as defaulting, business failure, etc., by the overseas customer—will be insured equally by FCIA and Eximbank. Political risks, on the other hand, will be insured solely by Eximbank. FCIA provides insurance short-term credit transactions up to 180 days (up to one year in special situations). Medium-term insurance on credits ranging from 181 days to five years is also available.

■ AID.—Of special interest to the American businessman doing business abroad is the Agency for International Development. AID encompasses functions formerly carried on by the International Cooperation Administration, the Development Loan Fund, and the Food-for-Peace program (Public Law 480). In general, AID makes an agreement with a country for goods or services necessary for the defense and development of that country, and consequently the Free World. The goods or services are bought through normal commercial channels with funds for payment made available through regular banking facilities.

The foreign customer notifies AID's Office of Small Business at least 30 days in advance of the order, which is placed with an American supplier. This office advises interested American businessmen of the goods or services to be bought, and the name and address of the customer, as well as other pertinent information. AID does not finance export sales, imports for resale, working capital loans, or loans for refunds or refinancing, unless financing is not available anywhere else in the Free World, including Eximbank.

AID has under its wing the very important, and often ignored, Office for Private Enterprise, which has two divisions. The Investment Development Division helps nations generate programs that will attract private investment, local and foreign. The Investment Guarantee Division provides guarantees against currency inconvertibility, expropriation, and losses resulting from war in those countries with which it has an investment guarantee treaty. IGD also covers investments of U.S. citizens or companies in new overseas projects that promote economic development or foreign trade. To qualify, such projects must have the approval of the local foreign government.

■ IMF.—Another key agency is the International Monetary Fund. Although IMF does not lend money to private business, it is an accurate barometer of a country's international credit standing. IMF is the largest source of quickly available international credit for member nations. When a country runs short of one of the key currencies—dollars, francs, pounds sterling—it can borrow from IMF, whose capital comes from gold and currencies paid into it on a quota basis by member countries.

■ IBRD.—The International Bank for Reconstruction and Development (World Bank) is another important source of financing, although it has not been used as effectively as it might have been by American business. The IBRD makes loans to governments, government agencies, and private business in its 74 member countries. American business benefits from the Bank's activities as supplier of goods and services to recipients of IBRD loans. The bulk of the Bank's loans are medium- and long-term, and are granted especially to basic industries and services. Loans usually are made for 5 to 25 years, and are granted to countries that cannot get capital at reasonable rates elsewhere. Private firms can obtain direct loans in local currency from the Bank for projects in member countries. But the Bank prefers to deal in hard currencies, government guarantees, and fixed-interest amortizing loans.

■ IFC.—The International Finance Corporation, created in 1956 by the IBRD to finance private enterprise in developing countries, is, on the other hand, more flexible and liberal than the IBRD. To be a member of IFC, a country must also be a IBRD and IMF member. IFC lends to, and buys into, private companies without government guarantees, does not lend to governments, and grants flexible terms to suit the needs of the borrower. IFC prefers industrial projects but will finance agricultural projects that support an industrial activity; it, also, will invest in expansion and modernization of existing facilities. There may be times when the American exporter will want to turn to IFC, instead of the Eximbank, to secure long-term credit for an overseas customer. Further, while IFC does not finance sales for American exporters, as does the Eximbank, an overseas customer can arrange financing with IFC, then be able to buy from the American exporter.

When IFC invests in a project, it advances part of the money as a loan at a fixed rate of interest, and part of the money on a contingent or capital-option basis. When the enterprise increases its earnings to a certain level, IFC takes its additional share in the form of increased interest charges, or by exercising stock options and then selling the stock on the open market.

■ IDA.—The International Development Association is another important government agency connected with international financing. Like IFC, it is an affiliate of the IBRD. It is managed by the IBRD's directors and staff, and only IBRD members are eligible for membership. IDA was created when the urgent need arose for an international monetary agency that would make funds available to less-developed countries, with less resulting strain on their balance-of-payments positions than would be caused by the more conservative terms of the IBRD. IDA financing is available to governments, public institutions, and private business. Government guarantees are not required. As in the case of IFC, however, loans are not made if funds are available at reasonable terms from other sources.

■ IADB.—The Inter-American Development Bank began operations in 1961 to help accelerate economic development in Latin America. It carries on ordinary banking operations for Latin America, similar to those performed by the IBRD, and its Fund for Special Operations functions much like the IDA. The Bank, designed to help private enterprise in Latin America, is anxious to attract private capital, and is primarily interested in granting loans and guarantees for projects related to economic development.

—Robert W. Young

BIBLIOGRAPHY

DYER, JOHN M. and FREDERICK C. DYER. *Export Financing: Modern U.S. Methods.* University of Miami Press, 1963.

ETTINGER, DR. KARL E. (ed.). *International Handbook of Management.* McGraw-Hill, Inc., 1965.

GILBERT, ROBERT A. *International Investment.* Simmons-Boardman Publishing Corp., 1963.

LEWIS, LESLIE LLEWELLYN (ed.). *International Trade Handbook.* The Dartnell Corp., 1965.

MARKHAM, JESSE W., CHARLES E. FIERO, HOWARD S. PIQUET. *The Common Market—Friend or Competitor.* New York University Press, 1964.

METZGER, STANLEY D. *Trade Agreements and the Kennedy Round.* Coiner Publications, Ltd., 1964.

SHANNON, IAN. *International Liquidity.* Henry Regnery Co., 1964.

STANLEY, ALEXANDER O. *Handbook of International Marketing.* McGraw-Hill, Inc., 1963.

WASSERMAN, MAX J. and RAY M. WARE. *The Balance of Payments.* Simmons-Boardman Publishing Co., 1965.

BUSINESS AND THE COMPUTER

EDP in the Modern World.—As every schoolboy must know by now, a computer is a device that translates raw data into meaningful, useful information. Its function is to amplify mental energy just as other machines amplify physical energy. This may sound mundane; it is, in fact, anything but that. What else among man's creations has had so profound an impact upon us in so little time? What other invention has undergone so rapid or dramatic a metamorphosis? Today's computers are thousands of times faster and more powerful than their recent predecessors. The "magic machine," comprehensible only to engineers and physicists, has evolved into a basic tool for manufacturing, banking, government, education, defense and space, medical research, marketing and management. Our lives are affected by the computer to a far greater extent than most of us suspect, yet we are only beginning to feel its impact and we are just beginning to use its power effectively.

The modern world is in the midst of a resounding information explosion. It echoes all around us—in the press, in the research laboratories, in our schools and universities. In the coming decade, we know that we are going to double the whole storehouse of human information. In the next ten years, man will learn more about himself and his environment than he has learned since 1946 (the beginning of the Age of the Computer), as much as he has learned since the first major rumblings of the Industrial Revolution in 1750—a greater harvest of knowledge, in fact, than all his gleanings since Stonehenge and the Valley of the Nile.

The electronic computer is the detonator of this information explosion. We are living in the most dynamic era of human history, thanks largely to the computer. We are all explorers with an electronic force at our disposal that can rocket us through centuries of progress in our own lifetime. Most important, it is a force with which we, unlike the explorers before us, can shape our objectives.

History of Computing.—Data have existed ever since man began to record his activities on the walls of caves. Man's unique penchant for abstraction led him to develop numbers systems that simplified the task of handling information. He found that with numbers he could predict natural events, establish values, and invent tools to help him to plan, trade and barter, and build. The Great Pyramids, the records of Phoenician voyages, enigmatic Stonehenge—these and a thousand other dusty remains of man's endeavors still testify to his mastery of mathematics and his ability to put his ever-accumulating knowledge and skills to work.

Surprisingly, the first significant instrument for figuring, the abacus, did not appear until sometime in the fifth century B.C. It wasn't until 300 B.C. that some long-forgotten but practical-minded Arabian devised a symbol to represent "zero." The first serious attempt at mechanizing computation was still two thousand years in the future.

That attempt came in the middle 1600's, as Europe awoke from its dark sleep to trumpets of discovery in the New World and rumblings of revolution in the Old. This was the age of Isaac Newton—a time of scientific revelation, and a time of invention.

The mathematicians of the 1600's gave serious attention to devices for simplifying computation and amplifying the usefulness of numbers. In 1622, the slide rule was developed by an Englishman, William Oughtred. A Scot, John Napier, invented logarithms and popularized a vest-pocket calculator. In 1642, Blaise Pascal, the French philosopher and mathematician, invented a gear-driven machine that added and subtracted. In the late 1700's, another Frenchman, Joseph Marie Jacquard, devised an automatic loom, capable of weaving complex patterns, that was controlled by a means destined to find a more significant application in computing machines—the punched card.

■ **BABBAGE'S ANALYTICAL ENGINE.**—Then, in the early nineteenth century, into Europe's crowded scientific pageant stepped Charles Babbage, English philosopher, practical scientist, mathematician, inventor, and eccentric genius. In 1831, after building a machine that solved algebraic problems, Babbage began working on a new machine, so advanced in concept even for that enlightened era, that it cost him his fortune, threatened his reputation, and consumed forty years of his life. He called it his Analytical Engine. As Babbage envisioned it, the Engine would be able to solve, part by part and in logical sequence, any conceivable arithmetic problem.

BABBAGE'S MACHINE, although never completed, anticipated many of the principal features in use in modern computers.

Its vast array of gears, axles, and cranks, powered by steam, was to perform up to 60 additions a minute.

The Analytical Engine shared four basic elements with today's most advanced computing systems: a memory for storing the raw data needed in any calculation; an arithmetic unit; a means of controlling the transfer of data back and forth between the arithmetic unit and the memory system; and provision for entering data and getting information out of the system. The Engine's memory was to have stored 50,000 digits. For controlling the flow of data into and out of the Engine, Babbage proposed to use punched cards similar to those developed by Jacquard. The most astounding feature of the Engine's design was its ability to make decisions, that is, to choose logically between alternate courses. This operation, known today as the "conditional branch," is an essential function in modern computers.

Babbage set perilously high standards for his Engine. But despite financial support from his government and forty years of his own efforts, the great Analytical Engine was never built.

■ **FIRST PRACTICAL ADDING MACHINE.**—Meanwhile, a demand arose for smaller calculating devices. In banking and in industry, swift expansion threatened to bury the pen-and-ink accountant under an avalanche of figure work. In Europe and the United States, inventors by the score went to work on a multitude of machines. Among them a man destined for prominence was William Seward Burroughs, whose trials and triumphs form a classic American story.

As a young bank bookkeeper in the 1880's, Burroughs saw the need for a machine that quickly and accurately could add long lists of figures, a job then still being done laboriously by battalions of clerks.

An engineer by instinct, Burroughs designed and built an adding machine, simple to operate, that listed the numbers it was adding on a paper tape. A company was formed in St. Louis to manufacture the machines. Fifty were produced and placed out on trial. By this time the project had taken ten years, consumed a fortune in speculative funds, and cost Burroughs his health.

Almost without exception, the machines failed after a few days' operation. Burroughs repaired them, but again they failed. One by one, the inventor cast them all from a second-story window onto a rubbish heap. Still unwilling to accept defeat, he began again. Burroughs improved his design, strengthened it, and devised a hydraulic governor to smooth its operation. New machines were made. They worked, and kept on working.

In 1925, almost a century after Babbage's efforts, Dr. Vannevar Bush and his associates at M.I.T. were at work on a large-scale mechanical analog computer, the "differential analyzer." Bush's machine was a complex, multilayered array of interconnecting rods and gears driven by electric motors. Installed at M.I.T., Bush's computer was used for years in solving differential equations. An improved model, further electrified and more precise, secretly calculated artillery trajectories during World War II.

■ **FIRST LARGE-SCALE DIGITAL COMPUTER.** —By 1944, a scant generation after Bush's initial work, an electromechanical digital computer bearing the formidable title of Automatic Sequence Controlled Calculator, Mark I, had been built and installed at Harvard. Mark I, the brainchild of Howard Aiken, used electromechanical relays similar to those in telephone switching exchanges.

But then, as the war headed toward its climax, events demanded an even greater rate of progress. A serious and bitter technological race had begun. Winning it would require the propelling energy of high-speed computation, and the secret lay in applying the same force that swiftly carried world news into American living rooms—electronics.

■ **FIRST ELECTRONIC COMPUTER.** —The first electronic computer, developed by John Mauchly and J. Presper Eckert at the University of Pennsylvania's Moore School of Electrical Engineering, went into operation early in 1946. Eighteen thousand vacuum tubes now did the work of reluctant gears and clacking switches. The computer, named ENIAC (Electronic Numerical Integrator and Calculator), performed 50 divisions, 500 multiplications, or 5,000 additions in a single second. It was estimated to work faster than 500 standard calculators manned by experts.

ENIAC was soon joined by other university- or government-built machines with such acronyms as EDVAC, SWAC, ORACLE, MANIAC, and JOHNNIAC (after the renowned physicist and computer pioneer John von Neumann). They became research tools for exploring nuclear energy, advanced electronics, and sophisticated weaponry.

Nor did the potential of computation and automatic data processing escape the sharp eyes of American businessmen. Perhaps the most famous of the early business machines was Eckert and Mauchly's Univac I (universal automatic computer), which was installed in 1951 by the Bureau of the Census. It labored there long and well, and now reposes in the Smithsonian Institution. Univac became the first mass-produced commercial computer.

■ **GROWTH OF COMPUTER USE.** —In 1955, only a few hundred computers were in operation in the United States. By 1960 their ranks had swelled to 4,500, and vacuum tubes had been displaced by transistors and similar miniature components that made the newer "second generation" systems faster and far more reliable. Computer "languages" such as ALGOL, COBOL, and FORTRAN, were being developed to make it easier for businessmen and scientists alike to communicate with their machines.

By the end of 1966, an estimated 40,000 systems were in service in the United States and abroad. The combined value of computing equipment, programs, and service delivered in 1965 came to roughly $6.5 billion. Industry estimates call for an annual delivery rate of some $10 billion by 1970.

In 1965, too, the "third generation" systems appeared, computers characterized by newly developed "integrated" circuits of microscopic size, by operating speeds often measured in nanoseconds (billionths of a second), by automatic operating systems which permit computers to control their own operations and even correct their mistakes, and by their ability to work on a number of unrelated programs and generate information for multiple users—all simultaneously.

Inside the Computer. —The foregoing discussion was about two types of machines, analog and digital. The slide rule and the speedometer are analog devices; they measure the relationship of one quantity to another. *Analog computers* do much the same thing, working with energy, pressures, distances, angles, and other physical quantities. Since these may be continuously changing or fluctuating, the computer's ability to generate a stream of comparisons makes it possible to examine trends and patterns.

In the electric analog computer, voltage, current, and impedance represent mathematically corresponding physical properties. For example, the rate at which petroleum flows through a pipe can be simulated by a voltage that varies as the rate of flow varies; the acceleration of an object or process can be represented by an electrical resistance that varies inversely to the rate of change. The analog computer is ideally suited for applications where changes in the input, that is, the quantities or occurrences being measured, can be described as continuous or smooth curves. *Digital computers,* on the other hand, work with problems in which quantities can be represented as numbers and where changes are described in increments or steps.

As might be expected, analog computers are at work principally in laboratory testing and analysis, in machine tool and automatic process control for industry, and in military service, where they compute trajectories or perform high-speed guidance functions.

Digital computers have more varied talents primarily because they deal with specific numbers; consequently, they are more widely used. In all subsequent discussion, the term "computer" will refer to digital machines.

Different uses call for different types of computers. The first machines were developed for scientific and engineering computation. Work being done today in supersonic airframe design or nuclear research typically calls for machines with great computational power. Most computers currently in use, however, are at work in routine or standardized data processing operations. For economic reasons, a different breed of computer was developed for these jobs in which the workload, in terms of input and output, is likely to be heavy but essentially repetitive. In commercial and Federal Reserve banks, for example, "data processing" systems handle a flow of 17 billion checks annually. This is a massive job of collection, distribution, accounting, and analysis.

More recently, the evolution of sophisticated information systems for management has brought about a third variety of computers in which data processing capability is melded with computing power. These computer systems are helping improve our understanding of how business operates and how it is affected by many crosscurrents.

Computers, whatever their use, display certain basic similarities. A discussion of computer applications will mean more if we first review these common elements—the "hardware" and "software"—that make up a computer system.

■ **HARDWARE AND SOFTWARE.** —Hardware refers to the computer's mechanical, electrical, magnetic, and electronic components. Software includes printed material, library programs, computer languages and compilers, executive routines, and other program elements that are required to make the computer do something useful. A "program," reduced to its simplest terms, is a sequential step-by-step set of instructions with which the computer solves a problem. We can "see" a program as represented by a flow-chart or a stack of punched cards; a program is meaningful to the computer only when it has been translated into electrical signals.

The modern computer retains the basic elements established by Babbage, namely, a provision for the input and output of data, a memory system, an arithmetic unit, and a means of controlling the transfer of data. *Figure 1* shows the relationship of these elements in the B5500 computer system.

■ **INPUT AND OUTPUT.** —The most common input devices are punched-card or punched-tape readers, magnetic-tape units, special typewriters, and bank-check sorter-readers. Output units include card or tape punches, line printers and listers, magnetic tape units and input/output typewriters. These are all items of hardware.

New input and output techniques are extending the computer's reach. Special sensing devices and data-communications units in the factory are collecting production data for computer analysis. Punched-card or typewriter units in warehouses advise the computer of orders received and shipments made, so that the computer can automatically bill customers and order the purchase or manufacture of replacement inventory items. In many savings banks, console units at tellers' windows transmit data directly to a computer that may be miles away, so that deposits or withdrawals can be posted simultaneously in the customer's passbook and in the computer's electronic memory.

Television-like display units are be-

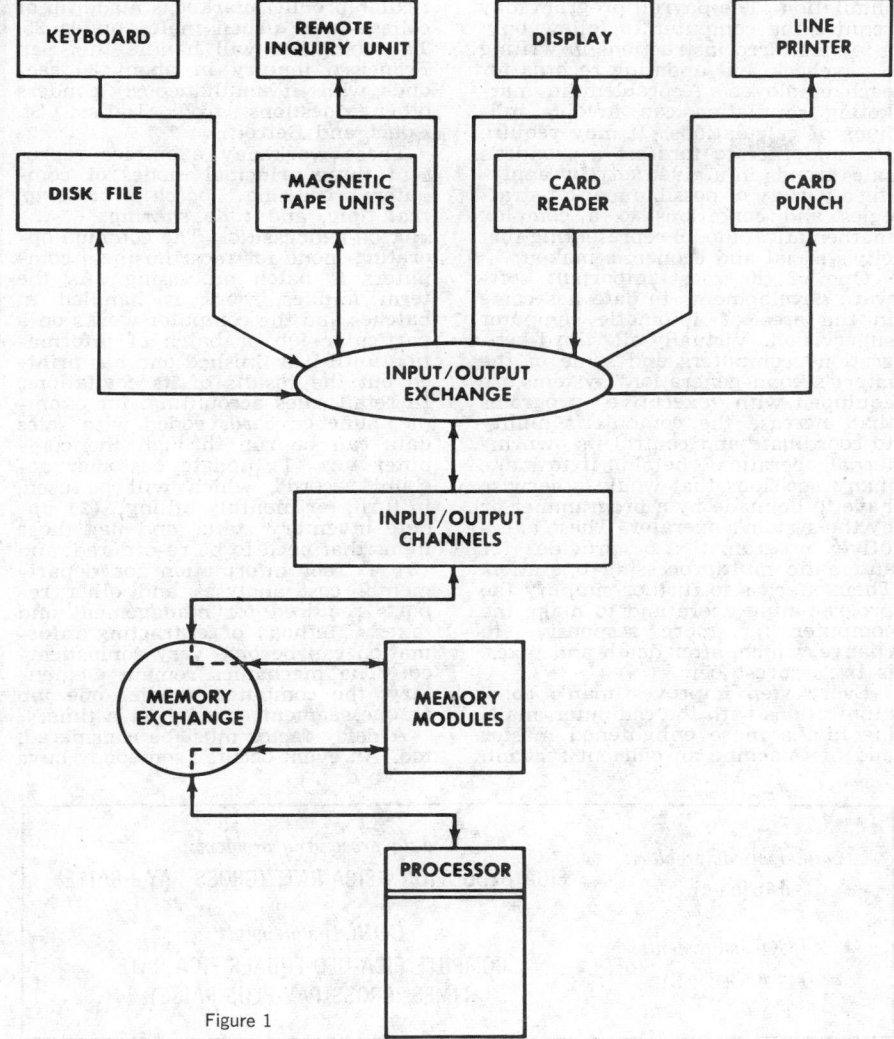

Figure 1

COMPUTER input channel transfers data from keyboard or tape through storage "memory" to processor; output of processed data is received as punch cards, tape, print, or display.

ing used in airline reservations systems, air traffic control, and continental defense applications. With "light pens" that can literally write on the display tubes, engineers can instruct a computer to amend mechanical drawings so that the effects of proposed changes can be instantly examined. Business managers will be able to evaluate marketing and production plans in much the same way. New optical devices that can read printed documents such as cash register tapes are helping to automate retail sales accounting. In some industrial setups, "slave" computers are acting as input and output devices for "master" computers.

■**MEMORY.**—Most computers have both main and auxiliary memories. Main memory is used for storing program instructions and segments of data needed at any given moment by the computer. Duration of storage is usually very brief, perhaps a few millionths of a second. Most computers now in use are equipped with "magnetic" core main memory systems. In these, many thousands of tiny

circular magnets store data in the form of magnetic flux. Some advanced systems contain very fast "thin film" memories in which microscopic dots of magnetic material, only a few molecules thick, substitute for magnetic cores.

Auxiliary memories are used for storing larger amounts of data for longer periods. Magnetic tapes and punched cards can store data indefinitely; however, if the information needed by the computer happens to be buried in the middle of a reel of tape or group of cards, valuable time may be lost in finding it. Many jobs call for data to be available in random fashion—automotive parts numbers or individual savings bank accounts, for example. In a relatively new development, the random-access disk file memory, the computer can select segments of data at random from a reservoir of facts and figures. In this device, data are stored magnetically on the surfaces of rapidly spinning disks that look like outsize phonograph records. Read/write heads positioned throughout the disk

file can locate and transmit data to the processor in fractions of a second.

■**ARITHMETIC AND CONTROL.**—In a computer, the arithmetic and control circuits are generally combined in a unit called the "central processor." This is where the actual processing of data occurs. Numbers are added or subtracted, multiplied or divided. Quantities are compared, conditions are examined, and decisions are made. When the computer "reads" a punched card or a segment of magnetic tape, it is translating patterns of holes or clusters of magnetic impulses into binary code, or what is known as "machine language." The processor responds to instructions expressed in machine-language statements. These are indecipherable to anyone not trained in machine-language coding, but a simple set of instructions, expressed in English, might go like this:

"Take the quantity stored in memory position 1001 and add it to the quantity stored in position 1002, then store the result in position 1003. Compare the new value of 1003 with the contents of location 1004. If higher, go to a series of program steps beginning in location 6000; otherwise, move a new value into location 1001 and repeat the process." It might take the computer ten or twenty millionths of a second to do this work.

Most computers are equipped with a single central processor. Some of the newer systems, however, are able to use two or more processors, and a few giant systems can incorporate a dozen or more central processors.

Originally, it was assumed that a computer would work on one problem or program at a time. (A program is a set of instructions that directs the computer to solve a number of related problems.) Today, however, many computers can handle several programs at the same time, a mode of operation known as multiprocessing. These newer computers automatically interleave programs in such a way that whenever processing is interrupted, as happens when a punched card must be read or a line is being printed, the processor will instantly switch to another program and work on it until the card-read or card-printing operation has been completed. The B5500 computer, for example, may switch from one program to another several hundred times each minute. This can increase the amount of work done by the system (its "throughput," to use the industry term) by fifty per cent and under some conditions by much more, with a resulting reduction in the cost of the jobs being processed.

Multiprocessing is one of the many functions of the computer's control structure. Within the processor, the control structure is comprised of electronic highways interconnecting with the arithmetic unit, memory system, and channels leading to the input and output units, in addition to circuits that act as traffic cops to maintain an efficient flow of data.

■**SOFTWARE.**—Without high-quality software to direct it, the best computer will provide only a fractional return on its user's investment. Manufacturers and users have cooperated in developing advanced software, and the effort has paid dividends to both parties. The development of standard computer languages, for instance, has greatly simplified the job of preparing computer programs and has helped extend the use of computers into exciting and profitable new areas. Software has become so important, in fact, that a "software industry" has evolved. A number of firms, some of international scope, have been built to handle specialized software needs of industrial and governmental users.

Until recently, communicating with a computer was a difficult and tricky business. The programmer had to specify every detail of every step the computer was to follow, and he had to express his instructions in the numerical code of machine language. Since the computer replied in machine language code, the programmer had to translate the results back into English before they made sense to anyone but himself. Hours or days could be spent in searching for a logical error hidden in long lists of numbers. The development, testing, and correction of even a basic operational program might occupy a group of programmers for several months. Any substantial change in the structure of a program required so much time and work that it was likely to be resisted strenuously. Clearly, this troublesome and costly communications gap had to be bridged.

In the late 1950's, about the time that the first transistorized "second generation" systems were in production, IBM introduced a computer language called FORTRAN (Formula Translation), while a comparable "higher level" language, ALGOL (Algorithmic Oriented Language), was being developed, principally in Europe. FORTRAN and ALGOL programs are written in terms of algebraic statements, with instructions such as "do," "if," "else," and "go to." They permit the ultimate user, the scientist or engineer, to prepare computer programs himself without concern for the complexities of machine-language coding.

FORTRAN and ALGOL were soon followed by a business data processing language called COBOL (Common Business Oriented Language). COBOL programs are written in a stylized form of English, greatly simplifying man-to-machine communications in commerce, banking and government.

Additional computer languages have been developed, but FORTRAN, ALGOL, and COBOL have been standardized and are in widest use. The translation from any of these higher level languages into machine language is accomplished by the computer using sets of instructions called "compilers." *Figure 2* shows how a mathematical statement can be expressed in ALGOL, and how an equivalent COBOL instruction can reflect a common data-processing problem.

Computer programs vary greatly in their degrees of complexity. They can range from a rather simple payroll routine to a complex exercise in

simulation. The payroll program may require the computer to follow only a few hundred instructions in writing a paycheck and updating records for each employee. A problem in marketing simulation can involve millions of calculations. It may require the computer to forecast a product's sales trends in a given city by applying a variety of possible market strategies and conditions to a complex mathematical model representing that city's social and economic makeup.

One of the most important software developments to date has come in the area of automatic computer supervision. Virtually all "third-generation" computers and some of the later "second-generation" systems are equipped with "executive" programs that increase the computer's ability to coordinate and control its own internal operations, helping it to make many decisions that would otherwise have to be made by a programmer or by the system's operator. These executive programs also provide for automatic multiprocessing operation. Their effect is to further simplify the programming chore and to make the computer far more responsive to change, which, after death and taxes, is life's surest bet.

Every step improves man's communications with the computer, making him a more enlightened master and his machine an efficient servant.

ticular product market is made up of college-level urban males under 35. The computer will handle this San Francisco inquiry in about 20 seconds, while it simultaneously ponders other questions from Dallas, St. Louis, and Detroit.

These workaday examples represent three principal modes of computer processing: *batch processing, real time,* and *time sharing.*

■ **BATCH PROCESSING.**—The common operating mode for most business computers is batch processing. As the term implies, work is handled in batches and the computer works on a particular job or batch of information until it is finished and has printed out the results of its cogitations. In retail sales accounting, for example, punched cards coded with sales data can be run through the computer to: (1) update customer account records, which will be used, in turn, for monthly billing; (2) update inventory status and flag those items that need to be re-ordered; and (3) extract information for departmental cost analyses and other reports required for management and taxes. Methods of extracting information can become very sophisticated. The mechanics remain elementary; the computer handles one job or one segment of a job at a time.

A delay factor must be considered, too. An event occurs (somebody buys

---

Figure 2

mathematical problem:
$$d = a(b+c)$$

ALGOL statement:
$$D := A \times (B+C);$$

data processing problem:
FICA DEDUCTION = FICA RATE (GROSS PAY + RAISE)

COBOL statement:
COMPUTE FICA-DED EQUALS FICA-RATE
TIMES (GROSS-PAY PLUS RAISE)

ALGOL computer "language" translates math (*left*) ; COBOL states business problem (*right*).

Processing Modes.—In Florida, as a multistage rocket lifts from its pad and points its nose toward an elusive point in the sky, a computer in a blockhouse near the launch site receives radar signals from the rocket, compares the "bird's" actual performance with an optimum flight plan, and radios steering commands to the rocket's control system.

In Chicago, a keypunch operator prepares a deck of punched cards representing the previous day's sales for a women's wear shop. From the input data on these cards, a computer bills customers, pays commissions to sales clerks, and prepares reports that will help the store's buyers analyze sales trends and will give its management the information needed for ensuring a satisfactory cash flow.

In San Francisco, an early-rising advertising man converses long-distance with his agency's computer in New York City. Using a direct-dial teletype, the adman has instructed the computer to review all prime-time TV spot availabilities in the southwestern states and to select the "best buys" for a client whose par-

a suit), a record is made (a saleslip and, later, a punched card are prepared), the computer subsequently processes this and other accumulated records, and the effect of the event is felt at some future time (the customer gets a bill, the buyer orders more goods, the store shows a profit).

■ **REAL-TIME.**—In contrast, a real-time system may use the results of its computations immediately to affect the status of one or more elements of a continuing operation. Input data can be received, examined, and used at once. As that rocket thunders aloft, for example, a continuous stream of radar information flows into the ground guidance computer in the blockhouse. Each input impulse triggers a series of computations: Is the rocket adhering to its flight schedule within acceptable limitations? If not, how must its steering mechanism act to bring it back on course? Deviations must be sensed and corrections made far more rapidly and delicately than the best human pilot could perform them.

The SAGE (Semi-Automatic Ground Environment) continental

BURROUGHS CORPORATION

BANK tellers use machines on counters to feed data on transactions to computer (see photo *below*) that adjusts accounts and signals machines to print new balance in passbooks.

air-defense system is an excellent example of real-time operations. A network of SAGE computers instantly alerts all responsible authorities to any hostile or unidentified aircraft or airborne objects approaching our continental boundaries. Input for the SAGE system comes from far-flung radar stations and coastal picket aircraft which survey the skies around the clock. The computers receive input continuously and directly. They detect, identify and, if necessary, call for split-second action as the event is taking place.

A real-time system may be as close as your neighborhood savings bank. In many branch banks today, a small machine at the teller's window, used for posting passbooks, is connected by telephone lines to a central computer. A customer's deposit or withdrawal is posted to his account, his accrued interest is totaled up, and an up-to-date balance is printed in his passbook. All this is accomplished in a few seconds, although the computer may be 50 miles away from the branch and may simultaneously be conducting business with other

branches, or even be serving a number of different banks. This system is said to operate "on-line" as well as in "real-time," because the many tellers' units are actually under direct control of the computer's central processing unit. Customers like this system because of its speed; bankers like it because it also saves money. Cash balances for every bank office are figured automatically, and because current balances are posted in passbooks there is no need to send the customer a periodic statement of his account. At the end of the banking day, the computer switches from real-time to a batch-processing mode and takes care of the necessary "back office" accounting. In each of these examples, the computer's response is synchronized with the needs of its users. This is the basic value of any real-time system.

■**TIME-SHARING.**—The next logical step is to equip the computer to serve a number of masters at the same time, thus increasing its utility and, consequently, its value. This brings us to the concept of "time-sharing." The San Francisco adman is 2,500 miles away from his agency's computer, but for practical purposes it might be right in his own office. With his teletypewriter, he can invoke any of a number of programs stored in the computer's large random-access memory. If his current objective is to purchase television spot announcements for a client, he will tell the computer what the product is, what stations he is interested in, whether the client wants his ad to appear within the body of a program or at station-break time, and what other requirements must be met. The computer will quickly search through encyclopedic amounts of rate and schedule data, check its ever-changing list of availabilities, match these up with a predetermined market profile for the particular product, and reply within a few seconds with a list of availabilities drawn up in order of

BURROUGHS CORPORATION

CENTRAL COMPUTER terminal (1) receives data from bank tellers (*above*) and passes it to processor (2), which checks customer's account in disk file memory (3), computes new account balance, and sends data to tellers within a few seconds. The system also processes data from these transactions for use in the bank's total operation. Magnetic tape units (4) record selected information for management reports that are reproduced on a high-speed printer (5). Punch card reader (6) and keyboard (7) are used to feed added data and instructions.

their predicted effectiveness. The objective is to provide the client with the best selection of TV spots available at that particular time.

But the computer is not limited to one conversation or job. While it is "talking" to the San Francisco office, it will receive and accept requests from other agency offices around the country. While it replies to one inquiry, it will be gathering and evaluating data to satisfy another. Concurrently, it may be simulating the market environment for an established consumer product, so that agency people can test the effects of competition, economic trends, or changes in advertising strategies and investments. It also may be at work helping to find out why a brand new product sold well in one control area and not so well in another. Thus, the computer is sharing its available time with a number of users, and it is at work on a diversity of projects within the company.

This particular computer operates on the multiprocessing basis that was discussed earlier. While only one program or problem is being computed at any instant in time, the machine may switch from one to another several times within a single second. It makes its own determinations on how to do this efficiently. This requires, in turn, an automatic and very efficient executive program. This is actually as much a technique of "resource-sharing" as it is of "time-sharing."

For a more literal example of time-sharing we can turn to MAC (Multiple Access Computer) in operation at M.I.T. Here, scientists, engineers, and instructors by the score communicate simultaneously with an immense computer system. The computer actually divides its processor time among contending users according to preestablished priorities. Input and output devices of various kinds are located at M.I.T.'s classrooms, offices, and labs. Because of the computer's great power and speed, the time lapse between inquiry and reply is slight, often undetectable by the human half of the relationship. In fact, each user gets the impression that he has sole use of the system, when, instead, he is sharing it with an unknown number of his colleagues.

The development of MAC and the lessons learned in its operation have led to financial, industrial, educational, and government time-sharing systems, and to considerable thought on how time-sharing can be exploited in the future.

■ **COMPUTER UTILITY CONCEPT.**—A hot topic in the rarefied atmosphere where advanced EDP techniques are debated is what is called the "computer utility concept." This refers to the likelihood that computer services will eventually be available publicly, roughly the same as water, electric power, and telephone service now are. Giant central time-sharing computer systems, perhaps with networks of smaller computers as message buffers and organizers, are pictured as being available for serving businesses of all sizes and types anywhere. Fees would reflect only the amount of computer time actually used by any subscriber. Conceivably, the subscriber could have computing- or data-processing power he might otherwise never hope to afford.

It is intriguing to contemplate the day when the grocer and druggist can bill their customers and restock their shelves automatically; when the doctor and attorney will have instant electronic access to libraries of data; when the small businessman can apply the same analyses and efficiencies to his affairs as his largest industrial brother. Even the man on the street will feel the change. We are already witness to the decline and fall of cash as a business medium. This may portend the day when suit designers further streamline trousers by eliminating all but one pocket, reserving that one for a single, all-purpose, computer-coded, cradle-to-the-grave credit card.

■ **MANAGEMENT INFORMATION SYSTEM.**—On a more tangible level, improvements in real-time and time-sharing techniques have added impetus to a new development in business computer usage—the management information system. The purpose of such a system is to gather all pertinent data about business operations as they occur, and then to let managers at every level know what's going on in time for them to act promptly and intelligently. Time is of the essence. You can't control what happened yesterday, and yesterday's facts and figures may be inadequate for today's situations. So a system that provides information in time for action holds messianic appeal. The technology necessary for such a system—high speed computation, vast random-access memory devices, comprehensive supervisory programs—is available. And a number of companies are at work building just such systems.

One of these, a $500 million-a-year manufacturer, has already instituted computer procedures for order entry and status reporting, production scheduling and inventory management, manufacturing control, accounting and marketing, and has included, as well, an advanced process-control system.

When the system is fully operative, a large electronic central file will receive information directly from field sales offices and plants; real-time computers will evaluate the information, update the files, and reply to the field with instructions. The system's computers, using mathematical models, will forecast sales and schedule production flow for each product; they will also specify the related machine and tool requirements. For the firm's accountants, the system will define the contribution to profit made by each product, sales territory, customer, plant, and machine. In the factories, many production processes will be computer-controlled. Such a system is very expensive. But it promises to pay off handsomely by making information available in time to influence the course of events, to take advantage of opportunities and to reduce or eliminate potential sources of difficulty.

Selecting a Computer.—In purchasing any "big ticket" industrial tool, whether it be a new punch press or a computer, one has to decide how well the purchase will "pay off" for the company. The stakes may be very high. The decision will affect not just one individual, but everyone else in the firm.

The principal reasons for installing a computer system are (1) economy through better use of the company's resources, and (2) improving management capabilities. Direct savings can often be made by transferring routine or clerical work to the computer, thus reducing the personnel force or switching people to jobs that computers cannot handle. Payroll, accounts receivable, and general bookkeeping operations are often the first to be assigned to the computer, but no machine can substitute for the human element in sales or customer relations, and many fabrication jobs still call for human judgment and dexterity. Indirect savings can be increased by establishing and following optimum procedures, as in inventory control. One electronics manufacturer reaped savings of several million dollars during the first year's operation of a computer-based inventory control system. The company did this by reducing its investment in inventory items and at the same time eliminating tie-ups caused by shortages of parts and subassemblies. Computer-produced management reports provide opportunities for savings, too, by keeping executives abreast of developments while there is still time for action.

Computers are available in an amazing variety of configurations and costs, from machines selling outright for less than $50,000 to giant systems that rent for $250,000 a month. Software and operating costs are just as wide-ranging. A company considering EDP operations must decide whether to purchase or lease its own system, or to buy EDP service from a data-processing center. The critical decision, however, is the decision on objectives.

■ **OBJECTIVES OF PURCHASER.**—What does a company want most from a computer? Economy? If so, it can try to cut costs by letting the computer take over routine work. This calls, first, for a closeup look at how data flow into and through the organization. Next, the company needs to estimate the dollar cost of new equipment, forms, and personnel, and weigh this against the savings from more efficient data handling.

Or should the objective be to improve the capability and effectiveness of the people who are directing the company's affairs? Here, the first step is a management-level study to spotlight the specific decisions that must be made in the conduct of the business, and to determine the relative value of the information needed for making those decisions. The content and format of the needed information, its accuracy, degree of precision, and its timeliness are the principal criteria for establishing management's "data base"—the foundation upon which a worthwhile information system can be constructed. These criteria will also help determine the dollar cost of the system. Before going further, management should conclude that the potential payoff warrants a serious, long-range investment in EDP programming.

■FEASIBILITY STUDY.—The next step is a feasibility study, an examination of the organization's structure, its environment, and all the variable elements that contribute to its "personality," to determine whether installation of an EDP system is feasible. The feasibility study will require a detailed analysis of how data should be handled, and it will generate plans for amending or revamping procedures to bring about a better "fit" with the logical capabilities of a computer. The study will establish recommendations for computing equipment based on the objectives of the company, and it will encompass a logical schedule for preparation, installation, and implementation of the computer. Later, the study will be used for evaluating the actual performance of the system, and this refers both to the machinery and to the company's ability to use it effectively.

It's not uncommon for a feasibility study to take several months to a year to complete, even when conducted for a small or medium-size firm. It must be logical, it must be complete, and it must have strong management support. Shortcuts at this stage will be paid for dearly after the system is installed and running.

In selecting specific equipment, there are basic considerations of equipment price or rental fees, operating speeds, memory sizes, and costs of operation and maintenance. These must be related to the work that the computer is to do. For example, raw speed is seldom the prime criterion for making the computer pay off; flexibility may be far more important.

Other considerations include a manufacturer's record of performance, his ability to provide programming and software support, local availability of a "back-up" system if the equipment fails, and his ability to provide a system fitted to the needs of a particular firm rather than his insistence on force-fitting the customer's operation to the computer. It may be important to choose a system that is "modular," that is, one that can be expanded or improved to handle increasing workloads without requiring basic changes to functioning computer programs. A requirement for real-time or time-sharing operations may be the deciding factor. Executive routines or "master control programs," which increase a computer's flexibility, are becoming available in some medium- and low-priced systems. These executive programs take on increasing importance as computers become more fully integrated in business operations.

Administration of EDP.—Data-processing operations will vary from company to company, reflecting the size of the computer installation, the nature of its activity, and the depth of the role that management has drawn for EDP to play in the company's affairs. A small firm equipped with a simple computer devoted to clerical duties may get by with an EDP staff of three or four people, whose chief functions will be to stuff punched cards into the machine at one end and tear off printed matter at the other. A few large corporations use computers by the score, and here the structures of the EDP departments are as diverse as the applications at which their machines are set to work. However, assuming a medium-size concern equipped with a medium-size computer, let us build a structure for the EDP function.

■MANAGER OF EDP.—To head the group we will appoint a Manager of Data Processing. He will be responsible for all aspects of the company's data processing and computing operations, starting with the feasibility study and continuing through the selection, installation, and implementation of the computer system. He will be responsible for the operation and administration of the system, including its personnel, its budgets, and its performance. He will either be an officer of the company or will report directly to a high-ranking officer. We will establish the EDP function as an independent service branch, so that it is equally accessible to all groups within the company.

Ideally, the Manager of Data Processing will be a good technician, a good administrator, and a good salesman. He must know enough about his equipment to organize workloads efficiently; be able to administer funds; establish and monitor performance standards; and manage people skillfully. He must be able to "sell" his services intelligently within the company, and elicit and maintain the support of top management.

■LINE AND STAFF JOBS.—Next, let us organize the data-processing department into three line activities and two staff activities, each reporting directly to the Manager. The line activities are tied to the day-to-day operation of the computer. A Supervisor of Operations will schedule operating personnel and see that work is received, processed, and delivered on schedule. A Supervisor of Programming will be charged with maintaining and improving current computer programs and with preparing new programs. The third line manager, the Supervisor of Systems Analysis, will conduct continuing studies of how information is generated and how it flows through the organization with an eye to improving or mechanizing this flow with the computer.

The two staff functions provide controls and services needed for efficient operation of the group. The Development Control Manager will be responsible for hiring and training personnel, developing methods and performance standards, evaluating and controlling the quality of the work done by the group, and administering budgets. The Operational Control Manager will maintain the company's library of computer programs, set up job schedules, coordinate and control the flow of data into and out of the department, and establish operating and time utilization standards. These supervisors and their staffs do not behave as separate entities; instead, their activities are interrelated and they act together as a cohesive group.

The departmental structure outlined here is idealized; the workaday world seldom permits such neat categorizing. In practice, the staff functions often are divided among the line supervisors and the Data Processing Manager, and titles and duties vary considerably from one department to another. Ironically, these EDP structures themselves are being affected by refinements in computer technology and by the way business computer users are redefining their objectives.

The Data Processing Manager, if he is to survive, will change with the times. He will assume the role of a knowledgeable, persuasive power salesman who works in diverse areas and at many levels within the organization to promote further logical use of the computer system. He will train himself both formally and by experience to a point where he can serve as a management problem solver, advanced system designer, and as an evaluator of his company's future development and needs.

This, of course, requires a change in the way some managements now view the data-processing function and their perception of how it can most effectively serve the total interests of the company. Almost without exception, the firms that presently benefit most from their EDP systems are those in which management looks upon EDP not as an isolated or esoteric tool but as the best available means of probing every aspect of their endeavors and uncovering the information they really need. They use EDP not to work faster, but to work more intelligently. Why, in their brief history, have computers helped compound progress, solve riddles, and create challenges as no instruments man has dealt with before? There are two essential reasons. First, they can perform great amounts of work in brief periods of time. Second, computers respond well only to sound reasoning; they force their users to think through every aspect of the problems at hand from starting point to conclusion. So far, at least, computers can only serve human logic, not substitute for it. This, perhaps, is their finest quality.
—Ray R. Eppert

BIBLIOGRAPHY

Bernstein, Jeremy. *The Analytical Engine: Computers—Past, Present and Future.* Random House, 1964.

Burck, Gilbert and the Editors of *Fortune. The Computer Age and Its Potential for Management.* Harper and Row Publishers, 1965.

Greenberger, Marvin, (ed.) *Computers and the World of the Future.* Massachusetts Institute of Technology Press, 1962.

Wiener, Norbert. *The Human Use of Human Beings (Cybernetics and Society).* Doubleday and Co., Inc., 1954.

Office Services.—Because of technological advances in office equipment and systems, fewer people are producing more work in a shorter time. As a result, many boring, time-consuming tasks are being eliminated. Some of the more recent advances include:

■ **TYPING AND STENOGRAPHIC POOLS.**—Today more than 200,000 dictating machines are sold in the United States each year. With business travel becoming more common, salesmen, technicians, and executives use these machines for field reports and correspondence, and mail or bring their tapes to the transcribing center. In the office there is a strong trend toward having large central transcribing machines available to executives, either by a special telephone system or through the regular telephone network. In one New York bank, more than 1,000 executives can dictate directly to a central group of machines and typists.

■ **COPYING AND DUPLICATING FACILITIES.**—Improved equipment affords even smaller offices the capability of printing and duplicating their own materials inexpensively, quickly, and simply. There are three basic types of machines that offices use for duplicating and printing: spirit, stencil, and offset. (Machines for smaller runs fall into another category.)

The spirit duplicator is the simplest, fastest, and least expensive for runs of up to 500 copies, but the quality of reproduction is relatively poor. In addition, this method cannot reproduce photographs.

Stencil duplicating machines are still the most versatile and the most widely used. The quality of the stencil copies is generally better than that of spirit copies, but not as good as offset work. From 1,000 to 3,000 copies can be run from one stencil and the machines are simple to operate. One new development is a device that makes stencils electronically, with an optical scanner.

Offset equipment, generally more costly, requires somewhat more skill to run than other types of duplicating equipment, but operation is being simplified. An advantage of offset equipment is that longer runs are obtainable than with spirit or stencil duplicators. Offset plates are made either by a photograph's electrostatic, or thermographic process, or by typing directly on paper masters. With metal plates, runs of up to 25,000 copies are possible.

The copying machine field is the fastest growing and most competitive of the office equipment industry. About 400,000 machines are in service and about $175 million worth of supplies are consumed by them annually. Early machines of this type, which required coated papers and chemicals to develop them, produced unattractive copies. Newer models use plain paper, the image is set thermally, and the copy closely resembles the original. Copy costs are about two or three cents each, and they are expected to decline as new techniques are perfected.

■ **OFFICE COMMUNICATIONS.**—Communication systems for office use are also being improved. Not long ago the telephone, the mails, and the messenger were the only means of transmitting oral or written messages. Then there developed such equipment as conveyor belts, pneumatic tubes, and the Telautograph to speed up transmission of written materials. Today closed-circuit television is linking many offices together. Likewise, facsimile reproduction equipment, which produces the familiar wire photos seen in newspapers, is being used by many offices. One interesting new development in this field combines xerographic printing and data transmission technology, with copies being produced on paper or even on offset masters for reproduction. A large telecommunications company has developed a new system which transmits photos, charts, and other documents over ordinary telephone lines, without special coaxial cables.

Teletypewriting is another written communications device which is familiar to most people, but it too is becoming more sophisticated. Basically, it is a typewriter connected through the public wire services to other typewriters. A message typed on one machine activates another (perhaps hundreds of miles away) through conventional telephone switching. These machines can now be equipped with photoelectric readers and tape punches for computers.

Records Management.—Our highly complex society has created what has been described as an "information explosion." An estimated 1.25 trillion pieces of paper are on file in the U.S. Filing and retaining unnecessary records costs an estimated $750 million a year. Studies have shown that only 1 to 15 per cent of retained records are ever needed, and that 90 per cent of those are less than one year old.

■ **STORAGE AND RETRIEVAL.**—Basically, there are three information storage and retrieval systems: manual, mechanical, and electronic. Manual systems need little explanation. They usually consist of drawers or trays with materials filed in them alphabetically, numerically, chronologically, or in some similar fashion.

Mechanical systems are often merely variations of manual systems, such as file trays that revolve horizontally or vertically to bring records to the operator. Other systems are becoming much more sophisticated. One microfilm equipment manufacturer has a machine that combines a camera-recorder, a selector-reproducer, and a film cutter for files which require frequent updating. One 25" x 19" x 20" cabinet can hold as much material as 50 ordinary four-drawer cabinets. Another manufacturer has equipment that can retrieve a document from a microfilm file of a million pages and copy it in 30 seconds. Perhaps the most dramatic system yet devised for condensing and re-trieving data is one that could reproduce the entire collection of books and pamphlets in the Library of Congress (270 miles of shelves) on cards which could be contained in six regular file cabinets. Inspection and correction of these records can take place at the micro-image level, and fast retrieval and reproduction are possible. Most of the new record-keeping systems combine microfilm processes with computers when actual documents must be viewed. If only data are needed, the vast memory storage of computers alone is usually relied on.

Office Equipment.—Conventional office equipment (typewriters, file cabinets, adding machines, dictating machines, and copying equipment) is being improved at a more rapid rate than ever before. New devices, undreamed of ten years ago, are becoming commonplace in the modern office. The business equipment industry has become a $5 billion-a-year giant in America and is expected to grow substantially as management struggles with greater complexity, higher costs, and the increasing need for speed.

■ **COMPUTER-ORIENTED MACHINES.**—Office machines used to function as separate units, but electronics has changed this pattern. Many office machines today are becoming input devices for computers rather than producing end products of their own. The following examples illustrate this point.

Adding machines are available which will print numbers on a tape that can be read by an optical scanner as well as by the human eye. The tape can then be fed directly into a computer. In the reverse situation, computers can print their results directly onto offset plates for fast reproduction on duplicating machines.

There are typewriters that can simultaneously produce a visual record and a punched card or magnetic tape for computer input, or for the preparation of other documents. Another machine with a computer-type memory device is able to produce statistical records and analytical reports as it performs its regular accounting functions. Likewise, almost all modern bookkeeping machines can be equipped to make punched or magnetic tapes for computers.

This emphasis on computers does not mean that offices without them cannot benefit from the technological advances just described. Computer service centers, which rent computer time to customers, are springing up everywhere, so no office need be deprived of the use of one. To circumvent the high cost of computers, some smaller companies are joining together to share them. Furthermore, all computer manufacturers are making strenuous efforts to bring their computers within the financial means of smaller companies. (See also *Business and the Computer,* page 1773.)

■ **OTHER EQUIPMENT DEVELOPMENTS.**—Not all the new office machines are computer-oriented, although most of their improvements are due to electronics. Eighteen or twenty different electronic calculators are on the market at this time, some with computer-type memory devices, programing features, and solid-state electronic circuitry that replaces mechanical parts, all in the interest of performing more complex calculations faster.

Several typewriters with memory devices are available, which permit pre-selection of paragraphs in hundreds of combinations. In this way, once the machine is set, letters, documents, and reports can be typed without any attention by the operator.

Office Space Planning, Layout, and Design.—Location of offices in relation to manufacturing facilities, other business and commercial establishments, transportation, parking and food services—all these must be considered in planning an office. Likewise, working conditions should be as attractive as possible, with a minimum of noise and dirt, and a maximum of lighting and ventilation. The prevalence of air conditioning today has substantially reduced a number of these problems. In many areas it is virtually mandatory if a company is to obtain employees.

■**IMPORTANCE OF WORK FLOW.**—In space planning and office layout, the most important factor is usually work flow. Office procedures, routines, sequences of operations, and work volumes should be carefully analyzed. Most

ARCHITECTURAL RECORD

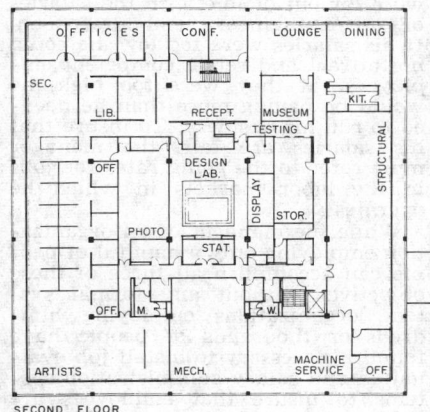

SECOND FLOOR

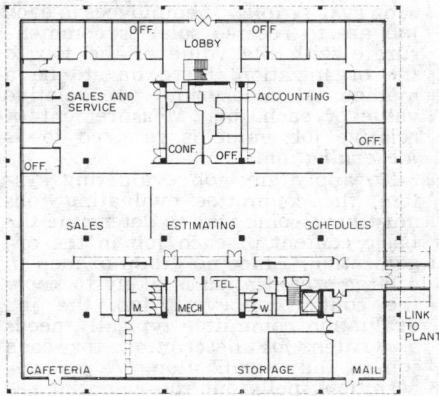

OFFICE plan groups staffs with related duties for efficiency, allows for storage and recreation for convenience and comfort.

offices have a number of different work processes or flows. Work stations should be arranged so that the largest volume flows the most smoothly and directly, with a minimum of backtracking and delay. Lesser routines can then be fitted into the main activities so as to cause the least disruption. With large volume, even the smallest savings of time for people or work to move through the office routine add up to substantial totals.

After basic work flows have been established and minor ones fitted in, other office requirements should be considered. Determination of space needed for corridors and passageways, reception areas, rest rooms, stock rooms, files, and reproduction equipment should be made. These should relate to the main traffic flow.

■**OFFICES, PARTITIONS, AND FURNITURE.**—Because of confidential work or conversations and the need for protection from distractions, some private offices are almost always required. Unless space is plentiful, however, pressure for private offices as status symbols should be resisted, because space utilization in a private office is only about 50 per cent of that in an open area. Furthermore, the cost of erecting, maintaining, and altering walls and partitions is substantial. Where walls and partitions are required, movable ones are usually best, for many organizations find that offices need to be relocated every three to five years. Modern furniture is gaining in popularity for the same reason, as it is adaptable to changing work conditions.

Development of Administrative Manuals. Administrative manuals usually cover one or more of the following subjects: policies, operating procedures, and rules and regulations. Manuals are a form of communication, and the larger the organization the greater they need to be formalized.

■**USES OF MANUALS.**—Manuals serve many purposes. The mere preparation of one usually reveals faults and inconsistencies in operations. Better ways of doing things are generally a by-product of manual preparation. They also assist in training new employees and in saving supervisory time.

Manuals help make procedures uniform and help maintain good work performance. They not only guide employees in their own jobs but show them how jobs are related and how their own fits into the broader operation. A well-informed employee is a more effective employee.

■**DANGERS OF MANUALS.**—Outmoded manuals, however, can do more harm than good. If changes in procedures are not carefully recorded in all manuals, some employees may continue to follow old ones, thus causing confusion and mistakes. Likewise, if revisions are not carefully checked for inconsistencies with other procedures, trouble is bound to occur. It is best, therefore, to centralize responsibility for manuals and establish good controls over the preparation and dissemination of changes.

The Systems and Procedures Approach. Responsibility for the systems and procedures function in a large organization is most frequently given to the controller, somewhat less often to the office manager. In a typical organization, the controller usually has the largest clerical staff and receives the function for that reason. Today, with controllers most often being responsible for the computer, it is more logical than ever that they have the systems and procedures function, although this is not universally prevalent.

While organizations have been systematically reviewing clerical operations for many years, the rapid development of computers has recently accelerated this work. Because computers must be fed logical and well-ordered material, and because input delays are expensive, systems and procedures analysis has been made more important by their advent.

■**BENEFITS OF SYSTEMS AND PROCEDURES WORK.**—Benefits to be derived from a good systems and procedures program are substantial and varied. The most obvious benefit, though sometimes not the most important, is cost savings. These savings come from the more efficient use of people and equipment, better distribution of work load, reduction of idle time, and the like. Improved service to customers may come about through faster processing of orders, or through better quality and accuracy of work. Management may receive more timely control reports and similar data on which to make prompt decisions and take action. These data may also be more accurate and comprehensive as a result of good systems work.

■**SKILLS AND APPROACH REQUIRED.**—Good systems and procedures analysts require special skills and attributes. They should have open minds, be observant and ingenious, have good judgment and good human relations, and keep themselves abreast of the latest techniques and equipment in their field.

In undertaking to improve a procedure, it is necessary first to gather all the pertinent facts, then to analyze them to find ways of improvement. Recommendations should next be developed and presented to management for decision. Following that, the changes should be installed and, after they have been in operation for some time, an audit or review of them should be made to see that they function as planned.   —Lynn A. Brua

BIBLIOGRAPHY

DICKINSON, A. LITCHARD. *Filing and Finding in the Office.* Business Press, 1965.
GAGER, A. H. *Practical Office Time Savers.* McGraw-Hill, Inc., 1957.
NEUNER, J. J. W. *Office Management.* South-Western Publishing Co., 1959.
SHARP, J. R. *Some Fundamentals of Information Retrieval.* London House, 1965.
TERRY, GEORGE R. *Office Management and Control.* Richard D. Irwin, Inc., 1965.

PERSONNEL AND HUMAN RELATIONS

Recruitment, Testing and Placement.— In modern business corporations, the job of keeping the company adequately staffed has generally been taken away from the local office manager and centralized in a division of the personnel department. Whether it is called employment, recruiting, or manpower procurement, the responsibility of such a division is to fill vacant positions throughout the company as they open.

As modern business has grown, so have its manpower needs. As businesses have expanded the volume of their operations, they have had to increase their staffs in order to meet greater production demands. Also, as companies have developed new products and services, they have had to develop new personnel who can produce them. Both kinds of business growth have created new jobs which the employment staff has had to fill with qualified personnel.

■**PERSONNEL TURNOVER.—**Whether businesses grow or decline, automate or maintain their traditional operations, turnover of personnel continues in every company. Long-service employees normally retire at 65; others die before they have reached normal retirement age. Thousands of women leave the labor force every year to marry and raise families. In the highly volatile economy of the United States since World War II, many changes have taken place in business. One symptom of these changes is the large number of people each year who change their jobs or their companies. Employees resign to get into another line of work, to move to another geographical area, to change their working hours, or to attempt to improve their opportunity for advancement in salary and responsibility. In other cases, job vacancies are created by management decisions to release employees for reasons of incompetence or poor attendance, or for failing in some way to meet company standards.

■**ATTRACTING JOB APPLICANTS.—**Various ways of obtaining applicants have been developed over the years, and companies are constantly striving to develop new ones. Among the most popular sources of new personnel are employment agencies, which help individuals to locate job opportunities for which they might be qualified. On the other hand, these agencies also help companies to find qualified applicants. *Employment agencies* do their work for a fee, which the applicant normally pays when he is successfully placed through the contact initially established by the agency. Other people seeking employment go out to call directly on the companies for which they would like to work. They simply go into employment offices and apply for jobs without introduction.

Companies attempt to make their job needs known in as many ways as possible. They frequently let their employees know about job vacancies. They are constantly in touch with employment agencies and government employment services to make them alert to current job needs. A number of companies place help-wanted ads in newspapers and other publications.

One of the very best sources for new personnel is school and college recruitment. Almost every major company in the country actively recruits at local high schools each June to attract graduates who do not plan to go on to college. Frequently such companies provide tuition refund plans and other devices to encourage these new employees to continue their education evenings. These programs are particularly attractive to students who wish to continue their education but cannot afford the expenses of a four-year college program. Each year many serious students are attracted to business by the opportunity to earn a living while going to college part-time.

■**THE EMPLOYMENT INTERVIEW—**Regardless of where an applicant comes from, his first contact with the prospective company will be with an employment interviewer. Typically, the applicant talks over with an experienced personnel interviewer his educational history and any work experience that he may have had. Frequently, applicants who have never worked before have little idea of precisely what kind of position they are seeking. An experienced interviewer ought to be able to develop an impression of the applicant's educational strengths and weaknesses and something about his outside interests. Such information provides insights into the kind of work that might be most profitable for the individual and the company to explore.

Whenever possible, interviewers will verify their impressions through appropriate tests. Tests in stenography, typewriting, and the operation of business machines are useful predictors of success. Other tests are given, where appropriate, to establish numerical facility, verbal facility, and clerical aptitudes. In addition, many companies rely on personality and interest tests to predict the likelihood of a candidate's success as a trainee. After the test has verified the interviewer's evaluation, he will probably arrange for the applicant to talk with a supervisor in the area of the business where a job is open that seems to fit the applicant's interests and qualifications.

This *departmental interview* is critical. In such an interview, the duties of the job are detailed in a first-hand way to the applicant. The prospective supervisor can measure the applicant's aptitudes and interests against the specific job while the applicant gains a detailed knowledge of the kind of work for which he is being considered.

■**SALARY ADMINISTRATION.—**The basic objective of any salary administration program is to pay each employee a "fair" salary. In modern industrial economics there is general agreement that salaries are "fair" when each employee is adequately compensated for the contribution he makes to the goals of the organization for which he works. Thus, when the manager of an organization says that his policy is to pay each employee a "fair" salary, he usually means that he has three objectives:

1. To insure that the more valuable a job is to the organization, the more the employees in that job will be paid as a group. For example, because the work performed by engineers in a manufacturing company is more valuable to the company than the work performed by draftsmen, the engineers will be paid more as a group than draftsmen.

2. To insure that within each job, the better the employee's job performance, the more he will be paid relative to other employees in the same job. Continuing the previous example, the draftsman who produces more engineering drawings of better quality than any of his co-workers is making a more valuable contribution to the organization and should be paid more than other draftsmen.

3. To insure that the salary level for each job is competitive with the salaries paid by other organizations for comparable jobs. It would do little good for a manager to insure that he paid his engineers more than his draftsmen, and that he paid each draftsman on the basis of job performance, if the salaries he offered were far out of line with the salaries of other engineers and draftsmen. If his salaries were too low, he could not attract and retain competent employees. If they were too high, he would be paying more than he needed to run his business. To insure that his salaries are fair, the manager must refer to the going rates for jobs in the labor markets in which he operates.

While the manager of an organization employing only a handful of people can accomplish all three of these objectives without any formal system, organizations employing hundreds or thousands of people have found it necessary to install job evaluation and salary administration systems to insure that employees are paid in line with these objectives.

■**JOB EVALUATION.—**If employees in each job are to receive salaries commensurate with the value of the job to the organization, there has to be a method of measuring the relative value of each job. Measurement of relative job value is referred to as *job evaluation.*

To apply any job evaluating system, the committee evaluating jobs must have some way to determine the basic content of each job in the organization. Since no group of men in a large organization is likely to know the content of every job, the job evaluation committee typically needs a written *job description* for each job in the organization. A job description spells out the essential responsibilities and tasks carried out by employees in the job. With these descriptions, the committee evaluates each job and assigns it a score.

KELLY SERVICES, INC.   KELLY SERVICES, INC.

PERSONNEL offices test (*left*) and interview (*right*) applicants to check their abilities.

There are several basic types of job evaluation plans. The *ranking method* is the simplest. Under this system, the job evaluation committee simply ranks or orders jobs according to their value. For example, a committee deciding that the engineer's job was substantially more valuable than the draftsman's might rank the engineer's job 12 and the draftsman's job 7. At the end of the process, each job is assigned a score. The more valuable the job, the higher its score. Jobs of equal value receive the same score.

As job evaluation has become increasingly used, more sophisticated evaluation systems have been developed and adopted. The *factor comparison system* is probably the most commonly used method of job evaluation today. Under this system, an attempt is made to identify the components or *factors* of the job which account for its value. For example, *knowledge* is a common factor in factor comparison plans. Next, *degrees* of each factor are defined, and points are allotted for each degree. Under this scheme, an engineer's job would be seen as requiring a greater degree of knowledge than a draftsman's so that the engineer's job would receive more points for knowledge than the draftsman's. Each job is evaluated factor by factor, the points for each factor are added, and the total deter-

Job Evaluation Score Points

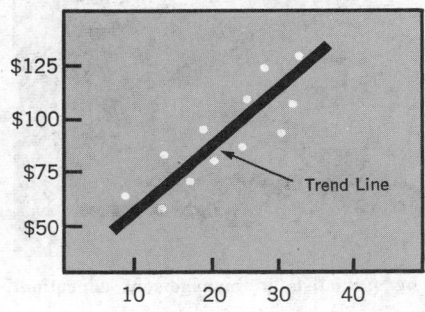

mines the relative value of each job.

■**SALARY DETERMINATION.**—After each job has been evaluated and given a score, it is necessary to relate these scores to dollars, thus determining the salary level that will be offered for each job. Usually, a *scattergram* is plotted to show the relation between the job evaluation score for a job, and the dollars paid for it.

The dollar value may, of course, be arrived at by using the average salary currently being paid by the organization for each job. Usually, however, it is at this point that the organization examines the labor market to determine whether its salaries are competitive. *Salary surveys* determine the average salaries paid by other organizations that compete for employees to fill the same jobs. These survey dates help management to decide what salaries it must pay to attract and retain the calibre of employee it wants.

After the scattergram is plotted, a trend line is calculated using the *method of least squares*. The trend line establishes the best average relationship between the point value of a job and the dollars that should be paid for it. Thus, the salary level that should be paid for a job evaluated at any given number of points can be determined by reading it off the trend line. For example, in the illustration above, the trend line indicates that a salary level of $75 should be established for each job evaluated at 20 points.

To plot the scattergram and determine the trend line, it is not necessary or practical to survey every job. A representative sample of jobs usually is sufficient. The salary levels of the remaining jobs, all of which are assigned an evaluation score, may be determined by referring to the trend line.

■**SALARY RANGES.**—After it has established a salary level for each job, management must decide whether to pay the job at a *single rate* or whether to pay employees within the job different salaries for different per-

formance. Jobs which allow employees little or no scope to increase their value through improved job performance (such as an usher) are usually paid a single rate.

However, the value of most jobs in an organization varies considerably, depending upon the employee's level of performance within the job. For this reason, organizations usually pay employees within the same job different salaries, according to performance. Where performance can be accurately measured in terms of items produced or processed, *piece rates* may be established. The more pieces produced, the higher the salary. More commonly, the management establishes *salary ranges* for jobs. For example, if it decides that the salary level for a draftsman should be about $7,000, the management may establish a salary range of $6,000–$8,000 for this job. Employees with relatively little experience are usually hired at or near the bottom (or minimum) of the range. As their job performances improve, they are given salary increases that raise them toward the range maximums. Workers are paid outside their range only in exceptional cases.

Employee Benefits and Counseling.—Employee benefit plans, often referred to as fringe benefits, might be simply defined as any benefits or compensation that employees receive over and above their regular wages or salaries. Here are some of today's most common benefit programs: pension, profit-sharing and cash-bonus plans; medical plans, including life, hospital and medical insurance as well as accident, sickness, and long-term disability benefits; stock-purchase plans; paid vacations and holidays; tuition-refund plans; and discount and recreational privileges.

■**GENERAL ATTRIBUTES.**—Although the specific package of benefits that a company or industry adopts may be tailored to its particular business or personnel, there are general attributes that should be present in any bona fide employee benefit plan:

1. The plan should be sponsored by management, or by employees with the acceptance and approval of management.

2. It should offer a benefit that would not normally have accrued to employees.

3. It should cover and appeal to a large number of employees and not a select few.

4. Generally, the employer meets part or all of the cost.

5. The plan should satisfy definite employee needs.

From management's viewpoint, an effective package of benefits should tend to achieve the following company objectives among employees:

1. Reduce unnecessary turnover.

2. Build a sense of security by providing a variety of protections for the employee and his dependents.

3. Build up morale and loyalty.

4. Increase efficiency and productivity.

5. Attract a better class of employees.

Employee benefit plans can be divided into three general categories: (1) benefits that offer security; (2) benefits that increase employee income; and (3) other meaningful benefits that have a tangible value or enhance working conditions.

■**SECURITY BENEFITS.**—1. *Pension plans.* These plans provide employees with periodic income for life after retirement.

2. *Life insurance.* Coverage may be in multiples of salary after several years of employment or merely a flat dollar amount. The employee has the right to designate a beneficiary or beneficiaries.

3. *Hospital and medical insurance.* These plans act as buffers against the heavy costs of illness or injury. Some plans have been written chiefly to absorb the normally higher medical costs of hospital care and surgery, while others are more comprehensive and cover a variety of services, including dentistry and psychiatry.

4. *Accident and sickness benefits.* These programs provide a continuation of all or part of wages during a period of disability. Accident and sickness benefits may be geared to just short-term absence from work due to non-occupational disability or, as is the present trend, provide as much as 50 to 60 per cent of salary during the entire period of a long term or even lifetime total and permanent disability.

Although the scope of benefits under any of these plans varies from company to company, a common feature is that eligibility to participate is normally based only on length of service. This may range from 30 days for medical insurance to 1 to 5 years of service for pension plans.

■**INCREASED-INCOME BENEFITS.**—Common in this category of employee benefit plans are the following:

1. *Paid vacations and holidays.*

2. *Cash bonus programs.*

3. *Suggestion systems* that pay cash to winning employees.

4. *Profit sharing.* Profit sharing is simply the formal agreement by a company to put aside, usually in a trust fund, a portion of its annual profits for proportionate division among employees. The plan may provide for deferral of payment of profit sharing funds to an employee until his retirement or severance, or may pay out money annually during active employment, usually after a waiting period of several years from entrance into the plan. Many plans combine deferral and cash payment.

5. *Employee stock purchase and thrift plans.* These are offered by management to employees as an incentive to save and also participate in the growth and financial success of their company through stock ownership. The employee accumulates, usually through payroll withholding, of a percentage of his salary, enough funds to purchase shares of company stock periodically. Often there are other investment choices available. The company sometimes contributes an amount matching all or a part of the employee's allotment as an incentive to participation.

■**OTHER BENEFITS.**—Typical of these benefits, which have tangible value or enhance the employee's working conditions, are the following:

1. *Educational and self-improvement programs.* The most common of these is the tuition-refund plan, in which the company reimburses the employee for part or all of the tuition costs for college or vocational courses taken voluntarily and which have a business orientation.

2. *Employee food services.* These include company subsidized cafeterias or free lunch programs, vending machines dispensing food and drink, and mobile food services such as coffee wagons that dispense food during "breaks" or rest periods.

3. *Medical services.* Emergency first aid, free annual physical examinations, and limited medical consultation can be provided through a fully equipped medical department staffed with a physician and nurses or through part-time medical professionals who are available several days a week or on call.

4. *Industrial recreation.* Company sponsored sports teams and a variety of other activities ranging from knitting to chess fall into this category. Organization and administration of these activities is normally handled by voluntary employee clubs. Equipment, materials, and space for meetings are often paid for by the employer.

■**ASPECTS OF ADMINISTRATION.**—Once a company installs its benefit plans, there are four basic aspects in the administration of the plans:

1. *The record-keeping function* may be a personnel department responsibility in smaller companies, but in larger firms with a number of plans in force, the vast amount of statistical information that must be maintained and kept current, as well as the meeting of insurance premium payment dates and the crediting of employee accounts under contributory programs, require the services of a department that can handle such detail.

The remaining aspects of plan administration as noted above are normally personnel department functions.

2. *Disseminating information* involves informing new employees about plans, interpreting plan provisions for new and old employees, explaining rights to terminating employees and the beneficiaries of deceased employees and the like.

3. *"Selling" the plan* is altogether different from merely providing facts about the plan. Employees must be constantly apprised of the merits of the plan and any recent developments affecting the plan. Periodic staff letters, notices on departmental bulletin boards, posters and spot articles in the company newsletter or magazine are effective means of maintaining employee interest and enthusiasm for the plan. Another successful method is to distribute to each employee, at least annually, a statement showing his dollar interest in the various company benefit plans.

4. *Continual review of a plan* entails periodic evaluation of its merits.

SUCCESS MOTIVATION INSTITUTE
TRAINING SESSION for salesmen is conducted by specialists in management education.

Skills Training.—Formal skills training within industrial and business organizations stems for the most part from World War II, when acute needs developed for training quickly large numbers of people to perform new jobs in aircraft plants, shipyards, textile mills, and dozens of other industries geared to the war effort.

Before that time, practically all industrial skills training programs were classified as *apprentice training.* They were most commonly found in the metal trades, and were aimed at turning out master craftsmen. Generally such programs extended over a number of years, and the specific provisions for conducting the program were defined in an apprentice agreement between the company and the union with jurisdiction over that trade.

Management Development.—A loose term that covers a wide range of activities, management development is aimed at helping managers to be more effective in their present positions or to prepare them for greater responsibilities. While planned programs for promoting such growth existed in a few companies before World War II, the real impetus for management development on a national scale came with the end of the war.

■**GUIDELINES.**—Since the late 1940's there has been a gradual evolution in the kind and quality of management development. While there is no general consensus on the content of the "best" management development program, professional training people generally agree on a few guidelines for effective management development. Briefly stated, these are:

1. All development is self-development.
2. Activities should be tailored to the man.
3. Developing requires action.
4. Controls can aid development.
5. Company climate affects development.
6. The boss is the key influence on development.
7. Development is a line responsibility.
8. Development is a long-range process.

These guidelines can be summarized in one general principle: what happens to the young manager on the job is far more important to his growth than the more formal off-the-job training courses. Organizations have taken a number of steps to enhance the manager's potential growth on the job. *Written position guides* specify the responsibility, authority, and accountability of the various management positions. Most importantly, they establish standards of performance for the manager against which his performance can be evaluated. *Performance appraisals* give a systematic way to evaluate a manager's performance in his job and assess his potential for advancement. Appraisals are prepared either by the manager's boss, or by his boss jointly with other individuals at the boss's level or higher who are closely familiar with the man's job performance. In the earlier years of performance appraisal there was an emphasis on assessing the man against a list of managerial traits (that is, judgment, initiative, planning, work relations, etc.) on a scale ranging from excellent to poor. More recently there has been a shift by many organizations away from abstract traits as a basis for appraisal to concern with how well a particular manager is meeting the performance standards for his particular job. The latter approach, concerned with the results a man is achieving in his job, is generally regarded as more conducive to real growth on the man's part than is a focus on abstract traits, which may be difficult to objectify.

As an integral part of the appraisal process, the *post-appraisal interview* is the occasion for the manager's boss and the manager to review the appraisal as a means of planning specific steps for the manager's growth and improvement.

To reinforce the results-oriented approach to analyzing the manager's performance, many companies have adopted a growth-planning technique called *management by objectives,* or performance planning, or target setting. At the beginning of a year the man and his boss agree on a few specific job goals for the man to achieve in the year ahead that will enable the man to do an even better management job than he is currently doing. The fact that the subordinate has a hand in establishing his own growth goals is held to be an important factor in motivating him to achieve these goals. At the end of the year the boss and the manager sit down to review achievement, to analyze constructively any failures, and to set new growth goals. In this framework manager development is a continuing process from year to year, stemming directly from the actual work situation.

Day-to-day *coaching* by a good supervisor can be one of the most potent growth forces in any manager's career. It takes the form of instruction, suggestion, questioning, and criticism to guide and motivate the subordinate. Other widely used on-the-job practices in manager development are assignments to challenging *special projects, task forces* and *job rotation.* The latter may consist of a series of relatively short-term assignments to several functions in the organization as an orientation program for prospective managers. More significant is the systematic assignment of high-caliber managers who have proved themselves in a broad range of assignments in the company, so that they become "generalists," individuals with the capacity to think in terms of the good of the company as a whole and not just a special function.

■**OFF-THE-JOB TRAINING.**—Important as these on-the-job developmental activities are in helping a manager grow, most large companies and government departments have recognized the need for supplementing these with planned off-the-job training. Many of the larger organizations conduct their own management courses, some primarily for middle-management levels or higher, others for lower-level supervisors.

■**THE CASE STUDY.**—The instruction and developmental methods in such courses include *lectures, panel discussions,* and *group discussions.* A training method of considerable significance is the *case study.* Pioneered by the Harvard Business School, the case study is based on the belief that a student of management can best attain managerial competence and understanding by analyzing and discussing actual problems. Generally each participant is given a written description of a concrete organizational problem. He is asked to study the case in private and outline what he considers to be the best solution. The entire group then comes together to discuss the adequacy of some or all of the proposed solutions and tries to identify the principles involved. Usually there is no one correct solution to the problem. The trainee is encouraged to be flexible, to explore alternative approaches, to learn how to question the situation to find out "What really is going on here?"

Business games have been called "case studies in motion." Most such games simulate a total business environment with several firms (trainee teams) competing in a common market. Game play is divided into play periods. In each period team participants must make a wide variety of decisions about all the aspects of company management—research, development, finance, production, and marketing. The consequences of each period of play are fed back to the several teams and new decisions must be made for the next play in the light of the new competitive situation. Computers have opened up the possibility of highly sophisticated and complex games with rapid feedback of results to the players. Playing time ranges from one day to several weeks.

■**HUMAN RELATIONS TRAINING.**—A major portion of managers' time is spent in dealing with people—giving instructions, coaching, motivating, reprimanding, trying to solve communications problems and misunderstandings. Human relations training was one of the first concerns of management and training professionals, and it has gone through a wide range of approaches.

Most radical but potentially perhaps the most productive of actual improvement in human relations skills is a complex process variously called *laboratory training, sensitivity,* or *T-group* training. It is in fact a laboratory in human relationships, the techniques for which were developed in the late 1940's. While there are differences among the behavioral scientists in their approach to laboratory training, the common element is a series of dilemmas or unfamiliar relationships which the group must work through toward a solution. The induced tensions and stresses promote behaviors that more closely approximate the participants' outside behavior than is true in most training settings. The training group acts as a mirror for each participant. He sees his own behavior more vividly than he has before. He learns at least tentatively how he may be more effectively himself, and gains a greater degree of acceptance of himself and others.

■**TEAM TRAINING.**—Individual growth experienced by participants in outside laboratory training has led some companies and government agencies to *organization development* or *team training*. Members of a managerial family work team in a division or department typically participate first in laboratory training. As a next step they meet together as a team to analyze their effectiveness, to identify work problems they may have together, and to set a few improvement goals for themselves in the way they manage their unit.

Manpower Planning.—This is the process of identifying the human resources that an organization will need in future years and of laying plans to insure that these needs will be met. Organizational planning for future *material* needs is now commonplace. The automobile industry predicts future demand for its products and builds new factories that will meet these predictions. The local school board plans the construction of new buildings by projecting the future population of school age children in its area. In both cases, organizations are planning for future material needs. Manpower planning involves anticipating future needs for human resources to operate the organization's facilities and the creation of plans to meet those needs as they arise.

The first phase of manpower planning involves the identification of future manpower needs. Two questions must be answered: (1) How many people will we need? (2) What kinds of people will we need?

To answer these questions, it is necessary to obtain from management a picture of the direction the organization will take in future years. Will activities of the organization expand? Remain about the same size? Or contract? Which activities are likely to become more automated? What new activities is the organization likely to undertake? What kinds of skills will be necessary to succeed in these new activities?

■**FUTURE PERSONNEL NEEDS.**—The answers to these questions give those responsible for manpower planning some basis for inferring the numbers and kinds of people the organization will need to meet its future objectives. In making these inferences, planners are especially challenged by the manpower problems that new or changing activities create. It is fairly easy to infer that currently successful activity, which might double in size but otherwise remain essentially unchanged, will require more manpower, but manpower with the same aptitudes and training possessed by personnel currently responsible for that activity. By contrast, it may be relatively difficult to visualize the kind of personnel necessary to conduct an activity with which the organization has had little or no experience.

■**PRESENT SKILLS AVAILABLE.**—After specifications of future personnel needs have been drawn up, it is necessary to take stock of the numbers and kinds of employees currently in the organization. With this skills inventory, manpower planners can identify those areas that currently have the proper numbers and kinds of personnel to meet future needs and those areas of the organization where current human resources do not match future requirements. In addition to cataloging present skills, an attempt should be made to obtain appraisals indicating the potential of the organization's current personnel for growth in the areas where future needs are anticipated.

■**COORDINATING PLANS.**—Having identified gaps between current human resources and future needs, the manpower planners are in a position to alert other members of the organization to anticipated future manpower needs and to work with them in laying plans to provide for those needs. For example, the manpower planning group would collaborate with the head of recruitment in determining whether the right numbers and kind of personnel will be in the labor market and available for employment when they are needed. It would collaborate with the individual responsible for training and development and with management to insure that candidates for anticipated openings are identified and given the proper training to prepare them for future responsibilities.

Thus by identifying future manpower needs, cataloging present manpower skills and coordinating the planning effort to fill any gaps which exist between present skills and future requirements, those responsible for manpower planning help management meet their goals by insuring that the necessary human resources will be available when needed.

Electronic Data Processing.—Not too long ago, personnel functions were handled manually by a staff of clerical employees. With the advent of electronic data processing, the potential of these machines became readily apparent in the operating areas of a company. As these high-speed machines became more sophisticated and their reliability was thoroughly proven, thought was given to possible other applications, such as the personnel functions of an organization. Instead of maintaining voluminous files on each employee, by gathering specific facts about each employee (such as name, address, education, position, salary and special skills), and by properly entering these data into the system, companies could eliminate much of the tedious routine associated with personnel activities and record keeping. (See also *Business and the Computer*, page 1773.)

Reduction of errors and rapid information retrieval are possible, as well as expanded and more varied information retrieval.

An electronic data processing system can be set up, for instance, that automatically prints a list of all employees hired on a certain month and year. Carrying this example a step further, the systems can be designed to automatically enroll these employees in various benefit programs when they become eligible for them. Depending on its size, the system might also prepare necessary documents (such as life insurance policies or medical enrollment forms) at the time the employee becomes eligible for the benefit.

■**OTHER COMPUTER USES.**—The output from the system is not limited to printed listings. The computer can also prepare punched cards or display the requested information on a viewing screen similar to a television screen. The viewing screen or other output device is attached to the electronic system but need not be located in the computer room. For example, a viewing screen might be physically located in the personnel department. In addition to the viewer, a printing machine will print the information in the area where the data are needed.

The ability to obtain output from the system in the personnel department at the time it is needed is helpful in many ways. For example, if the personnel department had available a position which would require a qualified lawyer, able to speak French and willing to travel, a properly programmed electronic system could search all employees' records and display the names of the qualified employees on the viewing screen in the personnel department. To manually search the thousands of files in a large corporation to determine which employees met the requirements would be an impractical, if not an impossible, task. High-speed electronic computers perform this task with such rapidity that the answers to such questions appear almost instantaneously.

Modern computer systems with their multi-task capabilities have become invaluable aids. Further uses of electronic computers by personnel departments are still being discovered and it would appear that, as in other fields, their uses will be almost limitless.

—Guy R. Byam

BIBLIOGRAPHY

FINLEY, ROBERT E. *The Personnel Man and His Job.* American Management Association, 1962.

FLEISHMAN, EDWIN A. *Studies in Personnel and Industrial Psychology.* The Dorsey Press, Inc., 1961.

HECKMANN, I. L. and S. G. HUNERYAGER. *Management of the Personnel Function.* Charles E. Merrill Books, Inc., 1962.

PIGORS, PAUL, and MYERS, CHARLES A. *Personnel Administration: A Point of View and a Method.* McGraw-Hill, Inc., 1961.

PIGORS, PAUL, and others, (eds.). *Management of Human Resources.* McGraw-Hill, Inc., 1964.

YODER, DALE. *Personnel Management and Industrial Relations.* Prentice-Hall, Inc., 1962.

ECONOMICS AND BUSINESS GLOSSARY

Abacus, a device for calculating, consisting of beads or balls strung on wires or rods set in a frame.

Abatement, the reduction or elimination of a claim, debt or tax. In tax payments, the reduction in whole or part of the amount levied but not yet paid.

Absentee Ownership, the ownership of, and derivation of income from, land or a business that the owner does not personally oversee. In contemporary usage, the term has been applied to the ownership of stock of a corporation by those who take no active part in its management.

Account, 1. A written record, usually in the form of debits and credits, of the business transactions of an individual or business unit. *Books of account* include journals, ledgers and other supporting records.

2. A statement of transaction during a specified period, as rendered, by a seller to a customer showing balance receivable or payable. Synonyms: statement, statement of account, invoice, bill (1).

3. In banking and finance, the amount of cash or the equivalent deposited in a bank or with a broker, subject to withdrawal or against which orders may be made. Examples: checking account, savings account.

4. The relationship between a manufacturer, wholesaler, retailer, bank, advertising agency, or some other business enterprise, with an individual customer, client, depositor, debtor, etc., particularly a relationship based on the extension of credit. Also, any regular customer or client.

An *account executive* is a business executive responsible for a particular client's account.

Accounting, 1. "The art of recording, classifying, and summarizing in a significant manner and in terms of money, transactions and events which are, in part at least, of a financial character, and interpreting the results thereof." (American Institute of Accountants)

2. The presenting or furnishing of a statement of accounts by one responsible for assets, cash, or a given assignment.

3. The work or profession of an accountant.

Accounts Payable, amounts owed to a creditor; on a balance sheet, those amounts (frequently listed as current liabilities) which are owed for the purchase of goods and services, including amounts due on notes, drafts, or on long-term installment purchasing contracts.

Accounts Receivable, amounts due from customers for goods sold or services rendered, but not including notes, drafts, or acceptances.

Accrued, 1. That which is earned but not yet due, payable, or collectible; applied to many items such as an asset, dividend, income, interest, or revenue.

2. Denoting a liability or expense incurred on or before a certain date which is payable at some future date.

Acid-Test Ratio, a liquidity ratio that shows the relationship between quick assets and current liabilities at any given time. Since the concept quick assets does not include inventories, the acid-test ratio is held to be a better index of a firm's operations than the current ratio. Synonym: quick ratio.

Active Market, in securities trading, a market characterized by frequent transactions; one in which the volume of trading is large, as distinguished from one which is dull, flat, narrow, or stagnant.

Actuary, 1. In general, one who is trained in mathematics or statistics; one who computes risks based upon the laws of probability and averages.

2. In insurance, a specialist who calculates the probabilities involved in any risk for which insurance is issued, and sets the appropriate rate to be charged for such insurance.

Ad Valorem Tax, a levy based on a fixed percentage of an item's dollar value (Latin, "according to value"). One of the two common levies upon imports; the other, *specific tax*, is a stated amount levied by weight or volume on each unit of the commodity imported. Other ad valorem taxes include property tax and sales tax.

Advertisement, a paid message that appears in a regular medium of communication. Its purpose is to sell a product, service, or concept. Synonym: advertising (1).

Advertising, 1. Any paid and openly sponsored form of nonpersonal public announcement or presentation of goods, services, or ideas, designed to induce the public to buy those goods or services or to accept those ideas. Advertising is a multiplied sales message, to be distinguished from a single sales letter. Advertising differs also from *publicity*, which does not

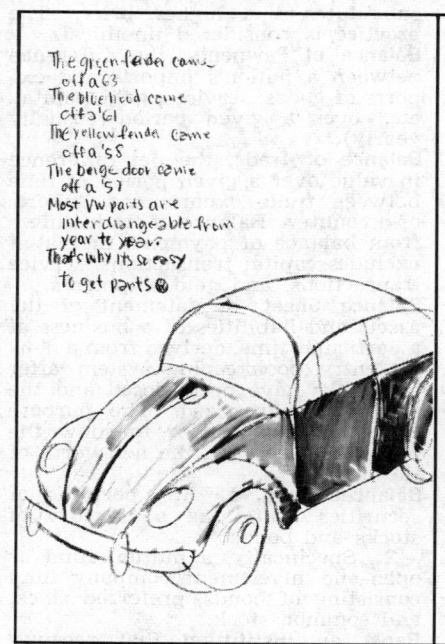

DOYLE. DANE. BERNBACH. INC.

THE PREPARATION OF AN ADVERTISEMENT

THE INITIAL IDEA, or copy theme, is decided upon, and a rough layout is made (A). The sketch is then made into a detailed layout (B), known as a comprehensive, and is given to the client for approval. The finished layout is reproduced on metal by a photoengraving process. (C) shows the advertisement in final form and as it will appear in national magazines and newspapers.

pay the medium (newspaper, magazine, radio, television, etc.) and does not necessarily identify the sponsor. See also *bait, classified, consumer, direct-mail, industrial, institutional, mail order,* and *outdoor advertising.*

2. The business or profession of designing, writing, and placing advertisements.

Affiliate, a business concern owned in whole or in part by another company; a branch; a subsidiary.

Agency Shop, a place of employment in which an employer agrees that all employees, whether union members or not, must pay union dues (or its equivalent in the form of a service charge) as a condition of employment. See also *closed shop, open shop, union shop.*

Agent, a person or company that acts for or in place of another (the principal) by authority. A *special agent* is authorized to act for a principal in the matter of a single act or transaction. A *general agent* is authorized to conduct all the business of the principal, or all business within a given function or territory.

Agribusiness, the production, processing, storage, and distribution of farm commodities, including both foods and nonfoods. It encompasses the manufacture and distribution of farm equipment, feed, fertilizers, and other supplies. By some measures, it also includes meat packing, grocery sales, and the production of textiles made from natural fibers.

Agricultural Economics, the study of the production and marketing of agricultural products and various farm programs.

Amalgamation, the uniting of two or more companies into one company. It may be a *merger,* the acquisition of one corporation by another in which one survives while the other loses its corporate existence; or a *consolidation,* in which both corporations are formed into a new company.

Amortization, 1. The gradual satisfaction, liquidation, or reduction of a debt (such as a mortgage or bond issue), usually by an installment or sinking-fund plan.

2. The gradual reduction in the book value of an asset having a limited life. In certain types of business with wasting assets, such as coal mines, the returns on investments are amortized by treating a part of the returns as a repayment of capital and the rest as interest.

Amortization is also applied to the process of calculating the value of securities which are sold for more or less than their face value, and the difference is charged over the life of the security.

Annual Report, a formal financial statement issued yearly by a corporation to its stockholders, summarizing the activities of the year and the financial condition of the company.

Annuity, an amount payable to a specified person or persons yearly, quarterly, or monthly, or at some other regular interval, for a definite or indefinite period, such as for a specified number of years, for life, or in perpetuity. An *annuity certain* is

paid for a fixed number of years, or for life, with a fixed number of payments guaranteed in any event. A *contingent annuity* has no fixed payment schedule, but is payable only when some uncertain event arises, such as the death of a named person while the annuitant is still alive. A *deferred annuity* provides for payment for a fixed number of years, or for life, to start at the end of a stated period.

Anti-trust, a term denoting any policy, legislation or action designed to protect trade or commerce from conspiracies to inhibit competition, or to protect against unfair business or monopolistic practices.

Appreciation, the increase in the capital or market value of any kind of property (stocks, bonds, goods, plant, equipment, real estate, etc.) above its value at some previous period; the excess of the present value over book value. (Opposed to depreciation.) For example, a stock purchased at $25 a share now selling at $30 has had an appreciation of $5 a share.

Arbitrage, the process of buying something (securities, negotiable instruments, currency or commodities) in one market and simultaneously selling it in another to take advantage of price differences.

Arbitration, the settling of disputes or differences between two parties, such as labor and management, by referring the matter to a third party, known as the *arbitrator,* who hears or receives evidence and then hands down a decision that, by previous agreement of the disputants, is binding upon both parties. See also *conciliation.*

Assessed Valuation, the value assigned to a given piece of privately owned property by local public officials, such as a board of assessors, as a basis for computing local property taxes.

Assessment, 1. A valuation placed upon property for the purpose of taxation.

2. A demand by a corporation that its stockholders pay a specified sum for each share of stock owned. When a corporation is organized, the stock is frequently issued for a fraction of the par value but subject to future assessments by the corporation as the need for additional capital arises. When a corporate reorganization takes place, shareholders frequently agree to an assessment to provide necessary working capital.

Assets, the property or resources of a business; the value of the things the business owns or has owed to it in contrast to the liabilities or amounts owed to others. The assets are carried on the left-hand side of a balance sheet, and the liabilities are carried on the right-hand side. The excess of assets over liabilities is called the *net worth.* See also *capital asset, current asset, fixed asset, frozen asset, liquid asset, quick asset, wasting asset.*

Association, a union of persons in a company, society, or some other group with the object of carrying on some common purpose. It is a general term and includes nonprofit or-

ganizations such as hospitals, trade unions and literary societies as well as organizations for profits, whether organized as partnerships, joint-stock companies or corporations.

Auction, a public sale of goods to the highest bidder, after a series of successively increased offers.

Audit, an examination and verification of accounts by a person who has had no part in their preparation. The accountant records the facts of his client's business, and the auditor goes over these accounts to determine if all the items shown actually exist, to see that the amounts charged are correct, and to determine whether the conclusions drawn from the records are valid and whether the transactions are legal.

Auditing, that branch of accounting that deals with the examination and verification of accounts; the vouching of the accuracy of a company's bookkeeping records.

Automation, the use of automatically controlled machines or processes (advanced mechanical equipment in combination with computers or other self-regulating controls) to perform calculating, research, record-keeping, and other tasks in offices, factories, stores, and the like.

Baby Bond, a bond with a par value of less than $100.

Backlog, 1. Unfilled orders on the books of a company.

2. An accumulation of unperformed tasks or unprocessed materials.

Bad Debt, a debt that is not collectible.

Bait Advertising, the advertising of certain articles (often either nonexistent or in very low supply) at bargain prices to entice customers into a store, in the hope of selling a substitute at a higher price. The practice is considered unethical.

Balance of Payments, the difference between a nation's imports and exports of goods, services, gold, capital, etc., over a given period (usually yearly).

Balance of Trade, the net difference in value over a given period of time between trade exports and imports of a country. Balance of trade differs from balance of payments in that it excludes capital transactions, service transactions, and gold shipments.

Balance Sheet, a statement of the assets and liabilities of a business at a particular time, derived from a double-entry bookkeeping system after the books have been closed and the accounts summarized. The purpose of a balance sheet is to show the financial status and the net worth of the company.

Balanced Fund, 1. Any portfolio of securities containing a mixture of stocks and bonds.

2. Specifically, a mutual fund or open-end investment company fund consisting of bonds, preferred stock, and common stock.

Bank, an institution that receives deposits of money and makes loans, its profits deriving from the interest on the loans made. A bank also borrows funds on its own account, issues currency under certain conditions, administers funds placed with it. Collectively, banks act as the administering unit of the entire financial system of a nation. *National banks* are federally incorporated under the National Bank Act and may have the word national in their titles. *State banks* are incorporated under the laws of the state and regulated by the state government. Any national bank, state bank, or trust company may become a member of the Federal Reserve System. *Savings banks* are primarily banks of deposit, paying interest to depositors, and are not required to keep a reserve. *Trust companies* are state incorporated and in addition to their general banking functions act as administrators and trustees either under the voluntary trust of a living person or as the executor of a will.

Bank Account. See *account (3)*.

Bank Deposit, funds placed in a bank to be kept in the customer's account and returned to the customer under stated conditions. See *account (3)*. See also *demand deposit*.

Bank Examiner, a government official who makes periodic examinations of the assets, liabilities, papers, books, and affairs of a bank for the purpose of auditing the bank statement.

Bank Holiday, 1. Any holiday on which banks are closed; legal holiday.

2. Those days on which all the banks are closed in time of financial panics.

Bank Note, a promissory note in the form of paper currency, issued by an authorized bank, and payable on demand, which circulates as money. As of August 1, 1935, all the bonds backing such notes were retired and no bank notes have been issued since.

Bank Reserve, See *reserve (2)*.

Barter, the exchange of one article for another; an exchange of goods without the use of money or credit. Primitive societies employed bartering before money came into use as a medium of exchange. Modern international trade, considered as a whole, is a system of barter, for there is no international money, and the imports and exports of a country tend to balance.

Bear, a dealer on a stock or produce exchange who believes that stocks or commodities are going to fall in price. The bear attempts to make a profit out of the falling market by short sales. See also *bull*.

Bear Market, depressed or declining market.

Bid, a statement, usually in writing, of an amount of money for which the bidder will do a certain thing or sell a specified amount of a product. When a government wants to buy certain goods or wants a certain structure built, specifications of the things wanted are made public, and the concerns desiring the contract submit sealed bids, usually accompanied by a certified check to guarantee the bid. At an agreed time the bids are opened, and the contract is rewarded to the *lowest* reputable bidder. In an auction, the bid is the oral or indicated statement of the price that the bidder is willing to pay for the article. The article goes to the *highest* bidder.

Big Board, nickname of the New York Stock Exchange.

Bill, 1. A written account of money owed for goods or services supplied, or for work done; an invoice.

2. A piece of paper money, such as a five- or ten-dollar *bill*.

Bill of Exchange, a written order requiring the person to whom it is addressed to pay a specified sum to a third person or his order, on demand or at a specified future time. Bills of exchange are used primarily in foreign trade and greatly facilitate the settlement of international balances by enabling a bank to counterbalance the debts between individuals in two countries. For example, Mr. Jones in the United States owes Mr. Wang in Japan $100, and Mr. Fu in Japan owes $100 to Mr. Smith in the United States. Instead of Mr. Jones paying Mr. Wang and Mr. Fu paying Mr. Smith, this double transfer of money can be balanced through the use of bills of exchange, the banks making the arrangement so that Mr. Jones pays Mr. Smith and Mr. Fu pays Mr. Wang, and no international transfer of funds is necessary. Synonym: draft.

Bimetallism, a monetary system in which both gold and silver are the standard money, and both are coined at a ratio fixed by law. The ratio is expressed in terms of weight (for example, 16 ounces of silver equals 1 ounce of gold, a ratio of 16 to 1). The United States, following the example of the countries of Europe, adopted bimetallism in 1792, the ratio being set at 15 to 1. This standard was abandoned in 1873, readopted in modified form in 1878, and abandoned for the gold standard in 1900.

Monometallism is a monetary system in which one metal, gold or silver, is the standard money. The gold standard was the accepted one from the abandonment of bimetallism until the economic depression of 1929, which caused all the nations of the world to adopt some sort of a government-managed currency. See also *gold standard*.

Black Market, a market that violates quota, price ceiling, or rationing controls or other public regulations; one that violates ethical practices.

Blue Chip, a common stock with a record of good earnings, regular dividend payments, and price stability; a stock that commands a high price in relation to the corporation's earnings because of its stability.

Blue Sky Laws, various state laws enacted to protect the public from frauds in the buying and selling of stocks, bonds, and other securities.

Bond, a device for borrowing money, issued as an evidence of indebtedness by a corporation or individual, bearing interest at a stipulated rate and having a certain number of years to run before it is to be redeemed. It is essentially a promissory note of the corporation that is not required to be paid for a period of years. Bonds of corporations or individuals (but not of governments) are usually backed by some security, such as a mortgage on the property that gives the owner of the bond the right to obtain repayment of his loan from a sale of the property if the corporation does not repay him. See also *baby bond, convertible bond, debenture bond, sinking fund bond*.

Bonded Warehouse. See *warehouse*.

Book Value, 1. Of securities, the total of the owners' equity as shown by the accounting records of the corporation; usually stated on a per-share basis to represent the value of assets applicable to the stock as

BIDS are signified by voice and raised hands on a selling floor in response to an offer.

shown on the books. (Distinguished from *market value*.)

2. In business, the net worth of a company; the excess of assets over liabilities.

Bookkeeping, the keeping of systematic, concise, and convenient records of the financial transactions of a business, to show what the transactions were, when they took place, and the amounts and sources of the gains and losses. *Double-entry bookkeeping* is the modern system with two entries for each transaction, one a debit and the other a credit. The essential books are the journal and the ledger, but for convenience in large establishments these books are divided to facilitate the handling of the entries. *Single-entry bookkeeping* is a simpler method, practical only in very small businesses, and only one entry is made for each transaction.

Boom, a sudden period of great prosperity, frequently caused by an outburst in speculation in land, commodities, or securities that causes a rapid rise in prices, an increase in activity, and large profits. A boom is often followed by an equally rapid recession (called a *panic* or a *bust*) accompanied by a sharp decline in business activity and large losses. The series of changes from boom through recession to boom again is called a *business cycle*.

Boycott, concerted action by a group that refuses to perform a customary act; a method by which a group of persons seeks to achieve the adoption of some program by refusing to have business or social relations with the persons opposing this program. The word is derived from the name of Captain Charles Cunningham Boycott (1832–1897), an English land agent in Ireland. Because of Captain Boycott's ruthless ejections of tenants, he was ostracized by his neighbors who even refused to sell him food and clothing.

The boycott has been widely employed in American labor disputes, but until recently was given little legal standing. A *direct boycott* is of one disputant against the other; this has received court sanction when no violence, coercion, or intimidation is involved. A *secondary boycott* is the use of pressure against third parties. Most forms of secondary boycott are considered unfair labor practices under the Taft-Hartley Act.

Branch, a subordinate or dependent unit or division of a business, as of a bank, factory, office or store.

Brand Name, a word or letter, or group of words or letters, composing a name or design that identifies the goods or services of a seller and distinguishes them from those of competitors; a trademark or trade name.

Broker, one who acts as a middleman negotiating the sale of an article between two others. Ordinarily, the broker does not possess the goods sold nor does he receive the goods purchased. The broker does not take any financial risk. He receives his profit from the commission paid by the party who first engages his services, although the payment of the commission is subject to any contractual arrangement desired by the par-

ties. Brokers are usually free lances in their relations with manufacturers, whereas selling agents or manufacturers' agents have continuous and permanent relations with the manufacturers for whom they sell.

Bucket Shop, a fraudulent stock brokerage office that purports to make stock purchases for customers, but in reality never does so. While the shop is solvent it pays out of its capital the customer's "profits" from the increase of stock prices. The shop makes its profits from the losses of the customer and from commissions for purported services. In effect, a bucket shop is a place where bets are placed on the rise or fall of stock quotations.

Budget, 1. In private business and in government, money designated for a particular purpose, as for advertising, sales, production, or research and development.

2. A written plan or program, or a specific part thereof, that covers the projected operation of a business, department, or activity over a specified future period of time.

Building and Loan Association. See *savings and loan association*.

Bull, a dealer or broker who believes that the market is going up and attempts to make a profit by buying the stock or commodities at the present price and holding them for sale later, when he expects the price will be higher. See also *bear*.

Bull Market, an advancing or rising market.

Business, 1. Any commercial, mercantile, financial or industrial activity designed to make a profit.

2. Any person, partnership, or corporation engaged in such activities; an enterprise.

3. Amount or volume of trade.

Business Cycle, a movement in business activity characterized by periodic changes or fluctuations from depression to prosperity and back to depression. It generally follows this progression: crisis, liquidation, depression, readjustment, revival, prosperity, speculation, crisis, etc.

Business Firm, according to the U.S. Office of Business Economics, a business organization under a single management. This may include one or more plants or outlets.

Business Industrial Goods, goods used in producing consumers' goods, or other business or producers' goods and services. Examples: land and buildings used for business purposes, factory or office equipment, operating supplies, etc. Synonym: producers' goods.

Business Savings, in government statistics, that portion of income produced by business which is retained during the year for addition to capital and surplus and not distributed to creditors, management, labor, stockholders or bondholders, or withdrawn by entrepreneurs.

Bust. See *boom*.

Buyers' Market, a market in which supply exceeds demand to the extent that buyers can bargain or set prices or terms of sale. See also *sellers' market*.

Buyers' Strike, an attempt by consumers to force lower prices by refrain-

ing, in protest, from buying in normal quantities.

Buying In, 1. The purchase of stock for the purpose of returning borrowed stock. In the case of a short sale the stock is borrowed for delivery to the buyer, and when the seller desires to complete the transaction, he buys in the stock and gives this stock for the stock that he previously borrowed.

2. At a public sale, the purchase of a property offered in order to protect the buyer's investment or other interest in the property.

Call, 1. A demand for payment of an obligation, especially a bank loan, which is payable on the lender's demand at any time.

2. In the securities or commodities market, an option or contract that permits the holder to buy a certain amount of a named security or given commodity at a stated price on or before a specified date. See also *put*.

3. An assessment on a stockholder or subscriber to pay additional capital, installment, or a subscription to capital.

Call Loan, a loan that is repayable on demand or call of the bank or other lender, or by the borrower.

Call Market. See *commodity exchange*.

Call Money, borrowed money that is returnable on call; funds available or loaned on call.

Capital, 1. In general, wealth, whether in money or property, owned and used to produce or create something of value; money invested; money that bears interest.

2. In classical economics, one of the three major factors of production, the others being land and labor.

3. In business, the money and credit needed to start and operate an enterprise; the total wealth or assets of a firm, including such intangible assets as securities, trademarks, patents, goodwill, etc.; the investment in a business. A distinction is frequently made between *fixed capital* and *working capital*.

4. In business, the excess of assets over liability; the net worth of an enterprise.

Capital Asset, an asset, tangible or intangible, that is held for a long term either as an investment or for use in production. *Fixed assets* include land, buildings, equipment, furniture, mineral deposits, timber preserves, and the like. *Intangible capital assets* include goodwill, patents, and trademarks. In commercial usage fixed asset and capital asset are used interchangeably.

Capital Gain (or **Loss**), the gain (or loss) realized from the sale or exchange of a capital asset at a price that is higher (or lower) than the original purchase or acquisition price.

Capital Gains Tax, a tax on the profit arising from the sale of a capital asset such as securities or real estate.

Capital Goods, goods such as equipment, machinery, tools, factories, etc., produced by man for use in further production. Synonym: producers' goods.

Capital Market, a general term for the entire system involved in the supply of and the demand for long-term investments.

Capital Stock, all shares representing equity or ownership in a corporation, including common stock and preferred stock. See also *stock*.

Capitalism, an economic system characterized by private or corporate ownership of the means of production, distribution, and exchange; by the freedom of the individual to contract with others and to engage in business activities of his choice; by private initiative and the profit motive and by the institution of credit. Synonyms: free enterprise, private enterprise.

Capitalization, 1. The value of the total outstanding stocks and bonds of a business enterprise.

2. The total investment of the owners in a business enterprise.

3. The equity of a corporation plus its long-term debt.

4. The conversion of income into a capital sum; to compute the present value of a periodic payment. For example, if the rent from a property is $100 a year, and the current interest rate is 5 per cent, to find the capital value of the property divide the rent by the interest rate; the capitalization is $2,000. Synonym: capitalized value.

Capitalized Value. See *capitalization* (4).

Carloadings, the total number of freight cars in the country loaded with revenue-paying freight during a certain period, usually a week. Freight-car loadings are an important indication of general business conditions and an important item in the calculation of business activity.

Carrying Charge, 1. An amount over and above the purchase price paid by the consumer to a retailer or other seller for the right to buy on an installment plan.

2. A recurring cost incident to owning or holding property, such as taxes, mortgage interest, rental, insurance, storage, etc.

3. The fee charged by a stock broker for carrying a customer's securities on margin.

Cartage, a charge made by a carrier for the transportation of goods to docks for reshipment or to their destination.

Cartel, a form of combination (1) among manufacturers or producers of raw material in the same or similar industries, by which independent firms or producers contract to regulate their output, prices, or markets; frequently, but not necessarily, an international combination.

Cash, 1. Currency and ready money, including coins and paper money; in a narrow sense, coins only.

2. In accounting, currency and negotiable instruments that can quickly be converted into cash, including certificates of deposit, postal money orders, traveler's checks, cashier or certified checks, drafts, bearer bonds, etc.

3. To convert into money, as to *cash* a check.

Cash Budget, 1. A budget that covers the planned needs of a business for funds over a specified future period of time, the sources—both internal and external—of these funds, and the estimated operating results.

2. In government, a budget that covers federal cash expenditures and cash receipts.

Cash Discount, a deduction made from a charge, debt, or account if the customer makes immediate payment, or pays within a specified period of time (usually within ten days of the invoice date).

Cash Market. See *commodity exchange*.

Cash on Delivery (C.O.D.), a method of shipping goods in which the carrier collects the payment for the goods at the time of delivery and remits the payment to the seller. If there is a large amount of goods, it is customary for the carrier to allow a reasonable time for the buyer to inspect the goods before collection is made. Synonym: collect on delivery.

Caveat Emptor (Latin, "let the buyer beware"), merchandising maxim summarizing the common-law rule that the buyer must examine, judge, and test his purchase to see that he is getting the quantity and quality expected.

Caveat Venditor (Latin, "let the seller beware"), merchandising maxim placing responsibility on the seller for any defects or deficiencies in items sold.

Certificate, 1. A formal written statement vouching for a certain matter, made by a person with authority and with a knowledge of the truth of the matter.

2. A document evidencing a debt or obligation (*certificate of deposit, certificate of indebtedness*) or ownership or share in equity (*stock certificate*).

3. A form of United States paper money (*gold certificate, silver certificate*).

Certificate of Deposit, 1. A formal, frequently negotiable and transferable, instrument issued by a bank evidencing an indebtedness arising from deposit of funds subject to withdrawal under specified conditions: on demand (*demand certificate*) or at or after a specified future date (*time certificate*). The latter usually bears interest.

2. A formal instrument, usually negotiable and transferable, issued by a trust company or other depository or agent for stocks or bonds deposited under terms of a reorganization, recapitalization, or other plan or agreement.

Certificate of Incorporation, an official statement by the proper state or federal authority of the incorporation of a business.

Certificate of Indebtedness, 1. A short-term negotiable instrument, usually interest-bearing, often unsecured, issued by a corporation or the U.S. government for temporary financing.

2. In general, any bond or other security evidencing debts, as distinguished from a stock certificate, which represents a share of ownership.

Certified Check, a check that is certified as good (both as to signature of the drawer and the availability of funds) by the bank on which it is drawn, and authenticated by the signature of an officer of the bank.

Chain Store, 1. One of several retail stores under the same ownership and central management, selling the same type of goods. (See also *retail store*.)

2. One of several independently owned but voluntarily associated stores joined together in some common activities, such as purchasing, promotion, and merchandising. Often the group is brought together by a wholesaler or manufacturer whose products are featured by the voluntary chain. Synonym: voluntary chain, voluntary group.

Chamber of Commerce, an organization of businessmen, representing the views of commercial, financial and industrial interests in a city or local area.

Change, 1. An equivalent amount of currency in a different form given in exchange.

2. The amount of money returned after making a payment with a piece of money greater than the price.

3. Small money or coins.

Channel of Distribution, the route or method by which goods are distributed from the original grower, manufacturer, or importer to the ultimate consumer, and the various businesses that are part of the distribution process.

Charge, 1. A debit to an account.

2. The cost of an item or service.

3. To purchase on credit, or without payment on receipt of goods. The seller debits the customer's account.

Charge Account, a credit account at a store, which permits a customer to buy now and pay later.

Cheap Money, money that has depreciated in value because of inflation.

Check, a bill of exchange or draft drawn upon a bank and payable on demand; the depositor thus orders the bank to pay his creditor from the fund on deposit to his account in the bank.

Checkoff, a voluntary arrangement under which the employer, by agreement with a labor union, deducts union dues and assessments from the pay of union members. The funds thus collected are turned over to the union.

Circulation, 1. The amount of money in active use at a given time; currency. (See also *money in circulation*.)

2. The average total number of copies of a publication issued, distributed, or sold over a given period of time. The circulation of a newspaper, magazine, or other periodical may be either gross or net. *Gross circulation* is the number of copies printed. *Net circulation* (sometimes called *net paid circulation*) is the number of copies actually sold.

Classified Advertising, advertisements in a newspaper or other publication arranged by categories like "lost and found," "help wanted," "room and board," "houses for sale," "used cars," etc.

Clearinghouse, an association for facilitating the settlement of claims between members, especially in banking. For example, when Bank *A* receives for deposit a check drawn on Bank *B*, *A* presents it to the clearinghouse for payment, rather than to

Bank *B*. By paying and balancing all claims of member banks, the clearinghouse eliminates the expense and inefficiency that would arise if each bank had to present claims individually to all other banks. A single payment by the clearinghouse is made to each bank and this settles all its claims against other banks.

Closed-End Investment Company, an investment company that has a fixed capital structure, or that issues capital stock only infrequently. The proceeds of the sale of capital stock are invested and reinvested in diversified securities. Once issued, the shares are traded in the over-the-counter market or on stock exchanges.

Closed Shop, a place of employment where the employer agrees to employ union workers only, and where employees must remain union members in order to retain their jobs. See also *agency shop, open shop, union shop.*

Coin, a piece of metal of prescribed size, shape, weight, and fineness stamped and issued by governmental authority for use as money.

Coinage, 1. The process of making legally authorized coins by combining pure metal and alloy in the stipulated proportions. All coinage in the United States is done by the U.S. Mint, which was authorized by Congress in 1792.

2. The pieces coined, collectively; coins.

Collateral, property that is pledged as security for the repayment of a loan. Collateral usually consists of stocks, bonds, negotiable instruments, warehouse receipts, negotiable bills of lading or trust receipts, although physical goods are frequently accepted. Ordinarily, collateral is given to the lender together with a promissory note. If the loan is not repaid, the lender may sell the collateral and use the proceeds to recoup his loss on the loan. If there remains any excess, it is given to the borrower. If the proceeds from the sale of the collateral are not sufficient to repay the loan in full, the borrower is still responsible for the unpaid balance.

Collect on Delivery. See *cash on delivery.*

Collective Bargaining, the process by which employees as a group, acting through their representatives, bargain with their employers for union recognition, wages, hours, conditions of employment, and allied matters. The power to bargain depends largely upon the power to withhold something that is desired by the other party. The employer has the power to withhold the work and the employee has the power to withhold his services. Collective bargaining necessitates some type of organization among the workers that is independent of the employer's control, such as a labor union.

When employers of a given industry, or segment of industry negotiate jointly with the union or unions representing the employees in the industry, the process is called *industry-wide bargaining.*

Collectivism, a planned economic system under government control, such as socialism or communism; or more specifically the general move-

ment away from the laissez faire doctrine and individualism. In all forms of society, there has been more or less social control of business activity, but during the nineteenth century there was a trend toward the laissez faire policy of no interference with business by government, as elaborated by Adam Smith in *The Wealth of Nations* (1776). From the beginning of the twentieth century, there has been an increasing movement toward a government-controlled economic order.

Combination, 1. The union or alliance of different individuals, organizations, corporations, trade associations, etc., for their mutual benefits. Such alliances formed to lessen competition are usually prohibited by law. See also *combination in restraint of trade, trust, pool, holding company.*

2. A business alliance or union; the bringing together of two or more business enterprises into one; an amalgamation. A combination may be a consolidation or a merger.

Combination in Restraint of Trade, any conspiracy, association, or combination (1) that obstructs the free flow of trade, or that attempts to monopolize or control production, traffic, or sale of any commodity, or that attempts to stifle free competition.

Command Economy, a mode of economic life based on a central authority—a political party or dictator—that determines which jobs people take, what goods will be produced, how they will be produced, and how the income and goods will be distributed. See also *market economy, traditional economy.*

Commerce, in general, the interchange of goods, property, or services, particularly on a large scale, nationally and internationally. *Intrastate commerce* is transacted wholly within the boundaries of one state, while *interstate commerce* is conducted between any place in one state and any place in another state.

Commerce Power, the power of the U.S. Congress under the Constitution (Article I, Section 8) to regulate trade between the states; the basis for all federal regulation of business.

Commercial Arbitration, the settlement of business disputes by arbitration.

Commercial Paper, any of various forms of short-term (usually one year or less), negotiable credit instruments that arise out of business transactions. Examples: bills of exchange, drafts, notes.

Commissary or **Commissary Store.** See *company store.*

Commodity Dollar. See *compensated currency.*

Commodity Exchange, an organized open market for buying and selling contracts for immediate or future delivery of standard primary products (such as coffee, grain, cotton, sugar, and metals). Prices are determined by market supply and demand. Membership of the exchange is closed; to obtain membership, one must be elected and purchase a seat, the price of which varies according to the particular exchange and business conditions. Samples and standard grades

NEW YORK COTTON EXCHANGE

COMMODITY traders bid at Cotton Exchange.

are traded, and the transfer of a warehouse receipt is treated as delivery.

A *cash market* or *spot market* in the exchange is where trading takes place for immediate delivery or very early delivery. The *to-arrive market* is for trading in commodities in the process of shipment or about to be shipped. The *futures market* is a market for trading in contracts to deliver a commodity at a specified future date. The *call market* is a market for bids and offers of certain grades of commodities.

Commodity Market, in general, regular trade in commodities, particularly through the commodity exchanges.

Common Carrier, an agency providing transport service, usually over fixed routes on definite schedules, for the general public. A common carrier may restrict classes of passengers or goods, but must accept all goods or passengers in these classes when accommodations are available and the fixed price for a particular service is tendered.

Common Stock, capital stock that does not have preference over other classes of stock, either in dividend payments or in ultimate distribution of assets, but that is usually the only class of stock with voting rights in the management of the company; dividend payments are unlimited after prior claims have been met. Common stock represents the holder's equity or ownership in the company.

Company Store, a retail store owned and operated by a company or governmental unit to sell primarily to its employees. Such establishments are usually found only in communities where there are no employees other than those of the concern owning the store, such as an army post, a mining town, or an industrial village owned by the industry. Synonyms: commissary, commissary store, industrial store.

Company Union, a labor union organized usually at the suggestion, and with the help, of an employer, and confined to units under the same management. The courts have upheld the National Labor Relations Board in declaring such unions illegal.

Comparative Economics, the study of different economic systems.

Compensated Currency, a monetary plan by which the gold content of the dollar would be changed with any change in the price level. Thus the gold represented by a gold certificate would always purchase the same amount of goods. The *compensated dollar* (sometimes called *commodity dollar*) is one of the many plans proposed to cure the evils of inflation and deflation. This plan has never been adopted, and since the world has generally abandoned the gold standard, there is little chance of its adoption, for the scheme requires a 100 per cent gold reserve. Synonym: managed currency.

Compensated Dollar. See *compensated currency.*

Competition, the struggle with others for a prize; particularly an open rivalry in the market between buyers and sellers of a good or service. In all economic systems competition serves as a driving force. Under capitalism, the prize for which men compete is usually wealth and the power and prestige that wealth brings with it. Under communism, competition is either for a recognition of merit in having served the state or for the power and prestige that come from an important position. The experience of Russia seems to show that some sort of a financial prize is necessary, at least in the nature of a wage differential.

Conciliation, the bringing together of two parties in dispute by a third party for the purpose of adjusting differences through compromise. See also *arbitration.*

Consol, in the securities trade, a term for a bond issue that is a consolidation of previous issues. The term is an abbreviation of *consolidated annuities.* For example, the various British government obligations were consolidated between 1750 and 1757 into annuity stocks, most of which bore 3 per cent interest. Interest was paid by the Bank of England, which held the stock, and if market conditions justified it, premiums were paid in addition to the fixed rate of interest. In 1888 and in 1903 the interest was reduced. The consols represented most of the national debt up to the time of World War I and were regarded as an index of the national credit.

Consolidated Annuities. See *consol.*

Consolidation, a combination (2) or *amalgamation* of two or more companies into a new one, which is the surviving company. In a *merger,* one existing and surviving company acquires one or more other companies.

Consortium, a group of representatives (especially, financial representatives) of various nations or private individuals in various nations bound together by an agreement to aid another nation, usually by extending loans or underwriting the government securities of the nation to be aided.

Constant Dollars, a method of expressing statistical series in a form that eliminates the changes in the purchasing power of the dollar. Usually the data are expressed in terms of dollars of some selected year or years.

Consumer, one who consumes, buys, or employs goods or services, rather than a product producer or distributor.

Consumer Advertising, advertising directed at the general public through mass media such as newspapers, magazines, radio, television, and billboards.

Consumer Price Index. See *cost-of-living index.*

Consumers' Cooperative, a retail store owned and directed by its own associated customer membership. Such stores are found largely in industrial communities, where the groups of workers are homogeneous in nature and where the incentive or necessity for saving is rather great, and in smaller communities for the purchase of feed and other farm supplies.

Cooperative stores are operated not for profit but for the benefit of the members of the cooperative association owning them. Some cooperative stores have at times returned savings direct to the members at time of purchase—through a policy of selling at lower prices than similar cooperative stores. However, the majority of successful cooperative stores use the *patronage-dividend* plan. By this method, the prices charged are quite similar to those at other stores of the neighborhood; but at the end of the year (or other accounting period) any profits remaining after the deductions for interest, sinking fund (if any), surplus account, and so forth are paid back to the members *pro rata* on the amount of their purchases. Thus, the individual or family who purchases a thousand dollars worth of goods from the store automatically receives a larger share of its profits than does the one purchasing only two or three hundred dollars' worth. The control of these cooperative stores, like the ownership, in most cases rests with the members. Many grocery stores and a few general merchandise stores are so operated in industrial sections of our cities. Students in several American colleges operate bookstores on a similar basis.

Consumers' Goods, merchandise bought and consumed by the general public rather than by industry (distinguished from *industrial goods*). Consumers' goods are sometimes classified as *convenience goods, shopping goods, specialty goods,* and *unsought goods.*

Contingent Annuity. See *annuity.*

Contingent Liabilities. See *liabilities.*

Convenience Goods, consumers' goods that are usually purchased frequently, immediately, and with the minimum of effort; distinguished from *shopping goods,* which are bought after comparing and considering the offerings of various retailers. Examples: tobacco products, soap, most drug products, newspapers and magazines, small packaged confections, many grocery products and, in general, many advertised brands of various products in constant use.

Convertible Bond, a bond that gives the owner the right to exchange the bond for some other security of the corporation, usually stock.

Corporation, a legal, private or public entity organized for the achievement of a common purpose, and treated by the law as a single person possessing rights and liabilities distinct from its constituent members or shareholders.

Cost, 1. The price paid to acquire, manufacture, accomplish or maintain something; charge (2); price.

2. In economics, the value, commitments, or payments to factors of production, including payments for capital, land, and labor, including management. The total costs of a business are frequently classified as *fixed costs* and *variable costs.*

3. That which is sacrificed in order to procure something.

Cost of Living, the money expenditures necessary for goods and services (food, clothing, and other necessities) that are needed to maintain a certain standard of living.

Cost-of-Living Index, a price index that measures changes in the cost of living over a period of time. The most frequently cited cost-of-living index is the consumer price index, designed by the U.S. Bureau of Labor Statistics to reflect changes in the prices of goods and services bought by the families of "typical" wage-earners.

Cost Plus, a price or a bid consisting of the cost of producing an article or doing work plus either a percentage of the total cost or a stated amount, which is the profit. If a contractor bids on the construction of a building "cost plus 10 per cent," this means that he will be paid the total cost of materials and wages plus 10 per cent of the total cost as his profit. Some arrangements, which call for cost plus a stated amount, are known as *cost plus a fixed fee.* The cost-plus bid is highly desirable when costs are subject to sudden fluctuations and when the construction involves a particular type of work, the cost of which is difficult to estimate.

Cost Plus a Fixed Fee. See *cost plus.*

Coupon, 1. In finance, a note or certificate of interest due attached to a bond. The coupon is cut from the bond when the interest is due and is then presented for payment. When a bond is sold *coupons off* (or *ex-coupon*), it means that the currently due interest payment will not be paid to the buyer. If the bond is sold *coupons on,* it means that the current interest payment is due the buyer. A bond sold with *coupons attached* has attached coupons for past due interest payments, and their value depends upon the condition of the business and the prospects of the past interest being paid.

2. In marketing, any certificate which is to be cut from an advertisement and used as an order form or to request additional information or secure a premium.

Craft Union, a labor union whose membership includes workers engaged in the same specialized craft or trade, or in several related crafts, regardless of the industry in which they are employed. Synonym: horizontal union. See also *industrial union.*

Credit Card, a small card issued by travel agencies, transportation companies, hotels, oil companies, restaurants, etc., giving the holder the right to charge goods and services to the issuing company.

Credit Union, a cooperative association organized to make small, short-term loans to its members at low interest rates. The source of funds for lending is from the members, who deposit savings at interest, or who purchase shares, or both.

Creditor Nation, a nation whose obligations to foreign owners of claims on it are less than the sum of all obligations due from foreign debtors (opposite of *debtor nation*). See also *balance of payment.*

Creeping Inflation, a slow but persistently upward movement in general price levels.

Crisis, a phase in a business cycle marked by a sudden drop in the volume of trade, profits, wages, and prices.

Cumulative Dividend. See *dividend.*

Currency, anything that circulates freely and is accepted as a medium of exchange, including coins, government notes, bank notes, etc.

Currency in Circulation. See *money in circulation.*

Current Asset, an asset that is either cash or could be converted within a relatively short period (usually one year or less) into cash or useful goods or services. Other examples: securities, goods and materials in inventory, accounts and notes receivable.

Current Debt, a business debt that is payable within the current fiscal year; a short-term debt. See also *funded debt.*

Current Liability, any liability that is due and payable within a relatively short period of time, usually one year or less. Examples: accounts payable, notes and acceptances payable, and accrued liabilities.

Current Ratio, a liquidity ratio that shows the relationship between total current liabilities. See also *current asset, current liability, acid test ratio.*

Dealer's Brand. See *private brand.*

Debasement, reduction in intrinsic value, especially of the metallic content of a coin below its face value.

Debenture, 1. An unsecured promise to pay made by a corporation. It differs from a promissory note in that the debenture is for a longer term.

2. A debenture bond.

Debenture Bond, a bond with a stated maturity date and rate of interest but with no security. It can also be a *convertible bond.*

Debit, 1. In bookkeeping, an entry made on the left or asset side of a ledger or account, recording either an addition to an asset or expense or a deduction to a liability, net worth, or revenue.

2. The amount so recorded; opposed to credit.

Debt, that which is owed by one person or organization to another, including money, goods, or services. See also *accounts payable.*

Debtor Nation, a nation whose obligations to foreign owners of claims against it exceed the obligations due from foreign debtors. (Opposed to *creditor nation.*) See also *balance of payments.*

Deficit, 1. A deficiency expressed in money; especially, that which is needed to make up the difference between receipts and expenditures, or between assets and liabilities. (Opposed to *surplus.*)

2. A loss in the operations of a business. (Opposed to *profit.*)

Deflation, a decrease of money in circulation below the needs of business, which brings about a fall in the general level of prices. *Inflation* results in a rise in the price level and, in terms of commodities, money is worth less. Deflation has the opposite effect, and prices fall.

Demand, 1. The total desire for the possession of a commodity of the individual members of the community. *Effective demand* is a desire for possession of an article by those who have sufficient money to make the purchase. Demand is accurately defined as "the entire complex of conditions, except price, which determines the amount of a commodity salable in a given market at a named price."

The demand at any particular time depends upon various factors: the value placed upon the particular commodity by the buyers, the purchasing power of the buyers, and the prices at which substitute and complementary goods are available.

Elasticity of demand is a measure that indicates how much demand will stretch in response to a change in price. Demand for an article is said to be elastic if the change in consumption is greater than the change in price. Luxury articles generally have an elastic demand. For example, if the price of candy is raised, then a great deal less candy will be purchased. But if the price of bread is raised, almost the same amount will be purchased. This is said to be an *inelastic demand,* since the change in consumption is less than the change in price. This inelasticity of demand makes any attempt at price control exceedingly difficult and frequently impossible. For example, the demand for agricultural products is generally inelastic, and approximately the same amount is consumed regardless of price changes. Thus, even a small overproduction may result in ruinously low prices; and if the prices are raised by artificial government action and there is any increase in the production due to this price rise, then the original price increase quickly becomes nullified or even reversed. For this reason, efforts to control the price of agricultural commodities by the government have included controlling the amount of production.

2. A request or call for payment of that which is due.

Demand Certificate. See *certificate of deposit* (1).

Demand Curve, a graphic presentation of a demand schedule.

Demand Deposit, a bank deposit subject to withdrawal at the will of the depositor without prior notice.

Demand Schedule, a tabulation of what people will pay for various products, and how much they are willing to pay over a differing price range.

Department Store, a retail store that is organized into separate units for purposes of promotion, service, accounting, and control or regulation.

The departmental organization is well defined; accounting records are kept by departments; and occasionally departments are leased, so that all parts of the store are not strictly under the same management.

The usual distinction between a department store and a *specialty shop* is that the department store carries more varied lines, and that dry goods are a main part of its stock. Department stores in large cities often have suburban branch stores that are specialty shops.

Depletion, the reduction or loss in value of an asset due to its being used up in whole or in part and not replaceable by human efforts; the exhaustion of natural resources, such as mineral deposits, oil, etc.

Depreciation, 1. In accounting, a reduction in the value of fixed assets such as buildings, machinery, furniture, equipment, tools, etc., resulting from wear and tear. In this sense, depreciation is distinguished from *obsolescence,* the reduction in the economic life of an asset due to changes in style, improvements in processes, technological progress, etc., and from *depletion,* the loss in value of an asset which is used up wholly or partly and is not replaceable by human efforts.

2. In economics, any shortening of the life expectancy of capital goods or assets, including not only losses due to wear and tear but also depletion, obsolescence and *deterioration* (the effect of the elements, breakage, or lack of maintenance upon the services of a limited-life asset.)

Depression, a phase of a business cycle marked by low activity in business, high unemployment, low production, little consumer buying, and contraction of credit.

Deterioration, a reduction in the value of a capital good or asset due to effects of the elements (exposure, fire, flood) breakage, or lack of maintenance. See also *depreciation.*

Devaluation, the assignment of a new and lower legal value to the monetary unit with the order that all contract obligations be settled with the new monetary unit. Devaluation is usually accomplished by an act of legislature. In most cases the name of the old monetary unit is maintained, but the bullion content is lowered.

Devaluation is a method of stabilizing the currency and increasing foreign trade by reducing the costs of commodities in terms of foreign money. The same result may be reached by increasing the amount of paper money, which reduces the value of the old money in circulation.

Diminishing Return, a general principle of productivity and a fundamental concept in economics: that increased effort and increased investment will not bring corresponding increase in production or profit beyond a certain point. The principle of diminishing return was first applied only to agriculture, and although it is now applied to all phases of production, it can best be explained in terms of agriculture. If increasing amounts of capital or labor are applied to a given unit of land, there finally comes a point in the production where the returns from the application of added amounts give a smaller return per unit. For example, a farmer may apply 30 pounds of fertilizer to an acre of land and get a yield of 14.9 bushels of wheat. If he applies 60 pounds of fertilizer he may get 17.3 bushels of wheat, and 90 pounds of fertilizer may increase the production to 18.9 bushels. However, although the total output is increasing, the percentage of each increase is decreasing. It is important to understand that this does not depend upon the declining fertility of the soil or the weather. The diminishing return is an economic phenomenon that occurs in any sort of agricultural or industrial production. Synonyms: law of diminishing return; law of variable proportions.

Direct Boycott, a boycott that bears directly upon the individual, group, or company against which the boycotters have a grievance, especially one in which a union refuses to deal with a company whose policies it opposes, but without involving the public. Synonym: primary boycott.

Direct Cost, a cost (for labor, raw materials, etc.) that can be readily identified with a specific process, operation, or unit of output; a variable cost. See also *indirect cost.*

Direct Mail, in advertising, any letters, folders, cards, literature, or other promotional material sent by mail directly to potential customers.

Director, one of a body of persons elected by the stockholders of a corporation to manage the affairs and set the general policies of the corporation. The board of directors selects the officers of the corporation.

Direct Tax, a tax that is collected directly and is not shifted or passed on to some other person on whom it is levied. Examples: sales tax, use tax. See also *indirect tax.*

Discount, 1. An amount taken off; a deduction made from a charge or debt, particularly for prompt payment; a cash discount.

2. A reduction in the list price or retail price granted to a particular customer or class of customers (*trade discount*), to purchasers of large quantities (*quantity discount*), or to purchasers who buy at other than the normal period (*seasonal discount*).

3. In banking, a fee charged by banks for lending money, deducted from the loan at the time the loan is made. When a bill of exchange or a promissory note is discounted at a bank, the right to obtain payment on the instrument is transferred to the bank for the present value of the note less a fee charged by the bank for this service. Discounting a note is practically selling it to the bank for its present value. Rediscounting by the Federal Reserve System is merely discounting a note for a banker. It is called *rediscounting*—discounting again—because the note has already been discounted once when the individual brought it to the bank.

4. The excess of the par or face value of a security over the amount paid or received for it. When securities are sold at less than par, they are said to be sold at a discount.

Discount House, a retail store that sells merchandise, especially brand goods, at low prices.

Discrimination, an unfair or unjust distinction, especially in charging higher rates to one person than another for a similar service. An unjustified or unfair price discrimination is considered an unfair trade practice and is forbidden by law.

Dishonor, to refuse or fail to pay a promissory note, draft, or bill of exchange when it is due or when it is duly presented for payment; to fail to accept a draft or bill of exchange when it is presented for acceptance.

Distribution, the branch of economic theory that deals with the analysis of the forces that govern the apportionment of goods and the value of production among those who perform services or provide the different necessary factors of production. One who contributes his capital to production receives a return called *interest;* one who uses his land for production receives *rent* for the land; and one who gives his labor in the productive process receives *wages.* The problem of distribution is to determine why the worker receives the amount of wages that he does, why the capitalist receives the interest that he does, and why the landowner receives the amount of rent that he does. What are the forces that determine how much of the total product shall be paid for each factor of production? As is the case with many economic problems, economists do not agree on any single theory of distribution. The marginal theory has been widely accepted, but it has been widely criticized and must certainly be modified by a consideration of the bargaining power of the owners of the various factors of production.

Dividend, a distribution of the profits of a corporation to its stockholders, a specified amount being paid for each share owned. Dividends are declared by the board of directors of the corporation, and the stockholders cannot compel the declaration of a dividend except by electing new directors. Dividends may not be paid out of capital. In England a dividend can be paid only in cash, but in the United States a dividend may be in cash, property, stock of the corporation or another corporation, bonds or scrip.

Division of Labor. See *specialization of labor.*

Dumping, 1. In general, selling large quantities of a product at very low prices in an attempt to gain a market advantage or to liquidate surpluses.

2. Specifically, selling a product in a foreign market below the price for which the same product is sold in the domestic market, or below the cost of production.

Durable Goods, products or commodities that have a continuous use over a period of time, usually three years or longer. *Consumers' durable goods* include such items as refrigerators, automobiles, pianos, furniture, jewelry, books, or TV sets. *Producers' durable goods* include a wide variety of machinery and equipment. See also *nondurable goods, semidurable goods.* Synonym: hard goods.

Econometrics, the application of mathematics to economics and the use of models to test economic theories.

Economic Growth, an increase in the amount of goods or services produced in a nation or area, coupled with an increase in output or income per capita.

Economics, 1. The study of people and their activities in the market.

2. The study of the production, distribution, and consumption of wealth.

3. "The study of human behavior as it relates scarce means, which have alternate uses, to given ends, such as maximization of income, usually employing price data in the comparison. Choice among 'given' ends, however, often involves choice among social policies and values, as well as guesses concerning future growth—thus going beyond a mere hypothetical national market."—David McCord Wright.

Elastic Demand. See *demand.*

Elasticity of Demand, a measure of the percentage change in the rate of buying commodities in relation to percentage change in price. See also *demand.*

Entrepreneur, one who undertakes an enterprise; an enterpriser; one who organizes the business, takes the risks, and receives the profits or losses of the business. The entrepreneur need not own the means of production; he may borrow capital, rent the land, and employ others to do the work. The entrepreneur was once dominant in economic life, but now his place has been taken by the corporation or the partnership. In recent years, the term has come to include people who are in business for themselves and small-scale enterprisers such as farmers, retailers and professional men who combine labor and management functions.

Equity, 1. The excess of a firm's total assets over its total liabilities; the net worth of a business.

2. The net investment that a person has in some enterprise or property.

3. The money value in a property in excess of claims against it.

Equity Capital, 1. The total investment in a business by all its owners, excluding amounts loaned by creditors.

2. In general, any security such as common or preferred stock.

3. Venture capital.

Escalator Clause, a clause in a union contract providing for automatic wage increases or decreases under specified conditions, especially in case of an increase or decrease in the government's periodically published cost-of-living index.

Estate tax, a levy against the wealth left by a deceased person; a tax levied against the entire, undivided estate itself, as distinguished from an *inheritance tax,* which is levied against the individual who inherits from the estate.

Ex-, a preposition meaning, in different contexts, out of, from, by, according to, formerly, or without. For examples, see *ex-coupons* under *coupon; ex-dividend* under *dividend; ex-interest* under *interest.*

Excess Profits Tax, a levy on business profits that are in excess of a fixed standard or which exceed those in previous years. The advantage of the excess profits tax is that it is based on ability to pay, and that it levies on business with extraordinary profits but spares those business undertakings that are developing or are only moderately successful. The objections to such a tax are based on its complexity, unfair discrimination, and excessive administration costs. In the long run, the tax falls mainly on businesses with fluctuating profits, taking a large part of the profits in good years but making no allowance for bad years.

Exchange, 1. The voluntary mutual transfer of goods and services of equivalent value. Exchange, with its problems of value, price, money, credit and marketing, is one of the central concepts of economics. In primitive society exchange takes place through barter, which becomes inconvenient when the society grows more complex. As specialization develops within the community, money develops as a medium to facilitate exchange. Under our present economic system, exchange does not take place directly between individuals but rather between enterprises. An individual works for a corporation or other enterprise and receives a salary for his services. The enterprise owns the article that is made, and this article is sold to another enterprise that in turn sells the article to the individual.

2. A place for the organized buying and selling of commodities or securities. See also *commodity exchange, stock exchange.*

3. A specialized fruit-growing and marketing company.

4. The process of settling accounts or debts between two parties residing in different localities without actually transferring money, by means of documents such as bills of exchange, drafts, notes.

Excise Tax, a levy imposed upon the manufacture, sale, or consumption of a particular commodity or upon the use of a particular service. Synonym: excise.

Exclusive Agency, a wholesaler or retailer in a given area who has sole rights (granted by the manufacturer) to sell a line, a brand, or a product.

Expense, any expenditure or charge incurred in the course of operating a business.

Face Value, the value printed on a financial instrument or document; par value.

Factor, 1. A commission merchant who advances funds to a consignor. A factor differs from a broker in having physical possession of the goods to be sold. Textile factors are specialized commercial bankers who finance textile mills and may also act as sales agents.

2. A person or firm that makes commercial loans on accounts receivable.

Factors of Production, the goods, services, or agents that combine to produce additional wealth or economic goods. The major factors of production are land, labor and capital. Sometimes a fourth factor, management or entrepreneurial ability, is listed.

Fair Market Value. See *market value.*

Fair Trade Law, any state law that permits a manufacturer to set a minimum retail sales price for his products.

Featherbedding, the practice of creating additional jobs even though the added employees are not needed and usually do not perform useful work; for instance, the hiring of an excessive number of "helpers" on construction jobs. Such practices are prohibited in the Taft-Hartley Labor Act.

Fiat Money, paper money with no actual backing, made legal tender by a fiat or decree of the government. Fiat money has no intrinsic value in itself and is not redeemable in any other kind of money or valuable metal. The Revolutionary War, for example, was financed largely with promissory notes of the Continental Congress. Although these notes were supposed to be redeemable in coin, there was no coin for the purpose. After the adoption of the Constitution, such money was redeemed at the rate of one cent for each dollar. The Civil War was largely financed by the issue of fiat money called *greenbacks,* but after 1878, the greenbacks were redeemed in gold.

Financial Statement, a summary of the financial condition of a business organization as of a certain time, or covering a stated period (usually a fiscal year), prepared for distribution to stockholders. The principal financial statements are the balance sheet, income statement and the statement of application of funds.

Firm, 1. A partnership or unincorporated association of two or more persons for carrying on a business; any organization combining the factors of production for the purpose of producing goods and services and selling them at a profit.

2. Unfluctuating or steady, as a market.

3. Not subject to negotiation or bargaining, as a price.

First In, First Out (FIFO), an accounting method for calculating the value of inventories, based on the assumption that the first goods received were the first goods used during an accounting period. Hence the valuation reflects the cost of the inventory most recently purchased, not the cheaper or more expensive inventories purchased at some time in the past.

Fiscal Year, any period of twelve consecutive months chosen as the basis for annual financial reporting, planning or budgeting; a corporation's accounting year.

Fixed Asset, any tangible asset held for a long term and used more or less permanently in the conduct of the business, as distinguished from one held for resale or consumption. Examples: land, buildings, equipment, furniture, fixtures. See also *capital asset.*

Fixed Budget, a budget set up for a given period of time and not intended to be modified or adjusted during the period covered; used primarily when sales and income can be predicted with a reasonable degree of accuracy (distinguished from flexible budget).

Fixed Capital, funds used to acquire those assets that are to be used over and over for a long period; sometimes, the asset itself (distinguished from working capital).

Fixed Cost, a cost that does not vary with volume of production, as distinguished from variable cost. Examples: rent, heat, light, property taxes, insurance, interest payments, maintenance.

Flexible Budget, a budget predicated on the variability of costs at different levels of operation; one that can provide automatic adjustments in response to changes in volume of business during the budget period. Synonym: variable budget.

Floating Debt, the indebtedness of a business which is not represented by securities; a debt consisting of short-term obligations such as accounts or notes payable and other current debts.

Foreign Exchange, 1. The mechanism by which payments are made between individuals in two countries that have different monetary units.

2. Specifically, the credit instruments used in settling accounts between persons residing in different countries.

3. The classical theory of foreign exchange is that if a nation exports more than it imports, the foreign exchanges will react favorably, specie will flow in, and prices will rise, checking exports and stimulating imports, until an equilibrium has been restored. Under modern conditions, when capital and services, as well as commodities, are transferred, and tariffs and numerous other restrictions are placed upon foreign trade and foreign exchange by the governments, this classical theory must be modified.

Foreign Exchange Rate, the price of a foreign monetary unit in terms of local currency. When the rate is $2.80 for one pound sterling, $2.80 in United States money must be paid for a pound sterling in English money. At this rate a person who wishes to pay a debt of £100 in England would have to pay $280 in United States currency plus commission charges by the banker. Foreign exchange is practically the only way in which debts abroad can be paid and the mechanism operates much as a clearing house between banks with the important difference that the banks are all using the same currency, while in foreign exchange different currencies are used and their relative values are constantly changing.

Fractional Reserve Banking, a system that permits commercial banks to keep only part of their assets in the form of reserves against deposits.

Free Coinage, the right to have any amount of metal made into coin by a government. The word "free" refers to the unlimited amount and does not mean that there is no charge.

Free Enterprise. See *capitalism.*

Free on Board (F.O.B.), all shipping and cartage expenses paid for getting the property to the carrier at the designated place and putting it on the carrier. If the price of an automobile is given F.O.B. Detroit, all freight and cartage charges have been paid up to the placing of the automobile on the carrier in Detroit. The automobile is free on board the carrier, but further freight charge must be paid by the buyer.

Free Trade, the commercial policy that does not restrict imports by tax levies or other barriers of free exchange such as quotas, import embargoes, exchange controls, subsidies to domestic producers, and the like. The argument for free trade is that each section should produce those products that can be grown or manufactured most cheaply and best and should exchange its products for others that it is not equipped to produce. Thus the total production of goods will be increased. The objections to free trade are generally that it does not aid local industry or make the nation self-sufficient, and that it does not prevent unfair trade practices, such as dumping, by other nations.

Freight, 1. The charge made for the transportation of goods by a carrier.

2. Loosely, the goods themselves.

Fringe Benefit, any non-monetary or indirect benefit received by an employee in addition to wage or salary compensation. Examples: paid vacations; accident, hospitalization, health, life or medical insurance; travel pay; recreational facilities, etc.

Frozen Asset, 1. An asset that is not readily convertible into cash, or one that can be sold only with great loss in value.

2. An asset that cannot be used because of government restriction or regulation.

Full Employment, the condition that exists when all who are willing and able to work can find employment without difficulty at prevailing rates of pay.

Fund, 1. Any amount of cash, securities, or other assets that can be converted quickly into cash.

2. Funds, money or cash available for use.

3. Money, or its equivalent, set aside for a specific purpose.

Funded Debt, the long-term indebtedness of a company or government evidenced by secured or unsecured, interest-bearing, promissory notes (bonds). See also *floating debt, current debt.*

Future, 1. A contract to deliver specified goods or securities at a certain time. An important part of a commodity market, especially grain exchanges, deals in futures.

2. In international trade, the purchase or sale of foreign exchange on the basis of a rate quoted as of some future date.

Futures Market. See *commodity exchange.*

Garnishment, attachment of an employee's wages in the hands of the employer by a creditor of the employee.

General Agent. See *agent.*

General Store, a retail store that carries a variety of nonrelated goods; usually operated in small towns and rural regions, but sometimes in the suburbs and industrial sections of large cities. Hardware, dry goods and groceries are usually carried.

General Strike, a simultaneous work stoppage by all, or almost all, the workers in a community or nation; sometimes distinguished from a generalized strike restricted to a single industry. See also *strike, sympathetic strike.*

Gift Tax, a federal or state excise tax on money or property donated by a living person. The donor pays the tax. See also *estate tax.*

Going Concern, a business or corporation that is operating or transacting its ordinary business and is expected to continue to do so in the future.

Gold Certificate, a form of U.S. paper money issued by the Treasury against deposited gold. It was in general circulation from 1865 to 1933. After 1933, it was issued in revised form, for use only by Federal Reserve Banks for reserve and transfer purposes.

Gold Exchange Standard, an elaboration of the pure gold standard, by which a country maintains its domestic currency at a parity with the standard money of a gold-standard country through the redemption of its money in bills of exchange in some gold-standard country in which bank deposits are carried.

Gold Standards, a country's standard monetary unit, which is defined or expressed in terms of a specified amount of gold of a certain weight and fineness. This basic unit of currency is freely convertible at home or abroad into that quantity of gold per unit of currency and is considered legal tender. Under the gold standard, the free export and import of gold for the settlement of international obligations is permitted.

Goods, 1. Any manufactured or processed items; merchandise or commodities handled in commerce.

2. Loosely, any item of inventory or asset, including fixed assets and items in process of production; as in the phrase goods and services. See also *capital goods, consumers' goods.*

Goodwill, one of the intangible assets of a business, consisting of the value of the business connections and the value of the probability that present customers will continue to buy from the same business or continue to buy an article bearing the trade name of the business.

Government Bond, a bond issued by a national government (especially an obligation of the United States government).

Grant-in-Aid, a sum of money or a subsidy from public funds given by a central government to a smaller governmental unit to assist in some type of public undertaking. Examples: money for road construction, education, old-age assistance, medical research, etc.

Gray Market, a market in which sales practices are not necessarily illegal but which are generally disapproved; especially the sale and purchase of scarce goods when supply and demand have been affected by abnormal conditions. See also *black market.*

Greenback, 1. Paper money issued by the United States during the Civil War, and not redeemable in silver or gold.

2. Any paper money. See also *fiat money.*

Gresham's Law, the general truth that, where two kinds of legal money of unequal value are in circulation and both are available for payments, the bad money tends to drive the good money out of circulation. This law is named after the commercial advisor to Queen Elizabeth, Sir Thomas Gresham, who was credited with having discovered the law. But it is now known that he was not the first to formulate it, for, in ancient Greece, Aristophanes pointed out a similar phenomenon. The explanation is very simple: people naturally prefer good money and keep it, but any bad money that comes into their possession is spent at the first opportunity. As everyone tries to keep the good money, it soon disappears from circulation, and the bad money becomes the general currency. The good money is often hoarded or is used for payments abroad.

Gross, 1. A measure of quantity; an aggregate of twelve dozen.

2. Before any deduction; total, overall, entire, complete; as in gross income, gross profit, gross sales; opposed to net.

3. To earn, make, or bring in (a certain amount) before deductions.

Gross Income, the total amount of money received by a business or individual for a given period from all sources, before any deductions for costs of manufacturing and selling and other expenses.

Gross Interest. See *interest.*

Gross Margin. See *gross profit.*

Gross National Product, the total output of goods and services of a country, stated at market prices for a given year. In the United States, as defined by the Department of Commerce, the total market value of the goods and services produced by the nation's economy, before deduction of depreciation charges and other allowances for capital consumption.

Gross Profit, the amount realized from sales, less the cost of the goods that were sold. Synonyms: gross margin, gross revenue.

Gross Profit Ratio, an operating ratio that shows the relationship of total operating costs to total gross sales.

Gross Revenue. See *gross profit.*

Gross Sales, total sales before deducting returns and allowances.

Group Banking, an arrangement by which two or more separately incorporated banks are brought under the control of a single corporation known as a *holding company.*

Group Insurance. See *insurance.*

Growth. See *economic growth.*

Growth Stock, the common stock of a company that is experiencing, or is expected to experience, substantial growth, well above the average for common stock in general.

Hard Goods. See *durable goods.*

Hard Money, 1. Metal coins, as distinguished from paper money.

2. Money fully backed by, and convertible into gold or silver, as distinguished from money backed solely by the credit of the government. Synonym: hard currency.

3. Loosely, cash assets, as distinguished from other quick assets.

Hedging, buying and selling at the same time with different dates of delivery, usually to guard against loss from a change in price. Hedging is a form of future trading in commodities, particularly cotton.

Hidden Tax, an indirect tax that is incorporated in the price of goods and services and, therefore, not apparent as such when paid.

Hoarding, the accumulation of supplies of scarce or critical items in times of shortage, so that others are deprived of their rightful share.

Holding Company, a parent corporation that owns all or most of the stock of other corporations, especially one organized for the express purpose of controlling or influencing the management of one or more other corporations through ownership of all or a majority of the securities of the corporation. A *pure holding company* is one whose assets consist almost entirely of the securities of other companies. A *mixed holding company* is both an operating company and a holding company. The holding company attempts to acquire control of an operating company with the least possible cash investment. Because of their abuses of power, Congress passed the Public Utility Holding Company Act (1935) designed to control the activities of the holding companies, particularly in the public utility field. The depression of the 1930's had wrecked many holding company structures, causing loss to many small stockholders. Companies in which a small group controlled widespread productive operations through the use of holding companies were broken up. The practice, generally, was forbidden by the imposition of restrictions on the issuance and sale of securities.

Horizontal Union. See *craft union.*

Hot Money, money deposited or invested abroad because of worries over devaluation, or a desire to escape high taxes, or to take advantage of higher interest rates.

Hypothecation, a pledge as security for an obligation without title or possession or right to title or possession, but only with the right to have the property sold to satisfy the claim in case of default.

Illegal Strike, a work stoppage by union members called in violation of a collective bargaining agreement or without consent of the union. Synonym: wildcat strike.

Imperfect Competition. See *monopolistic competition.*

Imports, the total of all tangible products brought into a country from abroad.

Improvements, changes in property to render it more useful, effective, pleasant, or valuable. Improvements include buildings or structures on the land, roads, curbs, sidewalks, drainage ditches or drains, sewage systems, gardens, and water mains.

Impulse Buying, purchasing by consumers on the spur of the moment instead of by previous decision, usually as a result of seeing a product in a display at the point of purchase.

Income, money, material goods, or services received or accrued during a given period of time; the benefits derived from the wealth and services of others. The value of the income is the sum of the values of these various benefits and services received, and for practical purposes it is usually expressed in money. Income in the economic sense is sometimes called *real income* in contrast to money income. *Money income* consists of the dollars received, but real income is the goods and services that can be bought with the money income. If the cost of living should go up and a worker receives the same wage, then his real income is lower, for with the same amount of money he is able to buy less goods and services.

Income Bond, a bond that pays interest only when it is earned in sufficient amounts to cover prior claims.

Income Statement, a summary of the income and expenses of a business, showing the revenues, expenses, and net income or net loss during the period (usually one year) covered by the report. Synonyms: operating statement, profit and loss statement.

Income Tax, a tax levied on individual and corporate net incomes.

Increasing Return, 1. A condition in which increased production results in increased profits on each unit because the cost of producing each unit has decreased.
2. The economic theory that enlarging the scale of operations expands efficiency.

Indenture, 1. In general, any formal contract (i.e., under seal) or agreement involving two or more parties.
2. Specifically, any agreement (e.g., mortgage, deed of trust, trust, etc.) between a corporation and a trustee that governs the conditions under which bonds are issued and names and empowers the trustee to act for all the bondholders.

Independent, in retailing, a store controlled by its own individual management as distinguished from a chain store or a branch. In production, the same term is used for a manufacturer, miner, or oil producer who is not connected with a dominant group.

Independent Union, a labor union that is not affiliated with any other national or international labor organization.

Index Number, a figure that discloses the relative change of costs, prices, employment, volume of production, business activity, etc., as compared with the magnitude at some specified time (the base period). The base is usually designated as 100. A general decrease in activity would be shown by a proportionally lower index number, and a general increase by a proportionally higher index number. For example, if the prices of all commodities increased 20 per cent over a normal base, the index number would be 120.

Indirect Cost, a cost that cannot be identified with a specific process, production, or unit of output. Examples: foremen's wages, upkeep, pro-rated charges such as power, heat, light, taxes, etc. See also *direct cost.*

Indirect Tax, a tax that is not collected directly but is shifted. The person paying the tax does not know he is doing so. Examples: manufacturers' excise taxes and custom duties. Opposed to *direct tax.* See also *hidden tax.*

Individualism, the doctrine that stresses the rights, desires, and needs of the individual in contrast to those of the state or of the people as a whole. The idea and the word itself originated with the Industrial Revolution. The physiocrats in France and Adam Smith in England urged that business be let alone, without government interference. However, government has always had some hand in business activity, especially through taxes, tariffs, and labor and industrial regulation. With the development of the modern economic structure, governments have been forced to take an increasing part in the regulation and control of business.

Industrial Advertising, advertising directed to industrial firms, as distinguished from consumer advertising.

Industrial Arbitration, the settlement of disputes between employers and workers by referring the matter to impartial experts, by whose opinions the parties have agreed to abide. See also *arbitration.*

Industrial Goods. See *producers' goods.*

Industrial Store. See *company store.*

Industrial Union, a labor union whose membership includes workers in a given industry, plant or group of industries regardless of the members' skill or craft. Synonym: vertical union. See also *craft union.*

Industry-wide Bargaining. See *collective bargaining.*

Inelastic Demand. See *demand.*

Inflation, a persistent upward movement in the general level of prices, occurring when the quantity of money increases faster than the quantity of real goods. See also *deflation.*

Inheritance Tax, a tax levied directly on the property received by an individual heir, as distinguished from an estate tax.

Installment Selling, a transaction on credit that gives the buyer the immediate possession of a purchase before payment is complete, under a contract that provides for periodic future payments. Usually, ownership of the purchase is withheld until all payments are completed.

Institutional Advertising, advertising aimed primarily at building up a company's name and prestige in the consumer's mind, rather than at selling a given product.

Insurance, the elimination of the risk of a large loss by the payment of a small, known cost by each of a large number of individuals who are exposed to similar risks. For example, anyone engaged in shipping faces the risk of having his ship sink and thus incurring a large loss. If all the shippers contribute to a common fund a sufficient amount to indemnify the owner for a ship that is lost, then every shipowner will have an annual small cost, called a *premium,* instead of the possible large loss that would result if his ship sank uninsured. For an insurance system to work, there must be a large number of individuals incurring the risk, and the risk must be of such a nature that the probabilities of its occurrence can be accurately determined.

Marine insurance was the earliest form of insurance, first issued in 1583. From this type, life insurance and fire insurance developed and were the only forms until recent times. *Life insurance* protects and provides for the family of a deceased, in most cases. *Fire insurance* assures the repayment for losses incurred by fire. *Group insurance,* one of the newer varieties, is taken out by an employer for the benefit of his employees, both parties usually contributing a part of the premium. Such insurance generally pays in the case of death or sickness and also provides for old-age pensions. In recent years, group insurance has been taken over by the United States government, especially under the provisions of the Social Security Act. Numerous other modifications of the principal older types of insurance have been developed in order to meet modern business and social conditions.

Intangible Asset, an asset that has no physical existence; one of value to a company through the rights and power it conveys. Examples: copyrights, franchises, formulas, patents.

Integrated Stores, large-scale retail outlets, each with many closely related parts under unit control. Examples: department stores, mail order retail divisions, chain stores.

Interest, a payment made for the use of capital and usually calculated as a percentage of the *principal,* the amount borrowed. Interest can be paid because capital is productive, and the borrower of the capital expects to produce and, thereby, earn, enough to pay the interest charge and also make a profit. The supply of capital available for lending in a community will depend on such factors as the general surplus of production over consumption, the distribution of wealth in the community, the social habits of saving, and the rate of interest being paid in the community. The demand for capital depends on the wants of the people, the rate of industrial and agricultural development, and the interest rate that is being demanded.

Gross interest, or interest as used in the general business sense, includes two elements besides the economic interest that has just been described. One element is risk: if there is a risk that the loan will not be repaid, the interest rate will be increased; if the credit of the borrower is so good that there appears to be no chance of default, the rate will be lowered. The other element is that of administrative costs: the interest rate charged must include the cost of investigating and collecting the loan, the cost of the bookkeeping, and various other administrative costs.

Interlocking Directorates, boards of directors of two or more corporations, especially those with allied business interests, having one or more directors in common. Through this method of control a community of interest may develop. Interlocking directorates in competitive interests are generally illegal.

International Trade, the exchange of goods and services between nations.

Interstate Commerce. See *commerce.*

Intrastate Commerce. See *commerce.*

Inventory, 1. An itemized, detailed, descriptive list of goods, goods in process, raw materials, and equipment with the number and value of each.

2. The supply of goods kept on hand by a business in order to meet needs promptly. Synonyms: stock, supply.

Investment, the act of directing the employment of funds into capital or claims on income. Investment includes the use of funds to build or maintain capital, such as lending money to a manufacturing company to buy new machinery; and it also includes the purchase of durable consumptive goods, such as a painting or piece of sculpture. Investment is based on the idea of future benefit: a person who lends or invests his money is depriving himself of its use at the present time, in order that he may have both the money invested and an additional sum at some future time.

The amount of funds that a community has available for investment is the excess of income over consumption. All of this fund may not be invested, as some individuals may prefer to hoard their money rather than invest it. The general factors to be considered in making an investment are the yield that will be received, the ease with which the investment can be sold, and the safety of the investment. It is not possible to realize all of these aims, for when the safety of an investment is high, the return is usually low, and when the yield on an investment is high, it is generally not very safe.

In order to protect investors, the United States government has passed a large number of regulations and has established the Securities and Exchange Commission.

Investment Bank, a financial institution that acts as an intermediary for business firms by marketing new issues of stocks or bonds through purchasing large blocks of such securities and selling them in smaller units to individuals or institutions. It is, thus, not a bank in the usual sense.

Investment Company, a financial organization that pools the investments of many individuals through the sale of shares or participating certificates and invests the collective funds in a diversified selection of securities. Synonym: investment trust. See also *closed-end investment company, open-end investment company.*

Investment Trust. See *investment company.*

Invoice, a statement of the amount, type, quality and price of goods delivered, usually sent to the buyer with the goods. It is not a bill or request for payment, but merely a statement as to goods delivered.

Iron Law of Wages. See *subsistence theory of wages.*

Jettison, the throwing overboard of a part of the cargo of the ship in order to save the rest. It is sometimes necessary to jettison some of the cargo when the ship must be lightened to weather a storm or to get off a shoal. The loss due to jettison is borne proportionally by the owners of the ship and of the cargo.

Job, 1. A piece of work, especially one of a defined character, undertaken at a fixed price.

2. A position or situation; regular, remunerative employment, especially a position that does not require professional or highly skilled training.

3. To serve as a middleman or jobber; that is, to buy or sell goods or merchandise in wholesale lots.

Job Analysis, the systematic compilation and study of work data in order to define and characterize each occupation, so as to distinguish it from all others for the purpose of recruitment, selection, training, promotion, etc.

Jobber, a middleman who buys from producers, wholesalers, or importers and sells to retailers. Originally, the term meant dealer in odd or job lots. Now it has almost the same meaning as "wholesaler."

Job Classification, a grouping of jobs into categories, following a job analysis, according to the type of work or the degree of skill required.

Job Description, a written statement (usually based on a job analysis) describing the essential features and requirements of a job.

Job Evaluation, a systematic procedure for measuring the relative value and importance of jobs in an establishment on the basis of their common factors. Its purpose is to determine wage and salary differentials or promotion requirements, to establish incentives, etc. Synonym: job rating.

Joint Account, 1. A bank account opened in the names of two or more persons and subject to withdrawals by each. Synonym: joint deposit.

2. A joint venture.

Joint Costs, expenses involved in the simultaneous production of two or more commodities or services.

Joint Return, a combined income tax report of the incomes of husband and wife.

Joint Venture, a business partnership or association of individuals or firms formed to carry out a single specific transaction or project. Synonym: joint account.

Journal, the book of original entry from which the accounts are posted into the ledger. The entry in the journal is a detailed description of the transaction. In modern bookkeeping the tendency has been to dispense with the journal and make the entries directly into the ledger, as the custom of making a formal and lengthy entry of the transaction has largely disappeared.

Jurisdictional Dispute, 1. A conflict between labor unions concerning the right of one of two or more unions to organize and represent the employees of a plant, trade, or industry. It frequently involves a craft union and an industrial union.

2. A controversy between unions over who should perform a particular type of work.

Kickback, the return of a portion of a fee, sales commission, or wages as a condition of obtaining the sale or employment.

Labor, 1. Work, toil, or effort; physical or mental productive work; especially, any type of paid work.

2. Collectively, those who work as employees, especially in manual capacities.

596   ECONOMICS AND BUSINESS GLOSSARY

3. Organized labor as a movement.

4. One of the three basic factors of production, the other two being land and capital.

Labor Contract, an agreement arrived at by collective bargaining between representatives of labor and management, covering wage rates, hours of work and other terms of employment, and conditions of work for a stated period of time.

Labor Economics, the study of the economic problems relating to labor, especially wages, working conditions, and collective bargaining.

Labor Force, 1. All persons in, or seeking, paid employment or self-employed persons.

2. Specifically, as defined by the United States Bureau of Census, all persons 14 years of age and over, not housed in a penal or custodial institution, who are gainfully employed and working at their employment, or who are gainfully employed but are temporarily not working, or who are working 15 hours a week without pay on a family farm or in a family business.

Labor Relations, relations between management and groups of employees, especially organized labor, including contract negotiations, collective bargaining, and concerted activities and grievance procedures.

Labor Theory of Value, a theory holding that the entire value of all products stems from the amount of human labor that produces them.

Labor Turnover. See *turnover.*

Labor Union, an organization of wage earners or salaried employees formed for the purpose of dealing with employers on matters concerned with grievances, labor disputes, rates of pay, hours of employment, or conditions of work. Synonyms: trade union, union. See also *company union, craft union, independent union.*

Laissez-faire, (French, let it go, let it pass), noninterference by government in business, letting business alone. The expression was probably first used in France by Vincent de Gournay (1712–1759), one of the founders of the physiocrats, among whom it became a central idea in the eighteenth century. The physiocrats rebelled against the system of regulation of industry and argued that, since manufacture and commerce do not produce wealth but are only instruments of distribution, they should not be taxed or hindered. This idea of a free and unhindered economic system was in accord with the idea of natural order of the universe, adopted and elaborated by Adam Smith. He did not use the term *laissez-faire,* but it was paramount in his doctrine. Adam Smith argued (1776) that the individual working for his own gain would strive to produce the best and most useful articles. Competition would force the individual to do this in order to survive and prosper. Therefore, the greatest production of goods would result when each individual was allowed to follow his own dictates. Smith declared that this was in harmony with the natural order. John Stuart Mill in his writings (1848) gave wide currency to the term *laissez-faire;* more recently it has been associated with the Manchester School in England.

The *laissez-faire* doctrine at first applied not only to government intervention but also to combinations of enterprises that aimed at a control of prices or production. This application of the doctrine was soon abandoned, and with the development of the modern economic system the *laissez-faire* doctrine has broken down in many particulars. Tariff barriers for example, are direct government aids to industry; the development of large industrial organizations, powerful enough to exert a considerable control over prices and production, has provoked a demand for state intervention. The opponents of *laissez-faire* insist that Adam Smith was wrong, for the greatest profit does not always result from serving the community. A high profit may result from the high-pressure selling of an inferior article, from the creation of an uneconomic demand, or from the exploitation of labor.

Land, all the natural resources not produced by man. To the economist the term includes not only the soil on the earth's surface, but the rivers and lakes; the natural resources under the surface, such as iron ore, coal and petroleum; the climatic conditions; and the animals and game on the land. Although some economists do not classify land separately but regard it as a type of capital, land is generally regarded as one of the factors of production. Land is the basis of all production, and combined with labor and capital, produces the world's wealth.

Landlord, an owner of land and improvements who rents them to others. The landlord pays the taxes and assessments, but repairs are a matter of agreement between him and his tenants.

Last In, First Out (LIFO), an accounting method for valuing inventories based on the assumption that the units sold or used are the most recently acquired or produced, and that the units on hand are those first acquired or made. The cost of articles sold or used, therefore, is current cost, whereas the items remaining in the inventory are those of an earlier date. See also *first in, first out.*

Law of Diminishing Return. See *diminishing return.*

Law of Variable Proportions. See *diminishing return.*

Layout, in advertising, a rough sketch or plan used to show the general arrangement of an advertisement and to give a working plan to the printer.

Lease, an instrument conveying property to another for a definite period, or at will, usually in consideration for rent or compensation.

Leaseback, a business arrangement whereby a company owning land or buildings sells its property to another company, private investor, or profit-making institution and simultaneously leases the property back under a long-term lease. Synonym: sale-and-leaseback.

Ledger, in bookkeeping, the essential final book in the double-entry system, in which are kept the records of the business transactions into various ac-counts. Entries in the ledger are made by posting from books of original entry such as journals or voucher registers. Under the system of double-entry bookkeeping each transaction of the business is shown by two entries in the ledger—one a credit under a certain account and the other a debit under another account. The ledger does not have to be a bound book; it is often a looseleaf book or card file.

Legal Tender, money, coin, or paper which must be accepted in payment of a debt.

Letter of Advice, a letter containing a notice or special information, usually from a consignor to a consignee, from an agent to a principal, or from a drawer to a drawee of a bill of exchange. It is customary for the drawer of a foreign bill of exchange to send a letter of advice to the drawee giving notice of the drawing of the bill and often containing other instructions or explanatory matter.

Letter of Credit, a letter from a bank, banker, or mercantile house, addressed to an agent or correspondent, requesting that credit be extended to the bearer for a certain or unlimited amount. The amount advanced is charged to the account of the drawer of the letter, or some other arrangements for payments are made in the letter of credit. Letters of credit are commonly used by travelers. The traveler pays the specified sum to the bank, and a letter of credit is issued for the amount paid. When he is traveling, the holder of this letter of credit presents it to agents or correspondents of the issuing bank, the requested funds are given, and the amount is noted on the letter of credit. A small percentage of the amount of the letter of credit is paid to the issuing bank for the service.

Leverage Ratio, any one of a number of ratios or relationships commonly used to measure the degree to which a business is financed by owners, or distinguished from funds provided by creditors. Examples: debt-to-equity ratio; current liabilities to net worth ratio.

Liabilities, the amounts owing or the debts of a business or individual. The liabilities are carried on the right-hand side of the balance sheet in contrast to the assets, which are carried on the left side. *Contingent liabilities* are obligations that will only arise under certain conditions. For example, if a manufacturer sells machinery with a guarantee, under ordinary circumstances there will be no obligation connected with this transaction; but if the machine should be defective, the seller will have to repay the buyer. The usual method of providing for contingent liabilities is for the accountant to set up a special reserve for contingencies.

License, 1. A right to engage in certain businesses, activities or occupations for which permission is necessary.

2. The document providing such a right; an official permit.

Lien, a legal claim upon real or personal property for the satisfaction of some debt or duty.

Life Insurance. See *insurance.*

Limited Company, a business association in which the liability of the stockholders is limited to the amount paid for the stock. In the case of "limited" banks of issue, only the unpaid portion of the shares is limited, and the liability of the shareholders is unlimited in respect to the notes issued. In contrast, a company of unlimited liability is one in which the owners are unlimitedly liable, and their entire personal estates may be taken to satisfy the debts of the company. English companies that are limited usually have the abbreviation "Ltd." as a part of their official style after the name of the company. In the United States, similar companies are called corporations.

Liquid Asset, any current asset, such as currency or any holding that can be converted quickly into cash without significant loss. See also *quick asset.*

Liquidation, 1. The process of converting property or securities into cash. A business in liquidation is being closed, and its property and goodwill are being converted into cash for distribution to creditors and owners.

2. Strictly, the process of finding actual value of uncertain obligations.

Liquidity Ratio, any one of a number of ratios or relationships commonly used to measure a firm's ability to meet its maturing debts on schedule. The most commonly used liquidity ratios are the current ratio, which shows the number of times current assets will pay off current liabilities, and the acid-test ratio.

Listed Security, a security that is listed, that is admitted to trading on a stock exchange.

List Price, the basic price of goods as listed in a catalogue; the price from which a trade, cash or quantity discount is allowed.

Lloyd's Register, in full, *Lloyd's Register of British and Foreign Shipping,* a publication containing the names and description of all British and certain foreign ships with a classification according to seaworthiness of the ship.

Loan, anything given to another on condition of return or repayment. If money or replaceable goods are borrowed, similar goods or a similar amount of money, but not the identical property, are returned. When other kinds of property are the loan, the identical article is returned unless it is stipulated otherwise. In medieval times, personal loans for consumptive purposes were made without any interest charge because the Church regarded interest as usury. Today, loans are made at a stipulated rate of interest.

Lockout, withholding of work by an employer from employees in order to gain concessions from the employees, or to coerce them into accepting the employer's terms (opposed to strike).

Lombard Street, a street in London on which many banks are located; the banking center of Great Britain. Lombard Street in London occupies a similar position to Wall Street in New York. The Jews of Lombardy (north Italy) were famous as bankers early in the ninth century. At the beginning of the fourteenth century many Lombard Jewish goldsmiths and bankers had settled in London, and this street was named for them.

Long and Short Haul, carrying freight over long and short distances. Proportionally unfair charges for long and short hauls on railroads and other common carriers and discrimination against shippers for short distances led to the passage of the Mann-Elkins Act in 1910. This act prohibited charging greater amounts for a short haul than for a long haul in the same direction and under substantially the same conditions.

Loss, an amount by which sales, revenues or other income falls below cost.

Loss Leader, an article, especially a popular item, sold deliberately at a loss in order to draw customers into a store in the hope of profitably selling them other items in stock.

Macroeconomics, the study of the economy as a whole; economics studies or analyses that consider aggregates of individuals or groups of commodities, such as total consumption, employment, or income. See also *microeconomics.*

Mail-Order Advertising, advertising designed to promote consumer purchases by mail directly from the advertiser.

Mail-Order House, a commercial establishment, retail or wholesale, that receives its orders and makes its sales by mail.

Maintenance of Membership, an arrangement or agreement between an employer and a labor union that requires members of the union at the time the contract is signed, or who subsequently join, to remain members of the union for the life of the contract or be discharged.

Managed Currency. See *compensated currency.*

Managerial Economics, the study of the effect of managerial decisions on production, employment, and prices.

Manufacturer's Agent, a broker who sells for one manufacturer or more, handling related but noncompeting lines of goods, usually on contract and in an exclusive territory. Sometimes the selling agents sell all the production of their principal, but usually the manufacturer's agents (as distinct from selling agents) handle only part of the entire output of the manufacturers that they represent. They are limited in their selling territory and in their power to set prices and terms. Unlike factors, the manufacturer's agents do not finance the mills nor do they perform any other function outside of selling.

Manufacturer's Brand, a brand used by the original manufacturer of the item, as distinguished from a dealer's brand. See also *national brand.*

Margin, 1. In accounting and marketing, the difference between the cost of goods sold and the total net sales income. Synonyms: gross margin, gross profit, gross revenue.

2. In securities trading, a deposit or advance by an investor with or to a broker; specifically, the amount needed to cover the difference between the amount of credit the broker is willing or permitted to extend to the investor and the amount of securities he purchases.

Buying stock *on margin* means that part of the funds for the purchase of the stock have been loaned by or through the stockbroker. The stockbroker may use the stock purchased as security on which to borrow from the bank. In case the stock falls in price, the owner must pay more of the purchase price, or the broker can sell the stock to recover the amount loaned. The Securities and Exchange Commission has the power to fix the amount of margin required.

Marginal Cost, the addition to total cost involved in producing one more unit of a product; the direct cost of producing the last unit of a run.

Marginal-Productivity Theory of Wages, the theory in economics that under perfect competition the laborer receives in wages an amount equal to the productivity of the least productive laborer in that type of work. The amount that the least productive worker adds to the total product is called the *marginal product.* It is not that the marginal worker is the least efficient, but that because of the law of diminishing returns, the marginal worker adds the least to the total product. To determine the marginal product, imagine that one worker is withdrawn; the decrease in the total product of all the workers caused by the withdrawal of this one worker is the marginal product. The employer will pay wages up to the value of the marginal product because there is this much added value in production.

This theory of wages has been widely criticized because it is based on the assumption of a perfect competition that does not exist; because production is due to an organic union of the various factors of production and the loss due to the withdrawal of one worker may be much greater than the marginal productivity assigned the worker; and because the theory does not take into consideration the relative bargaining power of the employer and the employee.

Marginal Revenue, the amount which the sale or production of one additional unit of product will add to the total income.

Marginal Utility, a basic economic doctrine that explains price on the basis of use-value, which in turn is dependent on scarcity. The key to the doctrine is the common fact that commodities are valuable in inverse relation to their available supply. Gold is more valuable than iron because gold is scarcer. If gold were discovered or produced in great quantities without any change in the demand, then its value would decline.

The marginal unit is the least important unit that is employed in production; and since all units are the same, and the most important unit can be replaced by a least important unit, both units will have the same value as the least important unit. This concept of the use-value of the single unit of a commodity, determined by the least important unit that is used, is now generally referred to as marginal utility.

Marine Insurance. See *insurance.*

Markdown, a reduction in price below the original retail price.

Market, 1. In economics, an ideal area

within which there is free competition and complete knowledge of buying and selling conditions so that the forces of supply and demand can converge to establish a single price. The market may be a single place in a small village, or it may cover the entire world. The theory of price based on a perfect market fails to express present-day conditions. The seller is not only anxious to sell his goods but he is also eager to maintain the price for future sales. Salesmanship and advertising not only facilitate the flow of goods, but also create a changed demand for the future. Monopoly conditions cause an entirely different situation from the theoretical perfect market. Monopoly interests tend to set the price at a point that will return the greatest profit and they may even destroy goods or dump them in a foreign country in order to prevent a lowering of the price in the home market. Even the market for agricultural products, which has been a relatively perfect market in the economic sense, has changed with the development of farmers' marketing cooperatives and government regulation.

2. In general, the place within which buyers and sellers are brought together, either face to face, or through some means of communication for the buying and selling or exchange of goods and services.

3. Trade or traffic in a particular commodity.

4. A body of persons carrying on an organized business of buying and selling securities as the stock market.

5. Current price.

Market Economy, a mode of economic life based on a system of free relations between buyers and sellers. In its purest form, market economy operates without a plan and with a minimum of controls. Buyers are free to buy what they want at the price they are willing to pay; sellers are free to sell or not to sell. See also *command economy, traditional economy.*

Market Research, the study of all problems relating to the transfer and sale of goods and services from producer to consumer, including all the activities enumerated as parts of marketing. (See *marketing.*) Advertising agencies, publishers of periodicals carrying advertising, commercial and industrial organizations—all were drawn by necessity into marketing research. The U.S. government, especially the Department of Commerce through its Census of Business, various regional and state organizations, and many universities and colleges continually make contributions to the data of marketing study and to its technique. Synonyms: market analysis, market research.

Market Value, the current, prevailing, or going price of a security, commodity, product, piece of property, etc., as indicated by current market quotations. In the United States, the Commissioner of Internal Revenue has recognized a judicial definition of fair market value as the price which property will bring when offered for sale by a willing seller to a willing buyer, neither being obliged to buy or sell. Synonyms: market price, fair market value.

Marketing, all business activities involved in the flow of goods and services from production to consumption.

Selling and buying, sometimes called *distribution* by businessmen, are only two of these marketing activities. The other activities include packaging, transportation, storage, financing, risk bearing, standardization, and market information. The middleman, who stands between the producers of goods on one hand and the consumers on the other, is the main factor in marketing.

Markup, the difference between the selling price and cost of an article, stated in monetary units or as a percentage of cost or retail price.

Mercantilism, a body of economic doctrine that arose after the decline of feudalism and influenced the government policy in France and England during the seventeenth century. Although mercantilism was attacked and discredited by Adam Smith (1776) and advocates of laissez-faire, some of its ideas still survive. Mercantilism seeks to have a nation sell more goods than it buys and through this so-called favorable balance of trade to increase the amount of gold bullion within the country. According to the mercantilists, this will increase the wealth of the nation. This economic school of thought supported a national economic policy as against the individual; it also favored free trade within the nation and tariffs to prevent the importation of foreign products. Adam Smith devoted about one-fourth of his *Wealth of Nations* (1776) to an attack on the mercantile policy. Fundamentally, the mercantilists were in error, because it is often impossible for a nation to sell more than it buys over a period of time, and because an increased amount of bullion within a nation would cause a rise in prices and act as a stimulation of imports and a check on exports.

Merchandising, coordination between production or purchase for resale on the one hand and selling on the other. In large retail stores, especially department stores, a *merchandising manager* supervises the activities of buyers for each line of goods and sees that the quantity, quality, and price range of goods bought are such as to assure maximum profits. From retailing the notion of merchandising—the function of buying (or producing) goods that can be sold quickly and profitably—has been extended to other branches of business.

Merger, a union of companies by which one company absorbs one or more companies with one surviving and the others losing their corporate existence. See also *amalgamation, combination, consolidation.*

Microeconomics, the economic study or analysis of small groups of people, individuals, and industries. See also *macroeconomics.*

Middleman, a person or business enterprise that intervenes in the process of sale between a producer and a consumer or between a producer of an article and a manufacturer who does further work on the article to prepare it for consumption. The middleman is a salesman who buys an article, not for his own use, but in order to sell it to a consumer. A typical middleman is the grocer who buys numerous groceries and performs a service to the community by having them available for sale.

Minimum Wage, the lowest wage payable to employees of a particular group by law or contract. The Fair Labor Standards Act establishes the legal minimum wage to be paid workers engaged in interstate commerce.

Mixed Economy, an economic system in which both publicly and privately owned enterprises operate simultaneously or exercise a degree of economic control.

Mixed Holding Company. See *holding company.*

Money, any article that is generally acceptable as a medium of exchange by the people of a community. The earliest forms of money were commonly used articles of merchandise, such as cattle, grain, skins of animals, special kinds of shells, knives, bricks of tea, or pieces of wampum. Precious metals such as gold and silver have been widely used throughout the world for money. As economic society progressed, the form of money changed, and it is still in the process of being changed. There are certain recognized attributes of good money. It must be generally accepted as money, small in size so that it can be easily carried from place to place, uniform, easily recognized, durable, and it must be easily divisible. It should also possess a stability of value. All these attributes of money are difficult to satisfy, and it has been almost impossible to find a money that has complete stability of value over long periods of time.

In addition to being a medium of exchange, money has other functions. It serves as a measure of value, a standard of deferred payments, a basis of credit, and a store of value. Furthermore, there are different kinds of money. *Standard money* consists of articles such as gold or silver that are valuable in themselves and will be readily accepted by the community. *Representative money* stands for or represents the actual coin. If gold is deposited with a government, and paper money is issued to the extent of the gold deposited, and the right is given to exchange the paper money for the gold at any time, this paper money is representative money. *Convertible fiduciary paper money* is paper money backed partly by a deposit of gold or silver and partly by credit. If, instead of the 100 per cent backing, there is a smaller percentage of specie backing, and if the holder of the paper money has the right to redeem it for the specie at any time, the paper money is of the convertible fiduciary type. Another type of money, in common use today, is *inconvertible paper money* or *fiat money.* This money cannot be converted into specie and is backed entirely or partially by the credit of the government.

Money in Circulation, all currency and coin not held by Federal Reserve

Banks or the U.S. Treasury in use at any given time. Synonym: currency in circulation.

Money Income. See *income*.

Money Market, a general term for the entire machinery involved in borrowing and lending short-term funds.

Money Supply, the total amount of money (coin, currency, bank deposits) in an economy; the sum of the cash and credit immediately available to business and the public.

Monometalism. See *bimetalism*.

MONOPOLIES like J. Pierpont Morgan's shipping combine were savagely attacked by cartoonists at the turn of the century.

Monopolistic Competition, the condition prevailing where there is a large number of sellers of identical or closely substitutable products. Synonym: imperfect competition.

Monopoly, 1. In economics, a market situation in which there is only one seller of a commodity or service.

2. An exclusive right, power, or privilege of engaging in a particular business; the exclusive possession of the trade in a given community; unified control over supply or distribution so complete that it makes possible the regulation of price.

Monopsony, in economics, a market situation in which there is a single buyer for a commodity.

Moratorium, an emergency act of a legislature or other official body suspending the payment of debts for a limited period. Moratoriums are enacted during times of financial crisis or panic.

Mortgage, a written conveyance of the title, but not the possession, of property, to secure the payment of a debt or the performance of some obligation, under the condition that the conveyance is to be void upon final payment or performance.

Mutual Fund. See *open-end investment company*.

Narrow Market, a market in which the volume of trading is limited; a dull, light or inactive market; usually applied to the stock market or parts of it. Synonym: thin market.

National Bank, a commercial bank that has been chartered by the office of the controller of the currency in the United States Treasury.

National Brand, originally, a term applied to a manufacturer's brand to distinguish it from a private brand (dealer's brand) on the grounds that it had wide, sometimes national, distribution as compared with a private brand. The distinction is becoming less clear with development of large wholesale distributing organizations and large retail chains.

National Debt, the indebtedness of a national government; specifically, the total of bonds, notes, certificates of indebtedness, bills, and other direct obligations of the United States government.

National Economics, the study of the collection and presentation of income data.

National Income, the total net monetary value of all goods and services produced in a country during a single year.

National Income Product, gross national product minus the costs of depreciation.

National Product. See *gross national product*.

National Wealth, in economics, the monetary value of the total national stock of both private and public goods, including land values.

Near Money, an asset that can be easily converted into money at par, yet cannot be spent directly. Examples: time deposits, United States bonds.

Negotiable Instrument, a credit instrument, payable unconditionally in a given sum of money at a fixed or determinable time and transferable upon endorsement or delivery.

Net, 1. The balance remaining after all possible deductions, offsets, or allowances from a gross amount, as applied to income, price, profit, etc.

2. To earn, make, or bring in a certain amount after deductions.

3. The earnings themselves.

Net Asset Value, in investment companies, the total market value of all securities held in the portfolio; usually stated in terms of value per share of outstanding stock.

Net Circulation. See *circulation (2)*.

Net Income, 1. That which remains from earnings and profits after all costs, taxes, expenses, property charges, interest, and allowances for depreciation and possible losses have been deducted.

2. Net profit.

Net Price, the price actually paid; the price of a commodity or article of merchandise after deducting all discounts, commissions, and allowances.

Net Profit, the amount realized from sales, less the cost of goods sold and all expenses of operating the business.

Net Worth, 1. In accounting, the excess of total assets over total liabilities.

2. Of a business, the equity of the owners, proprietors, or stockholders.

Non-Durable Goods, generally, consumers' goods and producers' goods that are normally consumed in use, or that are further processed by purchasers, and whose serviceability is limited to a period less than three years. Synonym: soft goods. See also *durable goods, semi-durable goods*.

Non-Operating Income, income from sources other than the operations for which a company primarily exists. Examples: dividends and interest from investments, income from oil and gas leases, patents, etc. See also *operating income*.

Note, 1. Any of various forms of credit instruments, consisting essentially of a written, unconditional promise to pay a sum of money at a specified future date to a named person, or to order, or to bearer.

2. A piece of paper money, such as a bank note.

3. A certificate, such as a gold certificate, or silver certificate, passing currently as money.

Notes Payable, in accounting, those current liabilities which are represented by promissory notes or other instruments of short-term indebtedness.

Notes Receivable, in accounting, those current assets which are represented by promissory notes or other instruments of short-term indebtedness.

Obsolescence, the reduction in the economic life of an asset due to changes in style or consumer demand, improvements in processes, technological progress, legislation, etc. See also *depletion, depreciation, deterioration*.

Odd Lot, a fractional amount of a security, or an amount of stock that is less than the unit of trading established by a stock exchange, usually less than 100 shares of stock or less than $1,000 in bonds.

Oligopoly, in economics, a market situation in which a few companies or sources control or dominate the market for a product or service.

Oligopsony, in economics, a market situation in which there are relatively few buyers.

Open-End Investment Company, an investment company that has a flexible capital structure and continues to sell additional shares to the public as demand requires. The proceeds of the sale of shares are invested and reinvested in diversified securities; thus a mutual fund is created. The price of the share is determined solely by the net asset value of the fund per share, plus a distribution fee or commission. Synonym: mutual fund.

Open Shop, a place of employment in which the employer can hire union or non-union workers alike, and in which there is no obligation for workers to join the union. In an open shop the employer may engage both union and non-union workers; he may give preference to either union or non-union employees; or he may employ non-union workers only. See also *agency shop, closed shop, preferential shop, union shop*.

Operating Income, income from the operations for which a company primarily exists. It does not include profits or losses from investments, the sales of real property, or other non-operating factors. See also *non-operating income*.

Operating Ratio, any one of a number of ratios or relationships used to analyze a company's operations. Examples: sales to merchandise ratio, sales to fixed assets ratio, sales to receivable ratio.

Operating Statement. See *income statement*.

Operations Research, the analysis, usually by applying of mathematical or scientific techniques, of a complex problem or operation in order to achieve more precise solutions. The term frequently implies the use of a team of experts skilled in different areas.

Option, an agreement or contract to buy (receive) or sell (deliver) certain property or named securities on specified terms within a stated period of time. Example: an agreement by the owner of a certain farm that for $100 paid the owner will sell the farm to another party for $10,000 at any time during the next year. If the buyer of the contract (option) does not choose to exercise his option, he loses only the amount ($100) he paid for it.

Order, a direction or request made in business; specifically, a direction to a stockbroker to buy or sell certain securities or any instructions to transfer or deliver goods.

Outdoor Advertising, display advertising, such as posters, billboards or illuminated signs, located out-of-doors.

Overhead, a general term for those costs of operating a business other than the direct costs of labor and material; costs incurred irrespective of the level of production; those costs which cannot be directly charged to the article produced.

Overproduction, a volume of production too great to be consumed. From the social point of view there can be no overproduction as long as any person that desires the article manufactured is without it. Thus, there can never be an overproduction of shoes as long as there is any person who lacks shoes, of wheat as long as anyone is hungry, of houses as long as anyone needs a home. But from the business point of view, overproduction exists when there is an excess of actual production over actual consumption. This point of view does not consider whether people need the article but whether they buy it. Overproduction results when there are more goods produced than can be sold. In this sense, overproduction is closely related to the business cycle and is one of the factors that brings on the stages of crisis and depression. Overproduction may be caused by unusually good crops, cultivation of additional land, more intensive cultivation, the expansion of industries and the invention of new processes. Or consumption may be decreased by a change of fashion, a saturation of the demand, emigration from the locality, excessively high prices, or a loss in purchasing power of the people.

Over the Counter, denoting transactions not consummated through an established securities exchange; applied to direct transactions between brokers, dealers and customers. Sometimes stock so traded, that is, unlisted stock, is called over-the-counter stock.

Panic, a sudden widespread financial fright marked by a wild effort to convert all securities into cash and to withdraw all deposits from the banks. A panic is generally the result of some commercial or business crisis and arises from the fear that banks will fail, and that securities will become practically worthless and should be converted into cash no matter what the loss.

Paper, negotiable notes, bills, etc. Collectively, commercial paper.

Par, a condition of equality between the face, or nominal, value and the market value of a share of stock, bond, bill of exchange, currency, or other instrument. In common usage, par is frequently used to mean the face value itself rather than the state of equality or relationship. See also *par value.*

Par Value, face value or nominal value; the value printed on the face of a stock certificate or bond instrument. Par value is not to be confused with *book value* or *market value.*

Parent Company, a company that holds a controlling interest in one or more subsidiary companies. See also *holding company.*

Parity, 1. In general, an equivalence in price, value, quality, or rate, or some other factor; especially the equality existing when two or more currencies are exchangeable for each other at the par or exchange rate.

2. In agriculture, a system of regulating prices of farm commodities, expressed as an equivalence of farm incomes and prices and those in the rest of the economy.

Partnership, an association of two or more persons who have under an oral, written or implied legal agreement pooled money, skills and labor to carry on business and share profits and losses.

Patronage Dividend. See *consumer's cooperative.*

Pay as You Go. 1. To meet costs or expenses as they occur.

2. To limit expenditures, particularly capital expenditures, to actual current earnings.

3. To pay income taxes at the time income is earned. See also *withholding tax.*

Personal Disposable Income, in government statistics, the amount of money that individuals have left after payment of direct taxes. When stated on a per-capita basis, it is a valid indicator of the standard of living.

Personal Income, in government statistics, the total current income received by persons from all sources, inclusive of transfers from government and business, but exclusive of transfers between persons.

Personal Savings, in government statistics, the excess of personal income over personal consumption expenditures and taxes and other payments to general government. It may consist of deposits in banks or savings associations, security purchases or the accumulation of life insurance reserves.

Picketing, posting striking workers at entrances to businesses to enlist public sympathy and agreement not to patronize the establishment.

Pit, the part of the floor of a commodity exchange devoted to trade in each of several particular commodities.

Planned Economy, an economic system in which some or all of the allocation of resources including land, labor, and capital, is directed by a central governmental authority.

Pool, 1. An agreement between business concerns to follow some special policy of prices, output, or division of territory. Such compacts cannot be enforced at law and are considered unfair trade practices, or agreements in restraint of trade.

2. A temporary combination of two or more persons to manipulate one or more securities. Securities trading regulations have practically eliminated pooling operations.

Portfolio, 1. An itemized list of securities and other investments of an individual, bank, or investment organization.

2. An itemized list or the total of outstanding loans, notes, bills, etc., held by a bank or finance company.

Preferential Shop, a place of employment in which the employer must give preference to union members over non-union members in hiring workers. Thus, if a union member is available and qualified he must be hired. See also *union shop.*

Preferred Stock, capital stock that has preference over other stocks of the same company with regard to dividend payments and any distribution of assets on liquidation. No dividends can be paid on common stock until the holders of preferred stock have been paid a stipulated amount. Preferred stock may be cumulative or non-cumulative. In *cumulative preferred stock* unpaid dividends accumulate until they can be paid; meanwhile, no dividends may be paid on other classes of stock. In *non-cumulative preferred stock,* dividends not paid one year do not become a liability of the company and hence will not have to be paid the next year.

Price, a measure in monetary terms of the exchange value of a good or service; the amount of money asked or given for the sale or purchase of something. See also *value.*

Price Cutting, selling goods at a price below what is recognized as a standard price, or below the manufacturer's suggested retail price.

Price Index, any one of several measures used to show an average price level of commodities over a stated period of time. See also *cost-of-living index.*

Primary Boycott. See *direct boycott.*

Priority, a preference in the right to have credit claims satisfied or to receive other benefits. A creditor who has priority has the right to have his claims satisfied in full before the claims of others are paid at all. A first mortgage, for example, has priority over a second or subsequent mortgage, and when the property is sold to satisfy the mortgage, the proceeds are used to satisfy the first mortgage. If anything is left, it goes to the second mortgage holder and on down the line.

Private Brand, a brand used exclusively by a distributor or dealer; distinguished from a manufacturer's brand and formerly from a national brand. However, since some private brands are now distributed nationally the distinction is fading. Synonym: dealer's brand.

Private Enterprise. See *capitalism.*

Producers' Goods, buildings, equipment, machinery, and all other manmade raw materials and resources that are used to produce other goods and services. Synonym: industrial goods. See also *consumers' goods.*

Product, in general, the result or end of any process of production or manufacture. Products have frequently and services. Synonym: industrial goods. See also *consumer goods.*

Production, 1. The act or process of creating, bringing forth, or making something; manufacture.

2. The creation of any good or service that people are willing to pay for; the creation of a utility which increases the want-satisfying power of goods and services. The economic process of society is directed toward obtaining things from nature and getting them to the consumer in a form ready to be used. All the steps in this process are regarded as productive if they add utility to the article. The farmer who grows food; the man who transports the food to the market; the warehouseman who stores food until it is wanted; the shopkeeper who sells the food to the consumer; the doctor, the lawyer, the teacher, the actor, the clergyman, the scientist—all create utilities when they render their particular services. All these are examples of production. The essential factors of production are land, labor, capital, and business enterprise. It is the working together of some or all of these factors that makes production possible.

3. The part of a business concerned with fabricating, assembling, or processing, and with related functions such as receiving, packing, shipping, storage, maintenance, and repairing.

4. Total output of an industry or firm; the thing produced; output.

Profit, 1. In economics (usually *profits*), the residual share of the product of an enterprise accruing to the entrepreneur after he has met his costs for capital, land, and labor (including salaried management).

2. In business, the portion of income remaining after all expenses are met; the excess of revenues over expenses, proceeds over cost, selling price over cost of acquisition, or other realized pecuniary gains. Profit may be expressed in various ways: *gross profit*, the amount realized from sales less cost of goods sold; *net profit*, the amount realized from sales less cost of goods and operating expenses.

Profit and Loss Statement. See *income statement.*

Profit Sharing, any one of various plans whereby employees receive a share, fixed in advance, of the profits of a company in addition to their regular wages.

Promissory Note, a written promise to pay a sum of money. Under the terms of the Uniform Negotiable Instruments Law, a promissory note, to be negotiable, must be in writing and signed by the maker, must contain an unconditional promise to pay a certain sum of money, must be payable on demand or at a fixed or determined future time, and must be payable to order or to the bearer.

Promotion, 1. An advancement to a position of higher rank.

2. The activities designed to advance, encourage, stimulate, or further interest in a person, organization, company, or cause or the interest in and sales of a product or service. See also *sales promotion.*

Progressive Tax, a tax that takes an increasing portion of the value assessed. Income taxes, for example, increase as income increases.

Property Tax, a tax imposed on the assessed valuation of real property, especially real estate.

Proportional Tax, a tax whose rate remains constant as the size of the base increases. Sales taxes, for example, are usually on a fixed percentage rate.

Prosperity, the phase of a business cycle marked by high levels of business activity, high production, little unemployment, active consumer buying, high capital investment, expansion of credit, etc. It is the peak of the cycle. See also *depression.*

Protest, a formal written statement, usually sworn to before a notary public, that a note or draft was dishonored when it was presented for payment, and giving other material facts regarding the note. The protest is sent to the maker and to the endorsers, and they become liable on the instrument.

Publicity, any action taken to obtain public interest, attention, or support for an organization, person, service, or product; especially, any news, promotional material, or information disseminated without specific payment to the medium (newspaper, radio, TV, magazine, etc.).

Public Utility, an enterprise so affected with public interest that the government has taken over its regulation or ownership. Public utilities include those enterprises that supply water, gas, electricity, telephone and rapid transit transportation. This classification is not fixed, however, and the list has been growing with the different economic needs of the community, and it changes from time to time and depends upon special circumstances. Some businesses are classed as affected with public interest on the basis of old common-law distinctions that granted certain rights and imposed certain liabilities on the enterprisers as common carriers. Other public utilities are so considered as the result of legislative action or judicial determination in recent times.

The distinguishing factor in most public utilities is their involvement with the public interest; because of this, they operate on the principle of decreasing cost and become natural monopolies. It has been found to be economically wasteful to force or even allow competition between public utilities. Because this monopolistic privilege has been given to them, the public utilities are closely regulated by the government, which usually goes to the extent of fixing the rates that they may charge.

Pure Competition, in economics, a market situation in which there are many sellers of an identical product or service.

Pure Holding Company. See *holding company.*

Pure Monopoly, in economics, a situation in which there is only one seller of a product.

Put, an option to sell certain securities at a certain price within a specified time. The other party to the option contract promises to buy the securities as agreed. A *call*, the opposite of a put, is an option to buy, with the other party agreeing to sell the specified securities at a certain price within a specified time if called upon to do so. A *spread* is the combined option of both putting and calling. A *straddle* is a special type of spread.

Pyramiding, 1. The use of unrealized profits from stock that has been purchased and held as the margin for the purchase of further securities. It is one of the most speculative methods of dealing in securities.

2. A means of gaining control of holding companies.

Quantity Discount, a percentage reduction in the list price of an item granted to encourage large purchases. Under the Robinson-Patman Act, such discounts are outlawed unless they can be justified by savings in handling, billing, packing, etc.

Quantity Theory of Money, a theory of the relationship between the amount of money in circulation and the price of commodities. The theory states that, if the velocity of the circulation of money and the quantity of goods remain the same, any increase in the quantity of money will bring a proportional increase in the price of goods. Expressed in the form of the equation $MV = PQ$, M is the amount of money, V is the velocity of circulation (or the number of times money is used in a certain period), P is the price, and Q is the total quantity of goods in the community. If an imaginary island has a total amount of money of $100, and each dollar is only used once in a period of time, and the total amount of goods on the island is 100 bushels of wheat, then the price of each bushel is $1. If the amount of money were doubled, the price of a bushel of wheat would increase to $2, or if the velocity of the circulation of money were doubled, the price per bushel would double as well.

The theory in this simple form is no longer accepted as an adequate explanation of price changes in our complex economic order, for it fails to take into consideration the important factors of saving and the function of credit. Furthermore, prices cannot be controlled by simply changing the amount of money in circulation, because other factors do not remain constant, the velocity of circulation is practically impossible to control, and the change in the velocity may offset any increase or decrease in the amount of money in circulation.

Quotation, a notification by a seller to buyers or the general public that certain goods are for sale at the price specified. A quotation is not necessarily a legal offer and is usually considered simply as an invitation to negotiate. In banking and security transactions, a quotation is the published price at which securities have been sold or are offered for sale. Stock quotations are in eighths of one per cent; quotation units in the commodity exchanges vary according to custom.

Quick Assets, in accounting, a current asset normally convertible into cash within a relatively short time, such as a month. Examples: cash, call loan, marketable security, or a commodity that is immediately salable at a quoted price on the open market. See also *liquid asset*.

Quick Ratio. See *acid-test ratio*.

Ratio, the numerical relation between two like quantities. The ratio is generally found by dividing the smaller quantity by the larger and is expressed in a percentage. Ratios are used in accounting to analyze financial statements. For example, the ratio of current assets to current liabilities is found by dividing the assets by the liabilities, which indicates the liquidity of the company.

Rationalization, in industry, any method, system, or means (such as scientific management) of making a task reasonable, intelligible, or simple, especially in order to reduce waste, inefficiency, or duplication.

Readjustment, the phase of a business cycle following a crisis, emergency liquidation, or depression, in which the normal equilibrium between supply and demand is being restored.

Real Income. See *income*.

Receipt, a written acknowledgment that money has been paid or goods or property have been received.

Recession, a period in business activity marked by a mild or gradual decline. It is not as severe or prolonged as a depression.

Rediscounting. See *discounting*.

Regional Economics, the study of the development of a specific geographical area.

Regressive Tax, a tax whose rate decreases as the tax base increases.

Regulation, in economics, some measure of control or guidance of private enterprise for the benefit of the general public.

Rent, 1. In economics, payment for the use of natural resources produced without the assistance of human labor. Rent in this theoretical sense may be *explicit* or *implicit*. If a farmer is actually a tenant and pays rent to the landlord, this is explicit rent. However, if the farmer owns the land, he, in effect, pays rent to himself, and this is implicit rent. In David Ricardo's (1772–1823) classical theory, rent is "that portion of the produce of the earth which is paid to the landlord for the use of the original and indestructible powers of the soil." But modern discussion has fairly well destroyed the older, and artificial, idea that rent was different from payment for the use of capital or other commodities.

2. In business, payment for the use of land or of any durable good, such as buildings, equipment, vehicles, etc.

Reorganization, the reconstruction of a corporation that is insolvent or threatened with insolvency. The interests of the bondholders, creditors, and stockholders are adjusted by agreement; the means of obtaining new capital are determined; and the new corporation takes over the franchise and business of the old one.

Representative Money. See *money*.

Research and Development, basic and applied research and engineering, as well as the design and development of prototypes and processes. Research is the quest for new knowledge in a field, and development is the application of that knowledge to meet specific objectives.

Reserve, 1. A special account set up on the books from profits or surplus or for a specific purpose. Usually a reserve is established to counteract losses that may reasonably be expected. The commonest accounts of this sort are reserves for bad debts and for depreciation, depletion and obsolescence. A *funded reserve* is a reserve invested in interest-bearing securities.

2. The amount of money kept available by a bank to meet demands of depositors. Synonym: bank reserve.

Retail, to sell in small quantities directly to consumers.

Retail Store, as defined by the United States Bureau of the Census, a business establishment engaged primarily in selling merchandise directly to personal, household, and farm users at retail.

Revival, the part of a business cycle marked by an upswing or a renewed business activity.

Right, in the securities market, a privilege given to a stockholder to buy at a fixed price and for a given period additional shares of the same stock in proportion to the number of shares of that stock he owns. Rights generally set the price below the current market price and can be traded on the open market if the stockholder does not wish to exercise them. See also *warrant*.

Right to Work, the right of an individual to work for a company without being compelled to belong, or not to belong, to a labor union. Right-to-work laws have been passed by many states, making it illegal for collective-bargaining agreements to contain union-shop, maintenance-of-membership, preferential hiring, or other clauses requiring compulsory union membership. The Taft-Hartley Law of 1947 outlawed the closed shop, and Section 14 (b) reaffirmed the right of states to pass right-to-work laws.

RETAIL sales may be made by specialized units of one department store like Macy's.

Risk, 1. In general, any element of uncertainty or chance of loss which is inherent in an activity. The term may be applied to the chance of loss from some particular hazard (fire, theft, explosion, etc.), or it may refer to economic uncertainty, such as changes in market demand due to consumer taste shifts, changes in price level, technological developments, shortages, and the like.

2. In insurance, the prospective amount of loss to which an individual, property, or goods may be exposed; the property covered by insurance.

Risk Capital. See *venture capital*.

Royalty, a payment of a share of the profits to the owner of a property for its use or exploitation. Royalties are commonly paid to the owners of coal mines, oil wells, forests, and patented articles, as well as to authors of books and to actors in television and movie productions. A royalty is usually set as a percentage of the profits or gross receipts.

Originally, a royalty was a payment to the Crown for use of royal lands. *Seigniorage*, the payment for coining money at the royal mint, was one kind of royalty.

Salary, a fixed compensation paid regularly for services of an executive, professional, or clerical nature. It is distinguished from wages, which are based usually on hourly rates or units of production and are paid largely for work of a manual nature.

Sale, 1. The transfer of ownership of property from seller to buyer; a contract between two parties, the seller or vendor and the buyer or purchaser, by which the former, in consideration of payment or promise of payment of a stated price, transfers to the latter the title and possession of property.

2. A special disposal or selling off of goods at reduced or bargain prices.

3. *Sales,* the total of recorded and reported amounts of goods sold during any given accounting period.

Sale-and-Leaseback. See *leaseback*.

Sales Management, the direction and control of all sales and sales-promotion activities, particularly personal salesmanship. Sometimes the sales manager controls advertising; sometimes there is an advertising manager. In either case the sales manager selects, recruits, trains and equips the salesmen; and sets quotas, allots territories, and decides sales policies.

Salesmanship, the art of selling; the personal presentation of goods, services, or ideas to prospective customers in such a way as to promote sales. Synonym: personal selling.

Sales Promotion, activities by a company designed to increase its sales. The term excludes direct advertising and selling itself, and includes promotional efforts such as design and distribution of novelties, store signs, displays, catalogues, circulars, and presentation of displays, sales demonstrations, and trade-show exhibits.

Saving, 1. Putting off consumption until a later time.

2. The flow of money or resources accumulated during a given period of time.

3. *Savings,* the stock of money or

resources set aside for future consumption or use, as a security against possible financial difficulty or to earn income. In government statistics, savings are classified as business savings or personal savings.

Savings and Loan Association, a cooperative association, formed under United States state and federal law, that promotes thrift and home ownership and accepts savings from its members in the form of share capital, invests its funds in mortgages and modernization loans, and permits withdrawals from share accounts similar to those allowed savings accounts in banks. Synonyms: building association, building and loan association, building society, homestead association (Louisiana), cooperative bank (New England), savings association.

Savings Bank. See *bank.*

Scarcity, the principal item in use-value. A great deal of economic theory is based on the concept of the scarcity of the factors of production: land, labor, and capital. In economic theory, man must strive to satisfy his needs and desires from the scarce elements provided. If there is a scarcity of land, man must learn to make more productive use of the land he has, or he must learn to grow food in chemicals without the use of land. If there is a scarcity of workers, man must learn to build machines to do the work. If there is a scarcity of capital, man must learn how to create more capital.

Many recent economists have pointed out that we have passed from an economy of scarcity to an economy of surplus or abundance. Originally, the problem of economics was to find the means to produce enough to go around; but now we have learned how to produce enough, and we must learn how to distribute it.

Scientific Management, the theory and practice of various principles directed toward a more efficient and rational method of production in industry. Scientific management is based upon research, investigation, experimentation, and analysis of each operation in the factory. It then coordinates and plans the entire activities of all the departments in the factory. Frederick W. Taylor (1856–1915) was the pioneer primarily responsible for the development of scientific management.

Seasonal Discount, a percentage reduction in the list price granted to encourage purchases at other than the normal season.

Seat, in the securities and commodities trade, a membership in an exchange including the privilege to trade there.

Secondary Boycott, a boycott in which a union attempts to persuade third parties to participate; a boycott carried on by workers not directly concerned with its outcome. Most secondary boycotts have been declared unfair labor practices by the Taft-Hartley Act.

Securities Exchange. See *stock exchange.*

Security, 1. In finance, any documentary evidence of the debt or equity ownership of a corporation or other business or financial organization. As defined by the Uniform Commercial Code, it is an instrument, whether payable to bearer or registered in an owner's name, of a type commonly dealt in on securities exchanges or markets, or commonly recognized as a medium of exchange. The Securities Act of 1934 listed the following as securities: notes, stock, bonds, debentures and trust certificates, evidences of indebtedness, voting-trust certificates, etc.

2. Safety from risk, the main objective of economic man.

3. Property pledged as collateral.

Sellers' Market, a market in which demand exceeds supply to the extent that sellers have such a favorable market position that they can raise their prices and still sell their goods. See also *buyers' market.*

Selling, the process of disposing of or transferring by sale; specifically the personal or impersonal process of assisting or persuading a prospective customer to buy a commodity or service.

Selling Agent, a type of broker under extended contract with a mill or manufacturer to sell the entire output of his principal, usually with full authority on prices and terms. Selling agents are usually paid a commission, as they are in business for themselves and often represent one or more manufacturers. The selling agent often helps to finance the production of mills he represents.

Semi-Durable Goods, generally consumers' goods and producers' goods that are not immediately consumed in use, but have a short useful life, usually from six months to three years. Examples: tires, clothing, shoes, hand tools.

Seniority, status gained by an employee's length of continuous service entitling him to priority to certain rights or privileges. Seniority may be considered, for example, in transfers, layoffs, rehirings, promotions, choice of shifts, etc.

Service, usually *services* (as in goods and services), any work or effort expended or performed to meet the needs or desires of others and by which no tangible product results. Examples: public utilities, such as telephone service, transportation, etc.; private education, laundry, dry-cleaning, repair work, professional activities by lawyers, physicians, dentists, etc.

Share. See *stock.*

Shopping Center, a group of retail stores in a more or less cohesive grouping (and sometimes, cohesive architectural style) in one place, supplying many basic shopping needs.

Shopping Goods, consumers' goods for which customers actually shop, for price or quality, or both, and purchase only after comparing.

Short Haul. See *long and short haul.*

Short Sale, the sale of borrowed stock or securities which the seller intends to buy later in order to "cover" purchases bought short. The short seller expects the price of stock to fall, and if it does, he is able to buy in the stock at a later date for a lower price, return this stock for the borrowed stock, and make a profit.

Silver Certificate, a form of United States paper money formerly issued by the Treasury against deposited silver. Its denominations were $1, $2, and $5. The issuance of two-dollar bills was discontinued in 1966. The Treasury discontinued the issuance of silver certificates in 1963, and all bills issued thereafter are Federal Reserve Notes.

Sinking Fund, a fund specially set aside at regular intervals to provide means for paying off a funded debt. The usual method is to pay annually a stipulated sum of money to sinking fund trustees who invest the principal and allow it to accumulate at compound interest until the time when the bonds mature. Then the bonds are paid with the assets in the sinking fund. The sinking fund may be derived from profits or from surplus, although in the latter case it is properly called *a sinking fund reserve.*

Sinking Fund Bond, a bond containing a provision that stated amounts or proportions of income will be paid each year into a sinking fund to provide for the redemption of the bond.

Social Insurance, government measures to provide relief or compensation for large groups of the general public for injuries or losses due to the uncertainties or hazards of life. Social insurance includes workman's compensation, and old age, survivors' and unemployment insurance.

Social Security, the principle or practice of providing through public welfare programs a degree of economic and social security to individuals or families. United States examples: old age and survivors' insurance, unemployment insurance, Medicare, public relief, family allowances, and public health services.

Soft Goods. See *non-durable goods.*

Sources and Use of Funds Statement. See *statement of application of funds.*

Special Agent. See *agent.*

Specialization of Labor, the organization and division of the process of production so that certain persons do a certain type or kind of work. Specialization has been divided into three main types: social specialization, geographical or territorial specialization, and technical specialization.

Social specialization involves a division of labor according to social classes. In early primitive cultures the men were generally engaged in occupations that took them away from the camp, such as hunting and fishing, and in making the implements for these activities. The women were more closely confined to the camp, caring for the children, gathering wild foods, tending the crops, and generally doing the arduous work. This social specialization has continued down to modern times. In addition to specialization between the sexes, which has become less important with the change in the status of women, there has developed the division of labor by trades and professions.

Geographical specialization denotes the specialization of production according to geographical or territorial sections. Nature herself is a specialist: certain parts of the world are better adapted to the growing of certain foods than others; certain natural resources are found only in particular parts of the world. Nearness to raw materials and to sources of power and the development of native skill have created special centers for producing certain goods. This geographical division of labor cannot develop without commerce, and the geographical division of labor is the basis of international trade.

Technical specialization means splitting the making of a commodity into a number of fractional operations and having each operation performed by a worker who does nothing else. Technical specialization is the most important type, and the term *specialization*, as it is commonly used, refers to it. This type began in the handicraft stage but it reached its important development only in the industrial stage in large factories using mass-production methods, and it is one of the most characteristic features of modern industry. Perhaps the best illustration of it at the present time is in the automobile industry, where one worker may do nothing but put a single bolt in the engine or a few tacks in the upholstery.

The advantage of technical specialization is that it brings increased production at a lower cost. The disadvantage is mainly in the monotony of the work and the possibility of increased exploitation of labor through speeding up the work. Increased production and decreased human work are results of specialization that are both desirable and permanent, but special adjustments and safeguards to protect labor must be taken. Synonym: division of labor.

Specialty Goods, consumers' goods that are not staple or common and are different in quality or some other respect from goods of the same general class; high-grade goods that the consumer prefers and that he will make a special effort to secure.

Specialty Shop, a retail store that carries specialty goods or a limited variety of goods in a single line. Millinery stores, men's hat shops, and hosiery stores are examples of single-line specialty stores. Some specialty stores have departments—but not so many as the typical department store and with a much more limited range in style and prices.

Specific Tax, a tax, such as an import duty or tariff, levied as a specific amount per unit of weight or volume rather than as a percentage of value. See also *ad valorem tax.*

Split. See *stock split.*

Spot Market. See *commodity exchange.*

Spread, a combined option of putting and calling. The term is also applied to a hedging operation in commodities that are sold on exchanges. See also *call, hedging, put.*

Standard Money. See *money.*

Standard of Living, the minimum of goods required by an individual or class to keep it in its usual status. A standard may allow merely physical necessities of life, or it may allow for physical comforts and certain

LOOK MAGAZINE

STRIKE issues and settlement proposals are debated by workers at a labor union meeting.

other needs, such as education and entertainment. The trend has been to consider the desirable minimum standard as one that demands both physical comfort and cultural opportunities. The recognized standard of living is constantly changing and progressing, and what is a rare luxury in one generation becomes a necessity in the next. Efforts to improve social conditions include the endeavor to make the minimum standard available to all and to raise this minimum standard.

State Bank. See *bank.*

Statement. See *account* (2).

Statement of Account. See *account* (2).

Statement of Application of Funds, a financial statement that shows the sources of funds made available over a specified period and their distribution; prepared from a comparative balance sheet. Synonym: sources and use of funds statement.

Stock, 1. A share in the ownership of a corporation, evidenced by a certificate. When stock is purchased, the buyer is really investing his money in the corporation and becomes a part owner of the corporation with the right to share in the profits and, usually, to exercise some control over the corporation's policies through the election of directors. Just what the stock means to its owner depends upon the terms of the contract with the corporation written on the stock certificate, the powers of the corporation in the charter the corporation received from the state and the actual method of management of the corporation. See also *common stock, preferred stock.*

2. Inventory.

Stockbroker, a broker who deals in securities.

Stock Certificate, the written evidence of ownership of one or more shares of stock of a corporation.

Stock Dividend, a dividend paid in the form of shares or fractional shares of stock of the corporation, instead of in cash.

Stock Exchange, an organized market for securities, where members buy and sell listed securities in accordance with established rules. The primary purpose of the stock market is to bring together all buyers and sellers and increase the marketability of the listed securities.

The London Stock Exchange is the greatest international market in the world. The New York Stock Exchange is one of the most important in the world, but it deals almost entirely in American stocks and lists few foreign securities. The stock exchanges in France and Germany are under rigid government control. The London exchange is a private organization managed by the members. The stock exchanges in the United States were privately managed until the Securities Exchange Act of 1934 brought the exchanges practically under the control of the government. Members of the New York Stock Exchange deal on their own account and also for their clients.

Only securities that are officially listed on the exchange can be bought and sold. Certain information must be filed with the Securities and Exchange Commission, and a stock must be approved by the exchange before it can be listed. The stock exchange has become one of the most important institutions in modern capitalistic economy, for it enables the securities of the government and private corporations to be distributed throughout the world and to remain readily marketable.

Stock Market, 1. One of the principal stock exchanges, particularly the New York Stock Exchange.

2. The entire business of buying and selling corporate securities.

Stock Right. See *right.*

Stock Split, the division of the issued shares of stock of a corporation into a larger number without changing the capital account but reducing the par or stated value of each share.

Straddle. See *put.*

Strike, a concerted suspension of work by a group of employees for the purpose of forcing a satisfactory settlement of an industrial dispute. Strikes are usually for the purpose of obtaining the right to bargain collectively or to obtain higher wages, shorter hours, and better working conditions.

Subsidiary, a company that is wholly or partly owned and controlled by another company. Synonym: subsidiary company.

Subsistence Theory of Wages, the economic theory that wages, in the long run, tended toward the lowest level that would support life. The basis of this theory was that labor was bought and sold like a commodity, and that the sole determinant of the value of labor was the cost of producing the labor supply. This cost of production was said to consist of the commodities—food, clothing, and shelter—that the laborer needed to exist, in addition to the cost of keeping up the labor supply, that is, the cost of rearing children to the working age. It was believed that if the workers received more than a bare living, there would be an increase in population, and the added numbers would again drag down wages to a bare subsistence. But if laborers received less than a bare subsistence some of the workers would die, and this shortage of labor would raise wages to the subsistence level again. Experience has shown that this theory of wages is no longer applicable to conditions in western nations. Population has not always increased when wages were raised. Synonym: iron law of wages. See also *marginal-productivity theory of wages.*

Supermarket, a large, limited-line, self-service, retail store specializing in groceries and small housewares.

Supply, the total available amount of any salable commodity; specifically, the total amount of an economic good that will be offered at any given price at any given time. Synonym: inventory. See also *demand.*

Surplus, 1. In general, that which remains above what is used or needed; excess.

2. In accounting, the excess of assets over the combined total of liabilities and capital.

Surplus Value, the theory of Karl Marx regarding the exploitation of labor. The basis of this theory is that labor is the only source of value and, therefore, all returns taken in the form of profits, rent, and interest are wrongfully taken from labor. Marx declared that the chronic oversupply of labor gives employers a monopoly advantage, and they can therefore deprive the laborer of what is justly due him. For example, if an employer hired a worker to build a boat that was sold for $100 over the value of the materials used in the construction, if the employer paid the worker $50, the other $50 retained by the employer would be surplus value created by the worker and wrongfully kept from him by the employer. This theory has been abandoned even by Communist economists, for the basic idea that all value is created by labor is not tenable. Value depends upon the utility of the article and its scarcity in relation to the demand for it. Furthermore, factors in addition to actual labor—land, capital, and enterprise—are now seen as productive.

Sympathetic Strike, a strike called by one union in sympathy with another, or to help another union enforce its demands.

Syndicate, an association of bankers for the purpose of carrying out some large financial plan. The commonest form is an underwriting syndicate formed for the purpose of ensuring the sale of a complete stock or bond issue. The syndicate buys the entire issue at a price under the estimated market value and then sells the securities to the public. Any of the issue that is not sold must be taken by the members of the syndicate.

Take-Home Pay, the actual amount of salary or wage received from an employer after all deductions for taxes, social security, insurance, etc., have been made.

Tangible Asset, an asset that has a physical existence. Examples: real estate, buildings, machinery, inventory, etc. See also *intangible asset.*

Tariff, 1. A schedule of fixed rates or charges.

2. A listing or schedule of the commodities on which import duties are levied.

3. A tax on imports.

Tax, any enforced contribution exacted from persons or property by the authority of a government, usually for the purpose of meeting the costs of government.

Tax-Exempt, 1. Released from the necessity of paying a tax in whole or in part.

2. *Tax-exempts,* a popular name for tax-exempt bonds, the income from which is exempt from certain taxes.

Technology, the art of combining productive resources to achieve given ends; the science or body of knowledge applicable to the production of goods.

Thin Market. See *narrow market.*

Tie-In Sale, a sale in which the buyer is required to accept one or more additional items to obtain the one he wants to purchase.

Time Certificate. See *certificate of deposit (1).*

Time Deposit, a bank deposit subject to withdrawal by the depositor only after advance notice or a stated period of time has elapsed. A savings deposit is one form of time deposit. See also *demand deposit.*

To-Arrive Market. See *commodity exchange.*

Trade Association, a group of competitors in industry or commerce united for common benefit and for the interchange of information and certain statistics.

Trade Discount, a percentage reduction in the list price granted to various classes of customers such as to wholesalers (by manufacturers) or retailers (by wholesalers). It is usually used as a means of adjusting prices to changed market conditions without the need to reissue new price lists.

Trademark, any device, symbol, diagram, name, word or words, etc., used by a manufacturer or distributor to identify the source, ownership, quality, or kind of a product or service, and to distinguish it from a competitive product or service.

Trade Union. See *labor union.*

Trading Stamp, a redeemable stamp given as a premium by a seller to a customer in the hope of increasing volume of sales. It is issued as a percentage of purchases and redeemable in merchandise at a store operated by the trading stamp company according to announced schedules.

Traditional Economy, a mode of economic life based on ancient customs and traditions. Primitive societies do not decide consciously what goods will be produced, how they will be produced, or how to distribute the products or income. All these things are done according to tradition. See also *command economy, market economy.*

Treasury Stock, stock issued by a company but later reacquired.

Trial Balance, in accounting, a listing of all debit and credit balances in a general ledger for the purpose of determining any errors.

Trust, any large company or combination of companies that is able to exercise effective control over markets or shut out competition through its great financial power. Originally, a trust was an organization formed to act as a *trustee,* that is, to act for the joint benefit of its members. See also *combination, monopoly.*

Trust Company. See *bank.*

Turnover, 1. The general act of any stock of capital, or inventory of goods, in relation to the volume of business. Merchandise turnover, for example, is the number of times that new merchandise must be purchased to replace the merchandise sold. If the entire stock of a storekeeper is disposed of twice a month, his merchandise turnover is twice a month. The higher merchandise turnover is, the better the business.

2. In personnel management, the number of times that positions in a business have to be refilled during a certain period (usually a year). The higher the labor turnover is in a factory, the greater are labor costs because it is necessary to train new workers, and there are losses from inexperience and slow work.

Underwriter, 1. In insurance, a company or individual that makes an insurance contract guaranteeing indemnity for loss if certain events occur; the insurer.

2. In finance, the person or corporation that guarantees the sale of certain securities by agreeing to purchase them on a set date at a set price. Usually, an investment bank buys new securities at a slight discount in return for the service of distributing the securities to other corporations and the investing public.

Union. See *labor union.*

Union Shop, a place of employment where the employer may hire union or non-union workers, but the non-union employees must join a union before a specified time (usually 30 to 60 days). See also *agency shop, closed shop, open shop, preferential shop.*

Unlisted Stock, stock that is not listed for trading on a stock exchange. See also *listed stock, over-the-counter.*

Unsought Goods, consumers' goods which customers do not yet want or know they can buy.

Urban Economics, the study of the economic problems peculiar to cities.

Usury, an excessive or illegal rate charged for the use of money. In the United States the maximum legal interest rate in each state is fixed by the legislature, and a rate that is higher than the legal interest rate is called usury.

Value, the value of an article may be defined as the power of that article to command other goods in exchange. The value of a table may be two chairs or ten meals. Price is merely an expression of value in terms of money. It greatly facilitates matters to have a common denominator of value, so that instead of saying that the value of a table is two chairs we can say that the value of the table is $10 and the value of a chair is $5. In speculating on the subject of value and price, the ancient Greeks distinguished two kinds of value, use-value or utility and cost. Adam Smith and the classical economists dismissed the idea of use-value as a cause of price. Using the famous illustration of water and diamonds, Smith declared that there was no relation between the utility of these two articles and their price: water, by far the more useful commodity, can be secured for nothing, but diamonds command a high price. The classical economists explained price on the basis of the labor cost of the article. The high cost of diamonds, they said, was due to the labor involved in obtaining them, and the low cost of water was due to the fact that no labor was involved in producing it. This theory has been generally abandoned, and modern economists have shown the importance of marginal utility, based on use-value that is dependent upon scarcity. The competition of various enterprises for the same factors of production causes the cost of labor in one factory to be determined by the amount that another factory manager is willing to pay the same laborer for his services in aiding in the production of another product.

Further factors in the question of price are the numerous conditions and prejudices that cause a buyer to purchase one article rather than another. In addition, any limitation of supply will influence price, and under monopoly conditions the price may be set arbitrarily at the point that will give the greatest returns. From the point of view of money, prices change in relation to the value of the commodities. High prices are related to cheap money, and low prices are related to dear money.

The price system is the general coordinating factor in our economic system. It encourages the enterprises that society desires and discourages those that society does not want. Paying the price for an article is like casting a ballot for that article and against other competing articles, for by the gain on the sale the one producer is given a basis to continue in business, and competing producers are restrained.

Variable Budget. See *flexible budget.*

Variable Cost, a cost that changes directly with changes in output. As production is increased, the variable costs increase, and vice versa. Examples: costs of materials consumed, direct labor, power, factory supplies, etc. See also *fixed cost.*

Variety Store, a retail store selling a wide variety of goods, usually in a low and limited price range. Such stores are largely self-service and have open-counter displays.

Venture Capital, money invested by stockholders or owners in a business enterprise, especially one in which there is a relatively large element of risk. Synonyms: equity capital, risk capital.

Vertical Union. See *industrial union.*

Vested Interest, an activity in which a large amount of capital has been put or which has been carried on for such a long period that the courts will not deprive the owner of the interest except for the public good or by compensating him.

Voluntary Chain Store. See *chain store* (2).

Voluntary Group. See *chain store* (2).

Wages, the price paid for the service of labor in a unit period of time; usually restricted to payments based on hourly earning rates, or on rates per unit of production, as distinguished from salary. Various theories of wages have been proposed from time to time and economic understanding of the factors influencing the wage rate is still developing. For a discussion of the principal theories, see *marginal-productivity theory of wages, subsistence theory of wages,* and *wages-fund theory.* See also *surplus value.*

Wages-Fund Theory, the economic theory that at any given time there is only a fixed sum of capital set aside for the employment of workers and that the only way wages can be increased is to reduce the number of workers or increase the amount of capital. The increase would come from profits, thus reducing savings which provide the capital from which the wage fund is derived. This theory was generally abandoned in the late nineteenth century and was largely replaced by the marginal-productivity theory of wages. See also *subsistence theory of wages.*

Wall Street, a street in the financial district of New York City. The term is used in a general sense to refer to the large financial interests of the country that have their offices in the financial section of New York City.

Warehouse, a building in which property is stored. A public warehouse is one that will accept goods offered for storage by anyone who pays the charges. The public interest in warehouses has brought them under government regulation. A *bonded warehouse* is one under the supervision of the government in which goods may be stored without the payment of customs duties. Goods brought into the country and intended for export are stored in bonded warehouses to avoid the payment of import duties.

Warehouse Receipt, a certificate listing and describing goods in a warehouse. It must be surrendered to secure delivery of the goods. While the goods remain in storage, the receipt is negotiable.

Warrant, a certificate giving a stockholder the right or option to purchase a stated amount of additional shares (either of the same or different class) at a specified price within a given time.

Watered Stock, stock issued by a corporation without receiving full value for it. One of the common methods of watering stock is to issue stock for property or services that are overvalued. If a corporation sells 1,000 shares of stock at $100 a share to investors and then gives another 1,000 shares of stock in payment for property and services really worth only $50,000, the stock is said to be watered, for the corporation has issued $200,000 worth of stock and has only received $150,000 worth of assets in return. The essence of watering stock is the over-valuation of assets, which may be done innocently or with intent to defraud.

Wealth, 1. Abundance of material goods; riches.

2. In economics, something that has exchange value. In order for a thing to be considered wealth in the economic sense, it must have four attributes: it must have utility, that is, it must be desired to satisfy human wants or needs; it must be scarce, that is, it must not exist in such abundance that anyone can have as much of it as he likes—air is not scarce and therefore not wealth; it must be material or concrete in nature; and it must be transferable so that it can be given to another person or its ownership can be transferred to another person. Money is not wealth because it is not useful in itself.

Wholesale Price Index, a price index designed to measure the changes in average prices paid by business firms for the commodities they buy. The U.S. Bureau of Labor Statistics issues indices for the prices of some 2,000 commodities.

Wholesaler, any middleman who is not a retailer, that is, does not sell to the consumer. Wholesalers sell goods for resale or for manufacture or remanufacture. In present usage *jobber* has the same meaning as wholesaler, though originally it meant one who owned and sold odd lots or job lots.

Wildcat Strike. See *illegal strike.*

Withholding Tax, any tax that is collected at the source, particularly a federal or state income tax collected for the government by the employer by withholding the amount of the tax from the wages and salaries of employees. See also *pay as you go.*

Working Capital, 1. The amount of capital needed to carry on a business, as distinguished from the capital invested in fixed assets. See also *fixed capital.*

2. In accounting, the excess of current assets over current liabilities. Synonym: net working capital.

Yellow-Dog Contract, a contract of employment by which an employee agrees as a condition of his employment that he will not join a labor union; generally illegal in the United States.

Yield, 1. The percentage of annual return on an investment; if $50 is received in annual dividends from an investment of $1,000, the yield is said to be 5 per cent.

2. In industry, the amount recovered from processing or refining.

—Donald T. Clark

Introduction to education   609
History of education   612
Philosophies of education   622
Educational structure   625
Curriculum   638
Educational statistics   644
Bibliography   647
College profile   648
Junior colleges   711

VOLUME EIGHT

EDUCATION

FUSCO/LOOK

Education

INTRODUCTION

This is an age of multiple revolutions. The ways in which we produce goods, educate our people, use our leisure, relate to our fellow men, and govern ourselves are subject to continual change. New ideas developed through scientific research are so quickly applied to daily life that even experts cannot keep up with the details.

Today the individual must seek education as a means not only to wealth and status but also to understanding. The uneducated man comprehends neither his personal nor his civic duties. Ignorance is a dead weight that presses down upon the United States and threatens its survival as a moral and political force.

Fifty years ago most people did not go beyond grade school. Industrial society still required plenty of hard labor; thus, a limited education was sufficient for the man who had to live by the sweat of his brow. The automation of the 1960's, however, while increasing productivity, is wiping out many unskilled occupations. Manufacturers and merchants demand trained workers to operate complex equipment. The factory hands, clerks, and elevator operators of yesterday are found in the unemployment lines of today. Even the machines that require human operators can be handled only by skilled technicians who have at least a high school education. Workers displaced by automation must either go back to school to receive new training or work only part-time, if at all.

The student who drops out of high school simply does not have the knowledge to hold a job in an age of advanced machine technology. He finds himself drifting from one dead-end job to another; he is unemployed, perhaps on public relief, in the intervals. The youth who is determined to go his own way will learn that he faces a life of needless poverty unless he gets at least a high school education.

There is some comfort in the fact that a smaller percentage drops out of school now than ever before. However, 7½ million dropouts will probably enter the labor market between 1960 and 1970. They will face very stiff competition from the 23 million graduating from high school during this decade, not to mention the three million housewives returning to work.

An additional problem is that the rate of job formation has decreased from about 1.9 per cent per year in the period 1947–1957 to about .9 per cent from 1957–1962. Fewer than ½ million new jobs are opening up each year—and none at all in the unskilled groups for which high-school dropouts are suited.

Struggle for Jobs.—The effects of the battle for jobs are already being felt. During the school session of 1962, there were 600,000–800,000 unemployed youths between the ages of 16 and 21. They represented about 7 per cent of the labor force, and 18 per cent of the total unemployed—and they stay unemployed longer than older workers. It is not unreasonable to expect that many, perhaps most, of the 7½ million dropouts in the 1960's will face long periods without work. Some of them will never find jobs. They will be hit hard at the very beginning of life, when hope should be at its highest and expectations should know no bounds. These young people must be brought back into the mainstream of education before they suffer a loss of faith in themselves, and perhaps in democracy.

Education is every bit as important to the nation as it is to the individual. Our mobile population needs good schools everywhere, not just in the suburbs. Overcrowded, understaffed schools whose teachers are poorly prepared, schools with modern stadiums but obsolete libraries injure not only the community but the entire nation. We have not demonstrated our awareness that education is the one investment that always pays off. Analysts estimate that more than 40 per cent of the growth in national productivity and almost 25 per cent of the increase in the gross national product in recent decades can be traced to a greater investment in education. Thus, educated manpower is more important to economic development than any other single resource.

Certainly, technicians and professionals are in great demand everywhere. Professional positions requiring 16 or more years of education are increasing more rapidly than positions in any other section of the labor force. Since 1952, jobs in this group have risen from 4,500,000 to 7,500,000. They will go up an additional 40 per cent to 10,700,000 by 1970. Not too many years in the future, the professionals will be the largest single group in the labor force. It should be obvious that people must be educated to meet the

increasing demands of such technical industries as electronics, aerospace, and atomic energy. To waste our resources of human brainpower is even more foolish than to squander our natural resources.

Whether education will receive the attention it deserves at the national level depends upon the force of public opinion mobilized to support it. People must be persuaded that education is the basic business of human society, that it enlarges the horizons of all who take it seriously, that it is a key element in the preservation of democratic values, and that we cannot maintain world leadership without educated minds. There are, unfortunately, too many people who do not take education seriously. To them it is a game, a means of keeping up with the Joneses. They want their children to "get an education," as they call it, but their interest is not so much in knowledge itself as it is in performance measured by the report card. We must educate, not pretend to educate.

It is difficult, if not impossible, to make up tomorrow for today's neglect. While we debate, the problem of the untrained, uneducated youth grows steadily more insoluble. More and more jobs are being automated out of existence. A report of the Fund for the Republic states that every job that can be automated by putting present knowledge to use will actually be automated within 20 years. If this forecast is accurate, thousands of additional occupations in middle management, the professions, and in the skilled trades will become obsolete.

It used to be that an occupation was taken up for a lifetime. Now, however, a young person may change occupations one or more times before he retires, and he may be required to retrain between jobs. Education is a lifelong pursuit, and it is abundantly clear that education cannot stop with a high school diploma or even a bachelor's degree.

Occupational Training.—If there were any further need to prove the importance of education in the economy, one could mention the Manpower Development and Training Act (MDTA). This legislation was passed by Congress in 1962 to provide occupational training for some of those who have been automated out of their jobs. It was found that many people applying for this training could not read, write, and count well enough to learn their new jobs. To solve this problem, some applicants are now taught reading, writing, and arithmetic as part of their training for jobs as auto mechanics, draftsmen, welders, electronics workers, and nurses' aides. This kind of education is bound to pay for itself many times over.

The lifetime difference in income between a man with a marketable skill and a man without one is about $50,000. The skilled worker earns more and spends more throughout his career. His job is probably much steadier. Therefore, skilled workers circulate more money in the economy, experience less unemployment, and are less likely to go on relief or spend time in jail. The result is greater prosperity for everybody: reduced unemployment insurance costs, lower welfare payments, and less crime and juvenile delinquency. To take one example, a special vocational education and counseling program under MDTA that was set up in the District of Columbia may eventually return as much as $45 million on an investment of less than $200,000 —a return of 22,500 per cent!

If we as a nation fully appreciated the importance of education today, we would offer modern vocational courses in all of our high schools. Every student should be able to get training in any occupation for which there is a market demand. If we fully appreciated the importance of education, we would provide better equipment and curricula to encourage potential dropouts to stay in school. We can never get them to stay if we offer courses that do not lead to jobs after school.

On the other hand, occupational training must not be weighted too heavily on the side of any specific job, because changing technology quickly outmodes this kind of information. Practical training must expose the student to many technical and general subjects. Such a student will always be able to find a job. He can move without delay to something else in his area if his job is automated. He will have a greater choice of jobs, will not suffer long periods of unemployment, and will contribute to and benefit from a much more flexible labor market.

If we really understood the value and importance of education in an age of technology, we would provide greatly expanded facilities for adults who want to return to school. More than eight million Americans 25 years and older have less than five years of schooling; more than 22 million have less than an eighth-grade education. Because they can barely read, write, and count, these people cannot find or hold jobs. They face a life of poverty and third-class citizenship. They are found across our nation, not just in one area or population group. In New York State, the number of adults who have less than five years' schooling is nearly 800,000. In Texas it is 672,000; in California, 505,000. In 15 states the figure exceeds 200,000. Eight states have 100,000–200,000.

Problems of Minority Groups.—Many of the poorly educated belong to minority groups that have not fully participated in democracy and free enterprise. They bear a heavy burden of past discrimination. Their fundamental problem is that they have not had free access to our better schools —or to any schools at all. President Kennedy stated the unpleasant facts in his civil rights message of June 1963. "The Negro baby born in America today, regardless of the section of the nation . . . has about one-half as much chance of completing high school as a white baby, one-third as much chance of completing college . . . one-seventh as much chance of earning $10,000 a year."

What is worse, the gulf is widening rather than shrinking because the Negro is out of work longer and more often than his white fellow citizen. The unemployment rate for Negro boys is 21 per cent; for Negro girls, 28 per cent. In some areas, the rates are much higher. This situation is more understandable when we remember that Negroes work mainly in unskilled, semiskilled, and service jobs that have high turnover and pay little. Some of these occupations are disappearing altogether. The economic costs of low Negro productivity are estimated at a staggering $14 billion to $17 billion each year.

Negroes and other minorities have a great potential that education could help them to reach fully. If the millions who are not well educated could go to school in their spare time, they would eventually add tens of billions of dollars to the economy. If a man or woman is unemployed for just one year, it costs the nation more in lost production and purchasing power than it does to send that individual to public school for 12 years. Therefore, no one should claim that we cannot afford adult education. The fact is that we cannot afford not to expand it. It should be given as high a priority as any other kind of investment in human resources.

Meaning of Education.—So far we have spoken almost entirely about the economic benefits and problems of education. But if education were only an economic matter, it would be a dull subject indeed. Actually, education expresses the ultimate beliefs of a people: their strengths and weaknesses, their values and priorities. In democratic countries, the condition of the schools is a reflection of the public attitude toward education; it is an index of support or apathy.

In the United States, education has had a practical flavor from the very beginning. The earliest schools were attached to religious congregations and were designed to produce ministers of the gospel. Later, when public grade and high schools were widely set up after the Civil War, agricultural, mechanical, and other vocational subjects often were taught. From 1920 until about 1950, a leading concern was adjustment, with emphasis on being a good citizen and getting along with one's fellows.

Today, however, a new value is being placed upon education. We now realize that the primary goal of education should be to inform, expand, and exercise our minds. If it fails to do that, it is wasting our time and the community's money. We have already seen that the individual who is not broadly educated is an outcast condemned to drift in a changing and uncharted world. There are too many people "at sea" today simply because of our neglect. Moreover, had we properly supported our schools in the past, we would now command far more knowledge and vastly greater powers of creative expression. Our civic character would be more praiseworthy, and democracy would be stronger in the great ideological struggle that is now raging throughout the world.

One of the chief values of liberal education is that it can cultivate a genuine cosmopolitanism. Education suited to the requirements of the present age would assure us an understanding and appreciation of other cultures; it would promote our participation in international cultural and economic activities. Without the perspective that such an education can give, we cannot hope to satisfy the requirements of world leadership.

We are engaged in a world struggle with totalitarian states whose emphasis is on iron discipline, collective action, and collective thinking. In such countries, the individual is little more than a tool of the government. If we are to compete successfully, we must do everything in our power to develop the potential of individuals, to show the superiority of a social system organized from the bottom up rather than from the top down. Through education we can develop a genuine individualism that encourages and protects independence in thought and action. In the past we have been so anxious to accommodate the student to his social and educational surroundings that we have endangered individualism. However, if our nation is ever to develop its true potential, we must use education to invest the individual with a sense of civic purpose and the mental and moral discipline required of a responsible citizen in a free society.

SIOUX CITY JOURNAL

HIGH SCHOOL dropout and what lies ahead.

Urging that education better satisfy our changing social needs and international obligations does not mean that the multitude of small tasks in our complex social order should be allowed to dictate school curricula. In the past, in trying to relate education to daily life, we too often dissipated our energies on trivia that have no rightful place in a pattern of formal instruction. Rather, a mastery of fundamental principles in the humanities, in the social and natural sciences, and in technology is the only goal that can mean anything to the individual, either economically or culturally, or serve the long-range interests of an advancing society.

Education in America is important, too, because it seems destined to become a major testing ground for one of the basic ideas inherent in democracy. This basic concept is that when the good of the individual is intelligently pursued, the general welfare is enhanced. The task of educators and of an informed public is to organize the educational system in such a way as to help the individual to achieve personal growth and understanding, to cultivate to the maximum his intellectual, moral, and aesthetic capacities. It is not enough to supply him with facts that often have only incidental or temporary importance. He must acquire the tools of learning; he must learn to read, to think, and to communicate. He must be creative when he applies his learning. He must be able to employ the scientific method. He must be detached and yet committed to human betterment. He must be tolerant, informed, and independent. Such a person will be genuinely free and will partake of the full range of world cultures. He will protect and perpetuate the institutions of a free society.

There are still too many people who consider education as training, as of only occupational, economic, or technological importance. It is true that we are called upon to provide new ideas to solve the growing scientific problems of our culture, but we must guard against the tendency to suppose that our well-being is served primarily by advances in technology, however vital or timely they may be.

Well-rounded Curriculum.—Knowledge is of value for its own sake as well as for its uses, and unless the sciences are supported in their own right, the capital of new information upon which technology draws will inevitably diminish. The social sciences, the humanities, and the fine arts are more important to personal fulfillment than the disciplines of physics and engineering that now make possible our military and political preeminence. The study of politics, history, and philosophy is fundamental to any self-governing society, and no nation can achieve anything worthwhile unless its character is expressed in great literature, music, and art.

Whatever some may believe, we cannot afford anything less than the pursuit of excellence. In the past we followed a laissez-faire philosophy of education. We tolerated mediocrity

FRANCIS KEPPEL, former United States Commissioner of Education.

because we were unwilling to pay the price of rigor and perseverance. We tried to tell ourselves that because all men are equal under the law, they must be held to a norm in school. This was a perversion of equality and a betrayal of the democratic spirit. Not all men are of equal capacity, but all should have the opportunity to develop to the fullest, so that each can make his contribution to our common life. There was never any sense in demanding the same average level of performance from everyone. Very slow learners and very fast learners were uncomfortable in this system and were deprived of their self-respect. The one failed and the other loafed. It is a tribute to the great importance of education that these undemocratic practices are being changed. Today we must educate the whole man, and gear our policies to that aim, freeing each man's full potential.

Planning for Tomorrow.—It would be foolish to deny that notable quantitative gains have been made in education over the years. Our literacy rate is now rising. We are spending more money on public education than ever before. Some of our schools are the best in the world. Nevertheless, we are reaching for better quality at all levels, realizing that we no longer need to devote precious time to meretricious frills in order to demonstrate our concern for the student or to prove our emancipation from the classical European pattern of education. We are focusing our attention on course content because one cannot know anything in general without knowing something in particular. We are finding that it is not necessary to abandon learning in order to reach the student. Indeed, the contrary is true; today's student often demands more than his teacher can give him.

The knowledge that must be taught today vastly exceeds the levels of two or three decades ago, both in quantity and in complexity. By the year 2000, the amount of information in the natural sciences alone will have increased a hundredfold since 1900. The students of today are learning more than students used to, of course, but they are still not learning enough. A variety of modern techniques are needed to teach them the facts and principles they must know. Teaching machines and programmed textbooks, educational television, new curricula and methods of organizing classes will all be important.

The great national debate on the nature and purpose of education can be attributed in part to the fact that we are a society of diverse groups, with interests that sometimes conflict and never wholly coincide. It also derives from our uncertainties and anxieties. What it shows most emphatically, however, is that our understanding of the importance of education is not complete. We shall have to spend much more on education if we are to make it the superb instrument of human welfare and progress that it should rightly be. More buildings, new equipment, more and better-prepared teachers, more scholarships, higher salaries, and expanded course offerings are vital.

Money alone cannot solve our problems, but without it we cannot solve them. If we do not spend more freely, we will become a second-rate nation. The Soviet Union has given us a good example. Ten per cent of the Soviet budget every year, or $8.9 billion, is devoted to all forms of education. This is a remarkable figure for a country still relatively poor.

In the past we have confidently assumed that our nation and its values would be preserved, come what may. We have believed ourselves to be on the side of right and that right would ultimately prevail. Now we are beginning to realize that a people must be strong and wise, as well as right, in order to survive. This is not a question merely of our contest with foreign powers. There is a feeling that scientific culture, though it was created by man, is a juggernaut out of control, that it has lost its human scale and is no longer responsive to human needs.

A partial answer to this analysis is that a scientific society came into being to satisfy certain needs and that it will last so long as it continues to satisfy them. If we want our 3,000-year-old Western tradition to endure in this world, however, we will have to provide a much greater investment in, and commitment to, education than anything heretofore envisioned. The time is coming when education will be the principal activity of mankind. In the words of Alfred North Whitehead, "The race which does not value trained intelligence is doomed. Not all your heroism, not all your social charm, not all your wit, not all your victories on land or at sea, can move back the finger of fate. Today we maintain ourselves. Tomorrow science will have moved forward yet another step, and there will be no appeal from the judgment which will be pronounced on the uneducated."

—Francis Keppel

HISTORY OF EDUCATION

In speaking of education and civilization, George S. Counts of Teachers College, Columbia University, once said: "An education can rise no higher than the conception of civilization that pervades it, provides its substance, and gives it purpose and direction." It is equally true that people cannot escape the imprint of the educational process to which they have been subjected; in a sense their destinies are shaped by the kind of education that they receive. By delving into the history of education, we can best see the results of the juxtaposition of education and civilization—what the consequences have been for society in the past and, more important, how future educators can best apply the lesson of history.

Education in the Primitive World.—The beginnings of education can be traced to the early tribes who accumulated a body of knowledge derived from their successful experiences in the struggle for survival. Much of what trial and error had proved reliable was retained and passed on to the young. In transferring skills from one generation to the next, primitive man became the first educator.

The prevalence of fear, characteristic of our earliest ancestors, was the impetus behind primitive man's educational pattern. From an inability to understand the phenomena of nature arose the customs and taboos. Those who showed an ability to propitiate the good and evil spirits became the *shamans* (witch doctors, medicine men, and priests), a respected tribal class that provided the rituals in which the young were instructed.

From his need to protect himself against marauders, primitive man evolved survival techniques that every child was expected to know before being accepted as an adult member of the tribe. Boys performed feats of strength and demonstrated their ability in hunting, fighting, fishing, weapon manufacture, and survival. Girls were examined for their knowledge of traditions, laws, dances, and the rituals for pacifying or enhancing spirit influences. The teaching during this period was done by priests and other elders; completion of the children's training session was celebrated with feasts and dancing.

The education of the primitive peoples was suited to their needs. It was only as man's needs became more complex that the educational process became more intensive and refined.

Education in the Eastern World

■**CHINA.**—A discussion of the intellectual side of Chinese life must necessarily center around the ideas of Confucius, whose teachings have affected the thoughts and activities of people in all parts of the world.

Confucius did not formulate his own system of thought; his writings are a distillation of the accumulated knowledge of centuries. The educational philosophy that Confucius' writings reveal is synthesized in a

NEW YORK PUBLIC LIBRARY

ANCIENT CHINESE scholar, locked in a cell, taking the thirteen-day government tests.

comment from his *Analects*: "To him who has no enthusiasm, I shall not open up the truth, and I shall not help anyone who cannot express his ideas." His disciples, however, did not follow Confucius' teaching precepts. Instead of drawing out the pupil, they forced him to learn through memorization.

The educational pattern was structured so that the child under seven was taught at home. He then attended an elementary school at which he learned to read and to copy the sacred books. Status was achieved by passing rigorous government examinations that lasted for thirteen days and were held in locked cells. As on the lower school level, the student was graded on his ability to memorize. Few persons studied for these tests because the preparation required wealth and time. Those who passed, however, were given the privilege of holding office.

The fatal drawback in Confucian education was its inflexibility and its commitment to the status quo. The avowed purpose of Confucius was to reform society by means of the moral standards and conventions of the ancients. This dedication to an established order paralyzed the imagination of the people. Thus progress came to a halt.

■**INDIA.**—One of the world's most stringent Hindu societies arose in India. Its limitations as the basis for an educational system resulted from its adherence to the caste system as an appropriate social structure. In the highest position were priests, followed by warriors and rulers. The third caste was made up of farmers, merchants, and artisans; in the last group were the *sudras,* or servants. All others were outcasts and untouchables. The priestly caste was given the responsibility of teaching; all boys received religious training, but further education was determined

by the limits of caste. According to Hindu thought, the members of different castes were as unlike as dog and cat. Each was made to serve a different purpose, and to suggest that they mingle or receive an equal opportunity was thought contrary to nature. In the highest castes the boy was first taught religion and later trained to be a merchant, an artisan, or a priest. His early education was received in the home, after which he made an intensive study of the sacred tracts. To become a priest, he spent another twelve years in college, learning by memorization and imitation. The studies, limited to ancient knowledge, were all in Sanskrit. Girls received no formal training, but were taught homemaking and child care by their mothers. All children were taught respect for rulers and parents.

The limited educational opportunities provided by Hinduism discouraged progress and produced a society entrenched in outdated custom and ritual. Only since World War II and the improvements in communications has this situation begun to change.

■**NEAR EAST.**—The Hebrews, the most literate people of their time, were the only ancients who gave educational opportunities to every member of society. Thorough religious training was essential for every member of the Jewish community because of the coalescence of spiritual and national ideas. Hebrew nationalism was fostered by a belief in an omnipotent God, Jehovah, who called upon the Hebrews to live a cooperative life of grace, thereby fulfilling their destiny as His chosen people.

Formal education began in a school attached to the synagogue, where scribes taught the children to read and write from the holy books. School was held from dawn to dark, with no vacations except on holy days. The students learned by memorization and repetition; writing was taught by having the child copy the scriptures on wax tablets. Discipline was harsh and in keeping with the advice of the Talmud: "Children should be punished with one hand and caressed with two." Elementary school was compulsory for all boys. Those who wished to go on began intensive studies of the whole body of written and oral law, known as the Torah. Rabbi Isidore Epstein of the Jews' College, London, stresses the importance of this study for the Jewish people: "Torah connotes the whole body of Jewish teaching, legislation, practices, and traditions that have proceeded from the interpretation and reinterpretation of the laws of the Bible according to the light of reason and the principles of righteousness, justice, and equity, as well as any modifications, made by the spiritual leader, that are applicable to changed conditions of life—economic, domestic, and social."

The education of women was geared toward training them for domestic and marital life. Their status in the Hebrew community was higher than that of women in any other society. The high regard in which Jewish women were held is explained by the Hebrew teaching that only in the married state could sanctity be realized. Both parents were responsible for a child's early training, and they were also required to continue their influence throughout his life. Thus no one could afford to be uneducated; the untrained were merely a burden to the community.

Scholars believe that this educational system preserved the unity of the Hebrew people and gave them the moral discipline that prevented their extinction.

Education in the Western World

■ ANCIENT GREECE.—The content of ancient Greek education was influenced largely by the Homeric poems (the *Iliad* and the *Odyssey*), which long remained the standard texts for elementary students. Children heard these stories in their home from elders and minstrels; thus a standard ideal of the gentleman and his role in society was transmitted from generation to generation.

School life was centered around the home, where girls learned their domestic responsibilities, or the court, where slaves taught the skills of the artisan. Craftsmen were highly respected and received their training as apprentices. Only the slaves were not formally educated. At puberty, noble boys joined their fathers to listen to the discussions of the elders in the council of nobles. The efforts of the classes were integrated to better serve the state. The slave cared for the land of the noble while the latter went to the wars, where he protected himself with weapons made by the artisan.

■ CITY-STATES.—With the formation of city-states, the Greek people were subjected to different influences that determined the direction of their educational system.

Sparta was dependent upon her military power to control her peoples as well as to defend herself against hostile neighbors. Thus Spartans were educated to become part of a military machine devoted to perpetuating itself. Intellectual and artistic ability were stamped out. At an early age males were taken by the state to begin their training as soldiers. They lived in barracks, were taught by officers, and spent most of their time with military comrades. Any development of individualism was curtailed. Instead, Spartans were taught only the arts of general utility—endurance of hardship, brevity of speech, and, where required, lying and stealing. Taught at home, girls learned to be as strong and courageous as their brothers.

Athens, on the other hand, was dedicated to the growth of individuality. Pericles, the ruler during the golden age of Athens, synthesized the state's philosophy of education: "In education we do not resort to laborious drilling from childhood on, but we get satisfactory results. We combine love of beauty with economy, and love wisdom with manliness. We blame not poverty, but laziness, and we expect a citizen not only to manage his own affairs but also to be an adequate judge of political questions. . . . In a word, our city as a whole is the school of Greece. . . ."

As opposed to his Spartan counterpart, the Athenian student became proficient in the Three R's, in gymnastics as well as in philosophy, grammar, music, and dancing. Discipline was mild, and the student was taught self-control. The aim of education was to develop the capacities of each individual, thus enabling him to make a social contribution.

■ ROME.—The education of the early Roman was a practical one, aimed at producing a well-informed servant of the state. After receiving early training at home, the youngster learned agricultural skills, the laws, the ballads, and the history of the people. Next he began the military training essential to every Roman boy in his future role as an active soldier. At all times he was reminded that to be a good Roman he must develop the virtues of bravery, dignity, prudence, justice, and reverence for the gods.

Once Rome triumphed, however, she was influenced by the cultures of her subject peoples, particularly the Greeks and the Hebrews. The pattern of education changed from one that molded every man similarly to one that gave a far broader education and trained men to serve society. An excellent school system was designed. The youngster learned his letters in an elementary school, and

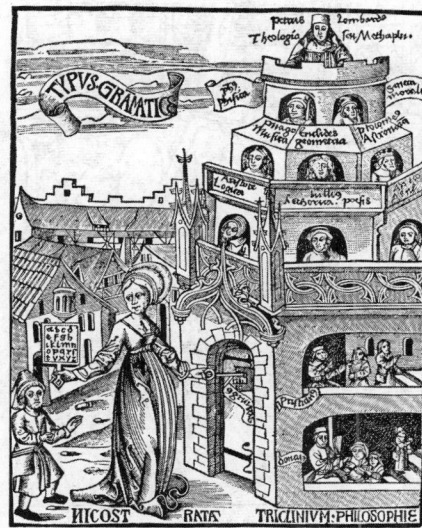

NEW YORK PUBLIC LIBRARY

TOWER OF KNOWLEDGE showing the progress of the curriculum in medieval Europe.

at ten he began his secondary studies —literature, geography, history, mythology, and the natural sciences. At sixteen he specialized in ethical and cultural studies, and at eighteen he entered a university, where he developed his practical skills.

The serious drawback of the Roman educational structure was that it educated the majority of its people for public service, rather than for education's sake. Consequently the society had no trained people to replace a corrupt ruling class, and the Roman state began its fatal decline. Had the state promulgated a school system for all the people, its history might have been very different.

■ MEDIEVAL EUROPE.—From about the sixth century through the eleventh century, the last stronghold of education was the Christian monasteries. Here the devotion to Christian doctrine was so strong that monks removed themselves from the external world to better contemplate the teachings of Christ.

These men formed groups under the leadership of one whose learning and piety they admired. One of their most important functions was to copy ancient manuscripts and thus keep learning alive.

Earlier the monastic orders had accepted as students only those who desired to join the community. However, the effectiveness of monastic instruction attracted the attention of the wealthy, who persuaded the monasteries to accept their sons as students or who invited the monks to establish schools in their courts.

Sporadically, during the early Middle Ages, the Church prodded its parishes to establish schools. Not until the eleventh century, however, did another type of school become more common than the *monastic school*. The *cathedral school* began to flourish because its notable teachers attracted students. Many of these schools became universities. Among them is the University of Paris, which had its

ALINARI-ART REFERENCE BUREAU

ROMAN SARCOPHAGUS depicting the elders using scrolls to educate a young Roman boy.

VICTORIA AND ALBERT MUSEUM

APPRENTICES were young boys trained in a specific art or trade by skilled masters.

origin in several cathedral schools of Paris. In the later Middle Ages more parish and secondary schools were established. The parish schools were also called *song schools* because music was incorporated in their elementary curriculum.

The feudal system gave rise to an unusual form of education. Knighthood, the aim of youth, was achieved only after a rigid preparatory course. From birth until seven, the boy was trained by his mother. He was then sent for seven years to the house of the feudal lord, where he was educated by the ladies of the court. After completing his training as a page, he became a squire for another seven years. Finally, at the age of twenty-one, he became a knight.

Because the Church was the most dominant organization of the age, great feudal armies voluntarily formed Crusades to regain the Holy Sepulchre from the Turks. These Crusades caused the breakdown of the small feudal kingdom; they also stimulated trade, the establishment of towns, and the rise of a merchant class.

This new commercial class grew very influential. Merchants organized towns free from the power of the nobility, and instituted schools for their children. The program of instruction for these youngsters was very practical and prepared them for work in commerce. They learned reading and writing, with emphasis on arithmetic, so that they knew how to calculate costs and prices. They received not only formal education in the administration of business, but also a practical education from the relatives whom they joined to observe the actual work. The elementary schools were supported by the merchants and were administered by priests. A significant educational innovation was the use of the vernacular as the language of instruction. Schools doing this were called *vernacular schools*.

■**RENAISSANCE EUROPE.**—Scholars agree that the period between the fourteenth and sixteenth centuries was the rebirth, the renaissance, of man. Its origins can be traced to the late Middle Ages, when the crusaders first linked the outside world with Europe.

Man began to stand up and look about. Commerce brought him quantities of goods that made life more comfortable; his demand for more goods encouraged greater trade and fostered organized manufacturing.

The scholar, too, looked up from his limited manuscripts at the wonders of the world and yearned to probe the mysteries of nature and man. Until then, his area of study had revolved around a view of man as a creature destined for fulfillment in the next world. Now man was becoming more secular and individual. He was pulling away from the dogmatism of the past and revolting against the autocracy of the clergy.

Interest in classical learning was revived. This revival first occurred in Italy, where many *court schools* were opened and supported by the nobility. Each noble, in the earlier period, organized a school only for his children. Later the children of his peers were accepted. These court schools were the forerunners of the modern boarding school. At the age of nine boys learned to read and write; for the following ten years they studied the classics, manners, morals, and the social arts. Girls remained in the home, where they were taught reading, writing, and court graces. Individual attention was given to every child, and the discipline was mild. The later *grammar school*, the *lycée*, and the *gymnasium* were modeled after the court schools.

In northern Europe the emphasis was less on aesthetic education and more on moral-social education. Here the individual was educated to help improve society. The classics, particularly religious literature, were taught, and students learned Greek, Latin, and Hebrew. Like the boys in the Italian court schools, these youngsters began at the age of nine and moved up in ten steps, or forms. The schools were supported by tuition and eventually became preparatory academies for the universities. History, geography, science, music, and art were later included in the curriculum.

The origins of elementary education for the ordinary people are also found in the Renaissance. Kings who fought Church control believed that the common man should be educated, and they patterned elementary schools after the vernacular schools of the merchants. It is believed that these institutions were the forerunners of the national and state school systems.

■**REFORMATION EUROPE.**—In the sixteenth and seventeenth centuries, man strained against his political, economic, and ecclesiastical shackles until he broke them. The Reformation was a result of Church and government competition for control, the impact of humanism, the emergence of the new sciences, the broadening of man's world view, and the strength of economics. In some countries these events brought a shift in power from the Church to the government and the merchants.

Despite the move toward greater materialism and secularism, the schools remained in the hands of the churches. Protestant leaders believed that all should be taught to read and write, and that they should receive instruction in manners, morals, and singing. Martin Luther, who was a prime advocate of change, believed in primary education for all boys and girls, but secondary study only for a selected few. The ideas of Luther and of other Protestant figures (Knox and Calvin) focused on education as a means for moral training. The Bible was the primary textbook, and the teaching of religion was of primary importance. Civic education was included in the curriculum, but the state was considered subordinate to the Church in all educational matters. The school system was twofold. In primary education the vernacular school of the Middle Ages was adapted for the masses and was supported by the state. The teachers were harsh, and children learned by memorization. Secondary education was restricted to sons of leaders and to those who desired to enter the ministry.

The progress made by the Protestant movement brought a counter-reformation by the Catholic Church. As part of its reform movement the Church encouraged the establishment of parish schools. A number of religious communities, or orders, took over this task. Among these were two that have made significant contributions: the Christian Brothers and the Jesuits. The former taught the children of artisans and the poor, while the latter confined their work to the secondary level. The orders' purposes were to teach religion and to prepare both lay and clerical leaders. The children entered the parish school, where they were taught the basic subjects and catechism. Few girls attended school until the teaching orders grew more numerous. (Girls were taught, however, as early as 1535 by Catholic sisters.)

On the secondary school level the

NEW YORK PUBLIC LIBRARY

JOHN AMOS COMENIUS, noted educator, formulated "ladder system" of education.

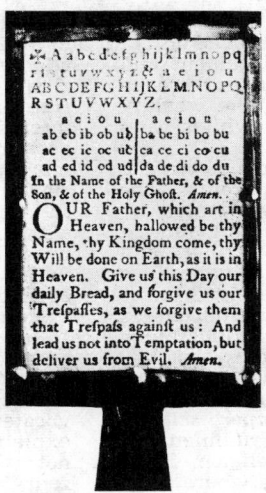

NEW YORK PUBLIC LIBRARY

ITALIAN picture poem (*above*). Eighteenth-century primer (*right*).

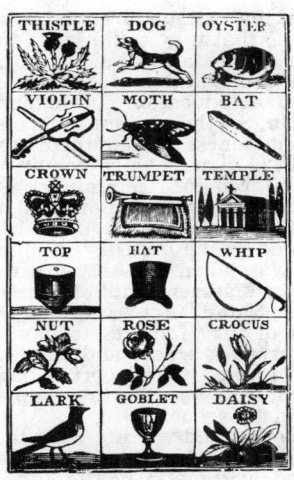

HORNBOOKS (*above*) and the New England Primer (*below*).

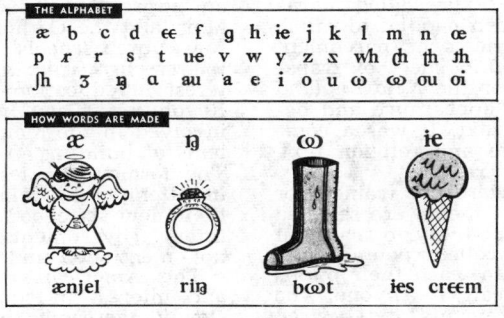

INITIAL TEACHING ALPHABET PUBLICATIONS, INC.

INITIAL TEACHING ALPHABET represents the 40 basic sounds of the English language.

student received an education that, while broad, was quite classical. Besides learning Latin, he studied Greek, logic, rhetoric, mathematics, ethics, metaphysics, and natural science. These were strongly tied to the religious writings of the Church Fathers. Discipline was strong, but not harsh. The Jesuit schools were open to all without fee, and the student continued his study as long as he met the standards of the Society. The Catholic orders made two significant contributions to education: a program for the preparation of their teachers and a very highly organized structure for school instruction.

Education attracted the attention of many leading thinkers of the Reformation period—Rabelais, Milton, Bacon, and Montaigne. Another was John Amos (Komensky) Comenius of Bohemia, who advocated patterning the educational program on the natural capacities of the child. Now our basic pattern, this approach is called the "ladder system." He suggested that the child move from one grade to another. Comenius believed that the child should be taught by his parents under the guidance of a teacher. At six the child would enter elementary school, to leave at twelve for six more years of secondary study. If he qualified, the boy would then enter a university at eighteen. He would remain there for another six years. Comenius also recommended a nationwide system of schools, with an elementary school in

every village, a secondary school in each city, a university in every province, and a research center to which scholars from all over the world would be invited. The doors, Comenius claimed, should be open to all without charge. His plan came to fruition only at the end of the nineteenth century.

■INDUSTRIAL-REVOLUTION EUROPE.—Until the latter part of the eighteenth century, goods were painstakingly produced by hand. Consequently, man had few leisure hours; his economic survival depended not only upon his own work but also upon that of his children. The time which in a later age would be allotted to education was given to production.

Beginning about 1760, there was a switch from hand to machine production, made possible by new inventions. With the growth of the factory system, workers and children found themselves exploited by the owner of the factory, the capitalist on whom they depended for employment. Gradually, however, the industrialized society produced organized groups determined to uphold the interests of the worker against the demands of his employer.

One of the demands of organized labor was the establishment of universal and free public education. In America this struggle was led by Horace Mann and Henry Barnard. By the second half of the nineteenth century, free public schools and compulsory attendance had been won.

Education in the United States

■COLONIAL AMERICA.—The settlements in colonial America clustered all along the eastern coast of the New World. The composition of each section differed; the educational pattern in each was characteristic of its people and their beliefs.

Most of the early settlers, from the Protestant countries, came to America because they desired greater religious freedom than was possible in the countries of their birth. Religion was uppermost in their minds, and the schools they established had one purpose—the training of future church members.

The schoolhouses of the colonial period were no more than shelters. There were no conveniences. The pupils sat on rough, backless benches without, in most instances, a desk board. The rooms were very cold, unsanitary, and dark. School began at 7 A.M. and was in session six days a week. The teacher was a harsh disciplinarian who freely used a whip and forced children to stand for hours. Although schools were open ten months of the year, the average pupil attended about four months. These conditions did not change until the eighteenth century, when newer European philosophies of education were introduced.

■NEW ENGLAND COLONIES.—The Puritans who settled in *New England* believed that the state should be built on a strong religious base. They were the first settlers in this country to require that all children be taught to read so that they could learn the precepts of the faith and know the law. The Puritans attempted to accomplish universal education through instruction in the home, but this method's ineffectiveness forced them, as early as 1642, to pass laws requiring that all children in a community be educated. By 1639 the Puritans had set up a secondary school for boys interested in the ministry. A significant step was taken in 1647 with the passage in Massachusetts of the Old Deluder Satan Act, requiring every town of fifty families to pay for the support of a school and each town of 100 families to support a grammar school. This was the first step to tax-supported schools.

Reading and writing were taught in all the schools, but only a few included arithmetic in the curriculum. Materials and teaching methods were poor. The first texts, called *hornbooks*, were wooden paddles to which were attached sheets of parchment covered with a thin sheet of transparent horn. Later the *New England Primer* made its appearance and became a popular text. It was a combination language and religion text, with emphasis on religion.

The teachers were not trained for their tasks. These men were selected not only for their ability to read, but also for their excellent penmanship, since they were to teach their pupils to write "artistically." Anyone who met these requirements and desired to teach could do so, provided he was approved by the local minister. Among tasks other than his teaching, the teacher took care of the church, directed the choir, rang the church bells, dug the graves, and in some instances was the town crier. Girls began their schooling in neighborhood homes and were admitted to the schoolhouse after the boys had left for the day or during the vacation periods.

■**MIDDLE ATLANTIC COLONIES.**—The peoples who settled in the *Middle Atlantic colonies* came with different traditions and backgrounds. Scots, Irish, Germans, Swedes, Dutch, English, Welsh, Finns, and French Huguenots—all Protestants but representing different churches—settled here.

The result of this national mixture was an educational pattern different from that of New England or the South. The desire to educate all children was not as strong as in other areas because the settlers did not appreciate the need for an education that embraced more than the techniques of food production and self-protection. As a rule, each religious denomination founded its own school, which it supported with church funds or private contributions; a minister was assigned to teach only reading, writing, and religion. Attendance, unfortunately, was irregular because children were required to remain at home and work on the land as soon as they could handle the tools.

■**SOUTHERN COLONIES.**—In the *southern colonies* great plantations were cut from the land. Although many of the families that settled here left England because of the rising power of the Puritan commonwealth, their underlying purpose was profit. The requirements for the management and operation of a plantation nurtured a society of three classes: the wealthy whites, the indentured whites, and the Negro slaves.

The education of the child was the responsibility of the parents. The children of the wealthy, tutored by teachers who lived with the family, were taught reading, writing, and numbers before being advanced to the classics. They also received introductory training in Latin and Greek, in science, history, and philosophy. After finishing these studies, the children were sent to England to complete their education. The children of the poor went to *pauper schools*, where they learned the rudiments of reading, writing, and religion. Some sections provided schools where these youngsters learned vocational skills in an *apprentice-training program*. In Maryland the Catholics established a few church schools.

■**AFTER THE AMERICAN REVOLUTION.**—Interest in education waned after the Revolution. The United States was involved in the many complex problems of building an enduring nation. The former colonies were entangled in attempts to define the rights of their new statehood and those of the infant government. Education was not mentioned in the Constitution.

The American resources, energy, and interest in education, however, slowly overcame the inertia of the postrevolutionary decades. An attempt to strangle a faltering government failed with the War of 1812. In the war's wake came a pride that again tied the American citizen to his democratic dream and that also gave birth to a national awareness.

The first *public high school* in the United States was opened in Boston in 1821. American educators were adopting the philosophies of Pestalozzi and Rousseau, and learning turned from memory work to motivation of interest in study. Science, drawing, geography, mental arithmetic, and music were introduced into the curriculum; and the teacher looked upon the youngster as a growing personality rather than as a child who needed to be disciplined. The first *normal school* for training teachers opened in 1823 at Concord, Vermont.

Manufacture and industry increased, and trade grew. This business activity stimulated the growth of an urban population, which in turn brought attention to education. Advocates of mass education spoke out, explaining that a democracy could not exist without an enlightened citizenry. The great battle for free schools began. In the meantime, numerous schemes were tried to promote the support of schools. Lotteries, land grants, and private contributions were used to support some schools, but all of these attempts failed. Although the suggestion that schools be tax-supported by each state was bitterly fought by the churches, it was finally realized this method was the only way to achieve mass education. DeWitt Clinton and Abraham Lincoln were among those who led the battle for free schools. By 1860 the American public school system was established in the populous states of the North and was being written into the constitutions of the new states. The concept that education was the right of every American child found fertile soil and took root.

■**AFTER THE CIVIL WAR.**—The free, tax-supported school spread westward; by the post-Civil War period, few communities were without a school. Only

ADDISON GALLERY OF AMERICAN ART

"SCHOOL ROOM," by an unknown artist of the 1830's, depicts rigid methods of discipline.

the South was slow in adopting the idea. However, in the wake of its reconstruction it, too, established public schools. Public funds for the erection of school buildings and financial support for educational programs created a new profession, teaching. States soon passed laws requiring training for those who desired to teach.

As the strength and wealth of the United States increased, the nature of the school changed. Most important in this changing nature was its acceptance as a new institution in the culture. School buildings were designed with attention to comfort, light, ventilation, safety, and beauty. Some of these buildings can still be found in the large cities. The number of textbooks increased. Pencils, paper, erasers, and blackboards became common tools. The curriculum, too, changed. Toward the end of the century, the states had passed compulsory attendance laws.

This period brought another significant change. Massachusetts gave rise to the public-supported high school when it passed a law requiring the maintenance of a high school by every town of 500 householders. Educational leaders, together with workingmen's associations, fought for free secondary education. This struggle was more bitter than that for the free elementary school. Not until 1872 was the battle won by the Kalamazoo, Michigan, decision that made the high school a part of the public school system.

■ SINCE 1900.—The battle for free public elementary and secondary schools was over by the turn of the twentieth century. The American people had established a national school pattern financed by the local school district and the state. In the early twentieth century American education developed from a narrow and somewhat rigid structure to one that encompassed all levels and walks of life. Considered a vital tool for democracy, education was also viewed as an institution that combined preparation for life in society with opportunities for individual growth. This philosophy was realized in the expansion of education.

The United States became an experimental ground for educational ideas. The thoughts expressed by Jean Jacques Rousseau, Johann Pestalozzi, Friedrich Froebel, and William James, Samuel Hall, Edward Lee Thorndike, and John Dewey were tried with various adaptations and ultimately gained at least partial acceptance in the educational continuum. America had grown tremendously, but was young enough to listen and to try. New faces appeared on the educational scene to lead the discussions for a more effective program. Among them were Franklin Bobbitt, W. W. Charters, Charles Judd, William H. Kilpatrick, William Reavis, George S. Counts, and Axtelle. The past had opened a new frontier, and America tried to see what could be made of it.

The *ladder system* became the educational organization. The child moved from one grade to the one above as he completed his studies. Each step

LIBRARY OF CONGRESS
KINDERGARTEN in the North-End Industrial Home, Boston, served working mothers.

MUSEUM OF MODERN ART
INDIVIDUAL attention, too often an educational luxury, helps motivate the child.

took a year and had its program of study. The sum of the steps equaled enough educational training to prepare the child for living in society. Beginning his schooling at six years, the pupil could finish his elementary program by age fourteen and his secondary education by age eighteen. Basically, this is still the educational pattern. The elementary school provides the child with his fundamental education; additional subject content and vocational preparation are given on the secondary level. The college and university offer a variety of programs for specialization.

Once this ladder pattern was established, Americans began to adapt it to suit the developing nature of the child and the changing American society. The basic design was extended and expanded. Kindergarten training was added. The Three R's of elementary school were strengthened by the addition of more subject matter— history, science, art, crafts, and music. The high school moved from a traditional classical curriculum to a comprehensive program that would give the youngster a broader background. The larger cities established technical-vocational high schools whose programs offered academic study with preparation for a vocation. The colleges changed from strictly liberal arts institutions to those emphasizing specialization as well.

In this century the 8–4 ladder system has been changing to the 6–3–3 scheme (primary, junior high school, and senior high school). The college pattern has changed to 2–2–1–3 (junior college, senior college, graduate, and advanced graduate). The adoption of these altered organizational patterns was encouraged by findings in child development research. The results of studies of the nature, needs, and development of the child were applied to teaching. The child was no longer viewed as a vessel into which

knowledge should be poured; rather, he was considered as one who could learn more rapidly if treated as an individual who must be guided by the teacher.

The strength of American education is largely dependent upon the teacher. At the beginning of the twentieth century the requirements for a teaching degree rose considerably, from a high school diploma or one year of college to a college degree. Those who prepare for teaching, in addition to the accepted courses of studies in liberal arts, now receive special training in psychology, sociology, child development, and teaching methods. Another prerequisite for a degree is practice teaching.

The American school system offers a complete education to a child. The schools have become an accepted part of our culture, and their support by public funds is unquestioned. In the course of the century the school system has met the challenge of an increasingly industrial society by the addition of technical and vocational programs to its curriculum; it has assisted in the assimilation of the children of millions of immigrants; it has broadened its scope and in many locales offers, besides the regular program, nursery education, after-school and evening activities, day camp and school camp programs, adult classes, special classes for the handicapped, and junior college study. In no other country has education permeated the society as successfully as it has in the United States.

Modern Schools and Changing Patterns
■ SCHOOL BUILDINGS.—When the graded school became common, city districts constructed two- and three-story plants. The rooms were placed around a light-well and balcony, with as many as 21 rooms plus a principal's office included in a single building. This type of school may still be seen

MARCEL BREUER & ASSOCIATES ARCHITECTS

A MODERN TREND in academic architecture is exemplified by this high school gymnasium-auditorium. Architects are designing separate buildings for each educational activity.

in the United States. Later an auditorium, a teachers' room, a playground, manual training rooms, music rooms, and domestic science rooms were added. This remained the basic school design until the 1940's.

■**ELEMENTARY SCHOOLS.**—The elementary school building is no longer the formidable, destruction-defying structure of three or four stories. The change in its architecture is due largely to Lawrence Perkins and Phillip Will who, with Eliel and Eero Saarinen, designed the Crow Island School of Winnetka, Illinois, in 1939. This one-story building provided a large classroom, an adjoining workroom, and access to a patio-work-play area. The ceiling height was lowered from twelve feet to nine feet, and light was diffused equally to every area in the room. Storage space, bookshelving, green chalkboard, a sink, and a lavatory were built into the classroom, which was fully exposed to natural light on two sides. At the time of its construction, this design was a bold break with the classic elementary school plant.

The modern elementary school is a low, one-story building housing an auditorium, a gymnasium, shower rooms, a cafeteria, art rooms, science rooms, music rooms, and a library. Each classroom is designed for a particular age group and contains equipment suitable for these children. Light-colored walls and desks, fluorescent lighting, heat and ventilation, green chalkboards, large bulletin boards, a sink, plenty of storage space, and even a small toilet for the little ones, complete the room. There is also equipped play space with allotted areas for all ages, as well as a parking lot and a bus station.

■**HIGH SCHOOLS.**—The high school building, too, has undergone great changes in design. The newer plans call for the construction of four wings,

one for each grade level, with shops, laboratories, gymnasium, auditorium, and administrative offices conveniently situated. The purpose is to house each age group together. Each wing contains the latest equipment, and there are playing fields for all sports and activities.

In an even more recent plan the academic, vocational, and physical education–auditorium spaces are housed in separate buildings that are attached. This design is a harbinger of one that will allow separate buildings for each educational activity within a large campus.

■**CITY SCHOOLS.**—Because of limited space, school planning is a problem in the big cities. The new buildings, some as high as nine floors, are equipped with elevators and escalators to speed the movement of students from class to class. Architects and educators are planning elementary schools on the first three floors of large apartment buildings. One board of education is toying with the idea of constructing a school on steel stilts to provide a play area under the building at street level.

Self-contained Classrooms and New Arrangements.—Self-contained classrooms are the more common arrangement in the elementary schools. Each teacher is assigned to a classroom, where he remains throughout the school year, teaching a class the various required subjects for that grade.

The high school is organized differently. Since all the high school subjects cannot be taught competently by one teacher, the classroom arrangement is by subject—English, science, mathematics, and so on. All the teachers who instruct in one area are in that particular department.

These two arrangements are highly modified plans borrowed from Europe, changed in America to meet the

demands of a growing school population. Essentially, the classroom arrangement has been patterned on the industrial assembly-line concept in order to expedite the flow of pupils.

■**DALTON AND WINNETKA PLANS.**—Further experimentation in the education field grew out of a dissatisfaction with the impersonality of an instructional organization that emphasized group teaching and showed little regard for the individual child. This was education, but hardly the kind that permitted a child to grow fully.

One of the first new experiments was the *Dalton Plan,* begun in 1919 in Dalton, Massachusetts, by Helen Parkhurst. Her plan was based on the principles of freedom, group interaction, and individual participation in learning. Each child contracted to do an assignment during the month and worked at it daily, assisted by his teacher. The plan worked within the traditional school organization.

A second innovation was the *Winnetka Plan,* sponsored by Carleton Washburne in Winnetka, Illinois. Here the pupil progressed at his own rate of achievement, often pursuing a different goal in each of his subjects (i.e., he might be well advanced in arithmetic, but retarded in the language arts). The idea was for the pupil to reach goals that would lift him to higher levels of learning. In the Dalton and Winnetka plans the pupil was always aware of his standing in each subject and had time to do individual study.

Today the organization of an elementary school classroom is more flexible. Although there is a specialized teacher for each class, the pupils are still involved in the activities of other classes. The teacher is assisted by specialists in art, science, physical education, music, and crafts. Some schools have introduced the teachers' aide plan, whereby nonprofessional persons are given the responsibility of clerical work, cafeteria supervision, monitoring, and other duties that decrease the time a teacher has for instruction. In some communities the local Parent-Teachers Association sponsors a volunteer teachers' aide program.

■**STAFF UTILIZATION PLAN.**—Although the high school continues to maintain a traditional pattern, some breakthroughs have occurred. One such change is the *staff utilization plan,* begun by J. Lloyd Trump. Its advocates believe that the high school of tomorrow will not have standard classes set to a rigid schedule; no longer will a subject be taught by only one teacher. This plan is organized around three activities: large-group instruction, individual study, and small-group discussion. The large-group activities are conducted for 100 or more students by a teacher specialist who is assisted by several general teachers. The student then has time to do individual study and to participate in small-group discussions conducted by the general teachers. In this plan more youngsters are taught in large groupings by fewer teachers, and they are given an opportunity to study alone and with small groups under teacher guidance. The atmosphere of freedom permits the student to develop his abilities.

Other Educational Innovations.—Begun in 1952, the educational television movement has steadily grown, with the Federal Communications Commission allotting a number of stations for educational purposes. Research findings show that television teaching is as effective as conventional teaching in the fields of music, general science, spelling in the primary grades, and English composition on the high school level. The medium is equally effective in teaching college courses, particularly general psychology, general chemistry, and business law.

Where educational television offerings are available, some schools have added them to their regular classroom programs. In New York City over seven hours of educational programs suitable for school children are telecast daily. Chicago and other large cities have regularly scheduled television lessons for pupils on all levels. In the Middle West, Purdue University sponsors a flying television station. From thousands of feet up, the programs can cover a wider area. New methods of filming and improved techniques in electronic transcription make it possible to distribute and retelevise the lessons.

Provisions for television are included in the design of the newer school buildings because closed-circuit television facilities enable educators to plan and present material that supplements classroom instruction. Only television sets connected to the circuit can receive the programs. With a coaxial cable as many as six different programs can be

carried simultaneously, so that six separate television courses can be conducted simultaneously during each instruction period.

Educational television has already proved effective in adult education. The Sunrise Semester courses of New York University, the program of the University of Pittsburgh, and a variety of classes from other educational television facilities have already made a considerable impact. Clearly, television as an educational technique has enormous potential.

■**LANGUAGE STUDIES.**—The teaching of foreign languages in the elementary schools has grown rapidly since 1950, but the idea is not really new. Cleveland, Ohio, schools had a large-scale program in the 1920's, as did, later, San Diego and Los Angeles, California, and some cities in New Mexico and Texas. Also, parochial schools for many years taught German, Polish, Italian, Lithuanian, and Greek as second languages to first- and second-generation children of immigrants.

The influence of World War II, the rising interest in intercultural understanding, and the desire for enrichment have encouraged the foreign-language movement. The teaching may begin anywhere between the first and sixth grades. Generally 15 to 20 minutes are devoted each day to language study. The "hearing-speaking" method is used (i.e., children are taught by listening and then speaking). In some programs writing and grammar are introduced in the fifth grade. Should this trend continue, it is possible that foreign languages as second languages will be taught on an elementary level. Thus the high schools will be forced to revise their programs, thereby re-

lieving the colleges of teaching the relatively elementary phases.

Critics of this movement state that the learning of two languages in childhood is detrimental to competence in either. Those who favor early learning of foreign languages explain that teaching the second language is not meant to develop a bilingual child, but only to aid the gradual development of an auxiliary language. The movement is faced by two important problems: a scarcity of competent language teachers and an already full elementary school study schedule.

Language study on the secondary level has taken a new turn. Until recently the modern languages emphasized reading competence, not speaking skill. The reverse is now becoming true, for there is a strong emphasis on speaking competence as the most important phase of language study. Electronics aids the high school in the form of the *language laboratory*. In the model language laboratory the students sit in booths equipped with earphones, microphones, and control switches. The instructor sits at a large control console overlooking the class. Within his reach are controls for transmitting tape recordings and for receiving the questions of the students. The teacher can communicate with all or any of the students, and lessons are transmitted from prerecorded tapes. This device permits a student to select any lesson, which is then automatically transmitted. He can also record his voice and play it back to evaluate his speaking competence. A government appropriation has financed the installation of such laboratories, over 5,000 of which are already in use in the public schools.

FAIRCHILD INDUSTRIAL PRODUCTS

LOOK MAGAZINE

FAIRCHILD MARK IV system (*left*) runs like a projector with program cartridges but functions like a television set with controls. Also used in language teaching is the laboratory (*right*), where each child is able to listen to taped lessons and then to his own voice.

26 To an Egyptian of 5,000 years ago, it didn't make any difference whether

he showed 13 as $\text{III}\cap$ or $\cap\text{III}$

Show two ways he could have shown 18. ***

$\text{IIIIIIII}\cap$ or $\cap\text{IIIIIIII}$ (any order)

27 Which of these choices has a value of 113?

(1) $\cap\text{IIII}\,\text{9}$ (3) $\text{II}\cap\text{I}\,\text{9}$ (5) all of these

(2) $\text{9III}\cap$ (4) $\text{9}\cap\text{III}$ (6) none of these

(5) all of these

28 In other words, the position of the numerals made no difference to the Egyptians.

If you take the numerals 9, $\cap$, and II and put them side by side

in any order, you will always get what value? *** (in our numerals)

112

LOOK MAGAZINE

TEACHING MACHINES (*left*) use programmed sheets such as the one above. These have a question and a space for the response; correct answers appear with a turn of the dial.

■TEACHING MACHINES.—Training devices, or *teaching machines,* have been in use for some time. The Link Trainer, a device that simulates the flight of an airplane, is used as a training aid by most airlines. A mock-up of an automobile has been used for many years in driver-training programs. Football, basketball, and baseball coaches have used many mechanical devices as teaching aids. Because of the shortage of instructors during World War II, the military forces used training devices to teach men to operate a radar set, to fire at moving targets, to learn the location of instrument controls while blindfolded, to handle the controls in dummy submarines, and to acquire the technique of bringing in airplanes on a mock-up carrier deck. Later the military developed machines for teaching elementary subject matter in arithmetic, electricity, accounting, and similar fields.

Sidney Pressey, a pioneer in automated teaching, presented teaching machines that tested students in several areas of study. He also developed several others that taught spelling, arithmetic, and other subjects by the drill method. He found that pupils liked to work with these machines that helped to save the teacher's time.

Teaching devices have become even more popular since World War II. Their cost, however, has made them somewhat expensive for common classroom use. Today this method of teaching is known as *programmed learning.* The machine is really a device that contains and controls the material as the student studies. The lesson to be learned is programmed, or written, to shape responses. If the answer is correct, the machine allows the student to go on to a higher level;

if the response is incorrect, he returns, depending upon the kind of error he has made, to material from which he learns enough to make a correct answer. The new method of programming is a contribution of Dr. B. F. Skinner who, with his students, has written very successful programs in spelling, arithmetic, mathematics, and other subjects.

In the past the teaching machine has been used in training people to solve problems. It is now used in all types of instruction. It appears that teaching by machine will find a place in the school because it saves so much of the teacher's valuable time. Its most important contribution, however, will be in its potential for systematizing study. Teachers, television, textbooks, encyclopedias, and films will, of course, still be necessary.

■DATA PROCESSING MACHINES.—Another school innovation is the use of *electronic data processing machines.* A great amount of information about the students is accumulated by a school during the year; but its processing, if done by hand, can take a long time. Too often it is never completed because of the shortage of time and skilled assistance. Electronic data processing machines can handle large amounts of information in a short period of time.

Some educators envision an "electronic school," in which the drudgery of correcting and grading papers, keeping records, writing report cards, obtaining and returning books from the library, will be eliminated. Each pupil will sit at a desk that has a panel of buttons and switches, a television screen, earphones, and a microphone. After the teacher has assigned a lesson, the pupil will study. In the course of this work, should he

desire further information about a certain aspect, he presses a button and speaks his request into the microphone. Instantly the page of the book he requires appears on the screen. The student may wish to view actual movies or photographs depicting some facet of his study. A flick of a switch, a spoken request, and the film appears on the screen. Next, he may want to acquaint himself with the sounds of a particular historical period and its music. Another order as he dons his earphones, and his request is fulfilled. He informs the teacher when he has completed his study, and receives a test paper. He answers the questions by pressing the proper buttons or by speaking into the microphone. Within seconds of the test's completion he and the teacher know his grade, with a complete rundown of his errors and a correction of his spoken words.

A specially designed room of this "electronic school" houses the equipment that sorts and controls the huge amount of knowledge necessary to its pupils. Included in this equipment are computers that record the answers of the pupils and quickly calculate scores, errors, and corrections.

Data processing is used in many schools today to schedule classes, to keep day-to-day accounts of expenditures, to determine the best bus routes, to find the most convenient sites for buildings, to record and report grades, and many other tasks.

At the same time that data processing machines are reducing clerical costs, they are also providing school administrators with day-to-day information about the achievement of each grade in all subjects, the daily attendance, and the patterns and trends of enrollment in the school

MCGRAW-EDISON COMPANY

EDISON RESPONSIVE ENVIRONMENT machines, used by kindergartners who teach themselves to read. They learn letters, then words and pictures, sentences, and finally stories.

district. A teacher or counselor who desires detailed information about a particular student and his achievement can have it almost immediately. Within minutes an instructor can have information about the progress of his classes, how they compare with others in the district and in the country, and their strengths and weaknesses. Data processing machines have considerably shortened the time needed to prepare analyses and have thus given teachers and administrators an earlier opportunity to study the various problems and decide on their proper solutions.

Perhaps the day is not far off when a pupil who is doing his homework may need more information for study. By merely dialing a number and making his request, he may be able to obtain the answer.

Measuring Knowledge.—Man has always had some yardstick for testing or measuring his abilities. Quite early in the existence of mankind, man observed the differences in the abilities and aptitudes of children. He sorted them out as potential warriors, fishermen, farmers, medicine men, and artisans, then proceeded to train them for these roles. The Romans, Greeks, Hebrews, Spartans, and other ancient peoples, after observing the boys, classified them according to the strongest tendencies they showed. As man's knowledge became greater, it was natural that he compare one man's knowledge with that of another and hold the more knowledgeable of them in higher respect.

■ **STANDARD INTELLIGENCE TESTS.**—But man was not satisfied; he soon wanted to know why and to what degree these ability differences among people existed. Not until the nineteenth century was a more precise measuring instrument developed. Alfred Binet formulated a test for determining the intelligence quotient of children. Through the work of Francis Galton, J. McKean Cattell, Lewis Terman, and Edward Lee Thorndike, the intelligence test was improved, and was used regularly in schools.

■ **CREATIVITY TESTS.**—Men still were unsatisfied. The striking differences among people in interests, abilities, ideals, social development, and emotional adjustment intrigued psychologists. Slowly the belief that each child is different from every other child was accepted, and teachers began to focus their attention on developing the child as an individual. Another new turn was made in testing. Havighurst and Davis showed that the I.Q. test used middle-class language not understood by rural and slum children and did not test these youngsters fairly. Wechsler formulated a test that measured more decisively the intelligence of any person, regardless of whether or not he could read. Torrance, followed by Getzells and Jackson, produced research findings that showed that the measurement of creativity is as good as, if not better and more important than, that of the I.Q. They contend that creativity is more indicative of intelligence than the ability to absorb and repeat knowledge. Another belief is that any child can be made bright by developing his curiosity and vocabulary.

USE OF TESTS.—Thousands of tests are used in the American public schools to assist the teaching staff. Achievement, I.Q., mental abilities, comprehension, attitude, interest, vocabulary, occupation tests, are only a few of them. In some school districts tests are given from the time a child enters kindergarten until he completes high school. Quite early an I.Q. test is given each child to determine how well he can do. As he continues in school, he is given an assortment of other tests that reveal how well he is progressing and whether he is working up to his abilities. A study of the test results gives teachers clues as to how the youngster can best be helped. Teachers, however, rely heavily on their own judgment coupled with the test findings, for they are aware that these instruments do not always correctly measure the youngster's knowledge and ability. The master teacher accepts these test findings as aids that help him to better understand the child, rather than as final results beyond which the youngster has no capability.

Tests are being used effectively by student counselors. The function of a counselor is to guide youngsters, particularly in high school, over the rough aspects in their schooling. A record of each student, containing his test results and other personal information, is kept on file. A study of the pupil's record aids the counselors in deciding on the guidance to give regarding study, choice of occupation, and selection of college.

—John S. Benben

LOOK MAGAZINE

CREATIVITY may be a better indication of a child's intelligence than the usual I.Q. test.

PHILOSOPHIES OF EDUCATION

Differences of Opinion in America.— Since its beginnings public education in America has been carried on in a context of competing beliefs and unresolved perplexities. The more complex the culture has grown, the more problematic has become the role of the "common school." Although it is over a century since such schools were founded, Americans have not yet agreed on whether "common" should be defined as "equal opportunity" or "equal excellence," with little agreement on the "truth" that must be taught to the young and less agreement on what constitutes the "real." Views conflict on the nature of the socially "desirable" and the "good," as well as on the values that the school is expected to pursue and the ideals toward which it is to strive. Despite this history of concern, philosophy of education is a twentieth-century product, observable mainly in the context of teacher-training.

These philosophies have differed in method and in concepts of learning and truth. They have set up divergent criteria in defining values; often they have differed in describing the nature of the persons to be schooled. But, whatever their ideational frameworks, they have shared a commitment to deliberate reflectiveness, a need for order, and a concern for seeing education as a whole.

Philosophy as a Discipline.—Philosophy represents a conscious effort to see things clearly and as a whole, to reflect on a wide range of experiences. It demands systematic thinking on the level of generality and on the level at which language and logic are examined and criticized. There are those who say that the discipline of philosophy is most adequately defined in terms of the questions to which it responds, as are most other disciplines.

Nature of Philosophic Questions.—What kinds of questions are philosophic? As in any discipline, they fall, roughly, into three categories: the analytic, the synthetic, and the normative or speculative. *Analytic* questions arise when the terms used in a given field are ambiguous or vague, or when theories are structured illogically. Such words as "common" and "equal" are considered, as are terms like "teaching," "learning," "thinking," "achievement," and others whose meanings need clarification if educational discourse is to proceed. Here, too, theories explaining education are examined—theories like those using "growth" as a premise, or "conditioning," or "training." Sometimes new theories are proposed and built.

Synthetic questions, on the other hand, deal with relationships of the many factors and forces in the field. When education is the object of study, such questions initiate organization of the various bodies of relevant factual information, both psychological and sociological. These are then brought into relationship with so-called *operative values,* the aspirations and

attitudes that affect program and policy in the schools. The philosophic purpose is to impose order upon a mass of discrete phenomena in order to compose an inclusive picture.

Most fundamental in the eyes of some philosophers are the *normative* questions, which promote the creation of values, and the *speculative* ones, which lead to the definition of possibilities and to views of the ideal. The school, more than most other social institutions, requires guidance by clear concepts of desirable social ends. Effective decision-making depends upon such concepts; without them educators cannot choose what knowledge and skills are to be taught or what methods are to be used in teaching them. The aims of schooling remain obscure when left to chance. Careful thinking must be done if a desirable way of life is to be delineated and if that delineation is to shape educational purpose and clarify instructional aims.

Approaches.—In the context of American society there is no single, official philosophy of education. In the discipline of philosophy itself there is no single approach to philosophic activity. Since philosophy of education was first defined as a discipline to be taught to teachers-to-be, four—and recently six—approaches commonly have been conceived as feasible alternatives. Originally, at the end of the nineteenth century, there seemed to be two definable points of view: traditionalism and the new education or progressivism. Forty years later *traditionalism* was subdivided into idealism, realism, and neo-Thomism, although the first two were occasionally linked as essentialism and the last coupled with Roman Catholic philosophy and labeled perennialism. On occasion, too, *progressivism* was subdued into the more traditional view, called "progressive," and an admittedly radical variant called "reconstructionism." After World War II, two additional positions began to suggest approaches to the educational activity: existentialism and logical empiricism, or analytic philosophy.

Dewey and His Predecessors

■**TRADITIONALISM.**—Philosophers, of course, have been concerned with education since the days of Plato.

Plato, St. Thomas Aquinas, John Locke, Jean Jacques Rousseau, and the other prominent philosophers who wrote about education tended, most often, to trace the implications of their general positions in order to define their ideas on learning and social life. Also, as in the cases of Plato and Rousseau, they usually confined themselves to discussions or descriptions of their conceptions of model systems and practices. Thus the discussions in *The Republic* and in *Emile* deal not with the problematic issues in contemporary educational activity but with ideal or imaginary schemes of what the writers thought education ought to be.

Men like Horace Mann and Henry Barnard, on the other hand, did concern themselves with the live issues in public education at the time. However, they developed their theories without specific reference to systems of philosophic thought. Their proposals, like the teachings of the earlier philosophers, provided background—and often matrix—for the educational philosophies to come.

■**PROGRESSIVISM.**—It was not until John Dewey confronted the unique complexity of nineteenth-century public education that philosophy of education began to emerge as an independent discipline. Dewey, as he pointed out in *My Pedagogic Creed,* was concerned with both the personal and social aspects of education. Beginning in 1894, he experimented with psychological theories of learning and behavior in the University of Chicago Laboratory School. At the same time he developed a conception of education as continuous with social life in general. The school, for him, was not to be a preparation for life, but "life itself," occurring in a deliberately created "miniature community" where children would learn how to deal with problems of cultural significance and personal relevance—and how to resolve them with the tools of reflective thought. The total enterprise was to be guided by a carefully developed notion of the "democratic" and the socially "desirable"; Dewey's educational work therefore was grounded in a philosophic point of view. As he said in *Democracy and Education* (1916), philosophy was "the theory of education in its most general phases," an articulation of what was involved in teaching the skills and habits most appropriate for settling the difficulties of contemporary social life. Dewey was not equipped to discuss education apart from the problems of knowledge, reality, and value.

This was largely because Dewey had a philosophic basis for his commitment to scientific method and to the naturalist conception of experience. Since his approach to instruction was new, or *progressive,* he had to defend it repeatedly and stimulate others to do so; the defense was couched in philosophic terms. His attack on the rigid, formalistic, classical education of the traditionalists was rooted in a charge that their theories were archaic, unsuited for the changing industrial society in which the schools were to play their part. Inevitably, the traditionalists counterattacked, generally on specific points. It was not until the fourth decade of the twentieth century that they found organized support.

Educational Philosophy in the 1930's.— In the intervening years philosophic questions about education had multiplied. Interest in them deepened as America's dynamic and unpredictable technology challenged the schools, and also as World War I undermined the belief that the world would be controlled by the rational minds of men. Economic difficulties were in the making; social relations were altering; moral confusions were deepening. In the flux and crisis of the 1920's and the 1930's, education was increasingly subjected to philosophic study in teacher-training institutions.

Influential colleges appointed faculty members who were deeply engaged in advancing Dewey's point of view, or *experimentalism*. They taught hundreds of students to think in the progressive tradition, to put their stress on the interrelations of school and society, to test values by their social consequences, and to orient themselves to the problematic, changing modern world. Despite prevailing opinion, this did not lead to a general reconstruction of American schools according to the progressive ideals. Administrators and policymakers sometimes used the language of progressives. Expanding knowledge of behavior, the ability to test capacity, the fluidity of the situation in which masses of young people were pouring into the schools—all these factors led to reforms and readjustments which occasionally corresponded to those proposed by the progressives. However, educational practice, then as now, was not proved to be the logical outcome of the prevailing theories about knowledge and value. There was little evidence that progressive teachers had themselves produced the changes on the educational scene.

The consequences for philosophy of education can be measured only through examination, once again, of teacher-training curriculums. Beginning in the 1930's, these consequences centered around the tendency to take an eclectic approach to the teaching of the discipline. *Eclectic* teaching meant the presentation of the full range of existing views in educational philosophy, views considered to be legitimate alternatives. It was held that a thoughtful comparison of the various approaches to each philosophical problem area would lead students to a critical examination of their own beliefs and assumptions. If they could be made aware and critical of their basic premises, it was thought, they might, if necessary, be able to reconstruct them. Each student was expected, after exposure to a survey of the field, to formulate a personal philosophy of education that would allow him to clarify his concepts of teaching and that would give him guidance when he was ready to play his part in the public schools.

The problem areas chosen for discussion were the traditional ones. The "nature of man" was dealt with, as were problems relating to the generic structures of "reality." There was the area of *epistemology*, having to do with the nature of knowledge; there was the area of *axiology*, involving the study and definition of values. Each philosophy of education was described in connection with those general areas. Within each, analytic, synthetic, and normative queries were dealt with implicitly or explicitly, depending on the bent of the philosophy concerned. More often than not, the presentation of an educational philosophy was preceded by a summary of the historic position from which it was reputedly derived.

■ IDEALISM.—Idealism was first discussed in its several historic manifestations. It might be traced back to Plato's conception of the realm of Ideas, which was to be apprehended through the dialogue, or by means of dialectical reasoning. The source might be identified in Christian philosophy, with its core belief in man's essential divinity. Alternatively, it might be located in Hegel's dialectical system and its culmination in Absolute Mind, or in Kant's vision of Pure Reason and the Will's autonomy.

Whatever origins were claimed, *idealism* as a philosophy of education placed its main stress on the spirit, on the untrammeled mind. The learner was conceived to be an essentially spiritual being whose self-realization involved a growing outward or upward toward union with the One— or the world community of souls, or the cosmic order, or the mind of God. The teacher, representing order and the unity of ideas, was to inspire the individual child to strive toward fulfillment. He was to set the child free for spontaneous self-activity and, at once, to nurture that freedom with the best of the human heritage—literature, history, philosophy, logic, and art.

Reality, according to the realist, was to be conceived as basically mental in character; for some, reality was identified with the encompassing Divine. Being mental, it was knowable by the liberated mind, or by intuition and imagination, which were to move through the mind's creations to apprehension of the All in All. There would be regard for scientific and spiritual truth in the classroom, since the mind's awakening depended upon the recognition of truth, on whatever level it was attained. However, in learning, the child would be engaged in reasoning more than in experiment; he would be helped to find his way through language, the symbol —through the Word.

Values were believed to inhere in the very structure of the moral universe. The teacher would reflect the best and the highest as he treated each pupil with care and regard, as he nurtured the child's spiritual potential, his uniqueness and dignity. His role would involve making each student aware of the part which each individual plays in the harmony of the whole. He would present models of dignity, courage, nobility, and beauty to each child, attempting to inflame him with a desire to reach beyond himself to join the world communion of free spirits.

■ REALISM—Realism can be traced back to the traditional materialisms, beginning with the atomism of the ancient Greeks. Hobbes belonged to this tradition, as did the empiricists John Locke and John Stuart Mill, as well as some of the nineteenth-century mechanists and naturalists. As a philosophy of education, therefore, *realism* laid its stress on structures, causal sequences, and connections in the lawful, material world as we know it.

For the realist, all depended upon training for intelligent acceptance of the reality that existed objectively, outside the minds of men. More important than individual flowering was an appropriate adjustment to "things as they really are." This adjustment was to be made possible by the selection of human capacities and tendencies whose cultivation was required by the constitution of the social and physical world. Among these was the power to exert effort in order to master essential knowledge. The realist would build a curriculum which would arouse children's interest in the "right" things.

Since the world could best be apprehended through mental activity, the realist would stress theoretical learning, understanding of accumulated knowledge, and respect for the truth—for its own sake. Values, for some realists, were inherent in the natural world; for others they were the objects of human interests, relative to particular societies. Depending on what interests were considered "right," certain values were more appropriate and more enlightened than others. Instruction in values would be similar to instruction in truth-getting; the objective would be adjustment to what was fundamental, what could be shown to be important in the meshes of social practice and natural events.

■ NEO-THOMISM.—There are points at which neo-Thomism was closely related to realism and other points at which it was related to idealism. A secular restatement of Thomist philosophy, it was oriented to higher education rather than to the public schools; however, its perceived implications made it one of the alternative positions. This philosophy stemmed from the thought of Aristotle and put its main stress on *self-actualization,* or the realization of those capacities which were "natural," those with which the individual was endowed. In spite of variations in capacity, human beings were believed to possess a common rational nature, which education was committed to release. Only if the mind was cultivated and set free could the individual realize his own capacities; only then could the intellect, unhindered by practical claims, pursue its proper quest. In the classroom this was to mean engagement in the liberal arts, or the great "conversation" of fine minds. It was to mean the pursuit of Truth in the "great books," movement toward moral certainty, and knowledge of the cosmic Absolute that imparted rational design to the world.

■ EXPERIMENTALISM.—There was a note of concern for the predetermined in all the traditional philosophies. For John Dewey and for the later experimentalists this signified a reliance on "spectator" knowledge, a concentration on passive learning of what adults—or authorities—considered right. Dewey had worked in the pragmatic tradition of William James and Charles Saunders Pierce, whose points of view had been distinguished by operational conceptions of meaning and truth. While their backgrounds were in the empirical tradition, experimentalists drew inferences quite different from those of the realists. Knowing as process and behavior was made focal. Meaning was defined operationally; the truth of a belief was sought in its consequences for experience.

Experience, for experimentalists, was the source of knowledge; it constituted the human being's "reality." The organism had in fact become human in an ongoing process of interaction with a physical and social environment. This interaction, or "transaction," with a dynamic world constituted experience; and human development demanded continuous reconstruction of it through intelligent reflection on the process. An individual could grow only as he perceived expanding meanings in his experience and as he made sense of his experience by coping with the novel predicaments of his life.

For education this meant a concentration on knowing as personal participation. The teacher, confronting diverse individuals, each with his own potential and his own experience with the common world, was to seek cues in each one's responses to the community life within the school. Each learner was to be guided by those cues, in terms of his own interests and curiosity, toward investigation of the problematic world. The curriculum, the heritage of accumulated knowledge, and the accumulated moral wisdom of the ages were to become resources to be consulted by each student as he sought, through deliberate inquiry, the answers to questions important to him. There was, therefore, no predetermined end to learning, since there was no end to the problems that would arise in experience. The objective would be to equip each student with skills appropriate to his capacities, with the ability to handle problems hypothetically and to live a life of intelligent participation, membership, and self-initiated growth.

Values, in no way objectively existent, were to be deliberately sought through the making of intelligent choices in the social world. The "good" was considered an emergent, defined by human beings in relation to particular life situations. At moments of doubt and conflict the person would be required to choose among alternative courses of action. An effective choice was one made after careful consideration of prevailing conditions (including existing value patterns) and anticipated consequences; the "good" appeared when resolution was achieved.

Dewey separated himself from both the "life-adjustment" movement in education and the extreme "permissivist" point of view, founded on either a theory of "felt needs" or "interest" spontaneously derived. In *Experience and Education*, written in the 1930's, he lashed out against the extreme progressivism which sacrificed commitment to experiment and belief in deliberate guidance to an unphilosophic and suspect notion of "freedom." Relativist and naturalist though Dewey was, concerned as he

was with developing an educational program appropriate to the cultural moment, he never belittled the role of subject matter in learning or the role of the teacher in guiding each child, by means of his own questions, toward mastery of relevant subject matter, membership in the community, and the expanding perception of life's meanings that signify "growth."

■**RECONSTRUCTIONISM.**—The traditionalists objected to the relativism of the experimentalist view, to its reputed preoccupation with practical results, and to its presumed neglect of essential theoretical learning. *Reconstructionism,* coming out of the progressive orientation, took issue with the concentration on methods and process. The world crisis, the reconstructionist held, demanded commitment and the definition of worthy goals derived from the known needs of human beings and societies. For him the public school was to be dedicated to social reconstruction, not simply to individual growth or to the cultivation of intelligence, which the experimentalist believed would transform the quality of social experience and, in time, create a richly democratic way of life. The reconstructionist attached more importance to the nonrational elements in culture, to the "group mind" and the uses of "social consensus." Not only would he orient the school to the problems of the environment; he would make it an agent for rebuilding the world.

The range of educational philosophies, then, extended from those preoccupied with the everlasting to those committed to advancing change. But eclectic presentation in the teacher education classrooms was not to last long after World War II. There were two significant reasons for the rise of "educational debate" in the United States and for the growing popularity of novel philosophic points of view.

After World War II.—The debate stemmed from charges that the public schools were insufficient, that they promoted mediocrity and neglected the "fundamentals" required by literate citizens. Representatives of positions linked to traditionalism mounted the attack; but most frequently it was couched in nonphilosophic terms, in language which the general public could understand. The response was, at first, defensive on the part of remaining progressives. Beginning in the 1950's, however, there was a general reformulation of the philosophic approach to education.

The revolution in the sciences did much to provoke it, as did the efforts among members of the learned disciplines to apply their specialized skills to a study of the public school curriculum. The "cold war" and the apparent need to compete with the Soviet Union generated further debate and investigation. At the same time, there was an increasing tendency among American educational philosophers to master the analytical techniques being perfected in the British universities. Some concentrated their efforts on language analysis; others worked with logical empiricism and attempted to purge edu-

cational discussion of its ambiguities, its value judgments, its unverifiable claims. Still others concerned themselves with the philosophy of science, which appeared, in the new scientific age, to hold promise of the methodological precision and clarity that educational discussion seemed to lack. In many colleges educational philosophy became a course in "analysis" of language, or the logic of theory-making, or the study of implications to be drawn from scientific "model-building." Philosophic training, in consequence, no longer involved exposure to a range of alternatives. Lacking reference to society at large or to matters of social moment, many courses now became modes of training in analytic skills.

■**EXISTENTIALISM.**—Simultaneously, interest grew in the "crisis philosophies," the world view called *existentialism.* Certain educational philosophers made this approach fundamental to their teaching of philosophic issues in education. Emphasis was placed on the difficulties of existence in a cosmos replete with injustice, lacking knowable evidence of purpose or moral support. Teachers holding this point of view were to concern themselves with the importance of individual choices and individual authenticity in a world threatening humanity today with conformity and dehumanization. In the existentialist classroom, literature was to receive primary attention, so that the learner, in his subjectivity, might engage in human predicaments vicariously and so discover what it would mean to choose himself in his "dreadful freedom" and achieve his identity, his "essence" in the open, dangerous world.

■**THE 1960'S.**—Invigorated by the analysts' concern for rigor and total clarity, and by the existentialists' sense of immediacy, educational philosophy opened a new chapter in the 1960's, in spite of attacks on teacher-training practices and on the discipline itself. If the "new education" meant primarily an incorporation of scientific findings into the educational process, this was being accomplished. If "traditionalism" signified, in part, a recognition of the need for structure, rigor, and purposiveness, it was finding acceptance among American schools. What remained was the need to develop a concept of education itself as a discipline, to apply philosophic method to the study of teaching operations and learning activities. Clarifying existing views of "thinking," "knowing," "explanation," "category," educational philosophy might be expected to bridge the gulf between science and the humanities, to integrate the many current researches into what human beings do when they reflect and when they learn. Applied at last within the schools, educational philosophy might be expected to clarify and articulate existing tendencies, to structure programs, to define desirable aims in a world where specialties multiply and problems never abate.

—Maxine M. Greene

EDUCATIONAL STRUCTURE

Rooted in the democratic system and essential to a pluralistic society, the pattern of American education has myriad facets and unequaled diversity. The "system" of education in the United States, if the term is at all appropriate, consists of two vast and complex subsystems—one public, the other private.

Free, universal, nonsectarian public education, as we know it in this country, is an indigenous product. More than 1,675,000 teachers, principals, and professors are regularly employed in public education in the United States. Private education, substantially smaller in the aggregate than public education, is nonetheless a great, ramified subsystem of educational enterprise. In 1964 public and private education together served better than 50 million of the 190 million in our population. The existence and continuance of both subsystems of education provide the means of schooling to which every American child has an inalienable right, and they assure that this right shall be exercised in the full freedom of the parents' choice. Through their own use as adults, and out of concern for their children's educational progress the people impel continual growth and expansion of the nation's schools, both public and private. In the course of such dynamic progress —and, it is reasonable to suggest, because of it—our public and private educational institutions are able to remain both separate and compatible.

Levels of Education.—As elsewhere in the world, the years of schooling in the United States are arranged in levels. Historically, there were three quite distinct groupings: *elementary school,* also known as primary school; *high school,* frequently referred to as secondary school; and *higher education,* which included everything that followed in public education. Nonpublic institutions also adopted these divisions. In many respects these basic groupings remain and give us the nomenclature of academic progression. Completion of elementary school is generally required for admission to the next level of schooling. In turn, enrollment for higher education is nearly always contingent upon a high school education, or whatever is equivalent.

The groupings are no longer as distinct as they were. Intermediate institutions now exist between elementary and high school, and between high school and the initial stage of higher education, called *college.*

Traditionally, elementary and high school education together demand 12 years of study. In some circumstances, students are able to fulfill the curricular requirements in 11 years or, if their proficiency and the educational resources warrant it, they may obtain some of the preliminary course work of higher education during the terminal high school year. State and local statutes in most areas fix the minimum age for a child's registration in the first grade of elementary school at six. Nearly all states require regular school attendance until a specific age, varying from 16 to 18. Thus, a child of six entering elementary school will be approximately 17 or 18 upon completion of 12 (plus or minus one) years of primary and secondary education. As many as half of the states now require completion of elementary school in order to be exempt from school attendance; 15 require completion of high school.

Public and Nonpublic Facilities.—Educational institutions at any of the three basic levels—elementary, secondary, and higher—are either public or private. Those that are public are supported and maintained at public expense. They belong to the state and are subject to both state regulatory and government operational control.

Nonpublic institutions, as all private schools are designated, may be subject to certain state regulatory controls, but their operational control belongs to an organization or a private individual. Their support does not come from tax revenue or other public funds. Depending upon the type of organization, level, purposes, and source of support, nonpublic institutions are variously termed parochial schools, independent schools, Latin schools, military schools, academies, seminaries, institutes, church-related colleges and universities, and private colleges and universities.

Public and nonpublic elementary and high schools together enroll more than 44 million students. Public and nonpublic institutions of higher education together enroll 4½ million.

At the primary and secondary levels, nonpublic schools sponsored and controlled by religious denominations are most commonly called *parochial schools.* Among the sectarian groups maintaining such schools are the Roman Catholics, Lutherans, Protestant Episcopalians, Seventh-day Adventists, Presbyterians, Friends, Methodists, and Orthodox Jews. Nearly 6½ million boys and girls, representing 14 per cent of the total number in grade school and high school in the United States, are enrolled in nonpublic institutions. All but 4 per cent are students in sectarian schools.

The Roman Catholic church estimates that 5½ million boys and girls are full-time students in its 10,600 elementary schools and 2,375 high schools. Approximately 85 per cent of all who attend nonpublic schools are enrolled at Catholic institutions. Schools of all other religious denominations together enroll about 11 per cent of the students in nonpublic schools.

In at least two cities—Dubuque, Iowa, and Manchester, New Hampshire—more than half of the children attending elementary and high school do so in Catholic institutions. In ten states no fewer than one of each five primary or secondary school pupils attends a Catholic school.

School Units—No single national pattern for the number of grades in a school existed in the early history of our public schools. Toward the end of the nineteenth century, nine-year elementary schools were common in New England, and seven-year elementary schools were general in the South. The earlier three-year high school course gave way to a four-year program. The predominance of eight-year elementary schools and four-year high schools in most of the country led to some standardization.

Near the turn of the twentieth century the junior high school movement began. It is now a part of the public school pattern in most of the United States. Most commonly the junior high school has included grades 7 through 9, but there are significant variations.

■**ELEMENTARY SCHOOL.**—At present, grades 1 through 6 are firmly established as the minimal province of the *elementary school.* Beyond the sixth year there are variations in the schooling patterns. In many localities a part of what was once called the *common school,* or the 8-grade elementary school, has been detached, either to constitute a new intermediate unit or to enlarge the high school

ROY DOTY

BREAKDOWN of sources of income received by public and private educational institutions.

LOOK MAGAZINE

KINDERGARTEN marks the beginning of a formal education, which continues through high school (*right*), college, and even graduate school.

program. It is usually grades 7 and 8 that are thus separated. In a small number of cases only grade 8 is detached. Conversely, in a number of private elementary schools, a ninth grade or ninth *form* (as their grades are sometimes called) has been part of the pattern or a recent addition.

The function of the elementary school, whatever its number of grades, includes teaching children the basic, or tool, subjects: reading, writing, arithmetic, and the subjects that extend from them.

■**THE JUNIOR HIGH SCHOOL.**—The intermediate unit between elementary school and high school is known as the *junior high school*. The elementary school is confined to grades 1 through 6, and similar accord exists with respect to grades 9 through 12 as the high school span; grades 7 and 8 have been the uncertain ones. With the exception of places where the older pattern of eight years of elementary school and four years of high school persists, and those in which there is a 6-6 pattern, public school systems use the three-unit plan of elementary, junior high, and senior high schools. More than half of all the communities in the United States now use the three-unit arrangement. The junior high school consists either of grades 7, 8, and 9 or of grades 7 and 8 alone. Junior high schools with grades 7 through 9 are twice as numerous as those with grades 7 and 8. In California there were a number of junior high schools that extended through grades 7, 8, 9, and 10. Virtually all have reverted to a three-year pattern.

The functions of the junior high school are generally agreed upon by educators. Its justification as an institutional entity, however, has been and still is the subject of much debate. The rationale of the junior high school is that its pupils, about 12 years of age, are adolescent, individualistic, and independent and thus must be treated differently from younger children in elementary school and differently from older ones in high school. The development of the junior high school has been described

as an outcome of greatly advanced understanding of child development, particularly that which took place during the first two decades of the twentieth century. It was then that adolescent psychology became a recognized branch of the behavioral sciences.

■**HIGH SCHOOL.**—The *high school*, or secondary school, has been the middle unit of schooling, preceded by elementary school and followed by higher education. During the nineteenth century a minority of those who completed elementary school went on to complete high school. Today the great majority of boys and girls do. The number of those going from high school to college is rapidly overtaking the number of those who do not. In the not too distant past, only a small minority went to college either directly or later.

The indicated change in the mean years of schooling for young people in America implies the enormous growth of the high school. This great expansion of secondary education is partly a consequence of the stricter compulsory schooling laws.

As the high school grew, it changed. In some respects the changes are as remarkable as the rate of growth. Different kinds of high schools came into being. The program was enlarged so that four years were required instead of three.

The typical American public secondary school is the *comprehensive high school*. As such it is uniquely a development of the United States. Several types of curricula, sometimes called *tracks* to denote direction and purpose, are used. These include academic or vocational, preparatory or terminal. That is, they emphasize either the liberal arts or studies directly concerned with employment skills and have one of two objectives: either to provide subject matter that anticipates and strengthens programs of higher education or to provide studies appropriate for a student not expected to engage in further formal education.

The *special high school* is distinct from the comprehensive high school.

It may be a commercial, technical, or, as with some private secondary institutions, a classical school.

A large category of high schools are the *vocational high schools*. Their programs include some of the so-called "general" courses offered in comprehensive high schools but emphasize work in shops of various kinds, mechanical drawing, electronics, printing, and training for various trades and crafts. The curriculum in many cases serves either as apprenticeship training or as preparation for entry into local industry.

The names of some high schools suggest the purposes they serve, all of them deemed to be within the realm of secondary education, at least by those localities in which they are established. There are the Boys' Trade and Technical High School in Milwaukee, the Polytechnic High School of San Francisco and, in New York, the High School of Art and Design, High School of Fashion Industries, Machine and Metal Trades High School, High School of Performing Arts, and the School of Printing.

The time span of high school programs varies according to the category of the school—comprehensive, vocational, or special—and to the state education laws. Thus, an area that has elementary schools with grades 1 through 6 and no junior high schools maintains high schools with grades 7 through 12. This is the 6-6 plan. Another area, utilizing junior high schools with grades 7 through 9, requires senior high schools with grades 10 through 12.

Patterns of Organization.—The Office of Education in the United States Department of Health, Education, and Welfare has determined the four most common patterns of public school organization in this country.

Approximately two-thirds of all the elementary schools in the United States contain grades 1 through 6. Of the remaining third, 22 per cent have grades 1 through 8, and 11 per cent have seven or nine grades.

High schools differ correspondingly. If no junior high school is involved,

BRIARCLIFF COLLEGE '64

CARTOGRAPHY, map making class at Briarcliff College, a private junior college for girls.

12 grades are divided between the elementary school and the high school. Where there is a junior high school, the 12 grades are divided among elementary school, junior high school, and senior high school.

Of the four most widely used patterns of public school organization in this country, the 6-3-3 plan is most popular. The 8-4 plan, with no junior high school, is next; nearly 25 per cent of all public education systems employ it. The 6-2-4 plan is third, with about 16.5 per cent of the schools arranged in this fashion. The last of the four most common patterns is 6-6, with an incidence of 14.5 per cent.

It was found that in large cities (at least 100,000 population) the 6-3-3 plan is the favorite. One-third of the elementary schools in the country (in towns of over 2,500) use it, as do two-thirds of those in large cities. In small communities the 8-4 pattern is dominant. About 30 per cent of the schools in the small communities have chosen this plan, and not quite 25 per cent have selected the 6-3-3 arrangement. In middle-size cities (over 10,000 and under 100,000 population) use of the 6-3-3 plan is almost 61 per cent; the 8-4 arrangement is used in 13.5 per cent of the middle-size cities.

None of the largest cities uses any one of three other major patterns— 6-2-4, 6-6, or 7-5. Except for about 5 per cent that have adopted the 6-2-4 plan, cities with populations of 25,000 to 99,999 also do not use them. In contrast, in cities of 2,500 to 24,999 about 19 per cent use the 6-2-4 plan, 13 per cent have adopted 6-6, and 6 per cent use the 7-5 arrangement.

From the standpoint of geography, the Northeast uses the 6-3-3 plan, to about the same extent as the nation as a whole. There is only a 5 per cent variation among all regions in their use of this setup. On the 8-4 plan, the disparity in percentages is larger: Northeast, 32.9; North Central, 16.7; South, 26.2; West, 18.4. The 6-2-4 plan figures are 10.7 in the Northeast, 21.5 in the North Central, 15.2 in the South, and 18.2

in the West. The 6-6 plan has 14.6 per cent adherence in the Northeast, 19 per cent in the North Central, 10.3 per cent in the South, and 15 per cent in the West. The 7-5 plan operates in 5.3 per cent of the schools in the Northeast, .9 per cent of the schools in the North Central, 3.7 per cent of the schools in the South and 5 per cent of the schools in the West.

A very few high schools, mainly in California, but also in Colorado, Indiana, Illinois, and Michigan, "extended" the high school program for a fifth year. However, all of these experiments and a good many others were either discontinued or altered significantly, so that nowhere is public high schooling *per se* prolonged beyond grade 12. In 1954 Pasadena, California, possibly the strongest proponent of the 6-4-4 plan of public school (six years of elementary school, four years of junior high school, and four years of junior college), abandoned it. Mississippi, too, during the same time was reverting to a more conventional pattern after a period of operating four-year institutions uniting grades 11, 12, 13, and 14. It is now unmistakable that administrators, faculty, and students, as well as the communities themselves, have rejected the concept that the junior college is an extension of secondary education. The separation of one from the other provides the irrefutable conclusion that the junior college is part of higher education in the United States.

Higher Education. — Educational programs whose prerequisites include approximately 12 years of prior schooling, or the equivalent, are in the realm of *higher education*. More than 2,100 institutions presently figure in this level of education in the United States. The dominance of publicly supported education that exists at the elementary and secondary levels extends to higher education despite the fact that private institutions outnumber public institutions at present. Public institutions enroll 59 per cent of the 4½ million college students in America.

In each of the past 12 years there has been a significant increase in the college student population. Estimates for 1970 point to an enrollment of over 6 million. Such projections take into account the larger birth rate in the period immediately after World War II; these children are now coming of college entrance age. And, of course, the proportion of young people continuing their education beyond secondary school is growing steadily. In addition, more adults than ever before are coming to evening college and university extension courses, as well as to summer schools.

A variety of educational institutions compose the spectrum of American higher education. Nearly all offer the student several programs from which to choose. Because some programs are sequential and because our age of specialization requires more and more preparation and training, the duration of higher studies is longer. The advances in particular fields of science and technology are so rapid that practitioners feel compelled to return to school.

In many occupational areas where an undergraduate college education previously sufficed for entry, graduate work is now expected. Men and women with postgraduate training find it necessary to return to universities and professional schools to remedy the effects of the rapid obsolescence of the knowledge with which they began.

As in the case of elementary and secondary education, the institutions of higher education are differently formed and differently named, with little consistency or standardization.
■**TECHNICAL INSTITUTE.**—Sometimes part of a junior college, more frequently independent, the technical institute provides programs of one to three years' duration. Two-year programs are most common. They generally prepare students for semiprofessional occupations, offering them "associate" degrees. The technical institute programs are most often related to engineering but also furnish training for business, health services, applied and graphic arts, and several other types of callings that are skilled but subprofessional.
■**JUNIOR COLLEGE.**—This type of institution, an American development of the twentieth century, is experiencing the most rapid growth of all units of higher education. By bringing post-secondary education to young persons in their own communities and requiring no commitment for more than two years of college work, it has greatly helped in handling higher education's unprecedented enrollment expansion.

Whether by design or by circumstance, many junior colleges are community-centered, serving the community in addition to being located there. Many two-year institutions are called *community colleges,* and the two names are used interchangeably—and even together, as the *community junior college.*

All community colleges, it may be said, are junior colleges; they provide two years of post-secondary, college-level study. All community colleges

LOOK MAGAZINE

HARVARD COLLEGE, Cambridge, Mass., as it appeared in 1776; etching by Paul Revere.

are publicly supported and publicly controlled, which is not true of all junior colleges. A fair number of the latter were established decades ago and as private institutions continue to serve students from a wide geographical area. The community colleges generally provide courses and programs for adults, as do a smaller but growing proportion of private junior colleges.

There are many forms of junior college, private and public. In recent years the private institutions have decreased in numbers and in student enrollment, while those in the public sphere have grown more numerous and appreciably raised their enrollment. Some of the private schools are primarily residential; other mainly accommodate local students. Some are church-related; others are independent. Only girls are enrolled in some of the nonpublic institutions. Public junior or community colleges are invariably coeducational, and few of them provide dormitory facilities.

The public two-year colleges fit into three categories with respect to their means of existence. They may be locally controlled and supported with or without state aid, wholly controlled and supported by the state, or sustained as two-year extension centers of four-year colleges and universities. Most states have junior colleges of more than one type.

A majority of the public two-year colleges profess to be comprehensive junior colleges with terminal programs, but the expectations of a growing majority of their students have caused these schools to stress work that will enable students to transfer to senior colleges. As community institutions, junior colleges have assumed cultural and civic responsibilities over and above the conventional courses leading to baccalaureate degrees (to be obtained from higher collegiate bodies). They look to the communities for suggestions and stimulation in planning their programs, and the communities look to the colleges for various services. They are multipurpose institutions in conception and in function.

There are more than 650 two-year colleges in the United States, of which approximately 150 are private. They represent 30 per cent of the American institutions of higher education and account for 14.1 per cent of their enrollment.

About 13 per cent—some 560,000—of the degree-credit students enrolled in all institutions of higher education in the United States are in two-year colleges. The proportion of males to females is close to three to one.

■**COLLEGE.**—Without the prefix "junior" or "community," the term *college* generally (but not always) means an institution of higher education that grants a baccalaureate degree for four years of work. Most of such institutions (about 800) are *liberal arts colleges.* (Liberal arts include English, classical and modern language studies, history, philosophy, mathematics, the social sciences, and the physical sciences.) A number of large universities have within them liberal arts colleges that attract a relatively small part of the total enrollment.

Another type of four-year institution offering baccalaureate degrees is the *teachers college.* Their number has decreased rapidly during the past two decades and is now under 150. Some have changed their purpose and have been renamed; others have had their purpose of training teachers diverted toward different programs or even to other schools. A few teachers colleges have been discontinued. They have gone the way of the *normal school,* which once had a large role in the preparation of elementary school teachers. Some *schools of education* in large universities operate what are in effect undergraduate teachers colleges but designate them merely as undergraduate divisions or

baccalaureate programs. Conversely, Teachers College, Columbia University, emphasizes graduate training in education.

The movement away from teachers colleges *per se* is the outcome of 50 years of warfare within higher education concerning the optimal curriculum for the prospective teacher—how much time should be devoted to liberal arts, fields of specialization, pedagogical courses, and practice teaching—and in which institutions and departments this work should be given.

Another type of college with a large if changing place in the realm of post-secondary education is the *college of agriculture.* A decade ago, 25 to 69 land-grant colleges, all in the western and northern states, were separate institutions with such names as *state college, college of agriculture and mechanical arts,* and *agricultural college.* In 28 states, the state university, as the land-grant institution, offered courses in agriculture and home economics, sometimes with separate colleges for the purpose. A few of the state colleges have become universities (Pennsylvania State, Michigan State University of Agriculture and Applied Science, Iowa State University of Science and Technology, and others), and some of the land-grant institutions have broadened their functions although their names are unchanged. At present the land-grant system comprises 47 universities in which agriculture, engineering, and home economics represent an essential part of the work; 5 major agricultural and mechanical institutions (Massachusetts Institute of Technology, Montana State College, South Dakota State College, Agricultural and Mechanical College of Texas, and Virginia Polytechnic Institute); and 16 higher education units established as agricultural and technical colleges for Negroes.

Although the present 68 land-grant colleges and universities represent only 3.4 per cent of the institutions of higher learning in the United States, they enroll 20 per cent of the nation's college population, award more than 20 per cent of all baccalaureate degrees, 25 per cent of all master's degrees, and 40 per cent of all doctorates. As many as 10,000 men and women earn undergraduate degrees in agricultural science and home economics each year in land-grant institutions.

Finally, there are the separate *theological colleges,* which account for a majority of the approximately 10,000 baccalaureate degrees awarded each year in this area. The rest are earned in theological and divinity schools associated with larger institutions.

Professional schools are more frequently parts of universities. However, the baccalaureate degree they offer, or have offered in the past, is different in some respects from that of the liberal arts college. It is a credential for a specific vocation. They may be public or private, degree-granting or nondegree-granting, responsible either to public agencies or to professional bodies with quasipublic authority, proprietary or non-profit, graduate or undergraduate or sometimes both.

Professional schools exist in nursing, engineering, dentistry, medicine, law, librarianship, education, pharmacy, religion, business, and a number of other areas. The only characteristic they have in common is their role in higher education.

■UNIVERSITY.—The *university* is an institution of higher education with a liberal arts college, a program of graduate study, two or more professional schools or faculties, and the power to grant degrees. Approximately 150 institutions in the United States are universities meeting these qualifications, enrolling nearly 1.7 million.

They are both public and private, and in each of these categories there are several types. In the public sector there are land-grant universities and other state universities that are not land-grant. There are state universities with several campuses—University of California in Los Angeles, Berkeley, etc.—some of which are full universities in themselves. There are municipal universities: University of Louisville (Ky.), University of the City of New York (N.Y.), University of Bridgeport (Conn.), and University of Akron (Ohio). There are private universities with large enrollments: Southern California (Calif.), New York (N.Y.), Harvard (Mass.), Washington (Mo.), Northwestern (Ill.), Notre Dame (Ind.). The University of California complex registers more than 60,000 students in eight locations; the University of Minnesota, 45,000. Among the private universities, New York University comes closest to these enrollments, with two campuses in New York City and about 33,000 enrollees.

In view of the fact that graduate schools are invariably parts of universities, there is no need to categorize them separately. They provide advanced work at the master's and doctoral levels. The professional schools of the universities constitute the other principal locus for advanced degree work.

Federal Government in Education.—No department in the federal government is comparable to a ministry of education in other lands. There is no reference to education in the Constitution; therefore, the federal role in this area has originated and grown within the restrictiveness of the Tenth Amendment and through the permissiveness of the "general welfare" clause of the Constitution. The Tenth Amendment provides: "The powers not delegated to the United States by the Constitution, nor prohibited by it to the States, are reserved to the States respectively or to the people." On the other hand, Article I, Section 8, Clause I of the Constitution provides: "The Congress shall have the power to lay and collect taxes, duties, imposts and excises, to pay the debts and provide for the common defense and general welfare of the United States. . . ."

Not without controversy in the past, or at present, has the federal govern-

ment's widening participation in promotion of this aspect of the nation's welfare been manifested. Upon leaving the presidency, George Washington urged his countrymen: "Promote, then, as an object of primary importance, institutions for the general diffusion of knowledge . . . it is essential that public opinion be enlightened." The Northwest Ordinance of 1787 set forth the policy "schools and the means of education shall be forever encouraged," which was followed as the nation grew.

Today every major agency of the United States government operates programs relating to education. Among these programs are the four-year colleges for each of the military services, distribution of milk and other food for school lunches, the support of scientific research, the conduct of a variety of financial aid programs for the assistance of graduate and undergraduate college students, and assistance to school districts that have been affected by federal activity.

Forty-two agencies of the federal government provide, in a single year, more than $2.2 billion in aid to education. Educational and training facilities operated directly by these agencies, or for them by other institutions, are but one aspect of the government's involvement in education. All government educational activities can be divided into five broad categories: education and training, research and development, facilities and equipment, financial assistance to individual students, and international education.

International education includes the full or partial subsidization of American students abroad; assistance to foreign students, teachers, and specialists studying in the United States; sponsorship of educational projects abroad; and exchanges of persons and information to contribute to the technological development of participating foreign countries. Most prominent among the federal agencies in international education is the *Department of State.* The International Coopera-

PIX, INC.

UNITED STATES Military Academy at West Point, oldest federal educational unit.

tion Administration and, more recently, the Alliance for Progress, figure in programs of educational and cultural exchange. They share the goal of furthering economic and social development in distant areas.

■FEDERAL AGENCIES.— The *Department of Agriculture* administers one of the largest federal programs of education and training through the Agricultural Cooperative Extension Service, which is under the direction of the land-grant colleges and universities. The objective of this program is to improve agricultural production, marketing efficiency, and rural living. Extension services of this nature account for more than half of some $110 million that the federal government annually appropriates for education in the agricultural sciences. At the elementary and secondary school levels, the Federal Extension Service operates the 4-H Club programs in cooperation with land-grant agricultural colleges.

The United States Department of Agriculture Graduate School in Washington, D.C., is not specifically related to agriculture, insofar as curriculum is concerned. It serves the general public, many of whom in that area are government employees. Study for credit is made possible through an arrangement with the University of Maryland.

A massive complex of educational and training enterprises supported by federal funds is operated by the agencies of the *Department of Defense.* The oldest unit among these is the United States Military Academy at West Point, New York, with more than 2,200 students in its corps. The Academy provides a four-year curriculum that includes the usual undergraduate subjects of mathematics, physics, chemistry, history, English, foreign languages, sociology, psychology, and economics, as well as an array of studies in the military sciences. The cadet at West Point graduates with an Army commission of Second Lieutenant. The Army maintains a Chaplains School to train ministers for that branch of service, the Special Services School, and the Command and General Staff School at Fort Leavenworth, Kansas, for officers of field grade and higher rank.

At the United States Naval Academy at Annapolis, Maryland, about 3,400 midshipmen receive a four-year education similar to that furnished by the Military Academy, but with emphasis on nautical and naval science. The midshipmen at Annapolis receives a commission as ensign, with assignment to either the Navy or the Marine Corps. The Navy provides graduate work for its personnel at Annapolis and, by special arrangement, at civilian institutions of higher education. At Newport, Rhode Island, the Naval War College offers a one-year course for officers.

The United States Air Force Academy near Colorado Springs, Colorado, with about 1,900 cadets, provides for Air Force cadets the same basic undergraduate education furnished by West Point and Annapolis, with the addition of specialized courses in the field of aeronautical science.

U.S. AIR FORCE

CADETS ON PARADE at the United States Air Force Academy near Colorado Springs, Colorado.

Each of the three branches of the armed services maintains Reserve Officers Training Corps programs at colleges and universities across the land. At their own institutions they provide a variety of training and drill exercises for their active reserve personnel. Two-week tours of duty are common.

The Department of Defense provides off-duty educational opportunities for members of the armed forces. Educational centers on military bases abroad are operated through contracts with American institutions of higher education. More than 100 such institutions provide on-base and on-campus courses for service personnel in the continental United States. The U.S. Armed Forces Institute provides correspondence study opportunities through 40 institutions at both high school and college levels.

The *Department of Commerce* provides training vessels, maintenance funds, and student subsidies for state maritime schools in four states: U.S. Merchant Marine Academy (N.Y.), California Maritime Academy (Calif.), etc. The U.S. Coast Guard Academy is located in New London, Conn.

The *National Science Foundation* administers large-scale programs designed to strengthen scientific education in elementary and secondary schools, colleges, and universities. High school teachers from thousands of institutions participate in academic-year and summer programs offered at hundreds of centers.

The *Atomic Energy Commission* supports conferences and institutes for college and university faculty members in biological science, industrial hygiene, and related fields. The manifold grant programs of the National Institutes of Health of the *Public Health Service* enable significant numbers of scientists, investigators, and clinicians to engage in further research training. They also make possible a pre-professional

preparation for such capacities.

The *Department of Justice* has a role in educating aliens preparatory to their naturalization. It is also concerned with the education of inmates of federal penal and correctional institutions. The National Police Academy and the Immigration Border Patrol Training School are within its purview.

■**THE OFFICE OF EDUCATION.**—Since 1953 the Office of Education, the primary education agency of the federal government, has been a subordinate part of the *Department of Health, Education, and Welfare.* In contrast to the Department of Defense, the Department of Agriculture, the Veterans Administration, and other agencies, its sole concern is education.

The *Office of Education* regularly performs tasks in three major areas: research, services, and administration of grants. In carrying out its assignments, the Office works with and through state, local, and private educational agencies. There is no overall federal policy with regard to education. Furthermore, the constitutionality of formulating and enacting such national policies is considered by some authorities to be debatable. Thus, separate acts of Congress and mandates of the executive departments serve to establish piecemeal what in most other countries would be a national educational policy.

In the absence, at least nominally, of an explicit national policy and a ministry of education, there has been the inevitable confusion of overlapping services, duplication of effort, and indirect remedial undertakings by a multiplicity of agencies, working sometimes in combination and at other times in less-than-splendid isolation. This has led, by its evident incoherence and wastefulness, to more authority for the Office of Education and to an increasing focus of educational responsibility upon that agency's officials and staff.

Sharp debate continues concerning

proposed measures to deal with important educational problems, with the matter of comprehensive federal educational policy, and with the Office of Education's rightful role. Two trends are apparent. Each year the federal government increases its financial assistance to many parts of the educational structure. Inescapably, some policy formulation ensues from the granting of aid. Is this, or is this not, "control"? As the demand for education increases and the public's interest in its "shortcomings" and "costliness" increases, pressure builds for a greater centrality of responsibility for coping with the resultant problems. As a consequence, the Office of Education grows and changes.

Some of the functions that the Office of Education performs are:

Research.—The office compiles statistical data concerning nearly all aspects of education in the country; designs and executes research projects and stimulates similar activity by other agencies, sometimes sponsoring the endeavors; inquires into special educational institutions and facility shortages.

Services.—Through conferences and consultation and through the dissemination of survey data, statistics, analyses, and reports of trends and innovations in education, the Office assists state and local education agencies: all the public ones and many private ones. It provides leadership and advisory services to the state departments of education, local school systems, higher education institutions, and professional organizations, concerning methods of instruction, preparation of teachers, educational legislation, teacher exchange, educational technical assistance programs, civil defense, and veteran education. In some of these fields, the work is done with or for other government agencies.

■**GRANTS.**—The Office administers a variety of financial aid programs. The purposes of some of these programs are: to identify and educate more of the academically talented; to increase numbers and training of personnel in the fields of science, mathematics, modern foreign languages, guidance and counseling, and technology; to educate and train more young people for farming, home economics, trades and industry, practical nursing, and distributive occupations; to extend public library services in rural areas; to assist local agencies in areas affected by federal activities in construction and operation of schools; and to increase the supply of capable and qualified teachers. The Office of Education assists the State Department and the International Cooperation Administration in their substantial programs of educational exchange, involving students, teachers, and specialists in scholarly areas.

Federal annual funds for the Office of Education have risen more than tenfold during the past decade and now exceed $500 million. Approximately 1,200 men and women, nearly all of whom are in the Civil Service, staff the Office's operations.

Their activities emanate from three major divisions, known as the Bureau of Educational Assistance Programs. At the head of the Office of Education is the commissioner of education, appointed by the President with the advice and consent of the Senate.

Within the States.—The federal government is a government of delegated powers; and since education is not one of the powers delegated to it, such function is reserved to the states. The authority of each state over its public education and, to a lesser degree, over its nonpublic education, is specifically derived from the provisions of its own constitution. The statutes and judicial determinations based upon the constitutions of the states have established over the years what is now commonly referred to as the state education systems. The body of law composed of the constitution, the statutes, and the judicial decisions in each state has shaped the organization and governs the operation of the school system.

The educational statutes of each state describe and mandate administrative machinery for carrying out its educational function. Although there are variations in the organization and procedures, the patterns are essentially the same. The state laws delegate to the local school districts the responsibility for the operation of their schools and place general supervision of the program in the hands of the state agencies.

■**STATE BOARD OF EDUCATION.**—Every state has some board of education; federal law requires such an entity if the state is to be eligible for financial aid to education. Forty-seven of the 50 states today have *state boards of education;* in 45 of these the board of education, in addition to exercising general control over elementary and secondary schools, is also charged with serving as the board for vocational education. Illinois, Michigan, and Wisconsin have vocational education bodies at the state level but do not use the board of education structure as such. Only two states besides the three mentioned have not designated their state boards of education as state boards of vocational education.

The responsibilities of the boards vary considerably beyond the areas of concern that are common to all. Some state education boards govern public institutions of higher education as well as the system of primary and secondary schools. In most states there are separate boards with responsibility for one or more institutions at the college or university level. During the past decade the total number of state boards of education of all kinds has fluctuated both up and down, but as many as 200 still exist.

Membership of state boards of education varies from 3 to 23 persons. Board members obtain their positions in various ways, and in some cases the board is composed of persons who attained membership in different ways. In more than half the states, appointment by the governor is either the sole or principal means of filling vacancies. Some boards are elected by the public or by legislatures. In a few states, one or more of the board members are chosen in conventions of local school board members.

A significant but diminishing number of members of state boards of education are in office by virtue of other positions they hold in state government. In the past they included elected state officials: the governor, secretary of state, and others. In 1920, a majority of the state boards of education had some ex officio members; by 1964, fewer than one-third of the bodies had any.

Other provisions concerning membership on state boards of education, apart from method of selection, have to do with distribution by congressional, judicial, or other districts; with political party association; with qualification or disqualification for employment in education; and with representation of designated callings.

The terms of office for membership on state boards of education vary considerably. They range from 2 to 13 years, with four-year terms most common. The usual arrangement is for staggered terms, to maintain continuity of work and to assure a nucleus of experienced members.

Typically, the *function* of the state board of education is that of policy approval and the general administration of state education laws. The degree to which either or both of these missions are fulfilled depends upon the system of educational administration in its entirety, and not upon the board alone.

The growing and changing panorama of public higher education in the United States contributes its own profile of a state board of education —in this case, a state board of higher education. A 1959 comprehensive study of state boards responsible for higher education disclosed that there were a total of 209 such boards. About half the number were carrying out functions involving more than one institution. They are designated as governing-coordinating boards because of their responsibility for multiple units of higher education. Such boards exist in 41 states. Almost half (358 of 748) of the institutional units of public higher education in the country identified in the study were under governing-coordinating boards. This situation reflects a growing conception of state-supported colleges and universities as integral parts of state enterprises in higher education.

■**STATE DEPARTMENT OF EDUCATION.**— Each state has a state department of education, headed by the chief state school officer. The decade between 1950 and 1960 saw a rapid expansion of state educational services and programs. There was a doubling not only of the professional personnel during this period but also a substantial broadening of the legal duties and powers pertaining to elementary and secondary schools.

The activities of state education departments—or departments of public instruction, as many of them are designated—have been classified as leadership, regulatory, and operational. The *leadership function* of the departments developed out of two areas of responsibility the bodies had —*statistical* (from inception to about 1900) and *inspectoral* (from 1900 to approximately 1930). These have also been termed *accounting and reporting functions.*

Until 1900 the professional complement of all of the state departments of education in the United States totaled less than 200. The current total of all personnel in the departments is greater than 15,000. Of these, 4,000 to 4,500 are on the professional and supervisory level.

In their leadership roles, the departments plan research, advise and consult with both subordinate agencies and the U.S. Office of Education, coordinate functions of intermediate supervisory groups and local districts, and manage the ever-increasing governmental activity—public relations.

The leadership role of the state education departments gave rise to the need for greater competency among the staff members. In turn, the quality of leadership has risen as a result of the "new breed" of educational specialists in the depart-

U.S. OFFICE OF EDUCATION

GUIDANCE and testing experts hold a meeting with members of the Office of Education.

LOOK MAGAZINE

SCHOOL SUPERINTENDENT representing a local community in Oregon meets with his board.

ments. No longer do the departments of public instruction abound with elderly, erstwhile superintendents mechanically measuring and recording compliance with regulations. An increasing number of persons on the state professional staffs are informed educators with recognized expertise in specific areas of subject matter and in teaching methodology. Most of the staffs today include specialists in elementary education, science education, curriculum, foreign language instruction, audio-visual aids, reading, junior colleges, teacher training, and other fields. With the assistance of skilled researchers, they initiate and execute significant studies. They carry on considerably more field consultation and demonstration than their predecessors.

In the *operational function,* some of the departments of public instruction have direct responsibility for teachers colleges; state trade schools; schools for blind, deaf, and otherwise handicapped young people; citizenship classes for the foreign-born; state libraries; museums; film censorship; licensing of educational personnel; and retirement systems.

Historically, the *regulatory function* is more basic to the state department's business than either its leadership or operational roles. More of it has statutory origin. In some respects the increasingly prominent leadership activity is an outgrowth of more effective handling of regulatory responsibility. The emphasis has shifted from annual "inspector-general" visitations in quest of infraction and irregularity to such cooperative endeavors as in-service training, subject-matter institutes, and conferences on school management. The regulatory requirements were designed to serve as minimal standards in protecting the lives and health of pupils, in assuring safeguarded and wise use of public monies, and in making and keeping the educational enterprise efficient. The difference between yesteryear and now is perhaps best

described as a change from policing to collaboration.

The question of control versus cooperation between state departments and school districts arises more frequently and more concretely than it does in federal-state relationships. Resolution of state-district differences frequently hinges upon interpretation of legislative enactments. The legal functionaries of both entities obviously play a large part in arriving at determinations. When the lawyers cannot settle the questions, either or both of the disputants can turn to the state courts. Federal-state education differences are often of a different nature because of the absence of constitutional authority at the national level. It is through the power of the national purse that the federal government at times makes educational policy and gains state acceptance.

A helpful perspective of the work of the state departments of education is provided by the data in a study published in 1950 by the U.S. Office of Education, ascertaining the quantity of professional staff time devoted to 33 "service areas" by the then 48 state departments. Nineteen of the 33 "service areas" averaged 1 per cent or more of the time of the professional staffs. In descending order the percentages were: vocational rehabilitation, 23.6; vocational education, 14.6; instructional services, 11.5; veterans education, 9.9; school lunch, 4.6; exceptional children and youth, 3.4; state and local public libraries, 3.3; finance and business administration, 2.5; higher education, 2; teacher certification, 1.8; adult education, 1.8; departmental office administration, 1.7; school plant, 1.5; surplus property, 1.3; guidance, 1.3; pupil transportation, 1.2; local school unit reorganization, 1.2; school health services, 1.

Veterans education undoubtedly occupies a lesser place today than it did just after World War II, while upward shifts can be seen in instruc-

tional services (post-Sputnik), school plant matters (post-war birth rate increase), and local school unit reorganization (desegregation rulings).

The importance of the *chief state officer* has grown considerably in the past several decades. Whether called *superintendent of public instruction, superintendent of education,* or *commissioner of education,* he is administrative head of the state department of education. He is also frequently the executive officer of the state board of education.

Developments have enhanced the prestige of the office and broadened the responsibility associated with top state education position. Modern superintendents, generally better equipped to handle the tasks than their predecessors, have enlarged the range of authority of the office. Now the standards for choosing chief state school officers are appreciably higher. The remuneration in these positions has increased, too, though not nearly as rapidly nor in proportion to the responsibilities. Despite the fact that quite a few large city superintendencies pay more than the average state superintendent's salary, an increasing number of able persons are attracted to service as state education chiefs.

Approximately half of the states still elect superintendents of education. This imposes a need for residence requirements, some campaigning, and the usual gamut of political considerations, none of which necessarily contributes to a choice of the most qualified person. In the rest of the states, the chief school officer is appointed, either by the board of education, as is true for some 22 states, or by the governor, as happens in 3 states. The tendency is undoubtedly toward appointment in circumstances of minimal political partisanship.

The duties of the chief education officer vary greatly from state to state. There are, nonetheless, some responsibilities that are common to all state superintendents: general supervisory authority over the state public school system; professional advice and guidance to the state board of education (frequently in the role of executive officer); administration of the state education department—appointments, promotions, removals, etc.; preparation of a budget for board approval and administration of appropriations therefrom; supervision of distribution of state funds to local school districts; interpretation of state education law and function as appeals officer; approval of plans for school sites and structures; supervision of certification standards and procedures for teachers, principals, and local superintendents; recommendation to the board of proposed legislation; general direction of school and district consolidation efforts; procurement of complete, accurate, and timely reports of various kinds from all public schools and districts of the state, and the periodic analysis and reporting of the resultant data, including publication; and leadership in advancing standards and means of training for educational personnel.

■**INTERMEDIATE ADMINISTRATION.**—In various ways and at different times most of the states have resorted to supervisory entities between themselves and the local school districts. These are the *intermediate administrative units.*

The county or its equivalent is an area for public school administration in all but 11 states—Alaska, Delaware, Hawaii, Idaho, New York, Connecticut, Massachusetts, Rhode Island, Vermont, New Hampshire, and Maine. Two basic types of county school organization exist among the 39 other states: the county unit system and the county intermediate unit. The latter is the predominant and traditional pattern of school system organization. It prevails in the Midwest, Great Lakes area, and in the Far West, where relatively small school districts are basic administrative units.

Two principal purposes of the intermediate administrative unit are to provide general supervisory linkage between the state department of education and the local school organization and to furnish specialized services that the local systems cannot maintain individually.

Where school districts are countywide, as in Florida, Nevada, and West Virginia, neither of the two main reasons for an intermediate administrative unit exists. Consequently, these states do not employ them. In New England and in New York the intermediate administrative units are composed of contiguous local school districts or town schools and are known as *supervisory unions* or *supervisory districts.* The local school districts that constitute the unions may or may not have individual superintendents, but are served in either case by the superintendent of the union or supervisory district, who is the chief officer of the intermediate administrative unit.

The main responsibility of intermediate units has not been, and is not, the operation of schools. They render consultative, advisory, and statistical services, and they exercise certain regulatory and inspectoral functions in behalf of the state department of education. Many of the agencies regularly supply several of the services included in the listing below (though not comprehensive, it is made up from reports of actual functions the units engage in): adult education; audio-visual equipment and operation; centralized purchasing; communication (ranging from handbooks to radio and television instruction); specialized instruction (for gifted, retarded, physically handicapped, homebound, etc.); financial services (accounting, auditing, reporting); health services (school nurse, doctor, dental hygienist); inservice education (teachers, principals, school board members, bus drivers, clerks); legal services; library services; professional personnel services (teacher placement, substitute pool, salary schedule development, policy coordination); pupil personnel services (attendance, guidance and counseling, testing, mental health clinic); pupil transportation

LOOK MAGAZINE

TRANSPORTATION by school buses is supervised by an intermediate administrative unit.

services (administration, coordination, bus maintenance); recreation; research; plant services (architecture, building, maintenance); special subject instruction (art, foreign languages, reading, science); trade and industrial education.

The most recent authoritative compilation of data concerning the personnel of the intermediate school agencies shows approximately 6,600 board members, 3,000 superintendents and other administrators, 2,600 instructional personnel, 1,300 other professional persons, such as attendance officers and health functionaries, and 3,500 secretaries, clerks, and other administrative assistants.

■**LOCAL SCHOOL DISTRICT.**—The *local school district* is the basic structural unit of public education. It is a civil subdivision of the state and is legally a quasi-corporation or quasi-municipal corporation. As a political division of the state, it has the authority to exercise such powers as are granted by the state legislature and the provisions of the state's constitution.

PROVIDENCE JOURNAL-BULLETIN

MOBILE LIBRARY offers books to rural areas.

These basic administrative units of education are generally responsible to the state, either directly to the department of education or through an intermediate administrative unit.

As units of state government, local school districts are usually separate from municipal government in the organizational sense. In a few states, municipal or county governments have some administrative authority, usually of a financial nature, over the districts. Districts enjoying fiscal independence are generally able to plan programs (of construction, for example) and implement them more swiftly than those requiring a sequence of hearings and approvals from other agencies. Fiscal independence in this connection is relative because revenue for public education expenses generally comes from several sources: the general appropriations by federal, state, county, and local governments; receipts from school taxes; income from leases of school land; income from permanent funds and endowments; interest; tuition; and charges. A school district that can procure tax funds from its own jurisdiction in an amount determined by its needs (over and above the formulae-fixed subsidies from federal, state, and other governmental entities) is said to have *fiscal independence.*

The total of local school districts in the United States is steadily diminishing. As reorganizations take place, districts are eliminated, consolidated, merged, and otherwise reduced in number. Only a very few states have added school districts during the past 30 years. In round figures, the totals of basic administrative school units have changed as follows: 1930, 130,000; 1940, 115,000; 1950, 85,000; 1960, 40,000. In 1964, there were fewer than 33,000 districts, with projected consolidations indicating only a very modest reduction during the current decade.

The local administrative units go by a variety of names: *city school district, common school district, county school district, union free high school district, town* or *township school district,* and so forth. One distinguishing feature of a district may be the level of schooling it provides: elementary school, high school, or sometimes junior college. The term *unified district* refers to a merger of elementary and secondary school jurisdictions. *Joint school district* signifies an amalgamation of two or more local districts, invariably neighboring ones. There are now many *community school districts*.

According to the U.S. Bureau of the Census, the responsibility for primary and secondary public education rests as follows: with independent school districts in 29 states; with county, city, or town government in 3 states; and with both independent and public agencies in 17 states. Hawaii is a single basic unit for school organization, as is the District of Columbia.

The main responsibility of the local district is the establishment and operation of primary and secondary schools within its area. In several states, one or more junior or community colleges are within the control of certain districts. Of the nearly 33,000 basic administrative units in existence, fewer than 29,000 are *operating* school districts. The rest operate no facilities whatsoever; they transfer pupils resident in their area to adjacent operating districts. The operating districts can be further divided as follows: about 19,000 maintain only elementary schools; close to 8,000 maintain both elementary and high schools; nearly 1,500 maintain secondary schools only; fewer than 300 operate junior colleges, either alone or in combination with their elementary and/or secondary programs.

Despite the enormous progress that has been made in strengthening districts by mergers and consolidations, nearly half of the existing basic administrative units have fewer than 200 pupils. Although the one-teacher, single-room school is rapidly becoming extinct in most states, a large number of very small school operations remain. This serves to explain the great need for, and importance

of, the services and program assistance that intermediate administrative units give to local districts.

■**LOCAL SCHOOL BOARDS.**—The policy-making body for a local school district generally has from three to nine members. It is vested with supervisory authority over the public educational program and facilities in its area at specified levels of schooling. The vast majority of board members—also known as *district trustees, directors,* and *committeemen*—are elected. The others are appointed by various government officials. All school board members are state officials, at least technically and legally, and are nearly always residents of the areas over which they have educational jurisdiction. Most boards are composed entirely of laymen, insofar as education is concerned. Seldom does any board have more than one member who is an educator.

All of these factors, taken together, lend the American school board its unique and manifestly democratic character. The schools are kept close to, and responsive to, the will of the people whose children they serve. Within the framework of state laws and state board of education regulations, the local board, via its policy-making role, manages the public education enterprise for the area. To a considerable extent, the quantity and quality of the educational program in a given community depends on the caliber of the board members.

Prevailing practices with regard to school board membership indicate that: members serve overlapping terms of from three to six years; in at least 42 states all or some of the local school board members are elected; in 33 states, all board members are elected; roughly 95 per cent of all local board members in the United States are elected; about 65 per cent of all board members have children attending school during their period of service; at least 22 states make no payment whatsoever for services as board members. In the other states nominal sums are paid,

either as stipends or at per-diem rates. Three-fourths of all who serve as board members receive no remuneration or reimbursement.

There are more than 147,000 men and women currently holding school board membership. Nebraska and Illinois each have about 11,000 board members. The District of Columbia has 9 and Hawaii has 10.

The *superintendent of schools* is in most cases the executive officer of the local board of education, and in virtually all instances he is the chief administrative officer of the school district. Much of what has been said about the relatively new status and authority of the state's chief school officer has a measure of application to the local superintendent of schools. The relationship *vis-à-vis* the board of education at both state and local levels is comparable. Perhaps the most significant single act of a school board is its selection of a superintendent. It is very likely that no factor can contribute as much to effective management of a school system (or do as much harm in the same context) as the ability or inability of board and superintendent to function cooperatively.

The board of education habitually looks to the superintendent to carry out policies they have determined. The basis for policy is frequently an accurate, detailed, and timely accounting of existing circumstances in the district schools, with recommendations for action on matters of concern—program, plant, faculty, or school enrollment. For both reports and recommendations, the properly functioning board looks to the superintendent, as they do to learn about the wide range of educational problems: those at hand, those that are imminent, and those that can be nipped in the bud.

The great variation in size of local districts suggests the different calibers of leadership needed for the superintendencies. As has been indicated previously, a city with a multimillion population sets very high standards for its superintendent. Those who serve in such offices are among the most skillful managers of educational enterprise in the country, and their salaries are commensurate. Only a small number of outstanding universities pay their presidents the amounts earned by the superintendents of city systems with hundreds of thousands of pupils.

At present there are more than 13,000 superintendents of basic administrative units. About 5,500 persons serve as assistants to superintendents.

Adult Education.—*Adult education* is based on the conviction that learning experiences must be designed to meet the needs and the interests of the mature person. For present purposes, it is appropriate to regard all persons beyond the age of compulsory education as adults. Thus, adult education can be viewed as an activity in which participation is usually voluntary.

In the 1930's the late Lyman Bryson, professor of education at Columbia University, defined adult

FARM SECURITY ADMINISTRATION

"LITTLE RED SCHOOLHOUSE" was a one-room school housing all the grades with one teacher.

education as ". . . all activities with an educational purpose that are carried on by people engaged in the ordinary business of life." This definition implies that adults are not full-time students and that their study is a supplementary pursuit.

The range and prevalence of adult education can best be judged by looking at the institutional arrangements for its provision and at the organizational and media channels through which it is sponsored and conveyed. It can also be identified by the subject matter with which it concerns itself, by the materials it uses, by the teaching methods employed, and by the objectives of the participants. A 1959 study entitled *Participation in Adult Education,* based upon the October 1957 Current Population Survey, Bureau of the Census and the Office of Education, found that over 8¼ million people in the United States were "definitely attending adult education classes." All of these were 14 years old or over and were not regularly enrolled in school; thus 7.8 per cent of the 105½ million "adults" in the population were attending classes.

Another large-scale inquiry into the nature and extent of adult education in the United States was made by the National Opinion Research Center of the University of Chicago during 1961 and 1962. This survey found that over 17 million adults were enrolled in some adult education activity during 1961–1962 and that more than 2½ million others were enrolled as full-time students.

■INSTITUTIONS.—Colleges and universities are the principal institutions for the education of adults. About 175 colleges and universities in the United States operate evening college or extension divisions. In addition, approximately 300 small liberal arts colleges provide some type of adult education.

Of nearly 2.7 million adults estimated to be engaged in college-sponsored study, the National Opinion Research Center judges that 900,000 are noncredit enrollees. A great majority of these students attend classes or programs of evening colleges and extension divisions.

Extension divisions are commonly part of public or land-grant institutions. They operate programs in several locations in their states as well as on their own campuses. The National University Extension Association (NUEA), whose membership includes nearly all institutions with sizable adult education operations, has a membership of about 80 universities. Approximately one-third of this number are private institutions with extension services either on their campuses or close by. Sometimes called *divisions of general education* or *schools of general studies,* their functions are similar to those of the land-grant institutions' extension organizations. The main purpose of both is to conduct noncredit undergraduate, graduate, and professional training classes, as well as short courses in various subjects.

Evening colleges generally serve adults who spend their days engaged

O. E. NELSON

PANEL DISCUSSION on India's foreign policy is conducted by an Indian exchange teacher.

in the ordinary business of life. The Association of University Evening Colleges (AUEC) includes in its membership almost all of the over 125 institutions with such programs for adults. The NUEA and the AUEC are the two organizations operating in the area of adult higher education. Much of the concern of their memberships is with standards, programs, and operations related to the education of nondegree, noncredit adult students.

Evening colleges and extension divisions are generally required to stand at least a substantial part of the costs of operation. In the extension divisions of private universities, student fees are usually higher than those of land-grant extension departments because little or no subsidy is provided. A few extension operations return to their institutions any income in excess of costs.

Extension and evening college programs for adults can be divided into four groups: informational, liberal, recreational, and vocational.

The most recent data concerning the adult education enrollees in jun-

ior college and community college programs indicate that they number over 160,000. Fifty-five per cent are female. An additional 50,000 persons take nondegree courses by mail from these institutions. Of these, 30 per cent are women and 70 per cent are men. Inevitably, as the number of public institutions of this type continues to grow, more of them will be serving greater segments of the adult population in their communities.

Much of the statistical data concerning the *Agricultural Cooperative Extension Service,* a relatively small facet of American education, cannot be separated from that compiled for land-grant colleges and universities. The land-grant institutions are the core of the Service, a tripartite agency composed of federal, state, and county extension services. Their annual budget is close to $200 million; the administrators and specialists of the Federal Extension Services, supplied almost entirely by the three levels of government, number about 250. Those in the state centers (usually land-grant institutions) and in the county services total more than

KATHARINE ENGLE CENTER

ART CLASS is one of the many adult education activities available to senior citizens.

15,000. There is at least one extension agent in every county.

The primary function of the Agricultural Cooperative Extension Service is an educational one; it supplies information on subjects relating to agriculture and home economics. A changing economy and the shift in population from rural to urban areas have greatly altered the role of its personnel and enlarged their educational mission. Most of the work of the county agent and of the home demonstration staffs involves leadership, education, and guidance. Each week, these experts work with hundreds of thousands of people, primarily those who live in the smaller communities and who are concerned with crop culture, livestock, and homemaking.

■ **ELEMENTARY AND HIGH SCHOOLS.**—The minimal figures for the current period indicate that at least 1,750,000 men and women are enrolled in public school education programs. Of 15,200 basic administrative school units, 832 reported that they were offering adult education programs.

Adult Registrations in Public Schools

Field of Instruction	Registrations (Thousands)
Americanization and citizenship	171
Literary education	47
Elementary education	38
High school academic education	411
Advanced academic education	50
Civic and public affairs	73
Personal development and group relationships	72
Family relationships	132
Homemaking and consumer education	459
Agricultural courses	106
Distributive education	89
Trade, industrial and technical courses	560
Business education	372
Fine arts	167
Techniques in practical arts and crafts	281
Health and physical education	190
Safety and driver education	117
Remedial education	9
In-service training for professional persons	65
Other	11

In the early years of public school adult education, there were two prime objectives. The first was to provide an opportunity for children who had left school and had gone to work to complete their formal education. The second was to enable immigrants to learn English. Both goals were achieved by many thousands of persons.

In the 120 years since the establishment of public evening schools, there have been many changes in the circumstances that lead adults to seek public education. Children no longer begin 10-hour-per-day jobs at the age of 11; they must be at least 16 years old to work 8 hours daily. Immigration no longer delivers thousands of uneducated people to our shores. Instead, the nation is now concerned

AMERICAN AIRLINES

STEWARDESS training class is one of the varied courses offered by proprietary schools.

with high school dropouts and with students who do not choose to continue their education on the college level. The old phrase "deficient in the rudiments" is no longer the sole prescription for enrolling persons who are beyond the compulsory school age. Public school programs for adults still offer basic English for those who may be literate in other languages or in none, and they continue to give citizenship courses to facilitate naturalization. However, they now offer a great deal more. The accompanying table lists a recent official tabulation of registrations in public school adult classes covering 20 fields.

■ **CORRESPONDENCE SCHOOLS.**—In *correspondence schools*, guidance comes through written communication between teacher and student. A syllabus, the standard material of all correspondence study, sets forth the objectives, subdivisions, and organization of the course. It suggests sources of information, makes assignments for reading and writing, explains difficult concepts, and provides

PENNSYLVANIA STATE UNIVERSITY

HOME STUDY by correspondence courses.

for evidence of the student's progress.

Over 50,000 persons take nondegree courses by mail from junior colleges. A recent survey reported that in 45 colleges and universities correspondence programs were taken by about 100,000 persons. Thirty-eight institutions reported 55,000 enrollments in high school–level courses. Since several hundred institutions offer such work, these figures can represent but a fraction of the total number of people involved in study by mail. One estimate places the number of persons engaged in correspondence study at 1¼ million. The United States Armed Forces Institute itself annually enrolls some 240,000 students in its own courses. In addition, other branches of the armed forces offer such work to an unspecified, but probably large, number of their members. Private correspondence schools indicate enrollments of more than 750,000 students.

■ **PROPRIETARY SCHOOLS.**—*Proprietary schools* are so called because they are independently financed and operated. Except for a small percentage with corporate nonprofit status, they remain in business as long as their income from tuition justifies continuance. Some are very profitable. They estimate an enrollment of over one million students, most of whom have had a high school education. Their programs include accounting, advertising, airline personnel, commercial and fine arts, design, dental technology, driving, electronics, engineering technology, insurance, interior design, languages, modeling, music, real estate, secretarial training, tailoring, typing and shorthand, and others.

Accreditation arrangements presently extend to only three groups among the proprietary schools—the independent schools of business, the home study or correspondence schools, and the technical schools.

■ **VOLUNTARY ORGANIZATIONS.**—About 2¼ million adults participate in educational activities sponsored by community organizations and closely related to the central purpose of the associations concerned. This particular category is quite broad and includes a variety of groups: League of Women Voters, National Congress of Parents and Teachers, American Red Cross, National Association for the Advancement of Colored People, the American Legion, Association of Junior Leagues, the Foreign Policy Association, the American Association of University Women, and a variety of service clubs.

Although these organizations are national and even international, their educational activities focus in communities. The educational programs under their sponsorship represent a major part of adult education in the United States.

■RELIGION-RELATED GROUPS.—The National Opinion Research Center estimates that 3¼ million persons attend classes, lectures, or discussion groups run by religion-related organizations; these educational programs are not always characterized by religion. Foremost in this group are the "Y" organizations—the Young Men's Christian Association, the Young Women's Christian Association, the Young Men's Hebrew Association, and the Young Women's Hebrew Association—whose combined membership exceeds four million.

"Y" organizations, with their more than 2,000 community establishments, sponsor informal adult education programs. Public affairs programs, health and physical education activities, workshops, seminars, and institutes for leadership development, as well as study offerings of a recreational, vocational, avocational, and spiritual nature are available at "Y" units.

Churches and synagogues provide group discussions and class meetings often dealing entirely with secular subject matter. As in the case of the "Y" organizations, some or all of this activity is open to the public at large, with no religious affiliation required.

There is also adult education that stresses the tenets, history, and traditions of a faith. Various missionary groups and some churches and synagogues emphasize this area and minimize or exclude secular education.

■BUSINESS AND LABOR.—The organizations and associations of management, industry, business, and labor conduct a great many programs of adult education. They also aid educational institutions in providing specialized offerings for the groups with which both are concerned. These aspects of adult education are not systematically established. Consequently, there is no easy method by which their efforts may be gauged.

Nearly all that they do in connection with adult education is closely related to the improvement of job performance. This is known as vocational training. The major management associations regularly offer courses in management development and supervisor training. They operate schools and institutes, usually staffed by employees of member companies. Some of the larger companies themselves engage in training and upgrading activities for their managerial and supervisory personnel. A few of the larger industrial concerns conduct training programs on company premises, on company time, and with faculty drawn from their own staffs. Several of these operations have enlisted the cooperation of institutions of higher education. This has resulted in the availability of highly specialized professional practitioners in temporary or full-time teaching assignments. Another result has been accreditation for company-provided course work.

In the technical sphere, private industry and its associations are doing more and more, although institutes of technology are still the major providers of training. Each year, hundreds of thousands of engineers, technicians, office employees, and semiskilled workers are beneficiaries of company-provided training programs. These opportunities are in addition to those that personnel can obtain at regular educational institutions at company expense.

Labor unions and their national and international affiliates have a notable history in adult education. About 14 million adults are members of one or another of the 75,000 local units in the 135 organizations that constitute the American Federation of Labor-Congress of Industrial Organizations (AFL-CIO). Another three million or four million are members of independent unions. Many of the larger local units, some city and state councils, and most of the national unions use the services of union education specialists. The programs that the labor organizations either operate themselves, subsidize, or encourage in other institutions can be divided into three categories: executive training of full-time appointed or elected union officers and staff; education and training of local leadership not employed by the unions; education of rank-and-file members.

Most of the formal training for career union personnel is done at a few universities with specially developed programs in labor-management relations. Similarly, during the past two decades, regular institutions have begun to play a part in preparing volunteers for union service at the local level. Not all national and international unions concern themselves with providing educational help for the general membership, but the majority do. Some of the larger international unions have large-scale programs, staffed with union educators and reaching into hundreds of local units throughout the country.

■LIBRARIES AND MUSEUMS.—Libraries have several ways of serving adults interested in education. Some have staff members with special training in work with adults, and some have separate departments devoted exclusively to the educational needs of the mature person. The library assistance provided adults is most often advisory. However, many libraries have regularly scheduled educational programs; these involve planned group discussions of specific books or of certain aspects of literature. Recordings, television and radio presentations, displays, subject-centered and theme-centered collections, lectures, concerts, and facilities for "Great Books" discussion groups are among the educational activities and provisions widely identified with libraries.

Museum programs also figure in adult education. Practically all of them build educational experiences around identification and explication of their treasures. Their curator staffs are educators by function and, in many instances, by training as well.

The growing cooperation between museums and art institutes on the one hand, and colleges, universities, and other educational institutions on the other, indicates a logical joining of talent, resources, and objectives. One of their common aims is the education of adults. Adult interest in the history, works, and practice of the visual arts has been accompanied and abetted by the educational vision of the institutes of art.

—Ronald Shilen

ROLLIE MCKENNA. MUSEUM OF MODERN ART

SCULPTURE CLASS for adults held at the People's Art Center of the Museum of Modern Art.

CURRICULUM

Every society, ancient or modern, primitive or industrially developed, has the problem of educating its younger members to take over the management of the society. The skills that have been developed by preceding generations must be passed on to a new group of young people. The accumulated knowledge and wisdom must be handed on. At the heart of the process of education in any society, therefore, is the problem of deciding what must be taught to the younger generation.

In a relatively simple, tradition-bound society in which the pace of change is slow, most of the cultural heritage can be passed on to almost all new members of the group. In such a society, decisions as to what to teach are not especially difficult. However, in a modern, industrialized nation, where new skills are always being called for, where knowledge continually proliferates, and where old values and traditions are challenged over and over again as new conditions develop, decisions as to what to teach are enormously complicated and require special knowledge and skill on the part of educators.

Only in our own century have such specialized knowledge and skill been developed in any systematic way. About the time of World War I certain educators became interested in improving the *curriculum* (a Latin word meaning 'racetrack') by utilizing a more scientific process to decide what should be taught in schools. Thus there emerged a new area of educational specialization now known as the *curriculum field*. In subsequent years, these new specialists have approached the study of their field with increasing sophistication.

Heritage of the Curriculum Field.—Pioneers attempting to improve the process they called "curriculum-making" or "curriculum construction" owed much to the preceding generations of educators. As in other modern countries, education in the United States had become an efficiently organized enterprise. Well-established traditions had developed as solutions were found for two key problems: (1) what information was to be presented (later referred to as the *scope* of the curriculum); and (2) in what order the information was to be presented grade by grade (later referred to as the *sequence* of the curriculum).

The question of scope was answered by deciding the list of school subjects that would be taught and selecting specific subject matter in each field. A textbook was then prepared to present the material in sequence.

With only one way of organizing the curriculum in mind—that is, around such subjects as history, chemistry, and arithmetic—those wishing to improve the curriculum had few choices. As conditions changed and the need appeared for something new in the curriculum, educators usually selected one of the following procedures:

1. A school subject was dropped in favor of a new one. For example, Greek as a high school subject gave way to modern foreign languages, and pedagogy was abandoned in the high schools as normal schools were developed to train teachers. Dropping a subject usually meant running counter to the vested interests of teachers prepared to teach it and of publishers with textbooks to sell. Another obstacle was the attitudes of parents who had studied the subject when they went to school.

2. New material was squeezed into an established subject, which was sometimes also renamed. An example is the shift from nature study to general science in the elementary school. This meant either dropping some subject matter formerly covered or treating more subject matter than before, sometimes in a more superficial manner.

3. Old subjects were retained and new ones added to the curriculum by lengthening the school day and/or reducing time for any one subject.

4. Certain subjects were designated as required subjects and others as electives. This system was used primarily in the high schools. Hopefully, every student learned what was necessary for all citizens, and individual students specialized in various subjects compatible with their aptitudes and interests.

All of the foregoing methods were employed by school systems in the United States to meet changes in the world and increases in knowledge. Perhaps the most popular of these methods was that of adding new subjects to the curriculum, as shown in the following table.

The elementary school had enlarged the scope of its curriculum in similar fashion. Compared with the reading and writing schools of colonial times, the curriculum of the typical elementary school of 1900 was rich indeed.

For most subjects, there was a choice of textbooks, which were relied upon to structure the scope and sequence of the subject.

Changing Definitions of the Curriculum.—The word "curriculum" was used in the nineteenth century to refer to the whole body of courses offered in a university or in one of its departments, but it did not come into general use with reference to elementary and secondary education until the early part of the twentieth century. At that time, the only way known for organizing what was to be taught was by school subject. Therefore, all early uses of the word were closely related to this view. For example, high schools that had had a college preparatory course and a commercial course began to speak of the college preparatory curriculum and the commercial curriculum. Each curriculum had a list of required subjects and recommended electives to be pursued by the student electing it. Although other meanings have developed for the word "curriculum" since 1930, it is still legitimate to use the word to signify a list of subjects that make up the entire course of study in an elementary or high school, or of one path through a high school (agriculture or home economics), or of one department, such as mathematics.

■CURRICULUM ANALYSES.—Later developments in the use of the term "curriculum" reflect changes within the curriculum field itself. Around 1920, Franklin Bobbitt, W. W. Charters, and others became interested in discovering what should be included in the curriculum through analyses of activities actually carried on by adults in society. As a result of the work of these early students of curriculum-making, a large number of school systems, such as those in the cities of Los Angeles and Denver and those of the state of Virginia, began to prepare *courses of study* for various subjects. These courses of study were intended to replace textbooks as the authoritative source for determining the scope and sequence of the curriculum. The documents usually began by listing the aims that had been established through scientific analysis and were geared toward preparing students for life activities. Next came outlines of the subject matter to be covered by students to achieve the aims. Often books and other materials to be used by the students were also listed.

Typical Elementary School Subjects, 1900			Development of High School Subjects of Study		
Major Emphasis	**Medium Emphasis**	**Minor Emphasis**	**Before 1800**	**1800 to 1850**	**1860 to 1875**
Reading	Spelling	Elementary Science	Latin (1640)	Arithmetic (1802)	Modern History (1869)
Literature	Writing	Play	Greek (1640)	Geography (1807)	Physical Geography (1870)
Arithmetic	Grammar	Physical Training		English Grammar (1819)	English Composition (1870)
Oral Language	Home Geography	Sewing		Algebra (1820)	Physical Sciences (1872)
Text Geography	History Stories	Cooking		Geometry (1844)	English Literature (1874)
Text History	Nature Study	Manual Training		Ancient History (1847)	Modern Languages (1875)
	Drawing				
	Music				

LOOK MAGAZINE

A TASTE FOR MUSIC is developed in a special class for these practicing young violinists. Extra-curricular activities which meet the needs of students' individual interests and abilities are the pride of a school, may include an orchestra and band.

School provides an opportunity to develop skills, to learn and grow together

A GEOGRAPHY PUPIL re-lives the voyages of explorers, and realizes the relation of the world to himself.

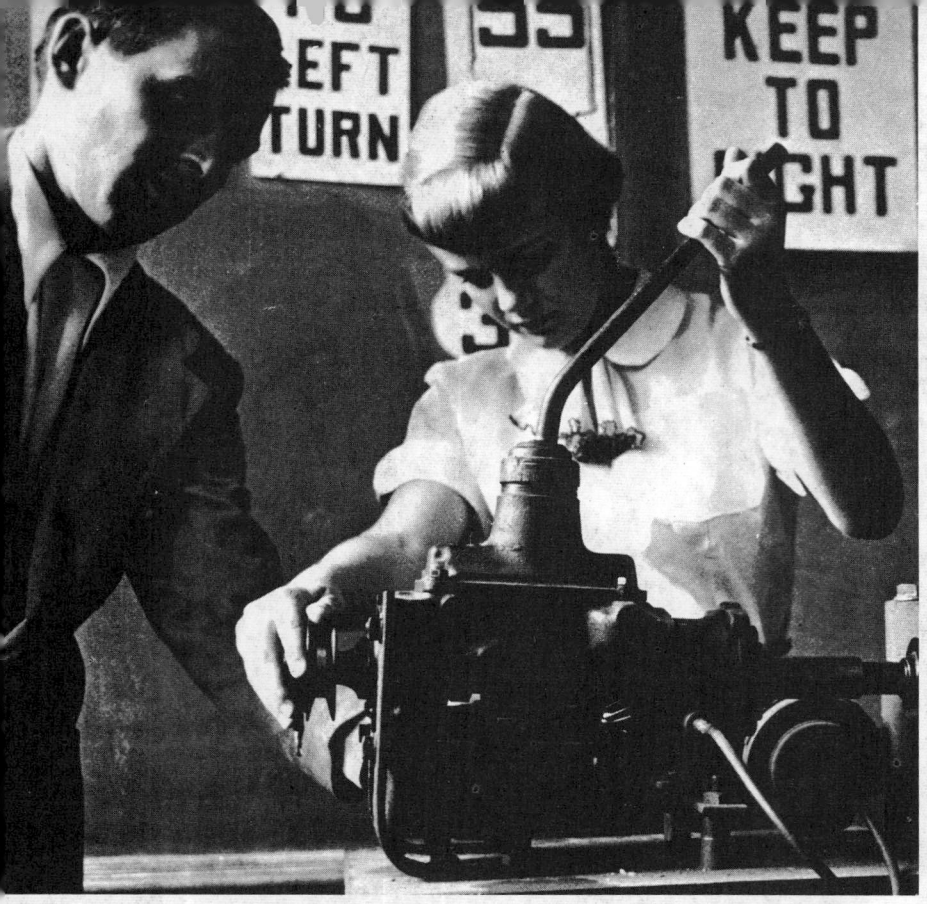

LOOK MAGAZINE PHOTO

THE ART OF DRIVING is taught in a class devoted to civic responsibility. An instructor explains the function and operation of an automobile gear shift.

WITH GUIDANCE from a faculty advisor, a young writer prepares an article for his school paper.

BIOLOGY AND CHEMISTRY students in today's school laboratories can, with dedication, become tomorrow's doctors and scientists.

The structure of one such course of study is revealed in the grid used to show the scope of work in the core curriculum. Down the left-hand side of the grid were the "major functions of social life": personal development; protection and conservation of life, property, and natural resources; production, distribution, and consumption of goods and services; communication; transportation of goods and people; recreation; expression of religious and aesthetic impulses; (for high school only) education; and extension of freedom. Across the top of the grid were the following centers of interest: for Grades 1 and 2, home, school, and community life; for Grades 3 and 4, adaptations of life to varied natural environments and to advancing physical frontiers; for Grades 5 and 6, effect of inventions, discoveries, and machine production upon our living; for Grade 7, social provisions for cooperative living; for the first year of high school, the effects of inventions and discoveries upon basic human needs; for the second year, the effects of agrarianism and industrialism upon everyday life; for the third and fourth years, the effects of democracy upon human relationships.

It was easy to think of such a document as the curriculum itself, since it was designed to replace the textbook as a curriculum directive to the teacher. The language of the day reflected this view of curriculum as a written course of study for one or more subjects. Books dealing with ways of revising the curriculum described elaborate procedures to be employed in preparing a course of study for three years of high school history or twelve years of English. In other words, curriculum now had a slightly different meaning assigned to it—the written course of study showing what to cover within a given subject or subjects.

High hopes were held for this method of curriculum-making, and its use spread rapidly. But a dozen or so years of experience with the "course of study movement" led to considerable disenchantment. By 1935, Caswell and Campbell quickly captured the attention of curriculum specialists when they proposed that the curriculum was not a mere document setting down an intended school program; the curriculum was what actually happened in the classroom.

■ **NEW MEANINGS OF CURRICULUM.**—The definition of curriculum as actual experiences under the direction of the school became a third meaning, one that is in current use along with the two already described. The new meaning was convenient for three reasons.

First, it adequately covered the various ways of organizing the curriculum with which educators were experimenting during the 1920's and 1930's. One could speak of a *subject-centered curriculum,* meaning that what was to be taught was organized around school subjects. One could speak of a *broad-fields curriculum,* or *fused curriculum,* meaning an organization in which related subjects had been brought together to make a new

whole. For example, the field of social studies was created out of geography, history, and other social sciences. The field of language arts in the elementary school encompassed reading, composition, penmanship, spelling, literature, and experiences in speaking and listening. One could also speak of a *unified curriculum,* or *integrated curriculum,* in which a unit of work, on a topic like "transportation" or "the Amazon River Valley" cut across subject boundaries and drew on many fields of knowledge (natural and social sciences, the arts, and the humanities).

The second advantage of thinking of the curriculum as all of the experiences within the school was that the multidimensional purposes of the modern school were now included in the curriculum. Experiences might be designed to promote democratic values and skills or to help an individual cope with his own feelings, relate well to other people, and develop social responsibility, whether or not a home base for these experiences could be found within a school subject. In other words, the new definition of curriculum made the term "extra-curricular" obsolete.

The third advantage of the new definition was that it focused the attention of educators on improving the actual operations in which students and teachers worked together. At the same time, it removed the false notion that a mere plan on paper guaranteed an adequate experience. While certain curriculum documents might have been useful as teaching guides, a change in the documents was not in itself a curriculum change. In the words of one writer: "To change the curriculum of the school is to change the factors interacting to shape that curriculum. In each instance this means bringing about changes in people—in their desires, beliefs and attitudes, in their knowledge and skill."

This view suggested that at least part of the energy that had gone into developing courses of study might be invested in in-service education of teachers and in the continuous planning of ongoing experiences. In fact, the teacher might plan certain aspects of the curriculum in the classroom with the help of the students, thus making education more meaningful to those being educated.

More recent work on the meaning of curriculum has centered on refinements within the concept of curriculum as the actual program of school offerings and the opportunities for experience thus afforded. Since the word continues to be used in three rather distinct ways, it is well to determine in what sense it is being used on a particular occasion. However, all meanings have two things in common: that they deal with what the school intends to teach and that they refer to more or less contained and organized experiences as opposed to unstructured and unexamined ones.

Scope of Today's Curriculum

■ **ELEMENTARY SCHOOL LEVEL.**—The curriculum of today's elementary school can no longer be described by merely

listing the subjects taught. Such a listing might show that attention is still given to the three R's (reading, 'riting, and 'rithmetic), but it could not reflect the fact that educators are no longer satisfied to establish minimum word-recognition skills in reading, minimum computation skills in arithmetic, and ability to write a fine hand and win a spelling bee. Now children are helped to become independent readers who can and do read for enjoyment but also have good reference skills, students who can vary their pace to suit different purposes in reading, and can also read critically. Certain concepts in geometry and algebra are taught along with arithmetic. The emphasis throughout is on understanding the nature of mathematics and the operations being performed as well as on uses of mathematics in modern society.

Children are still taught handwriting, but they are first introduced to a manuscript form (unjoined letters resembling print), which, compared with cursive writing, is easier for younger children to manage at their stage of physical coordination and has more transfer value for beginning reading. They are encouraged to maintain a mature form of manuscript for use throughout their lives, while learning to read and usually to write the cursive form from the middle grades onward. Handwriting is not learned for itself but, as is the case with spelling, grammar, and vocabulary, it is learned for use in both utilitarian and aesthetic written communication.

In social studies, which may appear under the separate subject labels of geography and history, the emphasis is on understanding people and their ways of life. A relatively new subject, elementary science, has been introduced, encompassing nature study (formerly the only science taught), and including also some simplified physical geography, physics, chemistry, biology, physiology, climatology, and astronomy. Most programs include opportunities to perform in art, music, and movement as well as to appreciate the accomplishments of artists in those fields. Health, safety, and physical education for use in building a sound body are also stressed.

In recent years many elementary schools have made foreign languages, usually French or Spanish, a part of the curriculum. Instruction may begin as early as kindergarten or first grade, but more commonly starts somewhere between the third and the sixth grades. Instruction is often carried on by a special teacher. Sometimes teaching is done by television.

■ **SECONDARY SCHOOL LEVEL.**—Throughout the junior high school years, the subjects typically pursued by all students are social studies (sometimes separated as geography in Grade 7, history in Grade 8, and civics or citizenship in Grade 9), English (including composition and literature), mathematics, general science, art, music, and physical education. Industrial arts for boys and home-making for girls are added features of most programs. Much work has gone into modernizing both science and mathematics; schools are being urged to include more content in social studies from a range of such social sciences as economics, sociology, and anthropology. English is being influenced by developments in the field of linguistics. Foreign languages, if not begun in the elementary school, are often introduced in Grade 7 or 8.

In the senior high school years, English is usually required in all grades. In the field of social studies, one year of American history is usually required, often with a second year of history or a course in problems of American democracy or some other social subject. Biology, chemistry, and physics, all responding to modernization, are available in most high schools. In the field of mathematics, algebra, geometry, trigonometry—and in some cases even calculus—are offered. Latin and one, two, or more modern foreign languages are available for those who elect them.

In the senior high school, as students begin to follow different curricula, different levels of courses may be offered. For example, those following a college preparatory route might have quite a different experience in English from those majoring in business. Since a much larger percentage of students go on to high school today than in 1900, the range of difference in student ability has increased markedly. Therefore, certain *remedial courses* are offered to help those of high school age who have not achieved the reading and writing skills necessary for courses geared to students with college potential. On the other hand, *advanced placement courses* are provided in some school systems to enable the most academically talented students to take college-level work while still in high school.

From this survey, it may be seen that schools in more recent years have changed the curriculum by adding or dropping courses, making new combinations of courses, providing different levels of the same subject, and updating the content of courses.

Organizing the Curriculum

■ELEMENTARY SCHOOL LEVEL.—Most elementary schools exemplify a combination of modes of curriculum organization. In most cases, the separate subject is the outstanding feature. Second in frequency of use is the broad field, such as language arts, social studies, science, or mathematics, the latter replacing straight arithmetic. Third is the unit of work cutting across subjects. Much time is spent on the so-called *tool subjects*, reading, arithmetic, spelling, penmanship, and composition. Reading and composition are used to reinforce each other; and spelling and penmanship are both taught individually and used in connection with composition. The program may include some simple science experiences—reading, observing, experimenting—and some health and safety instruction, which may or may not be correlated with the science being taught.

Social studies may be taught through a unit of work on such a topic as the postman, city traffic planning, or a new nation in Africa. Here the information included might come from social sciences, mathematics, and natural physical sciences. Art, music, and literature might also be sources of information, and these forms of expression might be used as the children communicate to others what they have learned. Separate periods for art and music not correlated with a unit of work are also provided almost daily, along with time for recreation, games, and exercise in a gymnasium or out of doors. An early-morning period for sharing happenings at home as well as current events in the local community and the wider world is a familiar feature that cuts across all subject boundaries and promotes oral discussion skills.

A snack period may provide simple experiences in practical arithmetic and the art of conversation as well as an opportunity for refreshment and rest. A time when the teacher reads or tells a story may not only develop taste in literature but also provide a change of pace in learning and an opportunity to experience the enjoyment of something along with others. Planning time allotments, handling of materials, and ways of approaching different parts of the program not only increase the efficiency of the immediate operation but also teach skills of planning and self-management. Time spent in delegating and fulfilling responsibilities for the care of the classroom and appearance of the school building and grounds is of special value in this connection. Skills of planning and self-management, and willingness to use these skills in community service, are also developed through a wide variety of service projects, such as operating a lost-and-found department or arranging an exhibit, for which time is periodically allotted in some schools.

Time is scheduled in short periods in some classrooms, in longer time blocks in others. Some of the time in an elementary school may be spent in specially equipped centers, often with a specialist in charge. A central library, a shop, a homemaking center, an art room, a music room, and a science laboratory are fairly common illustrations of such centers.

■SECONDARY SCHOOL LEVEL.—Even more than at the elementary school level, the separate subject is the most frequent way of organizing the curriculum on the secondary school level. A junior high school may have separate periods and teachers for reading, spelling, and English. Courses in world history and American history, geography, economics, and sociology are more frequently found in high school schedules than is the broad field of social studies. Except for the fused course, general science, separate subjects prevail.

To unify some of the experiences of the students, a few junior and senior high schools have experimented with a core of general education or a *common learnings course*, sometimes called a *core course*, in which social studies and English are often combined. A double or triple period in the school day is allotted for such a course. Within such a structure, a unit of work is often the form of curriculum organization employed. The unit method of organization is used to a limited extent within separate subjects and also in fused courses, and teachers of separate subjects usually attempt to point up the relationships of their subjects to other fields.

Changing the Curriculum.—When a change in the curriculum is brought about by introducing a new subject, such as French in the elementary school, several things are required. Of course, someone must be able to teach the new subject. The necessary materials for the students must be secured or prepared. Time must be found for the new subject, which means deciding whether the day is to be lengthened or whether time devoted to something else is to be shortened. The value of the new subject must be weighed against the value of whatever other service might have been purchased with the money—a trained librarian or school psychologist, for example.

If a new subject is introduced in the secondary school, such as advanced placement mathematics, again the qualified teacher must be found and appropriate materials purchased. In this case, since it is likely to be an elective subject, time may be found at the expense of another elective like art, thus affecting the balance of a student's program.

A change made by updating the content of a subject like mathematics or science may require special summer study by teachers or their in-service education during the school year, under the direction of a specialist from a college or university.

A change that involves new methods of teaching—such as helping students learn the skills of problem-solving or developing democratic values in connection with all their experiences at school—requires time and attention from teachers and supervisors alike, so that new insights may be developed and new teaching skills acquired.

Curriculum specialists advocate that all changes should be brought about through orderly processes, giving time to make thoughtful decisions, learn new ways of teaching, and secure new materials. Time is usually required for testing ideas on a small scale before they are introduced wholesale. Time and money are required for evaluating results to make sure that changes represent improvement.

■CURRICULUM SPECIALISTS.—The first step in such an orderly process is to assess carefully the direction to be taken in educating the youth. Here the views of laymen and educators alike are valuable, as they study people and conditions in the current society and decide whether the present direction of the society is desirable or is to be countered with education aimed in another direction. For example, does undesirable conformity seem to be on the increase and individual creativity on the decrease? Are children in affluent suburbs shoplifting "for kicks"? Are some students dropping out of high school and entering the labor market with insufficient skills for employment in an age of increasing automation? Are citizens of the United States at a disadvantage in their dealings with other people because they know no language other than their own?

It is the responsibility of curriculum specialists to see that teachers and other specialists in the school system join with laymen of appropriate competence to assess whether the curriculum is up to date and in harmony with the basic values of the society. It is also their responsibility to see that professional personnel study the adequacy of the present curriculum for moving toward such objectives and that they make plans for the most sound changes, considering the personnel and financial resources available. In this phase of the operation, where curriculum decisions are being made, lay specialists may be used as consultants; but decisions regarding what and how to teach are professional ones.

Further responsibilities of the curriculum specialist are to give leadership in planning and providing in-service education opportunities necessary to prepare teachers to implement curriculum changes, in selecting and putting to use new media and tools for instruction appropriate for the curriculum changes, and in gathering and appraising evidence on the worth of the changes after they are in operation.

Direction in the Curriculum Field.— Through the centuries there have been educators who were ahead of their times, who pointed the way to developments that are now almost taken for granted. The directions they have suggested and that are now well accepted are these:

1. There have been continuing attempts to make the curriculum more meaningful for each child. At first the attempts were crude, such as giving more time for the slower learner to accomplish the task and giving him repeated explanations. As our knowledge of the differences among individuals has increased, adjustments have been made in the time allowed for working on an aspect of the curriculum, in the amount of subject matter to be dealt with, in the level of skill to be reached, and in the very nature of the experience provided for different students. More and more it is recognized that individuals differ in the nature of their intelligence— that some are more gifted in social-influence skills, some in creating with words, some in spatial relationships, and some in logical thinking. Educators are becoming increasingly aware of the right of each individual to a curriculum that allows him to learn at his own pace and in his own way so that he can maintain a view of himself as a competent student.

2. There have been continuing attempts to provide a curriculum that has social significance, that is, one that deals with matters important to society. With so much that might be learned, it seems wise to select the content that is most relevant to the modern world. This is an especially important guide for general education. A wide range of choice for individual specialization is a further guarantee that important fields of knowledge and human creativity will be maintained and advanced.

3. There have been continuing attempts to provide for continuity in individual and group learning. Planning to close gaps between levels of the school—for example, elementary and junior high school—is one approach to the problem. Planning by a curriculum committee representing teachers from kindergarten through senior high school for a curriculum area like mathematics, science, social studies, or language arts is another approach. Diagnosing student achievement and keeping cumulative records of progress to aid the next teacher in planning for individuals is a third approach. Another approach is a deliberate plan to introduce, in early grades, certain concepts—say, from physics—returning to them in increasingly complex form in later grades. This is sometimes called a *spiral curriculum*. Planning major emphases as threads through the entire curriculum is a fifth and highly promising approach. The emphasis may be on the development of such significant concepts as freedom, social justice, and interdependence or on such basic skills as critical reading or problem-solving, with all teachers attempting, at their level and within their speciality, to contribute to the students' progress in developing such concepts and skills.

4. There have been continual attempts to provide for more integration in learning on the part of the individual student. Early in this century the term *correlation* was used to label teachers' attempts to point up the relationships between subjects, while still maintaining the identity of each separate study. The attempt to create a new whole by fusing several subjects into a broad field went even further. The unit of work that cut across several subjects and "integrated" experiences around a unifying theme, topic, or problem went even further. Many educators believe today that some of these attempts to integrate subject matter outside of the learner may have considerable value but that, with adult guidance, each individual can be helped to achieve an inner integration—a more unified view of the world and its knowledge—even though the curriculum may be made up of a combination of separate subjects, broad fields, units of work, and extra-class experiences. The use of major emphases as continuing threads should also contribute to a unified view. Most important of all for inner integration, however, is to put curriculum emphasis on development of students who are not only informed about other people, places, and conditions but who also care about these matters; who not only care but also take thoughtful and useful action to make the world a better place for all.

—Alice Miel

COOPER UNION SCHOOL OF ART AND ARCHITECTURE

INDIVIDUAL INSTRUCTION is given to art student in painting studio by instructor. Such methods of teaching enable students to discuss their individual problems and techniques.

ESTIMATED EXPENDITURES FOR PUBLIC SCHOOLS
1965–1966

Region and State	Total Current Expenditures for Public Elementary and Secondary Schools		Current Expenditures for Other Programs (Thousands)	Capital Outlay (Thousands)	Interest on School Debt (Thousands)	Total Current Expenditures, Capital Outlay, and Interest (Thousands)
	Amount (Thousands)	Per Pupil*				
The States and D.C.	$20,766,490	$532	$612,896	$3,431,840	$822,818	$25,634,046
New England	**1,119,545**		**14,255**	**130,075**	**20,886**	**1,284,761**
Connecticut	334,000	637	2,500	30,000	12,500	379,000
Maine	87,800	410	5,000	13,000	2,500	108,300
Massachusetts	517,000	530	6,000	52,000	—	575,000
New Hampshire	57,702	479	225	18,000	2,193	78,120
Rhode Island	81,450	576	425	14,075	2,893	98,843
Vermont	41,593	507	105	3,000	800	45,498
Mideast	**5,017,963**		**65,844**	**678,564**	**227,103**	**5,989,474**
Delaware	56,000	580	140	20,000	4,000	80,140
District of Columbia	76,324	578	4,016	17,569	—	97,909
Maryland	387,639	552	11,688	107,995	19,603	526,925
New Jersey	787,000	662	8,000	125,000	33,500	953,500
New York	2,560,000	876	30,000	375,000	105,000	3,070,000
Pennsylvania	1,151,000	565	12,000	33,000	65,000	1,261,000
Southeast	**3,534,110**		**99,848**	**544,905**	**108,526**	**4,287,389**
Alabama	283,000	355	1,500	26,000	10,000	320,500
Arkansas	154,763	376	1,305	30,900	5,068	192,036
Florida	506,348	439	40,743	162,700	13,658	723,449
Georgia	369,368	384	8,000	40,000	12,000	429,368
Kentucky	234,500	375	3,000	26,000	9,000	272,500
Louisiana	358,609	481	500	40,000	15,000	414,109
Mississippi	169,322	317	8,600	22,705	4,000	204,627
North Carolina	419,000	379	8,000	60,000	10,200	497,200
South Carolina	206,500	349	4,300	25,600	5,500	241,900
Tennessee	299,700	361	4,800	39,000	12,000	355,500
Virginia	386,000	424	15,000	62,000	10,500	473,500
West Virginia	147,000	367	4,100	10,000	1,600	162,700
Great Lakes	**4,116,294**		**80,200**	**730,000**	**172,000**	**5,078,494**
Illinois	1,125,000	591	35,000	160,000	46,000	1,366,000
Indiana	532,614	512	8,000	80,000	6,000	606,614
Michigan	950,000	523	25,000	225,000	57,000	1,257,000
Ohio	1,070,000	503	10,000	180,000	46,000	1,306,000
Wisconsin	438,680	575	2,200	85,000	17,000	542,880
Plains	**1,677,075**		**25,005**	**281,894**	**65,040**	**2,049,014**
Iowa	326,072	549	4,237	58,000	9,000	397,309
Kansas	245,384	511	3,738	30,581	8,000	287,703
Minnesota	433,458	577	5,530	84,243	24,284	547,515
Missouri	399,402	485	8,500	60,000	14,500	482,402
Nebraska	130,000	419	2,000	26,000	5,000	163,000
North Dakota	63,500	460	1,000	14,150	2,850	81,500
South Dakota	79,259	504	—	8,920	1,406	89,585
Southwest	**1,605,667**		**9,490**	**242,061**	**56,578**	**1,913,796**
Arizona	181,308	514	2,136	18,409	5,602	207,455
New Mexico	147,560	578	554	24,652	1,576	174,342
Oklahoma	265,799	481	1,800	34,000	4,400	305,999
Texas	1,011,000	449	5,000	165,000	45,000	1,226,000
Rocky Mountain	**556,179**		**10,172**	**122,386**	**24,000**	**712,737**
Colorado	232,000	513	7,500	50,000	13,500	303,000
Idaho	66,987	400	—	9,000	1,800	77,787
Montana	88,500	567	500	10,500	4,000	103,500
Utah	124,132	459	2,172	46,186	3,400	175,890
Wyoming	44,560	551	—	6,700	1,300	52,560
Far West	**3,282,656**		**315,015**	**719,974**	**148,685**	**4,466,330**
California	2,475,000	582	280,000	580,000	120,000	3,455,000
Nevada	55,222	528	544	1,179	3,700	60,645
Oregon	252,500	612	4,400	47,690	5,886	310,476
Washington	380,000	556	21,000	75,000	15,000	491,000
Alaska	41,827	775	1,439	2,225	1,917	47,408
Hawaii	78,107	515	7,632	13,880	2,182	101,801

Source: "Fall 1965 Statistics of Public Schools," circular #OE-20007-65, Office of Education, U.S. Department of Health, Education and Welfare.
* Per pupil in average daily attendance.

STUDENT ENROLLMENT IN VARIOUS LEVELS
OF HIGHER EDUCATION, 1965

Region and State	All Students in Survey	Students Taking Work Creditable Toward a Bachelor's or Higher Degree		Students in Undergraduate Programs Not Chiefly Creditable Toward a Degree	First-time Students Taking Work Creditable Toward a Bachelor's Degree	
		Number	Percentage of Change, 1964–1965		Number	Percentage of Change, 1964–1965
The States and D.C.	5,920,864	5,526,325	+11.6	394,539	1,441,822	+17.7
New England	386,574	365,990	**+13.2**	20,584	94,132	**+18.1**
Connecticut	84,048	79,372	+13.0	4,676	19,495	+33.4
Maine	22,999	21,244	+20.1	1,755	5,194	+16.9
Massachusetts	211,251	200,512	+10.9	10,739	51,258	+11.8
New Hampshire	20,480	19,581	+24.1	899	5,353	+20.0
Rhode Island	33,741	32,202	+20.2	1,539	8,686	+32.4
Vermont	14,055	13,079	+9.7	976	4,146	+10.4
Mideast	1,176,323	1,060,233	**+8.8**	116,090	211,633	**+7.5**
Delaware	13,167	12,334	+6.8	833	3,369	—.5
District of Columbia........	60,865	57,808	+3.8	3,057	7,457	—6.8
Maryland	98,594	96,430	+16.7	2,164	21,227	+19.7
New Jersey	129,684	127,868	+7.9	1,816	26,907	+2.8
New York	586,462	491,998	+8.3	94,464	89,748	+7.5
Pennsylvania	287,551	273,795	+8.6	13,756	62,925	+8.3
Great Lakes	1,125,951	1,078,154	**+11.7**	47,797	279,013	**+18.5**
Illinois	305,107	295,160	+9.6	9,947	73,469	+13.7
Indiana	142,113	141,409	+11.0	704	36,938	+22.3
Michigan	270,918	251,572	+14.6	19,346	65,234	+26.2
Ohio	278,506	266,363	+10.1	12,143	69,451	+12.2
Wisconsin	129,307	123,650	+15.0	5,657	33,921	+25.5
Plains	517,875	509,250	**+13.7**	8,625	149,973	**+15.3**
Iowa	86,588	85,328	+14.5	1,260	24,416	+15.2
Kansas	81,574	80,621	+12.2	953	24,401	+18.1
Minnesota	118,533	116,103	+10.6	2,430	32,709	+6.6
Missouri	135,652	133,806	+15.2	1,846	40,216	+17.0
Nebraska	49,805	49,252	+15.1	553	14,042	+24.2
North Dakota	22,470	20,904	+15.2	1,566	7,090	+26.2
South Dakota	23,253	23,236	+18.7	17	7,099	+14.4
Southeast	949,405	915,691	**+13.5**	33,714	272,365	**+21.5**
Alabama	67,151	66,515	+18.6	636	19,141	+41.7
Arkansas	43,026	42,541	+18.8	485	14,095	+23.9
Florida	141,591	130,320	+12.5	11,271	40,341	+21.5
Georgia	82,347	80,271	+19.0	2,076	20,711	+15.7
Kentucky	76,440	76,172	+16.2	268	22,600	+15.4
Louisiana	89,050	89,009	+7.4	41	22,063	+16.2
Mississippi	55,790	53,910	+15.8	1,880	17,977	+16.2
North Carolina	110,977	103,774	+10.9	7,203	30,958	+19.8
South Carolina	43,946	40,804	+6.6	3,142	13,277	+13.2
Tennessee	99,989	99,139	+13.4	850	26,809	+17.2
Virginia	91,696	86,431	+10.8	5,265	29,263	+29.1
West Virginia	47,402	46,805	+19.7	597	15,130	+36.6
Southwest	486,746	473,416	**+13.4**	13,330	130,445	**+23.0**
Arizona	72,503	69,429	+16.3	3,074	18,899	+11.0
New Mexico	30,388	30,006	+15.4	382	7,762	+20.8
Oklahoma	89,326	85,366	+12.8	3,960	23,969	+25.7
Texas	294,529	288,615	+12.7	5,914	79,815	+25.7
Rocky Mountain	184,419	179,373	**+14.2**	5,046	52,160	**+26.1**
Colorado	74,285	72,860	+14.0	1,425	19,914	+21.8
Idaho	20,788	19,805	+16.2	983	7,252	+30.1
Montana	20,308	19,976	+13.4	332	6,336	+27.8
Utah	58,323	56,334	+14.1	1,989	15,295	+29.2
Wyoming	10,715	10,398	+13.7	317	3,363	+27.5
Far West	1,079,946	930,593	**+10.2**	149,353	248,443	**+19.5**
Alaska	4,734	4,657	+12.3	77	1,727	+60.4
California	866,746	728,091	+9.0	138,655	189,017	+16.6
Hawaii	19,247	19,091	+20.2	156	3,841	+18.8
Nevada	8,039	7,935	+16.5	104	3,046	+121.8
Oregon	71,601	67,688	+14.5	3,913	20,309	+28.4
Washington	109,579	103,131	+13.9	6,448	30,503	+25.6

Source: "Opening Fall Enrollment in Higher Education, 1965," Office of Education, U.S. Department of Health, Education and Welfare.

PUBLIC SCHOOL ENROLLMENTS, TEACHERS, HIGH SCHOOL GRADUATES
1965

| State | Elementary Grades | | Secondary Grades | | Total Graduated[2] From High School |
	Pupils[1] Enrolled	Teachers[1,3] Employed	Pupils[1] Enrolled	Teachers[1,3] Employed	
The States and D.C.	26,415,834	955,658	15,727,670	740,930	2,362,100
Alabama	480,327	15,597	351,374	13,978	45,424
Alaska	41,800	1,554	17,927	1,127	2,258
Arizona	270,117	11,121	103,542	4,583	18,920
Arkansas	250,884	8,714	200,347	8,486	25,394
California	2,754,500	94,500	1,507,500	65,300	226,500
Colorado	287,999	11,297	198,785	10,519	26,749
Connecticut	367,801	14,575	206,997	10,395	31,729
Delaware	62,182	2,434	46,175	2,368	5,987
District of Columbia	92,665	3,213	51,351	2,404	4,709
Florida	687,806	25,382	532,775	22,468	61,190
Georgia	693,197	23,791	361,907	14,182	51,708
Hawaii	94,192	3,298	68,008	2,154	9,200
Idaho	92,215	3,560	81,481	3,701	11,518
Illinois	1,366,223	53,753	721,466	35,717	115,006
Indiana	693,100	24,541	431,624	20,543	66,348
Iowa	445,460	16,254	179,898	12,828	40,590
Kansas	365,501	14,802	141,457	11,917	28,000
Kentucky	436,599	16,293	228,447	9,768	35,233
Louisiana	505,113	18,252	297,479	13,136	39,269
Maine	148,631	5,717	73,875	3,416	12,661
Maryland	442,025	16,342	320,622	14,752	41,405
Massachusetts	616,000	24,550	404,500	20,454	63,364
Michigan	1,165,000	39,541	810,000	33,241	103,175
Minnesota	452,358	17,246	355,849	17,357	53,443
Mississippi	356,111	11,288	228,518	9,087	26,690
Missouri	703,635	24,668	260,716	12,372	51,261
Montana	109,292	4,950	57,473	2,705	9,941
Nebraska	194,844	8,790	123,902	6,641	19,886
Nevada	66,269	2,515	39,683	1,814	4,751
New Hampshire	83,007	3,239	45,850	2,290	7,775
New Jersey	847,000	35,000	439,000	24,000	78,000
New Mexico	153,780	5,916	113,920	5,074	13,453
New York	1,833,184	74,885	1,357,661	71,198	182,227
North Carolina	850,985	30,959	330,573	13,860	67,520
North Dakota	97,577	4,174	51,294	3,101	9,536
Ohio	1,395,481	49,440	874,627	38,587	132,612
Oklahoma	341,116	12,688	242,990	11,711	35,668
Oregon	274,830	11,968	173,697	8,876	29,988
Pennsylvania	1,226,421	43,716	963,408	45,293	143,200
Rhode Island	88,980	3,374	65,521	3,256	9,157
South Carolina	386,649	13,446	251,341	10,670	33,192
South Dakota	107,977	5,318	57,658	3,102	9,898
Tennessee	566,998	19,500	305,000	11,700	46,541
Texas	1,866,356	57,600	650,986	43,400	121,759
Utah	166,267	5,761	120,137	5,035	16,694
Vermont	55,639	2,278	28,615	1,605	4,452
Virginia	620,103	22,666	366,020	16,798	49,438
Washington	402,152	15,656	321,246	14,196	47,651
West Virginia	239,863	8,765	188,680	7,500	26,974
Wisconsin	519,698	20,457	339,403	18,026	58,829
Wyoming	49,943	2,289	36,365	1,959	5,226

Source: "Fall, 1965 Statistics of Public Schools," circular #OE-20007-65, Office of Education, U.S. Department of Health, Education and Welfare.
[1] Figures for fall, 1965.
[2] Figures for spring, 1965.
[3] Includes full- and part-time teachers.

BIBLIOGRAPHY

AMERICAN EDUCATION TODAY

CONANT, JAMES B. *The American High School Today.* McGraw-Hill, Inc., 1959.

CONANT, JAMES B. *The Child, the Parent and the State.* Harvard University Press, 1959.

DUPUIS, ADRIAN and CRAIG, ROBERT C. *American Education: Its Origins and Issues.* The Bruce Publishing Co., 1963.

HARRIS, RAYMOND P. *American Education: Facts, Fancies, and Folklore.* Random House, Inc., 1961.

HOFSTADTER, RICHARD. *Anti-intellectualism in American Life.* Alfred A. Knopf, Inc., 1964.

LIEBERMAN, MYRON. *The Future of Public Education.* University of Chicago Press, 1960.

MOLNAR, THOMAS. *The Future of Education.* Fleet Publishing Corp., 1964.

WOODRING, PAUL and SCANLON, JOHN (eds.). *American Education Today.* McGraw-Hill, Inc., 1963.

CAREER GUIDANCE

CUNNINGHAM, ED and REED, L. *Guide to Earning a Living.* Simon & Schuster, Inc., 1955.

DAVEY, MILDRED A. and others. *Everyday Occupations.* D. C. Heath & Co., 1950.

How to Create Your Career. National Vocational Guidance Association, 1956.

KING, ALICE GORE. *Career Opportunities for Women in Business.* E. P. Dutton & Co., Inc., 1963.

KITSON, HARRY D. *I Find My Vocation.* McGraw-Hill, Inc., 1954.

MAULE, FRANCES. *Executive Careers for Women.* Harper & Bros., 1961.

McLEAN, BETH BAILEY and PARIS, JEANNE. *The Young Woman in Business* (rev. 2nd ed.). Iowa State University Press, 1961.

MYERS, G. E., and others. *Planning Your Future.* McGraw-Hill, Inc., 1953.

Occupational Outlook Handbook: Employment Information on Major Occupations for Use in Guidance. U.S. Bureau of Labor Statistics, Department of Labor, 1959.

SEEMING, JOSEPH. *Jobs That Take You Places.* David McKay Co., Inc., 1950.

SMITH, LEONARD J. *Career Planning.* Harper & Bros., 1959.

U.S. DEPT. OF LABOR. *Occupational Outlook Handbook.* Superintendent of Documents, U.S. Government Printing Office, 1963.

Vocational Guidance Manuals (a series of 50 paperback books on specific occupations). Universal Publishing and Distributing Corp.

Vocational and Professional Monographs (a series of 59 paperback books on numerous occupations and professions). Bellman Publishing Co.

CHOOSING A COLLEGE

COX, CLAIRE. *How to Beat the High Cost of College.* Bernard Geis Associates, 1965.

FINE, BENJAMIN. *How to be Accepted by the College of Your Choice.* Channel Press, Inc., 1963.

GLEAZER, EDMUND J., JR. (ed.). *American Junior Colleges.* American Council on Education, 1963.

HOWES, RAYMOND F. (ed.). *Vision and Purpose in Higher Education.* American Council on Education, 1962.

IRWIN, MARY (ed.). *American Universities and Colleges* (9th ed.). American Council on Education, 1960.

LOVEJOY, CLARENCE. *Lovejoy's College Guide.* Simon & Schuster, Inc., 1961.

LOVEJOY, CLARENCE. *Lovejoy's Scholarship Guide.* Simon and Schuster, Inc., 1963.

NESS, FREDERIC W. (ed.). *A Guide to Graduate Study: Programs Leading to the Ph.D. Degree* (2nd ed.). American Council on Education, 1960.

QUICK, ROBERT (ed.). *Fellowships in the Arts and Sciences* (6th ed.). American Council on Education, 1962.

SULKIN, SIDNEY. *Complete Planning for College.* McGraw-Hill, Inc., 1962.

TURNGREN, ANNETTE. *Choosing the Right College.* Harper & Bros., 1952.

COMPARATIVE EDUCATION

BEREDAY, GEORGE Z. F.; BRICKMAN, WILLIAM W.; and READ, GEORGE H. (eds.). *The Changing Soviet School.* Houghton Mifflin Co., 1960.

BOWEN, JAMES. *Soviet Education.* University of Wisconsin Press, 1962.

RELLER, THEODORE L. and MORPHET, EDGAR L. *Comparative Educational Administration.* Prentice-Hall, Inc., 1962.

COUNSELING

BERDIE, RALPH F. (ed.). *Roles and Relationships in Counseling.* University of Minnesota Press, 1953.

ROBINSON, FRANCIS P. *Principles and Procedures in Student Counseling.* Harper & Bros., 1950.

CURRICULUM

FAUVRE, RONALD C. and BOSSING, NELSON L. *Developing the Core Curriculum.* Prentice-Hall, Inc., 1951.

KRUG, EDWARD A. *Curriculum Planning* (rev. ed.). Harper & Bros., 1957.

LEE, J. MURRAY and DORIS. *The Child and His Curriculum.* Appleton-Century-Crofts, 1962.

McINERNY, CHESTER T. *The Curriculum.* McGraw-Hill, Inc., 1953.

SMITH, B. OTHANEL; STANLEY, WILLIAM O.; and SHORES, J. HARLAN. *Fundamentals of Curriculum Development* (rev. ed.). Harcourt, Brace & World, Inc., 1962.

PHILOSOPHY AND HISTORY

ATKINSON, CARROLL and MALESKA, EUGENE T. *The Story of Education.* Chilton Co., 1962.

BRAMELD, THEODORE. *Education for the Emerging Age: Newer Ends and Stronger Means.* Harper & Bros., 1961.

BRUBACHER, JOHN S. *Modern Philosophies of Education* (3rd ed.). McGraw-Hill, Inc., 1962.

BRUBACHER, JOHN S. and RUDY, WILLIS. *Higher Education in Transition: An American History, 1636-1956.* Harper & Bros., 1958.

BUTTS, R. FREEMAN. *A Cultural History of Education.* McGraw-Hill, Inc., 1947.

COLE, LUELLA. *A History of Education: Socrates to Montessori.* Holt, Rinehart & Winston, Inc., 1950.

CONANT, JAMES B. *The Revolutionary Transformation of the American High School.* Harvard University Press, 1959.

MAYER, MARTIN. *The Schools.* Harper & Bros., 1961.

MEYER, ADOLPHE E. *An Educational History of the American People.* McGraw-Hill, Inc., 1957.

MONTAGU, M. F. ASHLEY. *Education and Human Relations.* Grove Press, 1958.

RUGG, HAROLD. *Foundations for American Education.* Harcourt, Brace & World, Inc., 1962.

ULICH, R. (ed.). *Three Thousand Years of Educational Wisdom: Selections from Great Documents* (2nd ed.). Harvard University Press, 1954.

PSYCHOLOGY

BRUNER, JEROME. *The Process of Education.* Harvard University Press, 1960.

CRONBACH, LEE. *Educational Psychology.* Harcourt, Brace & World, Inc., 1954.

FRANK, MARY and LAWRENCE K. *Your Adolescent at Home and in School.* The Viking Press, Inc., 1961.

GESELL, ARNOLD; ILG, FRANCES L.; and AMES, LOUISE BATES. *Youth: The Years from Ten to Sixteen.* Harper & Bros., 1956.

ILG, FRANCES L. and AMES, LOUISE BATES. *Child Behavior.* Harper & Bros., 1955.

LINDGREN, HENRY CLAY. *Education Psychology in the Classroom* (2nd ed.). John Wiley & Sons, Inc., 1962.

PRESSEY, S. L. and others. *Psychology in Education.* Harper & Bros., 1959.

RUGG, HAROLD. *Imagination.* Harper & Row, Publishers, 1963.

TEACHING

BOSSING, NELSON L. *Teaching in Secondary Schools.* Houghton Mifflin Co., 1952.

CHAUNCEY, HENRY and DOBBIN, JOHN E. *Testing: Its Place in Education Today* Harper & Row, Publishers, 1963.

HARRIS, ALBERT J. *How to Increase Reading Ability* (4th ed.). Longmans, Green & Co., Inc., 1961.

LUMSDAINE, A. A. and GLASER, ROBERT (eds.). *Teaching Machines and Programmed Learning: A Source Book.* National Education Association, 1960.

SLAUGHTER, STELLA STILLSON. *The Mentally Retarded Child and His Parents.* Harper & Bros., 1960.

STRANG, RUTH. *Helping Your Gifted Child.* E. P. Dutton & Co., Inc., 1960.

College Profile

SELECTING A COLLEGE

Advice to Students from the Executive Vice-President of the College Entrance Examination Board.

Introduction.—As young men and women of the United States, you enjoy opportunities for higher education unparalleled in the history of mankind. Nowhere else in the world do so many of college age have the chance to continue their education beyond the high school. And nowhere else is there such a variety of college possibilities available to you.

At the same time, because we as a nation believe in freedom of the individual and in local control of education, there is no master plan or national system for assigning you to colleges; there is no single formula for determining which college a particular student should attend. You are free to apply to almost any college, and colleges are free to adopt different admissions policies. For you as a student, then, the price of freedom is the responsibility for making a wise choice from among the diverse opportunities for higher education available to you.

There are a multitude of questions that you must face once you have decided that you want to attend college. For example: To commute or board? A two- or four-year college? Close to home or far away? A men's (or women's) or a coed institution? A small school or a large one? Public, independent, or church-affiliated? A specialized curriculum or the liberal arts? In the city, the suburbs, or the country? How much will it cost, how much can I afford, and how much financial aid am I liable to get? What are my chances of admission?

These questions cannot be answered separately, and there is no standard order in which they should be approached. In fact, many of them are not even separable from the prior question, "Should I go to college?"

Self-Evaluation.—Yet you have to begin somewhere. Fortunately, there is one factor that is basic to all of these questions—you. The place for any young man or woman to begin the process of choosing a college is with himself or herself. Because it is necessary to select a school that will meet your own particular needs, it is important that you pose the following questions for yourself.

■**GUIDING QUESTIONS.**—Why am I going to college? Is it because it is "the thing to do"? Because my parents expect me to? Because they went and want me to have the same advantage, or because they did not go and want me to have an advantage they did not enjoy? Because my parents did not go and I want to improve myself?

What do I expect from my college experience? Do I know what type of work I hope to do as an adult? Do I expect college to prepare me for it, or do I want to enter a profession that requires graduate school? Or am I unsure of how I want to earn my living and expect college to help me to make up my mind?

What kind of student am I? How intelligent am I? Do I work up to my capacity? Am I able to study on my own, or do I need close supervision?

Where do my academic abilities and interests lie? What subjects do I prefer? Do I do well in them? Do I do as well in ones that I am not particularly interested in? Are my interests and abilities consistent with what I think I want to follow as a career or with what my parents expect of me?

What are my nonacademic expectations for college? Are the spiritual, social, and extracurricular opportunities of equal or more or less importance as the academic training? Do I have a talent or skill I would like to develop or exploit?

What kind of person am I? Do I make friends easily? Do I want a campus where it is easy to make friends? Am I a "loner" or a "joiner"? Do I want to become one or the other? How do I react to authority? Do I dislike it but put up with it? Or am I a rebel? Or does it not make any difference?

■**PRECONCEPTIONS.**—When choosing a college, few, if any, of these questions can be answered profitably unless you have some idea of what is available to you. Therefore, as you begin to learn about yourself, you should also begin to learn about colleges. You cannot help but bring some preconceived notions to this task—preconceived from conversations about college at home, from what you have heard from college students or from your teachers, from what you have read, and perhaps from pipe dreams about growing up. More often than not, these notions are based on little more than fragments of information about a few particular institutions. To really understand the full range of possibilities open to you, you must put your prejudices aside and start with those sources of information that describe colleges in common terms.

Evaluation of a College.—The literature on college admissions is blessed with a number of directories that do this job in a variety of ways. The following *Cowles College Profile*, for instance, summarizes the academic or academically-related information that describes more than one thousand accredited, degree-granting, four-year institutions in the United States. More comprehensive data are included in the publications listed in the bibliography on page 76–3. A review of these books, some of which are bound to be available in almost any school, public library, or local bookstore, can serve three very useful purposes. First, it can serve to lay out the full range of higher education opportunities available. Second, it can serve to make more explicit or meaningful the questions—the perhaps vague and unformed questions—that have already occurred to you. Third, it can serve to help you formulate questions that may not have occurred.

For instance, the question "How are colleges classified?" may become "What are the differences among universities, liberal arts colleges, teach-

UNIVERSITY OF MICHIGAN NEWS SERVICE

STUDENTS head to and from class on the campus of the University of Michigan, Ann Arbor.

ers colleges, engineering institutes, technical institutes, and junior colleges? Or among state universities, state colleges, and community colleges?" Similarly, you may have wondered about the relative quality of institutions. After reading about various colleges, you might transform the general question "How good is a particular college?" into a series of inquiries that include the following: "Is the college accredited? What proportion of the faculty has doctoral degrees? What proportion of its alumni go on to graduate school? How many books are there in the library? What is the ratio of faculty to students? How much does it cost? What is the average ability or range of ability of the student body?"

Determining Your Qualifications. — In making judgments about a particular college, you will also refine your questions about yourself. For instance, you will come to realize that the question "How intelligent am I?" is not one that can be answered in absolute terms. Rather, you should concern yourself with the question "How bright am I in comparison with the other young people who have applied to, or have been admitted by, a particular college?" You will learn, too, how colleges measure brightness—that this is done in terms of school grades, standing in your graduating class, and the scores of your college entrance examinations. You will find that your school record, as indicated by the grades you have earned in classroom work and by the recommendations that your school will probably write for you, is the most important factor in determining your qualifications for college entrance. You will discover that test scores, although less important, do play a part in the process because they provide a common currency among the grading standards of different schools and because they indicate to colleges the instances where students appear to be working up to or below their capacities. It should become obvious to you that some colleges do not always select the brightest applicants, and also that "average" class standing or "average" test scores of admitted students does not mean "minimum." And you will then begin to ask "What are the other things that colleges look for besides academic ability? What are the factors that cause schools to reject students with above-average academic ability and performance and to accept some with below-average records? Do I want to go to a less demanding college, where I can be near the top of the class, or to a more demanding one where I will probably get a stronger program but will face the likelihood of low standing and run the risk of possible failure?"

At this point it should be clear that the process of choosing a college, even in its early stages, involves finding the right answers to the right questions. And, paradoxical as it might seem, discovering the right questions is usually harder than finding the right answers.

■**PERSONAL CONSIDERATIONS.**—As you answer the questions you have begun to pose for yourself, a general description of colleges in which you are interested will begin to emerge. The problem here is to avoid being trapped into a stereotyped definition, such as "a large, urban, coed university" or "a small, rural, men's college" or "a local community college." The best description of any college is one that gives proper weight to the importance of the questions asked and answered by each student.

College is primarily an academic experience, and the field in which you think you want to major could be a controlling factor in your decision. Or a wide variety of subjects offered could be important to you if you are not sure of the subject upon which you want to concentrate. If you have a special talent or skill, the availability of the appropriate extracurricular opportunities could be the most important factor in determining the type of college that appeals to you. Finding the right outlet for your abilities in music, art, drama, or athletics contributes, in many cases, to success in the classroom.

If you have difficulty keeping your mind on the books, colleges—large and small alike—that place emphasis on close supervision could provide a solution. Or, if you have trouble making friends easily, colleges that offer a planned program of social activities would be appropriate. On the other hand, if you find social activity too absorbing you might decide either that you need the seclusion of a men's or women's college or that at a coed university you would have to spend less time in doing what you would prefer doing anyway. For many students, the financial opportunities or barriers can be all-important. Here financial-aid opportunities and the possibility of commuting must be seriously considered.

In other words, as you begin to narrow the available college opportunities down to a general description of what you want from higher education, you must apply differential importance to the factors you are considering. You have to decide how much consideration to give to questions relating to career objectives, intellectual stimulation, extracurricular opportunities, social values, and finances.

■**COLLEGE CATALOGUES.** — Once you have determined the characteristics that describe the general type of college in which you are interested, assemble a list of specific colleges that meet your requirements and then begin a comparative exploration of their catalogues. In reading catalogues, keep in mind that what colleges say about themselves is bound to be written in the most favorable terms. With this caution, however, you will find the college catalogue full of important information about the college in general and about its requirements and procedures for application in particular. There can be both obvious and subtle differences in what similar colleges apparently want students to have studied in high school, and there are wide variations in pro-

cedures for making application. Note these variations carefully and, when you finally submit your credentials, follow the instructions to the letter.

Once you have begun to narrow the possibilities, it would be wise to turn from the written word to the other sources of information. These can include alumni of and students enrolled in particular colleges; college representatives, such as admission officers and faculty members; and, most helpful of all, secondary school guidance officers.

■**ALUMNI.**—In seeking to find out what a college is like from its alumni, keep in mind that their perceptions of their alma mater can vary widely. Some may be very recent graduates; others may have been out of school a long time. Of the latter, some will recall only "the good old days" and "the way college was when I was there," when in fact things may have changed a good deal. They have, in fact, in most institutions. Other alumni may actually be formal representatives of their college admissions office who are kept up-to-date and fully informed. In talking with alumni it is wise to take into account whether they represent one of these extremes or something in between.

■**STUDENTS.**—Students enrolled in a particular college can be a most valuable source of information. They can help not only by giving an inside view of the academic, extracurricular, and social aspects of their institutions, but also by recounting their own experience in making a choice of a college. But again, what they have to say must not be taken at face value. Account should be taken of who they are, what they are like, and what their degree of enthusiasm or disillusionment may be. The college student home for a vacation is probably more likely to be objective than the campus guide who has been chosen for his or her personality and school spirit.

■**COLLEGE REPRESENTATIVES.**—The college admissions officer or faculty member represents, of course, the best-informed source of facts about an institution. He not only knows the questions prospective applicants generally have on their minds, but he has had experience in interpreting these questions and in answering in a way that has proven useful to others. Like college catalogues, however, college representatives tend to put their institutions in their best light; that is part of their job. Nevertheless, more admissions officers are perceiving their role to be more than that of just a recruiter or gatekeeper and are acting as counselors to applicants about college-going in general.

■**GUIDANCE COUNSELORS.**—Your most important source of assistance will be your high school counselor. The person responsible for pre-college guidance in the local high school or prep school is the individual who has had the broadest experience with the types of problems that students face. Because he is trained in his profession, informed about college opportunities, and knowledgeable about the personalities and interests of the students he is counseling, the

FABIAN BACHRACH

GEORGE H. HANFORD, Executive Vice President, College Entrance Examination Board.

professional guidance counselor can be of great assistance to both you and your parents.

This is not to say that guidance counselors will relieve you of the burden of decision. Rather, their role is to assure that you know what source books are available, what other sources of information should be investigated, and what the questions are that you should ask about yourself and about colleges in order to make your *own* decision.

■SELECTING A COLLEGE INDEPENDENTLY.—Unfortunately, the opportunities for professional guidance from trained secondary school counselors of the kind described are not uniformly available throughout the United States. Where they do exist, full advantage should be taken of them; where they do not, the steps already outlined can serve as a substitute.

If you do not have the advantage of an intensive pre-college guidance program, you of course face a more difficult problem. Yet the application of initiative can result in an equally effective outcome—perhaps even a better one, because little has been handed to you ready-made. Probably your hardest task will be that of determining your chances of admission to a particular college. However, by comparing your school record, class rank, and test scores with published averages, you can make a rough estimate of your relative standing. By judicial questioning of college representatives, students, and alumni, you will be able to guess as to the nonacademic qualifications that particular colleges use in rejecting students with above-average academic records or admitting those with ones below average.

You will also find that when you write to a particular college out of your vicinity to seek information, or when you submit your application, the college will frequently put you in touch with a local alumni representative or make arrangements for an interview with an admissions offi-

cer either in your home town or in a city nearby.

For all students, of course, a visit to a campus is a desirable, but not essential, experience. Many students have gone through many enjoyable college years in settings they did not see until registration day.

The Final Selection.—By late in the junior year or early in the senior year of high school, you should have narrowed the field to a manageable number of college possibilities. You may have definitely decided by then upon dad's alma mater or the university across town or downstate or the local community college. It is more likely, however, that the choice is not yet this definite; perhaps there are a dozen or more places that appeal to you.

If you are wise, you will initially select a group of colleges with a wide range of selectivity. Some will appear difficult to get into; some, easy; and some, somewhere in between. Counselors, in fact, generally tend to suggest a minimum of three applications—that is, one in each category.

If at this point your reply is "Yes, but which three?" you would do well to remember the advice of one long-time admissions expert who said that choosing a college is somewhat like choosing a wife—that, in effect, at some point one has to stop being rational and let one's instincts or emotions make the selection. Yet once the choice has been made and you are enrolled, this analogy begins to break down. While in marriage society expects the affection to deepen and the union to last, rational observers of the contemporary college admissions scene have come to realize that the student who completes four consecutive years of college on one campus is the exception rather than the rule. It is true that many students "fall in love with" the colleges they have selected (whether these were the first, second, or third choice); but other students may not fare as well. Disillusionment may set in, finances may get tight, hopes and ambitions may change, and you may not finish what you started where you started it.

If this occurs, you, like the graduates of junior colleges, will have to make decisions about continuing your education. The junior college graduate is no second-rate citizen these days; in fact, the evidence indicates that successful junior college students tend to do better academically during their last two years at four-year colleges than the students who started in these schools. And the college drop-out has the same opportunity to prove himself in another setting.

■REFERRAL CENTERS. — There is also hope if you have been rejected by the colleges to which you have applied, despite formal pre-college counseling or because of inappropriate choices made on your own. In recent years, referral centers have been established to bring together the students who are still seeking admission to college late in their senior year of high school and the colleges that are still looking

for students. The three most widely-known, college-sponsored centers are:

The College Admissions Center
610 Church Street
Evanston, Illinois

The College Admissions Assistance
　　Center
41 East 65th Street
New York City, New York

The Catholic College Admissions
　　and Information Center
3805 McKinley Street, N.W.
Washington, D.C.

Admissions arranged through such centers have proven successful, despite the fact that the admitting college is not one of the ones to which the student originally applied.

Thus, while you have to take the matter of choosing a college with all seriousness, and while you should make your selection as though you are making an irrevocable decision, also realize that your entire educational future is not at stake. With the unparalleled scope and diversity of opportunities for higher education available in the United States, there are any number of "right places" for each young man and young woman who wants to attend college. If you ask yourself the right questions and answer them honestly, sooner or later the right door will open.

　　　　　　　　　—George H. Hanford

BIBLIOGRAPHY

COLLEGE GUIDES

CARTER, ALLAN M. (ed.). *American Universities and Colleges.* American Council on Education, 1965.
CASS, JAMES and BIRNBAUM, MAX. *Comparative Guide to American Colleges.* Harper & Row, Publishers, 1965.
GLEAZER, EDMUND J., JR. (ed.). *American Junior Colleges.* American Council on Education, 1965.
HAWES, GENE R. *The New American Guide to Colleges.* New American Library of World Literature, Inc., 1965.
HILL, ALFRED T. *A Directory of Small Colleges.* Council for the Advancement of Small Colleges, 1965.
KARL, DONALD S. (ed.) *The College Handbook.* College Entrance Examination Board, 1965.
LOVEJOY, CLARENCE E. *Lovejoy's College Guide.* Simon & Schuster, Inc., 1965.
U.S. OFFICE OF EDUCATION. *Education Directory, Part 3, Higher Education.* U.S. Government Printing Office, 1964.

PREPARING FOR COLLEGE

BOWLES, FRANK H. *How to Get Into College.* E. P. Dutton & Co., Inc., 1960.
LASS, ABRAHAM. *How to Prepare for College.* Washington Square Press, Inc., 1962.
SULKIN, SIDNEY. *Complete Planning for College.* McGraw-Hill, Inc., 1962.
WILSON, EUGENE S. and BUCHER, CHARLES A. *College Ahead.* Harcourt, Brace & World, Inc., 1961.

UNIVERSITY OF MICHIGAN

TUSKEEGEE INSTITUTE

MICHIGAN (*above left*), **TUSKEEGEE INSTITUTE** (*above right*), **HAWAII** (*center left*).

UNIVERSITY OF WISCONSIN

UNIVERSITY OF HAWAII

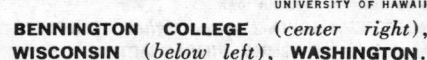

BENNINGTON COLLEGE (*center right*), **WISCONSIN** (*below left*), **WASHINGTON.**

BENNINGTON COLLEGE

UNIVERSITY OF WASHINGTON

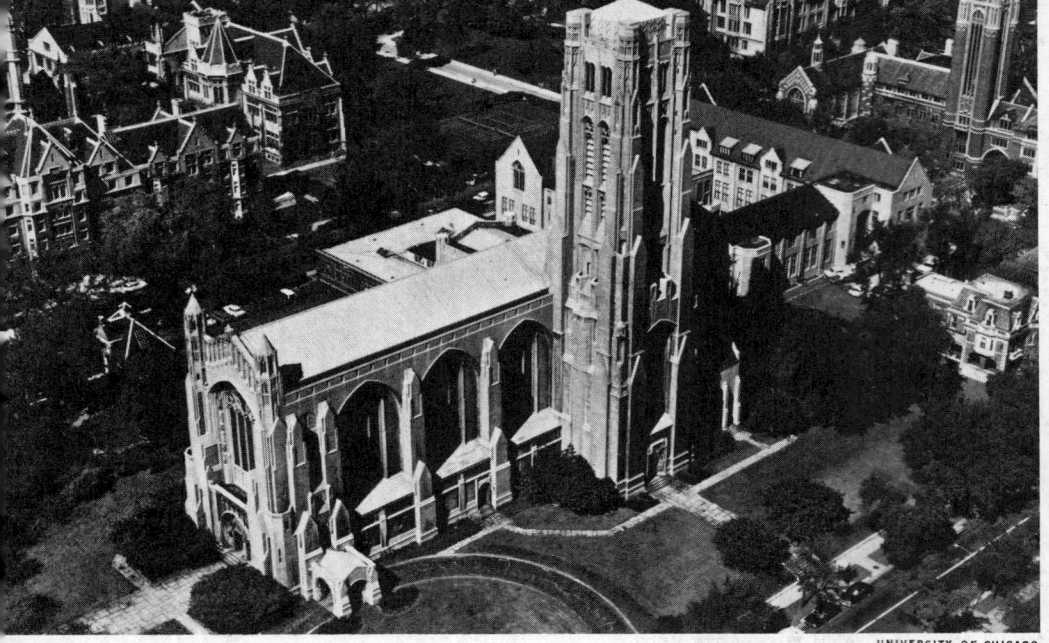

UNIVERSITY OF CHICAGO

TULANE UNIVERSITY

CHICAGO (*above left*), TULANE (*above right*), CALIFORNIA (Riverside) (*center left*).

UNIVERSITY OF CALIFORNIA, RIVERSIDE

UNIVERSITY OF NORTHERN IOWA

NORTHERN IOWA (*center right*), HARVARD (*below left*), SUNY BINGHAMPTON (*below right*).

STATE UNIVERSITY OF NEW YORK AT BINGHAMPTON

HARVARD UNIVERSITY NEWS OFFICE

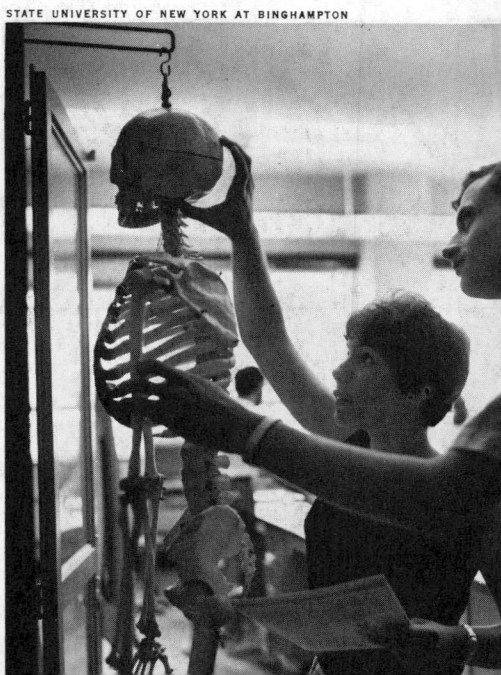

INTRODUCTION TO THE COWLES COLLEGE PROFILE

Purpose of the Profile.—The purpose of the COWLES COLLEGE PROFILE is to provide as much pertinent factual information on each college as possible within a limited amount of space. Each college is allowed only five lines in the table. In effect, this equalizes the large universities and the smaller colleges, for a university with 10,000 students is not allotted more space than a college with 800 students. Our aim is to present the basic data in chart form so as to facilitate comparisons of such things as geographic location of each college, costs of attending, size of each institution, entrance requirements, and special programs offered. This table is not meant to be a substitute for the college catalogues, nor is it meant to eliminate the need for interviews with high school guidance counselors, admissions departments, or college advisors. This PROFILE is only the first step; it should be used as an *introduction* to the entire process of finding and deciding upon a college that will best suit the student's individual needs.

Arrangement.—The PROFILE lists schools alphabetically within geographic areas that have been defined by the six regional accrediting associations of the United States. The geographic areas are arranged in the following order: New England; Middle States; Southern; North Central; Northwest; and Western. Each region is further subdivided: the states within each region are listed alphabetically, and the schools located in each state are listed in the same manner. For example, in the *North Central* region, which consists of 19 states, the first state listed is *Arizona,* and the first school in Arizona is *Arizona, University of.* A map of each region showing the school's location within a state accompanies each regional listing. There are many fine colleges within a moderate distance from the applicant's home; and the distance a student has to travel is a factor that is often given less thought than it deserves. For example, a student from a southern state might find himself unhappy in a college in the far West or in New England; or a student from New England might find that the South or the Middle West are very

different from his native region. Unless a student is prepared to make the adjustment to an area and to people quite unlike his own, he may be happier, and he may do better academically, in a college that is located fairly close to home.

Explanation of Statistics.—Most of the material in this table is clear from the column headings; there are several things, however, that require some explanation. Be careful not to misinterpret the statistics that refer to the high school rating and per cent of students accepted, the Scholastic Aptitude Test (SAT) and American College Test (ACT) scores, and the per cent of students receiving financial aid from the college.

■ **RANK IN HIGH SCHOOL.**—Concerning the high school rating, or the percent of college freshmen who graduate in a given fraction of their high school classes, remember that this figure can vary radically with the difference in quality of the high schools attended by the entering college students. A student who graduates, for instance, in the third quarter of his senior class in a well-equipped metropolitan public or private school is apt to be as well prepared for college as someone in the top quarter of a smaller, less endowed school.

■ **ACCEPTANCE.**—The per cent of applicants accepted at a college also varies, particularly when the college is in some way unique. Thus a student who is not ready to study art or music professionally might be urged by the admissions department at an art school or conservatory to attend a liberal arts college. Another example is that of colleges that have interim periods or "work periods" that allow a considerable amount of independent work; if a student is not prepared to deal with free time in a mature and worthwhile way, he may be discouraged from applying or rejected once he has applied.

■ **TEST SCORES.**—In reference to the SAT or ACT scores, remember that the figures given are *averages* and that the range of scores that make up these averages may be very broad. In the SAT scores, an average of 450 can mean that the accepted students' scores range from 300 to 600; the

ACT average of 21 might represent a range of from 18 to 24. Test averages are given for both mathematics and verbal exams.

■ **FINANCIAL AID.**—In reading the column that shows the per cent of students receiving financial assistance from the college and the average amount received, the problem of misinterpretation can again arise. In general, the per cent is fairly small, for the figure represents only those students who receive direct scholarship aid. In many cases, however, students work off loans from the college in campus jobs, or borrow money from the college to be paid back at a later date. It is possible, then, to have a scholarship, a loan, a job, or any combination of these three, from many colleges across the nation. The amount shown in the PROFILE is scholarship money, not money from loans or jobs, and, like the test scores, the amount is an *average* that can have a broad range. For a few colleges the actual range is shown.

■ **MISCELLANEOUS.**—In the last column of the table the information is varied. Two of the items listed are "per cent per area of study" and "cooperative programs." The former is a breakdown, by per cent, of the class of 1965 in each of several "major" fields —such as social sciences, natural sciences, humanities, and education. In certain instances the figures do not add up to 100 per cent; this is either because of mixed "majors," or because of a negligible per cent in one area. The cooperative programs with other institutions are most often 2-2, 2-3, 3-2, or 4-2 liberal arts-professional programs. By this type of arrangement a student may take two or three years of liberal arts, move on to professional study in another institution, and upon successful completion of a year or two, receive his B.A. or B.S. degree from the liberal arts college. For example, a student may take three years of liberal arts, transfer to a college of engineering, where after two successful years, he will receive a B.S. from the first institution and his professional engineering degree from the second. In this last column, the professional programs are abbreviated. The following is a list of abbreviations and what each represents.

ABBREVIATIONS

A	Army	**B.F.A.**	Bachelor of Fine Arts	**Jour.**	Journalism	**Oc. Ther.**	Occupational Therapy
AEC	Atomic Energy Commission	**B. Mus.**	Bachelor of Music	**Lib.**	Librarianship, library science	**Penn. State**	Pennsylvania State University
AF	Air Force	**B. Mus. Ed.**	Bachelor of Music Education	**LL.B.**	Bachelor of Laws	**Ph.D.**	Doctor of Philosophy
Alabama Polytech.	Alabama Polytechnic Institute	**B.S.**	Bachelor of Science	**m**	math	**Phys. Ed.**	Physical Education
Arch.	Architecture	**B.S. Ed.**	Bachelor of Science in Education	**M**	Marines	**Phys. Ther.**	Physical Therapy
B.A.	Bachelor of Arts			**Max.**	Maximum	**Psych.**	Psychology
B.A. Ed.	Bachelor of Arts in Education	**B. Th.**	Bachelor of Theology	**M.I.T.**	Massachusetts Institute of Technology	**ROTC**	Reserve Officer Training Corps
B. Arch.	Bachelor of Architecture	**bus., Bus.**	Business	**Med.**	Medicine	**R.P.I.**	Rensselaer Polytechnic Institute
		Cal. Tech.	California Institute of Technology	**med. tech.**	medical technology		
B. Art Ed.	Bachelor of Art Education	**Dent.**	Dentistry	**N**	Navy	**Teacher Ed.**	Teacher Education
		ed., Ed.	Education	**NASA**	National Aeronautics and Space Administration	**U. of Ill.**	University of Illinois
B.B.A.	Bachelor of Business Administration	**eng., Eng.**	Engineering			**U. of Penn.**	University of Pennsylvania
		For.	Forestry	**nat. sci.**	natural sciences		
B.D.	Bachelor of Divinity	**Georgia Tech**	Georgia Institute of Technology	**NSF**	National Science Foundation	**U. of Tenn.**	University of Tennessee
B. Ed.	Bachelor of Education	**home ec.**	home economics	**Nurs.**	Nursing	**v**	verbal
		hum.	humanities	**N.Y.U.**	New York University	**Vet. Med.**	Veterinary Medicine

Institution / Location / Founded / Affiliation	Enrollment M=men W=women	Projected enrollment in 1975	High school rating; % applicants accepted	SAT/ACT Averages m=math v=verbal	Annual Tuition; a. b. Room & Board; c. Out of State; d. Other State	% Students with $ aid; Average amount	Faculty-student ratio; % with Doctorates	Volumes in library in 1,000's	Endowment in $1,000's	Undergraduate degrees offered; Calendar; Per cent of students per field of study; Professional programs offered; Miscellaneous
ALABAMA										
Alabama, University of Tuscaloosa 1831 State	7472M 4503W	18000	42% in top 1/4 68%	22.1m 23.3v	a. $350 b. 700 c. 750	19% $600	1:16 66%	836	$11,700	B.A., B.S., B.F.A., B.Mus.; *Semester, summer sessions; Business, Dentistry, Engineering, Law, Medicine, Nursing, Teacher Education;* Coops in public administration with U. of Kentucky, U. of Tennessee; Air Force, Army ROTC required.
Alabama Agricultural and Mechanical College Normal 1875 State	652M 992W	3000	60% in top 1/4 57%		a. $260 b. 440 c. 410	60% $250	1:16 25%	71		B.S.; *Semester, summer session;* Education—54%, Home Economics—17%, Business Education—15%, Arts & Sciences—8%, Industrial Arts & Training—6%.
Alabama College Montevallo 1896 State	1015M 1248W	3500	70%		a. $200 b. 578 c. 410	20% $300	1:18 35%	100		B.A., B.S., B.Mus., B.Mus.Ed.; *Semester, summer session; Music.*
Athens College Athens 1822 Methodist	726M 294W	3000	24% in top 1/4 70%	M19m 18v W18m 20v	a. $790 b. 530	23% $250	1:17 48%	34	$1,600	B.A., B.S., B.S.Ed.; *Trimester;* Education—40%, Business—35%; *M.A.T.;* Two courses in religion, chapel attendance required.
Auburn University Auburn 1856 State	8921M 3722W	20000	75% in top 1/3 70%	M24.5m 21.3v W21.5m 22.6v	a. $300 b. 675 c. 600 d. 400	30% $200-750	1:17 43%	500		B.A., B.S., B.Arch., B.B.A., B.Mus.; *Quarter, summer session;* Arts & Sciences—28%, Education—24%, Engineering—22%, Home Ec.—3%, Chemistry—3%, Art & Architecture—7%, Veterinary Medicine—3%, Agriculture—7%; *Arch., Art, Eng., Forestry, Pharmacy, Teacher Ed., Vet. Med.;* AF, A, N, ROTC required.
Birmingham-Southern College Birmingham 1856 Methodist	443M 433W	1200	57% in top 1/5 72%M 85%W	M547m 526v W511m 519v	a. $900 b. 770	15% $100-1000	1:14 50%	93	$5,160	B.A., B.S., B.Mus., B.M.E.; *Quarter, summer quarter;* Natural Sciences & Math—26%, Humanities—18%, Education—12%, Social Sciences—10%, Business—10%, Music—5%; *Music, Teacher Education;* One course in religion required; Washington Semester.
Florence State College Florence 1872 State	1550M 1050W	5000	28% in top 1/4	19.2 (comp.)	a. $260 b. 540 c. 410	25% $300	1:22	77		B.A., B.S.; *Semester, summer session;* Education—49%, Phys. Ed.—2%, Science & Math—12%, Humanities—6%, Social Science—8%, Business—18%; *Teacher Education;* Army ROTC required for two years.
Huntingdon College Montgomery 1854 Methodist	350M 702W				a. $800 b. 800		1:12	67	$2,500	B.A., B.S., B.M.; *Semester, summer sessions;* 6 hours of Bible study, 3 convocations per week required.
Jacksonville State University Jacksonville 1883 State	2421M 1834W	8000	60% in top 1/2 96%		a. $260 b. 520 c. 410	10% $270	1:18	105		B.A., B.S., B.S.Ed.; *Semester, summer session;* Teacher Ed.—50%, Other—50%; *Teacher Education;* Army ROTC required first 2 years.
Judson College Marion 1838 Southern Baptist	400W	600	85% in top 1/2 88%	18.6m 20.4v	a. $650 b. 760	40% $261	1:12 43%	30	$1,105	B.A., B.S.; *Semester;* Humanities—42%, Social Sciences—28%, Education—17%, Business—7%, Natural Sciences—4%; *Music;* Coop—medical technology & nursing with Birmingham Baptist Hospital; Chapel attendance required; Degree 3-year program.
Livingston State College Livingston 1883 State	815M 328W	5000	10% in top 1/10 80%	M16m 17v W15m 16v	a. $261 b. 555 c. 411	25% $741	1:20	55		B.A., B.S.; *Quarter, summer session; Teacher Education.*
Oakwood College Huntsville 1896 Seventh-day Adventist	213M 220W	670	most in top 1/2 75%		a. $528 b. 650	2%	1:10 31%	21		B.A., B.S.; *Semester, summer session;* Social Sciences—34%, Business—26%, Education—23%, Natural Sciences & Math—16%, Humanities—3%, Home Economics—3%.
St. Bernard College St. Bernard 1892 Roman Catholic	473M 30W	800	28% in top 1/4 68%	499m 400v	a. $750 b. 825		1:15 30%	44		B.A.; *Semester, summer session; Medical Technology;* Coops—engineering with Auburn U., law with Howard College.
Samford University Birmingham 1842 Southern Baptist	1762M 1047W	3000	90% in top 1/2 86%		a. $720 b. 635 c. 816	40% $175	1:20 46%	176	$1,876	B.A., B.S., B.B.A., B.S.Ed., B.Mus., L.L.B., B.S.Phar.; *Semester, summer session;* Liberal Arts—32%, Business—14%, Sciences—16%, Pharmacy—10%, Law—14%, Teacher Ed.—30%; Coops—3-2 engineering with Vanderbilt U., 3-2 forestry with Duke U.
Spring Hill College Mobile 1830 Roman Catholic	688M 320W	1680	44% in top 1/3 57%	523m 508v	a. $1000 b. 950	8% $800	1:13 35%	150		B.A., B.S., B.S.C.; *Semester, summer sessions;* Natural Sciences—25%, Humanities—30%, Social Sciences—35%, Commercial Sciences—10%; *Teacher Training;* Army ROTC.
Stillman College Tuscaloosa 1876 Presbyterian	235M 431W	1200	most in top 1/2 69%		a. $720 b. 720	61% $425	1:13 30%	33	$1,100	B.A., B.S.; *Semester;* Education—18%, Social Sciences—21%, Humanities—18%, Natural Sciences & Math—24%, Business—19%; Coops with Indiana U. George Washington U., N.Y.U. Carnegie grant for experimental English program—$55,000; NSF grant for mathematics talent search—$25,000.
Talladega College Talladega 1867 American Missionary Association	159M 239W	950	77% in top 1/4 86%	M401m 340v W330m 319v	a. $550 b. 550 c. 125	61% $500	1:11 22%	45	$1,275	B.A.; *Semester;* Social Sciences—42%, Natural Sciences & Math—38%, Humanities—20%; Chapel attendance required once per week.
Troy State College Troy 1887 State	1600M 1400W	5000	83%		a. $300 b. 600 c. 150	35% $600	1:18 35%	74		B.A., B.S., B.S.Ed.; *Quarter; Teacher Education;* ACT scores required for admission.
Tuskegee Institute Tuskegee 1881 Private	1236M 1314W	3500	100% in top 1/2 72%	M405m 326v W341m 335v	a. $700 b. 650	15% $600	1:9 25%	151	$18,389	B.A., B.S., B.Arch.; *Semester, summer session;* Education—31%, Nursing—16%, Home Economics—13%, Mechanical Industries—11%, Social Sciences—10%, Natural Sciences—8%; *Engineering, Nursing, Veterinary Medicine;* Coops—3-2 engineering with UNCF colleges, U. Mich., and Wayne State; Air Force, Army ROTC required.

Institution / Location	Founded / Affiliation	Enrollment M=men W=women	Projected enrollment in 1975	High school rating: % applicants accepted	SAT/ACT Averages m=math v=verbal	Annual Tuition: a. b. Room & Board; c. Out of state; d. Other state	% Students with $ aid / Average amount	Faculty-student ratio; % with Doctorates	Volumes in library in 1,000's	Endowment in $1,000's	Undergraduate degrees offered; Calendar; Per cent of students per field of study; Professional programs offered; Miscellaneous

ALASKA

| Alaska, University of — College | 1917 — State | 1192M 687W | 5000 | 78% in top 1/2 65% | M21.0 W20.4 (comp.) | a. none b. $1158 c. 300 d. 141 | 35% $600 45% | 1:13 | 150 | | B.A., B.S., B.B.A., B.S.Ed., B.S.E., A.A.A.S.; *Semester, summer sessions;* Education—11%, Natural Sciences & Math—25%, Business—6%, Engineering—9%, Humanities—12%, Social Sciences—11%; *Engineering;* Army ROTC required for two years. |
| Alaska Methodist University — Anchorage | 1960 — Methodist | 289M 254W | 2000 | | | a. $960 b. 950 d. 80 | 40% $600 50% | 1:13 | 43 | $680 | B.A., B.S.B.A.; *Semester, summer sessions;* Social Sciences—54%, Humanities—16%, Natural Sciences & Math—26%, Business Adm.—4%; *M.A.T.* |

ARIZONA

Arizona, University of — Tucson	1885 — State	10390M 7136W	30000	85% in top 1/2 75%		a. none b. $835 c. 815 d. 269	16% $400 55%	1:20	1052	$1,136	B.A., B.S., B.Arch., B.F.A., B.Mus., LL.B.; *Semester, summer sessions;* Arts & Sciences—35%, Business—17%, Education—16%, Engineering—10%; *Arch., Bus., Eng., Jour., Law, Music, Nurs., Phar., Psych., Teacher Ed.;* Air Force, Army ROTC required.
Arizona State University — Tempe	1885 — State	12834M 7835W	25700			a. none b. $800 c. 815 d. 286	$300	1:20	597		B.A., B.S., B.Arch., B.F.A., B.Mus.; *Semester, summer sessions; Architecture, Business, Engineering, Music, Nursing, Teacher Education;* Air Force, Army ROTC optional.
Northern Arizona University — Flagstaff	1899 — State	3400M 2500W	13500	most in top 2/3 90%		a. none b. $575 c. 380 d. 207	20% $50-500	1:20	120		B.A., B.S., B.S.Ed.; *Semester, summer sessions;* Education—40%, Business—20%, Arts & Sciences—25%, Forestry—8%, Engineering—5%, Nursing—2%; *Teacher Education, Fine Arts, Business, Nursing, Journalism;* Coop—3-2 program in engineering.

ARKANSAS

Arkansas, University of — Fayetteville	1871 — State	5282M 2991W	12819	25% in top 1/5 80%	519m 483v	a. $200 b. 700 c. 270 d. 500	20% $475 56%	1:19	508	$505	B.A., B.S., B.Arch., B.Mus.; *Semester, summer sessions;* Engineering—23%, Education—21%, Business—16%, Natural Sciences—6%; *Arch., Bus., Eng., Law, Med., Music, Phar., Teacher Ed.;* Air Force, Army ROTC required.
Arkansas Agricultural & Mechanical College — College Heights	1909 — State	1129M 510W	3000	30% in top 1/4 85%		a. $200 b. 480 c. 270	24% $180-250 20%	1:20	40		B.A., B.S., B.B.A., B.Mus.; *Semester, summer session;* Education—38%, Business—30%, Sciences—10%, Forestry—10%, Arts—12%.
Arkansas College — Batesville	1872 — Presbyterian	226M 106W	600	35% in top 1/2 85%	M432m 390v W416m 411v	a. $1000 b. 900	39% $50-750 23%	1:15	43	$802	B.A.; *Semester, summer session;* Humanities—16%, Social Sciences—30%, Business—26%, Natural Sciences & Math—28%; 6 hours Bible study required.
Arkansas Polytechnic College — Russellville	1909 — State	1511M 693W	3500	45% in top 1/4 80%		a. $200 b. 590 c. 470	44% $380 20%	1:25	45		B.A., B.S.; *Semester, summer session;* Liberal Arts—46%, Business—21%, Education—23%; *Music, Teacher Education;* Army ROTC required.
Arkansas State University — State College	1909 — State	3148M 2010W	11054	most in top 1/2 84%		a. $200 b. 640 c. 470 d. 157	20% $300 44%	1:25	154		B.A., B.S., B.F.A., B.Mus.Ed., B.S.Ag., B.S.Ed.; *Semester, summer session; Music, Teacher Education;* Army ROTC required.
Harding College — Searcy	1919 — Church of Christ	645M 583W	1500	20% in top 1/4 90%	M21m 19v W18m 21v	a. $576 b. 544 d. 71	75% $100-400 29%	1:15	75	$13,000	B.A., B.S.; *Semester, summer sessions;* Natural Sciences & Math—29%, Education—24%, Humanities—14%, Business—13%, Religion—12%, Social Sciences—8%; *Teacher Education;* Coops—3-2 engineering, 4-2 engineering, 3-2 dentistry & medicine; 8 courses in Bible, chapel required.
Henderson State College — Arkadelphia	1890 — State	1740M 1160W	5500	75% in top 1/2 95%	M17.3m 17.3v W16.0m 20.0v	a. $200 b. 600 c. 470	12% $100 30%	1:23	65		B.A., B.S., B.S.Ed., B.Mus.Ed.; *Semester, summer sessions;* Education—31%, Natural Sciences & Math—22%, Humanities—18%, Business—12%, Social Sciences—11%; *Music, Teacher Education;* Army ROTC required.
Hendrix College — Conway	1884 — Methodist	459M 324W	1000	92%		a. $800 b. 700 d. 39	40% 40%	1:17	60	$5,884	B.A., B.Mus.; *Semester; Music;* Coop—3-2 engineering with Columbia; Two semesters religion.
John Brown University — Siloam Springs	1919 — Private	314M 181W	800	38% in top 1/5 90%		a. $550 b. 700 c. 100	20% $400 20%	1:16	27	$5,000	B.A., B.S., B.S.Ed., B.Mus.Ed.; *Semester;* Humanities—22%, Business—22%, Social Sciences—19%, Engineering—13%, Natural Sciences & Math—12%.
Little Rock University — Little Rock	1927 — Private	2065M 1173W	4500	25% in top 1/5 90%	M20m 19v W19m 23v	a. $600 b. no dorm d. 300	6% $250 27%	1:17	57	$5,000	B.A., B.S., B.Art Ed., B.Bus.Ad., B.Bus.Ed., B.Mus., B.Mus.Ed.; *Semester, summer session;* Teacher Education—11%, Business—25%, Natural Sciences & Math—18%, Social Sciences—22%, Fine Arts—6%.
Ouachita Baptist University — Arkadelphia	1886 — Baptist	767M 679W	2219	99%		$1450 Total	70% $500 30%	1:18	79	$2,000	B.A., B.S., B.S.E., B.Mus., B.Mus.Ed.; *Semester, summer sessions; Music, Teacher Education;* Army ROTC optional.
Philander Smith College — Little Rock	1877 — Methodist	231M 440W	1025	70%	M264m 240v W268m 279v	a. $574 b. 590 d. 35	61% $475 13%	1:18	48	$584	B.A., B.S.; *Semester.*
Southern State College — Magnolia	1909 — State	1360M 910W	4055			a. $200 b. 640 c. 470 d. 60	50% $400 12%	1:25	41		B.A., B.S., B.B.A., B.S.E., B.Mus., B.Mus.Ed.; *Semester, summer session; Teacher Education.*

Institution Location	Founded Affiliation	Enrollment M=men W=women	Projected enrollment in 1975	High school rating; % applicants accepted	SAT/ACT Averages m=math v=verbal	a. Annual Tuition; b. Room & Board; c. Out of state; d. Other	% Students with $ aid Average amount	Faculty-student ratio; % with Doctorates	Volumes in library in 1,000's	Endowment in $1,000's	Undergraduate degrees offered; Calendar; Per cent of students per field of study; Professional programs offered; Miscellaneous

CALIFORNIA

Institution	Founded/Affil	Enroll	Proj	HS rating	SAT	Tuition	%aid	Ratio	Vol	Endow	Notes
Azusa Pacific College Azusa	1899 Private	388M 344W	1200	15% in top 1/5 65%		a. $1050 b. 860 d. 100	85% $250 34%	1:20	38		B.A.; Semester; Social Sciences—35%, Education—30%, Music—20%, Bible—15%.
Biola College La Mirada	1908 Private	508M 649W	1700	100% in top 1/2 75%	M475m 475v W425m 500v	a. $1100 b. 750	50% $600 28%	1:17	80		B.A., B.S., B.Mus.; Semester; Bible—51%, Social Sciences—24%, Humanities—22%, Natural Sciences—3%.
California, University of—Berkeley Campus Berkeley	1868 State	9908M 6954W		most in top 1/8 63%		a. * c. $980 oos	6% $200- 600 90%	1:18	2800	$44,500	B.A., B.S., L.L.B.; Quarter (School of Law-Semester), summer sessions; Architecture, Business, Engineering, Forestry, Landscape Architecture, Law, Library, Optometry, Psychology, Social Work, Teacher Education; Air Force, Army, Navy ROTC optional. * None for state residents.
California, University of—Davis Campus Davis	1908 State	2771M 2008W	15000	100% in top 1/4 70%		a. $240 b. 920 c. 800	8% $200 70%	1:16	300		B.A., B.S.; Semester, summer sessions; Arts & Sciences—59%, Agriculture—24%, Engineering—8%, Veterinary Medicine—9%; Vet. Med.; Army ROTC required. All 5 campuses of the University of California system share an endowment of $152,000,000.
California, University of—Los Angeles Campus Los Angeles	1868 State	9586M 7901W	11100	most in top 1/8 52%M 48%W		a. $242 b. 998 c. 981	3% $582 85%	1:16	2422		B.A., B.S.; Quarter, summer sessions; Sciences—19%, Social Sciences—50%, Humanities—22%, Fine Arts—9%; Architecture, Business, Dentistry, Engineering, Law, Library, Medicine, Nursing, Public Health, Social Welfare, Education; AF, A, N ROTC optional.
California, University of—Riverside Campus Riverside	1907	2107M 1566W	8000	98% in top 1/5 74%	M575m 526v W522m 546v	a. $220 b. 940 c. 890 d. 38	14% $523 94%	1:12	350		B.A., B.S.; Semester, summer session; Social Sciences—44%, Natural Sciences & Math—37%, Humanities—18%; Study Abroad available through U. of California program.
California, University of—Santa Barbara Campus Santa Barbara	1891 State	5746M 5999W	14250	most in top 1/8 71%		b. $880 c. 981 d. 267	11% $550 95%	1:16	450		B.A., B.S.; Quarter, summer session; Social Sciences—37%, Humanities—19%, Natural Sciences—19%; Engineering, Education; Study abroad available through U. of California program; Army ROTC optional.
California Institute of the Arts Los Angeles	1962 Private	375M 375W	1250	50% in top 1/2 20%		a. $1100 d. 20	45% $750	1:20	100	*	B.F.A., B.Mus.; Six-terms (entire year); Fine Arts, Advertising Design, Fashion, Film Arts, Piano, Voice; Music, Art. * The Institute is endowed by the Walter E. Disney Foundation.
California Institute of Technology Pasadena	1891 Private	700M	700	99% in top 1/5 25%	775m 675v	a. $1800 b. 1000 d. 83	64% $100- 2000 90%	1:3	177	$80,000	B.S.; Quarter; Engineering—32%, Science—64%, Humanities—4%; Aeronautical, Civil, Electrical, Geological, Geophysical, Mechanical Engineering; 3-2 Liberal Arts program with certain colleges; Air Force ROTC optional.
California Lutheran College Thousand Oaks	1959 Lutheran	447M 470W	1500	91% in top 1/2 85%	514m 505v	a. $1425 b. 875	43% $400 46%	1:14	45		B.A.; Quarter, summer session; Teaching; 12 credit hours of religion required, chapel voluntary.
California State College at San Bernardino San Bernardino	1962 State	302M 320W	5000	all in top 1/3 80%		a. none b. $720	9% $707 93%	1:13	65		B.A.; Quarter, summer session; Humanities, Natural Science, Social Science; participates in California State Colleges International Program.
California State Polytechnic College San Luis Obispo	1901 State	5127M 1778W	12300	most in top 1/3 92%	525m 470v	a. none b. $849 c. 500 d. 100	65% $200 23%	1:15	169		B.S., B.Arch.; Quarter, summer sessions (2); Agriculture—22%, Engineering—35%, Applied Arts—28%, Applied Sciences—15%; Army ROTC optional.
California State Polytechnic College, Kellogg Campus Pomona	1949 State	4114M 1350W	10000	all in top 1/3 85%	M23.7 W21.9 (mean)	a. none b. 780 c. 600 d. 110	10% $200 25%	1:18	125		B.S.; Quarter, summer quarter; Agriculture—15%, Engineering—30%, Arts—7%, Sciences—19%, Business—16%, Social Sciences—15%, Physical Education—4%, Mathematics—4%; Teacher Education.
Chapman College Orange	1861 Disciples of Christ	451M 434W	1500	87% in top 1/2 79%	488m 486v	a. $1200 b. 865 d. 200	51% $575 52%	1:13	55	$1,063	B.A., B.S., B.Mus.; Semester, summer session; Social Sciences—50%, Education—22%, Humanities—13%, Fine Arts—4%, Natural Sciences—5%, Phys. Ed.—6%; Convocation attendance required; World Campus Afloat, Chapman College's Div. of International Education offers full semesters of college credit aboard globe-circling floating campus.
Chico State College Chico	1889 State	3372M 3077W	10930	30% in top 1/5 84%		b. $800 c. 540 d. 24	2% $200 57%	1:16	145		B.A., B.S.; Semester, summer session; Education—37%, Social Sciences—20%, Natural Sciences—9%, Business—9%, Humanities—8%, Industrial Arts—7%, Agriculture—6%, Engineering—4%; Nursing, Teacher Education.
Claremont Men's College Claremont	1946 Private	720M	800	70% in top 1/10 50%		a. $1700 b. 950 d. 70	33% $200- 2700 95%	1:11	500	$8,000	B.A.; Semester, summer session; Social Sciences—65%, Humanities—28%, Natural Sciences & Math—7%; Coop-3-2 management, engineering with Stanford; Army ROTC optional; One of the Claremont Colleges.
College of Notre Dame Belmont	1851 Roman Catholic	480W	875	80%	462m 489v	a. $900 b. 1100	64% $763 27%	1:8	56	$287	B.A., B.S.; Semester, summer session, intersession; Sciences & Math—15%, Bus. Adm.—9%, Languages—16%, Art & Music—14%, Social Welfare—14%, English—18%, History—9%, Social Science—4%; Teacher Education (Montessori Diploma—18%).
College of the Holy Names Oakland	1880 Roman Catholic	689W	800	90% in top 2/5 83%	450m 500v	a. $1050 b. 1100	40% $900 40%	1:12	62	$289	B.A., B.S., B.F.A.; Semester, summer session; Social Sciences—34%, Humanities—32%, Natural Sciences & Math—19%, Fine Arts—17%; Music, Lab. Tech., Teacher Ed., M.A.T. in Fr., Sp., Math.
Dominican College of San Rafael San Rafael	1890 Roman Catholic	542W	750	98% in top 1/2		a. $850 b. 1100	30% $500 45%	1:10	55		B.A., B.S., B.Mus.; Semester, summer session.

Institution / Location / Founded / Affiliation	Enrollment M=men W=women	Projected enrollment in 1975	High school rating; % applicants accepted	SAT/ACT Averages m = math v = verbal	a. Annual Tuition; b. Room & Board; c. Out of state; d. Other state.	% Students with $ aid; Average amount	Faculty-student ratio; % with Doctorates	Volumes in library in 1,000's	Endowment in $1,000's	Undergraduate degrees offered; Calendar; Per cent of students per field of study; Professional programs offered; Miscellaneous
Fresno State College Fresno 1911 State	4171M 3251W	11000	most in top 1/3	508m 490v	a. $132 b. $885 c. 720	30% $275 52%	1:16	223		B.A., B.S.; *Semester; Business, Journalism, Nursing, Teacher Education, Agriculture, Arts & Sciences, Criminology, Engineering, Health Sci., Home Ec., Indust. Tech., Social Work;* Study abroad avaliable through California State Colleges International Program; Air Force ROTC optional.
Fullerton, California State College at Fullerton 1959 State	4432M 3348W	10000	100% in top 1/3	518m 516v	a. $120 b. 1100 c. 300	15% $500 75%	1:15	150		B.A.; *Semester, summer session;* Social Sciences—34%, Humanities —25%, Business Adm.—23%, Fine Arts—8%, Natural Sciences & Math—5%, Education—5%; *Business Administration, Music, Teacher Education, Engineering.*
Harvey Mudd College Claremont 1957 Private	280M 13W	400	95% in top 1/10 40%		a. $1800 b. 1050 d. 200	75% $200-2800 98%	1:8	500	$1,500	B.S.; *Semester;* Natural Sciences & Math—67%, Engineering—33%; *Engineering;* One of the Claremont Colleges.
Hayward, California State College at Hayward 1959 State	2913M 2443W	16500	most in top 1/3		a. $97 b. no dorm	$100-400	1:17 60%	130		B.A., B.S.; *Quarter, summer sessions;* English, Education, Mathematics.
Humboldt State College Arcata 1913 State	2268M 1290W	7000	100% in top 1/3 75%	516m 499v	a. $90 b. 890 c. 720 d. 25	24% $600 54%	1:14	96		B.A., B.S.; *Semester, summer session;* Social Sciences—20%, Natural Sciences & Math—15%, Education—10%, Business—7%, Humanities—13%, Natural Resources—28%; *Nursing;* Coop-3-2 engineering.
Immaculate Heart College Los Angeles 1916 Roman Catholic	488W	725	51% in top 1/5 75%	491m 524v	a. $995 b. 1485	57% $1000 63%	1:12	100	$264	B.A., B.S., B.Mus.; *Three-term, summer session;* Humanities—61%, Social Sciences—15%, Natural Sciences & Math—17%, Dietetics—3%; *Music, Teacher Education;* Grants totaling $140,610 since 1960.
La Sierra College Riverside 1932 Seventh-day Adventist	782M 899W	1800	85%		$1834 Total	80% 39%	1:15	80		B.A., B.S., B.Mus.Ed.; *Semester;* Elementary and Secondary Education.
La Verne College La Verne 1891 Church of the Brethren	263M 272W	900	71% in top 2/5 75%	480m 473v	a. $1300 b. 840	50% $800 50%	1:15	44	$510	B.A.; *Semester, summer sessions;* Social Sciences—60%, Humanities—23%, Natural Sciences & Math—17%; *Pre-Med., Pre-Law, Teacher Ed., M.A.T.;* Junior Year Abroad in France or Germany.
Long Beach, California State College at Long Beach 1949 State	8931M 6136W	23209	100% in top 1/4 86%	22.2m 21.6v	a. $90 b. 808 c. 600 d. 61	15% $750 59%	1:17	193		B.A., B.S.; *Semester, summer sessions;* Education, Business, Engineering; *Teacher Education, Nursing, Ind. Tech., Physical Therapy.*
Los Angeles, California State College at Los Angeles 1947 State	7112M 5041W	20500	most in top 1/3	M515m 481v W465m 473v	a. $99 b. no dorm c. 300	4% $363 50%	1:17	214		B.A., B.S.; *Quarter, summer session;* Letters & Science—60%, Fine and Applied Arts—19%, Bus. Adm.—10%, Engineering—5%, Nursing—6%.
Loyola University of Los Angeles Los Angeles 1865 Roman Catholic	1406M 173W	1800	65%	531m 521v	a. $1250 b. 910	26% $500 61%	1:15	170	$2,085	B.A., B.S., B.B.A.; *Quarter, summer session;* Liberal Arts—51%, Business—17%, Natural Sciences—16%, Engineering—16%; *Law;* Air Force ROTC required.
Marymount College Palos Verdes Estates 1934 Roman Catholic	335W	800	28% in top 1/4 85%	500m 560v	a. $1050 b. 1000	25% $425 33%	1:11	47	$300	B.A.; *Semester, summer session;* Humanities—37%, Social Sciences—32%, Business—16%, Natural Sciences—15%.
Mills College Oakland 1852 Private	727W	900	85% in top 1/5 50%	585m 600v	$2985 Total	20% $1400 60%	1:11	142	$10,000	B.A.; *Semester;* Social Sciences & Educational Services—34%, Natural Sciences and Math—22%, Letters—24%, Fine Arts—20%.
Mount St. Mary's College Los Angeles 1925 Roman Catholic	1266W	1500	66%	475m 525v	a. $1000 b. 1100 d. 100	20% $450 34%	1:12	92		B.A., B.S., B.Mus.; *Semester, summer session;* Arts—80%, Natural Sciences—19%, Music—1%; *Music, Nursing, Social Work.*
Northrop Institute of Technology Inglewood 1942 Private	1384M 6W	1800	28% in top 1/4 65%	565m 468v	a. $945 b. 1008	18% $875	1:19	16		B.S.; *Quarter, summer quarter;* Engineering and Engineering Technology—100%; *Engineering.*
Occidental College Los Angeles 1887 Private	850M 625W	2000	84% in top 1/5 51%M 40%W	M653m 613v W625m 648v	a. $1500 b. 1000 d. 44	41% $1500 75%	1:14	190	$12,904	B.A.; *Three-term, summer sessions;* Social Sciences—35%, Diplomacy & World Affairs—7%, Biology—7%, Humanities—26%; Coop —3-2 engineering with Cal. Tech., Columbia; Air Force ROTC optional.
Pacific, University of the Stockton 1851 Methodist	1732M 1583W	4000	most in top 1/4 60%	M530m 540v W515m 550v	a. $1600 b. 1070	27% $600-2000 60%	1:14	136	$4,260	B.A., B.S., B.Mus., B.S.Ed.; *Semester, summer sessions;* Liberal Arts—86%, Pharmacy—9%, Education—3%, Engineering—2%; *Dent., Engineering, Music, Phar., Teacher Ed.;* The U. of the Pacific consists of "cluster colleges"—Raymond, Elbert Covell, Callison.
Pacific Union College Angwin 1882 Seventh-day Adventist	880M 778W	2000	90%		a. $1155 b. 765		1:12	73		B.A., B.S.; *Quarter, summer sessions.*
Pasadena College Pasadena 1910 Nazarene	691M 576W	1500	85%		a. $960 b. 700	35% $250 40%	1:20	100	$2,000	B.A.; *Semester;* Education—37%, Social Sciences—30%, Humanities—12%, Business—12%, Natural Sciences & Math—5%; 8 units of religion, chapel attendance required.
Pepperdine College Los Angeles 1937 Private	806M 542W	2500	70%	482m 471v	a. $1120 b. 850	21% $372-1488 75%	1:13	76	$1,350	B.A., B.S.; *Trimester, summer sessions;* Social Sciences—38%, Education—22%, Humanities—14%, Business—13%, Natural Sciences & Math—10%; Coop-3-2 engineering with Stanford; 4 courses in religion, chapel attendance once per week required.

Institution Location Founded Affiliation	Enrollment M=men W=women	Projected enrollment in 1975	High school rating; % applicants accepted	SAT/ACT Averages m=math v=verbal	Annual Tuition; a. Room & Board; c. Out of state; d. Other	% Students with $ aid; Average amount	Faculty-student ratio; % with Doctorates	Volumes in library in 1,000's	Endowment in $1,000's	Undergraduate degrees offered; Calendar; Per cent of students per field of study; Professional programs offered; Miscellaneous
Pomona College Claremont 1887 Private	607M 530W	1300	95% in top 1/5 30%M 25%W	M704m 659v W644m 667v	a. $1700 d. 65	40% $200-2850	1:10 78%	400	$16,667	B.A.; Semester, summer session; Social Sciences—32%, Natural Sciences & Math—36%, Humanities—34%; Army ROTC optional; One of the Claremont Colleges.
Redlands, University of Redlands 1907 Baptist	800M 600W	1500	90% in top 1/5 30%	M600m 580v W580m 600v	a. $1550 b. 900 d. 100	33% $100-1600	1:14 65%	146	$9,920	B.A., B.S., B.Mus.; Semester, summer sessions; Social Sciences—47%, Humanities—33%, Natural Sciences & Math—17%; Music; Coops—graduate studies with Claremont Colleges, Occidental, Whittier, Washington & U.N. Semester, programs in Europe & Mexico.
Sacramento State College Sacramento 1947 State	4083M 3494W	14000	100% in top 1/3 76%	M24.8m 21.3v W20.6m 22.3v	a. $102 b. 950 c. 602	12% $600	1:16 60%	250		B.A., B.S., B.Ed.; Semester, summer sessions; Liberal Arts—40%, Education—30%, Business—15%, Natural Sciences & Math—10%; Business, Music, Nursing, Teacher Education, Social Work, Engineering.
Saint Mary's College of California St. Mary's College 1863 Roman Catholic	900M	1035	65%	500m 500v	a. $1100 b. 990	30% $350	1:13 44%	70	$1,000	B.A., B.S.; Semester, summer session; Social Sciences—36%, Humanities—27%, Natural Sciences & Math—20%, Business—17%; Catholic students are required to take courses in theology.
San Diego, University of, College for Men San Diego 1949 Roman Catholic	500M	800	80% in top 1/2 58%	511m 502v	a. $1000 b. 900 d. 85	18% $250-1000	1:9 33%	52		B.A., B.S.; Semester, summer session; 12 units of theology courses required.
San Diego, University of, for Women San Diego 1952 Roman Catholic	676W	800	most in top 1/4 80%	550m 585v	a. $1000 b. 1550 d. 65		1:12 38%	51		B.A., B.S.; Semester, summer session; Social Sciences—43%, Humanities—40%, Natural Sciences & Math—11%; 18 units of philosophy, 8 units of theology, annual retreat required.
San Diego State College San Diego 1897 State	10357M 8162W	26000	100% in top 1/3		a. none b. $835 c. 600 d. 123	25% $525	1:17 67%	355		B.A., B.S., B.E.; Semester, summer session; Education—6%, Business—11%, Sciences—20%, Humanities—11%, Fine Arts—8%, Social Sciences—14%, Engineering—4%; Business, Engineering, Music, Social Work, Nursing, Teacher Education; Air Force ROTC optional.
San Fernando Valley State College Northridge 1958 State	7590M 6466W	20000	100% in top 1/3 82%	M530m 481v W452m 475v	b. $950 c. 500	7% $350	1:18 65%	221		B.A., B.S.; Semester, summer sessions.
San Francisco, University of San Francisco 1855 Roman Catholic	3940M 1974W	6747	77% in top 1/4 63%	543m 544v	a. $1072 b. 1000	33% $650	1:17 45%	156	$2,600	B.A., B.S., B.A.Classical; Semester, summer session; Social Sciences—40%, Business—19%, Nursing—5%, Humanities—13%, Sciences—9%; Business, Law, Nursing, Education, Theology; Coop—2-2, 3-2 engineering with U. of Santa Clara; 4 years of theology required of Catholics; Army ROTC required.
San Francisco College for Women San Francisco 1921 Roman Catholic	647W	750	100% in top 1/2 75%	450m 500v	a. $800 b. 1200 d. 100	30% $500	1:10 50%	135	$395	B.A., B.S.; Quarter, summer sessions; Social Sciences—47%, Humanities—37%, Natural Sciences & Math—13%.
San Francisco State College San Francisco 1899 State	7535M 6165W	14500	85% in top 1/5 80%	M531m 523v W479m 517v	a. $96 b. 880 c. 696	25% $48-1500	1:17 62%	350	$50	B.A., B.S., B.S.Ed., B.M., B.Voc.Ed.; Semester, summer sessions; Education—7%, Social Sciences—31%, Humanities—12%, Natural Sciences & Math—9%, Creative Arts—10%, Business—9%; Business, Chemistry, Medical Tech., Social Work, Nursing, Teacher Education; Air Force ROTC optional.
San Jose State College San Jose 1857 State	8806M 7378W	26000	100% in top 1/2 74%	M23.7m 20.1v W19.4m 21.5v	a. $91 b. 636-860 c. 691	25% $476	1:18 55%	344		B.A., B.S.; Semester, summer sessions; Humanities—42%, Sciences—24%, Business—16%, Engineering—14%; Engineering, Journalism, Music, Nursing, Occupational Therapy, Teacher Education; Study abroad available through International Program of California State Colleges.
Santa Clara, University of Santa Clara 1851 Roman Catholic	1600M 900W	2750	70% in top 1/5 70%	574m 563v	a. $1400 b. 1000	40% $200-1900	1:14 60%	155	$3,400	B.A., B.S.; Quarter, summer session; Engineering—11%, Business—23%, Sciences—25%, Humanities—41%; Business, Engineering, Law; 5 courses in theology; Army ROTC required.
Scripps College Claremont 1926 Private	500W	500	85% in top 1/5 30%	562m 618v	$2975 Total	30% $1114	1:11 66%	600	$8,064	B.A.; Semester; Social Sciences—39%, Art—29%, Literature—25%, Cross-concentrations—7%.
Sonoma State College Rohnert Park 1960 State	712M 784W	9000	most in top 1/3 80%	M506m 479v W467m 493v	b. $900 c. 600	13% $500	1:13 75%	75		B.A.; Semester, summer sessions; Social Sciences—54%, Humanities—22%, Sciences—6%.
Southern California, University of Los Angeles 1880 Private	4951M 2477W	11000	65% in top 1/5 62%	M598m 534v W516m 529v	a. $1500 b. 1000 d. 26	30% $825	1:15 89%	1100	$25,815	B.A., B.S., B.Arch., B.F.A., B.Mus.; Semester, summer sessions; Liberal Arts—35%, Business—20%, Law—6%, Fine Arts—4%, Education—6%, Engineering—11%; Arch., Bus., Chem., Dent., Eng., Law, Lib., Med., Music, Phar., Phys. & Oc. Ther., Pysch., Social Work, Teacher Ed.; AF, N ROTC optional.
Southern California College Costa Mesa 1920 Assemblies of God	292M 213W	1000	90%		a. $900 b. 860 d. 104	15% $350	1:21 52%	24	$225	B.A.; Semester; Social Sciences—27%, Humanities—16%, Religion—27%, Natural Sciences—1%.
Stanford University Stanford 1891 Private	4173M 1752W	6040	98% in top 1/5 23%	M690m 650v W640m 670v	a. $1575 b. 1140	40% $200-2700	1:10 97%	3000	$214,300	B.A., B.S.; Quarter; Social Sciences—54%, Sciences—18%, Humanities—17%, Engineering—9%; Business, Engineering, Journalism, Law, Medicine, Nursing, Physical Therapy, Psychology, Teacher Education; Foreign study programs; AF, A, N ROTC optional.
Stanislaus State College Turlock 1959 State	474M 474W	4200	most in top 1/3	530m 516v	a. $102 b. 900 c. 525	15% $481	1:15 71%	60		B.A.; Quarter; Social Sciences—30%, Education—10%, Humanities—14%, Natural Sciences & Math—15%, Business—3%; Study abroad available through International Program of California State Colleges in France, Germany, Italy, Japan, Spain, Sweden, Taiwan.
United States Intl. Univ.—California Western U. Camp. San Diego 1952 Methodist	1200M 800W	2500	90% in top 2/5 45%	540m 546v	a. $1425 b. 900	35% $450	1:18 72%	145	$2,852	B.A., B.F.A.; Quarter, summer session; Law, Education.

Institution Location Founded Affiliation	Enrollment M=men W=women	Projected enrollment in 1975	High school rating; % applicants accepted	SAT/ACT Averages m=math v=verbal	Annual Tuition: a. b. Room & Board c. Out of state d. Other state	% Students with $ aid; Average amount	Faculty-student ratio; % with Doctorates	Volumes in library in 1,000's	Endowment in $1,000's	Undergraduate degrees offered; Calendar; Per cent of students per field of study; Professional programs offered; Miscellaneous
Westmont College Santa Barbara 1940 *Private*	320M 353W	900	65% in top 1/5 55%	M567m 525v W526m 535v	a. $1365 b. 981 d. 174	56% $700	1:16 55%	58	$232	B.A.; *Quarter, summer sessions;* Education—19%, Social Sciences—35%, Humanities—20%, Natural Sciences & Math—10%, Psychology—16%; Daily interdenominational chapel attendance required.
Whittier College Whittier 1901 *Private*	825M 975W	2500	most in top 1/4 72%	525m 550v	a. $1260 b. 800	35% $500	1:16 50%	80	$4,000	B.A., B.Mus.; *Semester, summer sessions;* Social Sciences—60%, Humanities—20%, Natural Sciences—20%; Coops—3-2 engineering with U. of Southern California, Stanford, Colorado State, graduate study with Occidental, Redlands, & Claremont Colleges.

COLORADO

Institution Location Founded Affiliation	Enrollment M=men W=women	Projected enrollment in 1975	High school rating; % applicants accepted	SAT/ACT Averages m=math v=verbal	Annual Tuition: a. b. Room & Board c. Out of state d. Other state	% Students with $ aid; Average amount	Faculty-student ratio; % with Doctorates	Volumes in library in 1,000's	Endowment in $1,000's	Undergraduate degrees offered; Calendar; Per cent of students per field of study; Professional programs offered; Miscellaneous
Adams State College of Colorado Alamosa 1921 *State*	1283M 906W	3500	most in top 1/2		a. $315 b. 744 c. 450	50% 30%	1:20	110		B.A.; *Quarter, summer sessions;* Teacher Education.
Colorado, University of Boulder 1876 *State*	9588M 6093W	17460	56% in top 1/4		a. $286 b. 875 c. 1034 d. 86	20% $325	1:18 62%	935	$6,447	B.A., B.S., B.F.A., B.Mus., B.Mus.Ed.; *Semester, summer sessions;* Soc. Sci.—25%, Eng.—17%, Bus.—15%, Nat. Sci.—10%, Ed.—10%, Hum.—7%; *Bus., Eng., Jour., Law, Lib., Music, Psych., Social Work, Teacher Ed.;* Coop—exchange with U. of Erlangen, Ger.; AF, A, N ROTC optional.
Colorado College Colorado Springs 1874 *Private*	867M 585W	1500	50% in top 1/10 50%	590m 585v	a. $1700 b. 900	33% $870	1:12 57%	200	$10,000	B.A.; *Semester, summer session;* Social Sciences—36%, Natural Sciences & Math—22%, Humanities—16%, Business—12%; *Music;* Coops—4-2 sciences with Columbia, R.P.I., 3-2 forestry with Duke; Army ROTC optional.
Colorado School of Mines Golden 1874 *State*	1500M 14W	2200	40% in top 1/5 72%	640m 530v	a. $300 b. 681 c. 900 d. 100	15% $300-800	1:12 50%	113		B.S.; *Semester, summer sessions (work and academic);* Engineering; Army ROTC required for two years.
Colorado State College Greeley 1890 *State*	3376M 4161W	13740	100% in top 1/2 85%	21 (comp.)	a. $293 b. 810 c. 675	22% $700	1:20 46%	260		B.A., B.S.; *Quarter, summer quarter;* Teacher Education, Nursing; Air Force ROTC optional.
Colorado State University Fort Collins 1870 *State*	6578M 3607W	18000	57% in top 1/3 75%	M530m 470v W470m 480v	a. $336 b. 762 c. 921	15% $400	1:20 45%	340	$740	B.A., B.S., B.Ed., B.Mus.; *Quarter, summer session;* Arts & Sciences—61%, Agriculture—10%, Engineering—9%, Forestry—8%, Veterinary Medicine—7%; *Engineering, Forestry, Occupational Therapy, Teacher Education, Veterinary Medicine;* Air Force, Army ROTC optional.
Denver, University of Denver 1864 *Methodist*	3305M 2337W	8000	55% in top 2/5 58%M 73%W	M551m 515v W514m 528v	a. $1500 b. 900	50% $50-1500	1:17 67%	600	$12,548	B.A., B.S., B.F.A., B.Mus. B.Mus.Ed., B.S.B.A.; *Quarter, summer session;* Business—36%, Social Sciences—22%, Education—17%, Humanities—12%, Natural Sciences & Math—7%; *Bus., Eng., Law, Lib., Music, Psych., Social Work, Teacher Ed.*
Fort Lewis College Durango 1911 *State*	1030M 570W	2678	31% in top 1/3 68%	20 (comp.)	a. $300 b. 1100 c. 675 d. 180	25% $350	1:20 33%	50	$72	B.A., B.S.; *Trimester;* Natural Sciences & Math—34%, Humanities—30%, Business—26%, Social Sciences—9%; Coop—3-2 engineering with Colorado State University.
Loretto Heights College Denver 1918 *Roman Catholic*	940W	1200	30% in top 1/5 75%	475m 485v	$2500 Total	35% $500	1:12 31%	59	$153	B.A., B.S.; *Semester, summer session;* Humanities—38%, Nursing—20%, Social Sciences—28%, Education—50%, Natural Sciences & Math—8%; *Nursing, Teacher Education;* Courses in theology required.
Regis College Denver 1877 *Roman Catholic*	845M	1200	35% in top 1/4 65%	535m 510v	a. $1000 b. 950	60% $188	1:15 30%	50	$1,300	B.A., B.S.; *Semester;* Social Sciences—11%, Natural Sciences—23%, Business—28%, Humanities—38%; Coop—3-2 engineering with Marquette, St. Louis Universities.
Southern Colorado State College Pueblo 1933 *State*	2947M 1909W	9733	57% in top 1/2 95%	18.3 (comp.)	a. $291 b. 695 c. 540	10% $500	1:20 34%	60		B.A., B.S., A.A., A.A.S.; *Quarter, summer session;* Science & Math—18%, Humanities—28%, Social Science—27%, Business—14%, Education—11%, Ind. Arts—4%; *Music, Accounting, Nursing, Teacher Certification.*
Temple Buell College Denver 1888 *Baptist*	1100W	1200	40% in top 1/4 60%	496m 510v	$2850 Total	35% $750	1:13 52%	60	$27,000	B.A., B.S.Med.Tech.; *Semester, summer opera workshop;* Fine Arts—15%, Behavioral Sciences—35%, Humanities—25%, Natural Sciences—8%, Soc. Sciences—10%; Coop with Stanford for junior year in Asian Studies; Junior Year Abroad in Geneva, Madrid, Vienna.
United States Air Force Academy USAFA 1954 *Federal*	3140M	4100	59% in top 1/10 20%	676m 604v	a. none b. none		1:7 26%	240		B.S.; *Semester, summer term;* Natural Sciences & Math—31%, Social Sciences—4%, Engineering—36%, Military Science—2%, International affairs—17%, Mechanics—2%, Humanities—4%; *Engineering Science;* Coops in astronautics, international affairs, applied mathematics, management. Cadets earn monthly allowance.
Western State College of Colorado Gunnison 1901 *State*	1901M 991W	3300	90% in top 2/3 75%	not required	a. $201 b. 790 c. 450 d. 131	40% $500	1:22 42%	100		B.A.; *Quarter, summer session;* Teacher Education.

CONNECTICUT

Institution Location Founded Affiliation	Enrollment M=men W=women	Projected enrollment in 1975	High school rating; % applicants accepted	SAT/ACT Averages m=math v=verbal	Annual Tuition: a. b. Room & Board c. Out of state d. Other state	% Students with $ aid; Average amount	Faculty-student ratio; % with Doctorates	Volumes in library in 1,000's	Endowment in $1,000's	Undergraduate degrees offered; Calendar; Per cent of students per field of study; Professional programs offered; Miscellaneous
Albertus Magnus College New Haven 1925 *Roman Catholic*	686W	1000	72% in top 1/5 60%	550m 570v	$2300 Total $1000 Max.	30% 40%	1:10	51	$250	B.A.; *Semester;* Humanities—57%, Social Sciences—26%, Sciences & Math—17%; *Secondary teacher training, Theology;* daily Mass, annual retreat for Catholics; NSF grants totaling $60,000 since 1960.
Annhurst College South Woodstock 1941 *Roman Catholic*	380W	800	100% in top 1/2 52%	510m 522v	a. $800 b. 900 d. 100	27% $250	1:8 32%	25		B.A., B.S.; *Semester, summer session;* Humanities—74%, Sciences & Math—21%; *Business, Secondary teacher training;* Institute for the Teaching of English as a Foreign Language.
Bridgeport, University of Bridgeport 1927 *Private*	2543M 1944W	5000	78% in top 2/5 45%	520m 520v	a. $1050 b. 955	25% $750	1:15 39%	130	$2,000	B.A., B.S.; *Semester, summer session;* Business, Education, Engineering, Nursing; Grants totaling $5,000,761 since 1960.

Institution / Location / Founded / Affiliation	Enrollment M=men W=women	Projected enrollment in 1975	High school rating; % applicants accepted	SAT/ACT Averages m=math v=verbal	Annual Tuition; a. b. Room & Board; c. Out of state; d. Other state.	% Students with $ aid / Average amount	Faculty-student ratio; % with Doctorates	Volumes in library in 1,000's	Endowment in $1,000's	Undergraduate degrees offered; Calendar; Per cent of students per field of study; Professional programs offered; Miscellaneous
Central Connecticut State College New Britain 1849 *State*	1879M 2441W	8950	75% in top 2/5 60%	M516m 463v W495m 494v	a. $100 b. 630 d. 200	40% $200	1:16 35%	120		B.A., B.S.; *Semester, summer session;* Teacher Preparation—85%, Liberal Arts—15%; 6th year coop program with University of Connecticut, M.A.T.
Connecticut, University of Storrs 1881 *State*	4803M 3896W	21800	54% in top 1/5 25%	1060 (combined)	a. $190 b. 800 c. 590 d. 700 ($1290 oos)	13% $400		600	$1,411	B.A., B.S., B. Mus., B.F.A.; *Semester, summer sessions;* Business—12%, Education—11%, Engineering—6%, Liberal Arts & Sciences—45%, Other—26%; *Ag., Bus., Bus. Admin., Engin., Law, Nursing, Teacher Ed., Insurance, Phar., Social Work, Phys. Ed., Phys. Therapy, Fine Arts, Med., Dent. Med.;* New England Regional coop: Air Force, Army ROTC optional.
Connecticut College New London 1911 *Private*	1496W	2000	95% in top 1/5 48%	617m 623v	a. $1980 b. 1120 d. 50	22% $1200	1:11 57%	219	$6,055	B.A.; *Semester;* Humanities—37%, Science—18%, Social Sciences—38%, Foreign Languages—7%; *Teacher education;* Summer School of Dance; M.A., M.A.T. programs for men & women; Grants totaling $4,860,413 since 1960.
Danbury State College Danbury 1903 *State*	509M 891W	4175	63% in top 2/5 47%	489m 500v	a. $100 b. 630 d. 125	5% $225	1:13 32%	72		B.A., B.S., A. S.; *Semester, summer session;* Teacher Education—81%, Liberal Arts—19%; *Teacher Education.*
Fairfield University Fairfield 1942 *Roman Catholic*	1517M	2000	78% in top 1/2 28%	560m 545v	a. $1400 b. 1000	35% $450	1:15 40%	81		B.A., B.S.; *Semester, summer session;* Humanities—72%, Sciences—28%; *Education;* 4 religion courses required of Catholics.
Hartford, University of West Hartford 1957 *Private*	1521M 802W	3500	70% in top 1/2 55%	512m 504v	a. $1200-1675 b. 1000	40% $700	1:14 54%	130	$3,106	B.A., B.S.; *Semester, summer session;* Arts-Sciences—26%, Business Administration—30%, Engineering—10%, Education—18%, Art—7%, Music—7%, Other—3%; *Art, Business admin., Education, Engineering, Music;* Grants totaling $18,000,000 since 1958.
Saint Joseph College West Hartford 1932 *Roman Catholic*	582W	800	100% in top 1/2 58%	540m 555v	a. $1200 b. 1200	25% $500	1:10 52%	55	$293	B.A.; *Semester, summer session;* Teacher Education, Graduate Department; N.S.F. grants totaling $113,610 since 1960.
Southern Connecticut State College New Haven 1893 *State*	1645M 2825W	10000	100% in top 1/2 33%	M520m 498v W508m 510v	a. $100 b. 630 d. 85	32% $300	1:17 52%	140		B.A., B.S.; *Semester, summer session;* Education—47%, Liberal Arts—45%, Other—8%; *Teacher Education.*
Trinity College Hartford 1823 *Private*	1142M	1270	69% in top 1/4 34%	671m 631v	a. $2000 b. 920 d. 70	25% $100-1800	1:9 65%	460	$14,369	B.A., B.S.; *Semester, summer sessions;* Social Sciences—51%, Natural Sciences & Math—25%, Humanities—22%; *Engineering* (5-yr. B.S.) *Teacher Education;* Coop engineering with Columbia; Air Force ROTC optional.
United States Coast Guard Academy New London 1876 *Federal*	800M	1200	86% in top 1/5 7%	644m 576v	$300 Fee at Entrance	100% Total Cost	1:8 24%	75	Us Govt Endowed	B.S.; *Semester, summer term;* Standard curriculum for all cadets; Engineering or management—Social Science.
Wesleyan University Middletown 1831 *Private*	1350M	1547	93% in top 2/5 36%	686m 670v	a. $1800 b. 1075 d. 330	40% $1200	1:8 76%	570	$88,000	B.A.; *Semester;* Social Sciences—50%, Humanities—22%, Natural Sciences & Math—22%; *Public Affairs Programs, Center for Advanced Studies in Liberal Arts, Professions and Sciences;* Coop architecture & engineering with Cal. Tech. & Columbia; NSF grants exceeding $1,500,000 since 1960.
Willimantic State College Willimantic 1889 *State*	300M 550W	1500	95% in top 2/5 51%	485m 485v	a. $170 b. 630	20% $400	1:15 34%	50		B.A., B.S.; *Semester, summer session;* B.A.—15%, Teacher Education—85%; *Teacher Education.*
Yale University New Haven 1701 *Private*	4000M	4100	90% in top 1/10 25%	711m 697v	a. $1950 b. 1050 d. 500	50% $300-3000	1:7 85%	5000	$500,000	B.A., B.S.; *Semester;* Architecture, Art, Divinity, Drama, Engineering, Forestry, Law, Medicine, Music, Nursing; Army, Navy ROTC optional.

DELAWARE

Institution / Location / Founded / Affiliation	Enrollment	Projected	HS rating	SAT/ACT	Tuition	$ aid	Ratio	Volumes	Endowment	Degrees / Misc
Delaware, University of Newark 1833 *Private*	3019M 2399W	16000	80% in top 2/5 89% Del. 18% oos.	M570m 510v W520m 530v	a. $350 b. 805 c. 820 d. 855	22% $550	1:17 65%	500	$47,000	B.A., B.S.; *Semester, summer session;* Liberal Arts—41%, Education—18%, Business & Economics—13%, Engineering—13%, Agriculture—6%, Home Economics—6%, Nursing—3%; *Agriculture, Business, Education, Engineering;* Army ROTC required.
Delaware State College Dover 1891 *State*	508M 471W	1800	10% in top 1/5 40%		a. none b. $525 c. 350 d. 238	70% $308	1:13 22%	52		B.A., B.S.; *Semester;* Education—37%, Social Sciences—22%, Business & Commerce—23%, Other—18%.

DISTRICT OF COLUMBIA

Institution / Location / Founded / Affiliation	Enrollment	Projected	HS rating	SAT/ACT	Tuition	$ aid	Ratio	Volumes	Endowment	Degrees / Misc
American University Washington 1893 *Methodist*	2102M 2141W	6400	56% in top 1/4 59%	M557m 560v W521m 553v	a. $1550 b. 870	14% $763	1:14 56%	155	$3,686	B.A., B.S.; *Semester, summer session;* Social Sciences—35%, Fine Arts—8%, Law—12%, Humanities—11%, Education—13%, Business—15%, Natural Sciences—6%; *Business Administration;* Host for 92 colleges with "Washington Semester"; Given $1,282,250 since 1960 from Methodist Church of America.
Catholic University of America Washington 1887 *Roman Catholic*	1715M 948W	2500	60% in top 1/5 65%		a. $1400 b. 1000	23%	1:14 50%	700		B.A., B.S.; *Semester, summer session;* Architecture, Engineering, Law, Library Science, Music, Nursing, Psychology, Social Work.
District of Columbia Teachers College Washington 1851 *Municipal*	272M 631W	4000 *	37% in top 1/4		a. $70 c. 1126	40% $100	1:15 40%	92		B.S.; *Semester, summer session;* Education—55%, Physical Ed.—10%, Social Science—5%, English—10%, Math—10%, Science—5%, Foreign Languages—5%; *Teacher Education;* Grant from Office of Education for work-study program. * New college projected.
Dunbarton College of Holy Cross Washington 1935 *Roman Catholic*	483W	650	68% in top 2/5 65%	532m 543v	a. $1250 b. 1200 d. 120	16% $500	1:11 33%	50	$43	A.B.; *Semester, summer sessions;* Humanities—27%, Social Sciences—36%, Education—16%, Natural Sciences & Math—12%.

Institution Location	Founded Affiliation	Enrollment M=men W=women	Projected enrollment in 1975	High school rating; % applicants accepted	SAT/ACT Averages m=math v=verbal	a. Annual Tuition; b. Room & Board; c. Out of state; d. Other	% Students with $ aid; Average amount	Faculty-student ratio; % with Doctorates	Volumes in library in 1,000's	Endowment in $1,000's	Undergraduate degrees offered; Calendar; Per cent of students per field of study; Professional programs offered; Miscellaneous
Gallaudet College Washington	1864 Private	406M 360W	1300	45%		a. $500 b. 700	75% $400	1:7 20%	81		B.A., B.S.; Semester, summer session; Gallaudet is devoted solely to the teaching of the deaf; There are graduate programs for students who wish to become audiologists, speech pathologists, and teachers of the deaf.
Georgetown University Washington	1789 Roman Catholic	3130M 860W	4000	43% in top 1/10 39%	631m 624v	a. $1650 b. 1100 (room) d. 150	20% $1000 55%	1:8	620	$7,000	B.A., B.S.; Semester, summer sessions; Liberal Arts—33%, Foreign Service—28%, Business—13%, Law—10%, Sciences—9%; Dentistry, Law, Medicine, Nursing; Coops on graduate level with other area universities; Air Force, Army ROTC optional.
George Washington University, The Washington	1821 Private	2565M 2597W		62%-W 40%-M in top 1/5 70%	M590m 587v W569m 600v	a. $1700 b. 950- 1100 d. 10	13% $200- 2500 71%	1:17	410	$9,131	B.A., B.S.; Semester, summer session; Business Administration, Education, Engineering, Law, Medicine; 3-1 coop in medical technology with University Hospital.
Howard University Washington	1867 Private	3422M 2878W	13000	most in top 1/2 25%		a. $400 b. 710	27% $578 35%	1:15	363	$5,000	B.A., B.S.; Semester, summer sessions; Liberal Arts—74%, Architecture and Engineering—14%, Pharmacy—3%, Fine Arts—6%; Architecture, Dentistry, Engineering, Law, Medicine, Music, Social Work, Theology; Air Force, Army ROTC required.
Trinity College Washington	1897 Roman Catholic	988W	1500	70% in top 1/5 57%	600m 640v	a. $1400 b. 1200 d. 45	33% $100- 1250 50%	1:12	96	$833	B.A.; Semester, summer session; Social Sciences—49%, Humanities—33%, Natural Sciences & Math—18%; Coop program with Catholic University; 4 courses in theology required.

FLORIDA

Institution Location	Founded Affiliation	Enrollment M=men W=women	Projected enrollment in 1975	High school rating; % applicants accepted	SAT/ACT Averages m=math v=verbal	a. Annual Tuition; b. Room & Board; c. Out of state; d. Other	% Students with $ aid; Average amount	Faculty-student ratio; % with Doctorates	Volumes in library in 1,000's	Endowment in $1,000's	Undergraduate degrees offered; Calendar; Per cent of students per field of study; Professional programs offered; Miscellaneous
Barry College Miami	1940 Roman Catholic	615W	1500	45% in top 1/5 50%	485m 513v	a. $900 b. 1050	$200- 800 38%	1:11	55		B.A., B.S., B.S.Nurs.; Semester, summer session; Nursing, Social Work, Teacher Ed.; Weekly Mass, annual retreat required for Catholic Students only.
Bethune-Cookman College Daytona Beach	1872 Methodist	412M 563W	1200	65%	350m 325v	a. $900 b. 600	74% $475 40%	1:18	46	$1,675	B.A., B.S.; Semester, summer session; 4 hours of Biblical literature required; Junior Year Abroad program, Institute on Non-Western Affairs.
Florida, University of Gainesville	1853 State	12000M 6000W	16000	65% in top 1/5 50%		a. $300 b. 900 c. 750	5% $450 75%	1:20	1000	$2,500	B.A., B.S.; Quarter; Sciences, Liberal Arts; Architecture, Business, Education, Engineering, Forestry, Journalism, Law, Medicine, Nursing, Pharmacy, Agriculture, Health related prof., Phys. Ed.; Air Force, Army ROTC required.
Florida Agricultural and Mechanical U. Tallahassee	1887 State	1569M 1491W	5000	21% in top 1/2 69%		a. $200 b. 706 c. 400	12% $400 30%	1:14	149		B.A., B.S.; Trimester; Law, Nursing, Pharmacy, Teacher Education; Army ROTC required.
Florida Memorial College St. Augustine	1892 Baptist	170M 310W	1300	75% in top 1/2 70%		a. $650 b. 450 d. 110	91% $900 42%	1:19	52	$500	B.S.; Semester, summer session; Elementary Education—61%, English—15%, Music—17%, Social Sciences—18%.
Florida Southern College Lakeland	1885 Methodist	681M 729W	1800	67% in top 2/5 53%	517m 503v	a. $2040	34%	1:15	90	$1,688	B.A., B.S.; Semester; Business—25%, Education—15%, Social Sciences—23%, Humanities—19%, Natural Sciences & Math—20%; Army ROTC required.
Florida State University Tallahassee	1857 State	5061M 5066W	15000	70%		a. $260 b. 575 c. 660	25% $400 56%	1:28	689	$360	B.A., B.S.; Trimester; Business, Engineering, Library, Music, Nursing, Teacher Education; Coop—student exchange with U. of Mass.; Air Force, Army ROTC optional.
Miami, University of Coral Gables	1925 Private	9139M 5494W	16250	66% in top 1/2 80%	513m 500v	a. $1475 b. 850	65% $1000- 1500 65%	1:24	771	$17,500	B.A., B.S., B.B.A., B.Ed., B.Mus.; Semester, summer sessions; Education—33%, Arts—15%, Business—23%, Sciences—20%, Engineering—7%, Music—2%; Bus., Eng., Law., Med., Music, Nursing, Teacher Ed.; Air Force, Army ROTC optional. Research grants totaling $50,000,000 since 1960.
Rollins College Winter Park	1885 Private	550M 450W	1200	70% in top 2/5 52%	M579m 551v W548m 559v	$2675 Total	27% $1760	1:16	140	$6,000	B.A.; Quarter system; Coops—3-2 forestry with Duke U., 3-2 Engineering with N.Y.U., Columbia.
Stetson University DeLand	1883 Baptist	887M 755W	2500	67% in top 1/5 60%	M582m 540v W542m 553v	a. $1400 b. 850	42% $700 67%	1:15	148	$3,909	B.A., B.S.; Semester, winter study term, summer session; Law, Music, Teacher Education; Coops—3-2 engineering with Duke, U. of Florida, 3-2 forestry with Duke; Weekly chapel services required; Army ROTC optional.
Tampa, University of Tampa	1931 Private	1294M 661W	3000	most in top 1/2 85%		a. $1100 b. 990	29% $407 47%	1:25	85	$631	B.A., B.S.; Semester, summer session; A.B.—73%M, 27%W, B.S.—33%M, 67%W.

GEORGIA

Institution Location	Founded Affiliation	Enrollment M=men W=women	Projected enrollment in 1975	High school rating; % applicants accepted	SAT/ACT Averages m=math v=verbal	a. Annual Tuition; b. Room & Board; c. Out of state; d. Other	% Students with $ aid; Average amount	Faculty-student ratio; % with Doctorates	Volumes in library in 1,000's	Endowment in $1,000's	Undergraduate degrees offered; Calendar; Per cent of students per field of study; Professional programs offered; Miscellaneous
Agnes Scott College Decatur	1889 Presbyterian	750W	800	76%		a. $1700 b. 1000 c. 35	24% $575 70%	1:9	100	$11,900	B.A.; Quarter; Humanities—46%, Social Sciences—35%, Natural Sciences & Math—19%.
Albany State College Albany	1903 State	382M 713W	1229	most in top 1/2 85%		a. $315 b. 573 c. 330	80% $500 20%	1:17	33		B.A., B.S.; Quarter; Education—65%, Social Sciences—14%, Nursing—8%, Humanities—7%, Business—4%, Natural Sciences—2%; Nursing, Teacher Education.
Berry College Mount Berry	1902 Private	646M 602W	1800	80% in top 1/2 70%	M445m 415v W433m 445v	a. $900 b. 840 d. 60	17% $330 29%	1:19	55	$10,450	B.A., B.S., B.M.; Quarter; Natural Sciences—23%, Education—18%, Business—17%, Social Sciences—10%, Humanities—9%, Home Economics—7%; 9 quarter hours of religion, church services required; Grants totaling $2,000,000 since 1960.

Institution / Location / Founded / Affiliation	Enrollment M=men W=women	Projected enrollment in 1975	High school rating; % applicants accepted	SAT/ACT Averages m=math v=verbal	Annual Tuition; a. b. Room & Board; c. Out of state; d. Other state	% Students with $ aid; Average amount	Faculty-student ratio; % with Doctorates	Volumes in library in 1,000's	Endowment in $1,000's	Undergraduate degrees offered; Calendar; Per cent of students per field of study; Professional programs offered; Miscellaneous
Brenau College Gainesville 1878 *Private*	612W	625		425m 435v	a. $640 b. 980	12% $200	1:12 32%	24	$1,000	B.A., B.S.; *Semester.*
Clark College Atlanta 1869 *Methodist*	365M 633W	1200	65%	M363m 328v W332m 318v	a. $750 b. 603 d. 115	40% $600	1:12 30%	238	$1,737	B.A., B.S.; *Semester;* Arts—81%, Sciences—15%; Coop with Atlanta University Center; 6 semester hours religion and philosophy required; Center grant of $4,250,000 since 1960; Clark is a member of the Atlanta University Center, uses Center library.
Emory University Atlanta 1836 *Methodist*	1306M 897W	2200	57%M 44%W	628m 597v	a. $1650 b. 1000	30% $150-2000	1:10 75%	858	$100,000	B.A., B.S., B.B.A.; *Quarter, summer session;* Business, Dentistry, Law, Library, Medicine, Nursing, Teacher Education, Theology; One quarter Bible study required; Air Force ROTC optional.
Fort Valley State College Fort Valley 1895 *State*	362M 673W		25% in top 1/4 96%		a. $219 b. 450	11% $120-654	21%	39		B.A., B.S.; *Quarter, summer sessions;* Social Work.
Georgia, University of Athens 1785 *State*	6966M 4913W	20000	65% in top 1/3 78%	M529m 491v W505m 503v	a. $333 b. 780 c. 420 d. 450	15% $500	1:17 65%	680	$3,300	B.A., B.S., B.S.Ed., B.Mus., B.F.A.; *Quarter;* Agriculture, Business, Engineering, Forestry, Journalism, Landscape Architecture, Law, Music, Pharmacy, Teacher Education, Veterinary Medicine; Coop—3-2 engineering with Georgia Tech.; Air Force, Army required for 2 years.
Georgia Institute of Technology Atlanta 1885 *State*	6187M 90W	7750	80% in top 1/5 55%	634m 552v	a. $375 b. 800 c. 1065	15% $100-2000	1:15 66%	300	$1,373	B.S., B.Arch.; *Quarter, summer quarter;* Engineering—62%, Business—16%, Sciences—15%, Architecture—7%; Architecture, Engineering; Coops—3-2 engineering ed. with U. of the South, Davidson, Southwestern, U. of Geo., U. of Chattanooga; AF, A, N ROTC optional.
Georgia Southern College Statesboro 1908 *State*	1828M 2235W	7000	most in top 1/2 75%	482m 481v	a. $255 b. 570 c. 555 d. 48	15% $400	1:18 43%	95		B.A., B.S., B.S.Ed., B.B.A.; *Quarter, summer sessions;* Teacher Education.
Georgia Southwestern College Americus 1908 *State*	842M 491W	2900	87%		a. $ 85 b. 187 c. 110 d. 15	13% $507	1:20 30%	31		B.A., B.S., B.S.Ed.; *Quarter, summer Quarter;* Teacher Education, Business.
Georgia State College Atlanta 1913 *State*	4841M 3396W	25000	90% in top 1/2 75%	M488m 466v W445m 484v	a. $375 b. 800 c. 834 d. 50	1% $300	1:25 70%	185	$20	B.A., B.S., B.B.A., B.Mus., B.Vis. Arts; *Quarter;* Business, Music; Coop—B.S. in nursing with Medical College of Georgia; Army ROTC required; Grants totaling $409,596 since 1960.
La Grange College La Grange 1831 *Methodist*	300M 325W	850	most in top 1/3 60%	509m 505v	a. $1125 b. 675	20% $250	1:14 40%	39	$4,000	B.A.; *Quarter;* Grants totaling $2,500,000 since 1960.
Mercer University Macon 1833 *Baptist*	988M 614W	1600	35% in top 1/4 84%	525m 525v	$1920 Total	34%		100		B.A., B.S.; *Quarter;* Law, Pharmacy, Teacher Education; Army ROTC optional.
Morehouse College Atlanta 1867 *Private*	910M	1200	90% in top 1/4 30%		a. $750 b. 729 c. 110	40% $225-500	1:14 54%	275	$4,500	B.A., B.S.; *Semester, summer session;* Social Sciences—41%, Natural Sciences & Math—34%, Business—15%, Humanities—7%; Two courses in religion, chapel attendance required; Morehouse is a member of the Atlanta University Center, uses Center library. Grants totaling $3,000,000 since 1960.
Morris Brown College Atlanta 1885 *African Methodist Episcopal*	446M 695W	3000	75%	M350m 300v W300m 350v	a. $650 b. 585 d. 150	50% $500	1:15 36%	13	$800	B.A., B.S.; *Semester;* Social Sciences—39%, Education—22%, Natural Sciences & Math—13%, Humanities—10%, Business—8%; Coop—Morris Brown is a member of the Atlanta University Center, uses Center library. Grants totaling $239,500 since 1960.
North Georgia College Dahlonega 1873 *State*	744M 393W	1210	75%M 25%W	477m 468v	a. $309 b. 648 c. 330	22% $450	1:21 30%	70		B.A., B.S.; *Quarter;* Business—29%, Education—23%, Natural Sciences & Math—25%, Social Sciences—12%, Humanities—11%; *Business Administration, Teacher Education;* Army ROTC required.
Oglethorpe College Atlanta 1835 *Private*	400M 350W	2000	40%		a. $1100 b. 920 d. 80	$150-800	1:13 32%	28	$1,015	B.A., B.S.; *Trimester;* Liberal Arts—30%, Education—30%, Sciences —20%, Business—20%.
Paine College Augusta 1882 *Methodist*	266M 484W	800	most in top 1/4 85%		a. $650 b. 600	23% $354	1:13 18%	35	$378	B.A., B.S., B.S.Ed.; *Semester, summer session;* Liberal Arts—54%, Natural Sciences & Math—29%, Education—13%; Coops—faculty exchanges with Hamline U. and Carleton College.
Savannah State College Savannah 1891 *State*	661M 940W	2028	most in top 1/4 82%	M303m 264v W271m 294v	a. $255 b. 579 c. 330 d. 69	40% $450	1:20 30%	58		B.S.; *Quarter, summer session;* Education—57%, Natural Sciences—15%, Business Administration—7%, Social Sciences—10%, Technical Sciences—7%.
Shorter College Rome 1873 *Baptist*	347M 446W	1000	80%	M446m 420v W422m 431v	a. $700 b. 750 d. 150	20% $150	1:16	40	$1,046	B.A., B.Mus., B.S., B.S.Med. Tech.; *Semester, summer session;* Humanities—20%, Social Sciences—19%, Education—26%, Natural Sciences & Math—15%, Business—13%, Music—7%; *Music;* Grants totaling $454,000 since 1960.
Spelman College Atlanta 1881 *Baptist*	800W	1200	51% in top 1/5 89%	394m 377v	a. $750 b. 675	56% $350	1:17 23%	17		B.A., B.S.; *Semester;* Social Sciences—52%, Humanities—25%, Natural Sciences & Math—17%, Home Economics—5%, Physical Education—1%; Coop—Spelman is a member of the Atlanta University Center, uses Center library; 2 semesters religion, chapel, Vespers required.
Tift College Forsyth 1849 *Baptist*	550W	600	50% in top 1/4 94%	423m 425v	a. $585 b. 600	25% $450	1:15 35%	37	$1,500	B.A., B.S.; *Quarter, summer session;* Education—45%, Humanities —25%, Social Sciences—13%, Natural Sciences & Math—11%, Nursing—6%; Coop—nursing program with Georgia Baptist Hospital School; One course each in Old and New Testaments required; Kellogg Foundation grant of $10,000 since 1960.

Institution Location / Founded Affiliation	Enrollment M=men W=women	Projected enrollment in 1975	High school rating; % applicants accepted	SAT/ACT Averages m=math v=verbal	a. Annual Tuition; b. Room & Board; c. Out of state; d. Other state.	% Students with $ aid / Average amount	Faculty-student ratio; % with Doctorates	Volumes in library in 1,000's	Endowment in $1,000's	Undergraduate degrees offered; Calendar; Per cent of students per field of study; Professional programs offered; Miscellaneous
Valdosta State College Valdosta 1913 State	935M 1046W	5000	91%		a. $315 b. 591 c. 645	5% $325	1:19 31%	60		B.A., B.S., B.S.Chem.; *Quarter, summer session; Teacher Education (M.A.T.);* Coops in medical technology with area hospitals.
Wesleyan College Macon 1836 Methodist	707W	850	75% in top 1/4 66%	497m 516v	a. $1255 b. 775 d. 45	38% $500	1:12 38%	67	$4,000	B.A., B.S., B.F.A., B.Mus.; *Semester; Music, Teacher Education;* 6 hours of religion courses, weekly chapel required.
West Georgia College Carrollton 1933 State	1566M 1198W	6400	70%	M467m 426v W438m 446v	a. $255 b. 630 c. 585 d. 45	34% $400	1:19 33%	56		B.A., B.S.; *Quarter;* Education—25%, Social Sciences—45%, Natural Sciences & Math—14%, Humanities—11%; Grants totaling $2,118,544 since 1960.
Georgia College at Milledgeville Milledgeville 1891 State	1060W	1200M 1200W	65% in top 1/4 80%	450m 460v	a. $255 b. 600 c. 330 d. 100	40% $350	1:17 36%	90	$550	B.A., B.S., B.M.E.; *Quarter;* Education.
HAWAII										
Chaminade College of Honolulu Honolulu 1955 Roman Catholic	427M 241W	1000	73%	444m 426v	a. $800 b. 800	15% $91	1:16 18%	32	$8	B.A.; *Semester;* Social Sciences—57%, Natural Sciences & Math—18%, Education—10%, Business—8%, Humanities—7%; 8 hours of theology courses required of Catholic students.
Church College of Hawaii Laie, Oahu 1955 Latter-day Saints	515M 499W	1800			a. $200 b. 630 c. 200		1:15	27		B.A., B.S.; *Semester;* 16 hours of religion courses, attendance at devotional assemblies required.
Hawaii, University of Honolulu 1907 State	7505M 7267W	29300	67%		a. $170 b. 690 d. 63	16%	1:15 46%	500	$6,600	B.A., B.S., B.B.A., B.F.A., B.Mus., B.Ed.; *Semester, summer sessions; Engineering, Nursing, Social Work, Medicine, Public Health, Library Studies;* Air Force, Army ROTC required; The East-West Center for Cultural Technical Interchange is affiliated with the University of Hawaii.
IDAHO										
College of Idaho, The Caldwell 1891 Presbyterian	500M 335W	1100	64% in top 1/3 75%M 82%W	<u>22.0m</u> <u>21.0v</u>	a. $1300 b. 790	52% $730	1:16 37%	65	$1,172	B.A., B.S.; *Modified Semester, summer sessions;* Education—17%, Natural Sciences & Math—27%, Social Sciences—27%, Business—15%, Humanities—12%; Coop—3-2 engineering with Stanford, U. of Idaho.
Idaho, University of Moscow 1889 State	4115M 1845W	9100	75% in top 1/2 70%	M528m 468v W499m 494v	a. none b. $790 c. 500 d. 210	35% $50-1000	1:16 48%	300	$13,187	B.A., B.S., B.Arcn., B.Mus.; *Semester, summer session;* Liberal Arts—23%, Education—23%, Engineering—10%, Forestry—4%, Mines—2%, Agriculture—5%, Business—10%; *Engineering, Forestry, Law, Music, Teacher Education;* Air Force, Army, Navy ROTC optional.
Idaho State University Pocatello 1901 State	3128M 1649W	7500	most in top 3/4 90%		a. $280 b. 700 c. 500	25% $50-500	1:21 35%	400		B.A., B.S., B.B.A., B.Arch., B.Mus.Ed., B.M.T., B.S.Nursing, B.S.Pharmacy; *Semester, summer session;* Liberal Arts—45%, Education—20%, Business—10%, Pharmacy—6%; *Nursing, Pharmacy, Teacher Education, Business, Journalism, Dental Hygiene, Architecture, General/Nuclear Engineering;* Army ROTC optional.
Northwest Nazarene College Nampa 1913 Church of Nazarene	587M 527W	1400	80% in top 1/2 94%M 95%W		a. $800 b. 850 c. 72	15% $450	1:20 40%	52	$150	B.A.; *Three-term, summer session;* Coop—4-2 law with Willamette, U. of Idaho; 8 credit hours of religion, daily convocation, Sunday church attendance required.
ILLINOIS										
Augustana College Rock Island 1860 Lutheran	731M 766W	2000	85% in top 1/4 65%	M507m 560v W565m 580v	a. $1250 b. 1000 d. 100	68% $450	1:15 43%	130	$3,660	B.A., B.Mus., B.Mus.Ed.; *Semester, summer session;* Social Sciences—23%, Education—21%, Natural Sciences & Math—20%, Humanities—13%, Business—11%; *Music, Teacher Education;* Coop in engineering with Purdue, N.Y.U.; 4 courses in religion, chapel required.
Aurora College Aurora 1893 Advent Christian Church	528M 326W	1000	73% in top 1/2 70%		a. $1110 b. 820	35% $775	1:18 35%	55	$226	B.A., B.S., B.Th.; *Semester;* Education—26%, Social Sciences—15%, National Sciences—13%, Business—27%, English—12%, Theology—7%; Coop—3-1 medical technology; 6 hours religion required; Grants totaling $1,388,162 since 1960.
Barat College Lake Forest 1858 Roman Catholic	572W	700	100% in top 1/2 70%	480m 510v	a. $1000 b. 1200 d. 100	35% $900	1:10 53%	45		B.A., B.S.; *Semester;* Social Sciences—42%, Humanities—40%, Natural Sciences & Math—13%, Home Economics—5%.
Blackburn College Carlinville 1857 Presbyterian	268M 234W	800	70% in top 1/5 55%M 90%W	M552m 521v W538m 560v	a. $850 b. 300 c. 50	25% $70-850	1:13 45%	45	$3,500	B.A.; *Semester;* Natural Sciences & Math—42%, Social Sciences—32%, Education—15%, Humanities—11%; Coop—3-3 law with U. of Illinois, Washington U. in St. Louis; Weekly chapel required.
Bradley University Peoria 1897 Private	3200M 1500W	5000	38% in top 1/4 71%	M545m 474v W480m 491v	a. $1300 b. 900	30% $1300	1:17 45%	150		B.A., B.S., B.F.A.; *Semester, summer sessions;* Liberal Arts & Sciences—45%, Business—19%, Engineering—12%, Applied Sciences—10%, Education—8%; *Pre-Med., Pre-Dent., Sp. Ther., Music, Art, Int. Stud., Engineering, Music, Teacher Education;* Coop in education with U. of Indiana; Air Force ROTC optional.
Chicago, The University of; The College Chicago 1890 Private	1415M 989W	4000	81% in top 1/10 50%	665m 664v	a. $1980 b. 1270	55% $1310	1:9 100%	2504	$181,921 total University	B.A., B.S., B.F.A.; *Quarter, summer quarter;* Arts—79%, Sciences—20%; *Business, Law, Library, Medicine, Psychology, Social Work, Teacher Education, Theology.*
College of St. Francis Joliet 1925 Roman Catholic	850W	1200	most in top 1/2 80%		a. $600 b. 750	10% $500	1:12 35%	63	$200	B.A., B.S., B.Mus.; *Semester, summer session;* Social Sciences—40%, Natural Sciences & Math—28%, Humanities—26%, Medical Technology—7%; Coop—3-1 medical technology with St. Francis Hospital in Peoria, Illinois and St. Joseph Hospital, Joliet.
DePaul University Chicago 1898 Roman Catholic	3504M 1981W	15623	83% in top 1/2 73%	M523m 495v W484m 502v	a. $1140 b. no dorm	26% $600	1:15 58%	228	$2,093	B.A., B.S., B.M.; *Quarter, summer sessions; Business, Law, Music, Nursing;* 2 courses in theology required of Catholic students; Army ROTC optional.

Institution / Location / Founded / Affiliation	Enrollment M=men W=women	Projected enrollment in 1975	High school rating; % applicants accepted	SAT/ACT Averages m=math v=verbal	Annual Tuition: a. / Room & Board: b. / Out of state: c. / Other: d.	% Students with $ aid / Average amount	Faculty-student ratio / % with Doctorates	Volumes in library in 1,000's	Endowment in $1,000's	Undergraduate degrees offered; Calendar; Per cent of students per field of study; Professional programs offered; Miscellaneous
Eastern Illinois University Charleston 1899 *State*	3047M 2740W	9862	58% in top 2/5		a. $235 b. 840 c. 405	65%	1:13 60%	140		B.A., B.S., B.S.Ed.; *Quarter, summer session;* Teacher Ed.—77%, Business & Commerce—16%; *Med. Tech., Ind. Tech., Home Economics in Dietetics & Business.*
Elmhurst College Elmhurst 1871 *United Church of Christ*	700M 700W	2000	75% in top 2/5 50%	M522m 514v W518m 510v	a. $1300 b. 1000	36% $850	1:14 40%	65	$650	B.A.; *Semester, summer session;* Social Sciences—30%, Humanities—26%, Education—22%, Natural Sciences & Math—18%, Medicine—4%; Coop—3-2 engineering with N.Y.U., coop with Argonne Nat'l. Lab.; 6 hours religion required; Junior Year Abroad, Washington Semester.
Eureka College Eureka 1855 *Disciples of Christ*	300M 200W	785	22% in top 1/5 70%	22 (comp.)	a. $1200 b. 840 d. 100	40% $100-1200	1:15 40%	55		B.A., B.S.; *Quarter;* One course religion or philosophy, weekly chapel required.
George Williams College Downers Grove 1890 *Private*	453M 180W	1000	80% in top 1/2 60%		a. $1050 b. 900 c. 350	50% $1000	1:15 50%	37		B.A., B.S.; *Quarter;* Health & Physical Education—35%, Social Group Work—35%, General Studies—30%; George Williams students are educated for leadership in voluntary agencies, such as YMCA, YWCA, Boys' Clubs, settlement houses & recreation centers, as well as schools, government and welfare organizations.
Greenville College Greenville 1892 *Free Methodist*	442M 383W	1000	80%		a. $900 b. 830	33% $300	1:17 35%	58	$350	B.A., B.S., B.Mus.Ed., B.Th.; *Semester, summer sessions;* Education—25%, Social Sciences—20%, Religion—8%, Natural Sciences & Math—20%, Humanities & Fine Arts—12%, Business & Economics—15%.
Illinois, University of Urbana 1868 *State*	14062M 7560W	34000	75% in top 1/4	26 (comp.)	a. $170 b. 840 c. 750 d. 100	34% $100-500	1:12 66%	3751	$7,700 Total All Campuses	B.A., B.S., B.Arch., B.F.A.; *Semester, summer session;* Arts & Sciences—42%, Law—5%, Eng.—13%, Ed.—7%, Bus.—8%, Agriculture—8%; *Arch., Art, Bus., Dent., Eng., For., Jour., Landscape Arch., Law, Lib., Med., Music, Nurs., Phar., Psych., Social Work, Teacher Ed., Vet. Med.;* AF, A, M, N ROTC optional.
Illinois, University of —Chicago Circle Chicago 1964 *State*	6778M 4126W	25500	67% in top 1/4	24 (comp.)	a. $171 b. no dorm c. 750 d. 114	19% $100-500	1:18 55%	163		B.A., B.S., B.Arch.; *Quarter;* Architecture & Art—8%, Bus. Adm.—20%, Liberal Arts & Sciences—72%; *Architecture, Art, Business, Engineering, Teacher Education;* Army ROTC optional.
Illinois College Jacksonville 1829 *Presbyterian & United Church of Christ*	481M 327W	1000	65% in top 1/3 58%		a. $1050 b. 900	34% $801	1:15 50%	57	$3,500	B.A., B.S.; *Semester;* Social Sciences—44%, Economics & Business—27%, Humanities—16%, Natural Sciences & Math—13%.
Illinois Institute of Technology Chicago 1892 *Private*	2133M 115W	3000	75% in top 1/4 60%	642m 574v	a. $1600 b. 900	22% $625	1:10 80%	1000	$5,007	B.S., B.Arch.; *Semester, summer session;* Design—6%, Engineering—52%, Sciences—20%, Liberal Arts—14%, Architecture—8%; *Architecture, Art, Engineering;* Air Force, Marine, Navy ROTC optional.
Illinois State University Normal 1857 *State*	4049M 5650W	16770	60% in top 1/4	23 (comp.)	a. $225 b. 880 c. 390	80% $300	1:15 40%	350		B.A., B.S., B.S.Ed.; *Semester, summer session;* Education—49%, Humanities—17%, Social Sciences—10%, Health & Physical Education—9%, Natural Sciences & Math—9%, Home Economics—3%, Industrial Arts—3%, Agriculture—3%; *Teacher Education, Arts & Sciences, Applied Sciences & Tech., Business.*
Illinois Teachers College: Chicago-North Chicago 1961 *State*	693M 2105W	5000	most in top 1/2 60%		a. none b. no dorm c. $270 d. 120		1:18 40%	70		B.A.; *Trimester.*
Illinois Teachers College: Chicago-South Chicago 1869 *State*	713M 1463W	15000	75% in top 1/2 50%	M18.9 W18.3 (comp.)	a. none b. no dorm c. $413 d. 200	30% $600	1:16 44%	120		B.Ed.; *Trimester, summer sessions;* Teacher Education.
Illinois Wesleyan University Bloomington 1850 *Methodist*	750M 750W	1900	62% in top 1/5 70%	566m 552v	a. $1625 b. 920	49% $870	1:14 36%	90	$6,226	B.A., B.S., B.F.A., B.Mus., B.Mus.Ed.; *Semester;* Art, Drama, Music, Nursing, Teacher Education; Coops—3-2 engineering with U. of Ill., 3-2 forestry with Duke; One course in religion required.
Knox College Galesburg 1837 *Private*	725M 575W	2325	49% in top 1/10 71%	597m 577v	a. $2010 b. 1015	60% $687	1:14 61%	123	$10,429	B.A.; *Semester, summer session;* Social Sciences—36%, Natural Sciences & Math—22%, Humanities—32%, Education—10%; Coop—3-2 engineering with Columbia, Stanford; Advanced Army ROTC optional.
Lake Forest College Lake Forest 1857 *Presbyterian*	650M 600W	1250	70% in top 1/5 55%	M612m 587v W600m 615v	a. $1950 b. 1050	40% $1100	1:14 70%	100	$6,000	B.A.; *Three-term, summer session;* Humanities—48%, Social Sciences—40%, Natural Science & Math—12%; Elementary and Secondary Teacher training (no Ed. major); One course in religion required.
Lewis College Lockport 1930 *Roman Catholic*	1450M	2800	50%	21.3 (comp.)	a. $960 b. 800	34% $600	1:20 30%	37	$130	B.A.; *Semester;* Accounting, Biology, Chemistry, Economics, English, History, Management, Marketing, Mathematics, Philosophy, Political Science, Psychology, Sociology; *Dentistry, Engineering, Law, Medicine, Teacher Ed.;* Coop with College of St. Francis; 3 semesters of theology required of Catholic students.
Loyola University Chicago 1870 *Roman Catholic*	5247M 3260W	15000	55% in top 1/4	534m 543v	a. $1320 b. 950	25% $320	1:17 56%	461	$11,000	B.A., B.S., B.S.N., B.S.Ed.; *Semester, summer sessions; Business, Dentistry, Law, Medicine, Nursing, Social Work, Teacher Education, Humanities, Social Science, Arts;* Annual retreat required of Catholic students; Army ROTC optional.
MacMurray College Jacksonville 1846 *Methodist*	562M 552W	1300	50% in top 1/5 80%	M561m 530v W530m 540v	a. $1600 b. 865	41% $1200	1:15 53%	90		B.A.; *Semester, summer session;* Natural Sciences & Math—19%, Social Sciences—32%, Humanities—30%, Education—19%; 3-2 Engineering with Columbia U., U. of Illinois; Summer Abroad program, Foreign Languages, Europe & Mexico.
Millikin University Decatur 1903 *Presbyterian*	631M 482W	1700	47% in top 1/4 65%	M522m 486v W491m 481v	a. $1400 b. 900	30% $400	1:14 25%	92	$3,000	B.A., B.S., B.Mus.; *Semester, summer session;* Education—33%, Business—18%, Natural Science & Math—12%, Humanities—10%, Social Sciences—9%, Industrial Engineering—8%; *Music, Teacher Education.*
Monmouth College Monmouth 1853 *Presbyterian*	754M 502W	1600	80% in top 1/2 70%	M535m 493v W501m 499v	a. $1740 b. 860	30% $817	1:15 44%	100	$1,600	B.A.; *Three-term, summer session;* Coop—3-2 engineering with Case Institute, N.Y.U.

Institution / Location / Founded / Affiliation	Enrollment M=men W=women	Projected enrollment in 1975	High school rating; % applicants accepted	SAT/ACT Averages m=math v=verbal	Annual Tuition: a. b. Room & Board; c. Out of state; d. Other state	% Students with $ aid / Average amount	Faculty-student ratio; % with Doctorates	Volumes in library in 1,000's	Endowment in $1,000's	Undergraduate degrees offered; Calendar; Per cent of students per field of study; Professional programs offered; Miscellaneous
Mundelein College Chicago 1929 *Roman Catholic*	1200W	1500	48% in top 1/5 70%	504m 546v	a. $1150 b. 920	31% 29%	1:12 $390	58		B.A., B.S., B.F.A.; *Three-term;* Humanities—36%, Natural Sciences & Math—17%, Social Sciences—47%, 3-2 Engineering with Case Institute, N.Y.U.
National College of Education Evanston 1886 *Private*	50M 500W	1000	46% in top 1/4 50%		a. $1755 b. 1000	35% 52%	1:15 $1000	47	$550	B.A.; *Quarter, summer session;* Liberal Arts; *Education—98%; Teacher Education.*
North Central College Naperville 1861 *Evangelical United Brethren*	400M 400W	1200	60% in top 1/4 64%	M575m 530v W530m 530v	a. $1350 b. 900	45% 62%	1:13 $375	90	$3,000	B.A., B.Mus., B.Mus.Ed.; *Semester, summer sessions;* Humanities—28%, Natural Sciences & Math—22%, Social Sciences—20%, Education—20%; *Music, Teacher Education;* Washington Semester.
Northern Illinois University DeKalb 1895 *State*	6471M 6624W	22200	60% in top 1/3 70%	M24.0m 20.4v W22.5m 20.3v	a. $259 b. 888 c. 429	50% 51%	1:15 $233	364		B.A., B.S., B.S.Ed., B.Mus., B.F.A., Ph.B.; *Semester, summer sessions; Teacher Education.*
North Park College Chicago 1891 *Evangelical Covenant*	700M 600W	1800	45% in top 1/5 75%	M575m 525v W525m 575v	a. $1260 b. 900 d. 105	40% 32%	1:15 $600	75	$1,000	B.A., B.S., B.D., B.Mus.; *Three-term, summer session;* Social Sciences—45%, Humanities—27%, Natural Sciences & Math—16%, Nursing—9%; *Music, Theology.*
Northwestern University Evanston 1851 *Private*	3400M 2700W	6500	60% in top 1/10 50%	M644m 593v W583m 599v	a. $1800 b. 960 c. 60	22% 71%	1:11 $1500	1643	$204,000	B.A., B.S., B.Mus., B.Mus.Ed.; *Quarter, summer sessions;* Arts & Sciences—45%, Education—13%, Business—13%, Speech—10%, Engineering—9%, Journalism—6%; *Bus., Dent., Eng., Jour., Law, Med., Music, Teacher Ed.;* Navy ROTC optional.
Olivet Nazarene College Kankakee 1907 *Church of Nazarene*	875M 807W	2800	75% in top 1/2 75%		a. $800 b. 720	45% 33%	1:20 $100	63		B.A., B.S., B.Th.; *Semester, summer session;* Education—34%, Social Sciences—21%, Humanities—19%, Natural Sciences & Math—16%, Business—8%; 12 hours Bible and theology, chapel four times weekly required.
Principia College Elsah 1898 *Private*	347M 347W	700	40% in top 1/10 76%M 60%W	M582m 538v W562m 562v	a. $1938 b. 1200	25% 38%	1:13 $100-700	89	$6,900	B.A., B.S.; *Three-term;* Humanities—33%, Social Sciences—38%, Education—17%, Natural Sciences & Math—12%; Coop-3-2 engineering; Enrollment at Principia limited to children of Christian Scientists.
Quincy College Quincy 1860 *Roman Catholic*	850M 500W	2000	65%	450m 450v	a. $1000 b. 800	60% $500	1:10	110	$750	B.A., B.S.; *Semester, summer session.*
Rockford College Rockford 1847 *Private*	212M 259W	1000	20% in top 1/10 66%	541m 549v	a. $1400 b. 1000	38% 53%	1:12 $100-1100	60	$3,000	B.A.; *Semester plus January Interim, summer session;* Social Sciences—43%, Humanities—20%, Natural Sciences & Math—20%, Education—7%, Art—10%; Coop-3-2 dentistry, engineering, medicine, or law.
Roosevelt University Chicago 1945 *Private*	4071M 2768W	8000	most in top 1/2 58%		a. $990 b. no dorm	8% 39%	1:17 $420	172	$917	B.A., B.S., B.S.B.A., B.Mus., B.G.S.; *Semester, summer session;* Arts—57%, Business—25%, Sciences—15%, Music—3%; *Business, Music;* Coop—Jewish Studies program, College of Jewish Studies.
Rosary College River Forest 1901 *Roman Catholic*	850W	1200	48% in top 1/10 80%	527m 563v	a. $1000 b. 1050	20% 46%	1:11 $500	105		B.A., B.Mus., B.Mus.Ed.; *Semester, summer session;* Humanities—52%, Social Sciences—29%, Natural Sciences & Math—18%; *Library, Music;* Junior Year Abroad.
St. Procopius College Lisle 1887 *Roman Catholic*	758M	1200	90% in top 1/2 25%	520m 475v	a. $1000 b. 900	30% 40%	1:15 $252	65		B.A., B.S.; *Semester;* Coop-3-2 engineering with Marquette, Notre Dame.
Saint Xavier College Chicago 1847 *Roman Catholic*	1040W	1400	52% in top 1/5 75%	503m 528v	a. $1200 b. 900	48% $400	1:12	75		B.A., B.S. in Nursing; *Semester, summer session;* Education—30%, Nursing—25%, Other—45%; *Nursing;* Coop in teaching with U. of Chicago (MAT); Ford Foundation grant of $1,500,000, Public Health Institute grant of $650,000 since 1960.
Shimer College Mount Carroll 1853 *Private*	259M 159W	500	83% in top 1/2 75%	M615m 629v W587m 631v	$2720 Total	32% 25%	1:14 $1900 Max.	22	$300	B.A.; *Semester;* Humanities—33%, Social Sciences—33%, Natural Sciences & Math—32%; Junior Year Abroad.
Southern Illinois University Carbondale 1869 *State*	13454M 7017W	38000	40% in top 1/4 70%		a. $194 b. 800 c. 434	60% 60%	1:12	800		B.A., B.S., B.Mus., B.Mus.Ed.; *Quarter, summer quarter;* Business, Journalism, Music, Psychology, Teacher Education; Air Force ROTC optional.
Western Illinois University Macomb 1899 *State*	4037M 3168W	18931	80% in top 1/2 80%	23 (comp.)	a. $233 b. 774 c. 404	33% 47%	1:17 $350	153		B.A., B.S., B.B., B.S.Ed.; *Quarter;* Music, Teacher Education; Coop—3-2 engineering with U. of Illinois.
Wheaton College Wheaton 1860 *Private*	958M 846W		64% in top 1/10 61%	M608m 558v W585m 591v	a. $1320 b. 875	33% 42%	1:15 $417	146		B.A., B.S., B.Mus., B.M.Ed.; *Semester, summer sessions; Music, Teacher Education;* 14 hours Bible, daily chapel required; Army ROTC required for two years.

INDIANA

Institution / Location / Founded / Affiliation	Enrollment M=men W=women	Projected enrollment in 1975	High school rating; % applicants accepted	SAT/ACT Averages m=math v=verbal	Annual Tuition: a. b. Room & Board; c. Out of state; d. Other state	% Students with $ aid / Average amount	Faculty-student ratio; % with Doctorates	Volumes in library in 1,000's	Endowment in $1,000's	Undergraduate degrees offered; Calendar; Per cent of students per field of study; Professional programs offered; Miscellaneous
Anderson College Anderson 1917 *Church of God*	751M 669W	1750	40% in top 1/4 68%	450m 450v	a. $850 b. 660 d. 140	80% 50%	1:18 $660	70	$463	B.A.; *Semester, summer sessions; Teacher Education, Theology;* Attendance at chapel services twice per week required.

Institution / Location / Founded / Affiliation	Enrollment M=men W=women	Projected enrollment in 1975	High school rating; % applicants accepted	SAT/ACT Averages m=math v=verbal	a. Annual Tuition; b. Room & Board; c. Out of state; d. Other state.	% Students with $ aid / Average amount	Faculty-student ratio; % with Doctorates	Volumes in library in 1,000's	Endowment in $1,000's	Undergraduate degrees offered; Calendar; Per cent of students per field of study; Professional programs offered; Miscellaneous
Ball State University Muncie 1898 *State*	6211M 6472W	20988	38% in top 1/4 70%	M471m 422v W443m 439v	a. $300 b. 882 c. 501	13% $253	1:26 65%	300		B.A., B.S., B.A.Ed., B.S.Ed.; *Quarter;* Education—68%, Business—14%, Liberal Arts—7%; *Music, Teacher Education;* Coop—3-2 engineering with Purdue; Air Force ROTC optional.
Butler University Indianapolis 1855 *Private*	1220M 1172W	3200	50% in top 1/4 80%	517m 505v	a. $1250 b. 890	40% $625-1250	1:16 70%	180	$10,000	B.A., B.S., B.Mus., B.F.A.; *Semester, summer sessions; Liberal Arts & Sciences, Business Admin., Music, Pharmacy, Education;* Air Force ROTC optional.
DePauw University Greencastle 1837 *Methodist*	1250M 1150W	2400	46% in top 1/10 67%		a. $1750 b. 1000	25% $100-2750	1:15 70%	332		B.A., B.S.N., B.Mus.; *Semester; Music, Nursing, Teacher Education;* Coops—engineering with Case, Rose Polytechnic, Columbia, Purdue; Air Force ROTC optional.
Earlham College Richmond 1847 *Quaker*	583M 474W		60% in top 1/10 63%M 34%W	M608m 564v W590m 608v	a. $1830 b. 900 d. 150	45% $200-1700	1:14 60%	133	$3,156	B.A.; *Three-term;* Social Sciences—39%, Natural Sciences & Math—37%, Humanities—22%; Coops—3-2, 4-2 engineering with R.P.I., Case, University of Rochester; Attendance at 75% of weekly convocations required.
Evansville University of Evansville 1854 *Private*	1622M 1179W	3883	53% in top 1/4 74%	M530m 460v W475m 475v	a. $825 b. 765-795	50% $650	1:20 30%	74	$1,656	B.A., B.S., B.Mus.Ed.; *Quarter, summer sessions;* Education—41%, Liberal Arts—19%, Business—17%, Engineering—11%, Nursing—9%, Music—3%; *Music, Nursing, Teacher Education;* 10 hours Bible, Hebrew, or philosophy required; Air Force ROTC optional.
Franklin College Franklin 1834 *Baptist*	375M 225W	1000	57% in top 1/5 59%M 72%W	478m 491v	a. $1360 b. 870	33% $800	1:15 42%	75		B.A.; *Semester;* Social Sciences—37%, Education—23%, Humanities—22%, Natural Sciences & Math—20%; *Medical Technology, Teacher Education.*
Goshen College Goshen 1894 *Mennonite*	525M 575W	1500	most in top 1/2 90%	M525m 475v W475m 450v	a. $1240 b. 640	35% $600	1:15 45%	80	$250	B.A., B.S., B.D.; *Semester, summer session; Nursing, Teacher Education, Theology;* Coop—3-2 engineering with Purdue University.
Hanover College Hanover 1827 *Presbyterian*	509M 470W	1000	77% in top 1/5 66%	M579m 530v W584m 583v	a. $1280 b. 670	35% $460	1:15 68%	100	$6,000	B.A.; *Three-term;* Social Sciences—36%, Humanities—29%, Education—13%, Natural Sciences & Math—22%, Other—16%; Attendance at weekly chapel required.
Huntington College Huntington 1897 *United Brethren in Christ*	280M 255W	900	72%	M450m 420v W450m 420v	a. $930 b. 670	60% $50-930	1:13 25%	35		B.A., B.S., B.Th.; *Semester, summer session;* Education—45%, Social Sciences—29%, Humanities—12%, Natural Sciences & Math—10%, Business—4%; Attendance in church and two weekly assemblies required.
Indiana Central College Indianapolis 1902 *Evangelical United Brethren*	491M 477W	1400	52% in top 1/4 77%	450m 451v	a. $1100 b. 700	40% $400	1:12 20%	48	$600	B.A., B.S.; *Semester, summer session;* Education—39%, Business—15%, Social Sciences—14%, Humanities—12%, Natural Sciences & Math—11%, Nursing—4%; *Teacher Education;* Coops—engineering with Purdue, forestry with Duke.
Indiana Institute of Technology Fort Wayne 1930 *Private*	1307M 7W	2150	most in top 1/2 85%		a. $1050 b. 840 d. 60	5% $300	1:20 20%	35		B.S.; *Quarter;* Electrical Engineering—27%, Mechanical—26%, Civil—14%, Chemical—7%, Aerospace—12%, Math—4%, Chemistry—3%, Physics—2%.
Indiana Northern University Gas City 1963	180M 20W	800	75% in top 1/2 70%		a. $750 b. 1050 d. 25	10% $750	1:20 20%	5		A.B., B.S., B.B.A.; *Quarter, summer session;* Business Administration—90%, Electronics Technology—5%, Fire Technology—5%; *Business Administration;* Coops—Professional Art program with Art Institute of Pittsburgh, 2-2 Electronic Technology with Sams Technical Institute, Indianapolis.
Indiana State University Terre Haute 1870 *State*	5945M 4584W	18000	38% in top 1/4 85%	M464m 402v W423m 423v	a. $300 b. 882 c. 600	35% $250	1:18 54%	337		B.A., B.S.; *Semester, summer sessions;* Education—70%, Liberal Arts—30%; *Teacher Education, Business, Nursing;* Coop in engineering with N.Y.U., Rose Polytechnic Institute.
Indiana University Bloomington 1820 *State*	9605M 8734W	58000	30% in top 1/5 80%	*	a. $330 b. 1770 c. 960	50% $350	1:16 65%	1943	$791,331	B.A., B.S.; *Semester, summer sessions; Business, Dentistry, Journalism, Law, Library, Medicine, Music, Nursing, Optometry, Physical & Occupational Therapy, Psychology, Social Work, Teacher Education;* Air Force, Army ROTC optional. (Comb.) *State Res.—M—1026, W—977; Out of State—M—1120, W—1089.
Manchester College North Manchester 1889 *Church of the Brethren*	683M 664W	1500	80% in top 2/5 74%	514m 479v	a. $1200 b. 690 d. 105	40% $600	1:16 37%	76		B.A., B.S.; *Quarter, summer sessions;* Education—34%, Social Sciences—23%, Natural Sciences & Math—18%, Humanities—15%, Business—10%; *Teacher Education;* Coops—3-2 engineering and agriculture with Purdue University.
Marian College Indianapolis 1937 *Roman Catholic*	378M 689W	15000	45% in top 1/5 75%	496m 487v	a. $800 b. 760 d. 70	40% $400	1:15 25%	50	$67	B.A., B.S.; *Semester, summer session;* Arts—79%, Sciences—21%.
Notre Dame, University of Notre Dame 1843 *Roman Catholic*	5832M	7500	85% in top 1/3 58%	610m 562v	a. $1500 b. 850	30% $1200	1:11 61%	380	$37,126	B.A., B.S., B.B.A., B.Arch.; *Semester, summer session;* Arts—50%, Engineering—20%, Business—20%, Sciences—10%; *Architecture, Business, Engineering, Law;* 9 hours philosophy & theology required of Catholic students; Air Force, Army, Navy ROTC optional.
Purdue University Lafayette 1869 *State*	14103M 5383W	30000	62% in top 1/5 67%	578m 498v	a. $330 b. 945 c. 950 d. 100	18% $100-1600	1:11 75%	830		B.A., B.S.; *Semester, summer session; Engineering, Forestry, Pharmacy, Psychology, Teacher Education, Veterinary Medicine;* Air Force, Army, Navy ROTC optional.
Rose Polytechnic Institute Terre Haute 1874 *Private*	850M	1500	80% in top 1/4 50%	660m 540v	a. $1500 b. 875	45% $800	1:15 60%	31	$5,000	B.S.; *Quarter, summer quarter;* Mechanical Engineering—33%, Electrical—20%, Chemical—14%, Math—9%, Civil Engineering—10%, Chemistry & Physics—13%, Bioengineering—1%; *Engineering;* Army ROTC required.
Saint Francis College Fort Wayne 1890 *Roman Catholic*	269M 559W	1900	42% in top 1/4 84%		a. $600 b. 1000	20% $450	1:15 20%	55		B.A., B.S., B.S.Ed.; *Semester, summer sessions;* Elementary Education—46%, Liberal Arts—46%, Science & Math—9%.

Institution / Location / Founded / Affiliation	Enrollment M=men W=women	Projected enrollment in 1975	High school rating; % applicants accepted	SAT/ACT Averages m=math v=verbal	Annual Tuition: a. b. Room & Board c. Out of state d. Other state	% Students with $ aid / Average amount	Faculty-student ratio / % with Doctorates	Volumes in library in 1,000's	Endowment in $1,000's	Undergraduate degrees offered; Calendar; Per cent of students per field of study; Professional programs offered; Miscellaneous
Saint Joseph's College Rensselaer 1889 *Roman Catholic*	1319M 40W	1750	59% in top 1/2 75%	491m 457v	a. $1120 b. 700	25% $50-1500	1:14 35%	113	$412	B.A., B.S.; *Semester, summer session;* Liberal Arts; *Teacher Training;* Pre-professional programs; 3-2 engineering program available.
Saint Mary-of-the-Woods College Saint Mary-of-the-Woods 1840 *Roman Catholic*	660W	900	45% in top 1/5 80%	491m 510v	a. $1000 b. 850	30% $150-1500	1:14 41%	150	$1,200	B.A., B.S.; *Semester, summer session (members of the order only);* Humanities—25%, Education—21%, Social Sciences—11%, Natural Sciences & Math—13%, Fine Arts—20%, Home Ec.—6%, Business Adm.—5%; *Music.*
Saint Mary's College Notre Dame 1844 *Roman Catholic*	1215W	1500	61% in top 1/5 79%	525m 580v	a. $1200 b. 1250	16% $200-2000	1:12 35%	82		A.B., B.S., B.F.A., B.Mus.; *Semester, summer session;* Arts—65%, Sciences—30%, Fine Arts—3%, Music—2%; *Teacher Education; Medical Technology, Theology;* 16 hours theology required; Study Abroad program in Paris and Vienna.
Taylor University Upland 1846 *Private*	674M 577W	1750	most in top 1/2		a. $1200 b. 800	30% $100-2000	1:15 30%	67		B.A., B.S.Ed.; *Semester; Teacher Education;* Coop in engineering with N.Y.U., Purdue University, 5-year business with Indiana U.; Attendance at three chapel services per week required.
Valparaiso University Valparaiso 1859 *Lutheran*	2055M 1581M	5000	54% in top 1/5 80%	M571m 511v W528m 536v	a. $1100 b. 925 d. 150	41% $820	1:14 40%	191	$1,663	B.A., B.S., B.Mus.Ed.; *Semester, summer session;* Social Sciences—26%, Business—13%, Natural Sciences & Math—15%, Engineering—11%, Education—15%, Humanities—16%; *Engineering, Law, Music, Teacher Education;* 10 credits religion, daily matins, Sunday services required.
Wabash College Crawfordsville 1832 *Private*	888M	900	51% in top 1/10 87%	630m 577v	a. $1700 b. 850 d. 50	40% $1143	1:13 70%	168	$17,350	B.A.; *Semester;* Coop—6-year and 5-year engineering with Columbia University; One year religion and/or philosophy required.

IOWA

Institution / Location / Founded / Affiliation	Enrollment M=men W=women	Projected enrollment in 1975	High school rating; % applicants accepted	SAT/ACT Averages m=math v=verbal	Annual Tuition: a. b. Room & Board c. Out of state d. Other state	% Students with $ aid / Average amount	Faculty-student ratio / % with Doctorates	Volumes in library in 1,000's	Endowment in $1,000's	Undergraduate degrees offered; Calendar; Per cent of students per field of study; Professional programs offered; Miscellaneous
Briar Cliff College Sioux City 1930 *Roman Catholic*	753M 175W	1600	42% in top 1/5 85%		a. $700 b. 770 d. 75	50% $400	1:13 20%	45	$110	B.A., B.S., B.Mus.; *Three-term, summer session;* Arts—83%, Medical Technology—3%, Sciences—10%, Music—4%; 3-2 Engineering two-degree plan with U. of Iowa.
Buena Vista College Storm Lake 1891 *Presbyterian*	594M 231W	1500	35% in top 1/2 80%	M22.6 W21.7 (comp.)	a. $1200 b. 750	32% $100-1200	1:15 25%	40	$467	B.A., B.S.; *Semester, summer sessions;* Education—36%, Social Sciences—21%, Natural Sciences & Math—18%, Business—23%, Humanities—14%; 6 hours religion, chapel attendance required.
Central College Pella 1853 *Reformed Church*	564M 480W	1500	50% in top 1/4 65%	M519m 520v W491m 460v	a. $1130 b. 730	55% $400	1:14 44%	50	$1,800	B.A., B.Mus.; *Semester;* Social Sciences—34%, Humanities—21%, Elementary Ed.—16%, Natural Sciences & Math—21%, Physical Education—6%; Coop in home economics with Iowa State University; 6 hours religion, chapel attendance required.
Clarke College Dubuque 1843 *Roman Catholic*	1000W	1400	54% in top 1/4 89%	475m 500v	a. $1100 b. 1050	38% $500	1:14 25%	60	$459	B.A.; *Semester, summer session;* Social Sciences—31%, Natural Sciences & Math—29%, Languages—20%, Fine Arts—20%; *Teacher Education;* Coop—share facilities with Loras College, U. of Dubuque; Junior Year Abroad; 12 hours theology required.
Coe College Cedar Rapids 1851 *Presbyterian*	510M 445W	1200	69% in top 2/5 76%	M541m 527v W510m 542v	a. $1550 b. 900 d. 30	37% $550	1:13 50%	125	$6,960	B.A., B.Mus.; *Three-term, summer session;* Social Sciences—34%, Humanities—24%, Business—22%, Natural Sciences & Math—14%, Physical Education—6%; Coop—5-year engineering with Case Institute; Air Force ROTC optional.
Cornell College Mount Vernon 1853 *Private*	521M 466W	1000	73% in top 1/5 76%	M598m 543v W566m 559v	a. $1720 b. 890 d. 140	45% $100-2000	1:12 72%	143	$6,782	B.A., B.Mus.; *Semester;* Social Sciences—32%, Natural Sciences & Math—32%, Humanities—28%, Education—5%, Speech—2%.
Drake University Des Moines 1881 *Private*	2320M 1803M	5824	48% in top 1/4 56%	M24.1m 21.4v W20.8m 22.8v	a. $1200 b. 880	41% $800	1:16 51%	215	$4,820	B.A., B.S.; *Semester, summer session;* Journalism—6%, Pharmacy—11%, Business Administration—19%, Education—18%, Fine Arts—11%, Liberal Arts—30%; *Business, Law, Music, Pharmacy, Teacher Education, Theology;* Air Force ROTC optional.
Dubuque, University of Dubuque 1852 *Presbyterian*	506M 385W	1000	19% in top 1/5 90%	M508m 451v W476m 490v	a. $1180 b. 870 d. 80	34%	1:16 34%	80		B.A., B.S., B.S.B.A., B.Mus.; *Semester, summer sessions;* Social Sciences—32%, Natural Sciences & Math—19%, Humanities—21%, Physical Education—4%; *Teacher Education;* Coops—3-2 engineering, 2-3 nursing, share facilities with Clarke and Loras; 9 hours religion, chapel required.
Graceland College Lamoni 1895 *Latter-Day Saints*	495M 462W	1500	30% in top 1/5 82%		a. $965 b. 640	$780 Max.	1:18 24%	28		B.A., A.A.; *Semester, summer session;* Education—45%, Social Sciences—27%, Humanities—16%, Business—7%, Natural Sciences—4%; *Medical Technology.*
Grinnell College Grinnell 1846 *Private*	632M 559W	1300	88% in top 1/4 40%		a. $1925 b. 860 d. 115	45% $855	1:11 70%	173	$17,148	B.A.; *Semester;* Social Sciences—39%, Natural Sciences & Math—26%, Arts & Letters—35%; Coop—5-year engineering with Cal. Tech., Columbia, U. of Iowa; Washington semester, Argonne semester, Newberry Library program; Air Force ROTC optional.
Iowa, The University of College of Liberal Arts Iowa City 1847 *State*	7924M 5340W	15700	51% in top 1/5 88%	M27m 23v W24m 24v	a. $340 b. 915 c. 590	10% $100-1500	1:9	1226	$3,861	B.A., B.S., B.B.A., B.F.A., B.Mus.; *Semester, summer sessions;* Humanities—20%, Natural Sciences—16%, Education—16%, Social Sciences—15%, Business—14%; *Bus., Dent., Jour., Law, Med., Music, Nurs., Phar., Phys. & Oc. Ther., Social Work, Teacher Ed.;* AF, A ROTC optional.
Iowa State University of Science and Technology Ames 1858 *State*	9244M 3632W	17475	29% in top 1/10 60%		a. $345 b. 735 c. 930	15% $100-345	1:15 45%	600		B.S., B.Arch.; *Quarter, summer sessions;* Engineering—22%, Agriculture—22%, Natural Sciences & Math—7%, Education—8%; *Arch., Eng., For., Jour., Landscape Arch., Vet. Med.;* Air Force, Army, Navy ROTC optional.
Iowa Wesleyan College Mount Pleasant 1842 *Methodist*	516M 378W	1500	30% in top 1/5 78%		a. $1100 b. 820	45% $535	1:15 33%	41	$1,091	B.A., B.S., B.Mus.Ed.; *Semester, summer sessions;* Education—35%, Social Sciences—22%, Business—20%, Natural Sciences & Math—12%, Humanities—11%; Weekly chapel required; Iowa Wesleyan has study groups traveling to Egypt, Greece, U.S.S.R., Sweden, England, West Germany, France, Japan.

Institution Location / Founded Affiliation	Enrollment M=men W=women	Projected enrollment in 1975	High school rating: % applicants accepted	SAT/ACT Averages m=math v=verbal	Annual Tuition; Room & Board; Out of state; Other	% Students with $ aid / Average amount	Faculty-student ratio; % with Doctorates	Volumes in library in 1,000's	Endowment in $1,000's	Undergraduate degrees offered; Calendar; Per cent of students per field of study; Professional programs offered; Miscellaneous
Loras College Dubuque 1839 *Roman Catholic*	1600M	1800	86% in top 1/2 79%	23 (comp.)	a. $945 b. 1685 $250	33% 43%	1:15	160	$4,421	B.A., B.S.; *Semester, summer sessions;* Social Sciences—42%, Natural Sciences & Math—16%, Business—15%, Humanities—14%; Coop—3-2 engineering with U. of Detroit, U. of Illinois, Marquette, Notre Dame, U. of Iowa, N.Y.U., share facilities with Clarke & U. of Dubuque.
Luther College Decorah 1861 *Lutheran*	975M 870W	2500	66% in top 1/4 75%	549m 520v	$2085 Total $372	50% 50%	1:16	137	$1,200	B.A.; *Semester, interim period (3 weeks), summer session;* Social Sciences—37%, Humanities—22%, Education—23%, Natural Sciences & Math—13%, Fine Arts—5%; *Teacher Education;* 12 semester hours Bible study, daily chapel.
Marycrest College Davenport 1939 *Roman Catholic*	1065W	1500	most in top 1/2 80%	464m 471v	a. $850 b. 900 $200	13% 23%	1:13	56	$335	B.A., B.S.N.; *Semester, intersession (4 weeks), summer session;* Education—51%, Humanities—25%, Social Sciences—8%, Nursing—7%, Natural Sciences & Math—7%, Medical Technology—2%; *Teacher Education, Nursing, Med. Tech.;* Coop with St. Ambrose College; Summer or 1 or 2 sem. resident study U. of Salzburg, U. of Vienna.
Morningside College Sioux City 1889 *Methodist*	785M 568W	1850	44% in top 1/4 77%		a. $980 b. 710 d. 120	40% 36%	1:20	71	$1,500	B.A., B.S.; *Semester, summer sessions;* Music, Teacher Education; Coop—3-2 engineering with U. of Iowa, Iowa State; M. A. T.
Mount Mercy College Cedar Rapids 1928 *Roman Catholic*	635W	1095	42% in top 1/5 86%	308m 301v	a. $600 b. 900 $300	43% 16%	1:13	22		B.A., B.S.; *Semester;* Humanities—39%, Natural Sciences & Math—20%, Social Sciences—18%, Business—11%, Home Economics—11%.
Northwestern College Orange City 1882 *Reformed Church in America*	341M 282W	1107	most in top 1/2 90%		a. $940 b. 690 d. 40	40% $400 24%	1:17	36	$400	B.A., B.S.; *Semester, summer session;* Religion courses, chapel required.
St. Ambrose College Davenport 1882 *Roman Catholic*	1255M	1500	75% in top 1/2 63%	450m 450v	a. $1050 b. 950 c. 36	35% $854 25%	1:17	56	$1,052	B.A.; *Semester, summer session;* Social Sciences—28%, Business—26%, Natural Sciences & Math—21%, Humanities—10%, Education—1%.
Simpson College Indianola 1860 *Methodist*	483M 427W	1300	31% in top 1/5 77%	510m 498v	a. $1340 b. 800	55% $850 46%	1:13	70	$2,443	B.A., B.Mus.; *Semester, summer sessions;* Social Sciences—29%, Education—16%, Humanities—18%, Natural Sciences & Math—10%, Business—12%, Home Economics—4%, Fine Arts—5%; *Music, Teacher Ed., Med. Tech.;* One Religion course required.
State College of Iowa Cedar Falls 1876 *State*	3071M 3709W	12000	43% in top 1/5 72%	M26m 22v W23m 24v	a. $342 b. 700 c. 642	40% $400 35%	1:19	240		B.A.; *Semester, summer sessions;* Education—85%, Arts—15%; *Music, Teacher Education.*
Upper Iowa University Fayette 1857 *Private*	726M 328W	1500	82% in top 3/5 60%	21 (comp.)	a. $1200 b. 790	25% $425 32%	1:16	68	$924	B.A., B.S.; *Semester, summer sessions;* English & Fine Arts—13%, Natural Sciences & Math—16%, Business & Social Sciences—38%, Education & Psychology—33%; *Nursing, Library Science, Secretarial Science.*
Wartburg College Waverly 1852 *Lutheran*	735M 652W	1500	51% in top 1/2 88%	523m 529v	a. $1000 b. 700 d. 90	52% $550 42%	1:16	83	$481	B.A., B.S.Ed., B.Mus., B.Mus.Ed.; *Semester, summer session;* Arts—75%, Education—20%, Music—5%; *Music, Teacher Education;* Coops in Phys. Therapy, Med. Tech., Engineering; Grants totaling $712,000 since 1962.
Westmar College Le Mars 1890 *Evangelical United Brethren*	582M 534W	1400	60% in top 1/2 80%		a. $1000 b. 680 d. 110	43% $400 28%	1:16	65	$723	B.A., B.Mus., B.Mus.Ed.; *Semester (4-4-1), summer session;* Social Sciences—48%, Humanities—23%, Natural Sciences & Math—29%; *Teacher Education;* 4 hours in religion required. Grants totaling $141,341 since 1960.
William Penn College Oskaloosa 1873 *Quaker*	607M 251W	1200	50% in top 1/2 60%		a. $1000 b. 925 d. 74	50% $100-800 28%	1:16	55	$500	B.A.; *Semester, summer sessions;* Social Sciences—34%, Education—30%, Physical Education—20%, Natural Sciences & Math—17%; 9 hours Bible, religion, philosophy required.

KANSAS

Institution Location / Founded Affiliation	Enrollment M=men W=women	Projected enrollment in 1975	High school rating: % applicants accepted	SAT/ACT Averages m=math v=verbal	Annual Tuition; Room & Board; Out of state; Other	% Students with $ aid / Average amount	Faculty-student ratio; % with Doctorates	Volumes in library in 1,000's	Endowment in $1,000's	Undergraduate degrees offered; Calendar; Per cent of students per field of study; Professional programs offered; Miscellaneous
Baker University Baldwin City 1858 *Methodist*	468M 356W	1200	40% in top 1/4 90%	M451m 451v W418m 451v	a. $900 b. 800	35% $400 36%	1:14	67	$2,900	B.A., B.S., B.Mus.Ed.; *Semester, summer sessions;* Education—25%, Social Sciences—28%, Business—20%, Natural Sciences & Math—10%, Humanities—10%, Speech—7%; *Teacher Education;* 6 hours religion, philosophy required.
Bethany College Lindsborg 1881 *Lutheran*	240M 225W	800	37% in top 1/4 89%		a. $970 b. 710	30% $400 15%	1:11	37	$889	B.A., B.F.A., B.Mus.; *Semester;* Education—44%, Social Sciences—22%, Natural Sciences & Math—11%, Humanities—14%; *Music, Teacher Education.*
Bethel College North Newton 1887 *Mennonite*	300M 300W	1100	43% in top 1/5 95%	22.1m 22.1v	a. $1050 b. 700 d. 45	40% $300 40%	1:17	43	$1,233	B.A., B.S.; *Quarter, summer session;* Social Sciences—29%, Natural Sciences & Math—28%, Humanities—21%, Education—21%; *Teacher Education;* Coop—3-2 engineering with Kansas State, U. of Kansas, agriculture with Kansas State; 15 hours Bible, chapel required.
College of Emporia Emporia 1882 *Presbyterian*	586M 174W	1800	50% in top 1/2 76%	M439m 451v W320m 431v	a. $700 b. 800 d. 170	35% $420 40%	1:15	41	$710	B.A., B.S., B.Mus., B.Mus.Ed.; *Semester;* Education—60%, Business—20%, Other—20%; *Engineering, Medicine, Law, Medical Tech., Nursing, Veterinary Medicine;* Coop—3-2 engineering with U. of Kansas, Lafayette; 6 hours religion courses required.
Fort Hays Kansas State College Hays 1902 *State*	2884M 2080W	7200	28% in top 1/4 96%		a. $122 b. 700 c. 508	32% $302 14%	1:20	430		B.A., B.S., B.Mus.; *Semester, summer session;* Business—24%, Natural Sciences & Math—17%, Education—16%, Humanities—11%, Social Sciences—9%, Industrial Arts—6%, Agriculture—4%; *Music, Teacher Education.*
Friends University Wichita 1898 *Quaker*	376M 309W	1200	25% in top 1/4 85%		a. $800 b. 700 d. 100	32% $280 25%	1:12	40	$950	B.A., B.S., B.Mus., B.Th.; *Semester;* Education—60%, Other—40%; *Music, Teacher Education;* Coop—3-2 engineering with U. of Kansas, Kansas State, Wichita State; 6 hours Bible, chapel required; Grants totaling $125,000 since 1960.

Institution / Location / Founded / Affiliation	Enrollment M=men W=women	Projected enrollment in 1975	High school rating; % applicants accepted	SAT/ACT Averages m=math v=verbal	a. Annual Tuition; b. Room & Board; c. Out of state; d. Other	% Students with $ aid / Average amount	Faculty-student ratio; % with Doctorates	Volumes in library in 1,000's	Endowment in $1,000's	Undergraduate degrees offered; Calendar; Per cent of students per field of study; Professional programs offered; Miscellaneous
Kansas, University of Lawrence 1865 State	8631M 4842W	14000	48% in top 1/5	M572m 512v W519m 512v	a. $278 b. 737 c. 678 d. 400	15% $250-1400	1:15 55%	1100	$22,000	B.A., B.S., B.Arch., B.Art Ed., B.F.A., B.Mus.; *Semester, summer session;* Arts & Sciences—33%, Ed.—24%, Bus.—12%, Eng. & Arch.—12%; *Arch., Bus., Eng., Jour., Law, Med., Music, Nurs., Phar., Phys. & Oc. Ther., Psych., Social Work, Teacher Ed.;* Air Force, Army, Navy ROTC optional.
Kansas State College of Pittsburg Pittsburg 1903 State	3630M 1965W	8400	94%		a. $242 b. 700 c. 507	25% $600	1:20 31%	287	$210	B.A., B.S., B.F.A., B.Mus., B.Mus.Ed., B.S.Ed., B.S.B.A., B.S.T. & I., B.S.I.T.; *Semester, summer session; Music, Teacher Education;* Army ROTC required.
Kansas State Teachers College of Emporia Emporia 1865 State	2921M 2796W	8351	35% in top 1/4 95%		a. $235 b. 630 c. 500	5% $230	1:23 27%	250	$1,300	B.A., B.S., B.Mus. B.Mus.Ed.; *Semester, summer sessions;* B.S.Ed.—66%, B.A.—15%, B.S.Business—18%, B.Mus.Ed.—.8%, B.Mus.—.2%; *Music, Teacher Education.*
Kansas State University Manhattan 1863 State	7238M 3663W	18750	47% in top 1/4 80%	23.2m 22.8v'	a. $328 b. 800 c. 788	49% $550	1:16 49%	420	$3,379	B.A., B.S., B.Arch., B.Landscape Arch., B.Mus.; *Semester, summer session;* Arts & Sciences—27%, Engineering—17%, Education—15%, Agriculture—14%, Home Economics—8%, Architecture—14%, Commerce—10%, Veterinary Med.—4%; *Architecture, Engineering, Journalism, Music, Teacher Education, Veterinary Medicine;* AF, A ROTC optional.
Kansas Wesleyan University Salina 1886 Methodist	474M 245W	1630	40% in top 1/5 85%	21m 21v	a. $1100 b. 750 c. 80	40% $500	1:19 33%	53	$1,450	B.A.; *Semester, summer session;* Education—27%, Social Sciences—23%, Natural Sciences & Math—20%, Humanities—12%, Fine Arts—10%, Physical Education—8%; Coop-3-2 engineering with Kansas State, U. of Kansas; Washington Semester, U.N. Semester.
McPherson College McPherson 1887 Church of the Brethren	525M 310W	1200	52% in top 1/4 90%		a. $810 b. 750 d. 84	60% $100-750	1:17 40%	38	$1,021	B.A., B.S.; *Semester, summer sessions;* Education—60%, Other—40%; *Teacher Education;* Coop in engineering.
Marymount College Salina 1922 Roman Catholic	568W	800	44% in top 1/5 70%	19m 21v	$1620 Total	33% $850	1:10 42%	43		B.A., B.S., B.Mus., B.Mus.Ed.; *Three-term, summer sessions;* Language & Literature—12%, Math & Science—15%, Social Science—21%, Fine Arts—17%, Nursing—26%, Philos.-Theol.-Psych.-Ed.—9%; *Nursing, Teacher Education;* Generic baccalaureate program in Nursing.
Mount St. Scholastica College Atchison 1924 Roman Catholic	116M 531W	1200	most in top 1/2 83%	23 (comp.)	a. $600 b. 800 d. 60	53% $320	1:16 38%	55		B.A., B.S., B.Mus.Ed.; *Semester, summer session;* Science & Math—12%, Languages—7%, Sociology—11%, English—16%, Hist. & Pol. Sci.—9%, Phys. Ed.—6%, Home Ec. & Psych.—4%, Education—27%, Music—7%; *Music, Teacher Education;* 16 hours theology required of Catholic students.
Ottawa University Ottawa 1865 American Baptist	620M 408W	1125	60% in top 1/2 60%	M512m 458v W492m 486v	$1870 Total	28% $170	1:20 35%	55	$1,300	B.A., B.S., B.Mus.Ed.; *Semester, summer session;* Social Sciences—33%, Natural Sciences & Math—22%, Education—21%, Humanities—11%, Business—6%; Weekly chapel attendance required.
St. Benedict's College Atchison 1858 Roman Catholic	975M	1200	60% in top 1/2 60%	21.5m 21v	a. $900 b. 780	40% $200-800	1:14 32%	170		B.A., B.S., B.Mus. Ed.; *Semester;* Coop-3-2 engineering with Notre Dame, Kansas State, U. of Kansas; 16 credit hours of theology required; Grants totaling $38,970 since 1960.
Saint Mary's College Xavier 1923 Roman Catholic	799W	1000	53% in top 1/4 80%		a. $700 b. 750 d. 100	40% $350	1:15 35%	91		B.A., B.S., B.Mus., B.Mus.Ed.; *Semester;* Elementary Education—37%, Natural Sciences & Math—14%, Humanities—47%, Social Sciences—9%, Nursing Ed.—7%, Home Ec. & Dietetics—7%, Business—5%.
Saint Mary of the Plains College Dodge City 1952 Roman Catholic	294M 245W	900	55%		a. $500 b. 750 d. 90	37% $610	1:17 37%	27		B.A., B.S., B.Mus., B.Mus.Ed.; *Semester;* Elementary Education—11%, Humanities—47%, Business—18%, Natural Sciences & Math—10%, Social Sciences—9%; Coops in nursing and medical technology with St. Joseph's Hospital, Wichita.
Southwestern College Winfield 1885 Methodist	385M 362W	800	25% in top 1/5 89%		a. $850 b. 690	40% $180-500	1:17 42%	59	$3,100	B.A., B.Mus.; *Semester, summer session;* Education—32%, Business—18%, Music—5%, Natural Science—16%, Social Sciences—21%, Math—8%; Washington Semester, European summer travel, Asian-Pacific Seminar, U.N. Semester.
Sterling College Sterling 1887 Presbyterian	310M 317W	750	56% in top 1/2 89%	20m 20v	a. $900 b. 710	80% $428	1:15 46%	55	$1,500	B.A., B.S.; *Semester, summer sessions;* Education—45%, Social Sciences—27%, Natural Sciences & Math—13%, Humanities—8%; Coop-3-2 engineering with U. of Kansas.
Washburn University of Topeka Topeka 1865 Municipal	2595M 1552W	6000	90%	20.1 (comp.)	a. $385 b. 792 c. 600	60% $520	1:18 33%	85	$5,672	B.A., B.S., B.B.A., B.F.A., B.Mus., B.S.Ed.; *Semester, summer session; Law, Music, Teacher Education;* Coop—Washburn Semester at Copenhagen with Danish International Student Committee, Netherlands exchange program; Educational TV; Air Force ROTC optional.
Wichita State University Wichita 1895 State	7258M 3843W	15659	36% in top 1/4	21.2 (comp.)	a. $283 b. 725 c. 675	24% $50-1000	1:18 37%	262	$934	B.A., B.S., B.B.A., B.M., B.M.E., B.F.A., B.A.E.; *Semester, summer session;* University College—45%, Arts & Sciences—13%, Education—11%, Engineering—5%, Fine Arts—4%, Business—9%; *Engineering, Art, Business, Music, Teacher Education;* Air Force, Army ROTC optional.

KENTUCKY

Institution / Location / Founded / Affiliation	Enrollment M=men W=women	Projected enrollment in 1975	High school rating; % applicants accepted	SAT/ACT Averages m=math v=verbal	a. Annual Tuition; b. Room & Board; c. Out of state; d. Other	% Students with $ aid / Average amount	Faculty-student ratio; % with Doctorates	Volumes in library in 1,000's	Endowment in $1,000's	Undergraduate degrees offered; Calendar; Per cent of students per field of study; Professional programs offered; Miscellaneous
Asbury College Wilmore 1890 Private	480M 552W	1200	80% in top 1/2		a. $720 b. 430 d. 200		1:16 30%	70		B.A.; *Quarter, summer session; Teacher Education;* Attendance at church of student's choice required.
Bellarmine College Louisville 1950 Roman Catholic	1745M 105W	3000	most in top 2/3 75%	456m 499v	a. $900 b. 880 c. 1050 d. 30	40% $400	1:16 40%	45		B.A.; *Semester, 2 summer sessions;* Business—36%, Social Sciences—22%, Natural Sciences & Math—18%, Education—14%, Humanities—10%; Coop—coordinate with Ursuline College; 12 hours theology required. Air Force and Naval ROTC optional.
Berea College Berea 1855 Private	681M 780W	1500	75% in top 1/5 38%	M503m 454v W477m 476v	a. none b. $498 c. 121	100% to $700	1:14 33%	160	$38,117	B.A., B.S.; *Semester, summer session;* Social Sciences—18%, Humanities—17%, Natural Sciences & Math—19%, Education—10%, Home Economics—8%, Nursing—8%, Agriculture—5%, Bus. Adm.—12%, Ind. Arts—2%, Phys. Ed.—1%; *Nursing, Teacher Education.*

Institution Location	Founded Affiliation	Enrollment M=men W=women	Projected enrollment in 1975	High school rating; % applicants accepted	SAT/ACT Averages m=math v=verbal	Annual Tuition; a.; b. Room & Board; c. Out of state; d. Other	% Students with $ aid; Average amount	Faculty-student ratio; % with Doctorates	Volumes in library in 1,000's	Endowment in $1,000's	Undergraduate degrees offered; Calendar; Per cent of students per field of study; Professional programs offered; Miscellaneous
Brescia College Owensboro	1925 Roman Catholic	514M 563W	1480	most in top 3/5 75%	M21m 21v W20m 21v	a. $600 b. W720 M820	25% 30%	1:13	35	$300	B.A., B.S.; Semester, summer session; Humanities—15%, Social Sciences—20%, Education—25%, Natural Sciences—15%, Business—15%, Other—10%.
Campbellsville College Campbellsville	1923 Baptist	603M 476W	1500	90%		a. $570 b. 640	47% 30%	1:20	42		B.A., B.S.; Semester, summer session.
Catherine Spalding College Louisville	1920 Roman Catholic	124M 1708W	1800	85%	500m 550v	a. $800 b. 870	43% $773 25%	1:15	79	$123	B.A., B.S.; Semester, summer session; Nursing, Home Economics, Medical Technology, Social Welfare, Teacher Education; Coops—faculty and student exchange with Bellarmine, Nazareth, Ursuline Colleges, U. of Louisville; 12 semester hours of religion required of Catholic students.
Centre College of Kentucky Danville	1819 Private	386M 301W	1000	65% in top 1/5 75%	M591m 546v W548m 563v	a. $1350 b. 810 d. 90	38% $810 60%	1:14	81	$4,218	B.A.; Semester, summer session; Humanities—29%, Social Science—36%, Natural Sciences & Math—19%, Education—3%, Business & Economics—9%, Languages—4%; Chapel attendance once per week optional.
Eastern Kentucky University Richmond	1906 State	4785M 3187W	12000	most in top 2/5 82%		a. $200 b. 600 c. 540	34% $575 32%	1:18	177		A.B., B.S., B.B.A., B.Mus., B.M.E., A.A.; Semester, summer session; Music, Business, Law Enforcement, Nursing, Teacher Education; Army ROTC required for two years.
Georgetown College Georgetown	1829 Baptist	604M 588W	1500	40% in top 1/5 45%	498m 484v	a. $650 b. 615 d. 100	38% $345 31%	1:18	70	$1,253	B.A., B.S.; Semester, summer sessions; Humanities—31%, Natural Sciences—25%, Social Sciences—20%, Business—16%, Education—8%; 6 hours of Bible, chapel twice weekly, required.
Kentucky, University of Lexington	1865 State	8290M 5540W	19600	75% in top 1/2 80%	22.7 (comp.)	a. $281 b. 800 c. 820	12% $300 79%	1:17	1070	$440	B.A., B.S., B.Mus., LL.B.; Semester, summer session; Architecture, Business, Dentistry, Engineering, Journalism, Languages, Law, Library, Medicine, Music, Nursing, Pharmacy, Psychology, Teacher Education; Air Force, Army ROTC optional.
Kentucky Wesleyan College Owensboro	1858 Methodist	653M 347W	1200	50% in top 3/5 60%	450m 450v	a. $800 b. 750 c. 150 d. 70	25% $235 29%	1:18	50	$1,000	B.A., B.S.; Semester, summer sessions; Education—33%, Social Sciences—22%, Business—28%, Humanities—14%, Natural Sciences & Math—3%; 6 hours in religion required.
Kentucky State College Frankfort	1886 State	659M 567W		62%	12 (comp.)	a. $150 b. 440 c. 300	$400	1:18	32		B.A., B.S., B.S.B.A.; Semester, summer session; Teacher Education.
Louisville, University of Louisville	1798 Private	6215M 3097W	8570	most in top 1/2 70%	525m 498v	a. $1000 b. 760 c. 1500	35% $600 69%	1:17	427	$7,712	B.A., B.S., B.Mus., B.Engineering; Semester, summer session; Dentistry, Engineering, Law, Medicine, Music, Social Work, Teacher Education; Air Force, Navy ROTC optional.
Morehead State University Morehead	1922 State	3096M 2383W	12500	most in top 1/2 68%		a. $120 b. 580 c. 290 d. 60	24% $375 35%	1:21	125		B.A., B.S., A. of Applied Arts; Semester, summer and post-summer session; Teacher Education, Business, Music; Pre-professional programs.
Murray State University Murray	1922 State	3953M 2540W	9000	50% in top 1/2 85%	19 (comp.)	a. $240 b. 650 c. 580	12% $400 35%	1:22	130		B.A., B.S., B.Mus.; Semester, summer session; Music, Teacher Education, Nursing, Medical Tech., Agriculture, Home Economics; 3-2 Engineering coop with Vanderbilt U.; Army ROTC required.
Nazareth College of Kentucky Nazareth	1920 Roman Catholic	535W	800	53% in top 1/4 94%	400m 400v	a. $835 b. 710	25% $300 20%	1:11	39		B.A., B.S., B.Mus.; Semester, summer session; Sciences—75%, Arts—20%, Music—5%; Coop—limited cooperation and exchange with Catherine Spalding College.
Pikeville College Pikeville	1889 Presbyterian	442M 329W	1200	most in top 1/2 75%	17.6 (comp.)	a. $600 b. 650	39% $760 25%	1:18	45	$640	B.A., B.S.; Semester, summer sessions; Teacher Education, Music, Pre-professional; 6 hours Bible study, chapel attendance three times weekly required.
Transylvania College Lexington	1780 Disciples of Christ	450M 425W	1200	52% in top 1/4 65%	M516m 498v W495m 506v	a. $1350 b. 825	36% $725 50%	1:15	58	$1,338	B.A.; Quarter, summer sessions; Social Sciences—46%, Natural Sciences & Math—9%, Education—18%, Humanities—27%; Coops—University of the Americas in Mexico City, European semester in Aix-Marseilles, Junior Year Abroad, Washington Semester.
Union College Barbourville	1879 Methodist	507M 231W	1200	100% in top 2/3 60%		a. $1146 b. 680	40% $50-500 40%	1:13	47	$1,000	B.A., B.S., B.Mus.; Semester, summer sessions; Education—50%, Business—20%, Other—30%; Coops—3-2 medicine with U. of Louisville, 3-2 engineering with U. of Kentucky; One course in religion, weekly services required; Junior Year Abroad, Washington Semester.
Ursuline College Louisville	1938 Roman Catholic	564W	840	80% in top 1/2	476m 486v	a. $960 b. 980	18% $637 30%	1:10	44		B.A., B.S.; Semester, summer session; Social Sciences—33%, Education—33%, Natural Sciences & Math—14%, Humanities—20%; Coordination program with Bellarmine College.
Villa Madonna College Covington	1921 Roman Catholic	620M 340W	2000	80% in top 1/2 80%	22.2m 20.7v	a. $832 b. 890	30% $450 50%	1:14	51		B.A.; Semester, summer session; Business—28%, Natural Sciences & Math—16%, Social Sciences—14%, Humanities—13%, Education—29%; Coops—3-2 engineering with Notre Dame, U. of Dayton, 3-3 engineering with U. of Detroit; Attendance at services required of Catholics.
Western Kentucky University Bowling Green	1906 State	4813M 3280W	16000	80%		a. none b. 720 c. 480 d. 240	32% 38%	1:20	250		B.A., B.S., B.Mus.; Semester, summer session; Music, Teacher Education; Army ROTC optional.

Institution Location	Founded Affiliation	Enrollment M=men w=women	Projected enrollment in 1975	High school rating; % applicants accepted	SAT/ACT Averages m = math v = verbal	a. Annual Tuition; b. Room & Board; c. Out of state; d. Other	% Students with $ aid Average amount	Faculty-student ratio; % with Doctorates	Volumes in library in 1,000's	Endowment in $1,000's	Undergraduate degrees offered; Calendar; Per cent of students per field of study; Professional programs offered; Miscellaneous
LOUISIANA											
Centenary College of Louisiana Shreveport 1825 Methodist		608M 495W	1500	71%	488m 471v	a. $800 b. 750	50% $400	1:16 43%	77	$5,742	B.A., B.S., B.Mus.; Semester, summer session; B.A.—33%, B.S.—63%, B.Mus.—4%; Music; Coop 3-2 engineering with Arkansas, Columbia, Louisiana Tech., Texas A.&M.; 6 hours of Bible required.
Dillard University New Orleans 1930 Private		277M 591W		46% in top 1/4		a. $625 b. 575 d. 75	$100-600	1:14 28%	64		B.A., B.S.; Semester, summer session; Nursing; One semester religion course, two weekly chapel services, Sunday Vespers required.
Louisiana College Pineville 1906 Baptist		648M 620W	1500	most in top 1/2 90%		a. $580 b. 550	40% $200	1:20 30%	59	$2,600	B.A., B.S.; Semester, summer session; Education—46%, Social Sciences—17%, Humanities—9%, Business—8%, Math—4%; Teacher Education.
Louisiana Polytechnic Institute Ruston 1894 State		4810M 2414W	13336	99%		a. $180 b. 615 c. 780 d. 140	45% $300	1:24 35%	267		B.A., B.S., B.F.A.; Quarter; Education—24%, Business—25%, Engineering—18%, English—7%, Journalism—7%, Math—7%, Social Sciences—3%, Agriculture & Forestry—8%, Other—12%; Business, Engineering, Music, Teacher Education, Chemistry; Air Force ROTC optional.
Louisiana State U. & Agricultural & Mechanical College Baton Rouge 1860 State		8904M 5507W	19864	86%	20m 20v	a. none b. $745 c. 400 d. 220	33% $50-1000	1:19 51%	1030	$194	B.B., B.S.; Semester, summer session; Architecture, Business, Engineering, Forestry, Journalism, Landscape Architecture, Law, Library, Medicine, Music, Nursing, Psychology, Social Work, Teacher Education; Air Force, Army ROTC required for two years.
Louisiana State University in New Orleans 1958 State		3577M 2572W	10000	90%		a. no b. no dorm c. $400 d. 140	25% $300	1:19 52%	200		B.A., B.S.; Semester, summer session; Liberal Arts—30%, Sciences—15%, Reduction—30%, Business Adm.—15%; M.B.A., Teacher Education.
Loyola University New Orleans 1912 Roman Catholic		2549M 1407W	5500	64%M 86%W in top 1/3	M573m 548v W531m 559v	a. $1200 b. 900M 1000W	16% $800	1:9 40%	232	$6,574	A.B., B.S., B.B.A., B.Mus., B.Mus.Ed., B.Mus.Therapy; Semester, summer sessions; Arts & Sciences—39%, Bus. Adm.—17%, Music—2%; Business, Dentistry, Law, Medicine, Music, Teacher Education; Army ROTC optional.
McNeese State College Lake Charles 1939 State		2472M 1810W	9000	95%		a. none b. $640 c. 600 d. 170	26% $525	1:26 29%	85		B.A., B.S., B.Mus., B.M.Ed.; Semester, summer session; Education—53%, Natural Sciences—30%, Humanities—13%, Fine Arts—4%; Music; Army ROTC required.
Newcomb College New Orleans 1886 Private		2549W	(see Tulane)	73% in top 1/5 66%	587m 603v	a. $1500 b. 1250 d. 200	25% $1650	1:11 80%	951	(see Tulane)	B.A., B.S., B.F.A.; Semester, summer sessions; Humanities—44%, Social Sciences—29%, Natural Sciences—6%, Other—21%; Music; Newcomb College is the coordinate woman's college of Tulane University; Junior Year Abroad.
Northeast Louisiana State College Monroe 1931 State		3619M 2341W	15193	80%		a. none b. $664 c. 600 d. 148	43% $300	1:22 39%	107		B.A., B.S., B.Mus., B.Mus.Ed.; Semester, summer session; Education—25%, Pharmacy—27%, Business—14%, Pure & Applied Sciences—13%, Liberal Arts—8%; Music, Pharmacy, Teacher Education, Nursing; Army ROTC required.
Northwestern State College of Louisiana Natchitoches 1884 State		2751M 2452W	7000	70%		a. none b. $550 c. 600	50% $270	1:21 32%	140		B.A., B.S., B.Mus., B.Mus.Ed.; Semester, summer session; Sciences—53%, Arts—47%; Music, Nursing, Teacher Education; Army ROTC optional.
St. Mary's Dominican College New Orleans 1910 Roman Catholic		551W	800	100% in top 1/2 85%	450m 475v	a. $1015 b. 985	16% $200-800	1:9 31%	52		B.A., B.S.; Semester, summer session.
Southeastern Louisiana College Hammond 1925 State		3290M 1847W	8000			a. $180 b. 614 c. 600	25% $40-1000	1:20 20%	91		B.A., B.S., B.Mus., B.Mus.Ed.; Semester, summer session; Business & Accounting—29%, Education—15%, Natural Sciences & Math—13%, Social Sciences—17%, Humanities—5%, Agriculture—7%, Home Economics—4%, Music—3%; Music, Teacher Education, Nursing.
Southern University & Agricultural & Mechanical College Scotlandville 1880 State		2874M 3763W	9200 (Baton Rouge campus only)	80%		a. $130 b. 518 c. 600	65% $60	1:15 32%	186		B.A., B.S.; Semester, summer session; Education—62%, Liberal Arts—18%, Business—12%, Engineering—5%, Home Economics—4%; Law, Music; Army ROTC required.
Southwestern Louisiana, University of Lafayette 1898 State		4940M 3368W	14000	66% in top 1/2		a. none b. $600 c. 600 d. 130	40% $50	1:16 35%	285		B.A., B.S., B.Arch., B.Mus., B.Mus.Ed.; Semester, summer session; Humanities—32%, Education—30%, Business—19%, Engineering 10%, Agriculture—4%; Engineering, Music, Nursing, Teacher Education; Coop in library science with Louisiana State U.; Air Force ROTC optional.
Tulane University New Orleans 1834 Private		5690M	11039 inc. Newcomb	62% in top 1/5 66%	604m 559v	a. $1500 b. 950 d. 200	25% $1650	1:11 80%	951	$54,576	B.A., B.S., B.F.A., B.Arch., B.A.Engineering; Semester, summer sessions; Social Sciences—38%, Natural Sciences & Math—24%, Humanities—19%; Arch., Bus., Eng., Law, Med., Music, Public Health, Social Work; Air Force, Army, Navy ROTC optional.
Xavier University of Louisiana New Orleans 1925 Roman Catholic		452M 650W	1200	53% in top 1/4 85%		a. $700 b. 658 d. 188	40%	1:11 27%	94		B.A., B.S.; Semester, summer session; Music, Teacher Ed., Med. Tech.; Coop in engineering with Marquette, U. of Detroit, Notre Dame, Tuskegee Institute.
MAINE											
Bates College Lewiston 1864 Private		514M 419W	1200	80% in top 1/5 35%	M620m 603v W618m 640v	a. $1650 b. 850 d. 100	28% $748	1:15 45%	128	$6,938	B.A., B.S.; Semester; optional 2-month term permitting 3-year graduation; Social Sciences—48%, Sciences & Math—25%, Humanities—27%; Coop engineering with R.P.I.; Chemistry program certified by A.C.S.
Bowdoin College Brunswick 1794 Private		910M	925	94% in top 1/5 30%	644m 616v	a. $1900 b. 1050 d. 450	40% $1750	1:9 62%	317	$31,500	A.B.; Semester; Social Sciences—37%, Sciences & Math—41%, Humanities—22%; Army ROTC optional.

Institution / Location / Founded / Affiliation	Enrollment M=men W=women	Projected enrollment in 1975	High school ratings: % applicants accepted	SAT/ACT Averages m=math v=verbal	Annual Tuition: a. / b. Room & Board / c. Out of state / d. Other state	% Students with $ aid / Average amount	Faculty-student ratio: % with Doctorates	Volumes in library in 1,000's	Endowment in $1,000's	Undergraduate degrees offered; *Calendar;* Per cent of students per field of study; *Professional programs offered;* Miscellaneous
Colby College Waterville 1813 *Private*	788M 647W	1500	71% in top 1/5 33%	M640m 597v W616m 619v	a. $1750 b. 900 d. 400	36% $1500-1700 51%	1:15	250	$15,500	B.A.; *Semester, January independent study program, summer language session;* Social Sciences—48%, Humanities—37%, Natural Sciences—15%; *Teacher Education;* 3-2 Engineering with U. of Rochester, Exchange program with Fisk University; Air Force ROTC optional.
Farmington State College Farmington 1864 *State*	263M 427W	1500	35% in top 1/4 50%	470m 460v	a. $100 b. 708 c. 200 d. 150	17% $128 21%	1:14	36	$262	B.S.; *Semester, summer session;* Education—100%; *Teacher Education.*
Gorham State College Gorham 1878 *State*	459M 562W	2900	80% in top 1/3 59%	510m 490v	a. $100 b. 708 c. 200 d. 100	40% $350 25%	1:16	40	$14,500	B.S.; *Semester, summer session;* Education—98%; *Teacher Education, Liberal Arts;* Coop in course exchange with U. of Maine: NASA grant of $40,000 since 1960.
Maine, University of Orono & Portland 1865 *State*	4714M 2765W	12000	87% in top 2/5 60%	568m 547v	a. $400 b. 850 c. 1000 d. 150	25% $300 40%	1:15	455	$4,576	B.A., B.S.; *Semester, summer session;* Liberal Arts—43%, Business Admin.—9%, Education—19%, Technology—15%, Life Science & Agriculture—14%; *Business Administration, Engineering, Forestry, Law, Nursing, Teacher Education;* Coops with other New England state universities; Army ROTC optional.
Nasson College Springvale 1912 *Private*	452M 283W	1381	45% in top 2/5 58%	575m 575v	a. $1600 b. 950 d. 208	24% $200-800 36%	1:14	40	$1,067	B.A., B.S., A.A.; *Semester, summer session;* Social Sciences—31%, Business & Economics—15%, Sciences & Math—15%, Psychology—18%, Other—4%; Coop teacher education (M.A.T.) with U. of New Hampshire, European semester with Nasson faculty; Experimental New Division added 1966-67.
Saint Joseph's College North Windham 1915 *Roman Catholic*	230W	500	79% in top 1/2 60%	429m 463v	a. $ 900 b. 1000	22% $750 30%	1:14	20		B.A.; *Semester, summer session;* Social Sciences—30%, English—25%, Education—25%, Natural Sciences—8%, French—8%; *Teacher Education;* Sunday Mass required.

MARYLAND

Institution / Location / Founded / Affiliation	Enrollment M=men W=women	Projected enrollment in 1975	High school ratings: % applicants accepted	SAT/ACT Averages m=math v=verbal	Annual Tuition: a. / b. Room & Board / c. Out of state / d. Other state	% Students with $ aid / Average amount	Faculty-student ratio: % with Doctorates	Volumes in library in 1,000's	Endowment in $1,000's	Undergraduate degrees offered; *Calendar;* Per cent of students per field of study; *Professional programs offered;* Miscellaneous
Bowie State College Bowie 1867 *State*	200M 350W	1000	most in top 2/5 58%		a. none b. $550 c. 450 d. 55	33%	1:16	31		B.A., B.S. Ed.; *Semester;* Education—100%.
College of Notre Dame of Maryland Baltimore 1896 *Roman Catholic*	794W	1300	48% in top 1/5 65%	535m 570v	a. $1200 b. 1100	35% $400 35%	1:10	56	$750	B.A.; *Semester, summer session;* Education—16%, Science & Math.—25%, Humanities—44%, Social Sciences—15%; *Social Work, Teacher Education;* Coop exchange of teachers & courses with Loyola and Mt. St. Agnes Colleges; 12 semester hours of theology required.
Columbia Union College Takoma Park 1904 *Seventh-day Adventist*	496M 508W	1250	90%	17.8m 18.7v	a. $1000 b. 700	50% $150 21%	1:11	64	$159	B.A., B.S.; *Trimester;* Social Sciences—25%, Nursing—28%, Business—14%, Education—12%, Natural Sciences—10%, Humanities—5%; *Nursing;* Affiliation with Newbold College, Berkshire, England; Chapel required.
Coppin State College Baltimore 1900 *State*	173M 632W	1346	50%		a. $200 b. no dorm c. 450	$550 22%	1:16	46		B.A.; B.S.; *Semester;* Coop with Baltimore City Dept. of Ed., Coppin, Morgan, and Towson State Colleges in a Project Mission supported by Ford Foundation grant; Teacher education students have free tuition; Grants from U.S. Office of Ed. totaling $125,000.
Frostburg State College Frostburg 1898 *State*	615M 928W	3500	most in top 3/5 42%		a. $200 b. 675 c. 450 d. 110	12% $400 28%	1:16	63		B.A., B.S.; *Semester;* Teacher Education—80%, Liberal Arts—20%; *Teacher Education.*
Goucher College Towson, Baltimore 1885 *Private*	1024W 2M	1000	72% in top 1/5	625m 631v	a. $1600 b. 1350	20% $1200 60%	1:12	120	$8,262	B.A.; *Quarter;* Humanities—44%, Social Sciences—36%, Natural Sciences & Math—20%; *Elementary Education;* Coop with Johns Hopkins U.—exchange of courses; One course in either Old or New Testament required.
Hood College Frederick 1893 *Church of Christ*	750W	1250	87% in top 2/5 61%	579m 590v	a. $1600 b. 1100	40% $500-1500 45%	1:12	79	$2,600	B.A., B.S.; *Semester;* Social Sciences—36%, Humanities—30%, Education—13%, Natural Sciences & Math—5%; Faculty International Studies program supported by Ford Foundation; 6 hours religion & philosophy, weekly chapel required; Junior Year Abroad program at Strasbourg; Latin American Studies program.
Johns Hopkins University Baltimore 1876 *Private*	1750M	2000	62% in top 1/10 39%	700m 650v	a. $2000 b. 900	43% $100-2000 80%	1:7	1500	$150,000	B.A.; *Semester, summer session;* Social Sciences—29%, Natural Sciences—25%, Pre-Med.—17%, Humanities—12%, Engineering—16%, Business—1%; *Medicine, School of Advanced International Studies;* Coop with Goucher College; Army ROTC optional; Two Ford Foundation matching grants of $6,000,000 each since 1960.
Loyola College Baltimore 1852 *Roman Catholic*	862M	1200	30% in top 1/5 59%		a. $1100 b. 1000	49% $550 67%	1:12	69	$1,462	B.A., B.S.; *Semester, summer session;* Social Sciences—34%, Natural Sciences—30%, Business—36%; Coop—some exchange of students with Notre Dame of Md. & Mt. St. Agnes College; Army ROTC required for 1st year.
Maryland, University of College Park 1807 *State*	13066M 8771W	25000	47% in top 1/4 75%	32 (comb.)	a. $356 b. 890 c. 450	20% $400 72%	1:17	800	$10,750	B.A., B.S., B. Mus.; *Semester, summer session;* Dentistry, Engineering, Journalism, Law, Medicine, Nursing, Pharmacy, Psychology, Social Work, Teacher Education, Library Services, Phys. Ed.; Air Force ROTC optional. Coops—Nursing with Walter Reed Army Institution of Nursing, Pre-Veterinary Med. with U. of Georgia, Pre-Forestry, Pre-Theological.
Maryland State College div. U. of Maryland Princess Anne 1886 *State*	444M 246W	1084	70%		a. none b. $800 c. 700	60% $250 26%	1:13	30		B.A., B.S.; *Semester;* Sciences—77%, Arts—23%; Coop graduate program in education with U. of Maryland; Air Force ROTC required for 2 years.
Morgan State College Baltimore 1867 *State*	1792M 2143W	7000	40% in top 1/4 82%		a. $257 b. 655 c. 450	35% $600 41%	1:17	100		B.A., B.S.; *Semester, summer session;* Social Sciences—27%, Natural Sciences—24%, Education—20%, Humanities—19%; Coop—3-2 engineering with New York University; Army ROTC required; N.S.F. grants totaling $368,000 since 1960.
Mount Saint Agnes College Baltimore 1890 *Roman Catholic*	438W	650	66% in top 1/4 55%	549m 561v	a. $1000 b. 1000	41% $732	1:11	40		B.A., B.S.; *Semester, summer session;* Elementary Education—28%, Medical Technology—18%, Math & Natural Sciences—11%, Social Sciences—16%, Languages—6%, English—9%, History—8%, Speech & Hearing Therapy—4%.

Institution / Location / Founded / Affiliation	Enrollment 1975 M=men W=women	Projected enrollment in 1975	High school rating; % applicants accepted	SAT/ACT Averages m=math v=verbal	a. Annual Tuition; b. Room & Board; c. Out of state; d. Other	% Students with $ aid / Average amount	Faculty-student ratio; % with Doctorates	Volumes in library in 1,000's	Endowment in $1,000's	Undergraduate degrees offered; Calendar; Per cent of students per field of study; Professional programs offered; Miscellaneous
Mount Saint Mary's College Emmitsburg 1808 *Roman Catholic*	850M	1000	95% in top 1/2 20%		a. $1025 b. 900 $200	10% 25%	1:12	103		B.A., B.S.; *Semester, summer session;* Sciences—83%, Arts—12%; *Teacher Education.*
St. John's College Annapolis 1696 *Private*	196M 137W	325	55% in top 1/5 67%	635m 662v	a. $1950 b. 1050 $1050 Max.	29% 50%	1:7	50	$6,685	B.A.; *Semester;* Liberal Arts—100%—St. John's has a 4-year course consisting of 100 Great Books, languages, math, laboratory sciences, and music; Students may also attend St. John's new campus at Sante Fe, N.M., under the same curriculum and policies.
Saint Joseph College Emmitsburg 1809 *Roman Catholic*	650W	900	89% in top 2/5 55%	518m 540v	a. $900 b. 700 d. 90 $500	18% 25%	1:10	42	$403	B.A., B.S.; *Semester, summer session;* Nursing—37%, Humanities—23%, Natural Sciences—18%, Social Sciences—13%; *Education, Nursing, Social Work;* Coop in nursing with Providence Hospital, Washington D.C.
Salisbury State College Salisbury 1925 *State*	200M 435W	2315			a. $200 b. 550 c. 450 d. 75		1:12 34%	59		B.A., B.S.; *Semester, summer session;* Teacher Education—91%, Liberal Arts—9%.
Towson State College Baltimore 1866 *State*	1406M 2407W	10000	85% in top 2/5 50%	500m 500v	a. $200 b. 685 c. 450	10% $250 35%	1:16	100		B.A., B.S.; *Semester, summer session;* Teacher Education—70%, Liberal Arts—30%; *Teacher Education.*
United States Naval Academy Annapolis 1845 *Federal*	4200M	4500	70% in top 1/5 20%	670m 596v	pd. by govt. Salary: $152 per month	100% 30%	1:6	200		B.S.; *Semester, summer session;* All midshipmen take a basic course of study, plus one of 23 minors offered; All graduates receive B.S.— U.S. Naval graduate school in Monterey, California and selected other universities provide postgraduate training; Weekly chapel required.
Washington College Chestertown 1782 *Private*	323M 301W	800	63% in top 1/5 30%	M573m 539v W544m 563v	a. $1450 b. 900 d. 96 $200-2300	30% 50%	1:12	78	$1,500	B.A., B.S.; *Semester;* Arts—84%, Sciences—16%; Coops—3-2 programs in dentistry, engineering, medicine, law, nursing, veterinary medicine with any accredited professional schools.
Western Maryland College Westminster 1867 *Methodist*	405M 416W	1200	91% in top 1/4 33%	594m 575v	a. $1300 b. 850 d. 150 $800	55% 50%	1:11	77	$2,750	B.A., B.S.; *Semester, summer session;* Social Sciences—37%, Natural Sciences—29%, Humanities—28%; *Education;* Coop—3-2 engineering with Johns Hopkins & forestry with Duke; 3 semester hours of Biblical literature & chapel attendance required; Army ROTC required two years; U. N. Semester.

MASSACHUSETTS

Institution / Location / Founded / Affiliation	Enrollment 1975 M=men W=women	Projected enrollment in 1975	High school rating; % applicants accepted	SAT/ACT Averages m=math v=verbal	a. Annual Tuition; b. Room & Board; c. Out of state; d. Other	% Students with $ aid / Average amount	Faculty-student ratio; % with Doctorates	Volumes in library in 1,000's	Endowment in $1,000's	Undergraduate degrees offered; Calendar; Per cent of students per field of study; Professional programs offered; Miscellaneous
American International College Springfield 1885 *Private*	1163M 615W	1871	40%		a. $1200 b. 758	31% $288-671 40%	1:19	70	$863	B.A., B.S., B.B.A., A.A.; *Semester, summer session;* Liberal Arts—50%, Education—25%, Business—25%.
Amherst College Amherst 1821 *Private*	1210M	1200	76% in top 1/5 19%	a. $1700 b. 900 d. 550		40% $1500	1:8 73%	381	$67,433	B.A.; *Semester;* Coop course exchange with Smith, Mt. Holyoke, & U. of Mass; 3-2 program with approved engineering schools.
Anna Maria College Paxton 1946 *Roman Catholic*	500W	600	100% in top 4/5 58%	480m 500v	a. $800 b. 850 d. 150 $300-400	35% 10%	1:12	26		B.A., B.S., B.Mus.; *Semester, summer session;* Humanities—28%, Social Sciences—27%, Natural Sciences—24%, Education—20%; Coop in medical technology with Worcester hospitals; Five theology courses required of Catholics.
Assumption College Worcester 1904 *Roman Catholic*	400M	1000	60% in top 2/5 59%	531m 543v	a. $1200 b. 900 d. 175 $200-1200	20% 60%	1:10	75	$450	B.A.; *Semester, summer session;* Social Sciences—45%, Natural Sciences & Math—32%, Humanities—23%; Graduate Degrees (M.A., M.A.T.) in Liberal Arts; 2 Masses per week for Catholics; Junior year at University of Louvain, Belgium, for philosophy and French majors; Grants totaling $184,272 since 1960.
Atlantic Union College South Lancaster 1882 *Seventh-day Adventist*	455M 442W	1250	82%	M18.07m 15.07v W15.22m 16.57v	a. $1060 b. 700 $625	62% 29%	1:13	54		B.A., B.S.; *Semester, summer session;* Social Sciences—22%, Physical Sciences—7%, Natural Sciences—6%, Humanities—24%, Education—16%, Other—25%; 12-16 hours religious study, morning & evening services required.
Boston, State College at Boston 1852 *State*	1634M 2089W	7500	20%		a. $200 c. 600	35%	1:16	60		B.A., B.S., B.S.Ed.; *Trimester, summer session;* Education—60%, Liberal Arts—40%; *Teacher Education;* Air Force ROTC optional.
Boston College Chestnut Hill 1863 *Roman Catholic*	4811M 1403W	7000	64% in top 1/4 38%	639m 622v	a. $1600 b. 1050 $900	27% 62%	1:12	664	$7,400	B.A., B.S.; *Semester, summer session;* Social Sciences—40%, Natural Sciences—40%, Humanities—20%; *Business, Education, Law, Nursing, Social Work;* Army ROTC optional; Grants totaling $3,500,000 since 1960.
Boston University (B.U.) Boston 1839 *Private*	5401M 6776W	13920	75% in top 1/4 59% *	597m 602v *	a. $1550 b. 1050 d. 75 $400-2000	20% 46%	1:15	666	$18,000	B.A., B.S.; *Semester, summer sessions; Business, Engineering, Law, Medicine, Nursing, Social Work, Teacher Education, Theology, Journalism, Phys. & Oc. Therapy, Art, Music, Theatre, Public Relations, Communication Arts;* Air Force, Army ROTC optional. * College of Liberal Arts only.
Brandeis University Waltham 1948 *Private*	998M 874W	2000	88% in top 20% 20%	M685m 666v W650m 671v	a. $1900 b. 1100 d. 225 $200-3000	33% 90% +	1:6	405	$20,284	B.A.; *Semester;* Social Sciences—55%, Humanities—19%, Natural Sciences—18%, Creative Arts—8%; *Florence Heller Graduate School for Advanced Studies in Social Welfare;* Ford Foundation grants totaling $12,000,000 since 1960.
Bridgewater, State College at Bridgewater 1840 *State*	665M 1566W	4250	12%	M550m 525v W525m 550v	a. $200 b. 850 c. 600	25% $500 35%	1:15	60		B.A., B.S.; *Semester, summer session; Teacher Education;* Air Force ROTC optional.
Clark University Worcester 1887 *Private*	699M 483W	1800	70% in top 1/5 24%	M615m 600v W598m 620v	a. $1900 b. 1100 d. 200 $200-2900	40% 81%	1:14	265	$14,100	B.A., B.S.; *Semester, summer session; Teacher Education;* Coop art program with Worcester Art Museum School. Independent study period of 31 weeks in January.

Institution / Location / Founded / Affiliation	Enrollment M=men W=women	Projected enrollment in 1975	High school rating; % applicants accepted	SAT/ACT Averages m=math v=verbal	Annual Tuition; Room & Board; Out of state; Other	% Students with $ aid / Average amount	Faculty-student ratio; % with Doctorates	Volumes in library in 1,000's	Endowment in $1,000's	Undergraduate degrees offered; Calendar; Per cent of students per field of study; Professional programs offered; Miscellaneous
College of the Holy Cross Worcester 1843 *Roman Catholic*	2200M	2500	75% in top 1/4 60%	626m 606v	a. $1700 b. 1130 d. 400	45% $1000	1:11 50%	233	$4,700	B.A.; *Semester;* Humanities—36%, Social Sciences—36%, Natural Sciences—28%; Coop with Clark University; Air Force, Navy ROTC optional; Grants totaling $365,000 since 1960.
College of Our Lady of the Elms Chicopee 1928 *Roman Catholic*	671W	800	98% in top 1/2 40%	494m 490v	a. $800 b. 800 d. 75	34% $375	1:12 25%	33		B.A., B.S. in M.Tech.; *Semester, summer session;* Humanities—45%, Social Sciences—50%, Natural Sciences—5%; *Teacher Education, Social Work.*
Eastern Nazarene College Quincy 1900 *Nazarene*	437M 434W	950	23% in top 1/5 84%	492m 481v	a. $880 b. 674 d. 100	21% $110	1:15 45%	40	$293	B.A., B.S., B.Mus., A.A., A.S.; *Semester, summer & winter sessions;* Social Sciences—27%, Education—34%, Natural Sciences—19%, Humanities—18%; *Religion;* 12 hours religion & philosophy, services required; Grants totaling $36,000 since 1960.
Emerson College Boston 1880 *Private*	454M 618W	1200	97% in top 1/2 65%	450m 562v	a. $1784 b. 1000 d. 100	15% $500	1:15 25%	34	$175	B.A., B.S., B.Mus.; *Semester, summer session;* Speech, Speech Pathology, & Audiology—33%, Theatre Arts—25%, Broadcasting—16%, English—15%, Education—11%; Coop in music with Longy School of Music; Semi-monthly nonsectarian services.
Emmanuel College Boston 1919 *Roman Catholic*	1369W	1700	80% in top 1/4 60%	562m 590v	a. $1200 b. 1100	33% $400	1:10 37%	66		B.A., B.F.A.; *Semester, summer session; Teacher Education;* 12 credits of religion required for graduation.
Fitchburg, State College at Fitchburg 1895 *State*	709M 1014W	3000	85% in top 1/2 25%	505m 490v	a. $200 b. 1100 c. 600	20% $300	1:15 30%	50		B.A., B.S.; *Semester, summer session;* Education—85%, Nursing—14%, Arts—1%; *Nursing, Teacher Education, Liberal Arts, Med. Tech.*
Framingham, State College at Framingham 1839 *State*	463M 1440W	1600	15%	513m 518v	a. $200 b. 480 c. 600 d. 125	50%	1:16 30%	42		B.A., B.S., B.S.Ed.; *Semester;* Education—100%; *Teacher Education.*
Gordon College Wenham 1889 *Private*	279M 338W	800	84% in top 2/5 60%	M500m 500v W500m 550v	a. $1425 b. 1110 d. 160	40% $300	1:15 42%	50	$643	A.B., B.S.; *Trimester;* Social Sciences—28%, Education—35%, Humanities—19%, Bible—4%, Science—13%; *Graduate School of Theology;* NSF grant of $2100, AEC grant of $3,500 since 1960.
Harvard College Cambridge 1636 *Private*	4850M	5000	19%	705m 695v	a. $2000 b. 1170	34% $1360	1:7 95%	7500	$752,100	B.A.; *Semester, summer session;* Social Sciences—40%, Natural Sciences—32%, Humanities—23%; *Arts & Sciences, Business Administration, Dentistry, Design, Divinity, Education, Law, Medicine, Public Administration, Public Health;* Air Force, Army, Navy ROTC optional.
Jackson College Medford 1910 *Private*	961W	1000	85% in top 1/5 30%	640m 630v	a. $1900 b. 1110 d. 500	20% $2800 Max.	60%	350		B.A., B.S.; *Semester, summer session;* Classical Study Program in Naples, Paris, Tübingen, and London; Woman's college of Tufts University.
Lesley College Cambridge 1909 *Private*	565W	650	most in top 1/4 27%		a. $1700 b. 1000	12% $725	1:16 40%	40		B.S.Ed.; *Semester, summer session;* Education—100%; *Teacher Education;* Grants totaling $170,500 since 1960.
Lowell, State College at Lowell 1894 *State*	297M 1006W	3000	20%	503m 510v	a. $200 b. 650 c. 600	10% $400	1:16 36%	40		B.S.Ed., B.Mus.Ed.; *Semester;* Education—90%, Liberal Arts—10%; *Teacher Education;* Elementary Ed.—62%, Music—20%, English—9%, History—6%, Biology—3%.
Lowell Technological Institute Lowell 1895 *State*	2128M 118W	6000	most in top 1/3 40%		a. $200 b. 750 c. 600 d. 600	33% $300	1:13 25%	50		B.S.; *Semester, summer session;* Business, Engineering; Air Force ROTC optional; Science and research grants totaling $800,000 since 1960.
Massachusetts, University of Amherst 1863 *State*	5860M 4761W	19500	35% in top 1/10 33%	M588m 534v W566m 562v	a. $200 b. 798 c. 600 d. 136	45% $400	1:15 55%	400	$860	B.A., B.S., B.B.A., B.V.A.; *Semester, summer sessions;* Arts & Sciences—53%, Engineering—9%, Education—9%, Business Administration—13%, Agriculture—7%, Other—12%; *Bus. Admin., Chem., Dietetics, Education, Engineering, Forestry, Lands. Arch., Nursing, Phys. Ed.;* Coops—Amherst, Mt. Holyoke, Smith; AF, A ROTC opt.
Massachusetts, University of Boston 1964 *State*	1222M 929W	9000	33% in top 1/4 65%	M536m 506v W500m 512v	a. $200 c. 600 d. 80	33% $300	1:15 60%	35		B.A.; *Semester;* Humanities—32%, Social Sciences—40%, Natural Sciences and Math—28%; first graduating class in 1969.
Massachusetts Institute of Technology (M.I.T.) Cambridge 1861 *Private*	3657M 200W	3900	93% in top 1/10 38%	747M 673v	a. $1900 b. 1130	46% $100- 3600		960	$222,055	S.B., B.Arch.; *Semester, summer session;* Arts & Sciences—43%, Eng.—49%, Arch.—2%, Management—6%; *Architecture, Engineering, Humanities, Management, Science;* cross registration with Harvard, Radcliffe, & B.U.; Air Force, Army, Navy ROTC optional.
Merrimack College North Andover 1947 *Roman Catholic*	1001M 669W	1800	50%	550m 550v	a. $1300 b. 1000 d. 350	33% $1600 Max.	1:13 32%	53		B.A., B.S.; *Semester, summer session;* Arts—57%, Business Administration—16%, Natural Sciences—12%, Engineering—9%, Other—6%.
Mount Holyoke College South Hadley 1837 *Private*	1700W		65% in top 1/20 44%	600m 620v	a. $1850 b. 1200	63% $1450	1:11 67%	300	$30,000	B.A.; *Semester;* Social Sciences—26%, Humanities—52%, Natural Sciences—18%, Other—4%; *Nursing;* Coops with Amherst, Smith, & the U. of Mass.
North Adams, State College at North Adams 1894 *State*	247M 290W	2000	75%		a. $200 b. 540* c. 600 d. 30	25% $300	1:15 36%	38		B.A., B.S., B.S.Ed.; *Semester;* Humanities—31%, Elementary Education—36%, Sciences & Math—30%, Medical Tech.—3%; All programs are *Teacher Education.* *Women only.
Northeastern University Boston 1898 *Private*	9031M 2819W	12000	80% in top 2/5 45%	563m 502v	a. $1320 b. 1221	25% $1600	1:20 50%	173	$19,690	B.A., B.S.; *Quarter System;* Engineering—31%, Liberal Arts—27%, Business—24%, Education—7%, Nursing—4%, Pharmacy—3%, Phys. Ed.—4%; *Business, Engineering, Nursing, Pharmacy;* Coop Plan of Education; Army ROTC optional.

Institution Location Founded Affiliation	Enrollment M=men W=women	Projected enrollment in 1975	High school rating; % applicants accepted	SAT/ACT Averages m=math v=verbal	a. Annual Tuition; b. Room & Board; c. Out of state; d. Other	% Students with $ aid; Average amount	Faculty-student ratio; % with Doctorates	Volumes in library in 1,000's	Endowment in $1,000's	Undergraduate degrees offered; Calendar; Per cent of students per field of study; Professional programs offered; Miscellaneous
Radcliffe College Cambridge 1879 *Private*	1172W	(det. by Harvard)	90% in top 1/5 14%		a. $2000 b. 1240	25% $1700	1:6	135+ Harvard lib.	$16,285	B.A.; *Semester, summer session;* Humanities—48%, Social Sciences —38%, Natural Sciences—14%; *Professional Programs Available at Harvard;* Radcliffe shares faculty and curriculum with Harvard.
Regis College Weston 1927 *Roman Catholic*	910W	1200	58% in top 1/5 70%	550m 580v	a. $1200 b. 1100	27% $930 43%	1:12	74		B.A.; *Semester, summer session;* Social Sciences—24%, Humanities —40%, Natural Sciences—30%, Home Economics—6%.
Salem, State College at Salem 1854 *State*	1200M 1700W	5000	75% in top 1/4 20%	M550m 500v W510m 550v	a. $200 b. 1000 c. 600	20% $200 40%	1:15	55		B.A., B.S.Ed.; *Semester, summer session;* Teacher Education—70%, Liberal Arts—25%, Business Administration—5%; *Teacher Education.*
Simmons College Boston 1899 *Private*	1442W	1652	80% in top 1/5 32%		a. $1600 b. 1000 d. 400	24% $681 43%	1:12	119	$8,400	B.A., B.S.; *Semester, summer session;* Social Sciences—22%, Education—28%, Sciences—14%, Business Admin.—10%, Publication —12%, Nursing—9%, Home Economics—5%; *Bus. Adm., Ed., Nurs., Social Work;* Coops with New England Conservatory, Boston Museum School, Children's Medical Center, Greater Boston Hospitals.
Smith College Northampton 1871 *Private*	2300W		90% in top 1/5 40%		a. $2000 b. 1100	30% $2800 Max.	1:9 74%	500	$43,000	B.A.; *Semester, summer session (social work);* Humanities—43%, Social Sciences—40%, Sciences—17%; *Social Work;* Coop with Amherst, Mt. Holyoke, U. of Mass.
S. E. Mass. Tech. Inst. (S.M.T.I.) N. Dartmouth 1895 *State*	1564M 719W	7000	77% in top 1/2 54%	504m 471v	a. $200 no dorms c. 600 d. 55	14% $225 28%	1:12	60	$100	B.A., B.S., B.F.A., B.B.A.; *Semester;* Business & Industry—50%, Engineering—20%, Fine & Applied Arts—18%, Arts & Sciences— 12%; New Bedford Institute of Tech. and Bradford Durfee College became S.M.T.I. as of July 1, 1964.
Springfield College Springfield 1885 *Private*	1110M 475W	2000	32%		a. $1666 b. 800 d. 300	35% $500 46%	1:19	75	$4,500	B.A., B.S.; *Quarter, summer session;* Health, Phys. Ed., Rec.—49%, Teacher Ed.—22%, Arts & Sciences—29%; *Teacher Education, Phys. Ed., Community Rec.*
Stonehill College North Easton 1948 *Roman Catholic*	775M 475W	1750	87% in top 1/2 45%	M520m 520v W528m 528v	a. $1200 b. 900	35% $411 25%	1:21	54		B.A., B.S.; *Semester;* Humanities—61%, Business—21%, Sciences —18%.
Suffolk University Boston 1906 *Private*	1559M 339W	1500	50%	475m 475v	a. $1000	30% $400 34%	1:19	67	$280	A.B., B.S., B.S. in B.A., B.S. in Journalism; *Semester, summer session;* Elementary Education—6%, Social Sciences—29%, Sciences —11%, Humanities—12%, Business—41%, Journalism—1%, Secondary Teaching Minor—19%; *Law;* Evening Division.
Tufts University Medford 1852 *Private*	1800M	2920	79% in top 1/5 19%	650m 650v	a. $1700 b. 900 d. 75	31% $200- 2700 60%	1:10	319	$20,323	B.A., B.S., B.F.A., B.S. Ed.; *Semester, summer school;* Social Sciences—29%, Natural Sciences & Math—29%, Humanities—23%, Chem. Eng.—13%, Civil Eng.—27%, Elec. Eng.—36%, Mech. Eng.— 24%; *Dentistry, Engineering, Medicine, Theology;* 3 study-abroad programs; Air Force, Navy ROTC optional.
Wellesley College Wellesley 1870 *Private*	1783W		95% in top 1/5 30%	658m 679v	$2800 Total a. & b. d. $400	20% $1515 73%	1:10	380	$59,515	B.A.; *Three-term system;* Social Sciences—52%, Humanities—33%, Natural Sciences—15%; 2 units of Biblical history required; Grants totaling $3,166,262 since 1960.
Westfield, State College at Westfield 1839 *State*	479M 991W	3000	most in top 1/2 20%	514m 500v	a. $200 b. 384 c. 600	15% $300 28%	1:16	45		B.A., B.S. Ed.; *Semester, summer session;* Liberal Arts; *Teacher Education;* Coops with Fitchburg State College and East Central State College in Ada, Oklahoma.
Wheaton College Norton 1834 *Private*	1100W		85% in top 1/5 50%	602m 612v	a. $2300 b. 1000	18% $3200 Max. 64%	1:11	116	$7,000	B.A.; *Semester;* Social Sciences—35%, Humanities—35%, Other— 30%; *Teacher Education;* Junior Year Abroad available; Grants totaling $35,070 since 1960.
Wheelock College Boston 1888 *Private*	500W	550	77% in top 3/5 50%	536m 536v	a. $1700 b. 1000	12% $929 32%	1:15	31	$185	B.S. Ed.; *Semester, summer session;* Pre-school & Primary Education—100%; *Teacher Education.*
Williams College Williamstown 1793 *Private*	1224M	1250	82% in top 1/5 26%	677m 644v	a. $1800 b. 1000 d. 150	27% $1525 66%	1:9	275	$43,067	B.A.; *Semester, winter study program;* Social Sciences—55%, Humanities—23%, Natural Sciences & Math—22%; *Center for Development Economics (M.A.);* Ford Foundation grant of 2.5 million. Other grants totaling $16,853,000 since 1960.
Worcester, State College at Worcester 1874 *State*	595M 1019W	3300	45% in top 1/2 33%	500m 500v	a. $200 b. 500 c. 600 d. 100	6% $425 25%	1:16	48		B.A., B.S. Ed.; *Semester, summer session;* Education—56%, Social Sciences—13%, English—15%, Math—10%; *Teacher Education.*
Worcester Polytechnic Institute Worcester 1865	1360M	1700	90% in top 1/2 60%	665m 565v	a. $1800 b. 1000 d. 300	37% $800 40%	1:9	62	$18,000	B.S.; *Semester, summer session;* Electrical Engineering—28%, Mech. Eng.—26%, Chem. Eng.—15%, Civil Eng.—13%, Physics— 4%, Chem.—4%; *Engineering;* Coop in bio-medical engineering with Clark U; Army ROTC required for 2 years.

MICHIGAN

Institution Location Founded Affiliation	Enrollment M=men W=women	Projected enrollment in 1975	High school rating; % applicants accepted	SAT/ACT Averages m=math v=verbal	a. Annual Tuition; b. Room & Board; c. Out of state; d. Other	% Students with $ aid; Average amount	Faculty-student ratio; % with Doctorates	Volumes in library in 1,000's	Endowment in $1,000's	Undergraduate degrees offered; Calendar; Per cent of students per field of study; Professional programs offered; Miscellaneous
Adrian College Adrian 1859 *Methodist*	809M 674W	2000	95% in top 1/2 45%		a. $1200 b. 780	50% $600 50%	1:17	60	$2,500	B.A., B.S.; *Semester, summer sessions;* 6 credit hours in the department of religion required.
Albion College Albion 1835 *Methodist*	852M 805W	2000	80% in top 1/4 60%	590m 540v	$2420 Total	49% $733 47%	1:13	135	$8,321	B.A.; *Semester, summer session;* Humanities—29%, Social Sciences —39%, Natural Sciences & Math—32%; *Teacher Education;* Foreign study programs.

Institution / Location / Founded / Affiliation	Enrollment M=men W=women	Projected enrollment in 1975	High school rating: % applicants accepted	SAT/ACT Averages m=math v=verbal	Annual Tuition: a. / b. Room & Board; c. Out of state; d. Other	% Students with $ aid; Average amount	Faculty-student ratio; % with Doctorates	Volumes in library in 1,000's	Endowment in $1,000's	Undergraduate degrees offered; Calendar; Per cent of students per field of study; Professional programs offered; Miscellaneous
Alma College Alma 1886 *Presbyterian*	560M 553W	1550	76% in top 1/4	530m 530v	a. $1245 b. 850	70% $100-2000	1:15 66%	70	$2,000	B.A., B.S.; *Three-term;* Social Sciences—28%, Education—25%, Humanities—23%, Natural Sciences & Math—19%, Business—6%; Coop—3-2 engineering with U. of Michigan.
Andrews University Berrien Springs 1874 *Seventh-day Adventist*	792M 779W	2400	71% in top 1/2	46.8m 43.5v (comb.)	a. $1056 b. 720		1:15 55%	164		B.A., B.S., B.Mus., B.S.Art Ed., B.S.Eng., B.S.Med. Tech.; *Quarter.*
Aquinas College Grand Rapids 1922 *Roman Catholic*	350M 425W	2100	70% in top 1/2 65%	M480 W510	a. $760 b. 810 d. 30	60% $450	1:17 20%	55	$150	B.A., B.S., B.Mus.; *Semester;* Arts—65%, Sciences—88%, Business Adm.—33%, Music & Other—4%.
Calvin College Grand Rapids 1876 *Christian Reformed*	1720M 1514W	5000	90% in top 1/2	525m 500v	a. $930 b. 800	20% $200	1:20 50%	170		B.A., B.S.; *2 Semesters, January interim semester, summer sessions;* Liberal Arts—45%, Teacher Education—45%, Pre-professional—10%; *Teacher Education.*
Central Michigan University Mt. Pleasant 1892 *State*	3882M 4701W	14800	96% in top 1/3 72%	20.9 (comp.)	a. $300 b. 828 c. 600	17% $200	1:22 40%	286	$105	B.A., B.S., B.A.A., B.B.A., B.S.Ed., B.Mus.Ed.; *Semester, summer session;* Social Sciences—40%, Humanities—17%, Natural Sciences & Math—18%, Business—13%, Physical Education—7%; *Music, Teacher Education;* Army ROTC optional.
Detroit, University of Detroit 1877 *Roman Catholic*	4762M 1771W	8000	40% in top 1/4 82%	547m 512v	a. $1150 b. 780	25% $450	1:20 50%	284	$3,000	B.A., B.S., B.Arch.; *Semester, summer session;* Humanities—30%, Business—27%, Engineering—23%, Social Sciences—11%, Natural Sciences & Math—9%; *Business, Dentistry, Engineering, Law, Arch.;* 9 hours theology required of Catholics, 3 hours required of non-Catholics.
Detroit Institute of Technology Detroit 1891 *Private*	1640M 198W	3000	most in top 1/2 60%		a. $800 b. no dorm	4% $250	1:23 23%	38	$76	B.A., B.S., B.B.A.; *Semester, summer sessions;* Business—48%, Sciences—35%, Arts—17%.
Eastern Michigan University Ypsilanti 1849 *State*	5176M 5075W	23250	80% in top 1/2 63%	468m 450v	a. $300 b. 843 c. 600	25% $400	1:27 41%	189	$268	B.A., B.S., B.A.E., B.B.E., B.B.A., B.M.E., B.F.A.; *Semester, summer session;* Business—16%, Social Sciences—25%, Humanities—25%, Sciences—20%, Other—14%; *Music, Teacher Education;* Army ROTC required.
Hillsdale College Hillsdale 1844 *Independent*	609M 450W	1100	85% in top 2/5 24%	550m 540v	a. $1510 b. 890	22% $770	1:17 25%	60	$4,700	B.A., B.S.; *Semester, 9-week summer session;* Arts—76%, Sciences—24%; *Music, Teacher Education, Preschool Education, Business, Fine Arts.*
Hope College Holland 1851 *Reformed Church in America*	883M 792W	2400	52% in top 1/5 50%	M558m 502v W523m 527v	a. $1050 b. 850	43% $341	1:14 54%	100	$2,239	B.A., B.Mus.; *Semester, summer session, Vienna summer session;* Humanities—43%, Social Sciences—24%, Natural Sciences & Math—28%, Business—5%; *Music, Teacher Education;* 6 hours Religion, twice-weekly chapel attendance required.
Kalamazoo College Kalamazoo 1833 *Baptist*	635M 567W	1320	64% in top 1/10 55%	M633m 593v W608m 634v	a. $1095 b. 1125 d. 240	41% $100-500	1:17 55%	130	$9,593	B.A.; *Quarter;* Social Sciences—41%, Natural Sciences & Math—35%, Humanities—24%; Coop—3-2 engineering with U. of Michigan; Attendance at bi-weekly chapel—convocation required; Year-around program including career service, foreign study, senior independent project.
Madonna College Livonia 1947 *Roman Catholic*	5M 603W	900	60% in top 1/4 73%		a. $550 b. 700	32% $520	1:13 30%	43		B.A., B.S.; *Semester, summer session;* Humanities—25%, Natural Sciences and Math—15%, Social Sciences—28%, Home Ec.—2%, Medical Tech.—4%, Nursing—26%.
Marygrove College Detroit 1910 *Roman Catholic*	1544W	2000	75% in top 1/4	520m 540v	a. $900 b. 1125	26% $400	1:9	141		B.A., B.S., B.Mus.; *Quarter, summer session;* Social Sciences—32%, Humanities—46%, Natural Sciences & Math—14%, Home Economics—6%, Journalism—2%.
Mercy College of Detroit Detroit 1941 *Roman Catholic*	59M 1068W	2000	most in top 1/3 70%	M475m 470v W480m 480v	a. $770 b. 1160	60% $441	1:11 27%	50		B.A., B.S.; *Semester, summer session;* Sciences—42%, Arts—38%, Nursing—20%; *Nursing;* 4 courses in theology required of Catholic students, 1 course required of non-Catholics.
Michigan, University of Ann Arbor 1817 *State*	11251M 8662W		92% in top 1/4 55%	620m 575v	a. $348 b. 950 c. 1000	35% $340	1:15 82%	3584	$46,540	B.A., B.S., B.Arch., B.B.A., B.Mus.; *Three-term;* Social Sciences—36%, Humanities—32%, Natural Sciences & Math—20%; *Arch., Art, Bus., Dent., Eng., For., Jour., Landscape Arch., Law, Lib., Med., Music, Nurs., Phar., Phys. Ther., Psych., Social Work, Teacher Ed.;* AF, A, N ROTC optional.
Michigan State University East Lansing 1855 *State*	22891M 15216W		80% in top 1/4		a. $358 b. 873 c. 1025	40% $50-1500	1:19 70%	1200		B.A., B.S., B.F.A., B.Mus.; *Quarter, summer session;* Ed.—18%, Soc. Sci.—17%, Arts—15%, Bus.—14%, Nat. Sci.—10%; *Bus., Eng., For., Jour., Landscape Arch., Music, Nurs., Psych., Social Work, Teacher Ed., Vet. Med., Labor & Ind. Rel., Pub. Adm., Urban Plan.;* Air Force, Army ROTC optional.
Michigan Technological University Houghton 1885 *State*	3676M 304W	8600	75% in top 1/3 75%	M556m 466v W541m 531v	a. $300 b. 850 c. 750	59% $450	1:16 36%	108	$478	B.S., B.A.; *Quarter, summer quarter;* Engineering—65%, Business—13%, Sciences—15%, Forestry—6%; *Engineering, Liberal Arts, Medical Technology;* Air Force, Army ROTC optional.
Nazareth College Nazareth 1924 *Roman Catholic*	470W	1500	68% in top 1/3 75%	20.8 (comp.)	a. $850 b. 850 d. 30	40% $500	1:11 25%	40	$236	B.A., B.S., B.S.N.; *Semester, summer session;* Humanities—53%, Social Sciences—33%, Natural Sciences & Math—9%.
Northern Michigan University Marquette 1899 *State*	4384M 2513W	12000	24% in top 1/4 55%		a. $300 b. 884 c. 600	17%		100		B.A., B.S., B. Mus. Ed.; *Semester, summer session;* Teacher Education.
Oakland University Rochester 1957 *State*	1750M 1900W	12000	70% in top 1/4 80%	M610m 540v W540m 595v	a. $378 b. 890 c. 872	35% $585	1:20 70%	100		B.A., B.S.; *Three-semester;* Education—45%, Arts—38%, Business—7%, Engineering—10%; *Business, Engineering, Teacher Education.*

Institution / Location / Founded / Affiliation	Enrollment M=men W=women	Projected enrollment in 1975	High school rating; % applicants accepted	SAT/ACT Averages m=math v=verbal	a. Annual Tuition; b. Room & Board; c. Out of state; d. Other state	% Students with $ aid; Average amount	Faculty-student ratio; % with Doctorates	Volumes in library in 1,000's	Endowment in $1,000's	Undergraduate degrees offered; Calendar; Per cent of students per field of study; Professional programs offered; Miscellaneous
Olivet College Olivet 1844 *Congregational*	416M 304W	1000	40% in top 1/4 60%		$2000 Total	38% $900	1:15 30%	51	$203	B.A.; *Semester, summer session;* Social Sciences—47%, Humanities—26%, Natural Sciences & Math—26%; One course in philosophy and Bible, monthly convocation required.
Siena Heights College Adrian 1919 *Roman Catholic*	39M 726W	1050			a. $650 775 b. $300	25% 50%	1:15	56		B.A., B.S.; *Semester;* Social Sciences—43%, Humanities—40%, Natural Sciences & Math—15%; 8 hours in theology.
Spring Arbor College Spring Arbor 1873 *Free Methodist*	290M 310W	1200	60% in top 1/4 80%		a. $950 735 b. $300 d. 80	75% 37%	1:16	25	$100	B.A., B.S.; *Semester;* Education—65%, Other—35%.
Wayne State University Detroit 1868 *State*	11944M 9914W	31000	69%		a. $312 756 b. 750 c.	47%	1:19	992	$3,462	B.A., B.S.; *Quarter, summer quarter;* Engineering, Nursing, Occupational Therapy, Pharmacy, Arts, Social Sciences, Humanities, Physical Sciences, Teacher Education.
Western Michigan University Kalamazoo 1903 *State*	7445M 6751W	18800	69% in top 1/4 71%		a. $300 820 b. $275 c. 600	18% 44%	1:21	310		B.A., B.S., B.B.A., B.Mus., B.S.E. (Tech.); *Semester, spring and summer sessions;* Sciences—47%, Arts—38%, Business—13%; *Library, Music, Occupational Therapy, Teacher Education;* Army ROTC optional.

MINNESOTA

Institution / Location / Founded / Affiliation	Enrollment M=men W=women	Projected enrollment in 1975	High school rating; % applicants accepted	SAT/ACT Averages m=math v=verbal	a. Annual Tuition; b. Room & Board; c. Out of state; d. Other state	% Students with $ aid; Average amount	Faculty-student ratio; % with Doctorates	Volumes in library in 1,000's	Endowment in $1,000's	Undergraduate degrees offered; Calendar; Per cent of students per field of study; Professional programs offered; Miscellaneous
Augsburg College Minneapolis 1869 *Lutheran*	716M 720W	1800	64% in top 1/5 87%	M561m 496v W514v 503v	a. $1300 770 b. $996	52% 34%	1:18	77	$422	B.A.; *Three-term;* Social Sciences—33%, Natural Sciences & Math—22%, Humanities—21%, Education—41%, Business—5%, Religion & Philos.—5%; *Teacher Education, Med. Tech.;* Junior Year Abroad.
Bemidji State College Bemidji 1919 *State*	2009M 1231W	7000	most in top 1/2 99%		a. $240 660 b. $650 d. 45	48% 25%	1:20	65		B.A., B.S.; *Quarter, summer sessions;* Education—88%, Liberal Arts & Business—12%; *Teacher Education.*
Bethel College and Seminary St. Paul 1871 *Baptist*	455M 529W	1200	50% in top 1/5 89%	522m 502v	a. $1100 605 b. $400 d. 110	50% 34%	1:15	50	$50	B.A.; *Semester;* Social Sciences—39%, Humanities—11%, Natural Sciences & Math—11%, Religion—5%, Education—34%; *Theology;* 9 hours study of Christianity required.
Carleton College Northfield 1866 *Private*	780M 587W		95% in top 1/5 42%M 39%W	675m 655v	$2800 Total	45% $100-2500	1:12 75%	218	$20,629	B.A.; *Three-term; Teacher Education;* Coop—3-2 engineering with Columbia, M.I.T.
College of Saint Benedict St. Joseph 1913 *Roman Catholic*	492W	1050	60% in top 1/5 83%	500m 501v	a. $1100 800 b. $325 d. 40	48% 30%	1:11	48	$188	B.A., B.F.A.; *Semester, summer session;* Theol. & Philos.—1%, Humanities—29%, Education—36%, Social Sciences—13%, Natural Sciences & Math—17%, Home Economics—4%; Coop—tri-college program with St. Cloud State College, St. John's University; 14 credits theology required.
College of St. Catherine St. Paul 1905 *Roman Catholic*	1400W	1800	63% in top 1/5 84%	532m 541v	a. $1100 765 b. $583	32% 30%	1:13	147	$1,198	B.A., B.S.; *Semester, summer session;* Nursing—13%, Education—16%, Humanities—35%, Social Sciences—13%, Natural Sciences & Math—8%; *Nursing, Teacher Education;* Coop—area studies with College of St. Thomas, Hamline, Macalester; 15 hours theology.
College of St. Scholastica Duluth 1912 *Roman Catholic*	570W	1000	60% in top 1/3 80%		a. $750 795 b. $350 d. 35	65% 30%	1:10	57		B.A., B.S.; *Semester, summer session;* Education—36%, Nursing—23%, Social Work—10%, Medical Record Librarianship—7%, Dietetics—6%, Other—18%; *Nursing.*
College of Saint Teresa Winona 1907 *Roman Catholic*	1130W	1200	most in top 2/5 76%	506m 521v	a. $800 750 b. $200 c. 80	25% 25%	1:9	85	$500	A.B., B.S., B.S.N.; *Semester, summer session;* Education & Nursing 53%, Humanities—20%, Natural Sciences & Math—18%, Social Sciences—13%; *Nursing, Teacher Education, Medical Technology;* Coop with St. Mary's Hospital, Rochester.
College of St. Thomas St. Paul 1885 *Roman Catholic*	2150M	2500	41% in top 1/4 72%	536m 501v	a. $1150 950 b. $450	37% 37%	1:16	150	$7,111	B.A., B.S.; *Semester, summer session;* Social Sciences—32%, Business—30%, Natural Sciences & Math—22%, Humanities—12%; *Teacher Education;* Coops—3-2 engineering with Notre Dame, area studies with Hamline, Macalester, College of St. Catherine; 4 courses religion required; Air Force ROTC optional.
Concordia College Moorhead 1891 *Lutheran*	1062M 1173W	3480	65% in top 1/4 75%	565m 535v	a. $1100 700 b. $734 d. 18	61% 38%	1:16	100	$955	B.A., B.S., B. Mus.; *Semester, summer sessions;* Natural Sciences & Math—22%, Humanities—21%, Education—20%, Social Sciences—21%, Business—9%; *Music, Teacher Education, Hospital Admin., Home Economics, C.P.A., Chemistry, Medical Tech.;* 13 credits in religion, chapel attendance expected; Washington Semester, Junior Year Abroad.
Gustavus Adolphus College St. Peter 1862 *Lutheran*	785M 877W	2000	40% in top 1/10 80%	M583m 515v W533m 525v	$2200 Total	40% $100-1900	1:16 40%	102	$1,282	B.A.; *Semester, summer session; Music, Nursing, Teacher Education;* Coops—3-2 engineering, 3-1 medical technology, 2-2 nursing; 3 courses in religion required.
Hamline University St. Paul 1854 *Methodist*	561M 636W	1500	58% in top 1/5 80%	M572m 535v W523m 531v	a. $1320 870 b. $464	40% 49%	1:16	94	$12,075	B.A., B.S.; *Three-term;* Social Sciences—46%, Natural Sciences & Math—19%, Humanities—24%, Fine Arts—10%; *Music, Teacher Education;* Coops—area studies with College of St. Thomas, College of St. Catherine, Macalester; Washington Semester; United Nations semester; One religion course required.
Macalester College St. Paul 1874 *Presbyterian*	941M 924W	1850	82% in top 1/5 65%	M620m 592v W605m 621v	a. $1500 900 b. $100-1500 d. 34	47% 65%	1:14	150	$21,500	B.A.; *Three terms, one of which is 4-week interim, summer session; Teacher Education;* Area studies with Colleges of St. Catherine & St. Thomas, Hamline; One religion course.
Mankato State College Mankato 1868 *State*	4604M 3922W	15000	most in top 2/3		a. $285 720 b. $200 c. 429	25% 40%	1:20	175		B.A., B.S.; *Quarter, summer sessions; Teacher Education.*

Institution Location	Founded Affiliation	Enrollment M=men W=women	Projected enrollment in 1975	High school rating; % applicants accepted	SAT/ACT Averages m=math v=verbal	Annual Tuition: a. b. Room & Board; c. Out of state; d. Other state	% Students with $ aid; Average amount	Faculty-student ratio; % with Doctorates	Volumes in library in 1,000's	Endowment in $1,000's	Undergraduate degrees offered; Calendar; Per cent of students per field of study; Professional programs offered; Miscellaneous
Minnesota, University of Minneapolis	1857 State	6914M 5513W Col. of L.A.	52000 total university	42% in top 1/5		a. $255 b. 820 c. 840 d. 60	5% $315	1:23 60%	2072		B.A.; Quarter, summer sessions; Architecture, Business, Dentistry, Engineering, Forestry, Journalism, Law, Library, Medicine, Music, Nursing, Pharmacy, Physical & Occupational Therapy, Psychology, Social Work, Teacher Education, Veterinary Medicine; Air Force, Army, Navy ROTC optional.
Moorhead State College Moorhead	1887 State	2017M 1812W	6350	40% in top 1/4 82%	22 (comp.)	a. $252 b. 690 c. 360 d. 60	30% $550	1:20 47%	70		B.A., B.S.; Quarter, summer session; Education—68%, Liberal Arts —32%; Teacher Education.
St. Cloud State College St. Cloud	1869 State	4372M 3536W	13275	24% in top 1/5 95%	M20.9 W21.0 (comp.)	a. $191 b. 660 c. 292	23% $582 23%	1:25	108		B.A., B.S.; Quarter, summer sessions; Education—75%, Liberal Arts —25%; Teacher Education; Coop—tri-college program with College of St. Benedict, St. John's University.
St. John's University Collegeville	1857 Roman Catholic	1390M	1800	56% in top 1/5 69%	572m 532v	a. $1150 b. 840	43% $740 47%	1:13	155	$5,188	B.A., B.S.; Semester; Humanities—44%, Natural Sciences & Math— 25%, Social Sciences—22%, Business—5%, Fine Arts—4%; Coops —3-2 engineering, 3-3 architecture with U. of Minn., coop with College of St. Benedict, Army ROTC optional; member Central States College Assoc.
St. Mary's College Winona	1912 Roman Catholic	1050M	1500	55% in top 1/3 65%	23m 21v	a. $1050 b. 800	38% $400 33%	1:18	67		B.A., B.S.; Semester, summer session; Arts—81%, Sciences—19%; 3 courses in theology required.
St. Olaf College Northfield	1874 Lutheran	1255M 1249W	3000	77% in top 1/5 48%	M609m 562v W580m 580v	$2200 Total	40% $1000 54%	1:14	197	$2,401	B.A., B.S. in N., B.Mus.; Semester, one-month interim, summer sessions; B.A.—88%; Music, Nursing, Teacher Education; 3 semesters religion courses required; Foreign Studies program with interim, term or year abroad, Washington Semester; Air Force ROTC optional.
Winona State College Winona	1860 State	1867M 1252W	5000	95%		a. $240 b. 690 c. 384 d. 60	40% $600 30%	1:20	70		B.A., B.S.; Quarter, summer sessions; Teacher Education and Liberal Arts; Tri-college coop with St. Mary's and St. Teresa.

MISSISSIPPI

Institution Location	Founded Affiliation	Enrollment M=men W=women	Projected enrollment in 1975	High school rating; % applicants accepted	SAT/ACT Averages m=math v=verbal	Annual Tuition: a. b. Room & Board; c. Out of state; d. Other state	% Students with $ aid; Average amount	Faculty-student ratio; % with Doctorates	Volumes in library in 1,000's	Endowment in $1,000's	Undergraduate degrees offered; Calendar; Per cent of students per field of study; Professional programs offered; Miscellaneous
Acorn Agricultural and Mechanical College Lorman	1871 State	772M 1213W	3500	12 (comp.)		a. $186 b. 355 c. 341	40% $350 20%	1:12	34		B.S.; Semester, summer session; Education—60%, Liberal Arts— 42%, Vocational Education—17%.
Belhaven College Jackson	1883 Presbyterian	222M 333W	800	71% in top 1/5 88%	22 (comp.)	a. $750 b. 650	36% $280 33%	1:12	35	$1,052	B.A., B.S., B.Mus.; Semester; Music; Coops with Millsaps College, Joint Universities center; Two weekly chapel services required.
Blue Mountain College Blue Mountain	1873 Baptist	31M 393W	750	55% in top 1/2 97%		a. $450 b. 600	10% $100- 500 28%	1:11	29	$872	B.A., B.S., B.Mus.; Semester, summer session; Education—37%, Humanities—30%, Social Sciences—17%, Natural Sciences—8%, Home Economics—5%, Business—5%; 6 hours of Bible, five chapel services per week required.
Delta State College Cleveland	1924 State	1130M 1041W	3500	80%		a. & b. $825 c. 1125	25% $175 26%	1:20	63		B.A., B.S., B.S.Ed., B.Mus.Ed.; Semester, summer sessions; Education—60%, Arts and Sciences—15%, Business—25%; Teacher Education.
Jackson State College Jackson	1877 State	810M 1092W	5000	74%		a. $225 b. 465 c. 250	10% $184- 687 18%	1:19	35		B.A., B.S., B.Mus.Ed.; Quarter, summer session; Education—41%, Industrial Arts—28%, Humanities—14%, Social Sciences—10%, Natural Sciences & Math—9%.
Millsaps College Jackson	1890 Methodist	455M 470W	1500	75% in top 1/4 75%	24m 24v	a. $1000 b. 650	45% $300 33%	1:13	60	$3,200	B.A., B.M., B.S.; Semester, summer sessions; Social Sciences—48%, Natural Sciences—31%, Humanities—21%; Coops—3-2 engineering with Columbia, 3-2 forestry with Duke U.; 6 hours religion, one chapel service per week required.
Mississippi, University of University	1848 State	3560M 1562W	6000	55%		a. & b. $1160 c. 400	10% $600 45%	1:21	395	$1,228	B.A., B.F.A., B.B.A., B.Mus.; Semester, summer sessions; Business, Engineering, Law, Medicine, Music, Nursing, Pharmacy, Teacher Education; Air Force, Army, Navy ROTC required for two years.
Mississippi College Clinton	1826 Baptist	1098M 956W	2100	90%	21 (comp.)	a. $640 b. 600 d. 60	45% $500 38%	1:23	101	$2,250	B.A., B.S., B.S.Ed., B.Mus., B.Mus.Ed.; Semester, summer sessions; Arts—34%, Sciences—34%, Education—28%, Music—4%; Music, Teacher Education; 6 hours of Bible, chapel thrice weekly required.
Mississippi State College for Women Columbus	1885 State	2618W	4325	50% in top 1/4 97%		a. none b. $614 c. 315 d. 355	40% $450 33%	1:18	136	$189	B.A., B.S., B.F.A., B.Mus., B.Mus.Ed.; Semester; Humanities—25%, Education—23%, Social Sciences—14%, Natural Sciences & Math— 14%, Home Economics—12%, Business—9%, Library Science— 5%; Music; Bi-monthly chapel required.
Mississippi State University State College	1878 State	5806M 1321W	9028	75% in top 1/2 90%	22 (comp.)	a. $342 b. 670 c. 792	37% $800 49%	1:18	270	$442	B.A., B.S.; Semester, summer session; Business & Industry—24%, Engineering—23%, Education—23%, Arts & Sciences—18%, Agriculture—10%, Forestry—2%; Business, Engineering, Teacher Education; Air Force, Army ROTC required for 2 years.
Southern Mississippi, University of Hattiesburg	1912 State	2776M 1780W	8800	86%		a. $276 b. 477 c. 576	10% $50%	1:19	150		B.A., B.S., B.Mus., B.Mus.Ed.; Quarter, summer quarter; Music, Teacher Education; Army ROTC required.
Tougaloo College Tougaloo	1869 United Church of Christ	226M 304W	850	most in top 1/2 80%		a. $500 b. 495	60% $600 Max.	1:15	37		B.A., B.S.; Semester, summer sessions; Coop with Brown U.; 3 hours religion, one chapel per week required.

Institution / Location / Founded / Affiliation	Enrollment M=men W=women	Projected enrollment in 1975	High school rating: % applicants accepted	SAT/ACT Averages m=math v=verbal	Annual Tuition: a. b. Room & Board c. Out of state d. Other	Students with $ aid / Average amount	Faculty-student ratio / % with Doctorates	Volumes in library in 1,000's	Endowment in $1,000's	Undergraduate degrees offered; Calendar; Per cent of students per field of study; Professional programs offered; Miscellaneous
William Carey College Hattiesburg 1906 *Southern Baptist*	482M 330W	1500		M19 W18 (comp.)	a. $420 b. 475 $600-1200	53%	1:18	27	$325	B.A., B.S., B.Mus.; *Semester, summer sessions;* Social Sciences—24%, El. and Phys. Ed.—19%, Natural Sciences & Math—8%, Business—6%, Humanities—28%, Home Ec.—1%; One year of Bible, chapel twice weekly required.

MISSOURI

Institution / Location / Founded / Affiliation	Enrollment M=men W=women	Projected enrollment in 1975	High school rating: % applicants accepted	SAT/ACT Averages m=math v=verbal	Annual Tuition: a. b. Room & Board c. Out of state d. Other	Students with $ aid / Average amount	Faculty-student ratio / % with Doctorates	Volumes in library in 1,000's	Endowment in $1,000's	Undergraduate degrees offered; Calendar; Per cent of students per field of study; Professional programs offered; Miscellaneous
Avila College Kansas City 1916 *Private*	400W	1000	47% in top 1/4 80%	462m 480v	a. $800 b. 900	50% 28%	1:11	48	$100	B.A., B.S.; *Semester, summer session;* Education—24%, Nursing—26%, Humanities—27%, Natural Sciences & Math—19%, Social Sciences—4%.
Central Methodist College Fayette 1854 *Methodist*	537M 412W		80%		$1650 Total	$200-500 32%	1:15	72		B.A., B.S., B.Mus., B.Mus.Ed.; *Semester, summer session; Music;* Coops—3-2 engineering with Mo. School of Mines, Stanford, Vanderbilt, U. of Mo.; 6 hours religion, chapel required.
Central Missouri State College Warrensburg 1871 *State*	4179M 2852W	12000	80%	17m 18v	a. $203 b. 575 $31	12% 45%	1:24	136		B.A., B.S., B.B.A., B. Mus., B.Mus.Ed.; *Quarter, summer session; Music;* Coop—3-2 engineering with Missouri and Kansas Universities.
Culver-Stockton College Canton 1853 *Disciples of Christ*	524M 339W	1000	75% in top 1/2 70%		a. $1090 b. 780 $550 d. 100	30% 28%	1:17	78	$932	B.A., B.S., B.Mus.; *Semester, summer sessions;* Social Sciences—25%, Business—24%, Education—23%, Natural Sciences & Math—16%, Humanities—12%; Coop in engineering with U. of Missouri, 3-1 Medical Technology; Attendance at weekly assembly required.
Drury College Springfield 1873 *United Church of Christ*	620M 490W	1500	45% in top 1/5 81%	M524m 501v W497m 507v	a. $1100 b. 700-800 $600	31% 48%	1:14	89	$3,500	B.A., B.S., B.Mus., B.Mus.Ed.; *Semester, summer sessions;* Social Sciences—34%, Humanities—27%, Education—12%, Business—12%, Natural Sciences & Math—9%; *Teacher Education;* Coops—3-2 engineering, 3-1 medical technology, 3-1 nursing; Weekly chapel required.
Fontbonne College St. Louis 1917 *Roman Catholic*	962W	1200	80%		a. $1200 b. 900-1050 $450 d. 50	30% 21%	1:11	53		B.A., B.Mus.; *Semester, summer session.*
Harris Teachers College St. Louis 1857 *Municipal*	408M 890M	1500	most in top 1/2 65%		c. $700 d. 140 $220	12% 46%	1:22	47		B.A.; *Semester, summer session;* Education—100%; *Teacher Education.*
Kansas City Art Institute Kansas City 1885 *Private*	289M 171W	525	82%		a. $1000 b. 950 d. 200	39% 69% $470	1:12	11	$331	B.F.A.; *Semester;* Painting—36%, Graphics—36%, Sculpture—10%, Ceramics—8%, Industrial Design—10%; *Art;* The Kansas City Art Institute has a collection of 13,000 slides.
Lincoln University Jefferson City 1866 *State*	1223M 887W	4000	75% in top 1/2 96%		a. none b. $600 c. 200 d. 200	60% 25% $527	1:20	80		B.A., B.S., B.S.Ed., B.Mus., B. Mus. Therapy; *Semester, summer session;* Education—65%, Other—35%; *Music;* Army ROTC required.
Lindenwood College St. Charles 1827 *Presbyterian*	800W	850	98% in top 1/2 69%	517m 526v	$2535 Total $600	35% 40%	1:12	60	$8,660	B.A., B.S., B.Mus., B.Mus.Ed.; *Semester (4-1-4);* Humanities—36%, Education—34%, Social Sciences—19%, Natural Sciences & Math—11%; *Music, Teacher Education;* 6 hours religion or philosophy, Sunday vespers required; Junior Year Abroad, Washington Semester, Merrill Palmer, U.N. Seminar.
Marrillac College St. Louis 1937 *Roman Catholic*	369W	450	30% in top 1/5 85%	21 (comp.)	a. $300 b. 150 per mo.	21%	1:7	52	$104	B.A., B.S., B.S.Nursing; *Semester, summer session;* B.A.—52%, B.S.—12%, B.S.N.—36%; *Nursing;* Social Welfare Sequence, American Studies major.
Maryville College of the Sacred Heart St. Louis 1872 *Roman Catholic*	505W	770	36% in top 1/3 75%	514m 518v	a. $1250 b. 1300 $800	30% 35%	1:14	56		B.A., B.S., B.Med.Tech.; *Semester;* Humanities—40%, Social Sciences—30%, Education—16%, Natural Sciences & Math—11%, Med. Tech.—3%.
Missouri, University of Columbia 1839 *State*	11957M 6712W	25000	43% in top 1/5 75%		a. $330 b. 850 $500 c. 500	30% 41%	1:12	1250	$4,306	B.A., B.S., B.Mus.; *Semester, summer session;* Education—19%, Arts & Sciences—31%, Business—4%, Agriculture—7%; *Bus., Eng., For., Jour., Law, Med., Music, Nurs., Psych., Social Work, Teacher Ed., Vet. Med.;* Air Force, Army, Navy ROTC optional.
Missouri, University of Kansas City 1929 *State*	4748M 3143W	14000	44% in top 1/5 87%	505m 513v	a. none b. $850 $100 c. 500 1450 d. 375	10% 58%	1:19	250		B.A., B.S., B.B.A., B.Mus., B.Mus.Ed.; *Semester, summer session; Dentistry, Law, Pharmacy, Teacher Education.*
Missouri, University of St. Louis 1960 *State*	3446M 2357W	12500	30% in top 1/5 35%	22.5m 21.5v	a. $330 b. no dorm $450 c. 500 d. 30	5% 55%	1:24	32		B.A., B.S., B.B.A., B.S.Ed.; *Semester; Business;* The U. of Missouri at St. Louis graduated its first class in June, 1967; Army ROTC optional.
Missouri Valley College Marshall 1889 *Presbyterian*	545M 300W	1200	80% in top 1/2 60%	495m 500v	a. $950 b. 837 $600	50% 45%	1:19	60	$2,000	B.A., B.S., B.Mus.; *Semester, summer session;* Humanities—35%, Social Sciences—40%, Natural Sciences & Math—25%; Coop—3-2 engineering with U. of Missouri.
Northeast Missouri State Teachers College Kirksville 1867 *State*	3017M 2302W	7650	52% in top 1/3 75%	M20 W19 (comp.)	a. $140 b. 600 $606 c. 201	21% 41%	1:24	151		B.S.—18%, B.A.—2%, B.S.Ed.—53%, B.Mus.; *Quarter, summer session; Music, Teacher Education;* 3-2 engineering with U. of Mo., 3-2 osteopathy Kirksville College of O. & S.
Northwest Missouri State College Maryville 1905 *State*	2200M 1600W	6200	85%		a. none b. $650 $200 c. 200 d. 200	25% 30%	1:20	85		B.A., B.S., B.S.Ed., B.S.Med.Tech.; *Semester, summer session.*

Institution / Location / Founded / Affiliation	Enrollment M=men W=women	Projected enrollment in 1975	High school rating; % applicants accepted	SAT/ACT Averages m=math v=verbal	Annual Tuition; a. b. Room & Board; c. Out of state; d. Other	% Students with $ aid; Average amount	Faculty-student ratio; % with Doctorates	Volumes in library in 1,000's	Endowment in $1,000's	Undergraduate degrees offered; Calendar; Per cent of students per field of study; Professional programs offered; Miscellaneous
Park College Parkville 1875 *Presbyterian*	390M 188W	1200			a. $1210 b. 870 d. 150	65% $550	1:13 30%	72	$3,500	B.A.; *Semester;* Social Sciences—55%, Natural Sciences & Math—25%, Education—11%, Humanities—9%.
Rockhurst College Kansas City 1910 *Roman Catholic*	995M	1500	32% in top 1/4 77%		a. $950 b. 800	30%	1:12 28%	45		B.A., B.S.; *Semester, summer sessions;* Arts—35%, Sciences—30%, Business—35%.
Saint Louis University St. Louis 1818 *Roman Catholic*	4191M 2181W	7190	42% in top 1/5 65%	M24.0m 23.2v W22.5m 23.4v	a. $1400 b. 1000	28% $1100	1:6 72%	800	$20,228	B.A., B.S.; *Semester, summer sessions;* Humanities—34%, Social Sciences—37%, Natural Sciences & Math—29%; *Bus., Dent., Eng., Law, Med., Nurs., Phys. Ther., Social Work. Teacher Ed.;* 8 hours religion, annual retreat required of Catholic freshman & transfers; AF ROTC optional
Southeast Missouri State College Cape Girardeau 1873 *State*	3189M 2602W	7500	70%		a. $160 b. 600 c. 440	8% $325	1:22 30%	122		B.A., B.S., B.Mus.Ed., B.S.B.A., B.S.Ed., B.S. Nursing, A.A.Nursing, A.A.Data Processing; *Semester, summer sessions;* Education—66%, Business—15%, Natural Sciences & Math—10%, Arts—3%; *Teacher Education;* Coop in education with U. of Missouri.
Southwest Missouri State College Springfield 1905 *State*	3186M 2575W	11200	83% in top 2/3 94%		a. $200 b. 660 c. 280	16% $420	1:21 27%	156		B.A., B.S., B.F.A., B.Mus., B.S.Ed.; *Semester, summer session;* Humanities—28%, Social Sciences—20%, Education—19%, Business—20%, Natural Sciences & Math—13%; *Teacher Education;* Coop in education with U. of Missouri; Army ROTC required.
Stephens College Columbia 1833 *Private*	1950W	2300	25% in top 1/5 60%		$2900 Total	25% $100-1500	1:13 20%	75	$1,100	A.A., B.A., B.F.A.; *Semester, summer session (for B.F.A. candidates only); Music;* Attendance at weekly vespers services required; Summer Seminars Abroad, cooperating member Mid-Missouri Associated Colleges.
Tarkio College Tarkio 1883 *Presbyterian*	589M 195W	1300	most in top 3/5 75%	18 (comp.)	$2015 Total	35%	1:18 28%	42	$280	B.A.; *Trimester, summer session; Medical Technology;* 7 hours religion, daily assembly attendance required.
Washington University St. Louis 1853 *Private*	2148M 1535W	4200	75% in top 1/5 67%	630m 600v	a. $1900 b. 1125	33% $1200	1:8 80%	940	$125,000	A.B., B.S., B.F.A., B.S.B.A., B.Arch.; *Semester, summer sessions;* Arch.—5%, Arts & Sciences—67%, Business—5%, Engineering—12%, Fine Arts—8%, Nursing, Occupational & Phys. Therapy—3%; *Dentistry, Law, Medicine, Social Work, Teacher Education;* Air Force, Army ROTC optional.
Webster College St. Louis 1915 *Roman Catholic*	65M 850W	1500	40% in top 1/5 80%	498m 535v	a. $1280 b. 1100	40% $100-800	1:10 25%	32		B.A., B.Mus., B.Mus.Ed.; *Semester, summer session;* Humanities—46%, Education—11%, Social Science—33%, Natural Science—10%; *Music.*
Westminster College Fulton 1851 *Presbyterian*	650M	1000	40% in top 1/4 70%	550m 520v	a. $1600 b. 900	35% $800	1:12 65%	80	$2,500	B.A.; *Semester, summer session;* Natural Sciences & Math—35%, Social Sciences—30%, Humanities—35%; 6 semester hours religion, comprehensive tests, forum attendance requirement.
William Jewell College Liberty 1849 *Baptist*	612M 406W	1200	62% in top 1/4 60%	585m 590v 22.5 (comp.)	a. $1150 b. 800	40% $365	1:15 40%	92	$4,247	B.A., B.S.; *Semester, summer session;* Social Sciences—31%, Humanities—14%, Natural Sciences & Math—11%, Education—8%, Business—6%; Coops—3-2 engineering with Columbia, U. of Missouri, 3-2 forestry with Duke.
William Woods College Fulton 1870 *Private*	720W	900	33% in top 1/4 25%		$2550 Total	20% $500	1:11 33%	28	$600	B.A., B.S.; *Semester;* Coop with Westminster College (also in Fulton).

MONTANA

Institution / Location / Founded / Affiliation	Enrollment M=men W=women	Projected enrollment in 1975	High school rating; % applicants accepted	SAT/ACT Averages m=math v=verbal	Annual Tuition; a. b. Room & Board; c. Out of state; d. Other	% Students with $ aid; Average amount	Faculty-student ratio; % with Doctorates	Volumes in library in 1,000's	Endowment in $1,000's	Undergraduate degrees offered; Calendar; Per cent of students per field of study; Professional programs offered; Miscellaneous
Carroll College Helena 1909 *Roman Catholic*	464M 394W	1500	40% in top 1/4 86%M 97%W		a. $750 b. 660 c. 50	50% $900	1:15 18%	38	$2,500	B.A., B.S.; *Semester, summer session;* Social Sciences—39%, Natural Sciences & Math—22%, Humanities—25%, Elementary Education—14%; Coop—3-2 engineering with Notre Dame, Montana State, Gonzaga U.
College of Great Falls Great Falls 1932 *Roman Catholic*	498M 329W	1200	25% in top 1/4 80%	M20 W22 (comp.)	a. $800 b. 700	40% $250	1:20 25%	41	$87	B.A., B.S.; *Semester, summer sessions;* Grants totaling $203,800 since 1960.
Eastern Montana College Billings 1927 *State*	1586M 1255W	3114	95%	19.8 (comp.)	a. $330 b. 715 c. 937 d. 150	25% $100-900	1:25 30%	79		B.A., B.S.; *Quarter, summer sessions; Teacher Education, Biology, Chemistry, Math., Gen. Business, English, History.*
Montana, University of Missoula 1893 *State*	3472M 1826W	7753	85%	21.5m 20.9v	a. $359 b. 775 c. 967	21% $280	1:17 59%	400	$1,218	B.A., B.S., B.F.A., B.Mus.; *Quarter, summer quarter;* Liberal Arts—48%, Business—15%, Education—12%, Forestry—10%; *Business, Forestry, Journalism, Law, Music, Pharmacy, Teacher Education;* Air Force, Army ROTC optional.
Montana College of Mineral Science & Technology Butte 1893 *State*	502M 114W	998	41% in top 1/3 92%		a. none b. $765 c. 873 d. 265	33% $440	1:15 28%	35	$5	B.S.; *Semester;* Petroleum Engineering—8%, Geological—18%, Minerals—18%, Mining—14%, Metallurgical—5%, Engineering Sciences—14%, Geophysics—5%, Mineral Dressing—18%; *Engineering.*
Montana State University Bozeman 1893 *State*	4096M 2192W	8200	51% in top 1/3 90%		a. $375 b. 812 c. 982	15% $555	1:18 47%	400	$2,900	B.A., B.S.; *Quarter, summer sessions;* Agriculture—11%, Business—12%, Education—10%, Engineering—15%, Nat. Sciences & Math.—13%, Soc. Sciences—8%, Other—31%; *Architecture, Engineering, Nursing, Teacher Education;* Air Force, Army ROTC optional.
Northern Montana College Havre 1929 *State*	870M 418W	2125	50% in top 1/3 90%		a. $335 b. 725 c. 942	30% $210	1:19 18%	35		B.S.; *Quarter, summer session;* Teacher Education—55%, Assoc. degrees in Engineering Tech. and Nursing—10%, 2-year certificates & diplomas—35%.

Institution / Location / Founded / Affiliation	Enrollment M=men W=women	Projected enrollment in 1975	High school rating; % applicants accepted	SAT/ACT Averages m=math v=verbal	Annual Tuition; a. b. Room & Board; c. Out of State; d. Other	% Students with $ aid / Average amount	Faculty-student ratio; % with Doctorates	Volumes in library in 1,000's	Endowment in $1,000's	Undergraduate degrees offered; *Calendar*; Per cent of students per field of study; *Professional programs offered*; Miscellaneous
Rocky Mountain College Billings 1883 *Methodist, Presbyterian, United Church of Christ*	303M 179W	1090	95% in top 1/2 85%	20m 21v	a. $900 b. 750 d. 100	45% $500	1:14 50%	37	$830	B.A., B.S.; *Semester*; Arts—50%, Sciences—50%.
Western Montana College Dillon 1897 *State*	303M 179W	1090			a. $286 b. 630 c. 894		1:22 20%	32		B.S.; *Quarter, summer sessions*; Education—100%; *Teacher Education*.

NEBRASKA

Institution / Location / Founded / Affiliation	Enrollment M=men W=women	Projected enrollment in 1975	High school rating; % applicants accepted	SAT/ACT Averages m=math v=verbal	Annual Tuition; a. b. Room & Board; c. Out of State; d. Other	% Students with $ aid / Average amount	Faculty-student ratio; % with Doctorates	Volumes in library in 1,000's	Endowment in $1,000's	Undergraduate degrees offered; *Calendar*; Per cent of students per field of study; *Professional programs offered*; Miscellaneous
Chadron State College Chadron 1911 *State*	1029M 756W	3622	20% in top 1/5		a. $250 b. 696 c. 400 d. 20	33% $600	1:18 25%	80		B.A., B.S.; *Semester, summer sessions*; Education—80%, Liberal Arts—20%, English & Speech—19%, Natural Science & Math—24%, Social Science—13%, Business—10%, H & PE—13%, Ind. Arts—10%, Music—5%; *Teacher Education*.
Concordia Teachers College Seward 1894 *Lutheran*	540M 716W	2300	25% in top 1/4 75%		a. $635 b. 735	15% $150	1:14 30%	42		B.S.Ed.; *Semester, summer sessions*; Teacher Education—95%, General Studies—5%.
Creighton University Omaha 1878 *Roman Catholic*	1539M 1051W	4600	55% in top 1/4 89%	M25.2m 21.6v W22.0m 23.2v	a. $1070 b. 950	25% $331	1:15 40%	232	$5,270	B.A., B.S.; *Semester, summer session*; Social Science—21%, Business—20%, Humanities—32%, Natural Sciences & Math—11%, Nursing—6%, Education—3%; *Business, Dentistry, Law, Medicine, Nursing, Pharmacy, Teacher Education*; 4 semesters theology required for Catholic students; Army ROTC required.
Dana College Blair 1899 *Lutheran*	482M 329W	1500	25% in top 1/5 85%	22.2 (comp.)	a. $800 b. 700 d. 160	40% $50- 400	1:18 25%	50	$230	B.A., B.S.; *Semester, summer sessions*; Education—58%, Business—15%, Social Work—14%, Sciences—13%; *Teacher Education*; 6 hours of religion courses required.
Doane College Crete 1872 *United Church of Christ*	430M 230W	1000	95% in top 3/5 81%	M520 W490 (comp.)	a. $1050 b. 730 d. 170	54% $100- 800	1:15 35%	52	$4,077	B.A.; *Semester, summer sessions*; Coop—3-2 engineering with Columbia, 3-2 forestry with Duke, semester abroad program at University of Copenhagen, Denmark; 9 hours religion & philosophy, weekly chapel attendance required.
Duchesne College of the Sacred Heart Omaha 1881 *Roman Catholic*	416W	700	most in top 1/3 80%		a. $825 b. 975	33% $170	1:10 33%	35		B.A., B.S.; *Semester, summer session*; Humanities—27%, Social Sciences—27%, Natural Sciences & Math—13%, Nursing—11%, Home Economics—8%; 12 semester hours of theology required.
Hastings College Hastings 1882 *Presbyterian*	410M 340W	1000	24% in top 1/10 85%	524m 498v	a. $1150 b. 760 d. 100	60% $100- 800	1:13 50%	60	$2,500	B.A., B.Mus.; *Semester, summer session*; Social Sciences—33%, Humanities—29%, Natural Sciences & Math—18%, Physical Education—6%, Business—4%; *Music*; 4 hours religion, weekly chapel required.
Kearney State College Kearney 1905 *State*	2509M 1890W	9421	62% in top 1/2 97%		a. $250 b. 696 c. 400 d. 20	15% $500	1:21 30%	71	$60,000	B.A., B.S., B.A.Ed., B.S.Ed.; *Semester, summer session*; Education—90%, Liberal Arts—10%; *Teacher Education*; Coop—3-2 programs with the University of Nebraska in Law and Medical Technology.
Midland Lutheran College Fremont 1883 *Lutheran*	504M 381W	1400	40% in top 1/4 88%	22 (comp.)	a. $825 b. 685 d. 160	60% $400	1:15 28%	50	$640	B.A., B.S., B.S.Ed., B.S.B.A.; *Semester, summer session*; Humanities—30%, Social Sciences—29%, Business—18%, Natural Sciences & Math—18%, Physical Education—5%; *Teacher Education*.
Nebraska, University of Lincoln 1869 (M & W) *State*	17054	20000	48% in top 1/4 95%		a. $334 b. 725 c. 860	15% $304	1:18 65%	863	$10,000	B.A., B.S., B.F.A., B.Mus.; *Semester, summer session*; Architecture, Business, Dentistry, Engineering, Journalism, Law, Medicine, Music, Pharmacy, Psychology, Social Work, Teacher Education, Dental Hygiene, Medical Technology, Agriculture, Home Economics; *Air Force, Army, Navy ROTC optional*.
Nebraska Wesleyan University Lincoln 1887 *Methodist*	732M 741W	1700	48% in top 1/4 80%	535m 521v	a. $950 b. 775	39% $300	1:14 43%	83	$3,200	B.A., B.S., B.A.Ed., B.Mus., B.Mus.Ed.; *Semester, summer session*; Education—34%, Natural Sciences & Math—24%, Humanities—19%, Social Sciences—10%, Business—13%; *Music, Teacher Education*; 3-2 Engineering with Columbia, U.C.L.A. Latin American Studies.
Municipal University of Omaha Omaha 1909 *Municipal*	6142M 2940W	11000	20% in top 1/4 87%		a. $600 b. no dorms c. 820	20% $125	1:28 44%	300	$80	B.A., B.S., B.B.A., B.S.Ed., B. of General Studies; *Semester, summer sessions*; Air Force ROTC optional.
Peru State College Peru 1867 *State*	665M 376W	1800	55% in top 1/2 85%		a. $270 b. 650 c. 420 d. 50	30% $250	1:17 20%	75		B.A., B.S., B.S.Ed.; *Semester, summer sessions*; Education—90%, Liberal Arts—10%; *Teacher Education*.
Union College Lincoln 1891 *Seventh-day Adventist*	613M 588W	1400	93%		a. $1080 b. 700	50% $100	1:17 25%	70		B.A., B.S.; *Semester, summer session*; Business—15%, Education—15%, Home Economics—10%, Natural Sciences—8%, Health Science—20%, Religion—13%; *Nursing, Teacher Education*; 12 semester hours of Bible courses, chapel attendance required.
Wayne State College Wayne 1910 *State*	1408M 1282W	4000	65% in top 1/2		a. $250 b. 580 c. 400 d. 40	12% $200	1:20 34%	75	$3	B.A., B.S., B.F.A., B.Mus.Ed.; *Quarter, summer session*; Education—90%, Liberal Arts—10%; *Teacher Education*.

NEVADA

Institution / Location / Founded / Affiliation	Enrollment M=men W=women	Projected enrollment in 1975	High school rating; % applicants accepted	SAT/ACT Averages m=math v=verbal	Annual Tuition; a. b. Room & Board; c. Out of State; d. Other	% Students with $ aid / Average amount	Faculty-student ratio; % with Doctorates	Volumes in library in 1,000's	Endowment in $1,000's	Undergraduate degrees offered; *Calendar*; Per cent of students per field of study; *Professional programs offered*; Miscellaneous
Nevada, University of Reno 1874 *State*	4225M 2747W	10350	35% in top 1/5 83%	M21.5m 18.9v W17.0m 20.5v	a. $350 b. 820 c. 600	25% $200	1:16 56%	278	$2,138	B.A., B.S.; *Semester, summer session*; Education—13%, Engineering—21%, Agriculture—11%, Home Ec.—9%, Arts & Sciences—13%, Bus. Adm.—10%, Mines—19%, Nursing—13%; *Business, Engineering, Nursing, Teacher Education*; Army ROTC required for two years.
Nevada Southern University Las Vegas 1951 *State*	1595M 1297W	5500	39% in top 1/5 61%	M19.5m 19.6v W17.4m 21.6v	a. $322 b. 820 c. 600	20% $260	1:20 49%	75		B.A., B.S., A.A.; *Semester, summer session*; Business—26%, Education—23%, Natural Sciences & Math—22%, Social Sciences—11%, Humanities—8%, Fine Arts—6%, 2-year Assoc.—4%; *Nursing*; Nevada Southern is the Las Vegas campus of the University of Nevada.

Institution / Location / Founded / Affiliation	Enrollment M=men W=women	Projected enrollment in 1975	High school rating; % applicants accepted	SAT/ACT Averages m=math v=verbal	a. Annual Tuition; b. Room & Board; c. Out of state; d. Other	% Students with $ aid / Average amount	Faculty-student ratio; % with Doctorates	Volumes in library in 1,000's	Endowment in $1,000's	Undergraduate degrees offered; Calendar; Per cent of students per field of study; Professional programs offered; Miscellaneous
NEW HAMPSHIRE										
Dartmouth College Hanover 1769 *Private*	3110M	3100	86% in top 1/5 25%	681m 642v	a. $2075 b. 1000 d. 475	29% $1350	1:9 77%	937	$102,059	A.B.; 3-term, 3-course system, summer session; Social Sciences—47%, Natural Sciences & Math—22%, Humanities—20%, Business Administration—4%, Other—5%; Business, Engineering, Medicine; Air Force, Army, Navy ROTC optional.
Keene State College Keene 1909 *State*	712M 838W	2500	85% in top 2/5 35%	496m 472v	a. $300 b. 750 c. 800 d. 55	22% $410	1:21 25%	38		B.A., B.S., B. Ed.; Semester summer session & extension program; B. Education—82% (Elementary Ed., Secondary Ed., Home Ec., Industrial Arts), B.A. and B.S.—18% (History, Math, Psychology, English, Biology).
Mount Saint Mary College Hooksett 1934 *Roman Catholic*	300W	500	30% in top 1/4 60%		a. $1100 b. 1000 d. 100	20% $500	1:9 20%	26	$213	B.A.; Semester, summer session; Elementary Education—36%, Humanities—22%, Social Sciences—16%, Business—8%, Natural Sciences & Math—15%, Home Economics—3%; Coop with St. Anselm's College, Manchester, N.H.
New Hampshire, University of Durham 1866 *State*	3029M 2294W	5722	64% in top 1/5 36%	M583m 528v W541m 550v	a. $536 b. 780 c. 1375 d. 115	28% $590	1:13 43%	421	$3,718	B.A., B.S.; Semester, summer sessions; Social Sciences—24%, Humanities—17%, Engineering—12%, Natural Sciences & Math—21%, Education—10%, Agriculture—2%, Other—14%; Air Force, Army ROTC optional.
Plymouth State College Plymouth 1871 *State*	537M 843W	2000	87% in top 1/2 43%	501m 475v	a. $345 b. 750 c. 845 d. 150	35% $400 av.	1:19 29%	36		B.A., B.S.; Semester, summer session; Education—57%, Social Sciences—22%, Natural Sciences & Math—12%, Humanities—9%; Teacher Education.
Rivier College Nashua 1933 *Private*	470W	700	70% in top 2/5	500m 520v	a. $950 b. 850 d. 200	35% $400	1:11 25%	54		B.A., B.S.; Semester.
St. Anselm's College Manchester 1889 *Roman Catholic*	1116M 170W	1400	50%	500m 500v	a. $1400 b. 800	23% $400	1:13	66		B.A., B.S.; Semester; Social Sciences—53%, Natural Sciences & Math—35%, Humanities—12%; Nursing; Theology required of Catholic students, Catholic services available on campus.
NEW JERSEY										
Bloomfield College Bloomfield 1868 *Presbyterian*	650M 250W	1800	65% in top 2/5 50%	M510m 490v W480m 500v	a. $1080 b. 850	20% $173	1:17 30%	30	$1,050	B.A.; Semester, summer session; Social Sciences—44%, Business—20%, Humanities—22%, Natural Sciences & Math—14%.
Caldwell College for Women Caldwell 1939 *Roman Catholic*	725W	1050	68% in top 2/5 60%	500m 510v	$2,000 Total	25% $320	1:11 22%	48		B.A., B.S.; Semester, summer session (for Sisters only); Humanities—44%, Natural Sciences and Math—20%, Social Science—36%; Elementary, Secondary Education, Library Science, Medical Tech.
College of St. Elizabeth Convent Station 1899 *Roman Catholic*	944W	1182	44% in top 1/5 50%	520m 548v	a. $900 b. 1000 c. 75	14% $590	1:11 25%	45		B.A., B.S.; Semester, summer session (for Sisters only); Humanities—35%, Social Sciences—24%, Natural Sciences—23%, Home Economics—14%; W.K. Kellogg Foundation grant of $10,000, N.S.F. matching grant of $9,220.
Douglass College of Rutgers University New Brunswick 1918 *State*	2700W				a. $400 b. 800 c. 636	45%		130		A.B., B.S.; Semester, summer session; Music; Douglass students may take part in university activities & course offerings of Rutgers.
Drew University Madison 1866 *Methodist*	505M 563W	1200	56% in top 1/5 58%	572m 588v	a. $1650 b. 925 d. 100	26% $100-1650	1:14 66%	300	$13,513	B.A.; Semesters; Social Sciences—40%, Humanities—31%, Natural Sciences—29%; Theology; Coop-3-2 engineering with N.Y.U., & forestry with Duke U.; Brussels & London semesters, Washington Semester, United Nations and World Trade Semester in New York City.
Fairleigh Dickinson University Rutherford 1941 *Private*	3678M 2337W	8000	90% in top 1/2 60%		a. $1250 b. 1135	18% $200-1250	1:15 50%	350	$11,000	B.A., B.S.; Semester, summer sessions; Liberal Arts—57%, Education—18%, Business Administration—13%, Engineering—12%; Dentistry, Engineering, Nursing; Wroxton College in England for a Junior Year Abroad program; Summer program Cuernavaca, Mexico, Florence, Italy; Marine Biology St. Croix, Virgin Islands.
Georgian Court College Lakewood 1908 *Roman Catholic*	560W	900	52% in top 1/5 40%	550m 588v	a. $1200 b. 1035	18% $200-1375	1:12 48%	52		B.A., B.S.; Semester, summer session; Social Sciences—30%, Humanities—52%, Natural Sciences—18%; 14 credits in theology required.
Glassboro State College Glassboro 1923 *State*	1000M 2000W	8400	50% in top 1/4 33%	500m 500v	a. $150 b. 650	35% $450	1:10 65%	75		B.A.; Semester, summer session; Education—68%, Humanities—17%, Natural Sciences—7%, Social Sciences—8%; Teacher Education—100%.
Jersey City State College Jersey City 1927 *State*	800M 2000W	6200	90% in top 1/2 40%		a. $150 b. 818 d. 96	45% $400	1:16 33%	83		B.A.; Semester, summer session; Education—64%, Humanities—12%, Natural Sciences—13%, Social Sciences—11%; Teacher Education; Coop in nursing education with hospitals in Jersey City.
Monmouth College West Long Branch 1933 *Private*	2944M 1681W	6000	84% in top 1/2* 60%	498m 502v *	a. $1184 b. 900	20% $200-2200	1:25 29%	75	$105	B.A., B.S.; Semester; Sciences—70%, Arts—30%; Monmouth has some two-year academic programs which grant an A.A. *Liberal Arts Programs
Montclair State College Montclair 1908 *State*	1487M 2515W	8700	67% in top 1/5 33%	538m 542v	a. $150 b. 818 d. 100	22% $250	1:16 48%	90	$125	B.A.; Semester, summer session; Humanities—32%, Natural Sciences—20%, Social Sciences—13%, Physical Ed.—10%, Home Economics—8%, Industrial Arts—7%, Business—5%; Teacher Education.
Newark College of Engineering Newark 1881 *State & Municipal*	3760M 34W	5000		622m 509v	a. $440 b. 700 c. 826	10% $125	1:10 30%	50	$122	B.S.; Semester, summer session; Engineering—100%; Engineering; Air Force ROTC optional; Out of state candidates must be in top 1/10 of H.S. class and have S.A.T. scores of 650m, 550v.

Institution / Location — Founded / Affiliation	Enrollment M=men W=women	Projected enrollment in 1975	High school rating; % applicants accepted	SAT/ACT Averages m=math v=verbal	a. Annual Tuition; b. Room & Board; c. Out of state; d. Other state.	% Students with $ aid / Average amount	Faculty-student ratio; % with Doctorates	Volumes in library in 1,000's	Endowment in $1,000's	Undergraduate degrees offered; Calendar; Per cent of students per field of study; Professional programs offered; Miscellaneous
Newark State College Union 1855 — *State*	625M 2471W	7900	51% in top 1/4 54%	489m 509v	a. $150 b. 818	13% $450	1:16 36%	70		B.A.; *Semester; Teacher Education.*
Paterson State College Wayne 1855 — *State*	896M 3111W		33%		a. $289 b. 818	25%	1:16	80		B.A.; *Semester, summer session; Teacher Education—100%; Teacher Education.*
Princeton University Princeton 1746 — *Private*	3240M 3500		70% in top 1/10 20%	681m 640v	a. $1950 b. 1160	44% $1850	1:5 82%	2100	$136,905	B.A., B.S. Engineering; *Semester;* Liberal Arts—85%, Engineering—15%; *Architecture, Engineering & Applied Science, Woodrow Wilson School of Public & International Affairs;* Hosts for "Coop. Undergraduate Program for Critical Languages"; Washington Summer Intern program; A.F., A., N. ROTC optional.
Rider College Trenton 1865 — *Private*	2102M 1192W	4020	85% in top 2/5 40%	500m 500v	a. $1120 b. 1000 d. 280	12% $750	1:18 38%	125	$309	B.A., B.S., A.A.; *Semester, summer session;* Accounting—11%, Bus. Adm.—45%, Bus. Ed.—5%, Humanities—3%, Natural Sciences—3%, Secondary Ed.—4%, Secretarial—3%, Social Sciences—4%; *Business.*
Rutgers—The State University New Brunswick 1766 — *State*	5800M 7000		27%		a. $475 b. 900 c. 636 d. 126	35%	1:14 50%	1250		B.A., B.S.; *Semester, summer session; Business, Engineering, Journalism, Library, Nursing, Pharmacy, Social Work, Teacher Education;* Air Force, Army ROTC optional.
Saint Peter's College Jersey City 1872 — *Roman Catholic*	2900M 400W	5500	80% in top 1/3 50%	565m 545v	a. $1065 d. 90	30% $300	1:13 52%	74	$400	B.A., B.S.; *Three-term, summer session;* Social Sciences—30%, Humanities—16%, Natural Sciences—28%, Business—26%; Coop —3-2 engineering with University of Detroit; Army ROTC required.
Seton Hall University South Orange 1856 — *Roman Catholic*	4194M 120W	7843	56%	525m 501v	a. $960 b. 850 d. 100	$320- 800	1:14 39%	199		B.A., B.S.; *Semester, summer sessions; Humanities, Business, Physical Science, Social Science, Asian Studies, Sp. Ed.; Law, Nursing;* 2-4 semesters of religion required; Army ROTC optional.
Stevens Institute of Technology Hoboken 1870 — *Private*	1210M 1600		75% in top 1/4 55%	670m 570v	a. $1800 b. 920	55% $715	1:19 71%	58	$35,600	B.S. B. Engineering; *Semester, summer session;* Engineering—75%, Science—25%; *Engineering;* Army ROTC optional.
Trenton State College Trenton 1855 — *State*	966M 2313W	8500	70% in top 1/4 45%		a. $150 b. 818	33% $500	1:16 34%	150		B.A.; *Semester, summer session;* Education—98%, Liberal Arts—2%; *Teacher Education (M.A.T.).*
Upsala College East Orange 1893 — *Lutheran*	819M 709W	1800	53% in top 1/5	538m 530v	a. $1500 b. 850	20% $550	1:16 52%	100	$744	B.A., B.S.; *Semester, summer session;* Social Sciences—24%, Humanities—33%, Business & Accounting—25%, Natural Sciences —18%.

NEW MEXICO

Institution / Location — Founded / Affiliation	Enrollment M=men W=women	Projected enrollment in 1975	High school rating; % applicants accepted	SAT/ACT Averages m=math v=verbal	a. Annual Tuition; b. Room & Board; c. Out of state; d. Other state.	% Students with $ aid / Average amount	Faculty-student ratio; % with Doctorates	Volumes in library in 1,000's	Endowment in $1,000's	Undergraduate degrees offered; Calendar; Per cent of students per field of study; Professional programs offered; Miscellaneous
Albuquerque University of Albuquerque 1940 — *Roman Catholic*	775M 384W	1500	80% in top 1/2 65%		a. $900 b. 875	70% $800	1:15 20%	40		B.A., B.S.; *Semester, summer session;* Education—46%, Arts—22%, Business—24%, Sciences—7%, Medical Technology—1%; 3-2 Engineering program with U. of N. Mexico, N.M. State U., Purdue U.; Associate degree program began September 1967.
Eastern New Mexico University Portales 1934 — *State*	2400M 1600W	7500	90%		a. $320 b. 700 c. 720	33% $400	1:20 40%	150		B.A., B.S., Ed.S.; *Semester, summer session; Music, Teacher Education, Chemistry, Technology.*
New Mexico, University of Albuquerque 1889 — *State*	7958M 5021W	17500	80% in top 1/2 82%	22 (comp.)	a. $404 b. 808 c. 918	30% $400	1:21 66%	478	$395	B.A., B.S., B.B.A., B.F.A., B.Arch.; *Semester, summer session; Engineering, Journalism, Law, Medicine, Music, Nursing, Pharmacy, Teacher Education;* Air Force, Navy ROTC optional.
New Mexico Highlands University Las Vegas 1893 — *State*	1100M 600W	2000	25% in top 1/4 73%		a. $255 b. 228 c. 615	50% $500	1:20 55%	90		A.A., A.S., B.A., B.S.; *Quarter, summer sessions.*
New Mexico Institute of Mining and Technology Socorro 1889 — *State*	436M 117W	1500	85% in top 1/4 80%	580m 500v	a. $180 b. 700 c. 600 d. 91	35% $220	1:13 83%	55	$850	B.S.; *Semester, summer session;* Natural Sciences & Math—76%, Metallurgy—7%, Mining—7%, Petroleum—7%, Geography—3%.
New Mexico State University University Park 1888 — *State*	678M 363W	10000	100% in top 1/2 96%	M21.7m 18.7v W18.3m 21.1v	a. $260 b. 780 c. 510	48% $647	1:20 58%	180		B.A., B.S., B.F.A., B.Mus.Ed.; *Semester, summer sessions;* Engineering—32%, Arts & Sciences—26%, Education—18%, Agriculture & Home Economics—13%, Business—11%; *Engineering; Teacher Education;* Air Force, Army ROTC required.
St. John's College Santa Fe 1964 — *Private*	84M 55W	375	70% in top 1/5 71%	M597m 628v W514m 645v	a. $1950 b. 1050	35% $1327	1:8 41%		$32	B.A.; *Semester;* 4-year non-elective curriculum requires students to read and discuss Great Books of the Western World, Study Math., Lab. Sci., Lang., Mus.; Shares curriculum, governing board, President with St. John's College, Annapolis, Md.
Western New Mexico University Silver City 1893 — *State*	659M 498W	1715	80%		a. $130 b. 700 c. 310 d. 110	65% $50- 400	1:19 40%	50		B.A., B.S.; *Semester, summer sessions; Teacher Education.*

NEW YORK

Institution / Location — Founded / Affiliation	Enrollment M=men W=women	Projected enrollment in 1975	High school rating; % applicants accepted	SAT/ACT Averages m=math v=verbal	a. Annual Tuition; b. Room & Board; c. Out of state; d. Other state.	% Students with $ aid / Average amount	Faculty-student ratio; % with Doctorates	Volumes in library in 1,000's	Endowment in $1,000's	Undergraduate degrees offered; Calendar; Per cent of students per field of study; Professional programs offered; Miscellaneous
Adelphi University Garden City 1896 — *Private*	3731M 3205W	10000	38% M, 59% W in top 1/5 64%	M546m 513v W523m 524v	a. $1500 b. 1100 d. 110	20% $200- 1200	1:15 53%	150	$650	B.A., B.S., B.B.A., B.S. Ed.; *Semester, summer session;* Arts—63%, Business—21%, Science—11%, Education—5%; *Nursing;* Coop-3-2 engineering and architecture with Massachusetts Institute of Technology.

Institution Location	Founded Affiliation	Enrollment M=men W=women	Projected enrollment in 1975	High school rating; % applicants accepted	SAT/ACT Averages m=math v=verbal	a. Annual Tuition; b. Room & Board; c. Out of state; d. Other	% Students with $ aid Average amount	Faculty-student ratio; % with Doctorates	Volumes in library in 1,000's	Endowment in $1,000's	Undergraduate degrees offered; *Calendar;* Per cent of students per field of study; *Professional programs offered; Miscellaneous*
Alfred University Alfred	1836 *Private and Public*	1025M 475W	1600	57% in top 1/4 60%	M585m 510v W565m 570v	a. $1700 b. 950 d. 75	20% *$912* 50%	1:12	122	$5,900	B.A., B.S., B.F.A.; *Semester, summer session;* Liberal Arts—60%, Ceramic Science & Eng.—24%, Nursing—10%, Ceramic Art—6%; *Teacher Education;* Coop—3-2 engineering with Columbia University; Washington Semester; Army ROTC required two years; NSF grant of $58,170 since 1960.
Bard College Annandale-on-Hudson	1860 *Private*	307M 298W	650	62% in top 2/5 69%	M565m 600v W530m 600v	a. $2080 b. 920 d. 188	20% *$1200* 45%	1:11	91	$429	B.A.; *Semester, seven-week field period, Jan.-Feb.;* Languages & Literature—18%, Art/Music/Drama/Dance—32%, Social Sciences —40%, Natural Sciences & Math—10%; Coop—3-2 engineering with Columbia; NSF research grants totaling $14,000 since 1960.
Barnard College New York	1889 *Private*	1800W	2000	90% in top 1/5 45%	640m 679v	a. $1800 b. 1150	20% *$1400*	1:10	100+ Columbia lib.	$14,000	B.A.; *Semester;* Humanities—41%, Social Sciences—33%, Natural Sciences—26%; Coops with Columbia whereby a Barnard student can enter a professional school after 3 years and receive her B.A. after completion of first year graduate work.
Briarcliff College Briarcliff Manor	1903 *Independent*	675W	1000	25%	527m 537v	$3150 Total	5% *$400* 40%	1:13	37		A.B., B.S., A.A.; *Semester;* Humanities—55%, Sciences—45%; *Certification to teach first six grades.*
Canisius College Buffalo	1870 *Roman Catholic*	2198M 413W	3500	60% in top 1/5	574m 540v	a. $1250 b. 1100 d. 250	51%	1:13	115	$559	B.A., B.S.; *Semester, summer session;* Humanities—40%, Social Sciences—20%, Business Admin.—20%, Natural Sciences—20%; Coop—engineering with Detroit Univ.; Army ROTC required.
City University of New York— Brooklyn College Brooklyn	1930 *City*	5448M 6350W	17600		M621m 557v W568m 554v	a. none b. no dorm c. $425 d. 200	10% *$225* 80%	1:10	462	$146	B.A., B.S.; *Semester, summer session;* Social Sciences—24%, Liberal Arts—21%, Natural Sciences & Math.—32%, Education— 23%; Air Force ROTC optional.
City University of New York— City College New York	1847 *City*	11885M 4790W	18000			a. none b. no dorm c. $400 d. 100 fee	95%	1:15	800	$2,000	B.A., B.S.; *Semester, summer session;* Architecture, Business, Engineering, Teacher Education; Coop—pre-engineering students from other C.U.N.Y. units transfer to C.C.N.Y. after sophomore year; Army ROTC optional.
City University of New York— Hunter College New York	1870 *City*	2504M 7297W	8200*			a. none b. no dorm c. $400 d. 60 fee	10% *$600* 95%	1:19	362		A.B., B.S., B.F.A.; *Semester, summer session;* Nursing, Social Work, Teacher Education. *Separation of two campuses anticipated prior to 1975.
City University of New York— Queens College Flushing	1937 *City*	4346M 5758W	16000			a. none b. no dorm c. $400 d. 48 fee	70%	1:20	231	$29	B.A.; *Semester, summer sessions;* Social Sciences—38%, Education —24%, Natural Sciences & Math—18%, Humanities—16%; Coop— 3-2 engineering with Columbia and N.Y.U., 2-2 engineering with City College; Admission restricted to N.Y. State residents & U.S. citizens.
Clarkson Institute of Technology Potsdam	1896 *Private*	2150M 32W	3000	75% in top 1/4 75%	650m 550v	a. $1900 b. 900	50% *$200-2700* 50%	1:13	54	$5,645	B.S.; *Semester, summer session;* Engineering (Civil, Chemical, Electrical, Mechanical), Business Admin., Physics, Math, Chemistry, Industrial Distribution, Liberal Arts; *Engineering;* Army ROTC optional.
Colgate University Hamilton	1819 *Private*	1734M	2000	40% in top 1/5 32%	635m 610v	a. $1950 b. 1100	60% *$700* 70%	1:11	240	$18,880	B.A.; *Semester, summer session, January special studies period;* Social Sciences—43%, Humanities—30%, Natural Sciences & Math —27%; Coop—3-2 engineering with Columbia, U. of Rochester, R.P.I.; Off campus study groups in London, France, Washington D.C.; Air Force ROTC optional.
College of Mount Saint Vincent New York	1847 *Roman Catholic*	900W	1200	42% in top 1/5 78%	536m 566v	a. $1100 b. 1100 d. 140 fees	23% *$800* 33%	1:12	65	$500	B.A., B.S., B.S. Art Ed.; *Semester, summer session;* Humanities— 59%, Natural Sciences & Math—32%, Psychology—4%, Business —5%; Coop—interchange of facilities with Manhattan College; Aquatic Biology Institute in Nassau, Bahama Islands.
College of New Rochelle New Rochelle	1904 *Roman Catholic*	921W		67% in top 1/5 75%	589m 560v	a. $1600 b. 1200 d. 500	49% *$200-1500* 35%	1:12	87	$1,137	B.A.; *Semester;* Humanities—53%, Social Sciences—33%, Natural Sciences & Math—14%; 6 semester courses in theology; Junior Year Abroad in England, Ireland, Madrid.
College of Saint Rose Albany	1920 *Roman Catholic*	1095W		84% in top 2/5	550m 550v	a. $1100 b. 900	50% 35%	1:10	65		B.A., B.S.; *Semester, summer session;* Education—68%; *Social Work.*
Columbia College of Columbia University New York	1754 *Private*	2720M	4000	56% in top 1/10 35%		a. $1900 b. 1065	40% *$250-3000* 85%	1:8	4000	$204,000	B.A.; *Semester, summer sessions;* Columbia University has the following professional schools: *Architecture,* School of The Arts, *Business, Dentistry, Engineering, Journalism, Law, Library, Medicine, Nursing, Pharmacy, Psychology, Social Work, Teacher Education;* N ROTC optional.
Cooper Union New York	1859 *Private*	843M 158W	1100	15%	See Misc.	a. none b. no dorm d. $100 fee		1:8	90	$16,633	B. Arch., B.F.A., B. Engineering, B.S.; *Semester;* Engineering and Science—66%, Fine Arts—26%, Architecture—8%; *Architecture, Engineering;* Cooper Union is divided into the Schools of Art & Architecture, and Science & Engineering—S.A.T. requirements: Art & Arch.—560m, 560v; Eng. & Sci.—740m, 650v.
Cornell University Ithaca	1865 *Private & State*	6852M 2371W		80% in top 1/5 33%	682m 631v	a. See misc. b. $1200	78% *$1200* 90%	1:10	3000	$194,464	A.B., B.S., B.F.A.; *Semester, summer session;* Professional schools, some State contracted: Ag., Arch., Bus. & Public Adm., City Plan., Ed., Eng., Home Ec., Hotel Admin., Indus. & Labor Rels., Law, Med., Nurs., Vet. Med.; Coops with foreign univs.; AF, A, M, N ROTC optional. Annual tuition: Endowed divisions—$2050; Most state divisions—$675 (resident) $1075 (non-resident).
D'Youville College Buffalo	1908 *Roman Catholic*	1275W	1500	60% in top 1/5 51%	542m 578v	a. $1250 b. 1000 d. 30	44% *$415* 25%	1:10	58	$800	B.A., B.S.; *Semester, summer session;* Health Professions—34%, Education—25%, Social Sciences—35%, English—10%, Natural Science—15%, Humanities—25%, Foreign Languages—9%; *Nursing.*
Elmira College Elmira	1855 *Private*	1136W	1400	80% in top 2/5 68%	546m 560v	a. $1800 b. 1000 d. 70	25% *$100-1800* 60%	1:16	100	$3,136	B.A., B.S.; *Semester, summer sessions;* Social Sciences—35%, Education—31%, Humanities—14%, Natural Sciences—7%, Math— 9%, Speech Therapy—4%; *Teacher Education;* Coops—3-1 medical tech. with Sayre, Pa. Hospital, 2-3 nursing with Columbia, Cornell, Rochester, Western Reserve.
Finch College New York	1900 *Private*	400W	530	30% in top 1/4 40%		a. $2250 b. 1650	10%	1:9 60%	53		B.A., B.S.; Certification in Elementary Education; Third year abroad in Madrid, Rome, Paris, and London.

Institution / Location / Founded / Affiliation	Enrollment M=men W=women	Projected enrollment in 1975	High school rating; % applicants accepted	SAT/ACT Averages m=math v=verbal	Annual Tuition: a. b. Room & Board; c. Out of State; d. Other State	% Students with $ aid / Average amount	Faculty-student ratio; % with Doctorates	Volumes in library in 1,000's	Endowment in $1,000's	Undergraduate degrees offered; Calendar; Per cent of students per field of study; Professional programs offered; Miscellaneous
Fordham College Bronx 1841 *Roman Catholic*	2475M	2700	58% in top 1/5 50%	618m 607v	a. $1500 b. 1150	42% $862 65%	1:12	720	$9,400	B.A., B.S., L.L.B.; *Semester,* summer session; *Business, Law, Pharmacy, Social Work;* Coop—3-2 engineering with Columbia; Air Force, Army ROTC optional. Fordham College (men) and Thomas More College (women) comprise Fordham University, sharing faculty, Library and Endowment.
Good Counsel College White Plains 1923 *Roman Catholic*	506W	1000			a. $1000 b. 1000 d. 50	26% $475	1:12	44		B.A., B.S.; *Semester;* Humanities—50%, Social Sciences—24%, Natural Sciences—22%, Business—4%; Coop—honors seminar in history with St. Peter's College.
Hamilton College Clinton 1812 *Private*	830M	700	81% in top 1/5 34%	666m 638v	a. $1700 b. 1000 d. 150	40% $200-2850 70%	1:11	264	$15,600	B.A.; *Semester;* Social Sciences—15%, Humanities—57%, Natural Sciences & Math—28%; Coops—3-2 engineering with Columbia & M.I.T., R.P.I., U. of Rochester; Colgate Washington seminar; Princeton U. critical languages program for selected juniors; Honor system; A coordinate college for 600 women, Kirkland College, to open September 1968.
Harpur College Binghamton 1946 *State*	1216M 986W	6500	53% in top 1/10 45%	611m 605v	a. $400 b. 848 c. 600 d. 70	5% 75%	1:15	250		B.A.; *Semester;* Social Sciences—34%, Humanities—37%, Natural Sciences & Math—29%; Coop with SUNY at Cortland; Harpur College is the Liberal Arts College of the State U. of N.Y. at Binghamton; Semester abroad program at Neuchatel, Switz. and Salamanca, Spain; S. W. Asia, N. Africa, Russia, E. Europe area studies.
Hartwick College Oneonta 1928 *Lutheran*	709M 698W	1600	85% in top 2/5 50%	558m 537v	a. $1400 b. 900 d. 55	20% $1050 45%	1:15	65	$3,800	B.A., B.S.; *Three-term, one 3-wk. term for independent study,* summer sessions; Social Sciences—45%, Humanities—20%, Natural Sciences—22%, Nursing—9%, Medical Technology—4%; Coops with N.Y.U., Wayne State U., Wagner; Junior Year Abroad program, Washington semester, Hartwick Center at U. of Veracruz.
Hobart College Geneva 1822 *Episcopalian*	1062M		53%	610m 582v	a. $1700 b. 1000 d. 200	24% $962 53%	1:14	112	$4,194	B.A., B.S.; *Three-terms;* Social Sciences—25%, Humanities—50%, Natural Sciences—25%; Washington semester; Air Force ROTC optional; Hobart and William Smith are the coordinate men's and women's Colleges of the Seneca.
Hofstra University Hempstead 1935 *Private*	3072M 2152W	7000	33% in top 1/5 60%	547m 548v	a. $1600 b. 1150 d. 180	15% $1000 46%	1:17	189	$2,353	B.A., B.S., B.B.A.; *Semester, summer sessions;* Education—18%, Social Sciences—24%, Business, Marketing, etc.—18%, Humanities—23%, Natural Sciences & Math—12%, Engineering—5%; *Business, Engineering, Teacher Education;* Coop—pre-nursing with Cornell U., Columbia U., U. of Rochester.
Houghton College Houghton 1883 *Wesleyan Methodist*	501M 636W	1200	70% in top 1/4 73%	575m 525v	a. $1100 b. 770 d. 190	25% $250 40%	1:17	65	$352	B.A., B.S., B.Mus.; *Semester,* summer session; Liberal Arts—75%, Sciences—13%, Music—12%; *Music;* Coop in engineering with N.Y.U.; Daily chapel, 9 hours in division of theology required.
Iona College New Rochelle 1940 *Roman Catholic*	2486M	3000	most in top 2/5	524m 505v	a. $1200 b. no dorm	20% $500 30%	1:16	75		B.A., B.S., B.B.A.; *Semester,* summer session; Liberal Arts—58%, Business—33%, Sciences—9%.
Ithaca College Ithaca 1892 *Private*	1471M 1581W	3500	most in top 2/5 70%	M556m 535v W543m 552v	a. $1820 b. 1025 d. 150	37% $428 30%	1:16	90	$330	B.A., B.S., B.F.A., B.Mus.; *Semester, summer session;* Arts & Sciences—62%, Physical Education—15%, Music—14%, Physical Therapy—9%; *Music Ed., Liberal Arts, Business, Drama, Speech Pathology, Radio-Television.*
Keuka College Keuka Park 1890 *American Baptist*	744W	1200	95% in top 1/2 64%	529m 535v	a. $1650 b. 800 c. 40	25% $314 54%	1:13	50	$1,000	B.A., B.S.; *Quarter;* Social Sciences—36%, Education—20%, Nursing—18%, Humanities—20%; *Nursing, Teacher Education;* 5-week work-study period which involves community study, cultural study, vocational placements.
Ladycliff College Highland Falls 1933 *Roman Catholic*	575W	700	75% in top 1/4 35%	500m 523v	a. $900 b. 1050 c. 100	20% $200-500 25%	1:11	41	$20	B.A., B.S.; *Semester,* summer session; Humanities—50%, Social Sciences—30%, Natural Sciences & Math—20%.
Le Moyne College Syracuse 1946 *Roman Catholic*	929M 452W	1700	51% in top 1/5 35%	M580m 538v W584m 600v	a. $1400 b. 950	35% $400 35%	1:15	63	$895	B.A., B.S.; *Semester, summer sessions;* Arts—20%, Social Sciences—42%, Natural Sciences—23%, Business—15%, Humanities—6%; Coop in nursing with St. Joseph's Hospital, Syracuse.
Long Island University Brooklyn Center Conolly College Brooklyn 1926 *Private*	5086M 1992W	12000	54% in top 2/5 50%	481m 464v	a. $1408 b. 1100	11% $1032 44%*	1:18	105	$10,000*	B.A., B.S.; *Semester, summer session;* Humanities—8%, Social Sciences—15%, Natural Sciences—21%, Business—29%, Education—24%, Nursing—3%. *for entire LIU.
Long Island University Merriweather Camp. C. W. Post College Brookville 1954 *Private*	5818M 3180W	12000	34% in top 2/5 46%	532m 519v	a. $1408 b. 1100	5% $645 44%*	1:19	115	$10,000*	B.A., B.S.; *Semester, summer session;* Humanities—21%, Social Sciences—24%, Natural Sciences—27%, Business—27%, Education—1%. *for entire LIU.
Long Island University Southampton College Southampton 1963 *Private*	897M 538W	1600	25% in top 2/5 54%	472m 485v	a. $1408 b. 1100	5% $337 44%*	1:16	35	$10,000*	B.A., B.S.; *Semester, summer session;* Southampton College graduated its first class in 1967. *for entire LIU.
Manhattan College Bronx 1853 *Roman Catholic*	3520M	4050	48% in top 1/5 60%	610m 560v	a. $1400 b. 1050	45% $600 43%	1:15	125	$1,512	B.A., B.S., B.E., B.B.A.; *Semester, summer session;* Engineering—36%, Sciences—25%, Business—22%, Arts—13%, Physical Education—3%; *Business, Engineering, Teacher Education;* Junior Year Abroad; Distinguished Theology program; Air Force ROTC optional.
Manhattanville College Purchase 1841 *Roman Catholic*	24M 1319W	1800	72% in top 1/5 58%	598m 622v	a. $2000 b. 1000 c. 75	42% $200-2000 30%	1:8	140	$2,164	B.A.—97%, B.Mus.—5%, B.Sacred Mus.—2%; *Semester, summer session; Music;* Junior Year Abroad programs at U. of Madrid, L'Institut Catholique in Paris.
Marymount College Tarrytown 1907 *Roman Catholic*	849W	1000	56% in top 1/5 53%	559m 577v	a. $1500 b. 1200 c. 50	25% $750	1:14	55		B.A., B.S., B.F.A., B.Mus.; *Semester;* Humanities—52%, Social Sciences—40%, Natural Sciences and Math—16%; 3 credits per year required in theology; Junior Year Abroad programs in Barcelona, London, Paris, Rome, Quebec.

Institution Location / Founded Affiliation	Enrollment M=men W=women	Projected enrollment in 1975	High school rating; % applicants accepted	SAT/ACT Averages m=math v=verbal	a. Annual Tuition; b. Room & Board; c. Out of state; d. Other	% Students with $ aid; Average amount	Faculty-student ratio; % with Doctorates	Volumes in library in 1,000's	Endowment in $1,000's	Undergraduate degrees offered; *Calendar*; Per cent of students per field of study; *Professional programs offered; Miscellaneous*
Marymount Manhattan College New York 1948 *Roman Catholic*	550W	686	78% in top 1/4 60%	540m 771v	a. $1000 b. 90	30% $600	1:12	22	$285	B.A., B.S.; *Semester;* Fine Arts—23%, Humanities—26%, Social Sciences—31%, Natural Sciences & Math—20%; Teacher Ed. program for mentally retarded; Interinstitutional coop with CMRD of Bd. of Ed., Kennedy Child Center, N.Y. Blood Center, Museum of Natural History; Junior Year Abroad in London, Madrid, Rome, Paris; N.Y. State recommendation for Federal grant of $980,644 for library construction.
Medaille College Buffalo 1938 *Roman Catholic*	375W	800	most in top 1/2 90%		a. $850		1:11 50%	35		B.A., B.S.Ed.; *Semester, summer session;* Education—70%, Liberal Arts—30%; Teacher Education—the preparation of teachers for public and private, elementary and secondary schools.
Mills College of Education New York 1909 *Private*	465W	900	35%	450m 500v	a. $2000 b. 1200	20% $600	1:16 50%	35	$217	B.S.; *Semester;* Teacher Education—students qualify for N.Y. State certification; Mills operates children's centers in cooperation with the Department of Welfare.
Nazareth College Rochester 1924 *Roman Catholic*	1080W	1500	most in top 1/2 80%	551m 556v	a. $1300 b. 980 c. 30	25% $250	1:12 49%	80		B.A., B.S.; *Semester, summer session;* Coop program with St. John Fisher College.
New School for Social Research New York 1919 *Private*	26M 35W	500 see misc.			a. $1700	10% $300	1:12 50%	60	$1,143	B.A.; *Semester;* Social Sciences—46%, Humanities—54%; Undergraduate degree candidates are accepted at the New School only after two years of college—the projected growth figure of 500 includes only full time students, non-degree & degree candidates. There are 15,000 General Credit students.
New York University New York 1831 *Private*	6872M 4723W	15317	50% in top 1/5 65%	594m 590v	a. $1900 b. 1395 d. 100	24% $200-3600	1:14 65%	1650	$74,000	B.A., B.S., B.F.A.; *Semester, summer sessions;* Business, Dentistry, Engineering, Law, Medicine, Public Administration, Teacher Education. Coop 3-2 engineering with N.Y.U. engineering school; Air Force, Army ROTC optional.
Niagara University Niagara University 1856 *Roman Catholic*	1427M 479W	2000	35% in top 1/4 65%	525m 495v	a. $1224 b. 920 c. 100	24% $640	1:13 40%	85	$472	B.A., B.S., B.B.A.; *Semester, summer session;* Humanities—50%, Science & Nursing—25%, Business—25%; Nursing; Coop—3-2 engineering with University of Detroit; Army ROTC required first two years.
Notre Dame College of Staten Island Staten Island 1931 *Private*	476W	975	45% in top 1/5 75%	507m 527v	a. $1200 b. no dorm	16% $500	1:14 50%	35	$84	B.A., B.S.Ed.; *Semester, summer session;* Humanities—37%, Social Sciences—28%, Education—14%, Natural Sciences & Math—21%; NSF grants of $5,100, Atomic Energy Commission grant of $7,500 since 1960.
Pace College New York 1906 *Private*	6262M 1522W	10000	15% in top 1/4 25%		a. $1304 b. no dorm	5% $800	1:20 30%	130		B.A., B.S., B.B.A.; *Semester, summer sessions;* Business Administration; Teacher Education; Nursing; Pace has a branch campus at Pleasantville, N.Y.
Polytechnic Institute of Brooklyn Brooklyn 1854 *Private*	1588M 33W	2400	25% in top 1/5 70%	650m 550v	a. $1900 b. 800 c. 400	20% $725 Max.	1:10 77%	110	$5,500	B.S.; *Semester, summer session;* Electrical Engineering—40%, Mechanical—15%, Sciences—15%, Aerospace—10%, Chemical—10%, New programs (including pre-Medicine, Humanities, Social sciences)—10%; Engineering; Army ROTC optional.
Pratt Institute Brooklyn 1887 *Private*	1774M 984W	2850	70% in top 2/5 44%	*	a. $1700 b. 1000 d. 50-150	25% $750	1:9 30%	200	$14,500	B.S., B.Arch., B.F.A., B.Indus. Design, B.Engr.; *Semester, summer session;* Art—52%, Engr.—21%, Arch.—14%, Fashion—7%, Foods—6%. *Arch.—599m, 549v; Engr.—582m, 492v; Art—496m, 513v; Fashion—468m, 490v; Food Science—440m, 450v.
Rensselaer Polytechnic Institute (R.P.I.) Troy 1824 *Private*	3500M 100W	4100	85% in top 1/5 69%	710m 610v	a. $2050 b. 950	33% $100-2500	1:11 70%	115	$52,563	B.S.; *Semester, summer session;* Engineering—60%, Natural Sciences—30%, Architecture—5%; Architecture, Engineering; Coop with Albany Medical College in biology & medicine granting B.S. & M.D. after 6 years; Air Force, Army, Navy ROTC optional; Women housed in new dormitory.
Roberts Wesleyan College North Chili 1866 *Free Methodist*	264M 271W	950	34% in top 1/5 80%	M478m 463v W482m 464v	a. $860 b. 730 c. 60	30% $133	1:13 30%	40	$37	B.A., B.S.; *Semester, summer sessions;* Humanities—40%, Social Sciences—29%, Natural Sciences & Math—16%, Nursing—15%; Nursing; Non-sectarian chapel attendance required 3 times per week.
Rochester, University of Rochester 1850 *Private*	2082M 1379W	3500	89% in top 1/5 65%	M674m 613v W647m 640v	a. $2000 b. 1100 d. 150	30% $100-2000	1:12 70%	1000	$86,722	B.A., B.S., B.Mus.; *Semester, summer session;* Social Sciences—32%, Humanities—24%, Natural Science & Math—24%, Engineering—9%, Education—7%; Engineering, Medicine, Music, Nursing; Coop—student exchange with Howard U.; Air Force, Navy ROTC optional.
Rochester Institute of Technology Rochester 1829 *Private*	2861M 615W	5500	25% in top 1/5 40%	M552m 484v W498m 491v	a. $1560 b. 1260 d. 400	30% $675	1:14 17%	80	$21,000	B.S., B.F.A.; *Quarter, summer session;* Engineering—19%, Business—19%, Printing—18%, Photography—16%, Food Administration & Retailing—14%, Art, Design and Crafts—9%.
Russell Sage College Troy 1916 *Private*	1275W	1500	most in top 1/2 40%	550m 550v	a. $1400 b. 1100 c. 100	$200-1200	1:14 50%	100	$4,500	B.A., B.S.; *Semester;* Liberal Arts—75%, Other—25%; Nursing; Physical Therapy; Physical Education; Business and Retailing.
St. Bonaventure University St. Bonaventure 1855 *Roman Catholic*	1593M 359W	2000	28% in top 1/2 35%	519m 500v	a. $1100 b. 850 d. 100	10% $1200	1:15 30%	114	$110	B.A., B.S., B.B.A.; *Semester, summer session;* Humanities—54%, Natural Sciences—25%, Business—21%; Coop–3-2 engineering with U. of Detroit; Catholics required to take theology each semester and to make annual retreat; Army ROTC required.
St. Francis College Brooklyn 1884 *Roman Catholic*	1792M	2400	21% in top 1/5 54%	510m 490v	a. $1300 b. no dorm	35% $700	1:21 29%	53	$111	B.A., B.S., B.B.A.; *Semester, summer session;* Social Sciences—37%, Business—31%, Natural Sciences & Math—16%, Humanities—14%.
St. John Fisher College Rochester 1948 *Roman Catholic*	1130M	1500	59% in top 2/5 59%	547m 511v	a. $1300 b. 975 d. 100	25% $700	1:17 37%	51		B.A., B.S., B.B.A.; *Semester, summer session;* Humanities—59%, Business—22%, Natural Sciences & Math—19%; Coop—undergraduate program with Nazareth College, engineering program with U. of Detroit; Two-year NROTC or AFROTC with U. of Rochester.
St. John's University Jamaica 1870 *Roman Catholic*	5348M 3576W	10000		514m 504v	a. $1300 b. no dorm	14%		320		B.A., B.S., L.L.B.; *Semester, summer session;* Law, Business, Pharmacy; Asian Studies, African Studies.
Saint Joseph's College for Women Brooklyn 1916 *Roman Catholic*	674W	850	90% in top 2/5 77%	500m 525v	a. $800 b. no dorm c. 60	30% $230	1:9 33%	52	$78	B.A., B.S.; *Semester;* Social Sciences—14.5%, Natural Sciences & Math—15%, Humanities—28.5%, Education—42%; Theology courses, annual retreat required.

Institution Location / Founded Affiliation	Enrollment M=men W=women	Projected enrollment in 1975	High school rating; % applicants accepted	SAT/ACT Averages m=math v=verbal	a. Annual Tuition; b. Room & Board; c. Out of state; d. Other state	% Students with $ aid; Average amount	Faculty-student ratio; % with Doctorates	Volumes in library in 1,000's	Endowment in $1,000's	Undergraduate degrees offered; Calendar; Per cent of students per field of study; Professional programs offered; Miscellaneous
St. Lawrence University Canton 1856 Private	1039M 667W	2000	66% in top 1/5 40%	M616m 575v W615m 611v	a. $1800 b. 1030 d. 150	30% $100-2000	1:13 45%	180	$9,000	B.A., B.S.; Semester, summer session; Social Sciences—43%, Natural Sciences & Math—31%, Humanities—26%; Coop—3-2 engineering with Columbia, M.I.T., R.P.I., U. of R.; Junior Year Abroad—9%; Army ROTC optional.
Sarah Lawrence College Bronxville 1926 Private	550W		73% in top 1/4 15%	588m 641v	a. $2350 b. 1200	30% 60%	1:7	97	$1,645	B.A.; Semester; Sarah Lawrence has no "majors"; Junior Year Abroad program, summer session in Florence or Paris.
Siena College Loudonville 1937 Roman Catholic	1422M	1950	70% in top 1/4 60%	590m 560v	a. $1020 b. 950 d. 300	25% $640	1:14 30%	114	$500	B.A., B.S., B.B.A.; Semester, summer session; Humanities—62%, Business—38%; Coop—Inter-institutional Honors Colloquium with College of St. Rose; Theology required of Catholic students; Army ROTC required for two years; Grants of $50,000 from A.E.C. and N.S.F.
Skidmore College Saratoga Springs 1911 Private	1544W	2000	90% in top 1/5 58%	605m 610v	a. $1900 b. 1250	29% $730	1:12 65%	117	$2,500	B.A., B.S.; Semester; Liberal Arts—61%, Professional Programs—39%; Art, Business, Drama, Elementary Education, Music, Nursing, Phys. Ed.; Coop—exchange with Union College; Junior Year Abroad program.
State University at Albany Albany 1844 State	2251M 2887W	16500	98% in top 2/5		a. $501 b. 795 c. 675	60% $575	1:13 56%	300		B.A., B.S.; Semester, summer session; Humanities—38%, Social Sciences—23%, Natural Sciences & Math—20%, Business—19%; Business, Education, Library, Social Welfare, Nursing.
State University at Buffalo Buffalo 1846 State	5514M 3698W	20000	50% in top 1/5 30%	600m 600v	a. $400 b. 913 c. 600 d. 92	90% $400	1:12 65%	750		B.A., B.S., B.Ed.; Semester, summer sessions; Liberal Arts—59%, Bus. Adm.—8%, Education—5%, Engineering—11%, Med. Tech.—2%, Oc. Ther.—1%, Phys. Ther.—2%, Nursing—8%, Phar.—3%; Dentistry, Education, Law, Medicine, Pharmacy; Air Force ROTC optional.
State University at Stony Brook Stony Brook 1957 State	1910M 1592W	9000	84% in top 1/5 45%		a. $400 b. 815 c. 600 d. 600	33% $400	1:11 74%	300		B.A., B.S., B.Engineering; Semester, summer sessions; Humanities—19%, Engineering—11%, Social Sciences—37%, Science—33%.
State University College at Brockport Brockport 1867 State	1500M 2000W	5000	43% in top 1/5	571m 528v	a. $425 b. 772 c. 600		1:10 33%	120		B.A., B.S., B.S.Ed.; Semester, summer session; Teacher Education.
State University College at Buffalo Buffalo 1871 State	2514M 4385W	8400	26%		a. $400 b. 900 c. 600 d. 107	98% $500	1:15 40%	150		B.A., B.S.Ed.; Semester, summer session; Education—63%, Art—13%, Industrial Arts—10%, Home Economics—7%, Liberal Arts—9%; Teacher Education; Coop—semester of junior year in Siena, Italy available, and exchange program with the University of Puerto Rico, Costa Rica, England.
State University College at Cortland Cortland 1868 State	1127M 2208W	4500	51% in top 1/5 48%		a. $400 b. 855 c. 600 d. 115	95% $1426	1:13 34%	200		B.A., B.S., B.S.Ed.; Semester; Education—44%, Health, Rec., Phys. Ed.—30%, Social Sciences—10%, English—7%, Science—6%, Math—4%; Teacher Education (M.A.T.); Junior Year semester at various European Universities.
State University College at Fredonia Fredonia 1826 State	750M 1300W	6180	95% in top 1/2 35%		a. $425 b. 675 c. 625 d. 120	54% $600	1:14 45%	90		B.A., B.S., B.S.Ed.; Semester; Education—63%, Liberal Arts—24%, Music—13%; Music, Teacher Education.
State University College at Geneseo Geneseo 1867 State	3735M 4565W	8300	25%		a. $400 b. 800 c. 600 d. 25	95% $550	1:15 55%	110		B.A., B.S.Ed.; Semester, summer session; Humanities—17%, Sciences & Math—17%, Social Sciences—17%, Language & Lit.—4%, Fine Arts—10%, Psychology—7%, Education—24%; Teacher Education, Library.
State University College at New Paltz New Paltz 1885 State	1385M 2013W	5200	96% in top 1/2	588m 542v	a. $400 b. 820 c. 600 d. 125	17% $650	1:10 41%	150		B.A., B.S.; Quarter; Education—57%, Art Ed.—16%, Liberal Arts—27%; Teacher Education; African Studies, Asian Studies.
State University College at Oneonta Oneonta 1889 State	927M 2325W	5500	most in top 1/4 60%		a. $425 b. 820 c. 625	75% $450	1:16 30%	140		B.A., B.S., B.S.Ed.; Semester; Education—67%, Home Economics—9%, Liberal Arts—13%, Museum and Folk Culture—5%; Teacher Education; Coop—graduate program in museum work & folk culture with N.Y. State Historical Association.
State University College at Oswego Oswego 1861 State	1714M 2186W	9500	60% in top 1/5 49%		a. $400 b. 935 c. 600 d. 125	25% $475	1:16 40%	175		B.A., B.S., B.S.Ed.; Semester, summer session; Education—70%, Industrial Arts—19%, Liberal Arts—11%; Teacher Education.
State University College at Plattsburgh Plattsburgh 1889 State	996M 1489W	5974	most in top 1/3 44%	570m 530v	a. $400 b. 925 c. 1860 (oos total) d. 535	28% $500	1:15 35%	134		B.A., B.S.; Semester; Education—60%, Nursing—14%, Home Economics—5%, Liberal Arts—21%; Nursing, Home Ec., Education.
State University College at Potsdam Potsdam 1816 State	589M 1856W	5775	56% in top 1/5 45%		a. $400 b. 1000 c. 600	20% $400	1:14 30%	110		B.A., B.S.; Semester; Humanities—48%, Social Sciences—34%, Natural Sciences & Math—18%; Music, Teacher Education.
Syracuse University Syracuse 1870 Private	5773M 4093W	15942	56% in top 1/4 51%	592m 575v	a. $1620 b. 960 d. 100	37% $1250	1:16 66%	857	$38,765	B.A., B.S.; Semester, summer sessions; Humanities—56%, Education—15%, Business—10%, Art & Architecture—8%, Engineering—6%; Arch., Bus., Eng., Jour., Law, Lib., Music, Nurs., Teacher Ed.; Coops—3-2 eng., 3-3 arch. at Syracuse; AF, A, ROTC optional.
Thomas More College Bronx 1841 Roman Catholic	682W	1000	85% in top 1/2 45%	597m 640v	a. $1500 b. 1150	48% $860	1:12 65%	720	$9,400	B.A., B.S., L.L.B.; Semester, summer session; Business, Law, Pharmacy, Social Work; Coop—3-2 Engineering with Columbia. Thomas More College (women) and Fordham College (men) comprise Fordham University, sharing Faculty, Library, and Endowment.
Union College Schenectady 1795 Private	1356M	1650	79% in top 1/5 50%	662m 616v	a. $1800 b. 990 d. 133	45% $100-3000	1:11 68%	250	$32,000	B.A., B.S.; Term; Social Sciences—35%, Natural Sciences—34%, Engineering—22%, Humanities—9%; Engineering; Student exchange with St. Andrews University in Scotland and Technical Institute in Zurich, Switzerland; Air Force ROTC optional.

Institution Location / Founded Affiliation	Enrollment M=men W=women	Projected enrollment in 1975	High school rating; % applicants accepted	SAT/ACT Averages m=math v=verbal	a. Annual Tuition; b. Room & Board; c. Out of state; d. Other state	% Students with $ aid / Average amount	Faculty/student ratio; % with Doctorates	Volumes in library in 1,000's	Endowment in $1,000's	Undergraduate degrees offered; Calendar; Per cent of students per field of study; Professional programs offered; Miscellaneous
United States Merchant Marine Academy, Kings Point 1943, Federal	1000M	1250	90% in top 1/2 12%	620m 550v	a. none b. none	100% 8%	1:10	50		B.S.; Quarter; All midshipmen follow a prescribed course of study.
United States Military Academy, West Point 1802, Federal	3200M	4417	79% in top 1/5 30%	654m 581v	a. none b. none	8%	1:7	260		B.S.; Semester, summer session (military training); Engineering & Science—60%, Social Sciences & Humanities—40%; About 60% of USMA graduates attend civilian graduate schools under Army auspices. Some distinguished graduates proceed to graduate school immediately after graduation. Study must be in field Army requires.
Vassar College, Poughkeepsie 1861, Private	1600W	1650	87% in top 1/5	626m 650v	a. $1800 b. 1300 d. 40	28% $1500	1:10 67%	375	$60,000	B.A.; Semester; Social Sciences—46%, Humanities—38%, Natural Sciences & Math—16%; Teacher Education; Coops—summer internship in Washington, graduate study in classics in Athens or Rome; Old Dominion Foundation grant of $1,000,000, Ford Foundation matching grant of $2,500,000, since 1960.
Wagner College, Staten Island 1883, Lutheran Church in America	1332M 974W	3000	74% in top 2/5 62%		a. $1600 b. 1000 d. 50	75% $501	1:15 49%	70	$1,151	B.A., B.S., B.S.Ed.; Semester, summer session; Social Sciences—40%, Education—23%, Natural Sciences & Math—19%, Humanities—15%, Nursing—4%; Business, Education, Nursing; Coop in engineering with New York University; Grants totaling $1,400,000 since 1960.
Wells College, Aurora 1868, Private	615W	800	73% in top 1/5 40%	608m 618v	$3100 total	19% $836	1:10 64%	145	$5,546	B.A.; Semester, summer session (in German); Humanities—50%, Natural Sciences & Math—20%, Social Sciences—30%; Junior Year Abroad with Sweet Briar, Smith, Hamilton, Wayne State, Millersville State, N.Y.U.
William Smith College, Geneva 1908, Private	365W	1560 inc. Hobart	51% in top 1/5 50%	636m 626v	a. $1550 b. 1020 d. 300	25% $890	1:13 50%	105	$3,560	B.A., B.S.; 3-term, summer session; Social Sciences—55%, Humanities—25%, Natural Sciences—20%; William Smith & Hobart are the coordinate women's and men's Colleges of the Seneca.
Yeshiva University, New York 1886, Private	1023W 552W	1811	70%	602m 571v	a. $1500 b. 1320	75% $352	1:5 65%	400	$3,600	B.A., B.S., B.R.E., B.H.L.; Semester; Social Sciences—36%, Natural Sciences—41%, Humanities—23%; Education, Medicine, Psychology, Engineering; Coop—3-2 engineering with New York University.

NORTH CAROLINA

Institution Location / Founded Affiliation	Enrollment M=men W=women	Projected enrollment in 1975	High school rating; % applicants accepted	SAT/ACT Averages m=math v=verbal	a. Annual Tuition; b. Room & Board; c. Out of state; d. Other state	% Students with $ aid / Average amount	Faculty/student ratio; % with Doctorates	Volumes in library in 1,000's	Endowment in $1,000's	Undergraduate degrees offered; Calendar; Per cent of students per field of study; Professional programs offered; Miscellaneous
Agricultural and Technological College of North Carolina, Greensboro 1891, State	2197M 1398W	5080	50% in top 1/4 50%		a. $368 b. 552 c. 620	35% $400	1:16 24%	160	$20	B.S.; Semester, summer sessions; Social Sciences—22%, Nursing—5%, Humanities—20%, Natural Sciences & Math—13%, Business—13%, Engineering—13%, Physical Education—8%, Agricultural Science—3%, Home Economics—3%; Air Force, Army ROTC required.
Appalachian State Teachers College, Boone 1903, State	1990M 2427W	5378	50% in top 1/4 88%	445m 450v	a. $180 b. 396 c. 255 d. 193	56% $401	1:17 33%	137		B.A., B.S.; Quarter, summer session; Music, Teacher Education.
Asheville-Biltmore College, Asheville 1927, State	324M 216W	1800	60% in top 1/2 75%	M916 W934 (comb.)	a. $280 b. 950 c. 140	24% $300	1:14 55%	40		B.A.; Four-term, summer session; Humanities—38%, Social Sciences—36%, Natural Sciences and Math—26%.
Atlantic Christian College, Wilson 1902, Disciples of Christ	834M 691W	1800	69% in top 1/2 70%	M458m 415v W424m 422v	a. $865 b. 600	10% $494	1:18 30%	45	$800	B.A., B.S.; Semester, summer sessions; Sciences—72%, Arts—28%; Two courses in Bible, chapel attendance required.
Barber-Scotia College, Concord 1867, Presbyterian	15M 300W	600	80% in top 1/5 35%		a. $300 b. 410 d. 63	55% $250	1:12 24%	20	$800	B.A., B.S.; Semester; Education—45%, Social Sciences—19%, Humanities—15%, Natural Sciences—13%, Business—4%, Home Economics—4%.
Belmont Abbey College, Belmont 1876, Roman Catholic	650M 55W	1000	18% in top 1/4 40%	518m 610v	a. $600 b. 700 d. 100	31% $400	1:14 33%	62	$500	B.A., B.S.; Semester, summer session; Arts—93%, Sciences—7%; Coop—3-2 engineering with North Carolina State at Raleigh, Notre Dame, U. of North Carolina; 16 hours theology, attendance at religious services required.
Bennett College, Greensboro 1873, Methodist	662W	800	73% in top 1/5 48%		a. $715 b. 644 d. 61	52% $415	1:10 22%	53	$1,878	B.A., B.S.; Semester; Education—33%, Social Sciences—16%, Humanities—23%, Natural Sciences & Math—13%, Home Economics—10%, Med. Tech.—6%; Coops in law, nursing, special education with American University, Wayne State, Columbia University Teachers College respectively.
Catawba College, Salisbury 1857, United Church of Christ	536M 462W	1000	34% in top 1/5 53%	M505m 446v W478m 480v	a. $800 b. 695 d. 85	36% $334	1:13 25%	70	$2,500	B.A.; Semester, summer session; Humanities—35%, Social Sciences—20%, Business—25%, Natural Sciences & Math—20%; Coop—3-2 engineering with N.Y.U., 3-2 forestry with Duke U.; 6 semester hours religion, chapel & vespers attendance required.
Davidson College, Davidson 1836, Presbyterian	1000M	1000	75% in top 1/10 45%	650m 610v	a. $1400 b. 725	35% $100-2000	1:12 75%	130	$1,400	B.A., B.S.; Semester, summer session; Coop—3-2 engineering with Columbia, Duke, Georgia Institute of Technology; One religion course, attendance at some chapel services required; Army ROTC required for two years.
Duke University, Durham 1838, Private	2571M 1368W	6226	86% in top 1/5 45%M 30%W	642m 615v	a. $1637 b. 750	30% $200-2600	1:7 75%	1717	$55,672	B.A., B.S.; Semester, summer sessions; Social Sciences—44%, Humanities—19%, Natural Sciences & Math—21%, Engineering—9%, Nursing—7%; Engineering, Forestry, Law, Medicine, Nursing, Psychology, Teacher Education; Air Force, Navy ROTC optional.
East Carolina College, Greenville 1907, State	4474M 4360W	17550	34% in top 1/5 60%	485m 461v	a. $150 b. 630 c. 402 d. 249	21% $340	1:17 44%	300	$69	B.A., B.S., B.F.A., B.Mus., B.S.N., B.S.B.A.; Quarter, summer session; Education—24%, Business—20%, Natural Sciences & Math—17%, Humanities—15%, Social Sciences—6%, Home Economics—4%; Music, Nursing, Teacher Education; Coop in engineering with N.Y.U.; Air Force ROTC optional.
Elizabeth City State College, Elizabeth City 1891, State	411M 652W	1500	all in top 2/3 75%		a. $164 b. 548 c. 359 d. 158	70% $500	1:14 24%	53		B.S., B.S.Ed., B.A.; Semester, summer session; Humanities—10%, Social Sciences, Natural Sciences & Math—27%; Elementary Ed.—33%, Phys. & Bus. Ed.—30%; Teacher Education; Coop with East Carolina College, Greenville, N.C. for graduate courses (summer session).

Institution / Location / Founded / Affiliation	Enrollment M=men W=women	Projected enrollment in 1975	High school rating; % applicants accepted	SAT/ACT Averages m=math v=verbal	a. Annual Tuition; b. Room & Board; c. Out of state; d. Other	% Students with $ aid; Average amount	Faculty student ratio; % with Doctorates	Volumes in library in 1,000's	Endowment in $1,000's	Undergraduate degrees offered; Calendar; Per cent of students per field of study; Professional programs offered; Miscellaneous
Elon College Elon College 1889 *United Church of Christ*	885M 476W	1850	60%	M450m 475v W525m 525v	a. $900 b. 650	21% $545	1:18 25%	65	$1,500	B.A., B.S.; *Semester, summer session;* 6 semester hours religion, 1 chapel per week required.
Fayetteville State College Fayetteville 1877 *State*	415M 727W	1575	71% in top 1/3 82%	336m 314v	a. $100 b. 531 c. 300 d. 159	75% $275	1:16 26%	56		B.S.; *Semester, summer session;* Elementary Ed.—58%, Sociology—6%, P.Ed. & Health—4%, Hist. & Pol. Science—9%, English—6%, Biology—1%, Business Ed.—9%, Math—7%.
Greensboro College Greensboro 1838 *Methodist*	175M 435W	750	45% in top 1/5 33%	498m 508v	a. $940 b. 640 d. 300	30% $500	1:14 40%	48	$1,475	B.A., B.S., B.Mus., B.Mus.Ed.; *Semester, summer session;* Arts—88%, Music—8%, Sciences—4%; *Music;* Coop—member of Piedmont University Center, Winston-Salem; 6 hours of Bible study, attendance at chapel twice weekly required.
Guilford College Greensboro 1837 *Quaker*	930M 410W	950	73% in top 1/2 43%	522m 503v	a. $1000 b. 660	50% $210	1:18 40%	79	$6,710	B.A., B.S.; *Semester, summer session;* Social Sciences—50%, Natural Sciences & Math—16%, Education—16%, Humanities—12%; Coop—member of Piedmont University Center, Winston-Salem; 6 hours Biblical literature, twice-weekly chapel required.
High Point College High Point 1924 *Methodist*	570M 530W	1200	50% in top 1/4 41%	M521m 492v W517m 500v	a. $600 b. 630 c. 50 d. 184	30% $500	1:17 45%	64	$1,755	B.A., B.S.; *Semester, summer session;* Arts—70%, Sciences—30%; *Teacher Education;* Coop—member of Piedmont University Center.
Johnson C. Smith University Charlotte 1867 *Presbyterian*	494M 544W	1397	65% in top 1/5 60%	330m 310v	a. $700 b. 630	40% $250-500	1:15 20%	60	$2,000	B.A., B.S., B.D.; *Semester, summer session;* Education—70%, Natural Science & Math—20%, Humanities—10%; Coop—3-2 engineering with N.Y.U.
Lenoir Rhyne College Hickory 1891 *Lutheran*	587M 554W	1500	85% in top 1/2 45%	M460m 460v W460m 460v	a. $560 b. 580	20% $200	1:16 30%	50	$1,400	B.A., B.S.; *Semester, summer sessions;* Teacher Education, Medical Tech., Social Work.
Livingston College Salisbury 1880 *African Methodist Episcopal Zion*	305M 387W		all in top 3/5		a. $375 b. 400	$250	1:16	36		B.A., B.S., B.D.; *Semester, summer session.*
Meredith College Raleigh 1899 *Baptist*	850W	1200	90% in top 1/4 67%	525m 515v	a. $1000 b. 800	49% $275	1:15 36%	50	$1,072	B.A., B.Mus.; *Semester, summer session;* Arts & Music—8%, Business & Economics—10%, Humanities—21%, Home Economics—8%, Mathematics & Natural Sciences—18%, Social Studies—33%.
North Carolina, University of, at Chapel Hill Chapel Hill 1795 *State*	10359M 3797W	18000	76% in top 1/4 48%	592m 560v	a. $175 b. 500 c. 600 d. 340	39% $684	1:14 80%	1700	$14,087	B.A., B.S.; *Semester, summer sessions;* Liberal Arts—75%, Other—25%; *Business, Dentistry, Journalism, Law, Library Science, Medicine, Nursing, Pharmacy, Public Health, Social work, Teacher Education; Junior Year Abroad;* Air Force, Navy ROTC optional.
North Carolina, University of, at Greensboro Greensboro 1891 *State*	196M 3883W	8100	92% in top 1/4 66%	519m 520v	a. $175 b. 595 c. 600 d. 250	33% $50-1200	1:15 51%	256		B.A., B.S., B.F.A., B.Mus.; *Semester, summer session;* Arts—69%, Sciences—25%, Music & Fine Arts—6%; *Music, Teacher Education.*
North Carolina College at Durham Durham 1910 *State*	1070M 1581W	3000	100% in top 3/5 70%	337m 415v	a. $247 b. 465 c. 597 d. 73	75% $350	1:15 32%	144		B.A., B.S.; *Semester, summer session; Law, Nursing, Teacher Education;* Coop—faculty exchange with U. of Wisconsin, Duke University.
North Carolina State University at Raleigh 1887 *State*	7569M 795W	10101	79% in top 1/3 72%	577m 495v	a. $357 b. 766M 816W c. 782	19% $441	1:14 54%	371	$896	B.A., B.S.; *Semester, summer sessions;* Engineering—42%, Textiles & Design—16%, Agriculture—11%, Education—9%, Natural Sciences & Math—5%, Forestry—6%, Liberal Arts—11%; *Coops—Architecture, Engineering, Forestry, Landscape Arch., Teacher Education;* Air Force, Army ROTC optional.
Pembroke State College Pembroke 1887 *State*	902M 508W	4100	56% in top 1/4 83%		a. $150 b. 370 c. 500		1:17 33%	40		B.A., B.S.; *Semester, summer session;* Art—3%, Education—37%, Math & Sciences—11%, Business Admin.—15%, Languages—2%, English—7%, Social Sciences—14%, Home Ec.—3%, Music—2%.
Pfeiffer College Misenheimer 1885 *Methodist*	424M 418W	1000	30% in top 1/10 34%	474m 467v	a. $800 b. 700	41% $431	1:11 50%	50	$2,000	B.A., B.S.; *Semester, summer sessions;* Business—15%, Social Sciences—10%, Education—15%, Natural Science & Math—23%, Humanities—25%, Christian Education—7%, Music & Other—5%; Coop—member of Piedmont University Center, Winston-Salem; 9 hours religion, chapel required.
Queens College Charlotte 1857 *Presbyterian*	834W	950	60% in top 1/5 60%	518m 515v	$2500 Total	18% $563	1:12 34%	65	$3,500	B.A., B.Mus.; *Semester, summer session;* Humanities—44%, Social Sciences—37%, Natural Science & Math—19%; Washington Semester; Summer Study-Travel Abroad.
St. Andrews Presbyterian College Laurinburg 1858 *Presbyterian*	440M 515W	1400	60% in top 2/5 67%	M484m 456v W477m 480v	a. $1510 b. 885	33% $600	1:14 40%	40	$1,361	B.A., B.S., B.Mus.; *Semester, summer session;* Social Sciences—23%, Humanities—25%, Education—12%, Business—21%, Natural Sciences & Math—15%, Music & Fine Arts—7%; *Music;* Coop—3-2 engineering with N.C. State U.; Christianity & culture core program required.
Saint Augustine's College Raleigh 1867 *Episcopalian*	285M 447W	1200	95% in top 1/2 80%	308m 280v	a. $575 b. 420	20% $250	1:18 20%	30	$530	B.A., B.S.; *Semester, summer session;* Education—34%, Humanities—18%, Business—17%, Natural Sciences & Math—14%, Social Sciences—11%; Coop with Shaw University—course exchange; 3 hours Bible, 3 hours ethics, chapel services required.
Salem College Winston-Salem 1772 *Moravian*	587W	650	56% in top 1/5 55%	553m 539v	$2700 Total	13% $1070	1:11	69	$2,987	B.A., B.S., B.Mus.; *Semester;* Social Sciences—34%, Music—8%, Humanities—41%, Natural Sciences & Math—17%; *Music, Teacher Education;* Coop—exchange in course registration with Wake Forest College.
Shaw University Raleigh 1865 *Baptist*	269M 351W	1000	25% in top 1/4 50%		a. $600 b. 500 d. 143	61% $800	1:16 25%	28	$462	B.A., B.S., B.D.; *Semester, summer session;* Coop with St. Augustine's College, Raleigh.

Institution Location	Founded Affiliation	Enrollment M=men W=women	Projected enrollment in 1975	High school rating; % applicants accepted	SAT/ACT Averages m=math v=verbal	Annual Tuition: a. b. Room & Board; c. Out of state; d. Other state	% Students with $ aid Average amount	Faculty-student ratio; % with Doctorates	Volumes in library in 1,000's	Endowment in $1,000's	Undergraduate degrees offered; Calendar; Per cent of students per field of study; Professional programs offered; Miscellaneous
Wake Forest College Winston-Salem	1834 Baptist	1677M 725W	3700	85% in top 1/4 25%		a. $1000 b. 760	20% 70%	1:14	332		B.A., B.S., B.B.A.; *Semester, summer sessions;* Arts—53%, Sciences—17%, Business—9%; *Business, Law, Medicine;* Coops—3-2 engineering with N.C. State College, 3-2 forestry with Duke U.; Chapel services twice weekly required; Army ROTC optional.
Western Carolina College Cullowhee	1889 State	2084M 1580W	6000	88% in top 1/2 38%	M501m 453v W420v 460v	a. $150 b. 492 c. 402 d. 234	22% $325	1:19 40%	97	$110,000	B.A., B.S., B.S.Ed.; *Quarter, summer sessions;* Business—26%, Social Sciences—21%, Education—21%, Humanities—18%, Natural Sciences & Math—12%; *Teacher Education;* Coop—3-2 forestry with N.C. State University.
Winston-Salem State College Winston-Salem	1892 State	422M 1020W	3000	65% in top 1/4 73%		a. $100 b. 561 c. 300	65% $484	1:14 28%	62	$100	B.A., B.S.; *Semester, summer sessions;* Education—83%, Health & Physical Education—10%, Nursing—5%; *Teacher Education.*

NORTH DAKOTA

Institution Location	Founded Affiliation	Enrollment	Projected	HS rating	SAT/ACT	Tuition	% aid	Ratio	Vols	Endow	Degrees
Dickinson State College Dickinson	1918 State	760M 593W	2000	most in top 1/2 98%	19.2 (comp.)	a. $350 b. 496	35% $500	1:19 25%	35		B.S., B.A.—ADN.
Jamestown College Jamestown	1884 Presbyterian	293M 294W	1225	30% in top 1/5 70%	491m 496v	a. $1100 b. 900 d. 150	55% $700	1:12 22%	41	$1,750	B.A., B.S., B.S.Nurs.; *Semester, summer sessions;* Social Sciences—22%, Humanities—32%, Natural Sciences & Math—7%, Business—11%, Nursing—19%, Education—16%; *Nursing;* Coop—4-2 engineering with Stanford.
Mayville State College Mayville	1890 State	426M 295W	1200	90%	M20m 18v W18m 19v.	a. $240 b. 450 c. 450	30% $290	1:18 20%	35		B.A., B.S.Ed.; *Quarter; Teacher Education.*
Minot State College Minot	1913 State	787M 733W	2959	most in top 3/4 98%		a. $321 b. 550 c. 591 d. 75	25% $425	1:17 20%	83		B.A., B.S., B.S.Ed.; *Quarter, summer session;* Education—92%, Arts—8%; *Teacher Education, Medical Technology.*
North Dakota, University of Grand Forks	1883 State	4260M 2150W	10300	most in top 1/2 92%	M24m 20v W20m 22v	a. $375 b. 660 c. 819	25% $50-1000	1:20 37%	305		B.A., B.S., Ph.B.; *Semester, summer session;* Arts & Sciences—33%, Business—21%, Education—22%, Engineering—10%, Law—4%, Nursing—5%, Medicine—5%; Air Force, Army ROTC optional.
North Dakota State University Fargo	1890 State	3970M 1509W	7400	75% in top 1/2 85%	23 (comp.)	a. $360 b. 675 c. 804 d. 200	30% $400	1:20 40%	171	$2,700	B.A., B.S., B.Arch.; *Quarter, summer sessions;* Arts & Sciences—34%, Engineering—27%, Agriculture—15%, Home Economics—13%, Pharmacy—8%, Natural Sciences & Math—3%; *Engineering, Pharmacy;* Air Force, Army ROTC optional.
Valley City State College Valley City	1890 State	480M 437W	2700	85% in top 1/2		a. $150 b. 495 c. 360 d. 66	25% $390	1:20 17%	52	$850	B.A., B.S.; *Quarter, summer session;* Education—82%; *Teacher Education.*

OHIO

Institution Location	Founded Affiliation	Enrollment	Projected	HS rating	SAT/ACT	Tuition	% aid	Ratio	Vols	Endow	Degrees
Akron, University of Akron	1870 State	6962M 3765W	16000	43% in top 1/4 75%	M566m 484v W482m 469v	a. $456 b. 900 c. 1000	17% $175	57%	$245	$2,000	B.A., B.S., B.S.Ed., B.M.A.A., A.S.; *Semester, summer sessions;* Education—44%, Liberal Arts—25%, Business—22%, Engineering—7%, Fine Arts—2%; *Engineering, Law, Nursing, Education; Institute of Polymer Science Fellowships;* Air Force, Army ROTC required. Community & Technical College offers assoc. degrees in 14 fields.
Antioch College Yellow Springs	1852 Private	1014M 833W		78% in top 1/5 40%	M631m 629v W603m 637v	a. $1800 c. 628 d. 142	26% $471	1:8 55%	145	$5,466	B.A., B.S.; *Quarter;* Humanities—29%, Social Sciences—43%, Physical Sciences & Math—28%; *Engineering, Chemistry, Education;* Coop—4-1 Masters Degree program with U. of Chicago; Antioch has alternate work and study quarters, off and on campus, study abroad.
Ashland College Ashland	1878 Brethren Church	987M 791W	2800	30% in top 1/10 60%	495m 488v	a. $1056 b. 800	36% $318	1:14 26%	45	$957	B.A., B.S., B.S.B.A., B.S.Ed.; *Semester, summer session;* Social Sciences—10%, Education—51%, Business—19%, Humanities—8%, Natural Sciences & Math—12%; 4 hours Bible required.
Baldwin-Wallace College Berea	1845 Methodist	975M 975W	2400	55% in top 1/4 60%	M540m 500v W505m 515v	a. $1600 b. 870 d. 93	45% $700	1:19 55%	111	$4,186	B.A., B.S., B.Mus., B.Mus.Ed., B.S.Ed.; *Quarter, summer session; Music;* 5-6 quarter hours of history of religion required.
Bluffton College Bluffton	1900 Mennonite	311M 344W	800	84% in top 1/2 60%	M532m 470v W489m 500v	a. $1250 b. 800	20% $100-938	1:13 50%	40	$1,250	B.A., B.S., B.S.Ed.; *Semester, summer session;* Education—41%, Natural Sciences & Math—21%, Social Sciences—13%, Humanities—12%, Business—10%; Coop—3-2 engineering; 9 hours Bible study, chapel 4 times per week required.
Bowling Green State University Bowling Green	1910 State	5921M 5346W	19129	89% in top 1/2 74%	M23.7m 20.2v W21.5m 22.2v	a. none b. $850 c. 550 d. 520	35% $450	1:25 54%	460		B.A., B.S., B.F.A., B.Mus., B.S.Ed.; *Semester, summer sessions;* Education—26%, Humanities—21%, Business—14%, Social Sciences—14%, Natural Sciences & Math—14%; *Business, Music, Teacher Education;* Air Force, Army ROTC optional.
Capital University Columbus	1850 Lutheran	733M 765W	2000	69% in top 1/10 87%	M554m 496v W523m 515v	a. $900 b. 800 d. 100	35% $450	1:15 25%	70	$1,661	B.A., B.S., B.Mus., B.Mus.Ed., B.S.Ed., B.S.B.A., B.S.Nursing; *Semester, summer session;* Education—31%, Arts—27%, Sciences—17%, Nursing—10%, Music—8%, Business—7%; *Music, Nursing;* Air Force ROTC optional.
Case Institute of Technology Cleveland	1880 Private	1700M 20W	2000	51% in top 1/10 67%M 80%W	725m 650v	a. $2000 b. 1150 d. 400	35% $200-2600	1:8 93%	121	$30,000	B.S.; *Semester, summer research session (by selection);* Engineering—52%, Physics—14%, Metallurgy—12%; *Engineering;* Air Force ROTC optional.
Central State College Wilberforce	1887 State	1228M 1247W	3125			a. $335 b. 726 c. 635	33%	1:22 40%	70		B.A., B.S.; *Trimester; Music, Teacher Education;* Army ROTC required.

Institution / Location / Founded / Affiliation	Enrollment M=men W=women	Projected enrollment in 1975	High school rating; % applicants accepted	SAT/ACT Averages m=math v=verbal	a. Annual Tuition; b. Room & Board; c. Out of state; d. Other	% Students with $ aid; Average amount	Faculty-student ratio; % with Doctorates	Volumes in library in 1,000's	Endowment in $1,000's	Undergraduate degrees offered; Calendar; Per cent of students per field of study; Professional programs offered; Miscellaneous
Cincinnati, University of, Cincinnati 1819, Municipal	17262M 8325W	37439	65% in top 1/3* 70%	530m 504v *	a. $450 b. 975 c. 1050	10%	1:12	905	$33,897	B.A., B.S., B.B.A., B.F.A., B.Mus., B.S.Ed.; *Quarter, summer sessions;* Business—12%, Education—11%, Engineering—11%, Arts & Sciences—19%, Design, Arch., Art—8%, Music—4%; *Law, Med., Nurs. & Health, Pharmacy;* AF, A ROTC optional. * College of Arts & Sciences only.
Cleveland State University, Cleveland 1964, Public	5334M 2666W	15000	35% in top 1/4 76%	550m 480v	a. $495 b. 800 c. 990	18% $450 35%	1:21	100		B.A., B.S., B.B.A.; *Quarter;* Arts & Sciences—28%, Business—36%, Engineering—36%; *Engineering, Education.*
College of Mount St. Joseph on the Ohio, Mount St. Joseph 1853, Roman Catholic	1145W	1400	36% in top 1/4 83%	563m 597v	a. $900 b. 930 c. 100	36%	1:14 28%	72		B.A., B.S., B.Mus., B.Mus.Ed.; *Semester, summer session; Nursing.*
College of St. Mary of the Springs, Columbus 1911, Roman Catholic	265M 713W	2000	80% in top 1/2 71%	M500m 500v W492m 505v	a. $900 b. 900	40% $475 25%	1:14	41	$210	B.A., B.S., B.S.Ed.; *Semester, summer session;* Elementary Education—23%, Social Sciences—30%, Humanities—25%, Natural Sciences & Math—17%; Four years of theology required of Catholic students.
College of Steubenville, Steubenville 1946, Roman Catholic	550M 373W	1500	most in top 1/2 66%	465m 487v	a. $1200 b. 900	35% $560 17%	1:15	51		B.A., B.S.; *Semester, summer sessions.*
College of Wooster, Wooster 1866, Presbyterian	809M 690W	1500	65% in top 1/10 30%W 40%M	M605m 585v W570m 600v	a. $1700 b. 920 d. 100	40% $800 70%	1:12	350	$10,000	B.A., B.Mus., B.Mus.Ed.; *Semester, summer·session, summer session in Vienna;* Social Sciences—52%, Natural Sciences & Math—25%, Humanities—23%; *Music;* 6 credits of religion, four weekly chapels required.
Dayton, University of, Dayton 1850, Roman Catholic	4071M 1803W	8000	45% in top 1/4 60%M 40%W	525m 500v	a. $1000 b. 800 d. 150	50% $975 65%	1:18	200	$10,000	B.A., B.S., B.F.A., B.Mus., B.S.Ed., B.Engineering Tech.; *Trimester, summer term;* Arts & Sciences—40%, Education—22%, Business—20%, Engineering—13%; *Engineering, Teacher Education;* Army ROTC optional.
Defiance College, Defiance 1850, United Church of Christ	645M 339W	1200	60% in top 2/5 70%		a. $1350 b. 850	40% $50-1000 25%	1:15	50	$625	B.A., B.S.; *Semester (4-1-4);* Humanities—30%, Natural Sciences & Math—25%, Social Sciences—45%.
Denison University, Granville 1831, Baptist	947M 718W	2000	85% in top 1/5 80%M 56%W	M623m 565v W622m 617v	a. $1650 b. 960 d. 150	20% $125-2700 64%	1:13	155	$15,904	B.A., B.S., B.F.A., B.Mus.; *Semester;* Social Sciences—26%, Arts—8%, Humanities—42%, Natural Sciences & Math—24%; *Music;* Coops—3-2 engineering with R.P.I., 3-2 forestry with Duke, 3-2 graduate school with U. of Chicago; Air Force ROTC optional.
Heidelberg College, Tiffin 1850, United Church of Christ	568M 510W	1500	42% in top 1/5 71%	M556m 528v W525m 554v	a. $1520 b. 850 d. 100	40% $700 49%	1:14	94	$3,750	A.B., B.S., B.Mus.; *Semester, summer sessions;* Humanities—16%, Natural Sciences & Math—25%, Social Sciences—24%, Education—16%, Music—9%; Coops—3-2 agriculture with Ohio State, Med. Tech. and Nursing with Western Reserve, 3-2 forestry with Duke; 6 hours religion required, attendance required at convocations.
Hiram College, Hiram 1850, Disciples of Christ	583M 517W	1800	36% in top 1/10 73%	M574m 529v W554m 558v	a. $1615 b. 860 d. 160	33% $690 40%	1:14	98	$7,000	B.A.; *Quarter, summer quarter;* Natural Sciences & Math—20%, Social Sciences—38%, Humanities—15%, Education—11%, Fine Arts—15%; *Teacher Education;* One course in religion required.
John Carroll University, Cleveland 1886, Roman Catholic	2339M	2876	42% in top 1/4 79%	532m 502v	a. $1190 b. 900	24% $75-1500 41%	1:15	160		B.A., B.S.; *Semester, summer sessions;* B.A./B.S.—75%, Business—25%; *Teacher Education;* Coop in engineering with U. of Detroit; Army ROTC required.
Kent State University, Kent 1910, State	9536M 7667W	25000	39% in top 1/4 72%		a. $510 b. 789 c. 960	23% $300-600 49%	1:26	400		B.A., B.S., B.Arch., B.F.A., B.B.A.; *Quarter, summer quarter; Architecture, Business, Library, Music, Teacher Education;* Air Force, Army ROTC optional.
Kenyon College, Gambier 1824, Episcopalian	850M	825M 625W	69% in top 1/4 53%	630m 611v	a. $1760 b. 1000 d. 115	25% $100-2200 63%	1:11	192	$8,195	B.A.; *Semester; Theology;* Air Force ROTC optional.
Lake Erie College, Painesville 1856, Private	600W	715	44% in top 1/5 51%	535m 555v	$3000 Total	25% $100-1275 47%	1:12	60	$1,824	B.A.; *Trimester, summer session;* Junior Class spends winter term at one of 10 study centers in Europe (open to Lake Erie Students only).
Malone College, Canton 1892, Quaker	470M 554W	1500	45% in top 1/4		a. $750 b. 489 d. 50	$490 39%	1:16	33	$546	B.A., B.S.; *Semester, summer session;* Education—46%, Social Sciences—21%, Humanities—16%, Natural Sciences & Math—12%, Business—5%; Coop engineering with Ohio State.
Marietta College, Marietta 1835, Private	1013M 714W	1800	53% in top 1/5 62%	M556m 496v W539m 542v	a. $1400 b. 850 d. 50	23% $890 28%	1:18	136	$4,380	B.A., B.S., B.S. in Petroleum Studies; *Semester, summer session;* Natural Sciences & Math—32%, Social Sciences—41%, Humanities—26%; Coops—3-2 engineering with Case, Columbia, U. of Penn., 3-2 forestry with Duke, 3-2 natural resources with Michigan.
Mary Manse College, Toledo 1922, Roman Catholic	1517W	2000	85% in top 1/2 52%		a. $650 b. 790 d. 75	20% $300 15%	1:15	52		B.A., B.S., B.Mus.; *Semester, summer session.*
Miami University, Oxford 1809, State	5405M 4480W	12500	M70% in top 1/4 W80% in top 1/10 40%	M575m 550v W575m 580v	a. $540 b. 850 c. 500 d. 100	11% $50-1400 50%	1:18	500	$1,611	B.A., B.S., B.F.A., B.Mus.; *Trimester;* Arts & Sciences—42%, Education—30%, Business—16%, Fine Arts—5%, Applied Sci.—7%; *Art, Architecture, Business, Music, Teacher Education;* Coops—engineering with Case, Columbia, M.I.T., forestry with Duke; Air Force, Navy ROTC optional.
Mount Union College, Alliance 1846, Methodist	1614M 609W	1500	69% in top 1/4 70%	M554m 499v W522m 524v	a. $1605 b. 840	50% $100-1600 45%	1:16	125	$3,500	B.A., B.S., B.Mus., B.Mus.Ed.; *Three-term, summer session;* Arts—40%, Education—29%, Sciences—23%, Music—8%; *Music;* Coop in engineering with U. of Pennsylvania, Ohio State; 2 courses in religion, weekly chapel service required.

Institution Location / Founded Affiliation	Enrollment M=men W=women	Projected enrollment in 1975	High school rating; % applicants accepted	SAT/ACT Averages m=math v=verbal	a. Annual Tuition; b. Room & Board; c. Out of state; d. Other state	% Students with $ aid / Average amount	Faculty-student ratio; % with Doctorates	Volumes in library in 1,000's	Endowment in $1,000's	Undergraduate degrees offered; *Calendar;* Per cent of students per field of study; *Professional programs offered;* Miscellaneous
Muskingum College New Concord 1837 *Presbyterian*	710M 694W	1600	35% in top 1/10 40%M 45%W	M555m 505v W534m 535v	a. $1530 b. 840 d. 70	35% $830	1:14 44%	100	$6,583	B.A., B.Mus.; *Semester, summer sessions;* B.A.—75%, B.S.—9%, B.S.Ed.—14%, B.Mus.—2%.
Notre Dame College Cleveland 1922 *Roman Catholic*	619W	1000	90% in top 1/2 90%		a. $800 b. 880	20% $300	1:10 22%	45		B.A., B.S.; *Semester;* Social Sciences—23%, Humanities—13%, Sciences—27%, Home Economics—7%.
Oberlin College Oberlin 1833 *Private*	1335M 1113W	2600	68% in top 1/10 47%	656m 652v	a. $1750 b. 1060 d. 100	40% $100-3000	1:13 78%	630	$60,456	B.A., B.Mus.; *Semester, music summer session; M.A.T., Music;* Coop—5-year engineering with Case Institute, 5-year music in Oberlin Conservatory.
Ohio Northern University Ada 1871 *Methodist*	1638M 737W	2700	90% in top 1/2 77%	22.9 (comp.)	a. $913 b. 770	40% $700	1:16 37%	53	$2,400	B.A., B.S.; *Quarter, summer sessions;* Liberal Arts—69%, Engineering—7%, Pharmacy—9%, Law—13%; *Engineering, Law, Pharmacy.*
Ohio State University Columbus 1870 *State*	26718M 14489W	28000	73% in top 1/3 80%	M19.7 W21.5 (comp.)	a. $450 b. 825 c. 1008	20% $475	1:13 57%	1850	$19,842	B.A., B.S.; *Quarter, summer quarter;* Ed.—29%, Arts & Sci.—23%, Ag.—9%, Bus.—9%, Eng.—9%; *Arch., Bus., Dent., Eng., Jour., Landscape Arch., Law, Med., Music, Nurs., Opt., Phar., Phys. & Oc. Ther., Psych., Social Work, Teacher Ed.;* Air Force, Army, Navy ROTC optional.
Ohio University Athens 1804 *State*	9216M 5840W	20000	90% in top 1/2 88%		a. $495 b. 867 c. 990	35% $50-1250	1:20 50%	400	$1,250	B.A., B.S.; *Quarter, summer sessions; Business, Engineering, Journalism, Music, Teacher Education;* Air Force, Army ROTC optional.
Ohio Wesleyan University Delaware 1842 *Methodist*	1300M 1200W	2500	90% in top 1/2 70%	M598m 548v W570m 571v	a. $1700 b. 900	27% $300-1800	1:14 53%	300	$7,900	B.A., B.F.A., B.Mus.; *Three-term, summer session; Music;* Coops with M.I.T., Carnegie Tech., Case, R.P.I., Cal. Tech., N.Y.U., Drew University; Air Force ROTC optional.
Otterbein College Westerville 1847 *Evangelical United Brethren*	707M 686W	2000	31% in top 1/10	M518m 498v W520m 520v	a. $1405 b. 840	34% $650	1:15 30%	75	$3,052	B.A., B.S., B.Mus., B.Mus.Ed., B.S.Ed.; *Semester, summer session;* Humanities—50%, Education—32%, Sciences—14%; *Music, Teacher Education;* Coop—3-2 engineering with N.Y.U., 3-2 forestry with Duke; 6 hours of religion, weekly convocation required; Air Force ROTC optional.
Saint John College of Cleveland Cleveland 1928 *Roman Catholic*	638W	1270	56% in top 1/5 67%	500m 510v	a. $800 b. 870	33% $1000	1:8 25%	40		B.S.; *Semester, summer session; Nursing, Teacher Education.*
Toledo, University of Toledo 1872 *Municipal & State*	5754M 2449W	25000	70% in top 1/3 61%	M530m 495v W490m 489v	a. $544 b. 800 c. 960 d. 102	35% $50-2000	1:17 45%	300	$400	B.A., B.S., B.B.A., B.S.Ed.; *Semester, summer sessions;* Education—33%, Sciences—30%, Business—26%, Arts—11%; *Business, Engineering, Law, Pharmacy, Teacher Education;* Army ROTC optional.
Ursuline College for Women Cleveland 1871 *Roman Catholic*	468W	1000	91% in top 3/5	485m 520v	a. $800 b. 900	45% $370	1:10 30%	40		B.A.; *Semester;* Social Sciences—20%, Humanities—36%, Natural Sciences & Math—24%, Applied Arts—20%.
Western College for Women Oxford 1853 *Private*	500W	750	39% in top 1/4 84%	512m 504v	$2500 Total d. $35	26% $800	1:10 42%	60	$1,847	B.A.; *Three-term;* Social Sciences—21%, Humanities—49%, Natural Sciences & Math—16%, Home Economics—9%, Intercultural Studies—3%, Med. Tech.—1%, Phys.Ed.—1%; *Music.*
Western Reserve University Cleveland 1826 *Private*	1200M 1100W	2500	74% in top 1/5 70%	M624m 577v W581m 586v	a. $1650 b. 1000 d. 20	29% $1225	1:8 80%	876	$41,235	B.A., B.S., B.Arch., B.B.A.; *Semester, summer sessions;* Arts and Sciences—50%; *Business, Dentistry, Law, Library, Medicine, Nursing, Applied Social Sciences.*
Wilberforce University Wilberforce 1856 *African Methodist Episcopal*	411M 431W	1200	most in top 2/3 75%		a. $880 b. 690	$315	1:5 5%	33	$25	B.A., B.S., B.S.Ed., B.D.; *Trimester;* Soc.—25%, History—1%, Psychology—8%, Economics—12%, English—6%, Social Studies—4%, Biology—4%, Business—5%, Math—1%, Education—16%.
Wilmington College Wilmington 1870 *Quaker*	596M 328W	1000	37% in top 1/4 54%	497m 485v	a. $1120 b. 780 d. 105	16% $500	1:15 41%	56	$1,400	B.A., B.S.; *Quarter, summer sessions;* Social Sciences—36%, Humanities—20%, Natural Sciences & Math—18%, Education—16%, Business—10%; *Teacher Education;* Academic Honor System; International emphasis.
Wittenberg University Springfield 1845 *Lutheran*	1143M 1136W	2900	43% in top 1/10 61%	M579m 534v W565m 556v	a. $1605 b. 894 d. 144	41% $100-1600	1:14 52%	147	$11,489	B.A., B.F.A., B.Mus., B.Mus.Ed.; *Term, summer sessions;* Social Sciences—25%, Education—29%, Humanities—23%, Natural Sciences & Math—12%, Business—12%; *Music, Teacher Education, Theology;* Coop—3-2 engineering with Case, Columbia; 2 religion courses required; 4-year Honors Program.
Xavier University Cincinnati 1831 *Roman Catholic*	2270M	3000	71% in top 1/2 72%	525m 496v	a. $1200 b. 990	25% $250-1100	1:17 43%	136	$1,515	A.B., B.S. in B.A.; *Semester, summer sessions;* Business—30%, Social Sciences—37%, Natural Sciences & Math—17%, Humanities—15%; *Bus. Adm., Hospital Adm., Teacher Ed., Psychology;* 8 semester hours of theology required of Catholic students; Army ROTC required for two years.
Youngstown University Youngstown 1908 *Private*	8523M 3510W	20000	35% in top 1/3	460m 425v	a. $480 b. 900	9% $200	1:16	156		B.A., B.S., B.B.A., B.Mus.; *Semester, summer sessions; Engineering, Music;* Army ROTC optional.

OKLAHOMA

Institution Location / Founded Affiliation	Enrollment M=men W=women	Projected enrollment in 1975	High school rating; % applicants accepted	SAT/ACT Averages m=math v=verbal	a. Annual Tuition; b. Room & Board; c. Out of state; d. Other state	% Students with $ aid / Average amount	Faculty-student ratio; % with Doctorates	Volumes in library in 1,000's	Endowment in $1,000's	Undergraduate degrees offered; *Calendar;* Per cent of students per field of study; *Professional programs offered;* Miscellaneous
Bethany Nazarene College Bethany 1899 *Nazarene*	792M 759W	2600	75% in top 1/2	M19 W19 (comp.)	a. $600 b. 572	75% $285	1:25 51%	54		B.A., B.S.; *Semester, summer sessions;* Social Science—14%, Education—38%, Humanities—6%, Natural Science & Math—13%, Business—15%, Religion—14%; *Teacher Education, Theology.*

Institution Location	Founded Affiliation	Enrollment M=men W=women	Projected enrollment in 1975	High school rating; % applicants accepted	SAT/ACT Averages m=math v=verbal	a. Annual Tuition; b. Room & Board; c. Out of state; d. Other	% Students with $ aid Average amount	Faculty-student ratio; % with Doctorates	Volumes in library in 1,000's	Endowment in $1,000's	Undergraduate degrees offered; Calendar; Per cent of students per field of study; Professional programs offered; Miscellaneous
Central State College Edmond	1891 State	4704M 3148W	15000	most in top 3/4 60%	18.4 (comp.)	a. $216 b. 690 c. 524	20% $350	1:27 40%	125		B.A., B.S., B.M.E.; Semester, summer session; Teacher Education; Teaching—60%, Non-Teaching—40%.
East Central State College Ada	1909 State	1678M 1407W	5000	all in top 3/4		a. $216 b. 650 c. 296	28% $440	1:28 34%	63		B.A., B.S., B.A.Ed., B.S.Ed.; Semester, summer session; Teacher Education.
Langston University Langston	1897 State	600M 700W	2000	23% in top 1/4 95%		a. $216 b. 527 c. 512	65% $350	1:18 23%	94		B.A., B.S., B.S.Ed.; Semester, summer session; Natural Sciences & Math—25%, Education—30%, Social Sciences—17%, Home Economics—9%, Business—10%, Humanities—5%, Agriculture—3%.
Northeastern State College Tahlequah	1846 State	2861M 2219W		70%		a. $202 b. 650	40% $350	1:34 35%	110		B.A., B.S.; Semester, summer session; Teacher Education.
Northwestern State College Alva	1897 State	1028M 960W	3600	90%		a. $216 b. 576 c. 480	20% $400	1:32 33%	65		B.A., B.S., B.S.Ed.; Semester, summer session; Education—64%, Social Sciences—15%, Natural Sciences & Math—13%, Business—7%; Teacher Education.
Oklahoma, University of Norman	1890 State U.	10014M 5457W Total U.	26000	most in top 1/2 88%		a. $270 b. 740 c. 690		1:28 55%	1040		B.A., B.S., B.B.A., B.F.A., B.Mus.; Semester, summer sessions; Arts—26%, Business—19%, Engineering—18%, Education—16%; Arch., Bus., Eng., Jour., Law, Lib., Med., Music, Nurs., Phar., Phys. Ther., Psych., Social Work, Teacher Ed.; Air Force, Army, Navy ROTC optional.
Oklahoma Baptist University Shawnee	1910 Baptist	683M 785W	1800	70%		a. $600 b. 630	30% $350	1:11 37%	72	$2,900	B.A., B.S., B.Mus., B.Mus.Ed.; Semester, summer session; Music, Nursing, Hospital Ad.; 6 hours Biblical literature, semi-weekly chapel attendance required.
Oklahoma City University Oklahoma City	1904 Methodist	1724M 1114W	4000	58% in top 1/3 80%		a. $700 b. 580		1:13 60%	100	$2,000	B.A.; Semester, summer sessions; Law, Music; 6 hours of religion courses required.
							$50-600				
Oklahoma College of Liberal Arts Chickasha	1908 State	253M 754W	2400	most in top 1/2 98%	M18 W18.3	a. $300 b. 930 c. 690	15% $50-250	1:14 32%	56		B.A., B.S.; Trimester (summer session); Sciences—40%, Arts—20%, Teacher Education—40%.
Oklahoma State University Stillwater	1890 State	13500M 5800W	20000	90%		a. $270 b. 750 c. 690	3% $200-500	1:22 60%	980	$9,605	B.A., B.S., B.F.A., B.Mus., B.Mus.Ed.; Semester, summer session; Architecture, Business, Engineering, Journalism, Music, Teacher Education, Veterinary Medicine; Air Force, Army ROTC optional.
Panhandle Agricultural and Mechanical College Goodwell	1909 State	707M 460W	2733	20% in top 1/4 86%	16m 17v	a. $216 b. 540 c. 512	45% $400	1:24 22%	35		B.A., B.S., B.Mus.Ed.; Semester, summer session; Business—27%, Education—25%, Natural Sciences & Math—16%, Physical Education—11%, Social Sciences—10%, Agriculture—9%; Teacher Education; Army ROTC required.
Phillips University Enid	1907 Disciples of Christ	838M 627W	2000	25% in top 1/5	21.7 (comp.)	a. $930 b. 650	27% $300	1:18 42%	127		B.A., B.S., B.F.A., B.Mus.; B.Mus.Ed.; Semester, summer session; Education—43%, Liberal Arts—22%, Business—17%, Bible—12%, Fine Arts—6%; Music, Teacher Education, Theology.
Southeastern State College Durant	1909 State	1220M 985W	3000	90%		a. $168 b. 388 c. 416	30% $270	1:22 40%	84		B.A., B.S., B.Mus., B.S.Ed.; Semester, summer session; Teacher Education.
Southwestern State College Weatherford	1903 State	2573M 1607W	6887	20% in top 1/4 96%		a. $216 b. 552 c. 512	15% $600	1:23 33%	71		B.A., B.S., B.A.Ed., B.S.Ed., B.S.Pharmacy; Semester, summer session; Education—45%, Liberal Arts—33%, Pharmacy—17%, Med.Tech.—5%.
Tulsa, University of Tulsa	1894 Total M & W Presbyterian	3196	3660	90% in top 1/2 75%	M538m 500v W480m 500v	a. $675 b. 1925	27% $100-600	1:17 52%	225	$7,400	B.A., B.S., B.F.A., B.Mus., B.Mus.Ed.; Semester, summer session; Business, Engineering, Law, Music, Teacher Education; 3 semester hours of Biblical literature required; Air Force ROTC optional.

OREGON

Institution Location	Founded Affiliation	Enrollment	Projected	HS rating	SAT/ACT	Tuition	% aid	Ratio	Vols	Endowment	Degrees
Cascade College Portland	1918 Private	163M 141W	750	90% in top 1/2 90%	M459m 449v W443m 457v	a. $900 b. 954 d. 209	63% $570	1:12 30%	28		B.A., B.S.; Three-term; Social Sciences—19%, Humanities—63%, Natural Sciences—13%, Education—25%; Coops—3-1 Elementary Ed. with Oregon College of Education, 3-1 Medical Technology with U. of Oregon Medical School; Religion and daily chapel attendance required.
Eastern Oregon College La Grande	1929 State	793M 661W	1985	88%		a. $294 b. 787 c. 534	38% $510	1:20 30%	60		B.A., B.S.; Quarter, summer session; Education—79%, Liberal Arts—21%; Teacher Education.
George Fox College Newberg	1891 Quaker	190M 162W	600	94%		a. $990 b. 790	40% $400	1:13 25%	31	$1,000	B.A., B.S.; Term; Coops—3-1 teacher education with Oregon College of Education, major in art with Portland Museum Art School, medical technology with local hospital; 18 term hours of religion courses required.
Lewis and Clark College Portland	1867 Presbyterian	800M 750W	1750	75% in top 1/4	554m 553v	a. $1680 b. 870	35% $100-1680	1:14 60%	75	$2,500	B.A., B.S., B.Mus., B.Mus.Ed.; Three-term, summer session; Social Sciences—20%, Humanities—22%, Education—15%, Business—15%, Natural Sciences & Math—18%, Fine Arts—10%; Music, Teacher Education; 10% of student body in foreign study each year, Freshmen eligible.
Linfield College McMinnville	1849 Baptist	650M 576W	1350	most in top 1/4 40%		a. $1200 b. 800	31% $200	1:15 60%	55	$2,250	B.A., B.S.; Semester, summer sessions; Arts—60%, Sciences—40%; Music.

Institution / Location / Founded / Affiliation	Enrollment M=men W=women	Projected enrollment in 1975	High school rating; % applicants accepted	SAT/ACT Averages m=math v=verbal	a. Annual Tuition; b. Room & Board; c. Out of state; d. Other	% Students with $ aid / Average amount	Faculty-student ratio; % with Doctorates	Volumes in library in 1,000's	Endowment in $1,000's	Undergraduate degrees offered; Calendar; Per cent of students per field of study; Professional programs offered; Miscellaneous
Marylhurst College Marylhurst 1893 *Roman Catholic*	752W	950	38% in top 1/5 82%	457m 488v	a. $650 b. 840 c. 100	40% $650	1:12 20%	52	$215	B.A., B.S., B.Mus., B.S.Ed.; *Semester, summer session;* Arts—67%, Education—22%, Natural Sciences—11%; *Music, Teacher Education;* 21 hours of theology & philosophy of Catholics, 16 hours of non-Catholics required.
Mt. Angel College Mt. Angel 1888 *Roman Catholic*	155M 233W	1000			a. $900 b. 720	33%	1:11 15%	25	$30	B.A., B.S.; *Semester, summer session;* Education—50%, Social Sciences—32%, English—15%, Math—1%, Art—2%; Coops—teaching internship with U. of Oregon, medical technology with local hospital; 10 hours of theology required of Catholic students; ROTC with Willamette U.
Oregon, University of Eugene 1872 *State*	7840M 5210W	14000	92%	M540m 503v W493m 508v	a. $330 b. 780 c. 900	10% $300-400	1:18 55%	1145	$2,840	B.A., B.S., B.Arch., B.I.Arch., B.L.A., B.F.A., B.B.A., B.Ed., B.P.E., B.Mus.; *Three-term, summer sessions;* Liberal Arts—55%, Business—11%, Education—10%, Architecture—6%, Nursing—6%; *Arch., Bus., Dent., Jour., Landscape Arch., Med., Music, Nurs., Psych., Teacher Ed.;* Air Force, Army ROTC optional.
Oregon College of Education Monmouth 1882 *State*	1250M 1160W	3200	90%	442m 431v	a. $333 b. 720 c. 534	20% $200	1:22 33%	75		B.A., B.S.; *Quarter, summer session;* Education—95%, Liberal Arts—5%; *Teacher Education;* Air Force ROTC optional.
Oregon State University Corvallis 1858 *State*	8311M 4357W	18000			a. $369 b. 810 c. 999	40%	1:16	520	$700	B.A., B.S., B.S.Ed.; *Quarter, summer session;* Education—15%, Sciences—24%, Business—12%, Engineering—15%, Agriculture—8%, Home Economics—7%, Pharmacy—3%, Humanities & Soc. Sciences—13%; *Business, Engineering, Forestry, Music, Psychology, Pharmacy, Teacher Education;* AF, A, N ROTC optional.
Pacific University Forest Grove 1849 *Congregational*	613M 298W	1500	most in top 2/5 60%		a. $1300 b. 800	38% $500	1:14 55%	250	$5,000	B.A., B.S., B.Mus., B.Mus. Ed.; *Semester, summer session;* Liberal Arts—50%, Education—25%, Optometry—20%, Music—5%; *Optometry;* Coops—3-2 engineering, law, pharmacy, veterinary medicine, 3-4 dentistry, medicine.
Portland, University of Portland 1901 *Roman Catholic*	1036M 820W		75% in top 1/3		a. $1200 b. 850	50% $100-1000	1:14 40%	100		B.A., B.S.; *Semester, summer session;* Arts—52%, Business—17%, Sciences—16%, Engineering—12%, Music—3%; *Nursing;* 8 hours of religion courses required of Catholic students; Air Force ROTC optional.
Portland State College Portland 1955 *State*	4605M 3501W	10275	95%		a. $369 b. no dorm c. 999	25% $350	1:18 54%	189		B.A., B.S.; *Quarter, summer session;* Arts & Letters—20%, Bus. Adm.—16%, Education—13%, Science—20%, Social Science—31%; *Education, German, Social Work.*
Reed College Portland 1911 *Private*	627M 438W	1345	78% in top 1/10 74%	650m 675v	a. $2200 b. 790 d. 56	40% $100-3500	1:10 58%	250	$5,361	B.A.; *Semester, summer session (for secondary school teachers);* Sciences & Math—28%, Social Sciences—24%, Humanities—33%, Education (in M.A.T. program)—15%; Coops—5-year forestry with Duke, art with Portland Museum School, engineering with Cal. Tech., Columbia, R.P.I.
Southern Oregon College Ashland 1926 *State*	2180M 1238W	5000	most in top 1/2 92%	M496m 434v W449m 467v	a. $294 b. 760 c. 534	55% $350	1:21 38%	75		B.A., B.S., A.A., A.S.; *Three-term, summer session;* Education—40%, Liberal Arts—30%, Business—20%, 2-year terminal—10%; *Teacher Education.*
Warner Pacific College Portland 1937 *Church of God*	188M 156W	750	70% in top 1/2 90%	452m 432v	a. $810 b. 750 d. 90	60% $500	1:13 40%	33		B.A., B.Th., B.S.; *Quarter;* Social Sciences—39%, Religion—32%, Education—16%, Humanities—13%; Chapel attendance twice per week required; Grants totaling $503,000 since 1960.
Willamette University Salem 1842 *Methodist*	689M 533W	1700	most in top 1/4 65%		a. $1160 b. 800	35% $200-2100	1:14 50%	105	$8,143	B.A.; *Semester, summer session;* Social Sciences—60%, Natural Sciences & Math—26%, Humanities—14%; *Law, Music;* Coops—3-2 engineering with Columbia, Stanford, 3-2 forestry with Duke; One course in religion required; AF ROTC optional.

PENNSYLVANIA

Institution / Location / Founded / Affiliation	Enrollment M=men W=women	Projected enrollment in 1975	High school rating; % applicants accepted	SAT/ACT Averages m=math v=verbal	a. Annual Tuition; b. Room & Board; c. Out of state; d. Other	% Students with $ aid / Average amount	Faculty-student ratio; % with Doctorates	Volumes in library in 1,000's	Endowment in $1,000's	Undergraduate degrees offered; Calendar; Per cent of students per field of study; Professional programs offered; Miscellaneous
Albright College Reading 1856 *Evangelical United Brethren*	651M 475W	1200	50% in top 1/5 60%	M580m 528v W558m 540v	a. $1750 b. 850 d. 25	40% $460	1:12 34%	98	$2,552	B.A., B.S.; *Semester, summer session;* Social Sciences—23%, Natural Sciences & Math—25%, Business—9%, Humanities—32%, Home Ec.—11%; Coops—3-2 engineering with Penn. State, Buck-nell, U. Penn., 3-2 forestry with Duke U., 2-3 nursing with Reading Hospital; 9 hours religion, weekly chapel required.
Allegheny College Meadville 1815 *Private*	912M 592W	1800	70% in top 1/10 51% M 30% W	M615m 597v W598m 625v	a. $1850 b. 800	30% $560	1:13 60%	170	$8,120	B.A., B.S.; *Three-term, summer sessions;* Social Sciences—46%, Natural Sciences & Math—22%, Humanities—32%; Coop—3-2 engineering with Columbia; Air Force ROTC optional.
Alliance College Cambridge Springs 1912 *Private*	430M 120W	1000	20% in top 1/5 60%	M450m 450v W450m 450v	a. $1000 b. 750 d. 80	60% $400	1:12 30%	40	$3,000	B.A., B.S.; *Semester;* Social Sciences—38%, Natural Sciences & Math—40%, Business—10%, Humanities—12%.
Beaver College Glenside 1853 *United Presbyterian*	792W	1200	57% in top 1/5 54%	575m 580v	a. $1700 b. 1100 d. 75	17% $200-3100	1:12 40%	60	$230	B.A., B.S., B.F.A.; *Semester;* Humanities—33%, Education—28%, Social Sciences—24%, Natural Sciences & Math—15%; Coop—London Semester with College of the City of London.
Bloomsburg State College Bloomsburg 1839 *State*	1764M 1606W	6000	45% in top 1/5 60%	511m 485v	a. $300 b. 612 c. 600	30% $300	1:16 28%	90		B.S.Ed., A.B.; *Semester, summer session;* Education—90%, Arts & Sciences—10%; *Teacher Education.*
Bryn Mawr College Bryn Mawr 1880 *Private*	750W				a. $1550 b. 1150	32%	1:8	315	$20,300	B.A.; *Semester;* Pre-Med., Languages; Bryn Mawr has a graduate school of 350 men and women that grants a PhD.; Junior Year Abroad program.
Bucknell University Lewisburg 1846 *Private*	1693M 946W	3000	78% in top 1/5 42%	M653m 602v W645m 638v	a. $1750 b. 850 d. 150	51% $1150	1:12 56%	244	$14,269	B.A., B.S., B.Mus., B.S.Ed., B.S.B.A., B.S.Engineering; *Semester, summer session, summer institute for foreign students;* Arts & Sciences—69%, Engineering—18%, Business—13%; *Music, Engineering;* Coop—5-year engineering at Bucknell; Army ROTC optional.
California State College California 1852 *State*	2334M 1669W	6000	40% in top 1/4 65%	484m 472v	a. See misc. d. $544 d. 200	25% $360	1:20 25%	82		B.A., B.S. Ed.; *Trimester, summer session;* Teacher Education; Tuition—$290 teacher education, $340 liberal arts.

Institution / Location / Founded / Affiliation	Enrollment M=men W=women	Projected enrollment in 1975	High school rating; % applicants accepted	SAT/ACT Averages m = math v = verbal	a. Annual Tuition; b. Room & Board; c. Out of State; d. Other	% Students with $ aid / Average amount	Faculty-student ratio; % with Doctorates	Volumes in library in 1,000's	Endowment in $1,000's	Undergraduate degrees offered; Calendar; Per cent of students per field of study; Professional programs offered; Miscellaneous
Carnegie Institute of Technology Pittsburgh 1900 *Private*	2023M 1020W	3500	86% in top 2/5 50%	see misc.	a. $1950 b. 1000 d. 150	31% $950	1:9 70%	246	$59,900	B.A., B.S., B.F.A., B. Arch.; *Semester, summer sessions; Architecture, Art, Business, Engineering, Music;* Coop—interinstitutional exchange with Chatham College; Army ROTC optional; S.A.T. scores—Eng. & Science, 686m, 604v; Fine Arts, 549m, 562v; Margaret Morrison College, 586m, 578v.
Cedar Crest College Allentown 1867 *United Church of Christ*	655W	850	77% in top 1/5	568m 568v	a. $1500 b. 1100 d. 80	20% $800	1:12 40%	53	$1,486	B.A., B.S.; *Semester;* Liberal Arts—94%, Medical Technology—4%, Nursing—2%; 2 courses in religion required; Grants totaling $121,500 since 1960.
Chatham College Pittsburgh 1869 *Private*	660W	750	60% in top 1/5 55%	557m 601v	a. $1850 b. 1050 d. 50	35% $1400	1:11 60%	70	$8,250	B.A., B.S.; *Semester;* Humanities—45%, Social Sciences—35%, Natural Sciences—20%; Coop—interinstitutional exchange with Carnegie U.; Washington Semester.
Chestnut Hill College Philadelphia 1871 *Roman Catholic*	648W	700	64% in top 1/5 60%	546m 564v	a. $1300 b. 1000	20% $900	1:10 34%	71	$500	A.B., B.S.; *Semester;* Natural Sciences—30%, Humanities—53%, Social Sciences—17%; Junior Year Abroad program; Honors program.
Cheyney State College Cheyney 1837 *State*	787M 869W		48% in top 2/5	435m 448v	b. $612 c. 20/ credit d. 185	24% $203	1:15 21%	56		B.A., B.S.Ed.; *Semester, summer session; Teacher Education.*
Clarion State College Clarion 1867 *State*	1399M 1475W	5500	47% in top 1/5 25%	535m 509v	a. $275 b. 612 d. 50	40% $800	1:16 30%	125		B.A., B.S.Ed.; *Semester, summer session;* Education—70%, Liberal Arts—25%, Library Science—5%.
College Misericordia Dallas 1923 *Roman Catholic*	1315W	1600	most in top 1/2 57%	481m 488v	a. $800 b. 900 d. 100		1:15 25%	51		B.A., B.S., B.Mus., B.S.Nurs.; *Semester, summer session;* Education, Music, Nursing.
Dickinson College Carlisle 1773 *Private*	896M 477W	1500	74% in top 1/5 37%	M639m 623v W617m 642v	a. $1850 b. 950 d. 150	33% $1254	1:13 65%	158	$8,082	B.A., B.S.; *Semester, summer session;* Social Sciences—36%, Humanities—28%, Natural Sciences & Math—28%, Education—8%; Coop—3-2 engineering with Case, R.P.I., U. Penn.; Army ROTC optional; Grants totaling $895,000 since 1960.
Drexel Institute of Technology Philadelphia 1891 *Private*	4372M 956W	6000	85% in top 2/5 58%	620m 535v	a. $1200 b. 1065 d. 150	33% $400-600	1:17 45%	215	$12,527	B.S.; *Quarter, summer session;* Engineering & Science—67%, Business Administration—25%, Home Economics—8%; *Business Administration, Engineering, Science, Home Economics, Library Science.*
Duquesne University Pittsburgh 1878 *Roman Catholic*	2978M 2345W	10000	72% in top 2/5 68%	515m 506v	a. $1300 b. 870 d. 200	33% $550	1:11 47%	202	$600	B.A., B.S., B.Mus., B.Ed.; *Semester, summer session;* Arts & Sciences—30%, Education—22%, Business—17%; *Business, Law, Music, Nursing, Pharmacy, Teacher Education;* 8 credits religion required of Catholic students; Air Force ROTC required; Grants totaling $3,600,000 since 1960.
Eastern Baptist College St. Davids 1932 *Baptist*	245M 284W	750	65%	528m 532v	a. $1200 b. 800 d. 125	50% $600	1:12 25%	39	$1,200	B.A.; *Semester;* Elementary and Secondary Education—30%, Pre-Theological—15%, Liberal Arts.
East Stroudsburg State College East Stroudsburg 1893 *State*	915M 1203W	4000	most in top 1/2 14%	M518m 500v W488m 482v	a. $250 b. 612 c. 640 d. 100	30% $400	1:13 25%	50		B.A., B.S.Ed.; *Semester, summer session;* Education—61%, Health—30%, Liberal Arts—9%; *Teacher Education.*
Edinboro State College Edinboro 1857 *State*	1812M 2370W	8100	69% in top 2/5 53%	466m 476v	a. $250 b. 612	30% $750	1:20 20%	127		B.A., B.S.; *Semester, summer sessions;* Teacher Education—93%, Arts & Science—7%; *Teacher Education (Secondary, Elementary, Guidance).*
Elizabethtown College Elizabethtown 1899 *Church of the Brethren*	727M 632W	1900	99% in top 1/2 50%	525m 525v	a. $1390 b. 825	40% $600	1:20 20%	60	$1,000	B.A., B.S.; *Semester, summer sessions;* Arts & Sciences—45%, Business—20%, Education—35%; Coops—engineering with Penn. State, forestry with Duke University; Chapel attendance and 2 academic Bible courses required.
Franklin and Marshall College Lancaster 1787 *Private*	1600M	2000	91% in top 1/5 51%		a. $1900 b. 980	35% $1200	1:14 75%	191	$5,717	B.A.; *Semester, summer session;* Social Sciences—37%, Natural Sciences & Math—34%, Business—16%, Humanities—14%; Coops—3-2 engineering with R.P.I., Columbia, U. Penn., 3-2 forestry with Duke University; Special individual study & research programs for highly-talented students.
Gannon College Erie 1944 *Roman Catholic*	1926M	3500	24% in top 1/5 59%	518m 480v	a. $850 b. 700 d. 75	25% $400-600	1:20 35%	70	$250	B.A., B.S., B.Engineering; *Semester, summer sessions;* Science & Engineering—48%, Humanities—27%, Business—25%; *Engineering, Teacher Education;* Coop—fine arts & art ed. with Mercyhurst College; 6 semester hours theology, 15 hours philosophy required; Army ROTC required.
Geneva College Beaver Falls 1848 *Reformed Presbyterian*	797M 511W	1250	82% in top 1/2 60%	M505m 455v W460m 475v	a. $1150 b. 742	30% $400	1:16 31%	72	$3,200	B.A., B.S.; *Semester, summer session;* Education—25%, Business—20%, Natural Sciences & Math—20%, Social Sciences—15%, Humanities—4%; Coop—3-2 engineering with U. of Pittsburgh, N.Y.U.; Chapel attendance, 8 hours of Bible courses required.
Gettysburg College Gettysburg 1832 *Lutheran*	1200M 600W	2000	64% in top 1/5 50% M 38% W	M587m 545v W631m 618v	a. $1600 b. 810	22% $200-2500	1:14 43%	140	$1,841	B.A., B.S.Music Ed.; *Semester, summer session;* Social Sciences—35%, Humanities & Fine Arts—35%, Natural Sciences & Math—30%; Coop—3-2 forestry with Duke University; One academic course in Biblical literature & religion required; Air Force, Army ROTC optional; Asian Studies; *Teacher Training.*
Grove City College Grove City 1876 *United Presbyterian*	1311M 670W	1900	60% in top 1/5 35%	M587m 531v W578m 583v	a. $700 b. 825 d. 100	40% $500	1:18 45%	104	$4,000	B.A., B.S., B.Mus.; *Semester, summer session;* Social Sciences—25%, Business—20%, Humanities—14%, Education—14%, Natural Sciences & Math—14%, Engineering—13%; 6 hours of Bible required; Air Force ROTC required.
Gwynedd-Mercy College Gwynedd Valley 1948 *Roman Catholic*	600W	1000	80% in top 1/2 69%	470m 460v	a. $1000 b. 1300	25% $585	1:10 21%	26		B.A., B.S.; *Semester;* Liberal Arts—75%, Medical Technology—12%, Elementary Education—13%; Coop in teacher education with Villanova University. A.S.; *Semester;* Med. Sec.—33%, Secretarial—30%, Nursing—37%.

Institution / Location / Founded / Affiliation	Enrollment M=men W=women	Projected enrollment in 1975	High school rating; % applicants accepted	SAT/ACT Averages m=math v=verbal	a. Annual Tuition; b. Room & Board; c. Out of state; d. Other	% Students with $ aid; Average amount	Faculty-student ratio; % with Doctorates	Volumes in library in 1,000's	Endowment in $1,000's	Undergraduate degrees offered; *Calendar;* Per cent of students per field of study; *Professional programs offered;* Miscellaneous
Haverford College Haverford 1833 *Independent*	530M	700	80% in top 1/5		a. $1975 b. 900 d. 135	35% $200-3100 81%	1:10	250	$16,763	B.A., B.S.; *Semester;* Social Sciences—42%, Humanities—35%, Natural Sciences & Math—23%, Engineering—8%; Coop—undergraduate with Bryn Mawr, Swarthmore, U. Penn.
Holy Family College Philadelphia 1954 *Roman Catholic*	389W	650	72% in top 2/5 70%	475m 525v	a. $900 b. 900 d. 100	47% $437 30%	1:8	40		B.A., B.S.; *Semester;* Humanities—37%, Social Sciences—40%, Natural Sciences & Math—16%, Medical Technology—7%; *Education—Secondary Teacher Certification.*
Immaculata College Immaculata 1920 *Roman Catholic*	746W	1000	53% in top 1/5 61%	516m 534v	a. $1000 b. 1000	19% $350 30%	1:12	53		B.A., B.S., B.Mus.; *Semester, summer session;* Social Sciences—43%, Humanities—33%, Natural Sciences—24%; Grants totaling $93,000 since 1960.
Indiana University of Pennsylvania 1875 Indiana *State*	2552M 3384W	12500	80% in top 1/5 25%	M559m 502v W547m 542v	a. $280 b. 648 c. 600 d. 200	45% $450 35%	1:16	250		B.A., B.S.Ed.; *Semester;* Education—81%, Liberal Arts—19%; *Teacher Education;* Army ROTC optional.
Juniata College Huntingdon 1876 *Church of the Brethren*	653M 417W	1500	47% M 67% W in top 1/5 50%	M579m 525v W561m 545v	a. $1500 b. 850	30% $200-1250 39%	1:13	90	$2,864	B.A., B.S.; *Semester, summer sessions;* Social Sciences—33%, Natural Sciences & Math—36%, Humanities—21%, Education—13%, Teacher Ed.—10%; *Teacher Education;* Coops—3-2 engineering with Columbia, 3-2 forestry with Duke U.; One course each required in Humanities, Religion & Philosophy.
King's College Wilkes-Barre 1946 *Roman Catholic*	1600M	2000	54% in top 2/5	515m 495v	a. $1100 b. 900 d. 100	40% $500 35%	1:16	80		B.A., B.S.; *Semester, summer session;* Social Sciences—36%, Business—25%, Humanities—19%, Natural Sciences & Math—20%; *Teacher Education;* Coops—3-2 engineering with U. of Detroit, Notre Dame, Penn State; 13 credits theology required of Catholic students only.
Kutztown State College Kutztown 1866 *State*	900M 1800W	6000	75% in top 1/4 66%	M500m 525v W475m 550v	a. $250 b. 610 c. 630 d. 50	30% $250 38%	1:19	100		B.A., B.S., B.S.Ed., B.F.A.; *Semester, summer session;* Teacher Education.
Lafayette College Easton 1826 *Presbyterian*	1700M	2000	70% in top 1/5 35%	650m 600v	a. $1850 b. 920	33% up to $2900 55%	1:11	200	$37,000	B.A., B.S.; *Semester;* Liberal Arts—50%, Engineering—35%, Natural Sciences & Math—15%; One year religion course required; Army ROTC required 1 year.
LaSalle College Philadelphia 1863 *Roman Catholic*	3000M	3200	70% in top 2/5 50%	540m 530v	a. $1200 b. 900	40% $450 40%	1:16	118		B.A., B.S.; *Semester, summer session;* Liberal Arts—40%, Sciences—25%, Business Adm.—35%; Army ROTC required.
Lebanon Valley College Annville 1866 *Evangelical United Brethren*	480M 337W	1100	55% in top 1/5 54%	M571m 532v W569m 558v	a. $1530 b. 900	50% $340 50%	1:13	86	$2,247	B.A., B.S.; *Semester, summer session; Business Administration, Education, Music;* Coops—3-2 engineering with M.I.T., U. Penn., 3-2 forestry with Duke U.; One year of Bible study required.
Lehigh University Bethlehem 1865 *Private*	3100M	3200	76% in top 1/5 61%	680m 603v	a. $1800 b. 920	21% $1237 69%	1:12	440	$40,000	B.A., B.S.; *Semester, summer session;* Engineering—44%, Liberal Arts—32%, Business—24%; *Business, Engineering;* Coop—5-year liberal arts, engineering at Lehigh; Air Force, Army ROTC optional.
Lincoln University Lincoln University 1854 *Private*	700M 110W	1400	40% in top 1/4 52%	430m 423v	a. $720 b. 700 d. 200	75% 48%	1:12	110	$2,000	B.A.; *Semester, summer session;* 3-2 and 3-3 Engineering coop programs with Penn. State, Drexel Inst. and Lafayette College. Coop program with American U. and Franklin & Marshall College.
Lock Haven State College Lock Haven 1870 *State*	720M 930W	3200	90% in top 1/4 30%	495m 500v	a. $300 b. 600 d. 50	40% $600 30%	1:14	112		B.A., B.S.; *Semester, summer session;* Education—70%, Liberal Arts—30%; *Elementary Education—20%, Secondary Education—30%, Physical Education—20%.*
Lycoming College Williamsport 1812 *Methodist*	855M 576W	1600	42% in top 1/5 50%	M554m 509v W538m 541v	a. $1550 b. 900	35% $850 53%	1:15	69	$1,500	B.A.; *Semester, summer sessions;* Social Sciences & Math—24%, Humanities—33%, Business—14%; Coop—3-2 engineering with Bucknell, Penn. State, 3-2 forestry with Duke U.; Washington Semester, U.N. Semester, Junior Year Abroad.
Mansfield State College Mansfield 1857 *State*	600M 634W	4165	33% in top 1/5 33%	M497m 462v W494m 489v	a. $315 b. 612	25%	1:15	53		B.A., B.S.; *Semester, summer session;* Education—38%, Humanities—22%, Science & Math—10%, Home Ec.—17%, Social Science—10%, Public School Nurse—3%; *Teacher Education.*
Marywood College Scranton 1915 *Roman Catholic*	1420W	1850	80% in top 2/5	530m 545v	a. $900 b. 950	48% $600 20%	1:13	78	$261	B.A., B.S., B.Mus.; *Semester, summer session;* Liberal Arts—89%, Home Economics—11%; *Teacher Education;* Coop—3-1 medical technology with an accredited hospital.
Mercyhurst College Erie 1926 *Roman Catholic*	600W	800	75% in top 2/5 64%	498m 514v	a. $1000 b. 900 d. 100	42% $500 20%	1:12	25	$143	B.A., B.S.; *Semester;* Liberal Arts—68%, Home Economics—6%, Education—24%, Commercial Education—2%; *Teacher Education;* Coop—limited exchange of students & faculty with Gannon College.
Messiah College Grantham 1909 *Brethren in Christ*	213M 214W	800	45% in top 1/5 70%	M544m 482v W491m 479v	a. $1180 b. 684	50% $600 30%	1:16	35	$400	B.A., B.S.N., B.Th.; *Semester;* Liberal Arts—90%, Nursing—7%, Theology—3%; *Teacher Education;* Coops in Elementary, Business and Music Education; Chapel and 12 credits in religion required.
Millersville State College Millersville 1855 *State*	1406M 1704W	5800	50% in top 1/5 60%	M546m 505v W541m 535v	a. $300 b. 612 c. 636 d. 34	20% $350 32%	1:16	100		B.A., B.S.Ed.; *Semester, summer session;* Education—93%, Liberal Arts—7%, Sciences—3%; *Teacher Education;* Coop in medical technology with three Lancaster, Pa. hospitals, 3-2 Engineering with Penn. State U.
Moravian College Bethlehem 1742 *Moravian*	692M 482W	1200	41% in top 1/5 46%	M546m 503v W524m 538v	a. $1600 b. 900 d. 48	26% $900 42%	1:16	90	$4,368	B.A., B.S., B.D.; *Semester, summer session;* Humanities & Social Sciences—46%, Natural Sciences & Math—20%, Business—15%, Education—11%; *Theology, Medical Technology;* Coops—3-2 engineering, with U. Penn., Lafayette, 3-2 forestry with Duke.

Institution Location / Founded Affiliation	Enrollment M=men W=women	Projected enrollment in 1975	High school rating; % applicants accepted	SAT/ACT Averages m=math v=verbal	Annual Tuition: a. b. Room & Board; c. Out of state; d. Other	% Students with $ aid / Average amount	Faculty-student ratio; % with Doctorates	Volumes in library in 1,000's	Endowment in $1,000's	Undergraduate degrees offered; Calendar; Per cent of students per field of study; Professional programs offered; Miscellaneous
Mount Mercy College Pittsburgh 1929 *Roman Catholic*	920W	1400	43% in top 1/5 67%	504m 520v	a. $1200 b. 1050	42% $800 43%	1:13	70	$300	B.A., B.S.; *Semester, summer session;* Social Sciences—30%, Natural Sciences & Math—28%, Humanities—27%, Nursing & Speech Correction—18%; *Nursing;* 12 credits theology required of Catholics; Mellon Foundation grant of $293,550 since 1963.
Muhlenberg College Allentown 1848 *Lutheran*	808M 565W	1500	33% in top 1/10 33%	M610m 575v W590m 600v	a. $1750 b. 850	48% $100-1600 60%	1:12	106	$4,600	B.A., B.S.; *Semester, summer session;* Coops—3-2 engineering with Columbia, M.I.T., U. Penn., 3-2 forestry with Duke U.; 8 chapel services per semester, 2 courses in religion required.
PMC Colleges Chester 1821 *Private*	1384M 12W	2200	25% in top 1/4 57%	549m 514v	a. $1425 b. 1010-1150 d. 150	11% $566 44%	1:15	52	$648	B.A., B.S., B.S.B.A., B.S. Engineering; *Semester, summer session;* Business—48%, Liberal Arts—28%, Engineering—13%, Sciences—11%; Coop—exchange program with Chungang University, Seoul, Korea; ROTC required of cadets.
Pennsylvania, University of Philadelphia 1740 *Private*	4728M 2253W	7800	80% in top 1/5 39%	M672m 627v W638m 651v	a. $1770 b. 1000 d. 180	40% $1600 89%	1:9	2100	$166,000	B.A., B.S.; *Semester, summer sessions;* Social Sci.—31%, Bus.—19%, Nat. Sci. & Math—12%, Humanities—19%, Eng.—6%, Art & Arch.—7%, Ed.—2%; *Arch., Bus., City Plan., Allied Med., Social Work, Dent., Eng., Land. Arch., Law, Med., Nurs., Teacher Ed., Vet. Med.;* A, N ROTC optional.
Pennsylvania State University, The University Park 1855 *State*	15565M 6986W		69% in top 1/5 31%	M634m 548v W633m 595v	a. $450 b. 825 c. 1050	30% $350 46%	1:22	1000	$4,552	B.A., B.S., B.Arch., B.Arch.Eng.; *Term;* Liberal Arts—26%, Education—20%, Engineering—16%, Business—14%, Natural Sciences—8%; *Architecture, Business, Engineering, Forestry, Journalism, Landscape Architecture, Psychology, Teacher Education;* Study abroad in Eng., Fr., Germ., Italy, Spain; AF, A, N ROTC optional.
Pittsburgh, University of Pittsburgh 1787 *Private*	5340M 2791W	18600	63% in top 1/5 87%	M594m 537v W554m 552v	a. $1400 b. 1000	40% $100-1000 74%	1:12	998	$73,158	B.A., B.S.; *Trimester, summer session;* Liberal Arts—54%, Gen. Studies—10%, Engineering—19%, Education—11%, Pharmacy—2%, Nursing—4%; *Business, Dentistry, Engineering, Law, Medicine, Nursing, Pharmacy, Teacher Education;* Coop in engineering and sciences with Carnegie Tech.; Air Force, Army ROTC optional.
Rosemont College Rosemont 1921 *Roman Catholic*	650W	850	66% in top 1/4 52%	555m 567v	a. $1300 b. 1200 d. 118	17% $855 27%	1:8	75	$474	B.A.; *Semester;* Humanities—43%, Social Sciences—30%, Natural Sciences & Math—28%; 16 credits theology, Mass, annual retreat required.
St. Francis College Loretto 1847 *Roman Catholic*	900M 402W				a. $775 b. 800		1:17	59		B.A., B.S.; *Semester, summer session;* Coop—3-2 engineering with Notre Dame, U. of Pittsburgh, Penn. State, Villanova.
St. Joseph's College Philadelphia 1851 *Roman Catholic*	1791M	2150	58% in top 1/5 46%	589m 569v	a. $1075 b. 800	42% $755 37%	1:15	78	$6,271	A.B., B.S.; *Semester, summer session;* Social Sciences—27%, Business—28%, Natural Sciences & Math—26%, Humanities—19%; Air Force ROTC optional for two years; Coop in Engineering, Physics; Academy of Food Marketing; Latin American studies program.
St. Vincent College Latrobe 1846 *Roman Catholic*	993M	1000	46% in top 1/5 48%	540m 530v	a. $1140 (science) $1060 (non-sci.) b. 760	28% $750 25%	1:10	200	$263	B.A., B.S.; *Semester, summer session;* Social Sciences—40%, Natural Sciences & Math—26%, Humanities—24%, Business—10%; Coop—3-2 engineering with N.Y.U., Notre Dame, Penn. State, U. of Pittsburgh.
Scranton, University of Scranton 1888 *Roman Catholic*	1520M	2000	60% in top 2/5 55%	540m 503v	a. $1110 b. 800	43% $500 30%	1:14	103	$2,450	B.A., B.S.; *Semester, summer session;* Business—30%, Liberal Arts 22%, Social Sciences & Education—22%, Natural Sciences & Math—26%; Army ROTC required.
Seton Hill College Greensburg 1883 *Roman Catholic*	720W	850	75% in top 1/4 70%	523m 555v	a. $1100 b. 1000	30% $100-1100 37%	1:10	58	$450	B.A., B.S., B.Mus.; *Semester, summer session;* Humanities—40%, Social Sciences—32%, Natural Sciences & Math—17%, Home Economics Ed.—17%; *Music;* Two religion courses required of Catholic students.
Shippensburg State College Shippensburg 1871 *State*	1368M 1732W	6200	45% in top 1/5 34%	521m 491v	a. $300 b. 612 c. 640	33% $600 29%	1:15	148		B.A., B.S.Ed.; *Quarter, summer session;* Elementary Education—39%, Business—16%, Natural Sciences & Math—15%, Humanities—21%, Social Sciences—9%; *Teacher Education—95%, Arts & Sciences—5%.*
Slippery Rock State College Slippery Rock 1889 *State*	1905M 1312W	5600	41% in top 1/5 45%	510m 486v	a. $250 b. 612 c. 640 d. 60	45% $400 33%	1:14	98		B.A., B.S. Ed.; *Semester, summer sessions;* Education—87%, Humanities—3%, Social Sciences—6%, Natural Sciences & Math—4%; *Teacher Education;* Coop—3-2 engineering with Penn. State.
Susquehanna University Selinsgrove 1858 *Lutheran*	658M 467W	1500	most in top 1/4 25%	M565m 535v W585m 555v	a. $1300 b. 850 c. 200	40% $800 45%	1:13	60	$1,250	B.A., B.S.; *Semester, summer session;* Liberal Arts—75%, Sciences—25%; *Music;* Coop—3-2 engineering with U. Penn.; Twice-weekly chapel required; Grants totaling $1,265,000 since 1960.
Swarthmore College Swarthmore 1864 *Quaker*	546M 465W	1200	84% in top 1/5 30%M 20%W		$2860 Total a&b d. $190	30% $1100 70%	1:9	295		B.A., B.S. Engineering; *Semester; Engineering;* Coop with Bryn Mawr, Haverford and U. of Pennsylvania.
Temple University Philadelphia 1888 *Private*	1998M 1015W	12000	34% in top 1/5 50%	497m 503v	a. $920 b. 950 c. 1120 d. 130	27% $100-1000 50%	1:19	521	$5,356	B.A.; *Semester, summer sessions; Business, Dentistry, Law, Medicine, Pharmacy, Teacher Education;* Army ROTC optional.
Thiel College Greenville 1866 *Lutheran*	520M 495W	1300	68% in top 2/5 60%	M531m 497v W538m 546v	$2050 Total a&b d. $35	45% $560 43%	1:17	63	$1,000	B.A.; *Semester, summer sessions;* Humanities—38%, Social Sciences—37%, Natural Sciences—29%; *Medical Tech.;* Coops—3-2 forestry with N.Y.U., 3-2 forestry with Duke U.; 2 semesters religion courses, weekly services required; Washington Semester, Junior Year Abroad; Marine ROTC optional.
Ursinus College Collegeville 1869 *Private*	606M 456W	1500	91% in top 2/5 41%	M590m 560v W588m 590v	a. $1400 b. 900	50% $500 58%	1:14	75	$5,361	B.A., B.S.; *Semester, summer session;* Coop—3-2 engineering with U. Penn.; Chapel services required.
Villa Maria College Erie 1925 *Roman Catholic*	814W	1000	65% in top 2/5 70%	480m 481v	a. $950 b. 800	40% $100-1000	1:12	30		B.A., B.S.; *Semester;* Education—70%, Social Sciences—6%, Health Professions—21%; *Nursing, Dietetics, Medical Technology.*

Institution Location Founded Affiliation	Enrollment M=men W=women	Projected enrollment in 1975	High school rating; % applicants accepted	SAT/ACT Averages m=math v=verbal	a. Annual Tuition; b. Room & Board; c. Out of state; d. Other	% Students with $ aid; Average amount	Faculty-student ratio; % with Doctorates	Volumes in library in 1,000's	Endowment in $1,000's	Undergraduate degrees offered; Calendar; Per cent of students per field of study; Professional programs offered; Miscellaneous
Villanova University Villanova 1842 *Roman Catholic*	4200M 300W	5800	60% in top 1/4 35%		a. $1400 b. 1000	15% 23%	1:15	200		B.A., B.S., B. Engineering; *Semester, summer session; Engineering, Law, Nursing;* 6 semesters religion, annual retreat required of Catholics; Navy ROTC optional.
Washington and Jefferson College Washington 1781 *Private*	840M	1100	60% in top 1/5 45%	600m 560v	a. $1500 b. 930 $200-1500 d. 150	20% 55%	1:12	125	$11,000	B.A.; *Semester, summer sessions;* Natural Science—40%, Social Science—35%, Humanities—25%; One semester of religion & weekly convocation required; Army ROTC optional.
West Chester State College West Chester 1812 *State*	1814M 3145W	8800	41% in top 1/4 53%	509m 506v	a. $290 b. 612 $200 c. 680	50% 25%	1:17	150		B.A., B.S.; *Semester, summer session;* Education—76%, Music—10%, Liberal Arts—6%; *Music, Teacher Education;* Coop—exchange in courses and instruction with Cheyney State College.
Westminster College New Wilmington 1852 *United Presbyterian*	741M 646W	1500	81% in top 2/5 42%	M554m 507v W551m 533v	a. $1200 b. 778 $505	28% 42%	1:13	89	$3,700	B.A., B.S., B.B.A., B.Mus.; *Semester;* Liberal Arts—59%, Sciences—18%, Business—16%, Music—7%; *Music.*
Wilkes College Wilkes-Barre 1933 *Private*	1151M 816W	2300	92% in top 1/2 39%	M532m 501v W509m 506v	a. $1050 b. 1050 $450 d. 200	41% 32%	1:17	78	$3,716	B.A., B.S.; *Semester, summer session;* Sciences—43%, Liberal Arts—57%; Grants totaling $7,000,000 since 1960.
Wilson College Chambersburg 1869 *Presbyterian*	723W	1000	75% in top 1/5 40%	579m 586v	$2900 Total a&b $712	23% 55%	1:11	95	$4,939	A.B.; *Semester;* Social Sciences—32%; Humanities—58%, Natural Sciences & Math—10%; A course in Bible required.
RHODE ISLAND										
Barrington College Barrington 1900 *Private*	305M 372W	1340	25% in top 1/4 65%		a. $1260 b. 800 $500 d. 200	30% 20%	1:16	36	$303	B.A., B. Mus.; *Semester, summer session;* Biblical Studies—10%, Education & Psychology—51%, Fine Arts—2%, Humanities—17%, Natural Sciences & Math—5%, Social Sciences—15%; Chapel attendance required.
Brown University Providence 1764 *Private*	2450M		22%	690m 650v	a. $2000 b. 1080 $200-3100	45% 90%	1:4	1500	$70,000	B.A., B.S.; *Semester;* Social Sciences—41%, Humanities—34%, Sciences—25%; *Arts & Sciences Engineering;* Coop with R.I.S.D., Flexible curriculum, 6-year M. of Med. Sci., independent study, foreign study plans; Air Force, Navy ROTC optional.
Pembroke College Providence 1891 *Private*	1000W	1500	90% in top 1/5	686m 696v	a. $2000 b. 1050 $200-2800	45% 90%	1:4	1200	$70,000	Same as Brown University; Pembroke is the coordinate woman's college of Brown.
Providence College Providence 1917 *Roman Catholic*	2684M	3000	44% in top 1/5 57%	510m 500v	a. $1300 b. 900 $585	23% 25%	1:15	73	$900	B.A., B.S.; *Semester;* Humanities & Social Sciences—51%, Education—23%, Business—14%, Natural Sciences & Math—12%; Army ROTC optional.
Rhode Island, University of Kingston 1892 *State*	3225M 2189W	7600	38% in top 1/5 60%	M540m 481v W509m 494v	a. $250 b. 890 $330 c. 1000 d. 103	40% 59%	1:12	290	$67	B.A., B.S., B.F.A., B. Mus., A.S.; *Semester, summer sessions;* Education—23%, Business—17%, Engineering—16%, Liberal Arts—18%, Natural Sciences & Math—10%, Agriculture—6%; *Engineering, Nursing, Oceanography, Pharmacy;* Coop with other New England state universities; Army ROTC optional.
Rhode Island College Providence 1854 *State*	703M 1833W	3805	77% in top 2/5 61%	M527m 487v W500m 505v	a. $215 b. 875 $250-1200 c. 715 d. 45	40% 35%	1:13	80		B.A., B.S.; *Semester, summer session;* Education—50%, Humanities—19%, Natural Sciences & Math—11%, Social Sciences—14%, Industrial Arts—5%; *Teacher Education (M.A.T., M.Ed., C.A.G.S.);* Coop in ed. with B.U., U. of Conn.; A, AF, N ROTC optional; Science and research grants totaling $922,000 since 1960.
Rhode Island School of Design (R.I.S.D.) Providence 1877 *Private*	508M 451W	1000	30% in top 1/4 22%	605m 614v	a. $1800 b. 950 $853	31% 6%	1:10	37	$12,000	B.F.A., B.Arch., B. Landscape Arch.; *Semester;* Painting—10%, Arch.—17%, Art Ed.—13%, Graph. Design—11%, Illus.—10%, Interior Arch.—2%, Apparel Design—3%, Indus. Design—4%, Sculpture—5%, Landscape Arch.—2%, Textile Design—2%, Ceramics—2%; *Preceding Are Professional Depts.;* Recent grants total $75,000.
Salve Regina College Newport 1934 *Roman Catholic*	800W	1200	90% in top 1/2 16%	521m 543v	a. $1000 b. 900 $500 d. 300	24% 20%	1:10	40	$84	B.A., B.S.; *Semester, summer session;* Social Sciences—37%, Nursing—20%, Humanities—28%, Natural Sciences—15%.
SOUTH CAROLINA										
Benedict College Columbia 1870 *Baptist*	366M 695W	1300	85%		a. $400 b. 414 $150	25%	1:16	24	$504	B.A., B.S.; *Semester, summer sessions;* 6 hours religion, chapel, Vespers services required.
Citadel, The Charleston 1842 *State*	2001M		27% in top 1/4 58%	521m 470v	a. $350 b. 770 $200-1590 c. 672 d. 735	20% 28%	1:16	90		B.A., B.S.; *Semester, summer sessions; Engineering;* Air Force, Army ROTC required.
Claflin University Orangeburg 1869 *Methodist*	226M 489W	1000	50% in top 1/2 91%		a. $400 b. 450 $400 d. 200	25% 33%	1:20	30	$520	B.A., B.S., B.S.Ed.; *Semester, summer session;* Social Science—21%, Physical Education—13%, English—7%, Elementary Education—20%, Music—8%, Natural Science & Math—31%.
Clemson University Clemson 1889 *State*	4789M 469W	7410	89% in top 1/2 80%	541m 462v	a. $150 b. 750 $675 c. 650 d. 346	35% 60%	1:18	371	$434	B.A., B.S., B.Arch.; *Semester, summer sessions;* Engineering—26%, Education—3%, Arch—5%, Arts & Sciences—38%, Management & Textile Sciences—15%, Agriculture & Biological Sciences—13%; *Architecture, Chemistry, Engineering, Forestry;* Air Force, Army ROTC required for two years.
Coker College Hartsville 1908 *Private*	326W	500	30% in top 1/5 40%	425m 425v	a. $980 b. 775 $250 d. 135	30% 30%	1:10	45	$3,500	B.A., B.S.; *Semester, summer sessions;* B.A.—80%, B.S.—20%; *Music.*

Institution / Location / Founded / Affiliation	Enrollment M=men W=women	Projected enrollment in 1975	High school rating; % applicants accepted	SAT/ACT Averages m=math v=verbal	a. Annual Tuition; b. Room & Board; c. Out of state; d. Other	% Students with $ aid; Average amount	Faculty-student ratio; % with Doctorates	Volumes in library in 1,000's	Endowment in $1,000's	Undergraduate degrees offered; Calendar; Per cent of students per field of study; Professional programs offered; Miscellaneous
College of Charleston Charleston 1770 *Private*	206M 196W	850	68% in top 1/2 83%	M541m 520v W531m 520v	a. $1200 b. 1000 d. 60	47% $200-1000	1:14 48%	32	$1,000	B.A., B.S.; *Semester, summer session;* Humanities—40%, Nat. Sci. & Math—42%, Social Sciences—18%; Coop—3-1 program in medical technology with Medical College of S.C.
Converse College Spartanburg 1889 *Private*	750W	850	95% in top 1/2 50%	500m 500v	$2800 Total	23% $200-1800	1:10 40%	70	$1,600	B.A., B.Mus.; *Semester, summer session; Music;* Coop with S.C. School for the Deaf & Blind for training teachers of the deaf and blind; 3 hours religion, weekly chapel required.
Erskine College Due West 1839 *A. R. Presbyterian*	400M 300W	950	75% in top 2/5 50%	M507m 456v W496m 480v	a. $1100 b. 680 d. 110	25% $700	1:14 50%	50	$1,100	B.A., B.S., B.D.; *Semester, summer sessions;* Education—26%, Business—17%, Social Sciences—26%, Humanities—14%, Natural Sciences—17%.
Furman University Greenville 1825 *Baptist*	832M 685W	2500	72% in top 1/4 57%M 92%W	M549m 518v W557m 566v	a. $1000 b. 975	40% $450	1:15 65%	133	$7,400	B.A., B.S., B.Mus.; *Semester, summer session;* B.A.—83%, B.S.—13%, B.A.Mus.—4%; Coop in forestry with Duke University; Chapel attendance once per week required; Army ROTC required for two years.
Lander College Greenwood 1872 *Public*	185M 400W	1100	All in top 1/2 33%	475m 520v	a. $420 b. 525 c. 200 d. 450	25% $300	1:15 40%	40		B.A., B.S.; *Semester, summer session;* B.S. in Medical Technology; Associate degrees in Nursing and Secretarial studies.
Limestone College Gaffney 1845 *Private*	138M 520W	950	most in top 2/5 70%	450m 450v	$1885 Total	30% $250	1:11 37%	33	$990	B.A., B.S.; *Semester, summer session; Music, Med. Tech.;* No on-campus residence for men.
Newberry College Newberry 1856 *Lutheran*	535M 304W	1000	75% in top 1/2 62%	510m 475v	a. $985 b. 690 d. 100	38% $550	1:15 40%	50	$1,000	B.A., B.S.; *Semester, summer session;* Social Sciences—31%, Humanities—16%, Natural Sciences—15%, Education—17%, Business—21%.
Presbyterian College Clinton 1880 *Presbyterian*	520M 136W	900	25%	535m 510v	a. $970 b. 720 d. 110	35% $240	1:14 50%	60	$2,000	B.A., B.S.; *Semester, summer session;* Chapel services required; Army ROTC required for two years.
South Carolina, University of Columbia 1801 *State*	434M 334W	16300	30%M, 52%W in top 1/4 82%	M552m 478v W493m 492v	a. $410 b. 585 c. 960 d. 170	3% $100-700	1:20 42%	567	$1,835	B.A., B.S., LL.B.; *Semester, summer sessions;* Humanities—29%, Education—8%, Business—25%, Natural Sciences & Math—8%, Engineering—6%, Nursing—3%, Phar.—3%, Law—6%; *Business, Engineering, Journalism, Law, Music, Nursing, Pharmacy, Teacher Education;* Air Force, Navy ROTC optional. NSF grant for $550,650 since 1960.
South Carolina State College Orangeburg 1896 *State*	1031M 1078W	2500	50%	M375m 375v W375m 375v	a. $290 b. 410 c. 520	$234	1:11 29%	72		B.A., B.S.; *Semester, summer session;* Arts—35%, Science—60%; Army ROTC required.
Winthrop College Rock Hill 1886 *State*	3000W	4800	64% in top 1/4 68%	460m 448v*	a. $328 b. 575 c. 852	25% $400	1:21 43%	190		B.A., B.S.; *Semester, summer sessions;* Arts & Sciences—85%, Home Economics—11%, Music—4%; *Music.*
Wofford College Spartanburg 1854 *Methodist*	1000M	1000	47% in top 1/5 61%	540m 500v	a. $1325 b. 850	35% $1032	1:17 47%	85	$2,400	B.A., B.S.; *Semester (4-1-4), summer sessions;* Natural Sciences—28%, Social Sciences—28%, Psychology & Education—16%, Humanities—11%; Coops—3-2 engineering with Columbia; 3-2 forestry with Duke; 6 hours religion; Army ROTC optional.

SOUTH DAKOTA

Institution / Location / Founded / Affiliation	Enrollment M=men W=women	Projected enrollment in 1975	High school rating; % applicants accepted	SAT/ACT Averages m=math v=verbal	a. Annual Tuition; b. Room & Board; c. Out of state; d. Other	% Students with $ aid; Average amount	Faculty-student ratio; % with Doctorates	Volumes in library in 1,000's	Endowment in $1,000's	Undergraduate degrees offered; Calendar; Per cent of students per field of study; Professional programs offered; Miscellaneous
Augustana College Sioux Falls 1860 *Lutheran*	913M 1064W	3200	53% in top 1/4 79%		a. $1150 b. 660 d. 200	25% $200	1:14 40%	76	$744	B.A., B.S., B.S. in Nursing, B.Mus.Ed.; *Semester, summer sessions;* Education—19%, Natural Sciences & Math—11%, Humanities—19%, Social Sciences—6%, Business—11%, Nursing—6%, Phys.Ed.—5%, Music—4%; Coop—3-2, 4-2 engineering with U. of Denver, Stanford, M.I.T.
Black Hills State College Spearfish 1883 *State*	1200M 600W	2500	most in top 2/3 95%		a. $400 b. 618 c. 725	20% $500	1:21 28%	45		B.S., B.S.Ed.; *Quarter, summer sessions; Teacher Education.*
Dakota Wesleyan University Mitchell 1883 *Methodist*	456M 368W	1200	70% in top 1/2 75%		a. $775 b. 725 d. 70	40% $100-700	1:19 30%	34	$1,041	B.A., B.Mus.Ed.; *Semester, summer sessions;* Coop—1-3 nursing; One semester of religion courses, chapel attendance required; Grants totaling $250,000 since 1960.
General Beadle State College Madison 1881 *State*	610M 383W	1500	90%		a. $304 b. 550 c. 640 d. 60	45% $300	1:21 33%	35		B.S., B.S.Ed.; *Semester, summer session.*
Huron College Huron 1883 *Presbyterian*	414M 198W	1200	88%		a. $750 b. 680	57% $500	1:16 20%	39	$1,262	B.A., B.S., B.Mus.; *Semester, summer sessions;* 6 semester hours of religion courses, weekly chapel attendance required.
Northern State College Aberdeen 1901 *State*	1527M 1187W	4500	95%	20 (comp.)	a. $304 b. 558 c. 640 d. 31	80% $300	1:20 25%	77		B.S.; *Semester, summer session;* Education—80%, Liberal Arts—20%; *Teacher Education.*
Sioux Falls College Sioux Falls 1883 *Baptist*	432M 284W	1200	50% in top 1/4 80%	21.2m	a. $750 b. 662	49% $200	1:18 34%	45	$328	B.A., B.S.; *Semester, summer sessions;* Chapel and assembly attendance required.
South Dakota, University of Vermillion 1882 *State*	3200M 1300W	9200	94%	22.1m 21.5v	a. $285 b. 750 c. 640	30% $100-200	1:18 64%	300		B.A., B.S.; *Semester, summer session; Business, Law, Music, Teacher Education;* Army ROTC required for two years.

Institution Location / Founded Affiliation	Enrollment M=men W=women	Projected enrollment in 1975	High school rating; % applicants accepted	SAT/ACT Averages m=math v=verbal	Annual Tuition: a. b. Room & Board; c. Out of state. d. Other state.	% Students with $ aid / Average amount	Faculty-student ratio; % with Doctorates	Volumes in library in 1,000's	Endowment in $1,000's	Undergraduate degrees offered; Calendar; Per cent of students per field of study; Professional programs offered; Miscellaneous
South Dakota State University Brookings 1881 *State*	3014M 1556W	7071	most in top 1/2 95%	22.4 (comp.)	a. $325 b. 690 c. 850	19% $600 34%	1:15	166	$2,957	B.S.; *Semester, summer sessions;* Arts & Sciences—35%, Agriculture—25%, Engineering—20%, Home Economics—8%, Pharmacy—7%; *Engineering, Journalism, Nursing, Pharmacy, Teacher Education;* Air Force, Army ROTC required.
Southern State College Springfield 1881 *State*	683M 184W	1700	60% in top 1/2 85%		a. $304 b. 640 c. 615	40% $200-400 15%	1:20	32	$16	B.S.; *Semester, summer sessions;* Education—94%, Sciences—6%; *Teacher Education.*
Yankton College Yankton 1881 *United Church of Christ*	256M 117W	1200	31% in top 2/5 80%M 68%W	460m 462v	a. $790 b. 750	51% $200 25%	1:13	65	$1,402	B.A., B.S., B.Mus.; *Semester, summer session;* Education—40%, Social Sciences—23%, Humanities—35%, Natural Sciences & Math—12%, Business—9% (almost 4/5 of class in Mus./Phys./El./Sec.Ed.); *Music;* Coop—3-2 engineering with U. of Illinois.

TENNESSEE

Austin Peay State University Clarksville 1927 *State*	1909M 985W	5500	75% in top 1/2 80%		a. $165 b. 549-711 c. 225	35% $450 30%	1:20	72		B.A., B.S.; *Quarter, summer sessions;* Liberal Arts, Sciences, Agr., Bus., Home Ec., Ind. Arts, Teacher Ed.; *Dentistry, Med., Med. Tech., Phar., Law, Engineering.*
Belmont College Nashville 1951 *Baptist*	535M 547W	1600	most in top 1/2 50%	19 (comb.)	a. $720 b. 500	15% $300 33%	1:17	40	$610	B.A., B.S.; *Semester;* Arts—60%, Sciences—40%; Coop—pre-professional programs with the University of Tennessee.
Bethel College McKenzie 1842 *Presbyterian*	576M 236W	1100	most in top 1/2 65%		a. $675 b. 600	20% $500 34%	1:18	43	$1,000	B.A., B.S.; *Quarter, summer sessions;* Professional programs U. of Tennessee.
Carson-Newman College Jefferson City 1851 *Baptist*	884M 778W	2400	most in top 1/2 68%	21m 21v	a. $800 b. 640 c. 900	35% $40-800 32%	1:17	86	$1,375	B.A., B.S.; *Semester, summer sessions;* Social Sciences—35%, Education—24%, Humanities—17%, Business—14%, Natural Sciences & Math—8%; Coops—3-2 engineering & forestry; Two courses in Bible, chapel attendance required.
Chattanooga, University of Chattanooga 1886 *Private*	1079M 711W	2500	68%		a. $850 b. 750 d. 25	50% $100-1200 43%	1:17	90	$5,000	B.A., B.S., B.Mus.; *Semester, summer session; Music;* Coop—3-2 engineering with Georgia Tech., M.I.T., N.Y.U., U. of Tennessee, Vanderbilt, 3-2 Forestry with Duke; Army ROTC optional.
Christian Brothers College Memphis 1871 *Roman Catholic*	1050M	1500	80%	21 (comp.)	a. $750-900 b. 900	16% $500 30%	1:18	40	$170	B.S.; *Semester, summer session;* Engineering—47%, Business—27%, Natural Sciences & Math—9%, Humanities—18%.
David Lipscomb College Nashville 1891 *Church of Christ*	950M 934W	2400	80%	20.9 (comp.)	a. $960 b. 875	33% $400 48%	1:19	70	$2,207	B.A., B.S.; *Quarter, summer quarter;* Coop—3-2 engineering with University of Tennessee; 6 hours Bible study per year, daily chapel required.
East Tennessee State University Johnson City 1911 *State*	5169M 3442W	17900	most in top 1/2 82%	20 (comp.)	a. $168 b. 630 c. 333	10% $400 40%	1:19	166		B.A., B.S., B.S.Env. Hlth., B.S.Mus. Ed., B.S.Med. Tech., B.S.Nurs., B.F.A., A.A.Dental Hygiene & Nursing; *Quarter, summer sessions;* Liberal Arts—40%, Education—22%, Business—23%, Health—4%, Pre-professional—11%; *Teacher Education;* Coops in engineering with U. of Tennessee, in forestry with Duke; Army ROTC required.
Fisk University Nashville 1865 *Private*	397M 680W	1250	52% in top 1/5 79%	M413m 390v W411m 404v	a. $850 b. 715 d. 78	38% $437 48%	1:20	158	$9,609	B.A., B.S.; *Semester, summer session;* Social Sciences—27%, Natural Sciences & Math—39%, Education—8%, Humanities—6%, Music—2%, Other—14%; *Music.*
George Peabody College for Teachers Nashville 1785 *Private*	569M 1250W	2500	85% in top 1/2 60%		a. $1200 b. 700	40% $800 67%	1:10	1000	$6,388	B.A., B.S., B.Mus., B.Mus. Ed.; *Quarter, summer sessions;* Education—41%, Humanities—23%, Natural Sciences & Math—14%, Social Sciences—11%, Home Economics—7%; *Library, Music, Psychology, Teacher Education;* Army ROTC optional.
King College Bristol 1866 *Presbyterian*	184M 130W	550	83% in top 2/5 77%M 88%W		a. $1050 b. 700 d. 110	64% $300 44%	1:10	40	$2,000	B.A.; *Semester, summer sessions;* Coop—3-2 engineering with the University of Tennessee; 10 hours religion, daily chapel required.
Knoxville College Knoxville 1875 *Presbyterian*	390M 565W	1300	69% in top 1/3 65%	M400m 376v W378m 390v	a. $550 b. 625 d. 100	70% $550 35%	1:15	36	$968	B.A., B.S., B.S. in Commerce, B.Mus.Ed.; *Semester;* Education—53%, Natural Sciences & Math—15%, Humanities—9%, Social Sciences—22%; Coop—3-2 engineering with Lafayette, U. of Tenn.; student exchange with Macalester College, St. Paul, Minn.; One year Bible study, twice-weekly chapel required.
Lambuth College Jackson 1843 *Methodist*	476M 386W	1000	25% in top 1/5 80%	M550m 475v W500m 525v	a. $850 b. 600	40% $300 34%	1:17	40	$2,008	B.A., B.S.; *Semester, summer sessions;* Humanities—15%, Natural Sciences—25%, Social Sciences—60%; *Agriculture, Dentistry, Laboratory Tech., Law, Medicine, Ministry, Nursing, Pharmacy, Religious Education, Social Service;* 3-year residence plans for a degree.
Lane College Jackson 1882 *Christian Methodist-Episcopal*	396M 568W	1200	most in top 1/2		a. $450 b. 560	60% $475 35%	1:21	43	$500	B.A., B.S.; *Semester, summer session;* Coop—student exchange program with Nebraska Wesleyan University.
Le Moyne College Memphis 1870 *American Missionary Association*	218M 459W	900	most in top 1/4 70%	375m 400v	a. $550 b. no dorm	40% $200 35%	1:19	41	$308	B.A., B.S.; *Semester, summer sessions;* Education—41%, English—11%, Natural Science—25%, Social Science—23%; Coop with Grinnell College, Grinnell, Iowa, University of Iowa; Ford Foundation grant of $1,000,000 since 1960.
Lincoln Memorial University Harrogate 1897 *Private*	330M 251W	1200	52% in top 1/3 80%	18.6m 17.7v	a. $930 b. 765	75% $450 38%	1:19	50	$2,394	B.A., B.S.; *Quarter, summer session;* Education—60%; Coops in engineering and forestry.
Maryville College Maryville 1819 *Presbyterian*	421M 461W	1075	31% in top 1/5 43%	M497m 463v W466m 487v	a. $900 b. 780 d. 70	60% $285 33%	1:14	76	$3,500	B.A., B.S., B.S.Ed.; *Semester, summer session;* Social Sciences—33%, Humanities—40%, Natural Sciences & Math—15%, Arts—12%; 10 semester hours Bible, philosophy, religion, 4-day chapel required.

Institution Location	Founded Affiliation	Enrollment M=men W=women	Projected enrollment in 1975	High school rating; % applicants accepted	SAT/ACT Averages m=math v=verbal	a. Annual Tuition; b. Room & Board; c. Out of state; d. Other	% Students with $ aid Average amount	Faculty-student ratio; % with Doctorates	Volumes in library in 1,000's	Endowment in $1,000's	Undergraduate degrees offered; Calendar; Per cent of students per field of study; Professional programs offered; Miscellaneous
Memphis State University Memphis	1912 State	5663M 4073W	22000	most in top 1/2		a. $185 b. 825 c. 410 d. 300	4% $200 38%	1:19	200		B.A., B.S., B.B.A., B.F.A., B.Mus., B.S.Ed.; Semester, summer session; Sciences—57%, Business—19%, Arts—9%; Teacher Education; Air Force ROTC required.
Middle Tennessee State University Murfreesboro	1911 State	3374M 2387W	12500	90%		a. $185 b. 600 c. 410	30% 35%	1:18	100		B.A., B.S.; Semester, summer sessions; Teacher Education; Army ROTC optional.
Milligan College Milligan	1881 Disciples of Christ	501M 338W	900	80%		a. $575 b. 705 d. 60	30%	1:16	42		B.A., B.S.; Semester; Coop—3-2 engineering program available.
South, The University of the Sewanee	1857 Episcopalian	837M	1200	51% in top 1/4 66%	592m 562v	a. $1550 b. 790 d. 240	36% $1095 63%	1:13	163	$16,943	B.A., B.S.; Semester, summer session; Social Sciences—47%, Humanities—34%, Natural Sciences & Math—17%, Forestry—2%; Theology; Coop—3-2 engineering with Georgia Tech., Columbia, N.Y.U., 4-2 engineering with R.P.I.; Chapel required; Air Force ROTC optional.
Southern Missionary College Collegedale	1892 Seventh Day Adventist	560M 590W	1400	85%		a. $920 b. 637	23%	1:13	47		B.A., B.Mus.; Semester, summer session; Nursing.
Southwestern at Memphis Memphis	1848 Presbyterian	557M 433W	1200	77% in top 1/4 66%M 90%W	M585m 557v W582m 577v	a. $1500 b. 850	31% $750 75%	1:14	105	$5,500	B.A., B.S., B.Mus.; Semester, summer session; Social Sciences—39%, Humanities—41%, Natural Sciences & Math—17%; Music; Coop—3-2 engineering with Alabama Polytech., Georgia Tech., U. of Tenn., Vanderbilt; Two years Bible study required.
Tennessee, University of Knoxville	1794 State	17591M 8998W	35100	50% in top 1/4 80%	23.2m 21.2v	a. none b. $885 c. 450 d. 290	33% $500 60%	1:16	904	$4,000	B.A., B.S., B.Arch., B.F.A., B.Mus.; Quarter, summer quarter; Bus., Dent., Eng., Jour., Law, Med., Music, Nurs., Phar., Psych., Social Work, Teacher Ed.; AF, A ROTC required; Campuses at Memphis, Martin, Nashville, Tullahoma, Oak Ridge, Kingsport, Chattanooga.
Tennessee Agricultural & Industrial State University Nashville	1912 State	2467M 2234W	7000	89%		a. none b. $500 c. 165 d. 165	5% $165 28%	1:18	135		B.A., B.S.; Quarter, summer sessions; Education—52%, Social Sciences—21%, Natural Sciences & Math—12%, Engineering—8%; Music, Teacher Education; Air Force ROTC required.
Tennessee Technological University Cookeville	1915 State	3064M 1259W	8000	33% in top 1/4 86%		a. $165 b. 650 c. 330	4% $300 35%	1:17	200		B.A., B.S.; Quarter, summer sessions; Chemistry, Teacher Education; Coop in Engineering; Army ROTC optional.
Tennessee Wesleyan College Athens	1857 Methodist	460M 400W	1200	75% in top 1/2 75%	M19m 20v W18m 21v	a. $780 b. 720	50% $256 30%	1:17	42	$680	B.A., B.S.; Quarter; Education—40%, Humanities—25%, Business—18%, Natural Sciences & Math—9%, Accounting—6%, Social Sciences—2%; Coops—3-2 engineering with U. of Tennessee, 3-2 forestry with Duke; two weekly chapels required.
Tusculum College Greeneville	1794 Presbyterian	328M 222W	1000	20% in top 1/10 55%		a. $1025 b. 775	32% $50 30%	1:15	39	$2,500	B.A., B.S.; Semester; Social Sciences—40%, Education—30%, Natural Sciences & Math—14%, Undeclared—10%; Coops—3-2 engineering with Lafayette, 3-2 forestry with Duke; Convocation and vespers required.
Union University Jackson	1825 Baptist	450M 440W	1440	75%	M20.1 W19.3 (comp.)	a. $690 b. 640 d. 85	30% $300 30%	1:17	39	$810	B.A., B.S., B.Mus., A.A.Nursing; Semester, summer session; Arts—60%, Sciences—30%, Music—10%, Nursing—10%.
Vanderbilt University Nashville	1873 Private	2356M 1077W	4805	80% in top 1/4 50%M 40%W	M642m 605v W637m 631v	a. $1460 b. 1040 d. 200	31% $1150 74%	1:10	1000	$92,000	B.A., B.S., B.E., B.D.; Semester, summer session; Arts & Sciences—44%, Engineering—12%, Humanities—21%, Divinity—2%; Engineering, Law, Medicine, Audiology & Speech Pathology, Nursing, Psychology, Theology; Army, Navy ROTC optional.

TEXAS

Institution Location	Founded Affiliation	Enrollment	Projected enrollment	H.S. rating	SAT/ACT	Tuition etc.	% aid	Ratio	Volumes	Endowment	Description
Abilene Christian College Abilene	1906 Church of Christ	1719M 1356W	3500	41% in top 1/5 90%	M21.8m 19.7v W18.7m 21.3v	a. $832 b. 750	30% $490 39%	1:20	131	$5,000	B.A., B.S., B.S.Ed., B.S.H.E., B.S.M.E.; Semester; summer sessions; Education—48%, Religion—11%, Humanities—6%, Natural Sciences & Math—7%, Social Sciences—11%, Home Economics—6%, Business—13%, Agriculture—4%; Teacher Education; 15 hours Bible, daily chapel required; ROTC available on coop basis.
Angelo State College San Angelo	1928 State	1372M 1023W	6000	10% in top 1/4 90%	M17.9 W18.3 (comp.)	a. $100 b. 300 c. 150 d. 32	60% $160 22%	1:24	30	$25	B.A., B.S., B.B.A.; Semester, summer session; Business—29%, Education—22%, Liberal Arts—45%, Other—4%; Teacher Education, Medical Technology.
Austin College Sherman	1849 Presbyterian	590M 433W	1089	57% in top 1/4 72%	555m 543v	$2500 Total	39% $416 50%	1:12	84		B.A.; Semester (14-4-14), summer sessions; Social Sciences—28%, Humanities—18%, Education—21%, Natural Sciences & Math—28%, Business—5%; Coop-3-2 engineering with U. of Texas, Texas A.&M.,N. Y.U.
Baylor University Waco	1845 Baptist	3859M 2803W	7000	70% in top 1/4 79%	M24.2 W22.8 (comp.)	a. $800 b. 610	70% $455 40%	1:19	360	$25,000	B.A., B.S., B.B.A., B.F.A., B.Mus., LL.B.; Semester, summer session; Social Sciences—22%, Humanities—21%, Education—19%, Natural Sciences & Math—14%, Business—13%; Bus., Dent., Law, Med., Music, Nurs.; 6 hours religion, chapel required; Air Force ROTC optional.
Dallas, University of Dallas	1956 Roman Catholic	354M 504W	1600	53% in top 1/4 85%	M562m 540v W536m 509v	a. $950 b. 850 d. 200	40% $600 60%	1:11	60	$13,000	B.A.; Semester, summer sessions; Humanities—34%, Education—25%, Natural Sciences & Math—18%, Social Sciences—10%, Business and Economics—10%; 12 hours theology required of Catholic students.
East Texas Baptist College Marshall	1912 Southern Baptist	350M 350W	1200	33% in top 1/4 90%		a. $660 b. 540	50% $50-500 44%	1:18	55	$1,500	B.A., B.S., B.Mus.; Semester, summer sessions; Social Sciences—13%, Education—56%, Humanities—12%, Natural Sciences & Math—2%, Business—17%; 3 semesters Bible, chapel attendance required.

Institution Location	Founded Affiliation	Enrollment M=men W=women	Projected enrollment in 1975	High school rating: % applicants accepted	SAT/ACT Averages m=math v=verbal	Annual Tuition; a. Room & Board; b. Out of state; c. d. Other state	% Students with $ aid Average amount	Faculty-student ratio; % with Doctorates	Volumes in library in 1,000's	Endowment in $1,000's	Undergraduate degrees offered; Calendar; Per cent of students per field of study; Professional programs offered; Miscellaneous
East Texas State University Commerce	1894 State	4622M 3101W	15000	40% in top 1/4 85%		a. $174 b. 600 c. 574	20%	1:16 53%	315		B.A., B.S., B.B.A., B.Mus.; Semester, summer sessions; Teacher Education; Air Force ROTC required.
Hardin-Simmons University Abilene	1891 Southern Baptist	895M 859W	2500	41% in top 1/4 82%		a. $700 b. 710 $25-600	30% 33%	1:15	91	$3,000	B.A., B.S., B.B.A., B.Mus.; Semester, summer sessions; Education—28%, Social Sciences—25%, Business—17%, Natural Sciences & Math—14%, Humanities—9%; Music; Coop with McMurry College; 6 hours Bible, twice-weekly chapel required; Army ROTC optional.
Houston, University of Houston	1934 State	11662M 6011W	28282	51% in top 1/4 75%	M536m 486v W487m 498v	a. $100 b. 830 c. 400	25% $800	1:20 50%	380	$5,550	B.A., B.S., B.Arch., B.B.A., B.Accy., B.F.A., B.Mus.; Semester, summer sessions; Arts & Sciences—38%, Education—15%, Business—16%, Engineering—11%, Pharmacy—6%; Arch., Bus., Eng., Law, Music, Optometry, Psych., Teacher Ed.; Coops in South American Universities; Army ROTC optional.
Howard Payne College Brownwood	1889 Baptist	602M 509W	1200	28% in top 1/4 95%	15 (comp.)	a. $640 b. 775	10% $300	1:15 30%	80	$4,000	B.A., B.S., B.Mus.; Semester, summer session; Education—53%, Religion—30%, Business—15%.
Incarnate Word College San Antonio	1900 Roman Catholic	73M 1176W	1500	30% in top 1/4 50%	18m 20v	a. $800 b. 914 d. 450	25% $800	1:15 35%	68	$1,017	B.A., B.S., B.Mus.; Semester, summer sessions; Sciences—52%, Arts—33%, Music—3%; Music, Nursing, Teacher Education; Attendance at Sunday religious services required.
Lamar State College of Technology Beaumont	1923 State	4734M 3106W	20000	37% in top 1/4 85%	M491m 436v W444m 435v	a. $165 b. 720 c. 465	5% $425	1:26 43%	153	$99	B.A., B.S., B.B.A.; Semester, summer sessions; Education—26%, Engineering—19%, Fine & Applied Arts—7%, Liberal Arts—21%, Sciences—12%, Business—15%; Engineering.
Mary Hardin-Baylor College Belton	1845 Southern Baptist	107M 631W	1200	85% in top 1/2 90%	17.1m 20.1v	a. $480 b. 680 d. 145	60% $350	1:14 26%	57	$3,280	B.A., B.S., B.Mus.Ed.; Semester, summer session; Education—40%, Humanities—34%, Natural Sciences & Math—15%, Social Sciences—14%, Home Economics—14%, Business—7%; Music; Twice-weekly chapel services required.
McMurry College Abilene	1923 Methodist	974M 623W	1700	33% in top 1/4 92%	21.0 (comp.)	a. $650 b. 660	60% $200-700	1:19 50%	70	$2,500	B.A., B.S., B.B.A.; Semester, summer sessions; Education—55%, Liberal Arts—21%, Business—25%.
Midwestern University Wichita Falls	1922 State	1708M 1075W	4800	35% in top 1/4 95%	20 (comp.)	a. $100 b. 624 c. 400 d. 100	$180	1:24 41%	60		B.A., B.S., B.Mus., B.B.A., B.S.Ed.; Semester, summer sessions; Medical Tech., Music; Army ROTC optional.
North Texas State University Denton	1890 State	8173M 5800W	25000		457m 439v 18.1m 19.5v	a. $100 b. 520 c. 450		1:25 51%	500		B.A., B.S., B.B.A., B.Mus.; Semester, summer sessions; Business, Music, Teacher Education; Air Force ROTC optional.
Pan American College Edinburg	1927 State	1636M 1561W	6500	most in top 1/2 96%	18m 16v	a. $100 b. 693 c. 400 d. 100	40% $450	1:26 29%	63		B.A., B.S., B.B.A.; Semester, summer session.
Prairie View Agricultural & Mechanical College Prairie View	1876 State	1810M 1798W	5000	85% in top 1/2 75%		a. $100 b. 515 c. 400 d. 54	58% $400	1:18 22%	101		B.A., B.S.; Semester, summer sessions; Agriculture—3%, Arts & Sciences—63%, Engineering—9%, Home Economics—5%, Industrial Arts & Technology—15%, Nursing Ed.—5%; Teacher Education. Army ROTC required.
Rice University Houston	1912 Private	1484M 524W	2800	73% in top 1/20 33%	702m 666v	a. $1500 b. 1029 d. 83	50% $1800	1:10 72%	556	$80,102	B.A., B.S., B.Arch.; Semester; Arts and Sciences—80%, Engineering—9%, Communications—4%, Architecture—5%; Architecture, Engineering; Army, Navy ROTC optional.
Sacred Heart Dominican College Houston	1946 Roman Catholic	454W	700	37% in top 1/4 71%	460m 448v	a. $500 b. 840 d. 300	32% $500	1:10 15%	46	$535	B.A., B.S., B.Mus.; Semester, summer session; Nursing—34%, Education—27%, Humanities—22%, Natural Sciences—1%, Social Sciences—16%.
Saint Edward's University Austin	1885 Roman Catholic	800M 150W *	1200M 800W	82% in top 1/4 62%	M460m 460v W450m 470v	a. $900 b. 820 d. 70	15% $500	1:14 46%	47	$1,230	B.A., B.S., B.B.A.; Semester, summer session; Bus.—39%, Teacher Ed.—17%, Natural Sciences—16%, Humanities—14%, Social Sciences—14%; Coops with U. of Texas, Ibero-American U., Mexico City; 12 hours theology required of Catholic students; N, M ROTC optional. *Mary Hill College opened Fall 1966.
St. Mary's University of San Antonio, Tex. San Antonio	1852 Roman Catholic	3003M 533W	6000	most in top 1/2 75%	M450m 450v W450m 450v	a. $800 b. 800	15% $300	1:20 44%	145	$552	B.A., B.S., B.B.A., B.Mus.Ed.; Semester, summer session; Arts—69%, Business—20%, Sciences—10%, Music Education—1%; Law; 8 credits in theology required of Catholic students; Army ROTC required.
St. Thomas, University of Houston	1947 Roman Catholic	579M 450W	1500	most in top 3/4 86%		a. $820 b. 450 d. 150	25% $400	1:14 60%	30		B.A.; Semester, summer session; Coop in engineering with University of Texas.
Sam Houston State College Huntsville	1879 State	3888M 2941W	10000	30% in top 1/4 80%	M19m W20m	a. $100 b. 600 c. 400	10% $300	1:21 40%	225		B.A., B.S., B.B.A., B.Mus.; Semester, summer sessions; Sciences—66%, Business—22%, Arts—10%, Music Education—2%; Music, Teacher Education; Coop in engineering with University of Texas; Army ROTC optional.
Southern Methodist University Dallas	1911 Methodist	2809M 2125W	7567	58% in top 1/4 83%	M568m 517v W524m 524v	a. $1200 b. 910	33% $690	1:17 46%	871	$20,084	B.A., B.S., B.B.A., B.F.A.; Semester, summer sessions; Liberal Arts—56%, Business—28%, Engineering—11%, Arts—5%; Arts, Business, Engineering, Humanities & Sciences, Law, Music, Teacher Education, Theology; 6 hours religion or philosophy required; Air Force ROTC optional.
Southwestern University Georgetown	1840 Methodist	433M 382W	1000	83% in top 1/2 60%	527m 522v	a. $1025 b. 750	50% $100-550	1:13 40%	80		B.A., B.S., B.B.A., B.F.A., B.Mus.; Semester; Music; 3-2 forestry with Duke University; Two courses in Bible, weekly chapel required.

Institution / Location / Founded / Affiliation	Enrollment M=men W=women	Projected enrollment in 1975	High school rating; % applicants accepted	SAT/ACT Averages m=math v=verbal	Annual Tuition; a. b. Room & Board; c. Out of state; d. Other	% Students with $ aid; Average amount	Faculty-student ratio; % with Doctorates	Volumes in library in 1,000's	Endowment in $1,000's	Undergraduate degrees offered; Calendar; Per cent of students per field of study; Professional programs offered; Miscellaneous
Southwest Texas State College, San Marcos 1899, State	3545M 3035W	14500	73% in top 1/2 85%	20 (comp.)	a. $100 b. 720 c. 400 d. 70	25% $350	1:24 43%	150		B.A., B.S., B.B.A., B.Mus.; Semester, summer sessions; Teacher Education; Air Force ROTC optional.
Stephen F. Austin State College, Nacogdoches 1923, State	3831M 3031W	12000	50% in top 2/5 80%	20.2 (comp.)	a. $ 50 b. 630 c. 200 d. 38	16% $345	1:21 48%	133		B.A., B.S., B.B.A., B.Forestry, B.Mus.; Semester, summer session; Liberal Arts—45%, Education—25%, Natural Sciences & Math—11%, Fine Arts—6%, Forestry—4%; Teacher Education.
Sul Ross State College, Alpine 1920, State	1101M 768W	2560	25% in top 1/4 90%		a. $180 b. 625 c. 400	35% $250	1:25 33%	112		B.A., B.S., B.B.A., B.Mus.; Semester, summer sessions; Education—53%, Liberal Arts—22%, Business—12%, Range Animal Husbandry—6%.
Texas, The University of, Arlington 1895, State	8898M 2603W	25000	72% in top 1/2	500m 475v	a. $100 b. 700 c. 400 d. 74	40%	1:28	250		B.A., B.S., B.B.A., B.S.Engineering; Semester; Engineering—18%, Business Adm.—25%, Liberal Arts—33%, Sciences—24%.
Texas, University of, Austin 1881, State	17435M 9907W	35000	72% in top 1/4		a. $100 b. 732 c. 300 d. 44	52% $600	1:18 82%	1839	$489,000	B.A., B.S., B.F.A., B.B.A., B.M.; Semester, summer session; Arch.—2%, Arts & Sci.—38%, Bus. Adm.—13%, Communication—2%, Ed.—9%, Engin.—8%, Fine Arts—4%, Law—6%, Phar.—2%; Arch., Bus., Dent., Eng., Jour., Law, Med.
Texas, University of, at El Paso, El Paso 1913, State	4309M 2839W	14000		461m 449v	a. $100 b. 680 c. 400	18% $500	1:26 48%	200	$3,320	B.A., B.S., B.B.A., B.Mus., B.S.Med.Tech., B.S.Ed.; Semester, summer sessions; Education—20%, Business—17%, Social Sciences—17%, Natural Sciences & Math—18%, Humanities—17%, Engineering—11%; Engineering; Army ROTC optional.
Texas A. & M. University, College Station 1876, State	10000M 600W	15000	46% in top 1/4 81%	565m 468v	a. $100 b. 616 c. 400 d. 94	18% $50-800	1:18 45%	500	$2,500	B.A., B.S., B.B.A., B.Arch.; Semester, summer sessions; Liberal Arts, Science, Geosciences—39%, Engineering—37%, Agriculture—17%, Veterinary Medicine—7%; Veterinary Medicine; Air Force, Army ROTC optional.
Texas Christian University, Fort Worth 1873, Disciples of Christ	2255M 2502W	6200	50% in top 1/4 90%	518m 503v	a. $1200 b. 750 d. 39	25% $600	1:17 62%	550	$27,000	B.A., B.S., B.B.A., B.F.A., B.Mus.; Semester, summer sessions; Arts & Sciences—42%, Business—25%, Education—21%, Fine Arts—7%; Business, Music, Nursing, Teacher Education, Theology; 6 hours religion required; Air Force, Army ROTC optional.
Texas Lutheran College, Seguin 1891, Lutheran	380M 365W	1200	51% in top 1/4 74%		a. $800 b. 700 d. 110	40% $600	1:15 38%	70		B.A., B.S., B.B.A.; Semester, summer sessions; Coop—3-2 medical technology with any certified school of medical technology.
Texas Southern University, Houston 1947, State	1969M 2229W	5800	36% in top 1/4 100%		a. $100 b. 460 c. 400 d. 180	8% $225	1:19 33%	123		B.A., B.S., B.B.A., B.F.A., B.Mus.; Semester, summer sessions; Education—26%, Social Sciences—9%, Business—10%, Natural Sciences & Math—19%, Pharmacy—5%, Humanities—5%, Fine Arts—8%, Law—1%, Phys. Ed.—7%; Law, Pharmacy, Teacher Education; Coop in African Studies with Rice & U. of Houston.
Texas Technological College, Lubbock 1925, State	10970M 6798W	32100	most in top 1/2 75%	M509m 454v W457m 459v	a. $100 b. 720-990 c. 400 d. 44	6% $288	1:22 50%	850		B.A., B.S., B.B.A., B.Mus.; Semester, summer sessions; Arts & Sciences—41%, Business—23%, Engineering—14%, Agriculture—7%, Home Economics—7%; Arch., Bus., Eng., Music, Psych., Teacher Ed.; Air Force, Army ROTC optional.
Texas Wesleyan College, Fort Worth 1891, Methodist	1374M 896W	2500	20% in top 1/4 90%		a. $750 b. 675	25% $50-1200	1:19 35%	55	$3,000	B.A., B.S., B.B.A., B.Mus.; Semester, summer session; Music, Teacher Education; 6 hours Bible required.
Texas Woman's University, Denton 1902, State	4048W	7537			a. $100 b. 600 c. 400 d. 71	25% $400	1:18 50%	300		B.A., B.S.; Semester, summer sessions; Arts & Sciences, Education, Nursing, Home Economics, Health, Phys. Ed., Recreation, Fine Arts; Library, Music, Nursing, Occupational Therapy, Sociology, Teacher Education.
Trinity University, San Antonio 1869, Presbyterian	957M 1019W	2400	40% in top 1/5 84%M 79%W	M550m 524v W513m 523v	a. $1400 b. 920 d. 100	38% $475	1:13 70%	150	$31,500	B.A., B.S., B.Mus.; Semester, summer sessions; Business—8%, Social Sciences—19%, Speech & Drama—6%, Other—41%; Teacher Education; Two courses in religion required; Army ROTC required.
Wayland Baptist College, Plainview 1908, Baptist	350M 400W	1200	77% in top 1/2 95%	19 (comp.)	a. $630 b. 580	57% $200	1:14 33%	45	$2,803	B.A., B.S.; Semester, summer session; Social Sciences—27%, Humanities—21%, Education—19%, Business—7%, Math—6%; 6 hours religion, chapel attendance required.
West Texas State University, Canyon 1910, State	3698M 2402W	10000		18 (comp.)	a. $175 c. 475	19% $600	1:30	107		B.A., B.S., B.B.A., B.Mus.Ed., B.S.Med.Tech.; Semester, summer sessions; Teacher Education; Army ROTC optional.
Wiley College, Marshall 1873, Methodist	301M 324W	1250	75% in top 1/4 50%	M475m 450v W460m 485v	a. $550 b. 720 d. 129	50% $1000	1:16 45%	35	$1,000	B.A., B.S.; Semester.

UTAH

Institution / Location / Founded / Affiliation	Enrollment M=men W=women	Projected enrollment in 1975	High school rating; % applicants accepted	SAT/ACT Averages m=math v=verbal	Annual Tuition; a. b. Room & Board; c. Out of state; d. Other	% Students with $ aid; Average amount	Faculty-student ratio; % with Doctorates	Volumes in library in 1,000's	Endowment in $1,000's	Undergraduate degrees offered; Calendar; Per cent of students per field of study; Professional programs offered; Miscellaneous
Brigham Young University, Provo 1875, Latter-day Saints	10698M 8568W	20000	most in top 1/2 91%	22.4 (comp.)	a. $400 b. 705 c. 650	49% $200-1500	1:20 50%	650	$5,727	B.A., B.S.; Semester, summer session; Education—23%, Social Sciences—17%, Humanities—16%, Business—14%, Sciences—9%; Business, Engineering, Music, Nursing, Teacher Education; 16 credit hours religion required; Air Force ROTC optional.
College of Southern Utah, Cedar City 1897, State	1036M 586W				a. $210 b. 650 c. 315					B.A., B.S., A.A., A.S.; Quarter, summer session; Teacher Education. Students in top 3% of High School graduating class may receive full tuition award for 1 year.
Utah, University of, Salt Lake City 1850, State	9627M 4978W	23313	50% in top 1/5 66%	22.1m 21.2v	a. $375 b. 790 c. 690	18% $500-600	1:21 65%	1000	$1,727	B.A., B.S., B.F.A., B.Mus., B.Arch.; Quarter, summer quarter; Sciences—8%, Business—14%, Social Sciences—22%, Education—25%, Engineering—10%, Humanities—9%, Nursing—4%, Fine Arts—3%, Mines—3%, Phar.—2%; Arch., Bus., Eng., Law, Medicine, Music, Nurs., Phar., Psych., Social Work, Teacher Ed.; A F, A, N ROTC optional.

Institution / Location / Founded / Affiliation	Enrollment M=men W=women	Projected enrollment in 1975	High school rating; % applicants accepted	SAT/ACT Averages m=math v=verbal	a. Annual Tuition; b. Room & Board; c. Out of state; d. Other	% Students with $ aid / Average amount	Faculty student ratio; % with Doctorates	Volumes in library in 1,000's	Endowment in $1,000's	Undergraduate degrees offered; Calendar; Per cent of students per field of study; Professional programs offered; Miscellaneous
Utah State University Logan 1888 *State*	4022M 2542W	10000			a. $252 b. 680 c. 726 d. 75	18% *$500* 52%		500		B.A., B.S., B.F.A.; *Quarter, summer sessions;* Education—20%, Social Sciences—20%, Humanities—19%, Engineering—12%, Sciences—9%, Forestry—9%, Agriculture—5%, Family Life—6%; *Engineering, Forestry, Teacher Education;* Air Force, Army ROTC optional.
Weber State College Ogden 1889 *State*	5273M 2947W				a. $305 b. 675 c. 705	1:28 20%		75		B.A., B.S.; *Quarter, summer sessions;* Teacher Education; Army, Air Force ROTC optional.
Westminster College Salt Lake City 1875 *Presbyterian, Methodist, United Church of Christ*	386M 271W	1150	91% in top 1/2 84%	M457m 469v W453m 481v	a. $740 b. 750	50% $467 43%	1:19	30	$500	B.A., B.S.; *Semester, summer session;* Social Sciences—28%, Education—26%, Natural Sciences & Math—18%, Humanities—9%, Business—19%.

VERMONT

Institution / Location / Founded / Affiliation	Enrollment M=men W=women	Projected enrollment in 1975	High school rating; % applicants accepted	SAT/ACT Averages m=math v=verbal	a. Annual Tuition; b. Room & Board; c. Out of state; d. Other	% Students with $ aid / Average amount	Faculty student ratio; % with Doctorates	Volumes in library in 1,000's	Endowment in $1,000's	Undergraduate degrees offered; Calendar; Per cent of students per field of study; Professional programs offered; Miscellaneous
Bennington College Bennington 1932 *Private*	373W 11M	640	60% in top 1/5 29%	599m 653v	$3850 Total	24% $1157 27%	1:8	55	$825	B.A.; *Semester, work session (Jan.—March);* Literature—38%, Art—23%, Social Sciences—23%, Sciences—5%, Dance, Drama—3% each, Music—1%; Coop with Harvard in teaching (M.A.T.); Grants totaling $1,250,000 since 1960.
Castleton State College Castleton 1787 *State*	400M 450W	1000	85% in top 1/2 30%	M510m 497v W483m 521v	a. $340 b. 870 c. 840	15% $400 28%	1:15	35		B.S.; *Semester, summer session;* Teacher Education—90%, Nursing—10%; *Business, Nursing, Teacher Education;* Coop with U. of Vermont; Federal construction grant of $134,575 received since 1960.
Goddard College Plainfield 1938 *Private*	244M 272W	1000	26%	M559m 586v W510m 575v	a. $2200 b. 1000	40% $1300 28%	1:10	23		B.A.; *Semester, work session (Jan. & Feb.);* Social Sciences—51%, Education—23%, Humanities—14%, Natural Sciences & Math—12%; Ford Foundation—grants totaling $271,800, Natl. Inst. of Mental Health—grants totaling $88,464 since 1960.
Johnson State College Johnson 1827 *State*	271M 225W	800			a. $250 b. 865 c. 750	1:15 35%		19		B.S.; *Semester;* Education—95%.
Middlebury College Middlebury 1800 *Private*	827M 568W	1800	55% in top 1/4 33%M 20%W	M640m 618v W610m 650v	a. $1900 b. 1000	19% $100-1500 63%	1:13	175	$23,000	B.A.; *Semester;* Humanities—28%, Languages—11%, Social Sciences—33%, Natural Sciences—28%; *Fr., Gr., Ital., Rus., Span. language schools;* Coops—Arch., Lang., Med.; 3-2 Engr. with R.P.I., Columbia; Bread Loaf School of English; Graduate schools in Fr., Ger., Italy, Spain.
Norwich University Northfield 1819 *Private*	1167	2000	38% in top 1/4 55%	525m 490v	a. $1450 b. 780 d. 450	28% $100-2000 40%	1:15	85	$3,500	B.A., B.S.; *Semester, summer sessions;* Liberal Arts—38%, Business Admin.—26%, Engineering—24%, Science—12%; Voluntary chapel services; Army ROTC required—4-yr. ROTC participants receive $1300 govt. grants.
St. Michael's College Winooski Park 1904 *Roman Catholic*	1115M	1500	23% in top 1/5	525m 500v	a. $1350 b. 850 c. 150	30% $200-1150 25%	1:12	57	$536	B.A.; *Semester, summer session;* Humanities—40%, Science & Math—40%, Business—20%; 4 yrs. philosophy, theology.
Trinity College Burlington 1925 *Roman Catholic*	455W	700	75% in top 1/3 27%	475m 500v	$1750 Total	30% $200 25%	1:11	30		B.A., B.S.; *Semester;* Humanities—42%, Social Sciences—36%, Natural Sciences & Math—9%, Business—9%, Languages—6%; *Social Work;* Theology required of Catholics.
Vermont, University of Burlington 1791 *State*	2976M 2028W	7600	52% in top 1/5 45%	M575m 520v W540m 530v	a. $600 b. 870 c. 1800 d. 275	33% $575 70%	1:16	300	$10,700	B.A., B.S.; *Semester, summer sessions;* Arts & Sciences—48%, Engineering—21%, Education—15%, Nursing—5%, Agriculture—5%; *Engineering, Medicine, Nursing, Teacher Education;* Army ROTC optional.

VIRGINIA

Institution / Location / Founded / Affiliation	Enrollment M=men W=women	Projected enrollment in 1975	High school rating; % applicants accepted	SAT/ACT Averages m=math v=verbal	a. Annual Tuition; b. Room & Board; c. Out of state; d. Other	% Students with $ aid / Average amount	Faculty student ratio; % with Doctorates	Volumes in library in 1,000's	Endowment in $1,000's	Undergraduate degrees offered; Calendar; Per cent of students per field of study; Professional programs offered; Miscellaneous
Bridgewater College Bridgewater 1880 *Church of the Brethren*	457M 410W	1000	93% in top 1/2 68%		a. $1110 b. 735 d. 150	33% $350 35%	1:15	56	$832	B.A., B.S.; *Semester, summer session;* Social Sciences—31%, Natural Sciences & Math—27%, Humanities—19%, Business—11%; Coop in forestry with Duke University; 9 hours religion, philosophy, chapel attendance required for freshmen and sophomores; Study abroad in France or Germany available.
College of William and Mary Williamsburg 1693 *State*	1868M 1551W	3900	80% in top 1/5 15%	M614m 578v W612m 623v	a. $438 b. 720 c. 988	27% $350 50%	1:12	320	$3,311	B.A., B.S., B.Civil Law; *Semester, summer session;* Social Sciences—36%, Humanities—24%, Natural Sciences & Math—19%, Education—11%, Business—7%; *Law;* Coops—3-2 engineering, 3-3 architecture with R.P.I., Johns Hopkins, Columbia; Army ROTC optional.
Eastern Mennonite College Harrisonburg 1917 *Mennonite*	367M 369W	1000	39% in top 1/4 85%		a. $1100 b. 640 c. 1500	1:15 35%		41	$360	B.A., B.S., B.D.; *Semester, summer sessions;* 14 hours Bible, 2 hours philosophy required.
Emory and Henry College Emory 1839 *Methodist*	526M 340W	1250	53% in top 1/4	22.5 (comp.)	$1750 Total	45% $450 49%	1:13	85	$3,000	B.A., B.S.; *Semester, summer sessions;* Humanities—29%, Social Sciences—41%, Natural Science and Math—30%; Summer in Germany program with U. of Göttingen, Vanderbilt-in-France program with Vanderbilt U., summer theatre coop program, Asian Studies program, Mid-Appalachia Council; 6 hours religion, weekly chapel attendance required.
Hampden-Sydney College Hampden-Sydney 1776 *Presbyterian*	600M	600	60% in top 1/4 40%	580m 530v	a. $1400 b. 650	30% $750 75%	1:14	60		B.A., B.S.; *Semester;* Social Sciences/Humanities—70%, Science/Math.—30%.
Hampton Institute Hampton 1868 *Private*	911M 1219W	3000	most in top 1/2 60%		a. $800 b. 600 d. 100	20% $600 27%	1:15	103	$31,505	B.A., B.S., B.Arch.; *Semester, summer sessions;* Teacher Education—56%, Arts & Sciences—26%, Business—6%, Technology—4%, Home Economics—2%, Nursing—2%, Architecture—4%; Two hours religion, Sunday Vespers required; Army ROTC required.
Hollins College Roanoke 1842 *Private*	940W	1050	50% in top 1/4 28%	580m 620v	$2900 Total	15% $1878 66%	1:11	100	$8,000	B.A.; *Semester;* Humanities—51%, Social Sciences—34%, Natural Sciences & Math—15%; *Music;* Non-denominational chapel required once per week.

Institution Location / Founded Affiliation	Enrollment M=men W=women	Projected enrollment in 1975	High school rating; % applicants accepted	SAT/ACT Averages m=math v=verbal	a. Annual Tuition; b. Room & Board; c. Out of state; d. Other	% Students with $ aid / Average amount	Faculty/student ratio; % with Doctorates	Volumes in library in 1,000's	Endowment in $1,000's	Undergraduate degrees offered; Calendar; Per cent of students per field of study; Professional programs offered; Miscellaneous
Longwood College Farmville 1839 *State*	1644W	2400	81% in top 1/4 41%	489m 509v	a. $340 b. 615 c. 300	50% $300	1:16	88		B.A., B.S., B.Mus.Ed., B.S.Bus.Ed.; *Semester, summer sessions; Teacher Education.*
Lynchburg College Lynchburg 1903 *Disciples of Christ*	742M 646W	1500	92% in top 3/5 40%	400m 400v	$2100 Total	17% $800	1:16 40%	60	$2,500	B.A., B.S.; *Semester, summer sessions;* Arts—79%, Sciences—21%; Coop in Asian studies with Sweet Briar and Randolph-Macon Woman's College.
Madison College Harrisonburg 1908	225M 2425W	6000	63% in top 1/4 40%		a. $390 b. 495 c. 1300	45% $500	1:17 33%	135		B.A., B.S., B.Mus.Ed.; *Semester, summer session; Teacher Education;* Coop—2 year pre-nursing program with the University of Virginia.
Mary Baldwin College Staunton 1842 *Presbyterian*	700W	800	76% in top 1/5 50%	564m 565v	$2700 Total	33% $800	1:14 60%	75	$2,000	B.A.; *Semester;* Coops—Academic year in Madrid, India exchange, University Center in Virginia, Project Opportunity for Disadvantaged Youth; Two inter-denominational devotional services per week.
Mary Washington College Fredericksburg 1908 *State*	2015W		91% in top 1/4 55%	575m 581v	a. none b. $618 c. 600 d. 532	25% $300	1:13 50%	175	$350	B.A., B.S.; *Semester, summer session;* Humanities—76%, Sciences—17%; *Music;* Coop—3-1 medical technology with Medical College of Virginia, 2-2 nursing with U. of Virginia.
Old Dominion College Norfolk 1930 *State*	5453M 3327W	13413	55% in top 1/2 92%	M512m 470v W470m 480v	a. $400 b. 1100 c. 600	10% $240	1:19 38%	100		B.A., B.S., B.S.Ed.; *Semester;* Education—38%, Arts & Sciences—43%, Business—17%, Engineering—2%; *Business Adm., Engineering, Nursing, Education.*
Radford College Radford 1910 *State*	3150W	7000	65% in top 1/4 35%	528m 523v	a. $324 b. 504 c. 624	60% $500	1:15 35%	85		B.A., B.S.; *Quarter, summer sessions;* Teacher Education—85%, Liberal Arts—15%; *Teacher Education;* Special programs in Guidance, Home Economics, Health and Physical Education.
Randolph-Macon College Ashland 1830 *Methodist*	825M	900	50% in top 1/4 50%	575m 525v	$2200 Total	30% $800	1:13 50%	67	$3,000	B.A., B.S.; *Semester;* Social Sciences—60%, Natural Sciences & Math—15%, Humanities—25%; Coop—3-2 forestry with Duke University, member University Center in Virginia.
Randolph-Macon Woman's College Lynchburg 1891 *Methodist*	880W	1000	75% in top 1/5 68%	577m 593v	a. $1600 b. 1100	32% $775	1:11 59%	110	$3,276	B.A.; *Semester;* Social Sciences—42%, Humanities—27%, Natural Sciences & Math—22%; Coops—India exchange, member of University Center in Virginia, Asian Studies, computer center with Lychburg College and Sweet Briar. One course in historical religion required.
Richmond, University of Richmond 1830 *Baptist*	1280M	1500	90% in top 1/2 52%		a. $1050 b. 700	27% $100-1100	1:17 53%	161		B.A., B.S., B.Mus.Ed.; *Semester, summer session; Law;* Coop—3-2 forestry with Duke University, 3-1 in medicine and dentistry with any approved Medical School; 6 hours Bible required; ROTC optional.
Roanoke College Salem 1842 *Lutheran*	586M 371W	1500	58% in top 1/4 50%	M541m 506v W523m 518v	$2250 Total	35% $350	1:16 44%	65	$1,500	B.A.—72%, B.B.A.—10%, B.S.—18%.
Saint Paul's College Lawrenceville 1890 *Episcopalian*	154M 239W	700	80%		a. $550 b. 480 d. 145	68% $450	1:13 26%	42	$5,600	B.A., B.S., B.S.Ed.; *Semester;* Education—87%, Social Sciences—6%, Natural Sciences—4%, Humanities—3%; Coop—member of University Center of Virginia.
Sweet Briar College Sweet Briar 1901 *Private*	700W	800	53% in top 1/5 63%	621m 607v	$3100 Total	20% $200-2300	1:8 67%	123	$3,000	B.A.; *Semester;* Coops—study abroad with Smith, N.Y.U., Tufts, Wayne State, in Asian Studies with Lynchburg College and Randolph-Macon Woman's College, junior year in France sponsored by Sweet Briar.
Virginia, University of Charlottesville 1819 *State*	4424M 293W	7287	57% in top 1/5 51%	649m 587v	a. $452 b. 828 c. 1037 d. 243	25% $586	1:12 78%	1288	$82,163	B.A., B.S.; *Semester, summer sessions;* Arts & Sciences—59%, Commerce—10%, Architecture—3%, Engineering—13%, Nursing—9%, Education—6%; *Architecture, Business, Engineering, Law, Medicine, Nursing, Teacher Education;* Air Force, Army, Navy ROTC optional.
Virginia Military Institute Lexington 1839 *State*	1200M	1200	44% in top 1/4 43%	581m 534v	a. $240 b. 585 c. 710 d. 268	30% $100-1000	1:11 43%	137	$4,000	B.A., B.S.; *Semester, summer sessions;* Liberal Arts—40%, Engineering—30%, Sciences & Math—30%; *Engineering;* Sunday church attendance required; No student automobiles; Army, Air Force ROTC required.
Virginia Polytechnic Institute Blacksburg 1872 *State*	8400M 1000W	17000	80% in top 2/5 50%	588m 514v	a. $420 b. 525 c. 840	10% $500	1:12 60%	400	$500	B.A., B.S.; *Quarter, summer sessions;* Engineering—41%, Arts & Sciences—23%, Business—17%, Agriculture—10%, Architecture—7%, Home Ec.—2%; *Architecture, Education, Engineering;* Air Force, Army ROTC optional.
Virginia State College Petersburg 1882 *State*	958M 1249W	3600	65% in top 1/4 49%		a. $447 b. 456 c. 627	65% $558	1:11 25%	100	$183	B.A., B.S.; *Semester, summer sessions; Liberal Arts, Education, Home Economics, Industrial Arts, Agriculture, Commerce;* Army ROTC required.
Washington and Lee University Lexington 1749 *Private*	1386M	1400	60% in top 1/5 45%	635m 602v	a. $1400 b. 700	20% $100-2000	1:11 60%	202	$11,500	B.A., B.S.; *Semester;* Social Sciences—39%, Humanities—16%, Business—7%; *Business, Journalism, Law;* Coop—5-year engineering with Columbia, R.P.I.; Army ROTC optional; Grants totaling $1,203,663 since 1960.

WASHINGTON

Institution Location / Founded Affiliation	Enrollment M=men W=women	Projected enrollment in 1975	High school rating; % applicants accepted	SAT/ACT Averages m=math v=verbal	a. Annual Tuition; b. Room & Board; c. Out of state; d. Other	% Students with $ aid / Average amount	Faculty/student ratio; % with Doctorates	Volumes in library in 1,000's	Endowment in $1,000's	Undergraduate degrees offered; Calendar; Per cent of students per field of study; Professional programs offered; Miscellaneous
Central Washington State College Ellensburg 1891 *State*	2697M 2324W	7250	40% in top 1/5 65%		a. $57 b. 750 c. 171 d. 207-300	33% $600	1:16 45%	107	$5	B.A., B.S., B.A.Ed.; *Quarter, summer sessions;* Social Sciences—33%, Humanities—21%, Natural Sciences & Math—14%, Business—12%, Physical Education—8%; *Teacher Education;* Air Force ROTC optional.
Eastern Washington State College Cheney 1890 *State*	2464M 1703W	6700	65%		a. $264 b. 690-795 c. 471 d. 210	23% $662	1:18 35%	140		B.A., B.A.Ed.; *Quarter, summer sessions;* Social Sciences—15%, Science and Math—14%, Language & Literature—20%, Business—23%, Phys. Ed.—8%, Creative Arts—10%; *Music, Teacher Education;* Army ROTC required.

Institution Location / Founded Affiliation	Enrollment M=men W=women	Projected enrollment in 1975	High school rating; % applicants accepted	SAT/ACT Averages m=math v=verbal	Annual Tuition: a. Room & Board: b. Out of state: c. Other: d.	% Students with $ aid; Average amount	Faculty-student ratio; % with Doctorates	Volumes in library in 1,000's	Endowment in $1,000's	Undergraduate degrees offered; Calendar; Per cent of students per field of study; Professional programs offered; Miscellaneous
Fort Wright College of the Holy Names Spokane 1907 *Roman Catholic*	450W	600	41% in top 1/5 80%	443m 450v	a. $850 b. 800 d. 100	37% $600	1:12 25%	45		B.A., B.S., B.F.A., B.A.Ed.; *Semester, summer session;* Humanities—38%, Social Sciences—30%, Natural Sciences & Math—28%; *Teacher Education.*
Gonzaga University Spokane 1887 *Roman Catholic*	1566M 1007W	2900	61% in top 1/5 77%	531m 571v	a. $1000 b. 800	$387 35%	1:11	287	$7,700	B.A., B.S., B.B.A., B.Mus.Ed., B.Ed.; *Semester, summer session;* Liberal Arts—75%, Engineering—10%, Education—1%, Business—14%; *Law;* Army ROTC optional.
Pacific Lutheran University Tacoma 1890 *Lutheran*	980M 1035W	3000	54% in top 1/5 75%	M540m 499v W496m 509v	a. $1050 b. 800 d. 137	11% $100-900 45%	1:18	100	$500	B.A., B.S., B.B.A., B.F.A., B.N.; *Semester, summer session;* Education (*M.A.T.*), Arts, Business, Sciences; *Teacher Education;* Coop—3-2 engineering; Daily chapel attendance required; Army ROTC optional.
Puget Sound, University of Tacoma 1888 *Methodist*	1066M 930W	3000	94% in top 1/2 70%	530m 525v	a. $1150 b. 800	40% $700 50%	1:20	112	$5,000	B.A., B.S., B.Mus.; *Semester, summer session;* Business—29%, Social Sciences—16%, Education—15%, Natural Sciences & Math—9%, Other—31%; *Music, Occupational Therapy, Teacher Education;* 3 hours religion courses required; Air Force ROTC optional.
St. Martin's College Olympia 1895 *Roman Catholic*	545M 96W	1900	90%	M550m 550v W550m 550v	a. $950 b. 830 d. 60	20% $500	1:10 26%	50		B.A., B.S.; *Semester, summer session;* Arts—84%, Sciences—16%; Air Force ROTC optional by cooperative arrangement with the University of Puget Sound.
Seattle Pacific College Seattle 1891 *Free Methodist*	942M 1173W	2253	57% in top 1/5 73%	M552m 500v W487m 517v	a. $1068 b. 750 d. 147	37%	1:18	66	$655	B.A., B.S., B.A.Ed., B.S.Nursing; *Quarter, summer sessions;* Social Sciences—35%, Humanities—32%, Natural Sciences & Math—15%, Home Economics—5%, Nursing—4%, P.E.—4%; *Teacher Education;* Daily chapel attendance required; Grants totaling $783,487 since 1960.
Seattle University Seattle 1891 *Roman Catholic*	1914M 1685W	5745	50%		a. $960 b. 863	34%	1:15	100		B.A., B.Ed., B.Com.Sci., B.Engr., B.Nurs., B.Soc.Sci., B.A.Ed.; *Quarter, summer session;* Business, Education, Engineering, Nursing; 16 hours of theology courses for Catholics required, 2 hours for non-Catholics required; Army ROTC required.
Walla Walla College College Place 1892 *Seventh-day Adventist*	854M 852W	2500	55% in top 1/2 85%		a. $1200 b. 800	80% $400 25%	1:15	84		B.A., B.S., B.Mus.; *Quarter, summer session;* Music, Nursing; Twice-weekly chapel attendance required.
Washington, University of Seattle 1861 *State*	16427M 10004W	34900	50% in top 1/3 75%	575m 552v (out of) state only)	a. $345 b. 815 c. 825	20% $50-750 75%	1:14	1500	$51,474	B.A., B.S.; *Quarter, summer quarter;* Architecture, Art, Business, Communications, Dentistry, Education, Engineering, Fisheries, Forestry, Law, Library, Medicine, Music, Nursing, Pharmacy, Physical & Occupational Therapy, Psychology, Public Affairs, Social Work; Air Force, Army, Navy ROTC optional.
Washington State University Pullman 1890 *State*	5493M 3873W	14000	most in top 2/5 83%	345m 820v 825	a. $345 b. 820 c. 825	25% $100-1000 70%	1:15	950	$39,914	B.A., B.S., B.Arch., B.Mus.; *Semester, summer sessions;* Liberal Arts—42%, Education—15%, Business—14%, Engineering—12%, Agriculture—9%; *Bus., Eng., Music, Phar., Psych., Teacher Ed., Vet. Med.;* Air Force, Army ROTC optional.
Western Washington State College Bellingham 1899 *State*	2817M 3131W	10000	51% in top 1/4 82%		a. $264 b. 725 c. 471	14% $490 60%	1:16	155	$34	B.A., B.A.Ed.; *Quarter, summer sessions;* Teacher Education, Arts and Sciences.
Whitman College Walla Walla 1859 *Private*	603M 445W	1450	69% in top 1/5 78%	M606m 571v W580m 603v	a. $1500 b. 810	35% $100-2500 40%	1:14	126	$9,376	B.A.; *Semester;* Social Sciences—44%, Humanities—33%, Natural Sciences & Math—23%; *Music;* Coops—engineering with Cal. Tech., Columbia, medical technology with Seattle & Spokane hospitals, Rare languages with Princeton & Stanford, Student Exchange with Howard & Fisk Universities.
Whitworth College Spokane 1890 *Presbyterian*	560M 632W	1500	71%	M530m 512v W515m 520v	a. $1150 b. 750-800	33% $450 54%	1:18	60	$1,225	B.A., B.S.; *Semester, summer sessions;* Humanities—42%, Social Sciences—20%, Education—8%, Natural Sciences & Math—9%, Business—9%; Coop in medical technology & nursing with Seattle & Spokane hospitals; 6 hours Bible, tri-weekly chapel required.

WEST VIRGINIA

Institution Location / Founded Affiliation	Enrollment M=men W=women	Projected enrollment in 1975	High school rating; % applicants accepted	SAT/ACT Averages m=math v=verbal	Annual Tuition: a. Room & Board: b. Out of state: c. Other: d.	% Students with $ aid; Average amount	Faculty-student ratio; % with Doctorates	Volumes in library in 1,000's	Endowment in $1,000's	Undergraduate degrees offered; Calendar; Per cent of students per field of study; Professional programs offered; Miscellaneous
Alderson-Broaddus College Philippi 1871 *Baptist*	238M 272W	950	54% in top 1/4 65%	M520m 490v W485m 560v	a. $930 b. 670	42% $800 31%	1:15	35		B.A., B.S.; *Semester, summer session; Medical Technology;* Coop with Broaddos Hospital; Weekly chapel attendance required.
Bethany College Bethany 1840 *Disciples of Christ*	665M 437W	1200	25% in top 1/5 51%	531m 520v	a. $1400 b. 1000	33% $200-1200 54%	1:13	90	$8,372	B.A., B.S.; *Semester, summer session;* Natural Sciences—38%, Social Sciences—35%, Humanities—15%, Education—12%; Coops—5-year engineering with Columbia; 3 semester hours of Bible study required.
Bluefield State College Bluefield 1895 *State*	513M 432W	1900	48% in top 1/2 44%		a. $150 b. 550 c. 450 d. 245	35% $324 26%	1:23	40		B.A., B.S., B.S.Ed.; *Semester, summer sessions;* Teacher Education—80%, Technical Education—20%; *Teacher Education.*
Concord College Athens 1872 *State*	968M 945W	3783	40% in top 1/4 52%	18.8m 19.0v	a. $210 b. 694 c. 660	30% $600 23%	1:20	60		B.A., B.S.; *Semester, summer session;* Education—62%, Business—13%, Social Sciences—10%, Natural Sciences & Math—10%, Humanities—5%; *Teacher Education;* Coop—affiliation with University of Dakar, Senegal, West Africa.
Davis and Elkins College Elkins 1904 *Presbyterian*	397M 339W	1200	56% in top 2/5 51%	M495m 464v W493m 487v	$2400 Total	22% $500 48%	1:14	46	$600	B.A., B.S.; *Semester, summer session;* Natural Sciences & Math—21%, Social Sciences—25%, Business—13%, Humanities—21%, Education—20%; Coops—engineering with W. Va. U., forestry with Duke; 6 hours religion required; Air Force ROTC optional.
Fairmont State College Fairmont 1867 *State*	1377M 1125W	3000	30% in top 1/4 75%		a. $219 b. 669 c. 760	25% $350 25%	1:24	66		B.A., B.S., B.A.Ed.; *Semester, summer sessions;* Education—50%, Business—12%, Other—38%; *Teacher Education.*
Glenville State College Glenville 1872 *State*	763M 697W	2400	most in top 3/4 89%	18 (comp.)	a. $201 b. 648 c. 651	20% $450 20%	1:20	39		B.A., B.S.; *Semester, summer sessions;* Teacher Education—80%.

Institution / Location / Founded / Affiliation	Enrollment M=men W=women	Projected enrollment in 1975	High school rating; % applicants accepted	SAT/ACT Averages m=math v=verbal	a. Annual Tuition; b. Room & Board; c. Out of State; d. Other State	% Students with $ aid; Average amount	Faculty-student ratio; % with Doctorates	Volumes in library in 1,000's	Endowment in $1,000's	Undergraduate degrees offered; Calendar; Per cent of students per field of study; Professional programs offered; Miscellaneous
Marshall University Huntington 1837 *State*	3806M 3397W		20% in top 1/4 90%	18.8m	a. $ 50 b. 742 c. 350 d. 180	25% $600	1:24 31%	149		B.A., B.S., B.B.A.; *Semester, summer sessions;* Teachers College—45%, College of Arts & Sciences—45%, College of Applied Sciences —10%; *Teacher Education;* Coop in forestry with Duke; Army ROTC optional.
Morris Harvey College Charleston 1888 *Private*	998M 758W	2000	50% in top 1/2 50%	510m 490v	a. $600 b. 849 c. 400	45% $300	1:24 21%	50	$1,000	B.A., B.S.; *Semester, summer sessions.*
Salem College Salem 1888 *Private*	1046M 332W	2000	most in top 3/4 70%	18m 17v	a. $1000 b. 825	65% $750	1:20 20%	42	$451	B.A.; *Semester, summer session;* Social Sciences—34%, Physical Education—15%, Humanities—15%, Natural Sciences & Math—12%, Education—11%, Business—22%.
Shepherd College Shepherdstown 1871 *State*	702M 674W	3000	35% in top 1/4 68%		a. $206 b. 648 c. 656		1:19 33%	51	$150	B.A., B.S.; *Semester, summer sessions;* Liberal Arts—20%, Teacher Education—60%, Business Administration—10%, Home Economics —5%, Music and Art—5%; Washington Semester, International Education tours.
West Liberty State College West Liberty 1837 *State*	1415M 1013W	4100	78% above "C" average 60%		a. $150 b. 667 c. 600 d. 66		1:20 13%	56		A.B., B.S., A.A., A.S.; *Semester, summer sessions;* Education—52%, Business—23%, Liberal Arts—20%, Dental Hygiene—5%; *Teacher Education.*
West Virginia Institute of Technology Montgomery 1895 *State*	1721M 383W	2500	75% in top 1/2 72%	20.1m 18.1v	a. $219 b. 684 c. 450	35% $335	1:19 21%	48	$300	B.A., B.S., B.S.Engineering, A.S.; *Semester, summer sessions;* Education—33%, Engineering—31%, Business—17%, Liberal Arts—6%; A.S.—13%.
West Virginia State College Institute 1891 *State*	2010M 1136W	3648	70% in top 1/2 65%		a. $150 b. 576 c. 350 d. 250	14% $350	1:18 28%	76		B.A., B.S.; *Semester, summer session;* Education—64%, Arts—15%, Business—9%, Sciences—8%; *Teacher Education;* Coop—3-2 engineering with W. Va. U., Marshall U., W. Va. Institute of Technology; Army ROTC required for full-time male students.
West Virginia University Morgantown 1867 *State*	1841M 1187W	17000	50% in top 1/4	22 (comp.)	a. $231 b. 650 c. 761	30% $600	1:20 60%	700	$324	B.A., B.S.; *Semester, summer session; Business, Dentistry, Engineering, Forestry, Journalism, Law, Medicine, Music, Nursing, Pharmacy, Social Work, Teacher Education;* Air Force, Army ROTC required for two years.
West Virginia Wesleyan College Buckhannon 1890 *Methodist*	808M 790W	1800	66%M 75%W		a. $1100 b. 900 d. 200	37% $500	1:14 32%	80	$1,800	B.A., B.S., B.Mus.Ed.; *Semester, summer sessions;* Social Sciences —35%, Business—14%, Education—15%, Natural Science—9%, Home Economics—5%, Music—4%; Coops—3-2 engineering with U. of Pittsburgh, U. Penn., Bucknell, 3-2 forestry with Duke; Chapel required.
Wheeling College Wheeling 1954 *Roman Catholic*	494M 293W	1350	84% in top 1/2 70%	534m 531v 24.0m 23.4v	a. $1250 b. 1000	42% $600	1:16 45%	55		B.A., B.S.; *Semester;* Social Sciences—33%, Humanities—31%, Natural Sciences & Math—22%, Accounting—14%; Theology courses required of Catholic students.

WISCONSIN

Institution / Location / Founded / Affiliation	Enrollment M=men W=women	Projected enrollment in 1975	High school rating; % applicants accepted	SAT/ACT Averages m=math v=verbal	a. Annual Tuition; b. Room & Board; c. Out of State; d. Other State	% Students with $ aid; Average amount	Faculty-student ratio; % with Doctorates	Volumes in library in 1,000's	Endowment in $1,000's	Undergraduate degrees offered; Calendar; Per cent of students per field of study; Professional programs offered; Miscellaneous
Alverno College Milwaukee 1936 *Roman Catholic*	1502W	1900	92% in top 1/2 86%	500m 500v	a. $700 b. 840	14% $309	1:15 22%	63	$238	B.A., B.S., B.Mus.; *Semester;* Education—42%, Arts—31%, Nursing —10%, Music—7%, Medical Technology—3%; *Music, Nursing, Teacher Education.*
Beloit College Beloit 1846 *Private*	664M 752W	1800	68% in top 1/5 45%	M609m 592v W565m 598v	a. $2100 b. 900	30% $800	1:10 54%	185	$6,317	B.A., B.S.; *Trimester;* Social Sciences—45%, Natural Sciences & Math—28%, Humanities—22%, Education—5%; *M.A.T.;* Coop—5-year engineering with Columbia, 5-year forestry with Duke.
Cardinal Stritch College Milwaukee 1937 *Roman Catholic*	613W	900	most in top 1/2 90%	456m 467v	a. $680 b. 850	30% $200	1:8 32%	34	$119	B.A., B.F.A.; *Semester, summer session; Teacher Education.*
Carroll College Waukesha 1846 *Presbyterian*	570M 500W	1350	60% in top 1/4 50%	M558m 519v W518m 529v	a. $1350 b. 900 d. 140	25% $1000	1:14 50%	80	$2,200	B.A., B.S.; *Semester, summer sessions;* Social Sciences—20%, Natural Sciences & Math—25%, Business and Econ.—20%, Education—15%; *Teacher Education;* Coop—3-2 engineering with Marquette; Four hours of religion courses, weekly chapel attendance required.
Carthage College Kenosha 1847 *Lutheran*	875M 625W	1500	55% in top 1/4 60%	M22.3m 21.8v W21.9m 22.5v	a. $1400 b. 850 d. 20	35% $550	1:14 42%	61	$3,000	B.A.; *Semester;* Sciences—17%, Humanities—19%, Business—20%, Social Sciences—21%, Education—23%; Coop—3-2 engineering with U. of Illinois, Valparaiso U.; Six hours of religion courses, attendance at one weekly chapel service required.
Dominican College Racine 1946 *Roman Catholic*	300M 400W	1200	32% in top 1/4 82%	485m 493v	a. $850 b. 825	30% $650	1:13 15%	30		B.A., B.S., B.Mus.; *Semester;* Education—39%, Humanities—19%, Natural Sciences & Math—20%, Social Sciences—9%, Business —12%.
Edgewood College Madison 1927 *Roman Catholic*	756W	1000	43% in top 1/5 74%	484m 474v	a. $700 b. 1000	37% $275	1:10 30%	42		B.A., B.S.; *Semester, summer session;* Education—42%, Liberal Arts—50%, Medical Technology—4%, Business—4%; *Teacher Education, Business & Bus. Ed., Biological Research, Performing Arts.*
Holy Family College Manitowoc 1935 *Roman Catholic*	564W	650	most in top 1/2 90%		a. $550 b. no dorm d. 50	6% $400	1:10 33%	35		B.A., B.S., B.Mus.Ed.; *Semester;* Education—98%.
Lakeland College Sheboygan 1862 *United Church of Christ*	397M 198W	750	25% in top 1/4 76%	22 (comp.)	a. $1090 b. 950	60% $850	1:14 15%	38	$177	B.A., B.S.; *Semester, summer session, interim term of one month;* Sciences—60%, Arts—40%; Four credits in religion courses required.
Lawrence University Appleton 1847 *Private*	700M 550W	1500	87% in top 1/4 79%M 97%W	M653m 603v W626m 626v	a. $2725 b. 855	40% $1100	1:10 52%	165	$22,000	B.A., B.Mus.; *Three-term;* Overseas Center (Germany); Air Force ROTC optional.

Institution Location / Founded Affiliation	Enrollment M=men W=women	Projected enrollment in 1975	High school rating: % applicants accepted	SAT/ACT Averages m=math v=verbal	Annual Tuition; a. Room & Board; b. Out of state; c. Other d.	% Students with $ aid / Average amount	Faculty-student ratio; % with Doctorates	Volumes in library in 1,000's	Endowment in $1,000's	Undergraduate degrees offered; *Calendar;* Per cent of students per field of study; *Professional programs offered;* Miscellaneous
Marian College of Fond du Lac Fond du Lac 1936 *Roman Catholic*	19M 480W	800	84% in top 1/2 85%	19.2m 21.6v	a. $578 b. 800 $500	16% $500	1:11 30%	43		B.A., B.S., B.S.Ed., B.S.Nursing; *Semester, summer sessions;* Education—58%, Arts—10%, Sciences—3%, Nursing—26%.
Marquette University Milwaukee 1864 *Roman Catholic*	3951M 2823W	7545	42% in top 1/5 65%		a. $1250 $800	25%	1:13 44%	354	$8,909	B.A., B.S., A.S.Dental Hygiene; *Semester, summer sessions;* Liberal Arts—35%, Bus. Adm.—11%, Engineering—11%, Journalism—3%, Nursing—4%, Speech—4%, Med.Tech.—2%, Phys. Therapy—1%; *Dentistry, Law, Medicine;* 3-2 engineering; Ten credit hours of theology required of Catholic students; A, N ROTC optional.
Mount Mary College Milwaukee 1913 *Roman Catholic*	1219W	1400	47% in top 1/5	476m 490v	a. $785 b. 900 $150	20%	1:10 17%	70	$503	B.A., B.S., B.S.Ed.; *Semester, summer session;* Education—52%, Arts—20%, Occupational Therapy—10%, Medical Technology—4%, Social Service—8%; *Occupational Therapy, Teacher Education.*
Northland College Ashland 1892 *United Church of Christ*	550M 250W	1200	75%	M20m 19v W20m 21v	a. $1125 b. 720 $450	30%	1:14 30%	54	$1,500	B.A., B.S.; *Quarter, summer sessions;* Education—40%, Natural Sciences—20%, Social Sciences—20%, Business—15%, Art—5%.
Ripon College Ripon 1851 *Private*	605M 360W	1320	65% in top 1/4 75%	M590m 534v W553m 551v	a. $1835 b. 865 d. 450 $1150	35%	1:13 60%	83	$1,760	B.A.; *Semester;* Social Sciences—33%, Humanities—45%, Natural Sciences & Math—16%, Fine Arts—7%; Coop with Princeton in Critical Languages program, with U. of Chicago in humanities; Army ROTC required for two years.
St. Norbert College West De Pere 1898 *Roman Catholic*	966M 732W	2000	90% in top 2/5 50%	540m 510v	a. $1030 b. 780 d. 51 $800	35%	1:16 38%	64		B.A., B.S., B.B.A., B.Mus., B.S.Med.Tech.; *Three-term, summer session;* B.B.A.—24%, Sciences—17%, Arts—58%; *Teacher Education;* Coops—3-2 engineering with Marquette, 2-3 engineering with U. of Detroit; Theology courses required of Catholic students; Army ROTC required for 2 years.
Stout State University —Menomonie Menomonie 1893 *State*	1878M 1373W	6500	67% in top 1/2 96%	20.1m 19.5v	a. $292 b. 694 340 $600	40%	1:14 25%	70	$110	B.S.; *Quarter, summer session;* Industrial Education—33%, Home Economics Education—33%, Industrial Technology—16%, Clothing & Textiles—5%, Home Economics—5%, Dietetics—6%, Food and Nutrition—2%.
Stout State University Barron County Campus Rice Lake 1966 *State*	51M 42W	600	66% in top 1/2	19 (comp.)	a. $292 b. 694 c. 340 $500	20%	1:9 17%			
Viterbo College La Crosse 1931 *Roman Catholic*	604W	1300	91% in top 1/2 90%	22 (comp.)	a. $650 b. 800-850 $500	25%	1:11 30%	49		B.A., B.S., B.Art Ed., B.Mus.Ed., B.S.Nursing; *Semester, summer session;* Humanities—17%, Education—39%, Social Sciences—9%, Natural Sciences & Math—12%, Med. Tech—12%, Med. Rec.—9%.
Wisconsin, The University of—Madison Madison 1848 *State*	12207M 9678W	59000 Total Madison & Milwaukee	92% in top 1/2		a. $325 b. 920 c. 1050	33%	65%	1746	$15,568 Total Madison & Milwaukee	B.A., B.S., B.B.A., B.Mus.; *Semester, summer sessions;* Soc. Sci.—31%, Hum.—16%, Nat. Sci.—15%, Eng.—14%; *Bus., Eng., Jour., Law, Lib., Med., Music, Nurs., Phar., Phys. & Oc. Ther., Psych., Social Work, Teacher Ed.;* Junior Year in France, Germany; A F, A, N ROTC optional. Wisconsin-Monterrey program.
Wisconsin, The University of—Milwaukee Milwaukee 1956 *State*	6861M 5068W		83% in top 1/2		a. $325 b. 900 c. 1050	33%	47%	317		B.A., B.S., B.B.A., B.F.A.; *Semester, summer sessions;* Social Sciences—37%, Education—23%, Humanities—13%, Sciences—13%, Business—11%; *Engineering., Bus., Jour., Lib., Mus., Psych., Nursing, Social Work, Teacher Education;* Army ROTC optional.
Wisconsin State University—Eau Claire Eau Claire 1916 *State*	2671M 2655W	10000	48% in top 1/2 82%	M22.7 W21.6 (comp.)	a. $292 b. 680 c. 632 $680	40%	1:18 36%	135		B.A., B.S., B.S.Med.Tech., B.S.Nursing, B.Mus., B.Mus.Ed.; *Semester, summer session;* Education—40%, Liberal Arts—42%, Bus. & Econ.—12%, Nursing—6%; *Teacher Education, Nursing, Med. Tech., C.P.A.;* Coop—5-year engineering with N.Y.U., 5-year Engineering, Law, Med. with U. of Wis.
Wisconsin State University—La Crosse La Crosse 1909 *State*	2972M 2228W	7500	33% in top 1/4 79%	21 (comp.)	a. $300 b. 700 c. 650 $350	38%	1:15 46%	120		B.A., B.S.; *Semester, summer session;* Education—40%, Liberal Arts & Sciences—30%, Health & Physical Education—30%; *Teacher Education.*
Wisconsin State University—Oshkosh Oshkosh 1871 *State*	4345M 3922W	16000	71% in top 1/2 95%	21.5 (comp.)	a. $288 b. 700 c. 340 $510	20%	1:17 50%	171		B.A., B.S.; *Semester, summer session;* Letters & Science—50%, Education—37%, Business—13%; *Nursing, Letters & Science, Teacher Education.*
Wisconsin State University—Platteville Platteville 1866 *State*	2900M 1125W	6440			a. $300 b. 670 c. 690 $600	50%	1:17 40%	115		B.A., B.S.; *Semester, summer session;* Education—29%, Arts & Science—23%, Engineering—10%, Agriculture—12%, Industry—6%, Business & Econ.—9%, Med. Tech.—1%; *Teacher Education.*
Wisconsin State University—River Falls River Falls 1874 *State*	2337M 1210W	5400	45% in top 1/4 78%	M21.6m 18.3v W19.1m 21.0v	a. $210 b. 675 c. 341 d. 80 $450	35%	1:16 41%	95		B.A., B.S.; *Quarter, summer session; Teacher Education.*
Wisconsin State U.—Stevens Point Stevens Point 1894 *State*	3138M 1985W	9500	54% in top 2/5 92%		a. none b. $710 c. 340 d. 286 $400	33%	1:18 32%	128		B.A., B.S., B.Mus.; *Semester, summer session;* Social Sciences—14%, Natural Sciences & Math—14%, Humanities—13%, Home Economics—4%, Conservation—15%, Education—38%, Business—2%; *Teacher Education, Med. Tech.*
Wisconsin State University—Superior Superior 1896 *State*	1791M 988W	5500	40% in top 1/3 91%		a. $294 b. 660 c. 634 $350	52%	1:15 45%	125		B.A., B.S., B.F.A., B.Mus.; *Semester, summer session; Teacher Education;* Coop in engineering with N.Y.U.; Air Force ROTC optional.
Wisconsin State University—Whitewater Whitewater 1868 *State*	2386M 2087W	11873	63% in top 1/2 87%		a. $190 b. 660 c. 340 $264	25%	1:20 39%	90		B.A., B.S., B.B.A., B.Ed.; *Semester, summer session;* Education—56%, Business—23%, Liberal Arts—11%, Business Education—10%; *Teacher Education;* Coop—3-2 law and engineering with University of Wisconsin.

WYOMING

Institution Location / Founded Affiliation	Enrollment M=men W=women	Projected enrollment in 1975	High school rating: % applicants accepted	SAT/ACT Averages m=math v=verbal	Annual Tuition; a. Room & Board; b. Out of state; c. Other d.	% Students with $ aid / Average amount	Faculty-student ratio; % with Doctorates	Volumes in library in 1,000's	Endowment in $1,000's	Undergraduate degrees offered; *Calendar;* Per cent of students per field of study; *Professional programs offered;* Miscellaneous
Wyoming, University of Laramie 1887 *State*	3633M 2075W	8583	39% in top 1/4 86%	not required	a. $345 b. 830 c. 961 $518	51%	1:15 48%	396	$11,792	B.A., B.S., B.Mus., LL.B.; *Semester, summer sessions;* Education—31%, Engineering—15%, Business—10%, Humanities—7%, Social Sciences—11%, Sciences—10%, Law—3%, Nurs.—3%, Phar.—2%; *Bus., Eng., Law, Music, Nurs., Phar., Teacher Ed.;* AF, A ROTC optional. Coop Western Interstate Commission on Higher Ed.

UNIVERSITY OF COLORADO

NOTRE DAME (*above left*), **COLORADO** (*above right*), **ST. JOHN'S COLLEGE** (*center left*).

UNIVERSITY OF NOTRE DAME

ST JOHN'S COLLEGE

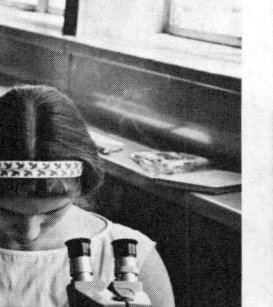

PRINCETON UNIVERSITY

FLORIDA (*center right*), **PRINCETON** (*below left*), **ALASKA** (*below right*).

UNIVERSITY OF ALASKA

UNIVERSITY OF FLORIDA

RUTGERS NEWS SERVICE

SHIELDS

RUTGERS (*above left*), **GEORGE WASHINGTON** (*above right*), **WAGNER COLLEGE** (*center left*).

MANUEL V. RUBIO

BROWN UNIVERSITY

OCCIDENTAL COLLEGE

BROWN (*center right*), **HARVARD** (*below left*), **OCCIDENTAL COLLEGE** (*below right*).

HARVARD UNIVERSITY NEWS OFFICE

JUNIOR COLLEGES: CHOICE AND CHANCE

Preparing For College.—If you are now attending a secondary school that offers several courses of study, you will know whether or not you are enrolled in a college preparatory curriculum. If you are attending an undifferentiated high school and are at all interested in college, one of the first things to consider is whether or not the course of study you are following in high school will qualify you for college entrance. This should be done in the ninth or tenth grade.

■ACADEMIC REQUIREMENTS. — Normally, and this qualification must be stressed, four years of English, two years of mathematics, and a unit each of history and science represent about the minimum that the least demanding colleges will generally accept; for many schools, two years of a foreign language is a desired prerequisite. Some technical, or otherwise specialized institutions, and some community colleges may demand less of this pre-liberal arts program, while engineering schools or pre-medical programs may require a good deal more in the fields of mathematics and science. A careful reading of the catalogues of the more selective liberal arts colleges and of the comprehensive universities will show that, while they often make exceptions for the brilliant student who was on the wrong academic track in high school, these colleges usually ask for the four years of English plus at least three of mathematics, two of either science or history or both, and prefer three or four years of a single foreign language over two years of one or two languages.

Meeting A Challenge.—American higher education is struggling today with a dual challenge. Not only must it provide quality education to an increasing number of students seeking college experience, but it must also meet the great diversity of individual interests and abilities of the young people and adults to whom an opportunity for education after high school is due. Communities and states across the country have found a way to solve the dilemma by using a resource that is known by a variety of names: the junior college, community college, or commuter college. This two-year institution may represent the chance and the choice that millions of Americans need today and will need even more tomorrow.

History of the Junior College.—Junior colleges were started around 1900. Early supporters hoped that this kind of college could provide the first two years of a four-year education in a setting that would give the maturing student a chance to reach his fullest capacity.

In recent years, these colleges have taken on a more responsible role in American higher education, for the nation has sought to extend the opportunities for education beyond the high school level and to produce men and women capable of filling jobs that were unheard of a decade ago.

The junior college has come to be recognized as a necessary link in the chain of education that leads from kindergarten to the specialized graduate program in the university; it stands between the high school and the four-year college or university.

In 1965 there were more than 720 junior colleges, enrolling well over one million students. Some 20 to 25 new institutions have been opened each year during the past ten years, and this rate of growth is likely to continue as more states incorporate the junior college idea into their higher-education plans. Some experts feel that two-year colleges will be enrolling half of all college students by 1975.

Functions.—For these students of the future, the junior college will be the starting point of a four-year college program, and, for many, an eventual graduate program. For others, the junior college will provide an avenue to responsible, rewarding positions in business and industry or in government work. For still others, primarily working adults, the two-year college will represent a means of preparing themselves for better positions or for retraining themselves in order to qualify for new occupations.

These are the functions that America's junior colleges have carved out for themselves—or that have been bequeathed to them—in light of the present and future educational needs of the country.

Private Junior Colleges.—Most of the early junior colleges were either independently supported or church-affiliated residential colleges. In 1965 there were 267 independent and church-related junior colleges in existence. Of that number, 168 had some connection with church denominations; and of these, 67 were affiliated with the Roman Catholic church. These private junior colleges concentrate on liberal arts and general

EDMUND GLEAZER, JR. Executive Director, American Association of Junior Colleges.

education and emphasize close student-teacher relationships. Some of the institutions are experimenting with the "occupational," or "semiprofessional," two-year program.

■COSTS.—The expenses of attending private junior colleges tend to be higher than those for public institutions, because the private colleges depend to some extent on tuitions and other fees to meet operating costs. The median cost for tuition and fees at private junior colleges is $526 per year, although the range is from $100 to $1600 annually. The residential student attending the private junior college must also expect to pay for room and board.

Public Junior Colleges.—While public community junior colleges developed more slowly in the first years of their existence, they now account for the greatest growth in the junior college field. In 1965 there were 452 public junior colleges, enrolling over 900,000 students. Many states are enthusiastically supporting the rapid growth of the two-year colleges. Florida, for example, which has junior colleges within commuting distance of 70 per cent of the population, eventually plans to have schools in every part of the state. California, an early developer of the junior college system, has about eighty colleges; these enroll approximately 85 per cent of all freshmen and sophmores attending college in California. New York, Michigan, Washington, Texas, Illinois, Maryland, and Massachusetts are among the states that have well-defined programs of junior college development. Several others—Ohio, North Carolina, New Jersey, Minnesota, Missouri, Arizona, Alabama, Georgia, and Pennsylvania—are in various stages of charting systems of public junior colleges.

■ORGANIZATION.—An important innovation in the field has been that of the establishment of multi-campus operations in major metropolitan centers. St. Louis Junior College, opened in 1962, now has three campuses; Chicago is opening its ninth branch; and Los Angeles has eight centers and plans to establish additional ones.

Public junior colleges are often organized under local boards of education that may also control the public school systems. The trend today, however, is toward the creation of colleges that have their own districts, boards, and officers; this gives the schools more autonomy and identity. In a few states, community colleges are operated as branches of state universities. The University of Kentucky, for example, has seven colleges operating in widely scattered communities.

■COSTS.—Tuitions at public community junior colleges are minimal since one of the primary aims of these institutions is to make college widely accessible. California institutions charge no tuition, but the median cost throughout the country of attending public junior colleges is approximately $200 per year. Since the public colleges operate largely for the commuting student, few of them maintain dormitories. Thus it is fairly inexpensive to attend a public junior college, providing the student is able to live at home.

Most junior colleges, both private and public, have scholarship and other student-aid programs; junior college students are also eligible for federal loans and scholarships.

Programs of Study.—While many jobs once available to the high school or vocational school graduate are diminishing in number, more sophisticated technical and semi-professional jobs are growing at an extremely rapid rate. These jobs require training beyond the high school level, but may not require a four-year baccalaureate education. The junior college has recognized this need and has moved to meet it.

The catalogues of many junior colleges contain programs of study in such varied occupations as radioscopy technology, data processing, missile technology, technical editing, and nuclear technology. Many professional fields need supportive personnel who can be trained in two years or less. For example, since the medical practice has become more refined and the demand for medical care has increased, most doctors and dentists today require a wide range of assistants. Many junior colleges now provide programs to train nurses, medical assistants, dental technicians, and even ambulance attendants. Other programs offered include law enforcement, social work, and fire and forest services. These courses of study train new personnel and also provide in-service training for those already employed.

In some fields of study, the courses offered are so broad and complex that they cannot be easily categorized. For instance, in the engineering and industrial technology category, the following programs are typical of those offered:

Aeronautical or Aero-Space Technology
Air Conditioning and Refrigeration Technology
Architectural Engineering Technology
Atomic Power Technology
Chemical Technology
Civil and Highway Engineering Technology
Computer Technology
Drafting Technology
Architectural Technology
Design Technology
Engineering Technology
Industrial Technology
Machine Technology
Petroleum Technology
Electrical Power Technology
Electronics Technology
Metallurgical Technology
Plastics Technology
Surveying and Topographical Drafting Technology

Not all junior colleges would offer courses of study in all of these subject areas, for the specific courses offered at each college depend upon where the college is located and the types of business and industry to which it relates its programing.

■**ADULT EDUCATION.** — An important role of the junior college is that of educating adults. Today education is considered a continuous process that offers the American citizen the opportunity for cultural enrichment as well as practical job training. With the increase in automation and the resultant displacement of workers from many kinds of jobs, many men and women have to be retrained. For many people, a few courses in a community college may result in job advancement.

An indication of the popularity of adult education programs is the fact that many community colleges enroll twice as many students in evening courses as they do in regular day classes. Often, part-time teachers are obtained from local business and industry to supplement the regular staff in teaching evening courses, particularly when the subjects are of a highly specialized nature.

■**DEGREES.**—Junior colleges offer associate degrees for those who successfully complete a two-year program. These degrees are receiving increasing recognition as junior colleges figure more prominently in the nation's higher education system.

Advantages of a Junior College.—The advantages of the community junior college are multiple. Through flexible admissions policies, these institutions will admit students who might not be accepted in universities where enrollment pressures have mounted to such a great extent that many young people of average scholastic achievement cannot get in. The community junior colleges also often offer repair courses, which help students to attain an academic level enabling them to proceed with normal college work or to enter occupational programs. Some colleges have achieved remarkable success in developing lagging or latent talent; they can cite cases where they have accepted students who have been "rejected" by other institutions and eventually have sent them on to great success at the same college or university that originally rejected them.

In addition to giving a chance to students with average or poor scholastic records, the community college offers an opportunity to the student who may have the scholastic background but not the financial means to enter a four-year institution located some distance from home. There are also many students of both high scholastic achievement and ample financial means who choose to attend a college in their home town for the first two years.

Another advantage of the junior college is that the primary function of its teachers is not to do research and to publish, but to provide as much individual attention as possible to the student. Unfortunately, junior colleges, like other institutions of higher education, are beset with increased enrollment demands, so that the classes cannot be kept as small as most administrators would like. Even so, the student-teacher ratio in most institutions is about 25 to 1.

Because of the great variety of students who enter junior colleges, there is an obvious need for superior counseling services. Most two-year colleges have large counseling staffs that assist students with such things as financial problems, curriculum planning, employment opportunities, and whether or not to transfer to other schools.

Outlook for the Future.—The junior college and the four-year institution are not competing with each other, but are closely cooperating in order to ascertain that an opportunity for post-high school education is available to as many people as possible. Many educational experts, in fact, predict that two-year colleges may eventually be the starting point for *all* beginning college students, with universities devoting most of their attention to the last two years and to graduate work. Even today, at least one-fourth of all students entering college start in a two-year college. A dramatic indication of the changing nature of American higher education is to be found in Florida. Florida Atlantic University in Boca Raton was established as a kind of two-year college in reverse: the university offers only the last two years of a four-year college program and does not offer a graduate program. Florida junior colleges are expected to send many of their graduates to Florida Atlantic University. A similar institution is being established in another part of the state. It is clear that in the future the junior college will figure more importantly in the scheme of higher education in this country.

—Edmund J. Gleazer, Jr.

ABBREVIATIONS

A. of God	Assemblies of God
A.M.E.	African Methodist Episcopal
Bapt.	Baptist
Byz. Cath.	Byzantine Catholic
C.	Coeducational
Ch. of Chr.	Church of Christ
Ch. of God	Church of God
Chr. Ch.	Christian Church
Com.	Community
C.N.J.	Church of the New Jerusalem
E.C.	Engineers' Council for Professional Development
Epis.	Episcopal
Ev. Un. Br.	Evangelical United Brethren
Free Meth.	Free Methodist
Ind. Np.	Independent, nonprofit
Indus.	Industrial
L.D.S.	Church of Jesus Christ of Latter-Day Saints
Luth.	Lutheran
Mennon.	Mennonite
Meth.	Methodist
M.S.	Middle States Assoc. of Colleges and Secondary Schools
N.C.	North Central Assoc. of Colleges and Secondary Schools
N.E.	New England Assoc. of Colleges and Secondary Schools
N.W.	Northwest Assoc. of Secondary and Higher Schools
Pent. Hol.	Pentacostal Holiness
Pil. Hol.	Pilgrim Holiness
Presby.	Presbyterian
Prot. Epis.	Protestant Episcopal
Rom. Cath.	Roman Catholic
S.A.	Southern Assoc. of Colleges and Secondary Schools
7 Day Adv.	Seventh Day Adventists
W.	Women
W.A.	Western Assoc. of Schools and Colleges

Institution	Location	Organized as Junior College	Registration or Accreditation	Enrollment	Type	Affiliation
ALABAMA						
Alabama Christian Col.	Montgomery	1942	State	164	C	Ch. of Chr.
Daniel Payne Col.	Birmingham	1953	S.A.	160	C	A.M.E.
Marion Inst., The	Marion	1917	S.A.	373	M	Ind. Np.
Northwest Alabama Jr. Col.	Phil Campbell	1963	State	131	C	Public
Sacred Heart Col.	Cullman	1940	S.A.	177	W	Rom. Cath.
Snead Jr. Col.	Boaz	1935	S.A.	578	C	Meth.
Southern Union Col.	Wadley	1923	State	238	C	Public
Walker Col.	Jasper	1938	S.A.	502	C	Ind. Np.
ALASKA						
Anchorage Comm. Col.	Anchorage	1954	N.W.	766	C	Public
Juneau-Douglas Com. Col.	Juneau	1956	N.W.	288	C	Public
Kenai Community Col.	Kenai	1964	N.W.	45	C	Public
Ketchikan Community Col.	Ketchikan	1954	N.W.	82	C	Public
Palmer Community Col.	Palmer	1961	N.W.		C	Public
Sheldon Jackson Jr. Col.	Sitka	1944	State	113	C	Presby.
Sitka Community Col.	Sitka	1962	N.W.	20	C	Public
ARIZONA						
Arizona Western Col.	Yuma	1963	State	1,014	C	Public
Cochise Col.	Douglas	1964	State	1,015	C	Public
Eastern Arizona Jr. Col.	Thatcher	1921	State	701	C	Public
Phoenix Col.	Phoenix	1920	N.C.	12,820	C	Public
ARKANSAS						
Arkansas State Col. Beebe Br.	Beebe	1932	N.C.	184	C	Public
Central Baptist Col.	Conway	1952	State	191	C	Bapt.
Fort Smith Jr. Col.	Fort Smith	1928	State	1,486	C	Ind. Np.
Shorter Col.	North Little Rock	1955	State	204	C	A.M.E.
Southern Baptist Col.	Walnut Ridge	1941	N.C.	372	C	Bapt.
CALIFORNIA						
Allan Hancock Col.	Santa Maria	1920	W.A.	2,318	C	Public
American River Jr. Col.	Sacramento	1955	W.A.	8,323	C	Public
Antelope Valley Col.	Lancaster	1929	W.A.	2,485	C	Public
Bakersfield Col.	Bakersfield	1913	W.A.	7,465	C	Public
Barstow Col.	Barstow	1960	W.A.	903	C	Public
Cabrillo Col.	Aptos	1959	W.A.	2,858	C	Public
Cerritos Col.	Norwalk	1956	W.A.	7,974	C	Public
Chabot Col.	San Leandro	1961	W.A.	4,927	C	Public
Chaffey Col.	Alta Loma	1916	W.A.	5,424	C	Public
Citrus Col.	Azusa	1915	W.A.	5,533	C	Public
City Col. of San Francisco	San Francisco	1935	W.A.	9,770	C	Public
Coalinga Jr. Col.	Coalinga	1932	W.A.	1,213	C	Public
Cogswell Polytechnical Col.	San Francisco	1930	E.C.	154	C	Ind. Np.
Col. of the Desert	Palm Desert	1962	W.A.	2,490	C	Public
Col. of Marin	Kentfield	1926	W.A.	3,479	C	Public
Col. of San Mateo	San Mateo	1922	W.A.	17,970	C	Public
Col. of the Sequoias	Visalia	1926	W.A.	2,047	C	Public
Col. of the Siskiyous	Weed	1957	W.A.	435	C	Public
Compton Col.	Compton	1927	W.A.	4,966	C	Public
Contra Costa Col.	San Pablo	1950	W.A.	4,632	C	Public
Deep Springs Col.	Deep Springs	1917	W.A.	21	M	Ind. Np.
Diablo Valley Col.	Concord	1951	W.A.	8,798	C	Public
East Los Angeles Col.	Los Angeles	1945	W.A.	9,770	C	Public
El Camino Col.	El Camino	1946	W.A.	13,589	C	Public
Foothill Col.	Los Altos Hills	1958	W.A.	8,995	C	Public
Fresno City Col.	Fresno	1910	W.A.	6,602	C	Public
Fullerton Jr. Col.	Fullerton	1913	W.A.	11,355	C	Public
Gavilan Col.	Gilroy	1919	W.A.	695	C	Public
Glendale Col.	Glendale	1927	W.A.	5,723	C	Public
Grossmont Col.	El Cajon	1961	W.A.	3,702	C	Public
Hartnell Col.	Salinas	1920	W.A.	2,595	C	Public
Humphreys Col.	Stockton	1947	W.A.	369	C	Ind. Np.
Imperial Valley Col.	Imperial	1960	W.A.	1,504	C	Public
Laney Col.	Oakland	1954	W.A.	5,252	C	Public
Lassen Col.	Susanville	1924	W.A.	265	C	Public
Long Beach City Col.	Long Beach	1927	W.A.	27,500	C	Public
Los Angeles City Col.	Los Angeles	1929	W.A.	15,989	C	Public
Los Angeles Harbor Col.	Wilmington	1949	W.A.	5,009	C	Public
Los Angeles Metropolitan Col.	Los Angeles	1950	W.A.	4,975	C	Public
Los Angeles Pierce Col.	Woodland Hills	1947	W.A.	10,004	C	Public
Los Angeles Trade-Tech Col.	Los Angeles	1949	W.A.	10,196	C	Public
Los Angeles Valley Col.	Van Nuys	1949	W.A.	13,723	C	Public
Menlo Col.	Menlo Park	1927	W.A.	351	M	Ind. Np.
Merced Col.	Merced	1963	State	2,181	C	Public
Merritt Col.	Oakland	1953	W.A.	6,583	C	Public
Modesto Jr. Col.	Modesto	1922	W.A.	6,370	C	Public
Monterey Peninsula Col.	Monterey	1947	W.A.	3,804	C	Public
Mt. San Antonio Col.	Walnut	1946	W.A.	10,861	C	Public
Mt. San Jacinto Col.	Beaumont	1963	W.A.	704	C	Public
Napa Jr. Col.	Napa	1942	W.A.	2,365	C	Public
Oceanside-Carlsbad Col.	Oceanside	1934	W.A.	1,734	C	Public
Orange Coast Col.	Costa Mesa	1948	W.A.	15,747	C	Public
Pacific Col.	Fresno	1961	W.A.	176	C	Mennon.
Palo Verde Col.	Blythe	1947	W.A.	388	C	Public
Palomar Col.	San Marcos	1946	W.A.	4,009	C	Public
Pasadena City Col.	Pasadena	1924	W.A.	12,918	C	Public
Porterville Col.	Porterville	1927	W.A.	880	C	Public
Reedley Col.	Reedley	1926	W.A.	1,408	C	Public
Rio Hondo Jr. Col.	Santa Fe Springs	1963	State	2,568	C	Public
Riverside City Col.	Riverside	1916	W.A.	7,322	C	Public
Sacramento City Col.	Sacramento	1916	W.A.	7,015	C	Public
San Bernardino Valley Col.	San Bernardino	1926	W.A.	10,182	C	Public
San Diego Jr. Col.	San Diego	1914	W.A.	15,542	C	Public
San Joaquin Delta Jr. Col.	Stockton	1935	W.A.	6,279	C	Public
San Jose City Col.	San Jose	1921	W.A.	8,756	C	Public
San Luis Obispo County Jr. Col.	San Luis Obispo	1964	State	458	C	Public
Santa Ana Col.	Santa Ana	1915	W.A.	5,325	C	Public
Santa Barbara City Col.	Santa Barbara	1946	W.A.	2,805	C	Public
Santa Monica City Col.	Santa Monica	1929	W.A.	11,415	C	Public
Santa Rosa Jr. Col.	Santa Rosa	1918	W.A.	5,957	C	Public

Institution	Location	Organized as Junior College	Registration or Accreditation	Enrollment	Type	Affiliation
CALIFORNIA (continued)						
Shasta Jr. Col.	Redding	1950	W.A.	2,487	C	Public
Sierra Col.	Rocklin	1914	W.A.	2,230	C	Public
Southwestern Col.	Chula Vista	1961	W.A.	3,019	C	Public
Taft Col.	Taft	1922	W.A.	1,075	C	Public
Vallejo Jr. Col.	Vallejo	1945	W.A.	3,533	C	Public
Ventura Col.	Ventura	1925	W.A.	8,738	C	Public
Victor Valley Col.	Victorville	1961	W.A.	1,216	C	Public
West Valley Jr. Col.	Campbell	1964	State	3,147	C	Public
Yuba Col.	Marysville	1927	W.A.	3,403	C	Public
COLORADO						
Lamar Jr. Col.	Lamar	1937	State	546	C	Public
Mesa Col.	Grand Junction	1925	N.C.	2,155	C	Public
Northeastern Jr. Col.	Sterling	1941	N.C.	1,151	C	Public
Otero Jr. Col.	La Junta	1941	State	706	C	Public
Rangely Col.	Rangely	1961	N.C.	153	C	Public
Trinidad State Jr. Col.	Trinidad	1925	N.C.	735	C	Public
CONNECTICUT						
Hartford Col. for Women	Hartford	1939	N.E.	190	W	Ind. Np.
Hartford State Tech. Inst.	Hartford	1946	E.C.	317	C	Public
Holy Family Seminary	West Hartford	1930	State	64	M	Rom. Cath.
Jr. Col. of Connecticut	Bridgeport	1927	N.E.	4,500	C	Ind. Np.
Manchester Community Col.	Manchester	1963	State	223	C	Public
Mitchell Col.	New London	1938	N.E.	1,368	C	Ind. Np.
Mount Sacred Heart Col.	Hamden	1954	State	43	W	Rom. Cath.
New Haven Col.	West Haven	1926	N.E.	2,373	C	Ind. Np.
Norwalk Community Col.	Norwalk	1961	State	792	C	Public
Norwalk State Tech. Inst.	South Norwalk	1961	State	1,264	C	Public
Quinnipiac Col.	Hamden	1929	N.E.	1,699	C	Ind. Np.
Silvermine Col. of Art	New Canaan	1960	State	58	C	Ind. Np.
St. Thomas Seminary	Bloomfield	1897	N.E.	175	M	Rom. Cath.
Thames Valley State Tech. Inst.	Norwich	1963	State	194	C	Public
Waterbury State Tech. Inst.	Waterbury	1964	State	191	C	Public
DELAWARE						
Wesley Col.	Dover	1917	M.S.	801	C	Meth.
DISTRICT OF COLUMBIA						
Immaculata Col. of Washington	Washington, D.C.	1912	M.S.	288	W	Rom. Cath.
Mount Vernon Jr. Col.	Washington, D.C.	1893	M.S.	216	W	Ind. Np.
Southeastern Univ.	Washington, D.C.	1940	State	225	C	Ind. Np.
FLORIDA						
Brevard Jr. Col.	Cocoa	1960	State	2,583	C	Public
Central Florida Jr. Col.	Ocala	1958	S.A.	1,096	C	Public
Chipola Jr. Col.	Marianna	1948	S.A.	944	C	Public
Daytona Beach Jr. Col.	Daytona Beach	1958	S.A.	1,587	C	Public
Edison Jr. Col.	Fort Myers	1960	State	940	C	Public
Florida Col.	Temple Terrace	1946	S.A.	354	C	Ind. Np.
Gulf Coast Jr. Col.	Panama City	1957	S.A.	1,028	C	Public
Hampton Jr. Col.	Ocala	1958	State	302	C	Public
Indian River Jr. Col.	Fort Pierce	1960	State	682	C	Public
Jackson Jr. Col.	Marianna	1961	State	80	C	Public
Jr. Col. of Broward County	Fort Lauderdale	1960	State	2,987	C	Public
Lake City J.C. & Forest Ranger School	Lake City	1962	State	679	C	Public
Lake-Sumter Jr. Col.	Leesburg	1962	State	576	C	Public
Manatee Jr. Col.	Bradenton	1958	S.A.	1,744	C	Public
Marymount Jr. Col.	Boca Raton	1963	State	196	W	Rom. Cath.
Miami-Dade Jr. Col.	Miami	1960	State	10,822	C	Public
North Florida Jr. Col.	Madison	1958	S.A.	706	C	Public
Okaloosa-Walton Jr. Col.	Valparaiso	1964	State	616	C	Public
Orlando Jr. Col.	Orlando	1941	S.A.	1,949	C	Ind. Np.
Palm Beach Jr. Col.	Lake Worth	1933	S.A.	3,623	C	Public
Pensacola Jr. Col.	Pensacola	1948	S.A.	3,435	C	Public
Polk Jr. Col.	Bartow	1964	State	1,067	C	Public
Rosenwald Community Jr. Col.	Panama City	1958	State	126	C	Public
St. Johns River Jr. Col.	Palatka	1958	State	1,665	C	Public
St. Petersburg Jr. Col.	St. Petersburg	1927	S.A.	5,978	C	Public
Suwannee River Jr. Col.	Madison	1959	State	328	C	Public
GEORGIA						
Abraham Baldwin Agr. Col.	Tifton	1933	S.A.	1,024	C	Public
Andrew Col.	Cuthbert	1917	S.A.	315	C	Meth.
Augusta Col.	Augusta	1925	S.A.	1,274	C	Public
Birdwood Jr. Col.	Thomasville	1954	State	90	C	Bapt.
Brewton Parker Col.	Mount Vernon	1927	S.A.	379	C	Bapt.
Brunswick Col.	Brunswick	1964	State	264	C	Public
Columbus Col.	Columbus	1958	S.A.	959	C	Public
Dekalb Col.	Clarkston	1964	State	763	C	Public
Emmanuel Col.	Franklin Springs	1935	State	253	C	Pent. Hol.
Emory at Oxford	Oxford	1929	S.A.	426	C	Meth.
Georgia Military Col.	Milledgeville	1930	S.A.	246	M	Public
Gordon Military Col.	Barnesville	1927	S.A.	300	C	Ind. Np.
Middle Georgia Col.	Cochran	1928	S.A.	946	C	Public
Norman Col.	Norman Park	1920	S.A.	459	C	Bapt.
Reinhardt Col.	Waleska	1889	S.A.	341	C	Meth.
South Georgia Col.	Douglas	1927	S.A.	750	C	Public
Southern Tech. Inst.	Marietta	1948	E.C.	1,180	C	Public
Truett-McConnell Col.	Cleveland	1947	State	336	C	Bapt.
Young Harris Col.	Young Harris	1912	S.A.	612	C	Meth.
HAWAII						
Maunaolu Col.	Paia, Maui	1950	W.A.	186	C	Ind. Np.
IDAHO						
Boise, Jr. Col.	Boise	1932	N.W.	3,055	C	Public
North Idaho Jr. Col.	Coeur d'Alene	1939	N.W.	744	C	Public
Ricks Col.	Rexburg	1915	N.W.	1,846	C	L.D.S.
ILLINOIS						
Belleville Township Jr. Col.	Belleville	1946	N.C.	844	C	Public
Black Hawk Col.	Moline	1946	N.C.	2,110	C	Public

Institution	Location	Organized as Junior College	Registration or Accreditation	Enrollment	Type	Affiliation
ILLINOIS (continued)						
Bloom Township Com. Col.	Chicago Heights	1958	State	1,143	C	Public
Canton Community Col.	Canton	1960	State	702	C	Public
Central YMCA Community Col.	Chicago	1961	State	2,427	C	Ind. Np.
Centralia Jr. Col.	Centralia	1940	N.C.	432	C	Public
Chicago City Jr. Col.	Chicago	1911	N.C.		C	Public
Amundsen Branch	Chicago	1956	N.C.	3,243	C	Public
Bogan Branch	Chicago	1960	N.C.	4,304	C	Public
Crane Branch	Chicago	1911	N.C.	2,601	C	Public
Fenger Branch	Chicago	1958	N.C.	1,366	C	Public
Loop Branch	Chicago	1962	N.C.	5,176	C	Public
Southeast Branch	Chicago	1957	N.C.	2,947	C	Public
Wilson Branch	Chicago	1934	N.C.	4,314	C	Public
Wright Branch	Chicago	1911	N.C.	9,147	C	Public
Danville Jr. Col.	Danville	1949	State	952	C	Public
Elgin Community Col.	Elgin	1949	State	1,544	C	Public
Felician Col., The	Chicago	1953	State	64	W	Rom. Cath.
Freeport Community Col.	Freeport	1962	State	540	C	Public
Immaculata Col.	Bartlett	1955	State	123	W	Rom. Cath.
Joliet Jr. Col.	Joliet	1901	N.C.	2,699	C	Public
Kendall Col.	Evanston	1934	N.C.	586	C	Meth.
La Salle-Peru-Oglesby Jr. Col.	La Salle	1924	N.C.	1,093	C	Public
Lincoln Col.	Lincoln	1929	N.C.	500	C	Presby.
Lyons Township Jr. Col.	La Grange	1929	N.C.	1,021	C	Public
Mallinckrodt Col.	Wilmette	1918	State	41	W	Rom. Cath.
Maria Jr. Col.	Chicago	1948	State	47	W	Rom. Cath.
Monticello Col.	Godfrey	1917	N.C.	276	W	Ind. Np.
Morton Jr. Col.	Cicero	1924	N.C.	2,123	C	Public
Mt. Vernon Community Col.	Mt. Vernon	1956	State	643	C	Public
Olney Community Col.	Olney	1963	State	295	C	Public
Peoria Col. of Bradley Univ.	Peoria	1946	N.C.	200	C	Ind. Np.
Southeastern Illinois Col.	Harrisburg	1960	State	350	C	Public
Springfield Jr. Col.	Springfield	1929	N.C.	743	C	Rom. Cath.
St. Bede Jr. Col.	Peru	1942	N.C.	113	M	Rom. Cath.
St. Mary of the Lake Seminary, J.C. Dept.	Niles	1961	State	309	M	Rom. Cath.
Thornton Jr. Col.	Harvey	1927	N.C.	2,089	C	Public
Trinity Christian Col.	Palos Heights	1959	State	197	C	Ind. Np.
Wabash Valley Col.	Mt. Carmel	1961	State	501	C	Public
INDIANA						
Ancilla Domini Col.	Donaldson	1937	State	77	W	Rom. Cath.
Vincennes Univ.	Vincennes	1873	N.C.	818	C	Public
IOWA						
Boone Jr. Col.	Boone	1927	State	176	C	Public
Burlington Community Col.	Burlington	1920	N.C.	518	C	Public
Centerville Community Col.	Centerville	1930	State	350	C	Public
Clarinda Community Col.	Clarinda	1923	State	290	C	Public
Clinton Jr. Col.	Clinton	1946	State	228	C	Public
Creston Community Col.	Creston	1926	State	254	C	Public
Eagle Grove Jr. Col.	Eagle Grove	1928	State	143	C	Public
Ellsworth Col.	Iowa Falls	1929	N.C.	635	C	Public
Emmetsburg Community Col.	Emmetsburg	1930	State	109	C	Public
Estherville Jr. Col.	Estherville	1924	State	311	C	Public
Fort Dodge Community Col.	Fort Dodge	1921	State	624	C	Public
Grand View Col.	Des Moines	1925	N.C.	1,026	C	Luth.
Iowa State Tech. Inst.	Ames	1960	N.C.	280	C	Public
Keokuk Community Col.	Keokuk	1953	State	245	C	Public
Marshalltown Community Col.	Marshalltown	1927	State	522	C	Public
Mason City Jr. Col.	Mason City	1918	N.C.	1,072	C	Public
Mount St. Clare Col.	Clinton	1918	N.C.	299	W	Rom. Cath.
Muscatine Community Col.	Muscatine	1929	State	543	C	Public
Ottumwa Heights Col.	Ottumwa	1925	N.C.	303	W	Rom. Cath.
Waldorf Col.	Forest City	1903	N.C.	460	C	Luth.
Webster City Jr. Col.	Webster City	1926	State	186	C	Public
KANSAS						
Arkansas City Jr. Col.	Arkansas City	1922	State	571	C	Public
Butler County Jr. Col.	El Dorado	1927	State	558	C	Public
Central Col.	McPherson	1914	State	155	C	Free Meth.
Chanute Jr. Col.	Chanute	1936	State	434	C	Public
Coffeyville Col.	Coffeyville	1923	State	753	C	Public
Dodge City Col.	Dodge City	1935	State	566	C	Public
Donnelly Col.	Kansas City	1949	N.C.	787	C	Rom. Cath.
Fort Scott Jr. Col.	Fort Scott	1919	State	315	C	Public
Garden City Jr. Col.	Garden City	1919	State	375	C	Public
Hesston Col.	Hesston	1924	State	287	C	Mennon.
Highland Jr. Col.	Highland	1937	State	512	C	Public
Hutchinson Jr. Col.	Hutchinson	1928	N.C.	1,266	C	Public
Independence Community Col.	Independence	1925	N.C.	483	C	Public
Iola Jr. Col.	Iola	1923	State	268	C	Public
Kansas City Kansas Jr. Col.	Kansas City	1923	N.C.	1,079	C	Public
Miltonvale Wesleyan Col.	Miltonvale	1930	State	119	C	Meth.
Parsons Jr. Col.	Parsons	1923	State	354	C	Public
Pratt County Col.	Pratt	1938	State	349	C	Public
St. John's Col.	Winfield	1893	N.C.	276	C	Luth.
KENTUCKY						
Alice Lloyd Jr. Col.	Pippa Passes	1923	S.A.	251	C	Ind. Np.
Lees Jr. Col.	Jackson	1927	S.A.	216	C	Presby.
Lindsey Wilson Col.	Columbia	1923	S.A.	494	C	Meth.
Loretto Jr. Col.	Nerinx	1936	S.A.	89	W	Rom. Cath.
Midway Jr. Col.	Midway	1944	S.A.	151	W	Chr. Ch.
Paducah Jr. Col.	Paducah	1932	S.A.	747	C	Public
Southeastern Christian Col.	Winchester	1949	S.A.	135	C	Ch. of Chr.
St. Catharine Jr. Col.	St. Catharine	1931	S.A.	210	C	Rom. Cath.
Sue Bennett Col.	London	1922	S.A.	253	C	Meth.
Univ. of Kentucky Com. Cols.						
Ashland Community Col.	Ashland	1957	S.A.	511	C	Public
Elizabethtown Community Col.	Elizabethtown	1964	S.A.	355	C	Public
Fort Knox Community Col.	Fort Knox	1958	S.A.	272	C	Public
Henderson Community Col.	Henderson	1960	S.A.	279	C	Public
Northern Community Col.	Covington	1948	S.A.	801	C	Public
Prestonsburg Community Col.	Prestonsburg	1964	S.A.	320	C	Public
Southeast Community Col.	Cumberland	1960	S.A.	338	C	Public

Institution	Location	Organized as Junior College	Registration or Accreditation	Enrollment	Type	Affiliation
LOUISIANA						
St. Joseph Seminary	St. Benedict	1893	S.A.	60	M	Rom. Cath.
MAINE						
Thomas Col.	Waterville	1956	State	178	C	Ind. Np.
Westbrook Jr. Col.	Portland	1925	N.E.	486	W	Ind. Np.
MARYLAND						
Allegany Community Col.	Cumberland	1961	State	400	C	Public
Anne Arundel Community Col.	Severna Park	1961	State	621	C	Public
Baltimore Jr. Col.	Baltimore	1947	M.S.	2,445	C	Public
Catonsville Community Col.	Catonsville	1957	State	1,050	C	Public
Charles County Community Col.	La Plata	1958	State	234	C	Public
Essex Community Col.	Essex	1957	State	576	C	Public
Frederick Community Col.	Frederick	1957	State	400	C	Public
Hagerstown Jr. Col.	Hagerstown	1946	State	558	C	Public
Harford Jr. Col.	Bel Air	1957	State	703	C	Public
Montgomery Jr. Col.	Takoma Park	1946	M.S.	2,778	C	Public
Mount Providence Jr. Col.	Relay	1960	State	79	W	Rom. Cath.
Prince George's Community Col.	Suitland	1958	State	1,174	C	Public
St. Charles Col.	Catonsville	1848	M.S.	187	M	Rom. Cath.
St. Mary's Col. of Maryland	St. Mary's City	1927	M.S.	227	C	Public
St. Peter's Col.	Baltimore	1950	M.S.	37	M	Rom. Cath.
Villa Julie Col.	Stevenson	1952	M.S.	117	W	Rom. Cath.
Xaverian Col.	Silver Spring	1933	M.S.	103	C	Rom. Cath.
MASSACHUSETTS						
Bay Path Jr. Col.	Longmeadow	1949	State	416	W	Ind. Np.
Becker Jr. Col.	Worcester	1942	State	634	C	Ind. Np.
Berkshire Community Col.	Pittsfield	1960	State	575	C	Public
Bradford Jr. Col.	Bradford	1902	N.E.	393	W	Ind. Np.
Cambridge Jr. Col.	Cambridge	1934	State	97	C	Ind. Np.
Cape Cod Community Col.	Hyannis	1961	State	484	C	Public
Chamberlayne Jr. Col.	Boston	1892	State	813	C	Ind. Np.
Dean Jr. Col.	Franklin	1941	N.E.	892	C	Ind. Np
Endicott Jr. Col.	Beverly	1939	N.E.	720	W	Ind. Np.
Fisher Jr. Col.	Boston	1952	State	464	W	Ind. Np.
Franklin Inst. of Boston	Boston	1908	E.C.	758	C	Ind. Np.
Garland Jr. Col.	Boston	1952	N.E.	357	W	Ind. Np.
Greenfield Community Col.	Greenfield	1962	State	492	C	Public
Holyoke Community Col.	Holyoke	1946	State	1,220	C	Public
Lasell Jr. Col.	Auburndale	1932	N.E.	696	W	Ind. Np.
Leicester Jr. Col.	Leicester	1940	State	227	M	Ind. Np.
Massachusetts Bay Com. Col.	Boston	1961	State	732	C	Public
Mount Ida Jr. Col.	Newton Centre	1907	State	560	W	Ind. Np.
Mount Wachusett Com. Col.	Gardner	1964	State	245	C	Public
Newton Jr. Col.	Newtonville	1946	N.E.	608	C	Public
Northern Essex Com. Col.	Haverhill	1961	State	713	C	Public
Pine Manor Jr. Col.	Wellesley	1911	N.E.	335	W	Ind. Np.
Quincy Jr. Col.	Quincy	1958	State	860	C	Public
Quinsigamond Com. Col.	Worcester	1963	State	557	C	Public
Wentworth Inst.	Boston	1911	E.C.	3,354	M	Ind. Np.
Worcester Jr. Col.	Worcester	1938	N.E.	2,401	C	Ind. Np.
MICHIGAN						
Alpena Community Col.	Alpena	1952	N.C.	576	C	Public
Bay De Noc Community Col.	Escanaba	1963	State	376	C	Public
Concordia Lutheran Jr. Col.	Ann Arbor	1963	State	461	C	Luth.
Delta Col.	University Center	1961	State	3,800	C	Public
Flint Community Jr. Col.	Flint	1923	N.C.	5,703	C	Public
Gogebic Community Col.	Ironwood	1932	N.C.	338	C	Public
Grand Rapids Jr. Col.	Grand Rapids	1914	N.C.	4,062	C	Public
Henry Ford Community Col.	Dearborn	1938	N.C.	8,652	C	Public
Highland Park Col.	Highland Park	1918	N.C.	2,301	C	Public
Jackson Jr. Col.	Jackson	1928	N.C.	1,857	C	Public
Kellogg Community Col.	Battle Creek	1956	State	2,150	M	Public
Lake Michigan Col.	Benton Harbor	1946	N.C.	1,587	C	Public
Lansing Community Col.	Lansing	1957	N.C.	3,121	C	Public
Macomb County Com. Col.	Warren	1954	State	4,175	C	Public
Michigan Christian Jr. Col.	Rochester	1959	State	210	C	Ch. of Chr.
Muskegon County Com. Col.	Muskegon	1926	N.C.	2,850	C	Public
North Central Michigan Col.	Petoskey	1959	State	365	C	Public
Northwestern Michigan Col.	Traverse City	1951	N.C.	1,122	C	Public
Port Huron Jr. Col.	Port Huron	1923	N.C.	2,447	C	Public
Schoolcraft Col.	Livonia	1964	State	2,153	C	Public
Suomi Col.	Hancock	1923	State	299	C	Luth.
MINNESOTA						
Austin Jr. Col.	Austin	1940	State	608	C	Public
Bethany Lutheran Col.	Mankato	1926	State	127	C	Luth.
Brainerd Jr. Col.	Brainerd	1938	State	318	C	Public
Crosier Seminary	Onamia	1926	State	52	M	Rom. Cath.
Ely Jr. Col.	Ely	1922	State	202	C	Public
Eveleth Jr. Col.	Eveleth	1918	N.C.	151	C	Public
Fergus Falls State Jr. Col.	Fergus Falls	1960	State	361	C	Public
Hibbing Jr. Col.	Hibbing	1916	N.C.	695	C	Public
Itasca Jr. Col.	Coleraine	1922	State	291	C	Public
Rochester Jr. Col.	Rochester	1915	N.C.	1,361	C	Public
Virginia Jr. Col.	Virginia	1921	N.C.	482	C	Public
Willmar Community Col.	Willmar	1962	State	657	C	Public
Worthington Jr. Col.	Worthington	1936	State	552	C	Public
MISSISSIPPI						
Clarke Memorial Jr. Col.	Newton	1919	S.A.	362	C	Bapt.
Coahoma Jr. Col.	Clarksdale	1949	State	517	C	Public
Copiah-Lincoln Jr. Col.	Wesson	1928	S.A.	543	C	Public
East Central Jr. Col.	Decatur	1928	S.A.	555	C	Public
East Mississippi Jr. Col.	Scooba	1927	S.A.	286	C	Public
Gulf Park Col.	Long Beach	1921	S.A.	333	W	Ind. Np.
Hinds Jr. Col.	Raymond	1922	S.A.	1,618	C	Public
Holmes Jr. Col.	Goodman	1925	S.A.	512	C	Public
Itawamba Jr. Col.	Fulton	1948	S.A.	714	C	Public
Jones County Jr. Col.	Ellisville	1927	S.A.	1,273	C	Public
Mary Holmes Jr. Col.	West Point	1932	State	176	C	Presby.
Meridian Jr. Col.	Meridian	1937	S.A.	373	C	Public
Mississippi Delta Jr. Col.	Moorhead	1926	S.A.	611	C	Public

Institution	Location	Organized as Junior College	Registration or Accreditation	Enrollment	Type	Affiliation
MISSISSIPPI (continued)						
Natchez Jr. Col.	Natchez	1954	State	210	C	Bapt.
Northeast Mississippi Jr. Col.	Booneville	1948	S.A.	737	C	Public
Northwest Mississippi Jr. Col.	Senatobia	1927	S.A.	820	C	Public
Okolona Col.	Okolona	1932	State		C	Prot. Epis.
Pearl River Jr. Col.	Poplarville	1922	S.A.	730	C	Public
Perkinston Col.	Perkinston	1925	S.A.	953	C	Public
Piney Woods Jr. Col.	Piney Woods	1932	State	151	C	Ind. Np.
Prentiss Normal & Indus. Inst.	Prentiss	1930	State	202	C	Ind. Np.
Saints Jr. Col.	Lexington	1954	State	30	C	Ch. of God
Southeastern Baptist Col.	Laurel	1958	State	110	C	Bapt.
Southwest Mississippi Jr. Col.	Summit	1929	S.A.	417	C	Public
T. J. Harris Jr. Col.	Meridian	1956	State	241	C	Public
Utica Jr. Col.	Utica	1954	State	433	C	Public
Wood Jr. Col.	Mathiston	1927	S.A.	134	C	Meth.
MISSOURI						
Christian Col.	Columbia	1851	N.C.	306	W	Chr. Ch.
Col. of the School of the Ozarks	Point Lookout	1956	N.C.	577	C	Presby.
Cottey Col.	Nevada	1914	N.C.	372	W	Ind. Np.
Crowder Col.	Neosho	1964	State	366	C	Public
Hannibal-LaGrange Col.	Hannibal	1918	N.C.	458	C	Bapt.
Jasper County Jr. Col.	Joplin	1937	N.C.	1,313	C	Public
Jefferson County Jr. Col.	Hillsboro	1964	State	297	C	Public
Jr. Col. of Flat River	Flat River	1922	State	481	C	Public
Kemper Military School and Col.	Boonville	1923	N.C.	229	M	Ind. Np.
Mercy Jr. Col.	St. Louis	1952	N.C.	77	W	Rom. Cath.
Metropolitan Jr. Col.	Kansas City	1915	N.C.	4,898	C	Public
Moberly Jr. Col.	Moberly	1927	State	188	C	Public
Missouri Western Jr. Col.	St. Joseph	1915	N.C.	845	C	Public
St. Louis Jr. Col. District	St. Louis	1963	State	4,999	C	Public
St. Mary's Jr. Col.	O'Fallon	1921	N.C.	143	W	Rom. Cath.
Stephens Col.	Columbia	1912	N.C.	1,834	W	Ind. Np.
Trenton Jr. Col.	Trenton	1925	State	135	C	Public
Wentworth Military Academy	Lexington	1923	N.C.	237	M	Ind. Np.
MONTANA						
Custer County Jr. Col.	Miles City	1939	State	265	C	Public
Dawson County Jr. Col.	Glendive	1940	State	349	C	Public
NEBRASKA						
Fairbury Jr. Col.	Fairbury	1941	State	324	C	Public
McCook Col.	McCook	1926	State	390	C	Public
Norfolk Jr. Col.	Norfolk	1927	State	483	C	Public
Scottsbluff Col.	Scottsbluff	1932	State	438	C	Public
York Col.	York	1959	State	255	C	Ch. of Chr.
NEW HAMPSHIRE						
Colby Jr. Col.	New London	1928	N.W.	546	W	Ind. Np.
Franconia Col.	Franconia	1963	State	152	C	Ind. Np.
NEW JERSEY						
Archangel Col.	Englewood Cliffs	1962	State	113	W	Rom. Cath.
Assumption Col. for Sisters	Mendham	1953	State	65	W	Rom. Cath.
Centenary Col. for Women	Hackettstown	1929	M.S.	639	W	Meth.
Immaculate Conception Jr. Col.	Lodi	1942	State	107	W	Rom. Cath.
Lutheran Collegiate Bible Inst.	Teaneck	1963	State	46	C	Luth.
Monmouth Col.	West Long Branch	1933	M.S.	2,722	C	Ind. Np.
St. Josephs Col.	Princeton	1914	State	38	M	Rom. Cath.
Tombrock Col.	Paterson	1956	State	27	W	Rom. Cath.
Trenton Jr. Col.	Trenton	1947	M.S.	1,528	C	Public
Union Jr. Col.	Cranford	1933	M.S.	1,417	C	Ind. Np.
Villa Walsh Col.	Morristown	1928	State	29	W	Rom. Cath
NEW MEXICO						
Alamogordo Community Col.	Alamogordo	1958	N.C.	468	C	Public
Clovis Community Col.	Clovis	1960	N.C.	213	C	Public
New Mexico Military Inst.	Roswell	1914	N.C.	377	M	Public
New Mexico State Univ.	Carlsbad	1950	N.C.	380	C	Public
Roswell Jr. Col.	Roswell	1958	N.C.	567	C	Public
NEW YORK						
Academy of Aeronautics	Flushing	1963	State	1,225	M	Ind. Np.
Adirondack Community Col.	Hudson Falls	1961	State	874	C	Public
Auburn Community Col.	Auburn	1953	State	2,030	C	Public
Bennett Col.	Millbrook	1935	M.S.	329	W	Ind. Np.
Borough of Manhattan Community Col.	New York	1964	State	485	C	Public
Briarcliff Col.	Briarcliff Manor	1933	M.S.	510	W	Ind. Np.
Bronx Community Col.	Bronx	1959	M.S.	6,105	C	Public
Broome Tech. Com. Col.	Binghamton	1947	M.S.	1,412	C	Public
Buffalo Diocesan Prep. Seminary	Buffalo	1931	State	93	M	Rom. Cath.
Cathedral Col.	New York	1903	M.S.	88	M	Rom. Cath.
Catherine McAuley Col.	Rochester	1954	State	195	W	Rom. Cath.
Cazenovia Col.	Cazenovia	1934	M.S.	415	W	Ind. Np.
Col. of the Holy Names	Albany	1961	State	64	W	Ind. Np.
Concordia Jr. Col.	Bronxville	1936	M.S.	421	C	Luth.
Corning Community Col.	Corning	1958	M.S.	1,760	C	Public
Dutchess Community Col.	Poughkeepsie	1958	M.S.	2,845	C	Public
Elizabeth Seton Col.	Yonkers	1961	State	331	W	Rom. Cath.
Epiphany Apostolic Col.	Newburgh	1889	M.S.	29	M	Rom. Cath.
Erie County Tech. Inst.	Buffalo	1947	E.C.	4,912	C	Public
Eymard Prep Seminary	Hyde Park	1927	State	28	M	Rom. Cath.
Fashion Inst. of Technology	New York	1944	M.S.	1,513	C	Public
Finch Col.	New York	1937	M.S.	300	W	Ind. Np.
Fulton-Montgomery Com. Col.	Johnstown	1964	State	324	C	Public
Hillside Hall Scholasticate	Troy	1954	State	38	M	Rom. Cath.
Hudson Valley Community Col.	Troy	1953	State	2,180	C	Public
Immaculata Col.	Hamburg	1957	State	87	W	Rom. Cath.
Jamestown Community Col.	Jamestown	1950	M.S.	1,170	C	Public
Jefferson Comm. Col.	Watertown	1963	State	515	C	Public
Jr. Col. of Albany	Albany	1957	M.S.	353	C	Ind. Np.
Jr. Col. of Packer Collegiate Inst.	Brooklyn	1845	M.S.	105	W	Ind. Np.
NEW YORK (continued)						
Jr. Col. of St. John's Univ.,	New York	1962	M.S.	647	C	Rom. Cath.
Kingsborough Community Col.	Brooklyn	1964	M.S.	468	C	Public
LaSalette Seminary	Altamont	1952	State	66	M	Rom. Cath.
Maria Col.	Albany	1958	State	205	W	Rom. Cath.
Maria Regina Col.	Syracuse	1961	State	319	W	Rom. Cath.
Mater Christi Seminary	Albany	1954	State	68	M	Rom. Cath.
Mater Dei Col.	Odensburg	1960	State	144	W	Rom. Cath.
Miner Inst.	Chazy	1957	State	57	M	Ind. Np.
Mohawk Valley Com. Col.	Utica	1946	M.S.	2,853	C	Public
Monroe Community Col.	Rochester	1962	State	3,176	C	Public
Nassau Community Col.	Garden City	1960	State	5,965	C	Public
New York City Community Col.	Brooklyn	1947	M.S.	9,344	C	Public
Niagara County Com. Col.	Niagara Falls	1963	State	1,505	C	Public
Onondaga Community Col.	Syracuse	1962	State	1,001	C	Public
Orange County Com. Col.	Middletown	1950	M.S.	3,407	C	Public
Our Lady of Hope Mission Seminary	Newburgh	1954	State	40	M	Rom. Cath.
Paul Smith's Col.	Paul Smiths	1946	State	827	C	Ind. Np.
Presentation J.C. of the Sacred Heart	Newburgh	1959	State	53	W	Rom. Cath.
Queen of the Apostles Col.	Harriman	1956	State	103	W	Rom. Cath.
Queensborough Com. Col.	Bayside	1960	M.S.	2,448	C	Public
Rockland Community Col.	Suffern	1959	State	1,864	C	Public
Sancta Maria Col.	Buffalo	1958	State	43	W	Rom. Cath.
St. Clare Col.	Williamsville	1957	State	36	W	Rom. Cath.
St. Joseph's Seraphic Seminary	Callicoon	1901	M.S.	71	M	Rom. Cath.
St. Pius X Prep. Seminary	Uniondale	1962	State	99	M	Rom. Cath.
Staten Island Community Col.	Staten Island	1956	M.S.	2,074	C	Public
State Univ. Agr. & Tech. Insts.						
Alfred	Alfred	1911	M.S.	1,735	C	Public
Canton	Canton	1907	M.S.	840	C	Public
Cobleskill	Cobleskill	1915	M.S.	1,096	C	Public
Delhi	Delhi	1915	M.S.	1,007	C	Public
Farmingdale	Farmingdale	1935	M.S.	6,718	C	Public
Morrisville	Morrisville	1938	M.S.	1,114	C	Public
Suffolk County Com. Col.	Selden	1960	State	3,505	C	Public
Sullivan County Com. Col.	South Fallsburg	1963	State	412	C	Public
Ulster County Community Col.	Kingston	1963	State	890	C	Public
Villa Maria Col. of Buffalo	Buffalo	1960	State	99	W	Rom. Cath.
Voorhees Tech. Inst.	New York	1961	State	428	M	Ind. Np.
Wadhams Hall	Ogdensburg	1924	State	46	M	Rom. Cath.
Westchester Community Col.	Valhalla	1947	State	3,655	C	Public
NORTH CAROLINA						
Brevard Col.	Brevard	1934	S.A.	417	C	Meth.
Central Piedmont Com. Col.	Charlotte	1949	State	2,768	C	Public
Chowan Col.	Murfreesboro	1937	S.A.	1,155	C	Bapt.
Col. of the Albemarle	Elizabeth City	1961	State	449	C	Public
Gardner-Webb Col.	Boiling Springs	1928	S.A.	932	C	Bapt.
Gaston Col.	Gastonia	1964	State	696	C	Public
Gaston Tech. Inst.	Gastonia	1957	E.C.	336	C	Public
Lees-McRae Jr. Col.	Banner Elk	1932	S.A.	510	C	Presby.
Louisburg Col.	Louisburg	1915	S.A.	663	C	Meth.
Mitchell Col.	Statesville	1856	S.A.	557	C	Ind. Np.
Montreat-Anderson Col.	Montreat	1959	S.A.	339	C	Presby.
Mount Olive Jr. Col.	Mount Olive	1952	S.A.	260	C	Bapt.
Oak Ridge Military Inst.	Oak Ridge	1933	State	52	M	Ind. Np.
Peace Col.	Raleigh	1918	S.A.	364	W	Presby.
Pineland Col.	Salemburg	1926	State		C	Ind. Np.
Sacred Heart Jr. Col.	Belmont	1935	S.A.	196	W	Rom. Cath.
St. Mary's Jr. Col.	Raleigh	1900	S.A.	275	W	Epis.
Warren Wilson Col.	Swannanoa	1942	S.A.	258	C	Presby.
Wingate Col.	Wingate	1922	S.A.	1,320	C	Bapt.
NORTH DAKOTA						
Bismarck Jr. Col.	Bismarck	1939	State	905	C	Public
Lake Region Jr. Col.	Devils Lake	1941	State	370	C	Public
North Dakota School of Forestry	Bottineau	1925	State	232	C	Public
North Dakota State School of Science	Wahpeton	1903	State	1,828	C	Public
OHIO						
Com..Col. Center, Lake Erie Col.	Painesville	1959	State	263	C	Ind. Np.
Cuyahoga Community Col.	Cleveland	1963	State	6,310	C	Public
Lorain County Community Col.	Lorain	1964	State	1,005	C	Public
Lourdes Jr. Col.	Sylvania	1957	N.C.	92	W	Rom. Cath.
Ohio Col. of Applied Science	Cincinnati	1919	E.C.	547	C	Ind. Np.
Sinclair Col.	Dayton	1924	E.C.	1,178	C	Ind. Np.
Univ. Col. of the Univ. of Cincinnati	Cincinnati	1960	N.C.	1,350	C	Public
Univ. Com. and Tech. Col.	Toledo	1938	N.C.	1,583	C	Public
Urbana Col.	Urbana	1924	State	160	C	C.N.J.
OKLAHOMA						
Altus Jr. Col.	Altus	1926	State	436	C	Public
Bacone Col.	Bacone	1927	State	467	C	Bapt.
Cameron State Agr. Col.	Lawton	1927	N.C.	2,027	C	Public
Central Pilgrim Col.	Bartlesville	1958	State	201	C	Pil. Hol.
Connors State Agr. Col.	Warner	1927	N.C.	519	C	Public
Eastern Oklahoma A & M Col.	Wilburton	1909	N.C.	875	C	Public
El Reno Jr. Col.	El Reno	1938	State	231	C	Public
Murray State Agr. Col.	Tishomingo	1923	N.C.	551	C	Public
Northeastern Oklahoma A & M Col.	Miami	1919	N.C.	1,712	C	Public
Northern Oklahoma Jr. Col.	Tonkawa	1920	N.C.	861	C	Public
Oklahoma Military Academy	Claremore	1919	N.C.	639	M	Public
Poteau Community Col.	Poteau	1932	State	133	C	Public
Sayre Jr. Col.	Sayre	1938	State	224	C	Public
Seminole Jr. Col.	Seminole	1931	State	80	C	Ind. Np.
Southwestern Col.	Oklahoma City	1946	State	135	C	Pent. Hol.
St. Gregeory Col.	Shawnee	1875	State	193	M	Rom. Cath.

Institution	Location	Organized as Junior College	Registration or Accreditation	Enrollment	Type	Affiliation
OREGON						
Blue Mountain Com. Col.	Pendleton	1963	State	430	C	Public
Central Oregon Col.	Bend	1957	State	638	C	Public
Clatsop Col.	Astoria	1959	State	336	C	Public
Concordia Col.	Portland	1950	N.W.	146	C	Luth.
Multnomah Col.	Portland	1931	N.W.	1,957	C	Ind. Np.
Oregon Tech. Inst.	Klamath Falls	1947	N.W.	908	C	Public
Portland Community Col.	Portland	1961	State	5,398	C	Public
Southwestern Oregon Col.	North Bend	1961	State	726	C	Public
Treasure Valley Com. Col.	Ontario	1962	State	574	C	Public
Umpqua Col.	Roseburg	1964	State	362	C	Public
PENNSYLVANIA						
Ambler Campus of Temple Univ.	Ambler	1952	M.S.	638	C	Ind. Np.
Baptist Inst. for Christian Workers	Bryn Mawr	1959	State	28	W	Bapt.
Eastern Pilgrim Col.	Allentown	1954	State	58	C	Pil. Hol.
Harcum Jr. Col.	Bryn Mawr	1915	State	620	W	Ind. Np.
Harrisburg Area Com. Col.	Harrisburg	1964	State	429	C	Public
Hershey Jr. Col.	Hershey	1938	M.S.	317	C	Public
Keystone Jr. Col.	La Plume	1934	M.S.	530	C	Ind. Np.
Lackawanna Jr. Col.	Scranton	1959	State	290	C	Ind. Np.
Manor Jr. Col.	Jenkintown	1959	State	185	W	Byz. Cath.
Mount Aloysius Jr. Col.	Cresson	1939	M.S.	428	W	Rom. Cath.
Northeastern Inst. for Christian Educ.	Villanova	1964	State	97	C	Ch. of Chr.
Novitiate of St. Isaac Jogues	Wernersville	1930	M.S.	93	M	Rom. Cath.
Penn Hall Jr. Col.	Chambersburg	1927	State	173	W	Ind. Np.
Pa. State Univ. Commonwealth Campuses						
Allentown Center	Allentown	1953	M.S.	136	C	Public
Altoona Campus	Altoona	1939	M.S.	1,168	C	Public
Behrend Campus	Erie	1948	M.S.	940	C	Public
Berks Center	Wyomissing	1958	M.S.	575	C	Public
Dubois Campus	Dubois	1935	M.S.	303	C	Public
Hazleton Campus	Hazleton	1934	M.S.	320	C	Public
McKeesport Campus	McKeesport	1948	M.S.	996	C	Public
Mont Alto Campus	Mont Alto	1963	M.S.	204	C	Public
New Kensington Center	New Kensington	1958	M.S.	1,064	C	Public
Ogontz Campus	Abington	1950	M.S.	1,979	C	Public
Schuylkill Campus	Pottsville	1934	M.S.	238	C	Public
Scranton Center	Scranton	1953	M.S.	353	C	Public
Wilkes-Barre Center	Wilkes-Barre	1953	M.S.	351	C	Public
York Campus	York	1953	M.S.	355	C	Public
Point Park Jr. Col.	Pittsburgh	1960	State	2,341	C	Ind. Np.
Robert Morris Jr. Col.	Pittsburgh	1962	State	2,700	C	Ind. Np.
Sacred Heart Jr. Col.	Philadelphia	1959	State	40	W	Rom. Cath.
Spring Garden Inst.	Philadelphia	1963	State	211	C	Ind. Np.
Temple Univ. Community Col.	Philadelphia	1948	M.S.	962	C	Ind. Np.
Temple Univ. Tech. Inst.	Philadelphia	1921	M.S.	1,691	C	Ind. Np.
Valley Forge Military Jr. Col.	Wayne	1934	M.S.	208	M	Ind. Np.
York Jr. Col.	York	1941	M.S.	1,554	C	Ind. Np.
RHODE ISLAND						
Johnson & Wales Jr. Col. of Business	Providence	1963	State	656	C	Ind. Np.
Rhode Island Jr. Col.	Providence	1964	State	325	C	Public
Roger Williams Jr. Col.	Providence	1948	State	704	C	Ind. Np.
SOUTH CAROLINA						
Anderson Jr. Col.	Anderson	1930	S.A.	696	C	Bapt.
North Greenville Jr. Col.	Tigerville	1934	S.A.	496	C	Bapt.
Palmer Col.	Charleston	1955	State	550	C	Ind. Np.
Palmer Col.	Columbia	1957	State	310	C	Ind. Np.
Spartanburg Jr. Col.	Spartanburg	1927	S.A.	550	C	Meth.
Voorhees Col.	Denmark	1929	S.A.	292	C	Epis.
SOUTH DAKOTA						
Freeman Jr. Col.	Freeman	1903	State	71	C	Mennon.
Presentation Jr. Col.	Aberdeen	1951	State	234	W	Rom. Cath.
TENNESSEE						
Cumberland Col. of Tenn.	Lebanon	1956	S.A.	320	C	Ind. Np.
Freed-Hardeman Col.	Henderson	1908	S.A.	637	C	Ch. of Chr.
Hiwassee Col.	Madisonville	1907	S.A.	409	C	Meth.
Lee Col.	Cleveland	1941	S.A.	600	C	Ch. of God
Martin Col.	Pulaski	1870	S.A.	259	C	Meth.
Morristown Col.	Morristown	1921	S.A.	252	C	Meth.
Owen Col.	Memphis	1954	S.A.	301	C	Bapt.
TEXAS						
Allen Academy	Bryan	1947	State	140	C	Ind. Np.
Alvin Jr. Col.	Alvin	1949	S.A.	1,144	C	Public
Amarillo Col.	Amarillo	1929	S.A.	2,314	C	Public
Annunciation Col.	Victoria	1959	State	24	W	Rom. Cath.
Blinn Col.	Brenham	1927	S.A.	850	C	Public
Cisco Jr. Col.	Cisco	1940	S.A.	435	C	Public
Clarendon Jr. Col.	Clarendon	1928	State	190	C	Public
Cooke County Jr. Col.	Gainesville	1924	S.A.	575	C	Public
Decatur Baptist Col.	Decatur	1898	S.A.	130	C	Bapt.
Del Mar Col.	Corpus Christi	1935	S.A.	3,010	C	Public
Frank Phillips Col.	Borger	1948	S.A.	620	C	Public
Henderson County Jr. Col.	Athens	1946	S.A.	745	C	Public
Hill Jr. Col.	Hillsboro	1962	State	489	C	Public
Howard County Jr. Col.	Big Spring	1946	S.A.	881	C	Public
Jacksonville Col.	Jacksonville	1918	State	121	C	Bapt.
Kilgore Col.	Kilgore	1935	S.A.	1,849	C	Public
Laredo Jr. Col.	Laredo	1947	S.A.	884	C	Public
Lee Col.	Baytown	1934	S.A.	1,787	C	Public
Lon Morris Col.	Jacksonville	1912	S.A.	335	C	Meth.
Lubbock Christian Col.	Lubbock	1957	S.A.	635	C	Ch. of Chr.
Lutheran Concordia Col.	Austin	1951	State	158	C	Luth.
Navarro Jr. Col.	Corsicana	1946	S.A.	945	C	Public
Odessa Col.	Odessa	1946	S.A.	2,162	C	Public
TEXAS (continued)						
Panola Col.	Carthage	1948	S.A.	390	C	Public
Paris Jr. Col.	Paris	1924	S.A.	502	C	Public
Ranger Jr. Col.	Ranger	1926	State	220	C	Public
San Angelo Col.	San Angelo	1928	S.A.	1,845	C	Public
San Antonio Col.	San Antonio	1925	S.A.	9,250	C	Public
San Jacinto Col.	Pasadena	1961	State	2,466	C	Public
Schreiner Inst.	Kerrville	1924	S.A.	208	C	Presby.
South Plains Col.	Levelland	1958	S.A.	879	C	Public
South Texas Jr. Col.	Houston	1948	S.A.	2,872	C	Ind. Np.
Southwest Texas Jr. Col.	Uvalde	1946	State	638	C	Public
Southwestern Assemblies of God Col.	Waxahachie	1944	State	369	C	A. of God
Southwestern Christian Col.	Terrell	1949	State	60	C	Ch. of Chr.
Southwestern Union Col.	Keene	1916	S.A.	245	C	7 Day Adv.
St. Philip's Col.	San Antonio	1927	S.A.	756	C	Public
Temple Jr. Col.	Temple	1926	S.A.	1,055	C	Public
Texarkana Col.	Texarkana	1927	S.A.	1,378	C	Public
Texas Southmost Col.	Brownsville	1926	S.A.	774	C	Public
Tyler District Col.	Tyler	1952	State	250	C	Public
Tyler Jr. Col.	Tyler	1926	S.A.	2,196	C	Public
Victoria Col., The	Victoria	1925	S.A.	1,189	C	Public
Weatherford Col.	Weatherford	1921	S.A.	653	C	Public
Wharton County Jr. Col.	Wharton	1946	S.A.	1,513	C	Public
UTAH						
Col. of Eastern Utah	Price	1938	N.W.	699	C	Public
Dixie Col.	St. George	1916	N.W.	554	C	Public
Snow Col.	Ephraim	1923	N.W.	560	C	Public
VERMONT						
Champlain Col.	Burlington	1878	State	740	C	Ind. Np.
Green Mountain Col.	Poultney	1931	N.E.	620	W	Meth.
St. Joseph Col.	Old Bennington	1963	State	126	C	Rom. Cath.
Vermont Col.	Montpelier	1936	N.E.	507	W	Meth.
Vermont Tech. Col.	Randolph Center	1957	State	264	C	Public
VIRGINIA						
Averett Col	Danville	1914	S.A.	498	W	Bapt.
Bluefield Col.	Bluefield	1922	S.A.	367	C	Bapt.
Christopher Newport Col. of Wm. & Mary	Newport News	1961	S.A.	781	C	Public
Clinch Valley Col. of Univ. of Virginia	Wise	1954	S.A.	301	C	Public
Ferrum Jr. Col.	Ferrum	1955	S.A.	802	C	Meth.
George Mason Col. of Univ. of Va.	Fairfax	1957	S.A.	169	C	Public
Marion Col.	Marion	1913	State	167	W	Luth.
Marymount Col. of Va.	Arlington	1950	S.A.	470	W	Rom. Cath.
Patrick Henry Col. of Univ. of Virginia	Martinsville	1962	S.A.	286	C	Public
Richard Bland Col. of Wm. & Mary	Petersburg	1961	S.A.	542	C	Public
Roanoke Tech. Inst.	Roanoke	1961	S.A.	322	C	Public
Shenandoah Col.	Winchester	1924	S.A.	519	C	Ev. Un. Br.
Southern Seminary Jr. Col.	Buena Vista	1927	S.A.	291	W	Ind. Np.
Stratford Col.	Danville	1930	State	310	W	Ind. Np.
Sullins Col.	Bristol	1917	S.A.	358	W	Ind. Np.
Tech. Inst., Old Dominion	Norfolk	1945	S.A.	318	C	Public
Virginia Intermont Col.	Bristol	1912	S.A.	549	W	Bapt.
WASHINGTON						
Big Bend Community Col.	Moses Lake	1962	State	1,302	C	Public
Centralia Col.	Centralia	1925	N.W.	1,095	C	Public
Clark Col.	Vancouver	1933	N.W.	3,327	C	Public
Columbia Basin Col.	Pasco	1955	N.W.	2,362	C	Public
Everett Jr. Col.	Everett	1941	N.W.	4,097	C	Public
Grays Harbor Col.	Aberdeen	1930	N.W.	1,241	C	Public
Highline Col.	Seattle	1961	State	3,184	C	Public
Lower Columbia Col.	Longview	1934	N.W.	1,915	C	Public
Olympic Col.	Bremerton	1947	N.W.	4,232	C	Public
Peninsula Col.	Port Angeles	1961	State	428	C	Public
Shoreline Community Col.	Seattle	1964	State	861	C	Public
Skagit Valley Col.	Mount Vernon	1926	N.W.	1,203	C	Public
Spokane Community Col.	Spokane	1963	State		C	Public
Wenatchee Valley Col.	Wenatchee	1939	N.W.	1,439	C	Public
Yakima Valley Col.	Yakima	1928	N.W.	2,841	C	Public
WEST VIRGINIA						
Beckley Col.	Beckley	1933	State	923	C	Ind. Np.
Greenbrier Col.	Lewisburg	1923	State	144	W	Ind. Np.
Potomac State Col. of W. Va. Univ.	Keyser	1921	N.C.	657	C	Public
WISCONSIN						
Concordia Col.	Milwaukee	1891	N.C.	167	M	Luth.
Milwaukee Inst. of Tech.	Milwaukee	1951	N.C.	7,944	C	Public
Milwaukee School of Engineering	Milwaukee	1903	E.C.	1,436	C	Ind. Np.
Univ. of Wisc. Fresh & Soph Centers						
Fox Valley Center	Menasha	1946	N.C.	499	C	Public
Green Bay Center	Green Bay	1947	N.C.	692	C	Public
Kenosha Center	Kenosha	1946	N.C.	558	C	Public
Manitowoc County Center	Manitowoc	1936	N.C.	305	C	Public
Marinette Center	Marinette	1935	N.C.	89	C	Public
Marathon County Center	Wausau	1947	N.C.	397	C	Public
Marshfield-Wood County Center	Marshfield	1964	N.C.	142	C	Public
Racine Center	Racine	1946	N.C.	480	C	Public
Sheboygan County Center	Sheboygan	1934	N.C.	277	C	Public
WYOMING						
Casper Col.	Casper	1945	N.C.	2,258	C	Public
Goshen County Com. Col.	Torrington	1948	State	161	C	Public
Northern Wyoming Com. Col.	Sheridan	1948	State	396	C	Public
Northwest Community Col.	Powell	1947	State	310	C	Public
Western Wyoming Jr. Col.	Reliance	1959	State	182	C	Public

VOLUME NINE

FOOD & AGRICULTURE

Food and agriculture   719

Agronomy   749

NORBERT KLEBER

Food and Agriculture

Agriculture and Civilization.—Civilization began when man started farming some ten thousand years ago. Before that, for perhaps a million years, people lived a wandering, precarious existence, hunting seeds and nuts and killing small wild animals for food. Agriculture permitted men to live settled lives and encouraged the development of industries and cities, necessary attributes for modern civilization.

Very likely one of mankind's greatest achievements—planting and harvesting crops—resulted from chance observation. A primitive woman may have noticed that grain-bearing plants grew up where grain had been spilled or stored. She then took the vital step of planting seeds, protecting the growing plants, and harvesting the crop.

Keeping animals probably began when primitive man tamed wounded or trapped animals, or when women saved and tamed young animals. Farming and animal husbandry developed together for a long period of time. The nomadic herding of livestock was a later development.

■ **ORIGINS.**—Agriculture originated first in the Middle East, probably in the grassy uplands where the wild grains and the wild animals first to be domesticated were found. By 5000 B.C., crops included wheat and barley, while sheep, goats, pigs, horses, and cattle had all been domesticated. The first farmers used tools of polished or chipped flint and obsidian.

Agriculture spread from the Middle East to the Danubian Basin, the shores of the Black Sea, the fertile crescent bordering the Arabian desert, and the valleys of the Indus River in India and the Hwang Ho in China. The crops, animals, and tools were much the same except in America, where agriculture probably was discovered independently.

Prehistoric man, drawing upon wild stock, developed all the major food plants and animals used today. Wheat and barley were domesticated in the Middle East. Rice and bananas were developed later in southeast Asia, and sorghum and millets in Africa. The New World saw the domestication of maize (corn) and potatoes. Food animals were domesticated first in the Middle East. Chickens were developed in southeast Asia, and turkeys domesticated in the New World.

■ **EARLY TOOLS.**—The first farming tool was a pointed stick, the digging stick. The food gatherers had used it to dig roots; the first farmers used it to dig holes for seeds. The spade was invented by the man who added a crossbar to his digging stick so that he could use his foot to drive it deep-

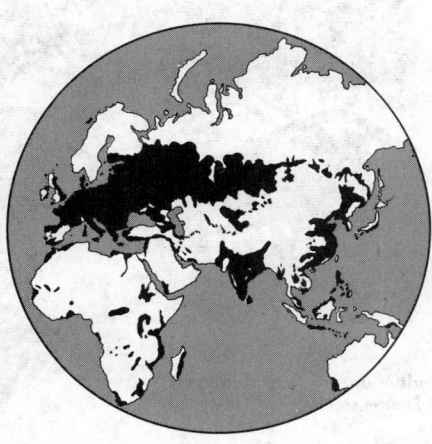

ABOUT TEN PER CENT of the world's land is under cultivation today. Much of the growing area is north of the equator.

er into the soil. A stick with a sharp branch at one end was the first hoe. Later, a sharp stone or shell was tied to the branch to give it a more effective cutting edge. Sharp stones set along one edge converted a stick into a sickle.

After animals were domesticated for food, they were soon trained to become beasts of burden. The next step, never taken by the American Indians, was to train animals to pull a heavy hoe through the earth—the beginning of plowing and cultivating by animal power. The Indians, perhaps because they had no animals for plowing, never adopted a *clean field* agriculture. Instead, they planted seeds in hills a few feet apart and cut the weeds only around the hills.

Nearly all prehistoric farmers in arid regions developed some method of irrigating their crops. Many also discovered the advantages of various types of fertilizer, from using farmyard manure to planting fish in hills of maize. They stored grain, seeds, and nuts for winter and also preserved meat and fish by salting and drying.

The discovery of metal and its uses, making the end of the Neolithic period, enabled farmers to have sharper, stronger blades for hoes, plow points, and sickles. The change came slowly and in some areas, particularly in America, did not take place until Europeans introduced the new tools.

When agriculture first appeared in recorded history, it already was well developed—all the basic advances in domesticating major crops and animals had been made. The rules men followed were based upon longtime observations and trial and error. For centuries, few changes took place.

Advances in Agriculture.—The transformation in English agriculture which took place during the eighteenth century paved the way for modern farming. The key to the change was the enclosure of former open-field farms and the conversion of much arable land into pasture. The rights of villagers to use certain lands in common were largely revoked, and many small landowners and laborers were forced out of farming. At the same time, many improvements in farming were made. Improved methods of cultivation were adopted and machines were more widely used. New crops and more productive varieties were introduced, and controlled animal breeding became possible.

Not all the improvements originated in England. Clover was introduced in Spain, turnip cultivation in Flanders, and new grasses in France. The Rotherham plow, with a coulter and share made of iron, may have originated in Holland.

■ **AGRICULTURAL LEADERS.**—The adoption of advanced practices was encouraged by a number of English agricultural leaders. For 150 years, British farmers learned from such men as Jethro Tull (1674-1740), Charles Townshend (1674-1738), Robert Bakewell (1725-1795), Arthur Young (1741-1820), Sir John Sinclair (1745-1835), and Thomas Coke (1752-1842).

Tull invented a grain drill and advocated more intensive cultivation and the use of animal power. Townshend improved crop rotation and stressed the field cultivation of turnips and clover. Bakewell developed better breeds of livestock. Young and Sinclair were influential writers, and corresponded with American leaders such as George Washington and Thomas Jefferson. Coke developed a model agricultural estate, working particularly with wheat and sheep.

■ **THE NEW WORLD.**—British technological improvements in agriculture gradually spread through western Europe and to the United States. Members of such groups as the Philadelphia Society for Promoting Agriculture and the South Carolina Society for Promoting and Improving Agriculture, both founded in 1785, were familiar with the new English practices and followed some of them. Longhorn cattle, developed by Robert Blakewell, were imported into the United States in 1783, while Henry Clay imported Hereford cattle in 1817. The first agricultural journal appeared in 1810, and John Stuart Skinner began publishing the influential *American Farmer* in 1819. Such periodicals brought some of the English advances to the knowledge of a wider group of American farmers.

The most important technological advance in American agriculture dur-

WORK-SAVING INVENTIONS that raised farm production are the McCormick reaper (*left*), Whitney cotton gin (*right*), and Deere steel plow (*insert*).

ing this period, however, had no relation to English agricultural change. It was, instead, English demand for cotton that led Eli Whitney in 1793 to invent the cotton gin. This practical device for separating the seed from the lint of short-staple cotton revolutionized Southern agriculture. Production of cotton increased from an estimated 10,500 bales in 1793 to 4,486,000 bales in 1861.

Extensive commercial production of cotton, made possible by the cotton gin, led to the expansion of the plantation system, with its use of slave labor. It also led to dependence upon the single staple crop. Cotton cultivation led to the rapid settlement of the region and returned large sums of money to the planters. It also encouraged the economic development of the entire nation by providing large sums for use in foreign exchange.

■**IMPROVEMENT OF PLOWS.**—Technical ingenuity was not confined to cotton. Many Americans were attempting to build better plows, fundamental to an improved agriculture. In 1793, Thomas Jefferson developed a moldboard, made according to a mathematical plan, that would offer little soil resistance.

The first patent for a plow was issued to Charles Newbold of New Jersey in 1797. The plow, except for the handles and beam, was to be of solid cast iron. Farmers distrusted the new plow, believing that the iron poisoned the soil and made weeds grow.

The next great improvement in the plow was Jethro Wood's cast-iron model, first patented in 1814 but greatly improved in 1819. The moldboard, share, and landside were cast in three parts. The interchangeability of the parts was one of Wood's major contributions to the development of the modern plow.

The cast-iron plow was successful

in New England and the Middle Atlantic states. But it would not scour in the prairies; the heavy, sticky soil would cling to the moldboard instead of sliding by and turning over. The steel plow was the answer to this problem. In 1833, John Lane, a blacksmith of Lockport, Ill., began covering moldboards with strips of saw steel. These plows succeeded in turning the prairie soil. In 1837, John Deere, a blacksmith of Grand Detour, Ill., began making a one-piece share and moldboard of saw steel. Deere became a successful manufacturer of steel and wrought-iron plows, which by 1860 had largely displaced the cast-iron plow in the prairies.

■**DEVELOPMENT OF THE REAPER.**—The mechanical reaper was probably the most significant single invention introduced into American farming between 1800 and 1860. It replaced much human power at a critical point in grain production where the work must be completed quickly to ensure saving the crop. By the American Revolution, the cradle had generally replaced the sickle and ordinary scythe for cutting grain. The cradle was a scythe with a light framework which gathered the stems and laid the grain down evenly.

Many inventors worked on animal-powered machines for harvesting grain. The first such machines in America efficient enough to find a market were patented by Obed Hussey in 1833 and Cyrus H. McCormick in 1834. In the struggle for business that followed, McCormick emerged dominant.

The Marsh harvester, patented in 1858, used a traveling apron to lift the cut grain into a receiving box where men riding on the machine bound it into bundles. Early in the 1870's, an automatic wire binder was perfected, but it was superseded by a twine binder late in the decade.

Other horse-drawn machines fol-

lowed the improved plows and the grain reapers. Threshing machines were first brought from Scotland, then a practical thresher was patented in the United States in 1837. Other American patents were granted in the 1840's and 1850's for an improved grain drill, a mowing machine, a disk harrow, a corn planter, and a straddle row cultivator. At the same time, improved crop varieties were being introduced from abroad, and the commercial fertilizer industry was just beginning.

American Agricultural Revolution.—The Civil War led to the first American agricultural revolution. Farmers found that the demand for farm products was so great and the labor shortage so pronounced that it seemed both possible and profitable to adopt the new machines and techniques developed in the preceding decades. The establishment of the land-grant colleges to teach agriculture and mechanical arts and of the Department of Agriculture, the provisions for Western settlement in the Homestead Act, and the chartering of the Union Pacific Railroad, all in 1862, were also made immediately possible by the war. Together, these changes marked a transition from subsistence to commercial agriculture and from hand power to animal power.

The first state agricultural experiment station was established in Connecticut in 1875. Congress provided in 1887 for a yearly grant to each state for the support of an agricultural experiment station. These stations, the state colleges, and the Department of Agriculture together brought science to farming. As a result, farmers obtained improved or new varieties of plants and breeds of animals, learned how better to fertilize their crops, feed their animals, and control many plant and animal diseases and pests. This became more prevalent after 1914, when Congress, by the Smith-Lever Act, provided for a county agent in each agricultural county. The county agent, college-trained, carried scientific knowledge directly to the farmers.

The farm machinery widely adopted after the Civil War was mostly horse-drawn, while various devices were used to transmit horsepower to such stationary machines as threshers. A considerable number of steam engines were built for farm use. These usually were mounted on wheels and could be moved from place to place by horses. By 1900, self-propelled steam tractors were being sold for use in agriculture, but their weight made them unwieldy.

The internal-combustion engine, which had been invented in Europe, was a more practical answer to the search for mechanical power. By 1890, a number of American companies were manufacturing stationary engines, some of which were mounted on wheels. John Froelich of Iowa built the first gasoline tractor on record that was an operating success. In 1892 he mounted a gasoline engine on a running gear equipped with a traction arrangement of his own manufacture. The tractor completed a 50-day threshing run. The first company in the United States devoted exclusively to the manufacture of tractors was established in Iowa City, Iowa, about 1903.

The change from animal power to mechanical power came slowly. Farmers already had horses and could grow the feed necessary to maintain them. It took another crisis, World War II with its manpower shortage and seemingly unlimited demand for farm products, to give impetus to the change.

Advances in Technology.—Technological changes, in most instances, resulted from the application of scientific theories to practical problems. This was true of hybrid corn, one of the greatest agricultural innovations in modern times. The theories of two European scientists, Gregor Mendel and Charles Darwin, were applied to the problem. In 1865, Mendel discovered and announced the basic laws of inheritance of specific characteristics, but the importance of his work was not recognized until about 1900. Darwin pointed out in 1876 that inbreeding usually reduced plant vigor while crossbreeding restored it.

■**IMPROVEMENTS IN GRAINS.**—A number of American scientists built upon the work of Darwin and Mendel. Those who contributed directly to the development of hybrid corn included William James Beal, George Shull, Edward Murray East, H. K. Hayes, and Henry A. Wallace. In 1914, Donald F. Jones, who had been appointed to the Connecticut Agricultural Experiment Station, devoted himself to developing a method for making hybrid corn practical. Within three years, drawing upon the work of his predecessors, he developed the technique called double-crossing. It has been used by commercial firms since. The first seed company devoted to the commercial production of hybrid corn

was organized in 1926. Mainly because of the use of hybrid seed, the per-acre yield of corn rose from an average 23 bushels in 1933 to 62 bushels in 1964.

The techniques used in breeding hybrid corn were successfully applied to grain sorghum in the 1950's and to semidwarf winter wheat for the Pacific Northwest in the 1960's. There have been gains, less spectacular, for other crops.

■**ADVANCES IN ANIMAL HUSBANDRY.**—Similar breeding techniques have been successfully applied to chickens, both as broilers and egg producers. Productive work has also been done with developing hybrid hogs. Crossbreeding has resulted in the development of new, useful breeds of beef cattle and sheep.

The dairy industry in the United States underwent a major change in the 1940's and 1950's. The changes have been due to several factors, such as the influence of markets, prices of milk and feeds, better knowledge of feeding, and the conquest of many pests and diseases. However, one of the most important has been the increased use of artificial insemination.

Artificial insemination as the best means of speeding up livestock improvement was demonstrated in Russia in the 1920's. The first dairy artificial-breeding cooperative in the United States was organized in New Jersey in 1938. It was found that instead of breeding only about 40 cows a year, artificial insemination made it possible for one bull to impregnate thousands of cows a year. Sires of proven ability to get high-producing offspring could be used to improve a dairy herd quickly. In 1943, the average American dairy cow produced 4,598 pounds of milk and 183 pounds of butterfat. In 1964, the figures were 7,880 and 292 pounds, respectively.

■**FERTILIZERS.**—The growth of the worldwide chemical fertilizer industry, able to supply farmers with the

elements needed for more effective production at reasonable cost, has helped bring about major changes in agriculture in many nations. It has been an important factor in what might be called the second American agricultural revolution. The Department of Agriculture has estimated that the increased use of fertilizer was responsible for 55 per cent of the increase in productivity per crop-acre from 1940 to 1955.

■**INCREASES IN PRODUCTIVITY.**—The unparalleled demand for farm products, a doubling of prices, and the shortage of manpower during World War II were basically responsible for the tremendous upsurge in production. The specific changes making up this technological revolution included the displacement of animal power by mechanical power, widespread progress in mechanization, greater use of lime and fertilizer, irrigation, adoption of conservation practices, use of improved varieties, better balanced feeding of livestock and poultry, and more effective control of insects and disease. The widespread use of agricultural chemicals has led some to label the contemporary period in agriculture the *age of chemurgy*.

The major key to progress in farming, with increases in productivity per acre and man-hour, was that technological innovations were adopted in combination. The farmer became a skilled manager and businessman, constantly seeking to find the most efficient and profitable combinations of technology. His success can be measured by the fact that in 1860 the American farmer produced enough food and fiber for 4.5 people; in 1940, for 10.7 people; and in 1964, for 33 people. In the 100 years from 1860 to 1960, the proportion of America's working population engaged in agriculture declined from 58 per cent to 8.3 per cent, and by 1964 to 6.5 per cent, but that percentage was providing abundantly for all Americans and millions of people overseas.

—Wayne D. Rasmussen

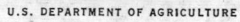
U.S. DEPARTMENT OF AGRICULTURE

HENRY AGARD WALLACE (*left*) developed hybrid corn and, as secretary of agriculture, aided other advancements in farming methods. Through research into new products and processes, George W. Carver (*right*) made contributions to the field of scientific agriculture.

FOOD AND AGRICULTURE GLOSSARY

Agricultural Chemistry, the application of chemistry to the efficient production and utilization of plants and animals of economic importance. While the definition refers mainly to farm crops and livestock, it may be extended to include forest and marine products, and indeed, to anything else that grows and is useful to mankind.

Together with genetics, improved farm equipment, and improved cultural practices, chemistry has played an important part in advancing modern agriculture to the status of big business. Various agencies of the Federal government are engaged in fundamental and applied chemical research, and in analytical and regulatory activities, that are of service to producers, handlers, processors, and consumers of agricultural commodities. Likewise engaged in this field are various state departments of agriculture, universities, and agricultural experiment stations; private institutions that conduct or foster chemical research and development; industrial processors of agricultural products; and manufacturers of agricultural chemicals.

Among the fields of application of agricultural chemistry are crop production; livestock and poultry production; storage, transportation, and marketing; food utilization; and industrial utilization of by-products.
—S. B. Detwiler, Jr.

Agricultural Engineering, the application of engineering principles to agricultural problems. The divisions are power and machinery, structures, electric power, processing, and soil and water.

The strong position of the United States in today's world is due to a prospering mechanized agriculture—an agriculture that produces food and fiber in abundance with less than 10 per cent of the gainfully employed labor force. The millions of workers thus released to other industries, services, and professions contribute to the remarkable industrial expansion and high standard of living.

Crops once thought next to impossible to be harvested mechanically have been mechanized recently. Typical examples are sugar beets, cotton, tomatoes, figs, prunes, and nuts. Research will extend mechanization to many other crops.

Production structures contribute to increased efficiency. A well-designed milking parlor permits one machine milker to handle up to 60 cows. A crew of 10 can feed 20,000 beef animals in a mechanized feed lot. Dehydrators and fruit and vegetable packing houses prepare products for final consumption.

Fully 95 per cent of the farms in the United States are electrified. In addition to the general improvement in living conditions, electricity operates much of the farmstead equipment. Pumping and heating water, brooding chickens and pigs, milking, refrigerating, and feed processing are now done electrically.

Other engineering contributions are in irrigation and drainage and soil conservation. The western third of the United States depends upon an irrigated agriculture. Drainage is as important in irrigated areas as in regions with abundant rainfall. Soil erosion, a menace to the land, can be controlled to a large extent by agricultural engineers.
—Roy Bainer

Agricultural Science, an interdisciplinary science that provides information on biological, physical, and socio-economic problems in the production, marketing, processing, and use of crops and livestock for food and clothing. Generally, it is divided into several separate but related sciences, each with its own professional groups. These include: plant sciences, animal sciences, engineering sciences, soil sciences, entomology, parasitology, and social and behavioral sciences.

Many persons who are agricultural scientists are also biologists, chemists, physicists, mathematicians, engineers, or economists. Agricultural science consists of portions of these and other basic sciences applied to crop and livestock production, marketing, and use.

Agricultural science includes *molecular biology,* the study of how viruses, bacteria, and molds change virulence due to changes in RNA or DNA, the chemical bases of living materials. Such changes must be understood in order to combat these organisms. It also includes *radio biology,* the use of isotopes to follow the physiology of nutrient assimilation, and of radiation to induce genetic change or insect sterility.

Systems engineering and *electronic data processing* have become a part of agricultural science. The combination of soil moisture, fertility, probability of rainfall, hours of sunshine, and known plant characteristics may be used to determine the best time to plant peas in Wisconsin or the amount, formula, and time of fertilizer application for Indiana corn. Automated equipment places the feed formulated to provide all nutrient requirements at least cost before Delaware broilers. The least-cost formulated feed may have been selected by means of linear programming, a method also used by economists to determine the best use of resources by an individual farmer to increase his income.

■ **EDUCATION AND RESEARCH.**—Agricultural science results from research in the laboratories of national governments, of universities, and of private institutions in many countries. In the United States, about 5,000 agricultural research scientists in the U.S. Department of Agriculture conduct research in many locations; about 10,000 do research in state agricultural experiment stations in the 50 states and Puerto Rico; about 10,000 do research in universities and col-

U.S. DEPARTMENT OF AGRICULTURE

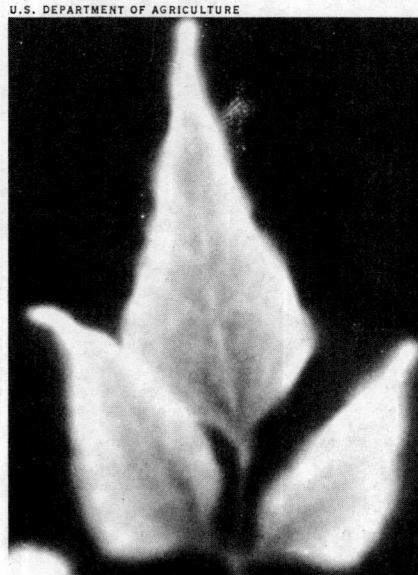

E. I. DU PONT DE NEMOURS CO.

RESEARCH brings agricultural knowledge as a scientist (*above*) studies chemicals' effects on plant development. At *left*, radioactivity records and controls plant growth.

SEAGRAM AND SONS. INC.

A SAMPLE of whiskey is drawn for quality checking by a tester using a "whiskey thief," which reaches to the center of the barrel.

JOSEPH SCHLITZ BREWING COMPANY

MALTING, initial step in brewing beer, begins with "steeping." *Above,* oxygen bubbles through barley and water in "steep tanks."

leges and in private research institutions, including the laboratories of many manufacturers of chemicals, food products, and textiles.

Many more agricultural scientists are engaged in teaching, extension service, regulatory work, and production. They take the technical information developed in research to the farms and factories where it is put to use. This has resulted in yields, per acre and per animal unit, double those of a hundred years ago. It has made fresh meat, milk, and eggs available the year round.

■**PEST CONTROL.**—*Entomologists, plant pathologists,* and *weed scientists* have developed means of controlling many insect pests, diseases, and weeds that limit the productivity of crop plants, trees, grasses, flowers, and shrubs. The wheat crop depends on the continued development of wheat stocks resistant to old virulent rusts and new virulent ones as they occur. Weeds are controlled on 75,000,000 acres in the United States by effective chemicals. Used according to prescription, these chemicals are innocuous to man and animals. Dramatic control of an animal pest, the screwworm fly, has been achieved by the production and distribution of radiation-sterilized males. Development of power machinery for planting, cultivation, and harvest has led to the displacement of the horse as a source of power, greatly reducing the amount of manual labor required for crop and forest production and livestock care.

Research in animal nutrition has led to the formulation of efficient diets that have cut in half the feed cost of producing broilers. *Nutrition research* has contributed to the improved health and production efficiency of all our livestock.

Research in animal disease has developed diagnostic tests and immunization methods that have made

possible the control of such diseases as *pullorum* in poultry, *brucellosis* and *tuberculosis* in cattle, *cholera* in swine. Research has developed effective parasiticides that protect our livestock against protozoan and worm parasites.   —T. C. Byerly

Alcoholic Beverages, potable liquids containing ethyl alcohol produced by enzyme action on sugars. There are three kinds of drink containing alcohol: wine, spirits, and beer. *Wine* is fermented from grapes or other berries and plants; *spirits* are distilled; *beer* is malted. Wine was first made by the ancient Egyptians. Grapes were later carried by the Romans to France, Spain, parts of Germany, and even to Britain. More recently, grapes have been grown in the United States, South Africa, and Australia. The cereals used to make spirits, except those made from wine, have spread over the world with the Caucasian population. Beer, known in the ancient East, was also made by the ancient inhabitants of northern Europe.

■**WINE.**—Grapes are used to make wine in commercial quantities. Other materials are generally used for home winemaking only. The grapes are crushed to express the juice, which ferments naturally because of the presence of skin fungi on the fruit, producing a chemical reaction. Two broad differences result from the color of the fruit—white and red grapes each produce wine of their own color with many intermediate and varying shades. The flavor varies from dry—that is, rather sour—to very sweet. The alcoholic content ranges between 9 and 18 per cent by volume and up to 25 per cent in fortified wines.

Champagne is a sparkling or bubbling wine, the sparkle being caused by bottling before fermentation is finished. Like many other wines, it is named after the place where it is

made: Champagne, Marne, France. *Asti spumante* is a sparkling wine made in Italy. Other French wines are *claret* from Bordeaux and burgundy from the province of the same name. Some light white wines are also made in France, but the German white wines, *moselle* and *rhenish,* from the grapes grown along the banks of these rivers, are perhaps the best known of this kind. *Tokay* is a famous Hungarian wine. *Chianti* and *lacrima christi* are well-known Italian products. Sherry comes from Spain, and *port* from Oporto, Portugal. The last is a fortified wine, that is, one to which brandy or alcohol is added. There are many other fortified wines. Wines of all these types are now made in the United States, principally in California and New York; in Australia, and in South Africa. Light white wines of the German type are now exported from Yugoslavia, as are Greek, Cyprian, and other wines formerly consumed locally.

■**SPIRITS.**—Brandy, whisky, rum, gin, and vodka are the best known spirits. Besides these, there is a variety of liqueurs, usually consumed after a meal. These drinks have a higher alcoholic content than wine, 25 to 50 per cent or more. Spirits are made by distillation; brandy from fermented grape juice, and the others from grain or potatoes.

Brandy, said to be first known in the East, was carried to Italy in the thirteenth century and known as *aqua di vita.* After this, it was made in the Netherlands, where it was known as *brandewijn,* the origin of its modern name. *Cognac* and *Armagnac* are made in those parts of France from which they take their names. Distilled drinks are made from the juice of other fruits, such as apples and cherries.

Whisky (or whiskey) originated in Scotland as *usquebaugh.* It has a high alcoholic content, ranging from about 40 to occasionally 75 per cent. It is made from cereals (rye, barley, maize, etc.) or potatoes. The grain is boiled to mash; then malt is added. Malt is grain sprouted in water, a process that changes the starch content to sugar. When the two are mixed, a chemical change from sugar to alcohol takes place, and this is separated by distilling.

Rum, which originated in the West Indies, is distilled from the fermented juice of sugarcane or from fermented molasses. All rums are colorless when distilled, but acquire color from the casks in which they are aged or from the addition of a coloring agent, such as caramel.

Gin is also distilled from cereals, chiefly barley. Various flavorings are added, the most favored being juniper oil. Gin contains from 25 to 50 per cent alcohol. It is the easiest spirit to fake, and substitutes (the renowned bathtub gin) are often sold.

Vodka is a Russian drink that is now being exported and becoming popular in western Europe and the United States. The materials used are roughly the same as those for other spirits, but the process and mixing are rather different.

■ **BEER, ALE, AND STOUT.**—These beverages are brewed, using barley or other cereal grain for malting, and then boiled with hops, after which yeast is added to the liquor to cause it to ferment. *Beer* is sometimes made from maize, and there is a story that Columbus was given maize beer by American Indians. Maize is also used by the natives of South Africa for making beer. *Lager* beer, a light beer, introduced to the United States by German immigrants in the nineteenth century, is the most popular type. A *dark lager* is made in southern Germany. *Ale* made in England is stronger and more bitter than lager. *Porter* is dark ale, and *stout* is a stronger ale. The color of the liquor is said to depend upon the tint of the barley used, though varied grain is often mixed before malting.
—G. E. Fussell

Alfalfa, a perennial *legume* sometimes referred to as the "queen of forage crops." It is the most nutritious of the commonly-grown hay crops, and richer in protein, minerals, and vitamins than either clover or timothy. It is utilized as pasture, hay, or meal.

Alfalfa is a particularly hardy plant, being drought-resistant as well as resistant to extreme heat and cold. It grows best in deep loam soils with porous subsoils that contain lime. If lime is not present in the soil, as is the case in most areas east of the Mississippi River, it must be added.

Alfalfa grows 2 to 3 feet high, with trifoliate leaves, purple or yellow flowers, and a long tap root that may extend 25 or 30 feet into the ground. It is subject to attack by *bacterial wilt, spotted alfalfa aphids,* and *alfalfa weevil.*

The center of production in the United States is the Middle West, with California, South Dakota, and Nebraska excelling in seed production.
—Robert G. Dunbar

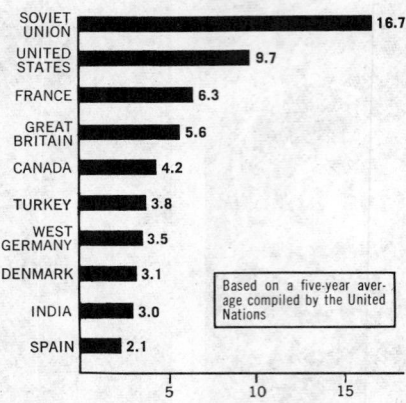

World Production of BARLEY in %

Country	%
SOVIET UNION	16.7
UNITED STATES	9.7
FRANCE	6.3
GREAT BRITAIN	5.6
CANADA	4.2
TURKEY	3.8
WEST GERMANY	3.5
DENMARK	3.1
INDIA	3.0
SPAIN	2.1

Based on a five-year average compiled by the United Nations

Barley, first brought into cultivation by prehistoric man, one of the two *cereals* that supplied the food necessary to allow civilization to develop, the other being wheat. There are two kinds of barley, two-row and six-row. Another, *Bere,* is called four-row, but its appearance is misleading. Today, barley is grown all over the world in subtropical and temperate climates. It will flourish in high altitudes, in poor soils, and in areas of low rainfall. Owing to its chemical composition, it does not make a satisfactory loaf, but can be made into a hard bread, which English consumers used to call *Barley bangers.*

The principal modern use of this cereal is malting for brewing. Pot and pearl barley are prepared for use in cooking, thickening soups, etc. The protein dissolves in water, and the solution (barley water) is often used in infant and convalescent diets. Barley grain and straw are used for feeding livestock, especially pigs.

There are several different strains useful for growing in particular places, some of which have been bred from a single ear. A good deal of work on breeding strains suitable for cultivation in the widely varied conditions of the United States has been done by the Bureau of Plant Breeding, Soils, and Agricultural Engineering.
—G. E. Fussell

Beekeeping or **apiculture,** the industry and hobby of raising bees and collecting the honey and wax they produce. Just how long man has kept bees is not known, but a cave painting in Spain, estimated to be at least 8,000 years old, shows a man robbing a bee cave. Not until the twentieth century, however, did man learn to control *swarming,* the bees' natural method of increase. Swarm prevention helps him harvest more honey from the bees.

When swarming occurs, the queen, a few drones, and 5,000 to 40,000 worker bees leave their home in a mass flight. They establish a new home in a hollow tree, a cave, or the wall cavity of a building some distance away.

The first step in the preparation of the new hive is wax construction. Hundreds of worker bees gorge themselves with nectar from flowers, and

wax glands on the underside of their abdomens convert the nectar into *white wax.* This is the structural material of the *comb,* or framework of the hive.

Honey is also prepared from nectar. Ripe honey, which is sealed in the wax cells, consists largely of a mixture of sugars. The honey serves as food for the bees.

Other cells are filled with pollen, or *beebread,* which is also collected from flowers and carried in pellets packed ingeniously by the bee on its hind legs.

Propolis, a resinous material on buds and scars of trees, is also collected and carried like pollen on the bees' hind legs into the hive. It is used to seal cracks and holes too small for the bee to pass through, and to keep out rain, wind, and small insects.

Within the hive, the queen lays thousands of eggs each day, one to a cell. After three days, the eggs hatch into *larvae,* after five days of feeding, these are sealed in their cells to pupate, or change into the form of the adult, a process that takes about three weeks.

Eventually, the queen ages sufficiently so that she no longer can continue her egg-laying at the required pace. The worker bees then select a few tiny larvae, enlarge their cells, and feed them a special glandular food called *royal jelly.* These larvae, which would have become worker bees after their pupal stage, instead develop into virgin queens. The first one to emerge, however, seeks out and kills the other virgins before they complete their pupation.

When the surviving virgin is about ten days old, she goes on her mating

U.S. DEPARTMENT OF AGRICULTURE

BEES SWARM by the thousands on a branch, as they attempt to build a new hive.

flight, and in the air mates with one to six drones, who exist primarily for this duty. She returns home to begin her lifetime task of egg-laying, never to leave the hive again except with a swarm. The now-ignored mother queen may remain several weeks before she finally disappears.

During all this time, the bees have been storing honey and pollen for winter use. The amount stored depends on the flowers in the area, the weather, and many other factors, but there should be at least 50 pounds of honey and several pounds of pollen.

With approaching winter, the flowers disappear, the drones die, and the queen reduces her egg-laying or ceases altogether. When the temperature goes below about 57° F, the bees form a tight cluster to conserve heat, maintaining a cluster temperature of about 92° F, even when outside temperature falls below zero.

This is the natural way of increase for bees, but it may not always be the best way from the beekeeper's point of view. The swarm may escape. It may leave at the beginning of a good period for storing honey, and before the colony is strong with bees again. Strong colonies are essential if much honey is to be stored.

The beekeeper has found that bees can be kept in multiunit hives with movable frames. These can be taken apart for examination, and if the bees are crowded, more room can be provided. If more colonies are desired, the hive can be divided after the main honey crop has been stored. The part of the hive that lacks a queen will promptly rear another.

When frames containing sheets of wax with embedded cell bases are placed in the hive, the bees will construct straight combs in them. When these combs are filled with honey, they can be cut out, or the honey can be centrifuged from the cells and the empty comb replaced in the hive to be filled again. The average amount of honey to be expected from a colony is about 50 pounds, although trained beekeepers often harvest many times that amount.

Persons unfamiliar with bees should always wear a veil or screen over head and face. When one is working with bees, smoke should be blown into the entrance hole and over the frames as they are exposed. Although the reason is unknown, smoke tends to keep bees away from the worker and discourage stinging.

With movable-frame hives, smoker, and veil, the beekeeper can regulate the colony so it will produce the maximum amount of honey for him, and he can increase the number of colonies as he desires.

—Samuel E. McGregor

Breeding, Animal, the improvement of the quality of domestic animals through breeding, observation, and selection. Little effective progress was made until the rediscovery (1900) of Mendel's laws of heredity and their application in animal breeding. Knowledge of genetics has rapidly increased since then. With this has improved our knowledge of *cytology* (the study of chromosome

AMERICAN ANGUS ASSOCIATION

CATTLE RAISERS learn new methods for managing their herds and to select the best stock to improve the quality of their cattle. Here judges examine Angus bulls to rate them on the special characteristics that mark superior breeding animals.

behavior), statistics, and interdisciplinary science, providing tools for describing populations and developing experimental methods and chemistry. Applied to the fundamental laws of genetics, such knowledge provides the basis for today's science of animal breeding.

■**SELECTION.**—In animal breeding, the basic problem is to identify those animals that have desirable characteristics and to use these in producing superior animals. The application of statistical theory to the fundamental laws of heredity has resulted in the development of techniques to establish the best procedures for selecting animals having the greatest genetic value for specific objectives. These procedures provide bases for evaluating the probability that differences observed will be repeated.

■**GENETIC IMPORTANCE.**—The expression of most traits of economic importance is determined by the combined efforts of *genotypic* (hereditary determiners) and environmental effects. Therefore, the degree to which the expression of a trait is determined by genetic versus environmental factors must be considered in deciding how to design the most efficient animal-breeding programs. Furthermore, procedures must be devised to estimate the genetic value of groups selected for reproduction.

■**MATING SYSTEM.**—Individuals selected in an animal-breeding program can be mated together in many different ways to reproduce a population. Thus, *mating system* refers to any set procedure used to mate selected individuals to reproduce a population. Where relationships have been established within a population, matings based upon these relationships may be carried out. Examples of mating systems based upon matings between individuals more closely related than the average of a population are *full-sib* or *half-sib* matings. Mating sys-

tems between individuals that appear more like each other or less like each other than the average of the population, ignoring relationships, are called *assortative* and *disassortative mating systems,* respectively.

■**ARTIFICIAL INSEMINATION.**—The practice of placing sperm cells in the female genitalia of animals by instruments rather than by natural service is known as artificial insemination. This method has been used widely in dairy breeding for animal improvement. Here it is possible to collect large amounts of semen from proven sires and to use this semen in producing calves from a very large number of females. Where rare bulls can be naturally mated to only about 100 cows a year, use of artificial insemination makes it possible for individual bulls to sire more than 10,000 calves a year. Management conditions have made this practice especially worthwhile for dairy cattle in the United States. In some situations this technique is worth considering for beef cattle, sheep, swine, horses, poultry, and fur-bearing animals. It may, someday, also be considered important from a eugenic standpoint for application to human populations.

■**PROBLEMS.**—It should be realized that there are problems in the application of breeding procedures in animal populations that are not apparent. Where breeding procedures are used to improve animals of economic significance, all groups (germ-plasm sources) which *may* have, but do not now have, significance must be reproduced each generation. If this is not done, sources that may be invaluable for adaptation to conditions of the future may be lost. Artificial breeding, specifically, storage of sperm cells and ova, may in the future provide cheaper ways of overcoming this problem.

—Laurence Baker

U.S. DEPARTMENT OF AGRICULTURE

A HONEY BEE leaves a cotton flower coated with the plant's pollen. Flying to other plants, the bee cross-pollinates the cotton.

Breeding, Plant, the improvement of the quality of crop plants through reproduction, observation, and selection. Little progress was made until the rediscovery (1900) of Mendel's laws of heredity and their application in plant breeding. Since then, knowledge of genetics and related sciences has increased rapidly.

■ **CROSS-POLLINATING SPECIES.**—The most extensive plant-breeding efforts to cross-pollinate crops of economic significance have been applied to corn, or maize. The basic procedures that have been applied to corn include the application of various mating systems, such as *self-pollination,* the development of inbred lines from open pollinated varieties; mass selection in improving germ-plasm sources prior to inbreeding; and the production and evaluation of very large numbers of experimental test crosses.

Due to differences in response to different environmental conditions, corn must be developed for each area that differs in length of day. Due to the increased yield obtained by crossing different sources of material, hybrid corn provides the main source of improved seed corn available today. With few exceptions, the primary objective in corn breeding has been to develop new crosses (hybrids) that yield more grain. Though disease and insect resistance is important and sometimes constitutes a problem, it has usually been provided through selection among indigenous sources of material.

■ **SELF-POLLINATING SPECIES.**—Until recently, breeding techniques for improving self-pollinating species were limited. The main sources of variability for traits requiring improvement were exotic materials or crosses of related species with existing species. Most self-fertilizing crops are not completely self-fertilized; therefore, limited crossing is possible to provide various sources of new material.

Self-pollinating crops that received attention were bread wheats, durum wheat, barley, rice, oats, and grain sorghum. Until recently, the potential value of first-generation hybrids of self-fertilized cereals was given little consideration. However, evidence now exists that increases of 30 per cent in yield may be possible through the development of such crosses. Other advantages, such as increased ease in improving quality, could be more important than increases in yield. A major obstacle still to be overcome in all small grains except sorghum is that cross-fertilization under field conditions must be possible before crosses can be produced in seed for wheat, rice, and barley. The problems probably are not insurmountable. Therefore, first-generation hybrids of many more normally self-fertilized cereals will be available in the future unless unforeseen difficulties appear.
—Laurence Baker

Cacao, the dried and fermented seeds of a green-leafed evergreen tree used in making cocoa and chocolate. Cacao, or cocoa, beans (*Theobroma cacao*) grow along the trunks and some branches of the cacao tree. The tree thrives in hot, rainy climates and is generally cultivated in lands 20 degrees north to 20 degrees south of the equator, where temperatures average between 65° and 75° F.

The tree is grown in shady areas, sometimes as an intercrop sheltered by leguminous trees or, as in some areas in Africa, by banana or rubber trees. In its early growth, the cacao tree is sometimes protected from winds by windbreaks. Most strains bear fruit from 3 to 5 years and produce for an average of 40 years, although some exceptionally hardy varieties have been known to live 200 years. The cacao tree bears its fruit, or pods, throughout the year, but the harvest is seasonal. The pods are carefully cut by hand from the trees, and then they are split. A good machete wielder can open as many as 500 pods hourly.

Of the many varieties of cacao, the main classifications are the *Criollo,* which produces a light-colored, thin-skinned bean used for fine chocolate; the *Forastero,* which is easier to cultivate on varied soils; and the *Trinitario,* a cross of the other two types. On a typical plantation in the Western Hemisphere, it is rare to find only a single species.

■ **COCOA AND CHOCOLATE.**—The most important products of the cacao bean are chocolate and cocoa. Prior to processing, the beans are weighed and blended, then roasted for one to two hours in large rotary cylinders. The beans turn a rich, brown shade and lose about 20 per cent of their weight. The remaining cracked *nibs* are conveyed to the mills, where they are crushed between large, steel-heated disks. The remaining viscous mass is called *chocolate liquor.* This liquor in a solidified state is used for cooking and is familiar as *bitter chocolate.* About 53 per cent of the liquor is the practical vegetable fat, *cocoa butter.* It lasts for years and melts at low temperatures, but remains solid at room temperatures. The 47 per cent residual is cocoa powder, used in chocolate-flavored foods and beverages. In manufacturing confectioneries, cocoa butter is added as an enriching agent. Breakfast cocoa contains 22 per cent fat; fine-quality chocolate requires a higher proportion of butter.

Cocoa, which is native to the American continent, was grown and used for many years by the Aztecs, Incas, Mayans, and Toltecs. Cortez and other Spanish explorers popularized its use on the European continent. By the seventeenth century, plantings were spread throughout the African colonial possessions. About 1828, a Dutchman, C. T. van Houten, developed a rich, palatable chocolate powder by removing some cocoa butter and adding an alkali to the mixture. About 50 years later, a Swiss invented the popular milk chocolate. Other notable manufacturers of chocolate include the Cadburys and Frys of Great Britain and the Baker and Hershey families of the United States.

Ghana is the world's largest producer of cocoa, exporting 38 per cent of the world total. About 45 per cent of the total United States cocoa imports are from Ghana. The United States consumes about 25 per cent of all the raw cocoa produced. The Common Market countries of western Europe import 35 per cent of the world total. In recent years, effective disease and insect control programs and favorable weather in producing countries were responsible for record production of cocoa, driving world market prices down. There is the possibility that production control, perhaps discovery of industrial uses for cocoa butter, and increased world consumption may reduce the gap between supply and demand in the world market.   —Marshall H. Cohen

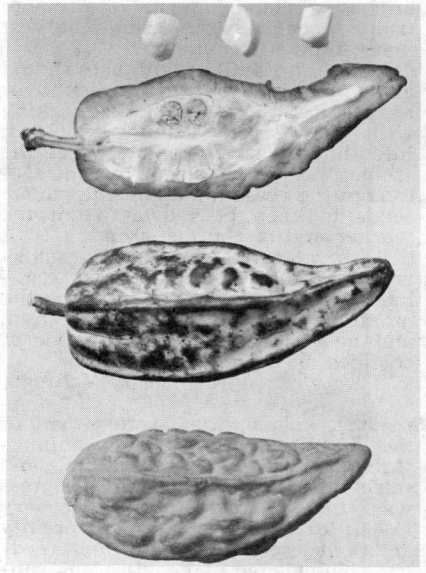

U.S. DEPARTMENT OF AGRICULTURE

CACAO was known to ancient Mayans, as the fossil below two modern beans shows.

Camel, a large herbivorous mammal used for riding, transport, meat, hides, and hair. The *Bactrian,* a two-humped camel, has heavy hair in the winter, hard foot pads, and short legs which fit it for cold and mountainous country. It is found in central Asia from the Black Sea to Manchuria, but cannot stand prolonged spells of great heat. The *Dromedary* has one hump, short hair, a long neck, long legs, and foot pads that hold the animal up in sand. It travels best on level sandy land and cannot move in mud. Dromedaries are found in North Africa, Egypt, Arabia, and India. They have also been successfully introduced into Spain and the Canary Islands, but unsuccessfully into Australia and the Americas.

Camels can metabolize the fat in their hump to get some water, but store most of their emergency water supply in one of their stomachs. They can go up to a week without water if they move slowly. Thick skin inside the mouth allows camels to eat nearly anything, including thorns, although they prefer brush, tree leaves, and fruit. Camels mate at any season and have a gestation period of about 12 months. The female usually produces one foal every other year. The working life of a camel is around 20 years. Camels are susceptible to *rabies, anthrax, tuberculosis, tetanus,* and *foot-and-mouth disease.* All these diseases can be prevented with vaccines. In addition, camels are particularly susceptible to the incurable and frequently fatal *trypanosomiasis* (sleeping sickness).

Camels are ruminants of the genus *Camelus,* which has two species, *C. Bactrianus* and *C. Dromedarius.*
—John T. Schlebecker

Casein, a heterogeneous compound protein derived from amino acids and containing primarily calcium, nitrogen, and phosphorus. Although the lack of uniformity limits its industrial applications, the casein compound is used in a wide variety of processes ranging from cheese-making to plastic manufacture. Casein constitutes the bulk of the curd of milk, and makes up about 3.15 per cent of the whole fluid cow's milk. It can be transformed into cheese, or *paracasein,* by the action of the enzyme *rennin.* For industrial uses, skim milk is treated with sulfuric acid, hydrochloric acid, lactic acid, and the casein is then washed, dried, and pressed. Dried casein is essentially a granulated jelly. It can be used to make a water-resistant wood glue, or a binder for various oil and latex paints. Lacquers sometimes also use a casein binder. Formerly large amounts of casein were used as a binder of paper coatings, but recently the use of casein for high-gloss paper has been declining in the United States. Casein can be hardened with formaldehyde to make plastics, but lately other chemicals have largely replaced casein. Since 1957, United States production of industrial casein has virtually ceased, although casein has been imported, chiefly from Argentina.
—John T. Schlebecker

AMERICAN ANGUS ASSOCIATION

BEEF CATTLE, such as the Angus breed (*above*) are, like dairy cattle, grazers. Angus cattle are highly adaptable to various climatic conditions and they produce the best beef. They are popular especially in the United States, Argentina, and in Scotland.

Cattle, herbivorous, horned, bovine mammals. The male is called a *bull,* the female a *cow,* a young cow a *heifer,* a castrated male a *steer,* and a young animal a *calf.* In the United States, cattle are raised for milk, meat, and hides. Cattle furnish the bulk of dairy products in the United States, as well as cattle meat, called *beef* or *veal.* Beef, the most popular of all meats in the United States, can be readily preserved, although most of it is sold as red (fresh) meat. Livestock and livestock products rank third as a source of farm income in the United States.

Most cattle are now sold at country selling points; central markets, such as Chicago and Omaha, handle only about 30 per cent of the total marketed. Beef slaughtering and processing have also been decentralized. Chain stores have been directly buying and slaughtering large percentages of cattle. Dairy processing has concentrated in fewer companies, both private and cooperative.

In the United States, the chief beef cattle have derived from British and Indian breeds, such as the English *Devon, Hereford, Red Poll, Shorthorn,* and *Sussex,* and the Scottish *Aberdeen Angus, Highland,* and *Galloway.* The Indian cattle include several *Zebu* breeds which Americans lump together under *Brahman.* Zebus have also been crossed with other cattle to produce various new fixed breeds, including the *Santa Gertrudis, Beefmaster,* and *Brangus.* The French *Charolaise,* and crosses from it, are becoming more important as beef cattle in the United States. The several breeds are valued for their adaptability to climatic and regional differences within the United States.

The dairy breeds of the United States all originated in Europe. The *Guernsey* and *Jersey* came from the Channel Islands, and the most popular, the *Holstein-Friesian,* came from the Netherlands. Dual-purpose cattle provide both beef and milk in commercial quantities. The *Brown Swiss,* the Scottish *Ayrshire,* the *Holsteins,* and the *Milking Shorthorns* are often considered to be dual-purpose.

Cattle are grass grazers, but high milk and meat yields are achieved by feeding silage. Dairymen and beef raisers increasingly supplement feeds with minerals, vitamins, and antibiotics. Antibiotics, however, should not be used as a feed supplement for lactating dairy cows for the drugs may enter the milk. Cows reach maturity in a year and can be bred about every three weeks thereafter, although breeding should not be permitted before the cow is 18 to 24 months old. The period of gestation averages 283 days, and the cow produces one calf, or infrequently two. The cow comes in heat 30 to 60 days after calving.

Some fatal cattle diseases, such as *anthrax* and *blackleg,* can be prevented by vaccination. *Tick fever,* once highly virulent in some places, has been controlled by dipping or spraying to kill the ticks. Dips and sprays have also been effective against arthropod-borne *anaplasmosis.* Vaccines can control *contagious abortion* (brucellosis) and *tuberculosis,* although the slight incidence of tuberculosis in the United States makes slaughter of diseased animals more practical. *Pneumonia* and *shipping fever,* although very common, can be cured with antibiotics. Dairy cattle particularly suffer from *mastitis,* which antibiotics can cure. Cattle succumb to a large variety of poisonous plants, for which the only prevention is poison-free pastures.

Cattle are ruminants of the genus *Bos,* with two living species, *B. longifrons* and *B. indicus.*
—John T. Schlebecker

AMERICAN JERSEY CATTLE CLUB

DAIRY CATTLE BREEDS originated in Europe and were brought to the U.S. by early settlers. The Jersey breed (*above*) gives the richest milk but the quantity produced is only half that of the Holstein, the first-ranking milk producer in America.

Chicken, an edible bird that is probably the most widely domesticated fowl in the world. Almost all *broilers,* or young meat chickens, have white plumage; they are crossbreds, produced from matings of special meat males and females. Usually one breeder produces the male line and another breeder, the female line. All chicks are produced in large incubators, some of which can incubate more than 50,000 eggs at one time. Many chicken producers have an integrated system, controlling the entire process from producing the hatching eggs to marketing the ready-to-cook broilers, TV dinner, or chicken pie. The margin of profit per bird is very small, but integration and large volume make it possible for the producer to market a product of excellent quality at a low cost to the consumer.

Poultry processing and marketing have benefited from technological development. Live birds are placed on a moving conveyor at one end of a plant, and when they reach the other end the birds are in ready-to-cook form. In a short period of time, the poultry is slaughtered, picked, eviscerated, washed, and chilled. Most of the operations are completely automatic and it is not unusual for plants to process 40,000 to 50,000 birds per day. Poultry is offered to today's consumer at an attractive price and in a variety of forms—chilled, frozen, canned, parts, boneless, cooked, and in combinations with other ingredients. (*See also,* Egg Production, page 1545.)
—Carl W. Hess

Chicory, an annual that grows from seed planted in the spring and best known for the use of its root as a coffee substitute or supplement. Although often regarded as a roadside weed in the eastern United States and Canada, chicory has long been cultivated in America. The base of the chicory

plant resembles the dandelion, but the stalk is longer, sometimes rising to a height of 5 feet, and its narrow, flat blossom is blue. Its spreading branches develop coarse-toothed and lobed leaves. These are valued as greens, used raw in salads or boiled. But the plant's long, fleshy root constitutes its most prized portion. Roasted and ground, it gives body, color, and long-lasting flavor to coffee. The plant originated in Europe and spread to other continents. It has been cultivated in the United States since the latter part of the nineteenth century.
—Charles E. Rogers

Chocolate. See *Cacao.*

Clover, an important group of annual and perennial plants of the *pea family* having trifoliate leaves and dense flower heads. There are several species, some of which can be recognized by the color of their flowers—red, crimson, or white. All are used as forage crops. Growing clover for forage brought about great progress in farming: livestock were fed better, especially in winter, and became more productive; the extra manure they produced was used to fertilize the land, increasing grain yield; clover root bacteria add nitrogen to the soil, an aid to fertility. This crop is very ancient; its uses were known in southern Europe in Roman times. However, it was neglected until the sixteenth century, when it began to be grown again in Spain. From there it was carried to Holland, and then to Germany and England about 1650. European settlers took the crop to the United States, where it became a grazing and hay crop.   —G. E. Fussell

Cocoa. See *Cacao.*

Coconut Palm, a tall tree with featherlike leaves, whose fruit—the coconut

—has made it nature's greatest provider to mankind in the tropics. Second only to the grasses among plants useful to man, it thrives in low-lying areas near the coast, 20° to 25° from the equator. The stem of the coconut palm rises to a height of 60 to 100 feet, with leaves growing only at its upper extremity. Within the graceful crown of leaves, the fruit ripens. A single tree may produce as many as 100 coconuts. Inside the outer husk of the fruit is found the familiar hard-shelled *nut.* It contains firm white meat and a white liquid, or *milk.* Dried coconut meat, which is known as *copra,* yields one of the world's most important vegetable oils.

Coconut oil is a product of importance in the modern technology of advanced nations. It is used in making candles, soap, shampoos, and detergents; as an element in synthetic rubber and in brake fluid for airplanes; and in the manufacture of tin cans, roofing plate, margarine, and shortenings. Shredded coconut meat supplies the coconut ingredient in cakes, pies, and confections. The husk surrounding the nut yields *coir,* a tough fiber that has many uses. Finally, young stalks produce a sweetish sap that is a source of sugar, alcohol, and alcoholic beverages.   —Charles E. Rogers

Coffee, a large, broad-leafed evergreen shrub, its seeds, and a beverage brewed from the roasted, ground seeds. The shrub belongs to the genus *Coffea* of the madder family. In plantations, its height is generally kept at 6 feet, although it can reach 14 to 20 feet. Coffee grows best in the temperate, tropical highlands. The fruit of the plant, the *cherry,* which ripens about six months after the plant's blossoming, is dried and depulped, and its green seed or bean is transported to consumer countries, where it is roasted and distributed.

The word *coffee* is from the Arabic *Qahwah,* and legend depicts the first user of coffee as an Arab physician named Rhazes around the tenth century. However, mention is made of its cultivation in Ethiopia as early as the sixth century. Its use as a stimulating beverage was popularized by Muslim priests, who found it beneficial during prolonged prayer ritual.

Coffee use was confined to the Middle East and Turkey until the seventeenth century, when traders, explorers, and patrons to the court of Louis XIV introduced it on the Continent. *Coffee houses* became a social institution in the seventeeth century, especially in England and Austria. Until then, all coffee was cultivated in Yemen and Ethiopia. About 1690, Dutch and French explorers introduced planting methods to Java and to the Western Hemisphere from Martinique to Brazil, which today is the world's leading coffee-producing country.

■**GROWING.**—Of about 25 species of coffee, the principal one is *Coffea arabica,* which grows best at altitudes between 2,000 and 6,500 feet in a rich terra cotta soil. Arabica coffees are grown in 58 of the 70 major coffee producing countries, but the most sought-after is the Brazilian *Santos.* Arabicas are subclassified into *Brazils*

PAN-AMERICAN COFFEE BUREAU

COFFEE BEANS must be sorted and graded by hand after they are dried and processed. Once this operation has been completed, the coffee is then packed for export and roasting.

and *Milds,* an example of the latter being the high-quality Colombian bean. Other species are the hardy *C. robusta* and the *C. liberica,* the former indigenous to Congolese Africa and the latter to West Africa. They are grown at low altitudes, from sea level to 2,000 feet. Robustas are increasingly used in producing instant coffee due to their lower cost and high caffeine content.

The coffee seed is frequently planted in nurseries under careful temperature control. The young tree is transplanted and shaded by corn plants or banana trees. The tree is pruned after two years and matures in six years. Average trees produce for 15 to 20 years, and yield about 2,000 cherries. The cherries are handpicked, dried, sorted, and bagged with little mechanization. However, Colombian Milds are depulped by a *wet process* in mechanically operated tanks. The *dry process* (sun-drying) is extensively used elsewhere.

■ **PROCESSING.**—Coffee should always be commercially roasted shortly before it is marketed and distributed. The green beans are placed in large, revolving cylinders for 15 minutes at 390°–422° F (some new machinery can do this operation at 500° F for 5 minutes). One process, called *wet roast,* includes a water-spraying operation. Cooling and further cleaning, or *stoning,* follow, and occasionally the rich brown beans are preserved with a light coat of molasses. Grinding and packing are the final operation. An exception is the processing of *instant* coffee, which requires a dehydration of the ground coffee, leaving the tiny soluble crystals. A pound of instant coffee requires three times as many beans as regular coffee. Coffee is finally bagged or canned in vacuum tins.

The economic importance of coffee in world trade is obvious: it constitutes 50 per cent of the export earnings of six Latin American countries and provides a livelihood for an estimated 13 million Latin Americans. Eighty per cent of Brazil's total exports was made up of coffee in 1964–65. Brazil normally exports half the

world's coffee. Increasing demand for African coffees has created an important source of earnings for this region. In 1964–65 African countries produced 16 million bags, or 43 per cent of the world's exportable production.
—Marshall H. Cohen

Corn or **maize,** a cross-fertilizing *cereal grain* that originated in Central and South America. The common hybrid *dent* corns of the United States Corn Belt were developed first by American farmers and then by plant breeders during the nineteenth century. However, they differ in morphology and performance from forms prevalent in other parts of the world. It is of interest to note that corn still furnishes 80 per cent of the calories and 70 per cent of the protein of certain Central American indians.

■ **CULTURAL PRACTICES.**—Until recently, corn was planted for the purpose of harvesting the grain primarily for animal feeding. Under these conditions, corn was usually planted in rows spaced 40 inches apart, and 12,-000 to 14,000 plants were planted per acre. With changes in the importance of various forms of livestock raising and crop production in the United States, the extent of the corn-growing area has changed. At the same time, innovations in growing conditions and harvesting methods have been applied. Today it is not uncommon to find corn planted in rows spaced 20

to 30 inches apart and planted in concentrations of 25,000 to 30,000 plants per acre.

■ **PHYSICAL CONDITIONS.**—Hybrid corn is now available to fit a range of maturity requirements. The growing season can range from 120 to 170 days. Warm humid weather is desirable, with 30 to 50 inches of rainfall evenly spaced during the growing season. However, although warm weather is desirable, consistent temperatures higher than 90° F can cause more damage than good to growing corn when large amounts of moisture are not available. Though rich loam is the best soil, any well-drained piece of land can be used to produce corn if it is in a good climate and is properly fertilized to provide the needed soil nutrients.

■ **VARIETIES.**—Several hundred varieties of yellow *dent* corns are now in use in the U.S. Corn Belt. The majority (80 to 90 per cent) is used for animal feeding, with a small amount (4 to 5 per cent) for starch and alcohol production.

Flint corns are harder and not as desirable for animal feeding. Even so, many varieties are still produced in the United States for special purposes and even more by many countries in South America, Africa, and the Middle East.

Pod corns, which are not cultivated extensively, have grains (kernels) enclosed in individual husks.

Sweet corn has a higher sugar content than other varieties and is more palatable for human consumption. It is produced throughout the U.S. Corn Belt and is marketed fresh, frozen, or canned.

Flour corns, which are soft and starchy, are grown chiefly in South America.

Popcorn is a type of corn with a hard surface and high moisture content in the endosperm. Steam generated in each kernel by quick heating causes it to explode, thus making it pop. It is also produced throughout the Corn Belt for human consumption.

■ **DISTRIBUTION.**—Most of the corn grown in the United States results from planting hybrid seed produced and distributed by commercial companies or released by universities. Such seed is made available throughout the corn-growing area of the United States through seedsmen. Corn is now grown in most areas of North America from Georgia to central Canada and from Colorado to the east coast. In addition, it is an important crop in Central and South America, South Africa, Europe, and the Middle East. Except for the United States, most countries of the world import some form of corn for animal and their livestock.

■ **TRADE.**—Corn has taken on a new level of importance in the world market. Though second to wheat for human consumption, it is a cereal feed grain of primary importance. The United States, Argentina, and South Africa are the major exporters of corn. The major importers are countries in western Europe and the Middle East, and Japan.
—Laurence Baker

World Production of CORN in %

UNITED STATES	44.4
SOVIET UNION	9.4
BRAZIL	4.2
MEXICO	2.6
YUGOSLAVIA	2.6
ROMANIA	2.6
SOUTH AFRICA	2.3
ARGENTINA	2.2

Based on a five-year average compiled by the United Nations

5   10   50

Cotton, a plant of the genus *Gossypium*, its fiber, and the fabric produced from the fiber. The plant belongs to the mallow family, which includes the okra, hisbiscus, and the rose of Sharon. Although cotton is a perennial shrub in climates where it is not killed by frost, its commercial production in nearly all areas necessitates planting a new crop annually for optimum quality and yield.

Boll segments and fiber found in caves of the Tehuacán Valley of southern Mexico indicate cotton was grown at least 7,000 years ago. And in India, seat of the ancient cotton industry, artisans many centuries ago achieved an unsurpassed degree of skill in spinning and weaving the fiber.

The comfort, launderability, and durability of cotton fabrics are due to the absorbency and strength of the fiber. It is formed when a hollow tube emerges from a cell in the seed wall—one tube from each of thousands of cells. Layers of cellulose fibrils build up in an orderly series of spirals within the tube. The fiber matures and, after the cotton boll opens, it dries into a flat, twisted, ribbonlike shape. The fibers interlock to form a fluffy white mass ideal for spinning into yarn.

While it is estimated that cotton has more than 10,000 uses, apparel and household items account for approximately 83 per cent of the total U.S. consumption. Large quantities of cotton are used also for making thread, bags, machinery belts, and medical supplies, and in automobiles.

Seed separated from the lint during the ginning process was once a waste product. Now all components—*linters* (short fibers clinging to the seed after ginning), *hulls*, and *meats*—are important by-products. Linters are a major source of cellulose for plastics and artificial fibers and are used for cushioning in furniture and mattresses. Hulls are used primarily for cattle feed. Oil is crushed from the meats. Refined cottonseed oil products include salad and cooking oils, mayonnaise, salad dressing, margarine, and shortening.

■**GROWING.**—There are many types of cotton, but cultivated varieties fall into two general categories—*upland* and *barbadense*. Upland cottons account for a major share of the world's production. Their fiber is shorter and coarser than that of barbadense cottons, such as Egyptian and Peruvian, and clings tightly to the seed.

Cotton is a commercial crop within limits of approximately 37° north latitude and about 32° south latitude in the New World. In the Old World, these extremes range from 47° north in the Ukraine to 30° south in Africa and Australia. With these wide variations, it is possible to find cotton being planted, cultivated, or harvested somewhere in the world practically every day of the year.

A growing season of at least 180 frost-free days is required for cotton. In the United States, planting dates range from early February in the Rio Grande Valley to late May or early June in North Carolina, Oklahoma, and Missouri, which are the upper limits of the Cotton Belt.

Within a week or two after planting, depending on temperature and moisture conditions, young seedlings emerge from the soil. A month to six weeks later, squares (flower buds) appear. In another three weeks the cotton blossom appears. After three days, the blossom withers and falls, leaving the young ovary attached to the plant. The ovary ripens, enlarges, and forms a pod called a *boll.* Inside the boll, the moist fibers grow and push out from the coating of the newly formed seed. Although the boll enlarges rapidly up to maturity, some time elapses before it opens and the fluffy cotton bursts forth. The interval from bloom to open boll is 45 to 60 days, depending on variety, soil fertility, moisture, and climate.

Cotton production has usually required a very large labor force, particularly during the peak seasons of weeding and harvesting. An exodus of workers from the farms of the U.S. Cotton Belt after World War II speeded mechanization. Man-hours required to produce a bale of cotton (500 pounds of lint) were reduced from 192 to 39 during the period 1940–1964. And in the 1965–1966 season, yield per acre reached a record 525 pounds, compared with 252 pounds in 1940.

■**HARVEST.**—In the 1966–1967 crop year, it is estimated that tractor power was used for virtually all of the land preparation, planting, and cultivation of cotton in the United States. Chemicals for weed control were used on an estimated 50 per cent of the acreage, and 78 per cent of the crop was harvested mechanically.

World cotton production increased from a pre-World War II average of about 32 million bales to an average of 51 million bales for the 1963–1964 and 1964–1965 seasons. The United States has harvested an average of 14.8 million bales of cotton annually since 1959, more than twice as much as Russia, the second largest producer. Significant quantities of cotton are grown also in mainland China, India, Mexico, Brazil, Egypt, Pakistan, and Turkey.

Cotton is grown in 19 states and is a major crop in 14 of them. Texas leads in cotton production, averaging about 4¼ million bales annually. Mississippi and California each produce an average of almost 2 million bales annually. Other major producing states, in the order named, are Arkansas, Alabama, Arizona, Tennessee, Georgia, Louisiana, South Carolina, Missouri, North Carolina, Oklahoma, and New Mexico.

Although textile consumption has been rising throughout the world since World War II, cotton has not shared proportionately; its percentage of the market declined from 72 to 54 between 1946 and 1964. Cotton's share of the U.S. market declined from 51 per cent of the total in 1947 to 41 per cent in 1964. Cotton's inability to compete effectively is attributed by industry leaders to price policies under government programs, rising costs, and greater research and promotion expenditures by competitors. —William L. Foreman

Cover Crops, grains grown to cover the soil and protect it against erosion. Their cultivation is an ancient farm practice, mentioned in the literature of pre-Christian Greece and Rome, as well as in ancient China. Buckwheat, oats, and rye were used as cover crops by colonial farmers in America.

INTERNATIONAL HARVESTER COMPANY

COTTON PRODUCTION, an ancient process, is performed almost entirely by tractor in the U.S. Other significant sources of this perennial shrub are Russia and Egypt.

Some crops among a score or more now widely used for the purpose are crimson clover, rye, and vetch.

Cover crops are often plowed under or disked into the soil as *green manure.* They add organic matter and often put nitrogen into the soil as well as improve its physical conditions. Millions of acres of cover crops are grown for green manure annually in southeast United States. Cover crops commonly utilized as green manure are alfalfa, soybeans, cowpeas, vetch, red clover, sweet clover, rye, buckwheat, and lespedeza. Colorful and exotic names of other cover crops often give us a clue to their origin, use, or appearance. Some of these are kudzu, sudan grass, Australian winter peas, hairy indigo, beggarweed, and the lupines—blue, yellow, and white.

While the main purpose of a cover crop is to prevent or reduce erosion, it may provide temporary grazing or a supply of grain. Cover crops are not as widely grown in summer as in winter, for land is more often used to grow cash crops. Annual rainfall of 20 inches or more is considered essential to the growth of a cover crop.

Agricultural experiment stations in all sections of the United States have supplied evidence of the effectiveness of cover crops. The U.S. Department of Agriculture offers cost-sharing payments through the Agricultural Conservation Program to encourage farmers to use cover crops. Also, in some surplus-reduction programs, farmers replace grains with such crops. Funds of the Commodity Credit Corporation are used to maintain reserve stocks of cover crop seed and to help the seed industry increase newly developed seed varieties for sale to farmers. —Charles E. Rogers

SCHAFFER AND SEAWELL, BLACK STAR
CAMEMBERT CHEESE is exposed to air during the many-day curing, or ripening, stage.

Dairy Products, any products derived from milk, chiefly cow's milk, but including the milk of goats, sheep, horses, reindeer, camels, and yaks. Organized dairying dates back to the third millenium B.C. in the Mesopotamian city-states, but it was unknown to the American Indian until 1607, when cows arrived with the Jamestown colonists. However, the growth of cities and the Industrial Revolution contributed to making it a full-fledged industry by 1900. In the United States, the leading dairy products—other than fluid milk—by volume of milk used in production are: 1) butter; 2) nonfat dry milk; 3) cheese; 4) ice cream; and 5) evaporated and condensed milk. In the United States during the past decade, per capita consumption of butter, evaporated and condensed milk, fluid milk and cream has decreased, while consumption of ice cream, cheese, and nonfat dry milk has increased. The consumption of cottage cheese has increased impressively because of its inclusion in many special diets. Although the per capita consumption of several products has declined, the total amount of milk used has risen steadily for many years. For the farmers of America, cattle and calves alone have produced more total income than have the various dairy products taken together. Dairy products brought substantially more income than any other major commodity, including bread grains, feed grains, and other livestock products.

Dairy-product processing was among the first of the industries to employ automation. Automation not only allowed economies, but more importantly, it allowed a marked increase in sanitary handling of an

Principal Varieties of Cheese

Name	Place of Origin	Type of Milk
Brick, Muenster	Germany	Cow
Brie	France	Cow
Caciovallo e.g. Provolone	Italy	Cow
Camembert	France	Cow
Cheddar	England	Cow
Cottage	America	Cow
Cream	America	Cow
Edam	Holland, Denmark, France	Cow
Emmentaler, Swiss	Switzerland	Cow
Gouda	Holland	Cow
Hand	Germany, Austria	Cow
Limburger	Germany, Belgium	Cow
Neufchâtel	France	Cow
Parmesan	Italy	Cow
Process	America, Denmark	Cow
Romano	Italy	Sheep
Roquefort, Gorgonzola (blue cheeses)	France, Italy	Sheep
Sapsago	Switzerland	Cow
Trappist	Canada, America	Cow
Whey-albumin cheeses e.g. Primost,	Netherlands,	
Ricotta	Italy	Goat, Cow

Source: Cheese Unlimited, N.Y.C.

easily contaminated food product. Nearly all milk, whatever its ultimate processing destination, is drawn from the cow by machine, pumped into stainless-steel tanks, cooled, and then pumped into bulk tank trucks with no human contact in the process and nearly no exposure to air. Tank trucks deliver the milk to automated processing plants where the milk is pasteurized and either delivered to the consumer as fluid milk or cream or changed into some other of the dairy products. Many creameries (butter factories) use a continuous process of butter manufacture wherein the milk, cream, skim milk, and buttermilk are untouched by humans except for testing and quality control. Many of the continuous processes no longer use churns in the strict sense of that term. Many cheese factories pump milk, curd, and whey from one process to another, and move the solid product about by conveyor belts. To some extent, however, cheese making still requires human handling at various stages of manufacture. In all manufacturing most of the equipment is made of stainless steel, and pasteurization is an important element. Ice cream and evaporated milk manufacture can be and often is fully automated, even to quality control by electronic devices.

In addition to the leading dairy foods, a variety of other products are made from milk. Some of these are: buttermilk, the liquid and solids left over after the butter has formed; casein, most of the solid element in milk, used in industry chiefly for glues and paints; whey, the liquid and solids left over after cheese has formed from curd; lactic acid, produced by the fermentation of milk sugar and used in food and industrial processes; and yogurt, a fermented milk with a consistency much like sour cream. —John T. Schlebecker

Duck, a web-footed swimming bird related to the goose and swan. Ducks are raised primarily for meat production in the United States, although in some European countries they are kept for egg production. The Khaki-Campbell duck reportedly lays as many as 350 to 360 eggs per year. The Pekin is the most popular breed in the United States. Others include the Rouen, Aylesbury, and Muscovy. Twenty-eight days of incubation are required for *ducklings* to hatch, except for Muscovy eggs which require 35 to 37 days. With proper care, ducklings grow very rapidly, reaching about 7 pounds at 8 weeks of age. A mature duck, or female, weighs about 8 pounds; the *drake,* or male, 9 pounds. At maturity and when fully feathered the drake, but not the female, has a few curled feathers at the base of the tail. The duck also has a much louder voice than the drake, except in the Muscovy breed. Ducks are not as susceptible to disease as most other types of poultry. Ducks are difficult to defeather in the home. They may be scalded by immersing them for 3 minutes in water heated to 140° F. The ratio of meat to bone is lower in ducks than in other types of poultry. —Carl W. Hess

Egg Production, the growing of fowl, principally chickens, for the primary purpose of laying eggs. The great majority of hens used are crosses of strains, of breeds, or of inbred lines. Under proper management, a hen can lay 240 or more eggs per year. The hens are usually kept in artificially lighted and ventilated houses on a litter floor or slatted floor or in cages holding from one to ten or more birds.

While many chicken breeds were used 20 to 30 years ago; today, only a few are used for commercial egg production. Leghorn or leghorn-type chickens lay white-shelled eggs. Heavies, such as Rhode Island Reds and Plymouth Rocks, lay brown-shelled eggs. Although some consumers prefer one or the other color, there is no nutritional or other difference between these breeds. The color of the yolk will also vary, depending on the feed used. For example, although complete, well-balanced commercial feeds are commonly used, large amounts of yellow corn or alfalfa in the diet will result in a deeper yellow.

Eggs are marketed by grade and size. Grade refers to quality (AA, A, B) and size refers to weight per dozen. Eggs weigh approximately 2 ounces each. Top quality eggs have a large amount of thick albumen (white) and high upstanding yolks, while low quality eggs spread when broken. In many modern egg-packing plants, eggs are automatically washed, graded, sized, and packed.

Eggs are also marketed as frozen or solid (dried) whole eggs, albumen, yolks, and various blends. These products are used in large quantities by institutions, bakers, and other food manufacturers. —Carl W. Hess

Fats and Oils, organic chemical compounds found in plants and animals and, therefore, in foods. As discussed here, fats and oils are *glyceride oils,* in contrast with mineral or petroleum oils. *Fat* is often used to signify a solid or semisolid product, such as that obtained from steam rendering of the fatty tissue of slaughtered animals, mainly cattle and pigs. *Oil* is often used to signify the liquid product obtained from vegetable seeds—such as soybeans, cottonseed, corn, peanut, safflower, linseed, or coconut —by heating and pressing or by extraction with a solvent, which is then evaporated. Purification by treatment with alkalai and bleaching earths and deodorizing under vacuum are usually applied to the crude oil to produce a bland edible oil. Since a semisolid fat will melt when heated, and a liquid oil will solidify when cooled, fats and oils are often considered together as glycerides. This is because they are both made up of chemical combinations known as esters of *glycerine* and *fatty acids,* or as *glycerides* of fatty acids.

Glycerine, or *glycerol,* is a viscous, water-soluble, colorless liquid containing three carbon atoms. Each carbon atom has a hydroxyl group attached to it that can combine with one fatty acid. Glycerine can therefore combine with three fatty acids to

U.S. DEPARTMENT OF AGRICULTURE

EGG PRODUCTION for one carefully bred and housed hen may total 240 a year.

make a *triglyceride ester* which is insoluble in water. The three fatty acids may be the same, but usually are different.

These fatty acids are made up of many carbon atoms joined together in a chain, with an acid group at one end. Each acid group is united with one hydroxyl group of the glycerol to make the ester group, as found in fats and oils.

The unsaturated fatty-acid glycerides of liquid vegetable oils, such as cottonseed or soybean oil, can be changed to saturated glycerides by adding hydrogen to the double bonds —a process known as *hydrogenation.* The resulting glyceride has more saturated glycerides, is semisolid, and is also more stable in resisting oxidation and rancidity. Such plastic shortenings are widely used commercially and domestically in baked and fried foods. Certain chemicals known as *antioxidants* may be added to fats and oils in minute amounts to retard oxidation and rancidity.

The liquid unsaturated vegetable oils are used for making salad dressings and mayonnaise, which are emulsions of the oil and water with vinegar, spices, and flavorings. A semisolid or plastic shortening, however, would not give the desired texture.

Fats and oils have the highest caloric value as a food, 9.0 calories per gram, carbohydrates and proteins each having only 4.0 calories. In addition, fats and oils are highly digestible. The body can synthesize fats from carbohydrates, but the fats that are eaten as such also become a part of the body fat.

Certain polyunsaturated acids are considered essential to proper nutrition, and the body cannot synthesize these essential fatty acids from carbohydrates. Linoleic acid, the most common essential fatty acid, is present in sufficient amounts in ordinary diets.

Water can react with oil to break the ester group to form glycerine and fatty acids. *Soaps* are made by reacting the fatty acids with an alkali, such as sodium or potassium hydroxide, or by having it present during the reaction with water. Certain soaps, when mixed with mineral lubricating oils, form greases.

Fatty acids differ as to the number of carbons joined in the chain (usu-

ally 12 to 18) and the way they are joined. Shorter chains make the acids and the oils lower melting. If each carbon in the fatty acid chain is joined to the next one in the chain by a single chemical bond, the fatty acid is said to be *saturated*—this makes the acid and the oils higher melting. If certain adjacent carbons are joined with two chemical bonds (a double bond), the acid is *unsaturated*—this makes the acid and the oil lower melting. For example, linoleic acid, which has two double bonds and 18 carbons, is lower melting than oleic acid, which has one double bond and 18 carbons. Oleic acid, in turn, is lower melting than the saturated stearic acid (18 carbons) or palmitic acids (16 carbons).

The animal fats have more saturated fatty-acid glycerides (mostly 18 and 16 carbons), which makes them semisolid at room temperatures, while the vegetable oils usually have more unsaturated acid glycerides, which makes them liquid.

The unsaturated acid glycerides are much more readily oxidized by the oxygen in air than the saturated glycerides. This is especially true if there are fatty-acid glycerides with two or more double bonds (*polyunsaturated acids*). Oxidation in edible fats and oils causes unpleasant tastes and odors.

The relationship of saturated versus unsaturated dietary fats is controversial. Some authorities believe that saturated fats lead to high levels of cholesterol in the blood, which may cause coronary thrombosis and atherosclerosis. Other authorities believe that this relationship has not been proven for humans.

Unsaturated oils—particularly linseed, soybean, and tung oil—find extensive use in paints, enamels, and varnishes. These oils all contain glycerides of fatty acids with two or three double bonds. The oils, often combined with a resin, and with pigments ground into them, dry on contact with the oxygen of the air due to oxidation and polymerization of the unsaturated acid groups. The polymerized oil becomes solid and holds the pigments as a strong paint film, which is used to protect and decorate wood and metal surfaces.
—Donald H. Wheeler

Fertilizer, a substance used in the cultivation of plants to enhance their growth. In addition to carbon dioxide and water, which green plants convert to carbohydrates, plants need a number of chemical elements for their growth. The plant obtains these essential elements through its roots from the soil. But a particular soil seldom contains as much of each of these essential elements as the plant requires. Even if a soil is extremely fertile, continuous harvesting of crops removes essential elements that have been taken up by the plants. Placing additional amounts of the essential elements in the soil in the form of fertilizer will thus improve the fertility of soil, or maintain it in fertile crop lands.

Organic fertilizers, such as animal manures, dead fish, and guano, have been used as fertilizers since ancient times. These materials are still used, but today most commercial fertilizers are synthetic products.

Nitrogen, phosphorus, and potassium are the three most important plant food elements. The percentage of each is usually specified for each lot of fertilizer sold. For example, a 4-10-6 grade fertilizer contains 4 per cent nitrogen, 10 per cent phosphorus pentoxide equivalent, and 6 per cent potash (potassium oxide equivalent). The designation of phosphorus and potassium by their oxide equivalents is a long established practice.

Three other elements are sometimes called secondary plant nutrients: calcium, magnesium, and sulfur. Boron, copper, iron manganese, molybdenum, zinc, and several other elements needed by plants in very small quantities are frequently added to fertilizers as trace elements.

Nitrogen is essential to plants, since it is a component of many chemical compounds made by the plant, including amino acids, the materials of which proteins are composed. Uncombined, or free, nitrogen makes up about 78 per cent of the volume of air, but in its free state nitrogen cannot be used by plants. It must first be combined with other elements to form compounds which can be used. Certain bacteria living in the soil are able to take nitrogen from the air and "fix" it into compounds available to higher plants.

Nearly all industrial processes for fixing nitrogen from the air involve making ammonia. This is done by combining nitrogen with another gas, hydrogen, at pressures as high as 1,000 atmospheres, in the presence of a catalyst. The ammonia formed is a gas at room temperature, but it can be compressed to form a liquid that can be stored if kept refrigerated or under pressure. With proper equipment, ammonia can be used directly as a fertilizer by injection into the soil. Much ammonia is converted into solution materials to make solid fertilizers, such as *ammonium nitrate, ammonium sulfate, ammonium phosphate,* or *urea.*

Phosphorus is a component of some of the key chemical compounds in all living cells. The chief source of phosphorus for fertilizers is phosphate rock, mined in Florida, Tennessee,

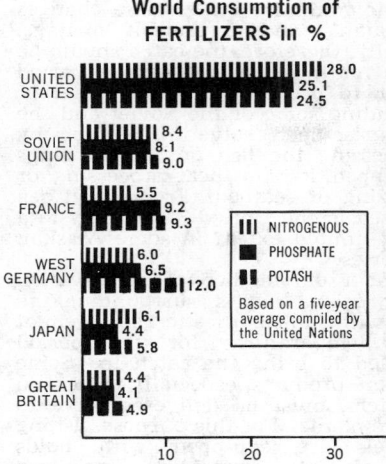

World Consumption of FERTILIZERS in %

	NITROGENOUS	PHOSPHATE	POTASH
UNITED STATES	28.0	25.1	24.5
SOVIET UNION	8.4	8.1	9.0
FRANCE	5.5	9.2	9.3
WEST GERMANY	6.0	6.5	12.0
JAPAN	6.1	4.4	5.8
GREAT BRITAIN	4.4	4.1	4.9

Based on a five-year average compiled by the United Nations

ALLIED CHEMICAL CORPORATION

NITROGEN compounds raise corn yield. Unfertilized plot (*left*) produced a small crop.

Idaho, Montana, Wyoming, and North Carolina. Outside the United States, the most important phosphate mining operations are in North Africa, West Africa, the Soviet Union, and various islands in the Pacific and Caribbean. Phosphorus in phosphate rock is in the form of *tricalcium phosphate,* which is often combined with calcium fluoride. Ground phosphate rock can be used as a fertilizer, but tricalcium phosphate is almost completely insoluble in water, so that phosphorus is not readily available to plants.

Treating ground phosphate rock with sulfuric acid to form a slurry, allowing it to harden, and then storing the mixture for a few weeks yields a solid product called *normal superphosphate.* In this mixture, the tricalcium phosphate has been converted into more soluble forms of phosphate that are readily available to the plant. *Triple superphospate* is a more concentrated phosphatic fertilizer, as is *diammonium phosphate.*

Potassium, essential to a number of chemical activities in the growing plant, is obtained from potassium compounds (collectively known as potash) mined in New Mexico, Canada, Germany, France, and elsewhere. It is also obtained from brines in California and Utah. *Potassium chloride,* often called *muriate of potash,* is the most common potassium material in fertilizers.

Today an efficient farmer has his soil analyzed and calculates exactly how much of each of the primary plant nutrients he needs. He can then order the exact type of fertilizer he wants, often made up specifically for his needs. The companies producing fertilizers tend to make more and more concentrated materials in order to save the cost of transporting inert matter. Special attention is also given to the form in which material is produced. For example, in solid fertilizers the trend is toward material composed of granules of uniform size, so that they will flow easily through application equipment with a minimum of dust.

The use of fertilizer is increasing at a tremendous rate in the United

States and in the rest of the world. As the world population increases it is necessary to use more and more fertilizer to produce crops to feed it. A great deal of effort is being expended by the United States, the highly developed countries of Europe, and Japan to increase the use of fertilizers in underdeveloped countries so that they may feed themselves.

—Albert S. Hester

Fiber Crops, providers of the basic materials for the manufacture of clothing, household goods such as sheets and towels, and commercial products such as bags, rope, and twine. Cotton is the leading fiber crop grown in the United States. Other fibers that are significant in world trade are flax, hemp, henequen, and sisal.

About 30 per cent of the world's cotton is grown in the United States. It ranks second among all U.S. cash crops. The fiber is used to make thread and cloth, and the kernel of the seed is crushed for oil, which is used for salad dressing, in cooking, and in making margarine, soap, paints, and lubricants. Cottonseed cake is a cattle feed, and cottonseed hull is utilized for roughage, fertilizer, and making fiberboard. Flax and hemp are also grown in the United States. The leading product of flax is linen thread. Linseed oil is made from the crushed seed of flax, and its straw is employed in papermaking. Hemp, a coarse, strong, and durable fiber, was used in pioneering times to make "homespun" cloth; today it is commonly used to make twine, rope, bagging, rugs, and sailcloth.

—Charles E. Rogers

Fish and Seafood, edible and industrially useful marine life. From a commercial standpoint, fish can be grouped into food fish, including shellfish, and industrial fish. Food fish provides about 10 per cent of the world's animal protein used directly for human consumption. Industrial fish are utilized in the manufacture of fish meal, fish oils, pet food, and fertilizers.

Tuna, salmon, and sardines are

among the important food fish consumed in canned form throughout the world. In the more developed countries, such food fish as ocean perch, haddock, flounder, redfish, herring, and cod are marketed either in fresh or frozen form as fillets, steaks, or dressed whole fish. In countries where refrigeration and other modern preservation methods are not as widely used, food fish in smoked, dried, or pickled, and cured forms are more prevalent.

Shrimp, lobsters, crabs, oysters, and clams are the principal shellfish species. These are distributed mainly in fresh or frozen form.

Industrial, or trash, fish include such species as menhaden, alewives, and anchovies. These, along with minor nonedible species of trash fish and the trimmings and waste from the preparation of food fish, provide the raw product for this growing segment of the fishing industry.

In 1964, U.S. commercial fishermen caught an estimated 4.5 billion pounds of all species. Of this amount, 35 per cent was landed on the northeastern and mid-Atlantic coasts, primarily in New England, 26 per cent in Alaska, Hawaii, and the Pacific coast states, and 36 per cent in the South Atlantic and Gulf states, with the remainder coming from inland lakes and rivers.

The world catch has doubled every ten years for the past several decades. The 102 billion pounds caught in 1963, however, is far short of the 440 billion pounds estimated to be available on an annual sustainable yield basis throughout the waters of the world.

In the United States, direct use of seafood for human consumption is considerably less important than the use of meats and dairy products. The annual per capita consumption is only about 10 to 11 pounds, compared with over 150 pounds of meat products. Nevertheless, the seafood industry is an important segment of the total food industry, both because of the present volume of production and because of its potential for satisfying future needs.

Because the production of food fish in the United States has remained relatively stable over the last 10 years, an increasing part of the U.S. supply of edible fish products is being supplied by imports. The population growth and purchasing power of the United States has provided a lucrative market for high-priced species sold by so many other fishing countries. Imports amounted to about 34 percent in 1964.

Commercial fishermen in the United States employ a variety of gear, methods, and seagoing vessels to catch fish and other marine species. Fish which tend to live in surface waters, such as salmon, tuna, and mackerel, are caught by means of nets, or hooks and lines. Bottom-dwelling species are caught with a variety of gear including nets, dredges, lines, and traps. The ships and boats used in the commercial fisheries also vary in design, tonnage, and size of crew.

The major problems in handling fishery products prior to consumption

are to minimize undesirable changes in quality and to prevent spoilage. Ideally, therefore, the catch should be held for the shortest possible period prior to processing. Some fisheries, including some of the Soviet and the Japanese fleets, solve this problem by processing the fish on factory ships equipped for the heat-processing or freezing of seafood. Freezing at sea is used in the United States only to a very limited extent in some Alaskan fisheries.

The usual method of preservation is by icing, that is, surrounding the fish with sufficient ice to keep them at low temperatures for the period needed to bring the catch in. Some marine products, especially crabs and lobsters, must be delivered alive to shore plants. For this purpose, fishing vessels are equipped with holds flooded with circulating fresh sea water in which the lobsters or crabs may be kept alive for several days.

■**PROCESSING OF SEAFOODS.**—Seafoods used for human consumption are sold in one of the following forms: fresh-refrigerated, frozen, precooked frozen, canned, cured or dehydrated. Fresh products are usually sold by the pound, without prepackaging, in locations close to the port of entry. Lobsters must be sold alive, and are therefore shipped in refrigerated containers filled with seaweed, and kept at a low temperature. Transportation by air has made it possible to market lobsters at great distances from where they are caught.

Much seafood is marketed as frozen products. These may be frozen fresh, as fillets, steaks, and individually quick-frozen shellfish, or precooked prior to freezing as fish sticks, various fish dishes, and precooked frozen shrimp.

Canning is the method of preservation applied to most of the fishery

TUNA RESEARCH FOUNDATION

TUNA, hauled by net onto fishing boats, is an important commercial fish. Most processed tuna goes to consumers in cans.

products processed in the United States. Products which are preserved in this manner include tuna meat, salmon, sardines, oysters, crab, and chowders based on fishery products.

Curing of fish by addition of salt and smoking is an old method of preservation, but is used in the United States only for a few specialty products. Dehydration by conventional drying methods is also used to a very limited extent, but recently there has been developed a considerable interest in freeze-dehydration, which is capable of producing high-quality dehydrated products. Shrimp, various precooked seafoods, and fish sticks and fillets are preserved by this method. Another new development is the use of atomic radiation to pasteurize fish and shellfish. Foods pasteurized in this manner retain their natural flavor and appearance, and may be kept at refrigerated temperatures for weeks whereas unpasteurized fisheries products are stable for only a few days.   —Marcus Karel

Flax. See *Rope,* page 1710.

Food Additives, chemicals that do not occur naturally in foods but are introduced in the course of food production, processing, or packaging. *Intentional additives* are chemicals added in controlled amounts with the purpose of achieving some desirable results. *Nonintentional additives* are contaminants introduced into foods as a result of manufacturing operations.

■**INTENTIONAL ADDITIVES.**—These are introduced in order to improve the safety, palatability, or nutritional value of foods. Additives inhibiting microbial spoilage are called *chemical preservatives.* Salt, organic acids, and certain other chemicals are used for this purpose.

Chemical reactions producing undesirable changes in foods are often controlled by addition of chemicals. Reactions with atmospheric oxygen are controlled by addition of *antioxidants,* notably ascorbic acid (vitamin C), tocopherol (vitamin E), certain phenolic compounds, and other reducing chemicals. Darkening of fruits and vegetables may be controlled by sulfites, and by ascorbic acid. Reactions involving metals present in foods may be minimized by the use of chemicals that tie up the metals in a nonreactive form. Chemicals effective for this purpose, called *chelating agents,* include salts of citric and phosphoric acids. Undesirable textural changes in certain types of foods may be prevented by addition of colloidal materials, such as carboxymethyl cellulose, which are known as *stabilizers.*

Additives may be used not only to prevent changes, but also to improve the initial quality of foods. Texture of meats, for instance, may be improved by adding plant enzymes such as papain (derived from the papaya plant), or bromellin (derived from pineapple). These enzymes tenderize meat, that is, they partially hydrolyze or digest it.

Taste and flavor may be adjusted to suit consumer preferences by means of synthetic sweetening agents, synthetic or natural flavor mixtures, and by flavor enhancers or potentiators. The last-mentioned category of additives has no characteristic flavor of its own, but is capable of enhancing natural flavors.

Color of foods may be improved by agents that stabilize or desirably alter natural pigments as the addition of sodium nitrite to meats or by addition of synthetic dyes.

Additives are often used to supplement the nutritional value of foods deficient in some vitamins, minerals, or other nutrients. For instance, bread, cereals, milk, and some baby foods are enriched with selected vitamins and minerals. Table salt is enriched by addition of iodides, which not only improve its handling characteristics but are also an important source of iodine, an element needed in the synthesis of the hormone thyroxin (produced by the thyroid gland).

■ NONINTENTIONAL ADDITIVES.—These may arise from agricultural practices—residues from pesticides, antibiotics for treating cattle, and similar agents; from manufacturing practices—as, metallic substances acquired from equipment used in processing foods; or packaging procedures—as, plasticizers or adhesives absorbed by foods from packaging materials. These additives serve no useful function, and their occurrence must be prevented or substantially inhibited to avoid possible health hazards.
—Marcus Karel

Food Engineering, the branch of engineering that deals with the development and operation of industrial processes aimed at the production of predictable and controlled changes in the chemical composition, physical characteristics, and biological properties of foods. These industrial processes and the associated controlled transformation of raw materials form the basis of food manufacturing and food preservation.

In designing and analyzing food processes, food engineering makes use of the concept of *unit operations.* A unit operation is an operation that may occur in any of a number of processes, often using different kinds of equipment, but that has a single physical basis and a single set of scientific principles, which apply independently of the process in which the operation is applied.

The purpose of engineering analysis of food processes is the quantitative determination of data needed for equipment design, for control of process variables, and for accurate prediction of process costs. The data obtained by the engineer may be the time needed to achieve a given effect under a given set of conditions, the size of equipment needed, or the specification of conditions such as temperature and pressure for a given process.

The complexity of the composition and structure of foods, and the stringent requirements with respect to wholesomeness and appeal of processed foods, present the food engineer with problems that call for extensive knowledge of scientific principles and the properties of foods. Food engineering must be concerned at all times not only with the efficiency of operations, but also with the effects of these operations on the foods and on the people who consume these foods. For this reason, graduate food engineers are not only trained in mathematical, physical, and chemical subjects, but are also prepared to consider the biological and biochemical problems that may arise in food processing.
—Marcus Karel

Food Manufacturing, the process of preparing farm produce for the consumer. This includes the slaughter of meat, fowl, and seafood, and the packaging of eatable foodstuffs.

■ MEAT-PACKING.—The conversion of livestock to meat, as well as to edible and nonedible by-products.

Most of the livestock used in the industry is produced west of the Mississippi River, and the major industry centers are located in Midwestern cities. The industry originated, however, on the East coast. At that time, the locally raised animals were slaughtered in nearby market cities, and surplus meat was salted and packed in barrels for export to the West Indies. This practice gave the industry its name, even though this method of "packing" is no longer practiced to any significant extent. During the nineteenth century, livestock raising moved progressively westward, and so did the industry. By mid-century the major meat-packing center was Cincinnati, Ohio. In the second half of the nineteenth century, with the rapid development of railroads, meat-packing plants were relocated at rail centers. The preeminence of Chicago as the meat-packing capital dates from that period. Chicago, Kansas City, Kans., Kansas City, Mo., and Omaha, Neb., are among the most important industry centers today.

Operations of the meat-packing industry include buying the livestock, slaughtering the animals, converting the carcasses to meat cuts and by-products, and selling these products. The animals are shipped to stockyards by railroad or truck and are held in pens. Prior to slaughter they are stunned. After slaughter the animal is eviscerated, and the carcass divided into two *sides,* which are then moved into a refrigerated room to allow rapid chilling. The viscera and other organs from each animal are collected in a separate container for inspection by a qualified representative of the Meat Inspection Division of the Bureau of Animal Industry of the United States Department of Agriculture. All meat that is moved in interstate commerce must be inspected, and the government inspection stamp guarantees that the animal was free from disease, was slaughtered under sanitary conditions, and that the carcass was wholesome at the time it left the packing plant. In addition, trained government graders may stamp carcasses with one of the official grades, which are based on the eating quality of the meat. The government grading is done only at the packer's request.

After chilling, the sides are divided into wholesale cuts. These are various portions of the carcass from which the retail cuts are prepared. The wholesale cuts for beef include round, sirloin, short loin, flank, rib, plate, chuck, brisket, and foreshank. For pork, they include hind foot, ham, side pork, loin, spareribs, shoulder, and jowl. The wholesale cuts are then shipped, leaving the final preparation of retail portions to the stores. Sometimes the sides are shipped, and all the cutting is done at the retail level. Most fresh meat is shipped at refrigerated temperatures; freezing is also used to some extent. Refrigeration at temperatures slightly above freezing is used also for preservation of meat products such as fresh ground meats, sausages, and a variety of cured products.

Other methods of preservation include heat processing, used for a variety of canned meats; freezing, used for many types of sausages and for certain precooked meat products; chemical preservation by salt, which is usually used in combination with refrigeration; and, more recently, irradiation and freeze dehydration.

A large variety of products forms the category of cured meats, that is, meats to which certain materials known as curing agents are added, frequently over a period of time, to alter the meat products with respect to their keeping qualities, flavor, and appearance. Originally the main purpose of curing was to allow meat to be stored at room temperature. With the advent of refrigeration, this purpose became secondary to the production of characteristic flavor and color. Curing processes vary greatly from product to product, and the curing agents vary according to the different processes. In most of the processes, however, the major components of curing mixtures are salt, nitrite, sugar, and flavoring agents. Some cured products are smoked to impart a characteristic and desirable flavor. Recently it has become possible to produce in meats a smokelike flavor without subjecting the products to actual smokehouse conditions.

In addition to the production of meats and meat products, the meat-packing industry is engaged in the production of a large variety of by-products. These include industrial raw materials, such as hides; chemicals derived from various nonedible portions of the animals, such as gelatin; and pharmaceuticals derived from the glandular organs of the slaughtered animals, such as dried thyroid glands of sheep which are used in treatment of goiter and other thyroid disorders in humans. Another important by-product of meat processing is animal fat, which is used for production of edible fats, such as lard, as well as for industrial greases.

■ POULTRY PRODUCTS.—Among meat products, poultry ranks third in quantity, surpassed by beef and pork products.

Poultry production centers are located in every major region of the United States. Modern poultry farming is based on scientific principles, utilizing technological advances in housing, disease control, sanitation, and feeding. The feeding practices are based on knowledge of nutritional requirements of birds, and the feed formulas include nutritional supplements, such as high-protein meals and vitamins.

Poultry is classified in accordance with the weight and age of the bird at the time of slaughter. Thus chickens may be classified as broilers or fryers, roasters, fowl, and cocks or old roosters. Turkeys are classified as fryer-roasters, young hens and toms, yearlings, and mature turkeys. The quality of individual birds is expressed by standards, ranging from A to C quality, established by the U. S. Department of Agriculture.

At a modern processing plant, the birds are put through a series of operations conducted in production-line fashion, with the birds carried on overhead conveyors. The major steps in processing include weighing, slaughter and bleeding, scalding (dipping in hot water to facilitate defeathering), defeathering, usually by automatic equipment, eviscerating, chilling, and grading. Additional steps depend on the manner in which the products are to be sold—fresh, frozen, cooked, canned, or dehydrated.

A large proportion of poultry is shipped fresh to retail channels. Fresh poultry is stored and distributed under refrigeration, packaged in boxes or in plastic bags. The storage life of refrigerated fresh poultry is limited, but recent research on the application of ionizing radiations and on the use of antibiotic dips indicates that the shelf life may be considerably extended.

Poultry to be stored for longer periods of time than are permitted by refrigeration is usually frozen. Birds to be frozen are usually placed in tightly fitting plastic bags, for proper packaging is necessary to maintain high quality in frozen storage. Freezing is usually done in air or by immersion in liquids.

In addition to uncooked poultry, processed as described above, large quantities are sold cooked. Cooked poultry products include a variety of canned items, such as chicken in broth, various stews and soups, and many others. A smaller quantity of cooked poultry items is available frozen; recently, interest has developed in the production of precooked freeze-dehydrated poultry dishes.

■**FRUIT AND VEGETABLE PRODUCTS.**—Most of the fruits and vegetables grown in the United States are harvested within a relatively short season. In order to assure a year-round supply, therefore, a large proportion of these crops is processed before delivery to consumers. Canning, freezing, pickling, and dehydration are the common methods of processing.

Modern production methods are aimed at maximizing the output per man-hour, which requires the introduction of mechanical devices for harvesting, and the mechanization of much of the processing operation. The mechanization of the agricultural practices, in turn, requires the use of herbicides, insecticides, fertilizers, and growth promoters. The efficiency of agricultural operations depends also, to a large extent, on selective breeding of suitable varieties of commercial crops. In recent years, the selection of varieties has been based not only on high yields and resistance to environmental hardships but also on suitability for mechanical harvesting and for processing. Suitability for mechanical harvesting requires a degree of sturdiness and, most important, uniform maturation times. Scheduling of the planting and harvesting operations is often based on the *heat unit system* in which each day of plant growth is credited with a certain number of units depending on the mean temperature of the day.

Generally, vegetables grown for processing are processed soon after harvest, thus minimizing post-harvest deterioration. Whenever delays occur, steps are taken to minimize deterioration, principally by rapid cooling of the crop and storage at low temperature. Some fruits, such as strawberries, are very susceptible to deterioration after harvest and must be cooled and processed rapidly. Other fruits, such as apples, pears, and oranges, may be stored for long periods of time without processing. In order to maximize their storage life, however, they are stored under strictly controlled conditions of temperature, relative humidity, and gas composition in the storage chambers. The preparation for processing of vegetables includes the following operations, most of which are also used in processing of fruits:

Cleaning: This involves washing with water containing disinfectants, brushing, and rinsing with water of potable quality.

Conveying: In most operations, conveying is mechanized. Depending on the nature of the material, this may include belt conveyors, vibrating conveyors, and many other devices.

Grading: Grading for size, appearance, and lack of defects requires some degree of manual labor. Many mechanical sorting devices for size grading, however, are used, and equipment has recently been developed for automatic color sorting and grading.

Peeling and Shelling: Many different methods may be used for this purpose. The simplest is manual peeling. Mechanical devices operate on the abrasion principle, chemical peeling methods (lye peeling), and loosening of the peels by steam with subsequent removal of the peel. Certain vegetables are flame-peeled. In this process, the product is exposed briefly to high-temperature combustion gases, which puffs and loosens the skins so they can then be removed by high-pressure water sprays.

Size Reduction: The fruits and vegetables are reduced to the desired form (slices, halves, purée) by various manual or mechanized methods.

In juice preparation, a number of different processes are available for pressing the raw material to release the juice, and for removing the undesirable components extracted with the juice. In some cases, the juices may be concentrated by the removal of a portion of the water. Vacuum evaporators of high heat-transfer efficiency are usually used, but some newer processes are based on removal of water as ice crystals in a process known as freeze concentration. The most modern process, not as yet completely developed, involves removal of water by diffusion through a membrane permeable to it but not to the dissolved sugars, flavor compounds, and other juice components.

The final processing and packaging of the fruit and vegetable products varies with the method of preservation. Products preserved by heat processing are usually packaged in cans.

Internal linings of the cans are chosen to assure best taste and appearance of the products and to prevent or minimize corrosion. Some fruit products may be packaged in aluminum cans or in plastic packages. Usually, the heat processing is conducted on the packaged product but, in the case of fluid products, it is often possible to heat the product in heat exchangers, and then to fill presterilized containers while the liquid is hot. This last method is known as *aseptic canning.* The amount of heat required to assure stability and safety varies with the product. Nonacid products, such as peas and many other vegetables, require the most heat since they are capable of allowing the growth of potentially deadly microorganisms, such as *Clostridium botulinum,* the causative agent of botulism—a form of food intoxication with high mortality rates. Most fruits, and some vegetables with high acidity, require only heating to temperatures close to boiling.

Other methods of preservation include freezing, dehydration, and fermentation. Fermentation is one of the oldest methods of preservation, and is still important in the preservation of cucumbers (pickles), tomatoes, peppers, and cabbage (sauerkraut). The fermented products are usually pasteurized in glass jars or cans.

Distribution of fresh fruits and vegetables without processing requires a degree of control of temperature and suitable packaging. Packages for fresh fruits and vegetables must allow gas exchange, since the plant materials are still "alive"—that is, they possess an active enzyme system that produces a high rate of respiration. When the normal respiration is inhibited by interference with gas exchange, the plants are subject to rapid spoilage. In the case of very actively respiring plants, the packages are perforated with holes to allow adequate gas exchange. —Marcus Karel

Food Preservation, the application of a process or processes that permit a normally perishable food to be stored for long periods without spoilage. Food spoilage means the loss of edibility due to formation of offensive changes in taste, flavor, texture, or appearance; loss of wholesomeness due to formation of toxins, extensive loss of nutritive value, or development of high concentrations of microorganisms. Spoilage may occur through chemical and physical processes, or through the growth and activity of microorganisms, such as bacteria, molds, and yeasts. Microbial spoilage is of greatest concern because it usually is rapid, and is most likely to result in conditions adversely affecting the health of consumers. Food preservation, therefore, is aimed primarily at the inhibition of microbial spoilage. Additional measures, such as exclusion of air and addition of chemical agents, may inhibit chemical deterioration.

Microbial spoilage may be prevented by *sterilization* of foods, that is, complete destruction of microorganisms present in foods, or by *inhibition* of growth of microorganisms by producing conditions unfavorable to their growth. Food may be sterilized by heating (thermal sterilization), by exposure to radiation (radiation sterilization), or by treatment with chemical agents (chemical sterilization).

Thermal sterilization is usually performed by exposing foods, packaged in hermetically sealed metallic containers, to temperatures of 240 to 250° F in pressurized vessels (canning) or by heating foods prior to packaging, and then packaging them under conditions preventing recontamination with microorganisms (aseptic canning). Newer methods of canning are aimed at improving the quality of foods, often by heating at very high temperatures for short periods of time.

Radiation sterilization is achieved by exposing packaged foods to radiations such as gamma rays from radioactive isotopes, X-rays, or high-energy electrons produced by electron accelerators. The type and amount of radiation used for food preservation are controlled to achieve sterilization without the production of any radioactivity in the food, and without impairing the safety of food. Radiation preservation, an outgrowth of postwar research interest in atomic energy, has recently received full recognition as a safe method of food preservation by the U. S. Food and Drug Administration.

Chemical sterilization is only rarely applied to food products. It is usually reserved for such items as clothing.

Food preservation without sterilization may be achieved by producing conditions unfavorable to microbial growth. Processes based on this principle include freezing, refrigeration, dehydration, chemical preservation, and fermentation.

Refrigeration, or storage of foods at temperatures slightly above freezing, is effective in slowing down microbial growth, but does not prevent such growth entirely. It is used, therefore, in combination with chemical preservation, or partial destruction of microbes (pasteurization) for products expected to have only a short storage life. Freezing prevents bacterial growth by crystallization of water and by low temperatures of storage. Although freezing can preserve foods with little impairment of their quality, it requires facilities for low temperature distribution and storage.

Dehydration reduces the water content of foods to low levels at which microbial activity ceases and chemical processes are greatly slowed down. It may be performed by a number of processes, ranging from the ancient technique of sun-drying to the most modern freezing dehydration.

Chemical preservation is based on addition to the food, or production in the food, of chemical agents that prevent microbial growth. The most commonly used agents include salt, acetic acid (vinegar), lactic acid, and other organic acids, and in some types of foods, high concentrations of sugar.

Fermentation, which in principle is identical to chemical preservation, is based on production of organic acid (usually lactic acid) by bacteria or molds either naturally present in the food, or introduced to it as a fermentation starter. Production of cheese, various sour milk products, pickles, and numerous other food products is based on fermentation, which is also vitally important in production of antibiotics.

■**FROZEN FOODS.**—The crystallization of water and the low temperatures of storage produce conditions that prevent spoilage of the food by microorganisms. These conditions are also effective in greatly slowing down most of the chemical reactions and physical changes that adversely affect the eating quality and nutritional value of stored foods. Best results are obtained when high-quality foods are selected for freezing, the food is frozen rapidly, and packaged in containers that prevent loss of water and of volatile flavors, and when the food is kept at temperatures below 0° F throughout its distribution and storage cycle. The food-spoiling microbes are not destroyed by freezing. It is essential, therefore, that after thawing, such foods be stored for only brief periods, preferably at refrigerator temperatures.

Freezing of foods by exposure to natural low temperatures is an old art, but modern food preservation by freezing began in the 1920's with the development of equipment for rapid freezing. At the present time, foods are frozen by one of the following methods:

Blast freezing in tunnels in which the food is exposed to air at temperatures below −20° F and air velocities of several thousand feet per minute; *plate freezing*, in which the food is cooled by contact with plates maintained at low temperatures; *immersion freezing*, in which foods are immersed in liquids such as brine or water-glycol mixtures maintained at temperatures of −20° to −40° F. Superior quality is claimed for foods frozen at these low temperatures.

Chief among foods preserved by freezing are concentrated orange juice, fruits and berries, vegetables, poultry, seafood, and a variety of precooked dinners. The growth in volume has been most spectacular for frozen juices, which increased in consumption from approximately two million pounds in 1946 to close to a billion pounds in 1960, and for precooked frozen dinners, which were virtually unknown in the 1940's but now account for a billion pounds annually. —Marcus Karel

Forests. See *Lumber Industry*, page 1698.

Fruit, any one of a large number of cultivated edible flower parts. Botanically, a fruit is usually considered the ripened ovary (or ovaries) of a flower (or flowers), with or without closely related parts. Some botanists prefer to designate it as basically the enlarged pistil of a flower. These definitions, however, include some plants that are classified as vegetables in economic terms (as, tomatoes and melons). We shall consider fruit to include perennial tree fruits and nuts, berries, and grapes. The main types of tree fruits are *citrus* (as, oranges), *pome* (as, apples), and *stone* (as, peaches).

The fruit industry in the United States is perhaps the most highly developed in the world. No other country produces such a quantity and variety of fruit so efficiently, and few, if any, have such an efficient fruit marketing system.

Fruit production has become highly specialized in the United States. Whereas at the turn of the century nearly every farm produced some fruit, today production is generally concentrated on specialized farms in fruit districts. These districts are usually identified by a temperate climate, good soils, and adequate rainfall or access to water. Mechanization is increasing; labor problems have led to special interest in mechanical harvesting.

In recent years, the value of fruit crop at farm level has been between

FLORIDA CITRUS COMMISSION

ORANGE PRODUCTION, a major part of the large, highly-developed U.S. fruit industry.

$1.4 billion and $1.8 billion. The retail value (including marketing charges and processing) is several times this figure. The leading fruit-producing states in terms of farm value are California (with about 40 per cent of the total), Florida (about 20 per cent), Washington, New York, and Michigan. Other important states include Hawaii, Oregon, Pennsylvania, New Jersey, and Virginia. The five most important U.S. fruits, in decreasing order of farm value, are oranges, apples, grapes, peaches, and strawberries. Nuts rate below peaches. Other leading fruits include grapefruit, pears, prunes, lemons, and pineapples.

The fruit crop is utilized in two ways, fresh consumption and processing. A major portion, about 60 per cent in recent years, is processed; this enables us to have nearly all types of fruit throughout the year. The major form of processing is canning, but freezing and drying are also important, particularly for certain crops, notably, frozen concentrated orange juice. A number of new processing techniques, such as freeze-drying, dehydro-freezing, and radiation treatments may become more significant in the future.

Total fruit consumption or use has averaged nearly 200 pounds per capita annually (this figure is in farm weight terms; it excludes nuts but allows for imports and exports). Overall, a slight downward trend is evident since World War II. This decline, however, may be more apparent than real because spoilage has been reduced by improved handling and increased processing. Even so, there has been increasing consumption of processed fruit as a substitute for fresh fruit. In either form, fruits add variety and enjoyment to the diet and are important sources of vitamins and minerals. —Dana G. Dalrymple

Fungicide. See *Pesticides,* page 1555.

Fur Farming, the raising of fur-bearing animals in captivity under conditions of controlled breeding, feeding, and care. Fur farming, sometimes called *fur ranching,* started in Canada at the end of the nineteenth century. Today most of the pelts from North America come from fur farms.

Fur farming is possible only with animals that breed well in captivity and present minimum problems in care and feeding. Beaver and muskrat, for example, require too much water to be profitably raised in captivity. Silver foxes and mink were the first animals to be raised on farms. Other fur farm animals are the fisher, marten, sable, nutria, skunk, raccoon, and chinchilla. The best chinchilla fur comes from wild Andean animals, but generally the fur of ranch or farm animals is superior to that of wild animals. Rabbits (conies) have long been raised for food, and more recently for fur.

Animals in captivity can be selectively bred to develop special colors of furs, such as the various mink mutations of pinks and even lavenders. In addition, furs from animals kept in captivity are more uniform in size and quality and can be used more easily in the garment industry.

Generally, the animals are kept in cages with wire mesh bottoms for ease of cleaning. The animals are usually separated to keep them from injuring one another. Some animals, notably mink, will kill their young if excited, so great care must be taken not to alarm them. All animals, if excited, are likely to damage their fur.

In captivity the animals are fed raw meat, poultry, and fish, with added supplements of cereals, citrus fruits, vitamins, and minerals. Fish of the carp family contain thiamine-destroying elements. Therefore, carp should be fed sparingly, if at all, for supplements cannot make up the thiamine deficiency, which results in *Chastek's paralysis.* Diseases such as distemper, abortion (*salmonellosis*), pneumonia, tularemia, and streptococcic septicemia either respond to antibiotics or can be prevented by vaccination. Some diseases, such as tularemia in mink, are difficult to treat because antibiotics can kill the animals. Anthrax is too dangerous to cure or treat and is too rare to require vaccination; it should be controlled by using great care in feeding and tending the animals. Avian tuberculosis has become increasingly damaging among rodents, but it can be controlled by making sure that the animals are fed uninfected pork or poultry. Most fur-bearing animals mate in the winter, although some, such as the muskrat and rabbit, produce several large litters a year.

When their fur is of best quality and size, the animals are killed painlessly by injection or electricity. The pelts are then removed, stretched, scraped, dried, and stored until sold. —John T. Schlebecker

NATIONAL FUR NEWS

MINK farming began in the nineteenth century. Today, a good brown pelt may bring $75; a pastel mutation as much as $125.

Gelatin, a purified form of glue, produced principally by the acid treatment of pork skin and the lime or alkaline treatment of calf hides and demineralized cattle bones. It is an easily digestible but nutritionally incomplete protein that is not coagulated by heat. In water, it forms gels that are easily dispersed by the addition of heat.

The properties of gelatin in water render it useful in gelation, emulsion stabilization, water-binding, foaming, solution clarification, and inhibition of crystal formation. These functions are utilized in various applications. In foods, gelatin is used in the preparation of desserts, confections, ice cream, whips, and jellied meats. Pharmaceutically, it is used in the formulation of emulsions, capsules, lozenges, suppositories, and cosmetic preparations, and as a treatment for nail defects.

Gelatin has a number of applications in the photographic, printing, electroplating, and tanning industries. It is also used to size (stiffen) paper and textiles, to fine (clarify) beverages, and to provide culture media for microorganisms. —Isaac J. Wahba

Gibberellic Acid, one of an expanding group of natural plant growth-regulating substances known as gibberellins. The nine closely related compounds that originally constituted this group are designated A_1 through A_9, the most widely known being A_3, or gibberellic acid. Gibberellins, produced by the fungus *Gibberella fujikuroi,* are obtained commercially by growing the fungus in a liquid culture medium and then extracting the gibberellins in a manner similar to that used in the production of antibiotics. In its natural habitat, the fungus attacks rice plants, causing abnormally long stems to develop, a disease known as *bakanae* or *foolish seedling.* The growth-accelerating factors were isolated in 1938 from infected rice plants in Japan. Responses to gibberellic acid have been studied widely in research with plants, since the acid accelerates stem elongation and induces other growth responses. It is used in crop production mainly to increase the size of some varieties of grapes, to improve the quality of navel oranges, and to increase the production of the enzyme alpha-amylase in malt. —John W. Mitchell

Goat, a hollow-horned, hoofed mammal that is similar to sheep. Males are called *bucks,* females *does,* and the young *kids.* Goats are kept for milk, meat, hides, hair, and sometimes work. In the United States, goats are kept primarily for milk, although some *angora* goats are kept for their hair. Goat's milk is easy to digest and is generally safe from tuberculosis, since goats rarely get this disease. The milk breeds used in the United States include the *Toggenburg, Nubian, Saanen, British Alpine,* and *French Alpine.* Goats usually mate in the fall or winter, but can mate anytime, and produce one or two young, with a gestation period of five months. The doe may be bred at eight months. Goats are browsers rather than grazers and will eat almost anything.

They can be especially destructive to young plants and trees because they eat bark. Goats suffer from *milk fever* and *mastitis,* both of which may be controlled by antibiotics. Pneumonia is usually cured with antibiotics, and anthrax can be prevented by vaccination. *Goat pox* and *brucellosis* are especially contagious and incurable, but they can be prevented by sanitation and the removal of diseased animals. Sulfa drugs work well on *actinomycosis,* an inflammation caused by a fungus. Worm parasites respond to treatment by vermifuges, such as copper sulfate, nicotine sulfate, and phenothiazine.

Goats are ruminants of the genus *Capra,* with four wild species, three domesticated species, and one species both wild and domesticated. In addition, *Capra ibex,* with several species, has never been domesticated.

—John T. Schlebecker

Goose, a web-footed swimming bird, related to swans and ducks, raised mainly for its meat. There is a limited demand for geese, probably due to the fatness of the meat. Geese are often kept by some to alert against intruders, or to weed cotton and berry fields. If not more than 5 to 7 geese per acre are used, and are removed before the berries ripen, they will not damage the crop. Of the numerous breeds, the Toulouse and Emden geese are the most popular. It is generally difficult to distinguish between the male and female. However, in Pilgrim geese the *gander,* or male, is white and the female, or goose, light gray. Goose eggs require 28 to 31 days of incubation for hatching. *Goslings* grow rapidly and reach 10–12 pounds at 10 weeks of age, and up to 25 pounds at maturity, depending on the sex and breed. The gander is usually several pounds heavier than the goose. Geese are long-lived—some up to 100 years—but females are normally not useful after 8 or 10 years. Ganders may have two or more mates but they usually remain faithful to the same one for life. Geese are costly, mainly because of low egg production and hatchability.

—Carl W. Hess

Grape, a vine-grown *fruit* ranging in color from greenish white to black. Grapes are the most important fruit produced in the world in terms of tonnage. Most of the production is concentrated in the Mediterranean area. On the basis of individual nations, Italy and France are the leaders, followed by Spain and the United States.

The U.S. produces 3 to 4 million tons, most of which is concentrated in California. In recent years, California has accounted for approximately 90 per cent of the crop, followed by New York, Michigan, Washington, Pennsylvania, and Ohio. Botanically, California grapes are of European varieties; others are generally American.

About one-sixth of production is sold for fresh consumption and about five-sixths for processing. The main forms of processing are: crushing for wine or juice; drying into raisins; and canning of white grapes. Crushing

takes a little over half of production, drying about a third, while canning is of relatively minor importance.

—Dana G. Dalrymple

Guinea Fowl, an edible bird characterized by a small, partially unfeathered head and a curved body. The Pearl guinea, with grayish plumage dotted with white, is the most popular variety of domestic guinea. Other varieties are the White and the Lavender. Guinea eggs hatch after 26 to 28 days of incubation. Young guineas, or *keets,* reach about 2½ pounds at 14 weeks of age, and at maturity weigh 3 to 3½ pounds. Guineas are used frequently in rural areas as guardians of the farmstead, for they produce harsh shrieks whenever strangers appear. They are considered a delicacy and are used as a specialty food.

—Carl W. Hess

Herbicide. See *Pesticides,* page 1555.

Horse, a domesticated, four-legged, herbivorous mammal best known for its use as a beast of burden, although its flesh is eaten in some cultures. Horses range in size from a few hundred pounds to more than a ton. Although a type of prehistoric horse once existed in North America, all horse stocks today are descended from animals that originated on the high plateaus of eastern Russia and Siberia. The currently accepted date for the domestication of the horse is approximately 5,000 B.C. From their native habitat they spread to the south and west. Successive invasions of the Arabs and the Moors brought these native strains into Spain, from which was developed the *Andalusian horse.* This was the horse brought to North and South America by the Spanish conquistadores and from which the South American *Criollo* and the North American *Mustang* are descended. English and Dutch settlers on the Atlantic seaboard brought horses from England and Holland to complete the basic stocks for the North American breeds, while a number of French horses were brought to eastern Canada.

Horses played a major part in the advancing American frontier, U.S. cavalry regiments eventually subduing the mounted Indian. In the wake of these battles came horse-drawn covered wagons, which in turn were followed by the horse-drawn plows that broke the plains to facilitate the sowing of food crops.

The peak of North American horse population was reached before World War I. After that, trucks began to replace horsepower in the cities. By the end of World War II, tractors had virtually driven horses off the farms. Today, the great majority of horses are used for sport—*thoroughbreds* for running and racing, *standardbreds* for harness racing, and *quarter horses* for working cattle, rodeo performances, trail riding, and pleasure riding. The standardbred horse is the only breed exported extensively by the United States; these horses are sent all over the world to provide breeding stock for harness racing. Other American breeds include the *American saddle*

horse, both three- and five-gaited, and the *Tennessee walking horse,* both of which are primarily horse show breeds. American breeds characterized by their color are the golden-colored *palomino* and the spotted *appaloosa.* Descended from the horse of conquistadores are horses of the *pinto* breed, which are marked in patches rather than in spots. One of the oldest American breeds is the *Morgan horse,* descended from Justin Morgan, a stallion foaled in the late eighteenth century and belonging to a Vermont school teacher of the same name. These horses are noted for their versatility in being able to perform all types of work.

Ponies are also bred extensively in this country, but the majority of them are imported from England, particularly the *Welsh* and the *Shetland;* the *Connemara* comes from Ireland. A native American breed is the *Pony of the Americas,* a small type of Appaloosa.

The gestation period of the horse is approximately 11 months. Given reasonable care, horses are generally free from disease, although they are subject to a number of respiratory ailments, most of them not fatal. Horses are also subject to sleeping sickness.

There has been a strong revival of interest in riding of all kinds in North America, and in fact throughout the Occident. —Alexander Mackay-Smith

Hydroponics, the science of growing plants in water or sand culture. In *water culture,* the plants grow with their roots suspended in a dilute solution of the essential mineral elements, contained in shallow tanks. They are supported above the water by wire netting or hardware cloth, which is covered with wood shavings, peat moss, or similar material in order to exclude light from the solution and maintain a high humidity around the upper roots. The solution must be renewed at intervals as water and elements are absorbed. It must be aerated to supply oxygen to the roots. In *sand culture,* the nutrient solution is applied frequently to containers of sand, or other inert media (vermiculite, perlite, haydite), in which the plants are growing. This method has been widely used in experimental studies of plant nutrition for many years.

A variation of the sand culture method, known as *sub-irrigation culture* is the only commercial application of hydroponics. Watertight beds are filled with a coarse medium, such as washed gravel. The nutrient solution is pumped into the beds or allowed to flow into them from overhead reservoirs, until the beds are filled to within an inch of the surface. The solution then flows out of the gravel to a storage tank. Since the only source of water and nutrients for the plants is from the films of moisture around the gravel particles, the cycle of filling and draining the beds must be repeated frequently.

The major handicap to economic food production by hydroponics is the cost of the installation. Some technical training and considerable experience are necessary for the efficient management of soilless culture crop production. Soilless culture was used to produce vegetables at certain United States Army bases oversead during World War II. Hydroponics continues to be an absorbing hobby for the home gardener. —Neil Stuart

Irrigation, the practice of making available to crops, pasture, lawns, and turfs a greater quantity of water than that retained from natural rainfall. It thus includes various flooding or ditching techniques for direct water application, called *gravity* or *low-pressure irrigation; overhead sprinkling* or *high-pressure systems* of varying design; *diking* of fields to obstruct the natural draining away of rainfall, as in rice paddies; and situations where groundwater tables are or can be made sufficiently shallow to permit the wetting of root zones from below.

Irrigation has played an important role in agricultural production since the dawn of history, as evidenced by the early civilizations in the Tigris and Euphrates valleys and the dynasties of ancient Egypt supported by the floodwaters of the Nile. Today about 400 million acres—about one-eighth of the world's arable agricultural land—are irrigated. Three-fourths of the total is in Asia, especially China, India, and Pakistan. North and Central America account for about 40 million acres, led by the United States with about 37 million acres of irrigated land. About 31 million acres of this is in crops, and 6 million acres in pasture. It has been estimated that the U.S. total eventually could reach about 75 million acres.

About 94 per cent of the irrigated land in the United States lies in the 17 western states, where the practice originated with aboriginal Indians, was taken up by the Spanish missionaries and by colonists from both Spain and Mexico, and was put on a sustained basis by the Mormon settlers who arrived in Utah in 1847. Rapid expansion through the West began about 1870 from a 32,000-acre project supported by Horace Greeley, near present-day Greeley, Colorado. Other large projects were started in about the same period near Riverside and Anaheim, California. But irrigation is also important in the Mississippi Delta states, in Hawaiian sugarcane areas, in Florida citrus groves, and on truck farms in New Jersey. Also, it is increasing in importance through most of the eastern states.

■**GRAVITY IRRIGATION.**—Methods of irrigation vary considerably from area to area and are closely related to the nature and proximity of water supplies. Gravity methods utilizing ditches, furrows, border dikes, and flooding are still employed on 90 per cent of the acreage in the older irrigated areas—the West, the Mississippi Delta, and Florida. About 55 per cent of this acreage is served by diversions from streams or reservoirs. Most of the remainder is supplied by pumping water from wells. While limited to nearly flat terrain and requiring considerable expense for land-shaping as well as considerable

BUREAU OF RECLAMATION, U.S. DEPARTMENT OF THE INTERIOR

FLOOD CONTROL in the Missouri River Basin Project of Montana performs the secondary function of aiding sugar beet production by diversion of water through irrigation systems.

volumes of water, gravity irrigation has the special advantage of requiring a comparatively small investment for irrigation equipment. Operating costs are largely for labor. Most of the needed reservoirs, canals, and land preparation were arranged through mutual irrigation companies or in recent years by the Department of the Interior's Bureau of Reclamation.

■**OVERHEAD IRRIGATION.**—Overhead or sprinkler irrigation is gaining rapidly in importance in all areas of the United States and in other countries too. More than 12 per cent of the irrigated acreage in the United States is now sprinkled, compared with 2 per cent in 1950. The most common system lifts water from wells or adjacent streams and forces it at high pressure into a main pipeline having several portable lateral lines, each with its own series of nozzles or sprinklers. The lateral lines are periodically disconnected and moved to a new valve point on the main line until the field is irrigated completely. To avoid uncoupling of lateral sections, the complete lateral may be mounted on large wheels and rolled to its new position. Or there may be a combination main and delivery line on lugged wheels in which some of the water pressure itself is used to inch the system along automatically. This is called a *hydraulic-move system.* Still another sprinkler system consists of a single large boom, or perhaps several booms, mounted on a trailer with giant nozzles along the booms and at the ends, operating much like an ordinary rotating lawn sprinkler. Some of these rigs can irrigate up to 5.5 acres per setting. Sprinkler systems are well adapted to both level and moderately sloping land but require a considerable investment in equipment. Their special advantages are complete control over rates of water application to match absorptive capacity of soils, uniform application to all areas, and portability.

■**SUBIRRIGATION.**—Subirrigation is possible with little expense under conditions where ground water tables are naturally shallow, as in the cranberry

bogs of Massachusetts and Michigan. Favorable conditions also can be created if the subsoil is impervious at a depth of 6 feet or more and if the surface soil is relatively permeable. A common technique is to surround large blocks of land with levees to prevent flooding, to install drainage systems, and then to pump excess water in wet seasons over the levees into the streams. In dry periods, the river water is siphoned or pumped back over the levees into ditches about one foot wide, 2 or 3 feet deep, and up to several hundred feet apart. The water is diffused through the root zone by capillary action, with downward percolation restricted by the impervious subsoil. Subirrigation can be very efficient as expenses for labor and operation are relatively small.

The role of irrigation in the U.S. farm economy is indicated by the fact that irrigated crops account for about one-fifth of the value of all harvested crops but only 8.5 per cent of the total crop acreage. In the order of their market value, the leading irrigated crops are cotton, vegetables, tame hay, potatoes, sugarbeets, corn, sorghums, barley, and wheat. Citrus and other orchard and vineyard crops also rank high. The value of the 6 million acres of irrigated pasture is difficult to estimate, but this acreage is an essential part of the feed base on many dairy farms and cattle or sheep ranches. —George A. Pavelis

Jute. See *Rope,* page 1710.

Meat Packing. See *Food Manufacturing,* page 1548.

Oats, a grain of the grass family, widely used as a source of human and animal food and an important source of straw. Oats rank fourth among the grain crops, next below wheat, corn, and grain sorghum. Despite the inroads of motor-propelled machines on farms, displacing the horses and mules that formerly were the main consumers of oats, this grain retains a prominent place in the farm economy. Now the oat crop is fed largely to dairy cattle, poultry, hogs, and sheep.

About 4 per cent of the billion-bushel annual United States crop goes into the manufacture of oatmeal for the breakfast table. Some oats are pastured and cut for hay or livestock bedding.

The oat originated in eastern Europe or western Asia. Among its principal growers today are the United States, the Soviet Union, Germany, Canada, France, and the United Kingdom. The type that is generally grown, known as the *common oat,* develops an upright pinnacle with branches falling about equally to all sides. Another type, known as *side oats,* has branches that fall to one side. Oat hulls vary in color according to variety. Some are white or gray, others are yellow, red, or black. The hulls are most often white in the sections of predominant U.S. production—the Corn Belt, the Great Lakes states, and the northern Plains. These areas taken together grow about three-quarters of the 25 to 30 million acres seeded annually in the United States. In the South, oats are usually red or gray. Most oats in cool climates are sown in the spring, but a fall-seeded crop will winter over in the warmer Southern states.

—Charles E. Rogers

Peanuts, a legume of the pea family, deriving the "nut" part of the name from the fact that the plant ripens its product within a shell. Though the peanut originated in South America, probably in Brazil, it has migrated to many parts of the world. China, India, West Africa, and the United States are leading producers. Except in the United States, peanuts are mainly crushed for oil, but here about 50 per cent of the crop goes into peanut butter. Most of the remaining nuts are roasted for direct consumption, used in candy and bakers' goods, or left in the soil to be rooted out by swine. *Peanut vines* produce hay equal in feeding value to clover. In the United States, the peanut is an annual plant grown mainly in the Southern states. Planted from the hulled seed in the spring, it develops *pegs* after blossoming. The pegs elongate and go into the soil where they produce the *groundnut,* as the peanut is sometimes called.

—Charles E. Rogers

Pesticides, any of various substances used by the agriculturist to destroy plant or animal pests. Most pesticides are manufactured chemicals that, by the nature of their purpose, must be lethal to some living organism. The utility of pesticides depends on the fact that there is a wide difference in reaction from species to species.

Specific terms are applied to pesticides according to the organism controlled. The Federal Insecticide, Fungicide, and Rodenticide Act, which regulates the marketing of pesticides or economic poisons shipped in interstate commerce, defines several such terms.

Insecticides are substances or mixtures of substances intended for preventing, destroying, repelling, or mitigating any insects that may be present in any environment. In the same manner, *fungicides* and *herbicides* are defined as substances intended for the control of fungi and weeds, respectively.

■**INSECTICIDES.**—Prior to 1940, agricultural pesticides were rather simple substances such as lime sulfur, arsenic acid, and Paris green (lead arsenate), as well as a few substances of plant origin such as rotenone and pyrethrum dusts. As a by-product of World War II, chemicals from a group developed for the purpose of destroying mankind were found useful in destroying insect pests. During this same period, it was discovered that the chemical *dichlorodiphenyl trichloroethane* (DDT) was very toxic to insects but relatively safe to man. These developments set the stage for a new era in the agricultural chemical industry. Today, there are four important groups of insecticides including chlorinated hydrocarbons, organic phosphates, carbamates, and botanicals.

The *chlorinated hydrocarbons* are organic chemicals that commonly contain chlorine, although they may contain fluorine, bromine, or iodine. There is a wide variation in the complexity of these structures, but the effects on the body are somewhat similar. Little is known of how these effects take place.

The fact that these compounds are soluble in animal fat accounts for scientists' concern regarding their storage in the body fat. Although the storage of DDT in human tissues has been studied for over 20 years, little significance has been associated with the storage except the obvious fact that it is proof of exposure and absorption of the compound.

The basic action of *organic phosphates* is similar within this group, but the degree of toxicity varies widely. In a very general way, these compounds disrupt transmission of nerve impulses, functions of the body over which we have little or no conscious control.

Carbamates affect the same systems of the body as do the organic phos-

phates. The major difference is that the effects of organic phosphates on the regulatory components of nerve transmission are either nonreversible, or only very slowly reversible, whereas carbamates are rapidly reversible in character. Carbamate compounds also vary widely in their toxicity both to man and insects.

Botanicals have a wide range of actions and toxicities. Nicotine is one of the most toxic to man, and pyrethrum is about the least toxic. *Rotenone,* which by laboratory evaluations is very toxic, is not a problem under practical conditions.

■**HERBICIDES.**—Chemicals of a nonspecific type, such as arsenic acid, had been used as herbicides prior to 1940. About this time, a number of relatively selective herbicides became available. These chemicals are, in general, much less toxic to man than the nonspecific types. *Dinitrophenols* are among the important herbicides toxicologically. Repeated exposure increases the chances of intoxication. Basically, these compounds increase the metabolic rate. Another important group of herbicides is the *chlorophenoxy acetic acid derivatives,* which include 2,4-dichloro phenoxy acetic acid (2,4-D). In plants these compounds function as hormones. The action in animals is thought not to be hormonal in nature, but the exact mechanism is not known. They are among the least toxic pesticides to man.

■**FUNGICIDES.**—There are a number of important agricultural fungicides. However, the two most frequently used classes are the dithiocarbamates and the organic mercurials. While many of the *dithiocarbamates* are irritating to the skin and eyes, they are not sufficiently toxic to be considered hazardous to use. For this reason, they have not been extensively studied as to mode of action. *Organic mercurial compounds,* such as phenyl mercuric acetate, are moderately to very highly toxic to man, since there is a general tendency to accumulate mercury in the tissue of the liver and kidney. Continued exposure to high concentrations of mercury from any source can produce serious injury.

—J. S. Leary, Jr.

Pheasant, an edible bird having a compact body, short unfeathered legs, and short rounded wings. The Ringneck is the most common of the pheasants. There are other popular breeds, such as Mongolian and Chinese, and ornamental breeds including Golden, Silver, Lady Amherst, and Reeves. In many sections of the country pheasants are popular as game birds and are raised for sports clubs. They are also used as a specialty food. Pheasant eggs hatch after 22 to 24 days of incubation. Pheasants are highly nervous and may injure their heads when raised in confinement. This is true even when the wing feathers of one wing are clipped or the last joint of one wing is removed to prevent flying. Most states in the United States restrict the raising of game birds, and require a permit or license for the raising or hunting of pheasants.

—Carl W. Hess

U.S. DEPARTMENT OF AGRICULTURE

SPRAYING soft-jet pesticides prevents or destroys various tree diseases.

Pigeon, a bird with dense fluffy plumage, a stout body and short neck, a small head, and a square or rounded tail. Young pigeons are called *Squab.* Of the many pigeon breeds, the King, Carneau, and Homer are the ones used for squab production. Squabs grow very rapidly and reach market age in about 4 weeks, depending on the size of the breed. *Homing pigeons* are raised by pigeon fanciers for racing. About 17 days of incubation are required for pigeon eggs to hatch. —Carl W. Hess

Poultry Products. See *Food Manufacturing,* page 1548.

Rice, a native grass of tropical Asia and the cereal food mainstay of the peoples of China, Japan, the mainland of southeast Asia, and the islands of the southwest Pacific. This is the *rice bowl,* where 95 per cent of the world's supply of the cereal is produced and consumed. There are thousands of known varieties, more than of any other crop.

Alone among the world's great crops, rice grows typically in a field of standing water, but the land must slope enough to allow a slight movement of the water. Irrigation is the prime requisite. Upland rice, grown without irrigation, constitutes a negligible part of the total harvest.

Most rice is grown in coastal plains and tidal deltas in tropical, semitropical, and temperate climates. Relatively high humidity and an average temperature of 70° F during the growing season of 4 to 6 months are necessary for best results. Heavy soil is desirable, and the subsoil must be impervious to water. Except in technically advanced countries like the United States, rice cultivation is done almost entirely by hand.

Seed is sown broadcast, and the seedlings that emerge are transplanted when they are 6 to 8 inches in height. They are planted in water 2 to 4 inches deep, in rows about one foot apart, to permit intensive cultivation. From the time the seedlings are transplanted until the harvest, they are supplied with heavy fertilization. Harvested rice is threshed by flailing or beating. It is then winnowed and the hulls removed. Afterward the clean rice is polished.

Communist China leads the world in rice production—about 80 million metric tons annually, according to an estimate made by the Food and Agri-

RICE CULTIVATION remains unchanged despite technological improvements in most of Asia, and many farmers still employ the primitive methods used by their ancestors for centuries.

and Japan falls into third place with 17 million. Some rice is grown on every continent. North America produced 4.5 million metric tons in 1964–65, the largest part—3.25 million tons —in the United States. The leading rice-producing states are Louisiana, Texas, Arkansas, and California.

About two-thirds of the world's exports of rice in 1964–65 were from six Asian countries: Thailand, Burma, South Vietnam, Cambodia, Taiwan, and South Korea. The principal importing countries also were Asian— Indonesia, India, Japan, Malaya, the Philippines, and Pakistan. The United States exported a record 2.1 million tons in 1964–65. India was the largest importer of U.S. rice. Increases in both acreage and yield among the principal importing countries of Asia have failed to bring about sufficient production to satisfy growing domestic needs. —Charles E. Rogers

Rye, a cereal of the grass family. Like many others, it probably originated from a wild species growing in the Near East. It is used largely as a bread grain in the Soviet Union and Germany. It flourishes in a variety of conditions, but when grown on good soil yields less profit than other crops. It is therefore cultivated mainly on the poor, light, dry land un-

crop to be consumed at an early stage of growth. If allowed to reach maturity, it is hard, dry, and unpalatable to stock. The straw is used for thatching, packing, and similar purposes. The crop is not important in the United States, where its annual production is comparatively small and is used chiefly to give flavor to the so-called rye bread. The grain is malted to make rye whiskey, and the straw is used for packing.

Rye is subject to a fungus disease, *ergot,* and if infected grain is made into bread, it can be a dangerous poison, sometimes causing death. Ergot is used, however, as an ingredient of drugs for medical purposes. —G. E. Fussell

Seafood. See *Fish and Seafood,* page 1546.

Sheep, horned, woolly mammals that are similar to goats. Males are called *rams,* females *ewes,* castrated males *wethers,* and the young *lambs.* Domesticated sheep are kept for wool, meat, fur, and hides. Outside the United States, ewes are sometimes kept for milk. Some sheep breeds produce higher-quality wool than others, and some produce meat more abundantly and rapidly. Meat animals must be raised comparatively near the point of consumption, because mutton cannot be pickled or smoked. Lambs are preferred for meat in the United States. Various breeds differ in their gregariousness. Sheep that are range-grazed should be gregarious, while sheep kept in farm pastures need not flock. The mutton types are best kept separate and need not be very gregarious.

Various crosses of breeds can be achieved to secure other desired characteristics, such as hardiness, rapid lamb growth, large lamb crops, and dual production of wool and meat. Wool breeds, sufficiently gregarious for herding, include the Rambouillet, Merino, Corriedale, Romeldale, Panama, Columbia, Targhee and the long-

World Production of RICE in %

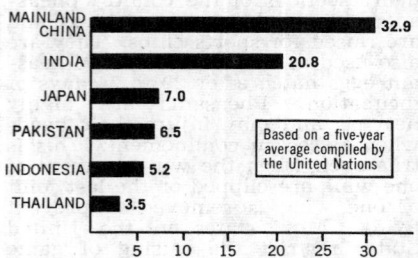

MAINLAND CHINA	32.9
INDIA	20.8
JAPAN	7.0
PAKISTAN	6.5
INDONESIA	5.2
THAILAND	3.5

Based on a five-year average compiled by the United Nations

culture Organization of the United Nations. The second largest producer is India with 55 million metric tons,

World Production of RYE in %

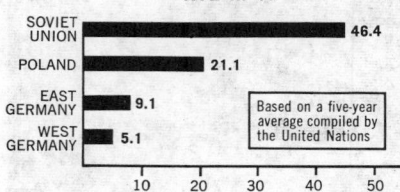

SOVIET UNION	46.4
POLAND	21.1
EAST GERMANY	9.1
WEST GERMANY	5.1

Based on a five-year average compiled by the United Nations

suited to producing high yields of wheat, characteristic of northeastern Europe. It is extremely winter-hardy and drought-resistant.

In Great Britain, rye is grown as a forage crop, sometimes as a spring

wooled Lincolns, Cotswolds, and Romneys. The meat breeds include the Hampshires, Suffolks, Oxfords, and Southdowns.

Sheep usually mate in the fall, and the lambs are born in the spring. The gestation is about five months, and the breeding life of a ewe averages seven years. Several of the most deadly sheep diseases, such as anthrax, blackleg, tetanus, and rabies, have effective vaccines. Crippling or fatal diseases, such as foot-and-mouth, listerellosis (circling disease), mastitis, and shipping fever respond well to antibiotics. Black disease, caused by liver flukes, can be prevented by chemical destruction of the intermediary snail hosts. Brucellosis and tuberculosis in sheep are very rare, and slaughter eradication works well. Liver flukes, long worms, and tapeworms all succumb to phenothiazine or other vermicides. Dips and sprays are effective against disease-carrying ticks and insects.

Sheep are ruminants of the genus *Ovis*, with four wild species-groups, one domesticated species-group, and many subspecies.

—John T. Schlebecker

Sisal. See *Rope*, page 1710.

Soils, earth composed of inorganic particles, organic matter, water, and air. They are formed by the weathering of rocks and the decay of organic material.

The formation of soils determines their classification into five broad soil belts, which in turn are divided into groups and subgroups. The *tundra soils* constitute the most northern of these belts; they are frozen much of the year and are available for cultivation only in the summertime. *Podzolic soils* have been formed mainly in the forested areas of eastern Canada, northeastern United States, and northern Eurasia. *Latosolic soils*, tropical and subtropical soils formed by the decay of forest and savanna vegetation, are extremely leached; the soils of the southeastern United States belong to this classification. *Chernozemic soils* are the product of prairie and steppe grasslands; they are relatively unleached and fertile. *Desertic soils* are those of the deserts; they are usually productive when irrigated.

■**CHEMICAL CONTENT.**—Plants need at least 16 chemical elements for growth and seed production: carbon, hydro-

gen, oxygen, calcium, nitrogen, phosphorus, potassium, sulfur, magnesium, iron, manganese, zinc, copper, molybdenum, boron, and chlorine. Of these, the first nine are the most essential. Carbon, hydrogen, and oxygen are obtainable from the water and the air, but the other elements or nutrients must be obtained from the soil.

The podzolic and latosolic soils of the eastern United States are usually deficient in calcium and consequently are more acid than alkaline. Since many plants are sensitive to acidity, these soils need the addition of calcium in the form of lime. To designate the soil condition, a pH scale from 0 to 14 is used. A pH factor below 7 indicates acidity; above it, alkalinity.

Nitrogen and sulfur are needed in the production of proteins, while phosphorus is necessary for photosynthesis and seed formation. Potassium is essential for such physiological processes as cell growth and the formation of starch and sugars.

These and other nutrients are added to soils deficient in them by means of crop rotation, green manuring, and the application of animal manures and commercial fertilizers. The inclusion of clover or alfalfa in a *rotation cycle* enriches the soil because of the action of nitrogen-fixing bacteria, which live in nodules on the roots of these plants. *Green manuring* is the plowing under of a growing, leafy crop, usually leguminous. Farmers have long used *animal manures*, but recently they have increased greatly their use of *commercial fertilizers*. In the years between 1942 and 1962, the consumption of commercial fertilizers in the United States more than tripled.

■**MOISTURE.**—The *moisture content* of the soil is of major concern to farmers. If there is too much, they must provide surface drainage by grading, terracing, and ditching or subsurface drainage by the construction of *tile* or *mole drains*. If the rainfall is normally sufficient, they must try to retain it by cultivation and by the destruction of weeds. If there is not enough, they must either conserve it or supplement it by irrigation.

In the United States, on the Great Plains and in the intermountain valleys farther west where annual rainfall is less than 20 inches, farmers and agronomists have developed a

type of moisture-conserving agriculture known as *dry-land farming*. It consists of the culture of drought-resistant crop varieties and of a system of alternate cropping known as *summer fallowing* in which every other year the land lies fallow in order to store moisture.

In arid regions, water is diverted from streams into ditches or pumped from wells and applied to the land by methods called *flooding, furrow, border, basin,* and *sprinkler irrigation*.

■**TILLAGE.**—To produce crops, the soil must be *tilled*. The first step in tillage is plowing, which loosens, granulates, and turns under organic materials. The seedbed is usually further pulverized by means of spike-tooth and disk harrows. Then crops are planted by means of planters and drills and, in the case of intertilled crops, cultivated during the growing season to reduce competition from weeds.

Loose soil, however, is subject to *erosion* by wind and water. On the Great Plains, where wind erosion is a problem, it has been checked by strip cropping and the creation of a stubble or trashy mulch. *Strip cropping* is the planting of grain in strips alternating with fallow, while *stubble mulch* is created by chisels and sweeps, loosening and granulating the soil but retaining the stubble from the previous crops on the surface. Erosion by water is retarded by *terracing, contour plowing,* and the planting of cover crops. —Robert G. Dunbar

Soybeans, an Asian legume or its seed. Soybeans originated in the Orient; in China they have been a staple food product for thousands of years. Introduced to America and grown in a small way in the nineteenth century, they were rediscovered as a valuable legume crop during the past half-century. Their rise to third place among cash crops in the United States took place after World War II. Adapted to temperate climate, with warm, humid growing seasons, this annual farm crop does well in tropical and subtropical areas as a hay and cover crop, though not for the development of beans. As a bean crop it is best adapted to the Corn Belt and the Great Lakes and Delta states.

Among the oilseed crops of the Western Hemisphere, soybeans hold first place. The annual value of the soybean crop in recent years has been nearly $2 billion. In the early 1930's, American farmers grew only enough soybeans to sell $10 million worth annually. About 700 million bushels were grown in the United States in 1965. Fifty per cent of the soybean crop in the United States before 1941 was grown for green manure, for grazing use, or for hay. Two-thirds of the crop is used to produce soybean oil and soybean meal. Over 25 per cent of the bean is exported.

The upsurge of soybeans during and since the 1940's is due to several circumstances. During World War II, supplies of fats and oils from the Far East were cut off, and margarine and shortening makers used soybean oil in place of imported oils. After the war, consumers were able and willing to

U.S. DEPARTMENT OF AGRICULTURE

PRIMARY SHEEP PRODUCTS are wool and mutton. The Hampshire breed (*right*) is more suitable for mutton, while the fine-fleeced Merino (*left*) is best used for wool.

M. FELDMAN

SUGAR CANE being dropped into a waiting wagon by a loader that crops a quarter-ton of cane. The new tractor, dubbed "Sugar Babe," has the capacity to pull four loaded trucks, or 65,000 pounds, to a sugar mill. This harvest is part of Florida's expanding sugar industry.

buy more livestock products, thus opening up a market for soybeans in mixed feeds. Recent rapid expansion of soybean crops in the United States has been aided by variety adaptation, and by advances in farm mechanization, marketing, and technology. Of the soybeans grown in the United States, 90 per cent is for food—in the form of oil for human consumption and soybean meal in mixed feeds for animals—and 10 per cent for nonfood products. In food industries, margarine and shortening take about one-third of the soybean oil produced annually; salad oil and mayonnaise, one-fourth. Nonfood articles include paints, varnishes, and lubricants; soaps, sprays, and cosmetics; oilcloth and linoleum.

Soybeans are eaten in many forms in China. *Bean curd* is the most common form, in addition to bean *milk*, which is pressed from the curd. The green leaves of the soybean find their way to the Chinese dinner table boiled as greens. The stalks are fed to pigs and chickens, or dried for fuel.
—Charles E. Rogers

Spices, aromatic vegetable products used primarily for seasoning and preserving food, and to a lesser extent for making perfumes, soaps, and lotions. The "true" spices, so designated by spice specialists, are pepper, vanilla, cloves, cinnamon, nutmeg, and ginger. Some spices come from the seeds, buds, flowers, and fruits of plants; others, from the bark, leaves, or roots. The harvested substance is usually ground, as is pepper, the most widely-consumed spice.

All true spices grow in the tropics, particularly in Asia and Africa. Cinnamon, cloves, nutmeg, pepper, and opium have been cultivated since medieval times in Ceylon, Malacca, and the Malabar Coast. For centuries these areas were exploited by Arabia, Venice, and Portugal, who amassed a great wealth by importing flavoring, meat preservative, and luxury spices to western Europe.

Measured by use and world trade, *pepper* is the leading spice and the United States is the leading consumer. Both black and white pepper are derived from a berry, known as *peppercorn,* that grows on a vine. India and Indonesia produce two-

thirds of the world's supply.

Vanilla comes from an *orchid,* which also grows on a vine. About two-thirds of the world production originates on islands off the southeast coast of Africa. Besides its well-known use as a flavoring, it is employed in the manufacture of chocolate, perfumes, and soap.

Cloves grow on trees that are native to Indonesia, though the bulk of world production now comes from Tanzania and the Malagasy Republic. While cloves have been used for centuries to flavor and decorate foods, two-thirds of the world's crop is now ground and mixed with cigarette tobacco.

Cinnamon, a popular flavoring, is derived from the bark of a tree grown in Asia. Its cousin *cassia* is similar, but is usually regarded as somewhat inferior. Trees that supply these spices belong to different but related species.

Nutmeg and *mace* grow on an evergreen tree—nutmeg is the seed, and mace is the membrane around it. Indonesia and the West Indies are the chief sources. Ground nutmeg has many uses in the food and beverage trade, and the oils of nutmeg and mace find their way into soaps, cosmetics, perfumes, confections, and pharmaceutical products.

Ginger, a pungent spice used widely for making ginger ale and for medicinal preparations, is derived from a root native to Asia. About one-half of the world's supply comes from India. Other sources are the west coast of Africa and Jamaica.

In addition to the true spices, there are many herbs and other plants that are commonly regarded as spices. Included among these are oregano, anise, caraway, cardamon, coriander, cumin, fennel, and mustard seed.
—Charles E. Rogers

Sugar, one of the carbohydrates, an important source of energy. Technically known as *sucrose,* it is produced commercially from sugarcane and sugarbeets. There are many types of sugar, notably *dextrose,* produced from corn, and *lactose,* produced from milk. Other sources of sugars are *honey, sugar maple trees, palm trees,* and *sorghum.* Sugars are produced in the leaves of green plants by photosyn-

thesis. Sugarcane and sugarbeets, which store sugar abundantly, have become the primary sources of sugar.

Sugarcane is a large perennial grass, which is produced in tropical and semitropical climates. Cuttings of the cane stalk, rather than seed, are used to propagate the crop. The cane attains heights of 10 to 20 feet. It is normally harvested 12 to 24 months after planting. For centuries, sugarcane was laboriously harvested by hand; today, the crop is often harvested by machine. The stalk is cut near the ground, and the top and the leaves are removed. The stalk or cane is shipped to a nearby sugar mill for processing. Normally, a number of crops may be cut from the same roots. It is not necessary, therefore, to replant every year.

The sugarbeet, a biennial plant, is produced in temperate climates. Normally, the crop is planted in the spring and harvested in the fall. Sugar is produced in its leaves and stored in its root. The crop is harvested by lifting the beet from the ground and removing the tops or leaves. Sugarbeet tops are fed to livestock. The root, or beet, is shipped to a nearby factory for processing.

Sugarcane is believed to have originated in the Orient, where its juice was valued hundreds of years before the birth of Christ. People are believed to have learned to produce sugar from sugarcane sometime about the fifth century. Much early trade revolved around sugar. Columbus introduced sugarcane to the New World on his second voyage.

The production of sugar from sugarbeets is a relatively recent development. In 1747, Andreas Marggraf, a German chemist, proved that sucrose could be extracted from sugarbeets. The world's first beet sugar factory began operating in Europe in 1802. The first successful sugarbeet operation was started in America in 1879.

Approximately 60 per cent of the sugar consumed in the United States is processed from sugarcane and sugarbeets produced by American farmers. The remaining 40 per cent is imported and then refined in the United States.

Per capita consumption of sugar in the United States is approximately 100 pounds a year. One-third of the sugar consumed is distributed through retail stores. The other two-thirds is distributed to food processors—bakers, bottlers, canners, confectioners, ice-cream manufacturers, and others—who use sugar as an ingredient in their products.

Sugar is an essential ingredient in many processed foods. In addition to its contribution as a sweetener, sugar can enhance the flavor, appearance, and texture of many foods. It performs many other purposes, one of which is that of a preservative.

—Nicholas Kominus

Sweeteners, Artificial, chemical compounds that are used for sweetening. They are also known as *synthetic, nonnutritive,* or *noncaloric sweeteners.* Artificial sweeteners have no nutritive value. They are primarily used in products for people who are overweight or have diabetes.

Saccharin, the first commercial artificial sweetener, is produced from coal tar. It was discovered by Ira Remson, an American chemist, in 1879. Its sweet taste, however, was discovered by Constantin Fahlberg, a German chemist working in Remson's laboratory, who obtained a patent on a process to manufacture saccharin. Commercial production began in 1901 in the United States.

Sodium cyclamate and *calcium cyclamate,* known as the cyclamates, are the major artificial sweeteners produced in the United States. Commercial production of the cyclamates began in 1950 in the United States.

Mixtures of saccharin and the cyclamates are also produced. *Cyclohexylsulfamic acid* is the third artificial sweetener to be used commercially in the United States.

Saccharin is generally considered to be 300 to 500 times sweeter than sugar. The cyclamates are considered to be 30 times as sweet as sugar.

Artificial sweeteners are produced in a number of plants located throughout the United States and many other countries. —Nicholas Kominus

Swine, omnivorous hoofed mammals that are a domesticated form of wild hog. The male is called a *boar,* the female a *sow,* the young female a *gilt,* the castrated male a *barrow,* the young a *pig.* In the United States, swine are kept primarily for meat and lard, with hides and bristles as side products. Hogs are especially desirable meat animals because pork can readily be preserved by pickling or by smoking. Furthermore, swine eat almost anything and can be raised under a variety of conditions. The animals also mature quickly and reproduce frequently with large litters,

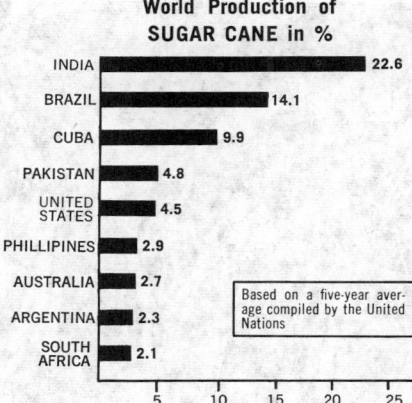

World Production of SUGAR CANE in %

INDIA	22.6
BRAZIL	14.1
CUBA	9.9
PAKISTAN	4.8
UNITED STATES	4.5
PHILLIPINES	2.9
AUSTRALIA	2.7
ARGENTINA	2.3
SOUTH AFRICA	2.1

Based on a five-year average compiled by the United Nations

so that they provide a large and steady supply of meat. Currently, hogs reach market weight in five or six months, and with recent advances in pig weaning and feeeding, sows can be bred three times a year. The gestation period averages 114 days, and sows come in heat about once every three weeks.

Various breeds of swine have different characteristics, although crosses are frequently preferred. Some breeds tend to produce more meat than others, but there are no distinctive meat or lard breeds. In general, the breeds which produce the most meat are the Yorkshire, Poland-China, Duroc, Tamworth, and Danish Landrace, and the recently developed American Landrace, Maryland #1, Minnesota #1, Minnesota #2, Beltsville #1, Beltsville #2, Montana #1, and Palouse. Other swine with varying advantages in size and hardiness are the Chester White, Berkshire, Hereford, and Spotted-Swine.

Swine gain best on formula rations containing corn, barley, sorghum, and alfalfa, with heavy supplements of vitamins, proteins, minerals, and antibiotics. Supplements should be added even when the swine are on pasture. Swine are susceptible to a wide range of diseases which, even when not fatal, sharply reduce rates of gain. Some diseases, such as brucellosis (abortion), atrophic rhinitis, influenza, and virus pneumonia, must be controlled by sanitation and sometimes by the slaughter of infected animals. Other diseases, such as erysipelas, leptospirosis, and hog cholera, can be prevented with vaccines. Swine parasites are mostly worms such as flukes, tapeworms, and roundworms. Roundworms cause the most trouble in the United States. Group treatment of swine produces the best

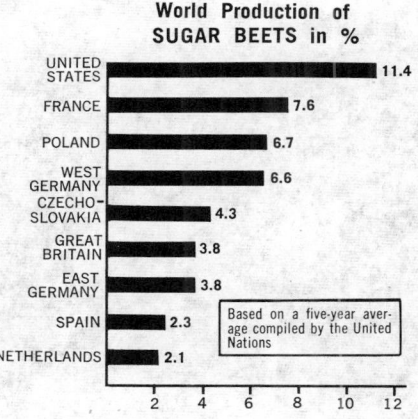

World Production of SUGAR BEETS in %

UNITED STATES	11.4
FRANCE	7.6
POLAND	6.7
WEST GERMANY	6.6
CZECHO-SLOVAKIA	4.3
GREAT BRITAIN	3.8
EAST GERMANY	3.8
SPAIN	2.3
NETHERLANDS	2.1

Based on a five-year average compiled by the United Nations

results. Treatment requires the use of dangerous chemicals and should be carefully undertaken. Effective vermifuges include phenothiazine, sodium fluoride, piperazine, and hydrocyin. *Trichina* are not serious in swine because recovery occurs rapidly as the worms enter the cyst state.

Swine belong to the genus *Sus,* with three species groups and several species subgroups.

—John T. Schlebecker

Tea, an evergreen shrub, its leaves, and the beverage brewed from these leaves. The tea plant, *Camellia sinensis,* whose leaves contain caffeine and tannin, grows widely in the humid tropics. Frequent rainfall, plentiful sunshine, and good soil fertility—conditions natural to Ceylon and India—are required for the best yields and quality. In Japan, organic fertilizers are widely used as plant nutrients, and yields have increased rapidly as a result. Tea is grown at varied elevations and on different terrains. Indian tea grows at elevations from 200 to 6,000 feet, particularly in the Darjeeling hill district. It is commonly grown on flat foothills in Latin America. In China, tea has been cultivated for centuries on almost vertical terraced banks, where natural irrigation can occur in areas of frequent rainfall. Tea is regarded as a plantation crop, but it is also frequently cultivated on small holdings and estates throughout Africa, Asia, and Latin America.

The three major varieties of tea are green, black, and oolong. Green, an unfermented leaf, is immediately toasted, while the black is fermented before being machine-toasted (Ceylon black dominates U.S. tea imports). Oolong is a semifermented leaf.

The tea plant reaches maturity 4 to 6 years after planting. Replanting is customary after about 60 yields per plant. The leaves are graded by size: the fine leaves near the end of the twig produce a high-quality tea, in contrast to coarse plucking.

India and Ceylon export 75 per cent of the world's tea, although 23 countries are rated as major producers. In 1964, India produced 823.8 million pounds of tea, 34 per cent of world production, and Ceylon produced 481.8 million pounds, or 20 per cent. About 92 per cent of the world's tea in 1964 was produced in Asia, while African and South American produc-

HAMPSHIRE SWINE REGISTRY

AMERICAN YORKSHIRE CLUB

SWINE provide a variety of pork and pork products. The Hampshire sow (*left*) is recognized as an excellent lard producer. The Yorkshire hog (*right*) is prized for its quality bacon.

U.S. DEPARTMENT OF AGRICULTURE

VEGETABLES are always available in U.S. markets. Cabbages (*right*) are grown in a climate good year-round, and snap beans (*center*) are bred for adaptability to fresh, frozen, or canned sales. Potato fields (*left*) produce the largest-selling crop.

tion, increasing in recent years, contributed the other 8 per cent.

The United Kingdom, the world's largest tea-drinking area, consumed 537 million pounds in 1964, half of it from India. Great Britain's tea consumption leads the world at 10 pounds per capita. In contrast, Americans, though increasing their consumption of tea and instant tea, used only 0.69 pounds per capita in 1964. United States tea imports, mostly from Ceylon, amounted to one-quarter of the United Kingdom's total.

Tea quotas had been controlled by agreement of producing countries under the International Tea Arrangement from the 1930's to 1955. Recently, prices of tea have been stable. Record world production of tea in 1964 resulted from widespread use of pesticides, fertilizers, and crop-substituting plans, such as Ceylon's "rubber into tea" replanting scheme.
—Marshall H. Cohen

Tobacco, a herbaceous plant of the nightshade family whose leaves are used extensively for smoking and chewing and as snuff. The origin of tobacco was well symbolized by the cigar-store Indian, a hallmark of tobacco shops in earlier generations. The American Indian introduced tobacco to the first white colonists in North America in the fifteenth and sixteenth centuries. He taught the Europeans how to use the leaf in forms common today—for smoking, chewing, and snuff. The fundamentals of cultivation were known by the Indian and passed on to the white man.

Today tobacco is grown in 22 states of the United States. Three-quarters of the crop comes from five states: North Carolina, Kentucky, Virginia, Tennessee, and South Carolina. There are six main classifications of tobacco leaf, according to the U.S. Department of Agriculture: flue-cured, fire-cured, air-cured, cigar-filler, cigar-binder, and cigar-wrapper. The United States leads the world in tobacco production and export, followed by China, India, the Soviet Union, and Japan. The world's annual harvest amounts to 9.5 billion pounds.

Labor input to grow an acre of to-

bacco exceeds 400 man-hours, contrasted with only 8 for wheat. Seeds are planted in seedbeds protected by cloth covering, and the seedlings that emerge are transplanted to the field in the spring, from March to May. After 90 to 100 days, the crop is harvested, then cured and sold at auction. It takes 1.25 billion pounds of domestic tobacco to manufacture the number of cigarettes produced annually in the United States—a total of 565 billion in all. —Charles E. Rogers

Turkey, an edible game bird native to North America, now almost entirely raised on farms. Of the many turkey varieties, only the Broad-Breasted Bronze, the Broad-Breasted Large White, and the Beltsville Small White are raised in commercial quantities. Much emphasis has been given by turkey breeders to wide breasts and overall meatiness. The Beltsville Small White is a relatively small, broad-breasted bird raised for use by small families. Marketed at about 5 months, the live *hens*, or females, weigh about 9 pounds; the *toms*, or males, about 16. The large

U.S. DEPARTMENT OF AGRICULTURE

BELTSVILLE TURKEYS, bred for small ovens, have extra meat on their bodies.

broad-breasted varieties weigh about twice as much or more when marketed. Turkeys were traditionally popular, chiefly for holiday consumption, although they are now available and used throughout the year. Reproduction in turkeys is relatively low due to poor egg production, fertility, and hatchability. Eggs hatch after 28 days of incubation. *Blackhead,* a major disease in turkeys, especially when kept with chickens, is caused by a microscopic parasite which attacks the cecum and liver. Pullorum and fowl typhoid used to cause heavy losses but these diseases now have been largely eliminated through blood testing. To help prevent losses from diseases and parasites, sanitary practices should be followed and chickens and turkeys should not be raised together. —Carl W. Hess

Vegetable, any one of a large number of herbaceous plants cultivated for food. The precise definition of a vegetable is troublesome. No single botanic or economic description is adequate or clear-cut. We shall consider vegetables as annual or semiannual crops (excepting asparagus or artichokes) that have an edible fleshy portion. Thus, some plants that botanically are fruit (as tomatoes and melons) are included.

As in few other nations of the world, fresh domestic vegetables are available the year-round in the United States. This is due to two factors: a wide range of climate, which permits vegetables to be harvested every day of the year somewhere in the country, and an efficient marketing system.

Vegetable production, like other phases of agriculture, is becoming more specialized. Therefore, production is becoming concentrated in fewer but larger farms. These generally are found in areas of temperate climate (excepting potatoes), good soil, and ample supplies of rain or other sources of water. Production is also becoming more mechanized; labor problems have led to special interest in mechanical harvesting.

The farm value of the U.S. commercial vegetable crop ranges widely from year to year but tends to average between $1.5 and $2 billion. The five most important states in terms of value of production are, in the order named, California (about 25 per cent of the total), Florida (about 10 per cent), New York, Idaho, and Maine. The latter two states are preeminent in potatoes. Other leading vegetable-producing states are Texas, Wisconsin, Arizona, Michigan, New Jersey, Oregon, and Washington. The most important single crop is the white potato, followed by tomatoes and lettuce. Other vegetables in approximate order of importance include snap beans, string beans, sweet corn, onions, cantaloupes, celery, cucumbers, carrots, cabbage, green peas, sweet potatoes, and watermelons.

Vegetables are either marketed fresh or shipped for processing. Some potatoes are also used for feed and seed. While more than half of the vegetable crop has been sold fresh in the past, processing is becoming more important. The most common forms of processing are canning and freezing; dehydration is of lesser importance. Potato products such as chips, shoestrings, and frozen French fries are of special significance. New techniques, such as freeze-drying, may play a greater role in the future.

Total vegetable consumption, or apparent use, is about 340 pounds per person per year; nearly one-third of this figure is represented by potatoes (these figures are in farm-weight terms, but allow for imports and exports). Consumption of fresh vegetables is decreasing while that of processed vegetables is increasing. Trends for the many individual vegetables vary: consumption of cabbage, for example, appears to be decreasing while that of salad vegetables, such as lettuce, has been increasing. Potatoes had been going through a long downward trend until a few years ago, when consumption leveled off.

—Dana G. Dalrymple

Wheat, the most widely cultivated *cereal*. It is grown around the world, with the Soviet Union, United States, China, Canada, and France leading in production. From 1955 to 1959 the average world production was 9.3 billion bushels, grown on 493,010,000 acres. Since wheat is a cool-season crop, most of these acres are situated

World Production of WHEAT in %

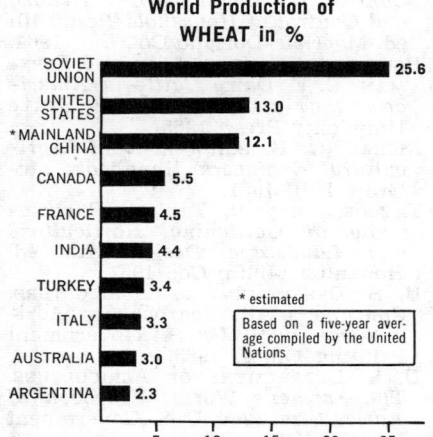

	%
SOVIET UNION	25.6
UNITED STATES	13.0
*MAINLAND CHINA	12.1
CANADA	5.5
FRANCE	4.5
INDIA	4.4
TURKEY	3.4
ITALY	3.3
AUSTRALIA	3.0
ARGENTINA	2.3

* estimated

Based on a five-year average compiled by the United Nations

LOOK MAGAZINE

WHEAT, the most widely cultivated cereal, is grown primarily in the climates of the Northern Hemisphere. Here, combines completely process a Kansas wheat crop.

in the Northern Hemisphere. The leading producers in the United States are Kansas, North Dakota, Montana, Oklahoma, and Washington.

Botanists count 15 species of wheat, of which three are generally grown in the United States—*common, durum,* and *club.* However, 95 per cent of the wheat produced in the United States belongs to the first-named species.

There are two principal types of wheat: *winter wheat,* planted in the fall, and *spring wheat,* planted in the spring. Another classification divides wheat into soft and hard varieties.

The soft varieties are grown in the eastern half of the United States and in the states of Washington, Oregon, and Idaho; the hard winter wheats account for most of the production on the central plains, while most of the wheat grown on the northern plains is of the hard spring varieties. When it was realized in the late nineteenth century that soft wheats could not withstand the temperatures and droughts of the plains, plant breeders sought adaptive varieties. Cerealists such as Mark A. Carleton of the U.S. Department of Agriculture learned that the hard winter wheats grown on the steppes of southern Russia were adaptable. He visited Russia and brought back a winter variety known as *Kharkov,* as well as a spring-grown durum wheat. In Canada, William Saunders and his sons bred a hard spring wheat known as *Marquis.* Using these varieties and others as parent stocks, wheat breeders have developed the wheats that now account for much of the nation's production.

Whatever the variety, the wheat plant consists of a root system, leaves,

stem, and heads or spikes. The roots ordinarily reach to a depth of 5–6 feet, while the stems vary from 2 to 5 feet. The heads bearing the kernels are usually 2 to 4 inches in length; the kernels are small and oval, consisting of a protective coating, a starchy endosperm, and the germ.

Wheat grows best on well-drained medium-to-heavy soils, especially silt and clay loams. Farmers living in humid areas prepare a seedbed by means of moldboard plows, spiketooth harrows, and disks; in the more arid Western states, they use adapted cultivators and blades. Farmers in both areas sow wheat by means of tractor-drawn drills.

Winter wheat, which is planted in September or October, is harvested in June and July, while spring wheat, planted in April, is harvested in July and August. Whereas 40 years ago most of the wheat crop was cut with a binder and threshed by a threshing machine, today more than 95 per cent of the crop is cut and threshed.

Wheat is subject to attack by rusts and smuts. Stem rust, which has been particularly destructive on the Great Plains, has been checked by the development of rust-resistant varieties, such as *Thatcher,* which was developed by the Minnesota Agricultural Experiment Station. Insect enemies include the Hessian fly, wheat jointworm, grasshopper, and the wheat-stem sawfly. To combat the attacks of the latter, Canadian cerealists developed the *Rescue* variety with solid rather than hollow stems.

Wheat is used principally for human consumption. The hard varieties, richer in protein than the others, produce flour that is used in the making of bread. Flour from the soft wheats is suitable for pastries, crackers, biscuits, and cakes. Durum wheat is used for the manufacture of macaroni, spaghetti, and vermicelli. Some wheat is converted into breakfast foods.

Wheat is nutritious. The average kernel contains about 70 per cent carbohydrates, 12 per cent protein, 2 per cent fat, 12 per cent water, 1.8 per cent mineral matter, and 2.2 per cent cellulose. The protein content of the hard wheats of the Great Plains may be as high as 15 per cent. A kernel also contains vitamins of the B-group, such as thiamine, riboflavin, and niacin.

Wheat is an important article of international trade. The United States exports more than half of its crop; in 1964 this amounted to approximately 675 million bushels. The other leading exporters are Canada, Australia, and the Soviet Union. Major importers are the United Kingdom, India, Japan, West Germany, and Brazil. (See also *Flour Milling*.)

—Robert G. Dunbar

Wool, a major textile fiber derived from the soft coat of a domesticated sheep. Its chief use is in outer apparel and household articles, such as blankets, with the manufacture of carpets and rugs utilizing a lesser amount. Wool is broadly classed as apparel or carpet quality. It is the seventh largest commodity in world trade.

U.S. DEPARTMENT OF AGRICULTURE

NEWLY SHORN SHEEP have surrendered their winter coat of wool in anticipation of the summer's warmth. These English sheep are raised primarily for high-grade mutton.

In the decade after 1955, world production of wool gained about 15 per cent to approximately 5.75 billion pounds (grease basis). Consumption rose by about one-fourth. Wool's share of total world fiber consumption dipped slightly, however, as the overall total rose and the use of newly developed man-made fibers increased.

Australia, which grows more than 1.7 billion pounds (grease basis) annually (almost entirely of apparel wool), is the world's largest producer, and has nearly 160 million sheep. Other leading producers of apparel-class wool, in order of importance, are New Zealand, Argentina, South Africa, the United States, Uruguay, and Great Britain. The Soviet Union is considered the second largest producer, and while its wool has been coarse, the output of apparel types is believed to be growing. Others in the coarse-wool category are The People's Republic of China, India, and Pakistan.

Wool has natural crimp and elasticity. It absorbs water vapor readily, but many wool articles resist wetting by liquid water. Wool dyes easily in a wide variety of fast colors. Wool garments impart a feeling of warmth, yet lightweight wool apparel is comfortable in hot weather. It has been said that if a fiber with wool's attributes had just been invented, it would lead the list of so-called miracle fibers. Also regarded as wool-type fibers are the specialty hairs such as mohair, cashmere, camel's hair, and vicuña.

Sorting of fleeces and scouring (washing) of the wool are the first steps in processing that leads to spinning. There are two spinning systems: woolen and worsted. The woolen system makes use of the shorter fibers. Woolen yarns are usually soft and lofty with relatively little twist and the individual fibers lie in all directions. In the worsted system, the aim is to lay the fibers as parallel as possible. The resulting yarn is firmer or harder and is given more twist than woolen yarn. Fabrics made of these two types of yarns are called woolens and worsteds.

Woolens, often used in sportswear and coats, lend themselves to a variety of colors and often have a woolly or hairy surface, which mutes and diffuses the colors and patterns. Fabrics usually made with woolen yarns include tweeds, meltons, coverts, and fleeces. Worsted fabrics, which usually are crisp and springy with little or no surface fiber, include serge, gabardine, and whipcord.

The United States, Great Britain, Italy, and Japan are among the largest manufacturers of wool. Though there has been a severe decrease in the number of mills and amount of wool machinery and a decline in cloth production since World War II, the American industry is regarded as the most efficient in the world, and it leads in the development of products made of wool blended with the new noncellulosic man-made fibers. For example, wool/polyester tropical cloth is the basic quality fabric for summer clothing. Producers make man-made

fibers especially for the various systems of textile processing, so the trend to blends is expected to continue. (See also, *Sheep*.)

—Gordon F. Graham

Yeast, a fungus growth consisting of tiny cells of vegetable matter that collect in a frothy, yellowish cluster. There are hundreds of species, widely distributed in nature, each strain possessing distinctive characteristics, properties, and uses. The most familiar species, *Saccharomyces cerevisiae*, is used to prepare cultures adapted specifically for the baker, the brewer, and the manufacturer of primary food yeast. Yeast has been utilized since ancient times as a leavening property in baking, as a fermenting agent in alcoholic beverages, and as a medicine and food. The ability of yeast to change sugar to alcohol makes it indispensable to brewers and distillers.

The yeast organism is grown in a suitable medium and harvested when a sufficient crop of cells has appeared. In former times it was grown from *wort* (an Old English word meaning herb, plant, or root) prepared from grains mashed in water. More recently, primary yeast has been cultivated from refuse material.

—Charles E. Rogers

BIBLIOGRAPHY

Anderson, Arthur L. and Kiser, James J. *Introductory Animal Science*. The Macmillan Co., 1963.

Bear, Firman E. editor. *Chemistry of the Soil*. 2nd ed. Reinhold Publishing Corp., 1964.

Bear, Firman E. *Earth, the Stuff of Life*. University of Oklahoma Press, 1962.

Borgstrom, Georg. *The Hungry Planet: the Modern World at the Edge of Famine*. The Macmillan Co., 1965.

Brewbaker, James L. *Agricultural Genetics*. Prentice-Hall, Inc., 1964.

Laverton, Sylvia. *Irrigation, its Profitable Use for Agricultural and Horticultural Crops*. Oxford University Press, 1964.

Leonard, Warren H. and Martin, John H. *Cereal Crops*. The Macmillan Co., 1963.

Mallis, Arnold. *Handbook of Pest Control; the Behavior, Life History and Control of Household Pests*. 4th ed. MacNair-Dorland Co., Inc., 1964.

Porter, A. R., Sims, J. A., and Foreman, C. F. *Dairy Cattle in American Agriculture*. Iowa State University Press, 1965.

Richey, C. B. editor-in-chief. *Agricultural Engineers' Handbook*. McGraw-Hill, 1961.

Taylor, Norman. *Taylor's Encyclopedia of Gardening, Horticulture and Landscape Design*. 4th ed. Houghton Mifflin Co., 1961.

U. S. Department of Agriculture. *Consumers All; Yearbook of Agriculture, 1965*. U. S. Government Printing Office, 1965.

U. S. Department of Agriculture. *The Farmer's World; Yearbook of Agriculture, 1964*. U. S. Government Printing Office, 1964.

Definition.—Agronomy is defined by the American Society of Agronomy as "the theory and practice of field-crop production and soil management." In several countries of Europe and South America, however, agronomy takes on a much broader meaning. In these countries, agriculture is divided into agronomy and animal science, with all phases of plant science, including horticulture, plant pathology, entomology, crop and soil science, combined into agronomy.

Agronomy is a specialized phase of several sciences. It includes soil physics (structural properties of the soil, aeration, and water movement), soil chemistry (physical and biochemical reactions that take place in the soil), soil microbiology (activities and decomposition products of microorganisms), soil fertility (factors affecting the availability of nutrients and the use of fertilizers), soil morphology and genesis (soil formation, classification, and survey), and soil conservation and management (controlling erosion and improving productivity).

History.—Technologically speaking, man has developed greatly; but he is still dependent upon the soil for many of his requirements. Although agronomy is very old, the greatest progress in it has been made only since the 1920's. There are myriads of problems yet to be solved.

The dawn of civilization is frequently recognized as the point at which man recognized that seeds could be planted and a crop grown. He quickly observed that plants grew better in some soils than in others. This was the beginning of soil science. Many references are made to soils and problems of crop production in very early literature. In the Greek epic the *Odyssey*, Homer (who is supposed to have lived at some time between 900 and 700 B.C.) tells how Odysseus, the far wanderer, was recognized at his homecoming by Argos, his faithful hound, who

was "lying on a heap of dung with which the thralls were wont to manure the land."

Acid soil conditions (sour soils), a major problem in many areas of the world today, were recognized by the Greeks between 800 and 600 B.C. They recommended application of *marl* (a mixture of clay and calcium carbonate) and shells to overcome this condition, a practice that was adopted by the Romans.

Theophrastus (c. 372–287 B.C.) recommended the abundant manuring of thin soils, but suggested that manure be used sparingly on rich soils. He was one of the first men to recognize the fertilizing value of saltpeter (potassium nitrate); he also recognized differences in the fertilizing values of manures, listing them in the following order of decreasing value: human, swine, goat, sheep, cow, ox, and horse. The importance of growing legumes to improve the soil condition for crops was advocated in the writings of Vergil (70–19 B.C.).

About 1500 interest began to develop in the study of the factors influencing plant growth. Francis Bacon (1561–1626) suggested that water was the principal nourishment of plants, with soil serving only as a support. This concept was substantiated by the famous Flemish physician and chemist Jan Baptista van Helmont (1577–1644), who conducted an experiment by placing 200 pounds of soil in an earthen container. In this soil he planted a five-pound willow tree. He shielded the container from dust and added only water. Five years later, the tree had increased in weight to almost 170 pounds, but the soil had decreased only about two ounces in weight. Van Helmont therefore concluded that water was the only nutrient needed for plant growth.

The discovery of oxygen by Joseph Priestley in 1774 stimulated Nicolas Théodore de Saussure (1767–1845), a Swiss naturalist, to begin studying the effects of air on plant growth.

As a result of this study, he was able to demonstrate that plants absorb oxygen and emit carbon dioxide (the process of respiration). He also showed that plants kept in an atmosphere lacking carbon dioxide will die, because they need the carbon dioxide for the process of photosynthesis. De Saussure also wondered about the origin of mineral salts found within plants.

Great advances toward answering this question were made by the brilliant German chemist Justus von Liebig and the two British scientists Sir John Bennet Lawes and Sir Joseph Henry Gilbert during the period 1840 to 1850. Through their efforts, information was gained about the elements required for plant growth. Liebig demonstrated that the plant obtains oxygen, hydrogen, and carbon dioxide from water and air. He also proposed the "law of the minimum," which states that plant growth (and subsequent yield of crops) is limited by the least plentiful nutrient element, providing all other nutrients are present in adequate quantities. Lawes and Gilbert showed that all plants require phosphorus and potassium and that all nonlegumes require nitrogen. They also established the famous Rothamsted Experiment Station—the first agricultural experiment station—which is still one of the outstanding research centers.

Soils.—There are so many definitions of soil that it is difficult to select any one as best. The following definition, however, is widely accepted by soil scientists: *Soil* is a naturally occurring body, three-dimensional in nature, formed at the earth's surface through the action of weathering processes on soil-forming materials (rocks and minerals), under the influence of climatic and biotic factors (plant and animal life). Soil is sometimes described as having the same relation to the earth that an orange peel has to an orange. The orange peel, however, is uniform in compo-

U.S. DEPARTMENT OF AGRICULTURE

SOIL SCIENTISTS at the turn of the century (*left*) lacked the tools and equipment to do as complete a soil study as today's specialists.

sition and thickness, which is not true of soil. Since the parent materials vary widely in composition and since the effects of climate, geologic age, *topography* (geographic features), and biotic factors are variable, soils vary. They may be reddish (because of iron deposits), such as those found in many tropical and subtropical areas (Brazil, India, Hawaii, and the southeastern United States), or they may be black, such as those found in many temperate areas (the northern part of the United States, Canada, and Russia). Soils vary in texture from coarse sand to fine clay; they may be shallow or deep. However, every soil consists of mineral and organic matter, water, and air. It is the link between the rock core of the earth and life on the surface.

The composition of soils varies with depth. A cross section of a soil reveals a series of zones, each somewhat different from the one above and the one beneath. Each of these zones is called a *horizon*, which is defined as a layer of soil, approximately parallel to the land surface, with observable characteristics. A typical soil has three major horizons: the A-horizon, the B-horizon, and the C-horizon. The *A-horizon* is the zone closest to the surface of the earth. Since water-soluble materials are carried downward through the A-horizon by soil water (a process called "leaching," the A-horizon is also called the "zone of leaching." The *B-horizon* lies directly below the A-horizon. Since soil water drains into the B-horizon from above and also rises into the B-horizon from below (high rates of evaporation cause the soil water to be drawn upward) to deposit water-soluble materials, this horizon is often called the "zone of accumulation." The *C-horizon* is a zone of partially broken and decomposed rock or mineral material. Some of the original *bedrock* (parent material) minerals may still be present, but most have been converted into other forms. The C-horizon continues downward to blend into the unweathered bedrock.

All three soil horizons develop from the underlying parent material. When the material is first exposed at the surface, weathering and decomposition proceed rapidly. While the decomposed material increases, downward-percolating water leaches out some of the minerals and begins to deposit them farther down. In this way, the A-horizon and the B-horizon are built up. As the weathering process continues, the bedrock material gives rise to the C-horizon; as time passes, the C-horizon reaches deeper into the bedrock and the B-horizon and A-horizon grow deeper.

Soil Classification.—The classification of soils is very important in identifying and associating their significant characteristics. For example, the thickness and characteristics of the horizons (depth of profile) will determine the amounts of nutrients and water that will be available to plants. Strongly acid or compact subsoils may not allow plant roots to penetrate deeply. Restricting the roots to the surface horizon greatly reduces the volume of soil available to plants as a storehouse of moisture in dry periods.

Soils with similar characteristics, such as parent material, topography, thickness of horizons, and presence of compact layers, may be grouped into a *series*. For easy identification, soil series are given names, usually a geographical term relating to the place where the soil is first defined. The soil series is, in turn, divided into soil *types* and *phases*. The *soil type* identifies the texture of the surface soil. The full name of a soil type includes both the name of the soil series and the textural class of the surface soil down to "plow depth," which is usually the upper six inches of soil. A *phase* indicates a specific condition important in the use and management of the soil. For example, in the soil classed as *Cecil clay loam, sloping eroded phase, Cecil* is the series name, *clay loam* denotes the soil type, and *sloping eroded* indicates that the surface horizon is not as deep as usual for this soil type and is on sloping land.

■**SOIL SURVEYS.**—There are several thousand kinds of soil, many of them surveyed and mapped. In the United States, soil surveys are made cooperatively by the Soil Conservation Service of the Department of Agriculture, agricultural experiment stations, and other state and federal agencies. The United Nations Food and Agriculture Organization (FAO)

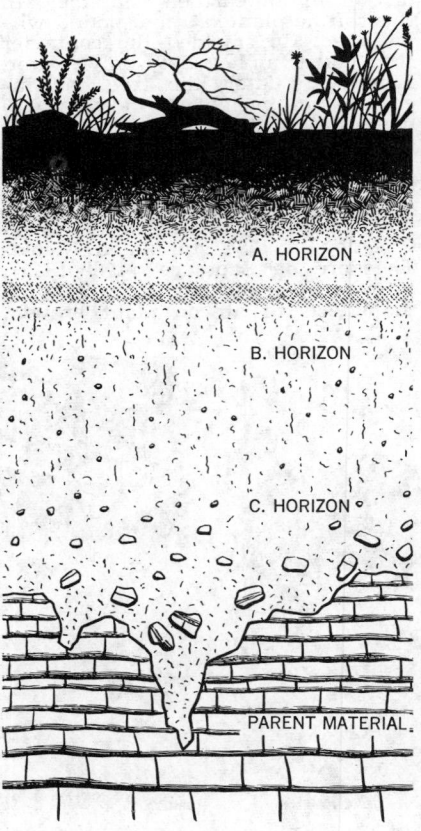

SOIL HORIZONS fall into three categories.

supports soil surveys in many countries as a step toward increasing food production. This group is also working on a world soil-survey program.

A land capability system has been developed by the Soil Conservation Service to aid farmers in planning their cropping programs. Land conditions, such as slope, degree of erosion, depth of topsoil, and drainage, greatly influence soil productivity and management requirements. As an aid in the selection of management practices, the soil series are grouped into capability classes, subclasses, and units. *Land capability classes* denote magnitude of hazards and limitations; *land capability subclasses* refer to kinds of hazards; and *land capability units* are management groupings for specific purposes.

There are eight land capability classes: I through IV are suitable for cultivation; V through VIII are better adapted to pasture, woodland, or wildlife uses. Each of the subclasses is designated by a letter to indicate the major kind of hazard. The letter *e* indicates an erosion problem; *w*, a water problem; and *s*, drought or low fertility. The capability unit is a division of the subclass and is designated by a number.

Soil Fertility.—Sixteen chemical elements are presently recognized as essential for plant growth. The test of essentiality is that a plant must have the element in order to complete its life cycle. Three of the essential elements—carbon, hydrogen, and oxygen—make up over 90 per cent of a plant. All three are obtained by the plant from water and air. The remaining thirteen essential elements are obtained from the soil.

Soil fertility includes the supply of the thirteen nutrient elements in the soil, plus the capacity of the soil to provide and transmit these elements to the plant over a period of time. Of the elements obtained from the soil, the primary elements—nitrogen, phosphorus, and potassium—are consumed in the largest quantities. The secondary elements are calcium, magnesium, and sulfur; the *micronutrients* (referred to as *minor elements* or *trace elements*), manganese, iron, copper, zinc, boron, molybdenum, and chlorine. The micronutrients are required only in very small quantities. Large amounts of several of these, including boron, manganese, and copper, will create a *toxic* soil condition.

■**FERTILITY MANAGEMENT.**—Soil-fertility management includes several objectives. One of these is to manage the soil in such a manner that during the growing season it will release amounts of nutrient elements adequate for the desired yield. A second objective is to avoid losses of nutrient elements through downward leaching by water, through excess uptake of the elements by plants, and through fixation by the soil into forms only slightly available to plants. A third objective is to overcome nutrient deficiencies and acidity in order that plant roots may utilize the maximum volume of soil.

LOUDON COUNTY, TENNESSEE - SHEET NUMBER 15

U.S. DEPARTMENT OF AGRICULTURE

COLOR CHARTS are used to identify the various soil layers. Once the soil scientist has classified the many soil layers in a region, he then prepares a special area map for use.

When soil fertility limits the yield obtained from a particular soil, one or more essential elements are deficient. The total amount of an element present in the soil does not indicate the amount available to a plant, for there are numerous factors that determine how much of a given element is able to be absorbed. These factors include moisture, aeration, acidity or alkalinity, presence of competing elements, and nature of the plant itself.

Since soils are developed through the weathering of rocks and minerals, geologic age influences soil fertility. Young soils usually contain mineral fragments that, with continued weathering, release nutrient elements for plant use. Very old, highly weathered soils, on the other hand, have more or less reached a state in which the rate of release of nutrient elements is slow. The number of years a soil has been cultivated also influences the fertility status. Poorly managed soil that has been permitted to erode may have very low fertility, even though it is geologically young. Well-managed soils, on which commercial fertilizers have been used correctly, may actually be much more fertile than they were in their virgin state, even though they are geologically old.

Contrasting soil situations are those in India and in the southeastern United States. The soils of India are young from a geologic viewpoint. They have, however, been farmed for centuries or more without any appreciable addition of commercial fertilizers. This has created widespread nutrient deficiencies. In contrast, the Piedmont region of the southeastern United States has some of the oldest soils, geologically speaking, in the world. These soils were highly weathered when the settlers first came to America—deficient in nitrogen, phosphorus, and potassium. Nevertheless, through judicious management and the proper application of various commercial fertilizers, many of these soils have been to some extent enriched and are presently relatively fertile.

Organic Content.—Organic-matter content frequently shows direct correlation with the fertility level of the soil. Organic matter accumulates in the soil through the centuries from plant and animal residues. Conditions conducive to good plant growth in virgin soil usually carry over into cultivated conditions. The breakdown of the organic matter releases nutrients accumulated by the native plants for use by the cultivated plants. Decomposition of organic matter is usually rapid during the first few years the land is under cultivation, then levels off. Erosion, of course, rapidly removes topsoil and organic matter, upsetting the equilibrium.

Soils developed under poor drainage conditions, such as *peat* and *muck*, are frequently very high in organic matter content. Such soils, however, are usually very low in minerals and also deficient in nitrogen. Draining such areas does not result in fertile soils, although good management and judicious use of fertilizer and lime can lead to good production.

Sandy soils do not usually contain as much organic matter as finer-textured soils do. Since nitrogen is released into soil through the decomposition of organic matter, sandy soils are frequently deficient in nitrogen. Pores are larger in sandy soils than in finer-textured soils, but the total pore space is less. This means that water will penetrate a sandy soil to a greater depth than it would a finer-textured soil. Thus, leaching of soluble nutrient elements, such as nitrogen in the form of nitrates, is more common in sandy soils than in silt loams or clay loams.

Toxic Soils.—Many soil conditions are toxic to plant growth. The more widespread natural toxic conditions (rather than those caused by the application of chemicals by man for the purpose of controlling such pests as weeds, insects, and nematodes) include acid, saline, and alkali soils.

Acid soils, old and highly weathered, are usually found in humid regions. They are low in calcium and magnesium and frequently are high in iron and aluminum, which form complex compounds with phosphorus. Some plants tolerate more acidity than others do. Blueberries, camellias, and azaleas grow better in acid soils, since iron and manganese are more readily available. Legumes, on the other hand, grow better in soils adequately supplied with calcium and magnesium and with a pH near neutrality. (A pH of 7 indicates neutrality; a pH above 7 shows alkalinity; and one below 7 shows acidity—thus, the lower the pH, the greater the acidity.) Acidity, as such, is not important to the immediate growth of plants unless the aluminum content is high enough to be toxic. If the aluminum content is low and sufficient nutrients, such as calcium and magnesium, are supplied, most plants can tolerate considerable acidity (to a pH of at least 4.0). Most plants, however, prefer a soil condition that is only slightly acid, where adequate quantities of calcium and magnesium are available (pH 6.0–7.0). The majority of nutrient elements are most available in a slightly acid soil.

A *saline soil* is one in which there has been such an accumulation of soluble salts that plant growth is reduced or stopped. Saline soils are most common in the drier regions of the world, where the rainfall is not sufficient to wash the soluble salts through the soil profile and into the groundwater. In the United States, most saline soils are found west of the Missouri River. Local areas in the more humid regions may also become saline. Severe windstorms, such as hurricanes, may cover tidewater areas with salt water. Salt accumulations in soils can also result from seepage from drainage ditches in which salt water has "backed up." Irrigation water may contain enough soluble salts to cause a saline condition if the salts accumulate in a particular area of the soil profile, such as the immediate surface. One of the most common localized saline conditions is caused by the improper application of fertilizer; the soluble nitrogen and potassium salts in the fertilizer may reduce growth or kill seedlings.

Good drainage through the soil profile is the first requirement for reclamation of saline soil. To reclaim such a soil, the soluble salts must be drained and washed from the profile to a depth of at least three feet. If the salts are predominately sodium, gypsum must be applied at the rate of two or three tons per acre before leaching. If the soil is *calcareous* (has excess calcium carbonate), it is likely to be deficient in phosphorus because calcium carbonate and phosphorus form tri-calcium phosphate, which is not readily available to plants.

An *alkali soil* has either a high degree of alkalinity (*p*H 8.5 or above) or a high percentage of exchangeable sodium (15 per cent or higher), or both, acting to reduce or stop growth of most crop plants. The exchangeable sodium, when present in sufficient quantities, causes the soil to run together when wet and to become hard when dry. Alkali soils usually evolve from saline conditions in which the soluble salts are predominately sodium.

To improve alkali conditions, the sodium must be replaced with calcium. Gypsum (calcium sulfate) is best for this purpose unless the soil is calcareous, in which case sulfur is used. As with saline soils, adequate drainage is necessary for reclamation of alkali soils.

Soil Testing.—Ever since Justus von Liebig (1803–1873) demonstrated that mineral elements are required for plant growth, there has been much interest in soil analysis as a method of evaluating soil fertility and ascertaining the nutrient deficiencies likely to occur. Early attempts at soil analysis were generally unsatisfactory, but much progress has been made since the 1930's. Today there is strong evidence that competent use of soil tests can make a valuable contribution to intelligent soil management. Soil tests are being conducted on all continents, and hundreds of thousands of soil samples are analyzed annually.

Information gained from soil testing is used in many ways. One of the more important objectives is to group soils into classes in order to formulate the best practices when adding fertilizer and lime. The amount of plant nutrients needed is related to the crop grown and the levels of available nutrients in the soil. A second important objective is to predict the probability of a profitable response to the application of plant nutrients. A third objective is to help evaluate soil productivity. The organic-matter content, level of nutrient elements, and *p*H of the soil have been found to be good guides in estimating the potential productivity of soils. Still another valuable objective is to determine

specific soil conditions that may be improved by the addition of soil amendments, such as manures, chemical fertilizers, and lime.

In conducting a soil testing program, there are six major phases that should be carefully considered. These phases are: securing representative soil samples (a poorly taken sample may be worse than none at all); adequate research to correlate the testing procedure with crop response on the type of soils to be tested; satisfactory chemical procedures (the technique used must be accurate and reproducible); interpretation of the results; recommendations based on the interpretation of the test results and other information that is available; and follow-up to see that the reports are understood and that the recommendations can be followed.

A wide range of values has been assigned to soil testing, from merely psychological to cure-all. The value of a soil test is as a good source of information that must be properly interpreted for use in soil management.

Soil Improvement.—Soil consists of inorganic (mineral) and organic matter, water, and air. The inorganic fraction of the soil usually constitutes one-half of the total volume of most surface soils. The organic portion is usually less than 5 per cent (it is higher in peat or muck soils). The remainder consists of water and air. The actual proportions of these four major components vary greatly with depth and type of soil. The proportion of air to water also fluctuates greatly within the same soil from season to season and even from day to day.

The inorganic fraction is frequently divided into size groups referred to as *separates*. The coarser material (larger than 2.0 millimeters) is classed as *gravel* or *stones*, and is not usually included in the discussion of particle size, except to designate a soil as "stony phase" if there are enough stones to warrant recognition. Particles less than 2.0 millimeters in diameter are grouped into *sand* (2.0 to 0.05 millimeters in diameter), *silt* (0.05 to 0.002 millimeters), and *clay* (less than 0.002 millimeters). Sand particles may be observed with the naked eye, but an electron microscope must be used to observe the fine clay particles.

Except for sand grains, soil particles do not usually occur singly. Instead, many fine particles may be grouped into a *cluster,* which is a secondary structural unit referred to as an *aggregate*. The aggregates may be arranged in *platy* blocks or cubes (often referred to as *granular* or *crumb*) or in *columns* (*prisms*). Arrangement of the individual grains or aggregates in the soil is referred to as *soil structure*. The size and shape of the pore space of the soil is largely determined by the structure. So are the movement of air and water through the soil and the capacity of the soil to hold water and air.

Improving the soil structure is a slow and tedious process. It is, therefore, better to maintain soil in a good physical condition than to try to improve the structure later. Freezing

and thawing, wetting (swelling) and drying (shrinkage) are important forces in determining soil structure. Aggregates, once formed, must be stable when wet. Soil organic matter, with products formed through activities of microorganisms, is very important in the stabilization of soil structure.

Soil structure is frequently destroyed by *compaction* with heavy machinery, such as rubber-tired tractors. Plowing or cultivating the soil when it is too wet will destroy good structure and result in a puddled condition. A driving rain on a freshly plowed field will have the same effect. One of the big problems in maintaining golf greens and tees is the compaction and puddling caused by avid golfers playing when the soil is wet. Working the soil excessively when it is dry, as with a disc, creates a loose, powdery condition that also destroys desirable structure.

Tilling the soil at the correct moisture level is very important in maintaining the desired physical condition. Rotation of sod with row crops gives the soil a "rest" and, through wetting, drying, freezing, and thawing, will improve the structure.

Natural Fertilizers.—Most "natural" fertilizers are organic, but there are also a few inorganic materials, such

Typical Analyses of Animal Manure

Animal	Pounds per Ton		
	Nitrogen (N)	Phosphate (P_2O_5)	Potash (K_2O)
Average barnyard (cattle and horse)	10	5	10
Sheep	21	6	20
Poultry	23	18	9

as sodium nitrate, that may also be classified as natural. Natural fertilizers include animal manures, bird or bat *guano,* fish meal, sewage sludge, and composts. Many other by-products may also be grouped as "natural," such as meat meal, bone tankage, dried blood, hair, wool, feather wastes, ground leather, horn meal, rice and peanut hulls, and tobacco stems. Seed meals, resulting from the removal of oil from seeds, are frequently used in fertilizers. Some of these meals are castor pomace, cottonseed meal, linseed meal, rapeseed meal, soybean meal, and peanut meal.

The mineral elements contained in the organic material were originally obtained from the soil. If the organic material is from an animal source, then the animal ate a plant or another animal that had eaten a plant. The plant obtained the minerals from the soil, and returning all of the plant remains to the soil from which it grew would not increase the mineral content of the soil. Placing organic matter grown on one soil upon another would increase the latter's fertility, providing none had been removed by other means.

Although animal manures are a good source of fertilizer, the only nutrients found in them are those present in the animal's feed. As the feed passes through the animal's digestive tract, certain portions are removed; no nutrients are added. The composition of manure is variable and depends upon several factors. One of these is the kind and amount of feed given the animal; feeds high in protein will result in manure relatively high in nitrogen. Another factor is the kind of animal: poultry manure is much higher in nitrogen and phosphorus than that of most animals. A third factor is the age of the animal; a young, growing animal removes more nutrients than does an old or mature animal. Likewise, a dairy cow producing milk will remove a different fraction of the feed than will a beef cow. Still a fourth factor is the amount and kind of litter used, such as straw or wood shavings.

Although the composition of manure varies greatly, as indicated above, the accompanying table shows the approximate composition of various types of manures. All organic fertilizers are decomposed by microorganisms in the soil, releasing the nutrient elements in a form that growing plants can assimilate. These forms are usually the same as those found in inorganic commercial fertilizers. For example, plants assimilate nitrogen as ammonium or nitrate ions, not as the proteins or amino acids found in the organic material. If temperature and moisture conditions are satisfactory (above 50° F.), decomposition takes place relatively rapidly, and the nutrient elements are released in sizable quantities within three weeks.

Chemical Additives.—The addition of chemical materials to soils is a very old practice. The application of *marl* (largely calcium carbonate), burned lime (largely calcium oxide), and saltpeter (potassium nitrate) was practiced several centuries before the Christian Era. No concentrated effort was made to utilize chemical fertilizers, however, until after the research of Justus von Liebig, Sir John Bennet Lawes (1814–1900), and Sir Joseph Henry Gilbert (1817–1901) was made known to the world. The amounts of chemical fertilizers consumed gradually increased, so that by 1905 the world consumption was about two million tons. A sharper trend did not begin until after World War I. The economic depression in the 1920's, followed by the severe depression and drought of the 1930's, created conditions that retarded the expansion of commercial fertilizer use. The most important chemical fertilizers used from 1905 to 1939 were sodium nitrate, ammonium sulfate, superphosphate (monocalcium phosphate), basic slag (a phosphorus-rich residue produced during the Bessemer process for making steel), and the potassium salts, potassium chloride and potassium sulfate.

During World War II several synthetic-nitrogen plants were built to produce material for explosives. Following the war, these plants began to produce fertilizers. New beds of phosphate rock and potassium salts also were developed. Economic conditions encouraged high crop production, and the use of chemical fertilizers increased at a fantastic rate. Since 1945 the increase in the consumption of chemical fertilizers has been at the rate of approximately 1,400,000 tons a year. The tonnage of chemical fertilizers manufactured has increased rapidly since 1945, as have the kinds of fertilizers available. The technology of fertilizer manufacture also has changed markedly, and even more significant developments are anticipated in the future.

All states of the United States and most countries of the world have laws governing the sale of commercial (chemical) fertilizers. The laws differ from state to state and from country to country, but they are similar in many ways. Almost all of the laws require that the product be labeled to show the percentage of the primary nutrient elements—nitrogen, phosphorus, and potassium—present. In most countries, including the United States, the order of listing the primary elements is nitrogen (N), phosphorus (as phosphorus pentoxide, P_2O_5), and potassium (as potassium oxide, K_2O). The phosphorus and potassium oxides are usually referred to as phosphate and potash respectively.

The *fertilizer grade* refers to a guarantee of the nutrient element content found in a fertilizer in terms of nitrogen, available phosphate, and water-soluble potash. A grade 5–10–15 fertilizer contains 5 per cent nitrogen, 10 per cent available phosphate, and 15 per cent water-soluble potash. The *fertilizer ratio* refers to the relative percentages of N, P_2O_5, and K_2O in the fertilizer. A grade 5–10–15 fertilizer has a ratio of 1–2–3; a grade of 5–10–10, a ratio of 1–2–2; and a grade of 10–10–10, a ratio of 1–1–1.

Understanding the fertilizer grade and ratio is very important in determining the proper fertilizer to purchase, the price to pay, and the rate of application. For example, a soil low in phosphorus requires a fertilizer grade in which the ratio of P_2O_5 to N and K is high. Many fertilizers have the same ratio but different nutrient content. For example, a 4–8–12 fertilizer has the same ratio as a 5–10–15; an 8–8–8, the same ratio as a 10–10–10. The cost per 100 pounds, however, should be different. Likewise, the rate of application should be different. Both the 4–8–12 and the 8–8–8 should cost only 80 percent as much as the 5–10–15 or the 10–10–10 respectively. The rate of application of the 5–10–15 or the 10–10–10 should be only 80 per cent that of the 4–8–12 or the 8–8–8. In other words, an application of 80 pounds of 10–10–10 contains as much nutrient material as 100 pounds of 8–8–8.

There is considerable variation in laws governing the labeling and guaranteeing of essential elements besides primary nutrients. Some states in the United States require labeling and a guarantee of all essential elements, which include the primary, secondary, and micronutrients. Other states require a guarantee only if the essential element is listed on the label.

There are many grades of fertilizers manufactured. In 1960, in the United States alone, over 1,600 grades of fertilizer were sold. The difference among the majority of these grades is not great; only 10 grades account for about 50 per cent of the fertilizer sold in the United States.

Only a portion of the fertilizer applied to the soil is used by plants in any one year. Nitrogen and potash are lost through leaching; some is assimilated by weeds; some, by microorganisms; and a portion reacts with the soil. The changes that the fertilizer undergoes after it is placed in the soil depend upon the condition of the soil. Soil condition also determines the residual effect of the fertilizer. In a broad sense, soils compete with plants for the fertilizer applied: the extent of competition is determined by materials in the soil that react with the fertilizer to change its availability. Iron and aluminum in the soil, for example, react with applied phosphate and greatly reduce its availability to plants. Thus, fertilizer applications should be based upon soil types as well as the economic returns that may be obtained from a crop.

Lime (calcium carbonate and magnesium carbonate) is not usually considered a fertilizer, although it supplies calcium and magnesium for plant use. It is generally applied to reduce soil acidity. Under normal conditions, soils tend to become acid through the formation of organic acids by the decomposition of organic matter, through leaching losses of calcium and magnesium, and other factors. Soils in semihumid or humid

Typical Analyses of Chemical Nitrogen and Natural Organic Fertilizers

Material	Nitrogen Content (Per Cent)	Material	Nitrogen Content (Per Cent)	Phosphate Content (Per Cent)	Potash Content (Per Cent)
Ammonium nitrate	33.5	Animal tankage	5.7–10.0	1.8–3.6	0.1–1.6
Ammonium nitrate-limestone mixtures	20.5	Dried blood	12.0–14.0	0.5–2.0	0.1–0.9
Ammonium phosphate*	11.0–21.0	Castor pomace	4.0– 6.5	1.0–2.0	1.0–1.5
Ammonium sulfate	20.5	Cocoa tankage	2.0– 2.5	1.0–1.3	0.6–3.0
Calcium cyanamide	21.0	Cottonseed meal	6.5– 7.5	2.0–3.0	1.5–2.0
Calcium nitrate	15.5	Fish tankage	6.5–10.0	4.0–8.0	0.1–1.1
Potassium nitrate	13.0	Garbage tankage	2.5– 3.3	2.0–5.0	0.5–1.0
Sodium nitrate	16.0	Tung meal	3.8– 4.4	1.0–1.5	1.0–1.5
Urea	45.0	Sewage sludge	1.5– 6.3	1.0–4.0	0.1–0.5
Anhydrous ammonia	82.0				
Nitrogen solutions†	16.0–49.0				

* Available phosphate (P_2O_5) content, 20.0%–53.0%.
† Aqueous solutions of ammonia with ammonium nitrate or urea, or both.

regions are likely to require an application of from one to two tons of lime per acre every three to five years.

For greatest efficiency, fertilizer and lime applications should be considered for a cropping system over a period of four to six years. This permits the residual effects of fertilizers and lime to be appraised and more fully utilized. Soil tests and soil survey reports showing the soil type are the best sources of information upon which to base a fertilizer-and-lime program.

Although the use of commercial fertilizers has increased many times since 1945, the amount presently used is only a small portion of that needed. Most soils, even virgin ones, cannot supply the amount of nutrients required for a large crop. The great increase in the use of commercial fertilizers has not been caused by "worn-out" soils, but by a greater yield potential than has ever before been attained. Improving plant nutrition is essential in improving human nutrition, since man's food is obtained directly or indirectly from plants. In order to attain ideal nutrition for the world as a whole, especially for the people in the underdeveloped countries, additional nutrients from chemical fertilizers must become available.

Crop Production.—In the production of crops, the principal interest is in the quantity and quality of yield in relation to the costs (input) of producing the yield. *Crop yield* can be expressed as a function of crop, soil, climate, and management. If an index value or numerical figure can be obtained for each of these variables, then the yield for a given set of conditions can be predicted. This is difficult, if not impossible, since there are so many variables involved. For example, the crop includes such variables as kind, variety, and thickness of stand (closeness of planting). For soil, consideration must be given to the nutrients, water, air, acidity, alkalinity, toxic elements, microorganisms, texture, depth of profile, type of clay, minerals, and many other factors. Precipitation, temperature, day length, light intensity, and wind are some of the climatic factors to be reckoned with. Management, as considered here, includes such factors as insect control, disease control, and weed control, and such seasonal cultural practices as planting, cultivating, and harvesting.

A low crop yield may be caused by defects in any one of the four factors listed above, in a portion thereof, or in a combination of them. The yield actually obtained is the result of the composite of all the factors. As yields increase, the composite of the factors involved must be more favorable. Production of 150 bushels of corn per acre requires the selection of a good corn variety (usually an adapted hybrid), a good stand, properly limed and fertilized soil, ample seedbed preparation, adequate pest control, and favorable climate. On the other hand, production of only ten bushels of corn per acre may occur with a poor variety of corn, a thin stand, little or no fertilizer, poor pest control, and adverse climate.

U.S. DEPARTMENT OF AGRICULTURE

WHEAT YIELD varies from county to county, depending on the condition of the terrain.

Man cannot control all of the factors involved in crop production, but research has given him access to the information and tools with which to make relatively high yields possible.

Unsolved Problems.—Although much progress has been made since 1945, prospects for the future are even greater. The solution of one problem through research usually results in the unfolding of many more; those not anticipated today probably will be the most important tomorrow. There are several problems at present, however, toward which more research should be directed.

One of these is the question of how to raise the productivity of soils to the level where high yields can be sustained. The concept that a virgin soil is in its highest state of productivity is erroneous; most virgin soils cannot support the productivity level that will be required in the future. Soil conservation will change from maintaining soils at the virgin level of productivity to improving the soil so that productivity may be maintained at a higher level. This will require improvement of both physical and chemical properties. Attention also will have to be paid to the microorganism population, which is a very important part of the soil.

More attention must also be given to higher-quality products. The amount of grass produced per acre is not as important as the amount of beef or milk that can be produced from the grass. Balancing of essential elements in the soil is important in obtaining good quality, but availability of the nutrients during various stages of plant development must also be considered. Likewise, nutrients cannot be considered alone, since moisture and other climatic factors are equally important.

Another problem that must be solved is how to achieve greater use of the soil for retaining water. With the rapidly increasing urban demand for water, both domestic and industrial, steps must be taken to utilize a much higher proportion of the annual precipitation. Construction of dams is helpful, but a bigger problem is the management of the watershed on which the precipitation falls. This includes not only farms, wooded areas, and rangeland, but roadsides, yards, and gardens as well.

As civilization develops, many "unnatural" products that come into use may contaminate the soil. Radioactive fallout from nuclear bomb testing is a good example. There are many others, however, such as the widely used insecticides, nematocides, herbicides, and other pest-controlling products. All of these may be very effective for the purpose for which they were originally developed, but their residue in the soil must be reckoned with—or serious damage may result. Reactions that take place in the soil must be ascertained and remedial practices developed where needed.

Waste disposal from cities and manufacturing plants is a big problem at present, and is likely to increase. Questions are being raised about the possibility of utilizing the soil for waste disposal without ruining it for other uses, particularly for crop production.

Land reclamation has been and is a very important phase of agriculture. It is likely to be even more important in the future. Not only will it be necessary to drain swampy areas and improve alkali conditions, as is being done now; man will also have to restore areas formerly used for roads or building sites. With a greater demand for food in the future, the reclamation of such areas is likely to be important.

—J. Walter Fitts

BIBLIOGRAPHY

AMERICAN SOCIETY OF AGRONOMY. *Advances in Agronomy.* Vol. 15. Academic Press, Inc., 1964.
BROMFIELD, LEWIS. *Out of the Earth.* Harper & Bros., 1950.
HIGBEE, EDWARD COUNSELMAN. *The American Oasis: The Land and Its Uses.* Alfred A. Knopf, Inc., 1957.
ISRAELSON, ORSON WINSO. *Irrigation Principles and Practices.* John Wiley & Sons, Inc., 1950.

VOLUME TEN

GEOGRAPHY

Physical geography	757
Cultural geography	767
Economic geography	771
Conservation	776
Maps	779
Bibliography	780

U.S. GEOLOGICAL SURVEY

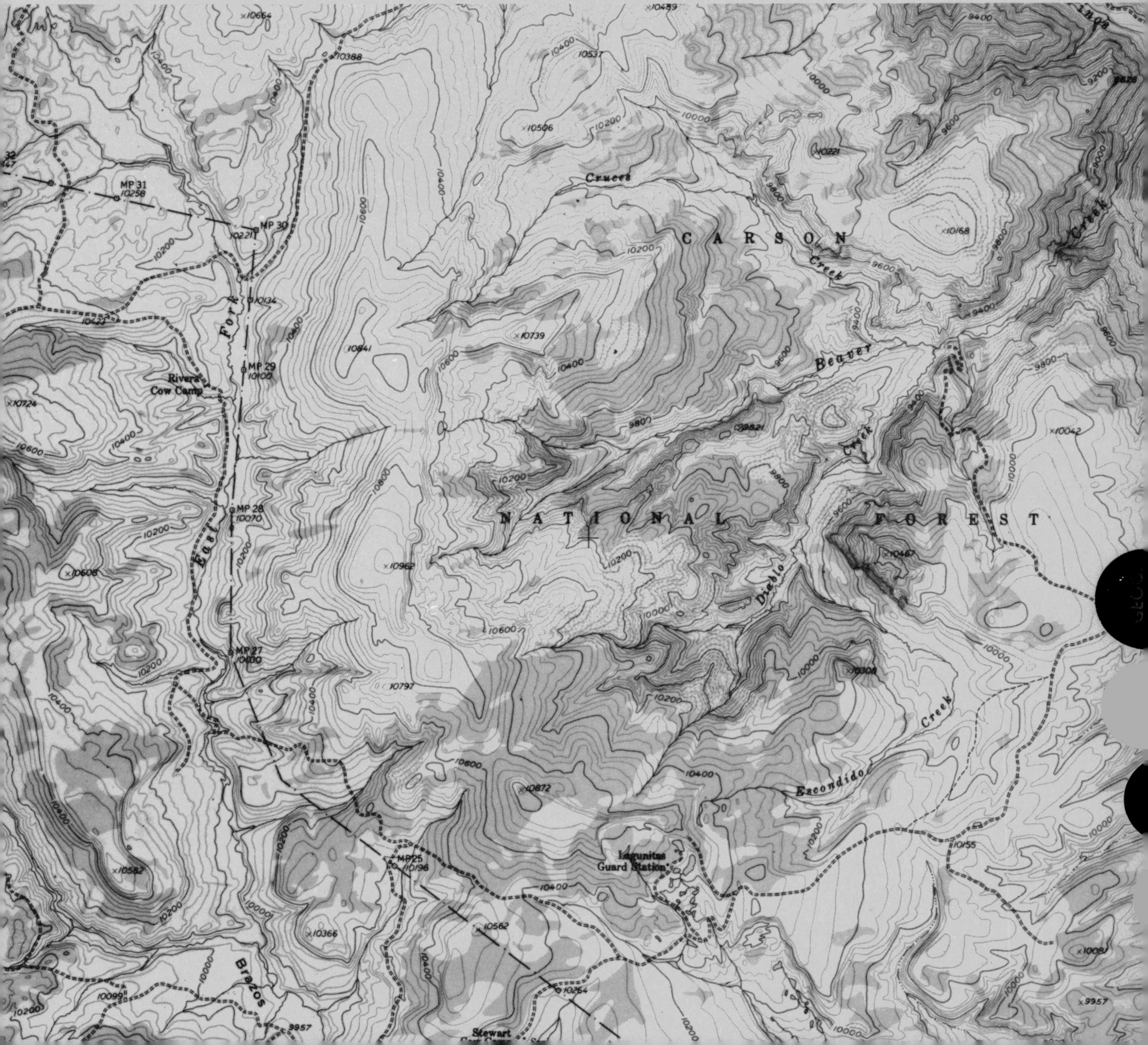

Geography

PHYSICAL GEOGRAPHY

As man reaches for the stars in his conquest of space, it is important that he understand his home planet, earth, in comparison with the other heavenly bodies. Unlike the stars, which are incandescent gaseous masses similar to our sun, the earth is a planet, a roughly spherical mass of material which describes a slightly flattened circle, or ellipse, around the sun along with eight other planets.

The word planet is derived from a Greek word meaning *wanderer*. The ancients recognized that a few stars in the heavens had paths across the sky that differed from the fixed circuits followed by nearly all of the other celestial bodies, including the sun. The planets seem to move across the background of stars because they are so much nearer and have paths comparable to that of the earth.

If the radius of the entire solar system, almost 3.7 billion miles, were reduced to one foot, the nearest of the millions of stars beyond the solar system that we have charted would be 7.6 miles away. If the sun were placed at the center of the same one-foot scale, the earth would have an orbit only ⅓ inch in radius, representing a mean distance of 92.9 million miles from the sun. Because the earth's orbit is an ellipse, it is about 3 million miles closer to the sun during January than in July.

EARTH

SIZE AND SHAPE. The earth is fifth in size among the nine planets, being larger than Mercury and Venus, the planets nearest the sun; Mars, between the earth and the sun; and Pluto, the planet farthest from the sun. The diameter of the earth is slightly greater at the equator (7,926.68 miles) than it is at the poles (7,-899.99 miles), because of a slight flattening at the poles.

The earth is far smaller than the largest planet, Jupiter, which has a diameter over 10 times that of earth and a mass more than 300 times as great. The sun, however, is by far the largest body in our solar system, for more than 100 earths could be strung along its diameter.

The total weight of the earth has been calculated at about 6,000 million, million, million tons, with an average density approximately 5.5 times that of water. Because the average density of rocks at the surface is only about 2.7, it is obvious that the interior of the earth must contain extremely dense material.

The great accuracy of location required for intercontinental rocket flights has led to increased refinements in the determination of the shape of the earth. Precise measurements made with the use of satellite rockets have revealed that, in addition to being flattened at the poles, the earth bulges slightly a short distance north of the equator and is thus somewhat pear-shaped. Such distortions from a perfect spherical shape, are relatively small, however, and would be difficult to see were the earth to be viewed at about the same distance as we see the moon.

COMPOSITION. Although man has scarcely pricked the outermost skin of the earth, the deepest penetration being an oil well about five miles deep, he has a considerable amount of information concerning the interior of the earth through the careful study of earthquake shocks as revealed in seismograph records.

The earth's crust varies in thickness from more than 20 miles under the continents to as little as 3 miles under the oceans. Near high mountains, it is believed to be somewhat thicker, perhaps as much as 40 miles.

The crust consists of two layers: an outer, *sialic* (*si*lica and *al*uminum) or granitic, layer; and, below this, a *simatic* (*si*lica and *ma*gnesium) or basaltic layer. Under continents the sial and sima are each 10 to 15 miles thick; under the oceans the sial thins out, disappearing completely in areas under the Pacific.

The surface separating the earth's crust from the mantle is called the Mohorovičić discontinuity, after the Yugoslavian seismologist who discovered it. The mantle is a relatively solid region approximately 1,800 miles deep. It probably consists of ferromagnesian minerals or sima and may be glassy in its upper portion. Below the mantle is the core.

The core has two parts. An outer zone 1,300 miles thick is composed of iron and probably is in a plastic or liquid state. An inner core, with a radius of 800 miles, is probably composed of solid iron mixed with nickel and cobalt in the same proportions as in metallic meteorites.

EARTH-SUN RELATIONSHIPS. Considering the range of temperatures in the entire universe, from the absolute zero of outer space, equal to –491°F, to the tens of thousands of degrees within the hottest stars, it is amazing that the surface of the earth has an absolute range of only about 260°F, and there are broad areas on earth where the temperature rarely varies more than 20°.

The reason for this unique condition, as well as many other phenomena such as day and night and seasonal changes, lies in the positioning and motions of the earth with respect to the sun. Before discussing these relationships it would be well to know something of the sun itself.

SUN

The sun is a rather ordinary star among the countless millions that have been observed in space. By our standards it seems immense, but many stars are much larger and some are smaller. It is also somewhat average in its temperature. There seems to be a rough correlation between size and temperature, with the smallest stars tending to be the hottest and most dense.

We are most concerned with the role of the sun as a body radiating energy in every direction. This radiant energy moves outward through space in waves that have a wide range of frequency and length. One band of such waves stimulates our eye retinas in the form of visible light. But there are many that are both longer and shorter than the light we can see.

Also issuing from the sun are vast streams of electrons that at times produce wild bursts of static on radios and may even interfere with many surface communication systems. The brilliant displays of the *aurora polaris* (termed northern lights in the northern hemisphere) are caused by the ionization of upper air atoms by incoming streams of electrons.

The distance between the earth and the sun allows the earth to intercept just enough solar radiation for the development of life as we know it. The atmosphere screens out the dangerous short wave-length radiation. Once absorbed by molecules on the earth, radiant energy may be transformed into other types of energy.

Nearly all of the energy found in any form at the surface of the earth has been derived from solar radiation, including the chemical energy of coal and oil, the hydroelectric power generated along our streams, the power of draft animals, and the energy within our own bodies. Were it not for the sun, the earth would be a lifeless, rocky orb, without soil or water.

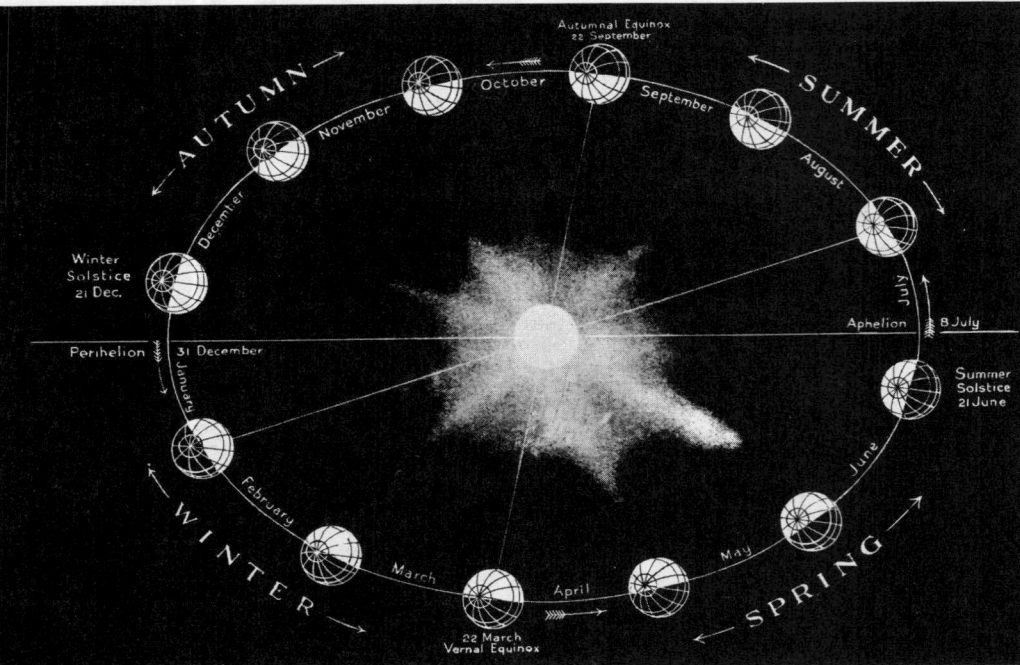

AMERICAN MUSEUM OF NATURAL HISTORY

SEASONS SHIFT as the earth's position relative to the sun changes, as shown in this drawing.

While it is true that the entire earth receives slightly more energy from the sun in January than in July, the influence of global temperatures is slight and overshadowed by more important factors. Latitude determines the seasonal changes in temperature and variations in the length of day and night, which become greater with increasing latitude.

These changes and variations are caused by the combination of several factors: the rotation of the earth on its axis once every 24 hours, the tilting of the earth's axis 23½° from the perpendicular to the orbital plane, and the constancy of the axial tilt at all positions in the earth's orbit.

There is little seasonal temperature change at the equator because day and night are always of virtually equal length, and the sun at noon never varies more than 23½° from the vertical. At the poles, on the other hand, days and nights are approximately six months long, and the sun shifts from being 23½° above the horizon to 23½° below it during the course of the year.

TIME AND LOCATION

The rotation of the earth on its axis, and its revolution around the sun, also provides a basis for keeping track of time and for locating places on the earth's surface. Our year of 365¼ days represents an approximation of the time it takes for the earth to complete one revolution around the sun. The true solar year is 365 days, 6 hours, 9 minutes, and 9.54 seconds.

The Egyptians and Mayans both had surprisingly accurate calendar systems compensating for the odd period of revolution. Monthly divisions also have long been used in the attempt to fit the lunar orbital cycle into the solar year. The moon moves into the same relationship with the earth and sun approximately every 29½ days. Thus, our 12 months represent divisions of the year that are close to the lunar cycle.

TIME ZONES. As the earth turns on its axis once every 24 hours, noon (when the sun is highest in the heavens) lies on the opposite side of the earth from midnight. The time of day, therefore, as measured by the position of the sun, changes continually as one passes around the earth in an easterly or westerly direction.

Appointments would be difficult to make and keep, except locally, were we to use solar time. For this reason, time zones approximately 15° of longitude in width have been arbitrarily determined.

Within each time zone the time remains constant. Adjacent time zones differ by one hour, since 15° represents 1/24 of the circumference of the earth. Because the earth rotates on its axis from west to east, the time zones are later to the east and earlier to the west of any given point. Eastern Standard Time, the time zone in the eastern United States, is one hour later than Central Standard Time, the next zone to the west.

INTERNATIONAL DATE LINE. Eventually, as one passes around the earth, a change in day must be made. This was first observed by the crew of the Portuguese navigator Ferdinand Magellan, who noted upon their return to Spain after traveling around the world from east to west that their ship's log had apparently lost a day. Had they sailed around the earth from west to east they would have gained a day. To correct this possible source of confusion, the international date line was established as the place where each calendar day begins.

The date line is located near the 180° meridian, one half of the world away from the Greenwich meridian, and zigzags from north to south through the Pacific Ocean, avoiding island groups. When a traveler crosses the date line from east to west, he moves ahead one day to make up for the hours he has set his watch back while traveling west through the time zones. When crossing the line going east, the traveler drops one day.

LONGITUDE AND LATITUDE. By comparing local sun time with the sun time along the 0° meridian, the meridian passing through Greenwich, England, longitude may be determined. If the sun, for example, is one hour short of being at its highest point at the same time that solar time is noon at Greenwich, the local position is 15° west longitude. Keeping track of Greenwich time today is done either by radio signals or by accurate time pieces such as chronometers.

Latitude, the angular distance north and south of the equator, is calculated by comparing the elevation of the sun above the horizon with what it would be at the intersection of the equator and the same meridian during the same moment. At night selected stars can be used for similar calculations.

EARTH HISTORY

No one knows for certain exactly when or how the earth came into being. The age of rocks can be estimated by carefully measuring the quantities of certain substances known to result from the decomposition of such radioactive minerals as uranium, however. The oldest rocks dated so far are about 2.7 billion years old. Yet none of these were part of the original crust, for heat and pressure altered them in later eons of time.

The age of the earth is presently estimated to be about 4.5 billion years. This agrees closely with the age of some meteoric material as shown by their content decomposition products of radioactive minerals.

ORIGIN. Many theories for the origin of the earth and its planetary companions have been proposed, but few of them are sufficiently comprehensive to explain the many puzzling details of the solar system. One of the most widely accepted hypotheses involves the generation of giant tidal waves in the incandescent solar atmosphere by the gravitational attraction of a passing star.

A long filament of gas, tapering at both ends, was drawn out too far to be pulled back into the sun. Its oblique motion carried it some distance, but the greater mass of the sun prevented its total escape into space. A close analogy can be found in placing satellites in orbit around the earth.

Condensation of the gaseous material, and gravitational attraction exerted by the condensed material on smaller masses near its path, led to the gradual growth of the planets. The earth is still sweeping in some meteoric fragments, but it is likely that the present size of the earth was reached during the first billion years or so.

Gravitational compression of the earth material as it grew in total mass, and the accumulation of heat resulting from the decomposition of radioactive material, led to the development of a molten or liquid core. Convectional currents in this and in the semi-solid or plastic outer portion shifted some of the lightest constituents to the surface as a kind of scum to form the outer crust. Areas of the earth's surface exhibiting interior heat losses and gains seem to indicate that the convectional movement of heat and material still continues.

The atmospheric gases may have resulted from rock fusion and ejection from deep within the earth. Some gases may have been gained by gravitational capture in space.

LIFE. Water, oxygen, carbon dioxide, sunlight, and the first oceans occupying the major depressions in the earth's surface were the requirements for the beginning of life.

The actual beginning is hidden, but the remains of lime-secreting algae have been found in sediments that radioactive uranium dating shows to be about 2.6 billion years old.

It is believed that life first appeared in the seas, perhaps along some warm, sandy shore. There, water rich in mineral salts, air with its carbon dioxide and oxygen, sunlight, and the possible catalytic action of rare minerals in the adjacent sand grains combined in this natural laboratory to form the first protoplasm, cell structure, and the first blueprint for genetic reproduction.

EARTH PULSE. Earth history, or at least the history of the outer crust, is essentially a long succession of alternate periods of instability and rest. These cycles have sometimes been referred to as the "pulse" of the earth. During the periods of instability, the crust buckled and warped, especially along what became continental margins.

Mountains and plateaus were lifted high above sea level, and volcanic activity was widespread in the areas of crustal weakness and cracking. The seas were confined largely to the ocean basins, and climatic changes were drastic. Pronounced glaciation at times covered large portions of the continents.

Under the continually changing demands of a dynamic environment, life forms changed rapidly. Some highly specialized forms were unable to adapt to the new conditions and died out completely.

These times of mountain-building, or orogeny, have been used as markers separating the divisions of geologic time. Major global orogenies separate the broad eras; the lesser ones, usually more local in occurrence, separate the periods and, within the periods, the epochs.

The intervening times of crustal stability were usually much longer than the orogenies. During these times erosion wore mountains down to plains, and deposition in other areas caused great troughs to subside under the weight of accumulated sediments. The seas frequently invaded the continental blocks along the coastal margins and through broad seaways into the interior plains.

Life forms spread over extensive areas of the earth and developed highly specialized characteristics in tune with the stable environments. Climates were much more uniform over the earth than they now are, and a distinct frozen polar region was rare.

GEOLOGIC TIME. The enormity of time measured on the geological time scale is difficult to comprehend. On such a scale mountains are but fleeting features on a continually changing stage. The Grand Canyon, awesome to behold as an example of the inexorable work of running water over vast periods of time, is a feature that has been developed only "yesterday" in the vastness of geological time, for it began to appear during the latter part of the Tertiary period, a mere 20 to 30 million years ago.

Using a base figure of 4.5 billion years for the age of the earth, and representing this as a quarter-mile race track, the length of time since glacial ice was rapidly receding from North America, about 10,000 years ago, would be equal to a distance on the track slightly less than the width of a dime standing on edge.

LITHOSPHERE

The solid outer crust of the earth has been altered many times since it was formed, and no remnant of the original unaltered crust has ever been found. Sometimes and in some places the crust was warped into huge folds or broad regional arches only to be worn down, or eroded, by running water, glacial ice, wind, or waves. At others, it was bent deep into the plastic sima, the dark, heavy sub-crustal material, under the weight of slow but continuous deposition, such as at the mouths of great rivers like the Mississippi or China's Hwang Ho, or Yellow River.

It is believed that such troughs or basins of deposition, subsiding for thousands of feet under the weight of erosional debris, at first push down on the underlying sima. After a certain critical point, the sima moves sideways toward the downward bulge, compressing its edges into great folds and slowly forcing up the entire basin.

This balancing process, termed isostatic compensation, has operated for billions of years to insure the continuation of the geologic processes of erosion, deposition, and crustal deformation, or tectonics. *Terra firma* (solid earth) is not an expression appropriate in the continuum of geological time.

Not all portions of the lithosphere are equally susceptible to tectonic forces. The most unstable portions have appeared to be the continental margins. Around the edge of the Pacific Ocean, for example, high mountains and ocean deeps are close together. The Pacific border is also the site of volcanic activity and earthquakes.

Some areas have been notably stable for long periods of time, however. Such areas are called shields because of their tendency to have broad, slightly convex surfaces somewhat similar to medieval European shields. The largest and most studied of these is the Canadian Shield, a huge mass of granite and other sialic rocks that covers a large part of Canada, dipping into northern New York, Michigan, Wisconsin, and Minnesota. Much of Africa is an ancient shield block.

CONTINENTS AND OCEAN BASINS

Earth scientists have been intrigued for many years by the apparent "fit" between North and South America on one hand, and Eurasia and Africa on the other. An associated feature of this pattern is a submarine ridge that runs the length of the Atlantic Ocean from north to south, describing an elongated S, which corresponds to the Atlantic shoreline of these continents.

Furthermore, if the American and Eurasian-African blocks were placed together, there would be an astounding conjunction of rock structures, strata ages, glaciated areas, fossils, and alignment of magnetic mineral particles in rocks. This conjunction seems to fit from the northern tip of Norway to the southern tip of Africa.

Another "fit" is possible, with Australia and Antarctica tucked together in the space now occupied by the Indian Ocean.

CONTINENTAL DRIFT. Early in the 1900s, Alfred Wegener, a German geologist, proposed a theory of continental drift. He suggested that during the Mississippian and Pennsylvanian periods all the continents were joined. But a rent appeared, and during the early part of the Mesozoic era the continents slowly moved, or drifted, apart toward their present positions. This may have been caused by slow-moving convection currents in a dense, plastic zone below the earth's crust.

Many objections have been found to the details of the Wegener hypothesis, and until recently it was generally not accepted by geologists. During the past two decades, however, new techniques of geophysical investigation have turned up much additional evidence to support the theory of continental drift, although the time and causes of its occurence are still subject to considerable debate.

CHARACTERISTICS OF CONTINENTS. The continental blocks, with islands, make up less than 30 percent of the earth's surface. Except for the southern tip of South America, each block has an ocean at its antipodal position (opposite side of the earth). The continental blocks also tend to have a triangular shape, with a broad side to the north and tapering to the south. It may be noted on a world map how many peninsulas point southward and how few extend northward.

Generally, the edges of the continental blocks lie below sea level. With few exceptions, there is a pronounced shelf zone bordering the continents which averages some 30 miles in width, and slopes gradually to a depth of less than 600 feet before the start of the continental slope. The continental slope plunges steeply into the ocean basins.

Crossing the continental shelf and slope in many places are submarine canyons, which may be as much as 10 miles wide and more than 6,000 feet deep. Some of these canyons appear to be extensions of valleys on the land

© National Geographic Magazine. Reproduced from the National Geographic Magazine by special permission

Thirteen Miles Above the Earth—A Vertical Photograph

This photograph, covering approximately 105 square miles, was made at a height of 72,395 feet above sea level (69,780 feet or more than 13 miles above the ground), over south-central South Dakota. The aerial camera mounted in the bottom of the balloon's gondola recorded the earth beneath. The geometrical cultivated fields and the straight section lines at the north (right side of picture) stand out in sharp contrast to grasslands and erosion channels carved by rain water draining into the South Fork of the White River, which extends diagonally across the lower part of the picture. Near the upper right-hand edge of the picture is shown the village of Parmelee with its small grid of streets. U. S. Highway No. 18, showing as a fine white line, enters Parmelee from the top of the photograph. The white irregular object a little over an inch in from the right margin is the official meteorograph suspended 33 feet below the gondola. The two shadowy lines extending inward from the top margin are ropes dangling from the side of the sphere and could have been formed during a glacial period when the sea level was lower than it is at present. There is also evidence that some of them could have been formed below the surface of the sea by turbidity currents or underwater avalanches.

VOLCANOES AND EARTHQUAKES

Volcanoes and earthquakes are associated with zones of crustal instability. Volcanoes occur where there has been a rupturing of the crust, permitting hot fluid rock, or magma, to rise along cracks or fissures. This magma originates within the crust itself.

It is not entirely understood why reservoirs of magma occur within the outer solid part of the earth, but suggested reasons include tensional stresses, which relieve the great rock pressures that normally keep the rock material solid despite temperatures of many thousands of degrees. There is also the possibility of the gradual accumulation of heat resulting from the breakdown of radioactive minerals.

VOLCANIC MATERIAL. The composition of volcanic material varies greatly, ranging from light-colored silicic lava that erupts explosively, contains large quantities of gases, has a relatively high temperature, is viscous or gluey, and piles up around the volcano, to the dark basic lava which erupts gently, has a low melting point, is relatively fluid, and may flow for miles.

The explosive volcanoes tend to build cone-shaped accumulations of ash and cinders, whereas the highly fluid and dark-colored lavas pour out onto the surface in broad sheets, forming immense dome-shaped masses such as the great volcanoes of Hawaii. During a volcano's eruptive period the composition of the lava may change and the volcano may produce both fragmental and fluid lavas during the same eruption.

EARTHQUAKES. The shock waves, or vibrations, produced by rock rupture are called earthquakes. When stresses accumulate over a long period, owing either to compression or tension, rocks eventually will break and slip along lines called faults. Certain fault lines may have active slippage along them for millions of years, and may produce cumulative displacements measuring miles in length and thousands of feet in height.

Most earthquakes take place well below the surface of the earth and their displacements may not be noticeable. Occasionally, however, a severe one near the surface produces sudden dislocations of roads, fences, or streams. Minor earthquakes also may result from severe volcanic eruptions or from the elastic rebound of the crust following the melting of huge continental ice sheets.

LANDFORMS

The physical features that make up the surface of the earth are the result of many different processes of change operating on a variety of materials for widely different periods of time. For these reasons no two hills or mountains look exactly alike, yet many of them have common proper-

ties by which they may be classified and understood.

Valleys, for example, may be produced by stream erosion, by the scouring action of a glacier, or by the solution of limestone by underground water. Each of these valley forms has distinctive characteristics whereby their origin can be deciphered. Furthermore, the pattern of stream valleys in a region of horizontal sedimentary rock layers will be different from the pattern in an area of metamorphic, or granite, rocks, or in Arctic climates the pattern will be different from that in the Sahara.

There is also a variation in the appearance of a stream from youth, when it has virtually no flood plain and the valley walls form a V in cross-valley profile; to maturity, when most of the falls and rapids have been eliminated and a flood plain begins to form; to old age, when valley-widening dominates downward cutting and oxbow lakes and natural levees are common.

Natural agents such as glaciers, waves, tectonic forces, weathering, and erosion produce specific types of landforms that can be recognized and classified.

The continental glacier that was retreating from North America 10,000 years ago left behind many characteristic landforms. Glacial deposition resulted in the hummocky belts of unsorted boulders and pulverized rock called moraines, the mounds of sand and gravel laid down by glacial meltwater called kames, the oval hills of unstratified clayey till called drumlins, and the low, winding ridges of sand and gravel that may extend for 100 miles or more in northern Canada and Scandinavia called eskers.

Glacial erosion also helped shape landforms such as the smooth, striated glacial pavements; the low, beveled rock mounds called roche moutonnées (sheep rocks), and the steep-walled basins called cirques formed by the headwall erosion of mountain glaciers.

Waves and currents in the sea produce their characteristic landforms such as notched sea cliffs; stacks, or rock columns left as erosional remnants; offshore bars or barrier beaches, such as the one on which Atlantic City, New Jersey is built; wave-filled terraces constructed off-shore by wave deposition; and spits and hooks, the sandy deposits extending out from the ends of coastal capes and promontories.

Tectonic forces produce anticlines, or upfolds; synclines, or downfolds; fault scarps, or cliffs resulting from slippage along earthquake faults; graben (from the German *Graben*, for ditch), or depressed crustal blocks bounded on at least two sides by faults. Volcanic activity may produce cinder cones, huge craters or calderas, sills or sheets of lava intruded horizontally between sedimentary rock strata, such as the New York Palisades, and dikes, lava intruded across and through rock strata.

Weathering and erosion in humid climates produce gently rolling plains or peneplains. In arid and semi-arid climates, plateaus with steep faces and pediments or slopes thinly veneered

with gravel are the common results. In the tropics isolated, steep-sided hills and mountains may rise abruptly from relatively flat landscapes. In desert areas temporary salt lakes, or playas, dunes, and broad, flat-topped hills, or mesas, are frequently encountered.

All these and many other landforms help to give variety to the surface of our planet, and to challenge scientists to interpret their various and changing shapes and compositions.

MINERAL DEPOSITS

Only a very small portion of the outer crust of the earth contains minerals that have an economic significance to man. In fact, of the thousands of individual minerals that man has found and identified, only a small number make up the bulk of the crust.

One single mineral, orthoclase, a pink or gray potassium aluminum silicate, is the primary mineral constituent of granite—the most abundant rock in the earth's crust. This one mineral probably constitutes one-fourth of the entire earth's crust. Although it has useful aluminum as one of its atomic elements, the aluminum is so tightly bound to its oxygen and silica companions that it is not commercially profitable to separate it.

Instead, nature performs this task by weathering and decomposing the shiny mineral into tiny clay particles. Under tropical or subtropical climatic conditions, most of the silica is leached out of the clay, producing an impure mixture of aluminum oxide and water known as bauxite, the principal ore of aluminum.

Most of the useful minerals are contained in relatively small exploitable deposits. As a general rule, the metallic minerals have more localized deposits than the non-metallic ones, and the richest metallic deposits are narrow veins of ore precipitated in rock fissures by thermal solutions.

In some localities valuable but lean materials have been concentrated into workable deposits. In one process of concentration the agents of erosion break down rocks, and as streams carry the sediment away, the heavier minerals fall to the floor of the stream channels. The placer deposits of gold, found in stream gravels, are an example of this.

Another process of concentration is secondary enrichment, in which new bodies of high-grade ore are derived from the oxidation of decomposed overlying masses of low-grade ore. Many copper and iron deposits are the result of this process.

Many valuable minerals are also scattered thinly in large rock masses, and as the small, localized deposits of high-grade ore are depleted, man has been forced to turn toward these massive deposits of low-grade ore. Some copper ores that are being worked economically today by mass-production techniques have such low-grade copper contents that they could scarcely be recognized as ore without careful quantitative analysis. For example, the average copper ore mined in the United States has a copper content of only about 0.9 percent. This is an indication of the world-wide scarcity of this metal.

Some minerals tend to be more concentrated in nature than others. Nickel, for example, is a fairly common mineral in the earth's crust, but it occurs in extremely small quantities and is mined in only a few widely scattered localities. Copper, on the other hand, is not so abundant, but it tends to be much more concentrated and is mined in many localities.

In general, the heavier metallic elements tend to be less abundant than such light metals as aluminum, sodium, or potassium. The heavier metallic elements, however, are likely to be more abundant in the sima rocks that have been brought to or near the surface by volcanic activity and are more easily separated from their compounds than the light metallic elements.

The mineral fuels—coal, petroleum, and natural gas—are almost always located in sedimentary strata. Coal represents ancient vegetation that accumulated under water in swamps and marshes and was later buried and compressed by sediments such as silt, clay, or sand. For this reason most coal occurs as broad sheets enclosed by sedimentary rocks.

Oil and gas are fluids and may flow from one place to another through permeable strata. They do not accumulate in commercial, exploitable quantities until they are trapped in some way, such as along the top of upfold or dome in rock strata which is overlain by shale or other impermeable rock.

SOILS

Solid rock forms the major portion of the earth's crust, but it is not in balance with environmental factors at the immediate surface. There nature tends to produce a balanced mixture of rock, air, water, and tiny life-forms which is called soil. Soil, therefore, is a natural substance that represents interaction among the four major global spheres—lithosphere, atmosphere, hydrosphere, and biosphere.

The properties of soils are exhibited not only at the surface but also for a variable distance below and are influenced by local variations in any of the environmental factors—climate, vegetation, bedrock, and relief of the land surface. Time is also a factor because the forces of erosion, weathering, and deposition are continually exposing new rock material or transferring fragmental rock debris to new locations.

Man himself has become an important agent in influencing the characteristics of soils in his search for food and fuel. So many factors influence soil characteristics that if one looks closely enough, soil differences may be seen every few feet.

SOIL CHARACTERISTICS. There are, however, broad features of soils that are similar over wide areas and that enable man to make, classify, and understand the development and best uses of soils.

In general, the youngest, or azonal, soils are composed of fragmental material that has recently been depos-

CANADIAN INFORMATION OFFICE

MINERAL DEPOSITS can be found by digging deep into the earth, as these uranium miners do.

ited. Their most distinctive properties are derived from the chemical composition of the included rock material. Intrazonal soils, somewhat older, have their principal properties largely determined by local conditions, such as wetness or limy parent material. The older, zonal, soils reflect the full effects of environmental factors and may be divided into major groups.

Tundra soil has a dark brown peaty surface over brownish-black soil, underlain by permafrost. Chernzem is a dark soil, high in organic matter, found in moderately humid regions under tall grasses. Desert soil is light-colored, porous, and low in organic matter. Podzol has a thick top layer of partially decayed organic material over a gray leached layer, underlain by a compact, dark reddish to yellowish brown layer. Podzols develop under forests or heaths in temperate to cold, humid climates.

Latosols are leached red and yellow soils which prevail in the tropics. Mildly acid solutions result from rainwater percolating through the soil, removing silica from the original rock particles and leaving behind concentrated iron and aluminum oxides common in crustal rocks, The reds and yellows are derived from iron oxides and are similar to the rust that forms on a piece of iron left outdoors.

In dry climates lime tends to accumulate in the subsoil, deposited by percolation from above or by capillary attraction from below. Evaporation releases this normally soluble and common substance and it accumulates much as the lime crust in a kitchen tea kettle. Poor drainage in dry areas often results in alkali or salty soils,

which are highly toxic to most plant growth.

Tropical soils are usually light-colored because bacteria destroy organic material. In temperate regions frost retards the development of bacteria so the soils generally contain more humus and are, therefore, dark.

ATMOSPHERE

The gaseous envelope that encloses the earth was little known until a few years ago when man decided to explore the rims of space. It is a highly complex part of the earth, and it is subject to continual change.

The atmosphere is many things. It is a huge heat-exchange mechanism, a filter for screening out dangerous short wave solar radiation, a means of transport for energy and water, a source of life-giving carbon dioxide for plants and oxygen for animals, an active agent in the breakdown of rocks and minerals, and a transportation medium for man himself.

The total thickness of the atmosphere is difficult to measure because the outer boundaries gradually blend into interplanetary space. We do know, however, that it extends at least 700 miles above the earth's surface.

At the earth's surface the average composition of the atmosphere by volume is about 75.5 percent nitrogen and 23 percent oxygen, plus small amounts of carbon dioxide, ozone, hydrogen, water vapor, dust, and gaseous impurities. There are also traces of several inert gases, such as krypton, neon, argon, xenon, and helium, which have no known function on the earth or in the behavior of the atmosphere.

VERTICAL DIVISIONS

Like the interior of the earth, the atmosphere is divided into layers.

TROPOSPHERE. The lowest layer, or troposphere, extends from the earth's surface to about 11 miles above the equator and to about 5 miles over the poles. The identifying characteristic of the troposphere is the decrease in temperature with altitude, or lapse rate, which averages about 3.3°F per 1,000 feet. Nearly all clouds and most of the mass of the atmosphere are contained in the troposphere.

A striking feature of the troposphere at increasing heights is the merger of the separate systems of the global wind pattern into one system of westerlies, although easterly winds persist to great heights in the low latitudes.

Tropopause. The upper boundary of the troposphere is called the tropopause. This boundary slopes downward near the poles and at times its surface is broken into step-like edges. There is a steep downward plunge of the tropopause in the midlatitudes which shifts between 25°F in winter and 40°F in summer.

Jet Streams. Near the slope is a narrow, westerly current of air called the jet stream. It averages 75 miles per hour (mph) in summer and 35 mph in winter, although it may reach speeds as high as 250 mph. Fluctuations in the speed of the jet stream appear to be related to the changes in solar energy accumulations on earth. The faster the jet stream flows, the more it kinks and loops. These irregular loops also seem to be linked to surface weather fronts.

There is some evidence for an easterly jet stream in equatorial regions. But it is not as strongly developed nor as regular in its occurrence.

STRATOSPHERE. The stratosphere, the layer above the troposphere, extends to approximately 50 miles above the earth. In the lower part of the stratosphere the temperature remains quite constant, near –67°F, as one ascends. Farther up the temperature tends to rise with increased altitude, and there is a tendency for the portion above the equator to have lower temperatures than portions over the poles.

It was believed for many years that the stratosphere was without much air movement because there is an unusually still zone in its lowest layer which is useful for high altitude flight. But rocket flights have revealed that this still zone is extremely narrow and that violent winds may be encountered above it.

Air flow patterns in the stratosphere seem to be almost the reverse of those in the troposphere. In the stratosphere easterly winds, complete with jets, prevail at middle and higher altitudes.

OZONOSPHERE. The ozonosphere is a zone lying between about 18 and 35 miles above the earth. It sometimes overlaps the stratosphere. The ozonosphere is characterized by an unusual concentration of ozone molecules, which are units of three oxygen atoms loosely linked together. Normally oxygen in gaseous form is in atomic pairs (O_2). Solar energy splits the ordinary double molecule into single atoms, which, in turn, combine with a double to form ozone.

Ozone has a strong affinity for absorbing ultraviolet radiation and reradiating it at longer wave lengths. Thus the ozonosphere acts as an automatic filter for short wave-length radiation. The greater the radiation, the greater is the manufacture of ozone and the greater its absorption. When the radiation level drops, so does the ozone content.

IONOSPHERE. The ionosphere forms the outermost and by far the thickest of the atmospheric layers, with a lower limit of about 35 miles during the day and about 60 miles at night and extending to more than 300 miles above the earth's surface. The temperature ranges from –90°F at its lower limit to as much as 2000°F at its upper limit.

The primary identifying feature of the ionosphere is the presence of several distinct layers. In each of these layers a large part of the atomic particles are ionized, which means that they have extra electrons attached to them. There also appear to be bands of free electrons.

At the outer edges of the ionosphere there is a danger zone for man —the Van Allen radiation belt. This is a zone of high energy neutrons, with enormous penetrating power. It varies in its concentration and appears to be open above both poles. This doughnut-shaped zone, while not strictly a part of the atmosphere, is a definite hazard to astronauts seeking to escape for the earth.

GLOBAL THERMAL BALANCE

The earth not only receives radiant energy from the sun, but it also re-radiates this energy into outer space. There is a close balance between incoming and outgoing radiation.

Considering the many different alterations that incoming radiation may undergo in the atmosphere or at the surface, even being locked up in coal or oil deposits for hundreds of millions of years, the continued existence of this balance is a remarkable feature of the earth. Had this balance not existed, our planet would have become progressively either hotter or colder.

Even more striking is the fact that the ratio between input and output of energy varies greatly from place to place, not only at the earth's surface but above it. The equatorial regions at the surface, for example, receive considerably more radiation than they re-radiate, and the high latitudes release more than they receive from the sun. The reverse situation seems to be true within the upper stratosphere and ozonosphere.

At the surface, the boundary between surplus and deficient energy lies at about 40° north and south latitude, shifting somewhat with the seasons.

To maintain a total balance in the face of latitudinal imbalances, energy must flow from low latitudes to high latitudes at the surface and vice versa in the upper air. The transportation of this energy takes many forms. It may be transported by ocean currents in the form of heat.

The main carrier of energy, however, is the motion of air, which moves vertically in air currents and horizontally in winds. This may involve direct heat transfer or the flow of warm air toward the poles and cold air toward the equator. It may also utilize the transfer of kinetic energy, the energy of motion, for mild breezes wafting poleward can become concentrated into howling blizzards in polar areas and then lose some of this energy by friction.

EVAPORATION AND CONDENSATION. By far the most efficient and effective means of energy is the evaporation of water from the warm oceans of low latitudes, the transportation of this water vapor by winds or air currents, and its subsequent condensation into liquid water at higher latitudes. This mechanism of heat transfer is very important to the global heat balance.

To vaporize water requires a surprisingly great amount of energy. For example, it requires about 540 calories to change one gram of water into vapor form, or 540 times as much as is needed to raise the temperature of one gram of water one degree Centigrade. In other words, it takes over five times as much energy to change boiling water to water vapor without a temperature change than it does to raise the temperature of water from the freezing point to the boiling point.

Condensation of water in a thunderstorm releases fantastic quantities of energy. The rain that falls to a depth of one inch on one single acre, or a plot about 200 by 200 feet, releases energy during condensation equivalent to the heat energy contained in 15,000 tons of coal. This heat was taken on somewhere—perhaps over a warm tropical or subtropical body of water such as the Gulf of Mexico.

Rain, of course, does not fall only in middle and higher latitudes. In fact, the equatorial regions are among the rainiest places on earth. This is caused by the fact that in those regions the transportation of heat is vertical, and the columns of rising air necessary for rain clouds may tower to heights of 30,000 to 45,000 feet. This is far higher than in middle latitudes. Meteorologists refer to the regions of net outflow as heat sinks, and it is clear that although the frozen wastes of polar areas constitute major sinks at the surface, others occur in the upper air above the low latitudes.

GLOBAL WIND PATTERNS

Wind, the horizontal component of air motion, is caused by the equalization of horizontal differences in air pressure. Therefore, variations in air pressure and in time are of prime consideration in understanding the global wind system both at and above the surface of the earth.

The source areas for the major surface winds are huge cells of high pressure, into which air descends from near the top of the troposphere and from which air diverges at the surface in huge spirals. The air does not blow straight from the center of these pressure cells, or highs, but obliquely, because of the deflective effect of the earth's rotation. This gives a rotational movement to the entire cell that is clockwise in the northern hemisphere and counterclockwise in the southern hemisphere.

HIGH PRESSURE CENTERS. The major high pressure centers are located in the subtropics with their centers roughly between 25° and 35° (the "horse latitudes"). They are permanent fixtures in the eastern third of the oceans, but tend to be located over the continental areas during the winter season.

The air flow along their equatorial sides is known as the trade winds (easterly winds); the flow along their poleward sides is known as the westerlies. Fluctuations in the number and shape of the subtropical highs determine the amount of wind that flows toward the equator on their eastern sides and poleward on their western sides.

There is a great interchange of air latitudinally when the cells are many and strong, as in the winter season, and little when the cells are few and elongated from east to west. The behavior of these subtropical highs is an important part of the heat exchange system of the earth.

Another high pressure source for surface air movement occurs during the winter over North America and Eurasia. The outward moving air there is extremely cold and shallow. It hugs the ground and moves into the westerly wind belt toward an area of lesser pressure. An analogy may be drawn with drops of water collecting under a dripping faucet and building up a mass that finally moves rapidly toward the drain.

FRONTS. The interaction between the cold air masses and the warm, often moist, westerly winds produce the storms and precipitation that release the energy that had been carried poleward. The fronts that appear on daily weather maps are the boundaries between air masses of different temperatures.

A cold front indicates that the strongest attacking air mass is the coldest of the two. A warm front occurs when warm air is attacking the weak side of a cold air mass. An occluded front is a situation in which one front overtakes another and destroys it, at least on the surface.

PRECIPITATION

Condensation and precipitation, or rain and snowfall, are important parts of the heat exchange system of the earth. The mechanics of precipitation are important in the understanding of this system for they greatly influence the distribution of precipitation over the world.

Condensation requires a tiny nucleus of some kind, such as a speck of dust, a tiny ice particle, or even a small bit of sea salt blown high into the air. It also requires cooling, because this decreases the capacity of air to hold moisture. If air is cooled enough, it may reach the dew point, which means that further cooling will cause the water molecules to pass from the vapor state to a liquid state,

WORLD CLIMATE REGIONS

Climatic Region	Characteristics	Location
Rainy Tropics	Enough rainfall for normal forest growth all year. Hot, little seasonal change in temperature.	5°S to 10°N, in places extending to 20-25° poleward on E. side of continents.
Wet and Dry Tropics (Monsoon Climates)	Pronounced seasonal variation in rainfall; dry season in low sun period (winter). Warm, little seasonal change in temperature.	Poleward of rainy tropics to about 15°.
Dry Climates (Arid and Semi-Arid)	Evaporation exceeds precipitation. Sharp daily changes in temp. Seasonal temp. changes increase with latitude.	15-30° on west side of continents, extending inland and poleward to 45-50°. Rare on E. side of continents.
Mediterranean Climates	Mild, rainy winters; arid summers.	West coast of continents to 50° and around Mediterranean Sea.
Humid Subtropical with Mild Winters	Rainfall throughout the year; hot summers, mild winters with occasional snow and frost.	E. third of continents between 25-40°.
Maritime West Coast Climates	Cool, drizzly summers; mild, rainy winters. Little sunshine. Thunderstorms rare.	West coasts of continents 40-65°.
Humid Continental with Hot Summers and Cold Winters	Rainfall throughout year; hot summers; cold, snowy winters.	N. Hemisphere only. N. Corn Belt and Lower Lake States in U.S.; NE China, Manchuria, and N. Japan.
Humid Continental with Cool Summers	Severe, snowy winters; cool, pleasant summers with some rainfall.	Northern U.S., southern Canada E. of 100° Long.; most of European Russia; Scandinavia E. of Atlantic coast; N. Manchuria.
Subarctic Climates	Long, very severe winters; short, cool summers.	A broad belt from N. Alaska to Labrador. N. Sweden and Finland east to most of Siberia.
Polar Climates	No frost-free season.	Antarctica; N. rim of N. Amer. and Central Eurasia. Extends south along E. coasts to 50°.

or condense. How much cooling is required depends on the amount of water in the air and its temperature.

Examples of condensation are seen on a glass of cold water in a warm room, on a bathroom mirror after a hot bath, and in the dew of early morning. Condensation in the free air by natural causes is represented by fog or clouds, the difference between the two being that fog occurs at ground level. The passage of warm air over a cloud surface may produce fog, and the rising of air, cooling as it rises, produces clouds.

In both of these examples little energy is involved because the amount of condensation is not great. The quantity of water in a fog blanket is not especially large because the droplets are so tiny.

A raindrop is quite another thing for it is usually a million times greater in total mass than the water vapor in fog or clouds. To obtain an increase in the rate of condensation in such a mass requires extremely rapid cooling by strong vertical air currents. The mechanism for such updrafts lies within the condensing water vapor. If very warm, moist air rises to the cloud level, the latent heat released will warm it, making it rise farther and faster to be further cooled, condensed, and so on in a chain reaction.

The air will continue to rise as long as condensing moisture maintains its temperature above that of the adjacent air. This cumulative chain reaction produces the rapid growth of rain drops. In unusually high columns of rising air, the drops may grow into hailstones by a series of ascents and descents in turbulent air.

Snow does not require as much condensational lifting as rain, and only a few degrees of cooling may be needed to produce snow flakes directly from vapor. Because cold air cannot hold much moisture, winter snowfall does not involve as much heat transfer as summer rain. On the average, about 10 inches of snow is equivalent to one inch of rain.

Rain and snow, therefore, occur in those parts of the world where there is air containing water vapor and mechanisms for making saturated air rise to the condensation or cloud zone. Such places include the side of a mountain facing a strong prevailing wind, or the front between contrasting air masses where warm air rises, or is displaced upwards, by colder air, or by local updrafts caused by unequal surface heating, as over a hot city street or a plowed field.

Rain is rare where downward air currents prevail, as in the regions of the subtropical high pressure centers, or where the air is extremely cold, as in polar regions. Warm air that is being chilled from below is stable and resists upward movement, whereas cold air that is being warmed from below is unstable and is easily triggered into upward movement.

REGIONAL CLIMATE

Climate is the average condition of the weather at a particular place over a long period of time. The word climate is derived from the Greek *klima*, which means incline or slope. The ancient Greeks thought that climate depended almost entirely on latitude, believing that the earth sloped away from the sun north of the Mediterranean Sea and, therefore, that the climate became colder to the north.

Many kinds of classifications of climate have been used but most of them have been based on average conditions of temperature and precipitation near ground level. The following table shows the principal climates of the world, their major characteristics, and general location.

HYDROSPHERE

Water makes up about 70 percent of the earth's surface, and the water area is called the hydrosphere. This area includes the water and ice in the oceans, rivers, lakes, and marshlands; ground water; and the water vapor in the atmosphere. Water fills tiny openings in rocks and soils, making itself available to living organisms almost everywhere except in desert areas or in frozen polar wastes.

HYDROLOGIC CYCLE

In the section of the atmosphere, it was noted how important the alternate evaporation and condensation of water was to the regulation of global energy balance, like a thermostat. This same process is also part of the hydrologic cycle, which is our continental water supply and drainage system. In the hydrologic cycle, water begins as atmospheric water vapor, passes into liquid and solid form as precipitation, falls to the surface of the earth where evaporation and transpiration through plants return it to the atmosphere as water vapor. Of course, the details of this process are far more complicated.

There are many detours, wanderings, and shortcuts, but every gallon of water on the surface of the earth is involved in this eternal cycle. Because water is so essential to man and is becoming more so with every passing century, the behavior of this cycle is of great importance.

Just as energy from the sun accumulates and is stored in vast underground oil and coal deposits, so too are there traps to intercept a portion of the hydrologic cycle. The great ice sheets of Greenland and Antarctica, remnants of much greater ones that existed thousands of years ago, are trapped water.

If these ice masses were to be melted, the global sea level would rise by some 150 to 200 feet, which would completely submerge most of the great cities of the world. Water may also be trapped in sedimentary and igneous rocks, in soils, and in the bodies of living things everywhere.

GROUND WATER. The part of the hydrologic cycle contained below the surface of the earth is called ground water. As rain falls, much of it soaks into the soil, filling the openings in both soil and rock. In most places there is a point below which all openings are filled with water.

The top of this saturated zone is called the ground water table. Where the water table meets the surface of the earth there may be lakes, swamps, springs, and streams. The water table rises and falls with changes in the amount of precipitation and tends to follow the general slope of the land surface.

Ground water is an important source of water for human use mainly because it is somewhat more dependable, is colder during summer periods, is usually cleaner, and is less susceptible to pollution than surface water sources. Its main disadvantage is that mineral salts it contains may make the water too "hard" or too salty for use. The quantity of ground water is also more likely to be limited for massive municipal and industrial use than the flow of large surface streams or the supply from lakes and ponds.

THE OCEANS

Fully 96 percent of all the water on earth is contained within the oceans. Not only are the oceans far larger than the continents, but they are also much deeper than the continents are high. There is considerably less local irregularity on the floors of the oceans than on the continents, but the major features, such as canyons and mountains, are much more impressive.

Far from being a featureless plain, the ocean floors are dotted with towering isolated pinnacles, called seamounts, which rise 3,000 feet or more above the floor; elongated ridges miles high; and, in some places around the margins of the ocean basins, great chasms or ocean deeps, which may plunge 20,000 feet or more below the level of the ocean surface.

COMPOSITION. In sea water the proportions of the various contained soluble salts remains relatively constant, despite wide fluctuations in total salinity. Sodium chloride represents about 70 percent of the soluble salts in the ocean. It is noteworthy that the same proportion of elements, although much more diluted, appears in human tears and blood plasma as appears in sea water. The source of so much sodium in the seas is an unsolved riddle to ocean scientists because the average composition of the rocks in the lithosphere does not show sodium and chlorine to be such dominant ions.

The most important substances in sea water to organic development are the dissolved gases of oxygen and carbon dioxide, and certain potash, phosphate, and nitrogenous salts that form plant foods just as they do in soils. The content of dissolved gases decreases with an increase in temperature. Thus, the polar seas have more life-giving oxygen and carbon dioxide than tropical waters, and hence are more prolific of life, especially during the long summer days when sunlight is available for photosynthesis.

Nitrates are a major requirement for life in the seas. Especially fertile "pastures" are found where an upwelling brings toward the surface the nitrate-rich waters which originate from the decay of life on the ocean floor. Such areas are found off the west coast deserts of the continents and in polar waters.

CIRCULATION. The circulation of water in the sea is in a complex system of great circular currents, or gyres, similar to the great currents of air that surround the subtropical highs. The direction of movement of the ocean gyres also resembles that of atmospheric high pressure cells in that they move clockwise in the northern hemisphere and counter-clockwise in the southern hemisphere.

The centers of the gyres are especially barren waters, high in salt, low in contained gases, and a deep blue in color. They lack the greens which mark the presence of tiny organic particles that are a sign of fertile waters. The center of the North Atlantic gyre is called the Sargasso Sea. The masses of floating seaweed and flotsam that collect in the gyre led early mariners to fear this strange ocean region as the graveyard of lost ships.

Not all the waters of the gyre rotate with the same speed. The most rapid currents are found on the western sides of the gyres. The Gulf Stream which forms the western edge of the North Atlantic gyre, has a speed at times as much as 5 miles per hour and has been called an "ocean river."

Although most of the water in the gyres makes its way slowly around and around the great circuits, a portion of it is discharged toward the polar seas, sometimes as marginal tongues and drifts, sometimes as great eddies. As the Gulf Stream begins its eastern path away from the east coast of the United States, it forms great loops, or meanders, in rough proportion to its speed, much as a garden hose bends and twists when the water is turned on full force.

At times the loops may cut across themselves, the detached loops heading slowly into the bordering sea as giant eddies. In such ways warm surface water is injected into polar waters. Cold polar water drifting equatorward is forced against the eastern coasts of continents and deflected to form slow, coastal currents, such as the Labrador Current, which flows southward along the Labrador and Newfoundland coast, and the Falkland Current, which flows northward along the Argentine coast.

The cold water meets warm water moving poleward at about 40° and flows under the warm water, eventually being added to the great surface gyres as the cold water gradually becomes warmed in low latitudes. As in the atmosphere, there is a complex mechanism in the sea involving "wheels within wheels," which runs our global heat transfer system and which is needed to remove the surplus heat of low latitudes.

BIOSPHERE

The biosphere is the zone of living organisms at or near the earth's surface, including parts of the lithosphere, hydrosphere, and atmosphere.

Since the beginning of life billions of years ago, countless forms of living things have spread throughout the world. Perhaps the most wonderful thing about life is that it has adapted to almost every environment found on earth.

Simple algae (single-celled plants) thrive in the hot springs of Yellowstone Park. Lichens fasten themselves to bare rock surfaces, requiring no soil and extracting their nourishment from the atmosphere. Underwater flash cameras have revealed life forms living in the ocean deeps without sunlight and under enormous water pressures. The Arctic tundra, frozen and windswept in winter, has a rich flora and fauna that lies waiting for the short summer season when the darkness disappears.

In the atmosphere, tiny grass seeds and thousands of plant spores and pollen particles ride the air streams a mile above the earth to be deposited in regions far from their place of origin. A close microscopic examination of a typical cultivated soil would show it teeming with life, with individuals continually being born, feeding, reproducing, adjusting their forms and activities to their special environments, and finally dying and adding their remains to the organic debris on which others will feed.

Nature has a remarkable way of working toward environmental balances, and the surface of our planet is a varied mixture or fusion of the four great spheres—lithosphere, atmosphere, hydrosphere, and biosphere. All of them are subject to change, and every change produces sympathetic alterations in each of the others. Some changes are global in scale and require millions of years to evolve; some are minute, taking only minutes to occur and involving only the most miniature characteristics of the environment.

Balances are thus relative in time, but they are no less real. The trend toward balances is especially evident in the biosphere. Life forms are very sensitive to environmental change, tending to form complex assemblages or communities that are nicely adjusted to the soil, the climate, the water supply, sunlight, and to each other, whether plant or animal.

Man is a culmination of the biosphere in two ways. First, he is the first organism to comprehend the totality of the environment and his own place in nature; and second, he is the only living creature to be able to consciously alter the environment to suit his needs. He can, if he so desires, sleep in cool comfort in the tropics, grow fresh strawberries in frozen Antarctica, or turn desert sands into luxurious market gardens.

One of the most highly specialized living organisms ever to appear on earth, man has become an independent variable, modifying the face of the earth wherever his needs require. There is no such thing as a completely natural environment anymore, except perhaps in those rare parts of the earth that are not as yet worth man's efforts to change them, such as the ocean depths, and the frozen polar regions.

Yet, with all his power and knowledge, man has much to learn of the complexities of organic balances, and his battles with living competitors for food and feed never ends.

THE LIVING PYRAMIDS

The plant and animal kingdoms, whether on land or in the sea, both are numerically arranged in the form of a truncated pyramid, or a pyramid whose tip has been cut off. The base of the pyramid, usually comprising by far the greatest total mass, is formed by the micro-forms, the tiny dwellers in the soil or in the surface layers of the sea.

Tiny plants and animals live together and depend on each other for their life cycles. As the life forms become larger, they become less numerous, but are no less a part of the dependent mass. The pyramid has no tip, because the requirement of mobility to obtain food places an upper limit on the size of living things.

PLANT WORLD. And so, within the plant world, the pyramid begins with the simple, single-celled algae, members of which form the green scum on stagnant pools, or band together in the oceans to form huge masses of seaweed, such as kelp. Soils everywhere are rich in micro-plant life, including the moulds or fungi whose *mycellia*, or mass of slender white threads may be seen entangling the needle litter beneath many pine forests. Such plants do not require sunlight and extract their carbohydrates from dead organic material.

Above the ground are other plants that attain various sizes in the competition for sunlight, water, and mineral foods. Some develop special devices to make effective use of the dim light on a shaded forest floor. Others thrive only in open sunlight, but require little water and so can meet competition. Some are water lovers, thriving in saturated bogs or along the edges of ponds. Competition eventually produces a mixture of large plants, or dominants, and smaller ones in each local environment.

The size of the dominants varies in different parts of the world and is related largely to the amount of water taken in through roots and the volume of water going out by transpiration through leaf and stem surfaces. The rainy tropics have large trees as dominants because of a plentiful supply of water the year round combined with warm temperatures all year to insure high transpiration rates.

In the tundra of Arctic regions, on the other hand, the plant life is rich and varied, but the dominants are small because of both low intakes and low discharges. Birches and willows that would have been trees a few hundred miles to the south here are stunted shrubs, a foot or two high. There is no liquid water for intake during the frozen winters, and transpiration rates are low because of cool temperatures, even during the short growing season. Nitrate deficiencies also contribute to the stunted growth of arctic plants, since micro-life forms are the usual source

of supply, and soils are acid and almost devoid of bacteria.

Some large portions of the continents have grasses and herbaceous (nonwoody) plants as dominants. Others have brush and scattered low trees—a woodland rather than a forest. Even the great deserts of the world are not without their flora and dominants, sparse though they may be.

The dominants are only at the tops of the pyramids. Living among them are the more numerous members of the assemblages, many of whom are too small to see or are hidden beneath the surface of the soil.

ANIMAL KINGDOM. The animal kingdom also has its pyramids which vary in constituent members with different environments. Some local pyramids are much larger than others and represent fertile regions, where conditions are favorable for life. Since most animal life feeds on plant life on one kind or another or on other animals, the animal pyramids closely parallel the plant pyramids on the land as well as in the sea.

Especially fertile regions, like the cold waters of polar seas, or the mid-latitude prairies (grass by virtue of fire and not climate), have supported massive communities of both plants and animals, especially before man inserted himself into the pyramid.

There are dominants and sub-dominants among the members of the animal communities as well as among the plant assemblages, and together they adjust themselves to each other in balanced relationships. Every plant and animal in an assemblage has its place and there are natural checks to their increase or decrease in numbers.

Man's experience in introducing new plants and animals into new environments without the customary checks and balances has forcibly illustrated this point. Some of his most serious ecological problems have been the result of such events, both intentional and accidental, as the introduction of the jackrabbit and prickly pear into Australia, the starling and Japanese beetle into the United States, and *lantana* (a flowering shrub) into the Pacific Islands.

MAN'S ROLE. The differences in plant and animal communities are somewhat like those of soils or climates. With close scrutiny, there are minute differences every few feet that can be noted, and these are changing rapidly as their micro-environments change. Then too, there are the great global plant formations—the tropical rain forest, the grasslands, the deciduous (leaf-shedding) forest, the coniferous (cone-bearing) forest, the tropical scrub woodland, the desert shrubs, and the tundra. Each has its own unique features, and its own assemblage of animals, large and small. Man is the only organism that roams them all, selecting here, destroying there—an independent, conscious force that will continue to alter the entire surface and to insert himself into every areal balance, whether local, regional, or global in scale.

—Joseph E. Van Riper

CULTURAL GEOGRAPHY

Culture is the total socially learned and shared behavior pattern of a human group. Each cultural group on the earth's surface has particular attitudes, degrees of technical ability and development, and ways of living which are called cultural traits. These traits determine the way people group themselves, their tools and use of raw materials, dominant food, and the degree of industrialization and its accompanying urbanization and specialization.

Cultural traits also determine the system of land tenure and use, the kinds of dwellings used, how houses and other structures are arranged and spaced to form hamlets, towns, and cities. People with the same cultural characteristics tend to modify the landscape in similar ways.

The cultural features which are encountered in wide variety around the world may be grouped according to geographical areas with a similarity of cultural traits within their borders. Depending on the basis for selection used, there are between a half-dozen and a dozen major culture regions in the world which exhibit sharp differences in culture traits; within these major culture regions are smaller areas of cultural distinctiveness called subregions.

Those who are raised in a particular culture region become so accustomed to living with their own culture traits that they accept them, while at the same time they are aware that people in other cultures do live differently. The small details of living, such as types of eating utensils or style of dress, are among the obvious cultural traits distinguishing one group from another.

If one goes back through history, however, he will discover that in some culture regions the cultural traits of today were not necessarily those of the past. For example, several centuries ago Europeans did not use knives and forks any more than they wore miniskirts or crew cuts.

Indigenous cultural traits are carried to other regions by trade, war, tourism, and the many modern means of communication. An example of this is the dominance of Islam in the Malayan subregion of the Oriental Culture Region; or the similarity of larger urban centers around the world. For culture traits change and evolve through time; and, as cultures develop, cultural traits are not only altered but may be spread and diffused in other areas.

Mankind has undergone a process of cultural evolution which has been extremely slow until the last few hundred years. Early man appeared almost a million years ago in Eastern Asia, Java, and Africa.

For thousands of years man used wood, bone, and stone implements. It was not until 3000 BC, when the people of the Middle East discovered the use of metals, that a basic cultural revolution was begun. First the use of copper, then the use of bronze (a harder metal, an amalgam of copper and tin), made possible more efficient tools and weapons for farming and hunting.

Another basic revolution in man's relationship to the land occurred when he domesticated plants and animals, thereby gaining greater control over his food supply. With the industrial revolution man developed and applied inanimate power on a large scale. This enabled him to transform the earth's surface to his own liking and to satisfy his own needs. He has plowed millions of acres, dug canals, mined large amounts of valuable minerals, and even destroyed vast areas by accelerating erosion.

ELEMENTS OF CULTURE

The elements of culture must take into consideration the population and its many characteristics—the number of people, their density patterns of population growth, whether they are sedentary or nomadic, how they group themselves, the degree of overpopulation or underpopulation. The formation of complex ethnic groups, the patterns of races, and modes of living all contribute to the formation of a distinctive culture region.

A second element is the combination of tools and their degree of complexity and the kinds of raw materials which they require. Between the most primitive tribe of the equatorial rain forest of Ecuador and the automated factory in California is a wide range of situations.

A third element of culture is the reliance upon a single dominant food. At one time in the Western Hemisphere it was maize (Indian corn); in northern Europe it was the white potato; in Asia, rice. These examples of the way in which one may speak of a rice culture or a potato culture demonstrate one of the characteristic features of major culture groups.

A fourth element is building material. In the dry zones, the earth itself has been used, as in the adobe houses of the southwestern United States; the Mediterranean area uses stone; in northern Europe and the United States wood has been used; central and western Europe use both stone and wood.

A fifth element of culture is population grouping, ranging from temporary sites to clustered settlements of hamlets, scattered settlements, and massive urban agglomerations.

A sixth element is the means of transportation and circulation of people and goods. They range from man and animal power to engines and rockets, from mule trails to railways and superhighways.

The cultural traits of some simpler societies dictate that each person be highly self-sufficient in terms of satisfying his own needs. This means that each person must be able to build his own house, hunt or cultivate his own food and prepare it, make his own clothing, and fashion the everyday implements that are required.

UNITED NATIONS

IN AFRICA simpler societies dictate self-sufficiency (*above*); others use modern technology, as in this Niger school (*left*).

UNITED NATIONS

In more complex societies cultural traits reflect a high degree of specialization with people concentrating on performing particular tasks and, in turn, benefiting from a multitude of specialized actions of other people. Because each person does only his task, there must be a medium of exchange, such as money, with which to obtain the specialized goods produced by others.

MAJOR CULTURE REGIONS

Within general geographic limitations specific cultural traits have developed, and although one region may share a religion or language family with another, the sum total of cultural traits has made each region unique. Six major culture regions can be recognized in the world—European, American, Dry World, African, Oriental, and Pacific.

EUROPEAN CULTURE REGION

The European culture region is limited on the west and north by the Atlantic and Arctic oceans; on the east by the Ural Mountains, Caspian Sea, Caucasus Mountains, and the Black Sea; and on the south by the Mediterranean Sea. It also extends across the Mediterranean Sea to North Africa and beyond the Urals across Siberia to the Pacific Coast. The region has been divided into three subregions: Mediterranean, European Plain, and Eastern Europe.

The primary cultural traits of this region include field agriculture and industrialization with its accompanying urbanization and high degree of job specialization. Some writers feel that the European Culture Region has also been characterized by an aggressiveness whereby these traits have been carried overseas and implanted among other peoples. European colonization has, in varying degrees, affected all the other culture regions.

The European region has been the center from which industrial society's ways have spread to most corners of the world. Industrialization began in Europe around the margins of the North Sea in the 1800s and 1900s. It meant the specialization of productive processes whereby raw materials were converted into manufactured finished products rapidly and in large quantities at low per unit costs. The keynote of industrialization is mass production.

The invention of new means of transportation, such as the railroad, automobile, and motor truck, meant that large population centers were possible because large quantities of food and necessities could be brought to nonagricultural urban residents. In the urban setting is the highest degree of specialization with the widest variety of occupational structure. In the less developed rural areas people are less specialized even as the professional people and stores which serve them are less specialized than in urban areas.

SUBREGIONS. A principal cultural subregion of Europe is the Mediterranean, where a degree of cultural unity was achieved south of the virtually continuous mountain barrier from the Pyrenees to the Black Sea. A second subregion is the great European Plain, which lies to the north of the mountain barrier and has as its focus the margins of the North Sea. The third subregion is the extensive plain of Eastern Europe, which includes the densely populated parts of the Soviet Union.

Between the subregions are relatively broad transitional zones where contrasting cultures come together. East-Central Europe is one such zone and has been termed the Shatter Belt because it contains elements of quite diverse cultures. Historically it has been an area of conflict, war, and political rearrangement.

AMERICAN CULTURE REGION

As a culture region, the western hemisphere, composed of the North and South American continents, is an offshoot of the European Culture Region. Small areas of indigenous culture still exist, but the distinctions within this region are primarily due to the differences among the Europeans who settled the Americas.

An outstanding cultural attitude of the American Culture Region is that natural resources are virtually limitless. During the 400 years of European influence in the western hemisphere, forests, soils, wildlife, and minerals have been exploited and used recklessly. Such an attitude was easier to understand in the early years when there was only a very sparse population in the entire hemisphere. Now there are almost 500 million people and the pressure of population on resources is already of alarming magnitude in such areas as the West Indies and parts of Central America.

Two major subregions were carved out during the colonial period—Latin America and Anglo-America. Latin America was settled by southwestern Europeans, primarily the Spanish and Portuguese. Anglo-America was settled by northern Europeans, primarily the English and French.

The Latin American subregion has the Spanish and Portuguese languages, Roman Catholicism, and laws and customs resembling those of southwestern Europe. In the North American subregion (Canada and the United States) English is the dominant language and Protestantism the dominant religion. The economic, social, and political customs are those of northwestern Europe.

LATIN AMERICA. There is great diversity of peoples within the Latin American subregion. In Ecuador, Peru, Bolivia, and Paraguay the population is largely Indian, and in some of the more inaccessible corners of Guatemala and eastern Mexico there are isolated tribes of Indians. The Caribbean and parts of Colombia and Brazil are heavily Negroid. Argentina and Chile are 90 percent European, and the other countries are mixed.

Most of the population is distributed along the coast; the interior is almost uninhabited. Urban clusters represent the twentieth century centers of innovation and industrializa-

GERMAN INFORMATION CENTER
EUROPEAN INDUSTRIALIZATION has spread to most areas of the world. Shown here, the purification of color pigments in a German factory.

tion, but there is little communication between them. The rural areas frequently reflect the more feudal type of society of 300 years ago.

NORTH AMERICA. In the North American subregion there is a degree of uniformity and standardization in terms of culture traits and the details of living. Small town life in the United States is pretty much the same regardless of location.

Cities are the centers of innovation, and the urban way of life has so developed that a suburban sprawl has occurred in which adjacent cities tend to coalesce. Thus, a megalopolis extends from Portland, Maine, to Richmond, Virginia. It is anticipated that in the last third of the twentieth century in the United States there will be megalopolis-type developments in southern California and most of Florida.

DRY-WORLD CULTURE REGION

South and southeast of the European Culture Region is a unique, broad, arid zone which acts as a barrier between the European Culture Region and the African Culture Region of Africa south of the Sahara, and the Oriental Culture Region. This "dry world" is one example of a culture region coinciding with a physical or climatic region.

The dry-world region extends from the Atlantic coast of North Africa deep into the Asian heartland to western Manchuria, in northeastern China. It includes the Sahara, Libyan, and Nubian deserts of North Africa and the Arabian, Anatolian, and Iranian plateaus, the Caspian Depression, the Tibetan Plateau, and the Takla Makan and Gobi deserts of Asia. The region is divided into Arab-Berber and Turkic-Mongolian subregions.

The inhabitants of the Dry-World Culture Region are traditionally nomadic, although there are densely populated areas around well-watered oases and river valleys. The characteristic traits of the region are pastoral nomadism, with its heavy dependence of man upon animals, and oasis farming.

There is a great contrast between areas with a small amount of water and those which have none. The climates of this region are too dry for field agriculture, and the natural resources are too scarce for industrial and technological development of any significance.

There are marked contrasts with the European and American culture regions in regard to moral codes, taboos, and tribal and political organizations, items which have little regard for political boundaries.

The two subregions are separated by the southern boundary of Turkey, the western boundary of Iran, and the Persian Gulf.

ARAB–BERBER. The Arab-Berber subregion of North Africa and the Arabian Peninsula is mainly Caucasoid, Muslim, and Semitic-speaking. The principal language is Arabic.

Rain falls mainly in the winter season. In the oases the date palm is the economic base. There are foreign cultural ties with adjacent African and European areas.

TURKIC–MONGOL. The Turkic-Mongolian subregion is Muslim to the west, Buddhist to the east. It is an Iranian (Indo-European) language area. There is some summer rainfall but a combination of low temperatures and aridity makes farming a hazardous proposition.

Foreign cultural ties exist mainly with the eastern subregion of the culture region.

AFRICAN CULTURE REGION

There is a striking boundary between the Dry-World Culture Region of North Africa and the African Culture Region south of the Sahara. This boundary cuts east-west across Africa from the mouth of the Senegal River to Khartoum in Sudan and then turns southeastward to the mouth of the Juba River. It marks the transition from dry climates and grassy steppes to subhumid and humid climates with dense, luxuriant vegetation.

The African Culture Region is too complex for simply delineated subregions. Instead, there are a number of

cultural landscapes, such as the low-lying tropical forest of Guinea, the drier western Sudan, the primitive areas of west-central Africa, the cooler plateau areas of East Africa, and the European-dominated southern Africa.

The African region is mainly inhabited by Negroid peoples who live in small permanent huts and houses. They depend upon simple hunting and gathering, pastoral nomadism in some areas, and primitive agriculture using hoes. Distinctive cultures developed in this region but not in complete isolation.

Stone Age cultures spread freely throughout the continent and ancient Egypt had close connections with this region. Influences from Southeast Asia are revealed through culture traits identical with regard to some food crops, domesticated animals, and house types. The Dry World's characteristic grazing economy spread deeply into Africa, and the Arab influence was so strong that the eastern Sudan became incorporated into the Dry-World culture area.

Not an area of written languages, the region was nevertheless highly advanced in some aspects of metallurgy, craftsmanship, and artistic development prior to the coming of Europeans in the 1800s. It attracted Europeans as a rich source of slave labor and raw materials and as an area that could become a colonial dependency of Europe.

In the middle of the present century many colonists were replaced by independent countries, although the European cultural imprint is still evident, particularly in southernmost Africa.

ORIENTAL CULTURE REGION

The Oriental Culture Region includes all of Asia south of the Soviet Union and the Dry World. It includes East Asia (China, Korea, Japan), the peninsulas of Southeast Asia, and the subcontinent of India. Physically, the continent of Asia is an area of sharp contrasts, containing the highest and lowest elevations, the coldest and possibly the hottest places, the rainiest and driest climates in the world.

Although three-fourths of Asia is almost devoid of people, more than half of the world's population lives on about 10 percent of the world's land area—along the southern and eastern coasts of Asia. The region is divided into the Indian, Chinese, and Malayan subregions, with a transitional zone that is comprised of Burma, Vietnam, and the intervening countries.

The Oriental Culture Region is more than 4,000 years old in some parts of northern China; from there this ancient culture spread into southern and eastern Asia. Another portion of this culture region had its origins in the Indus Valley of what is now Pakistan and spread to the Upper Ganges Valley in northern India. The common characteristic of the Oriental Culture Region is its great age, predating by many centuries European civilization. This gives the Orientals a feeling of cultural and spiritual superiority.

UNITED NATIONS

DRY—WORLD Nomads depend on their donkeys and camels for transportation and sustenance.

The region is marked by such traditional culture traits as willingness to accept an assigned place in a hierarchy of rank, as in the Indian caste system; little value placed on the individual; the importance of "saving face," or one's dignity; and the apparent acceptance of abject poverty without attempting to improve one's position.

INDIA. The Indian subregion has been traditionally an area of diverse peoples speaking many languages and occupying many different landscapes. There have been no unifying links in culture, tradition, or history. Even the name India is of foreign origin. These factors plus the cleavage between the many religions, their clear patterns of distribution, and the elaborate caste system of orthodox Hinduism have handicapped the rise of industrialization and the economic development of India.

In the Indian subregion the people are Mongoloid, Australoid, Negroid, and Mediterranean. The major language groups in northern India are Indic—a branch of Indo-European. In southern India they are Dravidian.

Europeans have been in contact with India for over 2,000 years. When Alexander the Great conquered northwestern India in 326 BC, he encountered a civilization already old. There was an extensive literature in written Sanskrit, religion and philosophy were highly developed, and architecture and craftsmanship were advanced. People wove fine cloths and fashioned metal tools and ornaments.

For hundreds of years Europe imported manufactures and other goods from India, such as spices, gems, oils, and silks. The voyages of discovery in the 1400s and 1500s were prompted by the search for a direct sea route to the rich eastern lands of India and other parts of the Oriental world.

CHINA. The Chinese subregion is unusual in that over half of it is unsuited for agriculture. Only about one-eighth of the land is presently under cultivation and must support a population of more than 700 million people. Thus each square mile of cultivated land must produce enough food to feed 3,000 people.

The Chinese subregion has such Dry-World Culture traits as the cult of family, patriarchal control, and the absence of a caste system. The rational use of land and gardening skills suggest the practice of oasis dwellers. A strong cultural trait is the traditional emphasis on ancestor worship, with the result that cemeteries occupy prime farmland.

The spoken languages and dialects are so varied that people from one part of the country cannot understand people from other parts. The written language is the same, however. The most widely spoken Indo-Chinese langauge is *Kuo-yü,* based on the language spoken in Peking.

Traditionally, Chinese society has been controlled by a system of ethics rather than by a system of laws. The People's Revolution and the subsequent communist political regime ruling China today have had uneven success in attempting to overthrow these traditional loyalties. There is a marked distaste for foreign innovations among most traditional Chinese and a fear of loss of face.

The Chinese have a world-wide reputation as traders and merchants. Functioning as commercial centers, cities have always been an important part of the Chinese landscape. Cities such as Canton and Shanghai have long been principal trade centers and points of contact with the rest of the world.

Japan is included as part of the Chinese subregion. A land of extremely high population density, it has become highly industrialized, high levels of productivity having increased Japanese standards of living by impressive margins. Major cities resemble cities the world over. In short, Japan is unique in its readiness to adopt Occidental, or Western, ideas.

MALAYA. The Malayan subregion includes the islands around Indonesia, or the East Indies, the Malayan Peninsula, and the Philippines. Over a long period of their early history, these peoples absorbed Buddhist and Hindu elements into their traditional culture patterns. Some time after the 1200s Islam was introduced. Today it is the most widespread religion in the area, with the exception of the Philippines, where Christianity is the major religion.

The principal source of livelihood is subsistence agriculture and the Europeans introduced modern farming.

At one time or another the Malayan subregion has been dominated by the Arabs, the Chinese, and the Europeans, and it still shows the influence of those peoples.

Between these three cultural subregions is a transitional zone similar in its diversity to the Shatter Belt of East-Central Europe. It includes the easternmost part of India, Burma, most of Thailand, Cambodia, Laos, and North and South Vietnam. This shatter belt has been invaded by very different kinds of people so that fragments of many different cultures now exist close to one another; lacking a basic coherence, stable political, social, and economic situations are most difficult to achieve.

PACIFIC CULTURE REGION

The Pacific Culture Region is composed of the continent of Australia, and Oceania (Melanesia, Micronesia, and Polynesia). Although it encompasses an enormous area, it has very few inhabitants. The early cultural roots were in Southeast Asia, but after its discovery and exploration in the 1500s, 1600s, and 1700s, Europeans colonized, exploited, and finally politically dominated this region.

Four main subregions—Polynesian, Micronesian, Melanesian, and Australian-New Zealand—can be distinguished on the basis of surviving aboriginal cultures and the degree of change brought by European influence. In the Polynesian subregion the outstanding cultural traits are subsistence farming and fishing, with copra as the main export. This subregion also includes the Hawaiian Islands—an anomaly because of their status as a part of the United States, commercial sugar and pineapple industries, and tourism.

The Micronesian subregion has a very small population and an economy based on subsistence farming and fishing. The Melanesian subregion is divided between subsistence farming, fishing, and commercial sugar cane and copra plantations.

The fourth subregion is composed of Australia and New Zealand—rich, remote outposts of the European Culture Region, indigenous elements having been all but obliterated. The European population is limited only by its small numbers in bringing this area completely into the industrialized world. Australia is pastoral, industrial, and highly urbanized. New Zealand is mainly agricultural and pastoral.

—Kempton E. Webb

UNITED NATIONS
IN THE ORIENTAL REGION, Indonesian farmers transplant young shoots in this rice paddy.

ECONOMIC GEOGRAPHY

The earth as a whole and the products of nature and of man's activities are too vast to be studied as a unit. A practical and logical approach is, first, by continents and then by natural units and, where they correspond, by political units, or countries, because this last division is that with which we are most familiar.

What then are the principal regions that contribute to the economic wealth of the world and produce the various raw materials and manufactured articles so necessary to our comfort? We cannot answer this question until we compare different areas and learn the climatic, economic, geographical and political causes for the distribution of the natural wealth of the world.

It is difficult to ascertain to what degree economic wealth produced by man's agricultural and industrial activities in a given area is due to location, fertility, climate and other natural influences, and to what extent it has been fostered by social, political, and governmental factors—by tariffs, treaties, landownership patterns, caste, or peculiarities historical development.

AUSTRALIA. The largest island in the world, nearly as large as the conterminous United States, Australia is a continent-nation. Pastoral and agricultural activities long prevailed, and Australia is still a leading world producer of wool, of which Britain imports a large share.

Australia's position as a gold producer has declined since 1910. Other mineral products are coal, silver, lead, copper, and tin. Australia is now a major manufacturing nation, as well as a leading producer of minerals. The climate, though generally hot and dry, is very favorable to human life; but the location of the island is unfavorable for world trade.

SOUTH AMERICA. Fourth in size of the continents, South America is handicapped by its location, for more than two-thirds of its area lies within the tropics and tropical rain belt. The present underdeveloped nature of much of South America may be attributed directly and indirectly to these facts: directly, because the efficiency of humans working in hot and humid climates is low; and indirectly, because it is almost impossible to cross the great forests resulting from these natural conditions.

The great forest of the Amazon basin is the largest equatorial forest in the world and one of the world's greatest sources of natural rubber. The Amazon River, in the northern part of South America, is the great, and was for many years the only, waterway system making it possible to penetrate the vast forests. No river equals the Amazon in volume and in number and size of tributaries.

Increasingly the Amazon region is being penetrated by highways, and air transport now links once inaccessible areas with the developed parts of South America.

Southern South America is separated by the Andes mountain system into two major countries and two major economic units—Argentina and Chile. Southern Brazil and northern Argentina, the northern part of this southern peninsula area of South America, constitute one of the world's leading food-exporting regions. Production is far beyond consumption, and the area around the Plata River (Río de la Plata) is one of the greatest surplus food producing regions in the world.

Argentina is a principal maize (corn) exporting country, supplying as much as half that commodity and also nearly half the linseed that enters international trade. Wheat is the principal export of Argentina.

This great food-producing region is also important as a grazing land for cattle and is one of the world's important sources of meat. Argentina exports considerable quantities of beef, wool, and mutton.

The wealth of Chile, a narrow country bounded by the Andes on the east and the Pacific on the west, is chiefly minerals. It ranks high as a world producer of copper, and a large share of its exports consists of nitrates.

The western coast of South America, including Peru, Ecuador, and Colombia, produces minerals chiefly, but Ecuador until very recently led the world in the production of the cacao bean, which is still a leading export. Colombia has important platinum mines and supplies a large part of the world's demand for that metal. The emerald mines at Muzo in the eastern Andes are famous.

Coffee makes up more than one-half the value of Brazil's exports. Other leading exports include cotton and cacao. Bolivia is the world's most important producer of tin and antimony. These and other metals account for practically all of the country's exports.

Venezuela ranks high in world oil production. The chief source is found in the Lake Maracaibo area, but newer fields in other areas are also significant. Venezuela's vast interior Orinoco region is important for its iron ore and hydroelectric power potential. This industry enables Venezuela to enjoy a healthy balance of trade.

Brazil occupies an area greater than that of the conterminous United States and lies almost completely in the tropics. To the climate and the volcanic soils, rich in iron, may be attributed the fact that nearly 70 percent of the world's coffee is grown in Brazil, nearly half the world's total coming from the state of São Paulo alone, where more than 3 million acres are planted in coffee. The Brazilian highlands in the east have vast mineral resources, with reserves of high-grade iron ore among the richest in the world.

To a large extent, South America is still a producer of raw materials. The continent as a whole lacks the capital and skills on a broad enough scale to launch needed development. It is hoped that funds available from the Alliance for Progress and other sources will aid South America to realize its great potential wealth.

Long-distance surface transport is difficult, as the vast interiors are almost impenetrable and the mountains of the west form great barriers to communication between the two coasts. There are no good seaports in the west and few in the east and south.

As yet, South America maintains its motto, "Down to the sea and away to the North," meaning that there is little internal trade, but raw materials of mine and farm are sent down the rivers, railroads, and highways to the sea and are then shipped to other countries, especially to Britain and the United States. From these countries South America imports manufactured goods: machinery, cotton textiles, iron and steel.

AFRICA. The Dark Continent, as Africa was long called, is gradually yielding to the inroads of modern industrial civilization. The handicaps of unhealthful coasts, a too regular coastline for good natural harbors, treacherous rivers, and a desert climate in many areas are gradually being overcome.

Africa is second to Asia in size and is cut by the equator about halfway in its length from north to south. In the northwest, an extension of the European Alpine system forms the Atlas Mountains. The rest of the continent is a plateau, separated from the ocean by a narrow coastal plain. This plateau consists of ancient rock,

CREOLE PETROLEUM CORP.

LAKE MARACAIBO, Venezuela, a major world source of petroleum, is dotted with oil derricks.

minerals from which supply the major portion of commercial wealth of the continent.

Internal trade and communication are difficult, one-third of the continent having no outlet to the sea. The rivers, although navigable for long distances, are treacherous with rapids and waterfalls. The Congo River in south-central Africa is an unsatisfactory waterway because the seasonal fluctuations in depth are so great. These conditions, however, give rise to vast potential waterpower—more than in any other continent.

Africa may be divided into three climatic regions, and its natural resources are determined by the differences between these regions. The north is dominated by the Sahara, greatest of the trade-wind deserts, an arid area contributing oil and natural gas to the economic importance of the continent.

The United Arab Republic (Egypt), a part of the Sahara, differs from the desert only because it has an irrigated valley as a result of the Nile floods. The people live only on the delta and banks of the river. Cotton is the chief crop, its long fiber commanding a high price; it constitutes a large share of the country's exports. Its biggest customer today, replacing Britain, is the Soviet Union. The bulk of Egyptian foreign trade is controlled by and moved through the port of Alexandria.

The second natural division is the equatorial region characterized by dense rain forests. The vegetation of Africa shades out gradually from this thickly treed area. In spite of its million or more square miles of forests, Africa as a whole exports little timber. Nearly half the forest area is in the equatorial zone, and the other half is farther south in the Congo (Kinshasa), the former Belgian Congo, and in Rhodesia. South Africa lacks sufficient timber and must import large quantities of wood.

The timber wealth of Africa lies in the mahogany, ebony, rosewood and other cabinet woods of the equatorial zone, although they have been developed very little. Timber is produced under serious disadvantages of high production and transport costs.

Rail charges are high on bulky commodities, and valuable timber stands are far from the coast. The cost of logging is great, especially because there are so many different species of trees to the acre and it is difficult to get trees out of the jungle. In addition, the tropical hardwoods in which Africa is most wealthy represent a negligible part of the world's trade in timber. To date, the economic importance of Africa's forests has been in by-products: palm oil, rubber, cork, gums, and dyes.

The equatorial zone harbors the cacao tree and is one of the important commercial sources of cocoa, producing about half the world's supply. At one time the bulk of the world's rubber came from the Congo basin and from the equatorial forests of the Amazon basin, but this production was rendered less valuable by the development of plantation rubber in Southeast Asia and by the production of synthetic rubber.

Of the major world commodities, Africa leads in the production of very few, mainly gold, diamonds, and exotic items such as ostrich feathers. South Africa is the leading producer of gold and diamonds. Since World War I and World War II South African industry has grown considerably. The mineral resources of the Congo (Kinshasa), Zambia, Rhodesia, Liberia, and other African nations are increasingly exploited.

The Congo's Katanga province and Rhodesia form one of the world's major copper-producing regions. South Africa has also risen to importance in the copper industry. Over three-fourths of that country's exports consist of products of the mine. Depletion of mineral resources could create a serious problem for the country. Large amounts of food are imported. Trade is chiefly with Britain and the United States. Britain, France, and Belgium still dominate the commerce of their former colonies.

Sheep raising is the chief agricultural industry of South Africa. Sheep number more than 45 million and wool is second to gold as an export. The Republic of South Africa comprises a territory wealthy in a few minerals, with areas of fertile soil and of ideal climate, and man has found it an agreeable place to live.

Africa is the leading continent in potential waterpower development and its mineral resources are great. The United States is a chief purchaser from South America but has little part in Africa's trade.

ASIA. Called the continent of diversity, the continent of extremes, Asia has the highest plateaus and the greatest extent of lowlands, the densest and the sparsest populations, the coldest and hottest climates (determined by physical features).

Some parts of the continent are 1,500 miles from the sea. The great Himalayas run from east to west and separate the southern and northern areas. Mountain masses occupy the center, far removed from the sea, with a continental climate subject to extremes in temperature.

Asia has the greatest population but still is the most sparsely settled continent. Nearly half the world's population is in the monsoon area of southeastern Asia, which includes India, China, Japan, Indonesia, and the Philippine Islands and constitutes a potent region in Asia's economic importance. With the investment of capital and the application of managerial ability, these people are joining the leading nations in the creation of economic wealth.

Asia is the leading food producer of the world, and undoubtedly takes first place also in the creation of the other elemental human needs of shelter and clothing, in spite of a relatively low standard of living. The continent leads in several of the world's major commodities, including vegetables, rice, tea, jute, silk, tin, and natural rubber.

India forms the southern peninsula of Asia, almost completely shut off from the rest of Asia by a wall of mountains.

The broad flat fertile plains make agriculture the essential occupation. The dense population causes serious food shortages at times, but production levels are rising with government aid. Cotton is grown chiefly for export to Britain and Burma. Manufactures are largely expert handwork, although India is fast increasing its production of machine-made articles.

Exports are raw cotton, rice, oilseed and tea; most of this trade is by sea. Imports are chiefly cotton goods (cotton clothing is sufficient in India's climate), metals, foodstuffs, gold, and silver. Cotton manufactures come mainly from Britain and Japan. The island of Ceylon, which lies south of India, exports tea, rubber, and coconut products.

The Malay Peninsula forms a part of the world's great tin-producing region, yielding over one-third the world product. (About 25 percent of the world's total comes from southeastern Asia.) The Malay Peninsula is also a leading rubber-producing region.

This plantation rubber replaced wild rubber (African and South American) in international markets. Half Malaya's exports consists of rubber. Imports are rice and manufactured goods from Britain and other nations. The Malay Peninsula contains the port of Singapore, one of the key distributing centers of the Orient.

Southeastern Asia, with its monsoon climate and heavy summer rainfall, is the great rice-growing region of the world. As a sugar producer, Java ranks below only Cuba and India. Java's sugar is too far removed from the leading sugar markets, the United States and Europe, to vie with the Caribbean crop. Rubber leads as an export, with sugar second. The trade of southeastern Asia is practically all seaborne. The political units trade with one another, but most of the foreign commerce is with Britain, the United States, and Japan.

Prewar China was noted for its silk industry. The present Communist regime has placed the emphasis upon rapid industrialization. Although once trading almost exclusively with the Soviet bloc, China has sought to overcome its chronic food shortage by contracting with Canada and Australia for massive grain shipments. The Chinese region of Manchuria, however, is one of the most important agricultural areas in the Far East. It is also rich in key minerals such as coal and iron.

Although its islands are cultivated intensively, Japan is becoming more and more dependent upon foreign supply of foodstuffs. The Japanese produce the greatest portion of the world's silk. Their textile output also includes cotton and woolen goods, although the raw materials for these products must be imported from abroad —cotton from the United States and India and wool from Australia. Synthetic fibers are also produced in large quantities.

Abundant waterpower is a decided asset to Japan's industry. Manufactured products include steel, chemicals, ceramics, wood products, precision instruments, and machinery. There is an extensive shipbuilding industry, and the Japanese have a considerable merchant fleet.

Closely allied with Japan since World War II, the United States supplies a high percentage of Japan's imports and accepts nearly as large a share of Japan's exports.

The Sea of Japan is one of the world's three leading fishing grounds, the total catch being extremely valuable. The industry employs more than 1 million Japanese, and fish is an important item in the Japanese diet.

North of the mountainous heart of Asia and south of the bleak Arctic Ocean is Siberia, that vast region which is a part of the Soviet Union. Long, cold winters and a sparse population charcterize this area; yet it has black fertile soils that give Asia the title "storehouse of the future." Wheat is the main crop

Although rainfall is limited, the cold climate prevents evaporation. The rivers freeze before they reach the sea in their northward course. Inaccessibility is the difficulty to be overcome and transportation is a critical problem. The long rivers are navigable to some extent, but have no outlet to the sea for boats.

Frozen streams offer the main handicap for the development of Siberia's billion or more acres of forest land. This great timber area stretches from northeastern Europe to the Pacific Ocean, and its wealth is still not entirely exploited. The Soviet Union's stand of forests is greater than that of any other country.

Mining is second to agriculture. Estimates have indicated that Siberia's coal basins equal half those of all Europe. The Soviet Union produces large quantities of platinum and manganese ore. It also has oil fields. As far as is possible, foreign trade is confined to immediate geographic

neighbors. The country is vast and products are diverse. It was only within the last few decades that the people learned to develop their natural resources with modern tools. Siberia is composed of many self-sufficient units of economic endeavor, and in the separate localities there is a marked absence of specialization.

Asia is indeed an economic frontier and a region of enormous possibilities. Large applications of capital and scientific enterprise with an inflow of the industrial civilization are developing the potential of the continent.

EUROPE. The continent of Europe is believed to be more productive than any other as it creates even more wealth than Asia and because in the northwestern portion mining and manufacturing are developed to such a high degree.

Of the world's principal commodities, Europe leads the continents in the production of more than half. The importance of northwestern Europe in population and industrial activity is due in large part to the fact that this is one of the few regions in the world with an ideal climate—one in which the average temperature for the coldest month does not go below freezing and for the hottest month is not above 70°. The climate is cyclonic in nature, bringing the stimulation of rapid but considerable short-range changes in temperature and in humidity.

In northwestern Europe industrial civilization has grown to great levels.

Before the recent development of the European Economic Community (or Common Market) Europe's political divisions, with accompanying tariffs and import quotas, made it impossible for natural geographic regions to operate as economic units. Neighboring European nations in the past often discriminated against one another's goods to their mutual disadvantage,

on the narrow grounds of protectionism. In this manner, ailing industry was perpetuated, and countries cut themselves off from their best markets, sources of materials, and labor forces.

The Marshall Plan successfully rehabilitated European national economies after the devastation of World War II. The next step for Europe was a customs union and the free flow of goods and services across the old political boundaries. This was finally effected by the Treaty of Rome, signed in March 1957 by Belgium, France, Italy, Luxembourg, the Netherlands and West Germany.

The spectacular economic success of the Common Market in a few short years has made Britain abandon its historic isolation from the Continent and seek membership. Other nations, including Greece, Ireland, Turkey, and Israel, are hopeful of allying themselves with this dynamic community.

Among the continents, Europe exceeds in size only Australia. European vegetation may be divided roughly into (1) the Mediterranean region, which includes Spain, Italy, and the southern coast bordering that sea; (2) the deciduous forests that cover an extensive area from Britain and northwestern Europe eastward across to the Soviet Union; (3) the coniferous forests that extend from Norway and Sweden eastward over northern Eurasia.

About one-third the world's coal is produced by Britain and West Germany. Romania and Poland are the big oil producers of Europe, and all European countries except the Soviet Union, Romania, and Poland are large importers of mineral oil. Fortunately, European waterpower is located in regions with coal deficits, and waterpower supplements coal as a source of power for the great industries of Europe.

France, Sweden, and Britain have considerable iron ore reserves, and the bulk of the iron and steel produced in the world is made in six countries, five of which are located in Europe.

Development of modern transportation has rendered the close natural association of iron and coal unnecessary for industry. Britain produces only about half of its requirements of ore and consequently imports large quantities. Spain is one of the major sources, as are the Lorraine fields in France. Spain exports large quantities of the ore to such countries as Britain and Germany.

More than half of the world's supply of zinc comes from the European countries (Belgium, Poland, France, and Germany). These countries are also large producers of lead. Aluminum is produced largely by countries with hydroelectric power—hence Norway's importance as an aluminum producer, although it imports the bauxite.

The Mediterranean countries with their cool moist winters and hot dry summers must overcome climatic handicaps as well as poor soils. Wheat, the hardy universal cereal, is the most important crop in this region. The countries of this area are

UNITED NATIONS
SHIPBUILDERS in one of the largest of Japan's many major shipyards assemble an ore carrier.

also outstanding producers of raw silk. France is one of the largest centers of raw silk and also has a great wool-manufacturing capacity. It is one of the world's greatest wine producers and has enormous iron ore reserves in the world-famous Lorraine deposits.

France ranks, with the United States, as a great producer of bauxite and it formerly was a large producer of antimony. The chief imports of France are coal and machinery and the exports consist largely of iron and steel products, silk, cotton, and woven fabrics.

Agriculture is the chief occupation of the people living in the Danube basin in southeastern Europe. Austria leads the other countries in this region in wool production. In the last few years, these countries have all increased their industrial output. The Danube countries also produce potatoes, sugar beets, barley, tobacco, and orchard fruits. Cattle, as well as sheep and horses, are bred.

West-central Europe includes the Netherlands, Germany, Switzerland, and Poland. The Netherlands is famous for scientific dairying and exports of cheese, butter, margarine, eggs, and meat. Chief occupations are dairying, shipbuilding, and ocean fishing. The Dutch are traditionally a seafaring and commercial people, but increasingly they are becoming a manufacturing people.

Germany is a nation of great scientific industrial activity, with a vast production of potash, phosphates, and nitrates. West Germany has become one of the world's most wealthy industrial states. Its export trade is chiefly with the neighboring countries of Britain, the Netherlands, Czechoslovakia, and Switzerland, and includes the factory products: steel manufactures, cotton, wool, and silk fabrics, beet sugar, chemicals, and dyes. The United States ranks high in supplying Germany's imports and in buying its goods, but German trade is heaviest with its partners in the European Economic Community.

Switzerland is world-famous for its scenery and its specialized manufacture of watches, clocks, and jewelry. It is among the leading countries in per capita foreign trade. Poland is a valuable mineral region, with great coal reserves and the most productive zinc mines in Europe.

In spite of its great crops, Europe must import food. This is due to the geographical specialization of agricultural production and also to the fact that all Europe lies in the Temperate Zone and cannot produce the variety of foods needed.

Europe grows about one-third of all the wheat in the world (excluding the Soviet Union); but all the big importers of wheat except Brazil and Japan are European countries, Britain leading. Of wheat, dairy products, and meat, Europe produces more than all the rest of the world; of barley, more than twice as much as the rest of the world; and of rye, twenty times as much. Europe formerly produced more than 40 percent of the world's sugar. Despite all this, Europe imports more food than the rest of the world combined.

The North Sea region is one of the world's three great fisheries. At one time, about a million tons of fish were landed by British, Norwegian, Dutch, and German fishermen.

Europe is self-sufficient in timber products. Except for the British-U.S. trade, most of the European timber trade is among the countries of the continent and not across seas. Europe has about 10 percent of the world's forest areas, three-fourths of which is coniferous forest. Finland, Sweden, Poland, Russia, Norway, Czechoslovakia, Austria, and Romania are important exporters of timber. The Soviet Union has the greatest potential capacity.

Scandinavia (Norway, Sweden, and Finland) is a part of Eurasia's great northern forest belt. Norway is noted for its water power, timber, and particularly fisheries. Fish and fish products represent a large proportion of Norway's exports. It is said that Norway is the only country in the world whose people could all get in their boats with all their houshold goods and sail away.

Coal represents nearly 90 percent by value of all the minerals products of the British Isles. The mineral next in value is iron ore. Britain no longer exports coal, except in negligible amounts, because reserves are only sufficient to meet domestic needs. Though an important iron and steel industry exists, Britain has to import much of the iron ore used. This is received principally from Spain and from Algeria.

In value, Britain's agriculture is second to its manufactures. Agricultural products of importance include potatoes, sugar beets, barley, oats, and wheat. Manufactured goods total about 80 percent of British exports. These include mainly cotton goods and woolens, and heavy goods,

such as machinery, iron, and steel. Food accounts for about half of the imports. Britain's trade balance is unfavorable but this excess of imports over exports has traditionally been balanced by invisible exports such as credits and tourist trade.

NORTH AMERICA. Ranking with Europe among the most productive continents, North America is third in size with an area of nearly 8 million square miles, the largest part of which lies in the North Temperate Zone.

Physical features of the continent fall into three groups: the Eastern Appalachians, the Great Plains, and the Rocky Mountain System. The last is the water divide of the continent, rivers flowing westward into the Pacific and eastward through the plains, the great granary of the world.

Main vegetation regions of North America include the hot wet forests of Mexico and Central America, cool temperate forests in the east, prairies in the center, desert land in the southwest, and coniferous forests in the north.

Although Canada has huge uninhabitable areas, it is believed to be capable of supporting many times its present population. Predictions are that, with the immense reserves of coal, asbestos, cobalt, and nickel, Canada will become the leading mineral-producing country of the world.

Canada is one of the leading gold-producing countries in the world. However, petroleum has succeeded gold as the country's most valuable mineral. Uranium fields discovered in the Blind River area, north of Lake Huron, are among the richest in the world. Most of the world's asbestos, cobalt, and nickel comes from Canada, which also produces important quantities of the world's copper, zinc, silver, and lead.

UNITED NATIONS
HUNGARIAN COLLECTIVE FARM. Eastern Europe's economy still relies heavily on agriculture.

Despite enormous coal reserves in western Canada, large quantities of the mineral are imported because the more thickly populated eastern section can obtain coal more easily from the United States. Large deposits of high-grade iron ore are being developed in Quebec and Labrador. Canada also has enormous waterpower facilities, both because of the natural topography and because of plentiful rainfall.

Canada's exports of pulp and paper are the largest in the world. Quebec Province is the chief source of asbestos production. There is a great cement industry in the St. Lawrence lowlands where the raw materials are found.

Canada is blessed with one of the world's greatest water-transportation routes—the St. Lawrence Seaway and the Great Lakes. Linked as they are by canals and locks, they give southern Canada a ready outlet to foreign countries and to ocean ports in the United States.

Canada is a great producer and exporter of paper products. Forests still cover 1 million square miles, and the total forestry value is greater than that of mineral products. The lumber industry is second in importance, and British Columbia produces more than one-third of the total output. Necessary conditions for a large-scale paper industry are found only in Canada, the United States, Scandinavia, the Soviet Union, and parts of Germany. The United States is the largest consumer per capita, using the total home production and four-fifths of Canada's output.

The Grand Banks of Newfoundland are one of three great fishing grounds of the world, the other two being the North Sea and the Sea of Japan.

Canada is said to be four extensions of economic United States into a frozen desert: (1) The fishing, timbering and mining of the provinces of western Canada are essentially like those industries in Oregon and Washington. (2) The grain-growing provinces of Canada are merely a part of the great prairie area of central United States, the spring wheat region being principally in Canada. (3) The so-called Ontario Peninsula is really a peninsula of Canada extending into the United States, with manufactures like those of Cleveland and Detroit and with agriculture similar to that of Ohio and Michigan. (4) The Maritime Provinces continue the industries of the New England States: lumbering, papermaking, and fruit growing.

Agriculture, including stock raising, is the chief occupation. Canada exports a large share of the world's wheat. Canada and the United States are the only important rye producers outside Europe. The Maritime Provinces are important for their fruit products, Nova Scotia being noted for apples, mostly exported to Britain.

Canada ranks high among world manufacturers, thanks to its cheap electric power. Exports are chiefly newsprint, wheat, wood, and wood products. Leading imports include agricultural and industrial machinery. Canada trades chiefly with the United States and Britain.

Alaska has great potential. Treaties between the United States, Japan, the Soviet Union, and Canada protect the great supply of seals in the Pribilof Islands, east of the Bering Sea.

The United States purchases the largest share of Mexico's exports, most of which are products of the mine, including petroleum, silver, lead, and zinc. Central America's significance lies in its fruits and other products commensurate with the tropical climate. Over three-fourths of the exports of the West Indies go to the United States and include bananas, sugar, tobacco, and bauxite.

Although the United States has an area roughly equal to that of Canada, the United States is far more favorably situated and has the capacity for supporting a much larger population. The rapid rise of the United States to a leading position among industrial nations was due to the possession of high-quality coal in great quantity and to the great ease with which it could be mined. There is an immense annual output of minerals, coal and oil competing for first place. Reserves are estimated to be equal to those of the rest of the world put together. The Pennsylvania anthracite field has the largest output of anthracite in the world. With the Appalachian fields, it yields nearly three-fourths of the United States' output of coal.

A large share of the world's supply of petroleum is found in the United States, but home and export requirements make it necessary to import oil. United States' exports of petroleum products have reached an impressive level. The United States also produces a large share of the world's iron ore, most of which comes from near Lake Superior.

The United States produces over half of the world's supply of copper and sulfur. It ranks high in gold production, along with South Africa and Canada. It is one of the greatest producers of lead and zinc—at least half of the world's supply. Over 70 percent of all bauxite was mined in the United States and the Guianas in 1946. The State of Arkansas is one of the greatest U.S. sources of bauxite.

Lumbering is the main industry of one-fourth of the states, but the lumber requirements make is necessary to import large quantities, chiefly from Canada. The United States is a major agricultural country, although relatively few of its people are employed in agriculture. Corn is the largest cereal crop. Of the huge production of wheat, never more than one-fourth is exported.

Most of the United States' demand for sugar is supplied by Hawaii and Puerto Rico, and nations in the Caribbean. About one-third of the world's tobacco is grown in Kentucky, North Carolina, and Virginia. Cotton leads as a commercial crop and is second in value among all crops. More than half the annual production is exported. Nearly half the world's cotton crop is grown in the United States. Canada and South American countries furnish the main markets for U.S. cotton cloth. The chief demands for cotton come from Japan, Britain, Germany, France, and Italy.

The United States leads the world in the manufacture of leather and imports large quantities of hides and skins in addition to its home supply. The great manufacturing region in the northeastern part of the country has an ideal economic climate of its own and the great natural resources of the whole country to draw from.

The United States ranks first among all countries in value of manufactured goods, which include textiles, leather, paper, rubber, chemicals, pottery, machinery, automobiles, and ships. Three-fourths of the world's automobiles are built here, and more than three-fourths of U.S. production comes from Michigan.

Vast as the foreign trade of the United States is, it is exceeded by its internal trade. Because the United States is still comparatively young in development, raw materials still make up a large part of exports, principally raw cotton, oil, tobacco, coal, meat, dairy products, and wheat. Other exports are iron and steel manufactures, motor cars, cotton, and copper manufactures, and wood. Imports include raw materials, coffee, tea, and cane sugar; European high-grade manufactured goods; and those minerals in which the United States is deficient.

The foreign trade of the United States is distributed widely. Exports go chiefly to Canada and Western Europe. Imports are mainly from Canada, Europe, and Latin America.

In spite of a lack of ideal climate in most of its area, the United States, with its 200 million people, has prospered greatly through the vigorous production of its natural fuels and other minerals and through the exploitation of its fertile soil and forest resources.

The United States and the other parts of the New World must inevitably settle to their rightful economic positions, based mostly on climate and annual appropriation of the sun's rays. We have greatly depleted our forests; we are depleting our minerals; we have turned regions that should never have been put to the plow into dust bowls; we have tended to exhaust our soil and to allow enormous portions of it to erode into uselessness. Conservation of national resources has been undertaken under various administrations, but it is not yet on a scale to ensure adequate conservation.

In economic geography, the relative importance of the continents or of other divisions of land bodies may be based on the relative importance of their economic productivity or wealth creation, or upon the number of people who are supported. On both counts, the Northern Hemisphere is much more important; and from both standpoints Eurasia far transcends in significance all other land areas combined. If one measures civilization by the yardsticks of educational attainment, health, per capita wealth, and so on, he finds that Britain, northern France, Belgium, the Ruhr, the Netherlands, and Denmark are the center of the world's highest civilization and the heart of the world's best climatic region, and that both desirability of climate and attainment of civilization fade gradually in all land directions at about the same rate.

CONSERVATION

Conservation is the wise use of a natural environment, the preservation and renewal of the quality and usefulness of natural resources. Man's past attitudes toward conservation can be seen in the land itself. The history of conservation is the history of the land.

Land History of the United States.—Roughly speaking, there have been seven phases in the land history of the United States. The first phase was the period of Indian stewardship, when a native people, restrained by their reverence for the land and by the limits of their knowledge, kept a rich and beautiful continent undefiled. The second phase was the period of early colonization, when immigrants, possessed of a higher technology, wrestled with the wilderness and subdued parts of it.

Walden (1854), the chronicle of two solitary years spent in the Massachusetts woods, Henry David Thoreau (1817–1862) lodged a powerful protest against man's way of life and his ruthless invasion and mishandling of nature. The book became a classic of American literature and is still widely read today as both literature and a testament to the beauties of the natural world.

In 1864 diplomat-scholar George Perkins Marsh (1801–1882) published *Man and Nature, or Physical Geography as Modified by Human Action*, which observed that man had become a geological force, capable of changing his environment either constructively or destructively. Marsh cited the man-caused damage of soil erosion, deforestation, overgrazing, and mineral depletion, and begged for the restoration of the harmony

tary of the Interior, was an early conservationist who is best remembered for his enlightened treatment of the Indians, preservation of the public domain, and the beginning of the system of national parks.

Legislative action during this phase included the establishment of Yellowstone National Timber Reserve during the administration of President Harrison and the setting aside in 1892 of 21 million acres of national land as a forest reserve system by President Cleveland.

■**PILOT PROGRAMS.**—The fifth phase did not begin until the turn of the century when, during the administration of Theodore Roosevelt, public conscience was aroused and a new concept developed—that part of the land should be publicly preserved, for its scenic beauty alone, in the form of national parks. John Muir (1838–1914) was instrumental in persuading the President to set aside millions of acres of forest land as national park areas. Roosevelt, a conservationist in his own right, appointed Gifford Pinchot (1865–1946), a professional forester, to head the U.S. Forest Service, and increased the forest reserve from 36 million to 100 million acres. The pilot conservation programs inaugurated during this period were most successful. Unfortunately, interest in conservation waned at the end of Roosevelt's term and remained dormant for two decades.

■**THE DEPRESSION.**—The sixth phase of our land history resulted from the Great Depression of the 1930's, when President Franklin D. Roosevelt made land rehabilitation and conservation programs part of the task of national reconstruction. To utilize the vast supply of unemployed labor, Roosevelt organized the alphabetic agencies: TVA (Tennessee Valley Authority), CCC (Civilian Conservation Corps), REA (Rural Electrification Administration), SCS (Soil Conservation Service), and AAA (Agricultural Adjustment Administration). These new agencies set out to refurbish the land. The dams and development projects that were instituted became hallmarks of the conservation effort. With the onset of World War II, however, resource projects were curtailed as all energy was diverted to the war effort.

■**SCIENTIFIC PROGRESS.**—The seventh phase of our land history began in 1942, when atomic physicists harnessed a new source of power with the successful test of the first atomic pile. This was the supreme conservation achievement of the century—the discovery of the availability of an untapped source of energy. Although it was realized that it would take many years of research before atomic energy could replace coal and oil as a practical and economically feasible power source, this achievement allayed fear of a natural-fuel shortage.

During and directly after the war, great strides were made in science and technology. Research brought new uses for such metals as beryl-

CULVER

PIGEON SHOOTS during the nineteenth century led to near extinction of the species.

■**MYTH OF SUPERABUNDANCE.**—As the frontier was pushed westward during the nineteenth century, the third phase began. The apparent superabundance of untouched resources found by settlers made Old World husbandry and resource replenishment seem unnecessary. These pioneers developed attitudes toward the land which led to an era of misuse and plunder. Americans went on a spree of waste, depleting the natural wealth of future generations by enhancing their own immediate prosperity. Resources were wantonly ripped, gouged, raided, and plundered. Forests were leveled, soil stripped, and streams needlessly polluted, exterminating numerous species of fish and wildlife.

■**CONSERVATION ENLIGHTENMENT.**—The fourth phase of America's land history had its beginnings in the work of the nineteenth-century naturalists, men of foresight who pioneered the conservation movement. In his book

which once had existed between man and nature. The book became known as "the fountainhead of the conservation movement."

Frederick Law Olmsted (1822–1903), a landscape architect, pioneered in the movement for public parks. The designer of many famous parks, monuments, world's fairs, and the grounds of the United States Capitol Building, Olmsted also participated in the development of Central Park in New York City. He strove in the face of almost insuperable political difficulties to make this, America's first public park, not only a work of art but also a successful municipal enterprise. *Public Parks and the Enlargement of Towns* (1871) and *A Consideration of the Justifying Values of a Public Park* (1881) were two of his works that proved milestones in America's public parks movement.

Carl Schurz (1829–1906), diplomat, soldier, and U.S. Senator and Secre-

U.S. DEPARTMENT OF AGRICULTURE

BARREN LAND resulted during the 1930's, when homesteaders' plows exposed portions of the Great Plains to the scourge of wind and rain.

lium, germanium, columbium, molybdenum, and titanium. Synthetic and substitute products were introduced, replacing available raw materials, while the usefulness of the raw materials themselves was enlarged. Research in agronomy, plant genetics, and plant pathology, combined with superior new fertilizers and pesticides, increased farm production; these developments made the granaries of American farmers overflow. Research in animal husbandry made American livestock the most productive in the world. Science encouraged the guardians of public and private lands to apply the tree-farming techniques fostered by the successors of Gifford Pinchot.

Past Progress and Present Problems.—
While scientific progress increased production, it created new conservation problems as well. Man's increasing ability to overpower the natural world also immeasurably enlarged his capacity to damage his environment. The introduction of new goods, machines, and processes fol-

lowing World War II resulted in many new waste products that served to befoul the land, air, and water.

■**CHEMICAL POLLUTION.**—Water pollution has become a serious problem, due mainly to enormous waste disposal difficulties, but also to national sloth. Expenditures on water treatment facilities are already more than $10 billion per year, yet an additional $6 billion will have to be spent for 10,000 new treatment plants to process and purify the ever-increasing load of polluted water.

Another pollution problem is caused by the wide use of pesticides, the chemical pest killers whose value in increasing farm production is indisputable, but whose poisonous properties linger in food and enter the bodies of fish, wildlife, and even man. Chemical insecticides are now applied to one acre in twelve in the United States each year. There is practically no place remaining in the continental United States where residues of these materials are not found. Studies have revealed that residues of the widely used insecticide DDT exist in

alarming amounts in the tissues of our wildlife. In one particular case more than 2,000 parts of DDT per million were found in the fatty tissues of pheasants collected near ricefields that were heavily treated with this insecticide. The tolerance permitted in domestic meats for human consumption is seven parts per million. Cases such as this one are not at all rare, and immediate action must be taken to stem the gradual poisoning of our environment.

■**LAND DESPOILMENT.**—The problem of litter has grown considerably since the war. Aided by industries that produce an incredible array of boxes, bottles, cans, cartons, gadgets, and a thousand varieties of paper products, our landscape litter problem has reached staggering proportions. Some idea of the cost of removing rubbish from public lands nationally can be seen in the case of Washington, D.C., where the government is currently spending $750,000 per year to remove trash and litter from the parks and monuments of our nation's capital. The solution of the litter

U.S. DEPARTMENT OF AGRICULTURE

CONTOUR FARMING was one of many solutions to the "dust bowl." Valuable topsoil was conserved and farm productivity increased as well.

problem lies in a change of attitude toward the land—a recognition by every American that he shares the responsibility for keeping America beautiful and clean.

The recent appearance of so many automobiles on the American scene accounts for more than one conservation problem. In addition to the air pollution or "smog" problem of many of our major cities, which in part is directly attributable to automobile exhaust fumes, more than 5 million battered cars are added annually to roadside junkyards, defacing the natural scenery and further adding to our landscape litter problem. More efficient exhaust systems that completely purify fumes before they are released to the air are helping to solve the smog problem; however, legislative action must be taken to stop the blight of our roadsides by unsightly junkyards.

Planning for the Future.—In addition to solving existing problems, the conservation movement must plan for the future to avert resource shortage.

■WATER.—As national growth strains water resources, efforts are being made to provide future generations with an adequate water supply. In 1900, 40 billion gallons of water were used daily in the United States. By 1964 this figure had reached well over 300 billion gallons, and recent surveys by the Department of Commerce estimate national consumption at over 450 billion gallons per day by 1975. Research is being undertaken to find methods of both extending already available water supplies and finding new ones. Diversion of water from areas of surplus to areas of shortage, the development of techniques for pollution control, and sustained-yield management of underground *acquifers*—the water-bearing layer of per-

LOOK MAGAZINE

DETERGENTS can pollute a quiet stream.

meable rock, sand, or gravel—are some methods of expanding the water supply we now have. Pilot projects, such as the *desalinization* (salt removal) plant at Point Loma, California, which turns 1 million gallons of salt water into fresh every day for the city of San Diego, are steps toward finding new water resources to supplement the available supply.

■POWER.—The wise use and management of available natural power is another program within the scope of conservation. In addition to building and maintaining the dams that harness the power of our rivers and the power lines that distribute the electricity produced, the government is conducting programs for the development of new natural-power sources. In the Passamaquoddy Bay area of

Maine, for example, efforts are being made to harness the daily ebb and flow of ocean tides, which reach up to twenty feet. The project envisions storing tidal waters in Passamaquoddy Bay on high tide and releasing the stored water through power station turbines into adjacent Cobscook Bay at low tide.

■PARKS.—Last, but not least, the providing of recreational facilities for future generations is another urgent aspect of present conservation planning. In 1940, while the population stood at 130 million, our national park system contained 22 million acres. Twenty years later our population had grown to a very mobile 183 million, yet park lands had increased very little. It is estimated that our population will have doubled by the year 2000, and with the total number of recreational visits to state and national forests in 1962 just short of 500 million, available outdoor facilities will be unbearably strained. It is necessary, therefore, for state and federal governments to take prompt action to save prime park, forest, and shoreline areas—of 21,000 miles of ocean shoreline only 7 per cent is presently reserved for public recreation—before they are preempted by other uses or are priced beyond the public purse. Part of this program should be the preservation, in their natural, unspoiled state, of those "natural" rivers having superior outdoor recreation values. The Allagash of Maine, the Suwanee of Georgia and Florida, the Rogue of Oregon, the Salmon of Idaho, the Buffalo of Arkansas, and the Ozark Mountain rivers in Missouri are all waterways that should be preserved as clean, wild rivers and a part of our rich outdoor heritage.

—Stewart L. Udall

U.S. DEPARTMENT OF THE INTERIOR

WATER POWER is harnessed on Washington's Columbia River as the 550-foot-high Grand Coulee Dam provides an inexpensive electricity source. The dam is also used for flood control, irrigation, and river regulation. This concrete structure is known as a gravity dam.

A map is a flat representation of the earth's surface, and the art and science of making maps is called cartography. It involves showing the surface of the earth and its features at a greatly reduced scale.

HISTORY OF MAPS

Map-making is as old as written records. A Babylonian clay tablet dating from about 2500 BC shows the arrangement of mountains and rivers in what is now northern Iraq.

Even most nonliterate peoples use and appreciate the value of maps. On their long sea voyages, Polynesian navigators carried maps made of slender wands and string to represent prevailing wave and current patterns in the sea. Shells were tied to the framework at appropriate spaces to represent islands. Long before Europeans discovered the western hemisphere, American Indian youths were trained to sketch simple maps in the dust with a stick.

ANCIENT MAPS. Accuracy in showing large portions of the curved earth surface on maps became a significant problem early in history. Well before the birth of Christ it had been clearly understood and demonstrated that the earth was a sphere. Attempts to measure the size of this sphere were made by the geographers, mathematicians, and astronomers of Alexandria, Egypt.

Eratosthenes. Some time after 250 BC Eratosthenes undertook to measure the distance between the cities of Alexandria and Syene (present-day Aswân) after calculating that the difference in solar elevation, or the angular distance of the sun above the horizon, between the two places was one-fiftieth of a circle. Fortunately, several of his errors cancelled each other and his results showed a circumference for the earth that was quite close to the correct figure of 24,902 miles.

Posidonius. A hundred years later the work was redone by Posidonius, who used the difference in the elevation of the star Canopus between Alexandria and the island of Rhodes in the Aegean Sea. Again errors compensated and his initial result was even closer to the actual circumference.

Unfortunately, Posidonius justifiably was worried about the estimated water distance between Rhodes and Alexandria and he arbitrarily reduced the distance. This time the errors did not cancel each other, and his figure of 18,000 miles was accepted and used for centuries without the realization that it was some 6,000 miles too small. Had Columbus known the true size of the world he might never have set out for the Indies in his small craft.

Ptolemy. Classical Greek cartography reached its peak in Claudius Ptolemy's *Mathematike Syntaxis* (also called *Almagest* from an Arabic translation of the 800s) and his *Geography*. In about 150 AD Ptolemy, working in the famous library at Alexandria, assembled the *Syntaxis*. It was based on the observations of the earlier astronomer Hipparchus and carefully explained the motions of the sun, moon, and planets, giving a celestial latitude and longitude for each of them.

Ptolemy supplemented his eight-volume *Geography* with an atlas containing maps of Europe, Africa, and Asia, and a map of the entire earth as then known on a stereographic projection. This new type of map-projection had curving lines for latitude and straight lines that met at the top for longitude, thus coming closer to showing the true shape of the earth's surface on a flat sheet than earlier maps.

Ptolemy's map looks strange today, not because he did not know what he was doing, but because of the crude instruments of his time, the lack of standard procedures, and because only a limited portion of the world was then known.

Latitude and Longitude. For many centuries the determination of longitude was an especially difficult problem for navigators and cartographers. Longitude is found by comparing the solar time at an unknown position with the solar time along a standard meridian. Each hour difference represents 15° of longitude.

In ancient times accuracy was almost impossible because of the lack of adequate portable timekeeping devices. Hourglasses were among the most common of the early clocks, but they were crude and subject to many human errors. Reasonably accurate portable timepieces did not appear until the 1500s.

Latitude was much less difficult to determine because it involved only the comparative measurement of the elevation of the sun or a star. For less accurate purposes, variation in the length of day and night during the course of a year constituted a rough estimation of latitude.

MEDIEVAL MAPS. Map-making degenerated to absurd levels in Medieval times. Attempts were made to construct maps to fit accepted Christian theology. The idea of a spherical earth was discarded and accuracy was incidental. Paradise consistently was shown in the east, Jerusalem was placed at the center of the world, and unknown lands were shown occupied by wierd beasts and supernatural creatures.

Even the shape of the world was made to fit religious symbolism. For example, the T-in-O maps showed the Mediterranean, Red, and Black seas in the form of a T or cross, with Jerusalem at the center. The cross opened out into the ocean which encircled the land and marked the rim of the world.

Other maps attempted to fit the arrangement of continents and seas into patterns similar to the form of the Holy Temple in Jerusalem. Fortunately, the Arabs had preserved the best of classical cartography and improved its accuracy. Their atlases were consulted in Europe during the 1500s.

RENAISSANCE MAPS. Increased navigation in the Mediterranean and the Atlantic led to the development of practical navigational charts between 1200 and 1500. Portolan charts, which appeared about 1300, probably were first drawn by the sea captains of Genoa. They showed coasts in remarkable detail and were adapted for compass navigation.

Until the 1500s, maps of any kind were rare things, drawn by hand, and usually the property only of the wealthy and powerful. There is evidence that some of the early navigators such as the Phoenicians had a supply of maps, but these were jealously guarded and were destroyed when no longer needed. Maps that could be obtained by the average person had to wait for the development of the printing press in about 1450.

MODERN MAPS. Within 100 years after the appearance of the printing press in Europe some 400 map-printing shops were in existence. The earliest major map production center was in the Netherlands, and the Dutch school of cartography became famous for maps of high quality. The great discoveries and explorations of the 1500s and 1600s kept map-makers busy with corrections and gradual increases in accuracy.

The growth of nationalism led to the development of large-scale national topographic maps in the 1700s and 1800s. Military men realized the enormous advantage of having detailed maps of the terrain in potential battle areas. Since 1900 there has been a veritable flood of maps, especially road maps, which high-speed color printing presses now turn out by the millions each year for the benefit of car owners everywhere.

The major characteristic of present-day cartography is the widespread development of maps portraying selected features of the earth's surface for special purposes. These include soil maps, air navigation charts, geologic maps, city maps, and even detailed maps of the ocean bottom and the moon. Today maps are everyone's tool.

SEMITIC MUSEUM, HARVARD UNIVERSITY

BABYLONIAN CLAY TABLET, the oldest map known, shows mountains on east and west.

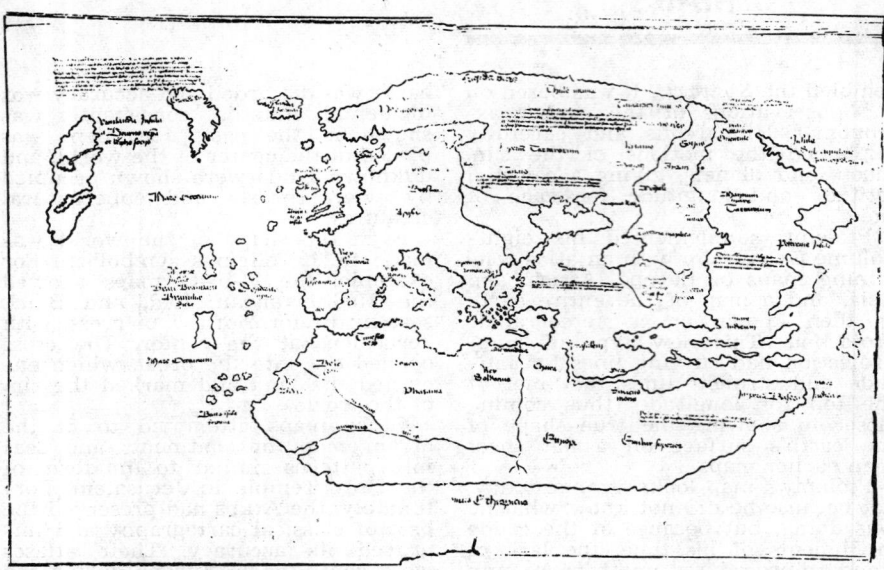

YALE UNIVERSITY

1440 WORLD MAP, based on Leif Ericson's voyage in the 1000s, shows North America at left.

MAP PROJECTIONS

A map projection is an orderly set of meridians of longitude and parallels of latitude on which a flat map may be drawn. The ancient cartographers recognized the problem of attempting to show the surface of a sphere on a flat surface. Although small globes were made from time to time, they were extremely difficult to construct accurately and were not easy to carry around. Once a grid system was devised, consisting of lines representing equal divisions of latitude and longitude, it was a relatively simple step to project this grid onto a flat sheet.

A flat map cannot reproduce all the properties of a spherical surface, but it can select certain properties at the expense of others. On the globe, meridians and parallels always intersect each other at right angles. This property may be preserved on a flat map, but areas are likely to be badly distorted.

Absolutely true scale in all directions (proportionate distance along all straight lines) can never be achieved on any map. The scale distortion may be insignificant on maps of small areas, but it can be very significant on world maps. The best that can be done on world maps is to reduce the distortion in selected areas or in certain directions.

Hundreds of map projections have been developed, and each has a special quality that serves a particular purpose. Many projections may be classified as cylindrical, conic, or azimuthal.

CYLINDRICAL. In a cylindrical projection the earth's meridians and parallels are projected onto a cylinder rolled around the equator of the globe. Meridians and parallels are straight lines intersecting each other at right angles.

The best known cylindrical projection is the Mercator projection, devised by Gerhardus Mercator, a Dutch cartographer of the 1500s. It consists of a single grid of straight lines intersecting at right angles.

The meridians are spaced evenly and proportional to their distance apart at the equator. They are thus pulled apart from their true spacing, except at the equator, since they should converge at the poles. The parallels increase in their spacing towards the poles in the same ratio as the meridians are pulled apart.

This projection was originally designed to aid mariners with its unique property of true bearings or compass directions between any two points. But although it preserves the actual shape of landmasses, it greatly distorts their relative size and that of the water areas between them. The distortion increases with higher latitudes. Greenland, for example, appears to be considerably larger than South America, whereas it is really only one-ninth as large.

CONIC. In conic projections the earth's meridians and parallels are projected onto a cone which touches the globe along a selected standard parallel. The cone is then cut from base to apex and rolled out flat. Meridians are straight lines radiating from the apex of the cone and parallels are concentric circles.

The best known conic projection is the Lambert conformal projection in which two "standard" parallels show true east-west distances. Between the parallels distances are slightly under scale; beyond them distances are slightly over scale.

AZIMUTHAL. In an azimuthal projection the earth's meridians and parallels are projected onto a plane tangent to a single point on the globe. All points have true compass directions from the center of the map and all straight lines radiating from the center have the same direction as the corresponding lines on a globe.

The most common azimuthal projection is the Gnomonic projection, in which meridians are straight lines and parallels are concentric circles. It is also called the "great-circle chart" because all great circles are shown as straight lines. This property makes the Gnomonic projection useful in laying out sailing and flying routes, although it greatly distorts sizes, shapes, and distances.

OTHER PROJECTIONS. There are many projections that are not truly related to these three types. They include the homolographic, the sinusoidal, and the interrupted homolosine.

The Mollweide Homolographic Projection shows the surface of the earth as an ellipse with parallels as straight lines more widely spaced near the equator than toward the poles. The central meridian is a straight line half the length of the equator. All other meridians curve out from the central meridian at equal intervals and converge at the poles. The scale differs along each meridian and each parallel.

In the sinusoidal projection all parallels are straight lines evenly spaced. The central meridian is a straight line half the length of the equator. All other meridians curve out from the center meridian at increasing intervals and converge at the poles. This squeezes shapes at the top, bottom, and sides. Only the distances along parallels and the central meridian are true.

The interrupted homolosine projection combines the homolographic for areas poleward of 40° with the sinusoidal for central areas. By interrupting the map in ocean areas and adding straight meridians near the center of each landmass, each continent appears to be at the center of the projection. This gives better shape and size to the continents.

This multitude of map projections makes it possible to select the kind of map property that is most useful.

—Joseph E. Van Riper

BIBLIOGRAPHY

BLAIR, THOMAS A. *Weather Elements*. Prentice-Hall, Inc., 3rd edition, 1948.

EYRE, S. R. *Vegetation and Soils*. Aldine Publishing Co., 1963.

FREEMAN, T. W. *A Hundred Years of Geography*. Aldine Publishing Co., 1967.

KING, C. A. M. *An Introduction to Oceanography*. McGraw-Hill Book Co., Inc., 1963.

MONKHOUSE, F. J. *A Dictionary of Geography*. Aldine Publishing Co., 1965.

PUTNAM, W. C. *Geology*. Oxford University Press, 1964.

STRAHLER, ARTHUR N. *Physical Geography*. John Wiley & Sons, 2nd edition, 1959.

TREWARTHA, GLENN T., A. H. ROBINSON, and E. HAMMOND. *The Elements of Physical Geography*. McGraw-Hill Book Co., 1961.

TREWARTHA, GLENN T. *An Introduction to Climate*. McGraw-Hill Book Co., Inc., 1954.

VAN RIPER, JOSEPH E. *Man's Physical World*. McGraw-Hill Book Co., Inc., 1962.

Theory of government	783
Government of the United States	785
Declaration of Independence	802
Articles of Confederation	804
Constitution of the United States	806
Law	812
Legal procedure	817
Labor legislation	827
Legal holidays in the United States	841
Parliamentary law	842
Government and legal glossary	849
Bibliography	914

VOLUME ELEVEN

GOVERNMENT & LAW

UPI

Government and Law

THEORY OF GOVERNMENT

What is Government?—Government is control. "Learn to govern your temper"—that means control. Trace the word back and you find that the Latin word to govern, *gubernare,* means to steer, to be pilot. The governor, *gubernator,* was the helmsman, responsible for the safety of all on board.

In a small boat with nearly everyone on board rowing there is no special need for a helmsman. In the small size ship of state everyone can help steer—the entire small community can meet and decide what is to be done. That would be a pure democracy. But it does not happen very often. Communities and nations are too big for a town meeting government. People are too busy, too indifferent, to spend the time and effort to be their own government. So most government is not direct self-government. A working definition is: government is public control by a few presumably for the benefit of the many.

Woodrow Wilson was a student of government before he became a statesman and in his great book *The State* he lists the eight essential functions of government:

(1) To keep order and provide for the protection of persons and property from violence and robbery.

(2) To fix the legal relations between man and wife and between parents and children.

(3) To regulate the holding, transmission and interchange of property, and the determination of its liabilities for debt or for crime.

(4) To fix the contract rights between individuals.

(5) To define crime and provide for the punishment of criminals.

(6) To provide for the administration of justice in civil causes.

(7) To determine the political duties, privileges and relations of citizens.

(8) To regulate the dealings of the state with foreign powers, to preserve the state from external danger and to advance its international interests.

In addition to these eight essentials, all modern governments have undertaken a whole series of service functions of the sort that might conceivably be carried on by private enterprise. This service field of government activity cannot be strictly defined, but we all recognize as familiar examples of government functions such things as the following:

Mail service
Fire protection
Health protection
Education

Road-building and maintenance
Conservation of natural resources
Information bureaus (e.g. census, weather reports, agricultural experimentation, geological and geodetic surveys).

One of the conspicuous trends of government at the present day is the expansion of these general service functions, and one of the main issues of modern political discussion is the degree to which this field ought to expand. Few people would hold, for example, that government operation of the postal system is an encroachment on the field of private enterprise, but many people object strenuously to proposals that the government operate the railroad system or the telephone and telegraph systems.

A second leading issue in the discussion of the proper field of government action arises from different interpretations of Wilson's function (3): "to regulate the holding, transmission and interchange of property, and the determination of its liabilities for debt and for crime." The extreme individualistic theory (the famous *laissez-faire* of the classical economists) limits government regulation of the holding and interchange of property to the government's guarantee of every man's right to do exactly as he pleases with everything he can get. The extreme totalitarian theory holds that the government can confiscate or abolish private property or specify in detail the use to which it is put.

Theory of government and the facts of government are quite different. Many statesmen have found that when they run a government it is necessary to do many things they would not approve in theory. Thomas Jefferson, for example, took advantage of the opportunity to buy Louisiana though his whole political philosophy assured him that the Constitution gave him no power to do anything of the sort. Lincoln boldly arrogated to the executive the right to proclaim Negro emancipation—as flagrant a case as any in American history of confiscating property without due process of law—justifying his action on the ground that it was a necessary war measure. Woodrow Wilson himself, though his political faith was that of the old Democratic party stemming from the ideas of Jefferson with its strong tradition favoring State rights and non-interference by government in the activities of business, sponsored the Clayton Anti-Trust Act, the Federal Reserve Law, the Federal Trade Commission Act and other pieces of legislation that

strengthened the control of the national government and interfered, his opponents said, with business.

Almost any government you examine closely will vary considerably from the eight essential functions laid down by Woodrow Wilson. In the history of the world there have been many forms of government, and today there are many variations in the character and nature of governments in different countries. We can understand these variations best by answering with actual examples certain questions suggested by our definition of government: public control by a few for the benefit of the many.

How complete is the control? Almost without exception the control exercised by governments today is more far-reaching than ever before. "The least government is the best government" was the maxim of Thomas Jefferson a hundred and fifty years ago. But about seventy years ago the young German Empire under Bismarck's iron rule introduced compulsory insurance for factory workers, tariff barriers to protect German industry and subsidies to steamship lines to improve German commerce. Germany had state socialism long before Hitler's National Socialism.

During most of the recent wars the governments of all combatant nations commandeered industry, rationed the inhabitants' food, fuel, and light, and set standards of pay and hours for workers. Public utilities (postal and telephone systems, railways, electricity, gas and water) are to-day regulated by many nations and completely controlled and owned by others. In Russia today the government is all-embracing, so that we have a new concept: the totalitarian state that controls education, business, religion —everything.

How are those in control *chosen* for the task of government? The few are chosen by the many—that is the ideal. But even when and where that is true, there are great variations in the meaning of "chosen by the many." Sometimes it is a direct choice—as we in the United States now vote for U. S. senators instead of having them chosen by the state legislatures as was originally provided by the Federal Constitution. Even this is a direct choice only in a qualified and modified fashion—for the party candidates for the Senate are chosen by party organizations, and the two or three names are then submitted to the many for their direct choice.

Candidates for President and Vice-President of the United States are chosen by party conventions, and from these candidates the President and Vice-President are actually elected by a plurality of the presidential electors. So it may happen that the choice of the Electoral College is not the people's choice. In 1888 Benjamin Harrison was made President by 233 electoral votes to 168 for Grover Cleveland, who received 100,000 more popular votes than Harrison (5,540,-329 to 5,439,853).

Though the King of England has not much practical control, he is the head of the government in theory. He is chosen by the accident of being the previous king's eldest son. Nevertheless, on several occasions in the past this regular succession has been set aside by Parliament, and it is really Parliament that fixes the qualifications of the king. In 1936 King Edward VIII was forced to give up the Crown by the political pressure of his ministers acting with the support of Parliament.

Occasionally in the last generation the choice of a governing head of a country has been by the oldest and most primitive of all methods—force of arms Mussolini was not elected Duce of Italy by popular vote. He led his Fascist Black Shirts—an organized force of a few thousands—in their march on Rome and made himself ruler. But Mussolini insisted that he ruled by consent of those whom he governed.

To whom are those who govern responsible? When Edward VIII was forced to abdicate it was made plain that the Crown of England is responsible to the Ministry and to public opinion.

Before World War II Japan had a constitution and a cabinet patterned on western models, but the government was not for the benefit of the many: the many were important only as subjects of the emperor, so government existed mainly for his glory.

Good government is especially necessary in this latter half of the twentieth century because machine production has knit the world together into an economic organism so complex, so subtly interdependent that a monkey wrench hurled into the machinery at one point may dislocate the lives of millions of people whole continents away. In brief, we know enough about chemistry and mechanics to build the framework for a rational and happy life. We also know enough about nuclear fission and fusion and poison gas and lethal microbes to shatter civilization to the chaos from which it has painfully evolved.

Our chance apparently lies in the rapid acceleration of progress in the social sciences—government, biology, economics, and sociology—and in the development and extension of an educational technique that will make us more sharply aware of our responsibilities and more ready to shoulder them.

Good government becomes more and more necessary because our populations are no longer predominantly rural. Our people live in huge cities, crowded together in communities such as the world never knew before. The day of individual work, for one's own needs, in one's own way, and in one's own time, has gone. Instead, men work in vast factories engaged in minute contributions to the finished article. Hundreds of thousands of men work underground digging the coal to feed the monster industrial machines. Millions of men, women and children toil anxiously to keep it going and the whole system is so inconceivably intricate and so closely articulated that dislocation in one part of its affects all the rest.

With it all has come the speeding up of life and the spirit of hurry and worry such as our grandfathers with all their lack of conveniences never dreamed of. The human race lives by schedule, according to a stereotyped routine. We hurry from birth to death goaded only to greater haste by our increasingly speedy conveyances, trying to catch up with the machinery which we have ourselves created. Truly this is a complex world. The life that men lived under the Roman Caesars with its horses, oxen, carts, and domestic hand labor, was more intelligible perhaps, than is our life now with its airplanes, its automobiles, its television, and its mass production.

Yes, government is necessary, and government officials who are honest and conscientious are most precious to any nation. In our democratic government every official has rights and privileges due his title, yet he is also responsible to the people who elect him to office or to the authority that appoints him. He is an agent with delegated powers. He is liable to removal from office, to defeat when he comes up for re-election, to trial upon impeachment. His continuance in office depends upon his good behavior.

Are there any rules that control those who govern? In countries (the United States, for example) with a written constitution that can be altered only by a long, elaborate process of amendment the rules are strict, rigid, difficult to change. In England the unwritten constitution may be altered much more easily and quickly —by an Act of Parliament that goes into effect immediately, as in 1911 when the veto power of the House of Lords was practically abolished. In France a National Assembly, composed of the members of the two houses, has power to amend the Constitution merely by majority vote.

What is meant by *benefit* when we speak of control for the benefit of the many? The preamble to our Federal Constitution proposes to "establish Justice, insure domestic tranquillity, provide for the common defense, promote the general welfare and secure the blessings of liberty to ourselves and our posterity." Liberty and freedom of the individual are benefits of government that we take for granted, though we recognize at the same time that individual liberty must necessarily be somewhat restricted for the public good—for example by forbidding adulteration of food or punishing fast driving.

What do we mean by *many* when we say government is for the benefit of the many? Government for the good of all the people is the ideal objective. How can this be secured? By a government that represents all the people! But in our own representative government the congressional district's representative at Washington is elected by the majority not by all the people in his district. Will he work for the benefit of the minority, those who did not vote for him? This question he must decide for himself. Certain types of government entirely disregard the benefit of the minority or even of a large class or of many large classes.

Types of Government

DESPOTISM, government by an absolute ruler. The term enlightened despot is often used, meaning an absolute ruler who rules for the benefit of his people.

TYRANNY, absolute rule of an autocratic and violent sort, often resulting from a forcible seizure of the government. This type of rule, by a tyrant or usurper, was common in ancient Greece where from time to time democracies were seized by ambitious men. Some Greek tyrants gave their subjects a very good government; but tyranny now implies cruelty and arbitrary use of power.

DICTATORSHIP, rule of a single person beginning in an emergency and sometimes chosen by legal methods, as in ancient Rome, to take complete command for public safety. In modern use dictator means one who exercises absolute authority in government or in any other sphere.

AUTOCRACY, the sole and undisputed government of a single ruler.

MONARCHY, government headed by a hereditary ruler, a king or emperor; *absolute,* if the monarch has complete power—or *limited,* if a constitution (or its equivalent) controls his actions (constitutional monarchy).

ARISTOCRACY, literally "rule by the best," is government by a small privileged class, noble or wealthy.

OLIGARCHY, government by a few and the sort of government in which only a small class have political rights.

DEMOCRACY, government by the people—*pure* or *absolute,* when the people govern directly and immediately as in a town meeting where every detail of government comes before all the people; or *indirect, representative* democracy, when the people delegate their authority to elected officials.

REPUBLIC, government by the people through their elected representatives; a representative democracy or a government by a select electorate (not necessarily all the people) which delegates power to its representatives.

COMMUNISM, a very radical and revolutionary form of socialism, is opposed to the property and profit principles of capitalism, and opposed to nationalism. The ideal of Communism is "from each according to his ability, to each according to his need." In practice, however, the worker is enslaved—helpless to achieve independence because he cannot acquire even minor wealth.

In FASCISM, a nationalistic government headed by an absolute dictator, the state is supreme. All opposition or dissent is suppressed by police authority. Industry and business are regulated, intellectual and recreational pursuits are controlled, and censorship of all forms of news is rigidly enforced.

Party Rule.—There were parties in ancient Athens—named Hillmen, Plainsmen and Shoredwellers, evidently regional classes of farmers. Our modern political parties originated primarily in economic classes with different views of the state and its relation to their business and other businesses. But there are two important facts to bear in mind about parties in government today: first, that the origin and original purpose of any political party are soon lost in modern politics; and that party organization plays an ever increasing part in government.

The change in party purpose and meaning is repeatedly illustrated in American government. Jefferson and the other leaders of the Democratic party defended State rights against centralization of power in the Federal government. During the 1936 presidential campaign the political descendants of Alexander Hamilton, who was for Federal aggrandizement at the expense of the states, were using the arguments that Jefferson used against Hamilton—and used them against the leaders of the Democratic party, in which Jeffersonian policies are traditional.

A generation ago in the United States it was a political maxim that there could be no healthy government without two parties of nearly equal strength—a minority, an opposition party, was as important as a majority, a party in power. Today in the Union of the Soviet party government means something it never meant before: the party *is* the State, no party but the party in power can exist at all. In Japan after World War II, sovereignty formerly vested in the Emperor was vested in the people. Parties immediately sprang up and Japan is now blessed with strong major and minor parties.

Need for Studying Government.—This changing concept of government, the wide variations between leaders of opposing parties, new practices in government here and abroad—all these are special reasons now for studying government. Never was it a subject of such varied interest.

It has always deserved more attention than it received. Government has not been as good as it should be, the representatives of the people have not been as wise as they should be. Why? One reason certainly is that the people have not cared enough or known enough or thought enough about their government.

GOVERNMENT OF THE UNITED STATES

About 115 years after the first voyage of Columbus to the New World the first English colony (Virginia, 1607) was founded in America; expansion was quite rapid, and ultimately the English nation planted thirteen colonies along the fringe of the Atlantic Ocean. American government had its origin in the actual experience of the hardy colonists in these Western outposts of civilization; for several generations they had been able to view the governmental policies of the mother country, take lessons from its triumphs and its mistakes and little by little transfer control of their destinies to their own hands.

The Colonial Period.—In origin, each of the English colonies was either a grant of privilege to an individual—like Pennsylvania to William Penn—or to a corporation, like Virginia or Massachusetts Bay. However, since those who settled in the colonies were brave, venturesome individuals, not desirous of asking favors of royalty, and since they were three thousand miles from the seat of a central government more or less indifferent to their interests, self-government quickly found roots in the soil of America.

When the American Revolution occurred, there was very little fundamentally new in political institutions in any of the colonies. Radically new governments were not set up—the old machines were used. The revolutionists of Rhode Island and Connecticut, where the governors, councilors and judges were not appointed by the Crown but created solely by the colony, found their colonial systems of government so well suited to their needs and ideals that they made no alterations in them other than casting off their allegiance to the king of Great Britain. The royal charter granted to Connecticut by Charles II in 1662 remained the constitution of that state until 1818, and the charter of Rhode Island, granted in 1663, remained in force until 1842. In all the states the distribution of representation, the suffrage, the qualifications for holding office and the legislative, executive and judicial institutions were continued after the Revolution without many radical alterations.

On the eve of the Revolution, the thirteen colonies had forms of government which presented striking similarity. Each had a governor, an assembly and a judicial system, and the common law of England, as far as it was applicable and had not been changed by legislation, was binding in all of them.

In eight of the colonies—Massachusetts, New Hampshire, New York, New Jersey, Virginia, North Carolina, South Carolina and Georgia—the governor was appointed by the king, recognized as the king's personal deputy and known as a *royal governor*. He was the highest executive official in the colony, charged with the preservation of peace and the advancement of the welfare of the colonists.

The governor, as the chief executive, supervised the enforcement of the laws and appointed, usually with the advice of his council, the important civil officers. He could, except in Massachusetts, remove any of the council and other officials for cause and direct them in their work. By virtue of his position as chancellor, he was head of the highest court in the colony, which handled appeals from lower courts and exercised important original jurisdiction in many matters. He also granted pardons and reprieves. He was commander in chief of the colonial forces, appointed the military officers of high rank, levied troops for defense of the colony and enforced martial law when this was necessitated by invasion or rebellion.

He had important legislative powers, including the right of veto. He appointed (except in Massachusetts) the members of the upper house of the colonial legislature and summoned, adjourned and dissolved the assembly.

But the royal governor was by no means an unlimited sovereign in his province, for he was bound by his instructions from the British government and by restraints which the assembly imposed through its power of controlling grants of money. Furthermore, complaints against his actions often were taken to the king in council across the sea. In Massachusetts the royal governor was somewhat limited by the colonial charter. He did not appoint the council or upper house and his appointments of civil officers required the consent of the council.

In Rhode Island and Connecticut the governor was elected annually by a general assembly composed of the governor, assistants and representatives chosen by the voters in each "city, town or place." In these colonies the governor did not stand out as a separate and distinct official. His duties were performed only in co-operation with both the assembly and council.

The executive authority in the proprietary colonies of Maryland, Pennsylvania and Delaware differed vastly from that of the other colonies. The proprietary colony was a vast estate, carved out of the royal domain and granted by the Crown to a proprietor. When the proprietor was in the colony he had the right to assume control of the executive authority there and when he was absent he vested it in a lieutenant-governor, who served in the capacity of agent for the real owner of the estate. The power of the governor in these colonies was less limited than in any of the others; but toward the end of the colonial era there was a gradual decline in his power, because the Assembly was winning control over measures appropriating money.

All the colonies had two branches in their legislatures except Pennsylvania, which had only one. In Massachusetts, Connecticut and Rhode Island the upper house was elected by the assembly; in the proprietary colonies the proprietor or his representative selected the councilors; in the other colonies the upper house or council was chosen by the king acting through the royal governor.

The council enjoyed the right to discuss and vote on all laws, and with the governor enjoyed executive and judicial functions. It advised the governor on important matters, and in conjunction with him formed the highest judicial tribunal in the colony.

In every colony there was an assembly of representatives chosen by popular vote; but, contrary to common impressions, there was nothing like universal manhood suffrage. In every colony there were restrictions on the suffrage, which were usually educational, property or religious qualifications.

The colonial assemblies from an early period of colonial history maintained that they possessed entire and exclusive authority to regulate their domestic affairs. In the matter of taxation they stoutly asserted their exclusive rights not only in formal declarations but also in actual resistance to the royal and proprietary governors. In addition to general legislative power, the assemblies usually exercised a large control over the executive department through their power to withhold the salaries of the officials.

The lowest colonial courts were those of justices of the peace who were generally appointed by the governor or in some instances elected by local freeholders, that is, owners of real estate. In civil cases these justices had jurisdiction over cases involving small amounts; in criminal matters they were allowed to try only the pettiest offenses against the law. In Massachusetts and a few other colonies the practice of uniting all of the justices of the country in a general court was followed; this court not only exercised criminal jurisdiction but supervised roads, bridges and similar affairs.

Above the justices of the peace there usually were the county courts whose judges were appointed by the governor, except in New Jersey where they were elected. In most colonies the county court had criminal jurisdiction over all except capital cases, but in Massachusetts, criminal matters were taken care of by the regular sessions of the justices of the peace. The county courts also had civil jurisdiction in cases involving less than certain amounts specified by law in each colony.

A high court was set up in each colony to decide weighty matters and appeals from the lower courts. In the royal colonies the governor, acting as chancellor, and his council generally composed this tribunal. In Massachusetts it consisted of a chief justice and four associates, appointed by the governor and council. In Pennsylvania the supreme court was composed of a chief justice and three associates, all chosen by the governor.

Of course, appeals always lay from the highest court in the colony to the king in council, and this power was frequently exercised just as certain cases are appealed to the Supreme Court of the United States at the present time.

Important Steps Toward Union.—(a) From 1643 to 1684 the Massachusetts Bay, New Plymouth, Connecticut and New Haven colonies formed the New England Confederation to strengthen their defense against the Indians, Dutch and French.

(b) In 1754 twenty-five members from seven colonies met at Albany to arrange a treaty with the Iroquois Indians and to consider other common interests. This Albany Convention adopted Franklin's plan for a permanent federation, but the members could not bind the colonies and the plan was rejected.

(c) In 1765, in consequence of the passage of the Stamp Act in Great Britain, at the instance of the Massachusetts house of representatives nine colonies sent representatives to the Stamp Act Congress at New York, which issued a declaration that the rights of natural-born English subjects belonged to the colonists, and framed petitions to the English government for relief.

(d) Further acts of England, especially the Townshend Acts (imposing additional duties on certain goods including tea), led to the formation of Committees of Correspondence among the colonists, who thus fostered unity of sentiment against England and for their common interests.

(e) The First Continental Congress was called by Massachusetts in 1774, after the English government had passed acts providing for the coercion of that colony. All the colonies except Georgia sent delegates to Philadelphia; they drafted the Declaration of Rights of the colonies, adopted articles of association, advised resistance, and provided in case of need for the meeting, May, 1775, of the Second Continental Congress.

(f) The Second Continental Congress met, delegates from all the colonies being present. In the meantime England had passed other measures of coercion and in attempting to seize the war supplies of the colonists, had brought on the battle of Lexington. It therefore became necessary for the Congress to make provisions for continuing resistance. In fact it became a governing body; and, with adjournments from time to time, until May 1, 1781, it directed the Revolutionary War and really organized and managed a new state. It issued the Declaration of Independence, recommended that the colonies provide for state governments and instituted relations with foreign countries.

(g) When the colonies declared their independence of Great Britain they also appointed a Congressional committee, composed of one delegate from each state, to draw up a form of union for all the new states. The Articles of Confederation thus drawn up were discussed for more than a year and were adopted by Congress in 1777.

Development of the Constitution of the United States

Failure of the Articles of Confederation.—When the Articles had been ratified by all the thirteen states (1781), it was confidently believed that the new nation had been satisfactorily launched upon its career. However, almost at once defects in administration became apparent. What had seemed admirable in theory to its framers failed when applied in practice to the many problems that had to be met. Because each state wished to maintain its "sovereignty, freedom and independence," Congress was hampered in all these ways:

(1) No important law could be put into operation until it had been ratified by nine of the states;

(2) Even when a law had been ratified by a state, Congress had no power to enforce its provisions there;

(3) Congress could pass laws for raising revenue, but could not force payment from objecting states;

(4) The states maintained their right to regulate interstate commerce among themselves and insisted upon independent action with respect to the regulation of foreign commerce;

(5) Amendment of the Articles to remedy defects was difficult: any proposed change had to be accepted by all the states;

(6) Taxation was a right reserved to the states; Congress could not legislate on the subject. Even expenses of war were to be met from a common treasury supplied by the several states.

Maryland and Virginia came into conflict upon the subject of the navigation of the Potomac River and Chesapeake Bay. Delegates from the two states met in the Mount Vernon Conference in 1785 and could not reach an agreement but decided to call a meeting of delegates of all the states for 1786 at Annapolis to discuss the commercial relations of the colonies.

At this Annapolis Convention only five states were represented—New York, New Jersey, Pennsylvania, Delaware and Maryland. They accomplished little but at the suggestion of Alexander Hamilton decided to ask the Congress to call a convention of delegates from all the states. The call was—

" . . . for the sole and express purpose of revising the Articles of Confederation and reporting to Congress and the several Legislatures such alterations and provisions therein as should, when agreed to in Congress and confirmed by the States, render the Federal Constitution adequate to the exigencies of Government and the preservation of the Union."

The Constitutional Convention.—This famous assembly met in Philadelphia beginning May 25, 1787, and George Washington was elected to preside. During the convention all the states except Rhode Island were represented and fifty-five of the sixty-five delegates named were present. The ablest and most notable men in the new republic were members. Months of discussion throughout the states had firmly convinced the nation that the Articles of Confederation could not be amended, so the convention began the consideration of an entirely new basic law.

It took four months of discussion and compromise to frame the new Constitution of the United States. There were conflicting views—between large states and small, between strong central government and State rights, between men who wanted a king in all but name and those with more democratic ideas.

The Constitution was adopted by the convention and signed on September 17, 1787. Of those who were present on the final day, only thirty-nine gave it the approval of their signatures and sixteen refused approval or absented themselves at the hour of signing. The document was submitted to the Congress and by it sent to the states for ratification, which occurred in the following chronological order:

Delaware, Dec. 7, 1787; unanimously.

Pennsylvania, Dec. 12, 1787; vote, 46 to 23.

New Jersey, Dec. 18, 1787; unanimously.

Georgia, Jan. 2, 1788; unanimously.

Connecticut, Jan. 9, 1788; vote, 128 to 40.

Massachusetts, Feb. 6, 1788; vote, 187 to 168.

Maryland, April 28, 1788; vote, 63 to 12.

South Carolina, May 23, 1788; vote, 149 to 73.

New Hampshire, June 21, 1788; vote, 57 to 46.

Virginia, June 25, 1788; vote, 89 to 79.

New York, July 26, 1788; vote, 30 to 28.

North Carolina, Nov. 21, 1789; vote, 193 to 75.

Rhode Island, May 29, 1790; vote, 34 to 32.

Divisions of the Constitution.—There are seven main sections, called Articles, as outlined below; each Article is subdivided into Sections and Clauses:

Article I. The legislative (lawmaking) department; qualification and election of members, the powers of Congress; powers prohibited to the states.

Article II. The executive department; election of the President of the United States; his powers and duties.

Article III. The judicial department; its organization and its powers.

Article IV. Relation of the states to one another and of the states to the United States.

Article V. Method of amending the Constitution.

Article VI. Declaration of the supremacy of the Constitution, affirmation of validity of contracts made prior to its adoption, and statement of oath or affirmation required of officials of the United States.

Article VII. Ratification of nine states to put the Constitution into effect.

Amendments. Some of the members of the Constitutional Convention believed that the new Constitution did not sufficiently safeguard the rights of the people, and they signed it only on the promise of the convention that the first Congress should present amendments covering such rights.

Accordingly, 12 amendments were proposed (Sept. 1789) and 10 were ratified by the end of 1790. These 10 are the Bill of Rights. Other amendments since adopted:

XI. Declared that a state shall not be sued in the United States courts by citizens of another state or of a foreign country (1798).

XII. Provided for electing the President and Vice-President on separate ballots by members of the electoral college (1804).

XIII. Abolished slavery (1865).

XIV. Defined citizenship in the United States, defining the status of the newly-freed Negro race (1868).

XV. Decreed equal voting rights for white and colored citizens (1870).

XVI. Authorized Federal taxation of income (1913).

XVII. Provided for election of United States Senators by direct vote of the people (1913).

XVIII. Prohibited manufacture, sale or transportation of intoxicating liquors (1920).

XIX. Gave women the vote (1920).

XX. Made the term of President and Vice-President begin on January 20 and of Congressmen Jan. 3 (1933).

XXI. Repealed 18th amendment (1933).

XXII. Limited the President to two terms or ten years in office (1951).

XXIII. Gave electoral college representation to District of Columbia (1961).

XXIV. Abolished poll tax for voting in federal elections (1964).

The Three Departments of the United States Government

Legislative Department.—In the organization of the United States government there must be a department whose business is the making of laws; it is called the legislative department. There is another which is charged with enforcing or executing the laws or statutes that the law-makers have enacted; this is the executive department.

Each of the above acts as a check upon the other. Every law passed by the legislative department must go to the Chief Executive for the purpose of approval before it can become operative. If in his judgment a measure that has been enacted is ill-advised, he may refuse to sign it, and this action is known as a *veto;* if it is vetoed, a proposed law is killed, unless the legislative department in each house can muster two-thirds of all its members to pass it again over the veto. This is not often possible.

The legislative department, in its upper house, the Senate, holds a check upon all important appointments to office made by the Executive. Each appointee to an important post must be approved by the Senate before entering upon his duties; if approval is withheld, he cannot serve.

The third branch of the government is the judicial department, which holds a check on the legislative, executive and administrative branches of the government through its ability to declare laws unconstitutional.

The Constitution declares (Art. I, Sec. 1) that "all legislative powers herein granted shall be vested in a Congress of the United States, which shall consist of a Senate and a House

of Representatives." The Congress, therefore, is the sole law-making power of the Federal government. Its two branches act as a check upon each other, for a bill, in order to become a law, must be approved by both in exactly the same phraseology; either house may withhold approval of a proposed act of the other.

The founders of the republic considered the Senators to be representative of the sovereign states of the union, and the Representatives the spokesmen of the masses of the people. The Senators have the longer terms—six years—and it was decreed (Art. I, Sec. 3) that they should be chosen by the state legislatures, and not by the people (this provision was altered by the 17th amendment in 1913); the Representatives, it was thought, would better reflect the wishes of the people if chosen directly by them and at frequent intervals, so their term of office was set at two years.

The Senate is a continuous body; its membership is so spaced that the terms of only one-third expire every two years (with the end of each Congress); there are always experienced

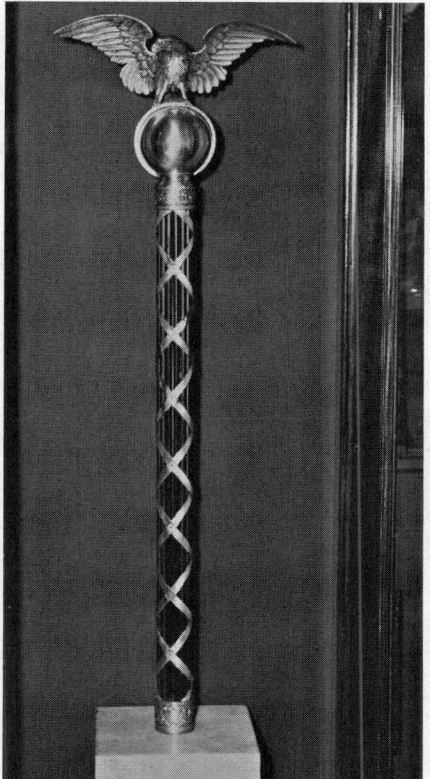

LIBRARY OF CONGRESS

MACE OF THE HOUSE OF REPRESENTATIVES is the only visible symbol of governmental authority in the United States. It is a 3-foot-high bundle of ebony rods (representing the States of the Union) surmounted by a silver globe above which is poised a silver eagle. When the House resolves into Committee of the Whole, the mace is moved to a low pedestal near the sergeant-at-arms. When a member of the House is considered out of order, the mace is "presented" to him, and order is restored.

men held over to each new Congress. The terms of all members of the House of Representatives expire at one time; election of all Representatives is for the term of one Congress only. It would therefore be possible that with every new Congress there might be a House membership entirely new and inexperienced; this never has happened for a majority of the members arc usually re-elected, and they return with the advantage of previous service.

The salary of both Senators and Representatives is $30,000 per year.

The Senate. Each state has two Senators, regardless of its area or population. The mandate of the fathers of the Constitution as to the manner of their election was changed in 1913 and now, like the Representatives, they are chosen by direct vote of the people, but to represent the whole state and not a separate part or district.

The Senate holds three powers that are denied to the House of Representatives: it has the power to approve or reject important appointments of the President to office; with the President it makes treaties with foreign powers and it has the sole power to sit as a court to try officials of the government impeached by the House of Representatives for misconduct. The Senate cannot originate a bill raising revenue; that power is reserved to the House of Representatives, because it more fully than the Senate reflects the will of the people. However, when a revenue bill reaches the Senate after passing the House, the Senate may amend it at will.

Qualifications of a Senator. To be eligible to election to the Senate, a person must have reached the age of thirty years, been at least nine years a citizen of the United States and live in the state from which he is chosen.

The House of Representatives. This is called the lower house of the Congress, but it possesses powers coordinate with those of the Senate, with the exceptions above noted. Though the Constitution limits the number of Senators to two from each state, no such limitation is placed upon the number of Representatives. The number of members of the House is determined in relation to the population and distributed among the states according to the population of the state, excluding Indians not taxed. The House is authorized to determine for itself after each Federal census what its number shall be for the next ten years. The population of the country is divided by the number of members of the House, to determine the number of people entitled to one Representative. Since 1912, the total membership has been fixed at 435. Based on the 1960 census, the ratio is one Representative for 410,481 inhabitants. The number of Representatives to which a state is entitled is determined by dividing its population by the unit of representation; but each state has at least one Representative. Nevada with about 285,000, Wyoming with 330,000, and Vermont with 390,000 population in 1960, each has one Representative although its population is less than the 410,481 unit.

CECIL W. STOUGHTON

CHAMBER OF THE HOUSE OF REPRESENTATIVES in the Capitol. Since 1857, members of the lower house have met here. Congress convenes in regular session on January 3 and, according to the terms of the 20th Amendment, in special sessions, if called by the president.

If a state does not make new congressional districts after a reapportionment that increases its representation, each additional Congressman to which the state is entitled is chosen *at large,* that is, he is elected by the voters of the whole state. Or if the representation is reduced and there is no redistricting the Representatives may be chosen at large—as in North Dakota which had three districts under the 1910 Census but only two representatives under the 1940 Census.

The House holds two powers that are denied the Senate: all bills for raising revenue (tariff and tax bills) must originate in the House, and the House has the sole power of impeaching government officials for misconduct. (The Senate tries impeachment cases.)

Qualifications of a Representative. He must be at least twenty-five years of age, must have been a citizen of the United States for at least seven years and must be an inhabitant of the state from which he is chosen. By custom each is selected from the congressional district he represents, unless he is a Congressman at large.

Officers of Senate and House. The presiding officer in the Senate is the Vice-President of the United States. The Constitution calls him president of the Senate. If he succeeds to the Presidency of the United States the Senate chooses a president *pro tempore.* Not being a member of the Senate he has no vote "unless they be equally divided."

The presiding officer in the House is the speaker, invariably chosen by the members from their number, though it would be legal to choose a nonmember. As a member of the House, he is entitled to vote on all occasions. The speaker is elected every two years, at the beginning of each new Congress. His salary is $43,000 a year, $13,000 more than other members of the lower House. He is leader of his party in the House. Each House has a sergeant-at-arms, who preserves order, a postmaster, doorkeepers and reporters of proceedings.

Powers of Congress. The general powers of Congress are:

To pass laws, to judge the elections and qualifications of its own members, to determine its own rules of procedure, to lay and collect taxes, duties, imposts and excises, to pay the debts and provide for the common defense and general welfare, to borrow money on the credit of the United States, to regulate commerce with foreign nations and among the several states and with the Indian tribes, to coin money and provide for certain substitutes for coin, and make provisions for controlling the value and purity of both, to fix standards of weights and measures, to establish uniform rules of naturalization, and uniform laws of bankruptcy, to establish and maintain a postal system with all needed equipment for efficient service, to make provision for the encouragement of inventors and authors by patent and copyright laws, to define and punish piracies and felonies committed on the high seas and offenses against the law of nations, to declare war and make full provision for carrying on war by land and sea, by regular

U.S. CAPITOL HISTORICAL SOCIETY

SENATE CHAMBER in the Capitol. Presided over by the vice-president, the Senate is made up of two senators from each state. The vice-president has no vote unless there is a tie. Above is a circular gallery for senators' families and members of the diplomatic corps.

the government to one man, the President of the United States. The Vice-President, who is elected with the President for a term of four years, has no executive authority.

The President is the only official of the government who must be a natural-born citizen of the United States.

The clause that no person shall be eligible to the Presidency "who shall not have been fourteen years a resident within the United States" excludes a natural-born American citizen who lives abroad; unless he is an ambassador or minister to a foreign country, since a public servant abroad is considered never to leave the soil of his country; wherever he may be, that spot is home territory. John W. Davis, Democratic candidate for the Presidency in 1924 had been U. S. Ambassador to Great Britain in 1918–21, but that did not disqualify him.

The President must be at least thirty-five years of age, the highest age requirement for any office in the government service.

The youngest man who has taken the oath of office as President was Theodore Roosevelt, in his 43d year; the oldest, William Henry Harrison, in his 69th.

From the founding of the nation in 1789 to 1873 the salary of the President was $25,000 per year. Increased in 1873 to $50,000 per year, it was again increased to $75,000 per year in 1909 and to $100,000 a year in 1949, with a tax-free expense account of $50,000 a year and a traveling expense allowance of $40,000 a year. An official residence, the White House or Executive Mansion, is also provided.

There is an election for President every four years. During the summer of this year each political party in its national convention nominates candidates for President and Vice-President. In each state the party names electors for these two candidates—as many electors as the state has representatives in both houses of Congress (Senators plus Representatives—so each state always has at least three electors). On presidential-election day in November the voters in each state vote for the state group of presidential electors. The entire number of electors chosen from all the states forms the electoral college, and this body elects the President and Vice-President.

The Electoral College. The total number of electors is the same as the number of Senators and Representatives in Congress. Since 1961 the number has been 538 (Senators, 100; Representatives, 435; D.C. 3). These 538 electors do not all meet in one place to cast their ballots. The process through which the President is elected (and with him, the Vice-President) is as follows:

On the first Tuesday after the first Monday in November the voters in each state choose their electors. When the result of that election in all the states is reported, nearly always it is known who is to be the new President and who the new Vice-President; for if a majority of the entire 538 electors chosen are Republicans, the Republican candidates are certain of eventual choice; if the majority is Demo-

army and navy or by militia, and to exercise exclusive jurisdiction over all districts that are acquired for the use of the Federal government in its civil or military capacities. Besides these special powers, the Constitution grants to Congress the right to make all regulations necessary to carry these into effect.

Every Act of Congress before it becomes a law must be submitted to the President for his veto or approval, as explained below under the heading *Duties of the President*. Any Act of Congress may come before the Supreme Court (see below) for a ruling on its constitutionality in connection with a suit on some matter under the law appealed from lower courts. There is no legal or judicial machinery for testing the constitutionality of an Act of Congress in itself—only as it affects an actual case in the courts between two parties and only on appeal. The particular clauses in the Constitution about the powers of Congress that have been most variously interpreted by the Supreme Court are: general welfare (Art.I, Sec. 8, Cl. 1), regulation of commerce between the States (Art. I, Sec. 8, Cl. 3) and the due process of law (5th and 14th amendments).

Scarcely less important than the powers granted to Congress are the restrictions placed upon it. It shall not suspend the writ of *habeas corpus* except in cases of rebellion or invasion if the public safety requires it; shall not pass bills of attainder or *ex post-facto* laws. No money shall be drawn from the treasury but in consequence of appropriations made

by law, and regular accounts thereof shall be published; no titles of nobility shall be granted by the United States, and presents and titles from foreign governments or rulers are forbidden to officeholders without the consent of Congress.

These prohibitions are all in the interest of the states and people against possible encroachments by the Federal government.

The several states are forbidden to enter into any relations with foreign states and are restricted closely in their actions regarding money, the law of contracts and some other important matters. Especially rigid are the provisions forbidding state interference with interstate or international commerce and relations with foreign powers.

Sessions of Congress. The Congress meets every year, formerly (under the original Constitutional provision) on the first Monday in December, but since 1934 (by the 20th amendment, adopted in 1933) on January 3rd. The life of each Congress is two years. Members are elected in November of even-numbered years. Unless they were called into special session they formerly did not take their seats for thirteen months after election, for each new Congress began in December of odd-numbered years. Now each Congress is organized two months following the election in November. There are two sessions of each Congress. Each begins on January 3 and each session may be a year in length.

The Executive Department.—The Constitution gives the executive power of

ABBIE ROWE

PRESIDENT JOHN F. KENNEDY, seated at his desk in the Oval Room in the executive (west) wing of the White House. Since 1909, this room has been used as the chief executive's office. The massive desk belonged to President Rutherford B. Hayes, and was a gift from Queen Victoria of England. Following Kennedy's election, the desk was relocated and restored. It is made from the timber of the British ship H.M.S. *Resolute.* In the background is the flag bearing the seal of the United States.

cratic, the Democratic candidates will be ultimately successful.

The electors meet in their respective state capitals on the first Wednesday after the second Monday in December to vote for the 2 officials to whom they are pledged. They send the report of their ballots to the Congress, and the two houses, meeting together, canvass the returns and announce the result. This formality completes the election, provided any candidates for President and Vice-President have received a majority (270) of the votes cast. If no one has the required number of electoral votes the procedure to be followed is that outlined in the 12th Amendment —the House of Representatives selects the President and the Senate selects the Vice-President.

The President- and Vice-President-elect, beginning in 1937, have taken office on the 20th of January under the 20th Amendment, which changed the date from March 4.

The Constitution originally provided that each elector vote for two candidates and that the person receiving the highest number of votes (if a majority) should be President and the next highest be Vice-President. In case of a tie or of no majority vote, the House of Representatives was to choose, voting one vote from each state, and choosing from the tie candidates or (if no tie) from the five highest on the list. The 12th Amendment to the Constitution changed this in 1804.

Duties of the President. The office of Chief Executive of the United States is one of the most powerful posts of authority in the world. Upon the President rest vast and ever increasing responsibilities.

He is commander in chief of the army and navy of the United States and of the militia of the states when called into military service of the nation.

He has the power to grant reprieves in cases involving Federal law and pardons for offenses against the United States except in cases of impeachment.

He makes treaties with foreign nations through the office of his secretary of state, but before a treaty may become effective it must be ratified by a two-thirds vote of Senators present in the Senate of the United States.

He appoints ambassadors, ministers and consuls to foreign countries, justices of the Supreme Court, all other Federal judges, members of his Cabinet, United States district attorneys and marshals, the three highest classes of postmaster and many other officers of the government, all with the consent of the Senate. Many minor appointments are made by Department heads, but the responsibility is his. Any appointments he makes during a recess of the Senate are valid without confirmation until the end of the next session of the Congress.

He makes reports to the Congress on the state of the nation, with recommendations as to needed legislature.

He calls special sessions of the Congress when emergency legislature cannot be postponed to a regular session; and he may adjourn both Houses if they disagree on the time of adjournment.

He receives ambassadors and ministers of foreign countries. An ambassador, representing the person of his ruler, is entitled to audience directly with the President at all convenient times.

He "shall take care that the laws be faithfully executed."

His power of appointing justices to the Supreme Court and other Federal courts with the consent of the Senate gives him a sort of control of the judiciary. His veto power gives him considerable legislative power. In these two respects his executive functions are not kept entirely separated from the judicial and legislative branches of the government.

The Constitution provides that every Act of Congress before it becomes a law must be presented to the President for his approval and signature. If he does not approve, he returns the measure with his objections to the House in which it originated for reconsideration. Then it can become a law only by a two-thirds vote in each House. If the bill is not returned within ten days, it becomes a law without the President's signature—unless Congress adjourns before the ten days are up, "in which case it shall not be a law." (The word *veto* is not used in the Constitution.)

The Vice-President has the same qualifications and is chosen for the same term and in like manner as the President. Unless the President dies or is removed or becomes incapacitated, the Vice-President's sole duty is to preside over the Senate. He may sit in the Cabinet by invitation of the President. He succeeds to the presidency if the President dies; and the members of the Cabinet succeed in the order of the establishment of their departments, beginning with the secretaries of state and of the treasury. The salary of the Vice-President is $43,000 a year. In political practice a candidate for the Vice-Presidency is usually chosen from a different part of the country and a different wing of the party than those of the candidate for the Presidency.

The Cabinet is not mentioned in the Constitution. The nearest it comes is (Art. II, Sec. 2, Cl. 1): "He (the President) may require the opinion in writing of the principal officer in each of the executive departments upon any subject relating to the duties of their respective offices." The executive departments were organized by law and not by the Constitution and the President's power of appointment is subject to approval by the Senate. It is a custom and not a law that has made the heads of departments a group of official advisers to the President.

The Cabinet consists of various secretaries: of state, treasury, defense, interior, agriculture, commerce, labor; also the attorney-general, the postmaster general, and the secretary of health, education, and welfare. They are (a) appointed by the President, confirmed by the Senate and

(b) serve really at the pleasure of the President, usually for his term unless their resignation is sooner brought about. (c) The members of the cabinet are the official advisers of the President and receive $30,000 a year.

Administrative Agencies. One of the most important developments in the Government has been the growth of the administrative agency under the control of the President, a cabinet officer or of Congress.

Industrial growth and the necessity for regulatory control of the railroads and other monopolistic corporations brought about the creation of the Interstate Commerce Commission in 1889. The Civil Service Commission had been created in 1883 to introduce some measure of control over the "spoils system" in the appointment of public officers and employees. The creation of these two independent agencies or commissions marked a departure from the long established system of national administrative organization.

Presidents Theodore Roosevelt and Woodrow Wilson urged administrative agencies as a means of achieving some of their objectives and many of the important boards and commissions now functioning had their beginning during that period. The Federal Reserve Bank, Federal Trade Commission, Tariff Commission, the Reconstruction Finance Corporation and numerous defense, labor conciliation and financial agencies were created to meet conditions arising from rapid industrial growth and from World War I. Another important agency, the Bureau of the Budget, was created in 1921 to try to bring economy and efficiency into national administration.

Agencies of this character multiplied rapidly during the early days of the New Deal to meet specific emergencies resulting from the worldwide economic depression of the 1930's. They also took over duties not specifically allocated elsewhere and fulfilled special functions necessitated by the expansion of the Federal government.

These were, primarily, functions and responsibilities hitherto not exercised by government or they related to responsibilities formerly belonging to the states. This action tended to centralize more and more power and responsibility in the federal government rather than in the state governments. It came about not only from a desire to make the Federal government more powerful and responsible, but also because the states either failed or were unable to meet the situations as they occurred.

An illustration of this action of a federal administrative agency is to be found in the handling of unemployment relief work during the early days of the New Deal. Individual states were either unable or unwilling to extend adequate unemployment relief benefits when needed. The Federal Government stepped in and through the CCC, WPA, PWA, FERA etc. extended federal relief, without regard to state lines, where it considered the need existed. Another example is to be found in the TVA and similar authorities developing natural resources extending over one or more states, for reclamation, conservation, electric power and other purposes. In the case of electric power, a "yard

SUPREME COURT BUILDING with twin rows of Corinthian columns surmounted by a pediment inscribed with "Equal Justice Under Law." On each side of the entrance is an allegorical statue. Here, the male represents execution of law. There are nine figures in the pediment. Center is the goddess Liberty with the scales of justice. Beside her are two guardians, Order and Authority, shown as Roman soldiers. Next are groups of two figures, Counsel. At each end is a recumbent youth, Research.

stick" of performance and value was created by the federal authority. Conformance by competitive private enterprise was obtained either by condemnation and purchase or by forcing the private company to meet the "yard stick" conditions.

In other cases Congress has created "independent" agencies, not subject to executive control, for a specific or general purpose. Such agencies are the Federal Trade Commission and the National Labor Relations Board. They are responsible only to Congress and have quasi-legislative and quasi-judicial functions. [On the other hand, when a cabinet minister finds himself not in agreement with the President, as was the case with Julius A. Krug, Secretary of the Interior, in 1949, he resigns.]

Among some of the important examples of administrative agencies are the Securities and Exchange Commission, Federal Reserve Board, Interstate Commerce Commission, Civil Aeronautics Authority, Maritime Commission, etc. In order to bring about closer integration and to eliminate duplication and overlapping of functions and responsibilities in administrative agencies, the Commission on the Organization of the Executive Branches of the Government was created in 1947. It was placed under the chairmanship of ex-president Herbert Hoover. After careful study the Hoover Commission rendered a series of reports. Some of the recommendations were adopted wholly or in part. As a result it is reported over

one billion dollars of annual expenditure for administrative agencies has been saved.

The Judicial Department.—This is the department of courts provided under the Constitution to adjudicate both civil and criminal cases arising from the execution of the laws of the United States. These courts have no connection with those established under authority of the various states.

The Constitution established the Supreme Court of the United States as the highest judicial power, and authorized "such inferior courts as the Congress may from time to time ordain and establish." All Federal judges are appointed by the President with the consent of the Senate and hold office during good behavior. Their salaries cannot be reduced during their term of office.

Supreme Court of the United States. This is now composed of one chief justice and eight associate justices. The Court had five justices until 1807, then six until 1837, up to ten in 1863. A law of 1866 to reduce the number to six was repealed in 1869 before the date on which it was to have gone into effect.

To become a member of the Supreme Court might well be the ambition of the greatest lawyers. William H. Taft declared that he would rather be Chief Justice of the Supreme Court than President of the United States. He achieved both posts. Upon the organization of the court in 1789 the Chief Justice received $4,000 a year.

the Associate Justices $3,500. These sums have been increased from time to time; today they are $40,000 and $39,500 respectively.

The Supreme Court is usually in session from October to May. It is housed in its own splendid building completed in 1936.

Powers of the Court. The Constitution declares the powers of the Supreme Court. Its jurisdiction includes:

All cases affecting ambassadors, other public ministers and consuls.

All cases of admiralty and maritime jurisdiction.

All controversies over which the United States shall be a party.

All controversies between two or more states.

All controversies between one state and citizens of another state or between different states, and controversies between the citizens of the same state claiming lands under grants of different states. But the Eleventh Amendment declares that this shall not extend to suits by a citizen of one state or a foreign state against another state.

All controversies between a state or the citizens thereof and foreign states, citizens or subjects.

In many countries the legislative body is free to enact whatever laws its members desire without any check. The whole American system is one of check and balance. The President may veto any act of Congress and it becomes law over his disapproval only by a two-thirds vote of each House of Congress. Besides, the Supreme Court has the power to declare an Act of Congress (or a statute of a state legislature) unconstitutional and therefore inoperative.

The Supreme Court has authority of two different kinds: *original jurisdiction* (over cases affecting ambassadors, other public ministers and consuls and cases in which a state of the Union is a party) or the power to hear these cases in first instance and finally; and *appellate jurisdiction* in other cases as determined by Congress, that is, power to give final decisions both as to law and fact in these cases after they have been tried in other courts.

The right of appellate jurisdiction is the source of the Supreme Court's power to declare an Act of Congress or a state statute unconstitutional. Only by implication and by custom it has this right—it is not definitely mentioned or given the Court by the Constitution. It is important to bear in mind that this power comes under the head of appellate jurisdiction and that the Constitution gives the Supreme Court "appellate jurisdiction . . . with such exceptions and under such regulations as the Congress shall make."

There have always been two schools of political theory on Constitutional interpretation in the United States. The strict cónstruction or State-rights view minimizes the national government, gives it no more than the Constitution unquestionably grants it and puts particular stress on the 10th Amendment which reserves to the states respectively or the people powers "not delegated to the United States by the Constitution, nor prohibited by it to the States." The nationalist or loose-construction interpretation adjusts the phrases of the late 18th century to 20th century conditions; considers that "general welfare" (Art. 1, Sec. 8, Cl. 1) includes modern legislation for social betterment; and makes the congressional power "to regulate commerce . . . among the several States" apply to almost all types of business.

The Supreme Court has from time to time seemed to interpret these and other phrases in the Constitution (especially "due process of law" in the 5th Amendment) now very strictly, now very loosely. The famous constitutional cases decided when John Marshall was Chief Justice, between 1801 and 1835, were definitely nationalist, construing the Constitution broadly and rousing the bitter opposition of Jefferson and others of the State-rights school. The famous Dred Scott decision in 1857 written by Chief Justice Taney was strict construction of the Constitution. During the last generation the Court has repeatedly curbed the efforts of Congress and state legislatures to pass laws for social betterment and the improvement and regulation of conditions of employment—the "due process" clause was interpreted to mean that there could be no legislation interfering with the liberty of contract. In the depression period of the 1930s the Court quashed New Deal legislation on the ground that it interfered with commerce that was inside a state and not interstate and that Congress had unconstitutionally delegated power to the President. Some decisions of this strict constructionist character were handed down by a divided court with the decision of a single justice making a law unconstitutional by 5 to 4 votes. The Court (which had been bitterly assailed in Marshall's day and in Taney's) was now criticized as reactionary and as assuming legislative powers. In 1937 President Roosevelt sponsored a measure to put new blood in the Court and increase its personnel with the hope of winning the Court's approval for his New Deal legislation. His own party split, many members refused to follow him and the measure was defeated.

Inferior Courts. The Constitution does not name these, but provides for —"such inferior courts as the Congress may from time to time ordain and establish."

United States District Courts number more than 100 with each judicial district an entire state or part of a state. They have original jurisdiction over offenses against the laws of the United States, and over certain classes of controversies between citizens of different states. Among the offenses of which the District Courts take cognizance are violations of the Federal laws connected with the revenue and postal laws, smuggling, counterfeiting and bankruptcy.

There are more than 150 district judges. The salary of a district judge is $30,000; he is appointed for life or during good behavior by the President of the United States with the consent of the Senate. Each of the District Courts has its district attorney, marshal and other officers who prepare cases for presentation to the bench and who execute the mandates of the judges.

The Circuit Courts of Appeals hear appeals from decisions in the District Courts; this function relieves the Supreme Court of the United States of much of its labor as the decision of the Circuit Court is usually final, only cases of high economic and constitutional significance going to the Supreme Court from the Circuit Courts. There are about forty-five circuit judges in the ten circuits into which the country is divided. The salary of a United States circuit judge is $33,000; his appointment follows the same course as that of a district judge. Originally the Justices of the Supreme Court rode the circuit as circuit judges.

Amending the Constitution is provided for in Article V. Two-thirds of both Houses of Congress may propose an amendment to the states. Or if legislatures of two-thirds of the states ask Congress to do so, it may call a convention for proposing amendments—this has never been done. An amendment proposed in either way becomes a part of the Constitution (a) when it is ratified by legislatures of three-fourths of the states or (b) by conventions in three-fourths of the states. When Congress proposes an amendment or calls a convention to propose amendments, Congress signifies which method—(a) legislature, (b) convention—shall be used by the states for ratification. But the method of ratification by legislatures has always been used.

Some amendments have been adopted to make it possible to enact laws that the Supreme Court had declared unconstitutional. The 16th Amendment authorizing Congress to tax incomes became a part of the Constitution in 1913, eighteen years after the Supreme Court of the United States had decided that an income tax law of 1894 was unconstitutional because it was a direct tax not "in proportion to the census" (Art. I, Sec. 9, Cl. 4). In 1924 Congress sent to the state legislatures a proposed amendment giving Congress power to "limit, regulate and prohibit the labor of persons under 18 years of age." This amendment was an attempt to secure legislation that the Supreme Court in 1918 and 1924 had declared unconstitutional. Although President Roosevelt and other influential men tried to get the amendment passed, the measure never received ratification from the states.

The Government of the States

The original thirteen states, at the suggestion of the Continental Congress, each in its own way and time adopted a state constitution. Under the Constitution (Art. 4, Sec. 4) the United States guarantees to each state a republican form of government. It is customary for Congress to pass an act permitting a territory to become a state under prescribed conditions of boundaries, population and so forth, with provision that it frame and adopt a constitution satisfactory to the Congress. These state constitutions are all modeled in part after the Constitution of the United States and of the older states. Of late years there has been a tendency to make them longer and to include subjects that were formerly left for action by the legislature. The process of amending state constitutions is almost continuous. Sometimes as many as two-thirds of the states in a single year are voting on proposed amendments. Each state government, like the Federal government, has three main departments—the legislative, executive and judicial.

Legislative Department.—The law-making department of the state is variously called legislature, assembly or general assembly. In Massachusetts and New Hampshire it is called the General Court. In most states it meets every other year, but every year in Arizona, Colorado, Georgia, Kansas, Massachusetts, Michigan, New Jersey, New York, Rhode Island, South Carolina, and West Virginia. The two houses, corresponding to the organization of the Federal Congress, are usually termed the Senate and House of Representatives. In Nebraska a constitutional amendment of 1934 established a single chamber legislature which first met in 1937; but there are few innovations in state government.

The upper house usually has fewer members than the lower and sometimes they are elected for longer terms. The total number of state legislators varies considerably in different states. New Hampshire has a senate with 24 members and a House from 350 to 400; New York has 58 Senators and 150 Assemblymen. Usually there is at least one representative for each county (in New England, each town) in the lower house of the state, and it is quite common for the rural parts of a state to be overrepresented and the cities to be underrepresented. The amount of state legislation is enormous—one authority estimates that in the 20 years from 1906 to 1926 over 850,000 measures were introduced in the legislatures of the 48 states and that 220,000 of these were enacted! But only a small part of this huge amount affects the political structure, for many legislative acts are appropriations or private, special and unimportant acts. Legislative councils in Michigan and Kansas since 1933 are specially organized committees to study the drafting of bills and furnish necessary information to legislators.

Executive Department.—The chief executive of the state is the governor elected for four years in 35 states and for two years in 15 states. Salaries range from $10,000 in Arkansas and North Dakota to $35,000 in New Jersey and Pennsylvania and $50,000 in New York. The average is $22,000. In every state except North Carolina the governor has the veto power. He makes comparatively few appointments to important offices, but his power lies in patronage grants.

The lower executives of each state are elected for the same term as the governor. They may include a lieutenant governor, secretary of state, treasurer, auditor, superintendent of public instruction, attorney-general and in some states a comptroller.

Judicial Department.—The supreme court is the head of the state system in most instances, and it has the power to declare statutes unconstitutional. They have been even more conservative in this respect than the United States Supreme Court. In a few states (Colorado, Florida, Maine, Massachusetts, New Hampshire and South Dakota) the Supreme Court is required to give opinions on questions submitted by the governor or legislature. In the organization of lower courts the state is divided into circuits (and at least one circuit court, known also as a county court, is provided for each county); the presiding officer is the circuit judge or county judge. The name of such courts is varied in a few states and in some there are additional courts to meet local needs, such as appellate courts, municipal courts, courts of general sessions, juvenile courts, etc. There are usually justices of the peace in each township.

Suffrage.—In general each state makes its own rules concerning who shall be allowed to vote in state and national elections. Three amendments to the Federal Constitution control this power of the states: the 14th (1868) which threatens with reduced representation in the lower House of the Congress any state that denies the right to vote for President to any of the male inhabitants of the state; the 15th (1870), forbidding denial or abridgment of the right of citizens of the United States to vote on account of race, color or previous condition of servitude; and the 19th (1920), that the right to vote shall not be denied or abridged on account of sex.

Most states set the voting age at 21 (18 in Georgia and Kentucky). All require a period of residence in the state—usually 1 year—and often a shorter period in the county or election district. Some states require the payment of a poll tax. About half the states have a literacy test and the others require that a voter must be able to understand and explain what is read to him. Louisiana and other southern states in an attempt to bar Negroes from voting and to keep the voting rolls under the control of election officers, exempted from the literacy test or alternative property ownership requirement "males entitled to vote on January 1, 1867, their sons and grandsons 21 years of age or over at the time of the adoption of the state constitution and citizens naturalized before 1898." Negroes could not enjoy these exemptions and might be excluded by the election officials as illiterates. The grandfather clause was declared unconstitutional by the Supreme Court. Other legislation by southern states tending to debar the Negro apparently is within the letter of the Federal Constitution. In New York the literacy test is conducted by school authorities and not by the election

officers. Paupers, persons of unsound mind and criminals are excluded from suffrage by varying state constitutional requirements.

State Administration.—For a score of years there has been an active movement to simplify and make more effective the elaborate and confused administration of the states. In 1917 Illinois adopted a scientifically planned organization of nine (later eleven) departments each headed by a director appointed by the governor with the approval of the senate. About twenty states have followed this general idea, mostly with less care and thoroughness than went into the Illinois plan.

The Political Divisions.—If a state were quite small, it would be possible to govern it with satisfaction from one central point. However, most states are large, and to attempt such an expedient would result in too much government near the focal point and too little control and attention at distant points. Therefore, each state is politically divided for the purposes of local self-government into counties (parishes in Louisiana), and the counties are divided into towns or townships.

The affairs of a county are entrusted to a sheriff, county clerk, county treasurer, state's attorney (or prosecuting attorney), assessor, register of deeds, superintendent of schools, coroner and surveyor; sometimes there is a comptroller, rather than treasurer. The sheriff and coroner are usually limited to two consecutive terms in office; others may be elected indefinitely. The legislative body is a board of supervisors, one member from each township, or a board of county commissioners of three or more members.

A township's affairs are in the control of a supervisor, treasurer, clerk, school inspector, assessor, justices of the peace and constables who are police officers with limited powers.

Municipal and local government has so many variations that it cannot be described in a few sentences. The old style of city government was in form something like the state government with an executive and two houses of a legislative body; and in fact it was usually controlled by the state government. The major changes in municipal government were: to simplify the legislative body; and to make the city independent of the state—to give the city home rule. A third objective has been to get away from party government in the cities, to keep elections there as free as possible from being swayed by presidential or congressional campaign issues —in short to give cities a businesslike rather than a partisan government. Cincinnati was one of the first American cities to employ a city manager rather than a mayor. Some of the other large cities which have city managers are: Dallas, Texas; Des Moines, Iowa; Hartford, Connecticut; Miami, Florida; Oklahoma City, Oklahoma; Richmond, Virginia; Rochester, New York; and Wichita, Kansas. One big advantage of having a city manager as the chief executive of the municipality, is that the elections can be held along non-partisan lines.

The Government of Territories

The United States has several outlying territories which have varying degrees of self-government. In 1958 and 1959 two former United States territories achieved statehood. The new states are Alaska (1958) and Hawaii (1959). The remaining territories can be divided into three main groups with varying degress of governing powers. These groups include: commonwealth, trusteeship, and non-self-governing.

Commonwealth. Puerto Rico, easternmost island in the West Indies, is a commonwealth freely associated with the U. S. It has its own constitution modeled after that of the United States, a locally elected government, and a

commissioner to the U. S. House of Representatives who does not, however, have any vote.

Non-Self-Governing Territories. American Samoa, the Canal Zone, the Virgin Islands, Guam, Midway and Wake Islands. In Samoa, the Canal Zone, and the Virgin Islands, the governor is appointed by the President. Guam has a limited self-government with the civilian governor operating under the supervision of the U. S. Department of the Interior. Midway and Wake Islands are primarily military bases.

The Trusteeships. Caroline, Mariana and Marshall Islands in the West Pacific. In 1947, the Security Council of the United Nations set up the Strategic Trust Territory of the Pacific islands,

and assigned these islands to the U. S.

Alaska was acquired by purchase in 1867. Hawaii was formally annexed after the independent kingdom of Queen Liliuokalani had been replaced by a republic. Puerto Rico and Guam were prizes of the Spanish-American War of 1898, as a result of which the United States exercised for a time a practical protectorate over Cuba. (The Philippine Islands were also annexed at this time but they received their complete independence in 1946.) The Panama Canal Zone came to the United States as a result of the revolution that set up Panama as a distinct republic separate from Colombia and made possible our building the Panama Canal. The Virgin Islands were purchased from Denmark in 1917.

THE WHITE HOUSE

CABINET MEETING in the Cabinet room of the White House. The cabinet is not mentioned in the Constitution, although it is stated that the president may require opinions from officers in each of the executive departments. Cabinet members are appointed by the president but must be approved by the Senate. They serve for the term of the president unless they resign. Seated around the table from left to right are: John Gronouski, former postmaster general; Arthur Goldberg, ambassador to the United Nations; Robert Mc- Namara, secretary of defense; Orville Freeman, secretary of agriculture; Willard Wirtz, secretary of labor; John Gardner, secretary of commerce; Nicholas de B. Katzenbach, attorney general; Dean Rusk, secretary of state; President Johnson; Henry Fowler, secretary of the treasury; Stewart Udall, secretary of the interior. Standing are presidential aides: Bill Moyers, Jack Valenti, Horace Busby, McGeorge Bundy, and Charles Schultze. Vice- president Hubert Humphrey is absent.

HISTORY OF THE U. S. PRESIDENTIAL CABINET

The cabinet is not mentioned in the Constitution, but Art. II, Sec. 2, Cl. 1 permits the president to "require the opinion in writing of the principal officer in each of the executive departments upon any subject relating to the duties of their respective offices." The executive departments were organized by law rather than by the Constitution. Custom, rather than law, has made the heads of departments a group of official advisers to the president, known as the cabinet.

Cabinet members are appointed by the president, subject to the approval of the Senate; approval is usually given as a matter of course. They serve at the pleasure of the president, usually for his term of office, unless their resignation is brought about sooner. The postmaster general is the only cabinet member whose tenure expires every four years. Their salary, determined by Congress, is now $30,000 per year.

Officially, cabinet members serve as department heads, with overall responsibility for departmental branches, including various boards, bureaus, divisions, commissions, offices, and services. Unofficially, they are members of the president's administrative family or council. They have no legislative function, and advise the president only on those matters that he brings to their attention.

President Washington repeatedly asked for advice (not always on matters connected with their departments) from department heads, particularly from Secretary of State Thomas Jefferson and Secretary of the Treasury Alexander Hamilton. In addition to being department heads, the two led diametrically opposed political parties, thus they were seldom in agreement in their advice to the president. Subsequent presidents have normally selected advisers from their own political party, although some advisers have been chosen from the minority party. Members of the cabinet often represent different parts of the country, minority groups, and various shades of political belief within the party.

From an original group of four members—secretaries of state, war, and treasury, and the attorney general (head of the department of justice)—the cabinet has grown to eleven. The war department is now represented by the secretary of defense, as is the navy department. The postmaster general, and secretaries of the interior; agriculture; commerce; labor; health, education, and welfare; and housing and urban development have also been added. The vice-president has sat as a member of the cabinet since 1921.

The law concerning presidential succession now states that in case of the death or incapacity of both the president and the vice-president, the succession as acting president should be in the following order: speaker of the House of Representatives, president pro tempore of the Senate, secretary of state, secretary of the treasury, secretary of defense, attorney general, postmaster general, secretary of the interior, secretary of agriculture, secretary of commerce, and secretary of labor.

Administration	State	Treasury	War	Justice (Attorney General)[2]	Navy[3]	Post Office[4]
Washington (1) *John Adams*	John Jay[1] Thomas Jefferson	Alexander Hamilton	Henry Knox	Edmund Randolph		
Washington (2) *John Adams*	Thomas Jefferson Edmund Randolph Timothy Pickering	Alexander Hamilton Oliver Wolcott	Henry Knox Timothy Pickering James McHenry	Edmund Randolph William Bradford Charles Lee		
John Adams *Thomas Jefferson*	Timothy Pickering John Marshall	Oliver Wolcott Samuel Dexter	James McHenry Samuel Dexter Roger Griswold	Charles Lee	Benjamin Stoddert	
Jefferson (1) *Aaron Burr*	James Madison	Samuel Dexter Albert Gallatin	Henry Dearborn	Levi Lincoln Robert Smith	Benjamin Stoddert Robert Smith	
Jefferson (2) *George Clinton*	James Madison	Albert Gallatin	Henry Dearborn	John Breckinridge Caesar A. Rodney	Robert Smith	
Madison (1) *George Clinton*	Robert Smith James Monroe	Albert Gallatin	William Eustis	Caesar A. Rodney William Pinkney	Paul Hamilton	
Madison (2) *Elbridge Gerry*	James Monroe	Albert Gallatin Geo. W. Campbell Alexander J. Dallas Wm. H. Crawford	John Armstrong James Monroe Wm. H. Crawford	William Pinkney Richard Rush	William Jones Benjamin W. Crowninshield	
Monroe (1) *Daniel D. Tompkins*	John Q. Adams	Wm. H. Crawford	John C. Calhoun	Richard Rush William Wirt	Benjamin W. Crowninshield Smith Thompson	
Monroe (2) *Daniel D. Tompkins*	John Q. Adams	Wm. H. Crawford	John C. Calhoun	William Wirt	Smith Thompson Samuel Southard	
J. Q. Adams *John C. Calhoun*	Henry Clay	Richard Rush	James Barbour Peter B. Porter	William Wirt	Samuel Southard	
Jackson (1) *John C. Calhoun*	Martin Van Buren Edward Livingston	Samuel D. Ingham Louis McLane	John H. Eaton Lewis Cass	John Berrien Roger B. Taney	John Branch	William Barry
Jackson (2) *Martin Van Buren*	Edward Livingston Louis McLane John Forsyth	Louis McLane William J. Duane Roger B. Taney Levi Woodbury	Lewis Cass Benjamin F. Butler	Roger B. Taney Benjamin F. Butler	John Branch Levi Woodbury Mahlon Dickerson	William Barry Amos Kendall
Van Buren *Richard M. Johnson*	John Forsyth	Levi Woodbury	Joel R. Poinsett	Benjamin F. Butler Felix Grundy Henry Gilpin	Mahlon Dickerson James K. Paulding	Amos Kendall John M. Niles
W. H. Harrison-Tyler	Daniel Webster Hugh S. Legaré Abel P. Upshur John C. Calhoun	Thomas Ewing Walter Forward John C. Spencer George M. Bibb	John Bell John C. Spencer James M. Porter William Wilkins	John J. Crittenden Hugh S. Legaré John Nelson	George E. Badger Abel P. Upshur David Henshaw Thomas W. Gilmer John Y. Mason	Francis Granger Charles A. Wickliffe
Polk *George M. Dallas*	James Buchanan	Robert J. Walker	William Marcy	John Y. Mason Nathan Clifford Isaac Toucey	George Bancroft John Y. Mason	Cave Johnson

1. John Jay served as secretary for foreign affairs under the Continental Congress, and unofficially served the department of state until 1790.

2. The attorney general has been a member of the cabinet since 1789, but did not head an executive department until the department of justice was established in 1870.

3. Department of the navy was included in the department of war until 1798.

4. The postmaster general became a cabinet member in 1829, but did not head an executive department until the post office department was established in 1872.

Administration	State	Treasury	War	Justice (Attorney General)	Navy	Post Office
Taylor-Fillmore	John M. Clayton Daniel Webster Edward Everett	Wm. M. Meredith Thomas Corwin	Geo. W. Crawford Charles M. Conrad	Reverdy Johnson John J. Crittenden	William B. Preston William A. Graham John P. Kennedy	Jacob Collamer Nathan K. Hall Samuel D. Hubbard
Pierce *William R. King*	William L. Marcy	James Guthrie	Jefferson Davis	Caleb Cushing	James C. Dobbin	James Campbell
Buchanan *J. C. Breckinridge*	Lewis Cass Jeremiah S. Black	Howell Cobb Philip F. Thomas John A. Dix	John B. Floyd Joseph Holt	Jeremiah S. Black Edwin M. Stanton	Isaac Toucey	Aaron V. Brown Joseph Holt Horatio King
Lincoln (1) *Hannibal Hamlin*	William H. Seward	Salmon P. Chase Wm. P. Fessenden	Simon Cameron Edwin M. Stanton	Edward Bates James Speed	Gideon Welles	Montgomery Blair William Dennison
Lincoln (2)-A. Johnson	William H. Seward	Hugh McCulloch	Edwin M. Stanton Ulysses S. Grant John M. Schofield	James Speed Henry Stanbery William M. Evarts	Gideon Welles	William Dennison Alex. W. Randall
Grant (1) *Schuyler Colfax*	Elihu B. Washburn Hamilton Fish	George S. Boutwell	John Rawlins William W. Belknap	Ebenezer R. Hoar Amos T. Akerman George H. Williams	Adolph E. Borie George M. Robeson	John A. J. Creswell
Grant (2) *Henry Wilson*	Hamilton Fish	Wm. A. Richardson Benj. H. Bristow Lot M. Morrill	William W. Belknap Alphonso Taft James D. Cameron	George H. Williams Edwards Pierrepont Alphonso Taft	George M. Robeson	John A. J. Creswell James W. Marshall Marshall Jewell James N. Tyner
Hayes *William A. Wheeler*	William M. Evarts	John Sherman	George McCrary Alexander Ramsey	Charles Devens	R. W. Thompson Nathan Goff, Jr.	David McK. Key Horace Maynard
Garfield-Arthur	James G. Blaine Frederick T. 　Frelinghuysen	William Windom Charles J. Folger Walter Q. Gresham Hugh McCulloch	Robert T. Lincoln	Wayne 　MacVeagh Benjamin H. 　Brewster	William H. Hunt William E. Chandler	Thomas L. James Timothy O. Howe Walter Q. Gresham Frank Hatton
Cleveland (1) *Thomas A. Hendricks*	Thomas F. Bayard	Daniel Manning Charles S. Fairchild	William C. Endicott	Augustus H. 　Garland	William C. Whitney	William F. Vilas Don M. Dickinson
B. Harrison *Levi P. Morton*	James G. Blaine John W. Foster	William Windom Charles Foster	Redfield Proctor Stephen B. Elkins	William H. H. Miller	Benjamin F. Tracy	John Wanamaker
Cleveland (2) *Adlai E. Stevenson*	Walter Q. Gresham Richard Olney	John G. Carlisle	Daniel S. Lamont	Richard Olney Judson Harmon	Hilary A. Herbert	Wilson S. Bissell William L. Wilson
McKinley (1) *Garret A. Hobart*	John Sherman William R. Day John Hay	Lyman J. Gage	Russell A. Alger	Joseph McKenna John W. Griggs	John D. Long	James A. Gary Charles E. Smith
McKinley (2)-T. Roosevelt	John Hay	Lyman J. Gage Leslie M. Shaw	Elihu Root William H. Taft	Philander C. Knox William H. Moody	John D. Long William H. Moody Paul Morton	Charles E. Smith Henry C. Payne Robert J. Wynne
T. Roosevelt *Charles Fairbanks*	Elihu Root Robert Bacon	Leslie M. Shaw Geo. B. Cortelyou	William H. Taft Luke E. Wright	William H. Moody Chas. J. Bonaparte	Chas. J. Bonaparte Victor H. Metcalf T. H. Newberry	George B. Cortelyou George von L. Meyer
Taft *James S. Sherman*	Philander C. Knox	Franklin MacVeagh	Jacob M. Dickinson Henry L. Stimson	George W. 　Wickersham	George von L. 　Meyer	Frank H. Hitchcock
Wilson (1) *Thomas R. Marshall*	William J. Bryan Robert Lansing	William G. McAdoo	Lindley M. Garrison	J. C. McReynolds Thomas W. Gregory	Josephus Daniels	Albert S. Burleson
Wilson (2) *Thomas R. Marshall*	Robert Lansing Bainbridge Colby	William G. McAdoo Carter Glass David F. Houston	Newton D. Baker	Thomas W. Gregory A. Mitchell Palmer	Josephus Daniels	Albert S. Burleson
Harding-Coolidge	Charles E. Hughes	Andrew W. Mellon	John W. Weeks	Harry M. 　Daugherty	Edwin Denby Curtis Wilbur	Will H. Hays Hubert Work Harry S. New
Coolidge *Charles G. Dawes*	Frank B. Kellogg	Andrew W. Mellon	Dwight F. Davis	Harlan F. Stone John G. Sargent	Curtis Wilbur	Harry S. New
Hoover *Charles Curtis*	Henry L. Stimson	Andrew W. Mellon Ogden L. Mills	James W. Good Patrick J. Hurley	William D. Mitchell	Charles F. Adams	Walter F. Brown
F. D. Roosevelt (1) *John Nance Garner*	Cordell Hull	William H. Woodin Henry 　Morgenthau, Jr.	George H. Dern	Homer S. 　Cummings	Claude A. Swanson	James A. Farley
F. D. Roosevelt (2) *John Nance Garner*	Cordell Hull	Henry 　Morgenthau, Jr.	George H. Dern Harry H. Woodring Henry L. Stimson	Homer S. 　Cummings Frank Murphy	Claude A. Swanson	James A. Farley
F. D. Roosevelt (3) *Henry A. Wallace*	Cordell Hull Edward R. 　Stettinius, Jr.	Henry 　Morgenthau, Jr.	Henry L. Stimson	Robert H. Jackson Francis Biddle	Charles Edison Frank Knox James V. Forrestal	Frank C. Walker
F. D. Roosevelt (4)-Truman	Edward R. 　Stettinius, Jr. James F. Byrnes George C. Marshall	Henry 　Morgenthau, Jr. Fred M. Vinson	Henry L. Stimson Robt. P. Patterson Kenneth C. Royall[5]	Francis Biddle Thomas C. Clark	James V. Forrestal[5]	Frank C. Walker Robt. E. Hannegan Jesse M. Donaldson
Truman *Alben W. Barkley*	Dean Acheson	John W. Snyder		Thomas C. Clark J. Howard McGrath James P. 　McGranery		Jesse M. Donaldson
Eisenhower (1) *Richard M. Nixon*	John F. Dulles	George M. 　Humphrey		Herbert 　Brownell, Jr.		Arthur E. 　Summerfield
Eisenhower (2) *Richard M. Nixon*	John F. Dulles Christian Herter	George M. 　Humphrey Robt. B. Anderson		Herbert 　Brownell, Jr. William P. Rogers		Arthur E. 　Summerfield
Kennedy-L. B. Johnson	Dean Rusk	C. Douglas Dillon		Robert F. Kennedy		J. Edward Day John A. Gronouski
L. B. Johnson *Hubert H. Humphrey*	Dean Rusk	C. Douglas Dillon Henry H. Fowler		Robert F. Kennedy Nicholas de B. 　Katzenbach		John A. Gronouski Lawrence F. O'Brien W. Marvin Watson

5. The department of war and the department of the navy became sub-departments of the department of defense, by Act of Congress, July 25, 1947.

Interior

Thomas Ewing
Thomas McKennan
Alex. H. H. Stuart

Robert McClelland

Jacob Thompson

Caleb B. Smith
John P. Usher

John P. Usher
James Harlan
Orville H. Browning

Jacob D. Cox
Columbus Delano

Columbus Delano
Zachariah Chandler

Carl Schurz

Samuel J. Kirkwood
Henry M. Teller

Lucius Q. C. Lamar
William F. Vilas

John W. Noble

Hoke Smith
David R. Francis

Cornelius N. Bliss
Ethan A. Hitchcock

Ethan A. Hitchcock

Ethan A. Hitchcock
James R. Garfield

Richard A. Ballinger
Walter L. Fisher

Franklin K. Lane

Franklin K. Lane
John B. Payne

Albert B. Fall
Hubert Work

Hubert Work
Roy O. West

Ray L. Wilbur

Harold L. Ickes

Harold L. Ickes

Harold L. Ickes

Harold L. Ickes
Julius A. Krug

Julius A. Krug
Oscar L. Chapman

Douglas McKay
Fred. A. Seaton

Fred. A. Seaton

Stewart L. Udall

Stewart L. Udall

The United States representative to the United Nations

In 1945, Congress authorized the president to name a representative of the United States to the United Nations, with the rank of ambassador. Henry Cabot Lodge, who served from 1953 to 1960, was the first representative to hold the rank of cabinet member. As a member of the cabinet, the representative attends cabinet meetings at which U. S. foreign policy is being determined and he plays a major role in formulating policy. From 1961 until his sudden death in 1965, Adlai E. Stevenson broadened the cabinet role of the representative, which varies with the presidential administration and the cabinet.

Roosevelt-Truman
Edward Stettinius
January, 1946—June, 1946
Herschel V. Johnson (acting)
June, 1946—January, 1947
Warren R. Austin
January, 1947—January, 1949

Truman
Warren R. Austin
January, 1949—January, 1953

Eisenhower (1)
Henry Cabot Lodge
January, 1953—January, 1957

Eisenhower (2)
Henry Cabot Lodge
January, 1957—September, 1960
James J. Wadsworth
September, 1960—January, 1961

Kennedy-Johnson
Adlai E. Stevenson
January, 1961—January, 1965

L. B. Johnson
Adlai E. Stevenson
January, 1965—July, 1965
Arthur J. Goldberg
July, 1965—

Establishment of U.S. Executive Depts.

State Previously Dept. of Foreign Affairs, July 27, 1789. Renamed, Sept. 15, 1789.	**Commerce** March 4, 1913. Previously Dept. of Commerce and Labor, created Feb. 14, 1903.
Treasury Sept. 2, 1789.	**Labor** March 4, 1913. A bureau of Dept. of Commerce and Labor in 1903.
War Aug. 7, 1789. Included Navy until 1798. Became part of Dept. of Defense, 1947.	**Defense** Sept. 18, 1947. War and Navy departments consolidated, with Army, Navy, and Air Force as subordinate departments.
Navy April 30, 1798. Became part of Dept. of Defense, 1947.	**Health, Education, and Welfare** April 1, 1953.
Interior March 3, 1849.	**Housing and Urban Affairs** September 9, 1965.
Agriculture May 15, 1862.	**Transportation** October 15, 1966.
Justice June 22, 1870.	
Post Office June 8, 1872. Post Office established Sept. 22, 1789.	

Agriculture

Norman J. Colman

Jeremiah M. Rusk

J. Sterling Morton

James Wilson

James Wilson

James Wilson

James Wilson

David F. Houston

David F. Houston
Edwin T. Meredith

Henry C. Wallace
Howard M. Gore

William M. Jardine

Arthur M. Hyde

Henry A. Wallace

Henry A. Wallace
Claude R. Wickard

Claude R. Wickard

Claude R. Wickard
Clinton P. Anderson
Charles F. Brannan

Charles F. Brannan

Ezra T. Benson

Ezra T. Benson

Orville L. Freeman

Orville L. Freeman

Commerce[6]

Geo. B. Cortelyou
Victor H. Metcalf

Victor H. Metcalf
Oscar S. Straus

Charles Nagel

William C. Redfield

William C. Redfield
Joshua W. Alexander

Herbert C. Hoover

Herbert C. Hoover
William F. Whiting

Robert P. Lamont
Roy D. Chapin

Daniel C. Roper

Daniel C. Roper
Harry L. Hopkins

Jesse Jones

Jesse Jones
Henry A. Wallace
W. Averell Harriman

Charles W. Sawyer

Sinclair Weeks

Sinclair Weeks
Fred. H. Mueller

Luther H. Hodges
John T. Connor

John T. Connor
Alex B. Trowbridge
C. R. Smith

Labor

William B. Wilson

William B. Wilson

James J. Davis

James J. Davis

James J. Davis
William N. Doak

Frances Perkins

Frances Perkins

Frances Perkins

Frances Perkins
Lewis B. Schwellenbach
Maurice J. Tobin

Maurice J. Tobin

Martin P. Durkin
James P. Mitchell

James P. Mitchell

Arthur J. Goldberg
W. Willard Wirtz

W. Willard Wirtz

Defense

James V. Forrestal

James V. Forrestal
Louis A. Johnson
George C. Marshall
Robert A. Lovett

Charles E. Wilson

Charles E. Wilson
Neil H. McElroy
Thos. S. Gates, Jr.

Robt. S. McNamara

Robt. S. McNamara
Clark Clifford

Health, Education, and Welfare

Oveta Culp Hobby
Marion B. Folsom

Marion B. Folsom
Arthur S. Flemming

Abra. A. Ribicoff
Anth. J. Celebrezze

Anth. J. Celebrezze
John Gardner
Wilbur J. Cohen

*created by L. B. Johnson Administration

Housing and Urban Affairs*

Robert C. Weaver

Transportation

Alan S. Boyd

---

6. Created in 1903 as department of commerce and labor. Renamed department of commerce in 1913, with creation of department of labor.

TABLE I. FACTS RELATING TO

No.	PRESIDENT'S NAME AND NUMBER OF ADMINISTRATION	BORN		PARENTS		PATERNAL ANCESTRY	FATHER'S OCCUPATION
		Date	Birthplace	Father	Mother		
1	George Washington, 1–2	Fri., Feb. 22, 1732	Bridges Creek, Va.	Augustine	Mary Ball	English	Planter
2	John Adams, 3	Wed., Oct. 30, 1735	Quincy, Mass.	John	Susanna Boylston	English	Farmer
3	Thomas Jefferson, 4–5	Tues., April 13, 1743	Shadwell, Va.	Peter	Jane Randolph	Welsh	Planter
4	James Madison, 6–7	Fri., Mar. 16, 1751	Port Conway, Va.	James	Nellie Conway	English	Planter
5	James Monroe, 8–9	Fri., April 28, 1758	Westmoreland Co., Va.	Spence	Elizabeth Jones	Scotch	Planter
6	John Quincy Adams, 10	Sat., July 11, 1767	Quincy, Mass.	John	Abigail Smith	English	Lawyer
7	Andrew Jackson, 11–12	Sun., Mar. 15, 1767	Near Monroe, N. C.	Andrew	Elizabeth Hutchinson	Scotch-Irish	Farmer
8	Martin Van Buren, 13	Thurs., Dec. 5, 1782	Kinderhook, N. Y.	Abraham	Mary Hoes (Goes)	Dutch	Farmer
9	William Henry Harrison, 14	Tues., Feb. 9, 1773	Berkeley, Va.	Benjamin	Elizabeth Bassett	English	Statesman
10	John Tyler, 14	Mon., Mar. 29, 1790	Greenway, Va.	John	Mary Armistead	English	Jurist
11	James Knox Polk, 15	Mon., Nov. 2, 1795	Mecklenburg Co., N. C.	Samuel	Jane Knox	Scotch-Irish	Farmer
12	Zachary Taylor, 16	Tues., Nov. 24, 1784	Orange Co., Va.	Richard	Mary Strother	English	Planter
13	Millard Fillmore, 16	Tues., Jan. 7, 1800	Summer Hill, N. Y.	Nathaniel	Phebe Millard	English	Farmer
14	Franklin Pierce, 17	Fri., Nov. 23, 1804	Hillsborough, N. H.	Benjamin	Anna Kendrick	English	Farmer
15	James Buchanan, 18	Sat., April 23, 1791	Near Mercersburg, Pa.	James	Elizabeth Speer	Scotch	Merchant
16	Abraham Lincoln, 19–20	Sun., Feb. 12, 1809	Hardin Co., Ky.	Thomas	Nancy Hanks	English	Farmer
17	Andrew Johnson, 20	Thurs., Dec. 29, 1808	Raleigh, N. C.	Jacob	Mary McDonough	English	Sexton
18	Ulysses Simpson Grant, 21–22	Sat., April 27, 1822	Point Pleasant, Ohio	Jesse Root	Hannah Simpson	English	Tanner
19	Rutherford Birchard Hayes, 23	Fri., Oct. 4, 1822	Delaware, Ohio	Rutherford	Sophia Birchard	Scotch	Merchant
20	James Abram Garfield, 24	Sat., Nov. 19, 1831	Orange, Ohio	Abram	Eliza Ballou	English	Farmer
21	Chester Allan Arthur, 24	Tues., Oct. 5, 1830	Fairfield, Vt.	William	Malvina Stone	Scotch-Irish	Clergyman
22	Grover Cleveland, 25	Sat., Mar. 18, 1837	Caldwell, N. J.	Richard Falley	Anne Neal	English	Clergyman
23	Benjamin Harrison, 26	Tues., Aug. 20, 1833	North Bend, Ohio	John Scott	Elizabeth F. Irwin	English	Farmer
24	Grover Cleveland, 27	Sat., Mar. 18, 1837	Caldwell, N. J.	Richard Falley	Anne Neal	English	Clergyman
25	William McKinley, 28–29	Sun., Jan. 29, 1843	Niles, Ohio	William	Nancy Allison	Scotch-Irish	Iron Mnfr.
26	Theodore Roosevelt, 29–30	Wed., Oct. 27, 1858	New York city	Theodore	Martha Bulloch	Dutch	Merchant
27	William Howard Taft, 31	Tues., Sept. 15, 1857	Cincinnati, Ohio	Alphonso	Louise M. Torrey	English	Lawyer
28	Woodrow Wilson, 32–33	Sun., Dec. 28, 1856	Staunton, Va.	Joseph Ruggles	Janet Woodrow	Scotch-Irish	Clergyman
29	Warren Gamaliel Harding, 34	Thurs., Nov. 2, 1865	Corsica, Ohio	George Tryon	Phoebe E. Dickerson	English	Doctor
30	Calvin Coolidge, 34–35	Thurs., July 4, 1872	Plymouth, Vt.	John Calvin	Victoria J. Moor	English	Farmer
31	Herbert Clark Hoover, 36	Mon., Aug. 10, 1874	West Branch, Iowa	Jesse Clark	Huldah R. Minthorn	Swiss	Blacksmith
32	Franklin Delano Roosevelt, 37 38, 39, 40	Mon., Jan. 30, 1882	Hyde Park, N. Y.	James	Sara Delano	Dutch	R. R. President
33	Harry S. Truman, 40–41	May 8, 1884	Lamar, Mo.	John Anderson	Martha Ellen Young	Scotch-Irish-Eng.	Farmer
34	Dwight D. Eisenhower, 42–43	Oct. 14, 1890	Denison, Texas	David Jacob	Ida E. Stover	German	Mechanic
35	John F. Kennedy, 44	May 29, 1917	Brookline, Mass.	Joseph P.	Rose Fitzgerald	Irish	Financier
36	Lyndon B. Johnson, 44	Aug. 27, 1908	Stonewall, Texas	Samuel Ealy	Rebekah Baines	Eng.-Scotch	Politician; rancher

TABLE II. FACTS RELATING TO

NAME	RESIDENCE WHEN ELECTED	TERM OF OFFICE		SUBSEQUENT CAREER	DIED	CAUSE OF DEATH
		From	To			
Washington	Mt. Vernon, Va.	Apr. 30, 1789	Mar. 4, 1797	Agricultural pursuits; appointed commander-in-chief (1798) because of threatened war with France.	1799	Acute laryngitis
Adams, J.	Quincy, Mass.	Mar. 4, 1797	Mar. 4, 1801	Member of Massachusetts Constitutional Convention of 1820.	1826	Natural decline
Jefferson	Monticello, Va.	Mar. 4, 1801	Mar. 4, 1809	Retired to his plantation at Monticello, Va.; devoted much time to the University of Virginia.	1826	Chronic diarrhœa
Madison	Montpelier, Va.	Mar. 4, 1809	Mar. 4, 1817	Retired to Montpelier, Va.; maintained active interest in education and politics.	1836	Natural decline
Monroe	Oakhill, Va.	Mar. 4, 1817	Mar. 4, 1825	Retired to private life in Virginia; served in Virginia Constitutional Convention in 1830.	1831	Natural decline
Adams, J. Q.	Quincy, Mass.	Mar. 4, 1825	Mar. 4, 1829	Member House of Representatives from 1830 to his death.	1848	Paralysis
Jackson	Hermitage, near Nashville, Tenn.	Mar. 4, 1829	Mar. 4, 1837	Retired to the Hermitage; maintained great interest in politics.	1845	Dropsy
Van Buren	Kinderhook, N. Y.	Mar. 4, 1837	Mar. 4, 1841	Renominated, 1840 and 1848, for the presidency.	1862	Asthma
Harrison, W. H.	North Bend, Ohio	Mar. 4, 1841	Apr. 4, 1841	Died in office.	1841	Pneumonia
Tyler	Williamsburg, Va.	Apr. 6, 1841	Mar. 4, 1845	Retired to his estate in Virginia; presided at the peace convention held in Washington in 1861.	1862	Liver trouble
Polk	Nashville, Tenn.	Mar. 4, 1845	Mar. 4, 1849	Died within 3 months.	1849	Chronic diarrhœa
Taylor	Baton Rouge, La.	Mar. 4, 1849	July 10, 1850	Died in office.	1850	Indigestion
Fillmore	Buffalo, N. Y.	July 10, 1850	Mar. 4, 1853	Chancellor, University of Buffalo.	1874	Natural decline
Pierce	Concord, N. H.	Mar. 4, 1853	Mar. 4, 1857	Traveled in Europe; retired to Concord, N. H.	1869	Stomach trouble
Buchanan	Lancaster, Pa.	Mar. 4, 1857	Mar. 4, 1861	Wrote defense of his administration.	1868	Rheumatic gout
Lincoln	Springfield, Ill.	Mar. 4, 1861	Apr. 15, 1865	Died in office.	1865	Assassinated by Booth
Johnson	Greeneville, Tenn.	Apr. 15, 1865	Mar. 4, 1869	Chosen United States senator in 1875.	1875	Paralysis
Grant	Washington, D. C.	Mar. 4, 1869	Mar. 4, 1877	Made tour of the world and retired to write his memoirs.	1885	Cancer
Hayes	Fremont, Ohio	Mar. 4, 1877	Mar. 4, 1881	Devoted his time to education, reforms and charity.	1893	Heart disease
Garfield	Mentor, Ohio	Mar. 4, 1881	Sep. 20, 1881	Died in office.	1881	Assassinated by Guiteau
Arthur	New York city	Sep. 20, 1881	Mar. 4, 1885	Died the year following his retirement.	1886	Apoplexy
Cleveland	Buffalo, N. Y.	Mar. 4, 1885 Mar. 4, 1893	Mar. 4, 1889 Mar. 4, 1897	Retired to New York to practice law; at the end of second term, retired to Princeton, N. J.	1908	Debility
Harrison, B.	Indianapolis, Ind.	Mar. 4, 1889	Mar. 4, 1893	Actively practiced law.	1901	Pneumonia
McKinley	Canton, Ohio	Mar. 4, 1897	Sep. 14, 1901	Died in office.	1901	Assassinated by Czolgosz
Roosevelt, T.	Oyster Bay, N. Y.	Sep. 14, 1901	Mar. 4, 1909	Headed scientific expeditions; wrote; active in politics.	1919	Heart trouble
Taft	Cincinnati, Ohio	Mar. 4, 1909	Mar. 4, 1913	Chief justice of U. S. Supreme Court.	1930	General breakdown
Wilson	Princeton, N. J.	Mar. 4, 1913	Mar. 4, 1921	Lawyer and writer.	1924	Heart trouble
Harding	Marion, Ohio	Mar. 4, 1921	Aug. 2, 1923	Died in office.	1923	Apoplexy
Coolidge	Northampton, Mass.	Aug. 2, 1923	Mar. 4, 1929	Writer.	1933	Heart trouble
Hoover	Stanford Univ., Cal.	Mar. 4, 1929	Mar. 4, 1933	Retired to private life.	1964	Natural decline
Roosevelt	Hyde Park, N. Y.	Mar. 4, 1933	Apr. 12, 1945	Died in office.	1945	Cerebral Hemorrhage
Truman	Independence, Mo.	Apr. 12, 1945	Jan. 20, 1953	Writer.		
Eisenhower	New York, N. Y.	Jan. 20, 1953	Jan. 20, 1961	Retired to Private Life.		
Kennedy	Boston, Mass.	Jan. 20, 1961	Nov. 22, 1963	Died in office.	1963	Assassinated
Johnson	Johnson City, Tex.	Nov. 22, 1963				

THE PRESIDENTS OF THE UNITED STATES

EDUCATIONAL ADVANTAGE	EARLY VOCATION	LATER VOCATION	RELIGIOUS FAITH	MARRIED	WIFE'S NAME	CHILDREN Boys	CHILDREN Girls	NAME
Common School	Surveyor	Planter	Episcopalian	1759	Mrs. Martha (Dandridge) Custis (1732–1802)	0	0	Washington
Harvard College, 1755*	Teacher	Lawyer	Unitarian	1764	Abigail Smith (1744–1818)	3	2	Adams, J.
William and Mary College, 1762	Lawyer	Lawyer	Liberal	1772	Mrs. Martha (Wayles) Skelton (1748–1782)	0	6	Jefferson
Princeton College, 1771	Lawyer	Lawyer	Episcopalian	1794	Mrs. Dolly (Payne) Todd (1772–1849)	0	0	Madison
William and Mary College	Lawyer	Lawyer	Episcopalian	1786	Eliza Kortwright (1768–1830)	0	2	Monroe
Harvard College, 1787	Lawyer	Lawyer	Unitarian	1797	Louisa Catherine Johnson (1775–1852)	3	1	Adams, J. Q.
Self Taught	Lawyer	Lawyer	Presbyterian	1791	Mrs. Rachel (Donelson) Robards (1767–1828)	0	0	Jackson
Kinderhook Academy	Lawyer	Lawyer	Reformed Dutch	1807	Hannah Hoes (1783–1819)	4	0	Van Buren
Hampden-Sidney College, 1790	Doctor	Soldier	Episcopalian	1795	Anna Symmes (1775–1864)	6	4	Harrison, W. H.
William and Mary College, 1807	Lawyer	Lawyer	Episcopalian	1813, 1844	First, Letitia Christian (1790–1842); second, Julia Gardiner (1820–1889)	3, 5	4, 2 }	Tyler
University of North Carolina, 1818	Lawyer	Lawyer	Presbyterian	1824	Sarah Childress (1803–1891)	0	0	Polk
Common School	Soldier	Planter	Episcopalian	1810	Margaret Smith (1788–1852)	1	5	Taylor
Common School	Wool carder	Lawyer	Unitarian	1826, 1858	First, Abigail Powers (1798–1853); second, Mrs. Caroline (Carmichael) McIntosh (1813–1881)	1, 0	1, 0 }	Fillmore
Bowdoin College, 1824	Lawyer	Lawyer	Episcopalian	1834	Jane Means Appleton (1806–1863)	3	0	Pierce
Dickinson College, 1809	Lawyer	Lawyer	Presbyterian	....	Unmarried	...	...	Buchanan
Self Taught	Farmer	Lawyer	Liberal	1842	Mary Todd (1818–1882)	4	0	Lincoln
Self Taught	Tailor	Politician	Liberal	1827	Eliza McCardle (1810–1876)	3	2	Johnson
West Point Military Academy, 1843	Tanner	Soldier	Methodist	1848	Julia Dent (1826–1902)	3	1	Grant
Kenyon College, 1842	Lawyer	Lawyer	Methodist	1852	Lucy Ware Webb (1831–1889)	7	1	Hayes
Williams College, 1856	Teacher	Lawyer	Disciples	1858	Lucretia Rudolph (1832–1918)	4	1	Garfield
Union College, 1848	Teacher	Lawyer	Episcopalian	1859	Ellen Lewis Herndon (1837–1880)	2	1	Arthur
Academy	Teacher	Lawyer	Presbyterian	1886	Frances Folsom (1864–1947)	2	3	Cleveland
Miami University, 1852	Lawyer	Lawyer	Presbyterian	1853, 1896	First, Caroline Scott (1832–1892); second, Mrs. Mary (Lord) Dimmick (1858–1948)	1, 0	1, 1 }	Harrison, B.
Academy	Teacher	Lawyer	Presbyterian	1886	Frances Folsom (1864–1947)	2	3	Cleveland
Allegheny College	Teacher	Lawyer	Methodist	1871	Ida Saxton (1844–1907)	0	2	McKinley
Harvard University, 1880	Writer	In politics	Reformed Dutch	1880, 1886	First, Alice Lee (1861–1884); second, Edith Kermit Carow (1861–1948)	0, 4	1, 1 }	Roosevelt
Yale University, 1878	Lawyer	Lawyer	Unitarian	1886	Helen Herron (1861–1943)	2	1	Taft
Princeton University, 1879	Lawyer	Educator	Presbyterian	1885, 1915	First, Ellen Louise Axson (1860–1914); second, Mrs. Edith (Bolling) Galt (1872–1961)	0	3 }	Wilson
Ohio Central College	Editor	Publisher	Baptist	1891	Florence Kling (1860–1924)	0	0	Harding
Amherst College, 1895	Lawyer	In politics	Congregationalist	1905	Grace A. Goodhue (1879–1957)	2	0	Coolidge
Stanford University, 1895	Engineer	Engineer	Quaker	1899	Lou Henry (1875–1944)	2	0	Hoover
Harvard University, 1904	Lawyer	In politics	Episcopalian	1905	Anna Eleanor Roosevelt (1884–1962)	4	1	Roosevelt
Kansas City Law School, 1925	Lawyer	In politics	Baptist	1919	Bess Wallace (1885–)	0	1	Truman
U. S. Military Academy, 1915	Soldier	University President	Presbyterian	1916	Mamie Geneva Doud (1896–)	2	0	Eisenhower
Harvard University, 1940	Reporter	Politics	Roman Catholic	1953	Jacqueline Lee Bouvier (1929–)	1	1	Kennedy
Southwest Texas State Teachers College, 1930	Teacher	Politics	Disciples of Christ	1934	Claudia Alta Taylor (1912–)	0	2	Johnson

*Date indicates graduation.

THE PRESIDENTS OF THE UNITED STATES

AGE AT DEATH	PLACE OF DEATH	PLACE OF BURIAL	WRITINGS OF THE PRESIDENTS	PRESIDENTIAL SOBRIQUETS	NAME
67	Mt. Vernon, Va.	Mt. Vernon, Va.	*Maxims; Transcripts of Revolutionary Correspondence.*	*Father of his Country; American Fabius.*	Washington
90	Quincy, Mass.	Quincy, Mass.	*Essay on Canon and Feudal Law; Defense of the American Constitution.*	*Colossus of Independence; Son of Liberty.*	Adams, J.
83	Monticello, Va.	Monticello, Va.	*A Summary View of the Rights of America; The Declaration of Independence; Act for Freedom of Religion.*	*Sage of Monticello; Long Tom.*	Jefferson
85	Montpelier, Va.	Montpelier, Va.	*Reports of Debates During the Congress of the Confederation and Federal Congress; Essays.*	*Father of the Constitution.*	Madison
73	New York city.	Hollywood, Richmond, Va.	*A View of the Conduct of the Executive; The People; The Sovereign.*	*Last Cocked Hat.*	Monroe
80	Washington, D. C.	Quincy, Mass.	*Poems of Religion and Society; Defense of Washington's Policy of Neutrality.*	*Old Man Eloquent.*	Adams, J. Q.
78	Hermitage, near Nashville, Tenn.	Hermitage, near Nashville, Tenn.		*Old Hickory; Caesar of the White House.*	Jackson
79	Kinderhook, N. Y.	Kinderhook, N. Y.	*Inquiry Into the Origin and Causes of Political Parties in the United States.*	*Little Magician; Wizard of Kinderhook.*	Van Buren
68	Washington, D. C.	North Bend, Ohio	*A Discourse on the Aborigines of the Valley of the Ohio.*	*Tippecanoe.*	Harrison, W. H.
72	Richmond, Va.	Hollywood, Richmond, Va.	*Dr. Updike Underhill*		Tyler
53	Nashville, Tenn.	Nashville, Tenn.	*Diary of James K. Polk.*	*Young Hickory.*	Polk
65	Washington, D. C.	Near Louisville, Ky.		*Rough and Ready.*	Taylor
74	Buffalo, N. Y.	Buffalo, N. Y.		*American Louis Philippe.*	Fillmore
64	Concord, N. H.	Concord, N. H.	*Some Papers of Franklin Pierce.*	*Purse.*	Pierce
77	Lancaster, Pa.	Lancaster, Pa.	*Résumé of My Administration.*	*Bachelor President.*	Buchanan
56	Washington, D. C.	Springfield, Ill.	*Orations.*	*Honest Abe; Great Emancipator.*	Lincoln
66	Carter's Station, Tenn.	Greenville, Tenn.	*Speeches.*	*Sir Veto.*	Johnson
63	Mount McGregor, N. Y.	New York city	*The Personal Memoirs of U. S. Grant.*	*Unconditional Surrender.*	Grant
71	Fremont, Ohio	Fremont, Ohio		*President de Facto.*	Hayes
49	Elberon, N. J.	Cleveland, Ohio	*Discovery and Ownership of the Northwestern Territory; Garfield's Words.*	*The Martyr President; The Dark Horse.*	Garfield
56	New York, N. Y.	Near Albany, N. Y.		*America's First Gentleman.*	Arthur
71	Princeton, N. J.	Princeton, N. J.	*Writings and Speeches.*	*Man of Destiny.*	Cleveland
67	Indianapolis, Ind.	Indianapolis, Ind.	*This Country of Ours; Views of an Ex-President.*	*Hoosier President; Son of His Grandfather.*	Harrison, B.
58	Buffalo, N. Y.	Canton, Ohio	*Speeches.*	*Prosperity's Advance Agent.*	McKinley
60	Oyster Bay, N. Y.	Oyster Bay, N. Y.	*The Winning of the West; The Rough Riders; The Strenuous Life; African Game Trails; The Great Adventure, etc.*	*Teddy; T. R.; The Rough Rider; Our Strenuous President.*	Roosevelt
72	Washington, D. C.	Arlington, Va.	*Four Aspects of Civic Duty; The United States and Peace; Ethics in Service, etc.*	*The Globe Trotter; The Judicial President.*	Taft
67	Washington, D. C.	Washington, D. C.	*Congressional Government; The State; A History of the American People; The New Freedom, etc.*	*The Scholar in Politics.*	Wilson
57	San Francisco, Calif.	Marion, Ohio			Harding
60	Northampton, Mass.	Plymouth, Vt.	*Have Faith in Massachusetts; The Price of Freedom.*	*Silent Cal.*	Coolidge
90	New York, N. Y.	West Branch, Iowa	*Principles of Mining; American Individualism.*		Hoover
63	Warm Springs, Ga.	Hyde Park, N. Y.	*The Happy Warrior; Looking Forward.*	*FDR.*	Roosevelt, F. D.
			Memoirs.		Truman
			Crusade in Europe.	*Ike.*	Eisenhower
			Profiles in Courage.	*JFK.*	Kennedy
46	Dallas, Texas	Arlington, Va.	*My Hope for America.*	*LBJ.*	Johnson

PRESIDENTIAL ELECTIONS AND INAUGURATIONS

Year	Presidential Candidates	State	Party	Vote Total	Electoral	Popular	Vice-Pres. Candidates Name	State	Facts Concerning Inauguration	Age at Inaug.
1789	**George Washington**	Va.	....	73	69[1]	....	*John Adams*	Mass.	I. **George Washington** was inaugurated President of the United States on a portico in front of the Senate chamber, Thursday, April 30, 1789, in the Federal building, facing Broad Street, in New York. The oath of office was administered by Robt. R. Livingston, chancellor of the state of New York, who exclaimed when the oath was taken, "Long live George Washington, President of the United States."	57
	John Adams	Mass.	....	...	34	....				
	John Jay	N.Y.	....	...	9	....				
	R. H. Harrison	Md.	....	...	6	....				
	John Rutledge	S.C.	....	.....	6	....				
	John Hancock	Mass.	....	...	4	....				
	George Clinton	N.Y.	....	...	3	....				
	Samuel Huntington	Conn.	....	...	2	....				
	John Milton	Ga.	....	...	2	....				
	James Armstrong	Ga.	....	...	1	....				
	Benjamin Lincoln	Mass.	....	...	1	....				
	Edward Telfair	Ga.	....	...	1	....				
	Electoral votes not cast	.....	....	...	4	....				
1792	**George Washington**	Va.	Fed.	135	132[1]	....	*John Adams*	Mass.	II. **George Washington,** for a second term, in the Senate chamber, Monday, March 4, 1793, in the Old Federal hall, in Philadelphia. Oath of office administered by William Cushing of Massachusetts.	
	John Adams	Mass.	Fed.	...	77	....				
	George Clinton	N.Y.	Rep.	...	50	....				
	Thomas Jefferson	Va.	Rep.	...	4	....				
	Aaron Burr	N.Y.	Rep.	...	1	....				
	Electoral votes not cast			...	3	....				
1796	**John Adams**	Mass.	Fed.	138	71[1]	....	*Thomas Jefferson*	Va.	III. **John Adams,** in the chamber of the House of Representatives, Congress hall, Saturday, March 4, 1797, in Philadelphia. Oath of office administered by Oliver Ellsworth, Chief Justice of the United States.	61
	Thomas Jefferson	Va.	Rep.	...	68	....				
	Thomas Pinckney	S.C.	Fed.	...	59	....				
	Aaron Burr	N.Y.	Rep.	...	30	....				
	Samuel Adams	Mass.	Rep.	...	15	....				
	Oliver Ellsworth	Conn.	Ind.	...	11	....				
	George Clinton	N.Y.	Rep.	...	7	....				
	John Jay	N.Y.	Fed.	...	5	....				
	James Iredell	N.C.	Fed.	...	3	....				
	George Washington	Va.	Fed.	...	2	....				
	John Henry	Md.	Fed.	...	2	....				
	S. Johnson	N.C.	Fed.	...	2	....				
	C. C. Pinckney	S.C.	Fed.	...	1	....				
1800	**Thomas Jefferson**	Va.	Rep.	138	73[1]	....	*Aaron Burr*	N.Y.	IV. **Thomas Jefferson,** in the Senate chamber of the Capitol, Wednesday, March 4, 1801, in the city of Washington. Oath of office administered by John Marshall, Chief Justice of the United States.	57
	Aaron Burr	N.Y.	Rep.	...	73	....				
	John Adams	Mass.	Fed.	...	65	....				
	C. C. Pinckney	S.C.	Fed.	...	64	....				
	John Jay	N.Y.	Fed.	...	1	....				
1804	**Thomas Jefferson**	Va.	Rep.	176	162	....	*George Clinton*	N.Y.	V. **Thomas Jefferson,** for a second term, in Senate chamber, Washington, Monday, March 4, 1805, by Chief Justice John Marshall.	
	C. C. Pinckney	S.C.	Fed.	...	14	....	Rufus King	N.Y.		
1808	**James Madison**	Va.	Rep.	176	122	....	*George Clinton*	N.Y.	VI. **James Madison,** in the chamber of the House of Representatives, Washington, Saturday, March 4, 1809. Oath of office administered by Chief Justice John Marshall.	57
	C. C. Pinckney	S.C.	Fed.	...	47	....	Rufus King	N.Y.		
	George Clinton	N.Y.	Rep.	...	6	....	John Langdon	N.H.		
							James Madison	Va.		
	Electoral votes not cast	.....	....	...	1	....	James Monroe	Va.		
1812	**James Madison**	Va.	Rep.	218	128	....	*Elbridge Gerry*	Mass.	VII. **James Madison,** for a second term, Thursday, March 4, 1813. Oath was administered by Chief Justice Marshall.	
	De Witt Clinton	N.Y.	Fed.	...	89	....	Jared Ingersoll	Pa.		
1816	**James Monroe**	Va.	Rep.	221	183	....	*D. D. Tompkins*	N.Y.	VIII. **James Monroe,** Tuesday, March 4, 1817. Oath administered by Chief Justice John Marshall, on a platform erected for the purpose, in front of the eastern portico of the Capitol at Washington.	58
	Rufus King	N.Y.	Fed.	...	34	....	John E. Howard	Md.		
							James Ross	Pa.		
	Electoral votes not cast	.....	....	...	4	....	John Marshall	Va.		
							Robert G. Harper	Md.		
1820	**James Monroe**	Va.	Rep.	235	231	....	*D. D. Tompkins*	N.Y.	IX. **James Monroe,** for a second term, in the House of Representatives, Monday, March 5, 1821. As March 4 came on Sunday he took the oath, administered by Chief Justice Marshall, at noon on Monday, March 5, 1821.	
	John Q. Adams	Mass.	Rep.	...	1	....	Richard Stockton	N.J.		
							Daniel Rodney	Del.		
							Robert G. Harper	Md.		
							Richard Rush	Pa.		
1824	**John Q. Adams**	Mass.	Rep.	261	84[2]	108,740	*John C. Calhoun*	S.C.	X. **John Quincy Adams,** in the hall of the House of Representatives, Friday, March 4, 1825. Oath of office administered by Chief Justice Marshall.	57
	Andrew Jackson	Tenn.	Dem.	...	99[2]	153,544	Nathan Sanford	N.Y.		
	Henry Clay	Ky.	Rep.	...	37	47,136	Nathaniel Macon	N.C.		
	W. H. Crawford	Ga.	Rep.	...	46	46,618	Andrew Jackson	Tenn.		
							Martin Van Buren	N.Y.		
							Henry Clay	Ky.		
1828	**Andrew Jackson**	Tenn.	Dem.	261	178	647,286	*John C. Calhoun*	S.C.	XI. **Andrew Jackson,** on the eastern portico of the Capitol, Wednesday, March 4, 1829. Oath administered by Chief Justice Marshall.	61
	John Q. Adams	Mass.	Nat. Rep.	...	83	508,064	Richard Rush	Pa.		
							William Smith	S.C.		
1832	**Andrew Jackson**	Tenn.	Dem.	288	219	687,502	*Martin Van Buren*	N.Y.	XII. **Andrew Jackson,** for a second term, in the hall of the House of Representatives, Monday, March 4, 1833. Oath administered by Chief Justice Marshall.	
	Henry Clay	Ky.	Nat. Rep.	...	49	530,189	John Sergeant	Pa.		
	John Floyd	Ga.	Ind.	...	11	....	Henry Lee	Mass.		
	William Wirt	Md.	Anti-M.	...	7	....	Amos Ellmaker	Pa.		
	Electoral votes not cast			...	2	....	William Wilkins	Pa.		
1836	**Martin Van Buren**	N.Y.	Dem.	294	170	762,678	*R. M. Johnson*	Ky.	XIII. **Martin Van Buren,** on the eastern portico of the Capitol, Saturday, March 4, 1837. Oath administered by Chief Justice Taney.	54
	Wm. H. Harrison	Ohio	Whig	...	73		Francis Granger	N.Y.		
	Hugh L. White	Tenn.	Whig	...	26	735,651	John Tyler	Va.		
	Daniel Webster	Mass.	Whig	...	14		William Smith	Ala.		
	W. P. Mangum	N.C.	Whig	...	11					
1840	**Wm. H. Harrison**	Ohio	Whig	294	234	1,275,016	*John Tyler*	Va.	XIV. **William Henry Harrison,** on the eastern portico of the Capitol, Thursday, March 4, 1841. Oath administered by Chief Justice Taney.	68
	Martin Van Buren	N.Y.	Dem.	...	60	1,129,102	R. M. Johnson	Ky.		
							L. W. Tazewell	Va.		
							James K. Polk	Tenn.	**John Tyler,** inaugurated 12 m., Tuesday, April 6, 1841, at Brown's Indian Queen hotel, Washington. Oath administered by Judge William Cranch.	51
							Thomas Earle	Pa.		
1844	**James K. Polk**	Tenn.	Dem.	275	170	1,337,243	*George M. Dallas*	Pa.	XV. **James Knox Polk,** on the eastern portico of the Capitol, Tuesday, March 4, 1845. Oath administered by Chief Justice Taney.	49
	Henry Clay	Ky.	Whig	...	105	1,299,062	T. Frelinghuysen	N.J.		
	James G. Birney	N.Y.	Lib.	...		62,300	Thomas Morris	Ohio		
1848	**Zachary Taylor**	La.	Whig	290	163	1,360,099	*Millard Fillmore*	N.Y.	XVI. **Zachary Taylor,** on the eastern portico of the Capitol, Monday, March 5, 1849. March 4 came on Sunday. Oath administered by Chief Justice Taney.	64
	Lewis Cass	Mich.	Dem.	...	127	1,220,544	Wm. O. Butler	Ky.		
	Martin Van Buren	N.Y.	F. S.	...	...	291,263	Chas. F. Adams	Mass.		
									Millard Fillmore, in the House of Representatives, 12 noon, Wednesday, July 10, 1850. Oath administered by Judge William Cranch.	50
1852	**Franklin Pierce**	N.H.	Dem.	296	254	1,601,274	*William R. King*	Ala.	XVII. **Franklin Pierce,** on the eastern portico of the Capitol, Friday, March 4, 1853. Oath administered by Chief Justice Taney.	48
	Winfield Scott	N.J.	Whig	...	42	1,386,580	Wm. A. Graham	N.C.		
	John P. Hale	N.H.	Fed. D.	...		155,825	George W. Julian	Ind.		
1856	**James Buchanan**	Pa.	Dem.	296	174	1,838,169	*J. C. Breckinridge*	Ky.	XVIII. **James Buchanan,** on the eastern portico of the Capitol, Wednesday, March 4, 1857. Oath administered by Chief Justice Taney.	65
	John C. Fremont	Calif.	Rep.	...	114	1,341,264	Wm. L. Dayton	N.J.		
	Millard Fillmore	N.Y.	Amer.	...	8	874,534	A. J. Donelson	Tenn.		

[1] Prior to 1804 each elector was entitled to vote for two candidates for President. The candidate with the greatest number of votes was declared elected President; the candidate with the next highest vote was declared elected Vice-President. [2] As there was no election the choice was decided by the House of Representatives.

PRESIDENTIAL ELECTIONS AND INAUGURATIONS—Concluded

Year	Presidential Candidates	State	Party	Vote: Total	Vote: Electoral	Vote: Popular	Vice-Pres. Candidates: Name	Vice-Pres. Candidates: State
1860	**Abraham Lincoln**	Ill.	Rep.	303	180	1,866,452	*Hannibal Hamlin*	Me.
	J. C. Breckinridge	Ky.	Dem.	...	72	847,953	Joseph Lane	Ind.
	Stephen A. Douglas	Ill.	Union D.	...	39	1,375,157	H. V. Johnson	Ga.
	John Bell	Tenn.	Amer.	...	12	590,631	Edward Everett	Mass.
1864	**Abraham Lincoln**	Ill.	Rep.	314	212	2,213,665	*Andrew Johnson*	Tenn.
	Geo. B. McClellan	N. J.	Dem.	...	21	1,802,237	G. H. Pendleton	Ohio
1868	**Ulysses S. Grant**	Ill.	Rep.	317	214	3,012,833	*Schuyler Colfax*	Ind.
	Horatio Seymour	N. Y.	Dem.	...	80	2,703,249	F. P. Blair, Jr.	Mo.
1872	**Ulysses S. Grant**	Ill.	Rep.	366	286	3,597,132	*Henry Wilson*	Mass.
	Horace Greeley	N. Y.	D. & L.	...	...	2,834,125	B. Gratz Brown	Mo.
	Charles O'Conor	N. Y.	Dem.	...	...	29,489	John Q. Adams	Mass.
	James Black	Pa.	Temp.	...	...	5,608	John Russell	Mich.
	Thos. A. Hendricks	Ind.	Dem.	...	42	....	Geo. W. Julian	Ind.
	B. Gratz Brown	Mo.	Dem.	...	18	....	A. H. Colquitt	Ga.
	Charles J. Jenkins	Ga.	Dem.	...	2	....	J. M. Palmer	Ill.
	David Davis	Ill.	Ind.	...	1	....	T. E. Bramlette	Ky.
	Electoral votes not counted	.....	....	...	17	....	W. S. Grosbeck	Ohio
							W. B. Machen	Ky.
							N. P. Banks	Mass.
1876	**Rutherford B. Hayes**	Ohio	Rep.	369	185	4,036,298	*Wm. A. Wheeler*	N. Y.
	Samuel J. Tilden	N. Y.	Dem.	...	184	4,300,590	T. A. Hendricks	Ind.
	Peter Cooper	N. Y.	Grb.	...	...	81,737	Samuel F. Cary	Ohio
	Green Clay Smith	Ky.	Pro.	...	...	9,522	G. T. Stewart	Ohio
	James B. Walker	Ill.	Amer.	...	...	2,636	D. Kirkpatrick	N. Y.
1880	**James A. Garfield**	Ohio	Rep.	369	214	4,454,416	*Chester A. Arthur*	N. Y.
	Win'd S. Hancock	Pa.	Dem.	...	155	4,444,952	Wm. H. English	Ind.
	James B. Weaver	Iowa	Grb.	...	...	308,578	B. J. Chambers	Tex.
	Neal Dow	Me.	Pro.	...	...	10,305	H. A. Thompson	Ohio
1884	**Grover Cleveland**	N. Y.	Dem.	401	219	4,874,986	*T. A. Hendricks*	Ind.
	James G. Blaine	Me.	Rep.	...	182	4,851,981	John A. Logan	Ill.
	John P. St. John	Kan.	Pro.	...	...	150,369	William Daniel	Md.
	Benjamin F. Butler	Mass.	People's	...	...	175,370	A. M. West	Miss.
1888	**Benjamin Harrison**	Ind.	Rep.	401	233	5,439,853	*Levi P. Morton*	N. Y.
	Grover Cleveland	N. Y.	Dem.	...	168	5,549,309	A. G. Thurman	Ohio
	Clinton B. Fisk	N. J.	Pro.	...	...	249,506	John A. Brooks	Mo.
	Alson J. Streeter	Ill.	U. L.	...	...	146,935	C. E. Cunningham	Ark.
1892	**Grover Cleveland**	N. Y.	Dem.	444	277	5,554,437	*A. E. Stevenson*	Ill.
	Benjamin Harrison	Ind.	Rep.	...	145	5,175,287	Whitelaw Reid	N. Y.
	James B. Weaver	Iowa	People's	...	22	1,041,028	James G. Field	Va.
	John Bidwell	Calif.	Pro.	...	...	264,133	James R. Cranfill	Texas
	Simon Wing	Mass.	S. L.	...	...	21,164	C. H. Matchett	N. Y.
1896	**William McKinley**	Ohio	Rep.	447	271	7,104,779	*Garret A. Hobart*	N. J.
	William J. Bryan	Neb.	Dem. }	...	176	6,502,925	{Arthur Sewall	Me.
	William J. Bryan	Neb.	People's }				{Th. E. Watson	Ga.
	John M. Palmer	Ill.	Nat. Dem.	...	...	133,148	Sim. B. Buckner	Ky.
	Joshua Levering	Md.	Pro.	...	...	132,007	Hale Johnson	Ill.
	Chas. H. Matchett	N. Y.	So. L.	...	...	36,274	Matthew McGuire	N. J.
	Chas. E. Bentley	Neb.	Nat.	...	...	13,969	J. H. Southgate	N. C.
1900	**William McKinley**	Ohio	Rep.	447	292	7,219,101	*Theo. Roosevelt*	N. Y.
	William J. Bryan	Neb.	Dem. & P.	...	155	6,357,054	A. E. Stevenson	Ill.
	James G. Woolley	Ill.	Pro.	...	...	208,187	Henry B. Metcalf	R. I.
	Eugene V. Debs	Ind.	S. D.	...	...	87,814	Job Harriman	Calif.
	Wharton Barker	Pa.	M. R. P.	...	...	51,585	Ignatius Donnelly	Minn.
	Jos. F. Malloney	Mass.	S. L.	...	...	99,613	Val. Remmel	Pa.
1904	**Theodore Roosevelt**	N. Y.	Rep.	476	336	7,623,486	*Chas. W. Fairbanks*	Ind.
	Alton B. Parker	N. Y.	Dem.	...	140	5,077,971	Henry G. Davis	W. Va.
	Eugene V. Debs	Ind.	Soc.	...	...	402,283	Benjamin Hanford	N. Y.
	Silas C. Swallow	Pa.	Pro.	...	...	258,536	George W. Carroll	Texas
	Thomas E. Watson	Ga.	People's	...	...	117,183	Thomas H. Tibbles	Neb.
1908	**William H. Taft**	Ohio	Rep.	483	321	7,637,676	*James S. Sherman*	N. Y.
	William J. Bryan	Neb.	Dem.	...	162	6,393,182	John W. Kern	Ind.
	Eugene V. Debs	Ind.	Soc.	...	...	420,393	Benjamin Hanford	N. Y.
	Eugene W. Chafin	Ill.	Pro.	...	...	241,252	Aaron S. Watkins	Ohio
	Thomas L. Hisgen	Mass.	Ind. L.	...	...	83,183	Jno. Tem. Graves	Ga.
1912	**Woodrow Wilson**	N. J.	Dem.	531	435	6,282,542	*Thos. R. Marshall*	Ind.
	Theodore Roosevelt	N. Y.	Prog.	...	88	4,114,585	Hiram Johnson	Calif.
	William H. Taft	Ohio	Rep.	...	8	3,480,479	James S. Sherman	N. Y.
							Nicholas M. Butler	N. Y.
	Eugene V. Debs	Ind.	Soc.	...	...	820,606	Emil Seidel	Wis.
	Eugene W. Chafin	Ill.	Pro.	...	...	181,762	Aaron S. Watkins	Ky.
1916	**Woodrow Wilson**	N. J.	Dem.	531	277	9,129,606	*Thos. R. Marshall*	Ind.
	Chas. E. Hughes	N. Y.	Rep.	...	254	8,538,221	Chas. W. Fairbanks	Ind.
	Allan L. Benson	N. Y.	Soc.	...	...	585,113	Geo. R. Kirkpatrick	N. J.
	J. Frank Hanley	Ind.	Pro.	...	...	220,506	Dr. Ira Landrith	Tenn.
1920	**Warren C. Harding**	Ohio	Rep.	531	404	16,152,200	*Calvin Coolidge*	Mass.
	James M. Cox	Ohio	Dem.	...	127	9,147,353	Franklin D. Roosevelt	N. Y.
	P. P. Christensen	Ohio	F. L.	...	...	265,411	Max S. Hayes	Ohio
	Aaron S. Watkins	Ohio	Pro.	...	...	189,408	D. Leigh Calvin	N. Y.
	Eugene V. Debs	Ind.	Soc.	...	...	919,799	Seymour Stedman	Ill.
1924	**Calvin Coolidge**	Mass.	Rep.	531	382	15,718,789	*Chas. G. Dawes*	Ill.
	John W. Davis	W. Va.	Dem.	...	136	8,378,962	Chas. W. Bryan	Neb.
	Robt. M. LaFollette	Wis.	Prog. & F. L.	...	13	4,822,319	Burton K. Wheeler	Mont.
1928	**Herbert C. Hoover**	Calif.	Rep.	531	444	21,943,328	*Chas. Curtis*	Kan.
	Alfred E. Smith	N. Y.	Dem.	...	87	15,430,718	Joseph T. Robinson	Ark.
	Norman Thomas	N. Y.	Soc.	...	...	267,420	Jas. A. Maurer	Pa.
1932	**Franklin D. Roosevelt**	N. Y.	Dem.	531	472	22,815,785	*John N. Garner*	Tex.
	Herbert C. Hoover	Calif.	Rep.	...	59	15,759,266	Chas. Curtis	Kan.
	Norman Thomas	N. Y.	Soc.	...	...	881,951	Jas. A. Maurer	Pa.
	William Z. Foster	Ill.	Workers	...	...	102,785	James W. Ford	Ala.
1936	**Franklin D. Roosevelt**	N. Y.	Dem.	531	523	24,476,673	*John N. Garner*	Tex.
	Alfred M. Landon	Kan.	Rep.	...	8	16,679,583	Frank Knox	Ill.
	William Lemke	N. D.	Union	...	...	882,479	T. C. O'Brien	Mass.
	Norman Thomas	N. Y.	Soc.	...	...	187,720	George Nelson	Wis.
1940	**Franklin D. Roosevelt**	N. Y.	Dem.	531	449	27,243,466	*Henry A. Wallace*	Iowa
	Wendell L. Wilkie	Ind.	Rep.	...	82	22,304,755	Charles L. McNary	Ore.
	Norman Thomas	N. Y.	Soc.	...	...	99,557	Maynard C. Krueger	Ill.
	Roger Babson	Mass.	Pro.	...	...	57,812	Edgar V. Moorman	Ill.
1944	**Franklin D. Roosevelt**	N. Y.	Dem.	531	432	25,610,946	*Harry S. Truman*	Mo.
	Thomas E. Dewey	N. Y.	Rep.	...	99	22,018,177	John W. Bricker	Ohio
	Norman Thomas	N. Y.	Soc.	...	...	74,787	Darlington Hoopes	Pa
	Claude A. Watson	Cal.	Pro.	...	...	72,295	Andrew Johnson	Ky.
1948	**Harry S. Truman**	Mo.	Dem.	529	304	24,104,836	*Alben W. Barkley*	Ky.
	Thos. E. Dewey	N. Y	Rep.	...	189	21,969,500	Earl Warren	Cal.
	Norman Thomas	N. Y	Soc.	...	...	132,138	Tucker P. Smith	Mich.
	Henry A. Wallace	Iowa	Pro.	...	...	1,157,100	Glen H. Taylor	Idaho
	J. Strom Thurmond	S. C.	S. R.	...	36	1,169,312	Fielding L. Wright	Miss.
1952	**Dwight D. Eisenhower**	N. Y.	Rep.	**531**	442	33,938,285	*Richard M. Nixon*	Cal.
	Adlai E. Stevenson	Ill.	Dem.	...	89	27,312,217	John J. Sparkman	Ala.
	Vincent W. Hallinan	Cal.	Prog.	...	...	140,138	Charlotta A. Bass	Cal.
	Darlington Hoopes	Penn.	Soc.	...	...	20,189	Samuel H. Friedman	N. Y.
1956	**Dwight D. Eisenhower**	Pa.	Rep.	531	457	35,582,236	*Richard M. Nixon*	Cal.
	Adlai E. Stevenson	Ill.	Dem.	...	73	26,028,887	Estes Kefauver	Tenn.
	Walter B. Jones	Ala.	S. R.	...	1	....	Herman Talmadge	Ga.
	T. Coleman Andrews	Va.	Ind.	...	...	167,826	Thomas H. Werdel	Cal.
1960	John F. Kennedy	Mass.	Dem.	537	300	34,226,925	*Lyndon B. Johnson*	Texas
	Richard M. Nixon	Calif.	Rep.		223	34,108,662	Henry C. Lodge	Mass.
1964	**Lyndon B. Johnson**	Texas	Dem.	538	486	43,126,218	*Hubert Humphrey*	Minn.
	Barry M. Goldwater	Ariz.	Rep.		52	27,174,898	William Miller	N.Y.

Facts Concerning Inauguration	Age at Inaug.
XIX. **Abraham Lincoln**, on the eastern portico of the Capitol, Monday, March 4, 1861. Oath administered by Chief Justice Taney.	52
XX. **Abraham Lincoln**, for a second term, on the eastern portico of the Capitol, Saturday, March 4, 1865. Oath administered by Chief Justice Chase.	
Andrew Johnson, in his rooms at the Kirkwood House, Washington, D. C., 10 A. M., Saturday, April 15, 1865. Oath administered by Chief Justice Chase.	56
XXI. **Ulysses Simpson Grant**, on the eastern portico of the Capitol, Thursday, March 4, 1869. Oath of office administered by Chief Justice Chase.	46
XXII. **Ulysses Simpson Grant**, for a second term, on the eastern portico of the Capitol, Tuesday, March 4, 1873. Oath administered by Chief Justice Chase.	
XXIII. **Rutherford Birchard Hayes**, privately in the White House, at 7:05 P. M., Saturday, March 3, 1877. Oath administered by Chief Justice Waite. The oath of office was publicly taken March 5, 1877.	54
XXIV. **James Abram Garfield**, on eastern portico of the Capitol, Friday, March 4, 1881. Oath administered by Chief Justice Waite.	49
Chester Alan Arthur, at his residence, N. Y., 2 A. M., Tuesday, Sept. 20, 1881, oath administered by Jno. R. Brady, justice of the N. Y. supreme court. Oath repeated at the Capitol, September 22, 1881; administered by Chief Justice Waite.	50
XXV. **Grover Cleveland**, on the eastern portico of the Capitol, Wednesday, March 4, 1885. Oath administered by Chief Justice Waite.	47
XXVI. **Benjamin Harrison**, on eastern portico of the Capitol, Monday, March 4, 1889. Oath administered by Chief Justice Fuller.	55
XXVII. **Grover Cleveland**, on eastern portico of the Capitol, Saturday, March 4, 1893. Oath administered by Chief Justice Fuller.	55
XXVIII. **William McKinley**, on the eastern portico of the Capitol, Thursday, March 4, 1897. Oath administered by Chief Justice Fuller.	54
XXIX. **William McKinley**, for a second term, on the eastern portico of the Capitol, Monday, March 4, 1901. Oath administered by Chief Justice Fuller.	
Theodore Roosevelt, at residence of Ansley Wilcox, Buffalo, N. Y., September 14, 1901, at 3:32 P. M. Oath administered by Judge John R. Hazel, of the United States district court.	42
XXX. **Theodore Roosevelt**, on the eastern portico of the Capitol, Saturday, March 4, 1905. Oath administered by Chief Justice Melville W. Fuller.	
XXXI. **William Howard Taft**, in the chamber of the United States Senate, Washington, March 4, 1909. Oath administered by Chief Justice Fuller.	51
XXXII. **Woodrow Wilson**, on eastern portico of the Capitol, March 4, 1913. Oath administered by Chief Justice Edward D. White.	56
XXXIII. **Woodrow Wilson**, on eastern portico of the Capitol, March 4, 1917. Oath administered by Chief Justice Edward D. White.	
XXXIV. **Warren Gamaliel Harding**, on the eastern portico of the Capitol, March 4, 1921. Oath administered by Chief Justice Edward D. White.	55
Calvin Coolidge, at home of his father, John C. Coolidge, Plymouth, Vt., August 2, 1923. Oath administered by his father.	
XXXV. **Calvin Coolidge**, on plaza of the Capitol, March 4, 1925. Oath administered by Chief Justice, Ex-President, Wm. H. Taft.	50
XXXVI. **Herbert C. Hoover**, on eastern portico of the Capitol, March 4, 1929. Oath administered by Chief Justice Wm. H. Taft.	54
XXXVII. **Franklin D. Roosevelt**, on rostrum in front of Capitol, March 4, 1933. Broadcast over radio. Chie Justice Hughes administered oath.	51
XXXVIII. **Franklin D. Roosevelt**, on east portico of the Capitol, January 20, 1937. Chief Justice Hughes administered the oath.	54
XXXIX. **Franklin D. Roosevelt**, on the steps of the Capitol January 20, 1941. Oath administered by Chief Justice Hughes.	58
XL. **Franklin D. Roosevelt**, on south portico of the Capitol, January 20, 1945. Chief Justice Stone administered the oath.	62
Harry S. Truman, in the red-draped cabinet room of the White House, April 12, 1945. Oath administered by Chief Justice Stone.	60
XLI. **Harry S. Truman** on East Portico of the Capitol, Jan. 20, 1949. Oath administered by Chief Justice Vinson.	64
XLII. **Dwight D. Eisenhower**, on steps of Capitol, Jan. 20, 1953. Oath administered by Chief Justice Vinson.	62
XLIII. **Dwight D. Eisenhower**, on the east steps of the Capitol, Jan. 21, 1957. Oath administered by Chief Justice Warren.	66
XLIV. **John F. Kennedy**, on the steps of the Capitol's east portico Jan. 20, 1961. Oath administered by Chief Justice Warren.	43
Lyndon B. Johnson, aboard the Presidential jet at Dallas airport. Oath administered by Judge Sarah T. Hughes.	55
XLV. **Lyndon B. Johnson**, on the steps of the Capitol's east portico, Jan. 20, 1965.	

JUSTICES OF THE U. S. SUPREME COURT

Name	Service: Term	Service: Years	Born	Died
John Jay, N. Y.	1789–1795	6	1745	1829
John Rutledge, S. C.	1789–1791	2	1739	1800
William Cushing, Mass.	1789–1810	21	1733	1810
James Wilson, Pa.	1789–1798	9	1742	1798
John Blair, Va.	1789–1796	7	1732	1800
Robert H. Harrison, Md.	1789–1790	1	1745	1790
James Iredell, N. C.	1790–1799	9	1751	1799
Thomas Johnson, Md.	1791–1793	2	1732	1819
William Paterson, N. J.	1793–1806	13	1745	1806
John Rutledge, S. C.	1795–1795	..	1739	1800
Samuel Chase, Md.	1796–1811	15	1741	1811
Oliver Ellsworth, Conn.	1796–1800	4	1745	1807
Bushrod Washington, Va.	1798–1829	31	1762	1829
Alfred Moore, N. C.	1799–1804	5	1755	1810
John Marshall, Va.	1801–1835	34	1755	1835
William Johnson, S. C.	1804–1834	30	1771	1834
Brock Livingston, N. Y.	1806–1823	17	1757	1823
Thomas Todd, Ky.	1807–1826	19	1765	1826
Joseph Story, Mass.	1811–1845	34	1779	1845
Gabriel Duval, Md.	1811–1836	25	1752	1844
Smith Thompson, N. Y.	1823–1843	20	1767	1843
Robert Trimble, Ky.	1826–1828	2	1777	1828
John McLean, Ohio	1829–1861	32	1785	1861
Henry Baldwin, Pa.	1830–1844	14	1779	1844
James M. Wayne, Ga.	1835–1867	32	1790	1867
Roger B. Taney, Md.	1836–1864	28	1777	1864
Philip P. Barbour, Va.	1836–1841	5	1783	1841
John Catron, Tenn.	1837–1865	28	1786	1865
John McKinley, Ala.	1837–1852	15	1780	1852
Peter V. Daniel, Va.	1841–1860	19	1785	1860
Samuel Nelson, N. Y.	1845–1872	27	1792	1873
Levi Woodbury, N. H.	1845–1851	6	1789	1851
Robert C. Grier, Pa.	1846–1870	24	1794	1870
Benjamin R. Curtis, Mass.	1851–1857	6	1809	1874
John A. Campbell, Ala.	1853–1861	8	1811	1889
Nathan Clifford, Me.	1858–1881	23	1803	1881
Noah H. Swayne, Ohio	1862–1881	19	1804	1884
Samuel F. Miller, Iowa	1862–1890	28	1816	1890
David Davis, Ill.	1862–1877	15	1815	1886
Stephen J. Field, Calif.	1863–1897	34	1816	1899
Salmon P. Chase, Ohio	1864–1873	9	1808	1873
William Strong, Pa.	1870–1880	10	1808	1895
Joseph B. Bradley, N. J.	1870–1892	22	1813	1892
Ward Hunt, N. Y.	1872–1882	10	1811	1886
Morrison R. Waite, Ohio	1874–1888	14	1816	1888
John M. Harlan, Ky.	1877–1911	34	1833	1911
William B. Woods, Ga.	1880–1887	7	1824	1887
Stanley Matthews, Ohio	1881–1889	8	1824	1889
Horace Gray, Mass.	1881–1902	21	1828	1902
Samuel Blatchford, N. Y.	1882–1893	11	1820	1893
Lucius Q. C. Lamar, Miss.	1888–1893	5	1825	1893
Melville W. Fuller, Ill.	1888–1910	22	1833	1910
David J. Brewer, Kan.	1889–1910	21	1837	1910
Henry B. Brown, Mich.	1890–1906	16	1836	1913
George Shiras, Jr., Pa.	1892–1903	11	1832	1924
Howell E. Jackson, Tenn.	1893–1895	2	1832	1895
Edward D. White, La.	1894–1910	16	1845	1921
Rufus W. Peckham, N. Y.	1896–1909	14	1838	1909
Joseph McKenna, Calif.	1898–1925	27	1843	1926
Oliver W. Holmes, Mass.	1902–1932	29	1841	1935
William R. Day, Ohio	1903–1923	19	1849	1923
William H. Moody, Mass.	1906–1910	4	1853	1917
Horace H. Lurton, Tenn.	1909–1914	5	1844	1914
Charles E. Hughes, N. Y.	1910–1916	6	1862	1948
Edward D. White, La.	1910–1921	11	1845	1921
Willis Van Devanter, Wyo.	1911–1937	26	1859	1941
Jos. R. Lamar, Ga.	1911–1916	5	1857	1916
Mahlon Pitney, N. J.	1912–1922	10	1858	1924
James C. McReynolds, Tenn.	1914–1941	27	1862	1946
Louis D. Brandeis, Mass.	1916–1939	23	1856	1941
John H. Clarke, Ohio	1916–1922	6	1857	1945
William H. Taft, Conn.	1921–1930	9	1857	1930
George Sutherland, Utah	1922–1938	16	1862	1942
Pierce Butler, Minn.	1922–1939	17	1866	1939
Edward T. Sanford, Tenn.	1923–1930	7	1865	1930
Harlan F. Stone, N. Y.	1925–1941	16	1872	1946
Charles E. Hughes, N. Y.	1930–1941	11	1862	1948
Owen J. Roberts, Pa.	1930-1945	15	1875	1955
Benjamin N. Cardozo, N. Y.	1932-1938	6	1870	1938
Hugo L. Black, Ala.	1937-....	..	1886	....
Stanley Reed, Ky.	1938-1957	19	1884	....
Felix Frankfurter, Mass.	1939–1962	23	1882	1965
William O. Douglas, Conn.	1939–....	..	1898	....
Frank Murphy, Mich.	1940–1949	9	1890	1949
James F. Byrnes, S.C.	1941–1942	1	1879	....
Robert H. Jackson, N.Y.	1941–1954	13	1892	1954
Harlan F. Stone, N.Y.	1941–1946	5	1872	1946
Wiley B. Rutledge, Jr., Ia.	1943–1949	6	1894	1949
Harold H. Burton, Ohio	1945–1958	13	1888	1964
Fred M. Vinson, Ky.	1946–1953	7	1890	1953
Tom C. Clark, Tex.	1949–....	..	1899	....
Sherman Minton, Ind.	1949–1956	7	1890	....
Earl Warren, Cal.	1953–....	..	1891	....
John M. Harlan, N.Y.	1955–....	..	1899	....
Wm. J. Brennan, Jr., N.J.	1956–....	..	1906	....
Chas. E. Whittaker, Mo.	1957–1962	5	1900	....
Potter Stewart, Ohio	1958–....	..	1915	....
Bryon White, Colo.	1962–....	..	1917	....
Arthur J. Goldberg, Ill.	1962–1965	3	1908	....
Abe Fortas. Tenn.	1965–....	..	1910	....

Bold-face type denotes Chief Justices.

PRESIDENTS OF CONTINENTAL CONGRESS

Peyton Randolph, 1774
Henry Middleton, 1774
Peyton Randolph, 1775
John Hancock, 1776
Henry Laurens, 1778
John Jay, 1779
Sam Huntington, 1779
Thomas McKean, 1781
John Hanson, 1782
Elias Boudinot, 1782
Thomas Mifflin, 1783
Richard Henry Lee, 1784
John Hancock, 1786
Nathaniel Gorham, 1786
Arthur St. Clair, 1787
Cyrus Griffin, 1788

SPEAKERS OF THE HOUSE OF REPRESENTATIVES

Congress	Years	Name	State	Born	Died
1	1789–91	F. A. Muhlenburg	Pa.	1750	1801
2	1791–93	J. Trumbull	Conn.	1740	1809
3	1793–95	F. A. Muhlenburg	Pa.	1750	1801
4–5	1795–99	J. Dayton	N. J.	1760	1824
6	1799–1801	Theo. Sedgwick	Mass.	1746	1813
7–9	1801–07	Nathaniel Macon	N. C.	1757	1837
10–11	1807–11	J. B. Varnum	Mass.	1750	1821
12–13	1811–14	Henry Clay	Ky.	1777	1852
13	1814–15	Langdon Cheves	S. C.	1776	1857
14–16	1815–20	Henry Clay	Ky.	1777	1852
16	1820–21	John W. Taylor	N. Y.	1784	1854
17	1821–23	P. P. Barbour	Va.	1783	1841
18	1823–25	Henry Clay	Ky.	1777	1852
19	1825–27	John W. Taylor	N. Y.	1784	1854
20–23	1827–34	A. Stevenson	Va.	1784	1857
23	1834–35	John Bell	Tenn.	1797	1869
24–25	1835–39	James K. Polk	Tenn.	1795	1849
26	1839–41	R. M. T. Hunter	Va.	1809	1887
27	1841–43	John White	Ky.	1805	1845
28	1843–45	John W. Jones	Va.	1791	1848
29	1845–47	John W. Davis	Ind.	1799	1859
30	1847–49	R. C. Winthrop	Mass.	1809	1894
31	1849–51	Howell Cobb	Ga.	1815	1868
32–33	1851–55	Lynn Boyd	Ky.	1800	1859
34	1855–57	N. P. Banks	Mass.	1816	1894
35	1857–59	James L. Orr	S. C.	1822	1873
36	1859–61	Wm. Pennington	N. J.	1796	1862
37	1861–63	Galusha A. Grow	Pa.	1822	1907
38–40	1863–69	Schuyler Colfax	Ind.	1823	1885
41–43	1869–75	James G. Blaine	Me.	1830	1893
44	1875–76	Michael C. Kerr	Ind.	1827	1876
44–46	1876–81	S. J. Randall	Pa.	1828	1890
47	1881–83	Joseph W. Keifer	Ohio	1836	1932
48–50	1883–89	John G. Carlisle	Ky.	1835	1910
51	1889–91	Thomas B. Reed	Me.	1839	1902
52–53	1891–95	Charles F. Crisp	Ga.	1845	1896
54–55	1895–99	Thomas B. Reed	Me.	1839	1902
56–57	1899–1903	D. B. Henderson	Iowa	1840	1906
58–61	1903–1911	J. G. Cannon	Ill.	1836	1926
62–65	1911–1919	Champ Clark	Mo.	1850	1921
66–68	1919–1925	F. H. Gillett	Mass.	1851	1935
69–71	1925–1931	N. Longworth	Ohio	1869	1931
72	1931–1933	John N. Garner	Tex.	1869	....
73	1933–1934	Henry T. Rainey	Ill.	1860	1934
74	1935–1936	Joseph W. Byrns	Tenn.	1869	1936
74-76	1936-1940	W. B. Bankhead	Ala.	1874	1940
76-79	1940-1947	Sam Rayburn	Tex.	1882	1961
80	1947-1948	J. W. Martin, Jr.	Mass.	1884	....
81	1949-1953	Sam Rayburn	Tex.	1882	1961
82-83	1953-1954	J. W. Martin, Jr.	Mass.	1884	....
84-87	1955-1961	Sam Rayburn	Tex.	1882	1961
87	1962-....	J. McCormack	Mass.	1891	....

THE DECLARATION OF INDEPENDENCE

With Original Spelling

IN CONGRESS, July 4, 1776

When in the Course of human events it becomes necessary for one people to dissolve the political bands which have connected them with another, and to assume among the powers of the earth, the separate and equal station to which the Laws of Nature and of Nature's God entitle them, a decent respect to the opinions of mankind requires that they should declare the causes which impel them to the separation.—We hold these truths to be self-evident, that all men are created equal, that they are endowed by their Creator with certain unalienable Rights, that among these are Life, Liberty and the pursuit of Happiness.—That to secure these rights, Governments are instituted among Men, deriving their just powers from the consent of the governed,—That whenever any Form of Government becomes destructive of these ends, it is the Right of the People to alter or to abolish it, and to institute new Government, laying its foundation on such principles, and organizing its powers in such form, as to them shall seem most likely to effect their Safety and Happiness. Prudence, indeed, will dictate that Governments long established should not be changed for light and transient causes; and accordingly all experience hath shewn, that mankind are more disposed to suffer, while evils are sufferable, than to right themselves by abolishing the forms to which they are accustomed. But when a long train of abuses and usurpations, pursuing invariably the same Object evinces a design to reduce them under absolute Despotism, it is their right, it is their duty, to throw off such Government, and to provide new Guards for their future security.—Such has been the patient sufferance of these Colonies; and such is now the necessity which constrains them to alter their former Systems of Government. The history of the present King of Great Britain is a history of repeated injuries and usurpations, all having in direct object the establishment of an absolute Tyranny over these States. To prove this, let Facts be submitted to a candid world.—He has refused his Assent to Laws, the most wholesome and necessary for the public good.—He has forbidden his Governors to pass Laws of immediate and pressing importance, unless suspended in their operation till his Assent should be obtained; and when so suspended, he has utterly neglected to attend to them.—He has refused to pass other Laws for the accommodation of large districts of people, unless those people would relinquish the right of Representation in the Legislature, a right inestimable to them and formidable to tyrants only.—He has called together legislative bodies at places unusual, uncomfortable, and distant from the depository of their public Records, for the sole purpose of fatiguing them into compliance with his measures.—He has dissolved Representative Houses repeatedly, for opposing with manly firmness his invasions on the rights of the people.—He has refused for a long time after such dissolutions to cause others to be elected; whereby the Legislative powers, incapable of Annihilation, have returned to the People at large for their exercise; the State remaining in the mean time exposed to all the dangers of invasion from without, and convulsions within.—He has endeavoured to prevent the population of these States; for that purpose obstructing the Laws for Naturalization of Foreigners; refusing to pass others to encourage their migration hither, and raising the conditions of new Appropriations of Lands.—He has obstructed the Administration of Justice, by refusing his Assent to Laws for establishing Judiciary powers.—He has made Judges dependent on his Will alone, for the tenure of their offices, and the amount and payment of their salaries.—He has erected a multitude of New Offices, and sent hither swarms of Officers to harass our people, and eat out their substance.—He has kept among us, in times of peace, Standing Armies without the Consent of our legislatures.—He has effected to render the Military independent of and superior to the Civil power.—He has combined with others to subject us to a jurisdiction foreign to our constitution, and unacknowledged by our laws; giving his Assent to their Acts of pretended Legislation:—For quartering large bodies of armed troops among us: —For protecting them, by a mock Trial, from punishment for any Murders which they should commit on the Inhabitants of these States:—For cutting off our Trade with all parts of the world:— For imposing Taxes on us without our Consent:—For depriving us in many cases of the benefits of Trial by Jury:— For transporting us beyond Seas to be tried for pretended offences:—For abolishing the free System of English Laws in a neighbouring Province, establishing therein an Arbitrary government, and enlarging its Boundaries so as to render it at once an example and fit instrument for introducing the same absolute rule into these Colonies:—For taking away our Charters, abolishing our most valuable Laws, and altering fundamentally the Forms of our Governments:—For suspending our own Legislatures, and declaring themselves invested with power to legislate for us in all cases whatsoever.—He has abdicated Government here, by declaring us out of his Protection and waging War against us.—He has plundered our seas, ravaged our Coasts, burnt our towns,

and destroyed the lives of our people.— He is at this time transporting large Armies of foreign Mercenaries to compleat the works of death, desolation and tyranny, already begun with circumstances of Cruelty & perfidy scarcely paralleled in the most barbarous ages, and totally unworthy the Head of a civilized nation.—He has constrained our fellow Citizens taken Captive on the high Seas to bear Arms against their Country, to become the executioners of their friends and Brethren, or to fall themselves by their Hands.—He has excited domestic insurrections amongst us, and has endeavoured to bring on the inhabitants of our frontiers; the merciless Indian Savages, whose known rule of warfare is an undistinguished destruction of all ages, sexes and conditions. In every stage of these Oppressions We have Petitioned for Redress in the most humble terms Our repeated Petitions have been answered by repeated injury. A Prince, whose character is thus marked by every act which may define a Tyrant, is unfit to be the ruler of a free people. Nor have We been wanting in attentions to our Brittish brethren. We have warned them from time to time of attempts by their legislature to extend an unwarrantable jurisdiction over us. We have reminded them of the circumstances of our emigration and settlement here. We have appealed to their native justice and magnanimity, and

we have conjured them by the ties of our common kindred to disavow these usurpations, which would inevitably interrupt our connections and correspondence They too have been deaf to the voice of justice and of consanguinity. We must, therefore, acquiesce in the necessity, which denounces our Separation, and hold them, as we hold the rest of mankind, Enemies in War, in Peace Friends.

WE, THEREFORE, the REPRESENTATIVES of the UNITED STATES OF AMERICA, in General Congress, Assembled, appealing to the Supreme Judge of the World for the rectitude of our intentions, DO, in the Name, and by authority of the good People of these Colonies solemnly publish and declare, That these United Colonies are and of Right ought to be FREE AND INDEPENDENT STATES; that they are Absolved from all Allegiance to the British Crown, and that all political connection between them and the State of Great Britain, is and ought to be totally dissolved; and that as FREE AND INDEPENDENT STATES, they have full Power to levy War, conclude Peace contract Alliances, establish Commerce, and to do all other Acts and Things which INDEPENDENT States may of right do.—AND for the support of the Declaration, with a firm reliance on the protection of divine Providence, we mutually pledge to each other our Lives, our Fortunes and our sacred Honor.

SIGNERS OF THE DECLARATION OF INDEPENDENCE

NAME	ORDER[1]	COLONY	OCCUPATION	BORN	BIRTHPLACE		DIED	AGE[2]
Adams, John	6	Massachusetts Bay	Lawyer	Oct. 30, 1735	Quincy	Mass.	July 4, 1826	90
Adams, Samuel	2	Massachusetts Bay	Brewer	Sept. 27, 1722	Boston	Mass.	Oct. 2, 1803	81
Bartlett, Josiah	9	New Hampshire	Physician	Nov. 21, 1729	Amesbury	Mass.	May 19, 1795	66
Braxton, Carter	51	Virginia	Planter	Sept. 10, 1736	Newington	Va.	Oct. 10, 1797	61
Carroll, Charles	31	Maryland	Lawyer	Sept. 20, 1737	Annapolis	Md.	Nov. 14, 1832	95
Chase, Samuel	44	Maryland	Lawyer	April 17, 1741	Somerset Co.	Md.	June 19, 1811	70
Clark, Abraham	14	New Jersey	Lawyer	Feb. 15, 1726	Elizabethtown	N. J.	Sept. 15, 1794	68
Clymer, George	38	Pennsylvania	Merchant	Mar. 16, 1739	Philadelphia	Pa.	Jan. 23, 1813	73
Ellery, William	22	R. I. and Prov. Plan.	Lawyer	Dec. 22, 1727	Newport	R. I.	Feb. 15, 1820	92
Floyd, William	5	New York	Farmer	Dec. 17, 1734	Brookhaven	N. Y.	Aug. 4, 1821	86
Franklin, Benjamin	46	Pennsylvania	Printer	Jan. 17, 1706	Boston	Mass.	April 17, 1790	84
Gerry, Elbridge	8	Massachusetts Bay	Merchant	July 17, 1744	Marblehead	Mass.	Nov. 23, 1814	70
Gwinnett, Button	40	Georgia	Merchant	1735	Down Hatherly	England	May 16, 1777	42
Hancock, John	1	Massachusetts Bay	Merchant	Jan. 12, 1737	Braintree	Mass.	Oct. 8, 1793	58
Hall, Lyman	47	Georgia	Physician	April 12, 1724	Wallingford	Conn.	Oct. 19, 1790	66
Harrison, Benjamin	54	Virginia	Farmer	April 5, 1726	Berkeley	Va.	April 24, 1791	65
Hart, John	13	New Jersey	Farmer	1711	Stonington	Conn.	May 11, 1779	68
Hewes, Joseph	35	North Carolina	Merchant	Jan. 23, 1730	Kingston	N. J.	Nov. 10, 1779	49
Heyward, Thomas, Jr.	56	South Carolina	Lawyer	July 28, 1746	St. Luke's	S. C.	Mar. 6, 1809	62
Hooper, William	23	North Carolina	Lawyer	June 17, 1742	Boston	Mass.	Oct. 14, 1790	48
Hopkins, Stephen	12	R. I. and Prov. Plan.	Merchant	Mar. 7, 1707	Providence	R. I.	July 13, 1785	78
Hopkinson, Francis	29	New Jersey	Lawyer	Oct. 2, 1737	Philadelphia	Pa.	May 9, 1791	53
Huntington, Samuel	11	Connecticut	Lawyer	July 3, 1731	Windham	Conn.	Jan. 5, 1796	64
Jefferson, Thomas	32	Virginia	Lawyer	April 13, 1743	Shadwell	Va.	July 4, 1826	83
Lee, Richard Henry	48	Virginia	Soldier	Jan. 20, 1732	Stratford	Va.	June 19, 1794	62
Lee, Francis Lightfoot	55	Virginia	Farmer	Oct. 14, 1734	Stratford	Va.	Jan. 11, 1797	62
Lewis, Francis	7	New York	Merchant	Mar. 21, 1713	Llandaff	Wales	Dec. 30, 1803	90
Livingston, Philip	3	New York	Merchant	Jan. 15, 1716	Albany	N. Y.	June 12, 1778	62
Lynch, Thomas, Jr.	43	South Carolina	Planter	Aug. 5, 1749	Winyah	S. C.	At sea 1779	30
McKean, Thomas	39	Delaware	Lawyer	Mar. 19, 1734	New London	Pa.	June 24, 1817	83
Middleton, Arthur	50	South Carolina	Planter	June 26, 1742	Middleton Pl.	S. C.	Jan. 1, 1787	45
Morris, Lewis	15	New York	Farmer	April 8, 1726	Morrisania	N. Y.	Jan. 22, 1798	71
Morris, Robert	24	Pennsylvania	Merchant	Jan. 31, 1734	Liverpool	England	May 8, 1806	72
Morton, John	16	Pennsylvania	Surveyor	1724	Ridley	Pa.	April 1777	53
Nelson, Thomas, Jr.	49	Virginia	Statesman	Dec. 26, 1738	York	Va.	Jan. 4, 1789	50
Paca, William	28	Maryland	Lawyer	Oct. 31, 1740	Wye Hall	Md.	Oct. 13, 1799	59
Paine, Robert Treat	4	Massachusetts Bay	Lawyer	Mar. 11, 1731	Boston	Mass.	May 11, 1814	83
Penn, John	18	North Carolina	Lawyer	May 17, 1741	Caroline Co.	Va.	Sept. 14, 1788	47
Read, George	41	Delaware	Lawyer	Sept. 18, 1733	Cecil Co.	Md.	Sept. 21, 1798	65
Rodney, Caesar	52	Delaware	General	Oct. 7, 1728	Dover	Del.	June 29, 1784	55
Ross, George	37	Pennsylvania	Lawyer	May 10, 1730	Newcastle	Del.	July 14, 1779	49
Rush, Benjamin	27	Pennsylvania	Physician	Dec. 24, 1745	Berberry	Pa.	April 19, 1813	67
Rutledge, Edward	34	South Carolina	Lawyer	Nov. 23, 1749	Charleston	S. C.	Jan. 23, 1800	50
Sherman, Roger	19	Connecticut	Shoemaker	April 19, 1721	Newton	Mass.	July 23, 1793	72
Smith, James	36	Pennsylvania	Lawyer	1719		Ireland	July 11, 1806	87
Stockton, Richard	10	New Jersey	Lawyer	Oct. 1, 1730	Princeton	N. J.	Feb. 28, 1781	50
Stone, Thomas	30	Maryland	Lawyer	1743	Poynton Manor	Md.	Oct. 5, 1787	44
Taylor, George	33	Pennsylvania	Iron Maker	1716		Ireland	Feb. 23, 1781	65
Thornton, Matthew	17	New Hampshire	Physician	1714		Ireland	June 24, 1803	89
Walton, George	53	Georgia	Lawyer	1741	Prince Edward Co.	Va.	Feb. 2, 1804	63
Whipple, William	20	New Hampshire	Merchant	Jan. 14, 1730	Kittery	Me.	Nov. 28, 1785	55
Williams, William	26	Connecticut	Statesman	April 8, 1731	Lebanon	Conn.	Aug. 2, 1811	80
Wilson, James	42	Pennsylvania	Lawyer	Sept. 14, 1742	Carskerdo	Scotland	Aug. 28, 1798	56
Witherspoon, John	21	New Jersey	Minister	Feb. 5, 1723	Yester	Scotland	Nov. 15, 1794	71
Wolcott, Oliver	25	Connecticut	Jurist	Nov. 20, 1726	Windsor	Conn.	Dec. 1, 1797	71
Wythe, George	45	Virginia	Lawyer	1726	Elizabeth Co.	Va.	June 8, 1806	80

[1] Order in which they signed. [2] Age at death.

THE ARTICLES OF CONFEDERATION

[NOTE. The text of the Articles reproduces the original in spelling and punctuation.]

To all to whom these Presents shall come, we the undersigned Delegates of the States affixed to our Names, send greeting.

Whereas the Delegates of the United States of America in Congress assembled did on the fifteenth day of November in the Year of Our Lord One thousand seven Hundred and Seventy-seven, and in the second Year of the Independence of America agree to certain Articles of Confederation and perpetual Union between the States of Newhampshire, Massachusetts-bay, Rhodeisland and Providence Plantations, Connecticut, New York, New Jersey, Pennsylvania, Delaware, Maryland, Virginia, North-Carolina, South-Carolina and Georgia, in the Words following, viz. Articles of Confederation and perpetual Union between the states of Newhampshire, Massachusetts-bay, Rhodeisland and Providence Plantations, Connecticut, New-York, New-Jersey, Pennsylvania, Delaware, Maryland, Virginia, North-Carolina, South-Carolina and Georgia.

ARTICLE I. The stile of this confederacy shall be "The United States of America."

ARTICLE II. Each State retains its sovereignty, freedom and independence, and every power, Jurisdiction and right, which is not by this confederation expressly delegated to the United States, in Congress assembled.

ARTICLE III. The said states hereby severally enter into a firm league of friendship with each other, for their common defence, the security of their Liberties, and their mutual and general welfare, binding themselves to assist each other, against all force offered to, or attacks made upon them, or any of them, on account of religion, sovereignty, trade, or any other pretence whatever.

ARTICLE IV. The better to secure and perpetuate mutual friendship and intercourse among the people of the different states in this union, the free inhabitants of each of these states, paupers, vagabonds and fugitives from justice excepted, shall be entitled to all privileges and immunities of free citizens in the several states; and the people of each state shall have free ingress and regress to and from any other state, and shall enjoy therein all the privileges of trade and commerce, subject to the same duties, impositions and restrictions as the inhabitants thereof respectively, provided that such restriction shall not extend so far as to prevent the removal of property imported into any state, to any other state of which the Owner is an inhabitant; provided also that no imposition, duties or restriction shall be laid by any state, on the property of the united states, or either of them.

If any Person guilty of, or charged with treason, felony, or other high misdemeanor in any state, shall flee from Justice, and be found in any of the united states, he shall upon demand of the Governor or executive power, of the state from which he fled, be delivered up and removed to the state having jurisdiction of his offence.

Full faith and credit shall be given in each of these states to the records, acts and judicial proceedings of the courts and magistrates of every other state.

ARTICLE V. For the more convenient management of the general interests of the united states, delegates shall be annually appointed in such manner as the legislature of each state shall direct, to meet in Congress on the first Monday in November, in every year, with a power reserved to each state, to recal its delegates, or any of them, at any time within the year, and to send others in their stead, for the remainder of the Year.

No state shall be represented in Congress by less than two, nor by more than seven members; and no person shall be capable of being a delegate for more than three years in any term of six years; nor shall any person, being a delegate, be capable of holding any office under the united states, for which he, or another for his benefit receives any salary, fees or emolument of any kind.

Each state shall maintain its own delegates in a meeting of the states, and while they act as members of the committee of the states.

In determining questions in the united states, in Congress assembled, each state shall have one vote.

Freedom of speech and debate in Congress shall not be impeached or questioned in any court, or place out of Congress, and the members of congress shall be protected in their persons from arrests and imprisonments, during the time of their going to and from, and attendance on congress, except for treason, felony, or breach of the peace.

ARTICLE VI. No State without the consent of the united states in congress assembled, shall send any embassy to, or receive any embassy from, or enter into any conference, agreement, alliance or treaty with any King prince or state; nor shall any person holding any office of profit or trust under the united states, or any of them, accept of any present, emolument, office or title of any kind whatever from any king, prince or foreign state; nor shall the united states in congress assembled, or any of them, grant any title of nobility.

No two or more states shall enter into any treaty, confederation or alliance whatever between them, without the consent of the united states in congress assembled, specifying accurately the purposes for which the same is to be entered into, and how long it shall continue.

No state shall lay any imposts or duties, which may interfere with any stipulations in treaties, entered into by the united states in congress assembled, with any king, prince or state, in pursuance of any treaties already proposed by congress, to the courts of France and Spain.

No vessels of war shall be kept up in time of peace by any state, except such number only, as shall be deemed necessary by the united states in congress assembled, for the defence of such state, or its trade; nor shall any body of forces be kept up by any state, in time of peace, except such number only, as in the judgment of the united states, in congress assembled, shall be deemed requisite to garrison the forts necessary for the defence of such state; but every state shall always keep up a well regulated and disciplined militia, sufficiently armed and accoutred, and shall provide and constantly have ready for use, in public stores, a due number of field pieces and tents, and a proper quantity of arms, ammunition and camp equipage.

No state shall engage in any war without the consent of the united states in congress assembled, unless such state be actually invaded by enemies, or shall have received certain advice of a resolution being formed by some nation of Indians to invade such state, and the danger is so imminent as not to admit of a delay, till the united states in congress assembled can be consulted: nor shall any state grant commissions to any ships or vessels of war, nor letters of marque or reprisal, except it be after a declaration of war by the united states in congress assembled, and then only against the kingdom or state and the subjects thereof, against which war has been so declared, and under such regulations as shall be established by the united states in congress assembled, unless such state be infested by pirates, in which case vessels of war may be fitted out for that occasion, and kept so long as the danger shall continue, or until the united states in congress assembled shall determine otherwise.

ARTICLE VII. When land-forces are raised by any state for the common defence, all officers of or under the rank of colonel, shall be appointed by the legislature of each state respectively by whom such forces shall be raised, or in such manner as such state shall direct, and all vacancies shall be filled up by the state which first made the appointment.

ARTICLE VIII. All charges of war, and all other expences that shall be incurred for the common defence or general welfare, and allowed by the united states in congress assembled, shall be defrayed out of a common treasury, which shall be supplied by the several states, in proportion to the value of all land within each state, granted to or surveyed for any Person, as such land and the buildings and improvements thereon shall be estimated according to such mode as the united states in congress assembled, shall from time to time direct and appoint. The taxes for paying that proportion shall be laid and levied by the authority and direction of the legislatures of the several states within the time agreed upon by the united states in congress assembled.

ARTICLE IX. The united states in congress assembled, shall have the sole and exclusive right and power of determining on peace and war, except in the cases mentioned in the sixth article—of sending and receiving ambassadors—entering into treaties and alliances, provided that no treaty of commerce shall be made whereby the legislative power of the respective states shall be re-

PAINTING BY JOHN TRUMBELL: LIBRARY OF CONGRESS

THE DECLARATION OF INDEPENDENCE was signed at Independence Hall on July 4, 1776.

favour, affection or hope of reward:" provided also that no state shall be deprived of territory for the benefit of the united states.

All controversies concerning the private right of soil claimed under different grants of two or more states, whose jurisdictions as they may respect such lands, and the states which passed such grants are adjusted, the said grants or either of them being at the same time claimed to have originated antecedent to such settlement of jurisdiction, shall on the petition of either party to the congress of the united states, be finally determined as near as may be in the same manner as is before prescribed for deciding disputes respecting territorial jurisdiction between different states.

The united states in congress assembled shall also have the sole and exclusive right and power of regulating the alloy and value of coin struck by their own authority, or by that of the respective states—fixing the standard of weights and measures throughout the united states—regulating the trade and managing all affairs with the Indians, not members of any of the states, provided that the legislative right of any state within its own limits be not infringed or violated—establishing or regulating post-offices from one state to another, throughout all the united states, and exacting such postage on the papers passing thro' the same as may be requisite to defray the expences of the said office—appointing all officers of the land forces, in the service of the united states, excepting regimental officers—appointing all the officers of the naval forces, and commissioning all officers whatever in the service of the united states—making rules for the government and regulation of the said land and naval forces, and directing their operations.

The united states in congress assembled shall have authority to appoint a committee, to sit in the recess of congress, to be denominated "A Committee of the States," and to consist of one delegate from each state; and to appoint such other committees and civil officers as may be necessary for managing the general affairs of the united states under their direction—to appoint one of their number to preside, provided that no person be allowed to serve in the office of president more than one year in any term of three years; to ascertain the necessary sums of Money to be raised for the service of the united states, and to appropriate and apply the same for defraying the public expenses —to borrow money, or emit bills on the credit of the united states, transmitting every half year to the respective states an account of the sums of money so borrowed or emitted,—to build and equip a navy—to agree upon the number of land forces, and to make requisitions from each state for its quota, in proportion to the number of white inhabitants in such state; which requisition shall be binding, and thereupon the legislature of each state shall appoint the regimental officers, raise the men and cloath, arm and equip them in a soldier like manner, at the expence of the united states; and the officers and men so cloathed, armed and equipped shall march to the place appointed, and within the time agreed on by the united

strained from imposing such imposts and duties on foreigners, as their own people are subjected to, or from prohibiting the exportation or importation of any species of goods or commodities whatsoever—of establishing rules for deciding in all cases, what captures on land or water shall be legal, and in what manner prizes taken by land or naval forces in the service of the united states shall be divided or appropriated —of granting letters of marque and reprisal in times of peace—appointing courts for the trial of piracies and felonies committed on the high seas and establishing courts for receiving and determining finally appeals in all cases of captures, provided that no member of congress shall be appointed a judge of any of the said courts.

The united states in congress assembled shall also be the last resort on appeal in all disputes and differences now subsisting or that hereafter may arise between two or more states concerning boundary, jurisdiction or any other cause whatever; which authority shall always be exercised in the manner following. Whenever the legislative or executive authority or lawful agent of any state in controversy with another shall present a petition to congress, stating the matter in question and praying for a hearing, notice thereof shall be given by order of congress to the legislative or executive authority of the other state in controversy, and a day assigned for the appearance of the parties by their lawful agents, who shall then be directed to appoint by joint consent, commissioners or judges to constitute a court for hearing and determining the matter in question: but if they cannot agree, congress shall name three persons out of each of the united states,

and from the list of such persons each party shall alternately strike out one, the petitioners beginning, until the number shal be reduced to thirteen; and from that number not less than seven, nor more than nine names as congress shall direct, shall in the presence of congress be drawn out by lot, and the persons whose names shall be so drawn or any five of them, shall be commissioners or judges, to hear and finally determine the controversy, so always as a major part of the judges who shall hear the cause shall agree in the determination: and if either party shall neglect to attend at the day appointed, without showing reasons, which congress shall judge sufficient, or being present shall refuse to strike, the congress shall proceed to nominate three persons out of each state, and the secretary of congress shall strike in behalf of such party absent or refusing; and the judgment and sentence of the court to be appointed, in the manner before prescribed, shall be final and conclusive; and if any of the parties shall refuse to submit to the authority of such court, or to appear or defend their claim or cause, the court shall nevertheless proceed to pronounce sentence, or judgment, which shall in like manner be final and decisive, the judgment or sentence and other proceedings being in either case transmitted to congress and lodged among the acts of congress for the security of the parties concerned: provided that every commissioner, before he sits in judgment, shall take an oath to be administered by one of the judges of the supreme or superior court of the state, where the cause shall be tried, "well and truly to hear and determine the matter in question, according to the best of his judgment, without

states in congress assembled: But if the united states in congress assembled shall, on consideration of circumstances judge proper that any state should not raise men, or should raise a smaller number than its quota, and that any other state should raise a greater number of men than the quota thereof, such extra number shall be raised, officered, cloathed, armed and equipped in the same manner as the quota of such state, unless the legislature of such state shall judge that such extra number cannot be safely spared out of the same, in which case they shall raise officer, cloath, arm and equip as many of such extra number as they judge can be safely spared. And the officers and men so cloathed, armed and equipped, shall march to the place appointed, and within the time agreed on by the united states in congress assembled.

The united states in congress assembled shall never engage in a war, nor grant letters of marque and reprisal in time of peace, nor enter into any treaties or alliances, nor coin money, nor regulate the value thereof, nor ascertain the sums and expences necessary for the defence and welfare of the united states, or any of them, nor emit bills, nor borrow money on the credit of the united states, nor appropriate money, nor agree upon the number of vessels of war, to be built or purchased, or the number of land or sea forces to be raised, nor appoint a commander in chief of the army or navy, unless nine states assent to the same: nor shall a question on any other point, except for adjourning from day to day be determined, unless by the votes of a majority of the united states in congress assembled.

The congress of the united states shall have power to adjourn to any time within the year, and to any place within the united states, so that no period of adjournment be for a longer duration than the space of six Months, and shall publish the Journal of their proceedings monthly, except such parts thereof relating to treaties, alliances or military operations, as in their judgment require secrecy; and the yeas and nays of the delegates of each state on any question shall be entered on the Journal, when it is desired by any delegate; and the delegates of a state or any of them, at his or their request shall be furnished with a transcript of the said Journal, except such parts as are above excepted, to lay before the legislatures of the several states.

ARTICLE X. The committee of the states, or any nine of them, shall be authorized to execute, in the recess of congress, such of the powers of congress as the united states in congress assembled, by the consent of nine states, shall from time to time think expedient to vest them with; provided that no power be delegated to said committee, for the exercise of which, by the articles of confederation, the voice of nine states in the congress of the united states assembled is requisite.

ARTICLE XI. Canada acceding to this confederation, and joining in the measures of the united states, shall be admitted into, and entitled to all the advantages of this union: but no other colony shall be admitted into the same, unless such admission be agreed to by nine states.

ARTICLE XII. All bills of credit emitted, moneys borrowed and debts contracted by, or under the authority of congress, before the assembling of the united states, in pursuance of the present confederation, shall be deemed and considered as a charge against the united states, for payment and satisfaction whereof the said united states, and the public faith are hereby solemnly pledged.

ARTICLE XIII. Every state shall abide by the determinations of the united states in congress assembled, on all questions which by this confederation are submitted to them. And the Articles of this confederation shall be inviolably observed by every state, and the union shall be perpetual; nor shall any alteration at any time hereafter be made in any of them; unless such alteration be agreed to in a congress of the united states and be afterwards confirmed by the legislatures of every state.

AND WHEREAS it hath pleased the Great Governor of the World to incline the hearts of the legislatures we respectively represent in congress, to approve of, and to authorize us to ratify the said articles of confederation and perpetual union. *Know Ye* that we the undersigned delegates, by virtue of the power and authority to us given for that purpose, do by these presents, in the name and in behalf of our respective constituents, fully and entirely ratify and confirm each and every of the said articles of confederation and perpetual union, and all and singular the matters and things therein contained: And we do further solemnly plight and engage the faith of our respective constituents, that they shall abide by the determinations of the united states in congress assembled, on all questions, which by the said confederation are submitted to them. And that the articles thereof shall be inviolably observed by the states we respectively represent, and that the union shall be perpetual. In Witness whereof we have hereunto set our hands in Congress. Done at Philadelphia in the state of Pennsylvania the ninth Day of July in the Year of our Lord, one Thousand seven Hundred and Seventy-eight, and in the third year of the independence of America.

State of New Hampshire—Josiah Bartlett, John Wentworth, jun^r, August 8th, 1778; State of Massachusetts Bay—John Hancock, Samuel Adams, Elbridge Gerry, Francis Dana, James Lovell, Samuel Holten; State of Rhode-Island and Providence Plantations—William Ellery, Henry Marchant, John Collins; State of Connecticut—Roger Sherman, Samuel Huntington, Oliver Wolcott, Titus Hosmer, Andrew Adams; State of New York—Ja^s Duane, Fra: Lewis, Wm Duer, Gouv^r Morris; State of New Jersey—Jno Witherspoon, Nathl Scudder, November 26, 1778; State of Pennsylvania—Robert Morris, Daniel Roberdeau, Jon. Bayard Smith, William Clingar, Joseph Reed, 22d July, 1778; State of Delaware—Thos McKean, Feby 22d, 1779, John Dickinson, May 5th, 1779, Nicholas Van Dyke; State of Maryland—John Hanson, March 1, 1781, Daniel Carroll, ditto; State of Virginia—

Richard Henry Lee, John Banister, Thomas Adams, Jno Harvie, Francis Lightfoot Lee; State of North Carolina—John Penn, July 21st, 1778; Corn^s Harnett, Jno Williams; State of South Carolina—Henry Laurens, William Henry Drayton, Jno Mathews, Rich Hutson, Thos Heyward, jun^r.; State of Georgia—Jno Walton, 24th July, 1778, Edwd Telfair, Edwd Langworthy.

THE CONSTITUTION OF THE UNITED STATES

[NOTE. The text of the Constitution printed here precisely reproduces the original document in spelling and punctuation. Comments and explanations are in smaller type.]

PREAMBLE

WE THE PEOPLE of the United States, in order to form a more perfect Union, establish Justice, insure domestic Tranquility, provide for the common defence, promote the general Welfare, and secure the Blessings of Liberty to ourselves and our Posterity, DO ordain and establish this Constitution for the United States of America.

Article. I.

Section. 1. All legislative Powers herein granted shall be vested in a Congress of the United States, which shall consist of a Senate and House of Representatives.

Section. 2. The House of Representatives shall be composed of Members chosen every second Year by the People of the several States, and the Electors in each State shall have the Qualifications requisite for Electors of the most numerous Branch of the State Legislature.

No Person shall be a Representative who shall not have attained to the Age of twenty five Years, and been seven years a Citizen of the United States, and who shall not, when elected, be an Inhabitant of that State in which he shall be chosen.

Representatives and direct Taxes[1] shall be apportioned among the several States which may be included within this Union, according to their respective Numbers, which shall be determined by adding to the whole Number of free Persons, including those bound to Service for a Term of Years, and excluding Indians not taxed, three fifths of all other Persons. The actual Enumeration shall be made within three Years after the first Meeting of the Congress of the United States, and within every subsequent Term of ten Years, in such Manner as they shall by Law direct. The Number of Representatives shall not exceed one for every thirty Thousand, but each State shall have at Least one Representative; and until such enumeration shall be made, the State of New Hampshire shall be entitled to chuse three, Massachusetts eight, Rhode Island and Providence Plantations one, Connecticut five, New York six, New Jersey four, Pennsylvania eight, Delaware one, Maryland six, Virginia ten, North Carolina five, South Carolina five, and Georgia three.

When vacancies happen in the Representation from any State, the Executive Authority thereof shall issue Writs of Election to fill such Vacancies.

[1] Partly superseded by Amendment XIV.

The House of Representatives shall choose their Speaker and other Officers; and shall have the sole Power of Impeachment.

Section. 3. The Senate of the United States shall be composed of two Senators from each State, chosen by the Legislature thereof, for six Years; and each Senator shall have one Vote.

Immediately after they shall be assembled in Consequence of the first Election, they shall be divided as equally as may be into three Classes. The Seats of the Senators of the first Class shall be vacated at the Expiration of the second Year, of the second Class at the Expiration of the fourth Year, and of the third Class at the Expiration of the sixth Year, so that one third may be chosen every second Year; and if Vacancies happen by Resignation, or otherwise, during the Recess of the Legislature of any State, the Executive thereof may make temporary Appointments until the next Meeting of the Legislature, which shall then fill such Vacancies.[1]

No Person shall be a Senator who shall not have attained to the Age of thirty Years, and been nine Years a Citizen of the United States, and who shall not, when elected, be an Inhabitant of that State for which he shall be chosen.

The Vice President of the United States shall be President of the Senate, but shall have no Vote, unless they be equally divided.

The Senate shall chuse their other Officers, and also a President pro tempore, in the Absence of the Vice President, or when he shall exercise the Office of President of the United States.

The Senate shall have the sole Power to try all Impeachment. When sitting for that Purpose, they shall be on Oath or Affirmation. When the President of the United States is tried, the Chief Justice shall preside: And no Person shall be convicted without the Concurrence of two thirds of the Members present.

Judgment in Cases of Impeachment shall not extend further than to removal from Office, and disqualification to hold and enjoy any Office of honor, Trust, or Profit under the United States: but the Party convicted shall nevertheless be liable and subject to Indictment, Trial, Judgment, and Punishment, according to Law.

Section. 4. The Times, Places and Manner of holding Elections for Senators and Representatives, shall be prescribed in each State by the Legislature thereof, but the Congress may at any time by Law make or alter such Regulations, except as to the places of chusing Senators.

The Congress shall assemble at least once in every Year, and such Meeting shall be on the first Monday in December, unless they shall by Law appoint a different Day.

Section. 5. Each House shall be the Judge of the Elections, Returns and Qualifications of its own Members, and a Majority of each shall constitute a Quorum to do Business; but a smaller Number may adjourn from day to day, and may be authorized to compel the Attendance of absent Members, in such

[1] See Amendment XVII.

Manner, and under such Penalties as each House may provide.

Each House may determine the Rules of its Proceedings, punish its Members for disorderly Behaviour, and with the Concurrence of two thirds, expel a Member.

Each House shall keep a Journal of its Proceedings, and from time to time publish the same, excepting such Parts as may in their Judgment require Secrecy; and the Yeas and Nays of the Members of either House on any question shall, at the Desire of one fifth of those Present, be entered on the Journal.

Neither House, during the Session of Congress, shall, without the Consent of the other, adjourn for more than three days, nor to any other Place than that in which the two Houses shall be sitting.

Section. 6. The Senators and Representatives shall receive a Compensation for their Services, to be ascertained by Law, and paid out of the Treasury of the United States. They shall in all Cases, except Treason, Felony and Breach of the Peace, be privileged from Arrest during their Attendance at the Session of their respective Houses, and in going to and returning from the same; and for any Speech or Debate in either House, they shall not be questioned in any other Place.

No Senator, or Representative shall, during the Time for which he was elected, be appointed to any civil Office under the Authority of the United States which shall have been created, or the Emoluments whereof shall have been encreased during such time; and no Person holding any Office under the United States, shall be a Member of either House during his Continuance in Office.

Section. 7. All Bills for raising Revenue shall originate in the House of Representatives; but the Senate may propose or concur with Amendments as on other Bills.

Every Bill which shall have passed the House of Representatives and the Senate shall, before it become a Law, be presented to the President of the United States; If he approve, he shall sign it, but if not he shall return it, with his Objections to that House in which it shall have originated, who shall enter the Objections at large on their Journal, and proceed to reconsider it. If after such Reconsideration two thirds of that House shall agree to pass the Bill, it shall be sent, together with the Objections, to the other House, by which it shall likewise be reconsidered, and if approved by two thirds of that House, it shall become a Law. But in all such Cases the Votes of both Houses shall be determined by Yeas and Nays, and the Names of the Persons voting for and against the Bill shall be entered on the Journal of each House respectively. If any Bill shall not be returned by the President within ten Days (Sundays excepted) after it shall have been presented to him, the Same shall be a Law, in like Manner as if he had signed it, unless the Congress by their Adjournment prevent its Return, in which Case it shall not be a Law.

Every Order, Resolution, or Vote to which the Concurrence of the Senate and House of Representatives may be necessary (except on a Question of Ad-

journment) shall be presented to the President of the United States; and before the Same shall take Effect, shall be approved by him, or being disapproved by him, shall be repassed by two thirds of the Senate and House of Representatives, according to the Rules and Limitations prescribed in the Case of a Bill.

Section. 8. The Congress shall have Power To, lay and collect Taxes, Duties, Imposts and Excises, to pay the Debts and provide for the common Defence and general Welfare of the United States; but all Duties, Imposts and Excises shall be uniform throughout the United States;

To borrow Money on the credit of the United States;

To regulate Commerce with foreign Nations, and among the several States, and with the Indian Tribes;

To establish an uniform Rule of Naturalization, and uniform Laws on the subject of Bankruptcies throughout the United States;

To coin Money, regulate the Value thereof, and of foreign Coin, and fix the Standard of Weights and Measures;

To provide for the Punishment of counterfeiting the Securities and current Coin of the United States;

To establish Post Offices and post Roads;

To promote the Progress of Science and useful Arts, by securing for limited Times to Authors and Inventors the exclusive Right to their respective Writings and Discoveries;

To constitute Tribunals inferior to the supreme Court;

To define and punish Piracies and Felonies committed on the high Seas, and Offences against the Law of Nations;

To declare War, grant Letters of Marque and Reprisal, and make Rules concerning Captures on Land and Water;

To raise and support Armies, but no Appropriation of Money to that Use shall be for a longer Term than two Years;

To provide and maintain a Navy;

To make Rules for the Government and Regulation of the land and naval Forces;

To provide for calling forth the Militia to execute the Laws of the Union, suppress Insurrections and repel Invasions;

To provide for organizing, arming, and disciplining, the Militia, and for governing such Part of them as may be employed in the Service of the United States, reserving to the States respectively, the Appointment of the Officers, and the Authority of training the Militia according to the discipline prescribed by Congress;

To exercise exclusive Legislation in all Cases whatsoever, over such District (not exceeding ten Miles square) as may, by Cession of particular States, and the Acceptance of Congress, become the Seat of the Government of the United States, and to exercise like Authority over all Places purchased by the Consent of the Legislature of the State in which the same shall be, for the Erection of Forts, Magazines, Arsenals, dock-Yards, and other needful Buildings;—And

To make all Laws which shall

be necessary and proper for carrying into Execution the foregoing Powers, and all other Powers vested by this Constitution in the Government of the United States, or in any Department or Officer thereof.

Section. 9. The Migration or Importation of such Persons as any of the States now existing shall think proper to admit, shall not be prohibited by the Congress prior to the Year one thousand eight hundred and eight, but a Tax or duty may be imposed on such Importation, not exceeding ten dollars for each Person.

The Privilege of the Writ of Habeas Corpus shall not be suspended, unless when in Cases of Rebellion or Invasion the public Safety may require it.

No Bill of Attainder or ex post facto Law shall be passed.

No Capitation, or other direct, Tax shall be laid, unless in Proportion to the Census or Enumeration herein before directed to be taken.

No Tax or Duty shall be laid on Articles exported from any State.

No Preference shall be given by any Regulation of Commerce or Revenue to the Ports of one State over those of another: nor shall Vessels bound to, or from, one State, be obliged to enter, clear, or pay Duties in another.

No Money shall be drawn from the Treasury, but in Consequence of Appropriations made by Law, and a regular Statement and Account of the Receipts and Expenditures of all public Money shall be published from time to time.

No Title of Nobility shall be granted by the United States: And no Person holding any Office of Profit or Trust under them, shall, without the Consent of the Congress, accept of any present, Emolument, Office, or Title, of any kind whatever, from any King, Prince, or foreign State.

Section. 10. No State shall enter into any Treaty, Alliance, or Confederation; grant Letters of Marque and Reprisal; coin Money; emit Bills of Credit; make any Thing but gold and silver Coin a Tender in Payment of Debts; pass any Bill of Attainder, ex post facto Law, or Law impairing the Obligation of Contracts, or grant any Title of Nobility.

No State shall, without the Consent of the Congress, lay any Imposts or Duties on Imports or Exports, except what may be absolutely necessary for executing it's inspection Laws: and the net produce of all Duties and Imposts, laid by any State on Imports or Exports, shall be for the Use of the Treasury of the United States; and all such Laws shall be subject to the Revision and Controul of the Congress.

No State shall, without the Consent of Congress, lay any Duty of Tonnage, keep Troops, or Ships of War in time of Peace, enter into any Agreement or Compact with another State, or with a foreign Power, or engage in War, unless actually invaded, or in such imminent Danger as will not admit of delay.

Article. II.

Section. 1. The executive Power shall be vested in a President of the United States of America. He shall hold his Office during the Term of four Years, and, together with the Vice President, chosen for the same Term, be elected, as follows

Each State shall appoint, in such Manner as the Legislature thereof may direct, a Number of Electors, equal to the whole Number of Senators and Representatives to which the State may be entitled in the Congress: but no Senator or Representative, or Person holding an Office of Trust or Profit under the United States, shall be appointed an Elector.

The Electors shall meet in their respective States, and vote by Ballot for two Persons, of whom one at least shall not be an Inhabitant of the same State with themselves. And they shall make a List of all the Persons voted for, and of the Number of Votes for each; which List they shall sign and certify, and transmit sealed to the Seat of the Government of the United States, directed to the President of the Senate. The President of the Senate shall, in the Presence of the Senate and House of Representatives, open all the Certificates, and the Votes shall then be counted. The Person having the greatest Number of Votes shall be the President, if such Number be a Majority of the whole Number of Electors appointed; and if there be more than one who have such Majority, and have an equal Number of Votes, then the House of Representatives shall immediately chuse by Ballot one of them for President; and if no Person have Majority, then from the five highest on the List the said House shall in like Manner chuse the President. But in chusing the President, the Votes shall be taken by States, the Representation from each State having one Vote; A quorum for this Purpose shall consist of a Member or Members from two thirds of the States, and a Majority of all the States shall be necessary to a Choice. In every Case, after the Choice of the President, the Person having the greatest Number of Votes of the Electors shall be the Vice President. But if there should remain two or more who have equal Votes, the Senate shall chuse from them by Ballot the Vice President.[1]

The Congress may determine the Time of chusing the Electors, and the Day on which they shall give their Votes; which Day shall be the same throughout the United States.

No Person except a natural born Citizen, or a Citizen of the United States, at the time of the Adoption of this Constitution, shall be eligible to the Office of President, neither shall any Person be eligible to that Office who shall not have attained to the Age of thirty-five Years, and been fourteen Years a Resident within the United States.

In Case of the Removal of the President from Office, or of his Death, Resignation, or Inability to discharge the Powers and Duties of the said Office, the Same shall devolve on the Vice President, and the Congress may by Law provide for the Case of Removal, Death, Resignation or Inability, both of the President and Vice President, declaring what Officer shall then act as President, and such Officer shall act accordingly, until the Disability be removed, or a President shall be elected.

The President shall, at stated Times,

[1] This paragraph in force only from 1788 to 1803; superseded by Amendment XII.

receive for his Services, a compensation, which shall neither be Increased nor diminished during the Period for which he shall have been elected, and he shall not receive within that Period any other Emolument from the United States, or any of them.

Before he enter on the Execution of his Office, he shall take the following Oath or Affirmation:—

"I do solemnly swear (or affirm) that I will faithfully execute the Office of President of the United States, and will to the best of my Ability, preserve, protect and defend the Constitution of the United States."

Section. 2. The President shall be Commander in Chief of the Army and Navy of the United States, and the Militia of the several States, when called into the actual Service of the United States; he may require the Opinion, in writing, of the principal Officer in each of the executive Departments, upon any Subject relating to the Duties of their respective Offices, and he shall have Power to grant Reprieves and Pardons for Offences against the United States, except in Cases of Impeachment.

He shall have Power, by and with the Advice and Consent of the Senate, to make Treaties, provided two thirds of the Senators present concur; and he shall nominate, and by and with the Advice and Consent of the Senate, shall appoint Ambassadors, other public Ministers and Consuls, Judges of the supreme Court, and all other Officers of the United States, whose Appointments are not herein otherwise provided for, and which shall be established by Law; but the Congress may by Law vest the Appointment of such inferior Officers, as they think proper, in the President alone, in the Courts of Law, or in the Heads of Departments.

The President shall have Power to fill up all Vacancies that may happen during the Recess of the Senate, by granting Commissions, which shall expire at the End of their next Session.

Section. 3. He shall from time to time give to the Congress Information of the State of the Union, and recommend to their Consideration such Measures as he shall judge necessary and expedient; he may, on extraordinary Occasions, convene both Houses, or either of them, and in Case of Disagreement between them, with Respect to the Time of Adjournment, he may adjourn them to such Time as he shall think proper; he shall receive Ambassadors and other public Ministers; he shall take care that the Laws be faithfully executed, and shall Commission all the Officers of the United States.

Section. 4. The President, Vice President and all civil Officers of the United States, shall be removed from Office on Impeachment for, and Conviction of, Treason, Bribery, or other high Crimes and Misdemeanors.

Article. III.

Section. 1. The Judicial Power of the United States, shall be vested in one Supreme Court, and in such inferior Courts as the Congress may from time to time ordain and establish. The Judges, both of the supreme and inferior Courts, shall hold their offices during good Behaviour, and shall, at stated Times, receive for their Services, a Compensation, which shall not be diminished during their Continuance in Office.

Section. 2. The judicial Power shall extend to all Cases, in Law and Equity, arising under this Constitution, the Laws of the United States, and Treaties made, or which shall be made, under their Authority;—to all Cases affecting Ambassadors, other public Ministers and Consuls;—to all Cases of admiralty and maritime Jurisdiction;—to Controversies to which the United States shall be a Party;—to Controversies between two or more States; between a State[1] and Citizens of another State;—between Citizens of different States;—between Citizens of the same State claiming Lands under Grants of different States, and between a State, or the Citizens thereof, and foreign States, Citizens or Subjects.

In all Cases affecting Ambassadors, other public Ministers and Consuls, and those in which a State shall be Party, the supreme Court shall have original Jurisdiction. In all the other Cases before mentional, the supreme Court shall have appellate Jurisdiction, both as to Law and Fact, with such Exceptions, and under such Regulations as the Congress shall make.

The Trial of all Crimes, except in Cases of Impeachment, shall be by Jury; and such trial shall be held in the State where the said Crimes shall have been committed; but when not committed within any State, the Trial shall be at such Place or Places as the Congress may by law have directed.

Section. 3. Treason against the United States, shall consist only in levying War against them, or in adhering to their Enemies, giving them Aid and Comfort. No Person shall be convicted of Treason unless on the Testimony of two Witnesses to the same overt Act, or on Confession in open Court.

The Congress shall have Power to declare the Punishment of Treason, but no Attainder of Treason shall work corruption of Blood, or Forfeiture except during the Life of the Person attainted.

Article. IV.

Section. 1. Full Faith and Credit shall be given in each State to the public Acts, Records, and judicial Proceedings of every other State. And the Congress may by general Laws prescribe the Manner in which such Acts, Records and Proceedings shall be proved, and the Effect thereof.

Section. 2. The Citizens of each State shall be entitled to all Privileges and Immunities of Citizens in the several States.

A Person charged in any State with Treason, Felony, or other Crime, who shall flee from Justice, and be found in another State, shall on Demand of the executive Authority of the State from which he fled, be delivered up, to be removed to the State having Jurisdiction of the Crime.

No Person held to Service or Labour in one State, under the Laws thereof, escaping into another, shall, in Consequence of any Law or Regulation therein, be discharged from such Service or Labour, but shall be delivered up on Claim of the Party to whom such Service or Labour may be due.

[1] See Amendment XI.

Section. 3. New States may be admitted by the Congress into this Union; But no new State shall be formed or erected within the Jurisdiction of any other State, nor any State be formed by the Junction of two or more States, or Parts of States, without the consent of the Legislatures of the States concerned as well as of the Congress.

The Congress shall have power to dispose of and make all needful Rules and Regulations respecting the Territory or other Property belonging to the United States; and nothing in this Constitution shall be so construed as to Prejudice any Claims of the United States, or of any particular State.

Section. 4. The United States shall guarantee to every State in this Union a Republican Form of Government, and shall protect each of them against Invasion; and on Application of the Legislature, or of the Executive (when the Legislature cannot be convened) against domestic Violence.

Article. V.

The Congress, whenever two-thirds of both Houses shall deem it necessary, shall propose Amendments to this Constitution, or, on the Application of the Legislatures of two thirds of the several States, shall call a Convention for proposing Amendments, which, in either Case, shall be valid to all Intents and Purposes, as Part of this Constitution, when ratified by the Legislatures of three fourths of the several States, or by Conventions in three fourths thereof, as the one or the other Mode of Ratification may be proposed by the Congress; Provided that no Amendment which may be made prior to the Year One thousand eight hundred and eight shall in any Manner affect the first and fourth Clauses in the Ninth Section of the first Article; and that no State, without its Consent, shall be deprived of it's equal Suffrage in the Senate.

Article. VI.

All Debts contracted and Engagements entered into, before the Adoption of this Constitution, shall be as valid against the United States under this Constitution, as under the Confederation.

This Constitution, and the Laws of the United States which shall be made in Pursuance thereof; and all Treaties made, or which shall be made, under the Authority of the United States, shall be the supreme Law of the Land; and the Judges in every State shall be bound thereby, any Thing in the Constitution or Laws of any State to the Contrary notwithstanding.

The Senators and Representatives before mentioned, and the Members of the several State Legislatures, and all executive and judicial Officers, both of the United States and of the several States, shall be bound by Oath or Affirmation, to support this Constitution; but no religious Test shall ever be required as a Qualification to any Office or public Trust under the United States.

Article. VII.

The Ratification of the Conventions of nine States, shall be sufficient for the Establishment of this Constitution between the States so ratifying the Same.

DONE in Convention by the Unanimous Consent of the States present the Seventeenth Day of September in the Year of our Lord one thousand seven hundred and Eighty seven and of the Independance of the United States of America the Twelfth. IN WITNESS whereof We have hereunto subscribed our Names,

Attest: William Jackson, Secretary; George Washington, President and deputy from Virginia; New Hampshire —John Langdon, Nicholas Gilman; Massachusetts—Nathaniel Gorham, Rufus King; Connecticut—William Samuel Johnson, Roger Sherman; New York— Alexander Hamilton; New Jersey— William Livingston, David Brearley, William Paterson, Jonathan Dayton; Pennsylvania—B. Franklin, Thomas Mifflin, Robert Morris, George Clymer, Thomas Fitzsimons, Jared Ingersoll, James Wilson, Gouverneur Morris; Delaware—George Read; Gunning Bedford, Jr., John Dickinson, Richard Bassett, Jacob Broom; Maryland—James McHenry, Dan of St. Thomas Jenifer, Daniel Carroll; Virginia—John Blair, James Madison, Jr.; North Carolina— William Blount, Richard Dobbs Spaight, Hugh Williamson; South Carolina— J. Rutledge, Charles Cotesworth Pinckney, Charles Pinckney, Pierce Butler; Georgia—William Few, Abraham Baldwin.

The Constitution was ratified by the thirteen original States in the following order: Delaware, December 7, 1787, unanimously; Pennsylvania, December 12, 1787, vote 46 to 23; New Jersey, December 18, 1787, unanimously; Georgia, January 2, 1788, unanimously; Connecticut, January 9, 1788, vote 128 to 40; Massachusetts, February 6, 1788, vote 187 to 168; Maryland, April 28, 1788, vote 63 to 12; South Carolina, May 23, 1788, vote 149 to 73; New Hampshire, June 21, 1788, vote 57 to 46; Virginia, June 25, 1788, vote 89 to 79; New York, July 26, 1788, vote 30 to 28; North Carolina, November 21, 1789, vote 193 to 75; Rhode Island, May 29, 1790, vote 34 to 32.

AMENDMENTS

Twelve amendments to the Constitution were proposed at the First session of Congress, held in New York City, on March 4, 1789. The first two were not adopted. The following 10 were ratified Dec. 15, 1791, and form what is known as the "Bill of Rights." The original proposal of these amendments was preceded by the following preamble and resolution:

The conventions of a number of the States having, at the time of their adopting the Constitution, expressed a desire, in order to prevent misconstruction or abuse of its powers, that further declaratory and restrictive clauses should be added, and as extending the ground of public confidence in the Government will best insure the beneficent ends of its institution.

Resolved,

By the Senate and House of Representatives of the United States of America, in Congress assembled, two-thirds of both Houses concurring, that the following articles be proposed to the Legislatures of the several States, as amendments to the Constitution of the United States; all or any of which articles, when ratified by three-fourths of the said Legislatures, to be valid to all intents and purposes as part of the said Constitution, namely:

The following ten original amendments were declared in force December 15, 1791.

Amendment I.

Congress shall make no law respecting an establishment of religion, or prohibiting the free exercise thereof; or abridging the freedom of speech, or of the press; or the right of the people peaceably to assemble, and to petition the Government for a redress of grievances.

Amendment II.

A well-regulated Militia, being necessary to the security of a free State, the right of the people to keep and bear Arms, shall not be infringed.

Amendment III.

No Soldier shall, in time of peace be quartered in any house, without the consent of the Owner, nor in time of war, but in a manner to be prescribed by law.

Amendment IV.

The right of the people to be secure in their persons, houses, papers, and effects, against unreasonable searches and seizures, shall not be violated, and no Warrants shall issue, but upon probable cause, supported by Oath or affirmation, and particularly describing the place to be searched, and the persons or things to be seized.

Amendment V.

No person shall be held to answer for a capital, or otherwise infamous crime, unless on a presentment or indictment of a Grand Jury, except in cases arising in the land or naval forces, on in the Militia, when in actual service in time of War or public danger; nor shall any person be subject for the same offence to be twice put in jeopardy of life or limb; nor shall be compelled in any criminal case to be a witness against himself, nor be deprived of life, liberty, or property, without due process of law; nor shall private property be taken for public use, without just compensation.

Amendment VI.

In all criminal prosecutions, the Accused shall enjoy the right to a speedy and public trial, by an impartial jury of the State and district wherein the crime shall have been committed, which districts shall have been previously ascertained by law, and to be informed of the nature and cause of the accusation; to be confronted with the witnesses against him; to have compulsory process for obtaining witnesses in his favor, and to have Assistance of Counsel for his defence.

Amendment VII.

In Suits at common law, where the value in controversy shall exceed twenty dollars, the right of trial by jury shall be preserved, and no fact tried by a jury, shall be otherwise re-examined in any court of the United States, than according to the rules of the common law.

Amendment VIII.

Excessive bail shall not be required nor excessive fines imposed, nor cruel and unusual punishment inflicted.

Amendment IX.

The enumeration in the Constitution, of certain rights, shall not be construed to deny or disparage others retained by the people.

Amendment X.

The powers not delegated to the United States by the Constitution, nor prohibited by it to the States, are reserved to the States respectively, or to the people.

Amendment XI.
(Ratified Feb. 7, 1795)

The Judicial power of the United States shall not be construed to extend to any suit in law or equity commenced or prosecuted against one of the United States by Citizens of another State, or by Citizens or Subjects of any Foreign state.

Amendment XII.
(Ratified July 27, 1804)

The Electors shall meet in their respective states, and vote by ballot for President and Vice-President, one of whom, at least, shall not be an inhabitant of the same state with themselves; they shall name in their ballots the person voted for as President, and in distinct ballots the person voted for as Vice-President, and they shall make distinct lists of all persons voted for as President, and of all persons voted for as Vice-President, and of the number of votes for each, which lists they shall sign and certify, and transmit sealed to the seat of the Government of the United States directed to the president of the Senate;—The president of the Senate shall, in the presence of the Senate and House of Representatives, open all the certificates and the votes shall then be counted;—The person having the greatest number of votes for President, shall be the President, if such number be a majority of the whole number of Electors appointed; and if no person have such majority, then from the persons having the highest numbers not exceeding three on the list of those voted for as President, the House of Representatives shall choose immediately, by ballot, the President. But in choosing the President, the votes shall be taken by states, the representation from each state having one vote; a quorum for this purpose shall consist of a member or members from two-thirds of the states, and a majority of all the states shall be necessary to a choice. And if the House of Representatives shall not choose a President whenever the right of choice shall devolve upon them, before the fourth day of March next following, then the Vice-President shall act as President, as in the case of the death or other constitutional disability of the President.—The person having the greatest number of votes as Vice-President, shall be the Vice-President, if such number be a majority of the whole number of Electors appointed, and if no person have a majority, then from the two highest numbers on the list, the Senate shall choose the Vice-President; a quorum for the purpose shall consist of two-thirds of the whole number of Senators, and a majority of the whole number shall be necessary to a choice. But no person constitutionally ineligible to the office of President

shall be eligible to that of Vice-President of the United States.

Amendment XIII.
(Ratified Dec. 6, 1865)

Section 1. Neither slavery nor involuntary servitude, except as a punishment for crime whereof the party shall have been duly convicted, shall exist within the United States, or any place subject to their jurisdiction.

Section 2. Congress shall have power to enforce this article by appropriate legislation.

Amendment XIV.
(Ratified July 9, 1868)

Section 1. All persons born or naturalized in the United States, and subject to the jurisdiction thereof, are citizens of the United States and of the State wherein they reside. No State shall make or enforce any law which shall abridge the privileges or immunities of citizens of the United States; nor shall any State deprive any person of life, liberty, or property, without due process of law; nor deny to any person within its jurisdiction the equal protection of the laws.

Section 2. Representatives shall be apportioned among the several States according to their respective numbers, counting the whole number of persons in each State, excluding Indians not taxed. But when the right to vote at any election for the choice of Electors for President and Vice-President of the United States, Representatives in Congress, the Executive and Judicial officers of a State, or the members of the Legislature thereof, is denied to any of the male inhabitants of such State, being twenty-one years of age, and citizens of the United States, or in any way abridged, except for participation in rebellion, or other crime, the basis of representation therein shall be reduced in the proportion which the number of such male citizens shall bear to the whole number of male citizens twenty-one years of age in such State.

Section 3. No person shall be a Senator or Representative in Congress, or Elector of President and Vice-President, or hold any office, civil or military, under the United States, or under any State, who, having previously taken an oath, as a member of Congress, or as an officer of the United States, or as a member of any State Legislature, or as an executive or judicial officer of any State, to support the Constitution of the United States, shall have engaged in insurrection or rebellion against the same, or given aid or comfort to the enemies thereof. But Congress may by a vote of two-thirds of each House, remove such disability.

Section 4. The validity of the public debt of the United States, authorized by law, including debts incurred for payment of pensions and bounties for services in supressing insurrection or rebellion, shall not be questioned. But neither the United States nor any State shall assume or pay any debt or obligation incurred in aid of insurrection or rebellion against the United States, or any claim for the loss of emancipation of any slave; but all such debts, obligations, and claims shall be held illegal and void.

Section 5. The Congress shall have power to enforce, by appropriate legislation, the provisions of this article.

Amendment XV.
(Ratified Feb. 3, 1870)

Section 1. The right of citizens of the United States to vote shall not be denied or abridged by the United States or by any State on account of race, color, or previous condition of servitude.

Section 2. The Congress shall have power to enforce this article by appropriate legislation.

Amendment XVI.
(Ratified Feb. 3, 1913)

The Congress shall have power to lay and collect taxes on incomes, from whatever source derived, without apportionment among the several States, and without regard to any census or enumeration.

Amendment XVII.
(Ratified April 8, 1913)

Section 1. The Senate of the United States shall be composed of two Senators from each State, elected by the people thereof, for six years; and each Senator shall have one vote. The electors in each State shall have the qualifications requisite for electors of the most numerous branch of the State Legislatures.

Section 2. When vacancies happen in the representation of any State in the Senate, the executive authority of such State shall issue writs of election to fill such vacancies: Provided, That the legislature of any State may empower the executive thereof to make temporary appointments until the people fill the vacancies by election as the Legislature may direct.

Amendment XVIII.
(Ratified Jan. 16, 1919)

Section 1. After one year from the ratification of this article the manufacture, sale, or transportation of intoxicating liquors within, the importation thereof into, or the exportation thereof from the United States and all territory subject to the jurisdiction thereof for beverage purposes is hereby prohibited.

Section 2. The Congress and the several States shall have concurrent power to enforce this article by appropriate legislation.

Amendment XIX.
(Ratified Aug. 18, 1920)

Section 1. The right of citizens of the United States to vote shall not be denied or abridged by the United States or by any State on account of sex.

Section 2. Congress shall have power to enforce this article by appropriate legislation.

Amendment XX.
(Ratified Jan. 23, 1933)

Section 1. The terms of the President and Vice-President shall end at noon on the 20th day of January, and the terms of Senators and Representatives at noon on the 3d day of January, of the years in which such terms would have ended if this article had not been ratified; and the terms of their successors shall then begin.

Section 2. The Congress shall assemble at least once in every year, and such meeting shall begin at noon on the 3d day of January, unless they shall by law appoint a different day.

Section 3. If, at the time fixed for the beginning of the term of the President, the President elect shall have died, the Vice-President elect shall become President. If a President shall not have been chosen before the time fixed for the beginning of his term, or if the President elect shall have failed to qualify, then the Vice-President elect shall act as President until a President shall have qualified; and the Congress may by law provide for the case wherein neither a President elect nor a Vice-President elect shall have qualified, declaring who shall then act as President, or the manner in which one who is to act shall be selected, and such person shall act accordingly until a President or Vice-President shall have qualified.

Section 4. The Congress may by law provide for the case of the death of any of the persons from whom the House of Representatives may choose a President whenever the right of choice shall have devolved upon them, and for the case of the death of any of the persons from whom the Senate may choose a Vice-President whenever the right of choice shall have devolved upon them.

Amendment XXI.
(Ratified Dec. 5, 1933)

Section 1. The eighteenth article of amendment to the Constitution of the United States is hereby repealed.

Section 2. The transportation or importation into any State, Territory, or Possession of the United States for delivery or use therein of intoxicating liquors, in violation of the laws thereof, is hereby prohibited.

Amendment XXII.
(Ratified Feb. 27, 1951)

Section 1. No person shall be elected to the office of the President more than twice. No person who has held the office of President, or acted as President for more than two years of a term to which some other person was elected President, shall be elected to the office of President more than once.

Amendment XXIII.
(Ratified March 29, 1961)

Section 1. The District constituting the seat of Government of the United States shall appoint in such a manner as the Congress may direct:

A number of electors of President and Vice President equal to the whole number of Senators and Representatives in Congress to which the District would be entitled if it were a State, but in no event more than the least populous State; they shall be in addition to those appointed by the States, but they shall be considered, for the purposes of the election of President and Vice President, to be electors appointed by a State; and they shall meet in the District and perform such duties as provided by the twelfth article of amendment.

Section 2. The Congress shall have power to enforce this article by appropriate legislation.

Amendment XXIV.
(Ratified Jan. 23, 1964)

Section 1. The right of citizens of the United States to vote in any primary or other election for President or Vice President, or for Senator or Representative in Congress, shall not be denied or abridged by the United States or any State by reason of failure to pay any poll tax or other tax.

Section 2. The Congress shall have power to enforce this article by appropriate legislation.

Amendment XXV.
(Ratified Feb. 10, 1967)

Section 1. In case of the removal of the President from office or of his death or resignation, the Vice President shall become President.

Section 2. Whenever there is a vacancy in the office of the Vice President, the President shall nominate a Vice President who shall take office upon confirmation by a majority vote of both Houses of Congress.

Section 3. Whenever the President transmits to the President pro tempore of the Senate and the Speaker of the House of Representatives his written declaration that he is unable to discharge the powers and duties of his office, and until he transmits to them a written declaration to the contrary, such powers and duties shall be discharged by the Vice President as Acting President.

Section 4. Whenever the Vice President and a majority of either the principal officers of the executive departments or of such other body as Congress may by law provide, transmit to the President pro tempore of the Senate and the Speaker of the House of Representatives their written declaration that the President is unable to discharge the powers and duties of his office, the Vice President shall immediately assume the powers and duties of the office as Acting President.

Thereafter, when the President transmits to the President pro tempore of the Senate and the Speaker of the House of Representatives his written declaration that no inability exists, he shall resume the powers and duties of his office unless the Vice President and a majority of either the principal officers of the executive department or of such other body as Congress may by law provide, transmit within four days to the President pro tempore of the Senate and the Speaker of the House of Representatives their written declaration that the President is unable to discharge the powers and duties of his office. Thereupon Congress shall decide the issue, assembling within forty-eight hours for that purpose if not in session. If the Congress, within twenty-one days after receipt of the latter written declaration, or, if Congress is not in session, within twenty-one days after Congress is required to assemble, determines by two-thirds vote of both Houses that the President is unable to discharge the powers and duties of his office, the Vice President shall continue to discharge the same as Acting President; otherwise, the President shall resume the powers and duties of his office.

LAW

Law is like life or matter or electricity—hard to define. Though we use it and benefit by it, we may not know its exact nature or be able to say just what it is. Some light on its meaning comes from the common phrase, "laying down the law." The words *law* and *lay* have the same root: law is something laid down. A statute is something laid down or established. Law is a system of rules or principles with authority.

Who lays down the law? What is the authority? The government is the obvious answer. Law is the rules laid down by the government.

Law and Right.—If we look at other languages, we find that *droit* is French for law—and that it also means right, straight, upright; the German word for law is *Recht*—and that it also means right, proper; and the Italian word is *diritto*—and that it also means direct, straight.

Etiquette tells us what is right. So does morality. So does law. Each is prescribed or established rules of conduct. They are alike because they all express the usages of some community at a particular time and place. In different communities, at different times, in different places there are all sorts of differences in the rules for politeness or righteousness or being a law-abiding citizen. The origin of all these social controls is custom. It is the custom of a dominant social class, especially in the matter of etiquette. Etiquette, standards of morals and law are all the rules of this class that set the standards and lay down the law. Law is more formally and definitely set. Like etiquette and morality it changes from time to time and is not the same in different places at the same time; but at any one time or place law seems more hard and fast and less open to question or difference of opinion than etiquette or morality. In politeness and goodness, we are governed considerably by the example of certain leaders; but, though it is true that our obedience to the law and our observance of it may depend on how others obey and observe it, the law has a force behind it that is different from any power that makes us polite or moral.

Law and morality and etiquette are all enforced partly by our desire to win the approval and avoid the disapproval of other members of the community. Law and morality unite to control much of the whole field of human conduct. For example, most modern societies consider it both immoral and unlawful to kill a human being (except in war, in self-defense or by police officers), to commit adultery, or to steal. More and more the law is coming to coincide with the rules of good conduct. This is seen in every field of law. In defining crimes and noncriminal wrongs, the law is becoming more interested in the intent, that is, in the spirit of the act and its purpose, which are the things that count in morality. In trade, law is becoming more and more severe on fraud and unfair practices. What used to be considered excusable business shrewdness is now discouraged by law. The old maxim of the law, *caveat emptor*, (let the buyer beware) has almost disappeared, so heavy are the obligations of fair dealing that modern law puts on the seller, so powerful are the laws' efforts to protect the buyer who used to be told that he must look out for himself.

With all these similarities between law and morality and etiquette, there are essential differences between these three methods of social control. Law refers to external action, whereas morality refers to the mind. Law imposes a norm to which all must conform, morality imposes an ideal standard toward which all should strive. The sanctions of law and morality are different—that is, the force that deals with violations of the controlling rules. Fear of disapproval may be the only reason for observing rules of etiquette or even certain moral rules, but it is seldom the only reason for obeying the law of the land. For a breach of etiquette, one is likely to suffer exclusion from certain social contacts. Immorality provokes vigorous and widespread criticism and a more complete social ostracism. For unlawful acts, the offender is tried by a court, pays retribution to an individual whom he has wronged and may be fined, imprisoned or even put to death. It is true that you can imagine instances of immorality where the punishment that the community informally imposes is more painful than the penalty for certain unlawful acts—like paying damages for trespassing or a fine for violating the ordinance against parking. However the penalties of law are more uniformly and impersonally administered; they are administered by public authorities and they are administered more publicly and the purpose of the law and the conduct it demands are generally approved.

Law and Public Opinion.—It is plain that law depends on custom. It is plain that the purpose of law is approved in general by the public. It follows that nothing seems to be law (effective law, anyway) that lacks popular support. The law against homicide is not much of a law in a primitive community where many murders are no more shocking to the frontiersman than bad table manners would be to us today. The 18th Amendment to the Constitution of the United States, prohibiting the sale, manufacture and transportation of intoxicating liquors was openly disobeyed by some citizens (including lawyers) because they thought the regulation of anyone's drinking habits was not a proper function of government. Other citizens disobeyed the same law because they believed that only a small minority had favored the Amendment. The repeal of the Amendment was certainly the result of public opinion. In a sense, public opinion makes laws, breaks laws and repeals them or renders them inoperative. Our statute books contain many laws that are dead letters. Some have gone out of date just because so long a time has passed since they were enacted. Some laws are on the statute books but have never been in force, because they were never intended to be enforced; they were passed as gestures, concessions to loudly expressed moral sentiment or

UNITED NATIONS

INTERNATIONAL COURT OF JUSTICE, the Hague, Netherlands, the judicial organ of the U.N.

attempts to pacify political opponents.

When a statute is repealed during the prosecution of a person accused of violating that statute, the prisoner is usually dismissed. The reason seems to be that as public opinion has changed enough to repeal the law now, the law could not have been really supported by public opinion when the accused violated the law. It often happens that a jury acts on the assumption that a law without popular approval is not a law to be enforced. Under the old English law a man who stole a loaf of bread was condemned to death; when the public revolted from this extreme punishment juries would often declare a guilty man innocent rather than have him punished by death. And the one who mercifully enables a dying person to end his suffering is guilty of murder, but the jury will usually decide that the "mercy killer" did not do the alleged act, in order to prevent what is thought to be an unjust punishment.

Changes in Law.—What sort of conduct must be regulated by law? The answer is constantly changing, and so the content of the law constantly changes. For example, the criminal law of England formerly protected a man's interest in an animal only if the animal was edible. Old crimes have ceased to be crimes under new modes of thought, and penalties are very different now from what they were in England two centuries ago when 160 crimes were punishable with death. Within a much shorter period some old forms of property have disappeared and new forms have become important—such as promissory notes, bills of exchange, corporate stock.

There has also been a great change in the authority back of the law—a change that corresponds roughly with alterations in the organization of society.

In primitive society, just because it is organized so differently from our own, it is hard to say what is law or even whether there is anything that can be called law—except criminal law. Conduct of all kinds is regulated by taboo. Judged by the apparent purpose of the taboos, many of them seem to be for the public good and in this respect they have one of the essential qualities of law—for example, taboos respecting foods may guard the public health and taboos about personal relations such as marriage may preserve good order inside one group or peace between different groups. But we cannot be sure that the taboos had the purpose we read into them. Besides, the punishment under taboo was merely predicted and there was nothing to make it come true but the frightened apprehension of the wrong-doer. No penalty was demanded and enforced by society.

In a theocracy, the priests who governed as the representatives of the tribal god learned the will of the god and told it to the tribe as a message from the god. Moses received the ten commandments from Jehovah on Mount Sinai in a thick cloud with thunders and lightning and "the whole mount quaked greatly." The penalties under the Mosaic law had an extra terror because the law came from the terrible mountain. How different are the authority and the source of law today in democratic states! The people's elected representatives enact the statutory law in national Congress and in state legislatures; and judges (many of them elected by the people) declare the rules of law that are not enacted and fix the actual meaning of the laws that are enacted. From day to day in this year a century and a half after the adoption of the Constitution the judges of certain courts have the power to decide the meaning of our Constitution.

Crime and Punishment.—In primitive society punishment was private vengeance. By custom of the community, with the approval but without the participation of the community, a man who was injured (or his group) took revenge on the wrong-doer (or on his group). The penalty was retaliation in the strict sense of that word, a punishment to fit the crime. Like injury, like penalty was the principle of *lex talionis,* the law of retaliation. In the Mosaic law the penalty is: "Eye for eye, tooth for tooth, hand for hand, foot for foot." Gradually private retribution was superseded by punishment set and administered by government.

In the Babylonian Code of Hammurabi, 1900 or 2000 years before Christ, there was no recognition of private vengeance: the state set penalties for different crimes—death by burning, drowning or gibbeting for different crimes—and the state exacted these penalties. There are two extreme opinions of scholars about this and other early codes that are full and minute in their list of punishments. One opinion says that from the earliest time it was recognized that certain wrongs were offenses against the state or community and that this is the reason for the many penalties in these codes. The other interpretation is that the community was interested not so much in punishing an offense against the public order (the wrong or crime) as in preventing the person or family that had been wronged from pursuing a private vengeance that would again disturb the public peace.

Whether it is a concept of long standing or merely a development in the gradual growth of civilization, the principal that a crime is an offense against the state is an essential of law as we know it. The act of the wrong-doer is usually one that directly injures another individual—stealing, homicide or fraudulent representations. It is also an injury and an offense to the state, prosecuted in the name of the people. Many offenses against an individual plainly threaten the public peace—larceny, robbery and the other wrongs just mentioned. Minor offenses, if they were left unpunished, would endanger the public peace by encouraging many further offenses. A thousand car drivers may ignore traffic lights if one who disregards a light goes unchallenged.

Often in sentencing a prisoner the judge says: "I must make an example of you"; and many penalties are inflicted mainly as examples.

COMPARATIVE LAW

In the 19th century, after Darwin had roused interest in evolution of animal and plant life and scholars began to study the relations of different languages, in England and Germany there sprang up the investigation of early law and an attempt to compare different legal systems, primitive and recent. Before this time the legal scholars had directed their attention toward finding natural law and perfect justice. Legal study had been deductive and in the 19th century it became inductive. The Grimm brothers to whom we owe the famous fairy tales studied early Teutonic law as well as myth. Sir Henry Maine (1822–88) wrote *Ancient Law* in 1861 and *Early Law and Custom* in 1883, drawing on his knowledge of primitive law in the village communities of India.

But neither ancient nor primitive legal systems have had any great influence upon our modern law. Finding the same ideas, the same methods, the same solutions or even similar punishments does not prove any relation or connection between the legal systems in which the similarities occur. No matter where or when the problem arises of protecting a loan to a debtor whose mere promise to pay is not enough, it is almost certain that the lender will say: "Give me your cattle or land for security." No matter where or when a creditor wants payment made at a point far distant from the debtor, the creditor is sure to say: "Give me an order on your friend who lives where the payment is to be made. Command him to pay it there." The chief value of comparative jurisprudence is that it discovers variations rather than likenesses, for the likenesses are so easy to explain.

Law of Babylon and Egypt.—Our knowledge of ancient law is steadily growing. Archeologists are unearthing legal records on Babylonian bricks, Assyrian tablets and Egyptian papyri. Two thousand years before Christ Hammurabi, king of Babylon, compiled a code that combined two earlier legal systems. It was discovered in 1901 and it proves that there was a complete system of commercial law (contracts, sales, pledges, suretyship), land law, wills, criminal law and some material on judgments and procedure. About early Egyptian law we know less, for we have no copies of codes; but there is abundant evidence in documents with legal allusions and legal meanings to make it plain that there was an elaborate system of commercial law in that land at an early date.

The legal material that is being uncovered by archeologists is valuable because it helps us reconstruct the early law of Babylon and Egypt—and because it helps to appraise the social conditions and ideals of the ancient world, for law deals with the fundamental interests of a nation.

The Jewish Law.—The Old Testament contains half a dozen codifications, usually dated in this order: the Decalogue (*Exodus* 20: 1–17; *Deuteronomy* 5: 6–21), the Covenant code (*Exodus* 20: 23; 23: 19; 24: 17–26), the curses of Mount Ebal (*Deuteronomy* 27: 15–26), the Deuteronomic Code (*Deuteronomy* 21–26), the Holiness Code (*Leviticus* 17–26), and the Priestly Code (most of the book of *Leviticus*). The Bible contains in its narrative portions very many scattered provisions of popular law or customs relating to family relations, landed property, inheritance, debtors, slaves and crime. This customary law manifestly comes from different periods in the development of Jewish culture. Some is from the stage of nomad life; some from that of settled tribal agricultural communities; some from that of urban civilization. Conflicts are observable between the living popular law and some of the high religio-ethical principles enunciated as ideals, rather than realities, in the codes.

Altogether the Jewish law of the Old Testament furnished admirable material for the historical study of law and other social institutions. It illustrates the relation between law and the dominant interests of society, which in this case are those of religion in a theocratic state.

Archeological discoveries are constantly revealing new connections between the Bible and the culture of the ancient Orient, and this is true of the law. Two qualities, however, characterize the Jewish law and set it apart from other Oriental systems. Particularly in its codes it has high religious and ethical principles, and is more humane (however deficient it may seem to us) than other ancient systems in its emphasis upon family purity, freedom of the person and relative protection of animals, slaves, aliens, debtors and the poor. Its second characteristic is that it has been almost wholly confined to the Jewish people; though it was never a world-law, it has remained a living law for a people scattered world-wide, in which respect it is unique.

Roman Law. The legal system of Rome began as the law of the City of Rome and so was called *jus civile* or city law. This early city law was primitive and crude, a body of rigid detailed rules that applied to citizens. After the expulsion of the kings in 509 B.C., the prolonged contest between the patricians and the plebeians led to a codification of the law in 451 B.C. Probably investigations were made into the laws of Athens and Sparta, and even a few enactments of Solon and other famous lawgivers may have been incorporated, but the main body of the law that was codified in *The Twelve Tables* was of Roman derivation. These tables related to judicial procedure, ownership, inheritance, torts and the sacred law.

Foreigners (*peregrini*) living in Rome, subjects but not citizens, were numerous and economically and socially important in the city even when it had barely begun its conquests. As early as 242 B.C. a special magistrate (*praetor peregrinus*) was appointed to try cases in which these foreigners were involved. As the foreigners at Rome came from all parts of the

FRANK J. DARMSTAEDTER

MOSES AND THE TABLETS OF THE LAW, an engraving by the Frenchman, Gustave Doré. Moses, the great leader and lawgiver of the Israelites, received the Ten Commandments on Mount Sinai. Included in the Old Testament, the Commandments have been adopted as moral law by many religions. The Bible contains various provisions of laws and customs that developed from various stages of Jewish culture.

world, the magistrates who tried their cases had to apply rules suggested by considerations of fairness and common sense and rules taken over from a commercial law that was current in the Mediterranean at that time. Thus the law applied to the *peregrini* was a general law of natural justice, based on considerations of equity and utility (*ex bono et aequo*). Because it applied to different nationalities (*gentes* in Latin) it was called the *jus gentium*.[1]

These two systems side by side at Rome, affected each other. The citizens' law became less formal, more businesslike and more equitable. The aliens' law became more precise and more sternly just. Soon citizens and subjects had practically the same private rights under the law—first in a general sort of way and finally in 212 A.D. by the Edict of Caracalla, which gave citizenship to all freeborn subjects and so made the same law for all Romans.

After another three centuries in 528–34 A.D., the Emperor Justinian had the Roman law summarized in three parts: a student's textbook, called the Institutes; a compendium of the jurist-made law, the Digest or Pandects (literally, all-embracing); and a Code of imperial rescripts (that is, special decisions by the Emperor). This compilation, the *Corpus Juris Civilis* or body of civil law, is by far the most famous and most influential law-book of the world's history. Scholars and statesman of the Middle Ages studied it with consequences of immense extent and immeasurable importance. More or less altered, everywhere more or less combined with local native custom and statute, it is the civil law that now rules most of the world that is not ruled by our own English common law.

The Roman law, quite apart from what it did in form, in code and in the actual content that passed into the civil law of modern times, contributed the idea of fair trial, proof of guilt, opportunity for the accused to meet his accusers and know their accusations. In the New Testament (Acts 25:16) a Roman provincial governor, Porcius Festus, states this principle: "It is not the manner of the Romans to deliver any man to die before that he which is accused have the accusers face to face and have license to answer for himself concerning the crime laid against him."

Roman law in its form and content greatly influenced the law of almost all nations of Europe. In the early 16th century Germany and most of the rest of Europe (but not England) took over the Roman civil law and discarded their own customary law, the folk law or common law that expressed their own native and local ideas. This adoption of Roman law was called the *Reception*. Of it a great English jurist, Frederick W. Maitland says: "The modern historian of Germany will speak of the Reception as no less important than the Renaissance and the Reformation with which it is intimately connected."

The Roman law is especially in-

¹ Later *jus gentium* came to mean international law.

teresting to us because today it governs most of the world. The great legal systems of the world are usually divided into: civil law (the legal systems based upon the Roman law); the common law; and the Mohammedan law. The civil law rules in the nations of Europe (except England), Egypt, the Union of South Africa and the African colonies of civil-law nations, Central and South America and our own state of Louisiana, Quebec, Japan and China (through their borrowing from the German law) and to some extent in the Asian colonies of civil-law nations.

In English law—and so in American law—Roman law has had considerable influence. The church or canon law was largely Roman and this canon law was the branch in which most of the Lord Chancellors of England were trained because they were churchmen. These chancellors in the Court of Chancery built up a system (called *equity* as distinct from English common law), which changed the English and American administration of justice quite as much as the rulings of the *praetor peregrinus* in Rome altered Roman law.

Anglo-American Law.—The law of the United States and of England is fundamentally Germanic rather than Roman. In the fields of equity and admiralty law and in the details of many other portions of English and American law there are Roman influences, but they are not basic and have frequently been exaggerated. When Roman law in the 16th century was more or less adopted and fused with native local law in most countries of Europe—what is known as the Reception—nothing of the sort happened in England. So English law is related to the native legal systems of continental Western Europe through the common Germanic elements of the continental nations' laws and the English law. All the absolutely fundamental doctrines of our property law, for example, are pure Germanic doctrines of the early medieval period; indeed, they are decidedly more so than the principles of the present property law of Germany, because that has so many elements of Roman law from the time of the Reception.

The phrase *common law* is likely to be misunderstood, because it is used in several different senses. It means Anglo-American law as contrasted with the Roman law and its present descendants, the civil law and canon law. It also means that portion of our legal system that is not equity. Sometimes Common law means our traditional or customary law as contrasted with our statutory law which is made by legislatures. The phrase *common law* refers to the origin of English (and so American) law in general customs common to the whole kingdom of England as distinguished from peculiar local and class customs which differed widely among themselves. This common legal custom was gradually formulated in the King's courts as distinct from local courts. It came about mainly as a process of genuine discovery, but in part by deliberate suppression of local

customs which the Crown was not for some reason bound to respect. The royal courts gave the Crown revenue and power. Royal justices traveled on circuit through the country, bringing the king's justice to every subject, expediting justice, making it cheaper than it would have been if litigants had been compelled to travel to the court at Westminster. They offered suitors the great advantages of jury trial, and gradually the king's justice displaced almost all local and feudal jurisdictions of a general nature. Statutory law also became of great importance in the medieval period. In the reign (1154–89) of Henry II the circuit system was established—judges taking the king's court to different parts of the realm—and the power of ecclesiastical courts began to be limited and lessened. In the reign of Edward I (1272–1307) there were many important statutes, especially about inheritance and transfer of real estate, with further limitations of the power of the Church and increase in the power of the Crown. Under Henry VIII the Act of Supremacy made the King head of the English Church and again reduced the importance of the ecclesiastical courts and increased that of the king's courts.

Colonial Law.

The English law has not always been so supreme in America as it is today. The Englishmen who settled our thirteen colonies wanted and found in America freedom from tradition. As Sir Guy Carleton said, it was "impossible for the dignity of the throne or peerage to be represented in the American forest." The colonists judged many English institutions to be unnecessary or unsuitable. They did not transplant bodily and immediately to American soil the legal system of the mother country. They lacked, at first, the books and the knowledge that would have made it possible; but they also lacked, at first, the desire to do so. Many of them had fled from England to find freedom from political or ecclesiastical constraints, and they may well have included in their distrust or enmity the courts as a part of the English governmental system and the law as the bulwark of the economic and social order of that country. Only three of the thirteen colonies *formally* recognized English law as governing, in fact, their administration of justice. Several explicitly denied its binding character and for a long time acted upon this denial. In Massachusetts, for example, there was for a time a sort of Bible Commonwealth under the Mosaic Code. Each of the colonies at some time used some sort of code, fundamental law or body of statutes chosen as meeting its particular needs. All passed their own laws and quarreled with the home government and its local representatives over lawmaking. Sometimes they violated English law and even their own charters. In early Massachusetts the government actually imprisoned men who wanted to appeal to English courts. Many important innovations in the law were thus made It was all an aspect of the growing away from England which culminated in the Revolution. Positive and general distrust of English institutions was largely confined to New England in the period of its early settlement.

English Law Paramount.

In the 18th century there was a constant development of local governmental institutions; there were clashing policies regarding trade and taxes, and bickerings with royal agents over the mother country's rights of political control; and these factors were sweeping the colonies toward the Revolution. But that began with a Declaration of Independence, which was from end to end an argument that the colonists here had been denied the rights of Englishmen at home. In the 18th century English lawbooks became more abundant. Scores of colonists were trained for the legal profession in England, especially after 1750. It became clear that for the regulation of the mutual rights and duties of citizens the common law had served our needs and could continue to serve them. Thus it happened that after Independence, all the original states at varying dates adopted the English Law, statutory and nonstatutory, as the basis of their own legal systems.

English and American law have countless differences in detail. Examine a particular technical point and often you can see no agreement, no relationship. You must remember that there are also countless agreements on other details. What is more important, there is a common mass of fundamental concepts, of general or basic principles; there is the same general classification of materials and the same technique of dealing with them.

American law does not entirely agree with itself. Aside from a few fields in which exclusive Federal jurisdiction creates uniformity, there is, speaking strictly, no American Law. Each state of our country has its own law, slightly affected by provisions of the Federal Constitution. But of course the resemblances between the state systems are very great, and we use the term *American law* to designate this vast mass of common concepts, rules and principles.

Documents of the Law.

English law differs from continental European law in having much more complete historical material for students of the law. The Anglo-Saxon records from the 6th century onward are numerous and inclusive and make it much easier to understand the essentially Germanic thought and institutions of early English law because they are written in the native tongue instead of Latin. And the *Year Books*, which are informal reports and colloquial discussions of actual cases in the king's courts from the late 13th century to the early 16th, are a unique record of medieval law and of a medieval language. No other country has anything like them. In modern times, too, the English and American "reports" of decided cases (almost wholly those decided in the courts of last resort alone) are unique for their fullness and vast bulk. At the present time they total between fifteen and twenty thousand volumes.

Codification.

Our law has such a huge bulk because it is uncodified—that is, it has not been boiled down and digested as Roman law was by Justinian; and the whole common-law system is based on the principle of *stare decisis, et non quieta movere,* which means, stand by decisions and do not reopen matters that are settled. Reports must be bulky to preserve the countless decisions that serve as precedents. The Romans were not excellent codifiers, but their modern followers have, in following their example of codification, improved its quality. All the civil-law countries have codified the principles of their law. Only a few states of our country have enacted their substantive law in general codes. But rules of legal procedure have been codified in nearly two-thirds of the states. By the adoption of Uniform Acts (prepared by the American Bar Association and State Commissioners on Uniform Laws) complete or nearly complete uniformity has been reached throughout the country in state legislation in certain fields of law, chiefly commercial, for example, the law of negotiable paper, sales, warehouse receipts, etc. In this indirect way some parts of American commercial law have become as well defined and as uniform as if the states had adopted a uniform commercial code. In England statutory statement of portions of the law has proceeded much farther than in the United States, and of course an Act of Parliament sets the law for all England, but the statutes of one state of our Union make law only for one state of the 48.

American statutory law, as well as the reporting of American court decisions, is immensely bulky. Just as thousands of decisions are handed down by our courts of last resort, so thousands of laws are passed by our state legislatures at every session. The decisions present a vast amount of duplication in the application of common principles to legal problems that constantly recur. In the immense output of legislation, too, there is a constant recurrence of similar problems. The significance of our legislation lies in the novel social problems with which it deals, and the opportunity presented for trying out variant public policies in different states. Novel problems of recent decades include regulating public utilities (railroads, gas and electric companies, etc.) and sales of corporate stock and bonds (*blue-sky* laws), workmen's compensation and social insurance (against old age, sickness or unemployment), formulating state labor policies, curbing fraud and unfair practices in trade, regulating automobile, truck and trailer traffic. Thus, much of our current legislation embodies the popular will of the day on issues of reform. During the last half century its quality has been greatly improved because the legislatures are employing experts to draft legislation and because nearly all our states now have legislative reference bureaus to aid legislators in the study of their problems and give aid in drafting bills. This lessens litigation, avoids invalidation of statutes by the courts on the ground that they are unconstitutional and insures more complete attainment of desired ends.

Equity.—In both England and the United States the legal system still consists of two distinct parts—the common law and equity. Equity was developed in England from the 14th century onward by the king's chancellor in his Court of Chancery, sitting as the king's representative to deal with petitions from his subjects. The early chancellors were all churchmen (no layman was chancellor until 1529), and these chancellors were all trained in the civil and canon laws that ruled in all church courts. The chancellor's court gave justice where it was not to be procured in the courts of common law because their rules were incomplete or rigid, because the principle of precedent was out of touch with the problems of the moment, because juries might be intimidated or for other reasons. Equity as a complement to our common law was like the benefit in Roman law from the *praetor peregrinus* who transformed the *jus civile* into the *jus gentium.* In both the English and the Roman system the older law was too formal, too inelastic and too narrow in its spirit. The reforming process both in Rome and in England was an emphasis upon essential fairness. The gradual absorption into our common law of the law merchant developed in international commerce and fairs by medieval merchants is another instance of the liberalization of our law and it is even more closely parallel to what the foreign praetor did at Rome.

In almost all of our states the same courts administer both legal and equitable relief. In all the code states—those with a code of civil procedure—there is only one form of civil (noncriminal) *action;* the distinction between actions at law and suits in equity has been abolished. But the distinction between law and equity is not abolished: those that originated in common law remain *legal* and those that were developed in chancery remain *equitable.* There is still some conflict between the principles of these two portions of our law; but in the long run the equitable principles generally prevail.

Equity looks through form to substance. It acts consistently on a plane of morality higher than that of the nonequity law. It is still a growing jurisdiction supplementing and humanizing the nonequity law. An English statute of 1783 and similar statutes in at least two of our states provide that, when the rules of law and equity conflict, equity shall prevail. It may be an actual advantage that the two systems of law and equity have not been fused, with equity in the predominant position; if equity is still far from perfect its doctrines should not be fixed for good and all. Many lawyers feel that equity is itself becoming too much a matter of rules and precedents. The substantive principles of the two systems have fused by a slow infiltration of equitable doctrines into all parts of the common law.

What's Wrong with the Law?—Popular criticism of the law and its administrators has for centuries been abundant (not more in our own than in other countries), and not at all confined to disappointed litigants. In our country it is directed today against the law, the judges, the bar and the administrative officials who enforce the judgments of the courts and provisions of the statutes.

The law is considered by many to be unduly conservative. Undeniably it lags behind social changes. Law is the embodiment of what purport, at least, to be society's pondered judgments on its fundamental interests. Our constitutions and statute-books record our theories of government, our standards of governmental organization. If our legislators truly represent us the laws they make must reflect our general attitudes toward agriculture, trade, industry and transportation. They embody our conception of men's basic mutual rights and duties, our measurement of the individual against society, our ideals regarding religion, education, personal freedom, personal security, the protection of youth and age and the succor of the physically and mentally infirm, our attitudes toward the problems of poverty and of labor—in short, the estimates of every kind which we make of our own day and forecast of our children's day. Nobody will deny that all these estimates need persistent scrutiny and occasional revision—that the law should constantly be criticized. This is true both of public law and of the substantive rules of the private law that reflect our conceptions of individualism and express the mutual rights and duties of individuals. It must be admitted, however, that our criticism cannot be very scientific or accurate. We may all agree that a law or institution works well or ill, but we cannot state mathematically how well or how badly. There is no established method of scientific measurement for that. On fundamentals the law is conservative—for it is the designed conservator of fundamentals. Courts in their opinions occasionally suggest desirable changes in procedure or in the substance of the law; our state attorneys general sometimes do the same. In twenty states Judicial Councils exist for improvement of the procedural law alone. All the states occasionally, in revising their statutes, have introduced improvements. Not one state has yet provided a permanent instrumentality that will continuously scrutinize the statutory law and the nonstatutory law (both substantive and procedural) with the duty of suggesting amendments. This should be done. The creation of such reformative agencies is probably near. Far less is wrong with the law, however, than with its administrators.

The judges, many critics of our law consider, should make more and better law. The judge's power to make law is based on his adapting rules and precedents of the past to the changing needs of today, and so the opportunity of a judge to make law is limited. The network of precedents covers the field of law. It has been well said that only within the interstices of this net can the courts make law, and that even then they make it by analogy. A judge's decision that is contrary to a prior and clear decision of a higher court or that disregards such a decision will be reversed on appeal, unless the higher court reverses its previous decision, which seldom happens. In another sense, however, every judge has daily opportunities to make law; for he may lessen the infinite obscurities in the opinions supporting earlier decision. Unintelligent opinions have literally filled the law with obscurities. There are some problems in property law, for instance, that have been recognized literally for centuries, but the treatment of them by the courts has not improved in all that time. A statement about such a problem by a court in 1900 or 1938 is no more modern than one from Coke on Littleton in 1629 or even one from Perkins's *Profitable Book* printed in 1530. The rule of *stare decisis,* the judge's compulsory habit of looking to the past for the rules which govern problems of the present—that is what makes of most judges somewhat stodgy conservatives. Another reason is that almost all judges, before they attain judicial office, are successful practitioners who serve important business interests, so that from these associations judges naturally acquire a conservative attitude on social and economic questions. It may fairly be said that too few judges have any considerable knowledge of economic problems or social conditions; that too few have the ability to make desirable adjustments of the law, that too many harbor a professional aversion to change. But all criticisms of judges are really criticisms of those who elect or appoint them. The bar generally ignores its duty to lead the people or the appointing officer to a proper choice; and politics and indifference are the causes for this state of affairs.

The same is true of all our public prosecutors and others who represent the state in the administration of the law. Surveys of crime conditions have been made in various cities and states. They have all shown in varying degree the powerful and baneful influence of politics at every step—in determining whether or not to arrest a suspect, whether to hold an inquiry before the grand jury, whether to indict him, whether to *nolle prosequi* (do not prosecute) the action, whether to parole him from prison, whether to pardon him. With rare exceptions the office of public prosecutor is given not to career men who know the law but to political neophytes who want to make that office a springboard to some other political position.

The educational and moral standards for admission to the bar are not sufficiently high, and disbarment proceedings after admission are much too infrequent. Law has come a long way in its thousands of years of slow development. The slow advance has been considerably accelerated in the last three centuries, maybe even more in the last century. There is hope for the future—especially if there is a more general interest in law and government with a growing sense of the responsibility each citizen has for making law more just and government more free.

LEGAL PROCEDURE

The more important principles of the law as they apply to our everyday lives may be summed up under the general head—rights under private law. And these may be classed as they are based on (1) status; (2) contract, including (a) negotiable instruments, (b) agency, (c) corporations, (d) partnership and (e) sale of personal property; (3) obligations imposed by law irrespective of agreement, which involve besides other rights a special consideration of real property, its ownership and transfer by deed, lease or will; (4) remedial rights and legal remedies, including court procedure.

(1) STATUS

Certain rights and duties exist between parties who bear a certain relationship to one another. The most striking illustration is family relationship. Rights and duties of husband and wife and of parent and child are created by the existence of those family relations and are confined to persons bearing that relation to each other. The relation of master and servant involves at common law certain consequences, and other consequences are often added by statute.

(2) CONTRACTS

Most of the ordinary transactions of business life involve applications of the law of contracts. The greater part of the law of agency, partnership, insurance, sales, negotiable paper and banking consists of specialized contractual law.

The simplest and also most accurate conception of a contract is a promise or a number of promises forming part of a single transaction to which the law attaches legal obligation. Promises of competent parties may be binding because of their form or because of their essential character. Contracts of the first kind are called formal, of the second kind, informal or simple contracts.

Requisites of Contracts.—Both formal and informal contracts may consist wholly of a promise or promises by one party only or of mutual promises by the parties. In the former case the contract is called unilateral, in the latter case it is called bilateral. Both formal and informal contracts require that the parties undertaking to contract shall have capacity for that purpose. Both types also may be invalidated by being opposed to statute or public policy; or by being induced by fraud, duress or essential mistake.

A contract is voidable when it may be avoided at the option of one of the parties. The term *void contract,* sometimes used for an agreement or promise having no legal effect, is a contradiction in terms. Being void, such an agreement is not a contract.

Incompetent Parties.—In order to protect certain classes of persons, their capacity to make a binding contract has been limited by law. They may be divided into the following classes: (1) infants; (2) insane persons; (3) drunkards; (4) married women; (5) corporations.

Infants. At common law, all persons under twenty-one years of age are infants. In a few states, however, by statute females are of age at eighteen.

An infant's contract for necessities is legally binding, but his other contracts are voidable by him. Necessaries consist of whatever, in view of his station in life, and his supplies from other sources, is essential for his welfare. An infant may avoid his contracts within a reasonable time after he becomes of age, and if he has not received property which he still retains, his power of avoidance is generally not limited in time, but in some states an infant who has received property can never avoid obligations without returning what he has received. Even for necessaries an infant is liable only for their fair value. He is liable for his torts or wrongdoings of a civil nature.

Insane Persons. Agreements of a person so insane as to be totally incapable of understanding what he is doing are generally void. If not insane to that degree, his contracts are generally voidable in the same way as the contracts of an infant. In some states, however, if an insane person not wholly devoid of reason has received fair consideration for his promise and the person with whom he dealt had no knowledge of the insanity, the contract is held valid.

Drunkards are under no positive disability unless their intoxication is so great as to deprive them wholly of the use of their mental faculties. In that event they are dealt with like insane persons. The fact, however, that a person is slightly intoxicated may render him more easily a prey to fraudulent persons; thus drunkenness is often a relevant fact in determining whether a transaction was induced by fraud.

Married Women. At common law a married woman could not contract or acquire a contract right or other personal property or retain the ownership of such rights or personal property that she had at the time of her marriage. Courts of equity, however, from an early day, have protected her separate estate and recognized her contracts relative thereto. This estate included all property both real and personal, which was settled upon her to her sole and separate use. The legal title to it had to be in some other person (who might be her husband), who held it in trust for her. The Married Women's Acts, which are in force in every state of the Union, have so far enlarged the rights and powers of married women that they are generally under no disability or only unable to contract with their husbands **or to** become surety.

Corporations are created by the state and have only the powers given them by their charters. They may make contracts, provided they act within the scope of their charters. Contracts attempted beyond that scope are *ultra vires* (exceeding legal power or authority).

Formal Contracts are of two kinds: (1) promises made as part of proceedings in court and (2) promises under seal. At common law the seal consisted of an impression on wax or a wafer attached to a written instrument. By statute, however, a mere scroll generally has the same effect as a common-law seal. By more comprehensive statutes, in some states seals are now wholly abolished, and in many other states if it is proved that there was not such consideration as is necessary for informal contracts, a promise under seal is not binding.

Informal or Simple Contracts depend for their validity upon a manifestation of mutual assent and sufficient consideration to support the promises of the parties. Informal contracts are at the present time of much the greatest importance everywhere, and in many states owing to the abolition of seals or a diminution of their legal effect all contracts are informal.

Mutual Assent.—Expression of assent to a contract, as a practical matter, can be secured only by an offer by one person and acceptance by the person to whom the offer is made. An offer to contract is a promise, in terms conditional on there being given in exchange for it another promise or some specified performance. Giving such other promise or performance is itself a manifestation of acceptance. Before such acceptance takes place, however, and making any subsequent acceptance ineffective, an offer may be terminated: (1) by revocation by the offeror; (2) by rejection by the offeree; (3) by death or insanity of either party; (4) by lapse of an unreasonable time for acceptance. An offer may be made not simply by spoken or written words but by acts manifesting the offeree's intention or by both words and acts. Thus an order given to a shopkeeper implies a promise to pay for the goods requested, if they are furnished.

An offer can be accepted only by the person to whom it is addressed. The method of accepting an offer for a unilateral contract is by doing the act requested in the offer. An offer for a bilateral contract is accepted by giving the promise that the offeror requested. The offeror may impose any conditions in his offer that he sees fit, and in order to form a contract the offeree must always comply with these conditions. When an offer is made by mail, an acceptance by mail, if properly addressed and stamped, takes effect when it is posted. The fact that it is lost in the mail is immaterial. The offeror, however, may make actual receipt of the letter of acceptance a condition of his offer. The rule in regard to acceptance by telegraph is the same as in the case of acceptance by post. Use of the mail or telegraph must have been expressly or impliedly authorized by the offeror in order to

make the mere despatch of a letter or telegram a valid acceptance. Use of that means in communicating the offer or general custom may give the requisite authority by implication.

Like an offer, acceptance may be indicated by acts as well as by words. A contract is called an express contract where the assent of the parties is manifested by oral or written words. An implied contract is one where assent is inferred from the acts of the parties. Obligations to pay for benefits received, though not created by any manifestation of assent, are also sometimes called implied contracts, but are better called quasi contracts.

Consideration.—Consideration means an exchange given for a promise. In order to support a promise there must be something given in exchange for it, and the exchange must be such as the law requires. Therefore, a promise to make a gift is not enforceable, though an actual gift accompanied with delivery of chattel property is effectual, since the donee then relies on possession of the chattel not on a promise. Consideration for a unilateral contract is legally sufficient if it is anything which the promisee was not previously under a legal obligation to do or give, and a *promise* of any such thing is sufficient consideration for a bilateral contract. Payment of all or part of an admitted debt or a promise of such payment is, therefore, insufficient consideration for a promise by the creditor. A promise, though conditional on the happening of an event which may never occur (such as a promise to pay money if a house burns) is, however, sufficient consideration for another promise. It is also immaterial that consideration for a promise is of little or no pecuniary value so long as the offeror requested it and the offeree was not bound to give it. It is a common error to suppose that inserting in a contract the clause "in consideration of one dollar" automatically makes a contract binding; but it must be borne in mind that the courts are always ready to find any additional promissory advantage beside the small consideration which will establish the intent.

Promises Binding Without Assent or Consideration.—There are very few promises which are binding without any acceptance by the promisee and without any consideration. Such are promises to pay a debt of the promisor, recovery of which has been barred by the Statute of Limitations or by discharge in bankruptcy.

Necessity of Writing.—An early English statute, called the Statute of Frauds, required certain contracts to be in writing, or a written memorandum to be made signed by the party to be charged, stating the terms of the contract, in order that such contracts should be enforceable. This statute has been substantially re-enacted in all the United States. The contracts that are thus required to be in writing are the following: (1) contracts by an executor or an administrator to pay damages out of his own estate; (2) contracts to answer for the debt or default of another;

(3) contracts in consideration of marriage, that is, contracts for marriage settlements; (4) contracts for the sale of any interest in land; (5) contracts which cannot be performed within a year from their formation; (6) promises to pay an antecedent debt that otherwise would be barred by the Statute of Limitations; (7) promises to accept a bill of exchange; and certain other contracts under the statutes of most American states, require a writing.

In some states also a writing is necessary to make enforceable promises: (1) to revive a debt barred by a discharge in bankruptcy; (2) to make a will or leave a legacy; (3) to authorize an agent for some purposes; (4) to pay commissions to real estate brokers.

Under the English statute, a written memorandum signed by the party to be charged was also required to make enforceable sales and contracts to sell chattels exceeding £10 in value, if no part of the goods were accepted and actually received by the buyer, and no earnest money or part of the price paid by him. There were thus alternative methods besides a written memorandum for making such transactions enforceable. About three-fourths of the United States have enacted a similar statute, but in these states the minimum amount necessary to bring the transaction within the statute varies greatly. In Ohio it is $2,500. In no other state is it higher than $500, the figure adopted in a number of States. In others it is $50.

Illegal Contracts.—An agreement to do an act which is prohibited by positive law or which is against public policy is illegal and cannot be enforced by a party who knew the facts making the agreement illegal. A party who has no reason to know such facts may, however, recover damages for breach of an illegal contract. Thus if a married man engages himself to an unmarried woman who does not know he is already married, she can maintain an action for breach of promise.

Wagering Contracts. In this country wagering contracts are not enforceable. They include not only ordinary bets but speculative transactions where the parties do not contemplate a delivery of goods or shares of stock bought or sold but merely payment of the difference between the contract price and a subsequent market price.

Sunday Contracts. Sunday contracts, as a rule, are prohibited by statute. At common law, however, they were enforceable. The statutes of the various states vary considerably, but all exempt from their operation contracts founded upon works of charity or necessity. Under these statutes, contracts not within this exemption are illegal. Formal contracts and negotiable instruments take effect on delivery. Therefore, bills of exchange, promissory notes, bonds, deeds and mortgages delivered on Sunday are illegal although signed on a secular day. But those delivered on a secular day are enforceable although signed on Sunday. An informal contract takes effect on acceptance of an offer. Therefore if an offer is made on Saturday and the acceptance is given on Sunday, the transaction is invalid; but an acceptance on Monday of an offer made on Sunday creates a valid contract.

Usury Statutes. Usury statutes obtain in nearly all of the states. Usury is interest contracted for or paid in excess of the legal rate. The purpose of the usury statutes is to protect debtors from overreaching creditors. They vary in the different states. A few make the entire contract void. Others make the interest void. Still others merely make the excess above the legal rate void. They apply to loans but not to sales. Hence they are not applicable where bills or notes are discounted by a third party. Nor, by the Law Merchant, do they apply where a banker in loaning money, deducts in advance the highest rate of interest allowable. Devices to cover an intent to obtain usury by commissions or bonuses are carefully scrutinized by the courts.

Contracts in Restraint of Marriage. Contracts which unduly restrain a person from marrying are against policy and void. Thus, a contract never to marry or not to marry any one but a certain person to whom the promisor is not already engaged is void. But a contract not to marry until of age is valid. And ordinarily a contract not to marry without the consent of the promisor's parents is valid.

Contracts facilitating divorce or separation of married couples are illegal, though after actual separation a contract fixing the amount of settlement is valid.

Contracts in Restraint of Trade. From early times contracts unreasonably restraining employees whose employment had terminated from exercising their skill were held to be illegal. A restraint was unreasonable which exceeded what was necessary for the protection of the promisee, as where it would prohibit exercise of the promisor's occupation in territory beyond the scope of the promisee's business. This is still law both in England and in the United States; and a similar rule invalidates contracts prohibiting competitors in a business or profession from exercising that business or profession beyond the extent necessary for the protection of the business purchased. The prohibition of contracts in restraint of trade has been extended, especially in the United States, to all contracts the tendency of which is to obtain a substantial monopoly, and statutes have been passed both by the Federal Government (the Sherman Law) and by many states making any transaction, whether by contract or by actual combination, illegal and in many cases criminal.

Contracts Obstructing Justice. Contracts by which a lawyer or other person undertakes to pay the expense of litigation and to receive in return a share of the proceeds of the litigation are generally, though not universally, held illegal. Contracts to refrain from prosecuting or disclosing a criminal offense are also illegal. An injured person may refrain from prosecuting but he may not bargain for consideration for so doing.

Contracts Tending to Political or Business Corruption. Lobbying contracts are illegal though contracts to argue in favor of legislation before legislative committees are valid. Contracts for procuring public contracts, for the appointment or compensation of officials, for procuring pardons or for the location of public buildings are also illegal, as are contracts to secure the election to office in a private corporation and contracts of agents or other fiduciaries for secret commissions or for any purpose which tends to impair fidelity.

Miscellaneous Illegal Contracts. Contracts with alien enemies are forbidden. Contracts already existing with them are suspended if they involve merely unilateral obligations to pay money or transfer property; but existing contracts which would require continued exchange of performance during war are wholly voided. Contracts to promote illegal acts or to indemnify one who performs them are prohibited. However, mere knowledge by a seller that the buyer intends to use goods purchased for an illegal purpose does not generally preclude recovery of the price. Revenue statutes and licensing statutes also may make contracts illegal.

Rules of Interpretation.—The ultimate purpose of rules for interpreting contracts is to ascertain their meaning, which often is not clearly expressed. To accomplish this the following rules are applied by the courts:

When the contract is in writing, its purport cannot be contradicted or varied by proof of oral agreements or conversations. This rule does not apply, however, where the writing is a mere memorandum of the contract or where the purpose in introducing oral testimony is to show fraud, illegality, mistake of expression, usage or custom or a condition precedent to the writing becoming effective. Nor does it apply to subsequent oral agreements. Nor to oral testimony whose purpose is to explain not contradict the meaning of terms.

When the instrument is partly written and partly printed and the written and the printed parts conflict, the writing controls.

In both oral and written contracts words must be interpreted in their plain, common meaning. If, however, the context or surrounding circumstances show that the parties intended to use them in a peculiar or technical sense, the words then take that special meaning.

When doubt exists as to the meaning of a word or clause, it is construed most strongly against the party using it.

When words or clauses are repugnant, those which are opposed to the manifest intention of the parties are rejected.

Subsequent acts of the parties may have a controlling influence in determining the meaning of their agreement. In no case, however, will they be allowed to defeat the plain import of their words.

The various parts of the instrument must be construed together. When there are several contemporaneous agreements relating to the same transaction, they must be construed in the light of one another. And when one or more other papers are directly referred to in the instrument as constituting an inducement to the contract, they are entitled to consideration.

Mistake. Where parties to a contract bargain on the assumption that an essential fact exists and it does not, the contract is voidable. The mistake must be mutual and relate to a vital fact that was assumed as a basis of the bargain.

Misrepresentation, as distinguished from fraud, is an innocent misstatement or nondisclosure of a fact. Though formerly this had no effect on a contract, the prevailing tendency is now to treat it as ground for voiding a contract. Mere nondisclosure, however, does not ordinarily have this consequence. There are, however, some exceptions to this rule. Where one party justifiably relies upon the other party for knowledge of certain facts, that other party in consequence is bound to exercise the utmost good faith. Such contracts are insurance contracts, and those made between parties occupying a fiduciary relation, such as guardian and ward, trustee and *cestui que trust,* attorney and client, principal and agent.

Fraud is a misrepresentation of a material fact, present or past, made with knowledge of its falsity or in reckless disregard whether it is true or false, which deceives the other party, to his injury.

Ordinarily, to constitute fraud, there must be the intentional use of deception or artifice to cheat another. There are, however, some exceptions to this rule. Where the deceiving party is duty bound to make a disclosure, where he takes steps to prevent a disclosure or where the concealment renders that which is stated false, the nondisclosure amounts to fraud. The effect of fraud upon a contract is to make it voidable at the option of the injured party.

Duress is actual or threatened violence or imprisonment which reasonably causes another to enter into a contract. It may be by one of the parties to the contract or by his agent. And it may be directed against either the other party to the contract, or his or her spouse or other near relative. It may consist of the threatened destruction of property, or, under oppressive circumstances, of the illegal detention of property. Its effect is to render the contract voidable.

Undue Influence. Undue influence is akin to duress. It consists in one of the parties to the contract taking an unfair advantage over the other party, who reposes confidence in him, possesses a weak intellect or is in distress. Like fraud, its effect upon a contract is to render it legally voidable.

Modes of Discharging a Contract.—Contracts are discharged: (1) by agreement; (2) by performance; (3) by impossibility of performance; (4) by breach; (5) by operation of law in a few less common ways.

Discharge by Agreement. The parties may agree that their contract shall no longer bind them. Such an agreement is called a *waiver, cancellation* or *rescission.* Express words of rescission are not essential. When the parties make a new contract which is inconsistent with the old one, the old contract is discharged. In such case if a third party is substituted for one of the original parties with the consent of all three, the new agreement is called a *novation.* A unilateral obligation, however, cannot be discharged by mere agreement. The same requirement of sufficient consideration for creating an unsealed contract exists for discharging contractual rights as for creating them. Where both parties are under an obligation, the mere agreement of each to surrender his rights is enough.

Discharge by Performance. Strict and full performance of a contract discharges it.

Performance may consist in payment of money or negotiable paper. In the latter case the performance may be absolute or conditional. Ordinarily, a presumption arises that the payee is entitled to sue on the original contract if the paper is not paid when due.

Rejection of tender or of an offer to perform may constitute a release. Thus, when a party offers to render services, deliver goods or do some other act which he is bound to perform and the tender is definitely refused, he is released if the contract is bilateral.

If, however, there is merely a unilateral obligation to pay money or render some other performance capable of subsequent fulfilment, a tender of what is due does not discharge the debt. Usually, however, it stops the accrual of interest, and also puts the burden of costs on the creditor in case he sues to recover the debt. Moreover, if any security for the debt exists, it discharges it.

Discharge by Impossibility of Performance. When impossibility of performance arises subsequently to the formation of the contract, it does not discharge it in every case. It does, however: (1) when the contract is one for personal services, and death or incapacitating illness supervenes; (2) when the continued existence of some specific thing or means of performance is essential to the performance and it ceases to exist through no fault of either party; (3) when the impossibility is created by domestic law; (4) in a few recent cases it has been held that a change in facts that were understood to be a basic assumption in the formation of the contract, entirely frustrating the object or value of performance of the contract, discharges it.

Discharge by Breach. Breach of the contract by one of the parties always gives the other party a right of action for damages, and if it is a material breach and the injured party so elects, it discharges the contract.

Other Methods of Discharge by Operation of Law. Contracts are discharged by operation of law: (1) by merger; (2) by cancellation or destruction of a formal contract; (3) by

alteration. Remedies under a contract may also be barred by a discharge in bankruptcy or by the Statute of Limitations.

Merger is the absorption or extinguishing of a lesser security by a greater, whereby the lesser ceases to exist but the greater is not increased. A contract under seal will merge a simple contract, and a judgment will merge a contract under seal. But a written contract not under seal will not merge an oral one because they are of equal grade. Each is merely a simple contract.

Cancellation or Destruction of a formal unilateral contract if done intentionally by the promisee discharges it.

Alteration of a written contract discharges it provided the alteration is material and is made fraudulently and intentionally by one of the parties to it or by his agent without the consent of the other party.

(a) NEGOTIABLE INSTRUMENTS

The law of negotiable instruments differs from the general law of contracts in that it is practically uniform throughout the United States. The Uniform Negotiable Instruments Law has been adopted, with only minor changes, in all of the states, the District of Columbia and American possessions.

Assignment of an ordinary contract does not fully substitute a new contract with the assignor for the original one. Negotiability gives substantially this effect.

An instrument to be negotiable must conform to the following requirements: (1) it must be in writing and signed by the maker or drawer; (2) it must contain an unconditional promise to pay a sum certain in money; (3) it must be payable on demand or at a fixed or determinable future time; (4) it must be payable to order or to the bearer; and (5) where an instrument is addressed to a drawee, he must be named or otherwise indicated therein with reasonable certainty.

Bills of Exchange.—A bill of exchange is an unconditional order in writing addressed by one person to another, signed by the person giving it, requiring the person to whom it is addressed to pay on demand or at a fixed or determinable future time a certain sum in money to order or to the bearer.

Bills of exchange are of two kinds: (1) foreign and (2) domestic. A foreign bill of exchange is a bill drawn in one state or country and payable in another state or country. A domestic or inland bill of exchange is a bill which is payable in the state or country in which it is drawn.

The necessary parties to a bill of exchange are the drawer, the drawee and the payee. There may be, in addition, indorsers and indorsees. After the drawee accepts the bill he is called the acceptor. By accepting the bill he becomes the party primarily liable.

Unless the drawer has directed that presentment be made for acceptance it is not essential in the case of bills payable on demand or on a certain date to present them for acceptance. It is customary to do so, however, with those payable at a specified time. Those payable a certain number of days after sight or demand must be presented for acceptance within a reasonable time.

The drawee is entitled to inspect the bill and to refrain from acting for twenty-four hours. This is to enable him to investigate the drawer's account before deciding whether he will accept the bill or not.

An acceptance which differs from the tenor of the bill may be refused by the holder; but if he consents to receive it, he can have no greater right.

Promissory Notes.—A promissory note is an unconditional promise in writing made by one person to another signed by the maker engaging to pay on demand or at a fixed or determinable future time a certain sum in money to order or bearer. If a note is drawn to the maker's own order, it is not complete until endorsed by him. The liability of the maker, unlike that of the drawer of a bill of exchange, is primary and unconditional.

Negotiation. A bill or note payable to bearer or payable to order and indorsed in blank is transferable thereafter by mere delivery. The transferor in such case impliedly warrants the genuineness of the signatures and the body of the instrument. He also impliedly warrants the capacity of the parties to make a contract and his title to the instrument.

When the instrument is payable to order and has not been indorsed or when it has been specially indorsed by naming the indorsee, any further transfer will require the indorsement of the indorsee. Without such indorsement the equitable title will pass but not the legal title.

Indorser. An indorser of a bill or note not only impliedly warrants all that a transferor by mere delivery impliedly warrants, but also, in the case of an unaccepted bill payable at a certain future time, that it will be accepted unconditionally by the drawee when duly presented for acceptance; and in the case of a promissory note or an accepted bill payable at a certain future time, that it will be paid at maturity if duly presented for payment or, if payable on demand, that it will be paid when demand of payment is made, if that demand is made within a reasonable time. And furthermore, that in case of dishonor, either by nonacceptance or nonpayment after due demand, he will pay the obligation if due notice of the dishonor is sent to him.

Where there are two or more indorsers they are liable *prima facie* in the order in which their names appear on the instrument.

A drawer of a bill or indorser of a bill or note is not liable unless the instrument is on presentment to the drawee or maker at maturity dishonored by him and prompt notice of the dishonor sent. Notice of dishonor may be oral. Ordinarily, however, it is in writing. It should contain statements showing: (1) a sufficient description of the instrument dishonored; (2) that it was presented for acceptance or payment; (3) that acceptance or payment was refused; (4) that it has been protested, if protest is necessary; (5) that the holder looks for payment to the party notified.

Protesting a bill or note consists in taking the necessary formal steps, usually by a notary public although it may be done by any respectable resident with two or more creditable witnesses, to establish and certify to its dishonor. It is essential that the same notary take all the steps required and that the certificate of protest be based upon his acts.

Protest is necessary only in case of bills or notes made in one state or country and payable in another. Presentment, notice and protest may be waived. Sometimes the waiver is written with an indorsement. Even after failure of the holder to exercise the required diligence to charge a drawer or indorser, a promise by him to waive the deficiency is effective.

A restrictive indorsement is one which restrains further indorsement of the bill or note. Title is vested in the indorsee as a trustee or agent. Thus, "Pay to John Brown for my use" or "Pay to John Doe for my account" are restrictive indorsements.

Checks.—A check is a bill of exchange drawn on a bank, payable on demand.

A checkholder, as a rule, may not sue the bank. The bank's duty is to the depositor, and it will be liable to him for failing to pay a properly drawn check when there are funds. When the check has been previously certified by an authorized officer of the bank, that operates as an acceptance and the bank becomes liable to the holder. When the holder of the check procures the certification, the drawer and the indorsers are released.

A check should be presented within a reasonable time. What constitutes a reasonable time depends upon the circumstances of the particular case. If through neglect to present within a reasonable time the drawer should suffer, as where the bank fails, the drawer is discharged to the extent of the injury suffered. One who takes an overdue check, like one who takes any overdue bill or note, is subject to equitable defenses of the maker.

When the fund of a depositor is attached, the bank, as a rule, may not pay his checks unless they have been certified before the attachment.

When a bank pays to a holder in due course a check whose signature is forged, it must bear the loss. And when it pays a raised check to such a holder, it also must bear the loss, unless the drawer's negligence in making out the check facilitated the forgery.

Holders in Due Course of negotiable paper are persons who take it in good faith, without notice of equities in the usual course of business, for a valuable consideration and before maturity.

As a rule, such a holder of negotiable paper takes it free from all equities. Negotiable paper is endowed with the capacity for transfer, and it is not the purpose of the law that, when it passes from hand to hand, its origin shall be scrutinized at the peril of nonpayment. In that way its valuable quality is not impaired or lost. The requirement is that the transfer shall be made with honest intent and belief by the purchaser that the paper is the evidence of an honest indebtedness. To constitute notice of an infirmity in the instrument or defect in the title of the person negotiating the instrument, the person to whom it is negotiated must have had actual knowledge of the infirmity or defect or knowledge of such facts that his action in taking the instrument amounted to bad faith.

(b) Agency

An agent is one who represents and acts for another who is called his principal. Agency is the relation which exists between such persons. The relation of agency may be created by agreement or by operation of law.

Creation by Agreement may be by appointment or by ratification. Appointment is a manifestation by the principal to the agent that the agent may act on his account and consent by the agent so to act. Ratification is the principal's adoption of an act by an unauthorized agent. To create the agency relation by ratification the following conditions must exist: (1) the doer of the act must profess to do it on behalf of an existing principal; (2) the approval of the act must be given with full knowledge of all the facts; (3) the act must be approved as a whole. It may not be approved in part and repudiated in part.

Creation by Operation of Law.—As a rule, the agency relation is created by agreement of the parties. There are, however, two important exceptions to this rule: (1) agency by estoppel or apparent authority; (2) agency by necessity. In these cases there is no assent of the parties. The relation is created by operation of law.

In the case of agency by estoppel (automatic bar) the principal by his act estops (or bars) himself from disputing the agency. As said by an eminent judge, "Where one has so acted as from his conduct to lead another to believe he has appointed some one to act on that belief, then, unless he interposes, he will, in general, be estopped from disputing the agency, though in fact no agency really existed."

An example of agency by necessity is that which arises where a husband improperly fails to furnish his wife with necessaries. In this case, as Chief Justice Holmes said, "it [the law] creates a compulsory agency."

Agents.—Agents are classified by the scope of their authority and also by the nature of their duties.

By scope of authority agents are either general or special. A general agent is an agent authorized to conduct a series of transactions involving a continuity of service, and a special agent is one authorized to conduct a single transaction or a series of transactions not involving a continuity of service.

By the nature of their duties, agents are either professional or nonprofessional. The former include brokers, factors, commission merchants, auctioneers and attorneys at law.

Capacity of the Parties. Any person who has legal capacity to act in his own right may act through an agent. And any person who has sufficient natural capacity to perform the act delegated to him may be an agent. Thus an infant or married woman may appoint an agent who will have the same powers as the principal, and an infant or other person incompetent to bind himself may act as an agent and legally bind his principal.

Appointment of Agents. Ordinarily, an agent may be appointed orally. In some cases, however, by statute, a writing is essential. At common law, to empower an agent to bind his principal by an instrument under seal, the agent's authority must be under seal. At present, however, as has been previously said, seals have been abolished in many states and even where they still have force the rule is subject to the following exceptions: (1) where the instrument is sealed in the presence of the principal by his authority; (2) where the instrument does not require a seal for its validity.

Duties and Liabilities of Agents. An agent must be loyal to his trust and obey instructions. He must not engage in enterprises antagonistic to the interest of his principal nor reap secret benefits at the expense of his principal. He must exercise due care and skill and keep regular accounts of his transactions connected with the agency. If he exceeds his authority as agent, he is liable to a third party with whom he deals as well as to his principal. And in all cases he is liable to third parties injured by his torts just as if he were not an agent.

Rights of Agents. An agent is entitled to the compensation agreed upon or to reasonable compensation where no sum is fixed by agreement. If the term is fixed and he is wrongfully discharged, he has the option of treating the contract as rescinded and recovering the actual value of the services rendered or of treating the contract as subsisting and recovering damages for the breach. If he should decide to do the latter, it is wiser to wait until the end of the term, since the damages are otherwise uncertain.

Liabilities of Principal. Besides the duties to the agent involved in the preceding statement of the agent's rights, it is the duty of the principal to give instructions to his agent what duties he is to perform, to furnish him with proper appliances and so forth. The acts of the agent within the scope of the agency are the acts of the principal, and the principal is liable to third persons for them.

Termination of the Agency Relation. The agency relation may be terminated as follows: (1) by act of the parties; (2) by expiration of the term; (3) by operation of law.

(1) The parties may terminate the relation at any time by mutual agreement. Moreover, as a rule, either party has the actual power to re-nounce the agency at any time. In doing so, however, he is liable in damages for breach of his contract. The only exception to this rule is where the agent's authority is coupled with a proprietary interest in the subject matter of the agency. In such case the principal cannot renounce the agency.

(2) When the agency is created for a definite period, it expires at the end of the term; if no time is specified it terminates at the end of a reasonable time.

(3) The chief causes by which the agency relation may be terminated by operation of law are: death, loss of capacity of principal or agent, impossibility, war, bankruptcy and accomplishment of the authorized act. There are certain types of agency, such as a power coupled with an interest, which are not terminated even by the death of the agent so interested.

(c) CORPORATIONS

A business corporation from a strictly legal point of view is an artificial person created by law and distinct from its members. Practically, however, it is an association of natural persons endowed with power by the legislature to carry on business enterprises in many respects as an individual.

How Corporations are Created.—In this country they are created by the legislature and as a rule under general statutes. Under these statutes the charter of the corporation consists of the certificate of incorporation, the articles of association and the statutory provisions.

Corporate Attributes and Powers.—As a legal entity, a business corporation has capacity within the limits fixed by its charter and by law to exercise the legal functions of a natural person.

Corporate Management.—The ultimate power in a corporation rests in its members. In a business corporation they are the stockholders. They choose a board of directors, and this board is entrusted with the direct management of the business. For carrying out this work a president, secretary and treasurer are usually chosen by the board. By-laws established by the corporation on its formation with subsequent amendments fix the duties of officers and other details.

Each stockholder is usually entitled to one vote for each share of stock owned and by statute may be permitted to cumulate them as he chooses. He may also vote by proxy. But voting power is often restricted in the charter to a special class or classes of stockholders.

The board of directors usually has a wide discretion in the management of the business. It has sole power to declare dividends and to fix the time and place of payment. As a rule, the majority of the directors constitute a quorum. The board has authority to select agents of the corporation but not to decide upon important changes in the company's business nor to determine whether the business shall be wound up or not.

Liability of Shareholders.—As a rule, the shareholders whose subscriptions are fully paid are not liable to the creditors of the corporation. But by statute in various cases where they participate in the wrongful diversion of the capital of the corporation to the injury of its creditors, they are liable to them. Shareholders in national banks are liable on insolvency of the bank to pay toward its indebtedness an additional amount equal to the par value of their stock.

Modes of Dissolving a Corporation.—A corporation may be dissolved in any one of the following ways: (1) by expiration of its charter; (2) by surrender of its charter with the consent of the state; (3) by legislative enactment, provided it is constitutional; (4) by judicial proceedings for the purpose of forfeiture owing to misuser or nonuser of its franchises.

(d) PARTNERSHIPS

A partnership is an unincorporated association of two or more competent persons who have agreed to unite their property, labor and skill (entire or in part) in carrying on a lawful business as principals for their joint profit.

The requisites of a partnership are: An agreement by two or more competent persons to carry on a lawful business as principals for pecuniary gain. The contract need not be in writing unless its terms bring it within the Statute of Frauds.

Classification of Partnerships.—Partnerships are sometimes classified as ordinary partnerships, limited partnerships and joint-stock companies.

Ordinary partnerships are divided into general and special partnerships.

A general partnership is one for carrying on a general kind of business or several kinds of business. A special partnership is one created to accomplish a single adventure.

A *limited partnership,* allowed by statute in a few states, is one having one or more general partners whose liability for the firm debts is not limited, and one or more special partners whose liability is limited. In organizing this kind of partnership the provisions of the statute must be carefully followed.

Joint-stock companies are partnerships with a capital stock divided into transferable shares. In the absence of statutory provisions they are governed by the articles of association, the by-laws, and the general principles of partnership.

Classification of Partners.—Partners are designated according to the relation that exists between them and the firm or between them and third persons. Thus, depending upon such relation, they are called ostensible, active, secret, dormant, nominal, general, special, incoming, retiring or liquidating.

Powers of Partners.—As a general rule, each partner for the purposes of the partnership business is an agent of the firm and of his copartners. The extent of the agency depends upon the nature of the business. In a trading firm a partner has implied power to buy and sell goods, execute commercial paper, borrow money, pledge or mortgage firm personalty, collect debts due the firm, lease premises, hire property, appoint agents, etc. He has no implied power, however, to submit controverted partnership matters to arbitration or make a general assignment for the benefit of creditors.

In the case of a non-trading firm the implied powers of a partner are more limited. Thus, he has no implied power to bind the firm by making, accepting or indorsing commercial paper. Such paper, therefore, is not enforceable even in the hands of a *bona fide* purchaser.

Rights and Duties of Partners to One Another.—Each partner, in the absence of an agreement to the contrary, has an equal right to share in the management of the business of the firm. And each has the right to have firm property applied to the payment of firm debts.

The partnership relation is one of great confidence and trust. For this reason the law requires that partners exercise toward one another the highest integrity and good faith. In the absence of agreement, a partner must not engage in transactions antagonistic to the firm's business or take secret profits at the expense of the firm. He must conform to the partnership agreement, keep accounts, exercise care and skill and consult with his copartners upon all proper occasions.

Liability of Partners.—Partnership obligations arising from contract are joint, while those arising from tort are joint and several. Each member of the firm is personally and unlimitedly liable, however, for all the firm debts. But a partner who is compelled to pay firm debts out of his separate estate is entitled to credit for the payment in an accounting with his copartners.

Partnership Property.—The property of the firm may be both real and personal. The legal title to the firm personalty may be held in the firm name. This is sometimes allowed by statute also as to the firm realty; but apart from statute it is not possible, and even though permitted it is not wise. This is owing to the fact that the firm is not a separate legal entity. The deed should run to all of the partners in trust for the firm. It may be held by any one, however, for the use of the firm. The interest of a partner in the firm property is a peculiar one. It is simply his share in the surplus after the debts are paid. And this is all the buyer gets where a partner's interest is sold by a separate creditor under a writ of execution.

Actions in Law and Equity.—Since the firm is not a separate legal entity, a partner cannot sue his firm at law. Nor can the firm sue him. Moreover, a partner cannot sue his copartner at law except as to transactions wholly distinct from the partnership business; and also as to matters which arise prior or subsequent to the partnership and which, though connected with it, are not partnership transactions. Thus, a partner may sue his copartner at law for breach of his agreement to enter into the partnership relation, to furnish capital, pay debts, indemnify him for expenses paid or reimburse him for capital advanced.

Dissolution of the Firm.—The partnership relation may be terminated either (1) by act of the parties or (2) by operation of law.

By act of the parties it may be by original agreement or by subsequent act; and by original agreement it may be by lapse of time or by the accomplishment of the object of the partnership.

By operation of law it may be by death, insanity, marriage of a female partner unless regulated by statute, bankruptcy, illegality or war between the countries of the partners. The circumstances under which each of these causes will effect a dissolution of the partnership relation are similar to those under which each of them will terminate the agency relation.

A court of equity may decree the dissolution of a partnership for (1) fraud in creating the partnership, (2) insanity of a partner, (3) gross misconduct of a partner or (4) hopelessness of success.

Notice of Dissolution Required. When the partnership is dissolved by act of parties, notice of the dissolution must be given not only to those who have had dealings with the firm but also to the public generally. The former must have actual notice transmitted to them, but for the latter a general notice in a newspaper of general circulation in the neighborhood, for a reasonable period, is sufficient.

Effect of Dissolution. When the partnership is dissolved by the death of a partner, the legal title to all the the firm personalty and to all realty the title to which was in all the partners jointly vests at once in the surviving partners, who hold it in trust for the firm. Moreover, the right of disposing of all the partnership assets, real as well as personal, vests in them. Firm creditors may proceed at law against the surviving partners. In case of their insolvency or in any case if by statute the liability of partners is joint and several, the creditors may proceed in equity against the estate of the deceased partner.

After dissolution, the partners may perform acts essential for closing up the business, but not with the view of creating new ventures.

SALE OF PERSONAL PROPERTY

The Uniform Sales Act has been adopted with only minor changes by most of the states, Alaska and Hawaii, and thus the sale of personal property in the major part of the United States is governed by this uniform law.

The Act defines a sale of goods as an agreement whereby the seller transfers the property in goods to the buyer for a consideration called the *price.*

Formalities of a Sale.—A sale or contract to sell may be oral or in writing; the price may be paid at once or promised on a future day; possession of the goods may be given the buyer immediately or retained for a time by the seller. But a contract to sell or a sale of goods of the value of $500 or upwards is not enforceable unless the buyer accepts part of the goods and actually receives them or makes a part payment, unless some note or memorandum in writing of the contract or sale be signed by the party to be charged. There is an acceptance of the goods when the buyer, either before or after delivery of the goods, expresses by word or conduct his assent to becoming owner of the specific goods.

When Title Passes.—When the title passes is governed by the intention of the parties. Unless a different intent appears the following are the rules for ascertaining the intent of the parties: If the goods are ready for immediate delivery, the law presumes that title passes at once. If they are not, the law presumes that title is not to pass until they are put in a deliverable condition. If the sale is on approval, the law presumes that title does not pass until the buyer has tried and approved them or has kept the goods and failed to give notice of rejection to the seller by the end of a fixed or reasonable time. In the case of a "sale or return," it passes to the buyer at once with the right to pass it back to the seller within the time agreed or within a reasonable time when no time is fixed, if he chooses to do so. Where the goods are shipped C.O.D. (Collect on Delivery) in accordance with an order or contract, the title passes to the buyer upon delivery to the carrier, but the buyer is not entitled to possession of them until he pays the price.

In many situations such as bankruptcy of one of the parties or a destruction of the goods by fire, the question whether title has passed to the buyer is very important. For example, goods in the possession of the seller may be destroyed by fire. If the title to the goods has passed to the buyer, the buyer must bear the loss, but if the title has not passed, the seller must bear the loss.

Duties of the Parties.—The duties of the seller are three-fold. He must furnish the thing agreed upon, transfer title to the buyer and give him possession of it. The duties of the buyer are to take delivery and pay the price.

Warranties.—An express warranty is any affirmation of fact of any promise by the seller relating to the goods, if the natural tendency of the affirmation or promise is to induce the buyer to purchase the goods, and if the buyer purchases the goods relying thereon. But no affirmation of the value of the goods, nor any statement purporting to be a statement of the seller's opinion shall be construed as a warranty. Unless there is a contrary intention, the law states that there is an implied warranty by the seller that he is the owner of the subject matter of the sale and that it is free from incumbrance. When the goods are sold by sample, he impliedly warrants that they shall conform to the sample; and when they are sold by description, that they shall conform to the description. When goods are sold by a manufacturer or dealer, he is generally held to warrant impliedly that they are free from latent defects. And when goods are selected by the seller to fulfill a particular purpose, the manufacturer impliedly warrants their fitness for that purpose.

Remedies of the Buyer.—When the buyer has paid for the goods and the seller refuses to deliver them, the buyer is entitled to recover the market value of the goods at the time and place of delivery together with interest. If he has not paid for the goods, he is entitled to recover the difference between the contract price and the market price at the time and place of delivery, provided the latter price is greater than the former together with interest.

Any breach of warranty gives the buyer a right of action for damages amounting to the difference between the value of the goods as they are and what it would have been had the goods been as warranted. As an alternative, in most states the buyer may rescind a sale if he can return the goods uninjured within a reasonable time.

Remedies of the Seller.—If the buyer fails to fulfill his duty, the seller may sue for the breach. If title to the goods has passed, he recovers the price. Also, if the goods are specific and not readily salable, he is allowed to notify the buyer that the goods are held for him; he can then, too, recover the full price. If title has not passed and the goods are readily salable, the seller recovers as damages the difference between the contract price and the market price. The seller is further protected by rights against the goods. Though title has passed, the seller, so long as the goods remain in his possession, has a lien on them unless he has agreed to give credit. A lien may be enforced by rescission of the transaction or by resale of the goods. Even if the goods have already been shipped to the buyer, the seller may, if the buyer proves to be insolvent, give notice to the carrier to stop them in transit. The carrier must comply if the goods have not been delivered, unless they have been shipped under an order bill of lading. In that event the carrier need not deliver to anyone without surrender of the document.

(3) OBLIGATIONS IRRESPECTIVE OF AGREEMENT

Obligations of this sort are customarily classified either: (1) as quasi contracts or (2) as duties to make compensation for torts.

Quasi Contracts.—These are so called because the remedy for their enforcement in English and American law has been similar to that granted for contracts.

Quasi contractual obligations include: (1) judgments, taxes, official and statutory obligations of various sorts, and (2) obligations arising from unjust enrichment; that is, the receipt of property or services that the recipient ought to pay for, though he has not contracted to do so.

Torts.—Torts are wrongs or injuries that give rise to a duty to make compensation to the injured party. A tort is a civil wrong and the remedy for a tort is a civil action brought by the party injured as distinguished from a crime where a criminal action is brought by the state. The same act may be both a tort and a crime; for example, if a man assaults and beats another, he may be punished by the state for his crime, but the person injured may also bring a civil action against the one who did the tortious act for damages.

Torts may be divided into two main classes: (1) intentional harm to persons, land and chattels, (2) negligence; but torts also include invasions of economic relations and transactions, defamation, interference with domestic relations and the invasions of other miscellaneous interests.

Intentional Harm to Persons, Land and Chattels. This class of torts includes intentional harmful bodily contact (battery), intentionally putting another in apprehension of harmful or offensive contact (assault), false imprisonment and intentionally causing emotional distress—except when such action is privileged as when the act was done in self-defense or when an arrest was being made. A trespass on land and the interference with the possession of chattels is a tort, except when such action is privileged as when consent is given.

Negligence. In determining what constitutes negligence the standard of a "reasonable man" is used. Negligent conduct is action that a reasonable man should realize involves an unreasonable risk of causing injury to another. Or negligence may be the failure to act when it is necessary for the protection or assistance of another and there is a duty to give this protection or assistance. If the injured person is also negligent (contributory negligence), this may prevent his recovering damages from the person who did the act causing the injury.

REAL PROPERTY

Land and whatever is permanently attached thereto, together with certain incorporeal rights relating to land, are called *real property.*

Definition of Estates.—An estate is an interest in land. These interests in land are of various types and durations and are expressed as different estates.

In Fee-Simple. This is the highest estate known to the law. It is an estate of inheritance, free from any condition and of indefinite duration.

In Fee-Tail. This is an estate of inheritance which is descendable only to particular heirs of the grantee and not to his heirs in general. It had its origin in the desire of owners of great estates to keep them intact to particular families by restricting the power of alienation. In this country it is looked upon with such disfavor that, where it is recognized at all, the restraint upon free alienation is limited by statute so that the immediate grantee gets a life estate and the second taker gets the remainder in fee.

For Life. An estate for life may be created by the parties themselves or, as in the case of dower, by operation of law.

For Years. An estate for years is an estate for a certain number of years and is a mere chattel interest, even if created for a thousand years. It may be limited to commence presently or at some future time. It does not descend to a deceased lessee's heir, but vests in his executor or administrator of the deceased in the same manner as other personal property.

At Will. This is an estate which the tenant holds at the pleasure of the lessor. Statutes almost invariably require a notice to quit, and the practical effect of these statutes is to convert estates at will into tenancies from year to year or from month to month.

By Sufferance. A tenant by sufferance is one who holds over after his term expires and is allowed by the owner to continue in possession. At common law he was not liable for rent beyond the term agreed unless the lease expressly so provided; but modern statutes frequently make him liable for double rent.

In Remainder. This is an estate which is limited to commence at a future time on the termination of a precedent estate created at the same time. It is either vested or contingent. A vested remainder is one in which there is an immediate fixed right of future enjoyment. A contingent remainder is one where no right of enjoyment accrues until the happening of some uncertain event which may never happen.

In Reversion. This is the residue of an estate left in the grantor or his heirs commencing in possession upon the determination of a particular estate granted. It is subject to the same incidents as an estate in remainder. Practically the only difference between these two estates is that a remainder is always created by act of the parties and a reversion always by operation of law.

In Severalty. This is an estate held by one person in his own right. Most legal estates in real property belong to this class.

In Joint Tenancy. A joint tenancy is an estate in which the grantees have the same interest, created at the same time, by the same conveyance and held by them by the same undivided possession. The most important incident of this estate is the right of survivorship, that is, on the death of one joint tenant, the survivors have the entire estate. This tenancy is chiefly used for partnership and trust property.

In Common. An estate in land held by two or more persons with interests accruing under different titles. They may acquire their title from different sources at different times, and acquire different shares.

By Entirety. This estate is created when a conveyance is made to husband and wife and the conveyance either states that they shall hold by entireties or is silent as to the manner in which they shall hold. They are not joint tenants, nor are they tenants in common. Neither party can dispose of his or her interest without the assent of the other; and upon the death of either, the estate survives to the other. This kind of estate is abolished by statute in some states.

Equitable Estate. An equitable estate is a right or interest in real property not recognized at common law but recognized and made available by courts of chancery. In general the holder of an equitable estate is entitled to the income or beneficial enjoyment of his equitable estate (which, like a legal estate, may be an estate in fee, for years or for life, joint or several, in remainder or reversion) while another person, typically a trustee, has the legal title to the property.

Modes of Acquiring Title.—Original title to property is acquired in the following four ways: (1) occupancy, (2) discovery, (3) conquest and (4) cession.

Derivative title is acquired in three ways: (1) by descent through consanguinity, affinity or adoption. (2) by act of the parties and (3) by operation of law. It is acquired by act of the parties either by public or private grant or by devise. Public grant is by patent or legislative grant. Private grant is by deed or by dedication.

Deed.—In its widest signification a deed is an instrument under seal written or printed; but the word is commonly used in the narrower meaning of a deed of conveyance of realty.

The two parties to a deed are the grantor and the grantee. If the grantor is married, his wife also should sign the deed. This is essential to convey her dower interest. Where the land conveyed is a homestead, it is essential in order to transfer her homestead right.

The premises should be accurately and minutely described. Reference should be made to prior deeds by which title was acquired by the grantor. If the land is described by metes and bounds and by specifying the number of acres and the two descriptions differ, the former will govern.

A quit-claim deed merely transfers all the right, title and interest in the land that the grantor has. A warranty deed, in addition to this, contains some or all of the following covenants of warranty: that the grantor is lawfully seized of the premises in fee-simple; that the premises are free from all incumbrances; that the grantor has good right to sell the same to the grantee and that he will; and that his heirs, executors and administrators shall warrant and defend the same to the grantee, his heirs and assigns forever against the claims of all persons whatsoever.

A deed is executed by the grantor signing it and annexing his seal. If the grantor is a corporation, the deed should be signed by its president or by some other officer authorized so to do. At common law the sealing of the deed was the most important act in its execution. In some states, by statute, sealing is not essential. In some states two witnesses are essential; in some, one; and in others, none. In order that the deed may be recorded, it must also be acknowledged.

To pass the title to the property, the deed must be delivered by the grantor or his agent to the grantee or to some one on his behalf.

A delivery of the deed by the grantor to a third party to hold until the grantee has performed certain conditions or until a certain time has elapsed does not pass the title until the condition has happened or the time elapsed. Such a delivery is called a delivery *in escrow.*

Recording a deed is not essential to pass title to the grantee, but if the grantor should make a second conveyance to an innocent purchaser, or in some states if the grantor's creditors without notice of the conveyance should attach the land, the latter purchaser or the creditors could defeat the original conveyance. To protect himself, the grantee should have the deed recorded at once. To do so gives constructive notice to the world that the title to the land is in him.

Wills Concerning Real Property.—Title to real estate as well as to personalty may be acquired by devise or will in all the states of the Union. To render a person competent to transfer title by this means he must be of full age and of sound mind and must act voluntarily.

In most of the states a will must be in writing, signed by the testator or by some person in his presence and by his direction, and attested by witnesses, who must subscribe their names in the presence of the testator. The form of wording a will is immaterial as long as its intent is clear.

Witnesses. Most of the states require two witnesses, but three are required in Connecticut, Maine, Massachusetts, New Hampshire, South Carolina and Vermont.

At 18 years males and females are competent to make wills in California, Connecticut, Hawaiian Islands, Idaho, Montana, Nevada, North Dakota, Oklahoma, South Dakota and Utah. At 18 years females (but not males) are competent to make wills in Colorado, District of Columbia, Illinois, Maryland, Missouri, Washington and Wisconsin.

In the following states persons of 18 years may dispose of personal property only: Alabama, Arkansas, Missouri, Oregon, Rhode Island, Virginia and West Virginia. In Georgia anyone over 14 years and in Louisiana anyone over 16 years is competent to make a will. In Colorado persons of 17 years, and in New York males of 18 and females of 16 years may dispose of personalty.

(4) REMEDIAL RIGHTS AND LEGAL REMEDIES

The law does not undertake to enforce specifically most legal duties created by status, contract, quasi contract, ownership of property or the law of torts. Instead, a right to recover appropriate pecuniary damages is given. The right of action allowed by law for breach of any legal duty may be called a remedial right. When a right *in rem* (in or against the thing) is violated by a particular individual the owner of the right *in rem* then acquires, besides his original right against all the world, a special right *in personam* (against the person) against the wrongdoer.

Thus an owner of land acquires a right *in personam* against a trespasser for the recovery of damages suffered by the trespass. So a right *in personam* may change its character when the right has been violated. The right of a servant to employment under a contract becomes a right of action for damages if the employer wrongfully discharges the servant. Both rights against the master are rights *in personam,* but the right of action arising on breach of the contract is different from the right to employment which existed under the contract when it was still unbroken.

Closely connected with the subject of legal rights and duties is the subject of legal remedies for their enforcement. The rules defining the rights and duties of persons has been called the substantive law and that defining the remedies and the procedure and proof, the adjective law. Adjective law may be divided into the law of procedure and of proof or evidence. Procedure in turn may be divided into civil procedure and criminal procedure; and civil procedure into procedure of law and in equity.

Civil Procedure.—The fundamental steps of civil procedure at law are the beginning of the action by a writ or notice to the defendant, pleading, trial, judgment and execution.

Pleading consists first of a statement of the plaintiff's case variously styled a *declaration* or *complaint.* This is followed by a *plea* or *answer* of the defendant denying some or all of the facts alleged in the plaintiff's statement, or alleging further facts or both. The answer is sometimes followed by other pleadings. The ultimate result of the pleading is that each party has set forth the facts on which he relies, and these facts have either been admitted or denied by the other party, thus clarifying and defining the issue that is to be tried before the court. If essential facts are denied, it is necessary to try the disputed question by means of proof.

Not only questions of fact but also questions of law may be involved in a dispute. The parties may agree as to the facts and dispute only whether on those facts the plaintiff has a right of action. Or the defendant may dispute the truth of the facts alleged by the plaintiff and assert that, even though the facts are as the plaintiff alleges, still the plaintiff has no cause of action. Questions of law are decided by a judge, and questions of fact are decided by the jury. In accordance with the judge's decision on questions of law and a jury's verdict on questions of fact final judgment is given by the court for the plaintiff or defendant. In the United States at the present day many questions of fact are decided by judges without the aid of juries, but owing to the provisions of state constitutions, this is generally impossible unless the parties waive their right to be tried by a jury.

Procedure in equity differs from procedure at law in various respects. The plaintiff's pleading is called a *bill* or *petition* and is fuller than is usual in a declaration at law. The defendant's answer also is fuller as to facts charged in the bill. There is no jury; questions of fact as well as of law are determined by the judge.

The most fundamental difference between *equity* and *law*, however, is in regard to the character of the final order of the court. When judgment is rendered at law in favor of the plaintiff, an execution for the amount of the judgment is put in the hands of a sheriff, who endeavors to satisfy the execution by seizure of the defendant's goods. The decree of the court of equity, however, is directed to the person of the defendant, ordering him on pain of imprisonment to do what the court directs. A court of law can give only a money judgment, a court of equity can effectively order a defendent to do many things besides the payment of money; and not only affirmative orders but negative orders or injunctions are possible and constitute one of the most important branches of equity jurisdiction.

In many states of America the procedure at law and in equity is now made substantially identical, and even in states where this is not so, the same court generally has jurisdiction of both actions at law and suits in equity, but the general constitutional requirement of jury trial in an action at law, involves the persistence of a difference between matters originally within equitable jurisdiction and other matters. Moreover, the distinction between equitable relief and legal relief is still necessarily observed.

Criminal Procedure.—This is, in the main, like civil procedure at law; the chief difference relates to the beginning of the proceedings. A person may be charged with crime by complaint made by any citizen to a magistrate, who, if he is satisfied that there is reasonable cause for the complaint and if he has jurisdiction to try cases of the sort, may proceed with the trial of the accused; otherwise, he may hold the accused for trial in the proper court.

Another method of beginning a criminal prosecution is by information filed by a prosecuting officer, but the commonest method for serious crimes is by indictment found by grand jury on a case presented to it by the prosecuting officer. The accused may then be arrested and held for trial either by confining him or by admitting him to bail. Those who give bail are regarded as private keepers of a prisoner and are bound to produce him when called upon to do so.

Greater particularity is required in the criminal pleading of the indictment than is necessary in civil actions. The defendant makes no answer or plea other than guilty or not guilty. The latter plea compels the government to prove everything essential to

COMMERCIAL LAW IN THE VARIOUS STATES

STATES AND TERRITORIES	LEGAL RATE PER CENT	ALLOWED BY CONTRACT PER CENT	INTEREST LAWS PENALTY FOR USURY	STATUTES OF LIMITATION JUDGMENTS YEARS	NOTES YEARS	OPEN ACCOUNTS YEARS
Alabama	8	8	Forfeit interest if not paid	20	6	3
Alaska	8	12	Double excess already paid recoverable; forfeit all interest not paid	10	6	6
Arizona	6	10	Forfeit excess if not paid	5	4	3
Arkansas	6	10	Forfeit principal and interest if not paid	10	5	3
California	7	12	Forfeit excess of interest if not paid	5	4	4
Colorado	8	12	Forfeit excess of interest if not paid	20	6	6
Connecticut	6	12	Fine or imprisonment or both, excess forfeited	None	6	6
Delaware	6	6	Forfeit excess whether or not paid	10	6	3
District of Columbia	6	8	Forfeit interest, whether or not paid	12	3	3
Florida	8	10	Forfeit interest if not paid; double excess recoverable if paid	20	5	2
Georgia	7	8	Forfeit excess, if not paid	7	6	4
Hawaii	8	12		20	6	6
Idaho	7	10	Forfeit interest whether or not paid	6	5	4
Illinois	5	7	Forfeit interest unless borrower is corporation	20	10	5
Indiana	6	8	Forfeit excess if not paid	20	10	6
Iowa	6	8	Forfeit interest if not paid	20	10	5
Kansas	6	6	Forfeit double excess whether or not paid	5	5	3
Kentucky	6	6	Forfeit excess if unpaid	15	15	5
Louisiana	5	8	Forfeit excess whether paid or unpaid	10	5	3
Maine	6	Any	No provision except for small loans	20	6	6
Maryland	6	6	[1] Forfeit excess if unpaid	12	3	3
Massachusetts	6	Any	No provision except for small loans	20	6	6
Michigan	5	7	Forfeit interest if unpaid	10	6	6
Minnesota	6	8	Forfeit interest if unpaid; forfeit excess if paid	10	6	6
Mississippi	6	8	Forfeit interest if unpaid; if more than 20%, both principal and interest	7	6	3
Missouri	6	8	Forfeit excess	10	10	5
Montana	8	10	Forfeit double amount of interest whether paid or unpaid	10	8	5
Nebraska	7	10	Forfeit interest	5	5	4
Nevada	7	12	Forfeit excess	6	4	4
New Hampshire	6	Any	No provision	20	6	6
New Jersey	6	6	[1] Forfeit interest	20	6	6
New Mexico	10	12	Forfeit double amount of interest whether paid of unpaid	7	6	4
New York	6	6 except call loans	[1] Forfeit of principal and interest if unpaid, excess if paid; misdemeanor; any rate allowed on collateral call loans of over $5,000	20	6	6
North Carolina	6	6	Forfeit interest if unpaid, and double interest if paid	10	3	3
North Dakota	6	10	Forfeit interest if unpaid, and double interest if paid	10	6	6
Ohio	6	8	Forfeit interest if unpaid	15	15	6
Oklahoma	6	10	Forfeit double interest whether paid or unpaid	5	5	3
Oregon	6	10	Forfeit principal and interest if unpaid	10	6	6
Pennsylvania	6	6	Forfeit excess whether paid or unpaid	5–20	6	6
Puerto Rico	6	12		5	3	3
Rhode Island	6	Any	Forfeit excess if unpaid	20	6	6
South Carolina	7	8	Forfeit interest if unpaid and double interest if paid	10	6	6
South Dakota	7	12	Forfeit all interest whether paid or unpaid; misdemeanor	10	6	6
Tennessee	6	6	Forfeit of excess whether paid or unpaid; misdemeanor	10	6	6
Texas	6	10	Forfeit all interest if unpaid; double interest if paid	10	4	2
Utah	8	12	Forfeit excess if unpaid	8	6	4
Vermont	6	6	Forfeit excess whether paid or unpaid	8	6	6
Virginia	6	6	Forfeit all interest whether paid or unpaid	20	5	3
Washington	6	12	Forfeit double interest if unpaid	6	6	3
West Virginia	6	6	Forfeit excess if unpaid	10	10	5
Wisconsin	6	10	Forfeit all interest if unpaid, and treble excess interest if paid	20	6	6
Wyoming	8	12	Forfeit interest if unpaid	21	5	8

[1] In Maryland, New Jersey and New York a corporation cannot set up usury as a defense.

make out the guilt of the accused of the crime charged.

In civil cases it is sufficient for one alleging facts in his pleading to prove them by a mere preponderance of evidence; but in criminal trials the government must prove the prisoner's guilt beyond a reasonable doubt in order to convict him.

Appellate Procedure.—Trials, both civil and criminal, are ordinarily conducted by a single judge, but appellate courts are established to revise the rulings of law made by trial judges if these rulings are questioned. When the trial judge makes a ruling of law, the party aggrieved by his decision may reserve the right to question the correctness of the ruling in an appellate court, which generally consists of from three to seven judges sitting together. If the ruling at the trial is held to be incorrect by the appellate court, a new trial is ordered.

Evidence.—A very important branch of the adjective law is that relating to evidence. Evidence includes all the means by which any alleged matter of fact, the truth of which is submitted to investigation, is established or disproved. It is an obvious rule of logic as well as of law that no testimony is admissible which is not relevant to the facts in dispute; but not all evidence which is relevant is admissible.

Indeed the law regarding evidence has been defined as consisting of rules excluding various kinds of logically relevant testimony; the most important of these rules is that which excludes hearsay evidence. Hearsay evidence is evidence given by one person regarding facts told to him by another person. Since the truth of hearsay evidence depends upon the veracity of the person who originally made the statement and not the veracity of the person in court,

such evidence is generally excluded. Because the original person making the statement was not sworn and is not before the court to be cross-examined, it is held that hearsay reports cannot be accepted as evidence.

Of vital importance also is that which excludes oral evidence of the contents of a written document when the written document is obtainable and which makes a written contract between parties a conclusive statement of the particular agreement. The rules of evidence grew up as an accompaniment of the jury system and, to a large extent, are designed to avoid the misleading of a tribunal composed of twelve men unlearned in the law and perhaps of no great education. A very common kind of legal errors carried from trial courts to appellate courts consists of erroneous rulings admitting or excluding proffered testimony.

LABOR LEGISLATION

Labor legislation is now customarily defined as the laws that are intended to improve the working and living conditions of wage earners and low-salaried employees. Most of the early laws concerned with labor had an entirely opposite purpose; namely, to restrict the freedom and activities of the workers.

Early English Attitude.—This restrictive legislation was a reflection in part of the mercantilist theory that dominated the economic thinking of the western world from the beginning of the wage system in the 14th century to the time of Adam Smith in the later part of the 18th century. The mercantilists viewed labor as the primary source of national wealth but deduced from this idea that the poorer the laborer and the lower his wages, the larger was his contribution to the national wealth. Low wages, substantially at the level of subsistence, were considered essential to national welfare. Such an atmosphere of thinking made it almost impossible that legislation should favor the worker.

The famous English Statute of Apprentices or Artificers, passed in 1563 in the reign of Elizabeth, authorized the justices of the peace to fix the wages, hours and terms of contracts of workers according to the scarcity of labor and the cost of living.

This law imposed severe penalties for nonobservance. In practice this meant fixing labor conditions primarily in the interest of the employer, although the statute did place a certain responsibility on the Government for the maintenance of a subsistence wage and for public relief for persons unable to obtain work. Broadly speaking, the attitude of mind expressed in the Statute of Apprentices in 1563 prevailed in England for more than 200 years and was carried into the American colonies as they were settled.

In the American Colonies

Even in the early years of these colonies a considerable body of law was concerned with labor, and with almost no exceptions this legislation was directed to control labor not to protect it. In New England this control took the form chiefly of restrictions upon the wages of skilled workers; in the middle colonies it took the form chiefly of a system of indentured servants, often referred to as white servitude, and farther south the effort was to solve the labor problem by the introduction of Negro slavery.

Restricting Wages.—Plymouth Colony and Massachusetts Bay Colony passed similar laws in 1630 fixing a maximum rate of pay. In Massachusetts Bay Colony:

It was ordered that Carpenters, Joyners, Brickelayers, Sawers and Thatchers shal not take above 2s. [approximately 48 cents at present exchange rates] a day, and 16d. [32 cents] a day if they have meate and drinke, nor any man shall give more, under paine of 10s. to taker and giver; and that sawers shal not take above 4s. 6d. ye hundred for boards, att six score to the hundred, if they have their wood felled and squared for them, and not above 5s. 6d. if they fell and square their wood themselves.

It was ordered that labourers shal not take above 12d. a day for their worke, and not above 6d. and meat and drink, under paine of 10s. (Massachusetts Bay Colony Records, Vol. I, p. 109.)

This law was not successful and later the General Court appointed a commission of 29 men, including Endicott, Winthrop, Bradstreet and Mather, "to bring into the next General Court their thoughts for the remediing of the same." (Massachusetts Bay Colony Records, Vol. I, p.223).

This communion of the best minds of Massachusetts Bay produced a policy of local option by which each town was advised and requested to control its own wage rate.

The Court, having taken into consideration the scarcity of money and the great abatement in the prices of corne, cattle and other commodities of the countrey, whereby

it is impossible that men shall bee able to give such wages to servants and other labourers and workmen as formerly, so as many think better to lay aside their busines and impliments (which would tende to the ruin of the Churches and the Commonwealth) than to spend the small remainder of their estates for the maintenance of others in such a way as will not afford them some equall recompence—it is therefore hereby declared that it is thought equall that all servants, labourers and workmen shall bee content to abate their wages according to the fall of the commodities wherein their labour is bestowed, and that they shall bee satisfied with payment in such things as are raised by their labour or other commodities which the countrey affoards, and that they are to be content to partake now in the present scarcity as well as they have had their advantage by the plenty of former times, and this Court shall account it great oppression in any that shall transgress the intention of this Order, and will have them proceeded with accordingly. (Massachusetts Bay Colony Records, Vol. I, p. 326.)

Although the General Court of the Bay Colony thus changed its policy from one of dictating a limit to what a workman might have for his work to one of thinking about what should content him, the court of Plymouth Colony retained its old legal rate of 2s. but had no greater success in enforcement. When the towns of the Bay Colony undertook to carry out what the colonial authorities had passed on to them to handle, the wage rates fixed by the towns were lower than those in the colonial statutes, but that was because a general depression and hard times followed the crop failure of 1640. Carpenters in Hingham were reduced from 2s. to 1s.10d., and wheelwrights from 2s.3d. to 2s. a day; but mowers kept the old rate of 2s. and common labor rose to 1s.6d. As late as 1651 Thomas Trusler of Salem was presented before the Essex County Court for "taking excessive wages from John Alderman, "10s.6d. for a day's work of 6 oxen and one man," but no fine is recorded. Later in the 17th century and about 20 years after the New England colonies had given up the futile effort to control a commodity so urgently

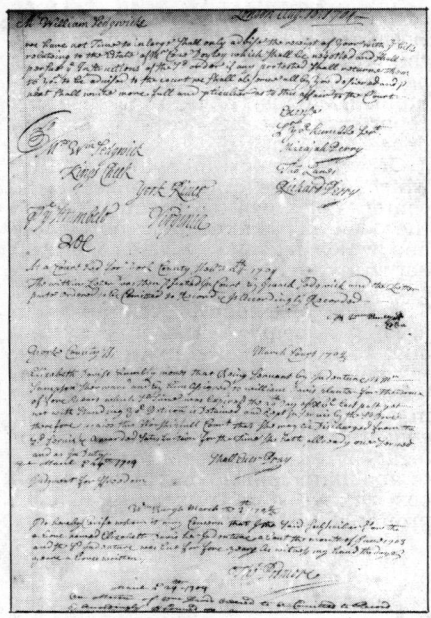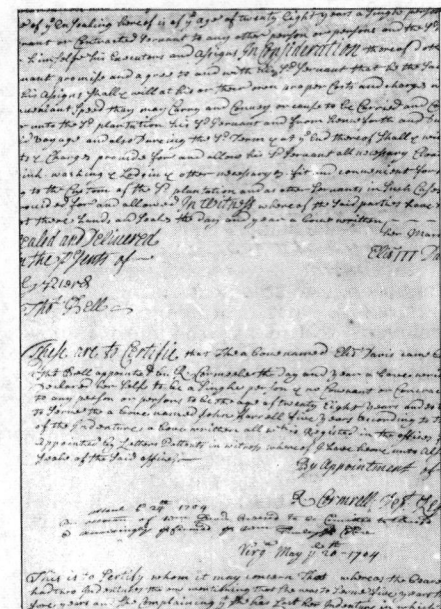

VIRGINIA STATE LIBRARY

CONTRACT for Elizabeth Davis, indentured to John Farrell. Filed in Virginia in May, 1704.

in demand as labor, Virginia attempted both impressment and wage fixing in its program of town building and succeeded only in driving mechanics out of the colony.

The many, constantly repeated efforts to control and regulate labor by legislative action were made inoperative by the continued scarcity of workers, especially in the skilled crafts, and by the abundance of land and the common desire to plant settlers upon it.

The tendency of craftsmen to become farmers was frowned upon in New England, since it was "more to the public welfare and the Glory of God to hold them to their trade;" and it was specifically legislated against in Virginia. Agents of the Virginia Company were instructed to establish tradesmen in towns in order "to remove them from temptation to plant on their own account."

Indentured Servants.—The old system known as *indentured labor* grew out of the demand for land and for laborers in the colonies and out of the overpopulation and extreme poverty of Europe. It was most prevalent in the middle colonies, although it was probably practiced to some extent in all the colonies.

White servitude took two different forms—labor under a specific contract called an indenture and under a less definite agreement embodied in legislation or in the *custom of the country*. An indentured servant was one who came to the New World under a contract with the planter who imported him into the colony or with the shipowner or merchant who transported him for the purpose of disposing of his services upon his arrival. British law required that all British subjects emigrating as servants, before they sailed, should execute indentures stipulating the number of years of service entered into and whether the labor to be

performed was a definite trade or any kind of work required by the other party to the contract. In consideration of his right to the servant's labor the master agreed to provide food, clothing and lodging for the stated period of time and generally to allow additional compensation in provisions, clothing and equipment upon the expiration of the term. This allowance came to be known as *freedom dues* and sometimes, particularly in the beginning, included land. These indentures were similar in form; in fact a printed form came into use as the system developed. They were officially recorded at the port of embarkation and had the full force of law in both England and the colonies.

Though the business thus created was in large part a legitimate form of assisted immigration, it led to evils both in procuring and in transporting that discredited the entire traffic. Systematic kidnaping of children and adults was carried on openly and flagrantly in English seaports. The alarming proportions assumed by this outrage at last compelled legislative action that influenced the indenture system as a whole but did not materially affect the kidnaping evil itself. The law requiring that indentures be executed and recorded before sailing was a direct result of the practice of kidnaping. This law probably checked the operations of the organized kidnapers to some extent, but a few years later merchants in the colonial trade appealed to Parliament for measures to protect their legitimate business of supplying the colonies with laborers. Parliament granted the request with an act making the stealing and transporting of children and adults a crime punishable by death without benefit of clergy.

The first laborers sent into the early settlements as indentured ser-

vants came chiefly from the great class of unemployed and unemployable unskilled workers and landless agricultural laborers—the unassimilable surplus population of Great Britain. Undoubtedly throughout the history of the indenture system in all the colonies the majority of the servant class that came from the British Isles and the Continent belonged to this unemployable group, and there were not as many ex-convicts as some historians have supposed.

The colonists opposed the introduction of convicts by every means within their power, but their efforts were not successful. Pennsylvania and Virginia controlled the matter to a considerable extent, but the other settlements were unable to do so. Maryland especially became the dumping ground for English jails and received more convicts than any other plantation in the colonies. An authority states that between 1717 and 1775 the number sent from Old Bailey alone was thought to be 10,000, and the whole number from various places in Great Britain and Ireland was estimated as at least 50,000.

The attitude of the American settlers toward the practice is shown in the many regulative and restrictive laws passed by the provincial legislatures and by the bitter attacks upon it in the early newspapers. Franklin fought it vigorously in his paper and in England.

After the emigrating servant, whether indentured or kidnaped, a free-willer or a convict, had survived the hardships and perils of the voyage, he became merely merchandise when the ship reached its American port. Prices varied according to age, skill, length of service and other considerations, but the average price for adults seems to have been about £15 to £20 ($72.90 to $97.20), though convicts were regularly sold by the contractors at £8 to £20 ($38.88 to $97.20) each. The price for which redemptioners were sold in Pennsylvania was gradually advanced during the 18th century, and as the price increased charges of passage were increased, so that the shippers put in a claim for a man's transportation that was substantially the market value of his services.

As settlement moved back from the seaboard, a new business grew up analogous to that of servant shipping. Dealers would buy up servants in blocks at the port of entry and take them inland for sale in the new settlements. The trade practices of these dealers seem to have earned for them their suggestive name of *soul drivers* and were in fact not unlike the better-known tactics of their contemporaries, the slave traders. The back country was depended upon largely to furnish the market for the criminal class that the more experienced buyers in the old settlements refused.

A servant became the property of his employer or master as soon as the sale of his services was effected. He could at any time during his servitude be resold for the remainder of his term without his own consent. In Pennsylvania, however, the law did not permit his removal from the colony after resale without his consent.

The legal character of the institution of white servitude was definitely fixed in all the colonies and was practically identical in all those where it was the predominating labor system. An indenture executed in England covering the term and kind of service, the obligations of both master and servants and the remuneration to be paid was regarded as a legal contract enforceable by the colonial courts.

Whether the servant was bound by an indenture specific in its terms or merely by the custom of the country, he had, as one writer puts it, "a legal as well as moral right to expect that provision would be made for his comfortable existence"; and, according to a contemporary, "the laws of Virginia take great care for the good usage of servants as to necessities, Diet and Clothes." Virginia law provided that a sick or disabled servant "could claim support and medical attention at his master's charge during servitude without any reciprocal right on the part of the master therefor."

Legally servants could always bring charges against their masters for mistreatment, violation of contract and the like; but they were themselves subject to punishment if they failed to prove their case. The laws themselves afforded almost unlimited opportunities for injustice and exploitation by providing for additional time in servitude as a penalty for countless infractions and misdemeanors. In its practical application, extension of time as a legal theory worked two ways: It was granted to the employer as compensation for damages in his claim against a servant who broke laws dealing solely with the master-and-servant relationship; and it was also granted even in criminal cases where the employer paid in money a fine assessed against a servant for violation of general laws having no connection with his status as servant.

Numerous laws were designed merely to protect the master in his right to his servant's time and labor. Chief among these were those prohibiting trading with a servant without his master's consent; prohibiting marriage of servants even to free persons without such consent, and relating to runaway servants. Offenses against all these laws were punished by extension of the period of servitude, the amount of added time in some instances was fixed by statute, in others, determined by the court.

Apprenticing children to trades followed in practically all particulars the indenture system, but there were two marked differences—the length of service and the fact that an apprentice could not be assigned or transferred to a master other than the original contracting party, except in case of the death of the master. Studies of the old colonial labor system make almost no distinction between actual apprenticeship and indenturing children, so that it is difficult now to draw the line. The record is clearer in New England than in other colonies, probably because bound servitude was less general among workers other than apprentices, and more trades were practiced.

As a general rule an apprenticeship lasted for seven years, unless the child was very young when bound. In that case the term expired when the boy became 21. The custom developed during the 18th century of giving both apprentices and indentured children six weeks' schooling throughout the year. Pennsylvania law made that compulsory in 1810.

Ten Dollars Reward.

RAN AWAY from the Subscriber, on the night of the 15th instant, two apprentice boys, legally bound, named WILLIAM and ANDREW JOHNSON. The former is of a dark complexion, black hair, eyes, and habits. They are much of a height, about 5 feet 4 or 5 inches. The latter is very fleshy, freckled face, light hair, and fair complexion. They went off with two other apprentices, advertised by Messrs Wm. & Chas. Fowler. When they went away, they were well clad—blue cloth coats, light colored homespun coats, and new hats, the maker's name in the crown of the hats, is Theodore Clark. I will pay the above Reward to any person who will deliver said apprentices to me in Raleigh, or I will give the above Reward for Andrew Johnson alone.

All persons are cautioned against harboring or employing said apprentices, on pain of being prosecuted.

JAMES J. SELBY, Tailor.
Raleigh, N. C. June 24, 1824.   26 3t

REWARD NOTICE appeared in Raleigh *Register* when Andrew Johnson, seventeenth president of the United States was an apprentice to a tailor and ran away.

The indentured system was widely used as a means of emptying European orphan asylums and almshouses. The vice-director of a Dutch colony on the Delaware River wrote thus to his commissioners in Holland in 1658:

The children sent over from the almshouse have safely arrived and were in sufficient request so that all are bound out with one and the other; the eldest for 2 years, the others, and the major portion, for 3 years, and the youngest for 4 years, earning 40, 60 and 80 guilders [$16, $24, and $32] during the above period, and at the end of the term will be fitted out in the same manner as they are at present. Please continue to send others from time to time but if possible none ought to come less than 15 years of age, and somewhat strong.

The bulk of indentured-servant traffic flowed into Virginia, Maryland and Pennsylvania, and the system was economically more vital to those colonies than to the others. The economic value of the indenture system became markedly different in the tobacco-growing South and in industrial Pennsylvania. In the first half of the 18th century the system declined in the plantation colonies almost as rapidly as it grew in Pennsylvania, and it lasted in the latter colony nearly a century after it was outgrown in Maryland and Virginia. As a labor policy white servitude continued in Pennsylvania for a quarter century after the establishment of the Republic. It took on renewed vigor after the Revolution, and indentured servants figure largely in the heavy immigration at the close of the 18th century. The last officially recorded registry of a redemptioner in Pennsylvania is dated December 1, 1831.

The system was never legally abolished. It died gradually as the economic conditions that had created it changed. As population increased, indentured immigrants were no longer necessary to an adequate labor supply, and with the introduction of machinery and the factory system employers found it cheaper to hire free labor by the day or as needed than to maintain servants by the year. One law, however, did affect the system materially. When imprisonment for debt was outlawed, and the master could no longer compel the servant to discharge his debt, the institution of indentured service received its legal death blow and necessarily died out without any special enactment.

Negro Slavery.—The stronghold of Negro slavery in the United States was in the southern states, where it was favored by the particular agricultural conditions existing there. Slavery thus became identified with a particular form of unskilled agricultural labor. As the prosperity of these sections depended so greatly on the efficiency of the labor supply, it would have seemed logical for the colonial and state governments affected to have enacted legislation protecting the slaves from exploitation and abuse. Actually this did not happen. The conception of the slave as a chattel without any legal or civil status was so dominant that practically no legislative measures for his welfare were anywhere taken. Such legislation as was enacted was directed to protect the slaveholder in his rights in his slave property.

Modern Protective Legislation

Origins.—As in all social movements it is difficult to set a precise date for the beginning of modern protective labor legislation. Its origins may be traced to the Industrial Revolution, which brought forth the factory system, and the French Revolution with its philosophy of humanitarianism. James Watt was perfecting his steam engine in the 1770s and '80s and his work, probably more than any other one thing, inaugurated the present power-machine age with its concentration of production in large units. It meant, among other things, the transfer of workers from the home and small workshop to communities built upon large-scale production, in which the working and living conditions of the employees were subject to many hazards and vicissitudes not previously experienced. Thus although power machinery brought a vast cheapening in production costs, it created employment conditions under which the worker was easily subject to exploitation and under which there was no form of collective action by the workers (indeed such collective action was for a long time forbidden by law) and the individual employee was practically helpless to protect himself. Thus arose the need for state protective measures to minimize, if not actually

LIBRARY OF CONGRESS

SLAVE AUCTION IN THE SOUTH, from a sketch by Theodore R. Davis. Negroes were judged by physical appearance, with greatest emphasis on strength. Slavery held no age barriers.

to prevent, some of the worst abuses of the new system. Unfortunately the economic philosophy of the time, carried over from the more primitive social organization of premachine days, was slow to recognize the altered conditions. In effecting a change in this philosophy the liberal, humanitarian ideas released by the French Revolution played a vitally important part. Their influence was slow in making itself felt in England and the United States, but gradually these new ideas of the human value of the common man spread sufficiently to influence the electorates and the legislators. The American Revolution was essentially political, and the Constitution of the United States that resulted therefrom was a political document. In it there is not even a reference to labor or to labor conditions. The French Revolution, on the other hand, was concerned with such topics as the rights of man with greater emphasis than ever before upon the rights of men in the lowly stations of life. Just as the American Revolution had profound aftereffects on the political thinking of the whole world, the French Revolution left an indelible impress on its social thinking.

Developments in Foreign Countries.—
England was the first country to make use of power machinery on a large scale. From the standpoint of national wealth and prestige, the results were marvelous, and England became the workshop of the world. But for the workers themselves the immediate results were disastrous. Men, women and children toiled incredibly long hours under dangerous and unhealthy surroundings. In the

mines women and men were used often in place of animals to drag the coal wagons, and sweatshop conditions of the worst kind developed in the textile industries. Intoxicated by the material benefits of low-cost production and its widening world markets, the country was for a long time heedless of the vicious conditions imposed upon the workers under the new factory system.

Just how bad conditions in the cotton mills were, especially as regards the child employees, is evident from the testimony before a parliamentary committee in 1816, as summarized in the recently published *Economic History of Europe since 1750* by Witt Bowden of the United States Bureau of Labor Statistics and Professors Karpovich and Usher of Harvard University. A cotton manufacturer stated that children as young as 5 years of age were employed; that the usual hours of work were 14, some mills requiring 15; and that some mills allowed no intermission for meals. A magistrate testified that the warm, humid, unventilated mills with cotton lint or *flew* polluting the air induced a condition that required the frequent administration of emetics. A physician whose father-in-law owned a large mill testified "with the greatest reluctance" that when the children first came to the mills, with the close, humid atmosphere and high temperature, they were seized with a mild fever and were subject to a subsequent debility. There was no protection from the machinery, and he had "too often" seen workers crushed to death, and the mangling of the hands of the children was "a very common thing."

He stated further that children, so far as he knew, were never allowed to sit down during working hours; that they frequently walked 2 miles from their homes to the mills; and that the factories in his community usually operated from 6 o'clock in the morning until 7 o'clock at night in summer, and from 7 until 8 in the winter. Among the workers he said, "scrofula is common indeed, and consumption extremely common."

In 1819 an act was passed (but never enforced) forbidding the employment of children under 9 years of age in the mills and limiting the hours of those from 9 to 16 years to 12 hours per day. The first effective child-labor law was enacted in 1833. It was applicable to children in textile mills, excluded children under 9 years of age and provided for the gradual introduction of a 9-hour day for minors. Equally important was the fact that this law provided for paid inspectors and machinery of enforcement.

Slowly there was a broadening of national sympathy and understanding. The hours of labor of children were still further reduced, women were similarly protected against excessively long working hours, factory acts provided for safer and more healthful working conditions in industrial plants, workmen's compensation laws were enacted, and these, with other similar laws, gave England before the end of the 19th century a comprehensive labor code. This was rounded out early in the 20th century by a series of social-insurance laws setting up a system of public social insurance for workers against the hazards of unemployment, sickness and old age.

Other European countries, as they became more and more industrialized, experienced substantially the same evil human effects as had England and undertook with varying degrees of rapidity and thoroughness to control the evils by public legislation. Germany was the first to adopt a broad program of social insurance, the program starting in the 1880s and being enlarged in the subsequent decades. This movement in Germany was the result in part of humanitarian impulses; but a dominating motive was the policy of Bismarck to fight the growing labor and socialist movement of his day by having the state take the lead in improving the conditions of the workers.

By the time of World War I practically all the industrial countries had more or less comprehensive labor codes. In this movement toward liberal labor legislation, a prominent place was taken by the British dominions of Australia and New Zealand, especially in the fields of shortened working hours and minimum working wages.

Following World War I the political upheavals in Italy, Germany, Russia and certain other countries resulted in the establishment of nondemocratic governments and a complete change in the character of their labor legislation. In Germany and Italy the power of unions was subordinated to that of the government in determining wages and working conditions. In Russia, where the private employing class was abolished and the Government was frankly in control of the working class, practically all legislation was directed to the welfare of labor; but individual workers and groups had to surrender much of their freedom in the interest of the collective state.

Legislation in the United States

In the United States protective labor legislation developed slowly. Although power driven industries, such as woolen manufacturing, developed early in the United States, they were localized and on a small scale. The country as a whole was generally agricultural until the closing years of the 19th century. The frontier was still moving slowly westward and vacant lands were available for energetic, ambitious workers who did not care to live in expanding industrial areas. Constitutional interpretation, the conservative attitude of courts and legislatures and the absence of an organized movement for protective labor legislation enabled employers to operate their plants much as they pleased, their only restraint being the law of supply and demand. When serious attempts were made by labor to secure a voice in the matter of wages, hours and working conditions through unionization, the employer was usually able to defeat these efforts by resort to the courts with the plea that such actions would infringe "freedom of contract" and "due process" clauses of the Constitution.

The lack of support for labor, whether organized or unorganized, was in large part due to the strongly entrenched philosophy of individualism which characterized the country and which held to the theory that any man who wanted to could make a living if he was willing to work. As industry grew in size, concentration and specialization, the individual worker had less and less freedom of action. Industries of various types such as automobiles, steel, rubber, textiles, etc., tended to concentrate in certain areas; the workers became skilled or semiskilled in repetitive work which characterized the particular industry and were valueless elsewhere. The assembly line of mass production was taking the place of the factories where individual workers exercised a variety of skills.

The depression of the 1930's struck these workers with devastating effect. Government as well as industry devised various schemes to help them. In some states legislation favorable to labor had been enacted, but federal legislation for the mass of workers was almost non-existent.

The inauguration of President Franklin D. Roosevelt in March 1933 and the announcement of the New Deal program marked the beginning of a promised attempt to restore normal economic and business conditions. Labor was in a period of transition and doubt. Early in 1932, the enactment of the Norris-LaGuardia bill had given to labor full freedom of association without interference by employers; contracts denying employment to members of labor unions, called "yellow dog" contracts, were outlawed and federal courts were prohibited from issuing injunctions in labor disputes except under carefully defined conditions.

Continuing the promise of the Norris-LaGuardia act, the Roosevelt administration adopted a policy of economic planning and control as embodied in the National Industrial Recovery Act. A first step toward meeting the demands of labor was the legalization of the right to organize as embodied in section 7a of the act, the basic purpose of which was to put people back to work. Less than six weeks after the act had been declared unconstitutional in *Schechter v. U. S., 1935*, the National Labor Relations act, popularly known as the Wagner act, became law. This act extended the provisions of section 7a and made more explicit certain rights and privileges guaranteed to labor, including not only "the right to self-organization," but also "to bargain collectively through representatives of their own choosing." Five unfair labor practices on the part of employers were prohibited, but there were no prohibitions on labor. The National Labor Relations Board (NLRB) was set up to hear all cases arising from the act, which obtained constitutional recognition in *NLRB v. Jones & Laughlin Steel Co., 1937*.

In 1935, the Social Security act became law with comprehensive provisions for unemployment insurance, old age pensions and other aids to the needy. The Fair Labor Standards bill, popularly known as the Wages and Hours bill, was prepared and finally became law in 1938. It provided for a minimum wage of 25 cents an hour rising to 40 cents in seven years, a 44-hour week to be reduced to 40 hours in three years, and it prohibited the labor of children under 16 in industries whose products entered into interstate commerce.

The Wagner act, the Social Security act and the Wages and Hours act, each validated by Supreme Court decisions, constituted an imposing program of social legislation, all of it highly favorable to labor. Moreover, the courts went on to exempt labor unions from prosecution under anti-trust laws and to remove other restrictions by generally upholding the right to strike, to boycott and to picket.

Because of an increasing number of strikes during World War II and as a direct consequence of a coal strike called by John L. Lewis in 1943 in an unusually arrogant manner, Congress, over a presidential veto, hurried to enact the War Labor Disputes act, popularly known as the Smith-Connally act. The specific authorization of a presidential power of injunction to halt strikes deemed against the public interest was included in the act. Strikes continued, but the president had some measure of control over the powerful labor leaders. The statutory expiration of the act and the continuance of strikes brought about the enactment, in June 1947, over a presidential veto, of the Labor Management Relations act, popularly known as the Taft-Hartley act. It was bitterly opposed by labor leaders and New Deal politicians on the ground that it set up "government by injunction" where labor was concerned; that it was, in fact, a "slave labor" law. The act also included a proviso, reluctantly accepted by many labor leaders, that certain officers of labor unions take an oath to the effect that they were not

NATIONAL CHILD LABOR COMMITTEE

DOFFERS IN A COTTON MILL in 1911. These young boys worked for very little pay.

then members of the Communist party as a condition precedent to the right of access of the particular union to the National Labor Relations Board. Strenuous, but unsuccessful, efforts were made by labor leaders to have the act repealed.

Such questions as industry-wide bargaining, pension and retirement benefits, labor monopoly exemption from federal anti-trust laws, etc. were the subject of public debate. Some urged legislation as a means of stabilizing labor-management relations on an equitable basis.

Child Labor Legislation.—In the United States as in most other countries the first important labor protective laws dealt with the regulation of the employment of children. The exploitation of children in factories was probably never as bad as it was in the British textile mills in the early 19th century, but conditions elsewhere were serious too. As early as 1848 Pennsylvania passed a law forbidding the employment of children under 12 in textile mills, but the law was not effectively enforced. This was also true of similar laws enacted in Rhode Island and New Jersey about the same time. A 14-year age limit became fairly general, gradually increased to 16 years. Today the entire United States including the District of Columbia as well as Puerto Rico, has child-labor laws. These laws usually set a minimum age for employment, with a higher minimum age for hazardous employment in dangerous jobs; they require employment certificates, limit hours of work, and prohibit night work. Twenty-three States, Alaska, and Puerto Rico, now have a basic minimum age of 16 for employment; two States have a 15-year minimum, and 22 States have 14-year minimums.

Comparatively early in the movement to restrict child labor, the idea was advanced that this was a fit subject for Federal control, and on two occasions Congress passed acts directed to this end, one based on the interstate power of the Federal Government and the other based on its taxing power. Both laws were declared unconstitutional by the United States Supreme Court. Finally, the Fair Labor Standards Act, commonly known as the Federal Wage and Hour Law, became law in 1938. It regulates the health, efficiency and well-being of most adult workers and has specific clauses relating to child labor. It sets a basic 16-year minimum age, provides for an 18-year minimum for occupations declared hazardous; and permits employment at 14 for certain manufacturing occupations outside of school hours.

Closely related to child-labor laws are compulsory school-attendance provisions. All States now require children to attend school at least until they are 16, some to 17 and 18, although various exemptions are permitted in the different States. While a number of States still permit children under 16 to be exempted from school attendance to enter employment, the most recent trend is against such exemptions. A chart on Page 1366 lists for each State the minimum ages for employment, the age up to which certificates are required, and the compulsory school ages.

Regulation of Women's Employment.—
Of recent years especially there have been two schools of thought among women's groups regarding the desirability of special protective legislation for women. Those who favor this type of legislation hold that women are more susceptible to injury from long hours, overstrain and industrial poisons than men are, and that injuries to them have a more serious social effect than in the case of men. Therefore, for the sake both of the individual woman and of society, the law should step in and protect women from undesirable conditions, especially since they are later entrants into industry than men, are less used to organization and are less able to protect themselves. The opponents of such legislation claim that it may easily become a handicap to the women it is intended to aid, making it impossible for them to enter the better-paid occupations and forcing them to crowd into already overcrowded, badly paid fields. Moreover, they point out that at present we have very little reliable information about the effect of given occupations or conditions upon women's health, and that much of our special legislation for them is based upon general impressions rather than upon ac-

BURTON BERINSKY, ILGWU JUSTICE

HAND FINISHING of dresses is a demanding task performed almost exclusively by women in the dozens of small factories that are found in the garment district of New York City.

curate knowledge. Where the advocates of protective legislation for women would forbid their employment in an occupation patently hazardous or carried on under evidently unhealthful conditions, the opponents of such legislation would devote themselves to prohibiting employment under such terms for any worker and would legislate specially for women only where it can be definitely proved that some condition harmless to men is injurious to women.

Hours of Labor. The movement for limiting the hours of labor for women followed closely upon the agitation for the regulation of working hours for children. In the 1830s and '40s protests against the long working hours for women as well as men, particularly in textile mills, where the daily hours of work were normally 12 or more, were made frequently by labor groups and efforts increased to secure appropriate legislation. Acts were actually passed in a few states, such as New Hampshire and Pennsylvania, which provided that 10 hours should be the normal working day for all workers in the absence of an express contract requiring longer hours. The employers, in general, immediately drew up contracts to that effect and in spite of a certain amount of resistance by the workers and a few strikes, were successful in their efforts and these laws therefore proved entirely futile.

The movement for shorter hours, like other social-reform movements, languished in the violent antislavery agitation for some time prior to the Civil War and was not seriously revived until the 1870s. The first effective law limiting the hours of women was that of Massachusetts in 1879. This law provided for a maximum 10-hour day and 60-hour week. The movement spread gradually to other states and was greatly strengthened when the United States Supreme Court in 1908 upheld the constitution-

ality of the Oregon 10-hour law for women. By the end of 1937 only four states—Alabama, Florida, Iowa and West Virginia—had no law of any sort regulating the working hours of women. Indiana has but one limitation of hours—that prohibiting the employment of women at night in manufacturing.

All other states, the District of Columbia and Puerto Rico have definitely forbidden the employment of women for more than a certain number of hours a day or week or have penalized all employment beyond certain specified hours by providing that it must be paid for at an increased rate. But in many states the number of industries or occupations coming under the law is so small as to affect only a small proportion of all wage-earning women in the state. No state has regulated each industry or occupation by the passage of all types of hour laws. California has the most inclusive hour legislation.

The general trend of the states is towards an 8-hour-day and a 48-hour week-limit as the maximum time a woman may be employed in one or more industries. The fact that the leading industrial states in the country, New York, Illinois, Ohio, Pennsylvania and California, have established the 8-hour day and the 48-hour week stresses the possibility and feasibility of all states having similar legislation in the near future.

In general the southern and midwestern states lag behind this trend in making the maximum a 9- or 10-hour day and a 54- to 60-hour week. The Women's Bureau of the U. S. Department of Labor is promoting standards and policies to improve women's working conditions, increase their efficiency and advance their opportunities for profitable employment. This Bureau is aiding women's working conditions in regulating the length of time for meal periods and rest periods and limiting industries to a 6-day work week. Women now have seating laws in practically every state. Over half the states have occupational limitation laws.

In regard to night-work legislation, about half the states place some limitation on the hours of employment of women in certain industries or occupations.

In some few additional states the laws do not prohibit the employment of adult women at night but regulate such employment either by limiting the number of hours that may be worked or by requiring the employer to meet specific working-conditions standards. The 10 P.M. to 6 A.M. hours are most commonly frowned upon.

Minimum Wages for Women. The first minimum-wage law for women was adopted by Massachusetts in 1912, and this was the effective beginning of a movement that spread very rapidly up to 1923, when the United States Supreme Court held unconstitutional the minimum-wage law of the District of Columbia, reversing an earlier decision and several favorable decisions by state supreme courts. As a result of this adverse action by the United States Supreme Court in 1923, many of the existing laws were repealed or became inoperative, and although efforts were made to redraft certain of the laws along lines that might be acceptable to the courts, little was accomplished in this field until after the decision of the Supreme Court in May 1937 in the so-called *Washington Case.* Here the United States Supreme Court, by a 5 to 4 decision, again reversed itself and declared the principle of a minimum-wage law for women did not violate the Constitution. Chief Justice Hughes, in handing down the decision of the Court, gave a very interesting statement of the social philosophy back of such legislation in the present age:

The principle which must control our decision is not in doubt. The constitutional provision invoked is the due-process clause of the fourteenth amendment governing the States, as the due-process clause invoked in the *Adkins case* governed Congress. In each case the violation alleged by those attacking minimum-wage regulation for women is deprivation of freedom of contract. What is this freedom? The Constitution does not speak of freedom of contract. It speaks of liberty and prohibits the deprivation of liberty without due process of law. In prohibiting that deprivation the Constitution does not recognize an absolute and uncontrollable liberty. Liberty in each of its phases has its history and connotation. But the liberty safeguarded is liberty in a social organization which requires the protection of law against the evils which menace the health, safety, morals, and welfare of the people. Liberty under the Constitution is thus necessarily subject to the restraints of due process, and regulation which is reasonable in relation to its subject and is adopted in the interests of the community is due process.

During the life of N.R.A. (1933–35) minimum wages were established for women as well as for men in all of the codes adopted.

Soon afterwards the Fair Labor Standards Act of 1938 was passed, which provided for minimum wages and maximum hours for all employees, including women, engaged in industries in or affecting interstate commerce. By 1948, 26 states had enacted minimum wage laws applying to

ASSEMBLY LINE in a factory. Crude methods and poor working conditions, along with long hours and low wages, were some of the reasons for the labor reforms of the 1920s.

women; 43 had enacted laws limiting daily and weekly working hours and 9 states required equal pay for equal work.

Because of the division of opinion between those who favored the stand taken by the U. S. Supreme Court in the Adkins case and of those who supported the opposite opinion expressed in the West Coast Hotel case, in 1942 a constitutional amendment, called the "Equal Rights Amendment" was proposed. This amendment proposed. "Men and women shall have equal rights throughout the United States and every place subject to its jurisdiction." This proposed amendment was not immediately acted on.

Homework.—Some 50 years ago the bad working conditions in the so-called sweatshop industries all over the world aroused a considerable wave of public feeling that culminated in two types of protective legislation for homeworkers. In Australia and later in Great Britain minimum-wage laws applying to homeworkers as well as factory workers were established. As a result, the number of homeworkers was decreased and their wages increased so that they more closely approximated factory standards. This principle of regulating industrial homework through minimum-wage legislation has prevailed in the majority of countries outside the United States.

Homework legislation in the United States has been of a different type. Investigations of sweated industries in New York, Pennsylvania, Massachusetts, New Jersey, Indiana, Mary-

land and Ohio in the 1890s revealed the same deplorable conditions among homeworkers that had been found in Australia and England. The result of these investigations was the passage of the so-called antisweating laws in a number of states. The aim of these laws, however, was primarily the protection of the consuming public from unclean products, and focused on an improvement of physical surroundings rather than on an improvement of actual working conditions.

Another factor influencing the trend of legislation was the fact that a New York law passed in 1883 prohibiting the manufacture of cigars in city tenements was declared unconstitutional on the ground that it was an economic and not a health measure. Up to the present time, though approximately one-third of the states have enacted minimum-wage laws, they have not been used extensively to control industrial homework. California and Wisconsin specifically refer to homeworkers in wage orders and Connecticut sets a minimum wage for homeworkers in the lace industry; but there is little mention of homework in the regulations of the other minimum-wage states.

At the present time about one-third of the states have statutes or official regulations governing industrial homework. Three laws (Connecticut, New York and Rhode Island) passed in 1935 and 1936 institute a stringent regulatory system attempting to raise labor standards as well as to compel sanitation and are aimed at the eventual elimination of homework. The laws and regulations in the other states, with the exception of California where homework regulations are a part of several minimum-wage orders, are the outgrowth of the anti-sweating laws mentioned above and, for the most part, are intended for the protection of the consumer.

The minimum straight-time hourly rate for all workers subject to the Fair Labor Standards Act in the continental U. S. is now $1.25. The Act does not require that employees be paid on an hourly basis. Any method of payment, for example price rates, may be used, provided the employee receives at least $1.25 an hour. Wage boards investigate and recommend that certain wages be set for certain industries, but not below $1.25.

Hours and Wages of Men.—Maximum-hour and minimum-wage legislation for women has been fairly frequent in the United States and still more frequent in the case of minors. But in the case of adult males little effort was made until comparatively recently to impose legislative restrictions of wages or hours except in public employment and in employments involving special hazards to the workers concerned or to the public. This was due partly to the fact that the courts almost invariably frowned upon such legislation in the case of adult males in private employments as violation of the principle of freedom of contract, and partly to the fact that the organized men workers were in general opposed to legislative fixing of minimum standards for themselves. Now the minimum is $1.25 per hour for all employment.

Constitutionality of Hours Legislation.—The first important decision of the United States Supreme Court on the constitutional question of the power of a legislature to fix a maximum number of hours of labor that persons may work in private employment was that of Holden v. Hardy, decided by the United States Supreme Court in 1898. In this opinion the court held that a legislature had such power in the case of employments that were particularly dangerous or unhealthful. In 1905, however, the United States Supreme Court was asked to pass on the constitutionality of the New York statute providing that no employees should be required or permitted to work in bakeries more than 60 hours a week and more than 10 hours a day. The court held: "The limitation of the hours of labor as provided for in this section of the statute, * * * has no such direct relation to and no such substantial effect upon the health of the employee, as to justify us in regarding the section as really a health law"; and "under such circumstances the freedom of master and employee to contract with each other in relation to their employment, and in defining the same, cannot be prohibited or interfered with, without violating the Federal Constitution." (Lochner v. New York.)

A change of attitude took place in 1917, when a statute of Oregon limiting the hours of labor of any person, whether man or woman, working in

MINIATURE PRECISION BEARINGS, INC.

PRECISION WORKERS in a modern assembly line. Following labor legislation, working conditions improved. In well-lit widely spaced, and comfortable factories, workers were able to increase output. Along with this came increased pay, better hours, and fringe benefits.

any mill, factory or manufacturing establishment for 10 hours a day and providing for overtime was upheld as constitutional by the United States Supreme Court. (Bunting v. Oregon.) In view of this decision it is generally considered that state legislatures have the power to fix the maximum number of hours for men at less than 10, particularly in view of the language of the court in a case upholding the validity of a California statute fixing the maximum number of hours for women at 8 hours. (Miller v. Wilson, 1915.) The court then said: "It is manifestly impossible to say that the mere fact that the statute of California provides for an 8-hour day, or a maximum of 48 hours a week, instead of 10 hours a day or 54 hours a week, takes the case out of the domain of legislative discretion."

Before the National Industrial Recovery Act of 1933 there had been no

Federal legislation attempting to fix minimum wages for men in private employment; so the constitutionality of such action had never come before the courts.

NRA Codes.—The National Industrial Recovery Act of 1933 represented a sharp break with American tradition as regards Federal legislative intervention in the matters of wages and hours of adult men. This Act provided, among other things, for the establishment for each industry or group of related industries of a "code of fair competition." Each code, to be worked out in consultation by the employers and employees in the industry and by the National Recovery Administration, was to provide for fixing minimum wages and maximum hours for all employees in the industry, men as well as women.

Prior to its being declared unconstitutional in 1935, the NRA had approved several hundred separate industrial codes covering the major part of American industry. There were wide differences between these codes in their labor provisions, but the great majority provided for a work week of not over 40 hours and for minimum hourly wage rates of between 32½ and 40 cents, inclusive.

The National Industrial Recovery Act covered only workers engaged in employments concerned with interstate commerce, for it was felt that this limitation would make the law constitutional. But in modern economic life it is very difficult at times to decide what industries or employments are interstate in character, and the Supreme Court has

ASSOCIATED PRESS

NATIONAL RECOVERY ADMINISTRATION flag being raised over New York Headquarters. This 1933 Act provided a "code of fair competition" for various industries. It covered only interstate commerce workers.

discussed various aspects of this question in a long series of cases without ever developing any precise distinction of universal applicability.

The decision of the Supreme Court that overthrew the NRA in 1935 involved so many constitutional questions that it still was not quite clear just how far Congress could go in this matter; therefore, the advocates of wages-and-hours legislation were not deterred from carrying their efforts to secure Federal legislation on the subject. At the 1937 session of the Federal Congress, new bills providing for the establishment of legal standards of hours and wages for all employees in all industries vested with an interstate character were under discussion and had wide support.

The character of the support for this type of legislation, however, had changed as time went on. In the earlier days the arguments for limitation of hours and for minimum wages had been based solely on the idea that too long hours and too low wages were detrimental to the health of workers. With the advent of the great depression of the early 1930s attention turned to the possible desirability of shorter hours as a means of spreading work and relieving un-

employment. This was one of the main arguments for the N.R.A.

The Fair Labor Standards Act established basic minimum wages and overtime payment requirements for employees engaged in interstate commerce or in work necessary to such production. This includes the production of goods which will move in interstate commerce. The Act also places restrictions on child labor by prohibiting the shipment of goods in interstate commerce if produced in any establishment where oppressive child labor has been employed.

The minimum straight time hourly rate for all workers subject to the Act in the continental United States is now $1.25.

There is no limit in the number of hours which may be worked in any one day or any one week, but one and a half the workers' regular hourly rate of pay must be paid for all hours worked over 40 a week.

A work week is seven consecutive 24-hour days. It may begin at any time of any day of the week, but no changes in the work week may be made for the purpose of evading the overtime provisions of the Act.

In the case of activities engaged in by employes after May 14, 1947, an employer is not liable for time spent outside the work day in such activities as walking, riding or traveling to and from the actual place of performance of the work of the employe.

Following World War II, the Labor-Management Relations Act of 1947 (Taft-Hartley Act) was passed. This Act guarantees the right of workers to organize and bargain collectively with their employers or to refrain from all such activities. To enable employes to exercise these rights and to prevent labor disputes which may burden and obstruct commerce, it places certain limits on the activities of employers and labor organizations.

The Taft-Hartley Act applies to all employes and employers engaged in industries affecting commerce between the states with the exception of agricultural laborers, domestic servants, Government employes and persons employed by a parent or spouse. Severe penalties are enforced for illegal practices.

Safety and Sanitary Conditions.—Legislation establishing standards of safety and health in industrial plants is so voluminous in state legislation and is necessarily so concerned with details that a summary review is impossible. In general the laws deal with such subjects as machine safeguarding, removal of dust, protection against poisonous substances used in various productive processes, toilet facilities, pure drinking water and seats for female workers. Some states attempt to incorporate the detailed specifications in the laws themselves; others leave a rather wide discretion to the factory inspectors and still others provide for special commissions or boards to work out the detailed rules and regulations in definite codes. All the states have some legislation in this field, some being extremely good and some very unsatisfactory. Always, however, it has

been found that in order to secure good safety and health standards in actual practice it is necessary to have a staff of trained inspectors to make periodical visits to the plants, to advise with the managements and to insist upon the enforcement of the laws.

Workmen's Accident Compensation.—Under the old common law, even under statutes establishing employers liability, a worker injured in the course of his employment had only a rather remote chance of receiving compensation. The injured worker or his family had recourse only through a damage suit against the employer. To secure damages in court under the common law, the worker was usually compelled to prove that his employer had not used reasonable care in protecting his employees against injury, that the injury received was not an ordinary risk inherent in the job, that the injury was not the result of negligence on the part of a fellow worker and that the injured worker himself was free from negligence. Even in those states where after 1885 employer-liability laws had been enacted, the injured worker was obliged to resort to the courts, where he still had to present his case in opposition to that of his employer or an insurance company.

In contrast to the principle that part of the responsibility for industrial injuries should be borne by the worker is the principle underlying workmen's-compensation legislation, which is that the cost of industrial injuries should be borne by industry as part of the cost of production.

The advent of legislation compelling the employer to pay benefits to his workers without suit or proof of negligence tended to make industry aware of the economic burden of this industrial hazard. The payment of premiums on workmen's-compensation insurance, coupled with a merit-rating provision, has made him conscious of a responsibility. It has also, in some instances at least, made it profitable for the employer to cut down on his accident rate.

Abroad, Germany in 1884 and Great Britain in 1897 and 1906 took the lead in the enactment of effective workmen's-compensation systems. Laws of Maryland (1902 and 1910) and of Montana (1909) were results of early efforts in the United States, but these were without adequate regard for either legal or economic principles. By 1911, however, a number of states had adopted more or less effective laws. All of the States and territories now have workmen's compensation laws, and Federal laws cover Government employees, longshoremen and harbor workers. Such legislation provides for payment of benefits to injured employees or to the dependents of those killed in industry, regardless of who was at fault in the accident. Recent trends in workmen's compensation legislation include increases in the amount of weekly and total benefits; payment of benefits for the entire period of disability, rather than for a specified number of weeks; coverage of all occupational diseases, instead of only specified diseases; and full payment of hospitalization, doctors' and nurses' fees, rather than a limited amount of money or time.

Scope and Character of Existing Laws.— In no case does a state compensation law cover all employments in the state. Certain employees are exempt specifically by the act or because the state has no jurisdiction over them. Employees engaged in interstate commerce are not covered by any state workmen's-compensation law because they are engaged in work that comes under the jurisdiction of the Federal Congress even though the Federal law creates liability but does not provide for compensation. Certain types of employees are not covered by the various laws. Some laws cover only employees engaged in hazardous work. Casual employees are usually exempt, and those engaged in certain occupations, such as agriculture and domestic service, are excluded from the benefits of most workmen's-compensation legislation.

Approximately one-third the compensation acts are compulsory; employers are required to comply with the terms. In the other two-thirds of the acts, an employer has the option of not accepting the act, but he is induced in most cases to accept by the provision that if he does not, then in any suit brought against him by an employee to recover damages for injury or death the employer is deprived of the common-law defenses of negligence of a fellow servant, assumption of risk and contributory negligence.

Most of the states specify that compensation shall not be paid for a period of time immediately following the injury. This waiting time varies from a minimum of 3 days to a maximum of 14 days in the various states, and the majority require a 7-day waiting period. This period for which no compensation is required to be paid has no relation to the requirement to provide medical and hospital care, as the employee is entitled to these immediately. Nearly all the states provide that if the disability continues a certain number of weeks, the payment of compensation shall be retroactive to the date of injury. This provision eliminates the danger of hardship being worked upon workmen who are permanently or totally disabled.

The amounts actually payable under the various compensation acts are determined by three factors— the rate, usually a percentage of the wages; the term or period of payment and in most states a fixed maximum weekly or total payment. The amount and method of payment also differ according to the type of injury. The acts prescribe certain payments in case of death and in case of permanent total disability and also have specific provisions covering permanent partial disability and temporary total disability. All compensation laws in the United States provide for medical aid to injured employees.

Two general methods are used in administering the workmen's-compensation laws: (1) by a special administrative commission or board created for the purpose of enforcing the provisions of the law; and (2) by the courts of the state. When administration is left to the courts it is usually because no other machinery for administration has been created and this law, like other laws, is enforced in the various state and county courts.

Administration by the courts exists in only a few of the states and these are mostly rural, in the south or midwest where manufacturing is at a minimum. The major difficulties of court administration have been summed up as: (1) delay of court procedure, (2) the cost of court procedure and (3) the unfitness of the courts for the settlement of compensation. A complete understanding of industrial conditions is essential in a successful administration of the laws. The vital factors in successful administration are the giving of prompt, honest and full compensation and immediate medical aid as required by the law. To achieve these purposes a special administrative board or commission is almost essential. Where the law is administered by a commission or board, appeals to courts are usually limited to questions of law, and determination of facts is left to the exclusive jurisdiction of the commission.

Under the great majority of the laws the cost of compensation falls entirely upon the employer, although in the states having a state fund some small part of the cost is shifted to the public. The laws provide for three general schemes for insuring the risk of liability based on industrial accidents: (1) state insurance fund, (2) private insurance companies and (3) self-insurance. Approximately 40 laws permit the employer to be a self-insurer.

All the states with the exception of a few far western ones, which depend on their farmlands for their livelihood, allow the employer to insure through private insurance companies. In these states, an exclusive state fund is maintained and employers coming under the coverage of the Compensation Act are required to insure their risk in the state fund; although even a few of these now permit self-insurance under certain circumstances. Other states maintain competitive state funds in which the employers may insure their risks, although insurance therein is not compulsory.

Walsh-Healey Act.—One other important Federal Act is the Walsh-Healey Public Contracts Act of 1936 which sets labor standards for work on Federal contracts. It sets basic standards for work done on U. S. Government contracts exceeding $10,000 in value for materials, articles, supplies, equipment, or naval vessels. It provides a basic 8-hour day and 40-hour week. Overtime is permitted provided that time and one-half the worker's basic hourly rate is paid for daily or weekly overtime, whichever results in greater compensation. This act sets a minimum age of 16 for boys and 18 for girls.

Unpaid Wages.—Another type of legislation affecting wages regulates the payment of wages and provides for the collection of unpaid wages. Forty-eight of the fifty States and Puerto Rico have some legislation covering the payment of wages. These laws set certain requirements as to the frequency of payment (usually semi-monthly), the medium of payment, the time of payment to workers separated from the pay roll, and the keeping of records. The best laws also include a provision authorizing the State labor department to take assignments of wage claims for the collection of unpaid wages for the employee. Sixteen jurisdictions now provide for this type of aid to a worker whose employer has failed to pay him.

Employment Agencies.—Another type of protection to the worker is the regulation of private employment agencies through which the worker often obtains his job. Such agencies are subject to regulation in 42 States and the District of Columbia. As is usual in all types of State laws, these laws vary considerably from State to State. Generally, however, the States require the agency to obtain an annual license, to post a bond, keep records, and to refrain from specified undesirable practices.

New Trends.—Newer trends in labor legislation included the enactment of equal pay laws, fair employment practice acts, and acts under which persons who are unemployed because of non-connected work illness, would receive benefits.

Laws prohibiting discrimination in rate of pay because of sex were first passed in 1919 in Michigan and Montana. No other States enacted this type of law until interest was aroused again during the Second World War. Now more than a dozen states have such laws.

Laws designed to eliminate discriminatory employment practices based on race, creed, color, or ancestry, were first passed in New York and New Jersey in 1945. Since that time many more States have passed such laws. The act forbids employers to discharge or discriminate against any person in regard to wages or other terms or conditions of employment because of race, creed, color, national origin, or ancestry. Employment agencies are also prohibited from discriminating on these grounds, and labor organizations may not exclude or expel from membership any person for these reasons. These acts provide for investigation of complaints of unlawful employment practices and the issuance of cease-and-desist orders by the agency administering the law. Review and enforcement of such orders by the courts are provided under all the acts. Laws against discrimination have also been enacted in Indiana and Wisconsin but these provided for voluntary rather than mandatory compliance.

The third new type of law, providing benefits for unemployment due to non-work-connected illness, was first passed in Rhode Island in 1942. Since then several other States have adopted such acts.

SOCIAL SECURITY

The Social Security Act is an offer by the Federal government to contribute on a 50-50 basis with each local state toward whatever social security legislation that state wishes to adopt. As the term is ordinarily understood, social insurance includes the various public systems, established on an insurance basis, for the protection of wage earners and low-salaried persons against such hazards as unemployment, sickness and old age. Workmen's accident compensation hardly comes within this category, being more properly conceived as a substitute for the old liability system under which the employer, theoretically, was responsible for accidents growing out of employment. Also old-age pensions, pensions for the blind and other forms of state help to the unfortunate are not properly to be included as forms of social insurance, as they represent direct gifts by the state. The Federal Social Security Act, however, included several kinds of aid or relief by the state; these, therefore, may be conveniently considered under the present heading.

The United States lagged far behind most other modern industrial countries in public social insurance. During the current century England and Germany have established comprehensive systems of unemployment, old-age and sickness insurance for low-paid workers; France has enacted a social-insurance law covering the major industrial hazards except unemployment, and many other European countries have set up more or less complete systems of this character.

In the United States the first significant legislation of this character was in 1932, when Wisconsin established an unemployment-insurance system. This was followed in 1935 by the Federal Social Security Act, which created a framework for unemployment insurance and old-age insurance and certain forms of Federal grants-in-aid to the indigent aged, to the blind, to the extension of public-health services, to vocational rehabilitation and to the welfare of children.

Public assistance is a Federal-State program. The Federal Government sets up certain standards for this and shares the cost of public assistance with every state that maintains these standards.

These regulations include (a) State-wide operation of an assistance program. (b) The distribution of public assistance on the basis of need. (c) No citizenship requirement, such as length of citizenship, which might exclude some U. S. citizens. (d) The right to a fair hearing before a State agency if a claim for public assistance has been denied. (e) Safeguards to keep confidential the names and other information about people applying for assistance. (f) Selecting on the basis of merit the personnel to administer a state agency's program.

Unemployment Compensation. — The provisions of the Social Security Act relating to unemployment compensation are very simple. All states establish a fund out of which to pay weekly benefits to men and women workers who are laid off or lose their jobs; they all require employers to contribute to this unemployment fund and in this way to take responsibility for unemployment, just as they pay for insuring their workers against accident to life or limb in the factory, shop or store.

The state laws are alike in certain other respects: If they have been approved by the Social Security Board and if the methods of administration meet the requirements of the Social Security Act, the Federal Government grants money to the state to pay the costs of administration. To be approved, a state law must contain certain provisions that will protect the state unemployment fund and safeguard the workers' interests.

Nevertheless, state laws vary considerably. They vary as to: (1) kind of employment funds; (2) workers covered; (3) benefit payments; (4) qualifications for receiving benefits; (5) state agency for administering the law.

Qualifications for Benefits.—To qualify for benefits, the worker must have had a certain amount of employment the year before. Some states require that he shall have been employed for 13 weeks within the year, others require 60 days, 90 days, 16 weeks, 20 weeks or 26 weeks. Some states that require 26 weeks allow as an alternative 40 weeks within the past 104 weeks. One state requires 90 days within 12 months or 130 days within 24 months. The various state laws differ on this requirement, as they differ on others, and the newer laws differ from the others in their method of calculating the amount of employment.

A waiting period for the worker is required in unemployment-compensation laws just as in workmen's compensation for accident; that is, he must wait as a rule two or three weeks after being laid off before receiving unemployment benefits. Some states require only two weeks; others require four weeks, and there are other provisions in some of the state laws.

Unemployed workers may be disqualified for benefits or their waiting period may be lengthened if they are discharged from the job for misconduct, if they quit voluntarily, or if they refuse to take a suitable job when one is available. Ordinarily benefits are not payable to workers on strike or unemployed because of a labor dispute; but there are several states in which benefits may be paid in such cases under certain circumstances.

Old-Age Assistance and Old-Age Benefits.—The Social Security Act sets up two systems for aiding the aged: One is designed to help the states to give immediate assistance to aged individuals on a basis of need; the other to provide annuities in the future to persons over the age of 65, based upon their wage experience. The two plans are complementary and may be described briefly as follows:

1. *Old-Age Assistance.*—A state may submit to the Social Security Board for approval its plan for old-age assistance. The Board is directed to approve such plans as conform to certain requirements as to eligibility, such as age, residence and citizenship, and to requirements as to state operation and standards of administration, intended to assure proper and efficient state action by the enactment and administration of laws that may reasonably be expected to provide assistance to needy aged individuals without discrimination. After the plan is approved, the state receives from the Federal Government an amount equal to one-half the sum expended for old-age assistance by the state with respect to individuals 65 years or older who are not inmates of public institutions. The Federal Government matches on a fifty-fifty basis every dollar spent by the state for old-age assistance. In addition the Federal Government pays for administrative expenses an amount equal to 5 per cent of the sum granted to the state.

2. *Old-Age and Survivor Insurance* provides benefits to a worker when he reaches sixty-five, providing he has worked in covered employment. It also provides survivor benefits to any worker's family when he dies, whatever the worker's age. Originally restricted to wage earners in private industry and commerce, it was extended January 1st, 1951, to include domestic and agricultural workers, and under certain conditions, employees of non-profit institutions, State and local government employees, and some Federal employees: also, the self-employed, except in certain jobs.

To qualify for benefits for himself and his family the worker must fulfill the following conditions:

(a) He must have worked on a job covered by the law.

(b) He must have received at least $50 in wages, or $100 in self-employment, in each of at least half as many calendar quarters as there are between December 31st, 1950, and the quarter in which he reaches age 65, or dies. Once he has earned 40 quarters of coverage, he becomes fully insured for life. If he does not have enough quarters when 65 to be fully insured, he may earn the additional quarters needed in covered employment or self-employment after 65.

Military service of 90 days or more from the beginning of World War II to January 1st, 1954, entitles the veteran to wage credits of $160 per month for such duty. A worker is "currently insured" if he should work half the last 3 years of his life on a covered job.

Monthly benefits are based on earnings up to $4,800 per year and vary according to the category (retirement, survivor, disability), in which the claim is made. Benefits are paid as long as the insured earns less than $1200 per year. If $1200 up to $2,080 is earned, only some monthly benefits are paid. If more than $2,080 is earned, no benefits are paid.

Children.—The Social Security Act makes provision for the protection of children who are in need of special assistance. It offers grants to states to assist in meeting the costs of: 1. aid to dependent children (mothers' aid), 2. maternal and child-health services, 3. services for crippled children, 4. child-welfare services.

Aid to the Needy Blind is provided for those who cannot see well enough to provide for themselves, who are not living in a public institution and are not receiving old-age assistance. These needy people who have not had an opportunity to build up social insurance rights or whose needs are greater than can be met by present social insurance benefits receive monthly allowances.

Servicemen's Readjustment Act (G. I. Bill of Rights). This Act provided veterans with readjustment allowances if unemployed and subsistence allowances for job training, apprenticeship and education. It also provided tuition payments for those attending school or college, vocational rehabilitation, and guaranteed loans to veterans for the purchase of homes, farms and business property.

LABOR ORGANIZATIONS

The existence of effective labor legislation is in large part due to the existence of effective labor organization, and the increasing scope of labor legislation has more or less followed the increasing strength of labor unions.

The earliest labor unions in the United States were local craft unions. The carpenters of Philadelphia organized as early as 1791; the shoemakers in the same city and the printers in New York, in 1794; and in 1795 a union of tailors was organized in Baltimore. These early organizations were all local and all of skilled workers in single crafts, as there was then little intercity competition and machinery had as yet done little to impair craft skill.

Probably the first movement toward a federation of crafts was in Philadelphia in 1827, following a strike among the building trades for a 10-hour day. This was followed by other efforts at federation, and in the 1830s there developed numerous workingmen's parties whose activities were chiefly political, with broad platforms including such items as free schools, universal manhood suffrage and the universal 10-hour day. These labor-political movements were not very successful, but with interruptions, such as that caused by the great panic of 1837, the workers' organizations continued for the most part to espouse political reform measures until the time of the Civil War, when the labor program changed to the more strictly labor objectives of shorter hours and higher wages.

In the 1860s there were several efforts to establish national labor unions, and in 1866 there was formed the National Labor Union, which at its crest had more than half a million members. Its program was very practical and it repudiated strikes except as a last resort. This organization lasted only a few years, and other efforts of similar character also had short lives, although having very definite influence in developing the trade-union spirit and in securing various forms of legislation for the benefit of labor. Out of these scattered movements a really powerful national organization, the Knights of Labor, finally emerged in 1869.

WIDE WORLD

WALTER REUTHER (*hatless, with vest*) is approached by Ford Motor Company police during a bitter union conflict in 1937. Active in the United Auto Workers, Reuther became its president in 1946. First president of the CIO, he is now vice-president of the merged AFL-CIO.

The Knights were at first a secret association with an elaborate ritual, and this secrecy led to much misunderstanding and hostility. There was really nothing to conceal in the organization, however, and in 1881 it gave up its cloak of secrecy. The organization won a few rather important victories in industrial matters and developed a membership of some 700,000 in 1886. This was the height of its power.

The Knights of Labor were organized on the basis of the one-big-union idea, including everyone in its membership, without regard to skill, color or creed. Its aim was a co-operative society, in which all classes should participate in a fuller life, and it did not place much weight upon opportunist methods. Its idealistic qualities led perhaps to its undoing, as it achieved too few immediate results to satisfy its membership.

A new organization with more immediate practical aims and built solely on craft unionism was growing up side by side with the Knights of Labor, and by the 1890's had completely superseded it as an effective force. By 1900 the Knights organization was practically dead, though the American Federation of Labor was developing greater and greater power, which has continued up to the present time. It gradually absorbed all the principal unions in the country except the railroad brotherhoods and up to 1936 experienced no serious split in its ranks and no serious rivalry as the mouthpiece of American Labor. In 1936 the separatist movement organized as the Committee on Industrial Organization occurred. The C.I.O. included a number of national unions, all organized on an industrial rather than a craft basis, which had previously been members of the A.F. of L. but were dissatisfied with the A.F. of L.'s organizational

policies. The A.F. of L. had always favored the craft type of union, and the C.I.O. unions felt that in the modern industrial world, labor, to secure its maximum efficiency, would have to organize more and more along industrial lines, especially in the large mass-production industries. In 1936 and 1937 it was very successful in organizing the steel, automobile and certain other industries along industrial lines. This meant conflict with many of the old craft unions, such as the machinists' and carpenters' unions, which already had local branches, embracing only members of their own crafts, in many of the mass-production industries. In 1955, the two great unions, each with about 7,000,000 members, merged. George Meany, President of the A.F. of L., was chosen leader of the new organization.

Labor Organizations and the Law.—In their early days labor unions were in constant conflict with the law. Strikes were frowned upon by the communities and by the courts, and the association of workers into groups for the purpose of pressing their demands upon employers was often treated as a conspiracy and the members were penalized. Gradually this attitude changed, and at the present time labor is everywhere granted the legal right to organize, and many states have laws protecting union labels, union cards and other expressions of union organization. Also, at the present time the legal right to strike is, in general, everywhere recognized, although there is still wide difference of opinion in the laws and courts as to the right of members of unions to picket plants that are being "struck"; but picketing not involving violence or physical intimidation is also accepted as legal in most jurisdictions.

The injunction was early used by employers as a weapon against the activities of labor organization. The labor unions bitterly resented this practice and in recent years have been successful in securing legislation by Congress and by several states forbidding the use of the injunction in labor disputes, except within rather narrow limits. In similar fashion the so-called *yellow-dog* contract has been made illegal in certain legislation of recent years. The yellow-dog contract requires the employee, as a condition of employment, to agree not to join a union while employed by that particular employer. It is a practice that the labor union charges is particularly vicious as it enables an employer to take unfair advantage of an employees' needs and thereby interferes with the employees' freedom of action.

Industrial Disputes.—Until the New Deal legislation beginning in 1933 there had been comparatively little effort on the part of the state or Federal governments to deal by law with the difficult problems of industrial relations and industrial disputes. At comparatively early dates, however, various states had provided for a system of state conciliation in cases of strikes and lockouts, and the Federal Government set up a special conciliation service in the United States Department of Labor when it was established in 1913.

As a result of the National Industrial Recovery Act of 1933 and related legislation, the need developed for a far more comprehensive system for the adjustment of labor disputes. The first major step in this direction was the creation in August 1933 of the National Labor Board. This Board functioned throughout the life of the NRA and successfully handled thousands of cases arising under that Act. This was done directly or through a series of subordinate regional and special industry boards. As a result of this earlier experience, Congress passed in July 1935 the National Labor Relations Act known as the Wagner Act, "designed to diminish the causes of labor disputes burdening or obstructing interstate and foreign commerce." A quasijudicial board of three members was created for the express purpose of settling labor disputes and guaranteeing the right of collective bargaining. In accomplishing the latter objective, the law declared certain activities of employers "unfair labor practices." Briefly these practices were: (1) to interfere with, restrain or coerce employees in organization or collective bargaining; (2) to dominate or interfere with the formation or administration of any labor organization; (3) to encourage or discourage membership in any labor organization by discrimination in the matter of hiring, term or condition of employment; (4) to discharge or discriminate against an employee because of the filing of charges against an employer; and (5) to refuse to bargain collectively with representatives of the employees.

Like Section 7 (a) of the National Industrial Recovery Act of June 16, 1933, the new National Labor Relations Act declared a similar purpose and object in enacting the statute: "Employees shall have the right to self-organization, to form, join, or as-sist labor organizations, to bargain collectively, through representatives of their own choosing, and to engage in concerted activities, for the purpose of collective bargaining or other mutual aid or protection."

The National Labor Relations Act, as thus briefly described, was directed toward a particular object—the establishment of conditions under which the principle of collective bargaining could be carried on under fair conditions. It was thus not a general act for the adjustment of all labor disputes; but as so many of the labor disputes of recent years have been due to controversy over the right of collective bargaining, the Act was of very great importance, and the board, in its short period of existence, handled a large number of important cases. This act, applying to labor relationships of employees engaged in work of an interstate character was upheld by the United States Supreme Court in April 1937.

From 1935 to 1947 the unions enjoyed the protection of the National Labor Relations Act. In 1947 however it was amended and became the Labor Management Relations Act, commonly called the Taft-Hartley Act. Since that time, organized labor has taken the position that the Taft-Hartley Act should be repealed outright, and the 1935 Wagner Act re-instated.

Taft-Hartley Act.—The changes made by the amendment to the Taft-Hartley Act were to prevent excesses by unions. For instance, the act now outlaws the closed shop; it permits union shop agreements but only with a union certified as a collective bargaining agent by the National Labor Relations Board. However, it is no longer necessary to submit a proposed union shop contract to a vote of the employees before it can be approved. It requires unions to file reports with the Secretary of Labor showing among other things, the names, compensation, and methods of selection of officers, dues and initiation fees, procedure for the conduct of internal affairs, and full financial data. In addition, it declares the following actions to be unfair labor practices on the part of unions: (1) to restrain or coerce employees in the exercise of rights guaranteed in section 7; to restrain an employer in the selection of his bargaining or grievance representatives; (2) to discriminate against an employee to whom membership in the union has been denied or terminated on some ground other than nonpayment of dues, or to cause an employer to discriminate against an employee; (3) to refuse to bargain collectively; (4) to engage in strikes and boycotts for purposes prohibited by the act; (5) to exact excessive initiation fees; (6) to exact compensation for service not performed or not to be performed.

Changes in administration were also made. The National Labor Relations Board was enlarged to 5 members; and the General Counsel, formerly under the Board's supervision, was given final authority with respect to the investigation and prosecution of unfair labor practice charges.

Injunctions.—The Taft-Hartley Act also qualified the provisions of the Norris-LaGuardia Anti-Injunction Act in some ways. This latter Act, passed in 1932, defines and limits the powers of the Federal Courts to issue injunctions in labor disputes. The injunction was in the past used by employers as a weapon against the activities of labor organizations. The unions bitterly resented this practice and worked toward getting legislation passed to prevent it, resulting in the passage of the Federal Norris-LaGuardia Act in 1932. This Act declares it to be public policy that the worker shall have full freedom of association, self-organization and designation of representatives of his own choosing to negotiate the terms and conditions of his employment, free from employer interference in these or other concerted activities for mutual aid or protection. It specifies that Federal Courts may not issue injunctions in labor disputes to prohibit workers from doing certain acts, including joining a union, assembling to act in promotion of their interests, refusing or ceasing to work.

In addition, the Norris-LaGuardia Act provided that contracts whereby a worker agrees not to join a union or to resign if he is a member are against public policy and unenforceable in Federal Courts. Previously such so-called "yellow dog contracts" were commonly used as weapons against unions.

With the passage of the Norris-LaGuardia Act, labor unions felt that an end had come to the evil of control by injunction. The Taft-Hartley Act, however, modified the provisions of the Norris-LaGuardia Act in that the National Labor Relations Board is directed to seek an injunction where it reasonably believes that an unfair labor practice involving certain jurisdictional strikes or secondary boycotts exist. In addition, it authorizes the issuance of an injunction upon application of the Board after the latter has issued a complaint charging an unfair labor practice, but before determination of the issues by the Board. The Act provides that the Courts shall not be limited by the Norris-LaGuardia Act in issuing injunctions in such cases.

State Labor Laws.—In addition to the Federal legislation discussed, State laws also regulate industrial relations. A number of the States have adopted anti-injunction acts modeled on the Norris-LaGuardia Act. Several States have comprehensive State labor relations acts of the Wagner-act type. On the other hand, a few States have acts that contain most of the basic features of the Taft-Hartley Act. In addition, many other States have laws dealing with some one phase of industrial relations, most of them being union-restriction provisions. These include anti-closed shop laws, prohibition of secondary boycotts and jurisdictional disputes; restriction of picketing and other strike activities, regulation of labor disputes in public utilities, and some even dealing with the regulation of the internal operations of unions.

While some of these anti-union provisions were passed in the decade preceding 1947, a larger number were enacted in 1947, the year the Taft-

Hartley Act was passed. In that year alone, 32 States enacted one or more laws placing restrictions on union activities.

The years 1948 to 1951 showed some reversal of this trend; although union-regulatory acts were passed in these years in some States, other States adopted legislation repealing or modifying union-restrictive legislation passed in 1947—a direct result of active efforts on the part of organized labor to convince the public of the undesirability of union-restrictive legislation.

Government Labor Departments.—The first state agency established for the purpose of enforcing labor legislation and in general looking after the welfare of the workers was the Bureau of Statistics of Labor of Massachusetts, created by a law of 1869. Other states followed this example, until at present practically all the States have agencies of this character, under varying titles, such as department of labor, and industrial commission. These agencies are usually vested with the duties of factory inspection and the administration of other labor laws.

In 1884 the Congress, chiefly as a result of the activities of the Knights of Labor, established the United States Bureau of Labor primarily for the purpose of collecting and disseminating statistical information of value to labor. In 1913 a United States Department of Labor was created with the full status of a government department and with its head a member of the President's Cabinet. The former Bureau of Labor was transferred to the Department as the Bureau of Labor Statistics. The United States Department of Labor is now divided into several bureaus or divisions, the names of which are indicative of their fields of activities—Bureau of Apprenticeship, Bureau of Employment Security, Bureau of Labor Standards, Bureau of Labor Statistics, Wage and Hour and Public Contracts Divisions, Women's Bureau, Bureau of Veterans' Reemployment Rights, and the Office of International Labor Affairs.

Public Employment Agencies.—The need for a public employment service is an outgrowth of the modern industrial system. The multitude of hiring establishments, the variety of occupations, and the wide range in the skills and abilities of workers result in a situation where it is almost sheer coincidence if the employer and the job-seeker get together directly at the exact moment when both are interested in what the other has to offer. The need for an organized method to bring them together is so universal, and the desirability of having access to a wide range of job opportunities and a wide range of qualified workers is so great, that only a public service operating on a coordinated nation-wide basis can meet the need.

Recognition of the need for such placement services emerged slowly just before the turn of the century. Beginning in 1890, a few states and municipalities appropriated limited amounts of money for the operation of one or more public employment offices. By 1900, five states had passed

such statutes and by 1933 some 27 states had established public employment offices in their principal cities. In addition, beginning in 1917, a sketchy program of employment information had been carried out by the Federal Bureau of Immigration and Naturalization to encourage alien immigrants to locate in centers of potential employment opportunity.

In 1933 the Congress enacted the Wagner-Peyser Act which established the United States Employment Service as a bureau in the U. S. Department of Labor. This bureau was charged with promoting and fostering a national system of employment offices "for men, women and juniors who are legally qualified to engage in gainful occupations; to maintain a veterans service to be devoted to securing employment for veterans; to maintain a farm placement service; to maintain the public employment service for the District of Columbia; and . . . to assist in establishing and maintaining a system of public employment offices in the several states and the political subdivisions thereof."

The Act provided that monies appropriated in the states for the operation of public employment offices would be matched (within specified limits) by Federal funds. By 1937 all states had accepted the provisions of this Act. The nation-wide system of state employment services was taken over by the Federal Government and operated on a national basis (as part of the War Manpower Commission) from 1942 until 1945 when the War Manpower Commission was abolished by Executive Order and its employment service functions were transferred to the Department of Labor. On November 15, 1946, responsibility for the operation of local employment offices was returned to the states and the responsibilities of the national bureau reverted to those functions relating to the development of policies, standards and effective operating methods. There are at the present time nearly 1800 full-time public employment offices in the United States through which part-time itinerant service is provided to some 2400 additional communities.

The program of the public employment service consists of six coordinated functions, directed toward the achievement and maintenance of a high level of economic activity and maximum employment, and effective placement service designed to bring workers and employers together as speedily and efficiently as possible.

International Labor Organization.—One of the most significant developments in the field of labor legislation was the establishment of the International Labor Organization at the close of World War I. This organization was created for the purpose of securing improved and uniform labor standards for the workers of various countries. The animating reasons as then set forth were: First, that injustice and hardship to large numbers of workers are potent causes of unrest and are thus perils to world peace; and, second, that the failure of any nation to adopt humane conditions of labor is an obstacle in the way of

other nations that desire to improve their own conditions.

The general conference of the International Labor Organization, which meets annually, is composed of delegates designated by each of the member states. Each state is entitled to four delegates, one representing employers, one the workers, and two the government concerned. Representation is thus tripartite, and this tripartite character carries through all the work of the conference, its committees, and also the governing body.

The function of the conference is to formulate proposals regarding labor standards. The proposals are referred to as draft conventions. It requires a two-thirds majority of the conference to adopt a draft convention. After a convention is approved it is submitted to the competent authorities of the member states for their attention. If a state ratifies a draft convention it is, of course, bound by its terms. In other words, the conference acts as a meeting ground for discussing and drafting proposals which may serve as a guide for action by the member countries. The conference has, however, an additional significance in that, representing as it does the various economic groups in a very large number of countries, any agreement arrived at by substantial majorities may be assumed to reflect in some degree the current of world opinion and may also have an influence upon such opinion and thus ultimately upon state action.

About sixty nations are members of the International Labor Office. The United States affiliated with the International Labor Organization in 1934. Since the first conference in 1919, the International Labor Office has adopted 98 Conventions and 87 Recommendations. These cover standards for wages and hours, vacations, child labor, recruitment and employment, industrial safety and health, social insurance, migration, condition of seamen, and many others. Although the United States has ratified only five of these Conventions, the major reason for this has been that many of the Conventions deal with subjects in whole or in part within the jurisdiction of the various States, rather than within the jurisdiction of the Federal government alone.

The revised constitution of the International Labor Office which went into effect in 1947 sets up a procedure for Federal-State countries like the United States, with States or Provinces having either sole responsibility for labor legislation and administration or sharing concurrent jurisdiction with the Federal Government. Under the revised International Labor Office Constitution, the Secretary of Labor refers to the Governors of the several States for action on such Conventions as are determined to be within State jurisdiction. State action to meet the International Standard may be through legislation or by administrative practice. The U. S. Department of Labor then has the responsibility of reporting to the International Labor Office what measures have been taken by both Federal and State Governments to meet the terms of the Conventions.

LEGAL HOLIDAYS

January 1. *New Year's Day:* In all the States, District of Columbia, Puerto Rico.

January 8. *Anniversary of Battle of New Orleans and Jackson Day:* In Louisiana.

January 19, *Lee's Birthday:* In Alabama, Arkansas, Florida, Georgia, Kentucky, Louisiana, Mississippi, North Carolina, South Carolina, Tennessee, Texas.

Lee-Jackson Day: In Virginia.

January 20. *Inauguration Day* (every 4 years): D. C., La. (Baton Rouge only).

January 30. *Roosevelt's Birthday:* In Kentucky.

February 12, *Lincoln's Birthday:* In all States, Virgin Islands, except Alabama, Arkansas, District of Columbia, Florida, Georgia, Idaho, Louisiana, Maine, Massa-

chusetts, Mississippi, New Hampshire, North Carolina, Oklahoma. Rhode Island, South Carolina, Texas, Virginia.

February 14. *Admission Day:* In Arizona.

February 22. *Washington's Birthday:* In all States, District of Columbia, Puerto Rico, Virgin Islands.

February or early in March. *Mardi Gras Day:* In Alabama, Florida (in counties where there are carnival associations), Louisiana (certain parishes).

March 2. *Texas Independence Day:* In Texas.

March 15. *Jackson's Birthday:* In Tennessee.

March 22. *Emancipation Day:* In Puerto Rico.

March 25. *Maryland Day:* In Maryland.

March 30. *Seward's Day:* In Alaska. (Not observed by Federal employees).

Good Friday: In California from 12:00 to 3 p.m., Connecticut, Delaware, Florida, Hawaii, Illinois, Indiana, Louisiana, Maryland, Minnesota. New Jersey, North Dakota, Pennsylvania, Tennessee, Puerto Rico, Virgin Islands.

Arbor Day. (Second Monday in April): In Utah.

April 13. *Jefferson's Birthday:* In Alabama, Missouri, Oklahoma.

April 19. *Patriot's Day:* In Maine and Massachusetts.

April 21. *San Jacinto Day:* In Texas.

April 22. *Arbor Day:* In Nebraska.

Oklahoma Day: In Oklahoma.

April 26. *Confederate Memorial Day:* In Alabama, Florida, Georgia, Mississippi.

continued on next page

continued from previous page

Easter Monday: In North Carolina and the Virgin Islands.

Fast Day: In New Hampshire (fourth Monday in April).

May 4. *Rhode Island Independence Day:* In Rhode Island.

May 10. *Confederate Memorial Day:* In North Carolina and South Carolina.

May 20. *Anniversary of the signing of the Mecklenburg Declaration of Independence:* In North Carolina.

May 30. *Decoration Day or Memorial Day:* In all States, District of Columbia, Puerto Rico, except Alabama, Georgia, Mississippi. In Florida *Memorial Day* for veterans of all wars; in Virginia, *Confederate Memorial Day:* In North Carolina and South Carolina for Federal Government offices only; Texas, not for banks.

June 3. *Jefferson Davis' Birthday:* In Alabama, Florida, Georgia, Mississippi South Carolina, Texas.

Confederate Memorial Day: In Kentucky, Louisiana, Tennessee.

June 11. *Kamehameha Day:* In Hawaii.

June 14. *Flag Day:* Throughout U. S.

June 20. *W. Virginia Day:* In West Va.

July 4. *Independence Day:* In all States, District of Columbia, Puerto Rico, Virgin Islands.

July 13. *Forrest's Birthday:* In Tennessee.

July 24. *Pioneer Day:* In Utah.

July 25. *Constitution Day:* In Puerto Rico.

Supplication Day: In the Virgin Islands.

August 1. *Colorado Day:* In Colorado.

August 14. *World War II Memorial Day:* In Arkansas.

Victory Day: In Rhode Island.

August 16. *Battle of Bennington Day:* In Vermont.

August 30. *Huey Long Day:* In Louisiana.

September 9. *Admission Day:* In California.

Labor Day: In all States, District of Columbia, Puerto Rico.

September 12. *Defender's Day:* In Maryland.

September 16. *Cherokee Strip Day:* In Oklahoma.

Indian Day (first Saturday after full moon in September): In Oklahoma.

October 10. *Oklahoma Historical Day:* In Oklahoma.

October 12. *Columbus Day:* In all States and Puerto Rico, except Arkansas, District of Columbia, Idaho, Iowa, Maine, Michigan, Mississippi, North Carolina, South Dakota, Tennessee.

October 18. *Alaska Day:* In Alaska.

October 31. *Nevada Day:* In Nevada.

November 1. *All Saints Day:* In Louisiana.

November 4. *Will Rogers Day:* In Oklahoma.

November 11. *Veterans' Day:* All States, except District of Columbia and Puerto Rico. In Delaware does not apply to educational institutions.

Election Day: (first Tuesday after the first Monday in November). In all states except Alabama, Connecticut, District of Columbia, Georgia, Kansas, Kentucky, Maine, Massachusetts, Mississippi, Nebraska, New Mexico, North Carolina, Utah, Vermont.

Thanksgiving Day: (fourth Thursday in November). All States, District of Columbia, Puerto Rico, Virgin Islands.

December 25. *Christmas Day:* In all States, District of Columbia, Puerto Rico, Virgin Islands.

December 26. In South Carolina.

PARLIAMENTARY LAW

Those rules, precedents and usages that are generally accepted for deliberative assemblies or organizations are called *parliamentary law.* Most of these rules had their origin in the English Parliament, although some have been changed to adapt them to the needs of other legislative bodies. The rules and usages of Congress have great weight as correct parliamentary law in the United States generally, but the legislature of each state has a code of its own containing the general rules, and special ones not commonly accepted but needed because of local conditions.

Besides the common parliamentary law recognized by deliberative bodies in general, any society or organization may make rules for its own government. When there are no special rules to the contrary, the body is controlled by the principles of common parliamentary practice, and these principles govern if there are no rules enacted by the body itself.

Uses.—Parliamentary law is needed in deliberative bodies in order that there may be a mutual understanding what may be done, that the rights of the body and of its individual members may be protected, and that business may be transacted speedily and in orderly fashion.

A gathering does not become a deliberative body until it is duly organized. This implies officers and members. There must be an officer to preside over the deliberations and a clerk or secretary to keep a record of the transactions.

Parliamentary practice presumes that ordinarily matters for discussion and decision emanate from some member or members of the meeting and that the discussing and deciding is done by the membership.

ORGANIZATION

Temporary.—At the time appointed for the meeting some one steps forward requests the meeting to come to order and, having secured attention, makes a motion that a certain person whom he names act as chairman; or he asks the assembly to nominate a chairman. And he puts motions or nominations to vote, until someone is elected to preside. The chairman then takes his place, and the organization is completed by the nomination and election of a secretary and any other necessary officers.

A Convention of Delegates. In the case of a convention of delegates (of a political party, for instance) a temporary organization is first made by electing a chairman and secretary *pro tem.* Then a committee on credentials is chosen to ascertain who are duly authorized to take part in the deliberations and the voting. This committee next reports the names of those who are found to have proper credentials and the doubtful or contested cases, on which it makes recommendations. No one without proper credentials is allowed to vote on the report of the committee or on any question until he is duly accepted as a delegate. The organization of the convention is completed by nominating and electing permanent officers.

It is then customary for some member to state briefly the object of the meeting, and business may be introduced at once. A committee is sometimes appointed to prepare resolutions while addresses are given to fill up the time. The committee reports as soon as possible or it may bring in its resolutions after a recess or at a subsequent meeting.

Permanent.—After a temporary organization is effected, the chairman calls upon some person who is taking a leading part in getting up the society to state the object of the proposed organization. A motion or resolution favoring the organization is next in order. If this motion is carried, a committee is appointed to draft a constitution or by-laws or both.

The constitution should contain five articles at least:

(1) name and object of the society,

(2) qualifications of members,

(3) officers, their election and duties,

(4) meetings of the society and

(5) how to amend the constitution.

At the second meeting the constitution is adopted, and after all have signed the constitution who wish to become members, by-laws may be adopted, and a committee is appointed to nominate permanent officers, to be elected then or at an adjourned meeting. Each permanent officer as he is elected, takes the place of the temporary one, and when all are elected, the organization is completed.

Nominations and Elections.—Generally the best way of making nominations is to place the matter in the hands of a committee created for the purpose, who, after due consideration, make the nominations and tender their report to the assembly. Then a motion is made and seconded to adopt the report of the committee. The names of the nominees are again read with a pause after each, to give opportunity for other nominations. Any member who is not satisfied with a nomination may move to substitute another name, and if this motion receives a second and is carried, the substituted name takes the place of the regular nominee.

A vote by acclamation may be taken upon each name before passing to the next. The more common way is to vote upon the names as a whole, after the entire list has been considered.

Sometimes the chairman is authorized by the assembly to make the nominations, and then the names are treated the same as if brought in by a committee.

Another way of nominating is as follows: Some member obtains the floor and says, "I nominate Mr. A" In the same way another member nominates Mr. B, and another Mr. C, and so on. When a number of candidates have thus been nominated, some member moves that the nominations close, and if this motion is seconded and carried, the chairman then takes the vote upon the names in the order in which the the nominations were made until one is elected. If there is more than one office to be filled, the same process must be gone through with for each office.

If the election is to be by ballot, and the names are on the ballots, each voter may cast his ballot as it is or may cross off names and write others in their places. If blank slips are used, each voter writes on his slip the names of the nominees or substitutes other names according to his choice. A majority of all the votes cast is necessary to a choice. If the office or offices are not filled at the first ballot, the voting must continue until the necessary officers are elected.

CONDUCT OF BUSINESS

Officers and Their Duties.—The presiding officer is generally known by the title of Chairman, President or Moderator. He should always be addressed by his title. In referring to himself he should use the third person: "It is the opinion of the chair."

It is his duty to call the meeting to order at the proper time, to announce in its order each item of business, to state all proper questions, to put them to vote, to declare the result of the vote, to see that the rules of debate are not violated, to preserve order, to state points of order or course of proceeding (by request or when he finds it necessary to do so), to receive all messages and other communications and announce them to the assembly and to act for the assembly in signing all papers.

He may sit while he is stating a question, but he should rise to put a question to vote or to speak to a question of order.

Vice-President. The vice-president acts in place of the president in his absence.

Clerk or Secretary. The recording officer, whether called clerk or secretary, keeps a correct record of the proceedings (the *minutes*) and reads them at the next meeting. In the absence of the chairman (if there is no vice-president present) it is his duty to call the meeting to order; to occupy the chair while the assembly proceeds to elect a chairman *pro tem.*; to read

papers to be acted upon when he is requested to do so; to call the roll of the assembly when that is necessary; to hand to the chairman of every committee appointed a list of the persons on the committee and a statement of the matter committed to them; to make out in order and hand to the chairman before each meeting the items of business for the meeting; to have at each meeting a list of all committees; to have the custody of all papers and documents; to sign his name to the minutes; and to authenticate by his signature (alone or in connection with that of the chairman) all the acts, orders and proceedings of the assembly. In some assemblies the secretary is appointed to act as treasurer also.

Treasurer. The treasurer has charge of the funds of the society and pays them out by order of the assembly, preferably on vouchers or orders signed by the secretary. His annual report should give the amount in the treasury at the beginning of the year, the amount received, the amount paid out and the balance on hand. This report should be examined by an auditor or by an auditing committee and compared with the itemized accounts kept by the treasurer and the receipts he has received for payments made. If it is found correct, it should be approved by a vote of the society.

Committees.—A committee for deliberation or investigation should be large and should represent all classes and localities. A committee for action should be small and should consist only of those who are in favor of the proposed action.

A committee may be nominated and elected, or the chairman may be authorized (by the constitution or by-laws or by a vote of the assembly) to appoint a committee or committees. The constitution or by-laws may also prescribe the number of members of which each committee shall be composed, or the number may be included in the motion if the appointment is ordered by the assembly.

In the event that different numbers are proposed, the number is decided by vote. The vote is taken first on the highest number proposed, and then upon the next and so on until a vote is carried.

A special or select committee is a committee appointed for a particular occasion.

A *standing* committee is one appointed beforehand, for all matters that may arise of the same nature.

The person first named on a committee is the *chairman;* he calls the members together and presides until the committee elects another chairman. In the absence of the first member the next in order who is present acts as chairman. The committee chooses a secretary, who is usually one of its own members but may be a non-member. It conducts its proceedings in the same manner as business is conducted in the assembly.

A committee must be assembled to do business, and a quorum must be present.

A paper referred to a committee must not be altered or rejected by them. The committee may present amendments written on another sheet;

they may recommend a substitution; or they may make any recommendation they see fit. The report of the committee is signed by all the members or by the chairman alone, and he makes the report to the assembly unless another has been chosen to tender it. Only that which has been agreed to by the majority can be incorporated in the report, but the minority may also tender a report if they choose. The minority report may be substituted for the report of the committee by a vote of the assembly. When the committee has tendered its report in full and the report has been accepted, the committee is thereby discharged, but it may be revived by having the whole report or some part referred back to it.

Sometimes the motion to adopt the report includes a recommendation "that the committee be discharged," but the recommendation is superfluous if the report is intended to be final.

Committees may *adjourn* from time to time until their work is completed. Then the motion is to *rise,* which means the same as to adjourn and is subject to the same rules.

Committee of the Whole. The object of resolving the assembly into the committee of the whole is to permit less formality in the consideration of a subject than under ordinary circumstances. The motion is, "That the assembly do now resolve itself into a committee of the whole, to consider," and so forth, specifying the subject. If this motion is carried, the presiding officer at once calls another member to the chair and takes his place as a member of the committee. The only motions in order are "to amend," "to adopt" and "to rise and report." Before going into the committee of the whole, the assembly may pass an order limiting debate, and this order cannot be changed in the committee.

When the chairman resumes his seat, the member who presided in the committee rises and informs the chairman that he is ready to report. The report may then be received, or the time may be fixed when it shall be received.

The clerk keeps the minutes of the proceedings of the committee if there is not an assistant clerk to keep them, but the only record he makes in the minutes of the assembly is the report as received from the committee. If at any time the committee becomes disorderly, the presiding officer may resume the chair and declare the committee dissolved.

The quorum of the committee of the whole is the same as that of the assembly.

Informal Action. Instead of going into a committee of the whole, the assembly may consider a question informally with the same freedom and the same restrictions as in the committee of the whole. In this case the chairman retains his seat and there is no motion to rise and report. The chairman brings the subject that has thus been considered before the assembly, and it is treated as if it were reported by a committee.

Any motion except "to amend" or "to adopt" puts an end to the informal action. A temporary memorandum is kept the same as in the committee of the whole, and the clerk enters only the chairman's report in the minutes.

Quorum.—A quorum of an assembly, a committee or a board is such a number as is competent to transact business; and unless the number is prescribed by the constitution or by-laws or by an order of the assembly, it consists of a majority of the members. The number may be fixed at much less than a majority. When a quorum is not present, the only action that can be taken is to adjourn.

Order of Business.—In the absence of special rules upon the subject, the regular order of business is as follows:

(1) Reading the minutes of the previous meeting.

(2) Reports of standing committees (boards of managers, trustees and so forth come under this head).

(3) Reports of special or select committees.

(4) Unfinished business.

(5) New business.

To take business up out of its order requires a suspension of the rules. A better way is to lay on the table business as it comes up, and thus reach a question that it is desirable to consider first.

Introduction of Business. New business must be introduced when there is no question before the assembly. It may be brought in in the form of a resolution or recommendation or in the form of a simple motion. The member rises, addresses the chairman by his title and, after being recognized by a bow or having his name announced, reads his resolution or recommendation and moves its adoption; or he makes a simple motion as suggested above. In either case another member seconds the motion.

Amendments and all other questions are introduced in the same way as new business. The table of motions shows when each motion is in order, and how the question may be treated.

The mover of a motion may modify it or withdraw it altogether before it is stated by the chair; but after it is stated he can do neither without the consent of the assembly. If a mover modifies his motion, the one who seconded it may withdraw his support or accept the modification.

Mere routine business may be transacted without the formality of a motion if no one objects.

Resolutions and Motions.—The following are typical forms:

Resolved, That fifty dollars of the funds of this society be appropriated to defray the expenses of its delegates at the general convention.

We recommend, That a committee of three be appointed by the chair to draft resolutions, or to make recommendations, respecting the establishment of a branch office in San Francisco.

First Member: Mr. Chairman, I move that the resolutions be adopted.

Second Member: Mr. Chairman, I second the motion.

A resolution or recommendation may have a preamble or preambles worded about as follows:

Whereas, It is desirable to procure only the best of material for our new building; and,

Whereas, We deem it necessary to send a man to personally superintend its selection; therefore,

Resolved, That . . . or We recommend, That . . .

The Motion.—The basis of business— the point for discussion and decision— is called the *motion.*

A motion is a formally-worded proposition presented in a deliberative body for its consideration and for its decision by vote.

A member having something to which he desires the meeting to agree makes a motion to that effect.

Before making his motion he must obtain the floor. To do this in an organized meeting he rises and, addressing the chairman, says, "Mr. President" (or whatever the title may be) and then waits for recognition. The chairman, hearing and seeing the member who has risen, recognizes him by pronouncing his name, "Mr. ——" or "The gentleman (or member) from ——," mentioning the locality he represents.

No member has a right to make a motion, discuss a question or address a meeting until he has thus addressed and has thus been recognized by the chairman. Then he has the floor.

Having obtained the floor, the member says, "Mr. President" (or whatever the title may be), "I move . . ."

Now it is necessary for another member to indicate his desire to have the proposition considered. This is called *seconding the motion.* To do this the second member may rise and, after securing recognition from the chair, say: "Mr. President, I second the motion." This is the better form. However, it is considered proper in ordinary assemblies for the person who seconds the motion to remain seated if he desires, and say simply: "I second the motion."

Stating the Question.—The presiding officer then says, "It has been moved and seconded that . . ." He reads the resolution or hands it to the secretary to be read by him. After stating or reading the motion, the president says, "The question is on the adoption of the resolution or motion just read." Or he may say, "You have heard the motion. Have you any remarks to make?" or, "Remarks are in order" or some equivalent expression. This is *stating the question.*

After the chairman has stated the question, the subject is open to discussion.

In routine work the chairman may often put a question without waiting even for a formal motion. This can be done only with common or universal consent only in regard to minor matters. Then this method saves time and does no injustice.

After a motion has been made and seconded and the question has been stated by the chair, the members may enter upon its discussion.

If a motion is not seconded, the chair should not state it but should say: "The motion is lost for want of a second."

Debate.—To debate a question the member must secure the floor in the same manner he would secure it for the purpose of offering a motion. The ordinary rule is for the presiding officer to give the floor to the member whose voice he first hears. When two or more address the chair at about the same time, the chair must decide who is entitled to the floor.

In such a case the member upon whose motion the subject was brought before the body or who presents the report, if he has not already spoken to the question, has the prior claim and should be recognized even if another addressed the chair before him. A member who has not spoken has priority over those who have.

Points of Order.—It is the privilege of any member to call attention to a breach of order in debate by obtaining the floor and saying, "I rise to a point of order." The chairman then says, "Please state your point of order." When the point is stated, the chairman decides whether it is well taken or not, and his decision is subject to appeal. When a question of order is raised, the speaker should at once take his seat and await the decision. Then if the decision is in his favor he may proceed; but if the decision is against him, and anyone objects to his speaking further, he cannot continue without permission from the assembly.

Limiting Debate.—It is the custom of bodies to limit the time of a speech and the number of times a member may speak to the same question.

The common parliamentary law is not to allow a member to speak more than once to the same question until all who desire have spoken.

If a member offers to speak a second time, and no one signifies a desire to occupy the floor, and there is no objection, the chair may permit the member to proceed. Otherwise to obtain the privilege of speaking a second time the question must be put to vote for the decision of the meeting.

An order limiting or closing debate can be adopted so that at the time specified all discussion upon it shall cease. As a body can limit the time of a speaker, it can also extend his time. The meeting can also extend the time of the debate.

In the discussion the speakers must confine themselves to the question before the body and avoid personalities or other improprieties.

The maker of a motion may vote against his motion but cannot speak against it.

Putting the Question.—If no one rises to speak, or the chairman thinks the debate has ended, he asks, "Are you ready for the question?" If then no one rises to debate it, he proceeds to put the question to vote.

In putting the question, the ordinary form will be for the chair to say, "The question is on the adoption of the motion [or resolution] you have just heard read. As many as are in favor of its adoption will say *aye.*" When the *ayes* have voted, he will then say, "As many as are of a contrary opinion will say *no*" or "All opposed will say *no.*" The chair, judging the comparative vote, will announce the result, stating that the motion is carried or lost. If he thinks the *ayes* are in the majority he says, "The *ayes* appear to have it." Then he pauses to see if anyone expresses doubt, and if no objection is raised, he says, "The *ayes* have it, and the motion is agreed to [is carried, or prevails]." If he think the *noes* are in the majority, he says, "The *noes* appear to have it," waits for an objection—and so forth.

Form of Voting.—The following are customary forms of voting:

viva voce (meaning by voice), ayes and noes;

show of hands, which are counted by the chairman or by tellers;

rising vote, the count of those standing being made by the chairman or by tellers;

voters pass between tellers, who count them;

yeas and nays;

by ballot.

Where a hand-vote is customary the chair may say, "Those in favor of the motion or resolution will hold up the right hand" and then "Those opposed will manifest it by the same sign." Excepting in a few cases a majority vote determines a question.

Discussion can be renewed even after the voting has begun, and up to the final voting of both sides.

Caution. Some chairmen make the mistake of saying: "All in favor of the motion say *aye*. Those opposed manifest it by the same sign." But the words "same sign" should be used only when the vote is being taken by a show of hands or other visible indication of the voter's preference.

When a motion is put to a vote the literal question before the house is: "Shall the motion be adopted?" The answer is either yes or no. When those in favor say "aye" (which is another form of the word *yes*), those opposed should say "no."

Division. When the chairman announces the result of a vote, any member may express a doubt as to the accuracy of the decision by rising and saying, "Mr. President, I call for a division of the house." If a member thus calls for a division, the presiding officer shall say, "A division is called for; those in favor of the motion will rise and stand until counted." After they are counted and the number is announced, he shall say, "Those opposed will rise," and they will be counted and the number announced. The chair or the clerk (or both) may count. After the announcement of the result, a member may press the doubt further by calling for a count by tellers, and even after that has been taken there may be a demand for the *ayes* and *nays*.

Ayes and Nays. The object of calling the *ayes* and *nays* is usually to place the names of the members on record so that it will be known how each man voted. At other times it is used as dilatory motion, and is made for the purpose of consuming time. In Congress one-fifth of the members present can order the vote to be taken by *ayes* and *nays*. In some bodies it is ordered on the call of a single member. Societies should have a rule stating what small minority may order the *ayes* and *nays*. In any meeting a majority vote can order the ayes and nays. When the ayes and nays have been ordered, the presiding officer will put the question in a form similar to the following: "As many as are in favor of the adoption of the resolution will, when their names are called, answer *aye* [or *yes*].

Those opposed will answer *nay* [or *no*]. The secretary [or clerk] will call the roll."

The roll is then called, and each member, as his name is called, rises and answers *aye* or *nay,* and the answer is noted by the clerk. When the roll call is ended, the clerk reads the names of those who voted in the affirmative and then those who voted in the negative. Errors may then be corrected. The clerk gives the number voting on each side to the chair, who announces the result.

The Ballot. Sometimes a vote is by ballot. It is common and most equitable in the election of officers.

The chairman appoints at least two tellers, who distribute slips of paper upon which the members write their votes. The tellers collect and count the votes and report the result to the chairman, who announces it to the meeting. In counting ballots all blanks are ignored. To announce an election the chair will say: "The whole number of votes cast is——; the number necessary for a choice is ——; Mr. A received ——; Mr. B, ——; Mr. C, ——. Mr. A, having received the requisite number, is therefore elected."

Tie Vote. When there is a tie vote the motion fails. The chairman, if a member of the meeting or authorized by constitutional law, however, has the casting or deciding vote in such a case, and, if he gives it for the affirmative, the motion prevails. He may even vote with the minority when his vote will make a tie, and thus defeat a measure, and he may vote in any case where his vote would change the result. Thus where a two-thirds vote is necessary, and his vote given to the minority would prevent the adoption of the question, the presiding officer can so cast his vote.

Classes of Motions.—Motions are classified according to their nature and purpose:

(1) The *principal* motion or *main* question by which the subject is brought before the body.

(2) Those which bear upon the main question. These are called *subsidiary motions,* and are as follows:

(a) to postpone indefinitely,

(b) to amend,

(c) to refer (commit or recommit),

(d) to postpone to a certain day or time,

(e) the previous question,

(f) to lay on the table.

(3) *Incidental questions,* so called because they are occasioned in a casual way during the consideration of other questions. From their very nature they must be decided before the questions which give rise to them. They include:

(a) suspension of the rules,

(b) withdrawal of a motion,

(c) reading of papers,

(d) objection to the consideration of a question,

(e) questions of order (including appeals from the decision of the chair).

(4) *Privileged questions,* so called for their pressing importance and need of immediate attention; therefore they may interrupt other proceedings. They are:

(a) calls for the orders of the day,

(b) questions of privilege,

(c) the motion to adjourn,

(d) the motion to fix the time to which to adjourn.

Order of Precedence. The motions below numbered 1 to 9 take precedence over all others in the order given, and any one of them, except to amend or substitute, is in order while a motion of a lower rank is pending.

(Letters refer to rules following)

Closing a meeting.	
1. To fix time to which to adjourn	B
2. To adjourn (in committees, to rise), or to take a recess, without limitation	A E F
Concerning orders, rules and so forth	
3. For the orders of the day	A E H N
To make subject a special order	M
To amend the rules	M
To suspend the rules	A E F M
To take up a question out of its proper order	A E
To take from the table	A E G
Questions touching priority of business	A
4. To lay upon the table	A E G
To bring up a question the second time.	
To reconsider debatable question	D E F Y
To reconsider undebatable question	A E F I
Questions of privilege.	
Asking leave to continue speaking after indecorum	A
Appeal from chair's decision touching indecorum	A E H L
Appeal from chair's decision generally	E H L
Question upon reading of papers	A E
Withdrawal of a motion	A E
Suppressing or extending debate.	
5. For the previous question	A E M
To limit or close debate	A M
To extend limits of debate	A
Deferring action.	
6. To postpone to a fixed time	C
To refer to committee.	
7. To commit (or recommit)	D
Modifying or amending.	
8. To amend or to substitute, or to divide the question	K
Suppressing the question.	
Objection to consideration of question	A H M N
9. To postpone indefinitely	D E

Rule A. Undebatable, but remarks may be tacitly allowed.

Rule B. Undebatable if another question is before the assembly.

Rule C. Limited debate allowed on propriety of postponement only.

Rule D. Opens the main question to debate. Motions not so marked do not allow of reference to main question.

Rule E. Cannot be amended. Motion to adjourn can be amended when there is no other business before the house.

Rule F. Cannot be reconsidered.

Rule G. An affirmative vote cannot be reconsidered.

Rule H. In order when another has the floor.

Rule I. A motion to reconsider may be moved and entered when another has the floor, but the business then before the house may not be set aside. This motion can only be entertained when made by one who voted originally with the prevailing side. When called up it takes precedence of all others which may come up, excepting only motions relating to adjournment.

Rule K. A motion to amend an amendment cannot be amended.

Rule L. When an appeal from the chair's decision results in a tie vote, the chair is sustained.

Rule M. Requires a two-thirds vote unless special rules have been enacted.

Rule N. Does not require to be seconded.

General Rules.—No motion is open for discussion until it has been stated by the chair.

The maker of a motion cannot modify it or withdraw it after it has been stated by the chair, except by general consent.

Only one reconsideration of a question is permitted.

A motion to adjourn, to lay on the table or to take from the table cannot be renewed unless some other motion has been made in the interval.

On motion to strike out the words, "Shall the words stand as part of the motion?" unless a majority sustains the words, they are struck out.

On motion for previous question, the form to be observed is, "Shall the main question be now put?" This, if carried, ends debate.

On an appeal from the chair's decision, "Shall the decision be sustained as the ruling of the house?" the chair is sustained if the vote for a tie.

On motion for orders of the day, "Will the house now proceed to the order of the day?" This, if carried, supersedes intervening motions.

When an objection is raised to considering questions, "Shall the question be considered?" objections may be made by any member before debate has commenced, but not subsequently.

HIGH SCHOOL LITERARY SOCIETY

Model for Organization.—The following is correct procedure in forming a literary society for a high school.

A group of students who are interested have met in a classroom. Mr. White, who has been active in bringing them together, takes his place on the platform, raps on the desk and says:

"The meeting will please come to order. Nominations for Temporary Chairman will be received."

Mr. Smith (rising): "I nominate Mr. Jones."

Miss Brown (either rising or seated): "I second the nomination."

Mr. White: "It has been moved and seconded that Mr. Jones act as Chairman. All in favor will say *aye*."

After considering the number voting *aye*, Mr. White says: "All opposed say *no*."

If he is satisfied that a majority have voted *aye*, Mr. White says: "The motion is carried. Will Mr. Jones please take the chair?"

If he is satisfied that a majority have voted *no*, Mr. White says: "The motion is lost. Other nominations are in order."

If more than one are nominated, Mr. White puts to a vote each name in the order nominated until one receives a majority.

Mr. Jones (or whoever is chosen) takes the chair and addresses the group:

"I thank you for the honor. I consider that it is greatly to our advantage to have a literary society in our high school and I trust we shall make it a source of credit to our school. Nominations for Secretary are in order."

Miss Ames (rising): "Mr. Chairman."

The Chairman: "Miss Ames."

Miss Ames: "I nominate Miss West."

Mr. Black (either rising or seated): "I second the nomination."

The Chairman: "Are there any other nominations?" (After a pause) "As there are no further nominations, we shall proceed to vote. It has been moved and seconded that Miss West act as secretary of the meeting. All in favor say *aye*." (After considering the number voting *aye*) "All opposed say *no*. The motion is carried. Will Miss West please take her place as secretary?"

Miss West does so and thereafter keeps a record of all motions made, seconded and carried, of officers elected, communications received and other business transacted.

The Chairman: "I shall ask Mr. Randall to state the object of this meeting."

Mr. Randall (rising): "Mr. Chairman."

The Chairman: "Mr. Randall."

Mr. Randall: "It has been evident for some time that a literary society is needed in this high school. It will give us a chance to learn many things which we cannot get from our regular studies—training in parliamentary law, the art of speaking in public, practice in debating. To that end I move the adoption of the following resolution, which I ask the Secretary to read."

He hands it to the Secretary, who reads it aloud:

> "RESOLVED, That a literary society be formed in this high school for the purpose of self-improvement of the members."

Miss Arnold: "I second the resolution."

(The person who seconds a motion or resolution need not rise nor address the chair. All others wishing to take part in the proceedings should first rise, address the presiding officer by his or her appropriate title and wait for recognition by the chair before speaking.)

The Chairman: "Are there any remarks?"

Several persons present speak for or against the resolution.

The Chairman: "Are you ready for the question?"

No one rises to speak, but several persons call out: "Question."

The Chairman: "You have heard the resolution, which has been duly moved and seconded. All who are in favor of the adoption of the resolution will say *aye*. All opposed say *no*. The resolution is adopted."

Miss Stewart (rising): "Mr. Chairman."

The Chairman: "Miss Stewart."

Miss Stewart: "I move that the Chairman appoint a committee of three to draft a constitution and by-laws, and to report at our next meeting."

Mr. Cox: "I second the motion."

The Chairman: "It has been regularly moved and seconded that the Chairman appoint a committee of three to draft a constitution and by-laws, and to report at our next meeting. Are there any remarks?" (Hearing none) "Are you ready for the question?" (Several say "Question") "All who are in favor of the motion will say *aye*. Those opposed say *no*. The motion is carried. I shall appoint Mr. White, Miss Ames and Mr. Green as the committee."

(Mr. White, being named first, is Chairman of the committee.)

Mr. Adams: "Mr. Chairman."

The Chairman: "Mr. Adams."

Mr. Adams: "I move we adjourn."

Miss Moore: "I second the motion."

This motion is not debatable, cannot be amended and takes precedence over all other business. It must be put to a vote at once unless a motion is made to adjourn to a fixed time or place.

Miss Turner: "Mr. Chairman."

The Chairman: "Miss Turner."

Miss Turner: "I move that we adjourn to meet again in this room two weeks from today at three o'clock in the afternoon."

Mr. Pope: "I second the motion."

This motion is debatable and may be amended.

Mr. Long: "Mr. Chairman."

The Chairman: "Mr. Long."

Mr. Long: "I move to amend the motion to read that we adjourn to meet one week from today at four o'clock in the afternoon."

Miss Clarke: "I second the amendment."

The Chairman: "The question is first on the amendment. Are there any remarks? All who are in favor of the amendment will say *aye*. Those opposed say *no*. The amendment is carried. The question is now on the motion as amended. Are there any remarks? All who are in favor of the motion as amended will say *aye*. Those opposed say *no*. The motion is carried, and the meeting now stands adjourned to meet again in this room one week from today at four o'clock in the afternoon."

If the amendment is lost, the Chairman will announce: "The amendment is lost. The question is now on the original motion." (Proceed in the regular order by asking for remarks and so forth.)

If the motion to adjourn is lost, it cannot be renewed until some business has been transacted.

One week later, at four o'clock in the afternoon, the second meeting is held, with the Temporary Chairman and Temporary Secretary still performing their respective duties as previously.

The Chairman: "The meeting will please come to order. The Secretary will read the minutes of the previous meeting."

The Secretary does so.

The Chairman: "You have heard the minutes. Are there any corrections or additions? If not, they will stand approved as read."

If corrections or additions are made, the announcement will be: "The minutes as corrected [or enlarged] will stand approved."

The Chairman: "The next order of business will be the report of the committee on constitution and by-laws, of which Mr. White is Chairman."

Mr. White: "Mr. Chairman."

The Chairman: "Mr. White."

Mr. White: "Your committee submits the following proposed constitution and by-laws."

He hands the manuscript to the Secretary.

The Chairman: "What is your pleasure? Shall we read the constitution and by-laws and vote upon their adoption as a whole? Or shall we read and vote upon them article by article?"

Miss Wood: "Mr. Chairman."

The Chairman: "Miss Wood."

Miss Wood: "I move that we vote

upon the constitution and by-laws as a whole."

Mr. Dean: "I second the motion."

The Chairman: "It is moved and seconded that the meeting vote upon the constitution and by-laws as a whole. All who are in favor will say *aye*. Those opposed say *no*. The motion is carried. The Secretary will read the proposed constitution and by-laws."

The Secretary does so.

Mr. Young: "Mr. Chairman."

The Chairman: "Mr. Young."

Mr. Young: "I move the adoption of the constitution and by-laws as read."

Miss Faris: "I second the motion."

The Chairman: "It is regularly moved and seconded that the constitution and by-laws as read be adopted. Are there any remarks? Are you ready for the question? All who are in favor will say *aye*. Those opposed say *no*. The motion is carried, and the constitution and by-laws are adopted."

If the motion to adopt as a whole is lost, or if no such motion is made, the following should be the procedure:

Miss Gale: "Mr. Chairman."

The Chairman: "Miss Gale."

Miss Gale: "I move that the constitution and by-laws be considered and adopted article by article."

The motion is seconded and adopted.

The Chairman: "The Secretary will read the first article." (The Secretary does so.) "Are there any amendments or additions?"

If members desire to amend or add to the article, motions to that effect may be made and seconded, and the Chairman will put them to a vote until the article is satisfactory to a majority of those present; and so on with the succeeding articles.

If there are no amendments or additions, the Chairman, after a pause to ascertain the fact, will say: "All who are in favor of Article I as read will say *aye*. Those opposed say *no*. The *ayes* have it, and Article I as read is adopted." (And so on with the other articles.)

Another method, equally proper, is for the Chairman to say: "Are there any amendments or additions to this article? Are there any objections? Hearing none, I will ask the Secretary to read the next article."

In either case, after all the articles have been read and passed by or acted on, they should be adopted as a whole.

Mr. Hart: "Mr. Chairman."

The Chairman: "Mr. Hart."

Mr. Hart: "I move that the entire constitution and by-laws (as amended, if that has been done) be adopted as a whole."

Miss Knox: "I second the motion."

The Chairman: "It is regularly moved and seconded that the constitution and by-laws as amended be adopted as a whole. Are there any remarks? Are you ready for the question? All in favor will say *aye*. Those opposed will say *no*. The motion is carried and the constitution and by-laws are adopted as a whole."

The Chairman: "We will now take a recess for ten minutes, during which

time all persons present who wish to become members of the new literary society will please sign the constitution and by-laws." (They do so.)

At the conclusion of the recess the Chairman raps for order again and says: "The next order of business will be the election of officers in accordance with the constitution. How will you have them selected? Shall we appoint a committee on nominations or shall we have nominations from the floor for each office?"

Mr. Burton: "Mr. Chairman."

The Chairman: "Mr. Burton."

Mr. Burton: "I move that the Chairman appoint a committee on nominations consisting of three members, who shall retire and report back to this meeting as soon as they have made their selections."

The motion is seconded and carried. The Chairman appoints Mr. Burton, Chairman; Miss Knox and Mr. Hart. They retire.

The Chairman: "While we are waiting for the committee on nominations to report, I suggest that we have expressions of opinion from several present as to what our proposed literary society should do." Various suggestions are made. The committee returns to the room.

The Chairman: "Is the committee on nominations ready to report?"

Mr. Burton: "Mr. Chairman."

The Chairman: "Mr. Burton."

Mr. Burton: "The committee on nominations recommends the election of the following as permanent officers of this literary society":

Mr. Burton may read the report himself or hand it to the Secretary, who reads it.

"For President, Mr. Hill; for Vice-President, Miss Pierce; for Recording Secretary, Miss Abbott; for Corresponding Secretary, Miss Early; for Treasurer, Mr. Noble."

Mr. Kane: "Mr. Chairman."

The Chairman: "Mr. Kane."

Mr. Kane: "I move that the candidates named by the committee on nominations be declared elected."

Miss Page: "I second the motion."

The Chairman: "It is regularly moved and seconded that the candidates named by the committee on nominations be declared elected. Are there any other nominations? As there are no other nominations, are you ready for the question?"

Mr. Foster: "Mr. Chairman."

The Chairman: "Mr. Foster."

Mr. Foster: "I rise to a point of order."

The Chairman: "Please state your point of order."

Mr. Foster: "My point of order is that the constitution provides that all elections for officers shall be by ballot. Hence the motion now before the house proposes a method of election that would be illegal."

The Chairman: "The point of order is well taken. The motion that the candidates named by the committee on nominations be declared elected is out of order."

Mr. Hopkins: "Mr. Chairman."

The Chairman: "Mr. Hopkins."

Mr. Hopkins: "I move that the Secretary be instructed to cast one ballot in favor of the election of the

candidates named by the committee on nominations."

Miss Cooper: "I second the motion."

The Chairman: "It is regularly moved and seconded that the Secretary be instructed to cast one ballot in favor of the election of the candidates named by the committee on nominations. Are you ready for the question? All who are in favor of the motion will say *aye*. Those opposed say *no*. The motion is carried, and the Secretary is so instructed."

The Secretary writes the names and offices on a ballot, and reports: "Mr. Chairman."

The Chairman: "Madam Secretary."

The Secretary: "The ballot has been cast in favor of the election of the following: For President, Mr. Hill; for Vice-President, Miss Pierce; for Recording Secretary, Miss Abbott; for Corresponding Secretary, Miss Early; for Treasurer, Mr. Noble."

(In practice, it is not necessary for the Secretary actually to write the names on a ballot, but it is sufficient if the Secretary states to the Chairman that the ballot has been so cast.)

The Chairman: "The ballot has been cast for the candidates named, and I declare them duly elected to their respective offices. Will Mr. Hill please come forward and take the chair, and will Miss Abbott please take her place as Recording Secretary of the meeting?" (They do so.)

If there are other nominations from the floor for any office, then the Secretary cannot be instructed to cast a ballot for that office. The Chairman takes up in turn each office for which additional nominations are made, beginning with the President, and says:

"Are there any other nominations for President? Hearing none, we will proceed to vote on the candidates in the order in which their names were proposed."

Or somebody may move that nominations be closed, which must be seconded and put to a vote. If carried, the Chairman proceeds:

The Chairman: "Mr. Hill, Miss Blake and Mr. Hood have been nominated for President. According to the by-laws, all elections for officers shall be by ballot. The Secretary will prepare ballots and distribute them to the persons present who are entitled to vote. All persons who have signed the constitution and by-laws are entitled to vote. Each member will write upon the ballot the name of the candidate for President preferred. Then fold the ballot and hand it to one of the tellers. The Chairman appoints Mr. Taylor and Miss Faris as tellers, who will collect the ballots and count them, and report the result of the vote."

If there are factions, the chair should appoint a teller from each faction, so far as possible.

The tellers collect and count the ballots. Mr. Taylor, having been named first, reports:

Mr. Taylor: "Mr. Chairman."

The Chairman: "Mr. Taylor."

Mr. Taylor: "The result of the vote is as follows:

Whole number of votes cast, 37; necessary to a choice, 18.

Mr. Hill received 19 votes; Miss Blake received 10 votes; Mr. Hood received 8 votes."

Or the tellers may hand the report to the Secretary, who reads it.

The Chairman repeats to the meeting the result of the vote, and adds: "Mr. Hill, having received a majority of all the votes cast, is duly elected President. Will Mr. Hill please take the chair."

If no one has received a majority, the Chairman says: "No one has received a majority of the votes cast. You will prepare your ballots again." And so on until one receives a majority.

The successful candidate for President takes the chair.

The same procedure is followed for the other candidates.

Instead of appointing a committee on nominations, all nominations may be made from the floor. When nominations are made from the floor, the procedure will be the same as it is when the committee on nominations makes its report.

The Chairman: "Nominations for President are in order."

Miss Page: "Mr. Chairman."

The Chairman: "Miss Page."

Miss Page: "I nominate Mr. Hill." (Nominations need not be seconded.)

Mr. Gray: "Mr. Chairman."

The Chairman: "Mr. Gray."

Mr. Gray: "I nominate Miss Blake."

Mr. Nolan: "Mr. Chairman."

The Chairman: "Mr. Nolan."

Mr. Nolan: "I nominate Mr. Hood."

The Chairman: (After a pause) "Are there any further nominations?" (No response.) "If there are no further nominations for President, I declare the nominations closed."

Or somebody may move that nominations be closed, and this motion is seconded and carried.

The Chairman: "You will prepare your ballots." (The votes are collected and counted by the tellers; they report the result to the Chairman, who announces it to the meeting, as already outlined.)

The same procedure is followed for all the officers.

If there is only one nomination, someone after being recognized by the Chairman may say: "I move that the Secretary cast one ballot for Mr. Hill for President."

If this motion is seconded and carried, the Secretary reports: "Mr. Chairman, the ballot has been cast in favor of Mr. Hill for President."

The Chairman: "The ballot has been cast for Mr. Hill, and I declare him duly elected President."

Model Constitution and By-Laws.—The constitution provides the framework, while the by-laws take care of the working details. The former is the carriage; the latter, the power. The line is not closely drawn, however, and often the whole may be merged and designated as either the one or the other.

The following is offered as a model that contains the main essentials:

CONSTITUTION

ARTICLE I

NAME. The name of this organization shall be the Adelphian Literary Society of the Springfield High School.

ARTICLE II

OBJECT. The object of the Society shall be the self-improvement of the members in public speaking, debating, essay writing, parliamentary law and kindred subjects.

ARTICLE III

MEMBERS. Members shall consist of two classes—active and honorary. Active members shall comprise students in good standing in their studies in the Springfield High School, who may sign the constitution and pay the required dues. Honorary members shall comprise teachers, alumni and guests, who shall not be required to pay dues.

ARTICLE IV

OFFICERS. The officers of the Adelphian Literary Society shall be a President, a Vice-President, a Recording Secretary, a Corresponding Secretary and a Treasurer, who shall be elected by ballot from the active members of the society at the last meeting in each semester of the school year. The officers shall assume office at the first regular meeting in each semester and shall serve for a term of one semester and until their successors shall be elected and take office. A vacancy in any office may be filled at any regular meeting for the balance of the term. The officers shall have the customary powers of such offices in parliamentary bodies.

ARTICLE V

COMMITTEES. There shall be the following standing committees, of three members each, to be appointed by the President:

Membership, Program and Entertainment.

The Membership Committee shall endeavor to secure desirable Members for the Society. All applications for membership shall first be passed on by the membership committee, who shall recommend to the Society such names as the committee approves.

The Program Committee shall arrange for the programs of each meeting.

The Entertainment Committee shall provide for special entertainment features not included in the regular programs.

Other committees, either standing or special, may be appointed as seems necessary. Unless otherwise provided for in the resolutions creating them, all special committees shall be appointed by the President.

ARTICLE VI

MEETINGS. Regular meetings shall be held at four o'clock in the afternoon of Wednesday of each week while school is in session. Where the regular meeting day falls on a holiday, the meeting shall be held on the day previous. Special meetings may be called by the President or by any five members, by posting notice thereof on the regular bulletin board of the High School, at least two days before the meeting is to be held. Such notice shall state clearly the time and place of the meeting.

ARTICLE VII

AMENDMENTS. Amendments to the constitution may be presented at any regular meeting, but shall not be voted on until the next regular meeting. A majority vote of all active members present at the meeting shall be necessary for adoption.

BY-LAWS

ARTICLE I

QUORUM. A majority of all the active members shall constitute a quorum. (If the membership is large, a smaller number than a majority may be declared a quorum.)

ARTICLE II

RIGHTS AND DUTIES OF MEMBERS. Active members may serve on committees and hold office. Honorary members shall have the right to be present at all meetings and may take part in the discussion of any question but shall not have the right to vote. They may serve on committees but shall not hold office.

New members shall be admitted in the following manner:

At each regular meeting the name of an applicant may be proposed by an active member. All names proposed shall be referred to the membership committee who shall report at the next regular meeting. If the committee's report is favorable, each name shall be voted on separately. A ma-

jority vote of all active members present is necessary to elect to membership.

ARTICLE III

DUES. The dues of active members shall be one dollar for each semester, payable during the first two weeks of the semester. If not paid within two weeks, the member shall stand suspended until the dues are paid. During suspension a member may attend meetings, but shall not take part in the program nor serve on committees nor hold office. If the dues are not paid by the end of the semester, the member's name shall be stricken from the membership roll. To become a member again his name must be proposed and passed on by the membership committee, and voted on by the membership as in the case of other applicants.

ARTICLE IV

RULES OF ORDER. All questions of parliamentary law shall be governed by *Robert's Rules of Order*, Revised Edition.

ARTICLE V

DUTIES OF OFFICERS. The President shall preside at all regular and special meetings, and appoint all committees not otherwise provided for. The Vice-President shall perform the duties of the President when the President is absent or otherwise unable to act. The Recording Secretary shall keep the minutes of all regular and special meetings in a book to be kept for that purpose. The Corresponding Secretary shall send out written notices and attend to such correspondence as may be required. The Treasurer shall collect the dues and pay such bills as have been approved for payment in open meeting. He shall keep an accurate record of all receipts and disbursements. He shall present a report at each regular meeting showing the balance on hand. At the end of his term of office he shall turn over all of the money, with his books and records, to his successor.

ARTICLE VI

ORDER OF BUSINESS. At every regular meeting, the order of business shall be:

1. Roll call
2. Reading minutes of preceding meeting
3. Program
4. Receipt of communications, bills, and so forth
5. Reports of standing committees
6. Reports of special committees
7. Unfinished business
8. New business
9. Adjournment

By a two-thirds vote at any regular meeting, the order of business may be set aside for that meeting.

The reading of the minutes may be dispensed with by a majority vote.

ARTICLE VII

AMENDMENTS. Amendments to the by-laws may be presented at any meeting, whether regular or special, but shall not be voted on until the next meeting, either regular or special. A majority of a quorum present at the meeting shall be necessary for adoption.

Abuses.—Parliamentary law was evolved as a means of giving fullest expression to all opinions and of insuring justice to all members of an assembly. However, it is not uncommon for individuals to take advantage of the wording of the law for their own advancement or that of the groups they represent. There have been several Speakers of the House of Representatives who crushed out all minority opposition and yet adhered strictly to the letter of parliamentary law. The simplest practice was to refuse to recognize members who were known to disagree with the majority. Such members were helpless to change the situation.

Members of the Speaker's own group were now and then ignored as a means of punishing them for some offense. In the Senate the most outstanding abuse of parliamentary law is for a member to filibuster, that is, to take advantage of the unlimited debate allowed by Senate rules and prevent transaction of any business by talking as long as he is physically capable.

Abandonment, the intentional relinquishment of rights or property. There must be both the intention and the external act. Therefore lost articles are not abandoned, and title remains in the owner. Abandonment of personal property gives title of ownership to any person who takes it. An inventor who dedicates his discovery to the public abandons title to a patent. Abandonment of persons bound by relationship is illegal. It becomes *desertion* if a family or any of its members are abandoned, and the law prescribes penalties.

Abdication, the act of a sovereign in renouncing his royal office. It may be voluntary, but more often the ruler is forced into retirement by political pressure. Below are listed some important abdications in the past 70 years:

Year	Ruler
1886	Alexander of Bulgaria
1889	Milan I of Serbia
1889	Dom Pedro of Brazil
1909	Abdul Hamid of Turkey
1910	Manuel II of Portugal
1912	Hsuan Tung of China
1917	Nicholas II of Russia
1917	Constantine I of Greece (restored, 1920)
1918	Ferdinand I of Bulgaria
1918	Charles I of Austria
1918	Wilhelm II of Germany
1918	All German kings and princes
1922	Constantine I of Greece
1923	George II of Greece (restored, 1935)
1925 and 1940	Carol of Rumania
1931	Alfonso XIII of Spain
1935	Prajadhipok of Thailand
1936	Edward VIII of Great Britain
1945	Bao Dai of Indo-China
1947	Michael of Rumania
1948	Wilhelmina of the Netherlands
1955	Norodom Sihanouk of Cambodia

Abduction, the act of taking away a woman, especially a girl in her teens, by fraud, undue persuasion or force. Kidnaping, originally the forcible taking away of a man, woman or child from his or her own country and sending him or her to another, now has the meaning of any forcible taking away or imprisoning.

Absent voting, the privilege of casting a ballot without appearing in person. More than half the states of the Union, beginning with Vermont in 1896, have laws permitting absent or absentee voting, especially for students away from home and for railroad men. The reasons for voting at home are: custom, local elections, state control of suffrage requirements and the necessity for careful scrutiny of voters. The absentee laws are drafted to prevent fraud and to ensure the voters' rights.

In Great Britain Acts of Parliament in 1918 and 1920 control and permit absentee voting and also voting by proxy.

Under the German Republic, a German citizen could vote anywhere in the Reich if he had an electoral certificate or *Stimmschein*.

Abstract of title, a brief statement of the documents and facts upon which title to land depends, made for the purpose of enabling the buyer to review easily the validity of the title. The abstractor does not guarantee title, but he is usually liable for damages resulting from an incorrect abstract.

Acceptance, the receipt of a thing offered by another with the intention of keeping the thing and the indication of such intention by some act.

Acceptance of goods upon delivery, not obligatory until the buyer has had a reasonably satisfactory opportunity to inspect them to find whether their quantity, quality and condition are satisfactory. According to the Sales Act acceptance by the buyer does not free the seller from obligation to make good any defects or shortcomings that appear later and could not reasonably have been discovered on preliminary examination; but to have a good claim, the buyer should inform the seller *within a reasonable time* after he discovers shortcomings or defects.

Accessory, one who aids in the perpetration of a crime but is not present when it is committed. If present, he is one of the principals. An *accessory before the fact* is one who has knowledge of the proposed criminal act and takes no steps to prevent it; an *accessory after the fact* has knowledge of the commission of a crime and helps to shield the offender.

Accidental president, a derogatory term for a chief executive not elected to that office but succeeding on the death of the President who was elected. The accidental presidents of the United States were Tyler, Fillmore, Johnson, Arthur, Theodore Roosevelt, Coolidge and Truman.

Acknowledgment, a formal declaration before a notary or competent court officer that the instrument is one's genuine and voluntary act or deed. The certification of the officer or notary on an instrument that it has been acknowledged is also called an acknowledgment. An instrument that has been acknowledged may be used as evidence in court or recorded without further proof of its execution.

Act, the finished and formally announced will of a legislature, including any necessary approval by the proper executive officer; a *statute*. The term *bill* is properly applied only to the draft of a proposed act.

Action at law, a proceeding in a court by which one party prosecutes another for the enforcement of a right, the redress of a wrong or the punishment of an offense.

Act of God, an inevitable accident or other happening that could not be foreseen or controlled and that is not caused or aided by man.

Administrative agency, a governmental body created by an executive act of the President or by an act of Congress. Some administrative agencies that are independent of the President are the Interstate Commerce Commission (1887), the National Labor Relations Board (1935), the Federal Trade Commission (1920) and the Tennessee Valley Authority (1933). Other important agencies such as the Hoover Commission, created by an act of Congress in 1947, or agencies located in one of the executive departments like the Federal Security Agency, 1939, are subject to the control of the President.

Administrative law, that branch of law that prescribes the manner of activity and the jurisdiction of the various officers and organs of the government concerned with administration.

Administrator, a person appointed by a probate, orphans' or surrogate's court to manage and distribute the estate of a person who has died without appointing an executor. Relations are usually entitled to first consideration for appointment, ranking above creditors. The administrator usually executes a bond for faithful performance of his duties; his remuneration is fixed by the court.

Admiralty, that branch of the law that deals with maritime questions and offenses. Admiralty jurisdiction in the United States is in the Federal courts. (Art. III, Sec. 2.)

Adoption, the act through court procedure by which a child becomes a legal member of another family and has conferred upon him in his new status all rights that can be claimed through natural relationship of parent and child including the right to inherit as if a blood descendant if the parent dies without a will. State laws about adoption vary widely. Some states permit adoption only by married couples, and some allow adoption of minors only.

Advertising restrictions, enacted into law during the period since 1912 in most states of the United States, forbid false representation (by circulation or publication) concerning property, services or securities offered to the public for sale. The police power of the Government is the sanction for these laws.

About 30 states have adopted the Printer's Ink Model Statute (drafted by an advertising publication named *Printer's Ink*) which provides that offering or publishing "an advertisement that is false, deceptive or misleading" is a misdemeanor.

Blue-sky laws in many states control the sale of securities.

Federal restrictions of advertising are of three kinds: postal restrictions, forbidding the use of the mails to defraud; Federal statutes with penalties for misbranding food and drug products; and the general powers of the Federal Trade Commission to issue desist orders against firms using advertising illegitimately.

Advisory opinion, an opinion by a state's highest court given for the guidance of the governor, the legislature or state official in regard to the constitutionality of a proposed measure. The opinion has no binding force since a court can legally deal only with a specific case brought before it. Colorado, Florida, Maine, Massachusetts, New Hampshire and Rhode Island are

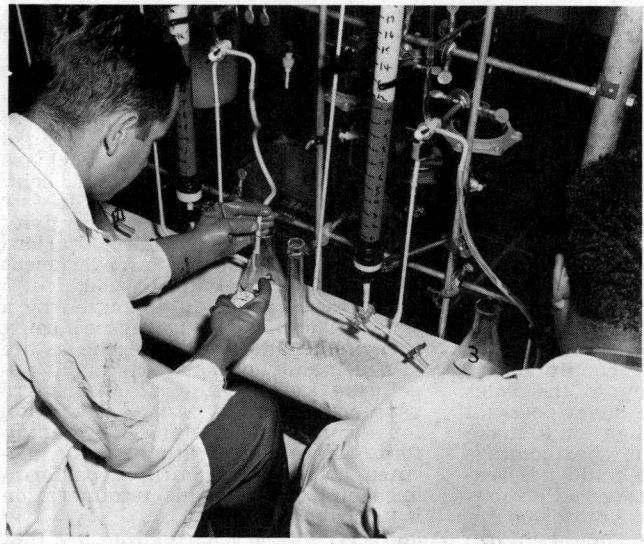

U.S. DEPARTMENT OF AGRICULTURE

RADIOSTRONTIUM being removed from milk by a division of the Department of Agriculture (*left*). Up to 98 per cent of *strontium 90*, a result of fallout, can be removed by passing it through ion-exchange resins to increase acidity and then returning to normal.

The U.S.D.A. Sedimentation Research Laboratory is concerned with sedimentation problems applied to conserving water and the fertility of soil. A hydrologist uses a gamma-ray density probe (*right*) to measure volume weight of sediment held in reservoirs.

some of the states that permit advisory opinions.

It has repeatedly been suggested that the Supreme Court of the United States should furnish advisory opinions about bills of dubious constitutionality, but the court has ruled that its jurisdiction is limited to "cases and controversies" by the Constitution (Art. I, Sec. 2, Cl. 1.).

Affidavit, a written statement sworn to before a notary, court clerk or other person authorized to administer oaths. If prepared by a second person, the declaration is read in full and if it is found to be correct, it is signed by the declarant, who then makes oath or affirmation that it is true.

Affidavit of defense, a statement made in the required legal form that the defendant has a good defense upon the merits of the case to the plaintiff's action.

Affirmation, a solemn declaration made by a person whose conscience or religion forbids him to take an oath. He affirms, rather than swears, that statements he is to make are true. An affirmation has the same effect as an oath, and one who affirms is subject to the penalties for perjury.

Affray (literally, fright, making afraid), a disturbance of the public peace by two or more people fighting and causing terror in a public place. It differs from a riot in that an affray is not premeditated.

Age has a definite bearing on one's legal status and responsibilities. Under 7, a child is assumed to be incapable of criminal intent; and between 7 and 14 the same incapability is presumed until the contrary is proved. An infant of 14 or more years is presumed to be capable of committing a crime just as an adult although the contrary may be shown. *Age of consent to marry,* formerly 14 for males and 12 for females, has been increased by statute in all but 11 states.

Full age, mature age, majority (as contrasted with being a minor or under age) is usually 21, though about one-third of the states set 18 years as the age of majority for women. In some states a female attains majority upon marriage even if she is not 21 (or 18).

The Constitution of the United States sets 35 years as the minimum age for President, 30 for senators and 25 for representatives in Congress.

Agency, the relationship that results where one party, called the *principal,* authorizes another, called the *agent,* to act for him in business dealings with third persons. An agent is distinguished from a servant only as a matter of degree, the agent generally having more authority and occupying a superior position to that of a servant.

Agriculture, Department of, an executive department of the Federal Government since 1889 with a Secretary who is a member of the President's Cabinet. From 1862 to 1889 there was a Department administered by a Commissioner. As early as 1839 Congress had appropriated money for studying farm conditions and for free distribution of seeds. The main object of the present department is "to acquire and diffuse among the people of the United States useful information on subjects concerned with agriculture."

The activities of the Department are concerned with all features of farming. Its major units are the Agricultural Research Administration (1942), concerned with the bureau of chemistry, soils, animal husbandry, dairy industry, entomology and plant quarantine, human nutrition and home economics, plant industry and agricultural engineering, research and experiment stations; the Commodity Credit Corporation (1933); Farm Credit Administration; Federal Land Banks; Farmer's Home Administra-

tion; Federal Crop Insurance Corporation; Forestry Service; Rural Electrification Administration; Soil Conservation Service; and the Bureau of Agricultural Economics.

Without any division of authority, the Department of Agriculture probably touches more people more often than any other department of the government.

Air Forces, Department of the, established as an executive department in the National Military Establishment, as a result of the military unification program. It was authorized by the National Security act, which officially began operation Sept. 18, 1947. It is headed by the Secretary of the Air Forces, who has no cabinet status. He is responsible to the Department of Defense, which consists of the departments of the Army and Navy and Air Force.

The U. S. Air Force includes air combat and service forces and is part of the Department of the Air Forces. Its primary responsibility is defending the United States against air attack, carrying on combat and bombing operations against an enemy, and providing joint amphibious and air operations. The United States Air Force is composed of the Regular Air Force, the Air Reserve, the Air National Guard and the Air Reserve Officers Training Corps.

Alderman, a representative of a ward in a city, council or board of aldermen, the lawmaking body of the municipality—or, in a few cases, the lower house of the municipal legislature. Some boards of aldermen are elected in part not by districts but from the city at large. Usually there are one or two aldermen from each ward, elected for one or two years; they usually serve without pay, but salaries are provided in large cities. The mayor is the presiding officer of the board of aldermen.

The board of aldermen was abolished in New York city in 1938, and a City Council with members elected by proportional representation was substituted.

Alias or Alias dictus (Latin, otherwise called), used in legal language before any name assumed by a man who wishes to hide his identity. If William Grant, a criminal, fears his name will lead to his apprehension, he may change it to Edward Jones, and the authorities will call him William Grant *alias* Edward Jones.

Alias writ, a second or further writ issued after the first has expired.

Alibi (Latin, elsewhere), a defence in criminal cases that the accused was somewhere else at the time of the crime. There can be no more convincing proof of innocence than a well-substantiated alibi.

Alien, a person living in one country but a citizen or subject of another country. He is under the jurisdiction of the country in which he is a resident and he is entitled to the protection of of that country's laws. Punishment is meted out to him for his misdeeds as if he were a citizen. There is an exception to this where aliens enjoy extraterritorial privileges, as most foreigners do in China and until 1936 did in Egypt. Under this treaty arrangement, the alien remains under the jurisdiction of the courts of his own nation.

Undesirable aliens were long excluded from the United States by immigration officials on the grounds of poverty, liability of becoming public charges, bad physical condition, illiteracy, Oriental race, harboring dangerous political views. The *quota* system of 1924 cut down on immigration by allowing only about 150,000 a year from Europe and setting as a maximum from each country 2 per cent of the number from that country who were reported in the U. S. Census of 1890. This made the quota higher for immigrants from northern, northwestern and western Europe because they had been the principal factors in immigration up to 1890.

All-Union Congress of Soviets (up to 1923 on the formation of U.S.S.R. called the *All-Russian Congress of Soviets*), the "supreme organ of authority" in Russia, replaced in 1936 by the Supreme Council. The Congress held few sessions and seems to have been a mere rubber stamp for the decisions of the Communist party. It met, about 1500 strong, in the capitals of the different republics in turn, dramatizing the power of the government. Under the 1936 constitution the Council of People's Commissars is responsible to the Supreme Soviet for the administration of departments or commissariats divided into two classes: All-Union People's Commissariats operating directly from the centralized government or by bodies which these Commissariats appoint; and the Union-Republic People's Commissariats, operating through commissariats of each republic. So half the administration is centralized and half is localized. The All-Union Commissariats—Federal Commissariats we might say— are Defence, Foreign Affairs, Foreign Trade, Postal and Electrical Communications, Railways, Water Transport, Heavy Industry, Defence Industry. The Union-Republican Commissariats are Food Industry, Light Industry, Timber Industry, Agriculture, State Grain and Livestock Farms, Finance, Internal Trade, Internal Affairs, Justice, Public Health.

Althing (*al*, general; *thing*, assembly), the lawmaking body of Iceland, established in 930 A.D. by the Constitution of Ulfliot and, except for the interval 1798–1874, in continuous existence ever since. Its membership is around 52 of which 41 are elected. The capital representatives and the 6 double-number members are chosen by proportional representation. Supplementary seats are distributed among political parties which have too few representatives in proportion to their voting strength. The prime minister and his cabinet are responsible to the *Althing*.

Ambassador, a diplomatic minister of the highest rank, considered to represent personally the sovereign or head of the nation sending him to another Power and having personal access to the head of the state to which he is sent. *Ambassador* in common use implies *ambassador extraordinary and plenipotentiary*, that is, with full powers; usually the letters of credence carried by the ambassador inform the other Power that the head of the state sending the ambassador will confirm anything done by him. Diplomatic officers of lower grade represent the country and not its ruler; some of them do not have full powers. Ambassadors are sent only to the greater Powers. In 1893 the U. S. Congress first authorized the President to send ambassadors (instead of ministers) to the Great Powers whose representatives in Washington were of similar rank. Most of the diplomatic representatives of the United States in foreign countries have the rank of ambassador and are appointed by the President subject to the approval of the Senate. The number in this rank varies from less than fifty to more than sixty. Most of them are career diplomats, that is, men who have made the diplomatic service their life work. In some cases, however, ambassadors are appointed as a reward for political services rendered. The salaries of American ambassadors are variable depending on the importance of their post. In addition, an expense allowance of varying size is allowed. Immediately after World War II, no ambassadors were accredited to either Germany or Japan until the peace treaties were signed. The Embassy, official residence of an ambassador, is considered to be the territory of the Power accrediting him, and is not subject to the laws of the country.

Amendment, improvement or more generally any alteration. In procedure the correction of an error in a writ, record or other judicial document. In parliamentary law a slight change in the form of a motion or a bill.

In constitutional law an amendment is rewriting a part of the constitution, Federal or state. The method of amendment is stated in the constitution. The Federal Constitution can be amended only by the legislatures or constitutional conventions of three-fourths of the states. Congress has the power to choose which method of ratification is to be used. Amendments to state constitutions may be proposed by constitutional convention or (in all states but New Hampshire) by the legislature. If the amendment is proposed by the state legislature, it is not effective until it is approved by popular vote—except in Delaware where amendments are in effect if they are adopted by a two-thirds vote of each house in two consecutive legislatures.

American party, a secret party formed in 1854 that sought to permit only Americans to hold office. Later it was merged with the Know-Nothing party.

Amnesty, forgetfulness of wrong, a declaration by a duly constituted authority that gives a group of offenders pardon for offenses and reestablishes them in all their civil rights. A memorable example of amnesty was the act of President Johnson in restoring all rights to those who had directly or indirectly participated in the Civil War. *Amnesty* is not a technical term of the law. In common use it implies two things that *pardon* does not: restoration to civil rights —general or full pardon; and usually the inclusion of a whole class or community.

Anarchism, the social theory that government is an evil and that an ideal community would have no government, for it would need no control. *Anarchy* is sometimes used in the same sense, but in distinction from anarchism, it means lack of governmental control—hence, chaos and confusion. The famous Russian revolutionist Mikhail Bakunin (1814-76) tried to secure anarchism speedily; the Frenchman, Pierre Joseph Proudhon (1809-65) thought it must come slowly. Other famous writers who have urged anarchist doctrines include William Godwin, "Max Stirner" (Kaspar Schmidt), Leo Tolstoy and Prince Peter Kropotkin.

Answer, the defendant's formal pleading or statement of defense in reply to the action of the plaintiff. It deals mainly with facts but may include the demurrer, which deals with law. The answer creates an issue between the two parties.

Anti-Federalists, American political party that opposed the adoption of the Constitution because it centralized power in the Federal Government. Later it became the Jeffersonian Republican party that was the forerunner of the present Democratic party.

Anti-Masonic party, an American political party formed as a result of the opposition to Masons following the disappearance of William Morgan in 1826. Morgan had been a Mason, resigned and published a book purporting to reveal the secrets of Masonry. After his disappearance it was alleged that he had been murdered by Masons. The Anti-Masonic party was organized to elect non-Masons to public office and was one of the factions forming the Whig party in 1834.

Appeal, the right of a defendant in a criminal case or a litigant in a civil suit, if he is defeated in the trial court, to ask that a higher court review the record of the case and ascertain whether errors in the trial justify another hearing or a reversal or amendment of the original decision. In the Federal system the United States Court of Appeals receives cases from the District Court, and the Supreme Court is the tribunal of final appeal. In the state judicial systems the courts vary, but from the township court of a justice of the peace and the county or circuit court appeals ultimately reach the state supreme court.

The system of appeal in our Federal courts makes it possible to carry to the Supreme Court of the United States any case involving the constitutionality of a statute. In this way the Supreme Court acquires the power of invalidating a law passed by Congress, the state legislature or any other legislative body within the state, if the Court declares the act unconstitutional.

Court jurisdiction is of two kinds: *original,* when a case goes to the court for first trial, and *appellate* or *review,* when the case comes to the court only on appeal.

In Great Britain the House of Lords is the court of last appeal, but only the law lords (who have had legal training and experience as judges) conduct the business of the House when it sits as a court of appeal. Until 1908 there was no appeal in general criminal cases from the verdict in the trial court. But after a remarkable series of official prejudices and mistakes that culminated in the wrongful conviction of Mr. Adolf Beck, the court of criminal appeal was established by the act of 1907 to rectify such errors. If an appeal against a conviction is allowed, the accused is acquitted and there is no power to grant a new trial. But on an appeal against a sentence, the court may quash the sentence, reduce it or even increase its severity.

Appearance, coming into court as a party to a suit, whether as plaintiff or defendant; the formal proceeding by which a defendant submits to the jurisdiction of the court by acting personally or through an attorney.

Appointment, the selection of public officials by a designated individual or small group as distinct from popular election. The power of appointment usually lies in the chief executive and is a relic of the royal prerogative. The President of the United States under the Constitution (Art. II, Sec. 2) "shall nominate, and by and with the advice and consent of the Senate, shall appoint ambassadors, other public ministers and consuls, judges of the Supreme Court and all other officers of the United States whose appointments are not herein otherwise provided for and which shall be established by law; but the Congress may by law vest the appointment of such inferior officers as they think proper in the President alone, in the courts of law or in the heads of departments."

Members of the Cabinet are appointed by the President (sometimes as rewards for service in the election campaign), and these appointments are usually unquestioningly approved by the Senate. The President's appointments to the judiciary and to posts in the foreign service are more likely to be questioned or even disapproved by the Senate. His appointments to local posts are largely prompted by the wishes of the members of Congress (especially of his own party) from the state where the office is to be filled. Postmasterships and other minor offices are likely to be political appointments formally in the President's power but actually dictated by party leaders. Appointments for political purposes have influenced American history, notably the appointments of President John Adams in 1801 intended to offset the power of the newly elected President Jefferson. One of the appointees was John Marshall, who as Chief Justice of the Supreme Court shaped the interpretation of the Constitution quite differently from the beliefs of Jefferson and Jackson.

In the separate states the governor has far less appointing power than the President since state department heads are usually elected by the people. There is a tendency toward more power for the governor in the newer state constitutions and reorganizations of the executive and administrative offices. In New York, for example, since 1927 (by a Constitutional amendment) the governor with the consent of the Senate appoints 14 administrative heads including the secretary of state, and there has been an attempt to organize a Cabinet of department heads to advise the governor.

Federal judges are appointed by the President with the consent of the Senate; but it is a peculiarity of the American system that many state and local judges are elected by popular vote. In Switzerland, cantonal judges of the lowest courts are elected by the people; and in France in the days of the Revolution, from 1790 to 1804, judges were elected— but these are exceptions to the general rule in Europe of appointed judges.

In 38 American states even the highest judges are elected; in Rhode Island, South Carolina, Virginia and Vermont, the legislature appoints the higher judges; in Delaware and New Jersey the major judges are appointed by the governor and senate; in Massachusetts all judges are named by the governor and his council.

In England the king in theory appoints the prime minister; actually he has no choice save to take the recognized leader of the party in power. The prime minister selects the other members of the Cabinet and the king's assent is necessary before they take office. All court officers—judges, justices of the peace, sheriffs and clerks—are appointed in England, and so are the permanent county and borough administrative officers.

It is a puzzling question whether a democracy benefits by having many of its officers appointed instead of being elected by the people. Possibly posts that require expert professional or technical ability are filled better by appointment, but everything depends on the wisdom of the appointer and his freedom from partisan bias.

The power of appointment usually implies the power of removal.

Apportionment, in U.S. constitutional law the allocating to states the number of representatives they shall have in the lower House of the Congress; and similarly in a state the determination of how many legislators shall form the state legislature. As total population changes there must be reapportionment to secure any semblance of fair representation. Reapportionment need not mean redistricting since legislators may be chosen at large, that is, to represent the whole state.

The original apportionment of the Federal House of Representatives is in Art. I, Sec. 2 of the Constitution; and that section provides that the apportionment shall be based on a census taken every 10 years as Congress shall direct. No reapportionment was made in 1920, but there was one in 1930. The following table gives the representation under each census.

State constitutions usually have similar provisions for apportionment and for redistricting the state for its own legislature. Often there is a provision that every legislative district must be compact and made up of contiguous areas. This is to prevent inequalities in districts and the forming of legislative districts that will give one party an unfair advantage over the other—as by making new districts so that the party will carry most of the districts even if it has not a majority of the votes in the whole state that is made up of the districts. (This tricky practice is called a *gerrymander.*)

In England and other European countries there is no legal provision for apportionment or redistricting, for there is no attempt to keep electoral districts approximately the same in population.

Appropriation, assignment to a particular purpose, especially setting apart money. In the law of debt appropriation is the act of deciding to what particular indebtedness any one payment on account shall be applied.

In government finance an appropriation is the authorization of specific expenditure or an entire series of annual or periodical expenditures classed by purpose, manner and amount.

The U. S. Constitution provides that "no money shall be drawn from the treasury but in consequence of appropriations made by law" (Art. I, Sec. 9, Cl. 7) and limits to two years appropriations to raise and support armies (Art. I, Sec. 8, Cl. 12). The power of appropriation naturally goes with the power of raising the revenue to be expended. As all revenue measures by Constitutional provision (Art. I, Sec. 7, Cl. 1) must originate in the House of Representatives, it has become the custom that all bills for spending or appropriating money also originate in the Lower House. That House since 1921 has concentrated the task of framing appropriation measures (formerly performed by 14 sepa-

Apportionment of State Representation in Congress

Not More Than One in Every	1788 30,000	1790 33,000	1800 33,000	1810 35,000	1820 40,000	1830 47,700	1840 70,680	1850 93,423	1860 127,381	1880 151,911	1900 194,182	1910 211,877	1930 280,674	1940 301,164	1950 344,587	1960 410,481
Alabama	...	...	...	1	3	5	7	7	6	8	9	10	9	9	9	8
Alaska	...	...	...	...	...	...	...	...	...	...	...	...	...	...	...	1
Arizona	...	...	...	...	...	...	...	...	...	...	1	1	2	2	2	3
Arkansas	...	...	...	...	...	1	1	2	3	5	7	7	7	7	6	4
California	...	...	...	...	...	...	2	2	3	6	8	11	20	23	30	38
Colorado	...	...	...	...	...	...	...	...	1	3	4	4	4	4	4	4
Connecticut	5	7	7	7	6	6	4	4	4	4	5	5	6	6	6	6
Delaware	1	1	1	2	1	1	1	1	1	1	1	1	1	1	1	1
Florida	...	...	...	...	...	...	1	1	1	2	3	4	5	6	8	12
Georgia	3	2	4	6	7	9	8	8	7	10	11	12	10	10	10	10
Hawaii	...	...	...	...	...	...	...	...	...	...	...	...	...	...	...	2
Idaho	...	...	...	...	...	...	...	...	...	1	1	2	2	2	2	2
Illinois	...	...	...	1	1	3	7	9	14	20	25	27	27	26	25	24
Indiana	...	...	...	1	3	7	10	11	11	13	13	13	12	11	11	11
Iowa	...	...	...	...	...	...	2	2	6	11	11	11	9	8	8	7
Kansas	...	...	...	...	...	...	...	1	7	8	8	7	6	6	6	5
Kentucky	...	2	6	10	12	13	10	10	9	11	11	11	9	9	8	7
Louisiana	...	...	...	1	3	3	4	4	5	6	7	8	8	8	8	8
Maine	...	...	...	9	7	8	7	6	5	4	4	4	3	3	3	2
Maryland	6	8	9	9	8	6	6	6	5	6	6	6	6	6	7	8
Massachusetts	8	14	17	13	13	12	10	11	10	12	14	16	15	14	14	12
Michigan	...	...	...	...	1	3	4	6	11	12	13	17	17	18	19	
Minnesota	...	...	...	...	...	...	2	5	9	10	9	9	9	9	8	
Mississippi	...	...	...	1	1	2	4	5	5	7	8	8	7	7	6	5
Missouri	...	...	...	...	1	2	5	7	9	14	16	16	13	13	11	10
Montana	...	...	...	...	...	...	...	...	...	1	1	2	2	2	2	2
Nebraska	...	...	...	...	...	...	...	...	1	3	6	6	5	4	4	3
Nevada	...	...	...	...	...	...	...	...	1	1	1	1	1	1	1	1
NewHampshire	3	4	5	6	6	5	4	3	3	2	2	2	2	2	2	2
New Jersey	4	5	6	6	6	6	5	5	5	7	10	12	14	14	14	15
New Mexico	...	...	...	...	...	...	...	...	...	...	...	1	1	2	2	2
New York	6	10	17	27	34	40	34	33	31	34	37	43	45	45	43	41
North Carolina	5	10	12	13	13	13	9	8	7	9	10	10	11	12	12	11
North Dakota	...	...	...	...	...	...	...	...	...	1	2	3	2	2	2	2
Ohio	...	...	1	6	14	19	21	21	19	21	21	22	24	23	23	24
Oklahoma	...	...	...	...	...	...	...	...	...	...	5	8	9	8	6	6
Oregon	...	...	...	...	...	...	1	1	1	2	3	3	4	4	4	4
Pennsylvania	8	13	18	23	26	28	24	25	24	28	32	36	34	33	30	27
Rhode Island	1	2	2	2	2	2	2	2	2	2	3	3	2	2	2	2
South Carolina	5	6	8	9	9	9	7	6	4	7	7	7	6	6	6	6
South Dakota	...	...	...	...	...	...	...	...	...	2	2	3	2	2	2	2
Tennessee	...	1	3	6	9	13	11	10	8	10	10	10	9	10	9	9
Texas	...	...	...	...	...	...	2	2	4	11	16	18	21	21	22	23
Utah	...	...	...	...	...	...	...	...	...	1	2	2	2	2	2	
Vermont	...	2	4	6	5	5	4	3	3	2	2	2	1	1	1	1
Virginia	10	19	22	23	22	21	15	13	11	10	10	10	9	9	10	10
Washington	...	...	...	...	...	...	...	...	...	1	3	5	6	6	7	7
West Virginia	...	...	...	...	...	...	...	...	...	4	5	6	6	6	6	5
Wisconsin	...	...	...	...	...	...	2	3	6	9	11	11	10	10	10	10
Wyoming	...	...	...	...	...	...	...	...	...	1	1	1	1	1	1	1
Total	65	106	142	186	213	242	232	237	243	332	391	435	435	435	435	435

rate committees) in a single Committee on Appropriations with 35 members and 13 subcommittees of 5 members each, dealing with appropriations for these 13 classes: (1) Agricultural Department, (2) Labor Department, (3) District of Columbia, (4) Executive Office and independent commissions, etc., (5) Interior Department, (6) legislative branch, (7) Defense Department, (8) Post Office Department, (9) State Department, (10) Treasury, (11) Commerce Department and (12) Justice Department. Each bill as drafted by a subcommittee must receive the approval of the entire committee before it is reported to the House. No appropriation may be considered by the Committee unless it has been recommended by the Bureau of the Budget.

The President may not veto single items in an appropriation bill, but governors of the states have that power.

In England appropriations are made by the House of Commons acting as a Committee of Supply—the action is said to be by the House in Supply. (By meeting as a committee the House frees itself from the strict rulings of the Speaker.) The Committee does not frame the appropriations but merely acts on the recommendations of the Government, that is, of the responsible ministry. The Committee may (1) vote the grant proposed, (2) reduce it or (3) reject it—but cannot increase it. Reduction or rejection is rare; it would show lack of confidence which might overthrow the Government, lead to a general election and lose present members their seats in Parliament. Appropriations voted by the Commons must be submitted to the House of Lords but become law at the end of a month (even if the Lords do not assent) upon receiving the assent of the Crown which is given as a matter of course. The appropriation act for yearly expenditures of the British Government is officially called the Consolidated Fund Act.

Arbitration, settling disputes by other authority than judicial tribunals or courts provided by law. The authority that arbitrates may be: (1) chosen by agreement of the two parties to the dispute—sometimes each party chooses one arbitrator and these two arbitrators select a third as odd man or umpire or arbiter with a casting vote; or (2) the arbitrators may be a board or commission created by statute or by a group like a trade association. The decision of the arbitrators is called an *award.*

There are three applications of arbitration: (a) in international affairs; (b) in commercial disputes arising in business relations; (c) in disputes between employer and labor.

International Arbitration may be by a special commission or board of arbitrators chosen by agreement between contesting nations or, under present conditions, by reference to the International Court of Justice, or World Court of the United Nations.

International arbitration has had a long history, but it is only since the middle of the 19th century that it has been used often for the settlement of disputes between nations. One of the early important cases was that of the Alabama Claims, growing out of British-American relations during the Civil War, which was legalized in the Treaty of Washington, 1871. This arbitration had a wide influence. Subsequently arbitration was accepted by the United States in relation to fisheries, boundary and claims disputes.

Impetus was given international arbitration by the Hague Conference of 1899 which created the Hague Court, officially known as the Permanent Court of Arbitration, later improved and strengthened by the Hague Conference of 1907. These conferences paved the way for the creation of the Permanent Court of International Justice, established after World War I by the 13th article of the Covenant of the League of Nations. Because of the ineffectiveness of this body, the World Court had little business of importance. Its functions were, to a degree, usurped by treaties designed to prevent war such as the Washington Disarmament Treaties, 1922, and the Briand-Kellogg pact of 1928. The Court was confined to cases "judicial in their nature." It was suspended in 1940 and was replaced by The International Court of Justice, or World Court, of the United Nations in 1945. This is a court of law dealing only with legal questions and is not concerned with political disputes. It has, in large measure, replaced the Hague Tribunal or Permanent Court of Arbitration set up in 1899.

Commercial Arbitration is the arbitration of business disputes. It was originally developed in the United States by trade associations and chambers of commerce. One of the first such tribunals was set up in New York City in 1768. In time, other large cities did likewise. In the early part of the 19th century several states passed legislation relating to business arbitration. The procedure is simple, agreements and awards are usually promptly arrived at and the procedure generally is economical and effective. For *Industrial arbitration*, see p. 1809.

Armaments, Limitation of, has been much sought after in recent years but in the absence of an accredited international commission for constant unhindered inspection no such plan could be carried out.

In the latter part of the 19th century when the great powers of the world were striving for the control of lands and peoples in Asia and Africa, armies were expanded and navies were built to provide the power to enforce colonizing claims. The international rivalries thus formed led to World War I. The Treaty of Versailles of 1919 imposed a limitation of armaments on the conquered central powers—Germany, Austria, Turkey and Bulgaria. Another step in this direction was taken by the Washington Disarmament Conference, 1921–22, which dealt largely with naval limitations and the situation in the Pacific. The resulting treaties established a naval ratio between the United States, Great Britain and Japan and prohibited the fortification of mandates, including those of Japan.

The false security following these treaties was but a prelude to World War II. Germany repudiated the Treaty of Versailles and re-armed. Japan secretly fortified its mandated island groups in the Pacific and ignored the naval ratio it had accepted. At the end of the second World War it was hoped that some effective program of limitation of armaments could be agreed on. Instead the nations of the world again started a mad race to re-arm to the fullest extent possible. The problem became more acute when the atomic and hydrogen bombs became actualities. No nation was willing to relinquish any of its sovereignty. Nor was any nation willing to give the U. N. the authority to enforce armament rules and regulations. One reason for the refusal of the various countries to plan an international disarmament program was the unfortunate result of a similar program after the first World War.

Arraignment, in criminal law, bringing an accused person before the court, calling him to the bar for the purpose of identifying him, reading the indict-

ment to him and requiring him to answer guilty or not guilty. If he pleads not guilty, a day is set for the trial giving him time enough to prepare his defense. If he pleads guilty, an early day is set for presenting sufficient evidence to provide a court record of the case and for pronouncing sentence.

Arrest, the taking of a person into custody in order that he may be held to answer for committing a criminal offense or be prevented from committing such an offense. Arrests may be made with or without a warrant, which is a duly issued authorization to make an arrest. It may be addressed to a peace officer or to a private individual. In most cases an arrest may be made by either a peace officer or a private individual without a warrant. A peace officer may arrest for a felony or a misdemeanor committed in his presence; or he may arrest one whom he has probable cause to believe is guilty of a felony. An officer may not arrest without a warrant for the commission of a misdemeanor if it is not committed in the officer's presence. An individual has the same power to make arrests, but where an arrest is made for a felony not committed in the presence of the person arresting, there must be a certainty the felony has actually been committed.

Arrest does not necessarily mean continued detention until the trial. The accused has the right to temporary liberty by furnishing bail for his appearance when he is called unless there are statutory provisions to the contrary.

Arson, the malicious and wilful burning of a house or outhouse belonging to another person. Only houses ordinarily used for human habitation and buildings within the curtilage (or immediate area of the house), such as barns, are the subject of arson. However, many states have extended by statute the definition and scope of arson.

The burning of one's own property is not arson, but if this is done with the purpose of defrauding an insurer it is a crime under particular statutes in some states. Twenty years or life imprisonment is the penalty in some states; death in others.

Article, a distinct part of a legal document. In the plural, articles often mean all the parts, all the provisos, all the items. So *Articles of Confederation* were the whole document under which the American Congress operated during the Revolutionary War and until the adoption of the Constitution. *Articles of Impeachment* are the complete list of charges brought in the indictment found by the House of Representatives. *Articles of War* and *Articles for the Government of the Navy* are collections of all rules and regulations for governing the army and navy. *Articles of Association* or *Articles of Incorporation* are the general written rules by which a corporation agrees to act and carry on its business. These articles must be approved by the Government before a charter is issued permitting the corporation to operate.

Article X of the League of Nations pledging members to preserve against external aggression the territorial integrity and existing political independence of all members was the main obstacle to its acceptance in the United States.

The Federal Constitution is cited by Article, Section and Clause.

Assault and battery. An *assault* is any unlawful offer or attempt to injure another with apparent present ability to carry out the attempt, which causes an apprehension of peril. A *battery* is any harmful or offensive touching of another. A battery is the consummation of an assault. However, there may be an assault without a battery and it is even possible to have a battery without an assault.

Assembly, gathering together. The right of peaceful assembly is guaranteed by the 1st Amendment to the Federal Constitution: "Congress shall make no law . . . abridging . . . the right of the people peaceably to assemble."

Unlawful assembly is the gathering of three or more persons with intent to commit a crime or to act in a way to endanger the public peace.

In constitutional law of many states of the Union the state legislature is called the General Assembly or the Legislative Assembly. (Etymologically *assembly* and *congress* both mean meeting, coming together.) The lower house in New York and California is called the Assembly, and in New Jersey, the General Assembly.

The lower house of the League of Nations was called the Assembly, and was composed of about 3 representatives from each member nation. The Assembly elected part of the Council or upper house.

Assessor, an official of township, village or city, elected or appointed to fix property values for purposes of taxation. It is not usually a salaried office; remuneration is for time actually employed. Often the same duty is performed by a board of assessors or tax board.

Assignment, any written transfer of interest or title in property. An assignment for the benefit of creditors is the voluntary transfer by the debtor of his property to an assignee in trust. The assignee is to use the property to pay the creditors and any surplus is to be returned to the debtor. A general assignment includes all the nonexempt property of the debtor; it is often made to a trustee who realizes for the various creditors.

Assize, originally a session or sitting of a court or legislative body. The only current use of the word is to mean the session three or four times a year in each English county of a judge of the High Court of Justice, called the *judge of assize,* or of a commissioner of assize appointed by the judge. This traveling court was instituted to determine issues of fact that would be heard at Westminster *nisi prius,* unless they were heard beforehand in the county. The trial is before a jury. Magna Charta in 1215 transferred assize courts from Westminster to the local county to remedy delay and save provincials the cost of coming to London.

In Scotch law an assize is a jury

trial of a criminal case or the jury in such a case. Historically the word has many meanings. The Grand Assize was a jury of 16 empowered to settle questions of ownership which had previously been decided by combat; it was one of the reforms of Henry II, King of England from 1154 to 1189, in whose time the word *assize* was also used of the ordinances issued by the King in his plan to introduce a system of royal justice to supersede local justice: the Assize of Clarendon in 1166 and the Assize of Northhampton in 1176 took jurisdiction in certain cases away from the barons and sheriffs and gave it to royal judges on circuit.

From the 12th century on there were in England *assisae venalium,* assizes of things for sale, the Assize of Bread and Ale in 1267, for example. These were limitations of price, weight and quality, especially for food, set by justices of the peace; usually the adjustment was to the price of grain.

Assumpsit, an action at law to recover damages for breach of a simple contract. It is so called from the Latin word used in the complaint, *assumpsit* (he undertook).

At large, said of a representative chosen by voters of the whole state (and not of a single congressional district) when a state is not redistricted after a new apportionment of its representation in Congress.

After the census of 1960, the following states elected congressmen at large: Maryland, 1 out of 8 Congressmen; Ohio, 1 out of 24; Texas, 1 out of 23; Alaska and Hawaii, 2 each, entire representation; and Delaware, Nevada, New Mexico, 1 each, entire representation.

Ambassador at large is the unofficial term applied to a representative of one country carrying on negotiations with various other nations.

Attachment, a writ issued by a court commanding the seizure of a person for contempt of court or ordering the taking of the defendant's property into legal custody to satisfy a demand of the plaintiff.

Attainder, in old English law, loss of civil rights after judgment of death with the additional penalty of forfeiture to the state of some or all of the convicted man's personal and real property and the denial of his right to transmit property to his heirs. In 1814 attainder was restricted to cases of treason and murder, and in 1870 the whole system of attainder was swept away.

Bills of attainder were legislative acts that declared certain persons attainted without any judicial trial. They came into wide use during the reign of Richard II and continued until 1688 but after that were seldom used.

The memory of the wrongs done under Bills of Attainder was fresh enough in 1787 to cause the framers of the Constitution of the United States to prohibit Bills of Attainder (Art. I, Sec. 9, Cl. 3).

Attorney, any substitute or agent appointed to act for another. An attorney *in fact* is an agent empowered by the authority given him which is called a *power of attorney*. An attorney *at law* is a lawyer practicing in the courts where he represents his principal or client.

Attorney general, the chief law officer of the United States and of each state. The Attorney General of the United States is the head of the Department of Justice, a member of the Cabinet of the President, the legal adviser of the President in all official matters and also of the heads of the various executive departments. His salary is $30,000 per year.

The attorney general of a state occupies a similar position. He is legal adviser to all departments in the state government and he appears for the state in all cases in the supreme court of his state to which his commonwealth is a party. In most states he is elected by popular vote; but he is appointed by the governor in New Hampshire, New Jersey and Pennsylvania, by the judges of the state supreme court in Tennessee and by the Legislature in Maine.

In Great Britain the Attorney General is almost always a member of the Cabinet.

Autonomy, self-government of a community. Canada and all other dominions of the British Commonwealth of Nations are autonomous.

Bail, to deliver an arrested person to his surety upon his giving security for the arrested person's appearance before the court when required. Bail also means the persons who become the sureties. The accused may place his own property in pledge, or the required bond may be furnished by another. Cash may be deposited in exactly the amount required; real estate must be worth twice the amount. Whenever a bondsman fears a bond may be forfeited by flight of the accused, he may deliver the accused to the court and ask for cancellation of the bond. Excessive bail is prohibited by the Eighth Amendment to the Federal Constitution. Even a person charged with a capital offense may be bailed if there are no constitutional or statutory provisions to the contrary.

Ballot, a means of secret voting; originally a small ball used for secret voting; the black ball for a negative vote is the source of the phrase, *to blackball,* in the sense of voting against, excluding from membership in a club. In ancient Athens a bit of tile or pottery (perhaps at an early date an oyster shell) was used in voting to banish a citizen, and from the word *ostracon,* oyster shell or tile, comes the word *ostracize,* the practice of banishing or blackballing.

Modern ballots are written or printed. When the candidates or the party organization supplied the ballots (the regular custom in the United States as recently as 1880), there were opportunities for trickery and fraud. Now official ballots, printed by government authority, contain only the names of candidates duly nominated.

Ballot reform has been secured by the Australian ballot, the voting machine, the Massachusetts ballot, the nonpartisan ballot and the short ballot.

The *Australian ballot,* was first used in 1856 in South Australia. This system of balloting requires that all ballots be printed at public expense and delivered to each polling place in sealed packages on the eve of election; the seals are unbroken until the polls open. A ballot, marked with the initials of a judge of election, is handed to the voter as he enters a closed booth, and he secretly marks his preferences among the nominees for office. Then he folds the ballot and returns it to the judges, who deposit it in the ballot box. This system makes it impossible for any other than an official ballot to be used.

In some parts of the world the ballot to be voted is placed in an official envelope and sealed; this used to be the rule in Germany.

When the Australian ballot was

LOOK MAGAZINE

FORMER ATTORNEY GENERAL Robert Kennedy on one of his many visits to a federal penitentiary. The Attorney General of the United States is the head of the Department of Justice, serves as a member of the Cabinet, and is legal adviser to the president.

first used the nominees of each political party were printed in separate columns (the party column ballot), and to vote for every nominee of one party a voter need only put a cross in the circle at the head of the column. To vote a split ticket, choosing candidates from different parties, the voter had to put a cross in a square before each name—so that a straight ticket was much easier to vote than a split ticket, especially if a party emblem appeared at the top of the column so that a voter could identify the party without reading any name on the ballot.

The voting machine is a mechanical device for recording votes secretly and counting them automatically. The names of nominees are arranged in party columns with the name of the party and of each nominee opposite a push-button. To vote a straight ticket for all nominees of one party, a voter pushes only one button, the one opposite the party name. To vote a split ticket, he pushes the button opposite each name that he favors. The machine automatically counts the votes for each nominee, so a minute after the polls close the results appear.

On the voting machines in New York, the names of nominees are arranged in horizontal rows by party. Over the name of each candidate is the party emblem and a small lever. This lever must be pulled down over the name of every nominee to be voted upon (only one lever for the same office will operate) and left in that position until the vote is registered as the voter leaves the booth.

Both the Australian ballot and the voting machine have the virtue of secrecy but the fault of hindering independent voting and encouraging party voting. The *Massachusetts ballot,* first used in Massachusetts in 1888, lists all candidates for the same office alphabetically under the name of the office. Usually the symbol of the party is printed after the name.

After the Australian form came into use, all official ballots were alike in one respect: there was only one ballot for a voter at any election, and it contained all the names of all candidates. It was a blanket or all-covering ballot. The natural result was a long and unwieldy ballot. To reform this situation there is a strong movement for a *short* ballot under a proposed new system of fewer elected officers and more positions filled by appointment. The theory is that the voter will make a more intelligent choice if he has only a few offices to fill.

The *nonpartisan ballot* carries the idea of the Massachusetts reform to its logical conclusion—it contains no party classification, no party symbols, no party identification. It was first used in city and local elections where national party affiliations have little meaning. Nonpartisan ballots for the election of judges are now used in Arizona, California, Idaho, Minnesota, Nebraska, North Dakota, Ohio, South Dakota, Washington, Wisconsin and Wyoming.

Written-in ballots are those bearing names not officially printed but added by the voter—an extreme sign of independence.

Bankrupt (from Latin, bank broken), a person or company whose assets admittedly do not equal liabilities that are due and payable and demand for which has been made. Bankruptcy may result from voluntary action of the debtor; or it may be forced by creditors when utter inability to pay is shown or when the debtor is discovered in an attempt to prefer one creditor above another or to remove assets or transfer them to another with intent to defraud his creditors.

The Constitution of the United States (Art. I, Sec. 8, Cl. 4) gives Congress the power "to establish uniform laws on the subject of bankruptcies," so there are no state laws except in regard to the insolvency of certain corporations that are not included in the Federal bankruptcy laws.

Action may be begun by an appeal to a Federal court by three or more creditors or if there are fewer than twelve by a single petitioner. The court appoints a receiver, and places the case in the hands of a referee in bankruptcy. All the assets of the bankrupt not exempted by law must be turned over to the receiver. All creditors present their claims, and in due time they are paid their proportion of all money realized, less expenses incident to the proceedings.

If a bankrupt honestly relinquishes his total assets, his discharge from bankruptcy frees him from claims for debts incurred prior to the beginning of the action.

Barnburners, the radical element in the Democratic party in New York state politics (1843-48) that opposed the extension of slavery and local public works. The name was derived from the story of the Dutchman who burned down his barn to get rid of rats, the implication was that the Barnburners would destroy their political party to achieve their ends and do away with corporations and public works to get rid of their abuses. In 1848 the Barnburners nominated Martin Van Buren for President, and this split in the Democratic party resulted in a victory for the Whigs. The Barnburners merged with the Free-Soil party and later the anti-slavery groups joined the Republican party.

Benefit of clergy, in medieval law, the privilege of all priests and clerks of the Church to be tried by a church court, which could not inflict capital punishment. In the 14th century in England anyone who could read the first verse of the 51st Psalm could claim benefit of clergy and be free of danger from the severe laws that made death a common penalty. In England benefit of clergy was not abolished until 1827 and (for peers of the realm) 1841. In the United States the plea of benefit of clergy was recognized for a time in a few states, but in most jurisdictions it was either not recognized or expressly forbidden by statute. In cases of capital crimes against the United States benefit of clergy was abolished by an act of Congress in 1790.

"Best Evidence" Rule, a rule pertaining to the introduction of evidence in a court; the highest degree of proof that is possible must be produced if such evidence is accessible. Thus a copy of a contract cannot be introduced in evidence if the parties have the original contract.

Bigamy, wilfully contracting a second marriage when the contracting party knows the first marriage still exists. If husband or wife has not been heard from for 7 years (5 years in Arkansas and Indiana), under the common law the presumption of death is raised, and a new marriage may occur with no taint of bigamy.

Bill, a draft or form of a proposed act or statute, submitted to a legislature for enactment into law. Sometimes the word is used to mean an actual statute—for example in the phrase *bill of attainder,* used in the Federal Constitution (Art. I, Sec. 9, Cl. 3). A *bill of pains and penalty* is a special act of the legislature that imposes a punishment less than death upon persons supposedly guilty of some great offence without a legal trial. Bills of attainder and bills of pains and penalties are forbidden by the Constitution of the United States and by the constitutions of most of the states.

The Federal Constitution prohibits the states issuing *bills of credit* (Art. I, Sec. 10, Cl. 1), that is, paper money issued by the state on the faith of the state, designed to circulate as a medium of exchange.

Bill often means no more than legal document.

A *bill of health* is a medical officer's certificate as to absence or presence of infectious disease on board a ship leaving port.

A *bill in equity* is a written complaint addressed to a court of equity containing the names of the parties in the suit, the facts of the case with an averment that they are contrary to equity and a prayer for relief.

A *bill of exceptions* is a summary of exceptions to the rulings of a trial judge, a preliminary to an appeal.

A *bill of indictment* is the charge presented to a grand jury, which becomes a *true bill* if the jury finds that it cannot be ignored.

A *bill of particulars* is a detailed statement of a plaintiff's claim or of a defendant's set off.

Bill of Rights, any formal declaration of the rights and liberties of a people. The most famous example is the Act Declaring the Rights and Liberties of the Subject and Settling the Succession of the Crown, presented by the English Lords and Commons in 1689 to the Prince and Princess of Orange before they became William III and Mary of England. A Declaration of Right, asserting the claims of Parliament against the usurpation of the Stuart kings, had been presented to William and Mary earlier in the year when the Crown was offered to them. The Bill of Rights besides arranging the succession to the throne (more formally done by the Act of Settlement in 1701) vindicated and asserted these rights:

That only by consent of Parliament can laws be suspended or executed, money be levied or a standing army be maintained; that Protestant subjects have the right of having arms for defense; that subjects have the free right of petitioning the King; that elections to Parliament must be free; that speech and debate in Parliament must be free and not "questioned in any Court or place out of Parliament"; that excessive bail ought not to be required nor excessive fines imposed nor cruel or unusual punishments inflicted; that Parliament should meet frequently—and a few other claims.

In the United States the main ground of opposition to the Constitution as drafted by the Convention of 1787 was that it did not specifically recognize and guarantee the rights of the people. Clauses 2, 3 and 4 of Article I, Section 9, on *habeas corpus, ex post facto* laws and direct taxation and the definition of treason in Art. III, Sec. 3, were in the right direction, but were not of sufficiently broad scope. Twelve amendments were submitted by the First Congress in 1789 and the ten that were adopted have been popularly called the *Bill of Rights.* They deal with such fundamental rights as freedom of religion, speech, press, assembly and petition; right to bear arms, due process of law, speedy jury trial, indictment by grand jury, no excessive bail or fines, no cruel or unusual punishments, no double jeopardy by retrial for the same offense, compensation for property taken for public use. The rights of the states are covered by the 10th Amendment reserving to them powers not delegated to the United States by the Constitution.

The constitutions of the individual states contain in almost all instances a Bill of Rights or a Declaration of Rights.

In January 1918 the Third All-Russian Congress of Soviets adopted in the new constitution of the Russian Socialist Federated Soviet Republic a declaration of rights calling for: nationalization of all land, forests, underground mineral wealth, waters, livestock and banks; workers' control and then national control of factories, mines, railways and other means of production and transport; repudiation of loans by the czarist Government, landlords and the bourgeoisie; and organization of a Red army.

In the 1937 constitution of the Union of Soviet Socialist Republics, Chapter X, headed "The Fundamental Rights and Duties of Citizens," lists these rights: to work; to rest and leisure; to maintenance in old age, sickness or loss of capacity to work; to education; to equal privilege for both sexes, all nationalities and races and "all spheres of economic, social and political life"; to freedom of conscience, freedom of worship and freedom of antireligious propaganda; to freedom of speech, press, assembly, street processions and demonstrations; and to unite in public organizations. Inviolability of person, of homes and of correspondence is guaranteed, and so is the right of asylum to persecuted foreign citizens. This remarkable Bill of Rights closes with a list of duties: "to maintain labor discipline . . . to respect the rules of socialist human intercourse . . . to safeguard and

fortify public, socialist property . . . to defend the fatherland."

Blackmail, extortion, a demand for money from a person on threat of public exposure or some other form of intimidation. To constitute blackmail, it is not necessary that the attempt at extortion be successful; the demand alone is a crime, but it is hard to punish; for victims, if they are guilty of the act alleged, usually hesitate to complain to the authorities.

Bloc, a group or combination for a special purpose, especially the union of legislative members of different parties. If the bloc controls the balance of voting power, it can prevent the passage of a measure it opposes and may be able to secure the passage of legislation it favors. The *farm bloc* in the Congress of 1921 worked for agricultural legislation.

In France where there are numerous political parties the bloc is the common method of uniting a number of small parties of the same general political philosophy to protect their interests. In France after World War I, the Bloc National was the combination of all the conservative elements that defeated the socialists in 1919. The Popular Front that came into power with Léon Blum in May 1936 and continued to govern France under Camille Chautemps, was a bloc of the leftist parties.

In international politics a bloc is a group of nations with a common cause for which they work without an actual treaty or general alliance.

Blockade, in international law and in war, obstructing any communication with a country and especially its ports to prevent its receiving materials of war or even food supplies. It is a fundamental principle of international law that a "blockade to be binding must be effective, that is to say, maintained by a force sufficient to prevent access to the coast of the enemy."

A *paper blockade,* announced by publication but not followed by force to make it effective, is in effect a warning to neutrals not to approach a forbidden zone.

Blue-sky laws, the popular name for statutes that regulate the issue and sale of stocks and bonds by demanding that certain conditions of security be shown prior to issue, thus offering some assurance of value to investors. When Kansas passed the first of these laws in 1911, the reason was that some companies were capitalizing the "blue sky!" Within 20 years after that time all the states except Nevada and Delaware passed blue-sky laws.

Board, originally the table at which an administrative group met and now the group itself, whether in private business or in government. In government some of the common uses of the term are:

Board of Trade, a department in the British government with jurisdiction in Scotland as well as England over private enterprise except labor and land transport, which have separate ministries. It administers the laws regulating merchant shipping and those relating to wrecks, maintains a register of shipping, has charge of lighthouses, controls patents and trade-marks, weights and measures,

administers the bankruptcy law, gathers important commercial statistics (including food prices and supplies) and authorizes municipal public utilities. It is a board only in theory; really it consists of a president and his staff. The president of the Board of Trade is usually a member of the Cabinet. (In the United States *board of trade* is not a government term but is sometimes used of local chambers of commerce.)

Board of Education, a local group in charge of schools, sometimes called *school board.* Usually there is a board for each school district, a county board and city and state school boards. In England *board* schools were those supervised by local boards elected by taxpayers; but in 1902 the school boards were abolished and local administration of schools was transferred to county and borough councils. The Board of Education in the British government is one of the great executive departments of the kingdom. Like the Board of Trade it consists of a president and his administrative staff. Its work is supervising, inspecting and co-ordinating the school machinery, making investigations and publishing reports.

Board of Health, the term applied to many state, municipal and local departments in charge of public sanitation and prevention of disease in the United States.

Board of Pardons, an advisory group in some states of the union sharing with the governor the right to pardon convicted criminals, or making recommendations to him on applications for pardon—an attempt to lessen the governor's power in this respect.

Board of Aldermen, the legislative power in many American cities.

Board of Estimate, in New York city under the charter of 1936 the administrative branch that must concur in all major legislation adopted by the Council to make it effective. It consists of mayor, comptroller (3 votes) president of the council (3 votes) and the five borough presidents with 2 votes each for the boroughs of Manhattan and Brooklyn and 1 vote for each of the other three boroughs. There are boards of estimate in other cities.

County Board, the legislative power in almost all counties of the United States including the parishes of Louisiana. A few counties in Virginia, California, Ohio, Texas and Nebraska have a county manager, selected by a board which is elected by the people; the manager appoints the principal county administrative officers. In some states there are *ex-officio* county boards, county judges and justices of the peace. Sometimes they are elected to represent the townships of the county; and sometimes they are elected at large from the whole county. In Connecticut the county boards (three members in each county) are appointed by the Legislature.

Federal Reserve Board (or Board of Governors), under the Act of 1913 setting up the Federal Reserve System, the eight members governing the system—two *ex officio,* Secretary of the Treasury and Comptroller General; and six appointed by the President with the consent of the Senate. The Board chooses three of the nine members on the governing board of each of the twelve Federal Reserve District Banks; and it supervises the Federal banking system and the bank-note currency of the United States.

The U. S. Department of Interior has a Petroleum Advisory Board, and the Department of Labor has the National Labor Relations Board and also the Textile Labor Relations Board.

Bolshevik (plural Bolsheviki), from the Russian meaning members of the majority party, as contrasted with *Mensheviki,* meaning members of the minority party. The split developed at a meeting of the Social Democratic Party in 1903 over Lenin's theory advocating an armed revolution of the proletariat and a centralized party. The more radical members of the party followed Lenin and formed the Bolsheviki; and the more conservative members formed the Mensheviki under Martov. With Leon Trotsky, Nikolai Lenin returned to Russia in 1917, built up the Bolshevik strength and engineered the "rule of the proletariat," which developed into the Soviet Republics. The Bolshevist group is now the official Communist party.

Borough, originally the same word as -burg or -burgh meaning fortress in names of cities.

In Great Britain, a parliamentary district, the unit to elect members of the House of Commons. A *pocket* borough was one controlled by a single person or family, as if it were in his pocket. A *rotten* borough was one with a very few voters, represented in the Commons in spite of the small population. By the Act of 1883 a *county* borough (sometimes with different boundaries from the old-time county) with a population of 75,000 or more is represented in the Commons. There are about 256 *ordinary* boroughs in Great Britain, smaller municipal units, chartered by the Crown and controlled by the county. The Government of London Act in 1899 set up in London 28 metropolitan boroughs, each governed like an ordinary borough.

In Connecticut, Minnesota, New Jersey and Pennsylvania a *borough* is a special form of municipal government like an incorporated village or town in other states.

In the city of New York the five boroughs (Manhattan, Brooklyn, Queens, Bronx and Richmond) are the political units, each having been an independent city or county before 1898, when Greater New York was chartered.

Budget, an inclusive list of the proposed expenditures and expected receipts of an individual, business or government for a specified period, usually a year. The governmental budget system originated in England. The budget is submitted to the House of Commons as a Committee on Ways and Means in the annual financial statement of the Chancellor of the Exchequer. Although it is considered by the Committee of the Whole, no serious changes can be made in the budget without up-

setting the Government and bringing about a general election.

In France each minister submits estimates for his own department. The Commission (or committee) of Finance passes on the budget; and this committee and the whole Chamber have power to alter the budget.

In the United States the business of government has only recently been put on a budget basis. The Budget and Accounting Act of 1921 created in the United States Treasury Department a Budget Bureau under a director appointed by the President but not removable by him. The President presents a budget to Congress with a special message something like the British Chancellor's budget speech. While it is the executive branch of the government that prepares the budget each year, the representatives of the people must approve it before it becomes final.

Six states—California, Louisiana, Maryland, Massachusetts, Nebraska and West Virginia—have constitutional provisions for a budget system; and all the other states have budgets now. The budget is made by the governor in California, Maryland, Massachusetts, Nebraska, Tennessee, Vermont and Utah, the tax commission in Louisiana, a department of finance (under a director appointed by the governor) in Illinois, a board of affairs in Wisconsin (governor, three appointees of the governor, secretary of state, two members from each house) and legislative committees in other states.

Municipal budgets in the United States preceded the Federal and state budget systems. In 1907 the New York Bureau of Municipal Research began to study budget methods. In city-manager municipalities the manager is usually director of the budget. In other cities the tendency is to give the responsibility of the budget to the mayor or to a smaller group than the city council or board of aldermen and to give the council power to reduce the budget estimate but not to increase it.

Bull Moose party, name applied to the Progressive party in 1912 when its leader, Theodore Roosevelt, declared that he felt "as fine as a bull moose."

Bureau, originally, a writing desk; then used of other furniture and of a business office, especially a minor business division of a government department.

In the French Government a *Bureau of Age* organizes each house of the French parliament when it first meets. The oldest member of the house acts as president and the six youngest members as secretaries. Then a Permanent Bureau is appointed—a president, four vice-presidents, eight secretaries and three questeurs—in each house to control procedure according to rule. The president of each permanent bureau has an important position in parliament and is a practical adviser to the president of the republic in cabinet crises.

In the United States Government there are over 50 bureaus, mostly divisions or parts of departments dealing with specialized activities. Some of the most important are:

In the Department of Agriculture,

Bureau of Agriculture Stabilization, Marketing and Foreign Agriculture, Soil Conservation, Animal Industry, Dairy Industry, Entomology and Plant Quarantine, Plant Industry, and the Weather Bureau.

In the Department of Commerce: Bureau of the Census, Bureau of Public Roads, National Bureau of Standards.

In the Department of the Interior: Bureau of Mines, Indian Affairs, Reclamation, Geological Survey, and Land Management.

In the Department of Justice: Federal Bureau of Investigation, Bureau of Prisons.

In the Department of Labor: Bureau of Labor Standards, Labor Statistics, Employment Security, Women's Bureau.

In the Department of the Treasury: Bureau of Customs, Bureau of Engraving and Printing, Bureau of Narcotics.

In the Department of Defense: Bureau of Medicine and Surgery.

In the Department of Health, Education and Welfare: Children's Bureau.

Outside of the departments is the independent Bureau of the Budget, established in 1921 to assist the President in preparing his budget, and later officially supervising its administration.

Bureaucracy, government by bureaus, a term used to describe a narrow rigid form of government hidebound and not responsive to public opinion; or a government in which administrative officers like bureau heads control the entire government and dictate its policy instead of limiting their activities to their own bureaus or departments.

Burgess, originally a citizen of a borough and sometimes the representative of a borough in the English House of Commons. The lower house of the Virginia legislature was called the House of Burgesses in colonial times. The members of this house are now called delegates.

Burglary, originally breaking and entering by night into the dwelling-house of another with the intent to commit a felony. Now most states do not limit burglary to night or to breaking into a dwelling, and all states have extended the common law definition. But to constitute burglary, there must be *breaking into;* if the one who steals enters through an open door, the offense is not burglary. Opening a window to gain entrance is sufficient breaking into. The penalty for this crime is imprisonment up to twenty years.

Burgomaster, the title of the mayor of a borough or city in Holland, Flanders or Germany.

Business law or **Commercial law,** those parts of the law that are often and directly applied to the conduct and direction of business and to the problems and disputes arising and resulting therefrom; especially the law of partnership, corporations, agency, contracts, negotiable instruments, insurance, sales, guaranty, lien and bankruptcy.

By-election, an election to fill a vacancy, held at a time other than the regular date. Death in office or transfer to another office is the usual reason.

Bylaw, originally a local law, the rule adopted by a village or town (from *by,* Anglo-Saxon for village, as in place names like Derby and Rugby); and now the local or special rules of a society or corporation to govern details of procedure not covered by its constitution or charter.

Cabinet, originally little cabin or cage, a case or cupboard and, by extension, a small room. Then (as in the case of the words board and bureau) those who meet in a small room, a group of advisers, especially advisers to an executive.

In both Great Britain and the United States the Cabinet has no constitutional authorization but is merely a matter of custom.

In England the Cabinet had its first beginning under Charles II (1660–85) when it became customary for the king to dismiss individual ministers who were objectionable to Parliament. William III (1688–1702), like Washington in the early part of his administration, first chose his ministers from both parties. But this plan did not work well, and in 1694 the king dismissed the Tory ministers and chose Whigs in their places. When the Tories became the dominant party, members of that party were chosen as ministers. Later the ministers began to meet together for purposes of conference with the king and consultation among themselves. In the years 1721 to 1742 under Sir Robert Walpole, an *inner cabinet* developed rapidly in importance, a small group (usually five) that was virtually in control of the Government.

In the middle of the 19th century the Cabinet took its present form and function. It is a group of the king's ministers (that is, heads of executive departments), all members of Parliament and responsible to the House of Commons; usually members of the majority party in the House of Commons and leaders of that party; always acting as leaders in legislation. All Cabinet members are members of the Privy Council and all are ministers. The Cabinet deliberates and advises; the Privy Council decrees; the individual ministers execute.

The life of a Cabinet depends on the favorable vote of the House of Commons. If the House votes against a Government measure (that is, one sponsored by the Cabinet), this lack of confidence may overthrow the Government and require a general election which chooses a new House of Commons. The decision to dissolve the house and call a new election lies with the Cabinet. If the new House has a different party in the majority, a new ministry (or Government) must be formed and a new Cabinet is chosen from it by the prime minister selected by the King.

Just what ministers or department heads shall be selected for the English Cabinet depends on the prime minister who is forming the ministry, on the personnel of the ministry and on other special controlling factors. The size of the Cabinet varies from ministry to ministry. During a war it is usually small—for greater effi-

BRITISH TRAVEL ASSOCIATION

NUMBER 10 DOWNING STREET, London, is home for the British prime minister in office.

ciency. In recent years the number of cabinet members has averaged about 17.

Until World War I most English Cabinets had been composed of members of a single party, but during the war and in several Cabinets since that war different parties have been represented in the same Cabinet. Another innovation brought by that war is the Cabinet Secretariat, a staff that keeps records of Cabinet meetings—formerly only the prime minister was allowed to take notes (so that he might give information to the king)—and plans the detail of meetings and communicates Cabinet decisions to ministers.

In the United States the development of the President's Cabinet had no historical relation to the growth of the English Cabinet. The Constitution (Art. II, Sec. 2, Cl. 1) allows the President to "require the opinion in writing of the principal officer in each of the executive departments upon any subject relating to the duties of their respective offices." President Washington repeatedly asked for written advice (not always on matters connected with their departments) from department heads, especially from his Secretary of State, Thomas Jefferson, and his Secretary of the Treasury, Alexander Hamilton. These two, besides being department heads, were leaders of two diametrically opposed parties—so that their advice seldom agreed.

From an original group of four members—secretaries of state, war and treasury and the attorney general—the Cabinet of the President of the United States has now grown to 10, with the War member now repre-

sented by the Secretary of Defense, and the Postmaster General, The Secretaries of the Interior, Agriculture, Commerce, Labor, and Health, Education, and Welfare, are added.

The Law concerning Presidential succession, passed in 1886, has been changed. It now states that in case of the death or incapacity of both the President and Vice President, the succession as acting President should be in this order: the speaker of the House of Representatives, President pro-tem of the Senate, Secretary of State, Treasury, Defense, Attorney General, Postmaster General, Secretary of the Interior, of Agriculture, of Commerce and of Labor.

Like other presidential appointments, those of department heads are subject to the approval of the Senate, but this is usually granted as a matter of course. Members of the Cabinet in the United States have no legislative function—they are officially department heads and unofficially members of the President's administrative family or council, advising him and discussing with him only the matters that he chooses to bring before the Cabinet meetings. They are (also unofficially) leaders of the majority party, usually representing different parts of the country and different shades of political belief within the party. The Vice-President has sat as a member of the Cabinet since 1921, beginning with Calvin Coolidge.

Cabinet government in other countries varies from both the British and the American pattern. In France the Cabinet functions only in leading and planning legislation, but the Cabinet members need not be members of either house of parliament, and the overthrow of a Cabinet by the unfavorable vote of the Chamber of Deputies does not end the session of the House of Deputies—a new Cabinet can come into office without a general election. So the Cabinet is much weaker than in England and is the creature of the Lower House.

In Japan the Cabinet is not responsible to the Diet and the selection of the Cabinet need not follow the popular vote.

Cadets (from the initial letters of Constitutional Democrats), the abbreviated name of the Russian Constitutional Democratic party, mostly middle class, that backed Kerensky's government in 1917.

Candidate, one who offers himself or is put forward by others for appointment or election to office. The word is supposed to come from the same root as *candid,* meaning gleaming white; the explanation is that Roman candidates for office appeared in spotless white togas.

From the number of candidates the vote of the people or the appointing power of President or governor chooses the official. How are the candidates chosen in the first place? The method varies. Caucus or committee of party leaders is one type of candidate maker. Then came the convention, more definitely representing the members of the party. Direct choice by the party members is the most democratic form of selecting candidates, and this method is called the *direct primary.*

Canon law, a body of ecclesiastical law that originated in the Church of Rome, relating to matters over which the church exerts or claims jurisdiction. England has a sort of national canon law, but the canon law as a system of jurisprudence never was adopted in America. Canon law still is important in countries where the established state religion is Catholic.

Traces of canon law still remain in the common law of England and many states of the United States—notably the exemption of church property from taxation and exemption of clergy from military service or jury duty. Even as recently as a century ago the English Church courts had jurisdiction in certain cases over marriage, wills, brawling in church and defamation.

Canton, the local name of any of the 22 members of the Swiss Confederation, corresponding roughly to an American state. In France a canton is a subdivision of an arrondissement—more like a ward than any other American division. There are about 3,000 cantons in the French Republic.

Capital punishment, the penalty of death visited upon those guilty of the greatest crimes. The word *capital* is from the Latin, and means *pertaining to the head;* as beheading was the old legal method of taking life, we find in this fact the origin of the term *capital punishment.*

Crimes punishable in some states by death include murder, abduction, arson, and rape. Treason to one's country is a capital offense. Alaska, Delaware, Hawaii, Maine, Michigan, Minnesota, New York, North Dakota, Rhode Island, and Wisconsin have no death

penalty. The method used in federal crimes requiring the death penalty is the same as in the state where the sentence is imposed. If the state has no death penalty then the Federal judge prescribes the method. In states where the death penalty is imposed the following methods are employed:

Hanging: Idaho, Iowa, Kansas, Montana, New Hampshire, and also Washington (or life imprisonment).

Electrocution: Alabama, Arkansas, Connecticut, District of Columbia, Florida, Georgia, Illinois, Indiana, Kentucky, Louisiana, Massachusetts, Nebraska, New Jersey, Ohio, Pennsylvania, South Carolina, South Dakota, Tennessee, Texas, Vermont, Virginia, West Virginia.

Lethal Gas: in an airtight chamber: Arizona, California, Colorado, Maryland, Mississippi, Missouri, Nevada, New Mexico, North Carolina, Oklahoma, Oregon, Wyoming.

Shooting or Hanging, at option of the prisoner: Utah.

In modern times capital punishment has been abolished in many countries in accordance with the present method of treating criminals, which stresses prevention, social causation and correction rather than punishment.

Cassation, annulment, quashing, making invalid, nullifying. The French Court of Cassation is a supreme court of appeal in ordinary court cases with three sections: *requests or petitions,* passed on to decide whether a civil case shall be heard on appeal; *civil,* deciding cases recommended by the petition chamber; and *criminal.* Each of these sections has a president. There are 45 other judges. A general president is in charge. When the court quashes or cassates the decision of a lower court, the case goes back for retrial to a lower court of the same grade as the one that first tried the case but not to the same court. Members of the court are appointed for life by the Council of State; the president gets 150,000 francs a year, the judges or councillors, 100,000 francs each.

Caucus (apparently a North American Indian word meaning talk, council or counselors), a party committee that plans policies and picks candidates. There was a Caucus Club in Boston in 1763. Between 1800 and 1824 party candidates for President and Vice-President of the United States were chosen by party members of Congress meeting "in caucus." This method was replaced by party nominating conventions. Congressional caucuses still select party members to serve on committees.

In England the Liberal party in Birmingham under the leadership of Joseph Chamberlain in 1867 was organized somewhat along American party lines with ward meetings of all voters of the party and with an active general committee. This method won three elections for the party and came to be called the *Birmingham caucus.*

In Australia the powerful Labour party decides its policy by caucus of party members of municipal councils, state or Federal legislatures. The of-

ficial Labour party in Australia is sometimes called the *caucus.*

Caveat emptor (Latin, let the buyer beware), a maxim of English and American law that the buyer acts at his own risk in the sales of personal property, in the absence of an express warranty, where the buyer has had an opportunity to inspect the goods and the seller is guilty of no fraud and is neither the grower nor the manufacturer of the article sold. The tendency of modern regulative law is to lessen this risk and give more protection to the customer. The civil-law maxim *caveat venditor* (let the seller beware) is just the opposite principle to that of the common law.

Caveat (let him beware) is a formal caution or warning given to a judge or public official against the performance of an act or a notice given to an officer not to do a certain act until the party giving notice is heard. The phrase is used in the general sense of a precaution for self-protection.

Censorship, government restriction of freedom of speech and freedom of the press, the theater and other public agencies.

The word *censor* is Latin in its origin. Under the Roman Republic the office of censor was created in 443 B.C. to relieve the consuls of the duties of making the census or registration list. So *censor,* related to *census,* meant originally one who values or assesses. The two censors (like the consuls) had to agree if their action was to be authoritative. They could exclude any citizen from the official list on the ground of bad morals; and so censorship came to mean supervision of public morals. The early Roman emperors retained the title of censor.

In early American political history there was a *council of censors* in Pennsylvania from 1776 to 1790 and in Vermont from 1777 to 1870. It had power to investigate the operation of the state government. A convention was called by the Vermont council in 1870 to amend the state constitution by omitting the clause that created the council of censors.

The Government still exercises the police power that excludes from entry to the country undesirable visitors or immigrants on the ground of moral turpitude (baseness) or of enmity to the established form of government. But this power is no longer called *censorship.*

In modern times censorship usually applies to freedom of speech (notably in political matters); to freedom of the press—with the two main subdivisions, newspapers and books; and to control of the theater, motion pictures and radio broadcasts.

The attempts of government to control these different forms of communication are not the only kind of censorship, for there is a sort of control by the general feeling of the community, and besides there is the constantly exercised control of the publishers and owners of newspapers, magazines and books and of the proprietors of theaters, the motion-picture companies (individually and jointly) and the radio broadcasting companies. This self-

UNITED PRESS INTERNATIONAL

RADIO FREE EUROPE

CENSORSHIP of the news in Korea is illustrated (*left*) by a Japanese newspaper that is being read by a Korean during the Korean War. Note that certain "disapproved" sections have been deleted with black ink. Censorship usually occurs in totalitarian states where all is controlled by the state. Behind the Iron Curtain very little outside news is received. Letters to Radio Free Europe (*right*) arrive daily. All are anonymous, and are identified by code names. Many are answered by supplying information on the air.

censorship is very effective; it is based on the practical standard of self-interest.

Church Censorship. Government censorship arose largely out of the traditions of the Roman law and the activities of the Roman Catholic Church, which were in part based on the principles of Roman law. In 1515 the Lateran Council of the Church forbade the printing of any book that had not been examined by the proper Church authority. Permission to print, the *imprimatur* (Latin, let it be printed), was the positive side of the Church censorship; the negative side was the *Index Librorum Prohibitorum* (list of forbidden books), dating from 1546, revised in 1900, and the *Index Expurgatorius* (purifying list), which tells what must not be read unless it has been expurgated or freed from dangerous doctrine or subversive matter.

A less formal sort of ecclesiastical censorship today is the *white lists* of books and plays recommended to Catholics.

Censorship in Great Britain. In England after the Reformation the power of the Church to control the press passed to the Crown, and printing was licensed by the Star Chamber or other governmental authority. During the English Civil War the Long Parliament passed in 1643 a strict licensing act that was the occasion for John Milton's *Areopagitica . . . for the Liberty of Unlicensed Printing.* Under the Stuart kings before and after Cromwell licensing was strict, and the freedom of the press was seriously impaired. But in 1695, a few years after the accession of William and Mary, the licensing act was not renewed, and since that date the English press (both newspapers and books) has been famously free.

There is no corresponding freedom of the theater in Great Britain. An act of 1737 required all plays to be submitted to the lord chamberlain; an act of 1843 gave this official power to forbid the production of any play; and an act of 1924 gave him further power. For more than 3 centuries it has been forbidden to represent on the stage any living Christian king; and rules about royalty on the stage postponed the public presentation of Laurence Housman's *Victoria Regina* in London for several years after it appeared in New York, and then it appeared only on special permission from the Crown.

Freedom of speech in Great Britain is practically unrestrained by any censorship. Hyde Park in London is famous as the scene of soap-box orations attacking the British Government.

Censorship in America. In early Colonial America there was the same strict supervision of books and newspapers that prevailed in England under the Stuarts and the Protectorate. The governors licensed the few presses in the colonies up to 1730, and religious books were under censorship until 1695. Newspapers were frequently suppressed. In 1734 the trial of John Peter Zenger for libel marked one step toward freedom of the press as it established the doctrine that a jury shall decide whether there has been a libel.

The Bill of Rights in the original amendments to the Constitution of the United States begins with the words:

"Congress shall make no law respecting an establishment of religion, or prohibiting the free exercise thereof; or abridging the freedom of speech, or of the press." (Article I).

Under the Constitution there can be no censorship of press or speech. But there is an old Latin proverb, *Inter arma leges silent,* that means constitutional guarantees vanish in wartime. In 1798 Congress passed the Alien and Sedition laws that permitted the President to deport editors of papers opposing the administration policy if they were aliens and that made it a crime to publish any attack on that policy. This exercise of censorship was a main factor in the speedy downfall of the Federalist party that voted these laws. But in other wars there have been similar removals of the Constitutional protection for freedom of speech and press. In the Civil War and again in World War I Congress and the Supreme Court made rules to punish those who criticized the administration and national policy. In 1920 Chief Justice Hughes recognized the extravagance of government censorship in wartime, saying: "We may well wonder whether constitutional government as heretofore maintained in this republic could survive another great war even victoriously waged."

Not merely war feeling but also any notably aroused partisan spirit is sure to result in some form of censorship. In the United States this censorship has often been demonstrated in various local-government activities against meetings and parades of minority groups, whether labor unions, Socialists or Communists. In 1938 several municipalities, notably Jersey City, refused licenses to such meetings and practically prohibited the distribution of pamphlets or circulars by members of these groups—on the ground that the people of the community resented the activities of these groups, and so any public meeting or speaking in which they took part would provoke disorder and endanger the peace of the community.

Local censorship is applied in other fields. Though a Federal official has the say whether a book printed abroad may be excluded from the United States because it is obscene, and the Post Office Department can exclude a book or pamphlet from the mails, it is the local police officials who decide whether a book or magazine may be sold on the newsstands, and it is the local authorities who say whether a theatrical show or a motion picture may be exhibited.

Censorship in Totalitarian States. In countries where one party is supreme, where the one supreme party is the state, censorship takes an extreme form. All exists for the state and party, all is controlled by the party. Hence freedom of speech and freedom of press are impossible. For example, until Hitler was beaten non-Aryan and anti-Nazi books were confiscated and burned in Germany. Charlie Chaplin's movie *Modern Times* was barred from the German movie houses. In Japan the Government attempted to censor and punish subversive thought. The totalitarian governments of Latin America exercise an equally complete censorship. Dictatorship and militarism both thrive on censorship—but the reason why is that dictatorship and militarism are one-party governments, and that tolerance and recognition of the rights of minorities are necessary to free speech and free press. The great dangers to free government today are: censorship that says, "You can't print that or say that" and propaganda that commands, "You must print this and you must say this."

Census, an enumeration or listing for taxation or other government purposes. In ancient Babylon, Persia, China and Egypt there were government censuses, some of them more than 4,000 years ago. At Rome population and property were listed every five years, and in 5 B.C. Augustus extended the Roman census to every part of the Empire, so Joseph and Mary, the mother of Jesus, went to Bethlehem to be taxed (Luke 2:1-5).

In 1085-86 William the Conqueror had a Grant Inquest of England made and the summary of this census appeared in the famous *Domesday Book.*

In modern times the first censuses were in French Canada (Quebec and Nova Scotia) in the middle of the 17th century. In the 18th century there were censuses in Sweden (1748), Denmark (1769) and Spain (1787). A census of the population of the United States is required every ten years by the Constitution (Art. I, Sec. 2, Cl. 3) to give a basis for representation in the House of Representatives and to apportion direct taxes. The first U.S. census was taken in 1790. The scope of the enumeration broadened with the inclusion of vital statistics and information on manufactures, agriculture, mining and fisheries. Since 1902 there has been a five-year census of electrical industries. From 1900 to 1920 a census of manufactures was taken every five years; after that, every two years.

The Bureau of the Census, a part of the Department of Commerce, was established in 1902 and is the major fact-finding and statistical service agency of the Government. The vital statistics functions of the Bureau were transferred to the Federal Security Agency in 1946. The Department of Commerce publishes the census reports and the *Survey of Current Business* compiled by the Bureau.

Central Intelligence Agency, coordinates the intelligence activities of the various departments and agencies of the U.S. Government in the interest of national security. The C.I.A. was established in 1947 under the National Security Council. Its director and deputy director are appointed by the President with the consent of the Senate. In 1965 William F. Raborn succeeded John A. McCone as Director.

Centralization and decentralization of government, two opposed theories and practices. In England and most European countries administration is much more centralized than in the United States. The Dominion of Canada has provinces that are somewhat comparable to the states of the United States, and the provinces have their own legislatures; but their chief executive is a lieutenant governor not elected by the voters of the province but appointed by the Dominion authorities. The U.S. Constitution reserves to the states all powers not expressly granted to the Congress and the United States—a decentralized government. In Canada all powers not specifically given to the provinces are reserved to the Dominion Government—a high degree of centralization.

The French department and the English county or borough have none of the governmental independence that there is in the American state. Even in the United States, decentralized as government is here, there has always been a centralizing tendency, always a school of statesmen who believed that the Union should be stronger than it had been and the separate states should be weaker.

Party differences in the United States have centered (in theory, at least) on this controversy between strong central government and State rights. Hamilton wanted a strong central government; Jefferson was afraid that Hamilton's ideas would endanger the states and the liberty of the people. The party in power, whatever its name and its platform, has always been for the strong centralized government; the outs have almost always urged the preservation of State rights. Jefferson and Jackson, opposed in theory to strong central government, actually strengthened the Federal power when they were in office. And in much later times, under the pressure of national economic problems the leader of the Democratic party in the New Deal increased the powers of the Federal Government at the expense of the State rights that his party has so long upheld. During Roosevelt's administration, his Republican opponents urged plans for decentralization.

Prime examples of centralization were the dictatorships of Hitler and Mussolini, who took unto themselves all power in the state. The Soviet Union with power concentrated in the hands of a single party has a highly centralized bureaucracy.

After World War II West Germany became a Federal Republic somewhat similar to the U. S., with a high degree of decentralization. Italy's corporate state delegates governmental functions to various economic groups.

The modern trend is towards increasing decentralization. As society grows more complex government must expand its services to provide adequately for the needs of citizens. Such broad administration is better accomplished at a local level.

Certiorari (Latin, to be certified, made more certain), a writ from a higher court to a lower, ordering the lower court to certify and return to the higher court the record in a particular case. It has been one of the most valuable and efficient remedies in the common law for correcting error.

Chamber, originally Latin *camera,* a vaulted room. The meeting place of the Italian lower house was called *camera* or *camara,* and the U.S. Senate meets in the Senate *Chamber.* By an extension it has come to mean those who meet in such a room, a branch of the legislature. A bicameral legislature has two chambers, two branches, the upper and lower.

Chamber of Deputies is the name of the Lower House in most Latin countries—France, Rumania, Brazil, Chile and others.

Chancellor, originally a clerk who sat at a chancel or latticed window and now a title of various high officials. The king's chancellor in England was a secretary of the king with special powers which gave rise to the system of chancery courts where petitioners came for equity that they could not find in courts of law. The *Lord Chancellor,* formerly head of the chancery court, now is president of the chancery division of the High Court of Justice and of the Court of Appeal.

A more important English official is the *Chancellor of the Exchequer,* practically a minister of finance, always a member of the House of Commons (since money measures must originate in that house) and c:

the Cabinet, in which he is often prime minister. Among the great chancellors of the exchequer were: Robert Walpole, William Pitt, W. E. Gladstone, Stanley Baldwin and Neville Chamberlain.

In West Germany, the Prime Minister has the title of Chancellor of the Federal Republic of Germany.

In the United States, in states that have a distinct system of equity courts, chancellor is the title of an equity judge and particularly of a presiding judge distinguished from the other equity judges who are called vice-chancellors.

Chancery or **Court of equity,** a court where equity jurisprudence is administered. Equity as a particular judicial system developed in England and was adopted in America with various statutory modifications. The system of equity that first appeared about the middle of the 14th century developed because many cases arose for which there was no remedy at the common law. Petitions seeking relief in such cases were made to the king who usually referred them to the chancellor. Later the petitions were addressed directly to the chancellor and a separate and distinct judicial system developed outside of the common law. The controversy between these two courts raged for two centuries but finally in 1616 the prerogatives of the equity courts were affirmed by royal decree.

Much of the English equitable jurisprudence was taken from the Roman civil law, since the early chancellors were officials of the church and learned in the canon law. Now equity courts no longer administer a sort of "natural justice" unhampered by any rules. Instead the courts of equity have become as hidebound as the common-law courts by rules of procedure and the principle of *stare decisis.*

In 1873 the rules of equity in England became a part of the law of the land and special equity courts were abolished, the chancery becoming a chancery division of the high court of justice.

The states of Alabama, Delaware, Mississippi, New Jersey and Tennessee have separate chancery courts; in the other states and in Federal courts the same judges hear cases at law and cases in equity.

Chancery courts originated the *injunction,* an order or a prohibition, and other methods of making a person do something for the benefit of a plaintiff besides pay money damages, which formerly had been practically the only redress at law for wrongs to person or property.

Charter, originally a little paper, from Latin *cartula,* diminutive of *carta;* hence, any legal document, deed or conveyance. In this sense the word is now used only in the phrase a *ship's charter,* meaning the lease of a vessel.

The many present uses of the term *charter* all agree in meaning a grant from a sovereign power. The *Great Charter* (Magna Charta) of 1215 wrung from King John by the barons is the most famous of charters.

The *charter colonies* in America (Massachusetts, Connecticut and Rhode Island) had royal charters for their government without any direct interference from the Crown such as the Crown colonies had.

A *chartered company* in Great Britain is a corporation with a special charter. The East India Company and the Hudson's Bay Company were chartered companies, and in the last two or three generations the chartered company in England became as popular as the corporation in America. In both countries a certificate of incorporation is called a *charter,* and a member of an association from its beginning is called a *charter member.*

A *chartered accountant* in Great Britain is a member of a certified association, roughly equivalent to the American certified public accountant (C.P.A.).

The *People's Charter* of 1838 in England was the summary of demands made by the *Chartist* reformers who wanted universal male suffrage, vote by ballot, annual parliaments and no property qualifications.

In the present system of local government in England new boroughs must be chartered by an order in council or by an Act of Parliament.

In American local government cities and other municipalities are usually chartered by the state legislature; but the home-rule movement attempts to take this power from the legislature and give it to the voters. In Missouri the state constitution of 1875 gives each city over 100,000 in population the right to frame its own charter—so that the charter is no longer a grant from a sovereign power. Arizona, Arkansas, California, Colorado, Florida, Maryland, Michigan, Minnesota, Nebraska, New York, Ohio, Oklahoma, Oregon, Texas, Washington and Wisconsin have made similar provisions for home-rule charters.

The Fascist *Charter of Labor,* proclaimed in April 1927 by the Fascist Grand Council of Italy, claimed for the Government control of labor and granted workers a six-day week and an annual vacation with pay.

Chattels (from the Norman French, meaning goods of any kind), a broad term denoting any property, movable or immovable, that is less than a freehold. Chattels are divided into two classes—chattels real and chattels personal.

Chattels real are interests that are annexed to or concern real estate and are less than a freehold. A lease of land for years is a chattel real.

Chattels personal are things that are movable and may be taken from place to place, such as animals, furniture, automobiles or clothing.

A *chattel mortgage* is a conveyance of some present legal or equitable right in personal property usually as security for a debt, but it may be as security for the performance of some act. In some states a chattel mortgage operates as a transfer to the creditor of title to the goods on the condition that if the debt is paid or the act performed title will revert to the debtor. In other states the mortgage is treated as security only. Title to the property does not pass; there is only a lien on the property. In either case the debtor retains possession of the goods unless he fails to pay the debt due, when the creditor may take possession of the property.

Checks and balances, the precautions against too great concentration of governmental authority in any one division of government. Some of the compromises of the Constitution resulted in balancing one interest with another: for example, the Senate represents the states and the Lower House represents the people. The power of vetoing legislation gives the President and the governors (of all states except North Carolina) a check on the legislative branch. The President's appointive power is checked by the requirement that his appointments must meet with the consent of the Senate. The power of the Supreme Court to declare Federal or state laws unconstitutional is a check on Congress and the state legislatures and is a control between Federal and state authority.

This whole American governmental system of checks and balances may be called a check and balance on the American theory of sharply separated governmental functions into executive, legislative and judiciary.

Cheka, abbreviation from the initials of *Cherezoychainya Kommisiya,* literally extraordinary commission, the agency set up in the autumn of 1918 to combat counterrevolution in Soviet Russia. This branch of the secret police was replaced in 1922 by the State Political Department (G.P.U.).

Citizenship, membership in a nation or city with consequent allegiance to its government and the right of protection by that government. Citizenship does not automatically or necessarily confer suffrage (right to vote) or other political rights; its rights are civic, and the department of political science that deals with the duties of citizens and the rights of citizenship is called *civics.*

A state defines citizenship for itself, and so the theories of citizenship vary in different countries. Nations that follow the Roman Law, such as France and Italy, follow the theory of *jus sanguinis,* which is that citizenship is determined by the nationality of the father, or if the child is illegitimate, by the nationality of the mother. England follows the theory of *jus soli,* that the nationality is determined by the place of birth. The United States applies both theories: *jus soli* to all children born in the United States; and *jus sanguinis* to children born of Americans traveling abroad, if the children return as minors to live permanently in the United States or make a declaration of citizenship at majority. Due to this difference between countries, it frequently happens that a person has dual citizenship, that is, he is a citizen of two nations.

Citizenship in the United States is acquired by birth or by naturalization. The 14th Amendment (1868) to the Federal Constitution declares: "All persons born or naturalized in the United States, and subject to the jurisdiction thereof, are citizens of the United States and of the state wherein they reside." Children of

U.S. citizens born on foreign soil are citizens. Aliens who are free whites (that is, full-blooded Caucasians) or of African descent may be naturalized, but not aliens of Japanese, Chinese or Hindu races. An Act of 1922 (amended in 1930 and 1934) makes a wife's citizenship independent of her husband's: an alien who marries a U.S. citizen does not become a citizen by reason of the marriage; and marriage to an alien does not deprive a woman of her U.S. citizenship—she may give it up only by a formal renunciation.

Citizenship by naturalization is presumed to lapse upon two years' residence in the country of original allegiance or five years' residence in any other foreign country.

City, in the United States, a local government unit with a larger population than a village, town or borough, but (like those units) governed by a charter granted by the state legislature.

In Great Britain large municipalities formerly were not cities unless they were cathedral towns, but this distinction no longer holds. The British cities and other municipal government units are governed by the provisions of general Acts of Parliament with only an occasional special law for the government of a single city.

In the United States there is little uniformity of government even in cities in the same state and of the same size, since the state legislature grants individual charters. If the charter originates with the city itself, it is called a *home-rule* charter.

American city governments, though they differ in many details, may be classed under three main heads—(1) mayor-and-council type; (2) commission plan; and (3) city-manager plan.

(1) Government by *mayor and council* is the older method with one executive and a legislature and administrative body, all elected by the people. Sometimes, in addition to the council there is a board of aldermen, so that the municipality has a two-chamber legislature. Most of the larger and older cities of the United States are governed this way, usually under a system of party elections. The city of New York under the charter of 1936 elects members of the Council by proportional representation.

(2) *Commission government* is by an elected board of three, five or seven members, each of whom becomes head of a city department. The general principle is the concentration of legislative and administrative powers in a small body. Commissioners are often elected on a nonpartisan ballot, and sometimes there is provision for recalling a commissioner. The method was adopted as an emergency measure in Galveston, Tex., during a severe flood, and the commissioners were appointed by the governor. The courts decided that this was unconstitutional, and then the commissioners were elected by the voters of the city not from districts but at large. Des Moines, Iowa, adopted a commission plan in 1907; Spokane, in 1911; New Orleans, in

1912; Jersey City, N. J., Portland, Oreg., in 1913; Newark, in 1917; and Omaha in 1923. Comparatively few cities have adopted the commission form of government since 1934; and some cities that had it gave it up and returned to the mayor-and-council form—for example, Buffalo (1916-28), Denver (1912-16), Lowell (1911-20).

(3) The city-manager government started in small cities in the South—Staunton, Va., in 1908, and Sumter, S.C., in 1913. It centralizes responsibility in a manager, usually a technical expert, who is hired by the city council or the city commission—that is, the system can be combined with either of the systems already mentioned. Often the manager comes from the outside. His post is not considered political but administrative like the head of a business organization. The larger cities that have managers are: Cincinnati, beginning in 1926; Kansas City, Mo., adopted in 1926; Rochester, N.Y., since 1928; Dayton, Ohio, after the flood of 1913.

City manager, see *City.*

City Planning is a form of municipal control made necessary by the growth of the modern city. In a growing community, areas change in character and use. Residential areas gradually change to industrial ones with accompanying low-rent slum sections. When the change is uncontrolled, as has usually been the case, unwholesome conditions may develop, particularly in sanitation, health and living conditions.

Another important reason for city planning is to improve traffic conditions. Most cities in the United States developed with narrow streets and no provisions for extensive automotive transportation. As a partial solution of the problem, one-way streets have been designated, traffic lights installed, street cars have been replaced by busses, pedestrian traffic regulated, railroads have either been elevated, gone underground or removed altogether from congested areas. Many slums and tenements have been replaced by modern apartments. The size and type of buildings have been regulated by zoning restrictions in order to reduce congestion, increase light and air, etc. Parks have been laid out for recreation and rest and all main traffic arteries, tunnels and bridges have been constructed in such a way as to reduce traffic congestion. Federal funds have frequently been made available for housing and roads as a part of desirable city-planning programs.

Civil death, the state of a person considered dead insofar as his civil rights are concerned, although he may be actually living. The property of a person civilly dead passes to his heirs as though he were physically dead. In some jurisdictions a person who has been convicted of murder or certain other serious crimes and sentenced to life imprisonment is civilly dead.

Civil law, in early times the law governing the citizens of the particular state (*jus civile*) in contrast to the

law applied in cases between citizens of different states (*jus gentium*); in the Middle Ages the Roman law of Justinian's Pandects as distinguished from the canon law of the Church; the law governing private relationships in contradistinction to the law governing public relationships; in present English usage those legal systems based on the Roman law in contrast to the common law. The civil law governs in all Europe, except England, and in those countries that were once colonies of European Powers.

Thus this general usage of the term *civil law* includes the law of such nations as Germany where the original Teutonic law was influenced by the Roman law, especially during the 16th century.

Civil Rights, claims to civil liberties given legal standing by statutes upheld in the courts. The acquisition of civil rights has been a long process of growth involving custom, legislative and judicial recognition, and enforcement, and has intertwined social, political, and economic relationships. Segments of society that are denied certain rights through custom or prejudice have struggled to obtain them.

The basis of civil rights in the U. S. is the Bill of Rights—the first ten amendments of the Constitution. These include the rights to a free press; to freedom of religion, assembly, and petition; to freedom from unreasonable search and seizure; to trial by jury, etc. Milestones in the struggle to secure civil rights were the Northwest Ordinance of 1787, establishing religious freedom, prohibiting slavery, and guaranteeing the basic rights of English liberty; the 13th, 14th, and 15th amendments, freeing the slaves and giving them the vote; legislation of the 1930's and 1940's, particularly the Social Security Act, the Wagner Act, the Taft-Hartley Act, and the Fair Labor Standards Act; and the Supreme Court decision of 1954, outlawing segregation in schools.

In 1964, the Civil Rights Act (1) made discrimination illegal in public facilities, (2) strengthened the 1954 Supreme Court decision requiring school integration by enabling the Attorney General to initiate suits on behalf of individuals, (3) established a commission to investigate violations of fair hiring practices, and (4) reduced certain voting qualifications. Federal legislation in 1965 banned all poll taxes as requirements for voter eligibility and provided for federal registrars to safeguard voter registration.

Many Negro demonstrations, supported by civil rights groups, brought civil conflicts in the mid-1960's as segregationists sought to slow school integration and Negro voter registration. In 1964 and 1965, riots in some cities with large Negro populations led to even further pressure for progress.

Civil service, the duties of all government employees not in the army, navy, legislative or judicial branches of the government; and (by extension) the whole body of civil servants. The phrase originated in India when that country was ruled by the British East India Company: the civil service of India then was the company's civilian employees, that is, those not in the army or navy.

In Federal, state and municipal governments the civil service breaks into two divisions: political appointees and those chosen on the basis of competitive examination or other set standards. *Civil service reform* is the effort to have no partisan, political appointments. An Act of Congress in 1883 created a Civil Service Commission of three members, appointed by the President with the consent of the Senate, not more than two to belong to the same party, to control examinations and appointments. The *classified* civil service, coming under the Commission, included in 1883 about 14,000 Federal employees. In 1956, the total number in the Civil Service was 2,500,000.

In the states there is still a considerable predominance of political appointments. In three-fourths of the states the civil service is filled with partisan employees who may be turned out after an election that is favorable to the other party. The general methods of the Federal civil service are paralleled in California, Colorado, Illinois, Maryland, Massachusetts, New Jersey, New York, Ohio and Wisconsin. Appointments are by competitive examination for most posts and by noncompetitive examinations for employees in certain crafts. Some posts are *exempt* from examination—deputies, chief clerks and some laborers.

Municipal civil service in the United States is coming under the control of commissions, usually of the city but sometimes of the state, which conduct examinations and make appointments.

In Great Britain the civil service is distinctly nonpolitical, permanent and (in comparison with our civil service or with the British ministry and department heads) technically expert. A civil servant is not permitted to be a candidate for political office, to serve on a party committee or to take any active part in politics.

In Germany under the old Empire the civil service was excellent, highly professional in its training and quite free from political taint. But the Nazi regime made loyalty to the party the test of civil fitness—and loyalty to the party was then the definition of loyalty to the German Government.

Closure rules, regulations limiting (literally closing) debate in a legislative body. In the U.S. House of Representatives it is always in order to move the previous question (that is, whether the discussion of the main issue shall be terminated and the matter brought to a vote); if the measure is carried it bars further debate and the question is then voted on. Another House rule, adopted in 1841, limits any member to one hour in debate on any measure, and a later rule forbids any but the mover, proposer or introducer of a measure to speak more than once on the same issue. Since 1806 the U.S. Senate has had no rule giving the right to move the previous question. In 1917 a rule was passed by which a two-thirds vote (after a petition signed by 16

Senators) may adopt an hour limit on speeches upon a certain measure. This closure is seldom used.

In the English House of Commons there are these methods of closure: *simple,* by motion carried that "the question be now put"; *guillotine* closure, by motion carried that debate end at a certain time, chopping off the discussion; *compartment* closure, by setting a limit on debate upon a certain part of a bill; and *kangaroo* closure, the selection (by the Speaker or the Chairman of the Ways and Means Committee) to single out the only amendments that may be discussed—jumping like a kangaroo from one to another.

Code Napoleon, the system of civil law, really the Five Codes compiled for the French nation by order of Napoleon Bonaparte after he became emperor and enacted between 1804 and 1810. It combined the principles of the Justinian Code and Roman law in general with the Germanic law of the northern provinces of France and certain principles resulting from the French Revolution. The Napoleonic Code became the basis of the laws of the Netherlands, Belgium, Louisiana, which was a French settlement, and the Province of Quebec in Canada.

Codes, systematization and orderly arrangement of the complete body of the law. Codes have been common in the development of Roman law and civil law—not in the history of English and American law. The British adopted a penal code for India in 1860 and other codes later. Seven states of the United States have reduced their laws to code form, and Louisiana since 1808 has had a code of civil law resembling the famous Code Napoleon. Other states and the Federal Government have compiled statutes in a form to which the term code is applied in a broad and general sense. California and the two Dakotas have attempted to codify the whole body of law. In New York codes on special topics—lien law, general business law, real property law—have been enacted as statutes. Codes of procedure are common in the United States, beginning with the important pioneer work of the New York code (often called the *Field Code* from its main author David Dudley Field 1805-94), which was adopted in 1848.

Coinage, the government's power of coining money; in the United States granted to Congress (Art. I, Sec. 8, Cl. 5) and denied to the states (Art. I, Sec. 10, Cl. 1). United States mints are located in Philadelphia, Denver and San Francisco.

In 1873 Congress stopped the coinage of standard silver dollars, and in 1900 the money system of the United States was put on a gold basis. In 1933 Congress called gold into the Treasury, ceased to coin gold and made contracts to pay in gold no longer binding. In 1934 the value of the dollar was reduced to 59.06 per cent of the previous gold content.

Colony, a territory away from but belonging to one of the independent and generally powerful countries of the world. Distant from the mother country, it remains dependent upon

or protected by it in various ways. The word *colony* is derived from the Latin *colere,* meaning to cultivate.

A colony is nearly always established in a region that is in a less advanced state of civilization. The purpose of colonization is to relieve overpopulation in the mother country, to exploit natural resources that have previously been ignored or used only in part or to further the interests of the mother country thru commerce.

Rome, Greece and other ancient powers acquired colonies by conquest and settlement. During the 19th century, Africa and Asia became for the powers of Europe, a source of colonies. Great Britain, France, Portugal and Spain were prominent. The latter two declined in power and lost control of most of their colonies. Belgium, The Netherlands, and Italy rose to economic if not military power through the ownership of colonies. Most colonial expansion was ended by World War I. Mandates under the League of Nations brought about changes in control of former German-held colonies. World War II practically ended colonial domination on a large scale. Almost the entire structure of British colonial power was swept away, most of the important former colonies becoming independent, and some of them voluntary members of the British Commonwealth of Nations. Much of the same thing happened throughout Asia to other colonial powers. The only large areas that now can properly be termed as colonial are in Africa whose countries because of the illiteracy, military weakness and the backwardness of their people are not able to resist. Even in Africa, the urge for self-determination and equality is weakening the control of foreign nations whose colonial powers have gradually given place to spheres of interest or most favored nations. A modern phenomenon is the domination by Soviet Russia of so-called satellite nations.

Cominform (formerly **Comintern**), abbreviation for "The Communist Information Bureau." The Cominform was generally regarded as a revival under another name, but with similar purpose, of the Communist International, organized by Lenin and his associates in Moscow, March 4, 1919. The Comintern was based on the Lenin conception of "democratic centralism," and was organized to keep close check on Communist parties and their members throughout the world. Its membership was made up of representatives from each national Communist party, its meetings were held in Moscow on call by the Russian head of the party, and its deliberations were carried on under the close supervision and control of the Russian Communist leaders. Stalin, who succeeded Lenin as head of the Comintern, used the organization as a means of preaching world revolution through infiltration, seizure of power by violence if necessary, and rule from Moscow through local puppets. On May 22, 1943, Russia, in the midst of World War II, dramatically announced the dissolution of the Comintern.

A threat to Communism arose first in the Marshall plan to aid European recovery and, second, in rumblings of revolt in the Russian satellite countries. The Comintern was revived, therefore, at a secret meeting in western Poland in September, 1947 as the Communist Information Bureau with Zhdanov, looked on by many as Stalin's heir-apparent, as its master. Its original members included Communist leaders from Russia, France, Bulgaria, Yugoslavia, Poland, Italy, Hungary, Czechoslovakia and Romania, nine in all. The first important act of the Cominform was the expulsion of the Yugoslav party because of the refusal of the Yugoslav leader, Marshal Tito, to attend a meeting in Bucharest in June, 1948. From being a Russian satellite country, Yugoslavia became an experiment in imperial Communism. Tito refused to change his policy and his revolt from Russian control seemed to constitute a threat to Russian domination of eastern Europe that could not be disregarded. In August, 1949 at Sofia and again in November, 1949, near Budapest in Hungary, the Cominform met, denounced Tito as a foreign tool and called on Communists the world over to join together and help overthrow him and his government. The Cominform worked to make all elements obedient to Soviet control. It was dissolved in 1956 when it was considered no longer practical.

Commerce, the exchange or buying and selling of commodities on a large scale between different places. The "commerce clause" of the Constitution delegates to Congress authority to regulate commerce "with foreign Nations, and among the several States, and with the Indian tribes." The meaning of *foreign* commerce demands no further explanation but the meaning of *interstate* commerce has been broadly interpreted by judicial decisions. In addition to the ordinary buying and selling of goods across state borders, the jurisdiction of the national government embraces transportation, communications, electric power, insurance, and other industries.

Besides the regulation of interstate and foreign commerce Congress has the power to prevent interference of such commerce even though it entails regulating persons and activities that are not in themselves parts of interstate commerce.

Although *intrastate* commerce is essentially controlled by the various states, there are occasions when Congress wields its powers in this sphere also. This occurs when the regulation of *intrastate* commerce is essential for the proper control of *interstate* commerce and when *interstate* and *intrastate* commerce and industry are inseparably intermingled.

Commerce, Department of, one of the divisions of the Executive Department of the United States, whose chief, the Secretary of Commerce, is a member of the President's Cabinet. The department was organized "to foster, promote, and develop the foreign and domestic commerce; the mining, manufacturing, shipping, and fishing industries; and the transportation facilities." It was the Department of Commerce and Labor from its organization in 1903 until 1913, when the new Department of Labor was established. In the Department of Commerce are the bureaus of Foreign and Domestic Commerce and of the Census, Coast and Geodetic Survey, Inland Waterways Corporation, National Bureau of Standards, Patent Office, Weather Bureau and Civil Aeronautics Administration and other bureaus.

Commercial law see *Business law.*

Commission, authority to act for a particular purpose, as an army officer's commission or a notary public's commission or the commission merchant who buys or sells on special orders and is paid on commission; and then by extension power that is delegated to a group or a board also called a commission.

In the Federal Government several boards with powers given by Congress are called commissions: the Interstate Commerce Commission (1887), the Civil Service Commission (1883) and the Federal Trade Commission (founded in 1914).

Some subdivisions of the Federal departments are headed by *commissioners.* In the Treasury Department there are commissioners of public debt, internal revenue, narcotics, and customs. The Department of the Interior has a commissioner of education, one of Indian affairs, one of general land office. The patent office in the Department of Commerce is under a commissioner. In the Department of Justice there is a commissioner of immigration and naturalization.

Commission government,, see *City.*

Committee, a group to whom a matter is entrusted or committed, particularly a group in a legislature with specific duties in examining, drafting and recommending bills for action by the entire legislative body. The small groups expedite the business of the whole house. This sort of legislative machinery seems to have originated in the English Parliament.

In the Congress of the United States and in the different state legislatures all bills are referred to committees, and no measure comes before the House unless it is favorably reported by the special committee that deals with that type of bill. In the House of Representatives a measure that is buried in committee (that is, not reported by the committee) can be brought to the attention of the House only on petition with signatures of 218 members (out of a membership of 435). Committees hold hearings on bills and sometimes conduct investigations on order of the House. The membership of committees is by parties, the majority party having the most members on each committee and supplying the chairman.

Often majority members of a committee meet and make plans without consulting the minority members, so that committee recommendations are likely to be partisan. Membership usually goes by seniority in the House: the older members are put on the more important committees and the chairmen are usually members of the longest service. U. S. Senators and Representatives seldom serve on more than two important committees. The choice of committee members is nominally made by the House itself; actually the members are discussed, selected, and named by the party managers or by a party caucus. The House of Representatives has 19 committees with 9 to 42 members on each. The most important of the committees in the House of Representatives is the Committee on Ways and Means, dealing with revenue bills which must originate in this House. It has 22 members and its chairman is the majority leader of the House. Other House committees are: appropriations, rules, banking and currency, commerce, rivers and harbors, military affairs, naval affairs, post offices, public lands, labor and pensions.

The U.S. Senate has 15 standing committees, each with 13 to 21 members. The Finance Committee in the Senate corresponds to the Ways and Means Committee in the House but has less power. The Senate Committee on Foreign Relations and that on Judiciary are particularly powerful because the Senate has powers that the House has not in foreign affairs and in approving judicial appointments. The Senate with its smaller membership and longer term of service for each member relies on committees less than the House of Representatives.

The *committee of the whole* is a peculiarity of parliamentary law. It is a meeting of the entire legislative body under committee rules that are less formal than those of the legislature, and it has a committee chairman in the chair instead of the regular presiding officer of the Chamber.

In the American state legislatures the system of committees is much the same as in Congress. A notable exception is the Massachusetts General Court (state legislature), in which committees must report back all bills. In the Nebraska Senate, the one-chamber legislature that first met in 1937, a much simplified system of committees was used with only 17 committees instead of the 70 in the former two-chamber legislature.

Steering committee is an unofficial but important group in a legislative body headed by the majority party's floor leader and composed of the more important members of the party. The group guides and manages the business of the House.

The English House of Commons is the source of the committee system. All money bills and all confirmations of provisional orders issued temporarily by government departments come before the House sitting as the Committee of the Whole House. When it considers appropriations the Committee of the Whole is called Committee of Supply (or House in Supply); and when it considers revenue measures it is the Committee on Ways and Means—which explains the use of that term in the U.S. House of Representatives. The House of Commons has four grand committees or standing committees, known by the letters A to D inclusive, and a fifth, the Committee on Scottish Affairs. They are not representative of party strength in the House, and they differ besides from American standing committees because they do not deal each with a specific type of legislation.

The House of Commons has about 20 *select* committees, with 15 members, each to investigate specific topics; members are usually named in the motion that proposes that particular committee.

In the organization of American political parties the committee is important. National political campaigns (for presidential elections and elections to Congress) are planned and run by a national committee for each party. State committees have members from each county or town or congressional district, and each of these members is chosen by the county committee of his party in primaries of local conventions.

Commodity Credit Corporation, The, was organized Oct. 17, 1933 under the laws of Delaware and was managed by the Reconstruction Finance Corporation. It became a part of the Department of Agriculture in 1939 and was permanently chartered July 1, 1948, under a Federal charter. It became part of the Commodity Stabilization Service of the Department of Agriculture in 1953. Its object was farm price support. To accomplish this it was authorized to engage in buying, selling, lending, storage, and related activities of specified agricultural products. Flexible price supports ranged from a minimum of 75 percent to a maximum of 90 percent of parity. In the first 23 years of buying and selling farm commodities, it showed a net loss of over 5 billion dollars. In that same time the CCC had loans of 2.3 billion dollars outstanding to support prices. Nearly one-half of this amount was on upland cotton. The loans in 1957 crops alone were estimated to be over 3 billion dollars.

Common carrier, one who undertakes to transport persons or goods for anyone who pays the recognized charge, fare or rate. The common carrier is liable for loss or damage not caused by the shipper, by enemies of the country or by an act of God. Especially over the railroads modern governments exercise a considerable control—ranging from full government ownership and operation in some countries to our own Federal supervision of freight rates and passenger fares and legislation on relations of railroads to their employees.

Common law, a term deriving its original meaning from the medieval judicial theory that the law administered by the king's courts was the customary or common law of the realm as contrasted with the custom of local jurisdiction; now used in various senses. (1) The system of law of England and the United States in contrast to other legal systems, such as the civil law or Mohammedan law. (2) That body of the law that is based upon custom and precedent and not upon legislative enactments. (3) The body of rules and remedies administered by common-law courts as distinguished from equity courts. (4) The law of the whole country as distinct from the special law of one region.

The American common law consists of the common law of England prior to 1607, or in some cases a later date, and certain English statutes enacted prior to the Revolution, in so

CENTRAL OFFICE OF INFORMATION, LONDON

HOUSE OF COMMONS in the English Parliament. Beneath the clock is the speaker's chair. To the left are the benches for the Government, with the ministers occupying the front row. The prime minister occupies the center aisle seat. To the right are the seats of the Opposition, with their leaders in the front row. The gallery directly above the speaker's seat is for reporters and women. The side galleries are for special members. All other persons are termed "strangers" and are seated according to rank.

far as this law was considered applicable to the conditions in America, modified by local custom and subsequent decisions of American courts. Since the laws of every state are different, there is no general common law in the United States today.

Common pleas, name of a court of record in some states having general original jurisdiction in civil suits.

Commons, House of, the lower house of the English Parliament, representing the mass of the people, the commons, as distinct from the two other estates or classes of the feudal period, the nobles and the clergy, whose part in English government was played through the House of Lords. When Parliament first separated about 1344 into these two houses, Lords and Commons, the Commons represented the shires or counties (knights of the shire) and the towns (burgesses of the towns). In 1407 King Henry IV agreed that thereafter all money grants should be approved by the Commons before the Lords considered them—an important first step in the growing importance of the House of Commons. In 1911 the Commons were empowered to pass money grants or public bills without the approval of the House of Lords. Long before this, in 1689, the Commons had made the Crown its servant by adopting the Bill of Rights.

The House of Commons now has 630 members. They need not be residents of the districts that they represent. Women have been eligible since 1918, and 21 women were elected between 1919 and 1929. Barred from membership are Roman Catholic priests, clergymen of the Church of England and of the Church of Scotland, peers of the realm, government contract holders, convicts, lunatics, idiots. 12 seats in the House of Commons represent universities. Oxford and Cambridge return two members each; four Scotch universities, two members in all. Each graduate of a university that has this privilege may vote for a member of the House to represent the university and also for a member to represent the community in which he lives. The communities—boroughs and counties—elect one member apiece, except that 12 large boroughs and the City of London elect two members. Women vote for representatives in the House of Commons—the law of 1918 gave the suffrage to women over 30; the law of 1928 to women over 21. There are about 34,000,000 qualified voters: 19,000,000 women and 15,000,000 men. The maximum term of office is five years, but an election for the House of Commons may be called at any time that an important measure proposed by the Cabinet is defeated in Parliament.

Commonwealth, the same word as commonweal or public good; in the specialized sense, the whole body politic, all the people of a state; also a name applied to certain forms of free government, notably to the state governments of Massachusetts, Pennsylvania, Kentucky and Virginia. Each of them is officially a commonwealth, not a state.

In 1952 Puerto Rico (formerly an organized territory) became a commonwealth freely associated with the United States.

England was a commonwealth and

not a kingdom from 1649, when Cromwell and his parliamentary army drove out the Stuart kings, to 1660 when the kingdom was restored.

The British Commonwealth of Nations was created in 1931 by the Statute of Westminster. It includes the United Kingdom of Great Britain and Northern Ireland, Canada, Australia, New Zealand, India, Pakistan, Ceylon, Ghana, and numerous other smaller countries.

Commune, a French municipal government, the smallest governmental district in the French political machine. There are about 38,000 communes in France, most of them with less than 500 inhabitants. The commune is governed by a council of 10 to 36 members (except in Paris with 90 and Lyons with 54) elected by wards in other communes that had more than 10,000 inhabitants and on a general ticket in the smaller communes. They serve six years and choose for a four-year term a mayor (*maire*) and an assistant (*adjoint*)—or in the larger communes several assistants. Paris is a commune in name, but has a government unlike other communes. It is subdivided into 9 sectors each having its own mayor. Lyons has a mayor but the Prefect of the Rhone controls the police. In French history the Commune was the government set up in Paris in 1792-94 by representatives of the communes; and this name was also given to the insurrectionary government of Paris in the spring of 1871 after the German troops had departed from the city.

Communism, a radical and revolutionary form of socialism, opposed to the property and profit principles of capitalism and to nationalism. The ideal of communism is "From each according to his ability; to each according to his need." The government of Soviet Russia set up in 1917 by the Bolshevist revolution was actually in the hands of the Communist party. The main objectives of that party, summed up in 1918 by the Congress of Soviets, were: abolishing private property, making all property national for the laboring masses to use; workers to control industry; all factories to be nationally owned; banks to be nationalized; debts of the old Russian Government to be repudiated; compulsory labor.

Communism, of which Soviet Russia is a present-day exponent, aims at world-wide revolution. After World War II, Russia not only had the task of rebuilding industries and towns, but of extending Communism to surrounding countries, to form a protective satellite ring. In China, the Communist forces have managed to drive the Nationalists from most of the country. The Chinese Communists have never taken direct orders from Russia, but they have signed treaties of support. Due to disturbed economic and social conditions after World War II, Communism gained control in many European countries.

Compensation, payment of money or an act ordered by the court to be performed by one person to another to indemnify or compensate the other for losses or damage. It often refers to payment for property seized for pub-

lic use. The 5th Amendment to the Federal Constitution provides that no private property "shall be taken for public use without just compensation" and the same clause requires "due process of law." By the 14th Amendment due process is made the rule for state laws so that compensation applies there too. Usually compensation must be market value of the property condemned or the equivalent of what the owner loses.

Compensation to workmen for accidents at work is the subject of a series of laws beginning in 1910 with a New York act declared unconstitutional in 1911.

Complaint, the formal statement filed by a plaintiff, his pleading to start suit against a defendant; also called a *petition* or *declaration.*

Composition with creditors, an agreement between a debtor and two or more of his creditors by which the creditors agree to accept a part payment in full satisfaction of the debt.

Conciliation may be a form of international procedure as evidenced in treaty obligations or it may be a means of bringing industrial disputants together to settle differences. Domestic conciliation courts exist in several cities and states.

Conflict of Laws, divergence between the laws of different states; and the branch of law that determines whether in dealing with a legal situation the law of some other state will be recognized, be given effect or be applied. A typical case involving a conflict of laws occurs if Mr. Jones and Mr. Smith have an automobile accident in New Jersey. Then Mr. Smith sues Mr. Jones in a New York court. The New York court must then determine whether it will apply the New York law or the New Jersey law in deciding the case. In this particular instance the New York court would apply the New Jersey law. A body of law governing various situations and determining when the law of another state should be applied has recently developed.

Conscription or **Draft,** compulsory enrolment for military service—ordinarily of men, but also of national resources, production and manufacture. Conscription means listing or cataloguing the resources of men, machinery and money—not forcing them into service. In World War II more than 24,000,000 men were enrolled in the United States, but not quite 3,000,000 were actually drawn (or drafted) from this list for service.

Conscription and the draft were first employed on a large scale in France during the wars of the Revolution and the Napoleonic campaigns because the Revolution in overthrowing the monarchy had destroyed the regular, professional army of France. From 1800 to 1813 more than two and a half million men were drafted into Napoleon's armies.

In American history, some of the colonies decreed the draft in the Revolutionary War; both North and South used it in Civil War, and in New York city the draft riots of July 13-16, 1863, resulted in the death of a thousand persons; in both World Wars a Selective Service Act con-

scripted the manpower of the nation. The Selective Service Act, the second peacetime draft in American history, was enacted in 1948. It was extended during the Korean Conflict and several times since then. In 1951 it became known as the Universal Military Training Service Act. Its administration is under the Selective Service System.

Conservation, government activity in maintaining and preserving natural resources—forests, water, soil, minerals, wild life. It was the policy of the United States Government in its early years to hasten settlement and private ownership by giving away public lands. Right after the Civil War this process was very rapid. The consequences were serious: uneconomic cutting of timber, overcultivation of crop lands and the misuse of grazing lands for raising crops. Floods and droughts were traced directly to these wasteful practices.

In 1876 a government forester was first appointed, and in 1921 certain public lands were set aside as forest reserves. The Newlands Reclamation Act of 1902 appropriated for building irrigation plants the income from the sale of arid lands in the West. In 1905 President Theodore Roosevelt persuaded Congress to give the control of public forests to the Forest Service, which was transferred from the Interior to the Department of Agriculture. In 1908 an Inland Waterways Corporation and in 1901 a National Conservation Commission made elaborate reports. There was bitter opposition to every attempt at Federal conservation, but in 1911 Congress authorized the purchase of forest land on watersheds of navigable streams in the eastern states so that the program was no longer limited to the public lands of the western states.

In the early 1930's severe floods and terrible dust storms and droughts coincided with a crisis of unemployment. A new conservation policy was created to meet the occasion, aided by the Civilian Conservation Corps or CCC.

Conspiracy, the agreement of two or more persons to accomplish something that is unlawful, or an agreement to perform a lawful act in an unlawful manner. A conspiracy to commit a crime is a different offense from the crime that is the object of the conspiracy. In order to complete the crime of conspiracy it is not necessary that any act should be done in pursuance of the agreement; the mere agreement constitutes the crime.

Constitution, the entire system of fundamental political institutions of a state. In the United States where a relatively large part of the fundamental institutions is embodied in written documents, the term is often confined to those documents—the Federal Constitution, drafted in 1787, ratified in 1788 and variously amended since; and the constitutions of each of the states. But these written constitutions are not complete descriptions of American government today. They do not tell all that we need to know about how the government is constituted. We can accurately say that a written constitution is the constitution of a government only in a partial sense. There is noth-

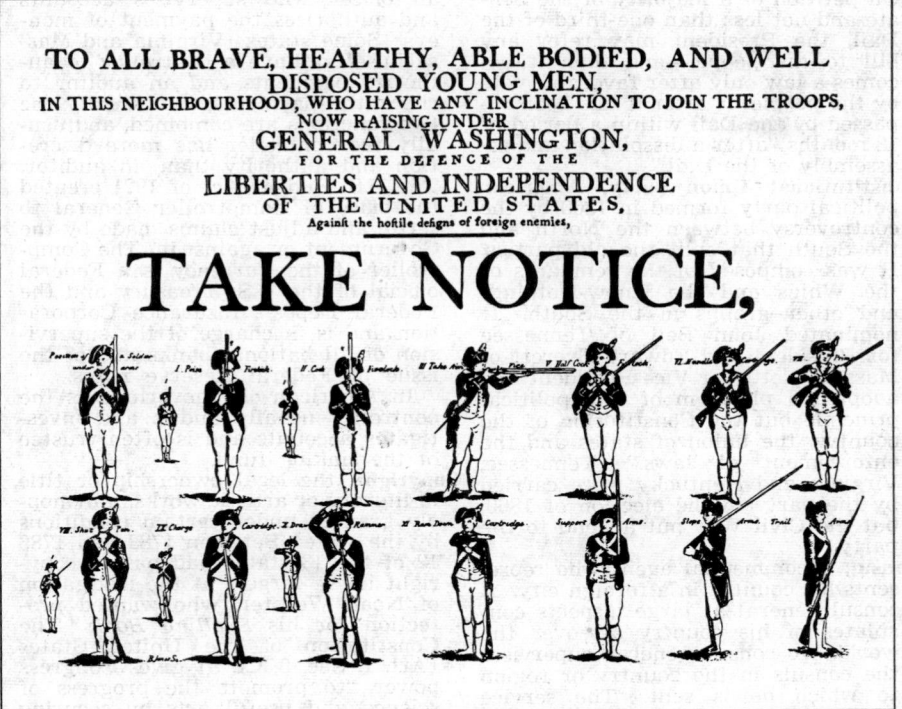

TO ALL BRAVE, HEALTHY, ABLE BODIED, AND WELL
DISPOSED YOUNG MEN,
IN THIS NEIGHBOURHOOD, WHO HAVE ANY INCLINATION TO JOIN THE TROOPS,
NOW RAISING UNDER
GENERAL WASHINGTON,
FOR THE DEFENCE OF THE
LIBERTIES AND INDEPENDENCE
OF THE UNITED STATES,
Against the hostile designs of foreign enemies,

TAKE NOTICE,

PLEA FOR SOLDIERS was posted in this form for enlistment during the Revolutionary War.

ing in our Constitution (or even in the laws that supplement it) about a Cabinet, parties, nominating conventions, congressional committees or many other important factors in our actual government.

In the United States not only the Federal Government has a written constitution, but each state likewise has such a constitution. Each of these constitutions establishes the method of government and also contains grants and limitations of power to the several departments of the state. The Federal Constitution gives certain powers to the national Government and denies certain powers to the individual states. Except in so far as powers are granted expressly or by necessary implication to the national Government, they are retained by the states. Both in Federal and state constitutions the individual is protected by certain fundamental rights. Laws passed in violation of a constitution are void, and whenever they are questioned they will be so declared by courts having jurisdiction.

In the United States and in each of the states the judicial interpretation of the written constitution so largely controls the government (Federal and state) that the term *constitutional law* is confined to court law in decisions interpreting, limiting and applying the constitution. There is nothing quite like this in the government of any other country.

The Supreme Court of the United States cannot decide on the constitutionality of any measure except in a suit brought before the court. Some state courts of last resort are occasionally asked for an advisory opinion on the constitutionality of a proposed law, but a ruling of this sort is hypothetical and not a binding, final interpretation or decision.

This power of the Supreme Court rests on two clauses in the Constitution: Art. III, Sec. 2, Cl. 2, giving the Supreme Court "appellate jurisdiction both as to law and fact, with such exceptions and under such regulations as the Congress shall make"; and Art. VI, Sec. 2, making "this Constitution and the laws of the United States the supreme law of the land . . . anything in the Constitution or laws of any State to the contrary notwithstanding."

The Federal supremacy laid down in the phrase last quoted is somewhat offset by the 10th Amendment: "The powers not delegated to the United States by the Constitution, nor prohibited by it to the States are reserved to the States respectively, or to the people." Repeatedly the supreme Court has ruled acts of Congress unconstitutional on the ground that they interfered with State rights.

The interstate commerce clause, Art. I, Sec. 8, Cl. 3, giving Congress power "to regulate commerce among the several states" has often been in controversy before the Supreme Court. Does commerce include manufacturing? Can the states legislate on "commerce among the several states"? Have the states power to tax commerce of that sort? In 1937 the Supreme Court upheld the right of the state of Louisiana to tax chain stores doing business in the state on the basis of the total number of units of the chain in the whole country.

The 5th Amendment declares that "no person shall be deprived of life, liberty or property, without due process of law." Repeatedly the Supreme

Court has had to decide in various cases what is due process of law and the Court has often declared laws unconstitutional on the ground that they are arbitrary and unreasonable.

The most broad and far-reaching powers of Congress have been claimed under the "elastic clause," as it has been called—Art. I, Sec. 8, Cl. 18, empowering Congress "to make all laws which shall be necessary and proper for carrying into execution" the powers of the Federal Government. "Necessary" and "proper" both admit of wide variation in interpretation. So does the phrase in Art. I, Sec. 8, Cl. 1, giving Congress power to provide for "the general welfare of the United States."

The British constitution is almost entirely unwritten, a matter of custom and gradual development. The documents that form a part of it are very few and date from many different periods. Under Cromwell as Lord Protector from December 1653 to May 1657 England had a written constitution in one single document, the Instrument of Government. Today there is nothing of the sort, and the scheme of government is based on historic documents like Magna Charta and the Bill of Rights; certain laws, like the Habeas Corpus Act of 1679, the Act of Settlement of 1701, the Parliamentary Act of 1911 and the Representation of the People Act of 1918; the principles of common law, mostly not in written form; and many conventions or customs, such as the peculiar relation of Cabinet and Ministry and Cabinet and Commons.

The constitution of the Fourth Republic of France is noteworthy in these respects:

The legislative assembly of the French Republic has two chambers, the National Assembly and the Council of the Republic, but the latter body is definitely subordinate, being limited to advisory and delaying powers.

The constitutionality of laws is determined before their promulgation by a special committee created exclusively for that purpose.

If two cabinet crises occur within an 18-month period, the Council of Ministers may decide to dissolve the National Assembly, after consulting the President of the Assembly.

The constitution created the French Union, a governmental structure composed on the one hand of Metropolitan France, her overseas departments and territories, and on the other hand of associated territories and states. The President of the French Republic is also the President of the French Union. Descendents of the ruling families of France are barred from the presidency.

In Germany and Italy Hitler's and Mussolini's dictatorships did away with any constitution in either sense of the word. The government was what the Duce or the Fuehrer declared it to be.

The Constitution of the U.S.S.R., adopted on December 5, 1936, provided for a federated state. Today the U.S.S.R. is composed of 15 soviet socialist republics (or union republics), each with its own constitution. The legislative power is the Supreme Soviet, elected for 4 years and composed of two chambers: the Soviet of the Union, one deputy for every 300,000 of population; and the Soviet of Nationalities, 25 deputies from each union republic, 11 from each autonomous republic, 5 from each autonomous region and 1 from each national area. (The union republics are made up of autonomous republics and regions and national areas.) The Supreme Soviet in joint session chooses a Presidium of 32 members. The Presidium is an executive committee of the Supreme Soviet and exercises authority between sessions of the Soviet. The Council of Ministers has the highest administrative authority in the U.S.S.R. Members are appointed by the Supreme Soviet and it is headed by a Chairman (Premier). It is empowered to issue decrees and executive directives to supplement existing legislation. Each republic of the U.S.S.R. has its own Supreme Soviet and Council of Ministers.

All men and women over 18 have the right to vote, and to elect members of each Soviet. The Communist Party is the only political party which is permitted to exist. Amendment to the Constitution is effected by two-thirds vote of each Chamber, sitting in session.

The 1937 Constitution of Ireland (Eire), formerly called the Irish Free State, established that country as a free, sovereign and independent state. The President must be 35 years of age, is elected for 7 years by direct vote of the people, is eligible for re-election once only and may be removed by the legislature on a two-thirds vote after certain formal investigation. The President appoints the prime minister (*Taoiseach*) and 6 to 14 other members of the government on the nomination of the legislature. The national parliament, called *Oireachtas*, consists of two houses, *Dail* and *Seanad* (or Senate), which meet at least once a year. Members of the Dail are chosen by universal suffrage from representative districts that may be revised every 12 years by the Oireachtas. Members of the Dail are chosen by Proportional Representation. The same Dail cannot continue for more than 7 years.

The Irish Senate has 60 members: 11 nominated by the Taoiseach; 3 elected by the National University of Ireland and 3 by the University of Dublin; and 43 to be elected from candidates listed on five panels for their knowledge and practical experience of: (1) language, literature, art, culture; (2) agriculture and fisheries; (3) labor; (4) industry, commerce, engineering, architecture; and (5) public administration and social service. These panels are to be formed "in the manner provided by law," and "provision may be made by law for the direct election by any functional or vocational group or association or council" of a certain number of senators on these panels.

The Irish President may refer any bill to the Supreme Court for a ruling on its constitutionality or the constitutionality of any part of the bill, but the President has no veto power.

On petition of a majority of the Senate and not less than one-third of the Dail, the President may refer any bill to the people—and then it becomes a law only after favorable vote by the people or after it has been repassed by the Dail within a period of 18 months "after a dissolution and reassembly of the Dail."

Constitutional Union party, American political party formed in 1860 by the controversy between the North and the South that split the old parties. It was composed of the remnants of the Whigs and the Know-Nothings and other groups in the South. It nominated John Bell of Tennessee for President and Edward Everett of Massachusetts for Vice-President and adopted a platform of "No political principle but the Constitution of the country, the union of states and the enforcement of laws." Tennessee, Virginia and Kentucky were carried by the party in the election of 1860, but the Civil War put an end to the party.

Consul, a commercial agent who represents his country in a foreign city. A consul general at large inspects consulates of his country all over the world. A consul general supervises the consuls in the country or region to which he is sent. The service studies foreign markets and seeks outlets for trade from the homeland; consuls also protect the interests of fellow citizens abroad. Vice-consuls and consular agents are subordinate to the consul in certain areas. Consular officers of the United States are appointed by the President with the approval of the Senate, but the consular service has been on a civil-service basis since 1906. By the Rogers Act of 1924, the consular service and the diplomatic service were consolidated into the Foreign Service under the Department of State.

Contempt, a disrespect shown to a court, wilful disobedience of its mandates or an attempt to tamper with the course of justice. Contempt may be punished by the court without any jury trial. In the United States legislative bodies also have the right to punish for contempt, especially failure to appear or answer at a session of an investigating committee of the legislature.

Contraband, originally forbidden or contrary to a ban or edict and in common use illegal in the sense of smuggled goods. Specifically in international law contraband (or contraband of war) means goods that cannot be shipped by neutrals to one belligerent without risk of seizure by the other belligerent. *Absolute* contraband includes guns, ammunition and explosives. *Conditional* contraband is material of doubtful or double use that might be intended for peaceful purposes—cotton, gasoline, horses, for example. During World War I cotton and rubber were considered absolute contraband. The seizure of neutral ships engaging in contraband trade always tends to embroil neutral nations.

Controller or **Comptroller** (the second form is the older spelling and is the more common in government use),

an officer who supervises accounts and authorizes the payment of moneys. Some states (Virginia and Massachusetts) have a controller to authorize payments and an auditor to check the payments, but usually the two functions are combined, and usually the controller has more discretion and authority than an auditor. The U.S. Budget Act of 1921 created the office of Comptroller General to settle and adjust claims made by the Government or against it. The Comptroller of the Currency is a Federal official of the U.S. Treasury and the Federal Deposit Insurance Corporation and is in charge of the supervision of all national banks and of the issue of Federal Reserve notes.

In American city governments the controller usually audits and investigates accounts and is often trustee of the sinking fund.

Copyright, the legal ownership or title in literary or artistic works, a monopoly granted under certain conditions by the state. Between 1783 and 1786 12 of the 13 states had passed copyright laws—largely at the instigation of Noah Webster, who wanted protection for his *Spelling Book.* The Constitution of the United States (Art. I, Sec. 9, Cl. 8) gives Congress power "to promote the progress of science and useful arts by securing for limited times to authors and inventors the exclusive rights to their respective writings and discoveries." The law passed by Congress in 1790 made duration of copyright 14 years from the date of publication and permitted renewal for 14 years. The present law permits 28 years of protection with renewal for another 28 years.

In Great Britain copyright is for the lifetime of the author and for 50 years after his death—an attempt to secure to the author's heirs the same monopoly. There have been various attempts to secure an agreement among all nations that will assure an unbreakable contract, so that with such need for an international copyright, the Universal Copyright Convention was established. The United States became a member in 1955, although not all the individual states acceded immediately to its terms. The international symbol of copyright is the letter "C" within a circle, accompanied by the name of the copyright owner and the date of publication. On a work of first publication this symbol assures protection in the countries which are participating in the Convention.

Coroner, a public official charged with inquests or investigating the causes of suspicious deaths. The coroner was an English Crown officer and in some English dialects he is called *crowner.* In the United States a medical examiner sometimes replaces the coroner, but he is still a county officer in many states, usually elected by popular vote but in a few instances appointed by the executive.

Corporative state, Mussolini's name for the government he developed for Italy: not the people but industry's employers and workers were represented. The people were regarded as producers rather than as citizens, and under this doctrine individuals have never, whether in Russia, Germany, or Italy, benefited. The Chamber of Deputies came to an end in 1936 and the National Council of Corporations, set up in 1934, took its place. Industry was divided into 22 category corporations, each with its own council representing the employers and the workers of that category of industry. The 22 councils had 824 members. In 1926 and 1927 all employers and workmen were organized—locally in syndicates and nationally into confederations that were later called corporations.

The real power in the corporative state was not these corporations nor their representatives who formed the legislature but the Ministry of Corporations, created in 1923 with Mussolini at its head. He was the president of each of the 22 councils and of the Council of Corporations.

Nationalization of some industries seems a part of the policy of the corporative state.

Council (from Latin *concilium*, something called together), an assembly or convocation, usually one that has advisory or lawmaking powers.

In the United States the word is seldom used for any governmental agency except the city council, a legislative body or one of two legislative bodies (the other being a larger group, the board of aldermen). In Maine the governor has an Executive Council to advise him; seven members elected by the legislature form its membership.

In some city governments the *common council* is the legislative department or the lower house of the city legislature and is usually composed of one or two representatives from each of several small political divisions called wards.

Abroad the term has a much wider and very varied use.

In England the Privy Council is of great historical importance. It originated with the Norman kings as a small group of advisers to the king, the King's Privy Council; a larger group at court was called the Great Council, and it developed into Parliament. The number of privy councilors has always included more commoners and new peers than members of the old nobility. The Cabinet members, present and past, belong to this Council. The Cabinet originated as a Privy Council group of committee and now has many of the powers that once made the Privy Council great. *Orders in council* are the only lawmaking power left to the Privy Council; they include summoning and dissolving Parliament, granting charters of incorporation and providing detailed applications for new Acts of Parliament to go into effect. *Committees of the Council* have important duties, especially the judicial committee (created in 1833), which advises the Crown on appeals to the King's Council from church courts, admiralty courts and the courts of the colonies—and so is actually a court of last appeal in these cases.

The Privy Council meets in full strength only on the death of the king and other ceremonial occasions.

The Council of State in France is made up of 64 members (39 in ordinary service, appointed by the President of the Republic, and 25 in ex-traordinary service). It gives technical advice to the Government on problems of administration, and it must pass on rules of administration before they become operative.

The Council of Ministers in the French Government is the official title of the Cabinet, which includes the heads of all 18 departments. The *President of the Council of Ministers* is the actual title of the French Premier, but the President of the Republic is in the chair when the council of ministers meets (usually twice a week) to transact business, especially foreign affairs and national defense. The same group meets at least once a week as a cabinet with the premier in the chair to plan policies.

BENITO MUSSOLINI, Fascist leader of Italy.

In France and Belgium a *conseil des prud' hommes*, council of experts (or discreet men), acts as an arbitration board in industrial disputes. Its decisions are final in cases under 300 francs; over that amount an appeal may be taken to the regular courts. The council is made up of employers and workmen in equal numbers.

In the Union of Soviet Socialist Republics the highest executive power of the state is held by the *Council of Ministers*. There is such a council in each union republic and one for the Union of Soviet Socialist Republics (U.S.S.R.). These councils are responsible to the supreme soviet of the Union Republic and the U.S.S.R., respectively.

In the early days of the church, Councils were important. One of the first of consequence was the Council of Nicaea, 325 A.D., at which Arianism, denial of the divinity of Christ, was denounced. The opposing doctrine of Athanasius was adopted and proclaimed as the Nicene Creed.

The Council of Trent, 1545, was summoned by the Pope to consider the question of reforming the Catholic church and to settle disputed questions of religious belief. No Protestants attended the meeting. The Council accepted the Pope as the head of the church, the Vulgate Bible was proclaimed the standard, deviation from the Church view in teaching was prohibited and certain beliefs of Martin Luther were declared accursed. The Council also authorized the first "Index of Prohibited Books."

The Vatican Council, 1869–70, a general Council of the Catholic church, the first since the Council of Trent, reaffirmed and deepened the traditional faith of the Church on the relationship of faith and reason and defined the dogma of *papal infallibility.*

The Council of Ministers of Fascist Italy, 1928–43, the *Council of National Defense in the United States,* 1916, and the *Council of Foreign Ministers,* 1945, also are examples.

County, an administration division of a state in each of the United States (except Louisiana where the corresponding term is *parish*). There are about 3,000 counties in the U. S., 3 in Delaware, 254 in Texas. One county in California, San Bernardino, has an area of more than 20,000 square miles —much larger than Belgium or Denmark or the Netherlands or Switzerland. Most counties are governed by a board, but a few have adopted the manager plan used in some cities. The typical county officer is the sheriff (originally shire-reeve, meaning county overseer), the local police officer, elected by popular vote except in Rhode Island, where the state legislature names the sheriffs. There are county courts in about a third of the counties of the United States. Almost all the counties have a prosecuting officer, the county attorney or district attorney, usually elected by popular vote. Counties have little legislative power but wide administrative functions, usually including the administration of justice, public-health regulations, poor relief, schools and tax collection.

In England the county is an old unit of government. The Anglo-Saxon name for it was *shire,* meaning district, a syllable that remains in the names of several English and Scottish counties— Lancashire, Lanarkshire, Devonshire. After the Norman conquest, shires were called *counties* because they were similar to the domains of counts on the continent.

The English Local Government Act of 1888 set up 62 administrative counties, dividing for governmental purposes the larger of the 52 historical counties or shires, incorporating each of the new counties and giving it an administrative council that is not a lawmaking body but sets tax rates and supervises schools, poor relief and highways. The council has two types of members: councilors, elected for 3 years, and aldermen who serve for 6 years, half of them going out of office every 3 years. The aldermen are chosen by the councilors; when they pick them from their own number, other councilors must be chosen at a special election.

County boroughs in England are the 80-odd cities, each over 75,000 in population, that have asked and received separate incorporation so that they are governed independently of the county in which they lie.

Coup d'état (French stroke or blow of state), violent seizure of power, Famous examples are: Napoleon Bonaparte's overthrow of the French Directory, November 9, 1799; Louis Napoleon's establishment of the Second French Empire in December 1851; and Mussolini's march on Rome, October 30, 1922.

Council of Europe, established in 1949, has 12 member states from western Europe. It consists of the Committee of Foreign Ministers and a consultative assembly. Its powers are advisory and it aims at political integration of democratic European forces.

Criminal law, a branch of public law that deals with crimes and offenses. It defines the various classes of actions that are contrary to the public peace and to the safety of individual or group members of society and declares the penalties that shall be visited upon offenders.

Crown, the authority and power of the English king and of his ministers. In this sense, the importance of the English Crown in government has been increasing in the last century though the personal power of the king has decreased. Certain powers of American governmental officers, especially the President and the governors of the states, are derived from the powers of the English Crown.

Legally the king is still the source of authority. Whatever is done in his name is done by the Crown if not actually by the king. All the extension of governmental functions in the last generation or so has meant more administrative activity for the Crown. The Crown is the executive—the king and his ministers have the same power in that respect that our president and state governors have. Pardon and reprieve are executive powers.

The Crown is increasingly important in the British Empire as well as in the United Kingdom. By the Statute of Westminster (1931) the United Kingdom and the Dominions formed the British Commonwealth of Nations, an association of free members, united only by their common allegiance to the Crown. Since 1926 the governor general of a British dominion has been the representative of the sovereign and legally the appointee of the king and not of the Government, that is, the Ministry or Cabinet.

Foreign relations, which in the United States are in the hands of the President and the Senate, are Crown powers in England. Treaties may be referred to Parliament, but that is not necessary.

The king-in-council, that is, the king and his Privy Council, make certain laws and have authority that is unlike anything in our American system. Other powers of the Crown that have no American parallels are: conferring honors and titles of nobility—usually done in fact by the king's ministers but always in the king's name; and acting as the head of the established churches of England and Scotland.

Damages, money compensation or indemnity for injury or loss. Originally the word meant (as it still does in the singular) the actual loss or harm suffered. Both penalties and damages in our legal system today are refinements of the early retaliation or *lex talionis,* as the Romans called it, which demanded an eye for an eye, a life for a life.

Damnum absque injuria is damage suffered without any violation of a legal right, and in such a case there is no cause of action by the person who suffers the damage against the person who caused it. Thus no damages may be recovered unless there has been a violation of a legal right.

Declaration, in common law pleading, the plaintiff's formal statement of his cause for complaint and demand for relief. In code practice this is called a *complaint;* in equity, a *bill;* in civil law, a *libel;* and in church law, the *allegations.* The declaration must contain the *count* or *counts,* that is, the cause of action; and the word *count* is sometimes used instead of declaration.

Declaration means also a statement made by a party to a transaction. Under certain conditions a declaration is regarded as original evidence and is admissible as such. It is similar to an admission.

Dying declaration is an unsworn statement by a person expecting to die, telling the cause of his death. It is admissible evidence in prosecution for murder or homicide.

Declaration of intention is the statement of an alien before a court that he intends to become a citizen and to renounce his allegiance to any foreign sovereign. It must be made 3 years before the alien is admitted as a citizen, but there are many exceptions to this rule. Some states require declaration of intention before an alien may secure title to real estate.

Declaratory judgment, a declaration by a court of the rights, status or other legal relations of a person; differing from other judgments because it does not order anything to be done. Such a declaration has the force and effect of a final judgment or decree.

Decree, the judgment or decision of a court of admiralty or equity; similar to a judgment of a court of common law. *Decree nisi* in English law is the conditional judgment that, after a certain time (usually not less than 6 months), a divorce will become absolute on motion, unless (*nisi* is Latin for unless) cause to the contrary is shown.

Deed, literally something done; any written instrument, signed, sealed and delivered; specifically an instrument for the transfer of title to real estate.

Defendant, the party sued in a court of law whether in a civil or criminal action. The other party to the suit is the plaintiff.

Defense, Department of, an executive branch of the U. S. Government created by the National Security act of July 26, 1947, amended August 1947. The Department of Defense is headed by a Secretary of Defense with cabinet status, and is the executive department of the National Military Establishment. The departments of War and Navy, together with the Department of the Air Force, (giving the Air Force an independent departmental status) are the military elements of the Department of Defense. Each division is administered by a secretary without cabinet status. The military head of the Department of Defense is the chairman of the Joint Chiefs of Staff. This arrangement grew out of the plan for a military unification of the armed services.

Del credere agency or **Del credere commission** (Italian, meaning of belief or of trust), a special agreement between an agent and his principal by which the agent undertakes to pay his principal for goods he sells if the purchaser does not pay; and the principal agrees to pay the agent additional compensation. The agent's undertaking is not required to be in writing since it is not a legal guarantee.

Delegate, a deputy; one with powers granted (or delegated) by another or by the people. The representative of a Territory in the Lower House of Congress is called a *delegate;* he looks out for the interests of his constituency but has no vote. In Maryland, Virginia and West Virginia, the Lower House is called the *House of Delegates.*

Delegated powers, any authority that comes by grant from another. The 10th Amendment (in the Bill of Rights) to the U. S. Constitution says: "The powers not delegated to the United States by the Constitution, nor prohibited by it to the States, are reserved to the States respectively or to the people." Orders in council and regulations made by government departments are the usual types of delegated legislation in England.

In France the Council of Ministers has power to set the details for the administration of certain laws. In Italy, when it was a Dictatorship, practically all legislative power was passed to Mussolini's Council of Ministers and Council of Corporations. In Soviet Russia the Presidium of the Supreme Soviet has constitutional power to "interpret existing laws and promulgate orders," and the Council of Ministers "issues decisions and orders on the basis and in the pursuance of the laws in operation and supervises their execution." This is not a delegation of legislative powers because they are conferred by the Constitution to the Council.

Delivery, in the legal phrase "signed, sealed and delivered," the transfer of the document or deed to the grantee or to a third party; the transfer of possession of a thing from one person to another. No particular form of procedure is necessary in a delivery. It may be done by an act or merely by words.

Democratic party, a political party in the United States. The antagonism between business and agriculture that had been shown in Colonial times and that had found expression in the Constitutional Convention came to a head in the heated debates that marked the passage of the first Revenue Act (1789), and the country gradually became divided into two major political parties. Thomas Jefferson headed the group that has now become the Democratic party. At first it was called the *Republican* party, then the *Democratic-Republican* party and in 1829 the *Democratic* party. Thomas Jefferson and his followers were sympathetic toward the French Revolution, opposed the concentration of power in the Federal Government and stood for personal liberty. It was the party of the farmers, the industrial workers, the poor and the radicals. The opposition group was the Federalist party led by Alexander Hamilton.

In 1800 the Democratic-Republican party was successful in electing Thomas Jefferson as President and he was again elected for the following term. As the power of the Federalist party declined, that of the Demo-

"A LIVE JACKASS KICKING A DEAD LION"

LIBRARY OF CONGRESS

DEMOCRATIC DONKEY, symbol of the Democratic Party, first appeared in *Harper's Weekly* in 1870. This political cartoon, by Thomas Nast, spoofed Edwin McMasters Stanton, secretary of war under Lincoln. A Unionist, Stanton had many enemies among the northern Democrats, or Copperheads. Stanton was named to the Supreme Court bench four days before his death in 1869.

cratic party grew. James Madison was elected for two terms and James Monroe followed for a similar period, being elected by an overwhelming majority. The split that had developed within the party led to the election of John Quincy Adams over Andrew Jackson in the bitter controversy of 1824. In 1829 Andrew Jackson became President and the radical Democrats came into power. After Jackson's second term another Democrat, Martin Van Buren, was elected. The Whigs were successful in 1841, electing Harrison and Tyler, but the Democrat Polk followed, and the Democrats were successful in every presidential election up to the Civil War time, except for the Whig victory under Taylor in 1848. By 1860 the Democratic party had divided into the northern and southern Democrats and did not return to power until the election of President Cleveland in 1892.

After the withdrawal of the Republican reconstruction policy in the South, that section became strongly Democratic and the "Solid South" has remained Democratic with the exception of the election of 1928. The radical program of the Populists was largely adopted by the Democrats who nominated Bryan and fought for the free-silver policy in 1896, but the Democrats were defeated. A split in the Republican party led to the election of Woodrow Wilson in 1912, but after World War I the Republicans again came to power. For a decade

the Democratic party showed little strength; then, largely due to the economic depression that began in 1929, the Democrats returned to power in 1932 under the leadership of Franklin D. Roosevelt with an overwhelming majority.

Demurrer, a written plea in behalf of a defendant, addressed to a court in a case at law admitting that the facts as disclosed are true but denying that they are sufficient to support the issue raised. If the demurrer is fully sustained by the court, the case is dismissed, but sometimes the complainant is permitted to amend the complaint to cover the points protested in the demurrer. The demurrer has been abolished in English higher courts, in equity cases in U. S. Federal courts (1913) and in the practice of New York and New Jersey. It is in general use in most state courts.

Department, a division of the executive branch of the Government of the United States. The Constitution (Art. II, Sec. 2, Cl. 1) says that the President "may require the opinion in writing of the principal officer in each of the executive departments," but these departments are not named or described in the Constitution. They have been created by statute, and by custom their chief officers are members of the President's Cabinet.

In the state governments there are many independent administrative agencies, each headed by an appointee of the Governor. Departments in New York State, for example, are Adjutant General, Advertising, Aeronautics, Agriculture, Banking, Budget, Conservation, Corrections, Education, Employment, Equalization of Assessments, Fish and Game, Forestry, Health, Highways and Public Works, Insurance, Labor, Libraries (Archives, History, Law, and State), Liquor Control, Mental Health, Mines, Motor Vehicles, Old Age Assistance, Park, Personnel, Police, Printing, Public Assistance, Public Utilities and Railroads, Purchasing, Taxation and Finance, Unemployment Insurance, Welfare, and Workmen Compensation.

The Constitution of the French Union provides for 98 departments. Originally 83 departments were set up in 1789–90 and since then 7 have been added to Metropolitan France. The remaining departments include 4 Algerian Departments and 4 Overseas Departments. Each department has at its head a prefect, nominated by the Minister of the Interior and appointed by the decree of the President of the Republic. Departments are divided into districts called *arrondissements*, and these again are sub-divided into *cantons*.

Dependency, a term loosely used for a province, territory or possession that is distinct and usually remote from the nation on which it depends. Dependencies of the United States are: the Panama Canal Zone, Virgin Islands, American Samoa, Guam, Wake and Midway Islands, and the Mariana, Caroline, and Marshall Islands.

The dependencies of Great Britain and other European Powers are more accurately called colonies, protectorates and trusteeships.

Deportation, the forcible removal from a country of one considered by its government an undesirable alien.

Deposition, the written testimony of a witness, in the form of questions and answers, given under oath (or affirmation), to be used in the trial of an issue at which the witness cannot be present. It cannot be used in criminal trials without the consent of the defendant.

Deputy, one to whom power is delegated or deputed, one appointed as a substitute. Any official assistant who has any of the powers of his chief is a deputy—*general deputy,* if he has all his principal's powers; *special deputy,* if he is authorized to act only for a particular purpose. There are deputy sheriffs, deputy collectors, deputy judges.

Chamber of Deputies is the name given to the lower house in the legislatures of most Latin countries—France, Mexico, the South American republics. The deputy has powers delegated by the people. The French deputies number more than 600. They are elected for 4 years by a majority vote on the first ballot or by a mere plurality at a second election if there is no majority on the first. Deputies must be 25 years old.

Devolution, a term used in England for the suggested plan to relieve Parliament of some of its responsibilities by transferring (devolving) them to other governmental agencies. These would be: (*a*) functional, new organizations set up to take over specific tasks, like health, education or social control; (*b*) regional and territorial, giving home-rule parliaments to Scotland and Wales and allowing more self-government to counties and boroughs.

Dictator, in ancient Rome an executive appointed for a special crisis, usually to repress disorder in the city. He had more power than the two chief magistrates (consuls) and did not share authority as the consuls did. He was nominated by one of the consuls, approved by the Senate and actually appointed by a law of the Comitia. Julius Caesar's selection as dictator in 48 B.C. for an indefinite period and his choice as dictator for 10 years in 46 B.C. were contrary to the original purpose of the dictatorship and were one reason for his assassination in 44 B.C. Originally a dictator laid down his office as soon as he had completed the task for which he had been named dictator. After Caesar's death Mark Antony in 44 B.C. passed a law abolishing the dictatorship.

In modern times a dictator is one who seizes power by force or by extending the authority he legally and regularly holds. In an even broader sense a dictator is one who exercises sole and autocratic power no matter how he came to power. Admiral Nicolas Horthy, Regent of Hungary, was often called a dictator, though he was formally elected governor of Hungary and then regent of the kingdom in 1920 after his army had taken the government from the Communists. In Russia, in Italy, and in Germany the control of the government by a single party (after the overthrow of a representative government in which two or more political parties had a voice) had given the party leader dictatorial powers in each country. It should be noted that Italy had a king who was practically a figurehead; and that Soviet Russia has a figurehead president under a formal constitution that does not recognize the supremacy of the Secretary of the Communist Political Party.

Dictators in Europe were largely an outgrowth of the confusion that followed the 1st World War and the growth of Communism in Russia, Nazism in Germany and Fascism in Italy. Portugal is another one-party government. The republic of Turkey was ruled by a constitutional dictator, Mustapha Kemal Ataturk, elected president in 1923. In Greece General Metaxas, head of the army, exercised almost dictatorial powers after the restoration of the monarchy.

In South America and Central America dictatorial governments set up by sudden revolutions have been common since the time that the republics there became independent of Spain. From 1908 to 1935 Juan Vicente Gomez ruled Venezuela. Franco has controlled Spain as Chief of State since 1939. In Cuba Batista interrupted a presidential election with a coup d'etat in 1952, and subdued a coup in 1957.

Diet, a legislative assembly, so called from its meeting on a set day—*dieta* in Latin meaning a day's journey, from *dies,* day. In German the corresponding word is *Tag*—as in Reichstag, the national or the imperial assembly; Landtag, the provincial assembly. In Denmark and Sweden the two-chamber legislature is called *Riksdag,* from the noun *dag,* day.

Under the Holy Roman Empire the meeting of the imperial councilors was called the Diet. Historically important are: the Diet of Worms in 1521 that declared Luther a heretic; the Diet of Spires (Speyer) in 1529 that banned Luther's teaching; and the Diet of Augsburg in 1530 that failed to settle the religious dispute over Lutheranism.

Diplomatic service, the organization of a government that handles foreign affairs and international relations; especially the personnel of that organization resident abroad.

The diplomat or diplomatist got his name from the diploma, an official document in duplicate (*diplo-* in Greek equals *dupli-* in Latin and *double* in English), which was the authority from his home government for him to act as its representative.

The importance of diplomacy in history may be suggested by what Benjamin Franklin did in France for the American colonies in winning support in the Revolutionary War; what Jefferson and his representatives did to purchase Louisiana and carry American territory to the Mississippi; or the part that Woodrow Wilson played in the First World War, the Treaty of Versailles and the League of Nations.

The diplomats of any Power are personal representatives of the executive of that Power—president or king

THE WHITE HOUSE

PRESIDENT JOHN F. KENNEDY in one of the rooms in the executive (west) wing of the White House. He is seated in his famous rocking chair. With him are French ambassador Hervé Alphand (*left*) and French foreign minister Maurice Couve de Murville (*right*).

—to the executive of the Power to which they are accredited. Under the United States Constitution (Art. II, Sec. 2, Cl. 2), the President, "by and with the advice of the Senate, shall appoint ambassadors, other public ministers and consuls" and (Section 3) "shall receive ambassadors and other public ministers."

In practice the diplomatic representatives of the United States are appointed from two major classes: members of the political party of the President-elect who have been of special assistance in the political campaign just ended—wealthy businessmen, journalists and politicians; and the trained diplomatic staff of the State Department. The political appointees in the first class seldom remain in their posts for more than a single presidential term, for they are almost certain to be replaced by the friends and followers of the next newly elected President. The career men stay in the service, being promoted to more important posts on merit and their record, independent of politics. In 1924 the Rogers Act combined the consular and diplomatic services into a well-organized Foreign Service.

In Great Britain a trained diplomatic service was begun in 1816 when one or two attachés (or assistants) were sent out with each ambassador or envoy. Younger sons of noble families were almost the only material considered for this service for many years, and up to 1919 no one could be a candidate in the competitive examinations for diplomatic posts unless he had a yearly income of £500. In 1921 the whole Foreign Service was reorganized and put under the Foreign Office.

The relative rank of diplomats was

defined in 1815 by the Congress of Vienna and in 1821 by the Congress of Aix-la-Chapelle, representing the principal European Powers; and those definitions have been adopted by the U. S. Department of State. There are three classes: ambassadors, legates or nuncios; envoys, ministers and others accredited to sovereigns; and chargés d'affaires who are accredited not to sovereigns but to ministers of foreign affairs. In each class the precedence at any capital or court goes to the diplomat of longest service to that country.

Secret diplomacy results in agreements or understandings between nations that are unknown to the people at large in the nations interested and to other nations. Such understandings brought Italy into the First World War on the side of Britain and France —and then blocked President Wilson's efforts to make a just peace. The first of Wilson's Fourteen Points was: "Open covenants of peace openly arrived at, after which there shall be no private international understandings of any kind, but diplomacy shall proceed always frankly and in public view." This ideal has not yet been realized.

Dissolution, breaking up; especially the power to break up a legislature by bringing its session to a close so that a general election is necessary. There is no such power in our American scheme of government.

In Great Britain Parliament may be dissolved by the king, which actually means that the Cabinet has this power. It is exercised so often that Parliament seldom serves the entire 5-year term for which members of the House of Commons are elected. If the Commons votes "No confidence," the Cabinet must dissolve

Parliament and there must be a general election. Sometimes the Cabinet hastens the dissolution of Parliament so as to have a general election at a time when it will be particularly favorable to the party represented by the Cabinet or when the party leaders are eager for an expression on public policy by the voters.

In France, the President of the Republic formerly had the power to dissolve the Chamber of Deputies with the approval of the Senate. Under the Fourth Republic, established in 1947, the President has broader powers than under the Third Republic, but he may not dissolve the Assembly.

District, a division for governmental purposes. Congressional and election districts are units for electoral purposes. A school district is a unit for administration of schools.

District courts, Federal courts of first instance, that is, those in which Federal cases are first heard.

District of Columbia, seat of the Federal Government of the United States; 70 square miles in area. The District was administered by a mayor and council until 1878, when Congress assumed legislative control; it has no popular representation, citizens of the District having no vote, but the 23rd Amendment, adopted in 1961, gives the District 3 electors in Presidential elections. Three commissioners—two residents appointed by the President and the Senate and one military officer named by the President—constitute an executive board in charge of administrative activities, with power to make ordinances regarding public welfare, health and safety. Congress devotes a few days periodically to a consideration of the affairs of the District.

Similar Federal districts for the national capital have been set up in Mexico and in Australia. Mexico City is in a Federal district (Distrito Federal, abbreviated D. F.), administered by the central Government. The city of Canberra, capital of the Commonwealth of Australia, is situated in a Federal Capital Territory of 940 square miles, originally a part of New South Wales and now belonging to the Commonwealth Government. It is administered by a commission of three, one going out of office each year. There is no private ownership of land; title is with the Government, which issues leases.

Division, a formal method of taking a vote in the English House of Commons. The vote is usually taken by calling for all those in favor to say "aye" and then for those opposed to say "nay." This voting by acclamation (all calling out at once) cannot be measured accurately. The presiding officer guesses by the volume of sound. If any member challenges the Speaker's announcement of the vote, there is a division. All members of the House are summoned, the aye-and-nay shouted vote is taken again and almost certainly challenged again, and all members are then ordered to division lobbies. Those voting *nay* march to a room at the Speaker's left and those voting *aye* go to a room on his right; as they march back into the House their numbers are counted

by four tellers appointed by the Speaker. This method is much speedier than the name-by-name rollcall in the U. S. House of Representatives.

In the Federal Government of the United States several administrative parts of the executive departments are called divisions: the Treasury Department has a Savings Bond Division, a Division of Tax Research, and a Legal Division; the Department of the Interior has a Division of Power, a Division of Oil and Gas, a Division of Geography, and a Division of Information; the Post Office Department has a Division of Budget and Administrative Services, a Division of City Delivery, a Division of Post Office Personnel, a Division of Clerical Service, and a Division of Typography.

Divorce, the legal dissolution of the relation of husband and wife and restoration to each of the previous condition of an unmarried person. In the United States divorce is not regulated by the Federal Government but by the various states; therefore the legal causes for divorce are far from uniform. A divorce is easiest in states with the lowest requirements for residence before suit—6 weeks in Nevada and Idaho, 60 days in Wyoming, 90 days in Arkansas, and 3 months in Utah; in Connecticut, 3 years' residence is necessary, and in Massachusetts, 5 years. Six months are required in 6 states, but in most states one or two years' residence is required.

There are over a dozen legal causes for divorce, ranging from drunkenness to the most serious marital charges. The Roman Catholic Church does not permit divorce, though it sometimes grants annulments; and some other churches refuse marriage to divorcees.

An *annulment* is a court decision that a marriage was void from the beginning. A *separation* is a mutual agreement not to live together, usually a contract with provision for support.

Dominion, a self-governing part of the British Empire or more properly of the British Commonwealth of Nations. The Balfour Report of 1926, reviewing the status of the different parts of the Empire after World War I, created the name British Commonwealth of Nations and suggested that its self-governing parts were in no way subordinate to each other or to the United Kingdom, "though united by a common allegiance to the Crown." Under the Statute of Westminister formulated in 1931, the British Parliament passes laws for the dominions only after consultation with the dominion parliament and only if the act expressly states that it applies to the dominion and that the dominion "requested and consented to" it. Legislation by dominion parliaments requires the formal assent of the governor general, which is given as a matter of course.

In international relations the dominions are free and independent. Most of them belong to the United Nations, and all are free to send ministers to other nations and to make treaties.

Double Jeopardy. The Fifth Amendment of the Constitution declares that no person shall be "subject for the same offense to be twice put in jeopardy of life or limb." Jeopardy means the danger of being convicted of a crime in a federal court. "Life and limb" has been liberally interpreted as any legal penalty imposed for a true criminal offense.

After a person has been placed in jeopardy he cannot be tried again by the federal government for the same crime. The law applies only in cases where the defendant has been tried by a petit jury. Therefore, the failure of a grand jury to indict is no guarantee that a person cannot be brought before it a second time and be subsequently indicted.

The privilege granted by the double jeopardy clause can be waived by the defendant himself, if he is convicted and requests a new trial. If he is again found guilty the decision is final and he has no chance to be granted another trial.

Drafting, see *Conscription.*

Duchy, the territory or dominion of a sovereign duke or duchess. If of considerable extent, it is generally called a grand duchy. Luxemburg, one of the smallest independent states of Europe, is a grand duchy bordering on France, Belgium and Germany. Made a duchy of the Holy Roman Empire by Charles IV in 1354, it was declared a grand duchy by the Congress of Vienna in 1815. Since 1919 it has been ruled by the Grand Duchess Charlotte. Until the regime of the National Socialist party in Germany, when all political subdivisions were rearranged and sovereignty was taken from the individual states of the Reich, such former grand duchies as Baden, Hesse, Oldenburg and Mecklenburg (Mecklenburg-Schwerin and Mecklenburg-Strelitz) played important parts. The rulers of Baden, however, had been known since the 11th century as *margraves*. Until 1917 the Republic of Finland was also a grand duchy of the Russian Empire, the czar himself holding the title of grand duke.

The Duchy of Cornwall and the Duchy of Lancaster are dukedoms of the British royal family. Cornwall was first held by the Black Prince, son of Edward III, who in 1337 was created the first English duke. Lancaster was bestowed 14 years later on the king's cousin Henry but reverted to the royal house on the marriage of Henry's daughter Blanche to John of Gaunt, Edward III's youngest son.

During the Middle Ages parts of Germany, Austria, Hungary, the Netherlands, Belgium, France and Italy constituted duchies that were powerful political allies or pawns. Among them were Normandy, Burgundy and Savoy in France, Brunswick, Saxe-Weimar and Saxe-Coburg-Gotha in Germany, Tirol in Austria, Brabant in Belgium and Tuscany in Italy.

Due process of law, regular court routine in distinction from special statute law enacted by a legislature. The U. S. Constitution in the Bill of Rights, Amendment 5, provides that "no person shall be deprived of life, liberty or property without due process of law." The Supreme Court of the United States frequently has to decide whether a law is valid or void on the basis of this constitutional clause. There is no definition of due process or of the application of the clause—except in particular cases.

Dumbarton Oaks, Wash., D.C., the site of a conference held Aug. 21 to Oct. 7, 1944, when representatives of the United States, United Kingdom, Russia and China met to discuss international organization for world peace. These talks resulted in proposals which substantially comprised the United Nations Charter adopted at San Francisco.

Easement, a limited right to the use of certain land of another for a specific purpose without profit. The most common example is the right to pass through the land of another to reach one's own property, there being no open public road; this is called a *right of way.* In England and in some states of the United States there may be a *negative easement,* such as the right to forbid a neighbor to build anything that will obstruct the light of windows.

Economic Advisers, Council of, was established in the Executive Office of the President by the Employment Act of 1946, approved Feb. 20, 1946. The Council was to assist the President through the Employment Act and make an annual Economic Report to Congress. It studies economic developments and trends; appraises the activities of the Federal Government as they have a bearing on the national economy; and develops and recommends to the President national economic policies to foster free competitive enterprise and to maintain employment, production and purchasing power. Basically, the Council was created on the theory that economic planning by government could control the business cycle and keep industry on a healthy, productive basis. This was to be accomplished, when deemed necessary, by a planned program of various public works.

Economic control, the regulation of business activities by government.

In the Anglo-American tradition of government, there has been economic control from the earliest times. About 1200, the fairs were strictly regulated by the Government, and they had to have a permit from the Crown. When the Black Death swept over Europe, it caused a great labor scarcity, and the Ordinance of Laborers (1349) and the Statute of Laborers (1351) in England declared that it was a duty to labor, fixed wages, gave a detailed regulation of the labor contract, abolished day-to-day employment and substituted term employment. It was made a criminal offense for a worker to take more than a certain wage or for an employer to entice a worker from another master. As early as 1299 records show a prosecution of a carpenter for combining with others of his trade to obtain a higher wage than was set by the ordinance of the City of London. In the Dyer's Case (1415) it was held that a contract not to use a craft for a half year in a

certain town was against public policy. In 1552 legislation was passed to prevent engrossing (the crime of buying food at wholesale to sell dear at retail), forestalling (buying goods before they had reached the public market) and regrating (like engrossing but including selling at a very high retail price). This legislation was not completely repealed until 1844.

The philosophy of Adam Smith in his famous *Wealth of Nations* became the accepted attitude during the 19th century, and many governments adopted an attitude toward business of *laissez-faire* or leave-it-alone.

The tariff has played an important part in American political history and shows the interrelation of politics and economics, but a more conscious effort to control for the public good seems to date from the end of the 19th century with President Theodore Roosevelt's advocacy of conserving national resources and his attacks on the trusts.

The confusion that followed World War I and the depression that came in the early '30s forced governments in all parts of the world to mix in business. The Soviet Russia, aiming to create a great industrial nation, took complete control of production and distribution and assumed ownership of all natural resources. In Italy and Germany, the State, becoming totalitarian, supervised business as never before.

The accession of Franklin D. Roosevelt to the presidency and the inauguration of the New Deal in 1933 was marked by a great increase in the scope of economic control by government. The first steps were the temporary closing of the banks, the reform of the banking system, the creation of the National Recovery Administration (NRA), of the Tennessee Valley Authority (TVA) and the Federal Emergency Relief Administration (FERA). These were followed by a vast program of governmental reform, and reorganization and expansion of economic control. Measures were enacted designed to stimulate industry, increase employment and care for those who could not find work. These initial steps were followed by agencies designed to correct abuses in the marketing of securities and in the management of public utilities in the electrical field, particularly in relation to holding companies. It was hoped that TVA would supply a yardstick with respect to rates for electricity. Attempts were made to control agriculture and to fix prices for agricultural products. Another important step taken by the New Deal was the establishment of a federal social security plan for unemployment as well as for old age.

Economic Coöperation Administration (ECA), created in April 1948 to administer the European Recovery Program (ERP) enacted into law by Congress as a result of the so-called Marshall Plan of economic aid to Europe. The purpose of the Marshall Plan was to fill the vacuum of war-torn Europe and to prevent the spread of Communism by removing the motivating causes—hunger and poverty.

The program to be carried out by the ECA had four general objectives: (1) the generation of a strong productive effort by each of the participating countries; (2) the creation of internal financial stability; (3) maximum coöperation between the participating countries; and (4) a solution of the participating countries' trading deficits with the American continent, particularly by means of exports.

Sixteen western European nations, forming the Committee of European Economic Coöperation were the initial beneficiaries of the plan. Among the notable exceptions were Spain, Russia and Russian satellite nations. Six billion dollars was authorized to be expended by ECA in the first year and up to 17 billion dollars in 4 years. To be successful the ERP required faith, mutual coöperation, enthusiasm and dollars.

The first phase of the ERP was essentially a subsidy to restore European productivity; the second phase aimed to make the money and credit the basis for a central fund to promote freer trade among the participating nations. American aid, as directed by the ECA, was used as an instrument for the economic integration of western Europe.

Election, choice, especially the choice of government officials by qualified voters. Elections vary as to type and method, but usually all have the same objective, the choice of a candidate for office. A *run-off* election is held in case of a tie vote or insufficient votes to qualify for election.

Electoral College, the indirect method of choosing the President and Vice-President of the United States by the vote of electors in each state, the number of electors equaling the state's representatives in Congress—one for each Senator and Representative. In the 1964 Presidential election, the representation of the states ranged from 3 apiece for Alaska, Delaware, Nevada, Vermont, Wyoming, and the District of Columbia, and 4 for 10 states, to 25 for Texas, 26 for Illinois and Ohio, 29 for Pennsylvania, 40 for California, and 43 for New York.

Embargo, an order of a state prohibiting merchant vessels from leaving its ports. The embargo as applied to ocean shipments is often important during wartime. An embargo has as its object that of damaging another country by depriving it of commerce. Also, a prohibition on the movement of traffic by rail, truck, airplane, etc. due to a strike or disaster such as a flood or fire.

Embezzlement, the act of an agent, servant or trustee in appropriating property that has been placed in his charge for safe-keeping or for disposal according to directions. Embezzlement is a statutory crime.

Emigration, see *Immigration.*

Eminent domain, the power of government to appropriate any property for the public use or public good. In England it is called *compulsory purchase.* The Bill of Rights in the Federal Constitution (Art. V) provides that "private property shall not be taken for public use without just compensation." Most state constitutions have similar provisions.

Empire (from Latin *imperium,* command, sovereignty, authority, government), a group of nations, states or peoples under a single central government. The Latin word first applied to military power. The derived Latin word *imperator,* first meaning a victorious commander, later came to mean head of the state, including its conquered parts. So in ancient history *empire* is used of a power built by arms: the Persian Empire, Alexander's Macedonian Empire, the Roman Empire. For the same reason *empire* usually means a far-flung rule. The French Empire was created by Napoleon's victorious armies. Before World War I there were three empires in Europe, each ruled by an emperor whose title was a modification of the Latin name, Caesar, the title of the Roman emperors. The Russian Empire had its Czar or Tsar. The Austrian Empire and the German Empire each had its Kaiser, but the German word *Reich,* which we translate empire, was used of the German Republic set up after World War I until the end of World War II; it is really a word meaning rule or state with no implication what sort of government is meant.

Japan was called an empire because its ruler was absolute and (like Alexander and the Roman Caesars) was considered divine. The ruler of Ethiopia is called emperor, although his kingdom has never been an extensive or divided empire.

The British Empire is now officially the British Commonwealth of Nations. The name *British Empire* came into use after 1876 when the Prime Minister, Lord Beaconsfield, added to Queen Victoria's official titles Empress of India; but there was never any official British Empire. Especially in the period of imperialism at the end of the 19th century the word *empire* was used of any nation that was eager to spread its influence and power by conquest or colonization.

Employers' liability, a legal term with two very different meanings: (1) the liability of an employer for injury done by his employee in course of his employment, as when a delivery truck of a store injures a pedestrian; and (2) the commoner use nowadays, the liability of an employer to compensate an employee for injuries received in employment.

Enabling act, a special statute authorizing a corporation or an individual to do something or to carry on some activity that otherwise would not be legal. For example, on March 23, 1933, the German Reichstag passed by a vote of 441 to 94 the Enabling Act (Law to Combat the National Crisis) sanctioning Hitler's dictatorship and giving him 4 years of power to do anything but abolish the Reichstag or Reichsrat and diminish the rights of the President.

Equity, in the broad sense, equality or natural justice; a system of remedial justice administered by the courts of equity or chancery.

Escrow (old law French for scroll), a deed or bond duly executed by the contracting parties (grantor and grantee) and placed in the hands of a third party, to be held by him until agreed conditions between the two parties have been satisfied. Once deposited, the escrow is beyond recall by the grantor. When conditions are fulfilled, the document is delivered to the grantee.

Established church, an ecclesiastical system recognized and specially privileged by government—for example the Anglican (Protestant Episcopal) Church in England and the Presbyterian Church in Scotland. There are established churches in the following countries: Bolivia and Peru (both Roman Catholic); Greece (Hellenic Eastern Orthodox); Bulgaria (Bulgarian Eastern Orthodox); Sweden and Finland (both Swedish Lutheran). The Roman Catholic Church was disestablished in France in 1905 and in Spain in 1933. In the different states of the German Empire there were established churches—some Protestant and some Catholic—until 1918 when the head of each state (and of its church) abdicated. Russia had an established church (the Greek Eastern Orthodox) until the Bolsheviks in 1918 separated Church and State and openly crusaded against religion. In pre-war Italy and Germany the government was bitterly opposed to any church authority—that the totalitarian state supersedes any authority but its own is the dictators' idea. But in Italy the state government in 1929 ended the 60-year-old quarrel of Church and State by recognizing the political independence of Vatican City, the residence of the Pope.

European Common Market or Euromarket was created by a treaty signed in Rome on March 21, 1957. Its member nations consist of France, West Germany, Italy, Belgium, the Netherlands and Luxembourg.

The chief aim of this body is to assist these nations in establishing bigger markets for their manufactured goods. Due to smaller populations Western Europe must produce on a more limited scale. Now that the manufacturers can be assured of a larger market, they can adopt more effective mass-production methods and therefore sell at a cheaper rate. In the past, the customs and tariff barriers erected by each nation to protect its small home market from a flood of outside goods, was an obstacle to growth. The European Common Market intends to reduce these barriers.

Excise or **Internal revenue,** tax levied on the manufacture, sale or consumption of goods within a country. It is a tax levied for doing something, as distinguished from a property tax, which is levied on something owned. Excise taxes include levies on tobacco, liquor, gasoline, sales, amusements and incorporation.

Execution, putting into effect a legal judgment, sentence or document. The special uses of the word are: (1) *execution of a judgment,* the seizure of a debtor's property to satisfy the judgment; (2) *execution of a criminal sentence,* especially capital punishment; (3) *execution of a deed or will,* making it valid by signing, sealing and delivering.

Executor, a person named by the maker of a will to carry out the terms of the will. Frequently two or more coexecutors are named. If the decedent leaves no will or if the executor he appoints cannot act, the probate court appoints an administrator. Under direction of the court, the executor or administrator discharges the obligations imposed in settling the estate; all his acts must be approved by the court.

Exemption, freedom or immunity from the general provisions of the law. A physician's instruments, a lawyer's library, the tools of any trade, the homestead of a farmer are exempt from seizure for debt (unless they are pledged by mortgage, or the exemption is otherwise waived); there are similar exemptions in bankruptcy. Editors and teachers are exempt from jury duty; ministers of the gospel, from military service.

Ex post facto (Latin, from what is done afterwards), retroactive, especially a law that makes a deed a crime that was not a crime when committed or increases the penalty for a crime or removes a lawful protection. The United States by constitutional provision (Art. I, Sec. 9, Cl. 3; and Art. I, Sec. 10, Cl. 1) forbids the passage of *ex post facto* laws, but this is interpreted only in the limited sense of applying to criminal or penal statutes. It does not apply to civil cases. The British Parliament still has power to pass *ex post facto* laws.

Exterritoriality or **Extraterritoriality,** literally being outside or beyond the local jurisdiction; privileges or immunities that make a foreigner free from the law of the land in which he lives. In Turkey, Egypt, Persia, Siam, Japan and China treaties or agreements (called *capitulations*) gave to citizens of western nations the right of exterritoriality so that they were not governed by local laws. In the East there has been a constant tendency to withdraw exterritorial rights. The first to abolish these exterritorial rights was Japan in 1892, and with the practical withdrawal of the capitulations in Egypt in 1936 China became the only nation remaining where such rights were enjoyed by foreigners. Since the establishment of the Communist People's Republic of China in 1949 and the withdrawal of Nationalist China to Formosa in 1950, the special privileges enjoyed by Great Britain, Japan, and the United States before World War II, no longer exist in China.

This immunity is always granted to diplomatic representatives of one country residing in another; there is a legal fiction that the ambassador's residence is a part of his own country and not of the country in which it is actually situated. Traveling royalty is immune from the laws of lands visited.

Extradition, the surrender by one authority, state or nation to another of a fugitive from justice. Not all crimes are subject to extradition; each treaty providing for mutual favors of this nature specifies what crimes shall warrant extradition. In countries where no treaties on the subject are in force, a fugitive from justice is safe. The Federal Constitution (Art. IV, Sec. 2, Cl. 2) requires extradition from one state to another "on demand of the Executive authority of the State from which he fled." Frequently, a governor has refused to honor such a request, and the Supreme Court has declared that no "clause or provision in the Constitution arms the Government of the United States with power . . . to compel the execution of this duty."

Fair Employment Practices Commission (FEPC), a permanent federal commission proposed to supervise employment practices and to act on complaints of failure by employers to follow the law in respect to discrimination in hiring, in employment, in hours, wages or working conditions. Some states, notably New York, have such a commission.

False Imprisonment, total restraint without legal authority, whether or not the restraining force is physical. The one who falsely imprisons another has committed a crime and may be punished by the state; he also has committed a tort and is liable to the injured party for damages. Miscarriage of justice by which a jury orders a defendent to prison when he is actually not guilty is not false imprisonment. The letter of the law has been followed, and the judgment is based on all evidence obtainable. If later evidence establishes the innocence of the prisoner, he has no redress, though he can secure his freedom and sometimes the state gives him compensation.

False pretenses, untrue representation of past or present facts with intent to defraud; a criminal offense if the fraud is committed.

Farm Credit Administration, a U. S. Government unit created in 1933 by President Roosevelt to replace the Federal Farm Board (established in 1929) that he abolished. The governor and two deputy governors supervise 12 Federal Land Banks (created in 1916) —in Springfield, (Mass.), Baltimore, Columbia (S.C.), Louisville, New Orleans, St. Louis, St. Paul, Omaha, Wichita, Houston, Berkeley (Calif.) and Spokane—that make loans on first mortgages; 12 Federal Intermediate Credit Banks, which rediscount farm and livestock paper for periods between crops; 12 Co-operative Banks that finance farm supply cooperatives; and the Production Credit Corporations and Associations, which constitutes a permanent production credit system.

Fascism, the principles of the Italian group or party called Fascisti or Fascists. The name is derived from the Roman fasces, a bundle of rods carried by the lictor, an officer attending magistrates. The fasces in ancient Rome symbolized the authority and power of the law. In modern Italy the followers of Mussolini took the name of Fascisti to signify that the law must be obeyed and that force would be used against radicals, Communists and Socialists and that the state is all-powerful in every field of human activity.

Federal Bureau of Investigation, a division of the Department of Justice charged with the general investigation of offenses against Federal laws, except counterfeiting, narcotics and other matters not within the jurisdiction of the Department of Justice. The FBI, organized in 1924, achieved prominence in connection with kidnapping cases and in the detection and arrest of those engaged in espionage, sabotage, and treason. It is responsible in matters pertaining to the internal security of the U. S., particularly in the detection and arrest of suboteurs and foreign agents.

Federal Communications Commission, a U.S. Government board of seven members created in 1934 to regulate interstate telephone, telegraph and radio broadcasting. The latter had been transferred from the Federal Radio Commission created in 1927. The Communications Commission requires periodical reports and the filing of rate schedules by all companies in its jurisdiction. It may prescribe rules and fix new rates and investigate any transactions of communication concerns. No extensions or construction of new plants or consolidation of companies (especially telephone) is allowed without the Commission's permission.

Federal Deposit Insurance Corporation (FDIC) organized on a temporary basis in 1933 and made permanent in 1935. Its chief purpose is to insure deposits of all banks entitled to the benefits of insurance under the act, to the extent of $5,000 on the deposits of each depositor. The FDIC pays off the depositions of insured banks closed without adequate provision having been made to pay depositors' claims. All bank members of the Federal Reserve system, are, under the law, insured under the permanent insurance plan. In January 1949 over 13,000 banks were insured by FDIC. All advances by the Federal Government to the FDIC have been repaid and since Sept. 1, 1948, it has been financed by its member banks.

Federal government, or Federation, a group of states united under a central government by a covenant or league that reserves some powers to the separate states. The term comes from the Latin word *foedus, foederis,* meaning league or covenant. The same root appears in the word *confederation* and in the title *Confederate States of America* adopted by the South in the American Civil War; but confederation has a very different meaning—a union for a particular purpose in which the states retain practically all power and governmental authority. In the Civil War the northern army was often called federal to distinguish it from the Confederate forces.

West Germany is a Federal Republic composed of 10 autonomous states. German writers on government call a federation a *Bundesstaat* or union-state.

The best known of federal governments is the United States of America where the federal union under the Constitution of 1787 succeeded the loose government under the Articles of Confederation.

The Commonwealth of Canada is a federal government in which the central government has all power not reserved to the provinces by the constitution—just the opposite of the U. S. Constitution which reserves to the states all power not expressly granted to the Federal Government.

The Commonwealth of Australia (1901) is distinctly federal with six states, one territory and a Federal Capital Territory like the District of Columbia.

Growing unrest in the colonial possessions of the great powers increased the desire for a greater measure of self-government, preferably within the structure of a stable government. This urge was particularly evident in the British colonies in Africa. Northern Rhodesia, Southern Rhodesia, and Nyasaland joined together in the Central African Federation. The Federation of Nigeria includes 3 regions (Northern, Western, and Eastern) and the quasi-federal territory of the Southern Cameroons. Kenya, Tanganyika, and Uganda proposed joining together in the East African Federation. In the West Indies, six British-held islands likewise were federated. As federations these groups anticipated membership in the British Commonwealth.

Federal Home Loan Board, a government agency set up in 1932 to assure small home owners of safe financing at low interest rates. It was created during the Hoover administration and later was greatly expanded. It supervised the Home Owner's Loan Corporation and the Federal Savings and Loan Insurance Corporation, both terminated in 1937. It was transferred to the National Housing Agency in 1942 and to the Housing and Home Administration in 1947, when its functions were assumed by the new Home Loan Bank Board.

Federalist party, the first American political party. Led by Alexander Hamilton, James Madison and John Jay, this group urged the adoption of the Constitution by the various states and was called Federalist because the Constitution was creating a Federal government. The first elections were nonpartisan, and it was not until 1800 that there was a distinct party alignment among the voters. However, John Adams, a Federalist, was elected in 1796 and from 1801 until its breakup about 1816-20, the Federalist party was the opposition party.

Federal Power Commission (FPC), originally authorized in 1920 to administer the Federal government's interest in water power on Federal property. It was reorganized in 1930 with five fulltime commissioners to control and supervise hydroelectric power plants on public lands or affecting navigation. The FPC is in charge of a national power survey and conducts electric rate surveys. The FPC regulates most interstate hydroelectric utilities under the Federal Water Power act of 1920 and has certain jurisdiction over rates and accounting practices of such public power projects as the Hoover dam, TVA, Fort Peck project, the Bonneville dam in Washington, etc. It is also concerned with the enforcement of the Natural Gas act of 1938 as it relates to the inter-

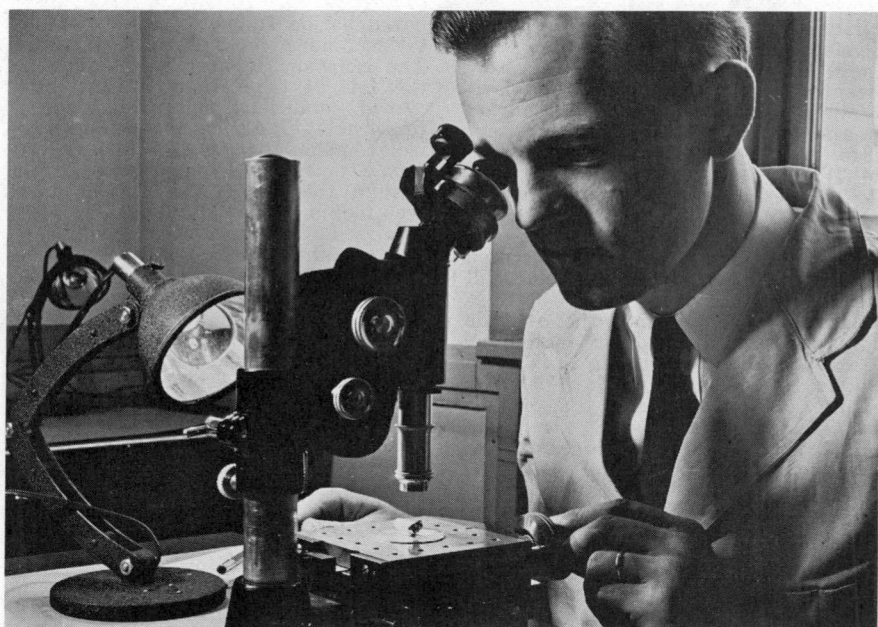

HAROLD RHODENBAUGH

F.B.I. TECHNICIAN studying a bullet under a microscope to measure the lands and grooves.

Federal Trade Commission, a commission of five members appointed by the President to investigate improper business management practices. It was interested especially in unfair methods of competition, monopolies and practices tending to lessen competition in interstate and foreign commerce. The commission was created on the recommendation of President Wilson by an act of Congress in 1914 and received additional powers from the Clayton Antitrust Act of that year and from the Webb-Pomerene act of 1918 (permitting concerns to consolidate for foreign trade). The Commission was also charged with enforcement of the Robinson-Patman act of 1936 which had to do with price discrimination, inter-locking directorates and other trade practices. In its efforts at enforcement the FTC, acting on a Senate resolution, made a thorough study of the public utility holding company and of its practices in pyramiding operating and underlying holding companies. Its report led to the Public Utility Holding Company act of 1935 with its so-called "death sentence" clause. Another consequence was the creation of the Securities and Exchange Commission which regulated the issuance of securities, the acquisition of utility assets, securities and "service contracts" and other intercompany transactions.

Another important activity was the action instituted related to the "basing point" practice long employed by some of the large corporations. Prices of products from any one of a number of plants were all based as to freight charges on a central point. The FTC required a revision of schedules and prices based on the actual point of shipment. This action was upheld in the lower courts and in the U. S. Supreme Court.

The Commission has power to issue an order to "cease and desist" from unfair practices. When an offender against such an order after signing a promise that he will not continue the forbidden practice vio-

state transportation and distribution of natural gas.

Federal Reserve System, a U. S. banking system set up by the Owen-Glass Federal Reserve act of 1913, effective Nov. 16, 1914. The law created 12 Reserve Banks in 12 districts with headquarters in Boston, New York, Philadelphia, Cleveland, Richmond, Atlanta, Chicago, St. Louis, Minneapolis, Kansas City, Dallas and San Francisco. The districts do not follow state lines.

The Federal Reserve System was established because of the great expanse of territory in the United States, the wide diversity of industries and the special position of agriculture, the need for an elastic currency that could be readily expanded when additional credit was required, and the need for centralized reserves that could be transferred from one area to another as needed.

The 12 Reserve Banks are privately owned by individual member banks, each being required to subscribe for Reserve Bank stock to the amount of 6% of its paid-up capital and surplus. The member banks in each of the 12 districts elect six (of nine) directors of their district Reserve Bank—three bankers and three persons engaged in commerce, agriculture or industry not officers, directors or employees of any bank. Three more directors (including the chairman who is called the Federal Reserve Agent) are appointed by the Board of the Federal Reserve system. The Board is aided by the Federal Advisory Council of 12 members, one from each district, elected by the district Boards of Directors.

Federal Security Agency, created April 25, 1939 for the purpose of grouping under one administration those agencies of the Federal Government concerned with the promotion of social and economic security, educational

opportunity and the health of the nation. It was replaced by the Executive Department of Health, Education and Welfare, April 11, 1953, which supervises such organizations as the Office of Education, Public Health Service, Social Security Administration, the Children's Bureau, and Vocational Rehabilitation.

Other Bureaus are those of Employment Security, Federal Credit Union, Old-Age and Survivors Insurance Bureau of Public Assistance. These are state initiated and state administered. Several federally-aided corporations including the American Printing Office for the Blind, Columbia Institution for the Deaf and Howard University are also under the jurisdiction of the Federal Health, Education, Welfare Dept.

BUREAU OF ENGRAVING AND PRINTING

CURRENCY is printed on this U.S. treasury press at the rate of 40,000 notes per hour.

lates this promise, the complaint is usually made public.

The Security Exchange Act of 1934 took away from the Federal Trade Commission authority to administer the Securities Act of 1933 and set up the SEC or Securities and Exchange Commission.

Felony, at common law, every crime that occasioned a total forfeiture of lands or goods and to which might be added capital or other punishment according to the degree of guilt. A felony is always a grave crime; lesser offenses are called *misdemeanors.* The various states have defined the terms by statutes, and there is no uniformity, so that the same crime may be a felony in one state and a misdemeanor in another.

Fictions, assumptions (true or false) that courts of law (especially in England) made and did not permit anyone to disprove. It is a legal fiction that everyone knows the law—necessary to uphold the maxim, "Ignorance is no excuse." The law of adoption is based on the fiction that a child becomes a member of a family to which it has no blood relationship. It was a fiction of English law that husband and wife are one person. That a corporation is a person is a legal fiction. It is a fiction of international law that a warship is a part of the country that owns it and that an ambassador's residence is not a part of the country in which it is situated. In another sense a legal fiction is "any assumption that conceals the fact that a rule of law has undergone an alteration." When legislation required public transfers of land, a legal fiction preserved the secrecy of titles by this method: the new owner sued to assure his title, and the old owner entered no defense, so that the court could do nothing but recognize the change of title. Blackstone said: "No fiction shall extend to work an injury, its proper operation being to prevent a mischief or remedy an inconvenience that might result from the general rule of the law." Legal fictions were long one method of changing the law in fact and in result though not in form or in theory.

Filibuster, originally a freebooter, buccaneer or pirate; and now, in the slang of legislative bodies, a person who holds up the course of legislative business by technicalities, privileges, prolonged speeches and other obstructive tactics. This method of delay also is called a filibuster, and the same word is used as a verb meaning to delay or obstruct legislative business.

Fine, in criminal law a penalty in money assessed against a defendant in a criminal case as a penalty for wrongdoing. In misdemeanors the amount is left largely to the judgment of the court; in felonies, the statutes declare what minimum and maximum fines shall be imposed, and they may be assessed in addition to sentence of imprisonment. The Constitution of the United States forbids excessive fines (Amendment 8).

Five-Year Plan, the government programs in Soviet Russia adopted for the agricultural, industrial and economic development of the Soviet Union.

Foreign Ministers, Council of, The, representing the five principal Allied powers in World War II, was provided for at the Potsdam conference in July, 1945. The Council was constituted to do "the necessary preparatory work for the peace settlements and to take up other matters . . . referred to (it) by agreement of the governments participating." China was represented at the first meeting and France in all but the second.

Foreign Policy determines the attitude of one sovereign nation to another or to the world as a whole. In the United States, foreign policy in the 175 years of its national existence has moved from isolationism at one extreme to full participation in world affairs at the other. The fundamentals of American foreign policy were self-determination, independence, noncolonization, nonintervention, nonentanglement in European politics, freedom of the seas and freedom of commerce. In large measure these fundamentals still constitute the basis of American foreign policy, with the notable exception of nonentanglement in European politics.

In the early years of its existence as a nation the United States took little interest in affairs elsewhere. As a matter of self-defense, President George Washington urged the country "to steer clear of permanent alliances." Subsequently, Thomas Jefferson gave currency to the expression "entangling alliances" rather than "permanent alliances." Twenty-five years later, President James Monroe, in his famous doctrine, reminded European powers that "we consider any attempt to extend their system to any portion of this hemisphere, as dangerous to our peace and safety." These two statements formulated the foreign policy of the United States for over 100 years. We would not interfere in the affairs of Europe and elsewhere; we would resent and fight against any interference in our own affairs or those of other nations of the western hemisphere. This policy of isolationism began to come to an end in the latter years of the 19th century, with the enunciation of the Open Door policy in China in 1899. The consequences of the Spanish-American war and the resulting American acquisition of the Philippines thrust the United States into international politics as a world power, and gave it authority and prestige as a colonial power. The period between the Spanish-American war and World War I was a period of alleged imperialism in American foreign policy. On the other hand, an interest in the preservation of world peace was evidenced by American participation in the peace conference at The Hague.

Participation in World War I and the initiative and leadership of President Woodrow Wilson in the creation and organization of the League of Nations divided the United States into two groups. The isolationist would reject the League of Nations and confine foreign relations to polite diplomatic activities; the opposition would join the League of Nations thereby pledging the United States to full participation in world affairs and to taking sides in important disputes. The isolationists won; membership in the League of Nations was rejected. World conditions, however, made it impossible to return to 19th century isolationism. Because of its size, economic power and importance to the rest of the world, the United States was forced to take some part in world affairs, as a matter of self-defense if for no other reason. Always an advocate of international peace and disarmament, the United States in 1922 as an important supporter of the Hague Peace Conferences, recommended an international disarmament conference at Washington at which the subject could be discussed. A limitation of armaments on a ratio basis and a variety of international agreements were made, followed several years later by the Briand-Kellogg pact of 1928 to outlaw war. In this period of the 1920's the national foreign policy had become "cooperation without entangling alliances."

International relations, affected by world-wide economic depression, the rise of Mussolini and his Fascists, Hitler and his Nazis and of the military party in Japan, again forced the United States to come out of its isolationism and to take its place as a world power. President Franklin D. Roosevelt re-stated the Good Neighbor policy of the United States with respect to the Latin American countries. He also moved to eliminate one element of friction in international affairs by means of the Hull reciprocal trade agreements. Support of Great Britain and later of Russia and China in World War II, led the United States into a deeper participation in European and Far Eastern affairs. President Roosevelt made further commitments at Casablanca, Teheran and Yalta, involving the United States in world affairs.

The formation of the United Nations to replace the outmoded League of Nations, was forcefully sponsored by the United States. This was done because of the increasing need for understanding between the nations of the world, because of the need for an organization dedicated to the principals of world peace and international cooperation. The United States has assumed an all-important position in world affairs. In 1956 the Panama Declaration demonstrated the solidarity of western hemisphere countries. The Eisenhower Doctrine of 1957 set forth the U. S. program for halting communism in the Middle East.

Foreign service see *Diplomatic service; Ambassador; Consul.*

Forgery, making or changing a document, especially imitating the handwriting of another person on any document with the intention to deceive or defraud. The most common forgeries are signatures on checks, notes and wills, but any secret alteration of any part of a document, even of a word, if a new meaning is given to the instrument, constitutes forgery if intent to defraud is shown. The crime is a penitentiary offense. In England forgery was a capital crime without benefit of clergy for two centuries after 1634. A clergyman was hanged for forgery in 1777, a banker in 1824.

Fraud, in its general sense, all acts or omissions involving a breach of legal duty that result in damage to another. In order to sustain an action for fraud there must have been: (1) a false, material representation that the maker knew to be false and intended should be acted upon; (2) the hearer must have been ignorant of the falsity of the representation and have relied on it as the truth, and there must have been a right to so rely; (3) a consequent and proximate damage due to the reliance on the false representation.

Freedom of speech and press, see *Censorship*.

Free-Soil party, an American political party that came into existence in 1847 largely in opposition to the extension of slavery into the new territory acquired from Mexico. It was composed of the Barnburners of New York, the antislavery Whigs and the members of the Liberty party. The party met in a convention at Buffalo in 1848, adopted a platform favoring a homestead law, a low tariff for revenue and internal improvements and nominated Martin Van Buren for President and Charles Adams for Vice-President.

Garnishment (from *garn*, a variant of warn), originally a warning to a person not a party to the action to appear in court. Now, a judicial proceeding by which the plaintiff seeks to subject to his claim certain property or money owed.

Genocide, the deliberate destruction of racial, national or religious groups because of racial or national intolerance. It has been outlawed by a U. N. convention adopted Dec. 8, 1948.

Gerrymander, the process of redistricting a state or other political division in such a manner as to give one party an unfair advantage over another. The term derives its name from Elbridge Gerry who was governor of Massachusetts in 1812. He had the election districts redistributed to the advantage of his party, and one district (a part of Essex County) had boundaries so eccentric that on the map the outline looked like a dragon.

Gestapo, a division of the German Nazi secret police which originated following Hitler's Munich Putsch in 1923. It took its name from the first two syllables of the German name of the organization—Geheime-Staats-Polizei. In its final form it was the result of the merger of Herman Goering's Prussian secret police and of local secret police elsewhere in Germany. In 1936 Heinrich Himmler was placed in charge of the entire secret police of Germany, including the Gestapo. In time it became active all over the world and was notorious for its methods and practices.

Government, Forms of. The forms which governments have taken in history have varied from the dictatorship, or one man rule, to the town meeting in which every man had a voice. The monarchy, the oligarchy or the aristocracy have characterized government where the mass of the people had

little voice in government. The dictatorship often assumes the pretense of popular support, but seldom accords it any voice in the government. In a constitutional monarchy, like the United Kingdom, the monarch has become merely a symbol. The British government is a government in which the ministry and the legislative bodies exercise the real control.

France is a republic with a cabinet form of government; the United States is a republic in which the president is independent of the legislative body so far as his tenure is concerned, but who has great power through the various instrumentalities of the government. Although Russia has the forms of a republican government it is controlled by one party—the Communist Party—dominated by a few men. Another form is that of the federated government presided over by a chief of state and his cabinet.

Governor, originally a pilot or steersman; now the chief executive of a state of the United States or the executive, representing the British Crown, in an English colony or dependency—tor example, North Borneo, Cyprus, Singapore, Fiji Islands, British Honduras, British Guiana, Bermuda, British West Africa.

Thirty-five states of the Union elect the governor for a 4-year term; 15, for a 2-year term. Many cannot succeed themselves. The governor is likely to be a leader of his party in the state and many Presidents of the United States have come to that office after acting as state governor—notably Cleveland, Wilson, and the two Roosevelts. The governor of New York receives an annual salary of $50,000; California pays $44,100; 44 states pay from $35,000 to $15,000; others vary from $13,750 to $10,000. Except in Mississippi, where there is something like the presidential electoral college, the governor is elected by popular vote.

The governor's executive and administrative powers in some states are limited by the fact that department heads are elected just as he is and are responsible not to him but to the voters. But there is a tendency to give the governor more power, and in states where there has been a recent overhauling of the machinery of government the new constitutions provide that the governor appoint department heads. In Maine the legislature elects a Governor's Council, and in Massachusetts a similar advisory body is elected by popular vote. In several states the governor has not the full pardoning power. North Carolina is the only state where the governor has not the power to veto legislation. In the other states a governor's veto may be overridden by a two-thirds vote, a three-fifths vote or (in a few states) by a mere majority. A few state constitutions allow the governor to veto separate items in appropriation bills, but in most states this is forbidden as in the Federal Constitution. Since 1908 the state governors have met in yearly conferences to discuss common problems.

The governors of English colonies

and dependencies usually serve for 6 years. The dominions have each a governor general, a Crown appointee and representative, who serves for a minimum term of 5 years. He has a veto power in theory but seldom or never uses it.

Greenback party, a political party in the United States, organized in 1875 to bring about the repeal of the Resumption Act by which greenbacks were to be redeemed in specie beginning in 1879. As a result of the panic of 1873 the West and South were suffering from credit restrictions, and they believed that the inflation of the currency would aid in the recovery. When the supporters of the greenbacks (fiat money) failed to dominate the Democratic convention, they withdrew and formed the Greenback party. Peter Cooper, who was nominated for President, polled only 81,737 votes.

After the labor troubles of 1877, labor organizations allied themselves and formed the *Greenback-Labor party,* which sent 14 representatives to Congress in 1878, and in 1880 James B. Weaver of Iowa polled 308,-578 votes as their candidate for President. After that the party showed a rapid decline, and its members returned to the old parties.

Guaranty, a contract by which one person agrees for a consideration to pay a debt if the debtor does not. Some states distinguish between surety and guaranty as follows: a guarantor pays when the debtor cannot, that is, the guarantor is secondarily liable and need pay only after a demand is made upon the debtor and refused; a surety pays when the debtor does not, that is, the surety is primarily liable and becomes responsible as soon as the debtor defaults. For most purposes the two words are synonymous.

Guardian (a variant form of *warden*), one appointed by a court to control the acts and manage the property of an infant (a person not yet of age), called a *ward.* He stands before the law as the legal parent but is not permitted to derive profit from the estate of the ward, except the compensation allowed for his services. All his acts are subject to court approval, and he is personally accountable for losses if he deliberately exceeds his authority. If an infant or person otherwise legally incapable has no legally appointed guardian, a *next friend* may act for him—that is, anyone not having an interest in opposition to that of the infant. Formerly when married women suffered from legal disabilities, they could sue only through a next friend.

Habeas corpus (Latin, *you shall have the body*), a legal writ issued by a court commanding public officials or private persons who have a person in detention to bring him into court to show cause why he is held. An application for it cannot be denied in times of peace; the Federal Constitution (Art. I, Sec. 9, Cl. 2) and most state constitutions declare that "the privilege of the writ of habeas corpus shall not be suspended unless when in cases of rebellion or invasion the public safety may require it." The writ is returnable immediately—there is no delay in bringing it to court. If sufficient cause for detention is not shown, he is set free. Historically, this writ was used to establish the right of personal liberty against the tyranny of nobles, king or courts.

Habitual criminals or habitual offenders, those repeatedly convicted of crime and considered a special menace to the public safety. In the United States, beginning with the Baumes act of 1926 enacted in New York, the mandatory penalty for a fourth conviction for felony is life imprisonment.

Hearing, formerly a proceeding in a court of equity in contradistinction to a trial in a court of law; now used for both. A hearing may also take place before an administrative board or a magistrate. It generally includes the right to introduce testimony and to argue the merits of the case.

Hiring halls are places where men are assigned to jobs aboard ships. They are usually controlled by the maritime labor unions and are considered to be "closed shops," because access to them is only accorded members of the union. This preference was held to be in violation of the Taft-Hartley Labor-Management act which prohibited the closed shop. The National Maritime Union (NMU) and other maritime unions opposed both the ruling of the National Labor Relations Board (NLRB) and a decision of the U.S. Supreme Court outlawing the hiring hall when operated by a labor union and prohibiting access to all but union members. The hiring hall was an outgrowth of the improvement in maritime labor conditions begun in 1915 by the La Follette Seaman's act and continued by the Jones act of 1920 and the Wagner act of 1935.

Home Office, a part of the British Government, a department under the Secretary for Home Affairs, who is usually a member of the Cabinet. The Home Office has many functions. Up to 1801 it handled all colonial affairs. It is still in charge of the Channel Islands and the Isle of Man, which are not colonies but Crown dominions; but its jurisdiction does not include Scotland.

Home rule, the right of cities to frame their own charters. As the city is a corporation, its charter or frame of government must originate with the state. In state legislatures the representatives of the county and rural districts are likely to outnumber those from the cities and are certain to outnumber the representatives from any one city. Hence it often happens that a municipal charter drafted and granted by a state legislature is dictated largely by the interests of the rural part of the state.

The various attempts to correct this condition may be classified as follows:

Constitutional provisions against special legislation attempted to make it impossible for a state legislature to draft a charter that applied to a single city, but the courts ruled that legislatures might charter cities by classes—and usually the largest city in a state is in a class by itself, so that this method is of no avail.

Sometimes the state constitution (in Illinois, for example) allows special legislation on city charters but makes it operative only after the charter has been approved by the voters of the city.

Sometimes the legislature gives a city the choice between different types of charter.

The method that is commonly called *home rule* goes even farther. It was first used in Missouri in 1875, and it permits the voters of a city (over 100,000 in Missouri) to decide whether they will adopt a charter submitted to them by a city board. The only stipulation is that the charter must be in harmony with the constitution and laws of the state.

Homicide, the killing of one person by another. *Justifiable* homicide includes: the acts of officers who kill offenders fleeing from justice, the case of persons who are killed in the necessary dispersal of a mob, the legal act of putting a condemned man to death. *Excusable homicide includes only* those cases in which a person kills another in defense of his own life or in which death results accidentally from the act of another person engaged in a legitimate task. *Felonious* homicide is a willful killing under such circumstances that the killer is punishable. It has two classes: murder, killing with malice aforethought, (premeditated), and manslaughter, when the killing is not premeditated.

Hoover Commission, the popular name given the Commission on Organization of the Executive Branch of the Government. Ex-President Herbert Hoover was appointed chairman of the commission which was authorized by Congress on July 7, 1947. The Commission submitted its findings in brief reports with certain recommendations, in 18 installments, January to April 1949. These reports related to certain suggested changes in the organization of the Executive Branch of the Government. They were received with general approval but the "chaos of establishments" set up by Congress was perpetuated so far as possible by an entrenched bureaucracy that favored changes in every bureau except its own. All suggested reorganization plans were submitted to the President and sent by him to Congress as promptly as possible. Some of the Commission's recommendations have been carried out but some have not. The Commission ceased to exist by statutory limitation, June 12, 1949, after all of its recommendations had been submitted to the President.

Housing, dwelling accommodations and the provision of those accommodations, especially as they are controlled and regulated by government.

The bad housing conditions in large cities and in factory towns and villages are due to many causes—poverty; immigration of a class with low living standards; a change in average standards of living that was far speedier than the rate of rebuilding and remodeling; and a housing shortage that became particularly severe during the two World Wars. Another cause has been the gradual depreciation of real estate values. Low-rent

areas often tend towards slum conditions.

The *housing problem* of inadequate and unsanitary dwelling makes it necessary for government to use its police power in setting certain minimum standards for new dwellings. The government has also helped finance private building projects.

A Tenement House law in 1867 for New York City forbade a tenement to cover all the lot—the law provided that there must be a 10 foot yard in the rear. Running water was required, but a backyard spigot fulfilled this requirements. Basement rooms for dwellings had to have a ceiling at least one foot above the side-walk level. The London County Council, created by the Local Government Act of 1888, investigated slums and began to build model tenements.

In the 1890's the reform that was started in New York spread to Boston, Philadelphia, Chicago and other American cities. They adopted laws to restrict and regulate new tenements. In 1901 New York established a Tenement House Department, and other cities followed. This department made regular inspections of tenements by city officials and enforced new regulations—water supply in each apartment, minimum size of rooms and minimum window space, maximum percentage of building lot to be occupied by building, maximum height of building. New state laws on housing —notably in Indiana, Michigan, Iowa and California—carried these restrictions much further. The City Code of Minneapolis during the years 1917 to 1919 made outstanding contributions in this line.

In the years during and following World War I, there was some public interest in housing, but it was largely confined to congested urban areas. The world economic depression of the 1930s saw an almost complete stoppage of home building. Then came World War II with only emergency housing programs. War time conditions had induced an acceleration in the marriage and birth rates and consequently an increasing need for housing.

The first effort at public housing on a large scale was provided for in the National Industrial Recovery Act (NIRA) and the organization of the Home Owners' Loan Corporation (HOLC) June 13, 1933. The aid however was primarily to save homes already constructed rather than to build new ones. These initial measures were followed by the National Housing Act of 1934, creating a national housing administration which had for its objectives the encouragement and the financing of housing construction and the providing of employment.

The first serious approach to the housing problem was made in 1937 when the U.S. Housing Authority was created under the National Housing Act. It was empowered to make loans over a period of three years to local housing agencies to cover the difference between an economic rent and the rent the low income groups could afford to pay. Provision was also made for loans for slum clearance and low cost hous-

POVERTY, and poor living conditions can be found in all sections of the U.S. (*right*). Cramped quarters accommodating many people may be due to many causes: housing shortage, a change in standards of living, low income, and large families. These constitute slums. Low cost housing development (*left*), are part of the slum clearance project. Financed by the government, they are designed to provide families with healthy living conditions at low cost and, at the same time, destroy inadequate and unsanitary slum dwellings.

ing. In all cases the Federal Housing Administration loaned money to state and local boards and authorities and in a sense underwrote the projects. All construction work was performed under the direction of these local housing agencies. Provisions for those better off but lacking funds had been made in the Home Owners' Loan Act of 1933.

There have been various groupings of the federal housing and local authorities. In July 1947 the Housing and Home Finance Agency was established to provide a single permanent agency responsible for the principal housing programs and to fulfill the functions of the Federal Government. This Agency was made up of

(1) The National Housing Council, a policy-making body.

(2) The Home Loan Bank Board under which were the Federal Home Loan Bank System for making loans to banks and through them to veterans, the Federal Savings and Loan Insurance Corporation for Savings, and the Home Owners' Loan Corporation, liquidated in 1936, for granting long term, low interest mortgage loans to home owners.

(3) The Federal Housing Administration for insuring accredited lenders of housing loans.

(4) The Public Housing Administration to liquidate war emergency public housing and to render financial assistance for low-cost housing and slum clearance.

In addition to Federal aid in housing, some states and cities have initiated housing programs on a large scale. Their function has been to advance the necessary funds to builders, at the same time maintaining a certain control as to occupancy and use. In 1965, the Department of Housing and Urban Development was established, with Cabinet rank.

Immigration, moving from one country *into* another. Moving from one's own country is *emigration*. The governments of both the countries involved are of course interested in this motion. They have, therefore, set up many forms of control.

All through the 19th century there was a continuous flow of migration from Europe to the New World with little or no control. The United States, Canada and, to a very little less degree, Central and South America are composed entirely of immigrants and descendants of immigrants. In the 10 years from 1847 through 1856 about 3,000,000 immigrants came to the United States, many of them driven from Ireland by the terrible potato famine or from Germany by the failure of the Revolution of 1848. After 1880 more immigrants came here from southern and especially southeastern Europe than from northern and western Europe, which had previously made the largest contribution. In the 10 years ending 1910 about 6,000,000 came from the south against 2,000,000 from the north; and in the next 5 years 3,000,000 (out of a total of 3,800,000) were from southern Europe.

In much the same way that American manufacturers persuaded Congress to put a heavy tariff on foreign-made goods, organized labor urged Congress to protect the American workingman by forbidding and limiting immigration. Chinese coolies had come to California at the time of the Gold Rush in 1849, and they had worked on the transcontinental railroads. In 1882 the first Chinese Exclusion Act was passed. In 1885 an Alien Contract Labor law forbade the entry into the United States of anyone under contract "to perform labor or service of any kind."

Later laws aimed to improve the quality of the immigration. An act of 1917 excluded illiterates over 16 years of age. Quota acts were passed in 1921, 1924 and 1929, limiting the number of immigrants from each country. The total number that can be admitted from Europe in any year is 150,000. The maximum from each country is 2 per cent of the foreign-born from that country that were in the United States at the time of the census of 1890 (when south European immigration had not yet set in.) As a result of these laws the number of English-speaking immigrants in 1927 was a little more than in 1914; but the number of non-English-speaking immigrants in 1927 was only about one-fifth as much as it had been in 1914.

All Asiatics (Chinese, Japanese and others) are excluded except students and professional men and their families.

The Chinese hurried into Australia at the time (1851) of the gold rush there, as they had come to California in '49. They were immensely unpopular. The different states adopted legislation against Chinese immigration, and one reason why the Australian federation was adopted was that the strong Labour party clamored for uniform laws against Chinese and Japanese throughout Australia. Both Chinese and Japanese as well as Asiatics who are British subjects are now excluded in effect by a law that refuses entry to anyone who cannot write from dictation 50 words in his own or some other language. Between 1905 and 1914 no alien passed this test.

In New Zealand a poll tax of £100 on immigrants of alien race keeps out Asiatics. In Canada the tax on Asiatics was set at $50 in 1886 and at $500 in 1904, and a law of 1923 permits the entrance of Asiatics only if they do not belong to the laboring class.

The home government in England, especially after World War I, made efforts to aid emigration to the different parts of the Empire. Up to 1926 (when there was no longer a demand for labor) the Dominion of New Zealand, co-operating with the London authorities, assisted immigration from Great Britain by free transportation or reduced rates. This assistance was granted only to a person whom a New Zealander of recognized standing agreed to employ. The last year this was in force (1926) more than 10,000 immigrants were assisted by the Government.

World War I produced new conditions affecting immigration into the United States. In 1921 an act of Congress limited immigration to a quota of 3% of the foreign-born based on the 1910 census; this quota was further reduced by the Johnson act of 1924 to 2% of the 1890 census of recorded foreign-born. This law, which favored immigrants from northern Europe, reduced annual immigration into the United States for permanent residence to about 150,000. This figure was increased in varying amounts by special amendments, one of the most important of which was that relating to the granting of temporary visas in excess of quota. This provision permitted a stay usually of six months before quitting the country.

An additional quota of Displaced Persons from European areas, made homeless because of World War II, was permitted. Those immigrants above the quota allowance were charged off or mortgaged against quotas for future years. The purpose was to find asylum for D.P.'s who had no homes and who desired to escape from conditions under which they had to live.

Immigration from Europe to the United States was restrained in some measure by the home countries, especially emigration from Russia and its satellite countries in eastern Europe and the Balkans. In the latter case emigration was prohibited by government decree.

Another immigration movement on a large scale was that of Jews from all parts of the world into the state of Israel where they established for themselves a homeland of which they had dreamed for many years.

Impeachment, an accusation of wrongdoing brought against a government official by an authorized legislative body. The constitution of the United States provides that the House of Representatives has the sole power to impeach an officer of the United States' government. A majority vote is required for impeachment. The Senate, acting as a judicial body, tries the case. The Chief Justice of the Supreme Court is the presiding officer. A two-thirds' vote of the Senators present is necessary for conviction. Andrew Johnson, the only President of the United States to be impeached (1868), was acquitted.

Imperialism, a policy of colonial expansion and overseas conquest, particularly for commercial purposes. The colonization of America by the Spanish, French, Dutch and English is one example of imperialism. Another is the division of Africa among the great Powers in the last part of the 19th century. The Spanish American War of 1898, England's war with the Boer republics of South Africa, the Japanese expansion into Korea, Manchuria and China and the Italian conquest of Ethiopia in 1934-36 are examples of imperialism in a violent form excused in each instance by the theory that the aggressor has a mission to civilize a more backward nation.

Indeterminate sentence, one that gives a minimum and a maximum term but leaves the precise time that must be served to administrative officers. A sentence of 1 year to 10 years means that the prisoner must serve at least 1 year but cannot be held longer than 10 years. The purpose—to permit a prisoner's release when his reformation has been effected—is a distinctive factor in the new and more flexible type of criminology.

Indictment (from French *inditer,* meaning to indicate or point out), a formal accusation of a crime against one or more persons, laid before a grand jury. When the grand jury finds sufficient evidence to warrant holding the accused for trial in court, the indictment is endorsed and called a *true bill of indictment.* Often the word *indictment* alone is loosely used for this finding of the grand jury.

Infant, one under legal age, a minor. Legal infancy ends the first instant of the day before a person is 21 years old. In a few states a girl comes of age at 18, except for voting. In most states an infant of 14 has reached the age of discretion, is held responsible for criminal acts and may choose a guardian. An infant cannot act for himself in court, so a guardian or next friend must act for him.

Information, a formal accusation by a prosecuting attorney or other government officer that is the basis for prosecution without any action by a grand jury. Some states of the United States have done away with the grand jury, and in these states information there takes the place of indictment. But the Federal Constitution and some state constitutions forbid any prosecution for "a capital or other infamous crime unless on a presentment or indictment of a grand jury, except in cases arising in the land or naval forces or in the militia in actual service." In England information by court officials has taken the place of indictment by grand juries as a preliminary to the trial of a criminal.

Initiative and **Referendum,** two forms of direct legislation by the voters of a state.

Initiative is literally the power or right to originate a law; because the Federal Constitution provides (Art. 1, Sec. 7, Cl. 1) that "all bills for raising revenue shall originate in the House of Representatives," we may say that the House of Representatives has the initiative in revenue measures. In the special sense initiative is the right (under certain state constitutions and a few city charters) of the people to originate laws by securing a petition signed by a certain number of voters or a certain fraction of the total number and then by voting on the proposed measure, which becomes a law if it receives the required majority.

Referendum means literally "to be referred." It is the practice of submitting for popular approval or disapproval a measure passed by a legislature.

These two methods of democratic legislation were known in Greece, but in modern times they seem to have originated in the Swiss cantons and in the Swiss Federal Government. In 1831 the canton of St. Gall adopted a method of referendum by which the voters might petition that a measure be referred to them. This was called a *facultative referendum* and sometimes a *veto.* The *compulsory* or *obligatory referendum* did not follow a petition: it was required by the constitution in the case of certain laws—they must be referred to the people and approved to become operative. Any measure now passed by the Federal Assembly must be referred to the people if 30,000 signers petition for the referendum, and then it becomes law only on a majority vote at the referendum election. The *initiative* was first used in the canton of Vaud in 1845.

In the United States the common method of amending state constitutions is by a referendum to the voters of the state after the action of the legislature. (Delaware does not require a referendum; two successive legislatures may amend the constitution. In New Hampshire the people vote every 7 years as to whether the constitution needs amendment; but amendments are adopted by the constitutional convention without reference to the voters.) In states where the constitution may be amended by a constitutional convention, the question of calling the convention is sometimes submitted to the voters. New York state requires the approval of the voters to amendments adopted by the convention; and most state constitutional conventions refer their amendments to the voters even if this is not required by law. In Oregon the state constitution may be amended: at a referendum election after approval by the legislature; by popular initiative; or by a referendum vote after a constitutional convention, which can be called only after the question has been referred to the voters.

Initiative and referendum on other than constitutional matters appeared in American state governments at the turn of the century: South Dakota (1898), Utah (1900), Oregon (1902), Nevada (1904), Montana (1906), Oklahoma (1907), Maine, Missouri and Michigan (all 1908), Arkansas and Colorado (1910), California and Arizona (1911), Idaho, Ohio, Nebraska and Washington (1912) were among the first.

The referendum was extensively used in Australia and New Zealand,

Injunction, a writ of court ordering the performance of an act that the court believes is essential to justice, or prohibiting an act that is believed to be contrary to equity and justice. A *preliminary injunction*

is issued to restrain the doing or continuing of the act alleged to be wrongful until the rights of the parties can be settled. It is issued only when the court believes that irreparable harm will result before the case is settled. A *full* or *permanent* injunction is issued after a hearing.

The injunction has been important in American labor history. Its use was begun in the 1880s and first came to general public notice in the Pullman strike of 1894 when it was used against Eugene Debs and his American Railway Union. The use of the injunction was bitterly fought by the American Federation of Labor, but without much success.

A clause in the Clayton Act of 1914 was hailed as putting an end to the injunctive process against labor unions, but subsequent Supreme Court decisions did not support this opinion. The Norris-LaGuardia Act (1932) imposed more rigorous restrictions on the courts, but it was not until the enactment of the National Industrial Recovery Act in 1933 and the Wagner Act (1935) that labor leaders felt free of the injunctive threat. Because of the abuse of power the right to use injunctions in labor disputes was restored first in the war-time Smith-Connally Act (1943) and then in the Taft-Hartley Act(1947). It has been exercised on several occasions recently, particularly in connection with coal and railroad labor disputes.

In personam and **In rem.** *In personam* means an action against a person; *in rem* means an action against the thing. An action *in rem* may be against a ship or other specified object to regain possession of it when the defendant cannot be found but the property is in the court's jurisdiction; or it may be an action regarding the status of a person, such as marriage, divorce or settlement. In such a case, the status is the thing that the legal action is directed to and not the persons. The more usual legal action is against a person or persons; actions in tort and contract are actions *in personam.*

Inquest, inquiry or investigation, especially the inquiry of a coroner's jury, actually seeing the corpse of anyone who has died in suspicious circumstances or (when a death certificate has been refused by a physician) hearing testimony of doctors and of lay witnesses and giving a verdict whether death was by natural cause, suicide or homicide. If the verdict is homicide, the coroner's jury tells at whose hands the death occurred or uses the phrase "at the hands of person or persons unknown." An inquest to fix damages is the inquiry of a jury appointed to determine the amount of damages in a case where there is no question of law. The word *inquest* is also used of the jury that holds the inquiry and of the jury's finding.

Insanity, an unsound mental condition. Insanity is not generally considered as a legal term. The law merely attempts to ascertain whether a person has sufficient soundness of mind to be competent to perform certain acts or to be responsible for acts committed.

BUREAU OF INDIAN AFFAIRS

OFFICE OF INDIAN AFFAIRS is concerned with the management of various Indian tribes. Federal schools enrolling Indian children teach English as a second language, since 82 per cent of the children are full-blooded Indians coming from homes where only the Indian language is spoken. In this Navajo classroom, listening skills are being developed.

The test of mental unsoundness is not necessarily the same in a proceeding to appoint a guardian for a person alleged to be insane and in a criminal action seeking to hold the person allegedly insane for his wrongful conduct. In criminal action in some states, the English rule (McNaghten's case, 1843) is applied: Did the accused know that the act he committed was wrong? In other states, insanity is interpreted as a mad, irresistible impulse, independent of any ability to distinguish between right and wrong.

Insolvency, the state of a person whose total property and other assets are insufficient to pay his debts; a general inability to pay debts when they are due. As used by the courts, the term is virtually synonymous with bankruptcy. Insolvency laws are state statutes governing insolvency; similar Federal regulations are called *bankruptcy* laws.

Interior, Department of the, one of the 10 executive departments of the United States Government, whose head, the Secretary of the Interior, is a member of the President's Cabinet. The department was organized in 1849, when it was called the Home Department, and it now contains the following important offices and bureaus: Land Management, Bureau of Indian Affairs, Geological Survey, Bureau of Mines, Bureau of Reclamation, National Park Service, Petroleum Conservation, Fish and Wild Life, Division of Territories and Inland Possessions, Bonneville Power Administration, Alaska Railroad, etc. Under the Connally "Hot Oil" Act (1935), the department is concerned with oil development, including production and distribution.

Internal Revenue (called *inland revenue* in England), the Government's income from domestic taxes as distinct from its income from customs or tariffs and from its income from its own property and services. The enormously increasing cost of government makes it necessary that total revenue should be much larger than it was before the year 1916. At the same time, the drop in international trade has made it almost impossible to increase the revenue from

customs taxes on imports. Hence, there has been an enormous increase in the amount of internal revenue as will be seen from these figures.

U. S. Customs and Internal Revenue Receipts by Fiscal Years

	Customs (Millions of dollars)	Internal (Millions of dollars)
1911	314.5	322.5
1916	213.2	512.7
1921	308.6	4,595.4
1926	579.4	2,836.0
1931	378.3	2,428.0
1936	386.8	3,512.9
1947	494.1	39,379.0
1949	384.5	40,308.0
1954	590	69,920.0

The main items in the 1954 internal revenue total were:

	(Millions of dollars)
Income Tax:	
Corporations	21,483
Individuals	32,433
Excess Profits	63
Estate and gift taxes	935
Alcoholic beverages	2,783
Tobacco	1,580
Stamp taxes	90
Manufacturers' and retailers' excise taxes	3,127
Miscellaneous	1,937

These figures are all national revenue. All local taxation produces another class of internal revenue.

The U. S. Treasury Department has commissioners of Internal Revenue, Narcotics and Customs. In England the Board of Inland Revenue, the Post Office and the Customs are in charge of the public revenue.

International law or **Law of nations,** the rules governing the conduct and relations of countries or states toward one another.

International law differs very materially from the acts of parliaments or national congresses and the laws of state legislatures but in general purpose resembles national or state law.

Rights of the states of the world demand recognition and protection. Chief among these rights is that of a nation to independence and the privilege of maintaining its own chosen form of government without outside interference, unless in the exercise of that right the security of neighbor states is threatened. A state must be assured of jurisdiction without interference from outside over its own territory and the people therein.

If the seas belong to all states in common, there must be recognition of the right of each to freedom of navigation. To safeguard the interests of all, the waters of the oceans and seas are considered a part of the mainland of each country for a distance of 3 miles from shore; the ships of no nation have a right to sail inside this 3-mile limit of other lands without permission, but of course except in time of war all vessels are welcome in territorial waters everywhere. All waters beyond this limit constitute the *high seas.*

International law has become more and more of a necessity as relationships between countries have grown closer. There is a need for close cooperation between the nations to codify and agree on certain laws. The International Court of Justice of the United Nations is attempting to fill this position. It functions as a judicial organ and its primary weakness lies in the fact that there is no police force to see that all countries abide by the rules agreed to. One favorable sign in this constant disagreement has been the fact that the International Law Association has continued to meet despite two World Wars. A law of nations can only exist if there is rational legal thinking on an international plane and if there is "an equilibrium, a balance of power between nations."

The sources of international law are numerous; they consist very largely in treaties made from time to time; in conventions or congresses of the powers wherein principles for international guidance are set forth; and in solemn declarations of a great power that in time other nations accept as a rule of international conduct. As an example of the latter, the Monroe Doctrine (United States, 1823) was denounced in Europe for many years, but the insistence of the United States in upholding its principles brought eventual recognition of its binding character. Great Britain once claimed the right to search foreign vessels and take therefrom seamen suspected of being English subjects on the theory "once an Englishman always an Englishman." The War of 1812 was fought in part in opposition to this right; and as a result of the war, the unwritten law of safety under any flag has not since been questioned.

A declaration of war brings into effect between the contending parties (known as *belligerents*) that branch of international law known as the *Laws of War.* Other nations, *neutrals,* not involved in the actual war, have new obligations imposed upon them. They must not give aid or comfort to any of the belligerents; if citizens of a neutral country violate neutrality they cannot count on their government to avert punishment.

Private International Law or *conflict of laws* is often considered as a

part of international law; but private international law relates to the reference by one state with the laws of another. Thus if a contract is made in Germany and an action on it is brought in the courts in New York, that court ordinarily will enforce the contract according to the laws of Germany. Therefore private international law is enforced by the courts of a nation and is part of the law of that nation and not properly the law between nations. International law is the *jus inter gentes;* the conflict of laws refers to the *jus gentium.*

Interpellation (French, challenge, interruption, question), in French legislative procedure a challenge to a ministerial policy by a formal question put by any member of the National Assembly. The question is written. It may not apply to the budget. To a question on foreign policy the Minister of Foreign Affairs may refuse an answer for reasons of state. The Chamber sets a date for the answer to an interpellation and debates and discusses the answer when it is given. If the vote after discussion is unfavorable to the explanation given in the answer, the ministry is forced to resign.

Interstate Commerce Commission, an independent Federal Government authority of 11 members (originally 5), serving 7 years with overlapping terms, appointed by the President under the Interstate Commerce Act of 1887 to regulate commerce between the states by rail. In 1885 the U.S. Senate had investigated railways, and the Act of 1887 was a result of this investigation. The Hepburn Act of 1926 gave the commission power to fix rates for interstate railways. A law of 1926 gives jurisdiction over interstate air commerce to the Secretary of Commerce; and in 1934 the Federal Communications Commission was created to control the telephone, telegraph and radio. The Commission has judicial powers—it can make decisions as well as enforce the law.

Intestate, without a will, leaving no formal will. When one dies intestate, the court appoints an administrator to apportion the estate among the lawful heirs.

Iron Curtain, a phrase first used by Joseph Goebbels, German Nazi propaganda minister, after the Yalta conference when he said: ". . . the Soviets will occupy the whole east and southeast of Europe. In front of this enormous territory an iron curtain will go down . . ." Winston Churchill gave currency to the phrase in a speech at Fulton, Mo. in the summer of 1946, as describing the wall of secrecy behind which the Russian Soviet Government operated and by means of which it could control information to the Russian people from the outside world.

Issue, in a legal action the controverted or material point of law or fact that a trial is to determine. When the issue is joined, that is, when pleading comes to the point where one side denies and the other affirms this matter in dispute, the case proceeds to trial.

Judgment, a decision rendered by a court in a case submitted to it; a legal award.

Judicial councils, state boards studying court procedure and the reorganization of the judicial system. The movement for reform by this means began in 1922, and several states have adopted it.

Judicial review, the power of a higher court to rule on the decisions of a lower court by reason of its appellate jurisdiction. In a special sense the term is limited to the lawmaking power of the courts, as their interpretations of statutes and their decisions on the constitutionality of laws actually create the fundamental law of the land.

Jury, a group, usually 12 in number, formally selected and put on oath to return a verdict or true answer on a matter in controversy. The jury is a part of the common-law system as distinct from equity. It is judge of the facts not of the law in any controversy. The origin of the English jury system seems to have been in the inquest of the Frankish kings in the 6th or 7th century. The custom was brought into England with the Normans—instead of trial by battle they used a method of sworn inquiry before a jury.

They right of jury trial is a part of free institutions throughout the British Empire and the United States. A man has the privilege of being tried by a jury of his peers, that is, of his equals, those of his own class.

A *grand jury* is a large group, usually 12 to 23 members, which examines accusations of criminal charges as a preliminary to trial. Trial follows the grand jury's true bill of indictment, a verdict that there is ground for action. The grand jury is a county institution. Some states of the United States have abolished the grand jury or limited its activities. In England grand juries no longer indict criminals, but court officials lodge an information.

The *petit* (or petty, small) *jury,* as distinct from the grand jury, tries and decides the facts of cases in court—unless the accused agrees to trial without jury. The term *jury* is ordinarily applied distinctively to this body. The petit jury is chosen from a sheriff's panel or list of possible jurors. In criminal cases, from those summoned for a term of court, the judge, the prosecuting attorney and the attorney for the defense choose 12 by a rather elaborate process of questioning. On formal exception or objection (by either attorney) to the service of any juror (called a challenge), that juror may not serve. Challenge may be *for cause,* with an expressed reason; or *peremptory,* without any reason being given. The number of peremptory challenges allowed varies in different cases. The procedure of examination, cross-examination and challenge of jurors often produces long delays in trials; but the foundation is an attempt to secure unbiased jurors and thus assure justice.

The 12 jurors must agree in their verdict; if there is no agreement, a new trial must be held. A constitutional amendment in New York state (1937) permits verdicts by 10 of 12 jurymen in civil cases.

Certain occupations are exempt from petit-jury duty—usually all government employees, clergymen, physicians, dentists, pharmacists, attorneys, members of the army, navy, marine corps or fire department.

A California statute in 1917 provided for drawing women on juries; and Connecticut, New Jersey and other states have similar provisions making this duty compulsory for women. Rhode Island law provides that women over 25 may be called on jury duty if the courthouse has suitable accommodations. In Maine no person is disqualified for jury duty "by reason of sex." Women are permitted on juries in 10 states and in the District of Columbia. New York by a law in effect in 1937 allows women to serve or to be excused on their request. South Carolina forbids women serving on juries. About half the states have no specific legislation on the point and have not altered the practice of having only men on juries even though the 19th Amendment has given women the vote and the state law has always said that "all legal voters" are liable to jury duty.

A *coroner's jury* holds an inquest (or investigation) on the cause of a death that seems not due to natural causes. The verdict of a coroner's jury is not an indictment but may be the basis for an indictment or information.

Justice, Department of, an executive division of the Federal Government since 1870. The head of the Department is the Attorney General, a member of the President's Cabinet since the first organization of the Federal Government (see *Attorney General*).

The Department is organized with bureaus and divisions as follows: Office of the Alien Property Custodian, Bureau of Prisons (Federal penal institutions), Immigration and Naturalization Service, Federal Bureau of Investigation (the FBI-men, see *Federal Bureau of Investigation*); these divisions—Antitrust, Claims, Criminal, Customs, Lands and Tax; and the Taxes and Penalties Unit. The Attorney General appoints a Parole Board of five to grant and revoke paroles of Federal prisoners; and the Pardon Attorney investigates applications for clemency and makes recommendations to the President in regard to them.

The Department is responsible for prosecuting Government cases against corporations, individuals, and states.

Justice of the peace, the lowest officer in the judicial system of a state. He is elected as a township official and has limited judicial powers. In states in which there are no periodical grand juries, he may hear evidence in criminal cases sufficient to determine whether the accused shall be held for trial in the county court and may fix the amount of bail to be required. He has full jurisdiction in the disposal of petty civil cases, but from his decisions appeal may be taken. Where there are regular grand juries, the justice of the peace in criminal cases can only bind an accused over to the grand jury.

In the United States the justice of the peace is usually an elected officer, but in a few states he is appointed by the governor.

In England the justice of the peace is "commissioned under the Great Seal to keep the peace," which explains the title. The first justice of the peace was appointed in 1323. Until a generation or so ago only the landed gentry and country squires were justices; but now they are commissioned from every walk of life and from both sexes.

Juvenile court or **Children's court,** a special tribunal to hear cases brought against minors (under 16 in some states, 17 in some, 18 in others). In such a court a child is not treated as a criminal. With his accuser and sponsors he meets the judge in a rather informal way. The judge has a heart-to-heart talk with the offender, and if he finds the child guilty, the youthful offender may be placed upon probation, and an effort is made to care for him in such a way that he will develop into a useful citizen. The court has power to commit the offender to an institution. The first juvenile court was established in Cook County (Chicago), Ill., in 1899. Within 30 years there were children's courts in every state but Maine and Wyoming.

Kidnaping, the crime of forcibly or fraudulently carrying away from its home a child or (by extension of the original meaning of kid for child) a grown person. It is one of the most serious offenses against peace and order; in some states it is a capital offense, in others it may be punished by life imprisonment. The kidnaping of Charles A. Lindbergh's son in 1932 resulted in a Federal law against kidnaping and the development of special crime-detection methods by government agents of the Federal Bureau of Investigation.

King, a ruler in a monarchy, whether it is absolute or constitutional or a dictatorship with only a faint trace of monarcy left.

Our word *king,* German *König,* Danish *konge* and the related Teutonic words seem to mean "descendant of the kin or nobility." The Latin *rex,* French *roi* and Italian *re* are all related to the Indian and Sanskrit word *rājā* (still used of Oriental princes in the form *rajah*); and the root idea seems to be guide, shepherd, pilot, with a figure of speech like that in the word *governor,* which originally meant steersman. In many early communities the king was chief priest or even a god in human form; and the early kings of Rome are half-mythical figures as important in religion as in government. So long as Church and State stayed closely related, the power of the Church made most European kings somewhat sacred, and there grew up the doctrine of divine right, which reached its high point in England with the Stuart kings. The English Civil War crushed that idea. After Cromwell English kings ruled under the authority of Parliament. English Common Law was largely the outgrowth of a long effort on the part of English kings to bring the courts and judges under the Crown. That law is the basis of our law in the United States. Many of the constitutional powers of the President of the United States and of the governors of states are immediately derived from the powers of the English kings—rights of appointment, power of pardon and veto, control of foreign affairs. So the history of kingship has a definite meaning even for our republican government.

There are not so many kings left in the world today, though several kingdoms have been set up since the World War of 1914–18. At the end of World War II several kingdoms, upon whose soil Russia had fought, found their affairs closely aligned with those of Russia; most are republics. The following is a list of countries which have kings: Afghanistan, Belgium, Denmark, Ethiopia, Great Britain (queen), Greece (restored 1935 with less power), Iran, Jordan, Laos, Libya (since 1951), Morocco, Nepal, Netherlands (queen), Norway, Saudi Arabia (a state since World War I), Sweden, Thailand, and Yemen.

World War I put an end to several kingdoms including those of Prussia and Hungary. The King of Portugal had abdicated in 1910 and the King of Spain followed in 1931. World War II ended the regent monarchy in Hungary and also the kingdoms of Italy, Yugoslavia, Bulgaria and Rumania.

Kingdom, a country or territory subject to the jurisdiction of a king. Most modern kingdoms are constitutional monarchies; that is, although executive and legislative authority is vested in the ruler, his power is limited by a constitution and his acts, to become effective, must be countersigned by a cabinet official or minister of state.

Know-Nothing party, a political movement in the period before the Civil War that worked for the election of native Americans to office. The waves of immigration during the 1840s and the concentration of Roman Catholics in the eastern cities led to a resurgence of nativism, and political organizations such as the *American party* aimed at keeping the foreign groups from control of the government. The Know-Nothing party was largely a secret organization and got its name because the members would reply to queries about the party, "I don't know."

Ku Klux Klan, originally a secret hooded organization formed in Pulaski, Tenn. in May 1866 as a youth organization. It soon developed into an agency for disciplining the negroes freed by the Civil War and also against those who supported them and used them. In 1867, at Nashville, Tenn., the Ku Klux Klan was organized as the "Invisible Empire of the South" and for several years operated solely for the purpose of curbing negro actions by intimidation. The Klan was formally disbanded in 1869, but its uniforms, rituals and methods were used by irresponsible men, often for selfish purposes. With the end of Reconstruction in 1877 the Klan practically disappeared. It was revived in 1915 as a product of World War hysteria, but was again disbanded in 1928. It was revived again in the 1940's and gained renewed notoriety in the 1950's and 1960's.

Labor, Department of, an executive division of the Federal Government, established independently in 1913. A Bureau of Labor was set up in the Interior Department in 1884; it became an independent bureau in 1888; and in 1903 a department of Commerce and Labor was organized. It comprises: Labor Statistics (domestic and foreign), Children's Bureau (but only as to child labor) Women's Bureau (promoting the welfare of wage-earning women), bureaus of Labor Standards, Apprenticeship and of Veteran's Reemployment Rights. It also includes the Wages and Hours and Public Contracts Division and the Office of International Labor Affairs. Many of its responsibilities were transferred to the Health, Education, Welfare Dept. The Department undertakes to promote the welfare of wage earners, improve their working conditions, and further their opportunities for employment.

Lame Duck Amendment, the 20th Amendment to the Constitution of the United States, proposed in 1932 and adopted in 1933, making the terms of Senators and representatives end on January 3 instead of on March 3. This put a stop to sessions of Congress in which there sat representatives or senators who had not been re-elected. Such members were called lame ducks because they were disabled, had lost the support of their constituencies. New members of Congress now take their seats within 2 months of their election instead of waiting more than a year until December of the year after their election.

Land. Government policies about distributing public land and the various forms of land tenure have been very important in politics and history. *Public land (ager publicus)* was a matter of constant controversy in the Roman republic where the state was constantly expanding by conquest of new territory, first in Italy and later in every part of the circle of lands around the Mediterranean. The common people received grants of this land sometimes as the result of efforts to reform the social conditions of Rome, sometimes as a gift or bribe to win favor for a political group. There were special grants to veterans of the Roman army.

The whole feudal system of Europe in the Middle Ages was based on the principle that land was held by grant from a superior. In England the Norman Conquest in 1066 introduced this system under which the king became owner of almost all lands, which he granted to his noble followers subject to the payment of certain dues and services. In turn the nobles could make similar grants. Lands thus granted were inherited by the oldest surviving male son; this practice is called *primogeniture*. The results of the feudal system still affect life in England and Ireland. Many large estates belonging to certain families for centuries were split up and parts of them sold in the depression years after World War I; but the evil absentee landlords, for example, English owners of great areas in Ireland managed by agents and rented to small farmers, has not been entirely abolished. In the 19th century much common land was taken over by Eng-

lish cities and boroughs, which bought off the nobles who had some claim to part ownership.

Free land was the bait that drew settlers to America. It was granted in one way or another by the English Crown—and the claim was one of conquest.

Even before the present government of the United States was set up, the Continental Congress passed laws governing the distribution of public lands in the Northwest. From the Land Ordinance of 1785 down to the Morrill Act of 1862, Congress granted lands for the support of schools and colleges. In 1785 a settler could buy 640 acres at $1 an acre. In 1796 the price had doubled. In 1820 the minimum area that could be bought was reduced to 80 acres and the price to $1.25 an acre. For 20 years after 1840 there was agitation for free distribution of lands. "Vote yourself a farm" was the slogan of demagogues. A bill for free grants was defeated in Congress in 1852. President Buchanan vetoed another in 1860.

In 1862 the Morrill Act granted lands for agricultural and mechanical colleges, and the Homestead Act threw open public lands to settlement in 160-acre units, by grown citizens and by aliens who had declared their intention of becoming citizens. The distribution undoubtedly checked radical and socialist tendencies by giving to those who might have become dangerously discontented the opportunity to hold land. In 1862 the Federal Government authorized building the Union Pacific Railroad and granted it 20 sections (that is, 20 square miles) for each mile of the railroad. In 1864 public lands with coal on them were put on sale at $25 an acre.

The states had long before abolished the right of primogeniture with the result that large estates were being divided from generation to generation instead of being kept intact in the possession of the eldest son. Now the western states passed homestead exemption laws, which made the free lands given to settlers free from seizure for debt. The land policy of the Federal Government and the state governments hastened the settlement of the West. In 1900 there was little public land left. The era of homestead distribution was ended. It had been extravagant and reckless. Valuable timber had been cut to clear land for the plow. Overplowing had produced erosion—good land gone bad. Many settlers had picked bad land in the first place. In 1895 the Federal Government transferred to the states arid land that was not fit for farming.

Two new policies appeared—conservation and reclamation—to attempt a remedy for extravagance and waste. A law of 1891 authorized the President to reserve lands covered with timber or undergrowth—and President Theodore Roosevelt brought the total of forest reservations up to 150,-000,000 acres. The Reclamation Act of 1902 created a Bureau of Reclamation in the Department of the Interior to reclaim desert lands by irrigation. Hoover Dam on the Colorado River,

the Grand Coulee Dam on the Columbia and the Central Valley project on the Sacramento and San Joaquin rivers in California are great public works supervised by this bureau. The work of conservation was expanded to a huge scale by the establishment in 1933 of the Civilian Conservation Corps, which put to work at conservation tasks hundreds of thousands of unemployed young men.

The Department of Agriculture is the government agency under which projects pertaining to flood control, soil erosion, reforestation, etc., have been initiated. Under the direction of the Secretary of Agriculture, new uses and capabilities of land have been established. He has also directed the formation of both rural and suburban resettlement projects.

The boldest and most comprehensive reclamation and conservation project is that of the Tennessee Valley Authority (TVA). It covers all aspects of the land question, particularly those pertaining to electric power and irrigation. The success of this project has furthered similar developments in other parts of the country, some as huge as TVA.

Larceny, carrying away personal property of another with the intent to appropriate it to one's own use without the owner's knowledge or consent. Most states include carrying away or *asportation* as a part of the definition of larceny, but there is a tendency to consider this an unimportant factor —Texas has abolished the rule that asportation is necessary to constitute larceny. Larceny differs from burglary because it is without breaking and entering. If the value of goods taken does not exceed $15 (in some states $25), the crime is *petit* larceny; if it is more than that amount, *grand* larceny.

Law merchant, the Norman English translation of *lex mercatoria* or *lex mercatorum,* the laws that apply to trade. During the Middle Ages throughout the commercial world of Europe the practices and customs of merchants constituted this law merchant, which was administered by a group of separate courts that operated side by side with the king's courts: the *pie poudre* courts (literally, dusty-foot courts) for itinerant merchants, which tried cases at every fair or market; and the staple courts held at staple markets selling wool and leather, where alien merchants were tried by juries of foreigners. Cases were tried speedily and on the spot, and this peculiar jurisdiction avoided the conflict that would otherwise have occurred between local and foreign law. Later the law merchant was administered by the common-law courts, and certain of its principles were adopted, especially those regarding negotiable instruments. Now the same term is used sometimes to apply to all laws dealing with trade— partnerships, joint-stock companies, agency, contracts, negotiable papers.

Leader, a literal translation of the official titles of the German dictator, *Fuehrer,* and the Italian, *Duce.*

In each house of the U.S. Congress

and in the state legislatures a *floor leader* is chosen by each party to have charge of the party in the legislature. The majority leader has enormous power and influence. With the minority leader he decides who shall speak on certain measures and how much time shall be allowed for debate. The floor leader of the majority party is head of an informal steering committee that controls the procedure of the House.

Lease, a written contract for the possession and profits of land and tenements for a fixed period of time, for life or during the pleasure of the parties. If tenure is for less than a year, the agreement may be oral. The privileges and obligations of each party are an essential part of the contract. The owner is the *lessor;* the one in possession is the *lessee* or tenant. The compensation to the lessor is *rent.* The lessee's holding is a *tenancy,* and the right of the landlord is called a *reversion.*

Legal tender, money offered at the right time and place, which the law compels one to accept in payment of obligations due him. Not all money is legal tender. One is not obliged to accept copper cents to an amount exceeding 25 cents. A tender of 50 silver half-dollars to extinguish a $25 debt is not legal; half-dollars are legal tender to the amount of $10 only. In spite of the law, creditors usually accept what is offered, unless the tender proves inconvenient to handle.

Legislation, lawmaking, usually in the restricted sense of making statutes or ordinances through a body called a *legislature,* assembly or council—usually a group representing the people. In a wider sense there is legislation by the courts as they interpret the law made by the legislature.

In most governments, the legislative power resides with the group that can raise and appropriate money; lawmaking includes taxation; lawmaking includes the authority to say how revenues shall be spent.

The lawmaking power of the executive, from the strictly legal point of view, consists only in his veto. This power has been constantly exercised by the President of the United States, by governors of states and by mayors of American cities The pressure of a strong executive exerted on the legislature may make the executive the lawmaker in fact if not in law, the legislature giving its stamp of approval on proposed legislation prepared and handed to it for affirmative action.

Early in the New Deal of the 1930's, for example, bills prepared at executive direction were sent to Congress and were often enacted without debate. Congress and the executive learned that such laws, many of them hastily and loosely drawn, to be effective should be sufficiently explicit to contain designated rather than general grants of power. During these years, Congress delegated so much of its power to the President that it became a "rubber stamp." Gradually, however, much of this delegated power was regained.

The field that is covered by legisla-

tion is constantly widening; social security, maximum hours, minimum wages, workmen's compensation, housing, farm subsidies, soil conservation programs are new subjects for legislation.

Interested special groups are always bringing pressure to bear on Congress and on state legislatures to act favorably on measures they approve and to vote against measures that these groups fear or disapprove. The voters have some powers of starting laws by the processes of *initiative* and *referendum.*

A development in the United States has been the growth in power and authority of the administrative or independent agency. Some of these bodies such as the National Labor Relations Board (NLRB) have become quasi-legislative and quasi-judicial bodies. They have indicated the legislation desired and then interpreted and enforced the legislation in accordance with their own desires and interpretat that of social and labor legislation, has thus been built up that has acquired the force and effect of law. Only rarely has legislation so interpreted been overthrown by the courts, both because the field of interpretation, particularly that of social and labor legislation, has been new and because the courts and the independent agencies have viewed the interpretations as desireable.

Delegated legislation is common in England. The Privy Council issues detailed applications of many acts of Parliament, and every department of the Government makes regulations that are law. In France, the Council of Ministers and the Council of State work out the methods of applying the laws passed by the National Assembly.

Legislature, the lawmaking body of a state, consisting of one or two branches (usually two), called the *Senate* and *House of Representatives.* In some states the name *General Assembly* is the legal designation. The presiding officer of the Senate is the lieutenant governor of the state; of the House, a speaker, chosen from the membership.

Lend-Lease, a system of mutual and reciprocal aid, initiated by the Lend-Lease Act of March 11, 1941, under which the United Nations operated during World War II. The act constituted an immense delegation of power to the President, but received the sanction of Congress. It was immediately marked by the lend-lease transfer of 50 old-age destroyers to Great Britain in exchange for 99 year leases to the United States of rights to naval bases in the Caribbean, Guiana, Newfoundland, and Bermuda. Also, vast quantities of military supplies were sent to Russia and other allied countries on the authority of the Lend-Lease Act.

During the period Lend-Lease was in effect, over $47,500,000,000. worth of supplies, munitions, grants and credits were made. By 1947 final settlements of Lend-Lease accounts had been made by the United States with all countries which had participated except China and Russia.

Libel (from Latin *libellum,* little book or pamphlet, handbill), a public or published defamation of character that exposed the person who is defamed to

contempt, ridicule or public hatred. Slander is mere spoken defamation. There can be no libel without *publication,* that is, the defamatory matter must be made known to persons other than the injured party. Truth is a defense against a civil action for libel, except (in some states) where a malicious intent is shown. Truth is not a defense in a criminal prosecution for libel, except where it has been so provided by statute. Other defenses of libel are: *fair comment,* honest and fair criticism of a public official, for example; *privilege,* absolute or qualified, the right of legislators or of witnesses under oath (absolute) or in a confidential relationship of lawyer and client (qualified privilege).

A person who has been guilty of libel or slander may be sued by the injured party for money damages or the state may bring a criminal action to punish the offender by imprisonment.

Liberal Republican party, formed in 1872 by Republicans who were opposed to Grant because of the corruption during his first term of office. Horace Greeley was nominated for President, but the other leaders charged political chicanery and failed to give their whole-hearted support. Grant was elected by a vote of 286 to 63 in the electoral college.

Liberty party, an antislavery political party formed by the Abolitionists in 1840 under the leadership of Joseph G. Birney and John G. Whittier, the poet. It showed some strength in local elections, but in 1848 it formed part of the Free-Soil party and later its leaders were instrumental in founding the Republican party.

License (from Latin *licet,* it is allowed; contrast *illicit,* meaning illegal), permission or authority to do a certain thing that would be illegal without such permission or authority. The permission may come from a private individual or corporation, as in the license of patent rights to a manufacturer, like the famous Selden patent (1895) licensed to most American makers of motor cars in 1903–11. Such licenses usually pay a royalty on sales or on units produced. The permission is often from the Government, which under certain conditions and fees allows the licensee to carry on a business that would be illegal without a government permit. The commonest sort of license from government authority is permission to manufacture and sell intoxicating liquors. Licenses are issued by appropriate authorities to permit fishing and hunting, keeping a dog, driving a motor car, running a hotel or restaurant, practicing such professions as medicine and dentistry.

Lien (French, a bond or tie), the right of a creditor who holds property of a debtor to retain possession until the debt is satisfied; in general, any charge upon property, real or personal, to satisfy a debt. If the debt is for material furnished or for wages due in the construction or repair of a building, the lien is called a *mechanics'* or *material man's* lien. A *carrier's* lien is for unpaid charges on freight; a *tax* lien is made for unpaid taxes.

Limitations, Statute of, a law that sets a period after which a claimant cannot sue. Most states require a defendant to claim benefit of the statute; some states make the limitation automatically operative. By Act of Congress "no person shall be prosecuted, tried or punished for treason or other capital offense, willful murder excepted, unless the indictment is found within 3 years next after such treason or capital offense is done and committed." There is no limitation of time within which a prosecution for murder may be commenced. Usually the periods are: 20 years for actions on real-estate title or on sealed contracts, 6 years for personal actions and 2 years for prosecutions of a misdemeanor.

Lobby, any small room or passage; particularly the entrance or waiting room of a hotel or public building; and specifically the public entrance to a legislative meeting place; by extension, the persons who congregate there, especially those who are not members of the legislature but wish to influence legislation. Their attempts to influence legislation are called *lobbying.* They take their most vigorous form when the lobbyist represents a large number of citizens, influential industries, organized labor, associated employers, religious and reforming organizations. Munitions makers try to influence laws about neutrality. Labor unions are eager to secure statutes about strikes and picketing and wages and hours—and so, for different laws on the same subjects, are employers' associations. Government employees and war veterans want pensions.

Lobbying is usually understood as personal influence brought to bear on legislators. But the activity of these pressure groups is various, and in the last few years it has developed into mass demonstrations in the capital city (national or state) of army veterans or farmers needing relief and organized letter or telegram campaigns to legislators.

The power of the lobby in a democratic country like the United States is great. It is responsible for the enactment of much legislation. Lobbies such as the labor lobby and farm lobby in turn break down into special interest lobbies within the group, such as the dairy industry, the live-stock industry, the corn and wheat farmers, etc. Other lobbies are concerned with public utilities, railroads, airplanes, sugar, oil, cotton and the like. There are also lobbies for favorable legislation on civil rights or in the interest of one or another minority group. In recent years, labor and other special interest lobbies who usually represent many thousands of voters have gained many more objectives than the so-called "capitalist" lobbies ever did. Such lobbies represented financial and economic power rather than votes. The power of the votes represented by lobbies and the funds available to them make it difficult to control their activities.

Local government, self-government by a municipality, varied and far from uniform in the United States. In most

CENTRAL OFFICE OF INFORMATION, LONDON

HOUSE OF LORDS, part of England's Parliament, is the highest court of appeal for Great Britain, but only nonhereditary law lords and hereditary lords who served as judges may act. The lord chancellor sits

European countries the government of cities and smaller administrative units is centralized and completely controlled by the national Government. English cities and counties have a uniform method of government laid down by Parliament, and they are immediately subject to the Board of Health. They receive grants from the national Government and raise some revenue by their local taxes.

Local option, a form of delegated legislation by which a certain measure goes into effect in any minor governmental unit only after it has been approved by the voters of that local unit. The sale of liquor and the adoption of daylight-saving time are subjects often referred to local voters giving them an opportunity to exercise home rule on a small scale.

As liquor licensing in the United States is controlled by state laws, but the actual administration is usually by local authorities and the proceeds of license taxes go in part to local government units, the question of local option naturally arose. Two county courts in Georgia in 1833 received from the legislature the right to grant or refuse liquor licenses. In 1838 Connecticut and Rhode Island gave the towns in those states the same power. Local option helped secure state-wide prohibition in many states of the United States; when the National Prohibition Amendment was adopted in 1919, more than two-thirds of the inhabitants of the United States already lived in dry territory, and this was largely due to local option. Norwegian towns in 1894 were

on the woolsack (an ottoman-like sack of red cloth stuffed with wool) in front of the sovereign's throne. The red leather benches on either side are for peers of the realm. At the far end is where verdicts are given.

empowered to stop the local sale of liquor, and only 13 still permitted its sale at the time national prohibition was adopted in Norway during World War I. Scotland had a form of local option from 1920 on.

The adoption of daylight saving time is another subject often referred to local voters giving them an opportunity to exercise home rule on a small scale.

Lords, English, Irish and Scotch noblemen with hereditary titles or with life titles. The hereditary titles descend from father to oldest son (sometimes to an only daughter) and were originally marks of the king's favor. These peers of the realm are not allowed to vote. The lords with hereditary titles are called *lords temporal* to distinguish them from archbishops and bishops of the Church of England, called *lords spiritual,* who have the title for life through their position in the Church. Another group of life lords are the law lords created by legislation since 1876 to sit in the House of Lords as lords of appeal in ordinary.

The House of Lords is part of the Parliament of Great Britain and northern Ireland, now far less important in governmental authority than the House of Commons with which it had equal power until 1911. In 1909 the House of Lords had refused its consent to Lloyd George's budget, which greatly increased taxation on land and other wealth. The Parliament Act of 1911 took from the House of Lords their power to block money bills: if the lords do not approve a tax, loan or appropriation measure within two years after the bill went from the House of Commons, it became a law without their approval. In January 1950, this period of suspensive veto was reduced from two years to one year.

The House of Lords is the highest court of appeal for England, Wales and North Ireland and for Scotland in civil cases; but all members do not act in this court, only the law lords who are nonhereditary members of the House and those hereditary lords who have served as judges.

The number of English hereditary lords in the House is not constitutionally limited. Peeresses (women with hereditary titles) may not sit in the House of Lords. There are 16 representative peers of Scotland. The lords spiritual number 26—the archbishops of Canterbury and of York and 24 bishops of the Church of England.

Many attempts have been made to reform the procedure under which the House of Lords operates. As it is an hereditary body and largely Tory in its outlook it was considered a block to social progress, especially when a Labor government was in power. Packing of the House by the appointment of members known to be in sympathy with the ruling party has been resorted to at times, but a reform of procedure is preferred.

Lynching, the extra-legal execution of an offender by a mob, has been long practiced in the United States. The term is thought to have been derived from a Virginia judge named Lynch.

Lynching is resorted to by local mobs because of the enormity of the crime alleged to have been committed, such as homicide or rape, because of the character or race of the perpetrator, and because of the failure of local law-enforcing agencies to restrain the mob or to impress on it the sureness of quick trial of the offender.

Since 1882 about 5000 persons have been lynched, of whom about 25% were white and the remaining 75% Negro. Lynching has decreased from a total of 130 in 1901 to almost nothing in late years.

Mandamus (Latin, we command), a writ handed down by the superior court, addressed to an inferior court, an official, an individual or a corporation, ordering the performance of some act or public duty therein specified. It refers to things the law requires to be done that have been neglected.

Mandate, a system of government by a trustee; the territory thus governed. Mandates under the League of Nations as provided for in the Treaty of Versailles, 1919, were assigned to various nations to be exercised over former German colonial possessions and former Turkish territories. There were 3 classes of mandates: (1) former Turkish territories to be made independent, including Palestine, Transjordania, Iraq, Syria and Lebanon; (2) German holdings in Africa; and (3) German Southwest Africa and former German possessions in the Pacific Ocean. None of these mandates was to be fortified. This prohibition, however, was violated by Japan in its mandates over the Marshall, Caroline, Ladrones and Pel-

lew islands, all of which were strongly fortified in great secrecy and became important Japanese bases in World War II. After the formation of the United Nations, mandates became known as Trusteeships. The United States, in 1947, was named to the trusteeship of the Marshall, Caroline and Marianna island groups.

Manslaughter, a killing of one person by another without the malice aforethought that characterizes murder. The crime may be voluntary manslaughter, committed in a sudden burst of temper, without desire to kill; or involuntary, when death results from negligence or unlawful act, as speeding in an automobile.

Martial Law, in American procedure, is control of the civil population through the use of military force, after the civil authorities have shown themselves ineffective in meeting an emergency situation. It may be declared by the President of the United States or by the governor of a state and in rare cases by a ranking military officer when such action, in his judgment, is necessary. Martial law is invoked to protect public and private property and to protect life. The Constitution of the United States provides that the Federal Government shall protect the States "on application of the Legislature or of the Executive (when the Legislature c a n n o t be convened) against domestic violence (Art. IV, sec. 4). At such time of martial law, however, "the writ of Habeas Corpus shall not be suspended unless when in cases of Rebellion or Invasion the public's safety may require it. (Art. I, sec. 9)." A famous case denying the right of suspension and military trial was passed on by the U. S. Supreme Court in *Exparte Milligan,* 1866, which Charles Evans Hughes summarized in the statement: "Outside the actual theater of war . . . the right of the citizen to normal judicial procedure is secure."

During a period of martial law, civil rights are usually suspended and trial is in the military courts. As soon as martial law is ended, the civil authorities assume control and those arrested are turned over to them.

At various times during and after the Civil War, martial law was established by Federal troops in some of the Southern states. In 1871 martial law was declared in South Carolina to enforce the 14th amendment. Martial law is usually invoked by the state governors to protect the life and property of the civil population after the civil authorities have failed to do so. Labor disputes and disasters, such as fires and floods, have been two principal reasons for the declaration of martial law. An example of the former was during the railroad strike of 1877 and again during the Colorado coal strikes in the early 1900's; an example of the latter was the declaration of martial law at the time of the San Francisco earthquake in 1906 and at Texas City, Texas, in 1947 after a disastrous explosion and fire. Neither military rule, as in the South during Reconstruction, nor military aid to the civil power is example of martial law, though it may lead to a declaration of martial

law. During recent years, there has been a reluctance on the part of the federal and state government to declare martial law in labor disputes no matter how desirable it may seem. Government seizure of property has not been infrequent, but in such an act there has been no suggestion of martial law.

Mayhem (originally the same word as maim, to disfigure or disable), inflicting an injury upon an adversary that makes him less able to defend himself.

Mayor, the chief executive officer of a city, except in those with charters for a manager or commission government. The word is variation of *major,* greater, superior; under the Frankish kings of the Merovingian line (500-750 A.D.) the major of the palace, *major domus,* superior of the house, became an important official.

In the United States, mayors are now elected by a popular vote, but it is only for a little over a century that this has been the rule. In colonial times, the mayors were appointed by the governor of the colony or in a few cities by the council of the city. The mayor's power has increased; he appoints and can remove many administrative officials and department heads; has executive and legislative power; and may be on the board of estimate or otherwise in financial authority.

Two to four years is the usual term of a mayor in a city of the United States.

Mediation, in international law the action of a third Power in attempting to compromise differences between two Powers. The Hague Conferences of 1899 and 1907 recommended mediation.

Mediation is frequently employed in industrial and labor disputes. Many states and large cities have mediation boards. The Federal Mediation and Conciliation Service, an independent agency authorized by Congress in the Taft-Hartley Act, 1947, was empowered to act in the name of the Federal government in industrial disputes. Its intervention was not to be mandatory but by agreement.

Military law, the body of regularly enacted rules that govern, regulate and control military forces in peace and war. It is enacted by the law-making body of the nation and is administered by courts of inquiry and courts martial independent of civil courts or of the writ of habeas corpus.

Militia, in general, a body of citizens enrolled and organized as a military force for periodical instruction, discipline and drill but not called into active service except in emergencies. In the United States since 1903, the militia includes all able bodied citizens and males of foreign birth who have declared an intention to become citizens, between the ages of 18 and 45. The organized militia is called the National Guard.

Ministry, the department heads of a government, a term used in Europe, South America and other places but not in the United States, where the executive heads of departments are usually called *secretaries* and the word *minister* is not used.

Minorities, in the United States, have come to have social, political and racial meanings and importance. On the basis of social and racial status and conditions, minorities have clamored for political representation, privileges, and social recognition. It is proper that the rights of minorities be respected and recognized by the majority. It is likewise proper that the minority recognize that the majority also has certain and specific rights that demand respect.

Minorities, increasingly, have demanded certain political rights that cannot and should not be denied them, such as equal application, with the majority, of the police power, of the right to vote, to education, to equality of taxation and before the law, etc. These rights are provided for in the Bill of Rights and in the 13th, 14th and 15th amendments to the Federal Constitution. Certain social privileges claimed as minority rights, such as freedom from discrimination, claims to social equality, etc. are more difficult of attainment because such relationships are difficult to achieve through legislation; their attainment is usually the result of education and association. Constitutional guarantees are not self-executing but may be made effective by legislation. Peaceful human relationships are not attained by legislation.

Political minorities are frequently in opposition to the ruling group, which may itself be a numerical minority which has seized power. This is illustrated in the Russian satellite countries in eastern Europe. The political minority at one time may be the political majority at another. This is often the case in the United States and Great Britain.

Misdemeanor, a minor crime, less serious than a felony and distinguished from it in some state statutes.

Monuments, National, natural features reserved by the Government for public use. Usually smaller than national parks, they contain historic or prehistoric relics, notable geologic formations and animal life, etc.

Mortgage, a conditional transfer of ownership (usually real estate) from one person to another as security for payment of a debt. If the debt is paid when due, the mortgage is canceled. If the debtor cannot pay, the holder of the mortgage may take possession or through a mortgage sale, called a foreclosure, realize money to liquidate the debt. In most states, a period of from 6 months to 2 years after foreclosure is allowed the debtor to redeem the property by paying principal, interest and costs. Mortgages must be recorded so that the history of the parcel of land may be complete; during the time that the property is mortgaged, it cannot be sold except subject to the mortgage. A *chattel mortgage* is a mortgage given on personal property pledged for payment.

Moslem League, The, a political organization for Indian Moslems, held its first conference in 1906 presided over by the Aga Khan. It grew out of the Indian nationalist movement of the 1890's. Ali Jinnah, later prime minister of Pakistan, became president of the League in 1916. The League continued as a political party when India became a Dominion and finally a Republic.

Murder, killing with malice aforethought, that is, with deliberate intent. The common law recognized no degrees of murder; but statutes and state penal codes distinguish between first and second degrees. Death or life imprisonment is the usual penalty for first-degree murder; for the second degree, the sentence varies in different states from 3 years to longer periods.

National Guard, The, was established as the organized militia by the Dick Bill of 1903. This law also provided that instruction and equipment should be furnished by the U. S. Army and that the organized units could be called into Federal service by the President. Provision was later made for sending it anywhere for service. In accordance with this amendment, National Guard units were sent to the Mexican border in 1916. By the Selective Service Act of 1917, National Guard units were drafted into the U. S. armed forces and as such served in France and became a part of the Army of the United States (AUS). By the Selective Service Act of 1940 National Guard units were mobilized into Federal service and remained in active service until the end of World War II, receiving replacements from volunteers and draftees.

NATIONAL PARK SERVICE, U.S. DEPARTMENT OF THE INTERIOR

STATUE OF LIBERTY in New York harbor.

During peace time, the National Guard units meet in their various home localities at intervals, usually attend military field manoeuvres and are subject to call by the governors of their state for riot, disaster or other emergency duties. Officers of all ranks, formerly elected by the membership, are appointed by the governor of the state. A National Guard Bureau in Washington insures both representation and a control and direction over training, equipment, etc.

National Labor Relations Board, an independent agency, created in 1935 to administer, interpret and apply the provisions of the National Labor Relations Act, known as the Wagner Act. The Board was originally composed of 3 members and its practices were so flagrantly partisan as to excite much

criticism and a Congressional investigation in 1939. The Board not only interpreted the Wagner Act, but also developed into a quasi-judicial and quasi-legislative body, in that many of its decisions based on its judicial attributes came to have the effect of law. Finally, in 1947, Congress enacted the Taft-Hartley Labor-Management Act which changed the powers and functions of the Board in a number of important respects. The membership was increased from 3 to 5 and a separation was made of the prosecuting and judicial functions by vesting final authority for investigation and prosecution in the Board's general counsel. The Board was required to treat affiliated and unaffiliated unions alike. Other added provisions related to jurisdictional disputes, injunctions, etc.

Nationalism, in its broadest sense, is a devotion to or advocacy of national interests or national unity and independence. This desire has been particularly manifest in the efforts of minorities within an empire or nation to gain their independence and to set up their own government. For example, the Jews and the state of Israel, the Irish and the Republic of Ireland, the Hungarians and their republic, the Indonesians of the former Dutch East Indies and the United States of Indonesia.

Nationality is primarily racial, political or institutional solidarity and is maintained in spite of dispersion, either from choice, necessity or from force. Large emigrant groups in a foreign country often continue to evidence their nationality in their native dress, customs or in other ways. Nationality may come to represent a fusion of many races and cultures, as in the case of the French; or it may represent definite characteristics and objectives.

Nationalization, the vesting of control and ownership in the state or nation, is a characteristic of the modern socialist and communist states. It has been practiced for many years in varying degrees and has been applied particularly to public utilities and services that are used by all the people of a country, such as the railroads, telephone and telegraph, electric power and light, banking, etc. It is the opposite of capitalism or private control and ownership. Because of the vast destruction of World Wars I and II, and accompanying impoverishment, nationalization, in one form or another, has come to characterize many modern states. Its extreme form is seen in Soviet Russia. At the other extreme is the United States, where most of business and industry is under private ownership and control, though subjected to an increasing degree of government regulation. At the half-way point is Great Britain which has nationalized banking, coal, public utilities, etc.

Naturalization, the process by which an alien (foreign-born person) becomes a citizen of the country of residence. Sometimes there is conflict between the laws of the country of birth and those of the land of residence in which citizenship is desired. In such cases the naturalization laws of the country of adoption usually are supreme.

NAZI RALLY IN NUREMBURG, Germany, 1938. The National Socialist German Workers' Party, founded in 1919, became, under the leadership of Adolf Hitler, an influential organ of propaganda. Methods employed by the organization included revolutionary terrorism and mass meetings designed to arouse nationalistic pride. Party doctrine called for denunciation of the Jews and belief in the supremacy of the Aryan race. Hitler, made chancellor in 1933, was soon endowed with dictatorial powers. The symbol of the Nazi Party, seen on the flags, was the swastika. The Party collapsed following World War II.

The requirements for naturalization are in these acts of Congress, but actual naturalization is not a legal but a judicial process with much latitude left to the courts. In several cases the courts have refused to naturalize applicants who refused to take up arms for the defense of the country—notably Rosika Schwimmer, a woman 49 years old, who could never have been expected to bear arms. She asked for naturalization and was refused by the Supreme Court.

The administration of the naturalization laws is in the hands of a Commissioner of Immigration and Naturalization (two distinct bureaus) in the United States Department of Justice.

An alien at least 18 years of age entering the United States with the intention to remain permanently may become an American citizen after 5 years in continuous residence, if he can prove himself worthy and can speak the English language. Three years after his arrival he may file a declaration before the clerk of a court that he desires to be *naturalized;* this may be done earlier, but no benefit accrues from haste. Two years thereafter, having been a resident for 5 years, he may petition any court of record for citizenship papers. Two witnesses must swear to the facts of his continuous residence and to his good moral character. He must renounce his previous citizenship and swear allegiance to the United States. A person may become a citizen of

some of the states of the Union before he can be a citizen of the United States, for some states recognize him as a citizen immediately after his declaration of intention.

A child of American citizens who is born while his parents are in a foreign country is a citizen, provided he returns to the United States for permanent residence before the age of 18 or makes a declaration when he comes of age. When a father is naturalized his minor children receive naturalization with him; his children over 18 years of age must prove a residence of but 1 year preceding naturalization; the mother must go through the naturalization process. An American-born woman who marries an alien does not lose her citizenship by that act. An alien who marries an American citizen must be naturalized to become a citizen. Aliens who have served in the army or navy of the United States are freed from the initial declaration of intention.

Navy, Department of the, an executive division of the Department of Defense, created by the National Security Act of 1947. It was established independently in 1789, having been a part of the War Department. The Secretary of the Navy is usually a civilian, but not a Cabinet member. The Department has some activities that are not primarily concerned with war, such as the astronomical work of the Naval Observatory which makes astronomical observations and prepares the Nautical Almanac, and the work of the Hydro-

graphic Office and Bureau of Navigation concerned with chart making, oceanography and hydrography. The U. S. Marine Corps is under the direction of the Secretary of the Navy. Among divisions of the department are the bureaus of Aeronautics, Construction and Repair, including Salvage, Engineering, Medicine and Surgery, Ordnance, Supplies and Accounts, and Yards and Docks.

Nazi, a popular abbreviation for a member of the National Socialist German Workingmen's party (*Nazionalsozialistiche Deutsch Arbeitsche*). The term came to be applied to all supporters of Adolf Hitler, especially before and during World War II. The original Nazi party was formed in 1918 and taken over by Hitler and six comrades in 1920. Its 25-point program came to be the establishment of the state as supreme with Hitler as its leader and *Mein Kampf* its guide. Among its objectives were complete socialization of all large-scale manufacturing, expulsion of the Jews from Germany, the proof of Aryanism as a qualification for office, the union of all Germans, and more land for German expansion. The party disappeared at the end of World War II and many of its leaders were tried by international courts for war crimes.

Negligence, lack of prudence and reasonable care in the exercise of a duty (or the failure to do what ought to be done) that may result in distress or injury to others. If a landlord allows the fire escape on his building to become unsafe, failure to remedy the defect after being warned makes him liable to the charge of negligence. Negligence that leads to loss of life is not only *gross* negligence but may be charged as manslaughter

Neutrality in international law may define the status of those states not belligerents or it may denote the policy of a state with reference to a war. In early U. S. history, neutrality, so far as national policy was concerned, was necessary, but private individuals might carry on their commercial activities in non-contraband goods, protected under international law by the doctrine of neutrality.

Neutrality, however, has become less practiced and observed, because large-scale wars involve peoples as well as nations and because submarines and airplanes either cannot or will not make any distinction between neutral and enemy ships.

During the American Civil War, the United States insisted that if Great Britain *were* not to become a belligerent she must strictly observe and respect the laws of neutrality. Because Great Britain aided the Southern Confederacy by fitting out ships for use against the United States, she was sued and the United States was awarded damages. In World War I, because German submarines attacked unarmed, neutral American vessels, the United States declared war. Between 1935 and 1939 the United States passed various neutrality laws for its protection in case of a second world war, but eventually she became a belligerent.

Nihilism, the doctrine or belief that the existing form of government, economic and social, should be destroyed.

The word was first used by the Russian novelist Ivan Turgenev in *Fathers and Sons* (1862) to describe the view held by Russian revolutionists of that time. The violence that marked the growth of nihilism in Russia, notably the assassination of Alexander II in 1881, was the inevitable result of the central idea of this group. It was violence not for the sake of violence but to secure a desired end. Many anarchists—that is, believers in no government—were nihilists; but not all the nihilists were anarchists, for some of them had constructive ideas for new government by the people and a parliament of the people, and some of them were Marxian Socialists and believers in the principles underlying the present Soviet rule.

No confidence, Vote of, the majority expression by a legislative body that the Cabinet is no longer trusted. This forces the resignation of the Ministry and a general election. The method originated in the English House of Commons and is essential in the English scheme of government by a Cabinet and Ministry responsible to the House of Commons. The defeat of a Government measure (that is, one backed by the Ministry) is a more frequent cause of the Ministry's downfall. In rare cases, the Commons may pass a vote of *censure* against some specific act of the Cabinet or of one of its members. The vote of *no confidence* or *want of confidence* applies to the general policies of the Cabinet.

In the French Parliament (and especially in the Chamber of Deputies) the ministers must answer questions (*interpellations*) by legislators, and after this answer the House may vote not to accept the answer and force the Ministry to resign.

Nolle prosequi (Latin, be unwilling to prosecute), a method of discontinuing a suit by the declaration of the plaintiff or of the prosecuting attorney. The words are often abbreviated to nol. pros. It is not equivalent to an acquittal and is not a bar to a new indictment for the same offense.

Nolo contendere (Latin, I am unwilling to contend), a plea by a defendant in a criminal action without pleading guilty or not guilty, making it possible for him to deny the truth of the charges in a collateral proceeding. In the third person the Latin is: *Non vult contendere*, he will not contend. This plea is permitted in only a few states. Usually the plea must be "guilty" or "not guilty."

Nomination, the choice of a candidate for office. Literally the word means naming. It can be used of a candidate for an appointive office, named (nominated) by the President or a governor and submitted for the approval of the U.S. Senate or a state legislature. The common use is of candidates for elective office: each party or group nominates its candidate for each office to be filled; then from these candidates the whole body of voters elects to the office. The different methods of nominating candidates for elective offices are described under the headings *Caucus, Convention, Primary, Petition.*

Nonresistance, the theory and practice of certain Christian and pacifistic groups that refuse to use force to meet violence and will not resist any authority no matter how unjust its actions. The proof texts are in the New Testament: Matthew 5:39, "Resist not evil: but whosoever shall smite thee on the right cheek, turn to him the other also"; and Romans 13:1,2, "Let every soul be subject unto the higher powers. For there is no power but of God; the powers that be are ordained of God. Whosoever therefore resisteth the power, resisteth the ordinance of God." The English Quakers in the second half of the 17th century created two serious problems for government: one by their refusal to take oaths in court and the other by their pacifism and nonresistance. Nonresistance often became passive resistance or civil disobedience (as Thoreau called it in an essay he wrote at the time of the war with Mexico). Tolstoi in Russia insisted that a true Christian will take no part in any activity of the state that is compulsory.

The idea of passive resistance is Buddhist even more than Christian—a commonplace in the Orient. The Hindu nationalist leader Gandhi advocated passive resistance in his Satyagraha (truth-grasping) campaign against the British Government in India beginning in 1919. Gandhi's followers lay down in the streets and blocked traffic. Bazaars were closed in protest against policies of the government—a strike of retailers called *hartal* in India. Gandhi insisted that truth not violence was the tool for resistance. Nonco-operation is another term applied to this method of opposing the government. It has always been particularly difficult for any government to deal with.

Notary public, a minor official who under seal of his office attests the validity of signatures to deeds, contracts, affidavits and the like and administers oaths in connection therewith. Notaries receive remuneration in fees for work performed. Appointment is by the governor of the state and in the District of Columbia by the President. The commission is usually for 4 years.

Oath, a solemn pledge that statements are true or that a promise will be faithfully executed, made under a sense of responsibility to God. The Constitution of the United States declares the form of oath required of the President (Art. II, Sec. 1, Cl. 8); other oaths are patterned largely upon it. Affirmation without swearing by God is an accepted substitute in the case of persons who have conscientious scruples against the oath.

Obiter dicta, literally things said in passing (*obiter,* from *iter,* a journey); incidental remarks in a judge's opinion not bearing directly on the case or on the point of law involved in the case —and, for that reason, not binding and of no force as a court ruling.

Office, originally a service or duty; then the place or room where the service is rendered; and the division or department of government rendering a service.

The principal administrative departments of the English Government are called offices: Foreign Office, War Office, Scottish Office, Colonies and Dominions Office, Office of Works and his Majesty's Stationery Office. What Americans call the Post Office Department is called the Post Office.

In the Federal Government of the United States, a number of subdivisions of the executive departments are called office: as the Patent Office and the Office of Business Economics in the Department of Commerce; also the General Accounting Office, the Government Printing Office, Office of Naval Research, Office of Technical Services in Commerce, Office of Labor Solicitor. The General Accounting Office is under the direction of the Comptroller of the U. S.

Office of Price Administration (OPA), created by Executive Order, April 17, 1941 and named Aug. 28, 1941. It was set up to avoid inflation, by price and rent control and stabilization, and to prevent speculation, profiteering, hoarding and price manipulation. This agency probably touched the American people more often at more points of daily living during World War II, especially through ration books and price and rent control, than any other government bureau. It was consolidated with other war agencies in the Office of Temporary Controls, Dec. 12, 1946 liquidated, June 1, 1947.

Orphans' Court, name given in Maryland, Delaware, New Jersey and Pennsylvania to a court with probate jurisdiction over wills and the administration of estates.

Pacifism, the principle of a movement that seeks the establishment of universal peace. It is especially directed against war and militarism. Pacifists are divided into various groups with different specific policies. Some groups oppose international war but do not oppose class war by oppressed groups to gain economic or political equality. Pacifists do not oppose a small disciplinary police force to maintain law and order.

Religion has been a strong force in the spread of the pacifist movement. Some groups, such as the Quakers and the Moravians, made pacifism a central doctrine in their religion and are exempted from military service by the United States. Members of other religious groups who are pacifists have sought exemption from military service on this religious basis. Others call themselves *conscientious objectors.*

Pardon, full forgiveness of a specific misdemeanor or crime and the restoration of liberty and civil rights to a criminal. The pardoning power is usually vested in the executive authority but in some states has been given to a board of pardons and parole. The President of the United States can pardon any offender against the United States not under impeachment charges. State authorities may issue pardons for all offenses against the laws of their states, but not for offenses against exclusive Federal laws, such as smuggling, counterfeiting, etc.

A pardon may also be extended by the Pope in the form of a Papal indulgence as foregiveness for an ethical or ecclesiastical sin.

Parks, lands reserved for public use under government control (national, state, county or municipal). There seem to have been public and private parks in many ancient civilizations—small, formal gardens in Egypt and Greece; and large reserves on mountains in ancient Persia that were called by the Persian word from which we get our word *paradise,* originally meaning an enclosure and coming to mean an ideal heaven. In Rome there were city parks, many of them originally public meeting places (like the Greek *agora* or marketplace) or drill grounds, such as the Campus Martius, a grassy field on the east bank of the Tiber.

But public parks were rare until the Renaissance and not really common until the 19th century. Many European cities that had been walled and fortified in the Middle Ages discarded the fortifications in the 18th and 19th centuries and built ring parks, concentric arrangements of boulevards and public walks—Coblenz, Cologne, Strasbourg and Vienna are examples. In France the Revolution at the end of the 18th century turned over many royal parks and estates of the rich nobility to the republican government. In England about the middle of the 19th century,

long after the royal parks in London and the vicinity had been made public in fact if not in name, there was a sharp controversy over common lands or commons—pieces of ground that had belonged to all the inhabitants of a community and had been farmed in common long before the Norman Conquest in 1066 introduced the feudal system of landholding under the Crown and the nobles. The great landowners as far back as 1235 and 1285 had received authority from Parliament (an assembly of barons only) to enclose parts of this land and take title to it. From 1845 to 1869 as property became more valuable about 600,000 acres of commons were enclosed by action of parliamentary committees. An act of Parliament in 1876 checked the continuance of enclosure. Many common lands were bought by the government and became parks—Epping Forest, for example, about 5,600 acres 17 miles north of London.

In the United States public parks seem to have originated from the common lands. In 1634 the Boston Common was made a public park. Throughout New England commons that were originally used for pasturing cattle and that were almost always in the center of the settlement near the church and other public buildings in time became public squares. City Hall Park in New York city was originally a commons.

Planned parks began in the 50s; Bushnell Park in Hartford, Conn., around the state capitol building, was begun in 1853, and in 1857 the property for Central Park, New York city (now 840 acres) was bought. Fairmount Park, Philadelphia, **3,600** acres, one of the largest parks inside city limits, was begun in 1867. In the '90s cities began to plan series, chains of parks, inside and outside the city; Boston and Kansas City both began a program of metropolitan parks in 1892.

County park systems started about the same time: Essex County, N.J., in 1895. With the development of the automobile, special passenger automobile highways with elaborate landscaping were built, such as the Westchester County parkways and those on Long Island, both leading into the city of New York.

State parks are variously administered—in New York by a Conservation Department—and they may be historic sites, scenic marvels, forests, game preserves or sites for camping, playgrounds and recreation. The New York State Adirondacks Park is a forest reserve of more than two million acres with free camping. It is the second largest forest preserve in the U. S. There are about 31 developed campsites in the area. Along the west bank of the Hudson is the Palisades Interstate Park with a total area of 52,279 acres, which is under the joint supervision of the regular State Park

NATIONAL PARK SERVICE, U.S. DEPARTMENT OF THE INTERIOR

GRAND TETON NATIONAL PARK, Wyoming, is famous for its Teton Range, mountains of rugged Alpine character, rising above Jackson Hole.

commissioners from New York and New Jersey.

The National Park System originated in the United States with the establishment of Yellowstone Park in 1872. The Hot Springs Reservation, in Arkansas, established in 1830, was made a national park in 1921. The National Parks of the United States, formerly limited to the Far West, now include several in the mid-East and East, such as Isle Royale, Great Smoky Mountains, Acadia and Everglades. Yosemite, Sequoia and Mount Rainier are, next to Yellowstone, the oldest parks in the system, which extends to Mount McKinley in Alaska, and to Hawaii on the islands of Hawaii and Maui.

The national park system contains approximately 23,400,000 acres of Federal land.

National monuments, administered by the National Park Service, include areas of historic, prehistoric and scientific importance. The service also administers *national historical parks, military parks, battlefield parks, historic sites,* and *parkways*.

Civil War memorials include the battlefield parks at Gettysburg and at Chickamauga. Important national parkways are the Blue Ridge (N.C.-Va.) George Washington Memorial (Va.-Md.) and the Natchez Trace (Tenn.-Ala.-Miss.)

The *National Forests* are scattered throughout the United States and Puerto Rico. Some of the forests overlap state boundaries. The total area is in excess of 188,000,000 acres. In both Idaho and California, there are more than 19,000,000 acres; in Montana more than 17,000,000; in both Colorado and Oregon, more than 14,000,000. The forests are under the Forest Service, and one of their uses is to provide popular outdoor recreation.

Municipalities, counties, states and the Federal Government of the United States all have *game reserves* and *bird refuges*. Under the supervision of the Fish and Wildlife Service, Department of the Interior, are preserves for bison, elk, deer, mountain sheep and migratory birds.

In Russia, Germany, Austria and Poland, huge new parks were made after World War I from confiscated royal lands. Poland has game preserves of scientific importance.

President Kruger of the Boer Republic in 1898 established a game reserve between the Sabi and Crocodile rivers. It has been enlarged from time to time, and in 1926 the Union of South Africa made it a national park about 220 miles long and 40 miles wide. It contains elephants, giraffes, antelope, buffalo and perhaps a few of the rare black rhinoceros. There are two large game reserves and two national parks in Kenya and three in Northern Rhodesia, one of which is the Victoria Falls Reserve.

In the Belgian Congo, there are four great parks, two commemorated in a 1937 issue of postage stamps. The Parc National Albert, about 780 square miles, has three volcanoes and includes gorilla country and rare fauna and flora. Another large game reserve is in the Luana Valley.

In Australia there are reserves for

CENTRAL OFFICE OF INFORMATION, LONDON

HOUSES OF PARLIAMENT along the banks of the Thames River, Westminster, London. The tower on the left is the 340-foot-high Victoria Tower. On the right is the famous Big Ben.

the peculiarly Australasian animals —kangaroos, wombats, duckbill platypus—especially in Tasmania, with a park near Hobart and a 160,000-acre game reserve in the Mount Field country. New Zealand has island refuges for sea birds.

Parliament, originally a conversation or parley; then a conference and the council held by the early kings of England after the Norman Conquest; and now any legislative body, specifically that of Great Britain and Northern Ireland. Parliament is the official name of the legislature in Canada, Australia and the Union of South Africa. In New Zealand the name *General Assembly* is used.

Parliamentary government is that type of government in which a legislative body has complete control over lawmaking and administration—especially the type modeled on the English system in which the control of the government is in the hands of ministers who are members of Parliament and responsible to it.

Parole (French, word, promise, word of honor), a conditional release from punishment on pledge of good conduct given by a prisoner. The paroled person must make periodic reports and must submit to certain supervision. For misbehavior the parole may be canceled and the person returned to prison.

Party, political, an organization of persons with the same general beliefs about policies the government should follow, formed for the purpose of securing the adoption of their policies by the government. The most distinctive function of the political party is that it nominates some of its leaders for public office and attempts to

secure the election of these candidates.

Party government, a system of government based upon the selection of public officials from the candidates nominated by political parties. In a democratic nation there are two or more parties, and each has its own candidates and platform. The successful party in an election attempts to enact its program; the defeated party criticizes what is being done and promotes a general discussion of the policies of the party in power. In time of national crisis, such as a war, the various political parties often drop their differences and join together in supporting a national policy. In the United States and England there have generally been two major political parties, but in some countries, such as France, there has been a large number of parties.

At the beginning of the national government of the United States two political parties developed, and although their names have been changed, the general composition and programs of the parties have persisted down to the present. The Federalist-Whig-Republican party, which has had as its standard bearers Hamilton, Webster, Lincoln, McKinley and Coolidge, has mainly represented the industrial and financial interests of the nation. The Republican-Democratic party led by Jefferson, Jackson, Bryan and Franklin D. Roosevelt has primarily represented the agrarian interests and small groups of importers and industrial workers. The Federalist-Whig-Republican group has generally stood for a high protective tariff, centralized banking and a currency based on gold, internal improvements and economic measures favorable to industrialists. The Republicans and Democrats have often agreed on policies and as often disagreed. After the Civil War, the Democrats as the opposition were out of office for long periods. During that time, the Republican reconstruction policies antagonized the southern states, and thus the Democratic party came to include the so-called Solid South. Republican presidents were mediocre and twice the Democrat, Grover Cleveland, was elected. The beginnings of the agrarian movement in the 1880s and the agitation of William Jennings Bryan and others for "soft" money gave the Republicans a close call in 1896, but the success of the Spanish-American War kept them in office until the party was split by Theodore Roosevelt's third party movement in 1912. Woodrow Wilson, a Democrat, was defeated in 1920 because of his insistence on American participation, without reservations, in the League of Nations. Franklin D. Roosevelt was elected President on the promise of a New Deal in the midst of economic distress and was re-elected 4 times. The two parties have come to agree on the general objectives of social security measures, aid to the farmer and other domestic issues, but have often disagreed violently on details. In foreign affairs, both during and after World War II, the two parties followed a bipartisan policy.

Under a dictatorship only one political party is permitted. In Germany, it was the National Socialist party; in Soviet Russia, the Communist; in Italy, the Fascist. In these countries, only a small proportion of the citizens were permitted to join the party.

Patent, a government grant to an inventor, securing to him for a stated time the exclusive right to make, use or sell any new and useful machine, process or composition of materials of his invention. It also permits the patentee to sell or authorize others to use his patent. Every article thus protected must be marked with the word patented and also the date of patent issue or serial number. False marking renders the offender liable to fine.

The government grant of a patent is in effect a contract by which the inventor reveals the specifications of his device so that the public can use it freely after the patent period expires; for this future release of his property right, the Government gives him a monopoly protection during the life of the patent. The term of the patent in the United States for *inventions* is 17 years from the date of the patent issue. In most other countries, the term runs from the date of application. Patents for *designs* run in the U.S. for 3½, 7 or 14 years, depending on which is requested in the application. Patents may be extended by Act of Congress.

The Patent Office, created under a Constitutional provision (Art. 1, Sec. 8), is one of the oldest branches of the Federal Government. It was established in 1790 and issued its first patent to Samuel Hopkins, July 21, 1790. The law was revised in 1793 and a new law was enacted in 1836 requiring better proof of a right to a patent, but also

giving the patentee more protection. Many of the world's greatest and most useful inventions have been developed under the protection of patents granted by the Patent Office. One feature of American patent law that is particularly noteworthy is the right of the patentee to file improvement patents without jeopardizing title to his original patent.

Patents reflect stages of industrial progress and have shaped American industrial organization and growth. Among important original patents granted by the Patent Office were those covering the cotton gin, the harvester, the electric telegraph, the incandescent lamp, the telephone and others. In recent years as industry has become more complex, many of the most valuable patents have been issued to corporations rather than to individuals. Since the first patent was issued, a total of 2,500-000 have been granted, 500,000 of them in the last 15 years.

Penalty, punishment for crime or wrong doing, based on a retributive theory of law. Retaliation, punishment in kind, an eye for an eye and a tooth for a tooth, was the primitive notion of penalty. Modern criminology and psychology try to reform and readjust the criminal, giving him useful and educational occupation in prison, putting him on parole before his term is finished if his behavior is good and sometimes suspending his sentence and putting him on probation under helpful supervision.

Pension, a regular payment on account of meritorious service, because of age or for other stated reasons. Pensions have come to take two aspects: (1) for services rendered under certain conditions and for certain periods of time and (2) social security payments made on account of age, industrial or other disability or because of physical condition or handicap. Only the service aspect of pensions was important until a few years ago. Recently the increasing complexity of modern life has given power to the individual, political and social, and has created a demand for consideration. Still a third aspect of pensions has manifested itself, in the industrial pension, which at times is demanded when wage increases are not forthcoming.

Military and federal pensions. The United States Government has granted pensions to participants in all its wars. These are usually classified (1) for injuries in service; (2) to persons having specified lengths of service combined with other qualifications, such as age, disability or indigence; and (3) for service alone, usually granted to aged survivors. Such pension grants to survivors and dependents have increased both in volume and coverage, because of the large number of service participants in World Wars I and II, and because of the political power and influence derived from these numbers.

The soldier vote was important in American politics for 30 years after the close of the Civil War; it became important again after World Wars I and II. The number, benefits and size of pensions increased correspondingly. Before 1861, the total cost of war service pensions was about $90,000,000. By 1918 it was over five billion dollars and

in recent years pension payments totaled about two billion dollars and about three million cases. In addition to veterans' pensions after World War I, there were periodic demands for "adjusted compensation" or veterans' bonuses. These payments were in effect pensions.

Another type of service pension is that granted either for disability or service to retired members of the armed forces and to government employees for fulfilling certain service requirements. Pensions are also paid by states, municipalities and private businesses, according to length of service and type of record. This applies particularly to teachers, firemen, policemen and long-time public employees. Many business concerns, including banks, insurance companies, etc. have pension-payment plans, most of which are contributed to regularly by both employer and employee.

Old Age. Prior to 1930, old-age pensions and annuities covered only a small percentage of the population. The average annual pension was about $520. The Social Security Act of 1935 providing old age insurance coverage was greatly extended by subsequent amendments, especially by the amendment of 1956. Both employer and employee contribute to the pension fund. Survivor benefits are also paid.

Mothers and Orphans. Most states provide for payments to widows and deserted wives with small children to support.

Industrial. Many industrial and business concerns have adopted some kind of pension plan for their long-service employees, with both employer and employee contributing. In such cases the pension may or may not be in addition to the Federal old-age pension provided for by joint social security payments. Recently, non-contributory pensions have been granted in lieu of wage increases. This means that the employer periodically pays into the pension fund an amount that, when added to the social security payments, will produce the agreed-on pension at the specified time. There are variations of these basic methods.

Another type of pension fund is that derived from unit payments on the product produced by the worker. This is the plan used by the United Mine Workers where each ton of coal produced is taxed, the payments going into a fund for pensions as well as other benefits.

Many problems are posed by the non-contributory pension plan with regard to its control, adequacy, the effect of the pension-fund payments on industry financing, the soundness of the plan and its safety and continuity. Actuarial experience in the field of non-contributory pension plans is slight. It is difficult to determine what is the proper basis on which to operate such a plan. In the end, these funds are created from the sale of the product manufactured and thus come from the consumer eventually in terms of increased prices.

Perjury, false swearing, wilfully false statements under oath or affirmation in a judicial proceeding. The offense is a felony in most states. *Subornation.*

of perjury consists in securing another to swear falsely as to a material fact in a case.

Persona grata and **Persona non grata,** terms used to indicate that the diplomatic representative sent from another country is acceptable or not acceptable. If the representative is acceptable to the government to which he is sent, the envoy is said to be *persona grata;* if he is not acceptable he is *persona non grata.*

Personal property, movable property and certain interests in land as distinct from *real property* or *real estate,* that is, land and buildings attached to it.

Petition, a formal written request by citizens made to some governmental authority. The first amendment of the U.S. Constitution stipulates that Congress shall not abridge the right of the people "to petition the government for a redress of grievances." But this right of petition does not necessitate a consideration of it by the Government. Under a rule of the House of Representatives passed in 1836, petitions may be tabled without being referred to a committee or receiving any further consideration. The right of petition was first granted in England by Magna Charta.

Nomination by petition is permitted by some state constitutions, especially for the nonpartisan nomination of judges. The law specifies the number of signers required.

In the U.S. House of Representatives a bill not reported to the House by the committee to which it has been referred may be brought before the House for consideration if it is ordered out of committee by a petition signed by 218 representatives (out of a total of 435).

Plaintiff, the party making complaint in a case seeking a remedy for an injury. In a real action he may be called a *demandant;* in a divorce case, a *libellant;* in equity, a *complainant;* but the general usage is to call the claimant in all cases the plaintiff. The other party is the defendant.

Planning, systematized efforts to secure recovery or economic progress by governmental activities. Governmental programs for economic control became necessary in the confusion and disaster of the period after World War I and particularly in the depression that began in 1929. Planning is distinct from the isolated occasional economic legislation of earlier periods, the tariff laws, for example, that protected American infant industries even in the early days of the republic.

Government planning on a big scale after World War I began in the new Russia with a Council of Labor and Defense working through its State Planning Commission or Committee (*Gosplan*) in 1923. Between 1923 and 1928 corresponding planning commissions were organized in each of the seven republics. In 1928 the first Five-Year Plan abolished the NEP, which in 1921 had adopted some elements of the capitalist scheme. The Plan undertook to mechanize and collectivize 63,000,000 acres of farms (about one-fifth of the total) by 1933; that is, to have them operated by machinery

TENNESSEE VALLEY AUTHORITY'S Norris Dam, on the Clinch River in Tennessee. This shows a portion of the switchyard and powerhouse. When spillway is opened, the water cascades 207 feet down its face, a drop forty feet greater than that of Niagara Falls. The dam helps to control seasonal floods on the Tennessee and Ohio rivers, aids navigation in months of low flow, and provides for electric power production.

and owned not individually but by the state or communist groups; to invest about $33,300,000,000 in agriculture, industry and education; to increase industrial output 136 per cent and farm products 55 per cent.

In the United States and, in fact, in most of the world, the policy of *laissez faire,* was usual. The growth in the power and volume of industry and the constantly increasing restrictions on freedom of movement to the individual made him increasingly the victim of violent swings in industrial activity.

In the early years of the 20th century, government planning was begun indirectly in the form of public control of business methods. This action was largely negative in that it decreed what could *not* be done by industry. Government itself did little or nothing, nor was it expected to do anything. The first steps at planning in the United States related to the conservation and reclamation of natural resources and were confined to the Public Domain. They included reforestation, irrigation, flood control, conservation of mineral resources, particularly oil and gas, and the control of water-power development through licensing.

The world-wide depression of the 1930s struck the United States with full force in 1932. Franklin D. Roosevelt was elected President in that year on the promise of a New Deal that would bring order out of the existing industrial chaos, put industry on its feet and restore employment to the millions who were jobless. The proposed program also promised higher wages, shortened work hours, "decent"

minimum wages, better working conditions and a reasonable degree of control over production and competitive practices. A planned economy was proposed to accomplish these objectives. It was to be carried out by legislative or executive authority and through the cooperative action of business and industry. This necessitated fact-finding to learn the true situation, planning for present and future needs, and the control of production to meet the conditions as revealed. As industry recovered, it was expected that governmental activities would be restricted, but planning as a guide for the present and the future would be continued.

The first large-scale governmental attempts at planning were the National Recovery Administration (NRA) relating to industry and the Agricultural Adjustment Administration (AAA) as applied to agriculture. When the legislation authorizing these activities was declared unconstitutional, substitute measures were enacted that in many aspects carried forward the planning already under way.

The most spectacular of these planned projects was carried out by the Tennessee Valley Authority (TVA) which involved all of the various phases of life and welfare in an entire region. This adventure in large-scale planning was later repeated in varied form elsewhere.

Coincident with the restoration of industry and employment, planned measures were enacted concerned with social security, particularly unemployment, old age and dependency The provision of adequate housing, on a large scale, was also an aspect of planning, carried on largely through close co-operation with the construction industry, in the form of financial guarantees to protect the builder, and of planning and location of housing projects. The capitalistic system has been preserved, subject only to a closer and more rigorous regulation by the government. Congress authorized a permanent Council of Economic Advisers, to keep the President advised, to recommend current steps to be taken and to have ready for emergencies a considered program of governmental planning. All of these activities, however, are carried on within the existing frame of government and industry. There is little public ownership.

Government planning on a large scale has been a characteristic of dictatorships in recent years. The Nazi government of Germany exercised planning on a large scale, primarily in its warlike aspects. The government expanded various social-welfare and housing plans, but was more concerned with the planning of strategic roads, the location and building of munitions factories and the provision of plants producing synthetic materials such as oil, rubber, etc. Japan and Fascist Italy also did extensive economic planning before and during World War II.

Planning lies at the base of the Russian Soviet economy. It involves government ownership of the instruments and means of production in two forms: (1) state property including all the elements of industrial production, such as land, minerals, water, forests, mills, factories, mines, rail, water and air transport, banks, communications, etc.

These plans of development included not only the entire economic field, but also all cultural, educational, scientific, housing, and public-health activities. They have gone far to centralize all activities in the government and to give it nearly complete control of the tools of productive living.

In Great Britain, government planning has been carried on extensively. The railroads, public utilities, coal, the Bank of England, health and housing activities, social security and welfare have been socialized. Resistance to this process of planning has, however, been vigorous.

Platform, a declaration of party principles, the basis on which the candidates stand, a formal statement appealing for votes. Party platforms are adopted at national conventions in presidential campaigns and by state conventions in state campaigns. In states where there is no nominating convention, a party convention or (in Wisconsin) a party council is authorized to draft the platform.

Party platforms are general and vague—in their promise of performance and in their praise of what this party has done and their condemnation of what the other party has done.

Political parties abroad occasionally issue manifestos or statements of policies, but there is nothing in foreign party organization just like the American platform.

Plea, any pleading, especially an allegation of fact or the answer of a defendant. In particular it is the answer of a defendant arraigned in a criminal case to the question, "Do you plead guilty or not guilty?"

Pleadings, the various written statements setting forth the case and claim of the plaintiff and the answer and defense of the defendant until issue is joined—that is, the point in controversy made plain.

Plebiscite, in Roman government a decree (*scitum*) of the common people (*plebs*), which was voted by the *comitia tributa* or tribal assembly. Now the term means a vote of the people on a statute or other measure submitted to them for their decision. Any referendum is a plebiscite.

In 1947 the U. N. granted Kashmir the right to hold a plebiscite to determine whether it would become part of India or Pakistan. So far India has prevented this.

Plurality, the largest number of votes cast in an election. A *majority* is more than half the votes cast. Thus, if there are only two candidates, the one receiving a plurality would also receive a majority of the votes; but if there are three or more candidates, the one receiving a plurality may not have a majority of the votes cast.

Plural voting, the right to cast more than one vote in an election. In Belgium until 1921, some voters had three votes apiece; in many German cities, especially in Prussia, certain citizens could cast more than one ballot; and throughout the United Kingdom of Great Britain and Ireland, there are two voting qualifications that give certain electors more than one vote in parliamentary elections. Before 1918 one voter could legally cast many more than two votes—if he owned property in more than two parliamentary borroughs; and before 1918 general elections were spread over a period of two weeks so that a landowner in different parts of the kingdom might vote on different days in different boroughs. The law of 1918 limited plural voting to two votes: a voter might cast his ballot (and so might the wife or husband of such a property holder) in the district where he owned a residence and in the district where he owned business property, if these were different constituencies; and as some members of the House of Commons represented universities, the degree-holders of universities who voted for these university members have that extra vote besides the one for a candidate from the voter's place of residence.

Pocket borough, see *Borough.*

Pocket veto, see *Veto.*

Point Four, a program, formulated by President H. S. Truman in 1949, for American aid to underdeveloped countries, including technical aid. It includes financial co-operation by beneficiary countries.

Police Power, the power of the state to regulate persons and property in the interests of the general public welfare. As this power conflicts with the rights of the individual and with property rights, in certain respects the police power is limited by the Bill of Rights in the Federal Constitution and in the state constitutions and by such legal principles as due process of law. The conflict between these two principles of law provides the material for many crucial cases before our Supreme Court. The modern trend is toward an extension of the police power at the expense of individual and personal rights that might be used in a way to endanger the public good. Police power ranks with taxation as one of the fundamental powers reserved to the states by the Tenth Amendment to the Federal Constitution. States may exercise police powers through the passage of state statutes which may relate to a wide variety of subjects, such as control of gambling, the enforcement of health, morals and safety regulations, traffic regulations and control, etc. The Pure Food and Drug Act and the Meat Inspection Act of 1906 are examples of the exercise of police powers by the Federal Government.

The Narcotics Control Act of 1956 authorized severe penalties for those who traffic illegally in narcotics and marihuana. The first offense carries a penalty of 2 to 10 years, the second offense, 5 to 20 years, the third or subsequent offense, 10 to 40 years. Offenders are liable also to a fine of up to $20,000. The penalty for unlawfully procuring heroin for persons under 18 is life imprisonment or even death, if the jury so decides. Procurors who are under 18 are subject to a prison term of not less than 10 years. Witnesses important to the state may receive immunity.

Poll tax, literally "head tax," taken from the old English word "poll," meaning head or individual. The verb *poll* means to list or count individuals, and thus to take a vote. *The polls* is an old phrase for voting place.

The tax is levied on the person of the taxpayer rather than upon his property, requiring equal contributions from all upon whom levied, without regard for ability to pay. It has been imposed for a variety of reasons, including the establishment of eligibility to vote.

The poll tax was introduced to America in early colonial times, and was retained in many states until 1965. The 24th amendment, sent to the states by the Congress of 1962, was ratified in 1964, and barred the tax in federal elections. In 1965 federal legislation barred the tax in all state and local elections.

The enactment and enforcement of the 1965 legislation has led to protests on the part of southern states over the invasion of states' rights. Some states have groups moving toward other restrictions for the purpose of voter control, such as higher requirements for educational background for voter eligibility. This has led to added efforts by civil rights groups to avert the imposition of such laws.

Populist party, a political party formed by farm and labor groups in 1891. Due to economic conditions, the farmers of the South and Middle West were getting poorer, and conditions were so bad that they were burning their crops for fuel. On the other hand, the financial and commercial interests in the East were getting richer. The Populist party in 1892 adopted a platform including free coinage of silver, a graduated income tax, plenty of paper money, government ownership of railroads, direct election of Senators, an eight-hour working day, postal banks and prohibition. James B. Weaver of

Iowa was its candidate for President in 1892 and received over a million votes. When the Democratic party declared for "free silver" in 1896 and nominated Bryan, the Populists gave full support, but Bryan was defeated.

Post-mortem (Latin, *after death*), a formal examination to ascertain the cause of death. Physicians in registration areas are required to report deaths of their patients to the authorities; if the cause is not known, medical examination of vital parts may disclose it.

Post Office Department, an executive branch of the Federal Government established in 1789 under authority of the Constitution (Art. I, Sec. 8, Cl. 7), which granted Congress power "to establish post offices and post roads." The department is under the direction of the Postmaster General who is a member of the President's Cabinet. This department has jurisdiction over all post offices and other services connected with the collection, transportation and delivery of the mails.

The postal service in America was first a private enterprise, but in 1639 Massachusetts took the first step toward the establishment of a governmental postal system. For practical reasons, the framers of the Constitution followed the practice in Europe and made the mail system a public monopoly.

The services of the Post Office Department have steadily expanded so that they now include free delivery of mail in towns of over 1,500 inhabitants or where the gross receipts of a post office amount to at least $5,-000 a year, registering and insuring mail, the money-order system, the parcel post, air mail and, since 1910, a system of savings banks. Special rates are granted to certain classes of educational literature. Government mail is carried free and so are certain special classes of mail, such as literature for the blind that does not carry advertising. Subsidies of the mail service are used to develop air and ocean transportation.

Universal Postal Union, a system organized under the Treaty of Paris in 1878, in which practically all nations agreed they were "a single postal territory," and established equal rates and rules for all.

Power of attorney, written authority to act for another. The delegation of power may cover all the interests of the principal, a *general* power of attorney, or only specified duties, a *special* or *limited* power. If the agent acts within the delegated powers, the principal is legally responsible for his acts; if those powers are exceeded, responsibility is shifted to the representative.

Practice and procedure, the manner and method of starting and conducting litigation, as governed by what is called adjectival law. Practice and procedure have been greatly simplified in the last century. In England the Judicature Act of 1925 (following acts of 1873) cut away a great deal of unnecessary technicality and legal circumlocution and delay. In the United States the reform of pro-

cedure began with the Field Code (named from its principal author, David Dudley Field), adopted in 1848 in New York State. The commission that reported this code had been instructed "to provide for a uniform course of proceeding in all cases whether of legal or equitable cognizance and for the abandonment of all Latin and other foreign tongues so far as the same shall by them be deemed practicable." By the end of the century this New York reform code had been adopted in 28 states and 2 territories. A few states still distinguish between common law and equity at least in the form of actions. New Jersey still has separate courts of equity and law. Louisiana practice is still based on the Civil Code.

All state constitutions make trial by jury an inviolable right, and this has served to keep some distinction between common law actions in which a jury may be demanded and equity actions with no jury.

The main steps in a legal action are:

notice to the defendant, usually by a *summons;*

filing of plaintiff's *complaint* or *petition,* which must be served on the defendant;

defendant's *appearance* entered or his *answer* filed, possibly with a counterclaim;

trial of the action;

after verdict or judgment, a defeated party may *appeal* to a higher court.

Precedent (from Latin, meaning going before), a judicial decision, method of procedure or course of action that once decided then becomes a rule or authority for other cases under similar circumstances. The English Common Law, lacking codes and statutes, was built on precedents. An ancient maxim is *stare decisis,* stand by decisions. The tendency of law by precedent is to magnify the past and lose touch with new conditions, but the courts frequently do not follow this maxim and overrule earlier cases. Equity once was one corrective of this tendency; new statutes and the adoption of modernized uniform laws or codes are other remedies.

Preferential voting, a system by which the voter marks his first, second and third choices on the ballot. Then, when the votes are counted, if one candidate has a majority of the first choices, he is declared elected. If no candidate has a majority of the first choices, the second choices are added in, and if this does not give any candidate a majority, the third choices also are counted to determine the successful candidate.

This method of voting is a definite advantage over the ordinary type and attempts to select a candidate by a majority of votes, rather than by a mere plurality. Preferential voting has been widely criticized because as much weight is given to the second and third choices as to the first choices, and the second-choice vote balances the first choice in the final tabulations. Furthermore, many voters have refused to cast more than

a first choice, which defeats the purpose of the system.

Premier, see *Prime Minister.*

Press, Freedom of. See *Censorship.*

Primary election, the selection by a political party of candidates for public office to run for election on the party ticket. This selection was originally made in a legislative caucus, in which the members of the legislature had a party meeting and determined who the candidate of that party should be. In the time of President Jackson this method was supplanted by the party convention, composed of delegates of the small units of the party. Though the convention method has been retained in nominating candidates for President and Vice-President of the United States, it has been generally abandoned for other purposes.

Direct primary is the present widely used method of selecting candidates for office by the party. A primary election is held at an officially designated time prior to every election, and the members of the various parties vote for the persons whom they desire to be the party candidates in the regular election. In most states the voter in a primary election receives only the ballot of his party, on which are names nominated by petition and spaces for any names to be written in. In Wisconsin, Montana and Minnesota *open primaries* are held in which the voter receives the ballots of all parties and secretly chooses one party ballot and votes on it, the other party ballots being destroyed. The person in each party receiving the highest number of votes for a particular office in the primary election is designated as the candidate of his party for that office in the regular election. In some states where there is only one strong party, and nomination in the primary amounts to an election, there is a special provision that if no candidate receives a majority of the votes cast, a special *run off* election is held between the two candidates with the largest number of votes.

The direct primary election has not achieved the hopes of its sponsors, and the selection of candidates still remains largely in the hands of the political machine. The direct primary has been further criticized because it costs the Government so much for printing the ballots, because it costs anyone so much to secure a nomination and because the public takes so little interest in the primary election. But the direct primary seems better than any of the old systems of selecting party candidates for local offices.

The party candidates for President and Vice-President of the United States are selected in national party conventions. The delegates to the party conventions were formerly assigned on the basis of double the combined number of Senators and Representatives of the state in Congress. Owing to the objections to this system recent modifications have been made. In 1932 the Democratic party ruled that the number of delegates of each state to the convention should include twice the number of Senators and Representatives serving in the 72d Congress, with additional delegates granted to those states that had secured additional representation in Congress under the Reapportionment Act of 1930; delegates from American possessions; and four delegates at large for each Senator in Congress. It recommended that half of such delegates should be women. The rules providing for the allotment of delegates to the Republican national convention are complex, allowing four delegates at large from each state, two additional delegates at large for each representative at large in Congress from each state, two delegates at large from certain possessions and three additional delegates at large for each state casting its electoral vote for the Republican nominee for President in 1928, with adjustments under the Reapportionment Act of 1930.

In some states a direct primary is used to select the delegates to the national conventions, and in about one-third of the states the voters can express their choices for presidential candidates. Other states select their delegates by a state convention.

In the Republican national convention a majority is necessary to select the party candidate for office, but in the Democratic convention a two-thirds vote is necessary. In both, if the necessary vote is not secured on the first ballot, the candidates with a small number of votes drop out and the balloting continues until one candidate secures the requisite number and is selected as the party candidate for President. The convention then proceeds to select a candidate for Vice-President.

Prime minister, the first minister or department chief, especially in a representative government with a Cabinet of which the prime minister or premier is head.

The office developed gradually in England. About 1717 the king no longer attended meetings of the Cabinet, and thus the way was opened for one minister to take the lead and act as presiding officer. Robert Walpole from 1721 to 1742 was actually the first prime minister though he had no such title. William Pitt, who was chancellor of the exchequer and first lord of the treasury from 1783 to 1801, claimed the title of prime minister and argued that there must be a "minister . . . possessing the Chief Weight in the Council and the principal place in the confidence of the king." The 19th century saw the growth of the office and its gradual shift from responsibility to the Crown to responsibility to the Commons. In England the prime minister is rarely the foreign minister; usually he is chancellor of the exchequer and almost always he is a member of the House of Commons now that the power of the House of Lords has been diminished.

The Premier of the French Republic—more accurately, the President of the Council of Ministers—is named by the President. In France there are many parties, and often there is no recognized powerful opposition to the retiring premier. Often the premiership is offered to several leaders before one accepts it and manages to form a ministry.

With the diminishing power of the sovereign in Great Britain, and other countries having a similar form of government, the prime minister has assumed increasing importance. Temporarily, he *is* the head of the government, though he must resign if his government fails to receive a vote of confidence on important measures.

There is no parallel in the government of the United States to the prime minister. The President forms his own Cabinet and this Cabinet is quite unlike any government group in England or France.

Primogeniture, a system of inheritance whereby, upon the death of the owner, his lands invariably become the legal property of his oldest male heir, thus remaining intact in the family. American government has disapproved of this system, which the legislatures have abolished, providing for the division of landed estates among the numerous heirs (with rules of distribution varying in the different states). The object and the effect have been to prevent the concentration of vast quantities of land in the possession of a privileged class.

Private law, that part of the law that is administered between citizens in contradistinction to *public law,* which deals with the public generally or some class of the public.

Privilege, originally a favor granted by a law to a private person (Latin *privus,* private, and *lex, legis,* a law) or a law applying only to a certain class; then any right or immunity not enjoyed by all persons. Now it generally means some peculiar right or favor granted contrary to the general rule. The 14th Amendment to the U.S. Constitution forbids a state to "make or enforce any law which shall abridge the privileges or immunities of citizens of the United States." Article IV, Section 2, of the Constitution reads: "The citizens of each state shall be entitled to all privileges and immunities of citizens in the several states." In the limited sense, members of Congress have "parliamentary privilege," that is, immunity from arrest in any civil case and freedom of speech during a session of Congress. *Privileged communications* are confidential as between husband and wife or attorney and client. The one who receives such a communication cannot be compelled to disclose it in court.

Privy Council, see *Council.*

Privy seal, the seal that the sovereign of Great Britain attaches to those grants and deeds that do not require the great seal. On all documents that do require the great seal the privy seal must be attached before they go to the Lord Chancellor who affixes the great seal. The custodian of the privy seal is the Lord Privy Seal, and he has cabinet rank.

Prize courts and **Prize law,** the jurisdiction and the rules governing captures at sea in time of war. (Prize is from French *prise,* taken; and is used in the phrases, prize crew and prize money.) Prize law is a law of might and force administered at the order of the executive and not upon principles of justice and equity. Controversy over prize money after the Revolutionary War called attention to the need of some authority greater than that of the courts in each state. Under the Federal Constitution the Congress has power to make rules concerning captures on land and water (Art. I, Sec. 8, Cl. 11) and Federal courts have authority extending to "all cases of admiralty and maritime jurisdiction." (Art. III, Sec. 2, Cl. 1.)

Probate court, the tribunal with jurisdiction over the estates of deceased persons, usually a separate and specific court. In some states it is named *orphans' court* or *surrogate's court.*

Probation, release of a convicted person on a suspended sentence under the supervision and guidance of a special officer called *probation officer* to whom the delinquent must report. The method is closely related to *parole.* In 1878 the city of Boston appointed several probation officers and now the system is in operation in every state of the union—less effectively in rural communities. Children's courts operate almost entirely on this principle of putting the delinquent on probation—testing, proving.

Process, a writ or mandate of a court calling a defendant into court to answer in an action, civil or criminal. A *process server* is a person who serves such a writ by presenting it to the person called into court.

Progressive party, a name given to a political party in the United States on three separate occasions in the 20th century. In 1912, Theodore Roosevelt disapproved of President Taft's policies, and when he failed to receive the Republican presidential nomination, organized the Progressive, or Bull Moose party. Roosevelt's candidacy so split the vote that the Democrat, Woodrow Wilson was elected.

In 1924, Senator R. M. LaFollette organized a Progressive party and was its presidential candidate. He campaigned for legislation favorable to farmers and laborers.

In 1948, Henry A. Wallace organized a Progressive party and as its presidential nominee campaigned for a civil rights program, for socialization of public utilities, and conciliatory talks with Russia.

Prohibition party, a political party favoring the prohibition of the manufacture, sale or transportation of alcoholic beverages and various other measures, such as woman suffrage and the direct election of senators. It was formed in 1869 by the Grand Lodge of the Good Templars in Oswego, N.Y. It has had a presidential candidate in every election since then, and although it has elected only one member to Congress and has never polled a large popular vote, it played an important part in securing the adoption of the prohibition amendment.

Proletariat, the workers; the classes of society who earn a living by working for wages. In ancient Rome it meant anyone who had less than 1,500 asses (coins of small value—at one time a dime, later a cent) and therefore was considered able to serve the state only by rearing children. It comes from a Latin adjective *proletarius* meaning belonging to children.

Propaganda, any information of a biased or exaggerated nature issued for the purpose of influencing public opinion. There is a deluge of propaganda from governments as well as from all sorts of organizations and individuals attempting to convert public opinion to some cause. In times of war, propaganda is extensively and painstakingly organized by the government in order to arouse the patriotism of the people and keep them united in support of the national program. A dictator uses a constant stream of propaganda to maintain his power and his popularity with the people. The word was originally used for the missionary work of the Roman Catholic Church; one of its administrative departments is the Congregation of Propaganda (*de propaganda fide,* literally, of spreading the faith), and a College of the Propaganda or training school for missionaries was established in 1627 by Pope Urban VIII.

Proportional representation, often abbreviated P.R., a method of choosing officials (especially legislative) so that minorities will be represented, and the number of officials from different parties will be as nearly as possible be related to the actual votes cast by the voters. In 1857 an Englishman, Thomas Hare, wrote a pamphlet outlining a method of securing this result that was highly praised in John Stuart Mill's famous book *Representative Government* (1861). P.R. never came into use in England, but in different forms it is in use in Northern Ireland, the island of Malta, some Australian and Canadian provinces, in Finland (election of President and legislature), the Netherlands, Sweden, Czechoslovakia (lower House of the legislature), Belgium (lower House) and part of the United States.

The Belgian system, named after its deviser, De Hondt or d'Hondt, provides for party lists of candidates. The voter casts a single vote for the whole party list. Each party gets a proportion of all seats in the Chamber in the same ratio as the party's total vote bears to the grand total vote. This method makes it possible for blocs or groups of small parties to secure seats in the legislature.

The Hare method is a single *transferable* vote for each voter. He marks on his ballot his preferences, putting 1, 2, 3 with the names of his first, second and third choices. He may put in as many numbers as there are candidates. Up to a certain *quota* number, enough to elect a candidate, all the first-choice votes for him are counted for him; but beyond that number ballots with first-choice for an elected candidate are not credited to him, but to the second-choice candidate—and so down the line. First-choice ballots for a candidate who does not poll enough votes to pass a certain minimum (usually equal to the number of names required on a nominating petition) are not counted for that candidate but are transferred to those marked for second choice. Carrying this out by transferring both from the top and the bottom of the poll results in every ballot being credited to an elected candidate. No vote (except on a defective ballot) is thrown away.

The *quota* of votes to elect may be set by law or may be arrived at by dividing the total number of votes cast by the number of candidates to be chosen. When the quota is set by law, the number of candidates elected will vary from year to year. In 1936 the City of New York adopted proportional representation, but after several years of trial this method of voting was abandoned because of its relative complication and also because it gave undue representation in the case of minorities.

In Kalamazoo, Mich., and in Sacramento, Calif., P. R. was adopted but declared unconstitutional. Cleveland adopted P. R. in 1921, but abandoned it 10 years later. It was also adopted in other cities and towns in the United States including Boulder, Colo. (1917), Cincinnati, Ohio (1924), Hamilton, Ohio (1925), Toledo, Ohio (1934), Wheeling, W. Va. (1935) and Yonkers, N. Y. (1938). As some cities abandoned the plan others adopted it.

Another system has been used in Illinois since 1870. Three state representatives are chosen from each senatorial district, and every voter has three votes. He may give them all to one candidate, divide them 1½ and 1½ between two candidates or give one each to three candidates. This is called *cumulative voting.*

France tried the Belgian system, but gave it up because it gave too much power to blocs and small parties. Another system, originated in Baden and adopted by the German Reich, went to pieces under Nazi rule. With variations, proportional representation has been used extensively in European countries.

In 1931 Yugoslavia adopted a variation of the "list system" as used in Belgium, but this was ended with the overthrow of the government in 1945 and the setting up of a Communist form of government.

Proportional representation as a method of electing a legislative or representative body has not made much progress in the United States.

Prorogation, act by which the sovereign terminates a session of the legislature. This act ends all pending legislation, and such matters must be reintroduced at another session to receive consideration. The king of England has this power, as did the king of Egypt before the abdication.

Protection, the system or policy of fostering and shielding home industry from foreign competition by imposing high taxes upon foreign-made goods imported into the home country. In the earliest days of the United States the Government adopted this method of aiding industry by preventing competition from foreign goods, and with the exception of a short period in the middle of the 19th century this protection policy was followed until the Franklin D. Roosevelt administration. The general principle of protection has been that the duty fixed on a foreign commodity should be determined by the difference between the cost of production at home and the cost of production abroad, but the application of this principle has been practically impossible, and tariff rates were often established much higher than necessary to equalize the difference in cost of production. This protection policy has been favored by the industrial and banking groups and has been a main doctrine of the Republican party. Economists are agreed that, in general, this policy of protection is a tax on the consumer, an especial burden on the farmer and economically undesirable, but the protection policy has been followed because of the pressure of manufacturing interests and because of a desire to develop national self-sufficiency as a measure of preparedness for war. Even England, which was traditionally a free-trade country and had grown and prospered without protection, changed its policy after World War I and adopted a protective tariff in 1932.

Under the Reciprocal Tariff Act of 1934, the President of the United States was authorized to make tariff agreements with individual foreign nations and to put these rates into effect without submitting them to the Senate for ratification. Negotiations, conducted with most foreign countries, resulted in a general lowering of tariff rates.

The Reciprocal Trade Agreements Act of 1951 suspended all concessions to "iron-curtain" countries. The law of 1955 gave the president increased latitude for raising and lowering tariff rates.

Reciprocal trade agreements are not automatically renewed as soon as they expire, but are extended each time by Congress for a specified number of years.

Protectorate, the relationship between a stronger nation and a weaker one in which the former protects and partially controls the latter, nearly always for the benefit of the stronger state. The term is also used to mean the weaker country in this relationship. The United States has exercised a protectorate over the Dominican Republic, Nicaragua, Haiti, Liberia and (from 1903 to 1934 under the Platt Amendment) Cuba. With the abandonment of an imperialistic policy, American marines were withdrawn from Nicaragua by President Hoover, and in 1934 President Franklin D. Roosevelt withdrew troops from Haiti and negotiated a treaty with Cuba abrogating the right of the United States to intervene in Cuba's internal affairs, but maintaining a naval base at Guantánamo Bay. Britain exercises a protectorate over Bechuanaland, Swaziland, the British Solomon Islands and the Protectorate of South Arabia.

Protocol, in diplomacy the preliminary draft, agreement or statement of principles that is drawn up to be used as a basis for the negotiating of the final treaty; a convention not requiring ratification to become operative.

Province, any large territory or administrative division of a nation. The Romans used the term for any conquered district, but modern provinces correspond roughly to the states of the United States. The subdivisions of Canada, China and Spain are called provinces.

Public debt, the obligations of a government (national, state or local). Obligations for moneys borrowed constitute a *funded debt* as distinct from the *floating debt* of miscellaneous charges payable on demand. The idea of a public debt is easy to grasp when one realizes that any government is a business concern of long standing and continuous existence. A government that is not continuous—like the Czarist rule in Russia or the Confederate States of America—is like a bankrupt business: its debts are not paid.

In 1861, the public debt of the United States was about 90 million dollars; ten years later, following the Civil War, it had risen to nearly $2,500,000,-000. In 1915 it had been reduced to about $1,500,000,000 but 4 years later, in 1919, it had risen to over $25,000,000,000. In 1932, about the beginning of the world-wide economic depression, it had been reduced to about 19,500,000,000. During the depression governmental activities raised it to over $37,000,000 in 1938. World War II expenditures increased it to about $250,000,000. In 1957 the public debt was estimated at over $270,000,000,000.

The mere fact that a state or city has or has not a large debt is not necessarily an indication of the soundness of its financial structure. It is similar to a corporation in this respect, for you cannot judge the worth of a corporation by the amount it owes—that is, its outstanding stock. A state or city that has borrowed a million dollars for slum clearance may be in a more prosperous condition than another state that refused to borrow and allowed the slums to continue.

Public Domain, The, originally embraced all the area to which the Government of the United States held the title by virtue of its sovereignty. The "original public domain" was made up on

HUDIBRAS AND RALPHO in stocks, from a satiric poem written by Samuel Butler.

1,442,200,320 acres of land and 20,232,-320 acres of water area. This included the states of Alabama, Florida, Mississippi and all states north and west of the Ohio and Mississippi rivers except Texas. This public domain was acquired as follows: 266,430,000 acres by treaty with Great Britain at the end of the Revolution and by cession of western lands by the states to the Federal Government; Louisiana Purchase (1803), 530,000,000 acres; Oregon territory (by discovery), 38,000,-000 acres; Florida purchase (1819), 46,000,000 acres; Mexican cession (1848), 339,000,000 acres; Texas cession (1850), 79,000,000 acres; Gadsden purchase (1854), 19,000,000 acres. The Alaska purchase in 1867 added 378,000,000 acres.

Public policy or **Public interest,** the general spirit or customs of the people, underlying principles, occasionally invoked by the courts. Contracts are sometimes declared illegal and void merely as being against public interest —for example, a contract under which for a consideration one promised not to marry for a certain number of years. Contracts *contra bonos mores,* against good morals, are void as a matter of public policy. Advertising a reward for the return of stolen goods "and no questions asked" is against public policy in some places and is forbidden by statute.

Public utility, a business that supplies a public service—gas, electricity, water, transportation, communication—and charges for that service prices set by the government or regulated by law. The courts have defined a public utility as a business "affected with public interest," and more and more industries are being held to come within this broad classification. The public utility, whether privately owned or built and operated by the government, tends to be a monopoly, and what it has for sale becomes a necessity. For these reasons and for the public interest in the service, utilities have been more and more regulated and controlled by government, which sets the rates to be charged and declares that there is an obligation on the part of the utilities to be reasonable in dealing with the public. It has been so in the past with ferries, hackmen and innkeepers; it is so now with light and power companies, railways, telephone and telegraph companies.

The degree of control varies. It is more obvious and simple perhaps in a government-operated utility—like the U.S. postal service; the British postal service, which includes telegraph and telephone; and the waterworks, ferries and public markets that are almost without exception owned by municipalities. In the case of privately owned and operated utilities, rate-making must be based on two considerations—advantage to the public and fair return to the private owner on his investment. This obligation of the rate-setting authority to the private owner of a utility is based on the general principles of equity and is specifically required by the due-process clause of the 14th Amendment to the Constitution of the United States.

In rate setting there are several puzzling and controversial steps:

Is valuation (determination of a base for the rate) to be the original cost or an estimated cost of reproducing the existing property at present building prices? The second may be fairer, but it is certainly much more difficult than figuring original cost. On the other hand the value may be more or less than the original cost.

If valuation means present value, how is depreciation to be figured? Is the decrease in the value of equipment and buildings continuous throughout its life—so that if a machine that costs $50,000 will last 10 years, it can be valued at $45,000 after 1 year's use, at $40,000 after 2 years and at $5,000 after 9 years?

What is a fair rate of return? Does it differ from time to time—and from place to place?

On all these questions there have been sharp differences of opinion between the utilities and the commissions that are authorized to set rates. When the disputes have been taken into court, the decisions there have not set any definite rule.

The New Deal with the creation and development of the Tennessee Valley Authority in 1933 for the manufacture and distribution of cheap electric current suggested a method of setting rates: if the Federal Government goes into the business of a public utility, it can secure a *yardstick* to measure the cost and the efficiency of the privately owned public utility. It is an obvious criticism that a government-owned utility paying no taxes can operate at much lower cost than a privately owned utility that must pay many taxes.

Public works, the construction of public projects with the especial purpose of the reduction of unemployment and the restoration of purchasing power. Public works have always been carried on in the United States but, until recently, they were on a small scale. The world-wide economic depression of the 1930's forced government to fill the void created by the collapse of industry and the resulting unemployment. To do this, a planned economy was set up in which public works were an essential element. Roads, public buildings, reclamation, flood control, river and harbor improvements, housing and other similar work, either by direct hiring by the government or by provision of funds and guarantees against financial loss to private industry, were all operated under public works.

States and municipalities also engage normally in public works, stepping up their programs to provide added public employment when needed. Such local government activities are usually concerned with roads, park systems, public building construction and similar undertakings. Federal or local public works programs can only be successful when based on careful long-distance planning.

Punishment, the penalty inflicted by a legal authority for the violation of the law. In primitive times a punishment was inflicted from a desire for vengeance; if a man killed another the murderer had to be killed. In more modern times the idea has been to protect society by making an example of the offender and thus deter others from violating the law. At present the motive is to reform the offender and make him a constructive member of society.

Pure food laws, legislation to prevent adulteration and to protect the purchaser of foods. This type of legislation began in 1892, and such laws are now in operation in 46 of the 48 states. The Federal Pure Food and Drug Act of 1906 forbade the manufacture, sale and interstate transportation of adulterated foods and drugs; set up a Food and Drug Administration in the Department of Agriculture and established Federal inspection of slaughterhouses and packing plants. In 1872 the U.S. Supreme Court in the New Orleans Slaughterhouse Cases had decided that the police power of the states was not invalidated by the 14th Amendment (forbidding state laws abridging privileges of citizens) and that strict regulation of the meatpacking business in New Orleans was constitutional. The Pure Food Drug and Cosmetic Act of 1938 greatly extended the power of the Federal Government to prevent adulteration.

Quorum, the minimum number of members of a body who, when assembled, are legally competent to transact business: a majority unless there is a provision to the contrary.

For a long time it was the practice for members of the minority party in the House of Representatives of the United States to refuse to answer the roll call in order to delay proceedings and thus cause an adjournment on the grounds that a quorum was lacking In 1890 Speaker of the House Reed held that members of the House actually in the chamber who declined to answer should be counted present; and it was made a rule of the House that, on demand of a member or at the suggestion of the Speaker, Representatives in attendance but refusing to respond when their names were called be counted present.

Quo warranto (Latin, by what warrant), a writ issued by a court demanding that a person or group of persons show cause why they continue in the exercise of public office, enjoy privileges their right to which is questioned, operate under a franchise which is disputed, or continue in the enjoyment of certain other specified liberties.

Radical, one who advocates an extreme and revolutionary change in the economic or political organization.

Rebellion, organized and armed resistance to a government or defiance of it or any lawful authority by persons subject to that authority. It is a means used to redress grievances by force or to seize power for a minority. Important rebellions are the Great Rebellion (1642–52), the English Civil War between Catholic Charles I and the Protestants led by Parliament; and the Boxer Rebellion (1900) in which certain groups of Chinese attempted to drive all foreigners out of their country.

Recall, the removal of elected officers by popular vote at an election called by a petition signed by a certain per-

centage of the voters. As an official is an agent of the people, this is an extension of the popular control of government.

In the United States, the recall was first adopted by the 1903 charter of Los Angeles, and then by Seattle in 1906. The following states have the recall: Oregon, (1908); California (1911); Arizona, Colorado, Idaho, Nevada and Washington (all in 1912); Michigan (1913); Kansas, Louisiana and North Dakota (all in 1914); Wisconsin (1926). Besides, it is in the charters of many commission-governed cities. It does not apply to judges in the states of Idaho, Louisiana, Michigan and Washington. In Kansas appointed state officials may be recalled. In general, recall laws guarantee a period of grace, usually 6 months, before they can be invoked. At the end of this period, petitions with the required percentage of voters may be circulated against the accused officials. The recall election takes place after the filing of the signed petition.

Reception, the adoption of Roman Law into many of the legal systems of Europe, notably in Germany in the 16th century. The law of The Netherlands also had the Reception and through it and other influences Scotch Law became Roman and has only gradually been assimilated to the principles of English Common Law.

Reciprocity, in international trade mutual agreement between nations for more favorable tariff schedules than those granted other nations having no such agreement.

Reclamation, the bringing of land under cultivation. This may refer to land that at one time had been under cultivation and had been abandoned, or it may refer to land that had not previously been cultivated, usually for lack of water. Fundamentally, the soil is rich, but the territory arid and lacking in rainfall. Reclamation of the land to a productive condition is usually accomplished by irrigation. The first law relating to swampland reclamation was enacted in 1849 and related to Louisiana. By 1860, fifteen states were receiving authorized grants.

The reclamation of arid or desert lands involved many extensive areas west of the Mississippi River and was the reverse of swampland reclamation.

Because the areas involved usually were located in several states and because reclamation involved the use of water from rivers and a large investment over a long period of time, such projects came to be directed, controlled and executed by the Federal Government in co-operation with the states involved.

Three general policies have been followed: (1) encouragement of individual initiative under the Desert Land Act of 1877; (2) encouragment and stimulation of state and corporate enterprise under the Carey Act of 1894; and (3) reclamation by the Federal Government under the Newlands Act of 1902.

Until recent years, much of the land reclaimed by irrigation was by private enterprise. Examples of the Federal Government co-operating with private,

city and state-owned corporations are the Hoover Dam on the Colorado River, the All-American Canal into the Imperial Valley of California, and the Columbia, Colorado and Missouri River basins. All such projects involve irrigation, flood control, the generation of electricity or a combination of such objectives.

Reconstruction Finance Corporation (R.F.C.), organized by special Act of Congress, Jan. 22, 1932, to increase the willingness and ability of financial institutions to lend money. The RFC was also authorized to lend money to banks of all kinds, to building and loan associations, agricultural credit corporations, mortgage and insurance companies, states and their political sub-divisions, and to other public agencies. Railroads were also included.

The R.F.C. was abolished July 30, 1953. It was replaced by the Small Business Administration, an agency with lending authority of $275,000,000, with no loan to exceed $150,000.

Recorder, title given to the public official in some states, who has charge of real estate and other records; also certain judges in New Jersey with criminal jurisdiction. In Pennsylvania the Recorder is called a prothonotary.

Red, an Anarchist or Communist. In the symbolism of colors, red has long been the color of the vestments worn by priests in certain Western churches at the feasts of the martyrs. Probably from the time of the French Revolution, red, the color of blood, has been used to stand for those who were willing to shed blood for their cause. Red has been universally adopted as the color of Communism and revolution. The term is frequently used to refer to a person holding extreme or violent revolutionary views; also to identify Communist supporters or sympathizers.

Referendum, the submission of an act passed by the legislature to the people, who must approve it before it becomes effective. The usual procedure is for a petition to be drawn up, signed by the requisite number of voters and submitted to a designated official to be placed on the ballot in the next election. Most of the states use the referendum for amending the state constitution; about half the states use the referendum for general legislation, and some 300 cities use it for municipal ordinances.

Reforestation, the replenishment of deforested areas with trees of economic or decorative value.

There were many early statutes encouraging tree planting, but permanent reforestation work was not begun until 1885, when New York State established a service to administer the state forests scientifically. About two-thirds of the states now have forestry departments, which, in addition to other duties, supply planting stock to citizens and establish state forests.

Regent, one who rules in the place of another, especially in the name and place of a sovereign. A regent takes the place of a child potentate or one who is absent or disabled. The Board of Regents in New York controls the state's incorporated educational institutions.

U.S. FOREST SERVICE

RESEARCH INSTITUTE OF FOREST GENETICS covering cones to protect them from squirrels.

Registration of voters, the entering in a registry before an election of the name, address, occupation, age, party affiliation of and similar information regarding each voter. This registration is used to determine the party of the voter at the time of the primary election, in New York and most other states; and at the regular election the registration is used as an aid in the prevention of fraudulent voting. Forty states require an unrestricted and general registration of voters; two states do not require any registration; and in the others registration is required in the more populous sections of the state.

Reich, German word meaning a country but including the idea of the government and the people as well as the geographical nation. It has been traditionally translated empire, but it is equally applicable to the German state whether it is a republic or a dictorship.

Relief, as now understood, is a temporary form of social welfare. The term first came into public use during the depression of the 1930's though public relief, for many years, had been extended to the poor and the sick and to the victims of flood, famine, fire and other similar disasters. Until recent years social relief was usually extended by private individuals and charities; disaster relief was furnished by such private or public organizations as the Red Cross, Salvation Army, by federal and state governments and by private individuals.

The inadequacy of the measures taken and the election of Franklin D. Roosevelt in a Democratic landslide in 1932 were followed by the creation of numerous federal relief agencies, most of them designed to be temporary. The Federal Emergency Relief Administration was created and extended grants-in-aid for both work and home relief; the Civilian Conservation Corps, the Civil Works Administration, the Works Progress Administration, the National Youth Administration and the Resettle-ment Administration were all created to provide relief in various forms. A beginning in putting relief on a permanent social welfare basis was made by the enactment of the Social Security act of 1935.

American relief to Displaced Persons and to the war torn countries of Europe was extended by UNRRA, the ECA and the IRO.

Removal, Executive Power Of, the authority to declare an office vacant usually residing in the authority that makes the appointment. The Federal Constitution is silent on the subject of removals. Several presidents have exercised the right, sometimes in opposition to Congress. In the case of states the power of the governor to remove from office is usually restricted.

Reparations, a modern term used to describe a payment in money or goods or both made by a vanquished people or nation to the victors. In ancient times this payment was called tribute. It was levied by stronger on weaker nations or tribes and was a means of financing conquests and the continuing military organizations required to keep conquered people in subjugation. It was also used as a means of preserving freedom and independence by buying off aggressors.

Early Practices. As time passed tribute gave way to military indemnities levied by victor on vanquished, as during the Thirty Years War. Oliver Cromwell imposed indemnity payments on the Dutch in 1654; Napoleon imposed both indemnities and military requisitions as a means of helping to finance his military conquests. Germany in 1871 imposed on France an indemnity of five billion francs; Japan, after defeating China in 1895, imposed an indemnity of $180,000,000. The Allied nations imposed an indemnity on China of $333,000,000 as a consequence of the Boxer insurrection in 1900.

World War I reparations were based on the princple that Germany was responsible for the war and that she should pay for the resulting damage and destruction incurred in the victorious Allied countries. The difficulty encountered was in the transfer of large money payments from one country to another. A Reparations Commission, appointed to administer the reparations and to devise means for their payment, fixed the German liability at 132,000,-000,000 gold marks, equivalent to $31,-500,000,000. This was an enormous sum of money to be taken out of a defeated country.

However, the question of inter-allied indebtedness, much of which had resulted from war loans made by the United States, became entangled with reparation payments. The United States maintained that the two should be kept separate, but European allies inisisted that the two were inseparable and proposed to meet their indebtedness to this country from German reparations payments. This method led to confusion and default.

Under the Dawes Plan (1924) and the Young Plan (1929) the payments were scaled down, and on July 8, 1932, the principal creditors of Germany agreed to a total payment of about $3,000,000,000. The threatened collapse of Germany in 1931 led to the Hoover Moratorium on both war debts and reparation payments. Beginning in 1932 all war debt payments, except by Finland, were defaulted. Hitler's rise to power in 1933 was marked by a repudition of the Versailles treaty of 1919 and brought all reparation payments to an end.

World War II. Because of the difficulties experienced with money reparation payments, the policy adopted at the Potsdam conference of 1945 was to require these payments to be made in the form of industrial facilities, agricultural products, etc. Germany would be required to compensate to the greatest possible extent for the loss and suffering caused her opponents. The money value of reparations was not fixed, but in the Potsdam agreement it was provided that "Payments of reparations should leave enough resources to enable the German people to subsist without external assistance." For all practical purposes there was no clear definition of the plan in its full extent. Percentages of a variable amount and character of industrial production equipment were allocated to Russia from the western zone of Germany as well as the right to make removals from the Russian-occupied eastern zone. On March 26, 1946, the Allied Control Council approved a plan for reparations and for fixing the level of Germany's post-war economy. This plan was subsequently modified, Aug. 29, 1947, and again in the Bonn agreement of Nov. 23, 1949. The Western powers strongly objected to Russia's indiscriminate dismantling in East Germany and Austria.

The peace treaties with Italy, Bulgaria, Hungary, Rumania and Finland provided for a definite amount of reparations to be paid by each country over given periods of time in the form of industrial equipment, production output, etc. The payments were specifically allocated.

Repeal, the revocation, abrogation or cancellation of a law or regulation. A statute is expressly repealed when a subsequent statute specifically states that the prior one is repealed; or a statute may be repealed by implication when a subsequent statute contains provisions contrary to the prior one. The term is especially applied to the repeal of the 18th (prohibition) Amendment of the Constitution, accomplished by the 21st Amendment, ratified in 1933.

Replevin, a legal action to regain the possession of personal chattels that have been taken unlawfully from the plaintiff. The plaintiff gives security for the property thus returned to him pending court decision. The writ for return and the action in court are both called *replevin.*

Reprieve, suspension for a stated period of the execution of any sentence (especially death sentence) upon a convicted criminal. It is issued by the President of the United States in cases involving Federal law and by the governor of a state or state board of pardon in other cases.

Republic, a state in which the sovereign power is vested in the citizens, who govern themselves through elected representatives. In a more general sense, a republic is any nation not governed by a hereditary ruler. The ancient Greek city-states were completely democratic and the citizens governed directly. In more recent times a state was termed a republic even though the right to vote was restricted to a small class.

Republican party, in the United States, the early name of the party that became first the Democratic-Republican party about 1800 and later the Democratic party as it is known today. The present Republican party arose out of the slavery issue, which caused a split in the old Democratic and Whig parties, and specifically in opposition to the Kansas-Nebraska Bill of 1854. The antislavery Whigs and the Free-Soil and Know-Nothing parties joined the new Republican party, and in 1856 it obtained a national organization and nominated John C. Frémont for President. He was defeated but received a creditable vote. Sectional bitterness increased, and the Republicans were belligerent toward the South. In 1858 the Republicans were victorious in the congressional elections and 2 years later their candidate, Abraham Lincoln, was made President. Lincoln was re-elected to office but a split appeared in the party, which became more apparent after Lincoln's assassination. Johnson was a conservative and favored a moderate policy toward the South, but the radical Republicans, led by Sumner, Stanton and Stevens favoring a stern attitude, became the dominant faction. U. S. Grant was the successful Republican presidential candidate in 1868 and was re-elected. Scandals during the Grant administration caused another rift in the party and the formation of the Liberal Republican party, which declined after showing some strength in 1872.

The disputed returns in the election of 1878 were held by Congress to have elected the Republican nominee, Hayes, but this election marked the end of the Republican domination in the South and the development of the *solid South,* which was not broken until the election of Herbert Hoover in 1928.

LIBRARY OF CONGRESS

"THE THIRD-TERM PANIC," by Thomas Nast, introduced the elephant as the Republican party symbol. It was based on Aesop's fable of "an Ass, having put on the Lion's skin, roamed about in the Forest, and amused himself by frightening all the foolish Animals he met with in his wanderings." The New York *Herald,* as the Ass, is frightening the creatures with shouts of Caesarism, the movement to run Grant for a third term. The elephant, a bulky Republican voter, is stumbling into a pitfall.

After the election of Hayes, there tended to be a similarity in the platforms of the two major parties, and both parties contained conservative and liberal factions. The Republican party was representative of the New England and middle western financial interests and the prosperous western farmers and showed its greatest strength in the Northwest.

In 1880 the Republican nominee, Garfield, was elected, but at the next presidential election Cleveland was successful and became the first Democratic president since the Civil War. In 1888 the Republican party was victorious and elected Harrison. In 1896 the Republican party stood for the gold standard and conservative economic policies, in opposition to the radical Democrats led by Bryan, and McKinley was elected. Theodore Roosevelt, also a Republican, was the next President, but his splitting of the party led to the re-entry of the Democrats to power, and it was not until after World War I and the desire for a return to *normalcy* that the conservative Republicans were successful and elected Harding, then Coolidge and finally Hoover to the Presidency.

From 1933 to 1952 the Republican Party was out of power. Its presidential candidates, Alfred Landon in 1936, Wendell Wilkie in 1940, and Thomas E. Dewey in 1944 and 1948, were each defeated. Republicans gained control of Congress in 1946, but lost it in 1948. The Party generally coöperated in a bi-partisan foreign policy, but opposed many of the domestic policies of the Democratic Party before Eisenhower's Election.

Requisition, any formal request or demand by virtue of some right; especially for the return of a fugitive from justice. In this special sense, the word is used of the demand from one nation to another or from the authorities of one state of the Union to those of another. The surrender or extradition by one state to another of a person accused of a crime is required by the Federal Constitution (Art. IV, Sec. 2, Cl. 2).

Restraint of trade, any act, contract or agreement that unduly hinders or limits its legitimate competition and the pursuit of business by another. Statutes prohibiting agreements in restraint of trade have been interpreted by the courts as meaning *unreasonable* agreements in restraint of trade.

It manifests itself in various ways such as imposing restrictions on freedom of contract, or by agreements among competitors. These agreements take the form of pools, cartels, corporate or labor consolidations, etc. The Sherman Anti-trust Act of 1890, the Clayton Act of 1914 and other similar legislation was aimed at such corporate practices, but labor unions, exempted by the Clayton Act, are still free of such restraints.

Revolution, a radical and fundamental change in the government, its personnel or policies, such as the substitution of one government for another or the adoption of a new constitution. The term is also used to mean a radical change in any field, for example, the Industrial Revolution that changed our methods of manufacture through the introduction of machinery that displaced hand work, thereby causing temporary unemployment.

Riot, an unlawful assembly of three or more persons with tumult and violence that causes terror and a disturbance of the public peace. It must be proved that there was a premeditated unlawful assembly, that there was actual violence and force of a nature to cause terror and that the defendant was a participant in the disturbance. The English Riot Act of 1714 declared anyone guilty of felony who did not disperse upon proclamation or order to disperse by the proper law officer. This proclamation was called *Reading the Riot Act*.

Robbery, depriving a person of anything of value by taking it in his presence or from his person by force or intimidation. Some states provide degrees of robbery, as simple robbery, robbery with a gun, robbery in the daytime, and fix different penalties for each. Personal contact, force and fear enter into robbery and not into larceny.

Rotten borough, see *Borough.*

Sabotage, the purposeful waste or destruction of an employer's property. By working slowly, putting emery in lubricants to ruin machinery, breaking machines or other property and similar methods, employees seek to force the employer to grant concessions. Foreign spies sometimes succeed in sabotaging ships or other armaments. The term is also applied to the action of businessmen who cause a scarcity of goods in order to increase their profits.

Sanctions (from the same root as sacred), originally what makes anything sacred, dreaded, authoritative; then, in a general sense, anything that makes moral judgments valid—custom, conscience, public opinion; in law, the penalty and fear or the reward and hope that make the law respected and obeyed.

In international law where there is no police power to enforce decisions, sanctions is a recognized term for the co-operative action of certain nations to curb, check or punish a power breaking the law of nations.

The League of Nations Covenant provided (Art. XVI) that if any member resorted to war in disregard of the covenant, "all other members of the League . . . undertake to subject it to the severance of all trade or financial relations." Such sanctions were invoked by the League when Italy invaded Ethiopia, but the method did not prevent Italy from conquering Ethiopia in disregard of the League.

Satrap, the ruler of a province in ancient Persia. The satraps had absolute power in their provinces and so frequently abused it that the term is now used to mean a petty despot.

Seal (from Latin *sigillum,* a little sign or mark), originally an impression in wax or lead of an identifying mark to validate a signature or to take the place of a signature on a document; now any formal mark with a signature, even a mere pen scratch after one's signature around the letters *l. s.* for *locus sigilli,* place for seal.

A *deed* was originally an instrument under seal, but now some states do not require a seal on the conveyance of real estate.

Secession, formal withdrawal from an association, usually by a minority group that is dissatisfied with the policies of the majority. South Carolina seceded from the Union in 1860 and was followed by 10 other southern states. **The Civil War** settled the question that had existed from the time of the Constitutional Convention whether a state could secede from the union.

Secret Police is primarily Political Police. It has long been employed by the heads of state for their own protection and that of their government and is a weapon constantly used by dictators.

The modern ancestor of the Secret Police was the political police organized by Joseph Fouche at Napoleon's direction. Russia's secret police goes back many years to the Ochrana and the Cheka of the Tsars. Their modern counterpart have been the OGPU, the NKVD and now the MVD. Hitler in Germany had his Gestapo, Mussolini organized the OVRA, while Japan had the notorious Thought Control. Usually these national secret police organizations have been world-wide in their operations "shadowing" individuals wherever they went.

Secret Service, a department of the government whose agents are charged with the detection of Federal crimes, especially those of a political or military nature. The secret police of some nations, such as the MVD in Soviet Russia, have become powerful instruments for oppression and for the prevention of political opposition. In the United States the Secret Service is a division of the Department of the Treasury and is charged with the protection of the President and his family, the suppression of counterfeiting, the investigation of violations of certain acts, such as the Farm Loan Act, the Gold Reserve Act and the Liquor Trading Act, and investigations of offenses against the Treasury Department as the Secretary of the Treasury may direct.

Secretary, a public officer whose duty is to manage and direct the affairs of a department of the government. In the United States the heads of the departments of Agriculture, Commerce, Interior, Labor, State, Treasury, Defense, and Health, Education, and Welfare, are secretaries, and with the Attorney General and Postmaster General they make up the President's Cabinet. In Great Britain there are five secretaries of state: for the Home Department, for Foreign Affairs, for the Colonies, for Scotland, for Commonwealth Relations. They are members of the Cabinet. Other Cabinet members are not called secretaries.

Securities and Exchange Commission (SEC), created by the Securities Exchange Act of 1934 and given additional duties under the Public Utility Holding Company Act of 1935. The Commission is charged with the supervision of registration of securities and the suppression of fraudulent practices in the sale of securities under the Securities Act of 1933; supervision of security transactions under the Securities Exchange Act of 1934; and the regulation of public utility holding companies under the Public Utility Act of 1935.

The Commission is composed of five members, not more than three of whom may be members of the same political party. The members are appointed by the President with the advice and consent of the Senate for a term of 5 years.

Security, freedom from foreign aggression or interference. The desire for security has played a major part in European politics, and nations have sought security by nonaggression pacts, alliances, fortifications, armaments and international organizations, such as the United Nations.

France has long sought security from Germany. This desire was a reason for the Maginot Line. Since the end of World War II, the democratic nations, particularly of western Europe and North America, have sought security against sudden attack in various defensive economic and military pacts. Russia, likewise, has sought security by erecting a screen of satellite nations between herself and western Europe and has attempted Communist infiltration into the governments of her alleged enemies. This was done according to the general plan of Communist expansion and in order to cause as much confusion and sabotage as possible.

Sedition, the act of agitating by action, speech or writing for overthrowing or resisting the government. During World War I, sedition acts were passed by most of the states, restricting freedom of speech and stipulating severe penalties for any acts of a seditious nature.

Separation of powers, a political doctrine in the United States that the powers conferred upon the Federal Government by the Constitution are divided among three distinct and unique departments: legislative, executive and judicial. The legislature makes the laws, the judiciary interprets them, and the executive enforces the laws. Although this theory is still recognized, there are many practical impossibilities in such a separation of powers. The appointing power of the President is shared by the Senate; the treaty-making power is shared between President and Senate; the President shares legislative power through his veto; and Congress has powers of creating inferior courts and fixing the number of judges. Regardless of the theory, the practical administration of affairs has often broken down this division. During the Reconstruction era Congress completely dominated the executive, and in times of national crisis, such as the World Wars and the depression of 1929, the executive has completely dominated Congress. Furthermore the development of numerous administrative agencies that act both judicially and legislatively has tended to break down this separation of powers.

Sergeant at arms, a minor official, either elected or appointed, whose duty is to maintain order in a legislature or a court. The U.S. Senate, the House of Representatives and state legislatures have such officers. In England there is a sergeant at arms in both houses of Parliament to keep order and make any arrests ordered by the Speaker.

Single tax, a plan by which all government revenue would be secured through the taxation of economic rent. Henry George (1839-97), an

American writer and economist who was the leading exponent of the doctrine, argued that poverty could largely be abolished if the Government would appropriate the amount paid for the use of land (economic rent) and the unearned increase in land values. Early economists, such as Ricardo and the Physiocrats, had worked out similar doctrines.

Smuggling, carrying goods illegally from one country and entering another country with them by stealth, to avoid payment of customs duties; or bringing persons into a country in violation of the immigration laws.

Socialism, a political movement that aims to abolish exploitation by means of the collective ownership and democratic management of the basic instruments of production and distribution. Modern socialism includes several aspects: a criticism of the capitalistic system; an idea of the future ideal state and a proposed means of achieving it; and a political movement to achieve its proposals.

The Industrial Revolution in the latter part of the 18th century and the rise of modern capitalism that accompanied it brought into practical politics the idea that there should be a redistribution of income so that the employee would obtain a more equal share of production. Shortly after the peace of 1815 Robert Owen, a prominent English textile manufacturer, proposed that "villages of co-operation" be established to alleviate economic distress and suffering. With a small group of workers who believed in his ideals Owen came to America and established a communal settlement at New Harmony, Ind., which failed after 3 years. About the same time in France, Saint-Simon, Louis Blanc and Proudhon were advocating socialistic ideas. These early socialists were all utopian idealists, and it was the German Karl Marx, working with Friedrich Engels, who gave socialism its practical theory and definite organization. The famous *Communist Manifesto* (1848), issued by Marx and Engels, and the first volume of *Das Kapital* (1867), written by Marx, are the classic statements of socialism.

In England the Fabian Society, formed in 1883 by George Bernard Shaw, Sidney Webb, Ramsay MacDonald and others, sought to achieve socialism by a gradual evolution within the existing political structure. The Independent Labor Party, founded in England in 1893, is a socialistic party and has been in power twice since World War I and continues to be a powerful opposition party. Among its leaders were Keir Hardie, Sidney and Beatrice Webb, Ramsay MacDonald, Philip Snowden and Arthur Henderson.

In the United States early advocates of socialistic ideas were Horace Greeley, editor of the *New York Tribune,* Arthur Brisbane and (in his early years) Charles A. Dana. Edward Bellamy's *Looking Backward* (1888), which sold over a million copies, created a great interest in socialism.

The *Socialist Party* was formed in 1900, has had a ticket in every election since then, but it is no longer a leading party in the United States. The best-known leader of the Socialist party was Eugene V. Debs (1855-1926), a great orator, leader and idealist, who was imprisoned because he opposed the participation of the United States in World War I. Other leaders included Morris Hillquit, labor lawyer and author; Victor Berger, long a representative from Wisconsin; and Norman Thomas, party leader and several times candidate for President. At times the Socialist party has received nearly a million votes, but it has never achieved power, except in a few municipalities, because it has not obtained the support of labor. However socialistic principles have frequently been adopted by a major party.

Social Security Administration, The, created by the Social Security Act. approved, Aug. 14, 1935, originally operated independently until it became a part of the Federal Security Agency, July 1, 1939. The original three man Social Security board was abolished in 1946 and its functions transferred to The Federal Security Agency, which later was replaced by the Department of Health, Education, and Welfare. Within the Department, the Social Security Administration conducts the various phases of the program. These responsibilities included administration of the Old-Age and Survivors insurance, unemployment insurance and public assistance together with most of the maternal and child welfare programs of the Children's Bureau. These were transferred from the Department of Labor in 1946, except those relating to child labor. In 1948 when the U.S. Employment Service was transferred from the Department of Labor and the Federal Credit Union was placed under the Federal Security Agency, direction of these agencies was delegated to the Commissioner of the Social Security Administration.

The Social Security Administration came to include five program bureaus. They are: (1) Old-Age and Survivor insurance; (2) Bureau of Employment Security which administers Federal aspects of the operation of employment offices and of Federal-State unemployment insurance; (3) Bureau of Public Assistance, responsible for Federal-State programs for old-age assistance, aid to dependent children and aid to the blind; (4) the Children's Bureau, responsible for developing standards for the care, protection and well-being of children, and for programs in connection with maternal and child health, crippled children and child welfare services; and (5) the Federal Credit Unions responsible for chartering, supervising and examining agencies concerned with widespread extension of credit to people of limited means.

The Social Security law was amended several times in various important aspects.

Social Welfare includes freedom from want and fear, and security of employment which may be both of a public and private nature. In recent years it has assumed great political as well as social importance. Until the world-wide depression of the 1930's, most social welfare work was, almost exclusively, financed and carried on by private agencies, individuals and local organizations. This was particularly the case in the United States where charitable work, as it was called, was directed by the churches, social settlements, the Salvation Army or private individuals.

In cases of widespread disaster, when temporary relief was required, the Red Cross was prominent.

The New Deal promised social security in the form of unemployment and old-age insurance, sickness benefits and the hope for better housing and living conditions. Employment when not available in private establishments would be provided for in public works; provision for old age was to be taken care of by contributory old-age pension benefits; sickness was also to be taken care of. The various forms of accident compensation in effect were continued and extended; recreation facilities and medical clinics were set up and a comprehensive housing program for the low-income groups was planned and got under way.

Many of these promises, in varying degree, were fulfilled by provisions in the Federal Social Security Act of 1935, by the Federal Security Agency in 1939 and by various emergency measures some of which were made permanent.

The Wagner Labor Relations Act of 1935 gave power and security to organized labor, but unorganized labor received only a small portion of protection.

Public as well as private welfare agencies also do what they can to take care of workers and their families when they can prove eligibility and need for help.

Solicitor General, in the United States chief assistant to the attorney general and the second ranking official in the Department of Justice; in England a Crown officer next in rank to the attorney general.

Soviet, a workers' or soldiers' council in Russia. The soviets were first organized during the revolution of 1905 and were merely committees of factory workers. The soviets were revived and strengthened by the Bolsheviks during the revolution of 1917 and served as administrative and propaganda units upon which the Communist state was organized. Each soviet was supreme in the determination of its local affairs and served as the basic unit from which representatives were elected to higher congresses, the highest of which was the Union Soviet Congress. Under the Constitution of 1937 this method of indirect election was abolished, and universal direct election was adopted.

Speaker, one who presides over a legislative or deliberative assembly, enforcing rules of procedure, maintaining order and regulating the debates. The Speaker of the House of Representatives is formally chosen by a ballot of the members of the House, although in reality he is selected by a caucus of the majority party, the members of the majority party agreeing to vote for the representative so selected. The Speaker is the leader of the majority party in the House and has considerable influence in securing the adoption of measures proposed by his party.

Spheres of influence, the area of a country weak and undeveloped in military defenses to which a powerful nation acquires pre-emptory rights to economic exploitation by agreement with other Powers. Theoretically the sovereignty of a nation is not impaired by the establishment of a sphere of influence, but actually the interested nation has a great power over the area and often proceeds to annex the area as a colony.

The term was originally used at the time of the partition of Africa, when various powers agreed among themselves that each should confine its economic and later political efforts to a certain area and leave other areas to other Powers.

Spoils system, placing members of the successful political factions in lucrative government positions as a reward for their service to the political party. The spoils system slogan, "To the victor belong the spoils," had long been a political principle—in ancient Rome, in England in the time of the Georges and in colonial America—but in the time of Andrew Jackson it became the open practice in national politics.

State, Department of, the executive division of the Federal Government concerned with foreign relations, known originally as the department of foreign affairs, was constituted July 29, 1789. The secretary of state is the ranking officer in the President's Cabinet and the first Cabinet member in the Presidential succession.

The department receives and sends diplomatic and consular representatives to the nations of the world, conducts negotiations with foreign powers, develops international policies, is keeper of the Great Seal of the United States, publishes the *Statutes at Large* and has other domestic and foreign duties.

The Department of State is organized into 19 Offices, each in charge of a Director. Among the principal Offices are those of American Republics, European, Far Eastern, United Nations and other Affairs. The department also exercises jurisdiction over Caribbean, South Pacific and Inter-American Affairs.

States' Rights, or state sovereignty, has had a varied meaning in American history and often has been a defense mechanism of a minority section within the Federal Union. At one time, it meant the right of the individual states within the federation of the United States to nullify Federal laws or to secede from the Union at discretion. This conception ended with the Civil War.

States' Rights were at first conceived as a constitutional device with which to restrict the activity of the party in power. Recently they have been used to oppose attempts to take away from local areas certain powers, functions and responsibilities that

some people claim belong exclusively to the state.

The Tidelands Oil Law gave coastal states the right to off-shore minerals discovered within their historic boundaries. The federal order for desegregation caused great resentment in the South. Federal aid to education is prevented by state claims that disposition of school funds is in the exclusive domain of each state.

The growing size and complexity of the Federal Government and the close integration of all parts of the country with one another have acted to decrease the powers and rights of the individual states and to increase those of the central government.

State religion, the officially established religion of the state. Due largely to the Protestant Revolution, the Roman Catholic ideal of "One World, One Faith," broke down, and in the 17th century the principle of "One Nation, one Faith" arose. The king and the ruling class forced their form of religion upon the people, and official churches were organized to teach the official religion. By the Edict of Nantes (1598) Roman Catholic France granted toleration to the Huguenots; and by the Toleration Act (1689) Anglican England granted religious toleration to the Dissenters. These acts merely allowed unmolested worship and did not grant full civil rights to those who were not adherents to the state religion, nor did it free nonconformists from taxation for the support of the established church. The United States has never had a state religion.

Statute, as distinct from common law, a law passed by a legislature, the Federal Congress or the lawmaking body of a state. Sometimes the word is used of ordinances decreed by a municipal or town body.

Subpoena (Latin, under penalty), a writ commanding the appearance in court of a person on a stated day and hour, especially to give testimony on a case then to be heard. The writ may not be disobeyed, except under penalty (*sub poena*). When the writ calls for books or records to be brought into court by the person summoned, it is called a *subpoena duces tecum* (bring with thee).

Subsidy, a governmental grant of financial assistance to an individual, corporation or foreign nation for a purpose that is believed to be beneficial to the grantor. In England during the later part of the Middle Ages Parliament granted subsidies to the king, and it was the control over these subsidies that finally gave Parliament control over the king. During the reign of Charles II (1630–85) a fixed grant collected from a land tax was substituted for the subsidy. In France the king's financial power freed him from dependence upon the States-General and enabled him to exert absolute domination. Important international historical subsidies were the grants by England to Denmark during the Thirty Years' War and to the enemies of Napoleon during the Napoleonic Wars.

The most important subsidies at the present time are those granted to private individuals and corporations.

The United States grants subsidies for the development of airplane service and the merchant marine. Strictly speaking the subsidy is only the amount granted in excess of the legitimate cost of the service. Thus when the United States Government makes payments for carrying mail by air or steamers, it is only a subsidy to the extent that the amount paid is in excess of the legitimate cost of carrying the mail.

A *bounty* is similar to a subsidy but is granted for a certain service that has been rendered. Before the Civil War bounties were granted to induce enlistment in the army, and in frontier communities bounties are frequently given for killing certain dangerous wild animals.

Suicide, the death by his own hand of a sane person who has reached the age of discretion. It is a criminal act, but naturally no law can be effective when an attempt at self-destruction succeeds. Unsuccessful efforts may result in legal action, though the law is seldom invoked.

Suit, a legal claim, petition or prosecution; by extension, a case tried in a court of law or equity to decide an issue between a plaintiff (bringing the suit) and a defendant defending it. There are, of course, many highly technical details in some cases at law, but the principal steps or stages in the simplest kind of case may be summarized as follows: bringing the case to court, together with the parties involved; the definite formulation of the issue to be decided; the trial or hearing; the judgment; the judicial review (in some cases); and the execution.

Summons, a writ commanding the sheriff or other authorized person to notify a party to appear in court and answer a claim against him.

Surrogate, a judge in the state of New York with jurisdiction over the probate of wills and the administration of estates.

Suspended sentence, delayed punishment of a criminal, postponing his penalty in an attempt at merciful reformation. The suspended sentence goes a step farther than the indeterminate sentence: it holds the penalty back; the indeterminate sentence makes the penalty appreciably less for good behavior.

Syndicalism (from the French *syndicat,* meaning trade-union), a theory and plan for the forceful overthrow of existing political and economic institutions through a general strike and the substitution of a socialistic government by trade-unions. The Syndicalists advocate direct action by means of strikes and sabotage. They work for a general strike that will make the nation helpless and allow the trade-unions to seize power. Like the Socialists, the Syndicalists condemn the capitalistic system, but unlike the Socialists, they urge direct action and argue that the state is always tyrannical and whatever government there is should be by the unions. Syndicalism had its origin in France and was mainly inspired by the writings of P. J. Proudhon (1809–1865). In the United States syndicalism is advocated by the International Workers of the World (I.W.W.), an organization formed in Chicago in 1905. Its remaining members were later absorbed into a subsidiary union of the CIO.

Taft-Hartley Act, The (Labor-Management Relations Act), became effective, June 23, 1947, over a presidential veto, and by amendment, replaced the Wagner Labor Relations Act which had been in force since July 1935. The important changes prescribed in the Taft-Hartley Act were those relating to the use of a Federal injunction to halt strikes deemed to be against the public interest, a broadened definition of unfair labor practices to apply to labor and management alike, restrictions on access to the National Labor Relations Board, requirements for a non-Communist oath by certain officers of labor unions, the denial of the exclusive closed shop and restrictions on political contributions. Preferential hiring, secondary boycotts and jurisdictional strikes were prohibited; collective bargaining in labor disputes and periodical financial reports were required. The act also provided for an independent Federal Conciliation and Mediation service and placed restrictions on certain labor practices. The act said nothing concerning labor monopolies nor did it contain any restrictions on industry-wide bargaining or featherbedding.

In 1951 it was amended to permit union-shop contracts without first putting them to vote of the employees.

Tariff, a system of customs duties or taxes imposed on imports from outside the United States. Tariffs are imposed for protection or for revenue or both. Advocates of free trade oppose a tariff for protection and urge tariff for revenue or none at all.

Taxation, the usual method of obtaining funds for public use by assessing persons who are subject to the jurisdiction of the Government. The broad powers granted to Congress by the Constitution (Art. I, Sec. 8, Cl. 1), "to lay and collect taxes, duties, imposts, and excises, to pay the debts and provide for the common defense and general welfare of the United States," are subject to constitutional limitations. Direct taxes must be apportioned according to the population (Art. I, Sec. 9, Cl. 4), and all taxes must be uniform throughout the United States (Art. I, Sec. 8, Cl. 1). The income tax was first declared unconstitutional because it was a direct tax and not apportioned, but the 16th Amendment (proclaimed in 1913) granted Congress the power to levy an income tax "without apportionment among the several states and without regard to any census or enumeration." Furthermore, Congress cannot tax articles exported from any state or give preferential rates to certain ports, and in some cases the Supreme Court has held that Congress cannot impose a tax that has for its main purpose some social measure, such as a tax on the owners of certain industries who employ children under a certain age limit.

Early Federal taxes were derived from import duties and a variety of internal excise taxes. In 1802 the internal revenue taxes were abandoned. There was a short period during the War of 1812 when taxes were again levied. There was an income tax law enacted in 1892, after a short trial during the Civil War. This 1892 law was declared unconstitutional. In 1909, Congress called the tax assessed against corporations an excise tax, even though it was measured by income. This was done to meet the court's objection. The Revenue Act of 1932 added a gift tax, manufacturers' excise tax and taxes on telephone, telegraph and radio messages, bank checks, pipe lines and safe deposit box rentals.

State and local taxes have generally been on land and a few articles of personal property, but many states have levied inheritance taxes, corporation taxes, liquor taxes and a general sales tax. Nearly half the states in the Union had some sort of tax on chain stores to prevent the growth of this form of distribution.

The income tax is levied according to the ability to pay. On small incomes there is no tax. And on some incomes only a 4 per cent normal tax. The normal and surtax apply to the same classes of income with one exception. Interest on certain U.S. Bonds issued prior to March 1, 1941 is subject to surtax only. The combined normal and surtax rates, at present, are graduated between 20 per cent on the first 2,000 dollars over exemptions, and 91 per cent on all incomes in excess of 200,000 dollars. These rates are adjusted, however, by the discounts allowed in computing the tax. The sales tax is easy to collect but it is not proportional to ability to pay, and is more of a burden on the poor than on the rich.

Tennessee Valley Authority (TVA), was created by an Act of Congress, May 18, 1933, to provide for the unified development of the water-shed of the Tennessee River for flood control, reforestation, fertilizer production, and soil erosion control; for the general conservation and development of the natural resources of the region; and for the economic well-being of its people. The economic base on which the structure rests is the development and sale of hydroelectric power produced as a by-product of the social welfare and economic programs. As a part of its power program, the TVA was given control of the dam and government nitrate plant at Muscle Shoals on the Tennessee River. Governor Franklin D. Roosevelt of New York, as a candidate for President, made the TVA part of his electioneering campaign. The legislative driving power of Senator George W. Norris of Nebraska secured enactment of the necessary legislation and the technical experience and advice of Arthur E. Morgan provided the initial engineering plan for the project. The operation is financed by Congressional appropriations. It pays no taxes and has the status of an independent agency, controlled by a three-man board of directors responsible only to Congress.

The operations of TVA cover an area, largely rural, of over 80,000 sq. mi. located in parts of seven states with a population of about 3,250,000.

Twenty-seven dams for flood control, power production and other purposes have been constructed and are now in operation on the Tennessee River and its subsidiaries. More are planned.

The TVA has never received direct constitutional approval, but only indirect, as the result of U. S. Supreme Court affirmation of actions in the lower courts. It has accomplished in large measure what it was set up to do. In addition, during World War II, TVA contributed the enormous quantities of electric power required at the Oak Ridge plant for the development of the atom bomb. TVA has become a model for similar undertakings elsewhere in the United States.

Territory, any large unit of land—a region or district. In the United States, a political division under control of the Federal Government that has not sufficient population to entitle it to become a state. When a territory is entitled to statehood, Congress authorizes it to frame a state constitution; after this has been adopted, statehood is proclaimed by the President. The general rule has been that statehood may be sought when a territory's population is great enough to entitle it to one representative in Congress. A territory is represented in Congress by a delegate; he may debate on questions pertaining to his territory but he has no vote. Alaska and Hawaii were both territories before they became our 49th and 50th states, respectively, in 1959.

Third Parties. Traditionally, the two-party system has characterized American political history. Third parties have risen usually because of temporary national issues or to support individual ambitions. Among these have been the Anti-Masonic party, 1826-36, the Know-Nothing party, 1852-1856, several anti-slavery parties, 1845-61, Greenback party, 1876-84, the Populist party of the 1890's, the Progressive parties of 1912-16, 1922-24 and 1948, and the States' Rights Democratic party or "Dixiecrats," 1948.

The Republican party originally was a third party, but became a dominant party because of mergers, absorptions and conditions growing out of the Civil War. The Democratic party has an unbroken history, under various names, ever since the Anti-Federalist party of Thomas Jefferson was organized in the late 1790's.

Tort (French, wrong, from Latin meaning twisted), a civil wrong, a breach of legal duty (other than under contract) that causes an injury to another. It differs from crime in that a crime is an offense against the state, to be adjudged by the state; a tort is an offense of neighbor against neighbor, but the same act may be both a crime and a tort. The law of torts embraces fraud, trespass, libel and slander, negligence, nuisance and the like.

Totalitarian, a government organized and operated upon the doctrine that the state and the state alone is sovereign in the legal sense and all-powerful in every department of the nation's political activity, social life and economic structure. Soviet Russia is an example. In the totalitarian state, opposition political parties are abolished, the parliamentary system is substantially eliminated, and open disputes between capital and labor are prohibited.

Treason, defined by the Constitution of the United States (Art. III, Sec. 3) as "levying war against them (the states), adhering to their enemies, giving them aid and comfort. No person shall be convicted of treason unless on the testimony of two witnesses to the same overt act, or on confession in open court. The Congress shall have the power to declare the punishment of treason, but no attainder of treason shall work corruption of blood or forfeiture except during the life of the person attainted." Under this constitutional definition of the crime, the acceptable evidence and the punishment were much more mild, general and just, than earlier treatment of traitors.

Treasury, the department of the government responsible for the collection, control and expenditure of the public finances. In the United States, the Treasury Department was established by Congress, Sept. 2, 1789, as an executive department of the Federal Government in charge of a Secretary who is a member of the President's Cabinet.

The Treasury Department has a wide variety of responsibilities and is made up of many important bureaus and commissions. Its principal branches are the office of the Comptroller of the Currency whose most important functions relate to the supervision of the nation's banks; the Bureau of Customs which collects duties on imports; the Bureau of Engraving and Printing; the Bureau of Internal Revenue having to do with the collection of all money from all sources within the nation, including the collection of income, excise and corporation taxes; the Bureau of the Mint which coins the nation's metallic currency; the Bureau of Narcotics having to do with the manufacture, taxing and sale of narcotics including the Fiscal Service of Accounting, the Bureau of Public Debt and the Office of the Treasurer of the United States. The Bureau of Federal Supply is concerned with supplies and services for the Executive agencies. The United States Secret Service and the United States Coast Guard also are under this department. The Secretary of the Treasury is chairman of the expenditures committee of many of the important national administrative agencies such as the Library of Congress, the Red Cross, Munitions Control Board, etc.

Trespass, any tort or civil wrong, accompanied by violence and force, however slight. In a more special sense trespass means illegal entry on the land or property of another; in theory such entry is forcible. In some states trespass on another's property has been made a criminal offense.

Trusteeship, international, a system of colonial or dependent territory administration provided for in the United Nations Charter. It replaces a similar system of mandates included in the League of Nations organization. It is administered by the Trusteeship Council of the United Nations.

Three kinds of trust territories are included: (1) territories formerly held under League of Nations mandates, but by unanimous consent of all concerned, transferred to a trusteeship status; (2) territories acquired from the Axis powers as a consequence of their defeat; and (3) dependent territories which the controlling states may elect to turn over voluntarily to the trusteeship of the United Nations.

The Trusteeship Council is made up of the U.N. members administering trust territories and an equal number who do not control such territories. Trusteeship agreements are made under the supervision of the U.N. General Assembly. The U.N. itself may also hold a trusteeship. Territories designated as "strategic areas" are the responsibility of the U.N. Security Council, all other Trusteeships are under the control and direction of the General Assembly. Trusteeships are intended to last only until the trusteed area is equipped to become self-governing. "The interests of the inhabitants of these territories are paramount"; trusteeships accepted by the United Nations are "a sacred trust."

Ultra vires (Latin, beyond the powers), transcending the authority given by law. The phrase is specifically used of action by a corporation that exceeds the privileges and powers given the corporation by its charter or by statute.

Unemployment, the state or condition of persons out of work. Persons who are unwilling to work, those who are permanently or temporarily incapacitated or workers engaged in a strike are not a part of the economic problem of unemployment.

Unemployment of workers as a group may be either temporary or permanent. *Temporary unemployment,* when the worker is out of a job for a time but ultimately finds a job, is caused by seasonal changes in production and is most evident among farm workers, dock workers, and those engaged in luxury trades. Another reason is the cyclical changes in business conditions bringing alternating prosperity and depression. Changes in industry resulting from changing demands and business failures also affect many jobs. *Permanent unemployment* of a large group is the result of our economic system and technological progress in industry. This may, however, eventually create more jobs than it abolishes. This is illustrated by the technological progress that produced the automobile industry at the expense of the carriage industry. In the end, many more jobs were created by the new industry than had previously existed.

The most serious period of unemployment in American history occurred during the world-wide economic depression of the 1930s which followed a decade of false prosperity in the years after World War I. During the 1930s unemployment varied from a high of over 15,000,000 to around 7,000,000 in the latter half of the decade. As war clouds gathered over Europe, war orders in American factories brought a general increase in business activity and put many people back to work.

During the period of World War II, employment increased greatly. A large number of women went into factories to take the places of the men who were drafted into the armed services. By 1943 employment in manufacturing production was over 14,000,000, nearly double that of 1939. This figure had decreased to about 12,000,000 by 1949. In that year, the total of men and women gainfully employed in all kinds of work was more than 57,000,000; 30% were women. Less than 25% of this total were employed in manufacturing production, the balance being employed in a wide variety of service industries, in agricultural and farm work, etc.

Generally speaking, unemployment is a characteristic of the capitalistic system, though it is not unique. Unemployment also occurs in a communistic state like Russia or in a dictatorship like Hitler's Germany. In such cases, the individual, theoretically, is the ward of the state. In a democracy like the United States, where freedom of contract exists, unemployment is an evidence of choice or is due to discharge, lack of business or any other of a variety of reasons. The individual, if employed in a "covered" industry or trade becomes eligible for unemployment insurance and other benefits. If the amount of unemployment becomes serious, government planned work, particularly on public works, roads, etc. is got under way, to take up the slack. This was a particular feature of the New Deal during the 1930s when the Government endeavored to create as much employment as possible for all the people out of jobs.

Unemployment during World War II was usually under 2,000,000, many of the unemployed being only temporarily out of work. Some were incapable of work and others out of work by choice. During 1956 the number of unemployed had increased to about 3,000,000. There were about 67,000,000 employed.

Unemployment insurance is managed jointly by the states and the Federal Government. The laws under which the worker collects unemployment insurance vary among the states. Above all, the worker must be willing to take a job in his field at prevailing wage rates.

There are also various bureaus of public assistance and relief operated by the various states and municipalities with the help of grants from the Federal Government.

Universal Military training in the United States has frequently been advocated, but never prescribed by law. It differs from the draft or conscription in that the draft is usually a temporary service requirement to meet a war-time emergency or a threat of war, whereas *universal military training* is a permanent peacetime policy and is for training purposes only. Both the draft and universal military training are compulsory systems of raising manpower for military purposes. Each requires registration and service or training under specific conditions regarding age, physical fitness, dependency responsibilities, etc. Service in the armed forces, however, is required only of

draftees and calls are made only to fill
authorized quotas. In the case of universal military training, all those enrolled in certain age groups would be
called up for military training in local
areas subject to physical examination.
Those called would not be members of
the armed forces, would not be liable
for overseas duty and would not be
subject to the same regulations as those
which govern the armed forces. Those
who had undergone or were undergoing
universal military training would not
be subject to draft for military service
except as a result of congressional
legislation.

Verdict (Latin, true saying), the answer
to the court by a jury to the question
of fact submitted in a trial. In Scotch
law, besides "Guilty" and "Not guilty,"
a third verdict is possible, "Not prov-
en," which does not relieve the accused
of being retried on the same charge.
The answer of a judge or referee on a
question of fact is not a verdict but
a *finding*.

Veterans' Administration, an independent
agency of the Federal Government,
created in July 1930 to unify the work
of all Federal bureaus administering
veterans' benefits. The Veterans' Administration is concerned with the
administration of the various so-called
GI bills relating to education and
rehabilitation, insurance, loans, medical benefits, readjustment service pay
allowances, pensions and compensation
for service-incurred disabilities. In
1949 pensions and compensation totaled $1,891,000,000 for about 3,000,000
cases. Total expenditures for the fiscal
year ending in 1949, in addition to
the insurance-refund allowances, were
about $6,800,000,000. Regional hospi-
tals and domiciliary centers as well as
regional and district offices throughout
the United States and possessions
provide for local access to the Veterans' Administration. Certain recommendations have been made relative
to the re-organization of the Veterans'
Administration to enable it to handle
the more than 15,000,000 veterans
using its facilities.

Veto (Latin, I forbid), the power of
invalidating a law, especially such
power lodged in a single official. The
Roman tribunes of the people—an
office established in the 5th century
B.C. to protect individuals from injustice—could overrule any act of the
senate or any decree of a magistrate
by saying *veto*, I forbid.

The French constitution of 1791
gave the king a veto power, but Louis
XVI's attempt to exercise this power
in June 1792 when the Assembly voted
to take away his royal guards was
one of the immediate causes of the
French Revolution.

In the Constitution of the United
States, the President's veto power is
defined in Art. I, Sec. 7, Cl. 2. His
veto may be overruled by a two-thirds
vote of each House. If he does not
return a measure within 10 days
(Sundays excepted), it becomes a law
if Congress is still in session; but if
"the Congress by their adjournment
prevent its return . . . it shall not be
a law." This last method is called
pocket veto. President James Monroe
in his two terms, vetoed only one act

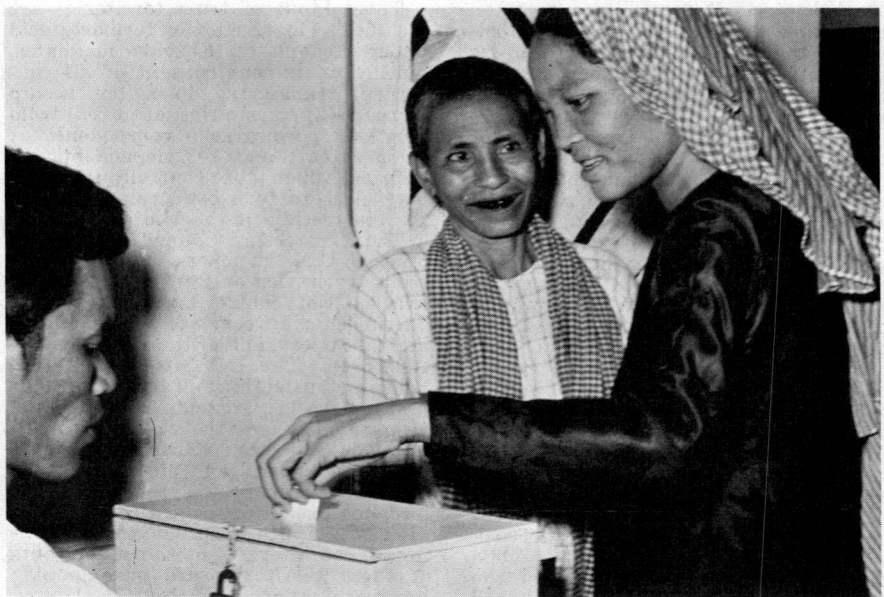

UNITED NATIONS

REFERENDUM in Cambodia, 1960, gave overwhelming vote of confidence to policies of Prince
Norodom Sihanouk, president of the Crown Council. A Cambodian woman registers a vote.

of Congress and had no pocket vetoes;
President Franklin D. Roosevelt, in
his 12 years and 3 months in office,
vetoed 371 acts of Congress and pocket
vetoed 260, a total of 631, the highest
number for any President.

All states of the Union except North
Carolina have power to veto an act
of the legislature; most of the state
constitutions permit "item vetoes,"
that is, vetoes of individual items in
legislative enactments, particularly
appropriation bills, without the necessity of vetoing the entire bill. This
same power has been recommended for
the President, but has not been adopted. If he objects to items in a bill, the
President must accept them or veto
the whole bill.

A somewhat similar power is exercised by the U.S. Supreme Court in
declaring that an act of Congress or
an action under a Federal law is void
because it is in violation of some
provision of the Constitution or is not
in accord with the intent of Congress
as interpreted by the court. In the
latter case, the act may be made constitutional by Congressional action.

The Charter of the United Nations
provides for the use of a veto to proposals objected to by members of the
Security Council. A unanimous vote
of the permanent members of the Security Council is required to secure
approval of measures brought before
it. In the early years of the U.N.,
Russia used her veto again and again.

Visit and search, the practice in war of
boarding and examining the papers of
a neutral ship to see if she carries
contraband (forbidden) cargo. If the
neutral merchantman is escorted by a
neutral warship, this creates the *right
of convoy*, freedom from visit and
search. Great Britain opposed this
theory of convoy but accepted it under
the Declaration of London in force
from 1906 to 1916. After 1916 the
right of convoy again became uncertain.

During World War I and more particularly during World War II, no
neutral ships if believed to be carrying
contraband goods, were spared by
German or other Axis submarines.
Because of this, neutral vessels, particularly American, were convoyed
even before the United States became
a belligerent.

Vote, the expression of a choice, preference or wish by one exercising the
right of suffrage. Voting is a method
of selecting public officials and determining controversial questions submitted to the voters. Vote is also used
to describe formal recording of the
expressed opinion of any group upon
a certain subject. In legislative assemblies, the vote may be by means of
a spoken word, a showing of hands
or other visible expressions of opinion;
but voting by large groups is usually
done by a ballot. In the United States
the individual state governments control the voting, subject to the constitutional provision that the vote shall
not be denied on account of race, color
or sex. In all states, except Georgia
and Kentucky where the voting age is
18, a person must be 21 years of age
to vote and he must be a citizen.
Those of unsound mind and those
guilty of certain serious crimes are
not allowed to vote. In addition, there
are varying requirements with respect
to residence, literacy, and registration.
Until federal legislation outlawed it in
1965, 7 states imposed a poll tax as a
voting prerequisite.

Voting Machine, see *Ballot.*

Wages and Hours Act, the popular name
applied to the Fair Labor Standards
Act of 1938. This was the culmination
of many years of effort to put a floor
under wages and hours in the form
of prescribed minimum wages and
maximum hours. This act provided
for a minimum wage of 25 cents an
hour which was raised to 40 cents an
hour in 1945. Effective, Jan. 25, 1950,

it was increased to 75 cents an hour and applied to workers protected by the 1938 Act. It has since been raised to $1.25 an hour. The basic work week was fixed at 44 hours in 1938, and reduced to 40 hours in 1941. Hours worked over the prescribed maximum are at overtime rates of pay. The act, which is administered by the Department of Labor, prohibited the labor of children under 16 in plants or businesses whose products entered into interstate commerce.

Wagner Act (National Labor Relations Act), July 5, 1935, contained many provisions of the National Industrial Recovery Act (NIRA) which was declared unconstitutional in 1935. It guaranteed to employees "the right to self-organization" and "to bargain collectively through representatives of their own choosing." Likewise, the act specified five unfair labor practices: (1) employers were prohibited from interfering with the employees' right to organization and collective bargaining; (2) they were prohibited from promoting company unions; (3) discrimination in employment was prohibited; (4) discharge of employees was prohibited because they made use of the provisions of the act in their own interest; and (5) employers could not refuse to bargain collectively with representatives of their employees. There were no prohibitions on employees, individually or collectively. The act gave great impetus to employee unionization. Freedom from restraint by anti-trust proceedings and the protection of the closed shop gave great powers to labor leaders. The constitutionality of the act was recognized by a decision of the U.S. Supreme Court, April 12, 1937, in upholding a decision of the National Labor Relations Board (NLRB) which interpreted and enforced the provisions of the Wagner Act. The act was replaced by the Taft-Hartley Labor-Management Relations Act of 1947.

War Department, The, one of the original parts of the executive Government of the United States, organized in 1789. It became the Department of the Army and a part of the Department of Defense, authorized in the National Security Act of 1947. There is one bureau in the department: the National Guard Bureau. The Office of the Chief of Staff includes divisions of Plans and Combat Operations, division of Information and the Army Comptroller. Under the General Staff of the Army are Personnel and Administration, including the Woman's Army Corps, the Intelligence, Organization and Training, Logistics and Plans and Operations divisions. Other divisions cover the Special Staff, including the National Guard, the Historical and Civil Affairs division, the offices of the Inspector General and the Judge Advocate General. Also under the General Staff are: the Administrative Services; the Technical Services, including the Chemical Corps, the Medical Department, the Quartermaster's, Signal and Transportation corps; the Ordnance Department, the Chief of Engineers and the Army Field Forces, which includes the combat units of the army.

LIBRARY OF CONGRESS

WOMAN SUFFRAGE, the right of women to vote on equal terms with men. Here women gather in front of the White House to protest to President Wilson and demand equal rights. Mrs. Emmeline Pankhurst, an early leader in the movement, was joined by Susan B. Anthony, Lucretia Mott, and Elizabeth Cady Stanton. They also advocated temperance. In 1920, the nineteenth amendment to the Constitution, stating that the right of citizens to vote could not be denied because of sex, was passed.

The administration of the army is divided into six army areas. The U.S. Military Academy at West Point, N.Y. is under the direction of the Department of the Army, as are other service schools.

The Secretary of the Army, though not a Cabinet member, is the chairman of the Arlington Memorial Amphitheatre Commission at Arlington, Va. The National War College, the Industrial College of the Armed Forces and the Armed Forces Staff College are schools of instruction and advanced study which are closely connected with the Department of the Army.

War, Laws of, are, in general, theoretical regulations that govern warfare. Like all international law, they differ from common or statute law in that there is as yet no enforcement agency with the power to impose penalties for violations. They usually rest on agreements between individual nations and are observed or ignored according to the moral and physical strength of the belligerents and the necessities of military position. Retaliation measures cannot of themselves halt violations. The laws of war as now constituted originated primarily at the Geneva Convention of 1864 that drew up rules for the humane treatment of prisoners of war. In general these regulations have been observed, though German treatment of war prisoners in World War II violated every known law of humanity, both physical and moral. The international peace conference at The Hague in 1899 and 1907 marked an advance in the formulation of laws of war that were reasonable and that seemed to have an enforceable basis. However, when war is under way the necessities of the belligerents and the morality of the leaders largely determine the extent of observance. During World War II, for instance, it was forbidden to bomb cities and terrorize non-combatants. No attention was paid to the prohibition. Likewise, submarines were used to attack vessels on the high seas without attempting to identify their nationality or the character of their cargoes. The use of poisonous gases and bacteria was forbidden by The Hague conventions and by several post-World War I conferences. They were not used by either side during World War II, because the advantages gained by their initial use by one side would soon have been overcome or neutralized as a result of their use by the other side. The most important weapons awaiting international control by laws are the Atom and Hydrogen bombs.

German treatment of Jews before and during World War II gave rise to the enactment by the United Nations, of a convention barring genocide. The War Guilt trials held at the end of World War II were unique because of the number of them and the percentage of convictions and executions. They set a precedent for future wars. One of the objectives of the United Nations is to become strong enough to prevent wars and to enforce laws of war agreed to by its member nations.

Ward, a minor or person otherwise not in full legal capacity (lunatic, for instance) under the protection of a court or of a *guardian* appointed by the court. The relation continues until the ward reaches majority or otherwise overcomes the legal incapacity.

Warrant, a writ issued by a court directing any peace officer to perform a specified act. Commonly a warrant means an order for arrest. A *search warrant* is an order to examine a house or other specified place for stolen goods, gambling apparatus, burglars' or counterfeiters' tools, etc. The Constitution of the United States (4th amendment) prohibits "unreasonable searches" and declares that no warrants shall be issued except "upon probable cause, supported by an oath or affirmation, and particularly describing the place to be searched and the person or thing to be seized."

Whig party, one of the main political parties in the United States in the second quarter of the 19th century. Its great leaders were Daniel Webster and Henry Clay, though neither was ever able to lead the party to victory. The various groups that opposed President Andrew Jackson, in 1836, formed an alliance, though there was a division on the choice of candidates. In 1840 the Whigs elected William Henry Harrison. Clay was defeated by James K. Polk in 1844, but in 1848 the Whigs elected Zachary Taylor. The Whig Party always contained diverse elements which were united mainly by opposition to the Democrats. When the slavery issue split the country, it likewise split the Whig party. Defeat in 1853 marked the virtual end of the party.

Whip, a member of a political party in a legislature appointed to enforce discipline among the members of the party, to secure the passage of legislation favored by the party and to secure votes against legislation opposed by the party. The party whip keeps members advised of pending legislation and sees to it that they are present to vote on important measures. He makes arrangements for *pairs* so that the voting outcome will not be affected by absences.

In Great Britain, the position is of tremendous importance; without the presence and activity of the party whip, Parliament could not function satisfactorily. The use of the party whip in the United States is very recent. The whip is chosen by a party caucus at the beginning of each Congress.

Witness, one who gives testimony about what he knows. A witness in court is summoned by a subpoena. He testifies only to what he knows or to what he has seen; the court is the judge of what testimony may properly be admitted. A witness is not required to testify to a matter that will tend to incriminate himself. Before beginning testimony, a witness is placed under oath or affirmation. If he utters false testimony, he is guilty of *perjury.*

Woman suffrage, the right of women to vote on equal terms with men. It was first proposed in the United States in 1848 at Seneca Falls, N. Y., in a general declaration of the rights of women. The early leaders of the movement—Susan B. Anthony, Lucretia Mott, Elizabeth Cady Stanton and others—advocated temperance and the abolition of slavery. The National Woman Suffrage Association was formed in 1869 to work for the adoption of a constitutional amendment,

and the American Woman Suffrage Association was formed in the same year to work with state legislatures. These two organizations were united in 1890 to form the National American Woman Suffrage Association. Leaders of the movement in this period included Anna Howard Shaw and Carrie Chapman Catt. In 1869 Wyoming was the first state to grant suffrage to women; in 1920 the 19th amendment to the Constitution of the United States became effective declaring that the right of citizens to vote shall not be abridged or denied on account of sex.

In Great Britain, the first petition in favor of woman suffrage was introduced into Parliament in 1867 by John Stuart Mill. A militant suffrage movement developed in England about 1903, but it was not until 1918 that women over 30 years of age were given the vote. In 1928 all women of voting age were given equal voting rights with men. Woman suffrage is now general throughout the world. The women of France and of Italy and Japan gained the right to vote following World War II.

World Court, The, is the popular name for the International Court of Justice of the United Nations, the successor to the Permanent Court of International Justice established as the World Court under the League of Nations covenant in 1920. Membership of the United States in the original World Court was long debated but was finally approved by the House of Representatives in 1925 and by the Senate, Jan. 27, 1926, with reservations. These amendments greatly reduced the authority and power of the Court. Largely because of the progressive impotence of the League of Nations and the lack of complete support by the United States, the World Court of the League of Nations had little of importance to do. It was suspended in 1940 when the League of Nations was dissolved at the outbreak of World War II.

The International Court of Justice was reconstituted in the charter of the United Nations in 1945. It was projected as one of the principal elements of the United Nations. With United States support it acquired both meaning and authority. The World Court held its inaugural meeting at The Hague, May 18, 1946.

The Court, which is the judicial organ of the United Nations, consists of 15 judges elected by the General Assembly and the Security Council of the United Nations. Members agree to accept the decisions of the Court; failure to do so makes the offender liable to action by the Security Council.

BIBLIOGRAPHY

GENERAL BOOKS

ARENDT, HANNAH. *Between Past and Future.* Meridian Books, 1963.
SCHLESINGER, ARTHUR JR. *The Politics of Hope.* Houghton Mifflin Co., 1963.

THEIMER, WALTER. *Encyclopedia of Modern World Politics.* Holt, Rinehart & Winston, Inc., 1960.

POLITICAL THEORY

ARISTOTLE. *Politics.* Translated by E. Barker. Oxford University Press, Inc., 1946.
CRANE, BRINTON. *The Anatomy of Revolution.* Random House, Inc., 1964.
CREEL, H. G. *Chinese Thought from Confucius to Mao Tse-tung.* University of Chicago Press, 1954.
GRIMES, ALAN P. and HORWITZ, ROBERT H. *Modern Political Ideologies.* Oxford University Press, Inc., 1959.
HOOK, SIDNEY. *Political Power and Personal Freedom.* Criterion Books, Inc., 1959.
MOORE, SIR THOMAS. *Utopia and a Dialogue of Comfort.* E. P. Dutton & Co., Inc., 1951.
PLATO. *The Republic.* Translated by Francis M. Cornford. Oxford University Press, Inc., 1945.

COMPARATIVE GOVERNMENT

United States

BINKLEY, WILFRED E. *American Political Parties: Their Natural History.* Alfred A. Knopf, Inc., 1958.
COHEN, BERNARD. *The Press and Foreign Policy.* Princeton University Press, 1963.
GOODMAN, WILLIAM. *The Two-party System in the United States.* D. Van Nostrand Co., Inc., 1956.
HOFSTADTER, R. *The American Political Tradition.* Random House, 1964.
JACKSON, ROBERT H. *The Supreme Court in the American System of Government.* Harvard University Press, 1955.
PELTASON, JACK W. and BURNS, JAMES M. *Functions and Policies of American Government.* Prentice-Hall, Inc., 1958.
ROSSITER, CLINTON. *The American Presidency.* Harcourt, Brace & World, Inc., 1956.
WHITE, THEODORE H. *The Making of the President, 1960.* Atheneum Publishers, 1961.
YOUNG, ROLAND. *The American Congress.* Harper & Bros., 1959.

Other Systems of Government

BEER, SAMUEL H. and others. *Patterns of Government: The Major Political Systems of Europe.* Random House, Inc., 1958.
EMERSON, R. *From Empire to Nation: The Rise to Self-assertion of Asian and African Peoples.* Harvard University Press, 1960.
FINER, HERMAN. *Major Governments in Europe.* Harper and Row, Publishers, 1960.
McDONALD, LEE CAMERON. *Western Political Theory: The Modern Age.* Harcourt, Brace & World, Inc., 1962.

UNITED NATIONS

BECKEL, GRAHAM and LEE, FELICE. *Workshop for the World: The Specialized Agencies of the United Nations* (rev. ed.). Abelard-Schuman Limited, 1954.
FENICHELL, STEPHEN. *The United Nations: Design for Peace.* Holt, Rinehart & Winston, Inc., 1962.

Physiology	917
Human anatomy	929
Diseases	940
Space biology	949
Public health	954

VOLUME TWELVE

HEALTH

PHOTOGRAPHED BY MORRIS WARMAN AT NEW YORK MEDICAL COLLEGE,
FLOWER AND FIFTH AVENUE HOSPITALS

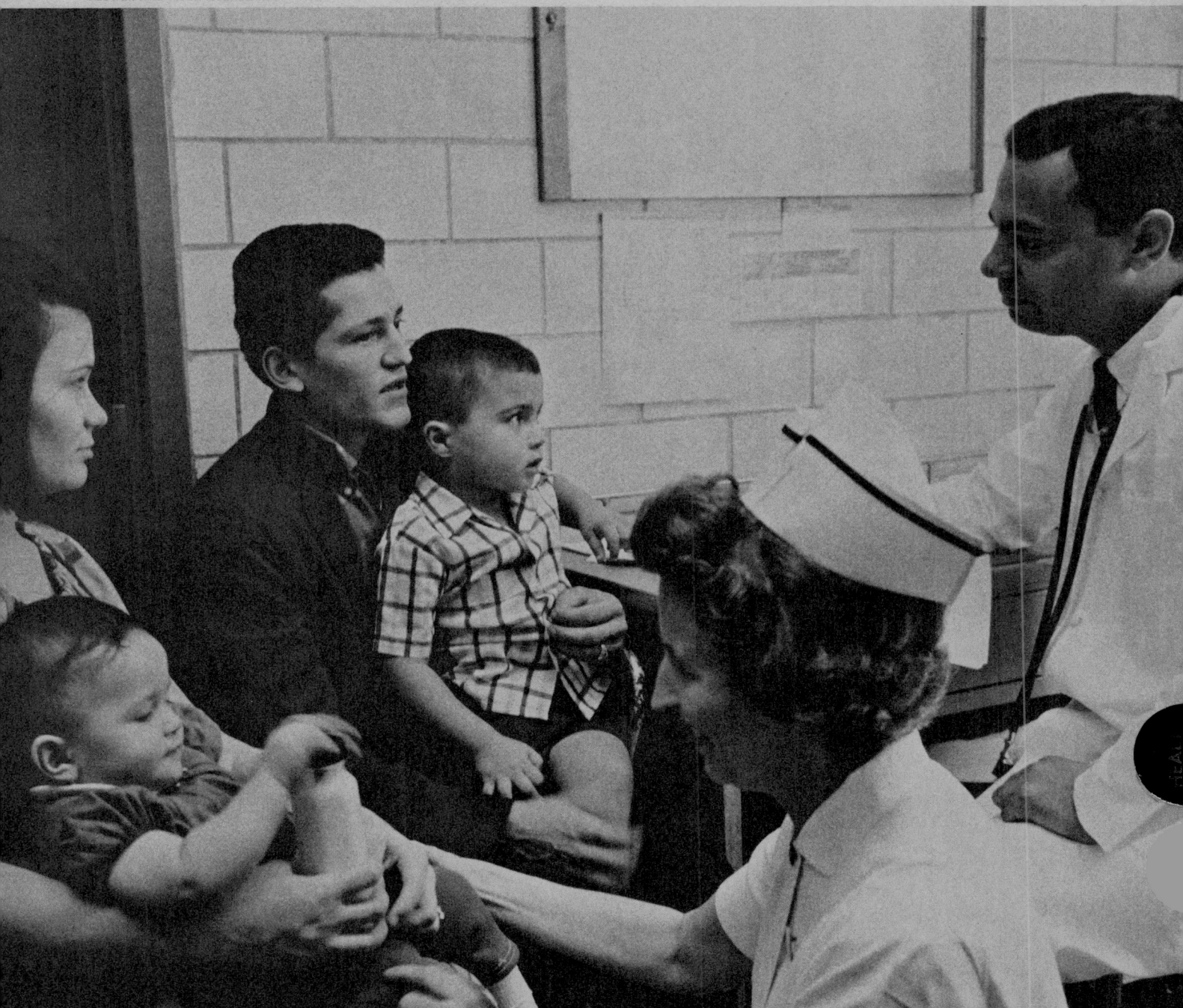

PHYSIOLOGY

The human body is composed of billions of microscopic units called *cells*. Each cell is a chemical factory capable of producing energy from food substances, of harnessing this energy, and of using it to build the materials it needs to function. Although all cells share these basic activities, each different type performs a unique function—nerve cells conduct impulses; muscle cells contract; kidney cells excrete waste chemicals; red blood cells carry oxygen; and so on. Groups of similar cells are gathered into *tissues,* and tissues of different types are united to form *organs* such as the liver, kidney, eyes, heart, and brain. Organs function as parts of larger *systems* such as the nervous, digestive, and circulatory systems. These systems compose the human body.

Structural Elements of the Body

■BONE.—*Bone* is the hard underpinning on which the soft tissues of the body rest. It is a complex, living tissue, consisting of a matrix of organic fibers with mineral crystals deposited throughout. Bone development begins in the embryo with the formation of a *cartilage* (elastic tissue) model; and as the embryo develops, centers of ossification appear. *Ossification* is the process of bone formation in which the *cartilage,* or elastic tissue, is replaced by hard, bony tissue. During body growth the regions of ossification enlarge until all cartilaginous tissue has been replaced by bone.

The hardness of bone tends to obscure the fact that it is a physiologically active tissue with important functions. Bone is constantly being destroyed and rebuilt, thus enabling the body's framework to reshape its structure according to the stresses it must bear. This aspect of bone activity is reflected by the disorder called *osteoporosis,* or softening of the bones. In this condition bone destruction proceeds at a normal rate, but synthesis of new bone tissue is slow. Osteoporosis may be caused by lack of normal bone stimulation as a result of inactivity, and occurs mainly in elderly or bedridden individuals.

The *calcium* salts deposited in bone are continuously being exchanged with calcium from the blood stream. In the disease called *osteomalacia*

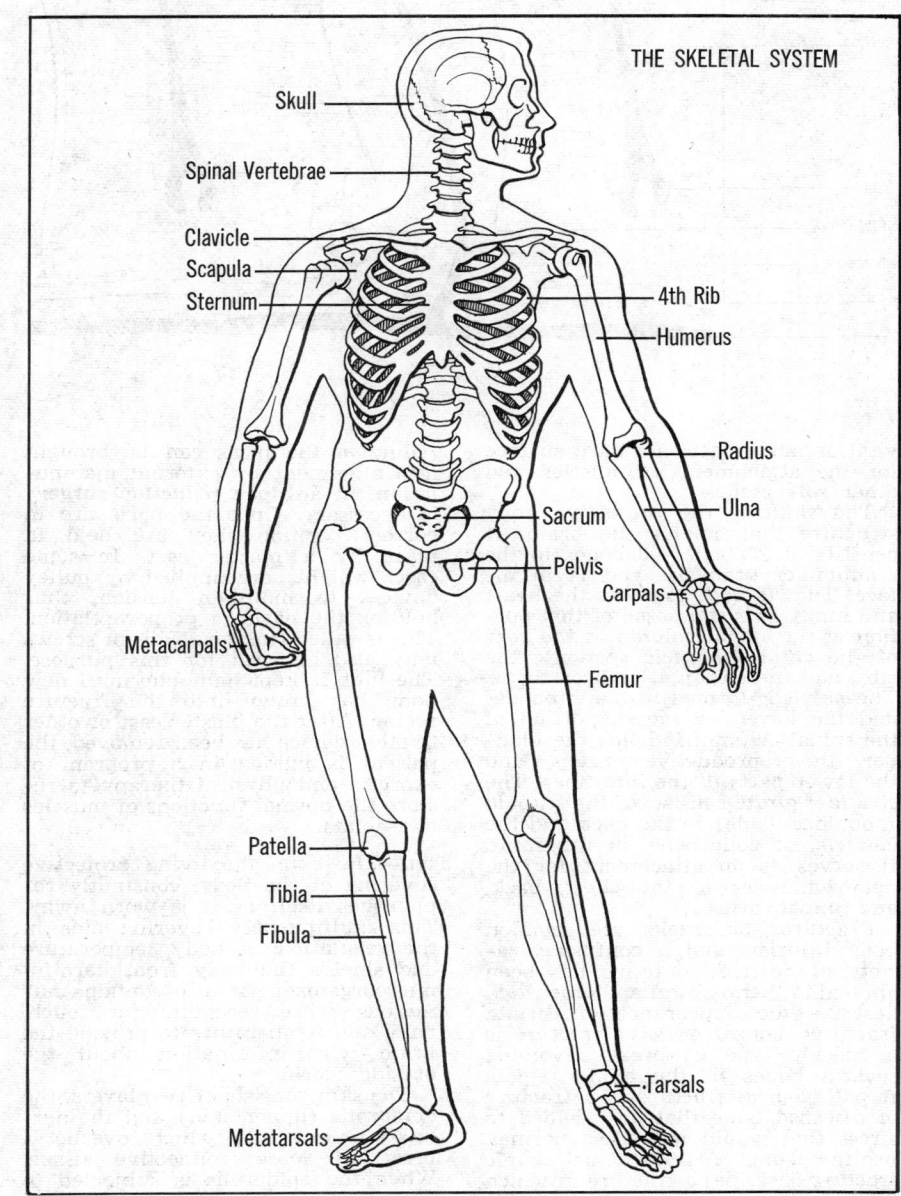

THE SKELETAL SYSTEM

Skull — Spinal Vertebrae — Clavicle — Scapula — Sternum — 4th Rib — Humerus — Radius — Ulna — Sacrum — Pelvis — Carpals — Metacarpals — Femur — Patella — Tibia — Fibula — Tarsals — Metatarsals

the exchange is unbalanced, resulting in the loss of calcium salts from the bone and a decrease in bone hardness. It may be caused by a dietary deficiency of *vitamin D,* a substance that promotes the absorption of calcium from the intestine. Without proper absorption calcium is withdrawn from the bone but is not replaced, leaving the bone soft and easily susceptible to fracture.

Another aspect of bone activity is the production of blood cells in the marrow of such bones as those of the spinal column and the ribs.

The body's framework is the *skeleton,* which consists of 206 bones, ranging in size from the small bones of the hands and feet to the massive *femur,* the long bone of the thigh. The bones are organized into various structures which encase and protect

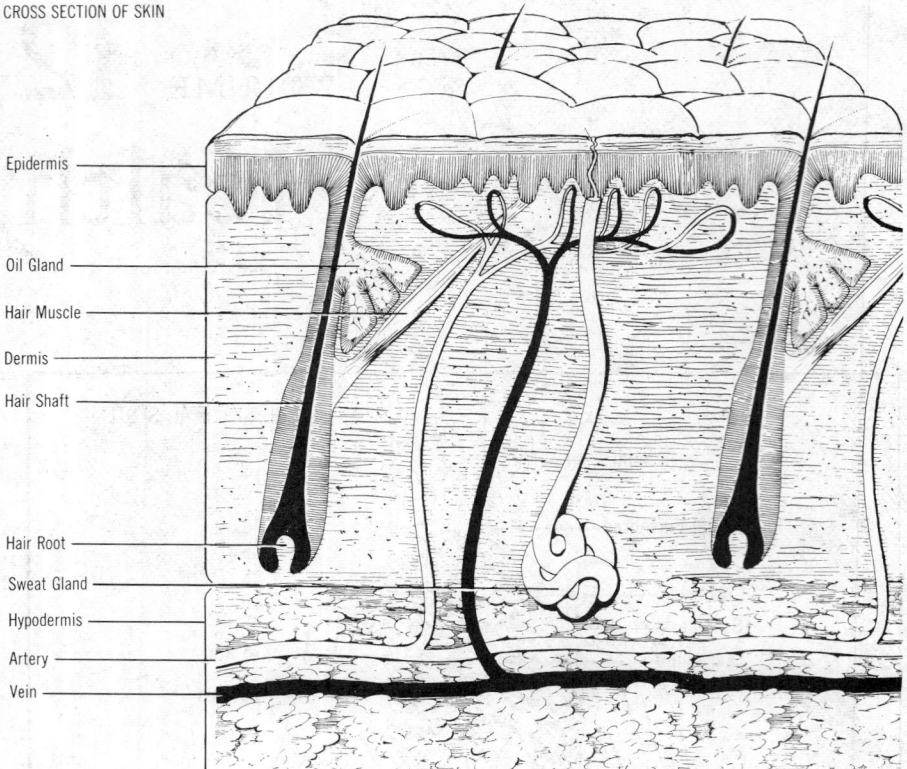

Epidermis

Oil Gland

Hair Muscle

Dermis

Hair Shaft

Hair Root

Sweat Gland

Hypodermis

Artery

Vein

vital organs or act as a hard surface for the attachment of muscles and other soft tissues.

The *skull* is the protective bony structure that shields the brain. It consists of 22 bones—8 bones in the cranium or braincase and 14 in the face. The *rib cage* encloses the heart and lungs. It is composed of that portion of the spinal column at the rear of the chest (*thoracic* section), the ribs, and the *sternum,* or breastbone. The *pelvis* is formed by the hipbones and the lower, or *sacral,* portion of the spinal column. It holds the bladder, the reproductive organs, and the lower parts of the intestines. The *shoulder girdle* consists of the *scapula* (shoulder blade) in the back and the *clavicle,* or collarbone, in the front. It serves as an attachment for the heavy muscles of the chest, back, and upper arms.

Fractures, or breaks, are common bone injuries; and a confusing variety of descriptive terms has been applied to them. *Spiral* and *greenstick* describe the appearance of certain fractured bones. A *Pott's fracture* is a specific type of break involving several bones in the ankle region. A *pathological fracture* is a fracture of diseased bone that has yielded to stress that would not affect normal, healthy bone. A *closed* or *simple fracture* describes a fracture in which the skin overlying the break is intact. In an *open* or *compound fracture* the skin is broken, and the injured tissues are exposed to air and dirt. Such fractures are very likely to become infected.

The basic principle of treating fractures is to *reduce* them—to bring the parts of the bone into normal alignment. The physician attempts to do this as quickly as possible, before too much swelling has occurred. Anesthesia is given to permit manipulation of the fracture. In a *closed*

reduction the parts can be brought into alignment by external manipulation. In an *open reduction* surgery is necessary. Once the parts are in correct position they are held in place by a plaster cast. In some cases weights are applied by pulley devices to maintain tension, thus holding the parts in proper relation. This is called *traction.* Nails or screws may also be used for this purpose. The limb is kept immobile until new bone has grown into the fracture region. After the plaster cast or other fixation device has been removed, the patient is guided in a program of exercise and physical therapy to restore the normal functions of muscles and joints.

Skin.—The *skin,* the living protective covering of the body, constantly replenishes itself as it is worn away. This multipurpose covering aids in the regulation of body temperature and shields the body from harmful microorganisms. It also contains numerous sense receptors for touch, pain, and temperature to provide the brain with information about the outside world.

The skin consists of two layers, the *epidermis* (upper skin) and the *dermis* (true skin), which overlie a layer of loose connective tissue. When the epidermis is subjected to irritation, it produces corns and calluses. It also contains the pigment-producing cells that generate a tan when exposed to the sun's ultraviolet rays. The epidermis has no blood vessels of its own, but receives nutrition from the dermis, which is divided into an upper *papillary* layer and a lower *reticular* layer. The papillary layer is convoluted; the overlying epidermis follows these convolutions, which are seen by the naked eye as fine lines and whorls. This is particularly evident on the

fingertips, where the ridged papillary layer forms distinctive patterns, or fingerprints, on the undersurfaces. The dermis contains sweat glands, sebaceous (oil) glands, nerve endings, and small blood vessels.

Through their secretion the sweat glands help regulate the body temperature—body heat is expended when sweat is evaporated from the skin. The warm-weather disorders of *heat cramp* and *heat stroke* are associated with the functioning of the glands. Heat cramps are caused by loss of large amounts of salt through the sweat. This disturbs the electrochemical balance of the body, resulting in painful muscular contractions. Heat stroke develops when the sweat glands cease to function. In this extremely dangerous condition the body temperature may rise above 105° F.

■ **HAIR.**—*Hair* is a skin appendage formed by an infolding of the epidermis. The hair grows outward from the *papilla,* an egg-shaped mass of cells at the base of the hair *follicle* (sac). Hair color varies with the amount of pigment, the greatest amount being present in black hair. Hairs on different parts of the body are constantly being replaced. The hairs of the scalp have a life span of from two to four years, while the hairs of the eyelashes may be replaced every three to five months.

Baldness, or loss of scalp hair, is common in men over twenty. It may begin as a receding hairline or a patch of hair lost at the top of the head. While most baldness is inherited, specific diseases, such as tuberculosis, and certain endocrine disorders or scalp injury may be responsible. Balding is usually permanent when the scalp is scarred by injury—by radiation exposure, for example. When scarring does not occur, hair will regrow if the cause is corrected. Treatment of baldness is feasible only when a specific disorder is responsible; inherited baldness cannot be successfully treated.

■ **SEBACEOUS GLANDS.**—The natural oiliness of the hair and skin is maintained by the *sebaceous glands,* which pour their oily secretion, called *sebum,* around the hair shaft. In *acne,* a skin condition particularly common in adolescence, the ducts of the sebaceous glands become blocked by accumulations of dirt and sebum.

■ **NAILS.**—*Nails* are horny plates that grow from a matrix at the rear of the nail plate; the growing nail glides forward over the nail bed. Disorders of the nail may be caused by damage to the matrix, by infectious diseases such as fungus, or by general body disorders which secondarily affect nail growth.

■ **TEMPERATURE CONTROL.**—The blood vessels of the skin are a principal means of body temperature regulation. When these vessels expand (*vasodilatation*), more blood is brought to the skin where it is cooled; when the vessels contract (*vasoconstriction*), blood is retained in the interior of the body, and heat is conserved. This contraction and expansion is largely under the control of the *autonomic* nervous system (see *Nervous System*) and responds to emotional factors and as to changes in the outside temperature.

■**SUBCUTANEOUS TISSUE.**—Beneath the skin is a layer of loose tissue called the *hypodermis,* consisting of connective tissue and fat. This is one of the main storage sites for body fat; in obese individuals it may be several inches thick. The connective tissue is a supporting network composed of cells, tough and flexible collagen fibers, elastic fibers, and a ground substance. The connective tissue of the skin and hypodermis is composed of loosely woven fibers; other types of connective tissue are elsewhere. *Dense connective* tissue, consisting of tightly packed fibers, is found in the intestines; *regular connective* tissue, made up of fibers aligned in definite patterns, is found in the *tendons*—the bands of tissue connecting muscle to bone.

Nutrition.—The human body has often been compared to a machine. This analogy, although useful to some extent, should be modified by the realization that the body is a machine which continually rebuilds itself. For this the body needs three kinds of materials: substances that provide energy, substances that can be used to build tissue, and substances which can initiate and facilitate the chemical reactions that produce energy and synthesize tissue.

The principal energy-rich foods in human nutrition are *carbohydrates* and *fats*.

■**CARBOHYDRATES.**—*Carbohydrates* are produced by green plants using the energy of sunlight. These substances, commonly called *starches* and *sugars,* are the ultimate source of energy for animals. Only plants possess the chlorophyll and similar light-sensitive pigments capable of trapping solar energy and storing it in the form of carbohydrates. Animals obtain their carbohydrates from cereals, vegetables, and fruits. Among the carbohydrate-rich foods in our diet are candies, ice cream, bread, spaghetti, and potatoes.

■**FATS.**—*Fats* are obtained from both plant and animal foods. Vegetable fats are found in olive oil, wheat germ oil, and various nuts. Animal fats are contained in milk, eggs, cheese, and meats. Fats are the principal form in which animals store energy-rich material in the tissues. In addition to being a source of energy, fats evidently are essential for other body activities. It has been demonstrated that skin disorders may develop if fats are not in the diet.

■**PROTEINS.**—Principal sources of tissue-building material are *proteins,* which are found in meat, milk, eggs, and fish. Proteins are the most complex chemicals in nature. They are composed of hundreds of thousands of building blocks called *amino acids.* Some 20 different amino acids are linked in various combinations to form the vast number of proteins found in nature. The importance of proteins in plant and animal life

cannot be overestimated. Every body cell, whether muscle, nerve, skin, blood, bone, or any other type, is composed of protein. Each plant and animal is composed of proteins that are unique in structure. In addition to the *structural* function which proteins have in the cells of living things, they also perform a vital role as *enzymes,* chemical agents that promote the thousands of chemical reactions occurring within the tissues.

■**MINERALS.**—For normal health the body requires certain *minerals* that may be used in structural tissue, in enzyme systems, in the synthesis of particular chemicals, or in various other body reactions. Among these essential minerals are calcium, phosphorus, iodine, iron, sodium, chlorine, and potassium. *Calcium* is contained in milk and cheese. In the body it is found in the bones and teeth. It is essential minerals are calcium, phosand for muscular activity. *Phosphorus* is also found in bones and teeth and is particularly important as a part of certain chemicals, most notably ATP (adenosine triphosphate) which makes possible energy storage and exchange in cells. *Iodine* is used in the synthesis of the thyroid hormone, which regulates the pace of body activity. *Iron* is essential for the manufacture of hemoglobin, the pigment of the red blood cells which carries oxygen to the tissues. *Sodium, chlorine,* and *potassium* are involved in the regulation of water balance and in nerve and muscle activity. Other minerals found

A CHART OF THE VITAMINS

Vitamin
1. *Food Sources*
2. *Functions*
3. *Daily Adult Requirement*
4. *Effects of Deficiency*

Vitamin A
1. Fish-liver oils, yellow and leafy green vegetables
2. Preserves night vision, integrity of skin
3. 5,000 I.U.
4. Night blindness, skin lesions

Vitamin B₁ (Thiamine)
1. Bran (coats of grain), yeast, meat
2. Helps body process foodstuffs for energy
3. 1.5 mg.
4. Beriberi, marked by loss of weight, body swelling, muscle wasting and weakness, nervous disturbances, heart damage

Vitamin B₂ (Riboflavin)
1. Yeast, liver, eggs, milk
2. Participates in energy-producing reactions and promotes growth
3. 2–3 mg.
4. Inflammation of tongue, lesions at corners of mouth and nostrils

Niacin (Nicotinic Acid)
1. Yeasts, meat, fish, peanuts
2. Various chemical reactions in cells of body
3. 20 mg.
4. Pellagra, marked by skin, digestive, and nervous system disturbances

Vitamin B₆ (Pyridoxine)
1. Liver, yeast, whole cereal grains
2. Functions in metabolism of amino acids
3. No minimum requirements set
4. Deficiency has been known to cause convulsions in infants

Pantothenic Acid
1. Yeast, liver, eggs, milk
2. Functions in energy-producing reactions and in synthesis of various chemicals
3. No minimum requirements set
4. No deficiency symptoms observed

Biotin
1. Liver, yeast, eggs, peanuts, milk
2. Participates in chemical reactions involved in tissue synthesis
3. No minimum requirements set
4. No symptoms of deficiency observed

Folic Acid
1. Widely distributed in animal and plant foods; also synthesized by intestinal bacteria
2. Synthesis of nucleic acids, cell formation
3. No minimum requirements set
4. Anemia

Vitamin B₁₂
1. Liver, lean meat, fish, milk
2. Manufacture of nucleic acids
3. No minimum requirements set
4. Pernicious anemia

Choline
1. Widely distributed in animal and plant tissues
2. Transportation of fat and formation of animal cells
3. No minimum requirements set
4. Accumulation of fat in liver; may aid in onset of cirrhosis

Inositol
1. Widely distributed in animal and plant tissues
2. Lipotropic agent
3. No minimum requirements set
4. Accumulation of fat in liver

Vitamin C (Ascorbic Acid)
1. Citrus fruits, raw leafy vegetables
2. Protects other vitamins from destruction in body
3. 75 mg.
4. Scurvy, marked by loosening of teeth, joint pains, hemorrhage

Vitamin D
1. Fish-liver oils, butter, egg yolk; also formed in body by action of sunlight on skin
2. Regulates absorption of calcium and phosphorus
3. 400 U.S.P. units
4. Bone disorders (rickets in children; osteomalacia in adults)

Vitamin E
1. Plant oils
2. Protects vitamin A from destruction in body
3. No minimum requirements set
4. Infertility, muscular dystrophy, or vascular diseases

Vitamin K
1. Synthesized by intestinal bacteria
2. Important in blood clotting
3. No minimum requirements set
4. Tendency to bleed easily

in the body include magnesium, sulfur, zinc, molybdenum, manganese, and cobalt.

■**VITAMINS.**—*Vitamins* are important in the enzyme systems which carry out essential chemical reactions. They are needed only in small quantities and generally must be supplied by the diet because they are not synthesized in the body. Vitamin K, which is synthesized by intestinal bacteria, is an exception.

Vitamins may be grouped in two categories: fat-soluble vitamins and water-soluble vitamins. The *fat-soluble vitamins*—A, D, E, and K—can be stored in the body and therefore do not have to be continuously supplied. *Water-soluble vitamins*—the B-complex vitamins and vitamin C—are not effectively stored in the body and must be regularly supplied through the diet.

■**NUTRITIONAL DISEASES.**—Nutritional disorders are of three types: those caused by a dietary deficiency of a necessary substance; those caused by the body's inability to absorb a substance; those caused by an excess of a nutrient.

The vitamin deficiency diseases are historically interesting for the role they have played in certain popula-

tions that have not had access to a sufficiently varied diet. *Scurvy*, for example, was a notorious scourge of sailors on long sea voyages where they had no fresh foods containing vitamin C. *Beriberi*, a disease caused by a deficiency of vitamin B₁, has long been prevalent in areas of the Far East where polished rice is the dietary staple. The protein deficiency disease *kwashiorkor* is found in certain areas of Africa where children are weaned on starchy foods.

In the disease called *sprue*, a disorder of absorption, the small intestine does not properly absorb nutrients. This may result in multiple vitamin deficiencies, *anemia* (a deficiency of red blood cells), and loss of weight. In *pernicious anemia* vitamin B₁₂ is not absorbed normally from the digestive tract because absorption is hindered by the absence of an intrinsic factor from the gastric juice. Red blood cell formation declines in the absence of the vitamin.

Vitamins A and D may be harmful if given in large doses over long periods of time. Excess vitamin A may cause bone and skin abnormalities. An oversupply of vitamin D may result in pathological deposition of calcium in soft tissues of the body.

Digestive System

■**TEETH.**—The first set of teeth—the *milk*, or *deciduous*, teeth—appear between the ages of six months and two years. These 20 deciduous teeth are replaced, beginning about the sixth year, with the 32 permanent teeth. Each tooth is capped by smooth, dense *enamel*, the hardest substance in the body. Underneath the enamel is the softer *dentine*, which is sensitive to heat and cold and is also less resistant to decay than the enamel is. The *pulp cavity* under the dentine contains the nerves and blood vessels of the tooth.

Decay, the most common dental disorder, is more common in children and adolescents than in adults. It begins on the outer surface of the tooth and spreads rapidly once it penetrates the hard enamel. If it is left untreated, decay causes inflammation of the pulp cavity, with excruciating pain, and eventual loss of the tooth. Another frequent tooth disorder is *malocclusion*, an abnormal positioning of the teeth. *Pyorrhea* is an inflammation of the gums which may be caused by irritation from deposits of tartar or by malocclusion.

■**SALIVARY GLANDS.**—There are three pairs of *salivary glands:* the *parotid glands*, which lie in front of the ears; the *submaxillary glands* of the jaw; and the *sublingual glands*, which lie under the floor of the mouth.

■**DIGESTION IN THE MOUTH.**—The first stage of digestion is initiated by the teeth, which grind the food and mix it with saliva containing the enzyme *salivary amylase*. This enzyme breaks down starches into simpler compounds. The food mass is then swallowed and propelled to the stomach via the *esophagus*, the long, tubular passageway connecting the mouth and the stomach.

■**DIGESTION IN THE STOMACH.**—In the stomach the food is kneaded and

mixed with gastric juices containing the enzyme *pepsin* and *hydrochloric acid*. Pepsin decomposes the long protein chains into smaller units called *peptides* and *proteoses*.

■**DIGESTION IN THE INTESTINES.**—The *intestines* are divided into two parts: the *small intestine*, a coiled tube about 21 feet long, and the *large intestine*, about 5 feet long. These terms "small" and "large" refer to the diameter of the intestines.

The small intestine is the major site of digestive activity. Here foods are broken down into simpler substances which can be absorbed by the body, thus completing the process which began in the mouth. In the small intestine fats are decomposed into *fatty acids* and *glycerol;* carbohydrates are decomposed into simple sugars; and proteins are decomposed into amino acids. This intense digestive activity is made possible by digestive enzymes secreted by the pancreas and by the intestinal lining itself. The liver contributes bile salts, which break fat globules into smaller particles that can be acted upon by fat-splitting enzymes. The products of digestion are absorbed through the intestinal wall by the blood and lymph streams and are distributed to the body cells. The undigested residue from the small intestine is moved by wavelike contractions of the intestinal wall (*peristaltic waves*), towards the large intestine. There water is absorbed from the residues, and the remainder passes to the *rectum* to be excreted.

■**PHASES OF DIGESTION.**—In the description of digestion given above, it is noted that at various points enzyme-containing secretions are poured into the digestive tract. An important aspect of digestion is the way that the flow of these secretions is controlled. With respect to enzyme flow, digestion is divided into three phases.

In the *psychic phase*, before the food is eaten, the flow of secretions from the salivary glands, stomach, and pancreas is stimulated by the sight or smell of food. This is effected by nerve pathways from the brain. The presence of food in the stomach during the *gastric phase* of digestion liberates hormones from the stomach lining that travel through the blood to stimulate glandular cells in the stomach. Then, in the *intestinal phase*, when food is in the small intestine, hormones are liberated from the intestinal lining to stimulate the stomach and the pancreas. Fatty substances in the small intestine stimulate the release of a hormone that inhibits digestive activity in the stomach.

Metabolism.—The process through which the body makes use of the end products of digestion is called *metabolism*. This process includes what happens to digested material after it enters the blood stream and the way in which the body uses food to build tissues and to produce energy.

■**LIVER.**—The *liver*, a major metabolic organ, has often been compared to a chemical factory because of its many functions. It is the largest gland in the body, comprising approximately

THE DIGESTIVE TRACT

Esophagus
Liver
Stomach
Pylorus
Pancreas
Large Intestine
Small Intestine
Rectum
Appendix

DIGESTIVE TRACT. Food is kneaded in the stomach and mixed with digestive enzymes; most digestion occurs in the small intestine.

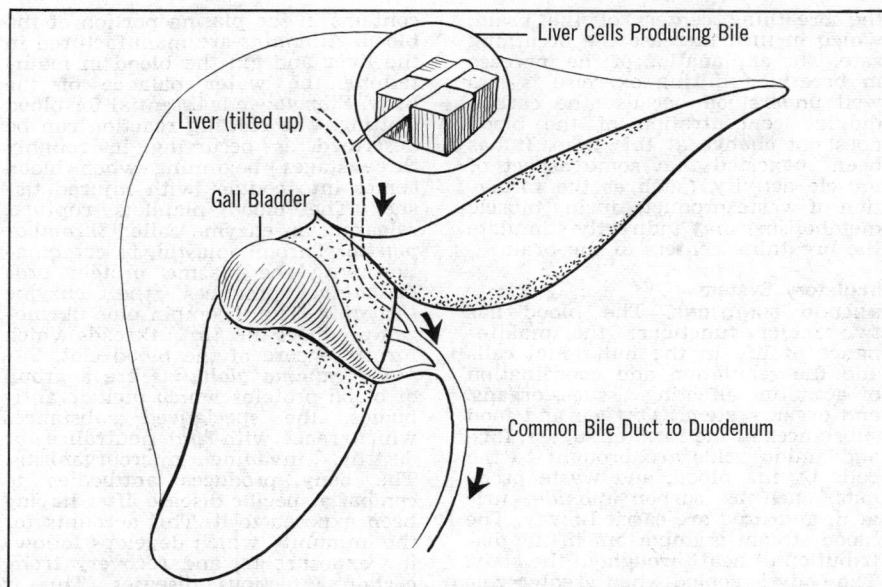

LIVER. Bile secretions flow from the liver to the gallbladder and the small intestine.

one-thirtieth of the body weight, or about five pounds in the average person. It lies on the right side of the body, immediately under the *diaphragm* (the disclike muscle which stretches horizontally across the body, separating the abdominal cavity from the chest cavity).

The liver is composed of two distinct types of cells—the parenchymal cells and the Kupffer cells. The *parenchymal* cells are the glandular, or secreting, cells, which perform most of the liver's metabolic activity. The *Kupffer* cells belong to the widely distributed *reticuloendothelial system* of cells, a system which plays an important role in the body's defense against infection. One of the main functions of this system is to remove bacteria and other foreign particles from the blood.

The liver plays a key role in the metabolism of carbohydrates, proteins, and fats. It stores vitamins and minerals and produces, among other things, the bile which is so important in the digestive process. Blood rich in digestive products from the intestine enters the liver by way of the portal vein. Sugars, the products of carbohydrate digestion, are stored in the liver in the form of the starch *glycogen*. Liver glycogen can be reconverted into other sugars and released into the blood as needed. If enough carbohydrates are not supplied in the diet, the liver can manufacture glycogen from other substances. *Amino acids*, the end products of protein digestion, are used by the liver as energy-producing substances. In this process a portion of the amino acid molecule is detached and converted into *urea*, which is excreted by the kidneys. Fatty acids which enter the liver are broken down into still simpler substances that can be more easily used for energy production. The liver also stores fats.

Bile is a liver product that contains both secretions and excretions. The secretions are manufactured by the parenchymal cells and contain bile salts, which aid in the digestion of fats. Bile also enables fats to be absorbed from the intestine. The excretions include the bile pigments, waste products derived from the breakdown of the hemoglobin of red blood cells. Bile pigments are produced by the Kupffer cells and also by other cells of the reticuloendothelial system. Bile is stored in the *gallbladder*—a small, pear-shaped pouch partially embedded in the undersurface of the liver—and is emptied into the small intestine through the *bile ducts*.

The liver manufactures certain essential *blood proteins*. Two of these, *prothrombin* and *fibrinogen*, are important in blood clotting; others (principally the *albumins*) contribute to the osmotic pressure of the blood. In this context *osmotic pressure* refers to the ability of the blood to retain water. This is attributed largely to the presence of large protein molecules that tend to draw water from the tissues into the blood, thus compensating for the leakage of fluid from the blood into the tissue spaces.

■**ENERGY PRODUCTION IN THE CELL.**— The energy-rich substances leaving the liver are principally sugars (*glucose*) and the products of fat breakdown. These are carried by the blood stream to all the body tissues, where they enter the individual cells. Here the energy-rich material is processed through a complex series of chemical reactions. The overall equation describing the process is: food substances + oxygen → carbon dioxide + water + energy.

In some popular treatments of physiology the statement is made that the body "burns" food as a fuel, thereby liberating energy. This suggests the inaccurate image of a stovelike device somewhere in the body being stoked with fuel and giving off heat. Actually each body cell burns its fuel in microscopic structures called *mitochondria*. The burning occurs in a series of reactions (the *Krebs cycle*), with small amounts of energy being liberated in the course of the series. This explains why the cells are not consumed by the violent reaction that would result if fuel combined directly with oxygen and ignited, as in the gasoline engine.

Respiration

■**RESPIRATORY PROCESS.**—Energy production in the cells requires oxygen. The process by which oxygen is taken

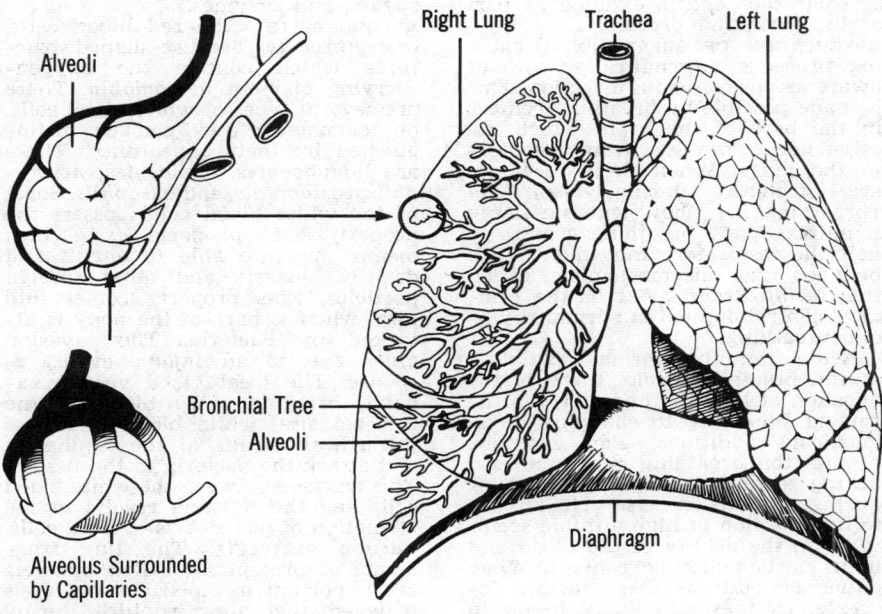

RESPIRATORY SYSTEM. Air enters the lungs through the trachea (windpipe) and passes through the successively smaller passages of the bronchial tree, ultimately reaching the alveoli, where there is an exchange of gases between the air and the blood stream.

into the body and used by the cells is called *respiration.* The mechanical work of breathing is accomplished principally by the *diaphragm,* a sheet of muscle which stretches across the lower boundary of the chest cavity. The size of the chest cavity increases as the diaphragm contracts, thus drawing air into the *lungs.* Air is expelled as the diaphragm relaxes. The muscles attached to the ribs also aid in breathing by slightly increasing and decreasing the size of the chest cavity.

Air is taken in through the mouth and nose and enters the *trachea,* or windpipe, a long, tubular structure which branches off at its terminal point into two main *bronchi.* In the lungs the bronchi divide into smaller and smaller branches, terminating in tiny saclike structures called *alveoli,* where the actual exchange of gases between the air and blood occurs. The surfaces of the alveoli are covered with thousands of minute blood vessels. The arrangement is such that only two fragile membranes separate a large sheet of moving blood from the air in the alveoli. At this point the blood surrenders some of its carbon dioxide to the air and absorbs oxygen from the air. This oxygen is bound in a loose chemical combination to *hemoglobin,* the pigment of the red blood cells.

The oxygen-bearing red blood cells are then carried to the farthest reaches of the body, finally arriving at the microscopic capillaries of the tissues, where a second exchange of gases occurs; oxygen leaves the capillaries to enter the tissue cells, and carbon dioxide enters the blood. Once it is inside the cells, oxygen is used in the burning of food substances to produce energy. The carbon dioxide entering the blood stream is a waste product of respiration and is carried in the venous blood to the lungs, where it passes into the air in the *alveolar sacs* and is exhaled as part of the breathing process.

■ **REGULATION OF BREATHING.**—Breathing proceeds automatically, without awareness or conscious direction. This is made possible by breathing centers in the base of the brain which receive nerve impulses from receptors in the lungs. When these receptors are stretched during *inspiration* (breathing in), they generate nerve impulses to the breathing centers to halt the inspiratory movement. It is believed that this mechanism, called the *Hering-Breur reflex,* is the principal control applied in normal rhythmic breathing.

Aside from this normal regulation of the breathing cycle, there is the question of how the body adjusts the rate of breathing to changing physiological conditions. For example, how is the breathing rate increased during ascents to high altitudes or during vigorous exercise? The answer to the question of high altitude seems to lie in the acidity of the blood and in its carbon dioxide content. When either or both of these factors increase, as they are likely to do in an oxygen-thin atmosphere, special *chemoreceptors* in certain arteries and in the brain relay impulses to the breathing centers of the brain, which in turn increase the breathing rate. The explanation of the increase in breathing during exercise is less well understood because the carbon dioxide concentration of the blood does not change at this time. It has been suggested that some aspect of muscle activity (such as the formation of waste products during muscle metabolism) may indirectly stimulate the breathing centers of the brain.

Circulatory System

■ **BLOOD FUNCTIONS.**—The blood has two major functions: the maintenance of life in the individual cells and the regulation and coordination of activities affecting tissues, organs, and organ systems. Oxygen and food substances in the form of sugars, fats, and amino acids are brought to the cells by the blood, and waste products, such as carbon dioxide, uric acid, and urea are carried away. The blood stream is important in the distribution of heat throughout the body. The body is cooled when greater volumes of blood flow to the blood vessels of the skin; heat is conserved when these vessels constrict, shunting blood to the deeper tissues.

The blood is a major line of defense against disease. It brings bacteria-fighting white blood cells to sites of infection. It also contains special proteins (*antibodies*) which neutralize disease-producing microorganisms. In addition to this, blood serves as a transportation network by carrying *hormones,* the secretions of the endocrine glands. These substances regulate certain important activities, such as metabolism and menstruation, and help the body adjust to sudden stress.

■ **BLOOD COMPONENTS.**—The fluid part of the blood, or *plasma,* is about 90 per cent water; but it also contains dissolved minerals, hormones, and such organic substances as fats, sugars, and enzymes.

■ **BLOOD CELLS.**—The red blood cells, or *erythrocytes,* are disc-shaped structures which contain the oxygen-carrying pigment *hemoglobin.* There are several types of white blood cells, or *leukocytes;* they can be distinguished by their appearance. These are *lymphocytes, monocytes, neutrophils, eosinophils,* and *basophils.* Some of the white blood cells possess the property of *phagocytosis,* which means they are able to engulf and destroy bacteria and other foreign particles. This property comes into play when a part of the body is attacked by bacteria. The invasion gives rise to an *inflammatory response.* The local blood vessels expand, bringing more blood to the infected site; white blood cells pass through the walls of the capillaries and attack the bacteria in the tissues. This warfare between the white blood cells and the bacteria results in the formation of *pus,* debris of dead cells.

■ **BLOOD PLATELETS.**—The tiny fragments of protoplasm called platelets are important in blood clotting. It is believed that they rupture during clotting, releasing enzymes that promote the formation of the blood clot.

■ **BLOOD PROTEINS.**—Blood proteins are contains in the plasma portion of the blood. *Albumins* are manufactured in the liver and aid the blood in maintaining the water balance of the body. *Fibrinogen* is essential for blood clotting. The clotting reaction can be described as occurring in roughly three stages, beginning when blood comes into contact with injured tissue: The blood platelets rupture, releasing an enzyme called *thromboplastin.* Thromboplastin, in combination with the plasma protein *prothrombin,* produces the enzyme *thrombin.* The thrombin plus fibrinogen produces the *fibrin* threads which form the core of the blood clot.

The *gamma globulins* are a group of blood proteins which include antibodies, the specialized substances which react with and neutralize, or destroy, invading microorganisms. The body produces antibodies to combat a specific disease after having been exposed to it. This accounts for the immunity which develops following exposure to, and recovery from, certain infectious diseases. This is also the principle on which *vaccination* works: a preparation is administered to cause the formation of disease-combating antibodies.

■ **BLOOD GROUPS AND TRANSFUSIONS.**—The blood of different individuals may differ in respect to the presence or absence of certain substances called *blood factors.* The most widely known factor system concerns the *antigens A* and *B* and their antibodies, *anti-A* and *anti-B.* The antigens and their respective antibodies are incompatible. For instance, if blood containing A is mixed with blood containing anti-A, the blood cells will *agglutinate,* or clump together. Antigens are contained in the cells; antibodies are found in the plasma. The blood of any human being will be in one of four *groups*—*O, B, A,* or *AB*—according to the presence or absence of these two antigens and two antibodies.

	Antigen	Antibodies
Group O	None	Anti-A; Anti-B
Group B	B	Anti-A
Group A	A	Anti-B
Group AB	AB	None

A fatal reaction may occur if a transfusion of the wrong type of blood is given to a patient. If group A blood is transfused into a group B patient, the anti-B antibodies of the transfused blood could agglutinate the recipient's blood cells (which contain the B antigen). This can result in chills, rapid pulse, and possibly kidney failure and death. For this reason the blood of both the donor and the patient are tested before a transfusion.

■ **Rh FACTOR.**—An additional and quite complicated blood factor is called the *Rh factor* (after the Rhesus monkey, which was used for the experimental work). The Rh factor is present in a majority of the population; such persons are called *Rh positive.* Individuals lacking the factor are called *Rh negative.* The occurrence of the Rh factor is associated with *erythroblastosis fetalis,* a disease of newborn infants of an Rh negative woman and an Rh positive man. If the child is

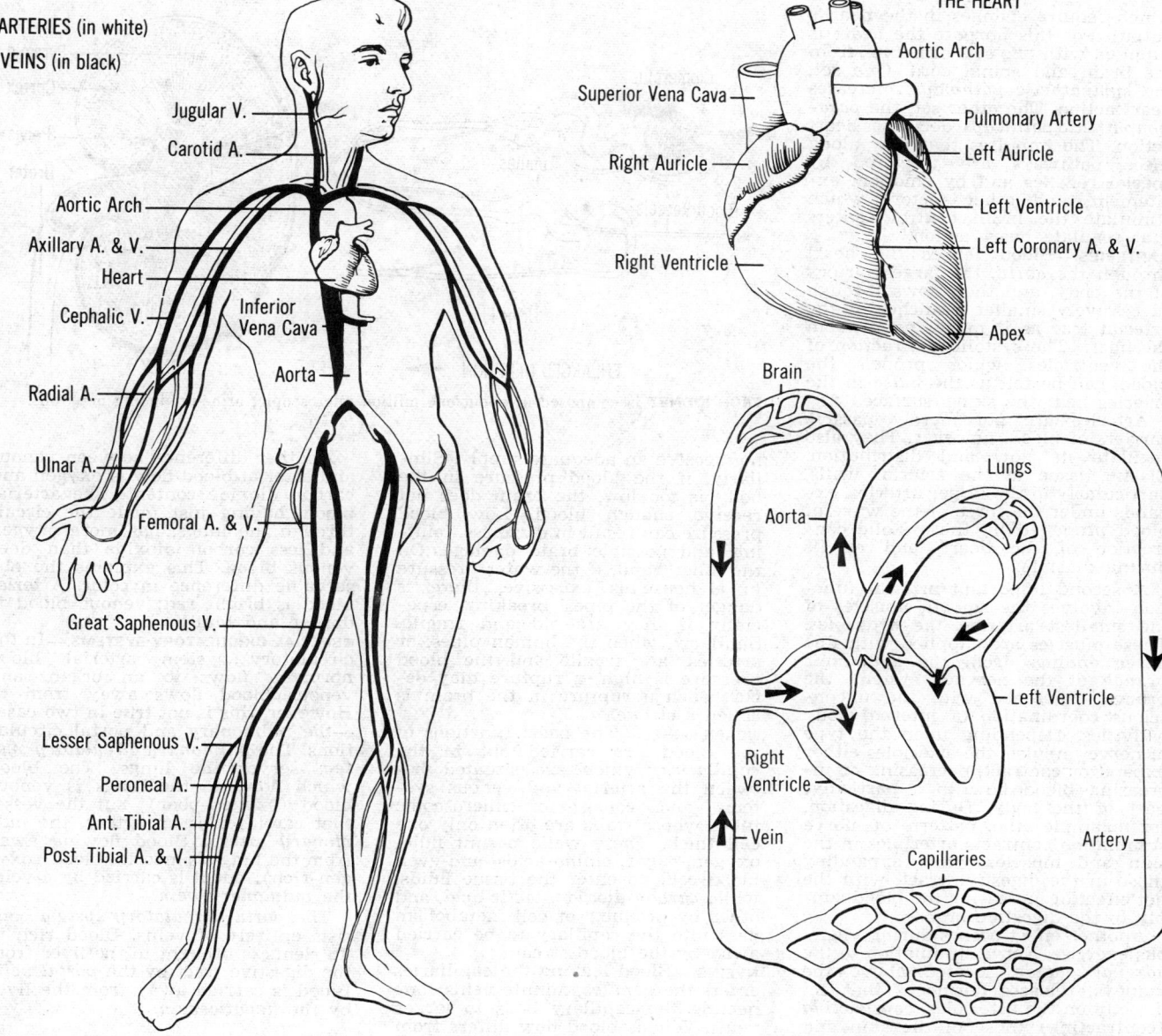

ARTERIES (in white)
VEINS (in black)

Jugular V.
Carotid A.
Aortic Arch
Axillary A. & V.
Heart
Cephalic V.
Inferior Vena Cava
Radial A.
Aorta
Ulnar A.
Femoral A. & V.
Great Saphenous V.
Lesser Saphenous V.
Peroneal A.
Ant. Tibial A.
Post. Tibial A. & V.

THE HEART

Aortic Arch
Superior Vena Cava
Pulmonary Artery
Right Auricle
Left Auricle
Left Ventricle
Right Ventricle
Left Coronary A. & V.
Apex

Brain
Lungs
Aorta
Left Ventricle
Right Ventricle
Vein
Artery
Capillaries

PULMONARY AND SYSTEMIC CIRCULATIONS

Rh positive, the mother's body may produce antibodies to destroy the fetus's red blood cells; the child is born with a severe anemia. Such children can be treated after birth with transfusions of Rh negative blood.

■BLOOD CIRCULATION.—The blood flows throughout the body in a closed circuit of vessels of varying diameter and structure. It is propelled through this circuit by the pumping action of the *heart*, a muscular organ about the size of the fist. The human heart consists of four chambers—two thin-walled *atria* (*auricles*) and two powerfully muscled *ventricles*. The heart can be considered as two synchronized pumps. The *right heart*, consisting of the right atrium and the right ventricle, receives blood from the great veins known as the *inferior* and *superior vena cavae*, and pumps this blood from the right ventricle to the lungs. The *left heart* receives

oxygenated blood from the lungs and pumps it into the arteries. The path of blood through the heart can thus be plotted as follows: the great veins —right atrium—right ventricle—lungs (via the *pulmonary artery*)—left atrium (via the *pulmonary vein*)— left ventricle—*aorta* (the largest artery of the body). As the blood passes through the lungs, it absorbs oxygen and surrenders carbon dioxide.

■DIASTOLE AND SYSTOLE.—Diastole and systole are the terms used to describe the principal phases of the heartbeat. *Diastole* is the relaxed phase during which the blood passes from the atria to the ventricles. During *systole* the ventricles contract vigorously, propelling blood to the lungs and the arteries. In these two phases the action of both halves of the heart are synchronized. During diastole both the left and right ventricles relax; during systole both contract.

■HEARTBEAT REGULATION.—The heart

beats regularly and automatically throughout life, adjusting its output to meet the changing needs of the body. This is possible because the normal heartbeat rhythm is controlled by bundles of specialized conductive tissue in the heart which act as a built-in timing system. Along the upper portion of the right atrium is the "pacemaker" of the heart (the *SA,* or *sinoauricular node*), which generates impulses at the rate of 60 to 90 per minute. These impulses spread along the walls of the left and right atria, stimulating contraction. At the *interatrial septum*, the boundary of the left and right atria, the impulse stimulates another structure, the *AV,* or *atrioventricular node*. This generates another wave of impulses that travels along the walls of both ventricles, causing them to contract.

However, since the system is purely a clocklike internal system, it is not sensitive to physiological conditions which require changes in the heart's output. For this purpose the heart is supplied with two sets of nerves from the brain and spinal cord. One set, the *sympathetic pathways,* increases heart action. The other set, the *parasympathetic pathways,* decreases heart action. The impulses that flow along these pathways are triggered by special reflexes and by emotion, excitement, and other factors which stimulate the brain control centers that regulate heart action.

■**ARTERIES.**—Blood leaves the heart through the *aorta,* the largest artery of the body, and then flows through successively smaller branches of the arterial tree as it moves away from the heart. The systolic contraction of the ventricles, which propels the blood, can be felt as the *pulse* in the arteries near the skin's surface.

Arteries are not merely passive carriers of blood, however. They also regulate its flow and distribution. Elastic tissue in the arterial walls, particularly in the larger arteries, expands under the force of the wave of blood propelled by the systolic contraction of the heart, and recoils during diastole.

A second important arterial function involves the smooth muscles of the smallest arteries, the *arterioles.* These muscles are supplied with fine nerve endings from the *autonomic branch* of the nervous system, the branch concerned with the unconscious coordination of internal body activities. Depending upon the type of nerve impulse, the arterioles either expand or contract, decreasing or increasing blood flow to a particular part of the body. During digestion, for example, the pattern of nerve stimulation contracts arterioles in the skin and muscles while expanding those in the digestive tract, with the net effect of increasing the blood supply to the digestive organs.

Another effect occurs during vigorous exercise. Nerve stimulation to the *adrenal glands,* located above the kidneys, releases hormones that act directly on the arterioles, *constricting* (contracting) those of the skin and *dilating* (expanding) those in the muscles of the trunk and limbs. This causes blood to be diverted to those muscles being used.

■**BLOOD PRESSURE.**—The terms used to describe blood pressure are *systolic* and *diastolic.* The first refers to the force, or pressure, of the blood during heart contraction. The second refers to the pressure of the blood when the heart is relaxed. Units of blood pressure are given in terms of millimeters of mercury, or the ability of the blood pressure to support a given amount of mercury in a glass tube.

Blood pressure generally increases with age. The average blood pressure of infants is usually about 80 millimeters of mercury systolic and 55 millimeters diastolic, or 80/55; the average figure for young adults is about 120/80.

The significance of blood pressure may be understood by an analogy between the circulatory system of the body and the plumbing system of a house. If the water pressure in a house is too low, the upper floors do

not receive an adequate supply. Similarly, if the blood pressure in the body is too low, the brain does not receive enough blood. Low blood pressure can result in dizziness, fainting, and possible brain damage. On the other hand, if the water pressure in a house is excessive, there is danger of the pipes' breaking, especially if they are old and fragile. Similarly, when the human pipes, or arteries, are fragile and the blood pressure is high, a rupture may occur. Such a rupture in the brain is called a *stroke.*

■**CAPILLARIES.**—The basic functions of the blood are carried out in the *capillaries,* which are situated between the arterial and venous systems and consist of microscopic tubes whose walls are often only one cell thick. These walls permit fluid, oxygen, sugar, amino acids, and even blood cells to enter the tissue fluids, while *carbon dioxide, lactic acid,* and other by-products of cell metabolism pass into the capillary to be carried away by the blood stream.

■**VEINS.**—Blood leaving the capillaries enters the *venules,* minute veins connecting the capillary beds to larger veins. Venous blood flow differs from arterial blood flow in several important respects. Blood in the veins is under considerably less pressure than blood in the arteries because the force of the heart's pumping action is not transmitted to the veins. For this reason arterial bleeding is much more dangerous than venous bleeding. When an artery is cut, blood spurts out with great force; and enough blood may be lost in only a few minutes to cause death. When a vein is cut, however, blood flows out slowly and steadily.

The low pressure of venous blood flow creates a problem in the return of blood to the heart. This is especially true with respect to the return of blood—against the force of gravity—from the lower extremities. To facilitate this movement, the veins are equipped with valves that permit the blood to flow in only one direction—toward the heart. In *varicose veins* these valves fail, permitting backflow of blood and the consequent appearance of saclike expansions of the venous walls.

Another difference between venous and arterial blood flow is oxygen and carbon dioxide content. The arterial blood, having just made the circuit through the lungs, has more oxygen and less carbon dioxide than does venous blood. This explains the observable difference in color. Arterial blood is bright red; venous blood is darker and bluish.

■**SPECIAL CIRCULATORY SYSTEMS.**—In the circulatory system arterial blood normally flows to an organ, and venous blood flows away from it. However, this is not true in two cases —the pulmonary and portal circulations. The *pulmonary circulatory system* serves the lungs. The blood which flows to the lungs is venous blood (oxygen-poor); but the vessel that carries it is an artery, the *pulmonary artery.* Blood flowing away from the lungs is arterial blood (oxygen-rich), but it is carried by a vein, the *pulmonary vein.*

The *portal circulatory system* consists entirely of veins. Blood rich in nutrients is brought to the liver from the digestive tract by the *portal vein.* Blood is carried away from the liver by the *hepatic vein.*

Lymphatic System.—The *lymphatic system* is a second circulatory system which returns fluids and proteins from the tissue spaces to the blood. As blood flows through the tiny capillaries of the tissues, fluids and proteins leak out. Without the lymph channels this material would collect in the tissues, producing fluid swellings known as *edema.*

The *lymph vessels* begin as small closed tubes in the tissues and join into larger vessels, eventually emptying into large veins in the chest. Lymph vessels are found in the skin, the muscle, and the linings of various organs. The *lymph nodes* distributed along the system contain cells that consume foreign particles and bacteria in the lymph fluid. This is an important defense mechanism against disease. Swelling of the lymph nodes is often a sign that the region which they drain is infected.

Reticuloendothelial System.—The cells of the *reticuloendothelial system* (*RE cells*) are widely distributed in the

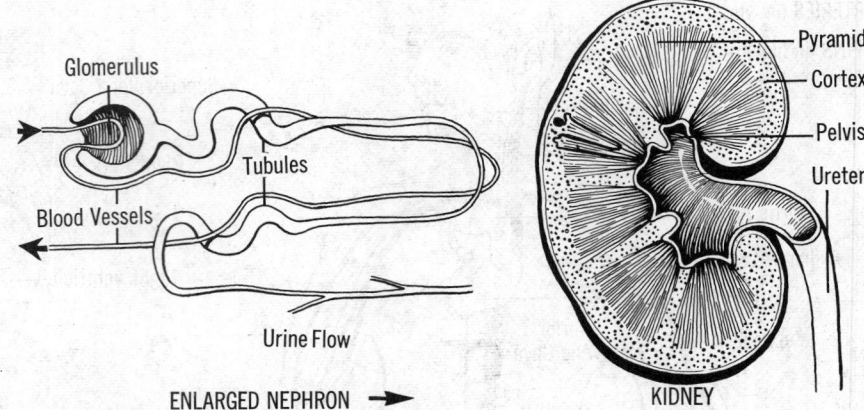

ENLARGED NEPHRON ➜   KIDNEY

EACH KIDNEY is composed of about one million microscopic, urine-producing nephrons.

body. They are found in the liver, in connective tissue, in the spleen, in the lymph nodes, and in certain glands. In addition to this "fixed" type, "wandering" RE cells travel in the blood stream to various parts of the body. All RE cells are scavengers, and as such play an important role in the body's defense against infection. They are able to *phagocytize,* to consume such foreign substances as bacteria. There is also evidence that RE cells participate in the production of *antibodies,* special substances that can destroy or neutralize invading microorganisms. In the spleen, liver, and bone marrow, RE cells consume old red blood cells and convert the hemoglobin into bile pigments, which are excreted with the bile.

Spleen.—The *spleen* is located on the left side of the abdomen underneath the diaphragm. This organ contains a rich network of blood channels, thus exposing a large volume of blood to the action of its cells.

The spleen acts upon the blood system in several ways. It manufactures white blood cells known as *lymphocytes* and destroys old red blood cells, white cells, and platelets circulating in the blood stream. Since it is part of the reticuloendothelial system, the spleen can also produce disease-fighting antibodies and is capable of phagocytizing bacteria and other foreign substances in the blood.

Kidneys.—Waste products are carried away from the body cells by the circulatory system. One of these wastes, carbon dioxide, is carried to the lungs, from which it is expelled. Other chemical wastes are disposed of by the *kidneys,* two bean-shaped organs embedded in the posterior abdominal wall. The kidneys are located one on each side of the vertebral column.

The basic functional unit of the kidney is the *nephron,* of which there are approximately one million in each kidney. The microscopic nephrons contain a filtering mechanism called the *glomerulus,* which leads into a long, twisted tubule. Blood enters the glomerulus, where virtually everything, except blood cells and large protein molecules, passes through to the long tubule. The material which enters the tubule is known as the *glomerular filtrate.* This is the first step of *urine* formation, which is essentially an indirect process based on the principle of selective reabsorption. Varying quantities of such substances as urea, sugar, salts, and most of the water are reabsorbed into the blood through the tubule wall. After a secretion of the cells lining the tubule has been added, the resulting urine leaves the tubule and passes through the *ureters* to the *bladder,* where it is stored until it is finally excreted.

Endocrine Glands.—The *endocrine glands* (as distinguished from the *exocrine glands,* such as the sweat glands of the skin) pour secretions directly into the blood stream. These secretions, known as *hormones,* serve as a means of long-distance control, enabling the body to coordinate its internal activities.

■**PITUITARY GLAND.**—The *pituitary gland,* or *hypophysis,* is a pea-sized structure situated under the brain. It is often called the "master" endocrine gland because of the control it exercises over other endocrine glands. The pituitary gland is divided into three parts: the anterior, intermediate, and posterior portions.

The anterior portion, or *adenohypophysis,* secretes hormones that stimulate the activity of other endocrine glands. Among these are the *thyrotrophic hormone* (*TSH*), which stimulates the thyroid gland, and the *adrenocorticotrophic hormone* (*ACTH*), which stimulates the outer layer of the adrenal glands. The anterior pituitary also secretes hormones that stimulate sexual development and regulate the menstrual cycle.

Secretion of many of these hormones is controlled by a chemical "feedback" principle. (This is a term borrowed from engineering, where similar principles are used in devices such as thermostats and governors.) Feedback control is illustrated in the secretion of the thyrotrophic hormone, which acts upon the thyroid gland. As the concentration of thyroid hormone in the blood declines, the pituitary secretion of thyrotrophic hormone increases. This stimulates the thyroid gland and elevates the blood concentration of thyroid hormone, which in turn inhibits further secretion of TSH by the pituitary gland.

Secretion of some pituitary hormones is controlled by stimulation from the brain. In emergency reactions, for example, the hypothalmus of the brain may stimulate the secretion of ACTH from the pituitary. ACTH in turn stimulates the secretion of *cortisone* and related hormones from the *adrenal cortex,* the outer portion of the adrenal gland. These *adrenocortical hormones* help prepare the body to meet the impending stress.

The functions of the intermediate portion of the human pituitary gland are not yet clearly understood. In lower animals it secretes a hormone that regulates the distribution of pigment in the skin (melohocyte-stimulating hormone, *MSH*).

The posterior portion of the pituitary, or *neurohypophysis,* secretes the *antidiuretic hormone* (*ADH*), which acts upon the kidneys to regulate the passage of water in the urine. It also secretes the hormone *oxytocin,* which stimulates contractions of the uterus during childbirth and milk flow from the breasts during nursing.

■**THYROID GLAND.**—The *thyroid gland,* located in the throat adjacent to the windpipe, or *trachea,* secretes hormones which regulate the rate at which the cells consume oxygen in the process of energy production.

Adjacent to the thyroid are the *parathyroid glands,* small brownish-red bodies that regulate the concentration of calcium in the blood. The action of the *parathyroid hormone* closely resembles that of vitamin D.

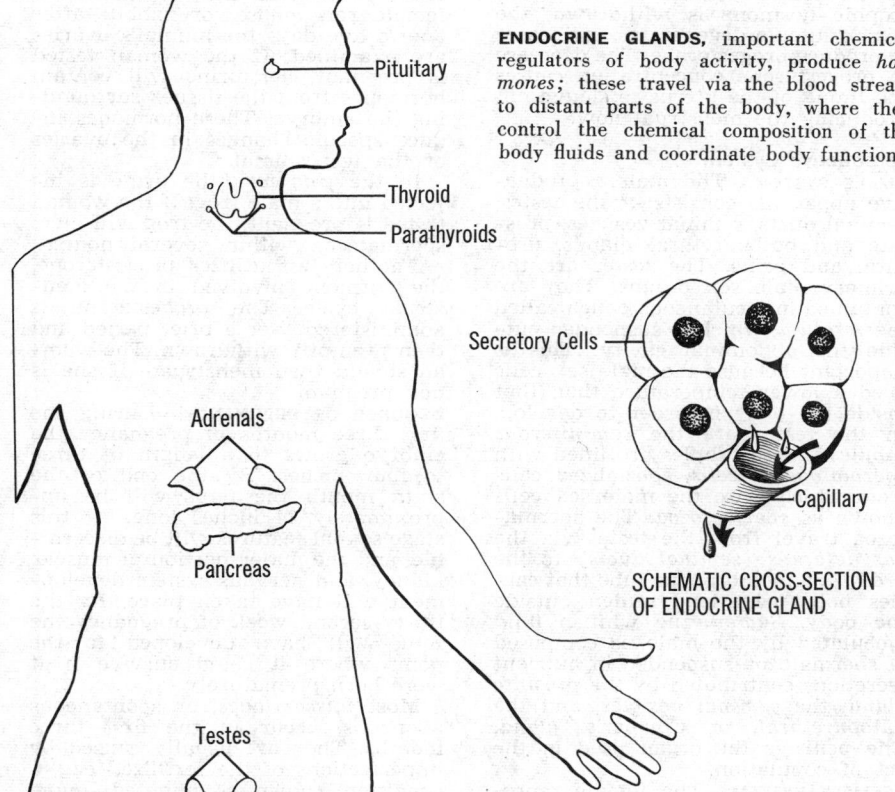

ENDOCRINE GLANDS, important chemical regulators of body activity, produce *hormones;* these travel via the blood stream to distant parts of the body, where they control the chemical composition of the body fluids and coordinate body functions.

Pituitary
Thyroid
Parathyroids
Adrenals
Pancreas
Testes

Secretory Cells
Capillary

SCHEMATIC CROSS-SECTION OF ENDOCRINE GLAND

Both substances regulate the calcium metabolism of the body.

■ADRENAL GLANDS.—The two *adrenal glands* are located one on each kidney. These small structures actually consist of two distinct glands.

The outer part of the adrenal gland, or *cortex,* produces three types of hormones: those involved in regulating the energy-producing activities of the body (including *cortisone*), those which regulate the mineral composition of the body fluids (principally *aldosterone*), and those concerned with the regulation of sexual characteristics (*androgens*). The group of adrenal cortex hormones is called *corticosteroids.* The release of these substances is controlled by ACTH, which is secreted by the anterior portion of the pituitary gland.

The inner portion of the adrenal gland, the *medulla,* secretes the hormones *epinephrine* (*adrenalin*) and *norepinephrine* (*noradrenalin*), which constrict small arteries and thus raise the blood pressure to prepare the body to meet impending stress. The secretion of these substances is controlled by direct nervous stimulation from the brain.

■PANCREAS.—The *pancreas* is both an endocrine gland and an exocrine gland because it secretes substances through ducts and also pours them directly into the blood stream. The exocrine portion of the pancreas is involved with digestion: the *acinar cells* secrete digestive enzymes into the *pancreatic duct,* which empties into the small intestine. The endocrine portion of the gland is involved in regulating the sugar level of the blood. For this purpose the *islet cells* (*islets of Langerhans*) secrete the hormones *insulin* and *glucagon.* Insulin lowers the blood sugar; glucagon apparently raises it. A partial or complete failure of the insulin supply results in *diabetes mellitus,* a disease which impairs the body's ability to utilize carbohydrates.

■SEX GLANDS OR GONADS.—The human sex glands include the *testes* of the male and the *ovaries* of the female. The testes produce *testosterone,* a hormone which promotes development of certain male physical characteristics. The ovaries secrete *estrogen,* the female sex hormone that influences the secondary sexual characteristics in women.

■PLACENTA.—The endocrine structure which appears only during pregnancy is called the *placenta.* It indirectly connects the blood stream of the mother with that of the fetus and also secretes the hormone *progesterone,* which regulates and maintains pregnancy. The placenta is passed from the body as the *afterbirth.*

■THYMUS.—The *thymus* is an enigmatic gland located in the upper chest. It reaches its maximum size at puberty and then begins to shrink. Evidence suggests that the thymus may play a role in the body's immunity mechanisms. Several hormones affecting growth have also been isolated from the gland.

■MENSTRUATION.—A simple listing of the names and locations of the endocrine glands and their hormones fails to give a full picture of their delicate interaction in the affairs of the body. An understanding of how hormones coordinate physiological activities can best be obtained from a description of the part they play in one body function, *menstruation.*

The pituitary gland initiates the menstrual cycle by secreting the *follicle stimulating hormone* (*FSH*), which causes the ripening of one of the egg-bearing follicles of the ovary. As this occurs, the ovary gradually increases its production of *estrogen,* the female sex hormone. Estrogen in turn stimulates development of the uterus lining, preparing it to receive the egg if it should be fertilized. Approximately halfway through the cycle (about the fourteenth day) the egg ruptures from the follicle, leaves the ovary, and travels down the fallopian tubes to the uterus. At this time the pituitary gland has already begun to secrete another hormone, the *luteotrophic hormone.* This causes the ruptured follicle, which is left behind in the ovary, to develop into the *corpus luteum* (yellow body). This in turn secretes the hormone progesterone, which joins estrogen in stimulating the uterine lining. Progesterone also acts upon the pituitary, inhibiting further secretion of the follicle-stimulating hormone. This prevents new eggs from ripening in the ovary.

The final stage of hormone control in the menstrual cycle presumably occurs when the concentration of progesterone in the blood reaches a critical level and inhibits secretion of the luteotrophic hormone. This sharply drops the progesterone level of the blood because, as the luteotrophic hormone is withdrawn, the corpus luteum degenerates and ceases to produce progesterone. The decrease in progesterone concentration causes the lining of the uterus to slough off, producing the menstrual flow.

Reproductive System

■MALE SYSTEM.—The male reproductive apparatus consists of the testes, seminal ducts, seminal vesicles, prostate and bulbourethral glands, urethra, and penis. The *testes* are the primary male sex organs. They are contained in a cutaneous pouch called the *scrotum,* which is suspended outside the abdominal cavity. This is important because the male sex cells need a lower temperature than that inside the body in order to develop. In the testes are the *seminiferous tubules.* These tubules are lined with *spermatogenic cells,* specialized cells from which arise the male sex cells known as *spermatozoa.* The spermatozoa travel from the testes via the *vas deferens* (*seminal ducts*) to the *urethra,* a membranous tube that carries both urine and semen outside the body. *Semen,* the whitish fluid ejaculated by the male, is composed of spermatozoa suspended in nutrient secretions contributed by the *prostate gland,* the *seminal vesicles,* and the *bulbourethral,* or *Cowper's, gland.* The *penis* is the organ used in the act of copulation.

■FEMALE SYSTEM.—The female reproductive apparatus consists of the ovaries, fallopian or uterine tubes, uterus, and vagina. The *ovaries,* or *female gonads,* are two small almond-shaped bodies located on each side of the body in a shallow depression on the lateral wall of the pelvis. An ovary is composed of about 50,000 ova-containing follicles. After the age of puberty the follicle-stimulating hormone (FSH) is produced, and one of these follicles matures during each menstrual cycle. It discharges its *ovum,* or egg, which then travels to the uterus by way of the *fallopian tubes,* two long, slender tubes connecting the ovaries to the uterus. The ovum is propelled through the fallopian tube by the action of *cilia* (tiny hairs) and smooth muscle. The *uterus* receives the egg and houses the fetus during pregnancy. It is a hollow, muscular, pear-shaped organ about three inches long, with a broad, flattened body above and a narrow, cylindrical part known as the *cervix* below. The *vagina,* a curved musculo-membranous canal, leads from the outside of the body to the cervix and receives the male penis during copulation.

Pregnancy begins when the female egg is fertilized by the male sperm. This usually occurs in the fallopian tubes. The fertilized egg then implants itself in the uterine lining and develops.

■PREGNANCY TESTS.—The most common sign of pregnancy is failure to menstruate. Several tests are available, however, to detect pregnancy in its early stages.

The most widely used pregnancy tests are the *Aschheim-Zondek test* and its modifications. The woman's urine is injected into an immature female rat, mouse, or rabbit; after one to five days the animal's ovaries are examined. If the woman tested is pregnant, her urine will contain hormones from the tissues surrounding the embryo. These hormones induce specific changes in the ovaries of the test animal.

In the *frog test,* the urine is injected into a male frog. If the woman tested is pregnant, the frog will eject spermatozoa within several hours.

Another test utilizes progesterone, the hormone involved in the menstrual cycle. The progesterone is administered over a brief period and then promptly withdrawn. The woman should then menstruate if she is not pregnant.

■COURSE OF PREGNANCY.—During the first three months of pregnancy the embryo grows to a length of three to four inches. By the end of the sixth month the fetus will be approximately 14 inches long. At this stage sexual features will be discernible, and the major portion of muscle, kidney, and nervous system development will have taken place. By the thirty-second week of pregnancy the fetus will have developed to the point where it could survive if it were born prematurely.

Most *miscarriages,* or spontaneous abortions, occur in the first three months. They are usually caused by imperfections of the fertilized egg, a condition known as *blighted ovum.* Spontaneous abortions after the first three months of pregnancy can be

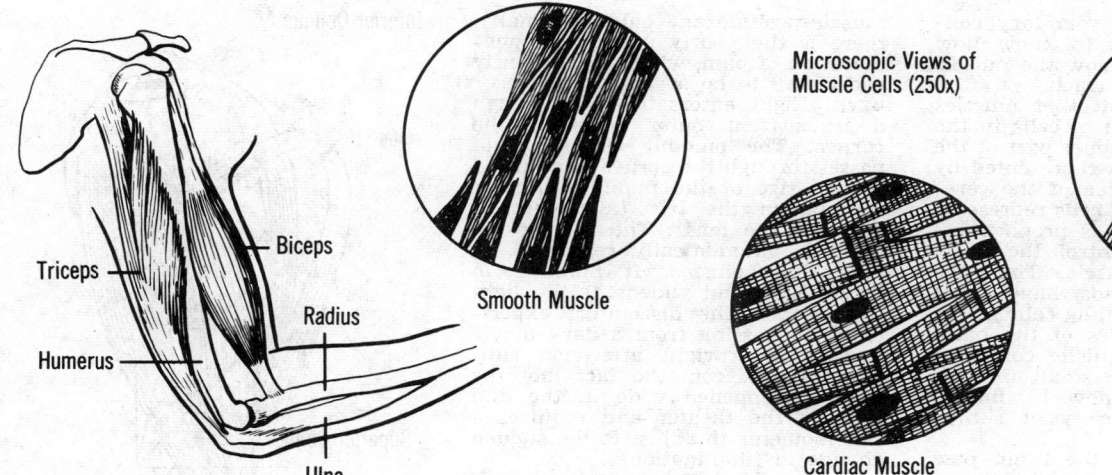

Microscopic Views of Muscle Cells (250x)

Smooth Muscle

Cardiac Muscle

Striated Muscle

Triceps
Biceps
Radius
Humerus
Ulna

MUSCLES. *Striated muscle* comprises the consciously controlled muscles of the trunk and limbs; *smooth muscle,* which is found in the walls of the digestive tract, in blood vessels, and in air passages, is unconsciously controlled by the autonomic nervous system; *cardiac muscle,* found only in the heart, is automatically controlled by the internal excitatory system of that organ.

caused by such disorders of the mother as syphilis, kidney disease, or a structural weakness of the neck of the womb, *incompetent cervix.*

An *ectopic pregnancy* occurs when the fertilized ovum becomes lodged in the fallopian tube, or some other site, instead of being normally implanted in the womb. Surgery is sometimes necessary to prevent serious injury to the mother.

Muscles.—There are three types of muscle in the body: skeletal muscle, attached to the bones of the arms, legs, trunk, and head; smooth muscle, found in blood vessels and the lining of the digestive tract; and heart muscle. The following discussion is limited to skeletal muscle.

.This type of muscle has been described by three different adjectives —skeletal, striated, and voluntary. *Skeletal* emphasizes the fact that these muscles are attached to the bones. *Striated* refers to the regular markings, or striations, of the muscle fiber that are visible under a microscope. *Voluntary* refers to the fact that these muscles are under the conscious control of the brain; they can be moved at will.

■MUSCLE STRUCTURE.—Muscle tissue can be described as fibers within fibers within fibers—rather akin to an electrical cable made up of smaller wires which are in turn composed of still smaller wires. Muscle is composed of parallel muscle fibers bound together in groups by bands of connective tissue. Each fiber is a separate cell with several nuclei distributed along its length. Each cell contains numerous *myofibrils* which extend the length of the cell. The myofibrils consist of short segments of the protein fibers *actin* and *myosin.* The clue to muscle contraction is believed to lie in the spatial arrangement of these protein fibers.

The functioning of muscle can be considered in relation to the questions of how muscles produce energy, how this energy is used for contrac-tion, and how muscle is controlled and stimulated by the nervous system.

■ENERGY PRODUCTION IN MUSCLE.—Energy production within the muscle occurs in two phases. One proceeds *anaerobically,* or without oxygen; the other requires oxygen. The principal source of muscle energy is *glucose.* During the processes of digestion and metabolism, carbohydrates (starches and sugars) are broken down into sugar (glucose) and absorbed into the blood. In the liver this sugar is stored in the form of the starch *glycogen,* which consists of thousands of sugar units. Liver glycogen is decomposed into sugar as needed and released into the blood stream, where it circulates to the muscles.

In the muscle cell, sugar is stored as *muscle glycogen.* When the muscle requires energy, this glycogen is broken down into its constituent sugar units. The muscle cells produce energy from sugar by breaking it down through a series of chemical reactions into *lactic acid.* In the course of these reactions energy is produced in the form of *adenosine triphosphate,* or *ATP.* This first phase of energy production is a "fast reaction" which does not require oxygen. The advantage of this is that muscles may be called upon to produce energy before the body is able to increase its oxygen intake.

The second phase of energy production involves the "burning" of lactic acid with oxygen. This phase occurs for the most part in the liver and requires another series of reactions, known as the *Krebs,* or *citric acid, cycle.* In the course of these reactions considerably more ATP is produced, along with the waste products, carbon dioxide and water.

It is helpful to place these chemical reactions in context, as they actually occur in conjunction with muscular activity. The case of a sprinter is a good example. A runner needs quick energy in order to race. While he is running, his muscles produce energy by breaking down muscle glycogen into sugar, which is then broken down into lactic acid. During this time he is said to acquire an "oxygen debt," referring to the extra oxygen he will have to breathe to rebuild the glycogen stores he has consumed. He repays this debt as his rate of breathing increases. At this time the second phase of energy production proceeds: lactic acid is transported from the muscle to the liver by the blood and is burned in the citric acid cycle, thus producing energy-rich ATP and more glycogen. This is generally described as the "second wind," the shifting of energy production to the *aerobic* or oxygen-consuming phase, once the rate of breathing has been increased.

■MUSCULAR CONTRACTION.—In order to understand muscular activity, it is necessary to know how chemical energy stored in ATP and in *phosphocreatine* (a high-energy phosphate that, like ATP, acts as the cell's immediate energy reserve) is converted into the mechanical energy of a muscular contraction. At one time it was believed that this resulted from the shortening of the actin and myosin fibers, but this hypothesis has been generally discarded in favor of what might be called the "sliding filament" theory of muscular contraction, which likens the muscle to a folding telescope opened to full length, with a spring inside tending to "telescope" it closed. The parts of the telescope lock in the open position by a rachet-like device. As the lock is released, the parts of the telescope are pulled together by spring action. This is roughly what is thought to occur in the muscle. The actin and myosin fibers are thought to lie in a telescoping arrangement, locked in position by bridges that cross between them. ATP may release these bridges, at which time the actin and myosin fibers slide together and lock in a new position.

■MUSCLE AND THE NERVOUS SYSTEM.—The large muscles of the trunk, limbs, and head are under voluntary control. It is important to know how this is achieved and how the muscle is stimulated to contract.

The voluntary control of muscles is under the direction of cells in the *cerebral cortex,* the upper part of the brain. Each muscle is represented by cells in the motor area of the cerebrum. The number of cells representing a specific muscle is proportional to the degree of control the brain exerts over the muscle. Thus the muscles of the hands have more representative controlling cells in the brain than do muscles of the back. This reflects the exquisite control a person has over the small muscles that enable him to move his fingers in such a great variety of skilled movements.

Nerve fibers from the brain pass down the spinal column, where they connect with the motor cells of the spinal cord. These fibers then leave the spinal cord through the spinal nerves, ultimately arriving at a *motor end plate* on a muscle cell. The nerve ending secretes a substance called *acetylcholine,* which alters the electrical properties of the membrane of the muscle cell. This triggers the muscle contraction, in which the energy contained in ATP somehow alters the spatial alignment of the actin and the myosin fibers.

Sense Organs.—It may be said that all the systems of the body exist for the sake of the nervous system. This incredibly intricate structure directs both the internal activities of the body and its interactions with the outside world. The *sensory receptors* are specialized structures that feed information into the nervous system. They include the *distance receptors* (eyes and ears), the *chemical receptors* (nose and taste buds), the *sensory receptors of the skin* that react to heat, cold, and pressure, and the *internal receptors* that maintain

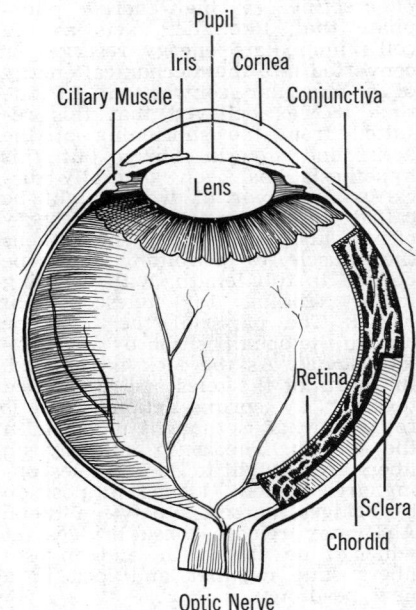

Pupil
Iris Cornea
Ciliary Muscle   Conjunctiva
Lens
Retina
Sclera
Chordid
Optic Nerve

THE EYE IN CROSS-SECTION

muscle position and balance. Finally, there is the poorly understood phenomenon of pain, which is frequently considered to be a sensation.

■**EYE.**—Light enters the eye through a transparent outer covering, the *cornea.* The amount of light that passes through the cornea is adjusted by the size of the *pupil,* a circular opening in the *iris* (a membrane covering the lens). The size of the pupil is automatically regulated by reflex mechanisms. It narrows in bright light and widens as the light grows dim. The discomfort experienced in passing from a dark movie theater into bright afternoon sunlight results from the fact that the pupil has opened wide in the dim light of the theater and requires a few moments to adjust to the sudden change in illumination.

Behind the iris is the transparent *lens,* an elastic body that is convex on both its front and back surfaces. The shape of the lens is adjusted by surrounding muscle that focuses light on the retina by altering the lens curvature.

The *retina* is the light-sensitive layer in the rear of the eye, where the image registers. Its structure is such that the actual light-sensitive cells (the *rods* and *cones*) are covered by two additional cell layers through which light must pass before it can activate impulses. The retina contains approximately 120 million rods, which serve for black-and-white perception, and 6 million cones, which distinguish color.

■**OPTIC NERVE.**—An image is transmitted to the brain by the *optic nerve,* which consists of about 1 million fibers. Before it reaches the brain, the optic nerve divides at the *optic chiasma.* This is a crossover point where the images from the right halves of both retinas travel to the right side of the brain, and images from the left halves travel to the left side of the brain. The visual impulses finally reach the *visual cortex* (the outer layer of gray matter of the cerebrum), located in the *occipital* (back) region of the cerebrum.

■**NATURE OF VISION.**—A simple description of the visual apparatus would make it seem as though the process of perception is well understood, whereas actually there are many unsolved problems in this field.

Vision is an active process. One point where the familiar analogy between the eye and a camera fails is in the idea that the visual image simply registers on the retina, from which it is communicated to the brain via the optic nerve. There is much evidence to indicate that the eye does not merely fix an object in focus, but moves about in definite patterns, "scanning" an object much in the manner of a photoelectric tube scanning an image broadcast on television. Much work in the field of vision concerns the nature of eye activity in the process of perception.

Still unanswered, too, is the question of depth perception—how things are seen in three dimensions. Some researchers feel that this is an inborn ability of the visual mechanism,

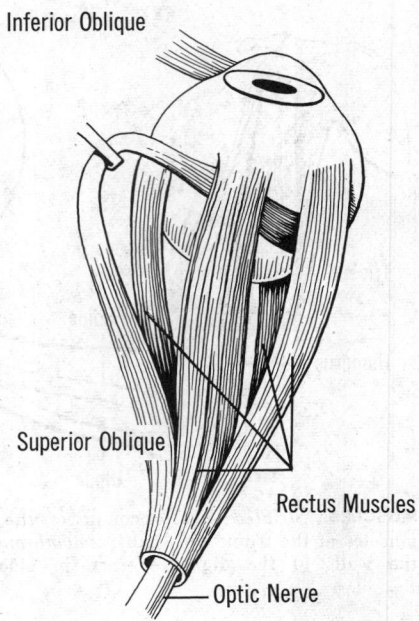

Inferior Oblique
Superior Oblique
Rectus Muscles
Optic Nerve

while others consider that it is learned in the course of development. One feature of depth perception, the fact that each eye sees a slightly different image, raises the additional question of *binocular fusion*—how the images from the two eyes are combined in the brain to form a single image.

■**COLOR VISION.**—The nature of color perception is another perplexing problem in the study of vision. Most theories of color vision propose the existence of specialized cone cells for the various colors. One of the best-known hypotheses, the *Young-Helmholtz theory,* proposes that there are three types of cones—one for blue, one for red, and one for green. All other colors would be created by stimulation in varying degrees and combinations of these three basic receptors. For example, yellow light would stimulate a specific number of red and green receptors. Impulses from these would somehow be mixed in the visual pathway or the brain to produce the experience of yellow. However, the Young-Helmholtz theory has been challenged by others. The *Ladd-Franklin theory,* for instance, proposes four types of receptors. As yet no completely satisfactory color theory has evolved.

■**EYE DISORDERS AND DISEASES.**—*Color blindness* is the inability to see a full range of colors. It is an inherited disorder which, according to the Young-Helmholtz theory, results from the absence, or failure to function, of one of the three basic cone types.

Blindness may be caused by disturbances to the visual mechanism at any point along the visual pathway. *Trachoma* is a viral disease which may cause a growth of tissue over the cornea; scarring of the cornea may result in blindness. *Cataracts* cause clouding of the lens and may be severe enough to blind the victim. A buildup of internal eye pressure occurs in *glaucoma,* at times

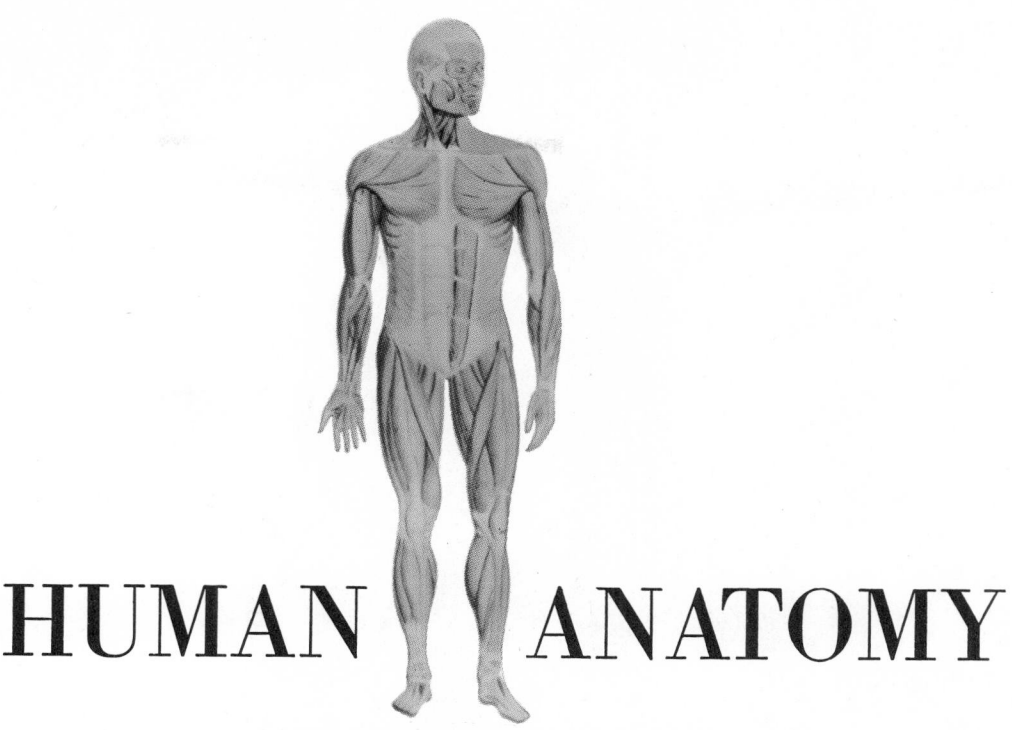

HUMAN ANATOMY

ILLUSTRATIONS BY RONALD KELLER

Prepared in consultation with
Charles N. Berry, Ph.D.
Seton Hall College of Medicine and Dentistry

This section on Human Anatomy is presented to help you to form a conception of the structure of the human body. The various structures of the body may be seen in their exact locations and in relation to the other structures. By the use of the transparencies one can determine these relationships in three dimensions—horizontally, vertically, and also in depth. In this way an understanding can be developed about the systems of the body and, therefore, about the total human organism.

Plate A shows the inside of the rib cage looking toward the front, while Plate F shows the inside of the skeleton looking toward the back. On the front of the first transparency (Plate B) most of the organs of the respiratory and digestive systems can be seen as viewed from the front. These organs include the trachea, the lungs, the intestines, pancreas, liver, and gall bladder. The thyroid glands (a part of the endocrine system) and the domelike diaphragm muscle are also seen. The back view of these organs is found on the reverse side of the transparency (Plate C). In Plate D are shown the principal parts of the circulatory system, plus the kidneys, suprarenals, and parts of the excretory system as seen from the front. In Plate E a back view of the same systems is shown.

By turning the transparencies and studying the organs and the systems that are contained from both the front and the back views, a more meaningful interpretation can be derived from the discussions in the text of the structure and functioning of the human body.

PLATE A

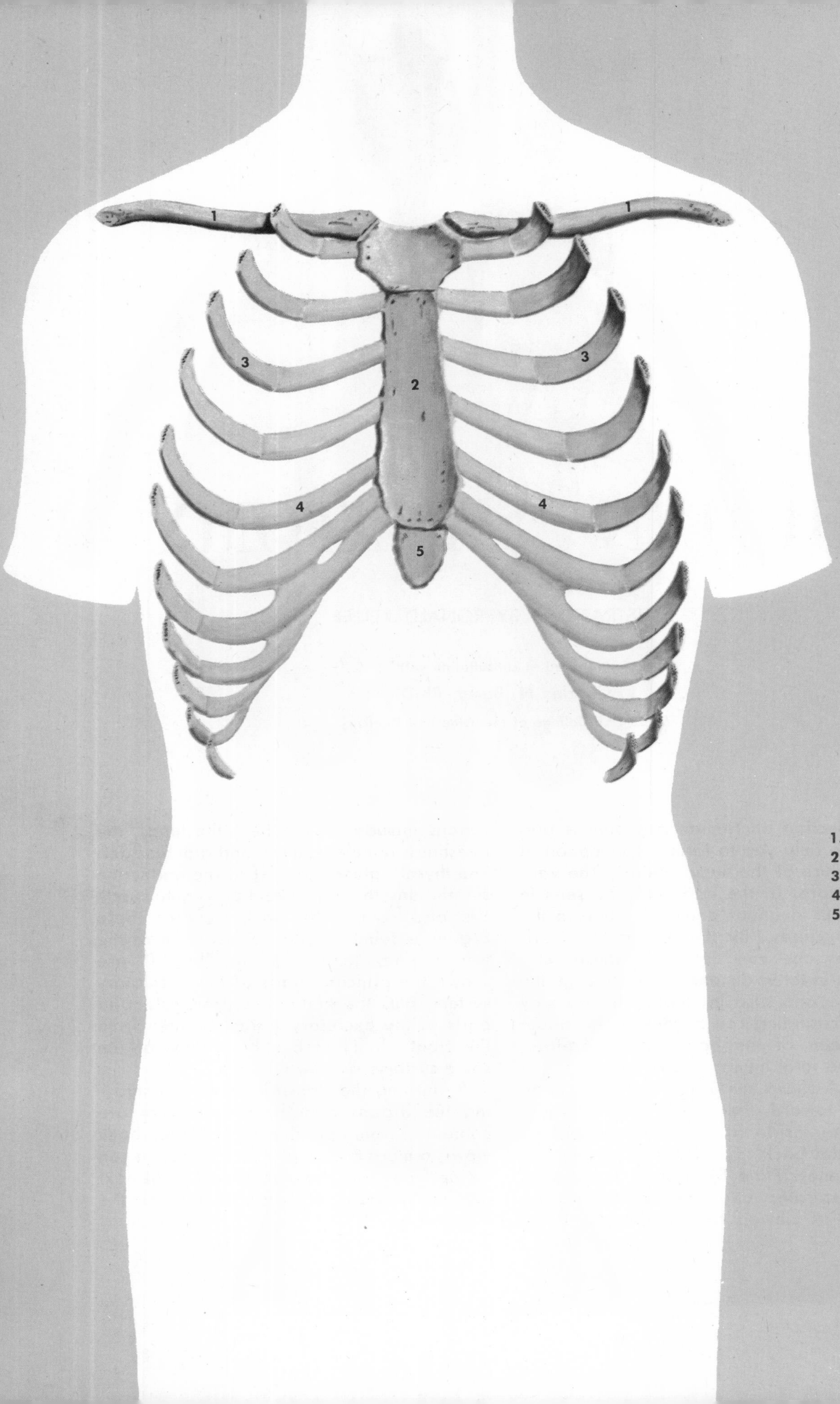

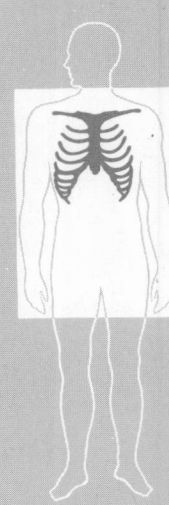

1. Collarbone (clavicle)
2. Sternum
3. Rib
4. Cartilage of the rib
5. Xiphoid process

© C. S. H. & Co.

PLATE F

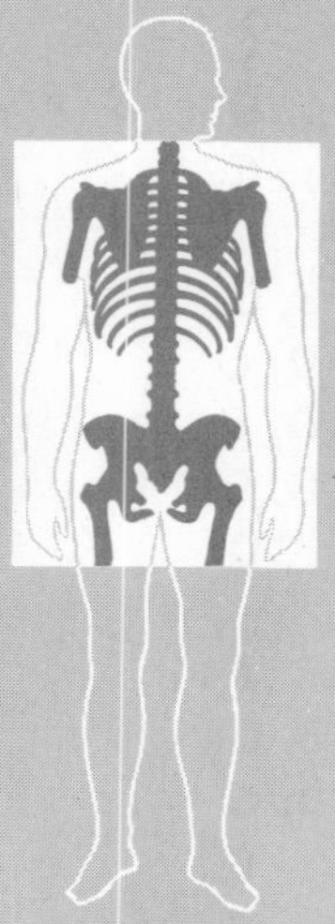

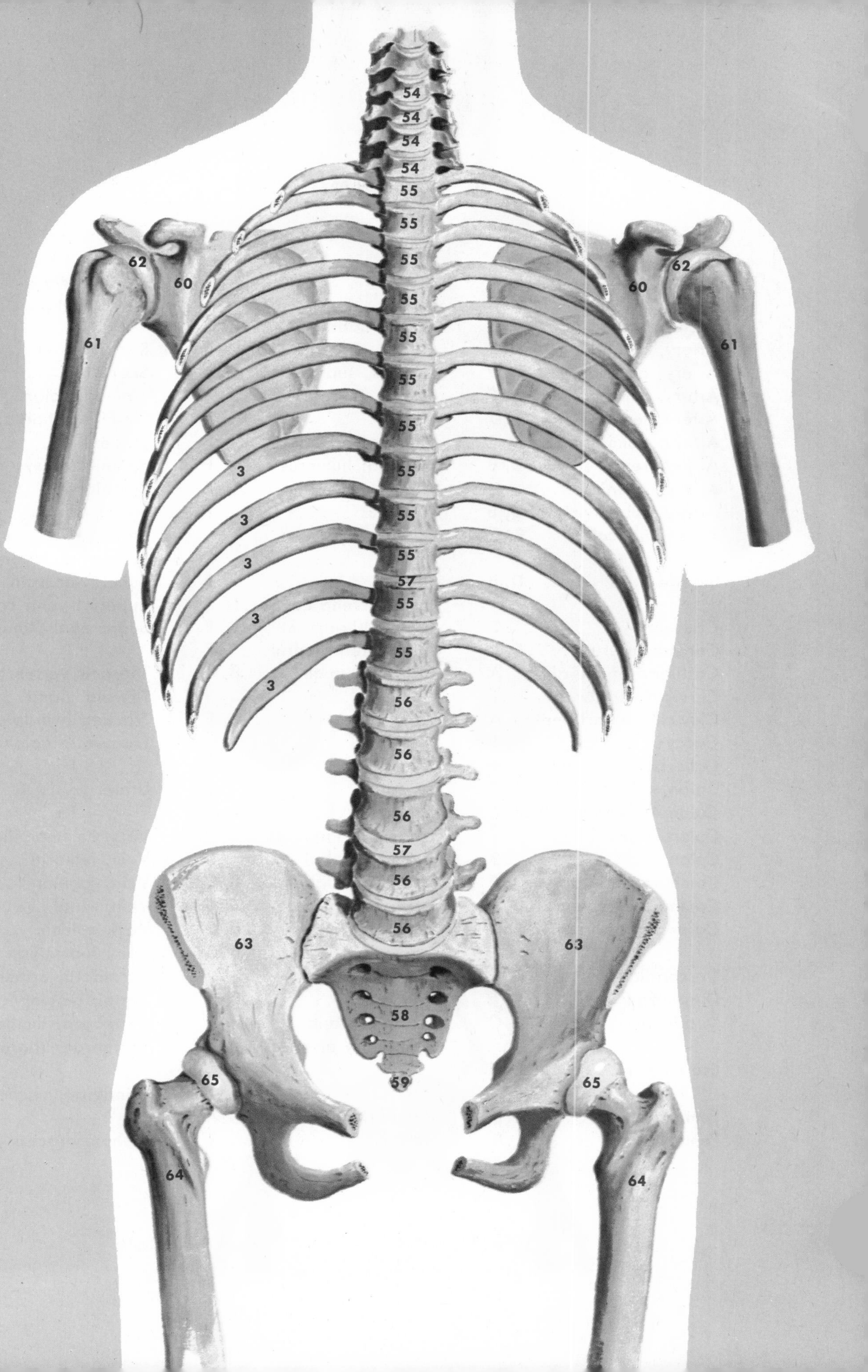

3. Rib
54. Cervical vertebrae
55. Thoracic vertebrae
56. Lumbar vertebrae
57. Intervertebral discs
58. Sacrum
59. Coccyx
60. Scapula
61. Humerus
62. Head of humerus
63. Ilium
64. Femur
65. Head of femur

© C. S. H. & Co.

INDEX

	Plate
Aorta	D, E
Appendix, vermiform	C
Arch of the aorta	D, E
Artery, carotid	D, E
Artery, coronary	D
Artery, common iliac	D, E
Artery, femoral	D
Artery, pulmonary	D, E
Artery, renal	D, E
Artery, splenic	C
Artery, subclavian	D, E
Ascending colon	B, C
Bladder	D, E
Caecum	C
Carotid artery	D, E
Cartilage of the rib	A
Cervical vertebrae	F
Clavicle (collarbone)	A
Coccyx	F
Collarbone (clavicle)	A
Colon, ascending	B, C
Colon, descending	B, C
Colon, sigmoid	C
Colon, transverse	B
Common iliac artery	D, E
Common iliac vein	D, E
Coronary arteries	D
Descending colon	B, C
Diaphragm	B, C, D, E
Duodenum	C
Esophagus	D, E
Femoral artery	D
Femoral vein	D

	Plate
Femur	F
Gall bladder	B, C
Gland, prostate	E
Glands, suprarenal	D
Gland, thyroid	B, C
Head of femur	F
Head of humerus	F
Heart	D, E
Humerus	F
Ileum	C
Ilium	F
Inferior vena cava	D, E
Inguinal ligament	D, E
Intervertebral disc	F
Intestine, small	B, C
Jugular vein	D, E
Kidneys	D, E
Larynx	B, C
Ligament, inguinal	D, E
Liver (left lobe)	B
Liver (right lobe)	B, C
Lumbar vertebrae	F
Lung, left	B, C
Lung, right	B, C
Pancreas	B, C
Prostate gland	E
Pulmonary arteries	D, E
Rib	A, F
Rib, cartilage of	A
Rectum	E

	Plate
Renal artery	D, E
Renal vein	D, E
Sacrum	F
Scapula	F
Sigmoid colon	C
Small intestine	B, C
Spleen	C
Splenic artery	C
Splenic vein	C
Sternum	A
Stomach	B, C
Subclavian artery	D, E
Subclavian vein	D, E
Superior vena cava	D, E
Suprarenal glands	D
Thoracic vertebrae	F
Thyroid gland	B, C
Trachea (windpipe)	B, C
Transverse colon	B
Ureter	D, E
Vein, common iliac	D, E
Vein, femoral	D
Vein, jugular	D, E
Vein, renal	D, E
Vein, splenic	C
Vein, subclavian	D, E
Vermiform appendix	C
Vertebrae, cervical	F
Vertebrae, lumbar	F
Vertebrae, thoracic	F
Windpipe (trachea)	B, C
Xiphoid process	A

Reprinted from HEALTH and FITNESS, by Meredith, Irwin and Staton
Copyright 1962 by D. C. Heath & Co.
By permission of the publisher.

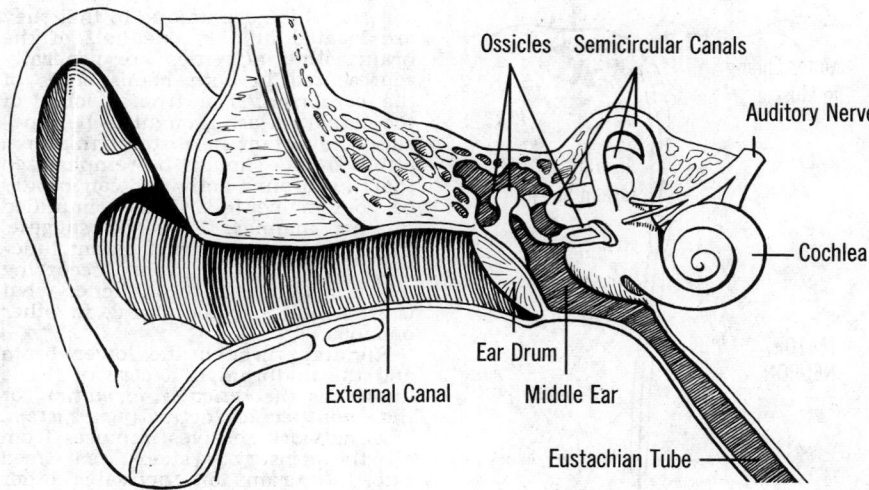

Ossicles Semicircular Canals

Auditory Nerve

Cochlea

Ear Drum

External Canal   Middle Ear

Eustachian Tube

THE EAR. Sound waves are ultimately converted into nerve impulses in the inner ear.

severe enough to blind by damaging the optic nerve. Glaucoma may be caused by blockage of the normal channels through which the eye fluid drains. Detachment of the retina caused by injury may produce blindness. Growing tumors may cut off sight by pressure on the optic nerve.

Treatment of blindness depends upon the cause and the structures involved. Damaged corneas can be replaced by transplanting new ones, and detached retinas can often be sewn back in place. Damage to the optic nerve and visual regions of the brain, however, is permanent.

■ **EAR.**—The *ear* is an organ of hearing and balance. The visible structure called the ear is actually only part of the *external ear*. It is joined to the *middle ear* by the *external ear canal*, which ends at the *eardrum*.

The middle ear contains three small bones—the *malleus, incus,* and *stapes* (also called the *hammer, anvil,* and *stirrup*)—so arranged that vibrations of the eardrum are transmitted through them in succession. The stapes transmits the vibrations to the inner ear at the oval window of the cochlea.

The inner ear consists of a spiral, snail-shaped structure called the *cochlea,* which is divided into three chambers, each of which extends the length of the structure. The middle chamber contains the *organ of Corti,* a delicate arrangement of hair cells and nerve fibers that converts the vibrations of the *cochlear fluid* into electrical impulses which travel along the *auditory nerve* to the brain.

The process of hearing can be understood as a translation of the physical properties of a sound wave into coded electrochemical nerve impulses. In brief, sound waves, which are vibrations of molecules in air, are transformed into vibrations of the eardrum. The movements of the eardrum are changed into vibrations of the bones of the middle ear. These are converted into movements of the cochlear fluid, exerting tension on the hair cells of the organ of Corti and finally generating nerve impulses in the auditory nerve.

■ **DEAFNESS.**—*Deafness* results from interference with the hearing process at any point. In *otosclerosis,* bony deposits fix the stapes in place, preventing them from transmitting vibrations to the inner ear. This condition can be corrected by freeing the stapes or by cutting a window between the middle and inner ear to permit vibrations to pass through. Damage to the cochlea or the auditory nerve, however, produces incurable deafness.

■ **BALANCE.**—Close to the cochlea in the inner ear are the *semicircular canals,* the organs of balance, consisting of three fluid-filled semicircular structures, each lying in a different plane. Within the open ends of the canals are the cone-shaped *cristae.* As the head is moved, the fluid in the canals drags against the cristae, bending them and generating nerve impulses to the brain. This stimulation, however, occurs only when motion begins or ends. When the body is spun at a fairly constant speed, dizziness results because the fluid and the cristae move together. Thus no stimulation is produced, and the brain receives no balancing signals. Ballet dancers avoid such dizziness by alternately increasing and decreasing their speed of rotation when executing pirouettes.

In addition to the aforementioned receptors there are also "gravity" receptors that are stimulated by changes in the position of the head.

■ **BODY SENSE AND BALANCE.**— The brain receives other types of information that enable it to maintain body balance. One source is the eyes, which perceive horizontal and vertical structures in the surroundings. Other information comes from sensory receptors located in the muscles and tendons. These are called *proprioceptors* and are activated when muscles contract and tendons stretch. Their signals inform the brain of the position and degree of muscular tension of the various parts of the body. This information aids in balance and also permits smooth, coordinated muscle action.

■ **SENSE OF SMELL.**—*Smell,* also called

olfaction, is one of the most primitive sensory mechanisms. In lower animals it affects behavior considerably. In man the sense of smell as a means of locating food and avoiding danger has yielded to the senses of sight and hearing.

The olfactory tissue is located at the upper rear portion of the nasal cavity. The olfactory cells are covered by a fluid layer that seems to dissolve odorous materials. However, the exact manner in which these materials excite nerve impulses is still not known.

The property of adaptation, common to all the senses, is particularly prominent in the sense of smell. When a person is first exposed to an odor (upon entering a room, for example) he senses it sharply. After a few moments, however, he ceases to smell it—the sense receptors have adapted to the stimulation and no longer report its presence.

■ **SENSE OF TASTE.**—The taste receptors are located on the surface of the tongue. There are four different types of taste cells corresponding to the four basic tastes—sweet, sour (acid), salty, and bitter. More complex taste sensations occur when two or more of these receptors are stimulated in various combinations. There is evidence that the different types of receptors are found in specific areas of the tongue—sweet and salt receptors on the tip, acid cells on the sides, and bitter receptors toward the back.

Flavor is a compound of the sensations of taste, smell, and also of touch, since there are also touch receptors in the tongue.

■ **TOUCH AND TEMPERATURE SENSATIONS.**—The skin has receptors that respond to mechanical pressure and temperature change. Impulses from these receptors travel to the brain, which has a type of map enabling it to identify stimulation as coming from a specific part of the body. The distribution of the various receptors over the body varies considerably. For example, more touch receptors are found in the tips of the fingers than in the skin of the back.

■ **PAIN.**—*Pain* is called a sensation since it involves receptors that transmit impulses to the brain. Pain differs from other sensations, however, in some important respects. It dominates consciousness, driving all other sensations into the background, and is not experienced in direct proportion to the stimulus. A sound grows louder as more energy beats upon the eardrums, but pain does not increase step by step in intensity as the stimulus is increased. For example, a severe razor cut may go unnoticed, whereas the pain from an injection can be heightened out of proportion to the injury. Pain is excited in several different ways. Other sensations are aroused by specific forms of stimulation, such as sound waves falling on the ear; but pain may be caused by tension and pressure in swollen tissues, by mechanical injury, or by chemical factors, such as are believed to be associated with the pain generated by strenuous muscle exercise.

There are other peculiarities associated with pain, such as the difficulty sometimes experienced in localizing it and the fact that the perception of pain is so strongly conditioned by social and cultural factors. From a strictly physiological point of view, it has been established that there are specific pain pathways in the brain and spinal cord.

Nervous System

■PERIPHERAL NERVOUS SYSTEM.—The sensations discussed above generally have their receptors in the outlying, or peripheral, regions of the body. The nerve impulses from these receptors enter the brain through either of two channels—the 12 cranial nerves or the spinal cord. The cranial nerves supply the structures of the head and neck. (An exception to this is the *vagus nerve,* which supplies the abdominal organs and the heart.) Entrance to the spinal cord is made through the spinal nerves. There are two spinal nerves for each segment or level of the spinal cord.

The cranial nerves and the spinal nerves, with their branches, constitute the *peripheral nervous system,* the system of nerve pathways linking the brain and spinal cord to the organs of the body. The peripheral nerves consist of *sensory (afferent) fibers,* which carry impulses to the brain, and *motor (efferent) fibers,* which carry impulses in the opposite direction. At various points along the peripheral pathways are structures called *ganglions,* collections of nerve cell bodies that act as relay stations. An incoming fiber ends on the body of a ganglion cell; another fiber conducts the impulse away from the ganglion.

■CENTRAL NERVOUS SYSTEM.—The *spinal cord* is a great nerve highway linking the brain to the rest of the body. Within its central *gray matter* are nerve cell bodies through which various linkages in the nerve pathways are made. Around the gray matter is *white matter,* consisting of bundles of nerve fibers grouped into ascending and descending tracts.

The *brain* is the most intricate structure known in nature. Although we can list the parts of the brain and attempt to describe their functions, this should not imply that man understands even a small fraction of what actually occurs in the brain.

The *medulla,* located at the base of the brain, is the point of entrance for the spinal cord and the location of the control centers that regulate heartbeat and respiration. The *cerebellum* is a rounded structure to the rear of the midbrain. It is a coordinating center for muscular activity. Here impulses from the spinal cord and cerebral cortex are integrated.

The upper part of the brain, the convoluted *cerebrum,* is divided into two *cerebral hemispheres.* The surface of the cerebrum, called the *cerebral cortex,* consists of several layers of cells that dip and twist in intricate folds. It is here that the centers for vision, hearing, touch, pain, and muscle control are located. It also contains the centers for

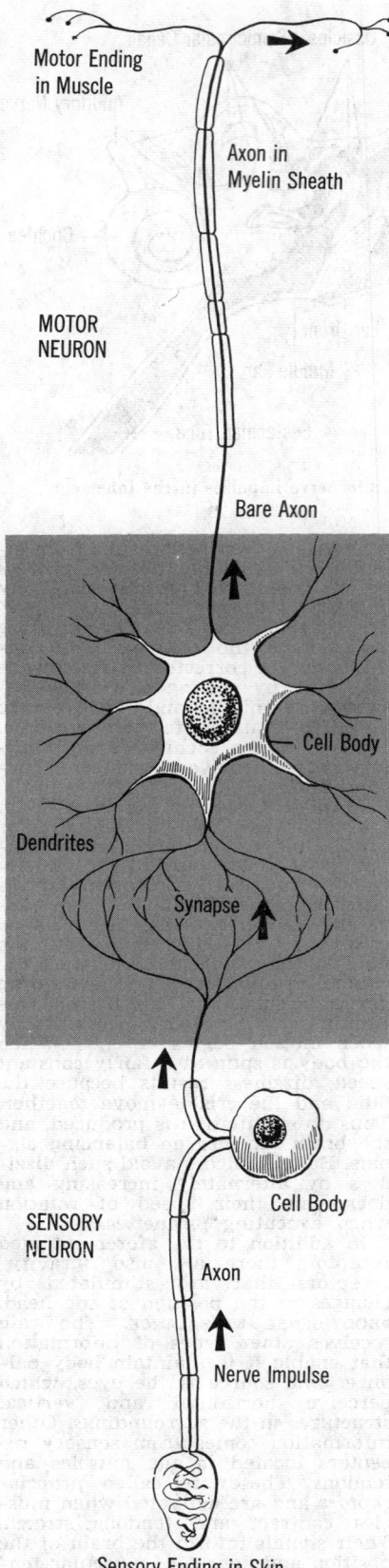

Motor Ending in Muscle

Axon in Myelin Sheath

MOTOR NEURON

Bare Axon

Cell Body

Dendrites

Synapse

SENSORY NEURON

Cell Body

Axon

Nerve Impulse

Sensory Ending in Skin

A NERVE CIRCUIT. Impulses from the skin travel to the spinal cord, then to muscle.

speech, which are unique in that they are located in only half of the brain; other activities are generally represented in both hemispheres of the cerebrum. The frontal lobes of the cerebrum are thought to be especially important in abstract thinking, although it should be emphasized that the brain's activities can hardly be compartmentalized and simplified in this manner. Evidence suggests that the brain to a great extent functions as a whole; events occurring in one portion greatly influence what is simultaneously occurring in other portions.

Running through the lower brain and the midbrain is a core of tissue known as the *reticular formation,* or the *nonspecific activating system.* This network receives impulses from all the sensory systems that feed into the brain and activates other portions of the brain and spinal cord. For this reason it is believed to play an important role in attention and consciousness. The reticular formation also feeds impulses into the *hypothalamus,* a key structure through which the brain controls the activities of the internal organs. The hypothalamus provides the connection to the autonomic nervous system.

■AUTONOMIC NERVOUS SYSTEM.—The nervous system not only regulates the activities of the body in relation to the outside world but also coordinates the activities of the internal organs. This second type of control proceeds without conscious direction and is made possible by special nerve pathways and cells organized into the *autonomic nervous system.* The system has two major divisions: the sympathetic nervous system and the parasympathetic nervous system.

The *sympathetic nervous system* includes centers in the middle of the brain and at its base. Its fibers extend to the various organs through the spinal nerves. These fibers end on smooth muscles in blood vessels and on glandular cells in the various tissues. When it is stimulated, the sympathetic nervous system helps to mobilize the body's resources for emergency action. This includes constriction of blood vessels in the skin and abdominal region and expansion of blood vessels in the muscles. Also, the heartbeat increases; and the movements of the digestive tract and the secretions of the digestive organs are reduced.

The *parasympathetic nervous system* generally produces effects which are the opposite of those associated with sympathetic activity. The parasympathetic fibers reach the organs largely through the vagus nerve and through the lower part of the spinal cord in the *sacral region.* When they are stimulated, the parasympathetic fibers slow the heartbeat and stimulate the movements and secretions of the digestive organs.

The autonomic nervous system exerts considerable control over the endocrine glands, and through this control the brain and nervous system achieve complete integration of body activity. One aspect of this control is the relationship between the hypothalamus and the pituitary gland, the "master" endocrine gland; pituitary secretions are regulated by the nervous system through the hypothalamus. The pituitary, in turn, regulates the secretions of the thyroid, adrenal, and sex glands. Thus the brain controls the endocrine system by regulation of pituitary secretions.

A second aspect of the nervous system's control over endocrine function is the direct nerve connection between the autonomic nervous system and the *adrenal medulla,* the inner section of the adrenal gland. This pathway is activated during times of stress, when nerve stimulation to the adrenal medulla liberates epinephrine and norepinephrine. These hormones increase heart action and otherwise prepare the body for vigorous exertion.

■**NERVE CELL AND NERVE FIBER.**—The structural element of the nervous system is a highly specialized nerve cell, the *neuron.* Knowledge of neuron function is still meager, but certain facts have been established.

An impulse passes from one nerve cell (A) to another (B) by way of a nerve fiber from A which ends on the cell body of B, or on a dendrite of B. (A *dendrite* is a branched structure attached to the cell body.) The gap which separates the nerve fiber of A from the dendrite or cell body of B is called the *synapse.* It has been established that at many synapses the fiber of cell A secretes a chemical transmitter substance which crosses this gap to act on the membrane of cell B, causing a series of electrochemical reactions in the membrane which generate a new nerve impulse in cell B. The impulse is called a *spike potential* and travels along the cell body of B like a spark along a trail of gunpowder, passing out of the cell body along the *axon,* the nerve fiber which conducts the impulse to the next cell. In some cells the axon may be several feet long, as in the large *pyramidal cells* of the brain that direct muscle movement. Axons from the body of the pyramidal cells extend down the spinal cord to motor cells in the anterior horn of the spinal cord. Nerves are thus collections of axons, each carrying its nerve messages from one cell to the next.

Facts on nerve cell function are: (1) The *all-or-none law* describes the fact that the nerve cell either generates a full nerve impulse or none at all, just as a bullet is either propelled from the barrel of a gun at its maximum speed or does not leave it at all. (2) All nerve impulses are alike. Nerve impulses generated by cells of varying type and size may differ from one another in the speed at which they travel or in their strength, but they all have the same electrochemical nature. This means that a nerve impulse communicating an odor to the brain along the olfactory pathway is essentially the same as a nerve impulse racing down the vagus nerve to stimulate the pancreas to secrete digestive juices. (3) *Inhibition.* An important class of nerve impulses in the nervous system are those which retard or inhibit nerve activity. Thus, an inhibitory impulse arriving at a synapse would lessen the likelihood that the next cell would be stimulated.

■**REFLEXES.**—*Reflexes* are comparatively simple patterns of behavior which are built into the nervous system. They do not have to be learned and require no conscious effort. They are often adaptive, and aid in functioning of the body or its protection.

The elements of a reflex are: the *receptor,* a sensory element such as the eye, ear, or the stretch-sensitive fibers which are coiled around certain muscle fibers; the nerve pathway between the receptor and the brain or the spinal cord; the connecting nerve pathways in the central nervous system; and the fibers that carry impulses away from the central nervous system to the muscles that put the reflex into action.

Although its importance is not generally appreciated, one of the most common reflexes operates every day of our lives. This is the *stretch reflex.* Distributed among the voluntary muscles of the body are stretch receptors that generate nerve impulses when they are put under tension. As a muscle relaxes, these receptors are stretched and give off impulses which enter the spinal cord, resulting in motor impulses that stimulate muscle contraction. This reflex maintains the tension of the muscles which hold the body upright. These receptors also temper muscular action, creating a smooth movement out of what might otherwise be a series of spasmodic jerks.

Other familiar reflexes include coughing, sneezing, blinking, and the diagnostic aid, the knee jerk.

—Martin Spencer and Daniel Monroe

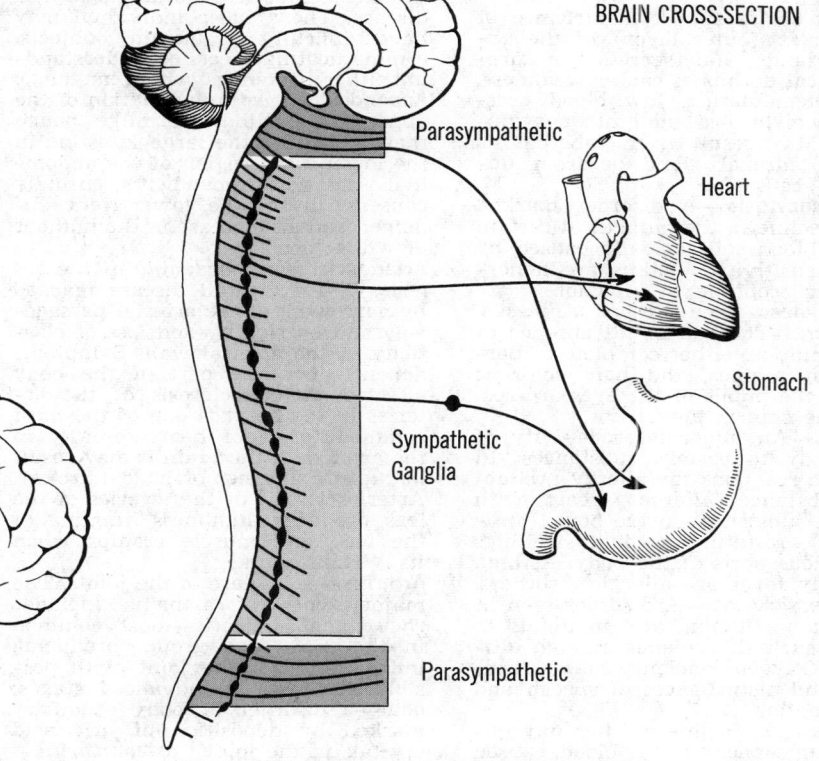

BRAIN CROSS-SECTION

Parasympathetic

Heart

Stomach

Sympathetic Ganglia

Parasympathetic

Cerebral Hemisphere

Cerebellum

Medulla

Spinal Cord

Sympathetic and Parasympathetic Nervous Systems

THE AUTONOMIC NERVOUS SYSTEM comprises the *parasympathetic system,* which slows the heartbeat, and the *sympathetic system,* which raises the sugar concentration in the blood, quickens the heartbeat, and mobilizes the body's resources for vigorous activity.

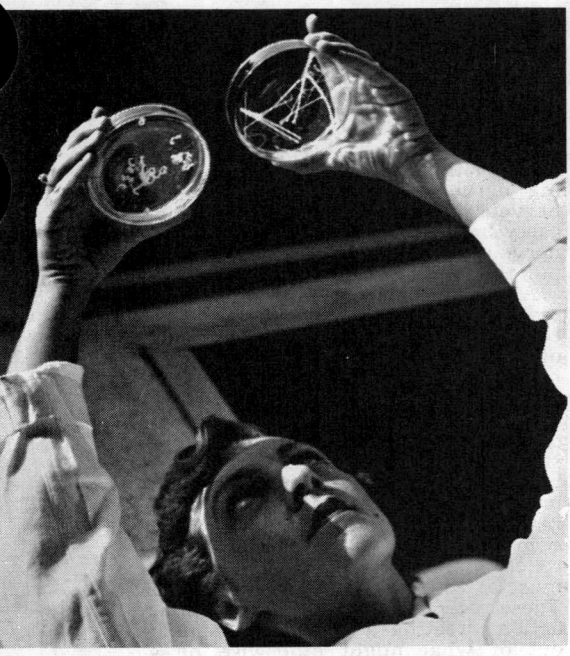

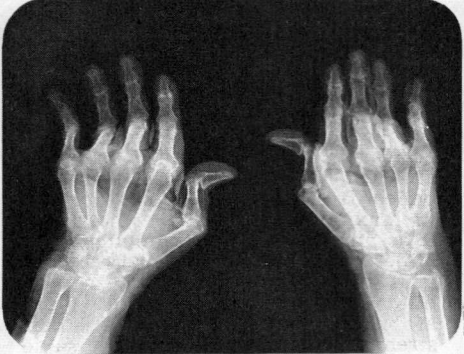

AMERICAN HEART ASSOCIATION AND WNEW–TV, CHANNEL 5

MEDICAL CARE requires the combined efforts of nurses, technicians and doctors. A technician examining a slide may be able to provide valuable information about the blood chemistry of a patient. The X-ray might aid the specialist in determining the extent of bone damage caused by arthritis. The surgeon operating on the young child (*right*) will require assistance from many individuals in order to perform a complex operation with relative safety.

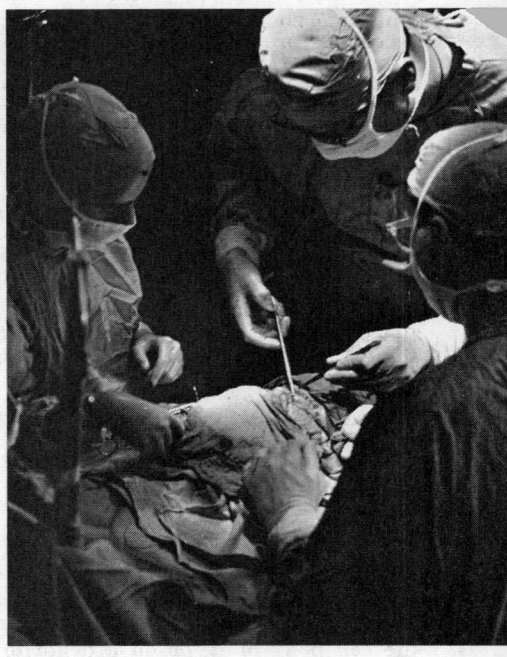

GLOSSARY OF DISEASES

(See also chart of infectious diseases.)

Acromegaly.—A pituitary gland disorder in which excessive secretion of growth hormone causes overgrowth of bone and tissues in face, hands, and feet.

Addison's disease.—A disturbance of the cortex (outer layer) of the adrenal glands. Undersecretion of adrenocortical hormones causes weakness, skin pigmentation, low blood pressure, weight loss, and other symptoms. May result from tuberculosis of the adrenal gland or from unknown causes.

Agranulocytosis.—A disorder marked by a decline in the number of certain white blood cells, usually caused by drug sensitivity. Victims are abnormally susceptible to infection.

Air sickness.—See *Motion sickness.*

Albinism.—The congenital absence of pigmentation, either complete or partial. In albinos, the hair color is white, the pupils of the eyes are red, and the skin is pink.

Allergy.—An abnormal sensitivity of the body to certain substances. In allergic reactions the allergy-producing substance (*allergen*) reacts with special substances in the body (*antibodies*), resulting in fluid swellings in various parts of the body. Asthma and hay fever are allergic disorders.

Altitude sickness.—A disorder seen in mountain climbing and in flights in unpressurized airplanes at high altitudes. Oxygen deficiency causes dizziness and disturbances of speech and coordination.

Anemia.—A decline in the oxygen-carrying capacity of the blood, caused by a decrease in the number of red blood cells or in the quantity of hemoglobin they carry. It may result from hemorrhage, excessive blood destruction, or damage to the blood-forming tissues. Anemia causes dizziness and shortness of breath.

Aneurysm.—A bulging or outpocketing in the wall of an artery, caused by structural weakness. It is seen in the later stages of syphilis and in arteriosclerosis (hardening of the arteries).

Aphasia.—A disorder of language functions, caused by brain injury or disease. The aphasic individual may have difficulty in naming objects, communicating ideas, or understanding either spoken or written language.

Appendicitis.—An inflammation of the appendix, a blind, wormlike pouch that opens into the large intestine in the lower-right region of the abdominal cavity. Appendicitis usually causes pain in the lower-right abdomen and an increase in the number of white blood cells.

Arteriosclerosis (*hardening of the arteries*).—An arterial disease marked by narrowing of the arterial passageway and by rigidity and loss of elasticity in the arterial wall. Symptoms depend upon the part of the body affected. Arteriosclerosis of the arteries in the heart is one of the most common forms of heart disease. In the arteries of the brain it may result in rupture and hemorrhage (stroke). Arteriosclerosis of the arteries of the legs produces numbness, tingling of the feet, and muscle cramps when its victims walk.

Arthritis.—A disease of the joints. The major types of arthritis include: *rheumatoid arthritis*—most common in the 30–40 age group, producing inflammation of the joint, with possible deformity in advanced stages; *gout*—a disorder of body chemistry marked by deposition of uric acid crystals in the joints; *osteoarthritis*—destruction of the joints, seen in elderly persons and possibly resulting from mechanical "wear and tear."

Asthma.—A breathing disorder. The most common type is *allergic bronchial asthma,* caused by sensitivity to such substances as pollen, wheat, chocolate, and various drugs. Asthmatic attacks exhibit shortness of breath, wheezing, and coughing.

Astigmatism.—A disorder of vision marked by an inability to focus properly all parts of the visual field. It is caused by differences in the refracting, or "light-bending," power of different parts of the visual apparatus.

Bedsores (*decubitus ulcers*).—Skin ulcers caused by prolonged pressure on such parts of the body as the heels, elbows, and back. Bedsores occur in bedridden patients who are kept in the same position for long periods of time.

Bell's palsy.—Paralysis of one side of the face, causing muffled speech, difficulty in eating, and tearing of the eye on the affected side.

Beriberi.—A nutritional disease caused by a deficiency of vitamin B_1.

Berylliosis.—Beryllium poisoning, caused by inhalation of, or contact with, beryllium fumes.

Blue baby.—A newborn infant suffering from congenital heart defects that interfere with the normal oxygenation of blood in the lungs. In such cases large amounts of oxygen-poor blood give the skin a bluish cast.

Botulism.—An often fatal type of food poisoning, caused by the consumption of improperly sterilized canned food contaminated with the anaerobic bacterium *Clostridium botulinum.*

Bronchiectasis.—A disease of the *bronchi* (the air passages to the lungs) in which the walls of the small bronchi are weakened and dilated. The disease may develop as a complication of lung infections. It produces coughing accompanied by bloody sputum.

Bronchitis.—An inflammation of the bronchi. *Acute bronchitis* may be caused by infection or by irritation from tobacco, chemicals, dust, and similar substances. Chronic bronchitis may be associated with lung diseases. Symptoms include coughing, wheezing, and shortness of breath.

Buerger's disease (*thromboangitis obliterans*).—A circulatory disease marked by progressive obstruction of the blood supply to the extremities. Occurs principally in smokers.

Bunion (*hallux valgus*).—A foot disorder in which the great toe points away from the midline of the body. The joint at the base of the toe is enlarged and deformed. The overlying skin is usually calloused. It is caused mainly by wearing narrow, pointed shoes.

Bursitis.—An inflammation of a *bursa* (fluid-filled sacs usually found at points of friction in the body, such as where tendons pass over bony prominences). *Subdeltoid bursitis* involves inflammation of the bursa in the shoulder region.

Cancer.—An abnormal, uncontrolled growth of cells. Occurs in plants, in human beings, and in other animals.

Car sickness.—See *Motion sickness*.

Cataract.—A clouding of the normally transparent lens of the eye, occurring mainly in the aged. Also a complication of *diabetes mellitus*.

Celiac disease.—A children's disease marked by interference with the absorption of nutrients from the intestine. Victims are undernourished and fail to grow normally.

Cerebral palsy.—Disturbances in muscular function and coordination caused by brain damage. It appears mainly in children and is associated with prenatal brain damage. In *spastic palsy*, the muscles contract vigorously, producing jerky, uncontrolled movements. *Athetoid palsy* is marked by constant, irregular, writhing movements.

Chilblain (*pernio*).—A redness, burning, itching, and blistering of parts of the skin, caused by repeated exposure to cold.

Cholangitis.—An inflammation of the bile ducts.

Chorea (*St. Vitus' dance*).—A brain disorder, marked by involuntary movements of the lips, cheeks, arms, and other parts of the body. It occurs as a complication of rheumatic fever (in children), pneumonia, and scarlet fever, and is occasionally seen in pregnancy.

Cirrhosis of the liver.—A scarring and degeneration of the liver that may be associated with alcoholism or liver infections. One serious complication is the weakening of certain large veins of the chest (*esophageal varices*), caused by obstruction of the blood flow through the liver.

Cleft palate.—Congenital openings in the *palate* (roof of the mouth) that join the nasal and oral cavities. Causes trouble in eating and speaking.

Clubfoot.—A congenital deformity of the foot and ankle. In most cases the toes point down and the foot is twisted inward at the ankle.

Colitis.—An intestinal inflammation that may be caused by infection, poisoning, or unknown causes. A major form of colitis is *nonspecific ulcerative colitis,* which occurs principally in young adults and produces pain, fever, diarrhea, and ulcers of the intestinal wall.

Cretinism.—A disorder of children in which a deficiency of thyroid hormone causes physical and mental retardation.

Cryptorchism.—Undescended testicle or testicles. The testicles usually descend during the seventh to the ninth month of fetal life. Failure of both testicles to descend usually causes sterility.

Cystic fibrosis.—An inherited disorder of the *exocrine* (duct) glands of the body (sweat glands, acinar cells of the pancreas, glands lining the bronchi). Characteristic symptoms include digestive difficulties, malnutrition, and chronic lung disease.

Cystocele.—A female disorder, marked by a rupture of the urinary bladder through the vagina. May cause backache and a burning sensation during urination.

Decompression sickness (*caisson disease, or the "bends"*).—Paralysis, loss of equilibrium, and pains in the muscles and joints caused by liberation of nitrogen bubbles from the blood. It occurs in individuals undergoing rapid reduction in air pressure, such as caisson workers, deep-sea divers, and others who work under increased air pressure.

Dermatitis.—An inflammation of the skin. May be caused by allergies, harsh chemicals, radiation, or overexposure to the sun.

Deviated septum.—A displacement of the partition (*septum*) that divides the nasal cavity. May interfere with breathing and speech.

Diabetes insipidus.—An endocrine disease marked by the passage of large amounts of urine. Caused by undersecretion of a pituitary hormone that regulates the reabsorption of water in the kidney.

Diabetes mellitus.—Disease caused by inadequate secretion of the pancreatic hormone insulin, with a consequent impairment of the body's ability to burn *carbohydrates* (starches and sugars) as fuel.

Diaper rash.—An inflammation and maceration of the diaper region in infants, caused by the action of urine on the skin.

Dwarfism.—Stunted growth, usually caused by disorders of the bones or of the endocrine glands. Types include *pituitary dwarfism,* in which body proportions are abnormal, and cretinism, in which both mental development and physical growth are impaired.

Eclampsia.—Convulsions and coma that may appear in certain disorders of pregnancy, called *toxemias.* Associated symptoms include swelling of the body, increased blood pressure, and abdominal pains.

Eczema.—A skin disorder marked by scaling, redness, itching, and blistering. In chronic cases, patches of skin become thickened and roughened.

Edema (*dropsy*).—A swelling of the body caused by accumulations of fluid in the tissues. May be caused by kidney disorders and circulatory disorders.

Elephantiasis.—A thickening of skin and underlying tissues. May be caused by interference in the circulation to a part of the body as a result of parasitic disease (*filariasis*), or by surgery.

Embolus.—A fragment of a blood clot or other substance that travels freely through the blood stream, eventually lodging in and obstructing a blood vessel. It may appear following blood clots in the vessels of the heart or after surgery. Emboli lodging in the blood vessels of the heart, brain, or lungs are highly dangerous.

Emphysema, pulmonary.—A lung disorder marked by expansion of the tiny sacs of the lungs (*alveoli*) where the exchange of gases occurs. It occurs in cases of bronchitis and interferes with respiration. It may result in coughing, shortness of breath, and, possibly, heart failure.

Epilepsy.—A brain disorder marked by convulsive seizures (*grand mal*) or by momentary faints or spells (*petit mal*), possibly caused by brain tumors, injury, or infection. In cases of *idiopathic epilepsy*, no observable cause can be ascertained. Such cases tend to appear in family groups.

Eunuchoidism.—A glandular disorder of males, characterized by female fat distribution, high-pitched voice, and other feminine changes in both the body and the psyche. It is caused by inadequate production of male hormones by the testes.

Exophthalmos.—A protrusion of the eyeballs, seen frequently in cases of hyperthyroidism.

Farsightedness (*hypermetropia*).—A visual disturbance in which the eye cannot focus properly. Distant objects can be focused by contractions of the muscle that controls the shape of the lens of the eye. Close objects can also be focused by this method, but at the cost of strain, eye fatigue, and headaches.

Fibroma.—A tumor of fibrous tissue, seen most often in the skin and subcutaneous tissue.

Fistula.—An abnormal opening between two body cavities (*internal fistula*) or between the body and the outside (*external fistula*).

Flat feet.—A depression of the long arch of the foot. It may be present congenitally, in which case the foot is usually strong and does not require treatment. Other cases develop as a result of mechanical strain to the normal foot.

Food poisoning.—A condition that usually results from consumption of food contaminated by pathogenic bacteria or by their secretions. The commonest type is caused by the *staphylococcus* bacteria, which may contaminate improperly refrigerated salads and pastries. Inadequately sterilized canned foods may contain the deadly *botulinum* bacteria.

Frostbite.—Tissue destruction caused by freezing. Frostbite depends not only upon the outside temperature, but also on how rapidly heat is conducted from the tissues by the wind. Thus, if the wind is sharp, frostbite can occur at temperatures as high as 23° F. The skin first becomes white and numb. Later, redness, blistering, and ulceration develop.

Gangrene.—Tissue destruction caused

by interference with the circulation to a part of the body. It may occur in arteriosclerosis, or through mechanical interference with the circulation, as when a portion of the bowel becomes twisted upon itself.

Gigantism.—Abnormal stature that may be caused by undersecretion of the sex hormones or by oversecretion of the growth hormones of the pituitary gland. In the first case, bone growth continues beyond the age at which it is usually halted by the sex hormones. In the second case, all the tissues of the body are stimulated to continued growth.

Glaucoma. — A visual disorder in which obstruction of fluid drainage from the eye causes an increase in internal pressure that may lead to blindness. Glaucoma occurs principally in older persons. Early symptoms are blurred vision, colored halos seen around lights, and headaches.

Glomerulonephritis.—A kidney inflammation seen primarily in young adults and children. Symptoms include puffiness of the face, swelling of the ankles, and high blood pressure.

Glossitis.—A redness and swelling of the tongue, arising from vitamin deficiencies, infections, anemia, or irritation.

Goiter.—An enlargement of the thyroid gland, often associated with a deficiency of iodine in the diet (*endemic goiter*). *Toxic goiters* cause oversecretion of thyroid hormone, resulting in weakness, tremors, and increased heart activity.

Gout.—A disorder of body chemistry in which crystals of uric acid are deposited in various tissues, particularly in the joint at the base of the great toe and in the earlobes.

Harelip (*cleft lip*).—A congenital defect of the face, characterized by a single or double fissure of the upper lip under the nostrils. Often seen with cleft palate.

Hay fever (*allergic rhinitis*).—An allergic reaction to certain air-borne pollens, or fungus spores. It often occurs in family groups, and causes sneezing, congestion of nasal passages, tearing, and itching of the eyes. Some cases improve spontaneously over a period of time, while others may develop into asthma.

Heartburn.—A burning sensation in the abdomen and chest, caused by leakage of stomach fluids into the *esophagus* (tubular passageway between the mouth and stomach).

Hematoma.—Swelling of a part of the body with blood that has escaped from the circulatory system. They are usually caused by injuries that rupture blood vessels. Hematomas disappear spontaneously, although hematomas on the surface of the brain (*subdural hematomas*) may persist and may eventually require surgery.

Hemophilia.—An inherited disorder of the blood-clotting function caused by the absence of certain essential proteins from the blood. The hemophiliac may suffer severe blood loss from trivial injuries, and at such times require transfusions of normal blood.

Hemorrhoids.—Enlarged veins in the anus or lower rectum, causing bleeding and pain during defecation.

Hernia.—A rupture of tissues through the walls of a body cavity. The commonest type involves the protrusion of the abdominal viscera into the inguinal canal, which normally connects the abdominal cavity and the scrotum.

Hirsutism.—An abnormal growth of hair, referring especially to the growth of a beard and the masculine distribution of body hair occurring in women suffering from certain glandular disorders.

Hives (*urticaria*).—Itchy swellings of the skin caused by allergic reactions to food, medicine, or infection.

Hodgkin's disease.—A disorder characterized by progressive enlargement of the lymph glands. Causes weight loss, itching, fatigue, anemia, and other symptoms attributable to pressure exerted on various tissues by the enlarged glands.

Hydrocephalus.—A disorder in which excessive quantities of cerebrospinal fluid accumulate within the cavities of the brain (*ventricles*). It may be caused by obstruction of the flow of cerebrospinal fluid by congenital malformations, tumors, or infections. In infants, hydrocephalus causes a characteristic enlargement of the head, accompanied by mental retardation.

Hydronephrosis.—A distention of parts of the kidney due to back-pressure of urine, resulting from obstruction of urine flow. It may be caused by tumors, congenital abnormalities, or stones. Severe cases may result in kidney failure.

Hyperthyroidism.—A disorder caused by excessive secretion of thyroid hormone. It produces rapid pulse, weight loss, diarrhea, and, in many cases, heart complications.

Hypogonadism.—Inadequate functioning of the sex glands, usually occurring in the male. In young boys, male sexual characteristics fail to develop. Instead, the body acquires a female fat distribution, weak musculature, and small genitalia.

Intestinal obstruction.—A disturbance involving interference with the passage of materials along the intestinal channel. It may be caused by a mechanical obstruction (tumors, scar tissue), irritation of the nerve supply to the intestines, or through interference with the blood supply to the intestinal wall.

Jaundice (*icterus*).—A yellowish tinting of the skin and eyeballs, resulting from an accumulation of bile pigments in body fluids. Bile pigments are produced from the hemoglobin of broken-down red blood cells and are normally excreted into the gallbladder and small intestine. Jaundice may be caused by obstruction of the bile ducts (*obstructive jaundice*), by liver disease (*hepatogenous jaundice*), or by massive destruction of red blood cells, leading to excessive production of bile pigments (*hemolytic jaundice*).

Ketosis.—A disorder of body chemistry, developing when the body uses fat as a principal source of energy. It may be caused by starvation or *diabetes mellitus*.

Leukemia.—A serious blood disorder involving overproduction of white blood cells. Principal changes are anemia, tendency to bleed, and susceptibility to infection.

Lichen planus.—Small, flat, purplish skin eruptions, usually seen on the wrists and above the ankles. It may spread slowly and persist for several months, but it is usually limited in extent.

Lipoma.—A tumor of fat tissue, usually seen on the back, neck, shoulders, or extremities. Lipomas are painless and grow slowly, sometimes achieving such size that they interfere with normal functioning by pressing on surrounding tissues.

Lupus erythematosus.—A disease of the connective, or supporting, tissues, marked by skin eruptions, joint pains, swelling of the lymph glands, and possible involvement of the kidneys, heart, lungs, digestive system, and nervous system. It occurs primarily in young women.

Lymphosarcoma.—A disease in which the lymph glands enlarge and produce massive numbers of certain types of white blood cells.

Melanoma.—A tumor containing the pigment *melanin*, which is normally found in the skin, hair, and eyes. Melanomas of the face and feet frequently become cancerous.

Ménière's disease.—A disorder of the balancing structures of the inner ear, resulting in attacks of vertigo, nausea, and hissing or ringing noises in the ear. It occurs primarily in elderly persons and is believed to be caused by fluid accumulations in the inner ear.

Morning sickness.—Nausea and vomiting that may occur in early pregnancy. It usually disappears by the end of the third month.

Motion sickness (*air sickness, sea sickness, car sickness*).—Nausea, dizziness, headache, and pallor, caused by continued rocking or up-and-down motions, and believed to result from interference with the body balance mechanisms.

Multiple sclerosis.—A nervous disease involving destruction of the fatty insulation that envelops many nerve fibers. The disease is marked by attacks of paralysis, disturbances of coordination, double vision, and other nervous symptoms that usually subside in days or weeks, only to recur later, usually with greater severity. The cause is unknown.

Muscular dystrophy. — An inherited disorder marked by a progressive deterioration of the voluntary muscles. Some forms of the disease attack children only.

Myasthenia gravis.—A disorder in which muscle weakness produces drooping eyelids, easy fatigability, and difficulties in eating and speaking. It is apparently caused by an interruption in the transmission of impulses from the nerves to the muscles.

Myxedema.—A disease caused by undersecretion of thyroid hormone in adults. Signs and symptoms include joint and muscle pains, voice changes, puffiness of the eyes, constipation, anemia, dizziness, and, occasionally, psychosis. (See also *Cretinism.*)

Nearsightedness (*myopia*).—A visual

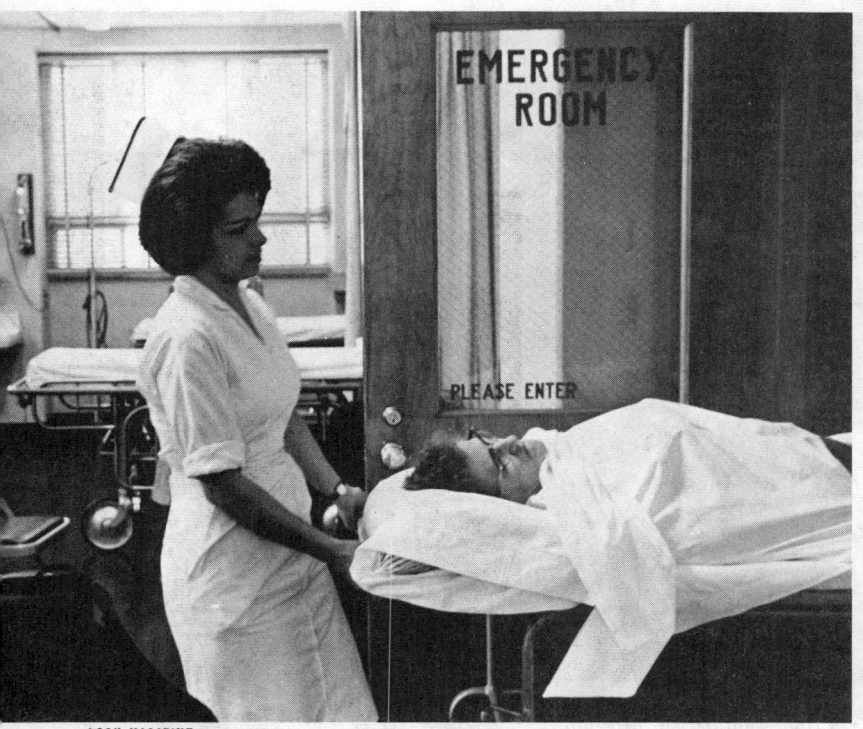

LOOK MAGAZINE

AMERICAN CANCER SOCIETY

HOSPITAL TREATMENT includes emergency care for new arrivals (*above left*), radiation therapy (*above right*), and surgery (*below*).

AMERICAN CANCER SOCIETY

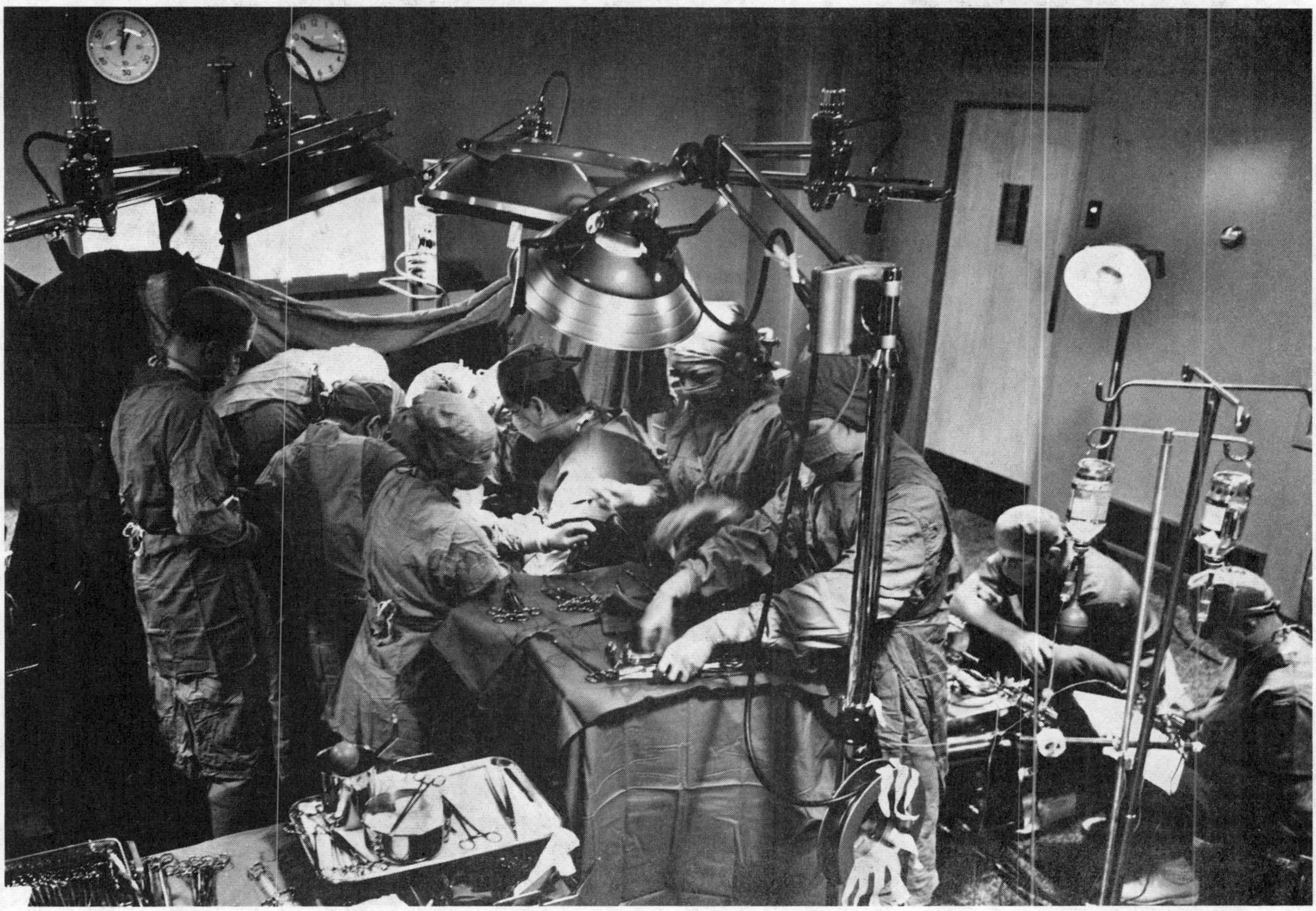

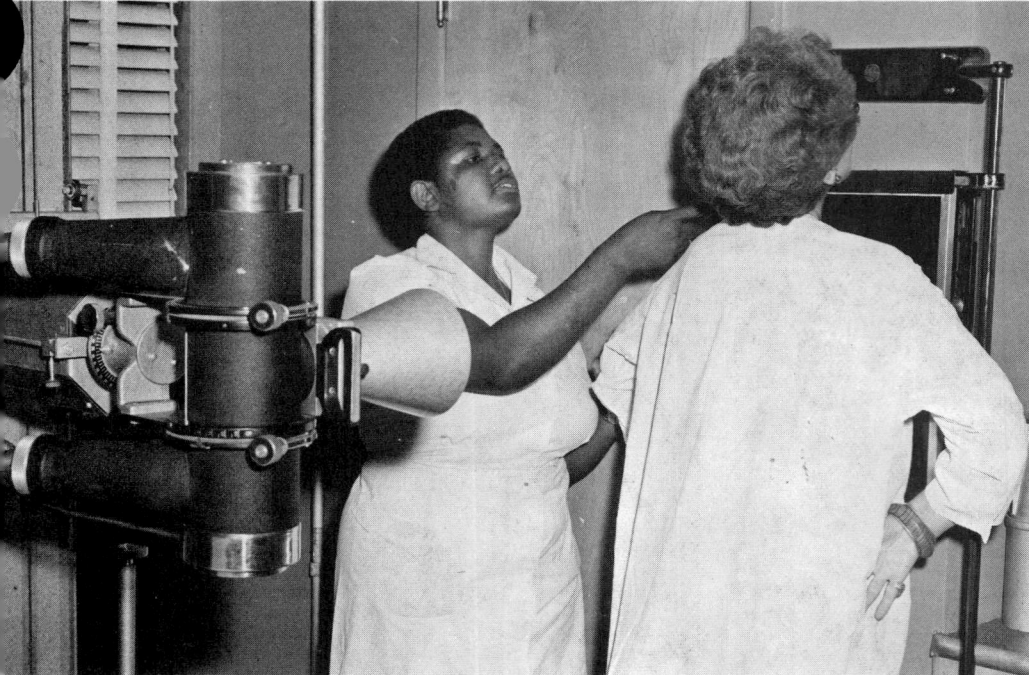

HEALTH INSURANCE PLAN OF GREATER NEW YORK

DISEASE PREVENTION. The x-ray machine (*above left*) and the scintillation detector (*right*) can give early warning. Vaccination (*below*) affords immunity.

UNITED NATIONS
AMERICAN CANCER SOCIETY

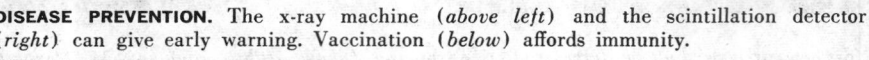

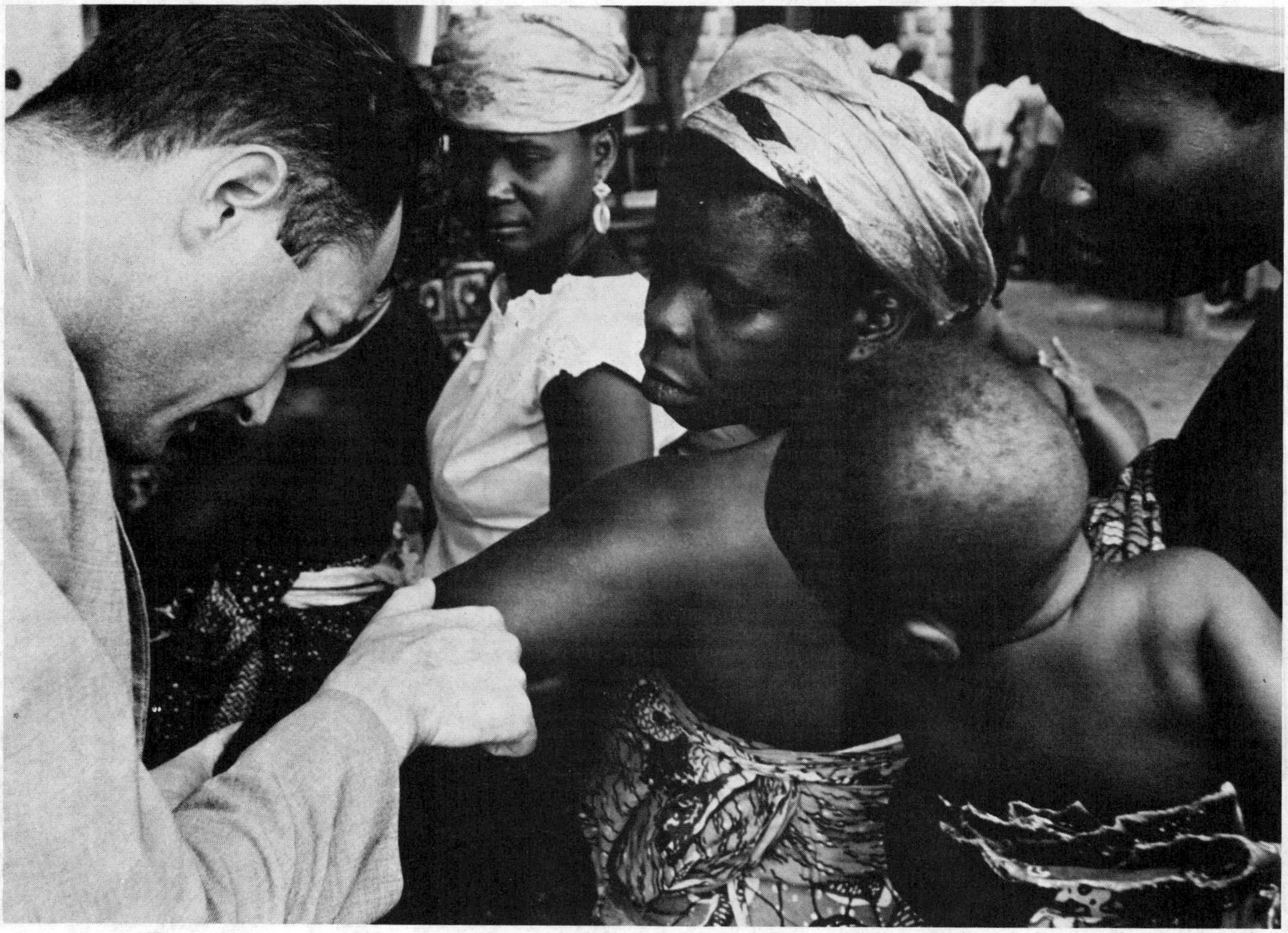

disturbance marked by difficulty in focusing distant objects. It usually develops between the ages of 9 and 13, becoming worse during puberty and then tending to stabilize.

Nephrosis.—A kidney disease marked by the excretion of proteins in the urine and by fluid swellings of the face, ankles, and other parts of the body.

Neuralgia.—A term describing intense shooting pain along the course of various nerves.

Neuritis.—An inflammation or degeneration of the *peripheral nerves* (those outside the brain and spinal cord). It may be caused by infection, poisoning, metabolic diseases, tumors, or by unknown causes. Symptoms include pain, tingling, numbness, muscle weakness, and, possibly, paralysis.

Night blindness (*nyctalopia*).—A disturbance of night vision, often associated with a deficiency of vitamin A in the diet. It may also occur as a complication of other eye disorders, such as nearsightedness and glaucoma.

Osteochondritis.—A bone disease of unknown cause, characterized by destruction of a limited section of bone. It occurs primarily in children and usually affects bones of the lower extremities.

Osteomalacia.—A loss of minerals from the bone, resulting in bone tenderness and *pseudofractures,* or splits in the bone without actual separation. Osteomalacia may be caused by deficiencies of calcium and vitamin D or by kidney disease.

Paget's disease (*osteitis deformans*). —A bone disease seen principally in older persons and marked by painful thickening and deformity of the bones of the skull, spine, pelvis, and thighs.

Parkinson's disease (*paralysis agitans*).—A nervous disorder marked by characteristic tremors and disturbances of movement. Occurs primarily in older persons.

Pellagra.—A disease caused by a deficiency of niacin in the diet and marked by disturbances of the skin, gastrointestinal tract, and nervous system.

Pheochromocytoma.—A tumor in the adrenal glands, or in various nerve centers in the body. The tumor secretes the adrenal hormones *epinephrine* (*adrenalin*) and *norepinephrine,* which raise the blood pressure and increase heart action.

Pityriasis rosea.—A skin disease, characterized by red, scaly, itching patches with lighter centers.

Pleurisy.—Inflammations of the membranes lining the chest cavity and covering the lungs (*pleura*). May occur as the result of a number of such infectious and noninfectious diseases as tuberculosis, rheumatoid arthritis, and rheumatic fever. Symptoms include chest pain and shortness of breath.

Pneumothorax.—The presence of air between the layers of the pleura. This may result from penetrating chest wounds or from various diseases of the lungs and may collapse the lung. May be induced to treat tuberculosis.

Polycythemia vera.—A blood disease, characterized by an increase in the number of red blood cells.

Prickly heat (*milaria*).—A rash caused by blocking of sweat gland ducts.

Psoriasis.—A chronic skin disease characterized by thickened red patches of skin covered by a silvery scale. It usually affects the elbows, scalp, and knees.

Pulmonary embolism.—An obstruction of a lung artery by a blood clot or other substance carried by the blood from another part of the body.

Purpura.—The appearance of hemorrhages in the skin and mucous membranes, associated with fragility of the capillaries or with a decline in the number of blood platelets.

Raynaud's disease.—A circulatory disorder, seen primarily in young women. It is marked by attacks of pallor, coldness, tingling, and pain in the fingers and toes.

Rectocele.—A female disorder in which the rectum presses against, or ruptures through, the wall of the vagina. It may occur after childbirth.

Regional enteritis.—An intestinal disease marked by scarring, thickening, and, possibly, by perforation of the intestinal wall. Usually appears in individuals under age 40.

Rheumatic fever.—A disorder seen most often in children and characterized by wandering joint pains, skin eruptions, abdominal pains, and, possibly, heart damage. Usually occurs some weeks following a sore throat caused by *streptococcus* bacteria.

Rickets.—A children's disease caused by a deficiency of vitamin D. Bones soften and fail to grow normally.

Sarcoidosis.—A disease in which nodules and scar tissue appear in the skin, lungs, bones, and other parts of the body. It may cause chest pain, shortness of breath, heart failure, and other changes, depending upon the organs affected.

Sciatica.—A radiating pain along the course of the sciatic nerve, which runs along the buttock and back of the thigh. It may be caused by spinal disorders, injuries, or tumors.

Scleroderma.—A disease of the connective tissue, marked by skin changes and, possibly, by disturbances of the lungs, blood vessels, intestines, and other organs.

Scoliosis.—A lateral deviation of the spine that may be caused by tumors, injury, paralysis, or a shortened leg.

Sea sickness.—See *Motion sickness.*

Scurvy.—A disease caused by a deficiency of vitamin C in the diet.

Serum sickness.—An allergic reaction to vaccines containing animal serums. It usually appears several days after the injection, and is characterized by skin eruptions and swellings of the face, hands, or feet.

Shock.—A circulatory collapse in which the effective blood volume is insufficient to carry out the normal functions of the circulatory system. It may be caused by extensive bleeding, by sudden expansion of the blood vessels, or by heart damage. Changes observed in shock are lowered blood pressure, pale, cold, and clammy skin, and weak pulse.

Sickle cell anemia. — An inherited blood disorder, marked by crescent-shaped red blood cells that tend to be destroyed easily, thereby causing clots to form in small blood vessels.

Silicosis.—An occupational lung disease, caused by inhalation of dust containing silica.

Slipped disc.—The displacement of an *intervertebral disc* (one of the cartilaginous structures that lie between the bones of the spine). It may be caused by strain or injury.

Spina bifida.—A congenital fissure of the back of the spinal column. In some bases the spinal membranes protrude through the cleft. In severe cases, disturbances of the nerve supply below the fissures may cause muscle weakness and neurological disturbances.

Sprue.—A disease in which food material cannot be properly absorbed through the intestinal wall.

Stroke (*apoplexy*).—Brain damage caused by a disturbance in the blood supply to the brain. May occur in arteriosclerosis and in some types of heart disease. Symptoms include paralysis and disturbances of speech and thought.

Tetany.—A state of extreme muscle excitability, usually accompanied by muscle spasms in various parts of the body. Associated with a decline in the concentration of calcium ions in the blood, it occurs in rickets and some kidney and intestinal disorders.

Thrombophlebitis.—A blood clot in an inflamed vein, usually in a limb.

Thrombosis.—A blood clot occurring in an artery or vein. It is often serious when the blood vessels of the heart, brain, or lungs are involved.

Torticollis.—A twisting of the neck to one side so that the ear approaches the shoulder. It may be either congenital or caused by injury to, or irritation of, the muscles and tendons of the neck.

Trigeminal neuralgia (*tic douloureux*). —A disorder marked by recurring attacks of severe pain along the trigeminal nerve of the face.

Tumor.—A swelling or growth in the body. *Benign* tumors do not invade healthy tissues. *Malignant* (cancerous) tumors invade adjacent tissues, causing cell destruction, and may spread to other parts of the body.

Ulcers.—Areas of destroyed tissue, affecting the skin or mucous membranes of the body. Skin ulcers may be caused by infection or by circulatory disorders. Ulcers of the gastrointestinal tract may be associated with oversecretion of gastric juice or may appear from unknown causes.

Uremia.—Changes in the concentration of urea, potassium, sodium, and other substances in the blood, seen in kidney disorders.

Varicose veins.—Veins that have become weakened and distended because of "incompetence" of the valves that normally prevent back-flow of blood. They usually occur in the legs or as hemorrhoids or varicoceles.

Vertigo.—Dizziness and loss of balance that may be caused by disturbances of the body's balancing mechanisms. Vertigo occurs in certain ear and brain disorders and also in motion sickness, where the usual visual balancing cues shift position.

—Martin Spencer and Daniel Monroe

A CHART OF INFECTIOUS DISEASES

Name of Disease
1. *Nature of Infecting Organisms*
2. *Special Geographic Distribution*
3. *Mode of Transmission*
4. *Groups Primarily Affected*
5. *Incubation Period*
6. *Signs and Symptoms*
7. *Prevention and Control*
8. *Remarks*

Actinomycosis
1. Fungi
3. Chewing, swallowing, or inhaling contaminated materials
4. Young males
5. Few weeks to a year
6. Draining wounds on head and neck, cough and abdominal pains if organisms attack lungs and viscera
8. Also occurs in cattle and other animals

Anthrax
1. Bacteria
2. Especially prevalent in Mediterranean region, Africa, and Asia
3. Skin contact with infected cattle hides, breathing infected dust, consuming contaminated milk or meat
4. Butchers, farmers, tannery workers, woolsorters
6. Skin—pustules
Lungs—cough, difficulty in breathing, prostration
Viscera—vomiting, pain, constipation
7. Vaccination of domestic animals; disinfection of animal products

Blastomycosis (Gilchrist's Disease)
1. Fungi
2. North America
4. Men between the ages of 20 and 40
6. Skin—abscesses, pustules
Lungs—cough, chest pain, fever
Bones—lesions
8. Also occurs in dogs, but no dog-to-man transmission has been established

Brucellosis (Undulant Fever)
1. Bacteria
3. Contaminated milk, direct contact with infected animals
4. Farmers and others who come into contact with infected animals
5. 10–30 days
6. Chills, backache, fever, headache, joint pains, loss of appetite and weight
7. Pasteurization of milk, elimination of disease in animals, human immunization
8. Disease occurs in goats, sheep, cattle, and other domestic animals

Candidiasis (Moniliasis)
1. Fungi
6. Attacks skin between fingers and toes, underarms, also mouth, nails, vagina, and lungs
8. Organisms may be present in mouth, skin, and intestinal tract without producing any signs of candidiasis

Chancroid
1. Bacteria
3. Sexual contact
5. 3–7 days
6. Ulcers on genitalia

Chicken Pox (Varicella)
1. Viruses
3. Through inhalation of infected airborne droplets
4. Children
5. 14–20 days
6. Rash, fever, headache, loss of appetite
8. Varicella virus is the same as that which causes herpes zoster (shingles)

Cholera
1. Bacteria
2. Far East
3. Consumption of contaminated water, food, milk
5. 1–6 days
6. Dehydration, diarrhea, weakness, possible circulatory failure
7. Purification of water supply, vaccination
8. Organisms produce a toxin which irritates intestinal wall; high death rate

Coccidioidomycosis
1. Fungi
2. Western and southwestern U.S., also parts of Central and South America
3. Organisms are carried by dust
4. 25–55 age group
5. 8–14 days
6. Usually attacks lungs; may also involve skin, nervous system, and viscera
7. Paving of roads and other dust-control measures
8. Disease is usually mild in Caucasians, but may be fatal in dark-skinned races

Cold, Common
1. Viruses
3. Probably transmitted by airborne droplets from nose and throat of carriers
5. 2–3 days
6. Sneezing, coughing, sore throat, possibly fever
7. Vaccines have been developed but their effectiveness is questionable

Cold Sores (Herpes Simplex)
1. Viruses
6. Single or multiple blisters on lips, eyes, or other parts of the body
7. Smallpox vaccinations sometimes prevent recurrences
8. Cold sores on eyes may produce scarring of cornea

Colorado Tick Fever
1. Viruses
2. Western U.S.
3. Ticks
5. 4–5 days
6. Fever, chills, headache, back and eye pain
7. Preventive measures against ticks
8. Only known tick-transmitted virus disease of Northern Hemisphere

Cryptococcosis (Torulosis)
1. Fungi
3. Contaminated soil
6. Attacks brain meninges, lungs, skin

Dengue Fever (Breakbone Fever)
1. Viruses
2. Tropical and subtropical regions
3. Mosquitoes (Aedes)
5. 5–8 days
6. Fever, headache, muscle soreness, pain behind the eyes
7. Mosquito control. A vaccine is available

Diphtheria
1. Bacilli
3. Airborne droplets from throat of carrier
4. Children
5. 2–4 days
6. Difficulty in breathing caused by diphtheritic membrane across the throat. Diphtheria toxin may attack heart and nervous system
7. Vaccine is available. Incidence of diphtheria has been greatly reduced since introduction of immunization
8. An antitoxin is available for treatment but must be used early if it is to be effective

Dysentery, Amebic
1. Amebae
3. Contaminated food
6. Attacks digestive tract causing diarrhea, weakness, nausea, vomiting; may produce liver abscesses
7. Sanitary disposal of wastes; hygienic handling of food

Dysentery, Bacillary
1. Bacteria
2. Most dangerous types occur in Orient
3. Contaminated food, water
4. Often occurs in epidemic outbreaks in institutions, military camps, and the like
5. Varies from 24 hours to several days
6. Violent diarrhea, fever, chills, cramps, nausea, vomiting. Develops more rapidly than amebic dysentery
7. Prevention of spread by treatment of those infected
8. Disease has been of historical importance in military campaigns: defeat of Persian army in 380 B.C. was in part ascribed to dysentery

Filariasis
1. Roundworms
2. Tropics and subtropics
3. Insects
6. Attacks skin, lymph vessels, eyes; massive swellings of arms or legs may develop
7. Sanitary measures to destroy insects
8. Some forms may cause blindness

German Measles (Rubella)
1. Viruses
3. Airborne droplets from respiratory passages of carriers
4. Children
5. 21 days
6. Skin rash, swollen lymph glands
8. German measles in pregnant women may cause serious damage to the fetus

Gonorrhea
1. Bacteria
3. Sexual contact
4. Young adults
5. 2–8 days
6. Attacks reproductive organs causing pain, fever, swellings. May result in sterility or permanent joint damage
7. Especially hard to control because of the difficulty of diagnosing the disease in women
8. Infants of gonorrheal mothers may develop eye infection while passing through the birth canal. To avoid this, drops of an antibiotic solution are routinely placed in the eyes of newborn infants

Hepatitis, Infectious
1. Viruses (type A)
2. Prevalent in Mediterranean region
3. Contaminated food or water; close personal contact with carriers
4. Children and young adults
5. 20–40 days
6. Fever, skin rash, weakness, fatigue, loss of appetite, chills, nausea, jaundice
7. Hygienic handling of food
8. Epidemics may occur in boarding schools and similar institutions

Hepatitis, Serum
1. Viruses (type B)
3. Transfusions of infected blood; contaminated needles used for injection
5. 60–160 days
6. Same as in infectious hepatitis (above)
7. Proper handling and source of blood supplies; adequate sterilization of needles

Histoplasmosis
1. Fungi
2. Especially prevalent in midwestern U.S.
3. Inhalation of fungus spores. Fungus is found in soil
6. Attacks lungs, causing fever, coughing, sweating, loss of weight

Hookworm
1. Roundworms
2. Tropical regions (*Necator americanus*)
Europe, North Africa, Far East (*Ancylostoma duodenale*)
3. Walking barefoot in infected soil, larvae penetrate skin of feet
6. Bronchitis, abdominal pain, anemia, weakness, pallor. In children causes physical and mental retardation
7. Sanitary disposal of excreta. Wearing of shoes

A CHART OF INFECTIOUS DISEASES (Continued)

Influenza
1. Viruses
2. Worldwide epidemics
3. Airborne droplets from carriers
5. 1–2 days
6. Chills, fever, pain behind eyes, muscle pains, sneezing
7. Vaccines give temporary immunity
8. Dangerous to old and debilitated persons, who may develop pneumonia

Leishmaniasis
1. Protozoa
2. Asia, Africa, Central and South America
3. Sandflies
6. *Leishmania donovani*—anemia, fever, chills, sweats, dizziness
Leishmania tropica—sores on skin, face, ears, neck, hands
Leishmania braziliensis — attacks mucous membranes of the mouth, nose, throat; may cause ulcerations
7. Elimination of sandflies; treatment of humans and dogs who carry the disease

Leprosy
1. Bacteria
2. Primarily in the tropics
3. Probably through infection of superficial skin abrasions
5. 2–4 years or more
6. Ulcers of skin, nerve damage, hair loss
7. Treatment of carriers
8. Sulfones now control most cases

Leptospirosis
1. Bacteria
3. Contact with field and swamp water contaminated by urine of infected animals
5. 7–10 days
6. Fever, vomiting, headache, congestion of eyes, muscle pains, small skin hemorrhages; in some types, jaundice
7. Eliminating rats and other carriers. Protective clothing to prevent organisms from entering the body

Lymphogranuloma Venereum
1. Viruslike microorganisms
2. In tropics and Mediterranean region
3. Sexual contact
5. 3–20 days
6. Genital ulcer, abscess, fever, joint pain, swelling, scarring of genitalia
7. Identification and treatment of carriers

Malaria
1. Protozoa
2. Temperate and tropical regions
3. Mosquitoes
5. Varies with type
6. Periodic attacks of chills, fever
Chronic malaria—listlessness, headache, fatigue, enlargement of spleen
7. Mosquito control, treatment of carriers
8. Malaria is the major parasitic disease of mankind

Mumps (Epidemic Parotitis)
1. Viruses
3. Direct contact; airborne droplets from mouths of infected persons
4. Children
5. 8–21 days
6. Attacks salivary glands, particularly parotid glands adjacent to ear. Causes pain, swelling, fever
7. A vaccine is available
8. Frequently produces inflammation of the testicles in adult males. In some cases sterility may result

Parrot Fever (Psittacosis, Ornithosis)
1. Viruses
3. Contaminated air droplets, feather dust from infected birds
5. 7–14 days
6. Fever, chills, headache, muscle pains. Eyes may become sensitive to light. Also pneumonia, insomnia, apathy
7. Treatment of infected birds; chemical prophylaxis of birds
8. Disease affects parrots, parakeets, ducks, pigeons, turkeys

Pinworm (Seatworm)
1. Intestinal roundworms
3. Contaminated food and drink. Pinworm eggs are carried in the air
6. Itching in anal region, poor appetite, weight loss
7. Worms may be removed by drugs
8. In some cases no symptoms observed

Plague (Black Death)
1. Bacteria
2. Asia
3. Rat flea transmits bacteria to man *Pneumonic plague*—bacteria are carried by airborne droplets from victims
5. 2–10 days
6. Swelling of lymph glands in groins and armpits. Chills, fever, delirium, headache, thirst. Hemorrhages into the skin and other parts of the body *Pneumonic plague*—attacks the lungs, producing a bloody sputum
7. Rat and insect control. Vaccines give temporary limited immunity
8. Disease is of historic significance, having caused devastating pandemics in Europe and the Orient

Pneumonia
1. Usually bacteria, but also viruses and fungi
3. Bacteria may be normally present in the body and attack when resistance is weakened by colds, malnutrition, exhaustion, or lung ailments
6. Coughing, fever, lung abscesses, aches, chills, chest pains, bloody or pus-laden sputum, loss of appetite
8. Drug-resistant staphylococcus bacteria cause many hospital cases of pneumonia

Poliomyelitis (Infantile Paralysis)
1. Viruses
2. Industrialized countries of temperate zones
3. Airborne droplets from carriers; contaminated food or other objects
4. Children and young adults
5. 3–35 days
6. May produce only fever and a mild feeling of illness. In other cases, sore throat, aches, headaches, paralysis. Viruses attack nerve cells controlling muscles
7. Vaccines are available
8. In underdeveloped countries where sanitary facilities are poor, infection usually occurs early in infancy when children are protected by antibodies received from the mother. This enables them to withstand the disease and develop permanent immunity

Q Fever
1. Rickettsiae
2. Western U.S., Australia, Italy, Greece
3. Inhalation of infected-tick excreta from animal hides and fleece
4. Animal handlers, woolsorters
5. 14–28 days
6. Chills, fever, headache, muscle pains, weight loss
7. Immunization; pasteurization of milk

Rabies
1. Viruses
3. Bites of infected animals
5. 10 days to several months
6. Fever, headache, burning and tingling sensations around the bite, difficulty in swallowing, breathing spasms, convulsions, fits. Invariably fatal unless injections of vaccine are given at once
7. Immunization of animals
8. Affects foxes, coyotes, jackals, wolves, skunks, and bats

Relapsing Fever
1. Bacteria
3. Ticks, body lice
5. About 7 days
6. Chills, fever, headache, vomiting, muscle and joint pain. Symptoms vanish and recur in cycles of decreasing severity
7. Control of parasites; spraying of homes and clothing with DDT
8. May occur in epidemic form

Rheumatic Fever
1. Bacteria
4. Children between the ages of 5 and 15
5. Develops some weeks after streptococcal infection of upper respiratory tract
6. Joint pains which move, or "migrate," from joint to joint in an unpredictable pattern, nosebleeds, abdominal pains, skin eruptions. Heart damage may be a serious complication
7. Antibiotics used to prevent recurrence
8. Disease is considered to be different from ordinary infectious diseases in that it develops *after* infection by bacteria. Apparently the signs and symptoms are not *directly* related to the presence of the bacteria in the tissues

Rickettsial Pox
1. Rickettsiae
2. Eastern U.S.
3. Mites
5. 1–2 weeks
6. Red, black-scabbed pimple in region of bite, fever, chills, headache, muscle pains, skin rash

Rocky Mountain Spotted Fever
1. Rickettsiae
2. Western Hemisphere
3. Ticks
5. 3–12 days
6. Headache, chills, fever, muscle-bone-joint pains, rash
7. Tick control; immunization
8. Occurs principally in spring and summer

Scarlet Fever (Scarlatina)
1. Bacteria
3. Airborne droplets from carriers, contaminated food and other objects
4. Children (rare in infants)
5. 2–5 days
6. Fever, headache, vomiting, sore throat, rash
8. Rheumatic fever or kidney inflammation may follow 2–3 weeks after recovery

Schistosomiasis
(Snail Fever, Bilharziasis)
1. Flatworms
2. Far East, Middle East
3. Infected water—organisms are carried by snails
6. *Intestinal schistosomiasis*—fever, abdominal pains, weight loss. In chronic stage anemia and irregular fever may develop *Vesical schistosomiasis*—bloody urine, ulcers of urinary tract, painful urination

Scrub Typhus
(Tsutsugamushi Disease)
1. Rickettsiae
2. Japan and South Pacific
3. Mites
5. 10–12 days
6. Skin lesion at bite; fever, chills, headache, skin rash
7. Control of mites

Shingles (Herpes Zoster)
1. Viruses
4. Adults
6. Attacks outlying (peripheral) nerves, causing inflammation, blistering, pain and tenderness along skin overlying nerve pathways, particularly of head and trunk. Serious eye complications if nerves in region of eye are involved
8. Virus of herpes zoster is the same virus that causes chicken pox. It is believed that the organism may be latent in the tissues and be reactivated by injury, medication, or tumors

(continued on next page)

A CHART OF INFECTIOUS DISEASES (Continued)

Sleeping Sickness
(African Trypanosomiasis)
1. Trypanosomes
2. Tropical Africa
3. Tsetse flies
6. Lesion at fly bite; fever, headache, enlarged lymph glands, weakness, muscle tenderness, physical and mental depression. Disease is most serious when central nervous system is attacked
7. Use of drugs to ward off infection in dangerous areas

Smallpox (Variola)
1. Viruses
3. Airborne droplets from carrier; contaminated clothing, eating utensils
5. 8–14 days
6. Fever, vomiting, headache, backache, skin rash
7. Vaccination
8. Scarring usually permanent. Vaccination has eradicated the disease in many countries, but pockets of smallpox still exist

Syphilis
1. Bacteria
2. Worldwide
3. Sexual contact, inheritance
5. *Primary stage*—3–4 weeks
   Secondary stage—4–6 weeks later
   Tertiary stage—20 or more years after original infection
6. *Primary stage*—lesion on genitals, mouth
   Secondary stage—skin eruptions, fever, sore throat, enlarged lymph nodes
   Tertiary stage—mental changes, heart disease, spinal cord damage
7. Educational program, early detection and treatment with antibiotics, prevention of congenital syphilis by treatment of pregnant mother
8. Decline in death rates of adults and infants, but disease not under control

Tapeworm
1. Flatworms
3. Contaminated beef, pork, fish
6. In many cases no symptoms. In others abdominal pains, digestive disturbances, nausea, anemia. Non-intestinal variety (hydatid disease) may attack liver, lungs, muscles; is contracted from infected soil or from contact with infected dogs
7. Proper cooking of meat, use of specific drugs, effective sewerage systems

Tetanus (Lockjaw)
1. Bacteria
3. Contamination of wounds with dirt containing tetanus spores
5. Varies from days to weeks to years

6. Violent muscle spasms. Death may result from interference with breathing. Tetanus toxin attacks nerve tissue
7. Immunization
8. Tetanus bacteria are frequently normal inhabitants of the intestinal tracts of man and various animals

Trachoma
1. Viruses
2. Near and Far East, southern Europe
3. Direct contact with carriers; contaminated personal articles
4. Children
5. Approximately one week
6. Tearing of eyes, sensitivity to light, scarring and ulceration of cornea and eyelids. May cause blindness
7. Treatment of carriers
8. Victims are susceptible to repeated attacks since no immunity develops

Trichinosis
1. Roundworms
2. Temperate zones
3. Contaminated pork
5. 1–4 days
6. No symptoms in mild infestations. In other cases nausea, diarrhea, vomiting, muscle pains, weakness, fever. Eyelids become puffy and hemorrhages appear under nails
7. Pork should be thoroughly cooked—30 minutes at 140°F. for each pound
8. Larvae become permanently encysted in muscles

Tuberculosis
1. Bacteria
3. Airborne droplets from carriers, contaminated milk
6. In early stage fever, fatigue, loss of weight. In later chronic stage also night sweating, bloody sputum, chest pains
7. Early detection and treatment of carriers; pasteurization of milk
8. Although a vaccine is available (BCG vaccine) and has been used for mass vaccinations its value for this purpose is not universally accepted

Tularemia (Rabbit Fever)
1. Bacteria
3. Contact with infected rodents, blood-sucking flies, and ticks; contaminated meat
4. Hunters, butchers, campers
6. Skin ulcers, eye inflammation or mouth ulcers, depending upon where the organisms enter the body; headache, fever, vomiting, chills
7. Immunization. Rabbit meat should be thoroughly cooked. Water from streams in infected areas should be avoided

Typhoid Fever
1. Bacteria
3. Contaminated food or water
5. 10–12 days
6. Headache, remittent fever, chills, nausea, cough, constipation, nosebleeds, "rose spots" on skin of trunk
7. Vaccination; detection and treatment of carriers; purification of drinking water

Typhus (Epidemic Typhus)
1. Rickettsiae
3. Body lice
5. 10–14 days
6. Chills, headache, aches, pains, fever, delirium, pink spots on skin later developing into hemorrhagic spots. Possibly gangrene of toes, fingers, or earlobes
7. Immunization, delousing procedures (using DDT)

Whipworm
1. Intestinal roundworms
3. Contaminated food or water
6. Mild infections go unnoticed. In other cases abdominal pain, nausea, vomiting, flatulence, headache, bloody stools, anemia, weight loss
7. Sanitary disposal of human wastes

Whooping Cough (Pertussis)
1. Bacteria
3. Airborne droplets from carriers
4. Children; females more often than males
5. 7–14 days
6. Explosive cough, convulsions, possible lung complications
7. Immunization
8. Epidemics have occurred in large cities at intervals of two to four years

Yaws
1. Bacteria
2. Tropics
3. Direct contact, organisms enter through the skin
4. Children living in crowded, unhygienic conditions
5. 3–4 weeks
6. Skin lesions. May attack bones in later stages
7. Treatment of carriers
8. The *Treponema pertenue*, which causes yaws, is identical in appearance to the *Treponema pallidum*, which causes syphilis

Yellow Fever
1. Viruses
2. Central and South America
3. Mosquitoes
5. 3–6 days
6. Fever, headache, backache, congestion of eyes, slow pulse, nausea, vomiting, hemorrhage from mucous membranes, jaundice; kidney failure in severe cases
7. Immunization; mosquito control

BIBLIOGRAPHY

BEST, CHARLES H. and TAYLOR, NORMAN B. *The Living Body* (4th ed.). Holt, Rinehart and Winston, Inc., 1958.

BURNET, MACFARLANE. *Natural History of Infectious Diseases.* Cambridge University Press, 1953.

CARLSON, ANTON J. and JOHNSON, VICTOR. *The Machinery of the Body.* The University of Chicago Press, 1953.

CLARK, RANDOLPH LEE and CUMLEY, RUSSELL W. *The Book of Health: An Encyclopedia for Everyone* (2nd ed.). D. Van Nostrand Co., Inc., 1962.

EDWARDS, LINDEN F. *Concise Anatomy.* McGraw-Hill, Inc., 1956.

EMERSON, CHARLES P., JR. and BRAGDON, JANE S. *Essentials of Medicine.* J. B. Lippincott Co., 1959.

GALLAGHER, J. R., GOLDBERGER, I. H., and HALLOCK, G. T. *Health for Life.* Ginn & Co., 1963.

GERARD, RALPH W. *The Body Functions.* John Wiley & Sons, Inc., 1941.

GOSS, CHARLES M. *Gray's Anatomy of the Human Body* (27th ed.). Lea & Febiger, 1959.

HICKMAN, CLEVELAND P. *Health for College Students* (2nd ed.). Prentice-Hall, Inc., 1963.

MITCHELL, PHILIP H. *A Textbook of General Physiology.* McGraw-Hill, Inc., 1956.

SCHIFFERES, JUSTUS J. *Healthier Living.* John Wiley & Sons, Inc., 1955.

SEXTON, W. A. *Chemical Constitution and Biological Activity* (2nd ed.). D. Van Nostrand Co., Inc., 1953.

STANLEY, W. M. and VALENS, E. G. *Viruses and the Nature of Life.* E. P. Dutton & Co., Inc., 1961.

SUNDGAARD, ARNOLD. *The Miracle of Growth.* University of Illinois Press, 1950.

YOUNG, CLARENCE and others. *The Human Organism and the World of Life.* Harper & Bros., 1951.

SPACE BIOLOGY

Areas of Study.—The new science of *space biology,* which is sometimes also referred to as *bioastronautics,* is concerned with the biological effects and the possible hazards that confront astronauts setting out on long missions through space. This science requires an ultra-careful study of the human body, as well as a physiological and psychological study of those people selected as astronauts. For this reason, the more specific term *space medicine* is often used, since animal studies, so far, are only incidental. Space biology must not be confused with *exobiology,* which is the study of life forms indigenous to celestial bodies other than the earth. Exobiology is only a theoretical science so far, concerned mainly with laying down its own foundations.

The problems encountered in space biology fall into two classes. One consists of those problems produced by the launching and operation of the sapcecraft. The other is comprised of those problems resulting from the environment of space, which differs fundamentally from the normal environment at or near sea level to which our bodies are accustomed. The problems associated with the operation of the space vehicle can further be divided into those associated with the *high-acceleration* phase that accompanies blast-off and reentry (or landing) and those accompanying the *zero-gravity,* or *weightless,* phase that is characteristic of orbital flight, whether the orbit leads around the earth or from the earth to the moon or another planet.

Gravitational Problems.—The letter *g,* used to describe the intensity of acceleration during blast-off, is an abbreviation of the word "gravity." It was chosen because the force the astronaut is subjected to is compared with the force due to gravitational acceleration at sea level. The normal force, designated as 1 g, to which we are subjected during our daily lives is the result of the earth's gravitational attraction. If the gravitational attraction were to be doubled, we would be subjected to twice the force, or 2 g; that is, we would weigh twice as much. The g-force experienced at any moment is the result of resisting the gravitational acceleration of the earth, since we are supported by the ground. If we were falling freely, without resisting the earth's pull, this g-force would disappear.

■ **CAUSE OF HIGH G.**—If a rocket rises vertically with an acceleration equal to that produced by the earth's gravitational field—that is, if it travels 32 feet per second faster at the end of every second—the astronauts in the space capsule atop that rocket will be subjected to a force of 2 g. One component of the 2 g force is caused by the acceleration of the climbing rocket, while the other is the result of the earth's gravitational field. The g-force acting on the astronaut's body is, therefore, always 1 g higher than is accounted for by the rocket's acceleration. All rockets are designed to operate with a constant thrust, which

means that the fuel consumption per second of powered flight remains constant. But since fuel consumption and thrust are constant, the acceleration must increase. For example, if the rocket lifted off with an acceleration of 1 g because the thrust of the rocket engine was precisely twice the weight of the rocket, the acceleration will be 3 g when the weight of the rocket, because of fuel consumption, has dropped to one half of the take-off figure. The astronaut will then experience a force of 4 g, 3 g of which is due to the rocket's acceleration and 1 g to the earth's gravity. Since the acceleration due to the earth's gravity decreases with increasing altitude, the g-force exerted by the earth is slightly less than 1 g when the rocket has climbed to an altitude of, for example, 50 miles. The difference for the first hundred miles is so small that it can be disregarded for practical purposes.

It is obvious, therefore, that the g forces on the body of the astronaut reach their peak during the last second of burning of the rocket fuel. At that moment the rocket is close to its minimum weight (the structural weight plus the payload weight) while the thrust is even slightly higher than it was at lift-off, because a rocket's thrust rises somewhat as external air pressure diminishes. For preliminary calculations it is assumed that the thrust of a given rocket engine in a vacuum is 16 per cent higher than it is at sea level. However, the actual increase is slightly different (but rarely by more than 1 per cent) because it is influenced by the design of the exhaust nozzle.

In the case of a two-stage rocket, the g-forces drop to zero when the

lower stage ceases burning and remain at zero until the second stage begins burning. Then another cycle of mounting g-forces, beginning at about 2 g, begins. The g-forces become zero during the interval between the burning of the first stage and that of the second stage because during this interval the rocket is effected by the gravitational pull of the earth and loses velocity.
■ **EFFECTS OF HIGH G.**—Before the first launching of a manned space vehicle, it had been calculated that the time from lift-off to insertion into an orbit around the earth would be on the order of five minutes. It was also calculated that the g-forces on the astronaut's body would average about 5 g, with a short-duration peak of over 8 g at the end of the first stage burning and a second short-duration peak of about 7 g at the end of the burning of the second stage. The question was, of course, how the human body would react to an acceleration of 5 g for a period of five minutes. No situation occurs on the ground that imposes a high acceleration for any length of time. The only periods of acceleration substantially higher than 1 g and lasting for more than a few seconds were experienced in making sharp banking turns in high-speed aircraft. Such turns were not made in the course of ordinary flying, but took place mainly in aerial combat during World War II. A rule of thumb arrived at during these experiences was that if the turn did not produce g-forces higher than 3 g they had no problem, but at 4 g or over they lost consciousness, or "blacked out." Fortunately, the blackout period usually lasted less than twenty seconds.

Although previous experience did

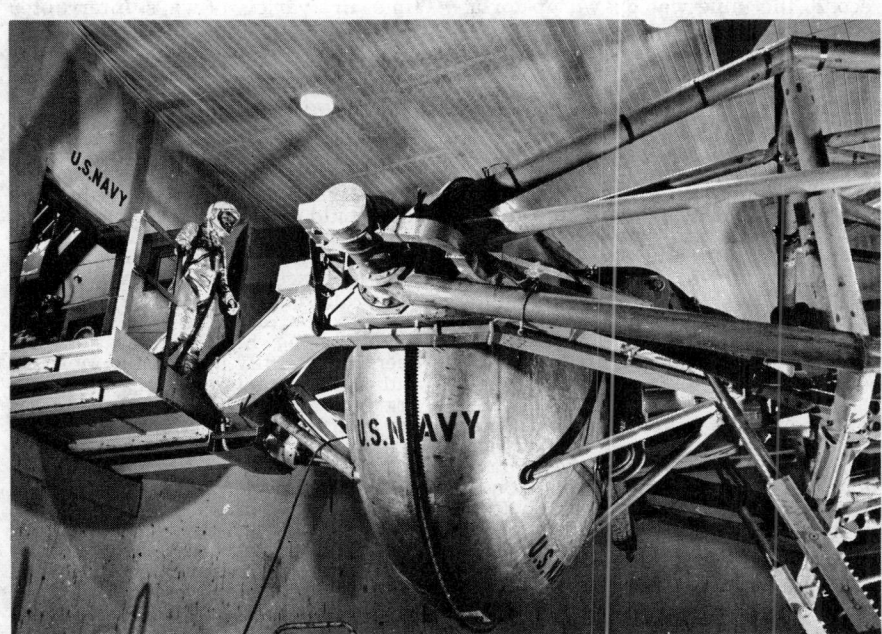

NASA

GIANT CENTRIFUGE is being used by astronaut Walter M. Schirra to test the effects of acceleration. Astronauts will experience acceleration during both launching and reentry.

NASA

WEIGHTLESSNESS is experienced in test flights prior to the astronauts' actual space flight.

not have more than a hint to offer, there was a way of investigating the problem. A rapidly spinning centrifuge could produce g-forces of the proper magnitude and duration. Preliminary experiments with small centrifuges showed that mice were usually killed by 25 g, but that hard-shelled insects (such as medium sized beetles) and very light insects (such as the common housefly) seemed not to be affected at all by the same acceleration. For the purpose of designing a centrifuge large enough to test people, a short table was drawn up. Although it was anticipated that a man would be put only into orbit, with an orbital velocity of 4.6 to 4.7 miles per second, the table was drawn up for a moon-flight, where a velocity of 7 miles per second is required. If it was assumed that the human body could not stand a higher acceleration than 3 g, the time required to reach a velocity of 7 miles per second was 9 minutes and 31 seconds. If 4 g could be used, the time shrank to 6 minutes and 21 seconds. If 5 g was possible, the time would be reduced to 4 minutes and 45 seconds; at 6 g it would be only 3 minutes and 48 seconds; and at 7 g it would be 3 minutes and 10 seconds. If a superman who could survive 10 g were found, only 2 minutes and 6 seconds would be needed.

While the first such centrifuge was being built, some thought was expended on the best position for the volunteer to be tested. The wartime pilots had, of course, been in a sitting position so that the g-forces acted along their spine, from head to buttocks. Theoretically there was a better position. The man should be placed on his back, with his head and shoulders slightly raised and his knees raised to about the level of the head. Then the g-forces would act from front to back and it seemed likely that higher accelerations could be endured in that position.

The actual tests, when they were

run, surprised everyone, from the volunteers who permitted themselves to be tested to the engineers and doctors who ran the tests. The series began with 3 g for 9½ minutes; no harmful effects were found, but the volunteers thought they had been left in the centrifuge for 20 minutes. In spite of these complaints a 4 g run was tried. This was easier on the volunteers; the shorter duration more than made up for the extra g. The 5 g and 6 g runs also proved to be easier on the volunteers than the 3 g run had been. When the 10 g run was tried, it was found to cause a physical hardship, but there was no "black-out."

These tests were repeated many times in a variety of ways. Interrupted tests were run to simulate the blast-off of a two- or three-stage rocketship. Tests of only 2 g for 25 minutes were run for the purpose of simulating a reentry into the atmosphere. The actual reentry imposes loads as high as those experienced in take-off, although for a slightly shorter duration. In the end it was clear that a healthy man could endure the acceleration required for going into space without any harm to his health. The centrifuge tests are now a standard item in the training of astronauts, and the position conceived as being the best for enduring high acceleration has been successfully used in the Mercury and Gemini manned-space-flights.

■**ZERO G PROBLEMS.**—Since the g-forces are the result of resisting acceleration (either gravitational or other forces) a spacecraft in orbit around the earth does not experience any g-forces at all. A capsule in orbit follows a path compounded of its own inertia and of the earth's gravitational attraction. One might say that it falls around the earth and, of course, every one of its parts, including loose objects in its interior, "fall" in the same direction with the same velocity.

While the absence of g-forces, called to "zero-g condition," was perfectly

explained from the point of view of the physicist, the physician could think of a large number of questions. What would zero-g do to the astronaut's heart? How would his lungs, stomach and intestines, inner ear, and brain and nervous system react? Would an astronaut be able to tell what was above and what below? Would he become completely confused—"disoriented" was the technical term—and be unable to work? And would he be able to sleep?

At first there seemed to be no answers to these questions and, again, previous experience offered no information. An approximation of zero-g (but only an approximation, because of air resistance) is experienced by a parachute jumper for the short time between leaving the aircraft and the opening of the parachute. It is experienced by a swimmer diving from a high board, and by a ski jumper during a long jump. But in each case the duration is measured in seconds, and the parachute jumper, the ski jumper, and the high diver always have their attention on other things. However, when the medical men concerned with the problem examined the operation of each organ, they found that gravity has very little to do with the functioning of the human body.

Inhaling, for example, is accomplished by expanding the chest so that the pressure inside the lungs is lower than the pressure outside the body. Exhaling is done by making the inside pressure greater than the outside pressure. Could an astronaut swallow without gravity? It was remembered that little boys drink a glass of water, or even eat food, while hanging by their knees from a bar, swallowing *against* gravity. And while there was no doubt that the sense of equilibrium was located in the ear, it was also known that it was not needed provided the man could see. As for the heart, it did have to lift the blood out of the legs and the abdominal cavity. It was soon realized, however, that the main work of the heart consists in overcoming the friction in the blood vessels; and that the friction would not be changed by zero-g conditions. There remained the two questions of how the brain and nervous system would function and whether an astronaut in orbit would be able to sleep.

Then a method of producing zero-g for a short time was devised. If an airplane went into a shallow dive, pulled out of it, and had the power shut down at the same time, it would fly through an arc on inertia only, like a projectile. While it was flying through that arc, the zero-g condition would prevail. After a few cautious experiments, such zero-g flights— which are now also a part of the training of an astronaut—were carried out in a long series of tests. First the ability of the test subject to stick a pencil accurately into the center of a paper target was tested. Then a few cautious swallows of water and then eating were tried. Everything worked well, although some practice was required for certain things. Just to be thorough, animal experiments were also carried out. These were done mainly with cats, for cats jump, are

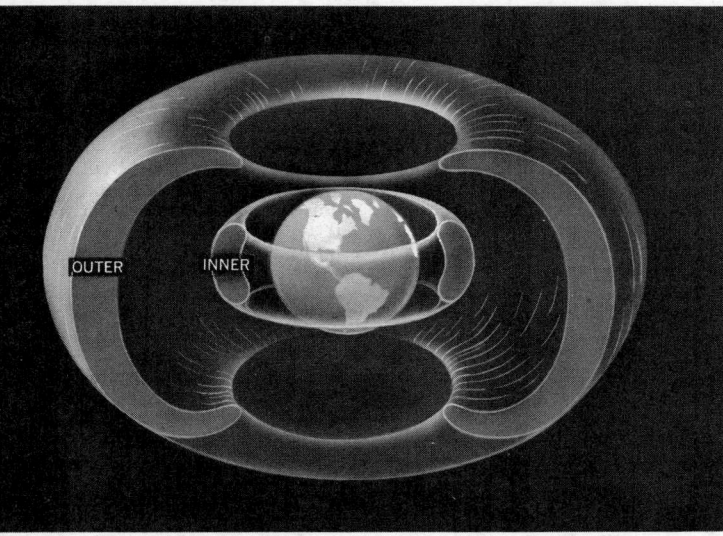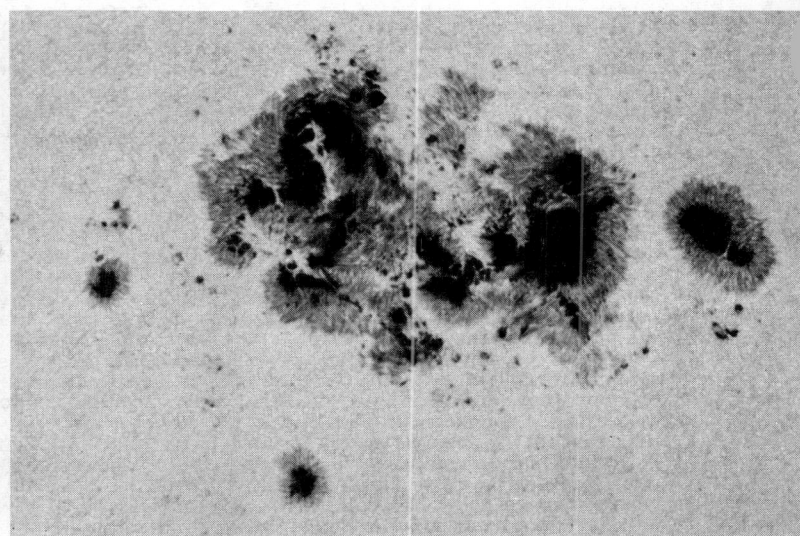

MOUNT WILSON AND PALOMAR OBSERVATORIES

VAN ALLEN RADIATION BELT extends to about 50,000 miles above the earth's surface. This belt is believed to be caused by trapped radiation from the sun. During sunspot activity (*right*), great amounts of solar flare radiation are emitted from the sun's interior.

versatile, and are not easily distracted from what they want to do. Only the question of whether they would be able to sleep could not be answered by these flights, for the condition of weightlessness in the initial tests lasted for only 30 seconds. The overall outcome of these weightless flights was that people could adapt well to the zero-g condition.

■**ANIMALS IN ORBIT.**—While the high-g and zero-g tests were being conducted, animals were sent up in the nose cones of rockets. A vertically rising rocket that is too slow to go into orbit will produce a high acceleration for about a minute. From then on, while it climbs to its peak by inertia only and while it is falling back, zero-g is obtained. It lasts from the moment the rocket engine cuts off to the moment the parachute attached to the animal capsule opens, which can be a period of six minutes and more. American scientists used rhesus monkeys, while the Russians used dogs (and later an assortment of animals, including hares, mice, and a few insects) for control purposes. Whenever the animals were recovered, they were in good shape, with the exception of one test animal that died of sunstroke because it was several hours before the capsule was found in the desert.

The first animal experiment in orbit was carried out by the Russians with their second artificial satellite, *Sputnik II*, which was launched on November 3, 1957. In addition to an artificial satellite identical to *Sputnik I*, the rocket carried an animal capsule holding a medium-sized female dog named Laika ("barker"), which lived in orbit for more than 150 hours. The dog's breathing, heartbeat, etc., were telemetered to the ground, and it was found that Laika's heartbeat was high above normal after the strain of the acceleration and stayed at a higher level for some time. Precisely the same observation was later made about human astronauts. However, it is interesting to note that during the

flight of *Gemini 5*, which lasted eight days, the heartbeat of astronaut Charles Conrad reached a greater frequency and stayed high for a longer time than that of astronaut L. Gordon Cooper, who had made a 1½-day orbital flight before.

Sputnik IV, which was orbited on May 15, 1960, may have carried an animal experiment too, but the capsule disintegrated upon reentry. *Sputnik V*, which was orbited on August 19, 1960, carried an animal capsule housing two dogs named Balka and Strelka, a few smaller animals, and microscopic life forms of various types. It was successfully de-orbited one day after firing and the animals were recovered. *Sputnik VI*, which was orbited on December 1, 1960, also carried two dogs, named Pchelka and Mushka, and smaller life forms; but this capsule burned up during reentry. *Sputnik IX*, launched on March 9, 1961, and *Sputnik X*, orbited on March 25, 1961, carried the dogs Chernushka and Zvezdochkar, respectively. Both were successfully de-orbited and the animals recovered.

■**MEN IN ORBIT.**—The Russians must have felt by that time that they had mastered the technique of de-orbiting, because their next space shot was a manned capsule, called *Vostok* ("east"). It went into orbit on April 12, 1961, with cosmonaut Yuri Gagarin aboard. The capsule was brought in for a landing a few hundred miles to the west of the lift-off area, so that Gagarin did not quite complete one orbit.

All these flights, however, had not answered the question whether a man could sleep when weightless. Gagarin's flight had lasted for only 108 minutes and it would be hard to tell whether an otherwise healthy dog had been deprived of sleep for twenty-four hours. Theoretical assertions ranged from the statement that weightlessness would make no difference at all, which turned out to be true, to the belief that a man might need only two or three hours of sleep per twenty-four-hour

period when weightless. The answer was supplied by the second Russian cosmonaut, Gherman Titov, who went into orbit in *Vostok II* on August 6, 1961. Titov completed 17½ orbits within 25 hours 18 minutes. He reported that he had eaten and slept but had felt "faintly nauseous" for the duration of the flight.

The flight of *Gemini 7* has shown that specially selected and trained men can not only live through two weeks of zero-g without visible harm, but can also perform a multitude of tasks accurately and efficiently. For still longer missions, however, such as a mission to Mars that would involve about 260 days in space for a one-way trip, special measures must be taken.

Environment of Space.—Man, when at home on the ground, is accustomed to what might be called a *particle environment*. The particles in question are the molecules of nitrogen, oxygen, and other gases that compose the atmosphere. Virtually everything we feel but cannot see—heat or cold, calmness or wind, and dryness or moisture—we are made aware of through the collision of these molecules with our skin. Only a strong sun in the sky reminds us that radiation is also present.

Space is not a particle environment, although microscopic and near-microscopic meteoric dust is found there. The roles of radiation and particles are more or less reversed in space when compared to the bottom of the atmosphere. At the bottom of the atmosphere man is in a particle environment with some radiation, while in space there is a radiation environment with some particles. Virtually all of this radiation, for a vehicle in the vicinity of the earth's orbit, originates in the sun.

There are two types of radiation. The first is the kind that comprises the electromagnetic spectrum, and which is usually labeled by its wavelength. The ordinary radio waves used for broadcasting are the longest, and next are the short radio waves used, for example, in radar sets. Infrared (or heat) rays come next, followed by the visible spectrum from red to violet, the ultraviolet, and finally the X rays. Since the sun is a weak radio star as well as a weak X ray star, the quantity of very long or very short waves it emits is small. Other stars produce a much higher percentage of very long waves—radar wavelengths and longer—and it may be assumed that there are also stars that produce an unusual percentage of X rays. This type of radiation from the sun is completely stopped by a very thin metal skin, comparable in thickness to the metal of an ordinary tin can. Since the skin of a space vehicle has to be thicker than that for structural reasons, it can be counted on to stop all wavelengths, including the X rays that naturally occur in space.

It is the second kind of radiation that poses problems. This type consists of *subatomic particles* that move through space at high velocities. Most of these particles are electrons, with a large admixture of protons (hydrogen nuclei). Of course, the energy of a proton depends not only upon its mass, but also upon the velocity with which it travels. The *cosmic rays* that puzzled scientists forty years ago turned out to be, in the main, very fast, and therefore very energetic, protons. Occasionally the nuclei of heavier elements are detected. These are collectively referred to as *heavy primaries;* it is believed that most of them did not originate in the sun but have come to the solar system from far distant places in space where a stellar catastrophe, such as a nova explosion, has taken place at some time.

Since the cosmic rays can penetrate many feet of concrete, there is no way shielding the astronauts in a space capsule against them. For a long time this was considered a major hazard to space flight. Both the United States and the Soviet Union have orbited numerous artificial satellites just for the purpose of detecting and measuring radiation in space. It is now known that the hazards lie elsewhere. The number of very energetic cosmic rays is small and every person sustains a number of hits of such particles in the natural course of events even when on the ground. The actual radiation hazards of space are twofold. One of these hazards, a solar flare, is a temporary event, while the other, the Van Allen belts, is permanent and fixed in space.

■SOLAR FLARES.—A *solar flare* is an especially bright spot on the sun, usually appearing in the vicinity of a sunspot group. The true nature of the sunspots is still not known, but a solar flare marks the spot where a large cloud of subatomic particles is injected into space. These clouds of protons and electrons, which often have a diameter several times that of the earth, constitute a truly major hazard to the life of astronauts. Fortunately, solar flares do not occur without any warning at all. In the first place there are years when the sun is relatively quiet and other years when it is more

active. These years of activity and inactivity constitute the so-called "sunspot cycle." There is, therefore, the possibility of a statistical prediction.

Even an individual and unexpected solar flare still has a built-in safety factor. The light emitted by a solar flare needs only about eight minutes to travel from the sun to the orbit of earth. The cloud of protons and electrons, however, travels more slowly than light, needing hours and sometimes days to reach us. There is, therefore, a warning period of at least a few hours. It may be mentioned that at some times a cloud of subatomic particles that was expected to strike the earth was never detected at all. This compels us to conclude that these clouds may not always travel in straight lines. Constant observation of solar phenomena, assisted in the near future by special sun-orbiting satellites, is expected to lead to a better understanding of all the factors involved, with the final result that reliable predictions will become possible.

■VAN ALLEN BELT.—The first artificial satellite orbited by the United States, *Explorer I,* which was launched on February 1, 1958, discovered the then unknown fact that the earth is surrounded by a radiation belt that begins at an altitude of about 500 miles above sea level. Almost a year later, on December 6, 1958, an attempt to send *Pioneer III* to the moon was unsuccessful in its main objective, but resulted in the discovery of another such radiation belt, about 12,000 miles out. They are now referred to as the inner and outer zone and have been named the *Van Allen belt* in honor of their investigator, James Alfred Van Allen. The inner zone forms a ring around the earth that reaches from about 40° North latitude to 40° South latitude. The inner zone is assumed to be more dangerous than the outer zone and could be easily avoided. All manned space flights performed so far have stayed in the clear space above the atmosphere and below the inner radiation zone, although Van Allen himself has stated that he does not

consider a quick penetration of the inner zone particularly dangerous. The outer zone is larger, more strongly curved, and apparently more diffuse, and it cannot be avoided by a spacecraft bound for the moon.

Because the belt is a mixture of electrons and protons that have been trapped by the earth's magnetic field, it is logical to assume that the trapped subatomic particles were originally members of solar flare clouds. The curved edges of the outer zone seem, from time to time, to touch the fringes of our atmosphere in the areas of the magnetic poles, and it is thought that this causes the auroras. Therefore, a particle that has been trapped in the outer zone does not stay there indefinitely, but the average time spent in the zone still has to be determined. Of the four bodies in space that have been investigated either directly or by space probe—the earth, the moon, Venus, and Mars—only the earth has been found to have a radiation belt. The conclusion is that of these four only the earth has a powerful magnetic field, but it is not yet known what factor is responsible for this condition.

Life Support.—Some aspects of life support are the same for missions of any duration. In each case the cabin temperature must be held within certain limits, with 70° Fahrenheit considered to be the ideal value. In each case the atmosphere of the cabin must be kept breathable, which is to say that it must contain about 20 per cent oxygen (if sea level pressure is maintained) and that excess moisture and carbon dioxide must be constantly removed. Sufficient food and drinking water for the astronauts must of course be available. The difference between the life support systems for short missions, up to ten days duration, and long missions consists in the engineering means by which these results are brought about.

■SHORT MISSIONS.—It is elementary to calculate the amount of oxygen, water, and food consumed per person during a twenty-four-hour period. This comes to about three pounds of food (pro-

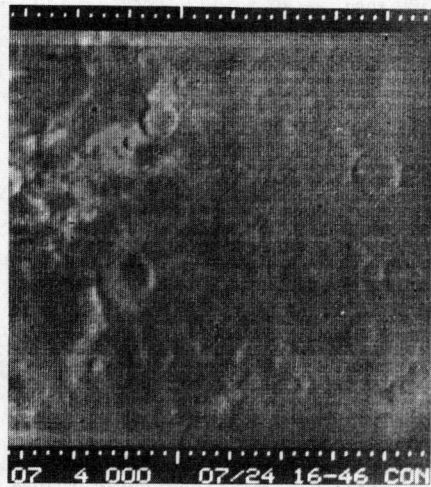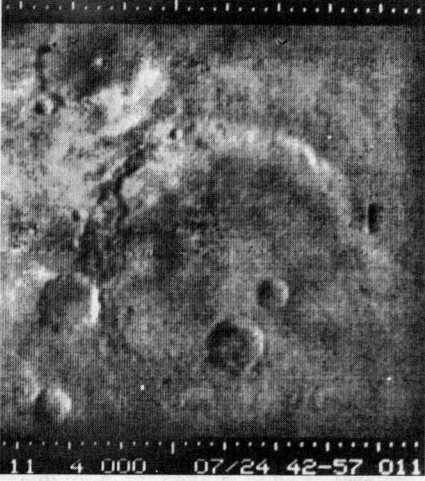

NASA

FIRST CLOSEUP PHOTOGRAPHS of Mars transmitted from the *Mariner IV* spacecraft. The photographs and the vast amount of data relayed from *Mariner IV* answered many questions about the distant planet; the data was invaluable for preparing the future manned trip to Mars.

cessed to eliminate all unnecessary weight and brought to the cheese-like consistency that is the most practical under zero-g), not quite a gallon of liquid, and less than a gallon of oxygen (if it is carried in liquid form). The main problem is the removal of waste matter. Here the ordinary body waste, which is caught and stored in plastic bags, is the simplest aspect. What is more difficult is the removal of the waste that contaminates the cabin atmosphere. Six-tenths of every quart of water a man drinks appears in the cabin atmosphere, partly through skin evaporation, but mainly by exhalation. Everyone knows how annoying high humidity is, so this water vapor must be removed, condensed into water, and stored. It is an interesting fact that a space capsule always ends up with more water than it started out with. Part of the food eaten by the men appears as water, the water being a type of by-product. The other waste material that contaminates the cabin atmosphere is carbon dioxide, which, while not poisonous in the strict meaning of the word, is quite insidious. Ground-based experiments with space-cabin simulators have shown that carbon dioxide, if not removed, results in lethargy and drowsiness. Test subjects simply insisted that they were going to sleep and refused to obey orders. Hence, the carbon dioxide content of the cabin atmosphere must be kept quite low (less than 1/10 of 1 per cent), and this is accomplished by absorbing the carbon dioxide with suitable chemicals.

For a short mission any attempt to reclaim something is meaningless, although it is, of course, likely that tests will be carried out on short missions *as experiments* in order to find good and efficient ways to do it. On a medium-short mission, one lasting more than one day but less than ten days, it is advisable to perform regular exercises in order to keep up the muscle tone. The stretching of rubber bands or steel springs is the simplest exercise, and adds the least weight. The astronauts could perform isometrics, the type of exercises that operate by playing one set of muscles against another set, but psychologically the stretching of springs or rubber bands, where the astronauts can see that something is going on, is a superior exercise.

The characteristic of the life support system for a short mission, then, is that it provides the astronauts with oxygen, food, and liquid in a *clean* atmosphere of a suitable temperature. But all the waste products are merely removed from circulation and stored to be brought back.

■ LONG MISSIONS.—The life support system for astronauts on a long mission has to do everything the short mission support system has to do, but it also has a few additional jobs. For example on a 250-day mission to Mars, boredom will be a very important factor. Even with the most rigorous system of inspection and testing, the working time of an astronaut will hardly be more than four hours per twenty-four-hour period. This means that entertainment, in the form of reading matter, music, and, if possible, movies, must be provided, all of it reduced to the smallest possible size and least possible weight. Another thing that has to be done is to provide what, for want of a better term, is referred to as *artificial gravity*. This could be done by separating the return stage of the rocket system, which would still be full of fuel, from the personnel capsule, connecting the two by a wire rope of adequate length, and then setting the two bodies to spinning around their common center of gravity. In this way centrifugal force would provide pseudo-gravity, which would make living more convenient. It is not necessary that this pseudogravity reach the value of 1 g, for one-third of 1 g would probably be sufficient.

For long missions it will also pay to do some reclaiming of waste matter, particularly of the carbon dioxide. There are chemical means of breaking down the carbon dioxide molecule (CO_2) into its components so that the oxygen can be re-released into the cabin atmosphere. The present methods are fairly clumsy, and it will be necessary either to refine them or to find a new one that can be used inside a spaceship. If external power is available—for example, solar energy collected by a paraboloid mirror mounted outside the ship—it would be comparatively easy to produce oxygen and hydrogen from the surplus water. The oxygen would be retained for breathing, while the hydrogen could be vented into space. A life support system for long missions would thus be characterized by reclaiming some of the waste matter and by jettisoning some of the other.

The ideal situation is, of course, what is known as a *closed ecological system*. Green plants take in carbon dioxide and give off oxygen during photosynthesis. Thus, to green plants carbon dioxide is food, just as is the more solid human waste. It is theoretically possible, therefore, to establish just the right balance, with plants absorbing the carbon dioxide, releasing fresh oxygen, and also utilizing the solid waste as fertilizer for growing edible fruits or parts. Such a completely closed system, however, is too heavy and requires too much room to be used in a moving vehicle. It is a good possibility, however, for a stationary establishment, such as a base on the moon or an outpost on Mars.

—Willy Ley

NASA

A GEMINI SIMULATOR, an essential instrument in the space program, provided training for the Gemini flight crew prior to the actual flight.

PUBLIC HEALTH

Public health, as defined by C. E. A. Winslow (1877–1957), is "the art and science of preventing disease, prolonging life, and promoting physical and mental efficiency through organized community effort for the sanitation of the environment, the control of community infections, the education of the individual in principles of personal hygiene, the organization of medical and nursing services for the early diagnosis and preventive treatment of disease, and the development of social machinery which will ensure to every individual a standard of living adequate for the maintenance of health."

Life Expectancy.—Accomplishments in the field of public health are reflected by the increase in life expectancy. In the United States the *average life expectancy* at birth is now 67 years for males and 73 for females. In contrast, it averaged only 50 years at the beginning of the twentieth century; a century ago it averaged only 40 years. Looking ahead, it is estimated that the average American born in the year 2000 will live to the age of 82, and one born in the year 2400 will normally reach the age of 100.

Although life expectancy has increased conspicuously in recent years, the natural span, or limit, of life has not changed appreciably. Barring "unnatural" death from disease or injury, man's lifetime is now, and always has been, about 100 years. This is the *biological limit* of human life. Although there have been reports of people living for 150 years and more, these cases lack scientific confirmation.

Traumatic Injuries. — Accidents are among the greatest public health problems in the world today, in terms of both disabilities and deaths. In the United States, accidents kill nearly 100,000 people each year and injure another 10,000,000. More than a third of these deaths and injuries are caused by motor vehicles, and another third occur in the home. Altogether, accidents are fourth on the list of the leading causes of death in the United States, being exceeded

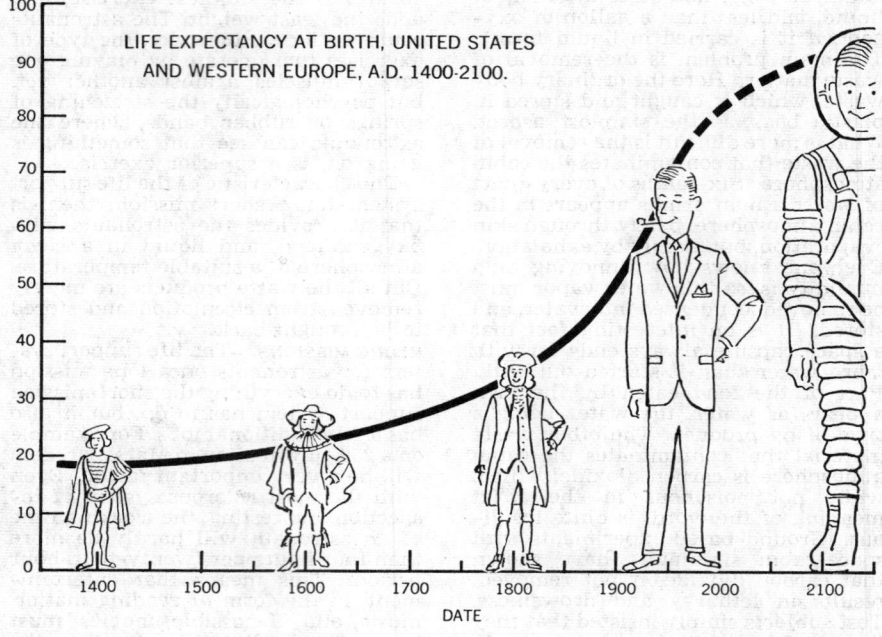

LIFE EXPECTANCY AT BIRTH, UNITED STATES AND WESTERN EUROPE, A.D. 1400-2100.

DATE

CAUSES OF DEATH IN THE UNITED STATES, 1961
(From data furnished by the National Office of Vital Statistics.)

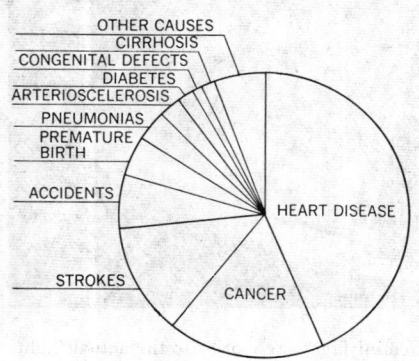

OTHER CAUSES
CIRRHOSIS
CONGENITAL DEFECTS
DIABETES
ARTERIOSCLEROSIS
PNEUMONIAS
PREMATURE BIRTH
ACCIDENTS
HEART DISEASE
STROKES
CANCER

only by heart disease, cancer, and strokes.

Among the other forms of violent death, suicides account for about 20,000 deaths each year and homicides for 9,000 more. Disasters, including fires, floods, windstorms, earthquakes, explosions, droughts, famines, epidemics, and extremes of heat and cold, account for about 1,000 deaths annually in the United States.

Wound Infections.—Accidental injuries are often complicated by invading microorganisms; these wound infections may prove more lethal than the traumatic injury itself. Such infections are responsible for about 4,000 deaths per year in the United States.

Staphylococci are the most common bacterial invaders but generally give rise to only localized lesions, described as *ordinary abscesses.* These specific microorganisms have proved susceptible to some of the newer antibiotics. However drug-resistant strains are emerging that are more difficult to control.

Streptococci are also fairly common secondary invaders. These bacteria tend to diffuse deeply into the tissues, leading to a generalized *sepsis* or *septicemia* (blood poisoning). Such complications of wounds were once so common that a minor scratch or simple surgical procedure would frequently prove fatal. At present, however, these infections are comparatively rare and can usually be controlled by the sulfonamides and antibiotics.

Tetanus (lockjaw) is still another type of wound infection. Although uncommon, it is a most excruciating affliction and ultimately kills half of its victims (250 deaths in the United States each year). Tetanus can easily be prevented by active immunization, provided it is initiated a month or

more before injury. The causative agent of tetanus is a microorganism present in ordinary soil, particularly soil fertilized with animal manure. When they are introduced into a puncture wound, in which most of the air is excluded, the organisms multiply and produce an extremely virulent toxin that then diffuses through the body, causing tetanic muscle spasms and other symptoms of the disease. At this point the only recourse is treatment with *specific antitoxin* (passive immunization), produced by actively immunizing animals and utilizing their serum. This treatment is not always successful, however, and the animal serum itself sometimes causes serious and even fatal reactions. In contrast, the *tetanus toxoid* used to produce active immunity is harmless because it is not an animal-serum preparation. Ideally, everyone should be immunized against tetanus as a child and thereafter should receive occasional booster shots. Such immunization will reduce the risk of this dread malady, but proper surgical management of wounds remains a necessity.

Infectious Diseases.—Progress in the extension of life has been due chiefly to the discovery of the specific causes and controls of infectious diseases. Recognition of microorganisms as a cause of disease and the application of control measures in the fields of environmental sanitation and immunization have advanced human welfare further during the twentieth century than has anything in the previous thirty centuries. Since those most susceptible to infectious diseases are infants and children, the life expectancy of the young has been increased about twenty years since the beginning of the twentieth century; that of adults over fifty, only about two years.

The conquest of disease has not only prolonged life but has also improved the general health of the individual during his entire life. An appraisal of the extent and degree of illness (*morbidity statistics*) is not as simple as counting the number of deaths (*mortality statistics*); nevertheless, there is abundant evidence of a tremendous improvement in man's general health. Even with this improvement, however, many health problems still remain to be solved. The World Health Organization lists the six major health problems as tuberculosis, malaria, venereal disease, malnutrition, mental illness, and environmental sanitation.

Airborne Infections.—Most of the common acute communicable diseases are classified as *contact infections* and *airborne infections,* as indicated by their modes of transmission. As a group they may also be described as *respiratory diseases,* because they involve various parts of the respiratory tract and are generally spread by discharges from the nose and mouth. They account for the largest proportion of disabling illness among persons of all ages, particularly among children. In the United States this group of diseases takes 100,000 lives

LOS ANGELES AIR POLLUTION CONTROL DISTRICT

AIR POLLUTION in cities such as smog-bound Los Angeles jeopardizes the public health.

annually. Control measures depend largely upon whether the causative agent is virus, fungus, or bacterium. ■INCUBATION PERIOD.—The *incubation period* of an infection is the time between its entry into the body and the appearance of the first symptoms. As a rule, *viral infections* have an incubation period of from 10 to 14 days (with the exception of the common cold, influenza, and cowpox, which have an incubation period of from one to three days). Most bac-

terial infections have an incubation period of from three to five days, with the exception of rheumatic fever, tuberculosis, and leprosy, which may evolve insidiously (without symptoms) over a period of many days. *Fungal infections* have an incubation period extending over a period of weeks.

■TREATMENT. — There is no specific treatment for most viral infections, but the majority of the bacterial infections and some of the fungal infections yield to the newer sulfonamides and antibiotics. Most viral infections produce a lasting immunity so that a second attack is unusual. But most bacterial and fungal infections do not produce a lasting immunity; repeated attacks can occur.

■CARRIERS.—The ultimate source of almost all infections is man himself, although animals may share a few of the bacterial and fungal infections. Viral infections usually arise from *active cases*—patients with obvious symptoms. Most bacterial and fungal infections arise either from active cases or from *carriers*—people who are infected but appear to be healthy.

Disease Control.—The control of infectious diseases involves an understanding of them and the application of the following measures.

■ISOLATION. — Patients with obvious symptoms should be isolated and precautions taken so that objects contaminated by them (*fomites*) are not contacted by others. Isolation rather than strict quarantine is now common practice, with a possible exception in cases of smallpox. Detection of healthy carriers (as in diphtheria) and *case-finding* (as in tuberculosis) are considered good public health practices. Likewise, the reporting of all cases of infectious

diseases to the local health department and surveillance by authorities to prevent epidemics are important control factors.

■DECONTAMINATION.—Contamination of the environment should be reduced. The practice of spitting must be condemned because *droplet nuclei* disseminated into the air by coughing and even by ordinary breathing are important factors in the spread of disease. Efforts should be made to provide proper ventilation, dust control, and the sterilization of indoor air by means of sunlight, ultraviolet light, and chemical aerosols. Avoidance of crowds, particularly indoors, is encouraged; avoidance of known patients and carriers is essential.

■RESISTANCE.—Resistance to infection should be maintained. Specific immunization for smallpox, diphtheria, poliomyelitis, whooping cough, and influenza should be a routine precaution. Vaccination against measles, tuberculosis, and certain respiratory diseases should also be considered. Although vaccination is compulsory in many countries, it is considered good public health practice in the United States to urge rather than to force immunizations. Other measures that reduce susceptibility to infections are adequate rest, exercise, recreation, and a proper diet. At the same time, allergies and other conditions that predispose a person to infections should be kept under control.

Problems of Nutrition.—Nutrition may seem to be an unimportant consideration to most Americans, but for two-thirds of the world's population the primary objective in life is getting enough food to maintain life. The world has never had enough to eat, nor will it in the immediate future. Even the modern miracles of science that have advanced food technology at a rate comparable to nuclear and space explorations have not kept abreast of the population explosion. Recent studies have revealed that at least 800 million people around the world are constantly faced with the prospect of starvation.

■MALNUTRITION.—The United States, in contrast, has such an abundance of food that millions of tons can be exported annually—and yet surveys indicate that the diets of more than half of the population are inadequate in some respect. Many people in the United States, through whim, fad, custom, or ignorance, become the victims of malnutrition. Nutritional deficiency diseases are very common, and even overt clinical cases are frequently observed; a surprising number of deaths are directly attributable to malnutrition.

■DIET.—An optimal diet must fulfill many criteria. It must, first of all, satisfy the appetite. Second, it must meet the caloric needs of the body in order to supply sufficient heat and energy for movement, thought, growth, and replacement of tissue. An average adult needs about 3,000 calories a day. (If this amount of calories was converted into heat energy, it would be enough to raise the temperature of eight gallons of water from 32° to 212° F.; if converted into work energy, it would be enough to lift a 150-pound person 60,000 feet.) An optimal diet must also contain the correct amounts and combinations of carbohydrates, proteins, fats, minerals, and vitamins. Most of these essentials may be obtained by eating a combination of dairy foods (including milk, cheese, ice cream, and butter), meats (including fish, poultry, and eggs), vegetables and fruits, and breads and cereals (particularly the whole-grain and enriched varieties).

■**VITAMINS.**—Although a diet made up of the above foods could fulfill the body's needs, it would not necessarily provide adequate amounts of certain minerals and vitamins—notably iron, iodine, calcium, and vitamins B_1, B_2, and C. A simple solution is to supplement natural foods with manufactured concentrates. Natural foods, however, are still the best source of vitamins and minerals; too often people take vitamins as a substitute for a balanced diet instead of using them only as a supplement.

■**EDUCATION.**—On the whole, proper nutrition depends largely upon the application of exact knowledge of food substances rather than upon the dictates of appetite, custom, habit, or fad. Although many public health agencies now disseminate diet information, education is badly needed.

Digestive Disorders.—An average, nutritionally correct diet may be inadequate for an individual who has an imperfect digestive system or defective endocrine system. As a rule, digestive and endocrine disorders are not readily controlled by the same type of organized efforts that are so effective in reducing infectious diseases and nutritional deficiencies. The control of digestive and endocrine disorders depends largely upon early diagnosis and appropriate treatment rather than upon specific preventive measures. Exceptions to this generalization are numerous, as may be illustrated by the many inflammatory diseases of the intestinal tract that result from the ingestion of irritants, such as foods that are too hot, too cold, too highly seasoned, or too coarse. Likewise, it is possible to control uses of excessive alcohol, laxatives, or cathartics. Emotional stress plays an important role in some digestive disorders; in others, heredity may be a significant factor.

Food Poisoning.—Afflictions associated with the ingestion of food can be serious and sometimes fatal. In recent years such afflictions have become less common, yet almost every person will experience at least one attack of food poisoning in his life.

■**STAPHYLOCOCCUS.**—At present, most cases of food poisoning are caused by a toxin that forms in foods contaminated by certain strains of staphylococcus bacteria. Nausea, vomiting, and abdominal cramps soon follow the ingestion of such contaminated foods. "Staph" food poisoning is associated mainly with prepared foods containing meat, eggs, or milk that have been seeded by the discharges from skin lesions, nose, or throat and

then have been allowed to incubate at room temperature. There is no specific treatment for this type of food poisoning and no immunization against it, although the hazard may be reduced by carefully protecting prepared foods from contamination, especially by refrigerating them.

■**BOTULISM.**—One type of food poisoning that has received much publicity because of its high fatality rate is botulism. Fortunately this disease is very rare. Botulism results from an enterotoxin produced by germs that remain viable in improperly processed canned foods. These germs are found in soil (particularly soils fertilized with animal manure) and are therefore usually associated with certain garden vegetables. The bacteria are spore-forming and cannot be destroyed by ordinary cooking; but the enterotoxin that they produce is heat-labile and can be destroyed by reboiling home-canned foods immediately before serving.

■**CHEMICALS.**—Another type of food poisoning can result from chemical contamination. Chemicals are often introduced into food unwittingly; for example, zinc poisoning can result from the ingestion of an acid food that was packed in a galvanized (zinc-coated) metal container. Chemical poisoning also occurs when a toxic chemical is confused with an edible one, as when cockroach powder is mistaken for baking soda.

The public has long been concerned with the detrimental effects of insecticides, preservatives, and other chemicals used in the production and processing of food products. In the United States this concern led to the enactment in 1906 of the Pure Food and Drug Act, and subsequently to its numerous amendments and to new laws. Enforcement of these regulations by the Food and Drug Administration (F.D.A.) and other federal, state, and local authorities, combined with the voluntary efforts of the food manufacturers themselves, has virtually eliminated any major hazard of food poisoning by chemicals.

■**PREVENTION.**—Extreme care in the procurement, processing, preservation, and preparation of food products is essential to the prevention of the various types of food poisoning and food-borne infections. Milk and meats deserve special attention because they deteriorate very rapidly. The pasteurization of milk by heating (143° F. for 30 minutes) is a practical means of eliminating disease-producing microorganisms that may have originated with the cow or have been introduced during later processing. Most meats are inspected by the U.S. Department of Agriculture's Bureau of Animal Industry, acting under the Meat Inspection Act of 1907. But even the most meticulous inspection of meat cannot guarantee its purity, and it is therefore imperative that all meats be cooked adequately before being eaten. The cooking of meats and other foods has probably prevented more illness than any other single public health measure. Proper refrigeration of foods is also important. However, refrigeration merely inhibits the growth of microorga-

nisms, and even frozen foods cannot be considered free of pathogens (disease-causing bacteria or viruses). In contrast, canned foods that are properly processed are sterile because they have been subjected to temperatures sufficient to destroy microorganisms. Even the spore-forming bacteria that cause botulism can be eliminated through the pressure-cooking routine in commercial canning.

Filth-borne Infections. — Typhoid fever and similar infectious diseases are spread from person to person, and occasionally from animal to man, by the contamination of food and drink by intestinal wastes. These diseases are among the most common and universally distributed of all afflictions, but prevail mainly in areas where sewage is improperly treated. Throughout history these diseases have plagued armies in the field and have often played an important part in determining the outcome of wars. Today the degree of civilization of an area can be measured by the incidence of filth-borne infections.

ANNUAL DEATH RATE PER 1,000 FROM DISEASE, INJURY, AND BATTLES; U.S. ARMY.
(From data furnished by the Surgeon General.)

■**AGENTS.**—Specific agents responsible for filth-borne diseases include the typhoid bacillus; the Salmonella that cause paratyphoid fever; the Shigella that cause the bacillary dysenteries; the Vibrio that causes Asiatic cholera; a number of viruses that cause polio, infectious hepatitis, and some forms of enteritis; many intestinal protozoa that cause the amoebic dysenteries; a formidable list of roundworms, including the common pinworm and hookworm; and flatworms, including the flukes and tapeworms.

■**CONTROL.**—Although immunization is of some value in the prevention of certain of the bacterial and viral filth-borne diseases, control measures are largely dependent upon the proper isolation of infected persons, sanitary disposal of body wastes, protection of food and drink from contamination, pasteurization of milk, and purification of water supplies. Treatment with the newer sulfonamides and antibiotics has some limited success, and some anthelmintic drugs are effective against certain of the worms. Prevention, rather than treatment, however, is the great challenge.

Water Supplies.—Communal water supplies are generally derived from lakes, rivers, and streams that are exposed to contamination by all types of filth, including the fecal wastes of animals and humans. Thus, all surface water must be considered as potentially dangerous and should be properly treated before ingestion. Procurement of an adequate supply of potable water is largely an engineering problem, but safety of the water is of immediate concern to health authorities.

■TREATMENT.—The usual treatment of a public water supply consists of these steps: aeration, chemical treatment, sedimentation, sand filtration, and chlorination. First, the water is aerated by spraying it into the air, where it loses objectionable tastes and odors. Chemical treatment follows, involving the addition of alum, lime, or other agents that cause the aggregation of suspended particles; these are then heavy enough to settle out. Next, the supernatant fluid is passed through a bed of sand and gravel to remove any remaining particles. Finally, a small amount of chlorine is added to purify the water as it flows to the consumer.

Sewage Disposal.—Proper sewage disposal is a major public health problem closely akin to that of a pure water supply. Here the problem is basically one of avoiding direct contamination of oneself, food, and drink with fecal wastes. This problem is largely controlled by the chemical treatment and removal of the solids from sewage, and the terminal disinfection of the effluent waters. While the water carriage system of waste disposal is commonplace today, the method is only about 100 years old. At present, about 25 per cent of the urban communities in the United States still have inadequate sewage treatment facilities.

Arthropod-borne Diseases.—More than half of all human misery and death may be attributed to insects and other arthropods.

■FLIES.—It is difficult to conceive of a better transient mechanical disseminator for disease germs, especially those of filth-borne diseases, than the ordinary fly. The fly's intestinal tract can carry a four-day food supply and still have enough room left for 20 million disease-causing pathogens. The bristled hair on the fly's body and its sticky foot pads can transport just as many pathogens. While many of the 100,000 known species of flies are transmitters of fecal-borne diseases, the common housefly is the greatest menace to human health because of its close association with man. In summer the housefly's life expectancy is about two months, but those that hibernate during cold weather may survive nine months or more. During her lifetime, a female fly will lay from six to ten batches of a hundred or more eggs, usually in the feces of man and animals or in decaying organic matter. The cycle from egg to larva to pupa to adult fly is about a week.

■INFESTATION.—Larvae, or maggots, of many species of flies are dangerous to human health because they invade living tissue, causing a condition known as *myiasis,* or fly infestation. Some eggs or larvae may be ingested with food or drink and develop within the human intestine, although

FLIES spread cholera and typhoid fever.

myiasis of the genital and urinary tracts is also possible. Many species of maggots invade the nose, sinuses, eyes, ears, and open wounds. Myiasis in any of these locations may produce festering, deep, disfiguring wounds that exude a bloody, foul pus.

■FLY CONTROL.—Control should begin early in the breeding season. Common methods within the home include the use of screening, flypaper, fly swatters, and insecticides. Ordinary cleanliness, however, is the most important control measure. Elimination of feeding and breeding grounds requires the proper disposal of garbage and body wastes. Insecticides, such as DDT, are useful in controlling flies, but environmental sanitation is more important.

■MOSQUITOES.—While most flies act as transient mechanical disseminators of filth-borne diseases, other arthropods also transmit disease. The bloodsucking *Anopheles mosquito,* for example, first infects itself and then infects a human host. Anophelene mosquitoes are *vectors* of malaria, a dread fever that leaves its victims frail, anemic, and wasted. Malaria attacks 100 million people yearly and kills more than a million. Fortunately, rigid control of the mosquito vectors has virtually eliminated this disease from the United States, but even temporary neglect of control measures would soon result in a resurgence of the widespread malaria epidemics

PHILIP GENDREAU

RODENTS transmit at least 18 diseases.

that once plagued the entire country. Other mosquitoes are vectors of yellow fever, dengue, filariasis, and some viral encephalitides (brain fevers). Of these, only the viral encephalitides are now of any great significance in the United States.

■OTHER ARTHROPODS.—Other arthropod-borne diseases are the flea-borne endemic typhus and bubonic plague. In addition, certain ticks are responsible for some spotted fevers, *Sarcoptes* mites are responsible for scabies (the so-called seven-year itch), and chiggers (immature harvest mites) are a common cause of skin irritation.

■RANGE.—Most arthropod-borne diseases are common in the tropics because the majority of insects and other arthropods flourish in warm regions and prevail in direct proportion to man's lack of control over them. (Louse-borne diseases are a notable exception. Lice flourish in the colder climes where more clothing is worn, thus providing the ideal circumstance for their propagation.)

■VECTOR CONTROL.—Control of all arthropod-borne diseases depends upon an exact knowledge of the habitat and life cycle of the vectors; the most effective control depends upon interrupting the vector's life cycle. Insecticides, fumigants, and repellents are useful. Of the insecticides, the *pyrethrums* are noteworthy because of their rapid "knock-down" effect, but DDT, although slower acting, is even more lethal. These chemicals, however, are dangerous and must be used very carefully.

■TREATMENT. — Specific treatment is available for a few of the arthropod-borne diseases. For example, quinine-like drugs are highly effective against malaria; and some antibiotics are useful against plague, yaws, and certain other diseases. For many of these diseases, however, there is no specific therapy; and for only a few, such as yellow fever, is immunization practical.

Animal-borne Diseases.—Animals are directly or indirectly responsible for transmitting more than 100 diseases; these are often transferred from the animal to a susceptible person by blood-sucking arthropods.

■RODENTS.—Rats and other rodents have always been a scourge of mankind, spreading terrible epidemics of disease and destroying or contaminating man's food. Rodents are responsible for the transmission of at least 18 diseases and, in the United States alone, destroy more than $2 billion worth of food and products yearly.

Rodent populations are limited primarily by the availability of food, so starvation should be a major part of any antirodent campaign. Rodent-proofing of buildings also limits the rodents' access to food and shelter, but poisoning is the simplest and most efficient method of control. The complete extermination of the species seems impossible, however, because wholesale killing gives the few survivors an easier life.

■LIVESTOCK.—One of the most significant animal diseases directly transmissible to man is *brucellosis,* a prolonged illness usually referred to as *undulant fever* and associated with cattle, goats, and swine. More than 5,000 human cases are reported each year in the United States; of these, about 80 are fatal. Transmission may occur by direct contact with infected animals or infected animal tissue, or by the consumption of unpasteurized milk and milk products. *Trichinosis* is an animal-borne disease that can be contracted from the ingestion of insufficiently cooked pork. *Tularemia,* a plaguelike disease, is usually communicated by direct contact with the tissue of infected rabbits. *Rabies,* or *hydrophobia,* is associated with the bites of certain infected animals, often dogs or bats.

Environmental Health Hazards.—*Radiation* is an important environmental health problem. There has always been some natural radiation in the environment, including that from radioactive substances found in rocks and soils, such as uranium and radium, as well as cosmic rays and other types of radiation from outer space. But man-made radiation, consisting of the radiation from medical and dental X-ray and fluoroscopic equipment and the much-publicized fallout from nuclear explosions, has become the major cause for concern in recent years. While overexposure to these types of radiation is potentially dangerous, the average person presently receives no more radiation from these man-made sources than from the natural sources. A number of research groups are now studying the effects of radiation on humans and animals. These studies center on the genetic effects (cell mutations) and long-term influences of both the natural and man-made forms of radiation.

■**PESTICIDES.** — Agricultural chemicals are another environmental threat to human health. Recent reports have asserted that pesticides are polluting rivers, destroying wildlife, and generally upsetting the balance of nature; however, many of these reports tend to give insufficient consideration to the benefits gained from the use of pesticides. Actually, modern agriculture depends heavily on the use of pesticides, and millions of people

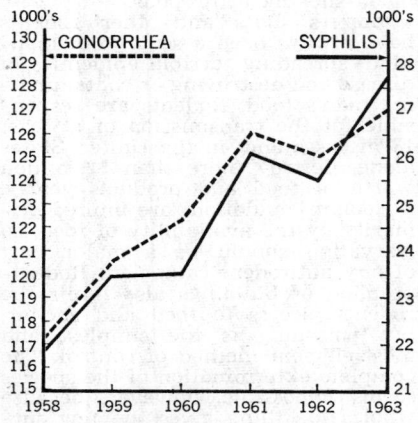

VENEREAL DISEASE has steadily increased in the United States. A major part of this increase was in the 15–24 age group.

are alive today only because of the chemicals used in suppressing the vectors of malaria, yellow fever, and typhus. At the same time, there are nearly 100 deaths a year in the United States that are caused by pesticides; most of these are the result of improper use. While pesticides at present constitute no great hazard, there still is need for continued government regulation of their production and use.

■**AIR POLLUTION.**—A major public health problem that increases with industrialization is *air pollution.* In the eastern sections of the United States, coal smoke and sulphur dioxide are the most common pollutants; in the western part of the country, pollutants arising from petroleum refining, chemical and metal manufacturing, and rubbish incineration are the major contributors. Automobiles are a ubiquitous source of impurities. Much thought is being given to the problem of air pollution, and most large cities now have active control programs.

■**CHEMICALS.** — Acute poisoning from ingested chemicals is a common medical emergency. During the first six months of 1961, 6,414 cases were reported in New York City alone. Internal medicines are the agents most frequently responsible; but topical medicines, cosmetics, detergents, insecticides, bleaches, solvents, disinfectants, and polishes are also involved. The number of potentially toxic substances in the home increases daily with the continuing advances in the synthesis and distribution of new chemical compounds. A *poison-control center* was opened in Chicago in 1953, and since then almost 500 more officially recognized centers have been established.

The first step in the treatment of poisoning cases is generally to empty the stomach by inducing vomiting. If the poisonous agent can be identified, the correct antidote can be given; for this reason, physicians usually request that the container with the remains of the poison be brought with the patient. It has been suggested that *ipecac* or a similar natural emetic be added to potentially dangerous preparations so that ingestion will induce vomiting at once.

■**GASES.** — Carbon monoxide is the most common poisonous gas, causing more fatalities than any other form of chemical poisoning (although many of these deaths are suicides rather than accidents). It is colorless, tasteless, and odorless; this imperceptibility, combined with the fact that the gas is found in the exhaust fumes of virtually every furnace, stove, and engine, makes carbon monoxide particularly dangerous.

Sociosexual Problems. — The venereal diseases are a major threat to health in every country of the world.

■**SYPHILIS.**—The most serious venereal disease is syphilis, an unremitting, progressive disease that caused 2,850 deaths in the United States in 1964.

The first symptom of syphilis is a painless, ulcerated sore, or *chancre,* on or near the genitals. Prompt treatment with penicillin at this stage

will render the individual noninfectious and will usually result in a complete cure; if neglected, the disease lapses into a secondary stage within a month. This stage is characterized by disseminated eruptions that may occur anywhere on the body and resemble many other skin conditions. The symptoms of secondary syphilis are often mild, but can be distressing. After about a year the disease lapses into a late stage characterized by destructive lesions, or *gummata,* which may affect any tissue or organ system of the body. Some complications of late syphilis include heart damage, blindness, paralysis, and brain damage. The late stages of syphilis are usually noninfectious, except in the case of a pregnant woman, who may transmit *congenital syphilis* to her child at this stage. Both the congenital and late forms of syphilis have, through the use of penicillin and other antibiotics, become uncommon in recent years in the United States.

■**GONORRHEA.**—A more common but less dangerous venereal disease than syphilis is *gonorrhea,* characterized by an inflammation of the mucous membranes of the genital organs. More than 1½ million cases are reported in the United States each year. Gonorrhea has a low case-fatality rate, but can produce a variety of serious complications, including infertility. In its early stages, gonorrhea may be easily controlled by penicillin and other antibiotics and by sulfonamides.

■**MINOR DISEASES.**—The three minor venereal diseases—*chancroid, lymphogranuloma venereum,* and *granuloma inguinal*—are "minor" only in contrast to syphilis and gonorrhea.

■**CONTROL.**—The control of venereal diseases centers on the detection and treatment of existing cases and carriers. Since infected persons are the only known source, or reservoir, early recognition and treatment of these cases offers the best chance of curbing the spread of infection. There is no active means of immunization, nor are convalescent cases immune to reinfection. The spread of venereal diseases can be lessened by the use of mechanical and chemical prophylaxes but depends upon social mores.

Maternity.—In addition to the prevention, control, and treatment of traumatic injuries and specific diseases, public health is concerned with the general daily welfare, physical as well as emotional, of the individual from the time of birth. Public health progress in the United States is reflected in the decrease in maternal and infant mortality.

■**MATERNAL MORTALITY.** — Before 1930 about 60 mothers died per 10,000 births; today maternal mortality is 2 per 10,000. (There were 1,350 maternal deaths in the United States during 1963.) The chief causes of maternal deaths, in descending order of magnitude, are hemorrhage, toxemia, abortion, infection, and ectopic pregnancy (a pregnancy outside of the uterus, as for example, in the Fallopian tube).

■**INFANT MORTALITY.**—There has also

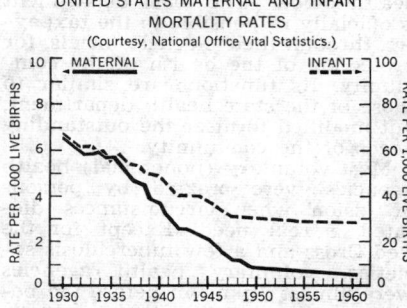

UNITED STATES MATERNAL AND INFANT
MORTALITY RATES
(Courtesy, National Office Vital Statistics.)

been a consistent reduction of infant mortality. In 1915 the death rate of infants under one year of age in the United States was about 100 per 1,000 live births; it is now less than 25 per 1,000. The majority of infant deaths occur within the first month of life as the result of (in descending order of magnitude) premature birth, congenital malformations, infections, and birth injuries. The extent of the existing infant mortality problem, however, may be judged from the 102,800 infant deaths in the United States in 1963 and from the fact that the toll is even higher in less developed countries.

■PREGNANCY.—A further reduction of infant and maternal mortality rates, as well as of birth abnormalities, can be insured if, as soon as pregnancy is suspected, the mother seeks competent medical supervision. Diet, rest, and moderate exercise are important during pregnancy, and an adequate intake of calcium, iron, protein, and selected vitamins should be carefully maintained for the benefit of both mother and developing child. This is particularly important, because during pregnancy eccentricities of the appetite may occur, resulting in vitamin deficiency. Extra precaution should be taken to avoid infectious diseases, particularly German measles, a disease that, when contracted during the first three months of pregnancy, may cause congenital abnormalities in the unborn child.

■CHILDBIRTH.—Birth complications affecting the infant are far more common than those affecting the mother. Of the 4 million births annually in this country, 80,000 (or 2 per cent) are stillbirths (babies born dead whose period of gestation was over 20 weeks). Since the hours of labor and childbirth and the days following delivery are very critical for the baby, modern facilities and expert medical attention are imperative.

■FEEDING.—Milk from the mother's breast has many advantages over a prepared formula, but breast feeding is not always possible, due to an insufficient milk flow, infections, or other complications involving the mother's breasts. When natural feeding is possible, it should be continued until the infant is six months of age. If a cow's milk formula is substituted, boiling the milk makes it safe and more digestible. Formulas usually consist of milk, water, sugar, and vitamin C and D supplements.

■EDUCATION.—Programs that aid in insuring the proper care of babies de-

serve a high priority in community public health efforts. Those not able to afford the services of a private practitioner should be able to obtain competent help from public clinics and health departments.

Childhood Health Problems. — Dental health is of particular concern to a growing child, but diseases associated with the teeth are not limited to any one age group. Although diseases of the teeth are rarely a direct cause of death, they do contribute to ill health. The health of the entire body depends upon the maintenance of sound teeth and, conversely, the soundness of the teeth depends largely upon the health of the rest of the body. Although at least 90 per cent of the people in the United States have significant dental disease, only 25 per cent of these are getting reasonably adequate dental care.

Dental caries (cavities), the most common dental disease, are a curse of modern civilization. Primitive people, sustained by relatively crude diets, suffered less tooth decay than does modern man. Some factors involved in dental caries are diet, oral hygiene, and mechanical defects.

■FLUORIDES.—The amount of fluorides ingested with food and drink has recently been shown to be of great significance; drinking water containing one part per million of fluoride dramatically reduces the incidence of dental caries, as has been demonstrated in numerous communities where the fluoride content of the water has been controlled at that level. Excessive fluorides found in some natural waters may give rise to a harmless condition known as *mottled enamel*, characterized by teeth that appear to be stained brown.

■EYES AND EARS.—The eyes and ears, vital to lifelong welfare, are very susceptible to various afflictions during childhood. It is important, therefore, that abnormalities be detected and treated at an early age, when chances for correction are greatest.

Loss of sight or hearing means personal tragedy to the individual and a burden to society. There are at present some 260,000 blind and 57,000 totally deaf persons in the United States; some impairment of vision is present in nearly half the population, and at least 3 million persons are handicapped by impaired hearing. Diseases of the eyes account for about 50 deaths in the United States each year, and diseases of the ears for about 600. Disorders of the nervous system can adversely affect the sensations of sight, sound, taste, smell, and touch. Protection of every part of the nervous system is one of the foremost objectives of preventive medicine and public health.

Mental Health.—Of every 100 American children of school age, 13 will fail to reach emotional maturity, 8 will be shattered by emotional breakdowns, 4 will be confined in mental hospitals for a time, and 1 will turn to crime. It is estimated that half of all the persons seeking medical treatment are suffering emotional upsets, while nervous disorders alone or in

combination with organic disease account for about 70 per cent of the medical cases being treated.

Of the 15 million United States draftees examined for military service during World War II, nearly 2 million (37 per cent) were rejected on the grounds of neuropsychiatric disorders; even after this initial screening, 39 per cent of all servicemen receiving medical discharges were classified as psychoneurotics. At present, more than 625,000 patients with nervous disorders occupy half the available hospital beds in the United States, and approximately 140,000 more need institutional care. Nearly 300,000 persons are admitted to mental hospitals annually; two-thirds of these are first admissions. This figure is expected to increase by 20,000 each year. Since the duration of treatment is usually so long, the burden of hospitalization would soon bankrupt most patients and their families. Therefore, the increasing responsibility for the care of the mentally ill has fallen to hospitals supported by public funds; at present, about 87 per cent of mental patients in the United States are cared for in state-maintained institutions. Although expenditures connected with disorders of the nervous system now exceed $200 million annually, another $500 million is needed to provide for a reasonable standard of treatment and care. Diseases affecting the nervous system account for 13 per cent of the deaths in the United States, collectively ranking second as the leading cause of death and being exceeded only by heart disease. Other deaths attributable to mental disorders during 1965 were 21,507 suicides, 10,712 homicides, and 2,665 fatal cases of alcoholism.

Problems of Later Life.—In 1900, 18 per cent of the people in the United States were over 45 years old; today 30 per cent are in this group, and estimates indicate that by 1980, 40 per cent of the population will fall into this category. At present, 10 million persons in the United States are over 65 years of age. Accompanying this rapid increase in the number

Fight
mental
illness

Help the mentally Ill

Join
and Support your Mental Health Association

NATIONAL ASSOCIATION FOR MENTAL HEALTH

POSTER urges all to fight mental illness.

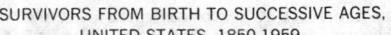

SURVIVORS FROM BIRTH TO SUCCESSIVE AGES,
UNITED STATES, 1850-1959.

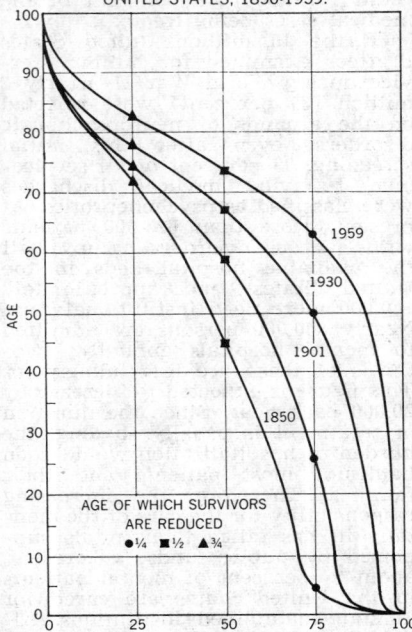

SURVIVAL CHART shows survivors from birth
to successive ages. People are living longer
today than at any time in history. In 1901,
18 per cent of the people in the United
States were over 45 years old; in 1964, 30
per cent of the people were in this group.

of older people has been a corresponding increase of chronic illness,
disability, degenerative diseases, and
physical and mental impairment.
Seventy per cent of those permanently disabled and 50 per cent of the
chronically ill are over 45 years old.
The most important illnesses of this
age group are heart disease, arteriosclerosis, high blood pressure, nervous and mental disorders, cancer,
arthritis, diabetes, kidney disease,
asthma, and tuberculosis.

The intensity of the problems of
later life has awakened an interest
in *gerontology,* the study of the aging
process, and *geriatrics,* medical care
of the aged. Numerous voluntary and
official health organizations have concerned themselves with various facets
of these problems. Notable among
these are the American Heart Association, the American Cancer Society, the National Tuberculosis
Association, and the National Institutes of Health—the research arm of
the U.S. Public Health Service.

Promoting Health.—Although the people of the United States are among
the healthiest in the world, sickness
produces widespread suffering and
a heavy drain on the nation's productivity. Numerous surveys indicate
that on any given day approximately
1 per cent of America's people are
disabled in hospitals, 4 per cent are
disabled at home, 20 per cent
are suffering from nondisabling ailments, and 65 per cent are semiwell
or subwell. Only 10 per cent of the
population enjoys really good health.

During 1962 a patient entered some
hospital in the country every 1.2
seconds; 7,028 hospitals registered
with the American Medical Association admitted 27 million patients who
spent a total of 512 million days in
the hospital. This meant an average
daily hospital census of over 1.4 million persons. One-third of these
hospitals are tax-supported; their
average daily census represents almost three-fourths of the total.

The present proportion of physicians to the general population is
greater in the United States, with its
1 physician for every 750 persons,
than in any other country except
Israel. The distribution of physicians
in the various states differs from 1
per 496 persons in New York to 1
per 1,459 in Mississippi. As a rule
there is a greater concentration of
physicians in large urban areas, paralleling the hospital monetary resources of the community.

■COST.—Part of the problem of getting
satisfactory medical care is the practical aspect of affording it. Those who
need medical care the most are usually least able to pay for it because
the ability to earn money to pay for
the necessities of life, including medical care, depends upon the individual's health. Each year the costs of
illness must be borne by the 5 per
cent of the population unfortunate
enough to need medical care, and not
every family is able to set aside
money for the time of sickness.

Not only has the present system
of fee-for-service failed to provide
adequate medical care for all persons
in the low-income group, but it has
also failed to distribute good services to rural dwellers and to draw
the public away from quack doctors
and patent medicines. Moreover, it
has failed to develop preventive medical services in proportion to their
importance, as judged by the fact
that less than $2 per capita is spent
annually for public health measures
while the average person spends
nearly $135 for curative measures.

In spite of these serious defects
in the present system of medical care,
progress during the last century of
American history has been spectacular. It is debatable whether such a
record could have been accomplished
under any other system.

■FUNCTIONS.—Functions of the various
state health departments are very
much alike. Whether carried out by
separate departments or bureaus,
their activities generally include
statistical tabulation and analysis,
control of contagious diseases through
laboratory diagnosis and public
health nursing in homes and clinics,
promotion of maternal and child hygiene, environmental sanitation, food
and drug control, industrial hygiene,
and health education.

Local health departments are official agencies of local governments—
city, county, or district. Their power
is embodied in the charter of incorporation, which establishes the local
governmental unit and is supplemented by local ordinances and the
state health code; this is done
through delegation of authority from
the state health officer to the local

health officer. The local department
is officially responsible to the taxpayers, through their elected officials, for
protection of the health of the community. Its functions are similar to
those of the state health department,
but modified to meet the outstanding
needs of the community.

Most voluntary (nonofficial) health
agencies were created by persons
of vision when circumstances dictated a real need. Except for the
Red Cross and a few tuberculosis societies, voluntary health agencies
were almost unknown before the beginning of the twentieth century.
Now there are more than 50,000 such
organizations.

Public Health Agencies.—Development
of state and local public health
agencies in the United States has
been gradual. The first local board
of health was authorized in 1797 in
Boston, Massachusetts, with Paul
Revere as its chairman. The first
state board of health was that of
Massachusetts in 1869; the last state
health department to be organized
was that of New Mexico in 1919.
Baltimore, Maryland, was the first
large city to organize a full-time
health department (1798), although
several smaller cities had established
part-time services earlier.

At present, no single agency of the
United States government is responsible for public health. Instead, many
agencies are individually concerned
with the health and welfare of the
people. The primary objective of most
of these is to provide services to the
various state governments in order to
aid them in carrying out their individual programs. Notable among
these are the Department of Health,
Education, and Welfare, the Department of Agriculture, the Department
of Defense, the Atomic Energy Commission, and the many branches of
the Veterans Administration.

The U.S. Public Health Service, a
major division of the Department of
Health, Education, and Welfare and
one of the oldest governmental
agencies, was organized in 1798 as
the Marine Hospital Service. Over
the years its responsibilities have
been extended to practically all
phases of medical care, preventive
services, and related research.

The first international public
health agency, the Egyptian Quarantine Board, was established in 1831
to control plague and other infectious
diseases then prevalent in the Mediterranean area. Its scope was enlarged with the opening of the Suez
Canal in 1869. The Pan-American
Sanitary Bureau, established in 1902,
was the first international health
agency to involve many nations of
the western world. International conferences held in Europe at intervals
beginning in 1851 culminated in the
establishment of the International
Public Health Office in 1909. The
Health Organization of the League
of Nations, organized after World
War I, was succeeded in 1948 by the
World Health Organization, a specialized agency of the United Nations.

—William Stiles

Study of history	963	Chronological history		
Archaeology	967	of the world	1027	
Ancient civilizations	972	Parallel outlines of		
Oriental civilizations	976	American History	1060	
The Middle Ages	982	Major wars	1071	
Modern Europe	986	Chronological tables of		
The United Nations	990	rulers	1078	
History glossary	994	Bibliography	1081	

VOLUME THIRTEEN

HISTORY

GREEK NATIONAL TOURIST OFFICE

History

INTRODUCTION

The word "history" means two distinct things. It means the past and all that happened in the past. It also means the record of the past—all the artifacts and monuments of the past and all that men have said and written of the past. Sometimes it is said that these things are much the same, that the past exists only in our record of it and that without such records there would be no past. But the past is not dependent upon us for its existence. It existed in its own right, and it happened even though historians failed to record it.

The historian who discovers new material about the past, who fills in some gap in our knowledge, does not create that past. But by discovering some lost ingredients or by illuminating dark areas, the historian can "remake" the past. History is there, it did occur, but the memory can be jogged, the consciousness can be stimulated, the image of the past can be evoked and sharpened and even changed. When the historian does these things, he makes history.

A people without an awareness of their history is like a man without memory—condemned to make the same discoveries that had been made in the past, invent the same techniques, wrestle with the same problems, and commit the same errors. History, in this sense, is the most essential ingredient of civilization. But memory is a fitful and constantly changing thing. History, however, is *organized* memory, and the organization is all important. As organized memory, history takes innumerable forms and serves almost innumerable purposes.

FORMS OF HISTORY

STORY. History is first a story. That was its original character, and that has continued to be its distinctive character. The "father of history," Herodotus, who wrote in ancient Greece during the 400s BC, had a story to tell—the struggle between the Greeks and the Persians—and he told it superbly. So, too, did his great successor Thucydides, who gave us the story of the Peloponnesian War. Livy and Tacitus, greatest of the Roman historians, were incomparable storytellers. So, too, are most of the great modern historians.

Although history is a story, it is not a made-up story. It is the story of what happened in the past or, more

accurately, of what the historian is able to recover and reconstruct of what actually happened, usually but a meager part of the whole story. History, thus, is a record.

RECORD. History collects and organizes the facts that are available and seem relevant, provides them with some kind of framework, and lays down guidelines for their presentation. It supplies order, harmony, and direction for what would otherwise be a chaotic assemblage of miscellaneous facts. Facts are the raw materials of history, just as marble is the raw material of sculpture, and the hand and mind of the historian are required to transform this raw material into something that has meaning.

The record has serious limitations, however, and so does the ability of the historian to organize that record. First, the record is incomplete. Much that happened in the past was not recorded, and much that was recorded was lost. There are, for example, immense gaps even in the records for the French Revolution and the U.S. Civil War. And what of the record of the American Indians before the coming of Columbus? What of the record of the peoples of Africa or of much of Asia? They had just as much "history" as had any other people, but very little of the record has survived.

The record is also lopsided and biased. We have no assurance that what was important always survived or that what survived was really important. Much of the record was destroyed, either by accident or by intent. Much of it has simply been lost. But even the records that have survived are often biased, indeed sometimes falsified. No two accounts of an automobile accident are alike, for example, and how can we expect 20 accounts of the Battle of Gettysburg to be alike? Each one will have its own point of view, its own bias.

We must also keep in mind that history is usually written by the victors, not by the vanquished. It is the Roman version of the conquest of Britain that has come down to us, not the British, and the European version of the conquest of the Americas, not the Indian.

History as record involves three processes. The first is the collection of relevant facts, but what seems relevant to one person may well appear irrelevant to another. The second is the organization of the facts into a coherent pattern, but no two patterns are ever quite the same. The third process is the interpretation of the facts and of the pattern, and no two interpretations are ever exactly alike.

None of these processes is wholly under the control of the historian, who usually uses facts others have gathered for him. He organizes these into patterns familiar to him from a thousand other books of history—the patterns of chronology, geography, politics, or race imposed upon him by his society. Even his interpretations depend on the frame of reference within which he writes. This is why a medieval and a modern historian interpret their material so differently, why a Chinese and an English historian may interpret their material so differently.

ART. The third quality of history is history as an art. History is a branch of literature, and most historical writing called "great" or put into the category of "classics" has literary and artistic distinction. Literary history is not just a matter of fine writing, however, for no amount of fine writing can make up for serious deficiencies in scholarship or in critical intelligence.

Literary style is a matter of the tone, the color, and the movement of the narrative. It is a matter of symmetry, concentration, unity and harmony, and the imagination that suffuses the whole. It is a matter, too, of artistic integrity, for although the style should be suited to the materials the materials should never be forced to fit the style.

PHILOSOPHY. The fourth aspect of history is history as philosophy. Most of the great historians have thought of history as "philosophy teaching by examples." It is only recently that historians have been tempted to discard this traditional function of history. But the public still wants philosophy with its history, and many of the most popular historians of our time, including Winston Churchill, Oswald Spengler, and Arnold Toynbee, wrote history as philosophy.

SCIENCE. No one can seriously dispute the claim of history to be story, record, art, and philosophy. But what of the claim to be a science as well? History is not a science in the sense that biology or chemistry are sciences. History cannot submit its data to scientific experiments, it cannot repeat its own experiments, and it cannot control its materials. Yet history tries to use the scientific method. It tests all things that lend themselves to testing and holds fast to what appears to have been proved true.

But the scientific method is valid only in the formal and somewhat elementary areas of history, never in the basic areas. History can prove by the scientific method that John Wilkes Booth did shoot President Lincoln in Ford's theater in Washington, D.C., on the night of Apr. 14, 1865. But the scientific method does not take us beyond that. Why did Booth do it? Who, or what, was responsible for his action? What were the consequences of the act? These, the really significant questions, cannot be answered scientifically.

TECHNICAL HISTORY. Disillusioned with the claims of scientific history, some modern historians have settled for what we may call technical history. The technical historian, much like a biologist or chemist, takes problems one by one, the smaller and more manageable the better, and works them out. He believes that if enough historians work tirelessly at enough problems, we may in time get a firm foundation from which to generalize safely.

Technical history distrusts the dramatic and detests generalizations. It avoids narrative, and its characteristic form is the monograph. It is impatient with the notion of history as literature and rejects the notion of history as philosophy.

USES OF HISTORY

What is the use of history? This question inevitably confronts everyone who proposes to read, study, or write history. In a practical way, history has no use. It is good for nothing that can be weighed, measured, or counted, and it will not guarantee any concrete results. But the same can be said for many other things society cherishes—for music, for art, for much of literature, for a rose garden or a Persian rug. Happily, there are other meanings to the term "useful."

History is useful in the sense that art, music, and poetry are useful—perhaps even in the sense that religion and philosophy are useful. None of these provides answers or guarantees results, but without these things life would be poorer and less meaningful.

REWARDS. If history does not have measurable use, it does have rewards and values; we may even call them pleasures. The first and perhaps the richest pleasure of history is that it adds new dimensions to life by extending our horizons and enlarging our experiences. It permits us to enter into the past, to project our vision back over thousands of years, and to enlarge our vision to embrace all the peoples of the earth.

This enlargement of experience carries with it a second pleasure, or reward. History provides us with great companions, and wherever the historian or the biographer has been, he has given new depth and range to our associations. History admits us to the company of a Thomas Jefferson and a John Adams and allows us to know them more intimately than their contemporaries did, for we can read their letters, diaries, and journals.

History also adds a new dimension to places. It allows the reader to travel in time as well as in space, to know not only contemporary Britain but Roman Britain, not merely the Florence of today but the Florence of Michelangelo. Finally, history enables us to know ourselves. Knowing yourself means knowing what you can do, and the only clue to knowing what a man can do is knowing what man has done.

LESSONS. It is far more difficult to go beyond pleasures of history to the lessons of history. For centuries men have sought in vain to learn the lessons that history taught. It is not that they failed to find lessons, or even "laws," but that they found so many. History "teaches" pretty much what historians or those in authority want taught, and so-called "laws" of history turn out, more often than not, to be the formulation of the desire or will of some dominant group—a church, a party, a nation.

Over the years history has been made to serve every imaginable cause. Southern planters used the history of Greece and Rome to justify slavery, and Adolf Hitler prostituted history to prove the superiority of the "Aryans," or the Germans, over all other peoples. But history has other and better uses than those of propaganda or self-justification.

PERSPECTIVE. History develops certain attitudes and encourages habits of thought. It reminds us that time is long and life is short; that each generation has deluded itself into believing that it was the end and object of history; that men have known crises before, and turmoil and war, and have survived; that those problems that loom so large on our own horizon may not even be visible on the larger horizon of history.

History reminds us that the world is large and not subject to our desires. It tells us that one people and then another, one nation and then an-

THE METROPOLITAN MUSEUM OF ART, GIFT OF J. PIERPONT MORGAN, 1911
EGYPTIAN BAS-RELIEF depicts a great civilization that flourished over 3,000 years ago.

other, has moved to the center of the stage and then moved off into the shadows. It warns us that our habits and standards and values have no cosmic validity and that we cannot impose our will upon history. It advises us to be humble and to be patient with the errors of men and the failure of their institutions. At the same time it advises us to be impatient with simple answers and solutions that deny the complexity and intricacy of the historical process.

History teaches tolerance. It teaches tolerance toward different faiths, loyalties, cultures, races, and civilizations, and thus teaches the necessity of freedom for inquiry, for criticism, and for dissent. History assures us that mankind is neither the creature of iron laws over which he has no control, nor the victim of chance. It tells us that if we are not the complete masters of our fate, neither are we wholly the victims of fate. The individual counts and society is important. A Muhammad, a George Washington, a Mahatma Gandhi did make a difference in the course of history.

PROBLEMS OF HISTORY

Like all fields of learning that have developed over the centuries, history bristles with problems. There are problems of the authenticity of documents, the authorship of papers or books, the credibility of witnesses.

There are additional problems of language, of interpreting texts, and of dating things. History also confronts us with the problem of interpretation —interpretation of the facts, of the causes, and of the meaning of events. Moreover, the historian himself is limited.

THE HISTORIAN. Try as he will, the historian can never be wholly objective or impartial. He is almost always a member of the upper or educated classes, and therefore represents a very small and very special group. How different would a history of the southern plantation system be if written by a slave? How different would be the story of the industrial revolution if written by an immigrant worker in a Pittsburgh steel mill.

Most historians also write, consciously or unconsciously, as members of a national group. Herodotus wrote of Greece as a Greek, and Tacitus wrote of Rome as a Roman. How different are histories of the United States written by Americans and by Russians, or histories of India written by Indians and by Englishmen.

The most difficult limitation on the historian is present-mindedness. We look at the past through the eyes of the present, judge it by our standards, and tend to forget that every "past" was the present to those who lived it. We fall into the habit of thinking that "Renaissance Man" should somehow live up to our notions of the Renaissance, that the Founding Fathers of the United States should always act out the role we have assigned them.

Closely related to the limitation of present-mindedness is the notion of inevitability. Because we know what happened in history, we are in the position of the reader of a mystery story who has read the last chapter first. Knowledge of the outcome discourages investigation into the causes of what we know happened.

All of these problems and limitations are the professional hazards to which the historian grows accustomed. More basic are two philosophical problems that have special fascination for the student of history—causation and judgment.

CAUSES. Why did history turn out the way it did? The search for the causes of things has long been a chief occupation of thoughtful historians. The Greek and Roman historians were inclined to ascribe whatever happened to the caprice of the gods. Medieval Christian historians saw whatever happened as the working out of the will of God.

The Enlightenment still explained history by a single cause, but it was the "law of nature," or sometimes "reason," in place of divine law. But the historians of the Enlightenment left no room for chance or for the role of the individual. It was the Romantic historians who introduced chance and emphasized the role of the individual—Thomas Carlyle, with his admiration for Frederick the Great; Jules Michelet, with his glorification of Joan of Arc.

The reliance on impersonal forces has continued to mark the search for causes. Some historians found the explanation of history in what they called "climate," a general term that embraced what we would include in the term "environment." Karl Marx founded a school of history that interprets most of the activities of men in terms of economic forces. The U.S. historian, Admiral Alfred T. Mahan, saw sea power as a determining force in history, and Henry Adams conjured up "force" to explain the happenings of history—first the force of religion, then the forces of coal and steam, and finally the force of the dynamo.

Beginning in the 1700s there came a "scientific" explanation—the doctrine of "progress." In the 1800s there appeared Charles Darwin's theory of evolution, which argued that through the operation of the law of the survival of the fittest there would come, in the end, a perfect adaptation of life to environment. Sociologists like Herbert Spencer and historians like John Fiske hastened to apply this thesis to history.

The evolutionists of the 1800s believed that man was the goal intended by "nature," not the production of any higher creature, and that the "perfecting of humanity" was to be the consummation of history. Gradually belief in progress and evolution faded, and the search for the causes of things continued. But the historians of the present recognize no sovereign explanation.

JUDGMENT. The second major philosophical problem of history is the validity of moral judgment. Should the historian expose "evil" and applaud "virtue"? Or should he seek to achieve complete objectivity, rigorously excluding personal, religious, national, and all other considerations that might affect his judgment? It is only in modern times that the question of moral judgment has come to the fore. Although the Greek historians did not concern themselves with it, judgment came to be one of the accepted functions of the historian with the Romans—Livy, Tacitus, and Plutarch.

Arguments for and against moral judgments are evenly balanced. Those who accept judgment as a proper function for the historian assert that it is the duty of the historian to hold up evil to reprobation and virtue to admiration. Those who reject the judicial function assert that the historian cannot pretend to objectivity or fairness, that he will never have all the evidence, and that there are no standards for judgment.

Moral standards vary from age to age and from society to society, and to apply the standards of our own time and society to wholly different times and places is grossly unhistorical. Those who reject the judicial function also assert that it is not the business of the historian to play God. Readers are perfectly capable of making their own judgments.

It is important not to confuse moral judgments with professional judgments, however. Within the field of his professional competence, the historian has the same responsibility as the judge, the physician, or the architect to give a professional opinion. The historian who has devoted years to the painstaking examination of the available evidence on a controversial issue, such as the origins of World War I, has not only the right but the obligation to give us the benefit of his professional judgment.

PHILOSOPHY OF HISTORY

Finally, we come to the vexatious question of the philosophy of history. The term itself is ambiguous. It may mean the philosophy the student brings to the study and interpretation of history. Or it may mean the philosophy the student reads out of history and to which he himself may conform. It may even mean both.

The very phrase "philosophy of history" conjures up the system-makers of the past who formulated full-scale philosophies of history and then demanded that history march to their commands. In the 500s, St. Augustine determined that history was the working out of the will of God, and in the 1800s, Georg Wilhelm Freidrich Hegel saw history as the history of freedom culminating in the present.

As we look at these and other philosophies of history we can only conclude that it is futile to try to compress the vast and complex stuff of history into any single framework. It is futile not so much because we have failed to solve the enigma of history, but because there is no solution and possibly no enigma except one of our own making.

If we cannot impose our patterns and our meanings upon history, perhaps history can impose some patterns and meanings upon us. For just as Everyman is his own historian, so Everyman is his own philosopher.

—Henry Steele Commager

HELEN BUTTFIELD

TEMPLE AT LUXOR, EGYPT, built in 1400 BC, was entered through these columns, which still stand and are important to archeologists.

Archeology (from Greek *archaia*, "ancient things," and *logos*, a "study" or "science") may be defined as the scientific study of the material objects left behind by ancient man. As the term is at present used, it comprises the study of nothing beyond the "works of men's hands," and it thus rejects such elements as ancient literature and the skeletal remains of early man. At the same time, the archeologist is obliged, from the very nature of the case, to make the greatest possible use of literary accounts, where they do exist, for the purpose of bringing light to bear on obscure archeological problems; and the evidence that is supplied by paleontology and many others of the sciences must not be neglected in archeological pursuits.

The field of archeological research is essentially the world, at least all parts of it where the foot of earlier man has trodden. In time, it covers the period that begins with the "eoliths," or the dawn stones, the first attempts of man at fashioning stones into hand implements, and ends with the Middle Ages. Indeed, it has been extended by some authorities to include the medieval period and even the modern world to the end of the 18th century.

The scope of archeological investigation is vastly more extensive in time if not in area than that of history. Hence, it is infinitely too vast to be comprehended by any single mind. Accordingly, archeologists are found divided into groups by periods or by geography: Classical (Greece and Rome), Egyptian, Mesopotamian, American, etc. Besides, archeologists devote themselves each to a special field of study: architectural, ceramic, numismatic or epigraphic, as they are interested in buildings, pottery, coins or inscriptions, respectively.

The purpose of archeology is to paint a clear picture of ancient cultures. For the prehistoric period (earlier than about 3500 B.C.), we are dependent entirely on the material things that the hands of man have fashioned. The historic age is illuminated by literary accounts, almost all so aristocratic in tone that they give a one-sided picture of the early civilizations. Archeology helps to correct this distorted view, for it investigates, quite impartially, the remains of temples and palaces and the ruins of the poor man's hut. In the archeological museum, we find, not only splendid sculptures and paintings, but humble earthen vessels, axe-heads, household utensils and many other objects that are useful rather than decorative.

Because it studies all available material that has been shaped by the hand of man throughout the ages, archeology is the most comprehensive and the most variegated of the sciences. It is the most useful aid that historical research can employ. On the material side, its discoveries furnish our museums with works of art that are often priceless in themselves and indispensable to a proper understanding of mankind's development in culture and civilization.

The course of man's existence upon earth may be divided into many periods. Of these the most important may be thus distinguished: (1) The Paleolithic, when the chief tools used by man were fashioned from stone by the process of chipping and flaking. The home of Paleolithic man was in the forest, in caves, or more commonly, in rock-shelters where the dampness of the cave was avoided. (2) the Neolithic, when the stone implements were ground and polished, as in the case of the American Indian cultures. In this era the arts of the potter originated, and agriculture came to be practiced in a small way. The dwelling of man was now the daub-and-wattle hut or the log cabin. (3) The Bronze Age shows distinct advance in the crafts and arts. The potter's wheel is invented and the Neolithic village is replaced, in some regions, by the town or city. (4) The Iron Age, when men came to appreciate the value of this metal which had, indeed, long been known but used mainly for ornament. This age merges with the Modern.

It is impossible to assign to these periods of time dates that are of much more than local significance. As an illustration, it may be noted that the Neolithic Age, which came to an end in Crete about 3000 B.C., persisted in America till the coming of the white men more than 4,500 years later. The cultures of the Americas never had either a Bronze or an Iron Age but skipped from Neolithic to Modern.

Chief among the materials that one may expect to find in an archeological excavation are pottery and architectural fragments. Archeological research on any period later than the Paleolithic is based on pottery. It is everywhere found, it is indestructible and it presents so many varieties of textures and decoration that it provides in itself a history of the cultural development of a given people. Architectural materials are to a considerable extent perishable. Nothing survives the action of time but stone, stucco, cement, mortar, terracotta and baked brick. The crude, or sun-dried, brick that was so much used in antiquity for building purposes comes to light almost invariably as a disintegrated mass of earth. Coins are of great importance, where they do occur, in establishing chronologies, but they are found little before 700 B. C. Dates are fixed by Carbon 14 dating, the astronomical dating of old sun temples and star temples, and the tree ring dating of Indian ruins. Paintings seldom survive, though the Bronze Age in Crete and Greece and the historical period of the Roman world provide us with sufficient examples of frescoes and mosaics to enable us to appreciate to some extent the details of this art. Weapons, offensive and defensive, household utensils and implements of agriculture are universally found. Inscriptions are of the greatest value to the historian and the student of social sciences, but they are found only among the remains of more advanced civilizations.

The method of discovering ancient sites is interesting. In the case of almost all the important cities of antiquity, the identity of their sites has never been lost; often, as with Rome and Athens, the original name has never been altered. But there are many lesser towns of the historical period, which were long ago covered up and the names forgotten. These we may identify through inscriptions found on the site. Light may be thrown likewise on the same point by the discovery of large numbers of coins the majority of which attest the ancient name.

But there are also many settlements, largely prehistoric, of whose name and fame we have no knowledge, although the exploitation of their ruins may prove of the highest archeological importance. Some of these, unsought by the explorer or excavator, we come to know of through the casual diggings of peasants who unearth objects of value that they offer to dealers in antiquities, and thus the secret is revealed. Sometimes the accumulated debris of the town forms a mound whose contours are unmistakable to expert eye.

Since World War I, air photography has proved useful in revealing the existence of ancient graves, earthworks, roads, systems of cultivation and even settlements. Where these are completely covered with earth, faint elevations and depressions may be left on the surface that will, in the early morning and late evening, throw shadows deep enough to be picked up by the camera of the airman. Ancient disturbances of the soil, for whatever purpose, seem to leave their inevitable traces in the plain, chiefly in the variegated colors of the vegetation, which the modern film and lens have no difficulty in differentiating. In a heavily forested country it is of course useless to attempt to photograph from the air.

The photographic process has been used with much success in Palestine and elsewhere in the Near East where so many objects of interest lie beneath a coating of sand. A recent report declares that a part of the original Mason and Dixon Line has been discovered in this way.

In excavating a site, the actual work of digging is performed, not by the so-called excavators, but by native workmen under the control of a native foreman. At the head of the party is the Director who must possess a working knowledge of the various types of material that are likely to be unearthed and some experience in the scientific principles of excavation. He is supported by a staff of experts, each of whom pursues some special task: surveying the site at all depths of progress, photographing the site and the finds, making drawings and plans.

KENAN T. ERIM

ARCHEOLOGISTS RECREATE a colonnaded market from columns excavated at a site in Turkey of an ancient Greek colony.

It is the desire of every archeologist that the site he is investigating may present an undisturbed system of stratigraphy. That is to say, that the spade may unearth a regular series of layers each of which houses the remains of its peculiar culture; and that it may not happen that the inhabitants have on occasion resorted to levelling the ground or to any procedure that results in confusing the various layers. When a layer or stratum containing a certain style of beads, pottery, figurines is replaced by one that shows materials of a wholly different type, the inference is that we have to do with an invasion and a resettlement of the site by outsiders. Frequently the hostile nature of their coming is heralded by traces of fire. Peaceful penetration reveals itself in other ways. It is clear that the record of the site must be read from beneath upward, or in an order that is the reverse of that in which excavation proceeds.

The immediate concern of the party is that records be kept of the progress of the excavation through (1) photography and (2) the surveyor's transit and endless measurements, with the results transferred to the chart. The exact distance between find and find must be recorded, their distance below the surface of the ground, and their distance above or below an ideal plane or *datum* level. Moreover, all recovered objects must be carefully preserved and catalogued immediately. The ideal excavation is so conducted that the excavators could, if called upon at a later date, restore every object found to its original position in the earth.

The second phase of archeological research is the work of a specialist in some particular field—architecture, pottery or sculpture—who devotes long and careful study to the accumulated material that belongs to his own department. Vase is compared with vase, coin with coin, sculpture with sculpture, and from the investigation there emerges a definite knowledge of each particular find, its chronology, importance, style and relation to other examples of the same type or to closely related types. This study is called *typology*.

The preliminary study of the excavated material is carried out partly —as with architectural remains and large and heavy sculptures—in the excavation itself, partly in an adjoining *excavation house*, which serves as a temporary shelter for the party of excavators. Publication of the new discoveries soon appears in the learned journals, generally in the form of brief summaries. Preliminary reports of a more detailed sort may be prepared entirely at the site of the dig, but these are seldom definitive. It is a matter of years—sometimes unfortunately many years—before the final publication of the material in large and sumptuous volumes. The knowledge thus acquired from the excavation of the site is gradually absorbed into the vast stream of historical and cultural research.

With regard to the final disposal of the various excavated objects this much may be observed: remains of buildings are, as a rule, left where they are found, though a particularly fine capital or moulding may be removed to a place of greater safety. Local museums absorb material of minor or local interest. The prize pieces are usually claimed by the national museums of the countries to which they belong. But as foreign scholars play such an important part in excavation, there is frequently an agreement by which a certain part of the spoils is assigned to the particular foreign institution that has assisted with money and expert advice.

When did the science of archeology originate? The answer to this question can be no more definite than one about the origin of the natural sciences. Each science moves from loose and vague beginnings in the direction of an ever increasing severity of accuracy. The *Society of Antiquaries* in England was formally constituted as early as 1717 and the *Society of Dilettanti* was founded in 1733. These learned bodies interested themselves in inquiries and theorizings that may be called archeological pursuits, though the methods employed seem to us today almost absurd. And it was not until the '70s of last century that such truly scientific organizations as the *Archaeogical Institute of America,* the *German Archaeological Institute,* and the English *Society for the Promotion of Hellenic Studies* came into being. As regards scientific excavation, it began not much, if at all, before the '90s.

We may now undertake a brief archeological survey of the most important regions of the earth. In Egypt, one of the two cradles of civilization, archeological activity began in the days of Napoleon. His great military expedition of 1798 was accompanied by a party of scientific men whose labors resulted in the first adequate description of Egypt and its monuments. The key to the ancient languages of Egypt was found through the discovery, in 1799, of what has come to be called the "Rosetta Stone."

Such was its importance that it was demanded of Napoleon and ceded by him to Britain in 1801 and is now in the British Museum. It bore three inscriptions: in Greek, demotic (the language of the common people) and hieroglyphics (the tongue of the priests and aristocracy), each written in its own characters. The Greek inscription contained a decree of the priests in honor of Ptolemy V (204–181 B.C.) and his queen. The others proved to be replicas of this decree, in the two current languages of the country. But in spite of what we might superficially regard as the obvious simplicity of the undertaking, it was not till 1821—and largely through the genius of the French scholar Champollion who compared this inscription with many others that he had copied—that the demotic and hieroglyphic versions were read by scholars.

A century of patient investigation in Egypt has thrown an extraordinary light on the ancient conditions of the country. In the popular mind, this culminated in the opening of the tomb of Tutankhamen in 1922. But in spite of the extraordinary wealth of its contents and the fact that its inner chamber had been veiled for over 3000 years from the eye of man, the discovery was hardly of first-class archeological importance. Considered much more important by the Egyptologist is the study of the Badarians—a Neolithic people who occupied the Nile Valley for perhaps 1500 years before the Egyptians.

One of the first great archeological undertakings was carried out in Mesopotamia, the second land to foster incipient civilization. Current archeological interest is centered, in the main, in this region and the territory lying to the east of it. The great Assyrian city of Nineveh, which was captured in 606 B.C., seems to have fallen so rapidly into oblivion that its very site was unknown two centuries later. This city was sought and found by the English archeologist, Sir Henry Layard, in the middle of the 19th century, and the excavations of Henry Creswicke Rawlinson and others, carried on sporadically over half a century, revealed to the world a new and distinctive civilization. An extended series of discoveries made known the course of the cultural and political history of the Mesopotamian valley during the 2,000-year-period that preceded the time of Christ.

The reading of the riddle of the cuneiform or wedge-shaped characters of the languages of Mesopotamia and Persia proceeded in a way somewhat different from that of the Egyptian. The inscriptions at the great Persian city Persepolis were copied and thus made accessible for study in 1765. The work of interpretation was carried onward by many scholars, notably those of Denmark, France and Germany. In course of time, it was recognized that the official inscriptions of Persia were trilingual—expressed in Persian, Susian and Babylonian.

The Persian was the first to be deciphered. Fortunately, the investigators were familiar, from literary sources, with the high-sounding titles arrogated to themselves by the Persian kings. It was observed that the inscriptions contained many instances of a certain word, in a short and a longer form. It was proposed that these might well stand for "king" and "kings" respectively, and when they occurred together, they signified "king of kings." After this beginning it was easy to infer—on historical grounds—that the king was Darius. Soon the name of his father Hystaspes and his son Xerxes was read, and much progress was made before Major (afterward Sir) Henry Rawlinson, who has been mentioned above, copied and interpreted the inscriptions of Hamadan and Behistun. By virtue of this man's extraordinary linguistic ability—he was not a professional scholar—the remaining difficulties were cleared away, and ancient Persian became an open book. The key to the cuneiform script having been thus found, it was not long before Susian and Babylonian yielded their respective secrets.

Shortly after World War I an expedition commenced operations on a site on the lower Euphrates, 100 miles south of Babylon. This was soon definitely identified as the "Ur of the Chaldees" which is so often cited in the Old Testament as the home of Abraham. The results obtained at Ur and in the surrounding terrain are the most remarkable in the present century. This was the cradle of the great Sumerian culture which preceded the rise of the Babylonian Empire and which outshone, in many ways, the culture of Egypt.

The Sumerians' origin is as yet unknown; all that can be said is that this people appears to have migrated from the northern highlands and to have settled a large portion of Mesopotamia before 3500 B.C. They seem to have been the first people to become expert in the smelting of metals. Their mythical ancestor was perhaps the Biblical Tubal-Cain, "an instructor of every artificer in brass and iron." They invented a military organization of great efficiency. Their objects of art, particularly those that are found in the royal tombs, are sumptuous beyond measure. Gold and silver cups, weapons of copper, silver and electrum (an alloy of gold and silver), mosaic standards and alabaster vases are found in these sepulchres. The sculpture is remarkably realistic, especially where it depicts animal forms.

Further to the east, the land of the Medes and Persians is gradually yielding up its secrets. Particularly is this true of the city of Persepolis where the great palace of the Kings has recently been unearthed by an American expedition. Far beyond the Persian plateau, in western India, the widespread influence of Sumerian culture has been clearly demonstrated, particularly by the excavations at Mohendyo Daro and Harappa. It is plain that there was intercommunication between western India and Mesopotamia in the third millennium before Christ. These early people of India had a well developed system of writing.

Turning westward, we find that archeological discoveries of the highest importance are being made in Syria. Two sites in particular claim our attention. At Ras Shamra, on the northern coast, there has been unearthed a curiously mixed culture that flourished more than a thousand years before Christ and that contains elements derived from Crete, Cyprus, Mesopotamia, Rhodes and places even more remote. The literary interests of the city are extraordinary; various alphabetical systems have been discovered and even dictionaries with Babylonian words and their equivalents in an unknown tongue in parallel columns. Eastward, on the banks of the Euphrates, at Dura-Europos, Yale University and the French Academy of Inscriptions and Letters started in 1928 to conduct a series of joint excavations.

Until captured in the year 256 A.D., Dura was an important frontier post of the Roman Empire. It was much influenced by the neighboring Parthians and their successors, the Persians. Both these peoples attained preëminence in military science, particularly in the invention of improved defensive armor. Armor has been found and excavations reveal a military mine and a countermine in which are the bodies of several Roman soldiers. Many fine frescoes and painted

THE METROPOLITAN MUSEUM OF ART
ARTISANS AT WORK: Egyptian wall painting from the Tomb of the Two Sculptors in Thebes.

tiles have been removed to the museum of Yale University.

In the ancient Holy Land, there has been an almost feverish activity since World War I and the consequent improvement of political conditions. Site after site that is mentioned in Scripture has been explored and excavated, and a flood of light has been thrown on the history and cultural conditions of the Hebrews and their predecessors in the Holy Land.

In northern Syria we encounter the southernmost fringe of the great civilization of the Hatti, the Hittites of Scripture, whose empire at its widest limits included most of the territory between Armenia and the Aegean Sea.

The most important centers of the culture were at Eyuk, Jerablus (the ancient Carchemish), Marash, Singjerli and Boghaz-Keui (the ancient Hattosas). The last is the capital, where some 10,000 inscribed tablets have been discovered. Among the most important work done in Turkey in recent years, are the diggings at Karatepe. Here was found a bi-lingual inscription which for the first time made possible the understanding of the mysterious Hittite language. The Hittites were powerful from 2000 to 1200 B.C. and rivaled Egypt and Mesopotamian Kingdoms. Like the Romans, the Hittites adopted and absorbed ideas and institutions from the many peoples with whom they came in contact. Notable among their artistic achievements are their relief sculptures, sometimes remarkably alike in enterprise and grotesquerie.

At Hissarlik, in northwestern Asia Minor, Heinrich Schliemann, the German Homeric scholar, began his excavations in 1870. This, he was led to believe, was the site of ancient Troy, immortalized in the *Iliad* of Homer. His view has been confirmed by recent excavations conducted by the University of Cincinnati The Homeric city, as it now appears, was the seventh in order, counting the strata from the bottom of the hill upwards—not the sixth, as was long believed.

The excavations of Sir Arthur Evans on the Island of Crete were among the most important of this century. The diggings were completed before his death and there is no work being done on the Island now. The excavations revealed a Bronze Age civilization contemporary with Egyptians and Sumerians. Palaces with ivory statuettes, the delicate and highly ornamented pottery, the objects of gold, bronze, and silver, bear evidence to the former existence of a people light-hearted and artistic, revelling in the joy of life.

In Greece itself almost all the ancient cities of importance have been excavated, at least in part, and we we are now well informed, through the spade and the manuscript, of the progress of the country from Neolithic times down to the Middle Ages. Almost every town now possesses its museum of local antiquities, while the most important of the artistic and portable finds are transported to the National Museum in Athens.

The Athenians have given much thought, of recent years, to the scientific restoration of the ancient temples. The Parthenon, the gem of the Athenian Acropolis, has had its fallen columns and parts of its entablature restored to their original place, and the experiment has been made of erecting in the eastern gable copies of statues that used to adorn that area but are now in the British Museum.

A great archeological project of modern times was the excavation of the Agora, the civic square of ancient Athens; and the reconstruction of its most important building, the Stoa of Attalus. The Stoa was the shopping center and favorite meeting-place of the Athenians. The work began in 1931, but most of the restoration was accomplished after 1945 by Homer Thompson, an American. As far as possible the same building materials were used as in the original Stoa. Dedicated in 1956, the Stoa became the official Museum of Athens, housing 100,000 coins and 65,000 relics.

Between World Wars I and II, Italy encouraged archeological research within the country. Since the second World War, however, not too much work has been done there. The excavations at Minturnae by the American School of Classical Studies brought to light many interesting objects. There was also extensive archeological work done in the northern and central parts of Italy.

LOOK MAGAZINE

RUINS OF THOLOS at Delphi, site of the ancient Greek temple to Apollo. This circular building of unknown purpose originally consisted of 20 Doric columns surmounted by an architrave and a frieze. The three columns shown were reconstructed in 1938.

The area of Rome that is richest in ancient monuments has been completely transformed. Two great thoroughfares have taken the place of the former maze of streets. Excavations proper have revealed much that is new, and the process of clearing ancient buildings of their modern additions has gone far toward making their details understandable. The temple of Vesta, Forum Romanum and the Theater of Marcellus have been partially restored so as to make clear to the observer the precise nature of the construction of the whole. The great Imperial Fora have for the first time been thoroughly excavated, cleared, and exposed to the public view.

The chief archeological interest of central Europe is the culture of the Paleolithic period, where its development may be studied to the greatest advantage. Public interest in this culture is twofold: in the curious and apelike skulls of the Stone Age men (whose study belongs to the domain of paleontology and anthropology rather than archeology), and in the extraordinary drawings and paintings, chiefly of animals, that have been found in caves that long ago served as human habitations. The first find was made in 1879 in the now-famous cave of Altamira in northern Spain. Experts doubted that the paintings were prehistoric until the discovery in 1895 of similar art in the cave of La Mouthe, in France. Since then more cave paintings have been found in various parts of France and Spain and in the "heel" of Italy.

There is little of the spectacular in the ancient remains found in the British Isles, but they present a unique record of the activities of man from the type of perhaps half a million years ago, down through the Neolithic, Bronze and Iron Ages, and finally the 400 years of Roman occupation. In all this vast expanse of time, there is no one age or period of outstanding pre-eminence such as we find in the cultures of southern Europe and the Near East; but seldom has fortune provided us with an archeological laboratory so complete in its equipment as the British Isles.

The relatively primitive conditions of life in aboriginal America render the greater part of North America comparatively uninteresting from the archeological point of view. The culture of both American continents is uniformly Neolithic, varied in the more progressive areas by an elementary knowledge of metals on the part of the natives. In New Mexico, particularly in the vicinity of Santa Fe, where the School of American Archaeology has its headquarters, the Indians achieved considerable distinction in the arts of pottery and building; but the advent of the white man interfered with whatever progress they might otherwise have made in these and kindred crafts. The descendants of these tribes have imitated the arts of their forefathers instead of improving on them.

A feature of American antiquarian lore is the repeated revival of interest in the story that makes the Norsemen the original discoverers of America. This is brought about through the discovery, from time to time, of inscriptions in runic characters and other materials alleged to be genuine memorials of the Norsemen's exploration of the country. Inscriptions of this sort have been found all the way from No Man's Land, an island near Martha's Vineyard, to Spokane, Wash. Many of these are forgeries; for example, the Norsemen's inscription at Kensington, Minnesota, was proved by Erik Wahlgren to have been faked. Several genuine weapons of ancient Scandinavian manufacture have been found to the south of Lake Superior, but whether by fakery or not no one is sure. Vikings' graves, axes, shields, and swords have been found in northern United States and southern Canada. Archeologists find it difficult to prove or reject these discoveries, and final judgment about their genuineness must be reserved.

South of the Rio Grande, the most important culture as yet unearthed is that of the Mayas of Central America, who were displaced by the Toltecs in the 8th century A.D. The Toltecs gave way about 400 years later to the Aztecs, who have long been known from their contacts with the Spanish conquerors of America.

Despite their Neolithic limitations, the Mayas may well be regarded as one of the miracles of prehistoric times. Truly amazing are their achievements in pottery, painting, carving in stone and architecture. They possessed a fairly effective system of writing and a calendar that is inferior only to the Julian system of 46–45 B.C. Whence did they come? The guess that makes them the descendants of the mound-building Indians of the Mississippi Valley is perhaps the most likely of the several conjectures that have been advanced.

Relatively little is as yet known of the archeology of South America, as only the northern fringe has been investigated in any detail. The artists of early Peru are known for their extraordinary skill in linear design, but to what extent they were originators and to what extent they may have drawn upon the Mayas for their inspiration cannot be determined without much patient investigation in the years to come.

And thus the great quest for the recovery of things of the past goes on, a quest that, from the nature of the case, can never end. We have accomplished as yet but a trifle of spadework, for the science has hardly progressed beyond its infancy. It will be the task of future generations to carry on the search, ever expanding and deepening the scope of their activities.

BARBACHANO TRAVEL SERVICE

TEMPLE OF KUKULCÁN, or El Castillo, at Chichén Itzá, Yucatán, Mexico. This temple pyramid was built between the eleventh and fifteenth centuries and is dedicated to the feathered serpent god, Kukulcán. It is considered an excellent example of the Toltec period, when Mayan art and architecture were greatly influenced by the culture of the Itza, an invading people from the north. Unlike Egyptian pyramids, which terminate in a point, the pyramids of the Mayas were flat on top to serve as bases for altars or temples. This ancient religious structure measures 197 feet at its base and rises in nine receding terraces to a height of 79 feet above its stone platform. A diagram of the structure of this temple appears below.

CROSS SECTION OF EL CASTILLO'S INTERIOR: *a*, outer stairway; *b*, outer terraced face; *c*, inner stairway; *d*, inner terraced face; *e*, vestibule; *f*, sanctuary of temple where jaguar throne reposes. The jaguar throne, carved from a single block of stone and painted red is studded with inlays of green jade. Here the ancient Mayas of the region sacrificed to Kukulcán.

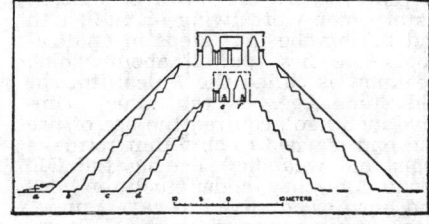

ANCIENT CIVILIZATIONS

Ancient history tells the story of man from his appearance on earth to the time of Christianity and the coming of the Germans in the Roman Empire. For convenience, it is usually divided into four parts—Prehistoric, Near Eastern, Greek and Roman. These civilizations overlapped in time and had a great deal of influence on one another. The center of activity in ancient times was the Mediterranean Sea. After the prehistoric Stone Ages, with the discovery of metals and the invention of writing, civilization began to develop rapidly in the the valley of the Nile and the fertile crescent formed by the coast of Syria and the great basin of the Tigris and Euphrates rivers. The lessons that the people in those areas learned were transmitted to the Greeks, who developed their brilliant culture in the lands surrounding the Aegean Sea.

Last among the great ancient peoples, the Romans entered the scene of history in the central Mediterranean peninsula of Italy and, after a brief period of growth and conquest, maintained control over the whole region around the Mediterranean, absorbing the culture of the East, remaking it to fit themselves and teaching it to the West. All ancient history treats a period when men were gradually mastering the methods of agriculture, industry and trade, political and social life and intellectual and artistic expression and were laying the broad foundations on which our own civilization rests. Most ancient peoples worshiped many gods; when Christianity won a victory over the pagan religions, the character of civilization was changed and the Middle Ages began.

Our information about antiquity comes first from the remains that have survived and are dug up by archeologists. Among these remains are tools, pottery, jewelry and clothing; the ruins or remnants of buildings, tombs, walls, roads and bridges; statues, reliefs, paintings and coins; and the skeletons and mummies of men themselves. These give us information about the appearance and the dress of the men and women of ancient times and about their abilities as workmen and enable us to picture the way in which they lived. In addition, we have, commencing with the time when writing began, all sorts of records written or incised on papyrus, stone, clay and the walls of buildings and tombs; and the works of literature that have come down to us. From them we are able to reconstruct the events and tell the story of the activities of the peoples of antiquity.

Prehistoric Times.—For many thousands of years before the dawn of written history men were living on the earth and taking the first steps in civilization. The first period about which we know is called the Paleolithic, or Old Stone Age. By that time, primitive men had acquired the use of fire and had learned to chip flint to make tools and weapons. During the Old Stone Age they added tools of bone and horn. They lived in caves, under overhanging rocks or in rude shelters; they gathered wild grains and fruits and secured their other food by hunting and fishing. Entirely dependent, therefore, on nature to supply their food, they worshiped gods who, they believed, helped them in their efforts to live. Skilled artists carved pictures on tools and painted likenesses of animals on the walls of their limestone caves. The examples found in the caves of southern France and northern Spain are often very beautiful.

In the Neolithic period or New Stone Age civilization took a great stride forward when men learned to farm and in some places learned at the same time to drain swamps and to irrigate dry lands. Animals were domesticated to serve men or to supply them with meat and milk. Storage receptacles were made of baskets and skins; then men learned to bake clay and make pottery. Weaving flax and wool led to the substitution of fabrics for animal skins as clothing. Chipped flint was still used for tools, but at this time hard stones were polished to make axes with fine edges and a variety of tools that had been impossible earlier. Houses were built; villages were founded and fortified, and complex social organizations were developed. Religions that sought to secure good crops and herds came into existence, and from the success of these agricultural experiences a strong belief in immortality developed.

When men learned to use metals—copper, bronze and later iron—the final stage in primitive culture was reached. At about the same time, priests worked out calendars to serve the farmers and devised systems of writing in response to the needs for records. Writing began with the drawing of pictures to represent objects and to tell stories. Then a picture came to be used to represent a sound (corresponding to a group of our letters), the sound of the name of the picture. Using several of these as parts of words, new picture groups made new words. Among the Egyptians, whose writing the Greeks called *hieroglyphics,* some characters were eventually used to stand for single consonants. Hieroglyphic writing contained all three—pictures of objects, of sounds and of single letters. The Egyptians wrote on strips pulled from the papyrus reed and pasted together. Later, they simplified their pictures, but they never developed an alphabet. Pictures were used also in Babylonia, and these in time came to represent syllables. The Babylonian writers drew with blunt-ended reeds on clay tablets that they afterwards baked. As a result, the picture element was lost. The lines thus drawn were wedge-shaped, and for this reason, Babylonian writing is called *cuneiform.* Shortly before 1000 B.C. the Phoenicians devised signs to represent single letters by using pictures to represent the first sound of the name of the object.

The Near Eastern Civilizations.—Written history begins with the great cultures of Egypt and Babylonia in the river valleys of the Nile and the Tigris-Euphrates. In these two regions of the Near East, the annual floods, when the river waters overflowed their banks and left a deposit of silt on the land, provided fertile soil. The needs of drainage (to draw off surplus water) and of irrigation (to wet the lands during the dry summer) required co-operation under strong and unified control. The rewards of labor, however, were very great, and men were able to accumulate wealth and to develop culture. Materials such as clay, stone, metal, wool and flax were at hand for the development of industry, and the rivers provided highways for trade.

Agriculture was the chief occupation, and men acquired skill in working the ground and producing wheat and barley and many vegetables. They tended goats, sheep and cows, ducks, geese and cranes, and used the donkey as their chief beast of burden. In addition, they snared wild birds, hunted animals and caught fish in the streams. They wove wool and linen for clothing and tapestries and made pottery, dishes and metal jewelry. In Egypt they made jars of the stone, which was plentiful, and used the papyrus reed not only for paper but for ropes, mats and even boats. Babylonia had little building stone or pottery but became famous for its fine carving of gems and seals and for its woolen goods. Trade passed not only on the rivers but on the roads developed through Syria and on the Mediterranean. The governments were all-powerful. In Egypt the king was regarded as a god; in Babylonia he was a priest-king, the earthly representative of the gods. Laws that regulated land ownership and tenantry, the practices of industry, and the methods of trade were developed and recorded. The code of Hammurabi, King of Babylon in the 20th century B.C., is the oldest surviving code of laws in the world. The people of both Egypt and Babylonia produced works of literature including much of great interest, as shown in the fragments that have remained—myths of gods and heroes, stories of adventure, collections of wise sayings, poems, prayers and hymns—the Egyptian works written in hieroglyphs on papyrus and the Babylonian, in cuneiform on clay tablets. In mathematics, these early people of the Near East could solve many problems. Geometry, earth measurement, was an Egyptian science. From the Babylonians, who used sixty, instead of ten, as a unit of measure, has come our sixty-minute hour. The Babylonians knew some astronomy—without a telescope they predicted eclipses and worked out a rather accurate calendar. Though these ancient people depended greatly on charms and prayers to heal the sick, they knew much about drugs and could perform many surgical operations. They worshiped many gods, for whom they built temples. The Babylonians made their temples of brick, building great towers (with setbacks like those of our skyscrapers) called *ziggurats;* to architecture they contributed the arch and the vault. The Egyptians used stone to erect great pyramids and temples with pillars and columns.

In Babylonia religion was devoted to the needs of life in this world, since the Babylonians had only vague ideas concerning a future life. They sought to learn the will of the gods and developed divination, the art of foretelling the future through various means, such as the examination of the livers of sheep, dreams, accidental occurrences and astrology, the study of the stars. As the Egyptians believed in immortality, they built great pyramids as tombs for their kings; later, they dug tombs with many rooms in the cliffs above the Nile. Around or near the royal tombs were the graves of their people. They mummified the body to preserve it; and they placed objects in the tombs and painted pictures on the sides to supply the soul with food and pleasure. To decorate the temples they made fine statues of stone or copper and carved many pictures on the walls.

The Semitic tribes of Syria, the Hittites of Asia Minor (first users of iron) and the people who lived in the Aegean region came under the strong influence of Babylonia and Egypt, and much of the culture of these later peoples shows a clear relationship to these two mighty, early civilizations.

Between the years 1100 and 800 B.C., the great powers of the East were weak, and the small states of Syria made good use of their chance for independence. The Phoenicians of Tyre and Sidon, inventors of the alphabet, possessed fine glass and woolen industries and carried their products and the goods of Babylon and Egypt throughout the Mediterranean and into the Atlantic. In southern Syria, the Hebrews, coming out of the desert and conquering both Canaanites and Philistines, established their little kingdoms. They possessed a religion of great spiritual and moral power that they had received from their leader, Moses. Their prophets developed this faith into a belief in one God, Maker and Ruler of all, who demanded good behavior, economic and social justice and true humility from all His worshipers. The collection of their historical books, laws, proverbs, psalms and prophetic writings that forms our Old Testament is our most precious heritage from antiquity.

The peoples of Syria were soon overwhelmed by the great empire of Assyria. The Assyrians, a martial, peasant folk of the Tigris valley, contributed much to military science, imperial organization and road building, and spread Babylonian culture over their domains. The Chaldaeans, who succeeded to their power in Babylonia, were celebrated in antiquity for their use of the older methods of divination and additions thereto particularly in astrology. Then, between 600 and 500 B.C., the whole East fell under the power of the kings of Persia, mountaineers from the plateau of Iran. Their imperial organization, with its satrapies (provinces), governors, inspectors, postal service and roads, completed the development begun by the Assyrians. Their religion,

THE METROPOLITAN MUSEUM OF ART

DELPHI, about 160 A.D. In the center is the Temple of Apollo, the sun god. The altar is to the right, in front of the large, dark statue of Apollo. In the background, to the left, is an open-air theater with the back of the stage to the camera. To the right is a two-story colonnade. The other buildings were dedicated to the ancient Greek city-states.

a dualism, that is, a belief in two gods, one a god of light and truth, the other an evil god of darkness and sin, greatly influenced later thought.

Near Eastern civilizations thus contributed to mankind the ways of doing and making things; the beginnings of literature, the methods of trade; the principles of law, thought and science; the first lessons in architecture, sculpture and painting; and both superstitious and glorious ideas of religion. In their life and thought, however, there was little emphasis upon man as an individual. Especially in the great empires of Egypt and Babylonia, men as individuals had little consideration; they were subject to all-powerful kings and without political rights, and at the same time they were looked upon as playthings of the gods, clay in the hands of the divine potter, not worthy in themselves.

The Greeks.—The keynote of Greek history is the dignity of the free man and citizen. The Aegean Sea, dotted with islands and bordered by the mountainous lands of the Greek peninsula and Asia Minor, was the center of the activities of the Greeks. Greece itself is a land of mountains that divide it into little valleys with thin but fertile soil. Yet in some of these little valleys and along the narrow coast of Asia Minor between the mountains and the sea, a culture so varied and brilliant developed that it was not equaled until the modern era. The mild climate of the Aegean area, the clear air and the magnificent scenery made it a pleasant place to live. Though the soil never supplied quite enough food for the people, it did provide fields and climate suitable

for grapes and olives. The good deposits of clay, the mines of iron, copper and silver, the mountains of marble and the herds of sheep and goats on the hillsides furnished abundant materials for industry. The Mediterranean Sea was an easy highway of trade with other lands, so that the surplus of goods might be exchanged for needed food. By this same sea route, the lessons that the Near East had to teach were carried to the Greeks.

In the first period or Aegean age, of which records have been only recently discovered by archaeologists, the people on the island of Crete learned under Egyptian influence how to make pottery and work in metals, how to paint pictures and how to build. They transformed what they learned into a brilliant life, centering around a great palace adorned with paintings. They made beautiful clay figures, exquisite gold cups and inlaid daggers. They enjoyed parties with music, dancing, boxing and bull leaping. The system of picture writing devised by these early inhabitants of Crete cannot be read today. Their culture was taught to the ancestors of the Greeks on the mainland, whose fortresses, palaces and tombs have survived in ruins. The Greek legends of heroes like Hercules and Theseus and the story of the Trojan War were later recollections of the deeds of men of those early times. They overthrew the Cretans, and in turn their civilization was destroyed about 1100 B.C. by the Dorians, a tribe of Greeks from the Northwest; but the lessons that they had learned from the Cretans and through them from the Egyptians were transmitted to the new conquerors and were never entirely forgotten.

In the centuries that followed the Greeks spread first across the Aegean to the islands and the coast of Asia Minor and then, after 800 B.C., into the western Mediterranean, particularly Sicily and southern Italy, and into the Black Sea region. During this time, they developed that characteristic Greek political institution, the city-state. This was a group of people claiming common descent, living in a limited area with a common political, economic and religious center—usually an easily defended hilltop. In these city-states the Greeks advanced steadily toward democracy. First they were ruled by kings; then by aristocratic landowners; then by wealthy merchants; sometimes temporary monarchies called *tyrannies* were established; but when they organized an army, the men who fought soon gained political power; and finally in many states all free citizens were admitted to a share in the government. This political development and the economic and cultural growth that went with it began in Miletus and the other cities on the coast of Asia Minor that came to be called *Ionia*. It spread rapidly to all parts of the world where Greeks lived.

Chief among the cities of the mainland were Sparta, which was famous for the military training it gave its boys and for the strength of its army; and Athens, whose leaders, particularly Solon (*c.* 639–559 B.C.), Cleisthenes (*c.* 507 B.C.) and Pericles (*c.* 495–429 B.C.), established Athenian democracy and laid the foundations of Athenian greatness. In the 5th and 4th centuries B.C., after the Greeks had defeated the Persians, Athens became the great city of the Greeks. Greek olive oil, wine, woolens, metal goods and pottery were everywhere in demand, and to aid in trade the Greeks developed the use of coinage.

This was also a period of great works of literature and art. In literature, the Greeks created and established the forms that we still use. In the early period, Homer (9th century B.C.) wrote epic poetry, telling heroic stories in poetic form; in the 7th and 6th centuries B.C. poets like Alcaeus and Sappho wrote lyrics, short songs of love or nature or war to be sung to the lyre; others wrote songs for choruses or for soldiers to sing. In the 5th century, the drama came into full maturity, as the great writers of Athens, particularly Aeschylus, Sophocles and Euripides, produced tragedies, and Aristophanes, comedies. In prose, the father of his-

tory, Herodotus, wrote a prose epic of the Persian Wars; and Thucydides, the first scientific historian, described the great war between Athens and Sparta. The service of the democracy led to the establishment of schools of oratory, and great orators made this a recognized branch of literature.

Architecture and art were closely linked with religion. The Greeks believed that nature around them was filled with gods and goddesses of human form. In honor of these deities, men held feasts and offered sacrifices, took part in athletic contests like the Olympic games and held dramatic competitions in which many of the great plays were produced. Temples in which the gods might live were built of marble. Learning much from the Egyptians, the Greeks used columns and pillars and created the Doric, Ionic and Corinthian orders of architecture. To adorn these temples they carved figures in relief and made statues of gods and goddesses, great men and victors in the athletic games. The marble that they used gave them greater freedom than was possible to their Egyptian teachers who, besides being conservative, had to work in harder stone. The Greeks, using living models and seeking lifelike beauty, soon overcame deficiencies in their skill and produced superb buildings like the Parthenon and many marvelous statues. When the experience of distant lands and the ideas that they adopted from Egypt and Babylon made some men doubt the stories of the gods, Thales (*c.* 640–546 B.C.), Pythagoras (582–500 B.C.) and other daring men like them tried to explain the nature of the universe and thus started the study of philosophy. Hippocrates (*c.* 460–377 B.C.), discarding magic and charms in healing the sick, began scientific medicine. Teachers called sophists laid emphasis upon the importance of individuals, and Socrates (469–399 B.C.) turned the attention of philosophers to the study of ethics. Plato (*c.* 427–347 B.C.), his pupil, who taught school and wrote masterly philosophic essays in dialogue form, composed a description of an ideal state; and Aristotle (384–322 B.C.) prepared the way for many of the sciences in his systematic treatises, which aimed to describe the universe and the nature of man, society and government.

In the succeeding centuries continual wars among the Greek city-states weakened many of them. The smaller communities fell under the power of Athens, Sparta or Thebes and finally all were conquered by the Macedonian leaders, Philip (382–336 B.C.) and Alexander (356–323 B.C.). The last important period of Greek history followed the Macedonian ascendancy. Differing from the earlier *Hellenic* period, it is called *Hellenistic* for now Hellenic culture was blended with Near Eastern culture. It was marked by the great expansion of the power of the Greeks into the Near Eastern lands, as Alexander conquered Persia and he and his successors settled colonies of Greeks wherever they went with a resulting interaction of Greek and Near Eastern civilizations.

VENTURE MAGAZINE

PARTHENON, on the Acropolis, a 260-foot hill in Athens, was built about 447–432 B.C., as a home for Athena, goddess of wisdom. Inside is a 40-foot-high ivory, jeweled, and gold statue of Athena, left hand on a shield and right hand holding a winged "Victory."

The chief characteristics of Hellenistic culture were cosmopolitanism and individualism, motivated by the conviction that "the educated man is a citizen of the world." The city-states declined, and in their places came federal leagues or great kingdoms that were ruled by kings who claimed to be gods, and in which life was as carefully regulated as in the days of the Egyptian pharaohs. Scientific agriculture, specialized industry and widespread trade brought wealth to many; but high costs and small rewards made life very hard for the lower classes, so that reformers talked of redividing the land or forming communistic states.

Poets composed poems in many elaborate meters on a variety of subjects displaying their skill and knowledge rather than any creative genius. Much emphasis was placed upon useful knowledge. The historian, Polybius (c. 205–123 B.C.), composed a history of Rome for the education of future generals and statesmen. Scientists advanced such studies as: geography, wherein they arrived at a fairly accurate measure of the size of the earth; mechanics—Archimedes (c. 287–212 B.C.) was a scientific inventor in the 3rd century B.C.; mathematics—Euclid (c. 330–275 B.C.) compiled the basic geometry textbook; and medicine—the doctors discovered basic facts about the nervous system. Architects built porticoes in the marketplaces, theaters and stadia. Sculptors carved portraits and statues to adorn the houses of great men or to celebrate the victories of kings. In philosophy, great ethical systems were developed: the Epicureans taught the avoidance of pain and a mechanistic, evolutionary philosophy; the Cynics emphasized the simple life, independence and self-control; and the Stoics taught endurance and obedience to the law of nature. The old religion broke down with the decline of the city-state, and men turned to Near Eastern religions, such as the worship of Isis, which gave promise of immortality as a reward for sufferings on this earth. This last great period of Greek history, the Hellenistic age, came to an end with the establishment of the Roman empire; but Greek culture, absorbed by Rome, continued to be a vital force in the world.

The Greek spirit was based upon the principle of freedom and upon confidence in the power of man. "Of all the wonders on earth, none is more wonderful than man," said Sophocles. Men, unafraid and free to explore and discuss, endeavored to solve the mysteries of the universe in their search after truth. "The object of our discussion," wrote Plato, "is not that either of us may gain a victory but that between us we may discover the most perfect truth." The Greeks sought for proportion also. The search of the artists for perfect balance in statues and in buildings is best exemplified by the Parthenon and its marbles. In ethics, the motto of the teachers was, "Nothing to excess," and they called moderation "the golden mean." Finally, in all things, the Greeks looked for beauty—in art,

HELEN BUTTFIELD

COLOSSEUM, the Flavian Amphitheater, was begun in 72 A.D. under Vespasian and dedicated in 80 A.D. under Titus. The columns are different on each story: first, Doric; second, Ionic; third, Corinthian. The seats are divided into three terraces. The lowest were cushioned marble, reserved for senators. Women were not allowed to sit on benches unless they were vestal virgins or members of the imperial family.

literature, religion and the life of man.

Rome.—The mission of Rome was to absorb Greek culture, to add to it law, order, organization and practical arts and to teach this new civilization to the West. In striking contrast to Greece, Italy has few good harbors. The valleys and coastal plain west of the Apennine Mountains are fertile, and their inhabitants were devoted to agriculture from early times. Rome occupied the strategic position in this region at the crossing of the Tiber. The Romans learned the first steps in civilization from their neighbors, the Etruscans, a people, possibly from Asia Minor, who lived north of the Tiber—lessons in organization, architecture and divination. About 500 B.C., the Romans freed themselves from Etruscan rule and with great speed advanced to the conquest of Italy, then of the entire Mediterranean world. Even the great monarchies of the East fell before the Roman legions.

Great factors in this triumph were the elements of the Roman government: the Senate, composed of experienced former magistrates serving as a body to advise and administer; the two consuls, generals of the army and chief magistrates with full power of command as executives; and the people who had the right to give or refuse assent in their assemblies and were trained to render effective obedience in the army. Behind these institutions was Roman character, based on tradition and discipline and noted for simplicity, courage and fidelity. The chief contributions of the early Roman Republic were the marvelous methods of road building and a system of law which tried to secure justice for all men, even for non-Romans.

The great conquests brought new problems. The government, well adapted to the rule of a city-state, was not suited to the management of an empire. The other Italian peoples had been admitted to Roman alliance; but the overseas dominions were organized into tribute-paying provinces like those of Assyria and Persia. Great wealth from booty and graft suddenly came to Roman governors and businessmen, who shamelessly exploited and robbed the provincials. The great military power entrusted to the governors, who commanded armies that were now composed of professional soldiers, was a menace to the state unless some method of control could be developed.

Great estates belonging to wealthy Romans and worked by slaves began to appear in Italy, and the small farming class, backbone of early Rome, was turned into a poverty-stricken city population. The new class of businessmen challenged the power of the Senate over the empire. Finally the new wealth and the absorption of Hellenistic culture by the educated classes broke down the simplicity and vigor of the old tradition. Self-seeking took the place of loyalty to the public service.

The failure of the Senate to solve these problems resulted in the Roman revolution, a series of events that began with an attempt to remedy agricultural conditions in Italy, reached its climax with the dictatorship of Julius Caesar in 46 to 44 B.C. and ended with the victory of Augustus in 31

B.C. and his establishment of one-man rule over the Roman Empire. The first great period of Roman literature came during the period of conquest and revolution. In the main it followed Hellenistic models, poems, plays, history, oratory and philosophic essays, though it was inspired by the Roman spirit. The chief writer of this period was Cicero (106–43 B.C.). His orations are read in our schools, his letters form our best source of information about the politics of his time and his essays provide us with much of our knowledge of Hellenistic philosophy.

The Roman Empire.—In the Roman Empire, the three streams of culture—Near Eastern, Greek and Roman—met and mingled. The widely diverse peoples of East and West were welded together in a common loyalty to an emperor who, like the Eastern kings, was worshiped as a god. Their world was well administered by the emperors, who kept the governors in hand, preserved order in the provinces and guarded the frontiers against barbarian invasions. Roman law was developed into a body of rules and practices so suitable to meet the needs of varied peoples that it remains today the foundation of many modern legal systems. Roads, built for military purposes, bound the empire together, and Roman officials, merchants and soldiers carried civilization to all corners of the empire. The West was well Romanized; but the East remained Greek in language and culture. Industry was highly developed, and trade spread over the empire and reached beyond its borders even to India and China. In agriculture, great estates, many of which belonged to the emperors, continued to appear; but on them tenant-farming took the place of slave labor. Though the poor still received starvation wages, the government provided them with free bread and shows (*panem et circenses*) and in some towns furnished free schools, libraries, hospitals and medical attendance. Slavery declined except in domestic service.

There was great building activity throughout the Roman Empire. *Fora*

(buildings with porticoes in which work was carried on) and temples were erected; elegant houses for public baths and arenas like the Colosseum were constructed; aqueducts brought water that was distributed to fountains and sometimes piped into houses; bridges on arches crossed the streams along the roads; and ornamental arches celebrated the triumphs of the emperors. The Romans employed concrete as building material and perfected the use of the arch, the vault and the dome.

Latin literature attained its highest peak in the Age of Augustus when Vergil composed the *Aeneid,* Horace, his *Odes,* and Livy, his history. Though there were great writers like Seneca, Tacitus and Juvenal in the period that followed, most authors, terrified by the power of despotic emperors and afraid to express themselves freely, paid more attention to form than to content. The best writing and thinking was in the fields of morals and religion. Stoic philosophy was taught by Seneca and Epictetus, and by the philosopher-emperor, Marcus Aurelius (who wrote his *Meditations* not in Latin but in Greek). In the field of religion the Near East was all-powerful. Isis-worship from Egypt, Mithraism (a Persian religion developed out of the early dualism) and the worship of the Great Mother of Asia Minor took the place of the old gods of Greece and Rome in the hearts of the masses. Judaism, expounded by the rabbis who interpreted the collections of Hebrew sacred writings, spread throughout the empire; but victory rested with Christianity, inspired by the memory of its Founder, with its high code of morals, its intolerance of wickedness and the willingness of its adherents to suffer martyrdom for the faith they had espoused.

The Decline of Ancient Civilization.—The great spread of Near Eastern religions and the eventual triumph of Christianity came in that dark period of human history in which ancient civilization declined. In the 3rd century of the Christian era, the generals of the armies began civil wars to contend for the imperial throne, and the

political structure crumbled. Diocletian and Constantine revived it for a time, but in 395 the empire was divided in two. The Eastern half, with its capital at Constantinople, lasted until 1453; but the Western, suffering under Germanic invasions, came to an end in 476. With the fall of the political framework and the destruction of peace and unity, economic life also collapsed. Coinage was debased, commerce almost stopped, industry languished, and the great estates tried to become self-supporting. In the effort to keep necessary services going, the government reduced the tenants to serfdom and made commercial and industrial activities hereditary, thus establishing castes, forcing men to carry on the crafts or trades in which they happened to be engaged, and compelling boys to succeed their fathers in the same occupations and in the same places. These burdens, in addition to the crushing load of taxation, proved too great for the middle-class people to bear, and they declined in wealth and numbers. In the end, the Roman world was composed chiefly of powerful landowners and a great mass of tenant farmers, who were almost slaves. The army, made up of peasants, declined in intelligence and discipline until it could no longer hold back the barbarians, and the Germans flooded the Western empire.

Amid general discouragement, art, architecture and literature went into almost total eclipse. Superstition took the place of intelligence; and men, convinced that the world was base, sought only escape from it. To this weary world Christianity brought its high fidelity and its promise of Heaven. Its triumph marked the end of classical civilization. The new age, called medieval, was Germanic and Christian; but the lessons that Rome had garnered from the East, from the Greeks and from its own experiences were never lost. The institutions, the law, the literature, the architecture and the art, in short, the whole product of ancient culture continued as the inspiration of later ages and it lives today as the foundations of our modern life.

ORIENTAL CIVILIZATIONS

The human race has produced three great civilizations and all of them originated in Asia. They are the Chinese, the Indic and the civilization of the Near East. These three civilizations developed independently of each other and, until modern times, had very little to do with each other. As a result, the Orient may be said to be divided into three distinct cultural areas: the Far East, dominated by Chinese civilization; the Middle East or the sphere of the culture of India; and, finally, the Near East, where our own civilization originated thousands of years ago.

THE FAR EAST

China.—Chinese civilization is unique in that it began and developed almost

without any influence from other countries. China is isolated from the rest of the world by huge deserts, mountain ranges and vast oceans and consequently had time in which to create its own type of civilization without being affected by neighboring cultures. The only outside influence on Chinese civilization has been Buddhism, which was introduced into China from India nearly 2,000 years ago. But even in this case the Chinese so changed and adapted the practice of Buddhism that it hardly can be distinguished from the other two religions of China, Taoism and Confucianism. This approximation of one religion to another in China may be explained by the fact that the Chinese always try to harmonize and

blend conflicting ideas in an effort to reach a workable compromise. This is true of other aspects of Chinese life as well as of religion.

Though Chinese civilization is not as old as that of Egypt, it is the oldest in eastern Asia. It began probably 4,000 years ago in the valley of the Wei river, near the great bend in the Hwang Ho (Yellow River), hundreds of miles from the sea. The first two dynasties, according to Chinese historians, were the Hsia (2205–1765 B.C.) and the Shang (1766–1122 B.C.), but the real history of China did not begin till the Chou (pronounced Joe) dynasty, which began in 1122 and lasted to 249 B.C. This dynasty produced the great philosophers for whom China is famous, Confucius

(Kung-fu-tse), Lao-tse, Mencius (Meng-tse) and others.

Confucianism; Taoism.—Confucius, who lived from 551 to 478 B.C., is one of the greatest thinkers produced by the Orient. He was not a religious thinker like Buddha, Christ or Mohammed, but a social reformer. As he himself said, "I am not an originator but a transmitter." He edited or compiled the Chinese "Classics"—the nearest Chinese equivalent of the Bible of the Christians and the Mohammedan Koran. They are made up of the "Five Canons" and the "Four Books", which contain the morals and philosophy that the Chinese people have followed consistently for the past 2,500 years. Lao-tse is supposed to be the author of the *Tao Te Ching,* a small book containing the main tenets of Taoism. Taoism, unlike the practical Confucianism, is largely negative in its teachings and emphasizes pacificism, mysticism and the importance of non-activity. Mencius is chiefly noted as the philosopher who adapted Confucianism to the political needs of the Chinese people.

The Chinese people are unlike most Orientals and similar to us in many ways. For instance nearly all Oriental nations have a fondness for mysticism and religious speculation, and have never succeeded in developing a democratic form of government but have been content to be ruled by despots. This is not true of the Chinese, who have succeeded in developing democratic ideas in government and social organization, and who have been more interested in material prosperity and comfort than other Oriental peoples. Throughout history we find the Chinese making valuable contributions to science and often anticipating the great mechanical inventions of our own times.

To the Chinese, the family is the all-important unit rather than the state. The interests of a Chinese are centered first of all in his family and family-clan, secondly in his own community. A Chinese believes that his first duty is to his parents. Home and ties of blood are the center of life. The individual is unimportant. Ancestors are worshiped as a part of religion. The idea of Chinese nationalism has been comparatively unknown until this century, but it is an idea that has grown like wildfire, especially among the young people and since Japan has menaced China's survival as a separate nation.

One of the greatest rulers produced by the Chinese was a man named Shih Huang Ti or the First Emperor, who overthrew the Chou dynasty in the 3d century B.C. He abolished the nobility and founded a form of government that lasted until 1912. Since his time Chinese society has been democratic, and the only two classes that have existed have been the educated and the uneducated. Since any poor boy with talent was allowed to compete in the government examinations and, upon passing them, could occupy the highest posts in the state, there was no distinction between rich and poor as far as the state was concerned. The "First Emperor" also built the Great Wall of China, de-

CHINA NEWS SERVICE

GREAT WALL OF CHINA, the longest fortification ever built. The first wall was built before 200 B.C. by the tyrannical emperor Shih Hwang-ti; the present one, during the Ming Dynasty (1368–1644). It was constructed to keep out the Mongols, northern barbarians.

signed to keep the northern barbarians in check. It is said to be the only man-made object on earth that can be seen from the moon. Chinese writing was revolutionized by the use of small brushes made of hair. The Chinese use the pictographic method of writing and express their ideas in the form of pictures greatly abbreviated. Their characters or ideograms are not letters of the alphabet but actually represent an individual drawing of an object. There are about forty thousand of these ideograms in the standard Chinese dictionary.

The Han Dynasty.—During the next dynasty, the Han (206 B.C.–220 A.D.), the Chinese again showed their genius as inventors. Paper as well as porcelain was invented. It was a period of military conquests that extended to the boundaries of ancient Persia. Trade followed Chinese arms, and for the first time in their history the Chinese came into contact with the cultures of India and the Near East. Before long an extensive trade was carried on by Chinese and Persian merchants, the Chinese exchanging their silk goods for iron and precious stones of the Near East. So proud are the Chinese of the Han period that they often call themselves the sons of Han rather than Chinese. This was one of the great periods in Chinese art.

In this period Confucianism became the basis of the Chinese State, and the Confucianist scholars became the only state officials. To China belongs the unique distinction of having raised the scholar to the highest rank in society and put all power in his hands. In no other country was learning so honored and respected as in China.

Korea.—It was during this dynasty that the little-known peninsula called *Korea* or *Chosen,* "the land of morning freshness," was conquered and Chinese civilization penetrated into it. The culture of the Koreans is older than that of any other Far Eastern people

except that of China, from whom they borrowed their earliest civilization about 1000 B.C. The founder of Korea was a certain Ki-tze, uncle of the last Shang emperor of China. When the Shang dynasty fell in 1122 B.C., this prince with his followers fled to what is now northwestern Korea and there set up a new state. Gradually, this state extended its rule over the rest of the peninsula until by the 4th century A.D. the whole of Korea accepted Chinese culture. Though the Koreans belong to a different racial stock, they became thoroughly Chinese in their culture, becoming more Chinese in some respects than the Chinese themselves. Thus when most Chinese adopted the foreign Buddhism, the Koreans disestablished Buddhism and adopted the Chinese Confucianism. The upper classes in particular use only Chinese in writing, while the lower classes use an alphabet of 25 letters (11 vowels and 14 consonants) derived from India by way of China. Korean writers use Chinese rather than the native language. When the Japanese annexed Korea in 1910, they tried to force their language and customs on the Koreans. They also established the political religion, State Shinto. After the collapse of Japan in 1945, the Japanese were forced out of Korea and almost all traces of their 35-year occupancy have vanished. The Koreans are skilled artisans and their metal work and porcelain is highly prized throughout the world.

Probably the most important part played by the Koreans in Oriental history was to transmit Chinese civilization to Japan. They were the first scholars and artisans in Japan and the only ones until the Japanese learned the secrets of Chinese culture themselves.

Buddhism.—Early in the Christian era, during the Han dynasty, Chinese merchants traveling to India by the old caravan route through Turkestan brought back with them the teachings of Gautama Buddha. Buddhism affected Chinese civilization in many details. It had an especially strong influence on the religious ideas of the Chinese. It brought the Chinese the concept of mercy and compassion and the promise of an afterlife. Its influence upon Chinese art and architecture was tremendous. Monasteries and convents were built everywhere, especially on hilltops. Bell towers or pagodas dotted the countryside. The Buddhists also advanced landscape gardening to a higher degree. But it was in the field of decorative art that Buddhism was most felt. The figure of the seated Buddha is familiar to all students of Chinese art as are the other Buddhist symbols of the net, the rosary, the swastika and the lotus.

Tea drinking, so characteristic of the Chinese today, originally was practiced only by the Buddhist monks who used tea as a stimulant to keep awake during the night while at prayer. The practice soon spread among the masses partly because unboiled water in China is not suitable for drinking.

Tang Dynasty.—The most brilliant period in Chinese history is the Tang dynasty (618-907). During these three centuries China was not only the largest and most powerful state in the world but the most civilized. The capital, Ch'ang-an, on the site of which stands the present city of Kaifeng, was more populous and richer than its only two rivals, Bagdad and Constantinople. To promote commercial relations with India and the Near East the Tang emperors set out on a series of successful military campaigns to the north, west and south. Central Asia and southeastern Asia were conquered and Chinese civilization planted there.

Cultural progress kept apace with the material prosperity of the Tang period. Learning was very widespread and in the reign of Wu Hou, an empress who left a convent for the throne, women were allowed to compete with men in civil service examinations and, on passing, were given high government posts. The Chinese showed their ability as engineers and inventors by building the Grand Canal, by erecting those beautiful half-moon bridges that adorn the Chinese landscape and especially by the invention of printing. This last-named invention came about from ink rubbings made on stone and wood carvings. The invention of printing facilitated a wider diffusion of learning and made possible a greater production of books, which formerly were copied painstakingly by hand. The *Peking Gazette,* sometimes called the oldest newspaper in the world, dates from this period.

Chinese Poetry and Calligraphy.—As might be expected from a period of so much literary activity, poetry, prose and painting rose to unexcelled heights. The greatest poet of China, Li Po, whose poems are familiar to every Chinese schoolboy, lived at this time. Two great schools of Chinese painting were founded. Chinese painting is different from that of the West in that the Chinese artist paints from memory and uses ink as a medium, painting with a brush on silk or some other highly absorbent material. Among the Chinese, painting is closely related to literature, especially to poetry. As a famous Chinese poet-emperor once said, "A poem in every painting, a painting in every poem." In China, calligraphy or the art of writing beautiful characters is more esteemed than the painting of pictures.

During the next great dynasty, the Sung (960–1280), China became weak politically but continued to make advances in philosophy and art. Sung pottery is famous throughout the world and much sought after by art collectors. This period witnessed the attempt of a statesman and scholar, Wang An-Shih (1021–86), to introduce into China many of the reforms that have only recently been begun in the western world—daily regulation of wages, old age pensions, state relief for the sick and unemployed, regulation of prices, and a form of income tax and other benefits of state socialism.

In 1280 the Mongols conquered China. Their rule ended in 1368 when a Chinese general expelled them from Peking and established a pure Chinese dynasty, named the Ming (Bright), a famous period of Chinese art. In 1644 this dynasty was overthrown by the Manchus who reigned until 1912, when China became a republic.

It was during the Tang dynasty (618–907) that China transmitted her culture to Japan. At first Chinese civilization entered into Japan indirectly by way of Korea, but by the 6th century A.D. Chinese emigrants began to arrive and to teach the Japanese the elements of their civilization.

Japan.—The origin of the Japanese is unknown, but they are composed of three main stocks—invaders from Manchuria and the Malay islands, and the original inhabitants of Japan, known to us today as the hairy Ainus. Japanese historians traditionally begin their history on February 11, 660 B.C. when Jimmu Tennō, the first emperor of Japan, ascended the throne; but in reality Japanese history begins only in the 6th century A.D. with the introduction of Buddhism into Japan by the great Soga family.

The Japanese owe the Chinese the same debt that we owe ancient Greece and Rome for our cultural heritage. From China came whatever knowledge the Japanese ever had of writing, law, government, medicine, mathematics, the calendar, social organization and agriculture. Although the actual origin of the Japanese language is not known, its ideographs were borrowed from Chinese. Japanese has differing spoken and written languages, and in the latter are still further distinctions—the archaic, classical, epistolary and other forms. All the Chinese culture came through the medium of Buddhism, which was made the official religion of Japan by the Prince Regent, Shotoku Taishi, who ruled from 593 to 621, one of the greatest Japanese who ever lived.

Even before the introduction of Chinese civilization, the Japanese displayed certain traits that marked them as different from the Chinese. They had developed the idea of loyalty to the country to an advanced degree whereas the Chinese emphasized only loyalty to the group or family. Then too the Japanese have always been a martial people ready to fight on the least provocation while the Chinese, thanks to Confucianism, are pacifists and resort to war only when all other means of settling a dispute are exhausted. Finally the position of the emperor in Japan is different from that which was occupied by the Chinese emperor. The Japanese emperor is a divinely descended ruler whereas the Chinese emperor merely represented Heaven and did not claim a divine origin. In other words, the basis of the Japanese state was aristocratic and rested on the clan, which was descended from a god, but the basis of the Chinese state was democratic and rested upon the family structure.

For a few centuries the Japanese were content to imitate their Chinese teachers in the arts of civilization but before long they began to create things in the Japanese spirit. The two outstanding characteristics of the Japanese artistic genius are simplicity and a delight in exquisite details. We see this on every hand in Japanese creations in art, literature, decoration and architecture. In literature the Japanese developed the short poem called the *hokku,* which depends for its meaning not on what it says but on what it suggests. The Japanese house, too, is a constant reminder of Japanese simplicity and delicacy. It is always constructed of wood—necessary in a land of earthquakes—and is simplicity itself. The rooms are almost bare of furniture; whenever an article is needed it is brought out from the spacious closets with which every Japanese house is provided and removed as soon as it is no longer required. The floor is covered with a thick matting called the *tatami,* which is kept scrupulously clean. In a corner of the main room is a raised alcove named the *tokonoma,* where a few ornaments are displayed and replaced with others in conformity with the occasion and time of the year.

There are few countries in the world as beautiful as Japan. Abundant rainfall, plenty of sunshine and a luxurious vegetation tend to make the Japanese landscape one that is not easily forgotten. Mountain and forest and roaring torrent or waterfall are nearly always in sight; as a Japanese proverb says, "One is always within earshot of water in Japan." The loveliness of Japan is reflected in the universal love of beauty that every Japanese has. No matter how poor or humble a Japanese may be there is always a garden around his home, even if it is no larger than a few square feet. The Japanese are "born" artisans; their skill and phenomenal patience are proverbial. They excel in landscape gardening, lacquer work and woodcarving. In decorative art, their influence throughout the world is second only to that of the French. The art of flower arrangement or *ikebana* has reached a degree of perfection unknown in any other country.

Shintoism.—Here, as in China, there is toleration of all forms of religious belief. The Japanese are nominally Buddhists but many of them are also Shintoists. Shinto was the primitive religion of Japan before the coming of Buddhism and Chinese culture. It is typically Japanese in being a very simple religion. It gives only one command, the necessity of being loyal to one's ancestors. This precept of loyalty to the departed binds all Japanese in a bond of unity, almost unknown in any other country today. Shintoism has about 800,000 gods in its pantheon, mostly the deified heroes of the Japanese. The chief deity of Shinto, which means the "Way of the Gods," is Amaterasu, the Sun Goddess, from whom the Imperial Family of Japan traces its origin. The lesser clans, in turn, claim descent from the lesser Shinto divinities.

The emperor of Japan, until the last century, ruled the country but did not govern it. This was done in the beginning by the regents but since the 13th century by the military commander called the *shogun*. Thus Japan early evolved a dual form of government; the religious power was held by the emperor or Tennō, sometimes referred to as the *Mikado* ("August Gate"), and the temporal power was wielded by the military overlord or shogun, who maintained his own court and state officials. This form of government lasted until 1868 when the Emperor Mutsuhito overthrew the shogun and added the temporal power to his religious duties. This strong central government brought about the adoption of Western techniques much more easily than was possible in China. The American Occupation after World War II prepared the way for the new Democratic government that emerged following the peace treaty in 1951.

The population of Japan increases at a terrific rate. Within the past 60 years it has doubled itself but so did the production of food in Japan due to more intensive cultivation. But today the limit of food production has been reached, and the Japanese have had to turn to industry to provide for the surplus population of their country.

Tibet.—China likewise taught other nations of eastern Asia her wonderful and ancient civilization. In addition to Korea and Japan, the Manchus, Mongolians and Tibetans accepted the main principles of Chinese culture. The entire northern frontier region of China is often referred to as Tatary. The word *tatar* comes from a Chinese word meaning barbarian or one who does not know how to speak Chinese.

Some Tibetans are settled dwellers of the valleys and some are wanderers in the arid mountains.

Lamaism.—Buddhism was introduced from India in the 7th century A.D. but Chinese civilization remained the basis of Tibetan cultural life. So thorough was the conquest of Buddhism, however, that a large part of

JAPAN NATIONAL TOURIST ASSOCIATION

KOFUKUJI TEMPLE, located in Nara Park, or "Deer Park," in Nara, the ancient capital of Japan. This beautiful shrine is sacred to both the Shintoists and Buddhists.

the population entered the monastic life. The Tibetan monastery is known as a *lamasery* and often harbors 10,000 monks or lamas. The most famous of these lamaseries is at Lhasa, the capital of Tibet, and is called the *Jokhang*. Far above Lhasa towers the Potala, the palace of the head or Dalai Lama. It is located on a high hill, like most Buddhist temples, and in construction resembles a modern skyscraper. A series of staircases leads up to the Potala from the city.

Lamaism is the religion of some 3,000,000 Tibetans and of 7,000,000 Mongols and other races. At the head of this vast horde are two Lama popes, the Dalai Lama and the Panchen or Teshu Lama. Theoretically both the leaders have the same spiritual and temporal powers, but as the Panchen Lama rules over less territory than the Dalai, his authority is smaller. Then, too, modern political influences have been at work, and the Panchen Lama was protected by China's nationalist government after he was compelled to flee from his monastery at Tashilhunpo in 1924. The Grand Lamas are regarded as "Living Buddhas," being the incarnations of Buddha passing from one existence to another. When one dies, his successor is sought from among the baby boys born at the time the leader passed away because it is believed that the soul of the Buddha has only passed into another existence. These infant claimants to the throne are weeded out, and the one selected by the priests and nobles begins a rigorous education to fit him to assume his duties.

What the Tibetans know of art and literature is the monopoly of the lamas. The most characteristic products of the lamaseries are the prayer wheel and the Tibetan prayer rug, much prized by art collectors.

Mongolia.—The Mongols like the Tibetans are followers of Lamaism, or the Yellow Religion, a corrupt form of Buddhism, which in Mongolia as in Tibet has lost much of its Indian character and has degenerated into a form of spirit worship. Until the 13th century the Mongols were content to live as nomads, being quite backward in civilization. But early in that century one of their chiefs, named Temuchin, formed them into a nation. In 1206 Temuchin raised his standard of nine yak-tails and took the high-sounding title of *Genghis Khan,* the Mighty One. He at once ordered the conquest of the world. The conquests of the Mongols have no parallel in all history. Genghis Khan and his successors succeeded in conquering all of eastern Asia (except Japan), all of central Asia, India (where they are known as the Moguls), Persia and the Near East and nearly all of Russia. Never before nor since has so much of the earth's surface been ruled over by one nation. The Mongols succeeded in breaking down all barriers between the Far East, the Middle East and the Near East, so that trade between the East and the West again was resumed after many centuries of inactivity. Travel between the West and the Orient began and the wonders of Oriental civilization were made known to the Europeans of the 13th century.

The most famous of the Western travelers to China were the Polos, Nicolo, Maffeo and Marco (son of Nicolo), merchants of Venice. Marco (1254–1323) later dictated an account of his travels and residence in the court of Kublai Khan in Khanbaliq, just north of Peking, and the capital of the Mongols, deserted after their expulsion. Marco Polo's book became one of the most widely read in the Middle Ages.

Kublai Khan, who conquered China in 1280, was the greatest Mongol emperor. He brought Chinese civilization to the Mongols and created the Mongolian system of writing, which is based on a script borrowed from Syria. He introduced many influences from Persia into China, notably the novel and the drama. Like all Chinese emperors Kublai Khan practiced religious toleration, extending official patronage to all religions, including Christianity.

The Mongol hurricane soon spent its force and gradually the Mongols retired to their homeland, north of the Gobi Desert, where they live now as simple nomads hunting and grazing their herds.

Manchuria.—Another Asiatic people who owe China whatever knowledge they have of civilization are the Manchus, who in ancient times occupied the valley of the Amur River, but during the Middle Ages moved into what is today southern Manchuria. They are more like Europeans than Chinese and Koreans in their physical appearance. Their eyes have not the slant produced by an eyelid fold that is characteristic of other Mongolian peoples. It is believed by many that the Manchus have a Persian strain in them, which probably accounts for their somewhat Caucasian appearance. Until the 16th century they were an unimportant tribe, but late in that century a chief named Nurhachu welded them into a nation and started them on a career of conquest. In 1644 they succeeded in conquering China, and they continued to rule the Chinese until 1912. The Manchus introduced into China the queue or pigtail, which they obliged all Chinese to wear as a badge of servitude. They contributed very little to Chinese civilization and were ultimately absorbed within the Chinese masses. Today, only a few nomadic tribes in Manchuria are able to understand the Manchu language.

Because Chinese civilization was so old and self-sufficient and because China is so large, westernization did not make the progress that it made, for instance, in Japan. The Chinese were historically unwilling to accept western ideas unless they could be modified to suit conditions in China. What they desired to do was to graft western civilization on the trunk of Chinese culture so that the base would remain, as before, purely Chinese. However, with the flight of the Nationalist Chinese regime to Taiwan in 1949 and the Communization of the mainland into a People's Republic of China, the future of Chinese culture becomes uncertain. The Communists have embarked upon radical programs to modernize and collectivize industry, agriculture, education—in short, the whole of society. What resistance Chinese traditions may offer cannot yet be determined.

THE MIDDLE EAST

India.—The second great cultural area of the Orient is India. In many respects India is the most Oriental of Asiatic lands. The principal religion, Brahmanism (or more commonly, Hinduism), has played a greater part in determining the civilization of the people than in other parts of Asia. Very little is known regarding the history of India until the coming of the Aryans, a white people related to the ancient Persians, sometime in the second millenium before Christ. Their sacred songs to the gods of nature, now known as the *Vedas,* form the earliest records we have of their civilization. In order to maintain their white supremacy over the aboriginal inhabitants called the Dravidians and to keep their blood unmixed, the Aryans organized the so-called caste system. This system was devised to prevent any admixture of the white race with the natives and is to be found in no other country. In the beginning the Aryans recognized only four castes: the Brahmans, priests and scholars; the Kshatriyas, nobles and warriors; the Vaisyas, farmers and merchants, and finally, the Sudras, serfs and slaves. Later, these four castes multiplied until today there are thousands of castes in India, which form the greatest obstacle to any feeling of unity or nationalism. The word *caste* is not Indian in origin but is a Portuguese word (meaning race or unmixed race) describing this peculiarly Indian institution. The Hindus themselves use two words denoting the same thing: one, *varna,* means color; the other, *jati,* refers to one's birth or family origin. Only the Hindus practice the caste system; it is abandoned when a Hindu becomes a Mohammedan or a Christian.

Buddhism; Brahmanism. — Throughout their history the Hindus have been distinguished for their religious thought. One of the most understanding religious leaders of the world was a Hindu born in northern India in the 6th century B.C. named Gautama, the Buddha, the Enlightened or Awakened One. He founded a school of religious thought that was primarily designed to reform Brahmanism and especially to overthrow the caste system. Although in essence both religions emphasize the necessity of escaping from material life and extinguishing desire, the Buddhists protested against the ritualism and extreme self-denial and self-punishment practiced by the Hindus. Buddhism is based upon the equality of all in the religious life, women as well as men. The aim of the Buddhists, to obtain eternal life, Nirvana, by extinguishing all desire for material existence, is attained by following the "Eightfold Path": Right Belief, Right Feeling, Right Speech, Right Actions, Right Means of Livelihood, Right Endeavor, Right Memory and Right Meditation. For a time Buddhism triumphed in India, and missionaries were sent to preach it in all parts of Asia. But in the 3d century B.C. its followers split into two halves; the northern school (Mahayāna, the "Great Wheel") professed to regard Gautama as a god; but the southern school (Hinayāna, the "Little Wheel") preferred to consider Gautama merely as a teacher. It was from the northern school that China received her most important religion. The schism in the Buddhist church gave the Brahmans an opportunity to rouse the people against the Buddhists; a reaction set in and before long Buddhism disappeared in India. The triumph of Brahmanism and of the caste system was complete. The only stronghold left to Buddhism among the Indians is the island of Ceylon, where thousands of pilgrims annually go to Kandy, the capital, to venerate the reputed "tooth of Buddha" in one of the local temples.

India is a land of strange customs and stranger religions. It is likewise a land of contrasts: mud villages huddle against marble palaces dazzling white in the sun. One of the noblest architectural monuments in the world is in India—the Taj Mahal at Agra, tomb of the favorite wife of a Mohammedan ruler of northern India. Owing to the power that tradition has over the mind of the Hindu, life in India goes on today much as it did thousands of years ago. The only changes brought in were those introduced by the Mohammedans and, in modern times, by the British.

India has at least half a dozen distinct cultural areas. The farther south in India one goes the more ancient are the ruins which one meets until at the tip of the peninsula the origins of extinct civilizations are lost in time. Southern India around modern Madras was never politically or culturally a part of India proper and was itself the source of the civilization of southeastern Asia, the Malay islands and the East Indies.

The region north of Madras is a plateau called the Deccan and is the home of the warlike Mahrattas. It is likewise a stronghold of the Mohammedans. The Nizam of Hyderabad, the Moslem ruler of this region, is one of the richest men in the world.

Proceeding northwards we come to the modern city of Bombay, one of the great commercial ports of the Orient. In it are to be found descendants of the Parsis or Zoroastrian Persians who fled before the Moslems. They still practice the ancient religion of Persia and many of them constitute the wealthy merchants of Bombay. Northern India is especially famous for the sacred river, the Ganges, where millions of pilgrims come annually to wash away their sins, especially at the holy city of Benares. At one of the mouths of the river is Calcutta, the second great modern city of India. Delhi, the capital of Hindu India, where the Durbars or meetings of the Indian princes are held, is also a great center of Hinduism. Yet, in the main, India is agricultural. There are over half a million villages in India and most of the people, as in China and Russia, make their living by tilling the soil. In India the smallest group is the self-contained more or less communistic village community that formerly was governed by meetings of the village owners and was collectively responsible for its taxes.

The Mohammedans conquered India during the Middle Ages and today form the warlike elements in Indian life. The English are responsible for the development of such modern cities as Bombay and Calcutta with their teeming populations. It was British rule that was responsible for the abolition of such practices as suttee, the sacrifice of a widow on her husband's funeral pyre.

The Indians learned many Western ideas, especially nationalism, from Great Britain. Hindus, educated in England, returned to India and began to agitate for an "India for the Indians." There was an Indian National Congress (an annual assembly of nationalistic Hindus) and a corresponding All India Moslem League. The leader of the nationalists was Mahatma Gandhi, who organized a movement of passive resistance against British rule. On February 6, 1935, Sir Samuel Hoare pledged a government policy, that would make India a Dominion. The dream was realized in 1947, when Pakistan and India became Dominions. India and Pakistan later became republics.

As bewildering as the religions of India are her many races and languages. Generally speaking there are three racial types in India. In the north and east are the Mongoloid peoples of Nepal and Burma. In the central part and all through the south are the Dravidians, descended probably from the same stock as the Australian aborigines. Only in the northwest, in the Punjab and in Kashmir does the white race predominate. There are seven principal languages in India and hundreds of dialects of these languages.

The Punjab (literally, five waters or five rivers), the fertile Valley of the Ind, has been much exposed to invasions from Persia and Afghanistan, hence its white population. But it is Kashmir that is the most colorful portion of northern India. It is often called the California of the Orient.

Burma.—The color of the wheat fields in the dry season gives Burma its name, the Golden Country. Situated in southeastern Asia, Burma has been influenced by cultural streams from both India and China. The region is a stronghold of Buddhism, which was introduced from India early in the Christian era. Burma, inhabited by a people of the yellow race, contains two cities familiar to all travelers in the Orient, Rangoon and Mandalay. The Burmese received Buddhism of the Hinayana type from Ceylon but their culture was obtained from China. Their contributions to civilization are negligible, but their happy and gay temperament has led many who know them well to call the Burmese the Irishmen of the Orient.

Burma is cut off from Pakistan by high mountain chains, with the result that the Burmese have been allowed to develop comparatively uninfluenced by their neighbors. Burmese women, for example, have equal rights with their men. Hindu women are still completely subservient, but in Burma women come and go as freely as men and often work for their living; sisters inherit equally with brothers and wives are copartners with their husbands in all enterprises. Likewise, there is no caste system because it is forbidden by the

Buddhist religion. Although educational standards in Burma, as compared with western countries, are very low, the people in general receive a much better education than most of their Asian neighbors. Monasteries, which are located in nearly every village, provide free schooling. After nearly three centuries of British control and occupation by Japan during World War II, Burma has at last become an independent and self-governing nation.

HARRISON FORMAN

ANKGOR WAT, a twelfth-century temple in Cambodia, was discovered in the jungle in 1860 and restored by the government. The stepped pyramid has five towers; the highest one is over 200 feet tall.

Thailand.—East of Burma are the Thai who, like the Burmese, also belong to the Mongoloid type but are more warlike and progressive. The Thai have never been conquered by the Chinese; nevertheless, they too possess the elements of Chinese civilization modified by certain influences from India. The Thai are very artistic, as their capital Bangkok with its bizarre palaces, dazzling pagodas and temples testifies. Thailand is one of the few Oriental countries which is still independent of any western Power, and up until the time when it became a limited monarchy, it was ruled by a typical Oriental despot.

Viet Nam, Cambodia, and Laos.—From the latter nineteenth century until after World War II, these countries were under French control, as the administrative federation of Indo-China, composed of the colony of Cochin-China and the four protectorates of Annam, Tonking, Cambodia and Laos. The population is mainly Annamese. Their religion, patterned after Confucianism, is of Chinese origin. Cambodians comprise the second largest

ethnic group. They resemble the Thais. Buddhism is their religion, and their culture is similar to that of India.

Malaya.—British traders and plantation owners became active in Malaya in the eighteenth century. However, it was only in the late nineteenth century that the British Government became officially interested in Malaya's development. Malaya is called the melting pot of Asia. Besides the major portion of native Malayans, there are a substantial number of Chinese, Thais, Indians and people from nearby islands. Mohammedanism is the dominant religion. The natives have their own language and literature. The Malayan Federation is a Dominion of Great Britain.

THE NEAR EAST

We shall now consider the most western of all Oriental civilizations, that of the Near East. The contributions of the Babylonians, the Assyrians and the Hebrews are really a part of the history of the western world, as is the role played by the Arabs in conserving and improving the science of Greece and Alexandria and introducing it into Europe through Spain. But the religion of the Arabs, Mohammedanism, had a tremendous influence upon near eastern civilization and it spread over much of eastern Asia. After the first wave of Arab enterprise had spent itself in the 7th century A.D. it was Persia that contributed most to Near Eastern civilization.

Persia (Iran).—The history of ancient Persia is closely bound up with that of Greece and is principally noteworthy for the governmental methods of Darius I and the amazing conquests of Cyrus the Great. After centuries of strife a Persian prince named Ardashir founded about 226 A.D. a purely Persian line of rulers called the *Sassanid* dynasty (from Sassan, Ardashir's grandfather). The Sassanids reigned until 641, and in these four centuries Persia became powerful and wealthy, and art and literature flourished. Zoroastrianism, the early Persian religion, which explained life as a conflict between the gods of good and evil, was revived and flourished until the Arabs conquered Persia in 641 and made it Mohammedan. Persia then did much to bring about the Golden Age of Islam or Mohammedanism (749–847).

Mohammedanism.—Mohammedanism or Islam is the third great religion of the Near East and was founded by Mohammed (*c.* 570–632). In the religion of Islam, he is known as a prophet, along with Adam, Noah, Abraham, Moses and Jesus. At 40 Mohammed announced to the world that he had received visions from God and was convinced that he was God's messenger. His revelations have been collected in the Koran, the sacred book of Islam, which is written in classical Arabic. Every good Moslem centers his life about the performance of five duties: the acceptance of the confession of faith, "There is no good but the true God (Allah) and Mohammed is his prophet"; prayer, five times in every 24 hours, with the face turned towards Mecca; almsgiving; observance of the sacred month of Ramadan by fasting from dawn to sunset, and the pilgrimage to Mecca, which he must make at least once in his lifetime. The Koran describes the coming of a judgment day and the heaven and the hell awaiting in the hereafter; eternal punishment is the fate of those guilty of hypocrisy (professing, without having, a religion), murder, theft, adultery, luxury, dishonesty and other derelictions. Drinking, gambling and usury are rigorously prohibited as a part of Mohammedanism.

Though in the main the Persians were converted to Islam, they did not lose their national consciousness. To protect themselves against the predominant Arab element in Islam, the Persians took advantage of the schism that split Islam into two parts. Those Mohammedans who occupy the eastern half of the Mohammedan world or Persia became known as the Shiites; those of the western or Arab division were known as the Sunnites. The former are regarded as schismatics by the orthodox Sunnites. During the period of the Eastern Caliphate (or Moslem government) when the capital was at Bagdad, the Persian family of the Barmecides (descendants of Barmek) was largely responsible for the period of learning and culture that we associate with the name of Harun-al-Rashid, the hero of *The Arabian Nights*.

Even after the Arab Caliphate fell and the Seljuk Turks in the 11th century took up the task of defending Islam against the Christians, the Persians continued to contribute to Near Eastern civilization. Two of Persia's

great men were the poet-astronomer Omar Khayyám, whose verses are familiar through the translations of Edward FitzGerald to most readers of English literature, and a schoolmate of Omar's, the famous Hasan ibn-al-Sabbah, the founder of the dreaded secret society of the Assassins, really a sect of Islam. Hasan was better known to the Crusaders as the "old man of the mountain."

The Iranians are famous throughout the Orient for their skill in the manufacture of rugs, and in bookbinding. From China they learned the art of landscape gardening, so that the principal cities of Iran, Teheran, Isfahan, and Tabriz, are as famous for their rose gardens as for their mosques.

Today Iran is slowly undergoing a transformation due mostly to its ruler, Mohammed Reza Shah Pahlavi. The influence of the Moslem religion and its conventions is checked and women are allowed more freedom. Even the name of the country, Persia (Arabic in origin), has been changed to Iran or land of the Aryans to emphasize that the Persians are not Semitic, as are the Arabs, but belong to the same linguistic stock as the Europeans.

Turkey in Asia.—Central Asia is the homeland of the Turkish people. Thousands of years ago the area was quite fertile and the center of great civilizations; but as the plains dried up, civilization drifted into China, India and the Near East and only the hardy Turks remained.

It is difficult to classify them in any cultural group. They have been exposed to both Chinese and Persian influences through the centuries. In spite of that no great civilization has

been produced by the Turks, who are important mainly as warriors. When they became converted to Islam, or Mohammed's religion, their prowess as fighters helped protect and even spread that faith. Wave after wave of conquering hordes have emerged from Turkestan: the Seljuk Turks, who conquered Persia; the Ottoman Turks, who once threatened even Europe; and the armies of Tamerlane, who established a brilliant but short-lived empire with its capital at Samarkand at the end of the 14th century. Samarkand had played an important part in the trade between China and Persia and rose to its height of glory under Tamerlane. He was buried in one of its numerous mosques.

The greatest figure of the Ottoman Empire (1289-1922) was the sixteenth century Sultan Suleiman the Magnificent, who consolidated the Empire's boundaries and stabilized its political and legal institutions.

It was the Ottoman Turks who, in modern times, of all Oriental people, penetrated farthest into Europe. Though they kept much of southeastern Europe under their political influences for centuries, their cultural influence in Europe was negligible for they made no attempt to force their Christian subjects to adopt Islam and Oriental culture. Gradually they were expelled from their European possessions. Today Constantinople, which the Turks now call *Istanbul*, is the only foothold of Oriental civilization in Europe. Thus, this city, once the bulwark of western civilization during the Byzantine period, now acts as a bridgehead from the Occident to the Orient, located as it is at the crossroads of the world.

THE MIDDLE AGES

The long period that separated antiquity from modern times is called the Middle Ages or the medieval period. It is, of course, impossible to limit such a period by precise dates, but for convenience we may assume that it began about the year 400 and ended about 1500. In these eleven hundred years there emerged, flourished and declined a civilization fundamentally different from that of the Greeks or Romans on the one hand and from that of our day on the other.

The first stage in the evolution of this new civilization was the fusion of Roman and German peoples and institutions that took place between the 5th and 8th centuries. At the beginning of this period Roman emperors still governed Europe; but they were unable to check the progress of internal decay or to prevent tribes of German barbarians from crossing the frontiers and settling in their choicest provinces.

After the year 476 there was no Roman Empire in the West; yet its institutions and traditions lived on. From Rome, the Middle Ages inherited many of their most characteristic features, notably the ideal of a single

great state under an autocratic emperor. Roman law and the Latin tongue likewise survived the Roman state, as did the Christian religion and the Christian Church.

Roman civilization, however, was profoundly modified by the German invaders. The Nordic physical type was transplanted to Gaul, Spain, North Africa, Britain and Italy itself. In some areas, as in Britain, German dialects displaced the native tongues. Many military and legal institutions of the Middle Ages seem clearly to have been of German origin; but historians do not agree how great the influence of the Germans was upon the economic and social life of the regions where they settled.

Politically, this period of fusion was one of great disorder. A number of petty German kingdoms occupied the territory of the former Roman Empire. The history of these kingdoms is a dreary tale of perpetual war, murder and rapine.

The Early Church.—The one force making for stability was the Roman Catholic Church, which already possessed an effective organization. The smallest administrative unit was the parish, supervised by the priest. Parishes

were grouped into dioceses, each diocese governed by a bishop. Dioceses in turn were grouped into provinces, each province being under an archbishop or metropolitan. Supreme jurisdiction over the entire system was claimed by the bishop of Rome, the Pope. The popes held that they were the successors of St. Peter, whom Jesus had designated chief of the Apostles and to whom he had given miraculous powers. Accepted in western Europe, papal supremacy was disputed in the East.

An important development within the Church was the rise and spread of monasticism. Christian monasticism originated in Egypt. The first monks were hermits who sought to save their souls by exiling themselves from society. As time went on, many of these hermits formed communities where they lived together in a monastery under the rule of an elected abbot.

Monasticism spread to the West in the 4th century. There St. Benedict of Nursia (480-543) gave it definite form by drawing up a famous set of rules for the government of a monastery. This Benedictine Rule defines the duties and obligations of the monk, divides his day between manual labor and divine service, and even prescribes what he shall eat, drink and wear. Practical and moderate, it proved immensely popular and became the generally accepted rule of western monasteries.

To overemphasize the services of the Church in this period is impossible. Its splendid organization, directed by such able popes as Leo the Great (pope, 440–61) and Gregory the Great (pope, 590–604), did much to preserve civilization. In the absence of efficient civil government, the Church assumed responsibility for education, charity and the care of the sick. The Benedictine monks were tireless missionaries and pioneers, working among pagan Anglo-Saxons, Frisians and Thuringians. Their monasteries were islands of order and peace in a sea of chaos and war. They sheltered libraries and scholars and frequently had model farms where the agricultural science of the ancients was still known and applied.

The Byzantine Empire.—Meanwhile in the Balkan Peninsula, Asia Minor, Syria, Palestine and Egypt, the Roman Empire, with its capital at Constantinople (formerly Byzantium), still held sway. In the 6th century, this Byzantine Empire experienced a revival of its former glory. Under Justinian (emperor, 527–65), northern Africa, Italy and even part of Spain were reconquered. Roman law was codified in the *Corpus Juris Civilis*. The great domed Church of St. Sophia was built. Justinian's successors, however, lost his western gains and had difficulty in holding the capital itself. In the 7th century the empire was beset by a new enemy, the Mohammedans.

Mohammedanism.—Mohammedanism takes its name from its founder, Mohammed (or Mahomet) (*c.* 570–632), a native of Mecca in Arabia. Despite many obstacles, Mohammed succeeded in converting many of the Bedouin tribes to his religious views, the essence of which is, "There is but one God, Allah, and Mohammed is his Prophet." His followers are often called Moslems, and the whole civilization of Mohammedanism is styled Moslem.

Under the successors of Mohammed, the caliphs, the Arabs became a great conquering power. They overran Persia, Syria, Palestine, Egypt and northern Africa. In 711 they began the conquest of Spain. Their advance into Europe was not checked until 732 when the Franks defeated them in the Battle of Tours. In 717 they failed in an attempt to take Constantinople. They had occupied most of the important islands of the Mediterranean, whence they proceeded to subject Europe to an enforced isolation by severing the trade routes with the East.

The civilization of Mohammedan lands between the 8th and 12th centuries presented a sharp contrast to the semibarbarism of Europe. The luxurious courts of the caliphs were centers of art and letters. The cities enjoyed material comforts and conveniences undreamed of in the West. Learned men translated the works of

BETTMANN ARCHIVE

JEAN MIELOT, a self-portrait in the scriptorium. Scriptoria, which were begun in 526 A.D., were the writing rooms in which the monks of the medieval church studied and copied many religious manuscripts. It is to this practice that we owe the preservation of religious works and numerous chronicles of the time that serve as sources of historical reference.

Greek philosophers and scientists into Arabic. Mohammedan scholars did much to advance mathematics, astronomy, chemistry and medicine. The time was to come when Europe would profit greatly from their labors.

The Rise of the Frankish State.—In western Europe the major political development between 500 and 800 was the expansion of the Frankish state. The Franks were a Germanic tribe. Under their king, Clovis (*c.* 465–511), they conquered all of northern and southwestern Gaul. It was under Clovis, too, that they were converted from paganism to Roman Catholicism, an event of great importance, for it gained the Frankish king the support of the people and the co-operation of the bishops and native population of Gaul.

The successors of Clovis extended his conquests to the southeast and across the Rhine into Germany. As time went on, however, the kings became utterly incapable. By the 8th century they were mere figureheads. The actual government was in the hands of one of their officials, the Mayor of the Palace. In 752 a mayor named Pepin deposed the reigning descendant of Clovis and assumed the royal title. The dynasty established by Pepin is called Carolingian, descendants of Charles, from Pepin's son Charles (Latin, *Carolus*).

The Age of Charlemagne.—Charles the Great or Charlemagne (742–814) is one of the most imposing figures in history. A mighty conqueror, he annexed most of Italy, much of Germany and part of northern Spain to the already extensive Frankish territories.

Certainly his dominions were imperial in extent, and on Christmas Day, 800, the Pope crowned him Roman Emperor. Thus the imperial tradition was revived and the Medieval Empire was born.

Charles the Great was more than a conqueror; he was a great ruler. His vast dominions were efficiently administered by local counts, who were held strictly responsible for their actions by agents sent out directly by the king. Education and learning were encouraged with such gratifying results that historians sometimes speak of a Carolingian Renaissance.

Unfortunately this promising reign was followed by two centuries of chaos. The successors of Charlemagne divided his realm and fought among themselves and with their nobles. To make matters worse, Europe was scourged by new invasions. Fierce, pagan vikings swept down from Scandinavia and harried the coasts and river valleys of Britain and Gaul. The Asiatic Magyars (ancestors of the Hungarians) plundered and burned their way across Germany. Mohammedan pirates laid waste the coasts of Gaul and Italy.

Feudalism.—The Carolingians were quite unable to defend their subjects. In its dire necessity, society turned to feudalism. People no longer looked to the central government for protection, but to local nobles who had castles and bands of armed retainers. The term feudalism comes from the custom of the fee or fief, called *feudum* in medieval Latin. A fief was land granted by one man, called the lord, to another man, called the vassal, which means servant or subject. The vassal swore allegiance to the lord and promised to render him military assistance and other honorable services. It is important to note that both lord and vassal were nobles. Very often a man was lord and vassal at the same time. He might be lord of A and vassal of B. In the 9th and following centuries most of Europe was divided into fiefs. This meant the virtual disappearance of the state and central government. The king became simply a great feudal lord. His own vassals owed him certain services, but the vassals of his vassals owed him nothing at all. Nor did the king have a monopoly of the functions that we associate with central government. Most feudal lords had political powers, such as the rights to try people in their courts and to coin money.

Physically a fief was one or more great estates or manors. The center of the manor was the lord's castle or manor house. Close by was a village in which the most conspicuous building was the church. Around the village stretched the fields and forests. The villagers received protection from the lord of the manor. In return for this and for the use of the lands they occupied, they had to devote part of their time to the cultivation of the lord's crops. They also owed him certain payments. Most of the peasants were serfs who could not leave the estate and were subject to a perplexing variety of obligations.

The Holy Roman Empire.—The 10th century was a dark one. In England, the successors of Alfred the Great (king, 871–901) were powerless to resist a new Danish invasion. In France the Carolingians were displaced in 987 by the Capetians, who were no more able to maintain order than their predecessors. In Spain the Mohammedans crowded the Christians into the extreme North. In Italy, while rival lords fought each other, the papacy became the pawn of Roman politicians. Only in Germany were conditions better. There the vigorous Otto the Great (912–73) put an end to the Magyar invasions and checked disintegration. He was even able to conquer northern Italy and to assume the title of Roman Emperor; but this Holy Roman Empire included only Germany and Otto's Italian conquests.

The Crusades.—The 11th century saw the beginning of a general recovery that was to reach its height in the two succeeding centuries. This recovery was greatly stimulated by the Crusades (1096–1270). A succession of vigorous popes, notably Gregory VII (pope, 1073–85), had reformed the Church and freed the papacy from lay control. A follower of Gregory, Urban II (pope, 1088–99), sought further prestige for the papacy by uniting Europe for the recovery of Jerusalem from the Mohammedan Turks so that it would again be in Christian hands.

With the blessing of Pope Urban the First Crusade departed for the East in 1096. The crusaders captured Jerusalem in 1099, but the four petty states they established in Palestine and Syria were constantly threatened with extermination. This was staved off for a long time by the dispatch of

THE METROPOLITAN MUSEUM OF ART

THE HARVESTERS, an engraving after a painting by Pieter Breughel the Elder. This sixteenth century painting is an excellent example of Breughel's ability to capture the atmosphere of peasant life. It depicts noontime in a Flemish field during the wheat harvest.

new crusades from the West; but in 1291, Acre, the last Christian stronghold, was captured by the Egyptians.

Judged by their direct accomplishments, the Crusades were a failure; yet their by-products were of vast importance. Trade between East and West was stimulated. Europe escaped from its isolation. With trade, money again came into general use; old towns increased in population and many entirely new towns appeared; a new social class, the townsmen, began to play an important role in history. Europe's intellectual horizon was greatly extended, for the new intercourse with the East was quite as much a matter of ideas as it was of spices and silks. It may be added that the Crusades led to the collapse of the Byzantine Empire, for in 1204 a crusading army captured Constantinople. Though the Byzantines recovered it in 1261, the empire had been so enfeebled that it fell an easy prey to the Ottoman Turks, who finally took the capital in 1453.

The Rise of Powerful Governments.—Economic revival was accompanied by revival of the state. Many feudal lords never came back from the Crusades and feudalism declined. Kings were now able to pay soldiers in money, instead of land, and in the townsmen they found valuable allies.

Thus the successors of William the Conqueror (king, 1066–87) in England created a strong government that curbed the power of the nobility at every turn. It is true that *Magna Charta* (1215) and the rise of Parliament in the 13th century limited the royal power; nevertheless an able and energetic king could still rule England in fact as well as in name.

A similar development took place in France. Such ambitious rulers as Philip Augustus (1180–1223) and Philip the Fair (1285–1314) extended the royal domain by annexing the lands of their vassals and created a corps of administrative officials to whom the king's will was law. When Philip the Fair died in 1314, France was well advanced on the road to absolutism.

The Hohenstaufen rulers (1138–1254) of the Holy Roman Empire also tried to increase the power of the central government. Unfortunately, they tried to do too much—to control Italy as well as Germany—and they were defeated by the Pope and his allies, the powerful Italian cities. As a result, neither Italy nor Germany had a strong central government until modern times.

The Culture of the Middle Ages.—In this period medieval civilization reached its full development. Translations from Greek and Arabic into Latin made the vast knowledge of the ancient and Mohammedan philosophers and scientists accessible to Europeans. Justinian's codification of the Roman civil law was rediscovered, and the autocratic principles of the Roman law helped the state to triumph over feudalism. Schools flourished and the universities were born. The earliest of these were in Bologna, Paris and Oxford. Crowds of students thronged the lecture halls of these institutions where they studied the seven liberal arts—grammar, rhetoric, logic, arithmetic, geometry, astronomy and music—or took advanced courses in medicine, law or theology.

Theology was considered the queen of sciences. To it the best intellects

BETTMANN ARCHIVE

KNIGHTS departing for the Crusades (1095–1272). This painting of the School of Bourguignonne, illustrates one of the many military expeditions to free the Holy Land.

of the day devoted themselves. The intensely formal and logical methods of the theologians and their philosophy were called Scholasticism. The greatest of the Scholastics or Schoolmen was St. Thomas Aquinas (c. 1225–74), who harmonized the teachings of Aristotle (384–322 B.C.) with the doctrines of the Church and reduced Catholic theology to a clear and logical system.

At this time the Middle Ages made their greatest contributions to literature and to art. Latin was still used in all formal literature but now there began to be a less formal literature in the vernacular or everyday language of the people. Epics recounting the exploits of Roland, King Arthur and Alexander the Great were composed in Romance and the Germanic dialects; but the supreme achievement of medieval literary genius was the *Divine Comedy* of Dante Alighieri (1265–1321), the first great work in Italian.

In architecture, the 12th century deviated from the heavy, stolid Romanesque building and created a new style, later called Gothic. By a liberal use of spires, gabled roofs and perpendicular lines, Gothic architecture creates the illusion of height. Its conspicuous features are pointed arches, ribbed vaulting and flying buttresses. The large windows are filled with the most exquisite stained glass that has ever been produced. Gothic architecture was primarily a style for churches, and its finest examples are such cathedrals as Chartres, Reims, Notre Dame in Paris and Amiens.

The Church in the Later Middle Ages.— The Church was the dominant factor not only in this brilliant intellectual and cultural development but also in all the life of medieval man. The primary purpose of the Church was saving souls, but in many ways the

Church had become like a great state: it was an involuntary association; a person was born into it and could not leave it. It taxed him, tried him in its courts and looked out for him in sickness or poverty. It was efficiently governed through the hierarchy of priests, bishops and archbishops, and at its head was the Pope, an absolute monarch. Innocent III (Pope, 1198–1216) was not content with supremacy within the Church. He vigorously asserted that the Pope was superior to all kings and emperors, and a number of important rulers were obliged to admit his claims. In short, the Church, originally a spiritual institution, in the 13th century was becoming a great superstate.

The intellectual ferment of the 12th and 13th centuries produced only critics of the clergy and rebels against the doctrines of the Church. Such rebels, called heretics, became very numerous. To defend itself against them the Church organized regular crusades, for example, against the Albigensians around Toulouse and Albi in southern France in the years 1209 to 1229. Another weapon was the Inquisition, a special court for the trial of heretics. More effective against heresy was a spiritual revival within the Church itself. The two great leaders in this revival were St. Francis of Assisi (1182?–1226) and St. Dominic (1170–1221, born and educated in Spain), who founded the Franciscan and the Dominican orders of friars. In many ways the friars resembled the earlier orders of monks, but their main aim was preaching to the masses and caring for them, rather than saving their own souls. Their unselfish devotion to society did much to check the spread of heresy and to give people fresh confidence in the Church.

Despite the success of the Church

in suppressing rebellion in the 13th century, the next two centuries witnessed an alarming decline in its prestige. Between 1309 and 1377 the popes made their residence at Avignon in France instead of at Rome. Rightly or wrongly they were suspected of being mere pawns in the political game of the French kings. This Babylonian captivity was followed by the Great Schism (1378–1417). The rivalry of two, and then three, claimants to the papal tiara perplexed and scandalized all Europe. Heresy grew rapidly under such notable leaders as John Wycliffe (c.1324–84) in England and John Huss (1369–1415) in Bohemia. In 1417 the Council of Constance ended the Great Schism, but untold damage had been done that the popes of the late 15th century were unable to repair. Interested in establishing their control over the Papal States and enamored of the literary and artistic splendors of the Renaissance, they were famous for military prowess, diplomatic skill and esthetic taste, but rarely for piety or moral leadership.

The Rise of National Consciousness.— Still more threatening to the Church was the growth of national consciousness throughout Europe. This was evident even in such politically disunited areas as Germany and Italy. It was most apparent in England and in France during the Hundred Years' War (1337–1453). In England the new dislike of the foreigner was shown in the substitution of English for French as the language of law and of literature. It is noteworthy, too, that Wycliffe's opposition to the papacy was quite as much patriotic as religious. In France patriotism developed somewhat more slowly, only revealing itself when Joan of Arc in the years 1429 to 1431 rallied it for the expulsion of the English.

Equally dangerous to the Church was the parallel rise of political absolutism. By 1500 what we of today should call dictatorship was established in many parts of Europe. The petty states of Italy had long been ruled by families of despots, the Sforzas of Milan and the Medici of Florence. In France the king had become absolute, thanks to the work of Charles VII (king, 1422–61) and Louis XI (king, 1461–83). In England, Henry VII (king, 1485–1509) was founding the strong monarchy of the Tudors. In Spain, Ferdinand and Isabella, having united Castile and Aragon by their marriage in 1469, were expanding the royal power at the expense of the Church, the nobles and the cities. There were even attempts to strengthen the central government of the Holy Roman Empire; but in Germany it was the princes and not the emperor who were to become absolute.

The Renaissance.— Not only was the Church's political position being challenged but a new secular culture threatened the older culture of the Church. The rise of this new culture —and the new culture itself—is called the Renaissance, which means rebirth. The essential characteristic of the Renaissance was boundless admiration for classical antiquity. The movement began in Italy, where it found its first great exponent in Petrarch (1304–74). Scorning Scholasticism, this Florentine devoted himself body and soul to the classics. He read them avidly, imitated them in his own writing and sought high and low for lost manuscripts of classical authors. His enthusiasm was contagious. He left numerous disciples and imitators. They came to be called Humanists because Greek and Latin literature were called the humanities or the more human literatures in contradistinction to the sacred literature of the Bible, theology and the Church. Princes, wealthy burghers and even popes came under their spell and proved to be generous patrons.

Enthusiasm for the glories of Greece and Rome spread from literature to art. In the 15th century the architects abandoned Gothic for the classical style. The sculptors studied and imitated the surviving examples of ancient statuary. The painters had no paintings from Greece and Rome to imitate, so they strove to make their pictures realistic and lifelike, which was quite in keeping with the classical ideal. A new epoch in the progress of art had begun.

In all this the Italian cities, especially Florence, took the lead; yet the Renaissance was not to remain an exclusively Italian movement. In the 15th century it spread beyond the Alps, to produce in the northern countries the great humanist Erasmus (c.1466–1536) and the great artist Dürer (1471–1528).

It would be a mistake to attribute all of the great achievements of the 14th and 15th centuries to the classical revival. Many other factors were at work. Thus it is difficult to find any direct connection between Humanism and the revolutionary invention of printing in the 1450's or the even more revolutionary voyages of exploration that resulted in the discovery of the New World.

Nevertheless the classical revival was a very significant event in history. In 1300 European life and culture had centered in the Church. By 1500 Europe was becoming secularized. The national autocratic state was claiming man's allegiance even at the expense of his allegiance to the Church. A culture emphasizing man and his works was displacing one that stressed the spirit and the world to come. The Middle Ages were in dissolution. Our own age was assuming its familiar form.

MODERN EUROPE

Prior to the modern age European society consisted of the privileged aristocracy and the dependent serfs or farmers. All these people lived in small self-sufficient economic units, the agricultural manor villages, which had little need for businessmen to serve as economic go-betweens. By the 12th century the merchants and traders began to attain power. The building of towns, the expansion of trade and the formation of kingdoms were some of the causes that explain their rise.

At the beginning of the modern period two great movements—the Commercial Revolution and the Renaissance—led the business and professional men (the middle classes) on to fortune. The Commercial Revolution (1400–1700) gave them an opportunity to weaken the opposition of the privileged nobles and clergy and to advance in wealth and social position. The discovery of America, the remarkable development of trade and industry and the influx of gold and silver led to the establishment of the modern capitalistic or profit system. Gold and silver became the common mediums of exchange; barter virtually disappeared; and the increase of trade that followed brought the rise of rich and influential businessmen, capable of directing governments as well as commercial enterprises.

Age of Discovery.—Great colonial empires arose as a result of the Age of Discovery. As overseas possessions were established, the center of economic activity passed from the ports around the Mediterranean to the Atlantic. Portugal, Spain, Holland, France and England engaged in trading activities and created huge empires. Kings, often backed by the wealthy middle classes, destroyed the political power of their aristocratic subjects.

In a way the Italian Renaissance between the 14th and 16th centuries promoted the rise of businessmen. Individualism and emphasis upon worldly things, the bases of a middle-class regime, were the fundamental reasons why Renaissance men attempted to imitate the ancients in art and living. Wealthy individuals of that time, the Medici in Florence, for example, took keen delight in becoming patrons of learning that would sanction earthly rather than spiritual ways of living.

This Renaissance was not limited to the Italian city-states. Wherever the Commercial Revolution made possible the rise of the middle classes, an intellectual revolution took place. Sixteenth-century England enjoyed a golden age (the Elizabethan period) that culminated in the plays of Shakespeare. Seventeenth-century Holland experienced a scientific, educational and artistic birth that made possible the beautiful paintings of Rembrandt. Germany inaugurated the Christian Renaissance that resulted in the Protestant Revolt.

Commercial Policies.—This religious revolution contributed to the rise of our capitalistic age. Stanch defender of the established order, the medieval Christian Church favored the hierarchy of classes and feared the anarchy of individualism. The subordination of the material to the spiritual side of life was its constant aim. Despite its emphasis upon otherworldliness, the Church possessed great wealth and so laid itself open to criticism. Something had to yield. Advocating a return to the doctrinal and administrative simplicity of the early Christian Church, Martin Luther in Germany, John Calvin in Switzerland and John Knox in Scotland in the first half of the 16th century led the Protestant Revolt and founded Protestant sects whose followers live today in all parts of the world.

These religious leaders contributed to the economic and political as well as to the religious movements of their day. Through their emphasis upon the right of the individual to work out his own salvation by hard work and clean living, they indirectly sanctioned the activities of businessmen. To many of their followers the test of salvation was economic success as well as moral perfectibility; but the outstanding result of the Protestant Revolt was the subordination of religion to politics as the dominant factor in life. Henceforth the individual owed allegiance to the monarch as well as to the Church.

By the 17th century some European kings were virtually dictators. Desirous of increasing their power by creating prosperous states they adopted a new doctrine of political economy—mercantilism. The essense of this belief was a money theory of wealth. Gold and silver were the sources from which the prosperity of the state was derived. Therefore, the acquisition of this money by selling the maximum amount of goods to foreign countries and by buying the minimum amount from them was the objective of these mercantilist rulers.

During the 17th and 18th centuries this mercantilist policy was adopted by the monarchs of nearly all countries engaged in commerce and industry. Spain used it to exploit her great empire; the Italian city-states and the German countries applied it with success; in Holland, England and France it experienced its greatest triumphs. During the reign (1643–1715) of Louis XIV, famous for his autocratic saying, *"L'état c'est moi"* ("I am the State"), France became the classical example of an absolute mercantilist state. As a result of her commercial expansion she created one of the largest colonial empires, became the dominant nation in Europe and was recognized as the cultural center of the world.

The Intellectual Leaders.—The old order however, was not adapted to the growing capitalist regime. Three defects and abuses present in absolute monarchy—feudal society, paternalism and mercantilism—aroused much criticism. By the 18th century an intellectual revolt took place. First the scientists, Francis Bacon, René Descartes and Isaac Newton, and then the publicists, Voltaire, Jean Jacques Rousseau and Adam Smith, led the opposition. Through their researches they evolved a scientific method and a philosophical point of view that tended to weaken the bases of the privileged classes and the absolute government itself. Affirming a belief in social progress, some of these intellectual leaders asserted that the decadent absolute monarchies and the degenerate feudalism would have to give way to a new order. They advanced the concept of natural law, denounced the theory of the divine right of kings and attacked social inequalities and religious intolerance.

As bitter opponents of the old regime the traders welcomed suggestions that would enable them to advance their interests. They accepted, therefore, the views of the 18th-century English economist, Adam Smith. Maintaining in his famous book, *Wealth of Nations,* that the true strength of a nation lies in the prosperity of its citizens, Smith claimed that unrestricted enterprise promotes the accumulation of riches by the individual. In direct opposition to mercantilism he asserted that government interference in business is useless and even harmful; that each man knows best how to acquire wealth, and if he were permitted to adopt a policy of self-interest the nation would become rich. This doctrine of *laissez faire* (leave things alone, do not interfere) constituted the expression of economic liberty.

The Revolutions.—Influenced by these views, men strove first for intellectual and religious liberty, later for political rights and eventually for economic freedom. A series of upheavals resulted from attempts to realize these aims. In England a civil war (1642–49) and the so-called Glorious Revolution of 1688 resulted in the supremacy of Parliament. In America the Revolution of 1776 brought independence to the Thirteen Colonies and led to the abolition of mercantilism in England. The French Revolution of 1789 overthrew the monarchy, abolished the nobility and established political control by the business classes.

Two important 18th-century developments insured the supremacy of the capitalistic system—the Agricultural and Industrial revolutions, both resulting from a technological revolution that put mechanical power to work on the farm and in the factory. Scientific methods applied to all phases of rural and town life practically revolutionized agriculture and industry in England. Wealthy farmers abolished the strip system and introduced new notions of farming and stock raising. The soil was drained and fertilized, crops were rotated and sheep and cattle were carefully bred. New labor-saving devices, the reaper, the loom and the power machine, the steamboat and the locomotive, were introduced into agriculture, industry and transportation. Utilization of steam power resulted in the construction of factories and the increased output of manufactured articles, and made goods cheaper, promoted demand and revolutionized transportation and communication.

Accompanying this transformation came a complete change in the economic system. The feudal regime disappeared. In place of a social structure in which the status of each individual was determined by birth, tradition and law and under which production was carried on to meet immediate needs, there was an attempt to set up complete equality in social and political life; manufacturing was for future needs and in great quantity; and the profit motive became dominant.

Rise of Middle and Lower Classes.—This capitalist regime benefited the businessmen first and then contributed to the rise of the wage earner by making him class conscious. The workers soon refused to submit to the evils brought about by the mechanization of industry. They formed unions to better their own conditions and fought against the political and social restrictions of the old feudal regime only less vigorously than did the businessmen themselves.

Led by the middle classes, many wage earners and peasants helped to destroy the old order in the French Revolution of 1789. The destructive excesses of the Revolution soon alarmed the moderate liberals. Opposed to the wars, corruption, inefficiency and radicalism of the republican government, they submitted in 1799 to the dictatorship of Napoleon Bonaparte as First Consul. In 1804 he became emperor.

Napoleon as Dictator.—As head of the French state Napoleon I sought to create a great empire in which men, though denied political liberty, might enjoy legal equality and careers would be determined by talent; but Napoleon failed to realize his ideas. In his attempt to bring glory and prosperity to France by dominating the Continent and by creating a world empire, he encountered the opposition of the greater part of Europe. His disastrous invasion of Russia (1812) and his defeat at Waterloo (1815) finally doomed the Napoleonic scheme.

The representatives of England, Russia, Prussia and Austria tried at the Congress of Vienna (1815) to reestablish the balance of power whereby no single nation could dominate Europe. The continental states also attempted to check the spread of such liberal ideas as nationalism, constitutionalism and individual liberty.

Unrest of the 40s.—Despite the opposition of the conservatives, nearly every European country was touched by the revolutionary tendencies of 1815–48. In England the passage of the Reform Bills of 1832 and 1867 resulted in the establishment of a democratic government. In France the revolutions of 1830 and 1848 led to the creation of the Second French Republic. In various European states constitutions were granted and serfdom abolished. In Denmark a moderate constitution was created in 1849. In the Netherlands the people first obtained national independence and then gained political rights. In Switzerland the problem was one of nationalism rather than democracy. In the Balkans nationalist movements resulted in the gradual decline of the Ottoman Empire.

These revolutions were important because they were preliminary manifestations by Western peoples of their desire for national unity, control of government and social equality—all necessary in order that the capitalistic system might find an environment in which it could flourish. Complete success, the establishment of the middle-class order, was not feasible at that time. Before this transformation was possible, the Industrial Revolution had to create, in the revolutionary centers, more numerous businessmen and workingmen.

Radical Movements.—A division between the middle classes and the wage earners often delayed the progress of liberalism. This division was accentuated by the rise of radical movements—especially Socialism. Attacking capitalism, Socialist leaders, the Frenchman, Louis Blanc (1811–82), and the German, Karl Marx (1818–83), urged the workers to obtain economic and so political supremacy also by seizing the agencies of production and distribution and consequently the government. Opposed to these ideas, after 1848, the middle classes often favored certain features of the old regime—the monarchy and the dictatorship for instance—rather than a socialistic order.

Between 1848 and 1870 the revolutionary movement resulted in bourgeois, rather than socialistic, reforms. Led by Count Cavour (1810–61) and other patriots and aided by France, the Italian people expelled the Austrians, created a United Italy and established a constitutional monarchy. At the same time the Germans, ably directed by Otto von Bismarck, gained unity in the form of an autocratic empire by means of three successful wars. Liberalism even penetrated reactionary Russia. In 1861 Czar Alexander II emancipated twenty-three million serfs and introduced other reforms that made Russia a little more like western Europe.

Cultural Progress.—Europe prospered as a result of these advances. The period 1848–78, the mid-Victorian age, marked a high point in English economic and cultural progress comparable to the Elizabethan period. By 1848 the middle classes ruled England. They had grown in numbers and in power, thanks to the Technological and Industrial revolutions that rapidly made Great Britain an industrial beehive. As in the period of the Italian Renaissance, this economic prosperity was accompanied by marked cultural and scientific progress. Brilliant books were written by such earnest writers as William Makepeace Thackeray, Robert and Elizabeth Barrett Browning and Charles Dickens; and astounding discoveries were made in the fields of physics, geology and biology by Michael Faraday, Sir Charles Lyell and Charles Darwin.

Literary, scientific and industrial achievements were not limited to England. Honoré de Balzac, the French novelist; Georg Wilhelm Hegel, the German philosopher; Leo Tolstoy, the Russian literary giant, and Henrik Ibsen, the Scandinavian playwright, are a few of the great European intellectuals of the 19th century. The Frenchman Louis Pasteur, who laid the foundations of bacteriology, was but one of a great number of investigators many of them German, who in the late 19th century made Europe the scientific center of the world and the

PIX INC. (PHOTO DALMAS)

NUCLEAR TEST BAN TREATY, signed in Moscow on Aug. 5, 1963, was the tri-power agreement to ban testing in space and under water. The principal signers were Britain's Lord Home, Russia's Andrei Gromyko, and the United State's Dean Rusk. Shown here are Sen. J. W. Fulbright, Sen. Hubert Humphrey, Adlai Stevenson, U Thant and Nikita Khrushchev.

starting point of an entirely new phase of science.

Industrial progress was especially marked in Germany. By 1914 she ranked only after the United States and England as a coal producer and ahead of England in the manufacture of iron. In shipping Germany was second only to England and in the electrical and chemical industries Germany took the lead. Despite a declining rural population, German scientists and technicians were able to increase Germany's crops by promoting careful soil preparation and by producing and using fertilizers and agricultural machinery. Their development of the sugar beet was a noteworthy achievement.

All this cultural and economic development, however, had its dark side. The rise of the capitalistic system and large-scale business led to a vast accumulation of capital that caused further growth and expansion of business enterprises. By 1870 diminishing profits at home and economic opportunities abroad caused businessmen to seek raw materials, markets and places for investments in the so-called backward lands.

Improved means of communication and transportation, especially the telegraph, steamship and railway, accentuated the spread of capitalism. By making the world relatively smaller these conveniences contributed to the development of profitable trade with distant lands. Vast sums were expended in the creation of these transportation facilities. To safeguard these and other business enterprises, capitalists soon urged their governments to assume direct or indirect control over remote parts of the earth.

Empire Building.—Between 1870 and 1914 European nations took possession of large parts of Africa and Asia. In Africa, Great Britain obtained control of the Suez Canal, Egypt, the Sudan and a large part of the South; France built a great Mediterranean empire in North Africa; and Germany, Belgium, Portugal, Spain and Italy gained smaller areas of African territory. In Asia, Russia greatly extended her Siberian Empire; England exploited her Indian Empire; and France, Germany and Holland had minor possessions. By 1914 the European states were ready to devour China, the last tender territorial morsel in Asia.

Unfortunately this new imperialism was accompanied by the brand of diplomacy that frequently results in wars. By 1914 Europe was divided into two hostile camps, maintaining a precarious balance of power. On the one side were the have-not nations—Germany, Austria-Hungary and Italy (the Triple Alliance)—all of which wanted additional lands and increased opportunities. On the other side the have nations—Great Britain, France and Russia (the Triple Entente)—already possessed generous shares of the world. Statesmen on both sides wanted peace and attempted to settle all imperialist rivalries; but the economic antagonisms and hatreds that constantly endangered the maintenance of peace could not be controlled.

World War I.—Upon the assassination of the heir to the Austro-Hungarian throne, the same patriotism and nationalism that had contributed so much to the rise of the new order caused men of all classes to rally to their governments, and Europe plunged into one of the greatest of historic tragedies, the first World War.

After four years of conflict (1914–1918) superior human and material resources enabled the Allies to defeat the Central Powers and to attempt another balance of power. Germany, Austria, Hungary, Bulgaria and Turkey were deprived of valuable territories and saddled with heavy debts; new states—Poland, Czechoslovakia and Finland—were created, and the League of Nations, designed to maintain peace, was established.

After the war a number of events then threatened the peace of Europe. With industries hopelessly dislocated and disorganized by war demands, tremendous losses of man power and property and enormous inflation of financial systems, the entire post-war world was indeed in a lamentable state. Economic conditions in the defeated countries were especially bad. Burdened with heavy debts, these countries, especially Germany, Austria and Hungary, faced virtual bankruptcy.

The Communist State.—In addition to these difficulties, capitalistic Europe faced for the first time a communist state in Russia after her overthrow of the aristocratic government in 1917. Determined to end capitalism as well as absolutism, this communist government under the guidance of Lenin confiscated property, nationalized industry and abolished the profit system. An earnest effort was made to carry out the radical ideas of Karl Marx.

After the war communism threatened to overthrow capitalism in other European states. In Germany, in Austria, in Hungary—wherever the aftermath of the war created intense social unrest—radicalism secured a foothold. Capitalism was not destroyed, however. Under the leadership of dictators who aroused patriotism, abolished democracy and regimented society, communism was held in check.

The Dictators.—Intense antagonism to the provisions of the peace treaty of Versailles, 1919, together with poverty and destruction in western Europe, made it possible for Mussolini to create a Fascist Italy and aspire to empire. Hitler in Germany seized dictatorial power, created the Nazi state and sought world power. Stalin in Russia, after the death of Lenin in 1924, destroyed his opponents and established himself as sole ruler. In Spain, a prolonged civil war brought into power Franco who ruled the country as a dictator. Dictatorial rule has always been possible where the people of a country are dissatisfied and restless—where the social and economic set-up is unjust—and when the government is too corrupt or too weak to make any constructive changes. The recent dictators of Europe have been examples of this desire of the people to raise their standard of living, and to adjust the social inequalities. Unfortunately, they found out too late, the price that must be forfeited for this promised security.

World War II.—In Germany, Hitler had been assuring his people of the supremacy of the "master race" and their right to rule the world. To fulfill his promises, he launched a military campaign against his unprepared neighbors in September 1939, just twenty years after the signing of the Versailles Treaty. Eventually, most of the nations of the world were drawn into the cauldron of destruction.

When the war ended in 1945, Hitler and Mussolini were dead, and the Japanese empire was destroyed. The United States and Russia emerged as dominant world powers, the one as the champion of democracy; the other as the propagator of world communism. The "hot" war between nations gave way to a "cold" war between world ideologies, each striving to gain the support of the people of the world. The one offered individual welfare and freedom; the other collective security and submission to the will of the state.

Great Britain and France, impoverished by war-time losses of men and property, joined with some of the smaller nations of northwestern Europe in negotiating security pacts underwritten by the United States and Canada. Stalin in Russia controlled most of the nations of eastern Europe as satellite countries. These acted as a buffer wall of protection against alleged aggression from the West.

In order to help the countries of Western Europe regain a stable political, economic and social status, the United States initiated the Marshall plan of aid to Europe. They sent food, fuel, clothing, medicines and money to the people. This aid helped the nations to repair their industrial and agricultural economies. Aid was not extended to those war-devastated countries under the control of Russia. These nations exist under a controlled press and radio, and a refutation of human liberties. Their economy and society were too unstable to allow the people to effectively protest the seizure of their government by Russia. As a country becomes more stable the people protest more violently and will eventually throw off the yoke of the unwelcome dictator.

The United Nations was formed in the closing days of World War II, in the hope of preventing future wars and to help stabilize the world. It also hoped to control aggressor nations. Russia is a member, but has frequently used her veto on important proposals for world peace.

The British empire based its security on an extended Commonwealth of Nations but encouraged the independence of its colonies. Monarchism virtually disappeared from the continent. The nations of the world again began the race to re-arm. In 1946 Russia vetoed a U.S.-sponsored atomic energy control plan. In 1963 a Partial Nuclear Test Ban Treaty was signed by Britain, the U.S. and the USSR.

ASSOCIATED PRESS
WORLD LEADERS, U.S. Pres. Johnson and Soviet Premier Kosygin, met at Glassboro N.J. in June 1967 to discuss global problems.

UNITED NATIONS

The United Nations is an organization of nations that have voluntarily joined together to achieve a just peace and to ensure harmony and welfare in the world.

Its headquarters are in New York City, in a striking building complex that has become one of the best-known landmarks of that city. The building, on international territory, has come to symbolize the ideals of peace and brotherhood to all peoples.

The official languages are Chinese, English, French, Russian, and Spanish; the working languages are English and French. During meetings, speeches are simultaneously translated into all the official languages.

The United Nations is financed principally by contributions from its Member States: these are proportionately based on each country's economic power and are assessed by the General Assembly. In 1964 the budget appropriation for ordinary expenses amounted to $101,327,600.

Origins and Aims.—The concept of the United Nations derived from the League of Nations, which was established after World War I but unfortunately was unable to prevent aggression. In the first years of World War II, most people, trusting in an Allied victory, looked ahead to a more successful world organization that could serve as a guide and rallying point for their hopes and needs. The first document that anticipated "the establishment of a wider and permanent system of general security" was the Atlantic Charter, issued on August 14, 1941, by Franklin D. Roosevelt and Winston Churchill. The name "United Nations" was soon devised by Mr. Roosevelt and first appeared in the *Declaration of January 1, 1942,* which was an Allied pledge to pursue the war to a victorious conclusion and to adhere to the principles expressed in the Atlantic Charter. In several other wartime meetings the main features of the future world organization were worked out; and a conference was convened at San Francisco on April 25, 1945, while the war was still in progress. At this meeting the United Nations Charter was drafted by fifty nations (to which Poland was soon added); it was approved June 26 and became operative on October 24, 1945. The Charter's preamble embodies the ideals and the hopes of mankind: "To save succeeding generations from the scourge of war, . . . to reaffirm faith in fundamental human rights, . . . to establish conditions under which justice . . . can be maintained, . . . to promote social progress and better standards of life in larger freedom. . . ." The purposes of the organization are the maintenance of international peace and security through effective collective measures, the development of friendly relations among peoples, the achievement of international cooperation in disparate fields, and the coordination of the activities of nations in achieving these objectives.

AMERICAN AIRLINES

UN SECRETARIAT building in New York City.

The United Nations does not purport to be a kind of world government. Indeed, it is well aware of its limitations and, in spite of much criticism, does not try to overstep the limits of the possible and the real. It has little power, but it has an immense moral force at its disposal. By means of able and unobtrusive diplomacy, it has relieved tensions in many crucial situations. Its role is that of an intermediary: it cannot impose solutions, but it is instrumental in bringing them about. Diplomatic exchanges of the highest importance take place in its corridors. The United Nations' action in Indonesia, Kashmir, Palestine, Egypt, and the Congo, among other places, has been highly commendable and may have prevented the outbreak of larger, destructive armed clashes. The United Nations, furthermore, provides a forum for the smaller nations, many of which are actively participating in the sphere of international politics for the first time, and gives them chances for new accomplishment, regardless of their size or military and economic power.

■**REGULATING PRINCIPLES.**—It is important to consider the principles regulating the United Nations' activities in order fully to appreciate its method of operation. These principles are based on the sovereign equality of all its members, and all members are pledge to fulfill their obligations under the charter in good faith. Member States are pledged to settle their international disputes by peaceful means, refraining from the threat or use of force against other states. They are also to give the organization assistance in any action undertaken by it in accordance with the charter. Even nonmember states should abide by the principles of the charter, at least to the extent necessary to maintain peace and security. In principle the organization cannot intervene in the internal affairs of a state. Any peace-loving nation that accepts the obligations of the charter and that, in the opinion of the organization, is able and willing to follow these principles, may join the United Nations.

Principal Organs.—The United Nations is composed of six principal organs: the General Assembly, the Security Council, the Economic and Social Council, the Trusteeship Council, the International Court of Justice, and the Secretariat. There are also a number of subsidiary organs that serve specific purposes.

■**THE GENERAL ASSEMBLY.**—The General Assembly is the principal organ of the United Nations—the real "town meeting of the world"—in which all Member States, regardless of size, power, political or religious creed, economic standing, or race, are represented. Each member has one vote, a principle that is also adhered to in the other United Nations bodies.

Decisions in the General Assembly are made by simple majority or by two-thirds majority, depending on the importance of the matter. The General Assembly meets once a year, but special and emergency sessions may be called by the Secretary-General.

The main functions of the General Assembly are to discuss and to recommend. Recommendations are directed to member nations, to the Security Council, or to both. The subjects to be discussed are "any questions or matters within the scope of the present Charter."

Other functions of the General Assembly are election of the six nonpermanent members of the Security Council and the entire membership of the Economic and Social Council; selection, independently of the Security Council, of the judges of the International Court of Justice; admission of new members; and appointment of the Secretary-General, the last two functions upon the recommendation of the Security Council. It also debates reports from the other organs of the United Nations, initiates studies, supervises trusteeship agreements, and considers and approves the budget.

The General Assembly prepares much of its work through its seven main committees, on which any Member Nation can be represented, and a variable number of smaller and special committees.

Originally, the General Assembly was essentially endowed with the limited powers of debate and recommendation, whereas the Security Council was given the "teeth." But the Cold War and the Korean War brought, as by-products, an almost perpetual split in the Security Council between the Soviet Union and the other permanent members. Because unanimity among the permanent

UNITED NATIONS

THE UN GENERAL ASSEMBLY normally convenes on the third Tuesday of each September.

members is required for action, this split frequently paralyzed the Council. The stalemate was partly overcome with a resolution—"Uniting for Peace," passed in the Assembly in November 1950—that declared that if the Security Council cannot act when a threat to international peace is apparent, the General Assembly is empowered to appropriate the matter within one day and recommend collective measures, including the use of armed forces.

■SECURITY COUNCIL.—Eleven Member States are represented on the Security Council, the organ on which the Member States have conferred primary responsibility for the maintenance of peace and security.

There are five permanent members: China, France, the Soviet Union, the United Kingdom, and the United States. Six nonpermanent members serve two-year terms; their election, held in the General Assembly, is staggered, so that half the nonpermanent membership is changed each year. Equitable geographic distribution is the principal basis of selection. In 1964, with the changing and growing composition of the membership of the United Nations, serious problems are arising due to the limited number of nonpermanent members on the Council. It seems that an enlarged membership, of at least fifteen, will more faithfully reflect the new situation; and there appears to be a consensus that changes in the Security Council, as well as in other organs of the United Nations, will most likely occur in the near future.

In the event of a threat to, or a breach of, international peace or an act of aggression, the Council can take enforcement measures in order to restore peace and security. All members are pledged to contribute to a military force at the disposal of the Security Council; in practice, however, the Council has been unable to accomplish this.

Besides enforcement powers, the Security Council has other activities: it may investigate any dispute or situation that might create a dangerous situation in the relations between two or more countries and may also recommend ways and means of peaceful settlement; it may establish plans for eventual regulation of armaments; and it may call on members to apply economic sanctions and sever communications and diplomatic relations in serious cases of infringement of the Charter that do not warrant the use of armed force. Finally, as mentioned above, it recommends the admission of new members to the General Assembly and, together with that body, elects the judges of the International Court of Justice, and recommends the appointment of the Secretary-General.

Because threats to peace may appear suddenly, the Security Council is so organized as to be able to function continuously. Security Council members, members of the United Nations, and the Secretary-General may ask for debate in the Security Council. Even nonmember states may, in certain cases, be invited to submit their problems.

Each member of the Council has one vote. On "procedural" matters, any seven positive votes will carry a measure; but on "substantive" matters, five of the seven votes must represent unanimity of the permanent membership—unless all five agree, no decision can be taken. This illustrates what, in common parlance, is known as the veto power.

■ECONOMIC AND SOCIAL COUNCIL.—The Economic and Social Council, commonly referred to as ECOSOC, is composed of eighteen members, six of which are elected each year to a three-year term by the General Assembly. Meetings of the Council are held as often as necessary; there are at least two sessions a year. It reaches decisions by majority vote.

The general objectives of this body are the worldwide attainment of higher standards of living and health; the promotion of international cooperation in scientific, educational, and artistic endeavors; and the universal attainment of human rights and fundamental freedoms.

The Economic and Social Council is the organ of the United Nations that examines and makes recommendations based on studies and reports prepared by the Secretariat. It is responsible, working under the authority of the General Assembly, for the economic and social activities of the United Nations; it calls international conferences when needed and prepares draft conventions for submission to the General Assembly; it give information and assistance to the Security Council and, upon request, may perform services for members of the organization and the specialized agencies.

The Council also is charged with maintaining most of the contacts with the United Nations' specialized agencies, such as World Health Organization and UNESCO. These, in turn, may participate, without vote, in the proceedings of the Council.

It performs many of its functions through commissions and committees, whose number and composition vary according to existing needs. Four regional economic commissions report to the Council—those for Europe, for Asia and the Far East, for Latin America, and for Africa.

Essentially, the technical and humanitarian aspects of the activities of this body tend to keep it removed from the public's attention, since the public is primarily interested in the political performances in the Security Council and the General Assembly. Although ECOSOC has no power to make binding decisions, either on the Member States or on the other organs of the United Nations, its influence is real; and the fact that it is not in the limelight may help it to obtain appreciable results.

■TRUSTEESHIP COUNCIL. — The success of the Trusteeship Council is shown by the fact that it is rapidly working itself out of existence, for its aim—self-government or independence for the eleven countries originally placed under its jurisdiction—has largely been attained. Only three territories remained as trusts by May 1964.

The Trusteeship Council originated in the Mandate Commission of the League of Nations. The Council's membership is composed of United Nations members that administer the trust territories, permanent members of the Security Council that do not administer trust territories, and a sufficient number of other members to ensure that the total membership is equally divided between representatives from administering and nonadministering states. The "balancing" group is elected by the General Assembly for terms of three years. In 1964, the Council had eight members.

The trusteeship system applies to former mandates of the League of Nations, to territories taken from former enemy states after World War II, and to others placed voluntarily under its jurisdiction.

Voting in the Trusteeship Council takes place by simple majority. Missions are sent on special or periodic visits to the trust territories; the Council evaluates their reports and those of the administering authorities, and then makes a report on each territory to the General Assembly, which discusses it and makes recommendations. The Council meets twice a year, but can be convened at any time upon the request of a majority of its members.

■ **COURT OF JUSTICE.**—The *International Court of Justice*, with its seat at The Hague, the Netherlands, is the only principal United Nations organ not located in New York. It clearly descends from the Permanent Court of International Justice of the League of Nations and is, similarly, the main judicial organ of the United Nations. It is regulated by a statute of the Charter: therefore, all members of the organization are automatically parties to the statute. Also, countries that are not members of the United Nations may, under special conditions, submit to the Court's decisions. Although submission to the judgment of the Court is voluntary, its decisions are binding.

The Court consists of fifteen judges elected by the General Assembly and the Security Council for nine-year terms, each organ voting independently. They are chosen for their ability and not, in principle, for their nationality; however, no two judges may be from the same state. The Court strives for representation of the main geographical areas and judicial systems. The jurisdiction of the Court includes all matters specified by the Charter, by treaties, and by conventions in force. The Security Council may bring a legal dispute before the Court; the General Assembly, the Security Council, and other organs and specialized agencies may ask the Court for advisory opinions on legal matters.

In specified cases, a state may be bound to submit to any and all questions and decisions of the Court if the opposing party also accepts the jurisdiction of the Court: this is called compulsory jurisdiction.

The Court bases its decisions on existing and recognized international customs, conventions, principles of law, and decisions handed down by highly qualified jurists. It has rendered decisions and expressed advisory opinions in several cases, but as of 1964 it had not exercised a role commensurate with its potential.

■ **SECRETARIAT.**—The Secretariat performs the vast administrative functions of the United Nations and is composed of a staff of international civil servants headed by the Secretary-General.

Today, the most important duties of the Secretary-General are in the sphere of international diplomacy. He is first the chief administrator of the Secretariat and thus administers the entire organization, but his facility at diplomacy has become increasingly important. Because his nomination is approved by the permanent members of the Security Council, his use of his powers of mediation and conciliation are facilitated. He is empowered to bring to the attention of the Security Council any matter that, in his opinion, threatens international peace and security. This privilege gives him the opportunity to play a substantial role in shaping international affairs.

At the beginning of each regular session, the Secretary-General makes an annual report to the General Assembly; it generally forms the basis of the opening debates. It gives the opinions of the Secretary-General on the main issues and is a very good source of information on the activities and accomplishments of the United Nations during the preceding year.

Another important aspect of the Secretary-General's activities is the "representational" function. He is the only individual able at all times to speak for the United Nations as a whole. He must also coordinate the activities of six principal organs, subsidiary organs, specialized agencies, and information offices. He must ensure smooth functioning of all these bodies, and counteract the many centrifugal forces that may weaken, if not disrupt, the organization. In sum, he is responsible for making the United Nations system work.

The role of the Secretary-General is to implement the functions assigned him by the Charter, but there is latitude to interpret the role in a very personal way. Each man's personality, experience, and philosophy bring a decisive contribution to the position.

As of 1964, three men have been Secretary-General: Trygve Lie of Norway (1946–1953); Dag Hammarskjöld of Sweden, whose term was abruptly ended when he died in a plane crash in 1961; and U Thant of Burma.

The Secretary-General and his international staff, in the performance of their duties, may not seek or receive instructions from any government or authority outside the United Nations. The hiring of staff members is based on performance, competence, and honesty, as well as personal merit; due account is also given to geographical balance. It should be emphasized that a member of a national delegation to the United Nations is not a Secretariat staff member, so his conduct is not ruled by the principles proper to the Secretariat staff. For professional and other high-level positions, the number of nationals from any country should be roughly proportional to the size of the financial contribution that country has made to the organization. For the remaining jobs, most of the personnel is recruited locally.

Related Agencies.—There are a number of specialized organizations that either have been created by the United Nations or have come to be associated with it.

■ **UN AGENCIES.** — Various kinds of technical assistance programs are administered or created by the United Nations. Many of these projects are carried out under the *Expanded Program of Technical Assistance* (EPTA), an international effort started in 1950 to help the underdeveloped countries. By 1964, 1,300 experts, in every field and from over 90 countries, had given technical assistance to about 150 countries and territories. Funds for EPTA are contributed voluntarily by governments, and more than $400 million has been pledged since 1950.

United Nations Children's Fund—UNICEF—was created in 1946 by the General Assembly to help requesting war-torn countries meet the urgent needs of their children. Since 1950 it has given help in health, nutrition, family and child welfare, vocational training, education, and other fields. It is supported voluntarily by governments and individuals.

Other agencies created by the United Nations include the *United Nations Relief and Works Agency for Palestine Refugees,* and *the Office of the United Nations High Commissioner for Refugees.*

■ **SPECIALIZED AGENCIES.**—Certain intergovernmental specialized agencies give highly technical help to their members. They have headquarters throughout the world, and their contact with the United Nations is through the Economic and Social Council. Membership in these agencies does not necessarily coincide with United Nations membership. In 1964 there were 15 such agencies.

The *International Atomic Energy Agency* promotes the use of atomic energy solely for peaceful purposes, giving technical assistance to developing countries, promoting exchange of technical information among all member nations, and developing international health and safety codes in the use of radiation.

The *International Labor Organization* (ILO) brings together govern-

UNITED NATIONS

UNICEF, United Nations Children's Fund, helps young people in all parts of the world.

ment, labor, and management in an effort to develop improved standards for working conditions; it assists governments in economic development and conducts research on basic labor problems.

The *Food and Agriculture Organization* (FAO) helps countries increase the quantity and quality of food produced through farming, husbandry, and fishing.

The *United Nations Educational, Scientific, and Cultural Organization* (UNESCO) works to broaden education, combat illiteracy, bring the benefits of science to all countries, and promote cultural exchanges to increase understanding between peoples.

The *World Health Organization* (WHO) directs and coordinates the improvement of the world's physical and mental health. It warns of epidemics, sets international standards for drugs and vaccines, aids in eradicating disease and in improving water supplies and sanitation, protects the health of mothers and children, and trains doctors and health workers.

The *International Bank for Reconstruction and Development* (World Bank) furthers economic development of its members through technical advice and loans for productive projects.

The *International Development Association,* affiliated with the International Bank, provides financial aid on terms bearing less heavily on balance of payments than do conventional loans.

The *International Finance Corporation* aids private enterprise in the less-developed member countries.

The *International Monetary Fund* (IMF) provides financial assistance to help member countries deal with short-term foreign payments. It promotes currency convertibility and freer trade conditions.

The *International Civil Aviation Organization* is responsible for the international standardizations of flight and ground equipment, procedures, and services. It codifies international air law.

The *Universal Postal Union* organizes and improves postal services and promotes international collaboration in postal matters.

The *International Telecommunication Union* promotes international cooperation in radio, telephone, and telegraphic communications and allocates radio frequencies.

The *World Meteorological Organization* promotes cooperation in meteorology and is particularly concerned with establishing a world-wide system of weather stations with a rapid exchange of weather data.

The *International Maritime Consultative Organization* promotes international cooperation in maritime navigation and provides machinery for consultation in shipping matters.

The *General Agreement on Tariffs and Trade* (GATT) functions to ease trade barriers and establish rules of fair trade.

The Work of the UN—Since its birth in 1945, the United Nations has more than doubled its membership. It has tried to settle the disputes of the world peacefully, but at times has used military force. It is continuing to try to control armaments and to aid peaceful uses of atomic energy.

■**GROWTH.**—One of the more amazing aspects in the history of the United Nations is the change in its membership. To the 51 countries attending the founding ceremonies at San Francisco, many have been added. Membership in May 1964 numbered 112 nations, and no doubt will continue to grow. All the countries admitted to membership from 1957 to 1964 were former non-self-governing territories. The contribution of the United Nations to the struggle against colonialism has been immeasurable; it culminated in the General Assembly's declaration of December 14, 1960, which solemnly proclaimed "the necessity of bringing to a speedy and unconditional end colonialism in all its forms and manifestations."

The changing composition of the United Nations membership has emphasized the important of voting blocs. Before the massive admittance of the newly independent nations, the nations of the West, of Latin America, and of the Communist sphere tended to vote in their own groups. The newly emerged Afro-Asian bloc has generally stood together on questions of colonialism and aid to underdeveloped countries, but on other issues it has deeply divided. The voting pattern of this powerful bloc shows that it is less homogeneous than was commonly believed.

■**MILITARY ACTIONS.**—The United Nations has occasionally used armed forces to repel aggression, as in Korea, and to maintain the peace, as in the Suez Canal, in the Congo, and most recently, in Cyprus.

On June 27, 1950, the Security Council made a historic request that all member nations provide military assistance to the Republic of Korea. Fifty-three states approved this action in principle, sixteen promised combat units, and five agreed to contribute medical units. In July a unified command was set up in Korea under the United Nations flag and United States leadership. An armistice was signed on July 27, 1953.

After the armed clash in the Suez Canal in 1956, and in order to prevent the possible recurrence of hostilities, the organization recruited a military force, called the *United Nations Emergency Force* (UNEF) and composed of troops furnished by several member nations, to be dispatched to the border between Israel and Egypt.

This force performed its task so well that it established a pattern that was followed in the Congo. Here, the ONUC (from the French, *Opération des Nations Unies au Congo*) was created, and it greatly contributed to maintaining some peace and stability in the former Belgian territory that had achieved independence in 1960.

In 1964, in an attempt to keep under control the potentially explosive situation in Cyprus, a similar force was created—the *United Nations Peace-keeping Force in Cyprus* (UNIFICYP)—and dispatched there.

Successful as these operations have been, they have produced huge strains on the United Nations' budget, which has had difficulty in recovering from the effects of these unforeseen and heavy expenditures.

■**DISARMAMENT.**—Finding methods of disarmament has been one of the most important concerns of the organization. The *Disarmament Commission,* in which all Member States participate, was created to study ways of bringing the arms race to an end. The desirability of general and complete disarmament was recognized by a unanimous resolution adopted by the General Assembly in 1959. In 1962, the Assembly advocated the peaceful use of all energies and resources that eventual disarmament would make available. A number of conferences have been trying to solve this problem.

■**DOCUMENTS.**—The United Nations has given birth to several historic documents that represent the aspirations of mankind and hope to guide human behavior in the future; two of these are the *Universal Declaration of Human Rights* and the *International Convention on Genocide.*

■**ATOMS FOR PEACE.**—The use of atomic power for peaceful purposes has been a main preoccupation of the organization. Great momentum was given to this striving when, in December 1953, President Eisenhower spoke before the General Assembly on "Atoms for Peace." Four years later the *International Atomic Energy Agency* was created to deal specifically with these matters.

The Future.—What is the future of the United Nations at a time when man, for the first time, has the power to destroy his planet? It depends upon the will of the peoples of the world. If their conscience is aroused and their efforts converge to find solutions to the problems besetting mankind, the organization can be instrumental in achieving these objectives. If, on the other hand, the foreign policies of the leading nations are solely self-interested and fail to tame the growing destructive power that science has given the world, there is little hope that the United Nations will ever attain the objectives for which it has been created.

—Sergio Barzanti

WORLD HEALTH ORGANIZATION

UN MALARIA TEAMS fight disease in Asia.

HISTORY GLOSSARY

ACHAEAN LEAGUE, a confederation of Greek city-states, formed originally in 280 BC to resist the domination of Macedonia. In the century from 245 to 146 BC the Achaean League developed into the nearest approach to a modern democratic federal government that was created in ancient times.

Including most of the important cities of the southern part of the peninsula except Sparta, the Achaean League was the strongest force for Greek unity during the period of its existence. In 146 BC the Roman conquest of Greece broke up the league.

ACTIUM, a great sea battle fought off the west coast of Greece in 31 BC between the forces of Anthony and Cleopatra on the one side and Octavius (later Augustus Caesar) on the other. At least 200 ships on each side were engaged. When the battle was at its height the Egyptian squadron of Cleopatra withdrew, leaving Anthony's fleet to fight it out alone. The superior mobility of Octavius's light galleys decided the issue; Anthony's fleet was set on fire and practically destroyed.

Anthony had personally made his escape following the withdrawal of Cleopatra's force. His action was stigmatized in ancient times as gross cowardice. The battle ended the long rivalry for the mastery of the Roman world and enabled Octavius to establish himself as emperor of Rome.

AGINCOURT, a famous battle of the Hundred Years War between England and France, fought on Oct. 25, 1415. An invading English army, commanded by King Henry V in person, numbering not more than 15,000, severely defeated over 50,000 French.

The victory had no immediate strategic results, as the English army was too small to undertake an extensive conquest. Its chief value to Henry V was to rouse the confidence and patriotic pride of the English nation and enable Henry to secure the support of Parliament for a larger-scale invasion a year later.

ALABAMA CLAIMS, claims entered by the United States against Great Britain for damages inflicted on American shipping during the American Civil War by certain Confederate cruisers. Chief among them was the *Alabama,* which had been constructed in England and allowed by the British government to take to sea in violation (as the United States alleged) of the international obligations of neutrality.

Following a long exchange, the two nations agreed by the Treaty of Washington (1871) to submit the question to a board of arbitration consisting of one American, one English, and three neutral commissioners. The Treaty of Washington also defined the obligations of neutrals in wartime with respect to the points in dispute.

The tribunal met in Geneva on Dec. 15, 1871, and after much negotiation it announced its decision on Sept. 14, 1872. The American contentions were in the main sustained, and damages of $15,500,000 were paid by Great Britain. The case is notable in the history of international relations as one of the earliest instances of a grave dispute being settled by peaceful means.

ALBIGENSES, a religious sect opposing the authority of the church and the priesthood that flourished in the south of France in the late 1100s and early 1200s. In 1209 Pope Innocent III, angered by the murder of a papal legate who had been commissioned to inquire into the extent of the heresy, organized the Albigensian Crusade to stamp it out.

Under the leadership of Simon de Montfort, a merciless war of extermination was carried out. Towns were sacked, and their entire populations butchered; more than 20,000 persons, the majority women and children, were the victims of these massacres. In 1229 the Treaty of Paris ended the military phase of the crusade, but hunting down and destroying the remnants of the sect continued into the 1400s.

ALEXANDRIAN LIBRARY, the most famous library of the ancient world. The library was founded in the early 200s BC by the Egyptian kings Ptolemy I and Ptolemy II. In the time of Julius Caesar (47 BC) the library is believed to have contained something like 700,000 papyrus rolls—roughly the equivalent of 100,000 volumes of modern print. These rolls would of course be of priceless value to modern scholars, but they have all been lost.

In 641 AD Alexandria was captured by the Arabs under the Caliph Omar. A story arose several centuries later that this caliph, as an act of religious fanaticism, ordered the books of the Alexandrian Library distributed to be burned as waste in the public baths. Few modern scholars believe this occurred. Gibbon, one of the first scholars to question the truth of the legend, points out that by the 600s the Alexandrian Library had probably already lost most of the most important works that it originally contained.

ALSACE–LORRAINE, two eastern provinces of France that were long a bone of contention between France and Germany. Seized by the French during the wars of the 1600s, Alsace-Lorraine was recaptured by Germany at the close of the Franco-Prussian War (1871).

Two hundred years of French rule had made the population, especially in Lorraine, predominantly French in language, customs, and sympathies. The Germans attempted to Germanize the provinces, making the study of the German language compulsory in the public schools and adopting various other measures calculated to wean the population from its French allegiance. These efforts were, on the whole, unsuccessful down to the close of World War I.

Throughout the period of German rule the recovery of the "lost provinces" was a fond dream of patriotic Frenchmen. By the Treaty of Versailles (1919) Alsace-Lorraine was awarded to France.

ANCYREAN INSCRIPTION, or Monumentum Ancyranum, a long inscription in Latin and Greek engraved on the walls of the Augusteum, a temple in the city of Angora (ancient name, *Ancyra*) in Asia Minor. The inscription relates the *Res gestae divi Augusti* (the deeds of the deified Au-

CULVER
ANDERSONVILLE PRISON held soldiers captured by the Confederacy during the Civil War.

gustus) and is of great importance as a historical source for the period of Augustus' career. The inscription is a copy from two bronze tablets, now lost, prepared under Augustus' own supervision and placed before his mausoleum in Rome.

ANDERSONVILLE, a military prison of the Confederate government established in southwestern Georgia in 1864. The prison consisted of a stockade 15 feet high enclosing 26½ acres of land through which ran a small brook. No barracks or other substantial shelters were provided, and the prisoners made shift as best they could by contriving rude tents of blankets and rags or burrowing in the ground.

By midsummer 1864 there were about 30,000 prisoners confined in the prison—the space available was less than 4 square yards to the man. Overcrowding, unsanitary conditions, undernourishment, and exposure produced a fearful mortality. Approximately 13,000 men died out of a total admitted of 49,500.

After the war the popular demand for vengeance found a scapegoat in Henry Wirz, the prison superintendent, who was tried before a military court and hanged. MacKinlay Kantor recounted the story of this disgraceful prison in his 1956 Pulitzer Prize novel, *Andersonville.*

ARABIA, the great peninsula of southwestern Asia, lying between the Persian Gulf and the Red Sea. Its history reaches back at least 4,000 years. The earliest records deal only with its northern section—the pathway from old Egypt around the end of the Mediterranean to Syria and Palestine, where the tramp of armies resounded during the conflicts between the Egyptian corner of Africa and western Asia.

The earliest known people to live in Arabia were the *Minaeans.* There are many references to them in the Old Testament. They had an extensive kingdom, as has been learned from inscriptions, and it is believed to have existed until about 650 BC. When Cambyses subdued Egypt in 525 BC, Arabia became Persian and was made a province. The Romans invaded the country in 24 BC and established a temporary and limited authority several times during the first centuries of the Christian era.

Outstanding in Arabia's later history is Muhammad (c.570–632). (The rise and spread of Islam from its source in Arabia is traced in the section on Medieval History.)

The strongest figure in contemporary Arabian history is Abdul Aziz Ibn Saud, proclaimed king in 1926, who then became known to the western world as the ruler of Saudi Arabia. Ibn Saud organized the Arabian tribes against the Ottoman Turks in World War I and later added Hejaz to his domain, soon called the Kingdom of Hejaz and Nejd. In 1932 it became known as the Kingdom of Saudi Arabia. Yemen is an independent neighboring nation in Arabia. There are several other small countries.

ARAB INFORMATION CENTER

ARAB LEAGUE nations' heads of state gather for a meeting at league headquarters in Cairo.

ARAB LEAGUE, a regional bloc of Arab states formed in 1945. Its members include the United Arab Republic (Egpyt), Iraq, Syria, Lebanon, Jordan, Saudi Arabia, Yemen, Libya, Sudan, Morocco, Tunisia, Kuwait, and Algeria. The League was organized to safeguard Arab interests in Palestine and to promote a unity of policy in respect to the disposal of petroleum deposits in the region. The League failed to prevent the organization of the State of Israel. It supported Egypt in the Suez Canal crisis in 1957–1958 and is engaged in a joint Arab project of reclaiming the headwaters of the Jordan. The league takes a neutral stand in the Cold War.

ARBELA, a decisive battle fought in 331 BC on the plains between the Tigris River and the mountains of Kurdistan, 30 miles east of Arbela, between the Macedonians under Alexander the Great and the Persians under Darius. The battle resulted in the complete defeat of the Persians, the overthrow of Darius and his dynasty, and Alexander's occupation of Babylonia.

Alexander's force of some 50,000 was faced by a Persian host of over 200,000 men. Alexander's tactical leadership demonstrated the futility of mere numbers when opposed by disciplined and skillfully led troops.

ARGONNE, a wooded region in eastern France, the scene of severe fighting throughout World War I. For more than four years it was held by the Germans, who had so fortified it that the position was considered impregnable. After long preparation, a final Allied effort was made to drive out the Germans. Nearly 900,000 American troops under the personal direction of General Pershing had the cooperation of the French in the attack. The struggle raged from Sept. 26 to Nov. 6, 1918, and ended with the evacuation of the Germans. Five days later came the Armistice and the end of the war.

ARIANISM, the doctrines professed by the followers of Arius, a deacon of Alexandria (c.256–336AD), condemned as heretical by the Council of Nicaea in 325 AD. The essential feature of Arianism was its denial of the equality of the person of the Son with that of the Father in its conception of the Holy Trinity. Arianism thus tended to a denial of the divinity of Christ.

In spite of its formal condemnation by the council, Arianism continued to flourish throughout the 300s, especially in the Near East, and the controversy repeatedly threatened to disrupt the church.

ARMADA, a word originally meaning any fleet of war vessels but usually applied specifically to the Invincible Armada fitted out in 1588 by Philip II of Spain for war with England.

The war was the outcome of a long course of intrigue conducted by Philip to possess himself of the English throne and re-establish Roman Catholicism in England. Finding all his efforts to gain his ends by diplomacy foiled by the shrewd counterdiplomacy of Elizabeth I, the English Queen, Philip gave up plotting and scheming in 1588 in favor of open force. Affairs had been brought to a crisis by the execution in 1587 of Mary Stuart, on whom hopes for a Roman Catholic succession had been centered.

The Invincible Armada was the most formidable naval force ever assembled up to its time—130 ships, 27,000 soldiers and sailors. In addition to the fleet itself a supporting army of 33,000 men was waiting in the Netherlands under the command of one of the ablest soldiers of the period, Alexander Farnese. To contemporaries it appeared that the fate of England was sealed.

The Armada, under the command of the duke of Medina Sidonia, arrived in the English Channel late in July 1588. It was immediately attacked by the English, whose smaller

NEW YORK PUBLIC LIBRARY

ELIZABETH I ruled England when a commercial and religious controversy with Spain led to the launching of the Spanish Armada.

and more mobile craft were able to work havoc among the ponderous and unmanageable Spanish ships without suffering any substantial loss themselves. Three engagements took place, each disastrous for the Armada, and the Spanish attempted to withdraw.

The English cut off retreat by way of the English Channel, and it was necessary to sail all the way around the British Isles to reach the open ocean. Storms accomplished what the English had left undone; more than half of the ships were lost at sea, and only 54, battered and bedraggled, reached Spain. The disaster broke Spanish sea power and marked the beginning of English maritime greatness.

ATLANTIC CHARTER, Aug. 14, 1941, a joint declaration of policy and war aims agreed upon by U.S. Pres. F. D. Roosevelt and Winston Churchill, prime minister of Great Britain. The meeting was held at sea and pledged the United States and Great Britain to no territorial changes and no separate peace with Nazi Germany.

The charter gave expression to President Roosevelt's doctrine of the Four Freedoms—freedom of speech and religion and freedom from want and fear. It was used as an objective of Allied victory and an international charter of rights. The Declaration was signed by 26 anti-Axis allies in Washington, D.C., Jan. 1, 1942. Because of its importance, much of it was included in the Charter of the United Nations.

AUSTRIAN SUCCESSION. See *Succession Wars.*

BABYLONIA, an ancient country that lies within the basin of two great rivers, the Euphrates and the Tigris. Thousands of years ago these streams entered the Persian Gulf by separate mouths. Since then the debris-laden floods have built up an alluvial plain

that has gradually encroached on the gulf until it now extends perhaps 200 miles beyond what was the shore line 6,000 years ago. A single mouth now takes care of the waters from both rivers.

Topography. The topography of the Babylonian country would seem proof that there was where prehistoric man first began to leave written records of his existence. Then, as today, his three most essential needs were food, shelter, and a certain degree of safety. There they existed in larger measure, or could be obtained with less effort, than elsewhere, except in Egypt.

The climate was mild and agreeable, the country was protected by high mountains to the east and north, while to the west stretched away a desert not easily crossed by enemies. Food was abundant and easy to obtain. The streams and the waters of the gulf swarmed with fish. Flooded every year by the waters of the streams, the fertile plain was covered by vegetation. There was an abundance of game, and the rich soil required but little cultivation to produce heavy crops of various grains or many kinds of fruit.

With nature thus making it possible for man to obtain food, shelter, and safety with little effort, it would seem that he devoted some of his leisure to recording the happenings of his life, the result being a crude form of picture writing. This writing developed into a more clear and concise system, the characters being incised on clay tablets. Thousands of these are in existence and they are the chief records of the early Babylonians.

These records show that Babylonia was a land flowing with milk and honey. It is not surprising that tradition should have located there the Garden of Eden, that primeval place "out of which God made to grow every tree that is pleasant to the sight and good for food." Agriculture reached a high state of development,

made possible by a stupendous system of dikes to protect the land in times of flood, coupled with canals for irrigating purposes and for transportation. The remains of this skillfully planned system still cover the land.

Among the various crops cultivated in the area were cereals, olives, grapes, citrus, and other fruits. Many kinds of vegetables were also grown. The fauna included both wild and domestic animals. In the mountains to the north were to be found lead, copper and iron, as well as sandstone, basalt, and alabaster.

Early History. The earliest records of Babylonia start about 4500 BC. This was the beginning of the dynasty of Opis. There is no knowing just how long the first inhabitants, the Sumerians, had been there, or if the Semitic tribes had already arrived.

Dynasty followed dynasty, king followed king, and war followed war. Babylonia continued to prosper, and its capital, Babylon, while often captured and occasionally destroyed, increased its magnificence until it ranked as the greatest city of the ancient world.

Babylon. The city of Babylon was in existence as early as 3800 BC, and was made the capital of all Babylonia about 2094 BC. It was captured five times during the next 1,300 years and utterly destroyed by Sennacherib, Assyrian king, in 689 BC. He not only razed every building but opened a canal and let waters of the Euphrates flow over the site. It was promptly rebuilt, again destroyed, and then rebuilt a third time.

The city was enlarged by Nebuchadnezzar (605–562 BC), and its safety was assured by high walls girding an area of about 12 square miles. The remains of these walls have been traced and they have a total length of about 15 miles.

Nebuchadnezzar endeavored to outdo the Egyptian pharaohs in the construction of huge works requiring an immense amount of labor. Perhaps his greatest achievement, next to the magnificent royal palace, was the celebrated Hanging Gardens (one of the Seven Wonders of the ancient world), built to please his wife, Amytis, who was homesick for the mountains of her native land. From the descriptions it is assumed that these were mounds or towers, the terraces covered with earth from which arose plants and trees giving the appearance of mountains covered with vegetation.

It is probable that Nebuchadnezzar also rebuilt the Tower of Babel mentioned in Genesis 11. Its site has been found, but all that remains is a large hole in the ground, where bricks used in the construction of the tower had been dug out for later and smaller buildings.

The Fall of Babylon. The passing of Nebuchadnezzar marked the end of the Babylonian Empire. A new kingdom, the Medo-Persian, had come into existence. Headed by an energetic leader, Cyrus, the Persians defeated the Babylonians and captured the city. Not favored as a capital by the Persians, its population decreased and its buildings decayed until finally its location was forgotten.

Babylonian Writing. The Babylonians devised a system of writing, termed cuneiform because the characters were marked on soft clay with a triangular tool so that they were wedge-shaped. The clay tablets were about 6 by 3 inches in size and perhaps an inch thick. Those bearing records of importance were preserved in libraries, the one found at Hippur containing over 30,000 tablets. These were deciphered by means of trilingual inscriptions; one of the best-known is the Behistun Rock, an inscription on a cliff in western Persia telling in three languages the deeds of Darius, a Persian king.

Scientific Achievements. The Babylonians contributed much to the advancement of astronomy. They foretold eclipses of the sun and moon,

divided the zodiac into 12 signs and mapped the constellations of the zodiac. They devised a calendar that divided the year into months, weeks, days, hours, and minutes, using a sundial for the hours of sunlight and a water clock for those of darkness. Other inventions were duodecimal numbers and measures of capacity, weight, and length.

Later History. Babylonia fell to the Greeks after the death of Alexander in 323 BC. The Parthians next had possession. It was captured by Ottoman Turks in 1638, who held it until the end of World War I. It was then mandated to Great Britain, along with much of the surrounding territory. In 1930 the mandate was relinquished and it is now the independent nation of Iraq.

BACON'S REBELLION, a revolt in the colony of Virginia in 1676 led by Nathaniel Bacon, a member of the governor's council, against the oppressive rule of Berkeley, the royal governor. Berkeley's oppressions included levying excessive taxes, unfairness in qualifying voters, and injustice in laying tobacco duties.

Revolt broke out in 1676 when he refused to take protective measures against the Indians.

Bacon had asked the governor's permission to lead the settlers against Indians who had attacked his plantation, but he was refused. Bacon then proceeded to defensive measures against the governor's orders; there was considerable fighting and Jamestown was burned. Bacon died in the midst of the rebellion; left without a leader, his followers abandoned their aims and the trouble subsided.

Berkeley felt it necessary to demonstrate his authority and hanged several of Bacon's lieutenants. His severity made an unfavorable impression on Charles II, king of England, who remarked, "The old fool has taken more lives in that naked country than I have for the murder of my father," and Berkeley was removed.

BALAKLAVA, a historic battle of the Crimean War (1854-56), in which Russia fought the allied forces of Great Britain, France, and Turkey. Because orders were misunderstood or incorrectly conveyed, a British cavalry force of 670 charged a large body of Russian cavalry protected by infantry and met appalling disaster; only 198 of the attacking column survived. "It is magnificent," said a French general who witnessed the action "but it is not war." The incident has been immortalized in Tennyson's poem, "The Charge of the Light Brigade."

BARBARY STATES, the four countries of North Africa that border the Mediterranean Sea. In ancient times they were called *Mauretania, Numidia, Africa Propria,* and *Cyrenaica.* These names were later changed to Morocco, Algeria, Tunis, and Tripoli. Today the last two are known as Tunisia and Libya (Italian spelling, *Libia*). The first three were settled by the Romans who ignored the native tribes; and the last by the Greeks and Phoenicians. The city of Carthage was founded by hardy voyagers from Phoenicia.

After the disintegration of the Roman Empire in the 400s and 500s, the North African coast was swept by the Arab Muslim conquest, and in the succeeding centuries it became the western stronghold of Muslim power. From the 1400s to the 1800s the region was infested by Moorish and Turkish pirates and by desperate adventurers from many countries, who terrorized shipping on the Mediterranean and exacted tribute from maritime nations.

These outrages were at their height in the 1500s and 1600s. Europe then was filled with stories of captures by the pirates, of slavery at the oars of their galleys, and of hairbreadth escapes.

Efforts by the European powers to suppress the pirate menace were unsuccessful until the 1800s. The lead was taken by the United States in its wars with Tripoli (1801-1805; 1812-1815). The power of the pirates was finally broken by the French conquest of Algeria (1830-1847).

BARTHOLOMEW, ST., MASSACRE OF, a massacre of Huguenots in France begun at midnight in the city of Paris on the morning of Aug. 24 (St. Bartholomew's Day), 1572, and carried later to the principal towns throughout France. From 20,000 to 70,000 Protestants were butchered in cold blood by bands of armed men acting under threats of execution by their superior officers.

The massacre was ordered by the weak Charles IX, urged on by his mother, Catherine de' Medici, who hated and feared both the religious opinions and the growing political power of the Huguenot faction and its leader, Gaspard de Chatillon Coligny. Coligny was one of the victims of the massacre.

The Massacre of St. Bartholomew is one of the outstanding horrors of the savage religious struggle of the second half of the 1500s.

BABYLONIAN TABLET illustrating the cuneiform writing system used in the ancient Near East.

BASTILLE, a name used in early times for any fortified castle but later applied specifically to a great eight-towered building in Paris that was used as a state prison during the 1600s and 1700s. Especially in the reigns of Louis XIV and Louis XV, the Bastille acquired an odious repute as the place of confinement of political prisoners.

Particularly notorious was the system of imprisonment by *letters de cachet*—orders for imprisonment issued in the name of the king by which any designated person could be seized and confined without any chance to face his accusers or to know the nature of the charge against him. "These orders signed by your Majesty are often filled in with obscure names of which your Majesty cannot possibly have heard. They are at the disposal of your ministers, and it would appear, in view of the great number which are issued, of their clerks as well. . . . The result is, Sire, that no citizen in your kingdom can be assured that his liberty will not be sacrificed to a private grudge; for no one is so exalted that he is safe from the ill will of a minister or so insignificant that he may not incur that of a clerk in the employ of the farm [tax collectors]. The day will come, Sire, when the multiplicity of abuses of the *lettres de cachet* will lead your Majesty to abolish a custom so opposed to the constitution of your kingdom and the liberty which your subjects should enjoy."

As is evident from this protest of a French court of law (1770), the arbitrary imprisonments through *lettres de cachet* aroused widespread resentment, and the Bastille, as representing this tyranny in visible form, was bitterly execrated by the populace. One of the first acts of violence of the French Revolution was the storming of the Bastille by a Paris mob, on July 14, 1789. The commandant was killed and his head impaled on a pike.

In the following year the old building was razed. Lafayette sent the key of the Bastille to George Washington with a note declaring that the spirit of liberty exhibited in America had inspired the French to overthrow despotism in their own land.

Modern scholars have pointed out that the Bastille was actually a much milder place of confinement than the popular hatred would lead one to suspect. Especially in the reign of Louis XVI (1774–1793) many extraordinary privileges were allowed and in some respects the Bastille might be better described as a club than as a prison. Fraternization was permitted among the prisoners, and they were supplied with excellent food and clothing. The popular horror stories were carried over from earlier times.

BAVARIAN SUCCESSION. *See Succession Wars.*

BENEDICTINE ORDER, the earliest of the great monastic orders of western Europe founded by St. Benedict (480?–543?). Disgusted by the worldly life that he observed in Rome, Benedict withdrew to Subiaco near Rome where he began a life of rigid renunciation. He soon attracted a group of devoted

FRENCH GOVERNMENT TOURIST OFFICE
BURGUNDY'S RURAL LANDSCAPE has undergone little change since the Middle Ages.

followers. About 515 he composed his *Regula Monachorum* or *Rules of Life for Monks* setting forth his ideals of the truly religious life. This work became the accepted rule of Western Monasticism. In 529 Benedict founded the first Benedictine monastery at Monte Cassino.

In the following two centuries the order grew rapidly, and became the most important agent in spreading Christianity over western Europe. To the Benedictines must also be credited the preservation of most of the literary classics of the ancient world that survived the long cultural darkness of the Middle Ages.

In the 1200s, the high noon of European monasticism, it is estimated there were as many as 30,000 Benedictine monasteries, many of these were abandoned with the rise of the great order of mendicant friars found by St. Dominic and St. Francis.

By the 1400s the number of Benedictine communities had fallen to about 15,000. With the Protestant Revolt and the decline of medieval ideals that accompanied the expansion of Europe in the 1500s and 1600s, the Benedictines lost the dominance of the religious and cultural life of Europe that they had had for centuries.

BENELUX, a customs union in western Europe, deriving its name from the first syllables of its members—Belgium, The Netherlands, and Luxemburg. This union became effective Jan. 1, 1948 and formed the basis for a military defense pact. It bound the Benelux countries, Great Britain, and France for a period of fifty years to united action in case of attack. This pact, signed Mar. 17, 1948 at Brussels, was supplemented by an agreement with the United States in London, June 7, 1948, and related to continued military occupation and economic control of Germany. To give the agreements more validity they were linked with United Nation's policy and with the Marshall plan.

BERING SEA CONTROVERSY, a disagreement between the United States and Great Britain over seal fisheries in the Bering Sea. The dispute was submitted to arbitration in 1893, with the result that the claim of the United States to jurisdiction over sealing in waters beyond its territorial domain was denied, and Great Britain was awarded damages.

The Pribilof Islands in the Bering Sea north of the Aleutian Islands are the principal home of valuable fur seals. As part of the Alaska Territory, these islands were subject to jurisdiction of the United States, but the United States assumed the further right of regulating sealing over the whole of the Bering Sea, claiming that only by such regulation could the ultimate extermination of the herd be prevented.

U.S. efforts to enforce this assumed jurisdiction led to diplomatic protests, and the whole question was finally referred to a board of eight arbitrators—two to be appointed by each of the interested powers and one to be appointed by each of four heads of neutral states: the president of the French Republic, the king of Italy, and the kings of Norway and Sweden.

In 1911 the United States, Great Britain, Russia, and Japan agreed by treaty to abolish pelagic, or open-sea, sealing, thus effecting by mutual agreement what the United States had unsuccessfully attempted on its own responsibility.

BLENHEIM, a decisive battle of the War of the Spanish Succession, fought Aug. 13, 1704, at Blenheim, Bavaria, between the French and Bavarian armies, commanded by marshals Tallard and Marsin, and the English and Austrian armies under the duke of Marlborough and Prince Eugene. The battle resulted in the heavy defeat of the French and Baravians. The losses of the English and Austrians amounted to 4,500 killed and 7,500 wounded; of the French and Bavarians, 11,000 surrendered as prisoners, and an unknown number (exceeding 10,000) were killed.

The battle is of historical importance because it gave a crushing blow to the vast military and political power of France, which had dominated western Europe for 30 years and appeared at the opening of the 1700s to be invincible. The war dragged on for nearly 10 years, but the tide of French ascendancy under Louis XIV had definitely been turned, and France was forced to take the defensive.

BOHEMIA, a central European region that in early days was under the sway of various groups; at one time it was an independent state, then a crownland of Austria-Hungary, and finally the western province of the nation of Czechoslovakia. The territory that became Bohemia was occupied by a tribe called the *Boii*, a Celtic people who in the century before the beginning of the Christian Era were driven out of Germany.

In the 500s a Slavic people, the Czechs, came from the east and made permanent settlements. They were converted to Christianity by the Germans and existed until the 1100s as vassals of Germany. The Germans then permitted them to organize a kingdom, and the next 100 years was the period of their greatest power.

The kingdom fell into the hands of the Hapsburgs, whose religious persecutions of the people had no small part in bringing on the Thirty Years' War (1618–1648). Bohemia suffered much during this war; lost two-thirds of its population, and for more than a century was completely stagnant. Then the old spirit of the Czechs was revived; it ultimately won recognition for Czech instead of German as the official language of the province. At the end of World War I the Czechs and Bohemia became part of Czechoslovakia. They have remained Czechoslovakian since then, and are now part of the Soviet bloc of East European states.

BREST–LITOVSK, TREATY OF, the treaty concluding a separate peace between Germany and the newly established Bolshevik government of Russia during World War I. The treaty was signed on Mar. 2, 1918, after revolution, economic collapse, and a succession of military defeats had made it utterly imposible for Russia to continue fighting. The terms of the treaty were harsh in the extreme, providing for wide annexations of territory, heavy indemnities and oppressive economic control by the Central Powers of Russian supplies of food, oil, and other material.

By the conclusion of a separate peace with Russia, Germany was able to free large bodies of troops for a final effort to win the war in the west before the growing American army in France should become strong enough to affect the issue. But with the diplomatic ineptitude that characterized their conduct of the entire war, the Germans failed to estimate at its true value the moral effect of imposing such ruthless terms on a defeated enemy. Throughout the Allied countries the treaty roused a hatred and determination for vengeance that played no small part in drawing up the crushing terms of the Treaty of Versailles at the end of the war. By one of the clauses of the Treaty of Versailles, Germany surrendered the gains it had made by the Treaty of Brest-Litovsk.

BUCCANEERS, pirates and adventurers who harried the West Indies and the coast of South America in the 1600s and attained through their numbers, unity, and organization almost the position of a recognized national power. The buccaneers were recruited chiefly from groups of English, Dutch and French smugglers, who carried on an illegal trade in slaves and merchandise with the Spanish possessions.

Increasing in strength, they established several strongholds on various West Indian islands and ultimately succeeded in virtually controlling the entire Caribbean basin and Gulf of Mexico. They allied themselves with foreign powers, helping the English to capture Jamaica in 1655 and taking sides in the English-French and English-Dutch wars. They chiefly preyed on Spanish commerce, however, and for this reason were not molested seriously by the English, the only power able to put them down. For half a century the buccaneers' plundering raids rendered life and property insecure in all the coast towns; probably the strongest factor in breaking them up at the beginning of the 1700s was the impoverishment of the communities that had supported them.

BURGUNDY, a powerful medieval kingdom located between France and Germany, and now a part of France. Its first known settlers were a Germanic people who migrated into Gaul; they did not mix with the natives they found there, but established their own kingdom. Their first conquerors were the Franks in the 500s. At that time France controlled Burgundy. But by marriage between a princess of Burgundy and a male of the House of Hapsburg it became Austrian. King Louis XI seized it for France.

BYZANTINE EMPIRE, known also as the Eastern, the East Roman, and the Later Roman Empire, which existed for more than 1,000 years with its capital at Constantinople. With Gratianus, Theodosius had been co-ruler of the Roman world and had been entrusted with affairs in the east. When Gratianus was killed in a battle with Maximus, a usurper, Theodosius began a campaign that made him sole emperor of the east and the west, thus uniting the great Roman Empire for the last time. Following his death in 395, the vast domain was divided between his two sons, Arcadius and Honorius, the former receiving the empire in the east, the latter the western Roman world.

Early History. With Arcadius, the independent history of the Eastern, or Byzantine, Empire began. Between 395 and 1453, when it came to an end, it was ruled by 107 emperors. Only a few of these are worthy of a place in a brief historical record; several were Westerners elevated to power during the crusades, and of these the first was Baldwin I. Of the 107 who ruled, 20 were assassinated, 18 were blinded or otherwise mutilated by their enemies, 8 died in battle, 12 were forced to abdicate, 12 died in prison or in monasteries to which they had fled for protection and 3 starved to death. There was a constant struggle for

ALINARI ART REFERENCE BUREAU

BYZANTINE MOSAIC shows a cotte, undergarment worn over the shirt—kneelength on men, longer on women—covered by a cote-hardie worn beltless, draped on the shoulders.

supremacy among warring hosts, and finally the power of the Ottoman Turks prevailed. Their leader, Muhammad II, captured Constantinople in 1453.

Preserver of Civilization. For centuries the service to the world that made the Byzantine period remarkable was not realized. It conferred two great benefits on western civilization. First the empire stood solidly between the non-Christian hordes of Asia and the growing civilization of Europe; it warded off attacks that, had they been successful, might have inundated Europe and retarded its advancement for hundreds of years.

Second, Constantinople (during most of the period also known as *New Rome)* was a repository of the learning of the world. It preserved the best in art and literature of the Golden Age of the Western Empire, and it became the home of the greatest scholars of the time. When the Imperial City fell, there was an exodus that carried to central and western Europe the best thought of the age.

CADE'S REBELLION, an uprising in England in 1450 led by an Irish adventurer, Jack Cade. The rebellion expressed the discontent of the lower classes with the misgovernment of the group of powerful noblemen who controlled the incompetent King Henry VI.

Shakespeare has dramatized Cade's rebellion in the second part of *King Henry VI* (Act IV).

CANNAE, a great battle of the Second Punic War, fought in 216 BC between the Carthaginians commanded by Hannibal and the Romans under the Consuls Caius Terentius Varro and Lucius Aemilius Paulus. The battle marked the high point of Hannibal's invasion of Italy and very nearly resulted in the destruction of Rome.

The Carthaginian force was about 40,000 infantry and 10,000 cavalry; the Roman was nearly twice as large. Hannibal's masterly tactics in the Battle of Cannae have been admired by military students ever since—In World War I the German General Staff spoke of attaining a "Cannae" as the leading aim of military plans.

The essential features of Hannibal's plan was a weak center and strong wings so as to entice the enemy into a position where he could be attacked from both sides. The plan was a thorough success. "Jammed and packed by their own mass and momentum between the hostile columns, helpless, unable to fight or fly, the men were hewn down where they stood. It was a carnival of cold steel, a butchery, not a battle."

The Roman army was almost annihilated; at least 50,000 were killed. Hannibal's loss was less than 6,000. That the Battle of Cannae did not result in the complete collapse of Rome proves better than anything else in their history the invincible fighting stamina of the Roman people.

CAROLINGIANS, a line of Frankish kings who succeeded the Merovingians, the first dynasty of the Franks. The name was derived from Charles the Great (Charlemagne). The first Carolingian king was Pepin, or Pippin, who was crowned in 751. Charlemagne, the first great Frankish monarch and the greatest in the line, was the son of Pepin. The dynasty ruled until 987, when it was succeeded by the Capetians.

CARTHAGE, the greatest of the colonies of ancient Phoenicia. Situated at a strategic point on the Mediterranean coast of Africa, with a fertile surrounding territory and a harbor large enough for many vessels, Carthage became the greatest maritime and commercial power of the ancient world and the political rival of Rome.

Little is known of Carthage's early history. In his *Aeneid,* Vergil repeats the legendary story of its founding by Queen Dido, and he links this story with his equally legendary account of the founding of Rome, giving a poetical explanation of the deadly warfare that later grew up between the two cities.

It is probable that Carthage was originally a small trading post established in the 800s or 900s BC. With the waning of Phoenician power in the east, Carthage carried on and expanded the Phoenician civilization in the west. It is likely that many of the wealthy families of Tyre and Sidon emigrated to Carthage in the 700s and 800s BC, when those rich Phoenician cities were attacked by the Assyrians. At any rate, Carthage grew rapidly both in population and wealth about this time, and had become, in the 500s, the commercial capital of the Mediterranean world.

CENTRAL TREATY ORGANIZATION, (CENTO), an extension of the Baghdad Pact originally signed in 1955, excluding Iraq, since the 1958 overthrow of its pro-Western regime. The members are Iran, Turkey, Pakistan, and the United Kingdom. Funds for nonmilitary programs have been contributed by Britain and the United States. The United States signed "bilateral agreement of cooperation" on Mar. 5, 1959, including the use of armed forces in case of aggression.

CHAPULTEPEC, ACT OF, a declaration of reciprocal assistance and American solidarity by the governments represented at the International American Conference on War and Peace in Mexico City, Feb. 4 to Mar. 8, 1945. The conference was called to provide for the security of the western hemisphere and resulted in an inter-American defense pact agreement subscribed to by the foreign ministers of the Pan American countries represented. It was later adopted by the Pan American conference held at Bogota in 1948.

CHARTISTS, a political movement for democratic reform that commanded many adherents in England in the middle decades of the 1800s. The so-called *People's Charter* was a six-point program demanding: (1) annual Parliaments; (2) universal manhood suffrage; (3) vote by ballot; (4) equal electoral districts; (5) abolition of property requirement for members of Parliament; and (6) salary payments for members of Parliament within the English government.

The Chartist movement first became of political importance in 1839, when great mass meetings were held and there was much talk of violence if the demands of the Chartists were not granted. The government refused any concessions, and rioting that followed was put down by force. In the year 1848, when revolutionary activity disturbed all Europe, the English Chartists made another attempt to overawe the government, but without success. With improvement of economic conditions the movement gradually lost influence.

Ultimately almost all the objectives of the Chartist movement were attained in England in the typically English way of slow evolution. The Chartists contended for sound and desirable principles, but they were poorly led, and their political ineptitude probably postponed the ends they sought rather than hastened them.

COMMONWEALTH OF NATIONS, a group of independent nations, united by their acknowledgement of the British Crown or by their recognition of the British sovereign as head of the Commonwealth. The members include Australia, Barbados, Botswana, Canada, Ceylon, Cyprus, Gambia, Ghana, Guyana, India, Jamaica, Kenya, Lesotho, Malaysia, Malawi, Malta, Mauritius, New Zealand, Nigeria, Pakistan, Sierra Leone, Singapore, Tanzania, Trinidad and Tobago, Uganda, the United Kingdom, Western Samoa, and Zambia.

The original members were the United Kingdom, Canada, Australia, New Zealand, the Union of South Africa, the Irish Free State, and the Dominion of Newfoundland. Newfoundland was joined to Canada in 1934. Ireland resigned from the Commonwealth in 1949, as did South Africa in 1961.

The term "Commonwealth of Nations" was probably first applied in

JUSTINIAN I codified his empire's laws.

1883 by the Earl of Rosebery. The idea seems to have been originated in 1839 by Lord Durham in his *Report on the Affairs of British North America*. The member nations' relationship was defined at the Imperial Conference of 1926 in London under the chairmanship of Lord Arthur J. Balfour. The resolutions there adopted were given legal effect by the Statute of Westminster, an act of the British Parliament of Dec. 11, 1931.

The general effect of this statute was to render the parliaments of the several dominions formally supreme in their own jurisdictions and thus to place them on a footing of equality with the British Parliament. This Parliament cannot legislate for the dominions without their previous consent, and dominion parliaments are free to make laws without reference to the law of the United Kingdom. The genius of the Commonwealth relationship is its flexibility.

CONSPIRACY OF CATILINE, an attempt led by Lucius Catiline in 63 BC to overthrow the Roman government and establish a reign of terror. The plot was detected and frustrated by the vigilance of the consul, Cicero, whose violent orations, *In Catilinam* (Against Catiline), are our principal source of information about the episode, and his connection with the case has probably invested it with a greater importance than it truly deserves. It is nevertheless interesting for the question of Roman constitutional law that it involved and for the light it sheds on political and social conditions of the last years of the Roman Republic.

CONSTANCE, COUNCIL OF, one of the great ecumenical councils (that is, representative of the whole church) of the Roman Catholic Church, summoned by the pseudo-Pope John XXIII in 1414. The council was called to consider serious questions then agitating the church, among which were the rival claims to the papal chair of three alleged popes (John XXIII, Gregory XII, Benedict XIII) and the doctrines being spread in central Europe by John Huss. The council was the largest and most brilliant held up to that time. More than 18,000 priests and 80,000 laymen assembled in the Swiss city to watch and to influence the proceedings.

CORPUS IURIS (Body of the Law), the great collection of Roman laws compiled under the direction of the Emperor Justinian about 530 AD. The importance of this work is described by the German scholar, W. S. Teuffel, as follows: "Though Justinian, in causing these collections to be made, besides the craving to immortalize his name, was governed by the autocratic idea of establishing mechanical uniformity, foreclosing controversies among lawyers and debarring the judge from the exercise of his individual opinion, still it was he who rescued the treasures of ancient jurisprudence, otherwise doomed to destruction, rendered possible an historical treatment of Roman Law, . . . and laid the foundation of all further development of that law."

BETTMANN ARCHIVE

CHRISTIAN CRUSADERS are shown disembarking at Egypt for their march on the Holy Land.

COUNCIL OF TEN, the supreme governing body of the Venetian Republic during the last 500 years of its existence (1310–1797). It had its origin in a secret tribunal set up to suppress a popular uprising early in the 1300s, but it soon succeeded in usurping all executive power.

The Council's arbitrary methods of government, enforced by secret arrests and condemnations, by assassinations, by a complicated espionage system that pried into private as well as public matters, have made it execrated by all lovers of democratic traditions. But in its favor must be pleaded the usual excuse of tyrannical government—that the alternative was intense factional strife amounting to anarchy.

CRÉDIT MOBILIER OF AMERICA, a joint-stock company created by the stockholders of the Union Pacific Railroad Company when that road was under construction, and later the railroad's fiscal agent in completing its building. The federal government had given the railroad vast tracts of land along its route and guaranteed large subsidies to enable construction to proceed.

The amount the government had guaranteed was nearly double the actual requirements, and the Crédit Mobilier reaped immense profits. Its stock in the year preceding the completion of the railroad in 1869 paid dividends of more than 400 percent. An inquiry into the matter promised scandalous developments. To quiet the investigation, blocks of stock were sold to government officials at much less than market value.

It was found that the vice-president (Schuyler Colfax), the Speaker of the House of Representatives, three senators, and a number of representatives held blocks of the stock. The disclosures created intense excitement, but

there was not sufficient evidence on which to base expulsions from Congress or to prosecute the offenders in the courts. Later investigations partly exonerated some of the accused persons.

CRUSADES, a series of great movements by the Christian nations of western Europe to wrest the Holy Land from the possession of the Muslims. The crusades are conventionally considered as beginning with Pope Urban II's appeal to the Council of Clermont in 1095 and ending with the recapture of Acre by the Muslims in 1291.

Sporadic revivals of the crusading spirit continued, however, throughout the 1300s with an increasing admixture of political motives as distinct from religious. It was not until 1453, when Constantinople was captured by the Ottoman Turks, that it became clear to everyone that no further effective effort could be made.

In 637 Jerusalem and the Holy Sepulcher had fallen into the hands of the Saracens, but for nearly 400 years Christians were permitted to make pilgrimages to the great shrine of their religion, and the Latin Church in Jerusalem was allowed liberty to worship. In the 1000s the Seljuk Turks swept westward from Asia, possessed themselves of the Holy Land and brought to an end the era of comparative good will. Stories of brutality and persecution and of extortionate levies on pilgrims began to reach western Europe.

In 1095 Alexius Comnenus, emperor of the Eastern Roman Empire, wishing to regain the provinces that had been taken by the Turks, appealed to Pope Urban II for aid. The opportunity was eagerly seized by the pope, who saw an opportunity to recover for Latin Christianity the Greek Christians of the east, and who strongly felt the humiliation and danger to both branches of Christianity of the rising power of the Muslims. Urban also realized that nothing could so strongly make for unity among the western nations as a holy war against a common enemy.

At this juncture Peter of Amiens, a priest called *the Hermit*, returned from the east, where he had seen and experienced many of the hardships endured by the Christians of Jerusalem. He was welcomed by the Pope, who made him leader of the propaganda that was to awaken Christendom to activity. Peter traveled throughout all western Europe.

Late in 1095 Pope Urban addressed a plea to the Council of Clermont that was the last word necessary to invoke the crusading spirit: "Go now and take the sword of the Maccabees and protect the people of God. . . . The barbarous Turks have planted their colors on the very shores of the Hellespont, hence they threaten war to all the states of Christendom. Unless you oppose a mighty barrier to their triumphant course, how can Europe be saved from invasion?"

The First Crusade was begun in 1096, with an enrolment exceeding 200,000. It was divided into two armies. The first marched under Peter the Hermit. He had no authority, and there was practically no discipline. It resulted in a ghastly tragedy, and Peter's army was destroyed. Many were killed on the way through Hungary and Bulgaria, on account of the outrages they committed on the inhabitants. The second army was under experienced commanders, like Godfrey and Baldwin; it captured Jerusalem, slaughtered the inhabitants, and its leaders set up a kingdom that endured until Saladin retook the city in 1187. Jerusalem then remained in the hands of the Turks until Gereral Allenby entered it at the head of British troops in 1917.

In all, there were four principal Crusades and five minor ventures. One of the most remarkable and most ill-advised was the Children's Crusade in 1212. About 30,000 French children, probably half of them under the age of 12, reached Marseille, where the waterfront stopped them. Many returned home, but thousands were lured upon boats with the promise of free passage to the Holy Land; several vessels were wrecked, and those that escaped storms sailed to Alexandria, where the children were sold into slavery. Another section of this crusade, 20,000 strong, started from Germany but got no farther than Geneva. Thousands died of exposure and hunger, and few children reached home again.

DAWES PLAN, a temporary settlement of the Allied claims for German reparations following World War I. Penalties of 32 billions were assessed. In 1929 with the Young Plan, they were substantially reduced. German payments ceased in 1931.

DECEMVIRATE, a commission of 10 men (Latin *decem,* ten, and *vir,* man) appointed in the early Roman Republic (c.450 BC) to draw up a written code of laws and thus end abuses of partisan interpretation of the traditional law by patrician magistrates. The decemvirate produced the code known as the *Law of the Twelve Tables,* which became the foundation of all later Roman law.

The accounts of Livy and Dionysius, almost our sole sources for the story of the decemvirate, were written more than 400 years after the events and contain, along with some kernels of historical truth, a large mass of legend and political falsehood. The very famous story of Virginia, slain by her own father to save her from falling into the clutches of the villainous Appius Claudius, is now regarded as an invention.

A more plausible view of Appius Claudius, the leader of the decemvirate, is given by G. W. Botsford, who regards him as a great liberal leader of patrician rank but of popular sympathies, not altogether unlike President Roosevelt in our own day. "It is far easier, however, to believe that these stories are aristocratic falsehoods for blackening the memory of the decemvirs than it is to imagine that the man who gave his country the priceless treasure of just laws could be himself a monster of injustice and cruelty."

DECISIVE BATTLES OF THE WORLD. In 1853 the English historian, Edward Creasy, published a famous historical book, *Fifteen Decisive Battles of the World,* which was an attempt to interpret world history in terms of great crucial military movements. Another English writer, Henry Hallam, had attracted Creasy's attention by writing of the Battle of Tours (732 AD): "It may justly be reckoned among those few battles of which a contrary event would have essentially varied the drama of the world in all its subsequent scenes." Taking this criterion of what constitutes a decisive battle, Creasy selected the following as the great turning points in world history:

The Battle of Marathon, 490 BC.
The Defeat of the Athenians at Syracuse, 413 BC.
The Battle of Arbela, 331 BC.
The Battle of the Metaurus, 207 BC.
The Victory of Arminius over the Roman Legions under Varus (Teutoburg Forest), 9 AD.
The Battle of Chalons, 451.
The Battle of Tours, 732.
The Battle of Hastings, 1066.
Joan of Arc's Victory over the English at Orleans, 1429.
The Defeat of the Spanish Armada, 1588.
The Battle of Blenheim, 1704.
The Battle of Pultowa, 1709.
The Victory of the Americans over Burgoyne at Saratoga, 1777.
The Battle of Valmy, 1792.
The Battle of Waterloo, 1815.

Since Creasy's day there have been other battles that seem of similar importance—the Battle of Gettysburg,

CORCORAN GALLERY OF ART

THE MAID IN ARMOR ON HORSEBACK, from the Joan of Arc series by Louis Maurice Boutet de Monvel. Charles VII entrusted Joan with an army; and she laid siege to Orléans, defeated the English at Patay, and brought Charles to be crowned at Rheims. Joan was captured by the Burgundians and sold to the English, who tried and burned her for being a heretic.

1863; the Battle of Sedan, 1870; the Battle of the Marne, 1914; and the Battle of Midway, 1942. A brief account of these battles will be found under their individual names.

DISPLACED PERSONS (DP's), the term used to describe refugees in Europe who found themselves without home or income because of property confiscation and exile due to conditions caused by World War II. Resettlement of DP's was under the UN Relief and Rehabilitation Administration (UN-RRA) until is ceased to exist. These functions were assumed by the International Refugee Organization (IRO). Religious, racial and economic problems handicapped the work.

EGYPT, located in the northeastern part of Africa. The earliest history of Egypt is obscure, but the beginning of its continuous civilization dates from about 8000 or 7000 BC. The story can be read in the archeological works discovered there, although the continuous written record does not begin until about 5000 BC.

Up to that time the country was inhabited by Cushites, a Hamitic people. They probably migrated from the plateaus of Central Asia by way of the Isthmus of Suez, the same route followed later by the Egyptians themselves. The small Cushite states existed for centuries before they were subdued by Menes, whose dynasty lasted for 800 years. From Menes to the Persian conquest in 527 BC, 26 dynasties are recorded. The Persian dynasty following this conquest was the 27th, and four more dynasties follow, the third ending in 332 BC with the conquest of Alexander.

Menes was the first monarch of whom there is actual record—and some scholars think this name stands for three different kings. He (or they) reigned about 5000 BC, was supposed to have founded Memphis, to have united upper and lower Egypt, centralized the government, and firmly established a new dynasty. The 31 dynasties, of which his was the first, have been grouped as follows, according to the historian Manetho: Dynasties I-X, Ancient Empire; Dynasties XI-XVII, Middle Empire; and Dynasties XVIII-XXXI, New Empire. Some of these dynasties, however, are of comparatively little importance.

The kings of Dynasties II, III and IV left the structures at which the world has marveled ever since. These include the vast Pyramid of Sakkara (the most ancient monument in Egypt) and the three pyramids and the famous Sphinx at Giza.

Later kings left inscriptions on their monumental works, and the translations of these have added much to our knowledge of this ancient state. Apparently each one of these kings (among them warriors who invaded the neighboring countries of Asia, but without noteworthy results) built a new capital city, none far from Memphis.

Succeeding dynasties saw a lessening of central power, for local princes usurped some of the powers of the kings. The Golden Age of Egypt,

when literature and art were at their height, began about 2000 BC. Kings of Dynasty XII extended their conquests southward; the new riches aroused the ambitions of princes who thirsted for power, and for about a century the country was the scene of civil strife. It was during Dynasty XII that the famous Lake Moeris and the Labyrinth were constructed.

Lack of strong central authority opened the way for conquest from outside and resulted in the period of the Hyksos, or Shepherd Kings, who made up the Dynasties XV, XVI and XVII. These foreign invaders came from Asia, but their exact origin is not certainly known.

They held power for about 100 years, the last surrendering to native rule about 1580 BC, on being driven out by Amenophis I, first ruler of the Great Theban Dynasty XVIII. He was the first Egyptian who made his country's power felt east of the Mediterranean, beginning a period of Asian conquests. He built up a united nation and conquered both Phoenicia and Palestine but did not live to consolidate his gains.

Under Amenophis I and his successors a desire for conquest arose, with a military caste that first introduced into Egypt the use of the horse in war. The Egyptians then became masters of the region extending from Ethiopia to the Euphrates.

Under Thothmes I and III the palaces of Karnak and Luxor were built, and Egypt ruled as far as

TRANS WORLD AIRLINES

THE GREAT SPHINX OF GIZA, which is located near the Pyramid of Khafre, is only a short drive from Cairo, Egypt's capital.

Nineveh. Between these rulers came Thothmes II, who shared his reign with Hatshepsut, his sister and queen. It was she who sent Egypt's first fleet abroad (to Ethiopia and Somali) about 1500 BC, to secure gold and incense for the temples. Another famous king of the same dynasty was Amenophis IV (about 1410 BC), son of Thothmes III. He substituted the worship of the sun for that of the god Amen. At his death, however, the old faith was restored.

Egypt was at the height of its glory and the beginning of its decay under Dynasty XIX, to which Ramses I and II and Mineptah (son of Ramses II and probably the Pharaoh of Exodus) belonged. Ramses I was the first ruler in Dynasty XIX, about 1350 BC. Ramses II (about 1330 BC) continued a war in Syria begun by his father and after 20 years ended it by marrying his enemy's daughter. He retained Palestine and a part of Phoenicia for his country.

The king, Ramses I, erected many monuments to himself, but he also removed kingly names from others and substituted his own, so as to give the impression that his exploits and prowess were far greater than they really were. Ramses II, son of Seti I, and known as *Ramses the Great*, is called the most brilliant figure in Egyptian history and is among Egypt's most famous builders.

He defeated the Hittites and made a treaty with them. Seti built the Temple of Amen at Thebes, called the most splendid single chamber ever built. Ramses II is charged with surrendering Egypt to the Assyrians, from whom the Greeks helped to free it again. This started a Greek settlement in Egypt.

Ten kings bearing the name *Ramses* ruled in Dynasty XX. Ramses III delivered his land from numerous raids of plunderers and in turn plundered parts of Syria and Palestine. This dynasty is marked by no outstanding accomplishments and in fact shows a weakening of power. No great figure appeared after Dynasty XX until, in Dynasty XXVI, Necho II (609–594 BC) conquered Syria again and killed Joshua. He lost his power, however, when Nebuchadnezzar of Babylon defeated him at Carchemish.

At home he built a canal that connected the Nile and the Mediterranean with the Red Sea; he built a fleet that he sent around Africa, manned by Phoenician sailors. The last ruler of this dynasty was Psammetich II, who was defeated by Cambyses (525 BC), and Egypt became a province of Persia.

This overlordship continued until 414 BC, when the Persians were expelled, but the same oppressors returned in 343 BC. Alexander the Great conquered the land in 332 BC and founded Alexandria, which became famous as the principal center of Greek civilization. On his death in the same year, Ptolemy, one of his generals, became ruler (323 BC) and raised Egypt to high rank.

Under this first Ptolemy, a wise, considerate ruler, Egypt, as a Greek state, was allowed virtual independence and attained a foremost place

UNITED NATIONS/UNESCO

THE GREAT TEMPLE OF ABU SIMBEL, in the Nile Valley of the United Arab Republic (Egypt). The temple is among the archeological treasures saved from the rising waters of the Aswan High Dam by the UN Educational, Scientific and Cultural Organization (UNESCO).

among the world's nations. Never had it been so prosperous; commerce flourished, the people were contented, and Alexandria became a cultural center. A succession of nine Ptolemys followed; the next to the last, Ptolemy XIII, left the kingdom to his daughter, Cleopatra, and his son, Ptolemy XIV.

Cleopatra's ambition made her sole ruler, but partly through her intrigues with the Roman general, Antony, the kingdom was lost. Rome occupied the country and Egypt's history as an independent nation was not regained for centuries.

Rome ruled Egypt until the fall of the empire, 476 AD. During the latter part of the Roman rule, Egypt was given little attention and, without the support of the empire, fell an easy prey to the Saracens in 641. Egypt became a highly important Muslim territory, with Cairo one of the leading Islamic centers. There followed first a period of Fatamid rule (969–1171) and then of Ambyite control (1171–1250). Hoping to lessen the grip of Islam, the crusaders had struck at Cairo but failed.

From 1250 to 1517 Egypt was controlled by the order of the Mamelukes set up by Saladin. They extended their power over a large part of Africa, Syria, and Arabia. In 1517 the Turks, under Selim I, defeated the Mamelukes, but they still remained a force to be reckoned with. When Napoleon invaded Egypt in 1798 he found the Mamelukes opposing him. He gained and held control until 1801, when he was expelled by the Turks, who were helped by the British.

In 1811 Mehemet Ali became ruler of Egypt by the massacre of the Mamelukes. Under his control Egypt progressed rapidly in civilization. He considerably extended its boundaries and (by the Treaty of London, 1841) was made Viceroy of Egypt, as a representative of the Ottoman Empire. The independent position of the rulers of Egypt was much strengthened in 1867 by an imperial decree, which established the succession of the descendants of Mehemet Ali, under the title *khedive* (king).

Still greater powers were granted in 1872, and in 1874–1875 Ismail Pasha, the ruler at that time, greatly extended Egyptian territory, annexing the Sudan to Darfur and finally reaching the shores of Victoria Nyanza. He favored the building of the Suez Canal. In 1874 Gen. Charles George Gordon was appointed governor general of the Sudan and did much to suppress the slave trade.

The finances of the country became so involved that they were placed under European management and the country under English and French control. In 1879 Ismail was forced by the French and British to abdicate and was succeeded by his son Tewfik. Arabi Pasha gathered an army of followers and revolted against European influence.

The rebellion was suppressed by the British army and navy, the French taking no part. As a result the dual control ended, and Great Britain became the practical ruler of Egypt, despite the occasional protest of France and other European powers.

METROPOLITAN MUSEUM OF ART

WALL PAINTING from the tomb of User-het, Thebes, shows his mother and wife receiving water. They are wearing the wide jeweled collar, bracelets, and headdress of the period.

Following the establishment of dual French-British rule about 1880, a serious revolt began in the Sudan under the leadership of a Muslim, Muhammad Ahmad, who claimed to be the mahdi, or redeemer. The rebellion was difficult to suppress. In 1883 a British army under Hicks Pasha was totally routed. General Gordon was taken and killed (1885).

The result was that the mahdi drove the Egyptians out of the Sudan and left the way open for future occupancy by the British. This was accomplished by an Anglo-Egyptian expedition commanded by Sir Herbert (afterward Lord) Kitchener, who defeated the forces of the khalifa, successor to the mahdi, at Omdurman, near Khartoum, Sept. 2, 1898. On Jan. 19, 1899, by agreement, the territory became a condominium, known as the Anglo-Egyptian Sudan. French attempts to question the British action in the area culminated in the Fashoda agreement on Mar. 21, 1889 in which France relinquished its claim to the basin of the Nile.

Although Egypt had long been nominally a tributary state of the Ottoman Empire, British influence had been paramount, a position recognized in the Anglo-French agreement of Apr. 8, 1904. At the outbreak of World War I, Great Britain established a protectorate over Egypt, terminated Feb. 28, 1922. On Mar. 15, 1922, the Sultan of Egypt, Hussein Kamil, was proclaimed King Fuad I. A new constitution was promulgated, Apr. 19, 1923; was suspended, July 19, 1928; and an amended constitution promulgated, Oct. 22, 1930.

Zaghlul, head of a nationalist committee seeking independence, kept Egyptian affairs in turmoil. Finally, a treaty of alliance between Egypt and Great Britain, made public in November 1927, brought affairs to a crisis. It was unacceptable to the Egyptians, and King Fuad, on July 19, 1928, dissolved the parliament, to rule by royal decree. The king's illness, however, forced consideration for popular demands. He died Apr. 28, 1936, and was succeeded by his son, Farouk I. On Aug. 22, 1936, a 20 year treaty of alliance was signed with Great Britain and full sovereignty was achieved.

FILIBUSTER, a term applied to pirates who plundered Spanish possessions in the Americas. Later it was used to describe private military expeditions into countries that were at peace with the country from which the expedition was launched. There are numerous instances of filibustering in which American citizens have been engaged.

In 1855 William Walker of Tennessee invaded Nicaragua with a small force, but later fled to Honduras for safety, where he was arrested and shot. From New Orleans a filibustering expedition went to Cuba, but its leader, Lopez, was shot, and his followers were dispersed.

In legislation a filibuster is a weapon used to delay action. It consists of long speeches to consume time, the use of dilatory motions and the like. It is a device of the minority members intended to confuse and defeat the plans of the majority.

FEUDAL SYSTEM, an institution based on ownership of land and the personal relationship of landlord and tenant that flourished in Europe throughout the later Middle Ages. It probably had its origin during the later Roman Empire. In theory, the king owned the land, retained the larger part and divided the remainder among his retainers.

Later the government was less stable, and eventually, to promote security, the ruler divided his vast estates among the nobles and the great warriors and gave them sovereignty over their lands. In return, these landowners pledged their fealty to the king, guaranteeing aid to him whenever he needed it, which included the raising of armies for his defense when war threatened.

The land of each retainer was called a fief. It was customary for holders of large fiefs to subdivide them in turn among their own retainers. The owner of a fief was known as lord, liege, or suzerain; the one holding it was a vassal, retainer, or liegeman. Each vassal gave his pledge of loyalty and military service, and in turn the lord pledged protection. At the bottom of the classes were the submerged serfs. These were the laborers, bound to the fief, who passed with the land at every change of masters.

From the point of view of modern civilization there is much to be criticized in the feudal state, but it was an admirable system for the times in which it existed, and for centuries it flourished in France, England, Germany, Scotland, and parts of Italy and Spain. The times were troubled, and every class of society found security in a system that afforded protection against the prevalent lawlessness.

Feudalism also proved a bulwark against outside foes. One historian declares, "It was the mailed feudal horseman and the impregnable walls of the feudal castle that foiled the attacks of the Danes, the Saracens and the Hungarians." The great weakness of feudalism was that it prevented the formation of strong central governments. Each lord was a sovereign over his fief. As it became necessary in the evolution of society to centralize control, the feudal state disappeared.

FLODDEN FIELD, a battle fought in Northumberland in the north of England, Sept. 9, 1513, between the army of James IV of Scotland and English forces led by the Earl of Surrey. King James died on the field, and his army lost close to 10,000 men; the English loss was less, but so worn were Surrey's victorious troops that they did not pursue the retreating Scots.

Of little historical importance, the battle of Flodden Field has acquired fame chiefly from the spirited description of it in the 6th canto of Sir Walter Scott's *Marmion.*

FRENCH REVOLUTION, the great political and social upheaval of France at the end of the 1700s that developed into the Napoleonic Wars and effected the transformation of the old European order. The French Revolution began with what appeared to be a peaceable meeting of the Estates-General in May 1789. The first stage of the Revolution was marked by a series of non-violent changes on social and political levels.

The second stage, the period of the elected Legislative Assembly (October 1791 to August 1792), was marked by the failure of the limited monarchy that had been established by the Constitution of 1791—a failure attributable chiefly to the uncooperative attitude of the king and his immediate circle and to the efforts of foreign powers to crush the Revolution by force.

The third stage began with the assembling of the National Convention in September 1792 and ended with the downfall of Robespierre, July 1794. It was marked by the substitution of violence for debate under the increasing threat of foreign interference, by the abolition of the monarchy, followed by the trial and execution of King Louis XVI, and by the Reign of Terror under the dictatorship of the Committee of Public Safety.

The fourth and final stage of the Revolution proper is that of the bourgeoisie's reaction and the establishment of the Directory under the Constitution of the Year III of the Republic (1745–1795).

METROPOLITAN MUSEUM OF ART

"THE BARRICADE" (*Liberty Leading the People* or *Liberty on the Barricade*) by Eugène Delacroix (1798–1863). "Liberty" was inspired by the events of the 1789–1795 revolution in France. This painting, possibly the last successful allegory to be put on canvas, is a combination of realism, historical painting, and political cartooning. What seemed a last chance for "Liberty, Equality and Fraternity" for the people of France became the foundation for Delacroix's document.

The Revolution did not end in 1795; in a larger sense the whole period of the Napoleonic Wars (1796–1815) is a part of the French Revolutionary epoch, and even after 1815 the ideas of the Revolution continued to dominate the political life of Europe. But the period from 1789 to 1795 may be taken as the period of the Revolution itself. Later developments are the results of the Revolution.

Long before 1789 it was evident to every observing contemporary that the state of affairs in France could not endure for much longer. Throughout the 1700s discontent had been growing both more intense and more articulate. The list of social and governmental abuses was long and impressive. The lower classes, peasantry and urban proletariat were crushed under a grinding poverty made worse by a grossly corrupt and unequal system of taxation. The educated upper middle classes, business and professional men, found intolerable the governmental restrictions of their business activities and the freedom from taxation enjoyed by the privileged orders—the nobility and the clergy. It was to these men—the bourgeoisie—that the philosophical radicalism of Voltaire, Rousseau, Montesquieu and the Encyclopedists appealed.

Even among the privileged there were many enlightened individuals who realized that reforms must be made. But Louis XV and Louis XVI, whose reigns preceded the Revolution were both incapable of taking any statesmanlike steps that might have brought about a peaceful change. Louis XV (1715–1774) was an utterly worthless debauchee, the sum of whose political philosophy was contained in the cynical answer to suggestions that the monarchy was in danger: "It will surely last as long as I; my successor may take care of himself." Louis XVI (1754–1793) was incapable of grasping political realities, although personally anxious for his people's welfare.

In 1788 the governmental mismanagement had brought affairs to a sorry pass indeed—the nation was bankrupt. Every imaginable financial expedient—short of reform of taxation—had been tried and had failed. In the emergency the king finally consented to a measure that had been demanded with increasing loudness for the past several years, the convocation of the Estates-General, an ancient representative body that had not met during the previous 175 years. It was hoped that in some way the Estates-General would be able to find a way out of the overwhelming difficulties of the government.

The Estates-General consisted of representatives of the three classes, or estates, of French society: the clergy (First Estate), the nobility (Second Estate) and the commons (Third Estate). The Third Estate was numerically the strongest; it had as many representatives as the First and Second Estates together.

It was of great moment to decide whether the vote in the Estates-General should be by head or by order; if the vote was taken by order the numerical strength of the Third Estate was nullified, since on most questions it was to be expected that the First and Second Estates, representing the privileged classes, would vote together. If the vote was taken by head, however, the Third Estate would be able to control matters.

The dispute about the method of voting brought about the first really revolutionary act of the Estates-General. Led by Mirabeau and Sieyès, the Third Estate broke away from the privileged orders and organized themselves into a new body—the National Assembly—which they boldly declared was the legal voice of France. They were joined by many of the clergy and by a few liberal nobles. After a feeble resistance the king acquiesced, and the National Assembly, dominated by the representatives of the Third Estate, became an effective legislative body ready to take up the task of reforming the French government.

It is a common error to suppose that the Third Estate was elected by and represented the great submerged mass of the French people—the 20,000,000 peasants, artisans and laborers. In truth the Third Estate represented not this vast lower class—voteless, illiterate, truly forgotten men—but the small, although strong and compact, group of business and professional men—the bourgeoisie. It happened that the aims of the bourgeoisie coincided at the moment with many of the inarticulate longings of the lower classes, who vaguely attributed all their miseries to the king, the nobles, and to the system on which these had grown fat.

The National Assembly remained in session from June 1789 until September 1791. In these years it brought about sweeping reforms. "No other body of legislators has even demolished so much in the same brief period. The old form of government, the old territorial divisions, the old financial system, the old judicial and legal regulations, the old ecclesiastical arrangements, and, most significant of all, the old condition of holding land—serfdom and feudalism—all were shattered."[1]

An entirely new consitution, resembling in some ways the Constitution of the United States and in other ways the governmental system of England, providing for a strictly limited monarchy under the effective control of an elective legislative assembly, was instituted. When the National Assembly dissolved itself, it seemed to many that the work of change was accomplished, and that an era of peace and prosperity was about to begin.

Unfortunately the legislative program of the National Assembly did nothing to relieve the economic distress of the people. A radical movement began to gain headway among the turbulent Parisian populace—a movement that soon found able leaders in such men as Danton, Robespierre and Marat. Even more dangerous to the stability of the new constitution was the reactionary move-

[1] Hayes, Carlton J. H., *Political and Social History of Modern Europe*, Macmillan.

ment that was stirring in the outside world.

Hundreds of nobles, called *émigrés*, had fled the country taking with them as much of their property as they could smuggle out, and they were actively raising a counter-revolutionary army of their own and were seeking assistance from foreign powers. Early in 1791 the king himself had attempted to join this exodus; he and the queen had been arrested in the midst of their flight and were now virtually prisoners in the Tuileries Palace in Paris. Thus the Legislative Assembly that met in October 1791 was confronted with grave difficulties.

In 1792 foreign intervention passed from threat to reality. An army of Austrians and Prussians, led by the insolent and reactionary-minded duke of Brunswick, began an invasion of France with the avowed purpose of "putting an end to the anarchy in the interior of France." This ill-timed announcement roused the whole nation to a fierce spirit of resistance. The Legislative Assembly lost control of the situation; a series of violent insurrections of the mob occurred in Paris. Finally on Aug. 10, 1792, the Legislative Assembly broke up after voting to authorize a new election on the basis of universal manhood suffrage for a National Convention.

The 40-day interval between the end of the Legislative Assembly and the meeting of the National Convention was a time of wild disorder. The radical leaders of the Paris mob, of whom Danton was the chief, gained control of the city. In an effort to terrify the Royalists who remained in France and if possible to deter further advance by the army of the Duke of Brunswick, Danton adopted a fearful policy. At his instigation more than 2,000 persons guilty or suspected of Royalist sympathies were summarily butchered in what became known as the September Massacres. The royal family was seized and placed under close arrest.

The newly elected National Convention met in Paris on September 21. In the meantime the Duke of Brunswick had been defeated at the battle of Valmy; Paris and the Revolution were temporarily safe from foreign attack. A great change in spirit had taken place; ideas that were radical in 1789 were now thought conservative; ideas that were conservative in 1789 were now proscribed. The first official act of the National Convention was to declare the monarchy abolished. Within a few weeks it was determined to bring the king to trial. The day of peaceful reform was over. The enemies of the Revolution, both abroad and at home, had forced it to defend itself, and it defended itself with a reign of terror.

So dramatic and horribly fascinating were the events of the next year and a half that in popular thought they are often represented as the whole Revolution or at least the most characteristic part of the Revolution. In reality the Reign of Terror, which began shortly after the establishment of the dictatorship of the Committee of Public Safety in the spring of 1793, was not a necessary part of the Revolution at all. It was an effort to preserve the accomplished Revolution from the attacks of the reactionaries. Given the situation that existed at the beginning of 1793—a newly established government threatened by agitation within and foreign enemies without—the Reign of Terror was the inevitable outcome.

In December 1792 Louis XVI was tried before the National Convention and condemned to death by a narrow vote. The conservative party in the Convention, called the *Girondists*, opposed the king's execution, and it seems possible that if they had steadfastly hung together they could have retained control. But many of their members were afraid to support what might be a losing cause, and these vacillators, as it turned out, held the balance of power.

Once the Girondists had lost a crucial test vote on the question of executing the king, their influence rapidly declined. After the Committee of Public Safety had secured control, the Girondists were liquidated or purged, to borrow the phraseology of contemporary revolution.

The Committee of Public Safety, under the dominance of Danton, Robespierre, and St. Just, remained in power until the spring of 1794. The executions of enemies and suspected enemies of the Republic went forward with shocking ferocity. Marie Antoinette, the widow of Louis XVI, was dragged before the Revolutionary Tribunal and after a mockery of a trial was sent to the guillotine.

Many of France's ablest men also perished, among them the chemist Lavoisier and the promising poet André de Chénier. In the provinces outside Paris an indiscriminate butchery, far bloodier and less controlled than the executions in the city, swept away thousands of victims, most of them quite innocent.

Yet it is easy to overestimate the extent of the Reign of Terror and to forget the desperate provocation that brought it about. No more than 3,000 persons were executed in Paris during the whole course of the Committee of Public Safety's control; perhaps 10,000 were slaughtered in the provinces.

Estimating the victims of the September Massacres at 5,000 and the miscellaneous butcheries before and after at 2,000, we may estimate that the total number of lives sacrificed to the Revolution did not exceed 20,000 —a fearful toll, to be sure, but fewer than the number of persons killed in many of the world's famous battles.

Early in 1794 the fury of the Reign of Terror against counterrevolutionaries had spent itself. The leaders were quarreling among themselves. Robespierre first got the upper hand, and Danton, along with his friend Camile Desmoulins, was arrested and sent to the guillotine. But in July 1794 Robespierre fell a victim to the savage passions he himself had set in motion. With his fall and execution the Reign of Terror ended.

The National Convention remained in session for a year after the fall of Robespierre. During this last period it was dominated by upper middle class sentiment—by the bourgeoisie.

BETTMANN ARCHIVE

ABRAHAM LINCOLN AT GETTYSBURG, 1863, during dedication ceremonies of the Gettysburg battlefield as a national cemetery for the soldiers who died during the Civil War.

Reforms in the interest of the lower classes were dropped.

The Constitution of the Year III (dating from the abolition of the monarchy, Sept. 22, 1792), was a typically bourgeois document. It restricted suffrage to taxpayers who had lived a year in one place, thus excluding 90 percent of the people from a share in the government, and was scarcely more radical in its social and economic orientation than the "great machine for the manufacture of Philistines" that Matthew Arnold called the British Constitution.

By the Constitution of the Year III the executive power of government was entrusted to a board called the Directory. The Directory ruled France until 1799, when it was overthrown by Napoleon. Thus the republic became a military dictatorship.

GETTYSBURG, a battle of the American Civil War, fought July 1–3, 1863, between the Confederate Army of Northern Virginia under Lee and the Union Army of the Potomac under Meade. The battle stopped Lee's second invasion of the North.

GIRONDISTS, a political party during the French Revolution, so named from the circumstance that many of its ablest leaders were from the department of Gironde in the south of France. The Girondists first gained prominence upon the convening of the Legislative Assembly elected under the Constitution of 1791, which provided for a strictly limited monarchy.

In the assembly the Girondists represented moderate republicanism —they favored a further diminution of the powers of the king, and most of them hoped for the ultimate abolition of the monarchy; but they were against the immediate extreme measures favored by the radicals. The National Convention that assembled in Paris in the fall of 1792 was a far more radical body than the Legislative Assembly of 1791. The Girondists, who

had been radicals the year before, were now the extreme conservatives. They sat on the right of the convention hall. On the left sat the radical extremists, led by such men as Robespierre, St. Just, and Danton. (This is the origin of our modern terms *right* and *left* for conservatives and radicals.)

In the struggle for control of the National Convention the Girondists were at first the dominant party; but their influence rapidly declined as the convention began more and more to reflect the threats and passions of the Paris mob. The crucial test came on the question of executing Louis XVI; the Girondists tried to prevent this violent measure but were outvoted (January 16, 1793). From this time forth they faced an increasingly powerful opposition that first deprived them of political influence and finally sent their leaders to the guillotine.

In June 1793 Girondist leaders were expelled from the National Convention. The party of the left, led by Danton, Marat and Robespierre, now in supreme control, inaugurated the Reign of Terror. Most of the Girondist leaders, including the famous Madame Roland, were executed in October of the same year.

GNOSTIC HERESY, a mystical cult prominent in the early history of Christianity. Its leading feature was a combination or fusion of Christianity with the mystical doctrines of Oriental and later Greek philosophy. The Greek word *gnosis*, from which Gnosticism takes its name, means knowledge; but the knowledge claimed by the Gnostics was not a scientific or rational knowledge but a secret revelation to be understood only by initiates.

The influence of Gnosticism on the development of early Christianity was undoubtedly great, both through the symbolism and ideas that were introduced into Christianity by the Gnostics, and through the opposition to Gnosticism as a competitor to

Christianity, which led the early Christian leaders to a more exact statement of the characteristic Christian doctrines to distinguish them from the Gnostic heresy.

GRANADA, the most important of the Muslim, or Moorish, kingdoms established in Spain by the Muslims. The Muslims were finally expelled in 1492 by the armies of Ferdinand and Isabella.

It is related of Bobadil, the Muslim leader, that as he left Granada he stood on a hilltop for a last view of his city, and that hill became known as the *Hill of Tears*. His sorrowful exclamation as he turned away from the enchanted land is remembered as the "last sigh of the Moor." Granada now forms three provinces in southern Spain.

GRAND REMONSTRANCE, a list of grievances adopted by the English Parliament in 1641 against King Charles I. It included protests against every illegal act of his entire reign. The monarch sent an evasive reply; this led to the Civil War, the execution of the king in 1649, and the period of the Commonwealth, in which Oliver Cromwell ruled the country.

GUELPHS, patriots of medieval Itay, opposed by *Ghibelline* support for the ruling German emperors and (after the liberation) the aristocracy.

HAMPTON ROADS CONFERENCE, a meeting of representatives of the United States government and of the Confederate States on Feb. 3, 1865, in the endeavor to reach terms of peace. The Union was represented by President Lincoln and Secretary of State Seward; Vice-President Stephens headed the Confederate delegation.

Lincoln refused to consider a treaty of peace and would not listen to any

VENTURE MAGAZINE

THE ALHAMBRA, at Granada, Spain. This palace, built by Moorish princes of the Nasrid dynasty, was begun by Muhammad I in 1248. Here the Court of the Lions, named for the fountain, is surrounded by arches with molded plasterwork on slender marble columns.

proposal short of surrender of the Confederate army, the abolition of slavery, and restoration of the Union. The conference was fruitless.

HANSEATIC LEAGUE, also know as the Hansa, a league of medieval German cities, united for protection of their commerce against robbers and pirates. In 1241 Hamburg and Lübeck agreed to protect the land route between the North and Baltic seas; this alliance is frequently referred to as the beginning of the Hanseatic League although temporary conbinations for commercial purposes had occurred earlier.

Bremen quickly joined, and at the height of its influence more than 80 cities, chiefly ports on the North Sea and Baltic coasts, were in the compact. The Hanseatic League was soon able to obtain special privileges for its merchants in foreign countries, and

thus practically to monopolize the trade of all northern Europe. The league maintained armed forces both on land and at sea, and conducted negotiations with foreign governments. It reached the height of its power and prosperity in the 1300s, when it conducted a war against King Waldemar IV of Denmark and obtained in 1370 a guarantee of freedom to trade and a cash indemnity.

With the shift of commercial routes in the 1400s and better government protection, the league declined, but Hamburg, Bremen, and Lübeck continued their relations. Under the German Empire they were permitted to retain their status as free cities.

HASTINGS, a battle fought on Oct. 14, 1066, at Senlac Hill near Hastings on the southern coast of England between an invading Norman force un-

METROPOLITAN MUSEUM OF ART

BATTLE OF HASTINGS, during which Norman invaders defeated English armies in 1066, is depicted in the Bayeux Tapestry, woven in Normandy.

der Duke William (later William I of England) and an English army under King Harold II. The invasion was undertaken by Duke William to make good a vague hereditary claim to the English Crown. The battle resulted in the complete defeat of the English after a desperate contest. Harold was killed, and all organized resistance to William collapsed.

The battle changed the course of English history, as it introduced a foreign domination of England that ultimately fused itself with the original English nation.

HELOTS, a class of state slaves or serfs in ancient Sparta. They had no citizenship rights, but in time of war they were pressed into military service, serving as light-armed troops for the most part, although in grave emergencies they might be organized as part of the regular army, in which case they were sometimes granted freedom as a reward for bravery on the battlefield.

In normal times they were dis- tributed among property owners to work as agricultural laborers.

General treatment of the Helots was harsh and cold-blooded. When their numbers increased so that they seemed a danger to the state, they were systematically massacred.

HOLY ALLIANCE, a compact entered into by the monarchs of Russia, Prussia, and Austria in 1815, after the downfall of Napoleon. Its published intent was to unite the governments of the signers into a Christian brotherhood, and in all their acts to exemplify the tenets of the Christian religion.

All other nations of Europe joined the Holy Alliance except England and Turkey; England refused, Turkey was not invited. Behind the professed reason for the alliance's existence was the determination of the powers to resist all popular efforts to liberalize governments and to stifle all movements that might endanger the thrones of Europe. The alliance, called by its enemies the *Holy Aggies,* had no influence after 1830.

HOLY ROMAN EMPIRE, the realm in central Europe whose ruler claimed to be legal successor of the emperors of ancient Rome. It bore the title *Holy* because the Empire was related to the church. The emperors claimed sovereignty over all the governments growing out of the empire of Charlemagne, but actually their influence was limited to the German strongholds and to Italy.

The Holy Roman emperors were elected by the German electors; when an emperor proved unusually strong, he was able to extend his influence widely enough almost to justify the name Holy Roman Empire for his realm. Voltaire, in commenting on the incongruity of the name, said the Holy Roman Empire was "neither holy, nor Roman, nor an empire." Napoleon's early victories destroyed whatever semblance of empire central Europe maintained, and the name had no meaning after 1806.

HUGUENOTS (apparently a French corruption of the German *Eidgenossen,* confederates, oath-comrades), the

name applied to the Calvinist Protestants of France by their religious opponents during the factional struggles of the 1500s and 1600s. They had many able leaders, such as Condé, Admiral Coligny, and for a time Henry of Navarre.

At the head of the Catholic party, below the throne, were the members of the Guise family. The throne gave active assistance to the Guise faction and helped to promote the Massacre of St. Bartholomew (Aug. 24, 1572). The Edict of Nantes (1598) placed Huguenots and Catholics on a plane of political equality; when it was rescinded (1685) and the Huguenots were deprived of religious liberty, many of them left France. Some emigrated to the American colonies, particularly to South Carolina.

JACOBINS, a political party during the French Revolution, originally the members of a club, or society, that met in the Jacobin convent in Paris. In the early stages of the Revolution (1789–1792) the Jacobins represented sentiment favoring moderate republicanism.

After the assembling of the National Convention, the Jacobins became the party of extreme radicalism; the Girondist purge early in 1793 placed the Jacobins in supreme control. The most famous Jacobin leader was Robespierre; after his execution (July 1794) the Jacobin party declined.

KOREAN WAR, an undeclared war, officially termed a "conflict" by the U.S. government, fought by South Koreans and various members of the United Nations, primarily the United States, against the North Koreans and the Chinese Communists. The Soviet Union furnished North Koreans and Chinese Communists with planes and other military supplies.

On June 25, 1950 (Korean time) a North Korean army crossed the 38th parallel and attacked South Korean troops. On the morning of June 27, President Truman ordered General MacArthur to support the South Koreans. That same afternoon the Secu-

rity Council of the UN asked that UN members give assistance to South Korea to force the invading army back to the 38th parallel.

On July 1 soldiers of the U.S. 24th Infantry Division landed in Korea. On July 7 the UN Security Council voted that all United Nations' troops be asked to fight under a common UN command. U.S. General MacArthur was chosen UN supreme commander.

From the beginning of the war until Sept. 15, 1950, the South Korean and UN forces were driven southward, even past Pohang. An amphibious landing by U.S. troops at Inchon on that day, however, suddenly forced the North Koreans into retreat, and in the next 70 days North Korean forces were pushed back almost to the Yalu River.

On Nov. 26, 1950, however, a well-equipped army of 200,000 Chinese Communists crossed the Yalu to counter-attack. They drove the UN divisions steadily back. By Jan. 20, 1951 the communists were 70 miles below the 38th parallel. The South

KOREAN WAR
1950–1953

With the Korean conflict, the "cold war" between the communist nations and the free world became a "hot war." While UN forces, composed chiefly of U.S. troops *(left)*, came to the aid of the South Koreans, Chinese Communist forces entered the war on the side of the North Koreans. The war ended when delegates from the United Nations and North Korea signed an armistice at Panmunjom, Korea, on July 26, 1953 *(bottom)*.

WIDE WORLD

Koreans then began another offensive which carried them across the 38th parallel on March 31. The UN forces were increasingly handicapped, however, because their planes were not allowed to cross into Manchuria to bomb air fields, nor were they allowed to bomb supply depots and rail centers in other parts of China. General MacArthur repeatedly objected to these limitations, and on April 11, President Truman removed MacArthur from all command, replacing him with Lt. Gen. Matthew Ridgway, who had been in command of the U.S. 8th Army.

Thereafter the fighting swayed back and forth. Communist troops in the field numbered about 300,000 and the UN troops about 300,000. Soviet-made MIG jet fighters were beginning to equalize the former air supremacy of the UN. On July 10, 1951, the first of many armistice negotiations were opened at Kaesong, with two representatives from each side.

The fighting continued, however, while the negotiators discussed cessation of fighting, evacuation of troops from Korea, exchange of prisoners, establishment of a buffer zone between North Korea and South Korea, and a commission to supervise neutral zones. There was disagreement in January 1952 over exchange of prisoners and inspection of prison camps.

The North Korean communists did not contest the seas. U.S. Naval units roamed at will through the Sea of Japan, the East China Sea, and the Yellow Sea. Frequently, UN battleships lay off shore and gave artillery support to ground troops. Amphibious landings were highly successful, and sometimes surrounded troops were rescued by sea.

Air supremacy was entirely in favor of the UN from the beginning of the Korean War until April 1951. The Soviet Union started to deliver MIG-15 jet fighters that month, and the B-29s which the UN forces had been using to bomb supply lines and railheads were of little use thereafter.

The F-80 Shooting Star, F-84 Thunder Jet, and F-86 Sabre Jet were not as fast as the MIG-15 and the later MIG-19, but they were better armored and had more fire power. It soon became necessary to use B-47 Jet bombers in place of the older B-29s. The communists soon supplied great numbers of jets and air power was therefore more balanced in 1953.

An armistice was finally signed at Panmunjom in 1953. The armistice was continued thereafter, and prisoners were exchanged. The result of the conflict was that the division of Korea was confirmed. An inspection team was agreed upon to maintain this armistice. The Korean conflict had united the West in stopping communist expansion.

LEAGUE OF NATIONS. During World War I the centuries-old plan of organizing nations into an association for the preservation of peace and the supervision of international affairs was warmly and actively discussed. It was advocated by former President Taft of the United States, by Sir Edward Grey and Lord Robert Cecil of England, by Léon Bourgeois of France and by Gen. Jan Christiaan Smuts of South Africa.

In the United States the League to Enforce Peace, the League of Free Nations Association, and other organizations were formed to familiarize the public with the idea. It received the approval in 1916 of President Wilson, who ultimately made it the cornerstone of his foreign policy.

Government commissions in the United States, Great Britain, and France studied alternative plans.

At Paris the Peace Conference approved the principle of a league Jan. 25, 1919, and a draft Covenant of the League on February 14. The final draft of the Covenant was approved April 28 and, largely because of the insistence of President Wilson, was embodied in the treaties of peace. The League of Nations actually began to operate on Jan. 10, 1920. It ceased functioning during World War II, but many of its ideas were incorporated in the United Nations Organization.

The basic machinery provided by the covenant consisted of the Assembly, the Council, and the Secretariat. The assembly represented the many member states, each of which, with three delegates, had a single vote. The Council was composed of the delegates of the four permanent members (Great Britain, France, Italy, and the Soviet Union) and of eleven nonpermanent members elected by the Assembly—three each year to serve for 3 years.

China was elected to represent the Far East after the resignation of Japan, formerly a permanent member of the Council. The other members of the Council in 1937 were Bolivia, Chile, Ecuador, Latvia, New Zealand, Poland, Romania, Spain, Sweden, and Turkey. The permanent Secretariat, with its staff of over 600 men and women, was headed by a Secretary-General appointed by the Council with the approval of the majority of the Assembly.

The membership of the League included most of the nations of the world, fifty-four states having such membership in 1938, after Guatemala, Honduras, Nicaragua, and Paraguay had resigned in 1937 and 1938. Germany, admitted in 1926, withdrew in 1935. Japan withdrew in 1935 in protest against the League policy toward the Japanese invasion of Manchuria

UNITED NATIONS

LEAGUE OF NATIONS HEADQUARTERS in Geneva, Switzerland, now houses European offices of the League's successor, the United Nations.

WIDE WORLD

UNITED NATIONS CHARTER was signed in San Francisco in 1945 by the United States Secretary of State and by the leaders of 49 other nations.

in 1931. The United States was not a member. The League Covenant provided that if the United States joined the League, it should have a permanent seat in the council.

The reasons why the United States did not join are many. Most important was the general objection in the United States to Article 10, binding "members . . . to respect and preserve as against external aggression the territorial integrity and existing political independence of all members of the League." This seemed likely to embroil us in European quarrels, and there was longstanding distrust of any foreign entanglement.

Lastly, at the time the question was raised at the end of World War I, membership in the League was a Wilson policy, and his political enemies opposed it on that ground.

The Assembly would deal at its meetings "with any matter within the sphere of action of the League or affecting the peace of the world." (Article 3.) The approval of two-thirds of the Assembly was necessary for the admission of a new state to membership in the League. "Any member of the League may, after two years' notice of its intention so to do, withdraw from the League, provided that all its obligations under this Covenant shall have been fulfilled at the time of its withdrawal." (Article 1.)

The Council had extensive powers to keep members of the League from going to war; and should any member of the League resort to war in disregard of its covenants, it was the duty of the Council "to recommend to the several governments concerned what effective military, naval or air force the Members of the League shall severally contribute to the armed forces to be used to protect the covenants of the League." (Article 16.) Provision was made to apply financial and economic sanctions against the "covenant-breaking state."

The Secretariat was divided into sections as follows, each specializing on the subjects indicated: political, financial, economic relations, communications and transit, minorities, mandates, disarmament, health, opium traffic and social questions, intellectual co-operation, legal, information. Very real and somewhat successful

efforts were made to have its members represent the small powers as well as the large and to have them regard themselves as officials of an international organization rather than of a national state. They were League employees and were paid by the League. Because the Secretariat was a continuing body, both the Council and the Assembly depended upon it for information bearing on the questions that arose, as well as for purely secretarial assistance.

The general function of the League of Nations fell into two main categories, "to promote international co-operation and to achieve international peace and security." (Preamble.) Although high hopes were entertained that the League would be successful in preventing wars, attention was centered more and more in the League's work for international co-operation in other matters. For such cooperation there were created a number of technical and advisory committees composed mainly of experts.

Commissions of the League aided in the economic restoration of Austria, Hungary, Greece and Bulgaria. The League helped restore more than half a million war prisoners to their homes in twenty-six different nations. The Refugee Settlement Commission aided in the settlement of homeless millions, notably in the repatriation to Greek territory of one and a half million Greeks who had lived in Turkey for generations.

Under League auspices there were summoned a number of economic conferences to deal with the problems of finance, trade, and tariffs. Even if it was not successful in more fundamental matters, the League obtained international agreements on customs formalities on the export of hides, skins, bones, meat and other animal products, on the suppression of counterfeiting, and on the unification of laws relating to bills of exchange, promissory notes, and checks.

A good measure of success attended efforts to standardize international practices for transportation by rail, rivers, canal or sea. The League's Public Health Organization fought typhus and cholera epidemics in eastern Europe and won the adoption of certain safeguards.

Aiding the League of Nations in its work of peace but technically independent of it was the Permanent Court of International Justice, established in 1921. Its judges were elected by the Assembly and Council of the League, meeting simultaneously; its budget was part of that of the League.

The court sat at The Hague. It could act for any two states that agreed to submit disputes to it; for those states that recognized its compulsory jurisdiction; and for states that signed treaties and international agreements that provided for the submission to the court of any dispute arising under them. The Council of the League could ask the court for advisory opinions.

The International Labor Organization also was connected with the League of Nations but was independent of it, so that nations outside the membership of the League could join the labor organization. Its procedure was to prepare recommendations and to draft conventions for adoption by member states on such matters as woman and child labor, nightwork, unemployment, labor exchanges, and the like. The International Labor Organization has been carried over to the United Nations.

The efforts in the direction of peace and security, however, were failures. In 1933 after long study of the Japanese seizure of Manchuria, the League recommended that the territory be returned to China and that China and Japan should arbitrate their disputes with the help of a League committee. Even more serious was the League's unsuccessful attempt in 1936 to keep Italy from its conquest of Ethiopia, a member of the League.

In 1938 Great Britain under Prime Minister Neville Chamberlain adopted the policy of going it alone—without the League—in attempts to reach a peaceable understanding with Germany and Italy. Thereafter the power and prestige of the League declined, and during World War II it ceased functioning. Many of its principles, however, were carried over to the United Nations.

LEPANTO, a great naval battle fought off the coast of Greece on Oct. 7, 1571, between the Spanish and Italian fleets under Don John of Austria and a Turkish squadron under Ali Pasha. The Turkish force was almost entirely destroyed, and the naval power of the Ottomans that had been threatening to convert the whole Mediterranean into a Turkish lake was shattered so badly that it never again became formidable to the Christian powers. "There was a man sent from God whose name was John," exulted Pope Pius V when the news of the great victory reached Rome.

G. K. Chesterton's poem, *Lepanto*, describes the atmosphere that surrounded this "Last Crusade."

LEWIS AND CLARK EXPEDITION, a military exploring expedition of what is now the northwest section of the United States. When President Thomas Jefferson purchased the Louisiana Territory from France in 1803, there was a general desire to learn something of the character of the new possession. Jefferson appointed his private secretary, Meriwether Lewis, to head an exploring expedition, and the latter chose his friend, Captain William Clark, to accompany him as second in command.

With a company of 45 they started from a point now St. Louis on May 14, 1804. The course of the Missouri River was followed for 1,600 miles until October, when the party halted for the winter. In the following April the expedition continued on its westward course; the Rocky Mountains were first seen in May 1805 and on November 7 the Pacific Ocean was reached.

Progress had been slow, because of making maps and surveys all along the route. Incredible hardships were borne unflinchingly. The return trip, over the same route, was more easily made, as the party floated down-stream on the Missouri, and St. Louis was reached September 23, 1806. The total distance traveled was about 8,500 miles. Exhaustive reports were made to the president and to the Congress.

By passing through Oregon country, which was not included in the Louisiana Purchase, Lewis and Clark established on behalf of the United States a claim to that important territory. The services of the members of the expedition were appropriately recognized. Lewis and Clark were given large tracts of land, and other associates were allotted smaller tracts. Lewis was made governor of the Louisiana Territory; Clark was appointed to the territorial militia with the rank of general and was made Indian agent in the Louisiana domain.

LIBERATION, WAR OF, the name given by the Germans to the national uprising against Napoleon in 1813–1814 that resulted in the freeing of the German states from French occupation and influence. Following Napoleon's invasion of Russia and the virtual destruction of his *Grande Armee* in the fall and winter of 1812, Czar Alexander I led an army over the Niemen into Germany, proclaiming that he had come to liberate Europe from Napoleon's despotism.

On March 17, 1813, the Prussian king, Frederick William III, called his country to arms in the manifesto *An mein Volk*. The patriotic movement that had been stirring all Germany under the leadership of Baron Stein now burst out in flame, and the whole nation rushed to war with wild enthusiasm. On October 16–18, 1813, the great Battle of Leipzig was fought, in which Napoleon was decisively beaten by a combined army of Prussians, Austrians, and Swedes.

LIBERTY BELL, one of the most revered relics of the Colonial period in the United States. It was made in England in 1752 for the Pennsylvania State House, but in transit to the colonies its tone was injured through accident, and it was recast in Philadelphia in 1753. At that time around its upper surface were cast the words, "Proclaim liberty throughout all the land unto all the inhabitants thereof" (*Leviticus* 25:10), a quotation singularly prophetic, as it was destined to perform that service for a new nation.

On July 8, 1776, it was rung to call the people of Philadelphia to listen to the first public reading of the Declaration of Independence. When British Troops occupied Philadelphia during the Revolutionary War the bell was taken to Allentown, Pennsylvania, and kept in the basement of a church. It was later restored to *Independence Hall.*

When the bell was tolled during the funeral services for Chief Justice Marshall, on July 8, 1835, it was so badly cracked that it has never been rung since. Iron supports have been riveted around the inside to prevent further cracking.

Since 1854 the bell has stood on a pedestal inside the front entrance to the hall, facing the small park that is Independence Square, where it is viewed by hundreds of people every day; and it has been exhibited at expositions and world's fairs—always with great enthusiasm.

LICINIAN ROGATIONS, a group of proposals for settling the long strife between the patrician and plebeian orders, and introducing necessary social reforms in the ancient Roman Republic. First offered by the tribunes, Caius Licinius Stolo and Lucius Sextius Lateranus about 377 BC, they were finally enacted into law after 10 years of agitation.

The Licinian-Sextian Laws mark a turning joint in Roman constitutional history comparable with the great Reform Bill of 1832 in England. In the later republic, especially after the Second Punic War (218–202 BC), the provisions regarding the public lands were disregarded, and the growth of great estates worked by slaves with the consequent impoverishment of the mass of the people became one of the main factors in the decline of the republic's stability and strength.

In the patrician-plebeian strife the Licinian-Sextian Laws stand for the decisive victory of the plebeians; after the passage of the laws the patricians rapidly lost their special influence and position, and by 300 BC the patrician-plebeian distinction was no longer of any political or social importance.

LITTLE ENTENTE, a series of agreements signed in 1920 by Poland, Czechoslovakia, Yugoslavia, and Romania, by which they pledged united action to uphold their liberties and to support France against Germany. The Little Entente put itself on record as opposed to a political union of Germany and Austria, as such action would establish a strong power so

JOHN MORRELL & CO.
LEWIS AND CLARK were guided by an Indian woman, Sacajawea, on western explorations.

near their own borders that their safety would be jeopardized.

The solidarity of the Little Entente began to weaken after the Nazi party obtained power in Germany. Germany reached an understanding with Poland and began to exercise increasing influence in the Balkan region, particularly Romania. The seizure of Austria by Germany in 1938 indicated to most observers that its political importance was nearly ended.

LOCARNO CONFERENCE, October 1925, held at Locarno, Switzerland, was an effort to bring peace and security to western Europe. The result was the pact of Locarno, a series of treaties providing for peace and arbitration. The practical consequences were (1) French evacuation of the Rhineland and (2) Germany's entry into the League of Nations. For the first time in history the great powers surrendered their absolute "right to make war." Early in 1936 when Germany crossed the Rhine and fortified the demilitarized zone, the Locarno pacts became scraps of paper.

LOLLARDS, the followers of John Wycliffe's religious reformation in England in the late 1300s and 1400s. The Lollard movement was political and social as well as religious and drew its chief support from among the peasantry. In religious teaching the Lollards anticipated many ideas of protestantism, particularly condemnation of images in churches.

LYDIA, an ancient kingdom in Asia Minor bordering on the Mediterranean Sea. Its story connects the age of myths with the facts of history. No one knows who its early inhabitants were; they may have been Aryans from central Asia or of Semitic descent, as the names of some of their kings suggest. There was mineral wealth in the land, particularly gold in the bed of the Pactolus River.

The people received the alphabet from the Greeks, who got it from the Phoenicians. In turn the Lydians gave the Greeks some of their ideas on religion. The greatest and the last of the kings of Lydia was Croesus, whose name is still a synonym for wealth. He was overthrown in 546 BC by Cyrus the Great, and Lydia became a Persian province.

In later times the Greeks, the Romans, and the Saracens occupied it, and at last Turkey in 1413. It remained in Turkey's hands as a part of Anatolia, which constitutes most of the area of the modern republic of Turkey.

MACEDONIA, an ancient land of uncertain territorial limits, lying northeast of Greece and north of the Aegean Sea. Not much is known of the Macedonians before 480 BC, when they were conquered by Persia and compelled to assist Xerxes in his invasion of Greece. After the Persian defeat in 479 BC, Macedonian independence was restored. The civilization of the country developed after the Greek pattern and reached a high state before the accession of Philip II in 359 BC. He became powerful

enough to put Greece under his control. His son Alexander the Great not only held his ascendency in Greece but put more than half of the known world under his dominion. At his death, Macedonia fell to Antipator, one of Alexander's generals. Macedonia was subjugated by the Romans in a series of wars ending in 146 BC.

When the Roman Empire was divided, in about 395 AD, Macedonia became a part of the Eastern Empire, and eventually, in the 1400s, it fell to the Turks. A long period of repression followed that aroused world concern and intervention; but not until the Balkan War of 1912 did persecution cease. Ancient Macedonia is now Albania and parts of Greece, Yugoslavia, and Bulgaria.

MANCHURIA, the nine northeastern provinces of China, was known during the period of Japanese control, 1931–1945, as Manchukuo. It was the land of the Manchus and the home of the Manchu, or Ch'ing, dynasty that ruled China, 1644–1911.

Manchuria is largely populated by Chinese who began to settle there in the late 1700s. It was a battleground during the Russo-Japanese war, 1904–1905. The Chinese Communists took over in 1947, and drove the Nationalist forces out. After the surrender of Japan in 1945, a treaty was signed with the Soviet Union providing for Soviet withdrawal from Manchuria and joint Chinese-Soviet control of Manchurian railways for 30 years and certain interests in the port of Darien.

MARATHON, a great battle fought in 490 BC between the invading Persians and the Greeks (Athenians and Plataeans). The plain of Marathon is on the east coast of Attica about 18 miles northeast of Athens. The Persian forces, supported by their fleet, occu-

pied the plain near the shore. The Greeks numbered about 10,000; the Persians, more numerous, around 20,000, were routed by the skillful tactics of Miltiades. The Greeks attempted to set fire to the Persian fleet, but the Persians succeeded in getting to sea with small losses. Herodotus gives the losses in the battle as 192 for the Greeks and 6,400 for the Persians.

Fearing that the Persian fleet would next attack Athens, Miltiades sent Pheidippides to announce the victory to the Athenians. Pheidippides' endurance is commemorated by the Olympic event, the *marathon,* in which a long-distance foot race is run over a distance of 26 miles 385 yards.

The victory broke up the first Persian attempt to enslave Greece and inspired the whole Hellenic race with new confidence.

MARNE, a series of battles along the River Marne in northern France, Sept. 5 to 8, 1914, between invading German armies and defending French and British troops. After four days of fighting the Germans withdrew and the war became one of fixed positions. The defeat broke up the German plan for winning quickly. Although the Allies did not immediately win the war, Germany lost it at the Marne.

MARSHALL PLAN, first proposed by Gen. George C. Marshall, American secretary of state, in a speech at Harvard University, June 5, 1947, as the basis for European economic recovery. During the summer of 1947, 16 European nations, forming the Commission of European Economic Cooperation, conferred to work out a schedule of needs and to determine what each nation could contribute to help. The plan, known as the European Recovery Program (ERP) was enacted

EASTFOTO

HARBIN, MANCHURIA. The brightly colored blankets that are being considered by the customers in this woolen factory are among the loveliest specialties of this region.

into law by Congress in April 1948 to be administered by the Economic Co-operation Administration (ECA). About six billion dollars was authorized to be expended in the first year and up to 17 billion in the next four years.

As a condition of U.S. cooperation, Marshall stipulated that the European nations receiving aid would have to increase their own industrial production so that they would become independent and not rely solely on U.S. aid. These payments were credited with helping to halt the spread of communism in western Europe.

MASON AND DIXON'S LINE, a line surveyed between 1763 and 1767 by two English surveyors whose names it bears, separating the states of Pennsylvania and Maryland. The survey was made to establish the boundary between William Penn's Pennsylvania and Lord Baltimore's Maryland, regarding which there had been dispute. The line would have no added historic significance had it not marked later, with extensions east and west, the line of division between the slave and the free states of the Union.

The surveyors marked the line with milestones; one side of each have the letter *P* and the other the letter *M*. Every fifth milestone contained the sculptured arms of Penn and Baltimore. Eventually nearly all the stones were stolen, to serve as foundation stones for buildings, doorsteps, and the like, but many were later recovered and restored to their positions.

MEDIA, an ancient land that is now the northwestern part of Iran. The inhabitants, the Medes, were allied to the Persians in religion and language. Media was a vassal province of Assyria from 811 BC, but shook off the Assyrian yoke about 708 BC, and the Medes made Ecbatana their capital. The site of this ancient city is now believed to be that of the modern town of Hamadan, where are the reputed tombs of Mordecai and Esther.

Most famous of Median kings was Cyaxeres, who reigned about 40 years (625–585 BC). In league with Nabopolassar, king of Babylon, he conquered Assyria in 604 BC, and extended their power westward to the Mediterranean and eastward to present-day Afghanistan and Pakistan.

Media held Persia in subjection until 549 BC, when Cyrus the Great conquered it, and Persia became the mistress rather than the vassal. This event marked the beginning of the greatness of the Persian Empire.

MEROVINGIANS, the line of Frankish kings who first governed Gaul after it was taken from the Romans. Clovis, the first powerful Merovingian monarch, in 486 took advantage of the dying Roman Empire to give battle for possession of Gaul. He gained a decisive victory. Clovis was the only important king of the dynasty. He divided his dominions among his four sons, and decadence set in. Ambitious officers finally pushed the last Merovingian from the throne, and in 752 the Carolingian line was established.

METAURUS, a battle fought in 207 BC near the Metaurus River on the northern Adriatic coast of Italy between the Roman legions under Livius Salinator and Gaius Claudius Nero and a Carthaginian and Gallic army under Hasdrubal, brother of the great Hannibal. In the battle the Carthaginian invaders were cut to pieces, Hasdrubal himself was killed, and the most dangerous crisis of the Second Punic War was successfully passed.

If the Carthaginians had won this battle, it would have been impossible to prevent Hasdrubal from joining his brother Hannibal with heavy reinforcements, and although it may be too much to say that in that event the fate of Rome would have been sealed, it is hard to believe that even the courage and stamina of the Romans could have survived another assault of the sort Hannibal had inflicted in 218–216 BC, when he had first appeared in Italy at the head of adequate forces.

There can be little doubt that the victory of Rome in its long life-and-death struggle with Carthage was the victory of modern civilization; however much we may admire the genius of Hannibal we must realize that the triumph of Carthage rather than Rome would have meant the ruin of all the best features of the Greco-Roman world.

"He who grieves over the battle of Zama" (the battle in which Hannibal was finally defeated by the Romans), "should carry his thoughts to a period 30 years later, when Hannibal must, in the course of human nature, have been dead, and consider how the isolated Phoenician city of Carthage was fitted to receive and to consolidate the civilization of Greece, or by its laws and institutions to bind together barbarians of every race and language into an organized empire, and prepare them for becoming, when that empire was dissolved, the free members of the commonwealth of Christian Europe." So Thomas Arnold describes the issue that was really at stake in the battle of Metaurus.

MIDWAY, BATTLE OF, Midway is an island in the Pacific, 1,200 miles northwest from Hawaii. It was the scene of one of the great naval battles of World War II. The fighting lasted from June 3 to June 6, 1942 and was the first decisive defeat suffered by the Japanese during the war.

MISSISSIPPI BUBBLE, a speculative scheme promoted in France from 1717 to 1720 by a Scotchman, John Law. In 1716 Law, a man of great plausibility and real commercial genius, formed a group of bankers and speculators who founded the Banque Générale with the general purpose of acquiring trading monopolies in the New World and in the Orient.

In the early 1700s the possibilities of commercial exploitation of the distant parts of the world seem to have cast a kind of spell over the minds of Europeans; contemporary with John Law's activities in France the famous South Sea Bubble was exciting the speculators of England. Law's operations expanded rapidly after the es-

tablishment of the Banque Générale. He began to issue large amounts of paper currency that was accepted at par and even above par throughout France.

Law obtained the confidence of the government and was actually made Comptroller General of Finance in January 1720. The inevitable crash came in May 1720. Many thousands of investors were ruined and a panic was precipitated. Law escaped from France but was not able to salvage anything for himself from the wreck.

NANTES, EDICT OF, an edict issued by Henry IV of France in 1598 granting limited religious toleration and equality of political rights to the Huguenots (French Protestants). The Edict of Nantes brought to an end the bitter and bloody religious feuds that had distracted France for more than half a century. It is famous for its farseeing and statesmanlike conciliation in an age when the spirit of conciliation was extremely rare. Its opening article declares a general amnesty:

We have, by this perpetual and irrevocable edict, established and proclaimed and do establish and proclaim,
I. First, that the recollection of everything done by one party or the other between March 1585, and our accession to the Crown, and during all the preceding period of troubles, remain obliterated and forgotten as if no such things had ever happened.

The Edict of Nantes remained in force until 1685, when it was revoked by Louis XIV. Its revocation was an act of cruel bigotry and a political blunder of the first magnitude, as its immediate result was to force the emigration from France of some 300,000 of her thriftiest and most substantial citizens.

NASEBY, a battle between the forces of Oliver Cromwell and King Charles I of England in the Civil War waged by Parliament against Charles. Fought June 14, 1645, it was a defeat for the royalists. The forces of the king were so badly routed that he could not put another army into the field.

NICAEA, COUNCIL OF, the first general, or ecumenical, council of the Christian church held at Nicaea in Asia Minor in 325 AD. The Council is chiefly noted for its promulgation of the Nicene Creed and its condemnation of Arianism.

Meeting under the aegis of Constantine the Great, the first Roman emperor to recognize Christianity, the Council of Nicaea was an enormous force both for the political and religious unity of the Roman Empire.

NORTH ATLANTIC TREATY, signed in Washington, Apr. 4, 1949, by the United States, Canada, and ten nations of western Europe, is a treaty of common defense in the event of an attack on any signator. The United States is permitted to furnish military aid to any signator under a "mutual aid" clause.

The North Atlantic Treaty Organization (NATO) coordinates the economic, political, and military activities of these nations, plus new members such as Turkey, Greece, and West Germany.

PALESTINE, the Holy Land of Christians, as cradle of the Christian religion and sepulcher of the Christ, and the country of the ancient Hebrews. During one long period of its ancient life, one section was known as *Canaan,* and the southwestern part as *Philistia;* the people, as *Canaanites* and *Philistines,* respectively. The latter first applied the name *Canaan* (the *Promised Land* of the Israelites) to the land west of the Jordan River. The modern development of Palestine is along the shore of the Mediterranean, north of Hejaz; the Sinai peninsula forms part of its western boundary.

The history of Palestine before the penetration by the Israelites in the 1200s and 1100s BC is little known. Babylonian, Egyptian, Hittite and Amorite battled for supremacy. The influx of Israelites that probably began about 1300 BC is the first historical event that we can trace that permanently affected the country.

About 1030 BC the Israelites formed a united kingdom under Saul, whose immediate successors were David and Solomon. About 100 years later it was divided into two kingdoms, Israel and Judah, northern and southern, respectively. The northern fell to the Assyrians in 722 BC; the southern, to the power of Babylonia under Nebuchadnezzar in 586 BC, when he captured Jerusalem. After each of these events, thousands of the Israelites were carried away captive.

When Babylonia was taken by Cyrus the Great of Persia, he permitted the Jewish exiles to return home (536 BC), and Palestine became a Persian province attached to Syria. When Alexander the Great swept into Asia, a large Greek emigration followed, and Greek influence persisted to the time of the Roman invasion. Jerusalem was taken by the Romans in 63 BC, and for about 100 years most of Palestine was again a part of Syria, then a Roman province. Palestine belonged to Rome or to Byzantium until 614 AD, when it fell again to Persia. Persia held it until about 635, when it came under Muslim control.

The Crusades temporarily interrupted Muslim rule, but the kingdom of Jerusalem, set up by the Crusaders in 1099, was retaken by Saladin after an existence of only 90 years. The Ottoman Turks held Palestine from 1516 to 1918, when General Allenby, at the head of a British force, captured Jerusalem, and for the first time in 400 years a Christian flag floated over the city.

Turkey had joined its fortunes with Germany in World War I. After the defeat of the Central Powers Turkey was stripped of its possessions in Asia outside of Anatolia, and the new states of Palestine, Syria and Transjordania were formed. Palestine was placed by the League of Nations under mandate to Great Britain, to be held until it was sufficiently advanced to merit an independent government.

One of the immediate results of freedom from Turkish rule was an increase in the demand for the creation of an independent Jewish state. Encouraged by the Balfour Declaration of Nov. 2, 1917, proclaiming Palestine as a Jewish homeland, Jews began migrating to the country for permanent settlement. This influx created friction with the more numerous native Arabs. The agitation was renewed at the conclusion of World War II. Partition of Palestine between Arabs and Jews, as adopted by the United Nations General Assembly, Nov. 29, 1947, was accepted by the Jews, but rejected by the Arabs. As a consequence of this action there was considerable fighting. The British mandate was voluntarily ended on May 14, 1948 and Palestine became the state of Israel, with the city of Jerusalem, partitioned between Arabs and Jews, under United Nations trusteeship. The Zionist movement, which began in the 1880s in Palestine and elsewhere, was an important element in bringing about the creation of the state of Israel.

PAN-AMERICAN CONFERENCES (INTER AMERICAN CONFERENCES). The Panama Congress of 1826, called by Simón Bolívar, was the first Pan-American conference. It was not repeated immediately. The United States, cultivating friendship and better relations with Latin American nations, was careful not to arouse suspicion or resentment. On Oct. 2, 1889, the first international conference of American states met in Washington, D.C. and the Pan-American Union was formed. Several such conferences have since been held.

The conferences had commercial and military as well as political objectives, and resulted in the formation of the Organization of American States (OAS) in 1948 at Bogotá. The Alliance for Progress charter was signed in 1961 at Punta del Este.

PHOENICIA, a great commercial and colonizing power of the eastern Mediterranean in ancient times. The earliest history of Phoenicia is unknown, but it was a flourishing country in 1500 BC, had a separate existence until after 850 BC, and its commercial supremacy was not lost until 500 years afterward. The infertile Phoenician land lay in a narrow strip from 10 to 15 miles wide along the eastern shore of the Mediterranean Sea for a distance of about 150 miles with moun-

UPI PHOTO

ARAB INFORMATION CENTER

ARAB INFORMATION CENTER

PALESTINE SHRINES include the Jewish Wailing Wall *(left)*, the Christian Via Dolorosa *(center)*, and the Muslim Dome of the Rock.

tains on the eastern border. The people, Semitic in origin, were obliged to turn to the sea for a livelihood, and Phoenicia rose to be the greatest maritime power of the very early centuries. At first their sailors did not venture farther than the Strait of Gibraltar, for they feared the unknown expanse of ocean beyond the Pillars of Hercules; but when the mariners had once sailed past that narrow channel, their argosies were seen wherever there were people with whom to trade.

The unexcelled dyes of Tyre and the silver and brass vessels beautifully wrought in Sidon were exchanged for tin from England, ivory from Africa, copper from Cyprus, and gold, incense and pearls from Arabia. A remarkable people, the Phoenicians acquired wide reputation for the manufacture as well as the dyeing of textiles, work in glass as well as in metals, mining, and the expert building of temples, tombs, and other structures. To protect their vast commerce they built a navy to patrol their lines of trade. Wherever they went, they absorbed a knowledge of the arts practiced and contributed of their own knowledge to other peoples. To facilitate communication, they invented (it seems likely) the first written alphabet, later adopted by the Greeks, and by the rest of the civilized world. Beginning about 850 BC, Phoenicia was taken in turn by Assyria, Babylonia, Persia, and Egypt, and in 332 BC, by Alexander the Great. It main-

tained its name until 64 AD, when, under Roman rule, it was merged with Syria. In the centuries following the Assyrian conquest of Phoencia itself, the great Phoenician colony, Carthage, was growing in importance as a trading power in the western Mediterranean on the north shore of Africa.

Readers of the Bible find numerous references to the two great Phoenician cities Tyre and Sidon. Hiram, King of Tyre, supplied the cedars of Lebanon with which Solomon built the Temple at Jerusalem; many of the master workmen employed in its construction were from Sidon. The Old Testament refers to the Phoenician territory as part of Canaan and gives to its inhabitants the name Sidonians.

PILGRIMS, the band of Separatists who sailed to America in 1620 and founded Plymouth Colony. They were of the original group of religionists who left England for Holland to secure freedom of worship. Governor Bradford, one of the devoted band, referred to them as "pilgrims and strangers on the earth," hence the first name came to be applied to all Plymouth pioneers.

Compact of the Pilgrims. In the cabin of the *Mayflower* on the evening before landing the 31 heads of families represented adopted and signed a solemn agreement that was to serve as a basis of their government in the New World. It has become known as the *Compact of the Pilgrims.* In text,

spelling, and punctuation the following is an exact copy:

In ye name of God, Amen. We whose names are underwritten, the loyall subjects of our dread soveraigne Lord, King James, by ye Grace of God of Great Britaine, France & Ireland King, Defender of ye Faith, etc. Haveing undertaken, for ye Glorie of God, and advancemente of ye Christian Faith and Honour of our King and countrie, a Voyage to plant ye first Colonie in ye Northerne part of Virginia, doe by these presents solemnly and mutually in ye Presence of God, and of another, Covenant & Combine our selves togeather into a Civill body Politick, for our better Ordering & Preservation & Furtherance of ye ends aforesaid; and by Vertue hereof to enact, constitute, and frame such just & equall lawes, ordinances, Acts, Constitutions & Offices, from Time to Time, as shall be thought most meete & convenient for ye generall good of ye Colonie, unto which we promise all due submission and obedience.

The 102 Pioneers. The world is indebted to William Bradford, second governor of Plymouth, for the names of the passengers on the *Mayflower* as published in his valuable *History of Plimouth Plantation.* These names follow in exactly the phraseology of the Bradford volume:

The names of those which came over first, in ye year 1620, and were by the blessing of God the first beginers and (in a sort) the foundation of all the Plantations and Colonies in New-England; and their families.

Mr. John Carver; Kathrine, his wife; Desire Minter; & 2. man-servants, John Howland, Roger Wilder; William Latham, a boy; and a maid servant, & a child yt was put to him, called Jasper More.

Mr. William Brewster; Mary, his wife; with 2. sons, whose names were Love & Wrasling; and a boy was put to him called Richard More; and another of his brothers. The rest of his children were left behind, & came over afterwards.

Mr. Edward Winslow; Elizabeth, his wife; & 2. men servants, caled Georg Sowle and Elias Story; also a little girle was put to him called Ellen, the sister of Richard More.

William Bradford, and Dorothy, his wife; having but one child, a sone, left behind, who came afterward.

Mr. Isaack Allerton, and Mary, his wife; with 3. children, Bartholomew, Remember, & Mary; and a servant boy, John Hooke.

Mr. Samuell Fuller, and a servant, caled William Button. His wife was left behind, & a child, which came afterwards.

John Crakston, and his sone, John Crakston.

Captain Myles Standish, and Rose, his wife.

Mr. Christopher Martin, and his wife, and 2. servants, who were Salomon Prower and John Langemore.

Mr. William Mullines, and his wife, and 2. children, Joseph & Priscilla; and a servant, Robert Carter.

Mr. William White, and Susana, his wife, and one sone, caled Resolved, and one borne a ship-bord, caled Peregriene; & 2. servants, named William Holbeck & Edward Thomson.

Mr. Steven Hopkins, & Elizabeth, his wife, and 2. children, caled Giles, and Constanta, a doughter, both by a former wife; and 2. more by this wife, caled Damaris & Oceanus; the last was borne at sea; and 2. servants, caled Edward Doty and Edward Lister.

Mr. Richard Warren; but his wife and children were lefte behind and came afterwards.

John Billinton, and Elen, his wife; and 2. sones, John & Francis.

Edward Tillie, and Ann, his wife; and 2. children that were their cossens, Henery Samson and Humility Coper.

John Tillie, and his wife; and Eelizabeth, their doughter.

Francis Cooke, and his sone John. But his wife & other children came afterwards.

Thomas Rogers, and Joseph, his sone. His other children came afterwards.

Thomas Tinker, and his wife, and a sone.

John Rigdale, and Alice, his wife.

James Chilton, and his wife, and Mary, their doughter. They had an other doughter yt was married, came afterwards.

Edward Fuller, and his wife, and Samuell, their sonne.

John Turner, and 2. sones. He had a doughter came some years after to Salem, wher she is now living.

Francis Eaton, and Sarah, his wife, and Samuell, their sone, a young child.

Moyses Fletcher, John Goodman, Thomas Williams, Digerie Preist, Edmond Margeson, Peter Browne, Richard Britterige, Richard Clarke, Richard Gardenare, Gilbart Winslow.

WIDE WORLD
MAYFLOWER REPLICA escorted by Navy blimp while sailing from Britain to Massachusetts.

BETTMANN ARCHIVE

MARY, QUEEN OF SCOTS, reigned in the 1500s.

SCOTTISH TOURIST BOARD

SCOTTISH HIGHLANDS peak at Ben Nevis, rising over an Invernesshire loch.

John Alden was hired for a cooper, at South-Hampton, wher the ship victuled; and being a hopfull yong man, was much desired, but left to his owne liking to go or stay when he came here; but he stayed, and maryed here.

John Allerton and Thomas English were both hired, the later to goe mr of a shalop here, and ye other was reputed as one of ye company, but was to go back (being a seaman) for the help of others behind. But they both dyed here, before the shipe returned.

There were allso other 2. seamen hired to stay a year here in the country, William Trevore, and one Ely. But when their time was out, they both returned.

These, being aboute a hundred sowls, came over in this first ship; and began this worke, which God of his goodnes hath hithertoo blesed; let his holy name have ye praise.

Early Distress. The Pilgrims landed where the city of Plymouth, Mass., now stands; they occupied an Indian settlement whose inhabitants had left after being greatly reduced in numbers by a pestilence. The first winter was one of incredible hardship. Disease, exposure to the intense cold and scarcity of food cost the colony half its members; among the dead was Governor Carver. Late in the spring of 1621 about 50 more Separatists from Holland joined the colony, and William Bradford was chosen as the second governor. Within the next few years there rose to fame in the annals of American history such names as Miles Standish, John Alden and Priscilla Mullins (spelled Mullines in Bradford's book).

PRAGMATIC SANCTION, a statement or decree relating to affairs of state, issued by the head of a government with the force of fundamental law. The one best known in European history was issued by Charles VI, Holy Roman Emperor, in 1713, declaring that in the absence of male heirs his domain should be inherited by his daughter Marie Theresa. The other Powers agreed to accept his will in the matter, but after the death of Charles (1740) they tried to prevent her accession; her efforts to win her rights led to the War of the Austrian Succession.

RECONSTRUCTION, the period in the history of the United States during which the states of the late Confederacy were being reorganized for admission again into the Union. The end of the Civil War left them without state governments, and they were ruled by Federal troops and political appointees from the North. This was the era of *carpetbag government*—power exercised by temporary, alien authority. Many abuses of power were inevitable, and there was rejoicing both in the North and the South when the last of the seceded states was given back to its own control. This was in 1877, at the beginning of the administration of President Rutherford B. Hayes.

ROUNDHEADS, an uncomplimentary name applied to the followers of Oliver Cromwell in England, because they wore their hair close-cropped. Their opponents, the followers of the king, were known as *Cavaliers* and were often distinguished by long, flowing curls.

RYE HOUSE PLOT, a plan developed in 1683 by English Whigs (successors to the Parliamentarians of Cromwell's time) to waylay and kill King Charles II and his brother and place a Protestant, the duke of Monmouth, on the throne. The assassination was planned to take place at Rye House, the country place of one of the conspirators. The burning of a house where the king was staying caused a change in his tour, and the plot failed. Several alleged conspirators were beheaded.

SALIC LAW, a code of the Salian Franks, promulgated in the 400s AD, which dealt with crimes, injuries and inheritances. What makes it important in history was one of its phrases: "No portion of Salic land shall come to a woman; but the whole inheritance of the land shall come to the male sex." This rule seemed essential because of

military duties owed to the king by landholders; but its provisions were later to be applied against women who inherited kingdoms, and several wars were fought to secure the rights of women to become sovereigns. The most important of these was the War of the Austrian Succession, in which Maria Theresa fought for the crown of Austria.

SCOTLAND, since 1707 a part of the United Kingdom, which later became the United Kingdom of Great Britain and Ireland. It was called *Caledonia* by the Romans, who occupied the island of Great Britain before the Christian era and had subjugated Scotland as far north as the Firth of Forth by the year 82 AD.

Early History. The Romans departed in 412 because their legions were needed for home defense, and the island was left to its native peoples. In Caledonia these came to be identified as the *Picts*, descendants of Celtic invaders, and they were dominant until the end of the 400s, when there was an invasion of Scots from Ireland. These people settled east of the domain of the Picts.

The Picts and the Scots, close neighbors, united in 844, Kenneth MacAlpin, King of the Scots, becoming ruler. The territory thus joined was called Albainn, but later it took the name Scotland, from the Scots. The daughter and successor of Kenneth married a king of the Celts, who were settled farther north, and from this family union of the states came a more formidable force to resist the onslaughts of the invaders from England, though the latter took and held numerous islands, including the Orkneys and the Shetlands.

Succeeding kings fought for territorial advantage, until Malcolm II (r.1005–1034) established the border between England and Scotland where it is today. With Malcolm's death the line of kings established by MacAlpin ended, and his nephew Duncan came to the throne. Duncan was murdered by Macbeth, who in 1040 made himself king. Shakespeare's *Macbeth* is a thrilling account of the events of the period but is not historically accurate. Macbeth, in turn, was slain by Duncan's son, who became king as Malcolm III in 1058. This king was English in sympathy, for he was married to a sister of Edward, an English prince. He introduced the feudal system into Scotland and joined the English to resist the coming of the Normans. When in 1066 William the Conqueror succeeded at the battle of Hastings in forcing Norman rule upon England, Malcolm welcomed to Scotland many who fled from William's new rule. Malcom's English marriage and the Norman Conquest resulted in the gradual introduction of English thought and mode of life into the country.

After the death of King Malcolm III, his three sons ruled Scotland in succession. Only one, David I (r.1124–1153), was important; by his wise and ambitious rule he so advanced his country that England's jealousy was intensified, which led to measures to humble the Scots. In 1175 William the Lion, successor to David, was defeated in battle, and Scotland became a vassal state of England. Fifteen years later Richard the Lion-Hearted was heavily bribed to induce him to relinquish his rights, but succeeding English kings continued to assert an overlordship.

In 1293 the regular hereditary succession to the throne failed. Robert Bruce and John of Baliol disputed for the throne. It was given to Baliol, who was the selection of Edward I of England. English dominance of Scotland was made more secure when Edward I ended Baliol's rule and appointed a Scottish governor.

The War for Independence. The Scots bitterly resented this English interference in their affairs and rose in rebellion under the leadership of William Wallace. In 1297 Wallace won the battle of Stirling; but in the next year the English won at Falkirk. Wallace was tried unfairly for his part in the uprising and executed in 1305. Then Robert Bruce, grandson of the Bruce just mentioned, appeared as Scotland's champion. At the battle of Bannockburn in 1314 he decisively defeated the English and drove them from the country. For the next 15 years Bruce ruled as Robert I and was succeeded by his son, David II. From the date of Bannockburn until 1328, when Scotland's independence was formally conceded, there was intermittent warfare of an indecisive character.

The Stuart Ascendancy. David II died childless, and Robert II, grandson of Robert Bruce, who had been high steward, came to the throne, beginning the succession of the House of Stuart, named for the former hereditary office of the founder. Robert III followed him, and then James I was crowned. He was followed in turn by others of the same name; James IV married the daughter of Henry VII of England, thus uniting the two royal houses. When Henry VIII became king, he made war upon James and defeated him at Flodden Field in 1513. In that year James V came to the Scottish throne. He was defeated in battle by the English in 1542 and survived only a few days. The throne was left to his infant daughter, known as Mary Queen of Scots. She married the worthless Darnley and thereby lost some of her loyal support; she then married Bothwell, not knowing in her bewilderment the best and wisest course to pursue. This further alienated her supporters, and she was obliged to relinquish the throne in 1567, when her infant son became king as James VI. Mary made an attempt to regain the crown, but was defeated and then fled to England, where for 19 years she remained a prisoner. Queen Elizabeth of England, being told that her own throne would not be secure as long as Mary lived, was persuaded to sign her death warrant, and Mary was beheaded in 1587.

Union of the Two Crowns. On the death of Elizabeth in 1603, James VI of Scotland, son of Mary Queen of Scots, became also king of England, and was crowned as James I of England. His son, Charles, succeeded him in 1625.

In the English civil war that resulted from Charles's effort to establish his personal rule, Charles was defeated and in 1649 was beheaded. The Scots named his son, Charles II, as their king, but Cromwell at once went to war with Scotland over this succession and Charles fled to France for safety. Upon Cromwell's death and the end of the Protectorate in England, Charles was welcomed back to England and ruled as king of Scotland and England until his death in 1685.

He was succeeded by his brother, who ruled as James VII of Scotland and James II of England. The English Revolution of 1688 drove him from the throne. Scotland joined the revolution to preserve its religious freedom, and when William and Mary were chosen sovereigns of England, the majority of Scots also accepted them. A small group that held out for James was crushed by William with great severity.

Political Union. In 1702 Anne, daughter of James VII of Scotland and James II of England, became the English queen. The relations between Scotland and England never having been satisfactory and the importance of a closer union being obvious to prevent furthur alienation and possible destruction of commercial ties, the subject of political union was broached. At first the Scots were strongly opposed to the idea but were finally won over. Accordingly the Scottish Parliament was permanently dissolved, the English Parliament was enlarged in number to admit Scottish members, and in 1707 the separate history of Scotland ended. Thenceforth the union was known as Great Britain.

SHAYS' REBELLION, an uprising in Massachusetts (1786–1787), led by Daniel Shays, who had been a captain in the Revolutionary War. Displeased with the callous attitude of the courts in foreclosing mortgages, with office-holders who drew salaries deemed excessive, and with high taxes and other administrative abuses, Shays led a band of about 600 malcontents in a threat against the supreme court of the state, sitting at Springfield. The court adjourned until the mob dispersed. A little later, about 1,200 strong, Shays' force advanced to the arsenal in the same city, to secure arms. The state militia scattered the followers of Shays and arrested the leaders. Fourteen were sentenced to death but were pardoned by Governor John Hancock. Shays escaped to Vermont and was afterwards pardoned.

SHILOH (OR PITTSBURG LANDING), BATTLE OF, one of the important battles of the Civil War, fought April 6 and 7, 1862. General U. S. Grant was advancing along the Tennessee River, heading for the important railroad center of Corinth, Miss., when he

LIBRARY OF CONGRESS

GENERAL U. S. GRANT, victor at Shiloh.

stopped near Shiloh Church to wait for reinforcements from General Buell at Nashville. General Albert S. Johnston led a Confederate army in a surprise attack and forced the Union troops to retreat.

The reinforcements that General Grant had been expecting arrived late in the first day of fighting and the Confederates were defeated on the second day. The losses by both sides were severe. The Confederates lost about 14,000 men and the Union forces about 13,000. The battle was important because it meant that the Southerners lost their control of Tennessee.

SIBERIA, the name given the great land area of the eastern Soviet Union. The section is divided into two parts. The Western Siberian region has a capital at Novo-Sibirsk and the Eastern Siberian region has a capital at Irkutsk. The land extends from the Arctic

Ocean to the Mongolian border and has vast agricultural districts and huge untouched mineral deposits.

The early history of the region is not known, but probably the first settlers in this remote part of the world were driven northward by marauding bands of Mongols or Tatars. These early settlements were victimized by cruel Turkish tribes. The Turks then set up a form of civilization which lasted for several centuries. Finally Genghis Khan conquered the country in the early 1200s. All semblance of civilization already established was destroyed. About 300 years later the settlers asked for recognition from the Russian government in Moscow. This was refused.

In the year 1581, a Cossack adventurer, Yermak, entered this region and defeated the Tatars. He died soon after, but was soon followed by other Russians. Eventually Russia controlled all the territory to the Pacific Ocean. Further expansion was opposed by China's Manchus until 1858, when a treaty was signed giving Russia even more territory and allowing Russia to develop the important Pacific seaport of Vladivostok.

In recent years the Soviet government has made an effort to encourage settlement in Siberia by Russian peasants—partly to offset the large influx of Chinese from the south and partly to begin developing the latent natural resources. The Trans-Siberian railway proved an important aid to colonization since it established a link between this rugged country and the outside world.

SOUTHEAST ASIA TREATY ORGANIZATION (SEATO), the administrative arm of the Southeast Asia Collective Defense Treaty signed at Manila in 1954. Its purpose is the defense of Southeast Asia against armed attack and subversive activities. The nations participating in the treaty are Australia, France, Great Britain, New Zealand, Pakistan, Philippines, Thailand, and the United States.

SPANISH SUCCESSION. See *Succession Wars.*

SUCCESSION WARS, four conflicts in European history that involved the Great Powers and kept the continent in turmoil for the better part of 80 years. In each case the cause centered about the succession to a throne.

War of the Spanish Succession. Charles II of Spain (r.1665–1700) was childless. The Powers noted three valid claimants to the crown as his successor. They agreed that of the three, Joseph Ferdinand of Bavaria should be chosen, because the power of France was already too great to permit a French prince to ascend the Spanish throne to join the countries of France and Spain in an alliance; but the chosen prince died, and the Powers selected Archduke Charles of Austria. Then Charles II of Spain died, and his will bequeathed the throne to Philip of Anjou, a French prince. The Powers protested; France was firm, and war was declared in 1701. It ended in 1714 with the defeat of France, but French diplomats, by

making concessions elsewhere, succeeded in keeping Philip on the Spanish throne. This war extended to the American colonies of the Powers and was known in American history as *Queen Anne's War.*

War of the Polish Succession. Polish nobles chose as king of Poland Stanislas Leszczynski, whose daughter Mary was the wife of Louis XV of France. Russia and Austria in 1733 declared war to prevent the succession. France was defeated two years later, and the father-in-law was denied the throne.

War of the Austrian Succession. When Charles VI of Austria died in 1740 he desired that his daughter Maria Theresa succeed him. The other Powers had agreed to abide by his wish, but when Charles passed from the scene, the Powers broke their word and tried to keep Maria from the succession. Prussia, Bavaria, Sax-

MARIA THERESA

ony, France and Spain joined in war on her. By an alliance with England and Holland, the coalition was defeated and Maria Theresa received the title of empress through her agreement that her husband, Francis of Lorraine, should become emperor. The American phase of this war was known as *King George's War.* The struggle continued from 1740 to 1748.

War of the Bavarian Succession. Maximilian III Joseph of Bavaria died in 1777 without an heir. Austria tried to control the succession, but Prussia had a like ambition and war was declared. The other Powers intervened after hostilities had continued during 1778 and 1779, and the two contenders relinquished their claims. There were no important battles in this war; and it was nicknamed the *Potato War* because the main operations concerned the provision of supplies for the opposing armies.

SYRACUSE, one of the outposts of early Greek colonization, founded by adventurers from Corinth (c.735 BC). Located on the island of Sicily, it became one of the most prosperous cities of antiquity. It was an important center of Greek literature and art from the 400s BC until its capture by the Romans in 212 BC in one of the

campaigns of the Second Punic War. Thereafter the power of Syracuse declined.

The present-day city of Syracuse is near the ruins of the old town. During the Peloponnesian War between Athens and Sparta (431–404 BC), the Athenians sent a great expedition to seize Syracuse. After a long siege (415–413 BC), the Athenians were disastrously defeated, and a large part of their navy was destroyed. The failure of the Syracusan expedition led directly to the final crushing of Athens by Sparta.

THERMOPYLAE, a narrow mountain pass in Thessaly, the scene of a battle (480 BC) in which the Greek defenders won imperishable glory. In 490 BC the Persian king, Darius, had been defeated at Marathon in an attempt to conquer Greece. Ten years later his son and successor, Xerxes I, renewed the war with an enormous army. A small force of 7,000 Spartans, Athenians, and lesser allies met the invader at the pass of Thermopylae.

For two days the attackers sought to force their way through but were held back. On the evening of the second day a traitor, Ephialtes, one of the defenders from Thessaly, disclosed to Xerxes' generals a secluded path by which they could get around the pass and attack the Greeks from the rear.

When Ephialtes's treachery was disclosed to Leonidas, the Spartan leader, he dismissed all of his followers except his Spartans, the Thessalians and Thebans, and with only 1,400 men made a valiant stand against the hosts of Xerxes. The Thebans surrendered; all the others died, and the road to Athens was open to the enemy.

TIBET, a region in Southern Asia but little known to the outside world. Not only is it difficult to reach because of its location in the Himalayas, but until recent years foreigners were forbidden to enter. Of its early history little is known. No strong figure dominated Tibet until the great Mongol conqueror, Genghis Khan, added it to his Asiatic empire. Kublai Khan, grandson of Genghis, established the Mongol dynasty in China, and its sway extended to Tibet. There followed a struggle for religious ascendancy; Buddhism, which entered from China, and shamanism, already rooted in the country, were supplanted by Lamaist Buddhism, brought from India, and this faith still dominates the lives of the people.

Great Britain attempted to establish diplomatic relations through its colony in India in 1774 and again in 1790 to negotiate a commercial treaty; but they were not successful, for Tibetans charged that the English had at times given comfort to Tibet's enemies. The frontier of the country remained closed to the British until 1903. Then, the Manchu dynasty in China being unable to maintain control in Tibet, another English expedition entered the country. It was opposed by the waning Chinese authority but resulted in a British-Chinese agreement for trade relations and a further stipulation that recognized Chinese sovereignty.

The Manchu dynasty was overthrown in China in 1911. That revolution severely shook China's hold on Tibet. It was later governed by a regent, acting for the Dalai Lama, a minor, who was the temporal and spiritual leader and was considered the 14th reincarnation of the first Tibetan leader. The religion of the country is Lamaism, a form of Buddhism modified by animism and primitive magic. The capital is the sacred city Lhasa.

In 1950 the Chinese Communists overran Tibet. Internal autonomy was promised, with the border defense conducted by Communists. In August 1954 a revolt of 40,000 farmers was ended by the Communists killing most of the rebels.

MONKMEYER PRESS PHOTO SERVICE

TIBET. These trumpets, sounded in a mountain-top temple during a Buddhist rite, are accompanied by instruments twenty feet long that give out a low, continuous rumble sound.

TOWER OF LONDON, originally an English fortress and prison in the days of feudalism. Its construction was begun in 1078 under the direction of William the Conqueror. The site selected was that of an earlier fortress that may have been built by Roman soldiers. Today the Tower comprises a group of buildings whose only use is as an armory, barracks, and museum. It contains the royal jewel stronghold, including crowns, scepters, and riches of gold and jeweled ornaments.

The Tower is of great historical interest. There Anne Boleyn, Lady Jane Grey and her husband Lord Dudley, Sir Thomas More, and Sir Walter Raleigh were beheaded, and here some of them are buried.

TRIESTE, a former Italian city, set up as a Free City, Jan. 10, 1947, under United Nations administration. In 1954 a pact was signed by Italy and Yugoslavia ending a nine-year dispute over the Free Territory of Trieste. Zone A was given to Italy. Zone B with a strip of Zone A, largely Slovene in population, was allotted to Yugoslavia. It remains a free port and is important because it is at the head of the Adriatic Sea, and therefore is natural and accessible outlet for the adjoining areas to the north.

TRIPLE ALLIANCE, THE, in European history, was used for mutual protection and to maintain a balance of power among conflicting states. There have been three such alliances: (1) in 1668, among England, The Netherlands, and Sweden to prevent Louis XIV of France from absorbing the Low Countries; (2) in 1717, among Great Britain, France, and The Netherlands in opposition to Spain; and (3) in 1882, among Germany, Austria-Hungary, and Italy to oppose Russian penetration into the Balkans. Italy withdrew from the Alliance during World War I to become an ally of Great Britain and France against Austria-Hungary, and in 1916 likewise against Germany.

UNCLE SAM, the personification of the United States, its people and its government as a tall, thin character with chin beard, dressed in garments of the early 1800s, clothing and hat being decorated with the Stars and Stripes, the national emblem. The nickname of *Uncle Sam* is believed to have originated during the War of 1812 when Samuel Wilson, a government inspector of beef at Troy, N.Y., was always called *Uncle Sam*. After the inspection of the beef, it was shipped to an army contractor named Elbert Anderson and was always marked "U.S.—E.A." A joking workman, being asked what those letters meant, replied that he did not know, unless they were for Uncle Sam and Elbert Anderson.

UNDERGROUND RAILROAD, the secret routes by which northern abolitionists aided slaves to escape to freedom in the North and in Canada. The whites along the routes, usually through Pennsylvania and Ohio, gave food and shelter to the fleeing Negroes. One who took personal charge of a slave in flight was known as a *conductor;* and all who gave money and other assistance were *stockholders;* thus the term *railroad* came to be applied to the enterprise. Probably 3,500 slaves were thus assisted to freedom within 30 years.

VERDUN, TREATY OF, the earliest important political treaty in modern European history. Charlemagne left his vast empire to his son Louis the Pious. When Louis died in 840, his three sons fought for the domain. In 843 an agreement was reached and reduced to writing whereby one son, Charles, received the region west of the Rhine River, which became the nucleus of modern France; Louis received the greater part of modern Germany, east of Charles' domain but separated from it; Lothair became emperor and received territory between the North Sea and the Jura Mountains, the southern part of which in later centuries became the foundation of present-day Italy and the northern part of which included Lorraine, which was to be disputed between France and Germany for more than 1,000 years.

VERSAILLES, TREATY OF, several international agreements, but especially the document that made the peace at the close of World War I. The Peace Conference was held in 1919 in the Hall of Mirrors of the Palace of Versailles, which had been the scene of the coronation of William I of Prussia as German emperor in 1871.

A great staff of specialists working in committees drafted separate parts of the treaty. Each committee made its part as severe as possible—fearing that other committees might be lenient. There was a tremendous pressure of public opinion on each of the Big Four—Clemenceau of France, Lloyd George of Great Britain, Orlando of Italy and Wilson of the United States—to make the terms severe. An English historian of the Conference, Dr. H. W. V. Temperley, calls the treaty "crushing and severe to a high degree" and he said of it: "No great diplomatic instrument has ever been so speedily modified, revised or altered." The treaty was signed on January 10, 1920.

By the terms of the treaty the League of Nations was set up. Germany lost all its colonial possessions throughout the world, including German Southwest Africa, German East Africa, Togoland, and Kamerun, and its "sphere of influence" in China in the Shantung district was restored to China. East Prussia was split into two parts to establish the Free City of Danzig and to give Poland access to the sea. Alsace and Lorraine, given to Germany after the Franco-Prussian War of 1870, were returned to France. The coal mines of the Saar Valley in Germany were ordered turned over to France for 15 years. Small territories, such as Schleswig and two on the border of Belgium, were given to Denmark, Belgium and Luxemburg. Nearly all the German navy was ordered delivered to the Allies, as well as a large part of the country's mer-

NEW YORK PUBLIC LIBRARY

PRINCE METTERNICH

chant marine. German sailors sank many of the war vessels after they had been delivered into British waters.

The Treaty of Versailles made Germany responsible for damages done the Allies during the war, but it did not set these damages. That whole question was further involved because each of the Allies wanted to pay its war debts out of funds to be secured from Germany. A Reparations Commission in April 1921 assessed Germany 132 billion gold marks (about 33 billion dollars) in 42 annual payments. When these payments were not made, the Dawes Commission (1924, headed by Charles G. Dawes of the U.S.) adjusted the payments to the German Reich's ability to pay based on a survey made by the Commission. Again the payments were not made, and the Young Plan (1929, headed by another American, Owen D. Young) worked out another method of payment; but Germany defaulted in 1931.

Whether reparation demands were too high or the world depression came too soon, the demands that grew out of the Versailles Treaty for a German indemnity were not met. Many other terms of the Treaty were made null and void by the passage of time. Hitler's remodeling of Germany created

a huge new war machine where the Peace Treaty had forbidden an army. The colonies that were taken from Germany were demanded back by Hitler, and many students of international affairs who wanted peace urged that the colonies should be restored. The League of Nations established by the treaty failed to check Japan in Manchukuo or Italy in Ethiopia.

VIENNA, CONGRESS OF, a notable assemblage of officials of the governments of Europe called to meet in Vienna in October 1814 to readjust the map of the Continent after the downfall of Napoleon. The monarchs of Russia, Prussia, Austria, Denmark, and Bavaria were present in person. The main work of the Congress was done by the representatives of Austria, Prussia, Russia, Britain, and (in spite of protests) France. Lord Castlereagh acted for Britain, Metternich for Austria, and Talleyrand for France. When the Congress finally adjourned in June 1815, many readjustments had been made in an effort to secure the balance of power in Europe and with no attention to the claims of nationalities.

The Austrian Hapsburg rule was restored, and Austria received as additional territory in the Tyrol Venetia, Dalmatia, Galicia, and Salzburg. The Prussian monarchy was restored, and to its domain were added a considerable portion of Poland, some of Saxony, and other land in Germany. A German confederation of 39 states was formed, with Austria at its head. The Netherlands, including what is now Belgium and the Netherlands, was set apart as a kingdom. Sweden's control of Norway was confirmed. The kings of Spain, Sardinia, Tuscany, and Modena were restored to their thrones.

WATERLOO, the last engagement of the armies of Napoleon, against the Allied Powers of Europe, fought near Brussels, on the field of Waterloo June 18, 1815. The French force consisted of 70,000 men and 246 cannon; the Allies, under the English duke of Wellington, had 67,600 men and 156 guns. The

COURVOISIER COGNAC.

NAPOLEON'S FAREWELL to the Imperial Guard at Fountainbleau, in a painting by Vernet.

battle raged all day without decisive result; about 7:30 in the evening the Prussian General Blücher arrived with overwhelming reinforcements for Wellington. The struggle was at once renewed with increased intensity, and Napoleon suffered a terrible defeat. He lost 30,000 men, killed and wounded; the allied loss was 22,000.

Napoleon had previously been exiled to Elba, but he had escaped and was warmly greeted by his old army. He had all Europe against him; France was exhausted; yet he tried once more, at Waterloo.

WHISKY INSURRECTION, an uprising of the farmers in western Pennsylvania in 1794. In the early national period settlers in widely scattered districts found it difficult to transport their corn and other grains to markets in the centers of population. Some of them, notably in western Pennsylvania, converted their grain into whisky, thus lessening the transportation difficulty, as what they then had to sell was much less bulky.

To make whisky was not contrary to law, but the government levied a considerable tax upon whisky. The Pennsylvanians objected to the tax and ill-treated the revenue officers sent to collect it. President Washington sent 15,000 militiamen to the region to enforce collection and the insurrection soon subsided. This was the first occasion that the government used its power to enforce a federal statute within a state; hence the in-

cident is important in the history of American jurisprudence.

WITENAGEMOT, a council of leading men in the Anglo-Saxon period of England, existing to give advice and assistance to the king. It was composed of thanes, bishops, abbots, and nobles. So great was their influence that under extraordinary conditions they could depose the monarch and elect his successor. After the Norman Conquest, William the Conqueror caused its name to be changed to the Great Council, and he continued to recognize the validity of the body. In the struggle for individual rights in England, the Great Council was destined to develop into the English Parliament.

WORLD WAR I, the great conflict of 1914–1918 among the principal powers, including the United States. This was the first war to involve so large a number of nations, to be so terrifyingly costly in men and material, and to be as comprehensive and destructive with its modern scientific methods. It was, therefore, known for many years as "The Great War."

Causes of the War. The war may be called in general terms a conflict between pan-Germanism and pan-Slavism—that is, ethnic ties bound together Germany and Austria on the one hand and Russia and Serbia on the other, and ethnic antipathies separated these two groups. The same phenomenon may be called the growth

of nationalism—the unrest in Serbia and the unwillingness of the Serbs to be a part of the Austro-Hungarian Empire in which they had no natural national place.

The rapid growth of the German Empire since its foundation in 1871 at the end of the Franco-Prussian War, the bitter feeling between Germany and France that resulted from this war, the fear and distrust that Russia in the east and Great Britain in the west both felt of Germany's growing military power, and its professed international policy of pushing toward the east (*Drang nach Osten*)—these facts are important in any list of the reasons for World War I.

The immediate cause was the assassination (June 28, 1914) at Sarajevo by a Serbian of the Austrian archduke and heir to the throne, Francis Ferdinand. The Austrian authorities made impossible demands on Serbia—apparently expecting to provoke a war that would crush Serbia without involving any other Powers. A great many historians consider that the German emperor attempted to restrain Austria and that he did not want war.

Who Was in the War. When Austria actually declared war (July 28), Russian forces mobilized; and (August 1) Germany declared war on Russia. Within three days France and Britain were on the side of Serbia opposing Germany and Austria—drawn in by their obligation to preserve the neutrality of Belgium, which had been guaranteed in 1839 by Great Britain,

WIDE WORLD

1914-1918

"The Great War," as World War I came to be known, was a global conflict lasting from 1914 to 1918. Germany and Austria were the two key forces fighting an alliance composed of Britain, France, and Russia, and, later, the United States and Italy. At left, German soldiers guard the Vistula River in Russia in 1916. Seen above are four representatives of the Allied governments at the Paris Peace Conference in 1919. They are (from *left* to *right*, top row first): British Prime Minister George, U.S. President Wilson, Italian Premier Orlando, and French Premier Clemenceau.

WORLD WAR I

France, Prussia, Russia, and Austria. Japan declared war on Germany in August 1914.

Turkey came into the war (September 1914) on the side of Germany and Austria against its old-time enemy Russia and in the hope of regaining lost territory. Bulgaria got offers from both sides in the summer of 1915 but in October declared war on Serbia. Romania declared war on Austria in August 1916. Greece finally joined the Allies in June 1917. Other Powers also came in nominally or actually against Germany, Austria, and Turkey—for example, Liberia, Honduras, and Siam.

Italy in 1882 had joined Germany and Austria in a Triple Alliance, but at the beginning of the war Austria had not consulted Italy, and so Italy declared its neutrality and soon afterward demanded certain cessions from Austria as compensation for disturbing the balance of power and as the price for continued neutrality.

The gains that Austria would not give Italy were promised it under the Treaty of London (Apr. 26, 1915) by the Allies (Britain, France, and Russia), and this brought Italy into the war (May 23) against its old friends of the Triple Alliance.

The United States was neutral during the early part of the war, and Woodrow Wilson was re-elected in 1916 because "He kept us out of war." President Wilson hoped to make peace, but early in 1917 the German policy of unrestricted submarine warfare brought the United States into the war (April 6) on the side of the Allies.

In the spring of 1917 Russia had practically dropped out of the war after a series of defeats at the hands of the Central Powers. These defeats coupled with internal revolution resulted in the abdication of Czar Nicholas II a few weeks before the United States came into the war. In November 1917 the Bolshevik government of Russia declared for peace.

Even this brief outline of the action of the different powers shows how wide the scope of World War I was.

Operations of the War. Operations were so varied that they cannot easily be described in a short summary. The German forces advanced through Belgium, defeated the French and the British in northern France, and threatened Paris but were checked at the Marne (Sept. 6–10, 1914). Thereafter the fighting on the western front was trench warfare with both armies dug in. On the east the Russians had been defeated by the Germans at Tannenberg (Aug. 27, 1914), but they mounted a strong offensive against the Austrians.

In 1915 the Allies made no gains and suffered many losses. They began the ill-fated move against Turkey in the Gallipoli campaign. In 1916 the battle of Jutland (May 31) was not a decisive victory for the Allies, but it kept the German fleet from causing further trouble. Fighting on the western front in France was indecisive with terrible losses.

The year 1917 was marked by the German policy of submarine warfare that finally brought the United States into the war against Germany. The land fighting in France was bloody, indecisive, a futile attempt to break up the entrenched lines of the opposing armies. The British use of armed tanks with caterpillar treads in November at Cambrai promised a break. In October and November the Italians were crushingly defeated by German and Austrian forces in a great battle at Caporetto.

In 1918 the American Expeditionary Force arrived in large numbers and in July at the second battle of the Marne defeated a huge German offensive. The Allied victories that followed finally broke up trench warfare. The Italians gained a victory in September on the Piave. President Wilson's Fourteen Points, a program for international justice, weakened German morale; and suddenly the war ended (Nov. 11, 1918).

WORLD WAR II. The entire series of compromises following World War I may well be called the Truce of Versailles. It was not as cruel as the Brest-Litovsk Treaty which Germany previously forced on Russia. The League of Nations lacked the force necessary to preserve peace, so much desired by the United States, Britain, and France and pledged by all important nations. During the 1930s the Allied nations depended upon love of peace and disarmament for collective

WORLD WAR II

The second great war of the 1900s began only two decades after the end of World War I. The Axis powers, led by Germany, Italy, and Japan, were ranged against the Allied powers, headed by Britain, France, the Soviet Union, and the United States. Adolf Hitler *(right)*, the German leader, unleashed the war, which was fought on land, sea, and in the air. A Japanese plane shot down at sea *(below, right)* narrowly misses a U.S. carrier. The U.S. atomic attack on the Japanese city of Nagasaki *(below, left)* ended the devastating war.

LOOK MAGAZINE

WIDE WORLD

WIDE WORLD

security, while Germany, Japan, and Italy were secretly building the greatest war machine of all time. In 1931 Japan took Manchuria. Germany withdrew from the League in 1933, and announced rearmament in 1935; Italy attacked Ethiopia in 1935 and soon conquered it.

The aggressors, Germany and Italy, joined formally with Japan in the Anti-Comintern pact in 1936. German troops entered the Rhineland in 1936. Japan attacked China in 1937. In 1938 Germany, deserted by England and State. Czechoslovakia, threatened by Germany, deserted by England and France after Hitler's Munich treaty promising no further aggressions, yielded to German rule in 1938. Bohemia and Moravia were next taken into the German Reich.

These German aggressions were accomplished without firing a shot. Britain and France did not consider any one of them of sufficient importance to justify a war. Hitler and Mussolini achieved tremendous popularity among their countrymen.

Germany signed a treaty of neutrality and friendship with Russia. In the Spring of 1939, Germany took Memel, and Italy, Albania. The above aggressions were of great strategic and military value. Germany next demanded Danzig and the Polish Corridor. Poland refused and on Sept. 1, 1939, Germany attacked Poland.

In Poland Hitler first revealed his blitzkrieg technique, a cyclonic highly mechanized attack and penetration. With powerful airforce protection, tanks knifing into and behind the Polish lines, followed by infantry and artillery, Germany conquered Poland and the Free City of Danzig in 17 days. Germany allowed Russia, who had not entered the war, to possess eastern Poland. England and France, who had guaranteed Poland's integrity, following many serious treaty breaches by Germany, German threats of war, and demands for more territory, declared war on Germany September 3, 1939.

In a surprise move in 1940 Germany captured Denmark and Norway. Germany next invaded and conquered the Netherlands, Belgium, and France, with England losing many men and materials of war. Italy entered the war on Germany's side just before France fell. France withdrew from the war. England's colonies gave tremendous aid. Each side attempted to blockade the other, England practically driving the Axis powers from the sea. The Axis destroyed many British ships with submarines, raiding ships, and bombing planes, and severely damaged English cities and military objectives with bombing planes. English bombers wrought much destruction on Axis military installations.

Hitler's next planned move was to take over the Balkans and North Africa and thus gain control of the Mediterranean. With Egypt and the Suez Canal in his control, the Nazis could move eastward into India where they expected to join hands with their Axis partner, Japan, and thus gain control of the riches of Asia and the South Pacific. Hitler and his Nazis,

he promised his people, would control the world for a thousand years. A grandiose dream, and one that failed of fulfillment by the narrowest margin.

For a time only the courage of Britain and the ineptitude and military weakness of Hitler's other Axis partner, fascist Italy, prevented him from carrying out his timetable of world conquest. British troops were pushed back onto the beaches at Dunkirk; Winston Churchill became prime minister of Great Britain and told his people he could only offer them "blood, toil, tears and sweat"; British airmen, the "few to whom the many owed so much," throughout the bitter summer of 1940 successfully defended London against desperate German air attacks. To this end had come western appeasement and indecision.

The Germans in June 1941, after successfully occupying the Balkans, turned on Russia and pushed Stalin's troops northward to Leningrad and Moscow and southward to the Crimea. Finland was forced to join the Axis. In his drive against the Russians, Hitler's legions overextended themselves; by the end of 1942 they were being driven back westward across the Russian steppes through ice and snow and bitter cold.

Mussolini's Italian forces, in 1940, had been driven out of Ethiopia and the Red Sea region. In Egypt and Libya the tide of war swayed back and forth. Malta was bombed continuously. In the 1942 summer, Field Marshal Erwin Rommel led the Germans and Italians in a brilliant victory over superior Allied forces, driving deep into Egypt about 100 miles west of Alexandria. Later, Rommel in turn was forced westward by British and Colonial troops led by General Bernard Montgomery.

During the years between 1937 and 1941 Japan had conquered much Chinese territory, and Hong Kong, and had sent many troops into the Malay Peninsula in 1941. While conducting peace negotiations in Washington, Japan, seeing her strategic opportunity, attacked the United States at Pearl Harbor, Hawaii, and other Pacific outposts Dec. 7, 1941. Terrific destruction was wrought on the United States fleet at Pearl Harbor.

The Allies had been fighting a delaying war because at first they were not prepared to do otherwise, and then because they needed time to mobilize their potential strength. The United States had developed into the world's greatest arsenal, furnishing under the Lend-Lease plan war supplies to all the Allied nations. The Axis aim had been to win the war quickly before the Allies could prepare, and to sink Allied ships, cutting Allied supply lines. But by 1942, with the United States in full production and the submarine menace rendered almost harmless by an effective convoy system, the Allies were able to take the offensive.

In November 1942, U.S. troops landed in North Africa. Before long they had defeated or captured most of the defending German and Italian troops, and then they crossed the Mediterranean to overrun Sicily and

Italy. Mussolini fled Rome and was murdered as he made his way northward toward Germany.

After suffering many defeats and losses, Russia won back much territory in 1943, and in 1944 inflicted terrific defeats on the Germans, Finns, Rumanians, and Bulgarians, capturing much territory. The Americans and English, through steady bombing of German cities and war industries, softened Germany, thus preparing for the invasion of western Europe. In Yugoslavia, Marshall Tito and his guerrilla army harassed the Germans.

On June 6, 1944, American and British troops landed on the French coast in Normandy to form a second front—the western front for which Stalin and the Russians had long clamored. The British and Americans swept eastward to and across the Rhine and into the heart of Germany.

U.S. troops poured northward through southern France into Alsace-Lorraine and Bavaria; other forces came up from Italy through the Tyrol and the Danube valley into Austria; the Russians drove westward into Germany, Austria, and Hungary; Budapest and Vienna fell; the Ruhr was taken.

In the spring of 1945 Allied troops driving from the west, the east, and the south forced their way into Berlin and on May 8, 1945 the Germans capitulated unconditionally. Hitler and many of his fellow Nazis were dead; others had fled or were prisoners. The war in Europe was over. But world peace had not arrived; Japan fought on.

After Pearl Harbor Japan had gone on to easy victory among the islands of the South Pacific and in Burma, Malaya, and at Singapore. India was threatened. Only in the Philippines had the Japanese suffered any delay, but it was not sufficient to hinder their conquests to the south. The "greater East Asia co-prosperity sphere" promised the Japanese people seemed to be within the grasp of their leaders.

The first set-back came six months after Pearl Harbor, in a naval-air defeat at Midway Island near Hawaii. In the Coral and Bismarck seas, and elsewhere in the vast expanses of the Pacific during the summer of 1942, Japan suffered severe losses. In August 1942 Guadalcanal was successfully invaded and held by U.S. troops. The Solomon Islands were soon taken, then Guam, Saipan, and Tinian.

In October 1944 Gen. Douglas MacArthur was back in the Philippines from where he had been driven two and one-half years before. Iwo Jima fell in February 1945 and the Allied leaders met at Yalta in the Crimea.

Okinawa fell, and early in August 1945 atomic bombs from American airplanes were dropped on Hiroshima and Nagasaki. On Aug. 14, 1945, Japan, driven from all its conquests in Burma, the Netherlands Indies and elsewhere to the south, surrendered. The formal capitulation took place on the American battleship *Missouri* in Tokyo Harbor, Sept. 2, 1945. The war finally was ended. All the pomp and glory and boasting of Nazism, Fascism, and of the Axis had come to this bitter end.

CHRONOLOGICAL HISTORY OF THE WORLD

Universal history may conveniently be treated in three principal divisions:

I. Ancient History, which begins with the earliest written records and terminates A.D. 476, with the destruction of the Roman Empire.

II. Medieval History, which extends from the fall of Rome, A.D. 476, to the discovery of America, 1492.

III. Modern History, which commences at the latter epoch and continues to the present time.

The events that mark the separation between the *first* and *second* periods, are the irruption of the Teutonic tribes, the consequent fall of the western Roman Empire and the foundation of the modern European states; between the *second* and *third*, are the extension of learning by the invention of printing, the taking of Constantinople, the maritime discoveries by Spain, Portugal and other European countries, with the more extensive use of firearms.

I. Ancient History may be subdivided into six periods:

1. The nebulous period, comprising the fragmentary accounts of the early Assyrians, Babylonians, Egyptians, Chinese, Hindus and Hebrews, down to 2000 B.C.

2. The Mosaic period, from the time of Hammurabi to 1200 B.C., during which history passes from the realm of legend to that of fact.

3. The Assyrian-Babylonian period, which witnessed a long series of Assyrian conquests, the zenith of Babylonia, the rise of Greece and Rome and the foundation of the Persian Empire—1200 to 529 B.C.

4. The Persian-Macedonian period, from 529 to 323 B.C., during which both the Persians and the Greeks reached their greatest achievements.

5. The Greco-Roman period, from 323 B.C. to the Christian era, saw the decline of the Greeks and the coming universal power of the Romans.

6. The period of the Roman Empire, from the time of Christ to 476, was notable for the foundation of Christianity, Christian persecutions, the division of the empire, Roman luxury and corruptions and the incursion of the Teutonic hordes.

II. Medieval History may be treated in the following five periods:

1. *First*, the foundation of the modern states of western Europe, A.D. 476–622, when the Saxons invaded Britain, 449; the Visigoths settled in Spain, 507; the Ostrogoths in Italy, 489; and the Franks began the formation of the French monarchy, 481.

2. The *second* comprehends the age of Mohammed, with the propagation of his creed and the establishment of the states that embraced his religion, to the Treaty of Verdun, 622–843.

3. The *third* embraces the period from the Treaty of Verdun, when the empire of the West was divided, to the First Crusade, 1096. In this interesting period the monarchy of Charlemagne fell to ruin, the Capetian dynasty began to reign in France, Italy was parceled out among a number of petty princes, and Otto commenced the long-continued struggle against feudalism in Germany.

4. The *fourth* is the romantic or heroic period of the crusades, 1096–1273, in which the Roman legal code, the foundation of modern jurisprudence, began to be studied.

5. The *fifth*, from 1273 to 1492, beheld the revival of the fine arts in Italy, the taking of Constantinople and diffusion of its learned men, the revival of letters, the discovery of America, 1492.

III. Modern History falls conveniently into five periods:

1. The period of the Reformation, including its commencement by Luther, 1517, till the termination of the long series of religious wars by the Treaty of Westphalia in 1648. This period produced many important changes in Europe.

2. The period from 1648 to the death of Louis XIV in 1715, during which Russia entered European politics, and Great Britain began to assume large influence on the Continent.

3. The period from the death of Louis XIV to the Congress of Vienna, 1815, which marked the fall of Napoleon. In this period the independence of the United States was established, Prussia advanced to the front rank of European powers, the French Revolution occurred and the world witnessed the rise and fall of Napoleon.

4. From the Congress of Vienna, 1815, to the opening of the First World War, the era of Industrial Revolution.

5. From the beginning of the First World War to the present time, a period of political and economic confusion.

PARALLEL OUTLINES OF HISTORY

FROM THE DAWN OF HISTORY TO THE TIME OF HAMMURABI, B. C. 5000-2000

Characteristics of the Centuries	Babylonia—Assyria	Egypt	Arts and Sciences	Literature
B. C. 5000-4000 Civilization develops in Mesopotamia and Egypt as farmers and pottery makers settle in cities.	5000(?). Susa, Kish and other Sumerian city-states develop in Mesopotamia.	4221(?). Sun calendar invented; earliest date in history.	5000(?). At this date the simpler industrial arts had made considerable advancement both in Babylonia and Egypt. Northern Europe was emerging from the last Ice Age and was thinly peopled by wandering barbarian (Celtic?) tribes.	No written language known.
B. C. 4000-3000 Bronze Age. Dawn of recorded history. Civilization spreads in Egypt, Mesopotamia and the Aegean area.	4000(?). Deluge destroys Kish. 3800(?). Nippur and Agade grow. 3500(?). Sumerian culture spreads. Lagash (Shinar), Ur and Tepe Gawra thrive. Elam a powerful tribe on Persian border. 3100(?). Semitic tribes settle in Asia Minor, including Canaanites in Palestine.	4000(?). Abydos capital of predynastic kings. 3400(?). Menes begins First Dynasty, uniting Upper and Lower Egypt with capital at Memphis. 3200(?). Third Dynasty; pyramid era begins. 3100(?). Fourth Dynasty; zenith of Early Egyptian Empire under Cheops and Chefren.	4000(?). Hieroglyphic writing in Egypt and cuneiform writing in Mesopotamia. 3500(?). Dravidian civilization develops in southern India. 3200(?). Zoser builds step-pyramid at Sakkara, Egypt. 3100(?). Era of the great pyramids and the Sphinx. 3050(?). Earliest known wheeled vehicle at Kish, Mesopotamia.	Tomb inscriptions of Egypt and clay tablets of Babylonia are oldest known literature.

TO THE TIME OF HAMMURABI, B. C. 3000-2000

Characteristics of the Centuries	Babylonia—Assyria	Egypt	Arts and Sciences	Literature
B. C. 3000-2000 Great migrations of Aryan peoples from their centers in southwest Asia. Chinese civilization evident.	3000(?). Isin thrives. 2750(?). Under Sargon of Akkad the first Babylonian Empire spreads from Syria to Persia. 2500(?). Erech and Kish thrive. 2350(?). Elam conquers Akkad and rules all Babylonia briefly. 2200(?). Ur drives out Elam and restores Babylonian power. Nineveh rises. 2100(?). Rival city-states battle for Babylonian rule. 2050(?). Hammurabi unites Babylonia.	3000(?). Fifth Dynasty encourages Sun worship, centered at Heliopolis. 2750(?). Disorder and strife stop Egyptian progress. 2350(?). Egypt reunited under 11th Dynasty; trade and art revive. 2200(?). Egypt trades with Crete; Egyptian and Aegean cultures mingle. 2100(?). Mathematics develops.	3000(?). Use of metal tools develops in Egypt and Crete. Knowledge of glass, papyrus, pottery and navigation spreads. 2700(?). Huang-Ti founds Chinese Empire; silk industry develops. 2500(?). Aryans spread into India, Persia and Asia Minor, taking the horse and ox to these lands. 2205(?). Yu founds Hsia Dynasty in China. 2200(?). Nammu builds great ziggurat at Ur. 2050(?). Religion and learning revive in Mesopotamia.	Proverbs of *Ptah-Hotep*, world's oldest book (papyrus). *Egyptian Book of The Dead.* *Code of Hammurabi.*

FROM HAMMURABI TO THE PERIOD OF ASSYRIAN ASCENDANCY, B. C. 2000-1200

Characteristics of the Centuries	Asia	Egypt	Europe	Arts and Sciences	Literature
B. C. 2000-1200 Spread of Phoenician and Aegean civilizations around the Mediterranean. Development of Chinese and Hindu cultures. Rise of Hittite and Hebrew states in Asia Minor and Aeolian cities in Greece. Decline and revival of Egyptian power. Laws of Moses.	2000(?). Aryan Hittites subdue Semitic peoples, settle in Asia Minor, and begin wars with Babylonia. 1900(?). Assyria rises to power. 1800(?). Time of Abraham. Hebrews migrate west from Mesopotamia. 1766(?). T'ang founds Shang Dynasty in China. 1750(?). Barbarian Kassites take Babylonia, where they rule five centuries, absorbing older cultures. 1500(?). Feudal system develops in China. 1450(?). Hindu (Aryan) kings at war in central India; Magadha the leading state. 1385(?). Hittites drive out Egyptians and rule Asia Minor. 1300(?). Era of the Exodus. 1280(?). Shalmaneser I revives Assyrian Empire, conquers Hittites, rebuilds Assur and Nineveh, founds Calah.	2000(?). Egypt declines as rival feudal lords battle for power. 1800(?). Hyksos (Semitic?) tribes from Asia conquer and rule Egypt, bringing in the horse and traces of Mesopotamian culture. 1580(?). Hyksos kings driven out by Egyptians. Thebes capital of New Empire. 1479(?). Thothmes wins battle of Megiddo; Egypt rules Phoenicia and Asia Minor. 1400(?). Zenith of New Empire in Sudan, Ethiopia and Asia Minor. 1300(?). Moses leads the Hebrews from Egypt. Era of the Ramses Pharaohs.	2000(?). Aeolian peoples settle in Greece. Phoenician traders ply the Mediterranean. 1700(?). Zenith of power of Crete; Cnossus and Phaestus centers of art and learning. 1500(?). Ionian and Doric cities grow on Greek mainland, while Troy, Mycenae and Tiryns dominate Aegean. 1450(?). Cnossus and Phaestus destroyed. 1350(?). Phoenician tin traders reach England. 1250(?). Thebes, capital of the Boeotians, rises to power in Greece.	2000(?). Industry thrives in Phoenician states, while art and learning are nourished in Crete and Babylonia. 1600(?). Linear writing used by Greeks. 1500(?). Monotheism spreads in Egypt. Era of cliff tombs there. 1330(?). Temples at Karnak and Abu-Simbel in Egypt.	Papyri of Egypt. The *Vedas* of India (oral form). Mythology of Greeks and Hebrews takes fixed form. Rise of Sanskrit languages in Asia. Chinese *Book of Changes.* Laws of Moses.

THE ASSYRIAN-BABYLONIAN PERIOD, B. C. 1200-700

Characteristics of the Centuries	The Hebrews	Africa	Asia	Europe	Arts and Sciences	Literature
B. C. 1200-1000 Heroic age of Greece; Hebrews reach their highest point of national power. Beginning of the Medo-Persian nations. Celts disperse over western Europe and into British Isles.	1180–1020(?). Era of the Judges. 1020(?). Samuel, last Judge of Israel. Saul, first king. Wars with the Philistines. 1010. Death of Saul; David becomes sole king.	1180–1050. Egypt divided. 1100(?). Utica founded.	1200(?). Phrygians (Greeks) invade Asia Minor, conquer Hittites. 1184(?). Troy taken by Greeks. 1123. Chow dynasty begins in China. Chinese in Korea. 1115. Tiglath-Pileser founds new Assyrian Empire, wins Syria. 1050. Bactrian Empire grows in Persia. 1020. Gaza rises.	1100. Alba Longa flourishes in Latium. 1050. Rhodes flourishes. 1020. Phoenicians have forts in Spain (Cadiz).	1150. Irrigation and architecture revive in Babylonia. 1115. Mariner's compass known in China.	Early Hebrew literature. Dictionary of Chinese completed by Pa-out-she.
B. C. 1000-900 Homeric age. Celts already in Britain, with bronze in use. Phoenician trade extended to India. Temporary decline of Assyria.	1000. Jerusalem becomes Hebrew capital. 975. Solomon anointed king. 960. Temple of Solomon.	975. Egypt ruled by Lybian (Negro) armies. 950. Shishak establishes 21st Dynasty, revives power of Egypt, wars with neighbors.	1000. Phrygians rule Asia Minor. 970. Solomon and Hiram, King of Tyre, form an alliance; also Solomon and Pharaoh. 950. Brahmanism develops in northern India.	1000. Phoenician alphabet comes into use. 970. Solomon extends his commerce to India; builds Palmyra, Baalbec and other cities.		TheZend-Avesta of Zoroaster.
B. C. 900-800 Accurate Assyrian chronology begins. Decline of Phoenician cities.	933. Division of Hebrews into kingdoms of Israel and Judea. 930. Egypt sacks Jerusalem. 885. Samaria capital of Israel. 875. Ahab and Jezebel. 850. Warfare with Philistines. 840. Athaliah rules Judea, Jehu in Israel.	850. Civil wars in Egypt between dynasty of Bubastis and priests of Amon. 845(?). Phoenicians found Carthage.	900. Bithynians enter Asia Minor, win part of Phrygia. 880. Assurnasirpal revives Assyrian capital of Calah. 850. Shalmaneser III rules at Calah. 840. Urartu grows in Armenia.	900. Hallstat culture of Celts develops in south France. 875. Rise of Sparta to power in Greece. 845. Rise of Argos in Greece. 820. Laws of Lycurgus.	900. The Rhodians advance the art of navigation.	Homer, Greek poet. Homer's poems brought into Greece. Hindu "Brahmanas."
B. C. 800-700 Ethiopian supremacy in Egypt. Assyrian conquests continue; Babylonia rises to height of its power.	790. Jehoash wars with Syria. 781–740. Reign of Jeroboam in Israel. 760. Era of Amos. 745. Kashta of Ethiopia takes south Egypt, founding 25th Dynasty. 733. Pekah, King of Israel, besieges Jerusalem. 721. Samaria taken by the Assyrians; Ten Tribes carried into captivity. 700. Hezekiah, King. Sennacherib invades Judah.	745. Kashta of Ethiopia takes south Egypt, founding 25th Dynasty. 721. Pankhi of Ethiopia takes all of Egypt.	800. Lydia grows in Asia Minor. 760. Carchemish grows in Mesopotamia. 750. Assyria controls Persia. 745–728. Reign of Tiglath-Pileser III; Assur his capital. 736. Tiglath-Pileser III conquers Syria. 721. Shalmaneser, King of Assyria, takes Samaria. 721. Media rises in Persia. 715. Cimmerii from Europe conquer Urartu and Phrygia. 705. Sennacherib rebuilds Nineveh, conquers Syria.	800. Etruscans (from Lydia?) settle in Italy. 776. First Olympic games. 763. Messenian wars in Greece. 760. Greek migrations to Italy and Africa begin. 753. Legendary date of founding of Rome by Romulus and the Tarquins; Sabine War. 734. Carthaginians found Syracuse in Sicily. 725. Cumae grows to power in Italy.	800. Metal coins used in Lydia. 790. Corinthians employ triremes, or vessels with three banks of oars. 763. Assyrians record eclipse of the sun. 721. Eclipse of the moon observed at Babylon. 710. Roman calendar reformed; year divided into 12 months.	Greek lyric poetry flourishes. Development of Upanishad philosophies in India. Greek lyric poetry flourishes.

THE ASSYRIAN-BABYLONIAN PERIOD, B. C. 700-529

Characteristics of the Centuries	Hebrews	Asia	Africa	Europe	Arts and Sciences	Literature
B. C. 700-600 Zenith and fall of Nineveh and Assyrian Empire. Media rises to power. Teutonic and Slav races migrate west and north from Aryan center.	670. Manasseh, king.	681–668. Chaldean King Esarhaddon takes Sidon, revives Nineveh, expands Assyrian Empire to zenith of its power.	670. Assyrians ravish Egypt. 660. Psammetichus founds 26th Dynasty; Memphis the capital. Egypt again independent. 621. Carthage grows to power. 610. Pharaoh-Necho, King of Egypt. 605. Necho loses Syria at Carchemish.	673. Tullius Hostilius, King of Rome, destroys Alba Longa. 658. Byzantium founded by Greeks. 640. Latins conquered by the Romans. 616. Tarquinius Priscus, King of Rome. 604. Illyria conquered by Macedon.	640. Spherical form of the earth and true cause of lunar eclipses taught in Athens. 621. Draconian code formulated in Athens. 610. Pharaoh-Necho begins a canal between the Mediterranean and Red Sea. A Phoenician fleet sails around Africa.	Iambic verse introduced. Greek alphabet adopted. *Deuteronomy.* Alcaeus and Sappho, Greek poets.
B. C. 600-500 Zenith and fall of Babylon. Long reign of Nebuchadnezzar; he ravages Egypt. The seventy years' captivity of Judah. Rise of Persia.	597. Conquest of Jerusalem by Nebuchadnezzar. 591. Ezekiel prophesies in Chaldea. 586. Captivity of Judah completed, Jerusalem destroyed, Temple burnt. 579. Jews carried to Babylon. **Persia** 560. Cyrus, King of Persia; Susa and Persepolis his capitals. 538. Cyrus takes Babylon, frees the Hebrews. 536. Persian Empire rules from Syria east to India. 535. Temple rebuilt at Jerusalem. 529. Death of Cyrus; Cambyses, King of Persia.	605. Medes raid Assyria, destroy Nineveh. Assyrians win Syria from Egypt. 594. Rise of Magadha Empire in India. 589. Babylon invades Phoenicia. Medes in Lydia and Armenia. 572. Nebuchadnezzar takes Tyre. 562. Croesus, King of Lydia, subjects Asia Minor, but is defeated by Cyrus. 538. Babylon taken by Cyrus.	594. Greek state, Naucratis, rises in Africa. 581. Egypt invaded by Nebuchadnezzar. 569. Amasis, Cyrene Greek leader, becomes King of Egypt. 550. Carthage rules the Mediterranean, takes Sicily. 536. Pythagoras visits Egypt. 535. Cyrus invades Egypt.	594. Solon, Archon of Athens. 578. Servius Tullius, King of Rome walls the city. 569. Roman and Etruscan cultures mingle. 550. Marseilles founded by Phoenicians. 541–527. Pisistratus, tyrant at Athens. 529. Miltiades rules Thrace.	594. Solon's code supersedes that of Draco in Athens. Jain philosophies in India. 569. Babylon's era of magnificence under Nebuchadnezzar. Gautama, Founder of Buddhism. Zoroastrian doctrines in Persia. 535. Lao-tse teaches in China.
						Poems of Anacreon.

THE PERSIAN-MACEDONIAN PERIOD, B. C. 529-323

Characteristics of the Centuries	Persia	Greece	Rome	Other Countries	Arts and Sciences	Literature
B. C. 500-400 Zenith of Persia; and the glorious century of Greece. Struggles of patricians and plebeians at Rome.	525. Cambyses conquers Egypt and makes it a Persian province. 521. Darius I, King of Persia and Egypt. 508. Darius extends his rule to the Indus. 500. The Ionians revolt and burn Sardis. 490. Darius sends an army into Greece. 487. Egypt revolts, and is subdued by Xerxes. 485. Xerxes, King of Persia.	527. Pisistratus dies, after seizing Athens. 510. Followers of Pisistratus expelled; Democracy established at Athens by Cleisthenes. 494. Themistocles fortifies Piraeus. 490. Battle of Marathon. 485. Themistocles builds fleet.	509. The Tarquins expelled from Rome; Etruscan War; the Capitol finished. 494. Tribunes of the people chosen. 471. *Lex Publilia* gives legislative authority to plebeian assembly.	525. Carthaginians in Spain (Cadiz). 500. Kingdom of Ceylon, India, founded by Vijaya. 490–400. Celts develop in France and Spain (La Téne). 480. Syracuse repels invasion of Carthaginians.	525. Library at Athens; era of Aristides and Heraclitus. 509. Establishment of a republic at Rome. 490. The Temple of Minerva built in Rome. 485. Zenith of Etruscan culture, excelling in music, drama and architecture.	Confucius, the Chinese philosopher. Pindar, the greatest of the Greek lyric poets. Aeschylus, Sophocles.

THE PERSIAN-MACEDONIAN PERIOD

Characteristics of the Centuries	Persia	Greece	Rome	Other Countries	Arts and Sciences	Literature
	480. Xerxes bridges Hellespont, invades Greece and wins at Thermopylae.	480. Greeks end Persian invasion, winning battle of Salamis.			480. Ancient Suez canal opened.	Tragedies of Euripides.
		479. Battle of Plataea ends Persian threat.	474. Etruscans defeated in naval battle by Hiero of Syracuse.			
		478. Athens founds Delian League.				Comedies of Aristophanes.
	465. Persia loses all Asia Minor; Artaxerxes king.	467-61. Leadership of Cimon. Rise of Pericles.	472. Beginning of *comitia tributa*.	465. Egypt declines under Persian rule.	465. Building of the long walls between Athens and Piraeus and Athens and Phalēron.	
		457-55. War of Spartans and Boeotians against Athens.	458. Cincinnatus, Dictator.	450. Patna grows in India.	450. Parthenon begun.	
	445. Nehemiah rebuilds Jerusalem.		450. Laws of the 12 Tables.		445. Herodotus in Egypt.	
		444-29. Athens under Pericles.	445. Patrician-plebeian marriage legalized.	435. Samnites rule southern Italy.	435. The battering ram used in war.	
			443. Censorship instituted.			
	431. Jews and Samaritans in conflict.	431. Peloponnesian War between Athens and Sparta.	435. Border wars.			
		430. Great plague weakens Athens.		415. Athens fails to win Syracuse.		
		413. Disastrous defeat of Athenians at Syracuse.				Sanskrit grammar, *Panini*.
		411. Athens governed by the "400." Alliance of Sparta with Persia.	411. Roman famine.			
		409. Alcibiades leads Greeks into Byzantium.		407. Carthage invades Sicily.	409. Hippocrates advances medicine.	Philosophies of Plato and Aristotle.
		404. Athens surrenders to Sparta after long siege. End of Peloponnesian War.	401. Rome conquers Veii.	400. Delhi founded.	400. Catapults used in war.	
B. C. 400-300	401. Greeks defeat Persians at Cunaxa.	404-03. Government of Thirty Tyrants at Athens.				
Decline and fall of Persia before Alexander the Great; Greek language and civilization extended all through Asia Minor. Roman wars with the Samnites. Internal quarrels of the Romans diminish.		400. Sparta, supreme in Greece, invades Asia.	390. Rome destroyed by the Gauls. Camillus dictator.			
	387. Greek cities of Asia made tributary to Persia.	399. Socrates executed.	376-367. Patrician-plebeian political struggle leads to Licinian Laws.			*Anabasis* of Xenophon.
	370. Persia and Egypt at war.	370. Predominance of Thebes; decline of Athens.		370. Persia and Egypt at war.		
		364. Death of Epaminondas at battle of Mantinea.			369. Celestial globe studied.	
		360. Macedonia grows under Philip II.			360. Philippics of Demosthenes delivered.	
	343. Persians sack Sidon.	343. Philip conquers Sparta, attacks Athens.	343. Samnian War, continued 53 years.	343. Persia conquers Egypt; last native Egyptian king flees to Ethiopia.		Orations of Demosthenes and Aeschines.
			340. War with the Latins.	340. Carthage again defeated in Sicily.	340. Aqueducts speed growth of Rome.	
	338. Royal family destroyed with poison.	338. Athenians and Thebans defeated at Chaeronea. Philip master of Greece.	338. Dissolution of Latin League. Latin settlements reduced to Roman dependencies.			
	336. Darius III., King.	336. Philip assassinated; Alexander the Great succeeds him.				
		335. Alexander conquers Greeks, sacks Thebes.			335. Caustic art invented.	Philosophies of Zeno and Epicurus.
	334. Alexander invades Persia.					
		333. Battle of Issus.				
		332. Alexander takes Tyre and Egypt.		332(?). Caledonian tribes united under Fergus.	332. Alexandria, Egypt, founded.	Mencius, Chinese teacher.
	331. Battle of Arbela. Darius defeated by Alexander, who takes Persia and marches east into India.					
		327. Alexander masters northern India.	327. Second Samnite War begins.			
		323. Death of Alexander. Wars of his generals for rule of his empire continues to 281. Perdiccas regent for Asia, Antipater for Greece, and Ptolemy for Egypt.				

THE GREEK-ROMAN PERIOD, B. C. 323-200

CHARACTERISTICS OF THE CENTURIES	ROME	GREECE	ASIA MINOR	EGYPT, CARTHAGE	OTHER COUNTRIES	ARTS AND SCIENCES	LITERATURE
	321. Roman army surrenders to the Samnites at Caudine Forks.						First work on mechanics written by Aristotle.
	320. Samnites defeated at Luceria.		320. Egypt holds Palestine.	320. Ptolemy I (Soter) carries 100,000 Jews into Egypt.	320. Magadha Empire in India grows under Chandragupta.		
		319. Cassander assumes the throne of Macedon, rebuilds Thebes.					
	317. Syracuse and Sicily usurped by Agathocles.					317. Commerce of Macedon with India through Egypt.	Idyls of Theocritus.
	312. War with the Etruscans.	315–301. War among ambitious generals, Antigonus, Lysimachus, Cassander and others.	312. Seleucus I takes Babylon, establishes Seleucid dynasty.		312. War between Syracuse and Carthage.	312. The Appian Way constructed.	
					306. Seleucids invade India.	310. Aqueducts and baths in Rome	
			301. Battle of Ipsus. Alexander's empire divided anew, into four parts: Syria, Macedon, Greece, Egypt.		301. Seleucids invade Asia Minor.		
				300. Golden Age of the Ptolemies.			
B. C. 300-200 Semi-Greek kingdoms built on the ruins of the Persian empire; in Egypt the Ptolemies; in Syria, the Antiochi. Many Jews at Alexandria. Rome mistress of Italy; then, victorious over Carthage, extends her influence to Greece and Spain. Peasant proprietors replaced by slaves in Italy.	295. Invasion of Celts repelled at Sentinum.	295. Athens and Thrace vie for rule of Macedonia.					Euclid, the celebrated mathematician.
						293. Sun dial erected at Rome.	
			291. Seleucus founds Antioch, Edessa and Laodicea.				
						290. The Colossus of Rhodes built.	
	290. Peace with Samnites. 286. Law of Hortensius. 281. War with Tarentum. 280. Italy invaded by Pyrrhus.		285. The Scythians invade Asia Minor.	285. Phoenicia united to Egypt.		285. Dionysius founds the solar year.	Ramayana, Epic, India.
		284. Achaean League against Macedonia.		283. Death of Ptolemy Soter. Ptolemy Philadelphus, King of Egypt.		283. Pharos lighthouse built at Alexandria.	The Septuagint begun at Alexandria.
	266. Rome mistress of all Italy. 264. First Punic War. 260. Great Roman naval victory at Mylae.	279. Invasion of Gauls repulsed at Delphi. 277. Antigonus of Macedonia and Pyrrhus of Epirus battle for mastery. 268. Second incursion of Gauls.	281. Antiochus Soter succeeds Seleucus and wars with Egypt.	269. Egypt allied to Rome.			Persian Chronicle written.
	255. Roman army under Regulus crushed by Carthaginians at Tunes.				266. Empire of Asoka rules all India.	266. Silver money coined at Rome.	Berosus, Babylonian historian.
	229. Suppression of Illyrian pirates. 225. The Gauls repulsed in Italy.	250. Parthia revolts from Macedon.	262. Invasion of the Gauls.	256. Greeks defeat Egyptian fleet. 246. Ptolemy Euergetes subdues Syria.	246. Ch'in Dynasty of China founded by Huang Ti. 226. Pergamum flourishes.	224. Archimedes makes known his discoveries in mechanics.	
	219. Hannibal takes Saguntum, and crosses the Alps.		226. Seleucus III, King of Syria. 223. Antiochus the Great, King of Syria.	236–229. Hamilcar Barca establishes Carthaginian colony and military base in Spain.			
	218. Second Punic War. Hannibal defeats the Romans at Ticinus and Trebia.	220. The Social War. Philip of Macedon joins the Achaeans against Sparta.		221. Ptolemy Philopator, King.			Plautus, Latin poet.
	216. Varro at Cannae totally defeated by Hannibal.	214. Alliance of Philip and Hannibal. Rome enters Greece, allied to Sparta.		217. Ptolemy defeats Antiochus at Raphia.	214. Burning of the Books in China.		Hebrew Scriptures translated.
	206. Carthaginians driven out of Spain. 204. Scipio carries the war into Africa.			205. Ptolemy Epiphanes, King. Egypt a Roman protectorate.	206. Han Dynasty in China founded by Liu Pang.	206. Gold coined at Rome.	
	202. Hannibal defeated at Zama. End of war.		203. Judea conquered by Antiochus.	202. End of second Punic War. Rome wins Spain.	202. Art of printing known in China. 200. Hun power grows in central Asia.	202. Art of printing known in China.	Ennius, Roman poet. Moschus, bucolic poet.

THE GREEK-ROMAN PERIOD—200-60 B. C.

Characteristics of the Centuries	Rome	Greece	Asia Minor	Egypt, Carthage	Arts and Sciences	Literature
B. C. 200-100 Greece, Macedonia, Carthage and Spain under Roman rule; decline of the Roman oligarchy; the Gracchi begin the democratic revolution which ends in the empire. Eastern luxury introduced among the Romans.	200. Second Macedonian war. Achaeans and Sparta join Rome against Macedonia. 200-150. War with Gallic tribes. Subjugation of Spain.	197. Philip defeated by Rome at Cynoscephalae. Rome controls Achaean League.	198. Jews assist Antiochus in expelling the Egyptian troops from Jerusalem. 190. Scipio of Rome defeats Antiochus at Magnesia. 188. Antiochus killed. Syria a Roman province.	198. Egypt loses her Syrian possessions to Antiochus. 181. Ptolemy VI at war with Syria.	198. Books, with leaves of vellum, introduced by Attalus, King of Pergamus.	Comedies of Plautus.
	188. Rome rules eastern Mediterranean. 179-178. Tiberius Sempronius Gracchus (father of the tribune) pursues policy of conciliation in Spain.	179. Perseus reigns in Macedonia.	172. Antiochus IV, King of Syria.	174. Cato's embassy to Carthage.		Epics of Ennius.
		171. Third war with Rome. 168. Rome wins Macedonia at Pydna.	170. Jerusalem plundered by Antiochus Epiphanes.		170. Paper invented in China.	First library opened in Rome. Book of Daniel.
	155. Romans unsuccessful in Spain against Gauls. 151. Third Punic War. Conquest of Carthage and of Corinth. Greece annexed to the Roman empire. 149-139. Bloody Spanish revolts under Viriathus. 134-133. Slave insurrections in Sicily.	146. Corinth destroyed by the Romans. Greece becomes a Roman province.	165. Judas Maccabeus expels the Syrians. 161. Jews make a treaty with Rome.	164. Egypt admits Roman supremacy. 152. Masinissa defeats the Carthaginians. 151. Joint reign of Philometer and Physcon in Egypt. 146. Carthage taken and destroyed by the Romans. 145. Ptolemy Physcon becomes sole King of Egypt.	162. Hipparchus teaches trigonometry. 146. Alexandria the center of commerce. 140. Clock wheels invented by Ctesibius.	Comedies of Terence. *De Agri Cultura* of Cato. Histories of Polybius.
	133. Spain becomes a Roman province after Numantia is destroyed. Unsuccessful reform effort of Tiberius Gracchus. 130. Rome expands into Southern Gaul.		134. Invasion of Judea by Syria during strife between Pharisees and Sadducees.	129. Physcon driven from his throne for cruelty. 123. Carthage rebuilt as Junonia.	133. Equestrian order a distinct class in Rome. 130. Revival of learning in China with spread of Buddhism.	
	123. Caius Gracchus, Tribune, reforms Roman laws and social system. His defeat and death at the hands of the senatorial party begins long political struggle. 113. First great migration of the German tribes, Cimbri and Teutons. 109. Rome occupies Numidia. 104. Teutoni defeat Romans in Gaul and cross Pyrenees. 101. Cimbri defeated by Marius at Vercellae.		103. Civil war in Judea; Aristobulus, king.		123. Romans found Aix in France. 110. First sumptuary law at Rome.	Doctrines of Buddha put in Pali language (Ceylon).
B. C. 100-55 The Romans govern all the countries around the Mediterranean. Corrupt rule of the Roman oligarchy is followed by civil wars and establishment of the empire.	91. Social war in Italy. Roman allies demand citizenship rights. 88. War with Mithridates of Pontus. 82. Sulla made dictator of Rome after civil wars. Proscribes political enemies. 75. Bithynia a Roman province; war with Mithridates renewed. 71. Servile War under Spartacus. 65. Syria becomes a Roman province. 65. Pompey clears eastern Mediterranean of pirates. Defeats Mithridates. 63. Catiline's conspiracy detected and suppressed by Cicero. 60. First triumvirate—Pompey, Crassus and Caesar. Caesar consul.		86. Mithridates takes all Asia Minor. 74. Rome conquers Mithridates. 63. Syria and Judea under Roman rule.	88. Rome dominates Egypt. 82. Revolt in Upper Egypt, Thebes destroyed.	98. Roman schools of oratory on Greek models instituted. 90. Rome grants citizenship to all Italians. 74. The Romans possess gold mines in Asia Minor, Macedonia, Sardinia and Gaul; and silver mines in Spain.	Libraries of Athens sent to Rome by Sulla.

THE GREEK-ROMAN PERIOD—60 B. C.-1 A. D.

CHARACTERISTICS OF THE CENTURIES	THE ROMAN EMPIRE	EGYPT, CARTHAGE	ARTS AND SCIENCES	LITERATURE
B. C. 55-1 A. D.	55. Caesar passes the Rhine, defeats the Germans and Gauls, and invades Britain. 53. Crassus defeated and killed at Carrhae in Parthia. 51. Caesar completes conquest of Gaul, which becomes a Roman province. Vercingetorix, last great Gallic leader, surrenders. 49. Civil war between Caesar and Pompey. Caesar, Dictator. 48. Battle of Pharsalia—Pompey defeated by Caesar. Death of Pompey in Egypt. 47. Caesar takes Alexandria and conquers Egypt and North Africa. 44. Caesar assassinated. Antony master of Rome. 43. Second triumvirate—Octavius Caesar, Mark Antony and Lepidus. 42. Battle of Philippi; defeat and death of Brutus and Cassius. 37. Herod, King of Judea under Rome. 32-31. War between Antony and Octavius. By the battle of Actium (31), Octavius acquires the empire. 30. Republic of Rome becomes a monarchy in fact though retaining republican forms.	55. Auletes restored by Rome after revolt. 51. Cleopatra shares Egyptian throne. 46. The African war. 45. Caesar rebuilds Carthage. 43. Cleopatra poisons her brother and rules alone. 36. Cleopatra obtains from Antony a grant of Phoenicia, Cyrene, and Cyprus. 31. Defeat at Actium. 30. Suicide of Antony and Cleopatra; Egypt passes to Rome.	50. A water mill erected on the Tiber at Rome. 45. Caesar introduces Julian calendar in Rome. 30. Direct trade of Rome with India. Silk and linen factories in the empire.	Cicero, *Orations, Essays, Letters.* Caesar, Julius, *Commentaries.* Lucretius, *De Rerum Natura.* Sallust, *Histories, Memoirs.* Catullus, *Poems* The Alexandrian library burnt. Vergil, *Georgics, Aeneid.* Horace, *Odes, Satires, Letters.*
	27. Titles of Augustus and Emperor conferred on Octavius. 23. Agrippa subdues all Spain. 19. Death of Vergil. 18. Parthians defeated. 15. Cantabria, Austria and other territory conquered by Drusus. 13. Augustus assumes the title of Pontifex Maximus. 11. Germany subdued by Germanicus. 5. Varus appointed Governor of Syria, and Cyrenius Governor of Judea. 4. Birth of Jesus four years before the so-called Christian era. Death of Herod.		27. Treasures of Egyptian art brought to Rome. The Pantheon built. 22. Pantomimic dances introduced on the Roman stage. 19. Aqueducts constructed by Agrippa. 12. Roman legions settled in fixed camps, which soon grow into cities—Bonn, Trier and Mayence. 8. Calendar corrected by Augustus. 4. Chinese adopt Taoism.	Livy, *History of Rome.*

PERIOD OF THE ROMAN EMPIRE, A. D. 1-61

CHARACTERISTICS OF THE CENTURIES	DEVELOPMENT OF CHRISTIANITY	THE ROMAN EMPIRE	ARTS AND SCIENCES	LITERATURE
1-100 A. D. Christianity founded amid persecutions. Roman Empire continues to expand.		1. Peace with the Parthians. 9. Varus defeated by Germans, halting Roman spread to north. 14. Augustus dies; Tiberius, Emperor. 17. Germanicus leads Roman armies into barbarian East.	1. Maya cities growing in Central America.	Ovid *Metamorphoses*, poems.
	25. Pontius Pilate, Governor of Judea. 26. John the Baptist begins his ministry. 27. Jesus baptized by John. 29. Twelve Apostles sent abroad. 33(?). Crucifixion of Jesus. 40. Disciples first called Christians at Antioch. 41. St. Peter, first Bishop of Rome. 50. Paul preaches at Athens. 60. Paul imprisoned in Rome.	26. Thrace invaded by Rome. 29. Agrippina banished. 37. Tiberius succeeded by tyrant Caligula. 54. Nero, Emperor; a profligate and tyrant. 61. Revolt of the Britons under Queen Boadicea.	26. The Druids in Germany. 50. Cologne founded.	Philosophies of Seneca.

PERIOD OF THE ROMAN EMPIRE—62–381 A. D.

Characteristics of the Centuries	Development of Christianity	The Roman Empire	Arts and Sciences	Literature
	64. First persecution of Christians by Nero. Paul visits Jerusalem. 66. Jews at war with Romans; Paul beheaded. 70. Destruction of Jerusalem by Titus. The Jews dispersed.	64. Rome burns; Nero blames Christians. 69. Vespasian, Emperor, reforms government and army.	64. Nero's golden palace built — of great extent.	Epictetus, *Discourses.* Tacitus *Germania, History, Annals,* etc. Pliny's *Natural History.*
	79. Cletus, Bishop of Rome.	79. Pompeii and Herculaneum destroyed by eruption of Vesuvius. 80. Agricola governs Britain, reduces Wales and enters Caledonia. 83. Rhine-Danube frontier fortified.	78. The Capitol at Rome rebuilt. Baths, bridges, the Forum built. Age of classic art.	Plutarch, *Lives of Illustrious Men.*
100-200 A. D. Zenith of Roman empire. The good emperors. Persecutions of the Christians continued.	95. Second persecution of the Christians by Domitian. 107. Third persecution by Trajan. 118. Fourth persecution by Hadrian. 134. Heresy of Marcion. 150. Canon of Scriptures fixed about this time.	98. Trajan, Emperor; Roman Empire at its greatest extent. 100. The Huns migrate westward. 117. Hadrian, Emperor; makes a journey through the provinces; visits Britain and builds there a wall from the Tyne to Solway Firth; Armenia and Mesopotamia abandoned. 138. Antoninus, Emperor; 145–152 defeats the Moors, Germans and Dacians; stops the persecution of the Christians. 161. Marcus Aurelius, Emperor; 169, war with Marcomanni 193. Army rules Rome, makes Septimius Severus Emperor. 196. Byzantium captured by Rome.	130. Great buildings of Palmyra. 132. Ptolemy, celebrated Egyptian astronomer and geographer. 164. Seleucia destroyed.	Quintilian *Rhetoric and Criticism.* Galen writes on medicine.
200-300 A. D. Emperors chosen by the army. Frontier tribes troublesome. Persecutions continue.	202. Fifth persecution under Septimius Severus. 235. Sixth persecution under Maximinus. 250. Seventh persecution of the Christians. 262. Paul, Bishop of Samosatia, denies the divinity of Jesus Christ. 272. Persecution of Christians under Aurelian. 283. The Jewish Talmud composed. Religious ceremonies multiplied. Pagan rites imitated by the Christians. 296. Monks in Spain and Egypt.	202. Septimius Severus revives Roman frontier defenses. 212. Caracalla, Emperor. Frontier wars renewed. 226. Artaxerxes begins the new kingdom of Persia. 232. Persian war. 222–235. Alexander Severus, Emperor. 235. War with barbarians on Rhine and Danube. 241. The Franks first mentioned in history. 251. Confederacy of the Franks established between the Rhine and Elbe. Irish kings rule at Tara. The Persians victorious in Asia Minor. 256–69. Goths invade Asia Minor and Greece. 261. Sapor, the Persian, takes Antioch, Tarsus and Caesarea. 264. Odenatus of Palmyra is succeeded by his wife Zenobia, who reigns as Queen, independent of Rome. 268. Claudius II defeats Goths. 270. Aurelian, a great warrior, becomes emperor; 271, defeats the Goths and Alemanni; 273, reduces Palmyra and takes Queen Zenobia prisoner; 274, Franks, Spain and Britain reduced to obedience; 275, Aurelian killed. 277. Probus, Emperor; 280, defeats the Germans; 282, defeats the Persians, takes Ctesiphon. 284. Diocletian, Emperor. Nicomedia his capital. With three sub-emperors he fortifies the frontier against barbarian invaders. 286. Diocletian divides empire. 291. The Franks spread over northwest Europe. 296. Diocletian sends ambassadors to China. Persians defeat Romans at Carrhae.	215. Caracalla grants right of Roman citizenship to all the provinces to increase tax revenue. 235. Alexandrian School of Philosophy founded. 261. Followers of Mani and Zoroaster active in the East. 276. Rome surrounded with a wall. 284. Diocletian's Baths.	Tertullian, *Apology, Tracts.* Origen, theologian. Plotinus's Neoplatonism.
300-388 A. D. Constantine moves the capital of the empire to Constantinople and professes Christianity. Rise of Christian monasticism. Great church disputes and growing corruptions. Increasing frontier troubles.	303. Persecution under Diocletian. 306. Persecution of Christians stopped by Constantine. 313. Edict of Milan issued by Constantine legalizing Christianity. 325. Council of Nicaea; Arianism condemned; Nicene Creed proclaimed. 356. First schism in Roman Church.	304. Diocletian resigns the empire to Constantius. 306. Constantine the Great, first Christian Emperor, defeats the Franks. 313–323. Constantine and Licinius joint emperors. 330. Constantine founds Constantinople as the new Roman capital. 337. Death of Constantine, and accession of his sons. 364. Division of the Empire between Valentinian and Valens.	330. Constantinople seat of art and literature. 364. Forts built on the Rhine.	*Zend-Avesta* finished. Eusebius's ecclesiastical history. Gothic Bible of Ulfilas.
		WESTERN EMPIRE — 364. Valentinian, Emperor. 368. The Saxons invade Britain, but are defeated by Theodosius. 375. Valentinian defeats the Germans, unites Empire after Valens dies. 379. The Lombards move south through Germany toward Italy. Other barbarian tribes move west and south across France. · **EASTERN EMPIRE** — 364. Valens, Emperor. 376. Hungary and South Russia invaded by the Huns. 379. Theodosius the Great becomes a zealous supporter of Christianity. He subdues the Balkan tribes.	375. Chinese culture and Buddhism reach Japan.	
	373. Bible translated into the Gothic language. Death of Athanasius. 381. Second General Council at Constantinople.			Latin (Vulgate) Bible of Jerome.

PERIOD OF THE ROMAN EMPIRE—388-476 A. D.

Characteristics of the Centuries	Development of Christianity	Western Empire	Eastern Empire	Arts and Sciences	Literature
388-500 A. D. Invasions of barbarians. Gradual breakdown of Western Empire.	392. St. Chrysostom, Patriarch of Constantinople, leads reform of clergy.	390. Insurrection at Thessalonica put down by Theodosius with great cruelty. 392. Theodosius becomes sole Emperor of the East and West. 394. Empire finally divided between the sons of Theodosius.	388. Theodosius defeats Maximus, and rules the Western Empire. 394. Egypt included in Eastern Empire.	392. Impulse given to the development of mathematics at Alexandria.	Chrysostom, *Homilies, Commentaries, Epistles.*
	402. Innocent I., Bishop of Rome.	401. Europe overrun by the Visigoths under Alaric. 406. Vandals settle in Spain and Gaul. 410. The Goths under Alaric sack and burn Rome. 412. Rise of the Vandal power in Spain. 413. Burgundian kingdom grows on the Rhine.	401. Pallava Empire rises in southern India.	413. Coptic church rises in Egypt.	Augustine, *Confessions, City of God.*
	416. The Pelagian heresy condemned.	420. The Franks form a kingdom, under Pharamond, on the lower Rhine. 424. Valentinian III., Emperor. 426. Britain evacuated by the Romans. 428. Romans defeated by the Franks and Goths.		420. China united, learning revives. 425. Theodosius establishes public schools and attempts the restoration of learning.	
	431. Third General Council at Ephesus. 432. St. Patrick preaches the gospel in Ireland. 435. Nestorianism prevails in the East.	433. Attila, leader of the Huns, begins warfare that gives him rule from central Asia west to the Atlantic. 439. The Vandals, under Genseric, form Kingdom of Africa, take Carthage and plunder Italy.	431. Armenia divided by the Persians and Romans. 437. Pannonia, Dalmatia and Noricum gained from the Western Empire.	435. Theodosian Code published.	
	443. The Manichaean books burned in Rome. 447. Eutyches asserts the existence of only one nature in Jesus Christ. 451. Fourth General Council at Chalcedon.	441. Roman territories invaded by the Huns, Persians and Saxons. 445. Famous embassy from Britain soliciting aid against the Picts. 448. Arrival of Saxons in Britain. 451. Battle of Chalons. Attila defeated by Romans and Goths. 453. Death of Attila; Hun Empire collapses. 458. Franks, under Childeric I, conquer as far as the Loire and take Paris. 468. The Visigoths under Eric establish their kingdom in Spain. 476. Odoacer, King of the Herulii, takes Rome, and the Western Empire ends.	442. Attila in Thrace. 450. Marcian, Emperor, refuses to pay tribute to the Huns. 457. War with the Goths. 465. Great fire at Constantinople. 474. Zeno, Emperor; a turbulent reign. 475. Theodoric becomes chief of the Ostrogoths and invades the empire.	450. Buddhism in Burma. 452. City of Venice founded.	Decline of Latin literature with barbarian invasions.

FROM THE FALL OF ROME TO THE AGE OF MOHAMMED, A. D. 476-511

Characteristics of the Centuries	The Eastern Empire	British Isles	Italy and the Church	France	Arts and Sciences	Literature
	480. An earthquake destroys greater part of Constantinople. 491. Anastasius I, Emperor. Rioting and war over accession.	484. Saxons and Angles settled in Britain. 490. Sussex and Wessex kingdoms formed by Anglo-Saxons.	484. Christians persecuted by the Vandals. 493. Italy conquered by Ostrogoths under Theodoric.	481. Clovis I, founder of the French monarchy. 486. Battle of Soissons gained by Clovis. 496. Christianity introduced into France.	486. Rise of the feudal system in France under Clovis.	Boethius's *Consolation of Philosophy.*
500-600 A. D. Great disorders in the West. Beginnings of feudalism; power of the clergy increases. In the East, the great reign of Justinian.	502. Invasions by the Persians.			510. Clovis makes Paris his capital.	507. Long wall of Thrace built to keep out Goths. 511. The Salic law in France.	

FROM THE FALL OF ROME TO THE AGE OF MOHAMMED, A. D. 514-617

Characteristics of the Centuries	The Eastern Empire	British Isles	Italy and the Church	France	Arts and Sciences	Literature
	514. Revolt of Vitalianus. Constantinople besieged unsuccessfully by rebels. 528-65. Reign of Justinian; zenith of Eastern Empire. 529. Belisarius defeats the Persians. 532. Riot over outcome of games at circus complicated by political dissension of "blue" and "green" factions. 30,000 killed. 536. Belisarius conquers Vandal Empire in Africa. 540. North Africa, Corsica, and Sardinia annexed to the Eastern empire. 552. Narses rules Italy for the Empire. End of the Ostrogoths. 558. A plague extends over Europe and Asia and lasts about 50 years. 563. Persia defeats the Empire in the East; zenith of Sassanid power in Persia. 565. Death of Justinian.	542(?). Death of King Arthur. 552. Celtic tribes united in north. 559. Saxon heptarchy begins. 563. St. Columba converts the Picts to Christianity. 575. East Anglia a kingdom. 597. St. Augustine introduces Christianity into Britain.	529. Order of the Benedictine Monks instituted. 536. Italy conquered by Belisarius, for Justinian. 539. Milan ravaged by the Goths. 552. Italy ruled by Eastern Empire. Ostrogoth Kingdom ends. 568. Italy conquered by the Lombards. 575. First Monastery built in Bavaria. 597. Gregory, Bishop of Rome, establishes the Papacy.	529. France wins Thuringia. 532. Burgundy conquered by Childebert. 536. Ostrogoths surrender Gaul to the French. 557. Church of St. Germain de Prés built at Paris. 558. Clotaire I unites France. 568. Feudal wars in France; power of the nobles grows.	514. Use of the burning glass in warfare. 529. The schools of Athens suppressed. 532. The Christian era instituted. Rebuilding of great Cathedral of St. Sophia. 536. Manufacture of silk introduced from China into Europe by monks. 550. Manuscript copying in monasteries receives great impulse from Cassiodorus and associates. 559. The Saxon laws promulgated. The king's authority limited by the Wittenagemot. 568. The feudal system established in Italy by the Lombards. Written laws compiled by the Visigoths in Spain.	Writings of Gregory the Great. Code of Justinian, *Corpus Iuris*. Persian literature thrives under the Sassanids. Greek the official language of the Empire.
600-700 A. D. Rise and rapid spread of Mohammedanism from Arabia to India on the east and Carthage on the west. Christianizing of Germany.	600. Eastern Empire spread over Hungary, Poland, and Prussia, under Tiberius II. 602. Invasion by the Persians, who win Asia Minor. 610. Heraclius takes Constantinople and makes himself ruler. 612. Syria ravaged by the Arabs. 614. Jerusalem taken by the Persians.	604. St. Paul's Church founded by Ethelbert of Kent. 617. St. Peter's (now Westminster Abbey) founded.	607. The Pantheon of Rome dedicated to Christianity.	612. France again united. Merovingians and Pepins rule.	607. Brahmanism rises in India. 617. Ethelbert publishes the first code of laws in England.	

THE AGE OF MOHAMMED TO THE TREATY OF VERDUN, A. D. 622-689

Characteristics of the Centuries	The Empire and the Saracens	British Isles	Italy and the Church	France	Arts and Sciences	Literature
	622. The Hegira, or Mohammed's flight from Mecca to Medina. 632. Death of Mohammed. 633. Saracens under Omar take Jerusalem. 673. Saracens, now ruling Asia Minor and all north Africa, fail to capture Constantinople. 680. Kingdom of Bulgaria founded.	622. Northumbria chief kingdom. 633. Mercia chief kingdom. 638. Irish and Scots at war.	625-640. Churches of Jerusalem, Antioch and Alexandria lost to the Christian world by the sweep of Mohammedanism. 664. Synod of Whitby establishes Roman Church in Britain. 680. The Sixth General Council at Constantinople.	628. Dagobert I builds the Church of St. Denis, the sepulture of the French kings. 638. Kingdom divided by Clovis II and Sigebert, King of Austrasia.	622. Painting flourishes in China. 633. Mohammedanism and the power of the caliphs established in the East. 673. Ravenna, Italy, center of classic revival. 678. Greek fire used in war. 689. Japanese laws codified.	*Beowulf*. *The Koran*. Caedmon's *Paraphrase of Scripture*.

THE AGE OF MOHAMMED TO THE TREATY OF VERDUN, 698-841 A. D.

Characteristics of the Centuries	The Empire and the Saracens	British Isles	Italy and the Church	France	Arts and Sciences	Literature
700-800 A. D. Christianizing of Europe continues. Hostile caliphates of Bagdad and Cordova. Mohammedan advance in the West checked by Charlemagne, who nominally restores the Western Roman Empire. Norse ravages begin.	698. Carthage destroyed by the Saracens. 698–716. Anarchic conditions. 709. North Africa subdued by the Saracens. 711. Saracens invade Spain and central Asia. Kingdom of Visigoths destroyed at battle of Guadalquivir. 717. Leo III, Emperor. Saracen attack on Constantinople repulsed. 726–842. Contest over image worship. 746. Saracens defeated by Constantine V. 755. Saracen caliph of Cordova rules Spain. 762. Caliph Almanzor builds Bagdad and makes it his capital. 785. Empire invaded by Harun-al-Raschid, Caliph of Bagdad.	700. Anglo-Saxon octarchy. 705. Law code of Ine of Wessex enforced. 735. Death of the Venerable Bede. 757. Rise of Mercia under Offa. 787. First recorded invasion of the Danes into England, Ireland and Scotland.	698. Picts adopt Christianity. 726. The Emperor Leo forbids image worship. 728. Ravenna rebels over edict prohibiting image worship. 752. The Pope dethrones Childeric, King of France. 754. Lombard invasion repelled. 756. Papal states founded. Donation of Pepin. 772. Adrian I appeals to Charlemagne for help against Lombards. 787. Seventh General Council of Nicaea. Image worship controversy continues. 795. Leo III, Pope, recognizes supremacy of Charlemagne. 800. Charlemagne reforms the Church.	700. Aquitaine, Burgundy, and Provence become separate dukedoms. 714. Charles Martel, Duke of Austrasia. 725. Charles Martel subdues Bavaria. 732. Franks defeat the Saracens at Tours. 751. End of Merovingian line of French kings. Pepin the Short, first of the Carolingian line. 774. Charlemagne, sole ruler of Franks, wins Lombard Italy and repulses the Danes.	698. Christianity greatly extended among the German nations in the north of Europe, but almost exterminated in Africa by the progress of Mohammedanism. 716. The art of making paper introduced by the Arabs. 740. Saracens encourage learning. Ignorance, profligacy, and misery in western Europe 785. Golden period of learning in Arabia under the Caliph Harun-al-Raschid. 793. Foundation of schools in monasteries and cathedrals by Charlemagne.	Golden age of Saracen literature begins. *Romance of Antar.* Alcuin's letters and biographies.
800-900 A. D. Norse ravages continue. Feudal wars. Charlemagne's empire falls to pieces.	800. Spain divided between Saracens of Cordova and Christians of Asturias. 803. The Saracens ravage Asia Minor. Aghlabide caliphs rule north Africa. 813–14. War with Bulgarians. 823. Saracens conquer Crete. 829. Theophilus, Emperor.	813. Egbert, King of Wessex, defeats the Britons. 827. The seven kingdoms united by Egbert. Invasion of the Danes. 840. Kenneth unites the Scots and Picts and becomes king of Scotland.	800. Charlemagne founds the new Western Empire and is crowned at Rome. 824. Christianity carried to Denmark and Sweden. 827. Saracens invade Sicily. 841. Rise of Venetian sea power and art.	800. Charlemagne founds the new Western Empire and is crowned at Rome. 817. Louis I divides the empire. 841. Norsemen conquer Normandy. Franks admit Norman independence.	800. Agriculture and horticulture encouraged by Charlemagne; and in Spain under the caliphs. 802. Arabian horses introduced into Spain. 813. Transient revival of learning under Charlemagne. The golden epoch of Arabian literature. 828. St. Mark's Church at Venice begun. 840. Feudal system in its zenith. Japanese art and trade thrive.	Beginning of the Icelandic skalds. Arabian histories of Mecca and Medina.

FROM THE TREATY OF VERDUN TO THE FIRST CRUSADE, 843-850 A. D.

Characteristics of the Centuries	The Empire and Saracens	The British Isles	Italy and the Church	France and Germany	Spain, Russia and Lesser Countries	Arts and Sciences	Literature
	844. Decline of the caliphate begins. Frequent wars between the Greeks and the Saracens.	844. Irish drive out the Danes. 850. Danes invade England.	843. Lothair King of Italy. 846. The Saracens destroy the Venetian fleet and besiege Rome.	843. Treaty of Verdun, Charles I. (the Bald), King of France. Ludwig I, King of Germany.	843. Ramiro I elected King of Oviedo. 845. Norsemen sack Paris and Hamburg. 850. Persecution of the Christians in Spain.	843. Hereditary nobility and the clergy dominant in matters of state. 850. Roman and common law introduced.	Orfrid's *Gospel Book.*

FROM THE TREATY OF VERDUN TO THE FIRST CRUSADE, 856-921 A. D.

Characteristics of the Centuries	The Empire and Saracens	The British Isles	Italy and the Church	France and Germany	Spain, Russia and Lesser Countries	Arts and Sciences	Literature
		856. Danes settle in England.	856. Louis II at Pavia rules Italy. 858-63. Advance of power of Papacy under Nicholas I. "False Decretals," a forgery, used to increase papal pretensions.			856. Moorish architecture develops.	Bible in Slavonian.
	858. Great war with Saracens. Caliph Omar devastates Asia Minor.			858. Invasion of France by the Germans defeated. 860-900. Seacoast towns and river settlements depopulated by constant pirate raids of Northmen.	860. Gorm unites Jutland and the Danish isles. 862. Ruric the Norman, Grand Duke of Novgorod.	862(?). Norsemen reach Iceland.	
	866. Greek Church separates from Rome. 867. Basil inaugurates the Macedonian dynasty, reviving the Empire. 875-76. Basil defeats Saracens in Cilicia. 878. Saracens driven out of Sicily. 886. Leo VI, Emperor. 890. Southern Italy subject to the Greek Empire.	867. The Danes conquer Northumbria. 878. Alfred the Great defeats the Danes. 886. Alfred takes London.	866. Schism of the Greeks begins. 867. Eighth Council at Constantinople. 877. Saracens take Syracuse. 890. Arnulf, Emperor of Germany, takes Rome.	870. Lorraine divided by France and Germany by Treaty of Mersen (Charles the Bald of France, Ludwig the German of Germany). 875. Rivalry for Imperial crown between Ludwig the German and Charles the Bald. 879. Louis III and Carloman reign jointly. 885. Paris besieged by the Northmen under Rollo. 898. Charles III, King of France. 899. Hungarians invade Germany.	867. Alfonso the Great in Spain. 873. Sancho Inigo, count of Navarre. 875. Harold, first King of Norway. 889. Arpad lays the foundation of Hungary.		*Translations* of Alfred the Great. *Anglo-Saxon Chronicle.*
900-1000 A. D. Norse ravages and conquests continue; also feudal wars. The people in terrible suffering.	907. Russian expedition against Constantinople. 921. Fatimite caliphs rule north Africa.	901. Edward the Elder the first to take the title of "Rex Anglorum."	901. The Normans in France become Christian. 921. Bohemia becomes Christian.	911. Northmen gain permanent foothold in Normandy. 912. Conrad I, Emperor of Germany.	901. Republics of Venice and Genoa founded. 914. Beginning of Golden Age of the Saracens in Spain.	890. Trial by jury; fairs and markets in England. 900. England divided into counties, hundreds, and tithings.	The *Elder Edda.*

FROM THE TREATY OF VERDUN TO THE FIRST CRUSADE, 925-1031 A. D.

Characteristics of the Centuries	The Empire and Saracens	The British Isles	Italy and the Church	France and Germany	Spain, Russia and Lesser Countries	Arts and Sciences	Literature
		925. Athelstane King of England.	940. Italy in anarchy. 955. Baptism of Olga, and conversion of Russia to Christianity. 959. St. Dunstan, Archbishop of Canterbury, attempts to reform the Church.	918-36. Germany ruled by Henry the Fowler. 936. Louis IV, King of France. Otto, German Emperor, expands his domain and repulses the Hungarians.	936. Asturias becomes León. 940. Ramiro, King of León, defeats the Moors at Simancas.	936. Printing used in China. 939. Cordova, in Spain, becomes famous as a center of science, learning, industry, and commerce. 941. The figures of arithmetic brought into Europe by the Saracens. Linens and woolens manufactured in Flanders.	
	941. Romanus gains a naval victory over the Russians. 959. Emperor Romanus II. 961. Crete recovered from Saracens by Nicephorus. 969. Fatimite caliphs rule Egypt and Syria. 975-1025. Period of greatest Byzantine power. Joannes Zimisces, Emperor (969-76) and Basil II (976-1025). Saracens, Bulgarians defeated.	943. Malcolm I, King of Scotland. 955. Dunstan, abbot of Glastonbury, rises to great power. 985. Danish invasion under Sweyn. 997-1015. Ravages of Northmen nearly continuous. Ethelred II, King. 1002. General massacre of Danes ordered by Ethelred.	961-67. Otto the Great of Germany invades Italy, captures Rome and deposes Pope John XII. After period of confusion and war, Otto's son Otto II is crowned emperor by John XIII. 989. Greek Christianity spread in Russia by Vladimir. 999. Hungary becomes a fief of the Church. Gerbert, scholar and mathematician, becomes Pope as Silvester II.	950. Bohemia annexed to Germany. 954. Hugh, Duke of Burgundy and Aquitane. 960. Hugh Capet, Duke of France. 964. Italy united to the empire of Germany. Beginning of Holy Roman Empire. Tuscany becomes a dukedom. 986. Louis V, last of the Carolingians. 988. Hugh Capet, King, and founder of the Capetian line of French kings.	955. Sancho I, King of León. 960. Sung Dynasty rises in China. 973. St. Stephen, King of Hungary, gives it written laws. 981. Vladimir the Great, the first Christian ruler of Russia. 985. Sweyn I of Denmark invades England. 989. Norsemen in Spain. 999. Vikings reach America.	982. Dublin a trade center. Vikings visit Greenland. 986. Venice and Genoa rule the Mediterranean.	Firdusi's *Book of Kings.*
1000-1100 A. D. Increasing and beneficent power of the Church exerted in the direction of order. Normans in Italy and Sicily. The Norman conquest of England. Quarrels between popes and emperors begin.	1005. Mahmud, Ghazni Emperor, rules Persia and north India. 1018. Bulgaria again reduced to a Grecian province.	1005. Malcolm, King of Scotland; Brian Boru, King of Irish. 1016. Edmund II and Canute, King of the Danes, divide rule of England. 1031. Canute subdues Scotland.	1024. John XIX, Pope.	1015. Empire at war with the Poles. 1024. Conrad II, Emperor. 1031. Henry I, King of France.	1015. Russia divided among the 12 sons of Vladimir. 1016. Canute II, King of Denmark. 1019. Norway conquered by Canute. Danish ascendancy. Baltic States Christianized. 1031. Caliphate of Cordova ends.	1024. Musical scale of six notes invented by Guido Aretius.	Avicenna's writings on philosophy and science.

Characteristics of the Centuries	The Church	Eastern Empire	The British Isles	France
1000-1100 A. D. Continued	1041. Normans at Apulia rule South Italy. 1047. Clement II attacks vice of simony in church. Beginning of great age of power of papacy (1046–1305). 1048. Leo IX the first Pope to keep an army. 1054. Excommunication of the Patriarch of Constantinople and the Greeks. 1059. Quarrel between the popes and the German emperors on question of investiture. 1059. Council under Nicholas II decrees that future nominations to papacy be made by the cardinal, i. e., the higher clergy, and that nominee should be of Roman clergy. 1066. Pope Alexander II.	1042. First invasion of the Seljuk Turks. 1043. The Russians invade Thrace and are repulsed by the Greeks. 1054. Theodora, last of the Macedonian dynasty. 1059. Turks and Slavs invade frontiers. 1067. Emperor Romanus III defeated and taken prisoner by the Turks, who rule Asia Minor, Mesopotamia and Persia.	1035. Duncan and Macbeth vie for Scottish throne. 1042. The Saxon line restored under Edward the Confessor. End of Danish rule. 1051. William, Duke of Normandy, visits England. 1066. Harold II, last Anglo-Saxon king, killed at the battle of Hastings. William the Conqueror, King of England and Normandy. 1070. Feudal system centralized under king. 1072. England controls Scotland.	1041. "Truce of God" enjoined by church limits feudal warfare to two days a week. 1060. Philip I. 1066. William, Duke of Normandy, wins the crown of England. 1070. Rise of the troubadours in Provence.
	1073. Quarrel of Pope Gregory VII (Hildebrand) with the Emperor Henry IV. 1077. Submission of Henry IV to the Pope at Canossa.	1074. Syria and Palestine subdued by Saracens.	1076. Rebellion in Normandy.	1073. Normans conquer Maine. 1079. Birth of Abélard.
	1084. Triumph of Henry IV over Gregory. The order of the Carthusians instituted by Bruno. Normans sack Rome. 1095. Peter the Hermit preaches against the Turks.	1081. Alexius I (Comnenus), Emperor. Robert Guiscard invades the empire and defeats Alexius. 1087. Christian kingdom of Jerusalem overthrown by Saladin.	1085. Stern repression of feudal turbulency by William. 1086. The Domesday tax survey. 1087. William invades France. 1093. Malcolm III, of Scotland, invades England and is slain. End of Gaelic rule in Scotland.	1087. War with England. Robert, Duke of Normandy, opposes William Rufus.

PERIOD OF THE CRUSADES,

Characteristics of the Centuries	The Church	Eastern Empire	The British Isles	France
1100-1200 A. D. Quarrels between popes and emperors continue; zenith of papal power; Frederick Barbarossa. Feudal wars lessen; advance in power of kings and of towns at expense of the feudal baronage. The Crusaders. Improved judicial arrangements in England.	1096. The First Crusade. 1100. Study of theology receives new impulse. 1122. Concordat of Worms settling dispute between Empire and Papacy over investitures. 1123. First Lateran or Ninth General Council. 1127. Pope Honorius II makes war against Roger, King of Sicily. 1139. Second Lateran or Tenth General Council. 1147. The Second Crusade begun by Bernard of Clairvaux. 1154. Pope Adrian IV, an Englishman. 1160. Albigenses begin to appear. 1167. Rome taken by Frederick Barbarossa.	1099. Invasion by the Crusaders. Battle of Ascalon. Jerusalem stormed by Godfrey of Bouillon. Establishment of kingdom of Jerusalem. 1104. Battle of Acre. 1109. Tripoli taken by Crusaders. 1124. Tyre taken by Crusaders. 1143. Manuel Comnenus, Emperor, makes peace with the Turks. 1156. Manuel invades Italy but is repulsed. 1172. Turks conquer armies of Manuel.	1100. Henry I, King of England, unites the Normans and Saxons. 1107. Henry quarrels with Anselm, Archbishop of Canterbury, on question of investitures. 1124. David I promotes civilization in Scotland. 1135-54. Reign of Stephen. Civil disorder rampant. 1154. Henry II, King of England. 1158-1164. Reforms of Clarendon; Thomas à Becket, Archbishop of Canterbury. 1168. English invade Ireland. 1172. Henry conquers Ireland.	1096. Many French noblemen take part in the First Crusade. 1147. Louis VII joins the Second Crusade. 1154. Half of France under English rule. 1159. War with the English. 1170. Rise of the Waldenses, heretic Christians.

CENTURY, 1035-95, A. D.

Germany and Italy	Spain	Russia	Lesser Countries	Arts and Sciences	Literature
1039. Henry III defeats the Bohemians and Hungarrians.	1035. Ramiro I, King of Aragon.	1036. Russia reunited by Jaroslav.	1035. Hardicanute, King of Denmark.	1035. Romanesque architecture develops.	
1053. Henry makes his son, Henry, King of the Romans.	1054. Saracens driven from Portugal.	1054. Russia divided. Civil wars and great distress.	1055. The Turks reduce Bagdad and overturn the empire of the caliphs.	1055. First age of scholastic philosophy.	Runic inscriptions.
			1060. Robert Guiscard, Duke of Apulia.	1062. Surnames first used among the English nobility.	
	1065. Alfonso, King of Castile and León.		1065. Jerusalem taken by the Saracens. 1067. Polish conquests in Russia. 1068. Olaf III, King of Norway. 1070. Khmer Empire flourishes in Cambodia.	1068. Shoeing horses introduced into England.	Anselm.
1072. Henry IV quarrels with the Pope over the investiture of bishops. 1073. Saxons revolt.	1073. Christian conquest of Spain under way.	1073. Kiev, Russian capital, raided by Slav nomads.	1073. Maya Empire flourishes in Central America; Chichen-Itza, center of science and architecture.		The Cid.
1076. Civil wars rend the Empire. Henry declares Pope Gregory VII deposed at Council of Worms. Gregory replies by excommunicating Henry. 1077. Henry humbles himself before Pope at Canossa. 1080. Henry degrades the Pope and triumphs.	1076. Time of the Cid.				Domesday Book.
	1085. Toledo taken from the Moors by the Cid.		1084. Bohemia made a kingdom by Henry IV of Germany.		Song of Roland.
1090. The Popes continue their struggle against the empire. 1092. Revolt of Henry's son Conrad.			1090. Sicily taken from the Saracens by Roger the Norman.	1090. Fortresses at Newcastle and Carlisle built.	
	1094. Pedro I, King of Navarre and Aragon. 1095. Pedro wins Valencia.				

A. D. 1096-1273

Germany and Italy	Spain	Russia	Lesser Countries	Arts and Sciences	Literature
			1096. Flanders spreads rule over the Dutch.		William of Poitou, troubadour.
	1104. Alfonso I, King of Navarre and Aragon.	1100. Feudal rulers vie for control.	1105. War between Normans and Slavs in Poland.	1100. Rise of Gothic architecture; era of cathedral building begins.	
1111. Henry V compels the Pope to crown him.					Omar Khayyám.
1119. War between Pisa and Genoa.	1118. Alfonso captures Saragossa.		1119. Charles the Good, Count of Flanders.	1118. Knights Templar instituted.	Scholastic philosophy reaches a high point under Abélard.
1125. Lothair II opposed by Frederick and Conrad, Duke of Swabia. 1134. Albert the Bear conquers Brandenburg. 1139. Dissensions of the Guelphs and Ghibellines.	1139. Saracens defeated at Ourique. Portugal becomes a kingdom.		1139. Independence of Sicily recognized.	1125. Inca kingdom rises in Peru. 1140. Gratian collects the canon law.	
1152. Frederick I, Barbarossa, Emperor of Germany and Italy.		1147. Moscow founded.	1150. Sweden welcomes Christians.	1150. Magnetic needle known in Italy.	Nibelungenlied.
1158. The Emperor Frederick becomes King of Bohemia. 1162. Siege and sack of Milan by Frederick. 1167. Rome taken by Frederick.	1157. Castile and León divided.		1158. Persia taken by the Mongols. 1167. League of the Italian cities.	1158. Bank of Venice established.	
1170. Lombard League holds north Italy against Frederick.	1171. Seville is capital of Arabic Spain.	1168. Russians conquer Kiev.	1171. Saladin, Sultan of Egypt, conquers Syria, Assyria and Arabia. Fatimite dynasty ends.	1168. Colleges of law, philosophy and theology at Paris.	

Characteristics of the Centuries	Italy and the Church	Eastern Empire	The British Isles	France
1200-1300 A. D. Rise of universities and of mendicant friars. Quarrels between popes and emperors still continue; Frederick II of Germany. Last crusades. English liberties recognized by the crown. Hanse League established. Great conquests of Tartars in Asia; they overrun Russia and establish a dynasty at Moscow.	1190. Third Crusade. 1198-1216. Pontificate of Innocent III. Papal power reaches greatest height. 1202. The Fourth Crusade. Constantinople taken. 1215. Fourth Lateran Council, against the Albigenses. Dominican order founded. 1226. Lombard revolt. 1239-48. Struggle of Pope Innocent IV with the Emperor Frederick. 1248. Ghibellines take Florence. 1267. Dominion of Italy passes to Pope Urban IV.	1189. Turks and Slavs overrun the Empire. 1204. The Crusaders plunder Constantinople. Empire divided between Baldwin at Constantinople, Theodore at Nicaea and Alexius at Trebizond. 1229. Christians take Jerusalem. 1242. Mongols invade the Empire. 1244. Jerusalem retaken by Turks. 1260. Emperor Michael Palaeologus recovers Constantinople. 1268. The Mongols invade Asia Minor and take Antioch.	1189. Richard I engages in the Third Crusade. 1193. John attempts to seize the crown in the absence of Richard. 1200. John, King of England. 1208-13. Quarrel of John with Innocent III. John excommunicated. England placed under interdict. 1215. Magna Charta signed at Runnymede. 1216. Henry III, King. 1226. O'Neills and O'Donnells take Ulster. 1242. War with France. 1258. Famous Parliament at Oxford, providing a council of barons. 1265. First Parliament with representative knights of shires. Civil war, led by Simon de Montfort.	1190. Philip Augustus one of the leaders of the Third Crusade. 1204. Touraine, Anjou and Normandy reunited to France. 1214. Battle of Bouvines, Philip II puts down independent barons. 1223. Louis VIII conducts crusade against the Albigenses. 1226. Louis IX (Saint Louis), King. 1244. Albigenses finally crushed. 1258. France expands. Treaty of Correil. 1267. Burgundy falls to the crown.

PERIOD OF THE RENAISSANCE,

Characteristics of the Centuries	Italy and the Church	Eastern Empire	The British Isles	France
1300-1400 A. D. Growth of cities and trade—especially in Italy, where also literature and art, inspired by Dante and Giotto, make progress. Popes at Avignon; papacy now terribly corrupt. Era of Wycliffe: his teaching spreads in Bohemia. Invention of gunpowder. Mariner's compass comes into use in the West.	1274. Fourteenth General Council at Lyons. 1282. The Sicilian Vespers, a ferocious massacre of the entire French population of Sicily. 1296. Struggle of the Church with France. Boniface VIII issues bull excommunicating all princes who tax the church or clergy. 1303. Boniface VIII arrested by agents of Philip IV of France. 1309. Seat of the popes transferred to Avignon. 1311. General Council at Vienna. 1320. A century of war begins between city states of Italy. 1339. Struggle in Rome between the Colonna and the Ursini. 1347. Democracy in Rome under Rienzi, last of the Tribunes.	 1299. Othman invades Nicomedia and establishes the Ottoman empire. 1303. Genoese control trade of Black Sea. 1309. Knights Hospitallers settle in Rhodes. 1320. Civil war. 1326. Orkhan, Sultan of the Turks, takes Nicomedia and Nicaea. 1346. Turkish Empire expands rapidly.	1273. Edward I. 1283. England and Wales united. 1290. Expulsion of Jews. 1291. Bruce and Baliol contend for the crown of Scotland. 1295. Model Parliament of Edward I. 1297. War between England and Scotland. 1300. Silverplate used in England. 1303. William Wallace beheaded. 1306. Robert Bruce proclaimed King of Scotland. War with England continued. 1311. Power of king restricted by Parliament. 1314. Scots defeat the English at Bannockburn. 1327. Peace. Independence of Scotland. Deposition of Edward II. 1338. Struggle for the French crown begins. 1346. Battle of Crécy. 1348. The Black Death.	1276. France at war with Castile. 1285. Philip IV, King. Strengthens monarchy. 1296-1304. Philip quarrels with Pope Boniface VIII over taxation of church property. 1297. Invasion of Flanders. 1302. First convocation of the States-General in France. 1304. War with Flanders. 1306. France the most powerful state in Europe. 1309. Papal residence transferred to Avignon. 1314. Dissolution of Knights Templars. Jacques de Molay, Grand Master, burned. 1136. Philip V. 1332. Revolt of the Flemings. 1338. War with England. 1346. Normandy overrun by England. 1348. The Black Death.

CRUSADES—Concluded

Germany	Spain	Russia	Lesser Countries	Arts and Sciences	Literature
1183. Italy independent by Treaty of Constance. 1190. Henry VI, Emperor and King of Italy, takes Sicily. 1212. Children's crusades. 1215. Frederick II, Emperor. 1215-1265. Ghibelline-Guelph dissension throughout empire. 1226. Teutonic Knights receive feudal powers. 1228-29. Frederick II conducts crusade. Makes treaty with Sultan. 1239. Frederick quarrels with Pope a second time. 1250. Conrad IV, Emperor; feudal barons at war. 1255. Beginning of Hanseatic League.	1188. Alfonso IX, King of León. 1212. The Christians gain the Battle of Navas de Tolosa. 1217. Ferdinand, King of Castile. 1230. Castile and León united by Ferdinand III, who takes large territory from the Moors. 1250. Alfonso the Learned. 1265. Portugal expands.	1186. Incursion of Huns and Poles into Russia. 1200. Riga founded. 1224. Mongolian invasion known as the "Golden Horde." 1236. Second Mongolian invasion. Moscow burned. 1238. Russian independence overthrown by the Tartars. Khan of Kiptchak, Grand Duke.	1186. Saladin directs all his efforts against the Crusaders, but is defeated. 1200. Finland becomes Christian. 1212. Feudal wars in the Netherlands. 1216. Tartary and China overrun by Genghis Khan. 1222. Hungarian liberty assured by Charter of Andrew II. 1242. Mongolian invasion of Europe under Batu Khan. 1258. Mongols win Bagdad. 1268. Kublai Khan builds Peking and makes it his capital.	1190. The Jews become the principal bankers of the world. 1200. Trade guilds rise to power in western Europe. 1200-1400. Age of scholastic philosophy. Nominalist-realist controversy. 1222. University of Padua founded. 1229. Cambridge University founded. 1234. China uses gunpowder in cannon. 1240-1340. Great age of Gothic architecture. 1247. First war fleet in Spain. 1265. Parliament in England.	*Arabian Nights.* Prose *Edda.* Period of the troubadours in France; the minstrels in England; minnesingers in Germany. Sadi, the Persian poet. Roger Bacon writes on natural science.

—A. D. 1273-1492

Germany	Spain	Russia	Lesser Countries	Arts and Sciences	Literature
1273. Rudolf, Emperor, founds House of Hapsburg, revives power of the Empire, quells feudal barons, and takes Austria. 1278. Rudolph defeats rival Ottaker. 1291. Swiss League formed. 1298. Albert I, Emperor. 1304. Rise of the Swiss towns. 1308. Henry of Luxemburg, Emperor. Switzerland independent. 1314. Louis of Bavaria and Frederick of Austria contend for the crown. 1322. Frederick of Austria defeated. 1338. Diet of Frankfort. The estates of the empire defy papal interdict. 1348. The Black Death.	1274. Crown of Navarre passes to France. 1291. James II, King of Aragon. 1300. Dissensions in the Moorish state. 1312. Alfonso XI, King of Castile and León. 1327. Arrival of 200,000 Moors to assist Granada. 1340. Moors defeated at Tarifa.	1290. Khan of Kiptchak wields strong rule in Russia. 1300. Moscow made the capital; Kremlin begun. 1318. Finland invaded by Russians. 1332. Ivan I revives the Russian state. 1347. Zenith of Novgorod.	1283. Pisa and Genoa at war. 1290. Wenceslas, King of Bohemia, takes Cracow. 1299. Foundation of the Ottoman Empire. 1306. Poland reunited. 1307. Swiss Republic founded. Legend of William Tell. 1315. Swiss defeat Austrians at Morgarten. 1319. The Oligarchy of Venice established. 1346. Poland revives under Casimir III.	1273. First patent of nobility granted in France. 1285. Institution of the three great courts of law in England. Cimabue, the first of modern painters at Florence. 1300. Rapid advances in civilization—revival of ancient learning—improvements in the arts and sciences—and general expansion of liberty. 1302. Mariners' compass invented at Naples. 1304. Universities rise in France, Italy and Portugal. 1311. Governmental reforms in England. 1326. Clocks constructed on mathematical principles. 1326. Advanced political theories of Marsiglio of Padua. 1346. Gunpowder used at battle of Crécy. 1347. Manufactures and commerce improve in England.	Thomas Aquinas systematizes theology. *Romance of the Rose.* *Divine Comedy* of Dante. Duns Scotus. Wycliffe's *Translation of the Bible.* William of Occam.

Characteristics of the Centuries	Italy and the Church	Eastern Empire	The British Isles	France
	1354. Rienzi killed; papal dominion restored.	1355. John Palaeologus, Emperor.	1356. Edward, the Black Prince, wins the battle of Poitiers.	1356. King John defeated and taken prisoner at Poitiers. 1358. Revolt of oppressed peasantry (*Jacquerie*).
	1372–79. War between Venice and Genoa. 1378. Schism of the West; Pope Urban VI acknowledged in England; Clement VII in France, Spain and Scotland.	1373. Treaty with the Ottoman emperor. 1381. The emperor a vassal of the Turks.	1376. Death of the Black Prince. English retreat in France. 1381. Wat Tyler leads peasant revolt.	1380. Charles VI, King. 1381. Nobles end independence of the cities.
	1389. Boniface IX and Benedict XIII, Popes.	1389. Bajazet, Sultan of the Turks, defeats Serbs. 1399. Turks win Greece. 1402. Bajazet defeated and made prisoner by Tamerlane, at the battle of Angora.	1385. The Scots, assisted by France, invade England. 1399. Henry IV, King. House of Lancaster begins. Revolts in Ireland. 1406. James I, King of Scotland.	1386. Fruitless attempt to invade England.
1400-1500 A. D. Turks take Constantinople. Revival of learning and advance of art in the west—especially in Italy. End of Tatar rule in Russia. Invention of printing. Gunpowder generally used in war. Formation of modern "middle classes." Maritime discoveries: The cape route to India; the New World. End of the Middle Ages.	1409. The Council of Pisa. 1414. Council of Constance. 1416. Huss and Jerome burned for heresy. 1429. Schism of the West ended. 1431. Medici rise in Florence. 1448. Liberties of the German church are restricted. 1454. Struggle between Cosmo de' Medici and the aristocracy. 1458. The French rule in Genoa. 1463. War of Venice with the Turks. 1469. Lorenzo de' Medici succeeds Piero at Florence. 1471. Increase of the power of the Medici. Rise of learning. Sixtus IV, Pope.	1414. Mohammed revives Turkish power. 1425. Emperor John VII visits Italy to obtain help against the Turks. 1431. Turks spread into southeast Europe. 1444. Vladislas, King of Poland, defeated and killed by the Turks. 1448. Constantine XII, last of the Greek emperors. 1453. Siege and capture of Constantinople by the Turks, ending the Eastern Empire. **Ottoman Empire** 1460. Greece subjected to the Turks. 1464. War with Hungary. 1480. Otranto taken. 1481. Bajazet II, Sultan.	1414. Henry V claims the French crown. 1415. Lollards suppressed. 1422. Death of Henry V. Ascension of Henry VI. War with France. 1444. Truce with France. 1450. Insurrection of Jack Cade. Richard, Duke of York, claims the throne. 1455. Wars of the Roses begin. 1460. James III, King of Scotland. 1461. Edward IV, King. House of York. 1470. Warwick restores Henry VI temporarily. 1471. Warwick and Lancastrians defeated at Barnet. 1475. Edward IV invades France. 1480. War between England and Scotland. 1485. Battle of Bosworth Field ends Wars of Roses. Tudor line begins with Henry VII.	1410. Civil war between Orléans and Burgundy. 1415. Defeat by the English at Agincourt. 1422. Henry VI proclaimed at Paris King of France and England. 1429. Joan of Arc saves Orleans. Charles VII crowned at Reims. 1431. Joan of Arc burned 1444. Henry, King of England, marries Margaret of Anjou. 1453. End of the Hundred Years' War, with England holding only Calais in France. 1461. Louis XI, King. Feudal nobles lose power to the crown. 1475. War between France and Burgundy. 1477. Artois and Burgundy united to France. 1491. Brittany united to the crown.

PERIOD OF THE REFORMATION AND

Characteristics of the Centuries	Italy and the Church	British Isles	Germany	Spain and Portugal	France
1500-1600 A. D.	1492. Alexander VI, Pope. 1498. Savonarola executed at Florence.	1492. Henry VII invades France.	1493. Maximilian I, Emperor.	1492. Conquest of Granada. Jews driven from Spain. 1498. Vasco da Gama reaches India via Cape of Good Hope.	1498. Louis XII. 1499. Conquest of Milan.

RENAISSANCE—Continued

GERMANY	SPAIN	RUSSIA	LESSER COUNTRIES	ARTS AND SCIENCES	LITERATURE
			1353. Establishment of the Ottomans in Europe.		Froissart's *Chronicles*.
1355. Promulgation of the Golden Bull regulating the selection of the emperor.					Boccaccio.
	1365. France at war with Navarre.		1359. Hungarian conquests on the Danube. 1369. Tamerlane makes Samarkand the capital of his new empire.		Wycliffe. Chaucer.
1378. Wenceslas (King of Bohemia), Emperor.	1380. Feudal wars in Spain; English invasions.	1380. Tatar war. Dimitri Ivanovitch checks them at the Don. 1382. Moscow burned.	1380. Venice rules the Mediterranean and grows wealthy from trade with the East. 1385. War between Austria and Switzerland.		
1394. The emperor imprisoned at Prague.		1395. Tamerlane invades Russia. Russia under the Mongol Tartars until 1480.	1386. Battle of Sempach. Swiss defeat Austrians. 1399. Invasion of India by Tamerlane.	1386. Jan van Eyck invented oil painting.	Petrarch.
1400. Rupert, Count of Palatine, Emperor.	1407. John II, King of Castile.			1400. Wood engraving develops.	
1411. Sigismund (King of Hungary), Emperor.		1410. Battle of Tannenburg. Poles and Lithuanians defeat Teuton barons. Power of Teutonic knights broken.	1409. Germans invade Scandinavia. 1414–18. Council of Constance.	1409. University of Leipzig founded. 1411. University of St. Andrews founded.	
	1416. Alfonso V, King of Aragon and Sicily.				
1419–1436. The Hussite wars in Bohemia.				1425. Arts promoted in Italy.	
	1430. War between Castile and Granada.		1430. Aztec Empire rises in Mexico.	1436. Public library, Florence.	
1438. House of Austria (Hapsburg) established. Albert II (King of Bohemia and Hungary), Emperor.		1441. Kiptchak Mongols divide Russia.	1444. Hungarians and Poles overwhelmed by Turks at Varna. 1450. Kingdom of Delhi enlarged.	1447. Library of the Vatican founded. 1450. Flourishing period of trade in western Europe, particularly in Flanders, New Netherlands, Belgium, and a portion of France. Gutenberg's printing press, first in Europe.	Thomas a Kempis, *Imitation of Christ*.
1453. Austria made an hereditary duchy by Emperor Frederick III.	1452. Civil war in Navarre, in which Castile and Aragon join. 1454. Henry IV of Castile.		1453. Poland's independence confirmed. 1454. Poland at war with the Teutonic order. 1456. Hunyadi defeats Turks at Belgrade. 1458. Hungary vigorous under Matthias Corvin.	1460. Copper-plate engraving invented.	
		1462. Ivan the Great takes the title of czar.	1466. Prussia a fief of Poland. 1468. Uzun Hassan, master of Persia. 1470. Sten Sture, Regent of Sweden.	1464. Post offices in France and England.	Villon's *Poems*.
1469. Invasion of the Turks.	1469. Marriage of Ferdinand of Aragon with Isabella of Castile.	1472. Ivan marries Sophia, niece of the Greek emperor.		1473. Printed musical notes. Large library founded at Ofen.	Malory's *Morte d'Arthur*.
1477. Marriage of Maximilian and Mary of Burgundy.	1479. Union of Castile and Aragon. 1488. Diaz claims Cape of Good Hope trade route for Portugal.	1479. Great invasion of the Tatars. 1481. Power of the Tartars annihilated by Ivan III.	1485. Matthias of Hungary takes Vienna.	1477. Watches made at Nuremberg. First book printed in England by Caxton.	

RELIGIOUS WARS, A. D. 1492-1648

RUSSIA	SCANDINAVIA	OTTOMAN EMPIRE	LESSER COUNTRIES	ARTS AND SCIENCES	LITERATURE
		1493. War with Egypt, Hungary and Venice.	1492. America discovered by Columbus.	1493. Printing press at Copenhagen. Era of discovery in the New World begins.	
			1499. Voyage of Amerigo Vespucci. 1502. Sufi sole Sovereign of Persia.	1502. St. Peter's and other great churches built.	More's *Utopia*.

CHARACTERISTICS OF THE CENTURIES	ITALY AND THE CHURCH	BRITISH ISLES	GERMANY	SPAIN AND PORTUGAL	FRANCE
1500-1600 A. D. The Reformation. Immense development of new life in Europe. Power of Spain, and her conquests in America. The monarchy strong in England.	1503. Naples annexed to the Spanish crown. Julius II, Pope. 1506. St. Peter's begun (Rome). 1512. Decline of Borgia power. 1513. Pope Leo X, patron of literature and the arts. Italy under foreign rule. 1520. Luther excommunicated. 1525. Spanish ascendency by the victory of Pavia. 1527. Sack of Rome by soldiers of Charles V. 1540. Order of Jesuits founded by Loyola. 1545. Council of Trent. 1550. Julius III, Pope. 1559. Termination of French wars in Italy. 1569. Florence a grand duchy. 1585. Pope Sixtus V restores the Vatican library.	1509. Henry VIII, King. 1512. War with France. 1513. Battle of Flodden Field; English defeat Scots. 1517. Wolsey, chancellor and cardinal. 1534. Act of Supremacy. Church of England established. 1536. Dissolution of monasteries by Henry VIII. 1543. Invasion of France. 1547. Formal establishment of Protestantism. Edward VI, King. 1553. Mary, Queen of England. Catholicism restored. 1555. Persecution of the Protestants. Ridley, Latimer burned. 1558. Elizabeth, Queen. Rise of the Puritans. Protestant church restored. Jesuits spread over Ireland. 1568. Mary, Queen of Scots, takes refuge in England. Irish unrest grows. 1576. English sea power develops under Drake and Hawkins. 1584. Raleigh's colony in Virginia. 1585. War with Spain. 1587. Mary, Queen of Scots, executed. 1588. Spanish Armada destroyed.	1503. Much of Italy yielded to native princes. 1512. Maximilian divides the empire into 10 circles. 1514. Peasants' revolt in Hungary. 1517. Beginning of the Reformation. 1519. Charles V, King of Spain and Holy Roman Emperor. 1521. Diet of Worms. Luther refuses to recant. 1525. Peasants' revolt crushed. 1529. Turks invade Germany, besiege Vienna. 1543. War with France. 1547. Schmalkaldic War. Insurgent German princes against Charles V. 1555. Peace of Augsburg establishes principle of *cuius regio eius religio;* each prince to decide the religion of his territory. 1556. Charles V abdicates. Empire separates from Spain. 1564. Maximilian II, Emperor. 1576. Rudolph II (King of Bohemia and Hungary), Emperor. 1585. Religious wars renewed.	1503. Spain rules Naples. 1510. Portuguese colonize Brazil, India and Java. 1516. Charles, King of all Spain and the Netherlands. 1519. Conquest of Mexico by Cortez. 1525. Spain and the Empire defeat France and win Italy. 1534. Spain takes Tunis. 1540. Lisbon the market of the world. 1547. The Inquisition set up. 1556. Philip II, King of Spain. 1564. Acquisition of the Philippines. 1567. Duke of Alva, Governor of the Netherlands. 1570. Revolt of Moriscos crushed. 1571. Battle of Lepanto. Spread of Turks halted. 1580. Portugal passes under Spanish dominion. 1588. Defeat of the Spanish Armada.	1510. Council of Tours. 1515. Francis I invades Italy. 1520. Field of Cloth of Gold. 1521. War with Spain and the Empire. 1525. Francis defeated and taken prisoner at Pavia. 1532-1544. Struggle for possession of Italy. Diplomatic intrigues of Francis. Growth of absolutism. 1547. Henry II, King; Catherine de' Medici, Queen. 1552. New war with Charles V. France expands. 1558. Calais recovered. 1562. Religious liberty granted to the Huguenots. Huguenot wars. Era of Catherine de' Medici. 1572. Massacre of St. Bartholomew. 1577. Religious war. 1580. Religious wars sap French strength.
1600-1700 A. D. The Thirty Years' War, at first a life struggle of Roman Catholics and Protestants, results in downfall of Spain and the ascendancy of France, which reached its zenith under Louis XIV. The battle of civil and religious liberty fought out in England under the Stuarts. Rise of modern science and philosophy.	1592. The Rialto and Piazza di San Marco built at Venice. 1600. Giordano Bruno burned for heresy at Venice. 1609. Leghorn becomes the emporium of the Levant trade. 1618. Conspiracy of De Bedmar to subject Venice to Spain.	1600. East India Company formed. 1603. Union of England and Scotland under James I. 1605. Gunpowder Plot. 1607. English settlement at Jamestown. 1609. Smuggling thrives as taxes are raised. 1618. Sir Francis Bacon, lord chancellor. 1620. Pilgrims sail in *Mayflower*.	1594. Turkish invasion renewed. 1608. Protestant union under Frederick the Elector. 1618. Thirty Years' War begins. 1620. Battle of Prague.	1598. Philip III, King of Spain. 1601. Portuguese reach Australia. 1604. Peace with England. 1609. Expulsion of the Moors. 1614. Golden Age of Art in Spain and the Netherlands. 1621. Dutch War.	1588. Revolt of Paris. 1589. House of Bourbon begins with Henry IV. 1590. Siege of Paris raised by the Spaniards. 1598. Edict of Nantes—toleration granted to the Protestants. Peace with Spain. 1608. Quebec founded. 1610. Henry IV assassinated. King Louis XIII. Marie de' Medici regent. 1614. Last assembly of the States-General. 1618. Thirty Years' War begins with France torn by court intrigues.

AND RELIGIOUS WARS—Continued

RUSSIA	SCANDINAVIA	OTTOMAN EMPIRE	LESSER COUNTRIES	ARTS AND SCIENCES	LITERATURE
			1506. Poland under Sigismund the Great.	1505. Trade thrives in the Netherlands.	Erasmus's *Praise of Folly, Colloquies.*
1510. Renewed Tatar invasions. Moscow extends rule over Russia.		1512. Selim I, Sultan.	1511. Cuba conquered. 1512. Florida discovered.		
	1513. Christian II, King of Norway and Denmark.	1514. Persians defeated; Kurdistan added to the empire.	1513. Discoveries of Balboa. 1516. Rio La Plata entered.		Italian literature flourishes; Colonna, Ariosto and Machiavelli.
		1517. Turks win Egypt.	1517. First patent granted by Spain for the importation of Negroes into America. 1519. Spaniards, under Cortez, conquer Mexico.	1517. Luther and the Protestant Reformation.	Sachs founds the German drama.
	1520. Christian, King of Sweden. His barbarities arouse rebellion in Sweden. Massacre in Stockholm. 1523. Gustavus Vasa, King of Sweden. Union of Kalmar dissolved.	1520. Soliman the Magnificent, Sultan. 1521. Belgrade taken.		1522. Circumnavigation of the globe by Magellan.	Luther's *Bible.*
		1526. Invasion of Hungary. Battle of Mohacs. Hungarians routed. 1529. Invasion of Germany. Siege of Vienna.	1526. Mogul dynasty in India founded by Baber.		Rabelais.
	1532. Union of Norway and Denmark. 1535. Reformation sweeps over all the Baltic region.		1533. Spain conquers Peru and Texas. 1537. Calvin establishes theocratic regime at Geneva.	1530. Jorgens invents the spinning wheel for flax. 1535. First English Bible printed.	Calvin's *Institutes of Religion.*
1547. Ivan the Terrible, Czar.			1545. Mines at Potosi discovered. 1548. Jesuits invade Japan.	1545. Vesalius makes important contributions to the study of anatomy. 1548. Orange trees introduced into Europe.	First English Prayer Book.
1552. Mongols quelled. Ivan extends his rule into central Asia and Siberia.		1551. Tripoli and Arabia taken.			Camöens's *Lusiad.* Copernicus's *Revolutions of the Celestial Bodies.*
			1553. Michael Servetus burned at Geneva. 1556. Akbar raises the Indian empire to its greatest splendor.		
	1560. Eric XIV, King of Sweden. 1563. Seven Years' War between Sweden and Denmark.	1559. Military power of the Turks at its greatest height under Soliman. North Africa conquered.	1560. Poland becomes a major power.	1559. Carriages introduced into Paris. 1560. Knives first made in England.	Fox's *Book of Martyrs.*
			1568. Revolt begins in Netherlands.		Tasso's *Jerusalem Delivered.*
1571. Russia devastated by the Tatars, and Moscow burned.	1570. Peace of Stettin.	1570. War with Venice. 1571. Battle of Lepanto. Turkish fleet destroyed.	1570. Siamese state breaks up. Akbar extends his Empire in India.	1573. Titian, colorist, painter, at height of fame.	Ronsard's *Poems.* Cellini's *Autobiography.*
1578. Alliance of Sweden and Poland against Russia.		1578. New war with Persia. Turks win Crimea.	1579. Beginning of the Republic of Holland.	1580. English make paper. 1582. Gregorian calendar introduced.	Spenser's *Faerie Queene.*
1585. Boris Godunov, Regent.	1588. Christian IV, King of Denmark.		1585. Persia acquires great power under Abbas the Great.	1586. Tobacco introduced into Europe.	Montaigne's *Essays.*
			1590. Japan rejects Jesuits, invades Korea.	1590. Microscope invented.	Shakespeare's *Dramas.*
1598. Boris Godunov begins a new dynasty. Peasants made serfs.	1600. Charles IX, King of Sweden.	1595. Power in Hungary declines; revolt of Wallachia.	1605. Jahangir, Mogul Emperor of India.	1600. First opera, Florence. 1606. Gilbert's electrical discoveries. 1608. Telescopes in Holland.	Bacon's *Essays.* Douay Bible. Authorized English version of the Bible.
1609. Poles invade Russia. 1613. Michael Fedorovich, Czar, founds the house of Romanov. 1617. Finland ceded to Sweden.	1609. Gustavus Adolphus, King of Sweden. 1611. War between Sweden and Denmark. 1616. Sweden dominates the North.		1609. Independence of the Netherlands recognized. 1616. China and Manchuria united.	1614. Napier invents logarithms. 1615. Coffee in Venice. 1616. Harvey discovers the circulation of the blood. 1619. Slavery introduced in English-American colonies. 1620. Thermometers invented.	Lope de Vega's *Dramas.* Cervantes's *Don Quixote.*
		1618. Great Persian victory at Shibi. 1620. War with Poland. End of internal wars.			

PERIOD OF THE REFORMATION

Characteristics of the Centuries	Italy and the Church	Great Britain	Germany	Spain and Portugal	France
1600-1700 A. D. Continued	1626. St. Peter's dedicated. 1628. War following death of the duke of Mantua. 1631. Influence of France increases. 1647. Revolt of Naples under Masaniello.	1625. Charles I, King. 1627. War with France. 1628. Petition of Right. 1637. Hampden resists collection of ship money. 1641. Grand Remonstrance of Parliament against Charles I. 1642. Long Parliament convened. 1645. Charles defeated at Naseby. 1647. Fox founds the Society of Friends. 1648. Imprisonment and trial of Charles I.	1628. Victories of Wallenstein. 1629. Edict of Restitution demands that Church property converted by Protestants be restored, thus renewing war. 1630. Gustavus Adolphus invades Germany. 1631. Capture and sack of Magdeburg by imperial soldiers of Tilly. 1632. Battle of Lutzen. 1640. Frederick William of Prussia. 1648. Treaty of Westphalia. Terrible devastation throughout Germany as result of Thirty Years' War.	1625. Naval war with England. 1639. Loss of the Japanese trade. 1640. Portugal regains independence. Revolts in Spain.	1624. Ministry of Cardinal Richelieu. 1627. War with England over the Huguenots. 1628. Siege of La Rochelle 1638. Invasion of Spain. 1640. Turin taken by the French. 1643. Louis XIV, King. 1648. Wars of the Fronde.

FROM THE PEACE OF WESTPHALIA TO

Characteristics of the Centuries	Italy and the Church	Great Britain	Germany	Spain and Portugal	France
1600-1700 A. D. Continued **1700-1800 A. D.** Astounding growth of the British Empire. Government in England more or less representing the will of the people. Development of manufactures in England. Inventions and discoveries. Immense advance in arts and sciences. Independence of the United States. The French Revolution, which powerfully influences social, political and intellectual progress for the next hundred years.	1658. Venice at war with the Turks to keep Eastern trade routes open. 1670. War between Genoa and Savoy. 1676. French yield Messina to Spain. 1685. Venice wins against Turks. 1689. Alexander VIII, Pope. 1690. Italian Protestants win toleration. 1693. 50,000 killed in earthquake and eruption of Mt. Etna, Sicily. 1706. French driven from Italy by Prince Eugene. 1707. All Spanish possessions in Italy abandoned.	1649. Commonwealth under Cromwell. 1652. War with Holland. 1653. Cromwell, Lord Protector. Ireland subdued. 1660. Charles II, King. Stuarts restored. 1663. First English newspaper. 1666. Great fire in London. 1668. Triple alliance of England, Sweden and Holland against France. 1670. Secret Treaty of Dover with France. 1672. War with Dutch. 1679. Habeas Corpus act passed. 1685. James II, King. Rise of the Whigs and Tories. Monmouth's rebellion. 1688. Revolution. 1689. William III, King, and Mary II, Queen. War with France. 1690. Battle of the Boyne. James defeated, returns to France. 1694. Bank of England formed. 1697. General peace. 1698. Irish begin export of linen. 1701. War of the Spanish Succession. 1704. Gibraltar taken by English. 1707. Act of Union of England and Scotland. First united Parliament of Great Britain meets. 1713. Peace of Utrecht. England acquires large American possessions. 1714. George I, King.	1658. Leopold I, Emperor. 1660. Turks push further into the Balkans and Hungary. 1673. War of Austria and France. 1676. General revolt of the Hungarians. 1680. Part of Alsace seized by France. 1683. Siege of Vienna by the Turks. 1686. Buda taken from the Turks. 1687. Joseph I, King of Hungary. 1690. Joseph I, elected King of the Romans. 1697. Victories of Prince Eugene over the Turks. 1701. Hague alliance. Hohenzollern dynasty founded in Prussia. 1707. The Allies defeat France. 1711. Charles VI, Emperor.	1654. Brazil recovered from the Dutch. 1655. War with England. 1660. Portugal and Spain at war. 1673. War with France to protect Holland, part of which is lost. 1683. War with France renewed. 1689. Revolt in Catalonia in favor of France. 1691. Incursion of the French into Aragon. 1700. Death of Charles II precipitates European war of Spanish Succession. 1701. Philip V, King. 1705. Barcelona taken by the Allies. 1713. Philip reunites Spain.	1649. Siege of Paris. 1653. Mazarin enters Paris in triumph. 1659. Peace of the Pyrenees. 1660-1683. Ministry of Colbert. 1667. War with Spain in the Netherlands. 1672. War with Holland. 1678. Peace with Holland and Spain restores tranquillity to Europe. 1680. France the most formidable power in Europe. 1685. Revocation of the Edict of Nantes. Huguenots flee France. 1688. War of the Allies against France. 1693. Naval defeat by English at La Hogue. 1697. General peace of Ryswick between France and the Allies. 1702. Invasion of Holland. Revolt of the Huguenots. 1704. Defeat at Blenheim. 1708. France ruined by constant war. 1713. Peace of Utrecht—perpetual separation of the crown of France and Spain. 1715. Death of Louis XIV; Louis XV, King.

AND RELIGIOUS WARS—Concluded

Russia	Scandinavia	Ottoman Empire	Lesser Countries	Arts and Sciences	Literature
			1628. Dutch East India Company thrives.	1626. Mogul rulers build superb temples in India. 1630. Gazettes first published in Venice.	Grotius's treatises on law. Descartes's Philosophies.
1632. War with Poland. Poles advance to Moscow.	1632. Christina, Queen of Sweden; Oxenstierna, Regent.	1632. Murad revives the power of the Sultan. 1637. Troubles on the Tatar frontier. Bagdad taken by the Turks. 1639. Last invasion of Persia.	1634. English take Bengal from Portuguese. 1639. Great naval victory of Van Tromp, of Holland, over the Spanish fleet at the Downs. 1640. Madras, India, founded.	1634. Japan withdraws from world contacts. 1635. French Academy founded by Cardinal Richelieu. 1639. Printing in America. 1642. New Zealand discovered.	
1645. Rapid progress under Alexis.	1645. Peace between Sweden and Denmark.	1645. War with Venice.	1645. Manchu Dynasty founded, China.		

THE DEATH OF LOUIS XIV. A. D. 1648-1715

Russia	Scandinavia	Ottoman Empire	Other Countries	Arts and Sciences	Literature
		1650. Janissaries rule the Empire.	1653. Peace brings prosperity to the Netherlands.	1654. Air pump invented.	Corneille's Tragedies. Milton's Poems.
1654. Russian victories in Poland and Ukraine.	1654. Charles X, King of Sweden. 1657. War between Denmark and Sweden. 1660. Arts and sciences flourish.	1661. War with Austria. 1662. Invasion of Hungary. 1664. Turks defeated at St. Gotthard by Germans. Morocco independent.	1660. Sobieski, Polish general, defeats the Tartars. 1666. Mogul Emperor Aurangzeb rules India.	1660. Western Europe adopts coffee. 1660. Royal Society founded in England. 1666. Canal of Languedoc built. 1667. Gobelin tapestry manufactured in Paris.	Molière's Dramas. Boyle's Skeptical Chemist.
1667. Peace with Poland. 1671. The Cossacks subjugated.	1671. Christian V, King of Norway and Sweden.	1672. Invasion of Poland.	1674. Sobieski, King of Poland.	1671. Foundation of the Academy of Architecture at Paris.	Bunyan's Pilgrim's Progress.
		1678. First war with Russia.	1678. Mahratta kingdom in India wins Mogul domain.		Locke's Essays. Bossuet's Sermons.
1682. Ivan and Peter, Czars.	1680. Diet of Stockholm. Sweden reorganized.	1682. War with Austria. 1683. Defeat at Vienna by the Poles under John Sobieski.	1686. Deccan, India, conquered.	1681. Museum of Natural History founded in London. Jardin des Plantes founded at Paris. 1684. Differential and integral calculus.	Racine's Tragedies.
1689. Peter the Great.		1687. Revolution in Constantinople, Soliman II, Sultan. 1690. Recovery of Belgrade from the Austrians.	1689. Mogul power at its height in India.		
1692. First trade with China.	1693. The King of Sweden declared absolute.		1695. Brussels bombarded by the French.	1692. First opera in London.	
1698. Rebellion of Streltsi crushed by Peter the Great. 1700. Peter the Great wars with the Northern Powers.	1697. Charles XII begins to reign. Denmark, Poland and Russia form an alliance against Sweden. 1700. Defeat of the Allies at Narva.	1699. Peace of Karlowitz. The Ottoman power in Europe broken.	1700. Chinese conquer Tibet.		Newton's Principia.
1703. St. Petersburg founded. Russian territory extended to the Baltic.	1702-1706. Charles XII sweeps Poland and Russia.		1704. Stanislaus I, King of Poland.	1703. Russian newspaper established at St. Petersburg.	
1708. Charles XII of Sweden invades Russia. 1709. Peter the Great defeats Charles.	1709. Charles XII routed at Pultowa. Swedish power broken.	1710. War with Russia.			Flourishing period of French literature.
1716. Finland conquered.	1715. Charles returns to Sweden.			1714. Rise of commerce in Austria.	

CHARACTERISTICS OF THE CENTURIES	ITALY AND THE CHURCH	GREAT BRITAIN	GERMANY	SPAIN AND PORTUGAL	FRANCE
1700-1800 A. D. Continued	1718. Sicily and Naples united.	1718. War with Spain. 1720. South Sea Bubble; financial panic.	1718. Quadruple alliance against Spain. 1720. Prussia grows under Frederick William.	1718. Spanish power wanes.	1718. The Quadruple alliance against Spain. 1720. Mississippi Bubble.
		1727. George II, King of England.		1725. Spain and Austria allied.	1726–43. Ministry of Cardinal Fleury.
	1730. Clement XII, Pope.	1739. War with Spain. 1743. Fall of Walpole.	1733. War of the Polish Succession. 1740. War of the Austrian Succession. Maria Theresa rules Bohemia and Hungary.	1734. Conquest of Sicily and Naples by Don Carlos.	1733. The Polish Succession involves France in war. 1740. The Austrian Succession brings war. 1744. War with England and Austria.
	1744. Italy invaded by the French and Spaniards. 1746. French and Spaniards driven from Lombardy by Austrians.	1745. Troubles in Scotland. Invasion of Young Pretender. 1756. Alliance with Prussia. 1760. George III, King.	1745. Francis I, husband of Maria Theresa, Emperor. 1756. Seven Years' War—Austria, France and Russia against Prussia and England. Frederick the Great, although reduced to desperate straits, ultimately triumphs.	1746. Ferdinand VI, King. 1755. Earthquake at Lisbon kills 50,000. 1756. New era of prosperity.	1747. War with Holland. 1760. Loss of all Canada.
	1762. Temporal power of the Popes restricted.	1762. War with Spain. 1763. Peace of Paris. Canada and East Louisiana won by England.		1762. Spain invades Portugal, wins Louisiana.	1764. Jesuits expelled.
				1767. Jesuits expelled from Spain.	1770. Marriage of the dauphin to Marie Antoinette.
	1773. Jesuits expelled from Rome.	1775. War with the American Colonies. 1776. British army takes possession of New York. Hessians hired for service in America. 1781. Surrender of Cornwallis at Yorktown. 1783. Treaty of Versailles. Independence of the United States acknowledged.	1772. First partition of Poland. 1778. War of the Bavarian succession. Bavaria seized by Germany. 1786. Death of Frederick the Great.	1783. California settled. 1788. Spain joins in war against England. 1788. Charles IV, King.	1774. Louis XVI, King. Turgot unsuccessfully attempts financial reforms. 1776. Franklin in Paris. 1778. Alliance with America. 1780. French, Dutch and Spanish leagued against English. 1783–87. Financial ministry of Calonne. Deficit increases. 1788. Financial crisis. States-General summoned.
		1793. First coalition against France directed by England.	1792. War with France. 1793. First coalition against France. Prussia wins part of Poland.		1789. French Revolution begins. 1792. War with Germany. France declared a republic. 1793. King and Queen beheaded. Reign of Terror. 1795. Napoleon Bonaparte commands the army.
	1796-1797. Napoleon's Italian campaign. 1798. Roman republic proclaimed by the French. 1802. Napoleon, President of the Italian Republic.	1798. Nelson destroys French fleet near Alexandria. 1798. Second coalition against France. 1801. Union of England and Ireland. 1803. Successful war in India.	1797. Napoleon's Austrian campaign. 1800. France defeats Austria.	1796. Spain joins France in war with England. 1803. Napoleon dominates Spain.	1796. War in Italy. 1797. Napoleon in Austria. 1798. Expedition to Egypt. 1800. Battle of Marengo. 1802. Napoleon, President of the Italian Republic. War with England. 1804. Napoleon I, Emperor of the French.
1800-1900 A. D. Industrial revolution. Democratic institutions spread in Europe. Rise and fall of Napoleon. Formation of German Empire. Colonization of Africa and Asia by European Powers. Rapid growth of the United States.	1805. Napoleon crowned King of Italy. 1808. Rome annexed by Napoleon to the kingdom of Italy.	1805. Napoleon defeated at Trafalgar. 1806. Fourth coalition against France. 1808. Wellesley invades Spain.	1804. The emperor of Germany becomes emperor of Austria. Holy Roman Empire ends. 1806. Confederation of the Rhine. 1809. Peace of Vienna.	1805. Battle of Trafalgar. 1808. Madrid taken by the French. Joseph Bonaparte, King.	1805. Battle of Austerlitz. 1806. Battle of Jena. 1807. War with Russia. Invasion of Portugal. 1809. Battle of Wagram. 1810. Continental peace except with Spain.
		1812. War with the United States.	1812. Austria in alliance with France against Russia. 1813. War of German Independence.	1812. Battle of Salamanca.	1812. Russian campaign. 1813. Battle of Leipzig.
	1814. Fall of Napoleon. Kingdom ceases. Jesuits re-established.			1814. Ferdinand VII restored.	1814. Allies enter Paris. House of Bourbon restored. Napoleon exiled to Elba.
	1815. Italian states revived; Austria dominates Italy.	1815. British defeated at New Orleans. Wellington victorious at Waterloo. The Allies enter Paris.	1815. German League. Congress of Vienna. Prussia wins more territory.	1815. American colonies set up independent republics.	1815. Hundred Days' War. Battle of Waterloo. Napoleon, defeated, abdicates.

THE FALL OF NAPOLEON, A. D. 1715-1815

RUSSIA	SCANDINAVIA	OTTOMAN EMPIRE	OTHER COUNTRIES	ARTS AND SCIENCES	LITERATURE
	1718. Charles XII invades Norway and is killed.	1717. Turks lose Belgrade.			Pope, Defoe and Swift.
1721. Peter assumes the title "Emperor of all the Russians."	1721. Peace of Nystadt ends war between Sweden and Russia.	1723. Turks and Russians attempt to dismember Persia.	1723. Jesuits expelled from China.	1721. Inoculation for small-pox introduced.	
1727. Treaty with China.					
1730. Peter II, last of the Romanovs, dies.	1730. Christian VI, King of Denmark.	1734. Turks driven from Persia by Nâdir Shah.	1733. Frederick Augustus II, King of Poland.	1728. Behring Strait discovered.	Montesquieu and Voltaire.
1740. Ivan VI, Czar.	1741. Swedes driven out of Finland by Russians.	1740. Renewed invasion of Turkey by Persia.	1739. India invaded by Persia. Delhi sacked.	1740. Linnaeus begins systematic teaching of natural history.	
		1745. Defeat of Turks at Kars.	1744. Hostilities between the French and English in India.		
			1746. Dutch take Java.		
1756. Russia joins Seven Years' War against Prussia.			1756. Calcutta taken by the Nabob of Bengal. English massacred.	1750. Franklin's discoveries in electricity.	Voltaire, Diderot and Rousseau.
1762. Catherine II reigns.			1761. China wins Mongolia.	1761. Potatoes first planted in France.	
			1765. Establishment of the English in India.		
1768. War with the Ottoman Empire.	1772. Despotism reestablished in Sweden by Gustavus III.	1768. Egypt independent under the Mamelukes.	1766. Power of the Mamelukes revived in Egypt under Rodyan and Ali Bey.	1767. First spinning machine in England.	Lessing, Burke, Blackstone, Goldsmith and Adam Smith.
1774. Revolt of the Cossacks.		1772. Poland dismembered.	1772. Poland dismembered.	1768–79. Voyages and discoveries in the Pacific of James Cook.	
1776. Potemkin dominates Russia.			1774. Warren Hastings first governor-general of India.	1769. Watt improves steam engine.	Kant's critical philosophy.
			1776. Lord Pigot governor general of the East Indies.	1774. Priestley discovers oxygen.	
				1781. Balloon invented.	Gibbon's History.
				1782. Lavoisier founds modern chemistry.	
1787. War with the Turks. Russia expands to the South.		1783. Russia takes Crimea.	1788. English take Australia.	1783. Fitch operates steamboat on Delaware River.	
		1787. Disastrous war with Austria and Russia.			
	1792. Gustavus IV, King of Sweden.				
		1794. Bulgaria devastated.	1794. Polish revolt quelled.	1793. Metric system of weights and measures.	Burns's Poems.
			1795. Final partition of Poland.	1796. Jenner discovers vaccination.	
1796. Unsuccessful war with Persia.			1797. Swiss revolution. Helvetian Republic declared.	1797. Malthus announces his doctrine.	Schiller's works.
		1798. War with the French in Egypt.			
1801. Alexander, Czar.	1801. After destruction of Danish fleet by English at Copenhagen Denmark and Sweden accede to the alliance between England and Russia.	1803. Insurrection of Mamelukes at Cairo.	1801. Shinto forces dominate Japan.	1801. Volta's battery invented.	Goethe's Dramas and Poems.
1804. War with Persia.				1804. Code Napoléon reforms French law.	
1805. Russia joins the coalition against France.			1806. Louis Napoleon, King of Holland.		
1807. Treaty of Tilsit.	1808. Finland invaded by the Russians.	1807. War against Russia and England.		1807. Fulton's steamboat.	Cuvier's Natural History.
	1809. Charles XIII, King of Sweden.	1809. Russians defeated.		1808. Lithography invented.	
				1810. First steamboat built in Europe.	
1812. Invasion of Napoleon. Moscow burned. French Grand Army destroyed in retreat.		1812. Mohammed Ali rules Egypt.	1812. The Poles declared a nation by Napoleon. Diet of Warsaw.		Chateaubriand.
		1813. Serbia invaded by Turkish army.	American war with England.		
	1814. Union of Sweden and Norway as two kingdoms under one monarch.	1814. Malta falls to England.		1814. Steam carriages and gas lights used in England.	
1815. The Holy Alliance formed.			1815. William I, King of the Netherlands.	1815. Safety lamp invented by Davy.	Wordsworth's Poems.

Characteristics of the Centuries	United States	Great Britain	Prussia, Austria	France	Spain and Portugal
1800-1900 A. D. Continued	1816. U. S. Bank incorporated.	1816. Bombardment of Algiers. The Bey compelled to abolish slavery.	1815-48. Era of reaction under Metternich.		1815. Union of Portugal and Brazil under John VI.
	1817. James Monroe, President.				1817. Slave trade abolished.
	1818. Great Lakes Treaty with England.	1820. George IV, King. Cato street conspiracy.	1819. Carlsbad Resolutions suppressing freedom of education.	1818. France joins in Holy Alliance.	1820. Revolutionary movement put down with help of Holy Alliance.
	1821. Monroe re-elected. Missouri compromise bill passed.	1821. Trial of Queen Caroline.	1821. Insurrection in Moldavia and Wallachia.	1821. Death of Napoleon at St. Helena.	
	1823. Monroe Doctrine.				
				1824. Charles X, King.	
	1829. Andrew Jackson, President.	1828. Wellington ministry. Irish disturbances.			
		1830. William IV, King. Difficulties with China.		1830. Algiers taken by the French. Revolution. Louis Philippe, King.	
		1832. Reform bills prevent serious revolts.			
		1834. Gradual abolition of Negro slavery in West Indies.	1833. Zollverein (German customs union) formed.	1833. Peerage abolished.	1833. Isabella II, Queen of Spain. Portugal a constitutional monarchy.
	1837. Independence of Texas acknowledged. Martin Van Buren, President.	1837. Victoria, Queen.			1837. The monasteries in Spain dissolved.
		1838-48. People's Charter agitation.	1840. Frederick William, King of Prussia.	1840-48. Reaction and corruption under Guizot.	
	1841. Death of Harrison, and succession of Tyler.	1840. War with China over the opium trade. War in Syria; Great Britain an ally of Austria and Turkey.			1842. Insurrection in Barcelona.
	1845. Texas annexed to the U. S.; Polk, President.	1845. Severe Irish famine.		1844. War with Morocco.	
	1846. War with Mexico. The Oregon Treaty with Great Britain, settling the northwestern boundary of the U. S.	1846. Repeal of the English corn laws.			1846. Civil war in Portugal.
	1848. Gold discovered in California.	1848. Civil war in Ireland. Habeas Corpus Act suspended.	1848. Revolution in Hungary. Francis Joseph, Emperor.	1848. Abdication of Louis Philippe, and a republic proclaimed. Louis Napoleon, President. Bloody insurrection in Paris.	
	1849. Zachary Taylor, President. Railroad from Boston to New York.		1849. New Constitution promulgated for Austria.		
	1850. Attempted invasion of Cuba by filibusters. Texas boundary settled. Fugitive Slave Law passed.	1850. The war in Lahore ended. The Punjab annexed to the British Crown. English forces defeated in South Africa by the Kafirs.	1850. Hanover withdraws from the Prussian alliance. New constitution for Prussia. Hungarian revolt under Kossuth put down.		1851. Death of Godoy, "Prince of Peace."
				1852. Louis Napoleon declared Emperor.	
	1853. Franklin Pierce, President.	1853. Kafir war ended.			
	1854. Treaty with Japan.	1854. Crimean War. Treaty of alliance with France.		1854. Crimean War against Russia.	
	1855. Panama Railroad completed.	1855. British fleet bombards and partially destroys Canton, China.			
			1856. Hungarians granted amnesty.	1856. Peace with Russia.	
	1857. Dred Scott decision. James Buchanan, President. Great financial panic.	1857. Rebellion in India begins. King of Delhi proclaimed Sovereign of India.			
		1858. Property qualification for members of Parliament abolished.			
	1859. John Brown's raid on Harpers Ferry.		1859. Austria at war with France and Sardinia.	1859. War with Austria.	1859. War with Morocco.
		1860. Rebellion in India subdued.		1860. Era of colonial expansion in Africa and the Pacific.	1860. Defeat of the Moors.
	1861. Secession of the Confederate States. Opening of the Civil war, 1861-1865. Abraham Lincoln, President.	1861. Dispute with United States over arrest of Mason and Slidell.	1861. William I, King. New constitution for Austria. Civil and political rights granted Protestants.		
	1863. Gettysburg; Vicksburg turns tide of war in favor of Union. Draft riots in New York city.			1863. The French occupy Mexico.	
			1864. Austria and Prussia at war with Denmark. Schleswig-Holstein seized.	1864. Maximilian accepts Mexican crown.	1864. Rupture with Peru.
	1865. Assassination of President Lincoln; Andrew Johnson, President.	1865. Fenian outbreaks in Ireland.			1865. Dispute with Chile. Valparaiso shelled.
	1866. Civil Rights Bill passed.		1866. Prussia and Austria at war. Battle of Sadowa. First parliament of the German Confederation.	1867. French forced to withdraw from Mexico.	

OF THE FIRST WORLD WAR—A. D. 1815-1914

Italy and Greece	Russia, Scandinavia	Other Countries	Arts and Sciences	Literature
1815. Kingdom of Two Sicilies restored.	1815. Poland united to Russia.		1815. The abolition of the slave trade by the Congress of Vienna.	Scott's *Novels*.
		1817. The Mahratta power completely overthrown in India by the British.	1817. Public schools established in Russia.	Byron, Shelley, Coleridge.
		1819. Bolivar, President of Colombia, South America. Peru and Guatemala independent. Brazil independent.	1819. The steamship *Savannah* makes the first trip across the Atlantic.	
1821. Austrian invasion of Italy. 1822. Greek revolution. Declaration of Independence.		1822. Iturbide, Emperor of Mexico.		
		1824. Mexico a republic.	1824. Inland navigation develops in Europe and United States. Railway opened in England.	Vast increase in periodical literature.
	1826. Nicholas I crowned at Moscow. War against Turkey.	1826. Missolonghi and Athens taken by the Turks.		
		1829. Venezuela independent.		Balzac's *Novels*.
	1830. Polish revolt put down. Armenia conquered.	1831. Belgium independent, Leopold I, King.	1831. Reaper invented. Faraday discovers electro-magnetic induction.	Poe's *Poems* and *Tales*.
1832. Kingdom of Greece founded.		1833. Santa Anna, President of Mexico.	1832. Trade-unions spread in Europe.	Hawthorne's writings.
		1839. Turkey at war with Egypt. 1840. William I abdicates as King of Holland.	1837. Morse patents the telegraph. 1840. Penny postage in England.	Emerson's *Essays*. Pushkin, Heine.
1843. King of Greece accepts a constitution.		1842. Insurrection in India. China opens treaty ports.	1842. Ether anesthesia introduced.	Victor Hugo's works.
		1845. China makes trade treaty with United States.		
1848. Rising of the great Italian cities in revolution.	1848. Revolt of Holstein against Denmark is supported by Frederick VII of Prussia.	1847. Soulouque, President of Haiti. 1848. Holland receives a constitution. Insurrection in Ceylon. Hungary declared independent.	1847. Great canal from the Durance to Marseilles completed. Railroad building in Germany. Sewing machine invented and patented.	Gogol, Flaubert.
1849. Victor Emmanuel, King. Rome surrenders to the French; Garibaldi leaves city. Bourbon rule begins.			1850. Great agitation on slavery in United States.	Longfellow's *Poems*. Darwin, Tennyson, Dickens and Browning.
		1851. Discovery of gold in Australia. Dutch expand in the East Indies.	1851. Daguerre makes important contributions to photography. Railway between Moscow and St. Petersburg opened.	George Eliot, Lowell and Ruskin.
		1852. Buenos Aires taken by the liberating army. War between the Turks and Montenegro.		
1854. Sardinia joins Crimean War.	1853. War declared against Turkey. 1854. War with France and England. Siege of Sebastopol.	1853. Turkish-Russian War. 1854. Commercial treaty between United States and Japan.	1853. Perry's expedition to Japan.	
1855. Important concordat between Italy and Austria.	1855. Alexander II, Emperor. 1856. Evacuation of Crimea.	1855. Santa Anna abdicates the presidency of Mexico. 1856. China at war with England and France.	1855. Bessemer's steel process patented.	Spencer's *Philosophy*.
1859. War with Austria.	1858. Partial emancipation of the serfs. 1859. Charles XV, King of Sweden and Norway.	1858. Massacre of Christians in Turkey. Suez Railroad completed.	1859. Telegraphic communication between India and England. Petroleum discovered in Pennsylvania.	Huxley, Renan and Dumas.
1860. Garibaldi lands in Sicily and assumes dictatorship. Sicily and Naples liberated.			1860. Pony express between Mississippi and Pacific Coast.	
1861. Victor Emmanuel II, King of Sardinia, first King of Italy.	1861. Russian serfs emancipated.	1861. Canton restored to the Chinese by the French and English.		
1862. Insurrection in Greece.			1863. Abolition of slavery in the United States.	Blackmore's *Lorna Doone*.
1864. Florence made the capital of Italy.	1864. Russia drives Caucasian tribes into Turkey. Schleswig-Holstein seized by Prussia and Austria.	1864. Nankin, China, taken by Gordon for the Imperialists.	1864. Red Cross organized at Geneva.	
1865. Ionian Isles made over to Greece.			1865. Antiseptic surgery introduced.	
1866. Austrian war. Venetia proclaimed a part of Italy.	1866. Inauguration of trial by jury in Russia. War with Bokhara wins Russia more of central Asia.	1866. Fenians invade Canada. Repulsed.	1866. Open-hearth steel process introduced. Successful Atlantic cable.	Meredith, Taine, Arnold, Wallace.

CHARACTERISTICS OF THE CENTURIES	UNITED STATES	GREAT BRITAIN	PRUSSIA, AUSTRIA	FRANCE	SPAIN AND PORTUGAL
1800-1900 A. D. Continued	1867. General amnesty proclamation. Alaska bought. 1869. U. S. Grant, President. Union Pacific railway opened for traffic. 1869–76. Era of reconstruction. Carpetbaggers. Ku-Klux Klan.	1867. Reform bills. 1870. **Irish Land Act** passed.	1867. Autonomy for Hungary announced. Emperor crowned King of Hungary. 1870. War with France. Battle of Sedan.	1869. New constitution promulgated. 1870. War declared against Prussia. Battle of Sedan. Surrender of Metz.	
		1873. Payment of Alabama claims to the United States. 1875. Suez Canal bought.	1871. King of Prussia proclaimed Emperor of Germany. 1871. William I, Emperor; Alsace-Lorraine taken.	1871. Capitulation of Paris. Peace ratified. 1873. Marshal Mac-Mahon, President. 1874. Cambodia taken.	1874. Alfonso XII, King. 1875. Civil war.
	1877. R. B. Hayes, President. 1879. Specie payment resumed. 1881. James A. Garfield, President, assassinated; Chester A. Arthur, President. 1885. Grover Cleveland, President. Apache Indian War. 1886. Haymarket riots, Chicago. 1889. Benjamin Harrison, President. Johnstown flood.	1877. Queen Victoria proclaimed Empress of India. 1885. Wars in Sudan. 1887. Queen's Jubilee. 1889. Great labor strikes.	1878. Congress of Berlin to settle eastern problems. Occupation of Bosnia by Austria. 1882. Triple Alliance, Germany, Austria, Italy. 1885. Germany acquires colonies in Africa. 1888. Accession and death of Frederick III. William II, Emperor.	1881. Protectorate of Tunis. 1883. Madagascar colonized. 1890. War in Africa.	
		1890. Stanley returns from Africa.	**GERMANY, AUSTRIA** 1890. Bismarck dismissed in Germany. 1891. Triple Alliance renewed. 1893. Anti-Jesuit law repealed. 1894. Treaty with Russia. 1895. Kiel Canal opened. 1896. Germans adopt new code of laws.	1891. Panama Canal scandals. 1894. Dreyfus convicted of treason. 1897. Fashoda incident.	1893. War in Morocco.
	1892. Homestead steel strike. 1893. Grover Cleveland, President. 1894. Coxey's "Army." Labor troubles. Severe business depression. 1897. William McKinley, President. 1898. War with Spain. Hawaii annexed. 1899. Cuba, Puerto Rico and Philippines won.	1894. Manchester ship canal opened. 1895. Federation of Australia effected. 1896. South African troubles begin. 1897. Queen's Diamond Jubilee. 1899. War with Boers in South Africa.		1899–1906. Dreyfus case agitates nation.	1898. Spain loses American war.
1900 to date Japan becomes a world Power. Great commercial expansion in France, Germany, Japan, Great Britain and America. Power of the press grows. World War involves the principal nations.	1901. Philippine revolt quelled. 1902. Cuban independence effected. 1904. Panama Canal work begun. 1906. Earthquake at San Francisco. 1908. Financial panic. 1911. Standard Oil Trust ordered broken up by Supreme Court. 1912. Theodore Roosevelt bolts Republican Party. Woodrow Wilson, Democrat, elected. 1913. Federal Reserve Act.	1901. Edward VII, King. 1902. Alliance with Japan. 1903. Irish land bill passed. 1908. Old Age Pension law adopted. 1910. George V, King. 1912. Minimum wage law.	1902. Czechs trouble Austria. 1904. German troops defeated in Africa. 1905. Germany disturbs Morocco question. 1908. Austria absorbs Bosnia and Herzegovina.	1904. Disestablishment of Roman Catholic Church. 1905. Morocco partitioned. *Entente Cordiale* with Great Britain. 1906. Dreyfus cleared. 1908. Morocco further invaded. 1913. Poincaré, President.	1902. Alfonso XIII, King of Spain. 1908. Manuel II, King of Portugal. 1910. Portugal becomes a republic.

CHARACTERISTICS OF THE CENTURIES	UNITED STATES	GREAT BRITAIN	PRUSSIA, AUSTRIA	FRANCE	SPAIN AND PORTUGAL
Era of educational and social philanthropies.	1914. Intervention in Mexico. 1915. Sinking of *Lusitania* alarms nation. 1916. Villa raids New Mexico. 1917. United States joins Allies in war. 1918. Men and money rushed to Europe. 1919. Prohibition in effect. 1920. Women granted the vote. 1921. Harding, President. 1924. Strict immigration law.	1914. Joins Allies in war against Germany. 1915. Naval victory over Germany. 1916. Irish revolt. 1917. Women granted the vote. Food shortage caused by submarine war. 1921. Irish revolt flames. 1922. Irish Free State formed.	1914. Germany and Austria in war against Allies. 1915. Submarine warfare begun. 1916. New drive to Paris pushed. 1917. Germans win in Russia. 1918. Republics formed in Germany, Austria. 1920. Horthy controls Austria. 1922. German Republic quells opposition. 1924. Reparation plan put in operation.	1914. Germans invade France. 1915. Bitter fighting in France. 1916. French power weakens. 1917. Armies in the trenches. 1918. World War ends. 1919. Peace arranged at Versailles. 1922. Order and trade restored after war. 1923. Military occupation of Ruhr. 1924. Serious inflation.	1915. Revolts in Portugal. 1919. New revolts in Portugal. 1921. Disasters in war in Morocco stir Spain.

OF THE FIRST WORLD WAR—Concluded

Italy and Greece	Russia, Scandinavia	Other Countries	Arts and Sciences	Literature
1869. Vatican Council opened at Rome. 1870. Rome is made the capital of Italy. Pope forcibly deprived of temporal sovereignty. Doctrine of papal infallibility adopted.	1867. Alaska sold to the United States. 1871. Electric telegraph between Russia and Japan.	1867. Egypt claims independence. Mexico evacuated by French; native rule restored. 1870. Fenian raid in Canada. 1871. Feudalism ended in Japan.	1868. Suez canal formally opened. 1870. Railway from Calcutta to Bombay. Mont Cenis Tunnel completed. 1873. European calendar introduced into Japan.	Turgenev, Dostoevski.
1878. Humbert, King. Leo XIII, Pope. 1882. Death of Garibaldi. Triple Alliance with Germany and Austria. 1885. War with Ethiopia. 1887. Alliance of Italy with Austria-Hungary and Germany. 1891. Triple Alliance renewed. 1893. Pope's Jubilee at Rome.	1877. Russian War against Turkey. 1878. Spread of Nihilism in Russia. 1881. Alexander III, Emperor, following assassination of Alexander II. 1885. Ship canal from St. Petersburg to Cronstadt opened. 1888. Central Asian railway opened. 1890–1892. Famine in Russia.	1876. First Chinese railway. Revolt against Turks in Bulgaria. 1877. Diaz, President of Mexico. 1878. Montenegro, Serbia and Rumania independent. 1882. Japanese constitution. 1883. Korea independent. 1886. Upper Burmah annexed to British India. 1890. First Japanese Parliament opened. 1893. Kruger, President of (Dutch) Transvaal in South Africa.	1876. Telephone invented by Bell. 1878. Edison's incandescent lamp. 1882. Pasteur finds disease bacilli. Panama Canal begun by French. 1884. Linotype machine. 1885. Revised version of Old Testament published. 1886. Statue of Liberty unveiled, New York harbor. 1889. Eiffel tower in Paris. 1891. Canadian Pacific Railway completed. Rotary steam turbine. 1892. Gasoline internal combustion engine. Electric induction motor.	Ibsen, Tolstoy, Björnson. Mark Twain, Whitman, Zola. Hardy, Chekhov, Gorki. Brandes's *Essays.*
1896. Ethiopia routs Italy at Adowa.	1894. Nicholas II, Czar. 1895. Jews driven from Russia. 1896. Census in Russia. 1897. Control of Siberia liberalized. 1898. Russia leases Port Arthur.	1894. China and Japan at war; Japan wins Korea and Formosa. 1895. Belgium acquires African colony. Cuban revolution begins. 1896. European states divide Sudan. 1897. Turko-Grecian war. 1898. United States annexes Hawaii. 1899. British and Dutch at war in South Africa. "Open Door Policy" in China adopted. 1900. Boxer outbreak in China quelled by foreign troops.	1895. X rays discovered. 1898. Radium discovered. 1901. First radio signal sent across Atlantic.	Mitchell, James, Howell. Kipling's *Stories* and *Poems.*
1900. Victor Emmanuel III, King of Italy. 1903. Pope Pius X. 1908. Sicilian earthquakes. 1910. Greek constitution revised. 1911. Italy wins Tripoli from Turkey. 1912. Greece wins larger area.	1902. Trans-Siberian Railway opened. 1904. War between Japan and Russia. 1905. Russia yields Manchuria to Japan. 1906. First Russian Duma.	1902. Cuba independent. 1903. Panama independent. 1904. Japan defeats Russia and begins era of Asiatic aggression. 1905. Norway independent of Sweden. 1910. Montenegro a kingdom. 1911. Revolt in Mexico. 1912. Balkan uprising drives Turkey from Europe; China becomes a republic.	1902. The Hague Arbitration Court opened. 1903. Wrights' airplane flies. Motion pictures developed. 1906. Simplon tunnel opened. 1909. Bleriot flies English Channel. 1910. Discovery of North Pole announced. 1911. South Pole reached.	Lagerlöf, Strindberg, Wilde. Tagore, France, Conrad.

TO THE PRESENT: 1914 AND AFTER

Italy and Greece	Russia, Scandinavia	Other Countries	Arts and Sciences	Literature
1914. Italy deserts Triple Alliance. 1915. Italy joins Allies. 1916. Italian armies defeated. 1917. Revolt in Greece. 1918. World War ends. 1919. D'Annunzio seizes Fiume.	1914. Russia joins Allies in World War. 1915. Russian armies disorganized. 1916. Death of Rasputin. 1917. Bolshevist revolt in Russia. 1918. Separate peace, Russia and Germany.	1914. Japan joins Allies in World War. 1915. Bulgaria and Turkey join Germany in World War; Armenians massacred. 1916. Rumania joins Allies but is conquered by Austria. 1917. British win Palestine. 1918. Hungary a republic. 1919. Czechoslovakia, Yugoslavia, Poland and small Baltic states independent. 1920. League of Nations organized.	1914. Panama Canal opened. 1919. First transatlantic flight.	Yeats, Wells, Shaw. Hamsun, Lewis, Cather.
1921. Revolts in Italy. 1922. Mussolini, Dictator of Italy.	1921. Peace in Russia. 1922. Soviet Union formed. Church suppressed.	1921. Mexican disturbances quiet. 1922. Egypt independent; Turks depose Sultan.	1922. Radio broadcasting develops.	

CHARACTERISTICS OF THE CENTURIES	UNITED STATES	GREAT BRITAIN	GERMANY, AUSTRIA	FRANCE	SPAIN AND PORTUGAL
Democratic institutions lose ground as Fascist and Communist states rise.	1927. Mississippi floods. 1929. Herbert Hoover, President; financial panic. 1931. Depression. 1933. F. D. Roosevelt, President.	1926. General strike. 1927. Autonomous Dominions. 1929. Unrest in India. 1931. Financial crisis. Gold standard abandoned.	1926. Germany admitted to League of Nations. 1927. Allies leave Germany. 1931. Severe economic depression. Hitler becomes popular leader. 1933. Nazi party carries Reichstag elections. Hitler receives dictatorial powers. Anti-Semitic activity. Censorship.		1927. Portuguese in revolt. 1931. Republic proclaimed. Alfonso XIII outlawed. 1933. Church property expropriated. Redistribution of land. Secularization of marriage, education.
	1935. W. P. A. established. National Labor Relations Act. Social Security Act.		1935. Saar Territory recovered. Compulsory military service breaks Treaty of Versailles.	1935. Sit-down strikes develop as new industrial warfare technique.	
		1936. George V died. Edward VIII King. Non-intervention policy in Spain. Edward VIII abdicates.	1936. Remilitarization of Rhineland. German-Japanese alliance. Rome-Berlin Axis formed.	1936. People's Front government of Léon Blum. Extensive program of socialistic legislation.	1936. Civil war breaks out. Loyalist republican government attacked by insurgents under Franco.
	1937. Labor troubles continue. Tension with Japan over war in Far East. U.S.S. *Panay* bombed and sunk.				1937. Italy, Germany aid insurgents. Loyalists aided by Russia.
		1938. Chamberlain policy of "European appeasement." Large-scale rearmament program pushed. Munich Pact averts war.	1938. Germany annexes Austria and Czechoslovakian border districts. Anti-Semitism, militant nationalism intensified.	1938. People's Front government fails in financial crisis. Daladier receives dictatorial powers.	
		1939. Declares war on Germany. Blockades German exports and imports.	1939. Germany invades Poland. Danzig returns to Reich. Germany at war with England and France. Germany and Russia annex Poland.		1939. Spanish war ends. Franco becomes head of government.
	1940. Neutrality maintained. National Labor Relations Board settles labor problems. National registration and conscription.	1940. Winston Churchill chosen Prime Minister. Wealth and labor conscripted.	1940. Germans capture Denmark, Holland, Norway, Belgium, and France.	1940. France conquered by Germany and Italy.	
World War II. The "Axis," Germany, Japan, Italy, Finland, Rumania and Bulgaria against almost all other nations of the world, the "Allies."	1941. Roosevelt, Pres.; Wallace, Vice-Pres. Lend-Lease Act aids England, China and Russia. Japan attacks U.S. at Pearl Harbor. U. S. joins Allies in World War II.				
			1942. Germany suffers heavy losses in Russia. Terrific aerial bombardment by England.	1942. Great suffering. Germany executes many Frenchmen in reprisals. German favorites, Laval and Darlan, in power.	
				1943. Darlan, aiding Allies assassinated. De Gaulle and Giraud lead free French in Africa, fight Axis.	1944. Spain and Portugal neutral in World War II.
		1944. Defeats German submarines. Bombs Germany. Fights Germans in Italy.			
1945. United Nations conquer Axis. Atomic bomb invented.	1945. Win World War II. Pres. Roosevelt dies. H. S. Truman, Pres.	1945. Win World War II. Labor Party wins.	1945. Surrender to United Nations.		
			1946. Chief Nazi leaders tried before International Military Tribunal at Nuremberg. Allies administer Germany.	1946. Left parties gain majority in Assembly.	
		1947. Independence given India and Burma. Princess Elizabeth weds Mountbatten.			
	1949. Atlantic Pact signed by 12 nations.			1949. Communists attempt to gain control.	
1951. Western world unites against Communist aggression. 1951. Korean War.	1951. General MacArthur relieved of Asiatic command.	1951. Conservatives regain control of Parliament.	1950. Konrad Adenauer chancellor of West German Republic.	1951. France signs Arms Aid pact.	1951. Spain and U.S. exchange ambassadors.
	1952. Corruption in Government. Taxes and living costs high.	1952. George VI dies. Elizabeth II becomes Queen.	1952. West Germany coöperates in Schuman Plan and NATO.		

TO THE KOREAN WAR

Italy and Greece	Russia, Scandinavia	Other Countries	Arts and Sciences	Literature
1924. Greece a republic.		1924. Kemal, Dictator of Turkey, westernizes the people.		
	1927. Industrial growth forced in Russia.	1927. Civil war in China. Iraq independent.	1927. Lindbergh flies Atlantic.	
1929. Temporal power of Pope restored.	1929. Finland thrives.		1929. Press censorship spreads. Sound motion pictures developed.	
		1931. Japan seizes Manchuria; sets up puppet state of Manchukuo.	1931. Air conditioning becomes popular.	Karel Capek
		1932. Revolution in Siam. Turkey joins League of Nations.		Noel Coward
	1933. Second 5-year plan begun. Liquidation of kulaks. Severe food shortage.	1933. Revolt in Cuba ends dictatorship of Machado.		H. H. Richardson (Australia)
1935. Italy attacks Ethiopia. Sanctions imposed by League of Nations.	1935. Repression of Trotskyist counterrevolution.	1935. War between Bolivia and Paraguay over Gran Chaco territory ended.	1935. Color motion pictures develop. Streamline railway trains.	Emil Ludwig Thomas Mann Stephen Vincent Benét
1936. Conquest of Ethiopia completed. Sanctions withdrawn. Italy intervenes in Spanish Civil War.		1936. Chiang Kai-shek rouses China against Japan.	1936. *Normandie, Queen Mary*, world's largest ocean liners. San Francisco - Oakland bridge opened. Boulder Dam finished.	Ernest Hemingway Eugene O'Neill Pearl Buck
1937. Italy withdraws from League of Nations. Acts with Germany in Rome-Berlin axis.		1937. Japan pushes invasion of China. Dictatorship in Brazil.		Maxwell Anderson
	1939. Russia enters into trade and friendship agreements with Germany. Divides Poland with Germany.		1939. Cyclotron invented for smashing atoms.	Robert E. Sherwood Carl Van Doren
1940. Italy joins in war on side of Germany. France conquered. Italy makes war on Greece. Italy suffers heavy losses in Greece, Albania and Africa.	1940. Norway attacked and conquered by Germany. Russia takes over Lithuania, Latvia and Estonia.	1940. Australia joins England in war against Germany. War continues between Japan and China. Japan wins more Chinese territory. Denmark, Holland and Belgium conquered by Germany. Axis dominates Balkans. Michael, King of Rumania, Carol abdicates and goes to Spain. Rumania and Japan join "Axis."	1940. World's wars make United States center of scientific research. Super telescope on Mount Palomar is built.	
	1941. Russia attacked and invaded by Germany. England and Russia become allies.		1941. Nylon, rayon and cellophane much used.	Countee Cullen Richard Llewellyn D. W. Brogan
		1942. Heavy fighting in Egypt and Libya. King Carol in Mexico. Japan conquers Sumatra, Java and Borneo. Chinese valiantly fight Japanese. Turkey, Switzerland neutral. Japan captures Malaya, Singapore, Burma and Sarawak.		
1943. Allies capture Libya. Heavy Italian casualties in Russia. Italy loses all African territory. Italy surrenders.	1943. Received lend-lease aid from U. S.			
	1945. Russia drives to Berlin and victory.			
	1946. Frederick IX king of Denmark.	1946. Japan administered by Gen. Douglas MacArthur, U.S.A., drafts new constitution making Emperor dependent on constitutional processes.		
1947. Both countries destitute. Italy loses Libya, Ethiopia, and Somaliland. George II dies. Paul crowned.		1947. Pakistan and India gain independence.	1947. Majority of scientists work for abolition of atomic bomb in war.	
		1949. Communists conquer China. Israel, a new nation, elected to United Nations. Eire becomes republic.		The Wall by John Hershey
			1950. Truman orders hydrogen bomb made.	
1951. Land reforms pushed in Italy.	1951. Gustav V of Sweden dies. Russia encourages Communist expansion in Asia.	1951. War in Korea. Japanese Treaty of Peace signed. Leopold III of Belgium abdicates in favor of son Baudouin.	1951. Television sweeps United States.	Kon-Tiki by Heyerdahl Par Lagerkvist
1952. Greece and Turkey coöperate in North Atlantic Treaty Organization.	1952. Russia continues "Cold War."	1952. Libya becomes independent. Seven Arab nations sign Collective Security Pact. Nationalist agitation in Iran, Tunis, Egypt, Morocco.		

Characteristics of the Centuries	United States	Great Britain	Germany, France and Low Countries	Russia and her Satellites	South European Countries
Free Nations are united against Communist aggression.	1952. Hydrogen bomb perfected.		1952. European coal and steel community (Schuman Plan) ratified.	1952. Purge trial in Czechoslovakia.	1952. U. S. extends military aid to Yugoslavia.
			1952. West Germany made free nation and member of European Community.	1952. Persecution of Jews in Russia and satellite nations.	
	1953. Dwight D. Eisenhower President. Price and wage controls removed.	1953. Disastrous floods. 1953. Queen Mother Mary dies.	1953. Jean Monnet of Luxembourg is leader of European Union.	1953. Stalin dies. Georgi Malenkov elected Premier.	1953. Tito of Yugoslavia visits England.
	1953. Dep't of Health, Education, and Welfare created, giving cabinet rank to Oveta Culp Hobby. James P. Mitchell becomes Secretary of Labor. Earl Warren appointed Chief Justice of Supreme Court.	1953. Coronation of Queen Elizabeth II.	1954. Holland, Belgium, Germany and Luxembourg ratify EDC.	1954. H Bomb exploded by Russia.	1954. Mario Scelba is Italian Premier.
	1954. With arms and money, the U.S. strengthens nations outside the Iron Curtain.	1954. British-made Atomic weapons delivered to British forces.	1954. Berlin Conference of Big Four Foreign Ministers ends in failure to re-unite Germany.	1954. More consumer goods made available to common people.	
	1955. U.S. Armed Forces protect Formosa. Great prosperity. Draft reduced. Yalta treaty made public.	1955. Improvement in British economy—highest trading rate in its history.	1955. French National Assembly ratifies West German re-armament within NATO. Faure succeeds Mendes-France as Premier of France.	1955. Malenkov resigns. Bulganin and Khrushchev in power. Food shortage in Russia.	1955. Italy approves German re-armament. Franco of Spain plans for succession of Juan Carlos to throne.
	1956. Eisenhower announces renewed foreign defense aid.	1956. Anthony Eden faces test as Prime Minister.	1956. Left and right gain in French elections.	1956. Albania, Bulgaria, Hungary and Rumania take seats in the U.N.	1956. Italy, Portugal, Spain are new members in U.N.
Unrest in Middle East.	1957. U. S. takes lead in trying to settle Middle East disputes.	1957. Great Britain ceases fighting in Egypt, but asks for international control of Suez Canal. Macmillan new Prime Minister.	1957. The Saar is integrated into West Germany. 1957. Six European nations sign treaty to become a single economic community.	1957. Revolts in Poland and Hungary suppressed. 1957. Sputnicks, earth satellites, and intercontinental missile launched by Russia.	
	1958. Huge budget for missiles and space satellites. Explorer satellite orbiting at 18,000 miles per hour.		1958. France receives first oil from Sahara desert.	1958. Groza dies in Rumania. Maurer succeeds him.	1958. Spain fights border warfare in Africa.
	1959. Christian Herter appointed Secretary of State.	1959. Conservative Party wins third successive election.	1959. European Common Market in effect. De Gaulle is President of France.	1959. Moscow Fair. Russia launches satellite that photographs moon, circles earth and moon.	John XXIII is new Pope.
Exploration of Space	1960. U.S. spy plane downed in USSR. American pilot Powers captured. Eisenhower visits 11 nations.		1960. France tests Atomic device, becomes fourth nuclear power.	1960. Khrushchev kills Summit meeting, but attends U.N. Assembly.	1960. Fanfani becomes Premier of Italy.
	1961. RB-47 pilots are greeted by President Kennedy after being shot down, then released by Russians.	1961. Queen Elizabeth II visits India as millions welcome her.	1961. De Gaulle seeks peace with Algerian rebel leaders.	1961. Crop failure reported in Russia. Soviet satellite shoots rocket towards Venus.	
	1962. Crisis over Cuban missile bases.	1962. Great Britain negotiates to join Common Market.	1962. France negotiates with Moslem N.L.F. in Algeria.	1962. Russia and China engage in ideological struggle.	1962. Italy's Fanfani asks support of Socialists.
	1963. Assassination of President John F. Kennedy.	1963. Security scandal. Home replaces Macmillan as prime minister.	1963. De Gaulle refuses Britain membership in Common Market.	1963. Moscow-Peking split widens.	1963. Paul VI becomes new Pope.
	1964. Johnson signs Civil Rights and Anti-poverty bills.	1964. Harold Wilson succeeds Home as prime minister.	1964. France recognizes Red China.	1964. Khrushchev replaced by Kosygin and Brezhnev.	1963. Saragat replaces Segni as Italian President.
	1965. Vietnam war escalated; voting rights bill passed.	1965. Queen Elizabeth makes state visit to W. Germany.	1965. W. German–Israeli diplomatic relations established; French-NATO breach.	1965. Soviet cosmonauts take first space "walk"; Moscow–Peking tension.	1965. Greek political crisis.

TO THE PRESENT

THE ARABIAN NATIONS	THE FAR EAST	OTHER COUNTRIES	ARTS AND SCIENCES	LITERATURE
1952. Farouk of Egypt forced to abdicate.	1952. Treaty between Japan and Nationalist China signed in Taipei, Formosa.	1952. Race riots in Africa.		The Sea Around Us, by Rachel Carson
1952. Iran disputes with Britain over nationalization of oil. Riots. Premier Mossadegh wins dictatorial powers.	1952. Syngman Rhee elected President of South Korea.	1952. Chaim Weizmann, President of Israel, dies. 1952. Senora Eva Peron, first lady of Argentina, dies.	1952. British jet crosses Atlantic twice in 8 hours.	Out of Red China, by Liu Shaw-tong
1953. Quarrel between Mossadegh and the Shah in Iran.	1953. China continues Korean War. U. S. Seventh Fleet no longer guards Strait of Formosa.	1953. Prime Minister Malan assumes dictatorial powers in Union of South Africa.	1953. Atomic power put to industrial uses.	The Mongol Empire, by Michael Prawdin
1953. General Naguib after 6 months in power in Egypt assumes dictatorial authority.	1953. Yoshida loses confidence vote in Japan. New elections in diet.	1953. Dag Hammarskjold of Sweden elected Secretary General of United Nations. 1954. Mau Mau terrorize Kenya.	1954. Element 99 created. 1954. Skull of Piltdown man declared a hoax.	From Here to Eternity, by James Jones
1954. Turkey and Pakistan agree to closer political, economic and cultural security.	1954. War continues in Indo-China and Malaya.		1954. French Bathyscaphe establishes new deep-diving record.	The Power of Positive Thinking, by Norman Vincent Peale
1955. Iraq discontinues diplomatic relations with Russia. Turkey and Iraq sign mutual defense pact.	1955. Pakistan becomes independent republic. Indonesia faces economic and political chaos.	1955. Southeast Asia Defense Treaty signed.	1955. Mt. Palomar 200 in. telescope proves that universe is expanding. Oriental art popular in Western world.	Out of My Life and Thought, by Albert Schweitzer
1956. Jordan, Libya take seats in U.N.	1956. Cambodia, Ceylon, Laos, Nepal are new members of U. N.	1956. President-elect Kubitschek of Brazil visits U.S.	1955. Salk polio vaccine administered.	Gift From the Sea, by Anne Morrow Lindbergh.
1956. Mobs riot in Jordan.			1956. Many expeditions explore Antarctica.	Marjorie Morningstar, by Herman Wouk
1957. Suez Canal cleared of sunken ships.	1957. U Nu resumes Premiership of Burma.	1957. Ghana and Tunisia become new nations.	1957. Atomic submarine Nautilus is refueled for the first time after travelling 50,000 miles.	
1958. Oil flows through Algerian pipeline from Sahara on way to France. Egypt and Syria become United Arab Republic.	1958. President Soekarno fights revolt in Indonesia after Dutch are driven out. Federation of Malaya becomes new nation, a Dominion.	1958. President Jimenez of Venezuela driven into exile. Larrazabal is provisional president. The West Indies becomes a new nation.	1957. Sputnicks, artificial earth satellites, launched by Russia, circle the earth every hour and a half.	
	1959. Chinese forced by Communists to live in Communes.		1959. Russia launches satellite that photographs moon and circles earth and moon.	Doctor Zhivago, by Boris Pasternak
1960. Turkish government overthrown as Army seizes power.	1960. India and Communist China quarrel over boundaries. Syngman Rhee is forced from power in South Korea.	1960. Belgian Congo becomes Republic. U.N. Forces sent to maintain peace. Nationalism sweeps Africa.	1960. Polaris ballistic missiles fired from submerged U. S. submarine.	Advise and Consent, by Allen Drury
1961. Nasser meets with African leaders in effort to create Arab - African bloc.	1961. Chaos in Laos.	1961. Civil war flares in Congo.		Hawaii, by James Michener
1962. Hereditary absolute monarchy overthrown in Yemen.	1962. Heavy Communist infiltration of South Vietnam.	1962. Uprisings against "Apartheid" in South Africa. Avalanche kills 3,600 in Peru. Western Samoa becomes an independent nation.	1962. Ballistic Missile Early Warning System (BMEWS) completed protecting America's skies.	The Agony and the Ecstasy, by Irving Stone
1963. Civil War in Yemen. Nasser desires pan-Arab unity.	1963. Buddhist protest in Vietnam; Diem regime toppled in military coup.	1963. Kenya becomes independent. Zanzibar unites with Tanganyika. New nation of Malaysia formed.	1963. Soviet and U.S. manned space flights.	James Bond novels, by Ian Fleming
1964. Nasser promotes Arab political unity.	1964. Turmoil in South Vietnam continues.	1964. Nyasaland becomes independent nation of Malawi; Northern Rhodesia independent as Zambia.	1964. First photographs of moon's surface taken by U.S. spacecraft.	1964. The Group, by Mary McCarthy
1965. Ben Bella ousted in Algiers; E. German ambassador visits U.A.R.	1965. Armed conflict over Kashmir; Singapore secedes from Malaysia; Vietnam war.	1965. Gambia becomes independent African nation; Dominican Republic revolt. Rhodesia declares independence from Great Britain.	1965. Eight-day U.S. orbit.	1965. Herzog, by Saul Bellow

1. PERIOD OF DISCOVERY AND EXPLORATION, 1492-1607

RULERS	SPANISH EXPLORERS	RULERS	ENGLISH EXPLORERS
1474–1516. Ferdinand and Isabella.	1492. Columbus discovers the Bahama Islands and Hispaniola (Haiti) 1493–1496. Columbus discovers Jamaica and other islands. 1498–1500. Columbus on his third voyage discovers the mainland of South America without knowing it. 1499–1507. Amerigo Vespucci visits the American coast. 1502–1504. Columbus further explores the coast on his last voyage. 1510. Spanish settle at Darien, in Panama. 1513. Ponce de León visits Florida; Balboa sees the Pacific.	1485–1509. Henry VII. 1509–1547. Henry XIII. 1547–1553. Edward VI. 1553–1558. Mary. 1558–1603. Elizabeth. 1603–1625. James I.	1497. The Cabots skirt the coasts of Labrador and New England. 1565. Hawkins visits Florida. 1576–1578. Frobisher seeks a Northwest Passage in Canada. 1577–1580. Drake, sailing around the world skirts the shores of South America, Mexico and California. 1583. English attempt a settlement in Newfoundland. 1584. English take possession of Virginia. 1587. Raleigh plants a colony at Roanoke Island, North Carolina, but it is lost; there Virginia Dare was the first American-born child of English parents. 1602. Gosnold explores the shores of New England. 1603. Pring explores the Massachusetts coast. 1606. English companies are formed to plant colonies in America.
1516–56. Charles I.	1515. Havana is founded; Cuban Indians are subdued. 1516. Rio La Plata is discovered by Solis. 1519–1521. Cortez conquers the Aztecs in Mexico; Magellan's ship makes the first round-the-world trip. 1520–1527. Spanish ships explore the Atlantic coast. 1525–1533. Pizzaro conquers the Incas in Peru. 1530. Spanish colonization of South America begins. 1534. Mendoza founds Buenos Aires. 1542. De Soto reaches the Mississippi River.		
		RULERS	FRENCH EXPLORERS
1556–1598. Philip II. 1598–1621. Philip III.	1540–1542. Coronado explores from Mexico north into Colorado. 1565. Spain settles St. Augustine, Fla., the oldest town within the present United Staes. 1605. Santa Fe, N. M., settled	1515–1547. Francis I. 1547–1559. Henry II. 1559–1560. Francis II. 1560–1574. Charles IX. 1574–1589. Henry III. 1589–1610. Henry IV.	1504. French fishermen visit the Newfoundland Banks. 1524. Verrazano explores the North Atlantic coast. 1534–1535. Cartier explores the Canadian shore and enters the St. Lawrence. 1562. Huguenots under Ribault settle in South Carolina, but the Spanish drive them away. 1567. French ships attack the Spanish fort at St. Augustine. 1603. Champlain arrives in the St. Lawrence. 1604. Champlain plants a colony in Acadia (Nova Scotia). 1605–1606. French continue explorations along the New England coast.
RULERS	PORTUGUESE EXPLORERS		
1495–1521. Emanuel I.	1500. Cabral discovers Brazil and enters the Amazon. Cortereal skirts the coast of Labrador. 1530. Settlement of Brazil begins.		

II. THE COLONIAL PERIOD, 1607-1783

ENGLISH AND DUTCH COLONIES	FRENCH COLONIES	SPANISH AND PORTUGUESE COLONIES
1607. First permanent English settlement in America, Jamestown, Va. 1609. Hudson River explored by Dutch. 1615. Dutch place forts on Hudson River. 1619. First representative government in America set up at Jamestown. 1620. Pilgrims land in Massachusetts. 1626. New Amsterdam founded. 1630. Boston founded. 1634. Maryland settled by Catholics. 1635. Connecticut Valley settled. 1636. Rhode Island settled. Harvard University, first in United States, founded. 1638. Swedes settle in Delaware.	1608. Quebec founded. 1609. Lake Champlain discovered. 1615. Lake Huron explored. 1630. English invade Canada. 1634. Lake Michigan explored.	 1620. Church quarrels disturb Mexico. 1630. Dutch win Brazil. 1634. Central American Indians subdued. 1636. Colonial trade monopolized by Spanish Crown.
1647–1664. Stuyvesant governor of New Netherland. 1655. Dutch conquer Swedish settlements. 1663. Settlement of Carolina arranged. 1664. New Jersey and New York taken by English, ending Dutch North Atlantic colonies. 1669. Locke's Carolina Constitutions drafted. 1675. Indian wars in New England. 1676. Bacon's Rebellion in Virginia. 1681. Pennsylvania granted to Penn. 1686–1689. Andros, royal governor of New England. 1690. Indians raid Mohawk Valley, New York. 1692. William and Mary College founded; Salem witchcraft delusion. 1701. Yale College founded; Captain Kidd hanged. 1704. Newspaper published in Boston. 1706. French and Spanish invade Carolina. 1711–1715. Indian wars in Carolina. 1718. Law's Arkansas project fails. 1729. Separation of North and South Carolina. 1733. Savannah, Georgia, founded. 1745. Indian wars in New York. 1754. Congress of Albany plans border defenses. 1754–1763. French and Indian War. 1759. Wolfe captures Quebec.	1642. Montreal founded. 1663. Traders and missionaries venture beyond Lake Superior. 1669. La Salle explores Ohio River. 1681. La Salle descends Mississippi River. 1699. Biloxi, Mississippi, founded. 1711–1713. English invade Canada. 1718. New Orleans founded. 1729. Indians raid Natchez settlement. 1743. Explorers sight the Rockies. 1745. English capture Louisburg. 1749. Forts built in the Ohio valley. 1755. English exile Acadians.	1638. Bogota founded. 1642. Spain conquers Chile. 1655. Portugal recovers Brazil from Dutch. 1681. Indian revolts in New Mexico and Arizona. 1689. Buccaneers ravage Spanish Main. 1692. Gold found in Brazil. 1711. French take Rio de Janeiro. 1733. Jesuit missions set up in Arizona. 1743. Pirates take Manila treasure fleet. 1749. Spain and Portugal agree on boundaries of their colonies. 1759. Brazilian trade expands. 1761. English take Havana.
1763. Peace; English win Canada and East Louisiana; Indians led by Pontiac alarm frontier settlements. 1765. English Stamp Act inspires colonial congress of protest. 1766. Stamp Act repealed but colonial unrest continues. 1767. English Townshend Acts stimulate colonial desire for liberty. 1768. English troops quartered in Boston. 1770. Boston massacre. 1771. Settlement begun in Kentucky and Tennessee. 1773. Boston Tea Party; Committees of Correspondence organized. 1774. First Continental Congress meets; Kentucky grows rapidly. 1775. American Revolution begins; battles, Lexington and Bunker Hill. 1776. Declaration of Independence adopted; British leave Boston but win New York; Virginia adopts first constitution; Washington takes Trenton. 1777. Lafayette arrives; British win Philadelphia; Burgoyne surrenders. 1778. British invade the South; France joins in war against England. 1779. John Paul Jones challenges English naval supremacy. 1780. English win the Carolinas. 1781. Articles of Confederation effective; Cornwallis surrenders. ending war. 1783. England and Europe acknowledge American independence.	1763. Spain wins Havana and West Louisiana, yields Florida to England. 1765. Spanish trading restrictions eased. 1766. Acadian exiles settle in Louisiana. 1767. Spain expels Jesuits from her territories. 1768. French in Louisiana attempt revolt against Spain. 1769. Spanish missions established in California. 1773. Destructive earthquakes in Central America. 1776. Viceroyalty of Buenos Aires set up, governing Uruguay, Paraguay and Bolivia. Tucson founded. 1780. Revolt in Peru. 1781. British take Guiana. 1783. Florida is returned to Spain.	

III. FROM THE END OF THE REVOLUTION TO THE CIVIL WAR, 1783-1861

THE UNITED STATES			CANADA	LATIN AMERICA AND THE WEST INDIES
POLITICAL EVENTS	ADMINISTRATIONS	SOCIAL AND INDUSTRIAL PROGRESS		
1785. Church disestablished in Virginia; foreign ambassadors appointed. 1786. Shay's rebellion in Massachusetts; Constitutional convention called. 1787. Constitution drawn up; disposal of Northwest Territory decided.	1783–1787. Confederation of independent states.	1784. First successful daily newspaper in America: Fitch's steamboat tried out. 1786. Cotton planting extended in the South.	1784. Tories fleeing United States colonize Ontario and New Brunswick. 1786–1796. Lord Dorchester, Governor-General.	1786. European rivalry in Guiana.
1789. Organization of the executive, legislative, and judicial departments of the new government. The first Congress meets in New York. 1790. First decennial census is taken. Congress decides to locate the national capital on the Potomac. Assumption of the public debts of the several states. Passage of the first excise law. 1790–1795. War with the Indians north of the Ohio. 1791. Organization of the Bank of the United States. Ratification of the first ten amendments to the Constitution. Admission of Vermont into the Union. 1792. Admission of Kentucky. Formation of the first political parties under the Constitution.	George Washington, President. John Adams, Vice-President. Thomas Jefferson, Secretary of State. Alexander Hamilton, Secretary of Treasury Henry Knox, Secretary of War. Edmund Randolph, Attorney-General. F. A. Muhlenburg, Speaker of the House. John Jay, Chief Justice, Supreme Court.	1789. Control over foreign commerce passes from the states to the Federal Government. North Carolina establishes the first of the state universities. 1790. Samuel Slater sets up cotton machinery at Pawtucket, R. I. First patent law is passed. 1790–1799. Rapidly increasing demand for cotton. 1792. Founding of Williams College.	1789 and 1793. Sir Alexander Mackenzie explores the Athabasca region. 1790. British Parliament appropriates £3,110,000 to reimburse the Loyalists for their losses in the American Revolution. 1791. Constitutional Act passed by British Parliament separating Canada into Upper and Lower provinces. French law was continued in Lower while English law was established in Upper Canada.	1789. Many Carolina planters move to Louisiana. 1791. Beginning of the negro insurrection in Haiti. 1792. Sugar first refined in Louisiana. The process was commercialized in 1794 by Boré.
1793. Cornerstone of national capitol laid by Washington. Genet's meteoric career as minister from France. 1794. Whisky insurrection in Western Pennsylvania. Jay Treaty with England. Wayne defeats the Indians. 1795. Treaty with Spain. Treaty at Greenville with the Indians north of the Ohio. 1796. Admission of Tennessee. Washington issues his farewell address, September 17. The French Directory issues a decree against American commerce.	George Washington, Re-elected President. John Adams, Re-elected Vice-Pres.	1793. Whitney invents the cotton gin; cotton production greatly stimulated. Establishment of a mint at Philadelphia. Rapid expansion of America. 1794. Mail boats and passenger boats are established on the Ohio. Founding of Bowdoin College.	1793. Legislature of Upper Canada provides for gradual abolition of slavery. 1794. Toronto made capital of Upper Canada. 1794–1795. Political disputes in Lower Canada. 1796. Surrender by Great Britain of military posts in United States Northwest Territory.	1794. Toussaint L'Ouverture becomes leader of the Haitian revolt. 1795. Subjugation and deportation of Jamaican maroons (descendants of runaway slaves). France takes Spanish part of Haiti.
1797. Special session of Congress to consider relations with France. The X. Y. Z. overtures. Constitution launched. 1798. Adoption of the Eleventh Amendment. Passage of the Alien and Sedition laws. The Virginia and Kentucky Resolutions. The Navy Department is established. Naval quasi-war with France. 1800. The capital is removed from Philadelphia to Washington. Treaty with France ends alliance of 1778.	John Adams, President. Thomas Jefferson, Vice-President.	1797. The first patent for a cast-iron plow is granted Charles Newbold of New Jersey. A financial panic. 1798. "Hail Columbia" is composed by Joseph Hopkinson. First salt manufactory established in Ohio. 1800. India rubber is imported into the United States.	1797. Beginning of construction of Sault Ste. Marie Canal. 1800–1812. Many Americans and Scots immigrate into Upper Canada.	1800. Transfer of Louisiana from Spain to France.
1801. John Marshall is appointed Chief Justice. 1801–1805. War with Tripoli. 1802. Spain withdraws the right of deposit at New Orleans. U. S. Military Academy established. 1803. Louisiana is purchased from France for $15,000,000. Admission of Ohio. Case of Marbury vs. Madison is decided. 1804. Adoption of the Twelfth Amendment. Hamilton killed in a duel by Burr. 1804–1806. Lewis and Clark expedition. 1805–1807. Conspiracy of Aaron Burr. 1806–1808. The European "Continental System" brings distress on American shippers. 1807. The Embargo Act passed.	Thomas Jefferson, President. Aaron Burr, Vice-President. Thomas Jefferson, Re-elected President. George Clinton, Vice-President.	1801. New York Evening Post is founded by Alexander Hamilton. 1802. The Du Pont powder works established. 1803. Tobacco is exceeded by cotton as an export crop. First shipment of anthracite coal from Lehigh to Philadelphia. Grain cradle is patented. 1805. Robert Fulton originates the marine torpedo. 1806. Passage of a bill for the construction of the Cumberland Road. Gas for lighting is used in Newport, R. I. 1807. Successful trip of Fulton's steamboat, the Clermont, from New York to Albany.	1803. Slavery made illegal in Lower Canada. 1806. Quarrels in Lower Canada between French and English over taxation. First French-Canadian newspaper, Le Canadien.	1802. French capture l'Ouverture. 1803. Great Britain reacquires British Guiana by treaty. France abandons effort to subjugate Haiti. 1804–1806. Dessalines Emperor of Haiti; massacre of White population. 1806. British attack Argentina. 1806–1811. Christopher, President (King 1811–1820) of Haiti.

III. FROM THE END OF THE REVOLUTION TO THE CIVIL WAR—Continued

THE UNITED STATES			CANADA	LATIN AMERICA AND THE WEST INDIES
POLITICAL EVENTS	ADMINISTRATIONS	SOCIAL AND INDUSTRIAL PROGRESS		
1808. Foreign slave trade ended.		1808. American Fur Company founded by J. J. Astor.		1808. Royal family of Portugal emigrates to Brazil.
1809. The Embargo Act is repealed and a nonimportation act passed. 1810-1814. The United States takes possession of West Florida.	**James Madison,** *President.* George Clinton, *Re-elected Vice-Pres.*			1809. Ecuador tries for independence. 1810. Revolutionary movements begin in Argentina and Chile. 1810-1815. Revolt led by Hidalgo in Mexico unsuccessful.
1811. Battle of Tippecanoe with the Indians. Henry Clay and John C. Calhoun first appear in the House of Representatives. 1812. War declared against Great Britain. Admission of Louisiana. War with Algerian pirates. 1813-1814. War with the Creeks. 1814. The Hartford Convention proposes amendments to weaken the Constitution.	**James Madison,** *Re-elected President.* Elbridge Gerry, *Vice-President.*	1811. The first steamboat leaves Pittsburgh for New Orleans. Beginning of an era of state banking activity. 1812. Invention of stoves built with grates to secure draft. 1814. Francis Scott Key composes "Star Spangled Banner."	1812. Canada remains loyal to England during American war. 1813. Lord Selkirk plants an agricultural colony on Red River.	1811. Paraguay declares independence. Revolution begins in Columbia and Venezuela. 1811-1812. Francisco Miranda, Dictator of Venezuela. 1814. Simon Bolivar, Dictator of Venezuela, is driven out by royalist army. 1815-1821. Guerrilla warfare in Mexico.
1815. Captain Decatur forces Dey of Algiers to renounce tribute. Treaty of peace with England ratified. 1816. Second Bank of the United States is chartered. Admission of Indiana. American Colonization Society founds Liberia. Increased agitation for internal improvements. First tariff primarily for protection is passed. 1817. Admission of Mississippi. Congress prohibits foreign vessels engaging in the United States coasting trade. 1817-1818. Seminole War. 1818. Admission of Illinois.	**James Monroe,** *President.* D. D. Thompkins, *Vice-President.*	1815. First ocean steamboat trip, New York to Norfolk. 1816. Church of the Disciples is formed. The first steamer on Lake Ontario appears. The first savings bank in America is opened at Philadelphia. 1817. First instruction of deaf mutes in America by T. H. Gallaudet, at Hartford, Connecticut. 1818. First steamer on Lake Erie, the *Walk-in-the-Water.*	1817. Bank notes issued at Montreal.	1817-1823. Bernardo O'Higgins, Director of the Chilean State, defeats Spain. 1818. Bolivar renews war for independence. 1819-1830. Civil war and confusion in Argentina.
1819. Admission of Alabama. Florida purchased by the United States. Financial panic. Maine separated from Massachusetts. Dartmouth College case, and case of McCulloch vs. Maryland decided by Supreme Court. 1820. Admission of Maine. The Missouri Compromise adopted. 1821. The second Missouri Compromise and the admission of Missouri.	**James Monroe,** *Re-elected President.* D. D. Thompkins, *Re-elected Vice-Pres.*	1819. Combination sail and steamship *Savannah* made transatlantic trip. 1821. New York Stock Exchange organized. First public high school in United States opened in Boston.	1820. Agitation in Upper Canada. Dalhousie College founded at Halifax.	1819. Republic of Colombia founded, comprising New Granada, Venezuela and Ecuador. 1820. Peru revolts. 1821. Independence proclaimed in Peru, Nicaragua, Salvador and Costa Rica. John VI. returns from Brazil to Portugal.
1822. The independence of South American republics recognized. 1823. President Monroe states the "Monroe Doctrine" in his annual message to Congress. 1824. Protective policy greatly extended by an act of Congress. Visit of La Fayette to the United States.		1822. Gaslight introduced into Boston. 1823. Champlain Canal, connecting the Hudson at Albany with Lake Champlain, opened.	1824. Founding of the Canada Co. to promote colonization in the district about Lake Huron.	1822. Brazil declares independence and makes Dom Pedro emperor. Iturbide declared emperor of Mexico. 1823. Revolt led by Santa Ana overthrows Iturbide. 1824. Mexico adopts federal constitution. Bolivar establishes Peruvian independence. 1824-1839. Federal republic of Central America.
1825. Presidential election is thrown into the House of Representatives and results in the choice of Adams. 1825-1831. Dispute with Georgia over Indian land cessions. 1826. Deaths of Thomas Jefferson and John Adams, July 4th. 1827. Convention between U. S. and Great Britain to settle northeastern boundary. Anti-Masonry has its rise. 1828. Tariff of Abominations passed.	**John Q. Adams,** *President.* J. C. Calhoun, *Vice-President.*	1825. Erie Canal is completed. 1826. The Quincy tramway, sometimes called the first railroad in the U. S., is built from Quincy to tidewater, 3 miles away. 1827. Baltimore & Ohio Railroad is chartered. First rail laid July 4, 1828. 1828. Webster's *Dictionary* issued.	1826. Bytown (later Ottawa) founded.	1825. Uruguay revolts from Brazil, achieving independence in 1828. Upper Peru separates from Peru, taking name of Bolivia. 1826. Panama Congress called by Bolivar, with a view to general Latin-American federation. 1828. Mexican civil war. Peru at war with Bolivia and Chile.

III. FROM THE END OF THE REVOLUTION TO THE CIVIL WAR—Continued

THE UNITED STATES			CANADA	LATIN AMERICA AND THE WEST INDIES
POLITICAL EVENTS	ADMINISTRATIONS	SOCIAL AND INDUSTRIAL PROGRESS		
1829. The Postmaster General made a member of the President's Cabinet. Spoils system adopted.	**Andrew Jackson,** *President.* John C. Calhoun, *Re-elected Vice-Pres.*	1829. Process of manufacturing galvanized iron is perfected.	1829. Opening of Welland Canal. 1829–1830. Discontent in the Maritime Provinces.	1829. Venezuela withdraws from Republic of Colombia. Slavery abolished in Mexico. 1829–1833. Santa Ana dictator in Mexico.
1830. West Indian trade is opened to American vessels. The Webster-Hayne debate in the Senate.		1830. Organization of the Church of Latter Day Saints (Mormons). Chloroform discovered. Carolina Railroad begun. B. & O. Railroad opened to traffic.	1830–1831. Efforts at conciliation in Lower Canada thwarted by Papineau.	1830. Ecuador separates from Colombia; Flores, first President.
1831. The Anti-Masonic party holds the first national nominating convention. Rise of the Abolitionists. Garrison publishes the *Liberator.*		1831. Opening of the first school for the blind. McCormick invents the first successful reaper.	1831. Disputes arise over Maine boundary.	1831. Upon abdication of Dom Pedro I., his son, Dom Pedro II., becomes Emperor of Brazil.
1832. National Republican party frames the first party platform. Black Hawk War. New tariff law enacted. Nullification in South Carolina. Jackson vetoes the U. S. Bank Bill.		1832. The Ohio River joined to Lake Erie by canal. First street railway in the U. S. commences in New York. Pork-packing industry begins in Chicago.	1832. Opening of Rideau Canal. Legislature formed in Newfoundland.	1832. Colombia adopts name of New Granada, with new constitution; Santander, President.
1833. U. S. deposits removed from the National Bank.	**Andrew Jackson,** *Re-elected President.* Martin VanBuren, *Vice-Pres.*	1833. Carolina Railroad completed. Ross Winans builds the first typical American passenger cars. Oberlin, Ohio, first coeducational college, founded.		1833. Santa Ana, President of Mexico. Chile adopts new constitution.
1834. Congress creates the Indian Territory. National debt is extinguished. Whig party first takes its name.		1834. McCormick patents an improved reaper.	1834. The Ninety-two Resolutions, a French Canadian declaration of rights.	1834–1839. Confederation of Peru and Bolivia under Santa Cruz.
1835–1842. Second Seminole War.		1835. Morse invents magnetic telegraph; Colt, the revolver. J. G. Bennett begins publication of New York *Herald.* Business panic.	1835. A royal commission investigates the governor and assembly of Lower Canada.	1835. Anglo-American settlers declare Texas independent of Mexico. 1835–1852. Rosas dictator in Argentina.
1836. Admission of Arkansas. Roger B. Taney is made Chief Justice.		1836. Friction match is patented. Wesleyan College founded, first in America for women. 1836–1838. Invention of the screw propeller.		1836. Massacre by Mexican troops at Alamo, Texas. Samuel Houston, President of Texan Republic, defeats Mexican Army at San Jacinto, and captures Santa Ana.
1837. Admission of Michigan. Great financial panic.	**Martin Van Buren,** *President.* R. M. Johnson, *Vice-President.*	1837. Massachusetts State Board of Education is organized with Horace Mann as secretary. Invention of the hot-air blast in iron smelting. Audubon's *Birds of America* issued.	1837. British quell insurrections led in Lower Canada by Papineau and in Upper Canada by Mackenzie.	
1838. "Underground railroad" begins aiding fugitive slaves to escape from the South. 1838–1839. "Aroostook War" between Maine and New Brunswick.		1838. First shipment of grain from Chicago. *Great Western* and *Sirius* cross the Atlantic. National Road opened to Illinois.		1838. Guatemala overthrows Central American Union. Emancipation of slaves completed in British colonies, Jamaica, Barbadoes, Bahama, Bermuda, Guiana, etc. 1838–1841. M. B. Lamar, President of Texas. 1839–1841. War between Peru and Chile.
1839–1847. Anti-Rent agitation in New York.		1839. Vulcanized rubber patented by Goodyear.	1839. With consent of both Canadas, Parliament passes Union Act on the Durham plan.	
1840. Passage of Subtreasury Bill.		1840. Adams Express Company begins operation between New York and Boston.		
1841. The Subtreasury Act repealed. 1841–1842. Quarrel between President Tyler and the Whigs.	**Wm. H. Harrison,** *President.* John Tyler, *Vice-President.* (Harrison dies April 4, 1841, and is succeeded by **Tyler**).	1841. Dorothea Dix begins her 40 years' crusade for the better treatment of the insane. Horace Greeley establishes the New York *Tribune.* First steam fire-engine built and used in New York.	1841. First Parliament of the United Canadas opens, June 14.	1841–1845. Samuel Houston again President of Texas.
1842. Dorr's Rebellion in Rhode Island. 1842–1848. Frémont's explorations of the West.		1842. Buffalo connected with the East by railway. First use of anaesthesia in a surgical operation by Dr. Crawford W. Long, of Athens, Ga.	1842. Webster-Ashburton Treaty adjusts boundary between Maine and New Brunswick.	1842. Second federation of Central America established. Paraguay independent.
1843. Bunker Hill Monument dedicated.		1843. Oregon Trail opened.	1843. Opening of McGill University at Montreal and King's College at Toronto.	1843. Dominican Republic separates from Haiti.
1844. First treaty with China secures commercial rights for U. S. Mobs drive Mormons from Illinois.		1844. Manufacture of iron rails in this country begins. First successful use of the telegraph.	1844. Toronto *Globe* founded.	1844. Lopez, President of Paraguay.
1845. Admission of Florida. Annexation of Texas by joint resolution and admission of Texas as a state. U. S. Naval Academy established at Annapolis.	**Jas. K. Polk,** *President.* Geo. M. Dallas, *Vice-President.*	1845. Petroleum discovered near Pittsburgh. Separation of Southern from Northern Methodist and Baptist churches, resulting from quarrels over slavery.		1845. English and French blockade Buenos Aires. 1846. Treaty with New Granada giving U. S. right of way across Isthmus of Panama.
1846. Oregon Treaty with Great Britain. Admission of Iowa. Wilmot Proviso fails.		1846. The sewing machine is invented by Elias Howe. Smithsonian Institution founded. First slate quarry in Vermont is opened.		1846–1861. Civil war in Ecuador.

III. FROM THE END OF THE REVOLUTION TO THE CIVIL WAR—Concluded

THE UNITED STATES			CANADA	LATIN AMERICA AND THE WEST INDIES
POLITICAL EVENTS	ADMINISTRATIONS	SOCIAL AND INDUSTRIAL PROGRESS		
1846–1848. War between Mexico and the U. S.		1846–1848. Great wave of immigration from Ireland.		
1847. Salt Lake City settled by Mormons.		1847. Richard M. Hoe invents the rotary printing press. Use of adhesive postage stamps authorized.	1847–1854. Earl of Elgin, Governor of Canada, pursues policy of pacification.	1847. Soulouque, a Negro, President of Haiti.
1848. Organization of the Free-Soil party. Admission of Wisconsin. Peace with Mexico; California, Arizona and New Mexico won.		1848. The Associated Press first organized. First school for the feeble-minded opened. Discovery of gold in California.		1848. Peace between Mexico and U. S.
1849. Creation of the Department of Interior. California applies for statehood.	**Zachary Taylor,** *President.* Millard Fillmore, *Vice-President.* (Death of President Taylor July 9, 1850. **Fillmore** becomes President.)	1849. Rush of goldseekers to California.	1849. Rebellion Losses Bill, to pay for property destroyed in rebellion of 1837, passed.	1849. Soulouque proclaimed Emperor of Haiti. War of Central American Federation against Guatemala. Confederation defeated.
1850. "Compromise of 1850" admits California and adjusts other slavery questions. Clayton-Bulwer Treaty with Great Britain ratified.		1850. First national labor organization formed. Government grant of land to the Illinois Central Railroad, for stimulating railroad building. First census of manufactures. 1850–1860. Period of railroad consolidation.	1850. Parliament House burned in Montreal riots.	1850. Cuba invaded by American filibusters under Lopez.
1851. Vigilance committees bring law and order to California.		1851. H. J. Raymond founds the New York *Times.* The B. & O. Railroad reaches the Ohio. Western Union Telegraph Company established. Hudson River and Erie railroads opened.	1851. Renewed agitation over clergy reserves. Parties split into factions.	1851. Second filibustering expedition against Cuba; Lopez captured and shot.
1852. Deaths of Clay and Webster.		1852. Publication of *Uncle Tom's Cabin.*	1852. Laval University chartered.	1852. Brazil ends the slave trade.
1853. The Gadsden Purchase from Mexico.	**Franklin Pierce,** *President.* Rufus King, *Vice-President.*	1853. N. Y. Clearing House established. Chicago is reached by rail.		1853. Republican constitution framed for Argentina; civil war until 1862.
1854. Commodore Perry secures commercial treaty from Japan. Native American party (the "Know-Nothings") becomes prominent. Ostend manifesto. Kansas-Nebraska Act.		1854. The Mississippi River is reached by rail from the East. Elevator patented by Otis.	1854. McDonald ministry settles the clergy reserves question, abolishes seigniorial tenure, and makes a reciprocity treaty with U. S.	1854. Castilla revolution in Peru; slavery abolished. Abolition of slavery completed in New Granada, Venezuela and Ecuador.
1855. Troubles in Kansas.		1855. St. Louis is reached by rail. Bessemer steel process patented. Panama railroad opened.		1855. William Walker, filibuster from U. S., invades Nicaragua.
1856. First Republican national convention. Civil strife in Kansas.		1856. First bridge across the Mississippi built at Rock Island, Illinois.	1856. Legislature for Vancouver Island established. Gold discovered on Fraser River, British Columbia.	1856–1857. Walker driven out of Nicaragua.
1857. The Dred Scott Decision. Mountain Meadow's Massacre in Utah. Great financial panic.	**James Buchanan,** *President.* J. C. Breckenridge, *Vice-President.*	1857. Attempt to lay first telegraphic cable across the Atlantic fails. First state school of agriculture, Lansing, Michigan.		1857. Mexico adopts a new constitution. 1857–1863. Civil war in New Granada.
1858. Lincoln-Douglas debates in Illinois. Admission of Minnesota. Second treaty with China ratified.		1858. Second attempt to lay cable successful temporarily. First transatlantic message. Gold discovered near Pike's Peak. Overland stage line organized.	1858. Governor is appointed for British Columbia. Ottawa made capital. Decimal coinage adopted.	1858. Soulouque dethroned, Haitian Republic re-established; regime of chronic disorder ensues.
1859. Admission of Oregon. John Brown's raid on Harper's Ferry.		1859. First petroleum well dug. Photolithography introduced.	1859. Reformers at Toronto demand separation of Upper from Lower Canada.	1859. End of civil wars in Argentina.
1860. Democratic party splits on slavery question. Lincoln elected over Breckenridge, Bell and Douglas. South Carolina secedes, Dec. 20.		1860. Salt first attains commercial importance in Michigan. Oil fever in the Allegheny River valley. Gold rush to Colorado. Pony Express starts.	1860–1864. George Brown urges a federation of all British North American provinces.	1860. William Walker is captured and shot in Honduras.

IV. PERIOD OF THE CIVIL WAR AND RECONSTRUCTION, 1861-1876

THE UNITED STATES			CANADA	LATIN AMERICA AND THE WEST INDIES
POLITICAL EVENTS	ADMINISTRATIONS	SOCIAL AND INDUSTRIAL PROGRESS		
1861. Admission of Kansas. Trouble with England over the *Trent* affair. Southern States form the Confederacy. Battle of Bull Run; blockade of Confederate ports. **1862.** Legal tender notes. "greenbacks." issued. Slavery abolished in the territories and District of Columbia. Seven Days, Antietam and Fredericksburg campaigns; Grant wins in the West; Farragut takes New Orleans. Treaty with Great Britain for the suppression of the slave trade. **1863.** Proclamation of Emancipation, Jan. 1. Draft riots in New York. Admission of West Virginia. National Banking Act passed. Chancellorsville, Gettysburg, Vicksburg and Chickamauga campaigns. **1864.** Fugitive Slave Act (of 1850) repealed. Admission of Nevada. Premium on gold. Modoc Indian War begins. Grant drives toward Richmond; battles at Wilderness and Spotsylvania. Sherman marches through Georgia.	**Abraham Lincoln,** *President.* Hannibal Hamlin, *Vice-President.*	**1861.** First message sent over transcontinental telegraph lines. **1862.** Passage of the Morrill Act to found agricultural colleges. Passage of the Homestead Act. Union Pacific railroad chartered. First use of ironclad ships in warfare. **1863.** Organization of the Brotherhood of Locomotive Engineers. Delivery of mail by carriers begins. **1864.** Postal money orders first issued. First sleeping-car is built. Northern Pacific Railroad chartered.	**1861.** Nova Scotia legislature asks for a general federation.	**1861–1864.** Dominican Republic temporarily subject to Spain. Bolivia in anarchy. Juarez, President of Mexico. **1862.** Napoleon III plans to erect Mexican Empire for Archduke Maximilian. **1863.** New Granada renames itself Colombia. Mexico occupied by French army. **1864.** Maximilian crowned Emperor of Mexico. War in Paraguay.
1865. Thirteenth Amendment ratified. President Lincoln shot. General amnesty is proclaimed, following the end of the war. **1366.** Civil Rights Bill passed over the president's veto. Organization of the Ku Klux Klan. Shoshone Indian War. **1867.** Plan of military reconstruction of the South adopted by Congress. Admission of Nebraska. Purchase of Alaska from Russia. Organization of the Grangers. **1868.** President Johnson impeached, tried and acquitted. Six southern states readmitted to representation in Congress. Fourteenth amendment ratified. Burlingame treaty with China signed. **1868–1874.** "Carpetbag" rule in the South.	**Abraham Lincoln,** *Re-elected President.* Andrew Johnson, *Vice-President.* (On death of Lincoln **Johnson** becomes President.)	**1865.** First organization of the Standard Oil Company. **1866.** First permanently successful Atlantic cable laid. Salmon canning on the Columbia River begins. Massachusetts passes an eight-hour law for children. **1867.** Beginning of the manufacture of steel rails in the U. S. Ground wood pulp first used for making paper. **1868.** Westinghouse airbrake first successfully applied. First Siemens-Martin open-hearth furnace built. Founding of Cornell University.	**1865.** Quebec legislature endorses Union Resolutions. **1866.** Union Resolutions endorsed by Nova Scotia and New Brunswick. Reciprocity treaty with U. S. expires; not renewed. Fenian raid from U. S. into Canada fruitless. **1867.** Canadian Union Act passed by Imperial Parliament, providing federation of all British North American provinces ratifying. Upper Canada, renamed Ontario, separated from Lower Canada, renamed Quebec. **1868–1872.** Sir John Young, afterward Lord Lisgar, Gov. Gen. Fenian raid repelled.	**1865.** Insurrection in Jamaica suppressed. U. S. protests against French interference in Mexico. **1865–1870.** Brazil and Argentina in alliance at war with Paraguay. **1866.** Spain shells Valparaiso, Chile. **1867.** French troops withdraw from Mexico. Native forces overthrow Maximilian's government and put him to death. Republic re-established. **1868–1878.** Cespedes insurrection in Cuba. Santo Domingo proposes to join United States.
1869. Organization of National Prohibition Party. Disbandment of the Ku Klux Klan. Woman suffrage, upon equal terms with men, established in Wyoming. **1870.** Fifteenth Amendment ratified. **1871.** First Civil Service Reform Bill enacted. Legal Tender Act is decided to be constitutional. "Tweed Ring" in New York is exposed. Treaty with Great Britain. **1872.** Act for removing political disabilities passes Congress. Geneva award of $15,000,000 to U. S. Modoc Indian War in California.	**U. S. Grant,** *President.* Schuyler Colfax, *Vice-President.*	**1869.** Passage of eight-hour law for federal employees. Invention of the refrigerator car. First transcontinental railroad completed. **1870.** Opening at Boston of first kindergarten in the U. S. Steel rails first used on railroads. **1871.** Hoe perfecting press completed. Texas Pacific Railroad begun. Great Chicago fire. **1872.** Invention of duplex telegraphy. Import duties on tea and coffee abolished. Yellowstone Park organized. Bonanza mines on the Comstock lode discovered.	**1869.** Dominion purchases the vast territory of the Hudson Bay Co. Newfoundland refuses to join the Confederation. **1870.** Manitoba enters Dominion as a province. **1870–1871.** Fisheries dispute with U. S. adjusted by treaty. **1871.** British Columbia joins the Confederation. Uniform currency provided. **1872.** Dominion Parliament offers subsidy to promote building of Canadian Pacific R. R. **1872–1878.** Earl of Dufferin, Gov. Gen.	**1869.** Filibusters invade Cuba. Asunción taken by the Allies. **1870.** Insurrection in Cuba. **1870–1890.** Blanco, Dictator of Venezuela. **1871.** Brazil provides for gradual abolition of slavery. Juarez, President of Mexico.
1873. Crédit Mobilier investigation by Congress. One-cent postal cards issued. The demonetization of silver. **1874.** Organization of the Greenback party. Democrats control the House of Representatives for first time since 1856.	**U. S. Grant,** *Re-elected President.* Henry Wilson, *Vice-President.*	**1873.** Great financial panic throughout the country. The Westinghouse automatic airbrake is introduced. **1874.** The Eads Bridge across the Mississippi at St. Louis completed. First trunk pipe line from oil regions to Pittsburgh. Barbed-wire manufacture begins.	**1873.** Prince Edward Island enters Dominion. **1873–1878.** Alexander McKenzie, Premier, with Liberal ministry.	**1873.** Slavery abolished in Puerto Rico. **1874.** Religious orders suppressed in Mexico.

IV. PERIOD OF THE CIVIL WAR AND RECONSTRUCTION, 1861-1876—Concluded

THE UNITED STATES			CANADA	LATIN AMERICA AND THE WEST INDIES
POLITICAL EVENTS	ADMINISTRATIONS	SOCIAL AND INDUSTRIAL PROGRESS		
1875. Exposure of the Whisky ring. Act authorizing the resumption of specie payments. 1876. Sioux War. Massacre of Custer's troops by Sitting Bull. Admission of Colorado. Great corruption found in War Department.		1875. Hoosac Tunnel is completed. Founding of Smith and Vassar colleges for women. *Tom Sawyer* issued. 1876. Export of dressed beef begins. Great Centennial Exposition at Philadelphia. Bell patents the telephone. Founding of Johns Hopkins University.	1875. Dominion Court of Appeals (Supreme Court) established. Mounted police organized in western territories. 1876. Intercolonial railway opened, tying Halifax to Quebec.	1876. Venezuela repudiates papal authority.

V. PERIOD OF ECONOMIC DEVELOPMENT, 1877-1896

THE UNITED STATES			CANADA	LATIN AMERICA AND THE WEST INDIES
POLITICAL EVENTS	ADMINISTRATIONS	SOCIAL AND INDUSTRIAL PROGRESS		
1877. The Electoral Commission decides the contested election in favor of Hayes. Withdrawal of troops from the South. "Molly Maguires" hanged in Pennsylvania. War with the Nez Percé Indians. 1878. Bland-Allison Silver Bill passed over the President's veto.	**R. B. Hayes,** *President.* W. A. Wheeler, *Vice-President.*	1877. Edison devises the phonograph. Great railroad strike at Pittsburgh. Pope bicycle built. Goodyear welt machine brought into use. 1878. Introduction of the probation system for criminal offenders. Introduction of incandescent lights by Edison. First telephone exchange.	1878. Election endorses Conservative "national policy" of protective tariffs. 1878–1883. Marquis of Lorne, Gov. Gen. 1878–1891. Sir John A. McDonald, Premier, with Conservative ministry.	1877. Porfirio Diaz leads a Mexican revolution and becomes President. 1878. Argentine and Paraguay boundary arbitrated. Cuban revolt quelled.
1879. United States Government resumes specie payment. Women permitted to practice before United States courts.		1879. French Atlantic cable laid. Steamboat traffic on the Mississippi reaches maximum. Organization of First Christian Science Church. 1880. Edison builds the first electric railroad at Menlo Park. U. S. takes first rank among the nations in agricultural products. 1880–1890. Decade of great railroad building.	1880–1881. Commission investigates Canadian Pacific R. R.	1879–1884. Chile makes war on Peru to acquire nitrate deposits. Chile victorious, Peru exhausted. 1880–1884. Gonzalez, President of Mexico. 1880. Buenos Aires becomes capital of Argentina.
1881. President Garfield is shot July 2. 1881–1884. Lieutenant Greeley's Arctic explorations. 1882. Congress passes act to exclude Chinese laborers for 10 years. Edwards law for the suppression of polygamy. Apache Indian War.	**J. A. Garfield,** *President.* C. A. Arthur, *Vice-President.* (On death of Garfield, **Arthur** becomes President.)	1881. Organization of the American Federation of Labor. International Cotton Exposition at Atlanta, Georgia. 1882. Reorganization of the Standard Oil Company as a trust. Tolls abolished on the Erie Canal. District school system abolished by Massachusetts. 1883. Brooklyn Bridge opened. First canneries for Alaska salmon established. Northern and Southern Pacific railroads completed. Standard Time adopted.	1882. Northwest Territory divided and organized. 1883–1888. Marquis of Lansdowne, Gov. Gen. 1883. Riots in Newfoundland.	1881. Treaty between Chile and Argentina divides Patagonia between them. 1882–1899. Heureux, President of Dominican Republic.
1884. Creation of the Bureau of Labor in the Department of the Interior. 1885. Apache War in New Mexico. 1886. Silver certificates authorized.	**Grover Cleveland,** *President.* T. A. Hendricks, *Vice-President.*	1884. Great floods in the Ohio Valley. Financial panic. 1885. Long-distance telephone and electric railway introduced. 1886. Railroad strikes and anarchistic riots in Chicago. Wire nails first manufactured. Statue of Liberty unveiled.	1885. Canadian Pacific R. R. completed. Riel Rebellion in the Northwest subdued. 1886. Dispute with U. S. as to jurisdiction and fishing rights in Behring Sea referred to arbitration. Vancouver founded.	1884–1911. Diaz, President of Mexico. 1886. Colombia adopts new constitution. Slavery abolished in Cuba.
1887. Passage of the Interstate Commerce Bill. 1888. The states begin the introduction of the Australian ballot. New Chinese Exclusion Bill enacted by Congress. 1889. Admission of North Dakota, South Dakota, Washington and Montana. Pan-American Congress meets in Washington. 1890. Admission of Idaho and Wyoming. McKinley Tariff Act. Sherman Silver Purchase Act. Sioux War; Sitting Bull killed. Passage of Pension Bill. 1891. Formation of the People's Party. Massacre of Italians in New Orleans.	**Benj. Harrison,** *President.* Levi P. Morton, *Vice-President.*	1887. First vestibuled Pullman train in service. Beet sugar first successfully produced in U. S. at Alvarado, Cal. 1888. Washington Monument finished. Great Blizzard in the East. 1889. Oklahoma is opened for settlement. Johnstown flood. 1890. The United States takes first place among the nations in the production of iron. Passage of the Sherman Anti-Trust Law. 1891. Opening of the cog railroad to the top of Pike's Peak. St. Clair railway tunnel opened. Weather Bureau organized.	1887. Liberal party agitates for reciprocity with U. S.; Conservatives oppose it.	1888. Final act of Brazil abolishing slavery immediately. 1889. Revolution in Brazil expels Emperor and establishes republic. 1890. Revolution and financial revulsion in Argentina. 1891. Civil war in Chile. U. S. sailors attacked Fonseca, President of Brazil.

V. PERIOD OF ECONOMIC DEVELOPMENT, 1877-1896—Concluded

THE UNITED STATES			CANADA	LATIN AMERICA AND THE WEST INDIES
POLITICAL EVENTS	ADMINISTRATIONS	SOCIAL AND INDUSTRIAL PROGRESS		
1892. Behring Sea dispute referred to arbitration.		1892. Great strike at Homestead Ironworks. Long-distance-telephone line between New York and Chicago formally opened.		
1893. Equal suffrage granted to women in Colorado. Settlement of the Behring Sea dispute. Repeal of law requiring purchases of silver. Chinese exclusion policy adopted. 1894. New treaty with Japan. Passage of the Wilson Tariff Act. Republic of Hawaii is recognized. "Coxey's Army" marches on Washington.	**Grover Cleveland,** *President.* A. E. Stevenson, *Vice-President.*	1893. Great financial depression. World's Columbian Exposition at Chicago. World's parliament of religions at Chicago. Edison patents the kinetoscope, first motion-picture machine. 1894. The U. S. attains first rank among nations in the volume of its manufactures. Great railroad strike from Ohio to the Pacific coast. Also miners' strike and "Debs insurrection."	1893–1898. Earl of Aberdeen, Gov. Gen. 1894. Imperial Conference at Ottawa of delegates from eight self-governing British dependencies.	1893. Naval revolt in Brazil. Insurrections in Argentina. 1893–1910. Zelaya, President of Nicaragua.
1895. Income tax declared unconstitutional by the Supreme Court. Special message of the President on the Venezuelan question.		1895. Harlem ship canal opened. The name "yellow journalism" first applied to sensational papers.		1895. Boundary dispute between Venezuela and Great Britain becomes critical. Cuban insurrection.
1896. Equal suffrage granted to women in Utah and in Idaho. Admission of Utah. Great agitation for the free coinage of silver.		1896. Sault Ste. Marie Canal completed. Niagara Falls electric power turned on in Buffalo, N. Y.	1896. Dispute between Manitoba and Dominion ministry over Catholic school rights. 1896–1911. Sir Wilfrid Laurier, Premier.	1896. Gen. Weyler administers Spanish reconcentrado policy in Cuba.

VI. PERIOD OF NATIONAL EXPANSION

THE UNITED STATES			CANADA	LATIN AMERICA AND THE WEST INDIES
POLITICAL EVENTS	ADMINISTRATIONS	SOCIAL AND INDUSTRIAL PROGRESS		
1897–1898. Decisions of the Supreme Court that railroad rate agreements violate the Anti-Trust Law.	**Wm. McKinley,** *President.* G. A. Hobart, *Vice-President.*	1897. The steel rail pool collapses. Sextuplex telegraphy invented. Universal postal congress meets in Washington. Union Pacific Railroad sold to the reorganization committee.	1897. Dominion Parliament gives British a preferential tariff. Discovery of gold in the Klondike. Rush of miners thither.	1897. Venezuelan boundary adjusted by arbitration. Weyler leaves Cuba.
1898. South Dakota adopts initiative and referendum. Annexation of Hawaii. Congress orders forcible intervention in Cuba; war with Spain follows. Battles at Manila, El Caney and Santiago quickly bring peace. Greater New York formed. 1899. War in the Philippine Islands, led by Aguinaldo, against American domination.		1898. Commercial treaty with France signed. Boston builds a subway. Method of mercerizing cloth is patented. 1899. Great commercial and financial prosperity. First juvenile courts organized in Chicago.	1898–1904. Earl of Minto, Gov. Gen.	1898. U. S. battleship *Maine* destroyed by explosion in Havana harbor. Cuba and Puerto Rico taken by United States. 1899. Cuba under protectorate of U. S. Venezuela boundary settled. Castro, Dictator of Venezuela.
1900. Congress passes act providing civil government for the Philippines. Civil government established in Alaska. American forces sent to China. 1901. Passage of Platt Amendment relating to Cuban independence. "Open-door policy" for China announced.	**Wm. McKinley,** *Re-elected President.* Theo. Roosevelt, *Vice-President.* (On death of McKinley, Sept. 14, **Roosevelt** becomes President.)	1900. Floods damage Galveston. 1901. Formation of the United States Steel Corporation. Pan-American Exposition held at Buffalo. Discovery of the Texas oil field.	1900. Rapid colonization of Canadian Northwest, largely by emigrants from U. S.	1900. Civil war in Colombia. 1901. War between Venezuela and Colombia. Pan-American Congress at Mexico.
1902. Civil government established in the Philippines. 1903. Alaskan boundary tribunal in London decides in favor of the United States. Creation of the Department of Commerce and Labor. Canal treaty with Panama ratified.		1902. Great strike of anthracite coal miners. The Carnegie Institution of Washington is established. 1903. Pacific cable completed. Wright brothers fly their airplane.	1902. Canadian-Australian cable laid. 1903. Joint commission on Alaskan boundary decides favorably on claims of U. S. New transcontinental railway authorized.	1902. Revolution in San Domingo. Destructive eruption of Mt. Pelée. 1903. Independence of Panama declared under guardianship of U. S. Panama Canal Zone organized.
		1904. Exposition at St. Louis. Work on Panama Canal commences. New York subway opened.	1904–1911. Earl Grey, Gov. Gen.	1904. Strained relations between Venezuela and U. S. Venezuela made to pay European debts.
	Theo. Roosevelt, *Re-elected President.* C. W. Fairbanks, *Vice-President.*	1905. Investigation of insurance companies in New York begins.	1905. Saskatchewan and Alberta become members of the Dominion.	1905. Movement to establish confederation of Canada and British West Indies. U. S. assumes protectorate of Dominican Republic.
1906. Riot at Brownsville, Texas. Military occupation of Cuba. Passage of pure-food and drug-inspection law. Interstate Commerce Commission given more power.		1906. Earthquake hits San Francisco.	1906. Life-insurance investigation in Canada.	1906. Pan-American Congress at Rio de Janeiro. Destructive earthquake at Valparaiso, Chile.

VI. PERIOD OF NATIONAL EXPANSION—Continued

THE UNITED STATES			CANADA	LATIN AMERICA AND THE WEST INDIES
POLITICAL EVENTS	ADMINISTRATIONS	SOCIAL AND INDUSTRIAL PROGRESS		
1907. Admission of Oklahoma. Pure Food Law in effect. 1907–1909. United States fleet makes a round-the-world cruise. 1908. The United States remits the Chinese Boxer indemnity.		1907. Jamestown Exposition. Financial panic.	1907. Demonstration against Japanese at Vancouver. Mine strikes.	1907. Finances of San Domingo put under supervision of U. S.
1909. Congress proposes income-tax amendment.	Wm. H. Taft, *President.* J. S. Sherman, *Vice-President.*	1908. Tunnels opened under East River and Hudson River, New York. Great strike of coal miners in Pennsylvania. 1909. Exposition at Seattle. Hudson-Fulton Celebration at New York. Peary reaches the North Pole.		1909. U. S. withdraws army from Cuba.
1910. Equal suffrage granted to women in the state of Washington. Passage of postal savings bank law.		1910. I. W. W. starts labor disputes.		1910. Pan-American Congress at Buenos Ayres.
1912. Admission of Arizona and New Mexico. Progressive party formed. 1913. Department of Labor created. Federal income tax and direct election of senators made effective.	Woodrow Wilson, *President.* T. R. Marshall, *Vice-President.*	1911. Standard Oil monopoly broken up. 1912. Moderate-priced automobile is marketed. 1913. Parcel Post service begun. Serious Ohio floods. Federal Reserve System created.		1911. Revolts in Mexico end Diaz control. 1912. Trans-Andean railway opened. 1913. New revolt in Mexico.
1914. U. S. declares neutrality in European War. A. B. C. powers mediate dispute between U. S. and Mexico. 1915. Sinking of *Lusitania* rouses sentiment against Germany.		1914. Panama Canal opened	1914. Parcel Post begun. Canada joins in World War.	1914. New revolt in Mexico leads to U. S. occupation of Vera Cruz. 1915. U. S. takes control in Haiti.
1916. Wilson continues appeals for arbitration and peace.		1915. Federal Trade Commission formed. Expositions in California. 1916. Great industrial expansion with war orders; 8-hour railway labor law.	1916. World War losses increase.	1916. Villa pursued into Mexico after U. S. raid.
1917. War declared against Germany. Military conscription adopted. First U. S. troops reach France, June 26.	Woodrow Wilson, *Re-elected President.* T. R. Marshall, *Re-elected Vice-Pres.*	1917. Liberty Loans issued. Government takes control of railroads.	1917. Woman suffrage and military conscription adopted.	1917. U. S. buys Virgin Islands from Denmark.
1918. 2,500,000 U. S. soldiers in France. U. S. men in battle, the Somme, St. Mihiel, the Argonne. Wilson proposes 14 Points for Peace. Armistice ends World War. 1919. Wilson goes to Europe to promote League of Nations, but Senate rejects it. National Prohibition effective.		1918. Food and fuel rationed by Federal authorities. Industry expands rapidly, especially munitions and shipbuilding. Aircraft industry develops. Daylight-saving time adopted. 1919. U. S. and English fliers cross the Atlantic. Steel and coal strikes.	1918. Draft riots in Quebec. 1919. Serious strikes.	1918. Several Latin countries join Allies in World War, but take little active part. 1919. Peace dawns in Mexico.
1920. National woman suffrage in effect. 1921. Formal peace with Germany ratified. International Conference on Armament Reduction at Washington. 1923. U. S. troops leave Germany.	Warren Harding, *President.* Calvin Coolidge, *Vice-President.* (On death of Harding in 1923, **Coolidge** becomes President.)	1921. Industrial pace slackens. Radio broadcasting begun. Home electrical appliances multiply. 1923. First New York-California nonstop airplane flight. 1924. U. S. Navy planes make round-the-world flight.	1923. Canada and U. S. make trade treaty.	1920. Bolivia and Chile threaten war. 1921. U. S. pays Colombia for rape of Panama.
1924. Japanese exclusion policy becomes effective. European immigration restricted. Oil land lease scandals. Ku-Klux Klan revived. 1925. Adjustment of European war debts undertaken.	Calvin Coolidge, *Re-elected President.* Chas. G. Dawes, *Vice-President.*	1925. Dirigible *Shenandoah* wrecked. Coal miners strike. 1926. U. S. Navy plane flies over North Pole. Exposition at Philadelphia. Sound motion pictures accepted.	1926. Great Britain makes Canada an autonomous Dominion. Ontario gold rush.	1924. Calles, President of Mexico. U. S. troops leave Dominican Republic. 1925. Machado, President of Cuba. 1926. Mexico takes for poor lands of the Church and great estates.
1927. Exchange of Ministers with Canada begun. 1929. Kellogg Peace Treaty put into effect, signed by 62 nations. 1931. European war-debt moratorium.	Herbert Hoover, *President.* Charles Curtis, *Vice-President.*	1927. Lindbergh makes first Atlantic solo flight. Serious Mississippi floods. 1929. Economic boom results in stock-market collapse. Byrd flies over South Pole. 1931. Economic conditions grow worse. Empire State Building put up.	1927. Government sale of liquor succeeds. 1929. Disputes with U. S. over rum runners. 1931. New Welland Canal opened.	1927. U. S. halts civil war in Nicaragua. Mexico takes oil lands. 1929. Tacna-Arica dispute ends. Revolt in Haiti. 1931. Many revolts in Latin America.
1932. Bonus seekers driven from Washington. New National Bank law. 1933. National Prohibition ended. "Lame Duck" Congress ended. Russia recognized. New Deal relief and employment programs started. Farm and home loan laws.	Franklin Roosevelt, *President.* John N. Garner, *Vice-President.*	1932. Reconstruction Finance Corporation attempts to halt industrial panic. 1933. National bank holiday. Gold standard abandoned. Tennessee Valley Authority created. Exposition in Chicago. Dirigible *Akron* wrecked.	1932. Empire Economic Conference, Ottawa. 1933. Newfoundland faces bankruptcy.	1932. Chaco War in South America. 1933. Revolt drives Machado from Cuba.
1934. Philippine independence law passed. Stock exchange and public utility regulation increased. 1935. National Social Security law adopted. Bank deposits insured. New Deal reforms checked when declared unconstitutional.		1934. Dollar devalued. Textile strikes cause riots. Droughts and dust storms. 1935. Economic recovery stirs. Federal emergency relief program is extended, using $4,500,000,000.	1934. Newfoundland under British control. Dionne quintuplets born. 1935. Central Bank of Canada opens. 1935. Conservative reaction wins elections. Mackenzie King, Prime Minister.	1934. American antiwar treaty adopted. U. S. leaves Haiti. 1935. Mexico takes more church property. Chaco war ends.

VI. PERIOD OF NATIONAL EXPANSION—Continued

THE UNITED STATES			CANADA	LATIN AMERICA AND THE WEST INDIES
POLITICAL EVENTS	ADMINISTRATIONS	SOCIAL AND INDUSTRIAL PROGRESS		
1936. New soldiers' bonus paid. Agricultural relief law found unconstitutional. Merchant Marine laws revised.		1936. Heavy tax program fails to meet national deficit. Shipping strike on Pacific.	1936. Canadian Supreme Court invalidates "New Deal" legislation of Bennett government.	1936. Monroe Doctrine replaced by Common Front policy.
1937. Presidential inauguration changed to January. Feeling against Japan develops.	**Franklin Roosevelt,** *Re-elected President.* John N. Garner, *Re-elected Vice-Pres.*	1937. Labor-union conflicts and sit-down strikes check recovery. Serious Ohio River floods. Price-fixing made legal.		1937. Vargas, Dictator of Brazil, suspends republican constitution.
1938. Secretary Hull denounces international anarchy; "contagious scourge of treaty-breaking." United States sponsors plan to relieve plight of European refugees.		1938. Business recession. Administration plans new recovery program. Severe floods in Southern California.	1938. Semi-Fascist movement gains ground in Quebec. Partial suppression of freedom of speech and press. Trade agreement with United States.	1938. Fascist-Communist agitation shakes South America. Mexico expropriates large foreign oil properties. Pan-American Congress stresses American solidarity.
1939. Trade agreements with Great Britain, Brazil and Turkey. Felix Frankfurter and William O. Douglas made Supreme Court Justices. Justice L. D. Brandeis retires.		1939. Roosevelt announces national health program. New York World's Fair and Golden Gate Exposition open.	1939. King George VI and Queen Elizabeth visit Canada and the United States. Lord Tweedsmuir, Governor General of Canada, dies. Canada declares war on Germany.	1939. Devastating earthquake in Chile. Brazil concludes trade agreement with United States.
1940. Murphy made Supreme Court Justice. Strict neutrality kept. Senator William Borah dies. Law, restricting sale of war supplies to belligerents to cash-and-carry plan, vigorously applied. Robert H. Jackson—Attorney General.		1940. Federal Housing Act assists private construction. National Labor Relations Board arbitrates business and labor disputes. Both World's Fairs open for second year. Aliens registered; National registration and conscription.	1940. No conscription. Volunteers go to war in Europe. Laws passed for collective bargaining.	1940. Mexico continues seizure of foreign-owned oil properties. Refuses arbitration.
1940–41. United States secures new aviation bases in Atlantic. Chief Justice Hughes and Justice McReynolds resign from U. S. Supreme Court. Harlan F. Stone new Chief Justice.	1941. Franklin D. Roosevelt, 1st third-term president; Henry A. Wallace, Vice-President.	1941. United States prepares tremendous defense program. Lend-Lease aid given England and Russia. Germany sinks many U. S. ships. Japanese credits frozen. U. S. troops defend Iceland.	1941. Canada speeds up aid to England.	1941. Duke of Windsor, Governor of Bahamas. England and Mexico renew diplomatic relations. Panama exiles ruler. Americas present united front.
Dec. 7, 1941. Japan attacks U. S. at Pearl Harbor. U. S. declares war vs. Japan, Germany, Italy.				
1942. All Central and South American countries, except neutral Chile and Argentina, cooperate with U. S. U. S. in total war. Japan captures Guam, Wake Islands, Philippines.		1942. Tremendous war production. U. S. aids allies, England, Russia, China and Australia. War time adopted. U. S. builds mighty Army, Navy and Airforce. Shortage of rubber and oil. Price ceiling to prevent inflation. Rationing.	1942. Canada makes mighty war effort in total war. Nation votes conscription for overseas.	1942. Argentina and Chile remain neutral. All others fully cooperate with U. S. in war effort. German submarines sink many ships.
1943. U. S. captures Guadalcanal, part of New Guinea, New Britain, Solomon and Gilbert Islands.		1943. U. S. leads world in production of materials of war.	1943. Canada imprisons tremendous number of Axis soldiers. Alcan Highway opened.	
1944. Defeats Japs in Pacific and Burma. Allies invade Europe.			1944. Canadians take important part in war.	1944. Dictator Ramirez replaced by Farrell in Argentina.
1945. Allies conquer Axis. Byrnes appointed Secretary of State.	1945. Franklin D. Roosevelt. 1st fourth-term president; Harry S. Truman, Vice-President. Harry S. Truman becomes president on death of Roosevelt.	1945. Post-war security conference at San Francisco. United Nations rule Germany and Japan. War criminals punished. Atomic energy discussed.	1945. Canadians aid in conquest of Germany.	
			1946. Uncovering of spy ring dominates the scene.	
				1947. Prosperity throughout Latin America and South America. Extensive colonization of Central Brazil.
			1948. Canada sends money and food to Europe.	
1949. Atlantic Pact signed by 12 nations. Marshall Plan aids Europe. Democratic Congress, U. S. fights Communism.	1949. Harry S. Truman inaugurated President. Alben W. Barkley, Vice-President.		1949. Newfoundland, 10th Province of Canada.	
1950. Korean War begins.				1950. Puerto Rico given self-government.
1951. General MacArthur relieved of Asiatic command.		1951. Prices and wages frozen. War mobilization of industries. Atomic power released for industrial uses.		
		1952. U. S. contributes troops and money to North Atlantic Treaty Organization.	1952. Vincent Massey becomes Governor General of Canada.	1952. Batista seizes Cuban Government.

THE UNITED STATES			CANADA	LATIN AMERICA AND THE WEST INDIES
POLITICAL EVENTS	ADMINISTRATIONS	SOCIAL AND INDUSTRIAL PROGRESS		
1952. Governor Adlai Stevenson of Illinois campaigns against Eisenhower for Presidency. 1952. High taxes and corruption in government become issues of Democrats vs. Republicans.		1952. Congressional committees investigate gambling and crime syndicates. Many racketeers are convicted. 1952. Korean War causes war economy and full employment.	1952. Canadian Treasury reports revenues estimated at four billion dollars, largest on record.	
1953. Complete change in Cabinet. John Foster Dulles is Secretary of State. Herbert Brownell is Attorney General. 1953. U. S. Seventh Fleet is withdrawn from Strait of Formosa. 1954 Senator McCarthy and Committee investigate Communists.	**Dwight D. Eisenhower** *President.* Richard Nixon, *Vice-President.*	1953. Price and wage controls are abolished. 1953. Department of Health, Education and Welfare created, giving cabinet rank to Oveta Culp Hobby. 1953. James P. Mitchell becomes Secretary of Labor. Earl Warren appointed Chief Justice of Supreme Court. 1954. Huge Hydrogen blasts surpass previous atomic explosions. Many attempts to correct juvenile delinquency. Vaccine for polio tried.	1953. Canadian troops fight in Korea. 1953. Large-scale prospecting for uranium and oil in Alaska and Canada. Huge oil deposits already discovered in Canada. 1954. Prime Minister St. Laurent makes global good-will tour.	1953. Rafael Trujillo, Dominican dictator, visits U. S. 1954. Venezuela sends iron ore to U. S. 1954. Reversal of tide of Puerto Rican immigration to U. S. 1954. Coffee shortage in Brazil.
1955. U.S. Forces protect Formosa. John M. Harlan becomes Supreme Court Justice. Yalta treaty made public. 1955. President suffers heart attack.		1955. American Federation of Labor and C.I.O. merge after a 20-year separation. 1955. Salk polio vaccine administered.	1955. Prosperity in Canada.	1955. Assassination of President Remon of Panama. President Magloire of Haiti and wife visit U.S. Princess Margaret visits British West Indies.
1956. Eisenhower's State of the Union message asks for more schools, social security, highways, farm aid. 1956. Democrats accuse Republicans of mistakes in foreign policy, and neglect of farmers.		1956. Admiral Byrd leads Antarctic expedition. 1956. Soil bank and other relief for farmers. 1956. South fights de-segregation.	1956. Canada exports surplus butter.	
1957. Eisenhower asks Congress for a definite commitment to stop any aggressor nation in the Middle East. 1958. McClellan committee investigates abuses by Labor Unions. Congress votes for missile experimentation and space satellites.	**Dwight D. Eisenhower** *Re-elected President* Richard M. Nixon *Re-elected Vice-President*	1957. Congress passes Civil Rights bill. Eisenhower uses Federal troops to enforce Little Rock's school integration. 1958. Robert Young, railroad chairman, kills himself, emphasizing difficulties of U. S. railroads.	1957. Canada takes leading part in United Nations affairs. 1958. John Diefenbaker, Canadian Prime Minister, institutes new economic reforms.	1956. Assassination of President Somoza of Nicaragua. 1958. Rebellion in Cuba. Fuentes wins Presidential election in Guatemala. The West Indies becomes a new nation.
1960. Flag has 50 stars with admission of Alaska and Hawaii. 1960. Kennedy and Nixon debate on television. Election of Kennedy, first Roman Catholic ever elected President.		1959. Congressional investigations of TV quiz programs and radio disk jockeys.	1959. St. Lawrence Seaway in full operation.	1959. Castro wins revolution in Cuba. 1960. U.S. breaks off diplomatic relations with Cuba and Dominican Republic.
1961. RB-47 flyers released by Russia, welcomed in U.S.	**John F. Kennedy** *President* Lyndon B. Johnson *Vice-President*	1961. Kennedy sends bill to Congress to raise minimum wages. Chimpanzee alive after space flight.	1961. Red China buys grain from Canada in biggest deal since World War II.	1961. Civil war imminent in Cuba. El Salvador ousts pro-Communist government.
1962. U-2 pilot Powers exchanged for Russian spy Abel. Spaceman Glenn orbits earth.		1962. Many mergers of banks, of railroads, and of airlines. Congress investigates stockpiling of strategic metals. Kennedy asks for gradual elimination of tariffs between U.S. and Common Market.	1962. Canada imports from Cuba and Red China, but exports 5 times as much.	1962. Crisis in Cuba; Russians remove weapons. Cuba expelled from Organization of American States.
1963. Test-ban treaty with Soviet Union. Kennedy assassinated. 1964. Congress passes tax-cut bill. Johnson elected President, Humphrey Vice-Pres. 1965. U.S. marines sent to quell uprising in Dominican Republic. 1966. Escalation of war in Vietnam. Bombing of oil depots at Haiphong.	(On death of Kennedy in 1963, **Johnson** becomes President) **Lyndon B. Johnson,** *President* Hubert H. Humphrey, *Vice-President*	1963. Aid-to-education bill. Civil rights march on Washington, August 28. 1964. Civil rights bill. Warren Commission Report. 1965. Voting Rights Act suspends literacy and other voting qualification tests. 1966. 17.3 million Americans over 65 sign up for the voluntary part B of Medicare.	1963. Pearson succeeds Diefenbaker as prime minister. Canada sells $500 million worth of wheat to Soviet Union. 1964. Secessionist movement in Quebec. 1965. New maple leaf flag raised for the first time February 15. 1966. Munsinger parliamentary scandal leaves Prime Minister Pearson facing universal demands for his resignation.	1963. Third year of Alliance for Progress. 1964. Many Latin American countries break with Cuba. 1965. Military uprising in Dominican Republic. 1966. Conservative ex-president Balaguer elected in Dominican Republic.

(The figures prefixed to the names of leaders, battles, etc., indicate to which of the two contesting parties the leader belonged, or by which the victory was won; they correspond to the numbers used in the column giving the names of the contesting parties.)

NAME OF WAR, CONTESTANTS AND DATES	CAUSE OF CONFLICT	LEADERS	CHIEF BATTLES AND INCIDENTS	RESULTS AND COMMENTS
Trojan War—c. 1200 B. C. (1) Greeks vs. (2) Trojans	Aegean Greek civilization opposes advance of younger Doric Greeks.	(1) Agamemnon, Achilles, Ulysses. (2) Hector.	(1) Siege of Troy.	Capture and destruction of Troy. Doric Greeks supreme.
Messenian Wars—c. 700–456 B. C. (1) Spartans vs. (2) Messenians.	Conflicting ambitions of city-states.		(1) Siege of Mount Ithome.	Messenians become Helots (slaves to Spartans).
Persian Wars—500–479 B.C. (1) Persians vs. (2) Greeks. a. First Persian Expedition— 493 B.C.	Aid given by Athens and Eretria to revolting Ionic Greek cities, leading to burning of Sardis, c. 497. Continued plans of Darius for subjugating Greece.	(1) Mardonius, Xerxes, Darius. (2) Miltiades, Leonidas, Themistocles, Aristides.	(2) Marathon (490). (1) Thermopylae. (1) Athens (burned). (2) Salamis. (2) Plataea.	Partial success against Macedonians and Thracians.
b. Second Persian Expedition —490 B.C.				The Athenians are victorious and the Persians retreat to Asia Minor.
c. Third Persian Expedition— 481–480 B.C.	Xerxes desires to avenge his father's defeat.			Xerxes retreats to Persia after his defeat at Salamis.
d. Fourth Persian Expedition— 479 B.C.	War continued by troops which Xerxes left behind.			All Persian invasions and attempts to subjugate Greece cease.
Peloponnesian War—431–404 B.C. (1) Sparta and Allies vs. (2) Athens and Allies. a. First Period—431–421 B.C. b. Second Period or Decelean War—413–404 B.C.	Envy of Sparta and her allies at Athens' growing power and influence. Discontent among some of the Athenian subject states. Athens leads the Ionic Greeks; Sparta, the Doric.	(1) Brasidas, Lysander. (2) Cleon. Alcibiades serves Athens, Sparta and Athens in turn.	(1) Invasion of Attica, Siege of Plataea, Amphipolis. (2) Mitylene, Sphacteria, Expedition against Syracuse. (1) Aegospotami, Surrender of Athens.	By the peace of Nicias (421) both sides are to restore conquests and prisoners but terms are imperfectly carried out. The Spartans tear down the walls of Piraeus and Athens. Athens becomes an independent ally of Sparta. Sparta is now supreme in Greece.
Gauls' Invasion of Italy—390 B.C. (1) Gauls vs. (2) Romans.	Growing power and ambition of barbarian Gauls conflict with Roman self-assurance.	(1) Brennus. (2) Manlius Capitolinus.	(1) Battle of the Allia. Sack of Rome.	Gauls retire on payment of ransom. The overthrow of Rome had no permanent effect on her fortunes.
Greek Sacred War—339–338 B.C. (1) Macedonians vs. (2) Athenians, Thebans.	Rivalries of Greek city-states give ambitions of Philip of Macedon an opportunity to develop.	(1) Philip of Macedon. (2) Demosthenes.	(1) Chaeronea.	Philip gains leadership of Greece. Henceforth Greece is under the control of Macedonia.
Samnite Wars—343–290 B.C. (1) Romans vs. (2) Samnites. a. First Samnite War—343– 341 B.C.	A duel between two rival races for supremacy in Italy. Campanians implore aid of Romans against Samnites.	(1) Fabius Maximus, Lucius Papirius Cursor. (2) Gaius Pontius.	(2) Caudine Forks. (1) Sentinum.	Indecisive.
b. Second or Great Samnite War—327–304 B.C.	The occupation of Palaeopolis by the Samnites. In 311 the Etruscan cities joined in the war against Rome.			Samnites sue for peace but retain their independence.
c. Third Samnite War—298– 290 B.C.	The Samnites enter Lucania and refuse to withdraw.			Samnites defeated but not crushed.
Wars of Alexander the Great in Asia—334–328 B.C. (1) Greeks vs. (2) Persians, Egyptians, Bactrians, Hindus.	A war of conquest, a scientific expedition and a journey of discovery.	(1) Alexander the Great, Nearchus. (2) Darius III.	(1) Granicus, Issus, Siege of Tyre, Arbela.	Alexander conquers Asia from the Mediterranean Sea to the Indus and begins the Hellenizing of the East. Founds Alexandria in Egypt. The empire breaks up after Alexander's death, 323.
Roman War with Tarentum and Epirus—282–272 B.C. (1) Romans vs. (2) Tarentum and Epirus.	Pyrrhus, having won supremacy in Greece, takes part in Italian wars against the growing power of Rome.	(1) Manius Curius. (2) Pyrrhus.	(1) Beneventum, Tarentum. (2) Heraclea, Asculum.	Pyrrhus returns to Epirus and his allies one by one submit to Rome, which is left supreme from Straits of Messina to the River Arno.
First Punic War—264–241 B.C. (1) Romans vs. (2) Carthaginians.	A struggle for supremacy in Sicily.	(1) P. Claudius Pulcher, C. Lutatius Catulus, M. Atilius Regulus. (2) Hamilcar Barca, Hanno.	(1) Mylae, Agrigentum, Ecnomus. (2) Drepana.	Carthaginians yield Sicily and pay indemnity. Carthage retains the Western Mediterranean and Rome is launched on her career of conquest.
Second Punic War—218–201 B.C. (1) Romans vs. (2) Carthaginians.	A duel to the death between Rome and Carthage. Pretext, Hannibal's attacks on Saguntum in Spain.	(1) Q. Fabius Maximus, Publius Scipio. P. Cornelius Scipio Africanus. (2) Hannibal, Hasdrubal.	(1) Syracuse, Capua, Metaurus, Zama. (2) Ticinus, Trebia, Trasimen, Cannae.	Carthage forced to give up Spain, to pay an annual tribute, to surrender her fleet, and to agree not to go to war without the permission of Rome.
Greco-Roman War—214–146 B.C. (1) Romans vs. (2) Greeks.	Alliance of Philip, King of Macedon, with Carthage.	(1) T. Quinctius Flamininus, L. Aemilius Paulus. (2) Philip of Macedon, Perseus.	(1) Cynoscephalae, Pydna.	Macedonia becomes a Roman province.
Third Punic War—149–146 B.C. (1) Romans vs. (2) Carthaginians.	Ambitious Romans uneasy until Carthage is completely destroyed.	(1) Scipio Africanus. Scipio Aemilianus.	(1) Siege of Carthage.	Carthage destroyed. Most of her territory becomes a Roman province of Africa.
Jugurthine War—111–105 B.C. (1) Romans vs. (2) Jugurtha of Numidia.	Jugurtha, disregarding intervention of Rome, captures Citra and massacres male population.	(1) Marius. (2) Jugurtha.	(1) Muthul, Citra.	Numidia divided. The war reveals the corruption and incapacity of the Senatorial Government of Rome.
Marsian or Social War—90–88 B.C. (1) Romans vs. (2) Italian Allies.	Italian socii (allies) are denied the right of Roman citizenship.	(1) Marius. Sulla.	(1) Asculum.	Roman citizenship granted to all Italian residents.
Three Mithridatic Wars—88–63 B.C. (1) Romans vs. (2) Pontines and Armenians.	Ambition of Mithridates VI and his massacre of thousands of Romans in his territory.	(1) Sulla, Lucullus. Pompey. (2) Mithridates.	(1) Chaeronea, Orchomenus, Cabira, Tigranocerta.	Reorganization of the East, Pontus, Syria and Cilicia become Roman provinces.

Gallic War—Wars of the Roses

Name of War, Contestants and Dates	Cause of Conflict	Leaders	Chief Battles and Incidents	Results and Comments
Gallic War—58–51 B.C. (1) Romans vs. (2) Tribes of Gaul.	Desire to extend the Roman Empire.	(1) Julius Caesar. (2) Vercingetorix. Ariovistus.	(1) Siege of Alesia.	Conquest and organization of Gaul by Caesar. Gauls Romanized; boundaries of the old world enlarged.
Second Roman Civil War—49–31 B.C. First Period, 49–45 B.C. (1) Followers of Caesar vs. (2) Followers of Pompey.	Struggle for mastery between Caesar, conqueror of Gaul, and Pompey, conqueror of the East.	(1) Caesar. (2) Pompey and his sons.	(1) "Crossing the Rubicon." Pharsalus, Thapsus, Munda.	Caesar is appointed dictator for life. He is the founder of the new monarchy at Rome.
Second Period, 43–42 B.C. (1) Friends of Caesar (Second Triumvirate) vs. (2) Caesar's Assassins.	Assassination of Caesar, 44 B.C.	(1) Antony, Octavius, Lepidus. (2) Brutus, Cassius, Sextus Pompey.	(1) Philippi.	Brutus and Cassius, defeated, commit suicide.
Third Period—31–30 B.C. (1) Octavius vs. (2) Antony.	A continued struggle for supreme power.	(1) Octavius. (2) Antony, Cleopatra.	(1) Actium.	Triumph of Octavius, end of the Republic and beginning of the Empire.
Jewish War—A.D. 66–70 (1) Romans vs. (2) Jews.	Revolt of the Jews against Rome.	(1) Titus, son of Emperor Vespasian.	(1) Siege of Jerusalem.	Destruction of Jerusalem and the temple.
Dacian Wars—86–107. (1) Romans vs. (2) Dacians.	Roman desire to expand.	(1) Domitian, Trajan. (2) Decebalus.		Dacia is made a Roman province. Roman conquest and Empire reaches its highest point.
Invasion of Roman Empire by Northern Barbarians—375–493. (1) Romans vs. (2) Teutons and (Huns) Teutonic Tribes; Visigoths, Vandals, Suevi, Franks, Burgundians, Ostrogoths, Alemanni, Jutes, Saxons, Angles, Lombards.	The Huns (Mongolians) press upon the Teutons, who are forced to seek new lands within the boundaries of the Roman Empire.	(1) Valens, Stilicho Aetius, Leo (Bishop of Rome). (2) Alaric, Walja (Visigoth); Genseric (Vandal); Hengist and Horsa (Saxons); Attila (Hun); Theodoric the Great (Ostrogoth).	(1) Battle near Chalons (451). (2) Adrianople, Sack of Rome. Visigothic kingdom of Tolosa (Toulouse), (415–507). Vandals settle in Africa (429–534). Burgundians occupy Rhone Valley (443). Angles, Saxons and Jutes invade England (449), Huns and Ostrogoths ravage Gaul. Huns destroy Lombardy. Vandals plunder Rome (455). Odoacer gains ascendancy in Rome. The fall of the Roman Empire (476).	Overthrow of the Roman Empire in the West, though it continued in the East until 1453. This blending of Roman and Teutonic elements under the influence of the Christian religion and what remained of classic civilization formed the civilization of the Middle Ages.
Saracen or Mohammedan Wars—709–1492. (1) Saracens (Arabs) vs. (2) Christian nations, Persia and Egypt.	Saracens are ambitious to found a world-wide Mohammedan empire.	(1) Tarik, Abderrahman, Mohammed II, Harun al Rashid, Abdallah. (2) Charles Martel, Constantine, Palaeologus, Ferdinand of Aragon, the Cid.	(1) Damascus, Jerusalem, Alexandria, Carthage (697), Xeres (Spain), Granada, Toledo. (2) Constantinople (716), Tours, Las Navas de Tolosa (1212). (1) Constantinople (1453). (2) Granada (1492).	The Saracens attempted to conquer and convert Europe at three different times between 710 and 1492. Their power began to wane from the latter date. The Saracens won Spain, all north Africa, Egypt, and central Europe as far as Vienna, but were badly beaten in France and later driven out of Spain.
Crusades—1096–1291. (1) European Christians vs. (2) Turks and Moslems. First Crusade—1096–1099.	The appeal of the eastern emperor for aid, the desire to recover the Holy Sepulcher from the infidels, the love of adventure, and hope of gain.	(1) Peter the Hermit, Godfrey of Bouillon, Robert of Normandy.	(1) Nicaea, Antioch, Jerusalem.	Jerusalem is subdued and a transient kingdom is founded.
Second Crusade—1147–1149.	Preaching of Saint Bernard.	(1) Conrad III of Germany, Louis VII of France.		Armies almost annihilated by hunger, disease and the enemy.
Third Crusade—1189–1192.	Capture of Jerusalem by Saladin.	(1) Richard I of England, Philip Augustus of France, Frederick Barbarossa of Germany. (2) Saladin.	(1) Acre.	The Latin Christians secure by treaty the privilege of visiting the tomb of Christ for three years without molestation.
Fourth Crusade—1201–1204. (1) Crusaders vs. (2) Eastern Empire.	Appeals of Innocent III. Through influence of the Venetians the Crusaders turn aside to attack Constantinople.	(1) Dandolo, Baldwin of Flanders.	(1) Sack of Constantinople.	Division of Eastern Empire. The Venetians get the monopoly of trade of the Aegean and Ionian seas.
Fifth Crusade—1228–1229.	Vow of Frederick II. of Germany. He goes under Pope's excommunication.	(1) Frederick II.		Frederick secures a truce for 10 years and the restoration of Jerusalem to the Christians.
Sixth Crusade—1248–1254.	Louis IX of France starts on a crusade via Egypt.	(1) Louis IX later St. Louis.	(1) Damietta. (2) Expedition to Cairo.	Louis is captured in battle and released on payment of heavy ransom and evacuation of Damietta.
Last, Seventh Crusade—1270–1291.	Louis IX goes against Mohammedans of Tunis, Prince Edward of England to Syria.	(1) Louis IX, Prince Edward.	(2) Acre, last Christian stronghold in Syria, falls (1291).	The results of the crusades were development of commerce, introduction of new customs, products and manufactures, increase in freedom of lower classes, especially townsmen, and the power of the Crown.
Hundred Years' War—1337–1453. (1) English vs. (2) French.	The conflict of interests of the French and English kings in Guienne, Flanders and Scotland. Edward III advances claim by descent to the throne of France.	(1) Edward III. Edward the Black Prince. Henry V. Duke of Bedford. (2) Du Guesclin, Charles V, Joan of Arc.	(1) Crécy, Calais, Poitiers, Agincourt, Treaty of Troyes. (2) Orleans (1429), Castillon (1453).	England loses all her land in France except Calais. During the earlier stage of this war about one-third of the population of western Europe perished from the Black Death.
Austro-Swiss War—1386–1388. (1) House of Hapsburg vs. (2) Swiss Confederation.	Hapsburgs assert feudal rights over the peasants of the Swiss cantons.	(1) Leopold III of Austria. (2) Arnold von Winkelried.	(2) Sempach, Näfels.	Independence of Swiss secured.
Wars of the Roses—1455–1485. (1) Yorkists (White Rose) vs. (2) Lancastrians (Red Rose).	Misgovernment under Henry VI encourages Richard, Duke of York, representing the second line of descent from Edward	(1) Richard, Duke of York. Edward IV. Richard III. (2) Duke of Somerset.	(1) St. Albans, Northampton, Towton, Barnet, Tewkesbury. (2) Wakefield, Bosworth Field.	Henry Tudor (Lancastrian in the female line) secures throne as Henry VII. By his marriage with Elizabeth of York he unites the warring factions

French Civil Wars—American Revolution

Name of War, Contestants and Dates	Cause of Conflict	Leaders	Chief Battles and Incidents	Results and Comments
	III, to claim the throne against Henry VII (third line).	Queen Margaret. Earl of Warwick ("Kingmaker"), first a Yorkist and then a Lancastrian. Henry VII.		and establishes an almost despotic rule in England.
French Civil Wars—1562–1598. (1) Catholics vs. (2) Huguenots (Protestants).	Massacre of Huguenots at Vassy is a signal for uprising.	(1) Duke of Guise, Henry III. (2) Catherine de' Médici. Condé, Coligny, Henry of Navarre (Henry IV).	(1) Dreux, Jarnac, Montcontour. Massacre of St. Bartholomew, Siege of Paris. (2) Arnay-le-Duc, Coutras, Arques, Ivry.	By the Edict of Nantes (1598) the Huguenots are given equal political rights with Catholics, limited freedom of worship, the possession of La Rochelle and other strong places as cities of refuge.
War of Liberation of the Netherlands—1565–1609. (1) Spain vs. (2) Revolted provinces in the Netherlands.	Political and religious tyranny of Spain. Duke of Alva enforces the Inquisition.	(1) Duke of Alva. Alexander of Parma. (2) William of Orange Jan van Olden, Barneveldt, Maurice of Nassau.	(1) Mechlin, Haarlem. (2) Brill, Siege of Leyden, "Spanish Fury" at Antwerp. Pacification of Ghent (1576). Union of Utrecht (1579). Declaration of Independence (1581).	By the peace of Westphalia (1648) the independence of the seven northern provinces, the United Netherlands, is recognized. The ten southern provinces continue under Spanish rule until 1713.
Thirty Years' War—1618–1648. (1) German Protestants and their Allies, England, Holland, Sweden and France vs. (2) Imperial German Catholics and their allies, Spain, Italy.	Religious and political disputes between Catholics and Protestants. The war passes through four phases—(1) Bohemian-Palatinate. (2) Danish. (3) Swedish. (4) Swedish-French.	(1) Frederick, Elector Palatine, Mansfield, Gustavus Adolphus (Sweden). Turenne and Condé (France). (2) Emperor Ferdinand II, Maximilian of Bavaria, Tilly, Wallenstein.	(1) Stralsund, Edict of Restitution, Breitenfeld, Lützen. (2) White Hill, Magdeburg, Nördlingen.	This war is closed by the peace of Westphalia. Alsace thereby goes to France, Switzerland is separated from the Empire and the Palatinate is divided. The secularized lands of northern Germany are secured to Protestantism while leaving to Catholicism, Austria, Bohemia and Bavaria. Germany is left desolate.
Civil War in England—1642–1649. **(1) Royalists (Cavaliers) vs.** **(2) Parliamentarians (Roundheads) allied with Scots (to 1647).**	Charles I attempts to force a personal government on England. His disputes with Parliament covered (1) taxation, (2) privileges of Parliament, (3) religion, (4) control of the militia.	(1) Charles I, Prince Rupert, Montrose. (2) Cromwell, Essex, Fairfax, Leslie.	(2) Marston Moor, Naseby, Preston.	The war determines the army leaders to bring Charles I to trial and execution (1649). A Commonwealth was then established without King or House of Lords but with Oliver Cromwell as Protector (1653 to 1659).
Spanish Succession; in America Queen Anne's War—1701–1714. (1) France, Spain and Bavaria vs. (2) Austria, England, Holland, Portugal, Savoy.	Acceptance by Louis XIV of the bequest of the Spanish dominion to his grandson, Philip of Anjou, in violation of the partition treaty to which he had consented.	(1) Vendôme, Villars, Leopold of Dessau. (2) Duke of Marlborough, Eugene of Savoy, Heinsius.	(2) Gibraltar, Blenheim, Ramillies, Turin, Oudenarde, Malplaquet.	By the peace of Utrecht in 1713 and that of Rastadt in 1714 Spain and the Indies go to Philip of Anjou; Naples, Milan, Sardinia and former Spanish Netherlands to the Austrians. England receives Newfoundland, Acadia and Hudson Bay Territory from France and Gibraltar from Spain.
Northern War—1700–1721. (1) Sweden vs. (2) Russia, Poland, Denmark, Saxony.	Peter the Great joins Poland, Denmark and Saxony for the purpose of despoiling Sweden, the first power of the North, of her Baltic ports.	(1) Charles XII. (2) Peter the Great (Russia), Augustus II of Saxony.	(1) Invasion of Denmark. Narva, Invasion of Saxony. (2) Poltava.	By the peace of Nystadt (1721) Sweden cedes large territories to Russia. Russia takes the place of Sweden as the foremost power of the North.
War of the Austrian Succession—1740–1748. (1) Austria, supported by Hungary, Bohemia, England, Holland and Saxony vs. (2) Prussia, France, Spain, Bavaria.	When Maria Theresa succeeded her father, Charles VI of Austria, Frederick the Great of Prussia seized Silesia. This precipitated a struggle for Austrian territories. At the death of Charles VI of Austria the right of Maria Theresa to the throne is contested chiefly by Frederick the Great of Prussia who seizes Silesia.	(1) Maria Theresa, George II of England, Charles of Lorraine, Duke of Cumberland. (2) Frederick the Great of Prussia, Saxe.	(1) Dettingen. (2) Mollwitz, Chotusitz, Prague, Fontenoy, Hohenfriedburg, Soor.	By the Treaty of Aix-la-Chapelle Silesia is secured to Prussia, which state now becomes a great European power. This war is one phase of the long rivalry between France and Great Britain for seapower and dominion in America and India.
Seven Years' War in America French and Indian War—1756–1763. (1) England, Prussia vs. (2) France, Austria, Russia, Spain, Sweden.	Maria Theresa wishes to regain Silesia. Hostilities between French and English in America and India. George II's concern for his ancestral territory of Hanover.	(1) Frederick the Great, Duke of Cumberland. Wolfe (America), Robert Clive (India). (2) Daun (Austria), Charles of Lorraine, Montcalm (America).	(1) Dresden, Rossbach, Leuthen, Zorndorf, Minden. (2) Kolin, Hohkirchen, Kunersdorf. *In America:* (1) Louisburg, Fort Duquesne, Quebec. *In India:* (1) Plassey, Wandewash.	The peace of Paris (1763) gives to England Canada, the supremacy in India, and certain islands, especially in the West Indies. Prussia retains Silesia. This war really founded the British Empire, which is based on sea power and colonial dominion.
American Revolutionary War—1775–1783. (1) English Colonies in America aided by France vs. (2) England.	Colonists' spirit of independence grew with imposition of taxes without their consent, interference with local self-government by English officers, and the development of different economic outlooks.	(1) Washington, Greene, Allen, Putnam, Montgomery, Schuyler, Arnold, Stark, Sullivan, Lee, Gates, Wayne, Campbell, Morgan, Lafayette, de Kalb, Steuben, Kosciusko, Rochambeau. (2) Percy, Howe, Pigot, Carleton, Clinton, Cornwallis, Burgoyne, Baum, Tarleton, Rawdon.	*1775:* (1) Bunker Hill, Ticonderoga. (2) Lexington, Quebec. *1776:* (1) Trenton. (2) Brooklyn, White Plains, Ft. Washington. *1777:* (1) Princeton, Saratoga, Bennington. (2) Brandywine, Germantown. *1778:* (1) Monmouth. (2) Savannah. *1779:* (1) Stony Point, Chemung. (2) Savannah. *1780:* (1) Kings Mountain. (2) Charleston, Camden. *1781:* (1) Cowpens, Eutaw Springs, Yorktown. (2) Guilford Courthouse.	England conceded the independence of the American colonies, to which was granted all territory east of the Mississippi except Florida and Canada. American success inspired oppressed people in Europe, especially France, to revolt against their rulers.

French Revolution—War of Italian Liberation

NAME OF WAR, CONTESTANTS AND DATES	CAUSE OF CONFLICT	LEADERS	CHIEF BATTLES AND INCIDENTS	RESULTS AND COMMENTS
Wars of the French Revolution— 1789-1799. (1) Revolutionary France vs. (2) Coalitions of England, Austria, Prussia, Holland, and Spain. The Empire, Russia. a. First Coalition—1792-1797. b. Bonaparte's Egyptian Expedition—1798-1799.	Intrigues of emigrés; horror of Europe at the execution of the king; French offer of aid to revolutionists in other countries. Bonaparte aims to attack Great Britain's power in India and dreams of conquering the East.	(1) Dumouriez, Kellermann, Jourdan, Hoche, Pichegru, Napoleon Bonaparte, Moreau. (2) Duke of Brunswick, Coburg, Charles of Austria. (1) Napoleon Bonaparte. (2) Nelson (England).	(1) Valmy, Occupation of Nice and Savoy, Jemmapes. Execution of king (1793). Annexation of Belgium, Fleurus, Lodi; Siege of Mantua. (2) Mainz, Neerwinden, Kaisersautern, Wurzburg. (1) Battle of the Pyramids. (2) Aboukir, Acre.	By peace of Campo Formio (1797) the French frontier is advanced to the Rhine, Venice is given to Austria and the Cisalpine and Ligurian republics founded in Italy under French control. Nelson's victory removes a serious menace to British power in India and cuts off the French in Egypt.
Napoleonic Wars—1799-1815. (1) France under Napoleon vs. (2) European Powers led by England. a. Second Coalition—1799-1802. b. Third Coalition—1805.	The mistakes of the government of the Directory and the prestige of Nelson's victory enable Great Britain to form the Second Coalition. In the later stages this series of wars was kept aflame by Napoleon's insatiable lust for power and England's determination to end his dominance. Napoleon's inability to match English sea power was his greatest weakness.	(1) Napoleon, Joubert, Moreau. (2) Suvarov, Melas, Archduke John. (1) Napoleon. (2) Nelson, Mack, Alexander I (Russia), Kutuzov.	(1) Marengo, Hohenlinden. Napoleon's passage of the Alps (Great St. Bernard). (2) Novi. (1) Ulm, Austerlitz. (2) Trafalgar.	Peace of Luneville with Austria (1801); peace of Amiens with England (1802); Surrender of England's conquests except Trinidad and Ceylon; Malta to be restored to Knights of Malta. As a result of his brilliant successes Napoleon in 1804 took the title Emperor of the French.
c. (Fourth) War with Prussia and Russia—1806-1807.			(1) Double battle of Jena and Auerstadt. Berlin decree. Friedland.	By the treaties of Tilsit (1807) Russia recognizes Napoleon's relatives as kings of Naples, Holland and Westphalia and consents to Napoleon's control of the Confederation of the Rhine and the grand duchy of Warsaw. Alexander and Napoleon combine to dominate Europe.
d. Peninsular War—1808-1814.	Rebellion of Spain against Joseph Bonaparte, whom Napoleon had placed on the throne.	(1) Soult, Massena. (2) Duke of Wellington.	(1) Corunna. (2) Talavera, Lines of Torres Vedras, Albuera, Salamanca, Vittoria, Toulouse.	French expelled from Spain and Portugal.
e. Fifth War with Austria—1809.		(1) Napoleon. (2) Archduke Charles.	(1) Aspern, Wagram.	Austria cedes territory.
f. Invasion of Russia—1812.	Alexander's refusal to enforce Napoleon's continental system, and other causes of dispute.	(1) Napoleon, Marshal Ney. (2) Kutuzov, Barclay de Tolly.	(1) Smolensk, Borodino. (2) Burning of Moscow. Retreat from Moscow.	Flower of the French Army lost. Napoleon's armor of invincibility forever tarnished.
g. War of Liberation—1813-1814.	The oppressed states of Germany rise against Napoleon's tyranny, Prussia taking the lead.	(1) Napoleon, Ney, Macdonald. (2) Frederick, William III, Francis I, Alexander I, Blücher, Bernadotte.	(1) Lützen, Bautzen, Dresden. (2) Dennewitz, Leipzig (Battle of the Nations). Allies enter Paris.	Driven from Russia in 1812, from Germany in 1813, Napoleon in 1814 was forced to surrender France itself. By the Treaty of Fontainebleau he was given the Island of Elba and an annual revenue of 2,000,000 francs.
h. Waterloo Campaign—1815.	Quarrels among the allies and dissatisfaction of French with Louis XVIII. tempt Napoleon to return from Elba.	(1) Napoleon, Ney. (2) Wellington, Blücher.	Napoleon lands at Cannes (March 1); enters Paris March 20. (1) Ligny. (2) Quatre Bras, Waterloo, (June 18).	Waterloo marks the final downfall of Napoleon. In the Congress of Vienna the allies reconstructed Europe, erecting barriers against democratic movements and liberal ideas.
War of 1812—1812-1815. (1) United States vs. (2) Great Britain.	Destruction of American commerce, blockading of American ports and impressment of American sailors as a corollary of the British struggle with Napoleon. Indian troubles on the frontier were partly inspired by British traders.	(1) Hull, Dearborn, Harrison, Perry, Macdonough, Jackson. (2) Brock, Ross.	(1) Thames, Lake Erie, Lake Champlain, New Orleans. (2) Detroit, Queenstown, Chryslers' Farm, Bladensburg.	Treaty of Ghent restored prewar situation, but England did not revive old claims. The war brought America industrial self-sufficiency and showed her naval power. Northwest U. S. boundary was definitely fixed.
War of Grecian Independence—1821-1829. (1) Greeks, aided by England, Russia and France vs. (2) Turks.	Revived feeling of Greek nationality, stimulated by a widespread secret society working for a restoration of a Greek empire at Constantinople.	(1) Ypsilanti, Diebitsch (Russia), Marco Bozzaris, Byron (England). (2) Ibrahim Pasha.	Massacre of Greeks at Chios. (1) Navarino, Adrianople. (2) Missolonghi.	The treaty of Adrianople, 1829, compelled Turkey to acknowledge the independence of Greece, which chose as king the Bavarian Prince Otto I.
Mexican War—1846-1848. (1) United States vs. (2) Mexico.	Boundary disputes, the annexation of Texas, and pressure of American pioneers westward.	(1) Taylor, Scott. (2) Santa Ana, Ampudia.	(1) Buena Vista, Monterrey, Cerro Gordo, Chapultepec, Churubusco. Mexico occupied.	Treaty of Guadalupe Hidalgo set Texas boundary, gave U. S. California, Utah, Arizona, New Mexico and adjacent territory.
Crimean War—1854-1856. (1) Russia vs. (2) Turkey aided by Great Britain, France and Sardinia.	The political status and future of the Turkish Empire. Immediate cause, the claim of Russia to a protectorate over all Greek Christians living under the sultan's rule.	(1) Menshikov, Gorchakov. (2) Canrobert, Pelissier (France), Raglan, Simpson (England).	(1) Balaclava. (2) Alma, Siege of Sebastopol, Inkermann.	In the peace of Paris (1856) Russia's claim to a protectorate is disallowed, the Danube is opened to navigation and the Black Sea is closed to war vessels of all powers.
War of Italian Liberation—1859-1861. (1) Sardinia-Piedmont and France vs. (2) Austria.	Rebellion of Italians against foreign rule; France joined to strike a blow at her old enemy, Austria.	(1) Victor Emmanuel, Napoleon III, Garibaldi. (2) Francis Joseph II, Gyulay.	(1) Montebello, Magenta, Solferino. Peace signed at Zurich, Nov. 10, 1859.	Victor Emmanuel, starting with Lombardy won Parma, Modena, the papal legations, Sicily and Naples, together with the title, King of Italy. Venetia followed in 1866 and the addition of Rome in 1871 completed the unification of Italy.

American Civil War—Balkan Wars

Name of War, Contestants and Dates	Cause of Conflict	Leaders	Chief Battles and Incidents	Results and Comments
American Civil War—1861–1865. (1) Federal Government of United States vs. (2) Southern Confederacy, consisting of: Virginia, North Carolina, South Carolina, Georgia, Florida, Alabama, Mississippi, Louisiana, Texas, Arkansas and Tennessee.	The underlying causes of the war were: (a) Conflict between the doctrines of state sovereignty and nationalism. (b) Sectional antagonism over numerous issues concerning negro slavery. The immediate cause was the secession of Southern States. The reasons for secession, as given by Southern leaders, were: (a) Northern hatred of slavery and slander of slaveholders; the political campaign against the slave-holding interest, and the endorsement of such exploits as the John Brown raid. (b) The misinterpretation of the Constitution by the North, the repudiation of the Dred Scott decision, and the enactment by Northern states of "personal liberty laws."	(1) Lincoln, Stanton, Grant, McClellan, Sherman, Sheridan, Thomas, Meade, Reynolds, Pope, Buell, Farragut, Porter. (2) Davis, J. E. Johnston, A. S. Johnston, Lee, Jackson, Beauregard, Stuart, Longstreet, Bragg, Hood, Hill, Van Dorn, Early.	*1861:* (2) Bombardment of Ft. Sumter, Bull Run. *1862:* (1) West Tennessee campaign, Shiloh, New Orleans, Murfreesboro, Antietam. (2) Jackson's Shenandoah Valley campaign, Seven Days (Richmond), Bull Run, Fredericksburg. *Monitor* and *Merrimac* fought first battle of ironclad ships; result a draw. *1863:* (1) Vicksburg, Gettysburg, Chattanooga. (2) Chancellorsville, Chickamauga. *1864:* (1) Sherman's March through Georgia, Atlanta, Nashville, Sheridan's Shenandoah Valley conquest. (2) Wilderness, Spotsylvania, Cold Harbor, Lynchburg. *1865:* (1) Siege of Petersburg, leading to Lee's surrender at Appomattox.	The Union was preserved. Slavery was abolished. Secession as a working program was shown to be impracticable. The war cost the lives of nearly one million able-bodied men. The national debt was increased to $2,750,000,000. An incalculable amount of property was destroyed. Foreign immigration was stimulated. The industrial development of the North was speeded. The South suffered a severe economic setback.
Austro-Prussian (or Seven Weeks) War—1866. (1) Prussia with smaller North German States, and Italy vs. (2) Austria, Hanover, Saxony, and South German States.	Friction over Schleswig-Holstein enables Bismarck to force Austria into a war for supremacy in Germany.	(1) William I, Prince Frederic Charles, Moltke, Victor Emmanuel. (2) Benedek, Archduke Albert, Gablenz, Prince Charles of Bavaria.	*In Bohemia:* (1) Soor, Königgrätz or Sadowa. (2) Trautenau. *In the West:* (1) Aschaffenburg. (2) Langensala. *In Italy:* (2) Custozza, Lissa.	Closed with the peace of Prague, Aug. 23, 1866, which authorized the re-establishment of the Federated German States, excluding Austria; Austria ceded Venetia to Italy, and her rights in Schleswig-Holstein to Prussia. Hanover, Hesse, Nassau also are annexed to Prussia.
Franco-Prussian War—1870–1871. (1) France vs. (2) Prussia supported by all German States including South.	Jealousy of France at Prussian gains and friction over Hohenzollern candidacy for the throne of Spain. Bismarck's falsification of the "Ems dispatch" tricked France into a declaration of war.	(1) Napoleon, Macmahon, Bazaine. (2) William I, Moltke, Prince Frederic Charles, Crown Prince Frederic William.	(1) Saarbrucken. (2) Weissenberg, Wörth, Vionville, Gravelotte, Sedan, Capitulation of Metz, Orleans, Capitulation of Paris.	Closed in 1871 with the Treaty of Versailles with the following results: (1) The French military power was destroyed; (2) the western frontier of Germany was rendered secure; (3) The German Empire was established; (4) Germany acquired Alsace and Lorraine.
Russo-Turkish War—1877–1878. (1) Russia vs. (2) Turkey.	Turkish misgovernment and revolts in her Christian subject provinces, which were barbarously put down ("Bulgarian atrocities") arouse all Europe, but Russia alone declares war.	(1) Grand Duke Nicholas, Gurka, Grand Duke Michael, Alexander II. (2) Suleiman Pasha, Osman Pasha, Mukhtar Pasha.	(1) Passages of the Danube at Shitova. Shipka Pass, Plevna, Storm of Kars.	By the peace of San Stefano Montenegro, Servia and Rumania become independent; Bulgaria remains tributary but receives a Christian prince; Russia obtains large indemnity and part of Armenia and also Bessarabia.
Chinese-Japanese War—1894–1895. (1) Japan vs. (2) China.	Rival claims to suzerainty over Korea.	(1) Ito, Yamagata, Oyama, Nogi. (2) Tso, Yeh, Wei.	(1) Yalu River, Port Arthur, Wei-hai-wei, Niuchuang.	Treaty of Shimonoseki, signed April 17, 1895, removed Korea from Chinese influence; ceded Formosa and the Pescadores to Japan, and awarded to the latter an indemnity of $180,000,000.
Spanish-American War—1898. (1) United States vs. (2) Spain.	Sympathy for the oppressed Cubans. A growing spirit of imperialism in America, fostered by propaganda. Blowing up of U. S. battleship *Maine*.	(1) Dewey, Sampson, Schley, Shafter, Roosevelt. Miles, Wood. (2) Montijo, Cervera.	(1) Manila Bay, Santiago, El Caney.	By the treaty of Paris, Dec. 10, 1898, Spain recognized the sovereignty of the United States in Cuba, and ceded to that country the Philippines, Puerto Rico and Guam, in consideration of $20,000,000.
South African or Boer War—1899–1902. (1) Great Britain vs. (2) Transvaal, Orange Free State.	Resistance by the Boers (Dutch) to the British Government in the Transvaal.	(1) Roberts, Kitchener, French. (2) Cronje, Botha, De Wet, Delarey.	(1) Siege of Ladysmith, Paardeberg. (2) Colenso, Spion, Kop, Vaal, Krantz, Magersfontein.	Boers surrendered May 31, 1902; are granted the right of self-government under British Sovereignty, and united with other self-governing British colonies in South Africa.
Russo-Japanese War—1904–1905. (1) Japan vs. (2) Russia.	Conflict of interests in Manchuria; growth of Russian power in Asia; pressure of population in Japan.	(1) Togo, Kurokl, Oku, Nodzu, Oyama, Nogi. (2) Kuropatkin, Alexieff, Makarov, Stoessel, Stakelberg, Linevich.	(1) Port Arthur and Chemulpo, Vladivostok, Yalu River, Dalny, Siege of Port Arthur, Mukden, Sea of Japan.	Closed Sept. 5, 1905, by Treaty of Portsmouth by which Korea passes under control of Japan, China regains Manchuria, and Japan is granted important railroad rights. Russian military weakness was shown, while Japan rose to rank as a major power.
Balkan Wars—1912–1913. a. First Balkan War— (1) Bulgaria, Greece, Serbia, Montenegro vs. (2) Turkey.	Turkish misrule and atrocities, combined with racial and religious hatred.	(1) Czar Ferdinand, Crown Prince Constantine, Gen. Savov, King Peter.	(1) Lule Burgas, Adrianople, Janini, Scutari, Kirk, Kilissa.	Albania, a new state, was formed; Turkey lost nearly all European territory; Serbia, Greece and Bulgaria were enlarged.
b. Second Balkan War— (1) Greece, Serbia, Montenegro, Rumania vs. (2) Bulgaria.	Bulgaria, dissatisfied with her portion, makes war on her allies.	(2) Nazim Pasha, Muktor Pasha.	(1) Siege of Adrianople; Rumania invades Bulgaria.	Bulgaria lost much of the territory won from Turkey.

First World War—Second World War

Name of War, Contestants and Dates	Cause of Conflict	Leaders	Chief Battles and Incidents	Results and Comments
World War I—1914-1918. (1) *The Allies:* Serbia, Russia, Great Britain and Dominions, France, Belgium, Japan, Greece, Rumania, Montenegro, Portugal, Italy, United States. (China, Brazil, Cuba and other countries declared war but did not participate.) (2) *The Central Powers:* Austria-Hungary, Germany, Bulgaria, Turkey.	Assassination of Archduke Francis Ferdinand of Austria-Hungary by a Serbian peasant was an excuse for a test of power between jealous nations whose enmity was kept alive by propaganda while manpower and economic strength were built up after past wars. German desire for economic and political expansion had been held in check by other nations giving her belief in the right of her cause.	(1) Joffre, Nivelle, Petain, Foch, French, Haig, Albert I, Grand Duke Nicholas, Allenby, Byng, Jellicoe, Beatty, Lyautey, Brusilov, Kerensky, Diaz, Cadorna, Putnik, Pershing, March, Bliss, Bullard, Sims, Benson. (2) Crown Prince William, von Tirpitz, von Hindenburg, Ludendorff, von Moltke, Mackensen, Falkenhayn, Burian, Enver.	*East:* (1) Przemysl, Ledz. (2) Tannenberg, Masurian Lakes, Dunajec, Warsaw, Kovno. *West:* (1) 1st Marne, 2d Ypres, Verdun, Somme, Arras, Cambrai, 2d Marne, Chateau-Thierry, Belleau Wood, St. Mihiel, Meuse-Argonne, Hindenburg Line. (2) Mons - Charleroi, 1st Ypres, Neuve-Chapelle, Artois, 3d Ypres, Picardy, Lys, Oise. *South:* (1) Gorizia, Piave, Bagdad, Jerusalem. (2) Caporetto, Dardanelles, Monastir. *Asia:* (1) Tsingtao. *Naval:* Helgoland, Jutland.	Germany lost her commercial position; surrendered her fleet; her military autocracy fell; her colonies passed to her opponents; Alsace-Lorraine and parts of Schleswig and of Silesia seceded. The map of Europe was made over; Poland, Czechoslovakia, Yugoslavia, Hungary and small states on the Russian frontier became independent. Italy recovered and redeemed her lost provinces. Europe became industrially stagnant; Russia starved and Germany, Austria and Italy were torn with internal disorders. Republics were established and monarchies fell.
Russian Revolutionary War—1917-1920. (1) Russian Bolsheviki (Revolutionists) vs. (2) White Russians assisted by troops and supplies sent by World War I Allies.	Overthrow of imperial government in Russia by Bolshevik Revolution caused Russia's withdrawal from World War I. Allies, fearing the spread of revolutionary ideas, angered by the Bolshevik repudiation of Russia's debts and wishing to rebuild a Russian opposition to Germany, sent expeditions against the Bolsheviks. Former Russian nobility and owners of property fought the revolution because it dispossessed them of their privileges.	(1) Lenin, Trotsky, Felix Dzerzhinsky Chicherin. (2) Yudenich, Kolchak, Denikin, Wrangel.	(1) Execution of Czar Nicholas and his family (July 16, 1918). (2) British and American expedition to Archangel. (3) Reign of Terror against counterrevolutionaries. Organization of the *Cheka* or secret tribunal for crushing opponents of the revolution. (4) Occupation of Vladivostok by Japanese. (5) Civil War in South of Russia and in Baltic area.	Foreign efforts to crush Communists failed. Russian people were united in patriotic determination to control their own affairs. Lenin and Trotsky emerged as Russia's strong men. Communist activity was dispersed over the capitalistic world.
Italo-Ethiopian War —1935-36. (1) Italy vs. (2) Ethiopia.	Disputes over border infringements between Ethiopia and Italian colony of Eritrea. Fundamental cause was Italy's desire for colonial expansion.	(1) Mussolini, Emilio de Bono, Pietro Badoglio. (2) Haile Selassie.	(1) Imposition of Sanctions by League of Nations. (2) Bombing of Ethiopian towns by air raids. (3) Capture of Addis Ababa with flight of Ethiopian ruler, Haile Selassie.	Ethiopian easily crushed by modern military equipment of Italians. Impotence of League of Nations to prevent conflict involving a great Power demonstrated. Italy obtained large undeveloped African territory as field of exploitation.
Spanish Civil War —1936-39. (1) Loyalists vs. (2) Insurgents. (3) Unofficial participation by Italy and Germany on side of Insurgents. Support of Loyalists by Soviet Union and France.	Counterrevolution by supporters of the old regime financed by powerful outside interests. Religious strife over attempted disestablishment of Roman Catholic Church. Economic and social strife between the Left and Right.	(1) Francisco Largo Caballero, Manuel Azaña, Juan Negrin, José Miaja. (2) Francisco Franco, Emilio Mola.	(1) Siege of Madrid. (2) Large scale aerial bombardment of civilian population in Madrid, Barcelona, Valencia. (3) Capture of Bilbao by Insurgents. (4) Drive to Mediterranean by Insurgents. (5) Submarine activity and naval blockades.	International tension among the great Powers. Testing of modern military equipment and new tactics of warfare. Franco gained control over all Spain.
Chinese-Japanese War —1937-1945. (1) Japan vs. (2) China.	Japanese expansionist ambitions; resurgence of nationalistic spirit in China under the leadership of Chiang Kai-shek, Chinese resentment at Japanese encroachment in North China.	(1) Juichi Terauchi, Kenkichi Ueda, Seishiro Itagaki, Fumimaro Konoye. (2) Chiang Kai-shek, T. V. Soong.	(1) Capture of Shanghai and Nanking by Japanese. (2) Destructive air raids on Chinese cities, particularly Canton. (3) Huge losses of property and life on both sides without decisive results.	Japan's unconditional surrender leaves China free but poverty-stricken. Formosa and Manchuria returned to Chinese.
Second World War —1939-1945. (1) The Axis: Germany, Italy, Finland, Rumania, Japan, Bulgaria, Hungary vs. (2) The Allies: Great Britain, France, Norway, Belgium, Holland, Greece, Yugoslavia, Russia, United States, China, and others.	Germany, Italy and Japan desire expansion.	(1) Axis: Hitler, Goering, Rommel, Brauchitsch, Runstedt, Loeb, Mussolini, Tojo, Homma, Yamashita. (2) Allies: Roosevelt, Churchill, Stalin, Voroshilov, Timoshenko, Budenny, Marshall, MacArthur, Gamelin, Weygand, Eisenhower, MacArthur, Montgomery, Alexander, King, Arnold, Pound, DeGaulle.	Germany conquers Norway, Holland, Belgium, Luxembourg, France, Yugoslavia, Greece and Hungary. Tremendous battle of Russia. Battle of Atlantic. Japan attacks United States at Pearl Harbor. Japan conquers much Chinese territory. Allies win battles of New Guinea, New Britain; Solomon, Gilbert and Marshall Islands; Atomic bomb raid on Hiroshima.	1945. Germany, Italy, Finland, Rumania, Bulgaria, Austria and Japan surrender.

Indo-Chinese War—

Name of War, Contestants and Dates	Cause of Conflict	Leaders	Chief Battles and Incidents	Results and Comments
Indo-Chinese War—1946-1954 (1) Republic of Viet-Nam and the French Union vs. (2) Communist Viet Minh organization recognized by Russia in 1950 and aided by Red China.	The Communists within Viet-Nam try to gain control of the government. They use guerilla tactics.	(1) Bao Dai, Emperor of Viet-Nam, Marshal de Lattre de Tassigny, General Raoul Salan, Henri Navarre, Paul Ely. (2) Ho Chi Minh, Vo Nguyen Giap.	(1) Guerilla warfare and terrorist tactics by Communists. (2) Battles of Vinhyen, Dongtrieu and Nghialo. (3) General Charles M. Chanson, French Commissioner for South Viet-Nam, killed by member of Viet Minh rebel forces. (4) French Marshal de Lattre de Tassigny dies. (5) Battle of Nason, 12,000 French Union regulars surrounded by 25,000 Viet Minh soldiers. (6) Battle of Dienbienphu fought 1954.	The first free elections in war-racked Viet-Nam were held in 1953. The Communists tried to interfere with the voting, using guns and kidnapping candidates. However, 80% of the registered voters upheld Emperor Bao Dai's anti-Communist government. Armistice was signed in 1954. in which North Viet-Nam was surrendered to the Communists, while South Viet-Nam remained free. Election to be held in all Viet-Nam in the future.
Malayan War—1948-1957 (1) Great Britain and Malayan Federation. (2) Malayan Communist organization.	In World War II the Malayan Communists, then known as Malayan People's Anti-Japanese Army, were accepted as allies by the British. At the end of the war, the Communists declared their intention of capturing power by any means.	(1) Sir Gerald W. R. Templer, High Commissioner. Sir Harold Briggs, Operations-Director. (2) Chin Peng, Manap Jepun.	Guerilla warfare begun. Retreating into jungle camps, the Communists paralyzed the country's life by terrorism and sabotage; murder of planters, ambushing police, derailing trains, cutting telephone wires. Sir Henry Gurney, High Commissioner, ambushed and slain.	By draining U. S., British and French strength in Asia, the Communists interfered with these nations' efforts in Europe. Proposed—The British Dominion of Malaya. Malayan guerillas retreat. Moscow ordered Reds to drop terror, concentrate on winning the people.
Korean War—1950-1953 (1) North Korea and Communist China vs. (2) South Korea and the United Nations.	North Korean Communists try to annex South Korea.	(1) Kim Il Sung, Choi Yong Kun, Mao Tse-Tung, Chou En-Lai, Nam Il. (2) Syngman Rhee, Douglas MacArthur, Matthew Ridgway, Lee Chong Chan, Paik Sun Yup, Van Fleet, Mark Clark.	(1) In the first 83 days, Communists drive southward to Naktong River. (2) U. N. forces advance northward 71 days, to Chongja. (3) Chinese Communists enter war and drive southward to 38th parallel. (4) Fighting slows down as peace negotiations begin July 10, 1951. (5) Armistice signed July 26, 1953. Fighting ceased July 27, 1953.	Korean war proved to be testing ground of jet planes, modern armor, etc. It united the West in stopping Communist world expansion.
Algerian War—1955-1962 (1) France vs. (2) Algerian Rebels (National Liberation Front) (3) Secret Army (OAS)	Algerian desire for greater degree of self-government and eventual independence from France.	(1) DeGaulle, President of France (2) Ferhat Abbas, Ben' Khedda, Ben Bella (3) Pierre Lagaillarde, General Raoul Salan, Jean-Jaques Susini	(1) In 1955, first serious outbreak of anti-French terrorism. (2) Massacre of male population of Melouza (identified with Nat. Lib. Front) by rival rebel faction in 1957. (3) In 1958, Nat. Lib. Front established provisional gov't. for free Algerian republic (4) April 22, 1961—generals' revolt against French gov't. (5) Civil authorities and military groups loyal to DeGaulle put down generals' revolt. (6) Cease-fire between Algerian rebels and French army, signed March 18, 1962.	The 1962 treaty at Evian-les-Bains, France, resulted in a cease-fire and a referendum in which the Algerian people voted for independence. The Evian accords were jeopardized in the conflict's final months by the opposition of the Secret Army, an underground organization composed of European settlers and dissident French officers. The flight of European capital and skilled manpower to France may be offset by promised French economic and technical aid as the newly independent Algeria is stabilized.
Vietnamese War—1954- (1) South Vietnam with U.S. aid vs. (2) North Vietnamese Vietcong guerrillas, aided by Communist China.	Chinese Communist expansion and effort to gain power throughout Southeast Asia. U.S. defense of non-Communist South Vietnam against Communist infiltration, protection of access to water- and airways between Indian and Pacific oceans.	(1) Premier Ngo Dinh Diem, until autumn, 1963; Premiers Minh; Khanh; Huong; Kuat, until June. 1965; Premier Nguyen Cao Ky. (2) Communist guerrillas from N. Vietnam, trained and aided by Chou En-lai's cadres.	(1) 1954 Geneva Conference decision to reunite N. and S. Vietnam thwarted by policies of Ngo Dinh Diem. (2) 1961, direct U.S. intervention in S. Vietnam. (3) In 1963, 9-year regime of Ngo Dinh Diem toppled in military coup, replaced by military junta under Duong Van Minh; regime of Nguyen Khanh replaced this. (4) In 1963, religious strife between Buddhists and Catholics continued. (5) Plaine des Jarres. Spring of 1964—Communists drive neutralists out. (6) 1965: February—U.S. officially began daily bombings to retaliate for Vietcong strike at Pleiku; June — first U.S. units used in actual combat; July—massive buildup of U.S. troops begun; first U.S. jet fighter hit by Russian S.A.M. missile. Nov.—Largest loss of American lives to date in battle of Ia Drang (approximately 280 killed). (7) B-52 bombers from Guam bomb N. Vietnam for first time, April, 1966.	

ASSYRIAN RULERS BEFORE THE PERSIAN CONQUEST

Early Babylonian chronology is uncertain; the dates shown indicate the approximate times the several dynasties were in power. Names of individuals are seldom definitely known.

B.C.
2500	Dynasty of Ur.
2300	First Dynasty of Babylon—11 kings.
2160	Dynasty of Sisku—11 kings.
1780	Kassite Dynasty—36 kings.
1203	Dynasty of Isin—11 kings.
1070	Seacoast Dynasty—3 kings.
1050	Betbazi Dynasty—3 kings.
1030	Elamite Dynasty—1 king.
1025	Second Babylonian Dynasty—19 kings.
730	Dynasty of Sape (obscure, merges into Persian Conquest.)

KINGS OF EGYPT

Early Egyptian chronology is uncertain; the dates shown indicate the approximate time the various dynasties were in power. Individuals of special importance in history or art are named.

B.C.
3400	I Dynasty, founded by Menes.
	II Dynasty.
2980	III Dynasty.
2900	IV Dynasty, includes Khufu (Cheops), Khafre, Menkure.
2750	V Dynasty.
2625	VI Dynasty.
2475	VII and VIII Dynasties.
2445	IX and X Dynasties.
2160	XI Dynasty.
2000	XII Dynasty, includes
2000	Amenhemet I.
1970	Sesostris I.
1935	Amenhemet II.
1906	Sesostris II.
1887	Sesostris III.
1849	Amenhemet III.
1801	Amenhemet IV.
1788	XIII to XVII, or Hyksos, Dynasties.
1580	XVIII Dynasty, includes
1557	Amenhotep I.
1547	Thothmes I.
1501	Thothmes II. and Thothmes III.
1448	Amenhotep II.
1420	Thothmes IV.
1411	Amenhotep III.
1375	Amenhotep IV.
1358	Tutankhamen.
1350	XIX Dynasty, includes
1315	Ramses I.
1313	Seti I.
1292	Ramses II.
1225	Merneptah.
1209	Seti II.
1200	XX Dynasty, includes
1198	Ramses III.
1090	XXI Dynasty.
945	XXII Dynasty, includes
945	Sheshonk.
745	XXIII Dynasty.
718	XXIV Dynasty.
712	XXV Dynasty, includes
688	Tirhakah.
663	XXVI Dynasty, includes
663	Psammetichus I.
609	Necho.
593	Psammetichus II.
588	Apries.
569	Amasis II.
525	XXVII Dynasty (Persian).
405	XXVIII to XXX Dynasties.
30	Egypt becomes a Roman province.

KINGS AND RULERS OF ENGLAND

A.D.
827	Saxon Heptarchy ends and seven kingdoms unite as England.
827	Egbert.
838	Ethelwolf.
858	Ethelbald.
860	Ethelbert.
866	Ethelred I.
872	Alfred.
901	Edward the Elder.

KINGS AND RULERS OF ENGLAND—Continued

925	Athelstan.
940	Edmund I.
946	Edred.
955	Edwy.
959	Edgar.
975	Edward II, the Martyr.
978	Ethelred II.
1016	Edmund II, Ironside.
1016	Canute.
1035	Harold I, Harefoot.
1039	Hardicanute.
1041	Edward III, the Confessor.
1066	Harold II.
1066	William the Conqueror.
1087	William II, Rufus.
1100	Henry I, the Scholar.
1135	Stephen (of Blois).
1154	Henry II, Plantagenet.
1189	Richard the Lion-hearted.
1199	John Lackland.
1216	Henry III.
1272	Edward I.
1307	Edward II.
1327	Edward III.
1377	Richard II.
1399	Henry IV of Lancaster.
1413	Henry V.
1422	Henry VI.
1461	Edward IV.
1483	Edward V.
1483	Richard III.
1485	Henry VII, Tudor.
1509	Henry VIII.
1547	Edward VI.
1553	Mary I.
1558	Elizabeth I.
1603	James I, Stuart.
1625	Charles I.
1649	Commonwealth.
1653	Oliver Cromwell, Protector.
1658	Richard Cromwell.
1660	Charles II.
1685	James II.
1689	William III and Mary II.
1694	William alone.
1702	Anne.
1714	George I.
1727	George II.
1760	George III.
1820	George IV.
1830	William IV.
1837	Victoria.
1901	Edward VII.
1910	George V.
1936	Edward VIII.
1936	George VI.
1952	Elizabeth II.

KINGS OF FRANCE

A.D.
448	Merovech.
456	Childeric.
481	Clovis, grandson of Merovech.
511	Thierry, Childebert, Clodomer and Clotaire I.
558	Clotaire alone.
561	Charibert, Gontran, Sigebert and Chilperic.
583	Clotaire II of Soissons.
596	Thierry II and Theodobert II, kings of Austrasia.
614	Interregnum.
628	Dagobert and Charibert.
638	Siegebert II and Clovis II.
655	Clotaire II.
660	Childeric II.
679	Thierry III.
690	Pepin Heristal, Mayor of the Palace.
692	Clovis III.
695	Childebert III.
711	Dagobert III.
714	Charles Martel.
715	Childeric II.
720	Thierry IV.
742	Childeric III.
752	Pepin the Short.
768	Charlemagne and Carloman.
814	Louis the Debonnaire.
840	Charles the Bald.
877	Louis II the Stammerer.
879	Louis III and Carloman.
884	Charles the Fat.
888	Eudes.
898	Charles III the Simple.
922	Robert, Usurper.
923	Rodolph.

KINGS OF FRANCE—Continued

936	Louis IV the Stranger.
954	Lothaire.
986	Louis V the Lazy.
987	Hugh Capet, Usurper.
996	Robert.
1031	Henry I.
1060	Philip I.
1108	Louis the VI the Gross.
1137	Louis VII.
1180	Philip II Augustus.
1223	Louis VIII the Lion.
1226	Louis IX (St. Louis).
1270	Philip III the Bold.
1285	Philip IV the Fair.
1314	Louis X the Quarrelsome.
1316	John I, 8 days.
1316	Philip V the Long.
1322	Charles IV the Fair.
1328	Philip VI of Valois.
1350	John II the Good.
1364	Charles V the Wise.
1380	Charles VI the Beloved.
1422	Charles VII the Victorious.
1461	Louis XI.
1483	Charles VIII.
1498	Louis XII.
1515	Francis I the Gentleman.
1547	Henry II.
1559	Francis II.
1560	Charles IX.
1574	Henry III.
1589	Henry IV the Great.
1610	Louis XIII the Just.
1643	Louis XIV the Great.
1715	Louis XV.
1774	Louis XVI.
1804	Napoleon Bonaparte, Emperor.
1814	Louis XVIII.
1824	Charles X.
1830	Louis Philippe.
1848	Second Republic, Louis Napoleon, President.
1852	Napoleon III, Emperor of the French.
1870	Third Republic.

KINGS OF GERMANY

A.D.
843	Louis or Ludwig the German.
876	Louis or Ludwig the Younger.
882	Charles the Fat.
887	Arnulf.
900	Louis or Ludwig the Child.
911	Conrad I.
918	Henry I the Fowler.
936	Otto I the Great.

In 962 Otto the Great secured the crown of the Holy Roman Empire; from this date until 1806 the list of Holy Roman emperors is nearly identical with the list of kings of Germany. But after 1556 (abdication of Charles V) the authority of the Holy Roman emperors was chiefly confined to the hereditary possessions of the House of Hapsburg. In 1701 the Elector Frederick III of Brandenburg assumed the title of Frederick I, King of Prussia. In 1871 William I of Prussia became German emperor.

KINGS OF PRUSSIA

A.D.
1701	Frederick I.
1713	Frederick William I.
1740	Frederick II, the Great.
1786	Frederick William II.
1797	Frederick William III.
1840	Frederick William IV.
1861	William I, crowned German Emperor 1871.

EMPERORS OF GERMANY AND KINGS OF PRUSSIA

A.D.
1871	William I.
1888	Frederick III.
1888	William II.
1918	German Republic established.

HOLY ROMAN EMPERORS

A.D.
800	Charlemagne.
814	Louis I the Debonnaire.
840	Lothaire I.
855	Louis II.
875	Charles II the Bald.
877	Interregnum.
881	Charles III the Fat.
887	Interregnum.
896	Arnulf.
899	Interregnum.
901	Louis III, of Provence.
905	Interregnum.
962	Otto I, the Great.
973	Otto II.
983	Otto III.
1002	Henry II. the Lame.
1024	Conrad II.
1039	Henry III the Black.
1055	Henry IV.
1077	Rudolph, killed in battle.
1080	Henry IV, reinstated.
1106	Henry V.
1125	Lothaire II.
1138	Conrad III.
1152	Frederick I, Barbarossa.
1190	Henry VI.
1198	Philip.
1208	Otto IV.
1212	Frederick II.
1250	Conrad IV.
1254	Interregnum.
1273	Rudolph of Hapsburg.
1291	Adolph of Nassau.
1298	Albert of Austria.
1308	Henry VII of Luxemburg.
1314	Louis IV.
1347	Charles IV.
1378	Wenceslas.
1400	Robert, Count Palatine.
1410	Sigismund.
1438	Albert II of Austria.
1440	Frederick III.
1493	Maximilian I.
1519	Charles V.
1556	Ferdinand I.
1564	Maximilian II.
1576	Rudolph II.
1612	Matthias.
1619	Ferdinand II.
1637	Ferdinand III.
1658	Leopold I.
1705	Joseph I.
1711	Charles VI.
1742	Charles VII.
1745	Francis I.
1765	Joseph II.
1790	Leopold II.
1792	Francis II, till 1806.
1806	Confederation of the Rhine. Francis II renounces title of Holy Roman Emperor and King of Germany and takes the title of Francis I, Emperor of Austria.

EARLY KINGS OF ITALY

A.D.
476	Odoacer.
493	Theodoric.
526	Amalasunta and Athalric.
534	Theodotus.
536	Vitiges.
540	Interregnum.
541	Totila.
552	Interregnum.
553	Tejas.
	End of Gothic Kingdom in Italy.

KINGS OF MODERN ITALY

A.D.
1861	Victor Emmanuel II of Sardinia.
1878	Humbert I.
1900	Victor Emmanuel III.
1946	Humbert II.
1946	Republic proclaimed.

KINGS OF MEDIA

B.C.
634	Cyaxares I.
595	Astyages.
559	Cyaxares II or Darius.
536	Cyrus the Great, who forms the Medo-Persian Empire.

KINGS OF THE PERSIANS

B.C.
559 Cyrus the Great.
529 Cambyses or Ahasuerus.
522 Smerdis or Artaxerxes.
521 Darius or Hystaspes.
486 Xerxes the Great.
465 Artaxerxes Longimanus.
425 Xerxes II.
425 Sogdianus.
424 Ochus or Darius Nothus.
404 Artaxerxes Mnemon.
361 Artaxerxes Ochus.
338 Arses.
336 Darius Codomanus.
330 Alexander the Great conquers Darius. End of Persian Empire.

GOVERNORS AND JUDGES OF THE ISRAELITES

The dates shown are not substantiated by modern research, but are the result of early Biblical study.
B.C.
1491 Moses.
1451 Joshuah.
1405 Othniel.
1323 Ehud.
1305 Shamgar.
1285 Deborah and Barak.
1255 Gideon.
1236 Abimelech.
1232 Tola.
1210 Jair.
1188 Jephthah.
1182 Ibzan.
1175 Elon.
1165 Abdon.
1157 Eli.
1137 Samson.
1116 Samuel.

KINGS OF THE JEWS

B.C.
1095 Saul.
1055 David and Ishbosheth.
1048 David.
1015 Solomon.
975 Division of the Kingdom.

KINGS OF JUDAH

B.C.
975 Rehoboam.
958 Abijam.
955 Asa.
914 Jehoshaphat.
889 Jehoram.
885 Ahaziah.
884 Athaliah.
878 Jehoash.
839 Amaziah.
810 Azariah.
742 Ahaz.
720 Hezekiah.
698 Manasseh.
643 Amon.
641 Josiah.
610 Jehoahaz.
610 Jehoiakim.
610 Jehoiachin.
598 Zedekiah.
588 Nebuchadnezzar destroys Jerusalem.

KINGS OF ISRAEL

B.C.
975 Jeroboam.
954 Nadab.
953 Baasha.
930 Ela.
929 Zimri.
929 Omri.
917 Ahab.
897 Ahaziah.
896 Jehoram.
884 Jehu.
856 Jehoahaz.

KINGS OF ISRAEL—Continued

841 Jehoash.
826 Jeroboam II.
773 Zachariah.
772 Shallum.
772 Menahem.
761 Pekahiah.
759 Pekah.
730 Hosheah.
721 Shalmanezer, King of Assyria, takes Samaria. End of the Kingdom of Israel.

PRINCES OF JUDEA

(Called the Maccabees)
B.C.
166 Judas Maccabeus.
161 Jonathan.
143 Simon.
135 John Hyrcanus.

KINGS OF JUDEA

B.C.
107 Aristobulus.
106 Alexander Jannaeus.
79 Alexandra.
70 Hyrcanus.
70 Aristobulus.
63 Hyrcanus restored.
40 Antigonus.
37 Herod the Great.
3 Archelaus.

A.D.
8 Judea becomes a Roman province.

EMPERORS OF ROME

B.C.
31 Augustine Caesar.

A.D.
14 Tiberius.
37 Caligula.
41 Claudius.
54 Nero.
68 Galba.
69 Otho.
69 Vitellius.
70 Vespasian.
79 Titus.
81 Domitian.
96 Nerva.
117 Hadrian.
138 Antoninus Pius.
161 Marcus Aurelius Antoninus and Lucius Verus.
170 Marcus Aurelius alone.
180 Commodus.
193 Pertinax.
193 Julian, 66 days.
193 Septimius Severus.
211 Caracalla and Geta.
217 Marcinus.
218 Heliogabalus.
222 Alexander Severus.
235 Maximinus.
236 Gordian the Elder.
236 Pupeinus and Balbinus.
238 Gordian the Younger.
244 Philip.
249 Decius.
251 Gallus.
253 Emilianus.
254 Valerian; Gallienus, his son.
260 Gallienus alone.
268 Claudius II.
270 Aurelian.
275 Tacitus.
275 Florianus.
276 Probus.
282 Carus.
283 Carinus and Numerianus.
284 Diocletian.
304 Constantius and Galerius.
306 Constantine the Great.
337 Constantine II, Constantius and Constans.
361 Julian the Apostate.
363 Jovian.
364 Empire is divided.

ROMAN EMPERORS OF THE WEST

A.D.
364 Valentinian.
367 Valentinian and Gratian.
375 Valentinian II and Gratian.
383 Valentinian II alone.
392 Eugenius.
394 Theodosius master of the whole Roman Empire, which is divided between his sons at his death, Jan. 17, 395.
395 Honorius.
423 Valentinian III.
454 Petronius Maximus.
454 Avitus.
455 Interregnum.
456 Majorian.
461 Severus.
467 Anthemius.
472 Olybius.
473 Glycerius.
474 Julius Nepos.
476 Augustulus.
476 Rome taken by Odoacer, at which event Western Empire ends.

ROMAN EMPERORS OF THE EAST

A.D.
364 Valens.
378 Interregnum of 5 months.
379 Theodosius the Great.
395 Arcadius.
408 Theodosius II.
450 Marcianus.
457 Leo the Great.
474 Leo II.
474 Zeno.
491 Anastasius I.
518 Justin I.
527 Justinian I.
565 Justin II.
578 Tiberius II.
582 Mauritius.
602 Phocas.
610 Heraclius.
641 Constantine III.
641 Constans II.
668 Constantine IV.
685 Justinian II.
695 Leontinus.
698 Tiberius III.
705 Justinian II restored.
711 Philip Bardanes.
713 Anastasius II.
716 Theodosius III.
718 Leo III the Isaurian.
741 Constantine V Copronymus.
775 Leo IV.
780 Constantine VI and Irene.
797 Irene alone.
802 Nicephorus I.
811 Michael I.
813 Leo III.
821 Michael II the Stammerer.
829 Theophilus.
842 Michael III.
867 Basil I the Macedonian.
886 Leo VI the Philosopher.
911 Alexander and Constantine VII. Porphyrogenitus.
919 Romanus I, Lecapenes, Christopher, Stephen and Constantine VIII.
945 Restoration of Constantine VII.
959 Romanus II.
961 Nicephorus Phocas II.
969 John Zimisces.
975 Basil II and Constantine IX.
1025 Constantine alone.
1028 Romanus III Argyrus.
1034 Michael IV the Paphlagonian.
1041 Michael V Calaphates.
1042 Zoe and Theodora.
1042 Constantine X Monomachus.
1054 Theodora restored.
1056 Michael Stratioticus.
1057 Isaac Comnenus I.
1059 Constantine XI Ducas.
1067 Romanus Diogenes.
1071 Michael VII Parapinaces, Andronicus I, Constantine XII.
1078 Nicephorus Botaniates III.
1081 Alexius Comnenus I.
1118 John Comnenus I.
1143 Manuel Comnenus.
1180 Alexius Comnenus II.

ROMAN EMPERORS OF THE EAST—Continued

1183 Andronicus.
1185 Isaac Angelus.
1195 Alexius Angelus.
1203 Isaac Angelus restored.
1204 Alexius Mourzoufle.
1204 Baldwin I.
1206 Henry.
1217 Peter de Courtenay.
1220 Robert de Courtenay.
1228 John de Brienne and Baldwin II.
1237 Baldwin alone.
1261 Michael Paleologus.
1283 Andronicus II.
1295 Michael IX.
1328 Andronicus III.
1341 John Cantacuzene.
1355 John Paleologus.
1391 Manuel.
1425 John Paleologus II.
1448 Constantine XIII.
1453 Constantinople taken by Turks, and end of Empire.

RULERS OF RUSSIA

A.D.
1328 Ivan I.
1340 Simeon.
1353 Ivan II.
1359 Demetrius II.
1362 Demetrius Donskoi.
1389 Basil III.
1425 Basil IV.
1462 Ivan III.
1505 Basil V.
1533 Ivan the Terrible.
1584 Feodor I.
1598 Boris Godonov.
1605 Feodor II.
1606 Demetrius the Pole.
1610 Ladislaus of Poland.
1613 Michael Romanov.
1645 Alexis.
1676 Feodor III.
1682 Ivan V and Peter I.
1721 Peter I took title of Czar.
1725 Catherine I.
1727 Peter II.
1730 Anne.
1740 Ivan VI.
1741 Elizabeth.
1762 Catherine II the Great.
1796 Paul.
1810 Alexander I.
1825 Nicholas I.
1855 Alexander II.
1881 Alexander III.
1894 Nicholas II.
1917 Abdication of Nicholas, last of the czars.

KINGS OF SPAIN

A.D.
1469 Kingdom of Spain formed by marriage of Isabella to Ferdinand V.
1516 Charles I.
1556 Philip II.
1598 Philip III.
1621 Philip IV.
1665 Charles II.
1700 Philip V of Bourbon.
1724 Louis I.
1746 Ferdinand VI.
1759 Charles III.
1788 Charles IV.
1808 Ferdinand VII.
1808 Joseph Bonaparte.
1813 Ferdinand VII resumes.
1833 Isabella II.
1870 Amadeo I.
1874 Alfonso XII.
1886 Alfonso XIII.
1931 Republic proclaimed.

KINGS OF SCOTLAND		KINGS OF SCOTLAND—Concluded		KINGS OF SYRIA—Concluded		KINGS OF SWEDEN—Concluded	
A.D.		1437	James II.	92	Antiochus IX Grypus.	1276	Magnus II.
843	Kenneth McAlpin.	1460	James III.	91	Philip.	1290	Birger II.
858	Donald I.	1488	James IV.	90	Demetrius Euchares.	1318	Magnus III.
862	Constantine I.	1513	James V.	85	Antiochus Dionysius.	1365	Albert.
877	Aed.	1542	Mary Stuart.	83	Tigranes.	1397	Margaret.
878	Eochaed.	1567	James VI who in	69	Antiochus Asiaticus.	1411	Eric XIII.
889	Donald II.	1603	became James I of England.	65	Syria becomes a Roman province.	1441	Christopher.
900	Constantine II.					1448	Charles VIII.
943	Malcolm I.					1458	Christian I.
953	Indulf.	**KINGS OF SYRIA**				1520	Christian II.
959	Duff.			**KINGS OF SWEDEN**		1528	Gustavus I Vasa.
963	Culen.	B.C.				1560	Eric XIV.
970	Kenneth II.	312	Seleucus I Nicanor.	A.D.		1569	John III.
987	Constantine III	281	Antiochus I Soter.	966	Eric the Victor.	1592	Sigismond I.
995	Kenneth III.	261	Antiochus II Theus.	994	Olaf.	1606	Charles IX.
1002	Malcolm II.	246	Seleucus II Callinicus.	1026	Edmund Jacobson.	1611	Gustavus Adolphus II.
1033	Duncan I.	226	Seleucus III Ceraunus.	1035	Edmund or Amand III.	1632	Christina.
1039	Macbeth.	223	Antiochus III the Great.	1041	Haakon.	1654	Charles X.
1057	Malcolm III.	187	Seleucus IV Philopater.	1056	Steinkel.	1660	Charles XI.
1093	Donald III.	175	Antiochus IV Epiphanes.	1060	Inge I.	1697	Charles XII.
1094	Duncan II.	164	Antiochus V Eupator.	1054	Halstan.	1718	Ulrica Eleonore.
1098	Edgar.	162	Demetrius I Soter.	1080	Philip.	1720	Frederic.
1107	Alexander I	150	Alexander I Balas.	1100	Inge II.	1750	Adolphus Frederic.
1127	David I.	145	Demetrius II Nicanor.	1130	Ragwald.	1771	Gustavus Adolphus III.
1153	Malcolm IV.	144	Antiochus VI Theus.	1133	Magnus I.	1792	Gustavus Adolphus IV.
1165	William.	143	Diodotus or Tryphon.	1144	Sverker II.	1809	Charles XIII.
1214	Alexander II.	139	Antiochus VII Sidetes.	1150	Eric X.	1818	Charles John XIV.
1249	Alexander III.	130	Demetrius II Nicanor.	1162	Charles VII.	1844	Oscar Frederic.
1286	Margaret.	126	Alexander II Zebina.	1168	Canute.	1859	Charles XV.
1292	John Baliol.	124	Seleucus V.	1192	Sverker III.	1882	Oscar II.
1306	Robert I.	123	Antiochus VIII Grypus.	1211	Eric XI.	1907	Gustavus V.
1329	David II.	97	Seleucus VI Nicanor.	1220	John I.	1950	Gustavus VI.
1371	Robert II.	93	Antiochus Eusebes.	1223	Eric XII.		
1390	Robert III.			1250	Waldemar.		
1406	James I.						

POPES OF THE ROMAN CHURCH

END OF PONTIFICATE, A.D.		END OF PONTIFICATE, A.D.		END OF PONTIFICATE, A.D.		END OF PONTIFICATE, A.D.	
St. Peter	67	St. Boniface IV	615	Benedict V	966	Innocent VI	1362
St. Linus, M.	76	St. Deusdeditus or		John XIII	972	B. Urban V	1370
St. Anacletus or Cletus, M.	88	Adeodatus I	618	Benedict VI	974	Gregory XI	1378
St. Clement I, M.	97	Boniface V	625	Benedict VII	983	Urban VI	1389
St. Evaristus, M.	105	Honorius I	638	John XIV	984	Boniface IX	1404
St. Alexander I, M.	115	Severinus	640	John XV	996	Innocent VII	1406
St. Sixtus I, M.	125	John IV	642	Gregory V	999	Gregory XII	1415
St. Telesphorus, M.	136	Theodore I	649	Sylvester II	1003	Martin V	1431
St. Hyginus, M.	140	St. Martin I, M.	655	John XVII	1003	Eugene IV	1447
St. Pius I, M.	155	St. Eugene I	657	John XVIII	1009	Nicholas V	1455
St. Anicetus, M.	166	St. Vitalian	672	Sergius IV	1012	Callistus III	1458
St. Soterus, M.	175	Adeodatus II	676	Benedict VIII	1024	Pius II	1464
St. Eleuterius, M.	189	Donus I	678	John XIX	1032	Paul II	1471
St. Victor I, M.	199	St. Agathonus	681	Benedict IX	1044	Sixtus IV	1484
St. Zephyrinus, M.	217	St. Leo II	683	Sylvester III	1045	Innocent VIII	1492
St. Callistus, I, M.	222	St. Benedict II	685	Benedict IX	1045	Alexander VI	1503
St. Urban I, M.	230	John V	686	Gregory VI	1046	Pius III	1503
St. Pontian, M.	235	Conon	687	Clement II	1047	Julius II	1513
St. Anterus, M.	236	St. Sergius I	701	Benedict IX	1048	Leo X	1521
St. Fabian, M.	250	John VI	705	Damasus II	1048	Adrian VI	1523
St. Cornelius, M.	253	John VII	707	St. Leo IX	1054	Clement VII	1534
St. Lucius I, M.	254	Sisinnius	708	Victor II	1057	Paul III	1549
St. Stephen I, M.	257	Constantine	715	Stephen X	1058	Julius III	1555
St. Sixtus II, M.	258	St. Gregory II	731	Nicholas II	1061	Marcellus II	1555
St. Dionysius	268	St. Gregory III	741	Alexander II	1073	Paul IV	1559
St. Felix I, M.	274	St. Zachary	752	St. Gregory VII	1085	Pius IV	1565
St. Eutychian, M.	283	Stephen II	752	B. Victor III	1087	St. Pius V	1572
St. Caius, M.	296	Stephen III	757	B. Urban II	1099	Gregory XIII	1585
St. Marcellinus, M.	304	St. Paul I	767	Paschal II	1118	Sixtus V	1590
St. Marcellus I, M.	309	Stephen IV	772	Gelasius II	1119	Urban VII	1590
St. Eusebius, M.	309	Adrian I	795	Callistus II	1124	Gregory XIV	1591
St. Melchiades, M.	314	St. Leo III	816	Honorius II	1130	Innocent IX	1591
St. Sylvester I	335	Stephen V	817	Innocent II	1143	Clement VIII	1605
St. Mark	336	St. Paschal I	824	Celestine II	1144	Leo XI	1605
St. Julius I	352	Eugene II	827	Lucius II	1145	Paul V	1621
Liberius	366	Valentine	827	B. Eugene III	1153	Gregory XV	1623
St. Damasus I	384	Gregory IV	844	Anastasius IV	1154	Urban VIII	1644
St. Siricius	399	Sergius II	847	Adrian IV	1159	Innocent X	1655
St. Anastasius I	401	St. Leo IV	855	Alexander III	1181	Alexander VII	1667
St. Innocent I	417	Benedict III	858	Lucius III	1185	Clement IX	1669
St. Zozimus	418	St. Nicholas I (the Great).	867	Urban III	1187	Clement X	1676
St. Boniface I	422	Adrian II	872	Gregory VIII	1187	Innocent XI	1689
St. Celestine I	432	John VIII	882	Clement III	1191	Alexander VIII	1691
St. Sixtus III	440	Marinus I	884	Celestine III	1198	Innocent XII	1700
St. Leo I (the Great)	461	St. Adrian III	885	Innocent III	1216	Clement XI	1721
St. Hilary	468	Stephen VI	891	Honorius III	1227	Innocent XIII	1724
St. Simplicius	483	Formosus	896	Gregory IX	1241	Benedict XIII	1730
St. Felix III or II	492	Boniface VI	896	Celestine IV	1241	Clement XII	1740
St. Gelasius I	496	Stephen VII	897	Innocent IV	1254	Benedict XIV	1758
Anastasius II	498	Romanus	897	Alexander IV	1261	Clement XIII	1769
St. Symmacus	514	Theodore II	897	Urban IV	1264	Clement XIV	1774
St. Hormisdas	523	John IX	900	Clement IV	1268	Pius VI	1799
St. John I	526	Benedict IV	903	B. Gregory X	1276	Pius VII	1823
St. Felix IV or III	530	Leo V	903	B. Innocent V	1276	Leo XII	1829
Boniface II	532	Sergius III	911	Adrian V	1276	Pius VIII	1830
John II	535	Anastasius III	913	John XXI	1277	Gregory XVI	1846
St. Agapitus	536	Landus	914	Nicholas III	1280	Pius IX	1878
St. Silverius, M.	537	John X	928	Martin IV	1285	Leo XIII	1903
Vigilius	555	Leo VI	928	Honorius IV	1287	St. Pius X	1914
Pelagius I	561	Stephen VIII	931	Nicholas IV	1292	Benedict XV	1922
John III	574	John XI	935	St. Celestine V	1296	Pius XI	1939
Benedict I	579	Leo VII	939	Boniface VIII	1303	Pius XII	1959
Pelagius II	590	Stephen IX	942	B. Benedict XI	1304	John XXIII	1963
St. Gregory I (the Great).	604	Marinus II	946	Clement V	1314	Paul VI	
Sabinianus	606	Agapitus II	955	John XXII	1334		
Boniface III	607	John XII	964	Benedict XII	1342		
		Leo VIII	965	Clement VI	1352		

BIBLIOGRAPHY

GENERAL ASPECTS

AMERICAN HISTORICAL ASSOCIATION. *Guide to Historical Literature.* The Macmillan Co., 1963.

BARNOUW, ADRIAN J. *The Pageant of Netherlands History.* Longmans, Green & Co., Ltd., 1952.

BAUMER, FRANKLIN L. (ed.). *Main Currents of Western Thought.* Alfred A. Knopf, Inc., 1952.

BLOCH, MARC. *The Historian's Craft.* Alfred A. Knopf, Inc., 1953.

BRINTON, CRANE, JOHN B. CHRISTOPHER, and ROBERT L. WOLFF. *A History of Civilization.* 2 vols. Prentice-Hall, Inc., 1955.

BRUUN, GEOFFREY and WALLACE K. FERGUSON. *A Survey of European Civilization, Ancient Times to the Present.* Houghton Mifflin Co., 1952.

DURANT, WILL. *Our Oriental Heritage.* 2 vols. Simon & Schuster, Inc., 1935.

GABRIELI, FRANCESCO. *The Arabs: A Short History.* Translated by Salvatore Atanasio. Hawthorn Books, Inc., 1963.

GUSTAVSON, CARL. *A Preface to History.* McGraw-Hill, Inc., 1956.

LANE, FREDERIC C., ERIC F. GOLDMAN, and ERLING M. HUNT. *The World's History.* Harcourt, Brace & World, Inc., 1962.

LANGER, WILLIAM L. (ed.). *An Encyclopedia of World History.* Houghton Mifflin Co., 1952.

MORRISON, SAMUEL ELIOT. *Vistas of History.* Alfred A. Knopf, Inc., 1964.

PALMER, ROBERT R. *A History of the Modern World.* Alfred A. Knopf, Inc., 1956.

RALPH, PHILIP. *Story of Our Civilization.* E. P. Dutton & Co., Inc., 1954.

SELIGMAN, EDWIN R. *The Economic Interpretation of History: A Classic Study of "Historical Materialism"—Its Origins, Its Applications, and Its Significance.* Columbia University Press, 1963.

SETTON, KENNETH M. and HENRY R. WINKLER, (eds.). *Great Problems in European Civilization.* Prentice-Hall, Inc., 1954.

STERN, FRITZ. *The Varieties of History.* Meridian Books, Inc., 1956.

ARCHAEOLOGY

CERAM, C. W. *Gods, Graves, and Scholars.* Alfred A. Knopf, Inc., 1962.

CHILDE, V. GORDON. *What Happened in History.* Penguin Books, Inc., 1946.

COTTRELL, LEONARD. *The Horizon Book of Lost Worlds.* Doubleday & Co., Inc., 1962.

MEIGHAN, CLEMENT W. *The Archaeologist's Note Book.* Chandler Publishing Co., 1961.

PIGGOTT, S. *Approach to Archaeology.* Harvard University Press, 1959.

SILVERBERG, ROBERT. *Lost Cities and Vanished Civilizations.* Chilton Co., 1963.

SILVERBERG, ROBERT, *Sunken History: The Story of Underwater Archeology.* Chilton Co., 1963.

ANCIENT HISTORY

BOTSFORD, GEORGE W. *Hellenic History.* Revised by C. A. Robinson, Jr., The Macmillan Co., 1956.

DURANT, WILL. *Caesar and Christ.* Simon & Schuster, Inc., 1944.

DURANT, WILL. *The Life of Greece.* Simon & Schuster, Inc., 1939.

GIBBON, EDWARD. *The Portable Gibbon: The Decline and Fall of the Roman Empire.* The Viking Press, Inc., 1952.

GODOLPHIN, FRANCIS R. B. (ed.). *The Greek Historians.* Random House, Inc., 1942.

KITTS, H. D. F. *The Greeks.* Penguin Books, Inc. 1954.

SCULLARD, HOWARD H. *From Gracchi to Nero: A Short History of Rome, 133 B.C. to 68 A.D.* Frederick A. Praeger, Inc., 1959.

SHOTWELL, JAMES T. *The Story of Ancient History.* Columbia University Press, 1961.

SWAIN, JOSEPH W. *The Ancient World,* 2 vols. Harper & Bros., 1950.

TOYNBEE, ARNOLD J. *Greek Historical Thought.* Mentor Books, 1952.

WILSON, JOHN A. *The Culture of Ancient Egypt.* University of Chicago Press, 1956.

THE MIDDLE AGES AND THE RENAISSANCE

ADAMS, HENRY. *Mont-Saint-Michel and Chartres.* Houghton Mifflin Co., 1936.

COULTON, GEORGE G. (ed.). *Life in the Middle Ages.* The Macmillan Co., 1935.

DURANT, WILL. *The Renaissance.* Simon & Schuster, Inc. 1953.

EVANS, JOAN. *Life in Medieval France.* Phaidon Publishers, Inc., 1957.

FROISSART, JEAN. *Chronicles of England, France, and Spain.* E. P. Dutton & Co., Inc., 1930.

HUIZINGA, JOHAN. *The Waning of the Middle Ages.* Doubleday & Co., Inc., 1954.

KELLY, AMY R. *Eleanor of Aquitaine and the Four Kings.* Harvard University Press, 1950.

LOPEZ, ROBERT S. *The Birth of Europe.* M. Evans and Company, Inc., 1966.

MARTINES, LAURO. *Lawyers and Statecraft in Renaissance Florence.* Princeton University Press, 1968.

OSTROGORSKY, GEORGE. *History of the Byzantine State.* Rutgers University Press, 1957.

PAINTER, SIDNEY. *The Rise of the Feudal Monarchies.* Cornell University Press, 1951.

PATER, WALTER. *The Renaissance.* Random House, Inc., 1964.

ROEDER, RALPH. *The Man of the Renaissance.* The Viking Press, Inc., 1923.

THORNDIKE, LYNN. *The History of Medieval Europe.* Houghton Mifflin Co., 1949.

WATT, W. MONTGOMERY. *A History of Islamic Spain.* Edinburgh University Press, 1965.

YOUNG, GEORGE F. *The Medici.* The Modern Library, Inc., 1933.

SEVENTEENTH, EIGHTEENTH and NINETEENTH CENTURIES

BRUUN, GEOFFREY. *Europe and the French Imperium, 1799–1814 (Rise of Modern Europe* series). Harper & Bros., 1938.

CARLYLE, THOMAS. *The French Revolution, A History.* E. P. Dutton & Co., Inc., 1929.

DURANT, WILL. *The Reformation.* Simon & Schuster, Inc., 1957.

HAYES, CARLTON J. H. *A Generation of Materialism, 1871–1900 (Rise of Modern Europe* series). Harper & Bros., 1941.

LEFEBVRE, GEORGES. *The Coming of the French Revolution.* Vintage Books, 1957.

NICOLSON, HAROLD. *The Congress of Vienna.* Compass Books, 1961.

ROBERTSON, PRISCILLA. *Revolutions of 1848. A Social History.* Princeton University Press, 1967.

TAYLOR, ALAN J. P. *The Age of Metternich, 1814–1848 (Rise of Modern Europe* series). Oxford University Press, Inc., 1954.

TAWNEY, RICHARD H. *Religion and the Rise of Capitalism.* Penguin Books, Inc., 1947.

AFRICA

BARBOUR, NEVILL (ed.). *A Survey of North West Africa (The Maghrib).* Oxford University Press, 1959.

BARTLETT, VERNON. *Struggle for Africa.* Frederick A. Praeger, Inc., 1953.

CARTER, GWENDOLEN. *Independence for Africa.* Frederick A. Praeger, Inc., 1960.

HATCH, JOHN C. *Africa Today—and Tomorrow: An Outline of Basic Facts and Major Problems.* Frederick A. Praeger, Inc., 1960.

HOPKINSON, TOM. *In the Fiery Continent.* Doubleday & Co., Inc., 1963.

MARQUAND, LEO. *The Story of South Africa.* Roy Publishers, Inc., 1955.

MARSH, ZOË and G. W. KINGSNORTH. *An Introduction to the History of East Africa.* Cambridge University Press, 1961.

MOOREHEAD, ALAN. *The Blue Nile.* Harper & Bros., 1962.

OLIVER, ROLAND and J. D. FAGE. *A Short History of Africa.* New York University Press, 1963.

ROTBERG, ROBERT I. *A Political History of Tropical Africa.* Harcourt, Brace & World, Inc., 1965.

THEOBOLD, ROBERT (ed.). *The New Nations of West Africa (The Reference Shelf* series). The H. W. Wilson Co., 1960.

WALKER, ERIC A. *A History of Southern Africa* (3rd ed.). Longmans, Green and Co., Ltd., 1957.

ASIA AND THE MIDDLE EAST

BOSWORTH, CLIFFORD EDMUND. *The Islamic Dynasties.* Edinburgh University Press, 1967.

BURTON, HUGH. *Japan's Modern Century.* The Ronald Press Co., 1955.

FAIRBANK, JOHN K., EDWIN O. REISCHAUER, and ALBERT M. CRAIG. *East Asia. The Modern Transformation.* Houghton Mifflin Co., 1965.

FRITERS, GERARD. *Outer Mongolia.* The Johns Hopkins Press, 1949.

GARDNER, CHARLES S. *Chinese Traditional Historiography.* Harvard University Press, 1961.

GIBB, H. A. R. *Mohammedanism.* Home University Library, 1953.

HALL, D. G. E. *A History of South-East Asia* (2nd ed.). St. Martin's Press, 1964.

HEARN, LAFCADIO. *Japan: An Attempt at Interpretation.* The Macmillan Co., 1904.

HOLLAND, WILLIAM (ed.). *Asian Nationalism and the West.* The Macmillan Co., 1953.

LATOURETTE, KENNETH S. *A Short History of the Far East.* The Macmillan Co., 1957.

LAWRENCE, THOMAS E. *Seven Pillars of Wisdom.* Doubleday & Co., Inc., 1936.

LENIZOWSKI, GEORGE. *The Middle East in World Affairs.* Cornell University Press, 1957.

LINDSEY, MICHAEL. *China and the Cold War.* Cambridge University Press, 1955.

LOW, SIR FRANCIS. *Struggle for Asia.* Frederick A. Praeger, Inc., 1955.

MORAES, FRANCIS R. *The Revolt in Tibet.* The Macmillan Co., 1960.

MURTI, B. S. N. *Viet-Nam Divided: The Unfinished Struggle.* Taplinger Publishing Co., Inc., 1963.

PAYNE, ROBERT. *Lawrence of Arabia.* Pyramid Publications, Inc., 1963.

REISCHAUER, EDWIN O. *Japan Past and Present.* Alfred A. Knopf, 1947.

SANGER, RICHARD H. *The Arabian Peninsula.* Cornell University Press, 1954.

SCALAPINO, ROBERT A. (ed.). *North Korea Today.* Frederick A. Praeger, Inc., 1963.

SPEAR, PERCIVAL. *A History of India,* (vol. 2). Penguin Books, 1965.

STEVENS, GEORGIANA G. *Egypt Yesterday and Today.* Holt, Rinehart & Winston, Inc., 1963.

TELLER, EDWARD and ALLEN BROWN. *The Legacy of Hiroshima.* Doubleday & Co., Inc., 1962.

THAPAR, ROMILA. *A History of India,* (vol. 1). Penguin Books, 1966.

WINT, GUY (ed.). *Asia: A Handbook.* Frederick A. Praeger, Inc., 1966.

WINT, GUY. *Common Sense About China.* The Macmillan Co., 1960.

EUROPE

BONJOUR, EDWARD and others. *Short History of Switzerland.* Oxford University Press, Inc., 1952.

BRENAN, GERALD. *The Spanish Labyrinth.* Cambridge University Press, 1950.

CATELL, DAVID T. *Communism and the Spanish Civil War.* University of California Press, 1955.

CARMICHAEL, JOEL. *An Illustrated History of Russia.* Reynal & Co., Inc., 1960.

CRAIG, GORDON A. *Europe Since 1815* (2nd ed.). Holt, Rinehart and Winston, Inc., 1966.

CHURCHILL, WINSTON. *The Second World War.* 6 vols. Bantam Books, Inc., 1962.

DILL, MARSHALL. *Germany: A Modern History.* University of Michigan Press, 1959.

FALLS, CYRIL. *The Great War, 1914–1918.* G. P. Putnam's Sons, 1959.

GILBERT, MARTIN and RICHARD GOTT. *The Appeasers.* Houghton Mifflin Company, 1963.

GUNTHER, JOHN. *Inside Europe Today.* Harper & Bros., 1961.

GUNTHER, JOHN. *Inside Russia Today.* Harper & Bros., 1958.

GUÉRARD, ALBERT L. *France: A Modern History.* University of Michigan Press, 1959.

HARCAVE, SYDNEY. *Russia: A History.* J. B. Lippincott Co., 1956.

HISCOCKS, RICHARD. *The Rebirth of Austria.* Oxford University Press, Inc., 1953.

HUSSEY, W. D. *The British Empire and Commonwealth, 1500–1961.* Cambridge University Press, 1963.

KENNAN, GEORGE F. *Russia and the West Under Lenin and Stalin.* Atlantic Monthly Press, 1961.

LANGSAM, WALTER C. *The World Since 1919.* The Macmillan Co., 1954.

LEDERER, IVO J. (ed.). *Russian Foreign Policy: Essays in Historical Perspective.* Yale University Press, 1962.

LEVINE, IRVING R. *Main Street, U.S.S.R.* Doubleday & Co., Inc., 1959.

LORD, WALTER. *Day of Infamy.* Holt, Rinehart & Winston, Inc., 1957.

MAUROIS, ANDRÉ. *An Illustrated History of England.* The Viking Press, 1964.

MONAT, CHARLES L. *Britain Between the Wars, 1918–40.* University of Chicago Press, 1955.

RIASANOVSKY, NICHOLAS. *A History of Russia.* Oxford University Press, 1963.

SCHERILL, FERDINAND. *History of Europe: From the Reformation to the Present Day.* Harcourt, Brace & World, Inc., 1951.

SETON-WATSON, HUGH. *From Lenin to Khrushchev* (rev. ed.). Frederick A. Praeger, Inc., 1960.

SHIRER, WILLIAM L. *The Challenge of Scandinavia.* Little, Brown & Co., 1955.

SHIRER, WILLIAM L. *The Rise and Fall of the Third Reich.* Simon & Schuster, Inc., 1960.

STAVRIANOS, L. S. *The Balkans Since 1453.* Holt, Rinehart and Winston, Inc., 1958.

STEINBERG, S. G. and others (edd.). *A New Dictionary of British History.* St. Martin's Press, Inc., 1963.

SUMNER, B. H. *Peter the Great and the Emergence of Russia.* The Macmillan Co., 1950.

TAYLOR, A. J. P. *Illustrated History of the First World War.* G. P. Putnam's Sons, 1964.

TAYLOR, A. J. P. *The Struggle for Mastery in Europe 1848–1918.* Oxford University Press, 1954.

THOMPSON, SAMUEL H. *Czechoslovakia in European History.* Princeton University, 1953.

TREVELYAN, JANET P. *Short History of the Italian People From the Barbarian Invasion to the Present Day.* Pitman Publishing Corp., 1956.

TUCHMAN, BARBARA W. *The Guns of August.* The Macmillan Co., 1962.

VERMEIL, EDMOND. *Germany in the Twentieth Century: A Political and Cultural History of the Weimar Republic and the Third Reich.*

Frederick A. Praeger, Inc., 1956.

VON RAUCH, GEORG. *A History of Soviet Russia* (rev. ed.). Frederick A. Praeger, Inc., 1958.

LATIN AMERICA

ALEXANDER, ROBERT J. *Latin-American Politics and Government.* The Macmillan Co., 1965.

BANNON, JOHN FRANCIS and PETER MASTEN DUNNE. *Latin America: An Historical Survey* (rev. ed.). The Bruce Publishing Co., 1958.

BEALS, CARLETON. *Latin America: World in Revolution.* Abelard-Schuman Ltd., 1962.

BENTON, WILLIAM. *The Voice of Latin America* (rev. ed.). Harper & Row, Inc., 1961.

FAGG, JOHN EDWIN. *Latin America: A General History.* The Macmillan Co., 1963.

HERRING, HUBERT. *A History of Latin America.* Alfred A. Knopf, Inc., 1961.

PARKES, HENRY BAMFORD. *A History of Mexico* (rev. ed.). Houghton Mifflin Co., 1960.

THOMAS, ALFRED B. *Latin America: A History.* The Macmillan Co., 1956.

UNITED STATES

ALLAN, FREDERICK L. *The Big Change: America Transforms Itself, 1900–1950.* Harper & Bros., 1952.

BEARD, CHARLES A. and MARY R. *The Rise of American Civilization.* The Macmillan Co., 1934.

BURNS, JAMES MACGREGOR. *Roosevelt: The Lion and the Fox.* Harcourt, Brace & World, Inc., 1963.

CATTON, BRUCE. *The Army of the Potomac: A Trilogy.* Doubleday & Co., Inc., 1962.

COCHRAN, THOMAS C. and WAYNE ANDREWS (edd.). *Concise Dictionary of American History.* Charles Scribner's Sons, 1962.

COMMAGER, HENRY S. (ed.). *The Blue and the Gray: The Story of the Civil War As Told by the Participants.* The Bobbs-Merrill Co., Inc., 1950.

COMMAGER, HENRY S. (ed.). *Documents of American History.* Appleton-Century-Crofts, 1949.

COMMAGER, HENRY S. (ed.). *Living Ideas in America.* Harper & Bros., 1951.

COMMAGER, H. S. and A. NEVINS. *A Short History of the United States.* Alfred A. Knopf, Inc., 1964.

GOLDMAN, ERIC. *Rendezvous with Destiny.* Alfred A. Knopf, Inc., 1953.

JONES, HOWARD MUMFORD. *O Strange New World.* The Viking Press, 1964.

MERK, FREDERICK. *Manifest Destiny and Mission in American History.* Alfred A. Knopf, Inc., 1964.

MORRIS, RICHARD B. *Encyclopedia of American History.* Harper & Brothers, 1953.

MORRISON, SAMUEL E. and HENRY S. COMMAGER. *The Growth of the American Republic.* 2 vols. Oxford University Press, Inc., 1951.

NEVINS, ALLAN and HENRY S. COMMAGER. *America: The Story of a Free People.* Little, Brown & Co., 1942.

STOWE, HARRIET BEECHER. *The Annotated Uncle Tom's Cabin.* Edited by Philip Van Doren Stern. Paul S. Eriksson, Inc., 1964.

HOMEMAKING

Homemaking	1085
Furniture	1093
Interior decoration	1102
Etiquette	1112

VINCE LISANTI

Homemaking

HOME MANAGEMENT

Those most immediately and personally concerned with home management generally answer to the name of "homemaker" or "housewife." But with the complexities of living today, a more exact designation might be "domestic engineer." The modern homemaker holds down a myriad of jobs that, at a glance, completely refute the current trend toward job specialization and work simplification. She is called upon at one time or another—and often simultaneously—to serve as short-order cook, gourmet chef, Scout leader, gracious hostess, expert on child care and guidance, comparison shopper, nutritionist, seamstress, and a Solomon at settling small-fry disputes. Additional roles of interior decorator, general handyman, financial wizard adept at stretching the household budget, first-aid corpsman, family social director, chauffeur, laundress, and cleaning woman also come within her domain.

The full-time housewife works an average of seven to eleven hours a day, seven days a week; a homemaker who also works outside the home spends about 75 to 85 hours a week at her two jobs. One might wonder why, in this age, the homemaker's hours need be so long. Both business and industry endeavor to lighten her work load through the development of new products—pre-packaged foods, work-saving appliances, and time-saving cleaning aids. Architects and designers strive to provide more efficient homes and easy-to-maintain furnishings. Yet the housewife nevertheless is most likely to start her non-stop day making coffee at 7 a.m. and end it by tidying the living room at 10 p.m. This paradox is the result of many factors. Gone is the live-in maid who cooked, cleaned, and took care of the children. A broom, a mop, a bucket of suds, and a dust rag no longer constitute the major cleaning aids. Today's list includes everything from automatic floor polishers to rug shampooers and electric can openers. Pre-packaged foods and wash-and-wear fabrics save time and energy, and lighten the work load immeasurably. Time otherwise consumed by paring vegetables or starching and ironing thus is freed for other activities. However, Parkinson's law now comes into play: "Work expands so as to fill the time available for its completion." There exist all to many homemakers who, given the gift of leisure time, exert themselves in the enervating pastime called make-work.

To plan an efficient program of home management, every homemaker first should evaluate her job as domestic engineer. The application of her findings will result in more effective use of time, energy, and the household budget. Also important is her use of imagination, experimentation, and—above all—sense of humor.

How to Schedule Work.—The most routine aspects of home management are the day-in, day-out problems of keeping the house clean, preparing meals, and doing a multitude of tasks that come under the catchall heading of "housekeeping." Some of these already have been mentioned, but any housewife could easily add another twenty or more household duties. Indeed, it has been estimated that the average homemaker copes with some 350 activities a week. These range from such major jobs as shampooing the living-room rug and washing floors to finding time to sew on a button. Somehow, time must be found for all the jobs to be done.

■ **WHAT WORK TO DO.**—The most logical answer to this domestic problem of finding time is to formulate a work schedule. A pencil, paper, clock or wristwatch, and enough patience to time a typical work week's activities are the requirements.

First, write down social and civic commitments and the time involved. Then rule seven pages, one for each day of the week, into three columns, and head the columns *Daily*, *Weekly*, and *Special*. For the next seven days, each job and the time it takes to do it must be jotted down in the correct column. For instance, making beds will be listed under *Daily*, scrubbing the kitchen floor under *Weekly*, and cleaning closets under *Special*.

By the end of the week, the time required for routine jobs should be fairly clear. The *Special* list naturally will be incomplete, but this can be rectified by expansion of the list to include all the usual jobs falling within this category.

A composite picture of the seven pages now can be made by combining the information into a single three-column list. It might resemble the accompanying sample outline.

■ **SCHEDULING**—From this master list a weekly schedule can be devised. Time slots should be left for engagements noted on the outside activities list and for coverage of special jobs.

Allow for a test period during which the effectiveness of the schedule can be analyzed and necessary changes made. In order to include changes in work patterns, the listing must be periodically reevaluated.

The early morning is the best time to do basic chores because energy is highest following a night's rest. Also, if the routine jobs have been completed by lunch time, at least part of the afternoon will be free for outside activities.

A balance of chores is another clue to efficient scheduling. It is better to alternate light tasks with tiring ones. Follow a strenuous chore, such as

Sample Home Program

Daily	Weekly	Special
Tidy kitchen: wipe stove, oven, counters, refrigerator, sink	Clean stove, oven, refuse can, sink	Wash and wax kitchen floor
		Defrost, clean refrigerator
	Straighten kitchen cupboards; take grocery inventory	Clean closets, drawers
Straighten bedrooms: make beds, dust, mop floors, carpet-sweep, collect laundry	Wash kitchen floor	Polish furniture
Tidy bathrooms	Tidy closets, drawers	Clean or have cleaned rugs, carpets, draperies, curtains, upholstery, slipcovers
Straighten rest of house: dust, mop, carpet-sweep	Clean bathroom: wash tub, shower stall, toilet, tiles, laundry hamper, floor	Wash blinds, windows, clean mirrors
Do laundry if large family or one with infants	Vacuum blinds, baseboards, floors, upholstery, carpets	Wash walls, woodwork
Spot-clean stains	Polish metalware	Wax wood floors
	Spot-clean woodwork	Wash or clean lampshades, wash light fixtures
		Clean, mothproof seasonal clothing, household goods

washing floors, with a less physically demanding occupation, such as updating the household accounts.

Schedules should not be influenced by old-fashioned routines. The time-honored day to do the family wash is on Monday; but in a household with school-age children, Mondays might better be dedicated to straightening up the house after a busy weekend. The Saturday shopping might better be done on a midweek day when the stores are less crowded or on an evening when the husband can watch the children.

One important aspect in schedule-making often is overlooked. The homemaker concentrates only on the jobs to be fitted into a competent work pattern, forgetting the need for time to recharge her energies. This is somewhat alleviated if the heavy and light jobs are alternated; but time also should be set aside during morning and afternoon for a definite change of pace, be it a coffee break, a brief nap, or reading.

Efficient Work Methods.—It could very well be that the ideal housewife should by nature be both practical and lazy, with a sense of, and appreciation for, order. These somewhat paradoxical attributes would combine neatly the essential ingredients for evaluating and effecting efficient work methods in the home. Laziness, if constructive, spurs one to devise time- and energy-saving short cuts. But it also is necessary to have a clear eye for the practical and orderly aspects of everyday living.

■ PREPLANNING.—Each job should be assessed in terms of its necessity. All too often there are tasks that easily could be deleted or combined with other jobs. The types and the number of possessions also are part of the problem—a great problem in the limited area of an apartment. A jumble of knickknacks creates a perennial dusting hazard. Better to sort them and store some. The key to sound work methods is the ability to organize and coordinate the three phases of doing a job: *preparation*, *performance*, and *completion*.

LOOK MAGAZINE

DISHWASHING is simplified if preplanned.

Preparation.—It is important to set about one task at a time, rather than embarking on a series of projects. This takes discipline, as it is easy to be distracted by the sight of other jobs that also require attention. But a succession of barely commenced projects have a tendency to remain half finished.

The work schedule is a worthwhile defense against this particular problem. Consult the list after breakfast to line up the day's work in orderly fashion. Next, gather the necessary equipment for the first chore of the day. Jobs requiring the same cleaning aids can be grouped together to avoid repetitious preparation. Thus, if the chore is scrubbing the kitchen floor, consider also doing the bathroom floor. Each requires approximately the same tools.

Efficient job preparation is accelerated by storing equipment at the point of use. For example, such basic cleaning supplies as sponge, bowl brush, scouring powder, and ammonia for cleaning wall tiles should be stored in the bathroom. Carpet

sweepers and vacuum cleaners must be used throughout the house. These items and other general equipment and supplies should be stored in a centrally located utility closet that is convenient to a maximum number of rooms. A kitchen closet or second hall closet can be designated for this purpose. Hang brooms, mops, dustpans, and brushes on hooks to leave floor space free for such items as carpet sweepers, vacuum cleaners, pails, and work basket.

The work basket should contain dust cloths, spot remover, sponges, whisk broom, furniture polish, liquid detergent, sponge, and any other small items generally used in cleaning. When properly assembled and maintained, a work basket saves both time and energy; all the oddments used in cleaning can be transported to the work area in a single trip.

Performance.—Time can be saved by doing certain chores on a mass-production basis. Consider the job of making lunch sandwiches for school-age children. The casual housewife tries to combine making breakfast and preparing the children's school lunches. The result is confusion, unimaginative box-lunch menus, and inefficient expenditure of time and energy. To do the job properly, make up school lunch menus by the week, noting the needed ingredients on the grocery list. Then, at a slack period during the weekend, prepare the sandwiches in bulk, wrapping each separately and noting the type of sandwich on the sandwich bags. The week's supply then can be frozen. This same approach can be applied to preparing other dishes: when making stew, double the recipe and freeze half for later use.

An inescapable fact about homemaking is that certain periods of the day are more prone to job pressures than are others. These periods generally occur about mealtime. The day usually begins with a rush of activities. Breakfast must be made, lunches packed, children readied for school, husband seen off to work, and the family pet fed. Each of these activities can be broken down into

LOOK MAGAZINE

TIME- AND LABOR-SAVING DEVICES are a boon to the housewife of today. Compare the modern electric appliances with those of yesteryear.

 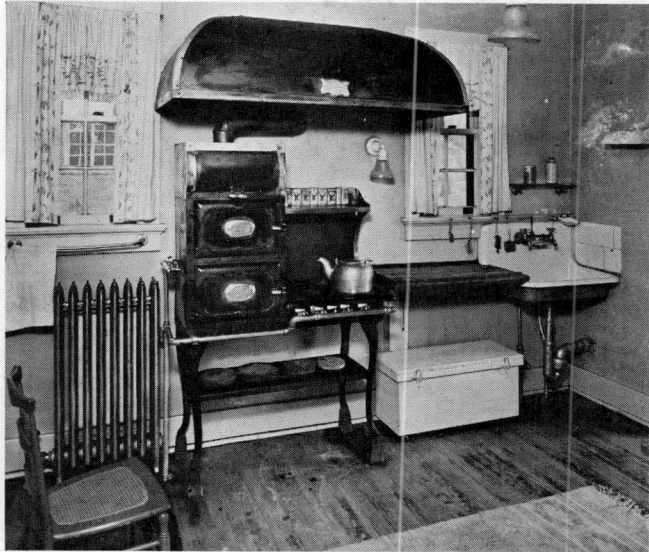

BETTMANN ARCHIVE

KITCHEN OF THE 1880'S, complete with a pump to draw water and a wood-burning stove; this was soon replaced by a gas stove (*right*).

individual steps. The breakfast table should be set with dishes, silver, dry cereal, and condiments as part of cleaning up after dinner. The breakfast menu for the next morning is checked, and the nonperishable foodstuffs placed on the kitchen counter. The necessary pots and pans for breakfast also are set out. A utility cart can be set up to carry items to the table in the morning, and then to clear the table in one trip.

Completion.—The completion, or clean-up, of a job is as important as preparation and performance. This part of the job can be broken down into three parts: maintenance of tools, storage of tools, and correct selection of the task to follow.

Tools must be in prime condition to give maximum service. They represent a considerable investment, and proper care will ensure longer life and satisfactory operation. Therefore each piece should be cleaned and, if necessary, oiled before storage.

Pertinent to home management is the ability to devise a schedule that employs a logical job sequence. Thus, if the living-room rug is to be vacuumed, it is only common sense also to do the adjacent floor areas. Again, the job of putting away the groceries has as its natural sequence the refilling of canisters and straightening of shelves. As this logical knitting of jobs evolves, changes should be made on your work schedule.

■**DIVISION OF LABOR.**—Home management should not be a one-man job. With the scarcity and high cost of labor today, it is not only reasonable but also necessary that each member of the family contribute to the efficient running of the home. How much of this should fall to the husband is a highly debatable, if not hotly disputed, question. Suffice it to say that chores that call for considerable strength or require a more mechanical turn of mind usually are better handled by the man of the family. The mother who continually picks

up after her children, makes their beds, and excuses them from helping with the lighter household tasks actually is doing them a distinct disservice. It is in their formative years that children learn the habits that they will carry into adult life. Taking an active part in family responsibilities also prepares children for their eventual adult roles. One family handles this by delegating a new responsibility to each child every year. Each, according to his age, is held accountable for certain chores. Each child gradually learns to take care of his possessions and to help in the running of the household.

■**WORK CONDITIONS.**—Work conditions will be more pleasant and less fatiguing if a few simple factors are remembered. Sufficient light, cross ventilation, and fresh air are essential for physical and mental well-being. Similarly, careful attention to the choice of comfortable work clothes and shoes insures easy movement. Dresses with large patch pockets are useful for holding stray items, and rubber gloves protect the hands.

The proper attitude also influences job effectiveness. To prevent the routine from becoming dull, be on the alert for better work methods. Check magazines and newspapers for information on new products and homemaking hints. Keep meals interesting by adding new recipes to the culinary repertoire. Maintain orderly lists of pending projects. These may be divided into such separate categories as *Call, Write, Do, Follow-up,* and *Buy.* Trying to keep a running mental list of all the things to be done leads to disorganization and discouragement. Conversely, a task checked off the list is a source of satisfaction.

1,095 Meals a Year.—Preparing three meals a day, 365 days of the year, adds up to a great deal of time in the kitchen. Indeed, the homemaker devotes proportionately more time to

kitchen work than to any other household task.

Kitchen work may be divided into four general areas: preparation of meals, cleaning up, storage, and grocery shopping.

■**PREPARATION OF MEALS.**—Meals may be planned either by drawing up weekly menus or by purchasing a variety of food in bulk so that meals can be prepared from an adequate stock. The success of each method depends on maintaining an all-inclusive grocery list. This should be kept in a convenient spot in the kitchen—on a bulletin board or cabinet door—for easy reference. Leave nothing to memory. If meals are planned weekly, select a time free from interruptions on a specified day to outline them. When this task has been completed, add to the grocery list the supplies necessary to cover the menus.

Try to shop for groceries only once or twice a week. More frequent shopping is wasteful in terms of time and energy, and also is indicative of careless planning. Before shopping, check the local newspaper for grocery specials and work sale items into your menus.

Excess time spent in meal preparation also can be curtailed. After consulting the menu, get out all of the necessary utensils and foodstuffs. When preparing fruits and vegetables, pare, slice, shuck, or peel them over newspaper so that the waste can be gathered up easily without soiling the work space.

Before storing groceries, prepare perishable foods for future use. Wash and clean vegetables and fruits. Meats should be cleaned and cut into meal-size portions (if these steps are necessary), then carefully wrapped for refrigeration or freezing.

One indispensable item is the kitchen timer; its uses are many and varied. It provides a sure way of timing cooking and frees the homemaker from constant checking and

LOOK MAGAZINE

KITCHENS OF TODAY are a homemaker's dream. They combine the latest technological developments with the beauty of contemporary design.

rechecking of the clock and food on the stove. It also can be used for many tasks outside the kitchen. For instance, an apartment dweller who uses community washers and dryers can use the timer to determine the laundry cycle.

■**CLEANING UP.**—Time and space are saved if things are cleaned and put away directly after use. Soaking cooking utensils facilitates the removal of grease. Knives, however, should never be left standing in suds, as prolonged immersion in some instances loosens the handle. When done by hand, dishes should be washed in the following order: glasses, silverware, china, utensils, and cookware. Let everything drain dry except the silverware, knives, and any utensils that tend to rust.

Combine the job of cleaning up with advance preparations for the next meal. Instead of storing items that will be needed again, put them aside for reuse. Leave kitchen counters cleared and clean. Good kitchen maintenance cuts down the need for heavy cleaning and makes big cleaning jobs easier to do.

■**STORAGE.**—The place and manner in which utensils, dinnerware, and foodstuffs are stored influence the efficiency with which kitchen chores can be performed. Ideally, items should be at point of use and within easy reach. Dinnerware should be stored close to the sink or dishwasher. The perfect solution is to have an openshelved pass-through from the kitchen to the dining room. The dishes, glasses, and silverware can be placed on the shelves from the kitchen side and later removed from the other side to the dining table. This arrangement also allows for easy serving and clearing away of dishes. Other items to be stored by the sink include water pitchers, vases, pots and pans, and vegetable and bottle brushes. Cooking utensils and brushes can be hung on pegs or hooks. The area below the sink is reserved for

storage of dishwashing supplies.

Nonperishable foodstuffs are stored near the work center. Mixing bowls, baking pans, and casseroles may be stored below the work center, with canisters on top of the counter. Above this should be hung spice shelf, knife rack, a wall-type can opener, and mixing utensils most often used. A pegboard is excellent for this purpose.

The place for skillets, pot lids, wooden stirring spoons, oven thermometer, deep-fat thermometer, and tea kettle is at the range. This also is the logical spot for a kitchen ventilating fan.

The kitchen should be functional, yet cheerful. Choose bright paint colors and gay fabrics. When painting the walls, remember that white and light shades of yellow, gray, tan, and green reflect the most light. Be sure the lighting is sufficient.

■**GROCERY SHOPPING.**—The grocery list should be organized before going to the store. A sample breakdown would be dairy products, fresh fruits and vegetables, meats and fish, frozen foods, household supplies, canned goods, and baked goods. List each group in the order that it appears in the store. This approach will save steps that otherwise would be expended in backtracking and crisscrossing the store.

Shop when store business is apt to be slow. Do not put it off until after five o'clock in the afternoon, as this is the time when business people must shop. Saturday excursions also are to be avoided. Although stores are not likely to be busy early on Monday mornings, try to avoid these hours. Stocks usually are depleted after the weekend rush, and supplies not yet fully replenished.

Many stores feature unadvertised specials that should be checked. However, avoid impulsive buying. Take advantage only of bargains that you really need. Otherwise, buy just those items that are on your grocery list.

Evaluating Family Standards.—The development of standards in the home results largely from a family's economic resources and its concept of comfort. In many cases, standards also are inherited from the parental home. However, whatever their origin, the standards by which a family lives should be subject to critical examination. Often, upon review, an established mode of living is found to be outdated or costly in terms of time, energy, or money.

■**SIMPLIFICATION OF HABITS.**—One question to ask is, "Do you do things through habit or by choice?" Take, for example, the matter of entertaining. If it somehow always involves elaborate preparations—polishing the silver, getting out the best china, drawing up a fancy, four-course menu—then chances are that having people in is a rare occurrence. Of course it is fun to give a special dinner occasionally, but the emphasis today is on informal living. How much better it is to have friends over more frequently and serve them a one-dish meal or brunch, or invite them to a picnic.

Revising family standards does not necessarily imply that they must be lowered. There are different ways of doing things, and often the substitute is as acceptable as the former method. Sometimes a family is forced to make temporary compromises in its way of living. If the homemaker is sick, then meals prepared from packaged or frozen foods and served on paper plates could be the order of the day.

Families with small children should consider purchasing plastic dinnerware for everyday use to avoid breaking expensive china. Plastic glasses and mugs for children, and plastic mats and paper napkins for the whole family will cut down the work load and household costs.

Another area that lends itself to work simplification is that of fabrics for clothing and household goods. Baby clothes come in a variety of

LOOK MAGAZINE

SHOPPING in supermarkets is fast, economical, and convenient; many homemakers, however, prefer patronizing the local specialty shops.

wash-and-wear materials: knits, seersucker, terry cloth, corduroy, and drip-dry cottons. Infants' stretch outfits are particularly desirable, as they require no ironing and fit well for an extended period of time. Sportswear and casual clothes for children and adults also are available in a wide range of wash-and-wear fabrics. When shopping, consider the amount of care and upkeep an article of clothing will require before making the final selection.

Use the same discretion when buying household goods. Eliminate ironing by buying drip-dry curtains; chenille, seersucker, corduroy, or drip-dry cotton bedspreads; paper guest towels for the bathroom; and no-iron sheets and pillow cases. Choose slipcover and upholstery fabrics that are crease- and stain-resistant, and blankets that are both machine washable and mothproof. Consider not only the eye appeal of clothing or household items, but also their long-term practicality.

Standards in cooking need not be adversely affected by the use of commercially prepared foods if they are selected judiciously. A whole meal out of a tin can be dreary. However, if a proper balance is struck between the use of prepackaged and home-cooked foods, the result can be more interesting meals.

Managing the Household Budget.—Nearly every family deals with a fixed income. Within this framework there are certain fixed expenses that most families must meet periodically: taxes (including state and federal income tax, unless wholly deducted from one's salary), rent or mortgage payments, life and health insurance, and church and charity contributions. In addition there are such variable expenses as heating costs, telephone and utilities, food (including cost of eating out), clothing, home and clothing maintenance, medical and dental expenses (unless covered by an insurance plan), car expenses,

commutation, recreation, and family welfare expenses. Needless to say, these are only the minimum expenses with which a family must cope. Not included are the costs that appear at different stages of family growth. Newlyweds must furnish a home. Later, a growing family brings added medical expenses, need for larger living quarters, perhaps the cost of having the children's teeth straightened, and a savings program for further education. Still later, the emphasis will shift to preparation for the retirement years.

■**PREPARING A BUDGET.**—In order to insure effective handling of family money matters, a plan or budget is essential. It may be kept in a notebook bought expressly for this purpose. Under the heading *Income* note all moneys that contribute to the family's annual income. (It is more realistic to deal with net income.) On a separate page, under the heading *Fixed Expenses,* jot down the outlays mentioned above. Checkbook stubs, if a checking account is maintained, present an easy way to determine these items. When added up, they will provide an exact figure for annual fixed expenses. Then, by dividing the total amount by 12, the amount of savings needed monthly to meet these payments is computed.

The total of the fixed expenses subtracted from the annual income determines the money available for *variable expenses.* Food is the largest item in this area, and it is difficult to reduce food costs to any large degree, although once-a-week shopping and observation of grocers' ads will help. A clothing budget can be determined by noting what clothing items must be replaced in the coming year for each family member. Then the individual items and their approximate costs are recorded in the notebook. The total figure indicates what the clothing budget for the year will be. One-twelfth of this amount may be put aside each month to cover clothing expenses as they occur. Savings can be realized by doing clothing and housewares shopping at

LOOK MAGAZINE

THE ICEBOX (*left*) had many disadvantages, but modern refrigeration is a convenience.

LOOK MAGAZINE

PICNICS, fun for the whole family, whether cooking on a sunny beach or roasting chickens on a snow-covered mountain in New England.

preseason, end-of-season, or white sales, or by exercising sewing skills.

■**RECREATION EXPENSES.**—This is a catchall heading that, when broken down, might include the following items: books, newspapers, magazines, hobbies, education, personal allowances, drugs and cosmetics, and recreation. Cost for each should be figured on a yearly and monthly basis.

One place where pennies dribble away is in day-to-day shopping. To discover just where they go, keep a small notebook in your purse and over a period of weeks jot down all purchases as they are made.

Two final figures must be included in the budget—the *rainy-day fund* and *savings.* The first is set aside to meet such unforeseen emergencies as prolonged illness, replacement of essential household items, and other unexpected major expenditures. Cost of home maintenance can be kept down by making repairs as soon as possible. Savings is an equally essential budget item that will allow eventual realization of family goals, whether they be a college education for the children, travel, or purchase

of an automobile or record player.

A working budget cannot be drafted overnight. The first outline should be subjected to review so that it may meet the family needs rather than dictate a rigid pattern of spending and saving. Even the accepted working budget should be reviewed.

Having now established how much must be set aside to cover budget expenditures, the next question is to determine where the budget money is to be kept. Checking and savings accounts may be opened, the first to cover such frequently recurring expenses as rent and utilities; the second to be used as a place of safekeeping for rainy-day funds and savings. The budget notebook, if kept up to date, will supply the necessary breakdown on disposition of the lump sums deposited in the bank accounts.

Another method for those who do not wish to maintain a checking account is the envelope system. Individual envelopes are marked *Rent, Food, Clothing,* and the like. Each pay day the specified amount is slipped into the correct envelope. However, a savings account should be

maintained for savings and emergency funds. This reduces the temptation to dip into growing funds and allows the money to draw interest.

If the desired balance between income and budget cannot be achieved, then drastic changes in family expenditures are necessary. These might include less expensive living quarters, reduction of large-scale purchases, sale of the family car, use of term insurance rather than straight life insurance, or an outside job for the wife. Before such steps are taken, the proposed remedy should be analyzed carefully. For instance, if the wife elects to work outside the home, will the salary earned appreciably offset the added expenses incurred? These would include a business wardrobe, cost of commutation and lunches, increased use of prepackaged food items, extra dry-cleaning costs, possible use of part-time houseworker, and hiring of a mother's helper for pre-teenage children. If the net income after expenses is negligible, then in all probability the wife's working is not the answer to the family's financial problems.

FINNISH NATIONAL TRAVEL OFFICE

INTERIOR DESIGN is an art form unto itself. Many rely on the advice of professionals, while others prefer to plan their own interiors.

FINNISH NATIONAL TRAVEL OFFICE

SCANDINAVIAN DESIGN is exemplified by this contemporary Finnish dining-room set.

Drawing up an effective budget should be a family project. Family goals must be defined and the development of each person considered. It is only through the cooperation of everyone that a working budget can be arrived at and maintained. Not only must the basic needs of the family be provided for, but provisions also must be made for future goals.

Apartment Living.—The trend today is toward urban living. For the vast majority of people this means setting up house in an apartment. Apartment living rarely is ideal, although it does have its virtues. On the one hand, there are no lawns to mow, no property taxes to pay, and no responsibility for building maintenance. However, life in an apartment can be fraught with problems.

Old buildings with sound-absorbing high ceilings and thick walls often need repairs. Many of the new buildings seem to have paper-thin walls and floors that act as sounding boards. In some instances the workmanship is slipshod and the appliances inferior. The first problem is that of choosing an apartment wisely. Other areas of concern, once the lease has been signed, include coping with architectural drawbacks and furnishing the rooms comfortably.

■**SELECTING AN APARTMENT.**—If possible, a couple should investigate prospective apartments together. Make up a list of questions to ask. These might include the following queries:

What are the terms of the lease?
Are any utilities included in the rent?
Are pets allowed?
What company manages the building?
Will the management paint? How often?
Will they replace worn-out appliances and fixtures?
Is the building rent-controlled?
Is the management willing to make necessary improvements or repairs?

Check all appliances, light switches, water taps, windows, and toilets to see that they are in proper working order. Since noise is a common complaint, run a simple test by having someone turn on a transistor radio in adjoining rooms and outside the apartment door. A radio set at average level should not be heard from room to room. (Remember that carpeting and draperies will help to muffle noises.)

■**CORRECTING STRUCTURAL DRAWBACKS.**—The apartment selected must have some winning aspects—a good-size kitchen, a spacious foyer, or a separate dining room—that prompted the choice. But chances are that closet and storage space are inadequate, room divisions unsuitable, some of the rooms too small, or exposed pipes a problem. Because the apartment usually is leased rather than owned, one must find inexpensive ways of surmounting these shortcomings.

Storage space can be increased through the purchase of ready-built closets. The less expensive kinds, made of heavy cardboard, are not attractive. However, a coat of paint of the same color as the walls and application of a stencil pattern will make them more acceptable. Curtaining off a room recess or the end of a room is another means of increasing the closet and storage space.

Poor floor planning can be corrected by installing room dividers. A long, narrow living room in an apartment bereft of dining space can be partitioned off at one end with a room divider to create a separate dining area. Dividers also may be used to create interesting effects.

Other methods of hiding or disguising architectural eyesores include the use of valances, screens, bracket-type bookcases, and draperies. The investment in most cases is small compared to the improvement.

■**FURNISHING AN APARTMENT.**—When furnishing an apartment, choose furniture that makes maximum use of the limited space available. The furniture should be simple in design and dual-purpose in construction. For example, use of chests and cabinets as tables means greater storage space. A large table can be used for both meals and paperwork.

Resist the temptation to overdecorate. Windows require some sort of treatment for purposes of decoration and privacy, but avoid piling one type of material on top of another. Venetian blinds, curtains, valance, and draperies festooning a single window are superfluous in terms of money and upkeep. Again, slipcovers serve a definite purpose in that they protect the upholstery and provide variety in the decorative scheme. Do not add another layer. Protective plastic covers may have their special uses, but often they are merely one more possession to take care of.

Fabrics should be chosen carefully. Slipcovers and upholstery fabrics should be tight-woven, with a smooth finish to resist the sooty dirt common to cities. Select patterned or striped materials for chairs or sofas, leaving the solid colors for pillows, cushions, and curtains. Curtains should be of a drip-dry material.

Area rugs represent a smaller investment than extensive carpeting. They also are easier to care for, less expensive to clean, and easier to remove. It is preferable to buy tweeds or patterns; solids tend to show every piece of lint and dirt.

When buying furniture, keep in mind that an apartment may be only a temporary home and that modern apartments are constructed on a much smaller scale than the average house. Therefore, do not crowd small rooms with oversized pieces. For example, an apartment normally does not lend itself to a full-size dining-room set. An attractive porch or dinette set scaled to the space available would be much more appropriate and later can be used in its rightful place.

Money and personal taste are two other important considerations. Purchase of "make-do's" is false economy. The piece bought as a temporary stopgap usually turns into an irritating lifetime possession.

—Virginia L. Robertson

BIBLIOGRAPHY

FINKE, MARY B. and HELEN KNOX. *Moneywise: The Intelligent Woman's Guide to Everyday Finance.* G. P. Putnam's Sons, 1950.

GILBRETH, LILLIAN M.; THOMAS, ORPHA MAE; and CLYMER, ELEANOR. *Management in the Home* (rev. ed.). Dodd, Mead & Co., 1959.

HOLT, SOL and MCCRACKEN, H. L. *Economics and You.* Charles Scribner's Sons, 1956.

JORDAN, DAVID F. and WILLETT, EDWARD F. *Managing Personal Finances.* Prentice-Hall, Inc., 1951.

MCDERMOTT, IRENE E. and WILLIAMS, FLORENCE. *Food for Better Living.* J. B. Lippincott Co., 1960.

STAR, MARY CATHERINE. *Management for Better Living.* D. C. Heath & Co., 1956.

HOME CANNING

The canning of food so that it can be stored for later use is based on two principles. The first is to provide enough heat to destroy the tiny organisms (molds, yeast, and bacteria) that cause food spoilage. The second is to prevent the re-entrance of these organisms by putting the food in a sterile container which is then perfectly sealed. The canning procedure is designed to accomplish these things and therefore should be followed very carefully.

Equipment. Glass jars vary in size and can be bought in half-pint, pint, quart, half-gallon, and the largest size, number ten, which is almost a gallon. These jars also come with various-sized mouths: small, regular, and wide. To seal the jars the caps have either rubber rings or automatic vacuum seals. In one kind of jar a wire bail is used to hold a glass top in place. This is called a *lightning jar.* On this type, the clamping bail is tightened to secure the glass top on the jar.

All jars must be of uniform thickness and free from nicks. Jars used from year to year should be checked for nicks and if some nicks are discovered, these jars should not be used for canning. Imperfect jars will not only be dangerous to handle, but if there are nicks on the lip of the jar, a proper seal cannot be made and the food will spoil.

Different types of caps can be used with the jars. Glass tops are used in the *lightning* jars and incorporate a rubber ring to seal the jar's contents. It is a good idea to replace the rubber rings rather than attempt to re-use them and take the chance of not sealing the jars perfectly.

Zinc screw caps have a porcelain lining which must not be cracked and the metal must be smooth and even. Rubber rings are used with zinc lids also. The seal on this jar-and-zinc-lid combination, is made at the point of contact with the rim of the lid and the glass lip just below the threads on the neck of the jar. The two-piece metal cap, a combination of a metal lid and a metal screw band, is the most commonly used closure for canning jars. The metal lid has a self-sealing compound on its edge and cannot be re-used.

Using any one of the above jar-and-lid combinations, fruit and vegetables may be processed in either a hot water bath or a pressure-cooker *canner.* Specific directions for the use of the pressure cooker will be supplied by the manufacturer. Before purchasing the canner, it is necessary to decide on the size of the jars to be used. The pressure cooker also varies in size. The pressure cooker finds special use in the canning of meats and non-acid vegetables which cannot be successfully processed by the hot-water-bath method.

If hot-water bath is to be used in canning, any large pot may be used that is deep enough to allow at least one inch of water to cover the top of the jars. A rack must be placed in the bottom of the pot to prevent the jars from bumping when the water boils. A hot water canner can be purchased complete with rack at moderate cost.

Methods. The two safest and widely used methods are *cold pack* and *hot pack* canning. In *cold pack* canning, the fruit or vegetables are cleaned and prepared as for cooking, then placed cold in the jars. The jars are then partially sealed and processed in a hot water bath or pressure-cooker. After the jars are removed from the canner, the seals are then tightened. In the *hot pack* method foods are packed boiling hot. The jars are then processed in either hot water or steam. The advantage of the *hot pack* method is that the jars can be completely sealed immediately and processed by the hot water bath method.

Procedure. The first step in either method is to wash the jars in hot, soapy water and rinse them in hot water. Leave jars in hot rinse water until ready for use. Cleanliness is essential.

Select only fresh and fully ripened fruits and vegetables for canning. Clean and prepare the produce as you would for cooking. Skins may be removed from tomatoes or peaches by placing them in hot water for about one minute and then putting them in a bowl of cold water. The skins are easily removed if this is done. If the *cold pack* method is used, the jars may be filled at this point.

In the *hot pack* method, precook the fruits or vegetables and use the water in which they were cooked to fill the jars. Berries and fruits may be packed in syrup that can be sweetened according to taste. A light syrup is made by adding one-third cup sugar to each cup of water and a thicker syrup can be made by using one cup of sugar to one cup of water. Fruits may also be packed in plain hot water if so desired. For vegetables, add one-half teaspoon of salt for every pint that is canned. The salt may be added as a last step in filling the jars.

Fill jars to within one-half inch of top using water in the *cold pack* method or the juices or syrup for the vegetables and the fruits in the *hot pack* method. Before sealing, release the air bubbles formed in the jars by running a knife or spatula down the side of the jar.

When the jars are filled, wipe the mouth of the jars clean and place the caps and rubber rings or the self-sealing lids in place. Zinc cap tops or screw-band tops are sealed tight at this time. Cold packs are not to be completely sealed at this time but are loosened one-quarter inch. *Lightning* jar bails are put in place but are not fastened until the canning is complete. The jars of food are now ready for the final processing.

Hot Water Bath Canning. The hot water bath may be used to process all fruits and acid vegetables. The canner must be filled with enough water to cover the jars with at least one inch of water. Remember to allow for the volume of the jars to be placed in the canner, since, if too much water is put in, it will spill over when the jars are placed in the canner. A good way to avoid this is to fill the canner about half full and keep a pot of boiling water on hand so that the canner can be filled to the desired water level after the jars are placed in the canner. The water must be kept at a "rolling boil" at all times. Make sure that the rack is in place and the jars do not touch each other. The water will stop boiling when the jars are placed in the canner, and the process should not be timed until the water starts boiling again. Tongs are very useful in removing the jars from the bath at the end of the required time period.

Pressure Cooker Canning. The pressure cooker should be used whenever meats and non-acid vegetables are canned. The non-acid vegetables include: asparagus, string beans, beets, corn, Lima beans, carrots, peas, and all greens. In the pressure cooker, these foods are processed by steam under pressure. The amount of pressure as well as the period of time is shown in the table below.

Final Steps. After processing, the jars are removed from the canner and the seals are completed on those jars that were only partially sealed. The bails on the *Lightning* jars are fastened also. To cool jars, place on towel or wooden racks away from all drafts. Inspect the jars from time to time to note leakage or bubbles that would indicate an improper seal. If an improper seal is noted, the contents of that jar must be recanned or used immediately. When jars are cool, they should be rinsed clean, labeled, and stored in a cool, dry place.

LOW-ACID VEGETABLES			FRUITS AND ACID VEGETABLES	
STEAM PRESSURE—240°F. (10 pounds steam pressure)	Half Pints and Pints	Quarts	BOILING-WATER BATH	Pints and Quarts
Asparagus	25 Min.	30 Min.	Apples (hot pack)	20 Min.
Beans, Butter and Lima	40 Min.	50 Min.	Apricots (hot pack)	20 Min.
Beans, Green, Snap and Wax	20 Min.	25 Min.	Berries	15 to 20 Min.
Beets	30 Min.	35 Min.	Cherries (cold pack)	20 Min.
Carrots	25 Min.	30 Min.	Figs	90 Min.
Corn, whole kernel	55 Min.	85 Min.	Grapes (cold pack)	20 Min.
Greens, all kinds	70 Min.	90 Min.	Peaches (cold pack)	25 to 30 Min.
Okra	30 Min.	40 Min.	Pears (hot pack)	20 to 25 Min.
Peas, Blackeye and Field	35 Min.	40 Min.	Plums and Fresh Prunes	20 Min.
Peas, Green "English"	40 Min.	40 Min.	Rhubarb	10 Min.
Potatoes, Sweet (wet pack)	55 Min.	90 Min.	Tomatoes	Quarts—45 Min.
Potatoes, New White "Irish"	30 Min.	40 Min.		Pints—35 Min.
Pumpkin and Winter Squash	60 Min.	80 Min.	NOTE: If using steam pressure, vent canner 10 minutes. Process fruits 10 minutes, tomatoes 15 minutes, at 5 pounds pressure.	
Squash, Summer	30 Min.	40 Min.		

Courtesy Ball Brothers Company

FURNITURE

A chair is a rest for the body when it is seated. A bed is a rest for the body in repose. A table is space for work. A cabinet is space to put things in when they are not in use. Some practical persons argue that improving ideas of usefulness and comfort gradually changed and multiplied the shapes of these first pieces of furniture, and so determined the history of all furniture design. Thus the matter might be dismissed if furniture had not been closely associated with the fine arts of all periods, if the habit of beautifying useful objects had not been common throughout human nature at all times. Domestic objects, especially, have been wrought age after age with loving care and skill. They are records of the manners and customs, and the taste, of the generations who used them. They belong to the art of the world. We might have attractive homes without taking the trouble to learn much of the history of furniture design. But that study is a part of a cultured person's background and is the basis for a developed taste in home decoration. It is best approached as a development of architectural and decorative influences.

Development of Furniture

Egypt.—Egypt mothered many of the arts, and to Egypt we are indebted for the first light thrown on furniture making. The dry air of Egypt has preserved material that gives us a fairly adequate idea of early Egyptian furniture. Excavations have brought to view examples of household equipment constructed of stone, metal and wood. Because the Egyptians believed that the souls of the dead would be aided in a future state by the presence of familiar objects of this life, burial places were filled with domestic furniture and utensils indicative of the rank, position and wealth of the deceased. In the tombs of kings have been found chairs, couches and tables made of ebony, cedar and sycamore and sometimes ornamented with horn, ivory, silver and gold.

The art of the Egyptians is symbolic, formal and full of restraint and vigor, at its best. Although largely derived from natural forms, it is highly conventionalized, stylized and refined. Motives common to much of the art, architecture and furniture are the lotus, the palm and the papyrus. Other important symbols are the scarab, the asp and the ram. Mythical figures with wings are seen in all the decorative arts, as are borders of frets, circles, triangles, scrolls, leaves, buds and flowers.

Our knowledge of this remote age which began at least 30 centuries before Christ, has been greatly increased by the careful representations of domestic life and of the processes used in all sorts of industrial occupations, painted on walls, carved in friezes and illustrated in ink drawings on papyrus scrolls. Most of our large museums contain originals or reproductions of these pictorial histories from tomb or palace walls, and with

them sometimes actual furniture and useful objects. There is a chair in the Cairo Museum that was taken from the tomb of a prince of the 18th Dynasty (1580–1350 B.C.). It is made of redwood, with a seat of woven cord, and has decorations in colored plaster. Like bedsteads and chests of the same great age seen in some American museums, it is remarkably akin to the design of our time. Through such survivals we know more about the life and the handicraft arts of ancient Egypt than of the life and art of peoples to whom we are more closely related in time and space, for example, western Europe in the Dark Ages.

Mesopotamia.—In Mesopotamia, the legendary cradle of the race, archeological explorations have revealed a buried city with art objects and

METROPOLITAN MUSEUM OF ART

EGYPTIAN CHAIR from Thebes, 1494 B.C. The back includes the household god, Bes, between symbols of stability and protection.

jewelry, household utensils and decorations in perfect condition. This city was built by the Sumerians 500 years before previously known history. Musical instruments and game tables, bowls and wall friezes have been uncovered as fine as the rare Egyptian work and not unlike it. In these two places, Sumeria and Egypt, the connected story of civilization began.

The land known as Sumeria became Babylonia, and Assyria too is in the Mesopotamian region. We have Bible stories of these countries, their kings and palaces, feasts and furniture. We know of the barbaric splendor of Assyria's red and gold ornaments, of the warlike and vainglorious pursuits of old Assyrian kings and of Babylon's parks and palaces. The palace of Nebuchadnezzar was surrounded by the famous hanging gardens that were one of the Seven Wonders. Many of our museums have sculptured friezes from the walls of those Mesopotamian palaces and domestic objects of stone and marble. Babylonian and Assyrian design is cruder than that of the Egyptians and it is not as well pre-

served by the climate. Animal forms are used with symbolic meaning; the bull, the lion and the griffin predominate and often have human faces. The kings are sometimes shown as god-men, warlike in Assyria and engaged in hunting pursuits in Babylonia. Animallike or godlike winged men are seen on objects of use, even on the domestic utensils that survive.

Among the Greeks.—The Greeks were the first to make beauty a way of life. The Egyptians had made their finest furniture and ornaments for tomb chambers and for use in some afterlife, but the Greeks thought only of making objects that should be both useful and beautiful in everyday life. The Greeks utilized to a certain extent motives used by the Assyrians and the Egyptians and purified their forms in a new development that gave the modern world its conception of proportion, order and beauty. The anthemion or honeysuckle, the laurel and acanthus occur frequently in decoration, together with borders known as the *egg-and-dart fret, guilloche, Greek-key scroll* and *dentil.* Our knowledge of this period and its domestic and industrial history is relatively complete. Through the study of Greek vases and their well-painted scenes, we gain much light on manners, customs and costumes. Down the centuries we have made intermittent use in interior architecture of the classic Greek motives. In the Greek theater of Athens, itself the model of some of our finest outdoor auditoriums, there are stone chairs still in place in the section reserved for personages of high rank. With the wooden chairs of ancient Egypt, these might have furnished the pattern for the first objects of their kind which were made by fine craftsmen for general domestic use in the modern eras.

Roman Ideals.—Carving, inlaying, veneering, sculpture, mosaic work and gold, made Roman art ornate and overdecorated. Greek forms and Greek ornament lost their characteristics of order and simplicity. Wreaths, festoons, garlands and emblems of wars and the chase were often so elaborate that the architectural character of interiors and furniture was lost beneath them. Where Roman and Greek ideas were fused, as in the city of Pompeii, unearthed in the 19th century, interiors and ornaments were finest. When Napoleon I remembered "the glory that was Rome," he ordered furniture designed after the forms used by the Caesars. The style that he thus established is not called Roman but *Empire.* The *curule* chair and the beds and divans still made under the influence of the Napoleonic period are our most notable inheritance from the Roman Empire.

East Meets West in the Arts.—Rome fell in 476 A.D., and from that date until the great age of cathedral building set in the story of art in the Western world is a story of the influence of Oriental ideals and especially of the

Byzantine art of the Eastern Empire.

This Byzantine art was the art of Europe during the great period when it was being Christianized and was submitting to the ideas of form and color that flowed in from eastward.

Romanesque art represents the turn of the current. Western ideas became vital and mingled more and more strongly with those of the East as churches, monasteries and communities grew up in Italy, France and England. It came first to Italy when builders revived engineering and architectural learning from the classic past and combined it with Byzantine styles. It developed later in countries to the north, where barbarian strains had come in and brought fresh kinds of design; and it was out of this later Romanesque design in France, England and Germany that the character of Gothic form first appeared.

Gothic Handicraft.—France and England are the important centers of Gothic art. The Romanesque style in decorative motives as well as in architecture made use of the tall, round arch form. Romanesque style gave place to Gothic style when builders learned the secret of pointing the arch and vault in support of buildings that rose high in the air. The religious enthusiasm of people, inspired by the Crusades and the attempts to win the Holy Sepulcher inspired new endeavors and new forms. Everything "reached towards heaven."

The leading decorative characteristics of the early Gothic style as applied to furniture designing were the pointed arch, the trefoil (three divisions), the quatrefoil (four divisions) and simple tracery. Furniture was massive, and Gothic motives were confined to ornament. Construction was at first little affected. The prominent features of the later Gothic style as expressed in furniture were the divided Gothic arch, the quatrefoil, the cinquefoil (five divisions) and an intricate scheme of tracery. The larger number of pieces in actual use at this period were chests of many varieties, cupboards, presses, stools, benches, chairs, bedsteads and bedstocks, the latter being built into the wall.

The Hall. During the 12th and 13th centuries, both in England and France, the hall was the main room in the house—in many cases the one room of the dwelling. In the homes of the nobility it was a lofty apartment that served the purpose of both kitchen and dining room and afforded the only living room. Meals were served on trestle tables. The lord and lady of the manor sat on a dais that elevated them a few inches above their guests.

Below the dais the long and narrow table was set with viands less costly than those served to the master and the mistress. Here were gathered the barons and the retainers. The placing of the salt divided the guests from the serving people, and the expression *below the salt* is one which has endured until today. On the dais were chairs with high backs and canopies. The canopies were convenient in case of rain, for the raftered roof was not always proof against the weather. Benches without backs for the guests

and stools for the servants constituted the rest of the dining-room furniture. Between meals the tables were placed against the wall, and the chairs drawn to the fire. It is interesting to note in passing that as circumstances of a very different kind cause architects to devote almost the entire main floor of many modern houses to one big living room, trestle tables are again used. They are separated into sections and disposed around the walls between meals, as are the benches sometimes used with them.

The Drawing Room. The 14th century added another room in the home of the affluent—a *withdrawing* room—the beginning of our modern drawing room. Here the mistress of the house with her ladies in waiting could retire when the music from the minstrels' gallery became too loud, or the jester's jokes too broad, or the drinking and fun too boisterous.

The 15th century was an important milestone in the march of progress. By this time the Gothic hall had lost its early character. It was large and often a meeting place for the owner and his friends. There are interiors in houses of Colonial America built after

METROPOLITAN MUSEUM OF ART

FRENCH GOTHIC CHAIR of the end of the fifteenth or beginning of the sixteenth century. The intricately carved back and low, legless seats are characteristic of Gothic furniture. The massiveness of the piece prevented its theft. Note the quatrefoil arch.

the idea of the medieval great hall. A tavern on the Hudson River, used by Washington as his headquarters during one part of the Revolution and now a museum, still has the great open hearth in the middle of the room, without a chimney to carry the smoke through the roof. As rooms multiplied, the hall ceased in turn to be parlor, kitchen and dining room. It was gradually approaching the great entrance hall of the 17th and 18th centuries. It retained its fine proportions and its lofty dimensions, but the raftered roof had given place to a beamed or vaulted ceiling. The big fireplace had grown more architectural, though still retaining its generous hearth. The rough walls were replaced by oak panels and fine tapestries imported from Flanders, the home of the great medieval weaving centers.

During this period, furniture was of two general types—movable articles that could be transported with ease and massive pieces that could be left behind with safety. It would be a bold thief who would try to escape with a heavily carved chair weighing several hundred pounds and made more unwieldy by a wooden canopy. In the same way the bedstead of the day was also quite immovable, for it, too, was well incased in wood and finished with a canopy. Both canopies had the same origin—namely, to protect the occupant from rain in case the roof should not be sufficient shelter. Though canopies survive in some bedrooms today, their practical necessity ceased when better building methods came into existence. When houses became watertight and airtight, furniture gradually assumed different aspects.

In the late 15th century, except in ecclesiastical chairs, the canopy was discarded. The evolution of the everyday chair form was completed. Flemish designers in the 16th century had an active hand in its further adaptation. They remodeled or revised the chair on new lines and sent it to England where, in the 17th century, it underwent other changes. It was the old Gothic craftsmen who took the crude pieces of the Dark Ages—the bench, the chest and the bedstock—and transformed them into things of beauty. In comparison with earlier efforts, they made these pieces of furniture articles of real comfort and convenience: Their constructive work was built for centuries rather than for years, yet the grace and charm of their carving, now almost as perfect as when it left their hands, still stand as models for the world.

The Renaissance in Furniture

Renaissance means a rebirth. The European Renaissance that came after the Middle Ages was marked by the energy and the creation that had resulted from the mingling of many races and strains and from a turning back to the Golden Age of classic antiquity for inspiration and for style.

Italian Renaissance.—The important city-states of Italy experienced the dawn of the Renaissance while Gothic inspiration was at its height in northern countries. Italy had no important Gothic Age but advanced direct into the newer expression from the Byzantine and the Romanesque styles that had developed more or less separately in the different principalities.

The Italian Renaissance falls into three distinct subdivisions, the *trecento* (1300–99); the *quatrocento* (1400–99) and the *cinquecento* (1500–99). The first century was one of beginnings. It produced the painter Giotto and was important for its fresh conceptions of painting and sculpture. The *quatrocento* witnessed an increasing return to Greek and Roman sources for design and decoration, and a climax of efforts which brought together in cathedral, palace or public hall the finest expressions of artist and artisan, who sought to achieve a new synthesis out of the combination of old and new motives, classic and modern details. This is a convenient period in which to observe a process active throughout history, the process by which architectural or other useful forms develop their decorations. The structural features and the ornaments associated together in any fixed style have not come into being at the same time. The Greeks had been developing their pure classical forms for ages before the decorative details we associate with them were fully developed. Specialists of this period or those who would be able to recognize the date of a piece of Renaissance furniture at a glance must pay particular attention to the persistence of medieval and Byzantine decorations almost down to 1500.

From 1400 to 1500 the increased use of classical detail may be observed. This was the age of Brunelleschi, Leonardo da Vinci, Michelangelo and the great Medici patrons of art. Great art and great literature familiarize us with the influences which, in the *cinquecento,* brought the period to its culmination. The *cinquecento* in Italy felt the full influence of the Roman revival.

The Renaissance raised furniture making to an equality with the other industrial arts. Pupils were apprenticed to a master and studied with him until they had perfected their craft, after which they opened workshops of their own. The pieces produced in these great studios united beauty with utility. For the first time in Europe designs were made with reference to their setting. The furniture of the private dwelling no longer suggested cathedrals or abbeys. It was made with a careful regard for the needs of the owner, his station and manner of living. Thus houses possessed a harmony that had hitherto been absent.

French Renaissance.—The French Renaissance really began in the 16th century under Francis I and extended to 1643 through the reign of Louis XIII. The Renaissance had begun to extend northward, and now a lively competition arose among these three monarchs. They summoned to their courts the great architects, painters, sculptors, woodcarvers and metalcraftsmen of Italy and Flanders. Francis inaugurated the French Ren-

aissance with its many important buildings and established a precedent of art patronage that in the succeeding centuries was equalled only once, when Louis XIV undertook the elaboration of the palace group at Versailles in the latter part of the 17th century. The reign of Francis at a more interesting period of the world's history and its art, from 1515 to 1547, represented extraordinary achievement. The combined reigns of the five succeeding monarchs completed the century and brought to a close the most important years of the French Renaissance. Of these sovereigns, Henry II and Henry IV alone were worthy successors to the great Francis I. They exerted a helpful influence on the fine and industrial arts and left much to testify to their taste and generosity. Each has been immortalized by a style named for him, the *Henry II* being the more celebrated.

Renaissance Details at first were combined with Gothic construction. It was not until the 16th century was well under way that the real force of the Renaissance was felt. France had been the birthplace of Gothic art and the transitional period was of longer duration than in Italy.

In the reign of Francis I, chairs became more varied in treatment. The cane design of Flanders was early adopted; the plain high Dutch chair became a favorite but was somewhat reconstructed. The French seem at all times to have been very much concerned about comfort, far more so than the English who were more or less indifferent to many of the refinements of life until the 17th century. And then it was by way of France that many minor comforts reached England.

As the 16th century advanced, French cabinets developed on high and narrow lines. Those of the Francis I period show carved panels, moldings and pilasters, but seldom anything ponderous—although at this time presses and armoires were built on heavy models. Distinctions between these pieces of furniture were always made in France, where subtle dividing lines were recognized. French furniture makers also made a distinction between designs for the *salon de famille* or family rooms and the *salon de compagnie* or rooms for more formal use, and this is the reason why so much French furniture that is brought to America is unfitted for modern living rooms.

Henry II in many ways did as much for France, artistically speaking, as Francis I. He did not build in the lavish way of his father, but two very clever women ruled his court, and each in different ways had a tremendous influence on the arts of the day. One was Catherine de' Medici, whose tastes were naturally Italian; the other, Diane de Poitiers, was easily the most remarkable woman of her time. Diane's emblem, the crescent, is found combined with Henry's monogram in one of the beautiful rooms in Fontainebleau. The chimney piece shows the early stages of the beautiful Renaissance pattern known as *strapwork,* a carved pattern of interlaced lines, so popular with workers in

stone, wood and silver in both France and England. It is seen in woodwork, in furniture, in bookbindings and in the Oiron pottery that is known as *Henry II ware.*

By the time of Henry IV (Henry of Navarre) a good deal of the beauty of early Renaissance ornament had disappeared. The simple arabesques, seen to such charming advantage in the Francis I style, and the equally simple strapwork of the Henry II style lost favor with decorators and woodcarvers. In this period the shell ornament that was destined to play such an important part in the decorative arts of France for nearly two centuries came into great prominence.

During the reign of Louis XIII came many changes in domestic comfort. The upholstered chair in the modern meaning of the term came into existence. It was an armchair, and the seat was lower and broader than in previous periods; and the upholstery, instead of being any rich and sumptuous material that the designer of the chair could command or the owner happened to possess, was an especially selected covering so designed as to correspond with other chairs or harmonize with the wall treatment. Window draperies also were selected with great care and were more than a mere protection against air and sunlight. The age of *upholstery* had arrived.

Wall treatment received especial attention and was carried to a very elaborate point in France during Louis XIII's reign. Simon Vouet, who bore the same relationship to Louis XIII that his famous pupil, Le Brun was to bear to Louis XIV, was responsible for most of the florid decoration of the day. Furniture makers were always a little behind the decorators, and though many of the wall schemes of the day are too ornate from the modern viewpoint, at least the beautiful chairs, tables and cabinets are well worth studying. Flemish influence was strong in the early part of the 17th century, probably because Rubens had visited the French court.

Characteristics of the French Renaissance.—The Renaissance had matured in France much later, and through a longer transitional period, than in Italy. Gothic art had come first to France and had been firmly rooted there. The ornament of the French Renaissance was in a lighter vein than that of the Italian and was much more original in design. It followed the same path of development, culmination and decline. Delicate arabesques and pierced shields were used by furniture makers and decorators. Later in the 16th century woodcarvers combined an interlaced ribbon or strap ornament with the lozenge and the cartouche, and this was followed by the introduction of the shell and the ornate scroll. From that date woodcarving lost much of its charm.

Flemish and Dutch Renaissance.—The Renaissance reached Flanders and Holland tardily. Gothic traditions lingered in the north, and the long transitional period lasted well into the 16th century. Holland was more independent politically than Flanders, and her work was less influenced by outside conditions. This fact makes Dutch work comparatively easy of identification, while that of the Flemish, being more mixed, sometimes raises a question. Spanish and French influences are more often present in the early Flemish work. Charles, King of Spain and Emperor of Germany, was also Count of Flanders and Duke of Burgundy. The intercourse between these countries and provinces grew decidedly intimate at this period. The Italian Renaissance had waned when the Flemish Renaissance was at its height.

When Italian influence reached Flanders it came by way of France, with a strong mixture of French feeling added. When this complex influence was carried into England it had gained another element in addition to the Franco-Italian, and this is one reason why the English Renaissance swings so far from the classic. In the 16th century, particularly, English work showed far more Flemish influence than either French or Italian. In the 17th century it was more Dutch than Flemish in feeling and remained so until the pendulum swung once more toward French designs, this movement giving way to the Classic Revival of the late 18th century. This was the period in which English household furnishings reached a high standard of excellence in the matters of simplicity, elegance and grace. It was the period that was reflected in the finest designs for furniture and decoration in America—the late Colonial or mahogany period.

Flemish Furniture. Primarily the Flemings were carvers. They were less bound by classic traditions than the Italians and maintained a simpler mode of living. Heads of men and women decorate many of their pieces, particularly in such articles as cabinets, cupboards and sideboards, and where there are large expanses of wood to be covered. But paneling, ribbon bandeaux, garlands of fruit and flowers, strapwork and kindred things are more harmonious in a modern dining room or living room than masks, animal heads or the human figure, clever as they may be in execution. The *linen-fold* pattern, sometimes called the *parchment scroll*, is found in much of the Flemish furniture of the 16th century and is one of the simplest and best patterns of that day.

Many Flemish details exist in our everyday furniture, but we have long since accepted them as entirely our own. They do not suggest to the casual observer anything bordering on period styles and have come down through long years of transforming and adapting. Flemish furniture makers rebuilt the beautiful Gothic chair, lowering the seat as well as the back, and substituting horizontal braces for the heavily carved arched braces of the 15th century. Flemish chairs were of several varieties, but two types were prominent—the upholstered chair with turned legs and braces and the carved chair with a cane back and a cane seat.

Dutch Furniture. Marquetry and inlay were favorite Dutch methods of ornamenting furniture during the 17th century. *Inlay* and *marquetry* are often confused, but they are quite different in workmanship and appearance. Inlay is of ancient origin and is made by filling in a depression cut from the surface of the wood. The Italian word is *intarsia* from a word that means to insert. Marquetry is of Renaissance origin and is, in reality, an overlay, a thin veneer of different woods fitted together to form a pattern. When the veneer is applied to the surface of the cabinet or other piece of furniture it seems a part of the construction. In the hands of an expert, marquetry offers great opportunity for varied and colorful effects. Dutch craftsmen have achieved marked success in this field.

But the especial importance of the Flemish and the Dutch Renaissance is the effect it had in the furniture making of England; for by this time (late 17th century) American furniture was beginning its history.

German and Spanish Renaissance.—Two phases of the Renaissance, German and Spanish, belong to the twilight of the great Classic Revival on the Continent. In Germany there was a long transitional period during which the lingering traditions of Gothic art died slowly. The early phases of the Renaissance show the grafting of the new upon the old. This mixture of Gothic and Renaissance was less successful in Germany than in France.

The best examples of German woodcarving of the early 16th century were of ecclesiastical origin and were more sculptural than architectural. Choir stalls and altar pieces were richly decorated in the manner of the day. In domestic furniture the combination of Gothic construction and Renaissance ornament was less harmonious.

The great presses and cabinets are the most characteristic pieces. Made of oak and walnut with carved panels and heavy doors, they are as substantial today as when they came from the hands of their maker. The plain surfaces are well distributed and the ornament, although it is elaborate, is neither heavy nor fantastic. The lock is usually concealed in the carving, and the key repeats the lines of the ornament. The ball feet are worthy of note, as they indicate a new feature of furniture making.

From her oriental colonies, Spain imported ebony and ivory and other costly adjuncts to furniture making. The elaborate metal work that today is the most interesting part of a great deal of this furniture is Spain's most important addition to furniture design.

Damascening, niello work (inlaying of black alloys) and kindred crafts had long belonged to Spain, following closely on the Moorish invasion. In Granada, the medieval city of the Moors, were fashioned many of the most elaborate chests and coffers, and long after the Moorish expulsion from Spain Granada still remained the center of fine cabinetwork. The Gate of Justice and the Gate of Judgment in the Alhambra were ornamented with many of the same motives used in minor metalcraft work and woodcarving. This is mainly an art of arabesque, developed by a people whose religion forbade them to use animal and human forms.

The Spanish cabinet, elevated on tall turned or carved columns, was a characteristic piece. One type is quite plain, apparently, but the whole front lowers at the turn of a key and reveals an exquisite inlay of ivory and metals with ornamental bosses. There are many variations of this beautiful style. Iron is used most attractively at times, and the inlay includes bone, horn, shell and occasionally painted decorations.

The influence of the Flemish cane chair on the furniture makers of

HISPANIC SOCIETY OF AMERICA

SPANISH VARGUEÑO, seventeenth century. Made of walnut, the vargueño is a cabinet-like combination of chest and desk. Similar to a desk, its front opens out on two supports, revealing a writing surface and inner chest with many carved and inlaid drawers.

Europe has been mentioned. The leather chair of Spain equaled it in importance. Both had high backs and carved legs and braces, but there the resemblance ended. The Spanish design consisted of a sturdy frame of oak, chestnut or walnut, a back completely encased in leather, turned stretchers, a carved underbrace and hoof feet. English furniture makers of the 17th century gained inspiration from both Flemish and Spanish models in their famous Jacobean designs of wood and cane.

The English Renaissance.—By the middle of the 17th century, French and Italian furniture, like the wall treatments of that day, became heavy and ornate. The vitality of the Renaissance in these countries had ended. It was the age of beautiful surfaces, but there was a growing insensitiveness to the values of art. Historically this effect has marked the decline of great styles, which may be seen to observe a cycle of developing forms, developing decoration, maturity and a period of decline in which surface effects are labored as the forms deteriorate.

When the classic wave reached England, it had gained and lost much on the way. There were French and Flemish influences—and English traditions too firmly planted to be uprooted.

Historic Periods. The characteristics of the 16th and 17th centuries in English designing may be summarized briefly:

First, the *English Renaissance* or *Tudor* style, which was a mingling of Flemish and Italian grafted upon Gothic.

Second, *Elizabethan,* showing greater unity. Strapwork and paneling were features of this period.

Third, *Jacobean,* covering nearly a century and including many types. Furniture was paneled and carved until the introduction of walnut, when veneer and marquetry became popular. Among Jacobean characteristics were the spiral leg, the rising panel and spindle ornaments. With the accession of William of Orange in 1688, Dutch influence prevailed, and English furniture was slowly developed on more graceful lines.

The English Renaissance, extending through the 16th and 17th centuries, a long period to sum up in a sentence, was nevertheless one that remained remarkably homogeneous through the era of international cross influences in Europe called *baroque.*

Queen Elizabeth was, of course, a Tudor, but gave her name to a style all her own. The term *Tudor* is usually applied to the reigns of Henry VII, Henry VIII and Mary. Elizabeth's long term ended in 1603 while Henry of Navarre was on the French throne. Her reign with that of the succeeding Tudors covered more than a century during one of the most interesting periods of style transition, an influence we still feel.

Strapwork is seen in many English cupboards of the late 16th century and also in chimney breasts and wall treatments. It is one of the most valuable contributions to design of the Elizabethan period and ranks with the linen-fold motive of an earlier day and with the rising panel of a later one.

Styles in English furniture were of slow growth, with much overlapping and intermingling. Of the kind noted during the Italian Renaissance, and it was not until Charles I ascended the throne that the popularity of certain Elizabethan patterns waned. Even then the outlines of furniture changed little. The court and livery cupboards were modified to suit a simpler scheme of carving; but oak was still the chief wood, and so long as it remained in use, massive furniture continued to be made. The Protectorate caused a break in the crafts, and by the time it was over and Charles II safely placed on the throne (1660), many new influences shaped and developed English handiwork.

Jacobean furniture is roughly divided into two parts—*Early* and *Late.* Early Jacobean preceded the Commonwealth, covering the reigns of James I and Charles I. Late Jacobean followed the Commonwealth, including the reigns of Charles II and James II. The Commonwealth or Protectorate period was too turbulent to be very productive of the arts and certainly produced nothing approaching a style, though the *Cromwell chairs,* simple in line, unornamented except by refined moldings, partly typify the spirit of the Protectorate.

After the Restoration, all English furniture became more graceful. Charles II had been brought up at the court of Louis XIV and quite naturally returned to England with French ideas of comfort and refinement.

The furniture of the Charles II period is worthy of its present revival. Designers of that period retained the best of the many motives bequeathed from the earlier part of the century and combined them with newer schemes. Paneling remained in favor but was diversified by nailhead and spindle ornaments.

The introduction of walnut brought about a decided change in English furniture. It made possible a lighter, more graceful construction and an entirely different scheme of decoration. Carving was largely superseded by marquetry, which was well adapted to walnut and to the Dutch designs which William introduced.

The William and Mary period is a brief but important link between 17th-century oak and 18th-century mahogany. During this period the revocation of the Edict of Nantes caused many Huguenots to take refuge in England. Some of them were of the craftsman class and readily found employment. This added another and very refined element in furniture designing.

Walnut was used during Queen Anne's time and continued in favor until mahogany was well established between 1720 and 1730. The cabriole or curved leg came into popular use in her day.

The Eighteenth Century

French.—When Madame de Maintenon wrote to a friend, "The king will have us buried in symmetry," she expressed characteristic features of the Louis XIV style. It was beautifully proportioned, formal, splendid, lacking in imagination and, from modern viewpoints, oppressively grand —like the monarch for whom it was named. The next Louis was to bury his court beneath ornament of gilt and paint before the balance swung back in the ill-starred reign of Louis XVI to a semblance of Greek simplicity and harmony.

Characteristics of Styles. French styles may be briefly characterized as follows:

Louis XIV was a formal rococo in which proportion and balance were the chief features. Important details were the shell, the classic acanthus, the ram's head, the mask and the satyr. In the early period, furniture was massive, and the designs of the Louis XIII style were perpetuated. Carving was largely displaced by marquetry and by chiseled mounts of metal. Boulle furniture belongs to this reign and is among the most valuable of the period. André Charles Boulle was a talented man; but his fame rests chiefly on a unique marquetry of tortoise shell and brass with which he ornamented furniture. Brilliant effects were obtained by lining the shell with color and by adding mounts of ormolu (a mixture of mercury and copper that gave brass the tone and texture of gold). Much French furniture of the time was thus embellished.

The period of French designing known as the Regency was the work of that brief time between the death of Louis XIV and the coming of age of Louis XV, when the duke of Orleans was Regent. It was characterized by extremes of ornament and is the least worthy of admiration of any of the French Periods.

In the Louis XV period balance and symmetry were less important in the eyes of the furniture makers than richness of ornament and flawless execution. Angles gave way to curves, and the talents of the goldsmith and the painter were employed in designing furniture that in workmanship and decorations have never been surpassed.

In the time of Louis XVI simplicity of construction and severity of ornament were dominant. Rococo details disappeared, and classic emblems replaced them. Important features were the fluted column, the bay leaf, the oak and the acorn, the bell flower or corn husk, the Greek band and the acanthus. Straight lines took the place of curves, and ornament was a means instead of an end.

The long reign of Louis XIV witnessed many changes and developments in furniture designing. The reign of the next Louis was briefer but long enough to make any one phase impossible; however, with Louis XVI the designing of the 18th century seems to have been crystallized. All the furniture of these three great epochs shows marvelous execution through extreme expressions of taste. Whether it be a Louis XIV cabinet, a Louis XV chair or a Louis XVI table, the workmanship is unsurpassed.

Metal played a very important part in many of the designs and added tremendously to their cost. All kinds of artists and craftsmen collaborated in furniture making. Furniture decorated with insets or porcelain, usually of Sèvres, formed one class of furniture; and fine upholstery of Beauvais and Aubusson were important accessories in the periods of both Louis XV and Louis XVI.

English.—In our devotion to English furniture of the late 18th century we are apt to overlook the rich legacy bequeathed to us by the early years of that century or to confuse it with other periods. It was a time of varied influences and designs, of many men working in many veins, of old ideas slowly giving way to new. It was full of picturesque vigor and of sturdy simplicity. Mingled traditions partly Dutch, partly Jacobean, persisted amid changing conditions.

The perpetuation of Dutch motives such as the cabriole leg and the web foot continued until the fourth decade of the century. The web foot or flat foot we find in most of the furniture of Queen Anne's time, and a charming adjunct it is to the designing of the day. Chippendale preferred the ball-and-claw foot that he used with distinction. He was one of the first English furniture makers to use the square leg and one of the first to adopt

FRENCH AND COMPANY, INC.

QUEEN ANNE side chair, on the left, is carved and inlaid walnut. These chairs were very comfortable, being upholstered and having shaped backs. The mahogany Chinese Chippendale, *second*, is an open armchair. The ball-and-claw foot was characteristic of Chippendale. Next is a Hepplewhite mahogany open chair of exceeding simplicity. Hepplewhite is noted for its stained wood and a characteristic back with an oval center. On the far right is a Sheraton armchair which is painted and decorated and has a cane seat.

the curving French leg of the Louis XV period; but he clung to the cabriole in its various forms until about 1740.

Chippendale was the first English furniture maker to have his name perpetuated by a style. Celebrated designers had preceded him, but their identity is submerged in that of their sovereigns. Chippendale raised his craft to such a point of excellence that his own name became associated with it.

What furniture of the 18th century would have been without mahogany is difficult to fancy. It is impossible to imagine Chippendale's designs in oak, just as it is impossible to conceive the heavy furniture of the 17th century executed in mahogany.

The chairs and settees from the Chippendale shop in Martin's Lane comprised many different styles. Among them were the early Dutch types with ball-and-claw feet and plain splats and these same Dutch types with pierced splats. (Splats are the single central upright parts in a chair back, a simplification of other forms, such as the ribbon backs, of this period.) These two distinct backs were also combined with straight legs, and later there were other variations. The curved leg of the Louis XV style was a favorite with Chippendale but was usually combined with an elaborate back.

There were several distinct *ribbon* styles, a rather uncommon one having an intricate leaf pattern carved with the ribbons. After 1740 the Gothic manner and the Chinese taste fascinated Chippendale, and about 1750 he became extremely rococo. It is important to realize that these incursions of new influence from far times and places are usually connected with important contemporary events. The English porcelain of the time, like the Chinese Chippendale furniture, tells a story of British trade in the East. It is only in the 20th century that the decorative arts of the Far East began to be assimilated and used to good effect in the industrial designing of the Western world.

Chippendale's great point of excellence as an industrial artist was his ability to take the designs he found at hand and so improve them that they took on new life and meaning. He adapted more than he originated; and in the end he lent his name and trademark to much more furniture than he made or even designed.

The Late 18th Century. Thomas Sheraton, George Hepplewhite and Robert Adam are the names that stand out brightest in the roster of the late 18th century. Robert Adam studied in Italy, and when he returned home he brought with him skilled artist craftsmen. Sir Christopher Wren, influenced by classic architects, had already set the stage; the time had come for an important period of English furniture design true to the Renaissance spirit.

We recognize the urn and the oval rosette as Adam; and we recognize certain motives like the acanthus, the ribbon band, the arabesque and the garland as both Adam and Louis XVI. There is a great deal of similarity between the two styles. We find in the English style a greater slenderness and a totally different treatment of the wood. The Adam brothers used carving very sparingly; many of their finest pieces have not a trace of it. They also brought to perfection painted furniture, employing Angelica Kauffman and other skilled pictorial artists for the finer work.

Many secrets of color learned during the Italian Renaissance went into Adam furniture, as so much of it was painted by Italian artists. A charming light green is often seen; there is also a burnished gold which almost equals vernis Martin, the celebrated French varnish.

Cane Furniture was designed by Adam and is today the type most frequently reproduced by American furniture makers. The chair back is usually oval, and the cane webbing follows the lines of the frame. Adam preferred the round leg. Hepplewhite chose the square leg. Most of the Sheraton furniture in America has the fluted leg. In the sideboards especially, it is a characteristic feature.

Inlaid Work. By the last decade of the century, the fancy was no longer for mahogany of any kind. Inlaid furniture of satinwood and painted furniture of satinwood represented the taste of the hour. Many writers have credited to Sheraton the introduction of satinwood. If this is true, he gave almost as much to the Adam brothers as they gave to him.

Sheraton. Sheraton's furniture creations may be divided into three classes—carved, inlaid and painted. His sideboards and chairs come usually under the first head; his cabinets and tables (the latter found in great variety in England) to the second; and to the third belongs a large portion of the work he did for the Adam brothers, which is extremely scarce in this country. Some of his inlay has as much color as if it had been executed with the brush.

Hepplewhite. Hepplewhite made masterly use of heart- and shield-shaped motives. Most of his chairs have shield backs, but it was in his dressing tables and kindred articles that this motive is seen in his most charming guise. Hepplewhite lacked the sound craftsmanship of Chippendale and Sheraton's fine sense of proportion. He understood little of the use of wood and nothing of carving and inlay, and there was little variety in his design. He used the one heart or shield shape over and over. But he had a fine intuition of form, and his popular success was so great that finally he employed many men to help him. His reputation was so well established that after his death in 1775 his widow successfully carried on his business for years.

Chippendale still held his field in chairmaking. Sheraton's sideboards, cabinets, tables and bedsteads are very commendable. Hepplewhite's sideboards and tables are also greatly to his credit. To Sheraton we accord a grasp of proportion and a feeling for restraint that were not equaled in his generation. He approaches the ideals of our own day—simplicity, proportion and reserve. Chippendale produced a far greater variety of designs, because variety of design appealed to him and because he lived at a time when fashions in furniture were extremely diversified. The last quarter of the 18th century was a remarkably unified period in English design, a fact for which Robert Adam is principally responsible.

The French Empire.—The Empire style marked the last of the great historic periods in furniture and decoration. It coincided with one of those recurrent returns to the decorative storehouse of classic art, and it was classical in a cold and restrained way, reflecting the personality of Napoleon, the man so closely identified with it. The Revolution had brought chaos to the industries of France that had flourished under the old regime. Cabinetmakers and metalworkers suffered imprisonment or death by the guillotine. Napoleon was insensitive to art values, but he sponsored a revival of craftsmanship and style and organized great public exhibitions with the idea of a courtly art, as in the time of the Louis. Court artist, architect and celebrated craftsworkers of the period worked together to produce a vast unified style with the letter "N" prominently marked on each piece. State suites in European hotels still contain such pieces from the days of Napoleon. Perhaps the whole effort would have been more important to us today but for the fact that already new industrial methods had weakened the old handicrafts of the Louis. Yet no monarch of the old regime had so dominated a style.

Designers of Louis XVI's day had revived classical design and made it an expression of elegance and refinement, in the reaction that followed the overornate style of the preceding period. But Empire artists exceeded all past efforts in using it to the glory of one man. The laurel leaves of the preceding style were rearranged and twisted into a victor's wreath. The fluted column upheld a torch. Roman and Grecian emblems were used lavishly. The craze for the antique transformed the dress of the day. Statesmen wore togas, and court ladies donned the gowns of Greek goddesses to match their background. Architects, decorators and furniture makers were imbued with the spirit of the hour.

The chief characteristics of the Empire style are still to be seen in tawdry side-street shops of most great cities, shops devoted to pseudo-art furnishings. They were reproduced on thousands of badly conceived objects of use and decoration. The commoner motives were the wreath, the torch, the Roman eagle, the Athenian bees, the Greek fret and the honeysuckle. After the campaign in Egypt the sphinx was added to the medley and became a conspicuous feature in both furniture and decoration.

Distinctive qualities of the furniture of the period are few and easily mastered. Constructively the plain column and the claw foot are the most salient features; decoratively the wreath and torch are most prominent. Marquetry was discarded, and plain surfaces were covered with ornamental mounts of chiseled metal. Chairs showed a square frame with a plain round leg.

In the plainer form the Empire style was full of dignity. It lacked the charm of the graceful Louis XVI style, but it had qualities of repose and stability that placed it far above some of its predecessors. One of the most interesting phases was the strong influence it exerted upon American furniture making of the early 19th century.

American Furniture

American furniture making described the same course as that of Europe. It differed in time and quantity; and new motives and materials gradually gave it a character of its own. Even when the new world craftsmen followed noteworthy English or French styles, they added stylemarks of their own. Today we value American Windsors more than those from England that provided the model; and we have Philadelphia Chippendale with its own unerring proportions and durable workmanship and its own fresh innovations of ornament.

The demand for old furniture, which has been increasing since the end of the 19th century, has brought to light much more information about our native product than we had before. Names of gifted 18th-century craftsmen have come to light and have been added to those of the great English cabinetmakers of that century. Goddard, Savery, Gillingham, Gostelow and Randolph are among them. John Goddard's block-front desks made in Rhode Island and the Philadelphia lowboys from the hand of William Savery justly merit fame. Demand for American antiques, coupled with interest in native folk arts and primitive paintings, has led gradually to systematic examination of all available sources of New World design, and has tended to multiply the names of designers and the styles for which they are responsible. Cabinetwork long attributed to English masters has been reclassified on the basis of this fresh research, which is still going on.

Periods.—Classifications of work done by American furniture makers from the 17th to the mid-19th century vary with various experts and have lately been the subject of much reordering as public taste tends more and more to turn back to our national background for old motives and new inspiration. *Founders' Colonial, Georgian Colonial* and *American Republic* are adequate labels.

The pioneers brought sturdy oak furniture from their native lands and used it as models for the first crude pine and hickory products. Gradually the forms were refined, more kinds of native wood were used and the numbers and kinds of pieces multi-

FRENCH AND COMPANY, INC.

LOUIS XV COMMODE. This deep-brown and polychrome lacquer commode is of the eighteenth century, (c. 1745). Designed by Pierre Rousell, its front edges assume a curvilinear form. Brown lacquer in commodes was rare, and Rousell was one of the very great ébenistés of the Louis XV epoch. The finest of Louis XV commodes were frequently characterized by bronze mounts extending from beneath the marble top to the feet.

FRENCH AND COMPANY, INC.

LOUIS XVI tulipwood and marquetry commode (*left*) mounted in bronze dore, by Alexis Delorme. A late Louis XVI, or directoire commode (*right*), is made of mahogany and mounted in bronze

dore. Attributed to Bernard Molitor, it is constructed along vertical lines and terminates in the fluted, straight legs characteristic of this epoch. The bronze mounts depict neo-classicism.

plied. The heavy medieval oak of English, Dutch and Flemish character persisted here and there. But plain painted or stained furniture of pine, maple and chestnut, with the later cherry and walnut, prevailed. This furniture was used in farm regions and in unpretentious homes until well into the 19th century and never passed entirely out of use. In museums, where it is enjoying a new season of appreciation, it is classified as Early American or *cottage* furniture. It is this that some authorities have given the very appropriate name *Founders' Colonial.*

Even before the end of the 17th century the English furniture of the period was being imported and used as models for new efforts. Demand for parlor pieces and fine furniture became much more general. The first half of the 18th century was a time of transition in our social, cultural and decorative tastes. Mixed influences in the mother country resulted in fresh Elizabethan, Jacobean and Dutch strains. The massive forms and elaborate carvings seen in some Early American furniture usually belong at their best to this time. The Queen Anne period brought lighter and more graceful adaptations, often in walnut. It continued many old style marks such as the cabriole leg and the webbed foot. This period has often been included in the general class of *American Georgian;* but no fresh source of inspiration prevailed, and there were no dominant new style characteristics till midcentury. Many elements of the international mixture that shaped the European baroque found their way into this earlier 18th-century American furniture; but traditional sources of English origin really prevailed until the coming of the great English cabinetmakers who followed Adam and ushered in the American *age of mahogany,* the *Late* or *Georgian Colonial.*

After the Revolutionary War the influence of Chippendale, Sheraton and Hepplewhite was still at its height and it weakened only gradually. Considerations, sentimental as well as political, then turned the eyes of the new nation to Paris. Thomas

Jefferson, third President of the United States, had studied architecture in France and had felt the same impulses towards Greece and Rome that were already at work in France. Jefferson revived and used Roman forms in a fresh American Renaissance. His public and private buildings may still be studied for a better understanding of form, proportion and balance. There was a brief post-Colonial period, during which these buildings and others they inspired, with transitional furniture, prevailed. The ideals of an American Republic that should resemble the republic of which Plato wrote accompanied the wide and general classic revival in our architecture that came about 1820. American Empire furniture, based upon the classic designs of Napoleon's craftsmen, came to its complete and final expression at this time. Like Jefferson's Roman Revival buildings, it was purer in form and more refined in detail than its models made for the French Emperor. But it was never a widely prevailing style during the efforts and experiments of the young republic to express itself in a homogeneous and appropriate manner.

19th-Century Currents. The influences of the Victorian era upon furniture and interiors overlapped with the American Empire style. Early Victorian furniture in walnut and rosewood often had something of the same sturdy construction and simple design; but in later phases, it was to mark a twilight of the gods in furniture design and domestic taste. The reaction swung back only slowly during the last half of the century to the honest Gothic creations of the Middle Ages for its inspiration. Thus came the Romantic revival that gave us mission furniture and indirectly influenced some of our prominent innovators of the present, notably Frank Lloyd Wright and some of today's industrial designers.

Founders' Colonial.—The straight chairs with banister or slat backs and seats woven of rushes are typical Early American. They were usually painted black, sometimes other colors. Plain deal tables with drop leaves and

square legs or gate-leg tables with turned legs belong to this period. The gate-leg style usually had eight turned legs, four of which swung around to raise and support drop leaves. American Windsor chairs and butterfly tables of rare and unusual charm are based upon Elizabethan models. The butterfly table is made of maple. Its name comes from the shape given the pair of flanges that replace the swinging legs of the gate-leg table. Chests, cupboards, benches and bedsteads, conspicuous in the limited Early American inventory, to which slope-top box desks and clocks with wooden works were added have a prim New World appearance in New England, Pennsylvania and Maryland. Early furniture was fine in the South and included more highboys, lowboys and cabinets, in a variety of hardwoods. Large chairs, small tables and utility stands soon appeared everywhere. The spinning-wheel and the loom, the cobblers' and the saddlers' bench were often considered part of the keeping-room equipment in the first days in New York, New England and Pennsylvania, when one great fireplace was the center of heat for all purposes. They are exhibited as furniture in modern museums and many sales galleries.

A paneled room of about 1740 is often typical of the Queen Anne or 18th-century transition style that may be studied in reproductions in American museums. It may contain inset cupboards paneled to correspond with the conventional rectangular divisions of the walls, and there may be a gate-leg table of walnut with a drawer and a walnut stand with drop leaves. Straight chairs with cabriole legs, sloped backs, straight arms and rush bottoms may be used alone, or a slim upholstered wing chair may accompany them. One of the most prized heirlooms of many American homes is a delicate Queen Anne lowboy of maple with the familiar cabriole legs and a slightly ornamental shaping of the drawer frames. The broken arch pediment, more familiar in Georgian Colonial, came at this time. So did the single fluted shell ornament set into some desks and lowboys for a century.

Georgian Colonial.—This furniture depended for its success upon the great supplies of West Indian mahogany then available. It could not have been developed so perfectly had not the shop practice of the American cabinetworkers served to prepare the way for its delicate forms and subtle ornament. The English architect of the Renaissance, Sir Christopher Wren, had helped to prepare the way for it when he revived classic architectural forms and made pattern books and working drawings that American architects had been using for a long time.

Architectural settings as well as craftsworkers' shops awaited the new era. These facts help to account for the Georgian flowering, the most homogeneous period in the history of American design until today. In furniture, the workmen made fresh adaptations but seldom departed far from the models set by Sheraton, Hepplewhite, Adam and the others; the fresh expression was that of a colonial dependency. But there was no later period in which the arts and crafts and industrial design of all kinds were so integrated ir a single style.

American Republic.—The Empire style in America followed the trend of the movement in France without many of the incongruities that developed there. Carved columns, claw feet, pineapple finials and ornamental brasses were the American style marks. Many of these are dismissed by the careless as Colonial detail; doubtless because this stream of influence is still difficult to free from the continuing traditions of the late Georgian. The American Empire style came between two periods of English influence that far outreached it in their effect upon the art and industry of the time. Both periods used some of the same forms and motives.

Duncan Phyfe was the single original furniture designer in America who made an impression upon the period. He was a Scotsman working in New York. His beautiful and now famous designs represent a conscious effort to improve upon the heaviness of Empire form and ornament. Insofar as he followed a model, it was Sheraton; but one of the chief distinctions of Duncan Phyfe's work is its individuality. A few museums devote rooms to it. Some of his followers in the Victorian era that was dawning designed equally elegant furniture using rosewood. But the taste of the times was fast becoming unfriendly to all sound principles of construction.

Eclecticism.—Heavy black walnut followed light and graceful rosewood carvings and was as elaborately ornamented. Ponderous tables soon supported marble slabs, and there were black horsehair upholstered chairs and sofas. The art impulse of the time expressed itself in Rogers groups, china dogs and chromo-lithographs. A little later dawned the era of golden oak, ushered in by the English reformer Eastlake and persisting in America after it was forgotten overseas.

FINNISH NATIONAL TRAVEL OFFICE

LIVING ROOM of a Finnish summer house is designed to adapt to natural surroundings. One chair (*left*) swivels on its metal base, while another (*right*) hangs from the ceiling.

TWENTIETH-CENTURY FURNITURE
BY BERNARD KARPEL

With furniture, as with other tools of living, the 20th century meant mechanization. The new industrial revolution put into the hands of designers and manufacturers such materials as metal tubing and bent woods, and encouraged large-scale production of standardized units. Human relationships were also modified. The home, traditional center of family and communal life, became smaller as education, entertainment and relaxation were supplied outside. Crowded cities and increased costs of living were influential in developing a type of furnishing which was compact and flexible.

Smaller families needed much less furniture, occupying less floor space. Fewer rooms meant more dual-purpose or built-in units. Lastly the jagged pace and complexities of metropolitan living favored shapes that were simple in structure and flowing in line.

Historically speaking, the use of the flowing line began with the beginning of the 20th century when *L'Art Nouveau* (in France) and *Jugendstill* (in Germany) exploited surface decoration as a substitute for structural considerations. Fortunately, short-lived, this departure was succeeded by the work of the Viennese, Werkstatte and Kunstgewenbe, which emphasized the artist-designed product. By the 1920s the French had taken a leading position in Europe and began influencing American design at the Paris International Exposition of 1925. Architectural in feeling, partly reflecting the cubist age, the French subordinated ornamentation to beauty of materials. By 1930, the Germans, Scandi-

navians and finally the Americans had begun to experiment with novel combinations of materials —and various new forms.

Significant landmarks are the invention of the first tubular metal chair in 1925 by Marcel Breuer of the Bauhaus faculty; the first cantilever chair, with jointed piping, by Mart Stam in 1926; the resilient chair of Mies Van der Rohe, 1927, which took advantage of the springy quality of closed steel tubing; the tubular armchair by Le Corbusier, 1929, adapted to a variety of sitting and lying positions without requiring mechanical adjustments; and the furniture by Alvar Aalto, 1932, which exploited the resiliency of bent or laminated plywood and its capacity, to follow free-flowing contours.

This sense of elasticity has been continued in recent designs; for instance, chairs for dining and relaxation with seats and backs fashioned of twine and webbing. Other furnishings, such as sofas, couches, even mattresses, manifest a similar historical and technical evolution from 19th-century ideas. Loose cushions on solid wood bases, leather and cloth stretched across rectangular, unbending frames, heavy stuffing over stiff-webbed foundations —- all these have yielded to manufacturing processes using compression coil springs, loose cushions on tension springs and buoyant sponge rubber on a plastic base.

At the beginning of the 20th century, sectional bookcases were introduced by Sears, Roebuck Company. Bruno Frank of the Deutsche Werkstatten in 1910 recognized the possibilities of this design principle, but it was Marcel Breuer who applied the unit idea to several types of furnishings, 1925-27. By 1930 two American designers, Donald Deskey and Gilbert Rhode, had on display furnishings of standard dimensions which could be arranged in a variety of ways. A recent manifestation of unit design is the storagewall, the work of George Nelson.

A series of storage bins that function as expandable closets and, at the same time, replace the conventional partition separating one room from another. The storagewall is an assymmetrical design which allows for personal variation. Its decorative beauty depends on structure rather than or-nament.

Furniture manufactured in the United States reflects an international character. In particular, the works of Charles Eames symbolizes experimental trends in American production.

His chairs are designed for and composed of molded plywood, adjusted to the natural contours and postures of the body; the metal frames are connected to the plywood forms by electronically-glued rubber mounts; seats and backs may be covered by foam rubber applied to the frame by electronic bonding.

Natural materials as well as synthetic finishes allow for chromatic variety. Seemingly radical shapes are derived from the combination of logical units manufactured by novel techniques. The result is a light, standardized, flexible chair, conforming in style and space requirements to contemporary architecture.

Furniture has travelled a long way from the symmetrical and static units of the 19th century with its stereotyped forms of decoration. The machine-made product, which Morris had laminated, was not to be denied but was humanized as it attained its own note of rational elegance.

Furniture as manufactured today falls into three general categories: *period reproductions*, still widely made and frequently ordinary in quality; *modern*, which is generally recognized by its simple line and complete lack of any ornamentation; and *borax*, cheap and overblown imitations of both period and modern furniture designs.

Furniture design cannot exist in a vacuum of esthetic considerations, but is subject, sometimes mercilessly, to the pressure of consumer taste. However, the activity of many designers of international reputation, the entrance of many large manufacturers into the modern field and the efforts of American museums to display and publicize modern design are greatly increasing public acceptance of the newer designs for furniture well-adapted to modern living.

INTERIOR DECORATION

Interior decoration is the art of making our homes beautiful; of creating settings suitable for the intimate daily life of the occupants. Whether the house be a mansion or a cottage, the planning of its contents and their arrangement should follow certain fundamentals. Natural taste reinforced by study will insure a harmonious and attractive home interior at moderate expense, but an unlimited outlay without these essentials may result in an opposite atmosphere.

Classical Influence.—Modern decorative practice began with the Renaissance in Europe and the revival of ancient art, that is, Greek art. From about 1600 to 1900 interior decoration, like architecture and painting of the time, was based upon ideas out of ancient Athens. Learning was revived also; and the scholarship and research that followed resulted in knowledge of the arts of all the other past periods. Through these centuries, *classic* art was the basis of styles not only in decoration but other arts as well.

Throughout this time there were occasional intervals of influence from other past periods: the *Roman* revival (classed with the Greek under the general term *classic*), the *Gothic* revival, and so on. But there was no new major style in the all-inclusive sense of the Gothic or the Greek. Art, architecture and other kinds of design relied upon adaptations and combinations of these earlier styles. The entire modern practice of their use is *eclecticism*—choosing here and there from the classical past. Gradually during the 20th century a new style is developing that appears to be taking its place among those great historic periods. It has begun to take form slowly as a revolt against borrowings and as a conviction that the machine-age way of life carries with it its own way of design. Past history is the best study of the slow process by which style revolutions come about.

French Styles.—Louis XIV built the Palace of Versailles in the 17th century. Interior decoration as a profession comes down from his time. He brought together the finest craftsmen of Europe to gild and paint and carve the interiors and fill them with sumptuous and glittering furniture, mirrors and jewellike ornaments. With the aid of the renowned Colbert he established centers for production of luxury wares. Gobelin, Aubusson, and Beauvais tapestries, Sèvres china, St. Gobain glass are all among the finest products of their kind ever made. For a century and a half the Versailles Palace and its contents were copied and imitated all over the world, and France became rich and famous as a producer of styles and of sumptuous merchandise. In spite of a general reaction against artificiality and ornateness, homes today are still full of reminders of that old king.

In the reign of Louis XV, extravagant decoration reached a climax. In the period of Louis XVI and Marie Antoinette, a quieter taste asserted itself as a reaction against extremes of vanity and folly in architecture, interiors and costumes. Many museums have recreated rooms from these periods and arranged them so that they may be compared. The ideal of classic style returned in the period of Louis XVI. In Napoleon's time a simpler use of Greek forms was introduced and became the basis of what we recognize as *Empire*. In 1925 Paris, still the world's recognized center of new styles and of decorative merchandise, was the scene of an international exposition of arts and crafts. From there *Art Moderne* was widely disseminated. It enjoyed a brief vogue in the United States under the name of *Modernistic,* but by 1930 it had largely passed. Today it is confused with the newer style that is based upon sounder and more permanent principles, called *Modernism* for lack of a better name. Mod-ernism in America has appeared and is making its way in interior design, largely as an independent development based upon changing industrial design and architecture.

English Decoration.—In England the heavy oak-timbered walls and furniture of the Middle Ages were slow to yield to Renaissance ideals. The 18th century brought an era of prosperity in which influences of the great Christopher Wren and of Adam and the fine furniture makers gave us what is still called "the golden age of home interiors." We have only to study this period to understand how the Georgian mansion came about and why Georgian interiors still contain what many people consider the most beautiful furniture available. American Georgian or *late Colonial* followed a similar course of development and produced a style that followed but did not imitate the English. This style still sets the standard for the average American home of taste and refinement, possibly because American culture arose out of the ideas that gave rise to the Georgian style.

Interrelation of the Arts.—In all these periods, in all countries, we find the art, architecture, interior decoration and costumes related to one another. The pointed arch of Gothic architecture was repeated in sculpture and furniture and also in the tall pointed headdress of the women and the sharply upturned points on the boots of all persons of rank. It is helpful in approaching the account of the 20th-century transition period to recall that the historic events of the time, great or small, determine the character of design.

Modernism or Functional Modernism came out of the industrial revolution. In this age when rapid, efficient machines are the basis of culture, we question classic decorations and painstakingly wrought handiwork on utilitarian objects. The result of functional design often appears over-plain, hard and cold. In some quarters at the height of the reaction all decoration and all ornament were rejected. Interiors today, where they depart from traditional use of period motives and styles, rely upon the beauty that is natural to the materials used. The grain of wood, the texture of fabrics, the polish of glass and metal are conspicuous. Large spaces, uninvolved masses and long horizontal lines bespeak the machine, as the Gothic product bespoke the cathedral.

Fortunately for us, there are unchanging principles common to all good design, capable of being applied under all varieties of changing custom and taste.

Elements Necessary for Success.—
Starting with the indispensable elements of all interiors, space, form and color, the decorator undertakes to achieve harmony, rhythm and unity. He uses the same principles adopted by the painter for this purpose. They are the principles of proportion, balance and emphasis. Scale and order are important in the decorator's dictionary; and among his ideals are simplicity, charm and originality. These ideals are hard to define—in people or in interiors—but they are instantly felt. Proportion, balance and scale may be achieved with almost mathematical accuracy.

Proportion. The Greeks were the world's masters of form. A study of Grecian architecture of the true classic period reveals subtleties of proportion that are amazing. Many modern efforts have been made to organize this *golden proportioning* into a modern system of design; but the decorator is concerned only with the broad principle of selecting and grouping objects in relation to interior space and to each other.

If the architect has done his work faithfully, it will not be necessary for the decorator to concern himself with the structural proportioning of the interior. In practice faulty dimensions must often be corrected or minimized, and architectural space divisions must be changed.

Balance is the principle by which repose is attained. There are two kinds of balance, symmetric and asymmetric. *Symmetric balance* is characteristic of all classic design. A Greek building façade or a wall in any classic-revival period represents two perfectly matching halves. The ancient Chinese and the modern Japanese have been masters of *asymmetric design,* which achieves its effect by more subtle means. It is sometimes called *occult balance.* In modern design of all sorts this asymmetric design is relied upon to produce an effect of vitality and interest and is called *dynamic balance* in contrast to the static effect of the more conventional symmetry. Modern designers say, "A seagull poised in flight is more beautiful than a sleeping cat"; and they speak of the balance that suggests movement.

Emphasis is based upon the natural habit of the eye to come to rest upon the most conspicuous object in view. Every picture, every room needs some strong point of attraction, some central emphasis to which attention returns again and again. Points of lesser interest must be calculated with this in mind. We have only to examine photographs of mid-19th-century parlors to see that so many points caused an atmosphere of unrest and confusion.

We might say that *scale* is a matter of the relative size of objects, and that *order* is the relative placing of those objects in a composition.

Rhythm, harmony and unity are often referred to as principles. They result from the principles of proportion, balance and emphasis. *Harmony* is attained by the successful blending or grouping of many elements. *Unity* results from carrying the results of this blending or grouping into a single effect. Rhythm is the interrelating of the parts: as the eye travels over any scene, it follows a *path of interest;* it moves and pauses before being brought to rest upon the central point of emphasis. If the decorator has been successful, this movement around a room becomes satisfying and pleasant. We understand the effect of movement and rest for the eye from analogy to the ear in listening to music. In decoration as in music, harmony, unity and rhythm are felt. Interior decoration is an art and a science, and these qualities are most apparent when the decorator is most an artist.

COLOR

The old discussion whether color or form is more important seems as futile as that of the hen and the egg. Sir Joshua Reynolds, founder of the English school of painting, and his contemporary, Gainsborough, became enemies through argument of the point. Romney was nearer right than either when he said that color and form need never be considered separately, and that line merely suggested the beginning of one color where another ended. Since the time of Cézanne, the French father of Modernist art, it has often been said that the eye actually sees little of forms except their color.

Color in History.—Color has always been a powerful agent in the hands of the decorator, never more so than today. It has been relied upon for beautiful effects, and gradually, in recent times, we have approached a more scientific understanding of its properties and influences. Something that is common to human nature finds its expression in color. The history of color is as long and as fascinating as the history of humanity. Scientists of our own day are studying paintings thirty thousand years old in ancient caves of prehistoric France and Spain. The animals and men and hunting scenes represented in these paintings are sometimes solid black, sometimes red or ochre and sometimes in a full range of polychrome colors, an effect that civilized man did not achieve again until the age of classic Greece.

The Egyptians used three-color combinations in unshaded tones: red, yellow and black; blue, white and yellow; black, yellow and white. Assyrian decorations were strong and barbaric with greater use of red. The Persians preferred blue. These three ancient nations, Egypt, Assyria and Persia, laid the foundations for the industrial arts of the western world. Persian blue, one of our precious possessions today, may be found in many forms. Rugs, pottery, enamels and illuminations show this matchless hue.

The Greeks first used shaded colors and made liberal use of purple and green. The lost *Tyrian purple* of history and romance seems to have originated in Greece and not in Tyre. It was a strange and beautiful dye, made from a shellfish found in the Aegean Sea. The secret of the dye has been lost since the days of the Roman Empire.

Roman color schemes are familiar to us because the Roman cities of Pompeii and Herculaneum have been excavated in modern times, and many public and private rooms have been completely uncovered. The deep flamelike hue called *Pompeiian red* was much used with white; and orange, black and white also are often seen in wall panels and furnishings. When the seat of Roman government was transferred to Byzantium by the Christian Emperor Constantine, the name of the city was changed to Constantinople, but the long period of rich Oriental art represented by this union of East and West is still called Byzantine. It is discussed at greater length in other articles in this volume. A brief Byzantine revival in recent times affected Continental Europe and the United States at the height of the modernistic vogue of the late 1920s.

Following the end of the Roman Empire came the Dark Ages, but this coming of Gothic culture was accompanied by the jewellike glow of the first cathedral windows, such as those at Chartres. The famous Gothic tapestries borrowed some of the color as well as the design of these windows. Gothic blues and greens and reds may be studied at their best in many museums. They were less gorgeous than the Byzantine colors of the preceding era and less sophisticated than those of the Renaissance that followed.

Brilliance and subtlety, depth and delicacy distinguished Renaissance schemes. Venetian red, Florentine blue, Neapolitan yellow belong to the story of the Italian Renaissance, when fine textiles and fine paintings were important to the backgrounds of a rich and regal way of life. From the Renaissance to the present the study of color is a part of the long story of period revivals and eclecticism that has already been reviewed. But color is a clue to lead us from period to period and from country to country. It will bring us safely through the mazes of styles and dates if we follow it with sufficient zeal.

Theoretical Color.—There are many theories of color. The spectrum theory based upon the rainbow or nature's colors has been used by the artist during much of the period of painting. It has been partially rejected in recent years as a result of scientific studies in various direc-

BLAINE AND BOOTH. INC.
ULF WAHLSTROM. W. AND J. SLOANE

FORMAL LIVING ROOM in a French country home (*left*) has a high, beamed ceiling and parquet wood floor. The ornate chandelier, fireplace, and period furniture carry out the traditional motif. The modern living room (*right*), with its sunken ceiling lights, open brass fireplace, and contemporary *objets d'art*, provides a striking contrast in design. Even the flowers are arranged along simple lines.

tions: the chemical nature of color; the analysis of light waves into the colors of the spectrum, and the length and behavior of these color waves; and the psychological reactions of normal people to color combinations.

The spectrum theory is worthy of careful study because it helps us to understand past art and decoration and to build theoretical color schemes. The modern artist and decorator say that artists' colors are not the same as nature's colors. Even though they show us why this is so, we nevertheless hold fast to the laws of color in nature, and their study is rendered fascinating by the use of color charts.

Color and Scientific Research.—Many modern researches in color and light are too technical to be readily understood by lay persons. We accept the scientist's evidence in this field, however, because his studies of the ray of light have given us the violet ray and the infrared ray. As the artist has taken the scientist's discoveries to the studio, he has made demonstrations that the Modernist decorator is more and more applying to his problem. A first principle is this: If colors affect one another, they are affected even more in a painting or in an interior by other considerations—space, changing light, relative areas of colored objects or surfaces and the texture or finish of the areas. The spectrum theory, because it is mechanical, may yield color schemes that are garish under one set of conditions and lifeless under another. Under the new compositional theories, a color unit is sometimes calculated under conditions like those in calculating a weight in engineering construction. We hear of *building* a color scheme, of the *weights* and *tensions* of colors, of their *dynamic interplay*.

The effects of modern color use are more familiar than the methods. Important national or international exhibitions include modernist interiors. These are seen also in many public and social buildings and in an increasing number of private homes. They are illustrated in fine color in yearbooks and magazines. Department stores of most cities have made demonstrations of them, sometimes successfully, sometimes deplorably. The total color reappraisal in process may prove as revolutionary as the discovery of mechanical perspective in the 15th century. Like that early discovery, it may not be codified into a set of working principles for the decorator for many years. If, meantime, we see conventional color schemes on every hand, that is because public style and taste are matters of slow change.

Color and Taste.—Even the members of one family seldom have the same likes and dislikes. Red pleases one and irritates another. Yellow strongly appeals to a third. A fourth may have a violent aversion to shades of brown or green. There is no arguing taste. But we no longer confuse taste and whim.

Colors have a psychological effect that is not measurable but is much better understood than by past generations. Under given conditions large groups of people react in given ways to certain colors and combinations of colors. Too much red overstimulates. Young ladies of the mid-Victorian era were flighty and hysterical; perhaps because their black walnut parlors were too full of red plush upholstery and big red roses climbing over wallpaper and carpet. Green is restful. Blue is depressing. We know from the poets that optimism is rosy, and melancholy is purple. Yellow is the color of the sun and is universally the symbol of warmth and life. Color combinations are now regarded as a play of these effects one against another in degrees and groupings suitable to the kind of effect desired. The strong, irritating character of red becomes pleasantly stimulating in certain combinations with a well-considered group of other colors. Color as well as music has its normal scale and range of emotional effects on the average person.

Practical Color Considerations.—Among the first questions that any decorator, professional or amateur, will ask are these:

1. What is the height, width and proportion of the room?

2. How much and what kind of light does it receive?

Historically, the best periods of decoration have been those in which colors have been so used that the effect was of more space and light, more harmony and repose. Designers know that through the use of color walls or parts of walls may be moved backward or forward in appearance, ceilings may be raised or lowered, and floors may be kept underfoot. Red comes forward, blue recedes. Yellow and light green, with a large range of other delicate tones, have the effect of increasing the sense of space. The ceiling of a room recedes into distance if it is made a delicate blue or pink; a cold blue or grey of medium tone brings the ceiling down. This one consideration often makes or mars an interior.

The problem of lighting is always important—both artificial light and natural light. The number and size of windows and the direction of light are all connected with color—how much color and what intensity of color are desirable. There is a marked difference in a room when it is hung with yellow-green and when it is hung with blue-green. Rooms with insufficient light are made more cheerful by the use of buff, light yellow, light green and warm grey. Occasional use of mulberry, gold or Venetian red accomplishes the same effect but requires skill. Silver, sapphire, jade and mauve are cool colors successfully used for sunny rooms. But most rooms are not sunny all the time—or dark all the time. Rooms facing east are dark in the afternoon, and rooms facing west have little direct light in the morning. Northwest rooms receive a clear, cold light most of the day and strong, bright light in the late afternoon, so that an ordinary, conventional color scheme that looks well for half of the day looks garish in the other half. This is largely true also of southeastern rooms.

There has been a gradual return to light neutral backgrounds for homes of all classes, but period rooms in natural wood or carved wood paneling are always the exception. Wallpaper of bright red or poisonous green is no longer used as it was in that recent period when all houses were tall and dark, most windows were narrow and slitlike, country houses were made darker by wide porches and thick, close planting, and city houses were crowded together. Then no colors appeared bright enough to lighten the interior gloom. Today the pendulum swings far in the opposite direction. The architect captures direct sunlight for every room. He diffuses and reflects all the daylight there is so that the interior has the maximum benefit of it at all hours. Many kinds of experts help architect, decorator and homemaker by devising systems of artificial illumination that recreate fixed degrees of daylight. At the same time the range of inexpensive colors in transparent hues has grown steadily more fascinating, and the decorator's knowledge of using these for subtle combinations has become more and more apparent.

Planning the Decoration.—The architectural style of any interior goes far toward dictating the decorative treatment. Fortunately the idea of a detailed architectural treatment for the walls of a room is now generally rejected along with the idea of bright and solid colors. Backgrounds are kept relatively neutral and uninvolved, even in period interiors where proportions, furnishings and general color scheme are as authentic as in a museum. It is therefore interesting to glance back briefly over the thousands of years in which the interior wall was treated as a problem in classic architecture.

From the Athens of Pericles to the Chicago of General Grant, the wall consisted of a dado, a frieze, a cornice and the space between. These members were originally subjected to the same principles of balance, proportion and harmony as the classic column with its base, pedestal, shaft and capital. The Romans misunderstood the principle and corrupted the proportions; but the practice continued with many modifications well into the 19th century. Marble, stone, wood, plaster and tapestry supplied the materials. Lastly, the dado and the frieze, and often the connecting vertical support at the corners were imitated in wallpaper. That was the period when wealthy Europeans were known to paint the end wall of an interior to simulate a trellised opening with another room beyond or even a window and a view.

The human hand that had played

the chief part in all things that man had made for use and beauty became relatively unimportant. It threatened to become useless for the great masses of working people, as machines multiplied, and factories grew larger and larger. The Romantic Revival was organized in England by people who saw that the whole countryside and the daily life were becoming ugly and unbearable through industrialization. William Morris and John Ruskin preached a return to the ways of the Middle Ages and the revived use of all the ancient handicrafts. The *Arts and Crafts Movement* helped re-educate a new age to the unchanging principles of good design. The interior decorator inherited from it certain fresh conceptions of utility and beauty, of form and function—and some of our finest conceptions of decorating informal rooms.

All interiors of our time are characterized by a certain atmosphere that derives from the current ideals of everyday life. They are modern in many ways, tangible and intangible. But when we consider the interior of the home that the Functional Modernist plans, we find a complete set of conditions that the decorator must make it his business to understand and respect. At first the new interiors were incomprehensible to decorators educated in traditional industrial and applied arts fields. A situation arose, apparently unique in the modern history of furnishing. The architects designed their own interior decorations and often the furniture and the accessories as well. It is only in the final years of the 1930s that decorative arists and designers of high repute began to work in both traditional and Modernist styles. Gradually manufacturers of furniture and textiles and department stores and special shops are becoming more able to provide the necessary designs for creating a good Modernist interior. Through the use of reliable books and magazines the amateur may arrive at his own sound plan of decoration.

Harmonizing Furniture and Background.—The interior and its furniture should be planned at the same time. Happy are those who can build and then buy suitable furniture. The logical sequence is first the walls, then the floors, then the contents of the room. But the complete scheme must be well in mind at the start to avoid serious and costly mistakes. Present conditions of mass-production manufacture and distribution make it fatally easy for the enthusiastic amateur to embark upon overambitious undertakings. Architectural units for schemes of all kinds are prefabricated, and often the practical aspects of the interior or the final effects will be sacrificed to some notion of picturesqueness. Besides, furniture from a worn-out or outgrown home must often be reconciled with new pieces in the same rooms. Pieces around which sentimental associations have gathered or substantial survivals representing now outmoded fashions in interiors may sometimes be remodeled with good effect either in establishments specializing in such work

or at home. But their haphazard use gives disturbing results.

The *what* and *how* of successful interiors are best determined by the amateur working with a good handbook as a guide. The distinction achieved by the skilled decorative designer or the "fun" enjoyed by the gifted amateur comes from the introduction of fresh and harmonious notes into the fixed limitations of a special kind of interior. It is important to see how the style of the room influences its contents in achieving an integrated effect. It is necessary to consider which rooms are suitable for special purposes.

American Styles.—The late Colonial or American Georgian house is favored by the homeowners in this country who represent the higher ranges of culivated taste; and so it is the most satisfactory type of interior to consider. Fine originals exist in many parts of the country with the furnishings that were designed for them still in place. Museums have carefully reconstructed many famous rooms of the period. Mahogany furniture in full range may be bought in antique stores and at auctions. All conditions make this a happy period to reproduce in intimate American living space. The influences of Wren and Adam upon interior architecture, and the influences of the fine craftsmen who shaped the Hepplewhite, Chippendale and Sheraton furniture flowed together in the American Georgian mansions that are probably the high watermark of American cultural expression. Perhaps the tradition has persisted because American heirlooms, insofar as there are any, come out of the Colonial interiors. The era that produced them was one of wealth and of cosmopolitan interests and foreign travel. Fine Oriental rugs, china, porcelains and metalwork belong in them.

The American interiors of an earlier time were often paneled in oak or pine according to their date. The architecture that we call *Founders Colonial,* so widely used in the restoration of old New England farmhouses and in new homes everywhere, makes typical use of exposed beams and woodpaneled walls in natural effect. Pine furniture is rightly used here in combination with maple, chestnut and the familiar American fruit woods in natural effect. The wide-board floors in these old houses often have taken on the finish of the ages.

The Elizabethan half-timbered house, in modern adaptation, usually has simple interiors of plaster with stained oak woodwork. The furniture should therefore be of oak in a sturdy and simple design and should be stained to harmonize with the exterior finish.

Mediterranean architecture, formerly seen in Florida and California only, has been adopted for homes all over the country. Its rough, tinted plaster walls with interconnecting archways instead of doors, its intimate warm and bright informalities make it ideal as a background for painted furniture in several colors. The colors here, as well as in the

MUSEUM OF MODERN ART

JAOUL HOUSE, by Le Corbusier, in Neuilly, France, uses open spaces and a tiled ceiling.

Norman house, should avoid the delicate effects and the elegancies of the occasional lacquered piece seen in a late Colonial or a formal French room.

Unity without Monotony.—To sum up: there is a prevailing unity in a well-conceived interior. The character, proportioning and treatment of the wall dictates the amount and kind and style of the furniture used. There are materials and finishes, forms and colors that are traditionally associated with every style of interior. But unity is not monotony. No one today would put fine mahogany furniture in a dark-oak interior or unpainted pine furniture against a formal Georgian wall, but even the amateur understands the advantages of diversifying tones and textures in finish and of alternating between Sheraton and Hepplewhite. A modern sense of fitness often aids us in placing a pair of fine Sèvres vases and a Persian embroidery on the same wall with an old Chinese portrait in a formal Colonial reception room where a gilt chair or an ornate cabinet full of small *objets d'art* would be fatal to the effect.

The Modernist Room may best be studied on the basis of an illustration taken from one of the soundest and most widely publicised homes built during the decade of steel-and-glass building design in America. This is one of the main floor rooms of a country house. Here, true to principle, walls tend to disappear. Large portions of the living floor are divided by short raillike partitions placed here and there as an aid to grouping the furniture. Large areas of the outside wall are of clear glass planned to enclose extensive panoramas of the landscape. In the work-

ing out of the color-and-exposure problem of this room, and again true to modern principle, one wall is of a contrasting color. The ceiling and portions of the side walls are finished in a synthetic material belonging to the group of chemical products called *plastics* with a shining surface especially planned to reflect light. The darker wall section is a warm brown tone, harmonizing with the floor finish but not attempting to match it. The fireplace is white. The floor covering is of light beige. The draperies are arranged to make a continuous covering for the wall spaces of glass and are slightly deeper in tone than the rug.

Use of Color.—The harmony of walls and furniture is realized through color. The rich brown of Circassian walnut in the grand piano and the low section of partition is repeated in lighter tone in the fireplace wall section. Both are balanced measurably by the use of unbroken areas of shining white in the wall and the fireplace and in the white furniture. Chairs and couches form a conspicuous part of the furniture. The white upholstery is alternated by the use of neutral tans and warm gold in solid color and by a couch covering patterned in horizontal stripes in an interesting interplay of many colors. The low tables and most of the other furniture are made of polished tubular metal. Table tops are glass. The harmony of walls and furniture is further realized here in terms of form and proportioning. The effect of unbroken horizontality depends on the relationship of all elements to a basic height line.

Everything that is done in designing a room of this character submits to the most rigid analysis according

to the principles of decoration with which we started. If the effect in the view shown appears formal and a little cold, remember that a part of the same general living space is devoted to a library, small and informal enough to be called a den.

The most successful woman decorator in the field of Functional Modernism explains how she designs a room with color: "With it we fortify or complement the existing architectural background, bringing some walls or lines forward by accenting them and making others recede by wiping them out with neutral tones. . . . We study the relative intensity of light as it reaches walls and then determine whether it is in the best interest of the room to bring forward a wall by projecting it more intensely into the light or to let it fall back into shadows." This designer confirms the practicability of new color theories and illustrates at least something of the new practice when she says that the client who insists upon a fuchsia-colored room does not really want a room with fuchsia-colored walls or hangings or furniture, but only a harmony of other colors with perhaps rare touches of the coveted hue, which afford the apparent effect of the flowers. The process is as subtle as that of a modern painter who undertakes to flood his landscape with the sense of sunlight or cold, clear dawn without falling back upon the palette of the academic painter. There is, of course, a perfect understanding, on the part of such designers, of key, rhythm and harmony, but particularly there is reliance upon the dynamic values of certain colors within the restful unity of the whole.

The Living Room.—Now that the word *parlor* has passed into disuse and *library* has lost most of its significance, the living room is the heart and center of the house. The architect often goes more than halfway toward making this the most cheerful, usable and attractive part of the interior when he bases his floor plan upon a study of the future occupants, their interests and their habits of work and play. The amount of main floor space devoted to this room is best determined by the architect's analysis. All that goes into the room and its arrangement and contents should conform also. Useful reference volumes, new books, magazines and newspapers, the telephone and the radio belong there; and the fireplace holds its ancient position of honor even where modern central heating and ideas of functional design prevail.

The living room is not a retreat for the quiet scholarly worker nor an appropriate laboratory or workroom for the amateur inventor or chemist. as some families suppose. Nor is it the ideal play place for the children. Its effect should be neither too formal nor too informal, as befits the center of the family's intimate home and social life. The furniture should be simple, durable and beautiful. Above all, the walls and furniture should never be permitted to become collecting places for trivial things.

In a Colonial living room an old landscape paper is sometimes very attractive. A paper in several colors is a decoration rather than a background and looks well with plain curtains and with rugs that derive their interest from texture rather than color pattern. Mahogany furniture of appropriate design and proportioning may be mingled with book cases and certain other pieces, stationary or movable, that are painted to match the ivory woodwork. A high, old-fashioned bookcase desk often looks well between two windows or where it will balance a door; it will afford protection behind its latticed glass for a few rare or delicately bound volumes.

Furniture as a Part of the Room. There is a growing practice in rooms of this character to recess the bookcases and made them a part of the architectural treatment; and this is in line with a wide movement towards furniture that is built into place. Properly planned and installed cupboards between the sections of recessed shelves are very useful in a large room. The extent to which modern cabinet work features can replace mahogany furniture successfully will depend on the degree of formality that is wanted and the experience of the planner. Millwork or precut designs for such combinations are nationally marketed by many producers who spend large sums of money in educating the public to the most satisfactory combinations and best schemes. Photographs and working drawings are sent to professional decorators and homemakers on request. They illustrate the Colonial period and many others.

Oak, walnut and maple offer endless possibilities in the living room. Unfinished furniture (as widely marketed as millwork) is especially helpful to the amateur who wants to avoid the effect of the conventional department-store suite. When such pieces are of good materials and workmanship, they may cost almost as much as those in the stock set. They must be finished to produce a harmonious, though not necessarily matching, effect. Above all, the finish must make the most of the natural beauty, grain and texture of the wood. The cheaper whitewoods are reserved for the rooms where paint is a suitable finish. Besides following a good formula and set of instructions in finishing, care and patience are necessary, and a workroom is highly desirable if the job is undertaken at home.

Choice of Furniture. New furniture for this or any other room where a strict period ensemble is not attempted is best when simplest. The room in careful period reproduction ought always to use only "fine" furniture that, if it is not actually old, is of expert handcraftsmanship. The popular, machine-made sets of furniture so widely sold imitate the hand effects or the style marks of the most elaborate periods, and so they display very poor taste. This is the reason why people, even those of moderate means, have turned back to the use of old things. If we follow our hobby as antique collectors with courage and judgment, we can often pick up old oak furniture for a living room at

BLAINE AND BOOTH, INC.

FORMAL DINING ROOM with round table and leather-upholstered chairs reflects the air of a French country home. The decorative mantel is a striking contrast to the bare floor.

prices comparing favorably with those paid for well-built mahogany furniture. We realize handsomely on such a hobby through the pleasure and the practical use we derive from an interior that is uniquely our own, even if our antiques do not actually increase in value with the passing of time.

Whether oak, maple or mahogany is used in one room, it should harmonize in a general way with the furnishing of other rooms in the same part of the house. Like mahogany, maple or walnut, oak is the proper wood for many different styles of interiors. This leads to the necessity of special study in the shapes and finishes that are suitable for combination with each other in any scheme we undertake to assemble without expert guidance. In one beautiful living room, for instance, the owner used Circassian walnut for the woodwork and a warm oil-finish ivory stain for the walls as a background for Italian walnut furniture of the 16th century. The curtains are rosy in tone, and rose color is prominent in the rug. Silver-blue, mignonette green, rose and ivory contribute to a color harmony that is soft and bright without being too elegant for a room of general use.

The Book Alcove.—A book alcove may appropriately be made a part of the structural design if the room is sufficiently large and has well-distributed light, and the furniture is substantially proportioned to the space. The character of the wood-

work and the style of the finish determine the atmosphere. The formal effect of the alcove as it is seen in the Bodleian Library at Oxford and at other famous English libraries is more suitable for the special than the general room, and so are the styles derived from the Spanish and Italian periods in which elaborate carving of oak was used. As a general principle, in contemporary furnishing, the bindings of the books are emphasized, and their often bright and beautiful color effects are made an important point of emphasis in the room. The cases, like the walls, tend to become neutral and unobtrusive in form and finish.

The Dining Room.—For many years the dining room was subjected to massive treatment, no matter what the other rooms were like. This theory gave us the beautiful, formal room hung in subdued leathers and furnished in carved oak. This is one of the most desirable state dining rooms that have come to us out of the past. When it is well executed, it has a true baronial dignity. Cordovan leather paneling and massive oak furniture produce a kind of somber beauty and a suitable setting for a table service of elaborately designed metal. The walls, though in rich and dense coloring, need not be gloomy under present conditions of lighting. But we do not often need baronial interiors in private American homes, even when expense is not the main consideration. The heavy silver and pewter plate "fit to set before a king" are better suited to glass cases in museums. The state dining room, according to present judgment, is better in clubs, hotels and institutions of state. Even in those places, where the effect is carried out in old Flemish, Spanish or Jacobean oak, there is still the danger of falling into the errors that led in the late 70s to some of our unhappiest interiors, little calculated to inspire modern "feast of wit, and flow of soul."

The dining room does not "go out on its own" except in the relatively few instances where a formal salon is furnished for social use; and some informal dining space is used for every day. Still keeping within the oak scheme, such dining rooms may be developed in Tudor as well as Jacobean, in Italian Renaissance as well as Spanish or Flemish style. They may be in the formal French styles or even Pompeiian or Byzantine if an expensive architect and an owner of cultivated taste combine their efforts with those of a decorator.

Less formal period dining rooms in Colonial, Louis XVI or American Empire effect may be made very attractive and may be harmonized with the entire interior scheme. Decorating and furnishing in one style and in a manner consistent with one period (even if not limited to that period), is more a matter of taste and care than of expense. A Louis interior costs much more than a Colonial interior of equal excellence, and an Italian Renaissance room more than one in Queen Anne style, not for the artistic values involved but because they require more consistency and are luxury interiors. The furnishings and fittings suitable for them are rarer and more costly, when they are good, and are often impossibly cheap and tawdry in modern reproduction. But today for the first time we can readily assemble any kind of interior we really need and find ourselves able to pay for.

Dining rooms offer fewer problems of consistency than almost any other rooms. The size and scale of pieces needed are well established in practice and have been subject to comparatively little variation down the centuries. Even in the cluttered periods, the dining room was less covered with bric-a-brac, and its walls were less abused by too many pictures than living rooms and bedrooms. Their general proportioning was less offensive, even when they suffered from overcrowding. Nevertheless many dining rooms even today strike us as too full of things. Their furniture may be beautiful, their color schemes harmonious, their walls and sideboards free of irrelevant decorations—still they produce an atmosphere of tiring confusion. We instantly feel the finer restraint and the greater atmosphere of repose in a room where a few inexpensive pieces are well placed; and we instantly feel disturbed where a set however beautiful is used in a space too restricted for it.

Little Rooms. The functions of the dining room tend to merge with those of the living room. Often some spe-

W. AND J. SLOANE

EARLY AMERICAN dining room is designed to reflect a warm and intimate atmosphere. China and glassware are displayed against the natural-grain wood of a traditional breakfront. The glow from the chandelier and the portraits on the paneled walls add charm.

cial part of the living room is devoted to the service of the family's meals. In larger homes there may be a breakfast nook and a dining porch, in addition to the regular dining room. The dining room often has a *bay* where informal luncheon may be served or a terrace for summer dining. Houses of conventional period design, even, make much of what the decorators sometimes call the *little rooms.* They are interesting centers of fresh experiment in the house because they may be redesigned with relative ease.

In one successful breakfast room, the furniture and woodwork were painted peacock blue. The paper had a white ground on which small, brilliantly colored peacocks were seen through a pleasant patterning of green foliage. A rug of Scotch weave covered the floor within six inches of the walls. It was green, with a well designed border repeating the peacock shades. The exposed part of the floor was also peacock blue to match the woodwork. White ruffled curtains were used. The narrow painted table had a runner of coarse canvas bordered by a design in green cross-stitching. On the narrow mantelpiece were a pair of dwarfed evergreen trees in blue miniature tubs. The furniture and color effects were carefully harmonized with the narrow space available, and the table was set with inexpensive peasant pottery in suitable color effects.

Another informal breakfast room was planned to make a place for six Early American chairs with rush seats, painted yellow and decorated with grapes. A round table of common pine was painted and decorated to correspond. A background for this crude but effective treatment was a paper of the 1820 period that gave the effect of paneling put on in small squares of green and yellow, each broken in the center to show a basket of fruit. The woodwork and the floor were painted green, and a large circular rug in black, green, gray and yellow completed the scheme.

Early American Suggestions. Interest in domestic life and taste of the pioneer Americans of three centuries is heightened by the present vogue for Early American pine furni-

ture, the recent interest in *primitive painting* and the knowledge that these things were not the property of any particular period but the possessions of the common people, familiar in farmhouses through several centuries. The pine furniture was painted in solid colors, and different colors were often used in one room. Floral and other decorations were used in New England, New York, Pennsylvania and the South, as paints became more common—red and black, at first, and later the polychrome colors seen on old Pennsylvania Dutch chests and bridal boxes.

In certain parts of the country, nothing could be more appropriate than a summer home dining room where old and new pine pieces are harmonized in a scheme of solid colors alternated. Blue, red, black, yellow and shutter green may be harmonized in a single interior if they are balanced with sufficient skill. The effect of a Colonial crazy quilt or an oval braided rug of the hit-and-miss variety will give a clue. Some Early American floors had solid colored borders painted on. Others made use of a spatter pattern covering the entire area of the wide oak, chestnut or pine space. This floor pattern, painted furniture, plain plastered walls, brick fireplace, hand-braided scatter rugs and some early native pottery will make an interior as attractive as it is sound for a house in the country. The blue of old wagon wheels keys a color scheme for the informal dining room by the sea; barn red for the farmhouse. The use must be wise and the effect subtly calculated; but it must be remembered that the colors and the combinations are pleasing because of their crude and naive blends, just as are Balkan embroideries or Scandinavian weavings.

A Modernist Dining Room. An interesting modernist dining room, at the other extreme, is in a city house where two of its walls are of glass brick. They are rounded together by a third wall, almost entirely of clear glass. The design shuts out the neighboring sights and frames the tiny garden. The glass-topped table stands upon four slim legs of tubular metal. The chairs are of metal with leather backs and seats in a combination of

BLAINE AND BOOTH, INC.

BEDROOM furnished in the style of a French country home is one of the latest trends in decorating. Lattice windows are flanked by two heavy wood chests under a high, beamed ceiling. The pattern of the decorative quilts is repeated in the draperies. Hand-crocheted afghans are folded at the feet of the beds. The large rooster atop the cabinet and the floral design of the chandelier add interesting notes to the decor of the room.

plain colors. The glass wall spaces are hung from ceiling to floor with adjustable draperies, straight-cut, plain-textured and almost neutral in tone. A room like this has little furniture. The table is a factory product, and one or two others like it may be brought in on special occasions. The view is the point of greatest emphasis. The gleaming table and its modern fittings merge into the design with it. The walls are of white arranged to diffuse light. The small, very modern fireplace without a mantel is a strong secondary note of emphasis, and there are few others except the specially designed lighting fixtures of polished white metal.

In more than one Modernist home of distinction wall partitions are movable, so that the living floor is sometimes practically one large unit, and at other times the dining space is closed off from general living space. Some walls roll quietly into place at the pushing of a switch. These movable partitions are very beautiful when they are made of light material such as is used in Japan. Heavy, soundproof curtains or clear, thick, unbreakable glass, set in folding panels of chromium or monel metal, are other materials for Modernist partitions.

The Bedroom.—Though the main living floor is always on display, the bedroom floors are private. The essentials in a bedroom are good ventilation, sunshine, freedom from disturbing sounds in the house and outside, convenient furniture, sufficient space and a pleasing appearance. When Mrs. F. D. Roosevelt went to Washington as First Lady, her White House bedroom was very large. She

had the dressing room of her suite made into sleeping quarters and the oversized chamber into a private office. No need, she said, for so much walking back and forth while one is dressing. Many bedrooms of the periods since the White House was built are too small for convenience and also for adequate treatment. Today we are again striking a happy medium.

The usual bedroom contains too many things. Photographs, knick-knacks and senseless little ornaments are strewn all over the place. If any part of the house should be simple in its appointments, it is the sleeping quarters. A few pictures and two or three interesting accessories are all that a bedroom ordinarily needs, and the accessories should be useful as well as beautiful. Another fault is the involved wall treatment. The wall finish may be plain or inconspicuously patterned. If it is plain, it should not be covered over with meaningless and ill-assorted pictures. If it is figured, care must be taken in the furnishing to avoid a crowded and confused effect. A rather bare scheme is required for figured backgrounds.

Where a figured wall is planned, the effect may be very interesting and pleasing if the paper is chosen with regard for the style of the furniture. There are many beautiful American, English and French patterns on the market. The same principles of harmony, emphasis and balance hold good here, and whatever scheme is adopted should prove restful but not monotonous, cheerful but not garish. Plain walls are often more pleasant when their texture is slightly rough. But recent restudies of the whole prob-

lem of color in its relation to light have resulted in the wide use of polished wall areas designed to reflect light and of other special plain surface treatments to create other special effects under artificial illumination. Many wall preparations are washable, a feature especially desirable in a sleeping room. Bedroom schemes may be carried out in many ways. Plain colors are pleasing in combination with chintz hangings. Success is not bound up with any one kind of treatment or by use of any particular period schemes. Whatever else it may have or not have, the bedroom calls for air, sunshine and order.

Rugs.—Better delay the scheme or let the floors go bare than make hasty, ill-advised selections. A wealth of material on almost every aspect of the subject is available. The history of the weavings with which civilized man has covered his floors is more fascinating than his use of color, because it is more closely associated with his growing ideas of domestic life and his art expression in other ways.

The *prayer rugs* of the Orient were originally objects of reverence, and their significance is mainly sacred in the East even today. Berber rugs have a strange pattern—bright but diffuse, with designs rich but abstract and formless—that is said to be a reconstruction of the effect derived from riotous fields of flowers seen in the native country. Swedish and Icelandic rugs woven in recent times for marketing throughout the western world take the peculiar character of their design and sometimes their motives from the days of the vikings. Our own hooked rugs, representative as they are of a minor, relatively unimportant activity, belong among American primitive arts or folk arts.

Rugs to complement the Room. At

METROPOLITAN MUSEUM OF ART

AMERICAN TEXTILES. This nineteenth-century rug from New England was made about 1825. It is composed of brown wool ground with a flower and a flowing vine design, as was the custom of this period.

one time in America no rug but an Oriental rug pleased us. For certain period rooms and certain effects we still accept no substitutes. We frowned upon all but plain unbroken weaves in floor coverings for a generation or two; but now we plan the coverings with full regard for the interior and its other contents. In the 19th-century period that produced red plush upholstery and wallpaper flowered over with red roses, carpets covered every inch of the floor space, and patterns of flowers and vines sprawled over every inch of the carpets. Now the 20th century turns to rugs and carpets designed with sobriety and thoughtfulness.

American carpet and rug manufacturers have a trade association through which information is being constantly developed regarding the best current ideas in style, design, color and popular taste. Rugs and carpets are woven in accordance with this research, and campaigns of advertising and education are carried on to help the homemaker in her choice of a particular covering for the floor of a particular room. The weight of the colors used sometimes appears more important than the pattern or actual color combination. Texture is emphasized as one of the means to a rich and subtle effect. The relative absorption of light of different weaves is stressed. For ordinary uses colors are almost never the bright and positive ones of the old times.

In a pleasant and varied color scheme of one new bedroom, white, with large areas of almost sapphire blue and touches of shell pink, the

MUSEUM OF MODERN ART

BULL IN THE SUN. This 85 x 116½-inch rug was designed by Arshile Gorky. Made of wool, it is probably done in the velvet weave, the simplest of carpet weaves. In this the pile is woven over wires; the pile yarns, however, remain uncut. The rug was designed in 1942.

METROPOLITAN MUSEUM OF ART

ORIENTAL RUG in silver brocade of sixteenth-century Persia. From a Moslem shrine in Iran, it shows a hunting scene.

large scatter rugs are all in one light color, a delicate jade green.

The rugs are woven with long, loose loop stitches, and the feet sink into them as into a bearskin rug. The magazines and Sunday newspapers constantly describe the new floor coverings of the best designers. The Metropolitan Museum (which has provided designers with study materials of all kinds, since the manufacturers' requirements in the styling of merchandise first took their revolutionary turn in the '20s) recently organized an international exhibition of modern rug designs. The trend seems established towards more color. American Modernist interiors until recently had almost exclusively made use of monotone effects in neutral colors for the floors. A newer phase equally avoids the naturalistic pattern of Oriental rugs from Persia and the geometric complications of the brief 1920–30 fad; but subdued patterns are returning.

Antique Rugs. Consideration of antique rugs as floor coverings is a subject apart from the study of fine collector's rugs. Aniline dyes and western influences have altered the old traditions and commercialized the old centers of weaving; almost every past style and kind of Oriental rug is imitated or reproduced for modern markets. We ignorantly place upon our floors rugs made to hang upon the wall. We incorporate into our decorative schemes fine designs that were approached by the Oriental only after he had removed his shoes. We grind precious symbolic patterns under foot.

The general classifications of Orientals are based upon geographical differences.

1. Persian designs are largely floral, and include among many others the Isfahan, Kermanshah, Kurdistan, Kashan, Meshed, Mosul, Saruk, Shiraz and Teheran.

2. The Turkish rugs of Asia-Minor are conventionalized patterns. Among them are the Anatolian, Bergama, Kaisarish, Karaman, Kurdish and Smyrna weaves.

3. Caucasians comprise the Baku, Cashmere, Dagestan, Derbend, Genghis, Kabistan, Karbagh, Kazak, Lezghian, Malgaran, Shirvan, Sumak, Tcherkess and Tzitzi. These designs are prevailingly geometric.

4. The Turkoman group from Afghanistan, Turkestan and Beluchistan includes, besides the weaves that take their names from these geographical subdivisions, the Bokhara, the Kashgar, Samarkand and Yarkand. They are designed upon the octagonal form.

5. Chinese rugs form a fifth class which has suffered from badly conceived imitations made in the West in recent times.

In deciding what kind of Oriental rug is suitable for the 20th-century interior, we must ask: Will it lie flat? Is the pattern two-dimensional or does it seem to rise in space? Is the composition one which may be viewed from any of its four sides or has it a top and a bottom? The Turkish, Turkoman and Caucasian examples are more geometrical than the Persian. It is the flatness and simplicity of the Bokhara design from the Turkoman or Turkestan group that has given it its tremendous vogue. The rich wine shades are well adapted to oak paneling, oak furniture and the color schemes often selected for living room and library. Certain old specimens are very valuable when they have taken on the bloom of iridescence that only time can give.

Modern Reproductions. The practical modern Bokharas compare favorably with the modern Kazaks, Kelims, Samarkands and Kabistans in weave, wearing qualities, color and price. The Persians were masters of color, their floral and animal forms still influence our fine arts, and their finest rugs are beyond price. Only a deep study of the subject or the advice of an expert should be relied upon in buying them. Rare hunting rugs or garden rugs or rugs in tree-of-life design have been reproduced in all their original colors, in modern wool and silk for use as wall decorations. They have an up-and-down design that gives them many of the values of a painting. They are especially effective in rooms where the floor covering is not too conspicuous.

The smaller Caucasian rugs contribute just the right note to a room now and then when thrown across a table. Early American rooms reconstructed in museums or pictured by eminent American painters show that this use is long established here.

Of the many famous and time-honored textiles now reproduced or imitated for everyday use, none is more noteworthy than the modern Persian rug, the Sharistan, woven on hand looms in this country. The designs are based upon traditional weavings of the 15th and 16th centuries, and made to order. Their peculiar, characteristic color harmony, suggesting the influences of time and sunlight, is entirely a matter of weaving, without washing or artificial aging.

Few people realize the extent to which the ancient weaving art has been revived in modern America. The famous tapestries of the Middle Ages were made in France. Famous rugs and hangings were made also in the France and Flanders of the 17th and 18th centuries, when Versailles, as we have seen, was made the center of western craftsmanship and decoration. The same kind of hand looms and the same traditions of design may be seen in use in New York today.

Pictures.—In many past times it has been truthfully said that the books, rugs and pictures make a room. Early in this century a general reaction set in against overcrowded rooms where the walls were literally lined with pictures. We are still fondly attached to inherited art, and the very ease with which all art of all pasts is reproduced in full color effect and the plentiful supply of fine modern etchings and lithographs at low prices make it fatally easy to misuse wall space.

The home decorator should have a compulsory history course in interior appearances in this one regard. The Louvre (the world's first public art gallery) and the palaces upon which it was modeled treated framed pictures as a wall covering, fitting them together with care. People who were artistic made the mistake of following this bad precedent that if one painting was a fine thing, a thousand paintings must be very much finer. Little by little for a hundred years, the canvases in museums have been thinned out, and a system of grouping has been established. Only gradually

in very recent decades, the museums have begun to think first of the individual picture and the total effect and afterwards of the number of things they must put somewhere. Cultured people no more show their love of art by making a display of it, than of their children or their jewelry. More than one decorative designer has built a room upon a single one of Van Gogh's colorful paintings or a Cézanne still life of the brighter period.

Choosing the Right Picture. The general principal to remember is: a picture must be carefully chosen and simply framed—and it must be in keeping with its environment. It must be submitted to the same test as the various other elements of the interior. The relation of periods of painting to periods of decoration is easily traced and applied. A good painting or a faithful color reproduction falls into a color relationship with other products of the same period, and less tangible relationships arise through the association of historic periods with each other. We look for classic marbles and classic themes in painting throughout the changing styles of the Renaissance era and associate with them certain classic color combinations. American portraits and the historic flower and botany prints are effective in Georgian rooms; and so are silhouettes, hunting scenes and many kinds of landscapes and painted studies of everyday life.

The familiar sentimental pictures that remind us of the appeal of mother love, the faithfulness of the old shepherd dog or the pathos of an aged and blind negro servant passed out of popular favor when the public first accepted post-Impressionist painting. Pictures that are marvelous in the detail with which they copy nature (as a photographic reproduction copies it) also have passed from favor among people of discriminating taste.

In general, we hang some one or two good paintings on the walls of a room where they form an appropriate part of the general scheme. Or if not paintings, prints. These should represent good art and good decoration. It matters little whether the room is planned as background for a treasured work of art or a work of art is chosen to fit into the scheme of the room. The picture must be suitable in size, scale, proportion and manner of framing to the room where it is hung if a truly pleasing, harmonious and discriminating effect is to be realized.

The fact that individuals often collect paintings in our day, and the additional fact that special interior planning is not prohibitive even in average homes, has made possible many private picture galleries. These have the atmosphere of the finest and most modern public picture galleries or some small special museums of recent planning. Pictures are the reason for the room's existence, but the pictures are arranged in a reposeful scheme, and confusion and crowding are avoided. Small sculptures or other three-dimensional accessories are used to aid the effect of balance, and a little simple furniture is added

to enhance appearance and comfort.

Picture Frames. Pictures, especially paintings, require frames when they are used in a planned interior decoration scheme. Gold frames were formerly correct and elegant and they are still almost indispensable for certain period rooms. Those of early Italian or 18th-century Georgian design are often beautiful. Those of the Louis XV and XVI period are almost always too elaborate for the average taste of the average home owner. Dull gold with a little Renaissance detail or perhaps some polychrome color is effective for reproductions of some Old Masters. It used to be important to graduate the width of the gold frame and the ornateness of the gilt carving to the grandeur of the subject. Today natural wood or wood stained in well-considered colors is preferable to gold frames. This sets the frame back and brings the picture forward. Some of the best artists of the modern world insist upon designing and even making the frames for their pictures—and the frames they make are most often plain unstained wood, sometimes with a little flat conventional carving, oftener without it.

If we really understand the principles of harmony, proportion and balance as they are applied to all the other aspects of a decorative scheme, we shall be able to use this understanding in choosing our pictures room by room and in putting them in frames that will emphasize their interest but keep them in their place as major points of emphasis.

AMERICAN MUSEUM OF NATURAL HISTORY

A PERUVIAN DOLL, dating from the fourteenth century, stands 32 inches tall. It is made of wood, wool, cotton, and fiber.

ETIQUETTE

Etiquette plays an important part in one's success. It comprises those rules and forms of conventional decorum that indicate what is proper in various contacts with one's fellow men and that have been developed among civilized peoples over many centuries. Many times what we consider to be the hallmarks of good breeding may be traced to the days of chivalry. The custom of raising the hat originated when knights, on accosting each other, raised the visors of their helmets to determine whether they were friends or foes. The custom of shaking hands originated in a desire to show a friendly feeling by indicating that one carried no concealed weapons, especially as one's left hand would generally be too weak to wield an effective blow. Many people still observe the custom of serving the hostess first, which may be traced to the desire of a medieval host to prove by having his lady taste each dish first that he did not wish to poison his guests.

The rules of etiquette are based on such qualities as courtesy, kindliness and consideration for the rights of others. They should be practiced from childhood until they become automatic. To speak in low tones and without boasting, to use accepted forms of speech, to talk too little rather than too much, to avoid superlatives and evident exaggerations—these are some of the marks of good manners and good breeding.

The foundation of etiquette is laid in the home. Thence its influence extends to every phase of the individual's life—to the school, to the church, to his work, to his social life and to his various contacts with strangers as well as friends. Etiquette is most useful in smoothing your contacts with others and making you, through observance of the social amenities, a more acceptable person.

Courtesy in the Home.—Every boy and girl should try to start the day right. Get up the first time that you are called rather than the third or fourth time. When you appear at the breakfast table, greet the family pleasantly. Observe the same punctuality at all other meals, taking care each time to wash your hands and comb your hair before you sit down to the table. When you take your place at the table, do so quietly without jerking or scraping your chair. Sit up straight, and don't tip your chair. Don't cross your legs under the table, and don't twine them around the legs of your chair or put your feet on the chair's rounds.

Contribute your share to the table conversation, modestly recounting events of the day at school or discussing some motion picture that you may have seen or some book that you have read. Don't interrupt or contradict when others are speaking. Try to avoid family arguments and mentioning troubles at meal time, as such expressions react on each individual nervously and impair digestion. Don't mention at the table any subject that is repulsive. The older members of the family should always be

careful about what they discuss at the table, as the younger children may cause embarrassment by repeating remarks they should not have heard.

When you leave school at noon or in the afternoon, go straight home so that your mother will not be worried by fearing an accident has befallen you. If you wish to go to a chum's home, first get your mother's permission.

Never tattle about your schoolmates to your teacher or about your brothers and sisters to your parents.

Be responsible for the appearance of your bedroom. Keep it orderly. Don't form the habit of leaving things around for your mother or the maid to pick up. Hang up each dress or suit in the closet, when you take it off. Leave your underclothes folded on a chair by your bedside and shine your shoes each night before you go to bed.

Leave each room, from the bathroom to the kitchen, in as tidy a condition as possible. Put back in the bookcase a book that you may be reading, and do not litter the piano with sheet music or leave the newspaper strewn in sections over the living-room floor.

Try to save your mother steps by answering the doorbell or telephone promptly. If the person wanted is not in, ask if you may take a message. Look for other ways, especially on Saturday, that you may assist your mother, such as dusting or running errands. Don't monopolize the telephone for your personal calls, and if you borrow the family car, do not keep it out too long without permission.

If you are a boy, be sure to rise when your mother or one of her friends enters the room and offer her a chair and remain standing until she is seated. Both boys and girls should rise on the approach of an older person. They are careful also to let this person, whether mother or grandmother, and, in the case of the boys, father or grandfather, precede them on entering or leaving a room and to hold the door open. Boys should pick up any article that the women may drop. Both boys and girls excuse themselves, if they leave the room. Excuses are offered also if one must pass in front of another person.

Respect the property of each member of your family, and don't borrow anything without permission. Return the borrowed article promptly and in good condition, and willingly reciprocate when the person from whom you have borrowed asks a favor. Respect for property extends also to the letters that your mother may receive and to the diary that your sister or brother may keep. Respect the privacy of others. Always knock on the door before you enter the bedroom of any member of the family; and never try to eavesdrop or overhear any conversation in which you are not included.

Be careful to thank a member of your family for a favor as graciously as you would a friend. Father will appreciate the fact that he is regarded

as something more than a pocketbook, and Mother will cherish your thoughtfulness, especially if she has sewed until the wee small hours on your graduation dress.

Both your mother and father will be glad of the good example that you set your younger brothers and sisters; for instance, you may share the candy stick that you have bought, offering the larger piece to your brother or sister.

Cultivate a family spirit and sense of loyalty by little attentions. Among these are remembering the birthdays of different members of the family, Mother's Day and Father's Day and observing occasional anniversaries, as well as Thanksgiving and Christmas.

The gathering of the family about the television screen in the evening not only provides the opportunity for closer association and better understanding among all, from the eldest to the youngest, but necessitates consideration of others in such matters as not obstructing another's view and deferring to others in the choice of program. The enjoyment of television entails good sportsmanship.

To indulge in tantrums so as to have your own way or to tease and impose on members of your family violates the rules of good breeding. Try always to be respectful, obedient and aboveboard in all your family relationships. If things do go wrong sometimes, don't criticize your family circle to outsiders; and never allow others to make disparaging remarks about any member of your family.

Deportment in Public Places.—On the street a girl speaks to another person; a boy lifts his hat when he greets a woman. If the boy and girl should be walking together, he raises his hat to the people whom she greets, whether or not he knows them.

A boy is careful to walk next to the curb; he takes a girl's arm only when he is steering her through a traffic maze. She may take his arm, though, if she needs support on slippery streets, over a rough road or in descending a flight of stairs. If the boy is walking with two girls, instead of walking between them he is still careful to keep his place on the outer side of the sidewalk. He raises his hat on taking leave of them at their destination.

When a couple are boarding a streetcar or bus, the girl gets on first; if the step is high, she may be assisted by her escort. On leaving the vehicle the boy gets off first and assists the girl to alight. The same holds true of a taxi or automobile, especially if there is no doorman. Since the advent of women in business the rule that a man should always offer his seat to a woman who is standing in a streetcar or subway train is not so strictly observed. However, he should be considerate of an older woman or of a young woman who may be holding a baby. If another man offers your companion a seat or picks up some article that she has dropped, tip your hat in thanks for this courtesy. The girl or woman should express her thanks verbally.

When a couple are attending the theater, the usher leads the way to the reserved seats. The girl follows the usher and in turn is followed by her friend. If there is no usher, the escort goes first to find the seats and then steps aside to let the girl enter, seating himself on or nearest to the aisle. Those who rise to let the couple pass should be thanked for this courtesy; care should be taken not to brush against them. The girl slips off her coat and removes her hat after she is seated. The boy may check his coat in the theater lobby before going to the seats.

Legitimate theater tickets should always be bought before the performance, and the girl's wishes should be consulted as to the kind of play that she would like to see. In the case of a theater party the host or hostess should determine before the party starts down the aisle the order in which the guests are to be seated, each young man following the girl for whom he has been chosen as partner. Ordinary afternoon dress is customary for the theater, although those who hold orchestra seats often like to dress—the girls wear dinner or evening dresses and the men tuxedos or "tails."

When a couple are dining at a restaurant, the headwaiter or hostess shows them to a table. The girl follows the headwaiter and in turn is followed by her friend. If there is no headwaiter, the young man goes first and selects a table. After choosing for the girl the more advantageous position he pulls out her chair and, when she is seated, helps her to remove her coat and arranges it over the back of her chair. If the girl is wearing an afternoon or simple dinner dress, she wears a suitable hat; but, if she is wearing an evening dress (and this is obligatory in many smart restaurants and night clubs in the large cities), she wears no hat and allows her friend to check her wrap. The boy should check his topcoat and hat at the entrance, or if the couple are dining informally, he may hang them on the nearest coat rack.

After the couple have scanned the menu, the young man gives his companion's order first and then his own. The *à la carte* dishes or those that may be ordered separately are printed on the left-hand side of the menu. The *table d'hôte* dishes or those that may be ordered at a set price for a dinner of four or five courses are printed on the right-hand side of the menu. A girl should be considerate of her friend's pocketbook and should not order too elaborate a meal, unless she is sure that he can afford it. Many a girl has not received a second invitation because she proved to be too expensive to entertain.

If two couples are dining together, one of the men will assume the responsibility of host and give all the orders. The seating arrangement is for the girls to face each other and for each man to sit at the left of the girl he is accompanying. If the party numbers more than four, the host or hostess indicates where each person is to sit. The men rise if someone stops at the table to greet someone in their party.

In first-class restaurants the host pays the waiter for the meal just after the bill has been presented, or if his party is very large, he may arrange with the proprietor to pay the bill afterward. In other restaurants one hands the bill to the cashier and pays him as one goes out. The customary tip left for the waiter is 10 per cent of the bill's amount.

When a couple are to attend a formal dance that is of a semipublic nature, the young man calls for the girl promptly at the hour stated, and she should not keep him waiting. Most girls appreciate a corsage, and the man should learn beforehand what color evening dress his companion will be wearing so that the flowers will blend nicely with it. If he is unable to find out, gardenias are always suitable. On arriving at the hall where the dance is held the couple greet the hostess and others in the receiving line, the girl going first and presenting her friend to those who may not know him. If the dance is given by a school society, for instance, the officers and faculty adviser may constitute the receiving line. Not until after the couple have passed down the receiving line does the girl remove her long gloves.

The young man always dances the first and last dances with his companion and generally asks her to reserve several other dances. He introduces to her any of his friends who may be present and endeavors to fill the rest of her dance program. He also escorts her to supper if special refreshments are served about midnight. If the girl's parents have asked that they return before the dance is over, say by one thirty, her escort makes sure that she is back by that time. Before leaving the couple must seek the hostess to thank her for a pleasant evening. The girl should apologize to any partners who have requested later dances on her program.

The following rules will aid you to improve your manners:

Don't call attention to yourself or to the group that you are with by laughing or talking too loudly.

Don't walk down the street four or more abreast and with arms linked.

Don't block traffic if you stop to chat with a friend on the street. Withdraw to one side or, better still, continue your conversation while you walk part of the way with your friend.

Don't stop to talk with anyone in a doorway; allow those who are coming out to do so before you enter.

Don't call to anyone in public unless it is an urgent matter.

Don't point and don't stare at another person, particularly a cripple or other unfortunate.

Don't discuss personal matters in public.

Don't walk along the street eating.

Don't replenish your make-up, comb your hair or clean your nails in public. If your morale needs to be improved by attention to these details, repair to a dressing room.

Don't read your neighbor's newspaper over his shoulder or surreptitiously from the side when you are riding on a streetcar, bus or subway train.

Don't indulge in any show of emotion in public, such as anger, embarrassment, unrestrained grief or hilarity. If you should be treated discourteously, don't descend to the churl's level with a crude retort.

Don't annoy others, especially in a theater or church, by whispering, giggling, fidgeting, rattling programs or returning for each act after the curtain has gone up. Moreover, don't attend if you have a cold, as continual coughing is annoying to the actors, the concert artist or the preacher and is disconcerting as well to the audience or congregation.

Don't litter the sidewalk or parkway. If you are reading a newspaper on the streetcar or subway train, don't leave the paper in your seat but carry it outside and deposit it in the nearest waste-disposal bin. When you are at the theater, don't toss your seat stubs carelessly aside in the lobby when you come out.

Excuse yourself if you brush against anyone on a crowded street or in a public vehicle.

When shopping await your turn and do not show impatience at any delay in being waited upon. Be courteous to the salesperson. Courtesy to all who serve us, whether public official or servants in the home, is a requisite of good manners. They are no less sensitive because their work calls for them to serve others.

Entertaining and Being Entertained.—A good host endeavors to invite those guests who will be congenial with one another. Instead of trusting to chance he plans every minute of the party so that there is never a lag in the conversation or games. He also tries to provide the kind of entertainment and refreshments that each of his guests will enjoy. At the outset he makes sure that all the guests are introduced to one another and generally suggests some game that will serve as an ice-breaker so as to make those who are shy or who are new in the group feel at ease. If there is dancing, the host should prevent stag and wallflower groups by insisting that every boy dance if he can. Many a boy is surprised at the latent possibilities of a shy girl, if she receives a little attention. The girl should try to overcome shyness and, if her dancing is a social handicap, she should take lessons to improve it.

The well-bred guest co-operates with the host to make the party a success. He arrives on time (except in the case of an informal tea when he may arrive any time during the hours stated). He shows enthusiasm about any form of entertainment that the host may suggest and instead of monopolizing any one person is attentive to all the guests. He is gay but never rowdy, for the person who tries to show off as the so-called life of the party generally turns out to be a bore to all the others. Making a double date for one evening should not be considered; it is discourteous to leave one party to go to another. Exceptions, of course, occur in holiday time.

When he takes his leave, each guest should find the guest of honor (or person in whose honor the party has been given) and express his pleasure in meeting him; also one should thank the host for a pleasant time. The host or hostess should shake hands with guests and respond with suitable sentiments of appreciation for their coming. If the guest is unable to pay a party call, he should send a gracious note expressing his enjoyment. A girl never pays a party call after she has been entertained with others at a party in a man's apartment.

When he is invited to spend a weekend or a longer period in a home, a guest should answer the invitation at once, and if he accepts, he should be explicit as to the time that he will arrive so that his friend may meet him. As a token of appreciation he should take a small gift for his hostess (generally the mother of the boy or girl he is visiting) and suitable gifts for small children in the family. He endeavors to fit into the family routine, offering to assist in the performance of certain home duties, and is even more careful about punctuality and neatness than he would be in his own home. He enjoys whatever entertainment is planned. If it is home movies or a visit to the nearby drive-in theater, when he himself prefers cards or conversation, he acquiesces.

The guest does not stay beyond the period for which he was invited unless he is especially urged to do so, for it is never wise to outstay one's welcome. As soon as he returns to his home, he writes a bread-and-butter letter expressing his thanks and appreciation. He is careful not to criticize his host or hostess or their friends either in their presence or to others, for one of the oldest rules of etiquette is loyalty to anyone whose hospitality one has accepted. The host and hostess also should be considerate in their attitude and comments and should not embarrass a guest in any way.

When he is invited to a luncheon or dinner, the well-bred guest answers the invitation promptly and arrives at least 10 minutes before the hour set. No hostess is expected to wait longer than 20 minutes for a tardy guest. The signal for all to repair to the dining room is when the maid or butler announces to the hostess: "Dinner [or luncheon] is served."

On entering the dining room women guests go first and the men guests follow. At a formal dinner, when the guests number more than eight, the hostess may indicate to each man who his dinner partner will be. The host takes in the woman guest of honor (the most important or the oldest woman), who is seated at his right. The man guest of honor (or *first gentleman* as he is called, if there is a woman guest of honor) serves as the hostess's dinner partner and is seated at her right. For such a formal dinner plain or gilt-edged place cards should be used. Otherwise the hostess may indicate where each person is to sit, congeniality being the determining point.

Each person stands behind his chair until the hostess is seated and then seats himself from the left side. It is customary for a man to arrange the chair of the woman at his right and

to push it forward as she seats herself. However, during the meal he is not supposed to confine his attentions entirely to her; he must talk occasionally to the woman at his left. Even if there has been some past unpleasantness between two guests, for the sake of the host and hostess they must appear to be good friends. At the end of the dinner the hostess rises, which is the signal for all to stand, and suggests that they repair to the television room, or to the living room for bridge or whatever diversion is planned.

At a more formal luncheon, generally at a hotel, and at a formal tea the women guests wear hats and remove their gloves only when they are served. In the case of a tea even the two friends of the hostess who pour tea at either end of the long table, do not remove their hats. Only the hostess and the girls who may assist her in passing the sandwiches and cakes are hatless.

Dinner dress is appropriate at a dinner in a home, especially if there is bridge, dancing or a musicale, or if the company is attending a play afterward. The issuance of formal rather than informal invitations generally indicates that the hostess expects her guests to dress formally. If her invitation comes over the telephone, she may indicate whether or not dinner jackets are in order, or the guest may ask if the dinner party is a dress affair.

An organization or society that is giving a formal dinner should have printed in the lower left-hand corner of the invitations, "Formal dress" or "Kindly wear dinner jackets," so that all the guests will be in formal attire. The women guests, of course, take their cue from this and appear in dinner or evening dress. At such a dinner the guests at the smaller tables start eating only after those at the speakers' table have begun.

The following important rules will guide you in proper table etiquette:

Eat your soup quietly and slowly, dipping the spoon forward or away from you. The spoon always remains in the soup plate when it is not in use.

Instead of buttering a whole slice of bread at one time, break it into small pieces and butter each piece (on the plate not in the hand) just before it is eaten.

Learn the acceptable way of eating spaghetti (wrapping it around the fork in Italian fashion), asparagus (eating the tips only), artichokes (pulling off one leaf at a time and dipping it in the sauce), celery and olives (eating them with the fingers rather than spearing them with a fork) and corn on the cob (holding the whole piece with the fingers).

Cultivate dexterity in handling the knife and fork. On finishing the meat or fish course lay them together on the right-hand side of your plate, the fork with the prongs uppermost and the knife on the outside.

At a formal dinner there are additional pieces of silverware that you should learn to identify. Among these are the oyster fork, fish knife and fork, canapé fork, dinner knife (steel blade), butter knife (which is laid across the bread plate when it is not

in use), salt spoon, salad fork, desert fork and spoon, coffee spoon, teaspoon and ice-tea spoon. Many households also have special breakfast silver, such as orange spoons.

When any dish is passed at the table, take the portion nearest you. This same rule applies to cake or cookies.

Don't take too large mouthfuls.

Don't chew with your mouth open.

Don't talk or drink with food in your mouth.

Don't pick your teeth.

Don't put hands, arms or elbows on the table except occasionally between courses.

Don't find fault with the food; if you are unable to eat any dish, leave it untouched without comment.

Don't continue eating after others at the table have stopped.

Don't push back your plate when you have finished or pile your dishes together.

Know how to use a finger bowl—first dip the fingers of the right hand and then the left and wipe them on the napkin.

Leave your napkin unfolded but laid carefully on the left side of the dessert plate. If you are staying several days in a household and receive a napkin ring, fold your napkin and insert it in the ring.

To Make Introductions Properly and Converse Easily.—A man is introduced to a woman. One may say in presenting him, "Miss Martin, may I introduce Mr. Collins?" The only men to whom a woman is presented are the President of the United States, a member of royalty, a foreign ambassador or a clergyman. In the case of a Roman Catholic cardinal or other dignitary such a form as "Your Eminence" is used. A Catholic priest is called "Father," but any Protestant clergyman, unless he holds a title or degree, such as bishop, dean, canon, Doctor of Divinity or Doctor of Theology, is addressed as "Mister." A doctor (physician, surgeon or dentist) and a judge are addressed by their titles, but in social life a woman who holds a Ph.D. or other academic degree is not addressed as "Doctor."

If the more abbreviated form of introduction is used, such as "Miss White, Mr. Black," emphasis is on the more important person's name. Moreover, one inquires of the man if he has met the woman but not of the woman if she has met the man. If the introduction occurs on the street, the woman bows, and the man raises his hat in acknowledgment.

Young women and girls are introduced to those who are older, as "Mrs. Smith, this is Helen Jones" or "Mrs. Smith, Miss Jones." Other permissible forms are: "This is my sister Ruth, Mrs. Smith" or in the case of a young married sister, "Mrs. Smith, my sister, Mrs. Johnson."

When a man or woman is introduced to several other persons, the usual form is to mention first the person's name and then the names of the persons to whom he or she is being introduced, as "Mrs. Robinson, Miss Jackson, Miss Roberts and Mr. Wilson."

Your friends, both boys and girls, are introduced to your parents with such phrases as "Mother, these are my friend Jimmy Reeves and his brother Joe"; or "Father, you know Frank Short, don't you?" If the introduction occurs in your home, you are careful to include the other members of the family in presenting your friends. You also use the full name, if you are introducing them to intimate friends and feel that they would be congenial, as "Mary West, Bertha Dickinson."

Generally each person who is introduced responds with "How do you do?" A cordial touch, however, is to add the name of the person, looking him squarely in the eyes and with a friendly smile. If you should not catch the name, do not immediately ask "What is the name?" Wait until you have an opportunity to inquire privately of the person who made the introduction and then take care to use the name the next time that you see your new acquaintance. However, if your own name is mispronounced, it is permissible to say: "I am sorry but you misunderstood my name. It is Clapp, not Platt."

Boys and men should shake hands when they are introduced to other boys or men. The younger one, though, waits for the older one to extend his hand. Boys and men also rise for introductions. Girls should rise when they are introduced to a woman or to a distinguished man; they remain standing until that person decides to be seated. If the introductions are made at a dinner table, it is not necessary to rise. A hostess rises to receive all introductions, to greet her guests and to say good-by to those who have to leave early.

Self-introductions may be made at, say, an alumni dinner, as it seems rude not to talk to your neighbors. It is also proper to approach without introduction and speak to anyone in such an intimate gathering as a tea at a friend's house.

The host or hostess or the sponsor making an introduction tries to find some topic of conversation that will be of interest to those who have been introduced. This, of course, should not be carried too far, but often an embarrassing pause after the "How-do-you-dos" may be saved by adding: "Mr. Minor has just returned from Florida," or "Miss Nolan is planning a trip to England this summer." On taking their leave the two acquaintances, if they have found each other congenial, may express their pleasure. One may say: "I am very glad to have met you," or "I trust that we shall meet again," and the other replies: "Thank you," or "I hope so, too."

The following are some rules of conversation that will make you more agreeable to others:

Take care not to monopolize the conversation. Don't interrupt when others, especially your elders, are speaking, and don't contradict them, argue with them or point out their mistakes. Be attentive so as not to ask them to repeat what they have said.

Don't indulge in unkind gossip or criticism. Try to discuss general topics, and be tactful in your remarks; avoid any subject that may later prove embarrassing—religion, politics and personalities are topics to avoid.

Try to avoid all nervous mannerisms, such as twisting your beads or tie or patting your elbow, and don't indulge in nudging, poking or slapping on the back the person with whom you are talking. Don't yawn if you find the conversation boring, and don't hum or whistle in the presence of others.

Learn to be a good listener. The person who manifests sincere interest in the pursuits of others is ever popular socially.

On joining a group first listen to their conversation, so as not to interrupt with some irrelevant remark. If the group is gathered about the outdoor barbecue, and the best way of broiling a steak is under discussion, keep to the subject in hand.

On Obtaining and Keeping a Position.— The fundamental qualifications of a good employee are good health, intelligence, technical excellence, honesty, sincerity, punctuality and a well-modulated voice; but today the applicant for a position must have more than these to offer. Many personnel managers consider that a carefully groomed appearance counts from 50 to 75 per cent in obtaining a position, and even after one is hired this standard must be maintained. The other important factors are loyalty, a pleasing personality, an understanding of human nature, the ability to get along with others, flexibility in adapting oneself to varied employment, good background, self-confidence and a sense of humor.

Your appearance is your front to the world, and you should try to look your best when you are making interviews. Cleanliness comes first. Start with a morning bath, and wear fresh underclothes. If you are a girl, be sure that you do not apply too much make-up (especially lipstick) and that your nails are clean. A tailored suit is always best for an interview. Later when you get the position you may wear spectator sports dresses that are semifeminine. Don't wear loud or unsuitable colors, gaudy jewelry or high-heeled shoes, and don't arrange your hair in a style that would be more suited to a ballroom than a business office. Be particular also about the use of a deodorant and a mouth wash, and save your perfume for use on social occasions. If you are a young man, you will shave carefully each morning, and you will be painstaking about such details as having your shoes well polished, socks that do not wrinkle or dangle, a spotless shirt and collar, buttons well sewed on, a suit free from spots, well-creased trousers, a tie that harmonizes with your shirt and socks and neatly combed hair.

If you are sent out on an interview by an employment agency, it is sufficient to present to the reception clerk the card of introduction that the agency gives you. If a friend or acquaintance is recommending you, he should send a letter of introduction in advance or should give you his card with some such notation as: "To Mr. Howard Pierce, Introducing Miss Cora Landon."

When you are admitted to your prospective employer's presence, remain standing until he asks you to be seated and then state your business briefly. Try to make as good an impression as possible with intelligent replies to the questions that he may ask about your dictation or typewriting speed and your educational qualifications. Watch your posture. Walk gracefully across the room and when you are seated, don't slouch or sprawl in your chair and, if you are a girl, don't cross your legs. Avoid discussing details of a personal nature or showing overanxiety about getting the position. On the other hand, don't show resentment at any personal questions the prospective employer may ask, such as the condition of your health and whether or not you live at home or are engaged to be married. If when you leave the interviewer says that there is no opening just at present but that he will keep your application in mind, don't show disappointment but try to be as friendly as when you entered. If he asks you to send him a letter stating your qualifications, do so within the next few days and express the hope that you will be remembered when there is an opening.

After you obtain the position, don't be disappointed if it is not so important a position as you had hoped it would be and if the salary does not come up to your expectations. Be glad to get the experience that may lead to a better and more remunerative opportunity later. A girl especially must realize that in the business world she will not receive as courteous treatment as she does socially.

The following rules of business etiquette should be observed daily:

Be punctual in the morning, take only your allotted time for lunch and do not be too eager to leave exactly at closing time.

Greet each person with whom you are closely associated with a friendly "Good morning" and "Good night."

If you are a young man, always remove your hat and always rise when you are addressed by your superior.

Don't chew gum when you are on duty, whether at a desk in an office or on the floor of a store.

Don't smoke unless you first find out that smoking is permitted.

Don't indulge in too much shop talk either with your friends or your business associates, and be careful not to reveal anything that is of a confidential nature.

Don't abuse the privilege of sick and emergency leave.

Don't use the firm's stationery and stamps for your personal mail.

Don't make too frequent use of the office telephone for personal calls, and don't allow your friends to call you too often.

Don't resent criticism and don't sulk if you are reprimanded.

Don't loiter in the dressing room when you must comb your hair, clean your nails or otherwise repair the ravages of the day.

Don't visit with your associates on office time. Save the description of your week-end until you go out to lunch with them.

Be willing to do your share, even though the job that you are asked to help out on is not your regular work.

Be loyal to the firm. Don't broadcast your notions about the inefficient way the business is run; and take extra care to do your own work so well that none of the inefficiency may be traced to you.

Remember that a business connection has no social significance; so take care, if you should see your employer and his wife dining at the Rainbow Room, not to intrude.

The Etiquette of Travel.—Travel has long been recognized as one of the finest educational means. Now that it is being made available to all by reduced or special train and bus fares in the United States and by European second- and third-class study tours it is essential that one know the accepted rules of conduct while traveling.

Whether one travels in a trailer or stays overnight in a motel, the same rules of good conduct prevail as when travelling by plane or stopping at the most expensive hotel. Courtesy smooths the way under all conditions.

The first thing to remember is that travel will bring you into contact many times with people whose ways of doing things are different from those to which you are accustomed. Unless you are able to overlook certain inconveniences, you will be continually disgruntled and unable to enjoy the things that you have gone to see.

When abroad, keep in mind that comparisons are always odious. Many a friendship has been nipped in the bud by the unthinking sentence: "We do it so much better at home." Sharp contrasts there are. It is often not easy to understand the reasons for differences in approach to similar problems; but each traveler should remember that he left home to broaden his knowledge and to enjoy himself, not to reform others. A few words of praise make each traveler a goodwill ambassador.

The nature of your trip will determine the kind and amount of clothing that you take; the well-bred person does not overdress. You may be off for a week at camp or the seashore, when you will want to relax in slacks or a play suit. When you attend a house party, more elaborate clothes will be required for teas and dances. When you travel through Europe, you will need suitable clothes for various occasions. Don't take too many clothes; two evening dresses will serve your purpose as well as six when you are on shipboard. At the country club or camp a young man can wear flannel trousers or slacks with his suit coat and look suitably dressed. Far too many trips are spoiled by taking along too much luggage at the start. Nice looking luggage is essential, and a collection of untidy lunch boxes and bundles should be avoided. The tips to porters and bellboys mount with extra luggage. Luggage on an airplane, of course, is strictly limited.

Air travel has now become as commonplace as travel by train, steamship or bus. The quickness of the plane trip eliminates certain details of other travel, and a more friendly spirit prevails in the air than among earthbound passengers. Conversation with a fellow passenger is regarded as a matter of courtesy, especially if one happens to be making his first flight. In general, however, the same etiquette applies to the airline as to other modes of travel.

As space is limited on a plane, reservations should be made early; but if cancellation is necessary, the money is refunded. Meals are served by the stewardess or steward, who is not tipped. Tipping is sternly prohibited by airline regulations.

The powder room on the plane corresponds to the dressing room on the train, and here as on the train, neatness is the chief requisite. As each woman takes her turn, she takes as little time as possible, and leaves the washstand and dressing table in perfect order.

When you are taking a long train journey, you will doubtless travel in a Pullman car. The person who occupies the lower berth has the privilege of riding face forward or facing the engine. If you are that person, remember it is courteous to offer to exchange your seat once in a while with the person who is riding backward or to invite him to sit beside you. When you are dressing in the morning you can help to relieve the congestion in the dressing room by putting on most of your clothes in your berth. When you are traveling, always carry your money and valuables in a belt or chamois pocket on your person, and don't leave them in your pocketbook under your pillow.

In the dining car courtesy requires that you greet your table companion or companions; but "Good morning" or "Good evening" is sufficient without further attempts at conversation. If a woman is traveling with a man, he should offer to take the seat nearer the engine so that he will ride backward.

Since traveling on a boat is like being on a floating hotel, you will be seeing the same people at each meal and on either side of your deck chair, and it is quite proper to introduce yourself and enter into conversation with them. If you have to share your stateroom with others, be careful not to encroach on the space that properly belongs to them; and if you return to your stateroom late at night after dancing, be quiet; don't disturb your cabin mates and those in the adjoining staterooms. When you are on deck, don't appropriate a deck chair that belongs to someone else; you are supposed to pay for and use your own.

On the last day of the voyage, distribute tips amounting to about 10 per cent of the passage money. If you have been a poor sailor and have had to have most of your meals in your room, the largest amounts go to the cabin steward and stewardess. Otherwise you remember the table, deck, bath and lounge stewards and others who have served you.

When you register at a hotel, sign your name and address. The proper form is "Lewis Clapp, New York, N. Y." or "Miss Ruth Johnson, Brooklyn, N. Y."; if a girl is staying at a girls' club, she drops the "Miss." A married woman signs herself "Mrs. Francis G. Short, Palo Alto, Calif." and a professional man, such as a doctor or dentist, writes "Dr. Eugene Baker, Ithaca, N. Y." When an entire family stays at a hotel, each child is registered separately. The parents' names come first and then the names of each girl and boy according to age, with "Miss" prefixed to the name of each girl over five, as follows:

Mr. and Mrs. James F. Reeves, Baldwinsville, N. Y.
Miss Mary Reeves
James F. Reeves, Jr.
Joseph Alan Reeves

While you are at a hotel, be sure that your door is kept locked, whether or not you are in your room. Leave the key at the desk every time that you go out of the hotel, and keep the room clerk and the telephone operator informed of your plans if you are expecting acquaintances to call. The dining-room waiter, the maid, bellboy and porter are tipped for any services.

In a first-class hotel you settle your bill on checking out. American-plan hotels have a rate by the day or week for room and three meals daily; European-plan hotels charge only for the room; the guest pays the waiter or dining-room cashier for the meals that he takes at the hotel. Many hotels require that one vacate the room by noon, if one has taken it for only one night. Otherwise notice should be given immediately after breakfast that one is planning to stay another day or several days.

The well-bred man removes his hat and does not smoke when he is riding in the elevator of a hotel or an apartment house.

When you call on a friend at a hotel, ask for him at the desk or telephone to his room from the lobby. Never walk in unexpectedly, no matter how well you may know him or the hotel attendants may know you. A young woman should receive men friends in the public rooms adjoining the lobby.

Funeral Formalities.—When you learn of the death of a friend or of some near relative of a friend, courtesy requires that you leave your card at the house and offer your sympathy to the next of kin. On the card that you send with flowers you should write, "With deepest sympathy" or "With heartfelt sympathy." Address the flowers to the member of the family you know best. They should be acknowledged with a personal word on a visiting card, if the recipient feels unable to write a note. A call of condolence is seldom returned. In the case of the death of an acquaintance send a card of sympathy by mail; if you knew the person sufficiently well, write a letter of condolence to his or her parents, brother or sister.

If the notice in the newspaper reads "Funeral Private," do not attend unless you are invited. It is quite proper to go if you are an intimate friend of either the deceased or of the family. Don't wear black unless you sit with the family but dress as inconspicuously as possible in something dark. If you are merely an acquaintance, you should sit near the back of the church or room in which the funeral service is held. Only intimate friends are invited to ride to the cemetery. If you are a young man and are asked to be a pallbearer at the funeral of a friend or the relative of a friend, only grave illness can excuse you from serving.

It is permissible to invite a friend who is in mourning to a concert a month or so after a funeral, but for at least 6 months one in mourning does not attend parties or gay affairs.

The Engagement.—As soon as a young man and a girl have decided that they will marry, the man should go to the girl's father or her guardian and ask consent. After he has announced that the girl has accepted his proposal of marriage, the young man should give a satisfactory explanation of his financial standing and prospects. He should postpone marriage until he can support a wife unless his own or the girl's father is willing to help the young couple to get a start.

The mother and sisters of the young man (or both parents) should call on the bride-to-be and her parents immediately after the girl's father or guardian has given his consent. If the bridegroom-elect is an orphan, his nearest relatives, such as an uncle and aunt, should go in the parents' place. If these relatives live at too great a distance, the welcome into their family may be extended by mail. The bride-elect and her mother return the call or send an appropriate letter acknowledging this courtesy. The call may be followed by dinners at which the two immediate families entertain each other.

If there has been a recent death in either immediate family, the engagement is announced quietly by telling only relatives and intimate friends. Otherwise a public announcement is made by the parents of the bride-to-be in the newspapers, and notes announcing the betrothal are sent to intimate friends. If a dinner or other kind of party is given to announce the engagement, the announcement may be made by the girl herself or by her mother as they introduce the fiancé who stands with them in the receiving line; or when the dessert course is reached during the dinner, the father of the bride-to-be may propose a toast to the betrothed pair, and a suitable reply is made by the young man.

The announcement of the engagement is followed by various parties and showers. The parents of the young man may give a dance or party so that their friends may meet their daughter-to-be. The girl's friends will invite those girls and women who know her very well to showers of various kinds—kitchen, linen and so forth. As to the selection of the engagement ring, the symbol since Roman times of betrothal, the young man should consult the taste of his fiancée whether she prefers the conventional solitaire diamond or some other stone. Superstition has built around certain jewels a romantic sentiment, such as "depth of true blue" for the sapphire and "warmth and ardor" for the ruby.

The Formal Wedding.—If a church wedding is decided on, the bride's parents must attend to such details as whether the date chosen is convenient for the clergyman who is to perform the ceremony and for the caterer. Weddings are never held in a Roman Catholic or Protestant Episcopal church on Sundays, Fridays or days in Lent, and among other denominations Sunday weddings are rarely solemnized in church.

The order for the wedding invitations is placed by the girl's parents about a month before the ceremony. One should be careful to invite only as many guests as the church will hold. The same holds true for the invitations to the wedding breakfast or other reception that may be held after the ceremony. A good safeguard is to use "R.S.V.P." (*Répondez, s'il vous plaît,* French for please reply) on the invitation to the reception, so that one can tell the caterer the exact number of guests who are expected.

Both the bride's mother and the bridegroom's mother decide whose names will be included among those who are invited only to the church and those who are invited to both the ceremony and the reception. Invitations are sent to intimate friends even hundred of miles away, as they not only carry news of the marriage but are a token of the esteem in which the friend is held. If the ceremony is a private one, announcements are sent afterward to persons on the visiting lists of both families and special friends of both the bride and bridegroom.

The wedding reception is held at the home of the bride's parents, grandparents or other close relatives, or it may be held in a hotel banquet room rented especially for the occasion. Only if the bride were an orphan would it be permissible to hold the reception at the home of the bridegroom's parents. The bride's trousseau must be provided by her family or herself.

The invitations, which the bride has addressed, aided perhaps by her mother and some of her friends, are mailed from 2 to 3 weeks before the wedding. Those who are invited to both the church and the reception, if they plan to attend, should send a wedding gift. This gift is sent direct by the store at which it was purchased and is addressed to the bride; with it is enclosed the donor's calling card. In the case of an informal wedding, it is permissible to use a wedding-gift card and to send a more personal gift to the bridegroom as well as to the bride.

The sooner the gifts are sent the better, because the bride will then have an opportunity to acknowledge them all before the wedding. Should she receive many gifts, she will find it wise to keep a list and to check off each entry as she writes her thank-you notes. If the gift is sent by a married couple, she uses the wife's name in her salutation and says: "Thank you for the exquisite present you and Dr. Blank sent me." In arranging the presents for the guests to see at the time of the reception it is customary to group together similar articles, such as all the silver on one table and all the china or glass on another.

At a formal wedding the bridesmaids are dressed alike, only their dresses or hats differing sometimes in color. The dress and hat of the maid or matron of honor may show more individuality, provided that they blend in coloring, material and general style with the dresses and hats worn by the bridesmaids. Only at an evening wedding are hats omitted. The flower girl is generally dressed in a period costume.

The bridesmaids carry their bouquets as if they were sheaves, holding them stem downward on the outer arm as they take their places in the procession. The bride furnishes her attendants with their bouquets, but they must furnish their own gowns, although the style and material and color are chosen by the bride. The bride shows her gratitude by presenting to each attendant some gift, such as a bracelet or other piece of jewelry, at the bridesmaids' luncheon or tea that is held a day or two before the wedding. The bridegroom likewise presents to his attendants some personal gift, such as cuff links or cigarette cases.

The bride's favorite sister is her maid or matron of honor, and her other sisters and one of the bridegroom's sisters serve as bridesmaids. If she has no sisters, she chooses for this honor the bridegroom's sisters and her most intimate friends. At an average wedding there are four to six bridesmaids. A bride may dispense with bridesmaids, if she wishes, but she retains the maid of honor to arrange her train and hold her bouquet.

The brother of the bridegroom usually serves as best man. If he has no brother, he may select the brother of the bride or his most intimate friend. His attendants are called *ushers* and are usually the same in number as the bridesmaids—from four to six. One of these should be a brother or cousin of the bride. The ushers wear light-gray gloves at a daytime wedding and white ones at an evening wedding. The bridegroom and best man wear white buckskin gloves. Cutaway coats, gray-striped trousers, high silk hats, black socks, gray ties, wing collars and white boutonnières constitute the traditional garb for bridegroom, best man and attendants at a formal daytime wedding. At a more informal wedding dark sack suits with white waistcoats and dark trousers may take the place of the morning suits. There still prevails the custom of the bridegroom giving a bachelor dinner two nights before the wedding day, at which his men friends drink the health of the bride and break the stems of their wineglasses.

For a formal wedding it is generally best to hold a rehearsal the day before. Everyone participates but the bride, for whom a substitute serves because it is considered bad luck for the bride to take part. The attendants have to be drilled in the pace decided on for the wedding march. The ushers who go first are followed by the bridesmaids, maid or matron of honor, flower girl and the substitute bride with the bride's father. The two shortest ushers lead the procession, and the two shortest bridesmaids are chosen to head the bridesmaids' section. Each pair in the procession counts a measure or four beats of time before following the pair in front of them. The bride and her father, though, must remember to count eight beats of time before starting up the aisle.

On reaching the chancel steps the ushers divide and assume positions on the steps or in front of the choir stalls that generally face each other. The bridesmaids, on reaching the chancel, also divide and take their positions on the inner side beside the ushers. The maid or matron of honor continues to the foot of the altar steps, where she stands on the left side opposite the best man. When the bride and her father reach the altar steps, the bridegroom, who has entered the chancel from the vestry with the clergyman and the best man at the first strains of the wedding march, steps forward and stands at the bride's right. The bride then takes the left arm of the bridegroom, and they ascend the steps of the altar, followed by the maid of honor and the best man.

At the proper moment in the ceremony the best man hands to the bridegroom the ring, which after the couple have pledged their troth is put upon the third finger of the bride's left hand. If the bride is wearing gloves, she slips off her left glove (or the hand of the left glove if she is wearing long gloves), when she gives her bouquet to the maid or matron of honor. To avoid any possible embarrassment at the actual wedding the best man should obtain from the jeweler a duplicate ring, which may be returned the day after the ceremony. Among his other duties on the wedding day is presenting the clergyman with his fee. He also acts as valet, travel and hotel agent and even expressman for the bridegroom.

Details for the Wedding Day.—About two hours before the hour scheduled for the ceremony, the bridesmaids, maid of honor and flower girl all meet at the bride's house, where they receive their bouquets. The automobile carrying the bride's mother leaves the house first, then the cars taking the maid of honor, bridesmaids and flower girl and last in the procession comes the automobile in which ride the bride and her father. This car waits in front of the church awning until the bride returns on the arm of her husband. The bridegroom and the best man arrive at the church at least 15 minutes before the hour scheduled and wait in the minister's study until word is received that the bride and her father have arrived. Just before entering the chancel the bridegroom removes his right glove and throughout the ceremony holds it in his left hand; or he may remove his gloves altogether and leave them in the study.

The women guests at a daytime wedding and at an evening wedding in an Episcopal church always wear hats; at a formal wedding the men generally wear high silk hats. The usher offers his left arm to a woman guest when he escorts her to her seat. The man who has accompanied her walks behind them. If the man has come alone, the usher walks beside him on the right. At a large wedding the usher may escort only the oldest woman (generally the mother). The younger women and girls follow according to age, and the same order of precedence is observed by the men and boys in the party, unless the father prefers to come last.

The head usher escorts the bride's mother to her pew on the left side of the church (facing the chancel) just before the wedding procession starts. The bridegroom's mother and father are seated with other relatives on the right side of the church, an usher escorting the mother to the section reserved for the bridegroom's relatives just before the bride's mother enters. No guest is seated in the main part of the church while the bride's mother is being escorted to her pew or after she is seated. After the bride's father has signified by placing her hand in the hand of the clergyman that he "giveth this woman to be married to this man," he descends the chancel steps and takes his place next to his wife in the pew reserved for them. If the bride has no near relative to give her away, her mother may answer the clergyman's query with "I do"; but in such a case the mother does not escort the bride; she walks alone in the wedding procession.

When the strains of the recessional sound, the maid of honor hands to the bride her bouquet, lifts her front veil if she has chosen to wear one over her face and arranges her train. The procession leaves in reversed order. The bride takes the bridegroom's right arm, and the couple are followed by the flower girl, maid or matron of honor, bridesmaids and ushers (or each bridesmaid may leave the church on the right arm of the usher who stood beside her during the ceremony). The best man, however, returns to the clergyman's study to collect the bridegroom's hat, gloves, stick and other belongings and hand them to the bridegroom before he and the bride step into the waiting vehicle. After the couple and the bride's attendants have driven away, the ushers escort to the door in the order of precedence the bride's mother, the bridegroom's mother and then the other women relatives. When they remove the white ribbons that mark off the sections reserved for special guests of the bride and bridegroom, the entire congregation leaves.

At the wedding reception the bride stands at the bridegroom's right; behind them is generally an elaborate setting of palms and flowering plants. The bridegroom's parents and the bride's parents stand in the receiving line nearest the door. On the other side of the couple are the maid or matron of honor, flower girl and bridesmaids. At a small wedding the ushers may present the guests to the bride and bridegroom. At a larger one a butler who stands at the door announces the name of each guest. What one says to the bridal couple depends on how well one knows them. The bride is wished every happiness, and the bridegroom receives congratulations. The bride presents her friends to her husband if they are unacquainted; and the bridegroom asks those guests who are his friends if they are acquainted with his wife.

On the bride's table in the dining room stands the wedding cake that the bride cuts, sharing the first piece with the bridegroom. In this cake are often hidden favors for the bridal attendants, such as a gold ring for the first to be married, a wishbone for good luck and so forth. At a large wedding, though, it is customary to present to each guest, on leaving, a small white box containing a piece of the wedding cake.

When the bride goes upstairs to change to her traveling clothes, the bridesmaids gather at the foot of the stairs so as to catch her bouquet, which she tosses to them when she has nearly reached the top, repeating the rhyme:

> Hail, there, pretty maidens,
> Standing all-arow!
> The one who catches this,
> The next bouquet shall throw.

The bridegroom also goes to the room reserved for him to change into the street clothes that the best man has left. When the couple are ready to leave, they descend the stairs together. Generally on the veranda the guests greet them with a shower of confetti, as they dash for the waiting car.

In the case of a home wedding there may be an improvised altar, and the procession may advance through an aisle marked off by white ribbons. The bride's mother receives the guests as they arrive. When she takes her place in the section reserved for relatives of the bride, it is the signal for the procession to start. It is very pretty if the wedding party descends a staircase, the ushers first, followed by the bridesmaids, maid or matron of honor, flower girl and the bride and her father. The clergyman and the bridegroom and best man, who have been waiting in an adjoining room, take their places as soon as the first strains of the wedding march are heard. After the ceremony, there is no recessional. The bride and bridegroom are first congratulated by the clergyman, who then retires. They receive their other guests where they stand.

If a bride chooses to be married in her traveling costume either at a church or her home, she dispenses with all attendants but a maid or matron of honor who is similarly garbed. The bridegroom is attended by only his best man.

In addition to paying the clergyman's fee and giving the ushers and best man their boutonnières and suitable gifts the bridegroom buys the bride's bouquet and ring. He is also responsible for furnishing the new home. All that the bride brings to it are her linen and silver, unless she has inherited some cherished pieces of antique furniture.

FORMS OF ADDRESS — RELIGIOUS, CIVIL AND MILITARY TITLES

Time-honored forms used in addressing notable people should always be observed; the schedule shows accepted usage.

PERSONAGE	LETTER SHOULD BE ADDRESSED	COMPLIMENTARY SALUTATION IN LETTER
Alderman (In the United States and Canada)	Alderman John Brown.	Dear Sir:
Ambassador	His Excellency, —— ——, Ambassador of Chile at ——; or To his Excellency, the Chinese Ambassador at ——; or To his Excellency, the Ambassador of the French Republic at ——. The words *His Excellency* may precede the personal name or hereditary or professional title. (*His Excellency* is usually abbreviated to *H. E.*).	Sir: or (with the personal title) My Lord: or Your Excellency:
Ambassador and his wife	Their Excellencies, the Ambassador of Peru and Madame ——; or Their Excellencies, the Chinese Ambassador and Madame ——. (*Their Excellencies* is usually abbreviated to *T. E.*)	Your Excellencies:)
Army Officers (In the United States)	The Commander in Chief, Army of the United States; or Major —— ——, U. S. A.	Sir: or (informal) My Dear Colonel Blank: or Dear Commander Blank: but, for officers below the rank of captain, Dear Mr. Blank:
Assemblyman	Assemblyman ——; or The Honorable —— ——, Member of Assembly.	Sir: Dear Sir: or My Dear Mr. Blank:
Assistant Secretary (Assistant to a Cabinet Officer)	The Assistant Secretary of the —— Department; or The Honorable —— ——; Assistant Secretary of ——.	Sir: or Dear Sir: or Dear Mr. Blank: (never Mr. Secretary).
Associate Justices	Honorable —— ——, Justice, Supreme Court of the United States; or The Honorable —— ——, Associate Justice of the Supreme Court; or Mr. Justice ——.	Mr. Justice: or, Sir: or My Dear Mr. Justice: or Your Honor:
Cabinet Officers (United States)	The Honorable the Secretary of War (or Labor, Commerce, etc.). The Honorable the Secretary of the Treasury. The Honorable the Postmaster General; or The Honorable —— ——, Secretary of Agriculture; or The Attorney General; The Secretary of State.	Sir: or Dear Sir: or My dear Mr. Secretary: or My dear Mr. Attorney General:
Cardinal	His Eminence Cardinal Blank; or His Eminence Paul, Cardinal Blank.	My Lord Cardinal: or Your Eminence:
Chief Justice of the Supreme Court of Canada	The Right Honourable Blank, P.C., Chief Justice of Canada.	Sir:
Chief Justice of the United States	The Chief Justice of the United States; or The Chief Justice of the Supreme Court; or The Honorable —— ——, Chief Justice of the Supreme Court of the United States; or (in social correspondence) Mr. Justice Blank; or (if to the Chief Justice and his wife) The Chief Justice and Mrs. Blank.	Mr. Chief Justice: or Sir: or (in social correspondence) My dear Mr. Chief Justice:
Congressman	The Honorable Henry F. Brown, House of Representatives, Washington, D. C.; or The Honorable William P. Brown, Representative in Congress, Albany, N. Y.	Sir: or Dear Sir: or My dear Mr. Brown:
Consul	To the American Consul at ——; or Mr. John Brown, United States Consul at ——; or John Brown, Esq., American Consul at ——.	Dear Sir:
Governor	The Honorable the Governor of ——; or The Hon. Henry Brown, Governor of ——; or (in Mass. and by courtesy in some other States) His Excellency, the Governor of ——; or His Excellency Henry Brown.	Sir: or Dear Sir: (see also *Lieutenant Governor*).
Governor-General of Canada	His Excellency, The Governor-General (official); His Excellency ——, The Governor-General (personal); or (if a royal duke) His Royal Highness, The Governor-General.	Sir: or My Lord: (according to rank).
Governor-General's wife (India and British Dominions)	Her Excellency —— ——.	Madame:
Judge (in Canada)	The Honorable Mr. Justice —— (if of a superior court or of the circuit court of Montreal); or His Honour Judge —— (if of a county court, court of sessions or district magistrates' court).	Sir:
Judge (in the United States)	The Honorable John Brown, United States District Judge (or Chief Judge of the Court of Appeals, etc.).	Dear Sir: or My Dear Judge Brown:
Lawyer	Mr. John Brown, Attorney at Law; or John Brown, Esq. (The form *Mr. John Brown, Esq.* is incorrect.)	Dear Sir: My Dear Mr. Brown:
Lieutenant Governor	The Honorable ——, Lieutenant Governor of —— (in a state of the U. S. A. and in South Africa); His Honour The Lieutenant Governor of —— (in other British dominions and colonies; if a title of nobility is held, it should be used first).	Sir: or Dear Sir:
Mayor (in Canadian cities and towns, and in English boroughs)	His worship, The Mayor of ——.	Sir: or Dear Sir:
Mayor (in English cities)	The Right Worshipful the Mayor of ——. (In London, York, etc., The Right Honourable the Lord Mayor of ——.)	Sir:
Mayor (in the United States)	The Honorable John Brown, Mayor of the City of ——; or The Mayor of the City of ——.	Sir: or Dear Sir: or My Dear Mr. Mayor: or (informal) Dear Mayor Brown:
Member of Parliament (or of a Provincial Legislative Council or of a Provincial Legislature, etc.).	To the usual form of address add M.P. (or M.L.C., or M.P.P., or M.L.A., etc.).	Sir:
Minister (Diplomatic)	The Honorable —— ——, Minister of Iran; or His Excellency The Right Honorable —— ——, Minister of ——.	Sir: or (with personal title) My Lord: Your Grace: or My dear Mr. Minister:
Naval Officers	The Admiral of the Navy of the United States; or Admiral ——, Commanding United States Navy; Captain John Brown, U.S.N.	Sir: or (informal) My dear Admiral Blank: Dear Captain Brown; but for officers below the rank of captain, Dear Mr. Brown:
Pope	To His Holiness Pope Pius.	Most Holy Father: or Your Holiness:
Premier of a Province of Canada	The Honourable ——, Premier of the Province of ——.	Sir:
President of a College or University	John Henry Brown, L.L.D. (or use the initials of his highest degree), President of —— University (or President, —— University); or President —— ——.	Dear Sir: or Dear President Brown:
President of the Senate of the United States	The Honorable, The President of the Senate of the United States; or The Honorable John Brown, President of the Senate.	Sir:

Forms of Address—Concluded

PERSONAGE	LETTER SHOULD BE ADDRESSED	COMPLIMENTARY SALUTATION IN LETTER
President of the United States	The President, The White House; *or* The President of the United States, The White House; *or* His Excellency, The President of the United States.	The President: My Dear Mr. President: *or* Mr. President:
Prime Minister of Canada	The Right Honourable ——, P.C., Prime Minister of Canada.	Sir:
Professor in a College *or* University	Professor John Brown; *or* John Brown, Ph.D. (or L.L.D., M.D., etc., using only the initials of his highest degree, if the degrees are in the same field), Professor of ——. (The title *professor* should not be assigned to teachers who have not attained professorial rank.)	Dear Sir: *or* My dear Professor Brown: *or* Dear Professor Brown: *or* My dear Professor:
Senator (in Canada)	The Honourable Senator ——.	Dear Sir: Dear Senator ——:
Senator (in the United States)	Senator Brown (unless there are two Senators Brown, in which case the first name or initial is added); *or* The Honorable Henry C. Brown, United States Senate, Washington, D. C.; *or* The Honorable James C. Jones, United States Senator, Harrisburg, Pa.	Sir: Dear Sir: My dear Mr. Senator: *or* My dear Senator: *or* My dear Senator ——: *or* Dear Senator:
Speaker of the House of Commons (Canada)	The Honourable ——, The Speaker of the House of Commons.	Dear Mr. Speaker:
Speaker of the House of Representatives of the United States	The Honorable The Speaker of the House of Representatives; *or* The Honorable Henry C. Brown, Speaker of the House of Representatives; *or* To the Speaker of the House of Representatives; *or* The Speaker.	Sir: *or* Mr. Speaker: *or* My dear Mr. Speaker:
Speaker of the Senate (in Canada)	The Honourable Senator ——, The Speaker of the Senate.	Dear Mr. Speaker:
Vice-President	The Vice-President; *or* The Honorable, The Vice-President of the United States; *or* The Honorable —— ——, Vice-President of the United States.	Mr. Vice-President: *or* Sir: *or* My dear Mr. Vice-President:

Titles of Nobility

PERSONAGE	LETTER SHOULD BE ADDRESSED	COMPLIMENTARY SALUTATION IN LETTER
Baron	The Right Honourable The Lord ——; *or* The Lord ——.	My Lord:
Baroness	To the Right Honourable the Baroness ——; *or* Right Honourable the Lady ——; *or* The Lady ——.	Madam:
Countess	To the Right Honourable The Countess of ——; *or* The Countess ——.	Madam:
Duchess	To her Grace, the Duchess of ——; *or* The Most Noble the Duchess of ——.	Madam: *or* Your Grace:
Duke	To His Grace, the Duke of ——.	My Lord Duke: *or* Your Grace:
Earl	The Right Honourable The Earl of ——; *or* The Earl of ——.	My Lord:
King	The King's Most Excellent Majesty; *or* His Most Gracious Majesty, King ——.	Sir: *or* May it please your Majesty:
Knight	Sir Henry W—— (initials of his order, if any, as K.C.B.).	Sir:
Lady	Lady ——; *or* (if the daughter of a viscount or baron) Hon. Lady ——; *or* (if the daughter of a duke, earl or marquis) Lady Mary ——.	Madam: My Lady: Your Ladyship:
Marchioness	The Most Honourable the Marchioness of ——.	Madam:
Marquis	The Most Honourable the Marquis of ——; *or* The Marquis of ——.	My Lord Marquis:
Prince of the Blood Royal	His Royal Highness Prince William.	Sir:
Princess of the Blood Royal	Her Royal Highness the Princess Elizabeth.	Madam:
Queen	The Queen's Most Excellent Majesty; *or* Her Gracious Majesty, The Queen.	Madam: *or* May it please your Majesty:
Queen Mother	Her Gracious Majesty Queen Alexandra.	Madam: *or* May it please your Majesty:
Viscount	The Right Honourable the Viscount ——; *or* The Viscount ——.	My Lord:
Viscountess	The Right Honourable the Viscountess ——; *or* The Viscountess ——.	Madam:

Introduction   1123
Energy and power
    sources   1129
Communications and
    transportation   1151
Materials and structures   1189
Machines and processes   1228
Bibliography   1290

VOLUME FIFTEEN

INDUSTRY & TECHNOLOGY

ARTHUR FREED

Industry and Technology

INTRODUCTION

Definition.—"The systematic interpretation of nature into a framework of law, we call science; the effort to convert experience and understanding to useful account is engineering," said Julius Stratton, president of Massachusetts Institute of Technology. Elmer Engstrom, former president of the Radio Corporation of America, has added: "Technology is the fruit of this process. It involves both science and engineering, and it depends on their free interaction."

These definitions, as we shall see, are extremely modern in character and primarily applicable only since the mid-twentieth century. In their light, the usual dictionary definition of technology as "industrial science" or the "systematic knowledge of the industrial arts" seems narrow. Historically, technology has been the sum of the tools, methods, experience, and comprehension of a society applied to its improvement, especially by increasing its total productivity. Engineering is the professional application of the tools, skills, and methods that comprise a society's technology.

Quite clearly, technology originated with early man's improvisation of simple stone tools and aids, which enabled him better to cope with his environment. Indeed, the conscious adoption of any form of technology to improve productivity, and to advance toward a more civilized state, is a significant distinction between human beings and animals.

Historically, the definition of technology tends to be influenced by its predominant form at any given time. Thus, the dictionary definition has been influenced by the Industrial Revolution (1750-1850) and the definitions of Stratton and Engstrom by the science-oriented technological revolution of our own time. For an appreciation of its total social significance, however, technology should be defined, in its broadest and deepest terms, as the human employment of any aid—physical or intellectual—in generating structures, products, or services that can increase man's productivity through better understanding, adaptation to, and control of, his environment.

Technology in Society.—The extraordinary development of technology in the twentieth century provides a remarkable perspective on the technological character of a society. The form and management of a society's technology at any time is intimately related to its goals. Indeed, the potentialities of its technology determine, in major measure, the goals to which a society can reasonably aspire. Thus, recent achievement provides an illuminating contrast to the technological levels of society only a few generations ago.

As a solitary human being acting alone, man can enjoy only the barest existence. Alone, he could live only as a wild animal, with a minimum of food, shelter, and protection. Only as he forms a social group can the productivity of the group as a whole be increased to provide more adequately for the needs of all. Through an organized society, each individual can do one or a few tasks more effectively; through learning, through mastery of tools and skills, and through articulation of the jobs done by each individual, the assembled group can provide most effectively for the society that it forms. Thus, perhaps one basic purpose of society is to increase the effectiveness of each individual—enable him to make a greater contribution to, and, thereby obtain greater benefit from, society. Technology is the means by which man's effectiveness can be significantly enhanced; it provides the methods and tools whereby he can multiply his skills and energies.

Of course, material well-being is not the sole purpose of a society. Certainly, government and philosophy, and art and literature are also among its aspirations. Yet man's spiritual and intellectual side cannot help but be blunted when the great mass of people have to struggle for bare existence in an uncontrolled and primitive environment.

Through most of history, improvements in individual productivity were relatively minor—the evolution from stone to bronze to iron for tools; a water wheel or a windmill for energy; a horse-drawn plow for turning the soil. None of these offered society much hope of dramatic improvement in the general standard of living. Under such primitive technologies, with their restricted levels of productivity, most men were destined to poverty with its inevitable brutality of the spirit. No ideology could substitute for inadequate technologies.

■**THE NEW SCIENCE.**—But in recent times, a radical change has taken place. Four centuries ago, dominated by the philosophies of René Descartes and Francis Bacon, science took a new turn. Speculation about nature was deemed useless, unless it could be verified by experiment. Gradually out of man's imagination, rigidly controlled by observation and experiment, a deeper comprehension of the behavior of nature was acquired. The process at first was very slow, but it quickened until, in the twentieth century, the detailed comprehension of natural phenomena has come with a rush. By his ingenuity man has penetrated deep into the vastness of space as well as into the inconceivably tiny atom, and by exploring the chemical structure of the living cell, he is beginning to expose the very secrets of life itself. Through his intuition and his artistic sense, man is connecting seemingly unrelated events of nature in a synthesis of the basic laws that govern these events—laws that, in turn, generate deeper insights and enable man to predict nature's most probable behavior in complex situations. Out of this more comprehensive science have arisen powerful new technologies, new ways to do new things far more effectively and often at a greater economy than ever before.

■**THE NEW TECHNOLOGY.**—In developing and learning to manage the new science-based technology, man has doubtless introduced a vast step-function in his level of civilization. The Stone Age, Bronze Age, and Iron Age represented distinct advances in man's social level as a consequence of new technologies, based on the discovery of new materials and tools that raised his level of opportunity and productivity. Yet each of these social developments was minor compared with the vast opportunity offered by today's science-based technologies.

Man has finally learned that the elimination of poverty can be achieved only through the tremendous increases in productivity that these new technologies can confer. The old engineering, derived from the total of day-to-day experience in the mechanical arts, simply had no hope of satisfying such goals for society. No idealistic philosophy could enrich a society of limited productivity, whose members derived their wealth from elementary technologies. Only by understanding nature in scientific and technological depth could man arrive at the high level of adaptation to his environment at which great advances in productivity could be realized.

The development of the remarkable science-based technologies in our time has enabled man to adopt new social goals with confidence. First, man can now visualize a level of productivity, conferred by the new science-based technologies, in which poverty can be totally obliterated.

Second, the development of new medical technologies represents the opportunity of healthful participation in society for a vast majority of its members. Since the American Revolution, life expectancy has risen from a mere 30 years to the Biblical goal of three score and ten, the major gain being since the turn of the century.

Third, with relief from the compulsion of satisfying daily and immediate needs, society can now establish new and major goals derived from man's age-old yearning for comprehension of the universe around him—goals such as the exploration of space, the moon, and the planets; the elucidation of the character of matter, or of the nature of life itself. As these goals are achieved and enlarged, they extend man's horizons and react in turn by enlarging still further the capability of his technological systems.

No nation can rise toward goals and aspirations which lie beyond its access to technological aids. The quality of its art, its literature, its music—the whole of its human attitudes—is dependent upon a sufficient measure of productivity to release men for such pursuits. But we must understand quite clearly that even a superb technology, suitably employed, cannot alone ensure a high level of cultural development. To employ a technology successfully, a people must be guided by a sense of purpose, a sense of morals and ethics, suitable to govern that technology for society's optimum benefit. However, without a suitable technological base, high cultural goals are beyond the reach of the great mass of people. With only primitive technologies at hand, man had little choice in selection of social goals. Only with the technological revolution of the twentieth century has the opportunity for choice of social goals been opened up. Unfortunately, the experience of the past offers few social guides to the successful management of the future.

Development of Technology.—The earliest record of technology is found in archaeology, where its tortuous development can be traced to the beginning of time. Indeed, the earliest suspected human remains—*Zinjanthropus,* found in 1959 by Louis S. B. Leakey 40 miles east of the eastern tip of Lake Victoria, Africa, and dated as 1,300,000 to 1,750,000 years old—are noted "as probably qualifying as man because his remains were found among stone tools." Thus, the acquisition of a technology of stone tools is considered a critical factor in the identification of early man as distinct from animals.

Archaeology usually divides man's development according to the character of his tools and their technological employment, following the suggestion of Christian Jurgensen Thomsen in 1836. Thus human history can be divided into three main stages: the *Stone Age,* when tools and weapons were made of stone, wood, bone, etc.; the *Bronze Age,* beginning about 2000 B.C., when tools of copper alloyed with tin came to dominate technology in advanced European, Asian, and African societies; the *Iron Age,* when iron began to be used as a basic element of technology, its significant employment dating from about 800 B.C., through earlier uses have been identified.

Thus, archaeology implicitly recognizes that the state of artistic, spiritual, and philosophical development of early civilizations is directly correlated to the technologies accessible to each civilization. While each of these human periods—stone, bronze, and iron—has been finely subdivided in terms of the intellectual development of each relatively isolated civilization, that development was essentially restricted by the character of its technology.

The development of technology down to the present century has been chronicled in many works. From the extraordinarily complex interactions in this development, certain broad generalizations can be preceived.

■**EARLY TECHNOLOGY.**—Man's original technologies were born of necessity by pure discovery and invention. These arose out of the need for shelter and clothing, more efficient and dependable supplies of food, and more adequate means of defense. As cities were formed, man needed water and sanitation, and roads and bridges for communication and commerce. Scientific knowledge was neither sufficiently advanced nor in the form necessary to contribute significantly to early technological progress. Indeed, it might be said that until technology could provide the means and materials for precise measurement and experimentation, modern science was inconceivable.

In its early stage, each technology developed as a "mechanic's-art" out of the gradually accumulated knowledge, skills, and experience of the ages. Technological processes and skills were transmitted by apprenticeship and through guilds (or their equivalent) until relatively recent times. Today's advanced engineering still bears many similarities derived from these early roots. But in the absence of broad and systematized knowledge of nature, provided by an advanced science, the value of these early technologies was slight.

However, the primitive character of early technologies should not cause one to underestimate the grandeur of man's early accomplishments. The great structures of the Greeks and the roads, bridges, and aqueducts of the Romans have influenced man's beliefs and actions. The great cathedral of Saint Sophia at Constantinople (Istanbul) has sustained for 1,600 years what was until very recent time the largest self-supporting dome ever constructed (and this in an active seismic region). Yet these magnificent works, like the Egyptian pyramids, were achieved by incredible employment of primitive labor and at dreadful human cost.

Another great root of technology lies in science, and this root has developed only as the "new" science has developed.

SMITHSONIAN INSTITUTION

TECHNOLOGY grew from pure science with such inventions as the deDondi astronomical clock of 1364 (*right*), a highly complex mechanism for measuring sidereal time, and the 1654 von Guericke air pump (*above*), which demonstrated the strength of a vacuum.

BURNDY LIBRARY

■**THE SIXTEENTH CENTURY.**—Science as we know it today—the rigorous exercise of human thought by observation, and more particularly by critical experiment—can be traced back a mere four centuries among the 70 centuries of recorded history. This new science seems to have arisen from the convergence of three major events toward the end of the sixteenth century. The first was the conception of the precise descripton of natural events by the application and development of the mathematics of the ancients. The second was the application of precise measurement in experiment to supply the data from which a mathematical description could be formulated. The third was the invention and use of the printing press for the rapid and widespread communication of scientific results and formulations. The scientific conceptions arising out of this convergence were guided by the recognition that the most simple and general synthesis of observed facts best approximated the truth.

Prior to this convergence, science was largely built out of the imagination, and technology out of crude empirical experience. While the ancients had made many casual astronomical observations, history awaited Tycho Brahe to bring them to really useful precision. At his magnificent observatory on the Danish island of Hveen (now Ven) during the last quarter of the sixteenth century, Brahe assembled the best astrolabes and calibrated circles, made to his specifications, which enabled him to measure the motion of the heavenly bodies with astonishing precision. On these measurements, the subsequent discoveries and developments in mechanics of Johannes Kepler, Galileo, and Isaac Newton were based. Galileo himself grasped the fundamental idea of measurement in his great work on mechanics and astronomy.

But, in a sense, the world awaited the critical thought of Bacon and Descartes, for both of whom experimental science, as opposed to the sterile scholasticism of the (medieval) universities, was the principal hope. Theory or hypothesis had its place in the new science, as a means to synthesize—to give direction to experiment and observation and to advance comprehension. But to experiment and to observe require means of measurement. So experimental science has grown out of the invention and elaboration of the instruments with which precise measurements could be made.

■**THE SEVENTEENTH CENTURY.**—The barometer of Evangelista Torricelli (1643); the telescope of Galileo (1609); the early thermometers of Galileo (1593), of Jan Baptista van Helmont (1630), and of Jean Rey (1632), which were followed by the precise instruments of Gabriel Daniel Fahrenheit (1724); the air pump of Otto von Guericke (1654); the pendulum clock of Christian Huygens (1656)—these and related developments represent the beginnings of the precise instrumentation out of which the new science was to grow. Although reasonably precise measure-

ments of mass and length had been made by the ancients, even these awaited the science of the sixteenth and seventeenth centuries for significant refinement.

As instrumentation grew more sophisticated, the interaction between science and technology became greater. Developments of the thirteenth and fourteenth centuries, including convex lenses by the glass workers of Venice, and the box compass, an invention of early navigators, prompted the dreams of Columbus. Throughout the subsequent growth of science, instrument makers drew on the skills of trade to supply the special materials, means of fabrication, knowledge, and manipulative capability derived from technological experience. In turn, the new means of measurement began to lift technology from the morass of empirical art to the solid foundations of science.

■**THE INDUSTRIAL REVOLUTION.**—In tracing the beginnings of the industrial revolution (1750), one historian has observed that "the industrial state, as now understood, did not exist, although the foundations for it had been well laid. . . . The wide use of power-driven machinery, although a basic factor, was not all-important. The application of science to technology played an increasingly effective part." The origins of this new and developing industry can be traced to the experimental developments of science—the beginnings of the heat engine out of a growing understanding of thermodynamics, of commercial chemistry out of molecular theory, and so on. Thus, the new roots of technology in science were beginning to form.

■**BEGINNINGS OF MODERN ERA.**—Before the twentieth century, however, the scientific roots of technology were slow to take hold. Consider the development of electric power. Only after electricity was lifted from the realm of parlor curiosity a mere century ago by the scientific theories and experiments of Henry Cavendish, Michael Faraday, Joseph Henry, Charles Augustin de Coulomb, Georg Simon Ohm, James Clerk Maxwell, and their successors could man conceive of unlimited energy transmitted from a distant source to await release at his command. Today living standards are directly proportional to the per-capita consumption of electric energy.

Basic technological inventions came directly out of the work of Faraday and Henry, and without much delay. Yet society's acceptance of controlled electric energy was painfully slow and labored. As one searches for the explanation, he finds many factors. Electrical technologists were few, for university training in engineering was in its infancy. Means of employing controlled energy awaited further research, invention, and development. Efficiency of application awaited the elaboration of nature by science. Above all, the public was not ready to buy on a scale sufficient to stimulate and enjoy the tremendous social benefits that electric power offered. Even as the twentieth century unfolded, electricity was viewed by most

people as a kind of plaything only distantly related to needs and aspirations.

So any analysis of scientific innovation must take into account that a society has a time-constant during which it exhibits severe resistance. How to shorten this time-constant would be worth some study. One suspects that constant and broad public exposure to the most advanced fronts of technology, such as the space program, may have a powerful influence in reducing public resistance to advanced technology as a whole. If this is so, perhaps the space program will be repaid many times over, merely by the advantages of earlier acceptance of new products and services that can mightily benefit society.

■**THE MODERN ERA.**—The turn of the twentieth century brought full development of the scientific roots of technology—a development that heralded the technological revolution whose full impact was to be felt by the midcentury.

The great inventors—Thomas Alva Edison, Henry Ford, the Wright brothers, Alexander Graham Bell, and Guglielmo Marconi—tapped the most elementary manifestations of science to create new industrial potentials, which, in turn, created altogether different kinds of industry and opened human potentials inconceivable before.

In the ensuing half-century, man's comprehension of the physical character of nature was revised completely and expanded enormously. He became able to deal with the minuscule—the atoms and nuclei from which matter is formed. As a result, all gross products of reactives could be predicted on the basis of a few equations.

With scientific groundwork laid, the full impact of the technological revolution became inevitable. Moreover, World War II had forced consummation of the marriage of science and technology so that the roots of technology by the midcentury were, for the first time, predominantly in science.

The Technological Revolution.—No social revolution is ever instantaneous, yet the rise of technological revolution at the mid-twentieth century was remarkably sudden when measured in the scale of human affairs. Perhaps its basic technical characteristic has been the development of electronics, whereby one can use sensors and amplifiers to detect and measure phenomena far beyond the capability of any human sense. This includes the modern computer, which can solve problems with incredible speed, can order the information, and produce results that could not otherwise be obtained in a lifetime.

Perhaps the most profound social consequence of the technological revolution has been the change in the character of the economy. Prior to and throughout the Industrial Revolution, man's principal effort, with the then primitive and empirical technologies, was to supply the basic necessities for living—food, clothing, shelter, and a minimum of protection and transportation. Even well into the twentieth century, the economy was primarily one of minimum necessity. Such an industrial economy is sharply population-limited to supplying the food that could be eaten, the clothes that could be worn, and so on. But the new science-derived industry of the present century enables man to adapt better to his environment. This new industry might primarily be called the "adaptive" industry, which, significantly, is not population-limited, for there seems to be no foreseeable limit to man's adaptation to, and command of, his environment. Already it forms more than half the economy, with no limit on its applicability in sight. To paraphrase Elmer Engstrom, in the 40 years from 1923 to 1963 the country has grown in population from 108 to 192 million, while its gross national product has multiplied nearly eight times from $80 billion to over $600 billion annually. The bulk of this greater product consists of goods and services that were entirely absent or relatively insignificant in 1923.

The actual process of transition from science to a suitable technology is not completely clear. One widely accepted public misconception should, however, be laid to rest. This is the idea that there is anything like a one-to-one correspondence between a scientific discovery and a consequent technology. A new technology depends on thousands of scientific advances articulated in the most suitable way. Jet aircraft technology, for example, depends on solid-state physics and physical metallurgy for materials of suitable properties; on progress in thermodynamics, fluid dynamics, and fuel technology; and on a wide variety of advances in communications and control. When it is said that a man can be sent to the moon in 1970, what is meant is that scientific progress on a thousand fronts now permits the development of a myriad of related technological processes, all of which must be suitably woven and articulated to form an adequate manned-space technology.

■THE RISKS.—The development of a new technology requires the combined efforts of the scientist, the engineer, and the entrepreneur who is willing to take risk. Adopting a new technological strategy presents many risks. Will the estimated combination of scientific resources produce the technological result anticipated? How can these be combined to produce the creative result visualized? How can the resulting product or service be made usable and marketable? How can the product or service be introduced so as to be accepted in areas in which it has either been unknown or previously offered in an inferior manner? The whole process involves a very special kind of imagination, faith, and creative genius, supplemented by a high order of education and manipulative dexterity. Access to a broad range of up-to-date scientific knowledge is imperative.

ABOVE: U.S. AIR FORCE   RIGHT: AMERICAN TELEPHONE AND TELEGRAPH COMPANY

GOVERNMENT AND INDUSTRY frequently join forces in technological ventures. Air Force research that led to the delta-winged bomber (*above*) has since been applied to the design of a planned commercial supersonic transport. The Telstar Communications Satellite (*right*), privately built and owned, was launched and is used by the government and industry.

For any technological strategy undertaken by an organization to be successful, the interval from its inception to its profitable exploitation should be about five years, certainly no longer than seven. To adopt longer strategies means the end is too fuzzy, the danger from alternative competing strategies too great, the cost of development too uncertain.

Thus, to initiate new technological strategies, an organization is usually staffed and equipped according to certain criteria. It must have intimate knowledge of the literature and practice of science, so that potential innovations can be recognized as they emerge from whatever combination of scientific sources. Government and industry must have access to groups of men so close to all working aspects of science that potential innovations fitting their general mission can be immediately recognized and interpreted. A central purpose of basic research in industry and government is to acquire a vanguard of men who are sufficiently informed over broad areas of science to recognize and to initiate new technological strategies out of the whole of scientific advance. From alternative strategies, selection can be exercised and decision made. This process appears to be most effective if that vanguard of strategy-makers actually participates in basic scientific research. Thus, most organizations in today's technology support a considerable effort in basic research.

Since innovation may arise from a synthesis of a wide variety of relatively unrelated scientific developments, the task of industrial or government laboratories is to articulate quite independent scientific discoveries or advances into a mission-oriented body of science and technology. This is possible only if the laboratory has full access to the total of basic scientific advance by intimate participation in it. It seems no accident that the formulation of Claude Shannon's information theory, which has revolutionized communications and data handling, should come out of the Bell Telephone Laboratories, though the scientific pieces from which it was constructed were diverse. Likewise, radar originated at the Naval Research Laboratory, though its ideas were derived from a multiplicity of scientific origins.

Finally, through its own facilities or through contact, the organization must have access to the capability for development and engineering that can bring the idea to fruition.

■ROLE OF THE GOVERNMENT.—Experience over the past two decades shows that the really great technological strategies, such as space exploration, Antarctic exploration, atomic energy, radar, aircraft navigation, and supersonic jet travel, must be initiated by government. It is of interest to observe that even in such a highly private business as rail transportation, no significant technological progress was made until the recent experimental program of the Japanese government and the more recent program of the United States. As the outstanding exception, the communications strategies of the telephone and telegraph companies represent great contributions by private initiative.

■ROLE OF PRIVATE ENTERPRISE.—On the other hand, smaller yet considerable technological strategies have come from private enterprise and have been produced in the most suitable form out of the competition of the marketplace. In a sense, the greater technological developments await the perfection by private entrepreneurs of the dozens of preceding technologies which make these possible. Experience indicates that the greatest success occurs in an open society with decentralized control, offering competitive opportunity for independent approaches to most suitable solutions.

Underlying the whole process of technological innovation is assumed a steadily expanding body of scientific knowledge to which it has access. Since, in basic science, the end result cannot be foreseen; since, in any event, the lead time from basic research to a product or service may often be too long, there is no broad

economic motivation for basic research other than the need for coupling science to technology, as previously described. Consequently, the support and encouragement for the exploration and elaboration of basic science must come primarily from government.

■ROLE OF THE UNIVERSITY.—In the Western system—for example, in the field of agriculture under the Morrill Act of 1862—basic research has been conducted at the universities, and at other advanced research institutions, largely with government support. This is a particularly efficient method, since the research can be coupled with the training of graduate and postdoctoral students and the advancement of the teachers.

The whole operation of systematically assimilating the resultant science into the technological process is still too new to be highly developed. Although the university cannot be expected to assume direct responsibility for innovation—which are properly assigned to industry and government—it can be expected to organize scientific knowledge in a form most readily digestible by society in its research for new industrial strategies.

Technology and Education.—The universities and professions were slow to recognize the new science as a legitimate branch of learning. Paracelsus' (1493-1541) attempt to introduce chemical science into medicine was instantly resisted. In England, the quarrel between the "new" scientists and the Oxford dons led to the formation of the independent Royal Society (1662). Not until the mid-nineteenth century did science and engineering achieve wider acceptance as legitimate subjects for university training.

As shown in the accompanying table, the onset of the technological revolution is graphically illustrated by the explosively rising demand for advanced education. This is doubtless the most remarkable social development in human history. Not only does it reflect the urgency for advanced education in a technological age, but it also represents a marked change in the tastes and desires of the marketplace for the quality and character of its products.

To meet this educational need, undergraduate institutions have been planted and have flowered in every state of the United States. There are between 3,000 and 4,000 such institutions, depending upon which categories are included. That these must double in their total capacity in the next two decades is no longer questioned.

However, as one views the national capability for graduate education, the picture is quite different. To advance its science base, and to transform that base into new and useful technologies, society quite suddenly has become aware that advanced graduate education is needed on a broad scale. If new technologies are to be made effective, highly educated leaders are needed in sufficient numbers—men whose insights can perceive the opportunities that nature offers and who can organize the environmental patterns to bring advantages to the great mass of our people. This requires training to the level of the doctoral degree, and continuing education beyond.

The first American doctoral graduate, Josiah Willard Gibbs, received his degree from Yale over a century ago (1863). Graduate education was later offered by Harvard, and Johns Hopkins was founded as a graduate university in 1876. The growth of American doctoral training was slow until the 1920's; until then a scholar still traveled to Europe to round out his academic development.

The period from 1920 to 1940 saw the emergence of the 25 graduate universities that now dominate the American scene. These universities set graduate opportunity as a primary goal, with distinguished faculties and emphasis on research as a part of a broad motivation toward graduate education. These universities now graduate the greater proportion of American doctoral graduates, of whom about 55 per cent specialize in science and technology. More, many more, such centers of graduate excellence are needed.

Recent critical studies by the National Academy of Sciences belie the oft expressed fear that increasing the numbers of doctoral graduates will dilute the intellectual quality of the doctorate. As nearly as can be ascertained, only about 2.5 per cent of those intellectually qualified for the doctoral degree ever achieve it. This represents an enormous loss of potential technological leadership.

Graduates in the United States

Year	Baccalaureate Graduates (per annum)	Doctoral Graduates (per annum)
1900	28,000	400
1920	50,000	700
1940	200,000	3,500
1960	450,000	10,000
1980	(estimated) 1,000,000	(?)

Problems of the Technological Age.—The achievement of virtually unlimited productivity, made possible by the new science-based technologies, presents society with a plethora of new problems induced by this wholly new situation. These include:

■POPULATION.—At the time of William Shakespeare, it took several hundred years for population to double. With disease, famine, and war, life was so uncertain that bare survival of the human race was always in question. With the science-based medical technologies of the present century, doubling time for populations is now 35 to 40 years. The hypothesis of Thomas R. Malthus (1798) has become a reality, the arithmetic of which cannot be refuted. Man must quickly find a solution to uncontrolled growth of populations, or he must surrender to widespread hunger, brutality, and death. Our basic resources of atmosphere, water, and materials must soon reach their limits if populations are uncontrolled. With reasonable control, these resources, manipulated with advancing technologies, can be made to support society indefinitely.

■WAR.—The powerful new technologies have created ultimate weapons of destruction. In acquiring the advantages of today's technology, man is faced with the necessity of developing new forms of social organization to keep these weapons under control. Here, society is severely hampered by the traditions of severely limited productivity and the outdated national objectives growing out of these antiquated traditions. In the present transition, the opportunities offered by the new technology must be defended against ignorance and chauvinism until they have a chance to be widely recognized and accepted.

■POLITICS.—To secure the advantages of the new technology requires major capital development and investment of an altogether new order. These depend, in large measure, on political stability and political evolution—not revolution. Likewise, large-scale political experiments over the past century have shown that individual incentive and opportunity, stimulated by competition, play major roles in optimizing the adoption of new technologies. Throughout history, men have deluded themselves into believing that political forms in themselves could achieve major social goals. From the new perspective, it can be seen more clearly that these goals can be achieved only through an adequate technology. But it is equally clear that realizing the potentiality of science-based technologies is possible only with suitably organized and reasonably stable and dependable political systems.

The outstanding success of the evolving Western political systems appears to be no accident. Decentralized economic systems, with such measure of centralized regulation and planning as is required for economic stability, seem to produce the optimum result. Overcentralized planning cannot forsee the power of technological change and generally suppresses advantageous development. Opportunity for the entrepreneur seems essential to the trial of new technological strategies.

■METROPOLITAN DEVELOPMENT.—The impact of the new technology in individual communities has had important consequences. Agriculture has become automated and industrialized to the extent that the open areas of the nation are being depleted of population. In the last decade, in Texas, for example, a half-million people have left the land for the cities. Texas' rapidly growing population is centered in nine or ten metropolitan areas.

The same tendency is manifested everywhere in the United States. In whatever way one may interpret this change in light of primitive and historic norms, the U.S. population will soon be centered in some 100 to 125 great and affluent metropolitan areas. And within the framework of present social concepts, employment for this concentrating population will have to be found in the new science-based technologies.

To measure the task ahead, it can be foreseen that each of these metropolitan centers must have a great graduate university at its hub. The university will be required to adopt new forms in its service to the whole community. As Clark Kerr has put it, in the new science-based society every metropolis will have to be a "city of intellect." With this must come viable city planning so that the metropolis remains both competitive and livable in the most artistic sense.

■POLLUTION.—Spreading to all nations, and with rising populations, the new technology can cause deadly pollution of the atmosphere, soil, and water, unless it is severely controlled. Strict pollution control must be accepted as a fully justifiable cost if national resources are to be preserved. With new levels of produc-

tivity, this cost can easily be absorbed. Moreover, with the new technology, no form of pollution need be tolerated, since solutions to every problem are conceivable.

■AUTOMATION AND INNOVATION.—The very basis for increased productivity of the individual is the increase in his control over whatever mechanism or process he may be directing. This is often called *automation*. As the degree of control of the individual is enhanced, the requisite level of training, skill, perception, and education to exercise that control is raised. At the same time, the number of persons previously occupied in the process is diminished.

To provide continued opportunity for employment of those displaced, further *innovation* from science is required. The day of the old-fashioned inventor is largely past; the source of innovation today is the highly educated scientist or engineer with the laboratory facilities to devise and develop new technological ideas and methods.

Thus, sustained employment involves the race between unemployment arising from automation and new opportunity offered by innovation. Success at every level in this race requires ever-enlarging opportunity for more adequate education and higher manipulative skills. This represents a serious problem for those who are displaced. To achieve the benefits of higher productivity offered by the new technologies, the community must provide opportunity for more advanced education and retraining in more advanced skills at every level of employment.

These are but a few examples of the utterly new problems that the new science-based technologies pose to society. As man finds the means to achieve his social goals, at the same time he acquires altogether new

problems. But it is of critical importance that he see these problems in their full perspective so that in searching for the solution he does not, metaphorically, kill the goose that lays the golden egg. The power of the new technologies creates a more delicate balance of social forces, in which ancient moralities and ethics must be evaluated and reevaluated in light of their new and far-reaching consequences.

Man or Machine.—Man's most basic aspiration is equality of opportunity for relief from want, disease, and brutality—affluence, if you like. He has now acquired the means to achieve that aspiration—a technology with which he can realize equality of opportunity. But this new technology can also be misused, particularly if it is employed in accordance with the norms of a more primitive civilization. In such a social framework, population increases, war, uncontrolled contaminants of living, unplanned metropolitan growth, and retention of unproductive and primitive pursuits can lead to serious and even destructive consequences. It must be realized clearly that the same technological base at once can free man and destroy him.

If man is to employ the new technology to achieve his goals, he must at the same time adjust his habits to control its potential abuses. He cannot destroy the technological base itself without at the same time destroying his hope of achievement. The focus, therefore, should be on the specific social adjustments that enable man to acquire the benefits and, at the same time, remedy the abuses.

The basic human problem ahead is whether man shall control the machine or fall slave to it. It is of little profit to try to destroy the machine and, with it, man's opportunity to rise to new heights of civilized opportunity. Equally, it would be of little profit to subordinate man to the very machine that can provide him his hope. To use the machine to lift man to new heights in the command of his environment and in the free exercise of his creative spirit is the great human problem of our time. It transcends all others. It cannot be solved by the oversimplified and time-worn clichés of the humanist, the scientist, or the politician. As man moves into the new technological age, with its enormous potentials for individual study and expression, creativity and freedom, he is confronted with problems, which, for the most part, have not been encountered before. At the same time, there are at hand altogether new opportunities for their solution. In this delicate social atmosphere, the solutions of the demagogue conceived "off the top of his head" or of the reactionary who relies too heavily on the past are unsuitable, even dangerous. The solutions will require deep and scholarly study, perception, and comprehension of both the machine—its uses and potentials—and of man—his hopes and aspirations. The humanist of the future must comprehend and encompass both.
                                    —Lloyd V. Berkner

BILLY DAVIS, LOUISVILLE COURIER-JOURNAL

MAN'S RELATION TO NATURE can easily be a destructive one in our technological age. Strip mining, for example, has resulted in large-scale soil erosion in parts of the country.

ENERGY AND POWER SOURCES

Manpower.—Man's control over nature and his environment took a major step forward when he first domesticated certain animals. This added enormously to his own limited energy. In time, however, man himself was displaced as a principal source of energy.

Man is a limited producer of energy. Thus, as long as man was dependent upon his own energy, supplemented by the contributions of his animate servants, his progress in meeting his requirements for food, clothing, and shelter was limited.

The Industrial Revolution.—The great expansion in man's productive power came with the development of his ability to harness mechanical or inanimate energy. This marked the start of the Industrial Revolution in England approximately 200 years ago. Only then did it become possible for more than a relatively small segment of the population to aspire to and achieve standards of material welfare above the bare subsistence level. This development has continued almost without interruption, so that the world as we know it today would be utterly inconceivable without the ubiquitous use of very large quantities of inanimate energy. This is likely to prevail even more in the world of tomorrow.

Sources of Energy.—There are currently four principal sources of primary energy; falling water (hydro), coal, oil, and gas. Rising in importance on the horizon is a fifth source—nuclear fuel, or atomic power. Minor primary energy sources, more or less exotic and negligible in their over-all economic value, are wind power, solar energy, and tidal power.

Perhaps the most versatile form of energy in use today is electric energy, but electric energy is not a primary energy source. It is a converted, highly refined form of energy. In the United States at the present time, approximately 20 per cent of the total energy used is converted to the electric form. Electric energy is particularly important in technologically and economically advanced societies and has contributed to their progress.

The great technological and economic progress that has taken place in the last two centuries can be viewed in terms of advancing technology and the development of energy-using machines and equipment.

In the United States, the commercial exploitation of mineral energy is roughly 200 years old. The bicentennial of the first commercial production of coal in Virginia was celebrated in 1959. The Titusville, Pa., centennial of the petroleum industry was celebrated a year or so before that.

At first, progress in the use of mineral energy was extremely slow. Even by 1850, in the United States, bituminous and anthracite coal occupied a relatively minor position in an already heavy energy-using country. Although coal was known and

ANSELL ADAMS

WATER was early man's prime source of power. The energy in a majestically free-flowing waterfall today can be harnessed to provide many kilowatts of electrical power.

in use prior to the Revolutionary War, approximately 90 per cent of the total energy, except that supplied by human or animal power, was still supplied by wood. The period before the Civil War was primarily a wood fuel economy.

Coal was not consumed in significant quantities until about 1860. Thereafter, it quickly began to replace wood as a railroad locomotive fuel and as a source of coke for the growing steel industry. The appearance of the automobile and the expanding automotive use of petroleum provided the major impetus for the growth in petroleum consumption; until then, petroleum had served primarily as a source of light and as a lubricant.

The increased use of natural gas over the past several decades received its greatest momentum with the development of welded seamless pipe. This made possible the extensive long-distance pipeline network that has been constructed largely since the end of World War II, and in turn the expansion of gas markets at locations remote from the source.

■**ELECTRIC ENERGY.**—Electric energy has many unique qualities, notably, ease of transportation and distribution, complete flexibility, cleanliness, safety, sensitive susceptibility to control, potential applicability to almost all energy-using processes, and the ability to be produced from every primary energy source. For these reasons, it has had an especially significant impact on our society since 1882, when Thomas Edison placed in commercial operation the first central-station power supply in the city of New York.

Since electric energy is a converted form of energy, limitations on primary energy supplies bear the seeds of limitations on electric-energy production. However, because electric energy can be produced from any primary energy source and because it is uniquely capable of potential application to any energy-using process, electrification offers an excellent route for solving the problems of the potential exhaustion of our mineral fuels. This prospect has been enhanced by the development of nuclear power—the first new primary energy source in almost 100 years. Its contribution to compensating for the depletion of the other primary fuels is limited primarily to its conversion to electric energy. The extent to which it can supplement older primary-energy resources depends, therefore, on the degree to which energy-using processes can be electrified. It is important to note, in this regard, that at the present time the largest single consumer of energy is transportation, and transportation is based almost entirely on petroleum.

Energy Consumption.—The growth in energy use in the United States reached the following balance for the year 1960: total energy consumption amounted to the equivalent of about 1,700 million tons of bituminous coal,

Energy Conversion Chart

From / To	Chemical	Elastic	Electrical	Gravitational	Heat	Kinetic	Nuclear	Radiation
Chemical			Electroplating / Storage Battery / Electrolysis		Blast Furnace / Refining			Photography / Photosynthesis
Elastic			Piezoelectric Crystal	Auto Suspension (Springs)	Thermostat / Expansion of Heated Metals	Trampoline / Diving Board / Tire Pump		
Electrical	Fuel Cell / Storage Battery / Primary Battery	Piezoelectric Crystal	Transformer / Motor-Generator / Rectifier	Hydroelectric Generators	Thermoelectric Generators	Phonograph Pickup / Generator	Nuclear Battery	Solar Cell / Photoelectric Cell
Gravitational		Auto Suspension (Springs)			Convection of Fluids and Gases	Clock Pendulum / Artillery Shell		
Heat	Combustion of Fuel / Heat of Chemical Reactions	Compression Ignition of Gases / Gas Cooling by Expansion	Heating Coils / Spark Plug / Thermoelectric Cooler			Friction / Impact	Fission / Fusion / Reactor	Infra-red Rays / High Frequency Cooker / Radiant Heating
Kinetic	Explosives / Rocket Fuels	Clock Spring / Slingshot / Trampoline	Electric Motor / Loudspeaker / Solenoid	Clock Weights / Falling Stone / Waterfall / Tides	Steam Engine / Turbine / Internal-Combustion Engine	Collision / Propeller		Radiation Pressure from Sun
Nuclear	No known method of conversion							
Radiation	Cold Light Emission (Firefly) / Chemical Laser		Fluorescent Light / Laser / Radar / Radio-Television	Gravitational Collapse	Light Bulb / Heated Surfaces		Radiation from the Sun / Nuclear Explosion	Fluorescence / Laser

of which coal itself accounted for about 23 per cent, petroleum 42 per cent, and natural gas 31 per cent. Hydroelectric energy provided the remaining 4 per cent.

By 1975, total energy consumption in the United States is expected to grow more than 60 per cent, to the equivalent of 2,750 million tons of bituminous coal. In that growth, coal is likely to increase its share to about 30 per cent of the total, petroleum should show a slight drop to 40 per cent, gas is likely to experience a larger decline to 25 per cent, hydroelectric power will provide about 3 per cent, and for the first time there will be a significant amount of nuclear power, providing the remaining 2 per cent.

In the year 2000, it is expected that changes in the relative importance of alternative sources of energy will still be gradual and relatively modest. At that time, of the projected energy equivalent of 4,000 million tons of bituminous coal, coal itself is likely to provide about 30 per cent; petroleum about 32 per cent; natural gas will have continued to fall, providing only 15 per cent; and hydroelectric power will provide 2 per cent. The major change expected for the year 2000 is the growth in nuclear power, which should provide the remaining 21 per cent.

The most significant aspect of these projections is that, despite the growth in total energy requirements by the year 2000 to almost 2.4 times the 1960 level, and despite the very rapid growth indicated for nuclear energy after 1975, the principal sources of energy for the United States will continue to be the fossil fuels, sup-

plying over 75 per cent of the total. The nuclear-energy figure shown for the year 2000 is based on the most optimistic assumptions about the rate at which nuclear energy can take its place in the economy. The nuclear-energy figure for the year 2000 may be lower, depending on developments within the fossil fuel industries.

In 1960, approximately 19.5 per cent of the total energy consumed in the United States was utilized in the production of the 753 billion kilowatt-hours (kwh) generated by the electric-utility industry. By 1975, even with expected improvements in the efficiency of converting mineral energy into electric energy, about 26 per cent of the total energy will be utilized for the production of about 2 trillion kwh. In the next quarter-century after that, electric-energy generation may be expected to triple to 6 trillion kwh and to account for 40 per cent of the total energy use. In this growth of electric energy, the role of coal will first expand, then gradually diminish as nuclear power increases in importance.

Energy Conversion.—The process of converting any of the primary sources of energy, particularly coal, oil, gas, or nuclear fuel, into electric energy involves a highly advanced and sophisticated technology. The preliminary process of heat release is followed by the conversion of the resulting mechanical energy into electric energy. It is a process that employs complicated machines and equipment to achieve a conversion efficiency of 40 per cent. This high degree of efficiency is the result of slow, painstaking research and de-

velopment that have been going on since the very inception of central-station electric power more than 80 years ago, when conversion efficiency was only about 5 per cent.

In essence, however, the process of converting the energy in mineral fuel to electric energy employs principles that date back to Michael Faraday's discovery of electromagnetic induction in 1831. The steam turbine that converts the thermal energy resulting from fuel combustion to mechanical energy dates back in its essential principles almost two centuries to Thomas Newcomen and James Watt. At the present time, more exotic ways of converting primary energy into electric energy are coming under increasingly intensive investigation. But these processes, too, are based on principles that have been known for more than 100 years. Four of these—thermionic generation, thermal-electric generation, fuel cells, and magnetohydrodynamic generation (MHD)—show particular promise of leading to advances in energy conversion. Each of these highly intriguing prospects depends on a different principle, but all have in common the aim of directly converting primary energy into electrical energy, without any intermediate mechanical device. While considerable progress has been made in the first three of these technologies, there has been no sign that any can be developed into a competitive, large-scale commercial energy converter in the near future.

Magnetohydrodynamics, the fourth of these new approaches, appears to offer more exciting possibilities. It offers the promise of great simplification of the electric generation process and the possible achievement of very high thermal efficiency—as much as a one-third improvement over the present highest efficiency of 40 per cent. Because of this promise, a considerable amount of research effort is going on today looking toward the development of MHD to commercial practicality.

Looking to the Future.—Whatever the results of present research into these more exotic energy-conversion devices, it is clear that total energy requirements by the year 2000 and during the intervening period will continue to necessitate very large amounts of fossil fuel. Thus, it will be essential to foster the continued development of an adequate supply of coal, oil, and gas for the long period during which nuclear power will gradually assume an increasing part of the total energy burden.

It is in the light of such an over-all outlook for energy requirements that the atomic program needs to be viewed, if an adequate supply of energy in the required forms is to be assured. The long-term promise of nuclear energy cannot be permitted to obscure the continuing importance of the fossil fuels. They must be able to provide, for some time to come, the far larger share of the total energy needs that nuclear power will not be able to satisfy even under the most favorable conditions.

Regardless of the progress made in new conversion technologies, these are unlikely to play a leading part in the supply of energy for the remainder of this century. Furthermore, they are only conversion devices and not new sources of energy. They will still require a supply of primary energy with which to carry out the process of conversion.

Thus, there is clearly a need for continuing concern for the supply and efficient utilization of the fossil fuels. For some time, they will continue to provide the greatest share of the total need for inanimate energy.

—Philip Sporn

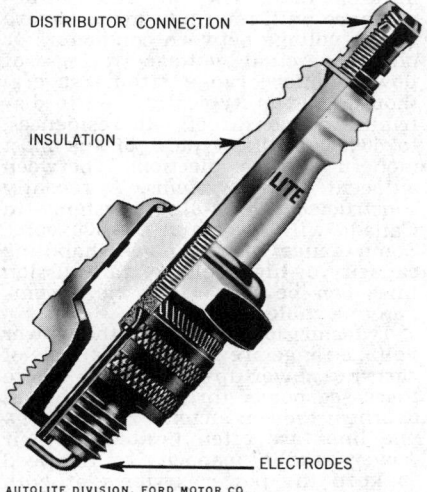

DISTRIBUTOR CONNECTION

INSULATION

ELECTRODES

AUTOLITE DIVISION. FORD MOTOR CO.

SPARK PLUG is shown in quarter section.

ENERGY AND POWER GLOSSARY

Automotive Electrical System, a complete power plant that produces and stores electricity, and delivers it as it is needed. Electric power is required for lights, radio, horns, windshield wipers, power seats and windows, heater and air conditioning blowers, and to turn the engine during starting. In addition, thousands of pulses of high-voltage electricity must be generated every minute to fire the engine's spark plugs. The electrical system used in most American automobiles operates on 12 volts. The electrical system also contains transformers, switches, contacts, relays, and fuses that distribute and regulate the flow of electricity. The complete electrical system actually consists of five interconnected systems—the generating, or charging system, the ignition system, the cranking system, the lighting system, and the accessory system.

■**GENERATING SYSTEM.**—The generating, or charging, system includes an alternator or generator, ammeter or warning light, voltage regulator, and battery. The generator converts mechanical energy from the engine into electrical energy. Either a *direct-current* (D.C.) *generator* or an *alternator* producing alternating current (A.C.) is used. Alternators are equipped with rectifiers to convert the A.C. to D.C. before it is used in the system.

Current from the generator is routed to the *voltage regulator*, which controls the generator's output. Located between the battery and the generator, the regulator operates to reduce generator output when the battery is fully charged and increase output when the battery is low. When the regulator is set correctly, just enough current is produced to keep the battery fully charged at all times. The *ammeter* (gauge), or warning light, provides a visual indication of whether the generator is charging or discharging.

Aside from the generator, the *battery* is the most important element of the generating system. The battery does not store electricity but converts electricity energy into chemical energy and stores it. When electricity is required, the chemical reaction within the battery is reversed to produce a flow of current at the terminals. A storage battery's capacity to store energy is limited; if current is not supplied continuously, the battery runs down or falls rapidly.

■**IGNITION SYSTEM.**—The ignition system, which consists of the ignition switch, coil, distributor, and spark plugs, receives electricity from the battery and creates a high-voltage spark at the electrodes of the spark plug. To bridge the gap at the plugs, a high voltage surge (20,000 to 30,000 volts) is applied across the electrodes. An additional function of the ignition system is to time and distribute the high-voltage surges exactly, so that the proper spark plug is energized at precisely the right moment.

■**CRANKING SYSTEM.**—The cranking motor is a heavy-duty electric motor that rotates the engine crankshaft during starting. Electric power for the cranking motor is supplied by the battery when the starter switch is turned on. Though similar to other electric motors, the cranking motor is specifically designed to operate for brief periods while heavily overloaded.

■**LIGHTING SYSTEM.**—The lighting system consists of the headlights, parking and tail lights, turn signals, emergency flasher, light switch, foot dimmer switch, instrument lights, and interior lights. The light switch is usually a two-position pull switch. The first position, or notch, illuminates the parking lights while the second notch turns on the headlights. The dimmer switch, which is located on the floor, switches the headlights to low beam to prevent blinding of oncoming drivers.

—Joseph J. Kelleher

Battery, Electric, a device that produces or stores electricity by chemical means. Typically, an electric battery has two electrodes: a positively charged *cathode* and a negatively charged *anode*. Both are immersed in an *electrolyte*, a chemical compound that dissociates into positive and negative particles called *ions*. Migration of the ions within the battery stimulates a flow of current in the external circuit connected to the battery. A battery often consists of a number of identical cells connected in series.

Batteries are of two basic types, primary and secondary. In the *primary cell*, the chemical substances are consumed during their useful life, after which the cell is discarded. The common flashlight battery is a typical primary cell that delivers only a predetermined amount of energy. *Secondary cells*, also called *storage batteries*, can be recharged many times before their components deteriorate.

Primary cells are further divided into wet and dry. In *wet cells*, the electrolyte is a liquid; in *dry cells*, it is a paste. The first battery, invented in 1800 by Alessandro Volta, was a primary wet cell consisting of copper and zinc disks immersed in a salt or acid solution. Most primary cells in use today are dry cells having a zinc anode in the shape of a cup that contains the electrolyte, ammonium chloride. The cathode is a carbon rod immersed in the zinc cup. A *depolarizer*, manganese dioxide, is added to the electrolyte to prevent accumulation of unwanted chemical substances on the electrodes that would stop the reaction.

A newer primary dry cell is the *mercury cell*, which was developed during World War II. It consists of a mercuric oxide cathode and a zinc anode in a potassium hydroxide electrolyte. It has longer shelf life and higher electrical capacity than the zinc ammonium chloride cell.

The *lead-acid cell* is the most common secondary cell in use today. Its

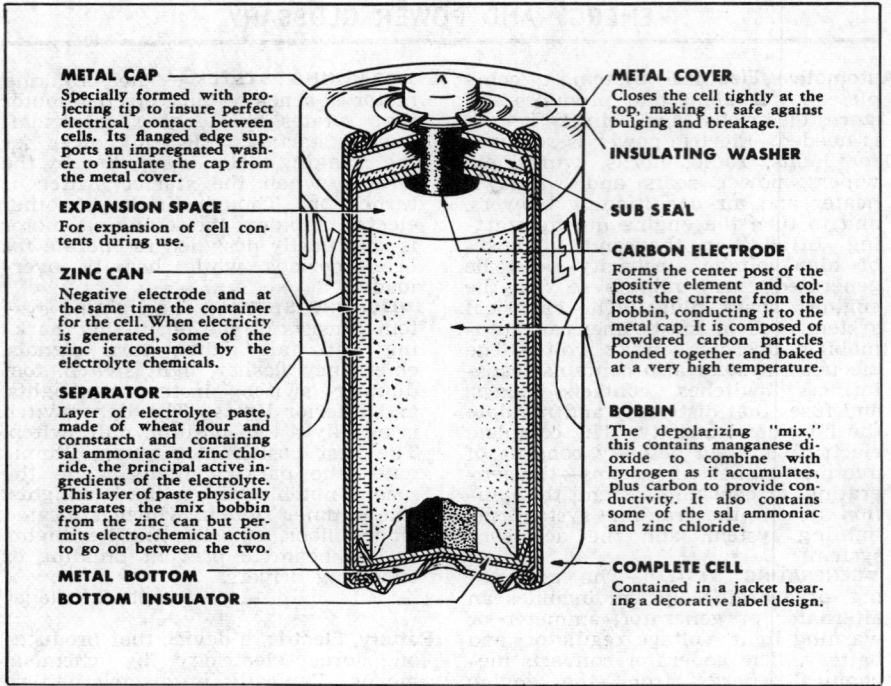

METAL CAP — Specially formed with projecting tip to insure perfect electrical contact between cells. Its flanged edge supports an impregnated washer to insulate the cap from the metal cover.

EXPANSION SPACE — For expansion of cell contents during use.

ZINC CAN — Negative electrode and at the same time the container for the cell. When electricity is generated, some of the zinc is consumed by the electrolyte chemicals.

SEPARATOR — Layer of electrolyte paste, made of wheat flour and cornstarch and containing sal ammoniac and zinc chloride, the principal active ingredients of the electrolyte. This layer of paste physically separates the mix bobbin from the zinc can but permits electro-chemical action to go on between the two.

METAL BOTTOM
BOTTOM INSULATOR

METAL COVER — Closes the cell tightly at the top, making it safe against bulging and breakage.

INSULATING WASHER

SUB SEAL

CARBON ELECTRODE — Forms the center post of the positive element and collects the current from the bobbin, conducting it to the metal cap. It is composed of powdered carbon particles bonded together and baked at a very high temperature.

BOBBIN — The depolarizing "mix," this contains manganese dioxide to combine with hydrogen as it accumulates, plus carbon to provide conductivity. It also contains some of the sal ammoniac and zinc chloride.

COMPLETE CELL — Contained in a jacket bearing a decorative label design.

EVEREADY

DRY CELL, rated at one and a half volts, generates electric energy through the electrochemical reaction between the zinc can and the pastelike depolarizing mix, called a bobbin.

positive plate is made of lead peroxide and its negative plate of lead. The electrolyte is dilute sulfuric acid. Like all secondary cells, the lead-acid battery is recharged by the passage of current through it in a direction opposite to the current flow on discharge. The lead-acid battery is low in cost, and its ability to supply high current for short periods of time makes it suitable for starting automobile engines.

The *nickel-cadmium secondary cell* can operate at low temperatures and, because no gases are given off during normal operation, it can be hermetically sealed. The positive plates are made of nickel oxide. The negative plates are made of cadmium containing a small amount of iron. The electrolyte is a solution of potassium hydroxide. Nickel-cadium cells are used in space vehicles and in specialized portable devices, but are too expensive for general automotive use.

Silver-zinc and *silver-cadmium* cells are small in size, light in weight, and perform well at high discharge rates. Despite their relatively short life, they are used in military and lightweight commercial equipment.

Another secondary cell in use today is the *nickel-iron cell,* which uses potassium hydroxide as the electrolyte. Called the *Edison cell,* it is used primarily in industry, where its high efficiency is of particular value.
—William C. Vergara

Diesel Engine, invented by Rudolf Diesel in 1892, is a particular type of internal-combustion engine. It differs from the gasoline internal-combustion engine (Otto cycle) in that the

fuel injected into the cylinder burns rather than explodes. No spark is required for ignition of the fuel of the diesel engine. Instead, the air in the cylinder is so highly compressed by the stroke of the piston that it reaches a sufficiently high temperature to ignite the fuel without a spark.

Only a slow-speed engine will follow the classic cycle conceived by Rudolf Diesel, and true diesels are large, heavy engines generally used to drive generators in electric power plants, railroad locomotives, or ships. Small, higher speed semi-diesel engines operate on a modified diesel cycle and are used to drive lighter equipment, including automobiles.

Although the original diesel engine increased mechanical efficiency, and enabled coal dust instead of liquid fuel to be burned, it was short-lived due to an Augsburg factory explosion. Required to revise it, Diesel then created a superior engine.

Diesels do not require high octane gasoline but generally use kerosene or heavier petroleum distillates as fuel. (See *Engine, Internal-Combustion,* page 1568.)   —Hunter Hughes

Power-Handling Capacity of EHV Lines

Voltage Rating	Typical Loads Carried in Megawatts (Millions of Watts)	Corresponds to the Average Consumption of:
115,000	120	Wichita, Kan.
230,000	300	Hartford, Conn.
345,000	550	Cincinnati, Ohio
500,000	1200	Montreal, Quebec
700,000	2900	Chicago, Ill.

Electric Power Transmission, the movement of electric energy from its point of generation to its point of use. The job of transmitting electric power has grown from the earliest direct-current (D.C.) transmission lines of several hundred volts, emanating from central community power stations of the 1890's, to today's vast alternating-current (A.C.) transmission networks, with some lines operating at hundreds of thousands of volts. These networks, or grids, extend hundreds of miles between terminals so as to interconnect almost all the major geographic areas in the United States and Canada.

The economic and technical forces that have encouraged higher voltages and greater transmission distances are not much different today than they were in the early stages of power-system evolution. One reason for this is that power companies have found it economical to generate power in large centralized plants, relying on more extensive transmission networks to deliver power to the ultimate commercial, industrial, and residential consumers. Another reason is that neighboring power companies (or regions) have found it economical to build transmission lines interconnecting their systems. This serves to reduce the number of spare generators required for emergencies; to take advantage of differences in time at which maximum power demand occurs; and to enable plants to be situated where generation is most economical, that is, at the source of fuel itself.

■CARRYING CAPACITY.—In general, the ability of a transmission line to carry power is proportional to the square of its voltage rating; for example, doubling the voltage increases the power-handling capacity by four. For a given voltage rating, the amount of power that can be transmitted is inversely proportional to the distance of transmission.

Power lines, in general, are three-phase. This means that three separate conductors are required, each operating at the same voltage with respect to ground, but each reaching the crest of its alternative voltage at a different time. They are rated in accordance with the route-mean-square (rms) voltage between conductors or phases. Actual voltage ratings of power lines range from several thousand volts, typically used to distribute power directly to residences, to 500,000 volts, typical of the most modern interconnections between adjacent power systems. A recently constructed inter-area system in Canada will operate at 700,000 volts. Some gauge of the power-handling capacity of high-voltage transmission lines can be seen from the accompanying table.

Transmission lines in the lower voltage range are generally capable of carrying power up to the point where increased power through them would overheat the conductors. Higher voltage lines are often limited in their power-handling capacity by the need to keep the power systems at both ends of the line in electrical synchronism. If too much power is carried, an electrical disturbance (such as a lightning stroke to the line) will cause the two systems to become unstable, that is, to lose synchronism. This is analogous to a long mechanical shaft coupling two motors. As long as the shaft is intact (even though twisted by the force applied), the motors must run at the same speed. If one machine tries to transmit too much torque to the other, the shaft will break, and the two machines will run independently.

■ECONOMIC FACTOR.—In general, the choice of voltage level for a transmission line is dictated by economics. Once the amount of power and the distance to be traversed is known, the most economic voltage level can be ascertained. As higher power levels and longer distances are required, higher voltage levels can be economically used—usually resulting in a decreased cost per kilowatt-hour of power transmitted.

Voltages as high as 1,000,000 volts have been proposed for use, and 1,500,000 volts may be technically feasible. Both voltages, however, are beyond the limits of present equipment.

With the exception of a few metropolitan high-voltage underground cables, virtually all transmission lines of 115,000 volts or more are carried on overhead wires. These wires are separated by porcelain insulators from the tower that supports them, and from each other simply by the air between them. By carefully designing cables that use oil and paper or, in some cases, synthetic insulation between wires, engineers have found that a spacing of 25 feet needed in open air can be reduced to several inches in a cable. This gain in compactness is achieved at a substantial increase in cost. A 345,000-volt overhead line that might cost $70,000 per mile using overhead construction would cost more than $1,000,000 per mile in metropolitan underground cable systems.

In the case of low-voltage distribution lines, the extra cost for underground cable is not nearly so great since the cable itself is much simpler

U.S. DEPARTMENT OF THE INTERIOR

ELECTRICAL POWER produced by the generating station at the Hoover Dam begins a 250-mile transmission to Los Angeles from these towers on the Nevada side of the dam.

and can be directly buried without specialized techniques or equipment. In new residential subdivisions, the cost of an underground system may be the same as that of an overhead system, or perhaps half again as much. Conversion of existing overhead distribution to underground is much more expensive, since virtually all equipment must be replaced.

■D.C. TRANSMISSION.—The technical limit of very-long-distance A.C. transmission lines is determined by keeping the two systems at either end of the line in synchronization. High-voltage D.C. transmission, therefore, has become increasingly attractive in the United States for long-distance, high-power applications.

On D.C. transmission lines, the power is (1) received as conventional A.C.; (2) converted to D.C. by huge mercury-arc rectifiers; (3) transmitted as D.C.; and (4) reconstituted into three-phase A.C. by an identical array of mercury-arc valves for delivery to the receiving system.

High voltage D.C. lines are capable of carrying immense blocks of power. The power flow over a D.C. line can be regulated virtually independently of the state of synchronism of the systems at the two ends. This is analogous to a fluid coupling in a mechanical system. Two high-voltage D.C. lines, each rated plus and minus 375,000 volts (750,000 volts between conductors), will soon link the Pacific Northwest with the city of Los Angeles and with the Hoover Dam in Arizona.

■ COMPETITIVE POWER SOURCES.—In the business world, high-voltage power transmission must be looked on as only one of several competing means of transporting energy. The energy that is ultimately delivered to a city can be converted from fuel resources

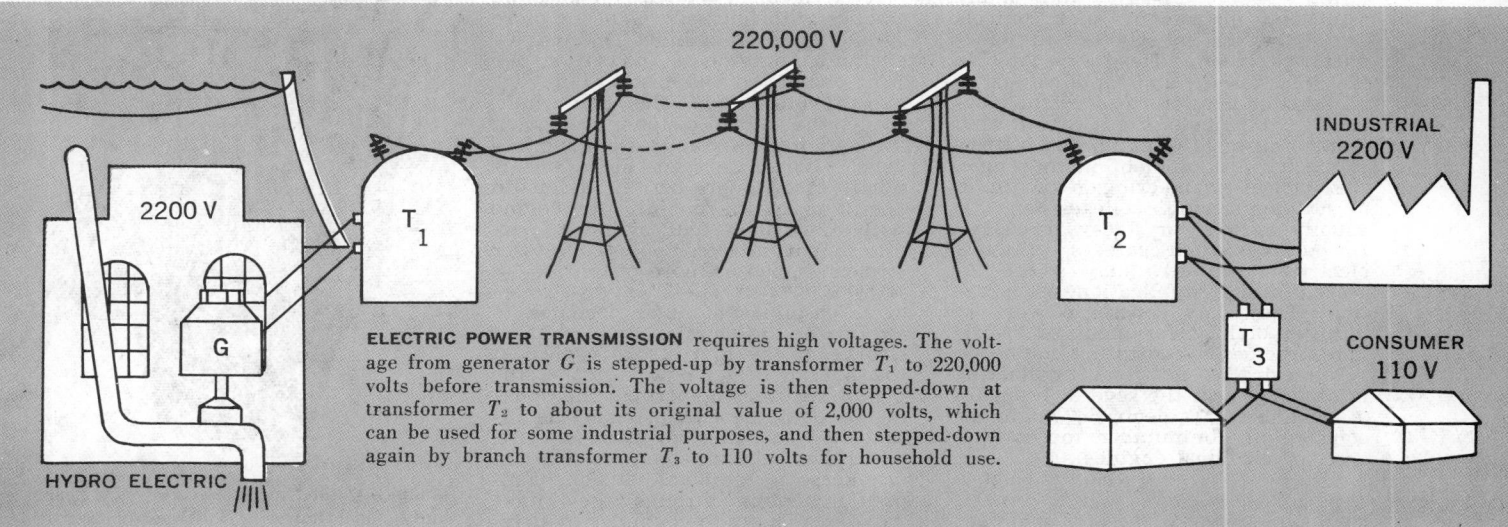

220,000 V

INDUSTRIAL 2200 V

2200 V

T_1

T_2

T_3

CONSUMER 110 V

ELECTRIC POWER TRANSMISSION requires high voltages. The voltage from generator G is stepped-up by transformer T_1 to 220,000 volts before transmission. The voltage is then stepped-down at transformer T_2 to about its original value of 2,000 volts, which can be used for some industrial purposes, and then stepped-down again by branch transformer T_3 to 110 volts for household use.

G

HYDRO ELECTRIC

hundreds of miles remote from the city and transmitted electrically to the urban load, or the fuel itself (coal, gas, oil, etc.) can be transported by rail or pipeline for use in generating the power locally.

Engineers sometimes talk of a day when each home will have its own power source (perhaps using atomic energy), thereby eliminating the need for power transmission altogether. There are some profound problems that make this appear quite unlikely. To begin with, all the progress in making power more economical has led to its generation in larger rather than smaller amounts. Secondly, the total-generating capacity in the United States is now only one-tenth as great as the sum of all individual maximum power demands of U.S. consumers. Extensive power transmission networks allow present-day systems to take statistical advantage of the fact that each consumer's maximum demand occurs at a different time. Individual home power units could not take advantage of this ten-to-one diversity.

—L.O. Barthold

Electrical Engineering, the branch of engineering dealing with the design and application of electrical equipment and electronic systems. The nineteenth century was a mechanical age, but with the invention of the electromagnet and the vacuum tube, electric power and electronic systems replaced many mechanical devices and made possible entirely new practical applications of the forces of electricity.

At the start of the twentieth century, electrical engineering was in its infancy, and electrical engineers dealt primarily with the design and operation of electric generating stations, transmission and distribution lines that delivered the electric energy to its point of use, and motors and electric lights that made use of the energy. This is still an important part of electrical engineering, but communication and electronics have become major aspects of electrical engineering. Telephone, radio, television, radar, X-ray, and many associated instruments and controls are all within the scope of the electrical engineers. He is responsible for the design and application of thousands of different pieces of electrical equipment, from complicated systems in huge research laboratories to electrical equipment in the home.

Electrical engineering is taught in most engineering colleges and is usually a four- or five-year course. In pursuing their careers, graduate electrical engineers may select research, design, application, or operation. They may choose to work in industry or in government, or in private practice as consulting engineers.

Numerically, electrical engineering is the largest of the several branches of engineering; electrical engineers considerably outnumber mechanical, civil, or chemical engineers.

—Hunter Hughes

Electroluminescence. See *Lighting,* page 1573.

Engine, Internal-Combustion, a prime mover in which the combustion of the fuel takes place within the engine rather than in an external furnace. Gasoline engines, gas engines, diesel engines, and semi-diesel engines, are all internal-combustion engines.

The internal-combustion engine considered here is the gasoline engine operating on an *Otto cycle,* named for the German inventor Nikolaus Otto, who patented and built (1877) the first practical engines of this type. It is today the commonest of all prime movers, powering all kinds of equipment from toys to aircraft, including the most obvious example, the automobile.

The gasoline engine derives its power from the explosion of a mixture of air and gasoline, as opposed to the diesel engine, in which the fuel burns rather than explodes. The air-fuel mixture, when ignited, expands rapidly in a cylinder, forcing a piston from the top of the cylinder to the bottom. The piston is attached to a crankshaft by means of a piston rod, and the crankshaft translates the lineal movement of the piston into rotary motion.

■**FOUR-STROKE CYCLE.**—The gasoline engine is designed to make use of either a two-stroke or a four-stroke cycle. In the four-stroke cycle, the piston strokes are: (1) *intake*—the piston moves down the cylinder drawing in, through an open intake valve, an explosive mixture of fuel and air; (2) *compression*—all valves are closed, and the piston moves toward the top of the cylinder, compressing the explosive mixture; (3) *power*—while all valves are closed, the mixture is ignited by an electric spark when the piston is near the top of the cylinder toward the end of the compression stroke; the resulting explosion drives the piston downward; (4) *exhaust*—as the piston reaches the end of the power stroke an exhaust valve opens, and on the return stroke the piston drives all exhaust gases from the cylinder to complete the series. It takes two full revolutions of the crankshaft to complete the four strokes.

It is customary to design gasoline engines with four, six, eight, or more cylinders. Four-cylinder engines, for example, provide a power stroke from one of the four pistons on every half revolution of the crankshaft, while the other pistons are going through intake, compression, or exhaust. It can be seen that a multiplicity of cylinders permits a smooth operation of the engine. An engine with more than four cylinders permits a partial overlapping of power strokes in two or more pistons.

■**TWO-STROKE CYCLE.**—The two-stroke-cycle gasoline engine is designed to eliminate the intake and exhaust strokes of the four-stroke cycle. At the bottom of its power stroke, the piston uncovers or permits the opening of both the exhaust and the intake valves. The air-fuel mixture, which has been precompressed in the crankcase or in an outside compressor, enters through the intake valve, *scavenges* the cylinder by driving out the exhaust gases, and is then

further compressed by the upward stroke of the piston. As with the four-stroke cycle, explosion results from an electrical spark, and the piston is driven downward on its power stroke.

Gasoline engines operating on the four-stroke cycle greatly outnumber those using the two-stroke, since automobile manufacturers have concentrated on four-stroke designs. There are, however, a few European manufacturers producing cars powered by two-cycle engines. Two-cycle engines have been used extensively in the United States for powering lawnmowers and similar light equipment. The average user is conscious of the difference only in that the two-cycle engine requires the addition of lubricating oil to the gasoline, whereas the four-cycle engine does not. In the United States, the trend is to the four-stroke cycle, even for small engines. However, the amazingly miniaturized, single-cylinder, model aircraft engine, with a cylinder smaller than a thimble, is a two-stroke design familiar to nearly every boy.

■**STROKE AND BORE.**—The number of cylinders has no direct relationship to the power or speed of an internal-combustion engine. A four-cylinder engine with a long piston *stroke* and a large *bore* (cylinder diameter) may have much more power than an eight- or twelve-cylinder engine with a short stroke and a small bore. Many of the great racing automobiles have four-cylinder engines. Equally great winners have six, eight, or twelve. It is a matter of the designer's preference. *Displacement* is a much more useful measure of

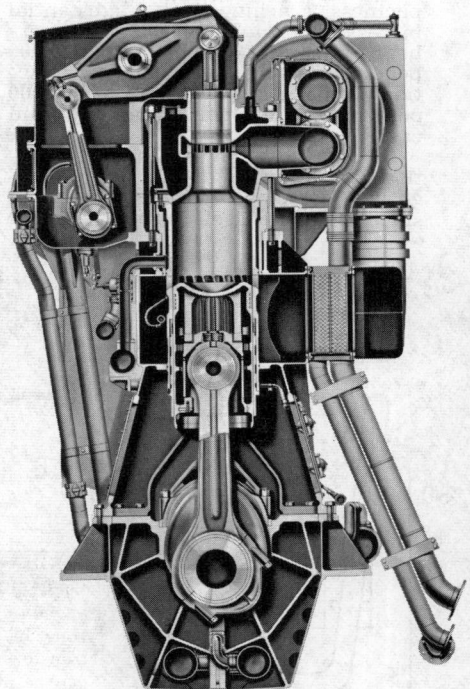

FAIRBANKS MORSE

DIESEL ENGINE in cross-section is a heavy-duty model delivering 1,000 horsepower per cylinder for marine or heavy industrial use.

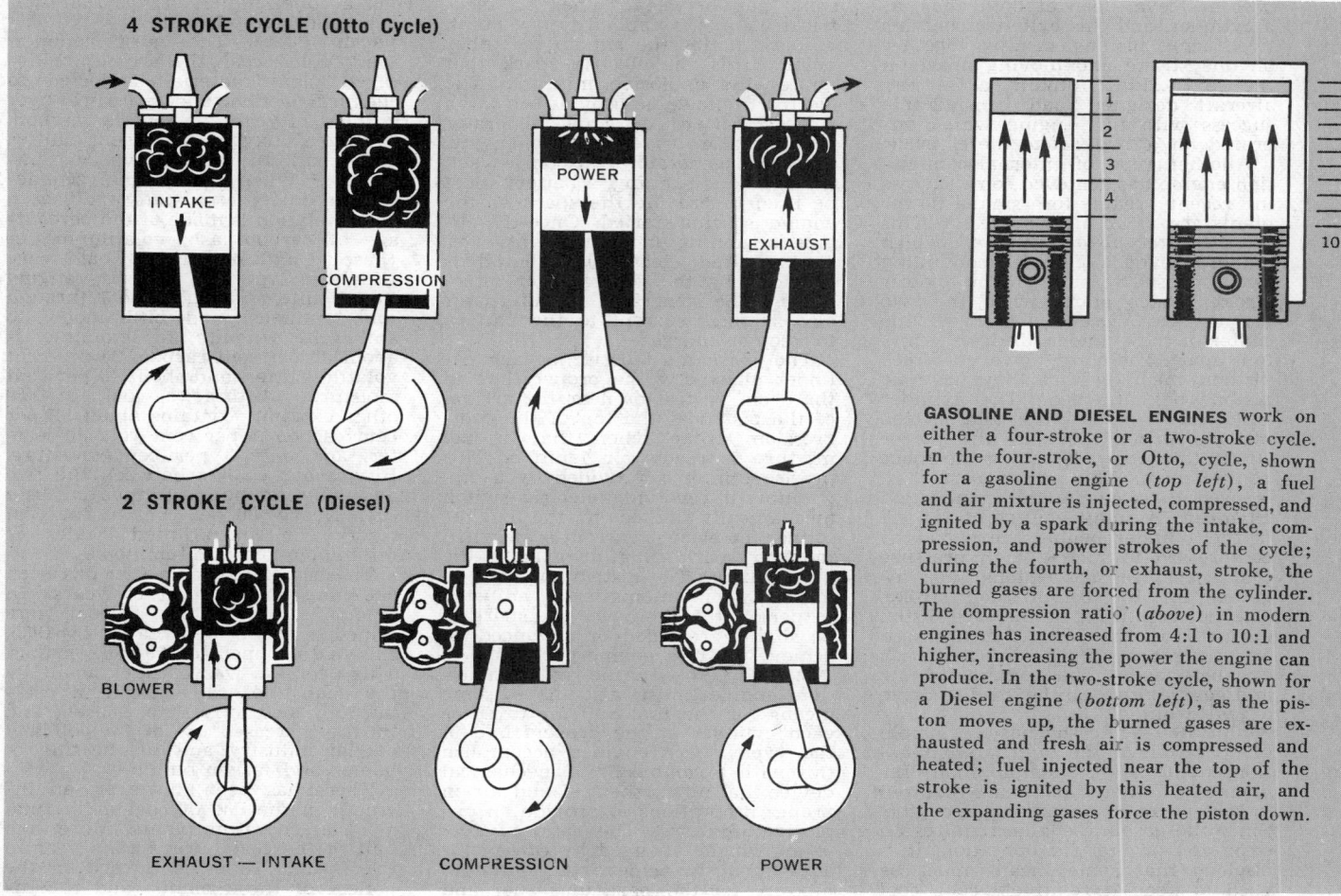

4 STROKE CYCLE (Otto Cycle)

INTAKE

COMPRESSION

POWER

EXHAUST

2 STROKE CYCLE (Diesel)

BLOWER

EXHAUST — INTAKE

COMPRESSION

POWER

1
2
3
4

10

GASOLINE AND DIESEL ENGINES work on either a four-stroke or a two-stroke cycle. In the four-stroke, or Otto, cycle, shown for a gasoline engine (*top left*), a fuel and air mixture is injected, compressed, and ignited by a spark during the intake, compression, and power strokes of the cycle; during the fourth, or exhaust, stroke, the burned gases are forced from the cylinder. The compression ratio (*above*) in modern engines has increased from 4:1 to 10:1 and higher, increasing the power the engine can produce. In the two-stroke cycle, shown for a Diesel engine (*bottom left*), as the piston moves up, the burned gases are exhausted and fresh air is compressed and heated; fuel injected near the top of the stroke is ignited by this heated air, and the expanding gases force the piston down.

power. When a piston moves in the cylinder from the bottom of its stroke to the top, its movement brings about a change in volume in the cylinder. The change in volume can be measured in cubic inches, as in U.S. practice, or in liters, as in European practice (a liter is about 61 cubic inches). This "working volume" of all the engine's cylinders combined is called the displacement of the engine. It can be seen that a four-cylinder engine in which there is a displacement of 100 cubic inches in each cylinder ($4 \times 100 = 400$) is larger, and all else being equal, more powerful than an eight-cylinder engine with a displacement of 40 cubic inches in each cylinder ($8 \times 40 = 320$).

■**COMPRESSION RATIO.**—The compression ratio is another factor influencing the power output and efficiency of a gasoline engine. The compression ratio is the ratio of the volume of the cylinder at the bottom of the piston stroke to the volume at the top. In modern automobile engines this ratio may be as high as ten or eleven to one, meaning that the maximum volume of the cylinder is ten or eleven times as great as the minimum volume, as measured with the piston at opposite ends of its stroke. These *high-compression engines* use the higher octane fuels.

■**CYLINDER ARRANGEMENTS.**—Internal combustion engines are designed with a wide variety of cylinder arrangements. The *in-line*, or straight, engine has all cylinders arranged in a line straight down the engine block. This is a common arrangement for four-, six-, and occasionally eight-cylinder engines. The V arrangement is more popular for eight-cylinder engines. It consists of two banks of four cylinders, each set at an angle with the crankshaft at the bottom. This is a compact design permitting the use of a shorter crankshaft. This V design is also used for twelve-cylinder engines and for the few sixteen-cylinder engines that have been manufactured.

In recent years the *horizontal design* has become popular for smaller (usually four-cylinder) automobile engines. This is a flat engine with half the cylinders on one side of the crankshaft and half directly on the other. This is a special type of V design in which the angle of the V has been increased to 180°.

The *radial engine* has been used largely for aircraft and is only now being replaced by the gas turbine and the turbojet. For many years it was the standard engine design for larger aircraft. In the radial engine the cylinders are arranged in a circle with

the crankshaft in the center. There is but one crank on the crankshaft to which a master rod from one piston is attached. The rods from the other pistons are connected by wrist pins to the large end of the master rod. There is always an odd number of cylinders.

During the last 75 years of intensive development of the internal-combustion engine, many engines with unusual cylinder arrangements have been built, but few offered any distinct advantages. One of the more interesting is the *rotary engine*, similar in appearance to the radial engine except that the crankshaft is stationary and the cylinders rotate about it. This was used for a few aircraft engines during World War I, but the rotation of the heavy engine in one direction made it difficult to keep the entire aircraft from rotating in the other.

The W engine has enjoyed some popularity as an aircraft engine, it being similar to the V but with an additional bank of cylinders between. The X is simply two V engines joined together, one above and the other upside-down below. None of these designs is popular today.

There are a few other internal combustion engine designs worthy of mention. The *opposed-piston engine* uses a sleeve, open at both ends, as a cylinder, and this cylinder contains two facing pistons, coming together on one stroke and moving apart on the next. Hugo Junkers, a German aircraft designer, had considerable success with this engine which operated on a two-stroke diesel cycle.

Another type of internal-combustion engine has achieved some success in recent years for small power plants and as an air compressor. This is the *free-piston engine,* which makes use of a cylinder containing two opposed pistons. The power stroke, which starts when the two pistons are close together at the center of the cylinder, drives the pistons apart. These are, however, "free" pistons, meaning that they have no piston rods attached. The cylinder is closed at both ends, and as the pistons spring apart in the power stroke they compress air in the space behind them. This air, or part of it, is used to scavenge the combustion chamber. A small volume of air left in the cylinder behind the pistons is compressed to such a high pressure that it bounces the pistons back together for the compression stroke. The power output of the free-piston engine is in the form of compressed air or compressed air combined with exhaust gases. The compressed air and gas mixture can be used to drive a gas turbine.

■ **COOLING.**—While the basic principle of operation of the internal-combustion engine is quite simple, many refinements and auxiliaries are required to achieve an efficient, reliable engine. Since the gasoline engine requires an explosion of fuel for operation, it is obvious that some means must be used to keep it relatively cool, cool enough to permit the lubricating oil to function efficiently. Engines are either *air-cooled* or *liquid-cooled.* For many years liquid-cooled engines were considered more satisfactory, but improvements in design have made the air-cooled design popular for smaller automobiles.

The *liquid-cooled engine* provides jackets around the cylinders through which the liquid flows, carrying off heat. The hot liquid flows or is pumped to a radiator consisting of finned tubes. A fan forces the air through the radiator. The cooling liquid is usually water to which alcohol or some antifreeze is added in cold weather. Occasionally other liquids, such as thin oils, are used as coolants. The principal advantage is the prevention of rust and scale in the cooling system.

The *aircooled engine,* provided with large cooling fins directly outside the cylinders, and with larger fans, manages to keep the cylinder temperature sufficiently low for efficient operation. This type of design is simple and ideal for propeller-driven aircraft, where the rapid flow of air over the cylinders provides excellent cooling

■ **IGNITION SYSTEM.**—An ignition system is also essential to a gasoline engine. The *spark* igniting the air-fuel mixture is provided by a *spark plug.* This plug, fitted into the top of the cylinder, has two points of copper with a small gap between. When an electrical voltage is applied to one point, a spark jumps the gap to the other point. It is the electric spark that ignites the explosive mixture. The electric voltage is provided from a *storage battery* or small generator or alternator driven by the engine. Since the generator runs only when the engine is running, a battery must be used to provide the spark as the engine is being started. Once the engine is running under its own power, the required electrical potential is provided by the generator or alternator. The generator or alternator also supplies current to the battery to keep it charged.

The spark must occur in each cylinder at exactly the proper time in the cycle, just at or near the arrival of the piston at the top of the compression stroke when the air-fuel mixture is ready for ignition. This precise timing is provided by a *distributor,* a revolving electric switch mechanically linked to the engine, so that the electric current is switched to each spark plug at exactly the proper time. The distributor may be manually or automatically adjusted to permit the timing of the spark to be slightly retarded or advanced to achieve the best engine performance.

■ **CARBURETION.**—An internal-combustion engine must also have some means for the fuel and air to enter each cylinder at the proper time in the cycle. Most engines accomplish this with a *combustor,* a mechanical device that mixes the fuel and air in proper proportions to provide an explosive mixture. The ratio of fuel to air can be changed by *carburetor* adjustment to achieve the optimum mixture for the particular fuel and the particular engine design. The air-fuel mixture from the carburetor is drawn into each cylinder on the intake stroke of the piston in a four-cycle engine or enters under pressure at the start of the compression stroke in the two-cycle engine.

■ **FUEL INJECTION.**—Some engines are designed to use *fuel injectors,* rather than carburetors. There is no premixing of air and fuel. Instead, the fuel is injected into the cylinder as air is being compressed on the upward stroke of the piston. This would appear to resemble the diesel engine, but with a high volatile fuel, gasoline, and with a spark ignition, there is still the characteristic explosion of the Otto cycle rather than the relatively slow burning of fuel characteristic of the true diesel.

■ **LUBRICATION.**—Lubrication is essential to the operation of the internal-combustion engine. Many types of lubricating systems have been designed, but all manage in some way to supply lubricating oil to the bearings of the crankshaft and to the walls of the pistons and cylinders, thereby reducing friction, and consequent overheating and wear.

Many useful accessories designed to improve engine operation or reduce engine wear have been developed. The *air filter* for the carburetor, the *supercharger,* and the *oil filter* are typical examples.

—Hunter Hughes

Fuel, a solid, liquid, or gas that will burn and give off heat.

■ **SOLID FUELS.**—The most common solid fuel is coal, the product of decayed plant material subjected to chemical action and pressure over millions of years. It contains carbon, hydrogen, oxygen, nitrogen, sulfur, and small amounts of various impurities. When coal is analyzed according to its *proximate analysis,* a determination is made of the percentage of carbon, ash, volatile matter (gases), and moisture. Coals vary widely in type and analysis, ranging from lignite, a low grade coal, through subbituminous, and bituminous, to anthracite. *Lignite,* for example, is about 30 per cent carbon, 25 per cent volatile matter, and about 40 per cent moisture. *Anthracite* coal, at the other extreme, contains about 92 per cent carbon, 5 per cent volatile matter, and only 3 per cent moisture. *Bituminous* coal is between the two and is by far the most important as a fuel. Nearly 80 per cent of the coal reserve in the United States is bituminous or subbituminous.

The use of coal as a fuel has been declining for the past 20 years. In 1947, 631 million tons of coal were mined in the United States; by 1965, this had dropped to 459 million tons. This decrease was brought about by the change of railroads from coal-burning locomotives to Diesels and by the increased use of fuel oil and gas in industry and for heating of homes and larger buildings.

There has been, however, an increase in the use of coal in thermal electric generating plants. More than half of the coal burned each year in the United States is burned in the boilers of these plants, and the increase has continued each year.

Lignite, also, is used primarily as a fuel for electric utility plants and its consumption may be expected to gradually increase. The outlook is less bright for anthracite, which has been burned primarily for space heating. Oil and gas have largely replaced it.

There are many other less important solid fuels. *Peat,* which is plant matter that has partially decomposed under water in a bog or swamp, is used as a fuel in many parts of the world. It is an important fuel in the Soviet Union and Ireland, where it is used in power stations as well as for heating. In most parts of the world it is produced as an agricultural additive to improve soil.

Wood is still an important fuel, since many homes have fireplaces, and a wood fire is pleasant if inefficient. Only in sawmills and the wood industries is it burned commercially.

Charcoal, generally produced by driving off the volatile matter in wood, leaving the carbon, is a minor solid fuel now formed into briquettes and used for outdoor cooking. It has some limited industrial uses.

Straw, tan bark, and bagasse (sugar cane from which the juice has been extracted) are burned in industrial boilers where they otherwise would be waste products, but they are not distributed and sold commercially as fuels. *Petroleum coke* is also burned

World Production of MINERAL FUELS

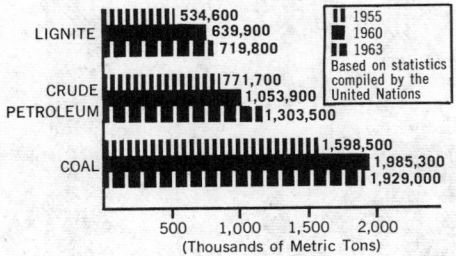

	1955	1960	1963
LIGNITE	534,600	639,900	719,800
CRUDE PETROLEUM	771,700	1,053,900	1,303,500
COAL	1,598,500	1,985,300	1,929,000

Based on statistics compiled by the United Nations

500   1,000   1,500   2,000
(Thousands of Metric Tons)

in a few thermal power plants, but it, too, is a minor solid fuel.

■ **LIQUID FUELS.**—Liquid fuels have increased enormously in importance during the twentieth-century. In 1900, liquid petroleum fuels were used to produce about 5 per cent of the energy output of the United States; by 1963 this had increased to about 35 per cent, largely at the expense of coal.

The most important liquid fuels are hydrocarbons produced by refining crude petroleum pumped from wells. A typical crude oil from a well contains about 85 per cent carbon, 13 per cent hydrogen, and some minor impurities. This kind of oil is refined by various processes to produce gasoline, kerosene, jet fuels, fuel oil, and many other products, such as lubricants and asphalt.

Gasoline is the most important of the liquid fuels, since it is used in most automobiles, trucks, and aircraft. Over 1.6 billion barrels of gasoline were produced in the United States in 1963. Today, natural gasoline refined from crude petroleum is combined with naphthas, natural gas liquids, and various other compounds and additives to produce a fuel suited to the modern internal-combustion engines.

Most *kerosene,* which is less highly refined than gasoline, is used as a fuel for jet aircraft, though there are other minor fuel uses. Military-grade jet fuel is a high-grade kerosene or a mixture of gasoline and kerosene.

Fuel oil is another product of crude oil refining. It is available in many grades and viscosities from thin Diesel fuel to heavy residual oils that are more solid than liquid and must be warmed before they will flow. The lighter *distilate fuel oils* are used as Diesel fuels and for smaller heating units. The heavier *residual fuel oils* are used in large heating units and as industrial and electric utility fuels.

Much recent research has been devoted to development of fuels for rocket engines. The United States has concentrated primarily on liquid fuels while continuing to investigate solid fuels. One important rocket fuel is kerosene and liquid oxygen (Lox). Liquid hydrogen-oxygen and hydrogen-fluoride serve as fuel for the upper stages of lunar launch vehicles now being developed. Nitric acid and alkyl-hydrazine mixtures are useful as fuels for some special requirements of spacecraft.

There are, of course, many liquid fuels other than those derived from crude petroleum. Considerable liquid fuel is extracted from natural gas. Oil can be extracted also from certain sands and shales, but neither of these sources has yet been exploited to any great extent. Alcohol is a good fuel but expensive. Liquid by-products of some process industries are used as fuels rather than being discarded as waste. So-called *black liquor,* a by-product of paper manufacture, is burned in papermill boilers, for example.

■ **GASEOUS FUELS.**—The use of *natural gas* as a fuel is growing rapidly—more rapidly than any other fuel. It is, like liquid petroleum products, composed primarily of hydrogen and carbon, and it, too, is taken from wells. After being processed, it is piped to the point of use. Natural gas, as a fuel, is used in industrial furnaces and utility boilers, but it has also become more and more popular for home heating and cooking and for heating commercial buildings.

The great advantage of gas is its simplicity of use. Solid fuels require large storage facilities and are difficult to handle. Coal varies greatly in burning characteristics, and when used in large utility boilers must be cleaned and pulverized. There is also the problem of ash removal and smoke. Coal's primary advantage is price, and even this advantage does not exist in all areas. Liquid fuels are ideal for moving vehicles and present less of a handling problem than solids, but they, too, must be stored in tanks prior to use. Gas, supplied to the user under pressure, requires no storage, no handling, and there is no ash or smoke. This accounts for the rapid increase in the use of natural gas as a fuel for heating homes and larger buildings.

Where natural gas is not available, *liquid petroleum gas* (LPG), consisting primarily of propane and butane, which are gas products of petroleum refineries, are sold in pressure tanks and used mostly as cooking fuels.

Gases other than natural gas are useful fuels. Before natural gas became so generally available, gas manufactured from coal and coke served as an important industrial and domestic fuel. Experiments have been conducted during the past few years for the gasification of coal in the mines so that the output of the mine is an industrial fuel gas rather than coal. A method for producing from coal gaseous hydrocarbon similar to natural gas, by a process known as hydrogenation, is under investigation. Gas fuels such as hydrogen and acetylene have specialized but limited use.

The term *fuel* now generally used with reference to uranium and plutonium in atomic piles producing heat, is technically incorrect, for there is no combustion involved in the nuclear reaction.

—Hunter Hughes

Fuel Cell, a versatile power source of great simplicity and high efficiency that converts energy from the reaction of a conventional fuel and air (oxygen) into low-voltage direct-current electric energy. Theoretically, a fuel cell can be built in almost any size and capacity. For practical purposes, however, individual cells are stacked in small modules, or *batteries,* and connected electrically in parallel. The major difference between fuel cells and conventional batteries is that the former operate continuously as long as fuel and an oxidizer are supplied and their electrolyte remains chemically unchanged, eliminating the need for recharging. Most fuel cells have no moving parts and require little or no maintenance. The noxious or toxic exhaust products associated with a combustion reaction—heat, smoke, and noise— are avoided. Water and/or carbon dioxide are the usual by-products.

The principle of the fuel cell is not new. Sir Humphry Davy first suggested it in 1802 and the first laboratory demonstration was by Sir William Grove in 1839. However, the fuel cell remained an electric power curiosity, by-passed by the steam engine, the internal-combustion engine, and nuclear energy, until the late 1950's. One of the first practical applications of fuel cells was on the

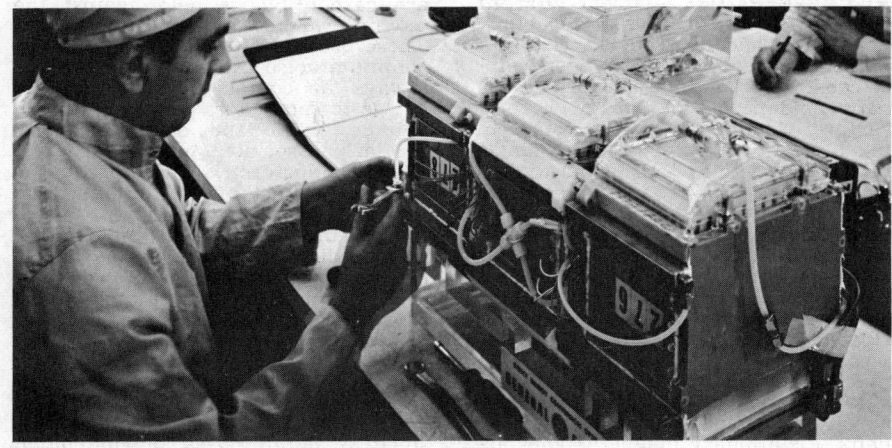

GENERAL ELECTRIC COMPANY

FUEL CELL MODULES (*foreground*) are connected with control equipment and enclosed in cylindrical cases during assembly of batteries that are used in the Gemini space program.

eight-day flight of the Gemini 5 spacecraft in August 1965, when two fuel cell batteries successfully provided prime electric power for the spacecraft.

The fuel cell reverses the well-known process of electrolysis. Instead of breaking water down into its components by passing an electric current through it, water is formed in a controlled reaction that liberates electric energy.

A typical fuel cell contains an anode and cathode, which are in contact with an electrolyte (acid or alkali) that acts as an ion-transfer medium. Fuel (normally hydrogen) is introduced at one electrode, and an oxidizer at the other. In an *acid electrolyte fuel cell,* the hydrogen reacts with the electrolyte at the anode, giving up electrons to the electrode and ions to the electrolyte. The ions migrate through the electrolyte to the surface of the other electrode, where they combine with electrons that have traveled through the external circuit and with the oxygen diffused through the electrode, to form water as a by-product. Individual cells are connected in series to produce the desired voltage, and are sized to give the needed current. Scaling up or down does not significantly change performance or efficiency.

The efficiency of fuel cells is far greater than that of conventional engines. By converting chemical energy directly into electric energy, the fuel cell is not subject to the thermal cycle limitation of conventional generating equipment. Unlike conventional engines, the fuel cell uses fuel only on demand and produces energy more efficiently at partial or no-load. Practical fuel cells can convert 60 to 70 per cent of chemical energy into electricity, an efficiency about twice that of a gas turbine.

Although recent development activity has brought forth a great variety of fuel cells, hydrogen and oxygen remain the most popular fuel-oxidizer combination. For general use, highly efficient fuel cells that consume a commonly available hydrocarbon fuel—such as natural gas, propane, or such liquid fuels as kerosene and gasoline—are being developed. Some use the hydrocarbon fuels directly; others use hydrogen extracted from the hydrocarbon by means of a reformer.

Eventually, fuel cells are expected to be used for a wide variety of ground and marine uses. Present applications are in military and space programs where the advantages of small size, low weight, and high efficiency outweigh high initial costs. Already proven on the Gemini spacecraft, fuel cells are also scheduled for the flight to the moon. Transportable fuel-cell systems, ranging in output from 10 watts to 15 kilowatts, could become the light, compact, all-purpose military electric power source. Silent and able to use military fuels and air at high efficiency, they may be used to power communications equipment, radar, and sonar or to charge batteries.

—Roy S. Mushrush

U.S. DEPARTMENT OF THE INTERIOR

GIANT GENERATORS use electromagnets to convert the mechanical energy produced by the Hoover Dam's water supply into electrical power for many areas of the West Coast.

Generator, Electric, a machine that converts mechanical energy into electric energy. It operates by providing relative motion between electric conductors and a magnetic field. Such relative motion, or "cutting," of lines of magnetic force generates electric voltage in the conductors. The conductors are joined in a systematic winding whose ends are terminated on the external frame. When these terminals are connected to an electrical load, the generated voltage causes electric current to flow through the completed circuit.

If the current from the generator flows continuously in one direction, it is a *direct-current* or D.C. *generator.* If the current rapidly reverses direction, it is an *alternating-current* or A.C. *generator.* The 60-cycle power systems in common use are supplied by A.C. generators, in which this cycle from positive to negative and back to positive occurs 60 times every second.

■ **D.C. GENERATORS.**—Direct-current generators are of two basic types, homopolar and heteropolar. The *homopolar* or *acyclic* D.C. generator is constructed with a uniform magnetic field perpendicular to its rotor surface. Conductors on the rotor cut magnetic lines uniformly in a single relative direction, thus generating a D.C. voltage. Connection to external load can be made by stationary contacts, such as carbon brushes sliding against collector surfaces on the rotor. Often the rotor is a solid metal piece that serves as the conductor. The acyclic D.C. generator, demonstrated by Michael Faraday in 1831, was the first type of generator.

The *heteropolar* D.C. generator, developed somewhat later than the acyclic generator, usually has several pairs of stationary magnetic poles arranged around the inner periphery of a magnetic yoke. The poles have electromagnet coils connected so that the poles are alternately north and south. The magnetic field passes from the north poles into the magnetic material of the rotor and then back to the stationary south poles. The rotor or armature has insulated conductors near the surface that pass alternately under north and south poles, cutting magnetic lines in two opposite directions. Thus is an A.C. voltage generated; if the conductors were connected directly to an electric load, A.C. voltage would flow. However, the heteropolar D.C. generator has a means of converting the A.C. to D.C. The usual conversion is by a *commutator* rotating with the armature. This is a cylinder comprised of wedge-shaped copper bars separated, one from the next, by thin strips of insulation. The individual copper bars are electrically connected to the armature conductors. Electrical contact is made with the commutator surface by means of *brushes,* which are carbon blocks held against the moving surface by spring pressure. These brushes are spaced around the commutator so that half of them are always in contact with bars connected to conductors generating north voltage, while the other half are similarly associated with south voltage conductors. Therefore, the switching effect of commutator bars sliding past brushes converts alternating-current voltage in the conductors to direct-current voltage at the stationary terminals.

Some small D.C. generators convert the A.C. to D.C. by means of rectifier elements mounted on the rotating armature. These generators usually supply magnetic field current to large synchronous machines.

Direct-current generators are classified as *shunt, series,* or *compound,* depending upon how the magnetic field is produced. The application determines which class should be

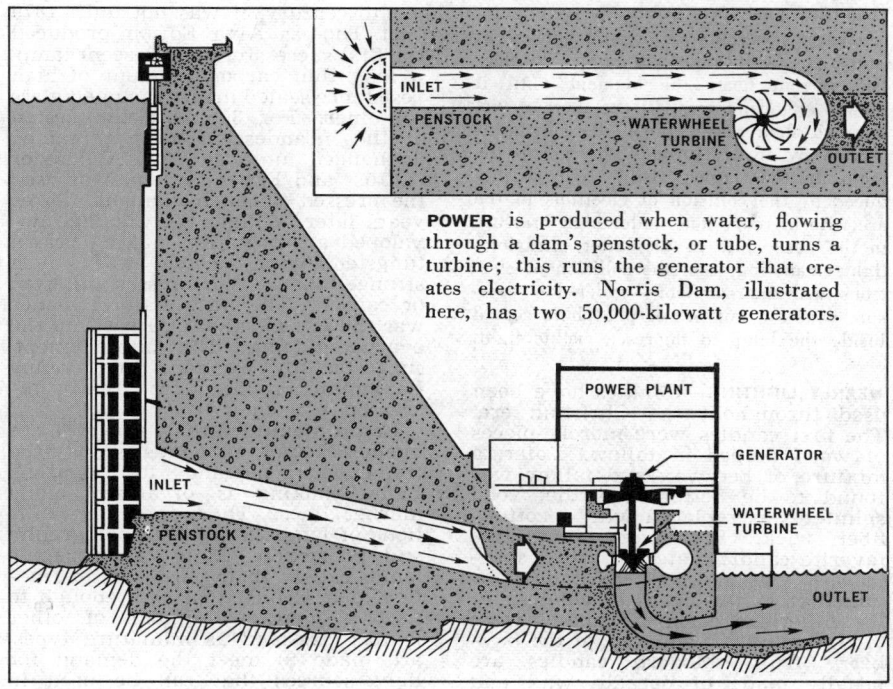

POWER is produced when water, flowing through a dam's penstock, or tube, turns a turbine; this runs the generator that creates electricity. Norris Dam, illustrated here, has two 50,000-kilowatt generators.

used. D.C. generators can be driven by any rotating prime mover, although engines, small turbines, and electric motors are most common. D.C. generators have industrial, utility, and transportation applications. The largest use is to supply power for D.C. motors, but electroplating, chemical refining, and others require bulk D.C. energy. Sizes range up to 6,000 kilowatts and 800 volts.

■ **A.C. GENERATORS.**—Alternating-current generators operate on the same principle of voltage generation as do the heteropolar D.C. generators. Indeed, the heteropolar D.C. generator is an A.C. generator until the commutator or other device changes the A.C. to D.C. The usual form of A.C. generator, however, has its electromagnetic poles on the rotor and its conductors for voltage generation on the stationary armature. This permits current to be taken off without large collector rings. However, a small collector is still needed to carry D.C. to the rotating electromagnets. The type of A.C. generator just described is the most common; it is often called a *synchronous generator* or an *alternator*. Two other forms of

A.C. generators, having lesser application, are the *inductor alternator* and the *induction generator*.

The inductor alternator has a toothed steel rotor that provides magnetic field variations simulating north and south poles. It is inherently limited to small power ratings and is best suited for generating high frequencies, that is, 180 to 10,000 cycles per second (cps).

The induction generator is simply an induction motor (see *Motor, Electric*) with its rotor driven faster than synchronous speed by a prime mover, thus feeding electric energy back into the power system to which it is connected. Because the induction generator requires a connected system for successful operation, it is limited to a few special applications.

The A.C. frequency generated by any alternator is determined by the formula: cycles per second =

$$\frac{\text{(number of poles)} \times \text{(revolutions per minute)}}{120}$$

Power systems in the United States and Canada are usually 60 cps. In other countries, however, 50 cps is often the standard frequency.

The principal use of A.C. generators is power generation for residential and industrial consumers. Large generators of two types are generally employed: *steam turbine-generators* and *hydroelectric generators*.

■ **STEAM TURBINE-GENERATORS.**—Steam turbine-generators, also called turbo-generators, are of the synchronous-generator type, and are directly connected to high-speed steam turbines. Because of the resulting large centrifugal forces, the rotor is a single-piece, high-strength forging slotted for the magnetic field coils. The result is a so-called *round-rotor field* instead of the *salient-pole field* previously described for synchronous generators. Progress in materials and

in mechanical and electrical design has been tremendous over the years, permitting larger and larger ratings of generators to be built. Units rated 500,000 kilovolt-amperes and higher have been installed. Voltages for the larger machines range up to 22,000 volts.

■ **HYDROELECTRIC GENERATORS.**—The hydroelectric generator, sometimes called *water-wheel generator*, is the other major type of large generator. It is a salient-pole synchronous generator, and the usual installation has a vertical shaft with the generator mounted above the prime-mover hydraulic turbine. The combined weight of the generator and turbine rotor plus the downward thrust of the water passing through the turbine is supported by a thrust bearing located near the generator. The speed of the generator depends upon the *head*, or height of fall, of the water and upon the type of turbine. Speeds range from about 50 rpm to 600 rpm for large hydroelectric generators, and ratings above 200,000 kilovolt-amperes have been furnished. The most common voltage rating is 13,800. The larger units may be 40 feet in over-all diameter when installed. Gas turbines and engines also are used to drive A.C. generators, but not to the same extent as steam and hydraulic turbines.   —H. D. Snively

Hydroelectric Power, the use of the force of falling water to generate electricity. There are two basic types of water power. The first utilizes the natural flow of rivers and must depend on the particular flow of a river at a given time. The second obtains water from a reservoir. The flowing water passes through turbines which power *hydroelectric generators* thus producing electricity.

The first hydroelectric plant was built in 1882 in Appleton, Wis. Several years later, George Westinghouse (1846–1914) developed a system of transmitting power across long distances by using alternating current. In 1896 current was generated at Niagara Falls, N.Y. and transmitted to Buffalo, a distance of 20 miles. (See also *Electric Power Transmission*, page 1566.)   —Joseph J. Kelleher

Lighting, the use of sources of illumination to facilitate seeing. The earliest form of artificial lighting was the open campfire, and this was succeeded by more sophisticated flame sources, such as candles, oil lamps, and gas lights. It was not until the last quarter of the nineteenth century that electric lighting systems became practical. Today, except in emergencies or in areas where electric power is not available, electric lighting is the universal source of artificial illumination. Electric lamps are relied on to supply the illumination needs of a highly complex technology. Electric lamps deliver lighting at standards of quality and quantity far beyond the possibilities of flame sources, and they do this safely and economically. Electric lamps are produced in thousands of shapes and sizes, with widely different performance characteristics.

World Production of ELECTRIC ENERGY in %

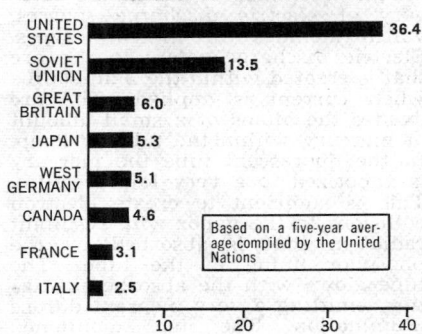

UNITED STATES	36.4
SOVIET UNION	13.5
GREAT BRITAIN	6.0
JAPAN	5.3
WEST GERMANY	5.1
CANADA	4.6
FRANCE	3.1
ITALY	2.5

Based on a five-year average compiled by the United Nations

10   20   30   40

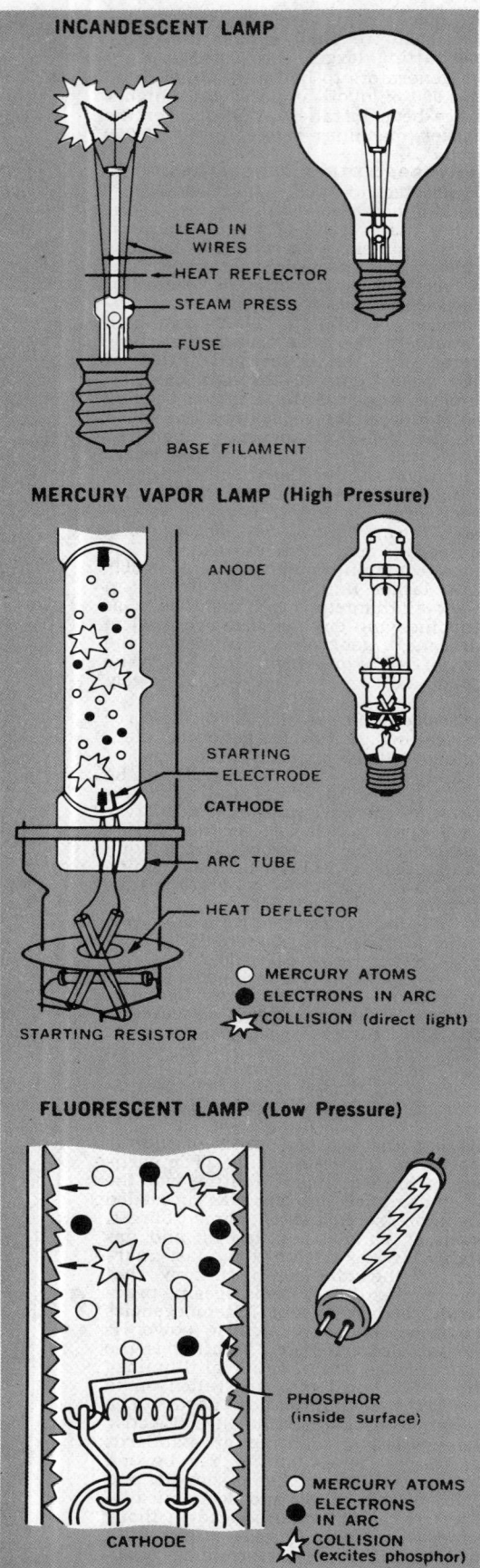

INCANDESCENT LAMP

LEAD IN WIRES

HEAT REFLECTOR

STEAM PRESS

FUSE

BASE FILAMENT

MERCURY VAPOR LAMP (High Pressure)

ANODE

STARTING ELECTRODE

CATHODE

ARC TUBE

HEAT DEFLECTOR

○ MERCURY ATOMS
● ELECTRONS IN ARC
✦ COLLISION (direct light)

STARTING RESISTOR

FLUORESCENT LAMP (Low Pressure)

PHOSPHOR (inside surface)

○ MERCURY ATOMS
● ELECTRONS IN ARC
✦ COLLISION (excites phosphor)

CATHODE

ELECTRIC LIGHTING SOURCES include incandescent, mercury vapor, and fluorescent lamps. In the incandescent lamp, the electric current heats the filament until it glows, or incandesces. In the mercury vapor and fluorescent lamps, the current is carried by an arc through the gas in the lamp. In the former, visible light is produced by the collision of electrons in the arc with mercury ions under high pressure in the gas, while in the latter ultraviolet light emanating from the collision of electrons with mercury ions under low pressure causes a mixture of phosphors coated inside the lamp to fluoresce visible light.

■**EARLY LIGHTING.**—*Candles* have been used throughout the Christian era. The first candles were merely pieces of wood dipped in tallow. Later, a mixture of beeswax and tallow was found to be better, and the wood splinter was replaced with a cotton-fiber wick. For many years the favorite candle material, called *spermaceti,* was a waxy substance obtained from the heads of whales. In the American colonies, candles were often made from the wax of the bayberry fruit. Modern candles are usually made of paraffin wax and stearin, a hardening agent derived from animal fats.

Primitive *oil lamps* were unsatisfactory because of their ineffectual lighting and smoky flame. In 1784 the French mathematician Jean Robert Argand equipped the oil lamp with a glass chimney, which provided for a better, steadier, less smoky light. During the period of oil lamp use, the chief fuel was whale oil.

For many years, gas was one of the most important illuminants used in cities. The early discovery of natural gas was made in England by Thomas Shirley in 1659, when he found gas bubbling through the water in a well. In the second half of the seventeenth century, John Clayton discovered that he could produce a gas that would burn by heating coal in a retort. It was another century, however, before gas came into practical use for illumination.

The first gas lights were merely open jets in which the flame burned with a deficiency of air. The light from the flame came from the incandescent particles of carbon that had failed to ignite. Later other substances were used with burning gas to give a whiter light. The *limelight,* for example, utilized lime (calcium oxide), but the materials found to be the best producers of light when heated to very high temperatures by a gas flame were the oxides of thorium, cerium, and zirconium. In 1885 the gas lamp was improved by Karl Auer von Welsbach's invention of a device, called the *Welsbach mantle,* by which a combination of these oxides could be suspended in the gas flame. The Welsbach mantle produced a brilliant white light and was responsible to a great extent for the adoption of gas lighting in towns and cities.

■**ELECTRIC LIGHTING.**—Although there had been experimentation with *electric* lighting since the early nine-teenth century, it was not until 1879 that Thomas Alva Edison produced the first successful incandescent lamp, a long thin carbon filament of high resistance sealed in an evacuated glass container. For 30 years the design of the incandescent lamp remained unchanged, until in 1907 Alexander A. Just and Franz Hanaman devised the pressed tungsten filament. Three years later, William D. Coolidge developed a process for making drawn tungsten wire, which was much stronger than either pressed tungsten or carbon. The next major advance was the introduction of a gas into the evacuated lamp. This improvement, suggested by Coolidge and Irving Langmuir, provided for greatly increased efficiency.

Lamp manufacture is a very large business today, as it must supply the tremendous demand for lighting. Lamp making is organized along market lines. Thus, there are millions of lamps made for photography and projection. Many photographic lamps satisfy their purpose in a fraction of a second, just long enough to take a picture. Millions of other lamps, classified as miniature types, are made to meet the demand for light sources that can be used in limited space for extended service; an example is the automobile lamp. Large lamps, both incandescent and fluorescent, used for general lighting service, account for the largest markets in terms of both numbers and dollars. Mercury lamps, widely used in industry and in outdoor area lighting, belong in the large lamp category.

■**TYPES OF LAMPS.**— *Incandescent lamps,* since Edison's day, have been the dominant source for lighting. The highly efficient fluorescent lamps, introduced in 1938, have by now created a strong and growing market for these sources. Nevertheless, incandescent lamps still account for well over half the money spent for large lamps. They are popular because of low installation cost and simplicity of operation. While they are made in many shapes, the typical incandescent lamp consists of a glass bulb enclosing a filament that is mounted on a glass stem; in the stem there are wires to carry current from the contact on the base to the filament. The instant the current enters the lamp the filament becomes incandescent, and thus produces light. Compared with the fluorescent lamp this process of light production is simple.

Fluorescent lamps are in the category of *electric discharge* sources, which includes the mercury types. Electric discharge refers to the arc that is created within the light source when current is applied. The arc excites the atoms of a small amount of mercury within the tube or lamp. In the fluorescent tube the mercury is vaporized to a very low pressure. This is sufficient to create electron collisions in the vapor with resultant radiation that is absorbed by the phosphor lining of the tube. The tube glows with the absorbed radiation, emitting a very pleasant diffuse illumination. The steps mentioned require several seconds in some fluorescent lamps to produce light. With the "rapid start" and "instant start" types the steps are telescoped by special design of the circuits.

Fluorescent lamps have greatly increased the scope of lighting service. Advanced standards of illumination, widely sought for stores, schools, offices, and factories, require economical fluorescent systems.

Incandescent and fluorescent lamps are often combined in general lighting installations. The two sources complement each other. Incandescent lamps are concentrated "point" sources, rich in red energy. Fluorescent lamps are diffuse, low-brightness sources, cool in effect and color quality, highly efficient and long-lived. In combination they provide versatile, satisfying illumination.

Mercury lamps, inherently producers of discontinuous spectrum concentrated in blue energy, offer economy of light production and long life. They are in demand for industrial and outdoor service where color quality may be less important than low-cost maintenance. Mercury lamps are high-pressure mercury vapor cousins of fluorescent lamps, and like them, are noted for efficiency. *Neon lamps* simply substitute neon gas for mercury vapor.

Lucalox lamps, made available in 1966, are the first general-purpose white light sources with efficiency in excess of 100 lumens per watt. These lamps belong to the family of high-intensity electric discharge sources that include the mercury types. Intense white light, produced in a slender, elliptical-shaped bulb, is made possible with the cigarette-sized Lucalox arc tube within the bulb. The ceramic arc tube permits the use of alkali metal vapors at much higher temperatures than have ever before been practical.

Electroluminescent lamps, available for commercial use, represent the most exciting development in illuminants in the mid-twentieth century. These are wafer-thin lights that can be made in almost any two-dimensional shape, from the size of a collar button to a rectangle measuring 12×14 inches. They are uniformly bright over the entire surface, and can be mounted on flat or curved surfaces. Electroluminescent lamps have a long, dependable life; they come in three colors—green, yellow, and blue—in addition to the standard white.

The operation of electroluminescent lamps is simple. Light emanates from crystalline powders, or phosphors, sandwiched between the lamp's two electrically conducting surfaces, one of which is translucent. When the lamp is connected to line voltage, the powders absorb the electrical energy and convert it into light with minimal heat. No auxiliary equipment is needed for operation. Some of the many uses for which these lamps are recommended include animated advertising displays; flashing or continuously lighted signs; decorative panels for aircraft, pleasure boats, and ocean liners; lighted railing for stairways; clock faces; lighted house numbers; courtesy lights in theaters;

and readout lamps for computers.

The principle of light production by electroluminescence has engendered much hopeful speculation about a larger role for lamps of this category. Architects dream of general lighting systems employing these sources in large panels for ceilings and walls. A great deal of investment in laboratory work has gone into the present product. As experience with present applications grows, and research developments are furthered, this new source may join the major general-lighting illuminants.

—James L. Tugman

Lightning, a high-voltage electric discharge in the form of a luminous, multibranched spark from cloud to ground, or within or between clouds. A typical lightning flash consists of from 2 to 40 separate strokes, at intervals of a few hundredths of a second, each consisting of tens of thousands of amperes of electric current. To the human eye, which cannot resolve the individual strokes, lightning appears as a single flash lasting about one second. The stroke is usually a mile or two in length, but may extend 50 miles or more on rare occasions. The electric power dissipated in a single stroke is in the range of several billion horsepower.

Lightning is produced by intense electric charges that occur during thunderstorm weather conditions. The central region of a thundercloud contains an intense negative charge, while the top and bottom contain intense positive charges. Lightning can occur within the cloud, or from cloud to cloud, when the insulation of air breaks down in response to these strong electric fields. Cloud-to-ground lightning occurs when the central negative portion of the cloud discharges to the ground below. Lightning is thought to be nature's way of returning positive charges from the earth to the upper atmosphere against the current that flows continuously from air to earth.

The several strokes along the lightning path heat the air, causing it to expand. Repeated expansion and contractions caused by the strokes generate intense sound waves, which we hear as thunder. *Heat lightning,* a reddish, luminous globe about a foot in diameter, is most mysterious of all. It may hover, explode, or quietly disappear.

—William C. Vergara

Magnetohydrodynamics, or *MHD,* a method of generating electricity in which an electrically conducting gas is forced to move past a magnetic field. The gas becomes conductive when it is heated to temperatures greater than 2,500°C, producing a mixture of electrons, ions, and molecules. This mixture, called a *plasma,* is forced past a magnetic field, thereby taking the place of the wires in a conventional electric generator. The major problem in *MHD* power generation is finding an electrical insulating material that can contain the white hot plasma over a period of years without breaking down. No such material has yet been developed.

—William C. Vergara

Motor, Electric, a machine that converts electric energy into mechanical energy. According to the "motor" principle, an electrical conductor carrying current in the presence of a magnetic field experiences a force that tends to move the conductor at a right angle to the field. An electric motor is constructed so that either the magnetic field member or the conductor member is stationary, while the other element becomes the rotor, free to rotate in bearings and coupled to the rotating mechanical load.

In construction, electric motors resemble electric generators. (See *Generator, Electric,* page 1572.) Most motors can operate as generators and vice versa; many practical applications require a machine to perform either function. A motor may be either D.C. or A.C., depending on which type is called for by the main power supply.

Direct-current motors are generally similar in construction to the heteropolar D.C. generator; they both feature a revolving armature and commutator and a stationary magnetic field. Incoming D.C. at the motor terminals flows into the armature conductors through the brushes and the commutator. The current-carrying conductors react with the stationary magnetic field to cause the rotor to revolve. The conductors thus contact positive and negative commutator brushes alternately. The sliding action of commutator bars past brushes performs the function of converting D.C. at the terminals to A.C. in the moving conductors, the exact reverse of its function in a D.C. generator.

A D.C. motor, like most other electrical motors, has an inherent ability to adjust itself to changing load de-

U.S. DEPARTMENT OF COMMERCE

FORKED LIGHTNING splits the sky during a summer electrical storm. Only about one electrical discharge in ten strikes the earth.

mands, as distinguished from many other mechanical drives. Since the motor has all the elements of a generator, it follows that the conductors are generating a so-called *back voltage* at the same time as they are experiencing the force that moves the rotor and drives the load. This back voltage, which always opposes the stationary terminal voltage in direction, is lower, and the difference between them is proportional to the load current. If the mechanical load increases, a motor will tend to slow down, thus reducing its back voltage, which is proportional to the speed. This will increase the difference between back voltage and applied voltage, and the motor will draw an increased current from the power line to match the new load demand.

D.C. motors, like D.C. generators, are classified as *shunt, series,* or *compound* according to how the electromagnetic field coils are supplied with current. In a *shunt* motor, the field winding is parallel to the armature circuit, so the magnetic field force does not vary appreciably with load-current changes. A *series* motor has its field winding in series with the armature, so its magnetic field strength changes directly with the load current. A *compound* motor has both a shunt and a series winding.

Shunt D.C. motors are widely used where it is desirable to have fairly constant speed, regardless of changes in mechanical load. Changes in armature current do not affect the magnetic field strength appreciably, and the motor will change speed only slightly with load changes. However, a big advantage of a shunt motor is that its speed is readily controllable by a *field rheostat,* an adjustable resistance in series with the field winding circuit. Increasing the resistance will reduce the field current and raise the motor speed; reducing the resistance will raise the field cur-

rent and lower the speed. These characteristics of good speed regulation under load and of simple speed adjustment make D.C. shunt motors desirable for many industrial applications. For example, large D.C. motors drive the main rolls of reversing and continuous metal rolling mills, where wide ranges of loads and of speeds are needed as the metal is processed from the hot ingot to the final product of thin strip or structural shape.

Series D.C. motors undergo a large drop in speed as the load current increases, due to the increased field strength. The driving torque increases rapidly, however, because the conductor current and the magnetic field strength increase together. This makes series motors particularly applicable in land transportation where this load characteristic is desirable; for example, a locomotive climbing a grade requires considerably more torque at a lower speed than it needs on the level run. The series motor also has excellent starting ability. However, the speed of a series motor is not adjustable by simple control methods.

Compound D.C. motors have characteristics ranging between those of shunt and series motors, depending upon the relative strength of the two field winding elements.

D.C. motors are usually powered from D.C. generators or from static rectifiers that convert A.C. to D.C. Small D.C. motors, such as those used in an automobile, can be powered from batteries. Ratings range from tiny units rotating at very high speeds to large, low-speed motors—for example, 7,000 horsepower (hp) at 50 revolutions per minute (rpm) for steel mill or marine applications. Voltages of less than 800 are customary.

Alternating-current motors are either *synchronous* or *asynchronous,*

depending upon whether they operate at exactly synchronous speed under all load conditions. Synchronous speed is determined by the formula:

synchronous speed (in rpm) =

$$\frac{120 \times \text{frequency (in cycle per second)}}{\text{number of poles}}$$

A *synchronous motor* has the same construction as a synchronous generator, with a stationary armature and a rotating electromagnetic field, usually salient-pole. An induction-motor type of winding on the pole surface permits self-starting of a synchronous motor having a three-phase or other polyphase armature winding. The motor locks into synchronous speed when field current is applied after it has been accelerated almost to speed by the induction-motor winding, which then ceases to carry current. Changes in load on the motor do not reduce the speed as on a D.C. motor, but do cause changes in the current and its so-called power factor drawn from the A.C. lines.

Synchronous motors are used where their constant speed, high efficiency, or other attributes are important. They are used as drive motors on A.C. to D.C. motor generator sets, and as drives for compressors, blowers, printing presses, centrifugal pumps, and many other devices. An increasing application for very large synchronous motors is in pumped storage hydroelectric units, where the unit acts as an electric generator during peak power periods and as a motor to pump water to a storage reservoir during off-peak periods. Units as large as 200,000 horsepower have been supplied for this purpose. A separate starting motor is sometimes used on such large machines instead of an induction-motor starting winding.

The most common *asynchronous motor* is the *induction motor.* The stationary member of an induction motor is like that of a synchronous

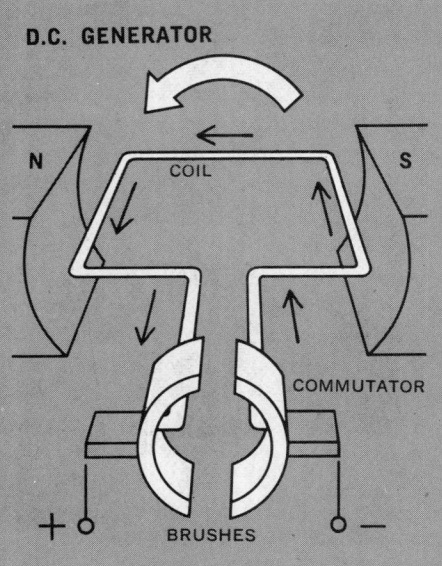

D.C. GENERATOR

N · S · COIL · COMMUTATOR · BRUSHES · + · −

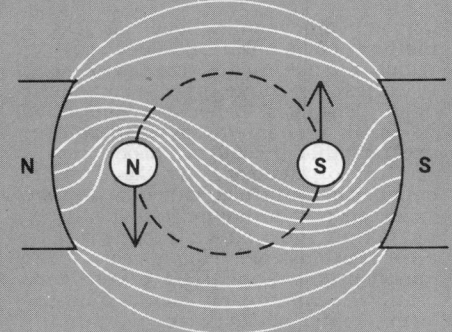

ELECTRIC GENERATORS produce an alternating current when a coil rotated in a magnetic field between the poles of a magnet (*below*), distorts the field. A direct-current generator (*left*) has a commutator, or split ring, to carry the current in only one direction; in an alternating-current generator (*right*) two slip rings change the flow alternately in opposite directions.

N · N · S · S

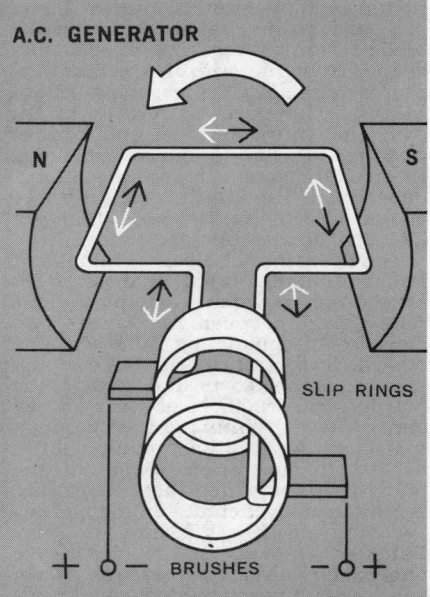

A.C. GENERATOR

N · S · SLIP RINGS · BRUSHES · + · −

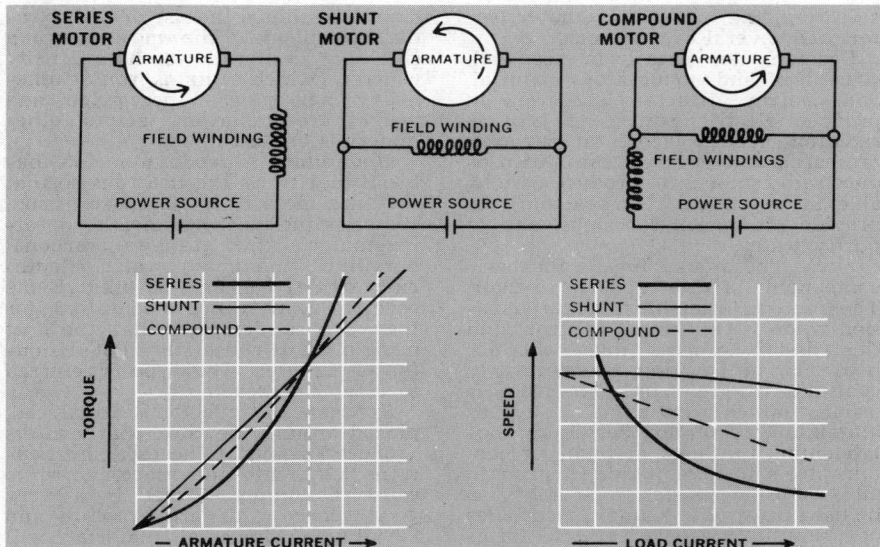

DIRECT-CURRENT MOTORS are classed by the manner in which their field coil is connected in the circuit. In a series motor (*top left*) the armature and field windings are connected in series; in a shunt motor (*top center*) they are connected in parallel; and in a compound motor (*top right*) the field winding is in two parts—one in series and the other in parallel with the armature winding. The increase in torque and decrease in speed of each type with increasing load are compared graphically at bottom left and bottom right, respectively.

motor. The rotor is either a *squirrel-cage* type or a *wound-rotor* type. The *squirrel-cage,* so named for its appearance, has an assembly of bare axial conducting bars embedded in the rotor surface and joined together at either end of the rotor by heavy conducting end rings. The *wound-rotor* has insulated conductors arranged in a polyphase winding, the ends of which are brought to collector rings on the shaft for external control purpose.

In either case, when power is applied to the stationary winding of a three-phase or other polyphase motor, a rotating field is induced that in turn cuts the rotor conductors, causes rotor currents to flow, and causes forces to be exerted on the rotor bars to turn the rotor. The rotor accelerates almost to synchronous speed but never quite attains it. If it did, no rotor current would flow and there would be no force to turn the rotor. The difference between actual speed and synchronous speed is called the *slip.* Slip increases with load and, depending upon the type of induction motor, is from 0.5 to 5 per cent of synchronous speed at rated load.

Wound-rotor motors with external control of their rotor windings are used where large speed adjustment is necessary. *Squirrel-cage* motors, rugged in construction and low in cost, are used in a variety of applications where approximately constant speed is needed but where speed adjustment is not required. Ratings up to 10,000 horsepower have been supplied. Wound-rotor motors over 40,-000 horsepower are in operation.

Another large class of asynchronous motor is the *single-phase induction motor.* It is usually small in power rating and designed for use where polyphase power is not readily available. A single-phase induction motor is not self-starting in the manner previously described, because a single-phase armature winding produces a pulsating field rather than a rotating field. It is customary to simulate the effect of a polyphase winding by a special starting arrangement that brings the motor up to speed, whereupon a single-phase motor will behave much as a polyphase motor. *Split-phase, capacitor, shaded-pole,* and *repulsion* motors are several types commonly used. Each name describes a starting method.

Series A.C. motors are asynchronous motors identical with series D.C. motors except that the field magnetic

structure is laminated instead of solid. Since the magnetic field and the conductor current change direction simultaneously at the A.C. frequency, this motor type behaves like a D.C. series motor. In fact, it is sometimes called a *universal motor* because it can be used on either A.C. or D.C. Applications are similar to those of D.C. series motors, in addition to considerable use in A.C. household appliances.

Fractional-horsepower motors are a class including all types of D.C. and A.C. motors less than one horsepower in rating. Most modern homes have from 10 to 50 fractional-horsepower motors performing various jobs.

Timing motors for electric clocks and other accurate timing purposes are A.C. motors of special construction, either *hysteresis motors* or *synchronous-inductor motors.*

—H. D. Snively

Neon Light. See *Lighting,* page 1575.

Nuclear Engineering, the branch of engineering that deals with the control and utilization of energy and radiations from nuclear sources. Perhaps the most common example of the work of a nuclear engineer is the nuclear reactor. In a nuclear reactor, the heat energy given off in the fission of uranium is converted into useful electric power. Examples of other things a nuclear engineer might design are food sterilization plants and thickness gauges. In a food sterilization plant, nuclear radiations (usually gamma rays from radioactive cobalt) are used to kill insects or bacteria in grain, bacon, and other food products, thus retarding spoilage. A thickness gauge can be built making use of the fact that the intensity of a beam of nuclear radiation is decreased in passing through matter. The amount of the decrease in intensity of a beam of beta rays, for example, can be used to measure the thickness of aluminum foil or the amount of tobacco in a cigarette.

The distinguishing feature of the formal education of a nuclear engineer is that it includes courses in reactor physics (the study of controlled nuclear chain reactions), atomic and nuclear physics, the handling and use of radioactive materials, radiation shielding, and the effects of radiation on materials. The nuclear engineer must also be skilled in other fields of engineering (e.g., electrical, mechanical, metallurgical, and chemical), in order to control, utilize, and understand problems associated with nuclear energy sources. —R. O. Wooton

Nuclear Power, energy that is obtained from nuclear fission and fusion reactions and from radioactive disintegrations. In a *fission reaction,* the nucleus of a heavy atom, such as uranium, splits into smaller fragments. In a *fusion reaction,* two nuclei of a light atom, such as hydrogen, combine or fuse to form a single, heavier nucleus. In a *radioactive disintegration,* the nucleus of an atom emits nuclear radiations in the form of gamma rays, beta particles, and alpha particles.

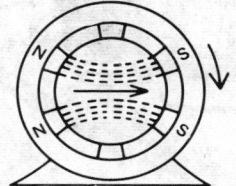 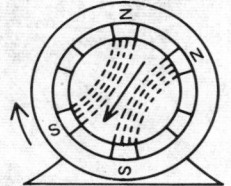 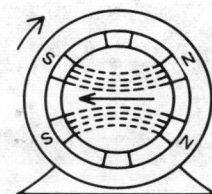

THREE-PHASE induction motor is a fixed rotor surrounded by a rotating magnetic field made by stator windings on three sets of poles. When the three-phase alternating current reaches the motor it moves through each winding, revolving the magnetic field.

The fission of uranium-235 is accomplished by bombarding the nucleus with a neutron, which splits the nucleus into two fragments of about equal mass. In the fission process a few neutrons are emitted, and energy is liberated. The energy liberated is the source of heat in nuclear reactors. The neutrons emitted can cause fissions in other uranium atoms, and a self-sustaining, or nuclear, chain reaction is possible. In addition to uranium-235, other isotopes of uranium and plutonium are readily fissionable by neutrons.

Fusion reactions are responsible for the heat generated by the sun and for the explosive power of the hydrogen bomb. Since about 1952, scientists around the world have been working intensively to attain a controlled fusion reaction, which could be used to generate electric power. Of primary importance for controlled reactions is the fusion of combinations of deuterium and tritium, which are isotopes of hydrogen. As of 1966, a controlled fusion reactor had not been built, and it is not known with certainty whether it is possible. It is a worthwhile effort for scientific research, however, since there is sufficient deuterium fuel in the oceans of the world to provide mankind with an essentially unlimited source of energy.

The nuclear radiations emitted in radioactive disintegrations possess energy of motion that can be converted into heat. This heat energy can be converted into electric power. Devices of this type have been built to provide power for marine life buoys and for space satellites.

—R. O. Wooton

Nuclear Reactor, a device that generates heat from the controlled fission of the atomic fuel. Since fission heat is accompanied by radiation, the reactor is a source of radioisotopes for research as well as for power. The reactor is divided into six basic sections: the *reactor core,* which contains the fuel; the *coolant;* the

shielding, the *moderator;* the *reflector;* and several *control rods.*

Reactors vary greatly in size, fuel, structural and moderator material, and coolant. Reactors are used to produce electric power, to provide radiation for experimental purposes (research and test reactors), to produce radioisotopes, to produce fissionable material (breeder reactors), to provide propulsion for ships, and to purify water.

Fuel. The atomic fuel is the basic component of the nuclear reactor. The fuel material must undergo fission when it captures a neutron, and this fission process must produce neutrons, in addition to energy, to continue the reaction. The fuel is usually mixed with a metal such as aluminum, zirconium, beryllium, molybdenum, tungsten, niobium, or certain steels to give it added strength and corrosion resistance. It may also be used directly as oxides or carbides of uranium in some ceramic forms with a minimal cladding (coating) for protection. The fuel and metal mixture is formed into spheres, pellets, or thin plates and is usually clad with the same metal that is used to mix with the fuel. The type of fuel and metal used depends upon the reactor temperature, the use of the reactor, or the reactor type. Fissionable materials used in nuclear reactors are uranium-233, uranium-235, and plutonium.

Coolant. A liquid or a gas is circulated through the reactor core as a coolant to transport the fission heat to energy conversion equipment, such as turbines. The most common coolant is high-purity water, but many other materials can also be used as a coolant. In order to increase reactor efficiency, the reactor is operated at maximum temperatures. The more recent high-efficiency reactors are using liquid metals such as mercury, sodium, or potassium as coolants. Organic liquids and high-pressure gases are also being used.

Shielding. The emission of high-intensity radiation accompanying fis-

sion necessitates the use of heavy radiation shields. The most common shielding material is high-density concrete, which contains iron or other heavy aggregate. Where size and weight are important factors, other materials are used.

Moderator. A moderator is a material that slows the neutrons so that they are more likely to cause fission. Water is the most common moderating material, but graphite (carbon), beryllium, and heavy water (deuterium oxide) can also be used. Some reactors do not have moderators, for they are so designed that the fast neutrons will cause sufficient fissioning of the fuel. This type is referred to as a "fast reactor."

Reflector. A reflector is a material, placed around the core, that scatters (reflects) some of the escaping neutrons back into the reactor core to cause fissioning. Water is a very good reflector, as are graphite and beryllium. Almost all materials will scatter some of the neutrons back into the reactor core, but the elements listed above are the most efficient.

Control Rod. The reactor control rod is a movable section of the reactor core that contains a neutron-absorbing material such as boron, cadmium, and other elements. Since neutrons cause fission, the insertion of a neutron-absorbing material reduces the fission rate and, therefore, the reactor power. The control rods are moved by electric motors and drive mechanisms.

■**OPERATION.**—To help describe the construction and operation of nuclear reactors, an example of a simple reactor system is given below.

One of the most common types of reactors in the United States is the pool-type research reactor. The reactor core is located near the bottom of a large pool of water that has been highly purified by distillation or by an ion-exchange process. All the water impurities are removed because most impurities become radioactive when bombarded by the neutrons

CONSOLIDATED EDISON

ATOMIC ENERGY produces electricity at a New York power station. Below this operating floor, a uranium oxide core is loaded into a reactor covered by water. By 1972 forty-one plants in the U.S. will use nuclear energy as an inexpensive, clean power source.

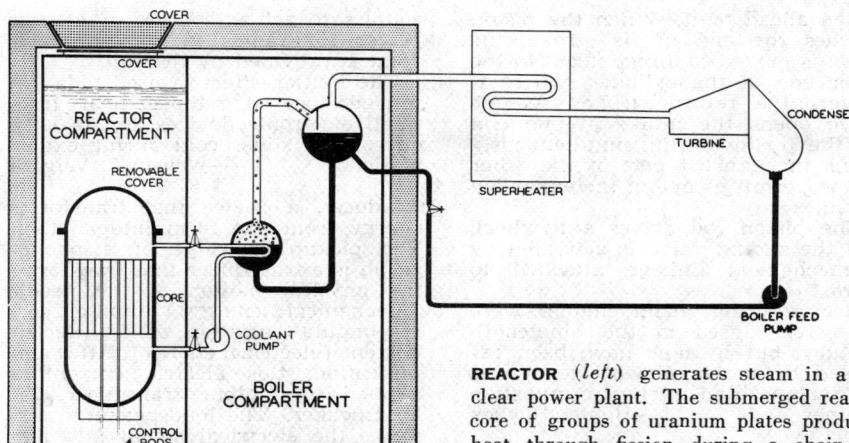

REACTOR (*left*) generates steam in a nuclear power plant. The submerged reactor core of groups of uranium plates produces heat through fission during a chain reaction which is set off by the partial removal of one neutron-absorbing control rod.

CONSOLIDATED EDISON

from the reactor. The pool water serves (1) as the reactor coolant, (2) as a neutron moderator, and (3) as a shield against the high-intensity radiation emitted from the core.

The pool water is circulated through the reactor to remove the heat generated. The water is raised in temperature as it passes through the core and must be cooled before it passes through the core again. The water is cooled by passing it through a "heat exchanger," which operates on a principle similar to that of an automobile radiator. Instead of passing air over the coils to cool the water, as in an automobile radiator, water is passed over the coils.

The reactor core of most of the pool-type reactors uses the plate-type fuel element. The uranium-235 is mixed with aluminum in thin plates and then clad with aluminum to form a plate about 1/16-inch thick. Ten to eighteen plates, spaced about 1/8-inch apart to allow water to flow between them for cooling, are grouped together to form a fuel element. Several of the fuel elements are brought together to make up the reactor core.

The reactor is controlled by placing a neutron-absorbing material (such as boron or cadmium) in the reactor core. If part of the neutron-absorbing material is removed, the reactor will begin to produce a self-sustaining chain reaction, which produces the heat. The reactor can be controlled by the neutron-absorbing material because neutrons, which are produced by fissioning, also cause the fissioning of the uranium. Therefore, absorbing some of the neutrons reduces the number of fissions.

A chamber situated in the reactor core measures the neutron intensity, which is proportional to the reactor power. The neutron chamber is connected to an automatic control device. When the reactor power goes up, the automatic control channel actuates the rod-drive motor and drives the control rod into the core, thereby absorbing more neutrons than before and, therefore, reducing the reactor power. If the reactor power drops below the pre-set power level, the automatic control system

actuates the control-rod drive motor in reverse and it pulls the rod further out of the core, increasing the reactor power.

■**REACTOR TYPES.**—Listed below are several reactor types with brief descriptions of the most common design features.

Research and Test Reactor. This type of reactor has a small core, usually measuring about two feet on a side. The core is fueled with highly enriched uranium (90 per cent or more uranium-235) and the structural material is aluminum or steel. The reactor, normally, is water-cooled and the high-power test reactor is pressurized to prevent boiling. The reactor is designed for experimentation on the effects of radiation on materials.

Power Reactor. The power reactor usually has very large cores, some measuring up to 20 feet or more in diameter. The fuel is normally uranium, slightly enriched (by a few per cent) in the uranium-235 isotope. The structural material is usually steel, and the core is contained in a steel pressure vessel. Pressurized water is the normal coolant, although sodium or organic coolants are sometimes used.

Submarine Reactor. This is a pressurized water reactor that uses highly enriched uranium in the metallic phase or as a ceramic (uranium oxide). The structural material is zirconium alloy or steel, and the core is small—only a few feet square.

Space Reactor. This type of reactor is very small, approximately a foot high and a foot in diameter, with a beryllium reflector. Liquid metals such as sodium or sodium-potassium alloy are used as the coolant to permit very high temperature operation.

Breeder Reactor. This type is a power reactor that has a uranium-238 blanket around it. The fission process in the core is by fast (high-energy) neutrons, as opposed to the usual thermal reactor that uses low-energy neutrons for fission. The fast neutrons collide with the uranium-238 atoms to create uranium-239, which decays to neptunium-239 and then to plutonium-239. The pluto-

nium-239 can then be used to fuel a nuclear reactor. The breeder reactor thus produces fuel even as it consumes fuel to produce power.

—L. O. Gunnels

Prime Mover, a mechanism that changes a natural energy source into mechanical energy in order to power a machine. The term is commonly applied to gasoline or diesel engines, steam turbines, steam engines, water wheels, windmills, and jet engines. The output of a prime mover may be used to rotate a shaft, move a machine element back and forth, or provide a jet for propulsion.

In a diesel-driven electric generator, the generator is turned by the diesel engine, which converts combustible fuel into mechanical energy. The diesel engine is the prime mover, while the generator uses the mechanical energy that is produced. Electric motors are not prime movers because their energy source, electricity, is not a natural source. (See *Engine, Internal-Combustion,* page 1568.)

—Joseph J. Kelleher

Solar Cell, a semiconductor device that generates electricity in significant quantities directly from sunlight. It differs from the older photovoltaic cell mainly in that it can provide a larger amount of electric power. The photovoltaic cell is used primarily as a control device, as in automatic exposure mechanisms for cameras. The solar cell finds its major field of application in power supplies for space vehicles, telephone stations, and portable radio receivers. A large panel of silicon solar cells has even been used experimentally to power an electric automobile.

A silicon solar cell is a thin wafer about twenty-thousandths of an inch thick. It is manufactured in sizes from 3/32-inch square to 1 1/4-inch in diameter. A solar cell weighs less than an equivalent volume of aluminum.

Silicon solar cells are useful for power applications because of their relatively high efficiency. Commercial solar cells are now available having conversion efficiencies between 10 and 13 per cent. This compares with about 11 per cent for the gasoline engine. A 26-square foot panel of solar cells has an electric output power of about 200 watts under solar illumination.

■**PRINCIPLE.**—The solar cell operates on the principle that when light energy strikes certain kinds of atoms, it will dislodge electrons from the atoms. In practice, the solar cell consists of a thin silicon wafer containing a small amount of a material such as arsenic. The surface layer has an additional admixture of boron or a similar material. The junction of the surface layer (boron-silicon) and the rest of the wafer (arsenic-silicon) forms a kind of electrical barrier. As light penetrates both layers, it creates negatively charged electrons and an equivalent number of positive charges (called *holes*) in each layer. The electric force at the junction of the layers drives the electrons to the arsenic side and the positive charges to the boron side. Conducting wires are connected to each layer, and electrons flow from the arsenic layer through the external circuit to recombine with the positive *holes* in the boron layer. This current provides the useful power of the cell.

A typical silicon solar cell having a useful area of one square inch will provide a voltage of about 0.4 volts and a current of 0.175 amperes under solar illumination. This amounts to about 0.07 watts. If higher voltages are required, a number of solar cells can be connected in series. The output voltage is then equal to the sum of the voltages of the individual cells. Additional current capacity can be obtained by using larger cells, or by connecting additional cells in parallel.

■IN SPACE VEHICLES.—The most dramatic application of solar cells has been in satellites and space vehicles, where they convert sunlight into electricity to power the vehicle's electronic equipment. The Telstar communications satellite carries 3,600 solar cells for that purpose. Other solar-cell powered space vehicles include the Tiros weather satellite, the Mariner Venus probe, the Orbiting Solar Observatory, Explorer satellite, and many others. When a satellite is in the shadow of the earth, it uses electricity from storage batteries that have been charged from solar cells. Solar cells are particularly useful in space vehicles because of their light weight and their ability to provide electric power indefinitely without using fuel.
—William C. Vergara

Steam Engine, a simple mechanical prime mover. Steam is produced, at the desired temperature and pressure, in an external boiler fired by coal, oil, gas, or some other fuel. Steam from the boiler is piped to the engine, which in its simplest form consists of a cylinder, valve, piston, piston rod, and flywheel.

At the start of a cycle, the steam enters one end of the cylinder through an intake port. The steam expands in the cylinder, forcing the piston ahead of it. When the piston reaches the end of its stroke, the valve is moved to direct steam to the other end of the cylinder, where it powers the return stroke. As the valve opens the intake at one end of the cylinder, it simultaneously opens the exhaust port at the other end to permit escape of the expanded steam.

The piston rod drives a flywheel, and the sliding valve is activated by a mechanical linkage attached to them.

Reciprocating steam engines were extensively used in the nineteenth century, but by now have been replaced by more efficient steam and gas turbines and internal-combustion engines.
—Hunter Hughes

Thermoelectricity, the generation of electricity by heating the junction of two dissimilar materials. When two wires made of different metals are joined at their ends, and the junctions are maintained at different temperatures, an electric current flows around the loop of wire. Such a device is called a *thermocouple*. The basic phenomenon is called the *Seebeck effect,* after Thomas Johann Seebeck who discovered it in 1821.

The opposite effect also takes place. If both junctions have the same initial temperature, and an electric current is passed around the loop of wire, heat is given off at one junction and absorbed at the other. This makes it possible to transfer heat from a cold body to a hot one, as in a conventional refrigerator. This phenomenon is called the *Peltier effect,* after Jean C. A. Peltier, who first demonstrated it in 1834. Both the Seebeck and Peltier effects are manifestations of thermoelectricity.

The Seebeck effect, in the form of thermocouples, has long been used to measure temperatures up to 3,000° F. This is possible because the voltage produced by a thermocouple depends in a known way on the temperature difference between the two junctions. Newly developed semiconductor materials with improved thermoelectric properties have enabled thermo-couples to act as sources of electric power for radios in remote areas. Heat is provided by the sun.

The Peltier effect is used today in refrigerators to remove heat from small electronic devices and to keep microscope slides cold during examination.
—William C. Vergara

Transducer, a device that transforms energy from one form into another. The pickup cartridge of a phonograph is a transducer that transforms the physical motion of the needle (mechanical energy) into a corresponding variation of an electric current (electrical energy). After amplification, this electric current is applied to another transducer, the loudspeaker. The loudspeaker transforms the electrical signal into mechanical oscillations that produce sound energy vibrations in the air. In a well designed transducer, the output signal must be proportional to the input signal. Otherwise, the output will be a distorted indication of the input information.

A power generator, which changes mechanical energy into electrical energy, is a transducer, as are a photoelectric cell, which transforms light into electricity, and a thermionic converter, which transforms heat into electricity. An important class of transducers is made of piezoelectric crystals, such as quartz, which transform mechanical stress into electricity. Another class is made of magnetostrictive materials, such as nickel, which are often used to transform electrical oscillations into mechanical vibrations.

Transducers are widely used in telemetry, especially in space vehicles, to obtain data for transmission to earth. They are also used in sonar systems to send sound waves into the water, and in the control of industrial processes for economy and safety. In such applications, transducers are designed to have electrical output signals because of the convenience with which they can be transmitted (by radio or wire) and then recorded and translated into accurate, numerical data.
—William C. Vergara

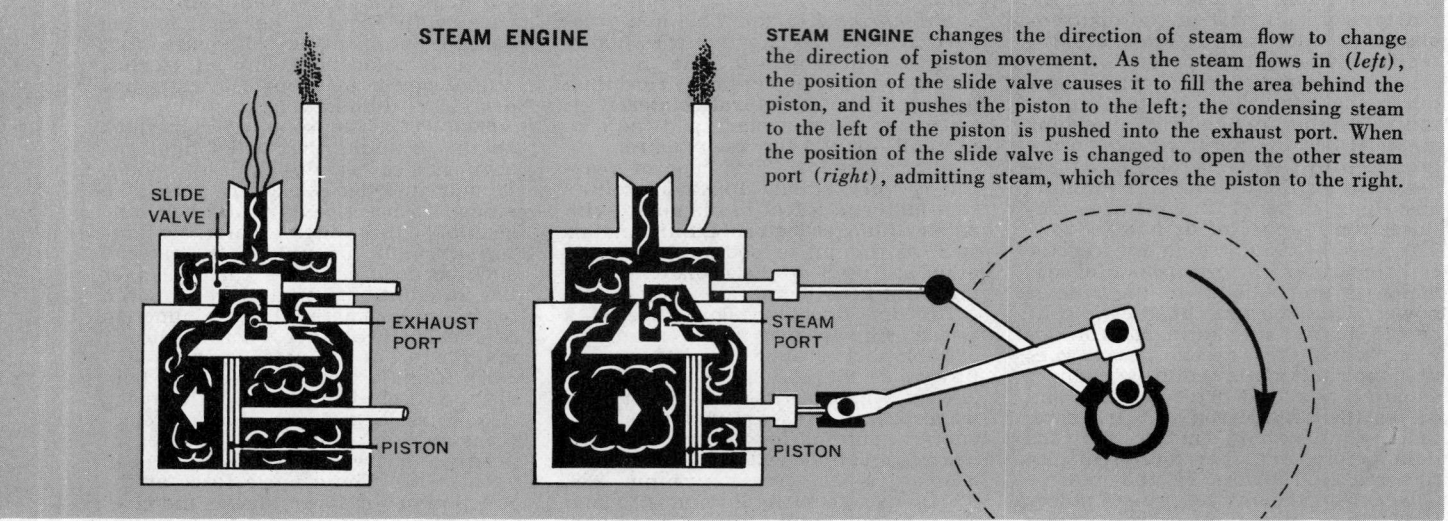

STEAM ENGINE

STEAM ENGINE changes the direction of steam flow to change the direction of piston movement. As the steam flows in (*left*), the position of the slide valve causes it to fill the area behind the piston, and it pushes the piston to the left; the condensing steam to the left of the piston is pushed into the exhaust port. When the position of the slide valve is changed to open the other steam port (*right*), admitting steam, which forces the piston to the right.

SLIDE VALVE

EXHAUST PORT

PISTON

STEAM PORT

PISTON

GENERAL ELECTRIC

STEP-UP TRANSFORMER is assembled, as its iron core and voltage-changing coils are lowered into place. Equipment for cooling the working mechanism circles the center tank.

Transformer, a device that transforms alternating-current (A.C.) voltage to a larger or smaller value.

A transformer that reduces a higher voltage to a lower one is called a *step-down transformer*; one that increases a lower voltage to a higher one is called a *step-up transformer*. The invention of the transformer in the late 1880's made possible the transmission and distribution of energy by electricity. Today, the transformer is utilized in almost every A.C. electrical circuit or system.

The most efficient type of transformer consists of a steel core around which are two or more windings of an electrical conductor. The input winding is designated the *primary*, and the output winding is designated the *secondary*. The secondary winding is normally located next to the core, while the primary winding is wound over the secondary but isolated from it. The core, which is laminated to reduce the electrical losses in the steel, provides a low-reluctance path for efficient magnetic coupling between the primary and secondary windings.

■**HOW IT WORKS.**—Since the transformer is a static device, an alternating-current voltage must be applied to produce the condition necessary to induce a voltage in the secondary winding. The ever-changing applied voltage (E_p) causes a current to flow through the primary turns (N_p), producing an electrical field. The flux of this field continually expands and compresses, and the primary windings convey this effect to the magnetic core. Since the secondary winding is located next to the core, this same flux causes the same volts per turn of windings to be produced in the secondary winding. Thus the desired secondary voltage (E_S) may be obtained by supplying the required number of secondary turns (N_S). The terminal voltages are therefore proportioned by the ratio of primary to secondary winding turns. This may be expressed mathematically as $E_p/E_S = N_p/N_S =$ turns ratio.

A transformer cannot create energy, and the output is limited to input minus losses. However, a transformer is usually very efficient, with losses of 0.5 to 1.0 per cent at full output, so that the input is almost equal to the output. This may also be expressed as $E_p \times I_p = E_S \times I_S$, where I is the current in amperes and the subscripts denote the primary and secondary currents respectively.

■**TWO MAIN TYPES.**—A transformer that has one primary winding, one secondary winding, and one core is classified as a *single-phase unit*. Many applications require more than a single-phase supply, because of the amount of power to be transformed or because of a need for a multiphase supply. In such cases, the single-phase unit may also be used by the proper connection of three units.

The *three-phase system* is almost universally used in the transmission of electric power. It carries three equal voltages situated 120 electrical degrees apart and normally varying at a rate of 60 cycles per second. In a three-phase system, a transformer must have the proper primary and secondary phase relationship as well as the proper voltage ratings.

The three-phase transformer may be made by winding three separate secondaries and three separate primaries on each of three legs of a single laminated core. However, a very popular type of transformer, called an *autotransformer*, has only one winding per phase. The primary voltage is applied to the winding, and the secondary terminal is tapped into the winding at the appropriate place to give the correct secondary voltage.

A transformer may also regulate voltage by using an automatic tap changer in one set of windings. A potential signal from the output is compared with a specified reference, and the load tap changer is automatically switched to the correct turns ratio to give constant voltage output. Typical tap ranges allow constant voltage output with an input of ± 10 per cent of rated voltage. Electric utility systems use many of these units to give constant-voltage service to their customers.

There are also transformers that use tap-changing mechanisms to shift the phase angle between the input and output terminals. This change in angle forces more or less power to flow over a given circuit, since power is the function of the sine of the angle between the system's input and output voltages. The phase-shifting transformer may require its circuit to carry more load, or it may limit the amount of power being trans-

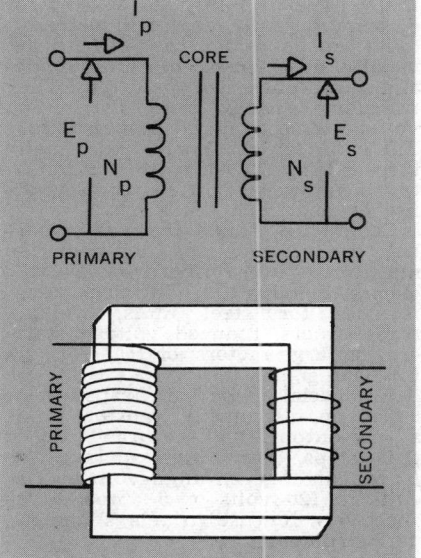

STEP-DOWN TRANSFORMER has more turns of wire on its input winding, or *primary*, than on its output winding, or *secondary* (*bottom*). As labeled in the schematic drawing (*top*), the primary voltage, E_P, primary current, I_P, and number of turns of wire in the primary, N_P, are related to the secondary voltage, E_S, secondary current, I_S, and number of turns in the secondary, N_S, as: $E_P/E_S = I_S/I_P = N_P/N_S$.

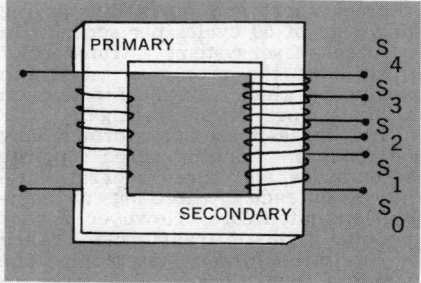

TRANSFORMER WITH A TAPPED SECONDARY, called an autotransformer, may be a step-up, step-down, or combination step-up/step-down, depending on the relative number of turns of wire in the primary and the tapped section of the secondary. As shown above, the number of turns in the secondary varies as connections are made between S_0 and the other taps; the range of the transformer can include other connections, for example, between S_1 and S_3.

mitted over a current-limited circuit such as an underground cable.

■ **HOW THEY ARE USED.**—Transformers have a variety of uses. Some of the more spectacular ones are found in the electric power industry. A generator step-up transformer might transform the output of a 1,000 megavolt-amperes (mva) generator from 25 kilovolts (kv) to 345 kv, 500 kv, or 700 kv for transmission over extrahigh-voltage (ehv) lines. Then autotransformers would be used to step down to 115 or 230 kv for transmission of the power into load areas. Here 25–200 mva bulk distribution transformers would again transform the voltage to 4 through 34.5 kv for distribution to homes or industry.

The distribution transformers are usually single-phase units for homes and three-phase for industry. They transform energy from distribution voltage to secondary voltages of 120/230 volts for the home and usually three-phase 277/480 volts for industry, commercial districts, or large office or apartment buildings.

Other uses range from the doorbell transformer in the home to multiphase transformers for electrochemical industries, furnace transformers for steel mills, welding transformers, reduced voltage starters for large motors, or transformers for neon signs.

A special type of transformer, called an instrument transformer, is a low-output, high-accuracy device that steps down high voltages or large currents on high-voltage circuits to 120 volts or 5 amperes respectively for use in relays, meters, or instruments.

The modern power transformer is a sophisticated apparatus. Trends indicate that banks larger than 1,500 mva will be required by 1970. At the present time, most large 500 kv and 700 kv banks must be composed of single-phase units, due to shipping limitations on size and to voltage clearances. Shipping limitations might require future large extrahigh-voltage banks to be made up of single-phase units.
—G. W. Alexander

Turbine, a machine that makes use of the pressure or velocity of a fluid to produce rotary motion. Turbines may be classified as hydraulic, steam, or gas, depending upon the fluid employed, and further classified as impulse or reaction types depending upon the manner in which the pressure energy of the fluid is converted to mechanical work.

Hydraulic turbines are large rotating machines used to drive electric generators for the production of power. The simplest type is the *impulse turbine,* or *Pelton wheel,* in which a nozzle directs a stream of water against buckets or cups attached to the periphery of a wheel. The velocity of the water from the jet provides the force to turn the wheel. This type of turbine works best with a high head (pressure) and is generally installed only where water is available at the top of a high hill or mountain for delivery through pipes to a turbine in a valley from five hundred to several thousand feet below. It is a high-speed machine.

The *reaction-type hydraulic turbine* is a slow-speed machine using a relatively greater volume of water than does the impulse turbine, but at lower pressure. The level of the water source may range from only a few feet above the turbine to as much as a thousand feet. A dam provides the water storage and the head for the turbine.

The reaction turbine makes use of a guide case and stationary vanes through which the water passes into vanes of a revolving wheel, or runner. Only part of the water pressure is transformed into velocity in the stationary vanes, its velocity continuing to increase in the vanes of the runner, providing a reaction pressure from which the turbine gets its name.

The *propeller turbine* is a variation of the reaction turbine, but it has fewer blades on the runner, and operates with a partial vacuum at discharge. It is best adapted to low heads and large quantities of water.

Steam turbines are also classified as impulse or reaction types, but most combine the two principles. Steam, in contrast to water, expands as it passes through a turbine. Therefore, an *impulse steam turbine* is one in which expansion of steam, with consequent increase in velocity, takes place only in the stationary blades or nozzles, while in the *reaction steam turbine* expansion occurs in both the stationary and the moving blades. The steam enters the turbine at a high pressure and temperature, and exhausts at a lower temperature and at a negative pressure, the vacuum being produced by a condenser.

Steam turbines vary in size from small machines with a single rotor producing a few horsepower to huge multistage machines driving power plant generators rated at several hundred thousand kilowatts. By far the greater part of the electric energy of the world is provided by steam-turbine driven generators.

In the past twenty years there has been a rapid increase in the use of *gas turbines.* These are somewhat similar in design to steam turbines, but they are powered by the expansion of compressed air and gases from burning kerosene or other hydrocarbon fuels. Part of the power output is used to drive an air compressor which provides the air required for combustion of the fuel within a combustion chamber. Gas turbines drive small and medium-sized electric generators, and are also used as aircraft (turboprop), railroad, and ship engines.

The first airplane generator was the *turbojet,* consisting of an axial or centrifugal air compressor and a gas turbine on one shaft, with a combustion chamber between them. With the innovation of this airborne power plant in 1939, the propeller, crankshaft, cylinder and piston became obsolete. Although many commercial and private airlines continue to use

MODERN STEAM TURBINE at the Widow's Creek steam plant of the Tennessee Valley Authority is capable of producing 500,000 kilowatts of electric power. Seven giant turbines at this plant are capable of producing more than 1,250,000 kilowatts of power, which is used in homes, farms, commercial establishments, and industries within the T.V.A. region.

propeller and piston-driven planes for maximum efficiency at low speeds, turbojets are invaluable for providing adequate thrust at transonic and supersonic speeds.   —Hunter Hughes

Ultrasonic Motor, a device for converting electric energy into vibrational mechanical energy, with the output exceeding 10,000 cycles per second. An ultrasonic motor is at the heart of every piece of ultrasonic equipment. Just as an electric motor takes electric energy and converts it to rotary motion, an ultrasonic motor converts electric energy to a reciprocating, or vibrating, motion. Ultrasonic vibratory motors are well suited to the age of automation and robot-controlled complexes, such as are found in space exploration devices. This is because ultrasonic motors have no gross moving parts, require no lubrication, and have the ruggedness needed to operate perfectly either under high stress or in a vacuum.

A typical ultrasonic motor has for its driving agency what is usually known as an electromechanical transducer. This transducer is generally nothing more than a specially fabricated piece of ceramic that is capable of generating vibrations from alternating-current electric energy by means of the piezoelectric effect. Or, instead, a stack of nickel laminations inside a coil of wire may be used. In this case, the magnetostrictive effect is used to convert the electric energy into mechanical vibrations. The transducer is coupled to a transmission member to convey the vibrations to the place where they are required to work.

Broadly speaking, ultrasonic motors are used for observing, testing, and analyzing, on the one hand, and for processing or manufacturing, on the other. The actual use of the motor determines its design very much as electric motor design is influenced by the use intended for it. In analy-

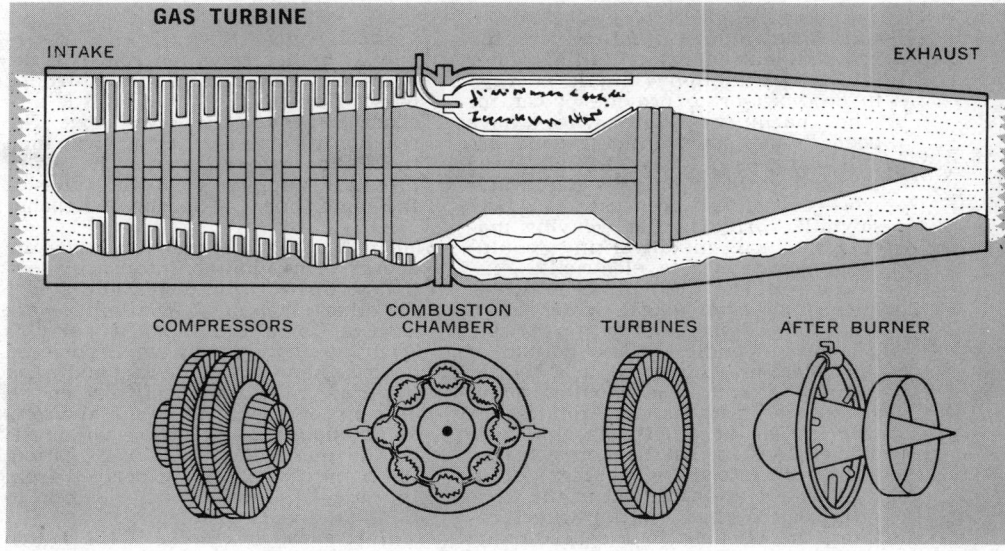

GAS TURBINE

INTAKE   EXHAUST

COMPRESSORS   COMBUSTION CHAMBER   TURBINES   AFTER BURNER

GAS TURBINES work on the principle of the expansion of air and gases occurring after fuel is burned and heat is generated in the combustion chamber. The heated gases strike a turbine wheel—which operates the compressor via a shaft—before escaping to propel the craft. The afterburner consumes any unburned fuel, furnishing additional thrust power.

tical applications, the ultrasonic motor vibrations are generally in the megacycle (million cycle) per second range; in processing, the motor frequency will be in the range from about 10,000 to 50,000 cycles per second.

■**ANALYTICAL USES.**—In the first area, often conceived generally as that of instrumentation, ultrasonic motors are used in sonar, with its various underwater uses; for flaw detection in large castings and forgings; for inspecting rails; for determining liquid levels in tanks; and for many other systems. With the advent of radar, the sonar idea was adapted to "seeing" what goes on inside the human body. As a result, new methods for detecting various kinds of cancer

have developed, along with spectacular advances in the fields of gynecology, eye and brain surgery, and the study of the action of the heart and other soft organs of the body.

■**PROCESSING APPLICATIONS.**—The second, larger area of use of ultrasonic motors is also proliferating rapidly. In the 1940's an ultrasonic machine tool was produced for cutting hard, brittle materials such as glass, ceramic, precious stones, and cements. This machine is used for die-making and in the fabrication of transistors, as well as in the field of glass and ceramic technology. In the 1950's, the use of ultrasonic motors attached to tanks filled with liquid was developed to a high point for all sorts of industrial cleaning problems. Such problems range from the cleaning of a tiny watch mechanism, to the in-process cleaning of rapidly moving sheets of metal on the production line. Dentists, too, employ ultrasonic instruments for cleaning teeth.

The 1950's and the 1960's have also brought new uses for the ultrasonic motor in wire-drawing, metal extrusion, metal and plastic welding, and other material-forming and assembly processes. To give one example, it is possible to push a metal screw into a solid plastic at room temperature with an ultrasonic motor. Immediately afterward, the screw may be unscrewed from the plastic, leaving behind a perfect thread.

Today the ultrasonic motor is where the electric motor was about 80 years ago. The 1970's and 1980's should see the rapid spread of the distribution of high-frequency, alternating-current power, just as 60-cycle, alternating-current power is now commonplace. As this expansion occurs, there will be an enormous expansion in the use of ultrasonic motors, not only in industry and medicine, but in the home as well where soon ovens may cook ultrasonically.   —Lewis Balamuth

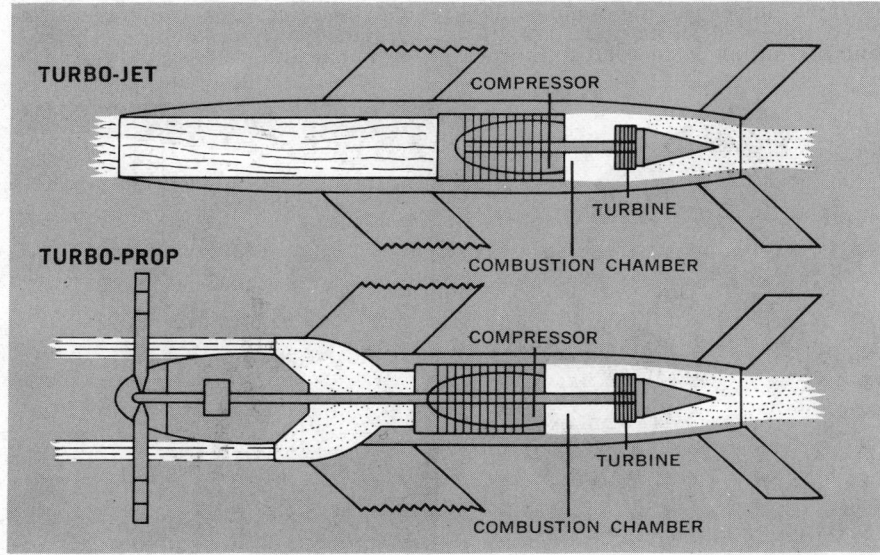

TURBO-JET

COMPRESSOR

TURBINE

COMBUSTION CHAMBER

TURBO-PROP

COMPRESSOR

TURBINE

COMBUSTION CHAMBER

COMMERCIAL AIRCRAFT TURBINES are of two types. In a turbojet (*above*), the escaping gas shoots out the rear of the engine, and the reaction to this force propels the plane. In a turbo-prop (*below*), the power of the escaping gas is used by a larger turbine to turn a propellor by means of a shaft, while the exhaust adds some thrust.

Water Wheel, a device that converts the gravitational energy of falling water into rotary motion (kinetic energy) to do work or to provide power for other machinery. Water wheels have been in use since antiquity and are still being used today. Initially used to grind grain or pump water, water wheels have also been used to power sawmills, drive textile weaving machines, turn metalworking equipment, and generate electricity.

The simplest form of water wheel is the *undershot wheel,* which has a series of paddles mounted on its rim. When the paddles at the bottom of the wheel are immersed in a swiftly running stream, the moving water strikes the paddles and rotates the wheel. The *overshot wheel,* a more efficient design, has buckets attached to or built into the wheel rim. All of the buckets are arranged in the same direction so that, as the wheel rotates, the buckets on the descending side open upward while those on the ascending side open downward. Water delivered to the top of the wheel by a pipe or sluice from a dam fills the buckets. As the wheel rotates, the descending buckets gradually empty as they reach the bottom of the wheel. The weight of the water in the full buckets on the descending side causes the wheel to rotate. The simple undershot and overshot wheels were frequently constructed of wood and some were as large as 70 feet in diameter.

Modern water wheels are of the impulse or reaction turbine types. The *impulse turbine,* or *Pelton wheel,* has buckets or blades around its rim that are struck by high-pressure jets of water. Water pressure in the jets is increased by positioning the impulse wheel as far below the supply reservoir as possible. Some hydroelectric plants have reservoirs located several thousand feet above the impulse wheel that drives the generator.

The *reaction turbine,* mounted horizontally, consists of a circular upper plate and lower ring connected by vertical vanes. Water from a reservoir at higher elevation is fed to the chamber surrounding the turbine, passes through the vanes, and is discharged through the lower ring. The reaction turbine is more efficient than the Pelton wheel because the water pressure is applied to all the vanes at the same time.   —Joseph J. Kelleher

Windmill, a device that converts the energy of moving air into rotary motion to do work or to provide power for other machinery. Windmills were used in China and Japan as early as 2000 B.C. These early wind-powered devices had vertical axes, and they powered mills previously driven by animals or men. Although the primary application for these windmills was in pumping water for irrigation, the name "windmill" is derived from the use of wind-driven devices to mill, or grind, corn.

Horizontal-axis mills of the Dutch type were in use in the eleventh century in Europe and in England by the twelfth century. Early horizontal-shaft windmills had simple canvas sails, stretched over wooden poles. These mills could not turn but were built facing the direction of the prevailing winds. Later, *post mills* were developed that allowed the operator to rotate the mill to face the wind.

The body of a post mill, containing the machinery and sails on a horizontal shaft, rests on a single heavy oak post mounted on a brick or stone foundation. A long tailpole projecting from the back of the body is used by the miller to turn the mill into the wind.

Tower mills, a later development, consist of a brick or wooden tower with a rotatable cap or roof. The sails and shaft are mounted in the cap, which turns as the wind turns. In 1745, Edmund Lee invented the fantail to keep the mill turned into the wind automatically. The fantail consists of a small windmill mounted at right angles to the main sails. When the wind shifts, it strikes the fantail, causing it to rotate. Linked to the mill by gears, the fantail drives the mill cap until the sails face the wind.

Experimental work to develop windmills for electric-power generation started in the 1880's and led to the development of the two-bladed, or propeller, windmill. Though many large aerogenerators have been built and tested, commercial applications are limited to smaller units, for isolated homes, with a capacity of about 3 kilowatts. The largest wind-driven generator ever constructed was a 1250-kilowatt unit built in the 1940's in the United States. Though research continues, it is unlikely that wind-powered devices will replace conventional power sources to any significant extent.

—Joseph J. Kelleher

BIBLIOGRAPHY

BLACK, PERRY O. *Audels Diesel Engine Manual.* The Howard W. Sams Co., Inc., 1964.

HALACY, D. S., JR. *The Coming Age of Solar Energy.* Harper & Row, Publishers, Inc., 1963.

HOGERTON, JOHN F. *The Atomic Energy Deskbook.* Reinhold Publication Corp., 1963.

KLEIN, H. ARTHUR. *Fuel Cells: An Introduction to Electrochemistry.* J. B. Lippincott Co., 1966.

LYTEL, ALLEN H. *ABC's of Electric Motors & Generators.* The Howard W. Sams Co., Inc., 1964.

MANDL, MATTHEW. *Fundamentals of Electric and Electronic Circuits.* Prentice-Hall, Inc., 1964.

MANN, MARTIN. *Peacetime Uses of Atomic Energy.* The Viking Press, Inc., 1964.

PURVIS, JUD. *All About Small Gas Engines.* The Goodheart-Willcox Co., Inc., 1960.

ROBERTSON, EDWIN C. AND HERBERT, ROY. *Fuel; the Conquest of Man's Environment.* Harper & Row, Publishers, Inc., 1963.

SHARLIN, HAROLD I. *The Making of the Electrical Age; from the Telegraph to Automation.* Abelard-Schuman Ltd., 1964.

ALLIS-CHALMERS MANUFACTURING COMPANY

WATER WHEELS are made in many sizes: the impulse, or Pelton, wheel (*left*) can produce 150,000 horsepower; the reaction, or Francis, type-turbine (*center*), can produce 35,400 horsepower; and the propeller-type runner (*right*) is rated at a lesser 44,000 horsepower.

COMMUNICATIONS AND TRANSPORTATION

Early Communications.—Ever since the dawn of history, every step in the growth of civilization has depended on man's ability to improve his techniques of communication in terms of: the amount of information conveyed; the distance over which it is sent; the time taken; the certainty of its arrival; and the number of people who could participate in the exchange simultaneously.

Improvement in response to each of these five challenges over the centuries makes up the history of communication—and the very building blocks for the growth of civilization. Today it is possible in one second to move thousands of words thousands of miles to millions of people. This is a long way from the limitations imposed by face-to-face communications at the dawn of history.

Progress has been achieved through a series of discoveries that continue to come at a fantastically accelerating rate. Each of these has brought new forces to bear on the development of civilization itself.

■**FIRE CODE.**—The signal fire, demonstrated in sending the news of victory back to Greece from Troy in 1084 B.C., was perhaps the first communication breakthrough. A single coded word, which could span land and water at a speed equivalent to 100 miles an hour, replaced the messenger who averaged 10 miles an hour. In the next 2,800 years, the signal-fire approach was perfected. First, scientific coding techniques were developed. The classical historian Polybius, in the fourth century B.C., devised a system of two sets of five lights each to send twenty-five individual letters and numbers, thereby increasing the amount of information that could be rapidly relayed by day or night over long distance.

■**EARLY ADVANCES.**—Then other modes of "transporting" information were developed, such as signal flags at sea, horns in the Swiss Alps, tom-toms in the jungle, and smoke signals on the plains. Even the ancient art of training homing pigeons was revived on grand scale by Napoleon's armies in the early nineteenth century. The latter made it possible to move more information—even a 1,000-word message from a moving army or ship—but the speed was not improved.

■**SEMAPHORE FLAGS.**—It was not until the close of the eighteenth century that another significant advance was made. By 1794 the mechanics of signal towers or flags had reached their ultimate effectiveness through the development by the French of the techniques of semaphore flags. Then, for the first time, *large* amounts of information, not just single words, could be relayed rapidly over long distances at an equivalent speed of 100 miles per hour.

The Nineteenth Century.—By 1800 the art of communication was beginning to be recognized as a significant element in the expansion of civilization. Books and journals were being regularly published; more and more people began learning more and more about others who lived far away. Increased communication among people created new problems in education and understanding, and demanded still more improvement in both the speed and volume of communications. In effect, "brainpower" was being developed, and man's muscles were soon to be multiplied through the Industrial Revolution, but the "nerve system" we call communication was still thin and weak. Society was beginning to need a "nerve system" capable of handling considerably more information and doing it faster.

LOOK MAGAZINE

RADIO aerial on high tower transmits electromagnetic waves which are then converted into audible signals by the receiving sets.

■**TELEGRAPH.**—In 1844 Samuel F. B. Morse demonstrated the magnetic telegraph by transmitting the message "What hath God wrought?" from Baltimore to Washington, D.C. At that moment the world witnessed the first of what turned out to be a series of communications innovations. Not only could news be sent at a rate equivalent to 1,000 miles per hour (counting the time it took to encode and decode the messages), but a sort of slow-motion two-way conversation was now possible.

Obtaining the acceptance or refusal of a potential political candidate while a convention remained in session, calling for rescue from attacking Indians or rampant floods, issuing crucial business orders to buy or sell on the market at a certain time—these were but a few examples of the new role of communications made possible by the magnetic telegraph. During the U.S. Civil War, the telegraph network was extended to span the nation. In 1868, ten years after a short-lived initial test, telegraph messages could be sent across the Atlantic by cable, thereby linking nations at speeds 100 times faster than before.

■**TELEPHONE.**—Then, in 1875, another discovery presaged a technological explosion in communications. While experimenting to devise a means of carrying several telegraph signals over one wire at the same time, Alexander Graham Bell happened to notice what seemed to be the transmission of sound by way of the reeds that he was trying to use to receive the separate electrical signals. He quickly diverted his efforts to this discovery; within a year he devised and demonstrated the telephone.

Bell's basic invention was the conversion of sound pressure waves into electrical energy and back again. After trials at short distances, telephone lines lengthened steadily, and by 1915 lines reach coast-to-coast.

Twentieth-Century: Radio.—New means for carrying electrical messages where wires could not be run, such as to ships at sea, were also being developed. The real impact of the "wireless" on communications was first demonstrated in 1899, when a lightship 12 miles off England used its radio to save all those aboard after being struck by another ship. Just two years later, in 1901, Guglielmo Marconi showed that the radio waves would follow the curve of the earth when he received the letter "S" transmitted in code across the Atlantic. At first radio, like the telegraph, could be used only with coded signals, but by 1906 the combined effect of Bell's invention and radio was achieved experimentally: Christmas music was played over radio and heard by receivers in the Boston area. By 1915 voice could be carried across the Atlantic, and around the world over a combination of radio and cable by 1935.

Radio also made it possible for one person to communicate with many at the same time on a one-way basis. Broadcasting, as we have come to call this application, started in 1920 with stations KDKA in East Pittsburgh and WWJ in Detroit. Music and news were offered to those experimenters who had receivers.

The invention of the triode vacuum tube by Lee De Forest in 1906 and development of the superheterodyne receiver by Edwin H. Armstrong in 1918 were important steppingstones in the rapid development of radio. By 1940, only 41 years after the first practical use of radio, long-distance two-way telephone and broadcast voice communications were a basic part of civilized society. They reached not only homes but also ships, planes, trains, and automobiles.

Within a span of less than a hundred years, communication had advanced from relaying a letter or a word at a time to the point where any two people could talk as in normal two-way conversation, though separated by thousands of miles. Not only could much more information be conveyed via the telephone—as much as one can generate in his speech—but the fine points of emotion—concern, love, or anger—and even personal recognition of the addressee's voice could enhance the communication. Presidents could now persuade kings directly when all else failed. Business contracts, subject to confirmation in writing, could be achieved on a worldwide basis as fast as political or economic circumstances changed. Vast audiences and whole nations could be entertained, informed, educated, and persuaded.

Television.—Such progress stimulated greater progress, and attention naturally centered on transmitting visual information. The basic truth in the saying that "a picture is worth 10,000 words" is certainly evident in the field of communications, whether measured in terms of effort required or the impact achieved.

In 1924 it first became possible to send a photograph via radio across the Atlantic, but it took 20 minutes. Only 40 years later a new picture could be sent over the same distance 60 times a second (the television rate)—an improvement of almost 5 orders of magnitude in speed, along with better quality and reliability. What happened in just four decades was the technological explosion of television. As in the case of voice transmission, the key lay in the invention and development of the device that would convert the "information" into an electrical signal and *vice-versa*. Vladimir Zworykin developed the "camera" tube (iconoscope) and Philo Farnsworth developed the "projector." In the 1930's television was still in the experimental stages, and it had to be put on the shelf during World War II. However, the tremendous technological strides made in electronics during the war rapidly advanced the television art between 1946 and 1950. Coaxial cables and microwave radio, products of World War II, became the work horses for carrying the high information content in broadcasting

pictures coast-to-coast by 1951. And in 1962 the Telstar communications satellite provided an adequately broad communication highway for carrying television signals across the Atlantic. In 1964 commercial videophone service (telephone with picture of caller) was established between Washington, D.C., New York, and Chicago. A year later, pictures of Mars were transmitted 150,000,000 miles to be seen within a few hours by millions of people.

Future Communications.—In the year 2000, history will consider these marvels of our day as but crude beginnings of whole new eras of communication experience. The explosion continues, and within another 40 years it is quite likely that *all* information will be distributed over a single cable to every home, in the same way that we now transport energy by a few wires for every need in the home. Over this "information umbilical cord" will come: visual contact with friends and salesmen; entertainment and cultural programs of a wide variety; and reference information and news in temporary display or printed form.

Perhaps the communication milestones of the future will involve experiments in receiving the information in three-dimensional form, including sensations of touch, smell, and taste. The ultimate in communications, in effect, enables one to become an "on-the-spot" witness—resulting in the experiencing of sensations without the actual movement of matter.

Such thinking is perhaps beyond comprehension today, but the recent trends must lead us to expect continuous achievement. The greater challenge is sociological and political, rather than technical. With the communications techniques of this era, we are playing with a powerful tool and dangerous weapon.

Communications assuredly can bring people to better understanding, but the power of broadcast radio over men's minds for the cause of hate was vividly demonstrated in the 1930's during the rise to power of a man who had once been an obscure house painter. Adolf Hitler made tremendous use of communications in rallying a super-nationalistic force in Germany, and he later used radio in controlling subjugated nations.

One could reasonably compare the development of voice radio communications to the first unleashing of atomic energy—the power of each for good or evil is truly comparable. The parallel can be continued through the development of the H-bomb and worldwide television. The latter, giving access to the minds of millions in different nations, has further multiplied human energy. So far, it has worked for peace, being kept under control of reasonable people. Whether we can keep it this way will depend upon our ability to discern that communications, now or in the future, is like many other of men's inventions in containing the potential to be either a powerful tool for good or a weapon for evil. —R. P. Gifford

Evolution of Transportation.—Transportation technology represents one of man's most spectacular achievements—his conquest of space and time. From its earliest beginnings, transportation has been the servant of man, not only for the movement of people and the exchange of goods but also for the transmission of ideas.

Our prehistoric ancestors relied upon their own leg muscles to move about and upon their own backs to transport goods from one place to another. The beginnings of civilization are concomitant with the domestication of animals, used as beasts of burden as well as for food. Furthermore, the first great civilizations—those in Mesopotamia, Egypt, and China—developed along waterways that served as an adjunct to transportation.

■THE WHEEL.—Every step upward in the level of civilization was linked with advances in transportation. One of the earliest—and certainly the greatest and most basic—of all transportation advances was the wheel. Prior to its invention, men pushed or dragged heavy objects on sledges, occasionally over lubricated boards to lessen the friction and ease the task. The inventor or inventors of the wheel, which first came into use about 3500 B.C., are unknown. However, without it men could scarcely have developed civilization beyond a certain point, for the difficulties of transportation would necessarily have limited the exchange of goods and the intercourse between and within communities.

■ROMAN ROADS.—Transportation is a system, for it includes not only the vehicle but the way over which it travels. The Romans built great roads, such as the Appian Way, that enabled them to conquer and rule a great empire. But the vehicles of classical antiquity were chariots, rude carts, and primitive wagons, drawn by men, oxen, or horses, whose pulling power was limited by inefficient harnesses. With the introduction of the horseshoe, rigid horsecollar, and tandem harness in the Middle Ages, the horse's tractive power could be more efficiently utilized even though the roads had deteriorated since Roman times.

■WATER TRANSPORT.—For centuries thereafter, few major advances were made in land transport, but water transportation improved greatly. The sternpost rudder, the fore-and-aft sailing rig, and navigational aids such as the mariner's compass and better charts enabled men to venture into the open seas in early modern times to discover new continents, to found great overseas empires, and to revolutionize commerce.

■NEW ROADS AND CANALS.—In the eighteenth and early nineteenth centuries, overland transportation again made great strides. Roadbuilding, which had languished since the decline of the Roman Empire, began to move forward again with the formation of turnpike companies and with new methods of road construction, associated with the work of Thomas Telford and John Loudon McAdam (Macadam roads) in Britain, and

Pierre Marie Jérôme Trésaguet in France. More immediately important for the beginnings of the Industrial Revolution was the creation of a network of canals, which provided the linkage between raw materials, factories, and consumers. The economic advantages of canals were shown in the Erie Canal. Before this canal was built, it cost $400 and took 20 days to move a ton of freight from Buffalo to New York City; once the canal was opened, it cost only $10 and took only 8 days. The Erie Canal opened the western lands of the United States by connecting them to the eastern seaboard, and it made New York the country's greatest port and largest city.

■ **STEAM POWER.**—Although water transportation still remains cheaper for bulk commodities than any other means, the canals soon fell victim to a new form of transportation—the railroad. Railroads were faster and could be built where canals were impossible. The railroad became the symbol of the new industrialized age of the nineteenth century. The steam engine was also applied to water transport, and the steamship with its increased speed, reliability, and cargo-carrying capacity drove sailing vessels into oblivion by the end of the nineteenth century.

■ **INTERNAL-COMBUSTION ENGINE.**—Yet, at virtually the same time, a new form of engine—the internal-combustion engine—appeared. This light, efficient, and portable power plant made private transportation possible in the form of the automobile. The internal-combustion engine revolutionized the transport of commodities, the movement of peoples, and the social life of the nation.

The internal-combustion engine also made possible the fulfillment of an age-old dream of mankind going back to the myth of Icarus—flight. Culminating the dreams and unsuccessful experiments of many generations, the Wright brothers' demonstration of flight by a heavier-than-air machine marked the beginnings of the aviation age. Yet for half a century man was atmosphere-bound if not still earthbound. Then, at the close of the 1950's, the development of rocket propulsion made it possible for men to venture into outer space. Having quickened transportation on the surface of the land and water, under water, and in the air, men could now think of travel throughout the cosmos.

Transportation and Technology.—Transportation developments are closely connected with those in other areas of technology. The locomotive would not have been possible without the steam engine, which was first developed to pump water from mines. Railroad development then provided a stimulus to other technological fields by vastly expanding the need for coal and iron in order to produce the locomotives and rails. Similarly, the internal-combustion engine, first designed as a stationary power source, proved applicable to automobiles and aircraft; these stimulated the rise of whole new industries, such as petro-

leum and rubber. In turn, these new industries increased the demand for transportation and, as in the case of petroleum, developed new types of transportation, such as pipelines for the transmission of petroleum products and natural gas. Similarly, new materials, new power sources, the miniaturization of components, and other innovations have resulted from the beginnings of aerospace travel.

Transportation also requires the development of auxiliary technologies. Bridges and roads are essential for land transport, ocean shipping demands ports and harbors, and airplanes must have airports and other auxiliary facilities. Furthermore, mass-production techniques, employed in all industries, derived from Henry Ford's assembly-line technique first applied to the automobile.

Transportation and Society.—More important than transportation's interrelations with other technologies has been its impact upon man, his physical environment, and his society. Because the major function of transportation is to move persons and goods from one place to another, men can utilize natural resources from all over the world and extend Western culture throughout the globe. Transportation makes it possible for each region of the world to specialize in what it can produce best, thereby enabling man to increase his productive capacity and his control over the natural environment. Furthermore, quick transportation covering the entire globe has enriched human life in the twentieth century.

The political configuration of a nation is also affected by its transportation. The transcontinental railroad served to unite the United States near the close of the nineteenth century. The railroad shrank the United States, in terms of travel time, and jet travel has similarly shrunk the entire world. International politics are also determined by transportation resources. Britannia's rule of the waves throughout the nineteenth century was dependent in large measure on Britain's superior naval transpor-

tation, in both mercantile shipping and military vessels. At a later date, the agelong rivalry between powers was to be affected by the airplane. And now, in the mid-twentieth-century, a still more advanced form of transportation—space flight—has become involved in the competition for world political prestige.

■ **URBAN DEVELOPMENT.**—Cities, the most populous environment for living in the twentieth century, are completely dependent upon transportation. For one thing, food has to be transported from the countryside to the urban population to keep it alive. For another, raw materials must be brought in to keep the city's factories going, while the finished products of the factories must be shipped to the consumers, many of whom live far away.

Not only did transportation make the city possible, but developments in intra-city transportation—which have been almost as revolutionary as the advances in long-distance transportation—enabled cities to become larger in area and population, to expand to the suburbs and exurbs, to develop into metropolises and now into megalopolises. From the beginning of recorded history, men had lived close to their work. The distances a man could walk in a reasonable time set the limits of city growth. Once street cars and other forms of urban transit came into use, working men could move into residential areas farther away from their work; the automobile expanded the area of the city even further.

■ **PROBLEM AREAS.**—Man's ability to travel quickly to all parts of the earth has had pronounced social and psychological repercussions. Transportation banishes isolation and increases the mobility of society. At an earlier period in history, a man's position in the social structure depended largely upon the status into which he was born and from which he could not easily escape. However, with economical and quick transportation, a man could strike out for himself in a new area and make his own place in society. This was

CULVER

ORVILLE WRIGHT became the first man to fly in a heavier-than-air craft during a test, on December 17, 1903, of the airplane that he and his brother, Wilbur, had designed and built.

certainly the case on the American frontier, and the ease with which Americans have moved about from one place to another has helped to mold a more democratic society.

That most depended-upon technological artifact of American society—the automobile—has influenced every aspect of life. It has done away with the traditional distinction between town and country inhabitants, helped to emancipate women, and made American society mobile and restless, always "on the go." Furthermore, the automobile has become one of the foundations of the American economy —it is estimated that one out of every eight American workers makes his living through the automotive industry, either directly or indirectly.

While transportation has led man to new triumphs and new opportunities, it has also presented him with new problems. Thus automobiles, which at first increased the speed with which persons could travel from home to factory, eventually became so numerous and created such great traffic jams as to decrease the mobility of the population. Parking difficulties, air pollution, and danger to the safety of pedestrians and of other drivers have become the concomitants of automobile transport.

Perhaps the cure for these problems is the application of more and better transportation technology. Efforts are being made to develop mass transportation for intra-city and inter-city use—coordinated transportation systems, involving the use of buses, elevated railways (monorail), and rapid transit and subway lines, are being considered for cities. For intermediate distances, one of the most publicized proposals is that of high-speed tube transportation which, for example, would carry passengers from Boston to Washington in 90 minutes in vehicles traveling at speeds up to 500 miles an hour through dual evacuated tubes. Helicopters, vertical takeoff and landing planes, and individual rocket belts are among the devices being investigated to increase still further the mobility of the population and the speed of transportation. At the same time, efforts are under way to increase automobile safety—by making the vehicles crash-proof, by improving road conditions, and by educating drivers.

Despite the problems, there is no doubt that transportation is going to develop further. In terms of the vast span of human history, transportation technology is still in its infancy. If the earth's age is taken as a 24-hour day, the time from the invention of the steam engine to the present would make up only 0.003 seconds of the 24-hour scale. Within the limited time of 200 years, man has evolved from reliance upon natural forces, such as the wind or animals, for transportation to dependence upon machines that carry him under the surface of the ocean, on the surface of the earth, above the earth, and outside the earth's atmosphere. Thus, transportation today provides both opportunities and challenges for the future.   —Melvin Kranzberg

COMMUNICATIONS AND TRANSPORTATION GLOSSARY

Aeronautical Engineering, the branch of engineering that deals with solving the problems of flight and with the design of aircraft. The principal flight vehicles are heavier than air —gliders, propeller-driven aircraft, helicopters, and jet aircraft. Lighter-than-air vehicles, such as balloons and dirigibles, play little part in modern aeronautics.

The physical basis for an airplane's ability to fly is known as *Bernoulli's principle.* According to this principle, a wing experiences a lifting force if its cross-sectional shape is designed to provide a higher air velocity above the wing than exists below it.

A second important factor in aircraft design is *drag,* the frictional force of air operating against the surfaces of the aircraft. Drag is overcome by the thrust of the propeller or jet to cause the wing or other airfoil to move through the air.

With the advent of jet and rocket propulsion, flight has become possible at supersonic speeds, greatly increasing the problems of aeronautical engineering. An aircraft flying at close to the speed of sound, about 760 miles per hour at sea level, begins to catch up with its own pressure or sound waves, producing a shock wave, or *sonic boom.* This considerably increases drag, while reducing the effectiveness of the plane's control surfaces. At supersonic speeds, the skin of the aircraft is heated greatly by friction with the air. At a speed of three times the speed of sound, the temperature of the skin can rise as high as 600° F.

The major tools of aeronautical engineers are the wind tunnel, in which flight conditions can be simulated, and the electronic computer, which solves the difficult mathematical problems that arise in their work.

—William C. Vergara

Airship, any powered, steerable, lighter-than-air craft. The two main types are commonly called *dirigible* and *blimp.*

Manned flight began in 1783 when the Montgolfier brothers of Annonay, France, discovered the lifting power of a bag full of heated air and devised the first man-carrying balloon. Jacques A. C. Charles' application of hydrogen as a lifting gas in 1784 greatly extended the capability of the free balloon. In the next hundred years, balloon flights became commonplace in Europe and America.

Free ballooning as a sport still has a few devotees. It also has certain limited scientific applications, such as high-altitude meteorological and aerological research, and some military uses, mainly for battlefield observation. As a practical navigation device, however, its utility is near zero. A free balloon drifts with the winds, and only by careful selection of predictable meteorological conditions can it be relied upon to travel for any distance in any desired direction.

■POWERED FLIGHT.—Prints dating from the late eighteenth and early nineteenth centuries show many ideas for aerial navigation. Among these are the application of sails or great sweeps (oars) to spherical balloons in an effort to guide them in desired directions independent of wind and weather. None of these arrangements had much success, for a truly steerable airship could not be contrived until lightweight power plants became available.

In September 1852, Henri Giffard, a French inventor, put up an elongated, hydrogen-filled balloon that carried a "car" containing a boiler, a steam engine, and a propeller. This demonstrated a certain controllability in a light wind, though it could not be called a complete success. The

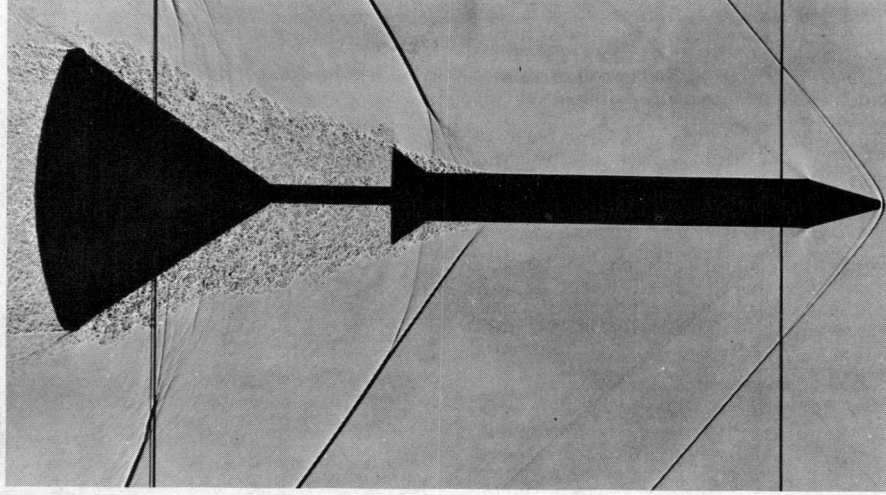

NASA

AERONAUTICAL scientists use a wind tunnel to test a model of an Apollo Launch Escape Vehicle at supersonic speeds by launching the device from a special gun. Air passing over the model produces progressive shock waves, which are recorded on a "shadowgraph" and appear as diagonal lines leading from the rocket's shadow in the photograph above.

first fully controlled airship flight occurred in August, 1884, when two French officers, Charles Renard and Arthur Krebs, flew the electric-powered dirigible *La France* on a circular course of five miles at Chalais-Meudon, near Paris.

In the historical development of the airship, two principal approaches were used: the *rigid, dirigible,* or *zeppelin* type of design, and the *nonrigid,* or *pressure,* ships. An intermediate, or *semirigid,* class also appeared briefly.

■RIGID AIRSHIPS.—Rigid airships are characterized by lightweight, fabric-covered external skeletons of metal that surround a series of independent lifting gas cells. To these hull structures are attached the control and passenger cabins, the power plant units, and the handling and docking devices. A rigid airship retains its external configuration whether or not the gas cells are inflated.

Count Ferdinand von Zeppelin built the first airship of this type, flown over Lake Constance near Friedrichshafen, Germany, in July 1900. Germany brought the rigid dirigible to a high state of development before and during World War I, when nearly 100 aircraft of this type were built.

■SEMIRIGID AIRSHIPS.—Semirigid airships are the least important of the three categories. None survived long in service. Such ships are characterized by an external structural keel from bow to stern that contains the crew and passenger quarters, and usually the power plant, and to which is attached a single, large, streamlined bag containing the lifting gas. If the gas escapes, the keel retains its shape, but the bag collapses.

France, Italy, and possibly Russia built several such ships in the 1920's and early 1930's. In 1921 the U.S. Army purchased one from Italy. Christened the *Roma,* it crashed and burned at Langley Field in February, 1922, ending American interest in the type. The most famous semirigid airships were the Italian-built *Norge* and *Italia.* In May, 1936, the *Norge* flew successfully from Norway to Alaska via the North Pole. An attempt to repeat the polar flight two years later ended in disaster.

■NONRIGID AIRSHIPS.—Nonrigid airships, or *blimps,* have been the most conspicuously successful type, and have been built and used in relatively large numbers. They have no rigid structural elements in the hull. The gas bag itself, under the internal pressure of the lifting gas, maintains proper aerodynamic shape and provides support for the attached cabin and power plant.

During World War I blimps enjoyed wide military and naval use by most major powers. By the end of the 1920's, however, active development had tapered off to near the vanishing point, except in the United States. Here, the U.S. Navy fostered a design and development program that came to a peak in World War II, then finally came to a halt twenty years later.   —S. Paul Johnston

Automobile. see *Motor Vehicle* and *Automobile Manufacturing.*

RYAN AIRCRAFT CORPORATION

SPIRIT OF ST. LOUIS was piloted across the Atlantic by Charles Lindbergh in May, 1927.

Aviation, the operation and use of flight vehicles within the earth's atmosphere. Where "aviation" ends and "space flight" begins is still subject to exact definition. For the present article, however, all forms of heavier-than-air craft designed to operate at altitudes to about 150,000 feet are considered to fall with the scope of aviation.

■FIXED WING AIRCRAFT.—The balloon flights of the Montgolfier brothers, Jacques A. C. Charles, and others in the late eighteenth century had freed men forever of being earthbound. Once the experimenters of the early nineteenth century had given up trying to emulate the bird (that is, the ornithopter) as a practical means to manned flight, the way was cleared for the accelerated development of the form of aircraft in most common use today—the *fixed-wing airplane.*

Sir George Cayley, the grandfather of aviation, established the basic theory and laid the experimental groundwork for modern aerodynamics in the period between 1799 and 1810. First he concentrated on *gliders,* experiments undoubtedly prompted by the observation that many birds soar and glide with rigid, outstretched wings for long periods. Cayley built gliders of all sizes, up to those with man-carrying dimensions. He postulated powered flight. He might, in fact, have evolved a successful airplane, had a lightweight engine then been available. Over 50 years were to pass, however, before a practical power plant for aircraft was available.

Meanwhile, many experimenters, including John Stringfellow, Félix du Temple, Alphonse Penaud, Clément Ader, Laurence Hargrave, and Sir Hiram Maxim, built models and constructed larger craft in many weird and wonderful forms. All of these, however, were largely unsuccessful as practical flying machines. Although most designers attempted to use steam as power for propulsion, it soon became clear that steam engine and boiler designs could not produce power/weight ratios compatible with flight requirements. The light and efficient internal-combustion engine had to be developed before practical flight was to be achieved.

Between 1896 and 1903 Samuel Pierpont Langley constructed several experimental small-scale *aerodromes,* which made extended power flights over the Potomac River below Washington, D.C. After years of such experimental aerodynamic research, coupled with a remarkable adaptation of a Balzer-designed gasoline automobile engine by Charles Manly, his assistant, Langley developed a man-carrying aerodrome that was ready for testing late in 1903. With Manly as pilot, two unsuccessful attempts were made to launch the machine from a catapult atop a houseboat on the Potomac River. Nine days after the second attempt, Orville Wright made the world's first power-driven, sustained, controllable airplane flight near Kitty Hawk, North Carolina.

The Wright Brothers. The achievement of the Wright brothers, Orville and Wilbur, was no happenstance. It was the logical result of painstaking study, research, and development over many years. Their basic interest in flight was stimulated by reports of gliding experiments by Otto Lilienthal in Germany. Their natural ingenuity and sound mechanical instincts led them step by step, from experimental kite and glider flying, through development of their own lightweight engine, to ultimate success on December 17, 1903. The longest of four flights made that day lasted 59 seconds and covered 852 feet from the takeoff point.

During the following two years, unnoticed by the press but never in secret, the Wrights built and flew improved machines, and developed their flying techniques at Huffman Prairie near Dayton. By the end of 1905 they were making fully-controlled flights (circles and figure eights) of as much as 38 minutes' duration.

■EARLY CRAFT.—European experimenters were also hard at work, but it was not until September 1906, that the first "hop" (21 seconds) was made by Alberto Santos-Dumont at Bagatelle, near Paris. In November, 1907, Henri Farman succeeded in staying in the air for a full minute in a Voisin biplane. During the following year progress accelerated rapidly. Many aircraft appeared in Europe and in America. Sponsored by Alexander Graham Bell's Aerial Experiment Association, Glenn Curtiss first flew the *June Bug* (1 minute, 43 seconds) at Hammondsport, N.Y., on July 4, 1908. On December 31, 1908, Wilbur Wright kept his *Model*

A biplane in the air over France for 2 hours, 23 minutes, 23 seconds.

At the beginning of World War I, the airplane was looked upon as an uncertain and unreliable substitute for battlefield scouts and observers. By the end of 1918 it had become a full-fledged tactical and/or strategic weapon. All major powers were engaged in extensive development programs, and the advance in performance was enormous. Heavy bombers were carrying substantial tonnages for hundreds of miles, and agile well-armed fighters were engaging in aerial combat at two-mile altitudes at speeds up to 130 miles per hour.

■ **POST-WORLD WAR I DEVELOPMENT.**— With the end of hostilities in 1918, other tasks for the airplane were quickly found. People began to realize its potential as a vehicle. A period of practical development ensued (1919–1940); it focused largely on civilian applications, and was based on expanding programs of scientific research in aerodynamics, propulsion, structures, materials, and devices for navigation.

The decade 1920–1930 was marked by many spectacular feats of pilots and planes, all laying the groundwork—both technically and with the public—for the widespread acceptance of the airplane as a practical vehicle in the 1930's. Among the more significant feats were:

May 8–31, 1919: the first eastbound Atlantic crossing, via Newfoundland and the Azores, by Lt. Com. A. C. Read in a U.S. Navy NC-4.

June 14–15, 1919: the first non-stop transatlantic crossing, Newfoundland to Ireland, by Sir John W. Alcock and Arthur W. Brown in a Vickers bomber.

May 2–3, 1923: the first non-stop U.S. transcontinental flight, by Oakley Kelly and John A. Macready in a Fokker monoplane.

April 6–Sept. 28, 1924: the first round-the-world flight, by two planes of the U.S. Army Air Corps.

May 8–9, 1926: the first round trip over the North Pole, by Richard A. Byrd and Floyd Bennett.

May 20–21, 1927: the first non-stop flight from New York to Paris, by Charles Lindbergh in *The Spirit of St. Louis.*

July 28–29, 1927: first non-stop flight from California to Hawaii, by Lester J. Maitland and Albert F. Hegenberger.

June 17–18, 1928: the first non-stop transatlantic flight by a woman, Amelia Earhart, with Wilmer Stultz and Lou Gordon aboard the Fokker *Friendship.*

Nov. 28–29, 1929: the first flight to circle the South Pole, by Byrd flying out of Little America.

■ **COMMERCIAL SERVICE.**—Although a few embryonic and intermittent passenger-carrying operations appeared in Europe shortly after the Armistice of 1918, precedence in the United States was given to the carriage of mail. Military airplanes were converted for this purpose simply by covering over the forward cockpit to form a mail compartment. During the 1920's a network of contract-operated airmail routes spread across the United States. Airway aids such as light beacons, radio-communication links, and improved weather-

reporting services came into being under the aegis of the U.S. Department of Commerce.

By 1930 scheduled passenger services were available between a number of cities, and a combined air and rail transcontinental service had begun. Encouraged by the growing demand for passenger accommodations, several manufacturers designed and put into production fast and efficient commercial aircraft. Notable among these were the Boeing *247*, Curtiss *Condor*, Lockheed *10*, and Douglas *DC-2* and *DC-3*.

What appeared to be a setback for commercial air transport in America occurred early in 1933 when President Franklin D. Roosevelt suddenly cancelled all airmail contracts on the grounds that certain frauds and collusions had been perpetrated by certain operators. This effectively shut down most commercial air services for a time. In the interim, the U.S. Army Air Corps was given the task of flying the mail. It was ill-equipped, under-staffed, and inadequately trained to cope with scheduled flying in the midst of severe winter weather, and a number of Army planes and pilots were lost. While shocking the nation, this tragic series of crashes pointed up the inadequacies of our air arm. During the following years, Congress granted increased funds for the procurement of planes and the training of pilots.

Airports, airways, and navigational aids kept pace with the expanding requirements of commercial air transport. By the mid-1930's, night-and-day air transportation for passengers and mail was commonplace in America. Parallel development, on a smaller scale, took place in Europe and in other parts of the world. Only the oceans stood in the way of a world-wide transportation system.

By 1937–1938 these last barriers began to yield. Exploratory operations by large four-engine flying boats over both the Atlantic and Pacific oceans demonstrated the feasibility of intercontinental cargo and passenger travel. By 1939 several limited commercial overseas services were in actual operation. The outbreak of World War II interrupted most civilian development in this direction. However, the tremendous wartime demands for overseas military air transport so accelerated the development of new long-range cargo aircraft and operational techniques, that a truly world-wide system of commercial air transport was to spring, almost full-grown, into being at the end of hostilities.

■ **WORLD WAR II AIRPLANES.**—The performance capabilities of the military aircraft of all countries improved considerably under the impetus of war, but in the end it was the sheer weight of numbers that predominated. In this area, Germany led the field by a wide margin in 1939–1940. By 1945, however, the United States had surpassed the rest of the world combined. Between 1943 and 1945, U.S. factories turned out almost 30,000 bombers, 40,000 fighters, 20,-000 trainers, and 13,000 transport and miscellaneous types.

Most of the planes used in World War II were developments of types designed in the late 1930's. Improvement had been continuous by increments. Almost without exception, airplanes were powered by gasoline engines equipped with air propellers. In 1943, however, another breakthrough was made with the advent of jet and rocket engines.

The application of direct thermal thrust to aircraft propulsion, either in the form of chemical rocket motors or of turbine-driven jets, immediately opened the way to vast improvement in performance. The so-called *sonic barrier* (Mach 1, which is equal to the speed of sound in air at any given altitude) no longer imposed a physical limitation on airplane speed. Furthermore, since reaction propulsion functions equally well in or beyond the earth's atmosphere, altitudes inaccessible to propeller-driven craft now came within reach.

The Germans flew the first experimental jet engine in August 1939. A Whittle-engined experimental *Gloster* flew in England two years later. The first U.S. jet flight occurred on Oct. 1, 1942, in a Bell *XP59A* aircraft powered by two General Electric turbojet engines. But the Germans made the first military application in production quantities. Some 1,300 Messerschmitt *ME-262* twin-jet fighters were built, and many saw service against American and British attacks in the last months of the war. Their performance was far superior, but their impact came too late to decide the outcome of the war.

■ **POST-WORLD WAR II DEVELOPMENT.**— By 1960, practically all military aircraft—except for primary trainers and certain special purpose slow-speed types—were powered by turbine engines, either by pure jets, for highest performance in speed and altitude, or by turbo-propeller combination, for long-range, heavy transport. Fighters tended to become almost missile-like in configuration, with small, almost embryonic wing and tail surfaces. Radar-controlled guided missiles replaced machine guns and cannon as armament. Mach 2 speeds became routine, and in some cases (for example, YF-12) Mach 3 has been attained. The ultimate in aircraft performance to date has been reached by the experimental X-15 rocket-powered airplane. This craft, which is air-launched from a B-52 bomber, has reached flight speeds of 4,100 miles per hour and altitudes (as a ballistic missile) of 350,000 feet. It has no immediate military application, but the lessons learned from its development have an important bearing on future development.

Although by 1965, with the advent of intercontinental guided missiles, the development of manned superbombers had practically ceased, large fleets of jet-powered heavy bombers—B-47's, B-52's, and B-58's in the United States, British *Vulcans, Victors,* and *Valiants,* etc.—came into inventories in the late 1950's. The range of such aircraft has been greatly extended by in-flight refueling from special tanker airplanes. A version of the Boeing 707 jet transport, the *K-135*, is in wide use as a tanker for the *B-52* bombers of the Strategic Air Command.

Probably the last of the large bombers (at least in the U.S.) is the *Valkyrie* (XB-70). Based on an Air Force requirement promulgated in 1954, the first of three prototype machines was flown on Sept. 21, 1964. This machine, with a take-off weight of some 530,000 pounds, is designed to fly at Mach 3 and to cover over 7,500 miles nonstop without refueling.

■NAVAL AVIATION.—Meanwhile, naval aviation was also developing according to its own special needs. In November 1910, Eugene Ely, a civilian pilot, took off in a Curtiss biplane from the deck of the *Birmingham*. Two months later, Ely landed on and took off from a wooden platform erected on the *Pennsylvania*. In 1911, Glenn Curtiss won the Collier Trophy for the development of the first practical float-type seaplane, the *A-1*.

Stemming from a World War I requirement for offshore patrol, initial naval interest (1918–19) centered on flying boats. Curtiss had built a prototype for Rodman Wanamaker for a transatlantic attempt in 1914, a project abandoned because of the outbreak of the war.

The development of flying boats, for both military and civilian purposes, followed a sporadic course throughout the 1920's and 1940's. Large two- and four-engine boats were used in great numbers for overseas and interisland transport in World War II. With the increased efficiency of large land-type transports and the availability of landing fields everywhere around the world, however, development of flying-boat types had been largely abandoned by the early 1960's.

Shortly after World War I, naval interest centered on the development of aircraft carriers, ships with long, clear decks for the launching and recovery of land-type aircraft. The record of U.S. naval carrier-based aviation in the Atlantic and Pacific during World War II is well known. It was a decisive factor in the defeat of Japan and made major contributions towards the outcome of the Korean War and subsequent peacekeeping operation around the world. The modern high-speed carrier with its complement of catapult-launched, high-performance jet aircraft carrying nuclear weapons and rocket missiles is one of the most powerful weapons systems available in the world today.

Attempts have been made in recent years to design a multipurpose aircraft to be used almost interchangeably over land and at sea—for example, the *F111* or *TFX*. By certain modification of equipment, it is expected to be used by both services. Its most interesting feature, however, is the incorporation of a variable-sweep wing. For slow flight speeds (takeoff and landing), its wings can be extended to an angle of about 90° to the fuselage, to give maximum span. Once the plane is in flight, the wings can be swung rearward to make an almost "delta" configuration for less drag and higher wing loading, the optimum condition for high-speed flight.

In passing, it may be pointed out that the variable-wing configuration described above is being given consideration in at least one of the *supersonic transport* (SST) design studies. The projected Boeing *733*, a 430,000-pound craft designed to carry 150 passengers over a 4,000-mile range at 1,800 miles per hour (Mach 2.7) at 60,000 feet, incorporates the variable-geometry wing. It is not anticipated, however, that a prototype will be ready for testing before 1970.

■ARMY AIRCRAFT.—Apart from Air Force and Navy, the ground forces have developed many requirements for fixed-wing aircraft. Hundreds of small, two-seat aircraft have been incorporated in regiments and divisions of ground troops for battlefield surveillance, artillery spotting, etc. Larger airplanes (single- and multi-engined) are in widespread use by the Army for rapid and efficient command and light-cargo transport. Rugged, slow-landing and steep take-off types are in service in rough terrain, where airfields are small or nonexistent. Also, ground-support and large-scale troop-transport requirements have fostered development of larger and faster cargo and personnel carriers by air and ground forces. Generally speaking, with modifications, the aircraft used are similar to those of commercial airlines. Modern civilian jet transports handle from 80 to 150 passengers at a time. Certain projected designs, primarily for the military, call for huge machines to carry upward of 500 troops. These, however, will probably not appear in service until the 1970's.

An interesting example of a highly specialized form of air-cargo carrier is the so-called *Super Guppy*, the *B-377PG*, which appeared in mid-1965. Its single purpose is to ferry very large rocket and space components from factories to firing sites. In reality, the craft is a *Strato-cruiser*, modified by the addition of a huge bubblelike superstructure over the length of the fuselage. This housing is large enough to enclose a Saturn V rocket, which is too large for transport by rail or over any U.S. highway. Four turbo-prop engines give this bulky and awkward-appearing flying machine a cruising speed of 250 miles per hour.

■BUSINESS AIRPLANES.—On the civilian side, a very wide variety of airplanes has evolved for both business and pleasure. Over 100,000 are in service in the United States alone. Here again, a detailed accounting is impossible. Types in current service range from single-seat motorless sailplanes to the large jet-powered transports which carry 100 to 150 passengers, in intercontinental service. The most prominent commercial transports are listed in the following table:

BAC VC10-1100	DeHavilland
BAC VC10-1150	Comet 4C
BAC 111-400	DeHavilland
Boeing 707-120	Trident IE
Boeing 707-320B	Douglas DC-7C
Boeing 707-420	Douglas DC-8-50
Boeing 720	Douglas DC-9
Boeing 727	Lockheed Electra
Boeing 737	Sud Caravelle 6R
Convair 440	Sud Caravelle
Convair 880	Super
Convair 990	Vickers Viscount 812

Since the end of World War II there has been a considerable upsurge in flying purely for fun, or for utilitarian purposes such as surveillance of large farm holdings. For this kind of flying, a number of excellent single-engined, two- to four-seat airplanes are available, either open cockpit or cabin types. Most are high-wing monoplanes (the biplanes of the 1920-30 period have practically disappeared) with tricycle landing gear (frequently retractable) and with automobile-like interiors. Prices range from $5,000 to $50,000, depending partly on the amount of navigation and communication equipment installed. The Cessna *150* and the *Piper Super Cub* are typical examples.

On an increasing scale, American business organizations are making use of fleets of airplanes for executive travel. Twin-engined light transports (propeller driven) with comfortable accommodations for five to eight passengers and a crew of two are available, fitted with the necessary radio and navigation instrumentation to permit their use on all U.S. and overseas airways. Such aircraft, depending upon the equipment installed,

LOCKHEED AIRCRAFT CORPORATION

SUPERSONIC TRANSPORT design shows the sleek lines that permit its huge size. When built in 1970, the aircraft will carry up to 266 passengers 1,800 miles an hour at low cost.

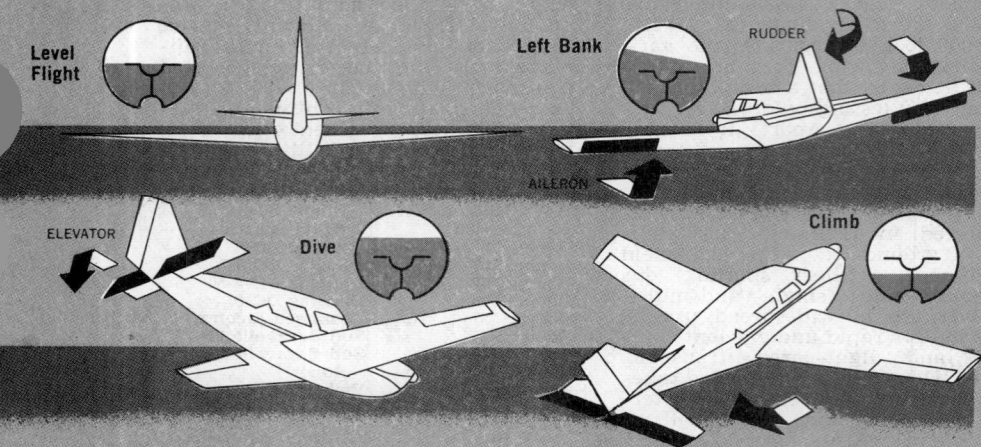

MANEUVERS, shown here as a pilot sees them on an artificial horizon (*insets*), are accomplished with air control devices. Ailerons alter the flow of air above or below each wing to bank the plane, while the rudder gives vertical stability. When air flows past a turned-down elevator, it causes a dive: a plane with elevator turned up climbs.

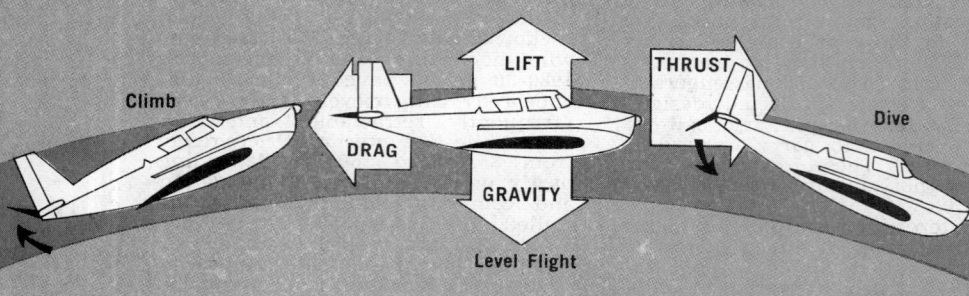

WINGS, or "air foils," create a partial vacuum above the wing's surface. Air pressure below the wing provides enough lift to overcome the force of gravity. Thrust, from jets or propellors, counteracts drag, or air friction, to move the plane forward through the air.

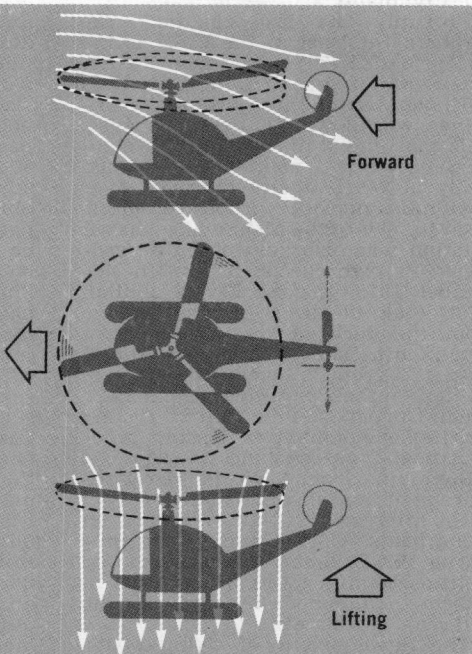

HELICOPTER rotor, with blades shaped as air foils, is both wing and propellor. In vertical flight (*bottom*) the blades' pitch, the angle at which they pass through the air, is increased to push air beneath the craft, causing it to rise; when pitch decreases, less air is pushed down, causing descent. A small tail rotor acts as a rudder to guide the craft and counteract torque from the main rotor (*center*). In horizontal flight the pitch of each blade varies according to the direction desired. Thus in forward flight (*top*) low front blades and high rear ones force air back and down.

range in cost from $30,000 to $80,000. More recently (1960–65), a number of high-performance jet-powered executive types have come on the market. Typical is the four-engined Lockheed *Jetstar,* which furnishes comfortable accommodations for ten passengers and a crew of two, and can cruise for about 2,000 miles nonstop at almost 500 miles per hour. Twin-jet types for similar service have been produced. Such aircraft are extremely expensive but can provide private executive transport at the same levels of comfort, speed, and safety available on modern airliners.

■ **VTOL CRAFT.**—The next stage in air-transport progress—still a long way off—will be the development of a VTOL (vertical take-off and landing) craft, which can convert in flight to a high-speed configuration, then reconvert to a zero-speed landing mode. Such aircraft, by combining the characteristics of the helicopter and the high-speed airplane, would eliminate the requirement for remote airports and all the difficulties and time delays now attendant upon ground transportation for passengers and cargo. Researchers have been working on the problem for many years, and a number of manufacturers in this country and abroad are developing prototypes. These are all small, experimental aircraft, but enough work has been done to indicate that some such configuration is feasible.

British and American designers (and doubtless those of the Soviet Union, although direct evidence is lacking) have long since been intrigued by the idea. The largest known example is the LTV-Hiller-Ryan *VHR-447* tiltwing transport, in which a relatively conventional wing and engine (four 2,800-horsepower turboprops) combination can be tilted vertically for a direct-thrust vertical takeoff, and, once in the air, the whole returned to "normal" flight position. To land, the procedure is reversed. The wing and engines are turned to the vertical configuration, and engine power progressively reduced to permit a vertical descent. This machine was test-flown late in 1964 and early in 1965. Other designers rotate only the power plants for vertical lift. Still other American and British types depend on the controlled deflection of the exhaust jet of a combination of turbojet engines for vertical lift and forward thrust. Although the concept has considerable promise for the future, the applications to date have not yet proven entirely satisfactory.

It is possible that such aircraft, by making city-center-to-city-center transportation available, and eliminating practically all ground time, might reduce the requirement for supersonic transports.

■ **ROTARY WING AIRCRAFT.**—One of the earliest conceptions of mechanical flight was sketched by Leonardo da Vinci in the late fifteenth century.

Many years later, Sir George Cayley experimented with helicopter-like toys made of corks, feathers, and a spring. About 1842, he drew up a design for a machine that incorporated many of the features of today's vertical risers. As with his work on fixed-wing machines, the lack of a suitable lightweight engine prevented him from designing an aircraft light enough to overcome the weight problem.

The advent of the lightweight gasoline engine and reports of the early airplane flights of the Wright brothers and others in the America and Europe stimulated renewed interest in the helicopter. It occurred to a number of contemporary experimenters that the inherent limitations of the airplane (long take-off and landing runs, high forward speed to maintain flight, relative instability, etc.) might be avoided by building movable-wing systems (that is, large propellers) rotating around vertical axes to develop vertical lift without forward motion of the entire machine. Eventually their theories proved tenable, but many years were to go by, and many unforeseen problems had to be solved, before a useful *helicopter* was to appear. In fact, it was not until the years immediately prior to World War II that practical flying machines of this type came into use.

Unaware of the complexities of the problem and of the difficulties of solution, however, many people in the first quarter of the twentieth century tried to build rotary-wing machines. Louis Breguet, Étienne Oehmichen, Paul Cornu, and Raoul Pescara in France, Igor Sikorsky in Russia, and Henry Berliner and George de Bothezat in the United States designed, built, and tested an extraordinary variety of complicated machines intended for vertical flight. Some of them managed to get a few feet off the ground before shaking themselves to pieces or going out of control. How to cope with gyroscopic forces and the differential lift produced in rotating-wing systems in forward flight was beyond the state of the aeronautical art of the period.

■THE AUTOGIRO.—It was a Spanish inventor, Juan de la Cierva, working in a somewhat different direction, who pointed the way to eventual solution. Instead of attempting true vertical flight capability by applying power to a rotating-wing or propeller system (as in a helicopter), Cierva combined a "free-wheeling" lifting rotor system with a conventional forward thrusting engine and propeller. No power is applied to the rotor. Under aerodynamic forces alone, the wing system produces lift by "autorotation" hence, his descriptive name, the *autogiro*.

VARIABLE SWEEP WINGS on F-111 plane fold (*left* to *right*) from takeoff position to the "full sweep" for supersonic flight.

GENERAL DYNAMICS CORPORATION

■THE HELICOPTER.—After many years as a designer and builder of large multiengined aircraft, Igor Sikorsky returned to his first love, the helicopter, in the late 1930's. In 1941 Sikorsky built and personally tested the VS-300 helicopter. This experimental machine had a single, articulated-blade lifting rotor, and three smaller rotors to provide stability and control. A year later, a more sophisticated design, the *R-4B*, with a single, large lifting rotor appeared and went into immediate production to supply a military demand. Although under active development by a number of manufacturers during World War II, helicopters played a relatively minor part. It was during the Korean War that this type of aircraft came into its own. The rescue of downed pilots and the evacuation of wounded under fire pointed up dramatically the possibilities of true vertical-lift machines.

Although their basic principles remain the same, modern helicopters have little resemblance to the fragile, open-framework Sikorsky *VS-300* of 1941. A detailed review of the stages of development is beyond our scope, but a few examples of modern helicopter trends will serve to indicate the degree of progress in the past 25 years.

There are many variations of the theme, ranging from the giant *YCH 54-A* Skycrane, designed to "straddle" and lift large and bulky loads of up to 20,000 pounds, down to small, two-place armed and armored attack helicopters to support troop movements.

The one- and two-place machines are generally powered by a single gasoline engine. Larger sizes including both military and commercial types are now almost universally fitted with single or multiple gas-turbine engines. Most designs depend on one lifting rotor (2, 3, or 5 bladed); some machines use twin-rotor systems, arranged fore and aft, and one design is built around twin intermeshing rotors, as in an eggbeater. Although the examples cited here are of U.S. origin, the same patterns can be found in the helicopters of other countries. The Soviet Union in particular has a very active helicopter program, matching the United States type for type, up to and including the huge *Flying Crane*.

■MECHANICS OF FLIGHT.—It is a fact that the automobile is more complicated in operation than the airplane. Although an airplane is physically easier to operate, a higher degree of skill is required. The airplane pilot is not troubled with a brake, clutch, or gears to change; in these respects he has an advantage over the automobile driver. In clear weather the pilot has only to watch the performance of his motor, keep his ship on an even keel, and follow his compass direction. He governs speed by feeding more or less gasoline to the engine with the throttle. He has two flying controls: a control stick (or wheel) for the hands and the rudder bar in small planes operated by the feet. For a finer attitude adjustment, *trim taps* are used.

The stick controls the *elevator* at the tail surface and the *ailerons,* movable flaps at the ends of the wings. Moving the stick forward causes the nose of the plane to dip; moving it back causes the nose to rise. When the stick is moved sideways, it operates the ailerons. When one aileron is depressed, it presents a flat surface to the rushing air and acts as a sort of brake, causing that wing to lift. The two ailerons work in opposite directions; when one is depressed, the other is lifted, so that one wing is pushed down and the other up. It is the action of the ailerons that causes a ship to heel over sharply in making a turn. Without the aileron action, a ship making a turn would simply skid sidewise through the air; a sharp turn could not be made and the plane could easily get out of control. But because the ailerons tip the wing so as to present a broad, flat surface to the air, the plane can "bank" around a very sharp curve, just as an automobile can turn a corner faster when the road is inclined than when it is flat.

The rudder bar controls only the rudder at the tail surface for right and left motion. When the pilot makes a turn to the right, he pushes down on the right rudder bar to turn the plane in that direction and at the same time moves the stick to the right to bring the ailerons into play and dip the right wing. Then, to *level out* he must use left rudder and move the stick a little to the left to bring the wings up to level again.

—S. Paul Johnston

Best-Selling Hard Cover Books*

Year	Fiction	Non-Fiction
1966	**Valley of the Dolls**, Jaqueline Susann	**How to Avoid Probate**, Norman F. Dacey
1965	**The Source**, James A. Michener	**How to be a Jewish Mother**, Dan Greenberg
1964	**The Spy Who Came In From the Cold**, John Le Carré	**Four Days**, American Heritage & United Press International
1963	**The Shoes of the Fisherman**, Morris West	**Happiness is a Warm Puppy**, Charles Schultz
1962	**Ship of Fools**, Katherine Anne Porter	**Calories Don't Count**, Herman Taller, M.D.
1961	**The Agony and the Ecstasy**, Irving Stone	**The New English Bible: The New Testament**
1960	**Advise and Consent**, Allen Drury	**Folk Medicine**, D. C. Jarvis
1959	**Exodus**, Leon Uris	**Twixt Twelve and Twenty**, Pat Boone
1958	**Doctor Zhivago**, Boris Pasternak	**Kids Say The Darndest Things!** Art Linkletter
1957	**By Love Possessed**, James Gould Cozzens	**Kids Say The Darndest Things!** Art Linkletter
1956	**Don't Go Near the Water!**, William Brinkley	**Arthritis and Common Sense**, Dan Dale Alexander

*According to retail sales. Courtesy, *Publishers' Weekly.*

Book Publishing, the procurement and processing of manuscripts and illustrations for publication in either hard-cover or soft-cover volumes. Book publishing in this century has become clearly differentiated from book printing and binding and from retail bookselling, all originally carried on as part of a single enterprise. The publisher's function is to finance the book, to publicize it, and to promote its widest possible distribution.

The publisher usually contracts with an author for the exclusive right to publish his book, in consideration of the payment of a percentage of the selling price as a *royalty.* In the case of textbooks, encyclopedias, and some other kinds of works, the authors may be commissioned by the publisher. The publisher may have, or the author may retain, the right to license translations and foreign editions of the work and dramatic, film, or broadcast versions. Income from such permissions and from the licensing of reprints and book-club editions is shared between the author and the original publisher.

Although a few publishers print their own works, usually the manufacture of a book is done under contract by a printing and binding firm, according to a design and specifications provided by the publisher and on paper supplied by him. (See *Printing* and *Bookbinding.*) Recent developments in manufacture, including the use of photo-offset lithography, of glued rather than sewn bindings, of high-speed presses, and of improvements in color printing have made possible the production of inexpensive paperbound editions and of popular art books and others with illustration in color.

The publisher seeks to promote the sale of books through visits of salesmen to wholesalers, bookstores, schools, and libraries, through advertising, and through the distribution of review copies and other means of publicity. An increasing proportion of sales is to schools and libraries.

Approximately 100 *book clubs,* a few very large clubs of a general nature and many smaller specialized ones, offer books to their members on a subscription basis at a reduced price. Several thousand books annually are reprinted in inexpensive paperbound editions and given mass distribution through newsstands, drugstores, supermarkets, and similar outlets. About 300 million copies a year are distributed in this form.

About 8 to 10 per cent of the total American book output is exported, of which scientific, technical, and medical books, college textbooks, and paperbacks are especially important. Canada is the largest single export market, but there is an increasing worldwide demand for American books.

In addition to the publishing of general *trade books* (fiction, poetry, children's books, and general works of broad interest), there are many specialized sectors of publishing producing school and college textbooks; dictionaries and encyclopedias; scientific, technical, medical, law, and business books; Bibles, missals, and other religious books; and other specialized works. The industry as a whole has expanded considerably in recent years, primarily as a result of the greatly increased enrollment at all levels of education, the growth of library service, and the general increase in reading as a part of the remarkable postwar cultural growth. Total sales of books in the United States rose from $750 million in 1954 to more than $2 billion in 1965. Of this sum, about 30 per cent represents textbook sales and about 20 per cent encyclopedia sales. Of the more than one billion copies of books distributed annually (including textbooks), more than 300 million are paperbound and nearly 100 million are sold through book clubs. About 28,000 different books were published in 1966, as compared with 12,589 in 1955. There are several hundred active book publishers, including church and university presses as well as commercial firms. They vary in size from small houses with only five or six employees to giant firms doing an annual business of more than $100 million.
—Dan Lacy

Canal, any open channel filled with water, used to convey water or shipping from one place to another. *Drainage canals* are built to carry off rainwater and waterborne wastes of all types, including domestic sewage. However, open sewage canals are now considered health hazards. *Water supply canals* bring water long distances, often passing through mountains in big tunnels. Large cities such as Los Angeles receive much of their drinking water via large canals. The canals that supply southern California also make possible the irrigated agriculture that thrives in the warm, sunny, semiarid climate.

■**NAVIGATION CANALS.**—Navigation canals for ships and barges represent man's first real large-scale transportation system, a natural outgrowth of using the rivers of the world to move passengers and freight from one place to another.

The Chinese started building the 1,000-mile Grand Canal about 500 B.C. The Babylonians linked the Euphrates and Tigris rivers with a canal at about the same time, but historians think this canal was originally built 1,000 years earlier and the Babylonians merely reconstructed the waterway. Late in the fifteenth century the *navigation lock* was invented, and engineers were no longer limited to building canals on level ground. The lock made it possible to lift shipping from a low level to a higher section. A *lock* is a large rectangular chamber, now usually built of concrete. Watertight doors, called gates, seal off each end of the lock chamber. To raise a ship, the gates on the high-level end are closed and big valves drain the water from the chamber so the water level in the chamber coincides with the water level in the low-level canal. The downstream gates are much higher than the upstream gates since they must extend below the surface of the low level to above the surface of the high level when the lock is full. When these big gates open, the ship enters the lock and the doors close behind it. Then different valves open, admitting water from the high-level canal to flow into and fill the chamber. The ship merely floats up as the water rises. When water levels coincide, the upstream gates open and the ship sails out. All this is done without pumping any water. It all flows by gravity and the only energy expended is that needed to open and close the lock gates and the valves. Using a series of locks, such as the Panama Canal does, huge ships are raised and lowered hundreds of feet.

Many countries of Europe have developed elaborate systems of canals, particularly in the Lowlands where they serve the dual purpose of drainage and navigation. Belgium and the Netherlands alone have about 7,000 miles of canals and canalized rivers. Nations with relatively limited seacoast, such as the Soviet Union, also have elaborate inland waterway systems. Much of this canal construction took place in the early 1800's before the advent of the railroads, which ultimately gave the waterways stiff competition in the transport of bulk materials. This same pattern developed in the United States, where the first canal was built in Massachusetts in 1793—a relatively short canal around some rapids in the Connecticut River. The Erie Canal linking the Hudson River with the Great Lakes at Buffalo was finished in 1825. In America, most of the canals were displaced by the railroads. The Panama and Suez Canals, which handle ocean-going ships, both cut thousands of miles off the ship lanes.
—William W. Jacobus, Jr.

Cinematography, the science and art of taking and projecting motion pictures. This is a two-part process which involves a motion-picture camera and a projector. The camera records the motion by taking a series of still pictures on a strip of film at precise intervals, usually 24 per second. The motion-picture projector flashes the still pictures on a screen at the same frequency at which they were recorded to produce the illusion of motion.

© WALT DISNEY PRODUCTIONS

SET IN MOTION, this series of *frames*, or still pictures, shows actress Julie Andrews levitating in the movie *Mary Poppins*.

■**CAMERAS.**—A motion-picture camera is simply a still camera which incorporates a mechanism to automatically advance the film past the lens and actuate the shutter. Every motion-picture camera incorporates a lens, shutter, gate, film-advance mechanism, and magazine. If sound is also being recorded, a *sound head* is added.

As in all cameras, the *lens system* gathers the light from the subjects and focuses it on the film. Many cameras mount several lenses on a rotating turret, enabling the camera operator to change lenses easily and rapidly.

Mounted between the lens and the film, *shutters* for motion-picture cameras consist of a pair of rotating disks with pie-shaped cutouts. To vary exposure time, the angular relationship between the disks is varied to change the size of the opening, while the rotational speed is held constant.

The film is held in the focal plane of the lens by the *gate*, which consists of the edge guides, aperture plate, and pressure plate. Lateral movement of the film is prevented by the edge guides while the pressure plate holds the film against the aperture plate positioned at the focal plane. The opening, or aperture, in the aperture plate defines the size and shape of the exposed area on the film for each picture.

Film movement through the camera is controlled by the *film-advance*, or *pulldown*, *mechanism*. Since the camera records a series of still pictures, the filmstrip moves intermittently. To advance the film, the pulldown mechanism uses a claw which engages perforations along each edge of the film. The claw pulls the film down, stops, withdraws from the perforation, and rises to repeat the cycle. As the claw rises, the shutter is opened, exposing the stationary film.

Magazines for motion-picture film consist of a pair of light-tight enclosures. Unexposed film is stored in one enclosure while the second collects the exposed film. The magazines are held in place by mechanical latches which allow fresh magazines to be attached to the camera as needed. At the usual exposure rate of 24 frames per second, a 1,000-foot film magazine can record approximately 11 minutes of action.

For *sound recording*, a microphone is used to convert the sound into electric signals which are amplified and applied to a lamp filament. As the sqund and the resultant electric signal strength vary, the intensity of the light produced by the lamp varies. This varying light intensity is focused by a lens system onto a narrow sound track on the light-sensitive film. After development, the sound track appears alongside the picture frames as a ribbon with transverse stripes of varying width and intensity.

■**PROJECTORS.**—The prime function of a motion-picture projector is to create the optical illusion of movement called *motion pictures*. The projector accomplishes this by flashing a series of still pictures on a screen. The in-terval between flashes is so brief that the eye retains the picture image during the periods the screen is dark. The viewer's eye is fooled into believing it sees motion while the viewer actually sees 24 still pictures every second.

To accomplish the desired effect, the projector incorporates a lens system, film-advance mechanism, light source, and, if sound pictures are to be shown, a *sound head*.

The *lens system* inverts the image on the film and focuses the picture on the screen. Moving the lens toward or away from the film focuses the picture for different projector-to-screen distances.

Motion of the film through the projector is controlled by the *film-advance mechanism*. The film is advanced in intermittent steps, frame-by-frame, at a rate of 24 frames per second. Inexpensive projectors of the amateur movie variety usually employ a clawlike device that engages the perforations on the film's edge. The pulldown claw pulls the film down one frame, disengages, and rises to repeat the cycle. More expensive projectors advance the film with a pair of sprockets driven by a *Geneva* mechanism. The sprocket drive has the advantage of distributing the load on the film over numerous perforations, reducing wear on the film and extending its useful life.

After the film has advanced the *shutter* opens, projecting the picture onto the screen. The shutter's function is to shut off light from the *lamphouse* as the film advances. This prevents the image from moving during exposure. Projector shutters usually consist of a rotating disk with cutouts or a pair of fanlike blades mounted on a shaft. Motion of the shutter is synchronized with the film-advance mechanism to allow light to pass only while the film is held stationary.

A powerful *light source* is required in the lamphouse to project the image on the film through the lens to the screen. Portable projectors for short distances rely on a powerful electric bulb or lamp. For motion-picture theaters, where the distance to the screen may be several hundred feet, a carbon arc or high-intensity mercury-vapor light source is required.

Sound for motion pictures is produced by the projector's *sound head*, which scans an optical track running along the film beside the picture frame. An *exciter* lamp projects a beam of light through the sound track to a photoelectric cell behind the film. Variations in the optical density of the sound track are converted into electric signals by the photoelectric cell to reproduce the sound recorded with the film. Silent-film projectors for home or amateur cinematography eliminate the sound head entirely.

Standard projectors are manufactured for 8mm, 16mm, and 35mm film. The 8mm film is really 16mm film which is split longitudinally during processing. Until recently, 8mm projectors were limited to silent pictures, but super-8 film now available provides space for a sound track. The 16mm projectors are widely used for scientific films, television news coverage, and instructional films.

Professional projection over distances exceeding about 100 feet require a 35mm projector, which is therefore used in all commercial motion-picture theaters. A wide range of other film widths has been used for special projection effects such as *Cinerama, CinemaScope, VistaVision, Todd-AO,* and many others. These films require either special projectors or multiple projectors synchronized to throw a single picture on very wide or curved screens. (See *Motion Picture Industry,* page 1602.)

—Joseph J. Kelleher

Clocks and Watches, instruments to indicate time and its passage, usually by means of a dial. Among the earliest of such devices was the *sundial,* whose origins are lost in history. Next came the *water clock,* which measured time lapse by a changing water level in relation to a scale. Its chief advantage was independence of of the sun. Some later water clocks operated mechanical almanacs. The most remarkable of these, made in China about 1100 A.D., embodied a water-activated escapement that foreshadowed the mechanical clock escapement of Western civilization. Another early method involved the burning of such substances as incense, wax, or oil, indicating time by measurement of the amount consumed.

The *sandglass* or *hourglass* of the Middle Ages consisted of two glass containers united at a narrow orifice through which the granular contents flowed from one container to the other. It had to be reset promptly at the end of a cycle to assure accuracy but was long popular at sea because ship motion did not affect its timekeeping. Today it is familiarly used as an egg timer.

The true mechanical clock appeared near the end of the thirteenth century. We know the details of an elaborate clock made by Giovanni de Dondi in 1364, which indicated many astronomical occurrences according to the Ptolemaic system. The timekeeping element consisted of a train of wheels driven by a weight and controlled by an escapement. This and subsequent escapements transferred the driving power to a balance wheel (later also to a pendulum). Teeth on the escape wheel—last of a series in the clock movement—acted on pallets, causing the balance wheel to oscillate and a hand to indicate elapsed time. To make clocks portable, a driving spring instead of a weight was applied during the sixteenth century. All clocks of this era kept time poorly and required frequent setting.
■**ACCURATE TIMEPIECES.**—In 1657, Christian Huygens of Holland successfully applied the pendulum, with its natural period of swing, to timekeeping, making possible the construction of fairly constant and predictable clocks. Soon a hairspring was added to the balance wheels, giving them a similar natural period of oscillation.

Application of these improved timekeepers to scientific tasks revealed many shortcomings. The greatest of these were overcome by improving the escapement and thermometrically compensating for gross errors caused by temperature variations.

Timekeepers of truly scientific utility were then possible, as demonstrated by John Harrison with his invention of chronometers for marine navigation. Practical instruments, with which the navigator could compute accurate longitude, date from the work of Thomas Earnshaw and John Arnold in the latter half of the eighteenth century.

The nineteenth century was notable for the refinement of manufacturing techniques and for the invention of designs for mass production. In clock manufacture the United States took the lead, beginning about 1816 with the work of Eli Terry. Clocks with wooden works were sold by the hundreds of thousands in the United States and surrounding areas; many are still in use. Their manufacture ceased, however, with the introduction of the stamped-brass clock about 1837, and the market for American clocks rapidly expanded overseas. The European industry was strongly affected by these developments and soon adopted American production techniques.

The nineteenth century also brought the introduction of precision *gravity escapements.* The most far-reaching scientific timekeeping advance of the century began in the 1890's with Charles Édouard Guillaume's alloys, which permitted the elimination of temperature compensators.

Further developments were made possible when electricity was applied to the old reliable pendulum or balance wheel. With the advent of electronics, additional refinement led to the quartz-crystal oscillator in which a resonant frequency was obtained and fed to a synchronous motor operating the hands. The *atomic clocks* of today's precision laboratories are similar but use a stream of particles as their resonant element. In watch design, the most radical advance has been the replacement of the balance wheel by a tuning fork.

—Edwin A. Battison

Communications Satellite, or *comsat,* an artificial earth satellite used to relay telephone, television, and similar signals between two earthbound stations. *Early Bird,* the world's first commercial communications satellite, was launched from Cape Kennedy, Florida, on April 6, 1965, opening a new era in international communications. After a series of tests and demonstrations, it went into commercial operation on June 28, 1965, linking North America and Europe. The event marked the first step toward the establishment of a worldwide network of satellites that will provide new channels of communication to many nations.

By the end of 1965, work was well underway on plans to install a new two-ocean commercial network using improved synchronous satellites larger and more powerful than Early Bird.

One of the new satellites would be located over the Pacific, expanding commercial service for the first time to the Pacific area, and a second satellite would be located over the Atlantic, supplementing and expanding service being provided by Early Bird. The satellites would serve the communications needs of NASA's Apollo moon-landing program, as well as offer services for other commercial uses. The system would be in operation by the fall of 1966.

Contract negotiations also were begun in 1966 leading toward the purchase of even more advanced synchronous satellites to be used in the developing global commercial satellite system in 1968.

International communications have been growing at a rate of 18 to 20 per cent a year. Radio and cable facilities have been constantly expanded to meet demands for more lines of communication to promote commerce and to exchange knowledge between peoples. But ever greater demands are being made.

The vast expanses of space offer one of the greatest potentials for satisfying this demand. Satellites can supplement, and greatly expand, the number of channels available for increased global communications. In addition, satellites can be used for different types of communication not now technically possible by existing transmission systems.

Early Bird has proven its versatility for all types of traffic: transmitting telephone calls, high-quality color and two-way black-and-white television, photographs, teletype, facsimile, data, and other communications between continents. Its commercial successors will vastly expand this capability to all parts of the world.

■**MICROWAVES.**—Advances in rocketry, in electronics, and in other technologies made possible the successful development of active communications satellites. Such spacecraft carry electronic equipment that can receive signals beamed to them by earth stations, amplify them, and repeat them to other earth stations.

Such satellites provide line-of-sight contact with the earth, receiving and repeating signals between earth sta-

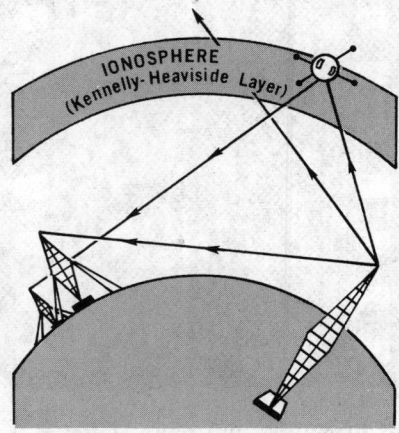

SATELLITES, by relaying microwaves between widely separated transmitters on earth, aid intercontinental communication.

tions over tremendous distances. They act essentially as radio towers in space. Because of their altitude, satellites can relay signals that otherwise would be blocked by the curvature of the earth. The signals used are microwaves which, like a beam of light, travel in a straight line. They can be transmitted through the air without being affected by lightning, bursts of radio activity associated with sun spots, or other atmospheric conditions that often disrupt ordinary radio signals.

■**TWO TYPES.**—Communications satellites are of two types, passive and active. *Passive comsats* contain no relaying signals; they merely serve to reflect signals between two points. *Active comsats,* which contain intricate electronic equipment, rebroadcast signals that are beamed to the satellite. The accompanying table lists the communications satellites that had been orbited by Jan. 1, 1966.

Communications spacecraft may be placed in medium-altitude orbits ranging from several thousand to about 12,000 miles, or synchronous altitude of 22,300 miles, Twelve or more medium-altitude satellites would be required to provide global communications coverage. Three synchronous satellites of sufficient power could provide coverage for nearly all the earth.

Early Bird is in a synchronous orbit; that is, its orbital speed keeps pace, or is synchronized, with the rotation of the earth. Thus it appears to hang in one spot in space. From its position on the equator above the mid-Atlantic 24 hours a day, it provides commercial communication service daily to the most heavily industrialized area of the earth.

As mentioned before, more advanced spacecraft are being developed for the developing global commercial system. Plans call for these advanced global satellites to weigh about 250 pounds and have a capacity for 1,200 or more voice channels—nearly three times the weight and more than four times the capacity of Early Bird.

■**COMSAT CORPORATION.**—The successful flight of Early Bird launched the Communications Satellite Corporation on its first commercial space venture

in partnership with many nations. Comsat is not a government agency but a shareholder-owned private company whose functions and responsibilities were specified by Congress in the Communications Satellite Act of 1962.

In conformity with this law, Comsat's stock is widely distributed. Ten million shares were issued and sold on June 2, 1964, to provide the initial financing for the corporation: half of the common stock to the general public and half to the U. S. companies authorized by law as communications common carriers.

Under the law, Comsat has a 15-member board of directors: six directors elected by public stockholders, six by carrier shareholders, and three appointed by the President of the United States, subject to Senate confirmation.

To implement the concept of a worldwide commercial satellite system serving all countries, the corporation by early 1966 had entered into international agreements with communications agencies in 48 other nations to share in the ownership and use of the space system. Comsat acts as manager of the system on behalf of the other members, and retains a majority interest.   —Matthew Gordon

Compass, an instrument that indicates the north-south direction. The *magnetic compass* consists of a magnetized needle mounted so that it can rotate freely in the horizontal plane. The needle aligns itself with the earth's magnetic field, and a scale, marked in degrees, is used to indicate bearings relative to the earth's north magnetic pole. Another type, the *gyrocompass,* obtains its directional properties from a spinning gyroscope.

■**MAGNETIC COMPASS.**—The earth acts as if it were a large permanent magnet, with magnetic lines of force extending between the north and south magnetic poles. These lines of force cause the magnetized needle in a compass to rotate until it points toward the magnetic poles. The magnetic compass does not point exactly toward the earth's geographic poles, however, because each magnetic pole is displaced about 700 miles from the

corresponding geographic pole. The error, or *variation of the compass,* varies from year to year and from place to place.

The *mariner's magnetic compass* consists of a round compass card, 7½ inches in diameter on which the magnetic material is mounted. The card, graduated in 360 degrees, is attached to an inverted cup. This, in turn, floats on a mixture of alcohol and water in a bowl. The compass bowl is mounted on gimbals for complete freedom of motion.

■**GYROCOMPASS.**—Unlike the magnetic compass, the gyrocompass points toward the geographic north pole. The heart of the gyrocompass is a spinning rotor, which is so affected by gravity that, as its axis tilts because of the earth's rotation, it experiences a continual force causing the axis to align itself with the north-south direction. A typical gyrocompass has a rotor several inches in diameter that spins between 6,000 and 20,000 revolutions per minute. The gyrocompass is used widely as an aid to ship navigation, with the more reliable magnetic compass backing it up.

An instrument called a *directional gyro* is used on many aircraft. It is not north-seeking but holds any preset heading with little error for periods up to half an hour. It must be reset periodically with the help of a magnetic compass. The *Gyrosyn compass* combines the functions of the directional gyro and the magnetic compass. It points toward magnetic north but does not oscillate during the maneuvers of the airplane as a magnetic compass would.

■**RADIO COMPASS.**—A radio compass uses radio waves to indicate the direction of a transmitting station of known location. It consists of a loop antenna, a radio receiver, and a direction indicator. When the loop is rotated so that it points toward the transmitter, it picks up the strongest signal. When the plane of the loop is at right angles to the station's direction, the received signal strength is a minimum. A scale attached to the loop then gives the station's direction with considerable accuracy. Modern designs eliminate the need for manual loop rotation in order to obtain a bearing. Electronic circuits monitor the broadcast signal and give continuous bearings of the station automatically. By reading the directions of two transmitting stations, the pilot can pinpoint his location on a navigational chart.   —William C. Vergara

Data Processing Systems, devices for the mathematical manipulation, storage, and retrieval of information. Data processing systems perform a variety of commercial recordkeeping and scientific tasks formerly done by hand. The type of equipment making up a data processing system can vary widely—from a single key-driven calculator to a powerful electronic digital computer linking up a score or more of individual units.

In all cases, the system involves three basic considerations. The first is input of source data, usually in the form of holes in cards or paper tape, magnetized spots on magnetic tape

Communications Satellites

Name	Nationality	Launch Date	Comment
Score	U.S.	Dec. 18, 1958	Broadcast Christmas message from President Eisenhower to the world
Echo 1	U.S.	Aug. 12, 1960	First passive comsat orbited
Courier 1B	U.S.	Oct. 4, 1960	First active repeater comsat orbited
Oscar 1	U.S.	Dec. 12, 1961	First amateur comsat; built by American Radio Relay League
Oscar 2	U.S.	June 2,1962	Amateur comsat; broadcast for 18 days
Telstar 1	U.S.	July 10, 1962	Active repeater comsat
Relay 1	U.S.	Dec. 13, 1962	Active repeater comsat
Syncom 1	U.S.	Feb. 14, 1963	Failed to function after orbiting
Telstar 2	U.S.	May 7, 1963	Active repeater comsat
Syncom 2	U.S.	July 26, 1963	First successful synchronous active repeater comsat
Relay 2	U.S.	Jan. 21, 1964	Active repeater comsat
Echo 2	U.S.	Jan. 25, 1964	Passive comsat; participated in first cooperative program with Soviet Union
Syncom 3	U.S.	Aug. 19, 1964	Synchronous active repeater comsat; used to telecast 1964 Olympic Games from Japan to the United States
Oscar 3	U.S.	Mar. 9, 1965	Amateur comsat; broadcast for 16 days
Early Bird	U.S.	Apr. 6, 1965	First commercial comsat; service initiated on June 28, 1965
Molniya 1	Soviet Union	Apr. 23, 1965	First Soviet comsat; active-repeater type
Molniya 2	Soviet Union	Oct. 13, 1965	Active repeater comsat

or disks, or characters printed on documents. The second is the planned processing of this data within the system—adding, subtracting, multiplying, dividing, comparing, storing, etc. The third is the output of an end result, usually in the form of punched cards, paper tape, magnetic tape or disks, visual display, or printed information on paper.

The most widely used data processing method today is the *punched-card system,* which involves the recording of data on cards in the form of punched holes or perforations. A perforation in a particular location, for example, may indicate the number "2" to the machine, while a perforation in another location will stand for the letter "A". Punched-card machines "read" these holes by means of small copper brushes or similar conducting devices. As a card passes under these brushes, an electrical circuit is created wherever there is a hole. This completed circuit then permits an electrical impulse to be routed through the machine where it is used in a predetermined, or programmed way.

■**DATA TRANSMISSION.**—The electronic movement of data from one location to another for the use of man or machine is not a new concept. Samuel F. B. Morse started it in May 1844 with his telegraph. In June 1876, at the Philadelphia Centennial, the public telephone made its debut in the United States. Since then, both the Western Union and American Telephone & Telegraph companies have transmitted untold billions of business messages.

In recent years the concept of data transmission has taken on new meaning. With the advent of electronic computers, and their voracious appetite for data, the need to maintain a flow of business information between remote offices and plants and a centralized data-processing installation has become acute. As a result, new input/output devices, along with higher-speed methods of communication, have been developed.

Input/output terminals today range from the teleprinter unit to devices that can accept punched-card or magnetic-tape data. For example, a wide range of teleprocessing devices have been introduced that are capable of "reading" punched holes in cards or magnetized spots on tape. These coded numbers and letters are translated into pulse signals on a device called a *Data-Phone.* The signals are then transmitted to a receiving station via regular telephone lines or private wire circuits.

Several types of transmission circuits are used today to move data from one point to another: low-speed wires, used mostly for teleprinter communications; voice-grade wires (regular telephone lines), capable of serving a wide range of input/output devices; and new wide-band, or high-speed, circuits that transmit by means of coaxial cable or microwave channels. This last category includes laser devices producing beams of coherent light that may be an important communications medium in the future.
                                        —Stanley Englebardt

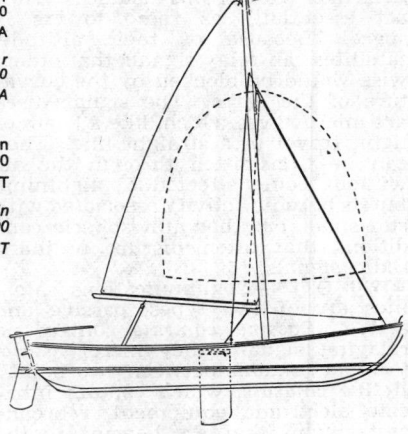

XEROX CORPORATION

XEROGRAPHY, using heat and electrically-charged paper and powder, reproduces in detail print, drawings and three-dimensional objects, as this photograph of a Xerocopy shows.

Duplicating Machines, copying machines used to reproduce or duplicate documents and drawings. The specific type of equipment employed usually depends on the material to be reproduced and the volume of copies desired.

The most familiar copying method, aside from use of carbon paper, is the stencil duplicating or mimeograph process. The word *mimeograph* was originally the trademark of the first manufacturer, but has since become a generic term to describe a particular duplicating process. Mimeograph utilizes stencil sheets made of porous paper covered with an ink-impervious coating. Typing or drawing on the paper with a sharp pointed object displaces the coating, exposing the porous paper backing. The stencil is then wrapped around an inked cylinder and rolled against paper. In this way, ink is forced through the openings onto the paper, and a duplicate of the stencil is printed. Mimeographing is an inexpensive technique, but it is limited to bulletins, forms, letters, and similar purposes.

An offshoot of the mimeograph process is the *spirit-duplicating method.* In this process, a special aniline-dye carbon paper is placed face-up beneath a sheet of coated paper. Typing or drawing on the coated paper produce a reversed copy on the back by the carbon paper. This master copy is then affixed to the drum of a duplicating machine, and the aniline dye is transferred to slightly moistened blank paper, which comes into contact with the master after entering the duplicator. The copies are extremely clear but limited in number.

Offset duplicating is also similar to the mimeograph process, but the equipment is generally larger, sturdier, and capable of turning out a much greater number of clear copies from a single master. The most important feature of offset duplicating is that the master copy can be reproduced from an original directly (without typing or drawing) by a photographic or electrostatic-transfer process. In this way there is no chance of human error.

The *electrostatic-transfer,* or *xerographic, process* uses an electrostatic force to deposit dry powder on copy paper ("xero" means "dry"). This involves exposing an original to an electrically charged plate. Where light strikes this plate, the charge is dissipated; but where opaque material, such as lines or letters, prevents light from coming through, the positive charge remains. The plate is then dusted with negatively charged particles, which are attracted to the positive ones. Positively charged paper is then placed over the plate and the negatively charged image transferred to it. The ink particles are fused to the paper by a heat process. The technique is extremely popular because almost any kind of original can be copied on almost any kind of paper.

An *infrared process* uses heat-sensitive paper that is placed on top of the original to be reproduced. Infrared light in the machine causes the carbon or metallic particles in the print on the original to heat up and transfer their image to the sensitized paper. No further chemicals or developers are needed.

The dry and moist *diazo processes* require translucent originals to be placed on top of azo-dyed paper. The pair are exposed to ultraviolet light. The paper is then developed either in ammonia vapor (dry process) or a special liquid (wet process).

The *dye-transfer process* utilizes a matrix sheet that is exposed to an original and then placed in an activator solution. After activation, the matrix is placed in contact with copy paper, and the dye in it is transferred. Up to five copies can be made from one matrix at low cost.

In the *silver-transfer* and *photographic copying processes,* the technique closely approximates standard photoprocessing methods. In both cases, the original is exposed to sensitized paper, which is then developed and printed. A more complex variation of this process is used to duplicate blueprints. —Stanley Englebardt

Electric Transit, mass transit facilities whose primary source of power is derived from electric generators. Electric-traction motors, powered by electric current from trolley wires and "third rails," have been the most desirable form of propulsion for mass-transit vehicles since the 1880's. From then until the great depression of the 1930's, electric streetcar lines and interurban lines were the major means of transportation, along with railroads. Trains running on elevated structures, originally steam-powered but later electrified, marked the beginnings of separated, right-of-way rapid transit in some of our largest cities.

The mass use of automobiles, starting after World War I, gradually brought on the demise of street railway and interurban lines. But electric transit systems in the form of rapid transit survived and lately have been flourishing due to their superior ability to furnish efficient access to congested urban areas. A single rail track can move as many people as 12 to 16 lanes of automobile highway in a given time.

Several types of electric transit are in use today or are being demonstrated for future use. All utilize electric motors to propel the vehicles and, in the more modern equipment, to slow them down by dynamic motor braking. Either direct-current or alternating-current power is obtained from the trolley wire or third rail, feeding the motors through speed-regulating controls.

■**STREETCARS AND TRAMS.**—Many cities of the world utilize modern versions of the old electric streetcar. But in the Western Hemisphere, they have virtually been abandoned because it is difficult to operate them efficiently in congested city streets. In Europe, there has been more interest in retaining a version of the streetcar, the *tram,* and converting it to private right-of-way operation.

■**TROLLEY BUSES.**—Also called "trackless" trolleys, these rubber-tired bus-like vehicles collect electric power from a double trolley wire overhead, but can maneuver independently of tracks. Now in limited use in some cities of the world, they too are slowly being phased out of service because of urban traffic congestion.

■**RAIL RAPID TRANSIT.**—Characterized by the *subway* and the *elevated,* this form of mass transit has maintained its usefulness over the years. Private right-of-way, fast schedule speeds, and the ability to run underground in subways through the heart of congested urban areas have enabled these rapid transit lines to survive despite increasing use of the automobile, and the tremendous public highway building programs. In this day of perpetual traffic jams and high parking rates, they have been increasing their ridership.

Rail rapid transit provides for the efficient movement of large numbers of people going in the same direction. For example, a single track in the Toronto subways carries 35,000 passengers per hour, the equivalent of 16 lanes of urban expressway.

Six metropolitan areas in the West-ern Hemisphere, have rail rapid transit in operation: New York, Chicago, Boston, Philadelphia, and Cleveland in the United States, and Toronto in Canada. In the Eastern Hemisphere, major systems are operating in London, Paris, Stockholm, Berlin, Hamburg, Madrid, Milan, Rome, Warsaw, Moscow, and Tokyo.

Completely new rail rapid-transit systems are also being built. In 1968, San Francisco will have the first section of its 75-mile long, 80-mile-per-hour system in operation. The Delaware River Port Authority is constructing an 11-mile system for the Philadelphia area, and Washington, D. C., will have a subway by 1971.

■**ELECTRIFIED COMMUTER RAILROAD SERVICE.**—Electrical MU (multiple unit) cars are used in certain major cities in the United States to provide rapid transit service for commuters. The largest commuter service railroad is the Long Island Railroad, connecting Long Island points with New York City.

■**MONORAIL.**—This class of electrical transit system is characterized by its single running rail or beam, in contrast with the two rails of conventional rail rapid transit. Two general types have been demonstrated: the *suspended monorail,* in which the passenger cab hangs down from the overhead beamway, and the *supported monorail,* in which the vehicle straddles the beamway. One of the earliest suspended monorail systems, built in 1901, is still in operation in Wuppertal, Germany. The monorail operating during the 1964–65 World's Fair in New York was also of the suspended type. The last supported monorail put in service was the line from Haneda International Airport to downtown Tokyo, approximately 8 miles long.

■**TRANSIT EXPRESSWAY.**—A developmental rapid-transit system was constructed in 1965 for demonstration in

ALWEG-SEATTLE MONORAIL INSTALLATION

MONORAIL car moves on horizontal rubber tires that grip the supporting beam, or rail.

South Park, Pittsburgh. On this prototype system, three unmanned vehicles run as single car units or coupled together into trains demonstrating multiple-unit operation completely controlled by computer. A test layout for speeds up to 50 miles per hour is provided by 9,340 feet of roadway in aerial, at-grade, single-track, and double-track configurations. Transit expressway is not a monorail but a dual rail system, with the vehicles running on top of the roadway. It is adaptable to subway construction.　　—Philip R. Gillespie

Electronic Engineering, the branch of engineering that deals with designing equipment, such as radio and television sets, by exploiting the existing knowledge of the electron. Electronic engineering deals with the emission of electrons from various substances and the control of the emitted electrons, by electrical or magnetic means, to perform useful functions. These include amplification of weak signals, counting operations in computers, modulation of broadcast signals, the generation of alternating-current signals, switching, and rectification. Electronic engineering differs, therefore, from the older field of electrical engineering, which is concerned primarily with the conduction of electricity in wires or solutions.

Radio and television are two everyday applications of electronic engineering. Equally important are microwave radio relay stations, which carry television signals and thousands of telephone conversations across the continents. Communications satellites make it possible to relay such signals around the world.

Electronic engineers design a wide variety of navigation equipment, such as loran and air traffic control systems, to help guide planes and ships to their destinations. The electronic automatic pilot enables a plane to fly along a preset course without help from the pilot.

Knowledge gained in the fields of communications and radar led directly to the electronic computer, which is having a tremendous impact on business, science, and industry. Computers process enormous amounts of data and make decisions more quickly, accurately, and economically than human beings. They also automatically control and optimize industrial operations.

Electronic engineering is vital to space programs, providing communication and remote-control equipment, as well as telemetry for storing and transmitting data to waiting ground stations.

The invention of the transistor has greatly reduced the size and power requirements of electronic equipment. It has also opened the way for microelectronic techniques that promise further to reduce the cost and size of electronic systems.

The field of electronic engineering is expanding dramatically both in importance and complexity. Its contributions to all phases of human endeavor should continue to increase greatly.　　—William C. Vergara

Elevator, an enclosed conveyance used to vertically raise or lower persons, merchandise, or vehicles from one level to another. The application of elevators goes back to the days of ancient Greece and Egypt, when they were used primarily to lift material. Today, elevators are still used to carry freight, but by far the major use is to carry passengers. The invention of the elevator was one of the factors that made the multistory building feasible, and the development of high-speed elevators contributed to the solution of the skyscraper. It is often said that more Americans ride each day in elevators than in any other form of public transportation.

The development of the modern elevator began in the middle of the nineteenth century. Most of the early elevators were hydraulic- or steam-powered. By the beginning of the twentieth century, however, electric elevators were being built, and this type proved capable of the high speeds that modern design calls for.

Both hydraulic and electric elevators are being manufactured today. The *hydraulic elevator* usually is restricted to buildings having no more than five or six stories and where speeds no greater than 200 feet per minute are required. *Electric elevators* are used for buildings of any height at speeds that may approach 2,000 feet per minute. Normal elevator speeds, however, are between 100 and 800 feet per minute.

■ **HYDRAULIC ELEVATOR.**—In a hydraulic elevator, the car is lifted by a hydraulic jack placed underneath the elevator in a hole approximately as deep as the height of the building. The grease rack that raises cars in the local gasoline station is a simple and familiar form of hydraulic lift.

■ **ELECTRIC ELEVATOR.**—An electric elevator is lifted by a drive powered by an electric motor. This machine is usually situated at the top of the elevator shafts. Several cables attached to the car are passed over the machine drive sheave (grooved drum) and then down to the counterweight which counterbalances the weight of the car. Friction between the ropes and drive sheave causes the elevator to move vertically as the machine rotates. Both the elevator car and the counterweight are guided in a vertical path through the building by rails or tracks.

■ **SAFETY DEVICES.**—Many safety devices are provided to protect the passengers. Among these are the speed governor, which stops the elevator in case of excessive speed by actuating a device on the car that clamps the guide rail; interlocks on the doors to prevent motion of the elevator unless the doors are closed and locked; and buffers or shock absorbers situated under the elevator to stop the car gently should it pass below the bottom landing. Many other electrical and mechanical devices are supplied to assure safe operation.

Originally, an attendant was required to operate an elevator, but since the 1950's almost all new elevators are automatic. Each passenger directs the elevator to the desired floor by pressing a button in the car. The operation of a group of elevators is regulated by a computer type of control to schedule their movement.

—P. L. Fosburg

Escalator, a moving stairway in which the steps move as a unit upward or downward under power at an angle of 30° to carry passengers. The escalator consists of an endless loop of steps attached to chains, all contained within a steel truss. The chains pass over sprocket-wheel assemblies at the top and bottom. An electric motor geared to the top sprocket wheels produces a continuous, even movement of the steps, which are supported by rollers traveling on inclined tracks. Enclosures, or *balustrades,* are provided on each side to form a railing and to conceal the mechanism. Along the top of each balustrade is a handrail that moves in synchronism with the steps. The step treads are grooved, and they mesh with comb-fingers at each end of the travel to protect the passenger as he enters and leaves the moving steps. The maximum allowable speed is 125 feet per minute. Most escalators, however, travel at a speed of 90 feet per minute.

The first true escalator made its appearance in 1900 at the Paris Exposition. Escalators are now used where a large number of people must be transported vertically for only a few floor levels, as in department stores, transportation terminals, and banks.

—P. L. Fosburg

Harbor, any sheltered body of water deep enough for ships and boats to anchor. Most harbors are situated where rivers empty into the sea in what is known as the river's *estuary.* Major harbors have facilities for loading and unloading both cargo and passengers; technically, this makes them *ports.* Harbors and ports often have shipyards where ships are built, launched, and repaired. Many harbors are designed for specific purposes, such as naval bases, small craft marinas, fishing ports, and commercial shipping terminals.

The most common type of harbor is a natural body of water, mostly surrounded by land, with access to the sea via a narrow inlet. Some harbors having the same characteristics are manmade. Usually, a harbor is constructed because the site offers convenient rail and highway connections. Most often, however, the natural harbor already existed and, because of this, the land transportation and port facilities followed. The majority of the world's major cities enjoy that status because of natural harbors. New York City, Rio de Janeiro, and Liverpool are typical harbor cities. But proximity to the sea is not absolutely necessary. New Orleans, Bremen, London, and Bordeaux, all situated far from the sea, are major ports because of their direct, deepwater channels leading to the sea.

In some parts of the world there are very few natural harbors, and ships must dock at piers and wharves which are unprotected from ocean waves, tides, and storms. Breakwaters, jetties, and seawalls are sometimes built to deflect the force of waves, thus creating an artificial sheltered area. However, these provide only limited protection for a limited period of time compared with that of a natural harbor.

The ideal harbor is deep enough to handle the largest ships, has space enough to provide all the docking and unloading facilities for both cargo and passengers, and provides a direct transfer to rail and truck transport. Efficiency is all-important at a commercial port. Like a railroad car, a ship standing idle while it is being loaded or unloaded does not make money for its owner.

—William W. Jacobus, Jr.

Highway Engineering, the branch of civil engineering concerned with the design, construction, and maintenance of roads. The Romans were probably the first to develop engineered highways—roadways built with foundations to sustain heavy traffic without deteriorating. But the art was lost for many years with the decline of the Roman Empire. For centuries, roads were made of dirt and gravel, until the advent of the automobile in the early 1900's.

Divided highways, an important safety development of the late 1930's, have evolved into today's freeways, superhighways, and expressways. By the separation of traffic moving in opposite directions, many accidents were prevented. But the early divided highway allowed traffic to enter or leave the road at almost any point, and service stations and other commercial establishments were permitted along the roadside without limitations. These conditions proved to be a major source of accidents, and engineers developed the *limited-access highway.*

Currently, the Federal government is sponsoring a national interstate highway program involving a vast network of limited-access roads, now under construction throughout the United States. The states, which actually handle construction, generally contribute only 10 per cent of the cost, while the Federal government provides the remainder. The U.S. Bureau of Public Roads oversees the design and construction of the interstate highways, which are regarded as the safest ever built. Access and egress are limited and curves and grades are very gradual. Interchanges are well lighted and provided with deceleration and acceleration lanes. Signs giving directions are large and clearly visible. Billboards and service stations are prohibited within the right-of-way. When completed, the interstate system will enable motorists to drive across the country on a single highway without encountering a single traffic light.

In cities, where traffic control is a major problem, traffic lights are a necessity and the computer has made it possible to completely integrate traffic systems, changing the timing of lights automatically in accordance with changes in traffic patterns.

—William W. Jacobus, Jr.

Lighthouse, a structure surmounted by a powerful light, used in marine navigation. Since the earliest days, the concept of a bright fire on a hill as a warning to ships at sea has been an accepted navigation and warning device. Whether it was recognized or not, the principle that the higher the light is situated the farther it will be visible, was an early proof that the earth was round. A light 10 feet high can be seen 8 miles away. A 50-foot light can be seen 12½ miles away. A lighthouse 1,000 feet high can be seen 40 miles off.

The earliest harbor planners knew that two lights were highly desirable for a safe entrance, for with two lights on which to base his position, the mariner by triangulation could know definitely where he was. Harbor lighthouses are known as *making lights* because they are the ones the ship's officer sees when he is "making" land.

Another type of light is the *warning light,* such as the famous Eddystone Lighthouse, which is used to mark an especially dangerous spot. *Coasting lights,* which lead the sailor along a coast, are still another type. *Leading lights* lead a ship up a channel or into a harbor.

■ LIGHT SOURCES.—The earliest lighthouses were probably wooden towers from which were hung crude metal baskets loaded with burning wood or coal. As far back as 300 B.C., one of the Seven Wonders of the World was the famed Pharos of Alexandria, a gigantic lighthouse structure said to have been over 100 feet high. It was built on a 400-foot cliff. Roman-built stone lighthouses were used through the Middle Ages.

After wood and coal, candlepower was the next source of light. Tallow candles were first used, then wax candles. The oil lamp that followed was a great improvement. Sperm oil was used at first, and then various vegetable oils. Petroleum came into use for lighthouses in the latter part of the nineteenth century. The electric light is today's standard where power sources are available, and the acetylene gas light is used in stations out of reach of electricity.

The lantern through which the light is projected is a vital part of the lighthouse. Ordinary glass came first, followed by cut glass of many varieties. The parabolic reflectors introduced at the end of the eighteenth century were an important step in the projection of light. Highly complicated and scientifically designed lenses have been developed to extend the range of the modern lighthouse.

Lighthouses are distinguished from one other by the intervals between the flashing of their lights. These are created by having a revolving lens, certain portions of which are blacked off to create the dark intervals.

The development of radar, loran, and other modern electronic safety and communications devices for ships has reduced the over-all importance of lighthouses. Many more lighthouses are being abandoned than are being constructed, but it will be a long time before the lighthouse is obsolete.

—Frank O. Braynard

America's Leading Magazines in 1966*	
Rank	**Circulation**
1 Reader's Digest	16,858,661
2 TV Guide	11,427,151
3 McCall's	8,566,910
4 Look	7,671,328
5 Life	7,449,865
6 Family Circle	7,051,231
7 Better Homes & Gardens	6,882,558
8 Saturday Evening Post	6,858,305
9 Ladies' Home Journal	6,804,779
10 Woman's Day	6,562,049

* Based on average circulation per issue through June, 1966; courtesy, Audit Bureau of Circulation.

Magazines, periodical publications that constitute a major medium of communication throughout the world. There are two major categories, general and special-interest, within which are many subcategories.

Magazines originated in the seventeenth century as book catalogues. Book publishers began adding brief descriptive material to certain books in their lists, and from these descriptions was developed the editorial content of modern magazines.

The *Journal des Savants,* published in France in 1665, has been considered the parent of all magazines, although the *Philosophical Transactions* of the British Royal Society shares the same date. *Weekly Memorials for the Ingenious,* published in London in 1681, may have been the first to accept contributions. As the editorial content broadened in scope and interest grew, periodicals such as *Athenian Mercury* (to which Daniel Defoe was a contributor) and Edward Ward's *London Spy* made valuable additions to the magazine concept.

In the eighteenth century, writers such as Joseph Addison and Sir Richard Steele wrote violent political essays for periodicals such as *Spectator* (1711) which attained a circulation of 4,000; *Tatler* (1709), *Guardian* (1712), and *Examiner* (1710).

The *Gentleman's Magazine,* published in 1731 in England, was the model for Benjamin Franklin's first magazine, which he called *The General Magazine.* The eighteenth and nineteenth centuries saw a rapid growth of periodicals. Charles Dickens, William M. Thackeray, and many other writers were magazine editors. In this same period many special-interest periodicals were introduced, including children's magazines such as *The Young Misses* (1806), *St. Nicholas* (1873), and *Youth's Companion* (1877). Other publications were devoted to art, science, and history. *The Pennsylvania Magazine* (1775–76) has both Robert Aitken and Thomas Paine as authors.

Today, in the United States, magazines are published as weeklies, biweeklies, monthlies, bimonthlies, quarterlies, and annuals. Some are general in format, offering articles, fiction, cartoons, and poetry, while others are noted for their treatment of the news, for photography, or for their coverage of specialized fields. Trade journals cover business, industry, and the professions.

Magazines could not be made available to the general public today at modest prices without advertising revenues. Production costs for any single magazine copy are usually far in excess of its subscription or newsstand sale price; for that reason, advertising revenue must be sought. In 1964, more than 7,500 companies spent almost $1 billion ($997,000,000) to advertise in general magazines. An additional $560 million was spent by advertisers in business publications.

A characteristic of United States magazines that distinguishes them from the majority of European periodicals has been their readiness to change their formats with the times. High-speed printing, color photography, and even three-dimensional printing were adopted first in this country; while British magazines, for example, have retained the same general appearance they had many years ago.

—Howard Watson

Marine Engineering, the branch of mechanical engineering concerned with the design and production of propulsion machinery. For almost all of recorded history, the science of marine engineering was limited to devices on ships having to do with cargo handling, hotel facilities for passengers, and engines of war. Propulsion was left to the winds. In the past 200 years, however, marine engineering has come to mean the science of ship propulsion, with all other applications of the term set aside into specialized fields under different categories. In two centuries, marine-propulsion machinery has moved through the inventive stage of the steam engine to today's wide assortment of power sources topped by the atom. Atomic power for ships has been pioneered by American science, as evidenced by the U.S. Navy's *Nautilus,* the first nuclear-powered submarine, and the *Savannah,* the world's first merchant ship to be driven by the atom. The Soviet Union has also constructed a nuclear-powered vessel, the ice breaker *Lenin.*

The use of nuclear power does not mean the end of the steamship, but rather its freedom from the restrictions of old-style fuels such as wood, coal, and oil. Now, once again as with the wind, the ship may sail indefinitely instead of being limited to the distance between coaling stations. To this degree, the atomic era is certain to be viewed as one of the major developments in marine engineering, although nuclear ships technically are still steamships.

The coming of automation to marine engineering was increasingly apparent in 1965, particularly in the American merchant marine. Direct bridge control of the ship's machinery was extended from tugboats, which have had it for some years, to large cargo ships and oil tankers.

Another evolutionary change that might be noted in marine engineering design was the placing of ship engines aft in large passenger ships and freight vessels, as in the British liners *North Star, Southern Cross,* and *Canberra,* and the twin Italian superliners *Michelangelo* and *Raffaello.*

—Frank O. Braynard

Marine Signaling, the method of communicating from one ship to another (or to shore), and the device or system of marking a channel or calling attention to a dangerous area. In one instance, the ship is the transmitter of information; in the other, the ship receives a communication or situation warning.

Marine signaling from ship to ship, or ship to shore, has become so mechanized as to virtually eliminate the need for knowing the traditional old-style manual methods. The day of blinker light or semaphore signaling is fast passing. These systems are still taught in maritime academies, but their use on shipboard has been all but abandoned. The various forms of radio communication have taken over, except in certain unmechanized craft, such as fishing boats. With many types of craft, the use of radio telephone has brought as much as a 50 per cent increase in efficiency of use and productivity.

Automation is also coming to the stationary markings that guide the mariner into a harbor or warn him of dangerous rocks. Although Coast Guard and similar craft are still required to maintain the vast network of *can* and *nun* buoys marking channels, the lighthouse and lightship are becoming automated to a surprising degree. Entirely mechanical lighthouses are commonplace today up and down the coasts of the United States.

Mechanical fog-warning systems and automated lightships are rapidly taking the place of man-operated equipment. The latest in mechanical signaling proposals is the turning-direction-signal system proposed recently for ships. One Navy transport has been so equipped. Another modern device is the signal light that would automatically glow when the ship's whistle is blown.

—Frank O. Braynard

Motion Picture Industry, the production of still pictures which, when shown in rapid succession, produce an illusion of continuous action. The production of motion pictures, in all but the socialist countries, is unique in that it is both an art and an industry. As an industry, it gives employment to more than 325,000 people in the United States alone (production and exhibition) and represents a capital investment of close to $3 billion in theaters, studios, and distribution facilities. As an art form, it reaches—and influences—upwards of 46 million people a week in the United States via theaters, untold millions more via television, and additional millions throughout the world.

The necessary interaction between patron and producer has profoundly affected the nature of the medium. Historically, the producer has always been close to his audience. Such industry veterans as Barney Balaban, Samuel Goldwyn, Spyros Skouras, Jack L. Warner, and Adolph Zukor were originally showmen. Their concept was to "give the public what it wanted." But rarely is the producer himself a film maker. To get a picture on the screen, he must rely upon the services of writers, directors, actors, art directors, composers, and a vast corps of technicians, all of whom take pride in their artistry and craft. These men are less inclined to accept the theory that "the public is always right." As artists, they often feel called upon to offer their own point of view.

■**INDEPENDENT PRODUCTION.**—Such are the tensions behind most film making. With the rise of independent production and the competition of television since 1950, traditional concepts of making movies to please everybody have not only been re-evaluated but revised. When control of production rested in the hands of eight major studios, most of them turning out 50 new films a year, there was little opportunity for the creative artist to experiment with themes or techniques. Increasingly, however, the new breed of independent producers has been seeking out directors and writers who have proved themselves at the box office, and offering them a virtual *carte blanche* to make the films of their choice. The studios, which have come to act more as distributors than as initiators, are quite willing to finance such projects if they have faith in the artists involved.

But perhaps the greatest change has come in the audience itself. Where once movie-going was a habit, accounting for upwards of 90 million weekly customers in the American market, the rise of television—and of box-office prices—has made for increased selectivity. People choose the films they want to see. Actually, with the sole exception of *Gone With the Wind* (1939), all of the all-time top-grossing pictures have been made since 1950, with a world's record gross foreseen for the 1965 production of *My Fair Lady*. While producers still dream of a picture that will please everybody, realistically they are willing to settle for a film that will attract some sizable segment of the mass audience. And with the advent of television, increasingly they are searching out themes unacceptable to the even wider mass audiences of that competitive medium.

■**FREEDOM OF SCREEN.**—As a result, and much to their chagrin, the film makers have found themselves in constant difficulties with censors, both legal and self-appointed. Censors function to protect the *status quo*, to preserve the moral standards of the past. Because of the tremendous immediacy of the film medium, it has always been particularly vulnerable to censorial attack. When films were produced in great quantities for the widest possible audience, this factor was taken into consideration. Not only did the studios support their Production Code Administration, which forced their films to hew to a safe, predetermined line, but they also had advisory staffs to apprise them of regulations abroad. In the changed situation, particularly after 1953 when Otto Preminger's *The Moon Is Blue* emphasized how outmoded such thinking was, the leading independent producers openly flouted their own industry's self-regulatory Code. In 1965, the Motion Picture Association announced plans to overhaul both the Code and its administration, bringing it more in keeping with contemporary standards and practices.

More important, beginning with *The Miracle* case in 1952, the U.S. Supreme Court has issued a series of opinions that have struck out every legal basis for state or community censorship of motion pictures except in cases of pure, hard-core pornography. Late in 1965 even the Catholic Legion of Decency, the pressure group most feared by the industry, announced a softening of policy. Henceforth, it was intimated, instead of condemning "indecent films," the Legion would put its emphasis upon support of "artistically and morally good" entertainment.

Less an endorsement than an acceptance of the realities of picture production, all such moves seemed to clear the way toward an acceptance of film classification, long practiced in Europe as an effective means of keeping children from seeing movies intended for adults. Indeed, without any legal obligation to do so, a number of producers have already released their films with "adult only" recommendations prominently displayed in marquee and newspaper advertisements.

The result has been a marked upsurge in films dealing with controversial, unconventional, or unsavory subject matter. Issues of the day—politics, nuclear warfare, integration—are handled openly and maturely. Similarly, sexual themes previously barred from the screen, including homosexuality and perversion, have been appearing with increasing frequency. Freed of the imperative to appeal to everyone, the film makers have discovered that they can speak forcefully and effectively to mass minorities.

In this, American directors and writers are approaching more closely the situation that prevails in most European countries. Because of spiraling production costs, the Americans will probably never be as free or as personal as Antonioni, Bergman, Fellini, Godard, De Sica, or Truffaut, to name but a few. But, like them, such directors as Blake Edwards, David Lean, Stanley Kramer, Stanley Kubrick, Otto Preminger, and George Stevens can make pretty much the films they want in the way they want to make them—a situation that obtains so long as they can demonstrate to the studios that finance them that audiences want to see such pictures in the first place.

In the socialist countries, this link between film audience and film maker is even stronger. Replacing the profit motive is social purpose, and preproduction committees (often made up of nonprofessionals) recommend or pass upon scripts on the basis of morality, practicality, and utility. Communication, always a vital concern for the film maker, under these circumstances becomes the primary consideration. (See also *Cinematography,* page 1595.)

—Arthur Knight

Motor Vehicle, a self-propelled conveyance used for passenger transportation or for hauling freight, and generally driven by an internal-combustion engine. The motor vehicle, while a comparatively recent development, had its beginnings in the eighteenth century. During the 1760's, the French military engineer Nicolas Cugnot constructed several workable steam-propelled vehicles. At about the same time, Francis Moore of London was also experimenting with steam propulsion. Richard Trevithick had several passenger-carrying steam vehicles running in England in the first decade of the nineteenth century; in the 1820's and 1830's, a number of heavy steam coaches were in use in that country. The use of these was discouraged during the 1830's by high tolls, and those remaining were practically legislated out of existence in 1865.

In the United States, Oliver Evans operated his *Orukter Amphibolos,* an amphibious dredge, in Philadelphia in 1805. Throughout the remainder of the nineteenth century, numerous Americans experimented with steam-powered carriages. Notable among them were built by Thomas Blanchard, Richard Dudgeon, and Sylvester Roper.

The internal combustion engine was first applied to a vehicle by the Frenchman Jean Joseph Étienne Lenoir, in 1863, in the form of a non-compression engine operating on ordinary illuminating gas. In Vienna the following year, Siegfried Marcus constructed a vehicle using an engine of the Lenoir type, but having a carburetor that would permit the use of liquid fuel. By 1876, the German Nikolaus Otto had developed his four-cycle engine, which was to become the power unit for nearly all the automobiles produced to this day. This type of engine was applied to vehicles in 1885, simultaneously yet independently, by the Germans Gottlieb Daimler and Karl Benz. In the United States, George Selden applied for a patent on a motor vehicle using a Brayton-type engine in 1879.

■**AUTOMOBILE DEVELOPMENT.**—By 1890 the times were nearly ready for the automobile. Practical steam cars could have been developed much earlier, but the lack of public acceptance and interest delayed the movement. Many historians agree with automotive pioneer Hiram P. Maxim, who felt that the bicycle was first necessary to give the public its first taste of private, independent transportation. Many American pioneers

produced experimental cars during the 1890's, among them the Duryea brothers, Elwood Haynes, A. L. Riker, R. E. Olds, Alexander Winton, Henry Ford, Louis S. Clarke, and the Stanley twins.

In this early period, steam, gasoline, and electricity were all used to propel vehicles. While steam and electricity were to see limited use for several decades to come, it became apparent very early in the twentieth century that the gasoline engine, through rapid improvements, was to be the ultimate choice as a source of power.

The automotive industry in the United States began early in the twentieth century to gain a small momentum. In 1901, the Olds Motor Works produced 425 curved-dash Oldsmobiles, the first notable instance of mass production. By 1903, more than 125 automobile manufacturers were able to produce and market more than 11,000 motor vehicles a year. A typical car of the period had a one- or two-cylinder engine located somewhere underneath the body, frequently under the seat. Horsepower varied from 4 to 10, which with a two-speed transmission generated speeds up to 20 miles per hour. Final drive was usually

SMITHSONIAN INSTITUTION

FORD MOTOR COMPANY

CHRYSLER CORPORATION

FRED MACKERODT

FORD MOTOR COMPANY

AUTOMOBILES, originally little more than self-propelled buggies like the Stanley Steamer (*upper left*), created a social revolution when Ford's Model T (*upper right*) put the American family on wheels. Today, sleek, luxurious cars like the Plymouth Barracuda (*above*), Chevrolet Camaro (*center right*), and Ford Thunderbird (*right*) fill the superhighways, parking lots, and "drive-ins" constructed for them.

by chain. The body frequently had only one seat, and steering was generally by means of a large, bow-shaped tiller.

By 1905, production had more than doubled; the pattern for the modern automobile was already apparent. A vertical engine, usually four-cylinder and rated between 15 and 30 horsepower, was placed in front, under a hood that was immediately behind the radiator. Bevel gears replaced the chains for the final drive. Equipped with two seats, wheel steering, and a three-speed transmission, some of the cars were capable of speeds up to 35 miles per hour. Production in 1909 went up to 127,000 vehicles, nearly double the 1908 figure. When the famous Model T Ford became available for $850, a trend was begun that put a serviceable automobile within the reach of all.

A few years earlier, in 1906, six-cylinder engines began to appear on the market. By 1910 the sixes were becoming common, though the four-cylinder models were to retain a substantial lead for some years to come. Selective transmissions had now taken a decisive lead over the progressive type. Steam and electric vehicles were being made only in token numbers, and it was obvious that they were about to pass from the scene. During the second decade of the century, some of the more significant advances were the electric starter, demountable rims to facilitate tire repairs, V-8 engines introduced by Cadillac in 1915, forced feed lubrication, and the widespread use of alloy steels.

The 1920's brought several innovations that made automobiles safer and more comfortable. The sedan, previously very expensive, now cost only slightly more than the open car. Balloon tires and hydraulic four-wheel brakes were introduced, and the end of the decade brought both safety glass and the synchromesh transmission. Horsepower varied between 25 and 35, and both four- and six-cylinder engines were common.

The six-cylinder engine gained a lead over the four during the 1930's and by the middle of the decade, streamlining was noticeable in body design. Power brakes became available on some models, and by the end of the decade, automatic transmissions were available in a few models. In the 1940's, advancement in automotive design was impeded by World War II, so the development and use of the automatic transmission did not become widespread until about 1950.

In the 1950's, tubeless tires and seat belts became common, and in 1953 the number of new cars equipped with V-8 engines exceeded the number with six-cylinder engines. Automobiles continued to grow larger and more powerful, causing some buyers to turn to the smaller foreign cars. This demand for smaller cars led the industry to offer a number of compact cars in 1960.

■COMMERCIAL VEHICLES.—In the commercial field, the development and use of motor vehicles was retarded during the early period, partly because of an attempt to adapt the passenger-car chassis to this heavier use. The general prejudice against motor trucks, for many years prevalent among business houses, was only deepened by the weaknesses resulting from this practice. In 1904, only 700 motor trucks were marketed in the United States.

The second decade of the twentieth century brought more substantial trucks. Tractors for street use were offered early in the decade in an effort to interest users who had a heavy investment in horse-drawn vehicles, for the tractors could replace the horses and front-axle assemblies and allow the vehicles to remain in service. In 1914, nearly 25,000 trucks were sold and the number of sales almost tripled in the following year. Except for a few very light models, trucks required solid rubber tires and, because of the condition of the nation's roads, were confined to use on city streets only.

The possibilities of cross-country motor transport were demonstrated soon after the United States entered World War I, when extreme congestion on the railroads forced trucks onto the highways. The war focused the attention of both designers and users on trucks. After the war, the nation's roads and the quality of pneumatic tires were improved, furthering the cause of motor freighting. During the depression years of the 1930's, merchants wanted to replace large inventories and bulk shipments by small, frequent deliveries. Thus began the trend to truck shipment on a large scale.

The development of the motorbus closely paralleled that of the truck. At first a novelty, open buses came into general use for sightseeing in cities. During the few years preceding World War I, a number of closed buses were introduced in cities on regular service lines. Like the truck, the bus moved out onto the open road following the war.

■MOTORCYCLES.—The invention of the motorcycle in 1885 is generally attributed to Gottlieb Daimler. It was not until the early 1900's, however, that the motorcycle became a practical means of conveyance. Used for private transport and traffic control, as well as for sport, the motorcycle today usually has one or two cylinders, an internal combustion engine that is air-cooled and gas-propelled, an electric ignition system and a three-speed transmission.

■VEHICLE STATISTICS.—Of the more than 170 million motor vehicles throughout the world, 86 million are in the United States. In 1962, the 200 millionth U.S. motor vehicle was produced, and in 1964 U.S. production totaled 7,745,492 passenger cars and 1,562,368 commercial vehicles. The U.S. imported 542,917 vehicles in 1964, and exported close to 300,000. A total of 12,400,000 wage earners, or one of every seven employed persons in the United States, depends on the motor-vehicle industry and related industries for his livelihood. American motorists drove 838 billion miles in 1964 and paid nearly 13 billion dollars in motor vehicle taxes.

—Don H. Berkebile

Moving Walk, a powered conveyance for moving passengers between two points either horizontally or along a slight incline. The moving walk has a high carrying capacity comparable to that of the escalator. The construction of a moving walk is also similar, except that the tread surface is flat and does not form steps. The tread surface is grooved and meshes with a combplate at either end of the walk. Moving walks can be used either on a horizontal plane, or at an angle of incline. Normally the maximum angle of incline is 10°, although under certain conditions the building code permits an angle as high as 15°. Normal operating speeds are the same as those for escalators, with the maximum speed usually being 120 feet per minute.

The first moving walk to gain attention was installed at the Columbian Exposition in 1892, but it did not become popular until the early 1960's. Moving walks are found most useful in buildings where large groups of people must move long distances horizontally and go up or down a short rise, as in transportation terminals, stadiums, and shopping centers. (See also *Escalator*.)

—P. L. Fosburg

Newspaper, a publication issued at regular intervals, usually daily or weekly, for the primary purpose of reporting current events. The first newspaper in the American Colonies, called *Publick Occurrences,* appeared on Sept. 25, 1690, in Boston. It was immediately suppressed by the authorities after the first issue because it had not been licensed and had dealt with political and military matters. No further attempt to publish a newspaper was made in America until 1704.

In 1965—275 years after the first publication—there were 1,763 daily newspapers in the United States, selling 60,412,000 copies every day, and almost 9,000 weekly or semiweekly papers, with circulations totaling 24,000,000.

After the *Boston News Letter* appeared in 1704 (the first regularly issued publication in North America), other weeklies were brought out, many under the name *The Gazette.* The first newspaper in New York City, the New York *Gazette,* appeared in 1725.

Another early arrival, the New York *Weekly Journal,* established by John Peter Zenger on Nov. 5, 1733, was to become the subject of the first libel suit brought in the Colonies, known as the "Zenger Trial." Zenger's arrest and imprisonment on

Largest Foreign Newspapers

Name	World-wide circulation:
Pravda	6,700,000
Izvestia	6,000,000
London Daily Mirror (A.M.)	4,951,488
Asahi Tokyo (A.M.-P.M.)	4,565,155
London Daily Express (A.M.)	4,329,128
Mainitchi Tokyo (A.M.-P.M.)	3,825,769
Yomiuri Tokyo (A.M.-P.M.)	2,711,066
London Daily Mail (A.M.)	2,423,424

Source: *Editor and Publisher*, 1966.

Largest American Newspapers

1965		1960	
New York News (A.M.)	2,097,578	New York News	2,021,395
Chicago Tribune (A.M.)	840,746	Chicago Tribune	869,958
Los Angeles Times (A.M.)	839,735	New York Mirror (A.M.)*	836,760
Los Angeles Herald Examiner (P.M.)	718,221	Philadelphia Bulletin (P.M.)	705,599
Detroit News (A.M.)	682,834	New York Times (A.M.)	644,175
Philadelphia Bulletin	672,235	Philadelphia Enquirer (A.M.)	618,902
New York Times	635,619	New York Journal-American	618,802
New York Journal-American**	535,310	Chicago Sun-Times	566,219
Philadelphia Enquirer	522,941	Chicago News	539,448
Detroit Free Press	509,410	Los Angeles Times	532,078

Source: Editor and Publisher.

*Ceased publication in October, 1963
**Merged on April 25, 1966 with the World Telegram and Sun and New York Herald Tribune to create the World Journal-Tribune (P.M.), and World Journal-Tribune (Sunday). Ceased publication May 5, 1967.

Nov. 17, 1734, was ordered by Governor William Cosby for defaming His Majesty's Government. Defended by Alexander Hamilton, Zenger was acquitted by a jury on Aug. 4, 1735, marking the dawn of that liberty which afterward revolutionized America and specifically established the tradition of freedom of the press, later guaranteed in the Bill of Rights.

The first daily newspaper published in the United States was the *American Daily Advertiser*, established in Philadelphia in 1784. New York City's first daily, known as *The Daily Advertiser*, was launched a year later.

Up until 1833, newspapers were mainly political organs espousing the cause of certain political parties and financed by them. In that year, James Gordon Bennett founded the New York *Herald* on purely journalistic principles, supporting it by revenues from readers and advertisers, and not beholden to any political party. Thus began the "independent" press as we know it today.

When the Revolutionary War began in 1775, there were 37 weekly newspapers in the American colonies. By 1835 there were 574 dailies publishing 2,601,000 copies per day, and about 4,500 weeklies and semiweeklies with a total circulation of about 11,000,000.

■MECHANICAL PROGRESS.—The introduction of the Linotype in the late nineteenth century enabled a printer to set a line of type by machine instead of by hand from individual characters. This brought about an industrial revolution in the printing field and a tremendous expansion in the number of newspapers, accelerated by the invention of the high-speed rotary press that replaced the slow and cumbersome method of printing directly from type on a flat-bed press.

At the end of World War I, there were 2,078 daily newspapers with circulations averaging 26,443,000 copies per day, plus more than 10,000 weekly newspapers. Since that time, rising production costs have brought consolidations and mergers, so that there are about 300 fewer dailies. But these are larger and stronger than their predecessors, and have twice as many readers.

The 1960's marked the beginning of another revolution in printing techniques and perhaps another expansion in the newspaper business. The offset press, used by several hundred small daily newspapers and many more weekly papers, was adapted for use in conjunction with photocomposition, thus eliminating the use of all hot metal. Larger presses were built for the large newspapers, and the trend promises to continue.

In addition, automation by computers was introduced into newspaper production. Some 24 large newspapers utilized computers in their composing room to set type. The device accepts a perforated tape from an ordinary typist and within seconds produces a second tape with lines justified (filled out to the full measure) and words hyphenated where necessary. The second tape, in turn, is used to operate automatic high-speed typesetting machines. One large computer can handle the requirements for several newspapers connected by wire. The number of newspapers using them for this purpose have increased steadily. The same computers can also be used for bookkeeping, payroll, and billing requirements, depending on the capacity of their memory storage units.

—Robert U. Brown

Phonograph, a device for recording and/or reproducing speech, music, or other sounds by means of lines mechanically introduced on a cylinder or disc. The idea of recording and reproducing sound by mechanics is more than a century old. Many inventors, among them a French scientist named Léon Scott, tried repeatedly but unsuccessfully to achieve it. Scott's device, which he called the *phonautograph*, came to public attention in 1857. It recorded sound in the form of an undulating line on a cylinder coated with lamp-black. The shortcoming that doomed the experiment was the inability to reproduce the recorded material.

Twenty years later, in America, Thomas A. Edison independently discovered how to reproduce sound, including the human voice. In so doing, he showed the way to the modern phonograph. The Edison method consisted of a grooved cylinder wrapped with tinfoil, stiffened with antimony; a diaphragm and needle, which rested on the foil; a mouthpiece to introduce sound; a funnel for outcoming sounds; and a crank to turn the cylinder.

Notable among the others who contributed to the development of the phonograph is Emile Berliner, who invented the microphone, the disk record, and the gramaphone. (See also *Sound Recording and Reproduction.*)

—John O'Brine

Photography, the recording of an image through the photochemical reaction of light on a sensitized surface. Photography is a versatile and useful means of communication and does not require the skill of an artist to capture a likeness. It can make a moment of history—of glory, or disaster, or achievement—a part of the lives of millions through its transfer to the printed page, the motion picture, or television screen.

Photography is a combination of chemistry, optics, and mechanics. It existed as an achievable reality in the minds of men for a hundred or more years before its actual birth. Strangely, the chemistry of the film and the optics of the camera were both known separately for many years before they were brought together.

■EXPERIMENTS WITH LIGHT.—The first recorded knowledge of the effect of light upon a chemical substance came in 1727 when Johann Heinrich Schulze, a German physician, discovered that chalk treated with a solution of silver and nitric acid would turn black when exposed to sunlight. He placed the mixture in bottles around which he wrapped stencils. Sunlight passing through the openings in the stencils turned that portion of the mixture black while the rest remained white.

Thomas Wedgwood, the son of Josiah Wedgwood, the famous English potter, made the first actual prints on paper, using sheets of paper coated with silver chloride which Karl Wilhelm Scheele and William Lewis had discovered had the same light-sensitive properties as Schulze's chalk. As negatives, he used silhouettes painted upon glass. He placed the glass plates upon the paper and made the exposure, the result of which was a black-and-white print that was the reverse of the image painted on the glass. In 1802, Wedgwood published a paper, in cooperation with Sir Humphry Davy, entitled *An Account of a Method of Copying Paintings on Glass, and Making Profiles, by the Agency of Light Upon Nitrate of Silver.* The pictures, however, were very fleeting; as soon as the "negative" was removed, the whole paper started turning black.

In 1839, William Henry Fox Talbot, at the suggestion of Sir John Herschel, developed a method of "fixing" the picture with the use of sodium thiosulfate, the *hypo* that is still used today for fixing photographic films and prints.

■EARLY CAMERAS.—The history of the camera goes back many years prior to the experiments in light-chemistry. Probably the earliest mention of a camera was made by Roger Bacon in 1267. Leonardo da Vinci, who died early in the sixteenth century, also described a *camera obscura*.

The camera obscura was a simplified camera. The first models, which were probably constructed in the sixteenth century, consisted of a lens at the front of a box that had a translucent screen at the focal point of the lens. When the box was aimed at a scene, an inverted image was projected on

FAIRCHILD SPACE AND DEFENSE SYSTEMS

SPECTACULAR picture of New York City and surroundings, above, was taken by a new aerial-photography camera that has a rotating prism covering a 180-degree panorama. The curvature is not the earth's, but is a geometric projection caused by the 180-degree span. The chief feature of panoramic cameras is their ability to take detailed photos at high speeds and low altitudes. The picture at left was taken outside an English castle with a fisheye lens and gives the effect of being at the bottom of a well. The photo at right was taken with a high-speed action camera with fast lens.

the screen. A thin sheet of paper was placed over the screen, and the screen was traced. Later, other lenses and mirrors were added to correct the image. More ambitious cameras obscura were made by using tents with a lens and mirror or prism at the apex.

■ BEGINNINGS OF PHOTOGRAPHY.—It wasn't until the early part of the nineteenth century that light-sensitive chemicals and the camera obscura were brought together to create the first real photographs. Joseph Nicéphore Niepce and Louis Jacques Mandé Daguerre, both Frenchmen, together discovered that when a silver plate of a silver-coated copper plate that had been exposed to iodine fumes, forming the light-sensitive silver iodide, was exposed in a camera obscura and the plate subsequently developed in mercury fumes, a positive picture of the subject was formed. When fixed with sodium thiosulfate, the picture became permanent. Many of these *Daguerrotypes* are still in existence, and even by present photographic standards are considered to be amazingly sharp.

The principal drawback to this method of photography was that there was no way of duplicating the pictures. There were no negatives. Each picture had to be separately exposed.

Talbot, who had discovered the method for "fixing" the light-sensitive chemicals, was also the first to create a negative process from which any number of positive pictures could be made with one exposure. This was called the *Calotype* (or Talbotype) process, In this process he used paper coated with silver nitrate which, after exposure, was developed in gallic acid and silver nitrate. This not only cut exposure from more

than an hour to less than a minute, but also yielded a negative print. Positive prints could be made by repeating the process but making the exposure for the final print through the first, or negative, print.

■ COLLODION PLATES.—To overcome the inadequacies of the paper negative, Claude Niepce de Saint-Victor in 1847 coated a sheet of glass with silver nitrate, using albumen to hold it in place. Collodion was later substituted for the albumen by Frederick Scott Archer of London.

The difficulty with this process was that a fresh wet solution had to be applied to the glass immediately before taking the picture. As a result, the photographer going into the field had to carry his darkroom with him —usually in the form of a tent— as well as all of his chemicals, glass plates, and processing trays. Mathew B. Brady first brought home to people the horrors of war in his Civil War photographs, traveling with a horse-drawn carriage equipped as a darkroom.

The first dry plates were made in England by Frank Charles Luther Wratten in 1877. These revolutionized photography by eliminating the need for the portable darkroom.

■ WORK OF EASTMAN.—Three years later, George Eastman, a book clerk of Rochester, N.Y., who had become interested in photography, began the manufacture of dry plates, developing faster mechanical methods of coating both plates and paper.

Up to this time, virtually all photographs had been made by men who were seriously engaged in photography either as portrait photographers or who saw in it other financial opportunities. Eastman felt that picture taking, if it could be made simple

e ough, would appeal to everyone. His belief was justified when, in 1888, he brought out the first simple amateur camera, which was advertised for years with the slogan, "You Push the Button, We do the Rest". The first camera contained a roll of sensitized paper upon which 100 circular pictures could be made. When the last exposure was made, the entire camera was returned to the manufacturer for the processing of the pictures and the reloading of the camera. It was with this camera that amateur picture taking—snapshooting—was born.

It wasn't until 11 years later that film itself came into being, when Eastman first produced a photographic emulsion that was coated on a flexible base. In 1895, he rolled strips of this film with an opaque paper to create the first daylight-loading film and made cameras available that would utilize it. This simplified and further popularized picture taking by making the film available almost anywhere and by eliminating the necessity for returning the camera to the manufacturer. It also brought into being an entirely new business— photofinishing.

■ COLOR PHOTOGRAPHY.—There still remained one major barrier to be hurdled if photography was to complete its role as a means of communication—color. James Clerk Maxwell, in 1861, had proved that color pictures were possible. At a Royal Institution lecture in London, he had shown lantern slides in color. The lantern slides had previously been tinted with transparent colors, but these were the first photographed and projected in color. They were pictures of colored ribbons of which he had made three exposures, one through a red solution, one through a green solution, and the third through a blue solution. Using three projectors, the slides were projected through the same colors and exactly superimposed on the screen to recreate the original colors of the ribbons.

Every color process since then has utilized the same principle. Early color photographs were made on three separate films exposed through appropriate colored glass filters, either one at a time or in *one-shot-cameras* in which, through an arrangement of prisms, all three films were exposed at once. Prints were usually made by making separate exposures from each of the three negatives on *stripping films*, which were then dyed, carefully stripped from their backing, and superimposed in register on each other on a white backing paper.

The Lumière process used dyed red, green, and blue starch grains over which the emulsion was coated. During development the film was exposed to white light, reversing the image and creating a positive transparency. Each of the tiny grains of starch had acted as a filter creating, when viewed unmagnified, the same effect as Maxwell's three slides had on the screen. The *Dufaycolor process* was similar, utilizing a red and green screen.

The first color film suitable for amateur use was made by two musicians, Leopold D. Mannes and Leopold Godowsky, Jr. This was Kodachrome film, which is made up of three layers of emulsion with dyes incorporated into them. The top layer is sensitive to blue light; yellow filter layer is beneath it, with a green-sensitive layer of emulsion under it; beneath that is a red-sensitive layer. Critically controlled processing is necessary to develop the three layers of emulsion, removing the silver and leaving only the three positive dye images. Placed on the market in 1935,

this film was first available only for use in amateur movie cameras. Later, it was made available for the amateur in the candid camera size of 35mm and in sheet film sizes for professional and commercial photographers.

Since then, other color films have been developed that are less critical in the processing stages and can be processed by the professional in his studio or by the amateur at home.

■APPLICATIONS.—Early photographs, both those taken by commercial and professional photographers, and those taken by the snapshooting amateur, were generally confined to people and places. It was not until later that science, industry, medicine, and education began to realize the full potential of photography as a means of communication and as a tool for their efforts.

Photography has invaded every field of human endeavor. Metals and chemical compounds are analyzed, and their analysis recorded on spectrographs and metallographs. The human body and giant heat exchangers for nuclear power plants are examined by radiography. Whole libraries are recorded on microfilm that can be stored in a desk drawer. Missiles and rockets are tracked across the sky by huge cameras. The planets and the far galaxies of space are explored by astrophotography. The authenticity of documents, postage stamps, and old masters is checked by infrared and ultraviolet photography. Motions that are too fast for the human eye to see are brought to a slow-turning halt by high-speed motion pictures. Photography is used to catch the bank bandit and the kitten at play. It has become an inseparable part of our life. As a means of communication, it speaks all languages with equal facility. —C. Grantly Wallington

Printing, the reproduction on paper or other substance of an image from an inked printing surface. Reproduction may be from a raised surface, as in *letterpress* printing; a depressed surface, an in *intaglio* or *gravure printing;* or from a level surface, as in *lithography* or *planography.* Although popularly associated with paper, printing is done on a variety of other materials—metal, metal laminated to paper, cloth, and plastic—and on objects of various shapes.

■LETTERPRESS PRINTING.—By this method, the portion of the printing surface which carries the image is raised above the nonprinting areas and only that surface is inked. Letterpresses take various forms and are constructed in sizes from small hand-operated presses to high-speed giants.

A *flat-bed cylinder press* also has a flat printing surface, or *bed,* but the sheet of paper is wrapped around an impression cylinder which rotates to press the paper against the inked printing form. By the addition of a second unit, a flat-bed cylinder press may be designed to print two colors on one side of the paper, or it may be constructed so that it turns the paper and prints both sides, in which case it is called a *perfecting press.*

A *rotary letterpress* consists of a cylindrical printing surface and a cylindrical impression cylinder between which the paper passes. If the rotary press prints on single sheets of paper it is called a *sheet-fed press,* which may run at speeds of up to 7,500 impressions per hour. If it prints on paper that comes from rolls it is known as a *web-fed press,* which may operate at speeds of more than 2,000 feet per minute. Both sheet-fed and web-fed rotary presses may print up to six colors during one pass through the press. Web-fed presses print both sides of the paper. Sheet-fed presses usually print only one side, but they also may be built to print both sides.

Letterpress printing may be done from metal type and engravings or it may be done from page plates, or *electros,* made from the original type and engravings. Rotary letterpresses always print from plates which are curved to fit the printing cylinder.

Letterpress illustrations may be reproduced from line or halftone engravings. A *line engraving* is made from artwork, such as an ink drawing, which is solid color with no shading. If an illustration contains continuous shading, such as a photograph or wash drawing, a *halftone engraving* is made. The artwork is photographed through a screen, or *grid,* of opaque lines at right angles to one another usually 60 to 200 per inch in each direction. The grid breaks up the artwork into fine dots of varying sizes, depending upon the intensity of the tone. In light areas the dots are almost nonexistent, while in extremely dark areas they are so large as to make an almost solid surface. The screened negative thus produced is etched on copper to furnish a printing plate which will reproduce the shading of the original artwork. Artwork or photographs in color are filtered to produce a plate for

HARRIS INTERTYPE CORPORATION

OFFSET presses use photographically treated cylinders to reproduce type and pictures. This web-fed, remote-controlled machine can print as much as 1,000 feet of paper a minute.

each of the primary colors—red, yellow, and blue—plus one for black for definition. When these four plates print together in perfect register, they produce an illustration in full color.

■ **GRAVURE PRINTING.**—Gravure, or *intaglio* printing, is the opposite of letterpress. Instead of a raised surface, minute wells etched into a copper cylinder carry the ink. The cylinder revolves in a trough of ink and is completely covered. A flexible metal scraper, called a *doctor blade*, wipes all the ink from the surface, leaving it only in the depressed wells. As the paper comes in contact with the cylinder, it draws the ink from the wells and deposits it in the areas to be printed. Gravure cylinders may be covered with a thin plating of chrome to give added strength for long runs. Like letterpress, gravure presses may be sheet-fed or web-fed. A web-fed gravure press is known as a *rotogravure press* and operates at speeds of more than 1,800 feet per minute.

Gravure cylinders are prepared photographically from type matter and illustrations. Photographs and wash drawings are handled in a manner similar to that used in making halftone illustrations for letterpress, except that all of the dots are the same size and shading is produced by varying the depth of the wells, thus controlling the amount of ink which each one will transfer to the paper.

■ **LITHOGRAPHY.**—Lithography, or planography, is based on the principle that oil and water do not mix. The perfectly level printing surface is treated photographically, so that the area which is to print will accept oil but not water. The entire plate is dampened, then inked. The printing image areas accept the ink, while the dampened nonprinting areas repel it. The most widely used form of lithography in use today is *offset*, in which a roller covered with a rubber *blanket* picks up the ink image from the lithographic plate and transfers, or *offsets*, it to the paper.

Offset presses may be either sheet-fed or web-fed. Like letterpresses, offset presses can be built to print up to six colors on both sides of the sheet with one pass through the press. A web-fed offset press can print more than 1,500 feet per minute. The offset process reproduces illustrations much as does letterpress except that no cuts are made. Screened halftones are put on film instead of copper and transferred photographically to the offset printing plate.

■ **OTHER PROCESSES.**—Other, less common printing processes include *silk screen,* in which the ink is forced through an open-weave mesh stencil; *flexography,* which is similar to letterpress except that it uses rubber plates; *collotype,* a photogelatin process which reproduces artwork in continuous tones; and *dry offset,* which uses no water and has a slightly raised image, but retains the step which transfers the image from the plate to a rubber roll, from which it is offset to the paper. Other recent developments are *three-dimensional printing* (see *Xograph,* page 1622); and *electrostatic printing* which, instead of pressure, rely on opposing electrical charges to attract the dry powdered ink to the paper.

■ **TYPE COMPOSITION.**—Since the invention of movable type in the fifteenth century, type has been set by hand. Most type now, however, is set by machine or photographically.

Intertype and *Linotype* machines cast a complete line in a single *slug.* Many of these machines are operated by punched paper-type tape which greatly increases their speed. The most dramatic recent development, however, is the computerized control of typesetting machines.

Monotype casts individual type characters. The casting machine is controlled by a punched tape produced on a Monotype machine.

Ludlow is a combination of hand and machine composition. The compositor sets individual matrices by hand and then places them in a Ludlow caster which produces a slug.

Photocomposition is similar in operation to hot-metal typecasting, but instead of the molten metal there is a photographic film, and the product, instead of metal type, is a film negative which can be used to make plates for any of the commercial printing processes.

Typewriter composition prints copy on paper to be photographed and made into printing plates. (See also *Printing,* page 1931.)

—Robert McGuire

Radar, the use of radio waves to detect a distant target and to determine its precise location. The term *radar* is an acronym for *RAdio Detection And Ranging.*

A radar set detects an object by means of radio echoes. A short burst, or *pulse,* of radio waves is sent out in a given direction. If these radio waves encounter an airplane, ship, or other solid object, a radio echo returns and is picked up by the radar set. These returning echoes show up as *blips* of light on the radar screen —a cathode-ray tube similar to the picture tube of a television set. Because of its motion, the blip of a target can be distinguished easily from those of fixed objects on the ground.

The target's direction is determined by sending out pulses in one direction at a time. The radar antenna rotates slowly, examining each segment of the search area in turn. When a moving target is detected, the antenna can be stopped "on target"—pointing directly at the object.

To measure the distance, or *range,* of the target, the radar set uses the fact that radio waves travel at a known speed. The farther away the target happens to be, the longer the length of time needed by the pulse to travel to the target and return. A radar set measures this time interval very accurately and converts it to miles or feet for the operator. By combining detection, direction, and range, a radar set gathers all the information needed to pinpoint moving targets.

—William C. Vergara

Radio, the use of radiated electromagnetic energy for various classes of communication, such as telegraphy, telephony, sound broadcasting, television, artificial satellites, navigation guidance, radar, telemetry, and remote control.

The common aspect of radio systems is the controlled radiation of energy into space from a transmitting antenna energized by the radio transmitter. This energy is propagated, often in a directed beam, to a radio receiver. Electromagnetic radiation is a natural phenomenon from substances at temperatures above absolute zero. Being random in nature, it is present in radio apparatus as "noise," which sets a limit to receiver sensitivity. The receiving antenna extracts energy from the passing wave, and, if enough is received to override the receiver's own noise and that of external ambient sources, natural or manmade, the signal can be received intelligibly.

Radio transmissions take place in the *radio spectrum,* which extends roughly from 10,000 to 150 billion cycles per second, or, in terms of electromagnetic wavelengths in free space, from 30 kilometers down to millimeters. The adjustment for a particular transmission on an assigned frequency is called *tuning,* which is familiar to every owner of a radio or television receiver. Many professional radio systems are pretuned to a fixed operating frequency.

All nations of the world follow a frequency allocation plan worked out by the International Telecommunication Union (ITU), organized in 1932, which superseded the International Telegraph Union, organized in 1865. Broad technical principles underlie the designation of different portions of the radio spectrum for various classes of service, namely: wave propagation characteristics; distances to be covered; whether directive or nondirective transmission; the amount of spectrum (bandwidth) needed for a particular type of transmission; time intermittency or continuity of transmission; and the seriousness of interference to a particular service. There are three ITU frequency allocation plans for three geographical regions of the world but, because of their nature, some bands of frequencies are uniformly allocated on a worldwide basis. Within the broad ITU plans, individual countries subdivide bands of radio frequencies in much greater detail to suit individual needs.

In the United States, allocations for nongovernment users are made by the Federal Communications Commission (FCC). Allocations for government radio frequency assignments are made by the Interdepartmental Radio Advisory Committee (IRAC).

All radio transmitters in the world have to be licensed by government authority, and license assignments are registered with ITU. There are rules concerning constancy of operating frequency, the class of transmission and the bandwidth employed, the avoidance of harmful interference, and also rules relating to many technical characteristics required for dis-

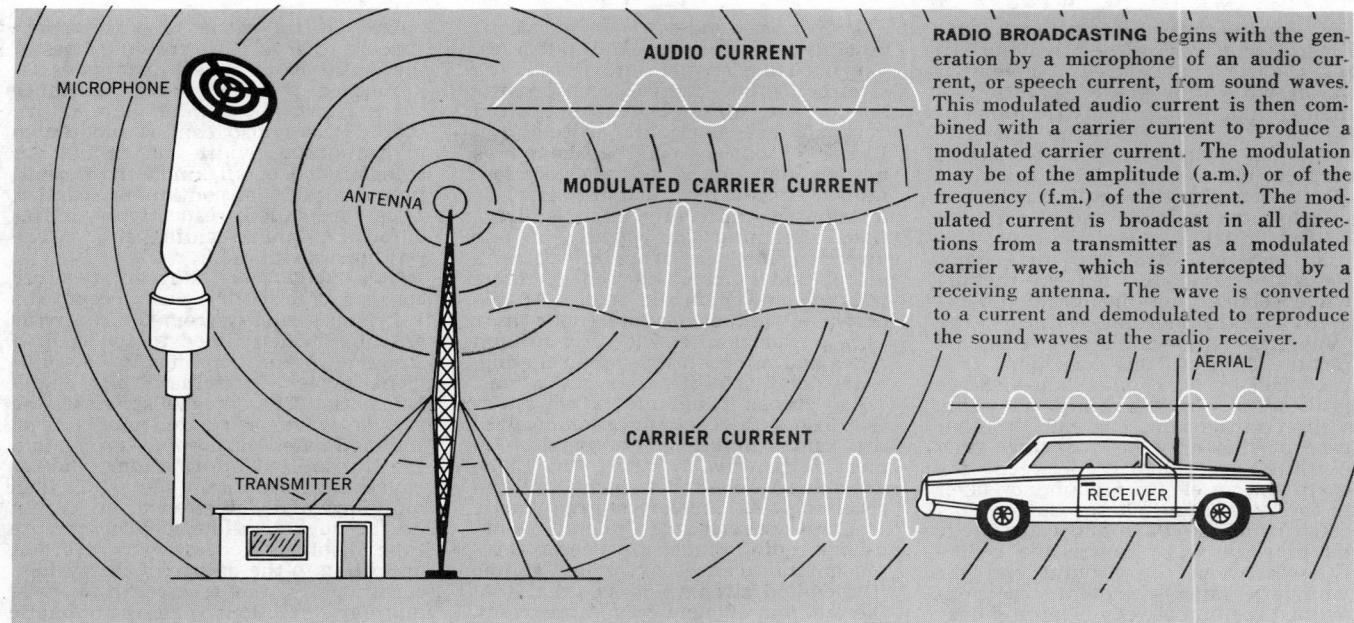

MICROPHONE

AUDIO CURRENT

ANTENNA

MODULATED CARRIER CURRENT

TRANSMITTER

CARRIER CURRENT

RECEIVER

AERIAL

RADIO BROADCASTING begins with the generation by a microphone of an audio current, or speech current, from sound waves. This modulated audio current is then combined with a carrier current to produce a modulated carrier current. The modulation may be of the amplitude (a.m.) or of the frequency (f.m.) of the current. The modulated current is broadcast in all directions from a transmitter as a modulated carrier wave, which is intercepted by a receiving antenna. The wave is converted to a current and demodulated to reproduce the sound waves at the radio receiver.

ciplined use of radio. Though unbelievably complicated, world use of radio is actually quite orderly.

Through its technical consultative committees, ITU continually promotes studies and tests that eventually lead to specific recommendations concerning new rules or arrangements. After formal adoption, they have the status of treaties, which in the United States require Senate ratification. Following this, FCC rules of compliance are promulgated essentially as law.

■ **RADIO WAVE PROPAGATION.**—There are four basic modes of radio wave propagation: *ground wave, skywave, quasi-optical,* and *optical.* As shown in the accompanying illustration, different parts of the frequency spectrum give best results in different modes, with overlap between them.

Ground waves. Frequencies below two to five million cycles per second (2 to 5 mc) can be propagated over the earth's surface as ground waves, which in some cases cover great distances if sufficient power is radiated. This is the only way the lowest frequencies are usable. Ordinary broadcasting amplitude modulation (AM) depends on ground-wave propagation for primary coverage. However, ground-wave distances decrease with

frequency because of earth curvature, so that above five million cycles per second, the losses limit distance so severely that it is more economical to employ other frequencies and propagation modes.

Skywaves. The upper atmosphere of the earth has various strata of ionized gas that bend and reflect some radio waves back to earth. Below one million cycles per second (1 mc), reflected *skywaves* are more bothersome than useful. But from 3 to 30 or 40 mc, the ionized strata, called *ionospheres,* act as efficient mirrors from which long-distance radio waves can be bounced by single or multiple reflection.

This frequency range, commonly known as *short wave,* is used for telegraphy and telephony over long distances, including international short-wave broadcasting. Variations in the ionosphere due to solar influences, and to the daylight-darkness changes, affect choice of best working frequencies and transmission reliability. Every short-wave broadcast listener knows how much variation in reception can occur from time to time. Nevertheless, this frequency range is of utmost utility for aviation, marine, transoceanic telephony and

telegraphy, sound broadcasting, navigation, and many other services that could not be realized economically by any other mode of wave propagation. However, all such services are confined to those employing narrow-band emissions, or bandwidths of less than 5-10 kilocycles, which is barely enough for acceptable telephony. Many long-distance circuits are limited to one or two hundred cycles' bandwidth, suitable only for slow telegraphy.

Quasi-optical Propagation. When the wave frequency is too high to be reflected from the ionosphere, the range of a station is limited to a relatively small distance beyond the horizon. Propagation into the transhorizon region is due to the phenomena of atmospheric refraction and diffraction over the curvature of the earth.

To best utilize these effects, as is done in typical frequency modulation and television broadcasting, the transmitting antenna is raised as high as feasible, and the radiant energy is concentrated toward the horizon. Hills and clusters of tall buildings in the wave path impair transmission by this mode. Reception is improved by using directional antennas (most

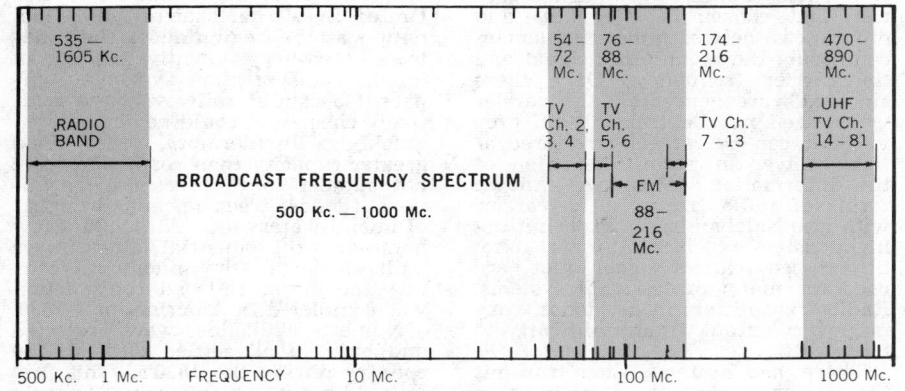

| 535 — 1605 Kc. | 54 – 72 Mc. | 76 – 88 Mc. | 174 – 216 Mc. | 470 – 890 Mc. |

RADIO BAND

TV Ch. 2, 3, 4 — TV Ch. 5, 6 — TV Ch. 7 – 13 — UHF TV Ch. 14 – 81

BROADCAST FREQUENCY SPECTRUM
500 Kc. — 1000 Mc.

FM 88 – 216 Mc.

500 Kc.   1 Mc.   FREQUENCY   10 Mc.   100 Mc.   1000 Mc.

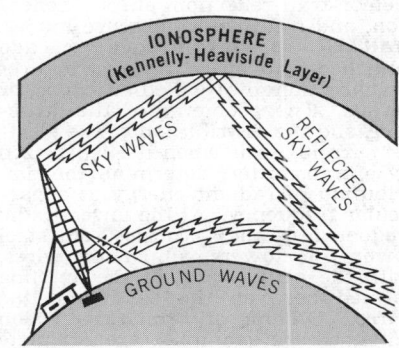

IONOSPHERE (Kennelly-Heaviside Layer)

SKY WAVES

REFLECTED SKY WAVES

GROUND WAVES

RADIO WAVES follow the curvature of the earth and are reflected by the ionosphere.

TV antennas are directional to some extent) and raising their heights. In television *fringe areas*, reception varies with atmospheric conditions—mainly the vertical distribution of humidity which causes the waves to bend downward and to penetrate further into transhorizon areas. It also varies when aircraft reflections interfere with direct reception, producing flutter in television images.

Exceptional distances are sometimes covered by superrefraction, when vertical humidity gradients exceed certain normal values. The "Venetian-blind" effect in a television picture is due to this condition. It is produced by occasional long-distance interference from another television station on the same channel. Another case of this may be a *surface duct* existing occasionally between the earth and an elevated boundary layer in the lower atmosphere. Such a duct often *traps* the wave and causes it to be propagated by successive reflections between the ground and the boundary layer—frequently a well-defined region between clear and hazy air. Cloud strata indicate similar conditions.

Optical Propagation. This term applies to propagation at still higher frequencies (500 mc or higher) where transhorizon propagation by diffraction almost disappears. These frequencies are useful only when applied to locations within line-of-sight. Though this is a serious limitation, it nevertheless provides a very wide usefulness. A number of extremely important services use optical transmissions, such as microwave radar, radio relaying of all kinds of telecommunications by means of a series of radio repeaters (most transcontinental television programs are carried this way), and satellite and space communications. For example, intercontinental satellite communication takes advantage of the great height of the satellite to give line-of-sight paths from the satellite to Europe and to North America. The satellite carries a repeater, which consists of "receive" and "retransmit" equipment that relays both ways.

Marginal Propagation Modes. It suffices merely to mention certain marginal and intermittent modes of wave propagation other than those discussed above, because they have some utility. They include tropospheric scatter, ionospheric scatter, meteor-trail reflection, auroral reflection, and a few more obscure modes.

■ **ANTENNAS.**—Radio waves are launched into space from structures (usually metallic) called antennas, or aerials. The geometry of the structure, and the distribution of the electric currents in it when it is energized by a transmitter, determine the distribution of radiant energy at a particular frequency. At the lowest radio frequencies, they consist of steel towers, or towers supporting wires, with the active parts of the antenna formed between the earth and the wires. Others, of which television antennas are examples, are complete structures held up in space on suitable supports, and connected to apparatus by a transmission line.

There are endless configurations possible for many special purposes, varying from simple auto "whips" to electromagnetic lenses, horns, paraboloids, etc., all dependent on desired vertical and horizontal directivity. Beams of energy can be shaped as needed for aiming at one location, fanned to cover a certain sector, or distributed uniformly in all directions. Beaming the power in one direction has the same effect as a searchlight, increasing the effective radiated power on the beam. At microwave frequencies, antennas may have power gains as high as a million times and are used for radio relaying, radar, and satellite communications.

Any transmitting antenna can function also as a receiving antenna with the same directional properties. In most microwave systems, the same antenna is used for transmitting and receiving. At the lowest frequencies (longest wavelengths), including ordinary radio broadcasting, the receiving antenna can be extremely simple if the field strength is so great that the antenna efficiency is unimportant. Modern broadcast receivers may only use a part of the power cord as an antenna. *Rabbit-ear* antennas often suffice for television reception. But in systems where economics determine the need for highest operating efficiency, the design of the receiving antenna must be elaborated to extract a maximum of energy from the wave to exclude electrical noise and interference as much as possible.

■ **RADIO TRANSMITTER.**—A transmitter consists of a source of electric oscillations of a required constancy at a specified frequency; amplifiers to attain a specified power; means for modulating the oscillations in such a manner as to carry the desired intelligence; and power supplies to energize the various portions of the transmitter.

The unmodulated radio frequency is called the *carrier wave*, or carrier. Modulation consists of interrupting or modifying its amplitude (AM), phase (PM), or frequency (FM) in accordance with telegraphy, telephony, television, or other form of communication. The information transmitted is contained wholly within the variations imposed on the carrier. It is even possible to transmit this information without the carrier in what is known as *sideband* transmission. Any form of modulation introduces other frequencies clustered around the carrier that consist of the sums and differences between the frequencies composing the modulating signal and the carrier frequency. Once these sidebands are generated, the carrier wave need not be transmitted, provided it can be correctly restored at the receiver to permit detection of the information. Most well-known forms of radio transmit the carrier with the sidebands, thus permitting inexpensive receivers to be used. Suppressed carrier techniques are used for many professional systems. Radio transmitters in use today vary in power output from milliwatts to megawatts.

There are systems that transmit the carrier wave in the form of short

pulses. *Pulse radar* uses the silent spacing intervals to receive echoes of the pulse from reflecting objects illuminated by the waves. Distance is measured by timing the return echo. Pulses also can be modulated in amplitude, width, or timing for transmission of all kinds of information, as with a continuous carrier. These are called, respectively, pulse-amplitude, pulse-width, and pulse-position modulation.

■ **RADIO RECEIVER.**—A radio receiver consists of circuitry that accepts the very small energy from the receiving antenna (when tuned to the desired frequency) and amplifies it to a sufficient power to actuate a detector efficiently. The detector separates the carrier wave or carrier pulses from the modulated variations that contain the transmitted information. The recovered information (signal) is then amplified and delivered to an output device, such as a loudspeaker, picture tube, display, teleprinter, or recorder, according to the nature of the system. Additionally, the receiver may have auxiliary functions such as automatic amplification control to compensate for fading, filters to exclude extraneous disturbances, impulse noise suppressors, and many others. The receiver must be adapted to the kind of transmission and the frequencies to be received, since it must work as a coordinated system with the radio transmitter. —E. A. Laport

Railroad, a system of land transportation with a permanent way, or track, of two parallel rails that support and guide vehicles fitted with flanged wheels. The chief advantage of this system is its ability to move heavy loads with a minimum of power because of the smooth running surface offered by the rails.

The rutways of ancient Greece and Rome can be claimed as the forerunner of the railway. Although primitive wooden railways were used in Central European mines during the sixteenth century—and probably earlier—the modern railway is essentially a nineteenth-century development. The Stockton and Darlington Railway in England was the first public railway. Opened in 1825, it ushered in the modern concept of the railway as a common carrier. Other similar enterprises followed, and England became the center of railway construction and technology.

■ **BEGINNINGS OF U.S. RAIL SYSTEM.**—The United States, an aspiring industrial nation at the beginning of the nineteenth century, urgently needed an inland transportation system. Compared to canals, railways were relatively cheap and could be constructed quickly. Furthermore, they had greater capacity than roads and were not subject to the seasonal disruptions (floods, freezing, and drought) of inland waterways. Although a few horse-drawn industrial lines were built earlier in the nineteenth century, no major railroad construction was completed in America until 1830.

Numerous rail lines were projected and built in all settled parts of the country during the 1830's. This first railroad boom, which produced nearly

UNION PACIFIC RAILROAD

A POWERFUL STEAM LOCOMOTIVE, the 4000, was one of the three largest ever built. It was first used to haul freight cars in 1941.

GENERAL MOTORS CORPORATION

AEROTRAIN, an American-built, lightweight diesel-powered passenger train, has ten coaches capable of carrying 400 passengers.

1,500 miles of track, did not end until the panic of 1837. Dull times slowed construction during the early 1840's, after which the system enjoyed another rapid growth. The New England states were united by a network of rail lines by 1850; the Midwestern system was virtually completed during the next seven years. Several lines—the Erie, Baltimore and Ohio, and Pennsylvania Railroads—connected the interior to the Eastern seacoast. The second boom was ended by the panic of 1857, a financial collapse directly associated with the overbuilding of railroads.

■ **THE TRANSCONTINENTAL RAILROAD.**—Interest in a railroad to the Pacific was heightened by the admission of California to the Union in 1850. While the first railroad bridge over the Mississippi River was completed in 1856 at Davenport, Iowa, the transcontinental railroad project did not proceed until the federal government agreed in 1862 to subsidize its construction. Work was started the next year by the Union Pacific in Nebraska and by the Central Pacific in California. The two companies, building toward each other, met at Promontory, Utah, on May 10, 1869, and the meeting was symbolized by

the driving of a *golden spike.* The completion of the transcontinental road spurred the construction of other Western lines, and by 1890 a nationwide rail system was complete. Railroad mileage continued to expand until 1915.

■ **STANDARDIZATION.**—While the national system was being completed, the question of a uniform gauge plagued the industry. The English *standard gauge* of 4 feet 8½ inches was used by many Eastern lines from the 1830's, but a variety of gauges was adopted throughout the country. The Erie chose the broad gauge of 6 feet; the Southern railroads, 5 feet; and the New Jersey lines, 4 feet 10 inches. In the 1870's and 1880's the narrow-gauge mania developed, but few major roads adopted the 3-foot gauge. The selection of 4 feet 8½ inches by the transcontinental railway in 1862 prompted other new roads to build on this width. The rebuilding of existing odd-gauge railroads was slow and costly, but by 1886 when the Southern railroads changed from 5-foot to standard gauge, nationwide conversion was virtually completed.

■ **ADVANCES IN THE SYSTEM.**—Between about 1870 and World War I, the railroads dominated land transporta-

tion in the United States. Long-haul road transport was nonexistent, river traffic languished, and canals were abandoned or reduced to low-tariff haulage. This concentration of traffic on one carrier proved too much for the rail system when demands for service exploded during World War I. In the crisis that developed, the industry was nationalized in 1918. Two years later the railroads were returned to private owners. In addition to being weakened by this experience, the railroads then also met aggressive competition for traffic. The motor truck began intra-city haulage not long after the war. Because of door-to-door delivery, trucks attracted much of the high-tariff freight. Automobiles, buses, and airlines cut deeply into passenger traffic. Pipelines and inland waterways, which developed during the same period, siphoned off much of the bulk traffic. The emergence of these competing forms of transportation, together with the great depression of the 1930's, struck a severe blow at the railroad industry. Many major roads were forced into receivership. Numerous secondary and short lines were entirely abandoned. Greatly weakened by these events, the railroads were none-

BALTIMORE & OHIO RAILROAD

PENNSYLVANIA RAILROAD

"TOM THUMB" (left) was an early experimental steam locomotive that carried passengers in 1829. At *right* is a modern electric engine.

theless required to transport the enormous traffic of World War II.

After the war, particularly in the 1960's, railroads have shown greater interest in revising their operations to suit the needs of shippers. Freight-train speeds have been markedly increased, with some "hotshot" freights offering overnight delivery between major cities. Special high-capacity cars, piggyback cars for truck trailers, multilevel automobile cars, and unit trains for efficient coal movements are among the more important reforms of recent years. Although much new equipment has been purchased, a less aggressive program has been pursued to attract passenger traffic, and its decline has been severe—down nearly 50 per cent since 1945. Heavy losses from operations, no longer compensated by equivalent freight business, have forced some railroads to abandon such service.

The railroad industry has made many efforts to streamline performance aside from new rolling stock. Centralized traffic control has speeded trains and eliminated unnecessary tracks. Dieselization has improved service and reduced fuel, service, and labor costs. Mergers between parallel roads eliminated duplicate facilities and personnel.

The railroad industry lost its monopoly in the 1920's, but its prospects are not all dark. Because of highway congestion and the inability of the airlines to carry freight at an economical rate, the railroad will undoubtedly continue as an efficient carrier for many generations.

■**LOCOMOTIVES.**—The steam locomotive, like the railway, originated in Great Britain. Richard Trevithick built the first steam locomotive in 1804 for the Pen-y-darran iron works in Wales. The machine proved too heavy for light track, intended only for horse-drawn wagons, but it encouraged other English mechanics to build locomotives. By 1820 the steam locomotive was recognized as a practical and economical form of motive power. Three years later, the world's first locomotive works was established at Newcastle by Robert Stephenson and Company. In 1829 this company completed the famous *Rocket,* a light, well-proportioned mechanism that incorporated all the basic features of subsequent steam locomotives—multitubular boiler, separate firebox, outside connection, and blast pipe exhaust.

The first locomotive in America, the *Stourbridge Lion,* was imported from England in 1829. Importation of British engines continued until 1841. American mechanics, however, quickly entered the field and produced a locomotive that was better suited to the uneven tracks of the cheaply built railroads. The West Point Foundry Association (New York City) built the first locomotive in the United States, the *Best Friend of Charleston,* in 1830. During succeeding years nearly 150 companies entered the field, but by 1915 the industry was dominated by three major companies—Baldwin, Lima, and American Locomotive.

■**AMERICAN STEAM LOCOMOTIVES.**—Because of inadequate capital, poor track, and steep grade, the pioneer railroads required flexible, cheap, and powerful locomotives. Simple, direct designs kept costs low—small wheels and high boiler pressures provided power, while leading trucks, bar frames, and equalizing levers offered a flexible running gear. All of these admirable features were incorporated in the eight-wheel, or *American,* locomotive. This machine was used for both freight and passenger service and proved so effective that it remained the standard wheel arrangement almost to the end of the nineteenth century. The development of heavier freight trains during the 1870's caused the decline of the *American* type for that service. More powerful freight locomotives, such as the *Mogul* and *Consolidation,* became common. During the same period, passenger train speeds were increased, and again heavier, more specialized locomotives replaced the *American* type.

The basic concepts of locomotive design were revised during the early years of the twentieth century. Faster schedules, heavier tracks, and more ample capital required a more sophisticated and scientific design. The most obvious change was an

Locomotives and Tracks in U.S.

Year	Engines	Track
1830	15	23 miles
1850	3,000	9,021 miles
1870	12,500	52,922 miles
1890	31,812	163,597 miles
1910	60,019	240,293 miles
1930	59,553	249,052 miles
1950	42,951	223,779 miles
1960	31,178	217,552 miles

Interstate Commerce Commission

enormous increase in size: whereas during most of the nineteenth century, few locomotives weighed over 30 tons, 60-ton locomotives were not uncommon by 1910. A wider variety of wheel arrangements and more specialized designs for each class of service were introduced. Locomotives became increasingly complex as more auxiliary equipment, such as stokers, superheaters, and feedwater heaters, was added to increase the machine's capacity and efficiency.

By the late 1940's steam locomotives were huge mechanisms, cluttered with numerous auxiliaries and intricate piping systems. The Union Pacific Railroad had a giant, 600-ton, articulated freight locomotive—the *Big Boy*—which was recognized as the largest steam locomotive ever constructed. Nevertheless, the last steam locomotives built in the United States (1953) continued to follow the basic design of the *Rocket* (1829). As a result of conservative design, poor thermal efficiency, together with several nonmechanical problems, such as labor and terminal costs, steam locomotives on U.S. mainline railroads were abandoned by 1960.

■**DIESEL-ELECTRIC LOCOMOTIVES.**—The diesel-electric locomotive succeeded steam as the principal railroad motive power by the early 1950's. First

used commercially by the Central Railroad of New Jersey in 1925, diesel-electrics were at first considered only for switching service. During the 1930's, several lightweight streamlined trains were built, and in 1935 the first freight diesel-electric was used on the Baltimore and Ohio Railroad. World War II interrupted the more rapid introduction of diesel locomotives. However, many major railroads began to convert entirely to this form of power at the war's end. By 1954, diesel-electrics were moving 80 per cent of the railroad traffic in the United States. The complete conversion took place in 1960.

The diesel engine drives a generator that supplies electricity to motors geared to the locomotive's wheels. Because of the electric transmission, it is possible to connect several diesel-electric locomotives, or units, thus forming a powerful locomotive under the control of a single crew. In recent years, heavy-duty hydraulic transmissions have been successfully employed for diesels.

■**CARS.**—The earliest railroad cars were small, four-wheeled and fabricated almost entirely from wood. Eight-wheel, or *double truck,* cars were introduced in 1831, and within a few years became the accepted model for both freight and passenger service. The basic form of American passenger car, with a center aisle, side seats, and an entrance at each end of the car was introduced at the same time. During most of the nineteenth century, such cars weighed about 15 tons and seated 60 passengers. The clerestory roof, a raised center section with windows for air and light, introduced in the 1860's, was a major innovation in car design. Wood construction continued until 1907, when all-steel coaches were introduced by the Pennsylvania Railroad. Steel passenger cars rapidly replaced weak, flammable wood cars. Lightweight streamlined cars appeared in the 1930's. Air conditioning soon became common.

A wide variety of freight cars—box, flat, hopper, gondola, tank, and others—was developed to handle the diverse products that must be transported. Of these classes, the boxcar is the most numerous, accounting for over a third of the 1,512,306 freight cars now in service in the United States. Wooden freight cars prevailed—although several thousand iron hopper cars were built from the 1840's through the 1880's—until the introduction of all-steel cars in 1897. The greater capacity of all-steel cars won rapid acceptance of this style of construction.

■**RAILS.**—A wide variety of rail types came into use during the first half of the nineteenth century. Strap rail, a thin bar of iron spiked to a longitudinal timber, was favored by most early roads because of its cheapness. This form of construction was not used by public railroads after the 1850's. More costly but more durable rolled rails were used on many of the better constructed pioneer railroads. For example, the Camden and Amboy was built with *T rails* in 1831, and the Philadelphia and Columbia with a form of chair rail known as *Clarence rail* in 1833. *Pear rail,* a squat form of T rail, and *U rail* were popular through the 1860's. After that time, however, "T" became the universal type of rail used on American railroads. Steel "T" rails were introduced during the 1860's and by 1890 were generally adopted by all major lines. Rail weight increased from 60 pounds per yard in the 1850's to about 120 pounds per yard at the present time; the heaviest rail in use weighs 155 pounds. Welded rails 1,500 feet long (standard rail length is 39 feet), now being widely installed, are free from troublesome rail joints and provide a smoother track. —John H. White, Jr.

Railroad Engineering, the design, construction, and maintenance of all physical properties needed for railroad operations. These include roadbeds, tracks, bridges, tunnels, stations, repair shops, locomotives, cars, signals, and rails.

A well-constructed track is fundamental to a successful railroad. Such a track is characterized by good alignment, proper drainage, easy grades, and generous curves. Grades rarely exceed two per cent, and curves are generally not sharper than a 1,000-foot radius on mainline railroads. Immense cuts, fills, trestles, and tunnels are required to maintain such a straight and level line. Railroad construction costs, accordingly, are high, but such roads are able to move heavy traffic with a minimum of power.

The track must be resilient to absorb and cushion the weight of passing trains. The wooden crosstie has been retained for this purpose although steel and cast concrete ties fitted with rubber cushions are being considered as the cost of wooden ties increases. Chemically treated wooden ties last as long as 40 years and remain the most popular type of railroad tie. Crushed stone is used by all major railroads for ballast.

At first, American civil engineers believed that the massive stone viaducts favored by British railways were the only design proper for railroad bridges. These structures were difficult and expensive to build. Wood was soon adopted because it was abundant, and a less costly bridge quick and easy to fabricate. Iron bridges of several patterns were used in the 1840's and 1850's, and by 1870 iron was the accepted material for railroad bridge construction. Late in the nineteenth century, iron was supplanted by steel.

Tunnels are avoided wherever possible because of their great cost. There are only about 1,400 tunnels on U.S. railroads. The first railroad tunnel in the United States was built by the Allegheny Portage Railroad, near Johnstown, Pa., in 1833. The Baltimore and Ohio Railroad built a short tunnel near Harpers Ferry, W. Va., in 1839–40. Many other short tunnels were then constructed. The first tunnel of major length was the 4.7-mile Hoosac Tunnel completed in 1875 by the Boston and Maine Railroad. The longest American railroad tunnel is the 7.7-mile Cascade Tunnel of the Great Northern Railroad. Today many railroads are eliminating tunnels by rerouting lines or by replacing tunnels with open cuts.
—John H. White, Jr.

Railroad Signaling, the system of semaphores and lights used to control railroad operation. There was little need for elaborate signals on early American railroads; traffic was light and trains rarely operated at night before 1850. Instead, the timetable, or the *time-interval system,* was the basis for train movements. By strict adherence to the schedules, each train on the line could be accounted for and would be in its proper place. This simple system worked well, even on single track line, as long as there were only a few trains. However, long delays often resulted; if one train was off schedule, other trains on the line could not proceed until it was accounted for. The introduction of telegraph dispatching in 1851 on the Erie Railroad greatly improved the efficiency of the timetable system.

The *space interval* or *block system,* where fixed signals are used, is a more positive method of traffic control. It was first applied on the Newcastle and Frenchtown Railroad (Delaware) in 1832. Manually operated ball signals at three-mile intervals governed train movements. This plan was not generally adopted until traffic increased to a point where the timetable system was inadequate for safe or efficient handling of train movements. The first important installation of the block system was on the United Railways of New Jersey, between Philadelphia and Trenton, in 1863. By 1876, the entire main line of the Pennsylvania Railroad was fitted with block signals, and within a few years most other major railroads had adopted the system.

All signals before Thomas W. Hall's *electric disc signal* of 1866–67 were manually operated. The principal manual signals were the *disc, ball, banner,* and *semaphore.* Automatic electric signaling enjoyed a rapid development after William Robinson's invention of the closed-track circuit in 1872. Because of inadequate electric motors and a dependence on batteries, the first automatic signals were mechanically driven by clockworks, whose action was in turn governed by an electric control. By 1893, more powerful yet compact electric motors permitted the automation of the long-favored semaphore signal. The semaphore, of ancient origin, remained the standard railway signal until about 1940, when it was superseded on many roads by light signals.

Centralized traffic control, or *CTC,* by which more than 150 miles of railroad can be controlled by a single operator, is the most important recent development in railroad signaling. It was first tested by the New York Central Railroad in 1927. By 1967, nearly 36,000 miles of road were operated by centralized traffic control. —John H. White, Jr.

River Engineering, a specialized science combining geology and engineering and devoted to the control and use of rivers, mainly for transportation purposes. It may also deal with the prevention of floods and of water pollution. The river engineer's task is twofold: first he must make the river navigable, deepening and widening its channel, bypassing its rapids, and straightening its curves; then he must try to maintain his handiwork, by far the more challenging job since rivers persistently resist man's efforts to harness them.

Despite dredging, revetments on river banks, and various control structures designed to keep river channels stable, natural forces, not completely understood, cause most rivers to *meander.* Straight reaches develop gradual curves. Winding sections become even more so, with the river always eroding its banks on the outside of the curve and depositing sediment on the inside. Floods often cause pronounced and sudden changes in river channels.

River engineers work to halt or at least slow down the natural river actions because they make navigation both difficult and dangerous. Some rivers are completely canalized, thus preventing many of the above problems. Relatively low dams, built at various points along the river's course, create what are called navigation pools, really reservoirs which together create a watery stairway. River flow spills over these dams and boats and barges go up and down level-by-level through navigation locks. Other navigation dams and locks are built to eliminate rapids and shallow stretches. For example, a dam just below the rapids forms a pool, inundating the rapids so river traffic may pass.
—William J. Jacobus, Jr.

Roads and Highways, thoroughfares for pedestrian, animal, and vehicular traffic. While paths and trails are as old as man, the first substantial, carefully engineered roads were built by the Romans. The influence of their heavy construction was felt down to the eighteenth century, when the modern science of roadbuilding originated. European road surfaces were frequently 18 inches thick until about 1775 when Pierre Trésaguet introduced a lighter construction into France. In England in the early years of the nineteenth century, two experienced road builders, Thomas Telford and John Loudon McAdam, improved the methods for building roads of broken stone. Telford's system, similar to that of Trésaguet, consisted of building a foundation of larger stones, which were then covered with several layers of smaller broken stones. McAdam felt that the foundation of larger stones had a detrimental effect, and built his roads to a depth of 10 inches with three layers of small stones, broken to a size which would pass through a 2-inch ring. Each layer was compacted by traffic before the next layer was applied, and in later years horse-drawn rollers, and eventually, steamrollers, performed the work of com-

UNITED STATES LINES

OCEAN MONARCHS, S.S. *America* (*foreground*) and S.S. *United States,* pass in the Hudson.

pacting. These men, particularly McAdam, also stressed the importance of proper grading and drainage, notably by raising the road above the surrounding terrain.

In the United States, the first long-distance section of broken stone and gravel surfacing was laid in Pennsylvania, on the Philadelphia and Lancaster Turnpike Road, between 1793 and 1795. In 1823 the first surface constructed according to the McAdam system was laid on the Boonsborough Turnpike Road between Boonsboro and Hagerstown, Maryland. During the mid-nineteenth century there was a general neglect of roads, particularly in rural areas. There were new developments, however, such as rock-breaking machinery and steam road rollers, yet the use of these did not become widespread until the end of the century.

In the 1890's many states began to enact road-aid laws, due in part to the efforts of the League of American Wheelmen. In 1893 the Office of Road Inquiry was established under the Department of Agriculture to begin studies on the management and construction of roads. During the first decade of the twentieth century several new constructions, used some years earlier for surfacing city streets, were introduced on rural roads. These were the various types of bituminous surfaces, such as coal tar, crude oil, and asphalt, and Portland cement concrete. The bituminous materials were more frequently used during the earlier years since they could be applied to old macadam roads without the necessity of building an entirely new road surface. The Federal government intensified its interest in roads during the 1920's; since that time, roads have continued to spread across the United States until they totaled 3,620,457 miles at the beginning of 1965. At the present time there is under construction a 41,000-mile National System of Interstate and Defense Highways. This system, scheduled for completion in 1972, will serve all of America's large cities. In the future, it is expected that national road mileage will not increase greatly, but emphasis will be directed toward better and safer roads.

—Don H. Berkebile

Ship, a seagoing vessel used for cargo and passengers or military applications. Nuclear power is opening vast new areas for maritime expansion. Atomic engines, by virtually eliminating the problem of air intake and exhaust, make possible the development of submarine ships of all types, with limitless size potentials. The entire area of underwater exploration and exploitation is becoming a billion-dollar industry. No longer must ships be tied to routes dictated by the location of bunkering stations. The commercial and military potential of atomic power in shipping is tremendous.

■**HYDROFOILS.**—Equally exciting are the new types of ships that have been developed in the postwar era. The hydrofoil has been perfected for short-haul coastal and lake use. With speeds of 50 to 70 knots, the effect of such ships on old schedules and transportation patterns is clear. In 1965, the U.S. Navy completed the Maritime Administration's *Dennison,* a 50-knot hydrofoil, which has been successfully tested. A hydrofoil vessel is equipped with stiltlike legs; it can rise out of the water and plane on these so-called *foils.* Speeds up to 100 knots are predicted, with possible application to major ocean vessels.

■**AIR-CUSHION VESSELS.**—Another major new ship type is the *surface-effect craft,* also known as the *hover-craft.* This vessel rides inches off the surface of the ocean, supported by an air cushion maintained by ducted fans. British ship architects developed this type of craft, two of which have been ordered for cross-Channel passenger and auto ferry service. The potential of the hovercraft is great, since it can ride not only over water but over flat land areas, suggesting door-to-door freight delivery to replace expensive cargo-handling steps at each seaport.

■**CARGO SHIPS.**—Ordinary cargo ships today are no longer so ordinary. Speeds, which for generations remained about 10 or 12 knots for the typical freighter, have now more than doubled. New liners vie for transatlantic freight speed records, breaking one another's marks as often as did the great clippers of a hundred years ago. Wider hatches for

better cargo handling, mechanical hatch covers, and heavier cargo-boom capacities allow quicker freight loading. Specialized types of cargo ships are another new phase of shipping. Liquefied gas carriers and tankers built to transport dozens of utterly different, often highly dangerous, cargoes are being built throughout the world.

In size, the oil tanker has attracted the most attention. As recently as World War II, a 16,000-ton vessel was considered a very large tanker. Today, orders for ships of 300,000 tons each have been given.

■**PASSENGER SHIPS.**—Modern transatlantic passenger ships are marvels of speed and comfort, largely because of the keen competition among the steamship companies and the maritime nations. Among British ships, the *Queen Mary* and the *Queen Elizabeth,* and among the French, the *France,* were built as the utmost in luxury liners. The *Queen Mary,* launched in 1934, has a gross tonnage of 81,237 tons. The *Queen Elizabeth,* launched in 1940, is the world's largest passenger ship, with an over-all length of 1,031 feet and a gross tonnage of 83,673 tons. Its engines generate 246,000 horsepower. The 83,000-ton *Normandie,* launched in 1935, was destroyed in a fire in New York Harbor in 1942. Its recent successor, the 66,348-ton *France* is the world's longest passenger ship; four feet longer than the *Queen Elizabeth.* Faster than either of the Queens is the *United States,* launched in 1952; it has 12 decks, two theaters, and two large swimming pools. With an over-all length of 990 feet and a gross tonnage of 53,329, the *United States* can carry 1,982 passengers in addition to its 1,000-man crew. Demonstrating the modern passenger ship's adaptability to wartime needs, the *United States* can be converted to a military transport ship capable of carrying 12,000 to 14,000 troops.

—Frank O. Braynard

U.S. NAVY

WORLD'S LARGEST aircraft carrier, the 86,000-ton nuclear-powered U.S.S. *Enterprise* is shown during construction in 1960.

Sound Recording and Reproduction, the processes whereby sound is converted, using microphones, to electric signals which are stored (recorded) in such a manner that they can be subsequently converted back to sound (reproduced), using loudspeakers. The difference in quality between the reproduced sound and the original sound determines the degree of fidelity, that is, high or low fidelity.

Sound results from vibrations in the air. It encompasses a range of audio frequencies that a human being is capable of hearing—normally from 20 to 20,000 cycles per second. A bass drum produces a low-frequency sound of about 100 cycles per second, while a violin can produce high frequency sounds up to 12,000 cycles per second. A male voice produces a range of frequencies between 100 and 10,000 cycles per second, while a female voice produces a range between 200 and 10,000 cycles per second.

There are three common methods of recording sound, each using a different medium for recording and storing sound information. These are modulated groove recording on phonograph discs, magnetic recording on audio tape, and modulated light recording on a photographic film.

The method of modulated groove recording on phonograph discs was invented by Thomas A. Edison in 1877. The medium originally used was a wax-covered cylinder approximately three inches in diameter. The magnetic recording system was invented by Valdemar Poulsen, a Danish inventor, in 1898. The medium used then was steel wire approximately 20 mils in diameter. No single person is credited with the discovery of the process of modulated light recording on film. Both the Radio Corporation of America and the Western Electric Company developed their own methods of sound-on-film recording in 1910.

■**MAGNETIC TAPE RECORDING.**—Most original performances are recorded by the magnetic process. The sounds produced by an actor or a singer or an orchestra's instruments are sensed by a microphone, or group of microphones, in which sound is converted to an electric signal. The electric signal is controlled, amplified, and directed to an audio magnetic tape-recording machine. In the tape machine, the electric signal acts upon an electromagnetic recording head, causing magnetization of a ¼-inch wide, 1½-mil thick magnetic audio tape as it passes over the head at a speed of 7½ inches per second. The magnetization varies in accordance with the original sound signal.

Audio magnetic recording is used because the tape can be more easily handled by the recording engineer. It can be edited (cut and spliced) to make corrections. Editing is not practical in either of the other recording methods.

Once the original recording is completed and stored on a reel of magnetic audio tape, it can then be dubbed (transferred) to the other media or duplicated on other reels of audio magnetic tape. The latter

COLUMBIA RECORDS

RECORDING session in a studio is taped and monitored by engineers in the control room.

process requires many tape recording machines to be fed from a playback machine on which the originally recorded tape is placed.

■**PHONOGRAPH RECORDS.**—The production of phonograph discs (or records) involves the following steps. First, a master disc recording is made, using the originally recorded tape as the source. That tape is placed on a playback machine similar to the one used in the production of audio tapes. The electric signal is picked up from the moving magnetic audio tape by an electromagnetic playback head, amplified, and directed to a phonograph-disc recording system. Such a system includes a powerful amplifier that feeds an electromagnetic cartridge, which in turn actuates a diamond-tipped cutting stylus. As the master phonograph disc rotates at a speed of 33 1/3, or 78 revolutions per minute, the stylus is moved from side to side in accordance with the original sound signal, creating a modulated groove (a groove of varying width). The groove is started from the outside and spirals toward the center. This master disc is used to produce a stamping mold *mother* from which copies of phonograph records, made of a vinyl plastic, are produced.

■**HIGH-FIDELITY REPRODUCTION.**—Audio tape and phonograph discs are the media most commonly used for playback or reproduction by high-fidelity enthusiasts. For reproduction purposes an *audio tape recorder* (capable of both recording and playback) is connected to an amplifier and loudspeaker system. The audio tape is placed (threaded) on the tape machine. The tape passes over an electromagnetic *playback head* located along the tape's path. The magnetization is picked up by the playback head and fed to a *loudspeaker* through a powerful *amplifier*. In order to reproduce a phonograph record, a *turntable*, upon which the record is placed, and a *tone arm* with a phonograph *pickup cartridge*, on which a *stylus* is mounted, are required. The stylus follows the groove and is moved from side to side in accordance with the recorded modulations, producing an electric signal at the output terminals of the cart-

ridge. The signal is fed to an *amplifier* and *loudspeaker* combination.

The phonograph pickup cartridge may be either an *electromagnetic* or a *crystal* type. In the crystal type, the material that responds in the cartridge is Rochelle salt or barium titanate (ceramic). In either type, the stylus is tipped with either sapphire or diamond, the latter being the more costly.

In a complete home high-fidelity reproduction system, a *preamplifier* is commonly used. This device is so arranged that it can accommodate many playback devices, including a radio tuner.

■**MODULATED LIGHT RECORDING.**—Modulated light recording on a system of photographic film is used with motion pictures. A light source is modulated (varied) in accordance with the sound signal. The light is directed to the unexposed film in the motion-picture camera while the camera is taking pictures. This sound signal is located on the film between the picture and the sprocket holes. After the exposed film is processed, it is ready for reproduction. In reproduction, light is passed through the film at the sound track position. The light intensity is varied by the modulation on the sound track and is directed to a photocell. The output of the photocell (an electric signal) is fed to a powerful amplifier and then to a loudspeaker.

■**STEREOPHONIC SYSTEMS.**—Stereophonic (dual channel) recording and reproduction differs from monaural (single channel) high-fidelity systems in that there are two channels, left side and right side. An original stereophonic recording, using left side and right side microphones, provides two separate but simultaneous electrical signals. On audio tape they are recorded on two parallel tracks, while on phonograph discs they are recorded on each side of the groove. In reproduction, both systems provide left and right side electrical signals that are fed to a pair of amplifiers and loudspeakers. Because the loudspeakers are physically separated, the listener is presented with a more realistic reproduction of the original performance.

—Emil P. Vincent

Stock Ticker, a telegraph machine that prints the quotations of stock or commodity sales. Each important stock or commodity exchange transmits reports of transactions on its *floor* over a separate ticker network provided and maintained by the telegraph company. To economize on transmission time, standardized abbreviations are used, such as *X* for United States Steel Corporation or *J* for Standard Oil Company of New Jersey.

At an exchange, reports of transactions are speeded to operators who use typewriterlike keyboards. The quotations typed by the operators are automatically combined in a stream of electric impulses flashing over the network, causing tickets in brokers' and other offices to print the quotations on a narrow tape flowing from the tickers.

The nation's exchanges have been provided with stock ticker systems by the Western Union Telegraph Company for about a century. At first, the tickers were slow and could not be brought into unison by central control, but were improved by Thomas A. Edison, a telegraph operator. He was rewarded with $40,000, and set up a shop to make tickers. This enabled Edison to start his career as an inventor.

About 1929 the old glass-domed ticker, initially developed by Edison, proved too slow to handle the volume of quotations on the New York Stock Exchange. A new ticker, with a speed of 500 characters per minute—about twice as fast as the old model—was installed in 1931. In 1964 that also had become too slow, and another ticker was put into use with a speed of 900 characters a minute.

The ticker system of the American Stock Exchange was improved at the same time. The older tickers are still used by the Midwest Exchange in Chicago, the Pacific Coast Stock Exchange, the Philadelphia-Baltimore-Washington Exchange, the Boston Exchange, and the grain, cotton, and other commodity exchanges.

—George P. Oslin

Submarine, a ship capable of running on or below the surface of the sea. Diesel engines are used for power while the ship is surfaced, and electric motors while it is submerged. Power for the electric motors is provided by banks of storage batteries. The batteries are charged by Diesel generators while the submarine is surfaced. Since the batteries can store only a limited amount of power, the submarines can operate submerged for only limited periods.

The invention of the nuclear power plant and its application to submarines led to the development of the first true submersible. Nuclear submarines can operate submerged indefinitely because their power plants do not require air to be mixed with the fuel. Nuclear submarines are driven by steam turbines connected to the propellers by reduction gearing. When the electric motor is used for propulsion, the turbines and reduction gearing are disconnected. As in conventional submarines, electric power is stored in banks of storage batteries. The batteries are charged by turbine driven generators or Diesel generators when the nuclear reactor is shut down.

Submarines have two distinct *hulls,* or bodies. The outer hull encloses the inner, or pressure, hull, which resists water pressure when the ship is submerged. The pressure hull is built up of cylinders and truncated cones reinforced with bulkheads and frames. Within the pressure hull are the crew's quarters, propulsion machinery, and battery storage areas. Watertight bulkheads divide the inner spaces to restrict flooding to local areas if the pressure hull is pierced.

Built into the space between the inner and outer hulls are the ballast and fuel-oil tanks. To prevent them from being crushed by water pressure, these tanks must be kept filled with fluid or compressed air.

A conning tower, or superstructure, mounted atop the submarine contains a bridge for operating on the surface. Protruding from the top of the conning tower are the periscopes, which provide visibility when the submarine runs just beneath the surface. Because the conning tower is outside the pressure hull, it is flooded during submerged operations. Pipes, fittings and valves atop the hull are enclosed in a free flooding enclosure.

A submarine dives by opening vent valves in the top of the main ballast tanks, allowing water to enter flood holes at the bottom. To surface, the vents are closed and compressed air is admitted to the tanks. This forces water out of the flood holes and enables the submarine to rise. Compressed air to blow the tanks is provided by compressors and stored in high-pressure bottles. Trim tanks are provided fore and aft to compensate for changes in weight as fuel oil and armament stores are consumed. The operation of leveling the submarine with the trim tanks is called *trimming.*

When running submerged, the submarine uses diving planes to control the angle of its motion. These planes are hydrofoils which can be tilted to develop vertical forces on the submarine. Conventional or Diesel-powered submarines have their diving planes mounted on the hull. Nuclear submarines have their forward diving planes mounted high on the sail or conning tower. When running on the surface, the planes of nuclear submarines are well above the water and look like aircraft wings.

Primitive submarines were built by Cornelis Drebbel in England and Le Son in France during the seventeenth century. A muscle-powered submarine, the *Turtle,* built by David Bushnell, was used against the British during the Revolutionary War. Robert Fulton's *Nautilus,* built about 1800, was similar in many respects to Bushnell's craft. After Charles Brun, Thorsten Nordenfeldt, Gustave Zédé, and others had constructed relatively unsuccessful steam- and electric-powered submarines, John P. Holland succeeded in building the first modern submarine. Named the *Holland* and purchased by the U.S. Navy on April 11, 1900, the craft was powered by a gasoline engine when surfaced and by electric motors when submerged.

By the end of World War II, the submarine had evolved into a large warship whose range and underwater capability were limited only by its need for Diesel fuel and air. This problem was solved by the application of nuclear power. The first nuclear-powered submarine, the U.S.S. *Nautilus,* was commissioned on Sept. 30, 1954. Since then, the United States has commissioned more than two dozen other nuclear submarines, and Great Britain and the Soviet Union have also launched vessels of this type.

—Joseph J. Kelleher

Telegraph, an electrical method by which information is transmitted to distant places and recorded. At one time, the term *telegraph* was applied to any system for sending coded messages. Thus, over the centuries, tele-

U.S. NAVY

U.S.S. LAFAYETTE, which is a nuclear-powered submarine, capable of cruising for extended periods without surfacing or refueling, undergoes sea try-outs in the Atlantic Ocean in 1963.

graph systems have transmitted signals by means of fire, smoke, colored sails, flags, drums, carrier pigeons, flashing shields in the sun, semaphore towers with movable arms, relay runners, and horsemen.

While a means of providing electricity was being developed, hundreds of men devised methods of sending electrical signals over a wire. Some used a wire for each letter of the alphabet; others used disks revolving in unison, with the same character visible when an impulse was sent; others used an electromagnetic needle that deflected to the right or left upon the arrival of electrical impulses.

In 1800, Alessandro Volta of Italy invented the electric cell, which for the first time provided a steady source of current. In 1829 Joseph Henry, a school teacher of Albany, N. Y., devised an electromagnet suitable for telegraph use. Sir Humphry Davy, Sir Charles Wheatstone and William F. Cooke, and others produced early electric telegraph systems.

Samuel F. B. Morse, an American artist, produced the first practical telegraph system to attain general use in the United States. The first line was placed in operation between Washington, D. C., and Baltimore, Md., on May 24, 1844, with the transmission of the words "What Hath God Wrought!" Licensed by Morse and his partners, 50 telegraph lines were built throughout the eastern states by 1851.

Most early lines used the Morse system, in which an operator opened or closed a key for short or long intervals. The combinations of these dots and dashes, the *Morse code,* indicated the letters of the alphabet and figures. Operators *read* messages by listening to the time intervals between clicks of a small iron bar in a *sounder* as it was attracted by an electromagnet, which was energized by the arriving electrical impulses.

In 1853 Wilhelm Gintl of Vienna developed the *duplex,* by which two messages could be sent simultaneously in opposite directions over a single wire. Thomas A. Edison produced the *quadruplex* in 1874, by which two messages in each direction could be sent simultaneously over one wire. Various printing telegraph systems, in which messages are received in printed form, were introduced in the 1890's. From this evolved the *multiplex system,* installed on most trunk lines in 1914. This permitted the simultaneous transmission of eight messages over one wire.

In the 1920's *teleprinters* were installed in the offices of some 30,000 companies, enabling them to send and receive their messages over a direct wire to the nearest main telegraph office. Many thousands of teleprinters also have been installed in branch telegraph offices and in private wire systems leased to large companies and the government.

In the 1940's fifteen high-speed message centers, each serving two or more states, were installed to mechanize the nationwide network. This eliminated manual handling at relay points. Each message is typed at the point of origin, and is switched through to its destination by the pressing of a button at only one point.

Facsimile telegraph systems were developed in the 1920's. An electric eye scans the handwritten or typed copy and flashes impulses over a circuit, causing a recorder to produce a facsimile of what was sent. The arriving current decomposes, or *burns away,* minute portions of the coating of an electrosensitive dry recording paper, and the message is ready for delivery. Facsimile systems are used by the U. S. Weather Bureau and the U.S. Air Force to send weather maps nationwide, and in other networks. Facsimile is also used by over 40,000 firms to send and receive 50,000,000 telegrams a year.

Installation of *frequency-modulation* (FM) *carrier systems* in the 1920's produced a vast increase in telegraphic capacity. With them, as many as 288 messages can be sent simultaneously over a single pair of wires. A number of frequencies are generated, and communications are sent over each frequency.

The first commercial microwave beam system was constructed in 1945, and such systems are now in nationwide use. A series of towers is built on high places, such as tall buildings or mountains, about 30 miles apart. Microwaves travel in a straight line. Reflectors on each tower catch the beam; the signals are strengthened and improved, then flashed on to the next tower. The beam is divided into voice-frequency channels, and an FM carrier system is placed on each channel, permitting 2,000 telegrams to be sent simultaneously over a single beam system. A 7,500-mile beam system was placed in operation in 1964, which added 80 million telegraph channel miles to the nationwide network.

Rapid growth in the use of computers in business management, with data transmitted from distant plants and offices to data centers, has required increasingly automatic and complex private-wire telegraph systems. This is the major growth trend of the telegraph industry in the 1960's.

The best known telegraph services are the *fast telegram, day letter, night letter,* and *telegraph money order.* Introduced in the 1960's was a dial-direct, subscriber-to-subscriber teleprinter exchange service called *Telex,* which produces instant direct connections with other subscribers by the dialing of a number.

—George P. Oslin

Telemetry, the process of making measurements at a distance with the help of sensing devices and radio, wire, or other means of communication. Telemetry is used to make measurements that would ordinarily be extremely difficult or impossible because of danger to human life, inaccessibility, or inconvenience. Telemetering systems range from the most simple (an outdoor-indoor thermometer with adjacent indicating scales) to complex instruments used to measure and transmit data from the upper atmosphere or from outer space.

Telemetry is used in space vehicles to sense environmental quantities such as temperature, pressure, and radiation, and to transmit the data by radio to the earth, where it is decoded and recorded. Sensing elements, or transducers, have been developed to measure: weight, time interval, angle, electric field strength, light intensity, temperature, velocity, atomic radiation, blood pressure, many other measurable aspects of the environment. The sensing elements invariably produce an electrical output signal, because telemetry transmissions are usually made by radio or wire. In practice, the signal from the transducer is applied to a wire line or radio transmitter that forwards the information to a distant receiver.

In addition to its role in space science, telemetry has been adopted for inventory control systems, airline reservation systems, stock quotation boards, and teleprinters used in telegraphy. Industry makes use of telemetry in the control of industrial processes, such as paper manufacture, pipeline flow, and the refining of crude oil. Telemetry is also used widely by meteorologists to gather weather data from the upper atmosphere.

—William C. Vergara

Telephone, a combination of devices by which sound is converted into electric impulses, transmitted, and reconverted into sound waves at the receiving instrument. The simple device Alexander Graham Bell invented in 1876 consisted of only a dozen parts. Although today's telephone contains more than 450 parts, the fundamental principle he discovered still applies.

The principle concerns the relationship between electric current and sound waves. Electric energy, supplied by a battery in a telephone central office, is carried to the telephone by a series of wires. When the handset is lifted, the battery sends a steady current through the *transmitter* (mouthpiece). When a person speaks, sound waves enter the transmitter and strike a diaphragm, which vibrates at various speeds, depending upon the variations in air pressure caused by the varying tones and loudness of the voice. As the diaphragm vibrates, it acts against a chamber filled with carbon granules, which move closer together or farther apart, depending on which way the diaphragm is moving. An increased air pressure momentarily packs the granules of carbon more tightly. This reduces the resistance of the carbon to the electric current flowing through it, and a stronger current goes out over the phone circuit. When a reduction in the air pressure allows the diaphragm to move outward, the granules separate slightly, so a weaker current is sent through the circuit. Thus the variation in the current takes on the pattern of the original sound waves.

The varying electric currents are

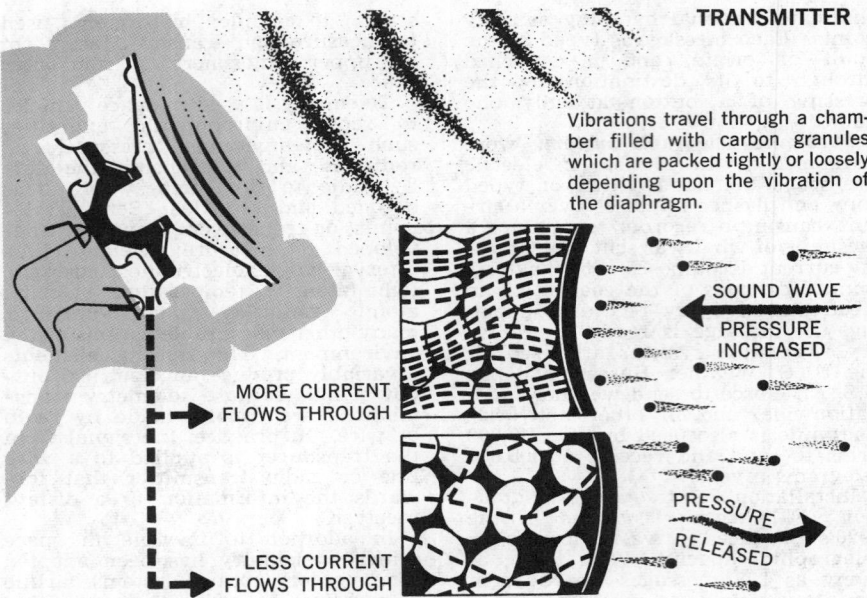

TRANSMITTER

Vibrations travel through a chamber filled with carbon granules which are packed tightly or loosely depending upon the vibration of the diaphragm.

SOUND WAVE
PRESSURE INCREASED

MORE CURRENT FLOWS THROUGH

LESS CURRENT FLOWS THROUGH

PRESSURE RELEASED

transformed back into speech sounds in the telephone *receiver* (earpiece), where two magnets regulate the movement of a thin circular metal diaphragm. One magnet is a permanent magnet that constantly pulls the diaphragm toward it. The other is an electromagnet, a piece of iron that becomes magnetized when electric current flows through a coil of wire wound around it. When the electromagnet is energized, it pulls the diaphragm away from the permanent magnet. The strength of the pull varies according to the pattern of the current set up by the distant transmitter. As the diaphragm moves in and out, it sets up new sound waves that are replicas of the original voice.

■ **SWITCHING.**—The usefulness of the telephone depends on the ability of users to be connected quickly and easily with one another. To accomplish this, each telephone is linked with a central office where connections to other telephones are made by switching equipment. Almost all telephones are dial-operated. Calls are switched automatically by four types of switching systems: step-by-step, panel, crossbar, and electronic.

Step-by-step equipment operates in direct response to the dial pulses generated by the user. *Panel* systems use the "common control" principle, in which the switches are operated by a common set of equipment instead of being under direct control of the dial. *Crossbar* switching involves crosspoint switches operated by a common group of equipment using the common control principle. Common equipment is used only long enough to set up the connection and is then released for other calls. *Electronic* switching, the newest system, is basically a digital data processor (computer) utilizing solid-state electronic devices. Each action takes only microseconds to complete because information is stored in magnetic "memories" rather than in arrangements of wires.

■ **TRANSMISSION.**—To get to and from a switching center, calls travel over wire, cable, and/or radio relay microwave systems. All long-distance channels use the carrier technique, by which many telephone conversations are carried simultaneously over a single pair of wires, coaxial cable, or radio relay. It is possible to carry as many as 16 simultaneous conversations over one pair of wires. Messages are transmitted by modulating alternating currents of different frequencies, *carrier frequencies.*

One form of carrier, called *coaxial cable*, consists of a copper wire held at the center of a metallic tube by insulating washers. Using the carrier technique, a pair of coaxial tubes—one for each direction of transmission—can handle as many as 1,860 simultaneous conversations. These cables may have 8, 12, or even 20 tubes.

Radio relay systems use superhigh frequencies, called *microwaves*, to transmit intelligence from point to point. Because microwaves travel in straight lines, they are usually aimed like a searchlight from one microwave tower to another. These towers, situated about 30 miles apart, amplify the signal. Generally, a clear line-of-sight path must exist between these amplifying stations. A microwave signal can be aimed so precisely that the same frequency can be used for transmission in different directions from the same station. One microwave carrier system, called *TH*, can carry as many as 11,160 telephone conversations or 12 television programs on one route. *Communications satellites*, such as *Early Bird*, are actually microwave towers in the sky.

Tropospheric scattter propagation, or "over-the-horizon" systems, use that portion of microwave energy that goes beyond the horizon and scatters downward to earth. A *feed horn* sprays the signal against a reflection screen, which beams it over the horizon in the direction of the receiving antenna situated several hundred miles away. The small portion scat-

tered downward is received by an antenna that resembles a huge drive-in movie screen. Here the signal is amplified and sent on to the next station or concentrated into a line-of-sight microwave system or other facility to reach its destination.

The first *undersea telephone cable* was laid between Miami, Florida, and Havana, Cuba, in 1921. The development of submarine repeater devices to amplify the signals made possible the first transatlantic telephone cable —between Scotland and Nova Scotia, via Clarenville, Newfoundland—in 1956. Later, cables were laid between Seattle, Washington, and Ketchikan, Alaska; Oakland, California, and Hawaii; Penmarch, France, and Nova Scotia; Miami and Puerto Rico; and Miami and Bermuda.

In 1963, new armorless cable was placed in service between Florida, Jamaica, and the Canal Zone, and between Tuckerton, New Jersey, and Cornwall, England. This type of cable was also used between the U.S. mainland, Hawaii, and Japan, via Guam, and between Guam and the Philippines. A fourth transatlantic cable, between New Jersey and France, was completed in 1965. These newly designed cables provide two-way communications over a single cable. This cable, with repeaters already spliced in, is placed by the 17,000-ton *C.S. Long Lines,* a specially constructed cable-laying vessel that lays cable while traveling at 8 knots.

■ **SERVICES AND PRODUCTS.**—In 1878, when the first telephone exchange opened in New Haven, Conn., 21 people signed up for service. Seven years later, the American Telephone & Telegraph Company (AT&T)— today the world's largest telephone

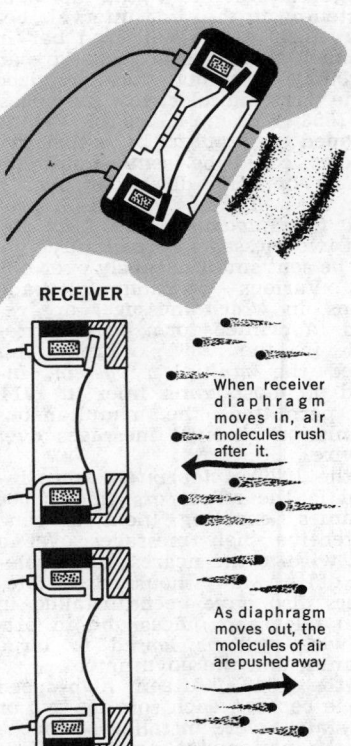

RECEIVER

When receiver diaphragm moves in, air molecules rush after it.

As diaphragm moves out, the molecules of air are pushed away

system—was established as a long-distance company. In 1900, AT&T's operations were expanded to include all telephone operations. This was the beginning of the Bell System, which today serves some 76 million telephones. About 2,600 non-Bell System companies cooperate with one another by interconnecting their lines and facilities, and their rates and functions are regulated by the Federal Communications Commission and locally, by state commissions.

Telephone Sets. Many different and distinctive telephone sets have been developed. Telephones with internal microphones and wall-mounted loudspeakers permit room-to-room communication. A microphone-speaker arrangement for door answering and a chime for the telephone bell are also available.

The *Speakerphone* permits "hand-free" telephoning and also enables a group to participate in a conversation. A sensitive microphone situated near the telephone picks up the speaker's voice. The answering voice is heard over a loudspeaker that can be adjusted for volume.

Among handset accessories is the *automatic card dialer,* which saves time by "reading" prerecorded telephone numbers and dialing calls. By the press of a telephone button, more than one outside line or extension may be held on one line, or transferred, while there is a conversation on another, and one may signal for a transfer or another extension. *Call director* telephones offer up to 30 outside lines—signaling, code dialing of extensions, transfer of calls, or by dialing a code, arranging a conference call.

Teletypewriter Exchange Service, which provides swift, written communications, is dial-operated and sends page and/or punched paper tape at speeds of 60, 75, and 100 words per minute.

Data-Phone service transmits data in any medium—punched cards, punched paper tape, magnetic tape, and facsimile material (such as maps and drawings, as well as handwriting)—over regular telephone lines. Data-Phone *data sets* accept information from various business machines, convert the information to electric signals for transmission over telephone lines and, at the receiving end, reconvert it to its original form. Speeds vary, although they usually range from about 100 to 2,500 words per minute.

Mobile telephone service provides communications between cars, trucks, trains, and ships and the nationwide telephone network.

Recent Developments. One example of improved service is *TouchTone* calling, which permits customers to push buttons instead of rotating the dial. These phones can also be used as data input devices. Electronic switching offers such advanced services as customer-dialed conference calls, abbreviated dialing (2 or 3 digits rather than 7 to 10), transferring incoming calls to another phone, and other features. *Picturephone* service was introduced in 1964.

—James M. Freeman

Teletypewriter, a device for transmitting typewritten messages electrically from one station to another where it is automatically typewritten again. The receiving instrument is especially interesting, as it appears to be operated by an invisible typist. All the operations of typing—including return of the carriage, spacing of lines, and operation of the type bars—are performed without the attention of an operator except for removing typed messages from the machine and providing it with new paper.

A keyboard printer is a particular type of teleprinter equipment. It is similar to a normal typewriter in that it has a keyboard consisting of alphabetic, numerical, and function keys and a printing mechanism. In addition, however, it has a device that generates electric signals. These signals are coded to conform with the character represented on the keyboard. When an operator types a character, a coded signal is generated and transmitted over a communication channel to a receiving teleprinter. At the receiving end, the coded signal is interpreted and the character is printed. Two or more operators at teletypewriters on the same circuit can converse simply by typing back and forth. The message appears as a page on the sending teletypewriter and is received as a page.

At the same time, punched paper tape can be created and used for future transmission, filing, or computer input. Using teletypewriter tape permits editing of errors, and it also provides for automatic transmission at speeds much greater than manual typing by an operator. As the operator types a character, a coded signal activates the punch which puts holes in the paper tape. These holes represent the coded form of the particular characters that were typed. Several codes are used, which provide five-, six-, seven-, and eight-level punched paper tape.

Punched paper tape transmission terminals consist of two units, a sender and a receiver. The sender consists of a paper tape reader and a signal generator. As the tape passes through the reader, the holes are read photoelectrically or by sensing pins that are connected to the signal generator. When the presence of a hole in the tape is sensed, an electric signal is generated. The operation is reversed at the receiver, which consists of a signal interpreter and a paper tape punch. As the electric signals are received from the communications channel, the pins in the tape punch are activated to punch holes accordingly to the paper tape.

Several types of teletypewriter are available: automatic send and receive page machine (ASR); automatic transmitter (ATR); keyboard send and receive page machine (KSR); keyboard typing reperforator (KTR); perforator (PERF); receive-only page machine (RO); receive-only typing perforator (ROTR); and reperforator transmitter (RT). The ROTR provides tape printed along the edge of the coded paper tape. Several models of each type are also available.

Teletypewriters are used to transmit messages over private-line services that connect two or more locations, as well as over the teletypewriter exchange network.

—James M. Freeman

Television, the electrical transmission and reception of transient visual images. In broadcast television, the picture is always accompanied by a sound transmission in the same channel.

Television transmission and reception form a "lock-and-key" system in that the transmitter and receiver must operate by a common set of rules. For example, television sets made for the United States signal are worthless in Great Britain, where transmission standards are different. This is in contrast to radio receivers, which can pick up any transmission to which they are tuned.

Television transmission in the United States is governed by the Federal Communications Commission, which issues a set of *Rules of Good Engineering Practice.* In the United States, television transmission occurs in three bands: the low very-high-frequency (VHF) band, the high VHF band, and the ultrahigh frequency (UHF) band. Each channel has a bandwidth of 6 megacycles (mc.) per second (sec.) disposed as shown in the accompanying table.

Disposition of Television Bands

Band	Channels	Location in Radio Spectrum
Low VHF band	2, 3, and 4	54— 72 mc./sec.
	5 and 6	76— 88 mc./sec.
High VHF band	7 to 13	174–216 mc./sec.
UHF band	14 to 83	470–890 mc./sec.

Other countries have allocated bandwidths of 6, 7, or 8 mc./sec. for their television channels.

VHF and UHF transmissions are normally limited in range to the horizon. This is why it is important that both the transmitting and receiving antennas be situated as high as possible.

For simplicity, an image can be considered as made up of points having different brightnesses. A television camera picks up this image, analyzes the brightness point by point, and converts the varying brightness into a picture signal, whose value varies accordingly. A *synchronizing signal* is also generated which, loosely speaking, establishes the location of each point in the picture. The receiver picks up both the picture and synchronizing signals. It then reproduces the brightness of each point in its proper location, thus reconstructing the image.

The output of the camera and the synchronizing signals occur in the frequency range up to about 4.0 mc., which are called *video frequencies.* The sound is *frequency-modulated* (FM) on a separate carrier radio wave higher in frequency by 4.5 mc. than the picture carrier. The complete signal is then transmitted on one of the channels listed above.

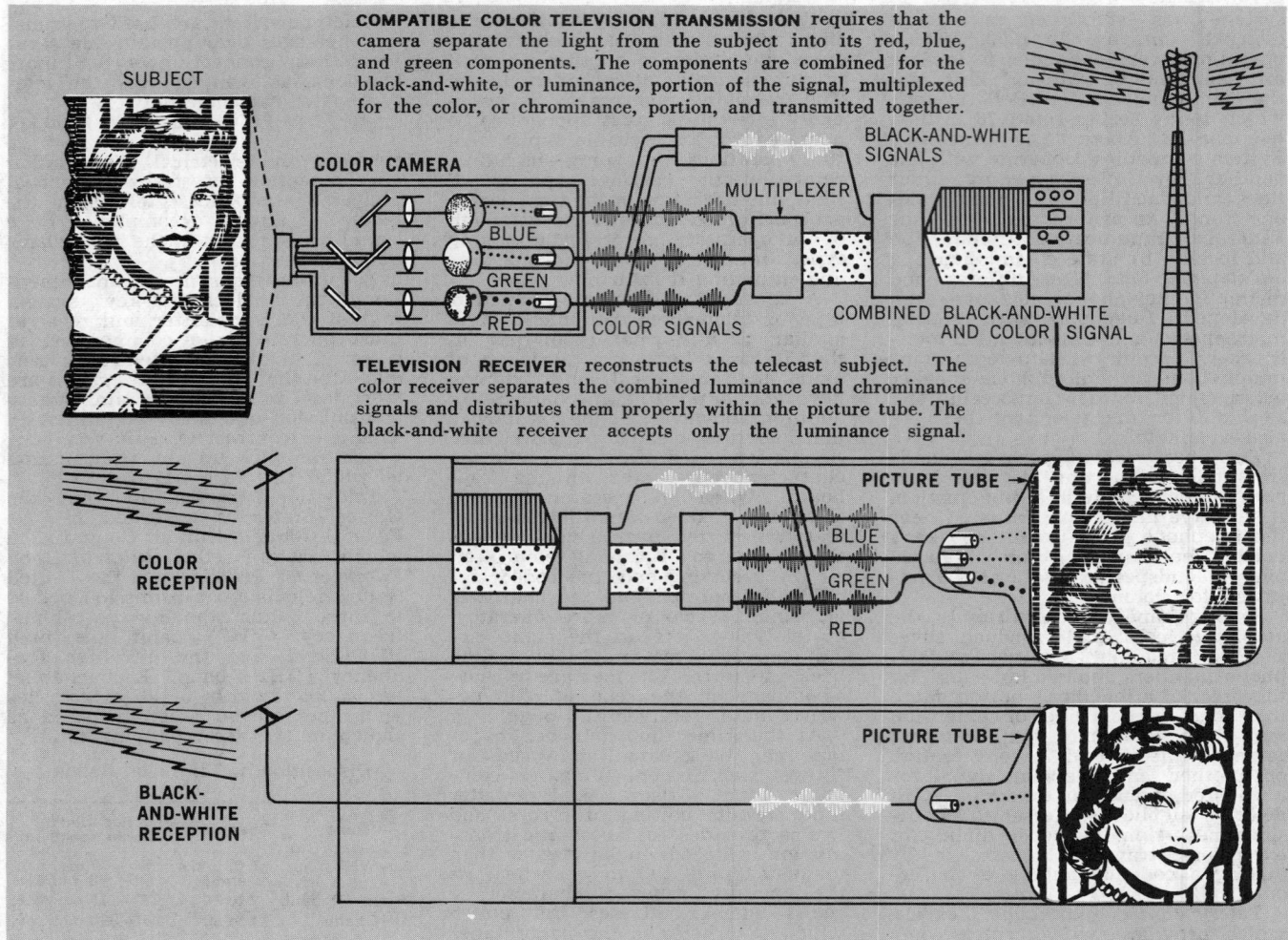

COMPATIBLE COLOR TELEVISION TRANSMISSION requires that the camera separate the light from the subject into its red, blue, and green components. The components are combined for the black-and-white, or luminance, portion of the signal, multiplexed for the color, or chrominance, portion, and transmitted together.

SUBJECT

COLOR CAMERA

BLUE

GREEN

RED

COLOR SIGNALS

MULTIPLEXER

BLACK-AND-WHITE SIGNALS

COMBINED BLACK-AND-WHITE AND COLOR SIGNAL

TELEVISION RECEIVER reconstructs the telecast subject. The color receiver separates the combined luminance and chrominance signals and distributes them properly within the picture tube. The black-and-white receiver accepts only the luminance signal.

COLOR RECEPTION

PICTURE TUBE →

BLUE

GREEN

RED

BLACK-AND-WHITE RECEPTION

PICTURE TUBE →

The receiver *antenna* picks up this signal and delivers it to the receiver which, in the United States, is of the superheterodyne type. The receiver selects the proper channel, detects and amplifies the signal, and separates the video, synchronizing, and sound signals from one another. The video picture signal is impressed on a cathode-ray tube. Within the tube it produces picture elements whose brightness is proportional to the strength of the picture signal and whose location in the picture is established by the synchronizing signal. The sound is treated in the usual manner of FM receivers.

■SCANNING.—At the camera, the picture is analyzed left to right and top to bottom, along a series of vertically displaced horizontal parallel lines, much as a person reads a book. This process, called *scanning*, is performed by a moving electron beam. When the beam has reached the right-hand edge of the scanning line, it quickly retraces to the left for the next line. When it has reached the bottom of the picture, it quickly retraces to the top for the next scan. The picture is blanked during retrace so that the retrace lines are not visible. In the United States, television pictures are resolved into 525 lines repeated 30 times per second; thus,

$525 \times 30 = 15,750$ lines per second. In Great Britain, the corresponding number is 405 lines repeated 25 times per second (10,125 lines per second); in Europe, it is 625 lines repeated 25 times per second (15,625 lines per second).

To reduce flicker, the number of *images per second* is doubled by an artifice known as *interlaced scanning*. The odd-numbered lines, of which there are $525 \div 2 = 262.5$, are scanned in 1/60 second, and the even-numbered lines are then scanned in the next 1/60 second. Each scan, taking 1/60 second, is called a *field*. Two successive fields comprise a *frame*, or a *picture*. The half-line left at the end of each field causes the lines of the next field to locate themselves halfway between those of the preceding field.

The power-line frequency, 60 cycles per second in the United States and 50 cycles per second in Europe, is the main factor determining the field frequency. Transmitting pictures at a rate of 60 fields per second on a 50-cycle power system, or vice versa, would produce a very annoying 10 cycles per second flicker unless expensive additional filtering were used. This difference in field frequency poses the greatest single problem in the international ex-

change of television programs.

■MODULATION.—The start of each line and the start of each field are initiated by distinctive synchronizing signals. In the United States, picture-black and peak-white are established by specific signal levels. The synchronizing signals and the pedestals on which they are placed occur at *blacker-than-black* levels, so that they, as well as the retrace lines, are invisible in a receiver whose average brightness is well adjusted.

As applied to the picture tube, black corresponds to zero beam current and increasingly positive signals on its control grid produce increasing brightness. However, the ratio transmission makes use of negative modulation so that peak-white, the brightest part of the picture, represents the lowest modulation level.

If a TV set is tuned to a channel on which no signal is being transmitted, the screen will be fully illuminated, or white, indicating a zero signal. A weak signal may produce "snow" indicating that the signal is not strong enough to effect the receiver's scanning beam.

Great Britain and France use positive modulation. Advantages can be cited for both types. The advantages of negative modulation are that noise cannot drive the signal below zero and, therefore, is less bright than for positive modulation, where it can produce brilliant white snow; it also provides fixed levels for black and for peak-white. The advantages of positive modulation are that noise cannot drive the synchronizing peaks below their level of zero volts and that reliable synchronization can be achieved more economically.

■IMAGE RESOLUTION.—In the United States, a bandwidth of 4.0 mc. is allocated for picture information. Including positive and negative half-cycles, this permits the transmission of $2 \times 4,000,000 = 8,000,000$ picture elements per second. Since there are 15,750 lines per picture, this corresponds to $8,000,000 \div 15,750 = 508$ horizontal picture elements per line. But since 85 per cent of the line period is reserved for picture and 15 per cent is reserved for synchronization, the number of possible picture elements is $508 \times 0.85 = 430$ per line. The picture face of a 23-inch tube is about 18 inches wide and 13.8 inches high. Therefore, the system is capable of resolving a picture element that is $18/430 = 0.042$ inch wide.

This means that a line can have any number of picture elements from 0 to 425, each 0.042 inch disposed in any order along the line. Assuming that 500 of the 525 lines are available for the picture and 25 lines for vertical retrace, the picture element is $13.8 \div 500 = 0.027$ inch high. While the vertical resolution is a function only of the tube size and the number of lines, the horizontal resolution depends on the bandwidth actually passed by the receiver.

As stated above, the sound is transmitted by FM on a separate carrier located 4.5 mc. above the picture carrier. The FM has a maximum deviation of ±75 kc. for regular FM broadcasting. Great Britain and France use AM for sound.

If the picture signal were transmitted by normal amplitude modulation, it would require two sidebands and occupy a total bandwidth of 8.0 mc., not including the sound. To save bandwidth, only part of the lower sideband is transmitted.

■CAMERA TUBES.—The camera tubes most used currently are the *image orthicon* and the *vidicon*. In both types, the image is focussed on a photosensitive surface, where it is stored as a potential image in the form of a surface distribution of electrical charges. This potential image is then discharged by a scanning electron beam that translates the charge distribution into a current proportional to the brightness of the consecutive points on the surface.

A synchronizing generator produces the synchronizing waveform that is added to the video signal for transmission to the receiver.

The locally generated horizontal and vertical synchronizing signals generate two sawtooth waveforms which respectively occur 15,750 and 60 times per second. The fast one is used for horizontal scanning and the slow one for vertical scanning of the camera in a manner identical to that described below for the cathode-ray tube display, called a *kinescope*.

■PICTURE TUBE.—The cathode emits a beam of electrons that is focused into a spot where it strikes the screen. The screen is coated with a phosphor, which emits light when it is struck by electrons. The brightness of the light spot depends on the energy with which the beam strikes the phosphor. This energy is controlled by the strength of the video signal, which in turn depends on the brightness of the corresponding spot at the camera.

The electron beam is made to scan in accordance with the synchronizing signals, which generate two sawtooth waves. One of these occurs 15,750 times a second and is applied to the horizontal deflection coils; the other occurs 60 times per second and is applied to the vertical reflection coils.

It is a law of electricity that a current (a moving electron is a current) going through a magnetic field is deflected at right angles to both the direction of the current and of the magnetic field by an amount that depends on the strength of both. Therefore, a set of coils that produces a vertical magnetic field of linearly increasing intensity (sawtooth) will cause the beam to move horizontally parallel to itself at a uniform rate. Another set of coils produces a horizontal field for vertical deflection. In this manner, the spot on the screen of the cathode-ray tube is made to scan horizontally and vertically, line-by-line and field-by-field, until the whole picture is covered.

The sawtooth wave is initiated by its synchronizing signal. To keep the initiation of the sawtooth, and therefore the start of the line, from being disturbed by noise or interference, a *fly-wheel circuit* is used that is unaffected by transient disturbances. The sawtooth is generated from a free-running oscillator at the normal synchronizing frequency. Its time relation (phase) is adjusted to correspond to the average phase of synchronizing pulse. Thus, the deflection is made essentially noise-free.

To prevent the average picture brightness from being affected by automobile ignition and similar noise, or by airplane flutter, the gain of the receiver is controlled by the average value of many synchronizing pulses, with the rest of the signal shut out. Because the synchronizing pulses occur only 15 per cent of the time, instead of 100 per cent, it is less affected by noise.

Black-and-white television requires the transmission of the "brightness" of successive points in an image. Color television requires that their *hue* and *color saturation* be transmitted as well. This is accomplished by adding a *color subcarrier*, within the black-and-white signal, which is doubly modulated, in *phase* and *amplitude* to transmit *hue* and *saturation* respectively. —Charles J. Hirsch

Typewriter, a mechanical device that produces printed copy a single character at a time as it is operated. Typewriters are either operated entirely manually or with the aid of an electric drive motor. Manual typewriters rely on the force of the operator's hand and fingers applied to the keys to operate the linkage and create the type impression. Electric typewriters are actuated by the motor which supplies the force necessary while the keys are simply control elements. Operators of manual machines must develop a uniform touch or pressure on the keys to produce letters of equal density. The electric typewriter has the advantage of producing uniform letter quality despite variations in the operator's touch or the force applied.

When the operator depresses a key, the printed character is produced by a block of raised type that strikes a carbon-impregnated ribbon, transferring the raised impression to the paper. The roller, or *platen,* around which the paper is wrapped, advances one character each time a key is struck. Normally, a cloth ribbon impregnated with ink is used. While the cloth ribbon is reusable, paper ribbons are good for only a single impression.

The average typewriter has approximately 43 keys, each with an upper and lower case letter selected by means of a shift control. Standard features also include adjustable margins, tabulators, and touch control.

Many special typewriters are available for specific jobs. Long carriage machines are made for the preparation of special documents such as accounting ledgers. The Varityper is a machine with easily interchangeable type faces, enabling a typist to produce copy with numerous type sizes, foreign language characters, and scientific symbols.

Though the typewriter has become an essential tool of industry and is found in many homes, it was not widely used until the 1880's. More than 150 years earlier, in 1714, a patent was granted by Queen Anne of England to Henry Mill for "an artificial machine or method for the impressing or transcribing of letters singly or progressively one after another, as in writing, whereby all writings whatsoever may be engrossed in paper or parchment so neat and exact as not to be distinguished from print." Though no model or drawing of Mill's design

TYPE sphere aids typing speed, accuracy.

exists, it is clear that he had attempted to produce a typewriter.

The first American patent for a typewriter was granted in 1829 to William Burt of Detroit. Burt's machine, called a *Typographer,* was never put into production. In 1843 Charles Thurber of Worcester, Mass., patented a typewriter that incorporated the first roller platen, a feature of almost all modern typewriters.

Serious development of a practical, commercially successful typing machine was started in 1867 in Milwaukee, Wis., by C. L. Sholes. His initial inspiration was an article in the *Scientific American* that described the invention of the *Pterotype* by John Pratt. The article pointed out the benefits of such a machine and the fame and fortune that its inventor could expect.

Sholes and two friends spent seven years building numerous prototypes until they had a practical working model. Sholes and his financial backer, James Densmore, then made an arrangement with E. Remington and Sons at Ilion, N.Y., in 1873 to put the typewriter into production. Remington, a well-known arms and sewing machine manufacturer, had the experience required to produce equipment consisting of numerous small parts.

A team of expert mechanics was put to work perfecting the details and readying the device for production. One problem was how to arrange the keyboard. Originally the letters were arranged alphabetically, but this proved impractical because the most frequently used letters were not the most accessible and the type bars frequently collided. Rearranging the keyboard in the same sequence as a printer's type case, in which the type is arranged for convenience, proved to be successful and this arrangement is still in use. The first commercial typewriter, Remington No. 1, was produced in September 1873.

This early machine was built into its own stand and used a foot-pedal carriage return. By 1876 a manual return replaced the foot pedal and the typewriter could be used on any table top. Remington Model No. 2 was designed and produced in 1878 as the first machine with both capital and lower-case letters.

In 1925 Remington produced the first electric typewriter, which was designed to produce copies of invoices and other multicarbon documents. By the end of World War II the potential of the electric typewriter to produce superior correspondence had become evident and numerous machines were being sold.

The most unusual electric model now available is the International Business Machine *Selectric,* introduced in 1961. This typewriter features a stationary roll platen and has the raised type characters on the surface of a plastic ball. When a key is depressed the ball rotates to the proper position and is depressed against the ribbon and paper. Character spacing is provided by the ball traveling along the platen and typefaces can be changed quickly by replacing the ball. —Joseph J. Kelleher

Xograph, the first mass-production process for achieving three-dimensional reproduction of a photograph that could be seen without viewing aids. The first photograph to be reproduced in this way was a black-and-white illustration for an article about Thomas A. Edison that appeared in *Look* Magazine on Feb. 25, 1964. A later issue of *Look* on April 7, 1964, contained a four-color advertisement produced by the same process.

To make an Xograph, a screen is placed in front of the film. The image is divided into hundreds of vertical parallel strips. After the film is processed, press plates are made in the conventional manner. In printing, a viewing screen is applied by coating the printed surface. The screen focuses on the vertical strips in the picture and provides the viewer with the illusion of depth.

The Xograph process was cooperatively developed by the *Look* Magazine division of Cowles Communications, Inc., and Eastman Chemical Products, Inc. A major technical breakthrough was the synthesis of *Epolene,* the plastic used for coating the viewing screen. Epolene has the required optical properties, is water-clear, adheres to paper, and has an optimum melting point for use on a high-speed press.

The original camera designed for this process was a 6-foot cube weighing half a ton. Later models became more mobile, consisting of three segmented parts: the camera proper, the control panel, and the electronic console. Their lenses are interchangeable from wide-angle to telephoto with a range of focus from 3 feet to infinity. The exposure may vary from 5 to 20 seconds. Although film size is 11 x 14 inches, the maximum of an Xograph is 8½ x 11 inches. The printing accuracy required is ten times normal.

Cowles Communications, Inc., publishers of *Look,* have organized a subsidiary, Visual Panographics, Inc., to make the process available commercially. It is being used by various companies for magazine covers and advertisements, books, counter displays, greeting cards, direct mail, post cards, and calendars.
—Marvin C. Whatmore

BIBLIOGRAPHY

BUCHSBAUM, WALTER H. *Fundamentals of Television.* John F. Rider Publisher, Inc., 1964.

CROWHURST, NORMAN H. *Stereophonic Sound.* John F. Rider Publisher, Inc., 1961.

FOSTER, LEROY E. *Telemetry Systems.* John Wiley & Sons, Inc., 1965.

GLASSTONE, SAMUEL. *Sourcebook on the Space Sciences.* D. Van Nostrand Co., Inc., 1965.

HAY, WILLIAM W. *An Introduction to Transportation Engineering.* John Wiley & Sons, Inc., 1961.

JANE'S ALL THE WORLD'S AIRCRAFT. S. Low, Marston & Co., Ltd., 1965/66.

LEE, MARSHALL. *Bookmaking; the Illustrated Guide to Design and Production.* R. R. Bowker Co., 1965.

MANDL, MATTHEW. *Fundamentals of Electronics.* 2d ed. Prentice-Hall, Inc., 1965.

MARCUS, ABRAHAM AND MARCUS, WILLIAM. *Elements of Radio.* 5th ed. Prentice-Hall, Inc., 1965.

RHODE, ROBERT B. AND McCALL, FLOYD H. *Introduction to Photography.* The Macmillan Co., 1965.

SCHNEIDER, HERMAN AND SCHNEIDER, NINA. *Your Telephone and How It Works.* 3rd ed. McGraw-Hill, Inc., 1965.

SIMON, IRVING B. *The Story of Printing; From Wood Blocks to Electronics.* Harvey House, Inc., 1965.

WOODS, ALLAN. *Modern Newspaper Production.* Harper & Row, Publishers, Inc., 1963.

VISUAL PANOGRAPHICS, INC.

THREE-DIMENSIONAL CAMERA was used to take the picture facing the title page. The special photographic process, called Xograph, was pioneered by *Look* Magazine. The unique optical equipment produces a print that is then coated with Epolene, a plastic material.

MATERIALS AND STRUCTURES

Introduction.—Structures have long constituted one of man's most evident and outstanding achievements in his efforts to adapt and shape the resources of his environment to the evolving material, social, and economic needs of civilized life. Seven of the outstanding structures of antiquity were known as "The Wonders of the World," and a number of the great constructions of the present century have been awarded similar distinction.

The needs that have challenged the skills and abilities of the master builder to provide such works have been varied. Meanwhile, the resources available with which to meet them, notably the materials, have likewise depended on the environment and age and are reflected in the scope and character of the structure provided.

Structural Requirements.—The varied needs of modern life pose a wide variety of structural problems, from buildings and bridges to dams, canals, and water supplies.

Over the centuries, the provision of shelters for homes and other buildings has evolved from the huts of primitive man to the most typically American structure of the present day, the "skyscraper." The predominantly agricultural way of life and economy of earlier centuries likewise prompted the construction of pioneer irrigation and drainage structures. Later, urban growth similarly demanded water supplies, streets, and other outstanding municipal works. The birth of trade and commerce has further challenged the skill of the structural expert in providing the essential arteries of transportation—roads, tunnels, bridges, canals, harbors, and river improvements. Successive improvements in vehicles, in more recent years, have required the building of the distinguished structures characteristic of the Railroad Age and of the current Highway Era.

Other needs, also, have long stimulated important technical advances. In the later Middle Ages, military interests led to the construction of one of man's most impressive structures: the medieval castle, the fortress-home of the Age of the Nobles. Two of man's outstanding structural achievements were inspired by religious motives: the massive pyramids of Egypt and, in sharp contrast, the daringly slender Gothic cathedral, "a bird-cage in stone" and quite as much a structural as an artistic triumph.

While many of these social and economic needs are thus as old as civilized life itself, the resources available to the structural expert have been vastly increased, notably in the last century and especially since the beginning of the twentieth century. As a result, modern works have set new records for size and scope.

Materials.—Among the physical resources available to the planner and builder, materials have played a vital role in meeting these challenges. Historians usually refer to the Stone Age (about 3500–3000 B.C.), supplemented

PUBLICITY CONSULTANTS, INC.

THE WORLD'S TALLEST skyscraper, New York's Empire State Building, rests on a steel framework that weighs 60,000 tons.

by an early use of copper and by the Bronze Age. About 1200 B.C., the Iron Age, in turn, followed a limited earlier use of meteoric iron. Actually, metals long remained scarce and costly, and were limited to tools, weapons, and fastenings. It was not until the eighteenth century in Britain that cast iron became available in quantity and at a cost that made possible its use a structural material. The world's first iron bridge was not built until 1779, at Coalbrookdale, England. Wrought iron followed with Henry Cort's puddling process about 1800 and the development of rolling processes to make bars and shapes. A century was to pass, however, before Henry Bessemer's method of producing steel led to the building of the first all-steel bridge in the United States in 1878.

From the structural standpoint, therefore, man was limited in materials to timber, stone, and brick—essentially the resources of the Stone Age—until well into the nineteenth century. In fact, it was not until the turn of the present century that another material, portland cement, was effectively developed to replace stone in construction.

■**CEMENT.**—The early Greeks had discovered that a mixture of Santorin earth (a volcanic ash from the island of Santorin) with lime produced a "natural" hydraulic cement which, unlike lime itself, would harden in

bulk or under water. The Romans, likewise, found that the volcanic ash pozzuolana produced a similar product. They were the first major users of a mixture of sand, broken stone, and cement (concrete) instead of stone or brick masonry.

These materials were of limited, local occurrence, however, and modern hydraulic cement did not become more widely available until the earlier years of the nineteenth century. John Smeaton in Britain had noted that cement made from limestone containing clay possessed hydraulic quantities and, about 1820, Joseph Aspden developed "portland" cement, so called because it resembled the famous limestone from the Isle of Portland. In the United States, the earlier "natural" cement had been introduced in building the Erie Canal, completed in 1825. Since portland was imported, it remained costly, and stone masonry, using a minimum of mortar, was standard until the birth of the American portland cement industry at the end of the nineteenth century. The New Croton Dam, built for the water supply of New York City in 1895–1907, was the last great stone masonry structure in the United States, the last in which natural cement was used, and the first in which portland was employed.

■**METALS AND CONCRETE.**—Alloy steels, aluminum, and other manufactured materials have also been developed, but their use has been confined largely to building construction. The combination of concrete and steel—reinforced concrete—however, has been widely used in recent years in "thin-shell" specialized engineering structures, such as airport structures.

Labor and Equipment.—These are the chief resources, other than materials, that have affected structural developments. As in the case of metals and cement, construction equipment long remained limited. Man-powered devices prevailed until steam power was applied to construction needs. The steam-powered pile driver, steam-driven pumps, steam drills, the steam shovel, and other modern devices gradually replaced ancient manpower equipment in the nineteenth century. This replacement of man by machine has been particularly characteristic of American practice.

In Europe, skilled labor generally has been plentiful while, relatively speaking, materials have been costly. In the United States, on the other hand, materials have been less costly while there has been a shortage of skilled labor, partly as a result of the availability of cheap land in the last century. Increasing labor costs, therefore, encouraged the development and use of machines. Here again, the change has been particularly rapid in the present century. It is interesting to note that, following the earlier use of steam shovels, there was a notable advance in rock drilling and the machine handling of excavated material when the Chicago Drainage Canal was built in 1892–1900, while the first New York subway, opened in 1904,

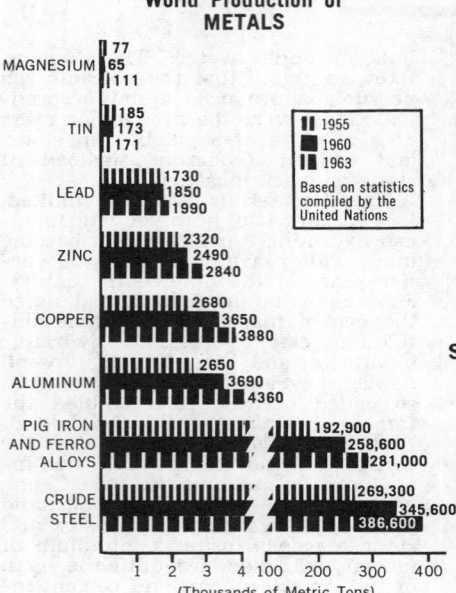

World Production of METALS

MAGNESIUM 77 / 65 / 111

TIN 185 / 173 / 171

LEAD 1730 / 1850 / 1990

ZINC 2320 / 2490 / 2840

COPPER 2680 / 3650 / 3880

ALUMINUM 2650 / 3690 / 4360

PIG IRON AND FERRO ALLOYS 192,900 / 258,600 / 281,000

CRUDE STEEL 269,300 / 345,600 / 386,600

1955 / 1960 / 1963
Based on statistics compiled by the United Nations

1 2 3 4 100 200 300 400
(Thousands of Metric Tons)

was the last great American pick-and-shovel and horse-and-cart construction project.

One result of mechanized construction is that it has speeded up operations and thus reduced the loss of income on expended capital. For example, the number of men and hoists that could be used on a stone-masonry work was limited. On the Croton Dam, the best record was 17,-188 cubic yards placed in one month. This was increased to 84,450 in placing the massive concrete of the Kensico Dam in 1913, while on the Grand Coulee Dam of 1939, with modern machines and belt conveyors, over 400,000 cubic yards were recorded in one month.

The advent of new materials and machine equipment has not only made possible far greater structures than the world has ever known but has also solved a problem that man for centuries was unable to meet. In building the stone arch bridges of earlier days, it was seldom possible with the equipment of the time to unwater, excavate, and build bridge piers more than 8 or 10 feet below water level. While few stone arches failed, foundation failures were frequent, as floods undermined the shallow piers. Today, open cofferdam foundations have been carried down to 80 feet or more below water level, using steel sheet piling and modern pumps and excavating equipment. Similarly, pneumatic and other methods make it possible today to provide adequate foundations under conditions that would have rendered such undertakings impossible a century ago.

These advances, involving major capital expenditures for equipment to avoid or reduce the costs of hand labor, and the emphasis on speed in construction have also brought about a marked change in the organization, planning, and management of construction operations. The building of many structures, such as stone arch bridges, has long required effective planning, direction, and skilled labor, but the earlier years of the rough-and-ready contractor bossing a group of husky laborers has given way to fully planned, scheduled, and organized construction operations under the direction of engineers who specialize in such work. As in industry and manufactures, engineered construction has become a major, exacting, and important field of engineering endeavor, and great works are completed today in far shorter time than was required for many minor undertakings in earlier years. (See *Construction Engineering,* Page 1638.)

Structural Mechanics.—While the major structural forms of the present day—the beam and column, the arch, retaining walls and dams, the truss, and suspension bridges—have long been known and used, their earlier design was based almost solely on an intuitive structural sense and judgment, matured through experience and observation. There was, in fact, little incentive to develop more fully rationalized and exact quantitative, mathematical and scientific techniques of design. Although this has led to greater safety and, especially, made a saving of materials possible, these values were earlier relatively unimportant. Minerals were both plentiful and inexpensive, but they were also far from uniform in their strength qualities. The loads to which earlier works were subjected not only were moderate, but many earlier structures would, by modern standards, be characterized as generously "over-designed." On the other hand, the development of more costly materials, of the truss and other forms, and the greatly increased loads of a Railroad Era inevitably led to a search to replace the earlier purely qualitative techniques by the far more effective and certain methods of the present day. The theoretical studies of engineering science, notably aided by physics, and coupled with practical testing, observation, and analysis by engineers, have been basic in planning and designing our modern record-breaking structures.

The ancient Greeks early noted that a stone beam failed by the breaking of its lower face in tension. In a few notable cases, they reinforced such beams with iron bars imbedded in the lower surface. Galileo, in addition to his purely scientific interests, studied the mechanics of beams and, although his observation was based on erroneous stress assumptions, noted that their strength varied directly with their breadth, but as the square of their depth. Later, the recognition of the elastic behavior of materials led to what became known as "the common theory of flexure," which Charles Augustin de Coulomb, the French military engineer, first expounded about 1780.

The problem of the continuous beam (one built over more than two simple supports) also attracted early attention. However, the first realistic and effective approach to this problem was prompted by the adoption, as the nineteenth century came to a close, of reinforced concrete, in which a notable saving of materials was secured through continuity in design.

■**DAMS AND WALLS.**—Another French engineer, Bernard Forest de Belidor, had advanced theories on retaining and quay walls to which Coulomb added some refinements that later workers, such as William J. M. Rankine in Britain, developed still further. Such walls are subjected to the action of widely varying and varied forces. Only in the last twenty-five years have many of the uncertainties of foundations and earth pressure been resolved and evaluated through the modern engineering science of soil mechanics.

Another retaining structure in which new records of height and size have been made in recent years is the masonry dam of the so-called gravity type. This type was late in development; the first rationalized, truly modern form did not appear until 1866. Even today, such uncertain factors as "up lift" still perplex the dam designer.

■**ARCHES.**—Similarly, although the basic action of the masonry arch has long been understood, the so-called spandrel-filled arch involves so many uncertain forces that design is based largely on arches that have been built by experience, and only an approximate checking through stress analysis is possible. The far later appearance of the modern ribbed arch, however, beginning with the stone Luxembourg span of 1898–1903 but later more fully exploited in reinforced concrete, has led to the development of the modern theory of the elastic arch and to the construction of many notable and daring spans.

■**TRUSSES.**—The truss, so widely used today, also has been known for centuries, but its first recorded use as a bridge form was about 1570. It was later carried forward by Swiss engineers. Nevertheless, the first iron bridges followed the early arch rather than the truss form, substituting cast-iron sections for the stone voussoirs. In the United States, however, the need for many inexpensive bridges and the abundance of timber led first to a remarkable timber truss era. Later, these spans gave way to iron trusses, and various forms were devised to provide for the more effective and economical use of this more costly new material. This advance required a more thorough knowledge and evaluation of the stresses in such framed structures. In 1847, a pioneer American truss builder, Squire Whipple, published the first text on truss analysis.

American engineers in the closing years of the nineteenth century were busy replacing earlier iron bridges with far heavier steel structures to meet the increasing locomotive loads of the Railroad Era. But new forms also were appearing. In 1917, Gustav Lindenthal set a new record with his "continuous" truss of two 775-foot spans for the Sciotoville (Ohio) bridge. The coming of the Highway Era, however, was to bring the great bridge spans of more recent years as well as interesting new truss and arch forms and record-breaking suspension spans.

■**SUSPENSIONS.**—The rise of the suspension bridge again demonstrates the vital role which materials have played in the evolution of structures. Crude suspensions of vines or ropes had been built in many lands, but the adoption and development of this form, which now far exceeds all others in record spans, awaited the advent of more permanent and stronger materials. The pioneer American bridge builder James Finley, in his first suspension of 1801, used links of wrought iron bars to form a "chain" suspension. Louis J. Vicat in France in 1830 adopted iron wire in lieu of bars and later developments have produced steel wire of remarkable tensile strength. The British engineer Thomas Telford reached a record 580-foot span in his "chain" suspension bridge in Menai (Wales) in 1826. Later great spans have been of wire and built in the United States. Washington A. Roebling, son of the American wire pioneer John A. Roebling, set a record in 1883 with the 1,595-foot Brooklyn span at New York. Finally, the cantilever span record of 1,800 feet was surpassed by the Ambassador bridge at Detroit of 1,850 feet in 1929. Within two years this was almost doubled by the completion of the 3,500-foot George Washington bridge in New York, and this, in turn, was followed in 1937 by the 4,200-foot Golden Gate at San Francisco, and the 4,260-foot Verrazano span at New York in 1965. Over 100,000 miles of wire were used in the 26-inch diameter cables of the George Washington span.

Inherently flexible "stiffening trusses" were early used in suspension bridges to avoid excessive local deflection by distributing loads. Such bridges thus became combination structures, and the involved mechanics of what, in effect, was a suspended truss, was not well developed until the earlier years of the present century. The susceptibility of such spans to aerodynamic action also led to some early failures. As spans increased, dead load mounts and stiffening were less necessary but the collapse of the Tacoma (Wash.) bridge in 1940, due to air action, again raised this problem. Today, modern design as well as modern materials make possible a still further span advance in one of the most spectacular structures of modern life.

Structural Engineer.—a specialist in the planning and design of a particular type of structure. As early as 600 B.C., the Greek historian Herodotus coined the title *architekton* for the builder of what would now be called an engineering work, a water-supply tunnel on the island of Samos. This "archtechnician" and the later Roman *architectus* were engaged in both architectural and engineering practice as we know them today. The first specialization arose from the term *ingenium,* or product of genius, which had been used as early as 200 A.D. to describe the engines of war of that day—catapults, battering rams, etc. By the late Middle Ages, the builder of fortresses became known as an *ingeniator*, or engineer. Military engineering became a specialty.

In the Renaissance, architecture began both to emphasize its "fine" art qualities and to draw away from the practical arts, while the rise of new needs, notably canals and other civic works that were unrelated to the artistic approach, tended further to divide the structural profession. It was not until 1802, however, that the last book to treat separately of both professions, architecture and engineering, appeared.

Not only did new engineering needs lead to this divorce, but the architect failed to follow the engineer in his use of new materials, in the development of more fully rationalized techniques of design, and in emphasis on utilitarian and economic values. In recent years architecture has been in transition, turning from a long-prevailing aesthetic approach to design, based on classical examples, to the search for a more practical evaluation of the artistic possibilities inherent in the new structural forms and materials, and to the effective utilization of new services developed by the engineer.

The structural engineer has continued to develop the scientific techniques of design and to further advances in materials, methods, and equipment, in seeking the fullest, most effective and economical use of all available resources in meeting the problems of his day. This involves a full and impartial analysis of the present and possible future needs and requirements of the structure he seeks to provide, and an equally objective evaluation of available resources in a balancing of alternate possibilities and costs. The professional structural engineer, therefore, requires not only special technical training, matured through experience, but also a keen sense of economic factors and values in seeking a synthesis leading to final plans and designs. —**James Kip Finch**

UNITED STATES STEEL

CATWALKS used by workers stringing steel suspension cables link towers of the Verrazano-Narrows Bridge under construction.

MATERIALS AND STRUCTURES GLOSSARY

Abrasives, materials of extreme hardness that are used to shape metal, wood, and stone by wearing away or grinding. Abrasive grains are used loose, mixed with oil to create a paste or slurry, compressed into wheels or blocks, or glued to a flexible backing such as cloth or paper.

In modern industry abrasives are used to polish, clean, cut, and machine materials such as wood, glass, stone, plastics, and ceramics. The high coefficient of friction of abrasive materials makes them essential in the formulation of nonslip paints and floor tile, brake linings, and clutch disks.

The grinding wheel of bonded abrasive grains has become a basic tool of the metalworking industry. Hand-held pneumatic or electric grinders are used to rough-grind and polish castings, welded joints, and metal stampings. Precision grinding machines are used to finish bearing surfaces, cam profiles, cylinder bores, printing-paper rolls, shafts, and pistons. An essential machine required for every metalworking shop is the tool grinder which is used to sharpen both hand tools and machine tool bits and cutters.

Abrasives may be divided into either natural or manufactured materials. Natural abrasives such as sand, emery, flint, sandstone, and silica have been used since the Neolithic period, which dates from 15,000 to 5000 B.C. The importance of abrasives in prehistoric cultures cannot be overestimated. Tribes or races that learned to cut grooves and drill holes in stones with abrasives had a distinct advantage over their neighbors. The holes and grooves enabled the prehistoric toolmaker to attach handles to his stone weapons securely, thereby producing a superior product. This seemingly simple advantage frequently enabled one tribe or race to conquer and dominate other peoples.

The first use of the grinding wheel was for the milling of grain. The wheel was mounted horizontally and driven by animals, water, or wind. Nearly 1,000 years passed before the grindstone was mounted vertically—on a horizontal axis—and turned by hand to sharpen or polish metal. Drawings in an illuminated manuscript known as the *Utrecht Psalter* (850 A.D.) illustrate the first recorded use of a grinding wheel for metalworking.

Since grinding wheels were produced from blocks of natural stone, grinding by this method was limited by the abrasive quality of the available stone. To take advantage of the wide range of natural abrasives available in granular form, metal and glass-workers in the fifteenth century began using wheels coated with grains. Tallow, wax, or oil was mixed with emery, garnet, or diamond dust and the mixture used to coat wood or metal wheels. Coarser grains of emery were used for metal removal while finer grains or dust, sometimes under pressure, could be used for polishing or light grinding.

The first synthetic abrasive, silicon carbide, was produced by Edward Goodrich Acheson in 1891. Sand (SiO_2), coke (C), sawdust, and salt are mixed and heated by graphite electrodes to 2,400° C. The basic chemical reaction is $SiO_2 + 3C \rightarrow SiC + 2CO$. The function of the sawdust is to create vent holes for the escape of gas and volatile compounds produced by the reaction of the salt with impurities. After firing, the silicon carbide is picked out and crushed to form grains of different sizes. Acheson called the crystals *Carborundum,* a trade name still in use.

The discovery of aluminum oxide in 1897 is credited to C. B. Jacobs. Abrasive aluminum oxide is made by crushing high-quality bauxite, calcinating it, adding coke and iron, and heating the mass to 2,100° C in an arc furnace.

Abrasives, both natural and synthetic, are generally classified as to hardness in terms of the Mohs scale, devised by the German mineralogist Friedrich Mohs. This classification rates talc as 1 and the diamond as 10. The accompanying table shows the relative hardness of some abrasive materials as ranked on both Mohs' and the Knoop hardness scales. The Knoop scale, developed by the American chemist F. Knoop, is a

Relative Hardness Scales

Substance	Mohs Hardness	Knoop Hardness
Talc	1	
Gypsum	2	30
Calcite	3	135
Fluorite	4	160
Apatite	5	400
Feldspar	6	550
Quartz	7	820
Topaz	8	1350
Aluminum Oxide	9	2000
Silicon Carbide	9 plus or 9.5	2500
Boron Carbide	9 plus or 9.75	2800
Diamond	10	6500

more precise method for the classification of hardness. Values are determined by pressing a uniform diamond pyramid into the material with a standardized load. The measure of the material's hardness is determined by the size of the indentation.

Grinding wheels are produced by mixing the desired abrasive with a binder, then compacting the mix in a press followed by firing in a furnace. After firing, the wheel is dressed and ground to final shape and spin-tested at high speed to check its structural soundness. Materials such as sodium silicate, rubber, shellac, and resinous compounds are used to bond the abrasive grains. Selection of a bonding agent depends on the grinding application. Rigid ceramics are required for precision grinding while rough hand grinding usually calls for resilient bonding materials such as shellac or rubber.
—Joseph J. Kelleher

Acoustical Engineering, the branch of engineering that deals with sound, particularly in theaters, auditoriums, churches, television studios, or other enclosed areas designed primarily for listening to music or speech.

One of the most important acoustical characteristics of a room is its *reverberation time,* the length of time needed for a sound impulse to fall to one-millionth of its initial intensity. A room lined with carpets, drapes, and other soft, sound-absorbing materials may have a reverberation time of a small fraction of a second. Such rooms, free of sound reflections from walls and floors, are sound-muffled or dead. A hard-walled gymnasium, on the other hand, may have a reverberation time of many seconds. In such rooms, sounds are reflected many times from wall to wall, reaching the listener at the same time as new sounds from the speaker and thus producing a confusion of sound.

Optimum reverberation times are somewhat less than one second for speech and between 1 and 3.5 seconds for music. The reverberation time of a room is controlled by lining walls and other reflecting surfaces with the required amount of sound-absorbing material. Recording studios, which must accommodate a wide variety of speech and music, are often equipped with removable wall panels of sound-absorbing and sound-reflecting materials.

Certain curved wall surfaces produce loud and soft sound regions in an auditorium. A sound-reflecting wall far removed from the speaker can produce a loud and annoying echo. Two parallel reflecting walls often produce a sequence of echoes, a phenomenon called *acoustical flutter.* These disturbing effects can be eliminated by careful design and by proper use of sound-absorbing materials.
—William C. Vergara

Adhesives, materials that can bond two other materials together by adhering strongly to the surfaces of both. In addition, the bond itself must be internally strong or else the bonding action will not be effective. Adhesives are usually applied in the form of solutions, emulsions, or soft gels, but they also can be applied as thin layers of solids that become fluid upon heating. (See also *Glue, Cement.*)
—John Price

Alcohols, a class of organic compounds composed of carbon, hydrogen, and oxygen and containing one or more hydroxyl groups (–OH). The suffix *-ol* or the prefix *hydroxy-* in the name of an organic compound indicates that it is an alcohol. Alcohols may be mono–, di–, tri–, or polyhydric, depending on how many hydroxyl groups they contain. In addition, alcohols are classified as *primary, secondary,* or *tertiary,* depending on whether the carbon atom to which the hydroxyl group is attached is linked with one, two, or three other carbon atoms.

The physical and chemical properties of alcohols depend on their molecular weight and the number and type of hydroxyl groups in the molecule. Alcohols are colorless, flammable, and toxic. Those of low molecular weight are liquids while those of high molecular weight are waxy-like solids.

Lower alcohols, such as ethyl alcohol, are generally employed as solvents, antifreezes, and extractants. Higher alcohols, such as cetyl alcohol, are used as antifoaming agents and evaporation retardants in reservoirs. The largest use of alcohols, however, is as intermediates in the production of other chemical compounds.

Fermentation of natural products, chemical syntheses based on hydrocarbons derived from petroleum or natural gas, and chemical treatment of natural fats and oils are the three most important sources of monohydric aliphatic alcohols. The fermentation of sugars and starches to produce alcoholic beverages has been carried out since the beginning of recorded history. However, fermentation is no longer the major source of lower alcohols, although it still is widely used. Synthetic processes are now used industrially to manufacture lower alcohols. These processes include oxidation, hydration, and oxonation of hydrocarbons; reduction of synthesis gas; condensation and reduction of aldehydes derived from alcohols; and reduction of animal fats and vegetable oils. For example, *methanol* (CH_3OH) the simplest alcohol, is produced by the catalytic reduction of synthesis gas (carbon monoxide and hydrogen). A major source of higher monohydric alcohols, which are used to make detergents, is the reduction of animal fats and vegetable oils, either by catalytic hydrogenation or by treatment with reducing metals.

Esters of the lower monohydric alcohols are used extensively as solvents for a wide variety of synthetic products. Esters from higher alcohols and dibasic acids are used as plasticizers for vinyl, cellulosic, and acrylic resins, and for synthetic rubber.

—John Price

Alkalies, substances that have marked basic—in contrast to acidic—properties. Chemically, they include the caustic hydroxides of lithium, sodium, potassium, rubidium, cesium, and (for practical purposes) ammonium salts. Commercially, the alkali industry is centered in the production of sodium carbonate (soda ash), sodium hydroxide (caustic soda), and chlorine—which is included because it is produced along with caustic soda by alkali manufacturers.

Caustic soda and chlorine are produced by the electrolysis of brine (sodium chloride) solutions. Chlorine is produced at the anode (positive electrode) and hydrogen, together with sodium hydroxide ($NaOH$), at the cathode (negative electrode). Anode and cathode products must be separated. This has led to the development of many ingenious cell designs. (See *Caustic Soda,* Page 1633.)

Sodium carbonate (Na_2CO_3), or *soda ash,* occurs in, and once was extracted from, plant ashes. Most commercial sodium carbonate is produced by the *Solvay process.* In an initial reaction, salt is converted to sodium bicarbonate, which precipitates and is separated. Heating the bicarbonate produces sodium carbonate.

Alkalies are used in the manufacture of glass, soap, various chemicals, cleaners, detergents, pulp and paper, water softeners, and textiles, and in petroleum refining. —John Price

Alloys, metallic substances composed of two or more chemical elements, of which at least one is a metal. Pure metals seldom possess sufficient strength for engineering purposes, such as building structures and machines. By adding the proper kinds and amounts of other chemical elements to pure metals, metallurgists create alloys that have mechanical, physical and/or chemical properties that are more suitable for a given purpose than the unalloyed metals.

■**ALLOYING METHODS.**—Alloys may be made by fusing (melting) the desired components together or by powder metallurgy. The *fusion method* is used to produce by far the largest proportion of alloys. When proper amounts of the constituents are melted together, they dissolve in each other. Upon cooling, the solution crystallizes to form a solid mass. Solidification of a pure metal or a compound occurs at a definite temperature. However, an alloy solidifies over a range of temperatures, and solid crystals of different compositions separate from the liquid at various temperature levels, according to a predictable pattern for a given alloy system. The kinds, sizes, and distribution of the crystals constitute the structure of the alloy. The structure of most alloys produced by fusion consists of crystals representing solid solutions, eutectics, intermetallic compounds, chemical compounds of metals with nonmetals (carbides, nitrides, phosphides, sulfides, oxides, etc.), or combinations of two or more of these. Their proportions depend upon the composition of the liquid solution and the degree of equilibrium attained.

In making alloys by *powder metallurgy,* powders of the required constituents are mixed and then pressed in molds at high pressure to form a *compact* of the desired shape and density. The compact is then heated to a sufficiently high temperature, usually in a furnace having a controlled atmosphere, to coalesce the powders, usually without melting any of the components. This heating operation is called *sintering.* Many alloys that cannot be made in any other practical way can be made by powder metallurgy.

The hardness, toughness, corrosion resistance, and other properties of an alloy depend upon its structure. The structure, and therefore the properties, of an alloy can in most cases be altered, sometimes over wide limits, by heat treatment (controlled heating

Principal Alloying Elements

Aluminum—deoxidizes; contributes lightness; restricts grain growth.

Chromium—strengthens and hardens; increases corrosion, oxidation and abrasion resistance.

Cobalt—increases hardness.

Copper—improves durability, machinability and high-temperature mechanical properties.

Manganese—increases shock resistance and hardness; counteracts embrittlement.

Molybdenum—increases hardness, hot strength and resistance to corrosion, abrasion and creep.

Nickel—strengthens and toughens steels.

Phosphorus—strengthens; improves machinability and corrosion resistance.

Silicon—deoxidizes; increases rust resistance, hardness and strength.

Tin—improves welding characteristics.

Titanium—inertizes carbon; reduces hardness; prevents austinite formation; prevents chromium depletion during long heating.

Tungsten—increases hot strength, abrasion resistance and hardness.

Vanadium—increases hardness in solution and tempering resistance; promotes secondary hardening and fine grain structure.

Zinc—improves durability, corrosion resistance and high-temperature properties.

Commercially Important Alloys
(Percentage Compositions)

Alloy	Carbon	Chromium	Copper	Iron	Lead	Manganese	Nickel	Tin	Zinc	other
Babbitt metal	—	—	4-5	—	—	—	—	90-92	—	Antimony
Brass	—	—	65-85	—	—	—	—	—	15-35	—
Britannia metal	—	—	4-16	—	—	—	—	80-94	1.5-5	Bismuth, Antimony
Bronze	—	—	80	—	—	—	—	10	0-10	Antimony
Carboloy	—	—	—	—	—	—	—	—	—	Tungsten-Carbide, Cobalt
Duralumin	—	—	4	—	—	trace	—	—	—	Aluminum, Magnesium
Inconel	trace	15	trace	7	—	trace	77	—	—	Silicon, Sulfur
Iron, cast	3.4	—	—	94.3	—	trace	—	—	—	Silicon
Iron, wrought	trace	—	—	98	—	—	—	—	—	Slag
Permalloy	—	trace	—	10-70	—	—	30-90	—	—	Molybdenum
Pewter	—	—	—	—	10-15	—	—	85-90	—	—
Solder	—	—	—	—	67	—	—	33	—	—
Stainless steel	trace	13-18	—	74-87	—	—	0-8	—	—	—
Sterling silver	—	—	7.5	—	—	—	—	—	—	Silver

and cooling cycles at temperatures below the melting point) alone, or by hot and/or cold working combined with heat treatment.

Some alloys can be wrought, that is, shaped by hot or cold working operations such as rolling, drawing, forging, or extrusion. Other alloys cannot be wrought or worked, and must be shaped by casting into molds or by powder-metallurgical methods.

■MAJOR ALLOYS.—Commercial alloys are divided into ferrous and nonferrous alloys. As the names indicate, the principal constituent of the ferrous alloys is the metal iron; the nonferrous alloys usually contain iron in very small amounts, if at all.

The principal *ferrous* alloys are the commercial forms known as cast iron and steel. *Cast iron* includes gray iron, malleable iron, nodular iron, and irons resistant to abrasion (chilled irons and white irons), corrosion (alloyed irons), and heat (also called alloyed irons).

Steel is a generic name for a very large number of cast and wrought ferrous alloys, including carbon steels, alloy steels, and stainless steels. The principal alloying elements, alone or in combinations, used for making alloy steels and alloy cast irons are boron, chromium, cobalt, niobium, copper, manganese, molybdenum, nickel, silicon, tungsten, and vanadium.

The most important commercial nonferrous alloys are based on aluminum, copper, lead, magnesium, nickel, tin, titanium, and zinc. Alloys of the precious metals (gold, silver, and the platinum group) form a special class that will not be considered here.

Cast and wrought alloys based on *aluminum* and *magnesium* and wrought forms of *titanium* alloys have a high strength-to-weight ratio. The aluminum and magnesium alloys are the most widely used of the lightweight alloys.

Copper-base alloys include brasses, leaded brasses, bronzes (including silicon bronze and aluminum bronze), copper-nickel alloys, and nickel silver.

Lead-base alloys include solders, arsenical lead, calcium lead, hard lead (lead-antimony alloys), bearing metals (babbitts), type metals (fusible lead alloys that melt at low temperatures), and terne metal.

Nickel is alloyed principally with copper, molybdenum, or chromium, or with all three, to make alloys resistant to many forms of corrosion. Iron, cobalt, and vanadium are also added to some of the alloys.

Tin provides the base for soft solders, pewter, bearing metals, and *white metal* for die castings.

Zinc is alloyed with aluminum and magnesium, or aluminum, magnesium, and copper, to produce alloys used for die casting.

Special-purpose alloys, not classified as ferrous or nonferrous but according to their uses or special properties, include permanent-magnet alloys, magnetically soft materials, alloys with high electrical resistance, electrical-contact materials, low-expansion alloys, hard-facing alloys, and numerous types of cast and wrought heat-resistant alloys.

—Harold McGannon

Aluminum, a metallic element, chemical symbol Al. It is the most abundant metal in the earth's crust (8.13 per cent), and is found in every continent except Antarctica. Aluminum occurs naturally only in a combined form. Its most common compound is aluminum oxide, which is most often found in clay, granite, slate, and marl. It is commercially produced from a gray-white or brownish ore called *bauxite,* which contains from 45 to 60 per cent aluminum oxide, or *alumina.* The ore was named after the town of Les Baux, France, where it was first discovered. Other important sources of ore are in British and Dutch Guiana, Italy, Jamaica, Australia, Hungary, and parts of Africa. Central Arkansas is the prime source in the United States.

Metallic aluminum is also found in *cryolite,* a sodium-aluminum fluoride used primarily as a bath material in the reduction of alumina to aluminum. *Corundum* is a crystallized alumina found in nature in the form of semiprecious and precious stones: amethyst, emerald, ruby, sapphire, topaz, turquoise, and lapis lazuli. Corundum and *alundum,* artificial oxides of aluminum, are abrasive materials and are used for making laboratory crucibles.

A mixture of granulated or powdered aluminum and iron oxide, called *thermit,* is used for welding. When the aluminum is activated by heating, it takes oxygen away from the iron oxide and forms aluminum oxide, leaving melted, pure iron that fills cracks and fuses the ends of the metals to be joined.

To produce aluminum, the bauxite is first ground and dried, then mixed with a solution of sodium hydroxide, which dissolves the alumina to form sodium aluminate. Silica, iron oxide, and other impurities in the bauxite are precipitated out of solution. Hydrated alumina crystals are used to seed the supersaturated sodium aluminate solution, and crystals of alumina form groups that become heavy enough to settle out of solution. After washing to remove traces of impurities, the alumina hydrate crystals are roasted at more than 2000° F to drive off the chemically combined water, leaving a fine white alumina powder. Then, alumina is dissolved in a bath of molten cryolite and aluminum fluoride in a steel container or cell lined with carbon. A carbon electrode is lowered into the mixture, and direct current (DC) power is applied, with the result that the oxygen of the alumina joins the carbon in the anode in the form of carbon dioxide while the metallic aluminum is freed.

■QUALITIES.—Aluminum is a soft, silver-colored metal with a melting point of 660° C, and a boiling point of 2500° C. Its most noted quality is lightness combined with high relative strength. It has approximately one-third the density of steel, copper, or zinc, and has high resistance to corrosion because it reacts in the air to form a thin surface coating of oxide that protects the remainder of the metal against further corrosion. Aluminum has high strength at low temperatures, making it particularly suitable for cryogenic uses. It ranks just below silver and copper as a conductor of heat and electricity and is being used increasingly as an electric conductor; on a pound-for-pound basis, aluminum's conductivity is more than double that of copper. It is nontoxic and can be easily rolled, hammered, pressed, drawn, or extruded into thousands of shapes and extremely thin thickness.

■INVENTIONAL FABRICATION.—Aluminum was first isolated in pure form by the Danish physicist Hans Christian Oersted in 1825, following unsuccessful attempts at chemically producing the metal by Sir Humphry Davy. It was Davy who called the metal aluminum, the name used in the United States, while it is called *aluminium*

REYNOLDS METALS COMPANY

IN A HYDRAULIC PRESS, aluminum is extruded into a specified shape for use in industry. Aluminum is so easily worked that it may be fashioned into a large variety of shapes.

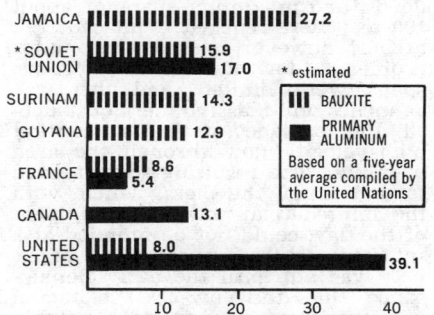

World Production of ALUMINUM in %

JAMAICA 27.2
*SOVIET UNION 15.9 / 17.0
SURINAM 14.3
GUYANA 12.9
FRANCE 8.6 / 5.4
CANADA 13.1
UNITED STATES 8.0 / 39.1

*estimated

BAUXITE
PRIMARY ALUMINUM

Based on a five-year average compiled by the United Nations

10 20 30 40

in the rest of the world. The first commercial production of aluminum was in France in 1855, using a chemical method developed by Henri Sainte-Claire Deville. Commercial production was greatly increased by the almost simultaneous discovery in 1886 of an electrolytic method of producing metallic aluminum, as the *Hall process*, by Charles Martin Hall, an American, and Paul L. T. Héroult, a Frenchman.

While most refining produces aluminum that is at least 99.5 per cent pure, a further refinement permits the production of "super purity" aluminum (99.99 per cent) used in making high-octane gasoline, as foil in the electronics industry, and in jewelry. Most aluminum, however, is used in alloy form. Copper, which permits the alloy to be heat treated, also increases strength and hardness, as do magnesium, manganese, and zinc. Corrosion resistance is provided by manganese and magnesium, while silicon lowers an alloy's melting point for improved fluidity for castings. Other alloying elements are beryllium, bismuth, boron, iron, lead, nickel, sodium, tin, titanium, and zirconium.

Extrusion—forcing heated cast billets through a die to produce an infinite variety of shapes—has become one of the most important methods of forming aluminum products. Castings also consume large quantities of aluminum. Forging or hammering and drawing for fine tolerances are other methods of forming aluminum. Plate, sheet, and foil are rolled in a wide range of thickness.

The building and construction industries use the greatest amount of aluminum for products ranging from foil insulation to door and window frames, siding, and anodized exterior facing products. Aluminum powder is used in paint form to protect other metals. The transportation industry is the second largest user of aluminum for truck-trailers, mobile homes, railroad cars, automobiles, and rapid transit systems. Pleasure boats and commercial vessels increasingly employ aluminum for hulls, superstructures, and other components. For many years, aluminum has been used in aircraft and aerospace applications as a lightweight structural material. Lightweight, air-transportable tanks, armored personnel carriers, and trucks use aluminum extensively.
—Robert H. Chamberlin

Aqueduct, a man-made channel or structure for carrying water. Aqueducts may be divided into two major types: the open channel, or grade-line, aqueduct, and the pressure-pipe line. Early irrigation ditches, or nearby streams, often served for public water supplies, but the Romans, the noted aqueduct builders of ancient times, built aqueducts that served not only the city of Rome but the entire Roman world.

Almost invariably these were grade-line works, artificial channels in which the water flowed as in a slow stream, although they were usually of the so-called *cut-and-cover* form, lined and covered with stone masonry. In crossing valleys, these channels were supported on masonry arches such as those carrying the lines to Rome and to Segovia in Spain. In general, these led to public fountains from which the people drew their needs. The Romans also used some lead pipes for delivery for baths and other services, and in a few rare cases built pressure lines down and across valleys, the so-called *inverted siphons,* in lieu of supporting arches.

Suitable metal, however, for such lines was lacking or costly and was later reclaimed for other purposes. Thus the grade-line type long remained standard; no major early pressure lines remain today, although it appears that one notable early, probably Greek, pressure line at Pergamon in Asia Minor may have been built of bronze pipe. Pipes of bored wood logs were later used for the supply system of the city of London as well as for several early American systems. The advent of a true Age of Iron in the eighteenth century, however, made cast-iron pressure pipe possible. The first such line in the United States was built in Philadelphia about 1820.

A number of European cities, notably in Britain, obtain their water through long pipe lines; especially long lines have also been built in Australia. In the United States, earlier works were usually of the cut-and-cover type. However, the 75-mile Catskill line built in 1914 for New York City was almost entirely a grade line and siphon work, while the 240-mile Colorado River aqueduct for a dozen cities in the Los Angeles area involved open canals, cut-and-cover conduit, siphons, pressure tunnels, and waterpower pumping plants to lift the supply over intervening mountan ranges. —James Kip Finch

Artesian Well, a natural source of water in which the water is forced to the surface by hydrostatic pressure. Two geological conditions are essential to create an artesian water supply. First, beneath the well site, there must be layers of water-bearing material entrapped between watertight, or *impervious,* layers of rock or clay. Second, at some location, the layers of entrapped water-bearing material must be elevated above the well site.

Elevation of the water-bearing material produces the hydrostatic pressure required to bring the water to the surface or above it. In some areas, springs are created when faults or cracks in the watertight layers allow the hydrostatic pressure to force water to the surface. If the water-bearing material is elevated far enough above the well site, the hydrostatic pressure is sufficient to shoot a column of water 100 feet or more above the well.

The conditions required for artesian wells are usually found in the valleys of mountain ranges or other hilly country. In the United States, the alternate layers of water-bearing and impervious material are elevated along the foothills of the Rocky Mountains. From there, the layers sweep downward under Kansas, Nebraska, Montana, and the Dakotas, creating a vast pool with sufficient hydrostatic pressure to force water to the surface. —Joseph J. Kelleher

Asbestos, a general name for the fibrous varieties of a number of rock-forming minerals. Products fabricated from various grades of these mineral fibers do not burn, and they resist chemical attack.

Traditional fine *amphibole asbestos* has high acid resistance and withstands temperatures up to 1,000° C. The other chief type, *serpentine asbestos,* is less resistant to heat and acid attack than the amphibole varieties, but it is used more because it is more abundant.

Mining methods are based on removing the host rock and milling. Open-cast mining is the most common, but underground systems also are used. Block-caving methods, used in Canadian mines, consist of undercutting huge blocks several hundred feet down, which are then progressively caved and loaded from the bottom.

After the fibers have been milled, they are graded by length. Those one-half inch or longer are used for textiles; shorter ones go to end products that are less exacting in their standards. Fiber grades are spun into yarns and woven into cloth. Brake linings, heavy packings and gaskets, electrical insulating materials, and protective clothing require the best fibers. Medium and short fibers are used in asbestos shingles, sheet gaskets, pipe, floor tile, less critical packings and gaskets, and as fillers for various other materials.
—John Price

Brass, an alloy of copper and zinc. Brasses are readily extruded, rolled, or forged, have good corrosion resistance, and can be joined by soldering or brazing. Brass is widely used for decorative trim, plumbing fixtures, electrical equipment, pipes and valves, musical instruments, automobile radiators, screws, cartridge cases, and hardware. The ratio of copper to zinc may be varied to control both the color and the malleability of the resultant alloy. An alloy of 80 per cent copper and 20 per cent zinc is very soft and has a golden-red color. A 60/40 copper-zinc ratio results in a yellow metal that is still malleable, while alloys with less than 50 per cent copper are white and become increasingly brittle with a rise in the percentage of zinc.

The more widely used brass alloys are frequently given trade names or names that reflect their application. Some common examples are *Muntz metal* (60 per cent copper, 40 per cent tin), *yellow brass* (66/34), *cartridge brass* (70/30), *low brass* (80/20), *red brass* (85/15), and *commercial bronze* (90/10). The addition of other metals results in a family of metals with names that are frequently misleading. The addition of a small amount of tin to molten brass produces an alloy called *nickel silver*, which contains no silver; while a manganese addition results in *manganese bronze*, which contains no tin. Small amounts of lead are often added to brass to improve its machinability. These *free-cutting brasses* (61 per cent copper, 3 per cent lead, 36 per cent zinc) are readily formed by automatic screw machines for many uses.

—Joseph J. Kelleher

Brick, a shaped, hardened block of clay used as a construction material. Bricks are among the oldest building materials still in common use today. Most are made of clay mixed with some sand, formed into rectangular blocks, and subsequently burned or fired until the clay particles fuse, forming a rigid, cohesive mass. Although brick may be of almost any size or shape, the standard U.S. brick measures $2\frac{1}{4} \times 3\frac{3}{4} \times 8$ inches. Materials other than clay are sometimes formed into similar shape and are also classified as brick.

Common brick, or ordinary building brick, consists of a clay and sand mix burned until the clay particles just begin to fuse.

Facing brick is similar to common brick, except that fewer imperfections are permitted, color variation is limited, and mechanical tolerances are more strict.

To achieve the abrasion resistance and weatherability demanded of a paving material, *paving brick* is fired until the clay particles fuse completely, filling all the voids in the sand-clay mix and rendering the finished product impervious.

Sand-lime brick is made of a mixture containing about 90 per cent sand with a large proportion of very fine grains and 10 per cent lime. Usually hydrated, high-calcium lime is used. The brick is cured in an *autoclave,* a closed vessel containing steam, at 100° to 150° F. The use of sand-lime brick in construction is identical to that of common brick.

Concrete brick is composed of ordinary Portland cement and aggregates formed into blocks, conforming to the standard sizes used by clay-brick manufacturers. Both regular and lightweight aggregates are used. *Refractory bricks* are masonry units manufactured especially for their resistance to heat. The production of refractory brick is similar to that of other brick, but the materials vary: flint clay, aluminum oxide, silica, and various mineral ores are used, depending upon the degree of temperature resistance needed, and upon the nature of the corrosive atmosphere to which they will be exposed.

—William W. Jacobus, Jr.

Bridges, structures providing support for the conveyance of traffic or other services over a valley, body of water, or road with openings for the passage of stream flow, navigation, or other traffic. Crude bridges were built by primitive people the world over, but the first notable bridge builders were the early Romans. In meeting their needs for roads to unite the Italian peninsula and their provinces, the Romans developed both timber and stone arch spans that were to remain the only practicable forms available until the late eighteenth century.

■**TIMBER BRIDGES.**—In many cases, bridges were built first as inexpensive timber structures and later replaced with more costly but more permanent stone arches. The first bridge over the Tiber at Rome, the Pons Sublicius (621 B.C.), made famous in the story of how Horatius held it against the Tarquins, was built of timber. Another early work, Pons Amelius (181 B.C.), was also of timber, but with stone piers. Timber bridges were likewise used in military operations, including Caesar's pile bridge over the Rhine and Trajan's timber arch over the Danube near Hungary's Iron Gate.

In addition to beam and arch forms, framed trusses must also have been developed early to support the roofs of temples and other buildings. Their first recorded use for a bridge, however, was by the Renaissance architect Andrea Palladio in 1570 in a remarkably modern form over the Cismone River. He noted that a friend had seen such a bridge in Germany. Later, Swiss engineers built a number of wooden bridges. This form was first extensively used and developed in the early nineteenth century in the United States, where they served for many highway crossings, often as *covered bridges* protected from the weather. Similar trusses and timber trestles were also used for early railroads. Later replaced with iron, these gave way to steel as the nineteenth century came to a close, when increasing loads demanded stronger spans.

■**STONE ARCHES.**—The arch appears early in ancient times in two forms: the *cantilever,* or so-called *false arch,* formed by horizontal overhanging stones, and the true circular arch of wedge-shaped blocks or voussoirs. Both apparently originated in the Near East and were used by the Assyrians. The Etruscans are credited with having introduced the true arch to the Romans.

The Pons Mulvius, now known as the Ponte Molle, which in 109 B.C. replaced a timber bridge on the Flaminian Way, a short distance above Rome, is said to be the earliest Roman arch still standing. It is of the standard Roman form having full-centered circular arches (with a rise equal to half the span) of unequal number, with a large, central span and substantial piers, aesthetically balanced and impressively stable. Its seven spans, each 51 to 79 feet, successfully carried heavy military equipment during World War II.

Many other notable bridges were built not only in Italy but also in the Roman provinces; for example, the high span (130 feet) over the Tagus River in northern Spain about 120 A.D. Here, with high stream banks, this form posed no obstruction to floods, and maximum spans of about 100 feet were reached. Full-centered arches, however, raised two major problems; for low-level crossings, spans were limited, and the arch haunches and massive piers obstructed the passage of floods, causing high-velocity flow through the arch openings. The resulting scour tended to undermine the piers, which, with the limited man-powered equipment of the day, could not be founded at a sufficient depth to avoid this danger.

It was not until the early Renaissance that the low-rise segmental arch was introduced in Italy, notably in the Ponte Vecchio at Florence of 1345 and the Castelvecchio bridge at Verona of 1356. This provided increased arch openings by making possible longer spans for low crossings, and a main span of 160 feet was reached in the latter work.

Conforming to the later aesthetic interests of the Renaissance, which regarded the abrupt angle between such arches and the piers as unpleasing, and believing also that some of the thrust could be more safely turned down to the pier, engineers introduced an elliptical form; an example is the Trinity Bridge at Florence in 1569. Known as the *anse de panier,* or basket-handle, this became a standard form and was widely adopted by the builders of the remarkable French highway system of the eighteenth century. Jean Perronet, the most famous of these French workers, finally revived the segmental form with slender columnar piers in his Pont de la Concorde over the Seine at Paris in 1791.

■**IRON AND TRUSS BRIDGES.**—A remarkable bronze truss of about 130 A.D. once supported the portico of the Pantheon in Rome. But it was destroyed in 1625, and it was not until 1779 that metal again appeared in a major structure. At this time, the advent of a true Iron Age in Britain led to the construction of a 100-foot cast-iron span at Coalbrookdale, and other more notable spans followed in the early nineteenth century. In general, the ancient arch form was used in these bridges, the voussoir stones being replaced by large cast-iron frames allowing larger spans. John Rennie's Southwark Bridge over the Thames at London in 1819 established a new arch record of 240 feet.

Wrought iron in quantity and at a cost making it available for bridges was later produced. By 1850, Robert Stephenson had completed the Britannia Bridge over Menai Strait in four unique spans of 230 to 460 feet, in which the trains traveled inside huge box girders.

Practice in the United States, however, centered largely in the truss forms. As earlier timber bridges were replaced by iron bridges, new truss forms emerged that were better suited to the economical use of the new material. By 1861, the plates and shapes now standard in steel construction had been developed, and the all-wrought-iron truss emerged. Steel later replaced wrought iron. It was first used with wrought iron in the United States in James Eads' famous St. Louis Arch in 1874. The first all-steel bridge was built in 1879.

British practice continued to favor solidly riveted plate constructions built in place, reflecting, it was said, boiler and shipbuilding techniques. It culminated in one of the wonders of the modern world, the Firth of Forth cantilever bridge of 1890, with its two great 1,710-foot spans. In the United States, designers adopted the so-called pin-connected forms of shop-fabricated parts that could be rapidly erected at low cost. It was estimated that by 1889, some 7,000 railroad spans of this type more than 100 feet in length had been built.

■ **SUSPENSION BRIDGES.**—Rope and similar suspensions were built by primitive peoples, but this was not a widely useful form of bridge until wrought iron became available. Bridges were then built using links of iron bars connected with pins. James Finley, an early American builder from Pennsylvania, pioneered in building "chain" suspensions, erecting the first in 1801. Twenty-five years later, the British pioneer Thomas Telford completed his Menai suspension bridge with a span of 580 feet, but the modern wire suspension was soon developed. Louis J. Vicat in France introduced the modern *spinning process*, using iron wires to build up suspension cables, in the Argental span of 1830. A Swiss, Joseph Chaley, reached 810 feet in 1834 at Fribourg, but the span record has since been held by the United States.

The outstanding American builder and wire manufacturer was John A. Roebling, an engineer from Germany, whose first suspensions carried wood troughs for canals over intervening valleys. His famous Niagara span of 822 feet was completed in 1855, and his even more famous Brooklyn Bridge of 1,595 feet at New York was completed after his death by his son, Washington A. Roebling, in 1883.

Not suited to heavy railroad loads, this form found increasing use with the advent of lighter modern motor traffic and, in 1929, when the Ambassador span of 1,850 feet was built across the Detroit River, finally took over the bridge span record. This, in turn, was followed by the great 3,500-foot George Washington span across New York's Hudson River in 1931, the 4,200-foot Golden Gate at San Francisco in 1937, and in 1965 by the 4,260-foot Verrazano-Narrows Bridge at entrance to New York Harbor.

■ **CONCRETE AND OTHER BRIDGES.**—As noted earlier, stone masonry found but rare and limited use in the United States. However, the birth of the American portland cement industry at the turn of the twentieth century made mass-produced concrete available at low cost, and several massive concrete viaducts were built. These included the Walnut Lane of 1908 at Philadelphia, the Rocky River of 1910 at Cleveland, and the great Tunkhannock on the Delaware, Lackawanna & Western Railroad in northern Pennsylvania in 1915 with ten 186-foot arches.

THE GEORGE WASHINGTON BRIDGE stretches 3,500 feet across the Hudson River.

Notable Bridges of the World

Name	Location	Type	Length in Feet	Date Completed
Ambassador	Detroit, Mich.-Sandwich, Ontario over Detroit River	Suspension Highway	span—1850 tot.—7400	1929
Bayonne	Bayonne, N. J.-Staten Island, N. Y. over Kill van Kull	Steel arch Highway	span—1652	1931
Bear Mountain	Peekskill, N. Y. over Hudson River	Suspension Highway	span—1632 tot.—2258	1924
Benjamin Franklin	Camden, N. J.-Philadelphia, Pa. over Delaware River	Suspension Highway	span—1750 tot.—8126	1926
Brooklyn	Manhattan-Brooklyn, N. Y. over East River	Suspension Rail, Highway	span—1595 tot.—6016	**1883**
Bronx-Whitestone	New York, N. Y. over East River	Suspension Highway	span—2300 tot.—4000	1939
Carquinez	Crockett-Vallejo, Calif. over Carquinez Straits	Cantilever Highway	span—2200 tot.—4482	1927
Chesapeake Bay	Delmarva Peninsula-Maryland mainland over Chesapeake Bay	Suspension Simple truss, Cantilever Highway	span—1600 tot.—7727	1952
Eads	St. Louis, Mo. over Mississippi River	Steel arch Railway	span—520 tot.—6434	1874
Forth	Scotland over Firth of Forth	Cantilever Railway	span—1710	1890
Fribourg	Switzerland over Sarine Valley	Suspension Highway	span—870	1834
George Washington	New York, N. Y.-Fort Lee, N. J. over Hudson River	Suspension Highway	span—3500 tot.—7800	1931
Golden Gate	San Francisco-Marin Co., Calif. over San Francisco Bay	Suspension Highway	span—4200 tot.—9217	1937
Greater New Orleans	New Orleans, La. over Mississippi River	Cantilever Highway	span—1575	1958
Hell Gate	New York, N. Y. over East River	Steel arch Railway	span—1017 tot.—18000	1917
Longview	Longview, Washington over Columbia River	Cantilever Highway	span—1200	1930
Mackinac	Mackinaw City-St. Ignace, Mich. over Mackinac Straits	Suspension Highway	span—3800	1957
Mid-Hudson	Poughkeepsie, N. Y. over Hudson River	Suspension Highway	span—1500 tot.—4072	1930
Plougastel	Brest, France over Elorn River	Concrete arch Rail, Highway	span—612	1929
Salazar	Lisbon, Spain-Seixal, Portugal over Tagus River	Suspension Highway	span—3,323 tot.—10,560	1966
Sando	Sweden over Angermanälven River	Concrete arch Highway	span—866	1943
Stockholm	Stockholm, Sweden over Stockholm Harbor	Concrete arch Rail, Highway	span—866	1943
Storstrom	Sjaellan I.-Falster I., Denmark over Storstrommen	Steel arch Rail, Highway	tot.—10432	1937
Sydney Harbor	Sydney, Australia over Sydney Harbor	Steel arch Rail, Highway	span—1650 tot.—3770	1932
Tappan Zee	Tarrytown, N. Y. over Hudson River	Cantilever Highway	span—1212	1955
Trans-Bay	San Francisco-Oakland, Calif. over San Francisco Bay	Suspension Cantilever Highway	span—2310 span—1400	1937
Triborough	Manhattan-Queens, N. Y. over East River	Suspension Highway	span—1380	1936
Verrazzano-Narrows	Brooklyn-Staten Island, N. Y. over The Narrows	Suspension Highway	span—4260 tot.—7200	1964

Attention abroad turned to reinforced concrete structures, and a far lighter, reinforced, open-spandrel form developed in the Swiss Langwies arch with a 315-foot span in 1915. This form has since been used for highway work in the United States, notably on the Pacific coast. However, the span record remains in Europe with such remarkable tours de force as the Plougastel Bridge at Brest, France, of 1929 with two 612-foot spans, and the Sando Arch at Stockholm with an 866-foot span, completed in 1943.

■MOVABLE BRIDGES.—Simple timber draw or beam spans, hinged at the inner end, were used over the moats of medieval fortresses and were early adopted for canal crossings in Holland to provide clearance for navigation. Similar modern steel rolling-lift bridges have been developed to meet needs of low-level crossing and navigation. Usually, the bridges are built in two section, meeting at the center of the span. The two arms rest on curved supports of the *rolling* or *trunnion* form, counterweighted and machine-driven. Other forms have also been developed, notably a *lift* type in which the entire span is counterweighted and lifted vertically between two end towers. The *swing* bridge, rotating on a circular track at the center pier of a two-arm span, is also widely used.

Needless to say, interruptions to traffic over or through such spans is unavoidable, and their use is usually limited to channels that carry only a small volume of shipping. Permanent spans are thus desirable. But in the United States, clearance requirements set by the Federal government may reach 200 feet or more on major navigable waters, requiring costly long, inclined approach spans. As a result, in many cases the alternative of tunnels has been preferred in recent years.   —James Kip Finch

Bronze, an alloy of copper and tin. Bronze is rarely used without the addition of elements. The most widespread use of *simple bronze* is for statuary (up to 20 per cent tin) and bells (up to 25 per cent tin). Conventional *binary bronze* contains from 3 to 10 per cent tin, with strength, hardness, and corrosion resistance increasing with the tin content. These alloys are widely used for commercial screening and springs. Minor additions of alloying elements can be used to amplify specific characteristics of bronzes. The alloy's corrosion resistance is dramatically improved by adding up to 3 per cent silicon to produce *silicon bronze*. Traces of phosphorus harden and strengthen bronze, while additions of up to 30 per cent lead improve its ductility and machinability. Many alloys commonly referred to as bronze contain no tin and are not truly bronzes. *Manganese bronze* contains 0.5 to 5 per cent manganese, copper, and other metals—but no tin. Another misnamed alloy, *beryllium bronze* (2 per cent beryllium, but no tin), can be strengthened by heat treatment, which makes it nearly three times stronger than structural steel.   —Joseph J. Kelleher

Building Construction, the erection of structures consisting of foundations, frames, walls, and roofs.

■FOUNDATIONS.—The foundation of a building is that part of the construction that ties the structure to the site upon which it rests. It must be able to support both the weight of the building itself, called the *dead load,* and the weight of the contents of the building—the furniture, fixtures, and occupants—called the *live load.* In addition, the foundation of a building must be capable of resisting lateral, or sideways, loads that tend to overturn the structure. Both wind and earthquakes impose significant lateral loads upon tall buildings.

Many types of foundations are used, depending upon the height, and hence the weight, of the building and the load-bearing capacity of the soil in the area in which it is built.

The science of *soil mechanics,* which is the study of the behavior of soils under load, is well advanced and engineers can quite accurately predict the pressures (in pounds per square foot) that any particular site can sustain. Thus, when the live and dead loads of a building have been calculated, it is a short step to determine the area of the footings that must be in contact with the soil to support the structure.

In the case of all buildings or poor soil conditions, these calculations may show that the area of the footings needed exceeds the total area of the base of the building. In such cases vertical structural members, called *piles,* which may be of wood, steel, or concrete, are driven into the ground until they reach solid bedrock, or the friction of the soil against the sides of the pile develops the required load-bearing capacity. The building's columns, which transfer vertical loads to the earth, rest atop these piles.

■FRAMES.—Until the turn of the century, the exterior and interior walls of a building—usually made of brick or other masonry material—carried the vertical loads to the ground. This type of construction was known as *bearing-wall construction.* Under this system, as taller buildings came into demand, the bearing walls at the base of a building had to be made considerably thicker. Seeking other solutions, engineers developed the skeleton frame with *columns* (vertical members) and *beams* (horizontal members) of steel or concrete. Both of these materials, being much stronger than the common brick they replaced, reduced the volume of material needed to support a tall structure and made possible the multistory commercial and residential buildings that are commonplace today.

■WALLS.—With the advent of the skeleton frame, the function of the exterior walls of a building was reduced to that of excluding wind and water from the interior of the building and minimizing the transfer of heat (outward in winter, inward in summer). By the early 1950's, architects were beginning to develop very thin, lightweight exterior walls, often referred to as *curtain walls.*

In this type of construction window glass comprises about half of the exterior wall area. For the remaining area many materials have been used, among them stainless steel, aluminum, porcelain enameled steel, precast concrete, and even architectural bronze. The choice of material for exterior curtain walls is determined by aesthetic appearance, weatherability, and cost.

Interior walls are more properly referred to as *partitions.* The most significant advance in interior partitions has been the development of demountable partitions for office buildings; these can easily be taken down and reused in a new location, thus permitting office arrangements to be changed to meet changing design requirements with little additional expense.

■ROOFS.—The roofs of most commercial, industrial, and high-rise residential buildings are flat, unlike the steeply pitched roofs of the typical small dwelling. Thus, they do not shed water as readily as pitched roofs and their construction requires considerable care.

The commonest roof construction for flat roofs is the built-up, multiply roof made up of alternate layers of heavy feltlike paper, and bitumen (tar). The *bitumen,* which is mopped onto the roof deck and onto the subsequent layers of felt, serves both as an adhesive to hold the felts in place and as a waterproof membrane. Often, built-up roofs are topped with a layer of a light-colored mineral aggregate that protects the roof membrane from accidental damage by the traffic of maintenance men. Also, because of its light color, the layer of aggregate increases the reflectance of the roof, thus minimizing the transmission of heat from the sun's rays during summer.

Elastomeric (flexible plastic) materials have recently been developed for roof surfaces. Although these materials possess certain inherent advantages over the conventional built-up, bituminous roof, the cost of the materials has limited their use to rather special applications.

■BUILDING CODES.—These are the statutory regulations governing the design and construction of buildings for ensuring the health, welfare, and safety of those who will ultimately occupy the building. The rules embodied in building codes are intended to ensure that the building's structural components, such as beams and columns, are adequate for the loads they must carry; that the building is protected against fire; that emergency exits are large enough for the speedy evacuation of a building in the event of any disaster.

Plans and specifications for a building must be submitted to the appropriate municipal officials, who will examine the design for compliance with the code before granting permission for construction to begin. Authority to enact and enforce building codes stems from the police power of the state government. But, in almost every case, this particular power is delegated to municipal authority.   —William W. Jacobus, Jr.

Calcimine, or *kalsomine,* a white or tinted wash made of glue, zinc white, and water, and used especially on plastered surfaces. It is one of the emulsion-type paints made from slated lime and water-washed clays. Like most water-thinned paints, calcimine is sensitive to water and is not washable. Addition of modified oils or resins that are water-soluble but that convert to an insoluble form when the water evaporates, can eliminate this defect. Calcimine was used extensively at one time because of its low cost. However, its use has dwindled over the years with the development of better, more durable paints.

—John Price

Camphor, a crystalline naturally gummy substance used as a medicine and plasticizer. Camphor occurs as colorless to white crystals, granules, or crystalline masses, or as colorless to white translucent tough masses or tablets. It has a characteristic penetrating odor and a pungent, aromatic taste. Camphor has been used for thousands of years as a component of incense and in various domestic uses because of its pleasant odor. Its first important chemical use was discovered a century ago—as a plasticizer for cellulose nitrate to produce *celluloid.*

Natural camphor is obtained by steam distillation from the leaves, twigs, and stems of the camphor tree, *Cinnamomum camphora,* which is found widely in China, Japan, and Taiwan. The trees reach maturity in 45 to 50 years, and camphor is extracted every 5 or 6 years. Because of the limitations on production of camphor by plantations, synthetic methods were developed to manufacture it from pinene, a turpentine derivative. Demand for camphor today has dropped off, however, primarily because of the replacement of cellulose nitrate by other plastics. Also, its use as a pharmaceutical has declined greatly.

Camphor is used widely in liniments and as a mild rubefacient, analgesic, and antipruritic. It is also used in photographic film and as an insect repellent, especially for clothes moths. —John Price

Calking and Sealing Compounds, a wide range of compositions used in the construction, manufacturing, and transportation industries. They are used to seal joints or voids against water or vapor, air and other gases, dust, sound, heat, and cold. Some compounds are applied after the structure is in place, as in masonry joints; others are applied during manufacture, as in automobile and trailer bodies.

Calks and sealants are usually supplied in knife- and gun-grade compounds. *Knife-grade* materials, the stiffer of the two, lend themselves to application with a putty knife. They are often supplied in extruded shapes ready for use. *Gun-grade* materials are extruded through an opening, using a hand- or pressure-operated gun. They are supplied in bulk form or in cartridges ready for use.

—John Price

Caustic soda, or *sodium hydroxide* ($NaOH$), one of the high-tonnage industrial chemicals. Consumption in the United States is approximately 5.5 million tons per year, and this amount is expected to increase.

Caustic soda and its companion product, chlorine, are produced by the electrolysis of brine (sodium chloride solutions). Chlorine is evolved at the anode (positive electrode), caustic soda and hydrogen at the cathode (negative electrode). Two variations are widely used in industry—the diaphragm cell and the mercury cell. The *diaphragm cell* keeps anode and cathode products separated by an asbestos diaphragm backed by an iron cathode. To minimize back-diffusion, only part of the sodium chloride is reacted in the anode cell. Caustic soda produced at the cathode is dried and separated from residual sodium chloride. In *mercury cells,* the cation (positively charged ion) forms an alloy or amalgam, which is pumped to another chamber, where it is reacted with water to produce caustic soda and hydrogen. The diaphragm cell is used more extensively, but mercury-cell use is growing, since this method produces a purer product at the same cost.

The chemical industry consumes nearly half of all U.S. caustic production. Pulp and paper manufacturers use substantial amounts of caustic and are expected to become increasingly important customers. It is also used in making rayon, aluminum, textiles, petroleum, soaps and detergents, and cellophane. —John Price

Cellophane, a transparent, flexible film, usually about one-thousandth of an inch thick, used principally for packaging food and other consumer goods. Invented in 1908 by Jacques Edwin Brandenberger, a Swiss chemist, cellophane was first made commercially in France. E. I. du Pont de Nemours & Company acquired the American rights in 1923 and four years later developed a means of moisture-proofing cellophane, a development that led to its wide use as a protective wrapping material.

The growth in use of cellophane coincided with, and contributed to, the development of the self-service merchandising concept in the United States. Since transparent film combines product visibility and product protection, it has facilitated the prepackaging of many commodities.

Cellophane is made from cellulose, which is derived from wood or cotton in a process that bears some resemblance to papermaking. Among the chemicals added during the process are caustic soda, carbon bisulfide, and sulfuric acid. Moisture-proofing is achieved by a coating of a lacquerlike substance or a synthetic resin. Cellophane manufacture requires a large investment, and a small-capacity plant is not profitable. There are three manufacturers of cellophane in the United States. About 300 other companies "convert" cellophane, that is, print it, make it into bags, or otherwise prepare it for ultimate use.

—E. I. du Pont de Nemours & Co.

Cellulose, the chief carbohydrate found in land plants. It forms the skeletal structure of the cell wall (hence its name) and occurs with polysaccharides and hemicelluloses derived from other sugars, such as xylose, arabinose, and mannose. In the woody part of plants, cellulose is mixed, and sometimes linked, with lignin. Wood normally contains 40 to 50 per cent cellulose, 20 to 30 per cent lignin, and 10 to 30 per cent hemicelluloses.

Commercial cellulose can be produced from cotton linters, but the main source is wood, particularly pine and spruce, from which it is removed by pulping methods designed to remove lignin and other noncellulosic constituents. In addition to mechanical and semimechanical processes that separate wood fibers for use in paper manufacture, there are three chemical pulping methods that are used widely. The most frequently used is the *kraft,* or *sulfate, process,* in which logs are debarked, chipped, and cooked at 160–170° C for 2 to 6 hours in a solution of sodium sulfide and sodium hydroxide. Sodium sulfide, added to the spent cooking liquor, is converted to sodium sulfide when the liquor is burned for recovery of sulfide. In the *soda process,* sodium hydroxide alone is used in the cooking liquor. In the *sodium sulfite process,* wood chips are cooked in a calcium bisulfite solution containing a large excess of free sulfur dioxide; lignins are converted to soluble lignosulfonates. Cellulose is used to prepare a wide variety of derivatives in the production of rayon.

—John Price

Cement, any substance that bonds materials together. In the broadest sense, glue, mucilage, epoxy, and paste are all cements, but more specifically the term applies to *hydraulic cement* used in construction. Hydraulic cement is a finely-ground, gray powder, which when mixed with water and sand makes mortar that will dry and hold together stones, bricks, or blocks of masonry. If a larger aggregate, such as gravel or crushed stone, is added to the mixture of water and sand the end product is a rocklike mass called concrete. (See *Concrete.*)

The Romans first discovered that a mixture of volcanic ash and lime, made by burning marble, would bond together rocks and cut stone for building their roads, aqueducts, and other structures. They called the material *caementum,* meaning, literally, pieces of rough uncut rock, in reference to the chips of marble from which the lime came.

Among the many things lost with the decline of the Roman Empire was the formula for making cement. A cement similar to that of the Romans was produced in England in 1756, that would harden under water just as the Romans' did. But the cement used today was not invented until 1824, when an English stonemason, Joseph Aspdin, found that by mixing the lime, silica, and alumina first, then burning and grinding the mixture, he could make a stronger cement. Since the concrete made with his cement looked very much like a rock formation on the Isle of Portland, Aspdin called his discovery *Portland cement.*

Today there are standard formulas for Portland cement, but for many years the various manufacturers used their own specifications and there were nearly a hundred different types.

Lime is the major ingredient of Portland cement, usually comprising about 60 to 64 per cent of the mixture. The lime is derived from limestone, oyster shells, or other natural rocks. *Silica,* obtained from blast-furnace slag, clay, or shale rock makes up 19 to 25 per cent of cement. *Alumina,* which is in the same slag, clay, or shale, comprises 5 to 9 per cent of the mixture.

Cement manufacture begins with the quarrying of the limestone. Huge crushers break the blasted limestone into small pieces about the size of chicken eggs. The crushed rock is then mixed with the silica-alumina-bearing slag, shale, or clay in big rotating cylinders called *ball mills.* Heavy steel or iron balls inside the cylinders batter the mixture into powder. This powder then goes to a tube mill that contains even smaller balls or pebbles of flint. The tube mill produces particles so fine that they can pass through a sieve that water cannot pass through.

Next, this finely ground powder is burned in great kilns as large as 15 feet in diameter and 400 feet long. This burning gives the material its binding quality, producing calcium silicates and calcium aluminates that react chemically with water to form a rocklike mass. The burning kilns also are long rotating steel cylinders, but these are lined with firebrick to protect the steel from temperatures as high as 3,000° F maintained at the lowest end of the kilns. The cement powder, which is sometimes mixed with water to form a soupy *slurry,* takes about two hours to pass through the kilns.

This tremendous heat, besides causing the chemical reaction, also causes the material to emerge from the kilns as *clinker,* larger pieces about the size of children's marbles. The clinker is cooled, a small amount of gypsum is added, and finally, more ball and tube mills regrind it. The end product, Portland cement, is so finely pulverized that 90 per cent will pass through a sieve with 40,000 openings per square inch.

Portland cement is modified in many ways for different purposes. Brick masons add more lime to the cement and sand, so their mortar is smoother and bonds better to the bricks. *Pozzolana,* siliceous material such as blast furnace slag, fly ash, or natural volcanic material, are also added to Portland cement, but mainly as a substitute for some of the more expensive cement when making concrete. There is a naturally occurring argillaceous limestone, which when burnt and pulverized results in natural cement. Natural cement is similar to Portland cement but is slower-setting and its quality is less dependable. A mixture of the two is sometimes used for special purposes.

Although cement traditionally has been packed in bags, most of it today is transported in bulk by huge rail tank cars, trucks, and barges. Cement is measured in barrels (bbl) rather than bags. A barrel of cement is 376 pounds. World production of cement is about 1.7 billion barrels annually.　　　—William W. Jacobus, Jr.

Ceramics, materials or products that are chemically inorganic (except metals or metal alloys) and are usually rendered serviceable by high-temperature processing. The raw materials for most ceramics are oxides and silicates, but many others are also used, including aluminides, beryllides, borides, carbides, nitrides, and silicides. Graphite and ceramic-metal composites are frequently classified as ceramics.

The usual product classification includes abrasives; cements, lime, and gypsum; electronic and technical ware; glass; porcelain enamel; refractories; structural clay products; and whitewares, which include dinnerware and plumbing fixtures. Pottery falls in either the technical or whitewares group, depending on its application.

Ceramic products range from single crystals, such as sapphire, through dense, polycrystalline, glass-free refractory materials, to glass-bonded crystalline aggregates and wholly vitreous (glassy) materials. A number of different manufacturing methods must be employed. Some products, such as volcanic glass (obsidian), depend upon the processes of nature.

Manmade ceramics came with the discovery of fire. Primitive men made simple bricks by adding water to clay to make it plastic and then shaping it by hand or in simple molds. These bricks were dried in the sun and finally hardened by firing.

The origin of such products is lost in the mists of antiquity. However, early man soon learned to refine and improve his raw materials and his forming, drying, and firing procedures. He found that mixtures of several clays often made it easier to attain the sizes and shapes he desired. Certain other materials, such as feldspar, served as fluxes, permitting firing at a lower temperature.

Even today many ceramics are made of three major components: mixtures of clays to provide plasticity; fluxes to assist in forming a glassy bond during firing; and a nonplastic or refractory material, such as quartz, to aid in glass formation and to provide a rigid skeleton.

■**PRODUCTS.**—Ceramic bodies are usually fabricated by extrusion, soft plastic forming, dry pressing, slip casting, hot pressing, or fusion casting. All but the last two are done at room temperature with raw materials of the proper composition, particle size, and size distribution. Some require the addition of as much as 20 to 30 per cent water. In every case the forming imparts an approximate shape and some degree of strength to the ware. If water has been added, this must be removed by a drying oper-

ation, and some shrinkage occurs. Further shrinkage, plus a very great increase in strength, develops when the ware is fired in a furnace or kiln at high temperatures ranging from 1,300° F for enamels to 3,300° F for alumina ceramics, or to even higher temperatures in special cases.

Ceramic products in general exhibit a unique combination of properties. They have great resistance to heat. Many have melting temperatures over 3,000° F. Most of them exhibit extreme mechanical hardness. Cubic boron nitride is as hard as diamond. Ceramic materials have very great intrinsic strength, but their normally brittle behavior is such that even careful design permits only a small fraction of this strength to be realized. Most ceramics are resistant to corrosive chemicals. (See also *Pottery,* Page 1654.)　—Charles J. Phillips

Charcoal, a porous solid material containing 85 to 98 per cent carbon. It can be produced by the ignition of almost any animal, vegetable, or mineral material containing carbon. *Activated charcoal* is produced by treating charcoal to give it a very large surface area, ranging from 300 to 2,000 square meters per gram of material. There are two types of activated charcoal: *liquid-phase* or *decolorizing* charcoals, which are light fluffy powders; and *gas-phase* or *vapor-adsorbent* charcoals, which are hard, dense granules or pellets.

Decolorizing charcoals are usually made from bones, wood, peat, lignite, soft and hard coals, tars and pitches, asphalt, petroleum residues, and carbon black. Liquid-phase charcoal is used to decolorize sugar solutions, to remove odor and taste from water supplies and to clarify solvents used for dry cleaning. It is also used in the reclaiming of rubber, pharmaceutical manufacture, food and beverage processing, and in purifying oils, waxes, plasticizers, and other chemicals.

Adsorbent charcoals are usually made from coconut shells, coal, peat, and petroleum residues. Gas-phase charcoals are used to recover volatile organic solvents from air, in the purification and separation of gases, and as a catalyst in the oxidation of various organic and inorganic compounds. Charcoal is activated by steam treatment, which tends to remove adsorbed hydrocarbons from the surface.

　　　　　　　　　　　—John Price

Chemical Engineering, the branch of engineering concerned with the application of the principles of chemistry, together with the principles of economics and human relations, to processes and process equipment.

The manufacturing processes used in the chemical industry are usually resolved into unit chemical processes and unit physical operations. Such steps, essentially, will be the same regardless of the particular branch of the chemical industry involved. In recent years, it has been realized that these processes and operations in themselves are not the true scientific fundamentals of concern to the chemical engineer. Accordingly, there has been increased emphasis on the so-called engineering sciences, including energy transfer, fluid dynamics, kinetics and mass, momentum, and thermodynamics.

Chemical engineers translate the results of laboratory research into large-scale commercial manufacturing plants. A recent survey of chemical engineers in the United States showed that 31 per cent are engaged in research and development work with private companies. Another 28 per cent are engaged in production and maintenance; 13 per cent in design and construction; 10 per cent in management and administration; 5 per cent in sales and technical service; and the rest are in government, laboratory and consulting work, teaching and other occupations.

Engineers are playing an increasing role in technical management of chemical process industries, many in major executive positions. But the primary consideration of a chemical engineer is the successful commercial development and operation of chemical processes to yield new and better products at lower costs.

The chemical manufacturing industries employ about 40 per cent of today's chemical engineering graduates; petroleum refining takes another 20 per cent, and process equipment and machinery firms about 6 per cent. The rest are employed in such chemical process industries as plastics, rubber, pulp and paper, drugs, nonferrous metals, glass and ceramics, paint and varnish, soap and detergents, synthetic fibers, textile processing, inedible oils and fats, explosives, leather, and food.

—John Price

Civil Engineering, the branch of the engineering profession dealing with the planning, design, and construction of public and private works and the structures, such as bridges, dams, tunnels, etc., incidental thereto, for railroad, highway, canal and harbor, water supply, power, flood control, irrigation, drainage, and similar needs.

For many centuries the three callings known today as architecture, civil engineering, and military engineering, which also included the limited mechanical interests of earlier days, were regarded as one profession. In ancient Egypt, this general "master builder" was known as *chief-of-works* and held an important position in the court. The Greek historian Herodotus was the first to refer to the builder of a water supply (about 530 B.C.) as an *architekton*. The Romans also used the title *architectus*. New interests developed during the Renaissance, however, ultimately led to the modern specialization. Notable among these interests were the advent of gunpowder and cannon, which introduced new techniques, and an emphasis on art and decoration in the design of buildings, which led to architecture being considered a "fine" rather than a practical art. Military workers adopted the title of *ingeniator,* to denote the ingenious builder of engines of war and medieval fortresses, and began to be known as military engineers.

The organization of the Corps des Ponts et Chaussées in 1716 and the famous Ecole in 1747 marked an important step toward the recognition of civil engineering as a separate profession. Architecture and civil engineering, however, remained closely allied throughout the great period of French leadership, and the last book to treat both professions as one appeared as late as 1802. Increased interest in works unrelated to artistic interests together with the rise of more exact mathematical techniques in design ultimately ended this long liaison.

Architecture and engineering had never been very closely allied in Great Britain, and about 1750 John Smeaton, the builder of the famous Eddystone Light, adopted the title *civil engineer* to distinguish his field from that of military workers. The British Institution of Civil Engineers was organized in 1818. However, Smeaton and others were also active in the development of the steam engine; this led to another division, and in 1847 the Institution of Mechanical Engineers was founded. The American Society of Civil Engineers followed in 1852.

Civil engineering, thus, has long been concerned with irrigation, water supply, drainage, highways and streets, canals, railroads, dams, reservoirs and aqueducts, bridges, tunnels, and other structures. While other engineering branches are devoted primarily to the production of consumer goods, civil engineering works are long-lived, permanent, capital investments. They require both an evaluation of benefits and costs and due attention to the forecasting and appraisal of possible future needs. Many also are public works.

The civil engineer produces no mass product. Each work involves individual planning and design to meet most effectively and economically the particular needs and conditions of the site and to take advantage of all available resources. Advances in engineering science have made more accurate design possible, but the wide variation in conditions to be met—from foundations to such adverse natural factors as floods and storms—requires judgment and skill based on practical experience.

—James Kip Finch

Clay, an earthy material that is plastic when wet but becomes hard when fired. It is composed mainly of fine particles of hydrous aluminum silicates and other minerals. There are many different types of clay with a wide range of plasticity—from *fat clay* (very plastic) to *lean clays* (barely plastic). Plasticity is affected by the type of clay mineral, particle size and shape, organic matter, soluble salts, adsorbed ions, and the amount and type of nonclay minerals it may contain.

Kaolinitic clays (these containing the clay mineral kaolinite) include china clay (also called paper clay or kaolin), ball clay, fireclay, and flint clay. Kaolin is white, has very fine particle size, and is nonabrasive and chemically inert. *Kaolins* are used in the manufacture of ceramics, paper,

rubber, paint, plastics, insecticides, adhesives, catalysts, and ink. *Ball clays* are composed mainly of kaolinite but are usually much darker than china clay. Ball clay is a fine-grained, very plastic, refractory bond clay, used in whitewares and some sanitary ware.

Fireclay is the term applied to clays that will withstand temperatures of 1,500° C or higher. Fireclays usually are light to dark gray, and contain minor amounts of illite and quartz impurities. Most fireclays are plastic, but some are nonplastic and very hard; these are known as *flint clays*. Fireclays are used extensively by the refractories industry. The foundry uses fireclay to bind sand into molds for casting metals.

Diaspore clay is a hydrated aluminum oxide, very hard and refractory, and is used to make refractory brick. Calcined diaspore clay is used as an abrasive.

Mullite, a high-temperature conversion product of many aluminum minerals, does not spall, resists heating and cooling exceptionally well, and is resistant to slag erosion. It is used in sparkplugs, laboratory crucibles, kiln apparatus, and other special refractories.

Bentonites, which contain montmorillonite, are formed by the alteration of volcanic ash. These clays are used in drilling mud, as a binder for metal-casting forms, to remove coloring matter from oils, and as an adsorbent for a variety of materials.

Attapulgite clays, also called *fuller's earth,* are hydrated magnesium aluminum silicates. They are used as adsorbents, decolorizers, and deodorizers.

—John Price

Coal, a combustible, carbonaceous material, formed beneath the surface of the earth from partly decomposed vegetable matter through a series of complex geologic processes. Although coal is termed a mineral, it differs from ordinary minerals in having an organic origin—that is, it was formed from the remains of living vegetation.

The material representing the first stage of the transformation of vegetable matter into coal is known as *peat.* It forms when plant materials accumulate under water or in a water-saturated environment where their decomposition is retarded. An accumulation of many layers of plant materials formed under such conditions is called a peat deposit.

The processes involved in the transformation of peat into coal are unknown, but it is thought that the conversion was caused mainly by pressures and heat exerted by accumulated overburdens and movements of the earth's crust. Over very long periods of time, this action resulted in both physical and chemical changes in the original plant materials, including a loss of moisture and evolution of carbon dioxide and methane, leaving an ever-increasing proportion of fixed carbon.

■VARIETIES.—Coals are classified according to degree of conversion, which is known as rank, into four general classes: lignite, subbituminous, bituminous, and anthracite.

Lignite, the lowest rank, has a high percentage of moisture and volatile matter and a low percentage of fixed carbon. It has a fibrous or woody structure and low calorific value (moist BTU of less than 8,300 per pound).

Subbituminous coal, which is similar to bituminous in appearance, contains more moisture and usually has a lower heating value. Better grades generally have calorific values ranging between 11,000 and 13,000 BTU's per pound, but the low grades are barely above lignite in heating value. Subbituminous coal also differs from bituminous in being entirely nonagglomerating or noncoking.

Bituminous coal, known as *soft coal,* has a volatile-matter content that ranges from 14 to about 40 per cent, and a calorific value of more than 11,000 BTU's per pound. Because of its wide range of volatile matter and fixed carbon content, bituminous coal is subdivided into three subclasses: *low volatile, medium volatile,* and *high volatile.* Low volatile bituminous approaches anthracite in dry fixed carbon and volatile matter, but the lower grades of high-volatile bituminous are only slightly above the subbituminous types in calorific value. Another distinguishing characteristic of some bituminous coals is their ability to agglomerate, or form coke. Not all bituminous coals have agglomerating properties, however. Varieties of bituminous range from the *banded,* which include the *bright* and *splint coals,* to the *nonbanded,* which are known as *cannel* and *boghead.* Differences in these types are attributed to the materials from which these coals were formed.

Anthracite is the highest-ranked coal. Known as *hard coal,* anthracite is characterized by its low moisture and volatile-matter content and its high fixed carbon. Subclasses range from *meta-anthracite,* which has 98 per cent or more fixed carbon, through *anthracite,* to *semi-anthracite,* which has properties lying between anthracite and low-volatile bituminous coals. Anthracite is dense, has a bright luster, and is uniform in texture. Its calorific value ranges between 13,000 and 14,000 BTU's per pound, somewhat less than the highest-grade bituminous coals. It is noncoking and, when burned, emits almost no smoke.

■**WORLD RESERVES.**—Coal is the world's most abundant and widely distributed energy resource. It is found on all continents, in virtually all geographic areas, and in most countries. The

UNITED ELECTRICAL COAL COMPANIES

STRIP MINING is speeded by this excavator, which can remove 3,500 tons of earth each hour. The excavator removes the top layers of earth; a power shovel then exposes the coal.

major reserves, however, are in Asia, North America, and Europe.

Data on world reserves vary greatly, but the total reserve in all areas, as estimated by the United States Geological Survey in 1960, was 5,115 billion short tons. Of the total, 49 per cent was in Asia, 34 per cent in North America, and 13 per cent in Europe. (The Asian total includes reserves in the European regions of the Soviet Union, for which there is no separate estimate.) The remaining 4 per cent was widely scattered in Africa, Australia, and South and Central America.

The United States, with an estimated 1,660 billion short tons, has the largest reserve. The Soviet Union and China, with 1,323 billion and 1,115 billion short tons respectively, are next in rank, while Germany with 316 billion and the United Kingdom with 188 billion short tons rank fourth and fifth. These five countries account for 90 per cent of the world's coal reserve. Because standards of thickness and depth of the deposits included in the reserve of individual countries vary, the figures above are not completely comparable. They do, however, reflect the approximate relative magnitude of the reserve in these countries.

It is estimated that 830 billion tons of the total United States reserve is

recoverable. This estimate is based upon the assumption that one-half of the reserve in the earth will be lost in mining while one-half will be recovered. The total includes 380 billion tons of bituminous coal, 224 billion tons of lignite, 218 billion tons of subbituminous coal, and 8 billion tons of anthracite. Approximately 40 per cent of the total reserve occurs in states east of the Mississippi River, principally in the Appalachian states, Indiana, and Illinois; the remainder occurs principally in the Great Plains and Rocky Mountain states.

■**PRODUCTION.**—In world production of coal, the United States ranks second only to the Soviet Union. Its output of 504 million tons in 1964 amounted to 17 per cent of the estimated 3,036 million tons of coal produced throughout the world; the Soviet Union produced 611 million tons that year. Virtually all of the United States production, however, was in coals of high rank, while about one-fourth (159 million tons) of the Soviet output was lignite.

The principal coal-producing states are West Virginia, Pennsylvania, Kentucky, Illinois, Ohio, and Virginia, accounting for about four-fifths of the total United States output. Only 5 per cent of the production comes from west of the Mississippi River, and this coal is mainly subbituminous and lignite.

Approximately one-half of the coal consumed in the United States in 1964 was used to generate electric power; about one-fifth was used for producing coke, one of the essential ingredients for manufacturing pig iron in blast furnaces. Most of the remainder was used for fuel by industrial plants and homeowners, although about 10 per cent of the production was exported. Of significance in the distribution pattern of bituminous coal in the past two decades is the change in the quantities used for residential heating and electric-power

World Production of LIGNITE AND BROWN COAL in %

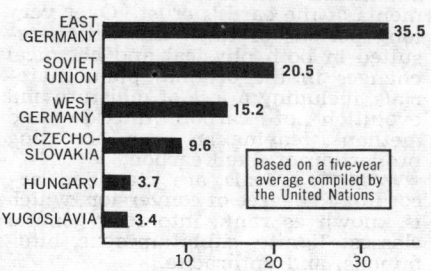

EAST GERMANY	35.5
SOVIET UNION	20.5
WEST GERMANY	15.2
CZECHO-SLOVAKIA	9.6
HUNGARY	3.7
YUGOSLAVIA	3.4

Based on a five-year average compiled by the United Nations

World Production of COAL in %

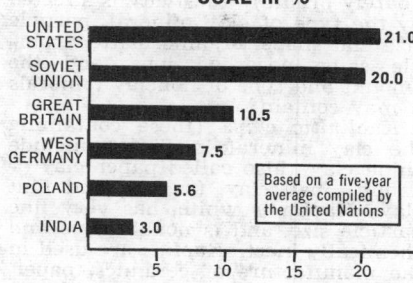

UNITED STATES	21.0
SOVIET UNION	20.0
GREAT BRITAIN	10.5
WEST GERMANY	7.5
POLAND	5.6
INDIA	3.0

Based on a five-year average compiled by the United Nations

generation. In 1944, 20 per cent of the coal consumed was used for residential heating and 13 per cent for electric power generation, but electric utilities now consume about one-half of the total distributed, while only 6 per cent is used for heating homes.

—Eugene T. Sheridan

Coal Tar, a black, viscous mixture of complex organic compounds, condensed from the volatile matter released when coal is carbonized. The yield and properties of tar vary greatly, but the composition of a particular tar depends principally upon the carbonization temperature and the length of time the coal was carbonized. Tars produced at high temperatures are characterized by large proportions of aromatic, hydrocarbon compounds, which result from the cracking of primary tars, formed at lower temperatures when the volatile matter was first evolved from the coal. Low-temperature tars are composed mainly of primary tars, which are aliphatic hydrocarbon compounds that have not been subjected to cracking. High-temperature tars contain high percentages of naphthalenes and anthracene oil, while low-temperature tars are rich in tar acids.

Virtually all coal tar in the United States is produced by high-temperature carbonization; approximately ten gallons of tar are recovered for each ton of coal carbonized. In some instances, tar is burned for fuel, but usually, it is separated into a number of fractions by several processes involving fractional distillation. In some plants, tar is distilled in batch stills from which the vapors pass into a fractionating column where successive distillate fractions are removed. Modern tar plants, however, use continuous stills that produce a series of distillate fractions simultaneously.

The crude fractions in tar, in order of increasing boiling points, are light oil, middle oil, heavy oil, and anthracene oil.

Light oil, composed of benzene and its homologues, represents from 3 to 5 per cent of the total products recovered. The volume of light oil in tar is too small for economical recovery at most plants, and this fraction usually is recovered with the middle oil. Virtually all the coke-oven benzene, toluene, and xylene—products commonly referred to as coal-tar crudes—are produced from light oil extracted from the coke-oven gas rather than from the light-oil fraction in tar.

Middle oil, composed of tar acids, tar bases, and naphthalene, accounts for about 15 per cent of the total products. Tar acids include phenol, the cresols, and xylenols, while the principal tar bases are pyridine, picoline, and quinoline. These compounds are the basic materials from which a wide variety of chemical materials are synthesized, including synthetic resins, drugs, vitamins, water-repellents, fungicides, weed killers, antioxidants, and rubber-curing agents. Naphthalene, which makes up about two-thirds of the tar bases, is used principally as a source of phthalic anhydride for the production of alkyd resins and many types of plasticizers.

The *heavy* and *anthracene oils,* combined, amount to 15 to 20 per cent of recovered products. The heavy-oil fraction, called *creosote oil,* is used principally in wood preserving. Anthracene oil usually is combined directly with the creosote, but it can be processed for the recovery of anthracene, phenanthrene, and carbazole. Anthracene, the most important of these, can be converted to anthraquinone, used for the synthesis of important classes of dyes and other organic chemicals.

The residue that remains after distillation is called *pitch.* Pitch is used mainly as a binder in the manufacture of carbon electrodes and for producing roofing materials, protective coatings, and fiber pipe. Approximately one-half of the coal-tar pitch produced in the United States, however, is used as fuel in steel plant furnaces.   —Eugene T. Sheridan

Coke, a hard, cellular, carbon residue, formed when coking coals are heated at high temperatures in coke ovens. Coke is irregular in shape, ranges in color from black to metallic gray, and is composed largely of carbon, although most coke contains about 9 or 10 per cent ash.

The process of converting coal to coke, known as carbonization, usually is accomplished in slot ovens and beehive ovens at temperatures above 900° C. *Slot ovens,* which are used almost universally for producing metallurgical coke, recover the volatile constituents of the coal, which subsequently are processed for the recovery of tar, ammonia, light oil, and gas. *Beehive ovens,* so called because of their shape, also produce good metallurgical coke but are used to a lesser extent, as they do not recover the volatile products.

Some coal is also carbonized at high temperatures in retorts, but the coke produced is not suitable for metallurgical use; it is used for domestic heating and for producing gas. Low-temperature carbonizing techniques produce only a char or semicoke, also unsuitable for metallurgical use.

Nearly 1.5 tons of coal are required to produce each ton of coke in a modern coke plant. A total of 89.2 million tons of coal were carbonized in the United States in 1964 to produce 62.1 million tons of coke. Of the total coke production, 2 per cent was produced in beehive ovens and 98 per cent in slot ovens.

Coke is one of the essential raw materials for producing pig iron, and about 90 per cent of all coke produced in the United States is used in pig-iron blast furnaces. Coke is used also in ferroalloy blast furnaces, in foundry cupolas, and for various other industrial purposes, of which the most important are chemical processing, the reduction of ferroalloys in electric furnaces, nonferrous smelting, and mineral wool manufacture. In past years, large quantities of coke were used for residential heating and for the production of producer gas and water gas, but these markets have been taken over by fuel oil and natural gas and only minor quantities are now used for these purposes.

—Eugene T. Sheridan

Concrete, an important construction material made by binding together sand, gravel, or crushed stone with hydraulic cement, which is a mixture of water and Portland cement. (See *Cement.*) In addition to being both fire- and weather-resistant, concrete is a very versatile building material. The initial mixture is plastic and easily workable into almost any shape. When concrete hardens, or *sets,* the sand and gravel, called *fine* and *coarse aggregate,* respectively, are joined together by the cement to form a rocklike mass which has great compressive strength. Well-made concrete, when broken for testing, fractures through the coarse aggregate, demonstrating that the concrete

TWA. EZRA STOLLER

CONCRETE adapts to a variety of uses and forms. For his Kennedy Airport TWA terminal, architect Eero Saarinen created graceful, soaring shapes from reinforced concrete.

is as strong as the rock it contains.

Engineers use concrete in almost every type of construction. The most obvious are highways, bridges, and dams. Less obvious, but just as important, are the massive foundations for skyscrapers, the mostly underwater piers that support the huge steel towers of bridges.

Although strong in compression, concrete is relatively weak under tension. To build concrete structures, such as buildings and bridges, in which the concrete is subject to tensile stresses, engineers embed steel bars in the concrete. Such concrete is called *reinforced concrete*. Reinforcing steel also is used to prevent cracks caused by expansion and contraction due to weather changes. A more recent engineering development is *prestressed concrete*. A prestressed concrete beam is made by putting the concrete member in compression longitudinally, by means of high-strength steel wire or strand. This can be done by casting the concrete around the strands, which are held in tension by jacks (*pre-tensioning*); or by leaving holes running through the beams, inserting the strands after the beam is cast, and then putting the beam into compression, (*post-tensioning*.) Both processes put the beam in a longitudinal compression so that it can better resist transverse tensile stresses.

By comparison, the concrete used for a massive gravity dam (one that relies on its own weight to hold back the water) is plain or *mass* concrete. There is no reinforcing; just enough Portland cement is used to bind it, and the coarse aggregate may be pieces of rock as large as 6 inches.

Aggregate used to make concrete is carefully processed. The particles, from the tiniest grain of sand to the largest piece of gravel or rock, must be clean, hard, and strong. Both fine and coarse aggregate are usually washed to remove any dust, silt, or other impurities that would interfere with the bonding reaction with the cement-water paste. Next, it is screened and carefully separated into various sizes. The quality and type of concrete depends on the proportion and gradations of the various aggregates. The ratio of cement to aggregate is also controlled. Most important is the water-cement ratio. Even when all other components of concrete are correctly proportioned, too much water reduces its strength very markedly. Concrete's strength is derived from the hydration reaction that takes place between the Portland cement and water.

There are many admixtures that are added to concrete at the time of mixing to impart special properties to the concrete, such as air-entraining agents, accelerators, retarders, antifreeze, damp-proofing agents, pozzolana, color pigments, and workability agents. Some of these admixtures accomplish more than one purpose. For example, calcium chloride added to concrete causes it to set faster by increasing the rate of hydration, but it also serves as an antifreeze for cold-weather concreting. *Retarders* do the opposite,

slowing the hydration rate and preventing flash-setting, which might occur under certain circumstances. *Air-entraining agents* put in the concrete mix increase the amount of air entrained in the concrete during mixing. Air-entrained concrete is highly resistant to freezing and thawing and the deterioration caused by the de-icing chemicals commonly used on highways during the winter. (See Cement.)

Pozzolana, siliceous materials such as diatomaceous earth, tufts, and pumicite, which occur naturally, or fly ash, ground blast-furnace slag, or calcined shale or clay, are being used in increasing amounts in concrete. Pozzolanas themselves are not cementitious, but when very finely pulverized will react with lime in the Portland cement to form compounds that are cementitious. Although pozzolanic concrete generally takes longer to attain its full strength, a large structure such as a dam may take five years to build, so this reduction in early strength is not important.   —William W. Jacobus, Jr.

Construction Engineering, the branch of engineering that deals with the building of structures rather than with their planning or design. Paralleling the mechanization of industry, that followed the advent of steam power, was a mechanization of construction that has transformed an ancient, primarily manual art into a highly developed modern engineering specialty. Engineers have long been responsible for the design and specifications for works and, notably in governmental projects, have also planned and directed construction operations. In general, however, the actual building of a project is carried out by a practical builder who is awarded the contract on the basis of the lowest bid.

In earlier years, the direction of laborers in the use of tools and materials constituted the major problem encountered by the contractor. Hand methods were long more or less standardized. Pick-and-shovel excavation, man-powered hoists, and horses and carts were the major construction resources. With the development of modern equipment and machine tools and emphasis on the rapid completion of a project, the selection of the most favorable methods and equipment for a specific construction and their comparative costs, the design of the plant, and the timing and scheduling of the sequence of operations involved, have led to labor-management problems in the field of engineering. Labor has been replaced by capital commitments in equipment. Construction has, in fact, become a highly divided specialty; companies specialize in fields ranging from foundation and underpinning operations, buildings, bridges, dams, and other structural needs, to highway work and subaqueous tunneling. Not only has the scale of modern works also tremendously exceeded those of earlier undertakings but the time required for their completion has been cut to a mere fraction of that prevailing about century ago.
—James Kip Finch

URIS BUILDINGS CORPORATION

FRAMEWORK of steel and mortar rises with the aid of an elevator (*left*) to lift tools.

Copper, an important nonferrous metal, one of the oldest metals known to man; symbol Cu. The discovery of the native form of copper about 8000 B.C. marked the beginning of the Bronze Age, after which this malleable metal was hammered into crude implements and weapons.

Early copper workings on the Sinai Peninsula have been dated as far back as 3800 B.C., and deposits on Cyprus were mined as early as 3000 B.C. These mines were valued possessions of empires that followed, and they were the main source of metal for the Romans. During this time the Egyptians developed the art of metallurgy, and the use of bronze (an alloy of copper and tin) became common.

Copper is widely used because of its chemical, physical, electrical, and mechanical properties. It has low chemical activity and combines in one of three valences: 2+ (cupric) is the most common, but 1+ (cuprous) is also relatively common; the 3+ valence occurs only in a few unstable compounds. With a specific gravity of 8.94, copper is a comparatively heavy metal. Its melting point is 1083° C, its boiling point 2595° C. The thermal and electrical conductivity of copper are both high, and only silver is a better conductor. Copper is one of the strongest of the pure metals. It is moderately hard, extremely tough and wear-resistant, and highly ductile.

Most of the world's copper is obtained from the sulfide ores—chalcocite, covellite, chalcopyrite, bornite, and enargite. Some is obtained from the oxide ores—cuprite, tenorite, malachite, azurite, and brochantite.

Michigan is now the only large-scale producer of copper in the United States. As the demand for copper has grown, the richer ores have been used up. The average U.S. ore now contains about one per cent copper, somewhat lower than that of other countries. However, flotation methods have been developed to upgrade the copper content of low-grade ores. Hence, known reserves will be sufficient to satisfy demand for a long time to come, although the use of lower-grade ores does increase production costs.

Flotation methods produce concentrates containing 20 to 40 per cent copper, and recent improvements promise to increase the yield. The concentrates usually are roasted to reduce their sulfur content (although this step can be bypassed with richer concentrates). Reverberatory furnaces have replaced blast furnaces for smelting concentrates, because they can smelt the finely-divided concentrate without sintering. Furthermore, these furnaces can use a wider range of fuels than can blast furnaces. Smelting yields *copper matte,* a molten solution of copper and iron sulfides, and a slag. The iron oxide is removed in a converter; the iron is further oxidized and formed into a slag by the addition of silica. The sulfur in the matte is oxidized to form sulfur dioxide, which passes off and leaves copper in the converter. When this copper is cast it forms cakes whose surface is roughened and blistered by the escaping gas, hence the name *blister copper.* It is 98 to 99 per cent pure copper. Blister copper is further refined in a furnace and cast into anodes containing 99.0 to 99.3 per cent copper. Electrolytic treatment further refines the metal to 99.98 per cent purity.

Most copper ores contain gold and silver, which are recovered along with other metals as by-products. When the ore is smelted, gold and silver dissolve in the matte. They remain with the copper through converting and furnace refining, and are recovered during electrolytic refining.

World Consumption of COPPER in %

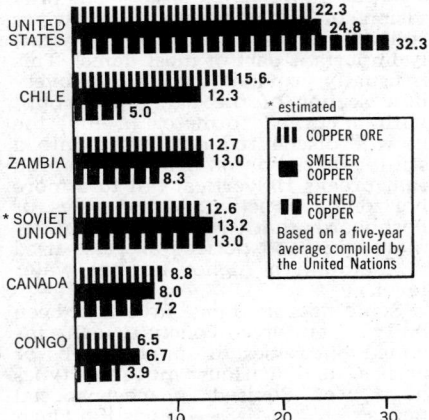

A significant amount of copper is produced by hydrometallurgy. The ore is leached with dilute sulfuric acid or a similar solvent without being concentrated. This process is used mainly for the oxide ores. But leaching does not remove gold or silver—an important part of the metallurgy of copper.

Copper is sold in several commercial grades. The American Society for Testing Materials designates material containing not more than 0.5 per cent of another element or elements as copper. These specifications cover three main commercial varieties: electrolytic, fire-refined, and lake copper. Copper also is specified by the method of processing: tough-pitch, oxygen-free, and deoxidized. Specific kinds of copper include casting copper, phosphorized copper, low- and high-residual phosphorous copper, silver-bearing copper, arsenical copper, selenium-bearing copper, and tellurium copper.

Copper is one of the few metals used more in its pure form than in alloys with other metals. Nevertheless, copper does combine with other metals to form a great number of commercially important alloys, of which brass (copper-zinc) and bronze (copper-tin) in their many varieties are among the oldest and most useful.   —John Price

Cork, the bark of the cork oak (*Quercus suber*), which is found in countries along the Mediterranean Sea. Portugal, Spain, France, Italy, Algeria, Morocco, and Tunisia are the main cork-producing countries.

The cork tree has two protective coatings: an outer bark (cork) and an inner bark. The cambium is inside the inner bark, and the cork can therefore be removed without damaging the tree. When the cork oak is about 20 years old—about 9 inches in diameter—cork is removed from the trunk of the tree. The bark grows back again at a faster rate and this *stripping* process can be repeated thereafter at 8 to 10 year intervals. After the cork is boiled, scraped, and dried, it is baled and sold for manufacturing operations.

Written records as far back as 400 B.C. tell of the use of cork. The early Greeks and Romans used it for fishing-net floats, stoppers, and inner soles of shoes. Residents of cork-producing countries for centuries have used cork slabs for roofs and floors.

Cork bark varies in thickness and the yield per tree ranges from 35 to several hundred pounds per stripping. Stripped cork is hauled to central stations where it is boiled in copper tanks for 30 minutes. Heavy weights keep it submerged. Boiling removes tannins, other water-soluble materials, and loose dirt. At the same time, the cork is softened and the rough, hard outside portion, called *hardback,* is loosened so that it can be scraped easily from the good cork. Boiling, scraping, and drying reduce the cork to about two-thirds its original weight, but the volume loss is only about 3 per cent.   —John Price

Dams, structural barriers to regulate the flow of or contain a river or stream. Low earth embankments or dikes have been built since ancient times to hold back water for irrigation or drainage. In earlier years in the United States, where timber was plentiful and funds limited, less costly timber and timber crib dams were also widely used. Larger dams of earth or masonry, however, are of recent origin. The first large masonry dams were built for irrigation in Spain in the late sixteenth century, but their modern forms are less than a century old. The greatest dams are products of the twentieth-century. Several other forms—arch, buttress, and movable—are also dams of modern origin.

■ **EARTH AND ROCK-FILL DAMS.**—Several earth dams more than 100 feet high were built before 1900. Usually constructed with a central core-wall of clay or concrete to provide water tightness and keep the lower slope reasonably dry, they were made of selected earth, deposited and compacted in place. However, because of the great disasters due to overtopping, such as the Johnstown flood of 1889 that resulted in the loss of over 2,000 lives, they were considered undesirable for higher structures. In the West, however, the *hydraulic-fill* method was developed and widely adopted; new height records followed. The 250-foot-high Fort Peck Dam on the upper Missouri, intended for flood control of the Mississippi and completed in 1940, involved placing more than 125 million cubic yards of earth and fill.

Rock-fill dams, which have a watertight diaphragm of steel or concrete, were also developed in the western United States in order to use local materials in remote sites. Composite forms of earth and rock-fill, such as the 400-foot-high Brownlee Dam on the Snake River (Idaho and Oregon), have also been built. A height over 500 feet was reached in the Swift and Trinity dams in Washington and California, respectively. A proposed Russian dam will raise this record to 735 feet.

■ **GRAVITY DAMS.**—The major requirements for a dam are tightness against seepage and stability against water pressure or possible overtopping and destruction by floods. The masonry gravity dam resists water pressure solely because of its weight. The first such dams simply were massive, generally rectangular blocks of masonry. As the mechanics of such structures were more clearly understood, however, the modern triangular, so-called *profile* evolved, increasing in width down from a minimum at the top. The Furens Dam of 1866 in France, 164 feet high, was the first of this rationally designed form. British engineers in India later built a number of similar irrigation dams of record height and length. A new record for height, 297 feet, was reached in the New Croton Dam built for the water supply of New York City in 1907, and the U.S. Bureau of Reclamation, established in 1902, later built a number of outstanding irrigation dams. The Grand Coulee Dam on the Co-

U.S. DEPARTMENT OF THE INTERIOR

HOOVER DAM on the Colorado River provides flood control, water and electric power.

Noted Modern Dams

Name	Location	Height in Feet	Length in Feet	Date Completed
UNITED STATES				
Anderson Ranch	Idaho-Oregon, Boise River	456	1350	1948
Ashokan	New York, Esopus Creek	252	4650	1912
Bull Shoals	Arkansas, White River	278	2349	1948
Center Hill	Tennessee, Caney Fork River	250	2160	1951
Cougar	Oregon, McKenzie River	515	1730	1965
Diablo	Washington, Skagit River	386	1180	1930
El Capitan	California, San Diego River	270	1200	1935
Flaming Gorge	Utah, Green River	502	1285	1964
Fontana	North Carolina, Little Tennessee River	480	2385	1944
Fort Peck	Montana, Missouri River	250	21026	1940
Friant	California, San Joaquin River	319	3488	1944
Garrison	North Dakota, Missouri River	210	12000	1954
Glen Canyon	Arizona, Colorado River	700	1560	1963
Grand Coulee	Washington, Columbia River	550	4173	1942
Hoover (Boulder)	Arizona-Nevada, Colorado River	726	1244	1936
Mansfield	Texas, Colorado River	270	5093	1942
Mud Mountain	Washington, White River	425	700	1948
Oahe	South Dakota, Missouri River	242	9360	1960
Owyhee	Oregon, Owyhee River	417	1010	1932
Palisades	Idaho, Snake River	260	2100	1966
Ross	Washington, Skagit River	545	1275	1949
Saluda	South Carolina, Saluda River	208	7838	1930
San Gabriel #1	California, San Gabriel River	355	1540	1938
Shasta	California, Sacramento River	602	3460	1945
Trinity	California, Trinity River	537	2450	1960
Wolf Creek	Kentucky, Cumberland River	240	5736	1948
FOREIGN				
Aswân	Egypt, Nile River	174	6900	1934
Aswân High	Egypt, Nile River	361	1630	Under construction
Bhakara	India, Sutlej River	680	1700	1960
Bin-el-Ouidane	Morocco, Wadi el Abid	440	950	1954
Burrinjuck	Australia, Murrumbridgee River	264	765	1913
Chambon	France, Romanche River	450	1080	1934
Grande Dixence #2	Switzerland, Dixence River	921	2480	1961
Karaj	Iran, Karaj River	590	1285	1962
Kurobegawa	Japan, Kurobe River	637	1434	1962
Mauvoisin	Switzerland, Drance de Bagnes	780	1750	1957
Mettur	India, Kaveri River	230	5000	1934
Sakuma	Japan, Tenryu River	512	1960	1956
Tres Marias	Brazil, Sao Francisco River	233	8400	1960
Volta	Ghana, Volta River	370	2100	Under construction
Wu-sheh	Taiwan, Wu-sheh Chi	374	699	1961

lumbia River, 550 feet, also a Federal power and irrigation work, today holds the record for volume, more than 10 million cubic yards of concrete, but the 921-foot-high Grande Dixence Dam, completed in 1966 in Switzerland, holds the height record.

So-called *rubble masonry*, large stones with joints filled with mortar and smaller stones, was used in earlier works, but the production of Portland cement on a large scale led to the wider use of mass-produced concrete. A so-called *cyclopean concrete*, large stones embedded in concrete, was adopted for the Kensico Dam (built 1910–1916) for New York City's water supply.

Large dams must be founded on rock sufficiently hard to support their thrust even under high water pressure. Adequacy of foundations, largely a matter of experience and judgment, thus is critical. Most failures have been due to foundation difficulties, and it may be said of dams that the risk of failure has been the price of progress. The possibility of uplift due to water pressure in the joint between foundation and structure has also received increasing attention in recent years; it may have contributed to some earlier failures.

■**ARCH DAMS.**—In order to save material, a dam in a narrow valley may be built as an arch with its axis vertical, convex upstream and abutting against solid and reasonably vertical canyon walls. Such an arch dam was apparently built as early as 1843, in the Zola Dam for the water supply of Aix in France. The arched form had been adopted in even the earliest Spanish gravity dams, however, with the idea that this would provide increased stability. Similarly, this plan was followed in early works such as the record-breaking Arrowrock Dam (Idaho), 350 feet high, of 1916. It was soon recognized, however, that in such an *arch-gravity* structure the development of arch action required special precautions to close all vertical joints if a saving in material was to be realized. This problem was met in the Hoover Dam on the Colorado River in 1936, an arch-gravity work that set a new height record of 726 feet. Even this record, however, has been surpassed by the 780-foot-high Mauvoisin Dam in Switzerland of 1957 and the 870-foot-high Vaiont Dam in Italy of 1961.

■**SPILLWAY AND OTHER DAMS.**—The provision of an adequate overflow or spillway to pass flood flows is a vitally important part of most dams. This is usually provided by a special overflow section of the dam, often built with a curved form, or profile; the flow is discharged downward into a stilling basin or onto a lower apron that breaks its vertical fall to a more horizontal direction. Crest gates or flashboards that can be cleared or removed in flood periods are also used to maintain a higher normal water level.

Some notable dams have also been built of reinforced concrete, using inclined buttresses to support slabs or arches, and various movable types have been devised to meet special needs.

—James Kip Finch

Explosives, substances or mixtures of substances that decompose suddenly to release great amounts of energy in the form of heat and expanding gases. They are used for destructive purposes in warfare, but their principal value lies in their peacetime use in mining, construction, road building, quarrying, land clearing, and other useful work. Commercial explosives have become so fundamental to the basic economy that their sales statistics are often considered an accurate indicator of the level of general business activity.

Explosives are useful tools because they concentrate immense force in small, easy-to-handle packages. The key to their power is the fact that they release all of their energy in extremely brief time intervals—usually a few millionths of a second. During its detonation period, for example, a stick of dynamite delivers as much energy as the entire electrical power industry of the United States is generating during that time.

There are two main classes of explosives: low (deflagrating) explosives and high (detonating) explosives. The former burn progressively over a relatively long period of time (though still for very small fractions of a second), whereas the latter act almost instantaneously.

Low explosives, which include black powder and smokeless powder, are now used largely for propellants, where their longer burning time provides a steady thrust to propel a bullet or missile. Other uses include fuzes, fireworks, and some special kinds of blasting.

High explosives include dynamite, TNT (trinitrotoluene), nitrocarbonitrates, and many compounds for special purposes. These are the so-called disruptive materials normally used for blasting today.

Rapid oxidation is the reaction that makes explosives function. A typical explosive compound contains both an oxidant and combustible elements, and it may include additives to prevent deterioration, to lower the freezing point, etc. It does not require air or any other external oxygen supply. Most explosives must be under confinement for proper performance, and many will simply burn if ignited.

In general, explosives used for military purposes differ from those used commercially. Dynamite, for example, is seldom used in military operations, and most military explosives are not satisfactory for civilian work. Some materials, such as TNT, that are primarily military do have limited commercial applications, usually as a constituent of a complex explosive material.

■**HISTORY.**—The early history of explosives is obscure. Some historians say that the Chinese used black powder several hundred years before the Christian era. In the seventh century, a Byzantine fleet is reported to have attacked enemy ships with Greek fire, a concoction of sulfur, rosin, pitch, and saltpeter, much like black powder, which burned with a roaring flame and reportedly had been known to the Greeks more than 1,000 years before. In the thirteenth century, the English chemist Roger Bacon set down the first known instructions for the manufacture of black powder, and by the next century it was being used as a propellant for firearms. In 1627, black powder was used in Hungary for blasting ore, the first known instance of useful work by an explosive.

Gunpowder was vital in colonial America and was one of the first commodities to be manufactured in the colonies. Black powder was probably used for blasting in New England by the early eighteenth century.

High explosives originated in 1845 with the discovery of guncotton by Christian F. Schoenbein in Basel, Switzerland. This was followed the next year by the Italian Ascanio Sobrero's invention of nitroglycerin, a major milestone in the history of explosives. Alfred Nobel in 1866 found a way to convert the unpredictable liquid nitroglycerin into a solid, stable material that he called dynamite. Dynamite, which has now been modified into dozens of different types, has been the leading commercial explosive for the past century.

■**NEW EXPLOSIVES.**—Research has been a characteristic of the explosives industry ever since the middle of the nineteenth century. One of the world's first industrial chemical research laboratories was established by Du Pont in Gibbstown, New Jersey, in 1902 to develop new explosives and improve manufacturing processes. Research on explosives led in time to a better understanding of chemistry, particularly organic chemistry, and helped create a base for the modern chemical industry.

Research produced a steady stream of improved and safer dynamites, new techniques for their use, and more efficient blasting accessories—fuzes, blasting machines, detonators, and similar devices. In 1935 a new type of explosive was introduced—*the nitrocarbo-nitrate* family, which is based primarily on ammonium nitrate, a chemical made from atmospheric nitrogen and a coal or oil derivative. Known as blasting agents, these materials are relatively inert and can be set off only by a strong explosive charge. They are not only safe but economical to use when conditions are appropriate. The most recent developments permit the use of fertilizer-grade ammonium nitrate as an explosive at substantial savings in cost. Other new forms of explosives include those in semiliquid or gelatin-like form, which can be loaded into the borehole by pumping, and metalized explosives in which powdered aluminum contributes added energy.

Explosives manufacturing processes vary, depending on the end product. In a typical dynamite plant, operations are conducted in small buildings isolated from each other to minimize hazards. Glycerin is treated in a continuous-process nitrating unit to form *nitroglycerin.* The liquid nitroglycerin is then mixed with ammonium nitrate or other solid materials —usually inert substances, such as wood flour, ground nut shells, and clays—to form a slightly moist, grainy mixture that is loaded into cartridges and shipped to the user.

There are approximately 20 manufacturers of explosives in the United States, operating plants scattered throughout the country. There are at least 20,000 large-scale regular users of explosives in the nation, and most manufacturers sell through a network of distributors. Explosives can be shipped by rail, truck, or other means under regulations of the Interstate Commerce Commission. Annual usage in United States in the 1960's exceeded 1,500,000,000 pounds.

—E. I. du Pont de Nemours & Co.

E. I. DU PONT DE NEMOURS & CO.

BLASTING AGENT is loaded into vertical holes in the face of a quarry; the explosion rips out 25,000 tons of sandstone, enabling miners to retrieve silica held by the rock.

Felt, a textile composition produced by pressure and friction instead of by customary spinning and weaving techniques. This process causes fibrous materials such as woolens, furs, and artificial staples to form a tough mat.

Fur (or *hat*) *felt* is made from cony, hare, muskrat, nutria, and beaver fur. Small amounts of synthetic fibers, such as protein fibers made from casein, corn, soybeans, or peanuts, sometimes are added. Felting is facilitated by a process called *carroting*—heating the fur while it is still on the pelt with certain oxidizing agents in acid solution. At first this was done with mercury in nitric acid. Fur thus treated turned yellow like a carrot; hence the name. However, mercury treatment is toxic and has been replaced by a method using chlorine compounds. *Wool felt* can be made without a chemical pretreatment. Woolen fibers are generally short to medium length. They are blended and then run through a series of processes: willying, blending, teasing, scribbling, carding, forming, hardening, milling, carbonizing, dyeing, and finishing. Batts of felt thus produced may be superimposed to increase thickness. Manufactured felts are used for upholstery, carpeting, billiard-table covers, padding for clothing, and for heat-insulating and silencing purposes. Impregnated synthetic-fiber felts are used for roofing, housing and shipping sheathing, and for pads under carpets.   —John Price

Fibers, Structural, threadlike substances useful as construction materials, including asbestos, rock wool, slag wool, glass wool, and lead wool.

Asbestos is the general name applied to a number of mineral silicates that are incombustible and can be separated into filaments. Largest sources of commercial asbestos are mines in Canada, the United States, and Africa. Asbestos appears in many forms and types, varying from long, soft, silky fibers with a definite orientation of the crystals to a short,

harsh, brittle mass fiber with random orientation of the crystals. Asbestos cloth is used for brake linings, clutch facings, gaskets, fireproof curtains, shingles, insulation, and fireproofing.

Mineral wool is the term applied to products known as rock wool, slag wool, and glass wool. Each of these materials is a fluffy, lightweight mass of intermingled vitreous mineral fibers composed of complex silicates. *Rock wool* is made from natural rock or combinations of natural minerals, which are melted and blown into fibers. *Slag wool* is made of iron, copper, or lead blast-furnace slags. *Glass wool* is made from conventional glass batch materials—such as silica sand and soda ash or borax—dolomite, and minor ingredients. Mineral wools are used as thermal insulation, sound-absorbing materials, and as a filter medium.

Lead wool consists of fine strands of metallic lead loosely wound into a rope. It is made by pouring molten lead through a fine sieve. The lead solidifies into fine strands as it falls through the air. Lead wool is used for plugging oil wells to prevent water seepage, and for other caulking purposes. It can be used under water or in gaseous locations where heat (which is not needed for lead-wool caulking) would be dangerous.

—John Price

Fibers, Synthetic, manmade materials used in the manufacture of textiles. In the modern world, the use of materials for clothing and other practical purposes has tended steadily away from natural substances toward synthetic replacements. This trend has resulted from the rise of applied technology which has created and made commercially practicable many synthetic materials with functional properties similar to those of their natural counterparts, and by the growth both in the number of people in the world and their standards of living. In response to an expanded demand for consumers' goods, synthetic products,

such as coated fabrics of various kinds, and plastic sheetings, such as vinyl, have replaced leather. Plastics in solid form have taken the place of wood and steel in many familiar uses, such as the handles of kitchen knives, knobs and handles, and the fittings of vacuum cleaners.

In no field has the trend toward synthetic materials been more pronounced than in textiles—the woven, knitted, or felted fabrics used since prehistoric times for clothing and home decoration. Synthetic textiles are purely a development of this century. As the century has advanced, their use has increased sharply to the point where they have outdistanced wool and silk and are fast catching up with cotton, in terms of poundage consumed.

■**CELLULOSE FIBERS.**—The first synthetic fibers were made from cellulose. These are rayon and acetate, known from their basic material as the *cellulose fibers. Rayon,* the first synthetic fiber, was developed experimentally in the latter part of the nineteenth century by Count Hilaire de Chardonnet in France and Charles F. Cross and E. J. Bevin in England. Commercial production of rayon, then known as artificial silk, was undertaken in the United States about 1910. In subsequent years, the manufacture of rayon as a textile fiber spread to virtually every industrialized country in the world. Rayon is made by a complex process in which pure cellulose is extracted from wood pulp, and to a lesser extent from cotton, by subjecting them to treatment with caustic soda and carbon disulfide. The result is a chemical solution which is pumped through a *spinneret,* a device that resembles a tiny shower-bath nozzle. The threadlike streams harden as they emerge, forming filaments that are gathered together into yarn. Among the trade names for rayon fibers are Cupioni, Fortisan, and Zantrel.

Acetate, the second synthetic fiber brought to wide use, is made, like rayon, from cellulose. However, different chemicals are added to the cellulose solution, with the result that acetate has somewhat different properties. Among the trade names for acetate fibers are Celaperm and Chromspun.

■**CHEMICAL FIBERS.**—The success of rayon and acetate for clothing fabrics and household and industrial uses spurred research into ways of making fibers by chemical means which would have functional properties even more desirable and versatile than those derived from the natural material, cellulose. It was discovered that certain polymers—the technical name for large molecules made by combining smaller molecules—have exceptional fiber-forming properties. In this research, Wallace Carothers is generally credited with the major effort that led to the first of the truly synthetic fibers, *nylon.* This fiber is created by a complex process from various chemical ingredients of which the most notable, for one form, are hexamethylene diamine and adipic acid. Another kind of nylon uses the chemical, caprolactam.

AMERICAN VISCOSE CORPORATION

RAYON fabric is woven from viscose filament cut into short lengths called "staple." After it is bleached, rinsed, and dried, the staple is baled and sent to spinning mills.

Introduced in 1939 by Du Pont, nylon was used during World War II for tow ropes for gliders and other military uses, where its great strength and durability were essential. When the war ended in 1945, as fast as its production could be expanded, nylon found its way into a steadily broadening variety of apparel. Today, nylon is produced in ever-increasing quantities for use in virtually every kind of apparel and decorative fabric.

The success of nylon led to increased interest in the profit possibilities of other synthetic fibers among large chemical companies in the United States, Europe, and Japan. In rapid succession since 1950, new synthetic fibers have been introduced, each with its own advantages for use in textiles. Among them have been the *acrylics*, fibers made largely from a chemical called acrylonitrile. Soft and bulky like wool, with wool's warmth, the acrylic fibers are also highly resistant to chemicals; when made into cloth, they offer good shape and crease retention. These characteristics along with quick drying give acrylic garments a high degree of easy-care convenience for consumers. Among the trade names for acrylic fibers are Acrilan, Creslan, and Orlon.

Another important group of synthetic fibers is the *polyesters*, fibers extruded from a chemical solution made up of dihydric alcohol and terepthalic acid. Blended with cotton or rayon, polyester fabrics have been second only to nylon in yielding apparel fabrics that are durable, wrinkle-resistant, and quick-drying. These qualities and easy maintenance are the basis of the popularity of the so-called *wash and wear* apparel. Among the trade names for polyester fibers are Dacron, Fortrel, Kodel, and Vycron.

Other synthetic fibers that have won acceptance in apparel are *spandex fibers*, such as Lycra, with *snapback* properties of stretch and recovery that give elasticity to corsets, brassieres, and bathing suits; the *elefin fibers* such as Royalene, made from a paraffinlike derivative of petroleum; and *glass fibers*, such as Herculon, which are extremely fine filaments of glass that have performed well in curtains and other decorative fabrics.

Along with the manmade fibers noted above, other fibers have been found advantageous in certain specialized textile uses. *Saran*, the generic name for vinylidene chloride fibers, is extruded as a stiff yarn with good chemical and flame resistance. Among its established uses are draperies and outdoor furniture fabrics. *Metallic yarns* are widely used for decorative effects in apparel and home furnishings fabrics. They are made by bonding aluminum foil between clear layers of plastic, or by vacuum depositing of aluminum on the surface of a plastic film.

The man-made textile materials have taken their place with cotton and wool as the principal materials for the endless variety of uses that the world's billions of people have for cloth. Indeed, it can be expected that, as the manmade fibers are improved by continuous research and testing, their use will almost completely supersede that of natural fibers. In this connection, it must be remembered that the major natural fibers, cotton and wool, are becoming more and more expensive to produce, while applied technology steadily reduces the cost of the synthetics.

—Jerome Campbell

Flux, a material added during soldering or brazing to improve the quality of the joint. *Soldering fluxes* remove oxide or other obstructing films so the parts will accept solder more readily. Activated rosin flux often forms the core of solder. Other fluxes include zinc chloride, ammonium chloride, and combinations of these. *Brazing fluxes* remove any oxides that may form during heating, brazing, or cooling and protect the joint from oxidation. Fluxes may be chemical formulations or protective and cleansing atmospheres. Borates and fluoroborates; chlorides of sodium, potassium, and lithium; borax and boric acid; and alkalis, together with wetting agents and water, are commonly used. *Protective atmospheres,* used in furnace brazing, include fuel gas, dissociated ammonia, hydrogen, inorganic vapors, or inert gases such as helium or argon.   —John Price

Fuller's Earth, a natural earthy material, usually a clay, that decolorizes mineral or vegetable oils. In ancient times, certain earths were used to clean raw wool by adsorption. The process became known as *fulling,* and the cleaning agent was called fuller's earth. The clay materials usually present in fuller's earth include attapulgite, montmorillonite, and kaolinite.

Fuller's earths apparently decolorize by selective adsorption of coloring matter and other impurities. These are held strongly within the clay structure and can be removed only by drastic treatment. Much fuller's earth is used to decolorize petroleum products, cottonseed oil, tallow, soy oils, and other products. For such applications the earth must not only decolorize, it also must not impart any taste or odor and must not retain too much oil that cannot be reclaimed. Some fuller's earths are used for oil-well drilling muds, insecticide carriers, and fillers. The main deposits of fuller's earth are in the United States, Japan, and England.

—John Price

Fur and Leather, pliable materials made from the hides, skins, or pelts of animals. Fur is a form of leather made from the skins of mammals, with part of the hair left on. Both fur and leather are processed so as to inhibit the decaying of the skin. The treatment alters the skin protein. It is necessarily less enduring for fur than for leather, since the hair cannot be destroyed in the process and the skins must be kept flexible and soft.

In *fur dressing,* the skins are first soaked in brine to soften the skin and to inhibit bacteria. The skin is then hammered with many needles to soften it, and the flesh is scraped off by hand with sharp knives. The pelt is then converted by *oil tanning,* called either *pickling* or *biting.* In these processes, the skins are soaked for several hours in solutions of chemicals such as sodium chloride, sulfuric acid, formaldehyde, and alum. This halts or delays putrefaction of the skins. The skins are then thoroughly dried, after which vegetable, animal, and mineral oils and greases are worked into the leather by a wooden piston *tramping machine,* or *kicker.*

The peltry is then rolled in circular vats with sawdust, which absorbs the oil and grease. The fur is combed, beaten, and sometimes sheared. Generally, the furs are dyed by rotating them in vats until the dyes are fixed. The dyes are usually anilines, although some furs, such as mouton, require vegetable dyes. Almost every type of mammal skin has been used for fur, but the favored fur animals come from a rodent family (beaver, muskrats, nutria, etc.), and the weasel family (sable, marten, mink, otter, kolinsky, etc.).

In contrast to fur, *leather manufacturing* removes all of the hair, and the hide or skin is more thoroughly preserved. Hide consists of the epidermis, dermis, and flesh, but only the dermis is used in leather. The hide, or skin, is first soaked in lime and water or various chemical depilatories. The hair and flesh are then scraped off by machine, and the hide is cut up to get pieces of uniform thickness in a process called *rounding.* Next, the hide is *bated* by washing with a weak acid solution (usually dilute sulfuric acid) and then by adding enzymes to the bating water. In bating, the enzymes destroy fat and oil and soften the hide. The hide is then pickled for a day or two in a chemical solution that further preserves the skin. After that, the leather is ready for *tanning.*

Tannin concentrates and extracts are usually used, and some sort of glucose is added to the tanning solution. Hides are often put in a series of vats with increasingly strong solutions so that the hides tan thoroughly and evenly. Tanning may take from several days to a year, depending on the tannin used and the type of leather desired. Tanning causes a reaction of the skin proteins with certain chemicals to produce a decay-resistant hide, although the exact nature of the reaction is not understood. Chrome is the only inorganic tannin of importance. Vegetable tannins, extracted from the bark, wood, or fruit of trees, are numerous. The most common sources of tannin are quebracho (44 per cent of the total used), chestnut wood extract (30 per cent), and mangrove (5.4 per cent).

After the leather has been tanned, it is colored and *fat-liquored.* Dyes and oils are worked into the leather in a vat, and the leather is then dried under increasing temperatures for nearly a day. *Sammying,* which consists of soaking and then milling in sawdust, completes the process. Next, the leather is finished; sometimes it is buffed or polished, sometimes shellacked or varnished.

One major virtue of leather is that it is porous, but it is also a poor heat

conductor. Nearly any skin can be tanned, including the skins of mammals, reptiles, birds, and fish. Cattle hides are the largest source of leather, and the shoe industry still uses most of the product. Luggage, clothing, and accessories are made of leather from the skins of ostrich, alligator, shark, and many other exotic animals.
—John T. Schlebecker

Gas, a combustible fluid supplied and utilized in the gaseous state as a fuel to produce heat, light, or power for domestic, commercial, and industrial applications. Each of the many types may be classified in one of three groups: natural gases, manufactured gases, or liquefied petroleum gases.

■**NATURAL GAS.**—The U.S. Bureau of Mines defines natural gas as a naturally occurring mixture of hydrocarbon and nonhydrocarbon gases found in porous formations beneath the earth's surface, often in association with crude petroleum. In the United States, this is the fuel used by over 95 per cent of the approximately 37 million customers who purchase gas distributed through street mains by gas utility companies. It was first discovered in the U.S. at Fredonia, New York, in 1821.

Natural gas is found in porous rock formations, not in cavelike spaces under the earth. Gas-bearing rock consists of carbonate rocks (principally limestone) or of sandstone, which act as a kind of rigid sponge holding the gas between the grains. The gas is trapped and held by a covering of impervious or nonporous rock.

The gas contained in these underground fields is obtained by drilling wells through the covering earth and cap rock and allowing the gas to be forced out by its own pressure. In 1964, 10,747 exploratory gas and/or oil wells were drilled in the U.S., and of these 16.7 per cent, or 1,796, were productive. Gas wells now average over 5,000 feet in depth and cost an average of about $100,000 each. Some approach three miles in depth.

Natural gas is found in 31 states, of which six states account for over 90 per cent of U.S. production. By order of rank these are: Texas, Louisiana, Oklahoma, California, New Mexico, and Kansas. Of the net U.S. production of 15,347 billion cubic feet in 1964, Texas alone was responsible for almost 42 per cent. The largest producing gas field in the world is the Hugoton, which extends from the Texas Panhandle, through Oklahoma, and into Kansas.

In 1964 the transportation of gas from the source to the ultimate consumers required 730,000 miles of pipelines, of which 9 per cent were located in the gas fields, 28 per cent were transmission lines, and 63 per cent were local distribution systems. This represents an increase of almost 60 per cent over 1954 statistics. In addition, new materials and techniques now permit the use of pipelines with much larger diameters—up to 42 inches. The first pipeline in the United States, built in 1872, was only two inches in diameter, and stretched five and one-half miles, from Newton to Titusville, Pennsylvania.

Natural gas, as distributed, usually contains 80 to 95 per cent methane (CH_4) and lesser amounts of ethane (C_2H_6) and propane (C_3H_8). Most of the remainder is nitrogen. The heating value ranges from 900 to 1,200 BTU's per cubic foot. With a specific gravity from 0.58 to 0.79, it is therefore lighter than air and dissipates rapidly in the event of leakage. As produced, it is basically odorless and colorless, but for safety reasons odorants are usually added, so that any leakage may be readily detected. The gas is nontoxic (nonpoisonous) to humans and animals, and not harmful to house plants.

Natural gas can be converted into a liquid by lowering its temperature to 250° F below zero and putting it under pressure. In this form it is called *liquefied natural gas,* and the process is referred to as *liquefaction.* It is done to facilitate storage and transportation, since the liquefied gas requires only 1/600 of the storage volume that would be necessary for its containment as a gas.

■**MANUFACTURED GAS.**—A manmade gas, manufactured gas is produced from coal, coke, oil, or by reforming natural or liquefied petroleum gases. The following are a few of the most widely used types:

Coal gas is made by the distillation of the volatile matter from coal in retorts. It is high in hydrogen and methane and has some carbon monoxide and illuminants. If steam is forced through the glowing coal or coke, it reacts chemically to form *water gas,* which consists of hydrogen and carbon monoxide. Since water gas burns with a blue flame, it is also called *blue gas.* Enrichment with a higher BTU oil gas increases the light-giving qualities, as well as the heat content per cubic foot. *Carbureted water gas* is made by enriching water gas with thermally cracked oil, natural gas, or liquefied petroleum gas. The major constituents are hydrogen and carbon monoxide. All of the gases made from coal or coke contain sufficient percentages of carbon monoxide to be poisonous if inhaled. As supplied by utility companies they have heat contents of 475 to 550 BTU's per cubic foot.

Oil gas is made by thermal decomposition (cracking) of oils, which may vary from naphtha to heavy residuum carbon oils. The volatile hydrocarbons and hydrogen formed may be controlled to provide mixtures that can supplement or replace 500 BTU manufactured gases or 1,000 BTU natural gases.

Acetylene gas (C_2H_2) is primarily used for metal cutting or welding operations and as an illuminant for lighting. It is formed by the action of water on calcium carbide (CaC_2). Today, however, much of it is made from *synthesis gas,* a mixture obtained by the partial burning of natural gas under controlled conditions. For storage and transportation, acetylene is dissoved in acetone under pressure and put into steel cylinders filled with porous packing.

■**LIQUEFIED PETROLEUM GAS.**—Referred to as *LP-gas,* liquefied petroleum gas is sometimes better known to the con-

sumer as "bottled gas," "tank gas," "LPG," or simply "propane" or butane." The hydrocarbon constituents are contained in natural gas, natural gas liquids, and crude oil, and consists of combinations of propane, butane, isobutane, propylene, and butylene. These hydrocarbons can be liquefied under moderate pressure at normal temperatures, but are gaseous when used at normal atmospheric conditions. When the gas is stored on the customer's premises, it is kept in liquid form in steel cylinders that may be replaced when they are empty or may be refilled from tank trucks. Some utility companies mix LP-gas with air and distribute it through their street mains.

The two major LP-gases, propane (C_3H_8) and butane (C_4H_{10}), both contain approximately 21,600 BTU's per pound. However, when drawn from the tank as a gas, propane has a heating value of 2,500 BTU's per cubic foot as compared with 3,200 for butane gas. The gases are heavier than air and are nontoxic.

In addition to its suitability as a fuel for home and industry, LP-gas is frequently used for automobile and other internal-combustion engines, and large quantities are consumed in the petrochemical industry as a raw material for making plastics and synthetic rubber. In 1964 approximately 12.4 billion gallons were consumed; this is a 100 per cent increase over the 1955 figures.
—Edgar A. Jahn

Glass, a hard, brittle, usually transparent or translucent material that does not crystallize as it solidifies. In the United States, the term *glass* is restricted to inorganic materials. In other countries, organic materials that possess the characteristic noncrystalline structure are called organic glasses.

The average composition of the earth's crust would make an acceptable glass. When cooled rapidly, magma solidifies to form *natural glass.* Among the rocks classed as glasses are obsidian, pumice, and tachylyte. Another form of natural glass is tektite, which is probably meteoritic in origin.

Glass is a noncrystalline, or amorphous, material. Its atomic structure is one of disorder or ramdomness (Fig. 1). To produce a glass, the ingredients must be present in the cor-

Fig. 1 — Fused Silica Glass

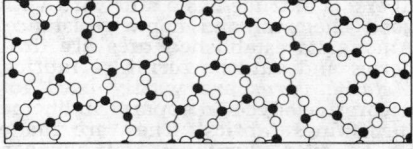

Fig. 2 — Crystalline Silica

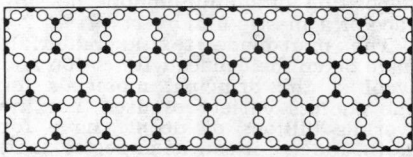

● Silicon   ○ Oxygen

Glass Characteristics and Products

Type	Characteristics	Typical Products
Soda-lime	Easily formed to many shapes Low in cost	Windows Bottles Lamp bulb envelopes
Lead-alkali	High clarity High refractive index High electrical resistivity	Art glass Thermometer tubing Optical parts
Borosilicate	Good heat, shock resistance High chemical durability	Laboratory ware Cooking ware Pipeline Boiler gauge glasses
Aluminosilicate	Good heat, shock resistance High service temperature	Ignition tubes High-speed aircraft windows
96 per cent silica	Excellent heat, shock resistance Good ultraviolet transmittance	High-temperature laboratory ware Spacecraft windows Furnace view ports
Fused silica*	Best heat, shock resistance Best ultraviolet and acoustical transmittance	High-speed wind-tunnel windows Ultrasonic delay lines.

* Fused silica, fused quartz, and silica glass are essentially the same material.

rect proportions. After these ingredients have melted and combined, the resulting fluid must be cooled rapidly enough so that randomness, which is characteristic of the fluid state, is frozen in. If the mixture of ingredients is not correct of if the cooling rate from the molten condition is too slow, the atoms will arrange themselves in a regular pattern that is characteristic of the crystalline solid state. (Fig. 2). Glass is sometimes called an undercooled fluid. Its structure is random like that of a fluid, but it is frozen and, therefore, has some of the properties of a solid, such as hardness and rigidity.

■CHEMICAL COMPOSITION.—The principal ingredient of most glass is silica sand. This is mixed with soda, lime, borax, alumina, potash, or any of several other materials. Nearly all of the known elements may be used in glass. More than 100,000 different glass compositions have been melted, and more than 1,000 kinds of glass are manufactured commercially. Almost all glass falls into one of six categories, which are based on chemical composition. The accompanying table contains a brief description of the characteristics of each type and some of the products made from each. *Soda-lime glass*, once known as *crown glass*, is the oldest type and still accounts for approximately 90 per cent of the glass produced today. It was first made about 4,000 years ago, but the exact date and place are still matters of speculation. Nor is it known how sand, soda, lime, and heat happened to be brought together by early man to form glass. *Lead-alkali glass*, once known as *flint glass*, was first made in 1675 and used for art glass because of its brilliance. The finest art glass is still made of this type; it is also used for optical parts, thermometers, and electric lamp parts.

While these older glass compositions are still used extensively, it is the four newer types (*borosilicate, aluminosilicate, 96-per-cent silica, and fused silica*) that have done most to increase the total number of glass products to nearly 50,000. Because of their improved heat resistance and chemical durability, these newer types perform under severe conditions that the older soda-lime and lead-alkali glasses could not withstand.

When additional strength is needed, glass may be tempered. This is a heat treatment that increases strength from two to four times. Soda-lime, borosilicate, and aluminosilicate glass may be tempered. Typical uses for tempered glass are automobile windows, doors for buildings, and food service ware.

Glass-ceramics are one of the more unusual discoveries of recent years. These materials are mixed, melted, and formed as glasses. Then they are converted, by a process of controlled nucleation and crystal growth, to polycrystalline ceramics. Because they are formed as glass, a greater range of shapes is possible than with other ceramic materials. After conversion, glass-ceramics are approximately four times as strong as glass. They were first used in nose cones for radar-guided ground-to-air missiles, and later for cooking ware.

Chemically strengthened glass is another discovery that opens still more possibilities for glass products. The process most frequently used involves the exchange of ions in the glass surface. After the ion-exchange treatment, the glass is up to ten times as strong as it was before. It can be bent and will withstand impacts better than any other kind of glass. It was first used as a rear-window material for convertible coupes. It is also used for laboratory ware, safety goggle lenses, and oil-well perforation capsules.

■NEW USES.—The growth of technologies in other fields continually provides new challenges and new opportunities for glass and glass-derived materials. For instance, space exploration spurred the development of spacecraft windows, low-loss antenna shields, and high-reliability electronic parts. The exploration of hydrospace (the depth of the oceans) makes use of submersible vessels and floats made of both glass and glass-ceramic materials.

Indeed, glass, once considered suitable only for windows and bottles, now appears to be a material with no limitations to its usefulness. Yesterday's limitations are a challenge stimulating today's and tomorrow's inventions. A typical example is photochromic glass. This material darkens automatically on exposure to light and clears when light source is removed. Such a glass shows promise for self-adjusting sunglasses and for control of sunlight in buildings and vehicles.   —George W. McLellan

Glue, an adhesive used for bonding separate pieces together. The term at one time referred solely to the high-molecular-weight protein extracts from hides, bones, and fish. However, the use of various protein glues as woodworking and furniture adhesives, and later as plywood adhesives, has tended to establish the term *glue* for all adhesives used by these industries.

Animal, vegetable, casein, blood albumin, liquid, and synthetic resin are the principal classes of woodworking glues. Of these, *casein*, which has a skim-milk base, is used most frequently in small workshops. *Animal glues* and *liquid glues* are used to some extent by cabinetmakers. The other glues require special equipment, such as heating facilities and presses, which tends to limit them to commercial use. Some *thermosetting resins* require temperatures higher than 300° F and pressures as high as 250 pounds per square inch, depending on the wood.

Animal glue is a crude, impure amber-colored form of commercial gelatin. It does not exist as such in the living organism, but is produced by the hydrolysis of animal collagen. It gelatinizes in aqueous solution. Animal glues are prepared by hot aqueous extraction from pretreated collagenous materials, chiefly animal hides and bones. Casein is the main protein of milk. It is made by coagulation by rennet or by acid precipitation.   —John Price

Granite, a natural plutonic rock formation with visibly crystalline texture, composed mainly of quartz and alkali feldspar with subordinate plagioclase and dark-colored minerals, such as biotite and horneblende. More generally, the term is applied to plutonic rocks rich in feldspar and quartz. Commercially, the term *granite* is extended to include any phaneritic rock rich in feldspar, with or without quartz and mafic (dark) minerals.

Because of its hardness, durability, and pleasing colors (flesh red, whitish, or gray), granite is an important building and ornamental stone. It occurs in a wide range of textures and structures.

Granite is thought to be formed by three processes—slow crystallization of deeply buried granitic melts; metamorphic recrystallization of volcanic or sedimentary rocks; and metasomatic transformation of various sedimentary or igneous rocks by introduction of certain elements, such as alkalis and silica, or by removal of others, such as iron, magnesium, and calcium.

—John Price

Gypsum, the most common of the sulfate minerals, hydrated calcium sulfate ($CaSO_4 \cdot 2H_2O$) which occurs naturally in many parts of the world. The white or slightly yellowish mineral is best known as the raw material, which when heated, loses almost all of its water to produce plaster of Paris. Gypsum is a very soft mineral and can be scratched with the human finger nail. Its hardness on Mohs' scale is 2.

The mineral is found in several forms: transparent crystals called *selenite;* a translucent, fine-grained mass called *alabaster;* a silky, fibrous form called *satin spar,* which looks somewhat like asbestos; a dull colored rock called *rock gypsum;* and an unconsolidated earthy form that is usually quite impure called *gypsite.*

Gypsum is widely used in the building industry to make many types of wallboard. In these applications the mineral is calcined (heated) to an even greater extent than for making plaster of Paris, removing even more of its water. The mineral is also used as a *retarder* in making Portland cement. Ground gypsum can be used as a fertilizer providing lime to the soil, but ground limestone has largely taken over its agricultural applications.

—William W. Jacobus, Jr.

Hydrochloric Acid, an aqueous solution of hydrogen chloride which attacks all common metals; also known as *muriatic acid;* chemical formula HCl. Pure hydrochloric acid is colorless; the acid containing impurities of iron, chlorine, or organic substances is yellow. Pure hydrogen chloride is a colorless, pungent gas at normal temperature and pressure. It fumes strongly in moist air and in concentrated form it is toxic if inhaled.

Basilius Valentinus is generally credited with the first production of hydrogen chloride, in the fifteenth century. The *Leblanc process,* invented by Nicolas Leblanc about 1790, was the first major commercial method of preparation. In this process, hydrogen chloride and salt cake (sodium sulfate) are produced as coproducts of the reaction of sulfuric acid and salt. Although the *Solvay process,* discovered by Ernest Solvay about 1863, has replaced the Leblanc process for making salt cake, the salt-sulfuric acid reaction is still important because of the industrial demand for both salt cake and hydrochloric acid. Hydrogen chloride is also produced by burning hydrogen in chlorine, which yields a high-purity product (99.7 per cent after purification) that is desirable for organic synthesis and in the manufacture of reagent-grade acid. This method is an outlet for chlorine obtained as a by-product in the manufacture of caustic soda. An increasing amount of hydrochloric acid is also produced as a by-product in the chlorination of organic chemicals, although contaminants such as chlorine, air, excess reactants, organic products, and moisture must be removed to yield a high-grade product.

Hydrochloric acid is used widely in industry for metal cleaning, sugar refining, synthetic rubber manufacture, glucose and corn sugar production, and reactivation of petroleum wells. It is also used in the production of metal chlorides, as a neutralizing agent, and in the production of organic chlorides.

—John Price

Iron and Steel, the two most important structural materials. Iron is the fourth most common element and the second most abundant metal in the earth's crust, of which it comprises 5 per cent. The core of the earth is believed to consist of iron and nickel, making iron the most plentiful element in the earth as a whole. Its symbol is Fe; atomic number 26, atomic weight 55.84, and melting point 1,535° C.

Iron occurs abundantly near the earth's surface in compounds (ores) that are widely distributed throughout the world. Its chief commercial ores are *hematite, magnetite, limonite,* and *siderite.* Iron rarely appears alone but is found free in meteorites, which usually also contain 7 to 15 per cent nickel. Meteorites were man's first source of iron, which he chipped off in small quantities as early as 4000 B.C. Although copper, bronze, lead, and some other metals were smelted before iron, iron was smelted sporadically over many centuries before the true Iron Age began.

■THE IRON AGE.—This term refers more to a stage of cultural development than to a period of time. The Iron Age originated in the Caucasus Mountains in a region known as Chalybia well before 1600 B.C., for by then the Hittites, whose tutors were the Chalybes, were skillful ironworkers. From the Hittites, the Iron Age spread to the Assyrians, Babylonians, Philistines, Egyptians, and other peoples of the Middle East, where it was well established by 1350 B.C. It spread eastward to China and India and was carried westward by the Phoenicians and the Greeks. It reached central Europe about 900 B.C. and Britain about 450 B.C.

Iron ore was smelted in primitive furnaces by means of charcoal kept burning under a forced draft from hand or foot-operated bellows. Oxygen in the ore combined with carbon in the charcoal to form carbon monoxide gas, releasing a relatively pure lump of iron intermixed with gangue from the ore that formed a slag. This was *wrought iron,* with a low carbon content. With some exceptions, it was the only form produced until the development of the blast furnace in the Rhine provinces in the fourteenth century.

■PIG IRON.—In the blast furnaces, taller furnace stacks and a more powerful draft from water-driven bellows enabled the process to produce molten iron, which could be cast in various forms. When the iron poured from the furnace, it was run into a large mold that fed a number of smaller lateral molds. Because this figuration resembled a sow nursing pigs, the iron became known as *pig iron.*

Pig iron contains about 4 per cent carbon and certain other elements, all of which tend to make it brittle. Pig iron can be converted into wrought iron by remelting and purifying it in charcoal hearths or puddling furnaces. Wrought iron is tough, ductile, and malleable. Although it was the chief form of iron for many centuries, it is little used today. *Cast iron,* as used today, is hard and has high wear and corrosion resistance; it lends itself well to casting in intricate shapes as well as in massive forms. Because of these properties, it is extensively used in pipes, rolls for rolling mills, engine blocks, cylinders and all kinds of machinery parts. The automotive industry is the largest user. Iron castings (including malleable iron) consume 5 to 10 per cent of the total pig iron production in the United States.

■STEEL.—Most of the pig iron is refined into *steel. Low carbon steel* contains less than 0.2 per cent carbon; *medium carbon steel* from 0.2 to 0.6 per cent; and *high carbon steel* from 0.6 to 1.8 per cent. All three also contain minimal amounts of other elements.

Alloy steels are those whose properties are enhanced by the presence of one or more alloying elements, chiefly manganese, molybdenum, nickel, chromium, silicon, tungsten, and vanadium. The major classifications are: high-strength low-alloy steels, constructional alloy steels, alloy tool steels, stainless steels, heat-resisting steels, and electrical steels. By varying the chemical composition, heat treatment, and other processing methods, manufacturers can produce carbon and alloy steels in a greater number of grades and for a wider variety of purposes than any other metal.

Because of its versatility, and the abundance of iron ore and other necessary raw materials in many parts of the world, steel has become the basic metal of industrial society. It meets over 95 per cent of civilization's metal requirements. (See also *Iron and Steel Production.*)

—Douglas Alan Fisher

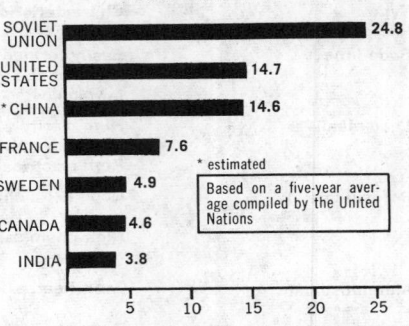

World Production of IRON ORE in %

SOVIET UNION 24.8
UNITED STATES 14.7
*CHINA 14.6
FRANCE 7.6
SWEDEN 4.9
CANADA 4.6
INDIA 3.8

* estimated

Based on a five-year average compiled by the United Nations

Kaolin, a fine, usually white clay resulting from the extreme weathering of aluminous materials, such as feldspar, that contain kaolinite as a main constituent. Kaolin remains white upon firing, and because of its excellent firing properties and refractoriness, is used extensively in the ceramics industry. It is also used as an adsorbent, as a filler or extender in paper and rubber products and pigments, and as an ingredient of medicines.

Kaolinite-type minerals form under acid conditions at low temperatures and pressures. Kaolinite is a principal component of lateritic soils. Its formation is retarded by the presence of calcium. In addition, the presence of a kaolinitic marine sediment is evidence of a kaolinitic source area, since this mineral does not form in the sea. Such a sediment also indicates a relatively rapid accumulation of material. —John Price

Kapok, the seedpod of a tree of the bombax family (*Ceiba petandra*), that grows in the American tropics, Philippine Islands, Java, Indonesia, Ecuador, West Africa, and Ceylon. The tree produces pods containing seeds covered with silky hair, called *silk cotton.* The fiber has a beautiful, silky luster, is almost white to yellowish brown in color, and is very light and fluffy. Fiber length ranges from three-fifths of an inch to one and one-fifth inches, and the diameter from 30 to 60 microns. Under a microscope, the fiber resembles a smooth, transparent tube.

Because of its buoyancy and moisture resistance, kapok is used extensively to stuff cushions, pillows, and mattresses, and for life jackets. It is also used widely as an acoustical insulating material. —John Price

Kerosene, a flammable hydrocarbon oil usually obtained by the distillation of petroleum. It is removed from the fraction of normal crude oils that boils between 350° and 550° F. It is refined so that it will have a specific gravity of about 0.80 and will remain liquid at temperatures down to about −25° F. Its chemical composition is usually confined to the stable paraffins and naphthalenes (molecules containing 10–14 carbon atoms).

The specifications for kerosene are rigid; otherwise, the material would not perform satisfactorily. The hydrocarbon composition must be paraffinic in order to avoid excess smoke when the liquid is burned. Viscosity must be about 2 centipoises to allow satisfactory feeding by a wick. The content of nonvolatile impurities must be held at a low level to avoid clogging the wick. Sulfur content must be less thn 0.2 per cent, and to reduce the hazard of explosion, a flash point of about 120° to 140° F is specified.

Kerosene, in addition to its use in lamps, is used for small cooking stoves and heaters, especially where more volatile gasoline is not suitable. It is also used as a solvent for insecticide emulsions and for paints. It is widely used as a fuel for jet engines and sometimes as a fuel for reciprocating engines. The specific impulse of kerosene is not high enough to allow it to be used as a modern rocket fuel, and it has been replaced by liquid hydrogen. About 5 per cent of the world's crude oil output is sold as kerosene. —John Price

Lacquer, any of various coatings for surfaces, produced by dissolving a cellulose derivative (usually nitrocellulose) and other modifying materials in a solvent, with a pigment added if desired. Lacquers dry by evaporation of the solvent. Use of highly volatile solvents produces extremely fast drying, and lacquers usually are applied by spray. Drying time can be extended enough to allow brush application, but such lacquers are not common. Nitrocellulose is not soluble in conventional paint thinners, so a mixture of solvents is used, usually containing esters, aromatic hydrocarbons, and petroleum thinners. Other cellulosic derivatives used in lacquers include cellulose acetate, acetate-butyrate, and butyrate—all of which are used where good weather resistance is required—and ethyl cellulose, which gives a flexible film but is too soft for many uses. Lacquers are used as the finish on automobiles and as coatings for furniture and other factory-finished items.

Originally, lacquers were produced from the juice of a tree of the sumac family. However, these materials, called Oriental or Chinese lacquers, are not commonly used today. —John Price

Lampblack, a complex mixture of substances with high carbon content and high molecular weight, prepared from the partial combustion of bulk liquid hydrocarbons. It is a fine powder with great tinting power, producing a dark blue-gray when mixed with zinc white in a 1:100 ratio. As a black pigment, lampblack is used in paint, enamel, lacquer, rubber, leather, concrete, printing inks, and paper. It is usually mixed to a stiff paste with such vehicles as drying or semi-drying oils, lacquer solutions, resin solutions, water, sizes, or unvulcanized rubber.

Lampblack has been used since antiquity. At one time the Chinese prepared it by burning chips of resinous wood and collecting the soot in chimneys. Raw materials for modern processing are creosote oil, with high aromatic and low phenol content, or high-grade petroleum fuels. Oils with high olefin content are preferred because they break down more readily and yield more product. The oil is burned with a deficiency of air to produce a soot that is collected in a settling chamber. —John Price

Lead, one of the oldest metals known to man; chemical symbol Pb. The earliest know specimen of the metal, a statue found at the Dardanelles, dates from 3000 B.C. It is a heavy metal (specific gravity 11.34) with a bright bluish color that tarnishes to dull gray. Lead occurs in nature usually in association with other metals, notably silver and zinc. Of the many minerals that contain lead, *galena* (lead sulfide), *cerrusite* (lead carbonate), and *anglesite* (lead sulfate) are commercially the most important. Galena is the most common of the three.

Commercial ores may contain as little as 3 per cent lead, although about 10 per cent is most common. Before smelting, the ore is concentrated to 40 per cent and zinc-bearing minerals, which interfere with smelting, are removed. Concentration is usually done by flotation. Sulfur is removed from the concentrate by roasting. Both pyrometallurgical and electrolytic methods are used to refine lead blast-furnace bullion.

In both methods, copper is first removed by cooling the melt below the freezing point of copper, and then skimming it. Most lead blast-furnace bullion is low enough in bismuth to allow pyrometallurgical refining in kettles and reverberatory furnaces. Tin, arsenic, and antimony are slagged at high temperatures by selective oxidation. Gold and silver are removed by the *Parkes process,* which utilizes their selective affinity for zinc. Residual zinc is removed with caustic by the *Harris process;* with chlorine, by the *Betterton process;* or by vacuum distillation. If at this point the bullion contains excess bismuth, it is treated with calcium by the *Kroll-Betterton* process. When bismuth content is originally high, copper-drossed bullion is cast into anodes that are electrolytically refined by the *Betts process,* which uses pure lead starting cathodes and an aqueous lead fluosilicate electrolyte. Precious metals and other impurities remain on the anode; high-purity lead is deposited on the cathode.

Lead is used in the manufacture of storage batteries. Tetraethyl lead is used as an antiknock additive in automotive fuels. Lead is used extensively in plumbing and piping and as a vibration isolator and ornamental trim in architectural applications. Because of its good corrosion resistance, lead is used in construction, especially in the chemical industry, and as a sheathing for underground electrical cables. Lead forms an oxide coating, which protects it from acid attack; hence, it is used in the manufacture of sulfuric acid. Alloys formed with copper, tin, arsenic, antimony, cadmium, bismuth, and sodium are all important commercially. Lead blocks radiation effectively; hence, it is used as a shield for X-ray equipment. Basic

World Production of LEAD in %

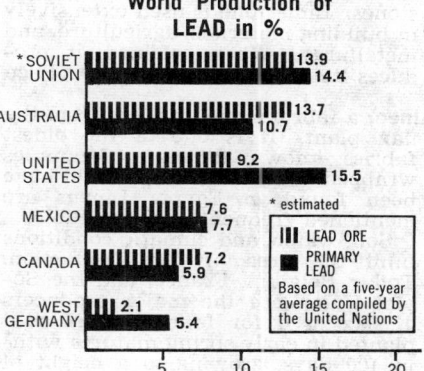

	LEAD ORE	PRIMARY LEAD
*SOVIET UNION	13.9	14.4
AUSTRALIA	13.7	10.7
UNITED STATES	9.2	15.5
MEXICO	7.6	7.7
CANADA	7.2	5.9
WEST GERMANY	2.1	5.4

* estimated

▌▌▌ LEAD ORE
█ PRIMARY LEAD

Based on a five-year average compiled by the United Nations

white lead (lead carbonate) is used widely as a paint pigment, and lead-bearing glazes are used in ceramics. Red lead (lead oxide) is used as a protective priming coat for metal surfaces. Lead alloys are used in soldering and welding. The metal is used in ammunition. Because lead compounds are highly toxic, precautions must be taken to prevent lead poisoning.   —John Price

Lime, a general term for many different products of calcined limestone, such as quicklime and hydrated lime. *Quicklime* is made of calcium oxide ($CaCO_3$) in vertical-shaft kilns to drive off carbon dioxide. It is often treated with water to make *hydrated lime,* or calcium hydroxide, $Ca(OH)_2$. This process is called *slaking,* but *slaked lime* usually refers to material with water in excess of that needed to form the hydroxide. *Milk of lime* is a suspension and solution of hydrated lime in water. *Hydraulic lime,* made from limestone containing silica and alumina, sets under water.

Lime is used in mortar, stucco, and plaster by the building industry; as a refractory for lining open-hearth furnaces; as a soil additive, for agricultural purposes or to stabilize roadbeds; as a raw material for making glass and other chemical products; and in water purification, sewage treatment, pulp and paper manufacture, refining of sugar and petroleum, and tanning.   —John Price

Limestone, a sedimentary rock composed primarily of the carbonates of calcium and magnesium. It is formed chiefly by accumulation of organic remains, such as shells or coral. Fossils contained in limestone have provided much knowledge of invertebrate paleontology and, hence, of the evolution of life and the history of the earth. More specifically, the term limestone applies to carbonate rocks dominated by the mineral calcite ($CaCO_3$), as opposed to dolomite, $CaMg(CO_3)_2$.

Limestones are composed largely of calcium oxide (CaO), and carbon dioxide (CO_2). Magnesium also is a common constituent; if it exceeds 2 per cent, the rock is termed *magnesian limestone.* Small amounts of aluminum and silica often are present. Iron oxide may be present, either as carbonate or in minerals such as clays. The chief minerals in limestone are aragonite and calcite, and dolomite in the dolomitic limestones. Limestone is used extensively in building materials, agriculture, and metallurgy. When calcined, it produces lime.   —John Price

Linen, a fabric made of fibers from the flax plant. It is one of the oldest fabrics known to man. Mummies wrapped in linen 4,000 years old have been found in Egypt. Linens are mentioned frequently in the Bible.

Soil, water, and climatic conditions limit the area of flax production. Today Belgium, France, and the Soviet Union are the major producers of flax used for fabrics. Flax seed planted in early spring matures within 100 days, growing to a height of about three feet. Harvesting machines pull the plant up by the roots, leaving the long fibers intact. After drying and seed removal, the fibers have to be dislodged from the woody core of the plant and the pectic gum that holds them together. Called retting, this process involves soaking in chemically treated water.

Linen manufacture combines art, science, and craft. Several technical mill operations are required to crush straw, separate waste, and comb and draw the fibers before they can be spun into yarn. The spinning, wrapping, and weaving methods are not essentially different from those employed for other fibers, though linen requires endless care, precautions, and control of moisture.

Belgium and Ireland are the main producers of the linen fabrics used in the United States. The well-known traditional linen weave is widely used for clothing, table linens, and drapery fabrics. Linen is often dyed in distinctive shades or printed with patterns. In addition, a large variety of weaves are made in linen—intricate novelties, heavy and patterned textures, intricate sheer casements, rich velvets, and smooth damasks.   —Dorothy Sparling

Lubricant, a substance capable of reducing friction between surfaces. Lubricants are one of the essential commodities of our civilization. Automobiles, aircraft, ships—in fact, all machinery—would stop running without lubricants. Since prehistoric times man has been aware of the need for lubrication and has used a wide range of substances to reduce friction. The axles of chariots found in Egyptian tombs have traces of lubricant which, upon analysis, proved to be mutton or beef tallow.

In common experience, lubricants are usually associated with oil or some other liquid. However, gases and solids are also used, especially at extremely high temperatures, or where replenishment of liquid lubricants is impractical.

Until recently, all lubricants were of animal or vegetable origin. Mutton and beef tallow, goose grease, fish oil, cottonseed oil, castor oil, and other vegetable oils were the only lubricants available in quantity. Though some petroleum products were in use prior to 1859, the drilling of Col. E. A. Drake's well in Titusville, Pa., in that year signaled the birth of the petroleum industry. Though mineral petroleum products make up the bulk of the lubricant supply, synthetic lubricants and chemical additives are becoming increasingly important.

Petroleum is the source of a wide variety of lubricants ranging from light machine oils to heavy gear oil. Different lubricants are produced by various refining processes which extract the specific fluids from crude oil.

Straight petroleum oils are classified according to their viscosity. General practice calls for the use of the lowest practicable viscosity since the lighter fluid produces less friction and improved cooling. Changes in viscosity with temperature—as temperature rises the viscosity drops—require heavier oils to be used for high temperature operation and lighter oils at low temperature.

Multigrade oils have been developed by the use of additives which enable the oil to provide proper lubrication over wider ranges of temperature and operating conditions. The Society of Automotive Engineers (SAE) has set standards for the different viscosity ranges and assigned ratings. For example, SAE 10W oil has a viscosity of 60 to 90 centistrokes while SAE 30W has a viscosity of 180 to 280 centistrokes. Multigrade oils for auto lubrication are frequently designated as SAE 10W-30, indicating a viscosity range of 60 to 280.

Additives improve the lubricant's general qualities or produce some characteristic required for special applications. Viscosity-index improvers are added to produce the widely used multigrade lubricants. To enable oils to operate at low temperatures, pour-point depressants such as metallic soaps are added. Antioxidants are used to increase the resistance of oil to oxidation by the atmosphere, thus retarding the development of acids and sludges. Antifriction and anti-wear additives, such as molybdenum disulfide, assure lubrication during start-up or under extreme operating conditions. Detergents or dispersants prevent the buildup of sludge and carbon deposits by keeping particles of carbon suspended in the lubricating fluid.

Synthetic oils developed during World War II as a substitute for mineral-based lubricants have proved superior in some applications. Their primary advantage is that they have a larger operating range than petroleum lubricants. Another advantage of the synthetics is that water-based lubricants can be formulated for use where fire hazards are present.   —Joseph J. Kelleher

Magnesium, a silvery white metal, chemical symbol Mg. It is the lightest structural metal, its specific gravity being 1.74, only two-thirds that of aluminum. Magnesium is the sixth most abundant element, making up about 2.5 per cent of the earth's crust—only iron and aluminum are more abundant among the structural metals. More than 60 minerals contain magnesium, but only a few are commercially important. In the United States, *brucite* (magnesium hydroxide), *dolomite* (calcium magnesium carbonate), *magnesite* (magnesium carbonate), natural brines, sea water, and sea-water bitterns are the important sources of magnesium.

The electrolytic and silicothermic processes are the two most important methods of producing magnesium in the United States. The electrolysis of magnesium chloride to yield chlorine and magnesium is the basis of the *electrolytic process.* Sea water, which contains about 0.13 per cent magnesium, is the main raw material, although magnesite, dolomite, and natural brines also have been used. Sea water is pumped into large set-

World Production of MAGNESIUM in %

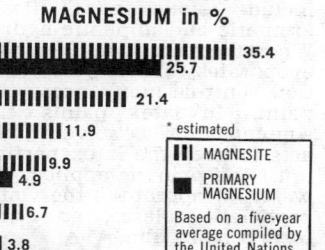

* SOVIET UNION 35.4 25.7
AUSTRIA 21.4
* MAINLAND CHINA 11.9
ITALY 9.9 4.9
* CZECHO-SLOVAKIA 6.7
NORWAY 3.8 12.8
GREAT BRITAIN 3.8
CANADA 6.5
UNITED STATES 7.0 42.8

10 20 30 40

* estimated

||| MAGNESITE
■ PRIMARY MAGNESIUM

Based on a five-year average compiled by the United Nations

tling tanks where it is mixed with lime obtained by roasting oyster shells. The lime converts the magnesium into insoluble magnesium hydroxide, which is filtered out and treated with hydrochloric acid to produce a magnesium chloride solution. The water is evaporated, and the dry magnesium chloride is transferred to electrolytic cells that break it up into magnesium metal and chlorine.

In the *silicothermic* or *ferrosilicon process*, ferrosilicon (an alloy of iron and silicon) is mixed with calcined dolomite ore and pressed into small briquets. These briquets are charged in a steel retort and heated under vacuum to about 2,200° F. The silicon reduces the magnesium oxide, which is formed when the dolomite is calcined, to a vapor of magnesium metal, which condenses in the cooler end of the retort. Magnesium is removed from the retort in the form of crystals, which are melted and cast into ingots.

Magnesium is very active chemically. It can displace hydrogen from boiling water, and many metals can be prepared by reduction of their salts and oxides with magnesium. The metal reacts with most nonmetals and acids, but it reacts slightly, if at all, with alkalis and many organic chemicals. Magnesium serves as a catalyst for organic condensation, reduction, addition, and dehalogenation reactions. It has long been used to synthesize complex organic compounds by the *Grignard reaction*. Magnesium has excellent working characteristics and can be cast, fabricated, and machine tool worked by virtually every metal-forming method known.

Because of its light weight, magnesium was first used on a large scale for structural applications in the aircraft industry. Since then it has been used to make a wide variety of industrial equipment, household goods, office equipment, and sporting goods. It is an alloying element with aluminum, zinc, and certain other nonferrous elements. Magnesium is used as an oxygen scavenger in the production of nickel and copper alloys and as a powerful reducing agent for the production of titanium, zirconium, beryllium, uranium, and hafnium.
—John Price

Marble, a stone material widely used for monuments, structures, and art objects. Geologists define marble as metamorphic rock composed of recrystallized limestone or dolomite. However, stonemasons regard any limestone that is hard enough to take a polish as marble. Early architects recognized marble's value as a structural stone because of its beauty, durability, and its capability of being carved effectively.

Marble does not have the open pores and small cavities of limestone, and therefore can be polished. Pure *calcite* or *dolomite marble* is white, and was considered to be the most beautiful variety by ancient architects. But impurities, which often occur in marble, give it many beautiful colors. This colored marble—often banded or mottled in gray, black, green, and shades of yellow, red, and pink—is cut into thin slabs and used as decorative facing stone for both the exterior and interior of buildings.

The Greeks and the Romans were famous for their architectural uses of marble and some of the most beautiful marbles are still quarried in Italy. Vermont has the most abundant deposits of marble in the United States, although it also occurs in California, Tennessee, New York, Georgia, and Texas. Marble is quarried in huge blocks and then cut into usable pieces and slabs with diamond-toothed saws and ingenious toothless saws. The latter, called *gang saws,* are merely a series of parallel steel bands, which saw back and forth on a block of marble as a slurry of sand and water flows over them. Although slower than the diamond saw, the gang saw eventually wears its way through the block, slicing it into slabs like a giant egg slicer.
—William W. Jacobus, Jr.

Mechanical Engineering, the branch of engineering that deals with the design of equipment that generates, transmits, or uses power. The mechanical engineer actually fits no precise definition—he may design supersonic aircraft; develop new ways to harvest, pack and ship farm crops; or work as the chief of a drilling crew on an oil-well rig.

The general concept of the profession is that the mechanical engineer works with equipment in motion rather than at rest. His work involves machines rather than stationary structures. The first society of mechanical engineers was formed in Britain in 1847. In 1880 John E. Sweet, professor of practical mechanics at Cornell University, called a meeting of 30 prominent American engineers to form an organization of mechanical engineers. The meeting was held in the offices of the *American Machinist,* a journal for machinists, and the group founded the American Society of Mechanical Engineers (ASME).

Though the term is less than 100 years old, mechanical engineering has been practiced since antiquity. The caveman who used a pole to pry loose a heavy stone discovered the principle of the lever, a basic mechanical device. The Greek mathe-

matician and physicist Archimedes was one of the first mechanical engineers, for he discovered the laws of mechanics and applied them to the theory of simple machines, such as the lever, pulley, and wedge. Leonardo da Vinci was another genius who applied mechanical engineering to the design of toys and military equipment far in advance of his day.
—Joseph J. Kelleher

Nitric Acid, a corrosive liquid inorganic acid, chemical formula HNO_3. The pure material fumes strongly in moist air and is miscible with water in all proportions.

Nitric acid has been known since the Middle Ages, when it was called *aqua fortis.* It was first prepared about 1100 A.D. by heating potassium nitrate with copper sulfate. Henry Cavendish, in 1785, synthesized the acid by treating sodium nitrate with sulfuric acid. The process has been used industrially, with Chile saltpeter as the source of potassium nitrate. Early in this century, various processes were developed to produce nitrous oxide (NO)—which can be converted to the acid by adding water—by subjecting air to an arc discharge. Modern synthesis depends on the catalytic oxidation of ammonia or the formation of nitrous oxide from air in a regenerative furnace.

Nitric acid is a strong monobasic acid. It reacts readily with alkalis, oxides, and basic materials to form salts. Reactions with ammonia to form ammonium nitrate and with sodium carbonate to form sodium nitrate are widely used in industry. It is also used extensively as an oxidizing agent and as a nitrating agent, forming esters and nitro compounds with organic materials. Nitric acid is one of the constituents of *aqua regia* (hydrochloric acid is the other), which is used to dissolve gold and platinum—the ratio is three parts nitric to one part hydrochloric. Nitric acid, when converted into inorganic and organic nitrates and nitro compounds, is used in fertilizers, explosives, dye intermediates, and various synthetic organic compounds.
—John Price

Nonferrous Metals, metals that do not contain iron in any significant amount. The most important metals from the standpoint of industrial consumption in the United States are aluminum, copper, lead, zinc, sodium, nickel, tin, magnesium, antimony, and titanium. Others of lesser importance are uranium, cobalt, silver, mercury, bismuth, molybdenum, beryllium, tungsten, zirconium, gold, tantalum, and niobium.

Most nonferrous metals are extracted from their ores and concentrates by chemical reactions that take place at high temperatures. This method, called *pyrometallurgy,* is one of the oldest known methods for recovering metals from ore minerals. However, electrometallurgy is used for recovering most aluminum, magnesium and some zinc; *hydrometallurgy* is used for some nickel.

Reduction of ores and concentrates results in two or more products: the reduced metal and a residue compound of unreduced *gangue* minerals (silicon dioxide, aluminum oxide, calcium oxide, and ferrous oxide) and the oxidized form of the reducing agent. Before the extractive process is complete, the reduced metal must be separated from this material. High-temperature processes can make this separation in several simple ways, provided the products can be liquefied or selectively vaporized.

Pyrometallurgy of nonferrous metals takes place in three steps: preparation, reduction, and refining.

Preparatory processes convert the raw material (the ore or an ore concentrate) into a chemical form suitable for further processing. One important process, the roasting of sulfides, consists of burning metallic sulfides in air or oxygen to convert them to metallic oxides, sulfates, or both together with sulfur dioxide. Another method, *sintering*, consists of consolidating finely divided particles into relatively large aggregates that are then reduced. Oxides of titanium, zirconium, and other refractory metals are prepared for reduction by *chlorination*, converting the oxides to metal chlorides. *Drying* and *calcining*, to remove free water and to decompose hydrates and carbonates, is another preparatory method.

Reduction consists of changing compounds to the metallic state and separating the free metal from the residue. Pyrometallurgical reduction requires a reducing agent, a substance that will combine with the unwanted element in the metal compound.

The volatile metals (zinc, cadmium, and mercury, and alkali and alkaline-earth metals) are reduced to the gaseous form of the metal. The gaseous metal can be condensed to a liquid or solid in a condenser separated from the reactants and residue, there simplifying purification. Most other nonferrous metals are reduced to a liquid metal in a blast furnace. Tungsten and molybdenum are reduced to solid metal because their melting points are so high. Titanium and zirconium also are reduced to solid metal because no container can hold the liquid metal without contaminating it.

Volatilization, drossing, and slag-refining are the three main purification methods. *Volatilization* is used where either the metal or its impurity can be removed as a gas. *Drossing* consists of bringing the base metal to a temperature at which the impurity becomes insoluble and can be physically removed. *Slag-refining* is the addition of a slag or molten salt that selectively absorbs impurities.

—John Price

Paint, a liquid that contains a binder, a pigment, a solvent, and small amounts of additives. When a thin film of this mixture is applied to a surface, it hardens and adheres tenaciously, so that it protects and decorates that surface. Paint has been used by man for centuries; cave paintings have been dated as old as 20,000 years.

As late as the beginning of the twentieth century, paints were made from naturally occurring ingredients by skilled craftsmen, each of whom developed his own formula. However, modern paints based on technical research, new ingredients, and standardized production methods were developed after World War I.

Paints can be classified according to end use—for example, exterior, interior, house, household appliance, furniture, automotive, or marine; or by composition—for example, enamel, varnish, or lacquer. The end use determines the composition and method of manufacture of the paint. Those used on exterior surfaces are formulated with durable binders and color-retentive pigments to withstand sun, rain, wind, and extreme temperatures. Finishes for interior surfaces must provide decorative effects and also resist abrasion, washing, and the effects of chemicals, atmosphere, —and temperature. In either case, the coat of paint must provide a suitable base for application of successive coats in the future.

A *varnish* is a transparent or clear liquid made by cooking rosin, gums, or other resins with oils. An *enamel* is a very smooth, fine-textured film. A *lacquer* is a paint that dries simply by evaporation of the solvent; it is generally fast-drying. *Shellac* in an alcohol solution is used for floors and other wood surfaces.

The *binders* used most frequently are vegetable oils, rosin, gums, shellac, and also alkyd, phenolic, epoxy, vinyl, acrylic, and styrene-butadiene resins. Vegetable oils such as linseed, soya, and castor oils are used as binders for exterior house paints and also as modifying components of alkyd resins, which are used for many exterior and interior house paints and for automotive and appliance paints. Phenolic, vinyl, and epoxy resins are used to provide chemical resistance and toughness to many appliance finishes, and for protection of chemical plants. Acrylic resins are used to provide extreme durability for automotive and appliance finishes, as well as for exterior house paints. Latex emulsions of styrene-butadiene, vinyl, and acrylic resins are used for many water-based interior and exterior house paints. Many of the resins used in appliance and automotive finishing require heat or catalysts, or both, for curing to a tough, dry film.

Pigments include many naturally occurring minerals, such as iron oxide, talc, marble, diatomaceous earth, and barytes, as well as manufactured forms, such as titanium dioxide, zinc oxide, lead and zinc chromates, lead sulfate, copper phthalocyanine (green and blue), toluidine red, molybdate orange, and ultramarine blue. Those which provide color and opacity are generally classified as *prime pigments;* titanium dioxide white pigment is probably the most important and most widely used. Those which do not add color or opacity are known as *extenders;* they are used to provide or control glass, adhesion, abrasion resistance, and durability.

Solvents are added to keep the binder in solution as a liquid so that

paint can be easily applied. Solvents include ketones, esters, alcohols, and aromatic and aliphatic hydrocarbons. When the paint is applied, the solvent evaporates, and its speed of evaporation controls many properties of the paint. In latex paints, the water content is not a "solvent" but merely acts to keep the latex particles apart until the paint is applied. When the water evaporates, the latex resin particles coalesce, or combine, to form a paint film.

Additives are used in paint to provide various properties: driers to speed drying time; flocculating and thickening agents to control flow and application; inhibitors for stability in the paint can; and fungicides to control mold and mildew growth.

Paint is manufactured in batch lots. The process starts with the grinding or dispersing of the pigment in a mixture of solvent and binder. In this operation, the pigment particles are reduced to the desired size and are coated with the binder solution. The grinding mill provides impact or shear force, or both, to disperse the pigment in a solvent vehicle. Then the remainder of the binder solution, solvents, and additives are added, and the mixture is blended until it is homogeneous.

Paints are applied by brushing, rolling, spraying, dipping, flow-coating, and many adaptations of these, including electrostatic spraying, reverse roller coating, curtain coating, and airless, steam, and hot spraying. The method used for any particular application depends on the kind, shape, and size of the surface to be coated, the application speed desired, the film thickness required, and the viscosity of the finish itself.

—Oliver R. Volk

Petrochemicals, chemicals derived from crude oil or its fractions, or from natural gas. Basically, petrochemicals are compounds of hydrogen and carbon, but a vast number of these chemicals also incorporate oxygen, sulfur, nitrogen, chlorine, or other elements. For many years, coal was the chief source of synthetic organic materials. Today, however, most organic chemicals are made from petroleum and natural gas.

The petrochemical industry is made up of many different chemical and petroleum companies. It is generally considered to have started about 1918 with the production of isopropanol, or rubbing alcohol, from refinery gases. The subsequent development of catalytic processes for making high-quality gasolines and of a high-temperature thermal-cracking process provided large quantities of many important chemical building blocks and spurred rapid growth in the chemical industry. In the United States in 1964, petrochemical production amounted to almost 80 billion pounds, worth some $8 billion.

Petrochemicals are used in manufacturing an almost limitless number of products. Synthetic rubber, man-made fibers, plastics, paints, detergents, and fertilizers are some of the petrochemicals that have shown the most spectacular growth. Synthetic rubber from petroleum supplies about three-fourths of the rubber needs of the United States. Petrochemical-based synthetic fibers, including nylons, polyesters, polypropylenes, and acrylics, contribute greatly to modern living. Plastics such as polyethylene, polypropylene, polystyrene, polyesters and polyvinyl chloride have created enormous new markets for squeeze bottles, packaging films, foam insulators, utensils, boats, piping, flooring, synthetic leather, luggage, and so on. Petrochemicals appear in paints as solvents, resins, driers, and emulsifiers. Synthetic detergents for both home and industrial uses owe their great effectiveness to petrochemical ingredients.

Petrochemistry plays a key role in feeding the world's rapidly increasing population. It makes possible large quantities of low-cost nitrogenous fertilizers essential for efficient food production. It is also a source of herbicides, insecticides, and fungicides that, when properly used, control agricultural pests without danger to mankind. Indirectly, it contributes greatly to food production by freeing land that would otherwise be required to grow natural fibers and rubber. In the future, petrochemistry may provide food directly. A new process, awaiting development, shows promise of producing a high-protein, high-vitamin food concentrate from petroleum.

—C. C. Garvin

Petroleum, a complex mixture of hydrocarbons of widely varying properties obtained from natural oil wells. Crude oil, the raw material for gasoline, heating oil, lubricants, synthetic fibers, plastics, and a host of other

World Production of CRUDE PETROLEUM in %

	%
UNITED STATES	31.4
SOVIET UNION	14.8
VENEZUELA	13.8
KUWAIT	7.5
SAUDI ARABIA	6.0
IRAN	5.2
IRAQ	4.3
CANADA	2.6

Based on a five-year average compiled by the United Nations

petrochemical products, is a plentiful resource found in North and South America, Europe, Africa, Asia, and Australia, and under the sea on the continental shelves. Although the world has large oil reserves, new reserves are constantly being sought.

Exploration begins with the petroleum geologist, who examines areas that might be expected to contain oil. He looks for porous sedimentary rocks, such as sandstone, limestone, and dolomite, because oil collects in the pore spaces in these rocks. He also looks for places where oil might be trapped. Such places of entrapment might include upward folds or arches in the rock layers, fractures in the earth's crust where porous layers have been cut off against nonporous layers, and buried porous lenses, such as beach sands, which pinch out between nonporous layers. The geologist studies maps and reports showing the rock formations that occur at the earth's surface, aerial photographs that reveal sur-

face features over large areas, and data obtained from wells already drilled in the area that may indicate the nature of the underlying strata.

If the geologist's preliminary studies indicate favorable rock structure, more advanced work involving *geophysics* is then undertaken to learn more about the nature of the rocks below the earth's surface. The geophysicist's chief tools are the *gravimeter*, the *seismograph*, and the *magnetometer*. The gravimeter measures differences in the pull of the earth's gravity from place to place. The seismograph measures the speed and intensity of artificial shock waves reflected from subsurface formations. The magnetometer measures variations in the earth's magnetic field. From studying the data gathered with these tools, the geophysicist can tell much about the nature and structure of the subsurface formations.

■**DRILLING.**—If this preliminary geological and geophysical work indicates that there may be oil in the rocks below the earth's surface, an exploratory hole is then undertaken, for it is only by drilling that oil can be discovered. Drilling may be accomplished by the *cable-tool* or the more common *rotary* method.

In cable-tool drilling, a heavy bit and stem on the end of a cable are alternately raised and dropped so that the bit pounds and pulverizes the rock. At intervals, the tools are removed and water is flushed into the hole so that the drill cutting may be bailed out. The cable-tool method is used primarily for drilling shallow holes in soft formation.

Most oil wells are drilled by the rotary method, using an augerlike bit attached to the lower end of a "string" of connected lengths of steel drill pipe. The drill pipe and bit are rotated by a turntable at the surface; as it turns, the bit bores through the rock. As the hole deepens, lengths of drill pipe are added at the top of the string. *Drilling mud,* composed of water, clay, and chemical additives, is pumped down through the inside of the drill pipe, forced out through the bit, and returned to the surface carrying rock cuttings from the well. The cuttings are studied under the microscope by the geologist in order to learn more about the rocks penetrated by the drill. In both drilling systems, a tall derrick supports the equipment that must be lowered into the well.

During the past 25 years, techniques have been perfected for deflecting the drill from the vertical into a gradual curve as the hole goes deeper. *Directional drilling* can penetrate rocks inaccessible by vertical drilling, such as oil deposits lying under built-up urban areas. Directional drilling is also used in offshore areas where as many as 30 wells can be drilled from a single platform, each one directed to a different part of the oil field.

■**OFFSHORE.**—Drilling under the sea involves specialized techniques and equipment. The drilling platform or vessel must be able to withstand storm winds and waves, and all equipment must withstand exposure

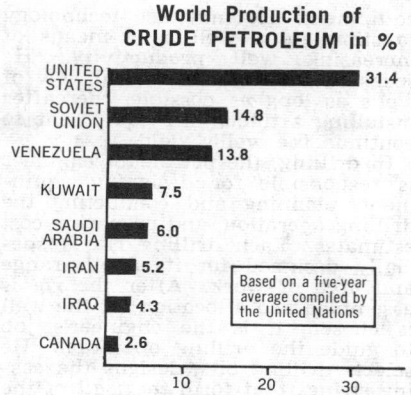

PAN AMERICAN PETROLEUM CORPORATION

ROTARY RIG for oil-well drilling drives a screw-shaped bit into the ground when derrick pulleys drop this huge block, which carries the bit at the end of its "string."

to salt water. Some drilling platforms are large, permanent, self-contained units, spacious enough to house personnel and supplies; others are only large enough to support the drilling equipment, with crew and supplies housed on a floating tender. Mobile drilling platforms include some that have legs which can be extended to the bottom for support, others that float freely and must be kept in position by complex navigational manuevers, and still others that may be partly submerged for greater stability. Wells have been drilled as far as 130 miles from shore and in water as deep as 600 feet.

■ **RESERVES.**—An exploratory well in an area where no oil has been produced is called a *wildcat.* It may cost from $50,000 to $3 million to drill, yet eight out of nine wildcats drilled in the United States are unsuccessful, or dry holes. If oil is discovered in a wildcat, additional wells called *development* wells are then drilled in order to outline the size and characteristics of the oil field.

Oil reserves in a field are estimated from this more detailed drilling. Reserves are described as *proved* or *probable,* depending upon how reliable the estimates are. Proved reserves are the amount of oil and gas that can be recovered economically under present conditions. A few decades ago, as little as 20 per cent of the oil in a field was recoverable, but modern recovery techniques developed through petroleum engineering have increased this to more than 80 per cent for some fields.

■ **DISTRIBUTION.**—A vast network of pipelines carries most of the world's crude oil, natural gas, and petroleum products on its initial steps to market. In the oil fields, gathering lines of perhaps 2-inch diameter lead from wells to storage tanks; larger pipelines lead into trunk lines that may be as much as 30 inches in diameter. The trunk lines move the oil to refineries or to shipping points, and also move refined products to market. Pumping stations keep the oil moving through the pipelines at a speed of 2 or 3 miles an hour. These stations may be as far apart as 150 miles, depending on the terrain and the type of oil to be moved.

Tankers play an important role in the transportation of oil, particularly in hauling oil from the Middle East and South America to Europe and North America. Barges transport much oil on inland and coastal waterways, and railroad tank cars also carry many petroleum products. Tank trucks that supply the neighborhood service stations and bring heating fuels to millions of homes are the final link in the transportation chain.
—Zeb Mayhew

Petroleum Engineering, the application of mathematics and natural sciences to the task of extracting crude oil and natural gas from the earth. The petroleum engineer is concerned with the planning and developing of oil and gas fields, with solving all problems of drilling and completing the wells, and with selecting the most suitable producing methods and equipment. He may use technology to stimulate a well as a means of increasing well productivity. He seeks to prolong the natural flow of wells as long as possible, thereafter installing artificial lift equipment to continue the well's yield.

In drilling, the petroleum engineer is responsible for designing equipment, planning and conducting the drilling operation, and preparing cost estimates. Each drilling rig is specially designed for its depth range and area of work. After the rig is assembled and a location for the well is chosen, it is the engineer's job to guide the drilling operation. He selects drilling bits, designs the casing strings that form the *wall* of the bore hole, and specifies the type of *drilling mud* to be pumped down the hole to lubricate the bit, to lift the rock chips out of the hole, and to subdue high pressures.

Reservoirs of oil and gas consist of interconnected pore spaces in underground rock such as sandstone and limestone. The petroleum engineer studies the reservoir to determine its extent and its physical characteristics. By analysis of cores of the reservoir rock and the contained fluid, and by the study of pressure and other measurements, he determines where wells should be drilled and how best to remove the oil and gas from the reservoir.

Oil is driven out of reservoir rock by the pressure of expanding gases associated with the oil, by the pressure of water surrounding the reservoir, or by a combination of the two. It is the job of the petroleum engineer to determine which driving force is present and to plan the most efficient use of such natural forces. He may find it necessary to inject gas and/or water to supplement the natural energy in order to maintain the driving forces or pressure at economically desirable levels.

Often when wells become old and production rates approach uneconomic limits, *secondary-recovery* techniques are employed to obtain still more oil. This consists of injecting even more gas or water into the reservoir and driving the oil to the wells. Other added recovery techniques are being developed in the petroleum industry's laboratories and being tested in the field. They include the use of additives to improve water displacement efficiency, *miscible displacement* using a solvent, and thermal methods. The latter include steam injection and combustion in the reservoir to improve flow properties of heavier oil. The engineer is responsible for carrying out these various additional recovery operations.   —Douglas Ragland

Plastics, synthetic organic materials that can be molded or cast in a variety of intricate shapes. Almost all plastic materials and modern synthetic textile fibers are made from resins. Resins, in turn, are made from chemicals derived from coal, petroleum, natural gas, and other sources.

The first plastic was *cellulose nitrate,* or *celluloid,* invented in 1868 by John Wesley Hyatt, a printer in Albany, New York. A prize had been offered for the invention of a material that could replace ivory in making billiard balls. The suppression of the slave trade from Africa had also taken the profit out of the importation of ivory, which was used not only for billiard balls but also for women's combs, piano keys, and knife handles. Hyatt noted that the end of the Civil War had left surpluses of guncotton, or nitrocellulose, which is a mixture of cellulose fibers, nitric acid, and sulfuric acid. By experimenting, he found he could mix this material with camphor to obtain a whitish solid material that could be pressed into blocks and then machined to the desired shapes. The only trouble was its extreme flammability—the material had to be machined under water. Manufacturers in Leominster, Mass., who specialized in products of ivory, bone, horn,

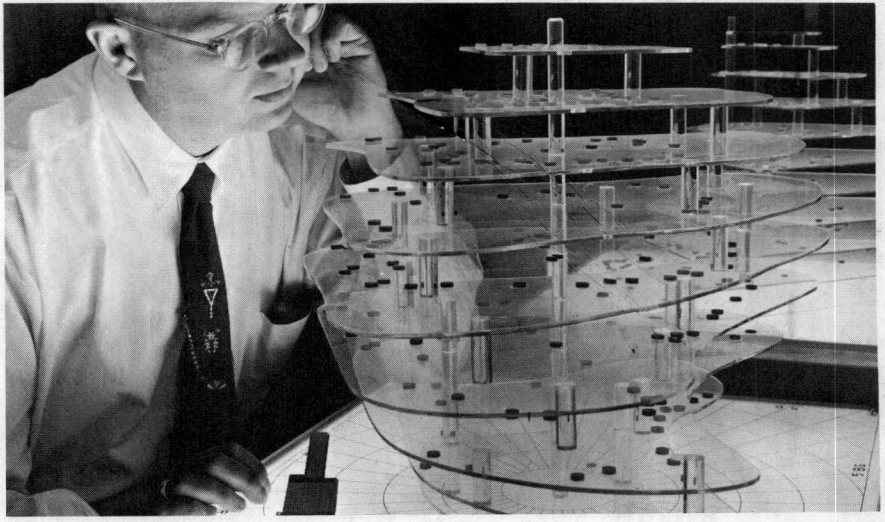

E. I. DU PONT DE NEMOURS & CO.

COLORS IN PLASTICS are analyzed for hue, lightness, and saturation to determine mathematically the proportion of dye to add to the material to obtain the desired color.

Common Plastic Materials

Plastic	Year	Common Uses	Outstanding Properties
Acrylonitrile-Butadiene-Styrene (ABS) (thermoplastic)	1948	Pipe and pipe fittings; football helmets; utensil and tool handles; automotive parts.	High impact and tensile strength; resistant to alkalies, salts, and many aliphatic hydrocarbons.
Casein (thermosetting)	1919	Buttons and buckles; game counters; adhesives; toys.	Takes a brilliant surface polish and withstands dry cleaning.
Cellulosics (thermoplastic)			
Cellulose Acetate	1927	Spectacle frames and toys.	Relatively light; among the toughest of plastics; good insulators; available in a wide variety of colors.
Cellulose Acetate Butyrate	1938	Steering wheels and tool handles.	
Cellulose Propionate	1945	Telephone hand sets.	
Ethyl Cellulose	1935	Electrical parts.	
Cellulose Nitrate	1868	Shoe heel covers.	
Epoxy (thermosetting)	1947	Protective coatings for appliances; adhesives; printed circuits.	Good flexibility; excellent resistance to corrosion.
Melamine (thermosetting)	1939	Tableware; laminated surfaces; buttons; hearing-aid cases.	Hard and scratch resistant; unaffected by detergents.
Nylon (thermoplastic)	1938	Tumblers; slide fasteners; brush bristles; fishing line.	High impact, tensile, and flexural strength; can be boiled and steam sterilized.
Phenolics (thermosetting)	1909	Radio and television cabinets; electric insulation; handles; dials; knobs.	Hard, rigid, and strong; excellent electrical insulators.
Polyesters (thermosetting)	1942	Impregnate cloth or mats; reinforced plastics for boats and automobile bodies.	Highly resistant to most solvents, acids, bases, and salts.
Polyethylene (thermoplastic)	1942	Flexible ice cube trays and toys; squeezable bottles; bags for packaging.	Strong and flexible; highly resistant to chemicals.
Polypropylenes (thermoplastic)	1957	Heat sterilizable bottles; packaging film and sheets; valves.	Good heat resistance; excellent resistance to chemicals.
Polystyrene (thermoplastic)	1938	Refrigerator food containers; instrument panels; wall tile; portable radio cases.	Good dielectric qualities; can be produced with a smooth surface or a special texture.
Urea (thermosetting)	1929	Lamp reflectors; appliance housings; electrical devices; stove knobs and handles; buttons.	Hard and scratch resistant; unaffected by cleaning fluids; good electrical qualities.
Urethanes (thermoplastic and thermosetting varieties)	1954	Foams used for cushioning, sponges, and appliance insulation; solids used in abrasive wheels, bristles, and tire treads.	Foams have good shock and sound absorption and heat insulation; solids have unusual abrasion and tear resistance.
Vinyls (thermoplastic)	1927	Raincoats; inflatable water toys; phonograph records; electric plugs; floor and wall coverings; upholstery.	Strong and abrasion resistant; fade resistant colors; resist penetration of water.

and tortoise shell, adopted Hyatt's new material and, despite many fires and explosions, made their town the first center of the plastics industry. Today, cellulose nitrate clings to only one exclusive market—dice for gamblers, who seem to prefer it for its weight and "feel," and perhaps also for superstitious reasons.

The second plastic was invented in 1909 by Leo Hendrik Baekeland, a Belgian chemist living in New Jersey. He mixed phenol, a coal derivative, with formaldehyde, an embalming fluid, to produce phenol-formaldehyde. This black substance, very difficult to burn and impossible to melt, proved to have good electrical properties. The inventor called it *Bakelite*.

New plastics developed slowly in the next decade. About 1915, *cellulose acetate* was evolved from the flammable cellulose nitrate by substituting acetic acid for the nitric acid. The new material had celluloid's qualities of appearance and formability but without the fire hazard. Later, it was found that cellulose ace-

tate could be extruded as a thread. This fiber found textile uses as *rayon*.

■**MODERN PLASTICS.**—Other resins were invented, creating new plastic materials for fibers, paints, and adhesives. At first, they were based on cellulose, but then resins were discovered that could be made from petrochemicals. Today, there are more than 30 basic kinds of resins, each with as many as 10,000 varieties. There now are more different kinds of plastic, with a wider range of predetermined properties, than the combined varieties of metal, wood, glass, rubber, and leather. They run the gamut from plastics that melt like wax to those that can stand thousands of degrees of temperature; from those that bend like tissue paper to those that, reinforced by glass fibers or asbestos, can be formed into plastic boats, automobile bodies, and aircraft parts.

Not only can plastics be made from resins to exact engineering strengths and resistances, but several different plastics can be made out of

a single raw material. The first *polyethylene* made in England before 1936 was derived from corncobs; today it is made from natural gas or petroleum. In India, which still lacks petrochemicals, sugar is converted into alcohol and polyethylene is made from that. One petrochemical gas, ethylene, can be made into four different kinds of plastics and resins by changing the manufacturing processes.

Thermoset plastics are those that *cure*, or harden, in heat, like waffles or hard-boiled eggs, and cannot be remelted and molded over again. *Thermoplastics* are those that melt in heat and harden in cool temperatures, like wax candles, and can be remelted and remolded. Between the two, in recent years, have come some, like the *urethanes*, which may be made to accomplish either effect.

■**APPLICATIONS.**—All plastics are light in weight. Steel weighs three times as much as aluminum, and aluminum weighs three times as much as plastics; therefore, steel weighs nine times as much as plastics. On the basis of per-cubic-inch production, more plastics are made than aluminum and all other nonferrous metals put together. In 1965, 11.5 billion pounds of plastics were produced in the United States, and by 1970 a production of more than 16 billion pounds is anticipated.

Plastics may be molded into products and parts; extruded like toothpaste into films and pipe, used for coating papers and fibers; foamed into insulation and heat-and-cold-resistant products such as drinking cups; laminated to other materials or to each other; cast into sheets like glass; formed from sheet into automobile bodies and housings for business machines; and blow-molded into bottles for bleaches, detergents, and milk. The thermoplastics have *plastic memory*, that is, after they are taken as flat sheets and formed into shapes, they return to flat sheet form, or try to, when heated. This quality is useful in making skin-pack for hardware and other items. Plastics can be painted, although most of them are colored through by pigments added during manufacture. They are warm to the touch, being good thermal insulators, and they are easily cleaned. Some are resistant to certain chemicals, such as cleaning fluids, but not to others. All may be made flame-resistant, but some require additives to assure this. Thus, the selection of the proper plastic for a given application is a job for a chemist working with a designer and a process engineer.

Most plastics are *polymers*, that is, they are made of individual units joined together into chains. The individual unit is called a *monomer*, and it is composed of hydrogen and carbon and some other elements that must be removed. The monomer is heated in kettles or in continuous processes, and the extraneous elements and as much hydrogen as possible are removed to produce the polymer. The more carbon and the less hydrogen, the stronger and better the plastic. The polymer may be in powder form or may be fed through an extruder and chopper to make pellets that are used for molding and extrusion. All thermoplastics, with the exception of the cellulosics, are polymers. Polymer science is the science of plastics today. Nylons are *polyamides,* acetals are *polyacetals.* The carbon and hydrogen atoms in the molecules are fused to make long, strong chains of molecules, which become plastics and resins.

When two or more different monomers are made into a single superstrong plastic, the product is a *copolymer.* When three different monomers are used, the result is a *terpolymer. Quadrapolymers* are made from four different monomers.

■**PROCESSES.**—Plastic materials are processed in a number of ways. The thermoplastics are *injection-molded* by melting the pellets or powders and squirting them into a cold mold where they harden into pieces. The *melt* was formerly pushed into the mold with a ram, but is now extruded with a screw, using *adiabatic,* or frictional, heat to melt it for flow. In the case of rigid vinyl, carbonates, and ABS (Acrylonitrile-Butadiene-Styrene) polymers, this is important because these plastics can degrade in properties if held in melt condition for too long a time. The higher the heat resistance of the polymer, the better the end product will be, but the more difficult it will be to process and the more sophisticated the machinery required to process it into a product or product part.

Extrusion works like a toothpaste tube with a corkscrew in the cylinder. The materials melt in the screw and are pushed out of a die (flat, round, or profile-shaped) into a cold and frequently water-quenched bath, where the material becomes solid and available for further processing. These dies produce film, sheet, and pipe, and are used for coating paper, textiles, and metals.

An extruded sheet may be thermoformed. It is reheated and sucked or blown into a mold to make, for example, the interior door of a refrigerator.

Casting is usually done from the liquid monomer. This, or extrusion, is usually how acrylic pieces are made. *Foaming* may be done by casting or by extrusion, depending on the material and the purpose of the product. Thicker sections usually are made by casting with the use of a catalyst or foaming agent. *Calendering* is done on huge and expensive machines and is largely used for soft vinyls for upholstery. *Coating* may be done by either calendering or extrusion, with the plastic spread over the paper or cloth, woven or nonwoven. Coating of metals or other materials may be done by heating the metal piece, dipping it into a bath of plastic powder or liquid, pulling it out, and letting it cool. Nylons, vinyls, and epoxies have been used in this manner, which is called *fluidized bed coating.*

The thermoset plastics can only be molded (except when they are catalyzed or self-heat-cured) by *compression molding,* or *transfer molding.*

The cold powder is put into a high-frequency heating chamber (which softens it) and poured into a hot mold; after a short time, the press is opened and the phenolic, melamime, or urea part is taken out.
——Hiram McCann

Plywood, a cross-banded assembly of layers (*plies*) of wood or of veneer with a lumber core. The plies are joined by an adhesive. Usually, the grain of one ply is approximately at right angles to the grain of the next ply. An odd number of plies generally is used.

Plywood, compared with other wood products, has greater uniformity in strength in the direction of its two major axes and is more apt to preserve its dimensions with changes in its water content. It has increased resistance to end checking and splitting and a greatly reduced tendency to twist and warp.

Thin hardwood veneers often are used with cores of less costly softwood in the manufacture of furniture and wall and ceiling panels. Plywoods made of inexpensive woods are used extensively in concrete forms, sheathing, subflooring, boxes, and crates. Molded, die-pressed, or bag-molded plywoods are used in the manufacture of boat hulls, aircraft parts, chairs, and similar shell-like constructions. ——John Price

Potash, a generic term applied to any potassium salt sold for its potassium content. Chief salts used commercially are potassium chloride, potassium sulfate, and a mixture of potassium sulfate and magnesium sulfate. At one time a potassium compound, potassium carbonate, was produced frcm solutions leached from wood ashes evaporated in iron pots; hence, the term *pot ashes.* In 1857, soluble potash minerals were recognized as valuable for fertilizer use, and these minerals since have been the source of potash for fertilizer and chemical use.

Usually the potassium content of minerals is stated in terms of potassium oxide (K_2O) because it was originally thought that potassium was effective as a fertilizer only in this form. More recently, there has been a move to quote potash content in terms of the element potassium rather than the oxide. Although there are many potash-containing minerals, most of the world's known reserves consist of sylvite, carnallite, kainite, langbeinite, niter, and polyhalite.
——John Price

Pottery, one of man's oldest uses of ceramic materials. It is quite possible that the art of basketmaking led to the first use of clay as a lining. By some unknown set of circumstances, it was then discovered that moist clay could be shaped by hand, without weeds or grasses as a support, and, when heated, would become permanently hard and durable. The methods used to make pottery today are not fundamentally different from those used thousands of years ago. In fact, at a very early stage, primitive man decorated his pottery with

quite elaborate painted and incised designs. The study of pottery fragments, called *potsherds,* permits archaeologists to assess the stages of development of ancient peoples.

Cruder, less pure clays are used to make stoneware, earthenware, art ware, flowerpots, and similar objects. China and porcelain are special types of pottery in which several types of purer clays are employed. The beauty of the pottery made in China during the Chou dynasty (1122–249 B.C.) has, in fact, led to the very use of the term "china." Later, the Chinese developed porcelain by adding feldspar to the clays. Both china and porcelain are hard, translucent, and nonporous, even without a glaze coating. Earthenware, on the other hand, is porous and must be glazed to become impervious.

Regardless of differences in raw materials, all pottery is made by one of three methods: pressing, jiggering, or casting.

Pressing is used only for irregularly shaped objects. The moist clay is shaped by hand pressure or by pressing into plaster molds.

Jiggering, used for making symmetrical objects, involves the use of a *potter's wheel* or its equivalent. Moist clay of the proper weight is placed on the revolving wheel and shaped by hand or by a jiggering tool. Heated dies are often used to assist in spreading the clay to the proper shape, and a water mist may be used for lubrication. The manufacture of plates, cups, and bowls by this method is now quite highly automated.

Casting involves the use of a clay slip—a suspension of clay particles in water with a consistency somewhat like that of paint. This slip is poured into a plaster of paris mold of the proper shape. The mold absorbs much of the water from the slip next to it. When this layer is thick enough to permit handling, the excess slip is poured out, and the mold is opened. This green ware is then dried and fired. Drying and firing must also be used for pressed or jiggered ware. ——Charles J. Phillips

Quartz, an important rock-forming mineral that occurs as a subordinate constituent of many igneous, metamorphic, and sedimentary rocks; chemical composition, silicon dioxide (SiO_2). The most important and widespread of all minerals, it is the main constituent of sandstone, quartzite, and unconsolidated sands and gravels. Ordinary quartz is colorless and transparent, with a vitreous luster. *Amethyst* is a purple or bluish-violet; *citrine* is orange-brown, produced by heat treatment of amethyst. *Rose quartz* is a massive type found in pegmatites. Quartz also may be smoky yellow to dark smoky brown, varying to brownish-black and almost opaque.

Quartz may be classified into two broad categories: *coarse crystalline,* in which individual grains are visible to the naked eye, and *fine crystalline,* in which grains are visible only under a microscope. Fine-crystalline quartzes are further divided into two main groups based on particle shape. The *fibrous* variety includes chalcedony, carnelian, and agate, and the *fine granular* variety includes flint and jasper. —John Price

Reservoir, a basin for the storage of water. Reservoirs are essential to the effective and economical control and utilization of water resources for almost every need—from irrigation to flood control, from domestic or industrial water supply and water power to transportation by river or canals. In early *basin irrigation*, low earth embankments were used to retain flood waters for later release to lower areas. Similar, so-called *tanks* of notable size were built quite early in India. Reservoirs of greater size, particularly those formed in river or stream valleys, however, required both the construction of higher dams and provision for the passage of flood flows.

It appears that such constructions were first undertaken in Spain in the sixteenth century. In recent years many huge reservoirs of this type have been built, especially in the United States. These include such outstanding works as the Hoover and Grand Coulee irrigation projects of the U.S. Bureau of Reclamation and those for the water supply of several of our larger cities, such as the numerous basins on the Catskill and Croton watersheds for New York City.

Reservoirs of smaller capacity are also built to help equalize demand or meet emergency needs. The domestic use of water varies throughout the day. When possible, it is usually economical to provide *equalizing reservoirs* large enough to carry peak loads, and thus permit the main supply aqueduct to be designed for average load.

In hydroelectric developments, sufficient *pondage* is desirable to store flow during low-demand hours for later use in carrying peak loads. Reservoirs are likewise essential in river canalization projects, and the provision of a summit water supply is a critical requirement for canals that pass over a divide. *Pumped storage* has been a more recent development in the power field; in the hours of low electrical demand, water is pumped to a high-level reservoir from which it can later be released to provide electric power in time of heavy demand.

Reservoir capacity is usually measured in *acre-feet*, that is, one foot of water over one acre, which is equivalent to 43,560 cubic feet or about 325,000 gallons. Lake Mead, formed by the Hoover, or Boulder Canyon Dam, holds a little over 30 million acre-feet; but, by far, the largest storage is provided by the Kariba Dam in Rhodesia, which contains 130 million acre-feet.
—James Kip Finch

Rosin, a solid resinous material obtained from the oleoresinous wood of pine tree stumps. It contains chiefly resin acids and smaller amounts of nonacid compounds. It varies in color from pale yellow to dark red or darker, depending on the source and the method of collecting and processing. It is translucent and brittle at ordinary temperatures, has a slight odor, and tastes like benzine. It is insoluble in water but is soluble in most oils and organic solvents.

Rosin may be used in its natural form, known as *unmodified rosin,* or it may be given chemical treatment (hydrogenation, disproportionation, or polymerization) to increase its stability and improve its physical properties. After such treatment the material is known as *modified rosin.*

Three commercially important methods of obtaining rosin are solvent extraction of pine stumps, turpentining of living trees, and separation from tall oil. Rosin products are used in paper sizing, lubricants, insulation, linoleum, adhesives, soldering fluxes, binders, soaps, and finishes.
—John Price

Rubber, any of a wide variety of natural and synthetic hydrocarbon materials that are commercially valuable for their highly elastic, moisture-resistant, electrical insulating, and wear-resistant properties. Slightly less than one-half of the rubber now consumed in the world is in the form of *natural* or *crude rubber* obtained from the sap of tropical plants. About 99 per cent of the world's supply of natural rubber is produced from a milklike sap called *latex,* which is released by "scarring" or tapping the bark of a tree (*Hevea brasiliensis*), of the castor-bean family. Less than one per cent is produced from *Guayule,* a plant native to Mexico.

Prior to the 1900's, most rubber came from the Amazon basin in Brazil, where *brasiliensis* grew. However, in 1876, Henry A. Wickham, later knighted for his enterprise, conceived the idea that rubber trees could also be made to grow on coffee plantations in India, where the climatic conditions were similar. He succeeded in carrying back from Brazil to England nearly 100,000 *Hevea* seeds, which were promptly planted in the Kew Botanical Gardens near London. About 3,000 of the trees survived and were transported to Britain's southeastern Asian possessions of Ceylon, Malaya, Sumatra, and India, where they were transplanted and grew well. Today, about 45 per cent of the world's natural rubber production of 2,200,000 long tons is grown in Malaysia, 28 per cent in Indonesia, 10 per cent in Thailand, and 7 per cent in Africa (Liberia and Nigeria).

Other areas that produce natural rubber include India, Vietnam, Brazil, Cambodia, Brunei, Territory of Papua in New Guinea, and Burma. Newer plantations have been planted in the Philippines, Guatemala, Costa Rica, and Mexico. It is interesting to note that, almost without exception, all natural rubber plantations are within 15 degrees north or south of the equator.

■**SYNTHETIC RUBBER.**—Since natural rubber is a polymer (a long chain of simple molecules), researchers saw an opportunity to duplicate it by joining simple chemical compounds, called monomers, together in a similar manner. Many different manmade polymers were made with general characteristics similar to those of natural rubber, but each having specific properties superior to it, as in resistance to chemicals, oils, sunlight, or heat, or in lower permeability to gases.

As early as 1879, a French chemist, Guy Bouchardat, used isoprene, a five-carbon molecule (C_5H_8) derived from natural rubber, and succeeded in converting it into a somewhat rubberlike substance. However, only in relatively recent years has science been able to exactly duplicate the polymer structure of natural rubber, using isoprene made synthetically from petroleum.

Necessity was proved the mother of invention twice in the history of the development of synthetic rubber. First, the Germans developed a rubber substitute, although a not-too-successful one, called *methyl rubber,* when their rubber supplies were cut off during World War I. Little work was done in the next twenty-five years except on an experimental basis. Again in World War II, when the Allied forces were cut off from their supply of natural rubber by the Japanese, a large-scale rubber industry was created, this time with complete success, by the United States. Today, large rubber and petroleum companies are spending millions of dollars to synthesize new monomers and rubberlike polymers.

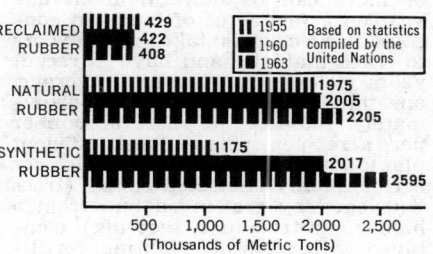

World Production of RUBBER

RECLAIMED RUBBER: 429, 422, 408

NATURAL RUBBER: 1975, 2005, 2205

SYNTHETIC RUBBER: 1175, 2017, 2595

■■ 1955 ■ 1960 ▮ 1963
Based on statistics compiled by the United Nations

500 1,000 1,500 2,000 2,500
(Thousands of Metric Tons)

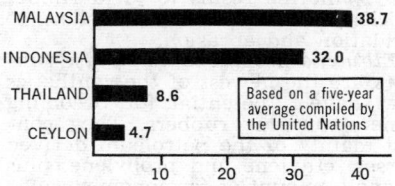

World Production of NATURAL RUBBER in %

MALAYSIA: 38.7
INDONESIA: 32.0
THAILAND: 8.6
CEYLON: 4.7

Based on a five-year average compiled by the United Nations

10 20 30 40

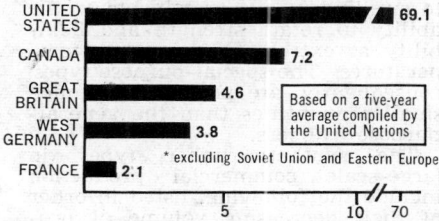

World Production of SYNTHETIC RUBBER in %

UNITED STATES: 69.1
CANADA: 7.2
GREAT BRITAIN: 4.6
WEST GERMANY: 3.8
FRANCE: 2.1

Based on a five-year average compiled by the United Nations

* excluding Soviet Union and Eastern Europe

5 10 70

A synthetic rubber plant with an annual capacity of 50,000 long tons or more can be built in about one year on a few acres of land. In contrast, *Hevea* trees take seven years to reach maturity and have in recent years yielded, on an overall average, one-third of a long ton (approximately 700 lbs.) of natural rubber per acre per year. Some efficient plantations yield 1,000 pounds per acre annually. Selected clones (trees developed by grafting a bud from a high-yield tree to a seedling) combined with scientific planting, fertilization, and tapping techniques, have yielded as high as 2,000 to 3,000 pounds per acre in a year.

Two-thirds of all the natural and synthetic rubber consumed in the United States goes into the manufacture of tires and other automobile products, which utilize rubber's characteristic properties of elasticity, shock absorption, and outstanding resistance to moisture and wear. Rubber's excellent electrical resistance make it useful for electrical insulation on wires and cables, and it is molded into miscellaneous mechanical goods. Its high resistance to abrasion, when compounded with other filler materials such as carbon black or clays, has won it a market in shoe products, flooring, and athletic goods. It can also be used in its latex form or dissolved in solvents to produce dipped goods, to impregnate paper or textiles, to serve as an adhesive, or to be whipped with air into a foam used in mattresses.

■**TYPES OF SYNTHETIC.**—A *general-purpose rubber* is one that has large-volume application, such as the manufacture of tires and commonly used molded articles. *Special-purpose rubbers* are polymers designed for specific applications that require distinctive properties, such as resistance to swelling in oils or solvents or the ability to retain strength and flexibility at extreme high or low temperatures. The special-purpose types, consequently, are produced in much smaller quantities than the general-purpose rubbers.

The synthetic-rubber types in large-scale commercial production include the following, listed in order of their decreasing volume of production:

Styrene-butadiene or S-type (SBR) rubbers constitute about 70 per cent of all the synthetic rubbers produced in the United States. They are copolymers of the petrochemical monomers butadiene (about 75 per cent) and styrene (about 25 per cent), and are used principally for making passenger-car tires and for other general-purpose molding uses.

Neoprene (CR) was the first synthetic rubber made in volume in the United States. It is called a special-purpose rubber today. Its use is confined principally to applications that require resistance to oil and gasoline, or for products that are exposed to sunlight or oxidation, such as hose, electrical insulation, gaskets, etc. Its monomer, chloroprene, is made from acetylene and hydrogen chloride.

Butyl rubber (IIR) is produced by copolymerizing the petroleum-derived monomer isobutylene and a small amount of another unsaturated hydrocarbon, such as isoprene, which permits this rubber to be vulcanized. As this rubber is not unsaturated to the extent natural or SBR are, it resists heat, aging, oxidation, and acids, and is a good electrical insulator. Its outstanding property of impermeability to gases ideally suits it for use in automobile inner tubes, which is its largest present application. It is used also in vibration mounts because of its ability to absorb shock.

A new group of synthetics is known as *"stereo" rubbers.* Their monomer units are lined up in the polymer in regularly repeated arrangements rather than at random as in most synthetic rubbers.

Polybutadiene (BR) was the second stereo rubber to be introduced. It is a highly elastic and abrasion-resistant rubber that duplicates natural rubber in its low heat-buildup characteristics. It is supplanting *Hevea* rubber in heavy-duty truck tires, and it improves the wear of SBR in passenger tires, so it is classified as a general-purpose rubber.

Polyisoprene (IR), the first stereo rubber, was introduced in 1954. The production of polyisoprene marked science's first success in chemically duplicating the natural rubber molecule and, as a result, essentially duplicating all its processing and end-use characteristics. For this reason it is like natural rubber, a general-purpose rubber.

Buna N, or N-type (NBR) rubbers are copolymers of butadiene and acrylonitrile. They are similar to neoprene in being highly resistant to oils, gasoline, and numerous solvents and are, therefore, classified as a special-purpose rubber. They can also be used in blends with polyvinyl-chloride resins to yield rubber stocks that are highly resistant to oxidation and abrasion.

Ethylene-propylene (EPDM) rubbers are the newest of the synthetics that have a potential for becoming general-purpose rubbers. They consist mainly of the petroleum-derived gasses, ethylene and propylene, plus a small amount of termonomer, sufficient to permit vulcanization. These rubbers have excellent resistance to ozone, sunlight, and weathering. EPDM rubbers have a very good flexibility at low temperatures and high electrical-insulation properties. In addition to their good potential for tires, they are being used increasingly in electrical insulation, auto parts, footwear, hose, sponge, and coated fabrics.

■**CONSUMPTION.**—The United States in the mid-1960's consumed about 2 million long tons of rubber, or about 22 pounds for every man, woman, and child. Approximately 75 per cent of this total was made up of synthetic rubber. Highly industrialized nations of Europe consume only 10 to 15 pounds per capita. Less developed countries, such as India and China, use only a fraction of a pound per person.

Rubber consumption in the United States continues to expand at a rate slightly over 3 per cent per year. Despite the fact that it has grown more than half again as large in the ten-year span from the mid-1950's to the mid-1960's, U.S. consumption continues to take a smaller percentage of the world's total. Until the late 1940's the United States consumed approximately two-thirds of the world total; by the mid-1950's, consumption had dropped to about half of the world total; by the mid-1960's, it had dropped again to less than 40 per cent of the world total. This trend reflects the much more rapid growth in the other industrialized nations.

Rubber was already a billion-dollar-a-year business in the United States when it initiated the large-scale production of synthetic rubber at the start of World War II. Including the production of synthetic rubber and all fabrication operations, the rubber industry has since grown to an $11 billion-a-year industry encompassing almost 1,500 companies. Many of these companies are expanding into diversified, but often related, fields of chemicals, plastics, metals, and textiles, and even into nuclear energy and space. (See also *Rubber Manufacture.*)

—Clayton F. Ruebensaal

Salt, the chemical compound sodium chloride (NaCl). In the United States, salt is produced in the South, chiefly in Louisiana, and in such Northern states as New York, Michigan, and Ohio. A more recent, and increasingly important, source of salt for the United States is the Bahamas.

Refined salt produced in the United States is obtained from underground mines. Salt in these mines is dissolved in water to form brine, from which it is recovered aboveground by evaporation. Salt from the Bahamas is so-called *solar salt,* which is produced by the evaporation of sea water. Northern rock salt usually is 95-97 per cent pure, southern rock salt better than 99 per cent pure, and solar salt 99.6 per cent pure. The recent trend has been toward shipping bulk salt from the mines to regional depots, where it is dried, crushed, screened, and packaged for final use.

Two-thirds of the U.S. salt output is used by the chemical industry. The largest single use is as raw material for the production of chlorine and caustic soda. Salt is used extensively for deicing roads and highways. It is also used in the meatpacking, tanning, food processing, rubber, oil, metal, and paper industries, as well as for seasoning foods and as an animal feed supplement.   —John Price

Sand, a loose, granular material made up of small particles of minerals or of rock and minerals. There are no generally accepted particle-size limits for sand, although geologists use a maximum of 2 millimeters and a minimum of 1/16 millimeter. Most sand is formed naturally by the disintegration of rocks. Many deposits contain varying amounts of clay and silt; some contain pebbles.

Sand is used in construction as a fine aggregate for concrete, mortar, and plaster. *Black sands,* such as

those in Florida, contain *ilmenite* (iron titanium oxide) and *rutile* (titanium dioxide) in sufficient quantities for commercial production. *Green sands* contain *glauconite,* an iron potassium silicate, and have been used as fertilizer because of their potash content. *Silica sands* are composed almost exclusively of quartz (silicon dioxide)—most contain more than 95 per cent, some more than 99 per cent. Silica sand is used in glass making, as molding sand, refractory sand, filter sand, and grinding and polishing sand; it is often called *industrial sand.* Natural molding sand contains enough clay and other bonding material to form molds in which metal is cast. Synthetic molding sand contains added amounts of *fire clay, bentonite,* or other bonding materials.
—John Price

Sandstone, a sedimentary rock consisting usually of quartz sand united by some cementing medium such as silica, iron oxide, or calcium carbonate. Often, many other minerals and even fragments of other rocks are included. Sandstone may take the form of *shale,* which is composed of particles smaller than 1/16 millimeter in diameter, or *conglomerate,* a form containing fragments larger than 2 millimeters in diameter. However, sandstone usually occurs in particle sizes between these two limits.

There are four generally recognized classes of sandstone: *arkose, graywacke, subgraywacke,* and *orthoquartzite.* Distinctions among these classes are made on the basis of mineral content and texture. Sandstone particles vary greatly in composition, including such common minerals as quartz, feldspar, and several clay minerals. Several other minor minerals are found in smaller quantities, including garnet, tourmaline, zircon, rutile, staurolite, magnetite, pyrite, and chromite.

Sandstones with silica cement are used for structural purposes. Some sandstone, such as *novaculite oilstone,* has been quarried to make grindstones, pulpstones, and sharpening stones.   —John Price

Sanitary Engineering, the branch of engineering concerned primarily with public health. A specialist in the more general field of civil engineering, the sanitary engineer is engaged primarily in meeting two basic problems of urban life: water supply and the disposal of street drainage and of domestic and industrial wastes. These have become more pressing and difficult problems with accelerated municipal and industrial growth.

In early centuries, water was obtained from rivers and irrigation ditches. As early as 700 B.C., a supply was brought by tunnel to Jerusalem from a spring outside the city walls. The Greeks followed with several similar works, and the Romans built aqueducts not only for Rome but throughout the Roman world. In many later cities, however, shallow wells were also used locally for supply. Drainage received some early attention, but early "sewers" were, in effect, only street storm-water drains.

Cesspools were used for domestic sewage, contaminating local well supplies until recurring cholera epidemics, as in Paris and London in the mid-nineteenth century, forced attention to this problem.

One of the first modern sewage systems was built in Hamburg, Germany, by a British engineer in 1850. Other, notably British, workers followed and by 1900 the relative advantages of "separate" and "combined" systems for drainage and domestic sewage were debated. While local wells were eventually abandoned, contamination through the practice of waste disposal in nearby streams led to typhoid epidemics that were common in American cities until early in the twentieth century. However, after Robert Koch discovered the typhoid bacteria in 1883, filtration to clarify turbid waters was developed and further perfected to provide an almost perfect "bacterial efficiency." The use of chlorine to kill bacteria followed and is widely adopted today. Nevertheless, many cities still face the problem of sewage and waste disposal and will ultimately be forced to provide suitable plants to treat their wastes.

In general, sewage plants are designed to accelerate the action of the natural factors that ultimately lead to the clarification of polluted waters. This usually involves the provision of conditions leading to the rapid growth of the beneficial bacteria that break down organic matter, as through the *activated sludge* process. This is followed by aeration to restore oxygen content. Industrial wastes which also vary with the industry, constitute a major problem. Manufacturers will undoubtedly be forced to give this source of pollution increasing attention in the future. The sanitary engineers thus face challenging problems, requiring not only the effective design of notable structural and mechanical works but also a thorough understanding of bacterial science and chemistry.
—James Kip Finch

Sericulture, the production of silk by raising silkworms. Silk has been a shining symbol of elegance and beauty ever since Hsi-ling-shi, the 14-year-old bride of Emperor Huang-ti, who ruled over China about 2640 B.C., first disclosed the secret of the silk cocoon. For nearly 3,000 years, the Chinese successfully guarded this secret. After that, silkworm eggs were smuggled into Persia, and that was the end of China's monopoly. Japan also got hold of the eggs and today is by far the largest producer of raw silk, with Red China, India, and South Korea next. In moderate quantities, raw silk is also produced in Italy, in the Near East, and in the Soviet Union.

Silk is a natural or live fiber, the filament which a silkworm spins for its cocoon. The silkworm is actually the caterpillar of the silkmoth (*Bombyx mori*) and its cocoon is the shell it constructs to protect itself during its growth from caterpillar to chrysalis (or pupa) to moth. A single cocoon is made of a continuous filament of silk, which the silkworm extrudes from its body. Along with the silk filament, the silkworm emits a gummy substance called *sericin.*

Sericulture involves the care of the little animal that produces the silk filament from egg through to cocoon. The breeder moths are selected with the utmost care. The eggs undergo many tests to ensure perfect, disease-free worms. They are put in cold-storage under strict governmental supervision until spring, when the mulberry trees begin to leaf. Then they are incubated until they hatch, in about a week, into tiny antlike silkworms. These have to be kept under rigidly clean conditions on trays that must be constantly refilled with the freshest mulberry leaves every two or three hours, for the silkworms eat voraciously day and night for five weeks. During this time they grow to about 70 times their original size. When the silkworm has eaten its fill, it creeps to straw that has been provided for it in individual cells and begins spinning its cocoon.

In the natural course of events, the worm inside the cocoon would develop into a chrysalis and the latter into a moth. The moth would then burst the cocoon and break the single long silk filament into many short ones. Therefore, it is necessary to destroy the worm inside the cocoon to enable the silk to be reeled off in one strand. This is done by stifling the worm with heat.

The next process is the unwinding (or reeling) of the cocoon, today mostly done by machinery. Hot water in basins is still used to melt the sericin, making it possible to unwind the cocoon. Because a single filament is far too fine for reeling, several cocoons are unwound at the same time. Their filaments are drawn together by passing them through a tiny porcelain eye, and the melted sericin now glues the silk filaments into a single thread. Later, the silk is re-reeled and twisted into skeins. The sericin is boiled off, either before or after weaving, to uncover the natural beauty of the silk. —Hans Vaterlaus

Slate, a dense, fine-grained rock produced by the compression of clays, shale, and other rocks so as to produce a characteristic cleavage. The chief minerals of slates are muscovite, chlorite, and quartz. Lesser constituents include tourmaline, rutile, epidote, sphene, hermatite, and ilmenite.

In the United States, slate is quarried in Maine, New York, Vermont, Pennsylvania, Maryland, and Virginia. The major slate-producing areas overseas are in England, North Wales, Scotland, Ireland, France, Bohemia, and Germany.

Slate is still processed by hand with a chisel and mallet. Big slabs are split along cleavages into separate slates whose thickness depends on the size required and the quality of the rock. Slates are trimmed to final size by hand or by machine-driven rotating knives. Slates are commonly used for blackboards and are used widely for roofing in thickness of about 5 millimeters. —John Price

Soaps and Detergents, substances used widely for cleaning, washing, and textile processing. They produce their effects by changing the surface tension of a solvent. Soaps actually are a special class of detergent, although the latter term is usually applied only to synthetic materials.

Soaps are the alkali-metal or ammonium salts of straight-chained carboxylic acids, the molecules of which usually contain 10-18 carbon atoms. Metallic soaps are akaline-earth or other metal salts; they are insoluble in water and find use in nonaqueous systems, especially as additives in lubricating oils and rust inhibitors. Soaps are prepared from naturally occurring triglycerides (animal and vegetable fats) by hydrolysis. At one time this was done by the action of water and alkalis, such as sodium hydroxide (NaOH) and potassium hydroxide (KOH), on fats in a soap kettle at high temperature. More common now is the direct hydrolysis of fats by water at high temperature. This allows isolation and rectification of the fatty acids, which are neutralized to form soap.

Rapid development of synthetic detergents has cut heavily into the use of soaps, except in toilet bars. A branched-chain detergent, alkylbenzene sulfonate (ABS), has been one of the most widely used materials in the synthetic group. However, ABS is not sufficiently biodegradable—efficient sewage-treatment plants degrade only 40 to 60 per cent of influent ABS. As a result, rivers and even drinking water supplies are contaminated with foam from residual detergent materials. Linear alkylate sulfonate (LAS) and linear alkylphenols (LAP) have been tried as an alternative. These materials, which have straight carbon chains in place of the branched chains in ABS, improve biodegradability. Under favorable conditions, sewage treatment will degrade more than 90 per cent of influent linear detergents. However, under anaerobic conditions LAS and LAP are not appreciably easier to degrade than ABS. Furthermore, at least one-third of the United States population discharges sewage into essentially anaerobic cesspools and septic tanks. Under unfavorable soil conditions, waste detergents leak into groundwater supplies. Synthetic primary or secondary alcohols, products that degrade faster than LAS or LAP, are therefore being considered as possible substitutes. —John Price

Sulfur, a commercially important, non-metallic element that makes up less than 0.1 per cent of the earth's crust; chemical symbol S. Although sulfur was discovered before recorded history, it was not until 1777 that Antoine Laurent Lavoisier first recognized it as an element. The largest known free-sulfur deposits are in Texas and Louisiana, where sulfur is found associated with limestone and cap rock formations over salt domes. It is also found near volcanic regions in Japan, Sicily, and Mexico.

The *Frasch process,* developed in 1891 by Herman Frasch, is used to extract sulfur from underground de-

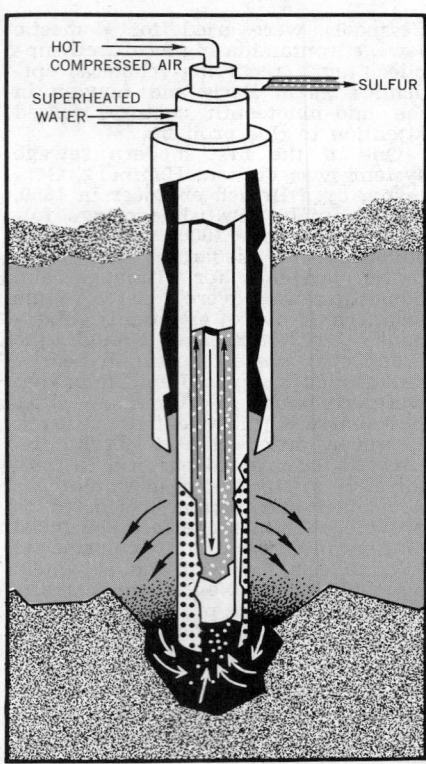

FRASCH PROCESS uses compressed air and superheated water to obtain sulfur for the fertilizer, petroleum, and other industries.

posits such as those in Texas and Louisiana. A hole is drilled down to the deposit, and three concentric pipes are lowered into the ore bed. Superheated (165° C) water forced down the largest pipe melts the sulfur, which has a melting point of 112.8° C. Hot compressed air is pumped down the smallest pipe, and a frothy mixture of water, air, and molten sulfur—99.5-99.9 per cent pure—is forced to the surface through the intermediate pipe.

Another major source is so-called *sour gas,* a natural gas containing hydrogen sulfide. Most natural gas is sweet, but the natural gas in France and Canada must be sweetened before it can be marketed. Large quantities of sulfur are obtained as by-products of the sweetening process.

The largest single use of sulfur is in the production of sulfuric acid, which is widely used in the fertilizer industry. Other uses are in paper manufacturing and bleaching; in the manufacture of titanium and other pigments; in pickling steel; in the production of nylon, rayon, and other cellulosic fibers; in petroleum refining; in rubber vulcanizing; and in a wide range of chemical manufacturing processes. —John Price

Sulfuric Acid, a strong, colorless, oily mineral acid, also known as *vitriolic acid* or *oil of vitriol;* chemical formula H_2SO_4.

Sulfuric acid is produced on a large scale by two processes: the *contact*

process and the *lead-chamber process.* The contact process, the more important of the two, produces acid of any desired strength, whereas lead-chamber acid is relatively dilute (60-78 per cent), hence less useful.

In the contact process, sulfur is burned or iron pyrites roasted in air to produce sulfur dioxide (SO_2), which is then oxidized to sulfur trioxide (SO_3) in the presence of a catalyst (vanadium pentoxide or platinum). Sulfuric acid is produced by the reaction of sulfur trioxide and water. Addition of more sulfur trioxide produces *oleum* (polysulfuric acid, $H_2S_2O_7$), which can be treated with water to produce acid of any desired concentration. The lead-chamber process involves oxidation of sulfur dioxide by nitric acid in the presence of water. The reaction is carried out in one or more large lead-lined rooms.

The concentrated acid is a strong oxidizing agent, especially at high temperatures. It reacts with metals, carbon, sulfur, and other oxidizable materials. Because of its high boiling point, it can react with salts at high temperatures to liberate volatile acids such as hydrochloric acid (HCL). The concentrated acid is a strong dehydrating agent and reacts vigorously with water, producing much heat. It also extracts hydrogen and oxygen to form water from organic materials, decomposing them and leaving carbon.

The major use of sulfuric acid is in the fertilizer industry. Phosphate fertilizers are made by treating insoluble phosphate rock with sulfuric acid. It is also used in the manufacture of ammonium sulfate, another fertilizer. Petroleum refining consumes large quantities of the acid, as does the manufacture of such chemicals as sulfates, nitric and hydrochloric acids, drugs, dyes, and explosives. It is used to pickle steel, to make storage batteries, paints, plastics, and various textiles, and has wide applications in the metallurgical industry.

—John Price

Tin, a metal first used by man more than 4,000 years ago; chemical symbol Sn. *Cassiterite* (tin dioxide) is the only tin-bearing mineral of commercial importance. There are no high-grade tin ores; most of the world's tin comes from low-grade alluvial deposits, which average 0.5 pound of cassiterite per cubic yard (3,000 pounds). Deposits containing up to 4 per cent tin are found in Bolivia and Cornwall, England.

Cassiterite is recovered from deposits by dredging, water jets, and gravel pumps on level ground, hydraulic methods where a head of water is available, and open-pit mining. The fine grains of cassiterite are 2½ times as dense as gravel, so concentration is a simple matter of screening and gravity separations. Concentrates usually contain 70-77 per cent tin, and lower-grade concentrates are upgraded before further treatment. Sulfur, arsenic, lead, antimony, and bismuth are removed by roasting. The addition of salt to form volatile or soluble chlorides helps to remove lead and silver. Excess iron and copper are leached with hydrochloric acid.

Primary smelting is carried out between 1,200° and 1,300° C, during which the amount of reducing agent is limited to give incomplete reduction. This produces metallic tin with low iron content. The resulting rich slag is treated further to remove most of the tin. Crude smelted tin is partly melted to remove iron, copper, and other impurities that form solid compounds appreciably above the smelting point of tin. Refined metal from most smelters is more than 99.8 per cent tin. Secondary tin from metal scrap amounts to about one-third of the total tin consumed in the United States. Most of it comes from tin-bearing alloys, which smelters rework into alloys and chemicals. Much high-purity tin is recovered by the detinning of tinplate scrap with a hot caustic solution and electrolytic treatment.

Half of the tin consumed is used in alloys. Soft solders are alloys of tin and lead, containing 20-70 per cent tin. Lead-free solders (with silver, antimony, or zinc instead of lead) are used for special applications. *Bronzes* are the most ancient of alloys and are still important structural metals. True *copper bronzes* include wrought *phosphor bronzes* (up to 10 per cent tin) and leaded-tin *cast bronzes* (5-10 per cent tin). *Babbitt metal,* used in bearings, is tin containing 4-8 per cent of copper and antimony. Other tin alloys include *pewter, Britannia metal,* and *type metal.*

Pure tin can be applied to all the common metals as a coating by hot-dipping or electrodeposition. Tin protects metal surfaces that oxidize or corrode easily. Tin-coated steel (tinplate for cans) is still an important product for tin, although other metals and plastics are taking over some of

television, and electronics industries. Tin-copper coatings are used for jewelry, handbag frames, wire goods, and hardware because of their lustrous finish.   —John Price

Titanium, a silvery-gray paramagnetic metal; chemical symbol Ti. It is stronger than steel but much lighter; its specific gravity is only 4.5, about 56 per cent that of steel. Titanium retains its properties from −320° to 1,000° F. With low electrical and thermal conductivity, it has outstanding resistance to corrosion in oxidizing media, and is impervious to atmospheric or salt-water corrosion. The most important sources of the metal are *rutile* (titanium dioxide) and *ilmenite* (a combination of iron oxide and titanium dioxide).

Titanium dioxide is widely used as a white pigment for exterior paints and as a whitener and filler in paper. Titanium metal, because of its low weight and high strength, has been used extensively in jet engines and airframes. The metal's corrosion resistance is valued in equipment, especially in the chemical and petroleum industry.

Titanium was discovered independently by William Gregor (who called it menaccanite) in 1791 and Martin Heinrich Klaproth in 1795. Jöns Jakob Berzelius first isolated crude titanium in 1825, but is was not until 1906 that M. A. Hunter separated enough metal for study. W. A. Kroll, in 1928, made the first metallic titanium and, in 1937, invented the process that bears his name—dry, high-temperature reduction of titanium halide with magnesium. Titanium production presents several formidable problems. The liquid metal seems to be a universal solvent; it dissolves or is contaminated by every known refractory. The metal must be reduced from its ore with extremely high purity. since contaminants destroy its

Tunnel, any underground passageway. Natural structures, such as long caves created by running water, fit this description, but from an engineering viewpoint, they are not tunnels. Civil engineers designate as a tunnel an underground passageway built without removing the overlying soil and rock. This rules out structures built by digging a trench, building the tunnel tube and then refilling the trench. This purist definition ignores the fact that the end product is a manmade underground passageway, a tunnel. Oddly enough, the first major tunnels driven by modern man were for boats. Since water transportation was most important, large tunnels were driven through hills for canals. The Languedoc Canal in France contained a tunnel built in the late seventeenth century. The first large tunnels in the United States were built for canals, but the railroads quickly superseded water transportation. By 1850, more than 50 tunnels had been built for railroads in the United States. Most of these were relatively short—less than a mile—and it was not until the 1860's, when power rock drills were developed, that longer hard-rock tunnels were driven.

■CONSTRUCTION.—Tunnel construction even today remains both difficult and dangerous. Paradoxically, tunneling is most difficult in rock or earth that is easy to dig through. Driving a tunnel through the soft, silty bottom of a riverbed, material that can be dug with a garden trowel, is far more challenging for engineers than blasting through solid granite. The rock tunnel is apt to be a self-supporting structure, whereas the subaqueous, so-called *soft-ground tunnel* must be supported completely with a steel and concrete lining.

Conventional *hard-rock tunneling* involves drilling holes with air-operated drills into the rock face. In a large tunnel many holes are drilled to prescribed depths in a set pattern. Explosives placed in the holes are detonated electrically, blasting the section of rock into small pieces. Machines remove the broken rock, called *muck,* and drillers return for another round. If the rock is weak and fractured, crews install steel or wood supports as the tunnel progresses. Depending on its purpose, and the quality of the rock, tunnels sometimes are lined with concrete. Softground tunnels, such as the under-river type, are usually shield-driven. The work area, called the *heading,* is often kept under air pressure. A tunneling shield resembles a huge barrel with its ends cut out. Its forward end has a strong cutting edge that forms the tunnel's outer perimeter, cookie-cutter fashion, as mammoth hydraulic jacks push the shield forward. Workmen, called *sandhogs,* excavate—usually by hand—within the shield as it moves ahead. Other crews at the rear of the shield install *liner rings,* sectional steel or concrete rings bolted to the ring behind it. A liner ring is installed when the shield is not advancing and its jacks are retracted. Once the ring is in place, the jacks bear on that ring to ad-

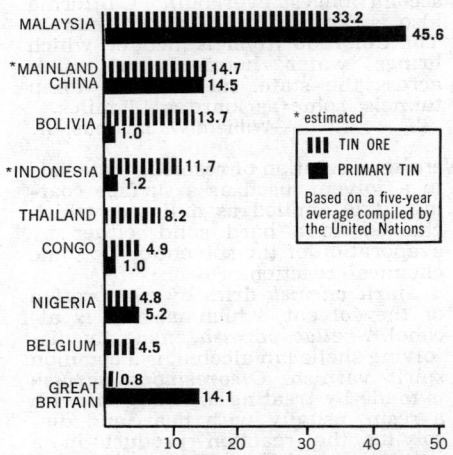

World Production of TIN in %

MALAYSIA	33.2	45.6
*MAINLAND CHINA	14.7	14.5
BOLIVIA	13.7	1.0
*INDONESIA	11.7	1.2
THAILAND	8.2	
CONGO	4.9	1.0
NIGERIA	4.8	5.2
BELGIUM	4.5	
GREAT BRITAIN	0.8	14.1

* estimated

■■■ TIN ORE
■■■ PRIMARY TIN

Based on a five-year average compiled by the United Nations

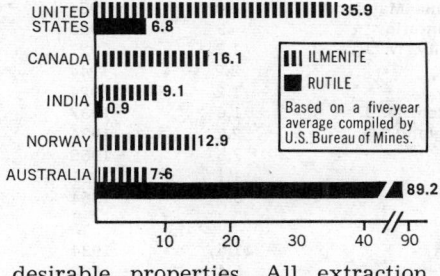

World Production of TITANIUM CONCENTRATES in %

UNITED STATES	35.9	6.8
CANADA	16.1	
INDIA	9.1	0.9
NORWAY	12.9	
AUSTRALIA	7.6	89.2

■■■ ILMENITE
■■■ RUTILE

Based on a five-year average compiled by U.S. Bureau of Mines.

the market. Hot-dip tin coatings are applied to copper wire and sheet and to steel and cast-iron parts.

Tin-cadmium coatings, which resist salt vapors, are widely used in the aircraft industry, and tin-zinc coatings are used widely in the radio,

desirable properties. All extraction and ingot melting must be done in vacuum or under a protective helium or argon blanket to prevent absorption of atmospheric nitrogen and oxygen.

The first step in reducing the metal from its ore is to chlorinate an oxide-carbon mixture to obtain titanium tetrachloride, which is treated with magnesium metal in a heat-resistant steel vessel at red heat under an inert-gas blanket. This yields commercially pure spongy titanium metal, which is further purified by remelting.   —John Price

vance the shield still further.

Water is one of the tunneler's major problems even in hard rock, but particularly in soft ground. Pumping compressed air into the tunnel, so the air pressure in the tunnel is greater than the pressure of the water in the soil being tunneled through, makes it possible to tunnel through very unstable soil. But working under air, sometimes two and three times normal atmospheric pressure, is very dangerous. Like deep-sea divers, sandhogs can work under such pressures for only limited periods. The body must be gradually returned to normal pressure or men suffer the diver's disease, the *bends,* which can be fatal. Also, a tunnel under air pressure can have a *blowout* in which the pressurized air in the tunnel works through the soil and bursts out into the river, causing the tunnel to flood with river water and mud.

Two recent developments have eased somewhat the plight of the tunneler. Giant tunneling machines with rotating cutterheads are taking the place of the sandhogs and blasters. These machines can work in harder and harder rock, as new steels are developed for the cutting teeth. By combining the boring principle with that of the shield, machines are now available that mechanically can bore through soft ground under air pressure. Engineers in the last decade have developed a sophisticated version of one of the oldest tunneling methods. The *cut-and-cover,* or *trench-type,* tunnel is built by digging a trench, building the tunnel in the trench, and then backfilling. The technique is used to build large tunnels in deep water. The tubes for the tunnel are built in dry docks. The mammoth steel and concrete sections

THE PORT OF NEW YORK AUTHORITY

THE LINCOLN TUNNEL'S third tube, under construction, reveals its casing of cast-iron cylinders. The tunnel provides a 1.6-mile roadway deep beneath the Hudson River.

have ends capped off. Dredges excavate a trench in the river bottom and the tube sections are floated into position and sunk into place. Divers connect the tubes and their caps are removed forming a continuous tunnel.

■**NOTABLE TUNNELS.**—Japan has begun construction of a 22.6-mile undersea tunnel to connect the islands of Honshu and Hokkaido. Besides using tunnels to breech water barriers, the world's engineers have long been busy driving tunnels through mountains for railroads and, more recently, highways. The Alps are literally riddled with tunnels. The longest vehicular tunnel, the 7.25-mile Mont Blanc Tunnel, was opened to traffic in 1965. Some famous rail tunnels in the Alps are the 12.3-mile Simplon Tunnel; the 11.5-mile Apennine Tunnel; and the 9.3-mile St. Gotthard Tunnel.

Auto tunnels are usually quite short because of the ventilation problem caused by exhaust gases. After Mont Blanc, the next longest is England's 2.4-mile Mersey Tunnel. New York City has the next three longest highway tunnels: Brooklyn Battery, 1.7 miles; Lincoln, 1.6 miles; and Holland, 1.6 miles.

The longest tunnels that have been built are for water supply. The world's longest is the Delaware River Aqueduct, a 14-foot diameter rock tunnel 85 miles long. Another tunnel, also part of New York City's huge upstate water supply system, is the 44-mile West Delaware Aqueduct, the second longest ever built. California also is famous for its water tunnels. The Colorado River Aqueduct, which brings water hundreds of miles across the state, has over a dozen tunnels, some as long as 18 miles.

—William W. Jacobus, Jr.

Varnish, a solution of resinous materials in a solvent, used as a surface coating. It is applied as a liquid, which changes to a hard solid, either by evaporation of the solvent or by some chemical reaction.

Spirit varnish dries by evaporation of the solvent, which usually is alcohol. *Shellac varnish,* made by dissolving shellac in alcohol, is a common spirit varnish. *Oleoresinous varnish* is made by treating a drying oil with a resin, usually with heat, and dissolving the reaction product in a petroleum solvent. These varnishes dry by evaporation of the solvent and by polymerization of the drying oil.

Varnish coatings protect wood from abrasion, staining, and weathering, and reduce the penetration of water and other liquids without obscuring

Notable Vehicular and Railway Tunnels

Name	Location	Length in Miles	Date Completed
VEHICULAR			
Baltimore Harbor	Baltimore, Md.	1.2	1957
Brooklyn Battery	New York, N. Y.	1.7	1950
Chesapeake Bay	Delmarva Peninsula-Virginia Mainland	2.0	1964
Detroit-Canada	Detroit, Mich.-Windsor, Ontario	.9	1930
Holland	New York, N. Y.-Jersey City, N. J.	1.7	1927
Kanmon	Japan	2.2	1944
Liberty Tubes	Pittsburgh, Pa.	1.2	1924
Lincoln	New York, N. Y.-Weehawken, N. J.	1.6	1937
Mersey	Liverpool-Birkenhead, England	2.2	1934
Mont Blanc	Italy-France	7.5	1965
Sumner	Boston, Mass.	1.1	1894
St. Bernard	Italy-Switzerland	3.4	1964
RAILWAY			
Arlberg	Italy	11.5	1934
Apennine	Austria	6.4	1884
Arthur's Pass	New Zealand	5.3	1912
Grenchenberg	Switzerland	5.3	1915
Hoosac	Hoosac, Mass.	4.8	1873
Loetschberg	Switzerland	9.5	1913
Moffat	Winter Park, Colo.	6.2	1928
Mont Cenis	France-Italy	8.5	1871
Mt. Royal	Montreal, Canada	9.0	1916
Roger's Pass	British Columbia	5.0	1912
Severn	England-Wales	4.5	1886
Shimizu	Japan	6.1	1930
Simplon	Switzerland-Italy	12.3	1905
St. Gotthard	Switzerland	9.3	1881
Tanna	Japan	4.9	1934
Vosges	France	7.0	1937

the wood's grain or changing its color significantly. Varnishes protect masonry from damage by moisture penetration and freezing. They are also used as insulation coatings for wires and as vehicles for paint. *Asphalt varnishes,* which contain a bituminous material and a drying oil in a solvent, are used for insulation and as a heat- or corrosion-resistant coating for metals. —John Price

Waxes, unctuous, viscous to solid substances used for protective coatings. Waxes fall into two broad categories: those produced from petroleum, and those derived from animal or vegetable sources. *Petroleum waxes* make up about 90 per cent of all wax used in industry. They may be either crystalline or microcrystalline. *Crystalline wax* is made from distillate lubricating fractions; *microcrystalline wax* is made from residual lubricating fractions of crude oil. Crystalline waxes melt at 120° to 150° F; microcrystalline waxes at 150° to 175° F. Petroleum wax is used to coat paper products and to blend with other waxes in candle manufacturing. It is used in the manufacture of electrical equipment and in many polishes for home and industry. Softer waxes, such as *petroleum jelly,* are used for medicinals.

Animal and *vegetable waxes* are esters of high-molecular-weight monohydroxyl alcohols and carboxylic acids. They are found in the cuticles of plants, in honeycombs and other insect cellular fabrications, as a coating on leaves of many trees and grasses, in the bodies of various land and marine animals, in seed envelopes, on the hair of animals, and associated with certain bacilli. Crude waxes often are mixtures of various organic substances of such complexity that it is impossible to separate completely and identify all components. Basically, however, waxes are known to be simple esters of steroidal or open-chain alcohols composed of an even number of carbon atoms (usually 24-36) esterified with acids of similar carbon content. Waxes are characterized by: *solidification point,* which is not necessarily the same as their melting point; *acid value,* which is the amount of free acid present, as measured by the number of milligrams of potassium hydroxide needed to neutralize free fatty acids present in one gram or substance; *saponification value,* the number of milligrams of potassium hydroxide needed to complete saponification of one gram of material; *iodine value,* which measures the degree of unsaturation—it is the number of grams of iodine absorbed by 100 grams of material, and the *Reichert-Meissel value,* which is a measure of the amount of low-molecular-weight acids present.

Carnauba wax, a coating on the leaves of the Brazilian palm *Corypha cerifera,* is one of the most important vegetable waxes. It is hard, has a relatively high solidification point (remaining solid in hot weather), repels water, and can be polished to a high luster. It is used extensively in floor and automobile polishes. *Japan wax* comes from the fruit coat of sumac berries. It is tough and can be kneaded without crumbling. *Spermaceti wax,* another commercially important wax, comes from the head of the sperm whale. *Lanolin* is purified wool wax or grease; it is used in salves and jellies, and in certain soaps and cosmetics. —John Price

Zinc, a malleable, ductile gray metal; chemical symbol Zn. It was discovered in Europe during the Middle Ages, although it was known much earlier in Asia. Zinc is 25th in order of abundance among the elements, making up 0.004 per cent of the earth's crust.

Pure, freshly polished zinc is bluish-white and lustrous. It tarnishes

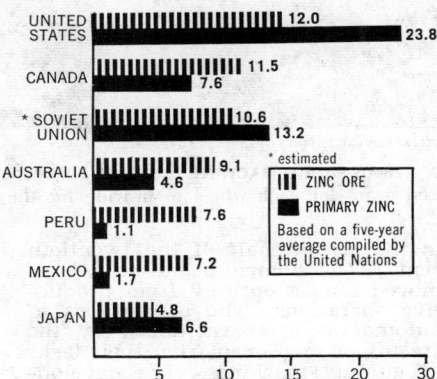

World Production of ZINC in %

UNITED STATES	12.0	23.8
CANADA	11.5	7.6
* SOVIET UNION	10.6	13.2
AUSTRALIA	9.1	4.6
PERU	7.6	1.1
MEXICO	7.2	1.7
JAPAN	4.8	6.6

* estimated

▍▍▍ ZINC ORE
■■■ PRIMARY ZINC
Based on a five-year average compiled by the United Nations

superficially in moist air, taking on its usual grayish color. Pure zinc is malleable and ductile enough to be rolled or drawn, but small amounts of contaminating metals can render it brittle. Zinc is a good conductor of heat and electricity, although its conductivity is only one-fourth that of silver, the best metal in this respect. Zinc is fairly active chemically. Its electromotive force is higher than that of hydrogen, so it will displace hydrogen from acid solution, liberating it as a gas, while zinc is dissolved to form Zn^{++} ions.

The chief zinc ores are *zinc blende* or *sphalerite,* and *marmatite* (both zinc sulfide). Other ores include *calamine* (a hydrated zinc silicate), *smithsonite* (zinc carbonate), *willemite* (zinc silicate), *zincite* (zinc oxide), and *franklinite* (an oxide of zinc, iron, and manganese). Much zinc is also separated as a by-product during the processing of iron ores.

Zinc is usually refined from its sulfide ores. Concentrates shipped to smelters contain 50 to 60 per cent zinc. Usual impurities are iron, lead, and cadmium. Sulfide ores are roasted before smelting to convert zinc to the oxide. Low-grade ores of the oxide type sometimes are concentrated in a rotary kiln, where the ore is mixed with enough coal to reduce the zinc oxide. Before pyrometallurgical extraction, concentrates are sintered to bring them to the proper density and particle size.

Several different processes have been developed to smelt zinc; the *horizontal retort* (Belgian) process;

the *vertical retort* (New Jersey) process; the *electrothermic* (St. Joe) process; the *blast-furnace* process; and the *electrolytic* process. The first four processes depend on the highly endothermic reaction by which carbon reduces zinc at 1,000° C or more, which is above the metal's boiling point. Enough carbon must be present to prevent oxidation of the carbon beyond the monoxide, since carbon dioxide will reoxidize the zinc vapor during the condensing step.

In the electrolytic method, zinc is produced from zinc sulfate solution. Anodes are made of lead alloy, cathodes of aluminum sheets, from which zinc is stripped periodically. This method produces high-purity zinc directly, whereas zinc produced by the carbon-reduction method must be refined to yield a high-grade product. One widely used method entails fractional distillation in reflux refining columns. Two lead columns remove lead, iron, and other high-boiling impurities, and a cadmium column removes cadmium and other low-boiling impurities. The purest grade of zinc, special high-grade, is more than 99.99 per cent pure.

The most important use of zinc is as a protective coating for other metals. Galvanizing is the process of coating iron or steel with zinc by immersion, electrolytic deposition, spraying, or treating with powdered metal near its melting point. Zinc is also used in brass and die-casting alloys and in dry cells. Rolled zinc is used in roofing, gutters, and flashing. —John Price

BIBLIOGRAPHY

BALL, MAX W. *This Fascinating Oil Business.* Bobbs-Merrill Co., Inc., 1966.

BRADY, GEORGE S. *Materials Handbook.* 9th ed. McGraw-Hill, Inc., 1963.

COOK, J. GORDON. *The Miracle of Plastics.* Dial Press, Inc., 1964.

CULLEN, ALLAN H. *Rivers in Harness; the Story of Dams.* Chilton Co., 1962.

DAVIES, J. D. *Structural Concrete.* The Macmillan Co., 1964.

GIES, JOSEPH. *Bridges and Men.* Doubleday & Co., Inc., 1963.

LEONARDS, GERALD A. *Foundation Engineering.* McGraw-Hill, Inc., 1962.

McGUINNESS, WILLIAM J. and others. *Mechanical & Electrical Equipment for Buildings.* 4th ed. John Wiley & Sons, Inc., 1964.

McMILLAN, PETER W. *Glass-Ceramics.* Academic Press, Inc., 1964.

MERDINGER, CHARLES. *Civil Engineering Through the Ages.* Society of Military Engineers, 1963.

SALVADORI, MARIO and HELLER, ROBERT. *Structure in Architecture.* Prentice-Hall, Inc., 1965.

SANDSTROM, GOSTA. *Tunnels.* Holt, Rinehart & Winston, Inc., 1963.

STAMM, ALFRED J. *Wood and Cellulose Science.* The Ronald Press Co., 1964.

STOUT, EVELYN E. *Introduction to Textiles.* 2d ed. John Wiley & Sons, Inc., 1965.

MACHINES AND PROCESSES

Evolution of Machines.—The history of machines may be said to begin with the introduction of complex machines in classical antiquity. In the Greek and Roman period it was human muscle that supplied the power to drive machines. In the Middle Ages human beings began to be replaced by nonhuman power sources, and machines became larger and more elaborate. This innovation continued to develop until the eighteenth century, when a new and more flexible power source—the steam engine—appeared. The steam engine was rapidly followed by the mechanization of the textile industry and by the introduction of machine tools. The Machine Age was further accelerated by the advent of electric power toward the end of the nineteenth century, and progress in invention and development of power-driven machinery has continued.

However, with the early 1950's came a remarkable advance, the *Age of Automation,* characterized by the automatic operation and direction of the machine and the computerized supervision of complex manufacturing processes. The Age of Automation, increasingly freeing man from production, will continue for the foreseeable future.

Role of Machines.—Machines contribute more to modern living than any other single feature of twentieth century society, yet there is no simple definition of machine. As mechanization encompasses a host of activities, it is impossible to formulate a definition that would apply equally, say, to the essential nature of both a drill press and a computer. A general understanding of the function of machines can be gained from the fact that they have long been adjuncts to man's feeble and fallible hands, and that more recently they have begun to add power to some of his similarly slow and erring thought processes.

The machines of antiquity served to modify or concentrate human effort to accomplish a desired end, such as lifting a heavy block of stone up to its position in a building wall. As mentioned in the section on energy and power sources, men of the Middle Ages developed remarkable sources of nonhuman power, and these were linked with machines to extend still further the effectiveness of hand tools.

With the advent of machinery that did not depend on human muscles, man became the guide or director of machine operation, in both a physical and an intellectual sense. He could channel the newly invented power sources into work that man alone could never accomplish. For example, it is impossible to conceive of a system that would directly use the million human beings that would be necessary to supply the power used by a modern jet aircraft.

Just as the Middle Ages began to see men freed from the drudgery of supplying power, such as walking all day and every day on a treadmill, so

INTERNATIONAL BUSINESS MACHINES CORPORATION

A RENAISSANCE MACHINE designed by Leonardo da Vinci was a car with a set of springs and gears for each wheel to provide for the difference in rotation when turning a curve.

in the second half of the twentieth century have men begun to be removed almost entirely from productive operations. The present era of automation is characterized by the freeing of men even from their tasks of guiding machines. The development of automatic controls, thus, is at least as important as the medieval invention of nonhuman power sources in terms of freeing men for the pursuit of more intellectual forms of activity.

■**ANCIENT MACHINES.**—The beginnings of the evolution that led to modern automation lay in the mist of prehistory, for early man had invented two of the classic five simple machines—the lever and the wedge, or inclined plane. Neolithic man then produced the wheel and axle. In historic times, the Greeks invented the pulley and the screw.

Antiquity also saw the invention of the first of the complex machines, all of which were constructed of wood. These included three complex devices employed in food manufacturing: pumps for irrigation, grain mills to produce flour, and presses used in making wine and olive oil. Looms were developed to weave fabric to clothe people, and remarkable man-powered cranes were constructed to build large buildings for shelter and social activity. Other interesting complex machines of antiquity, which had their origins in prehistory, were the potter's wheel, which may have preceded the wheel and axle on carts, and the bow-string drill.

The Greeks also invented heavy missile-throwing machines that were the ancient forerunners of modern ballistic missiles. By the close of the classical period, man had developed complex machines to produce food, to clothe and house himself, and to help him enforce his political aspirations on other groups.

Medieval Industry.—Up until the tenth century, medieval industry was largely domestic. There was little or no improvement of ancient machines or invention of new machines. However, from the tenth to the twelfth centuries there were improvements in ancient machines, accompanied by the introduction of sources of nonhuman power. Then again, from the tenth to the fourteenth centuries, few advances were made in food production and textiles, although the spinning wheel appeared at this time.

Most machines invented and developed in the later Middle Ages were associated with mining, metallurgy, and construction. These included mechanically operated bellows, saws, the pole lathe, toothed wheels for gearing, and the development of many applications for that all-important device, the crank, first used in the ninth century.

Improvements, made possible largely by the new power sources, were made in ancient cranes. Similarly, larger boring machines were developed, which were used at the end of the Middle Ages to produce cannon. At the same time, there were further developments in missile-throwing war machines, exemplified by the introduction of the counterpoise-powered trebuchet—a beam with a sling holding a rock at one end and a heavy counterpoise weight at the other.

One highly significant achievement of medieval technology was the mechanical clock, a spring-driven series of gears that kept time more accurately than earlier devices. A mechanical clock was built in Milan in 1335, and the Italian Jacopo de Dondi improved the design in 1344. As a large mechanism was easy to construct, most early timepieces were tower clocks like that made by Henry de Vick in 1379 for the Paris Palais de Justice.

FORD MOTOR COMPANY

EARLY MASS PRODUCTION in the automobile industry employed devices like this "body drop," used on a 1914 Ford assembly line to speed the manufacture of Model T cars.

widely used in modern computers.

Associated with early inventions of the Industrial Revolution was the extensive introduction of machine tools, which are metal-cutting tools. Until the middle of the eighteenth century, machinery was still being built by the carpenter. With the advent of the Industrial Revolution, metal began to be used in construction of machines. To work metal, new machine tools were required. Machine tools were powerful, and they were accurate—without them, the Industrial Revolution would have slowed down in the first half of the nineteenth century.

Typical machine tools are the drill press, metal screw-cutting lathe, planing machines, turret lathes, gear-cutting machines, precision grinders, and milling machines. Most of these devices were invented in the first half of the nineteenth century, and most of them operate with a shearing action of a sharp tool. Metals continued to be machined in this manner until the 1950's, when nontraditional machining techniques began to come into use, including laser machining, ultrasonic machining, plasma-torch cutting, and electrical-discharge machining.

Between 1400 and 1700 no important new power source was developed. However, looms, pumps, and mills were extensively improved, and new machines were invented, including knitting machines, clocks, screw-cutting lathes, and printing presses.

Without a doubt the most important of the new machines was the printing press, for it facilitated a remarkable spread of knowledge, beginning in the last half of the fifteenth century. Printing was also important from the mechanical point of view because it was the first process to mass-produce a product having interchangeable parts. A book was printed on sheets of paper that were folded into signatures—a signature usually contained 4, 8, 16, or perhaps 32 pages. Each signature was labeled, the first often being *A*, the second *B*. However, each *A* signature was like every other *A* signature, so that a book could be assembled by using any of the *A* signatures as the first in the book. The basic requirement for interchangeable manufacture is accurate production so that each part is like every other. Since each sheet was printed from the same type, all were exactly alike; therefore, it made no difference in which copy of the book a given sheet was used. However, it was not until the nineteenth century that manufacture using interchangeable parts was extended to other industrial operations.

The Industrial Revolution.—The Industrial Revolution, which began in the eighteenth century and has extended to modern times, was initially associated with James Watt's invention of an efficient steam engine and many new types of power-driven machinery. New power sources—improved water wheels, water turbines, and steam turbines—followed the

Watt steam engine, and new machines were developed.

There was little use for complex machines in agriculture until the eighteenth century, when there was an increasing demand for improved agricultural production resulting from an increase in population that has continued through the present day. New machines in the eighteenth century were varieties of seed drills, which mechanized planting. In the nineteenth century, reapers and threshers were developed to mechanize the harvest. More recently, mechanical harvesting techniques have been applied, particularly to fruit but also to field crops.

In the early decades of the Industrial Revolution, the introduction of new textile machinery spurred the revolution forward more than any other type of development. Powered spinning machines led to the invention of powered machines for preparing textile fibers for spinning. Not only were power looms invented, but also figure-weaving looms on which the design could be mechanically woven. These figure-weaving looms used large punched cards, the direct forebears of the punched cards so

Mass Production.—Aside from book printing, mass-production processes did not come into wide use until the early nineteenth century. Among the first persons to use such procedures were Eli Whitney in the manufacture of muskets and Eli Terry in the production of wooden clocks. In Whitney's musket factory, uniform parts were produced by machine, and these parts were assembled into individual muskets by filing and other fitting procedures. However, it was not possible to interchange parts among these finished muskets. With the advent of machine tools, which worked accurately and produced finished parts, it was possible in 1819 for John H. Hall of the Harpers Ferry Armory to start mass production of a breech-loading rifle employing the system of interchangeable parts. Mass production with interchangeable parts soon came to be known as the *American System* and spread to other areas of manufacture. Today it is almost universally employed, except that the computer is now making it possible to employ mass-production techniques that are entirely mechanized but that yield nonidentical products.

Assembly-line processing was an-

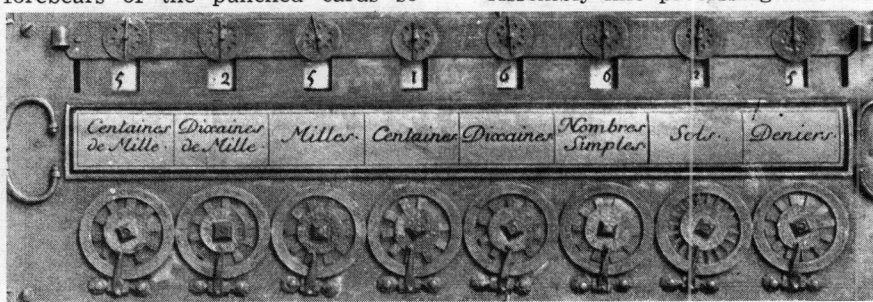

INTERNATIONAL BUSINESS MACHINES CORPORATION

MECHANICAL CALCULATING MACHINE, devised by Blaise Pascal in 1642, was the first one known capable of adding, subtracting, multiplying, and dividing with accuracy.

other important innovation in nineteenth century manufacturing. Assembly-line procedures were probably first introduced in pork packing houses in Cincinnati, Ohio, in the 1860's, and these slaughterhouse procedures, in turn, helped to influence Henry Ford to introduce his famous assembly-line automobile manufacture in 1913. Since Ford's successful employment of the assembly line, it has been widely used in manufacture and, recently, has been extensively automated.

■AUTOMATION.—Automation has been characterized by the introduction of automatic control and the electronic digital computer. Automatic controls employing the feedback principle first appeared in the eighteenth century on steam engines and windmills. An example was the fly-ball governor which James Watt adapted from windmill-driven flour mills to control the speed of a steam engine. Watt attached the device to the engine throttle; as engine speed increased, the device closed the throttle, thereby reducing speed. Thus, there was a *feedback* of information from engine speed to control to throttle to engine speed. Controls that use such feedback in "closed loops" are true automatic controls.

Although automatic controls were first known in the eighteenth century, it was only in the twentieth century that they began to be used extensively in continuous processes, for example, in chemical plants. Subsequently, self-regulating automatic control of machine-tool operation was introduced. In this technique, known as *numerical control,* numerically coded instructions on punched paper tape or punched cards are fed into a reading device in the machine, and the information in the tape or cards guides the machine through its task without the aid of human operators. Numerical control has eliminated human error, freed many workers from tedious and repetitious tasks, and has further improved the speed, safety, and accuracy of machine production.

The automation of business methods has been accomplished largely through the electronic digital computer. Although automatic controls had been little used here, data-processing computers have been extensively introduced since 1955 into business procedures, replacing human workers to an amazing extent in such operations as invoicing, accounting, paying, and inventory maintenance.

The computer, also, has been recently introduced into manufacturing processes. Numerical control directs a machine to produce a given product. Computers are employed to direct the several complex machines that will yield the desired product. Here, as the circumstances of machining may vary due to the condition of the tool or of the metal being machined, the computer corrects the process so that the final product is uniform. Numerical control had already replaced the machine operator. The computer is now replacing the supervisor of the operators.
—Frederick G. Kilgour

MACHINES AND PROCESSES GLOSSARY

Air Pollution, the contamination of the atmosphere with injurious substances. The effects of air pollution are serious. Through injury to vegetation and livestock, corrosion and soiling of materials and structures, lowering of property values, and interference with air and surface travel, air pollution costs billions of dollars each year in economic damage in the United States alone. Of even greater concern are its adverse effects on human health. Episodes of extreme pollution have contributed directly to sickness and death. More importantly, studies conducted over the past decade have produced a growing body of evidence that the long-term effects of exposure to ordinary levels of air pollution adversely affects the health of many and may result in chronic disease and premature death. Among the major illnesses which have been linked with air pollution are bronchitis, asthma, lung cancer, emphysema, and even the common cold. The unmistakable upward trends in the factors which contribute to the contemporary air-pollution problem—increasing urban population, increasing industrialization, greater demands for power produced by the burning of fossil fuels, more and more dependence on automobiles, trucks, and buses to meet rising transportation needs—these and other trends of growth leave no doubt that the potential scope and severity of the problem will intensify unless the nation substantially and rapidly augments its efforts to control the sources of air pollution.

The technical means for controlling, or limiting, the discharge of most pollutants to the air are available today. Through such devices as filters, scrubbers, centrifugal separators, electrostatic precipitators, or such means as industrial process modification or fuel substitution, the majority of sources can be adequately controlled. On the other hand, means for controlling the discharge from fossil-fuel burning processes or from motor vehicles, are either not presently available or are only partly effective. To bring such sources under fully adequate control will require substantial augmentation of research and development efforts by

both industry and government as well as public awareness.

The determination of the U.S. federal government to control air pollution is clearly expressed in the Clean Air Act of 1963 and the Clean Air Act Amendments of 1965. These new federal authorities include strengthened research and technical assistance activities, a matching-grants program which offers substantial financial stimulation for the creation or improvement of state and local regulatory control agencies, a federal abatement program focused primarily on interstate pollution problems, and the regulation, nationally, of auto exhaust emissions.

If the United States expects to fully meet the challenge of air pollution, great strides must be taken in the application of controls to pollution sources. The forces that shape the contemporary environment make certain that the problem will otherwise continue to worsen.
—Vernon G. MacKenzie

Assaying, the procedure used to determine the portion of pure or precious metal present in an ore sample. Unlike complete analysis, assaying usually determines only the proportion of certain valuable constituents to the whole sample. In essence, assaying procedures are adaptations of ore-treatment procedures designed to separate the valuable and waste portions of a mineral specimen.

Fire assaying, which is used for precious metal ores, makes use of the fact that the gold, silver, or platinum in a sample will dissolve in lead when submitted to high heat in a reducing atmosphere. In this process, litharge (a lead oxide), silica, and other materials are added to an *assay ton* (29.166 grams) of the sample. In the reducing atmosphere the litharge is reduced to lead, and the gold, silver, or platinum in the sample combine with it and sink to the bottom. The silica, borax, and nonvaluable portions of the ore become liquid at this high temperature. The lead button containing the precious metals is weighed and then submitted to a high temperature in an oxidizing atmosphere. This drives off the lead, leaving as residue a bead

U.S. PUBLIC HEALTH SERVICE

AIR POLLUTION, a serious problem in many cities today, is caused by vehicle exhaust fumes and by smoke that factories, like those above, pour over congested city areas.

containing only the gold, silver, or platinum. This is weighed and treated with hot nitric acid. The nitric acid dissolves the silver in the button. The difference in weight of the bead, before and after treatment by nitric acid, is the weight in grams of silver in the original sample. The remainder is gold and platinum. The weight in grams of gold or silver in an assay ton of sample represents the number of ounces of gold in a ton of the material of which the sample is supposed to be representative.

There are quicker methods than fire assaying for analysis of any ore material. The assay office can determine everything present in the ore material by chemical means or through the use of equipment such as the spectroscope, in which characteristic colors given by different elements are compared to calibrated standard samples. In assaying radioactive material, a scintillometer may be used to compare the radioactivity of the sample under analysis to a calibrated series of samples to determine the percentage of radioactive material in the sample. —J. C. Fox

Automatic Control Systems, assemblies of devices to maintain a desired physical state, such as temperature or speed, without the need for human intervention. Such systems make it possible for a rocket to travel a precise path to a distant planet or for a home to be automatically and safely kept at a comfortable, even temperature. Automatic control systems play an important role in technology, and give people more leisure time while increasing their comfort and safety.

Automatic control systems for space rockets or even for industrial processes can be extremely complicated, but they are based on the same principles as simple systems. Almost any measurable thing that can be controlled by hand can also be automatically controlled.

An elementary automatic control system is made of three main elements: a *sensor,* which measures whatever is to be controlled; a device to determine what must be done if the measured value does not meet specifications; and a *servo,* which causes a corrective action to be taken. A typical *sensor* is an electric thermostat that turns on a switch connected to a heater when the room temperature falls below a certain point. In this case, the device that determines what is to be done is the wiring of the system itself, causing the heater to be turned on. The *servo* in this case could be a valve that permits fuel to flow to the heater. Heat continues to warm the room until the thermostat signals a shutoff of the heaters. Such a control system is called an *on-off system,* and the difference between the turn-on and turn-off temperatures is called the *differential.*

A fundamental concept is *feedback,* a communication link between the servo, which brings about the corrective action, and the sensor, which commands the servo. In the simple example above, the feedback is

through the air in the room. The thermostat commands the heater to come on; the heater warms the air; and the heated air, in turn, feeds this information back to the thermostat—hence, feedback. In some complex systems, feedback can be achieved in ways other than through the controlled medium.

An automatic control system of a different type is illustrated by one of the oldest control systems, the speed governor of a steam engine. It permits gradual increases or decreases in control rather than all or none, as with an on-off control. This is called *proportional control.*

Special problems in automatic control arise if great precision is required. If, for instance, it should be

BURROUGHS CORPORATION

AUTOMATED devices process data from tape.

necessary to control the temperature of a room to within a fraction of one degree, the simple arrangement described above would not be adequate, no matter how sensitive or accurate the thermostat. There would be too much time delay in response of the system. When the thermostat turned the heater on, some time would elapse before the temperature rose in the room. By the time the thermostat turned the heater off, the temperature would have continued to rise for a while. As the temperature again fell, the thermostat would turn the heater on again, but too late to prevent a continuing dip in temperature. Any simple control system, no matter what it is controlling, has this tendency to swing rhythmically. This is called *hunting.*

Hunting can be eliminated by adding a device that will respond to the rate at which the controlled medium is changing. Such a control arrangement, called a *rate* system, has many applications. Airplanes and rockets have *rate gyros* that generate electrical signals according to how fast the vehicle is changing direction. These signals go to a computer, which in turn operates servos for steering. Such systems are called *rate damping* systems, and they permit smooth, even flight.

The ultimate in a control system is achieved when the sensors measure those things that would cause the change in what is controlled,

rather than measure the controlled medium itself. The reason is that a sensor which is sensing the controlled medium cannot do anything until a change occurs, and that change is the very thing the control system is supposed to prevent. This fundamental is the basis for very elaborate automatic control systems.
—John V. Sigford

Automation, a term denoting a wide variety of automatic procedures. To some, it is "the automatic handling of parts between progressive production processes"; to others, it is "an evolutionary extension of mechanization" or "a new technological revolution (that is, a second industrial revolution) with far-reaching social and economic effects."

Actually, a good case can be made for each of these definitions. The earliest so-called automated factories were those which used mechanical methods to move parts from one production machine to another. An automated refinery operation, for example, was one in which remotely controlled pipelines were used to move petroleum products between distillation towers. An automated factory was one that utilized conveyor belts or similar devices to pick up parts at one machine and move them along to the next production operation.

In the 1950's and early 1960's the term "automation" was applied to the growing family of numerically controlled production machines that operate from instructions punched into tapes or cards. Although an operator is still required to set up the tapes and supervise the machine, the actual milling, cutting, or drilling operations are performed automatically.

In a sense, the trend to numerically controlled machines is an extension of the Industrial Revolution of the eighteenth and nineteenth centuries. Originally, all machines and tools were operated and controlled directly by man or animals. The basic change effected by the Industrial Revolution was to replace muscle power with steam and, later, electricity. But the machines themselves were still operated and controlled by man.

Today we find man stepping further and further into the background as tapes or cards, often produced automatically by computers, control and run production machines while the operator functions primarily as an overseer.

All of this has contributed to the "technological revolution" that is sweeping industry today. In the office, we have the increased use of data-processing systems to take over many of the tedious clerical chores formerly handled by clerks; in the factory, we have the growing use of mechanical and electronic devices to manufacture, test, and transport products; and in science, we have a growing dependence on computers to perform computation tasks formerly done by hand—or not done at all. Among the results of these changes has been an increase in leisure time and an improvement in our standard of living. —Stanley L. Englebardt

Automobile Manufacturing, the production of motor vehicles, primarily those powered by an internal-combustion engine and designed to transport two to nine passengers. Although precise details are clouded by conflicting claims, it is generally agreed that production of automobiles in volume began in the early 1890's in western Europe. In the United States, series production of both electric and gasoline automobiles was under way by 1896, when the Pope Manufacturing Company of Hartford, Conn., produced 500 electric and 40 gasoline carriages in one year.

By 1897 Ransom E. Olds and Alexander Winton founded companies to build gasoline-powered cars and the Stanley brothers were building steamers, but only Pope could qualify as a volume producer.

Two important events in 1899 changed the picture radically. The Olds Motor Works moved to Detroit, and then the factory burned down. The only thing saved was the prototype of a low-priced car designed by Olds. By concentrating on the single-cylinder buggylike car, the company achieved instant success. In 1901, about 600 Oldsmobiles were produced; in 1902, production jumped to 2,500; in 1903, the number reached 4,000; and in 1905 a total of 5,000 units rolled from the plant. At that time Olds and his backers severed relations, and production of the economy model was halted.

■**MASS PRODUCTION.**—Although the Olds company had achieved substantial volume, its manufacturing methods were still based on skilled craftsmen producing one car at a time. The big change started in 1903 when Henry Ford, after several false starts, founded the Ford Motor Company and put his personal stamp on automobile production. He concentrated on developing a car suitable for the mass market, and then on cutting manufacturing costs. By 1907 the prototype of the *Model T* had been developed, and the most famous car ever built was offered to the public in 1908. In 1909, Ford stopped production of all other models and concentrated all his efforts on the Model T. By 1914 a complete assembly-line had been perfected that reduced chassis assembly time from 12½ hours to 1½ hours. The success of the effort to cut manufacturing costs was reflected in the rapid drop of the retail price. In 1912, a Model T sold for $600, and as production increased, costs decreased so the retail price could be dropped even further. Ford had produced 6,000 units in 1908, but by 1916 production soared to 577,000 Model T's and the price was down from $850 in 1908 to $360. A total of 15,007,003 Model T's had been built when production finally stopped on May 31, 1927.

■**ASSEMBLY-LINE METHODS.**—By the time Ford shut down to retool for a new model in 1927, the manufacturing processes developed to cut the cost of the Model T had been adopted by the entire industry. Assembly methods employed in the auto industry today can be traced to the basic con-

GENERAL MOTORS CORPORATION

MASS PRODUCTION of automobiles requires quick repetition of highly specialized tasks.

cepts that were in use at Ford as early as World War I. Work is moved past the operator on an assembly line while parts are stacked near at hand or delivered as needed by conveyors. The basic rule—never stop the assembly line—must be followed to get the most from continuous production. If a mistake is made, an operation missed, or a defect discovered, it is bypassed and corrected at the end of the line. Stopping the line would immediately idle every worker on it and result in complete loss of production.

Each operator performs one relatively simple task that is repeated on each piece of work. This reduces the need for skilled operators to assemble even complex equipment, since each worker need only know how to perform his simple, repetitive task.

The final assembly line in an auto plant, where thousands of parts are joined to produce a complete automobile, represents the culmination of several years' effort. Hundreds of cars are produced on the final assembly line each day, yet the dramatic assembly operation represents only a small portion of the total effort that goes into making a new car. The uninterrupted flow of vehicles from the assembly line reflects years of planning, engineering, and scheduling by specialists who have worked out thousands of details.

■**PRODUCT PLANNING.**—All work starts with a product-planning group that evaluates market research data and then, working with other departments, proposes a new model program to company management. New models proposed by product planning must provide what the customer wants, be manufactured at a competitive cost, be competitively priced, and return a profit for the capital invested.

A proposed new model is described in a *paper program,* or *package,* specifying in detail the targets and limits for the new model. The limits include the physical dimensions, total weight, carrying capacity, and power requirements. Targets include the total manufacturing cost and delivered price of the new car.

Production experts then examine the plan in detail to make sure that every part of it is practical from a manufacturing standpoint. Cost analysts and cost estimators examine the proposed product to determine manufacturing costs.

The final product plan, or package, is then presented to the product planning committee for approval. This is the signal to begin detailed styling and engineering work.

■**STYLING.**—Hundreds of sketches are prepared to develop new and interesting styling ideas, for the overall automobile as well as its different parts. From these sketches, coherent styling ideas gradually emerge. The most promising designs are developed into full-size clay models to get a three-dimensional basis for more effective selection of the final appearance.

Finished to a glossy smoothness, the clay is covered with plastic paint, and exterior trim is added. When the model is complete, it is difficult to tell the difference between the clay *mock-up* and a real automobile.

As the exterior is developed, interior styling is worked on by specialists in textiles, color, fashions, and plastics. Development of the car's interior must be integrated with exterior styling so that the two will harmonize. Design details are developed by artists who sketch ideas for seats, instrument panels, and other interior parts.

The most promising interior designs are blown up to full-size drawings and then developed into full-size models called *trim bucks,* before a final selection is made. Trim bucks are full-size models of the interior seating arrangement, with actual paints and fabrics used to show the proposed interior exactly as it will appear in the finished automobile.

■**ENGINEERING.**—While the design is being developed, engineers draw plans for each of the more than 13,000 operating parts that will go into the car. In designing a specific automobile and its many parts, engineers refer continually to the basic package document as approved by the product planning committee. This

GENERAL MOTORS CORPORATION

ON ASSEMBLY LINE front end parts are attached to a car body (*left*) and rear suspension is readied for placement (*right*).

is to be sure that the car will end up within the original objectives that govern construction, weight, cost, performance, and ease of manufacture.

The development of an individual part or assembly begins with an engineer's ideas in the form of sketches. While working out the basic design he keeps in mind the other parts with which it must be assembled, the work it will have to do, and the amount of space in the car available for it. The engineer's job is to make sure that all the pieces of the jigsaw puzzle fit in the spaces allotted to them—and that they all work when joined in final assembly.

Whenever a new model is mass-produced, production men frequently encounter delays, adjustments, and problems that are caused by the production process itself. In 1957, the Ford Motor Company adopted an idea that enables production engineers to discover and correct troubles in advance. The idea was a *pilot plant* that produces a few sample cars. A complete assembly line is set up in the pilot plant, with the same tools, templates, and forming devices, the same gauges, and the same skills that will be used to mass-produce the car on actual production lines. Ford's pilot plant has become a standard operation where the "bugs" are worked out of new car assembly methods well before production begins.

■ **FINAL ASSEMBLY.**—Hundreds of suppliers now begin to deliver raw materials and subassemblies, ordered well in advance, to the final assembly plants. Steel is shaped into car bodies from dies that took years to produce, while engines are machined and built from iron castings.

The first step in assembling a car is building the body. The various sheet-steel parts of the car body—*floor, roof,* and *side panels*—are stamped into shape on giant presses and then welded together on the longest feeder line in the assembly plant. Framing fixtures hold the panels in place while electric welding machines spot-weld parts together.

The welded body is mounted on a conveyor or wheeled dolly for further processing. Seams in the body metal are filled with molten solder, which is ground down to blend with the steel, forming smooth surfaces. The *doors* and *deck,* or *trunk lid,* are added and fitted; then all metal surfaces are ground smooth and the body thoroughly cleaned.

Moving along the conveyor system, the body is phosphate-coated in a dip tank to prepare the metal surfaces for painting, joints are sealed with vinyl and asphalt sealers, and protective layers of primer are sprayed on and baked in an oven.

On a parallel assembly line the *front end,* though a part of the body, is built up separately. This subassembly consists of the *front fenders, radiator, grille, headlights,* and *fender aprons* at the sides of the engine compartment. After being painted and trimmed, the front end is moved to the final assembly area, where it is added after the main body structure is secured to the *frame,* or *chassis.*

Trimming an automobile's body is the installation of the upholstery lining, instrument panel, electrical wiring, glass, interior hardware, heater, radio, and accessories, and the application of ornamental chrome. Particular care must be exercised during this subassembly because paint, trim, and upholstery are easily scratched, torn, or soiled.

Actual assembly of the complete automobile begins when a frame is lowered onto the moving assembly line. Subassemblies fed from conveyors or stockpiles close to the line are added in a carefully programmed sequence. The *front suspension, springs,* and *shock absorbers* are among the first parts to be added as the frame advances along the line. Then the *rear springs* and *rear axle* are bolted on. These subassemblies are usually manufactured at other plants and delivered to the final assembly plant. At the *engine drop,* completely assembled and test-run *engines* are lowered onto the frame—in the industry this operation is referred to as *decking the engine.*

With *fuel feed lines, brake lines,* and other connections installed, tightened, and inspected, the chassis enters a booth where *transmission oil* and *hydraulic brake fluids* are added. Beyond the booth, *wheels* with *tires* already mounted and inflated roll down inclined chutes from overhead assembly areas, and are fastened by power wrenches that tighten all five wheel bolts at once. Next a huge *body shim gauge* is lowered onto the chassis to check attachment points on the frame for possible misalignment before the body is added. The *body drop* refers to the operation where painted and trimmed bodies are lowered onto the frame.

Then the complete *front-end subassembly* is swung into place and bolted to the body and chassis. With the front end in place, the *hood* is installed and fitted. Assemblers check the operation of both hinges and latches, and adjustments are made to guarantee smooth operation and a good fit. Finally seats, built up on separate subassembly lines, are installed as the car moves toward completion. After an inspector has checked all previous inspection reports and given a final approval, an employee enters the car, turns the ignition key, and moves the car under its own power for the first time.

The car is driven a few feet to an inspection station where headlight beams are adjusted and front-wheel alignment is checked and set. At the next station, the car is checked on a dynamometer: with the engine running and the car in gear, the rear wheels rotate at varying speeds on rollers set into the floor, while the front wheels remain motionless. This test is a functional check of the complete drive line.

Checked throughout all the assembly operations, the car is then subjected to one final inspection. First a high-pressure water spray test checks for leaks, then a paint check under bright lights, and final examination of operating parts is made before the finished car is driven to a storage yard. Within 48 hours the car will be on the way to a dealer.

—Joseph J. Kelleher

Bearing, a friction-reducing support for a rotating shaft or spindle. Bearings vary in size and type from tiny jewels in watches and miniaturized instruments to huge roller bearings used on heavy machinery.

The simplest bearing is the *plain cylindrical journal bearing* exemplified by a wheel turning on the axle of a wagon or by a machine shaft turning in a cylindrical support. For ideal operation, there should be no metal-to-metal contact between the shaft and sleeve. A lubricant, such as oil or grease, prevents metallic contact by building up a wedge as the shaft turns in the sleeve. This wedge of lubricant separates the shaft from the sleeve and greatly reduces friction and heat. The heavier the bearing load and the slower the speed of rotation, the heavier the lubricant required.

Ball bearings, in their simplest form, consist of an *outer race* fitted into the sleeve and an *inner race* fitted onto the shaft. Carefully ground steel balls occupy the space between the outer and the inner races. There is point contact of the metal, since the bearing load is actually transferred to the steel balls, each of which touches the outer and the inner races. Ball bearings require some lubrication, but they depend upon the free rolling of the balls for their effectiveness rather than upon the lubricant. It is particularly important that they be lubricated lightly, for over-lubrication will cause heating and bearing damage.

The *roller bearing* is a variation of the ball bearing and is particularly suited to heavy loads. It uses cylindrical rollers rather than balls, and thereby provides a line contact of metal rather than a point contact. *Needle bearings* are similar to roller bearings, but the individual rollers are of much smaller diameter.

The plain cylindrical journal bearings, ball bearings, and roller bearings described are all designed to reduce the friction of a shaft turning on its support or a wheel or lever turning on its axis. Another type of bearing is the *thrust bearing,* which takes a load directly along the line of the shaft. Minute jewels may be used as *thrust bearings,* while at the other extreme, thrust bearings support the main shafts of huge hydroelectric turbines. There are thrust bearings to handle various types of loads between these extremes.

Often it is necessary to combine both types of loads, and some bearings are designed to handle a thrust as well as a radial load. The *tapered roller bearing* is a good example. In addition, there is a wide variety of special bearings designed to handle unusual conditions.

A number of materials are used in the manufacture of bearings. Steel, cast iron, and bronze are common bearing materials, and Babbitt metal and lead alloys are frequently used as bearing linings. Nylon and other plastics can be used for both sleeve and thrust bearings, while special applications call for the use of special materials.
                                                                                        —Hunter Hughes

 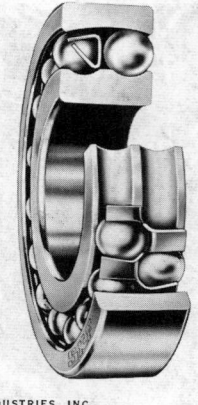 

MARLIN-ROCKWELL CORPORATION   SKF INDUSTRIES, INC.   FEDERAL-MOGUL CORPORATION

BALL BEARINGS (*left; center*) and plain roller bearings (*right*) are used mainly for radial loads, to reduce friction between an axle and its wheel or a shaft and its support.

Boiler, a closed vessel in which water under pressure is converted to steam by the absorption of heat from the combustion of fuel. Boilers are designed to absorb as much heat as possible from the fuel burned. The ratio of the heat absorbed by the water and steam to the heat input of the fuel per unit of time is known as *boiler efficiency.*

There are two general types of boiler: the *fire-tube boiler,* consisting of many tubes through which hot gases pass to heat the surrounding water; the *water-tube boiler,* in which water passes through the tubes and is heated by surrounding gases. Although used extensively, the fire-tube boiler is limited by its design to low pressure and low capacity. Water-tube boilers are used more frequently because they may be designed for either low or high operating temperatures and pressures, and for higher capacities.

Records indicate that certain properties of steam were recognized earlier than 100 A.D. At about that time, Hero of Alexandria invented a primitive boiler-turbine known as *Hero's engine.* The earliest form of water-tube boiler was patented in 1766 by William Blakey, a contemporary of James Watt, but the first successful water-tube boiler as we now know it was developed in 1788 by James Rumsey, an American. Stephen Wilcox, in 1856, was the first to use inclined tubes—the forerunner of modern water-tube boilers.

The first boilers were fired with coal by hand and, until the early 1900's, operated at pressures only up to 100 or 200 pounds per square inch. Now, practically all boilers are fired by mechanical means.

Boilers are designed for many purposes: small package boilers, shipped ready to be installed for heating or process; large package or field-erected boilers for industrial plants; and huge high-pressure boilers for electric utility companies. These last may be 20 or more stories high and produce up to 8,000,000 pounds of steam per hour, at temperatures of 1,050° F and above, and at pressures as high as 5,000 pounds per square inch.

During the last several years, the *once-through boiler,* which can be operated above or below *critical pressure* (3,206 pounds per square inch), has been used successfully by many large utility companies. The once-through boiler is, in essence, a number of parallel tubes through which fluid is pumped and to which heat is applied along their entire length. Water goes through once and comes out as superheated steam. Operation above critical pressure results in a higher efficiency. Improved efficiency is the boiler designer's constant aim.   —Margot Valentine

Bookbinding, the folding and gathering of printed sheets, sewing or gluing them together in proper order, and enclosing them in covers of paper, cloth, leather, or other material. Books usually are printed in sections consisting of multiples of four pages up to as many as 64 pages per section. The individual pages are arranged on the press so that when the printed page is folded, the pages fall into consecutive order. These folded sections are called *signatures.* Flat sheets go to folding machines to be made into signatures, while presses that print from rolls usually have a built-in folder and deliver folded signatures.

When all the sections for a book are printed and folded, endsheets are pasted to the first and last sections. Endsheets are four page signatures of strong paper that will eventually attach the book to its cover. In certain books, added strength is obtained by reinforcing the endsheets with a cloth strip at the fold.

The sections then are ready to be put together. A gathering machine picks up the sections in sequence and assembles them into a complete book. The gathered sections go into a sewing machine that fastens them together with strong thread. Books that are expected to receive hard use may be reinforced by sewing the sections to a cloth tape.

From the sewing machine, the book goes into a machine known as the *smasher.* This machine reduces the bulk at the back caused by the folds and the sewing. Next the book is trimmed on three sides. A rounding and backing machine then gives the backbone and fore edge their familiar rounded shape. The next machine glues a paper liner and a muslin reinforcing strip, if required, to the backbone. The processes described up to this point are known collectively as *forwarding*.

While the body of the book is being put together, other machines are making and decorating the cover or case. The most common cases are made of strong boards (a type of cardboard material) covered with cloth or paper, and sometimes both.

The cases and books are brought together on a *casing-in* machine that glues the endsheets firmly and accurately to the cases. A *building-in* machine next forms the cover around the book under heat and pressure. A final inspection completes the binding process. —Robert L. McGuire

DISC BRAKE

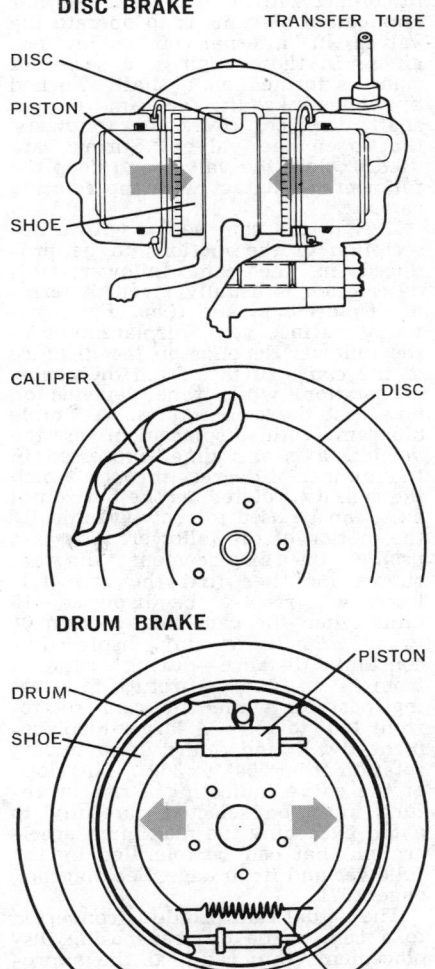

AUTOMOBILE BRAKES may be of two types, disk or drum. In disk brakes (*center*) a caliper straddles the disk above and behind the hub; when the brakes are activated, pistons within the caliper (*top*) force the shoes against the disk and friction slows the wheel. In drum brakes (*bottom*) pistons force the shoes evenly against the drums to create friction inside of the wheel; a spring releases the brake-shoes.

Brake, a device to slow or stop a machine or control its speed. This is generally accomplished by friction between a stationary and a moving part, which converts the energy of motion into heat.

The *block brake* is nothing more than a block, or shoe, bearing against a rotating wheel. Pressure is applied with a lever.

The *band brake* makes use of a band of asbestos fabric or other heat-resistant material passed around a wheel or drum. One or both ends of the band are attached to a lever in such a manner that a movement of the lever will tighten the band and the resulting friction will slow or stop the wheel.

Internal brakes, extensively used on automobiles, consist of brake shoes, covered with asbestos fabric linings, which can be brought to bear upon the inside of a metal drum. Automobile brakes are activated hydraulically. Foot pressure on the brake pedal moves a piston in a master cylinder. This transmits hydraulic pressure through brake fluid (a light oil) to wheel cylinders located inside the brake drum of each wheel. Increased fluid pressure in each wheel cylinder moves a small piston outward, and the piston forces the asbestos-covered brake shoes against the inside of the brake drum, stopping the wheels and the car. The use of hydraulic pressure to activate the brakes assures that an equal force will be applied to each wheel when the brakes are applied.

Cone and *disk brakes* depend for their action on the friction created by contact between a stationary cone or flat disk and a rotating member against which it is forced. Disk brakes have long been used on aircraft and recently been adapted for automobiles in a somewhat modified design. The automobile disk brake consists of a steel disk secured to and rotating with the wheel. The rectangular friction pads, one on each side of the disk, are actuated by hydraulic pressure so that they press against the disk, creating friction and stopping the car. Disk brakes are usually applied to the front wheels, but some cars have brakes on all four wheels.

Many automobiles are now equipped with *power brakes* in which a vacuum from the engine intake manifold supplements the foot pressure of the driver on the brake pedal, making braking easier.

Lifting equipment, such as cranes, hoists, or elevators, require special braking systems. They are frequently equipped with cone or disk brakes designed so that they will engage if the load should start to descend when it should be rising or stopped, or if it descends more rapidly than desired.

A completely different principle is applied in *eddy current brakes,* sometimes used for stopping heavy machinery quickly. A magnetic flux created by electrically excited poles causes eddy currents in the rotating rim. These currents convert the flywheel energy into heat, stopping the wheel. —Hunter Hughes

Brazing, the process by which metal parts are joined by heating and the space between them filled with a molten, nonferrous filler metal. If the parts are closely fitted, the filler metal will flow by capillary attraction between the base metal surfaces. A chemical flux or cleaning agent is used to assure that the filler alloys, *wets* the base metal, which is heated but not melted. Brazing is distinguished from soldering by the higher temperature required (over 800° F) and the greater strength of the brazing filler. Many different brazing methods are used to join a wide variety of metals and, in some cases, to join metals to specially coated ceramics or glass. The most common method is *torch brazing,* in which a gas torch is used to heat the base metal and melt the filler. Among the most useful filler metals are alloys of copper and silver with added traces of cadmium, nickel, phosphorus, and tin. Fillers of such alloys are used to braze mild steel, stainless steel, precious metals, nickel, and copper alloys. Aluminum brazing requires an aluminum filler alloy with 4 per cent copper and up to 13 per cent silicon. Liquid, powder, or paste fluxes are used to protect the joint from oxidation and to remove oxides formed during heating.
—Joseph J. Kelleher

Cable, or *wire rope,* is made up of iron or steel wire twisted into strands, which are then twisted around a core of hemp or other suitable material. Normally the wires are twisted in one direction to form the strands and the strands are twisted in the other direction around the core. The wire strands may be twisted either to the right (*right lay*) or to the left (*left lay*). If the wires and strands are twisted in the same direction, the wire rope is known as *Lang lay rope.* It is possible to combine the two, using a Lang lay for strands around the core and a regular lay for an additional outer layer of strands. This diminishes the tendency for the cable to spin or lash when used as a hoisting rope.

Wire rope is available in many varieties, varying in size, strength, and design. Standard wire rope is made up of six strands twisted about a hemp center with 19 wires in each strand. The more wires used in each strand, the more flexible the rope. Extra special flexible hoisting rope has six 61-wire twisted strands to attain maximum flexibility.

Iron wire rope is tough and flexible, but when more strength is required, the wires are made of steel. *Steel cables* for suspension bridges or tramways are usually made with six strands of high-strength steel and have wire cores.

Wire rope is used in many types of elevators, hoists, derricks, dredges, scrapers, or other material-handling equipment. It is also used for guying poles, stacks, and tall antenna.

Without wire rope, engineers could not have designed the long-span suspension bridges that are such a vital part of transportation systems.
—Hunter Hughes

Calculating Machines, mechanical, electric, or electronic devices used to speed computation. The *abacus,* the oldest and most widely used calculating machine on earth, was devised some 2,000 years ago. In the United States, Canada, and Europe, the abacus is little more than a curiosity, but in vast areas of Asia it is the only known counting device.

The abacus (from *abax,* an ancient Greek word for slab) was a direct result of early methods of counting. When primitive man satisfied his needs for food and shelter, he began seeking ways of expressing himself. He wanted to tell his family and neighbors "how many" animals he had killed on a hunt, "how many" children he had, and so forth. Thus, symbols were developed to indicate "one," "several," and "many." The next step was a big one—devising symbols to express specific quantities. The first two symbols were, quite naturally, a "two" and a "five" —"two" because man had two hands, and "five" because he had five fingers on each hand. By combining the symbols for hand and fingers, he could express many different specific quantities.

The abacus makes use of this two-five, or biquinary, notation system. The Chinese abacus, or *suan-pan,* for example, consists of a series of rods and wires on which beads are strung. There are seven beads on each wire, separated by a divider into a set of five on the bottom and two on top. Thus, the number "seven" can be expressed by one bead from the top (equalling five) and two from the bottom.

But the abacus had its shortcomings. It couldn't carry over tens from one line to the next. As man expanded his mathematical horizons, this became a problem.

■**ADDING MACHINE.**—In the seventeenth century, Blaise Pascal, as a young man working in his father's tax office, in Rouen, France, invented a gear-driven machine the size of a shoe box on which sums could be added by means of a series of notched wheels. The machine could perform addition and subtraction and was capable of carrying tens automatically.

Pascal's adding machine was primitive by today's standards, but the principles on which it was based have not changed. Modern adding machines and desk calculators all owe their origin to Pascal's device of three centuries ago.

■**SLIDE RULE.**—Another form of calculating device is the slide rule. This, however, is an analog device, in contrast to digital machines. The analog calculator simulates an actual problem by using a model that operates according to equivalent physical quantities. The slide rule, for example, doesn't actually add numbers. Instead, it adds the lengths proportional to them. The scales printed on the rule, however, permit reading the numbers themselves.

The slide rule, which was developed by the Englishman William Oughtred in 1632, was the forerunner of many analog devices designed to measure (and calculate) specific quantities. Among these devices are the *planimeter* for measuring areas, the *speedometer* for measuring speeds, and the *differential analyzer* for solving intricate problems in calculus.

■**CALCULATOR.**—Digital machines, on the other hand, deal with basic arithmetic and can be used for any problem that involves these terms. This was the reasoning behind the attempt of the Englishman Charles Babbage to build a "difference engine" in 1822. In effect, Babbage drew up plans for the first digital computer. His projected machine could do complex calculations and print out results. There was to be a "memory" made up of punched cards, and the machine was to have an arithmetic unit, called a "mill," in which to store this data. Output, according to Babbage's plans, was to be set up automatically in type, thus avoiding transcription errors.

Babbage was 130 years ahead of his time. Unfortunately, the device was to be set up automatically in type, technology, and the machine just couldn't be constructed.

In 1887 Herman Hollerith, of the U.S. Bureau of the Census, crystallized Pascal's and Babbage's ideas in his punched-card system. By working out an electromechanical method for recording, compiling, and tabulating census facts, he initiated a paperwork revolution. Within a few years a wide range of industries were using his punched-card techniques for accounting and record-keeping tasks.

■**COMPUTER.**—During the 1940's, several electronic machines were con-

INTERNATIONAL BUSINESS MACHINES CORPORATION

TABULATOR devised by Herman Hollerith in 1887 for the Census Bureau was based on the Jacquard automatic loom and used metal needles to sort punched data cards. The needles touched a charged surface through the holes, creating a current that activated an instrument that totaled the figures and made a record of the final data.

structed. The earliest simply linked up banks of vacuum tubes to existing punched-card machines in order to speed up the calculating process. In 1948, however, International Business Machines Corporation introduced a machine that could store its operating instructions internally, and this machine led to the beginnings of the "computer era."

Since that time, scores of computers have been introduced to perform a large number of functions. While these digital machines are infinitely faster and more flexible than the original abacus, they operate according to the same age-old principles.
—Stanley Englebardt

Cam, a disk, plate, surface, or roller which, when rotated or moved, controls the motion of a *follower* that is in contact with it. The most familiar application of cams is to operate the valves in internal-combustion engines. In these engines, a series of cams is formed on a shaft. Turned by the crankshaft, the cams on the shaft displace *lifters,* or followers, that open the valves. Springs are used to close the valves and keep the follower in contact with the rotating cam.

Design of a cam *begins* with a description of the motions to be produced in the cam follower; this description is usually given in terms of *displacement* and *time.* For a rotating surface cam, displacement of the follower depends on the distance of the cam's surface from the center of rotation, while time depends on how fast the cam rotates. A simple diagram with displacement as the vertical axis and time, expressed in the number of degrees through which the cam has rotated, as the horizontal axis, can be used to show graphically the motion of the follower. The cam *profile* or displacement diagram shown indicates that the cam follower will *rise*—or be displaced—10 units when the cam rotates from 0° to 40°, *dwell*—or stay displaced a constant distance—during rotation from 40° to 100°, and return to starting position while the cam rotates from 100° to 150°. A larger displacement, dwell, and return occur during rotation from 200° to 360°. The slope of the curve indicating a rise or return must be selected carefully to avoid exceeding the maximum acceleration that can be tolerated by the follower and its linkage. See diagram, page 1671.

The actual cam profile is converted to a cam shape by transposing displacements into radii, at the appropriate angular positions, around the cam's center of rotation. After the radii are laid out, a smooth curve is drawn between their ends to describe the shape of the cam. Where the displacement-time diagram indicates a rise, the cam's surface will be a curve of increasing radius. A dwell period results in a curve of constant radius, while a return curve is one of decreasing radius.

Cams are widely used for vending-machine mechanisms, machine tools, power transmission, and control mechanisms.
—Joseph J. Kelleher

Camera, an instrument for taking photographs. All cameras, from the most complicated to the simplest, are basically alike. All are light-tight boxes, with a front opening for light to enter (the aperture), a lens, a shutter, and a view finder.

For a good picture, the film must be properly exposed. Too much light will cause an excessive buildup of the silver in the film, making it too dense to print properly. Resulting prints or transparencies will be too light. If not enough light reaches the film, the result will be a print or transparency that is too dark.

The *shutter* may be likened to a window shade that can be raised and lowered; the speed at which this takes place determines the amount of light it will admit. In a camera, a fast shutter speed is also used to "stop" the motion of objects being photographed, by not allowing a long enough exposure for movement to blur the image.

The *aperture,* which usually consists of an *iris diaphragm* or, in simple cameras, holes of varying size, can be compared to the iris of the eye. If the light is too brilliant, the aperture closes; in dim light, it opens wider to admit more light.

The *lens* focuses an image on the film much as the lens of the eye focuses it on the retina. The larger the lens, the more light it will admit, thus permitting higher shutter speeds and at wider apertures.

In *simple* or *box* cameras, the aperture is fixed, and the lens and shutter are preset by the manufacturer to produce good pictures under ordinary picture-taking conditions. Unless an auxiliary lens is added, such a camera is unable to make a sharp picture at distances of less than six feet. It cannot make pictures under adverse lighting conditions, nor is the shutter speed fast enough to stop motion. When flash is added, however, the picture-taking range is considerably broadened.

Roll-film cameras, which take cartridges of film 35 mm wide, make up the vast majority of cameras on the market today. *Still-film cameras,* recently introduced, take a preloaded plastic cartridge that needs only to be dropped into place in the back of the camera. The cartridge has a notch on one edge which, in some models, engages a finger in the camera and thus adjusts the camera to films of different speeds. The simpler models of this type accept films of only one speed.

These cameras, like many other types on the market today, incorporate built-in exposure meters that in

SINGLE-LENS REFLEX CAMERA: (1) film speed set, (2) exposure meter lens, (3) setting marks, (4) exposure pointer, (5) central contact, (6) rewinder, (7) diaphragm stop, (8) diaphragm set, (9) shutter set, (10) shutter, (11) release key.

many cases are linked to the diaphragm (or aperture control) and shutter to provide automatic exposure control.

Studio cameras and *press-type cameras* generally use sheet film which is inserted in holders. (This must be done in a dark room, since the film is unprotected.) The holder is clamped to the back of the camera by spring clamps; the film in the holder is protected by a slide which is removed just prior to the exposure. The slide is replaced after the exposure and before the holder is detached from the camera.

Reflex cameras, which in recent years have been finding increasing favor with newspaper and magazine photographers, are of two types: twin-lens and single-lens.

The *twin-lens reflex* has a viewing lens with mirror and ground glass located directly above the taking lens. The ground glass shows the image to be photographed usually in full negative size. The image is clearly visible because the viewing lens is never stopped down to reduce the light. The image is also visible before, during, and after the exposure. Except at very close range, the image shown on the ground glass is exactly what the camera will see. Most of these cameras usually use roll film and provide pictures approximately 2¼ inches square. The larger picture, particularly when color is used, is preferred by many magazine editors.

The *single-lens reflex* usually uses 35 mm film. The ground glass in these cameras shows the image exactly as the camera will see it, even in ultra close-ups or when the camera lenses have been changed. This is accomplished through the use of a mirror, angled at 45° behind the lens, which reflects the image upward onto a ground glass. When the shutter release is pressed, the mirror springs out of the way, allowing the light image to reach the film. These cameras also use a focal-plane shutter in most cases, which prevents any light from reaching the film even though the taking lens is open.

The *focal-plane shutter* is a cloth or metal screen or shade that moves horizontally or vertically directly in front of the film. The amount of light reaching the film is controlled by the width of a slot in the curtain.

The *automatic* or *electric-eye cameras,* which have become so popular in recent years, operate on the same principle as any other camera. The single major difference is that they incorporate a sensitive photoelectric cell. The cell averages the amount of light on the subject at which the camera is aimed and converts that light into electric energy. This power actuates the lens and shutter settings in direct proportion to the amount of

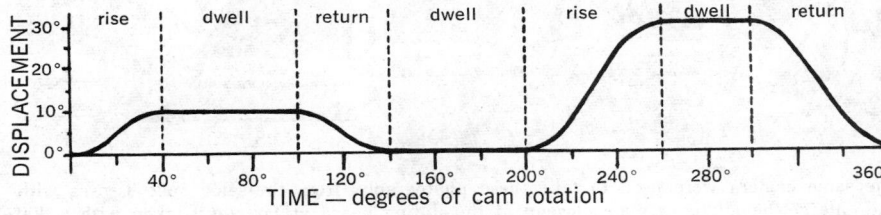

CAM PROFILE describes the motion of a cam "follower," a valve lifter, for example.

energy created by the light reflected from the subject. Such automatic cameras enable almost anyone, regardless of his knowledge of photography, to enjoy the advantages of an adjustable camera while maintaining much of the simplicity of the box camera.

The more advanced cameras usually have some provision for changing the lenses, so that the user can switch from a normal lens to a wide-angle or telephoto lens at will. Many of the newer single-lens reflex cameras incorporate a photoelectric cell within the camera that measures the amount of light striking the mirror. This offers an advantage: when lenses are changed, as when a telephoto lens is added, the light measured is only that which the camera sees through that lens and which will reach the film.

Another feature, which has been added to some cameras in recent years, is the *motorized film advance*. Whether it be an electric motor or a spring-wound motor, it advances the film automatically and cocks the shutter at the same time. With such cameras, whole series of pictures may be made in a few seconds.

Flashholders are built into many modern cameras, including some of the least expensive ones. They are synchronized to the shutter so that the bulb does not fire until the shutter is fully open. The latest type includes provision for a four-sided, sealed-in plastic "cube" containing four miniature bulbs. The cube turns as each exposure is made, placing a new "side" in position. When combined with a motorized film advance, the photographer is enabled to make four fully illuminated flash shots in rapid sequence.

Motion-picture cameras function on the same principles as still cameras which are described above. (See *Cinematography*.) The film, which is usually 8 mm or 16 mm, is drawn past the lens by a spring- or battery-powered motor. Recently, amateur cameras have been made with *zoom lenses*, which allow the focal length to be altered from telephoto to wide-angle—or vice versa—while pictures are being taken.

—C. Grantly Wallington

Camera Accessories, devices that facilitate the taking of photographs with a camera. Many items that were listed as accessories with older-type cameras are now built directly into the instrument, although they will still be required separately with certain types of camera. Included among such accessories are flashholders, range finders, and photoelectric exposure meters. Most professional photographers will continue to use them as separate accessories because of the greater flexibility and accuracy they offer.

The *flashholder,* as its name implies, is made up of a case for the batteries, a reflector, and a receptacle for the flashbulb. It is connected to the camera's shutter through a cord and a plug on the face of the camera or the side of the shutter. Its advantages over the built-in flashholder are that a number of such units can be connected together for more intense light or to cover a wide area; the reflector can be removed or aimed at the ceiling to provide diffuse illumination, and it may be held away from the camera for a better lighting angle. Some units are of the focusing type for photographing distant subjects. *Electronic flash* provides intense light with maximum convenience. The flashholder itself may be attached directly to the camera or held in the photographer's hand. Instead of a flashbulb, it contains a high-intensity tube that is flashed by a battery or power source frequently carried on a strap over the photographer's shoulder. It eliminates the need for carrying flashbulbs and provides an extremely intense light for a very short period of time, the flash of which is fast enough to stop rapid motion. Many studios are equipped with permanent high-powered units.

Separate *range finders* provide an accurate measure of distance by bringing two views of the subject from different angles into coincidence. This is accomplished with lenses and prisms, one of which is movable.

The separate *photoelectric exposure meter* offers several advantages. It is usually larger, thus will pick up more light rays reflected from the subject and give a more accurate measurement. It can be aimed to exclude some parts of the picture, such as large sky areas which, when the light is averaged, might indicate more light than is actually on the subject of the photograph. By aiming it at a similar nearby object with the same selectivity as the subject, a reading can be obtained for the distant object. One type of meter is also designed to read incident light, and is most frequently used by professional photographers. Held in front of the subject, it measures the amount of light reaching it.

Other useful accessories include *sun shades* to protect the camera lens from the direct rays of the sun that otherwise might spoil the picture; *tripods* to keep the camera steady on longer exposures and to hold it in position while the subject is being arranged; and *field cases* to protect the camera while traveling or for carrying it while keeping it convenient for use.

For black-and-white photography, a set of *filters* can add dramatic value to many pictures. A yellow or amber filter, generally designated as a *K2* filter, will darken blue skies and bring out clouds. A red filter will provide skies that are almost black with very dramatic white clouds. Filters are not used to any great extent in amateur color photography, although a *skylight*, or ultraviolet filter, can be useful in reducing the blue of distant haze in the mountains or at the seashore. It is also useful to protect the lens from sand or salt spray at the seashore, since it does not require any increase in exposure.

Probably one of the most useful accessories to the amateur photographer is the *close-up lens* that permits him to make close-ups of flowers, pets, and people. These lenses are available in different powers covering medium close-ups and extreme close-ups. They are easy to use and add to the camera's versatility.

Other accessories for specialized photographic work include *microscope adapters, copying stands, polarizing filters, ultraviolet* and *infrared filters,* and *light-balancing filters* for extreme accuracy in color rendition.   —C. Grantly Wallington

E. LEITZ, INC.

LENSES of different focal lengths attached to the same camera were used to take these photographs from the same spot. Lenses with greater focal lengths close in on distant objects and enlarge them. The extreme closeup of the sliding board at far *right*, taken with a 400 mm telephoto lens, is an 8X enlargement of the sliding board in the background of the far *left* picture, which was taken with a 21 mm lens.

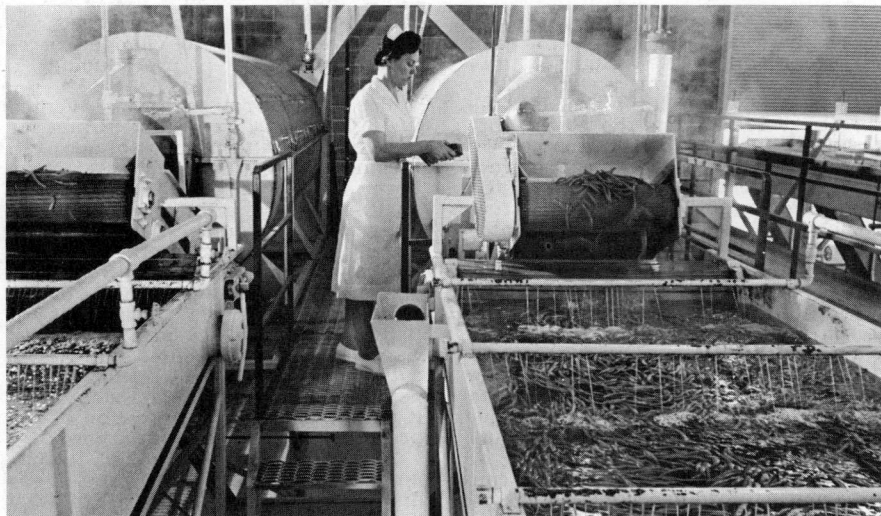

GENERAL FOODS CORPORATION

FREEZING is an important method of food preservation today. *Above*, green beans are blanched to destroy decay-causing enzymes, cooled, then packaged (*right*) for freezing.

Canning and Preserving, processes for protecting food from deterioration and decay and making it available for future consumption. Such food should retain desirable flavor, color, and texture, as well as its original nutritional value. *Canning* protects food by sterilizing and excluding air: *Preserving* protects food by adding substances such as salt or sugar, by removing moisture, or by fermentation.

Man probably first preserved food by *drying*, even before he learned to farm. Seeds and nuts, dried by the rays of the sun, would keep through the winter. Meat and fish could be preserved in the same way.

Cooking, after man discovered fire, made food more appetizing and was also a means of preservation, since heating killed some of the microorganisms and enzymes that caused spoilage. Preserving meat by *smoking* was an outgrowth of cooking.

Salt was used for flavoring before man learned that meat soaked in salt brine or rubbed with salt would keep for weeks or months. *Brining*, later called *pickling*, became a favorite way of keeping fruits and vegetables for winter use. The preserving properties of sugar were also known in ancient times, and the making of jam and marmalade was widely practiced.

Fermentation, the natural process of chemical change in food, was observed and used thousands of years ago. Fruit juices, when fermented, resulted in wine, a safe beverage in areas of uncertain water supply. Vinegar, a product of fermentation, was useful for pickling meats, fish, fruits, and vegetables. Fermented cabbage, or sauerkraut, was widely used. The fermentation of milk, which does not keep well, resulted in cheese, which does keep well. Bread—that is, the fermented sourdough bread developed by the Egyptians 5,000 years ago—came to be called the staff of life. It was nutritious, easily carried from place to place, kept for months without spoiling, and, with water, could sustain life for long periods.

■**HISTORY OF CANNING.**—For centuries, these outgrowths of natural processes were the only means that man had for preserving food. Then, in 1810, a French chemist and confectioner, Nicolas Appert, developed canning. Although the theoretical basis for canning was not known until Louis Pasteur observed the relationships between microorganisms and food spoilage some 50 years later, Appert's ideas are still valid. He placed wholesome food in clean, metal containers, which were then sealed and boiled for a sufficiently long time to prevent spoilage.

Canning spread rapidly. In 1810 an Englishman, Peter Durand, patented a can of iron coated with tin. Today's cans are primarily steel, with a thin coating of tin.

Commercial canning began in the United States with the production of pickles, ketchup, and sauces in Boston in 1819 and the canning of seafood in Baltimore in 1820. The first canners found that it was necessary to keep the cans in boiling water for five or six hours. In 1860, a canner found that adding calcium chloride to water raised its boiling point from 212° to 240° Fahrenheit, sharply reducing required cooking times. The invention of the *retort*, or *pressure cooker*, in 1874 was an even more important step. It gave the canner accurate control of temperature during the processing operation.

■**MECHANIZATION.**—Reduced cooking times meant that many more cans could be processed in a given period. This in turn led to the development of machines that would do many of the tasks formerly done by hand, such as shelling peas, cutting corn from the cob, and cleaning salmon. At the same time, can making became entirely mechanized. The modern open-top can, closed by crimping with a rubber sealing compound, speeded mechanical filling and sealing.

Glass jars have been most widely used for home canning, although tin cans have also been adapted for home use. Home canning of all types of food was greatly encouraged by home economists, state extension-service workers, and others from about 1900 to World War II as a means of utilizing home garden products, providing better diets, and reducing the cost of living on farms. Many farm women still can and preserve at home for winter use. However, the increasingly commercial character of farms, the low cost of commercially canned foods, and the widespread use of freezers have made home canning less important than it was before World War II.

Since World War II, commercial canning has been challenged by other methods of processing, particularly freezing and new types of drying. However, the production of canned foods has continued to grow, although with shifts among particular foods and in the geographical areas in which the canning is done.

The quality of raw materials is of primary concern to the modern canner. Canners work closely with farmers to secure a uniform product of a particular quality. This may take the form of contract farming, in which price, grade, and tonnage are agreed upon before the crop is planted. The canner may specify that particular seeds are to be used and particular cultivating practices are to be followed.

■**PROCESSING.**—Speed in processing, preserves some of the flavor, color, and nutrition that would otherwise be lost and, at the same time, tends to cut unit cost.

After the product to be canned reaches the plant, it is inspected and graded. Instruments measure such qualities as firmness, maturity, and color by mechanical, chemical, or electronic means, although much grading and sorting is still controlled by skilled human labor. Washing, peeling, trimming, grinding, and cutting machines have replaced virtually all hand labor in these processes.

The raw material may undergo preliminary cooking or blanching before the cans are automatically filled and sealed. Some large canneries then place the cans on moving belts that move through the cooking and cooling processes in one operation. Most canning is done with the retort or pressure cooker. The time required for processing depends mainly on the chemical and physical makeup of the food, as well as on the size of the container. After cooling, the cans are labeled and boxed for shipment.

Special techniques have been developed for some products. For example, certain soups are pumped through high-temperature heat exchangers into separately sterilized cans, which are then sealed under aseptic conditions. The goal of such procedures is to reduce processing times.

Some canners have adopted standards developed by the U.S. Department of Agriculture and pay for grading by the department. Others maintain their own grading systems. However, most canned goods do not carry any public indication of grade.

A new method of food preservation, called *irradiation, cold sterilization,* or *radiation sterilization,* is being tested by industrial and government laboratories. The food is exposed to nuclear radiation from a radioactive material or is bombarded with high-energy electrons. Although these techniques destroy microorganisms, they do not destroy enzymes, so objectionable flavors tend to develop in the food. However, bacon prepared by irradiation was purchased by the federal government in 1966 for military use.

—Wayne D. Rasmussen

Carburetor, a device that mixes air with gasoline or other internal-combustion-engine fuels in the correct ratio for complete combustion at all engine speeds. A secondary function of most carburetors is to control the engine's power output by throttling, or metering, the air-fuel mixture admitted to the cylinders.

The simplest type of carburetor consists of a tube with a *venturi,* or tapered restriction, in which a *jet,* or fuel-spray nozzle, is mounted. Fuel is supplied to the jet from a constant-level fuel chamber at atmospheric pressure. When the engine piston moves down, a partial vacuum is created in the cylinder, sucking air in through the carburetor. The speed of the air is increased as it passes through the venturi. Reduced pressure in the carburetor then allows atmospheric pressure on the fuel to force it through the nozzle into the airstream. The air-fuel mixture continues to flow into the cylinder until the piston starts to move upward in the compression stroke.

Automobile carburetors are far more complex, since their engines operate through a wide range of speeds and loads. To function properly, these carburetors incorporate a number of additional features.

For starting, a *choke,* or butterfly valve, is used to restrict airflow to the carburetor, thus increasing the suction on the fuel flow. A *throttle valve* between the carburetor and cylinder controls the volume of air-fuel mixture reaching the cylinders. Linked to the accelerator pedal, the throttle valve adjusts the power output and, thus, the speed of the vehicle in response to the driver's foot pressure. An acceleration pump in the carburetor provides momentary fuel enrichment when the accelerator pedal is depressed rapidly. The pump, linked to the throttle, increases the responsiveness of the engine during acceleration by maintaining the correct fuel-air ratio when the throttle is opened suddenly.

Carburetors for large engines may incorporate several tubes or throats in a single housing. Each tube may be equipped with identical jets, plus choke and throttle valve operating in unison, or the accelerator linkage can be constructed to operate each throttle valve in sequence as additional power is required.

—Joseph J. Kelleher

Cathode-Ray Tube, a device in which a beam of electrons is used to provide a pictorial representation of the current or voltage in a circuit. It is familiarly known as a television *picture tube,* or *kinescope.* It makes use of electric or magnetic fields to deflect a beam of electrons. These originally were called *cathode rays* because they are emitted by a negatively charged electrode, or *cathode.* After leaving the cathode, the narrow electron beam strikes a fluorescent screen on the face of the tube, where it forms a bright spot of light, called the *scanning spot.*

In a television set, the scanning spot moves from side to side and from top to bottom, quickly covering the entire area of the picture tube. This is similar to the way a typewriter covers a page with print. The picture is formed by changing the number of electrons in the beam as it moves from point to point on the screen. This causes the brightness of the scanning spot to change correspondingly, thereby producing a picture.

The cathode-ray tube was invented in 1897 by Karl Ferdinand Braun for the study of alternating voltages. In the modern *oscilloscope,* the electron beam scans from the viewer's left to right, producing a line of light on the screen. The voltage under study causes the beam to deflect vertically, in the course of time, in precise agreement with the magnitude of the voltage. In this way, the track of light represents the variation with time of the voltage under study. The cathode-ray tube is also an indispensable part of all radar sets, where it is used as a visual indication of the presence and location of targets.

The cathode-ray tube had its beginning with the Crookes tube, a gas discharge tube devised by Sir William Crookes about 1897. It consists of a completely enclosed vessel having two metal electrodes sealed through the walls. When a voltage is applied to the electrodes, and the tube contains a partial vacuum, a glow discharge takes place in the tube. This discharge is produced by collisions between cathode rays and gas particles in the tube.

■**X-RAY.**—In 1895, Wilhelm Roentgen discovered that X-rays are produced in the Crookes tube when the electron beam strikes a positively charged electrode, called the *anode.* The invisible X-rays, unlike cathode rays, are able to leave the tube and darken a photographic plate some distance away. They are produced whenever high-speed electrons strike the atoms of an anode. The energy of impact causes the atoms to vibrate violently, and to emit a high-frequency, short-wavelength light. This invisible radiation is electromagnetic in nature and, therefore, similar to ordinary light, infrared light, and ultraviolet light. X-rays differ only in having much shorter wavelengths,

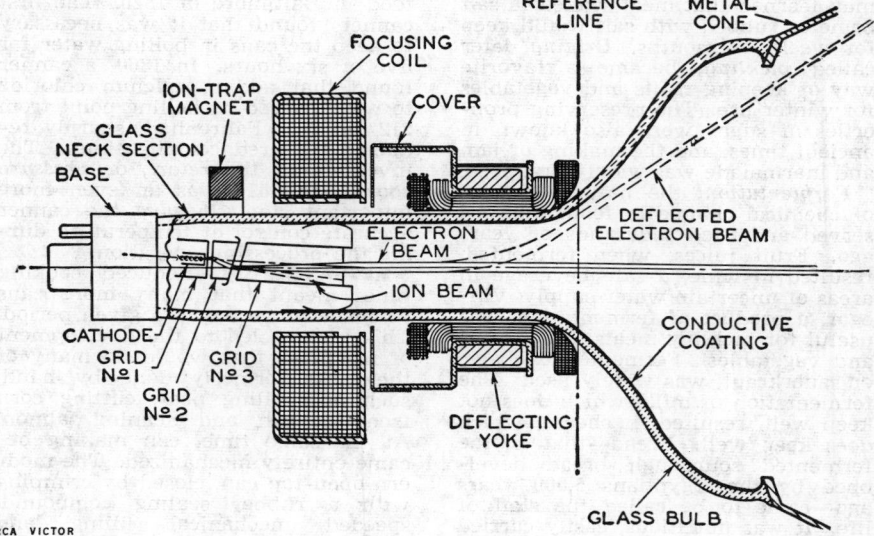

RCA VICTOR

THE KINESCOPE, or the internal structure of the television tube as it receives the electron beams in the home. The owner adjusts the focusing coil to obtain the best picture.

JERRY SOALT, ILGWU "JUSTICE"

GARMENT pattern is placed by marker (*above*) to utilize maximum fabric, and the cloth is cut along the pattern markings (*lower right*). After a seamstress (*upper right*) has sewn these pieces together, detail work and careful pressing will finish the garment.

which permit them to penetrate, to a greater or lesser degree, various substances that are opaque to ordinary light.

The modern *X-ray tube*, or *Coolidge tube*, invented by William D. Coolidge in 1913, has a hot tungsten filament, which gives off many electrons, and an anode, or target, of tungsten or another metal. Many thousands of volts are used to accelerate the electrons from filament to target. The filament temperature determines the number of electrons in the beam, and the voltage between target and filament determines their speed. The greater the speed, the more penetrating the X-rays. X-rays are used to produce shadowgraphs of the human body and to discover flaws within metal castings and other structures that cannot be studied by ordinary light.

■**TV CAMERA TUBES.**—Cathode rays are also an indispensable part of the *iconoscope,* an early television camera tube. This tube consists of a plate—about 4 by 5 inches in size and holding millions of tiny photoelectric cells—and a narrow beam of electrons that scans the cells. An image of the scene is focused by a lens on the light-sensitive plate, where each tiny cell generates a voltage proportional to the amount of light falling on it. The mosaic of cells creates an overall pattern of voltages that corresponds precisely to the pattern of light in the image. As the electron beam scans the mosaic of cells, it neutralizes the voltages and generates a picture signal in the form of a varying current of electricity.

The *image orthicon* is a generally superior television camera tube. It is more sensitive than the iconoscope and produces less distortion in the brightness of the image. It differs from the iconoscope in that the image is amplified electronically within the tube. A satisfactory picture signal can be produced, therefore, with less illumination on the scene.

—William C. Vergara

Clothing Industry, the manufacture of ready-to-wear apparel. The clothing industry traces its modern beginnings to the sewing machine, invented by Elias Howe in 1846 and improved by Isaac Singer in 1851, and to cutting equipment introduced in the 1870's and 1880's. Before that time, clothing worn by working-class people was made chiefly of coarse homespun by the women of the family. In the United States, only the rich could afford the services of custom tailors or dressmakers or imported garments from England and France.

Actually, manufacture of men's apparel preceded that of women's by almost a half-century. Production of men's clothing in quantity started in the early years of the nineteenth century, when firms made up hand-sewn but inferior *slop clothes* for sailors visiting waterfront shops in East coast ports.

The census of 1860, the first to take notice of the industry, reported 188 factories doing an annual volume of about $7 million and employing fewer than 6,000 "male and female hands." Ninety-six manufacturers turned out cloaks and mantillas. Among other major manufactures were hoop skirts and corsets.

In the 1880's and 1890's, immigration of craftsmen from central and eastern Europe hastened the pace of the industry's growth.

It was not until 1890, however, that female apparel increased its share of total garment production to 50 per cent. Wholesale volume in the women's wear section of the industry had jumped to $174 million by 1900. Factories had sprung up in Chicago, Cleveland, and Baltimore, as well as in the East coast ports of New York, Philadelphia, and Boston. By 1914, manufacture of women's wear had far exceeded that of men's wear.

It was not until 1908 that the separate dress was created by joining a skirt to a bodice. Sportswear and other casual clothes, born in the 1920's, came into their own in the 1950's, partly as a result of suburban living.

American manufacturers became aware of the Parisian couture just before World War I. Since then, except for the World War II period when the United States industry was thrown on its own resources, France has held a premier position in originating fashions. However, a number of American designers are also in the forefront among fashion leaders.

Newly important as a contributor to the fashion world, and always significant as a producer of attractive clothing for all social levels, the garment industry today is big business as well. In 1966 there were 8,225 men's, women's, and children's clothing manufacturers employing 609,000 workers on a $2,480,000,000 payroll and doing a $10,350,000,000 wholesale business.

During the past few years, the women's and men's apparel trades, traditionally among the last refuges of small business, have tended to join the ranks of big business by means of diversification of products, mergers, acquisitions, and public stock issues. More and more firms are cutting across women's ready-to-wear lines into accessories and even into men's wear, and vice versa.

—Samuel Feinberg

Clutches, mechanical devices used to engage and disengage rotating machine elements. They can be classified as either positive clutches or friction clutches.

Positive clutches cannot slip and have no friction elements. They cannot be engaged until both shafts are stopped or are rotating at the same speed. The simplest form of positive clutch consists of a pair of mating *dogs*, or *jaws*, that mesh. A shift lever or pedal is used to slide one of the jaws along its shaft, engaging or disengaging the opposite member. *Splines*, or *keys*, are used to transmit rotary motion between the sliding jaw and its shaft.

Friction clutches are widely used in automobile transmissions or wherever the speeds of the rotating elements differ. Motion is transmitted through a friction surface that permits slippage until the speeds of the rotating elements are equal. In the automobile, the clutch is mounted on the flywheel and transmits power through a flat friction disk splined to the driven shaft. The disk is located between a spring-loaded pressure plate and the flywheel of the engine. In the engaged position, axial force is applied by the springs to clamp the disk between the pressure plate and the flywheel. The disk is faced with specially compounded friction material riveted or bonded in place. These clutches are operated dry in most applications. Wet clutches, filled with a fluid, are used for heavy equipment, such as earth movers or caterpillar tractors; the fluid helps dissipate the heat produced by slippage.

Hydraulic clutches, or *fluid couplings,* use fluid to transmit motion between rotating shafts, end to end. These clutches have finned rotors enclosed in a fluid-tight housing filled with liquid. The vanes on the driving rotor impart a rotational motion to the fluid that is transmitted to and drives the vanes of the driven rotor. Smoothness and torque conversion are the advantages of the hydraulic clutch, which can tolerate wide differences in speed between the input and output shafts. These clutches are widely used in automatic transmissions for automobiles, trucks, buses, and military vehicles.

One-way, or *overrunning, clutches* permit transmission of rotary motion in one direction only. This freewheeling action allows the driven shaft to rotate faster than the driving shaft when a second source of power is applied or when the input slows down or stops. Spring-loaded *sprags,* or *balls,* are used to produce a wedging action between the input and output. When the overrunning clutch's input shaft rotates, the balls climb a ramp or the sprags tilt, wedging themselves between the driving hub and a driven sleeve. There is no slippage as long as input-shaft speed exceeds output-shaft speed. Once the speed of the output shaft exceeds that of the inputs, the balls are driven down the ramp to disengage or the sprags are tilted to free the sleeve. These one-way clutches operate automatically and

are frequently used to convert reciprocating motion to intermittent unidirectional rotation.

—Joseph J. Kelleher

Cofferdam, any temporary structure built to exclude earth and water from an excavation so that work may be done in the dry. The term, coined by civil engineers, stems from the structure's resemblance to a *coffer,* a little-used name for the rectangular chamber of a navigation lock, which in turn is shaped like a coffin. Cofferdams are commonly associated with marine construction such as bridge piers, canal locks, and dams.

A coffer formed by dams, hence cofferdam, is not to be confused with a *caisson,* although they often look alike and basically accomplish the same thing. A caisson is a chamber, sometimes very large, that is usually sunk by excavating within it, in order to gain access to the bed of a stream or other body of water. If the chamber is closed on top and the water is excluded by air pressure, it is called a *pneumatic caisson.*

Cofferdams are built in many different ways. The simplest version is an earthen dike built from the shoreline of a body of water to enclose a specific area. Pumps remove the water within the enclosure and work proceeds as though on dry land. Since earth dikes are often too temporary, especially in moving water such as a river, engineers have developed cofferdams with protective timber or steel sheeting on at least the riverward side of the structure. Early cofferdams often were formed of a series of *timber cribs* filled with rock and earth. Another common type of cofferdam consisted of two parallel rows of timber or steel sheeting filled with earth and linked by steel rods.

The most common cofferdam used today is the cellular steel sheetpile structure. Pile drivers form large circular cells by driving steel sheetpiles (long narrow pieces of steel with interlocks on their long edges so they can be locked together) into the river bottom. When filled with a granular material such as sand or gravel, each cell stands as an independent structure. When dozens of these are linked together and the construction site is enclosed with what looks like a row of giant tin cans, water can be pumped out. After the construction is completed the cells are removed.

—William W. Jacobus, Jr.

Compressors, devices that compress air or gas by decreasing its volume. This can be accomplished by machines referred to as either positive-displacement or dynamic compressors. *Positive-displacement compressors* can be classified as either *piston* or *rotary machines. Dynamic compressors* fall into the general classification of *centrifugal* or *axial flow machines,* and *jet blowers* or *air ejectors.*

■**PISTON COMPRESSORS.**—Piston compressors admit a quantity of the gas to a closed space where the pressure is increased by reducing the volume as the piston reciprocates. They work from slight vacuum (negative pressures) to several thousand

pounds per square inch (psi) pressure. The capacity in cubic feet per minute pumped depends upon the bore and stroke of the piston and the speed at which it is reciprocated. For pressures from 1 to 100 psi, single-cylinder compressors are adequate, while multiple-stage compressors—two, three, or four cylinder machines—can produce pressures up to 5,000 psi or higher. When more than one stage of compression is required, *intercoolers* are used between stages. Intercoolers, or *heat exchangers,* cool the gas as it travels from the discharge part of one cylinder to the intake of the next.

The simplest forms of piston compressor are the hand-operated insecticide sprayer and tire pump. As the operator pumps the handle back and forth, air is admitted to the cylinder and then is compressed as the moving piston reduces the volume of the cylinder. Piston compressors are commonly employed to supply air for paint sprayers or pneumatic tools and in household refrigerators.

■**ROTARY COMPRESSORS.**—Rotary compressors consist of a casing enclosing either a pair of impellers with intermeshed lobes or a single rotor with a series of sliding vanes arranged radially around the center of rotation. The rotors of *dual-impeller units* are symmetrical and interconnected by gears to rotate in opposite directions. As the impellers rotate, air trapped between the lobes and the housing is forced from intake to the exhaust port. *Sliding-vane compressors* consist of a slotted rotor inside a cylindrical housing. Vanes in the slots of the eccentrically mounted rotor are spring-loaded to contact the inner surface of the housing. As the rotor is turned, air trapped between the vanes is compressed as the space between the eccentrically mounted rotor and the housing walls decreases. Rotary compressors are used to supercharge internal combustion engines, for general blower service, or wherever high volume of gas must be moved at low pressure.

■**DYNAMIC COMPRESSORS.**—Dynamic compressors operate by accelerating and diffusing the gas passing through the machine. These compressors consist of a bladed rotor enclosed in a stationary housing. The blades on the rotor accelerate the gas inside the housing in the same way a fan blade accelerates air. The housing guides the gas or air to the rotor, changes the kinetic energy of the gas leaving the rotor blades into pressure, and directs the gas to the outlet.

In *centrifugal compressors,* the gas enters the machine at the center or hub of the rotor and moves radially toward the discharge ports. Gas flowing through *axial compressors* follows a relatively straight path parallel to the rotor shaft. Depending upon the pressure and volume required, either a single-stage or multistage axial compressor is used. The best-known application for these compressors is the aircraft gas turbine or jet engine. In these engines, ten or more sets of blades may be used to achieve the desired compression. —Joseph J. Kelleher

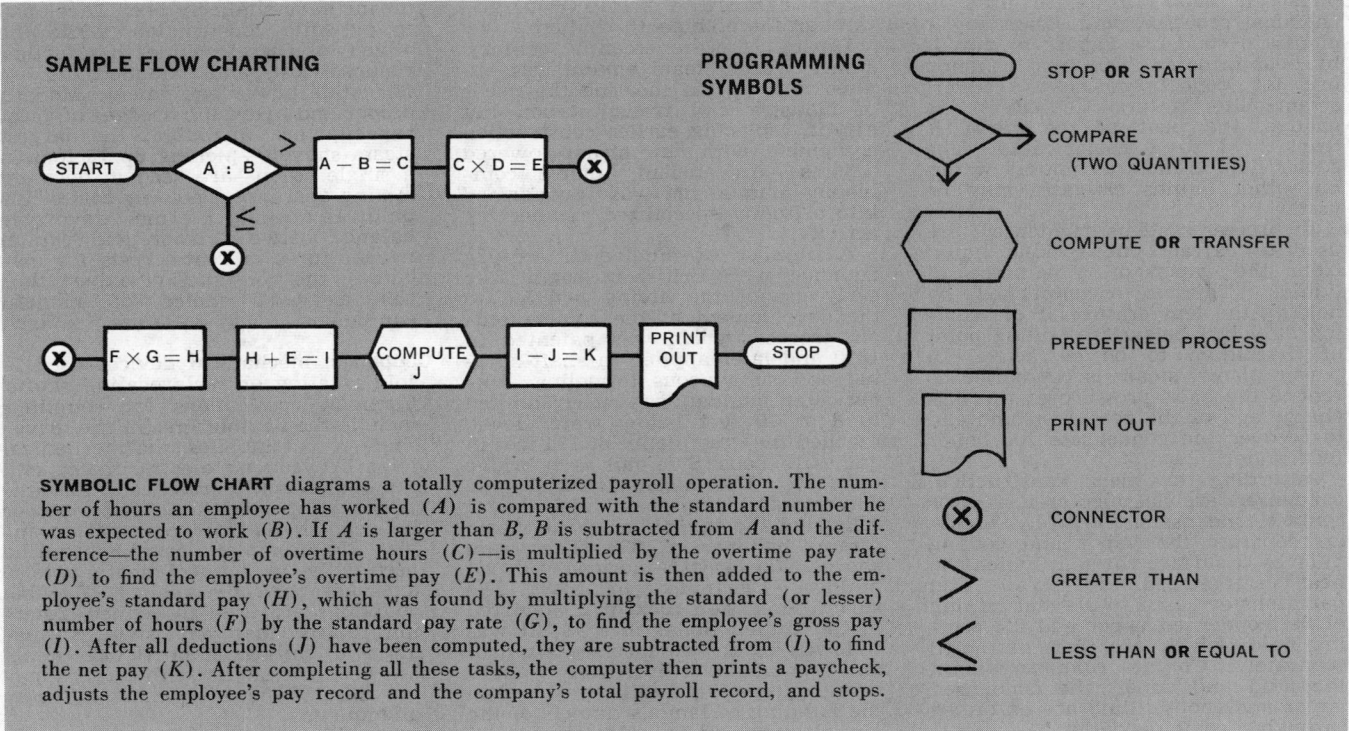

SAMPLE FLOW CHARTING

PROGRAMMING SYMBOLS

STOP **OR** START

COMPARE (TWO QUANTITIES)

COMPUTE **OR** TRANSFER

PREDEFINED PROCESS

PRINT OUT

CONNECTOR

GREATER THAN

LESS THAN **OR** EQUAL TO

SYMBOLIC FLOW CHART diagrams a totally computerized payroll operation. The number of hours an employee has worked (A) is compared with the standard number he was expected to work (B). If A is larger than B, B is subtracted from A and the difference—the number of overtime hours (C)—is multiplied by the overtime pay rate (D) to find the employee's overtime pay (E). This amount is then added to the employee's standard pay (H), which was found by multiplying the standard (or lesser) number of hours (F) by the standard pay rate (G), to find the employee's gross pay (I). After all deductions (J) have been computed, they are subtracted from (I) to find the net pay (K). After completing all these tasks, the computer then prints a paycheck, adjusts the employee's pay record and the company's total payroll record, and stops.

Computer, an electronic or mechanical device that accepts information, performs a mathematical or logical operation on it, and then reports the results in either a visual or machine-readable manner.

■**ANALOG COMPUTERS.**—The most common form of computer—often not recognized as such—is the analog device, which accepts continuous measurements to produce continuous solutions to mathematical equations. A classic example is the automobile speedometer, which converts the turning of a cylindrical shaft (the axle) into a numerical approximation of speed in terms of miles per hour. Another is the slide rule, which is based on the fact that two numbers can be multiplied by adding their logarithms. On the slide rule, however, we don't actually add numbers—instead we add the lengths proportional to them.

■**DIGITAL COMPUTERS.**—While the analog computer performs its calculations by measuring, the digital computer actually counts. The principle behind the digital computer evolved through the ages: first, in the form of the abacus, developed some 2000 years ago and still widely used; later, as a crude adding machine invented (1642) by the Frenchman Blaise Pascal; and, still later (c. 1670), as a primitive desk calculator built by the German mathematician and philosopher, Gottfried Wilhelm von Leibniz.

These earlier counting devices were dependent on manual effort—fingers moved beads or punched keys that turned notched wheels. In 1880, Herman Hollerith invented the punched-card technique, which substituted electric power for manual effort. While these electromechanical

devices weren't true computers, they were capable of performing a wide range of calculating tasks.

In 1947, J. Presper Eckert, Jr., and John W. Mauchly of the Moore School of Engineering, University of Pennsylvania, built a counting device called the Electronic Numerical Integrator and Computer (ENIAC). Instead of using electricity to move mechanical components, ENIAC employed thousands of switches, which were turned on or off by vacuum-tube-generated electronic impulses. This proved to be the first electronic digital computer.

The term "digital" is derived from counting on our fingers, or "digits." Because we have ten fingers, most computation is based on the familiar decimal system. Computers, on the other hand, use switches or other components which can be only in a state of "on" or "off," "yes" or "no," "0" or "1." For this reason, most digital computers are based on the binary counting system, which utilizes only two digits, 0 and 1. (See *Arithmetic*, page 1086.)

Although ENIAC could perform 5,000 additions per second (by using electronic impulses that move at the speed of light) its *program*—the series of instructions that tell the machine how to perform a particular job—was preset by means of wires. Thus, it did not have a high degree of flexibility.

■**PROGRAMMING.**—In 1948, International Business Machines Corporation introduced the Selective Sequence Electronic Calculator. The most important feature of this machine was its ability to store instructions magnetically and thus modify them as dictated by the developing stages of work.

Today there is a wide range of stored-program computers performing virtually every type of scientific and business task. Instead of vacuum tubes they use transistors or, in the latest models, microelectronic components. Although the specific method of data handling varies from model to model, all operate in basically the same manner.

A set of instructions tells the machine exactly how to perform a particular job, for example, process a payroll, update a file, or perform an engineering calculation. Then raw data are recorded in one of several media: punched cards, magnetic tape, direct access disk files, or simply in typed or magnetic ink characters. This information is fed into the system through an *input* device. There it comes under the control of the stored program and is processed accordingly. This may involve addition, subtraction, multiplication, division, or some similar mathematical or logical operation. The system's *output* then reports the results in the form of punched cards, magnetic tape, or printed media, or by display on a cathode-ray tube or some similar visual device.

Most digital computers today are used for routine office jobs as payroll, accounts receivable, or the like. Many, however, are applied to extremely sophisticated tasks, such as simulating real-life systems (human blood factors, war games, business operations) or continually monitoring complex physical systems (petroleum refineries, manufacturing processes). In these latter cases, the input to the digital computer often comes directly from an analog device by means of analog-to-digital converters. —Stanley Englebardt

Condenser, Vapor, a device used in chemical processes and steam power plants to condense vapors to liquids by heat transfer. The most common use for condensers is to convert steam into water. To effect the change, the heat of the vapor is transferred to a cooler fluid. The cooler fluid is most commonly water, but other liquids or gases may be used.

In process systems, condensers are used to extract one specific liquid from the vapor of a mixture of liquids. This is accomplished by holding the temperature of the cooling fluid just below the boiling point of the liquid to be extracted. In power plants, steam is condensed to reduce the back pressure at the discharge end of the power turbine and to recover the condensate for boiler feed water.

According to their construction, condensers are classified as surface or contact condensers. *Surface condensers* separate the vapor and cooling fluid by a surface through which the heat is transferred. Pipes, plates, and partitions are used to prevent mixing of the condensed vapor and the cooling fluid, which are then extracted separately. *Contact condensers* mix the fluid and vapor; the condensed vapor and cooling fluid are extracted through a common outlet.

—Joseph J. Kelleher

Construction Equipment, machinery used in the building of structures and roads. Until the advent of steam power, construction equipment was limited almost entirely to man-operated hoists, pumps, and similar devices. Labor was the major resource, works were long in building, and limitations—such as founding bridge piers at sufficient depth to prevent scour during floods—led to many failures.

The ancient Egyptians had developed no important equipment but, with plentiful labor, built huge temporary earth inclines in erecting their great stone constructions, such as the pyramids. The man-powered hoists and pumps of the Greeks and Romans remained little changed through the eighteenth century.

During the nineteenth century, James Watt's steam engine was applied not only in meeting the needs of industry and transportation but also in replacing earlier construction equipment with new steam-powered devices. An ancient, almost completely manual art was transformed into a highly specialized engineering activity.

A number of nineteenth century advances were British in origin. The early use of the diving bell led to the development of the compressed-air process, which was patented in 1830 and later applied in shaft-sinking and subaqueous tunneling. Underwater foundations, earlier limited to 8 or 10 feet below water level, reached the great depth of 136 feet in James B. Eads' St. Louis arch bridge of 1869. The steam-powered pile driver was likewise a British device following the invention of the steam forging hammer in 1838. The steam shovel, "the great American railroad builder," originated in 1838. The steam percussion rock drill appeared in the United States in 1849. It was followed by the compressed-air drill and, combined with Alfred Nobel's new explosive, dynamite, was used in the building of famous tunnels of the period, such as the Hoosac Tunnel (Massachusetts) of 1866. Nevertheless, other major advances were to come primarily in the United States in the earlier years of the twentieth century. The construction of the Chicago Drainage Canal (1892–1900) and the first New York subway of 1904 were largely pick-and-shovel undertakings.

Various factors contributed to this movement. One was that the increasing cost of labor emphasized labor-saving equipment. Another, at the turn of the century in 1900, was the introduction of the gasoline engine, which was to replace the horse-and-cart and to find increasing application in many construction devices, including pumps, scrapers, rollers, and loading and other equipment. Belt-conveyors and other mechanical means have similarly been developed to expedite construction, while the advent of Diesel engines has further reduced costs and extended the use of mobile power equipment. Modern dipper and hydraulic dredges of great capacity are available; the largest steam shovels—picking up 15 tons in a single scoop—are used in open-pit mining operations, notably coal stripping. In seeking the most favorable balance between labor and capital expenditures or rental costs for machines, the construction expert thus has a wide choice of modern equipment.   —James Kip Finch

Couplings, mechanical devices used to join rotating or reciprocating shafts. Common applications for couplings include the flexible link in the driveshaft of automobiles, the mechanical joint between an electric motor and the equipment it drives, and the universal joint used to transmit power between shafts intersecting at an angle. Rigid, or plain, couplings can be used only to connect shafts whose axes are perfectly aligned. Flexible couplings are used to connect rotating shafts that are slightly misaligned. Universal, or Hooke, joints are used for shafts with large angular misalignment or changing misalignments.

Rigid couplings consist of a sleeve or collar which slips over the joint between two shafts and is clamped or keyed to each. Flanged, rigid couplings have a hub, which is keyed or pressed on the shaft, and a larger diameter flange with a circle of bolt holes. When being mounted on each shaft, the flanged couplings are aligned and then bolts are installed in the holes.

Flexible couplings transmit power between shafts whose axes are not precisely aligned. The misalignment may be offset, angular, or a combination of both. An additional benefit of flexible joints is their ability to absorb or *damp* vibrations produced by speed variation or unbalanced rotating machinery. As the name implies, flexible couplings frequently consist of rigid hubs or spiders

...highways, canals, dams, and other massive projects proceeds quickly with the help of huge earth-movers such
...load many tons of dirt, transport it to a desired location, and spread it into an evenly graded surface.

AQUA·CHEM., INC.

DESALINIZATION PLANTS make salt water potable. The "flash evaporator" (*bottom*) converts 800,000 gallons a day. A desalter provides water for ship *Michelangelo* at sea.

clamped to each shaft and linked together by flexible material. The flexible material may be thin steel disks, steel springs, rubber impregnated canvas, or solid rubber.

The simplest form of flexible coupling consists of a pair of steel hubs joined by a solid-rubber sleeve. The rubber element is molded or clamped onto the hubs to form a solid, one-piece coupling.

One of the oldest couplings known is *Oldham's double slider coupling*, which incorporates the basic features from which most flexible couplings have been developed. These couplings consist of two hubs and a central plate. Ribs on opposing faces of the central disk mate with slots in the hubs. Lubrication is essential in Oldham's couplings because the ribs slide in the slots as the coupling rotates. For low-power, low-speed applications, a plastic such as nylon may be used for the central plate. This assures silent operation and eliminates the lubrication problem.

Universal joints are used to transmit power between shafts with large angular misalignment. These joints consist of a pair of yokes connected by a cross, or spider. Universal joints are widely used in automobile power trains. Common practice calls for the installation of two universal joints in the driveshaft that transmits power to the rear axle; this permits uninterrupted power flow to the rear wheels when the axle bounces up and down over bumps.
                                                 —Joseph J. Kelleher

Cybernetics, the science of communication and control. Cybernetics seeks a general theory of the way in which systems control themselves in the performance of a useful task. Such theories should apply equally well to any field of human activity or study: engineering, biology, physics, economics, business, or even baseball.

From the point of view of cybernetics, a system is any collection of items that influence one another as the system performs its function. A system usually consists of smaller subsystems, and is, in turn, often a part of a larger system. For example, a machinist and his tools form a system that produces parts by machine. The machinist's system, in turn, is a part of a larger system, the machine shop. The machine shop, in turn, is part of a still larger system, the factory. In the field of engineering, a system might consist of a jet

aircraft. In business, it might be a company that operates a fleet of such aircraft. In politics it might consist of the internal government of the United States, or a collection of all the world's nations and the way they interact to produce good will or war.

The most successful systems known are those found in nature's living things—vision, muscular control, life itself. The secret of this success seems to lie in the way such systems control themselves and communicate among their various parts. By studying such systems, *cyberneticians* hope to discover nature's basic principles of control so they can be applied to manmade systems of all kinds. A major contribution might then be made in the field of international relations. The system of nations normally accepts only force as a means of control. Perhaps the more subtle methods of control used in nature may one day offer a more peaceful and successful kind of regulation of international affairs.
                                                 —William C. Vergara

Desalinization, also known as desalination, methods of making seawater, and other polluted sources of water, fit for human and industrial uses. Desalinization has gained added momentum as the world faces an increasingly critical water shortage. This shortage is caused by four major factors: a fast-growing population; an even faster rise in the industrial use of water; the growing pollution of waterways; and maldistribution of water with respect to concentrations of population and industry.

Although millions of dollars are being spent to find new approaches, the long-proven method of *distillation* continues to be dominant. Virtually all seawater desalinization facilities in practical operation today

are based on the principle of evaporating water and leaving the brine (or other pollutants) behind.

More recently, significant advances have been made in *multistage flash distillation*. In this process, the pure distillate is obtained by evaporating the seawater at progressively higher vacuums and lower temperatures. This method has steadily brought down the cost of producing potable water to where engineers now talk of its soon approaching the cost of water purified by conventional chemical methods—which in turn are becoming higher as levels of pollution rise and the cost of treatment and distribution increase.

For many years the highest efficiency achieved in multistage flash distillation was about 10 to 1—that is, 10 pounds of pure water were produced for every pound of steam required to raise the temperature of the seawater to the flash point. However, in 1966, the Office of Saline Water, a part of the U.S. Department of the Interior, announced that it had given a contract for the construction of a new high-ratio multistage, multi-effect distillation plant at San Diego, Calif., that would achieve a ratio of 20 to 1—thus doubling the efficiency of this type of plant. This is expected to permit a substantial reduction in the cost of output water, and to hasten the day when desalinization becomes an economically practical solution to the world's growing need for water.

Research into other methods, such as *reverse osmosis* and *freezing,* continues. Furthermore, *electrodialysis* is being constantly improved as the method of choice for situations where the water supply has a relatively low concentration of pollutants—on the order of 5,000 parts per million or lower.
                                                 —Gordon F. Leitner

Dies, tools used to form or cut parts or shapes from a wide range of materials. To form parts, the material is stressed beyond its yield point until it takes a permanent set. To cut parts or punch openings, the material must be stressed in shear until it fails. *Forming dies* are used to bend, emboss, forge, draw, or form rigid material that can be permanently deformed. *Cutting dies* are used to cut out blanks for forming, to punch holes, or to cut either rigid or flexible stock to shape.

For high-volume production of complex shapes, *progressive dies* are used. A progressive die consists of as many as ten or more individual dies combined and mounted in a single press. As the workpiece passes from die to die, successive forming operations take place until the part is completed. The brass base of a light bulb, for example, is formed in a seven-step, high-speed progressive die.

In operation, dies are mounted in a press that exerts the force needed to form or cut the workpiece. Mechanical, hydraulic, or pneumatic presses may be used, depending on the force needed and the speed of operation. The basic method of feeding material to the dies is by hand. To increase the speed of operation, coil stock and automatic feeders are frequently used.

To cut soft sheet stock, steel rule dies are used in a press called a *clicker machine.* The machine consists of a wooden table over which a hydraulically operated arm is suspended. The sharpened steel rule die is placed on the material by hand, and the arm is lowered by hydraulic power to cut out a piece of stock. Clicker machines and steel rule dies are widely used to cut leather, canvas, sheet rubber, and gasket materials.
—Joseph J. Kelleher

Diving, entering the water and descending to a great depth, to accomplish a specific purpose, such as salvage. Diving was practiced in ancient times, at first without equipment and then with the aid of a *diving bell.* Diving bells originally consisted of a bell-shaped metal housing which retained the air inside when it was lowered into the sea. Divers could enter the open bottom of the bell to replenish their air without returning to the surface.

Drawings from the fourth century A.D. show Roman divers with watertight helmets attached to leather tubes leading to the surface. In 1240 Roger Bacon wrote of "instruments" which allowed men to walk on the bottom of the sea. The first practical diving suit was devised in 1819 by Augustus Siebe, who attached an air pump to a metal helmet. The complete diving apparatus consisted of the metal helmet attached to a leather jacket. Air from the pump was fed to the helmet through flexible tubes and kept the water below the diver's chin. One drawback of the original Siebe suit was that the diver had to remain standing or water would fill his helmet and he would drown.

After many experiments, Siebe developed a closed diving dress in 1830 with a helmet equipped with air inlet and regulating outlet valves. The principles developed by Siebe are still in use today, though numerous improvements have been made.

Modern diving suits with helmets require an air pump, metal helmet and breastplate, flexible air tube, weighted boots, lead weights, and a lifeline. When fully dressed before submerging, the diver is encumbered by several hundred pounds of equipment and cannot move without aid.

When submerged, the diver adjusts the regulating valve on his helmet, which controls the air entering the suit, until the buoyancy created by the air in the suit equals the weight of the equipment; this allows the diver to move freely. Plate glass windows in the helmet allow the diver to see while he is submerged. Divers generally breathe only compressed air. However, for dives deeper than 300 feet, a mixture of gases is necessary for greater resistance against water pressure.

The conventional diving suit and helmet are being rapidly replaced by self-contained breathing apparatus, known as *scuba,* devised by Jean Costeau, a French oceanographer. The diver is supplied with air from tanks strapped on his back and is free to swim or work unencumbered by air hoses or lifelines. Breathing tubes connect the compressed air tanks to the diver's mouthpiece. A demand valve on the pressure tanks admits air to the diver's mouthpiece each time inhalation drops the pressure. When the diver exhales, the air is discharged into the water.

Scuba diving has become a popular sport in Europe and the United States, where amateur divers use the equipment for spear fishing and exploring. Professional divers use the equipment for underwater repair, salvage, and rescue work. After much experimentation with air-gas mixtures replacing ordinary air, divers have descended successfully to depths of 750 feet. Because of its simplicity and mobility, scuba equipment has almost completely replaced the older hard-helmet diving suits.
—Joseph J. Kelleher

Dredging, the process of deepening, widening, and maintaining harbors, rivers, and canals. One of the first machines designed specifically to dredge a river channel was a sort of continuous chain with buckets at-

U.S. NAVY   SILVER SPRINGS, FLORIDA

DIVING EQUIPMENT (*left*), including metal helmet, suit, shoes, air hose, and air supply, weighs several hundred pounds; the less cumbersome self-contained scuba unit (*right*) consists of a watertight glass face-mask, rubber foot fins, and an aqualung.

ELLICOTT MACHINE CORPORATION

DIPPER DREDGES are used for the removal of heavy earth materials from shipping channels. The dredge shown here can reach to a depth of 47 feet below the water level.

tached at intervals. As the chain took inverted buckets to the bottom, full ones came to the surface and emptied into a barge at the top of the cycle. This dredge was invented in the early 1700's. As large excavating machines were developed for dryland excavations, marine engineers adapted them for dredging from barges.

The *dipper dredge,* a sort of underwater steam shovel, was among the earliest types of large dredging devices. The booms and rigging were adopted so the shovel could dip well below the surface. The buckets were enlarged and designed so some water leaked out as they emerged.

Huge dipper dredges still do much dredging, but they are being displaced by *hydraulic suction dredges.* These work like mammoth vacuum cleaners sucking the silt and sand from below the surface with pumps. For work in relatively firm material, hydraulic dredges are equipped with rotating cutterheads on the end of the suction pipe.

Hydraulic dredges range in size from small portable models that can be disassembled and moved overland, to the U.S. Army Corps of Engineers' big *hopper dredges.* These are full-scale seagoing vessels which—although they dredge hydraulically—are called hopper dredges because of their huge holds. The holds are filled with dredged material, taken to sea, and dumped through the bottom of the hold, as in hoppers.

Clamshell buckets mounted on cranes are also used for dredging. Another common method used for small-scale work is the *dragline,* a large steel scoop attached to a crane by two cables. One, running to the top of the crane boom, is used to cast the bucket into the water. The other, attached to the mouth of the scoop, is tied directly to the crane's winch; as it is reeled in, it pulls the scoop or dragline toward the crane, and thus fills it.   —William W. Jacobus, Jr.

Dyeing, fixing colors uniformly in textile materials. Although man has dyed textiles since prehistoric times, he was forced until 1856 to rely on a mere handful of colors derived from plant and animal sources. In that year, the synthesis of the first coaltar derived dye by William H. Perkin, a British scientist, marked the beginning of the synthetic dyestuff industry. Today, thousands of different chemical compounds of varying brilliance, fastness, and depth are available as dyes. None is effective on all textile fibers. Some work well on animal fibers, such as wool; others on vegetable fibers, such as cotton; and still others on one or more of the many synthetic fibers, such as nylon.

Dyes are classified into four general categories. *Direct dyes* dissolve in the dyebath and are taken up directly by the fiber. *Developed dyes* are taken up by the fiber but need further chemical treatment to yield their final shade. *Mordant dyes* have an affinity not for the fiber itself but for another substance (usually metallic) that is first applied to the fiber. *Pigment colors* are very fine colored powders dispersed into an emulsion that is linked to the fiber by an adhesive substance.

Within these four categories are many specific classes and subclasses of dyes. *Vat dyes* have maximum fastness to light and laundering and are usually applied to cotton and rayon. *Basic dyes* are used on cotton, silk, and wool where bright shades are desired, but they usually have poor fastness to light and washing. *Sulfur dyes,* another class used on cotton, possess very good fastness to washing but only moderate to good lightfastness. *Acid dyes* are used extensively on wool, silk, and nylon; they offer low cost, brightness, and easy application, and fastness to light and washing ranges from good to very good. *Disperse dyes* are applicable to manmade fibers, such as polyester, nylon, and acetate, and have

enjoyed a steady growth along with that of the fibers themselves during the past decade; while fastness properties are good to very good, these dyes often require special treatment to ensure fastness and uniformity on polyester and nylon. *Reactive dyes* are the newest class of dyes; these actually form a chemical union with either cellulosic or wool, depending on the structure of the dye; as a result, they feature very good fastness and bright shades.

Textile materials can be dyed in four basic ways, each related to a stage of textile manufacture.

In *raw stock* or *silver dyeing,* fibers are dyed in loose form, before they are drawn and twisted into yarn. This method, used mainly for wool, results in uniform dye absorption and colorfastness. The well-known expression *dyed in the wool* originally referred to fabric made of fibers dyed this way.

Yarn dyeing includes *skein dyeing,* in which loose hanks of yarn are dyed in a bath; *beam dyeing,* a method of dyeing warp yarns that are later woven with filling; and *package dyeing,* in which yarn is dyed while on tightly-woven spools. In each case, the operation is designed so that the dye penetrates to the innermost section of the mass of yarn to ensure a uniform color throughout. Yarns dyed by these techniques can be used for knitting or as components of yarn-dyed woven fabrics, such as plaids.

Piece dyeing involves the application of dyes to woven or knitted fabrics. (In some cases, complete garments, such as hosiery or sweaters, are dyed in piece form.) Piece dyeing is the most flexible and most economical method of dyeing, especially since most textile products are subject to the whims of fashion. The availability of piece dyeing permits the fabric merchant to maintain large stocks of undyed fabric, portions of which can be dyed on order to the specifications of the end-product manufacturer, and in whatever shades may be popular at a given time. Piece dyeing is carried out continuously or semicontinuously on various types of machines, either in open-width or rope form. Recent developments in machinery for piece dyeing have included faster speeds for economy, higher temperatures and pressures for better dye fixation, and the use of automated devices for greater uniformity and lower labor costs.

In *solution dyeing,* pigments are added to the liquid polymeric solution, from which a synthetic fiber is spun. The color, therefore, is well-fixed throughout the fiber. An economic disadvantage is that mills which make the fiber into fabric or yarn must maintain a very large inventory of differently colored fibers to satisfy customer demands for various colors. Thus, this method is used chiefly for synthetic fibers that are difficult to dye in yarn or piece form, or in cases where the color of the end-use item is of minor importance from the standpoint of fashion.
                              —Francis A. McNeirney

Electric Furnace, a heating chamber in which electric energy is the "fuel." Electric furnaces may be classified into two large groups, resistance furnaces and arc furnaces, according to the principles of heating employed.

Resistance furnaces may operate on the principle of indirect heating or direct heating. With *indirect heating,* electric current is passed through special resistors in the form of coils, rods, or grids or baths of molten salt that have high electrical resistance and are heated by their resistance to flow of the current. The heat generated is used to heat the furnace and the material in it by radiation, convection, and/or conduction. In the case of *direct heating,* current is made to flow through the material to be heated, and heat is generated in the material by its own electrical resistance. This may be accomplished by applying contacts to the piece to be heated, making it part of a low-voltage circuit, or by using the induction principle. *Induction heating* is accomplished by passing a high- or medium-frequency alternating current through a coil surrounding (but not in contact with) the material to be heated.

Arc furnaces are of three general types: indirect, direct, and a combination of the two.

Indirect-arc furnaces heat solely by radiation from the arc, using alternating current. One type employs two horizontal electrodes in a cylindrical furnace that rotates about the horizontal axis of the cylinder. An arc is maintained between the ends of the electrodes within the furnace above the heated material.

Direct-arc furnaces of the type employed principally for melting and refining ferrous metals use three vertical electrodes and three-phase alternating current. Current passes through an arc from one electrode to the bath of molten metal, passes through the bath, and arcs from the bath to another electrode to complete the electrical circuit. These are known as *series-arc furnaces.* Another type of direct-arc furnace is the *single-arc furnace,* employing alternating current in which the current arcs from one electrode to the bath, passes through the bath, and out through an electrode in the bottom of the furnace.

Consumable-electrode furnaces are direct-arc furnaces for remelting and refining metals under vacuum; they use direct current. In these furnaces, current passes through an electrode made of the metal to be melted, and an arc is maintained between the end of the electrode and a small pool of molten metal in the bottom of a water-cooled mold. Heat generated by the arc causes continuous melting of the end of the electrode. The melted metal drops into the pool and forms an ingot as the metal cools and solidifies in the mold.

The third type of arc furnace, the *combination arc and resistance furnace,* uses both arc radiation and the heat generated by current passing through the refractory bottom of the furnace to heat the charge.

—Harold McGannon

Electrical Measuring Instruments, devices that measure electrical quantities such as voltage, current, power, electric charge, or energy. They are used to obtain quantitative information about the status or performance of an electric circuit. Common measuring instruments include ammeters, voltmeters, and wattmeters.

The *d'Arsonval galvanometer* is a basic electromechanical device for measuring or detecting weak electric currents, and is the sensing element of many electrical measuring instruments. It consists of a small coil of fine wire suspended on bearings between the poles of a permanent magnet. If a current flows through the coil, it produces a magnetic field that interacts with the magnetism of the permanent magnet, causing the coil to rotate. A pointer attached to the coil indicates the amount of current flowing. In the absence of a deflecting current, a light spring returns the pointer to zero.

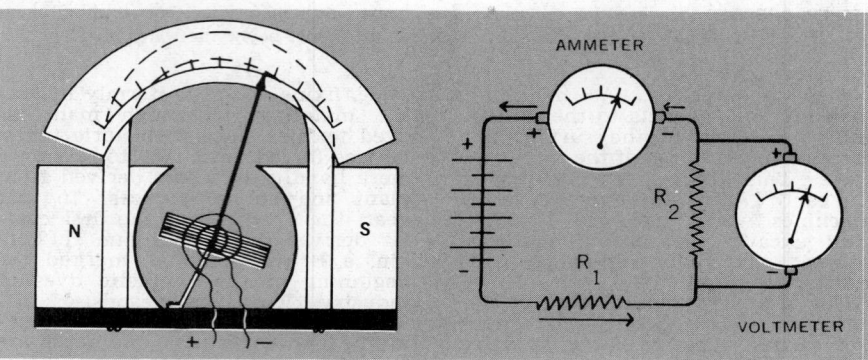

MOVING-COIL GALVANOMETER detects electrical currents with the use of a permanent magnet, whose field fills the gap between its north and south poles, and a coil attached to a spring in that gap. As current passes through the coil, it induces a magnetic field that is repelled by that of the magnet, and the needle is deflected. The spring returns the pointer to the zero position when the current ceases.

AMMETER, a modified galvanometer, measures in amperes the electricity flowing through a circuit. Only part of the current enters the device's magnetic field, but the magnet controlling the indicator is balanced to record the actual strength. Thus, even a current strong enough to destroy the mechanism can be measured. A *voltmeter* is a galvanometer linked to resistors (R_1, R_2) that limit the force of the measured current.

The ordinary *direct-current ammeter* is merely a sensitive galvanometer that has a shunt of very low resistance connected across the terminals of the coil. The shunt allows a predetermined fraction of the current to bypass the coil. The galvanometer's scale is calibrated in *amperes* to indicate the true current flowing in the circuit, even though only a small fraction of that current actually flows through its coil.

The galvanometer is also used as a *direct-current voltmeter* by connecting a large resistance in series with its coil. The resistance limits the current through the coil to a safe amount, and the scale is calibrated to read in *volts.*

The galvanometer is also the heart of the *ohmmeter,* a useful instrument designed to measure, in units of the *ohm,* the electrical resistance in a circuit. In operation, the unknown resistance is connected in series with a galvanometer and a battery of known voltage. The current that flows through the galvanometer, therefore, depends upon the magnitude of the unknown resistance. A scale, calibrated in ohms, gives that magnitude directly.

The galvanometer finds another application as the indicating element of the *potentiometer,* a voltage-measuring instrument that draws no current from the voltage source being measured. The unknown voltage source is balanced against a known, variable voltage, and any difference between the two will cause the galvanometer to deflect. Equality between the two voltages is achieved when the galvanometer reads zero.

The *Wheatstone bridge,* named for Sir Charles Wheatstone, is used to measure electrical resistance independently of any variations of the voltage source. It consists of three known resistances, an unknown resistance, a battery, and a galvanometer. The four resistances are connected in series, the four connections forming a square. The battery is connected to a pair of opposite points of the square, and the galvanometer to the other pair of opposite points. The bridge is balanced by adjusting the known resistances until the deflection of the galvanometer reaches zero. It is then possible to calculate the magnitude of the unknown resistance. The same fundamental principle is used to measure electrical inductance or capacitance in alternating-current circuits.

The *electrometer* is an extremely sensitive voltmeter that draws much less current in its operation than do moving-coil galvanometers. The first electrometer consisted of a sealed jar containing a metal rod to which were attached two small strips of thin gold foil. An electric charge causes the gold leaves to repel one another and their movement, measured against a calibrated scale by a microscope, gives the magnitude of the unknown voltage. An *electroscope* is merely an electrometer without a calibrated scale. Modern electrometers use electronic techniques to achieve even greater sensitivity. The latter are 100 million times as sensitive as the best galvanometers. The *Geiger-Müller counter* contains an electronic electrometer that indicates radioactivity levels when radiations from radioactive material enter the ionization chamber of the instrument.

The *fluxmeter* measures the magnetic strength of a magnet, electromagnet, or other source of magnetism. It consists of a search coil connected to a sensitive, moving-coil galvanometer. The coil of the galvanometer is suspended by a fine quartz or silk fiber that minimizes the forces tending to return the pointer to zero. In operation, the search coil is brought close to the magnet under test, and the deflection of the galvanometer indicates the change in magnetic flux, which is a measure of the strength of the magnet.

The direct current *wattmeter* indicates the product of voltage and current in a circuit, hence the electric power. The unit of measurement is the *watt*. The wattmeter is, essentially, a combination of a voltmeter and an ammeter, so arranged that the pointer indicates the product of the number of volts applied to a circuit and the number of amperes flowing through the circuit. The *watt-hour meter* indicates the total amount of energy consumed by a circuit. The usual alternating-current residential type uses a rotating disk whose speed of rotation depends on the power passing through the meter. A counting mechanism records the energy consumed in units of *kilowatt-hours*.

The *oscilloscope* is a versatile measuring instrument that presents a visual indication of the voltage existing in a circuit. It is used primarily for alternating-current measurements to show how the voltage varies in the course of time. This information is presented in visual form on a cathode-ray tube, similar to the picture tube in a television set.

—William C. Vergara

Electron Microscope, a device that uses electrons to form an image. Its development is encompassed by that of *electron optics,* a branch of physics.

The electron microscope, essentially, is an evacuated tube, or *column.* At one end is the *electron gun,* which accelerates freed electrons. The resulting electron beam is directed by electromagnetic and electrostatic fields (*lenses*) into the *specimen chamber.* After interaction with atomic nuclei of the specimen, the electrons are directed by more lenses, finally hitting a fluorescent *viewing screen* or photographic emulsion at the other end of the column. Here the image is formed from the waves associated with the electrons. Magnifications up to 200,000X and resolutions down to a few Angstroms (1 Angstrom = 10^{-8} centimeters) may be obtained.

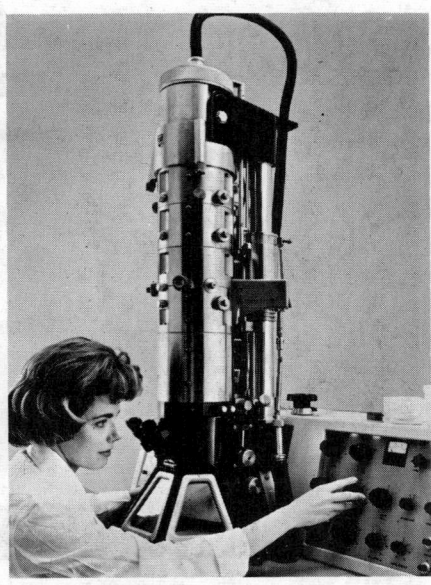

PHILIPS ELECTRONIC INSTRUMENTS

RADIO CORPORATION OF AMERICA

ELECTRON MICROSCOPE (*left*), capable of magnifying an object up to 500,000 times, is used to study molecular structure of solids. The electron micrograph (*right*) was taken through an electron microscope. It shows some zinc oxide crystals magnified 65,600 times.

Electron microscopy (and the co-technique of electron diffraction on the same instrument) has wide application. It is an indispensable and sometimes ultimate tool in such varied fields as biological ultrastructure, polymer chemistry, and metallurgical research on thin films (solid-state physics). More than 3,000 electron microscopes are employed throughout the world in research institutions, universities, hospitals, and private industry. Both use and demand are increasing each year. (See also *Microscope,* page 1703.)   —John W. Coleman

Electronic Industry, the design, manufacture, and sale of electronic equipment. This equipment includes television sets, radio receivers, radar sets, communication equipment, and countless other electronic marvels made possible by modern engineering.

Progress in the electronic industry has been particularly rapid as a result of automation and the impact of electronics on production methods. In 1966 it ranked fifth among the leading U.S. industries. Almost every area of the industrial and national economy has been affected by the growth of electronics. In 1965, the industry had sales of approximately $18 billion with an annual growth rate of about $1 billion per year. This was about 2.6 per cent of the gross national product. By contrast, the electronic output of the rest of the world was about $10 billion in 1964.

The largest user of electronic equipment is the U. S. government, which purchased about $9.6 billion worth in 1965. Most of this money was spent on electronic equipment for aircraft, missiles, rockets, and space vehicles. This includes radar sets for tracking, automatic flight-control systems, telemetry equipment to relay data to ground stations, and

general communication and navigational systems. Because of the high speed of modern aircraft, increasingly complex electronic equipment is needed to aid the pilot in the safe and efficient control of the plane. For unmanned missiles and rockets, even more sophisticated systems are required to provide the necessary guidance and control.

Consumer products accounted for sales of $3.1 billion in 1965. In addition to radio and television sets, consumers purchased phonographs, tape recorders, and a wide variety of hi-fi components.

American industry is another large user of electronic equipment, with purchase of some $5.1 billion in 1965. The largest part, $1.9 billion, went for computing and data-processing equipment. These electronic systems assist in almost all phases of business activity, from inventory control to payroll calculations. Electronic computers are even used to design other pieces of electronic equipment. Electronic equipment is used to control industrial processes, to measure and test a variety of products, and has many applications in the fields of communications and data processing.

Though relatively small in volume, about $212 million in 1966, *microelectronics* is probably the fastest-growing electronic field. Microelectronics replaces a radio tube or transistor and its usual complement of other parts with a tiny microelectronic package smaller than a pencil eraser. Microelectronic circuits have also proven to be more reliable than the parts they replace. As their cost comes down, microelectronic circuits are expected to find their way into all areas of electronics. Microelectronics will then be as important to the electronics industry as the transistor itself.

—William C. Vergara

Electroplating, the process of coating an object made of metal or other electrically conductive material with a layer of another metal or alloy through the use of an electric current. In modern practice, electroplating has either an aesthetic or a more functional aim, such as to improve the corrosion resistance of a product or to ensure low resistivity through electrical contacts. Often the functional and the aesthetic purposes are combined, as in the "chrome" plating of automotive bumpers and other components.

Fundamentally, the process is quite simple and requires a minimum of equipment: an object to be plated; a piece of the metal with which the object is to be plated; a special bath or solution in which both the object and the piece of metal are immersed; and a source of direct current. Plating begins when the negative terminal of the current source is connected to the object to be plated, and the positive terminal is connected to the piece of plating metal.

The *bath* is a solution of a chemical compound of the plating material. At the negative terminal, which is also the part to be plated, the metal in solution becomes deposited on the surface of the object. Simultaneously, more metal is dissolved from the metal at the positive terminal, replenishing the bath. The speed at which these reactions occur varies in direct proportion to the magnitude of the current. In addition, some baths have been found to be more efficient than others, so that a number of proprietary mixtures for baths have been developed.

Metals commonly used for plating are gold, silver, copper, nickel, chromium, tin, zinc, and cadmium. It is not uncommon to cover the same part with successive electroplated deposits of the same or of different metals. For instance, some of the better chromium-plated parts are coated first with copper, then with nickel, and finally with chromium. Others may receive two different deposits of nickel, and so forth.

Integrity of the coated layer is important, as it must act as a barrier to prevent the basis metal from coming into contact with the atmosphere or with other sources of oxidation and corrosion. Cleanliness of the part being plated is essential, as it permits good adhesion of the deposit and eliminates the source of holes in the plated metal. Even so, the deposit later almost always contains minute pores that are likely, sooner or later, to establish a connection between the corroding atmosphere and the basis metal.

To eliminate this possibility, high-quality electroplating includes one or two buffed layers. After each layer has been deposited, the part is washed and dried, and then vigorously buffed so as to smear the deposit. This smearing action bridges over the pores, effectively sealing them and ensuring the protection of the basis metal.

Certain metals adhere more tenaciously to some basis metals than do others. As the total protection pro-

WESTERN ELECTRIC COMPANY

ETCHING creates electronic circuits (*left*) as well as works of art. Circuit pattern at *right* is photographically etched on plastic film before size reduction and printing.

vided by electroplating is in part dependent on the thickness of the total plate, there is little lost in dividing this layer into a number of sublayers —as in the copper-nickel-chromium sequence. On the other hand, there is much to be gained, since the various sublayers are chosen for high adhesion to each other and to the basis metal and for their ability to resist different sources and types of corrosion.   —Felix Giordano

Engraving, the art of removing metal, especially from plates and cylindrical or other continuous surfaces, by means of shallow cuts. The purpose of engraving is to alter the original surface for decorative or utilitarian purposes.

A mechanical method of engraving is used to inscribe messages on the inside of rings, on watches and other jewelry, on plaques and trophies, and on similar articles. Engraving is also used to produce plates for printing paper currency, postage stamps, bonds, deeds, and other legal documents. In industry, the process is used to produce identification lettering on tools and dies and for the production of master rolls required in various types of embossing.

Much engraving is performed by hand, with tools which the master engraver himself fashions as he needs them. Where the purpose of engraving is to reproduce a master pattern of letters or other line work, a pantograph machine is used. The master pattern is fixed in place, and the lines in the master are traced with the machine's follower. A graver on the machine reproduces the master pattern in smaller size onto the metal surface. In some instances the graver is replaced with a rotating tool, which facilitates cutting through some harder metals but reduces the engraving's edge sharpness.

Engraving is sometimes used as a finishing operation to sharpen the edges of cuts produced in metal surfaces by mechanical or chemical action. Such a finishing operation produces a plate with all the working characteristics of one produced by engraving alone, and at a significant reduction in cost. (See also *Graphic Arts,* page 1925.)   —Felix Giordano

Etching, an engraving process by which metal or glass is removed by chemical action. In some instances, as when etching is to prepare a metal surface for microexamination, the etching action is required to be very shallow. In most instances, a deeper etching action is needed, as in the production of printing plates, and the chemical milling of relatively large surfaces, especially of magnesium, aluminum, and similar metals.

The chemical, or *etchant,* used varies with the material to be etched. Etching time is regulated by the activity of the etchant and the desired depth of etch.

Parts to be etched are prepared by masking out the areas in which no etch is desired, then either immersing the parts in the etching solution or spraying the solution on them. The spraying process is often used in the production of printing plates, as it reduces the amount of undercut at the edges of the masked-out area. When the etching is completed, the masking material is stripped from the surface of the part, which is thoroughly cleaned and dried.

Masking material may be applied locally by hand. More often, masking-out is achieved through a photomechanical process by applying the masking material over the entire surface, then exposing it through a plate negative of the desired design. This exposure activates the sections of the masking coat that are exposed to light, so that subsequent immersion in water or special solutions washes it off, leaving the coat only where no etching is desired.   —Felix Giordano

Farm Machinery, or *agricultural implements,* the tools used on the farmstead for crop and animal production. Farm machinery includes tractors, plows, planters, harvesters, and similar equipment. Today these implements and motor vehicles amount to more than 20 per cent of the value of physical assets on farms. Over $2.5 billion of farm machines and equipment is shipped each year by manufacturers. Farm machines are primarily responsible for the high level of agricultural production in the United States today. Less than 7 per cent of our population live on farms today, compared with 40 per cent only 35 years ago.

The *tractor* is the power unit that replaced the horse on farms. Tractors and electric motors today supply the power that makes it possible for one man to produce enough food for himself and 32 other persons. This ratio is still 1 to 2 or 3 in most countries of the world.

About 4.5 million tractors are used on U.S. farms today. Each farm worker has 40 or more horsepower at his disposal. Tractors sold about the time of World War II were mostly less than 35 horsepower (hp). In the middle 1950's, only 30 per cent of the tractors sold were less than 35 hp, and 20 per cent were over 50 hp. In the middle 1960's, only 12 per cent were less than 35 hp, and 40 per cent were over 50 hp. In fact, many present-day agricultural tractors are in the range of 90 to 130 hp.

Hydraulic steering, comfortable seats, improved safety features, air-conditioned or heated cabs, remote-controlled hydraulic cylinders for lifting implements, and power-shift transmissions are now commonly found on farm tractors. The modern three-point hitch, (a device at the rear of the tractor for attaching implements) has hydralic lift control and automatic load and depth control; that is, the implement depth is automatically adjusted to a load the tractor can pull through the earth. Lights for night work and safety lights for highway travel are standard equipment on most tractors today.

Plows and other ground-working implements are generally attached to and lifted by the three-point hitch. A rear wheel raised and lowered by a hydraulic cylinder, controlled from the driver's seat, is sometimes placed on the implement to assist in lifting a portion of the weight for turning or transport. Modern tillage equipment is pulled at speeds up to 5 or 6 miles per hour (mph) and will cover 10 to 50 acres a day, depending on the size of tractor and width of implement.

Modern *planters* range from 2- to 12-row units. They may be pull-type with wheels or mounted on a tool bar attached to a three-point hitch. Planters may be equipped with fertilizer, insecticide, fungicide, and herbicide applicators in addition to the seeding mechanism. Hoppers or spray tanks are used, depending on whether the chemical is granular or liquid.

In the Corn Belt, planters are often pulled behind a disk or spring-tooth harrow. This is referred to as a minimum-tillage operation. Another minimum-tillage practice is referred to as "mulch planting"; planters are designed to plant in last year's stalks (mulch) without first plowing or disking. This practice is found mostly in the Great Plains, where moisture must be conserved in the soil.

Cultivators equipped either with sweeps or with rotary hoe wheels are used to till crops at speeds from 2 to 12 mph. However, the number of cultivations is often decreased today by the use of herbicides sprayed on or mixed in the soil at planting time. Selective herbicides are available for some crops that completely eliminate the need of cultivation for weed control. On sloping land, however, cultivation still may be needed to prevent water runoff. After crops are up, chemical herbicides may also be sprayed on weeds and grass with special applicators to protect the crop from the direct spray.

Harvesters for most major and many minor crops are highly perfected. Self-propelled models now account for 85 per cent of sales of grain combines, compared with 25 per cent in the early 1950's. Today's larger combines cut, thresh, and deliver grain to transport trucks as they travel through the field, and often harvest as much as 75 acres in a single day. There are approximately one million combines in use on farms in the United States.

Corn is harvested with both combines and conventional *pickers.* The corn head for combines has been available since 1956, yet already more corn heads than conventional pickers are sold each year. Corn heads on combines pour the shelled corn in the bin mounted on the machine. Pickers put corn ears (generally shucked) into trailers pulled behind the tractor and picker. Shelled corn harvested with combines often has to be dried with heated air before it is put in barns or silos for storage.

Hay balers are used to put up about 75 per cent of the annual 100 million tons of forage (excluding silage). Modern balers pick the hay up after it has dried in the sun and compress it into neatly formed packages approximately $14 \times 16 \times 30$ inches. Attachments are available to throw the bales into trailers pulled behind the machines. Bales can be dumped or mechanically conveyed into storage with a minimum of handling. It is estimated that approximately 375,000 balers are in use. About 500,000 have been produced and sold since the mid-1950's. The average life of this machine is about seven years or less, depending upon the amount of use and type of terrain.

In the irrigated desert areas of California, Arizona, Nevada, and New Mexico, a new method of packaging hay into small cubes has come into use. Present technology limits this method of harvest to these dry weather areas. The cubes are $1\frac{1}{4} \times 1\frac{1}{4} \times 2\frac{1}{2}$ inches (so-called "bite-size"). The machine picks up dry alfalfa, sprays a small amount of water on it, and compresses it into these cubes at a rate of about 5 tons per hour. These cubes are easier to handle, transport, and feed than the larger conventional bales.

INTERNATIONAL HARVESTER COMPANY

HARVESTING TECHNIQUES have advanced considerably. In the nineteenth century, men labored behind a horse-drawn reaper (*left*) to bind and stack grain. Today, one diesel-powered combine (*right*) not only cuts, but binds and stacks grain in one continuous operation.

INTERNATIONAL HARVESTER COMPANY

INTERNATIONAL HARVESTER COMPANY

MODERN MACHINERY has increased productivity on the farm. Automatic planting machinery (*left*) results in a mechanical precision in the sowing of seeds that could never be achieved by men. A pick-up baler (*right*) collects, binds, and deposits hay in a continuous operation.

Cotton has been conquered by mechanical picker and stripper-type harvesters. *Cotton pickers* have several hundred rotating spindles that engage the cotton lint and twist it from the burs that hold it on the plant. Another mechanism unwraps (doffs) the cotton from the teeth on the spindle, then air-blows it up to the carrying basket. In the drier areas of Texas and Oklahoma, *stripper-type harvesters* use long rotating nylon brushes to remove both cotton and bur from the plant. The burs are later removed at the cotton gin prior to the cleaning and removing of the lint from the seed.

Vegetables now harvested with machines include radishes, carrots, beets, green peas, and spinach. However, melons, celery, cauliflower, lettuce, and broccoli are proving more difficult to conquer mechanically.

Tree fruits such as almonds, walnuts, pecans, filberts, prunes, and cherries may be removed from trees by *boom* or *cable shakers*. Some are caught on canvas conveyors, while others are swept up off the ground.

Farmstead buildings and equipment are undergoing a rather rapid change to facilitate mechanization and automation. Electric service on farms and the availability of numerous types of controls and servomechanisms make automatic operations for conveying, processing, and feeding a reality. Automated poultry, dairy, and livestock feeding operations are leading the way.

—H. F. Miller

Fasteners, mechanical elements used to hold two or more parts together. Thousands of different types of fasteners are available, ranging from the common wire paper staple to large structural bolts several feet long. In general, fasteners can be classified as *threaded* or *plain*. Threaded fasteners include machine screws, cap screws, wood screws, nuts, bolts, and studs. Plain fasteners include nails, rivets, pins, and staples.

Wood screws with recessed or slotted heads are available in standard sizes. These screws are produced in lengths from ¼ inch to 5 inches and with flat, round, or oval heads.

Self-tapping screws are used in metal assembly work, and tap or form a thread in a drilled hole. In addition to slotted and recessed heads, self-tapping screws are available with hexagonal heads. These screws are widely used in joining plastic and metal assemblies for household appliances, such as refrigerators and washing machines.

Set screws fit into tapped holes and are available in a wide range of sizes, in either square head or headless types and with flat, cone, cup, oval, or dog points. Either a slot or socket is used to drive the headless types. The most common applications of set screws are lock or position sheaves or impellers on rotating shafts.

Machine screws are classified according to the style of head and/or the type of drive used to install them. Thus, round, flat, fillister, oval, truss, binding, and pan-head machine screws have slotted or recessed heads and are turned by a flat-blade or Phillips-head screwdriver. Hexagonal-head machine screws are turned by conventional wrenches or external sockets.

Bolts are most easily differentiated from screws by the addition of a nut. Bolts are installed in drilled holes and hold two or more parts together by the clamping force created as the nut is tightened. Produced with either round, square, or hexagonal heads, bolts are available in a wide range of diameters, lengths, and styles. The more common styles include machine bolts, stovebolts, and stud bolts.

Used as permanently installed fasteners in castings, stud bolts, or *studs*, are threaded at both ends. One end of the stud is screwed into a tapped hole while a nut is installed on the other end. The nut may be removed and assembled many times without damaging the thread in the soft casting.

Nails are the most common type of plain, or unthreaded, fastener and have been in use for thousands of years. Most nails fall into two categories: *wire nails*, as the name implies, are cold-formed from lengths of wire and are of standard circular cross section; *cut nails* have a rectangular cross section and taper from

head to point. Though hundreds of different types of nails are available, house carpenters use only *flat*, or *common*, nails and *finishing* nails. Flat-head nails are used for fastening the structural members of the house, while finishing nails are used on the trim work.

The length of nails is given in terms of pennies, which is a holdover from the days when nails were sold at so many pennies per hundred. The penny system, with *d* used as the symbol for pennies, now designates only the length. For example, 2d nails are 1 inch long; 3d, 1¼ inch; 4d, 1½ inch; up to 10d for 3-inch nails.

Rivets are made in a range of head styles and sizes for joining everything from pot handles to structural steel. They are fitted into a drilled or punched hole and headed by hammering or pressing. Solid rivets of aluminum alloy are used by the millions to fasten the components of a modern jet aircraft. Rivets are also widely used in high-speed assembly operations where they are inserted into the part and headed by automatic equipment.

When only one side of a part is accessible, a *blind rivet* is frequently used. Blind rivets are usually hollow and are set by pulling an oversize mandrel through the hole. When a fluid-tight joint is required, the mandrel is broken off in the rivet, plugging the hole.

Pins are inserted in pre-drilled holes for a great number of fastening operations. Plain round pins are pressed into slightly undersized holes to produce an interference fit. Tapered pins, with a taper of ¼-inch per foot, are used where disassembly of the part may be required.

Roll pins and the *Spirol pin* are made by rolling a strip of steel into a C-shaped sleeve or coil. Compressed and inserted into an under-size hole, the coiled pin expands against the walls to hold the pin securely. These pins are used as fasteners, hinges, shafts, or dowels.

Stapling, or *wire stitching*, is an outgrowth of the staples used to fasten paper together. Equipment is now available to staple sheet steel up to 1/16-inch thick. The process can be used to fasten metal to metal, or metal to rubber, cloth, wood, or plastics. The staples are preformed or supplied in wire reels, cut to length, and formed in the gun. Stapling or stitching is widely used in the automotive industry to attach trim materials to body panels.

—Joseph J. Kelleher

Fire Detection, methods of sensing fire in its early stages to alert people of its occurrence, so it may be quickly controlled and damage held to a minimum. Mechanical, electrical, and electronic equipment are customarily used for the purpose, but in its broadest sense the term would include the employment of watchmen and guards to signal discovery of fire.

A typical fire-detection system includes fire detectors placed at prescribed ceiling locations throughout the structure to be protected. These are connected to a control unit, which in electrical systems energizes the detection circuits. When a detector senses a fire, an audible or visible alarm is automatically given, either on the premises or at an alarm center operated by the fire department or privately. Detectors may be actuated by heat or by smoke or other gaseous product of combustion.

Heat detectors of the fixed-temperature type most commonly are thermostats utilizing the different coefficients of expansion of two metals under heat to close electrical contacts. There is also thermostatic cable employing two tensioned steel wires separated by a covering which melts at the rated temperature. Other heat detectors operate on the rate-of-rise principle, functioning when the rate of temperature increase at the detector exceeds a stated number of degrees a minute. One form uses pneumatic tubing in which pressure builds up as heat reaches the tubing, and the pressure is applied to a diaphragm. Another form operates on the thermoelectric principle, employing two sets of thermocouples so arranged that one set is exposed to convection and radiation while the other is shielded. There are also detectors combining the fixed-temperature and rate-of-rise principles.

The melting of a fusible element by heat is used to actuate a detector employing compressed gas as the energy source for the alarm mechanism, and a mechanical unit using a spring-wound motor to sound the alarm.

Customarily heat detectors are set to operate at 135 to 165 degrees (Fahrenheit) temperatures, but where normal ceiling temperatures exceed 100 degrees higher settings are used.

Smoke detectors most commonly employ photoelectric cells in which the change in current resulting from partial obscuring of a photoelectric beam by smoke is measured and an alarm tripped when this obscuration reaches a critical value. A flame detector also uses a photoelectric circuit which is responsive to changes of light intensity resulting from the flickering of flames. Ionization and resistance-bridge types of detectors are responsive to both smoke and gaseous products of combustion.

■**FIRE EXTINGUISHER.**—The extinguisher is a device containing a liquid or powder to be discharged on a fire, and capable of extinguishing a fire in its early stages. Basically a fire extinguisher consists of a container, an extinguishing agent, a pressure-producing device or agent, and a discharge orifice or hose and nozzle. A good extinguisher can be put into operation quickly and with reliable effectiveness.

Many types have been developed. To designate their suitability, fires have been divided into four principal classes: A, B, C, and D.

Class A fires, which involve ordinary combustible material, are extinguished by the cooling action of water or water-based liquids or by certain dry chemicals. Extinguishers for this purpose include manually operated *pump tanks; water* or *anti-freeze water solutions,* stored under pressure; or *soda-acid extinguishers,* actuated by mixing sulfuric acid with a sodium bicarbonate water solution. Special dry chemicals for Class A fires have a monammonium phosphate base.

Class B fires, which involve flammable and combustible liquids, need a blanketing-smothering or flame-interrupting effect for extinguishment. Extinguishers for this purpose employ *dry chemicals* (having a base of sodium bicarbonate, potassium bicarbonate, or monammonium phosphate) discharged by an expellent gas; *carbon dioxide* stored under pressure as a liquid and discharged as a gas; *foam* generated by mixing aluminum sulfate and a sodium bicarbonate water-based solution; or *bromotrifluoromethane,* a liquefied gas.

Class C fires, which involve "live" electrical equipment, must be extinguished with a nonconductive agent to avoid shock hazard to the user. *Dry chemical, carbon dioxide,* and *bromotrifluoromethane* extinguishers employ such agents and are useful for these fires as well as for Class B fires.

Class D fires, which involve combustible metals, require special extinguishing agents that will not react with the particular metal involved. There are a number of commercial extinguishers suitable for use on magnesium, zirconium, titanium, or sodium, and some special powders, applied by scoops, and some liquids which are effective on metal fires.

Extinguishers employing *carbon tetrachloride* or *chlorobromomethane* have also been used on Class B and C fires, but these are gradually being replaced because they are not as efficient and produce irritating and toxic vapors. Also available, but not currently in widespread usage, are *loaded-stream* (alkali-metal salts in water) and *wetting-agent extinguishers.*

Portable extinguishers are tested and labeled by Underwriters' Laboratories (UL), Factory Mutual Engineering Division (FM), and Underwriters' Laboratories of Canada (ULC). The labels certify that the device meets exacting requirements of construction and performance. Standards on the installation, maintenance, and use of extinguishers are issued by the National Fire Protection Association. —Deuel Richardson

FIRE TRUCKS are equipped with high-powered pumps and hoses, chemical foam, and rotating extension ladders to allow firemen to attack a fire effectively from a variety of angles.

Fire Prevention, measures directed towards preventing the occurrence of fire. Fire prevention differs from fire protection, which refers to the methods of providing for fire control or fire extinguishment. Prevention methods take three general forms: laws and regulations, inspection programs, and public education.

Fire-prevention laws and regulations control the types of materials, wiring, and equipment—such as those for heating and air conditioning—used in buildings; the storage and handling of flammable liquids and gases; the use of explosives and fireworks; and other common fire hazards. Arson is also a subject of such laws. The laws and regulations may originate with the state or the locality, and administration is customarily in the hands of a state or local fire marshal or similar officer. The great majority of fire prevention laws and regulations derive from standards and codes developed by the National Fire Protection Association.

Inspection programs are carried on, usually by fire departments, in order to discover and correct hazardous conditions before they cause fires. Schools, hospitals, and other public buildings may be inspected monthly for this purpose, and commercial and industrial structures at least once or twice yearly. An increasing number of fire departments inspect multiple residential properties on a regular schedule, and also are instituting inspections of private dwellings, which can be entered only by consent of the occupant. There is also a great deal of valuable self-inspection by occupants of buildings of all types.

Fire-prevention education is based on the premise that people are the principal causes of fire, and that public awareness of and interest in reducing fire hazards is a necessary adjunct to laws and inspections.

U.S. FOREST SERVICE

"SMOKEY" is a symbol of fire prevention.

Many private and public agencies engage in this activity, and a substantial number of commercial and industrial concerns provide employee education in avoiding and correcting fire hazards. Such activity usually climaxes during Fire Prevention Week, observed annually in October, but most programs now have year-round emphasis. —Deuel Richardson

Firearms, weapons that discharge a projectile by means of an explosion. The first firearms were developed in Europe about 1300. The first of these were *cannon,* large tubes closed at the breech end and pierced with a little hole called a *vent* from the top of the tube to the bore near the breech. To fire one of these weapons, a glowing wire or a burning coal was thrust into the vent to ignite the powder inside the tube. By 1350, smaller versions of these guns designed to be held in the hand had appeared. Known as *hand cannon,*

they were fastened to a wooden pole, the forerunner of the modern stock, so that they could be held more easily. Soon the vent was moved from the top of the barrel to the right side, and a ledge to hold a supply of priming powder was added beneath it. To fire these improved guns, the shooter used a glowing wick called a *match,* which he held in his right hand. Shortly after 1400, a pivoted arm was added to the gun to hold this match. Before 1475, the first true gunlock, the *matchlock,* appeared, complete with a trigger to operate the pivoted arm.

About 1500, a new era in the history of firearms opened with the invention of the *wheel lock.* This lock produced a spark by holding a piece of iron pyrites in contact with a revolving rough-edged wheel. Guns could now be used with one hand, and *pistols* became practical for the first time. At almost the same time, another form of lock developed that produced a spark by striking a piece of flint against steel. Several versions of this mechanism appeared in various parts of Europe during the next century. They included the *snaphaunce,* the *Scandinavian snaplock,* the *miquelet,* and terminated with the invention of the true *flintlock* in France about 1610.

In 1807, Alexander Forsyth developed a system for igniting the powder charge in firearms by using a compound that exploded when struck a sharp blow. This invention paved the way for the *percussion cap* and the later *metal-cased cartridge,* both of which appeared before 1825. Successful *rimfire cartridges* are usually considered to date from the Smith & Wesson design in 1858, and the *centerfire type* was perfected in the middle 1860's.

Rifling, the system of spiral grooves in a gun barrel that causes the bullet

GUN MANUFACTURING has come a long way since Eli Whitney built smoothbore muskets with interchangeable parts. The entire group of parts making up the firing mechanism and chamber of the M-16 rifle, now in combat use *(top)*, is interchangeable with the same system on the assault rifle *(center)* and on the submachine gun *(bottom)*. To ease military supply problems further, all three weapons can fire the same, standardized ammunition.

to rotate and thus travel straighter, first appeared in central Europe about 1500. Muzzle-loading rifles were slow to load because the bullet had to fit tightly and could not be dropped in loosely as in the *smoothbore*, which used a cartridge consisting of a charge of powder and a bullet wrapped in paper. Finally, in the 1840's, an elongated bullet with a hollow base was developed that could be dropped loosely down the barrel but would expand when fired so that it fit tightly. It was called the *minié ball* after Claude Étienne Minié, one of the men who helped perfect it. The rifle had been used for military purposes from the beginning, but with the minié ball it became a practical arm for all troops, and the smoothbore disappeared except for shotguns and some highly specialized weapons.

From the very beginning, some guns were made to load at the breech as well as at the muzzle. Some used threaded holes with screw plugs; others used moving breechlocks. The problem was to develop a tight gas seal that would not stick and jam. Over the years there were a number of more or less successful solutions of this problem, including the pattern of John H. Hall, which was issued to American troops in 1819 and became the first breechloading military weapon issued on a large scale. The real solution, however, came with the development of the metallic cartridge that not only held the load but also sealed the breech when it was fired.

Repeating firearms also appeared early, shortly after 1500. Some piled shots on top of each other in one barrel; some used multiple barrels that were either stationary or revolving. The true *revolver* appeared before 1600, and there were even two magazine types using loose powder and ball in the early 1600's. Successful revolvers were developed in the early 1800's with such percussion cap weapons as the Colt, but magazine repeaters had to wait for the metallic cartridge to become practical. About 1860 *lever-action rifles*, such as the Henry and the Spencer, paved the way for the later Winchester. The *bolt-action rifles* with box magazine was invented by James P. Lee in 1879. Automatic weapons came next. The first practical *auto-loading* pistol, the Schonberger, was manufactured in Austria in 1892. Rifles followed, then machine guns. Now almost all military and some sporting arms are automatic or at least semiautomatic. —Harold L. Peterson

Flood Control, the erection of dams, walls, and levees to prevent rivers from overflowing their banks. To protect himself from floods, the flood plain dweller builds walls and levees, at least around the cities and towns, and sometimes for many miles along rural riverbanks. Hydrologists measure winter snowpack in the mountains to get some idea of how much water the spring freshet will bring. Nevertheless, floods are unpredictable, for it is not possible to predict with certainty how much rain will fall and how fast snow will melt.

Still, man has made progress toward harnessing the rivers. As a general rule, floods are seasonal and rivers do not leave their banks all year long. Hence, the principle of a flood-control dam.

Engineers build dams in the upper reach of a river and its tributaries to create reservoirs. The flood-control reservoir is unique in that much of the time, especially during the flood season, its water level is kept low by letting normal river flow pass the dam. When a flood develops as a result of heavy rains or rapidly melting snow, gates in the dam are closed and the reservoir traps the floodwaters. One such reservoir may not do the job on a large river—a series of reservoirs must be built. Between them, they store most of the extra water. When the high river flow returns to normal, the stored floodwaters are released gradually allowing the river to reach normal depth.

This method can be called *true flood control*. The waters are trapped upstream and prevented from surging downriver, out of control, and from causing serious damage. Although the flood is not really prevented, damage is minimized by confining the high water upstream. —William W. Jacobus, Jr.

Flour Milling, the process of converting wheat and other cereals into meal. Finely ground meal is called *flour* especially when made from wheat. Milling is one of the world's oldest industries, going back to Neolithic culture in Europe.

Milling is almost completely automated; modern plants require the attention of very few skilled millers. The white, inner portion of the kernel, called the *endosperm*, is mechanically separated from the *bran*, or outer layers, and from the *germ*, which is the embryo of the new plant, in the middle. The process consists of continual grinding, called *gradual reduction*, and sifting which produces flour and a by-product called *millfeed*, made up of the coarser particles. Millfeed is used in the livestock industry. About 73 pounds of white flour are extracted from 100 pounds of wheat, although more can be obtained if coarser flour is desired.

Millers make flour from different types of wheat, depending upon ultimate usage. Strong, high-protein wheat flours are used by bread bakers; soft wheat flours by cake and cookie bakers; and extrahard durum wheat flours by spaghetti and macaroni manufacturers. Specialty flours are made from rye, corn, and barley. American flour is exported to more than 100 countries.

White flour is *enriched* with vitamins and minerals, to government specifications, to replace those lost in the milling process. Enrichment, introduced in 1941, adds to the nutritional value of the product.

The larger millers make cake mixes, breakfast foods, and snacks, all having a processed cereal base.

■**HISTORY.**—In early times, grain was milled by rubbing it between two stones. Next came *millstones*, op-

erated in pairs. They were large, flat, and corrugated to provide an abrasive action. The bottom, or *nether*, millstone remained stationary while the top, or *runner*, stone rotated on a vertical axis. The grain was fed into an opening in the center of the upper millstone. As the stone turned, the grain gradually worked its way to the outer edges to emerge in ground form. The product was then sifted to remove the coarser particles, which sometimes were ground. The millstones were powered by hand labor, later by animals, and subsequently by water, wind, and steam power. Today most are electrically driven.

In the 1870's, the milling process was revolutionized. The Minneapolis millers, the leaders of the industry, introduced a new system of milling, developed in Hungary, involving the use of special cast-iron rolls, cylindrical in shape and corrugated.

By 1900, there were about 8,000 flour mills in the United States. Gradually, centralized operation was found to be more economical, with the result that today there are about 400 mills in the United States capable of producing a total of 95 millions pounds of flour every 24 hours. About 200 of these mills produce 85 per cent of the flour.

Buffalo is the largest milling center in the United States, with Kansas City, Mo., ranking second. Minneapolis, once the largest producer, is the headquarters of five of the nation's largest milling firms.

Though some of the larger mills have been closed, new ones have opened elsewhere. The trend is toward the erection of plants in areas of growing population, such as California, or in areas where transportation rates are more favorable to the markets served. Most remaining older mills have been completely modernized and re-equipped.

■**PROCESS.**—Essentially, the milling process still involves the use of three main machines: the roller mill, the purifier, and the sifter. In recent years, other machines have been developed for *impact milling*, and the separation and fractionation of flour by *air classification*. All are refinements and improvements of the basic process. Air conveying of stock, using pneumatic systems, is a major feature of modern mills.

The flour production process is divided into four main parts. First, the wheat is received and stored in elevators alongside the mill. Next, it is cleaned and conditioned, that is, it is prepared so that the separation of the endosperm from the bran can be efficiently performed. Some wheats are too hard and dry; others too soft and wet. Then comes the milling operation itself, after which the flour is moved to the warehouse where it is packed in sacks or placed in huge bins preparatory to conveying in bulk by trucks and railcars.

Throughout the process, chemists are continually checking the product for quality, and sanitarians inspect for purity and cleanliness. —George Swarbreck

Frozen Foods. See *Food Preservation*.

Furnace, an enclosure in which heat is generated by burning a fuel, or in some other manner. The heat produced in a furnace must be removed in some way for external use or made use of within the furnace itself.

The burning of fuel in a home furnace produces heat, which is then distributed through ducts as hot air or through pipes as hot water or steam. A furnace used to produce steam is known as a *boiler furnace.* The largest of these, which are designed for steam power plants, have walls lined with pipes through which water flows as it is being converted to steam. Smaller furnaces are frequently lined with firebrick or other refractories that will withstand high temperature.

Furnaces burning gas or liquid fuels are fired through burners or atomizers, and the exhaust gases are removed through a chimney or stack. Coal-fired boilers may be fed by various types of stokers or through pulverized fuel burners. If coal is to be burned, provision must be made for the removal of ashes.

Industrial furnaces of various types are used in iron and steel and other industries as part of the production process. A *blast furnace,* for example, is a tall column in which coke is burned on the hearth and hot gases pass upward through limestone, coke, and iron ore. This produces pig iron. *Open-hearth furnaces* and *electric furnaces* are also used in the steel industry.

Electric furnaces are available in many different designs. Some of them, particularly the *arc furnace,* operate at extremely high temperatures.   —Hunter Hughes

Furniture Manufacturing, the production of home and office furnishings. The furniture manufacturing industry originated with the early cabinetmakers and carpenters who handfashioned chests, cupboards, tables, benches, bedframes, and chairs. Early American designs were copies from European sources, principally English, Dutch, French, and Swedish, with certain differences due to the skill and facilities of the makers and the tastes and needs of the users.

Markets, manpower, and materials have influenced the formation and relocation of furniture manufacturing centers. Grand Rapids, Mich., no longer dominates in this respect. Jamestown, N.Y., and Gardner, Mass., are of lesser importance. Chicago and Rockford, Ill., are no longer significant furniture manufacturing centers. New York City is still important, particularly in upholstered and custom furniture. The Los Angeles area has grown extensively, especially in the manufacture of upholstered goods. Fort Smith, Ark., and northern Mississippi have expanded in industry importance, and Indiana accounts for substantial volume, being especially noted for cabinets and desks. The dynamic growth has been in the Southeast, commonly known as the High Point, N.C., area. Big, modern factories are situated in southern Virginia, central and western North Carolina, and eastern Tennessee.

The industry's products are diverse: wood and metal household and office furniture, both upholstered and unupholstered; mattresses and bed springs; public building furniture; partitions and fixtures. Hence, manufacturing practices vary. Depending on the product, operations may include cutting, machining, or fabricating wood or metal parts; making plywood or plastic laminated panels; assembly and fitting of parts; sanding and finishing of surfaces; cutting and sewing of upholstery fabrics; springing up of seating units and installation of padding and upholstery covers; handling of incoming materials and supplies; and expediting production and shipping to conform with sales requirements. Transportation poses unusual problems because furniture is rather bulky and easily damaged.

Production techniques also vary with furniture type and style. Upholstered furniture production lines are seldom conveyorized, but can be. Finishing departments of wood and metal furniture factories usually are equipped with conveyors. Precision, high-production woodworking machinery and powered hand tools are widely used.

Marketing requirements determine the kind, style, and price of furniture to be made. Designers are often employed to do the styling. In a larger company, product engineering is performed by a separate department, while in a smaller firm the plant superintendent may decide how the furniture is to be made.

To improve efficiency, furniture plants usually establish time standards for performing certain jobs. A per-piece rate is then paid the worker, or he is given a bonus for producing quantities above the standard, provided he meets quality requirements.

Most furniture manufacturers depend on vendors for metal and plastic parts, hardware, springs, turnings, carvings, fasteners, upholstery filling and covers. Metal furniture manufacturers do their own fabricating, at least in part.

New materials have brought about changes in furniture construction and processes. Particle board, a pressed board composed of wood flakes and fibers glued together, has almost completely replaced edge-glued lumber for cores of panels with veneer or plastic laminate surfaces. Hardboard, a thinner, dense panel of pressed wood fibers, has replaced plywood in many case and mirror backs as well as on drawer bottoms. It is also used for exterior surfaces to be painted or printed to resemble wood grain.

Although the industry consists of a large number of small manufacturers, its overall volume constitutes big business. For example, consumers spend as much on furniture and household equipment, including radio and television, as they do on automobiles and parts. With a rapid increase in new household formations, the industry expects to achieve dramatic growth by 1975. Along with this expansion will come unprecedented changes in the industry, both in the factory and in the marketplace.   —Raymond A. Helmers

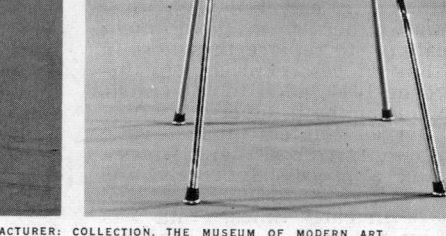

CHARLES EAMES, DESIGNER; HERMAN MILLER, MANUFACTURER; COLLECTION, THE MUSEUM OF MODERN ART   KNOLL ASSOCIATES, INC.: EERO SAARINEN, DESIGNER

FURNITURE of molded plastic (*left, right*) and plywood (*center*) can be beautiful, functional, and practical for mass production.

ILLINOIS TOOLWORKS, INC.   "PRODUCT ENGINEERING"

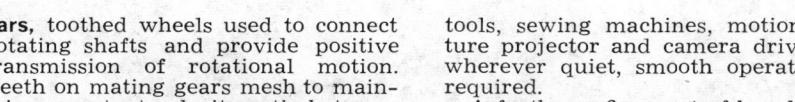

GEAR and pinion (*above*) have skewed axis for greater power. Bevel gear is at *right*.

Gears, toothed wheels used to connect rotating shafts and provide positive transmission of rotational motion. Teeth on mating gears mesh to maintain a constant velocity ratio between the driven and driving elements.

Spur gears have their teeth cut parallel to the gear's axis of rotation and can only be used to connect parallel shafts. *External spur gears* have teeth pointing away from the center of the gear, while the teeth of *internal spur gears* point toward the axis. A *rack and pinion* is a pair of spur gears with one gear, the rack, considered to be a circle of infinite radius. The rack and pinion converts rotary motion into linear motion, or vice versa.

Although most gears are circular, noncircular gears—which produce velocity ratios that change in a precise manner—are employed for special applications.

Helical gears have their teeth running on parallel axes but cut obliquely to the gear axis. Cutting the teeth obliquely increases the length of each tooth, and the contact between mating teeth proceeds from one edge across the tooth face to the opposite edge. Helical gears run more quietly than spur gears, especially at high speeds. *Herringbone gears* have double helical teeth of opposing twist, eliminating the axial thrust produced by single helical gears.

When shafts cross at an angle of less than 90°, *crossed helical gears* are used to transmit motion. Crossed helical gears have less load-carrying ability, because the teeth make point contact rather than line contact, as in conventional helical gears.

When shafts cross at right angles or intersect, *bevel gears* are used to transmit motion between them. *Straight bevel gears* have teeth which, if extended inward, would come together at the center line of the intersecting shafts. *Spiral bevel gears* with curved and oblique teeth overcome the limitations of straight bevel gears and provide gradual engagement, eliminating impact. These gears are employed for machine tools, sewing machines, motion picture projector and camera drives, or wherever quiet, smooth operation is required.

A further refinement of bevel gears is the *hypoid gear,* which is used to transmit motion between intersecting shafts that are neither parallel nor intersecting. These gears run smoothly and quietly and are widely used in automobile differentials. Reduction ratios of up to 60 to 1 are possible with hypoid gear sets, but due to the sliding tooth action, their efficiency is lower than bevel gears. The sliding action of these gears requires a special hypoid fluid for their lubrication.

—Joseph J. Kelleher

Guided Missile, a class of weapons characterized by the fact that they are self-propelled and that their flight-path can be changed, either by radio commands from a guidance center or by built-in (on-board) devices. While propulsion by rocket is the most common, it can also be by pulsejet, turbojet, or ramjet. However, not every rocket is a guided missile, and unguided bombardment rockets must be considered a special type of artillery. Missiles are classified according to their purpose: for example, an *air-to-air* missile is fired by one aircraft against another, and a *ground-to-air* missile is fired from the ground or from shipboard against aircraft. The most numerous group, the *ground-to-ground* missiles, are subdivided according to their range: *tactical missiles,* with ranges from 50 to 150 miles; *intermediate range ballistic missiles* (IRBM), with ranges from 500 to about 2,500 miles; and *intercontinental ballistic missiles* (ICMB), with ranges of more than 4,000 miles. Naturally, the longer its range, the larger the size of a missile, for most of the take-off weight is fuel. The trend in military missiles is in the direction of solid fuels. Though much more expensive than liquid fuels, a solid-fuel missile is not only more convenient to handle, but also can be launched on very short notice. (See also *Astronautics.*)

—Willy Ley

Gyroscope, a wheel universally mounted on bearings so that its axis can be made to point in any desired direction. The gyroscope is a useful device because, when spinning rapidly, its axis of rotation tends to maintain its initial direction despite the presence of forces that would otherwise change that direction.

Imagine a spinning gyroscope mounted, as in the accompanying illustration. Because of gravity, the spinning wheel tends to fall. But because of its rotation, the wheel revolves instead about the vertical direction Y-Y'. This slow rotation about Y-Y' is called *precession.* If pressure is applied about the vertical axis (V), the gyro, instead of turning vertically, turns or "precesses" about its horizontal axis (H).

In a practical gyroscope, the wheel (heavy for its size) and its axle are mounted within three gimbal rings. Three sets of low-friction bearings minimize the external forces that can affect the spinning wheel. A small motor produces the wheel's rotation, and the axis of the wheel constantly maintains any preset direction despite the motion of the airplane or ship to which the gyroscope's frame is attached. The rotors, or wheels, of directional gyroscopes vary from about one inch in diameter to several inches, and they spin at velocities up to 6,000 revolutions per minute. The tendency of a gyroscope to maintain a constant direction is called *gyroscopic inertia.*

■**AUTOMATIC PILOT.**—Gyroscopes are the heart of automatic-pilot systems used on modern aircraft. In practice, a computer, a number of servomechanisms, and other electronic equipment are used to take advantage of the gyroscope's directional properties without disturbing their delicate balance. In the automatic pilot, a vertical gyroscope controls ailerons and elevators, while a directional gyroscope is used for rudder control. With the help of these gyroscopes, which resist deflective forces, the automatic pilot enables a plane to fly a preset course without human assistance.

■**GYROCOMPASS.**—A gyrocompass is a

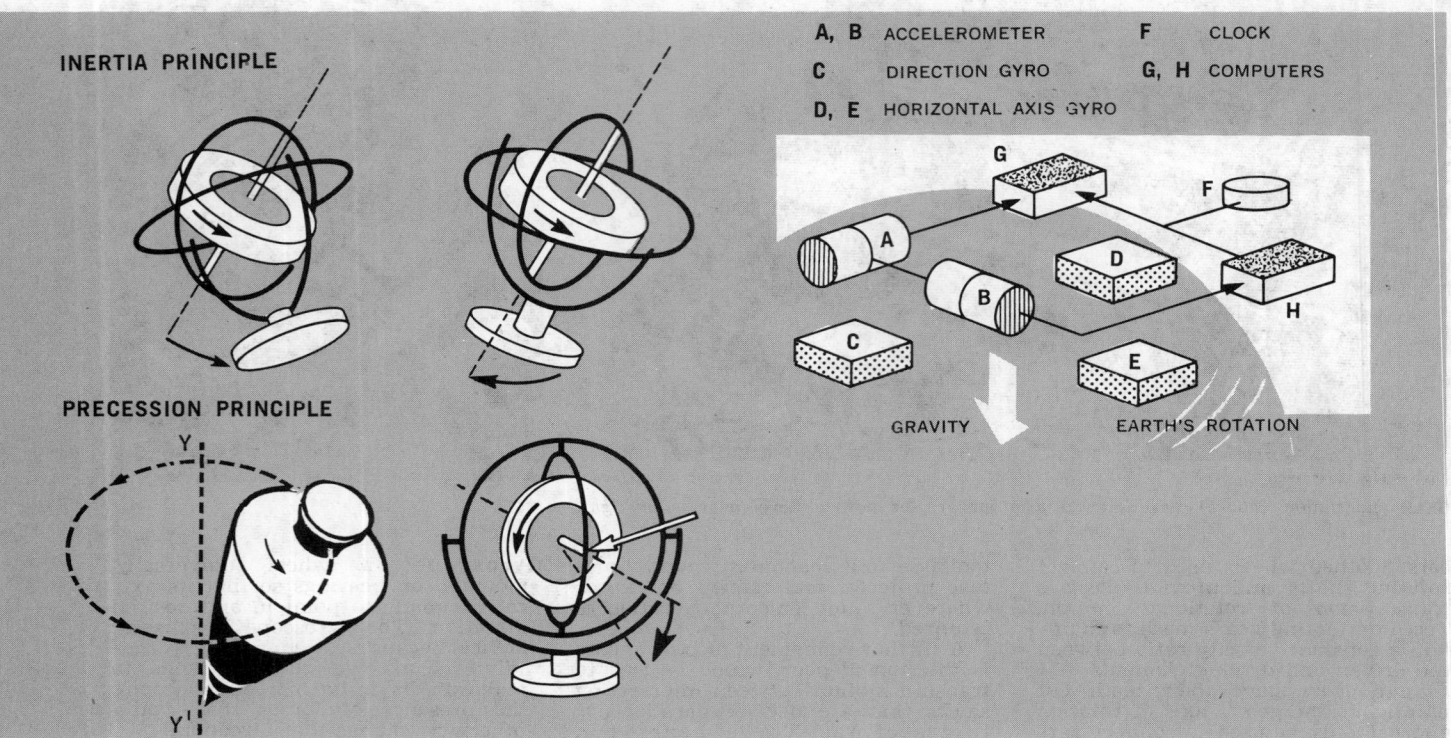

INERTIA PRINCIPLE

PRECESSION PRINCIPLE

A, B ACCELEROMETER   F   CLOCK
C   DIRECTION GYRO   G, H COMPUTERS
D, E HORIZONTAL AXIS GYRO

GRAVITY   EARTH'S ROTATION

more complicated device than the directional gyroscope. It makes use of the earth's rotational motion to cause precession of the gyroscope until it points in the north-south direction. The gyrocompass is widely used on planes and on ships where the presence of steel renders the magnetic compass unreliable.

■ **INERTIAL GUIDANCE.**—Gyroscopes make it possible for rockets, missiles, and submerged submarines to navigate accurately by means of inertial guidance or dead reckoning. Devices called *accelerometers* are used to measure the acceleration of the vehicle. With this information and the elapsed time, computers can calculate the distance traveled.

In order to operate accurately, the accelerometers must be kept at right angles to the force of gravity at all times. Otherwise, serious errors would be introduced because the devices cannot tell the difference between gravitational effects, which they should ignore, and vehicle accelerations, which they should measure. To eliminate this source of error, accelerometers are mounted on a platform which is stabilized in the horizontal plane by a pair of gyroscopes. This keeps the accelerometers horizontal, or perpendicular to the force of gravity. A third directional gyroscope keeps the stable platform pointing in the desired direction, regardless of the motion of the vehicle. Similar methods are used in the inertial guidance of torpedos.

■ **GYROSCOPIC STABILIZER.**—The marine gyroscopic stabilizer is a device that reduces the rolling of a ship by counteracting the forces produced by waves against the hull. As each wave strikes the ship, the stabilizer goes into operation, thereby preventing large oscillations from building up. The heart of the stabilizer is a massive gyroscope fastened to the structural members of the ship. The rotors of such gyroscopes are often over 10 feet in diameter. Gyroscopes and accelerometers are also used in the sensitive apparatus of Gyrofin ship stabilizers. This method uses the speed of the ship through the water to prevent rolling.

—William C. Vergara

Heating Systems, equipment for the maintenance of a closed space—office, home, or shop at a comfortable temperature during cold weather. The amount of heat supplied and the method of application depends on the outside temperature and the heat loss through the enclosure.

When planning a heating installation or plant, a heat balance must be calculated. This involves estimates of the heat lost through the walls of the structure to be heated and average temperature outside the structure. Finally the temperature to be maintained in the structure is selected depending on its occupancy and use. Heat lost through the walls depends on the type of construction, insulation, number of windows, and leakage and ventilation losses.

Once a heat balance has been calculated. This involves estimates heating units can be selected.

■ **STEAM HEATING.**—In steam heating, a boiler burning coal, natural gas, or oil converts water into steam. A system of pipes carries the hot steam from the boiler to cast-iron radiators or nonferrous convectors in the specific locations to be heated. The water that condenses within the radiators or convectors is returned to the boiler to be reused. Steam heating systems are relatively inefficient and require considerable maintenance, but are less expensive to install than hot-water systems.

■ **HOT-WATER HEATING.**—Hot-water heating systems are similar to steam systems except that the heat-transfer medium is a liquid rather than a gas. Water, heated in a boiler, circulates through the closed system to the radiators and convectors and, after giving up most of its heat, returns to the boiler. Hot-water heating systems are more expensive than steam systems to install, but are more efficient.

■ **HOT-AIR HEATING.**—A hot-air heating system requires ducts and blowers to carry warmed air to individual grills, from which it passes into the space to be heated. In some systems, the room air is returned into the system for reheating, for a system of this type is less expensive to operate—although more costly to install—than one requiring the introduction of outside air. Hot-air systems require considerable space for duct work and blowers. However, since the same ducts can also be used for central air conditioning, these systems are becoming more popular.

■ **ELECTRIC HEATING.**—An electric heating system relies on the generation of heat in resisting elements at each location to be warmed. Electric systems are the least expensive to install, have quick response and quiet operation, and permit a different temperature to be easily maintained at each location. However, the cost of operation is prohibitive except in localities where electric power is very cheap. (See also *Refrigeration,* page 1710.)

—Joseph J. Kelleher

Household Appliances, electric- or gas-powered devices used primarily in the home to ease the workload of homemakers. Although electricity became widely used by 1910, it served chiefly for lighting and power. By 1918, electric home refrigerators and ranges were developed and marketed, and electrical household appliances gained general acceptance. America's gas industry was born in 1816; a vast network of pipelines now crisscrosses the country. It is believed that the first gas range in the United States was introduced in 1840; 100 families were using gas ranges by 1859. In 1895, an instantaneous gas water heater with thermostatic control, the first automatic home appliance, was invented.

Since the introduction of the first electrical and gas household appliances there has been a flow of new products to the marketplace, interrupted only by World War II. Among the electrical appliances now in use are those for food preparation, such as the blender, can opener, ice crusher, food mixer, drink mixer, food chopper, juicer, and slicing knife. Cooking appliances include gas and electric ranges, gas-fired grills, and portable electric cooking utensils, such as the fry pan, griddle, toaster, coffee maker, waffle baker, egg cooker, broiler, table oven, saucepan, pressure cooker, corn popper, baby-food warmer, and bottle warmer. There are electric refrigerators, freezers, and combination refrigerator-freezers, as well as laundry appliances to wash, dry, and iron clothes.

Appliances for housecleaning include, in addition to several styles of vacuum cleaner, the floor polisher, rug shampooer, floor scrubber, upholstery shampooer, and furniture buffer. For other household chores there are electric and gas dishwashers, electric waste food disposers and gas incinerators, electric starters for charcoal fires, and defrosters for refrigerators. Household appliances now also include beauty and personal care products. The electric shaver was among the first of these; now

there are hair dryers, toothbrushes, manicure sets, vibrators, and massagers. One of the newest gas appliances is a toilet with a gas-fired unit for complete disposal of human waste without the use of sewers or plumbing.

■**NEW DESIGNS.**—There have been many refinements in appliances since their introduction. Extensive use of thermostats and other controls that sense a condition and respond to it has made appliances automatic to varying degrees. In some cases, appliances are programmed to permit the operator to control several factors with the push of one button.

The development of new materials for appliance construction has affected design. For example, seamless plastic door liners for refrigerators can now be formed with shelves and storage compartments for butter and eggs. More efficient insulating materials, such as foamed-in-place plastic, have made possible the larger-capacity refrigerators that fit the floor space of older thick-walled models. Anodized aluminum, stain-resistant porcelain enamels, glass, ceramics, stainless steel, and copper are among the materials used, in addition to steel, in the manufacture of household appliances.

Colored appliances have been on the market for many years. The number of colored major appliances sold annually has increased steadily since the early 1950's. Pink, turquoise, and yellow have been popular; wood tones, brushed stainless steel, and copper finishes have also been used extensively, although white still accounts for a sizable part of the market.

In the years following World War II, people were eager to buy any appliances that were available, and the builder market, with its demands for low prices and simple, low-cost installation, became an important factor in the appliance business. Consumers had many more appliances in their homes than ever before, but there were not enough trained appliance servicemen. The result was a rising wave of complaints about ap-

pliance breakdowns, the high cost of repairs, and the delays and other annoyances involved in getting repairs. Consumers became more selective in their purchases, seeking more reliable performance. Manufacturers responded with greater effort than ever before to design appliances with less probability of breakdown and with more readily accessible, more easily replaced or repaired working parts. Manufacturers, distributors, and dealers also increased their efforts to train service personnel and to reduce the time needed to obtain parts.

■**RANGES.**—Electric ranges require 230-volt, 3-wire service. Gas ranges may be fueled with natural or liquefied petroleum (bottled) gas, and many also use 115-volt electric service for clocks, timers, and lights. Oven thermostats are standard equipment; thermostatically controlled burners for surface cooking are available. Various oven control systems are also available; some use a delay, cook, and stop sequence; some cook and hold; some delay, cook, and hold.

Electronic ranges, which use microwave energy to cook food, require 230-volt, 3-wire electric service. They have been well accepted commercially but have gained only a small share of the domestic market. Electronic cooking is much faster than conventional cooking by heat, but cooking time increases with the amount of food to be cooked. The oven in such a device stays cool unless a heating element is used for browning. Any nonmetallic plates, containers, or wrappings may be used.

A range may be free-standing with one or two ovens, or oven and broiler, beneath the range cooking surface, or it may consist of one or two wall ovens, or oven and broiler, and a separate drop-in range top. The range may be wall-hung or stacked on a base cabinet with an oven at eye level and the cooking units or burners below it at counter level, or it may be a free-standing console with an eye-level oven over the range top and another oven below it.

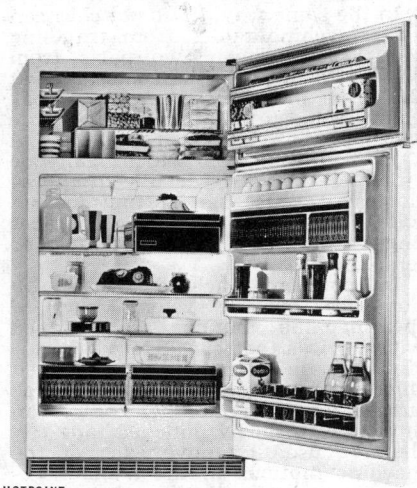

HOTPOINT

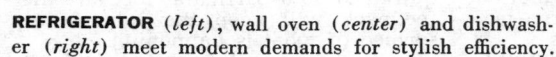

REFRIGERATOR (*left*), wall oven (*center*) and dishwasher (*right*) meet modern demands for stylish efficiency.

■**REFRIGERATORS AND FREEZERS.**—All of the refrigerators, freezers, and combination refrigerator-freezers now on the market are electric. Gas refrigerators did not prove competitive with electric models and are no longer being promoted in the United States.

A refrigerator may have a compartment for relatively short-term storage of frozen food. Such a compartment is separated from the fresh-food storage compartment by a chiller tray or drawer. The freezer compartment of a combination refrigerator-freezer is completely insulated and positioned separate from the fresh-food compartment. The freezer may be above, below, or on the side of the refrigerator section; in some models, the refrigerator is at eye level, with the freezer below it, under a counter-height work surface. Freezers, whether separate chest or upright models or in combination with refrigerators, maintain zero-tone temperatures that are suitable for freezing and long-term storage of frozen foods. There are manually defrosted refrigerators and freezers, automatically defrosted refrigerators, and refrigerators and freezers that are free of frost within the food compartments.

Thermoelectric refrigerators, unlike conventional refrigerators, do not use compressors but rely on the cooling effect produced by the flow of electric current through the junction of two dissimilar metals, the so-called *Peltier effect.* They are in limited production. Thermoelectric refrigerators are quiet and durable. At present, the high cost of materials used in them makes it economically unsound to produce the large sizes generally required for home use.

■**LAUNDRY APPLIANCES.**—A *washer* is a power-driven machine for washing fabrics in water. If automatic, as are the majority sold in the United States, it fills with water at a selected temperature (or as near to it as the water delivered to the washer permits), washes, rinses, extracts water, and stops—all by one setting of the controls without further attention by the user. A semiautomatic washer requires that controls be reset for one or more operations after the original setting, although the fabrics need not be removed. *Spinner washers,* in which items are washed in one container and removed to another for rinsing and water extraction, and *wringer washers* equipped with power-driven rollers for extracting water by squeezing, are still being made.

A *dryer* is a power-driven device for drying fabrics by evaporation through the use of various combinations of heat, air flow, and tumbling. Electricity or gas may be used as the heat source. Dryers may be time-controlled, with the drying time preselected by the operator, or they may be automatically controlled, with the drying time determined by measurements made by the machine.

Automatic ironers are being manufactured, but annual sales are low. *Hand irons* may be dry or combination steam-dry models; some steam-

AMERICAN SUGAR REFINING COMPANY

ELECTRICAL CONTROL DEVICES that represent automation, are the heart and nervous system of many industrial processing centers. A technician in the control room can observe and regulate both the material flow and the product quality at each stage of the process.

dry irons can also spray fabrics. Thermostatic control of irons is standard; in some models, steam can be produced at the low sole plate temperatures required for ironing thermoplastic synthetic fabrics.

■**DISHWASHERS.**—Dishwashers may be built in or portable, serve to wash, rinse, and dry dishes. Most models are electric; there is a gas dishwasher which so heats the water for the final rinse that the dishes dry without additional heat. The trend has been toward larger capacity, better washability due to improved water distribution and more effective detergents, and choice of cycles.

■**VACUUM CLEANERS.**—Vacuum cleaners utilize straight suction or a combination of suction and power-driven beaters and brushers to loosen and pick up dirt. The trend has been toward uprights with more easily used attachments for above-floor cleaning and toward suction cleaners (tanks and canisters) with better rug-cleaning performance, often achieved by power-driven brushes. Lightweight vacuum cleaners for quick pickup cleaning are often used as second cleaners in the home. Centrally installed vacuum cleaning systems for home use are gaining in importance.

■**SPECIAL FEATURES.**—Detachable thermostatic controls on many types of cookware make them both automatic and immersible. Nonstick coatings and other easily cleaned finishes are widely used. Cordless electric appliances, with rechargeable cells or batteries of cells, offer increased mobility and, in some cases, safety, although the amount of power that can be stored is limited. Available cordless appliances include toothbrushes, shavers, food mixers, ice crushers, and vacuum cleaners.

—Rose Marie Burnley

Industrial Control, the automatic regulation of machinery for safety, consistency, speed, or to enable operators of very complicated machinery to keep track of all the motions. Electric switches or relays, hydraulic devices, electric circuits, and/or pneumatic devices, are combined to create the control systems. For example, if a large press has two operators and there are four widely-spaced start buttons so connected that the ram of the press will not come down against the die unless all four buttons are pushed at once, it will take four hands pushing start buttons to make the press operate. This is a good safety device, which prevents one operator from starting the press before the other operator is ready.

In the same way, *limit switches* can keep machine tables from traveling too far; can keep two parts from coming together in the same place at the same time; and can stop a machine from cutting threads in a hole that has not yet been drilled.

Tracer controls, which can be either electric or hydraulic in operation, will cause the cutting tool to follow the same path that a tracer finger follows along a pattern or template.

In modern machine tools with numerical control systems, each of the machine motions is equipped with devices that can determine precisely where the machine is and feed this information back to the control. Instructions fed to the control in numerical form by punched tape can then be used to move each of the machine motions in the manner required to do a particular job, and the feedback will keep the control informed of what is happening.

—Anderson Ashburn

Industrial Engineering, the branch of engineering concerned with the planning and control of industrial production operations and the measurement and reduction of their cost. The rise of industrial engineering has been largely an American development, growing out of the struggle to secure increased production in view of ever-increasing labor costs. Some of the basic ideas may be traced far back to ancient times, however. The Greeks recognized that specialization —for example, having one worker make only the soles and another the uppers of sandals—led to increased output. Adam Smith in his *Wealth of Nations* (1776) emphasized the importance of such specialization. More recently, the development of mass production and interchangeable manufacture has also contributed to the movement toward what has been characterized as *engineered production.*

Frederick Winslow Taylor (1856–1915) is usually regarded as the father of scientific management, or industrial engineering. In the 1880's, he undertook studies for the Midvale Steel Company of Philadelphia. Taylor advised that special attention be given to selecting workers with special skills, and that they be directed and guided in their work to secure the more effective operation of their tools and machines and greater production. He also suggested that similar studies be made of management. Frank B. Gilbreth (1868–1924) pioneered in what were known as *time and motion studies,* leading to the reduction of movements on the part of the worker in carrying out his operations.

Opposed at first by both labor and management, efforts have continued to reduce costs and increase production through studies not only of manufacturing operations but also of the selection of tools and machines and all phases of management and operation. It is becoming more widely recognized that higher pay for workers can result only in the inflation of prices unless increased pay is accompanied by increased production. These methods and ideas are also receiving increased attention in foreign lands where labor conditions earlier had discouraged such advances. —James Kip Finch

Instrumentation, the use of instruments for the measurement and/or control of complex systems and processes. A system might consist of a jet aircraft or, a satellite-tracking radar system, and a process might range from a municipal water-purification plant to a steel mill. Instrumentation is a basic factor in automation, where it substitutes the precision of a machine for the judgment or performance of a human operator.

The instrument panel of a car is an example of instrumentation in its simplest form. The operator can observe the speed, water temperature, oil pressure, and fuel level of the vehicle on suitable meters or indicators. With this information, he can control the car efficiently. A more complex system would include recording and control instruments in a central place so that the operator could supervise an entire industrial process. In its most advanced form, an instrumentation system would be completely automatic, requiring little or no human attention. Any failure of the system to function correctly would be brought to the attention of an operator by a signal.

Instruments used in industrial processes vary in complexity from simple pressure gauges to sophisticated interferometers that measure dimensions by means of light waves. In chemical plants, where production is on a continuous flow basis, instruments measure and control flow rates and chemical composition. In modern factories, computers control the operation of machines from the raw material stage to the finished product.

In modern technology, instrumentation is most advanced in the field of space exploration. Complex instrumentation is used to control the velocity and trajectory of a spacecraft and to maintain communication between the spacecraft and the ground. Precise measurements are made of conditions in the spacecraft and automatic corrections are made to the vehicle's temperature, attitude, and orbit. The future will see greater use of instrumentation as man achieves greater efficiency in his daily work. —William C. Vergara

Iron and Steel Production, the processes by which iron is purified and alloyed to produce steel. The *Bessemer process* was the first to answer the Industrial Revolution's need for inexpensive, mass-produced steel. William Kelly, an American, and Henry Bessemer, an Englishman, a few years apart independently conceived of refining molten pig iron into steel by subjecting it to a strong air blast. They correctly theorized that oxygen in the air blast would burn off the excess carbon in the iron and also burn out most of the other undesirable elements formed during combustion.

The process developed by Bessemer gained the wider acceptance of the two, and became identified with his name. As it was finally developed, the *Bessemer converter* was somewhat pear-shaped, with many small holes in the bottom for the admission of the air blast. It requires about 20 minutes to make a heat of steel in the Bessemer converter, and capacities range from 5 to 25 tons of steel per heat. The first production of Bessemer steel in the United States dates from 1864. Within a few years, the Bessemer process became the major steel producer in this country, a position it held until it was overtaken in 1908 by the open-hearth process.

■**OPEN-HEARTH PROCESS.**—The open-hearth process, developed by the Siemens brothers in England and the Martin brothers in France, became known abroad as the *Siemens-Martin process* but is more commonly called the open-hearth process in the United States. It is so called because the elongated, saucer-shaped hearth is open to the sweep of the flames that refine the steel.

The furnace is regenerative in that the hot gases from combustion of the fuel are passed through regenerative brick chambers where they give up part of their heat. The direction of the gas flow is reversed periodically, and the incoming cold air for com-

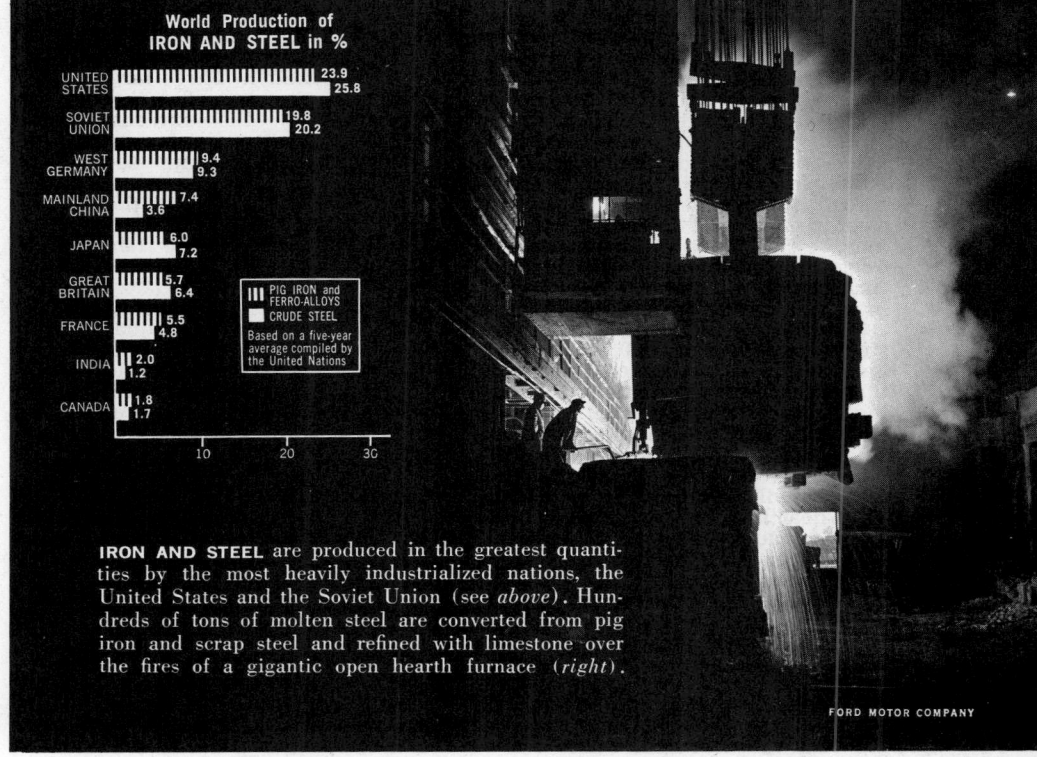

World Production of IRON AND STEEL in %

	PIG IRON and FERRO-ALLOYS	CRUDE STEEL
UNITED STATES	23.9	25.8
SOVIET UNION	19.8	20.2
WEST GERMANY	9.4	9.3
MAINLAND CHINA	7.4	3.6
JAPAN	6.0	7.2
GREAT BRITAIN	5.7	6.4
FRANCE	5.5	4.8
INDIA	2.0	1.2
CANADA	1.8	1.7

Based on a five-year average compiled by the United Nations

IRON AND STEEL are produced in the greatest quantities by the most heavily industrialized nations, the United States and the Soviet Union (see *above*). Hundreds of tons of molten steel are converted from pig iron and scrap steel and refined with limestone over the fires of a gigantic open hearth furnace (*right*).

FORD MOTOR COMPANY

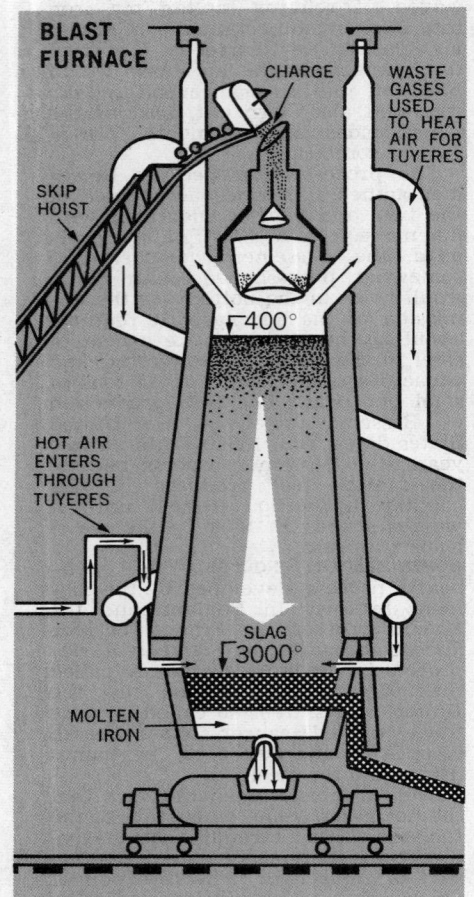

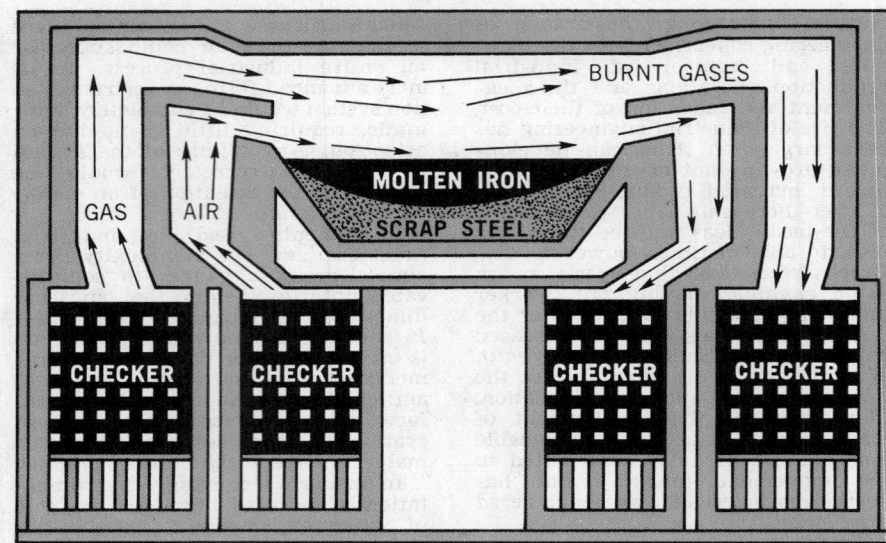

OPEN HEARTH FURNACE (*above*) is charged with melted iron, scrap steel, iron ore, and limestone. Brick "checkers" heat fuel gas and air before they are burned over the hearth. Waste gases are reused in other checkers to heat fuel and air entering the furnace.

STEEL is made in an electric furnace (*right*) with a charge of scrap steel, iron, and iron ore (*top*). Lowered electrodes oxidize impurities; then the slag is poured from the tipped furnace (*center*). Molten steel is removed by tipping the furnace to the other side. In a Bessemer converter (*far right*) the charge is molten iron (*top*). Air is blasted through to remove impurities (*center*) and the converter is tipped on its trunnions to remove the steel.

BLAST FURNACE (*left*) is charged by cars moving along a hoist with iron ore, coke, and limestone. The charge melts, reacts, and settles to the bottom, where the slag floats atop the molten iron.

bustion is led through the heated brick chambers, absorbing some of their heat. The air thus heated then joins the flames, raising their temperature higher than could be obtained with cold air.

The open-hearth furnace is generally charged with about equal parts of molten pig iron and steel scrap. Limestone is added to draw off waste matter in the form of slag. The open-hearth furnace produces a heat of steel in about 8 to 10 hours. The time may be shortened by the injection of oxygen. Capacity of the largest furnaces is 600 tons per heat, but most range from 200 to 300 tons.

After first exceeding Bessemer steel production in 1908, the open-hearth process continued to gain at the expense of the former, accounting at times for 90 per cent of American steel production. Its proportion in the mid-1960's was 72 per cent, while that of the Bessemer process had dwindled to 0.5 per cent. The open-hearth process became dominant because its method, though slower, permitted closer control over the composition of the steel. It was also favored because its larger capacity, greater versatility, and the generally higher quality of its steel.

■**ELECTRIC ARC PROCESS.**—The third major steel producer is the electric arc furnace, which refines steel by the heat generated from an electric arc and the electrical resistance of

the steel bath itself. It owes its development chiefly to Dr. Paul Héroult of France, who produced his first steel by the process in 1899.

The electric arc furnace resembles a huge teakettle. Three large graphite electrodes, entering through the roof, convey the current to the charge, which consists almost entirely of steel scrap with small amounts of slag-forming material. The chief advantage of the electric arc furnace is the high degree of precision with which the temperature and composition of the bath can be regulated.

Originally, its use was reserved for a limited range of high-quality alloy steels, but the electric arc process has become a versatile instrument for a much wider range, including carbon steels, which constitute over half of its production. The electric arc furnace produces practically all the stainless, tool, and special alloy steels used in the chemical, automotive, aviation, machine tool, transportation, food processing, and many other industries. Electric arc furnace production in the United States in the mid-1960's was over 13,000,000 tons annually, or 10 per cent of total steel production. Capacities range from 3 or 4 to 150 and 200 tons per heat.

■**BASIC OXYGEN PROCESS.**—A relatively new process rapidly being adopted around the world was developed in Linz-Donawitz, Austria, and is

known as the basic oxygen, or L-D, process. It was introduced in Canada and the United States in 1954. The vessel used somewhat resembles a Bessemer converter, but without the air holes in the bottom, since the oxygen is injected from above through a lance into the charge, which consists of about 70 per cent molten pig iron and 30 per cent scrap. The oxygen readily dissolves in the metal and rapidly oxidizes the silicon, manganese, phosphorus, sulfur, and carbon. The carbon is oxidized to form carbon monoxide gas, which causes vigorous boiling of the entire charge. Phosphorus, sulfur, and nitrogen content are generally lower than in open-hearth steel.

Advantages of the basic oxygen process are speed, lower installation costs than for an open-hearth furnace of equal productivity, and close control of the refining process. It can produce steel of open-hearth quality for a wide range of products at a rate of 300 tons per hour, compared with about 50 tons per hour in the open-hearth furnace. It can produce carbon, alloy, and stainless steels.

There were basic oxygen converters in 26 nations in the mid-1960's, with 70,000,000 tons annual capacity. Planned additions indicate a world output of more than 120,000,000 tons before 1970. In the mid-1960's, basic oxygen capacity in the United States was nearly 23,000,000 tons annually,

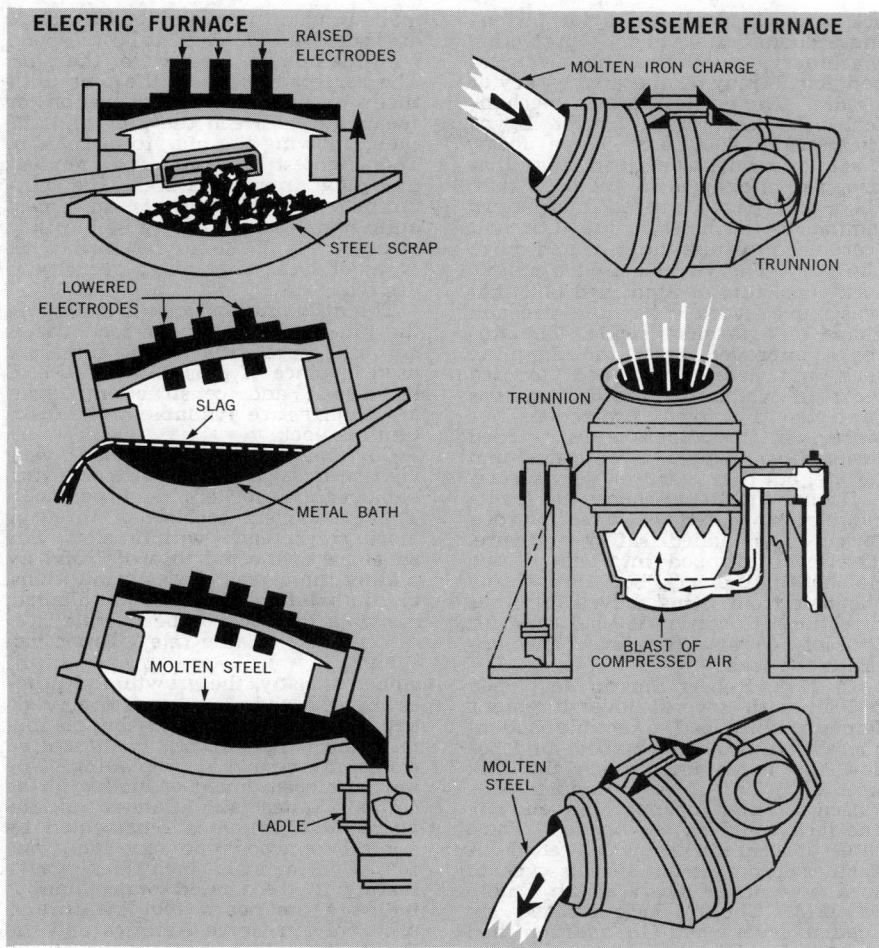

ELECTRIC FURNACE

RAISED ELECTRODES

STEEL SCRAP

LOWERED ELECTRODES

SLAG

METAL BATH

MOLTEN STEEL

LADLE

BESSEMER FURNACE

MOLTEN IRON CHARGE

TRUNNION

TRUNNION

BLAST OF COMPRESSED AIR

MOLTEN STEEL

or 17.5 per cent of the national capacity. An additional capacity of 20,000,000 tons is planned. Projections of future production indicate that the basic oxygen process will replace the open hearth process as a major steel producer in the United States by the mid-1970's.

■ DIRECT CONVERSION PROCESSES.—In recent years, a large number of processes aimed at supplanting the blast furnace by converting iron ore directly into steel, or into iron that could be used for steelmaking, have been investigated, and some have won commercial application. They have employed every known kind of apparatus and utilized all possible fuels, but in the end they have proved to be uneconomical. The blast furnace remains unchallenged as an efficient producer of iron for making steel.

One successful new process does not manufacture steel but refines steel that has already been made. This process was developed in response to the insistent demands of the space age for steels of greater strength and heat resistance than are produced by existing methods. Minute amounts of certain compounds or elements that are not injurious to steel under ordinary conditions may have deleterious effects in steels destined for the severest service. The worst offender is hydrogen. Minute quantities of this gas dissolved in

steel—4 to 8 parts per million—may later cause microcracks that can lead to failure of a vital part when it is subjected to great stresses, such as those resulting from high speeds at elevated temperatures. The residual hydrogen, as well as oxygen and nitrogen, can be reduced in steel by exposing it in liquid form, under certain conditions, to the suction forces of a state of vacuum.

Refining steel by the agency of a vacuum was known and practiced early in the century, but languished for want of a compelling need for it. Originally, the principle was applied to melting an already highly refined steel within a vacuum. The constant state of vacuum, maintained by powerful pumps, quite literally sucks the gases from the melted steel. The need for removing gases from large masses of steel, particularly from ingots intended for forging generator shafts and turbine rotors, led to techniques for degassing steel while it is still in a molten state. Some of the degassed ingots weigh as much as 250 tons.

Vacuum degassing, or *vacuum casting,* as the process is called, is being done on an increasing scale. Its main purpose is to reduce the hydrogen content of the steel, although nitrogen and oxygen are simultaneously removed. The operation begins with a ladle of molten steel, freshly tapped from an open-hearth or electric fur-

nace. The ladle is placed over a tank in which a vacuum has been created. The molten steel is allowed to pour slowly from the ladle through the vacuum chamber into an ingot mold below. In its passage through the chamber, the liquid steel separates into droplets, exposing the maximum surface of the steel to the sucking action of the vacuum pumps, thus facilitating the withdrawal of the gases. As much as 9,600 cubic feet of gases may be withdrawn from a ton of steel. Steels melted or cast in a vacuum are "cleaner" and stronger than those produced in the atmosphere. They have improved mechanical properties at high temperatures, greater ductility, and a high degree of uniformity in quality. The electrical industry now specifies vacuum-cast steel for all critical applications.

Another new process of major significance to the steel industry is *continuous casting.* It is characteristic of the trend to simplify processes, aided wherever possible by computer systems, with the object of reducing costs. The continuous casting of semifinished steel, such as slabs and billets, dispenses with the ingot, the reheating furnaces, and the primary and secondary rolling mills.

In principle, continuous casting is simplicity itself. It was first applied successfully to some nonferrous metals, but steel presented a number of obstacles. These obstacles have been sufficiently overcome to permit continuous casting of semifinished steel on a low-volume output, but not as yet on a high-volume basis to compete economically with the operations it is designed to replace. The main obstacle to large-volume production is inherent in the thermal characteristic of steel: its relatively slow cooling rate. In brief, steel does not solidify and issue from the machine fast enough, and with assured regularity, by any method yet devised, for "mass" production.

Machinery for continuous casting is a vertical structure, because the molten steel must flow downward into the mold and continue into a vertical cooling chamber. In some methods, the ladle containing the molten steel must be hoisted to a considerable height. In other methods, the finishing end of the machine is in a deep pit, with a correspondingly lower height to which the ladle must be raised. In a third method, a curved mold and cooling chamber make it possible to build a machine of reduced height.

The steel flows from the bottom of the ladle into a receptacle, serving as a reservoir, directly above the mold. The mold is made of copper and is water-cooled. As the steel pours from the reservoir into the mold, it is chilled, forming a shell one-quarter to one-half inch thick. Rollers grip the outwardly hardened casting and draw it downward, where it passes through water sprays, which perform most of the cooling. After the casting has become completely solid, it is cut by oxyacetylene torches into desired lengths. Stainless, tool, alloy, and carbon steels have been successfully cast.   —Douglas Alan Fisher

Jigs and Fixtures, devices used to hold the work during machining operations. The basic function of a jig or fixture is to reduce *set-up time,* that is, the time a machinist needs to position and clamp the workpiece on the machine. The additional function of a jig is to guide the tools precisely during the machining so that each workpiece is identical. Fixtures, however, merely hold the part without guiding the tools. The cost of jigs and fixtures is offset by the savings made in labor and machine time.

Both jigs and fixtures usually have a base plate with hardened stops and buttons that locate the part precisely. Buttons are used to locate horizontal surfaces—three buttons are needed to define and determine a plane surface—while steel pins or stops locate vertical surfaces. Jigs are usually equipped with a hinged upper plate into which hardened steel drill bushings are inserted. The bushings guide the drills, reamers, and cutters used to machine the production parts.

Depending on the application and the number of parts to be machined, jigs and fixtures are constructed of cast iron or fabricated of steel weldments with hardened steel inserts at wear points. Aluminum and magnesium are also widely used because they can be easily machined and are lighter to handle. The aircraft industry, which frequently requires large jigs for wings or airframes, uses fiberglass reinforced with steel tubes as the base for the steel wear points and bushings. —Joseph J. Kelleher

Kiln, in general usage, any large chamber in which heat is produced for baking, drying, melting, or firing. In ceramic practice, however, a distinction is often drawn between a *furnace,* in which actual melting occurs (as in a glass furnace), and a *kiln,* which may reach very high temperatures but does not actually melt the ceramic body. All ceramics, except glasses, must be fired in a kiln so that physical and chemical reactions will occur and give the ware strength and hardness.

Kilns are constructed from insulating and refractory brick. They are heated by gas, fuel oil, or electricity. In *periodic kilns* the ware is set in place, brought to the maturing temperature, cooled, and withdrawn. This inefficient method required days or sometimes weeks to complete. Modern *continuous kilns* are usually tunnel-shaped. The ware rides through on metal and refractory cars, starting in a low-temperature zone, passing into a zone of maximum temperature, and finally entering a zone of decreasing temperature before it is removed. The tunnel kiln reduces firing time as much as 75 per cent and controls temperature changes more efficiently. As a result, it can provide a higher quality product at a much lower cost.

Many ceramics require two firings. The *bisque,* or *biscuit,* firing fixes the size and properties of the body. The *glost* firing is performed after a glaze has been applied and fuses this glaze permanently to the ware.
—Charles J. Phillips

Lock, a mechanical device for fastening doors and lids, protecting machinery, or controlling electrical contacts. It may be operated by key or by dial. The earliest known mechanical locks were made by the Egyptians about 2000 B.C. These locks, made of wood, contained pegs that dropped into holes in the lock bolt. Keys with pegs arranged in a pattern similar to the holes in the lock bolt were used to raise the pegs and move the bolt. The Greeks used a simple lock consisting of a notched bolt that was moved with a key the size and shape of a farmer's sickle. The Romans improved upon the Egyptian lock and later developed *warded locks* in which the mechanism was protected by fixed projections, or wards. In the Middle Ages, warded locks became more complicated and ornate, but they were not very secure.

During the Renaissance, the *lever-tumbler* appeared in some warded locks as an added safety measure. The lever dropped into one of two notches in the lock bolt, preventing the bolt from being moved in either direction. However, it was easy for a thief to raise the lever and operate the lock.

In 1778, Robert Barron developed a lock with several lever-tumblers. Each tumbler had a double action; there were projections above and below the notch into which the lock bolt slid, and if any tumbler was raised too high or not high enough, the lock could not be opened. Thus, a very accurate key was needed. A further improvement in this type of lock was made by Jeremiah Chubb in 1818. Chubb's lock utilized six regular levers and, in addition, had a special "detector" lever that indicated to the owner if the lock had been tampered with.

■**MODERN LOCKS.**—The *pin-tumbler cylinder lock* was invented by Linus Yale, Jr., in 1865. With modern improvements, it is still considered the most secure key-operated locking device. This lock consists of an inner plug and outer shell. The plug is connected to the lock bolt or latch, which moves when the plug is rotated. In the locked position, metal pins are pressed into holes in the plug by springs and other pins called drivers, preventing the plug from being turned. There may be from three to seven pins, and these pins are

made in from six to ten lengths. Keys are cut with notches to correspond with the number and size of the pins. The correct key raises the pins until their top ends form a separation, or shear line, between the plug and the shell, allowing the plug to be rotated. The slightest variation will prevent the plug from rotating. The pin-tumbler cylinder permits an almost unlimited number of possible key changes. It is used for nearly all types of lock where high security is desired.

The *disk-tumbler lock* is similar to the pin-tumbler cylinder lock but is not as secure. Flat metal discs are used in place of pins, but because of its design and construction, fewer key changes are available in the disk-tumbler lock.

Combination locks provide very high security and are used on safes, bank vaults, lockers, and padlocks. The mechanism consists of three or more rings, each with a slot. The rings are connected to a dial and by dialing the correct series of positions, or *combination,* the slots are aligned, allowing the lock to be operated.
—Eaton Yale & Towne Inc.

Lumber Industry, the growth and processing of wood. *Lumber* is the product of the sawmill and the planing mill, and is not further manufactured except by resawing or planing. The unit of measurement of lumber in the United States and Canada is the *board foot,* which is represented by a piece of wood one foot long, one foot wide, and one inch thick. Originating in the United States lumber industry, the board foot measure is used only in North America and the Philippines. Elsewhere in the world, the common units of measurement are the *cubic meter,* the *cubic foot,* and the *standard* (or *Petersburg standard*), which is equal to 1,980 board feet.

Timber is a term loosely applied to standing trees or certain products made from them, such as large pieces used in construction of buildings, bridges, and ships.

The lumber and timber most important in construction and other industrial uses are *softwoods,* such as pine, spruce, hemlock, cedar, cypress, fir, and redwood. The term *softwood* bears no relation to the hardness of the wood; it refers to the coniferous,

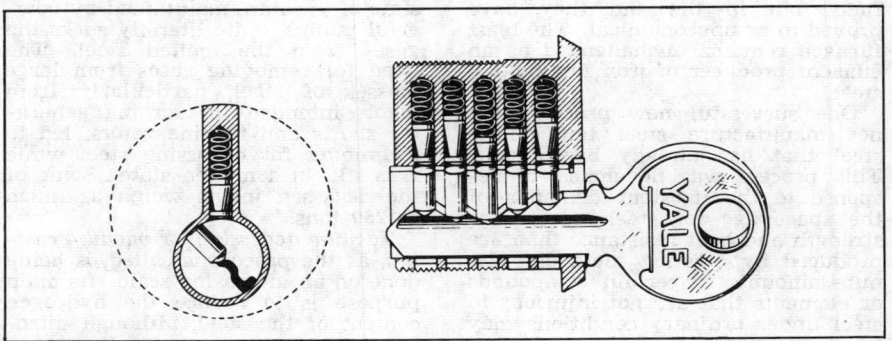

EATON YALE & TOWNE INC.

CYLINDER LOCK will turn only when the five steel pins are raised to a position in which the division between the two halves coincides with rim of cylinder. Then (*left*), it opens.

WEYERHAEUSER COMPANY

LUMBER is "engineered"-molded (*right*) into arches and trusses that are capable of supporting heavy roof loads. At *left*, a lathe "peels" a sheet of veneer off of specially selected log sections. The veneers are then cut to desired size and bonded together to produce plywood.

or needle-bearing trees. The *hardwoods* include the broadleaf trees that usually shed their foliage in the fall; they are used principally in fine veneers, furniture, flooring, and interior paneling in houses. Oak, birch, gum, maple, mahogany, and poplar are among the hardwoods.

■**LUMBER PRODUCTION.**—The United States and Canada together account for 33 per cent of the world's lumber production. The Soviet Union and its satellites account for 32 per cent, while western European countries produce 20 per cent. In 1959, the chief lumber-producing countries of Europe were France, Sweden, West

World Distribution of FOREST LAND in %

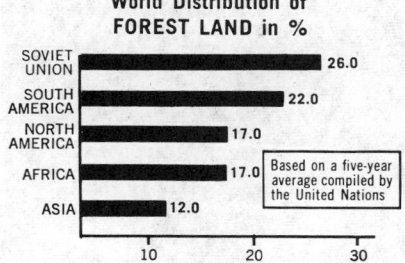

SOVIET UNION	26.0
SOUTH AMERICA	22.0
NORTH AMERICA	17.0
AFRICA	17.0
ASIA	12.0

Based on a five-year average compiled by the United Nations

Germany, Poland, and Finland, in that order. Peak lumber production in the United States was reached in 1909, when U.S. mills manufactured 45 billion board feet. Current annual production is approximately 35 billion board feet.

The United States lumber industry originated in the northeastern states about 1631, and then shifted to the mid-Atlantic states about 1860. From there it moved to the Great Lakes states, and, near the end of the century, to the south. After 1920, it moved to the western states, which lead in production today. *Second-growth,* timber that has grown in the regions first cut over, is reviving the lumber industry in the northern and

southern states of the eastern United States.

■**FORESTS AND FORESTRY.**—The United States has 758,865,000 acres of forest land, which is about one-third of the total land area of the 50 states. About 509 million of these acres are classed as *commercial forest land,* land capable of growing repeated crops of commercial timber and available for that purpose. The other 250 million acres are made up of unproductive land, as well as productive forest land withdrawn from commercial use for parks, game preserves, and the like.

Forestry, the scientific management of forests for continuous production of high-quality trees, is further advanced in Europe than anywhere else in the world. In Germany, France, and the Scandinavian countries, forestry has been practiced for centuries.

Economic conditions have combined with effective nationwide forest-fire prevention and control measures to render the practice of forestry attractive to private owners in the United States only within the past two decades. Generally the government-owned forest lands are well managed, as are the industrial ownerships, while farmers and other small landowners have been slow to adopt forestry measures.

An important development in United States forestry was the inauguration in 1941 of the *American tree farm system* by the forest products industry. The tree farm program gives public recognition to forest owners who dedicate their woodlands to the growing of repeated crops of trees for commercial use. Since the tree farm system was started, more than 29,500 tree farms containing nearly 67 million acres of well-managed, tax-paying private woodlands have been certified.

—Charles A. Gillett

Machine Tools, power-driven devices that cut or shape metal and other materials. Machine tools are essential to the manufacture of a host of products ranging from safety pins to automobiles, from watches to elevators. In the United States, for example, there are more than three million machine tools operating in thousands of factories. About 75 per cent of these are for metal cutting and 25 per cent are for metal forming.

Metal-cutting machines function in different ways. *Lathes* rotate the work, while cutting tools, which are stationary except for a feeding motion, cut the metal away in the form of chips. Lathes come in many different sizes and variations of design and function to produce parts that are shaped like shafts, cups, cones, or disks. When the cut is made on the outside of the part, the machining operation is called *turning;* when it is made on the inside, it is called *boring.*

Metal-forming machines consist principally of a variety of presses for shaping metal, but also include machines for bending, twisting, rolling, hammering, punching, and shearing.

Milling machines rotate the tool, a cutter that usually has a number of cutting points or teeth. The work is mounted on a reciprocating table and fed past this rotating cutter. By milling, it is easy to machine flat surfaces. Controlling the cutter position with a template and trace makes it possible to mill intricately shaped surfaces of dies and molds.

Planers cut flat surfaces by moving the work past a fixed tool. A succession of strokes can machine a large, flat surface. The same operation, on a smaller scale, with the tool moving instead of the work, is done in a machine called a *shaper.* If the planing or shaping operation is done with a tool that has many teeth, each making a small additional bite into the work so that the entire operation is performed in one stroke of the cutter, the tool is called a *broach;* the machine itself, which must have extreme rigidity and power, is called a *broaching machine.*

Drilling machines cut holes in solid material by feeding a rotating drill into the work. Drilling machines range from simple single-spindle machines, in which the drill is rotated by power but fed by hand, to complex automatic machines which drill hundreds of holes simultaneously in a prescribed pattern.

Grinding machines use an abrasive wheel, disk, or belt to cut material from the surface of the metal. Various types of grinding machines are built to duplicate all the actions of other types of cutting machines. The abrasive wheel, however, must always be moving at high speed. In cylindrical grinding, for example, the work rotates just as it does in a lathe, but the grinding wheel also rotates at the same time that it is fed across the work. Grinding can produce extremely fine, mirrorlike finishes. It can also make deep, rough cuts which are described as *abrasive machining.*

Other types of metal-cutting machine tools are built for special purposes such as sawing, gear cutting, honing, lapping, and polishing.

Some machine tools are loaded and controlled manually by a skilled machinist. These are often used in the manufacture of tools for other machines, and are called *toolroom machines.* Production machines often have automatic cycles, but may still be loaded and unloaded by hand. The operator may also make adjustments to correct for tool wear, changes in the material, or other conditions.

A number of successive operations can be performed by a line of machines working in tandem. These can be separate machines linked together by handling equipment, or they can be a single *transfer machine* in which the different stations are built around a rotating table or along a transfer mechanism that takes the work from station to station.

Some transfer machines perform just two related operations, such as drilling a hole and then cutting threads in it. Others perform hundreds of operations on a complex part, such as an automobile engine block and other automotive components, or an electric motor housing.

Conventional automatic machines are generally inflexible—they will only make one part or a few closely related parts. A transfer machine for an engine block may have to be scrapped when the particular design it makes is no longer in demand.

In recent years, a new kind of automatic control has been developed that is more flexible. Called *numerical control,* or *tape control,* it performs a sequence of operations in response to instructions fed to the machine in numerical form, usually by punched or magnetic tape. With these machines, automatic operation can be used in the production of small quantities of parts.

—Anderson Ashburn

Material Handling, the science of moving, packaging, and storing substances in any form. Frederick Winslow Taylor, the pioneer industrial engineer, called it "the blood stream of the factory." Material handling, in civilian terms, corresponds roughly to the logistics of military science. The techniques of modern material handling have replaced the "hernia methods" of lifting, carrying, and placing.

By proper handling, the smallest particle of a bulk material (such as coal) up to large heavy units (such as machine tools) can be moved in the most economical manner. It is an engineering science governed by axioms, laws, and economics—just like any other engineering specialty. Inasmuch as the packages and containers in which articles are shipped have an important bearing on the manner of handling before and after shipment, packaging occupies a large place in material-handling science. Material-handling engineering aims at the development of integrated methods, which move raw materials from the receiving department right through the processing plant to the boxcar, ship, airplane, or truck in the most economical manner.

Material handling offers important opportunities to reduce costs, increase production, save time and materials, reduce losses from breakage and pilferage, reduce injuries to personnel, and increase the utilization of cubic space. It has been called industry's chief area of unexplored cost savings.

■EQUIPMENT.—The *fork-lift truck* is the most familiar material-handling device, but it is not the only one. A wide variety of equipment is used in modern material-handling systems, notably the various *industrial tractors,* used to pull long trains of *trailers. Powered hand trucks* come under this general heading. Simple, manually-operated *floor trucks* on wheels or casters are also used to great advantage. An important auxiliary to fork-lift trucks is the *pallet,* which may be of wood, aluminum, steel, magnesium, plastic, cardboard, wood and steel, or wire. There is a trend toward use of unit loads, whereby a pallet is loaded with a given number and arrangement of packages at the manufacturer's plant, secured to the pallet with steel strapping, and delivered to its destination as a unit.

Conveyors of all types are important material-handling tools. The *rubber conveyor belt* is the wheel horse of the bulk-handling industries. The *roller skate wheel conveyor* is available in a variety of lengths that can be joined together. In the field of vertical material handling, the *electric hoist* finds many uses. The *overhead traveling bridge crane* has long been a fixture in plants where heavy lifts are common. Although there is a trend toward the single-story plant, *electric and hydraulic elevators* form an important part of the material-handling system in multistoried plants.

■SYSTEMS.—Material-handling systems are not new. A specialized mechanical-handling system was used to unload bags of cement from ships during the construction of the Pan-

ama Canal in 1912. Other specialized systems have been in existence for a long time. The industrial truck had its start early in the twentieth century when an electric motor powered by batteries was bolted onto an ordinary baggage carrier in a railroad terminal. Subsequent refinements have led today to the fork-lift truck capable of handling almost anything with one of many special attachments. It can be said that material handling only began to come into its own during World War II.

It is the opinion of specialists in this field that great opportunities lie ahead. Already promising development work is being done to apply atomic energy to material handling. Automatic warehouses are being developed in which a key would be punched in a central office to release a part from a bin to fall by gravity onto a conveyor belt, which would take it with other items on an order to a central packaging point.

These are examples from the most progressive segments of industry. There is still much time and money to be saved by the application of standard equipment used more conventionally. —Eaton Yale & Towne Inc.

CLARK EQUIPMENT COMPANY

FORK-LIFT TRUCK with triple-stage upright that extends on rollers from 12¾ feet to 15¾ feet and can lift up to 4,000 pounds.

Metal Coating, the art of coating a metallic surface with a layer of another metal, primarily to protect it from oxidation and corrosion. The coating metals are chosen from among those that are electropositive with respect to the basis metal.

A number of processes have been in use for many years to coat iron, steel sheet for roofing and other outdoor uses, and for the production of tinplate used in canning.

The basic process, still most often used, is *hot-dip galvanizing,* in which the iron or steel sheet is coated with a layer of zinc. In this process, the sheets are thoroughly cleaned by pickling, then washed and passed through sal ammoniac on their way to the pot of molten zinc. The process is continous, with the zinc-coated sheets passing through rollers as they come out of the zinc bath.

An alternative method is electroplating which is based on electrolytic action. In this process the steel is used as the negative electrode (cathode) and the zinc as the positive electrode (anode). An electric current is then sent from the anode to the cathode through a solution of a zinc salt (electrolyte). This causes the zinc to deposit on the negative pole or steel. The main advantage is that the steel is not heated, and thus does not distort. Limitations are the slow rate of coating and the relative sponginess of the coating obtained.

Two processes are used to deposit a layer of tin on sheet steel. Both are *hot-dip* processes, similar to that used in hot-dip galvanizing. In one process, the sheet usually passes through three tin baths, each purer than the one preceding it. In the other, the sheet is first passed through zinc chloride, then through the molten tin. In both processes, the coated sheet is finally passed through rollers that govern the depth of the deposited layer.

Another heat process for coating steel sheet with zinc is known as *sheradizing.* In this process, the zinc is not molten but is in the form of a fine powder, which is deposited on the sheet. The sheet is then heated until the powder melts to form the zinc coat.

All these processes were developed for coating sheet metal in large quantities, and they require expensive installations. To coat parts after manufacture, an electrolytic process has long been the only practical system. Recently, however, Minnesota Mining & Manufacture Company has developed a mechanical plating process adaptable to the coating of ferrous parts with zinc, tin, lead, or cadmium. The parts are degreased, descaled, and etched, then are coppered in various solutions, preparatory to plating. They are then loaded in a barrel together with tiny glass balls that act as a mild abrasive, the required amount of plating metal powder, a compound to promote the action, and water. The barrel is then tumbled at a surface speed of about 110 feet per minute for 45 minutes, after which the parts are separated from the glass balls, washed, and dried.

—Felix Giordano

Metal Shaping, any of various processes used to change the dimensions of a metal without chip removal. These processes include casting, forging, stamping, rolling, extruding, spinning, and drawing.

■**CASTING.**—Casting, in which molten metal is poured into a mold and allowed to cool and solidify, is one of the oldest forms of metal shaping. Since unusual shapes with a high degree of complexity can be duplicated by this method, a wide variety of casting processes have been devised.

Sand casting, in which the mold is a cavity in compacted sand, has been used to form metal objects for more than 4,000 years. The first step in sand casting is the creation of a wood or metal pattern in the shape of the part to be produced. The second step is to pack sand around the pattern and then to remove the pattern, leaving the mold. Pouring molten metal into the cavity left by removing the pattern is the third step. After the metal has cooled and solidified, the sand is broken away from the casting. Practically any metal can be cast in sand molds. The principal limitations of sand casting are a rough surface finish, a minimum section thickness of $\frac{1}{8}$ inch, and minimum tolerances of $\pm \frac{1}{16}$ inch.

Shell molding, a variant of sand casting, uses a mixture of sand and resin as the mold medium. The sand-resin mixes are formed over a polished metal pattern and hardened in an oven. Castings produced in shell molds have very smooth surfaces and can reproduce fine detail. At a cost little more than for sand castings, shell molded parts can be produced with tolerances as small as ± 0.004 inch and with sections as thin as $\frac{1}{16}$ inch.

Permanent mold castings are produced in reusable molds of refractory material for production runs in substantial volume. The molds are made in several parts to allow removal of the finished casting. The complexity of parts cast in permanent molds is limited, since the molds must be easily removable. Because of the chilling effect of the molds, permanent-mold cast parts have excellent mechanical properties. Hollow castings, called *slush castings,* can be made in permanent molds by pouring off liquid metal after a shell has formed on the mold surface. Permanent-mold cast parts have excellent sand castings in finish and density, can be held to closer tolerances (± 0.025 inch), and have a finer metal grain structure. While both ferrous and nonferrous parts are made by permanent mold casting, aluminum and magnesium account for the highest volume.

Die casting involves the injection of molten metal into closed steel dies clamped together under pressure. The dies are mounted in a machine that incorporates a heated reservoir for the metal, hydraulic rams to open and close the dies, and an injection system to feed the molten metal under pressure. In operation, the dies are closed and clamped by the hydraulic cylinder, molten metal is injected, and pressure is retained until the castings cool. The dies are then opened by the hydraulic cylinder, and the castings are ejected by pins in the dies. Machines capable of up to 100 shots (cycles per hour) are available, depending on the size of the part.

Although the surface finish of die-cast parts is excellent and rarely requires finishing operations, application of the process is limited by the problem of removing the part from the die. Complex multipart dies provide some design flexibility, but such dies are expensive, substantially increasing the die cost per part. Although usually applied to small parts, die casting is now being used for parts as large as automobile engine blocks weighing 80 pounds. Machines are available that can cast zinc parts weighing as much as 200 pounds.

Primary benefits to be derived from die casting are the close tolerances that can be held and the high production rates. With ordinary zinc castings, tolerances can be held to within ± 0.001 inch per inch of part length. Closer tolerances can be held if required, but die costs will then increase. Zinc, aluminum, magnesium, copper-base alloys (brass), lead, and tin are the metals most commonly used for die casting.

Centrifugal casting takes place in a rapidly rotating mold, relying on centrifugal force to produce a part with greater accuracy and improved physical properties. Symmetrically shaped parts, such as railroad car wheels, engine cylinder liners, sleeves, gear blanks, and pipe, are ideally suited to centrifugal casting. The mold consists of a metal flask, lined with sand or a refractory material, that resists the centrifugal forces. To cast pipe, the flask and its liner are rotated around its horizontal axis while a measured amount of molten metal is poured into one end. Centrifugal force holds the molten metal against the mold until the metal solidifies. A critical factor in centrifugal casting is selection of the correct spinning speed. Excessive speed produces highly stressed parts that will fracture easily, while slow speeds prevent the metal from adhering to the inside of the mold. Though any metal can be centrifugally cast, the process is most widely used to produce cast-iron pipe and large plumbing fixtures.

Lost wax, or *investment mold, casting* is a precision casting process widely used to produce parts from alloys that are difficult to machine. The process was developed 3,500 years ago, but it was not until the Renaissance that it was rediscovered by Italian metalworkers. Investment molding starts with a wax duplicate of the part to be cast. The wax pattern is placed in a box or flask which is filled with a liquefied refractory plaster. The mold is then baked in an oven to melt out the wax and harden the refractory material. Liquid metal is poured into the cavity left by the wax and allowed to cool. The mold is then broken away to free the castings. Because lost-wax cast parts can be used without machining,

UNITED STATES STEEL CORPORATION

FORD MOTOR COMPANY

ROLLED STEEL (*left*) is tempered as it passes through this machine before being plated with tin. Presses (*above*) shape flat steel sheets for use in the production of automobiles.

the process is widely used to cast the so-called superalloys. These alloys are used for gas-turbine blades, metal-cutting tools, extrusion dies, and pump impellers handling abrasive compound.

■**FORGING.**—Forging, as old a metal-shaping process as casting, consists of heating the metal and hammering it by hand or machine to the desired configuration. Flat dies are used to work heated billets to approximate shape; closed impression dies are used to produce a given shape for a specific part. In either case, forging has the advantage of compacting the material to improve its grain structure and mechanical properties. Steel forgings are widely used for automobile and truck axles, engine crankshafts, connecting rods, and gear blanks.

Drop forging is performed by either a steam or board hammer. Steam hammers are lifted and driven downward by steam pressure; board hammers rely entirely on gravity to deliver the hammer blow. Board hammers are built up to 4-ton capacity, while steam hammers are capable of delivering 25-ton blows. One advantage of the steam hammer is speed, for it can deliver 300 or more blows per minute. Dies for the part being forged are mounted in dovetails cut in the press's hammer and anvil.

Several progressive dies are usually required to forge a part to its final shape. Separate trimming presses are used to remove the *flash* (excess metal extruded around the parting line of the dies as they close) from the forging. For close tolerance, a high-pressure coining process is used to bring the finished forging to exact dimensions.

Forgings are produced in sizes ranging from a few ounces to several tons. Because they can be worked easily, straight carbon steels are the most commonly forged metal. Brass, bronze, aluminum, magnesium, and titanium are also formed by forging to improve their mechanical strength. Alloy steels, too, are forged, but they require additional skill and the design and use of special dies.

Upset forging, press forging, and cold-headed parts are variations of the basic forging operation, and each has its advantages. *Upset forging* uses bars of metal that are gripped between stationary jaws and impacted by the moving die. Common products of the upset-forging process are bolt heads, rivets, and other fasteners. *Press forging*—either hot or cold—starts with a slug of steel that is squeezed to make the metal flow into all recesses in the die. Progressive dies are usually used, mounted in either hydraulic or mechanical presses. *Cold heading* is similar to upset forging, but stock is fed from reels of wire to fully automatic machines. Production rates for smaller cold-headed parts can reach as high as 450 parts per minute.

■**ROLLING.**—By passing the metal between two rolls, which may be either plain or grooved, a wide variety of shapes—such as bars, plates, rods, sheets, slabs, and strips—can be produced. The rolls rotate at the same speed but in opposite directions. As the metal passes between them, it is reduced in thickness and increased in length. (The slight increase in width may be disregarded.) Rolling at atmospheric temperatures is called *cold rolling,* while rolling above the critical temperature of the metal is called *hot rolling.*

■**COLD PRESSING.**—Metal powder parts are made by compacting fine metal powders in a press, then sintering or oven-brazing the compact. The advantage of the process is that unusual metallurgical combinations can be obtained and the density of the part closely controlled. Porous parts can be produced by mixing in materials that dissolve when the compact is sintered. This process is used to produce extremely fine filters and porous bushings that retain lubricants, often used in sealed electric motors.

■**PRESS FORMING.**—Press forming involves a range of operations that include blanking, pressing, stamping, and drawing. Many different types of dies are used for press forming, depending on the metal, the thickness of the part, and the quantity of parts

required. For long production runs, such as automobile body panel, matched steel dies are used; but for limited production runs, dies of softer metals, plastics, and even wood are satisfactory. When the softer materials are employed for shallow draws, a rubber pad or blanket replaces the upper die. This is common practice in the aircraft industry where short runs of thin, soft aluminum are required.

Blanking involves deformation of the metal beyond the shear point to produce a clean, sharp break at right angles to the surface. *Pressing, stamping,* and *drawing* operations deform the metal beyond its plastic limit to produce a permanent set. For deep drawing operations, progressive dies are required, and the stock is annealed between draws. Nearly all ferrous and nonferrous alloys can be stamped, but springy materials are avoided.

■**EXTRUSION.**—Extrusion is a process similar to the squeezing of toothpaste from a tube, with heated metal instead of the paste. Most extrusion machines rely primarily on pressure to generate the heat needed although the billet is frequently preheated before insertion in the press. The press consists of a cylinder with a hardened die at one end and a hydraulic ram at the other. The ram applies tremendous pressure on the billet to raise the metal's temperature. Under pressure, the heated metal becomes plastic, flowing through the shaped dies in a continuous length. The extruded metal is cut to length and machined, forged, or otherwise processed to create finished parts.

Formerly, extrusion was limited to lead, copper alloys, aluminum, magnesium, zinc, and other soft metals, but recent advances have made it possible to extrude steels and other hard or high-temperature metals. Although the steels extrude easily, die life is short and special lubricants are required. For some steels, powdered glass is used as a lubricant.

■**OTHER METHODS.**—Although the most common methods of shaping metals have been described, hundreds of other processes are used by industry. Many of these operations involve highly specialized equipment that cannot be adapted to the general metal-shaping field. Among the more exotic procedures that show promise of wider application are explosive forming, high-energy-rate forming, and magnetic forming. *Explosive forming* shapes thick sections or ultrahard alloys on a single die, which is submerged in water and subjected to extreme hydraulic pressure by an explosion. *High-energy-rate forming*, with closed dies, employs a press driven by the sudden release of compressed gas. The energy applied to the metal slug in a few milliseconds induces plastic flow that results in close tolerance parts with improved grain flow. *Magnetic forming* relies on a burst of electromagnetic energy to compress or expand tubular sheetmetal parts on a mandrel or die. This process is limited to ferrous metals or other magnetic alloys.

—Joseph J. Kelleher

Methods Engineering, the branch of engineering that deals with the minimization of the cost of labor involved in performing repetitive jobs in factories or offices by the improvement of work methods. Each operation required to finish a given job or piece of work is analyzed, and unnecessary operations are eliminated. Methods, working conditions, and equipment are standardized, and the operator is trained to work according to a standard pattern. Once the job has been standardized, the time needed for an operator to complete the job is measured. Finally, a pay schedule is computed that provides an incentive for the worker to achieve or exceed the standard measure of performance.

Before any *methods study* is undertaken, the cost of making the study must be determined and balanced against the potential savings. For new jobs, a method is devised to accomplish the work, and then alternative ways of accomplishing the job are sought and evaluated. Motion studies—for which personal observation or motion pictures are employed—are then made if the job is repeated frequently, and the cost can be justified.

Once the work method has been refined as far as possible and standardized, the job is measured by *time study*. Using a stop watch, the engineer observes a typical operator, timing each movement. All the times are added, and allowances are made for stock handling, unavoidable delays, and personal needs to set a standard time for the specific job. These time standards are used to determine compensation or the work volume to be accomplished during a specific time interval.

—Joseph J. Kelleher

Microscope, an optical device that enlarges the image of small objects. The simplest microscope, therefore, is the ordinary magnifying glass. Normally, people see small objects best when they are held about 10 inches from the eye. At 8 or 9 inches the objects appear fuzzy, since the human eye cannot focus at the shorter distance. A microscope brings the object image closer to the viewer's eye while keeping it in focus. *Simple microscopes* consist of a single lens, like a magnifying glass, or several lenses which act as a single positive lens.

A *compound microscope* has two lens systems, each acting as a single positive lens. Compound microscopes have their *objective lens system* mounted at the bottom of a tube and an *eyepiece lens system* at the top. The magnification of a compound microscope is the product of the magnification of the objective lens system and the eyepiece. With an eyepiece magnification of 5 and an objective magnification of 25 the final magnification is 125, usually expressed as 125X.

The *resolving power* of a microscope is the limit of its useful magnification. This defines a microscope's ability to make very small details clearly visible. If a microscope magnifies an object beyond its ability to resolve detail, the image in the eyepiece becomes blurred. Additional magnification will increase the size of the image, but the image also becomes increasingly blurred.

Binocular microscopes have two eyepieces so that the viewer can use both eyes to observe the image. As a result, the operator has depth perception and eye strain is reduced. The image from the single objective lens is split, by a prism system, and divided between the two eyepieces like a pair of binoculars.

Proper illumination is essential for good viewing of highly magnified objects. When the object being viewed is transparent, illumination is provided by an adjustable plane mirror on the base of the microscope which reflects light up through the specimen. A plane mirror is used, with a small light source, to provide parallel rays in the illuminating beam. For intense illumination, a concave mirror or a system of condensing lenses provides a concentrated cone of light. Opaque objects require illumination from above. This is usually accomplished by a light source built into the microscope tube and focused on the specimen through the objective lens system.

Though simple magnifying lenses were used in China and the East before the Christian Era, it was not until about 1600 that a Dutch spectacle maker, Zacharias Janssen, produced a compound microscope that was 6 feet long and contained two lenses. Though the compound microscope had numerous advantages, the baffling problem of optical aberration which distorted the image and created colored fringes restricted development. Anton van Leeuwenhoek, the man who is credited with developing microscopy into a science, used a simple microscope for his studies. The problem of aberration was not fully solved until about 1850 when Charles Chevalier developed an achromatic lens eliminating the color fringe. (See also *Electron Microscope*, page 1683.)   —Joseph J. Kelleher

Mining, the process or business of extracting geologic materials from the earth's crust. All mining, whether it be by open-pit methods or underground, consists of three operations: breaking the ore, loading the ore, and transporting the ore to the treatment plant.

Whether a mineral deposit is mined by surface or underground methods (or both) depends on a number of factors. Among them are the proximity of the deposit to the surface, the unit value of the minerals to be recovered, the physical characteristics of the material to be mined, and the safety of personnel engaged in mining the deposit.

Surface mining entails the removal of all material overlying the ore body, plus the removal of enough more of this *overburden* to make an opening with sides sloping at an angle flat enough so there will be no sliding of the material from the walls into the pit. Thus, with the safety of the workmen in mind, surface mining requires the ore body to be stripped of its overburden and then be removed.

Overburden does not always have to be broken. When it does, depending on its consistency, it can be broken with a *ripper* or drilled and blasted. A ripper works like an oversized plow, pulled by a powerful tractor. If the overburden requires drilling and blasting, a churn drill, a percussion drill, or a rotary drill, may be used.

The *churn drill* is a heavy blunt drill that is raised and allowed to fall at the end of a wire rope, very much as the dasher moves in an old-fashioned churn. In *percussion drilling*, the sharp end of a steel drill is held against the bottom of the hole, and a sharp blow struck against the other end of the drill rod. The energy is transmitted through the rod to the point, which breaks off a chip of the material being drilled. The drill is raised, turned, and the process repeated. In *rotary drilling*, the drill bit armed with hard material, frequently diamond, is pressed against the bottom of the hole and twisted mechanically. As it turns, the material at the bottom of the hole is ground off.

With all three types, the ground or broken material from the bottom of the hole is removed to avoid wasting energy. It may be washed out with water or blown out with air. The holes drilled will vary from 3 inches to 3 feet in diameter. They may be vertical or at an angle, and anywhere from 3 feet to more than 100 feet long.

When a round of holes has been drilled, they are loaded with explosives and filled with stemming. Holes are drilled in a regular pattern calculated to distribute the explosive throughout the rock mass so the energy liberated when the explosive is detonated will be most effective. The object of drilling and blasting is to break the material into sizes easily handled by the loading and hauling equipment. At the same time, it is not efficient to break it into pieces smaller than necessary.

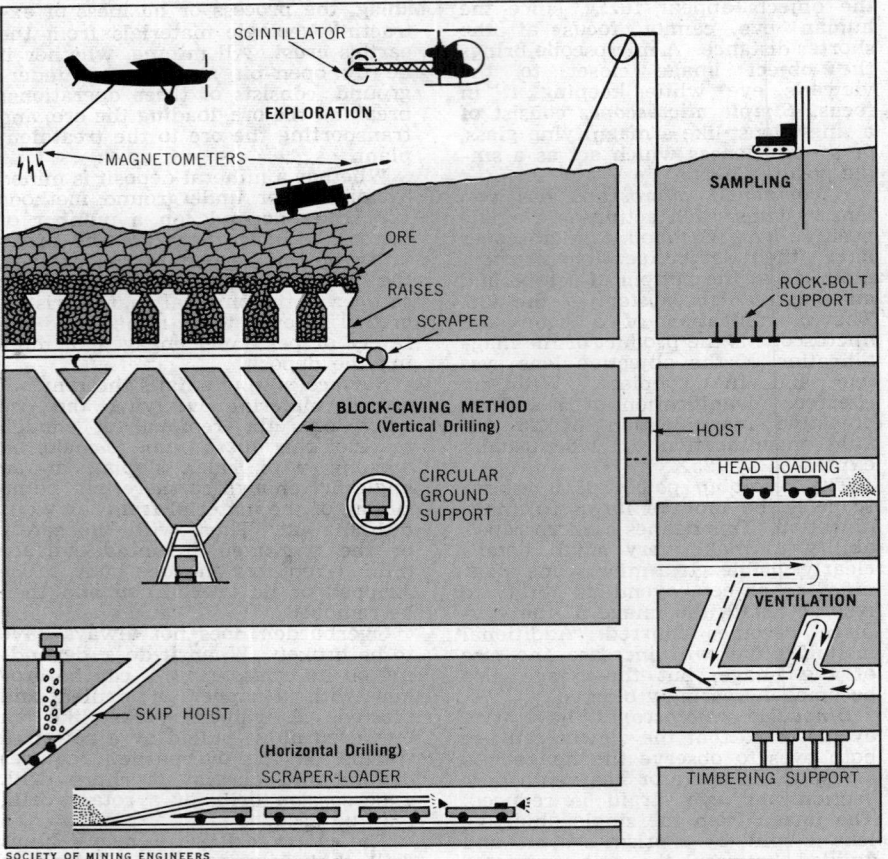

SOCIETY OF MINING ENGINEERS

MINING begins with geophysical exploration. Measuring instruments such as *magnetometers*, recording distortions in the earth's magnetic field that indicate possible ore deposits, and *scintillators*, reacting in the presence of radioactivity, are carried over an area by aircraft. Following the aerial survey, ground crews pinpoint deposits with similar devices and drill or blast holes for samples. If further search locates rich deposits, shafts are lowered and supported by beams and rock bolts, hoists are rigged for carrying men and ore, and a ventilating system is opened. This schematic drawing shows the *block-caving* method of mining, used primarily to obtain copper and molybdenum. Vertical "raises" and horizontal drilling knock the support away from ore-rich strata, and scrapers push the fallen ore through chutes or onto conveyor belts, then into mine cars. It is then transported for processing. A mine of the scale illustrated here may take ten years, from surveying to removing the first ore, to be put into operation.

Explosives used are dynamites of various strengths. Mixtures of ammonium nitrate and fuel oil, commonly called *ANFO*, have displaced the more expensive nitroglycerine-base dynamites to a large extent. Nuclear explosives have not yet been used in stripping operations, but the time may come when they are.

After the overburden has been broken, it is loaded into some means of transport. Loading is accomplished by several types of equipment. Mechanical shovels powered by electricity are most common. Some of these giant shovels with buckets of 200-ton capacity can pick up this load a third of a city block from the operator and deposit it on a spoil pile a block away in the other direction. In one day they use enough electric current to supply a city of 30,000 people. Huge draglines that sit on the bank above the cut can reach farther than the shovel and discharge farther away. However, bucket capacity of the dragline is less than that of a shovel of equal size. Where the character of the overburden permits, bucket-wheel excavators are coming into increased use. These also are gigantic, with a series of 20-cubic-yard buckets mounted on the periphery of a suitable wheel, discharging their loads onto a 6-foot-wide endless belt. The belt in turn discharges onto a stacker or conveyor belt, which may carry the waste material a mile or more before discharging it on the spoil pile.

Transport, as has been mentioned, is sometimes provided by conveyor belts. With the big shovels a more common type of transport is the off-highway truck. Again, these may be tremendous in size. Capacities of 70, 100, and more cubic yards are not uncommon. In many cases, transportation away from the shovel is accomplished in railroad dumpcars of 50- to 100-ton capacity.

Given proper conditions, *stripping* can be accomplished with bowl scrapers. These self-loading transports are used on hauls up to 5 miles when the material to be moved is uniform, relatively soft, and easily dug. Capacities run up to 36 cubic yards. Once the overburden has been removed, mining of the mineralized, valuable portion of the deposit begins. This follows the same general pattern as that of overburden removal, but the equipment is usually not so big. The pit is carried down in a series of benches that may range from 30 to 100 feet in height. The overall slope is maintained at an angle that will preclude slides. Usually, the ore material is more difficult to break than the overburden. Hence, a greater number of small holes are drilled closer together, loaded, and blasted to break a given amount of material. Transportation is by railroad cars, trucks, or conveyor belts. Every mine presents a different problem so the combinations of equipment used to load and haul the ore from its place in the earth to the concentration plant are almost infinite.

Unlike surface mining, *underground mining* does not require the removal of all material overlying the ore body. It does demand its support. To reach the ore body entails the sinking of one or more shafts, the driving of many horizontal openings and secondary vertical openings in or under the ore body, and the support of all the overlying material while the ore is being removed. All this must be carried out with strict attention to safety while the work is going on.

In underground mining, also, the cycle of breaking, loading, and transporting is basic. As in surface mining, the combinations of men, methods, and machinery used are almost infinite. In the simple, unmechanized *coyote-hole mine,* one or two men using hand drill, sledgehammer, and wheelbarrow, mine small amounts of material. In large mechanized mines, as much as 50,000 tons of material per day may be produced by hundreds of men using many complicated machines to break the ore, load it on trucks, rail cars, or conveyors, transport it to a central shaft, and there hoist it to the surface and the ore treatment plant. Mining methods may be classified on the basis of the amount and kind of support provided for overlying material.

Open stoping denotes large openings from which the ore is removed completely, with little or no provision for support. *Room and pillar* mining is characterized by parallel openings driven off a tunnel with pillars of ore left in between. When the limits of the ore body have been reached, the pillars are mined *on the retreat,* allowing the mined-out portion of the mine to cave in behind the work. In the *block-caving* method, blocks of the ore are undermined and allowed to cave. The broken material is then drawn off into cars below the caved areas and hauled away.

Shrinkage stoping is room-and-pillar mining adapted to steeply inclined ore bodies. Mining begins at the bottom of the *room,* which in this case is called a *stope.* The ore is broken overhead from the top of the stope and enough drawn out to leave room in which miners can work. Then, standing on top of the broken ore, the miners take out another cut from the ore over their heads, and again enough is drawn out from the bottom to leave room for the miners to work on the next cut. This is continued until the next level above is reached. At that time all the remaining ore in the stope is drawn off and, depending on the character of the material overlying the ore body, the empty stope is filled or allowed to stand open. When a series of parallel stopes with pillars between has been completed and the empty stopes filled, work begins on recovering the pillars.

In *cut-and-fill stoping,* work begins as it does for shrinkage stoping, but all the ore is drawn out and replaced by filling material. The miners then stand on top of the filling material to take the next cut. When all the ore is drawn off, another layer of fill is introduced, and the process is repeated. —John C. Fox

Ore Treatment, the step in which run-of-mine ore is converted into a concentrate that is a salable product. In general, this means that the valuable constituent in run-of-mine ore delivered to the plant must be separated from the nonvaluable component. Ore treatment usually entails coarse crushing, fine grinding, and separation. Nature seldom, if ever, produces two mineral deposits that are exactly the same.

In coarse crushing, large chunks of material coming from the mine are broken into sizes more convenient to handle in the fine grinding machines. In the fine grinding circuit of the mineral treatment plant, the material is reduced to the grain size of the valuable material. Ideally, fine grinding proceeds only to the point necessary to liberate the valuable mineral from the waste material.

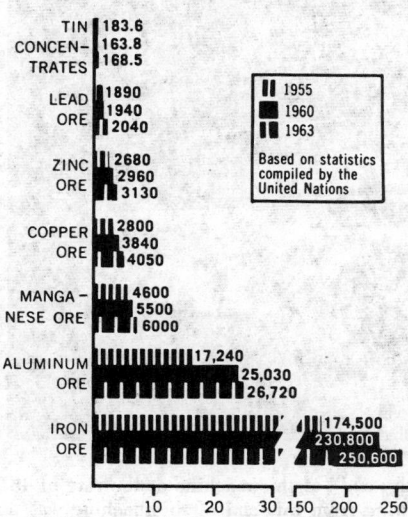

World Production of METAL ORES

	1955	1960	1963
TIN CONCENTRATES	183.6	163.8	168.5
LEAD ORE	1890	1940	2040
ZINC ORE	2680	2960	3130
COPPER ORE	2800	3840	4050
MANGANESE ORE	4600	5500	6000
ALUMINUM ORE	17,240	25,030	26,720
IRON ORE	174,500	230,800	250,600

Based on statistics compiled by the United Nations

10 20 30 150 200 250
(Thousands of Metric Tons)

OPEN-PIT MINING often requires blasting to remove rock from over the ore layer. Here workmen at an Arizona copper mine carefully set an explosive charge at the edge of the pit. When the ore has been exposed, it is scraped away and transported to a refinery.

From this point on there are a number of different methods of separating the two, depending on the chemical or physical properties of each.

Probably the first property used by man to separate the metalliferous portion of the rock mined from the waste portion was the difference in specific gravity. Nature herself uses this method in concentrating gold, tin, platinum, etc., in placer deposits. This is the same process used by the Forty-Niners with their gold pans and sluice boxes. It depends on the fact that a moving stream of water will carry away light (low specific gravity) material and will drop heavy (high specific gravity) material as it loses velocity. In the *jig,* an upward pulse is given to water through a bed of mixed heavy and light material. This pulse must be strong enough to lift and separate the lighter grain, allowing the heavier grains to work their way to the bottom, where they are drawn off periodically.

A multiplicity of separations is obtainable by feeding finely ground ore to a *hindered settling column.* This is a closed vertical tube through which a column of water rises at a given velocity. The speed of the water is controlled so that all but the heaviest material in the charge is carried up and over the top into another hindered settling column in which the water is flowing upward, again at a speed that will allow the heaviest constituent remaining to settle to the bottom. This cycling continues until only the finest, lightest material is discharged from the last column in the battery. The heavier portions are drawn off at the bottom of the tubes.

Shaking tables also make use of the difference in specific gravity between the various portions of the material under treatment. In shaking tables, a moving blanket of water is allowed to flow down an inclined table over a series of riffles while a horizontal motion is imparted to the whole table by pushing it forward gently, then jerking it back faster. Ground ore is fed at the top of the

table and carried down over the riffles by the blanket of water. Separation is achieved through a combination of the differential horizontal motion, the force of gravity, and the carrying power of the water. Heavier material comes off at the end of the table nearest the point at which ore is fed, while lighter material comes off at successive points along the lower edge of the table in different bands, separated according to the specific gravities of the materials that make up the mixture.

In the *heavy-medium method* of separation, the ore is fed into a receptacle containing a heavy liquid, the specific gravity of which is greater than that of the lighter portion of the ore and less than that of the heavier portion of the ore. The light material rises and the heavy material sinks, thus achieving a separation.

Flotation is a variation of the gravity principle. It uses the tendency of an air bubble to stick to the grains of one of the materials making up the mix, thus buoying it up. A stream of air is introduced into the bottom of a tank, called a *cell,* containing a water and ore mixture that is kept in constant agitation. Air bubbles attach themselves to one constituent but not the other; while one is carried to the top, the other falls to the bottom. The material to which the air bubbles are attached rises to the surface, forming a froth that is scraped off the top and collected.

Treatment or conditioning of the mixture with chemicals before addition to the cell, and the addition of other chemicals to the cell, can affect the propensity of air bubbles to attach themselves to grains of mineral. Thus, where the specific gravity of the materials is very close, one can be floated and the other depressed through the addition of proper chemicals to the system. Flotation is used to separate the valuable constituents from the waste rock in ores of copper, lead, zinc, molybdenum, and many other metallic ores. It is also used for a number of the nonmetallics and occasionally for coal.

Some materials will dissolve in a solution in which others will not dissolve. This property is used to effect a separation of valuable and waste portions of an ore. For example, in the cyanide process for gold recovery, when a charge of crushed and ground gold ore is allowed to come in contact with a potassium cyanide solution, the gold forms a complex ion with the cyanide and goes into solution. The rich liquor so formed is then drawn off and passed over powdered zinc. The zinc has a stronger affinity for cyanide than does the gold and displaces it from the gold cyanide solution, allowing the gold to precipitate. Nickel has a strong affinity for ammonia, forming the nickel-ammonia complex. This property is employed to separate nickel from some of its ores by allowing it to come in contact with an ammonium carbonate solution. The nickel ammonia carbonate solution is then heated to drive off carbon dioxide and ammonia and allow a nickel oxide to precipitate.   —John C. Fox

Paper, matted or fiber sheets (usually vegetable, although sometimes mineral, animal, or synthetic) formed on a fine screen from a water suspension. Paper derives its name from *papyrus,* a sheet made by pasting together thin sections of an Egyptian reed (*Cyperus papyrus*) of the sedge family, used in ancient times as a writing material.

A subdivision of paper is *paperboard.* The distinction between paperboard and paper is not sharp but, broadly speaking, paperboard is heavier, thicker, and more rigid than paper. In general, all sheets 0.012 or more inches thick are classified as paperboard.

Paper, as we know it, was invented in China in 105 A.D. by a young scholar named Ts'ai Lun. He pounded the inner bark of the mulberry tree into pulp, added water, and dried the flat, matted sheets in the sun for several days.

The first major improvement was made in 1798 when a Frenchman, Nicholas Louis Robert, patented a machine for making paper in a continuous sheet. Both linen and cotton rags were used then, but these were so scarce that papermakers searched continuously for a cheaper, more abundant raw material.

A firm of London stationers, the Fourdrinier brothers, added improvements to Robert's machine. The paper-forming sections of today's papermaking machines still bear the Fourdrinier name. In 1840, a German named Friedrich Keller patented the first practical methods of making paper from wood. He used a machine in which sticks of wood were held against a grindstone. Water was added to the separated fibers to make pulp.

In 1857 an American chemist, Benjamin Tilghman, patented the sulfite process of making wood pulp, using chemical treatment of the wood fibers. This development was followed in 1884 by discovery of the sulfate process by a German chemist named Carl Dahl.

The paper industry in America began with a small mill, built by William Rittenhouse near Philadelphia in 1690, which used rags at the basic material. Discovery of methods of using wood resulted in the establishment of a large number of mills in northeastern and eastern states where vast forests of spruce and fir—then favored woods—were to be found. Today the pulp industry uses almost all species of native trees; consequently, pulp and paper mills are located in nearly all forested sections of the nation.

There are 362 pulp mills and 806 paper mills in 44 states and the District of Columbia. These are the mills that make pulp paper from which consumer goods are made. Mills that make the paper and paperboard into end products, such as book paper, shipping containers, writing paper, envelopes, and grocery bags are termed *converting mills.* There are more than 4,000 such mills in the United States.

■**MATERIALS.**—Most pulp manufactured in the United States is made from wood. Waste paper also is used, by processes that remove ink and other impurities before repulping. Pulp from this source is used chiefly in the manufacture of paperboard. Rags, one of the earliest sources of fiber for pulp, are still used to some extent—in paper money, for example. Some straw is used for making coarse papers, and small quantities of coarse grasses and bagasse, the crushed stalks of sugarcane, are used.

■**MANUFACTURE.**—The several processes for making wood pulp are much alike in principle. The fibers are separated and arranged in new patterns and in combination with other substances to make different products. This is done either chemically or mechanically. The method chosen depends on the type of wood used and the requirements of the end product.

Bark is first removed from the logs, sometimes by hand labor in the woods, but usually by machines or jets of water at the mills.

In plants using the *mechanical pulping* method to make what is called *groundwood pulp,* sticks are reduced to fibers by huge, rough-faced grinding stones. Because lignin is not removed, papers made by this method do not generally keep their brightness and strength as long as papers made from chemical pulp. However, groundwood paper has certain qualities desired for various printing processes. Paper on which newspapers are printed consists largely of groundwood pulp. So are the lower grades of tablet paper and other papers that do not require unusual strength or durability.

In the *chemical processes,* wood fibers are separated from their lignin binder by cooking in any one of several chemical solutions. The most common are *sulfite* (usually an acid calcium bisulfite solution), *soda* (a caustic soda solution), or *sulfate* (a modification of soda with sodium sulfide). Special sulfite and sulfate pulps, called *dissolving pulps,* are used in the manufacture of cellophane, explosives, plastics, and rayon.

Paper made from hardwoods by the soda process is noted for its fine texture and excellent printing qualities. Hardwood fibers are much shorter than softwood fibers. When pulped by this process and mixed with longer fibers, hardwoods make high-quality magazine and book papers that are well adapted for the reproduction of photographs.

Originally, the sulfate process was used mainly for the pulping of softwoods, especially pine. Now the process is used in pulping both softwoods and hardwoods for *kraft* papers, which are used for wrappings, grocery bags, and other durable papers requiring strength. Envelopes for heavy mail, corrugated

KIMBERLEY-CLARK CORPORATION

NEWLY MADE PAPER is wound into a roll at the "dry end" of this machine at the rate of 13 miles per hour. The continuous sheet of paper flowing from this end of the machine was a slushy mixture of pulp and water at the machine's "wet end" only a few moments earlier.

board, and *tag stock* are among the paper products made from sulfate pulp. By bleaching, the uses of this pulp have been broadened in recent years to include tissue, writing, printing, and many other kinds of paper, including bright white grades.

Another way of making wood pulp combines mechanical and chemical methods in what is called the *semichemical process.* It was developed particularly for the pulping of hardwoods, but it has many variations. The pulpwood chips are cooked in a mild chemical solution, and the fibers are then separated mechanically. Semichemical pulps produce stiff resilient products and are used in making corrugated paperboard, egg cartons, and other items.

In each of the chemical methods, pulpwood sticks must be chipped before they are cooked. Rotating knives slice across the logs, cutting off chips from ⅜ to 1⅛ inches long and about ⅛ inch thick. An endless conveyor belt carries them to storage above chemical cooking vats, called *digesters.*

These digesters operate on the same principle as a kitchen pressure cooker. Wood chips in chemical solution are cooked with steam until reduced to a wet, pulpy mass. It is this cooking that dissolves the resins and gluelike lignin and causes the fibers to separate.

No matter which process is used, wood pulp requires additional treatments—washing and sometimes bleaching—before it can be made into paper or other products. *Washing* removes leftover dirt and uncooked or unbroken pieces of wood, and it separates fibers according to size. *Bleaching* gives pulp the desired degree of whiteness and also further purifies it.

All of the processes prescribed thus far take place in the pulp mill. Pulp not used immediately may be shipped or stored. In this event, most of the water is extracted from the screened stock. Then the pulp can be made into sheets, which can be placed in bundles or *laps* until it is shipped to a paper mill and converted into consumer products.

The United States is the world's largest producer of paper and paperboard. Mills produced 43.3 million tons of paper and paperboard in 1965 with 1966 production expected to reach 45.2 million tons. Per capita consumption of these products in the U.S. in 1965 was estimated at 500 pounds.
——Charles A. Gillett

Petroleum Refining, the process by which crude oil is converted into usable finished products. It is the manufacturing phase of the oil industry. The methods employed vary widely from one refinery to the next, depending on the crude processed, the nature and location of the market, the type of equipment available, and other factors. However, for simplification, it may be considered that most refining processes fall into one of four basic categories.

The FIRST type of process is *fractionation,* or distillation, This method of physically separating the crude's compound according to their boiling points was the earliest refining process, and it is employed to this day. It was originally accomplished in *shell stills,* networks of drums and pipes in which heated crude, one batch at a time, was separated into gases, raw gasoline, kerosene, light heating oil, heavy fuel oil, and other products. The *continuous-battery system* was evolved from the original process. In this system, the crude was introduced at one end of a series, or battery, of shell stills and was separated into various distillates as it passed through the battery.

Today, crude oil is run through hot coils of pipe in a large furnace, then into a tall steel cylinder known as a *fractionation tower.* As the petroleum vapors rise in the tower, they condense on trays according to the temperature at which each becomes liquid again. The various *fractions* of the crude, or *cuts,* each of which is characterized by a carefully controlled boiling range, can therefore be drawn off from the tower at different levels.

The SECOND basic type of process, this one essentially chemical, consists of transforming, or *converting,* certain of these cuts into products of higher commercial value to meet consumer demands. There are many ways of doing this, but all consist fundamentally of altering the molecular structure of the components. In some cases, the molecules may be *cracked* (broken into smaller molecules) to form lighter, more valuable products. In other cases, small hydrocarbon molecules are combined to form larger molecules in reactions called *polymerization* or *alkylation,* or molecules of hydrogen are combined with hydrocarbon molecules in a reaction called *hydrogenation.*

The most widely used conversion process is *cracking.* The type of cracking first invented (and still used) employs only heat pressure and is called *thermal cracking.* A later development involves the use of a catalyst, a substance that helps other substances to change chemically without itself becoming part of the final product. This is called *catalytic cracking.*

Nearly all fractions produced by the processes mentioned above contain certain objectionable constituents or impurities. The THIRD basic process is, therefore, *treating* or *purification.* Treating comprises the removal of the unwanted components, or their conversion to innocuous or less undersirable compounds. Examples are the catalytic sweetening processes, in which the sulfur compounds that are corrosive and give the product a foul, objectionable odor are combined with hydrogen to form a gaseous material and thus separated from the fraction that is being treated. The sulfur subsequently may be recovered for use or sale.

The FOURTH and last basic category is *blending* of the finished cuts into commercially salable products such as motor gasoline, kerosene, lubricating oils, and bunker fuel oil, according to their specifications.
——Clifton Garvin, Jr.

Pharmaceutical Industry, the industry engaged in the research, development, and production of drugs for the relief and cure of illness. In a sense, the pharmaceutical industry dates back to earliest recorded history. Priest-physicians of ancient Persia were called *magi,* the source of the word "magic." They used herbs to combat disease demons, or *drogues,* the source of the word "drug." Ancient Greek and Roman physicians prepared their own drugs, but in Egypt there were separate druggatherers who acquired medicinal herbs, often from far-off lands.

The first known apothecary shop was opened in Arabia in 754 A.D. While most of the remedies used by the ancients were worthless, they did stumble upon some useful ones, including quinine, cocaine, and opium.

Apothecary shops spread across Europe. The Benedictine Monastery on Monte Cassino in Italy had one with its hospital in 1086. In 1597, monks of the monastery of Santa Maria della Scala founded a pharmacy in Rome that continued to sell herbal remedies into modern times.

Paul Ehrlich, an assistant of Robert Koch, led a great medical breakthrough in Germany and coined the word *chemotherapy* for his treatment of illness with drugs, opening new areas for the pharmaceutical industry. In 1910, after 606 trials, Ehrlich developed an arsenic compound that cured syphilis effectively. The compound, first called "606" and later salvarsan or arsphenamine, was the first to cure an infectious disease in man. Important new products were added to the industry with the development of insulin, the lifesaver for diabetics, and vitamins—first from natural then from synthetic sources.

The mass production of pharmaceuticals in the United States began in 1778 when Andrew Cragie, a prominent Boston physician, opened a laboratory in Carlisle, Pennsylvania.

The modern pharmaceutical industry divides its products into two categories: *ethical drugs,* which are sold by prescription, and *proprietary drugs,* which are sold over the counter without prescription. After World War II, the U.S. pharmaceutical industry came into its own. In 1946, ethical drug sales were $424 million. By 1960 they had topped $2 billion, and it is estimated that sales in 1970 will reach nearly $5 billion. The investment in research into new drugs has grown spectacularly, too, from a little more than $25 million after the war to more than $200 million by 1960. By 1970, research spending is expected to reach $450 million.

Products of the U.S. ethical pharmaceutical industry fall into seven basic categories. *Antibiotics* and *sulfonamides* are agents used to treat infectious disease. *Vitamins* are used to treat and prevent malnutrition and *hemanitics* to cure blood deficiencies. *Endocrines,* including corticosteroids and steroid sex hormones, are used to regulate body functions. *Barbiturates* and *tranquilizers* induce sleep and calm emotional disturbances; the

CHAS. PFIZER & CO., INC.

ANTIBIOTIC CREAM will fill these tubes. Research facilities and mass output of modern drug firms aids the control of many painful, dangerous and once untreatable diseases.

increased use of tranquilizers has slowed the use of barbiturates. *Antihistamines* are used mainly for treating allergies and colds. *Biologicals* are immunizing agents, such as the vaccines for preventing poliomyelitis and influenza. Acetylsalicylic acid (aspirin) and other *analgesics*, many of which are sold as proprietary drugs, are also incorporated into ethical preparations.

One of the most spectacular developments in recent years has been the perfecting of synthetic hormone products as oral contraceptives. Research is continuing in this field, and several new products are now in the final testing stages.

As the pharmaceutical industry has produced drugs to control tuberculosis, pneumonia, diphtheria, and many other infectious diseases, research has switched its attention to diseases affecting older persons. Atherosclerosis (so-called hardening of the arteries) has been the target of extensive investigation. Much has been learned about this degenerative process, but so far no real breakthroughs have been made, although several helpful materials have been produced.

Cancer, metabolic diseases, mental illness, and diseases of the kidney, heart, and other vital organs all are being given close attention in the laboratory. —John Price

Photoelectric Devices, light-actuated devices designed to convert light into electric energy. They are used to measure illumination, for counting and sorting, and in the automatic control of machinery.

The *photoelectric cell* is an evacuated electron tube containing two electrodes: an electron-emitting electrode, called the *cathode,* and an electron-collecting wire, called the *anode.* The cathode is often a metal plate covered with a layer of silver that contains an alkali metal such as cesium. In other cells, the light-sensitive coating is placed on most of the inside surface of the glass, leaving an opening, or window, for the

admission of light. When light strikes the silver-cesium coating, electrons are emitted from its surface. An external voltage source of about 100 volts is connected between the anode (the positive terminal) and the cathode (the negative terminal). This voltage causes the emitted electrons, called *photoelectrons,* to enter the positively charged anode. The movement of these electrons through the external circuit constitutes the output current of the cell.

In practical use, a photoelectric cell converts a change in illumination into a change in electric current. This current change can then be used to control a motor in the performance of various useful tasks.

Some photoelectric cells are filled with a gas such as argon. Initial photoelectrons then strike gas particles, dislodging additional electrons on impact. This process increases the useful current of the cell as much as a hundredfold. Nevertheless, the current produced in such cells is still quite small. The *photomultiplier tube* increases the current still further. In this tube, the initial photoelectrons are sent down a long, narrow cylinder. The photoelectrons strike the inner wall of the cylinder many times as they move through it. At each such impact, several additional electrons are knocked out of the atoms of the cylinder. This process increases the number of free electrons up to a million times in such tubes. This makes it possible for extremely low light levels to generate relatively large amounts of current.

The photoelectric cell depends for its operation on the *photoelectric* effect, discovered in 1887 by Heinrich Hertz, the first scientist to experiment with radio waves. The photoelectric effect is the ejection of electrons from a material as the result of irradiation with light. The effect has two important characteristics: the number of electrons emitted depends on the light intensity falling on the material; the energy or speed of the emitted elec-

trons depends on the frequency (or color) of the light and not on its intensity. Each metal has a minimum or threshold frequency below which it will not emit photoelectrons. The alkali metals—sodium, potassium, rubidium, and cesium—emit more photoelectrons than do other metals under the same conditions.

The *photovoltaic cell* is also capable of transforming light into electricity. All practical photovoltaic cells consist of a junction of dissimilar semiconductor materials. In the *selenium photovoltaic cell,* a layer of pure selenium metal is deposited onto a metal baseplate. A small amount of cadmium or cadmium oxide is then deposited on the surface of the selenium forming the desired junction. Wire leads are then connected to the two materials of the cell. When light strikes the cell, a current flows from the selenium layer, through the external circuit connected to the cell, into the cadmium layer. The silicon solar cell operates in much the same way. Selenium cells are widely used in photographic exposure meters, automatic exposure devices for cameras, and for the measurement of illumination.

The *photoconductive effect* is also sometimes used in light-sensitive systems. Photoconductivity involves an increase in the electrical conductivity of a material resulting from illumination by visible or infrared light. In some substances, such as lead sulfide, lead telluride, and lead selenide, the incident radiation causes an increase in the number of free electrons in the substance. This makes it easier to send an electric current through the substance. Another type of photoconductive cell is made of two dissimilar semiconductor layers in a manner similar to the selenium photovoltaic cell described above. In fact, many photovoltaic cells can be made to function as photoconductive cells merely by connecting their terminals to a battery. The resulting current then changes in accordance with the amount of light received by the cell.

Photoconductive cells are often used in infrared missile tracking systems. This is possible because the exhaust of a missile gives off most of its energy in the infrared region. Photoelectric devices are also used to control street lights, to produce sound signals from the sound track of movie film, to sound fire alarms, and to do many other important tasks efficiently and effortlessly.
—William C. Vergara

Pottery Industry. See *Ceramics,* page 1634.

Production Engineering, the branch of engineering concerned with the preparation of a new product for manufacture, the supervision of the manufacturing plant during production, and the collection of data for use in solving problems in the first two areas.

Preparation for production involves selecting a product worth producing and analyzing critically the details of the design. This includes the simplification of the design wherever possible, the setting of tolerances and size variations of the component parts, and consideration of whether standard hardware can be used. Estimates of labor, material, and tool costs are then made. These estimates are derived from past records gathered during the data-collection phase of the operation. After tools are designed and materials are requisitioned, initial production and performance tests are made of the manufactured product to evaluate the success of the production planning.

Supervision of the manufacturing plant during production involves the formulation of production schedules and follow-up. This requires procurement of material, production schedules for component parts, training of manufacturing personnel, setting of wage incentives, quality control, equipment maintenance, and correction of the initial production design. The last element involves cost reduction and cost control. Cost reduction efforts often require developmental changes in the initial product design, or production plan, in order to reduce manufacturing costs.

The third element, data collection, requires the recording of design standards, manufacturing capacity, factory cost accounting, time and motion studies, labor and equipment studies, and product performance in the field. Accurate data collection is essential if the experience gained in manufacturing existing products is to be transferred to the new products.

—Joseph J. Kelleher

Pumps, devices that move, lift, or compress liquids, gases, or mixtures of both liquids and gases. These machines can be defined as either displacement pumps or accelerating pumps. *Displacement pumps,* either piston or rotary, work by drawing fluid into a casing and displacing it by the movement of mechanical elements. *Accelerating pumps,* either rotary or jet, work by accelerating the fluid with mechanical elements or a stream of fluid.

■**DISPLACEMENT PUMPS.**—The group referred to as displacement machines consists of piston, gear, vane, or screw pumps. These pumps are positive displacement units; that is, for each rotation or reciprocation cycle a fixed amount of fluid is displaced or moved.

Piston pumps consist of a casing or cylinder in which a piston is reciprocated by a power source. During the suction stroke, the piston moves away from the cylinder head, admitting fluid; during the pressure stroke, the fluid in the cylinder is displaced, or forced out. Check valves in the inlet and exhaust ports maintain unidirectional flow through the pump cylinder.

Gear pumps consist of a pair of meshed gears rotating in a housing shaped like a figure eight. Inlet and outlet ports are located at the midpoint of the housing. As the gears are rotated, fluid is trapped between the periphery of the gear teeth and the housing and is moved to the discharge end of the pump. As the gears mesh, fluid between the teeth is displaced and forced out of the discharge port.

Vane pumps have cylindrical rotors, equipped with sliding vanes, eccentrically mounted in a cylindrical housing. Retained in slots in the rotor, the vanes are spring-loaded to press against the housing walls. With the rotor mounted eccentrically, the space between the rotating vanes decreases as the vanes pass from the intake to the exhaust port. Spring-loading the vanes prevents leakage and makes it unnecessary to use check valves.

Screw pumps, as their name implies, incorporate right- and left-hand intermeshed helices on parallel shafts connected by gearing. As the helices are turned, fluid is displaced axially from inlet ports at each end to a discharge port at the center. These units are used primarily to pump oils and other fluids with good lubricating qualities.

■**ACCELERATING PUMPS.**—Grouped under the classification of fluid accelerating devices are centrifugal, axial-flow, and jet (injector) pumps.

Centrifugal pumps have an impeller, shaped like a ship's propeller, which is mounted in a housing. The fluid flows through the housing in a straight line parallel to the impeller's axis of rotation. These pumps are used to move large volumes of fluid at low pressure.

Jet, or *injector, pumps* employ a small, high-velocity stream of gas or liquid to move a larger volume of fluid. These pumps are primarily applied as feed-water injectors on steam boilers, where a small portion of the stream generated can be employed as the operating fluid. Among the advantages of such pumps are the durability and simplicity that come from having no moving parts.

—Joseph J. Kelleher

Quarrying, the removal of large deposits of rock, usually by the open-pit method, for use in construction, road building, the manufacture of cement and lightweight aggregates, other industrial purposes, or arts and crafts. Methods of quarrying differ depending upon the physical characteristics of the rock and its ultimate use. In quarrying building and monumental stone it is desirable to obtain large unbroken blocks, which later may be cut, dressed, and polished to the desired dimensions. Careful cutting and blasting are necessary to avoid shattering the rock. Quarrying the softer rock is usually done with a *channeling* machine. This machine cuts or saws a large block of rock from the main formation without breaking it. Such careful methods are not needed when the rock is to be crushed, as for road building, for making concrete, or for use as a flux in the steel industry. For such purposes, the rock is usually broken loose by explosives, and hauled to a processing plant where it is crushed, recrushed, conveyed over screens for sizing, and often washed to meet all market requirements.

—Michael Trojan

Quality Control, the process of maintaining production within the control limits that have been established for an operation. Many complex factors in materials, machines, and conditions of operation interact to cause slight variations in the "identical" parts produced. Variations may be slight, but they always exist. Two steel shafts may seem to be 3 inches in diameter, when one is really 2.99 and the other 3.01. Or two may seem to be 2.9998 inches, when one is really 2.99976 and the other 2.99984 inches. Each part will have some tolerance, or allowable variation, that will depend on the application. For example, the tolerance in diameter of the main shaft in a jet aircraft engine will be very small, but that for the diameter of a stewardess' call button in the same plane can be quite large. If a large number of parts are inspected and their size is plotted on a chart, the variations will fall into a pattern called the *normal distribution.* The largest number will be near the center, with a rapid or gradual falling off away from the center. By a combination of sampling inspection and mathematical analysis, it is possible to tell whether the distribution is abnormal because of some defect in the manufacturing process, or the center of distribution is drifting in one direction or the other because of changes.

Quality control is not the same as inspection. Inspection is a method of separating good and bad parts. Quality control is a method of studying the product to detect incipient defects in the process and correct them, preferably before bad parts are produced.

The process of quality control was developed by Walter Shewhart at the Bell Telephone Laboratories in 1924. It is now standard practice in many manufacturing plants, often in combination with other forms of inspection procedures.

—Anderson Ashburn

Radiation Detectors, devices that indicate the intensity of radioactivity by counting the number of subatomic particles that they encounter.

The *Geiger-Müller counter* consists of a positively charged wire enclosed by a negatively charged cylinder. An electron speeding through the cylinder collides with gas particles, knocking other electrons free. The process continues rapidly until an "avalanche" of negatively charged electrons flows into the positively charged wire. This produces an electrical impulse that causes a pointer to deflect or a clicking sound to be emitted. The greater the intensity of the radiation, the greater is the motion of the pointer, or the louder the clicking sound. Geiger-Müller counters find wide application in prospecting for nuclear materials and in nuclear safety programs.

The *scintillation counter* is a more accurate detector of nuclear radiation. When a radiation particle strikes certain materials, such as zinc sulfide, a faint flash of light is given off. This light flash falls on the surface of a material that emits electrons when struck by light. These electrons, in turn, pass through an electron multiplier tube, which produces an electric current large enough to be measured. Thus, a short pulse of electricity from the counter indicates that a charged particle has passed through the scintillator. Scintillation counters are widely used in nuclear physics laboratories.

Recently, radiation detectors called *image intensifiers* have been developed that amplify the light flashes from the scintillating plate without destroying the image. This makes it possible to take photographs of the actual track of the charged particle in the scintillator.

—William C. Vergara

Refrigeration, the removal of heat from an enclosed space and the maintenance there of a controlled temperature lower than that of the surroundings. Refrigeration for the preservation of food and other perishables has been in use for centuries, but mechanical methods have been developed only within the past 75 years.

From America's beginnings, "ice harvesting" was carried on during cold months on frozen lakes, ponds, and rivers. Until the early 1900's, such natural ice was the major source of the cooling employed in "cold storage" as well as in household "iceboxes."

The earliest mechanical refrigeration machines were the "ice makers," whose product supplemented the sometimes unreliable supply of natural ice (following a winter warmer than usual). The first machines used ammonia and brine as refrigerants, in both the compression cycle and the absorption cycle, which differs from the compression cycle only in the way the pressure is increased between the evaporating coils and the condenser. (For description of refrigeration cycle, see *Physics.*)

The absorption refrigeration cycle is a two-pressure, heat-operated cycle that makes use of a vaporizable liquid as the refrigerant and a second liquid as the absorbent. The liquid refrigerant vaporizes in the evaporator, taking in heat at low temperature, and is compressed by a heat-operated device to such a pressure that it condenses at a higher temperature in the condenser.

■ **MODERN REFRIGERATION.**—By the 1920's, mechanical refrigeration had made great strides. Then, the household refrigerator replaced the old icebox, and the iceman's daily visit became a thing of the past.

Today, mechanical refrigeration is essential to many processes and products. It has contributed to the nation's health through its use in the development and storage of drugs. It has made feasible the storage of sections of living tissue used in surgery, as well as whole blood, preserved in *blood banks.* It is responsible for the entire frozen food industry, established between 1940 and 1950, which makes out-of-season foods available all through the year.

Its applications extend to transport vehicles—railway cars, trucks, and trailers that carry frozen products from packing houses to home freezers —as well as to fixed installations. It has contributed immeasurably to the national defense program through provision for rocket fuels as well as many other defense needs.

Today, new areas of refrigeration are in process of development—for example, *cryogenics*, which involves the behavior of matter at temperatures below —250° F. —L. N. Hunter

Rope, a large, strong cord made of twisted or braided fibers or wires. Cordage, some of which is still made by hand, is commonly manufactured on specially designed machines, in three steps: spinning the yarn, forming yarns into strands, and laying the strands into rope.

Fibers that have been combed and drawn (*staggered*) to form a continuous sliver, or loose bundle, are spun or twisted into a *yarn*. The length, strength, and thickness of fibers vary widely, as do the machines. The pins of the combs and the *reach* of the drawing rolls must suit the fiber that is being worked. Short fibers, such as cotton and wool, require close, fine pins. Jute and flax need fine pins but their longer fibers require a longer reach. Manila hemp and sisal, which are coarser and longer, require coarse pins and a still longer reach. The spinning machines, too, vary with the size or weight of the yarn being spun. Yarn is usually *right twist,* although for some special ropes it may be *left twist.*

The strength of yarn is derived from the strength and quantity of the fiber and from the friction between fibers after twisting. Yarn may be used for *tying twine.* One of the largest uses is in agriculture as *binder* or *baler twine.*

Stranding is the next step in the manufacture of rope. Two or more yarns, sometimes several dozen, are gathered together and twisted to form the strand. This is usually left twist, since the strand twist must be opposite to the yarn twist. The strand is principally used in the manufacture of rope. Probably the most familiar strand to the layman is *butcher's twine.*

Rope is made by twisting or *laying* together strands, again in the opposite direction, usually right lay. Diameters range from $\frac{3}{16}$ inch or smaller, sometimes called *twines,* up to about 3 inches, sometimes called *hawsers.* Much of the tonnage produced goes to the marine, fishing, and pleasure boating trade. Among the other uses are scaffold rope, rigger's falls, tents, and cores for wire rope.

Cables are three ropes twisted together in a fourth step; they may be used in the marine trade or in oil- and water-well drilling.

Other constructions use braided and plaited cordage. These are *over-and-under* methods that offer advantages in certain applications. Braided clotheslines, fishing lines and large plaited hawsers for ships are the most common examples.

■ **MATERIALS.**—Ropes are made from animal sources, such as hair, sinew, and leather, and hand-crafted by primitive peoples. Rope is also made from mineral sources—for example, asbestos rope and packing, and wire rope from iron, steel, and copper. Wire rope has replaced much fiber cordage, for it resists crushing when overwound on drums on heavy machines. However, wire rope lacks elasticity and the ability to absorb shock loads.

Vegetable fibers, such as Manila hemp (abaca), cotton, jute, and sisal are used for cordage throughout the world. Most of the fibers used are cultivated crops, and the quantity and quality of production vary with the conditions of soil, weather, and disease. The fiber must be separated from leaf or stalk by cleaning away pulp and pith. Jute, for example, is retted (or rotted) in water, and the pulp is washed and beaten out by hand. The fiber is then dried. As a result of increased labor costs in areas where most fibers are grown, the price of vegetable fiber has been rising. Therefore, gummed paper tape, steel or wire strapping, and other materials are replacing many traditional vegetable fibers.

Synthetic fibers, such as nylon, polyesters, acrylics, and polyolefins, are growing in use. Although usually higher in cost per pound than natural fibers, they are more economical, as they do not rot, and are stronger per unit of weight and size.

—H. Davis Daboll

Rubber Manufacture, the treatment of natural and synthetic rubbers to form useful end products. Rubber manufacturing can be traced back to ancient civilization. From a tropical tree (*Hevea brasiliensis*), Amazon natives obtained a liquid, later known as natural rubber *latex,* which they used to make crude waterproof clothes, footwear, and balls. In the modern era, rubber manufacturing is generally traced back to a Scotsman named Charles Macintosh, who discovered that waterproof garments can be produced by inserting a thin layer of rubber between two layers of fabric.

Undoubtedly, the most important discovery in the whole history of rubber manufacturing was made by Charles Goodyear, who in 1839 discovered *vulcanization.* Considering that he experimented for nearly ten years, it is likely, as many historians believe, that he arrived at this discovery through trial and error. However, legend persists that he accidentally dropped a mixture of rubber, white lead, and sulfur on a hot stove. When the mixture cooled, it was found to snap back to its original shape. The characteristic of snapping back to the original shape even in extreme cold, and the fact that it was no longer sticky at high temperatures, were the important qualities imparted to rubber by vulcanization.

The first rubber goods factory in the United States was established in 1832 in Roxbury, Mass. After the discovery of vulcanization, other factories sprang up rapidly. At first these were primarily in New England; it was not until about 1870 that rubber manufacturing began in

FIRESTONE TIRE AND RUBBER COMPANY   GOODYEAR TIRE AND RUBBER COMPANY, INC.   FIRESTONE TIRE AND RUBBER COMPANY

TIRES, made of several parts, are joined together on a revolving drum. In the picture at left, the operator is applying the first ply. A "green" or uncured farm tractor tire, *center*, is hoisted into a curing mold, where it will be shaped into one like the suspended tire. The cured tires, *right*, are being conveyed to the last inspection site, where they will receive a series of final quality checks.

Akron, Ohio, which has since become the rubber capital of the world. Today, rubber manufacturing facilities are spread broadly over the United States, from New England to southern California.

By far the best-known and most important product of the industry is the pneumatic rubber tire. Approximately 40 per cent of the dollar value of the industry is in tire products. In addition to the pneumatic tire, a great variety of industrial and consumer products are manufactured from rubber. Conveyor belts, rubber hose, printing rolls, and chemical tank liners are among the more important industrial products. Rubber footwear, raincoats, foam rubber for automobile and furniture upholstery, and latex rubber thread are among the more important consumer products. Rubber continues to become increasingly more useful in sporting goods, ranging from golf balls to scuba diving suits. A major new use for rubber is developing in rubberized roads. The rubber is blended into the asphalt paving mixture, with the result that surface cracking of the road is eliminated in cold weather and the asphalt surface is prevented from softening in hot weather.

■**MIXING.**—The first major step in manufacturing a typical rubber product is *mixing the compound*. In this step, the rubber is masticated in roller mills or large internal mixers, the best known of which is called a *Banbury*. While the rubber is being masticated, vulcanizing chemicals, reinforcing fillers, antioxidant chemicals, and processing oils are mixed uniformly with the rubber. It is significant that sulfur, the chemical used by Goodyear, is still the most common vulcanizing chemical, although zinc oxide and organic chemical accelerators have replaced the white lead that he used.

Among reinforcing fillers, the most important industrially are the carbon blacks. Their use in rubber compounds is necessary to achieve the good wear resistance in today's tires. The function of antioxidants is to slow down the aging process; without them, rubber products would get sticky and crack. The processing oils are added to make the rubber softer and easier to form. Reclaimed rubber is also frequently used as a processing aid and as an extender to reduce the cost of the compound.

The second major step in the manufacturing process in the *fabrication* of the rubber into a form suitable for vulcanization. This is done by the processes of calendering, extruding, or molding.

■**CALENDERING.**—Calendering is the process by which rubber is formed into a flat sheet by passing the mixed rubber compound between heavy steel rollers. A calender has much the same appearance as a mill but generally has three or four rolls rather than the two rolls of a mill. Typically, the rubber is preformed into a sheet of approximately the correct thickness by squeezing it between the first and second roll of the calender; it is then formed into a sheet between the second and third roll. In the calendering operation a fabric can also be passed between the rolls, with the result that the rubber is deposited evenly upon the fabric surface. A 4-roll calender can be operated to coat rubber simultaneously on both sides of the fabric.

■**EXTRUDING AND MOLDING.**—By extrusion, such products as tread rubber for tires, inner tubes, hose, tubing, and strips for window seals are produced. The *extruder*, or *tuber*, as it is sometimes called, consists of a screw that rotates inside of a heated cylinder to force a previously warmed compound through a die or orifice. The final shape of the rubber product is dependent upon the opening in the die. In the *molding* operation, rubber is forced by compression into a heavy steel mold.

■**FABRICATION.**—In the fabrication of complex rubber parts such as a pneumatic tire, the various elements of the final product are shaped separately and assembled before vulcanization. For example, in the production of a pneumatic tire, the carcass fabric is first prepared by a calender operation. Then bead wire bundles are prepared by extruding rubber over wire, which is finally coiled into bundles of the right diameter. The tread and sidewall of the tire are formed by extruding a rubber slab of appropriate shape. The tire is assembled by wrapping plies of calendered fabric around a revolving building drum, around the end of which bead wire bundles are then placed. The edges of the calendered fabric are wrapped around the assembled bead wire bundles, and the tread and sidewall slab are then applied over the carcass fabric. The whole process of assembling the tire is accomplished in several minutes by an experienced tire builder. The assembled tire, still in the shape of the drum on which it was built, is finally placed in an automatic forming press, in which it is inflated into its final shape as the press closes and the vulcanization process begins.

The familiar inner tube used in many tires is shaped by an extrusion process. The rubber is extruded from a tubular die, cut to appropriate length, and formed into the shape of the tube by splicing the free ends together. The valve is inserted, and through it the tube is inflated after it is placed in a hot mold for final shaping and vulcanization.

Rubber or canvas shoes are assembled from flat pieces of rubber that have been formed by calendering. The sheet rubber is cut to appropriate size and built by hand on lasts that permit the composite layers of fabric and rubber to be formed to the desired shape and size. After the sole is affixed to the upper with a strip of *foxing* (an adhesive strip that combines the upper with the sole), the shoe is ready for vulcanization.

■VULCANIZATION.—The final step in the production of rubber products is the all-important *vulcanization*. This is most commonly accomplished by heating the assembled rubber part in a mold. The heat causes the sulfur to set up cross-links between the rubber chains of molecules. This process of cross-linking is responsible for developing the permanence of shape of the vulcanized product. Not all rubber products, however, are vulcanized in a mold. Rubber shoes, for example, are vulcanized in large pressure vessels containing steam and ammonia. Other rubber products, such as golf balls, are vulcanized in an atmosphere of sulfur chloride. Rubber products may also be vulcanized by atomic radiation without the necessity of using sulfur.

■LATEX.—Several important commercial products are made directly from liquid latex rubber by processes quite different from those described above; for example, gloves and balloons are formed by dipping. In the production of foam cushions for upholstery, mattresses, and pillows, the latex is whipped with air and molded into the desired shapes. Another important product of latex is Lastex thread. The latex is formed into a thread and, in a continuous process, is covered with textile fibers. Lastex thread has been widely used in bathing suits and other elastic clothing.

Many exciting new rubber products are being manufactured for use in space and underwater technology. Pressure suits, inflatable space stations, living chambers for ocean engineering work, buoys, and supply hoses require new properties and new techniques for their fabrication. (See also *Rubber*.)

—Marvin C. Brooks

Safes, containers designed to protect valuable articles from theft or fire. There are two types of safes: money safes and fire-resistant safes. The *money safe* is usually square with a circular door, constructed of fire- and drill-resistant metal, and is used for the protection of money, jewels, and valuable documents against theft, holdup, and burglary. For protection of the contents against fire, the money safe is welded into a record safe. To prevent it from being carted away easily, the money safe may be encased in a steel-covered reinforced concrete block.

A *fire-resistive record safe* is a container with the prime purpose of protecting its contents against fire. It is usually rectangular in shape with a rectangular door, having an inside and an outside metal shell with heat-resistive insulation between the shells. To be approved by the Underwriters' Laboratories, Inc., a record safe must pass a rigid fire-exposure test, a drop or impact test, and an explosion hazard test. The Underwriters issue labels of approval for three types of record safes: one that will withstand four hours' exposure to heat reaching 2000° F while the inside cannot exceed 350° F.; one for two hours' exposure at 1850° F; and one for one hour exposure at 1700° F.   —Ken Roberts

FORDHAM UNIVERSITY

SEISMOGRAPHIC RECORD is traced on a paper wrapped around a rotating cylinder.

Seismograph, a device for detecting and recording, visually or audibly, ground vibrations—especially those caused by earthquakes. As the definition implies, there are two parts to a seismograph, a detector and a recorder.

The *detector* is usually referred to as the *seismometer*, or *pickup*. It is essentially some form of pendulum, that is, a mass (the pendulum *bob*) lightly suspended from a frame attached to the ground. The principle involved is that the mass, because of its inertia, tends to stay at rest while the framework is jolted by ground vibrations, thus setting up a relative motion between the stationary mass and the framework.

In one modern seismometer, the mass is a heavy cylindrical magnet suspended by fine piano wires attached to the frame. Fixed to the base of the frame is a circular coil fitting snugly but freely into the circular magnet. If a ground vibration or wave passes under the seismometer, the coil moves with the ground into or away from the magnet, which remains stationary because of its inertia. Such motion of a coil in a magnetic field produces an electric current in the coil (the principle of the generator), and this current is led off to the recorder, where it is recorded visually or audibly (on tape).

Whether the magnet is the suspended mass and the coil is fixed to the base, or the coil is the suspended mass and the magnet is fixed to the base, makes no difference. Both methods are in equal use today. Such a seismometer may be set up vertically (so as to oscillate vertically), in which case it will respond to vertical ground vibrations; or it may be set up horizontally, in which case it will respond to horizontal vibrations. A complete seismic setup calls for three such seismometers. One is set up vertically, one horizontally on a north-south axis, and one horizontally on an east-west axis. Such an orientation makes it possible to determine the direction from which the vibrations come to the observatory.

The *visible recorder* is usually a drum around which is wrapped a sheet of photographic paper or stylus paper. For *photographic recording*, the current from the pickup is led to a moving-coil galvanometer, where it causes a mirror attached to the moving coil to reflect light from a fixed source back and forth on the drum in keeping with the ground motion. In the *stylus* type (pen and ink or hot-wire stylus), the current is amplified and led to a needle-type galvanometer. The stylus or pen, which is attached to the needle, then traces out the ground motion as the drum rotates. The drum is driven by a synchronous motor, and minute and hour marks are impressed on the record by a clock. Audible recording is done on tape.   —Joseph Lynch

Servomechanism, a combination of elements that control a source of power automatically in order to perform a desired function. All servomechanisms use *feedback*, the same process that helps to control the air temperature in our homes. Suppose the thermostat is set at 70° F. The furnace goes on automatically when the temperature falls below 70° F, and turns off when the temperature rises to about 72° F. The heating plant is merely a source of heat whose effect is to raise the air temperature in the home. This effect—the air temperature—is "fed back" to the thermostat and compared with its temperature setting. Any difference between the two is used to control the source of power, the furnace.

The same principle is widely used to control automatic machinery. Imagine a sheet of steel being pressed to a desired thickness between a pair of rollers. The thickness of the sheet is measured automatically and compared with the desired thickness. Any difference between the two thicknesses controls a motor that increases or decreases the roller spacing to provide the desired thickness.

Servomechanisms are also used to control high-speed aircraft where human reactions would be too slow. They are used in electric-power generating equipment to control voltage and frequency. They control the speed of motors, the temperature of the cooling water in automobile engines, the rate of fuel injection in missiles, and the automatic pointing of guns and radar beams. A servomechanism, in short, is the heart of any self-adjusting process or machine.   —William C. Vergara

Sewing Machine, a device for continuous stitching or sewing. The invention of the sewing machine cannot rightly be credited to one man. In 1790 Thomas Saint, an English cabinetmaker, patented a device for stitching shoes and boots, but his idea was never put to practical use. Others who devised sewing machines during the nineteenth century were Baltasar Krembs in Germany; John Duncan in Scotland; Josef Madersperger in the Austrian Tyrol; John Dodge of Monkton, Vt.; Barthélemy Thimmonier in France; and Henry Lye of Philadelphia, Pa.

About 1832, Walter Hunt of New York built the first sewing machine based on a lock-stitch principle. In this machine, an eye-pointed needle pushed a loop of thread through and beneath the fabric, where a bobbin carried a separate thread through the loop. Hunt, however, he did not apply for a patent. Elias Howe began to work on a sewing machine and was led to the same discoveries as those of Hunt; he patented his machine in 1846. In Boston in 1850, Isaac Merritt Singer, a journeyman mechanic, made the first sewing machine capable of sewing continuously. He was granted patents in 1851 and began to manufacture machines.

Today, more than 4,000 different types of sewing machines are made. Electric models for home use, whether portable or in cabinets, may be of the straight-stitch or swing-needle (zig-zag) varieties. Swing-needle machines can do straight stitching and many variations of zig-zag decorative stitching. One type can also do a chain stitch.

—Rose Marie Burnley

Shipbuilding, the construction of waterborne vessels. Archaeological artifacts recovered in the Mediterranean Sea and in Lake Nemi, Italy, have shown that wooden shipbuilding and boatbuilding were well developed as far back as 50 B.C. It was not until the early nineteenth-century that steel was used in ship construction. Today, wood, steel, fiberglass, and alloys are all used for shipbuilding. Eventually, plastic hulls may be produced for vessels exceeding 60 feet in length although, at present, plastic hulls are still in the process of development.

The art of shipbuilding consists of two phases: design and construction. The factors determining ship design are: the use to which the ship will be put; the speeds required of it; and the depth of the harbor where it will be constructed. These must be considered because they affect a ship's length, beam, depth, hull design, and means of propulsion.

Once such factors are determined, the preliminary designs for the ship may be made. Either a *line-drawing* or a *half-model* of the ship is prepared. The art of drawing ship plans developed slowly. The earliest English manuscript on the subject,

known as *Fragments of Ancient English Shipwrightry,* is commonly dated about 1586. Plans were usually drawn on parchment until late in the seventeenth century, when paper gradually came into use. Drafting methods employed in preparing a lines plan showing hull form have changed slightly since 1800. The practice of first making scale drawings of the form of the ship and then "laying down" the full-sized drawings of the shape of the frames and end profiles of the hull was first described in Mediterranean records of the fifteenth and sixteenth centuries.

The use of the half-model as a substitute for a lines plan is supposed to have developed in England as early as 1700. A solid block of wood was shaped to represent one side of the proposed hull. From this, the forms of the cross sections were taken and transferred to a plank or to drawing paper along the hull profile as developed in the block model. The half-model has the advantage of representing the hull-form in three dimensions. Hence, a half-model is sometimes made from the lines plan for study purposes by naval architects. Often, the design is tested in a model tank.

Before construction is started, the line drawing or half-model is reproduced in a full-size drawing. Called *lofting,* this reproduction is done in the *mold-loft,* a large room in which at least the forward and after halves of the hull can be drawn full-size on the floor. Lofting is closely tied to the use of plans or half-models, for only by using such plans can the small-scale design be reproduced to actual size. In large ships, the lofting is very extensive and requires much detailed work—some yards even use photographic methods of lofting. With the completion of *templates,* full-size wooden or paper patterns made in the mold-loft and complete even to drill holes to show the exact position of holes to be drilled or punched in the finished pieces, the actual construction of the ship may be started.

■**INTERNAL MEMBERS.**—The major structural members of ship may be divided into two classes: those that run lengthwise in the ship, and those that are set at right angles to its length. The chief function of the transverse frames is to withstand the pressure of the water. If a ship had adequate transverse frames and could always operate under ideal conditions in which there were no wind or waves, and the load could always be properly distributed, the longitudinal framework would not have to be very strong. Actually, much of the ship's weight may have to be supported by small areas along its length, as when it rides across a wave or when bow and stern are lifted together by two waves. This produces enormous stresses tending to cause the ship to sag, or "break its back."

Therefore, the most important structural member of a ship is its *keel,* the backbone of the ship, which is designed to provide longitudinal strength. It runs from stem to stern at the bottom of the vessel and is usually built to form a continuous structure from one end to the other. Extending upward from the keel to the upper deck for the full length of the vessel is a strong framework, often made of steel, called the *keelson.* Together, keel and keelson form a structure very similar to a bridge and thus provide much of the longitudinal strength of the ship.

■**CONSTRUCTION STEPS.**—The first step in the actual construction of a ship is the preparation of the *berth,* or bed, on which it rests during the building. This must be very solid and strong in order to support the enormous weight placed upon it. First wooden blocks, called *keelblocks,* are laid. The next step is the erection of bulkhead frames across the middle of the keel, beginning the main transverse structure of the ship. Many other transverse frames are then spaced at other points along the keel. If heavy material or preassembled parts are to be installed, overhead cranes, running on elevated

ABOVE—BETHLEHEM STEEL CORPORATION

TANKER (*above*) with a 27,200,000-gallon capacity takes shape in a shipyard berth five months after the keel-laying. At *left,* a ship's screw dwarfs men working in a drydock.

tracks on both sides of the *ways* (forms upon which the ship rides into the water) transport them and hold them in the exact positions desired until they can be bolted in place. Bolting holds the parts only temporarily until it is convenient to rivet them firmly into position.

When construction of the keel and bottom framing are completed, the floors, bulkheads, and additional frames are installed. Calking, installation of some machinery parts, and tests for watertightness complete the building-berth process. The ship is then ready for launching.

Usually a ship is launched stern-first although, in some parts of the world, the vessel is either set up with the bow to the water and launched bow-first or placed parallel to the shore and launched sidewise. A fourth method of launching is floating: the ship is built in a dry dock, below sea level; water is admitted into the dry dock, gradually floating the ship.

Once floating, the ship is taken to an *outfitting dock,* or *builder's wharf,* and its construction is completed. Deck structures and interior joinerwork are fitted, machinery installed, and, in the case of sailing vessels, masts stepped. With such equipment in place, the ship is given dock and sea trials before delivery to the owner. —Howard Chapelle

Shoe Manufacture, a highly mechanized industry, employing over 230,000 workers and producing more than 50,000,000 pairs of shoes each month in the United States. Yet it was long assumed that, because of the complex processes involved, shoemaking would always be done by painstaking handicraftsmen.

In the seventeenth century, when shoemaking as an industry first appeared in North America, it was customary for a cobbler to make regular trips around the countryside, living with each family in turn until he had completed a year's supply of shoes for everyone. As recently as 100 years ago, a good shoemaker, with tools which had changed little since their use by Egyptian artisans in the fourteenth century B.C., could average at the most five or six pairs of shoes a week. By contrast, the giant industry today turns out 70 pairs of shoes a week for each worker. This is accomplished by use of machines wherever practicable and also by the separation of the shoemaking process into small increments, each performed by a skilled craftsman.

The modern shoe industry was born in 1862 with the introduction of the McKay Sewing Machine, the first machine with the capability of stitching the shoe upper to the sole. The increase in mechanization has been rapid, until at the present time there are more than 300 different kinds of machines, some relatively simple, some highly complex. Depending upon the type of operation which they perform, their rate of productivity varies from a few hundred pairs a day to several thousand. There is now not a major operation in shoemaking which is not done better by machine than it once was by hand.

■**MANUFACTURING PROCESS.**—A shoe may undergo as many as 382 different operations in its manufacture and be composed of up to 290 separate items. After the initial step of cutting the upper from a pattern by means of dies, the shoe goes to the Upper Fitting Room, where the lining uppers, box toes, counters, and straps are assembled and permanently attached to one another by stitching, lacing or cementing (adhesive bonding). Other operations are often accomplished here like perforating, eyeletting, lacing, pinking and splitting or rubbing to a uniform thickness. Next, the fitted upper along with other parts of the shoe, including insoles and outsoles, counters, welting, heels and box toes, are assembled in the Stock Fitting Department. Then the assembled shoe undergoes the very important process of lasting.

A *last* is a form, formerly of hard maple wood, but now predominately of plastic, which reproduces the shape of the human foot and determines the exact style and size of the finished shoe. Lasting is a series of operations designed to create a new three dimensional shape from a two dimensional piece or pieces of material. When using leather upper and lining material they are thoroughly moistened, then stretched over the last, attached to the insole, and dried.

The next step accomplishes the attaching of the outsole to the upper. Shoes are traditionally divided into three general types, depending upon the method used for this step. The largest category, in which the sole is attached by cement, accounts for over half of the total shoes produced, including nearly all women's shoes. The second are the stitched shoes, including the Goodyear Welts, the Littleway Lockstitch and McKay constructions, and the Stitchdowns. Third is the vulcanized shoe—including both work and tennis type shoes. A fourth category, vinyl injection molded to fabric or leather uppers, must now be added because of its growing importance.

After attaching of the outsole the shoe is ready for heel attaching (where required) and finishing. By the time it reaches the shipping room it may have passed through 200 different pairs of hands. —Alice Regensburg

Silk Manufacturing, the production of textiles from raw silk. The art of weaving was developed in China more than 4,000 years ago. It then found its way to the Near East and, much later, reached the European continent. By the twelfth century, Italy had become the silk center of the West. In France, silk weaving was begun in 1480 during the reign of Louis XI, although it had been introduced in England somewhat earlier during the reign of Henry VI. Strangely enough, it was not until 1810 that the first silk mill was built in America. The industry did not really prosper, however, until a protective tariff was instituted during the Civil War. Today, the United States imports more raw silk than any other country in the world.

When the raw silk is reeled off from cocoons, it is not strong enough to be woven into anything except the sheerest material. Therefore, depending upon the fabric to be woven, two, three, or four silk threads are thrown together. This is done by *throwsters.* Much of the raw silk used for filling, called *tram,* is thrown with a certain twist. The silk yarns are woven on looms very much like those used for cotton. Automatic power looms have long since taken the place of hand-weaving methods in practically all the leading countries.

One of the outstanding features in silk weaving is the Jacquard loom, invented by Joseph Marie Jacquard of Lyons, France, in 1801. Jacquards are composed of a multiple of different weaves forming definite patterns, such as flowers or kindred motifs. The creation of these patterns is by the use of intricate perforated strips of punched cardboards operated in conjunction with the loom (similar to IBM machines). It is on these Jacquard looms that the brocades, brocatelles, damasks, and heavy fabrics for evening wear are woven.

Today, most of the raw silk is consumed in the *haute couture;* that is, in evening dresses where brocades, satins, crepes, chiffons, and georgettes are mostly used, and also in cocktail dresses, in which prints and shantungs are predominant. The demand for silk is also strong for cravat fabrics, as well as for upholstery and curtain materials. —Hans Vaterlaus

Simple Machines, the most elementary mechanical devices, one or more of which are the basis of all complex machines. The simple machines include the inclined plane or wedge, wheel and axle, pulley, and lever. The inclined plane or wedge becomes a *screw*—which itself is often classed as a simple machine—when it is wrapped around a cylinder, while *gears* are a form of wheel and axle. The pulley is found in cranes and hoists while the lever is found in its commonest form in an ordinary crowbar.

The function of the simple machines is to change either the magnitude or the direction of applied forces. When prehistoric man used a log or branch to move a large stone, he was unknowingly applying the *principle of the lever* to multiply the force available in his muscles.

As shown in the accompanying illustration, the force *F* applied on the log by the prehistoric man is multi-

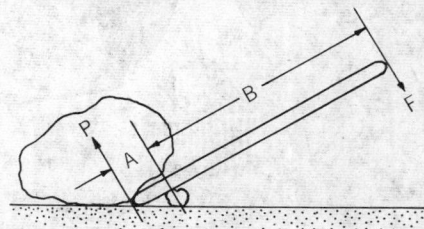

plied into a much larger force P applied to stone. If the distance B is six times longer than the distance A, the force P is six times greater than the force F applied by the man.

This example of a simple machine also illustrates the principle of *conservation of energy*. To lift the stone one inch, the user must exert a force over a distance of B/A inches. Simply expressed, a simple machine can convert a small force applied over a large distance into a large force acting over a small distance.

The *actual mechanical advantage* (AMA) of a simple machine is expressed as the ratio of the force produced to the force applied. In the case of the prehistoric man's lever, the AMA equals P/F.

Not all simple machines multiply the applied force. Some just alter its direction. When a rope is passed over a simple pulley, the input force applied F must be equal to the load it lifts.

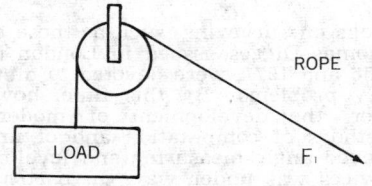

To reduce the force needed to lift the load, an axle or differential pulley is added to the simple pulley. In either case, the force needed to lift the load is reduced but it must be applied over a larger distance than the load moves. To lift the load one foot, the force F_2 must be applied for

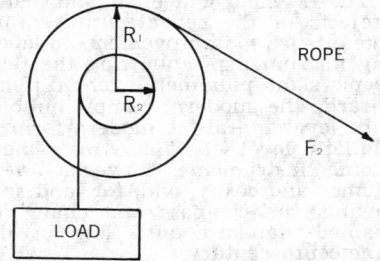

a distance equivalent to the ratio of the radius of the large pulley R_2 to the radius of the axle or small pulley R_1. The AMA of the system equals R_2/R_1.

In actual machines, friction exists and work must be exerted to overcome the friction. The *theoretical* efficiency of an actual machine equals the ratio of the useful work produced to the work input. The actual efficiency equals the *work out/work in*.

Because ideal machines have no friction, their efficiency is 100 per cent. The *ideal mechanical advantage* (IMA) of a simple machine is the ratio of the distance the input force moves to the distance the output force moves. The IMA therefore equals D_{in}/D_{out}.

In an actual machine the IMA is larger than the AMA because of frictional losses and the efficiency of an actual machine is the ratio AMA/IMA. Actual efficiency can be expressed as work out/work in, $F_{out} \times D_{out}/F_{in} \times D_{in}$, or AMA/IMA.
—Joseph J. Kelleher

Soldering, the joining or coating of metals with low-temperature alloys. Mechanical joints made with solder are liquid-tight and gastight, but have little mechanical strength. Depending on the alloy used, solder coating provides improved corrosion resistance, good electrical conductivity, and improved appearances. The most common soldering alloys consist of lead and tin and are available in wire, foil, bar, or ingot form. Soldering takes place when the low-temperature alloy is brought in contact with the heated base metal, where it melts and flows over the surface. The base metal can be heated with a soldering iron, gas torch, or oven, depending on the size of the work and area to be soldered. *Dip soldering*, which involves immersing the parts to be coated or joined in a bath of molten alloy, is used in high-volume manufacturing processes.

To assure adequate adhesion of the solder to the base metal, a *flux* is used to remove oxide coatings and to lower the surface tension. Rosins, zinc chlorides, sal ammoniac, and acids are common fluxes. With the exception of rosin, fluxes should be neutralized or washed away to prevent corrosion of the base metal. *Hollow wire solder* filled with rosin is widely used to join wires in electrical equipment.
—Joseph J. Kelleher

Spinning, the twisting of fibers to make a continuous thread or yarn. Spinning is an art older than recorded history. Spun yarns have been found amid the ruins of ancient civilizations, and hieroglyphs and cave drawings thousands of years old depict men and women spinning yarn by hand. Aborigines in all parts of the world have developed markedly similar methods of spinning.

Spun yarn is composed of a strand of fibers arranged in parallel form and twisted to provide cohesion and strength. Among the most commonly used natural fibers are cotton, wool, silk, flax, and jute. Today, many commercially produced synthetic fibers are spun into yarn on conventional machines.

All spinning was done by hand until about two centuries ago. The fibers were drawn from a supply of stock, loosely wrapped upon a rod which the spinner held under his arm. The fibers were paralleled and formed into a slightly twisted strand by the spinner using the fingers of both hands. A *spindle*, which also served as a yarn carrier, was suspended by the yarn and rotated to provide further twist. As the spun yarn accumulated, it was wound upon the spindle and secured so that it would not unwind as the spindle was again set in motion, and the drafting (drawing out) of the fibers resumed.

The *spinning wheel* or *Saxony wheel*, invented by Johann Jurgens of Brunswick, Germany, in the sixteenth century, was the first machine for spinning yarn from fibers. The *spinning jenny*, employing the principles of the Saxony wheel but equipped with a number of spindles, was invented by James Hargreaves in 1764.

The drafting of fibers with revolving rolls is the invention of James Wyatt, who built a spinning machine in 1730. Lewis Paul, an associate of Wyatt, patented a spinning machine in 1738 and a better model in 1758.

However, Richard Arkwright was the first to develop machine spinning on a commercial basis. Between 1769 and 1775, he patented carding, drawing, roving, and spinning machines. The mills he built and equipped with machines of his own design marked the beginning of what has come to be known as the Industrial Revolution.

The first spinning machine in America was a spinning jenny built by Christopher Tully in 1775 and installed in the Philadelphia mill of Samuel Wetherill.

The *mule frame* was invented by Samuel Crompton in 1779. *Cap spinning* was patented by Charles Danforth in 1828, and John Thorp patented *ring spinning* in 1830. Ring spinning is the predominant system throughout the world today.

A modern spinning frame may have 400 or more spindles. The rapidly revolving rolls take each inch of stock and draft it out into ten, twenty, or even into hundreds of inches of yarn. The spindles rotate at speeds up to 15,000 revolutions per minute to twist the yarn and wind it onto *bobbins* or tubes. (See also *Weaving*, page 1720 and *Tufting*, page 1717.)
—Wilmer Westbrook

Spring, mechanical elements that store energy when displaced or deflected. A spring may be made of any elastic material and can take any shape. Although springs are usually made of metal, they can also be made of wood, plastic, glass, or rubber. Springs may be classified according to their shape as coil, torsion bar, leaf, spiral, or disk.

Coil springs are produced by winding a wire around a rod or mandrel to form a helix. Tension springs frequently have the ends of the wire formed into hooks that can be easily connected to machine elements. Compression coil springs are wound loosely, or with space between the coils, to allow for contraction. The ends of compression springs are ground flat, perpendicular to the axis, to assure uniform deflection of the coil during loading.

Torsion bars consist of a rod, shaft, or tube that is loaded by twisting. Energy is stored when one end of the bar is held while the other end is rotated. Torsion bars are used as the springing element in some automobile suspensions.

Leaf springs are cantilever beams that deflect when loaded. Although a single leaf can be used, the usual arrangement is to add several leaves of varying lengths to the main leaf. The deflection characteristics and load-carrying ability of the main leaf can be adjusted by varying the length and number of the auxiliary leaves. One advantage of leaf springs is their ability to resist loads in two directions.

Spiral, or *watch, springs* are wound in an Archimedean spiral in a flat plane. When a watch spring is wound, the force deflects the coils, decreasing the space between successive turns. As the spring unwinds, the energy stored by winding is used to operate the clockwork.

Disk springs, also called *Belleville springs,* consist of a conical washer that deflects when an axial load is applied. These springs occupy very little space and support large loads with little deflection. Several disk springs can be stacked to increase their capacity.

Although springs are used in many ways, their primary function is to store energy. Common examples are clocks and wind-up toys, in which energy is stored by a mechanism that deflects the spring. As the spring returns to its original shape, the energy is released to move the clock hands or drive the toy. —Joseph J. Kelleher

Sugar Processing, the sequence of processes involved in producing sugar from sugarcane and sugar beets. Sugarcane deteriorates rapidly after harvesting. It must, therefore, be promptly processed at a nearby sugar factory or mill. At the factory, the cane is chopped into pieces and passed through huge rollers that crush it, thereby extracting the juice. The fibrous cane residue that remains is called *bagasse.*

Impurities are removed from the juice by heating and adding lime. A syrup develops as water is evaporated from the juice. The syrup is boiled under a vacuum, and a mass of sugar crystals and molasses develops. The sugar crystals, which are separated from the molasses in a centrifugal, are surrounded by a film of molasses and a number of impurities. The mass of crystals is referred to as *raw sugar*—a coarse, sticky, brownish substance.

Molasses and sugarcane bagasse are by-products of sugarcane processing. Molasses is used primarily for livestock feed, and bagasse for fuel at sugar mills and to produce paper.

Raw sugar is shipped to cane sugar refineries where it is converted into a variety of refined sugars. During the refining process, molasses is separated from the raw-sugar crystals. The crystals are dissolved in water to produce a syrup, which is then filtered to remove impurities. Next, the syrup is concentrated by evaporation and boiled under vacuum until refined-sugar crystals develop. These crystals are separated from the syrup by centrifugals and are dried and packaged.

Refined beet sugar is produced in factories that process the sugar beets —not in separate refineries. These factories are located in the sugar beet producing regions. The beets are washed and sliced into thin strips called *cossettes.* The sugar is removed from the cossettes by a diffusion process. The juice is then processed into sugar in a manner similar to the cane-sugar process. Beet pulp and beet molasses are by-products of beet-sugar processing. Both are used as livestock feed.

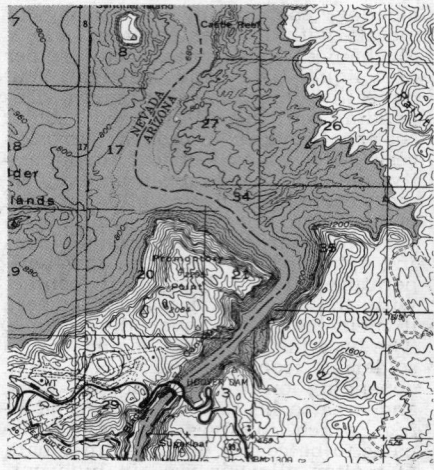

U.S. GEOLOGICAL SURVEY

TOPOGRAPHIC MAP (*left*) of Lake Mead area was plotted from aerial photograph (*right*).

Approximately 70 per cent of the sugar consumed in the United States is cane sugar; the remainder is beet sugar. Many varieties of refined sugar and styles of packaging are required to meet the demands of consumers. Refined sugar is distributed to food processors in packaged, dry bulk, and liquid forms.

In a number of places throughout the world, crude sugars are still produced for local consumption. These sugars are referred to as noncentrifugal sugars. —Nicholas Kominus

Surveying, the science of locating points on or near the earth's surface. The need for surveying arose in the earliest days of civilized life, and tomb pictures show the ancient Egyptians measuring fields with coils of rope. Similarly, the aid of these so-called *rope-stretchers* and of simple plummet levels was required in laying out the foundations for such great sloping works as the Pyramids.

The Greeks, endeavoring to rationalize earlier rules, created *geometry,* or *land measurement,* and applied their findings to more involved problems—such as surveys for tunnels carried out from two headings or requiring alignment and grade between intermediate shafts. The Romans, in turn, adopted these Greek advances and used the *groma,* or surveyor's cross, a cross-arm sighting device for setting out right angles and in laying out rectangular land plots which, it is said, inspired the American public-land system. For leveling, the *chorobates,* or plummet or water-trough leveling device, was apparently adopted in preference to the Greek *dioptra,* an angle-and-level instrument described by Hero of Alexandria. Surveying, however, was long to remain a simple art, based on similar triangles and right angles. Angle measurements were possible, but there appears to have been little early need or use for such measurements.

The advent of gunpowder and the rise of military engineering in the late Middle Ages and early Renaissance introduced problems of range and elevation. The first printed books on surveying, such as those of Thomas Digges, issued in London in 1556 and 1571, were devoted to military problems. By this time, however, the development of modern methods of computation and of improved angle-measuring and leveling devices was under way. In particular, the *enclosure* movement in Britain led to increased interest in land surveying. Although the graphical method of the "playne table" often sufficed, there was an increased use of the surveyor's *chain,* developed by Edmund Gunter, and of the surveyor's compass.

The French aqueduct and canal projects of the seventeenth century likewise led to improvements in leveling instruments. Following the telescopic-sight plummet level of Henri Picard, the modern dumpy bubble-tube level appears in modern form in Mallet's level of 1702. Angle-measuring instruments, however, were clumsy and costly, and, for land surveying, the compass and chain remained standard until late in the nineteenth-century.

A simplified form of the European *theodolite* was developed in the United States early in the nineteenth century, and this American *transit* remains today the standard American angle-measuring instrument. Equipped with *stadia hairs,* it is also used for smaller topographic surveys.

A major division is made between *plane surveying* and *geodetic surveying.* The latter, extending over large areas, involves the most accurate measurements required in surveying —so accurate that allowance must be made for the curvature of the earth. Carried out largely by government agencies, it provides the basic control for the more detailed topographic maps published by all major nations. The U.S. Coast and Geodetic Survey furnishes basic data to the U.S. Geological Survey, which issues maps— usually at a scale of about one mile to the inch—of most of the country. Aerial photographic surveys are increasingly used in map making.

Surveying provides essential data for the design and layout especially

of civil engineering works, and is therefore often undertaken by engineering offices. However, land surveying is usually regarded as a specialty. Land surveyors are licensed by the states, and their activities are limited to this field alone.
—James Kip Finch

Systems Engineering, the branch of engineering dealing with the optimal integration of a variety of machines, instruments, and other devices in order to perform a complex function. Systems engineering is interdisciplinary in nature, requiring a knowledge of all branches of engineering science that might bear upon a specific task.

The design of a satellite surveillance system is a typical application of modern systems-engineering techniques. Such a system might involve search radar sets to detect satellites, tracking radar sets to determine the satellites' precise locations, computers to calculate their orbits, data-processing equipment to reduce raw data to usable form, and a communication network to connect a number of ground stations located hundreds or thousands of miles apart. These and many additional subsystems, such as timing devices, hydraulic equipment, antennas, facilities, buildings, television networks, etc., are selected by systems engineers for their ability to perform a necessary function within the system. Where a needed subsystem does not exist, the systems engineer has it designed and built to his specifications. Many subsystems, in turn, are so complex that they too must be designed as individual systems with major electronic, electrical, pneumatic, and hydraulic components. The radar sets mentioned above would certainly fall into that class.

Systems engineering now plays a vital role in the design of military and commercial aircraft, in space programs, in the design of chemical processing plants, in communication and navigation networks, and in a great variety of complex systems made possible by modern technology.
—William C. Vergara

Transistor, an electronic device, made of a semiconductor material, capable of amplifying or switching electric signals. The transistor was invented in 1948 by William Shockley, Walter H. Brattain, and John Bardeen, scientists of the Bell Telephone Laboratories. Their invention was the greatest contribution to electronics since the invention of the vacuum tube, and for this feat they were awarded the Nobel Prize in physics in 1956.

The *junction transistor* consists of a tiny crystal of semiconductor material, usually of the chemical elements silicon or germanium. The crystal is extremely small in size, about 20-thousandths of an inch square and perhaps 6-thousandths of an inch thick. The crystal is initially of high purity. Small amounts of impurities are then diffused into the crystal at high temperature, a process called *doping.* This produces a sandwich within the crystal consisting of three layers of slightly different semiconductor material. Wires are then attached to each of the three semiconductor layers. These form the output electrodes of the device and are called the *emitter, collector,* and *base.*

Transistors can amplify electric signals because a small electric charge applied in the base electrode controls a much larger charge moving from the emitter to the collector. Unlike the vacuum tube, the transistor requires no heating; furthermore, the transistor operates on a fraction of the power required by the vacuum tube.

Closely related to the transistor is the *junction diode.* It differs from the transistor in that it consists of only two semiconductor layers instead of three. It has the important property of allowing current to flow only in one direction through the crystal. Diodes are widely used in electronic computers, radio receivers, and other electronic equipment.

In 1952 William Shockley developed the theory of a new semiconductor device which has come to be known as the *field effect transistor.* Its main advantage over the junction transistor is the extremely high electrical resistance it presents to the applied signal source. This means that it draws practically no current from the signal source. In that respect, the field effect transistor is similar in operation to the vacuum tube, but the transistor is more efficient.

The *silicon controlled rectifier* is another important transistor-like device. It is made of four parallel semiconductor layers in a single crystal of silicon. Electrodes are attached to three of these layers. The silicon controlled rectifier is used widely in rectification, the transformation of alternating current to direct current in electronic equipment. As a rectifier, it replaces large bulky vacuum tubes and performs the function with great simplicity and efficiency. It is also used as an "on-off" switch, controlled by momentary pulses of current, and as an amplifier which can increase the strength of a signal up to 10,000 times. It is used in battery chargers, in current-limiting circuit breakers, in electronic light flashers, and for speed control of electric motors. The light-sensitive silicon controlled rectifier is used for automatic lamp switching and in many applications in which light must actuate or influence an electronic circuit. A large number of other types of light-sensitive transistors are available for specific applications.

Until recently, the transistor has been unable to function well in extremely-high-frequency circuits. A new discovery, however, called the *metal base transistor,* may make it possible for transistors to be used at frequencies up to 10,000 megacycles per second or higher. Like the junction transistor, the metal base transistor consists of a three-layer sandwich. It differs in that the middle layer is made of a metal instead of silicon. This central metal layer is attached to the base electrode of the transistor, hence the term metal base transistor.

The future appears bright for new and improved types of transistors. Transistors capable of operation at frequencies up to thousands of megacycles are now being perfected. The vision of high-speed, light-actuated devices is now a reality and optical computing and amplifying systems may soon be developed.

One of the most promising new technological developments is known as *microelectronics.* The transistor has given electronics a tiny replacement for the older, larger, and less efficient vacuum tube. Lately, electronics engineers have begun to learn how to reduce the size of other electronic components, such as *resistors* and *capacitors.* This means that entire electronic circuits can be manufactured in a tiny package no larger than an aspirin tablet. One method of fabricating such circuits involves the diffusion of impurities into various portions of a tiny crystal of silicon. In this way, the resistors and capacitors are formed in or upon the silicon crystal concurrently with the formation of transistors. Although microcircuits are still technological infants, they are revolutionizing the electronics industry much more rapidly than did the transistor.
—William C. Vergara

Tufting, a variation of the sewing process used in the production of carpets, rugs, bedspreads, robes, blankets, and wearing apparel.

Carpets are the most important tufted fabric, with 300 million yards produced in 1964—a jump from 21 million yards in 1951, when the first figures were recorded by the U. S. Department of Commerce. During this short time, tufted carpets have replaced most woven carpets, and now more than 80 per cent of all carpeting produced in the United States is tufted.

In the tufting process, a piece of yarn threaded through a needle is pushed through a woven fabric (jute for carpets), caught by a latch and held, and withdrawn through the fabric. On some machines the loops of yarn are cut, producing *cut pile.* Other machines do not cut the loop, and the fabric is *loop pile.* Machines can be interchanged to make both types.

Machine output is high—about 15 times as high as on looms that make woven carpet. One tufting machine 12 or 15 feet wide produces 600 yards of carpeting in one 8-hour day. A machine runs at 550 *courses* (stitches) a minute. Machine gauge (distance between needles) is ⅛, ³⁄₁₆, or ⁵⁄₃₂ inch.

The yarn comes from a creel at the back of a machine that holds an average of 1,600 yarn ends. On machines that run the same style of carpeting for long periods, it is more economical to use yarn on beams, as in weaving. Latex backing is applied to all carpets. It locks the yarn tufts securely into the jute backing, gives carpets dimensional stability, and makes them nonskid.

■HISTORY.—Tufting began in 1895, when Catherine Evans (later Whitener), a Georgia farm girl, made a hand-tufted bedspread patterned after an old heirloom bedspread. She made this bedspread by drawing designs on unbleached muslin with a dinner plate and a ruler. Then she sewed stitches along the pattern with cotton yarn, and cut the heavy yarn between each stitch. She made a second hand-tufted bedspread as a wedding gift in 1898 and sold her first bedspread in 1900 for $2.50. Soon she enlisted the help of her neighbors to fill orders for her handiwork. Within ten years, women throughout the area were making bedspreads by the hundreds from her patterns.

Early bedspread operations were conducted in the home. Groups of people bought cotton sheeting by the case and tufting yarn from local mills. As bedspreads found a ready market, sheets marked with patterns were sent to distant rural communities and individual farmhouses. Women—and sometimes men and children—in the families tufted the bedspreads and clipped the stitches.

Many people worked to perfect tufting machines. The first machines were made from converted household sewing machines with single needles. Then came multineedle machines with gooseneck heads open at one end. About 1940, a few tufting machines were built with a fixed support at each end and a needle bar between; they tufted fabric in continuous rows 40 to 50 inches wide. Soon these machines were used to tuft fabrics for robes and small cotton rugs. By 1950, machines were being built to make cotton pile carpeting 9 to 12 feet wide. All of these machines were developed by local people around Dalton, Ga., and Chattanooga, Tenn. Britain has a high concentration of imported tufting machines producing carpets, and is now manufacturing some of its own machines.

Machines with electrically controlled pattern attachments produce many varieties of imaginative patterns from natural and manmade fibers in unlimited bold or soft classic colors.　　　—Richard B. Pressley

Vacuum Tube, a device consisting of several metallic structures in an evacuated glass chamber, capable of amplifying or switching electronic signals. The modern vacuum or electron tube, the triode, was invented in 1906 by Lee De Forest. This was actually a modification of an earlier device, the Fleming valve, or diode, invented by John A. Fleming in 1904.

De Forest's *triode* consists of three essential elements: a metal plate, called the *anode;* a wire filament or cylindrical electrode, called the *cathode;* and a wire-mesh screen, called the *grid.* A glass tube or envelope from which air is evacuated encloses the three elements and gives the structure its name, *vacuum tube.* The triode differed from Fleming's *diode* only in the presence of the grid; this, however, was enough to make the triode a significant advance.

In operation, the cathode is heated red hot and boils off electrons which form in a cloud around the cathode. Some of these electrons are attracted into the plate, which is connected to a positive voltage. In order to reach the plate, however, the electrons must first pass through the openings in the wire-mesh grid. The grid in a vacuum tube acts like a Venetian blind. A blind controls the amount of light that passes through it by varying the openings between the slats. A grid controls the flow of electron current from cathode to anode by varying the amount of charge on the grid. It is a well-known electrical principle that negative charges repel one another. Therefore, if the grid's charge is made sufficiently negative, few electrons can get through to the plate. As the grid's charge becomes less negative, a greater number get through. Since a very small amount of charge on the grid controls a much larger flow of charge (electrons) to the plate, the vacuum tube is able to amplify signals.

Vacuum tubes are often equipped with additional electrodes to alter their characteristics and make them more suitable for high-frequency or other special applications. The *tetrode* contains a second grid, and the *pentode* contains three grids.

Vacuum tubes are used in applications unsuited to transistors, such as high-power transmitters and the extremely-high-frequency circuits of some radar and communication systems. They are also used in applications where transistor costs are still too high, although this economic advantage seems temporary at best.

The most critical element in the Telstar satellite is a device called a *traveling wave tube.* It is a special type of compact and rugged vacuum tube that can amplify electronic signals at extremely high frequencies. For such purposes, the vacuum tube is still unrivaled by the tiny transistor. As transistor technology advances, however, use of the vacuum tube will be increasingly limited to specialized applications for which no transistor is yet available.

　　　—William C. Vergara

Valves, mechanical devices used to control the flow of liquids and gases through pipes or bored passages. According to their application, these devices can be classed as on-off, throttling, or check valves. *On-off valves* allow either uninterrupted flow or provide complete blockage. For such service, *gate* or *plug valves* are commonly used. *Throttling valves* modify the flow by partially blocking the passage, reducing the pressure and volume of fluid passing the valve. *Globe valves* are commonly used for throttling applications. A common application of such throttling valves is the water faucet. *Check valves* limit flow through a pipe to one direction and are widely used in pumps and compressors.

Gate valves and *globe valves* are produced in brass, bronze, cast iron, alloy steel, and stainless steel for pressures up to 5,000 pounds per square inch and temperatures up to 1,200° F. Most sizes are regularly stocked and have been produced to meet material and dimensional standards set by the American Society of Mechanical Engineers (ASME). These valves are generally fitted with flanges or threaded ends for mechanical connection, but special ends are also provided to allow the valves to be welded or sweated to pipe or machinery.

Poppet valves are used where rapid operation and high pressures are encountered. Common applications include internal-combustion engines, intake and exhaust valves, and hydraulic equipment control valves. The primary advantage of the poppet valve is that only a small movement of the valve stem is required to initiate or halt fluid flow.

Reciprocating pumps and compressors use check valves to maintain fluid flow in only one direction. Air or gas compressors employ *reed* or *plate check valves* consisting of thin metal elements operated by the pressure of the gas that is being pumped. During the suction stroke, the flexible metal plate or reed is lifted from the valve seat by the incoming air. During the compression stroke, the plate or reed is clamped to the intake valve seat by the pressure of the air in the cylinder.

Pump check valves are also operated by the pressure differential that exists between the intake and discharge ports of the pump. The design of the valve used is determined by operating pressures and by the type of liquid that is to be pumped. To simplify service, both compressors and pumps frequently use interchangeable intake and discharge valves.　　　—Joseph J. Kelleher

Voting Machine, a mechanical device for automatically recording and totaling the votes of electors. Voting machines are used only in the United States and in Trinidad and Tobago, West Indies. Most of the world still uses paper ballots marked by the voter and deposited in a sealed ballot box for counting after the polls close.

The Meyers Ballot Machine, invented by Jacob Meyers, was the first voting machine used in an official election; it was introduced at Lockport, N.Y., in 1892. These early machines were difficult to operate and not entirely reliable. Development of the Keipers roller interlock in 1912 offered the first practical means of controlling operation of a voting machine to limit electors to one vote for an individual candidate and no more than the legal number of votes for any single office.

Today's voting machine contains thousands of complicated parts, with space for as many as 500 candidates and referendum questions. It provides fast, accurate election results. A major feature is the protection it affords the elector against accidentally invalidating his own ballot.

When a voter enters the machine, it is locked and cannot be operated until an election official releases a latch on the outside of the machine. The voter then moves a large handle that closes the curtains and activates the machine so he can vote in secrecy. On the face of the voting machine, candidates' names are listed in party rows or in groups under the office they are seeking. The voter moves a small lever next to the name of the candidate of his choice, setting the machine to record a vote for that candidate.

After his ballot is cast, the voter pulls back the large lever that in one step records his vote, returns the candidate levers to their original positions, and opens the curtains. At the same time, a paper roll is advanced to hide any write-in vote and to present clean paper for the next voter.

Election officials obtain voting results as soon as the polls close by locking the machine and uncovering the counters. The votes for each candidate are read from the counters and entered on official election return sheets.

Ninety-nine per cent of the voting machines are made by two companies. Recently, ballot-marking devices and counting equipment have entered the election market. This equipment permits voting on a punched card ballot for tabulation by electronic machines. The special electronic counting systems use paper ballots marked with a fluorescent ink. To date, these devices have been used mostly on an experimental basis.   —Howard Burr

Water Treatment, the improvement of the quality of water to make it suitable for use. Water treatment is required for nearly all of the 22 billion gallons of water passing through municipal systems and 160 billion gallons used by industry each day in the United States.

Major forms of treatment include clarification and filtration to remove

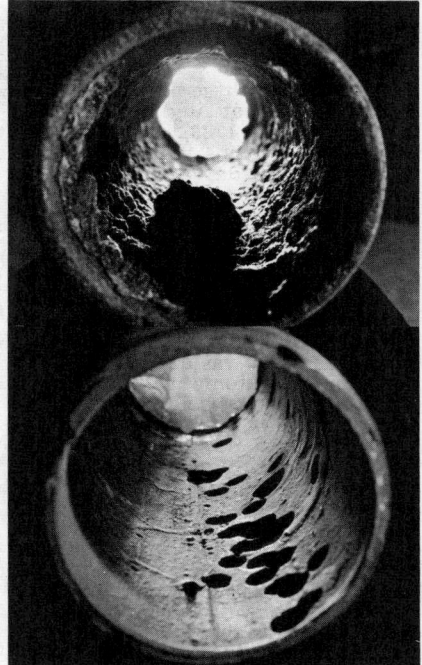

CALGON CORPORATION

WATER treated chemically stops oxidation that clogs (*top*) and pits (*bottom*) pipes.

solid matter; sterilization to prevent disease; softening to remove hardness; demineralization to remove all types of dissolved solids including the "hardness" of water; aeration or deaeration to remove gases; and the use of chemicals to prevent corrosion and scale formation. Generally, the more a water supply is purified, the greater is its cost to the user.

In *clarification,* water is retained for several hours in large settling basins to allow matter to drop to the bottom, where it collects as sludge. In modern plants, continuously operating equipment removes the sludge deposits. Hundreds of tons of sediment daily may settle out of water supplies withdrawn from turbulent rivers for a typical large community.

Coagulant materials, such as alum, ferrous sulfate, and lime, or organic polymers, are often mixed into the water to speed the settling of small particles. Coagulants attract and entangle particles suspended in the water, causing the formation of tiny clusters, or *floc,* which become heavy enough to drop relatively quickly.

Filtration of water through sand beds or anthracite generally completes clarification by removing fine particles of matter and bacteria that did not settle out. Filtration follows the *softening* treatment where mineral salts must be precipitated out of solution.

In *sterilization,* a biocide—usually chlorine—is added to the water in small quantities to kill disease-causing, or pathogenic, bacteria. Under some circumstances, chlorine dioxide gas is used to sterilize water because of its lesser tendency to accentuate objectionable tastes and odors in drinking water.

Softening of water is the reduction or removal of hardness, caused by the presence of calcium and magnesium salts that can deposit as scale in boilers, cooling water systems, domestic hot-water heaters, and other equipment. A common method of softening water is the addition of lime and soda ash to precipitate the calcium and magnesium salts. Cold lime-soda softening is conducted at normal water temperatures; in hot processes, the temperature is at the boiling point (212° F) or higher. Zeolite softener equipment uses ion-exchange materials to remove calcium and magnesium ions.

Demineralization removes dissolved salts of all types, including hardness, to produce water of distilled quality. Various types of equipment used follow the principle of removing cations (positively charged ions), such as calcium, magnesium, and sodium, in one operation, and anions (negatively charged ions), such as sulfate, chloride, and silica, in another.

Aeration, the mixing of air and water by spraying or forced air, removes dissolved gases such as hydrogen sulfide (which is the cause of a "sulfur" taste) and carbon dioxide (which causes corrosion). It also helps precipitate iron and manganese and increases biochemical oxidation in sewage treatment.

Where the corrosive effect of oxygen is undesirable—notably in boiler systems—oxygen, carbon dioxide, ammonia, and other gases are removed by *deaeration.* Water is heated to its saturation temperature (which varies with the operating pressure), the steam and water are mixed, and the gases are vented from the system. Deaeration of cold water is accomplished by vacuum.

Many other types of water treatment are used to solve specific needs. In boilers, phosphates prevent scale by precipitating calcium as a nonadherent sludge. Organic materials, such as tannin and lignin, disperse the sludge in the water so it can be removed by "blowdown." Corrosion control is effected in boilers with caustic soda, and in condensate return systems with volatile alkalies or filming amines that coat metal surfaces with an impervious film. Sodium sulfite and other oxygen-scavenging chemicals are often used to remove any oxygen remaining in the boiler water.

Municipal systems and once-through cooling systems frequently use sodium and sodium-zinc glassy phosphates to prevent scale deposits and reduce corrosion and "red water" caused by the precipitation of iron. Recirculating cooling systems use sodium-zinc glassy phosphates, or zinc ion with chromate, to control corrosion and scale deposits. Algae and other slime growths in cooling and process systems are controlled with biocides, such as chlorine, copper salts, quaternary-ammonium compounds, and potassium permanganate. Biocide materials are often alternated to overcome resistance developed by many organisms within the system.

■POLLUTION CONTROL.—Treatment of water *after* use, before it is discharged, has become a matter of public interest because heavy waste accumulations have caused serious pollution of many bodies of water. In 1964 in the United States, municipal and industrial systems dumped into rivers and lakes organic wastes equivalent to the untreated sewage of about 160 million persons.

Modern municipal sewage treatment plants can remove about 85 to 95 per cent of organic solids, and nearly all of the bacteria. So effective are these processes that, in Baltimore, a large steel company receives its service water supply of up to 150 million gallons per day directly and economically from that city's sewage treatment plant.

Industrial wastes are often more complex, and treatment depends on the specific waste materials being discharged by each plant. These may range from oils to acids to heavy metals to organic wastes. Treatment methods include sedimentation, coagulation, filtration, flotation, skimming, and oxidation.

The use and reuse of water within the same plant before it is ultimately discharged as waste is a practice that can be economically attractive in locations where initial treatment of raw water supplies is costly.
                                —Anthony E. Pizzuto

JACQUARD LOOM, *(left),* was invented in 1801 by a Frenchman for weaving intricate patterns. The complicated mass of threads that is being fed into the machine from the top determines the pattern. The finished fabric can be seen at the bottom of the machine.

NAVAJO woman weaving a blanket on primitive loom held together with rope.

MODERN HIGH-SPEED looms are just like simple looms but are automatic.

Weaving, the interlacing of two sets of yarns to form a fabric. The concept of weaving has not changed for centuries—some historians say for more than 6,000 years. The operation of a hand loom is based on age-old principles of weaving—the principles still used in modern looms.

First, the many parallel strands of yarn come from a *beam,* which is a large model of a simple sewing spool. These multiple strands of yarn, called *ends,* are the *warp.* It is not uncommon to weave fabric from a beam of more than 10,000 individual warp ends of synthetic fiber. Such a warp is 3,000 or more yards long.

The second part of fabric is the *filling,* the strands of yarn that interlace the warp ends to form the *fabric.* Filling is placed at right angles to the parallel warp ends in continuous rows. Filling yarn is usually placed on a *bobbin;* an average bobbin contains 4,000 yards of yarn.

In the hand loom, the weaver moves the treadle with his feet to move the warp yarn up and down, a process called *shedding.* The long needlelike fingers that support the warp ends are *heddles.* The shafts that support the heddles are *har-*

nesses. Pattern possibilities increase as the number of harnesses are increased. When one harness is at its lowest position and the second is at its highest, an *open shed* is created. Between each harness movement, the weaver throws a wooden shuttle containing a small bobbin of filling yarn through the open shed, a process called *picking.* After each shedding and each picking, the weaver pulls a handrail holding comblike teeth toward him to push the filling into the woven fabric, a process called *beating up.* The weaver continues this process over and over to weave fabric. Working steadily, the hand weaver of today, like the weaver of centuries ago, produces fewer than 20 picks a minute.

■**MECHANIZATION.**—With this same slow process, all fabrics were woven from prehistoric time until the textile industry of England pioneered the Industrial Revolution in the eighteenth century. Weaving developments during this great period of invention were most often met with passive resistance or even violence. But they created millions of new jobs, increased standards of living, and improved working conditions.

The first of these inventions was the fly shuttle patented by John Kay in England in 1733, which is still used in most looms today. However, weavers of that day thought it would put them out of work. Consequently a mob broke into Kay's shop, smashed everything, and would have killed him if two friends had not smuggled him out in a sheet.

About 1787, Edmund Cartwright, a minister of the Church of England, patented the first practical power loom. His loom was also the first one that stopped automatically when the yarn broke. Cartwright set up his first factory at Doncaster, using a bull to supply power. He replaced bull power with power from a steam engine shortly afterward.

The American textile industry began in 1790 when Samuel Slater built a loom and started manufacturing cotton cloth in Pawtucket, R.I. Slater, who was from England, built the loom from his memory of the design of looms there.

During the last part of the eighteenth century, Joseph Marie Jacquard, a mechanic of Lyons, France, turned his talents to improving the way of raising harnesses in looms for figure weaving. About 1801, he perfected the harness motion that bears his name today. But his invention also brought violence. Silk weavers of France, fearing that it would deprive them of their livelihood, broke up his device, and he had to flee to save his life. The device was declared public property in 1806, and Jacquard was rewarded with a pension and a royalty on each machine. By 1812, there were 11,000 looms with jacquards in France.

Engineers consider the jacquard one of the most perfect machines ever made. Today the principle and the essential parts are the same as Jacquard originally conceived them.

In 1894, James L. Northrop, an American, invented the rotary battery that changes bobbins of filling automatically. Before this time, weavers had to put up bobbins manually into shuttles on looms that changed shuttles automatically, or had to stop the looms to change bobbins in shuttles. Northrop's invention, like Jacquard's, is used in today's looms and is a marvel of precision—it changes bobbins with looms running at top speed.

Even though weaving today is based on principles thousands of years old, looms are quite efficient. *Fly-shuttle* looms run at 210 to 220 picks a minute. With the newest devices that transfer filling automatically, one weaver, one fixer, and one utility man can operate 100 looms for a total output of 10 yards of fabric 50 inches wide every minute. These looms often run more than a week without stopping. Loom efficiency in well-run mills is 98 per cent, with only 2 per cent second-quality fabric.

There are 2.6 million looms in the world today, including nearly 400,000 in the U. S. The world's total is dropping each year by about 25,000 looms because newer looms are wider, faster, and more productive. The only exception is in Asia, where looms are increasing at about the same rate that they are decreasing in other sections. Even with fewer looms, United States fabric production is gaining.

■**TYPES OF LOOMS.**—Looms are divided into three classes: cotton, manmade fiber, and woolen.

Three shedding motions are being used in today's looms: (1) cam motions with up to six harnesses, primarily for cotton fabrics with plain or twill designs; (2) dobby motions with 20 and 25 individually controlled harnesses, for cotton and manmade-fiber fabrics with fancy designs; and (3) jacquards for all fibers, with every warp end in the pattern controlled individually, for fabrics varying from brocades to woven portraits as intricate as any painted on canvas.

Loom picking today is much as it has always been. New metals enable picking parts to stand the pressure of high-speed looms. Looms are divided into types: *single-shuttle* looms for only one color or type of filling, and *multishuttle* (box loom) for four colors, or from four to seven colors with each color separate.

Northrop's rotary battery is still used in about 50 per cent of all looms, because the filling yarn and bobbins come directly from the spinning frame to eliminate rewinding, which has to be done with other systems. Three new systems for handling filling at looms have been developed the past 10 years, two of them in the U.S. and the third in the U.S. and many other countries.

The first system, the so-called *loom winder*, winds filling on the loom from a package of yarn weighing up to six pounds. The first production installation was made early in 1956. Today this system is being used in more than 100,000 looms throughout the world.

The second system is an *automatic filling magazine* that holds 96 bobbins. The loom changes these bobbins automatically. The system is being improved to handle bobbins directly from spinning frames. The economic aspects of the device are better than looms with rotary batteries.

The third system is known as *shuttleless looms*. Filling is inserted through the warp shed with flexible steel tapes much like a flexible steel ruler. This principle, *rapier* (swordlike), is not new, but U. S. mills have had such looms only since 1960. Economically, shuttleless looms are much better than fly-shuttle looms, but the range of fabrics that can be woven is limited. Speed is 230 picks per minute on looms 50 inches wide, a gain of about 50 per cent over fly-shuttle looms.

Another weaving system, called a *weaving machine*, is being used for wide looms (90 inches) weaving woolen and worsted fabrics. Filling is fed by a series of small shuttles (up to 16 of them, 3⅛ inches long) from large packages of yarn on the machine. The machine uses four colors of filling. The shuttles are picked through the warp shed one at a time by torque from a highly flexible steel rod. The looms are about 40 per cent more productive than fly-shuttle looms of equal width. (See also *Spinning* and *Tufting*.)

—**Richard B. Pressley**

Welding, the general term for a number of processes by which two or more objects or parts are joined to form a single, continuous whole. In practice, the term is applied only to those processes in which heat is utilized to produce the joint. The term is further restricted to joints involving only materials identical with or closely related to those of the parts being joined. In this sense, soldering, brazing, and adhesive bonding are not considered welding processes.

Traditionally, welding was restricted to metallic materials, but more recently the term has been extended to cover plastics as well. Not all materials can be welded either to themselves or to one another.

Most welding processes involve melting and resolidification of the materials in the area to be joined. Exceptions are forge welding and, more recently, friction welding. In *forge welding,* the materials are heated to the plastic point and are joined together by the application of external force, as might be exerted by the blows of a hammer, the method normally used by blacksmiths. *Friction welding* is very similar to forge welding, except that the heat is generated by friction of the two parts against each other automatically.

■**FUSION WELDING.**—All other methods of welding are classified as *fusion welding.* They differ from one another only in the way fusion of the mating surfaces is obtained.

In *gas welding,* heat is generated by the combustion of gases; the flame is applied to the areas to be joined until local melting occurs. The molten metal is restrained from flowing off and, on becoming solid, unites the parts. Often, additional metal, as from welding rods, is used to fill the space between the parts being joined. Gas-welding processes include air-acetylene, oxyacetylene, and oxyhydrogen, which produce flames of progressively higher temperatures as are needed with metals of progressively higher melting points.

Thermit welding is a process in which aluminum powder is mixed with the oxide of the metal to be welded and is packed around the joint. Heat is applied to some of the mixture, starting a chemical reaction in which the aluminum powder becomes aluminum oxide while the original metal oxide is reduced to pure metal. The reaction produces intense heat that melts the ends being joined. The aluminum oxide floats to the top and is later removed.

Arc welding includes a number of processes in which an electric arc is established between an electrode and the parts to be welded. Electrodes are either carbon or metal, and the processes are known respectively as carbon-arc and metal-arc welding. In *carbon-arc welding,* the consumed carbon is generally volatilized and does not become a part of the weld. Some metal-arc processes involve the use of an electrode, generally tungsten, which does not melt and therefore does not become part of the weld. Other *metal-arc welding* processes use an electrode that is of substantially the same material as the parts being joined, is melted in the process, and becomes part of the weld.

In *induction welding,* the welding heat is obtained by the flow of an induction current in the region of the weld. The resistance of the work to the flow of this induced current causes the metal to heat to the welding point.

Resistance welding also uses an electric current. The parts to be welded are brought into close contact with each other, and a current of high amperage and low voltage is caused to flow through them. Air gaps and surface oxides in the area of the weld act as resistances to the flow of current, resulting in localized heating, with melting of the metals, closing of the air gaps, and expulsion of the oxides. Typical welding techniques based on local electrical resistance are *resistance spot welding, resistance seam welding, projection welding, flash welding, upset welding,* and *percussion welding.*

■**NEWER METHODS.**—New welding techniques are electroslag welding, plasma-arc welding, and electron-beam welding.

Electroslag welding is used for depositing large amounts of metal, as might be needed to fill a large space between steel parts. Molten slag is placed between the parts, and electrodes of the metal to be welded are immersed in the slag. A current is then caused to flow through the electrodes. The slag, acting as a resistance, causes the electrodes to melt, the molten metal dropping to the bottom of the opening and gradually solidifying. The slag then rises in the opening, and, as more of the electrode metal is fed into it, continues the process, ultimately filling the gap.

In *plasma-arc welding,* the filler metal in the form of wire or powder is fed into a plasma jet and volatilized, to be condensed and solidified on the ends of the parts to be welded, thus effecting the joint.

In *electron-beam welding,* a flow of electrons is focused on the surfaces to be joined, causing them to melt to a shallow depth. The weld is produced by the solidification of this molten metal upon cooling.

Plastic materials are welded either by the friction process or by localized melting with a hot iron.

—Felix Giordano

Wood Finishing, the process of adding a protective or decorative coating to wood products. Wood finishing is an ancient art, dating back more than 2,000 years when balsams, pitches, shellacs, and oriental oils were used to adorn and protect wood surfaces. Although these purposes remain basically the same, there is quite a difference in the materials and their application today. Wood products that are factory-finished include furniture, wallboard and paneling, some flooring, and a variety of special products.

Paneling and other items with a flat surface can be production-finished on conveyor lines. These wood surfaces may require only two coats (with an intermediate buffing) applied by a *curtain coater.* This machine forms a veil or curtain of finishing material of proper viscosity, through which a panel passes on a conveyor belt to receive a coating.

Hardboard panels may first be given a ground-color coat in a *reverse roller coater,* which forces the pigmented material into the pores. It is then imprinted with a wood grain by an intaglio-type printing plate. A top coat is then applied by a curtain or roller coater, or by mechanical reciprocating spray guns. A dry film, such as polyvinyl with a wood grain or decorative pattern, can be applied to hardboard by high-pressure rotary-press equipment.

Furniture is almost always assembled before finishing, so automatic mechanical methods of finish application are not practical. Skilled operators with spray guns do the work. There are conventional guns that operate under air pressure. Mixing jets of air and fluid causes the material to atomize. By adjusting or changing the tip of the gun, the operator can form different spray patterns.

Hot spray brings the finishing material to the gum in a heated state and, therefore, contains less solvent. Airless spray systems bring the hot fluid to the gun under high fluid pressure, without compressed air. This material is atomized as it leaves the nozzle. *Electrostatic sprays,* used in coating metals and other materials that are electrical conductors, have been used little in coating woods, for a coat of material containing an electrical conductor must first be applied to the wood. Small parts, such as legs, may be *dip finished.* Viscosity must be controlled and the rate of withdrawal accurately timed to achieve a uniform coat.

Appearance plays an important part in furniture finishes. Dyes or pigments are added to materials to produce certain color effects. Woods sometimes are bleached, then stained, thereby enhancing the grain pattern with a uniform color without interference from the original colors in the natural wood, which vary from piece to piece.

Style requirements account for variations in finishing procedures. Artisans, working with dyes, pigments, and deft hands can produce truly artistic finishes to excite the most perceptive furniture buyer or interior designer. Distressing, spattering, antiquing, and padding to accent grain are some of the techniques.

Nitrocellulose lacquer is still the most popular material for furniture topcoats. It is easy to apply, has good stability, dries and rubs easily, and can be repaired with little difficulty. Amine and epoxidized lacquers, as well as alkyd urea synthetics, are also used for their better heat and mar resistance. However, they have less stability and are more difficult to apply or repair.

Polyester finishes, used in Europe in recent years, produce a very hard, mirrorlike finish, but have not become popular in America. Polyurethane materials have not been used for wood finishes, as they are difficult to apply and lack suitable color stability. However, this material may become important if technical problems can be overcome, because it offers a very durable surface.

—Raymond A. Helmers

Woodworking Tools, instruments used to facilitate mechanical operations on wood. Because wood is a universal material, used in some manner by virtually every industry and also in the education and hobby fields, the tools range from simple chisels to giant multipurpose machines costing tens of thousands of dollars. In wood products manufacturing, heavy-duty, high-speed machines are required. In smaller shops, including those involved in custom manufacturing, smaller, less sophisticated tools are needed. School shops, crating departments, pattern and sample shops, and cabinetmakers use machines in the middleweight class. Hobbyists have similar types of tools, but in the lightweight class. For construction work and maintenance, tools must be portable.

■**CROSS-CUT SAWS.**—In manufacturing, rough lumber or panels are first cut to specified lengths by powered *cut-off saws,* which are stationary units. The cutting stroke is automatic at the touch of a foot pedal, and there are both *overcutting* and *undercutting* types. *Swing saws* are manually pulled into the wood by the operator. Some machines are built with extra long stroke to cut wide panels. *Multiple panel saws* have two or more saw blades, and pieces are fed by a moving slat bed. In smaller shops, the *radial arm saw* is the mainstay for cross-cutting lumber and panels. It also may be adjusted to rip, miter, groove, or dado.

In construction and maintenance, the portable electric *circular saw* is important. A combination rip and cross-cut saw blade permits this tool to serve a double purpose.

Blades for production cut-off saws are usually carbide-tipped for long runs between sharpenings. In cutting plywood, panels, or plastic laminate that might splinter or chip easily, a fine-toothed saw blade is required.

■**RIP SAWS.**—Rip sawing (cutting wood parallel to the grain) calls for a blade that gives a slicing, raking cut. In production plants, special machines perform this work. They have power feeds and are adjustable as to width and depth of cut. *Gang rip saws* have two or more blades that cut the board into multiple strips of similar or varying widths.

■**PLANING AND JOINING TOOLS.**—In volume manufacturing, heavy-duty *facing planers* remove rough surfaces, level up twists and warps in the boards, and equalize their thicknesses. Usually, rough planing precedes ripping. If the stock is to be edge-glued, the rip saw may provide a suitable surface, but usually some of the boards must be jointed (planed edgewise). *Production jointers* have automatic power feeds and board turnovers. In the custom plant or hobby shop, simple hand-fed jointers are used.

■**EDGE-GLUING AND LAMINATING TOOLS.**—Panels for solid wood construction or wood cores are made of strips of wood, glued edge-to-edge. They are produced in *panel-making machines,* which cure the glue by steam heat or high-frequency radio waves. Some types of panels may be made on mechanical rotating clamps, with the adhesive curing at factory temperature. Small shops use hand-operated *cabinet clamps.*

A press is required to make plywood or laminated panels. *Hot presses,* often used in making plywood, may have one or more openings, may make panels 4 x 8 feet or larger, and are opened and closed by hydraulic pressure. Steam under high pressure is forced into the hollow platens, providing the temperature required to cure the adhesive. Similar *cold presses* can be equipped with radio-frequency generators to cure the glue.

Laminating presses need less pressure. Many of these operate on compressed air. Panels are compressed, and stacks are secured between mechanical clamps and removed from the press. The glue then sets overnight at room temperature. Other laminating is done with contact cement. The decorative surface and the core are passed through a *pinch-roller press* that squeezes the elements together. Smaller plants and shops use air-type and pinch-roller presses.

A key machine for fabricating panels is the *double-end tenoner.* It is a continuous-feed machine with adjustable width, equipped with saws, cope, tenon heads, and arbor motors. Virtually any kind of machining of ends or edges of flat stock can be done by this machine. It can tenon, groove, saw, miter, edge-shape, dado, and even edge-sand. Top surfaces can be contoured by cutter heads on a long shaft.

Another multipurpose machine, not limited to flat stock, is the *double-end sawing, boring, and chucking machine,* which operates on cycles. Typically, it grasps the work piece, miter-trims both ends, bores or chucks each end, bores multiple holes in top or sides, and releases the piece. This equipment is widely used in making parts for chairs and upholstery frames.

Single-end tenoners and *miter-saws* are used in smaller shops.

■ **SHAPING AND ROUTING TOOLS.**—Both *single-* and *double-spindle shapers* are used in large and small factories, especially on short runs. A jig or fixture holds the work piece or pieces, one edge of which serves as a pattern guide for the part as it rides against the shaper collar. Automatic shapers clamp the work piece, rotate it to the cutting head, and return it to the operator after the cut is made. Contour profilers perform similar operations. The piece is clamped on a moving table that takes it past a cutterhead, which moves in and out to conform to the pattern. Serpentine drawer fronts are typical parts made on this machine.

Routers can do similar work, but they have a rotating spindle above the work table. This allows the bit to be lowered into the work, and interior as well as exterior patterns thus can be cut in various patterns to specified depth. One make of router has an optical tracer that follows a simple drawing of a part. This in turn guides the travel of the router bit, automatically machining the part. Other routers have been equipped with automatic controls guided by magnetic tape. Numerical positioning control has been used on a router of still another design. Small shops and plastic laminators use portable high-speed routers and trimmers.

■ **MOLDING TOOLS.**—*Molding machines* have one or more cutterheads that produce a continuous pattern lengthwise on a piece of wood. They vary in size, capacity, and speed of operation. In the same family of equipment are *flooring and center-match siding machines.* They take rough lumber and make center- and end-match strip flooring automatically.

■ **BORING AND MORTISING TOOLS.**—*Multiple boring machines* are made in horizontal and vertical models. A boring machine can become a *mortiser* by installing a hollow chisel mortising bit. Smaller shops use *drill presses,* some equipped with multiple spindle attachments. Where portability is required, the *hand electric drill* is used.

■ **OTHER TOOLS.**—There is a wide variety of tools and equipment whose names are synonymous with their functions: band saws, single- and double-end dovetailers, automatic and back-knife turning lathes, single and multiple spindle carvers, embossers, wood benders, veneer clippers and splicers, dowel machines and dowel drivers, corner block machines, chair seat machines, and other tools for home or industry.

■ **SANDING TOOLS.**—*Multiple-drum sanders, wide-belt machines,* and *stroke sanders* are used for production sanding of flat surfaces. A sophisticated arrangement might have a wide-belt machine to cut down and even up the bottom of a panel. Another wide-belt machine would rough-cut down the top, while a third would give it a finer sanding. A final polish would be given by a stroke sander. One type of automatic stroke sander has a pneumatic platen that allows for slight variations in the wood surface, reducing the number of sand-throughs of the veneer.

There are automatic machines to sand moldings, irregular shapes, and turnings. There also are small machines with pneumatic drums or shaped wheels, and sanders whose belt follows a hand block, the shape of which conforms exactly to the molded part to be sanded.

Portable sanders come in models with rotating belts or disks. There are air- and electric-powered units whose pads have either reciprocating or orbital action. These are similar to the polishing machines used to rub finishes of wood products.

■ **CUTTING TOOLS.**—Home craftsmen and wood sculptors still use *chisels* and *turning tools,* such as *skews, gouges, round-nose chisels,* and *parting tools.* But power tools and machines have replaced these instruments in industry. *Bits* and *cutters* must be engineered for high-speed production. Power-boring bits include *spur bits, augers, countersinks, chisel bits, router bits, hole saws, plug cutters, wing cutters,* and *hollow chisel mortisers.*

The design and engineering of cutters and cutterheads for high-speed production is a demanding science. Electronic balancers and optical comparators are used by toolmakers to assure safe operation and efficient cutting.

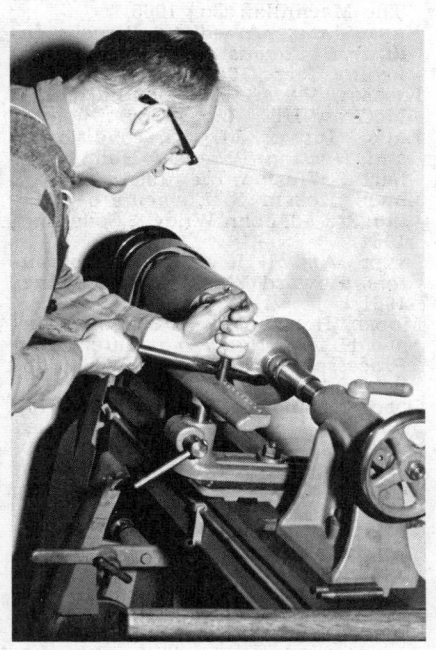

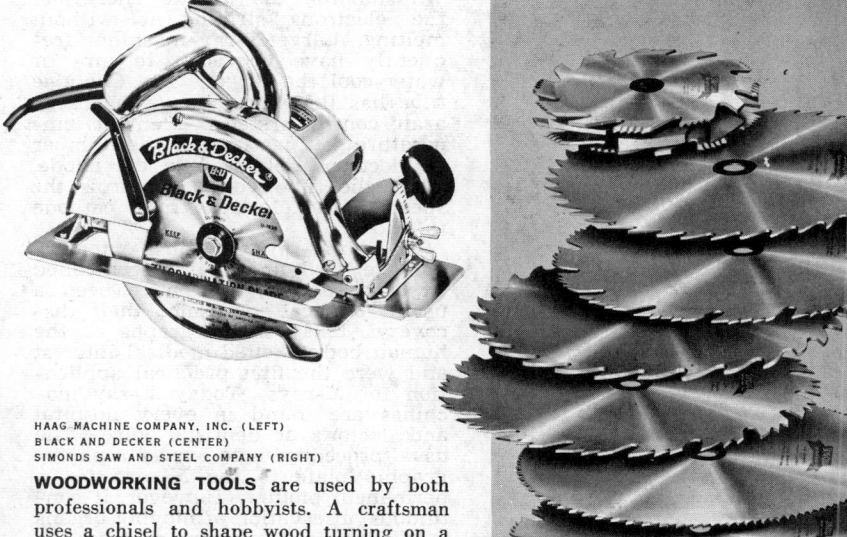

HAAG MACHINE COMPANY, INC. (LEFT)
BLACK AND DECKER (CENTER)
SIMONDS SAW AND STEEL COMPANY (RIGHT)

WOODWORKING TOOLS are used by both professionals and hobbyists. A craftsman uses a chisel to shape wood turning on a lathe (*left*). Electric saws (*above*) perform a variety of tasks with planer, rip, and combination blades like those at *right*.

Different wood species and types of cuts require specific cutting angles and optimum number of knife marks per inch for top efficiency. Cutterhead bits and knives may be made of high-speed steel, carbide-tipped or solid carbide, depending on requirements in use. Bits have a shape contoured end to end, so that they will retain the same cutting shape, sharpening after sharpening.

■**FASTENING TOOLS.**—Fastening tools in woodworking have progressed from hand devices to power-operated *staplers, hammers, tackers, nailers,* and *screwdrivers.* These tools drive nails up to two inches long into the hardest woods. One stationary-type machine makes its own fasteners from wire and drives them into the wood, even countersinking and blind fastening. Another drives corrugated fasteners, and there is a portable tool that does likewise. One tacker operates on electric power, although most use compressed air.

Air and electric screwdrivers and impact wrenches are useful woodworking tools. There are automatic screwdrivers and automatic nailing machines that can draw fasteners from a hopper through hollow flexible tube and drive them at the press of a trigger.

Portable power drills and screwdrivers, especially for building, maintenance, and hobby use, are available in cordless units. They are fitted with rechargeable nickel-cadmium batteries.

—Raymond A. Helmers

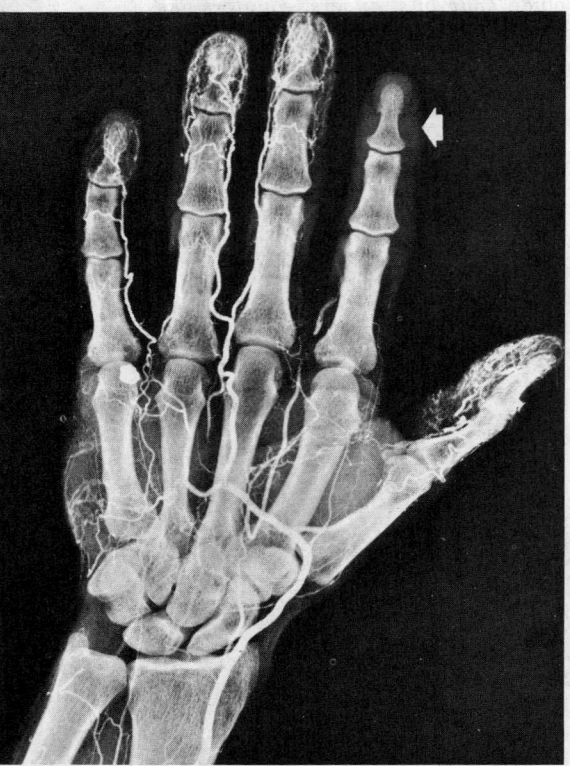

LOOK MAGAZINE

X-RAY shows a circulatory block in the index finger (*arrow*); injected radio-opaque material appears only in the other fingers.

X-Rays, high-frequency electromagnetic radiation produced in a vacuum tube when high-speed electrons—accelerated by high voltage—strike a metal target. X-rays are invisible to the human eye. The wavelength of this radiation is about 10^{-7} to 10^{-11} cm, which is about one ten-thousandth the wavelength of visible light. The rays can be detected by photographic plates, Geiger counters, ionization chambers, and chemically coated fluorescent screens.

X-rays were discovered by Wilhelm Roentgen in 1895 while he was experimenting with the *Crookes tube.* Roentgen noticed that a fluorescent screen coated with barium platinocyanide lighted up when electrons from the Crookes tube struck the screen. When Roentgen discovered that the screen glowed, even when the tube was totally encased in a paperboard box, he was baffled, until he realized a new kind of ray—completely different than visible light or ultraviolet light—was being produced. When he announced his discovery, Roentgen labeled them X-rays because X stands for the unknown in scientific research. For his discovery and development of X-rays, Roentgen in 1901 received the first Nobel Prize in physics.

Early X-ray, or Crookes, tube consisted of an evacuated glass tube with a concave cathode and metal anode, or target. A high voltage (30,000 to 40,000 volts) was applied between the anode and the cathode to accelerate electron flow from the cathode to the target. Electrons striking the target were decelerated and their energy absorbed by the atoms of the target. The affected atoms vibrated violently and gave off a high-frequency short-wavelength radiation—the X-ray.

The modern X-ray tube, developed by William D. Coolidge in 1913, uses a hot tungsten filament as a source of electrons, or cathode. The target, or anode, consists of a solid molybdenum or tungsten block capable of withstanding the kinetic energy of the electrons striking it without melting. Large X-ray machines frequently have provision to air- or water-cool the target. The *Coolidge tube* has the advantage of two separate control systems—filament temperature settings control the number of electrons delivered to the anode, while the tube voltage controls the speed of the electrons from cathode to anode.

Though X-rays can cause extensive damage to humans if uncontrolled exposure occurs, they have been a useful medical tool since their discovery. Early shadowgraphs of the human body excited medical interest and were the first practical application for X-rays. Today X-ray machines are found in every hospital and doctor's or dentist's office. The usual procedure is to expose a photographic plate to the X-rays for a permanent picture. However, if continuous observation of moving organs is required, a fluoroscope replaces the negative. High-voltage X-ray machines are frequently used for treatment of cancerous growths that

cannot be removed by surgery. *Lead shielding,* which X-rays cannot penetrate, is used to protect personnel from dangerous overexposure during operation. *Film badges* and *dosimeters,* which record the amount of X-ray exposure, are carried to provide an additional safety check for the operating technicians.

—Joseph J. Kelleher

BIBLIOGRAPHY

AINSWORTH, JOHN H. *Paper, the Fifth Wonder,* 2nd ed. Thomas Printing & Publishing Co., 1964.

BERNSTEIN, JEREMY. *The Analytical Engine: Computers—Past, Present and Future.* Random House, Inc., 1964.

CROUSE, WILLIAM H. *Automotive Mechanics,* 5th ed. McGraw-Hill, Inc., 1965.

D'ARCANGELO, AMELIO M. *A Guide to Sound Ship Structure.* Cornell Maritime Press, 1964.

DEGARMO, E. PAUL. *Materials and Processes in Manufacturing.* The Macmillan Co., 1962.

DOLAN, EDWARD F. JR. *The Camera.* Julian Messner, Inc., 1965.

FISHER, DOUGLAS A. The *Epic of Steel.* Harper & Row, Publishers, Inc., 1963.

GREGORY, EDWIN and others. *Steel Working Processes; Principles and Practice of Forging, Rolling, Pressing, Squeezing, Drawing and Allied Methods of Metal Forming.* Transatlantic Arts, Ltd., 1964.

HOWARD, WILLIAM E. AND BARR, JAMES. *Spacecraft and Missiles of the World.* Harcourt, Brace and World, Inc., 1966.

HUNTER, MAXWELL W. *Thrust into Space.* Holt, Rinehart & Winston, Inc., 1965.

JOHNSTON, BETTY J. *Equipment for Modern Living.* The Macmillan Co., 1965.

KELLER, A. G. *A Theatre of Machines.* The Macmillan Co., 1965.

KENT, JAMES A. editor. *Riegel's Industrial Chemistry.* Reinhold Publishing Corp., 1962.

KISSAM, PHILIP. *Surveying Practice.* McGraw-Hill, Inc., 1966.

LAUB, JULIAN M. *Air-conditioning and Heating Practice.* Holt, Rinehart & Winston, Inc., 1963.

LEWIS, ROBERT S. *Elements of Mining.* 3rd ed. John Wiley & Sons, Inc., 1964.

LYTEL, ALLAN H. *ABC's of Computers.* Howard W. Sams & Co., Inc., 1961.

MOORE, HARRY D. AND KIBBEY, DONALD H. *Manufacturing Materials & Processes.* Richard D. Irwin, Publisher, 1965.

ODDO, N. and E. CARINI. *Exploring Simple Machines.* Holt, Rinehart & Winston, Inc., 1965,

PETERSON, HAROLD L. *A History of Firearms.* Charles Scribner's Sons, 1961.

TWORT, ALAN C. *A Textbook of Water Supply.* American Elsevier Publishing Co., 1964.

USHER, ABBOTT P. *History of Mechanical Inventions.* Beacon Press, 1959.

Nature of language	1293
Learning to read, write, and spell	1298
Grammar	1303
Punctuation	1311
Figures of speech	1314
Writing and composition	1316
Importance of correct English	1320
Words and phrases often misused	1322
Public speaking and debate	1326
The study of foreign languages	1329
Classifications of languages	1333
Dictionary of abbreviations	1338
Bibliography	1340

LOOK MAGAZINE

VOLUME SIXTEEN

LANGUAGE & GRAMMAR

Language and Grammar

NATURE OF LANGUAGE

Our everyday speech is a thing that we are apt simply to take for granted without stopping to reflect about it; but when we do begin to think about language, we soon realize that far from being a commonplace thing it is a mystery—mysterious in its origin and mysterious in its infinite potentialities. It is no wonder that the ancients thought it of divine origin. When, however, we take a modern scientific attitude toward human speech, one of the first things observed is that language is not a natural thing like breathing or walking, but is something that has to be taught and learned. We speak rightly of our mother-tongue, because most of us do indeed first learn to speak as our mothers teach us. Afterwards we enlarge and extend our acquaintance with language by imitating the speech of the various members of the family, of our playmates and of other persons whom we meet in our daily life.

Language a System of Symbols.—This learning process is necessary for each generation, because, as a little reflection reveals, no natural connection exists between words and what they stand for. What we English-speaking folk call *bread,* the French call *pain,* and the modern Greeks, *psomi.* Likewise, the animal that we call *horse* is in German called *Pferd,* in French *cheval,* in modern Greek *alogo,* names utterly at variance with one another. Each language is a particular system of sound symbols.

We call a horse a *horse* because in the community where we were brought up it is the custom to name it so; and if we did not conform to the custom but used a word of our own, we should not be understood. When King Richard in Shakespeare's play cried out, "A horse! a horse! my kingdom for a horse!" he would certainly have lost all chance of saving himself had he used any other word but *horse,* for he was speaking to Englishmen. Language is, then, an arbitrary and conventional system of sound symbols by means of which the members of a given speech community, occupying a greater or less extent of territory, communicate with one another or, as it were, signal to one another their desires, thoughts and feelings.

From a slightly different point of view we may say also that language or speech is a form of human behavior in response to stimuli, since there can be no language without a social group whose members interact and stimulate one another to linguistic response.

The speech community may be distinct from the nation or political state. In Canada, for example, there are two principal speech communities, the English and the French; and in Great Britain besides the English-speaking groups there are the Welsh speech community in Wales and the Gaelic speech community in the Highlands of Scotland. On the other hand, in the case of some of the great, historic languages the speech community may far transcend the boundaries of nations. Our own English speech community is rapidly becoming almost a world-wide linguistic unit.

Language is the peculiar possession of man. Many animals, to be sure, do signal to one another by cries and other utterances in a way that is akin to language, and so we speak loosely of a cat language or bird language. Such sound signs, however, are not articulate speech in the true sense. When Homer speaks of human beings, he calls them "men who have articulate speech."

The origin of language is quite unknown; its beginnings lie too far back in the misty past of prehistoric ages. Among the various interesting theories is the idea that men first learned to talk by imitating the sounds that other animals make, sometimes called the bowwow theory; again, that human speech developed from the natural cries of joy, sorrow, surprise or some other emotion, which is known as the pooh-pooh, or interjection, theory. We have no means of proving these theories, however, and perhaps the most probable view is that language came into being by a very slow process in response to varied stimuli of early man's environment. This modern scientific view was anticipated by the Roman poet, Lucretius, and probably by his master, Epicurus.

Whatever its origin, there can be no question of the unique importance of language in the ascent of man from savagery and barbarism. It has been said that man is the only *tool-using* animal. Of all his tools, language is certainly the most useful. In his evolution the possession of this wonderful instrument has given him the edge on other animals. Man has not the strength of the tiger or the speed of the ostrich; so only by associating together in tribes have human beings been able to overcome their physical inferiority; and tribal life is largely dependent on language.

As tribes develop into states the importance of language increases rather than diminishes. To the Greeks, the common possession of their beautiful Greek speech was the very closest bond. All non-Greek-speaking peoples they called *barbaroi,* barbarians, stammerers, makers of strange sounds. Latin became the imperial language of an imperial people, and of all the conquests by the Romans none was so important for the future of civilization as the conquest by the Latin language. Modern nations, too, cherish their languages as the highest expression of national culture.

In the complexity of modern civilization language has indeed become the indispensable cement of human society. The study of languages, therefore, in the truest sense is the most *social* of all studies; and to the individual, as well as to the nation and to the world, language is of supreme importance as the vehicle of thought and the medium of one of the highest, if not the highest, of the arts —the art of literature.

The Sounds of Language.—Language, as we have said, is primarily a system of sounds. The letters or other signs with which it is written are only symbols. This distinction is of fundamental importance; for instance, it is not a question of how you pronounce the letter *a,* but rather of what sound or sounds the letter *a* is a symbol. In the English language, the letter *a* represents various sounds, as is quite clear if we think of the words *father, man, tall, fate, America.* The combination of letters *ough* represents altogether different sounds in the words *bough, tough, although* and *through.*

To gain a clear idea of language we must learn something about how speech sounds are produced. A wonderful music box, called the *larynx,* is in our throats. It is a veritable stringed instrument, such as a violin, for in the larynx are two flat, whitish membranes stretched horizontally from back to front, which are made to vibrate when the breath coming from the lungs is forced between them, producing the sound that we call *voice.* Not all speech sounds have voice, but all vowel sounds do and also some of the consonant sounds. These marvelous membranes, the vocal cords, to whose varying vibrations we owe not only all the beauty of the singing voice but also the melodious and ringing qualities that give charm to a well-modulated speaking voice, can actually be seen in a phonetics laboratory by means of an instrument called the *phonolaryngoscope.* If you have not access to such an instrument, you can convince yourself of the existence of the vocal cords by pressing a fingertip against your Adam's apple as you pronounce the vowel *a* (as in *father*), for the vibration of the vocal cords will be distinctly felt.

PHOENICIAN	EARLY GREEK read from right to left	LATER GREEK read from left to right	LATIN
			A
			B
			C G
			D
			E
			F V Y
			Z
			H
			I
			K
			L
			M
			N
			X
			O
			P
			Q
			R
			S
			T

Adapted from James Henry Breasted: Ancient Times

The Evolution of the Alphabet

The modern European alphabet, which is used in writing English, is simply the Latin alphabet with *I* split into *I* and *J*, and *V* split into *V*, *U* and *W*

The larynx, with its vocal cords, is by no means the only organ of speech, though it is one of the most important. E. H. Sturtevant says, "Speech is produced by the expulsion of the breath through the passages of the throat, mouth and nose, while these are modified in various ways." In the broadest sense, therefore, various parts of the body including the diaphragm, lungs and windpipe have to do with the production or modification of the breath stream. In a narrower sense, however, the organs of speech are the larynx, including the vocal cords, the pharynx (a cavity between the epiglottis, or lid of the larynx, and the mouth), the mouth, including the lips, teeth, roof and tongue, and finally the nasal cavity.

When the breath has free and uninterrupted passage through the throat and the mouth or the mouth and nose, the speech sounds produced are vowels. All other speech sounds are consonants (from Latin *consonans, consonantis,* sounding with). No sharp line, however, can be drawn between vowels and consonants. In pronouncing the vowel *i* in machine, the front of the tongue is raised and brought near the palate, still leaving room for the free passage of the breath; but if the tongue is raised still higher, so that audible friction is produced as the breath escapes, the sound becomes a consonant similar to the *ch* in German *ich.* So, too, whispered vowels are not true vowels, but approach the nature of consonants.

Voiced and Unvoiced Sounds.—All speech sounds may quite accurately be classified as either *voiced* or *unvoiced.* This is because the parts of the larynx are so flexible that the vocal cords may either be stretched taut leaving only a narrow space between them or left slack. When the vocal cords are stretched, as the breath is expelled through the throat it causes them to vibrate and so produces the musical sound called voice; when the vocal cords are relaxed, leaving a wider passage between them, there is no such vibration, hence no voice. The space between the vocal cords is called the glottis. All speech sounds that are accompanied by vibration of the vocal cords are called *voiced;* those not so accompanied are called *unvoiced, voiceless* or *breathed.* All true vowels are voiced. Consonants go largely in pairs, like the following, the first of which in each pair is voiceless, the second, voiced: *p, b; t, d; k, g; f, v; th* (as in *thin*), *th* (as in *this*)*; s, z; sh* (as in *she*), *zh* (as in *vision*)*;* but the *m, n* and *ng* are always voiced.

Consonants are also classified according to the manner of production and the place of articulation. So mobile are the organs of speech that by modifying their shape and position at an infinite number of places an infinite variety of speech sounds may be produced. In any one language, however, only a limited number of speech sounds is used. In pronouncing certain consonants the breath stream is first completely stopped and then suddenly released, as in making the sound *p* or *b* we first shut off the current of air by pressing the lips firmly together. When the lips are parted, the air behind them is expelled with a faint explosive sound. Similarly, in producing the sounds *t* or *d* the breath stream is temporarily stopped by placing the blade of the tongue against the ridge above the upper teeth; and in pronouncing *k* or *g* (in *go*) the breath stream is stopped by raising the back of the tongue toward the soft palate. Such consonants are called *stops, explosives* or *mutes.* In producing certain other consonants the breath stream is only partially obstructed and a narrow passage is left free through which the breath escapes with a slight rubbing sound. Such consonants are called *fricatives* and include the English *w, f, v, th, s, z,* and *y; l* and *r* also may be classed as fricatives.

All speech sounds that are formed with the nasal passage open are called *nasals.* If both mouth and nasal passages are freely open, we have nasal vowels like those we hear in the French words, *bon, bien.* In English, nasal consonants such as *m, n* and *ng,* are produced by having the nasal passage open (through raising the uvula), while the mouth passage is closed. The nasal consonants and also *l* are so sonorous that they sometimes take the place of vowels and form the chief elements in a syllable; thus we have syllabic *m* in *prism,* syllabic *n* in *heaven,* syllabic *l* in *table.* Consonants are also characterized according to the place of articulation as: *labial* (formed by the lips), *p, b, m, wh* and *w; labiodental* (formed by placing the lower lip against the upper front teeth), *f, v; dental* or *alveolar* (formed by putting the tongue between the upper and lower front teeth or against the ridge above the upper teeth), *th, t, d, n, l, s, z, sh, zh, r; palatal* (formed by raising the surface of the tongue toward the hard palate), *y* in *yield* or *yes;* and *velar* (formed by raising the back of the tongue toward the soft palate or velum), as *k, g, ng.* The sound of *h* is hardly a true consonant; it is merely a more or less forcible emission of breath through the open glottis, and is sometimes called a *glottal.* All these matters will be made clearer by studying the accompanying table of English consonants.

TABLE OF ENGLISH CONSONANTS

	Labial	Labio-Dental	Dental, or Alveolar	Palatal	Velar
Stops: Voiceless	p		t		k
Voiced	b		d		g
Fricatives: Voiceless	wh	f	th (thin) s, sh		
Voiced	w	v	th (this) z, zh l, r	y	
Nasals: Voiced	m		n		ng

The distinguishing qualities of vowels result in part from the position of the tongue as the sounds are being articulated and in part from the varying shape of the pharynx, which acts as a kind of resonating chamber. Vowels produced when the front of the tongue is raised more or less toward the hard palate are called *front vowels*, those articulated by arching the back of the tongue toward the soft palate are known as *back vowels*. Usually the *i* and *e* sounds are front vowels, *o* and *u* sounds are back vowels, and the various *a* sounds occupy a middle position. Vowels are distinguished also as *open* or *close* according to the degree of openness of the passage left between the tongue and the roof of the mouth as their various sounds are uttered. This distinction is rather difficult to seize, since the position of the tongue in pronouncing vowels is very fluctuating. The above classifications of vowels will be made clearer by a glance at the following vowel triangle.

```
                 Front      Back
Close  (machine) i            u  (rule)
         (tire)  i          u    (pull)
          (say)  ay      ow      (low)
          (ten)  e         o     (obey)
          (mat)  a      aw       (saw)
Open     (task)  a       a       (father)
```

Each language has its characteristic sounds, or *phonemes,* which are represented more or less inadequately by alphabetic symbols. So it often happens that two or more letters are employed to represent a single sound, as in the French word, *beau, eau* representing a simple *o* sound. On the other hand, a sound that is really complex may be represented by a single alphabetic character, as in German *zu,* in which *z* stands for *ts.* Among combinations of letters in English that represent single sounds are: *ph* (*f*), *th* (voiced or unvoiced), *ng* (a velarnasal sound with no real *g* sound in it), *ck* (*k*) and *sh* (a kind of sibilant, or hissing, sound); whereas, the single letter *j* (as in *judge*) stands for *dzh,* and *x* (as in *ox*) stands for *ks.* As an example of the arbitrariness of English spelling, note that the two final sounds of the word *judge* (represented by *dge*) are the same as the two initial sounds (represented by *j*).

The English *ch* serves as symbol for three different sounds or combinations of sounds: for *k* (as in *character,* a word borrowed from the Greek), for *sh* (as in *charade,* of French origin) or, most commonly, for *tsh* (as in both the two beginning and the two final sounds in *church*). The same combination of characters, *ch,* in German *ach* and Scottish *loch* is the symbol of a single guttural sound that is nonexistent in English. Similarly, *ch* in German *ich* and the letter *chi* in ancient Greek represent a palatal sound that is not found in English. The combination *gh* in English spelling, though not so variable a symbol as *ch,* still may represent the single fricative *f* (as in *rough*) or may represent a guttural sound that existed in Old English but is now lost (as in *through*). Obviously, then, every language has its own sounds, of which letters are only the imperfect symbols.

The Alphabet.—Our modern alphabet seems very simple. We speak of a child's learning his A B C's as the very beginning of education. Yet in spite of its apparent simplicity the alpha-

Hebrew	Greek	Russian	Gaelic
א.....(a)	Α α.....(a)	А а.....(a)	Ꭺ ᴀ.....(a)
ב.....(b)	Β б.....(b)	Б б.....(b)	ʙ ʙ....(b)
ב.....(v)	Γ γ.....(g)	В в....(v)	c c....(c)
ג.....(g)	Δ δ.....(d)	Г г.....(g)	ᴅ ᴅ....(d)
ד.....(d)	Ε ε.....(ĕ)	Д д.....(d)	e e....(e)
ה.....(h)	Ζ ζ.....(z)	Е е.....(ĕ)	ꜰ ꜰ....(f)
ו.....(v)	Η η.....(ē)	Ж ж....(zh)	ᵹ ᵹ....(g)
ז.....(z)	Θ θ...(th)	З з.....(z)	ʜ ʜ....(h)
ח.....(kh)	Ι ι......(i)	И и.....(ē)	ı ı.....(i)
ט.....(t)	Κ κ.....(k)	К к.....(k)	ʟ ʟ....(l)
י.....(y)	Λ λ.....(l)	Л л.....(l)	ᴍ ᴍ...(m)
כ.....(k)	Μ μ.....(m)	М м.....(m)	ɴ ɴ....(n)
כ.....(kh)	Ν ν.....(n)	Н н.....(n)	O o....(o)
ך..(kh *final*)	Ξ ξ.....(ks)	О о.....(o)	p p....(p)
ל.....(l)	Ο ο.....(ŏ)	П п.....(p)	ʀ ʀ....(r)
מ.....(m)	Π π.....(p)	Р р.....(r)	ꜱ ꜱ....(s)
ם..(m *final*)	Ρ ρ.....(r)	С с.....(s)	τ τ....(t)
נ.....(n)	Σ σ ς....(s)	Т т.....(t)	u u....(u)
ן...(n *final*)	Τ τ.....(t)	У у.....(u)	
ס.....(s)	Υ υ.....(u)	Ф ф.....(f)	
ע.....(ē)	Φ φ.....(f)	Х х...(kh)	
פ.....(p)	Χ χ...(kh)	Ц ц.....(ts)	
פ.....(f)	Ψ ψ....(ps)	Ч ч.....(ch)	
ף...(f *final*)	Ωω.....(ō)	Ш ш.....(sh)	
צ.....(ts)		Щ щ.(shch)	
ץ..(ts *final*)		Ы ы...(ay)	
ק.....(k)		Ь ь...(*final*)	
ר.....(r)		Э э.....(ĕ)	
ש.....(sh)		Ю ю...(yu)	
ת.....(t)		Я я.....(ya)	
ת.....(s)		Ѳ ѳ.....(f)	
		Й й...(*final*)	

Principal Alphabets with English Equivalents
Hebrew is nearest the Phoenician original. Greek was derived direct from the Phoenician. Russian is modified and developed from Greek. The Gaelic of Ireland is a simplified Roman

bet is the culmination of a very long evolution and is one of the most marvelous and far-reaching achievements of the human mind. We hear words as wholes. When we hear the word *man,* for instance, we do not naturally separate the sound of *m* from the sound of *a* or the sound of *a* from that of *n.* To become conscious of the separate sounds, or phonemes, of a given language, and so feel the need of a separate symbol for each sound involves a very difficult feat of abstraction.

Our modern English alphabet came

to us directly from the Romans who in turn got it from the Greeks. Its pre-Greek history, in spite of recent discoveries and researches, is still obscure. It must have had an Eastern Mediterranean origin, and it is probable though not certain that it was a development from the Egyptian hieroglyphics. Other theories connect it with Babylonian cuneiform, the Cyprian syllabary or the Minoan writing of Crete. The most probable development may be sketched as follows. In very early times (before 3000 B.C.) the Egyptians developed from their sacred picture writing a series of signs that were used with phonetic value, that is, to represent sounds. From ideograms (signs for ideas) they invented phonograms (signs for sounds). This had come about because the sign ⌣, for example, could stand not only for water but also for the sound *n*, since *n* was the most prominent sound in the Egyptian word for water. (Our N still has the shape of conventional water ripples.) Similarly the picture sign representing the mouth (◯) also had the phonetic value *r*. Thus, in the time of the Old Kingdom (3500–2700 B.C.), the Egyptians had already evolved a series of twenty-four alphabetic signs. These signs stood only for consonants, no indication for the vowels being used. The Egyptians did not perceive the priceless value of their discovery; they continued to use their old pictorial signs, standing for ideas, along with the phonetic signs.

From Egypt use of the alphabetic signs apparently spread to the neighboring peninsula of Mt. Sinai. In 1906 some very early inscriptions (about 1500 B.C.), written in a purely alphabetic script, were discovered in the Sinaitic peninsula by Sir W. Flinders Petrie. This Sinai script seems intermediate between Egyptian hieroglyphic and the early Semitic alphabets. The Greeks had settled in the Aegean basin probably long before 1500 B.C., and apparently borrowed an early type of Semitic alphabet either from the Phoenicians or from some other Semitic peoples with whom they came in contact in Asia minor. This seems fairly certain because the names used by the Greeks for their letters, *alpha, beta, gamma, delta,* and so forth, correspond closely to the Semitic names seen in the Hebrew alphabet—*aleph, beth, gimel, daleth.*[1]

From whomever the Greeks obtained the alphabet, they improved and completed it by using a few characters of the Semitic alphabet for which there were no sounds in Greek speech, for the vowels, so that these sounds no longer had to be guessed in reading.

The Greek alphabet was carried to Italy by colonists, was adopted by the Latins and adapted to their language, and through the medieval Latin manuscripts this Latin alphabet was transmitted to modern European nations. Modern Greece, however, still uses the ancient Greek alphabet, and Russia and a few other Slavonic peoples use the Cyrillic alphabet derived directly from the Greek.

Inflected Languages.—Perhaps the most distinguishing feature of early Indo-European speech—that language of

[1] These names make plain the change from picture writing to signs that stood for a single sound. *Aleph,* the Semitic word for *ox,* was represented by the picture of an ox head, which was read *aleph;* then the picture became the sign for the first sound in the word and this sign also was called *aleph. Beth,* Semitic for house, was expressed by the picture of a house, which became also the sign for the initial sound in the word; so that the Semites called their letter B by the name *beth.*

When the Greeks acquired these letters, they adopted with slight changes most of the Semitic names, though the names meant nothing in Greek. Thus Semitic *aleph* became Greek *alpha* and finally the English A; and Semitic *beth* became the Greek *beta* and finally the English B.

which most European languages, including our own English, are modern developments—is that each word not only carried its core meaning but in many instances also showed by its form its relation to the other words in the sentence. Thus in Greek, a typical Indo-European language, the word *pateres,* meaning *fathers,* indicates by the ending *-es* that it is the subject of the sentence; another form of the same word, *pateras,* shows by

THE METROPOLITAN MUSEUM OF ART

BABYLONIAN INSCRIPTION. This clay tablet bears a form of early writing called cuneiform, taking its name from the wedge-shaped form of its characters. It served as a means of writing for about 2,500 years.

the ending *-as* that it is the direct object of a verb; *pateron* expresses the possessive, *fathers'* or *of fathers;* and *patrasi* means *fathers* as the indirect object, *to* or *for fathers.* A language that indicates by such changes in form the relation of the word to other words in the sentence is called an *inflected* language and this modification of words to show their construction, or syntactical relationship, is called *inflection* (from Latin *inflexio,* a bending).

Even among inflected languages there is a great difference in the degree of inflection. The early Indo-European speech was highly inflected: a single verb had several hundred different forms. The tendency in the development of the various Indo-European languages, as they departed farther and farther from the parent speech, has been toward greater simplicity. Languages with a relatively large amount of inflection are sometimes said to be synthetic (from Greek *synthetikos,* putting together) because they put together in a single word several distinct ideas. In Latin, for example, the one word, *videbimus,* combines a verbal idea *vide-* (see), the idea of future time, *-bi-* (shall) and that of the first person plural, *-mus* (we). It means see-shall-we, or, as

we say in English in three separate words, we shall see. Similarly, the word *videras* combines *vid-* (seen), *-era-* (had) and *-s* (you, singular)—seen-had-you, or you had seen. Ancient Greek and ancient Sanskrit, the classic language of India, are more highly synthetic than Latin, Sanskrit being the most synthetic of the three.

Most of the modern Indo-European languages, being less highly inflected, are said to be analytic (from Greek *analytikos,* tending to break up). In French, for instance, the verb is partly synthetic and partly analytic. Two words, *nous verrons,* are used to express the idea *we-shall-see.* The idea *we* is a separate word, *nous,* and is implied also in the ending *-ons;* but *shall* and *see* are inextricably blended in one word, *verrons. Tu avais vu* (you had seen) in modern French is fully analytic: *tu* (you, singular), *avais* (had), *vu* (seen). French is also completely analytic in expressing the syntactical relation of nouns, prepositions being used instead of the ancient case endings. French personal pronouns are inflected, but the only noun and adjective inflections retained in French are those expressing gender and number, as in *doux* (sweet) when modifying a masculine singular noun, but *douce* when modifying a feminine singular noun; *cheval* (horse), *chevaux* (horses).

Verbs are more fully analytic in German than in French; compare *wir werden sehen* (we shall see). But German nouns and adjectives are inflected; for example, as subject of a verb, the form is *der gute Mann* (the good man); as direct object of a verb it becomes *den guten Mann;* and as possessor, *des guten Mannes.* English as spoken today is still less highly inflected than either German or French, though in the time of King Alfred, Old English was as highly inflected as modern German.

In Alfred's code of laws he translates into Anglo-Saxon the Ten Commandments. Here is the Fourth Commandment—from a manuscript about 1,000 years old: Gemyne thæt thū gehalgige thōne ræstedæg; wyrceath ēow siex dagas and on tham siofothan restath ēow. The interlinear that follows points out some of the inflected forms:

Gemyne Mind	**thaet** that	**thu** thou (possessive, *thīn;* objective, *thē*)
gehalgige make holy (*ge-* with an adjective forms a verb—like *be* in *belittle*)	**thōne** the (objective singular masculine of the demonstrative)	**ræstedæg;** restday; (singular, stem *dæg*)
wyrceath work (*-th,* plural ending)	**ēow** you (objective plural of *thū,* thou)	**siex** six	**dagas** days (plural has stem *dag-*)
and and	**on** on	**tham** the (dative singular of the demonstrative)	**siofothan** seventh	**restath** rest	**ēow.** you.

Conjugation of Verbs.—The various forms used in inflecting the verbs of any language can be grouped together in *conjugations* and the verbs are said to be *conjugated.* Latin has four regular conjugations, presenting certain differences of inflection. The conjugations are made up of *moods* and *tenses* of the verb, with the forms used for each person (*I, you, he, we, you, they*) in each tense. A mood (or mode) expresses a certain way of looking at the action. In Latin, the indicative mood states a fact; the subjunctive mood expresses will or wish and various other ideas; the imperative mood expresses a command or entreaty; and the infinitive mood is a noun form of the verb. In Greek and in some other languages another mood, called the optative, is used to express a wish and in several special uses. In modern languages the terms *potential* mood and *conditional* mood are sometimes used. In English, a verb phrase, such as *I might go,* is said to be in the potential mood; and *if I should go* is in the conditional.

Tenses express the time of an action or state as past, present or future and also very often certain other aspects of the verbal idea. Thus the imperfect tense in Latin describes the action not only as past but also as continuing; for example, *audiebat* (he was listening), imperfect, is distinguished from *audivit* (he heard), historical perfect. This important distinction is reflected in the modern Romance languages. In French, for instance, the imperfect tense, *elle chantait* (she was singing), is contrasted with the past definite, *elle chanta* (she sang).

In Latin the indicative mood has six tenses: present, imperfect, future, perfect, pluperfect (past perfect) and future perfect; and the subjunctive mood has four, lacking the future and future perfect. Greek has a special tense called the *aorist,* an indefinite past that expresses the action of the verb simply as occurring without any implication about its continuance.

Declensions.—The inflections of nouns, pronouns and adjectives are called *declensions* and such words are said to be *declined.* The name *case* is given to each of the different forms assumed in declension. As an illustration we may take the Latin noun, *rex.* The nominative (subject) case in the singular is *rēx* (king); the genitive (possessive) case, *rēgis* (king's or of a king); the dative (indirect object) case, *rēgī* (to or for a king); the accusative (direct object of a verb) case, *rēgem* (king); and the ablative (chiefly used with certain prepositions) case, *rēge.*

Other important terms used with regard to inflection are root, stem and ending. Root may be defined as the simplest element, or base, from which a word derives; stem, as the part of a word to which the endings are appended. Root and stem are sometimes but not always identical. *Vid* (see), for example, is the common root of the Latin verb forms, *vidēbimus* and *vidērās,* previously cited. An ending, or termination, is a syllable or syllables added to modify the meaning of a stem. In the word *vidēbimus* (we shall see), *vidē-* is said to be the present stem of the verb, *videō* (I see), and *-bimus* is the future ending for the first person plural. Similarly, *rēg-* is called the stem of the noun *rēx,* and a given form (e.g., *rēgī*) may be separated into the stem *rēg-* and the ending for the dative case, *-ī.* Sometimes,

however, stem and ending are so completely fused that they cannot be separated.

Etymology.—Knowledge of the roots of words is important, as often we can recognize the meaning of a new or strange word if we know its root through having seen or used it in another word. A knowledge of Latin and Greek roots is a great help to understanding English scientific and literary words.

In the English words *microscope, telescope, telephone, telegraph, phonograph,* you readily recognize the meaning of several roots: *micro-,* small; *tele-,* far; *-scope,* see; *-graph,* write; *-phone,* sound. Even if you had never before seen or heard the word *microphone,* you could analyze the two parts or roots as meaning *small* and *sound* and have some conception of its full significance—that a microphone enlarges small sounds as a microscope enlarges small visions.

TABLE I

English	Old English	German	Dutch	Danish
man	mann	Mann	man	Mand
father	fæder	Vater	vader	Fader
mother	mōdor	Mutter	moeder	Moder
brother	brōthor	Bruder	broeder	Broder
sister	sweostor	Schwester	zuster	Soster
house	hūs	Haus	huis	Hus
bread	brēad	Brot	brood	Brod
water	wæter	Wasser	water	Vand
one	ān	ein	een	een
two	twēgen, twā	zwei	twee	to
three	thrīe	drei	drie	tre
seven	seofon	sieben	zeven	syv
eight	eahta	acht	acht	otte
nine	nigon	neun	negen	ni
foot	fōt	Fuss	voet	Fod

Analyzing the word *etymology* itself, you know that the root in the last two syllables means science of, because you know the words *biology* (science of life), *theology* (science of God) and other such words. The first part of etymology means true thing, so etymology is the science of true meanings.

Relation of English to Other Languages.—The English language, originally a West Germanic dialect, is still Germanic in its structure. It is thus closely related to the other modern Germanic languages: namely, Dutch, German, Danish, Norwegian and Swedish. Through cultural relations of the English people in historical times our language borrowed so many words chiefly of Latin origin, either directly from the Latin or through French as an intermediary, that its vocabulary was transformed. It has been well said that modern English

might be more accurately characterized as an Anglo-Latin, rather than an Anglo-Saxon, language. English has also borrowed a great many words from the Greek language, especially words of significance in the fields of art, science and philosophy. The Greek element in English has been rapidly increasing in recent times, as thousands of scientific terms and names of modern inventions have been taken into English from Greek sources.

The accompanying tables will clarify these vocabulary relations. Table I gives the cognates (words found in two or more languages that have descended from a common parent speech) in several kindred Germanic languages of fifteen common English words.

Table II indicates the vast enrichment of English through derivatives from Latin, Greek and other sources; it gives also the corresponding Greco-Latin derivatives in three modern Romance languages, showing our common cultural linguistic heritage.

The following are examples of English borrowings or derivatives from less common sources:

zenith, from Arabic *samt*
nabob, Urdū *nawwāb,* deputy governor, from Arabic *nā' ib*
pundit, Sanskrit *paṇḍita,* learned
fakir, Arabic *faqīr,* poor; poor man
azure, Old French *azur,* from Persian *lajward, lāzhward,* from Latin *lapis lazuli* (*l* dropped as if it were the article *l'*)
wigwam, American Indian word
wampum, American Indian word
gas, word coined by a modern scientist
ampere, from the name of a French scientist.

Change of Meaning.—The letters of the alphabet came from Greece, Phoenicia and Egypt. The sounds we speak in certain words today have a definite relation to slightly different sounds in cognate words in Latin, Greek or Sanskrit thousands of years ago. Do words themselves mean the same now as then or have their meanings changed? Are there any general principles that govern this change?

The meanings do change. Though no rules of change exist, certain fairly well-defined types of change may be recognized.

Meanings become broader and more general—*manufacture* once meant making by hand (from Latin *manus,* hand, as in *manual*); now it means merely *making* and, as the commonest form of making now is making by machinery, the word has assumed that meaning.

Meanings become specialized or

TABLE II

English	Greek	Latin	French	Italian	Spanish
human		humanus	humain	umano	humano
divine		divinus	divin	divino	divino
reason		ratio, rationis	raison	ragione	razón
spirit		spiritus	esprit	spirito	espíritu
art		ars, artis	art	arte	arte
state		status	état	stato	estado
nation		natio, nationis	nation	nazione	nación
civil		civilis	civil	civile	civil
liberty		libertas	liberté	libertà	libertad
medicine		medicina	médicine	medicina	medicina
music	μουσική	musica	musique	musica	música
drama	ζρᾶμα	drama	drame	dramma	drama
theater	Θέατρον	theatrum	théâtre	teatro	teatro
philosophy	φιλοσοφία	philosophia	philosophie	filosofia	filosofía
physics	φυδικά	physica	physique	fisica	física
arithmetic	ἀριθμητική	arithmetica	arithmétique	aritmetica	aritmética
history	ἱστορία	historia	histoire	storia	historia

narrower—*antique* means old; and so did another form of the same word, *antic.* Then antic was narrowed down to mean the queer old clown in the comedy. Because the clown cut capers and did grotesque things, those capers were called *antics.*

Meanings are sometimes altered by usage; one generation interprets a word favorably; the next unfavorably. The original meaning of *imp* was bud or shoot; hence it came to mean son or offspring. A 16th-century prayer book refers to praying for the king and "his beloved son Edward, our prince, that most angelic *imp.*" Nurserymen still use *imp* to mean a plant graft; but the expression, *imp of Satan,* gave *imp* unpleasant connotations, so that it now means a small devil or mischievous person, an offshoot of Satan!

An example of a lowly word coming to mean something admirable is the modern English word *knight,* from Old English *cniht,* meaning a male servant.

The branch of language study that deals with the meanings of words and their changes is called *semantics.* The comparative study of different languages to trace their similarities and relationships, the precise recording of sounds and the attempt to discover how they have changed, the investigation of roots and of inflectional endings and the analysis of changing significances—all these make up the new science that is only a century old and that, like most sciences, owes much to the central notions of biology—evolution, growth, change, similarity. We never stop learning our own language so long as we are mentally alive. Through countless generations our mother speech, as well as many a tongue from which it has borrowed and to which it is related, has grown and goes on growing and changing like the living organisms we study in botany or zoology.

LEARNING TO READ, WRITE, AND SPELL

Man alone, of all animals, has a language that he can *speak, read* and *write.* Our language, heard, spoken and read, is so familiar to us from childhood that we seldom give a thought to how different our life would be without it. Imagine for a moment how the world would seem if you should awaken some morning unable to speak, read or write or to understand the speech of anyone else. Now imagine everyone else in this same condition and you can see that our schools, trade, industry, commerce and every other activity of modern life would stop as if by magic. This can never actually happen, but the imaginary picture shows how dependent we are upon the language skills of speaking, reading and writing. The great importance of teaching these skills properly in school and at home has induced teachers and research workers to devote years to studying *how* children learn to talk, read, write and spell. They have determined what will handicap or retard a child and the best way to remove these handicaps. They have found that learning the language skills is like learning golf, tennis or swimming—there is a right way, and there are many wrong ways to do it. If the right way is followed, the average child learns rapidly and enjoys the satisfaction of accomplishment. If a wrong way is followed, he learns more slowly, he is discouraged and sometimes, like slicing in golf, learns a cumbersome, inefficient method of reading or writing that hinders him all the rest of his life. Let us look at the results of some of these researches on how we learn the language skills.

Learning To Talk.—At birth an infant makes babbling, gurgling sounds that are the beginning of spoken language. When he wants something, he cries; when he is satisfied, he remains quiet. During the second year, as his bones, muscles and nerves mature, he gains more control over his tongue, lips, vocal cords and other organs of speech. At the same time he constantly hears the speech of others, both of children and adults. He finds that whenever candy is in sight, somebody makes the peculiar sound, *candy.* He then finds that if he makes that peculiar sound when no candy is in sight, as often as not somebody produces some. He makes the sound to get the candy, and if he always gets it simply by saying "ca" or "can" or "cannie," he will be very slow in learning the right sound. Sometimes in talking to a child, parents use the child's sound to refer to certain objects. When they do so they are deliberately teaching him incorrect sounds or baby talk. They are tripling his job of learning, for he must unlearn the wrong sound before he can learn the right one.

This process of learning, or associating a certain word or sound with each object or activity, continues month by month and year by year. The average child has at least as many words in his speaking vocabulary as indicated in the table[1] below:

Age of child	Number of words in vocabulary
2½	700
3	1,100
3½	1,500
4	1,900
4½	2,000
5	2,500
5½	2,700
6	2,800

Some children have difficulty in learning to talk and those who stutter and lisp have not learned to make the sounds of speech correctly. It is estimated that in the United States there are 1,000,000 stutterers and 10,000,000 who lisp or have other speech disorders. These irregularities seriously affect a child's mind and feelings, and many scientific studies have been carried on to discover the cause and cure for such speech defects. It has been found that there are four times as many boys as girls who stutter; that stuttering usually begins when the child is four or five years old; that it becomes more and more fixed as the child grows older and that it is very much easier to remedy the defect in its early stages than after the stutterer reaches the age of sixteen or seventeen. Left-handed children who are required to become right-handed are very likely to become stutterers after the shift to the nonpreferred hand. The reason for this is found in the physiology of the brain and nervous system. It is too technical to be discussed here; but the evidence clearly shows that many, perhaps a majority, of stutterers are not using their left hands, as they preferred when they were babies. Extensive training in the use of the originally preferred hand is usually followed by a marked improvement in speech.

Lisping and difficulties in articulation are other disorders of speech that interfere with the process of learning to talk. These are sometimes due to poor organs of speech, such as crooked teeth or harelip, but more often to slovenly habits of using the tongue and lips. One condition, known as a *lateral lisp,* is caused by speaking with the tongue in one side of the mouth rather than in the center where it belongs. One can easily demonstrate this to himself by uttering a few words with his tongue in one side of the mouth cavity. This condition is treated by calling the child's attention to the position of his tongue and training him to hold it in the center of his mouth when he speaks.

Another difficulty in learning to talk arises when one speech sound is substituted for another. This occurs when the child in the early stages of speech happens upon a wrong setting of his vocal organs for a certain sound and learns this wrong setting so well that it becomes a part of his speech. Many children four or five years old pronounce *s* for *f.* It is unfortunate that such substitutions stay in the child's speech for years when they can be eliminated in a very short while by proper instruction. If the parent or teacher will tell the child to bite his lower lip and blow, he cannot avoid saying *f.* The production of most of the other sounds of speech is equally simple.

Poor hearing also is sometimes the cause of difficulty in learning to talk. The organs of speech of a deaf mute are usually quite perfect, but he cannot use them properly because he has never heard the sounds of speech uttered by other people and therefore is unable to produce these sounds himself. Children who are hard of hearing often confuse various sounds, mispronounce others and produce jumbled speech; but to them because their hearing is inadequate *their speech seems all right.* Such children must be taught how to use their tongue, lips and other vocal organs if

---

[1] *Since individual children accomplish all their learning at their own rate, any such table as the one above should be taken only as an indication of the average.*

they are to produce the sounds of speech correctly.

The importance of giving the child proper instruction when he is learning to talk has only recently been recognized. Most adults of today learned to talk by hit-or-miss methods. Their speech was like Topsy in *Uncle Tom's Cabin*—it "just growed." As a result we have entirely too large a number of speech defectives, even in the more advanced sections of the country. The next generation will see the number of such defectives reduced to a fraction of what it is at present. Many school systems, particularly in the larger cities and the more progressive communities, are employing a specially trained teacher who devotes all his time to the prevention and correction of disorders of speech.

Learning To Read.—Reading and speaking are similar in many ways—both are language skills; both involve associating a symbol of some kind with objects and situations and activities. In the case of speech, this symbol is the word we hear, but in reading it is the word we see. When the sound *candy* is associated with something good to eat, an element of speech has been learned. When the printed or written letters *candy* are associated in the same manner, an element in reading has been learned. We may define reading as the process of associating various combinations of letters with specific objects, situations and activities.

Ordinarily speech is well along in its development before reading is begun. The child must therefore associate two things with the printed symbol that he meets in his reading lesson—namely, the object itself and the sound that stands for it. For example, a child may be taught that the printed word *candy* stands for the sound *candy* and hence for something good to eat. Twenty-five years ago reading was taught almost entirely by this method. It is now realized that learning to read in this manner results in word reading or word sounding. Each word must be implicitly pronounced before its meaning is fully grasped. It is the natural result of a method that associates the sound of the word with the printed symbol and with the meaning.

The newer method of teaching reading eliminates the middle step. The child is taught to associate the printed symbol with the meaning and to pay little attention to the sound of the word. This is accomplished by presenting the words in meaningful groups, phrases and short sentences. The material deals only with situations and activities that are familiar to the child from his past experience. The very first lessons introduce reading as a thought-getting, not as a word-sounding, process.

Even with the most improved methods of instruction all children do not learn to read with the same ease. Among a thousand children taken at random from the sixth grade, a few—perhaps ten or a dozen—do not read any better than the average first-grade pupil. At the other extreme, a few very good pupils read as well as the average high-school graduate. The poor readers have been carefully studied because a majority of failures in the lower primary grades are due to difficulties in reading. Children differ in intelligence just as they do in height, weight or strength, and if a child is very low in mental ability he is likely to be poor in reading as well as in other school subjects. It has been found, however, that a great many children who are retarded in reading are not at all below normal in intelligence. What are some of the things that may cause a child of normal or even above normal intelligence to have difficulty with his reading? They may be specified under several headings:

1. FAULTY VISION.—Reading is a *visual* skill. Everything we read comes to us through our eyes. If a child has poor eyes, he is likely to be a poor reader. The two eyes must work together like a well-trained team of horses. For most efficient vision, the eyes must look at exactly the same point at the same time. Some children have what is known as *overconvergence*, which means that the eyes turn in slightly more than they should. In extreme cases this is cross-eyedness and is very obvious; but in mild cases it is not obvious and simply reduces the child's reading efficiency. The opposite condition is known as *underconvergence*, which means that the eyes do not turn in as much as they should. A third state, known as *lateral imbalance*, occurs when the right eye sees a word higher or lower than the left eye sees it.

Another visual defect is *astigmatism*. The eye is really very similar to a small camera, with a lens in front and a surface similar to a film in back. If the lens is thicker on one side of the eye than it is on the other, vision is astigmatic—the image on the back of the eye is distorted, and the eye muscles are under constant strain trying to force the image into its normal shape. *Far-sightedness,* the inability to focus sharply on near objects, subjects a reader to constant strain because what he sees is fuzzy and out of focus.

Most of these visual defects may be remedied by muscle exercises or properly fitted glasses. The important thing is to discover the defect before it has handicapped the child's reading. Many school systems now give visual tests to all pupils and advise those who have serious defects to consult a competent eye specialist.

2. FAULTY PERCEPTION.—Sometimes a child will have difficulty in remembering and recognizing words even though his vision, as far as the eyes are concerned, is quite satisfactory. The word *cat,* for example, may have no meaning to him even though he has seen it many times before and can readily name the letters c-a-t. This happens when the relation between the visual symbol and the object has not been thoroughly learned.

In ordinary reading one does not look at every word but at groups of words. The eyes stop four or five times in reading across a line of print on a page of standard size. Each stop or fixation lasts about a quarter second and the movement or jump from one fixation to another requires only about one twenty-fifth second. It has been shown by experiment that during this jump the eye sees practically nothing—that perception of the words takes place only during fixation. One must therefore recognize the meaning of several words—perhaps an entire phrase—in the quarter second while the eye is looking at only a single word in the center of the phrase. These experiments show why word reading is inadequate, and why a good reader must be able to understand several words at a glance. Several methods have been worked out to improve this ability. One of the most common is to present cards by the flash method. Each card contains a short sentence or group of words. The card is presented for just an instant, and the child does not have time to read each word. This kind of practice develops ability to grasp the meaning of several words at a single glance.

Another kind of difficulty in perception is known as *reversals*. Some readers will read a word like *bid* as *did,* reversing the letter *b* and seeing it as *d*. Reversals may result in whole words being read backwards. For example, *saw* may be read as *was* and *not* as *ton*.

Reading Activities at the Pre-primer Level.— While the boys and girls are receiving instruction in the basal pre-primer program it is essential to carry on certain types of activities that build a readiness for the next level of reading instruction and that ensure mastery of the pre-primer reading skills.

A. WHAT ARE THE PRE-PRIMER READING SKILLS?—

1. Learning how to use picture clues as an aid in reading the text.

2. Learning how to use the context or the sense of what the other words are saying to figure out words.

3. Being able to detect likenesses and differences in word and letter forms.

4. Being able to recognize words by noticing the configuration or pattern of the word.

5. Mastering the basic sight vocabulary to be taught.

6. Developing the understanding that reading is simply talk written down and carries meaning just as the spoken word.

7. Developing a liking for reading, a desire to read and favorable attitudes toward reading.

8. Getting training in noting likenesses and differences in initial consonant sounds—orally.

9. Getting training in recognizing rhyming words orally.

B. DEVELOPING A LIKING TO READ, A DESIRE TO READ, AND FAVORABLE ATTITUDES TOWARD READING.—

1. The teacher's own enthusiasm about the children's learning to read has a favorable effect on the child's reading efforts.

2. A library table or corner which is attractive and many opportunities for the children to look at and handle the books.

3. A daily story time for the children to listen to stories read by the teacher.

4. A feeling of security and achievement is a must. Patience must be used for children who have difficulty learning the words.

5. Extra reading experiences through

news charts, experience charts, signs, labels, captions and printed text accompanying pictures, records such as room responsibilities, things to remember or summarizing after a discussion.

C. LEARNING TO LISTEN ATTENTIVELY.—

The following suggestions for training the children to listen attentively for a definite purpose can be effectively used at pre-primer level—

1. During story time expect the children to listen. Use stories that are not too long and that have attractive pictures to hold their interest.

2. Records can be effectively used to develop good listening habits. When the children respond to parts of the record such as imitating an airplane, the teacher knows they are following what is being listened to.

3. Using slide films can be helpful to increase the attention span of the children because they are interested in this type of material.

D. DEVELOPING THE IDEA THAT READING IS SIMPLY TALK WRITTEN DOWN AND CARRIES MEANING JUST AS THE SPOKEN WORD DOES.—

This is an idea that should be instilled into the boys and girls from the very beginning. Comprehension of what is read is necessary. If children realize that reading is talk written down they will more likely be looking for not only what it says but also what it means.

This idea can easily be developed in an incidental way by telling the children, by writing down the talk following trips and discussions and such ideas.

Learning how to use the punctuation marks to help us get meaning and to read as we talk is important.

E. DEVELOPING WORD-ATTACK SKILLS.—

First of all, the Guidebook suggestions that go along with the pre-primer level should be carefully studied and used by the teacher.

Besides the Guidebook, however, there are many possibilities for making sure the children are mastering the basic reading skills taught at pre-primer level. This is the foundation for later independence in reading.

1. Teach the children how to use pictures and the sense of what's being read.

2. There should be training in careful looking at words to notice likenesses and differences in word forms.

(a) Matching the words that are alike.

(b) Crossing out a word that is different.

(c) Finding a word in a line the same as the first one.

(d) Finding words and phrases in a list like the one at the top and underlining them.

(e) Use the pre-primer vocabulary and words that are alike in some way as—and, can, run

    like, little, look

3. Call attention to how words look to help remember words as—

(a) "something" is a long word
"he" is a short word

(b) can⎱ alike at beginning,
cat⎰ different at the end.

4. Mastery of the sight words being taught is the chief word-analysis skill at this level.

Following is a list of the pre-primer sight words that teachers should make sure the children can recognize quickly in any setting—

look	see	funny
jump	run	come
up	down	and
go	work	can
play	help	little
big	is	the
my	I	blue
make	yellow	red
find	said	for
want	here	we
one	three	a
two	you	not
it	to	me
where	in	away

It is not necessary to drill on the nouns because they are used less frequently and can easily be figured out by picture clues, the context, and later by sounding. The first two means are helpful at pre-primer level.

Suggestions that can be effectively used at pre-primer level to ensure mastery of the basic sight vocabulary are—

(a) Blackboard games such as— Reading the words that the teacher has written on the balloons.

(b) A fishbowl game using these words is good.

(c) Post a chart of words being studied.

(d) Find appropriate pictures to put up that can make use of these words in the accompanying caption or printed text. Use simple sentences at this level, i.e.,—

    This is Dick.

    He is big.

    He sees the car.

(e) In oral reading situations only be satisfied with having the words read correctly. This will instill accurate and careful looking at words.

(f) Give much practice in phrase reading—flash card idea:

    in the house

    to me

    can not go

5. A beginning is made in using structural analysis.

6. During the pre-primer level there should be much auditory training in hearing likenesses and differences in words, in initial consonant sounds and rhyming words. The Guidebook gives many suggestions. These can be supplemented by listening games as—

(a) I am thinking of a word that starts like big. It is made of glass and we put milk in it. What is it?

    big bottle

(b) Say yes if the words begin alike. Say no if the words do not begin alike—

    red run (Yes)

    no go (No)

    see sun (Yes)

F. DETERMINING READINESS FOR THE PRIMER LEVEL OF READING.—

1. Is the child anxious to read the next book?

2. Does he recognize words easily in context?

3. Can he read fluently in pre-primers?

4. Can he express himself in clear simple sentences?

5. Does he seem to enjoy the stories, be able to relate the ideas of the

text and pictures to get the meaning and read with expression?

6. Can he get an average score on the pre-primer basal test? Children who score low on this test should go through the Junior Primer.

First-Grade Reading Program. Goals.—

1. To get the children to like to read and to have an interest in reading.

2. To get the children to look for meaning in whatever is read; to realize that reading is talk written down and carries meaning just as the spoken word does.

3. To get the children to be able to listen effectively for a purpose.

4. To develop good work habits and paying attention to the task at hand.

5. To develop visual discrimination and perception.

6. To develop auditory discrimination of gross likenesses and differences in words, initial and final consonant sounds and rhyming words.

7. To get the children to acquire a basic sight vocabulary.

8. To stimulate the mental ability of all pupils in keeping with their maturity through an enriched program that provides for vocabulary growth and a common background of experiences.

9. To be alert for any signs of defects, deficiencies or maladjustments—

    physically

    emotionally

    socially

    mentally

and to use the help of the special services as needed.

First-Grade Reading Program. Standards of Achievement.—

1. All pupils must *satisfactorily* complete the primer level of reading for promotion to grade 2.

2. All pupils who have sufficient mental ability, maturity, and freedom from factors that hinder reading progress should complete the basal first reader.

3. First graders ought to know the names and recognize the printed forms of the ABC's—in random order—by the end of the year.

4. First graders by the end of the year ought to have the know-how of figuring out words by using:

(a) Picture clues.

(b) Context clues—the sense of what the other words are saying, and their own experience background.

(c) Careful looking at words from left-to-right and noticing how the word begins.

(d) Be able to use simple punctuation to get the meaning and for expression as well as proper phrasing.

(e) Quick recognition of a basic sight vocabulary.

(f) Structural Analysis.

    ————s for plural

    ————'s for ownership

    ————ed

    ————ing

PRE-PRIMER SIGHT VOCABULARY

look	see	and
run	come	go
jump	up	down
funny	away	work
play	help	find
can	the	is
little	big	said
it	one	two
three	not	want

a	at	I
in	red	to
we	yellow	blue
for	my	you
make	me	here
where		

PRIMER

pretty	eat	are
get	four	with
what	yes	now
do	will	ride
put	who	too
no	this	that
white	did	saw
good	stop	have
they	out	please
new	he	thank
soon	went	she
our	ran	all
came	am	on
must	so	laugh
some	say	black
but	like	there
was	fast	

FIRST READER SIGHT VOCABULARY

take	your	first
then	know	live
let	very	as
them	call	his
read	sleep	found
him	were	which
made	ate	after
us	wish	five
give	old	her
when	open	again
of	buy	how
an	be	had
has	well	many
could	fly	going
ask	think	from
or	every	may
why	over	just
once	round	green
any	try	brown

After completing the first reader, children should be able to attack words through initial and final consonant substitution.

A READING COMPREHENSION TEST

The crow's beak is wonderful. Of course, lips are better on people in many ways than beaks would be; but we cannot do one-tenth as many things with our mouths as the crow does with his. To be sure, we do not need to, for we have hands to help us. If our arms had grown into wings, though, as a bird's arms do, how should we ever get along in this world?

( ) 1. Crows are usually black.
( ) 2. Crows have beaks, and people have mouths.
( ) 3. Crows can do many more things with their beaks than people can do with mouths.
( ) 4. Crows are always getting into mischief.
( ) 5. The crow's arms have grown into wings.
( ) 6. People do not need beaks because they have hands to help them.
( ) 7. People fly in airplanes.

MONKMEYER

A LEFT-HANDED CHILD should write with the left hand and not be forced to change.

( ) 8. The crow eats a great deal.
( ) 9. Crows have feathers.
( ) 10. We do not need beaks because we have hands.

In this test, the amount of time is constant for all children, and those having the greatest ability to comprehend what they read are quickly spotted by their ability to identify the statements according to the above instructions.

Learning To Write.—The developing child must learn not only to talk and to read but also to write. Writing also is a language skill; it involves associating various objects and situations with words that are written. What we know of the activities of the past is largely dependent upon the preservation of what men and women of those times wrote. In the modern world much writing is done by means of the typewriter and therefore the development of a high degree of skill in handwriting is perhaps not so important as it once was, yet an inquiry among a number of business firms in a large city indicated that even today many employers demand a certain skill in handwriting before an applicant will be employed.

The modern trend places the importance on usefulness rather than perfection. Writing is developed along with reading, spelling and composition. This by no means implies a disregard for systematic learning or even of drills and practices. Self-analysis is encouraged as the child progresses. Since this analysis should be made in all his written work, the goals for mastery must be clear and definite.

Writing is done at the blackboard or on large sheets of paper with a blunt pencil. The child's earliest writing is much larger than it will be later on, because the muscles of his hands and fingers have not yet developed so he can make the finer movements necessary in ordinary writing.

From the beginning care is taken to provide each child with a comfortable seat so that he may sit squarely facing the desk with his head erect, his feet flat on the floor, the elbows two or three inches from the body and his trunk reasonably erect. We are apt to think that writing is done only with the hand and fingers; really it is done with the entire body. Psychological experiments have shown that when any part of the body is subjected to excessive strain or muscular tension, the effect irradiates or spreads to other parts of the body. A body position that is in any way uncomfortable or demanding, not only unduly tires the child but actually reduces the efficiency of the muscles of the fingers and hand.

A left-handed child should be allowed to write with his left hand. To insist that all children learn to write with the right hand is most unwise, for a child who is naturally left-handed if he is forced to use his right hand is very likely to develop a disorder in speech or reading; and he may never learn to write very well with his right hand because he is handicapped from the start. If the schoolroom is equipped with table-arm chairs, a certain number of them having the table on the left arm should be provided.

The paper is placed directly in front of the child and tilted about 30 degrees to the left. The pen is held easily and lightly in a position that is natural to the form of the individual hand. The movements in writing are of two kinds—across the page and up and down. Accordingly there must be two kinds of hand movements. The sideward movement is one of the most important aspects of writing. If it is not even and smooth, the letters will vary in slant, their spacing will be uneven, and their proper formation will cause undue exertion. The sideward movement is properly made by swinging the arm like a pendulum or lever with the fulcrum at the elbow or the resting place of the arm on the table. The movement should be even and smooth, not jerky or abrupt. Many books on teaching handwriting give exercises to develop the proper sideward movement of the arm and to maintain it while the activities of the fingers and hand take place.

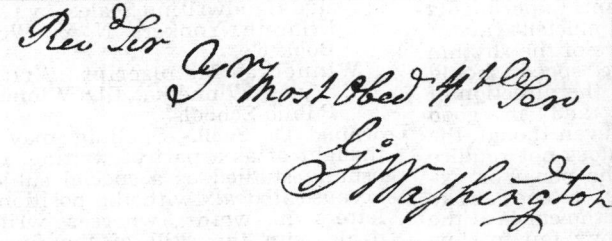

LOOK MAGAZINE

GEORGE WASHINGTON'S SIGNATURE (*left*) is a sample of the fancy writing of that period. Today, however, handwriting is by no means obsolete; every student's language skills include penmanship. The child begins with block printing and then progresses to script.

MANUSCRIPT WRITING. — In manuscript writing which resembles printed symbols, the letters—disconnected and simplified—are formed by straight lines, parts of circles, and circles. It is an old form of writing and was introduced in the United States in 1922. Within the past few years, a number of scientific investigations have been made to ascertain the relative merits of this system of writing. Experiments conducted by Gates and Brown, Conard and Offerman, Beach, Grill, and Kerr substantiate the advantages claimed for the teaching of manuscript writing. Listed among the most important advantages are: it facilitates learning to read and spell; it is easier for the child to learn; it is more pleasing to read; it is more rhythmical to write; it reduces eye strain.

Two important surveys strongly favor manuscript writing in the primary grades. The findings of Freeman's study indicate that 84 per cent of 727 schools use manuscript writing in the first and second grades. The opinions expressed favor manuscript writing and indicate that its advantages greatly outweigh its disadvantages.

Polkinghorne's survey of current practices in teaching handwriting reveals that: 1) 93.1 per cent of schools begin handwriting instruction in the first grade; 2) 89.3 per cent use manuscript for beginning writing; 3) 17.6 per cent teach manuscript in all grades; 4) 66.4 per cent change to cursive in third grade or above; and 5) 65.4 per cent use a commercially prepared system of writing.

When to change from manuscript to cursive is a controversial question. Some educators suggest it be done in the second and third grades, others in the intermediate grades, and some advocate its use throughout the entire school system. The change is begun by demonstrating the close relationship which exists between the cursive and the manuscript alphabet. Many teachers start with the child's spelling words and show the connecting strokes that the cursive forms add to the manuscript.

CURSIVE WRITING. In cursive writing the letters are joined together and slant is added. Researches made on the comparative speed and quality of both forms of writing reveal contradictory conclusions. Gates and Brown found that manuscript was more suitable to primary-grade children and cursive to children in the grades above. When the demand is for speed alone, cursive is superior.

FOUR STAGES IN LEARNING TO WRITE.

1. *Writing readiness.* The teacher observes the child to determine whether he is ready to learn how to write. The proper time to begin depends upon the child's desire to write, his need to write, and his ability to handle the necessary materials.

2. *Beginning writing.* In the first and second grades the child's beginning writing consists of brief and simple writing experiences. The process is made easy enough to insure some

measure of success. Proper motivation results in greater effort and better writing. At this time, emphasis is placed on correct letter formation and moving the hand across the page in the right direction. Practical experiences are stressed through writing names, labeling drawings, writing "get-well" cards, et cetera — all of which are integrated with the reading and social studies programs. Writing materials include the blackboard, beginner's pencil with medium soft lead, and one-inch ruled paper. Later as the child advances, he uses a regular pencil and the spacing on the ruled paper is gradually reduced.

3. *Rapid progress.* The third stage occurs in the intermediate grades. The aims of instruction are to improve writing skills, to increase speed, and to continue the improvement of legibility. Individualized practice periods based upon the diagnosis of writing needs are of supreme importance. The learner proceeds at his own rate and the teacher concentrates on the particular needs of each pupil.

4. *Refinement.* The final stage is the period of refinement and generally occurs in the upper elementary grades. Dictation exercises are valuable to test speed and legibility and to develop the habit of listening, thinking, and writing. When the pupil has mastered the essentials which make for legibility and a reasonable amount of speed, he is encouraged to develop his own individual slant and style. His writing tends to become more regular, unified, and rhythmical in terms of pressure and speed of the writing stroke.

The vertical or up-and-down movements are largely formed by movements of the fingers. At one time an attempt was made to teach writing by forcing the arm to make both the sideward and up-and-down movements. Experiments have shown that the arm movements are poorly adapted in most persons to the proper execution of the vertical stroke. To execute the up-and-down movements properly by moving the arm requires a great deal of practice, and only a few children ever develop enough skill to write satisfactorily in this way. Most children revert immediately to finger movements as soon as the writing lesson is finished, and if only arm movements have been practiced during the lesson, the time has been wasted. The theory of modern education is to teach what the children later use, not what they may or ought to use.

As in other skills that involve activity, the rhythm of writing movements is very important. Experiments have shown the most efficient rate of writing and the nature of the rhythm for each letter. The speed should slow down whenever the direction of movement changes, and in good writers this happens even though the letter being written does not require a complete stop of the pen. For example, in the letter *m* the stroke should slow down for the curve at the top. A poor writer may fail to slow down at such places or he may tend

to slow down in other places where the speed of the movement should remain unchanged. The proper rhythm and timing for each letter can be developed most readily by counting exercises that have been carefully worked out to follow the timing used by the best writers. Ordinary rapid counting is of little use, because the rhythm of each letter must be dealt with separately.

The practice period should always deal with the whole process of writing, but the pupil's attention should be centered on one or more specific movements that he is seeking to improve. It is very important to practice these movements in the normal writing situation. If they are practiced separately, the child will master them quickly but the learning will not carry over to normal writing. Consider, for example, the smooth, swinging movement of the forearm in moving across the page. This can be quickly mastered by itself, but unless it is learned in the actual writing situation, it does not become a part of the total combination of movements.

METHOD OF TEACHING WRITING. The objectives of teaching writing are: a) To make the child conscious of the importance of good writing. b) To have the child write legibly and with sufficient speed to meet his present needs and future requirements. c) To equip the child with methods of work so he will attack his writing problems intelligently. d) To diagnose writing difficulties and to provide suitable remedial measures. e) To permit each child to progress at his own rate of learning. f) To emphasize the importance of expressing ideas in legible writing. g) To help the child develop a critical attitude concerning the quality of all his written work.

Testing. The steps in testing include the following: a) Select a short stanza or paragraph the children have learned by heart. b) Provide pupils with writing paper. c) Give clear directions to the children. d) Make sure they begin and end at the time designated. e) Use a stop-watch or a watch with a second hand.

Measurement of handwriting. Writing scales are available to help the pupil evaluate his progress in writing. From time to time the scale may be placed on the bulletin board so every child can compare a specimen of his writing with those on the scale. Some of the most commonly used are:

Ayres Handwriting Scale, by L. S. Ayres. New York: Russell Sage Foundation.

Metropolitan Manuscript and Cursive Handwriting Scales, by G. H. Hildreth. Yonkers, N. Y.: World Book Co.

Winnetka Manuscript Writing Scales. Winnetka, Ill.: Winnetka Public Schools.

Learning To Spell.—Spelling may be thought of as a part of writing. It is usually studied as a special subject, because it deals with the position of letters in words, whereas writing deals with the skill of the fingers, hand and arm in forming the letters of words. A child begins to learn spelling when he begins to read and write. In his first reading he recognizes a word because he sees the pattern of letters; and it is this pattern that makes up the spelling of a word. Also in his earliest writing he learns the correct position of the letters, and this is really a lesson in spelling. Research has shown that special instruction in spelling by itself is necessary if many words are to be learned thoroughly. There has been a great deal of carefully conducted and rigid experimentation on how children learn to spell. Until fifty years ago, spelling lists for school children were compiled with very little study. It was felt that if a number of new words were presented each day or each week, the child would learn these with equal readiness and would thereby acquire a satisfactory spelling vocabulary. In contrast to this approach, every modern spelling course is based upon the results of extensive research.

Anyone who teaches spelling must recognize the following problems: 1) What words should a child learn to spell, and when should he learn them? 2) How can the child master these words? 3) How can the child develop self-reliance in spelling words not taught in school?

THE WORDS WHICH A CHILD NEEDS. Valid research should be consulted to determine the spelling words which a child needs. The researches of Horn, Anderson, Ayres, Cook and others show what words adults write most often. The investigations of French, Paul McKee, Fitzgerald and others indicate words most useful for child writing in life outside the school. The studies of Jones, Brittain, Breed, and Rinsland present information upon school writing. Jones's famous One Hundred Demons have served Americans for 35 years.

A basic life spelling vocabulary of about 2,650 words by Fitzgerald comprises approximately 95 per cent of the running writing of child and adult. A list of 350 basic spelling words, selected from this larger list, is most important for teaching beginning spelling to children. Because these 350 words account for 75 per cent of the words used by children and 41 per cent of their spelling mistakes, they should be mastered.

THE AIMS OF SPELLING. The child under guidance should:

Learn to spell the words in a valid list.

Learn to use these words in writing.

Develop a desire to spell with 100 per cent accuracy.

Develop an effective judgment as to the correctness of spelling in written work.

Acquire a method for learning new words necessary for writing in school and in life outside the school.

TEST BEFORE TEACHING. Because of the great variation in the abilities of normal children, testing in one form or another is the only way to determine which words of a lesson a child does not know. A preliminary test on the words of a week should be given to determine which words a child must study, and which he does not need to study.

MOTIVATE THE CHILD TO STUDY. When the child understands that the words he studies are the words he needs in writing and when he recognizes that the method he uses guides him to successful results, he will desire to study spelling.

TEACH AN EFFECTIVE METHOD OF STUDY. Important factors in teaching the spelling of a word are: a) meaning, b) pronunciation, c) presentation, d) imagery, e) recall, f) writing the word.

a. Meaning. The child must know at least one meaning of a word before he can write it sensibly. Generally, the child knows a meaning of a word that he needs; if he does not, he should be aided in learning a meaning by using the word in a sentence, by discussing it, or by looking it up in a dictionary.

b. Pronunciation. Correct pronunciation is important in learning to spell. The teacher may pronounce the word for the child or guide him to use the dictionary to determine the pronunciation from accent and diacritical markings.

c. Presentation. The word may be presented visually, in context or in a list. Words presented in a story or in sentences are meaningful. Visual presentation is supplemented when the child listens to teacher pronunciation and analysis, when he uses the word in a sentence, and when he writes it meaningfully.

d. Imagery. The child must form an image of the word. Visual, oral, auditory, and kinesthetic approaches to imagery have been used successfully. Space is too meager here to indicate the comparative values of each approach. However, despite the individual variations in imagery, the normal child will be helped by seeing, hearing, saying, and writing the word.

e. Recall. Recall is a test of imagery. It may be visual to check the syllabication and the sequence of the letters; it may be oral to check the spelling of the word. It should be motor to check the writing of the word.

f. Writing the word. The mastery of the spelling of the word may be checked by testing and also by writing the word in school and life situations. Every writing activity is a test of a child's ability to spell the words that he uses.

g. Summary. In learning to spell, it is safe to say that the child should see, hear, speak, and write. *The Five Steps of Learning to Spell a Word* which may be fitted to the language level of the learner should be mastered and used in sequence.

1) *Meaning and pronunciation.* Look at the word. Pronounce the word. Use the word correctly in a sentence.

2) *Imagery.* See and say the word. See the syllables of the word. Say the word, syllable by syllable. Spell the word.

3) *Recall.* Look at the word. Close your eyes and spell it. Check to see whether your spelling is correct. (In case you made an error, do steps 1, 2, and 3 again.)

4) *Writing the word.* Write the word correctly. Dot the i's. Cross the t's. Close the o's. Check your writing to see that every letter is legible. Check your spelling.

5) *Mastery.* Cover the word and write it. If it is correct, cover the word and write it again. If it is correct, cover it and write it once more.

GRAMMAR

A knowledge of the rules and principles of English grammar gives one basic help toward correct expression. It does not take the place of hearing and reading and speaking one's language; but it does add assurance and precision to speech. As a musician tunes his ear to good music by listening intelligently but becomes a good musician himself by diligent practice, so all of us may become fluent and skilful in the use of English not only by associating ourselves with good literature and those who speak correctly, but by speaking and writing according to accepted rules of good usage.

Grammar is based upon the classification of words into parts of speech and the relation of these parts of speech in sentences. Each language has its rules of grammar. However, when we speak of grammar without naming a foreign tongue we refer to our own language.

There are eight different parts of speech: Noun, Pronoun, Verb, Adjective, Adverb, Conjunction, Preposition, Interjection. *Nouns* and *Verbs* are far more important than the other parts of speech, as they are used to make the base of the sentence. *Pronouns* serve as substitutes for nouns. *Adjectives* and *Adverbs* are used to modify or add to the meaning expressed by nouns and verbs. *Conjunctions* are used as connectives. *Prepositions* express a relationship between a noun and some other part of the sentence. *Interjections* are words that express our emotions or feelings. They have no grammatical relation to other parts of speech used in a sentence.

Each part of speech will be discussed under the following headings: Definition, Kinds, Forms, Syntax or Construction. *Definition* means the identification of one part of speech as distinguished from another. *Kinds* are the classifications of the various parts of speech. *Forms* are the changes made to indicate different uses or meanings, they are sometimes called the *inflections* of a word. *Syntax* means the relation of words, phrases and clauses to other parts of the sentence. In a grammatical sense *construction* means the same thing.

A study of the structure of the sentence as a whole will follow the study of the parts of speech in their various uses. This process is called *Sentence Analysis.*

PARTS OF SPEECH

NOUNS

Definition: A noun is a word used as the name of a person, a place, a thing, an action, a condition or a quality: *John, Maryland, house, jumping, happiness, charity.*

Kinds: Proper, Common, Concrete, Abstract, Collective.

A *proper* noun is the name of some particular person, place or thing: *Henry, Boston, Tuesday, June.*

A *common* noun is the name of a member of a class of persons, animals, places or things: *girl, town, church, tree, music, sleep.*

A *concrete* noun names something that occupies space or may be perceived through the senses: *tree, stick, stone, desk, water, sky.*

An *abstract* noun is the name of a quality, a condition or an action: *greatness, cruelty, hardihood.*

A *collective* noun names any group or collection of persons, animals or things taken as one: *army, tribe, crowd, herd, team.*

Forms: Nouns may be inflected as follows: *Number* (Singular, Plural); *Gender* (Masculine, Feminine, Neuter); *Person* (First, Second, Third); *Case* (Nominative, Objective, or Possessive).

Singular number means one; *plural* number, more than one. The plural of a noun is usually formed by adding *s* to the singular (*boy, boys; tiger, tigers; rose, roses*) or, if the noun ends in *s* or the sound of *s* (*ch, sh, x, z*), by adding *es*: *dress, dresses; church, churches; box, boxes; waltz, waltzes.*

Nouns ending in *y* preceded by a consonant, change *y* to *i* and add *es*: *quantity, quantities.*

The following nouns ending in *o* add *es*: *cargo, hero, buffalo, potato, tomato, volcano.* Many nouns from foreign languages ending in *o* add *s*: *solo, alto, piano, basso, soprano.*

Many nouns ending in *f* or *fe* change *f* or *fe* to *v* and add *es*: *leaf, life, knife, thief, wife.*

Some nouns form their plurals irregularly: *child, children; foot, feet; man, men; ox, oxen; mouse, mice; goose, geese.*

Certain nouns use the same form for both singular and plural: *sheep, deer, trout* and in some senses *hair, fish, fowl.*

English has taken over the plurals of many foreign words along with the singular. Both in spelling and pronounciation, the English fashion is to be preferred where a choice is given.

Singular	Plural
alumnus (mas.)	alumni
alumna (fem.)	alumnae
analysis	analyses
animalculum	animalcula
antithesis	antitheses
appendix	appendixes, appendices
automaton	automatons, automata

axis	axes
bacillus	bacilli
bacterium	bacteria
bandit	bandits, banditti
basis	bases
beau	beaus, beaux
cactus	cactuses, cacti
cherub	cherubs, cherubim
crisis	crises
curriculum	curriculums, curricula
datum	data
dilettante	dilettanti
erratum	errata
focus	foci
formula	formulas, formulae
fungus	fungi
genius	geniuses, genii
genus	genera
gymnasium	gymnasiums, gymnasia
hippopotamus	hippopotamuses, hippopotami
hypothesis	hypotheses
index	indexes, indices
larva	larvae
madame	mesdames
medium	mediums, media
memorandum	memorandums, memoranda
monsieur	messieurs
nebula	nebulae
oasis	oases
phenomenon	phenomena
radius	radii
seraph	seraphs, seraphim
stimulus	stimuli
tableau	tableaus, tableaux
terminus	termini
thesis	theses
vortex	vortexes, vortices

Gender is a term referring to the form of word used to indicate sex. *Masculine* gender means male; *feminine,* female; *common,* either sex; *neuter,* absence of sex. The difference in gender may be indicated by the use of a different word: *man, woman; sir, madam; son, daughter; boy, girl; buck, doe.* Sometimes the difference in sex is shown by a prefix: *he-goat, she-goat; manservant, maidservant.* Sometimes a suffix effects the change: *hero, heroine; executor, executrix; count, countess; duke, duchess.*

Person is the term that indicates the speaker, the person spoken to or the person spoken of. Nouns are not inflected for person; personal pronouns are inflected for person: *I* am; *you* are; *he* is. Observe also that the different forms of the verb *be*—*am, are, is*—indicate person.

Syntax or Construction: Its case indicates the use or syntax of a noun or a pronoun in a sentence.

A noun is always in the *possessive case* when it implies ownership or a possessive relationship: *Edith's* book; *cow's* horns; the *year's* events; *Longfellow's* poems. The possessive of most singular nouns is formed by adding the apostrophe and *s.* Certain nouns ending in *s* or the sound of *s* take only the apostrophe: for *conscience'* sake, *Moses'* law. Plurals ending in *s* take the apostrophe only: boys', ladies', horses', babies'. Plural nouns not ending in *s* form the possessive by adding *'s; men's, children's.*

A noun or a pronoun is in the *nominative case* when used in the following relationships:

Subject of the sentence: *John* came. *I* went home.

Predicate nominative: John is *captain.* It was *she* who called.

Direct address: as Come here, *John.*

A noun or pronoun is in the *objective* (or *accusative*) *case* when used as follows:

Direct object: He wrote this *letter.* We saw *them.*

Object of a preposition: We walked to the *station.* They spoke to *us.*

Indirect object: I told *Betty* a story.

A noun or pronoun is called the *direct object* and is in the *objective case* when it is directly affected by the action of the verb: Henry tore his *coat.* A noun is an *indirect object* when it is less directly affected by the verb action: I told *Betty* a story. Here *story* is the direct object. The indirect object may be expressed with the preposition *to*: I told a story to Betty.

PRONOUNS

Definition: Pronouns are words used as substitutes for nouns: *I, he, my, that, who.*

Kinds: Pronouns may be Personal, Demonstrative, Relative, Interrogative, Indefinite.

A *personal pronoun* is one that indicates by its form the first, second, or third person; that is, the speaker, the person spoken to, or the person, place, or thing spoken of: *I, you, he, she, it.*

Demonstrative pronouns are always *definite,* and point specifically to the person, the place, or the things to which they refer: *This* is my bike; *That* was a beautiful car; *These* are my bracelets; *Those* were the days! In the sentence Our school is larger than theirs, the word *our* is an adjective: *theirs* is a pronoun, standing for their school.

A *relative pronoun* (*who, that, which, what*) is one in the subordinate clause that refers to a noun in the principal clause and establishes a relationship between the subordinate and principal clauses. The relative pronoun *that* is used to refer to persons, animals and things. The man *that* was elected was my uncle. The horse *that* was injured has been shot. The book *that* I bought was written by Mark Twain. *That* is preferred when the relative clause is restrictive; *who, whom* and *which* are used in *nonrestrictive* clauses. *Who* refers to persons only: This man, *who* was so kind, lives next door. *Which* (used to refer to animals and things) is a *nonrestrictive* relative pronoun used to introduce clauses that add new meanings: The house, *which* I approached, was large. The whale, *which* is the largest of mammals, lives in the ocean. Such clauses should be separated from the rest of the sentence by commas. *What* is sometimes a *condensed* or *indefinite relative* pronoun: He bought *what* he wanted. Expanded, this sentence might read: He bought *that which* he wanted.

An *interrogative pronoun* is one used in asking a question: *who, whom, which, what. What* is he doing? *Which* one is needed?

Indefinite pronoun.—When we desire to convey an indefinite or general impression, we avoid the use of a noun and often employ instead an indefinite pronoun: *nobody, something, someone.* Indefinite pronouns point out persons and things, but do so less definitely than do the demonstrative pronouns. Other examples of the indefinite pronoun are: *neither, several, one of many, none, some, everything, few, either, everybody, each, anything, nothing, anybody, anyone, all, any. Someone* is coming. *Nobody* lives here. *Something* should be done. *Several* came to her rescue. *Few* ever reach the summit.

Distributive adjective pronouns are singular in grammar and logic but have a plural suggestion. They must be used with singular verbs and other singular pronouns: *Every* man does *his* best. *Each* must do *his* duty.

Forms: Some pronouns are inflected for gender, number and case—especially the personal pronouns and the relative and interrogative pronouns that refer to persons.

PERSONAL PRONOUNS

First Person

	SINGULAR	PLURAL
Nom.	I	we
Gen.	my *or* mine	our *or* ours
Acc.	me	us

Second Person

	SINGULAR	PLURAL
Nom.	you	you
Gen.	you *or* yours	your *or* yours
Acc.	you	you

Third Person

	SINGULAR			PLURAL
	Mas.	Fem.	Neuter	All Genders
Nom.	he	she	it	they
Gen.	his	her *or* hers	its	their *or* theirs
Acc.	him	her	it	them

Old Style

	SINGULAR	PLURAL
Nom.	thou	ye *or* you
Poss.	they *or* thine	your *or* yours
Obj.	thee	you

Note that the genitive may be either an adjective or a pronoun. *My* (adjective) hat. The hat is *mine* (pronoun). *His* (adjective) hat. The hat is *his* (pronoun).

Relative and Interrogative Pronouns have a very simple declension:

	SING. AND PLURAL	SING. AND PLURAL
Nom.	who	which
Poss.	whose	whose
Obj.	whom	which

Syntax or Construction: The pronoun must agree with its antecedent (that is, the noun to which it refers) in *person* and *number.* The case form depends upon the use or syntax. For example, one may say: Robert, *who* came yesterday, lives in Boston. Robert, *whose* home is in Boston, came yesterday. Robert, *whom* we saw, lives in Boston. The person and number of the relative pronouns here used agree with the antecedent Robert, but the case forms are changed as the use is changed. Note that agreement in person is shown only by the form of the verb in the relative clause and only if the pronoun is the subject of the verb. Robert, who *is* here, was in Boston yesterday. I, who *am* here now, was there yesterday.

ADJECTIVES

Definition: An adjective is a word used to modify (describe or limit) the meaning of a noun or pronoun: *good, fast, glad, twelve, southern.*

Kinds: Descriptive (Proper and Common). Limiting, Numeral, Possessive.

A *descriptive* or qualifying adjective denotes kind or quality: a *blue* sky, a *good* girl, a *pleasant* day.

Limiting adjectives restrict the meaning of the noun: a *few* girls, *many* buildings. The *Articles* (*a, an, the*) are included in this class of adjectives. It should be remembered that *a* is used before words beginning with a consonant sound; *an* before a vowel sound: *a* top, *an* Indian.

A *numeral* adjective points out or indicates number of quantity: *Six* days, *Third* street. Numeral adjectives are of two kinds: *cardinals* (those used in simple counting), one, two, three; and *ordinals* (those indicating rank or succession), first, second, third.

A *possessive* adjective is one that signifies to whom the noun belongs: *his* football, *her* bicycle, *their* house, *my* book.

Forms: Adjectives are not inflected for number except in the case of numerals and certain pronominals: *this, these; that, those; my, our.* Adjectives have no person, gender or case. They are inflected, however, for *comparison.* This change indicates the degree of limitation or quality expressed. The *positive* degree is the simplest form: *large, beautiful, little.* The *comparative* degree denotes a degree higher or lower than the positive: *larger, more beautiful, less confident.* The *superlative* degree denotes the highest or the lowest degree that can be expressed: *largest, most beautiful, least confident.* The comparative and superlative forms are made by adding *-er* or *-est* to the positive or (usually in words with several syllables) by using *more* and *most* or *less* and *least.*

Syntax or Construction: An adjective may be used to modify nouns and pronouns directly (as illustrated above); indirectly or appositively (The girls, *all dressed up,* went to the party); to complete the meaning of a verb (They are *afraid*); and to complete the predicate and modify the object (He painted the fence *white*).

VERBS

Definition: A verb is a word used to assert something about a subject. It is the part of speech of prime importance, for without an asserting word there could be no sentence. Examples of commonly used verbs are *run, think, swim, buy, see, go.*

Kinds: Verbs are classified as Transitive or Intransitive; Regular or Irregular; Principal or Auxiliary; and Linking.

A *transitive* verb expresses action that is received or seems to be received by some person or thing. This receiver may be used as an object: John bought a *book* (active); or as subject: A *book* was bought by John (passive).

An *intransitive* verb is one the action of which is not received: the wind *blows;* we *walked* briskly.

A *regular* verb is one that forms its past tense and past participle by adding *d* or *ed* to the present: *walk, walked, walked.*

An *irregular* verb is one that forms its past tense and past participle irregularly: *go, went, gone; bring, brought, brought; burst, burst, burst.* (Irregular verbs are sometimes called *strong* forms; and regular verbs, *weak* forms.)

An *auxiliary* verb is one that is used as a helping verb: I *have* run; the bread *was* baked; I *may* come; I *might* go. *Have, was, may* and *might* are here used as auxiliaries with the principal verbs *run, baked, come, go.*

A *linking* verb is one used to connect or link a subject with a predicate nominative or a predicate adjective: This *was* the man; he *is* happy. The principal linking verbs are *be, become, seem, appear, grow.*

Forms: Verbs have Voice, Mood (or Mode), Tense, Person and Number.

A verb is in the *active* voice when it represents the subject as acting: John *caught* the ball.

A verb is in the *passive* voice when it represents the subject as acted upon: The ball *was caught* by John.

Mood (or Mode) means the manner of assertion made by a verb.

If the speaker asserts a fact or asks a question, he uses the *Indicative* Mood: I *walk;* Is he *walking?*

If the speaker commands or entreats, he uses the *Imperative* Mood: *Leave!* Please *go* at once.

If he expresses a wish, a prayer, a doubt, a supposition, a condition contrary to fact, a likelihood, a concession, a purpose, he uses the *Subjunctive* Mood:

May Thy will be done. (wish or prayer)

If the day *should be* clear, we shall go (doubt or supposition).

If he *had taken* my advice, he would have passed (condition contrary to fact).

If I *were* he, I would take the position (condition contrary to fact).

I *had gone* (or *should have gone*) but for you (likelihood).

Though he *slay* me, yet will I trust him (concession).

Answer briefly, so that you *be not misunderstood* (purpose).

Note: The distinctive forms of the subjunctive are gradually passing out of use. The nursery rhyme says: if this *be* I; but in ordinary speech we say: If this *is* I. The King James Version of the Bible says: Though he *slay* me, yet will I trust him; but everyday speech would use, not the distinctive subjunctive form *slay* for the third person singular, but the auxiliary: even if he *should slay* me.

Verbs are inflected according to *tense;* that is, the time indicated by the verb. Following are examples of the various tenses:

Present: *I move*
Past: *I moved*
Future: *I shall move*
Present Perfect: *I have moved*

(action completed in present time)
Past Perfect: *I had moved* (action completed in past time)
Future Perfect: *I shall have moved* (action to be completed in future time)

This simple distinction can be made between *shall* and *will:* to express simple future time *shall* is used with the first person and *will* with the second and third persons; to express determination *will* is used with the first person and *shall* with the second and third persons. *I shall go* means I am going; and *he will go* means he is going—a simple future. But *I will go, he shall go,* imply "no matter what."

Finite and *Infinitive Verbs.*—Finite verbs possess the properties of voice, mood, tense, person, and number. They must be distinguished sharply from the so-called infinite verb-forms—infinitive, participle, and gerund—which are not limited as to number or person or mood.

The conjugation of a verb is the orderly statement of all its persons and tenses in both voices and numbers, in all moods, as the following table shows:

Conjugation of the Verb "Be"
Principal Parts
Present Infinitive: to be
Past Tense: was
Past Participle: been

INDICATIVE MOOD
Present Tense
SINGULAR	PLURAL
1st Person, I am	We are
2d Person, You are	You are
3d Person, He is	They are

Past Tense
I was	We were
You were	You were
He was	They were

Future Tense
I shall be	We shall be
You will be	You will be
He will be	They will be

Present Perfect Tense
I have been	We have been
You have been	You have been
He has been	They have been

Past Perfect Tense
I had been	We had been
You had been	You had been
He had been	They had been

Future Perfect Tense
I shall have been	We shall have been
You will have been	You will have been
He will have been	They will have been

SUBJUNCTIVE MOOD
Present Tense
(If) I be	(If) We be
You be	You be
He be	They be

Past Tense
(If) I were	(If) We were
You were	You were
He were	They were

Present Perfect Tense
(If) I have been	(If) We have been
You have been	You have been
He have been	They have been

Past Perfect Tense
(If) I had been	(If) We had been
You had been	You had been
He had been	They had been

IMPERATIVE MOOD
Present Tense
SINGULAR	PLURAL
Be (you)	Be (you)

Infinitives
PRESENT	PRESENT PERFECT
To	To have been

Participles
PRESENT	PAST OR PERFECT	PRES. PERFECT
Being	Been	Having Been

Gerunds
PRESENT	PRESENT PERFECT
Being	Having been

Conjugation of the Verb "See"
Principal Parts
PRESENT	PAST	PAST OR PERFECT PARTICIPLE
See	Saw	Seen

ACTIVE VOICE
INDICATIVE MOOD
Present Tense
SINGULAR	PLURAL
1st Person, I see	We see
2d Person, You see	You see
3d Person, He sees	They see

Past Tense
I saw	We saw
You saw	You saw
He saw	They saw

Future Tense
I shall see	We shall see
You will see	You will see
He will see	They will see

Present Perfect Tense
I have seen	We have seen
You have seen	You have seen
He has seen	They have seen

Past Perfect Tense
I had seen	We had seen
You had seen	You had seen
He had seen	They had seen

Future Perfect Tense
I shall have seen	We shall have seen
You will have seen	You will have seen
He will have seen	They will have seen

SUBJUNCTIVE MOOD
Present Tense
(If) I see	(If) We see
You see	You see
He see	They see

Past Tense
(If) I saw	(If) We saw
You saw	You saw
He saw	They saw

Present Perfect Tense
(If) I have seen	(If) We have seen
You have seen	You have seen
He have seen	They have seen

Past Perfect Tense
(If) I had seen	(If) We had seen
You had seen	You had seen
He had seen	They had seen

IMPERATIVE MOOD
Present Tense
See (you)	See (you)

Infinitives
PRESENT	PRESENT PERFECT
To see	To have seen

Participles
PRESENT	PRESENT PERFECT
Seeing	Having seen

Gerunds
PRESENT	PRESENT PERFECT
Seeing	Having seen

PASSIVE VOICE
INDICATIVE MOOD
Present Tense
1st Person, I am seen	We are seen
2d Person, You are seen	You are seen
3d Person, He is seen	They are seen

Past Tense
I was seen	We were seen
You were seen	You were seen
He was seen	They were seen

Future Tense
I shall be seen	We shall be seen
You will be seen	You will be seen
He will be seen	They will be seen

Present Perfect Tense
I have been seen	We have been seen
You have been seen	You have been seen
He has been seen	They have been seen

Past Perfect Tense
I had been seen	We had been seen
You had been seen	You had been seen
He had been seen	They had been seen

Future Perfect Tense
I shall have been seen	We shall have been seen
You will have been seen	You will have been seen
He will have been seen	They will have been seen

SUBJUNCTIVE MOOD
Present Tense
(If) I be seen	(If) We be seen
You be seen	You be seen
He be seen	They be seen

Past Tense
(If) I were seen	(If) We were seen
You were seen	You were seen
He were seen	They were seen

Present Perfect Tense
(If) I have been seen	(If) We have been seen
You have been seen	You have been seen
He have been seen	They have been seen

Past Perfect Tense
(If) I had been seen	(If) We had been seen
You had been seen	You had been seen
He had been seen	They had been seen

IMPERATIVE MOOD
Present Tense
Be (you) seen	Be (you) seen

Infinitives
PRESENT	PRESENT PERFECT
To be seen	To have been seen

Participles
PRESENT	PAST	PRESENT PERFECT
Being seen	Seen	Having been seen

Gerunds
PRESENT	PRESENT PERFECT
Being seen	Having been seen

Progressive Form, Verb "See"
(Action thought of as continuing or "progressing")

ACTIVE VOICE
INDICATIVE MOOD
Present Tense
1st Person, I am seeing	We are seeing
2d Person, You are seeing	You are seeing
3d Person, He is seeing	They are seeing

Past Tense
I was seeing	We were seeing
You were seeing	You were seeing
He was seeing	They were seeing

Future Tense

I shall be seeing	We shall be seeing
You will be seeing	You will be seeing
He will be seeing	They will be seeing

Present Perfect Tense

I have been seeing	We have been seeing
You have been seeing	You have been seeing
He has been seeing	They have been seeing

Past Perfect Tense

I had been seeing	We had been seeing
You had been seeing	You had been seeing
He had been seeing	They had been seeing

Future Perfect Tense

I shall have been seeing	We shall have been seeing
You will have been seeing	You will have been seeing
He will have been seeing	They will have been seeing

SUBJUNCTIVE MOOD
Present Tense

(If) I be (*or* am) seeing	(If) We be (*or* are) seeing
You be (*or* are) seeing	You be (*or* are) seeing
He be (*or* is) seeing	They be (*or* are) seeing

Past Tense

(If) I were seeing	(If) We were seeing
You were seeing	You were seeing
He were seeing	They were seeing

Present Perfect Tense

(If) I have been seeing	(If) We have been seeing
You have been seeing	You have been seeing
He have (*or* has) been seeing	They have been seeing

Past Perfect Tense

(If) I had been seeing	(If) We had been seeing
You had been seeing	You had been seeing
He had been seeing	They had been seeing

IMPERATIVE MOOD
Present Tense

Be (you) seeing	Be (you) seeing

Infinitives

PRESENT	PRESENT PERFECT
To be seeing	To have been seeing

Participles

PRESENT	PRESENT PERFECT
....	Having been seeing

Gerunds

PRESENT	PRESENT PERFECT
....	Having been seeing

The Conjugation of a Regular Verb
CONJUGATION OF THE VERB *Move*
IN THE ACTIVE VOICE
Principal Parts

PRESENT TENSE	PAST TENSE	PAST PARTICIPLE
move	moved	moved

INDICATIVE MOOD
Present Tense

SINGULAR	PLURAL
1st Person, I move	We move
2d Person, You move (thou movest)	You move
3d Person, He moves	They move

Past Tense

I moved	We moved
You moved (thou movedst)	You moved
He moved	They moved

Future Tense

I shall move	We shall move
You will move (thou wilt move)	You will move
He will move	They will move

Present Perfect Tense

I have moved	We have moved
You have moved (thou hast moved)	You have moved
He has moved	They have moved

Past Perfect Tense

I had moved	We had moved
You had moved (thou hadst moved)	You had moved
He had moved	They had moved

Future Perfect Tense

I shall have moved	We shall have moved
You will have moved (thou wilt have moved)	You will have moved
He will have moved	They will have moved

SUBJUNCTIVE MOOD
Present Tense

(If) I move	(If) we move
you move	you move
he move	they move

Past Tense

(If) I moved	(If) we moved
you moved	you moved
he moved	they moved

IMPERATIVE MOOD
Present Tense

Move (you or thou)	Move (you)

Infinitives

PRESENT	PERFECT
To move	To have moved

Participles

PRESENT	PERFECT
Moving	Having moved

PASSIVE VOICE
INDICATIVE MOOD
Present Tense

1st Person, I am moved	We are moved
2d Person, You are moved (thou art moved)	You are moved
3d Person, He is moved	They are moved

Past Tense

I was moved	We were moved
You were moved	You were moved
He was moved	They were moved

Future Tense

I shall be moved	We shall be moved
You will be moved (thou wilt be moved)	You will be moved
He will be moved	They will be moved

Present Perfect Tense

I have been moved	We have been moved
You have been moved (thou hast been moved)	You have been moved
He has been moved	They have been moved

Past Perfect Tense

I had been moved	We had been moved
You had been moved (thou hadst been moved)	You had been moved
He had been moved	They had been moved

Future Perfect Tense

I shall have been moved	We shall have been moved
You will have been moved (thou wilt have been moved)	You will have been moved
He will have been moved	They will have been moved

SUBJUNCTIVE MOOD
Present Tense

(If) I be moved	(If) We be moved
You be moved	You be moved
(Thou be moved)	
He be moved	They be moved

Past Tense

(If) I were moved	(If) We were moved
You were moved	You were moved
He were moved	They were moved

IMPERATIVE MOOD

Be (you, thou) moved	Be (you) moved

Infinitives

To be moved	To have been moved

Participles

PRESENT	PAST	PERFECT
Being moved	Moved	Having been moved

Synopsis of a Verb:—A table of all forms of verb in a given person, number, voice and mood is called a *synopsis*.

Third Person, Singular Number, Active Voice, Indicative.

THIRD PERSON, SINGULAR NUMBER, ACTIVE VOICE, INDICATIVE
Mood of Verb "See"

Present Tense	He sees
Past Tense	He saw
Future Tense	He will see
Present Perfect Tense	He has seen
Past Perfect Tense	He had seen
Future Perfect Tense	He will have seen

SUBJUNCTIVE MOOD

Present Tense	(If) He see
Past Tense	(If) He saw
Present Perfect Tense	(If) He have (*or* has) seen
Past Perfect Tense	(If) He had seen

INDICATIVE MOOD
IN THE THIRD PERSON, SINGULAR NUMBER, PASSIVE VOICE

Present Tense	He is seen
Past Tense	He was seen
Future Tense	He will be seen
Present Perfect Tense	He has been seen
Past Perfect Tense	He had been seen
Future Perfect Tense	He will have been seen

SUBJUNCTIVE MOOD

Present Tense	(If) He be (*or* is) seen
Past Tense	He were seen
Present Perfect Tense	He have (*or* has) been seen
Past Perfect Tense	He had been seen

Note two other verb forms, the *infinitive* and the *participle*. The *infinitive* is not a mood. It does not assert action; it names action: *to move, to be*. *To*, when used with a verb, is called the sign of the infinitive and should not be separated from its verb. The *participle* names action and therefore has the property of both a noun and a verb.

Syntax or Construction: A verb may stand alone or in verb phrases. The infinitive is a verbal noun. It may be the subject of a sentence (*To run* is good exercise), the direct object (He tried *to play*) or appositive (It is good exercise *to run*). The participle has all the uses of the adjective: *Reading* exercises, *running* water, *past* performances, *hurried* preparation. The present participle is often used as a noun and is called a *gerund*. The gerund may be used as subject, direct object, predicate nominative, appositive or object of a preposition: *Running* is good exercise. *Driving* a car recklessly results in accidents.

The benefit of *running* a long race is better wind. The danger of *driving* recklessly is great. The gerund is sometimes used in the plural: His *comings* and *goings*. The genitive is sometimes used: Reading for *reading's* sake.

Principal Parts of Common Irregular Verbs

Present	Past	Past Participle
am	was	been
arise	arose	arisen
awake	awoke	awakened
bear	bore	borne
beat	beat	beaten
bet	bet	bet
begin	began	begun
bind	bound	bound
bite	bit	bitten
blow	blew	blown
break	broke	broken
bring	brought	brought
buy	bought	bought
catch	caught	caught
choose	chose	chosen
cling	clung	clung
come	came	come
creep	crept	crept
cut	cut	cut
dig	dug	dug
do	did	done
draw	drew	drawn
drink	drank	drunk
drive	drove	driven
eat	ate	eaten
fall	fell	fallen
feed	fed	fed
find	found	found
fight	fought	fought
flee	fled	fled
fling	flung	flung
fly	flew	flown
forget	forgot	forgotten
forsake	forsook	forsaken
freeze	froze	frozen
get	got	got *or* gotten
give	gave	given
go	went	gone
grind	ground	ground
grow	grew	grown
hang	hanged *or* hung	hanged *or* hung
have	had	had
hew	hewed	hewn
hide	hid	hidden
hit	hit	hit
hold	held	held
hurt	hurt	hurt
keep	kept	kept
know	knew	known
lay	laid	laid
lead	led	led
lie	lay	lain
ride	rode	ridden
ring	rang	rung
rise	rose	risen
run	ran	run
see	saw	seen
seek	sought	sought
sell	sold	sold
shake	shook	shaken
shine	shone *or* shined	shone *or* shined
shrink	shrank	shrunk
sing	sang	sung
sink	sank	sunk
smite	smote	smitten
speak	spoke	spoken
spin	spun	spun
spring	sprang	sprung
stand	stood	stood
steal	stole	stolen
stick	stuck	stuck
sting	stung	stung
stink	stunk	stunk
stride	strode	stridden
string	strung	strung
strive	strove	striven
swear	swore	sworn
swim	swam	swum
swing	swung	swung
take	took	taken
teach	taught	taught
tear	tore	torn
tell	told	told
think	thought	thought
throw	threw	thrown
weave	wove	woven
win	won	won
wind	wound	wound
wring	wrung	wrung
write	wrote	written

ADVERBS

Definition: An adverb is a word used to modify a verb, an adjective or another adverb: He went *quickly;* he did *very* well.

Often adverbs are formed from adjectives by adding the syllable *-ly: wise, wisely; quiet, quietly; soft, softly.*

Kinds: As to form, adverbs are simple *(gladly);* compound *(outside);* phrasal *(arm-in-arm).*

Adverbs express *manner.* They may be classified as they express *degree, negation, time and order, place and motion:*

Degree: very, too, hardly, little, enough, almost, partly, quite. He gave me *too* little; the record is *partly* true.

Negation: no, not, never. He *never* spoke the truth.

Time and order: again, last, first, secondly, always, yesterday. He was *first* on the list. John is *always* late.

Place and motion: there, in, out, below, up, down, here, hence. He placed the book *there;* I slid *down.*

Forms: Adverbs have no person, number, gender or case; but like adjectives they have three degrees of comparison—Positive, Comparative, Superlative: *carefully, more carefully, most carefully; quickly, less quickly, least quickly.*

Syntax or Construction: Adverbs tell how, when or where; they qualify verbs, adjectives or other adverbs: She sang *sweetly;* her song was *very* sweet; she sang *very* sweetly.

PREPOSITIONS

Definition: A preposition is a word used with a noun or pronoun to show the relation of the noun or pronoun to some other word or words in the sentence: Go *to* school; come *to* me.

Kinds: There are three kinds of prepositions:

Simple: at, by, for, in, but, with, of, from. He came *into* the house; she brought Mary *with* her.

Compound: beside, underneath, without, within, into, notwithstanding, providing, concerning. He sat down *beside* her; Harry came *without* any money.

Phrasal: instead of, out of, on account of, in spite of, because of. You go *instead of* George; we went *in spite of* the rain.

Forms: Prepositions are not inflected.

Syntax or Construction: A preposition with its object is called a prepositional phrase. When the phrase modifies a noun or pronoun it is called an *adjective phrase:* The work *of the day* is done. When it modifies a verb, an adjective or an adverb it is called an *adverbial phrase:* The boys have gone *to school.*

CONJUNCTIONS

Definition: A conjunction is a word that connects words, phrases or clauses: John *and* Mary; down the street *and* into the house she went; he came *but* she did not see him.

Kinds: There are two kinds of conjunctions, Co-ordinate and Subordinate.

Co-ordinate conjunctions connect words, phrases or clauses of equal rank: *and, likewise, also, however, nevertheless, but, still, or* and the pairs *either* and *or, neither* and *nor.*

Subordinate conjunctions connect clauses of unequal rank, that is, connect a subordinate clause to a main clause, for example:

Where, wherever, whence, whither (indicating place)—Go *where* you please.

When, whenever, while, until, before, after (indicating time)—I shall go *when* it is time.

As, how (indicating manner)—He plays the game *as* the rules require.

For, since, because (indicating cause)—He went *because* he was told to.

So that, lest, in order that (indicating purpose)—I scolded him *in order that* he might learn to obey.

If, unless, provided (indicating condition)—*If* it rains, I shall not go.

Though, yet (indicating concession)—*Though* it seems unlikely, I believe it.

Than (indicating comparison)—John is taller *than* William.

Forms: Conjunctions are not inflected.

Syntax or Construction: Conjunctions may be used to introduce noun, adjective and adverbial clauses as well as to connect words and phrases: *Whatever was said* is all right (noun clause); He *who would succeed* must work (adjective clause—usually introduced by the relative pronouns); The carpenter works *when he feels like it* (adverbial clause).

INTERJECTIONS

Definition: An interjection is a word used to express sudden or strong feeling: *Alas! Oh! Pshaw!*

Interjections have no division into kinds and forms, nor do they have any syntax or construction.

SENTENCE ANALYSIS

A sentence is a group of words expressing one complete thought. Every sentence has two parts, a subject and a predicate. In the sentence, The city of Honolulu is warmed by the trade winds of the Pacific, *city* is the simple subject and *The city of Honolulu* is the complete subject. The simple predicate is *is warmed,* and the complete predicate is *is warmed by the trade winds of the Pacific.* The subject of a sentence is that about which something is said. The predicate is that which says something about the subject. The main word in the subject is a noun or pronoun; the main part of the predicate is a verb or verb phrase. The simple subject or simple predicate and modifiers make the complete subject or the complete predicate. The word *substantive* is the name given to a noun or pronoun or to any word group that is used in place of a noun. An *appositive* is a noun or its equivalent, set alongside a noun or its equivalent, to name it in other words.

Phrases and Clauses.—A *phrase* is a group of words used as a single part of speech and that has neither subject nor predicate. It may be prepositional, as *of the house;* participial, as *having written a letter;* or infinitive, as *to go.* Any of these forms may be used as an adjective, an adverb or a noun; for example, *To suffer in silence* is the hardest test (infinitive phrase used as a noun); The boy *in the fifth seat* recited (prepositional phrase used an an adjective); They ran *to overtake us* (infinitive phrase used as an adverb).

A *clause* is a group of words that contains a subject and predicate. It is a *principal* clause if it is used to make a simple sentence or to help make a compound sentence or a complex sentence. Clauses may also be *subordinate.* Such clauses are used as nouns, adjectives or adverbs in complex sentences. *The lightning flashed and the thunder roared* is a compound sentence made up of two principal clauses. *That my friend has lost his watch is true* is a complex sentence that contains a subordinate clause used as subject of the principal clause. *The man who is honorable is respected* is a complex sentence made up of a principal clause, *The man is respected,* and a subordinate clause, *who is honorable,* used as an adjective.

Sentences containing but one subject and one predicate are called *simple* sentences: The man rode a horse. *Complex* sentences contain one principal clause and one or more subordinate clauses: I will come when he goes. *Compound* sentences are made up of two or more principal clauses: The rain fell and the game was stopped.

Sentences are also classified as: *Declarative,* if they merely state facts: James hurt his foot. *Interrogative,* if they ask questions: Will he come? *Exclamatory,* if they express emotion: What an awful calamity! *Imperative,* if they voice a command: Come at once!

The *analysis of a simple sentence* consists of finding the subject and predicate, telling the word and phrase modifiers of these elements and analyzing the phrases used as modifiers.

Beyond the other side of the garden I heard a loud noise. This is a simple, declarative sentence. The subject is *I,* without modifiers. The complete predicate is *heard a loud noise.* The verb is *heard;* the noun *noise* is the direct object of the verb and is modified by the article *a* and the adjective *loud.* The predicate verb is modified by the prepositional phrase *beyond the other side,* used adverbially. *Side* is the object of the preposition *beyond* and is modified by the article *the* and the adjective *other* and by the prepositional phrase *of the garden,* used

adjectively. *Garden* is the object of the preposition *of* and is modified by the article *the.*

The analysis of a *complex sentence* consists of stating the kind of sentence, principal clauses, subordinate clauses (kinds, relation to the principal clause), complete and simple subjects of each principal clause, complete and simple predicates of each principal clause, phrases, word modifiers of each principal clause; subjects, predicates, phrases, word modifiers of each subordinate clause.

When he turned abruptly to his right, he saw the beautiful and imposing sunset.

This is a complex declarative sentence, consisting of one principal and one subordinate clause. The principal clause is *he saw the beautiful and imposing sunset.* The subordinate clause is *when he turned abruptly to his right.* This is an adverbial clause of time, modifying the verb *saw* in the principal clause. *When* is a conjunction connecting the subordinate with the principal clause.

The complete subject of the principal clause is *he. He* is also the simple subject. The complete predicate is *saw the beautiful and imposing sunset. Saw* is the simple predicate. *Sunset* is the direct object of the verb *saw. Beautiful* and *imposing* are adjectives modifying *sunset. And* is a conjunction connecting *beautiful* and *imposing.*

He is both the simple and complete subject of the subordinate clause. The complete predicate is *turned abruptly to his right. Turned* is the simple predicate. *Abruptly* is an adverb modifying *turned. To his right* is an adverbial phrase modifying *turned.*

The *analysis of the compound sentence* consists in finding the co-ordinate members and the conjunctions connecting them and in analyzing each co-ordinate member as a simple or a complex sentence.

The leaves are falling, and the swallows will soon be gone. This is a compound declarative sentence. The first co-ordinate clause is *The leaves are falling;* the second co-ordinate clause is *the swallows will soon be gone. And* is the co-ordinate conjunction. *Leaves,* modified by the definite article *the,* is the simple subject, and *are falling* is the predicate. In the second clause *swallows,* modified by *the,* is the simple subject; and *will soon be gone* is the complete predicate. *Be gone* is modified by the adverb *soon.*

Parsing.—To parse[1] a sentence is to give each word in the sentence its classification as a part of speech and its form or inflection.

Turning abruptly to his right, he saw the beautiful and imposing sunset. *Turning*—verb, regular, intransitive, active, participle, present, modifies the subject *he. Abruptly*—adverb, manner, positive, modifies *turning. To*—preposition, simple, used in phrase *to his right,* modifying *turning. Right*—noun, common, third,

singular, neuter, object of preposition *to. He*—pronoun, personal, agrees with antecedent (understood) in third, singular, masculine. *Saw*—verb, irregular, transitive, active, indicative, past, agrees with its subject *he* in third, singular, predicate of sentence. *Beautiful*—adjective, descriptive, positive, modifies the noun *sunset. And*—conjunction, co-ordinate, connects the two adjectives *beautiful* and *imposing.*

Diagrams.—Sometimes the relation of the parts of speech in sentences may be understood better by means of diagrams. Following are illustrations of simple forms of the diagram:

1. *Subject and predicate.*—

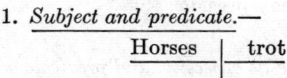

2. *Subject, predicate and direct object.*—

3. *Object complement and adjective.*—

4. *Adjective phrase.*—

5. *Adjective clause.*—

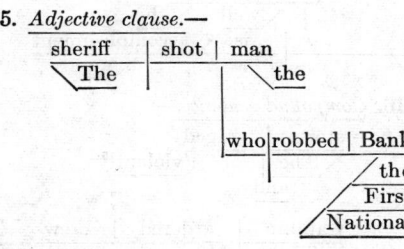

6. *Compound subject.*—

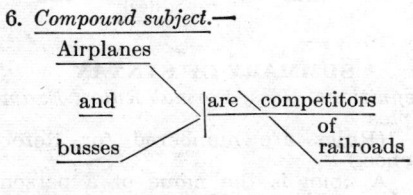

7. *Compound predicate.*—

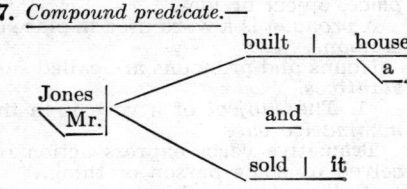

8. *Indirect object and adverb.*—

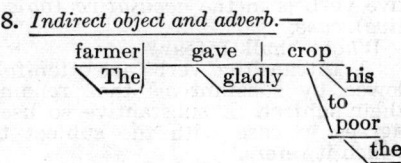

---

[1] To parse seems to have meant originally answering the question: "Quae pars orationis?" or the shorter form "Pars?" meaning "What part of speech?" Latin was long used in grammar classes—whether the language studied was Latin or English.

9. *Adverbial phrase.*—

soldiers | fought | battles
Many \ during \ severe
war
the

10. *Adverbial clause.*—

carpenter | works
The \ where
work | is provided

11. *Noun clause.*—

Whoever | comes
\ first
∧ | may preside

12. *Participle as adjective, and predicate adjective.*—

Roses | are \ beautiful
\ having
\ fragrance

13. *Gerund and predicate noun.*—

Running | is \ exercise
\ good

14. *Infinitive as adjective.*—

We | brought | lunch
\ our
to
eat

15. *Infinitive as noun.*—

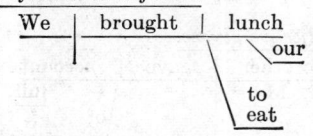

To
play | piano
well \ the
∧ | is \ accomplishment
\ an

16. *Compound sentence.*—

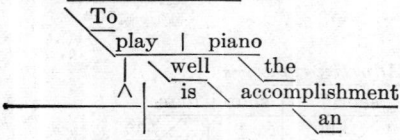

storm | raged
The \ violently
and

Captain | ordered | crew
The \ on \ the
deck

SUMMARY OF SYNTAX

Definitions, Uses, Formal Rules, Examples

(Rules are numbered for Reference.)

A *noun* is the name of a person, place, object or idea.

A *pronoun* is a word used in place of a noun.

Nouns and pronouns are called *substantives.*

1. The *subject* of a verb is in the *nominative case.*

Transitive verbs express action received by some person or thing.

2. The direct *object* of a transitive verb is in the *accusative (objective) case.*

Whom shall I fear?

3. Intransitive verbs are often followed by substantives that rename their subject. A substantive so used agrees in case with the subject to which it refers.

It is *I. Whom* do you take me to be?

A substantive that helps to complete a verb but renames the object of the verb is in the *accusative (or objective) case.*

The class elected him president.

4. The *object of a preposition* is in the *accusative (or objective) case.*

Give it to *me.* The cat is under the *stove.*

5. An indirect object is in the *accusative (or objective) case.* (Dative object.)

Bring *me* a chair.

Infinitives and participles do not really assert action or being, but they imply it, and in this sense may have subjects.

6. The subject of an infinitive is in the *accusative (or objective) case.*

She has *me* to protect her.

We thought *him* to be honest.

7. An appositive is a noun or pronoun used as explanatory of or equivalent to another noun or pronoun.

8. An appositive takes the case of the substantive to which it is attached.

The book was his, *Peter's.* (Posessive)

'Tis I, *Hamlet,* the *Dane.* (Nominative.)

Give it to me, your *brother.* (Accusative or objective.)

9. A noun or pronoun *independent by address* is in the *nominative case.* (Vocative.)

"*Men of Athens,*—Him declare I unto you."

"*Mr. President,* I rise to a point of order."

10. A noun or pronoun used *independently with a following adjective, adverb or phrase* may best be regarded as in the objective case, since it is virtually the object in a prepositional phrase from which the preposition is omitted.

Hat in hand, he stood waiting.

Beard unkempt, clothes threadbare, he looked down and out.

Fences down, weeds everywhere, the place was desolate.

11. Nouns or pronouns showing ownership are in the *genitive (or possessive) case.*

John's farm, *your* shoes.

12. When an inanimate thing is personified, the *gender* of its noun or pronoun is *determined by custom.*

She's a good old boat! (Feminine.)

The *sun* is hiding *his* head. (Masculine.)

13. *Collective nouns* are *plural* when their units act separately as individuals; *singular* when the units act together as one. *Plural titles* are in this sense *singular nouns.*

The class has had its picture taken. (All together.)

The class have had their pictures taken. (Each person by himself.)

The Newcomes is by Thackeray.

14. *Nouns used adverbially* to measure time or distance are in the *accusative (or objective) case.* (Adverbial objective.)

We walked an *hour,* traveled four *miles.*

15. A *substantive* used as an exclamation is commonly held to be *nominative.* But if the exclamation repeats an idea already used, it will take the case of the term repeated.

We shall be rich. We! think of that!

"We'll make you do it!" *Me!* I guess not!

16. A *pronoun* must agree with its antecedent in *number, gender* and *person.* Collective nouns take singular pronouns when the units act separately.

The Ship of State has refused to obey *her* rudder.

That is *he whom* you seek. (All three are in 3d person, masculine gender, singular number.)

The *case* of a pronoun does not depend upon its antecedent, but upon its use in the sentence.

A *verb* is a word which *asserts.* (Tells something of its subject.)

17. A verb agrees with its subject in person and number.

I *am*	She *goes*
You *are*	They *go*
He *is*	

18. A compound subject with *and* takes a singular verb if the idea of the combined subject is of *one* thing; if the compound subject is made of parts acting separately, the verb is *plural.*

Blaine and Cleveland *were* of opposing parties.

The sum and substance of the matter *is* this.

19. A *distributive* subject with *each, every, everyone, either, neither,* etc. requires a verb in the *singular:* a *disjunctive* subject with *either-or, neither-nor* takes a verb in the *singular* if the substantives are singular.

Either the book *or* the teacher *is* wrong.

Each of us must use *his* own judgment.

20. *Nouns plural in form* but singular in meaning commonly take a verb in the *singular.*

Hydraulics *is* a practical study nowadays.

Mumps *is* contagious.

The news *is* discouraging.

21. When the subject acts upon an object, the verb is in the *active voice.* When the subject is a receiver or product of action, the verb is *passive.*

The hunter *shot* the deer. (Active.)

The deer *was shot* by the hunter. (Passive.)

22. The *indicative mood* is used in questions and in simple assertions of facts or matter thought of as possible fact.

Were you there?

You *were* there.

If you *were* there, I did not see you.

(See subjunctive mood, rule 24.)

23. The *subjunctive mood* expresses a *wish,* or a *condition contrary to fact.*

Would he *were* here!

If he *were* here, we would know about it.

(Implying denial. He has not been here.)

24. The *imperative* mood states a *command* or request.

Please *go* at once.

The subject of an imperative verb is *you* understood; the you is seldom expressed, unless the mood is emphatic.

25. *Infinitives* may be used as *subject, object* of verb, *attribute complement, object of preposition, appositive, adjective modifier, adverbial modifier* or in an *independent phrase*.

26. Gerunds(verbal nouns in *ing*) have the *uses of nouns* together with the power of implying action, being or condition.

Examples have been given under *uses of Verbals*.

27. *Participles* may be used as *adjectives, adverbs, subjective complements, objective complements, following a preposition* or in *absolute phrases*.

28. The comparative degree of adjectives and adverbs, not the superlative degree, is used in comparing two persons or things.

He is the *taller* of the two; in fact, the tallest of the three.

29. A *co-ordinating conjunction* connects words, phrases or clauses of like rank, grammatically independent of each other.

I shall come if I can *and* if the weather is good.

30. A subordinate conjunction joins a dependent clause to a principal one.

Make hay *while* the sun shines.

31. Interjections commonly have no grammatical relations in the sentence. In certain constructions, however, the interjection seems to have a phrasal modifier.

"Ah! for the pirate's dream of fight!"

32. Verbs *become, feel, look, seem, smell, taste, sound, grow* take an *attributive complement* to describe the subject and an adverb to modify the assertion of the verb.

He grew *tall*: poisonous mushrooms taste *good*.

"He looks *well*" may describe his own condition, and so the word *well* may be a predicate adjective relating to the subject; or the sentence may mean that he *searches thoroughly*, in which sense *well* is an *adverb* modifying *looks*.

33. Assertions of Simple Futurity take the form.

I, we   shall
You   will
He, they   will

Assertions of Strong Purpose, Promise, Threat, Consent

I, we   will
You   shall
He, they   shall

34. Adjectives should not take the place of adverbs, nor adverbs the place of adjectives.

35. The six tenses of English verbs in the Active Voice, Indicative Mood, are built up from the *principal parts* as follows:

Present Tense, Past Tense as in *Principal Parts. Future Tense, shall* or *will* (Rule 34) with *Present Infinitive* (less "to").

Present Perfect, have or *has* with *Past Participle Past Perfect, had* with *Past Participle.*

Future Perfect, shall or *will* (Rule 34) with *Present* Perfect, the *have* form.

36. The six tenses of English verbs in the Passive Voice, Indicative Mood, invariably use the past participle of the given verb, preceded by an appropriate form of the verb *be*.

37. *Gerunds*, being verbal nouns, are modified by *adjectives* and *possessive pronouns*.

Now do it without *my* (not me) watching you.

Common Errors in Syntax.—(Numbers refer to rules in the preceding summary. Correct forms are given first.)

This is the *better* of the two—not this is the *best* of the two. (28)

You and *I* did it—not *you* and *me* did it, nor *me* and *you*. (1)

We boys will be there—not *us* boys will be there. (1)

It was *I, she, he, they*—not *me, her, him, them*. (2)

We believed it to be *her, him, them* —not *she, he, they*. (3)

Between you and *me*—not between you and *I*. (4)

She is tailer than *I* (am)—not she is taller than *me*. (1)

It was known to be *he*—not *him*. (3) *He* agrees with *it*.

Let *everybody bring his* own lunch —not *their* own. (13) (16)

We should all bring *our* lunches. (Action concerted.) (16)

Every boy and girl should do *his* best. (16) *Their* would be incorrect.

Each of us *has his* problems—not *have their*.

The actor *whom* you saw was Otis Skinner—not *who*. (2)

Whom did you call for?—not *who*. (4)

Whom did you select?—not *who*. (2)

Who do you suppose it is? (3) *Who* agrees with *it*.

Who do you think I am?—not *whom*. Agrees with *I*.

Whom did you take me to be? (3) *Whom* agrees with *me*.

The tree looks *beautiful*—not *beautifully*. (32)

The apple tastes *good*—not *well*. (32)

The tune sounds *harsh*. (32)

Roses smell *sweet*—not *sweetly*. (32)

She looks *charming*—not *charmingly*. (32)

We *shall* be drowned if we go there —not *we will* be. (33)

I *shall* be pleased to help you—not *will* be. (33)

The senate *has* adjourned—not *have* adjourned. (13)

There *are* all sorts of graft in town—not there *is* all sorts. (17)

Here *are* wealth and beauty—not here *is*. (17)

Neither of the men *shows* signs of giving in—not neither *show*. (17)

In both cases, there *are* bad birth and misfortune—not there *is*. (17)

One class of poets *believes* in symbolism—not *believe*. (17)

He is one of the best *actors that have* ever been here—not *has*. (16) (17)

Let *him* who will come—not let *he*. (2).

I *saw*—not I *seen*. (35)

I *did*—not I *done*. (35)

We *have gone*—not *have went*. (35)

We *were*—not we *was*. (17)

You *began* it—not you *begun* it. (35)

The wind *blew*—not the wind blowed. (35)

The glass is *broken*—not *broke*. (35)

We *have come*—not *have came*. (35)

He *has drunk* a glassful—not *has drank*. (35)

I've *forgotten*—not *forgot*. (35)

Have *spoken*—not have *spoke*. (35)

Somebody *has stolen* my hat—not *has stole*. (36)

Say it *slowly*—not *slow*. (32)

We can do that as *easily* as you please—not as *easy*. (32)

We chose the foreman *who* we thought could handle the men—not *whom*. (1)

Now skate without *my* helping you —not *me* helping. (37)

We ought to keep still about *his* being here—not *him* being. (37)

PUNCTUATION

Definition.—The word *punctuation* is derived from the Latin, *punctum*, a point. Punctuation originally consisted only of dots or points and still means marking with points. Internal punctuation separates words, phrases and clauses according to their interrelations and their meaning, which may be completely altered by inserting a mere comma. External punctuation separates the sentences themselves: with a period (.) after a declarative sentence; a question mark (?) after an interrogation; an exclamation point (!) after an exclamatory sentence; and a colon (:) after a transitional sentence.

Origin and Development.—Ancient Greek inscriptions were in continuous lines without punctuation and without spacing between the words. Points were first introduced to indicate the major pauses; but as early manuscript books were read mostly by scholars, punctuation was considered almost unnecessary.

The first system of very simple pointing by dots or tiny circles came into use in Alexandria in the 4th century B.C. The grammarian Aristarchus (d. *c.* 150 B.C.) amplified the meaning of the single dot by varying its position, placing it high to serve as a full stop; midway with the line for a slight pause (subsequently indicated by the comma); and low on the line for a semistop.

The introduction and spread of printing necessitated an accurate and more extended arrangement of arbitrary signs of punctuation. The famous Italian printer, Aldus Manutius (1450–1515) of Venice perfected for use in printing a system of pointing practically the same as we use today. The art of printing multiplied the number of readers, and those with little education were helped to quicker understanding of the printed page by careful punctuation.

Double punctuation or the use of two points together (such as the period, colon or comma with the dash or parentheses) was long practiced but is now avoided except in certain instances with the second of a pair of dashes or parentheses. The period and dash are still used together following a paragraph heading and between a quotation and its source (on the same line):

> **Ancient Egyptian Culture.**—The tombs of the kings . . .
> Life is real, life is earnest.—LONGFELLOW.

Two Styles in Modern Pointing.—Punctuation may be *close* and stiff, with points inserted wherever possible; or it may be *open* and easy with only the points necessary for clarity. Open punctuation is now considered the best usage, though in textbooks, laws and technical matter there is still a tendency to use many points. Close punctuation was governed by rhetoric; points were used according to natural pauses. Open punctuation is mostly grammatical to emphasize sentence structure and meaning. The rules that are given here are illustrated by examples of the correct use of punctuation.

The Period

Use the period or full stop—
After sentences other than direct questions and exclamations.

> He asked what I intended to do. (The indirect question is never followed by a question mark.)

After most abbreviations.

> The contract between Mrs. Harriet Blank and Mr. Henry Block, entered into Jan. 10, 1940, in Los Angeles, Calif., will expire at the end of a year.

After Roman numerals used to enumerate.

> I. Addition.
> II. Subtraction

Between a whole number and a decimal.

> The increase was 2.5 times what it was last year.

In a series of three to indicate an ellipsis.

> This book, . . . widely discussed, is ultramodern.

In a series of four (suspension periods) after an unfinished sentence.

> "Wait a moment so I may. . . ." She collapsed before she could complete the sentence.

Through a full line to indicate the omission of a line, paragraph or stanza.

> "My country 'tis of thee
> Of thee I sing." · · · · · ·

In close succession (leaders) connecting items with their prices in a statement or in tabular matter.

> 2 Dining chairs $15.00
> 4 Cushions 12.50

Do not use a period—
After most contractions (as distinct from abbreviations).

> Special classes meet on the 2d and 4th Tuesdays. Rob't Andrews, Sec'y, spoke.

After the abbreviation *cent* for centum.

> The bank paid 3 per cent interest.

After chemical symbols.

> Water, H_2O, occurs frequently in chemical compounds.

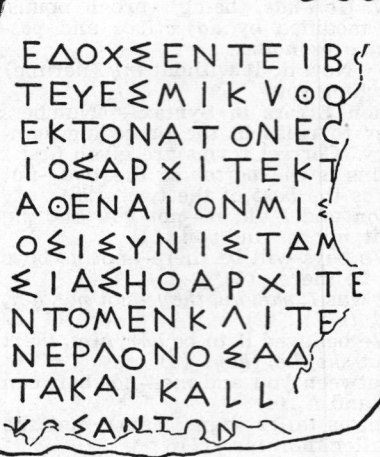

HARVARD UNIVERSITY PRESS

GREEK INSCRIPTION, part of a building commissioner's report in 409 B.C., shows words run together without punctuation.

After Roman numerals that do not enumerate.

> The Louis XIV period is described in Vol. IV, *The History of Furniture.*

After book sizes.

> The publisher decided upon 8vo for one book and 4to for the other.

In display headlines or titles.

> THE PRACTICE OF TYPOGRAPHY

After a signature in a letter.

> Sincerely yours,
> Margaret Manners

After items in lists.

> We send you the following goods—
> 3 Pairs of gloves
> 2 Felt hats
> 12 Turnover collars

Interrogation Point

Use the question mark—
After a direct question.

> (1) What would you have me say in reply?
> (2) Did prohibition prohibit? was the debated question.
> (3) The topic discussed was: Who will be the next president?

After an uncertain date.

> The Italian, Cristoforo Columbo (1446?–1506), we call Christopher Columbus.

In parentheses after a word or phrase to express doubt of the accuracy of the term.

> His accomplishment (?) was the ability to move his ears voluntarily.

Do not use a question mark—
After an indirect question.

> He inquired whether I wished to go.

After an interrogative sentence expressing a request.

> Will you please let us know immediately.

Exclamation Point

Use an exclamation point—
After expressions of surprise, alarm, appeal, command or other strong emotion.

> O Jane! how could you!
> Fire! fire! the house is on fire!
> Help! help! I am sinking!
> Awake! arise! flee to save yourselves!
> Bravo! Encore!

NOTE: In Spanish, inverted interrogation or exclamation points precede such sentences and the regular points follow them.

Do not use the exclamation point—
Too freely, as repeated exclamations weaken the effect.
After the vocative O. (It is not separated by any point from the word that follows it.)

> O Lord, Thy will be done.

Quotation Marks

Use double quotation marks (" ")—
To enclose a short direct quotation (borrowed expression).

> "Give me liberty; or give me death."

At the beginning of all paragraphs and also at the close of the final paragraph of a long quotation in text type. (Quotation marks are not used if the quoted matter is set in smaller type.)

> "It is a foul to strike a ball with both hands or to touch the ball twice in one attempt at batting.
> "Since only the server can score, fouls by the hand-in forfeit the ball, while fouls by the hand-out score for the server.
> "The officials of handball are a referee and a scorer."

For the titles of poems, ballads, hymns and short stories. For the names of ships, either double quotation marks or italics may be used.

> "The Raven"   "Lead, Kindly
> "Drink To Me Only   Light"
>   with Thine Eyes"   "The Queen Mary"
> "The Black Cat"   or *The Queen
>   Mary*

Use single quotation marks (' ')—
To enclose a quotation within a quotation.

> "Lives there a man with soul so dead
> Who never to himself hath said,
> 'This is my own, my native land!'?"

Do not use quotation marks—
For Bible excerpts.

> Thy rod and thy staff, they comfort me.

For adages or proverbs.

> A stitch in time saves nine.

In Foreign Composition.—In both French and Spanish, instead of our regulation quotation marks, guillemets (« ») are used; they are centered on the line and separated by a space from the words following the first pair and preceding the last.

> « D'abord il faut faire quelques achats », répondait la femme.
> « Nuestro grupo de románticos—dice—, aunque leyera y estudiara asiduamente . . . »

In German the first pair of quotation marks are a pair of normal commas on the line, and the closing marks are inverted commas superior to the line.

> Der Mann sagte: „Gestern im Theater sah ich ein gutes Drama."

The Colon

Use a colon—
After a transition preceding explanatory, defining and enumerating expressions.

> Among those who attended the function were the following: Senators Brown and White, General Jones, the Reverend Mr. Wright and members of the local press.

After the salutation in a letter.

> My dear Mr. White:

After a word introducing a long quotation.

> In his *Origin of the Species*, Darwin says:
> In the future I see open fields for far more important researches. Psychology will be securely based on the foundation already well laid by Mr. Herbert Spencer, that of the necessary acquirement of each mental power and capacity by gradation. Much light will be thrown on the origin of man and his history.

Between figures indicating chapter and verse in a biblical quotation.

He quoted John 3:16.

Between figures expressing time in hours and minutes.

The appointment is for 4:15 P.M.

Between numbers of volume and page in references so cited.

The article appeared in *Harper's*, 15:129.

Do not use a colon—
After such introductory words as *namely* and *for instance* (use a comma).

(1) His suggestion, namely, to go abroad, was most welcome.
(2) Different methods were established; for instance, that of rating students by intelligence tests.

The Semicolon

Use a semicolon—
To separate independent clauses without a conjunction.

Elizabeth insisted; her husband agreed.

To separate long co-ordinate clauses that include commas or have a conjunctive adverb.

The argument began quietly; but it soon reached a point, though with no such intention on the speaker's part, where many in the audience were rising in excitement; consequently the problem was to calm the disturbance.

To separate phrases and clauses introduced by a colon.

The rise in the city's population is shown by these figures: 1936, 459,763; 1938, 601,356.

To separate items in lists or references for which the comma is insufficient for clarity.

Atlantic Monthly, XI, 3–7; XV, 56.

Before the introductory phrases *that is, for example, for instance, to wit.*

A local advantage was extensively advertised by the Chamber of Commerce; that is, the abundance of iodine in the garden vegetables of the region, said to benefit the health of consumers.

The Comma

Use the comma—
Between words, phrases or clauses in place of a connective.

They bought apples, peaches, plums and pears.
In school, in college and in business gracious manners to all alike reveal good breeding.
The boys ran, the girls followed.
The rich and the poor, the high and the low, the well and the sick, received courteous consideration.
Red, green, blue or yellow may be used for the markers.

Between antithetical clauses.

The higher the altitude, the lower the temperature.

Between proper names of different persons.

For Robert, John obtained numerous favors.

Between unrelated numbers.

In 1938, 75 students won scholarships there.

Between the hundreds, thousands and so on in numbers having more than three digits.

1,500; 5,908,762.

Between words repeated for emphasis.

Realization of his hopes now seemed close, close at hand.

Between the parts of an inverted name in a bibliography or list.

Whittier, John

Between the parts of a date line.

Wednesday, June 23, 1940.

Between the two words where an ellipsis occurs.

Coffee needs cream; tea, lemon.

After the mild interjection *Oh.*

Oh, I wish I were in a sunnier clime.

After a conditional, temporal or other dependent clause that precedes the main clause.

(1) If you will come, we shall be glad to see you.
(2) When he heard the doctor's words, he became hopeful of recovery.
(3) As you cannot be induced to break the contract, nothing is to be gained by further discussion.

After an inverted expression.

What we see, we believe.

After a participial or absolute phrase.

Being without funds, he could not complete the course.

After an expression that otherwise would cause ambiguity.

Some time before, she applied for the position.

After the complimentary closing in a letter.

Cordially yours,
James Sutter

Before titles or their abbreviations following personal names.

Don Macarthur, Esquire; Upton Simms, Ph. D.

Before the connective in a compound sentence in which the subject changes in the second clause.

She conceded the point, and he knew she was right.

Before a short direct quotation.

The professor said, "Psychology should be applied in business and social contacts."

Before and after a nonrestrictive phrase or clause.

(1) The watchman, asleep in his chair, was unaware of the intruder.
(2) The driver, who was not licensed, caused an accident.

Before and after a word or phrase contrasted with what immediately precedes.

Honor, not gain, should be the first consideration.

Before and after a parenthetical word, phrase or clause.

(1) They decided, however, to continue the journey.
(2) His record, in general, received approval.
(3) Business integrity, as you will soon realize, is a valuable asset.

Before and after an appositive.

Miss Holmes, the teacher, was highly recommended.

Before and after a vocative.

To be sure, Edith, you are free to go.

Do not use a comma—
In page numbers of more than three figures:

The definition is on page 2569 in *Webster's Dictionary*.

Between figures expressing units of weights and measures.

The purchase included 2 lb. 8 oz. of glue and a dresser 2 ft. 5 in. high; delivery was made 3 hr. 15 min. after the sale.

Between figures designating a year.

Egypt had a great civilization as early as 5000 B.C.

Between two adjectives modifying each other and a noun.

She wore a brilliant blue costume.

Before *and* or *or* in series.

Her mother chose her wardrobe, books and associates.

Between appositive nouns the first of which is common, the second proper.

The scientist Einstein came to live in America.
The play *Abie's Irish Rose* ran for years.

NOTE: If the order is reversed, commas are used before and after the second noun (*see above*).

After a main clause followed by an adverbial clause completing the meaning.

She was happy because her lover had come back.

After introductory adverbs or adverbial phrases.

Undoubtedly he was mistaken in his estimate of many of his contemporaries.

Before or after a restrictive clause.

The man who would believe that is certainly a fool.

NOTE: *In close punctuation* (as distinct from the open style) *the comma is used—*
Before *and* or *or* in series.

(1) They selected roses, tulips, and hyacinths for the garden.
(2) John's gift was to be books, a radio, or a bicycle.

After an introductory adverb or adverbial phrase.

Inexorably, time and the law effected his removal.

To separate an independent clause used as subject or as predicate.

(1) Whatever is, is right.
(2) The principle recommendation is, the firm is reliable.

The Dash

Use a pair of dashes—
To set off an abrupt break in thought or construction.

If he must know—although nothing will be gained by it—then tell him.

To set off explanatory terms or phrases.

Edison's inventions—the electric light, the phonograph, a cooling system and numerous other inventions—were revolutionizing.

Use a single dash—
Before a final summarizing.

Subtle qualities of mind, appreciation of the finest shades of color, variations of form and expression and keen susceptibilities—these abilities made him an artist of the first order.

Before the source of a quotation.

Life is real, life is earnest.—LONGFELLOW.

Before an anticlimax, a climax or any surprise.

"Die and endow a college—or a cat."

Between a run-in question and answer.

Q. Were you present?—A. Yes, I was there.

Between the year of one date and the month of a succeeding date:

August 9, 1939—March 2, 1940.

Instead of repeating the name of an author in an index or a bibliography.

Wells, H.G., *The Outline of History*, 250
—, *Mr. Britling Sees It Through*, 252

After a side heading.

THE BABYLONIANS.—Their architecture reveals. . . .

To indicate an uncompleted word or sentence.

He supplied the ending of the word *ho—* in the game.
"Come here, Honoré, why—" She did not finish speaking.

To indicate time as continuing (after a given date).

Statistics, 1937—, are now available.

To indicate the omission of *to* between months or years or between page numbers (in these instances, the shorter dash is used).

May–September, 1939 (but, *From* May *to* September, 1939).
The subject is explained on pp. 7–10.

To indicate the omission of hundreds in consecutive years or page numbers.

He was in college 1936-38 but did not return.
Look up the references on pp. 103–9; 211–16.

Parentheses

Use a pair of parentheses to enclose—
An interpolated phrase when the break in the sentence structure is very definite.

The change voted (not unanimously) will soon be effective.

Explanatory phrases in court examinations and similar proceedings.

District attorney (to the witness):
Q. Have you seen this before (holding up Exhibit A)?
A. (After examining the object) I think—
Counsel for the defense (interrupting): I object.

Explanatory word not a part of a title.

The article appeared in *The* (Georgetown) *Times.*

Meanings of words.

The use of guillemets (French quotation marks) is limited.

A reference, whether in the body of a sentence or at the end.

The angle ABC (*see* Fig. 4) is a right angle.
Proof is given in this chapter (pp. 1–3).

Figures or letters that designate divisions in a sentence or treatise arranged for study.

The experiment requires (1) a Bunsen burner, (2) distilled water and (3) a large retort besides the chemicals.

Brackets

Use a pair of brackets to enclose—
An explanatory note not the author's.

[The opinions expressed are the author's and do not represent the policy of this periodical.—Editor.]
"America is active in peace." [Applause.]

An editorial note in a quotation.

"They [the Republicans] are enlisting their best speakers for the campaign."

The correction of an error.

He came on Friday, the 14th [13th].

Parenthetical matter within parentheses.

(He says [*see* his *History of New York*] that Hudson was here at an earlier date.)

Continued and concluded lines.

[*Continued on page 75*]
[*To be concluded*]

Do not substitute brackets for parentheses.

The Brace

Use the brace—
To group words, lines or figures relating to a preceding term or statement.

Main topics { Religion
Politics
Sociology

To group terms or figures for a summary.

1st ward 910 }
2d ward 1,007 } Total, 2,512
3d ward 595 }

The Apostrophe

Use the apostrophe—
As a sign of the possessive.

Cat's eye   Lewis and Clark's expedition
Cows' horns   For Jesus' sake

(*Its*—the possessive of it—*theirs* and similar pronouns have no apostrophe.)

To show contraction or omission.

Don't (colloquial)   mornin' (dialect)
I'll
it's (it is)   '80s

NOTE: *In close punctuation the apostrophe is used—*
To form the plural of figures, letters and years.

The 5's and 3's look much alike.
Mind your p's and q's.
First study the three R's.
In retrospect, the 1890's are most amusing.

(There is a growing tendency to omit the apostrophe in all these cases.)

Do not use the apostrophe—
In firm, institution or association names that otherwise would take the possessive form.

Teachers College Educators Association
Merchants and Mechanics Bank
(Exception: Young Women's Christian Association.)

Before abbreviated words that have become common colloquial usage.

phone   cello
possum   cellist
varsity

The Hyphen

Use a hyphen (-) *between—*
Compound adjectives or nouns and between double vowels.

(1) She wanted to take a round-the-world trip.
(2) The author attempted a cross-section of life.
(3) The clauses were co-ordinate.

Two syllables of a word divided at the end of a line, when lack of space necessitates its conclusion on the next.

The museum was open to the public free except on Monday.

Diacritical Marks.—Symbols to aid in pronunciation are called *diacritical marks.* They include the acute accent (as in *résumé*) and the grave accent (as in *Molière*) marking different pronunciations in French and used in English for many borrowed French words. The grave accent is also used to show that a syllable is pronounced, as in *blessèd, armèd.* The acute accent is commonly used in dictionaries to show which syllable has the stress; for example, *quin'-tu-plets,* to show that the first not the second syllable is accented.

The diaeresis (¨) in English indicates that the second of two vowels is pronounced separately. It is omitted when the word is divided between the vowels at the end of a line. (A hyphen, to separate double vowels, as in co-ordinate; is often used in place of the diaeresis.) In German the sign (¨) is called an *Umlaut.* The diaeresis or sometimes a tiny *e* is used over *a, o* or *u* to show that the *a* is really *ae,* the *o* really *oe,* the *u* really *ue,* and should be so pronounced; as in *Männerchor* or *Männerchor* for Maennerchor, *Müller* for Mueller.

The circumflex (^) over a vowel originally showed a rising and a falling accent. In most French words taken over in English a vowel with a circumflex stands in a syllable where a consonant has dropped out; as in *fête* (which was *feste* [*feast*] in Old French); and *bête* (which was *beste* [*beast*] in Old French).

The tilde or til is used in English words from Spanish or Portuguese, especially proper names. The tilde (~) in Spanish words is written over the letter *n* to show that it has a palatal sound: *cañon* is pronounced *canyon.* In Portuguese the same sign, called *til* in that language, is used over a vowel to show that it has a nasal sound; for example, *bõ* is pronounced like the French *bon;* and João is Portuguese for John.

The breve (˘), indicating a short sound, and macron (-), the long sound, are used to show pronunciation.

The cedilla (¸), which gives the *s* sound to *c,* is used in French to show that the letter *c* is not pronounced like *k,* as it otherwise would be before *a, o, u;* for example, *façade* and *François.*

FIGURES OF SPEECH

Figures of speech are pictures in words. *Figure* in this phrase does not mean number but pattern, design or picture. Figures of speech are picturesque expressions used for the purpose of making language more striking and more effective. Literal speech is language that says just what it means. Figurative language conveys or implies meaning by the use of imaginative comparisons, of skilfully devised phraseology or of contradictory inference. Poetry is full of figurative language, and so is our everyday speech with its nicknames and proverbs. An old name for figures of speech is *tropes,* which originally meant turns or twists. There is a famous verse:

His mouth he scarce could ope
But out there flew a trope.

A SIMILE expresses likeness between persons or things that are in most respects unlike. The comparison is definitely expressed, usually with the words *like* or *as,* sometimes by *than* and *seem.*

As the hart panteth after the water brooks, so panteth my soul after thee, O God.
—*42d Psalm.*
My love is like a red, red rose—*Old Song.*

Once let slavery get planted in a locality by ever so weak or doubtful a title, and in ever so small numbers, and it is like the Canada thistle or Bermuda grass—you cannot root it out.   —*Abraham Lincoln.*

A METAPHOR implies a likeness between two persons or objects usually unlike, without using any special words to indicate the comparison, but just by calling one the other. Omitting *like* or *as* from a simile usually leaves a metaphor; and the insertion of those words in a metaphor produces a simile.

Thy word is a lamp unto my feet, and a light unto my path.   —*19th Psalm.*

The Lord is my shepherd.—*23d Psalm*.
We are no other than a moving row
Of magic shadows-shapes that come and
  go.   —FITZGERALD, *Rubaiyat*.

In the last resort all men talk by signs. To talk by statues is to talk by signs; to talk by cities is to talk by signs. Pillars, palaces, cathedrals, temples, pyramids, are an enormous dumb alphabet, as if some giant held up his fingers of stone.—G. K. CHESTERTON.

An ALLEGORY is an elaboration of a metaphor into a lengthy narrative, as in Bunyan's *Pilgrim's Progress*, which is based on the metaphor: A man's life is a journey through this world to Heaven.

A man had a plain strong-bow with which he could shoot far and true. He loved his bow so well that he would needs have it curiously carved by a cunning workman. It was done, and at the first trial the bow snapped.   —From an old German legend.

PERSONIFICATION attributes human life or characteristics to inanimate objects; it speaks of these inanimate objects as if they were human or personal. "Necessity is the mother of invention" is both metaphor and personification.

Laughter holding both his sides.
  —JOHN MILTON in *L'Allegro*.
The sea waves sobbed with sorrow.
  —WHITTIER.

His life was gentle, and the elements
So mix'd in him, that Nature might stand up
And say to all the world, This was a man!
  —SHAKESPEARE.

The FABLE is an extension of the figure of personification, a simple story or anecdote in which animals or inanimate objects talk and act like human beings, and which ends with a moral that applies to the story. In the Old Testament there is a famous fable in the 9th chapter of the book of Judges, how the trees chose a king. Some fables have been condensed into a phrase, like "dog in the manger" to mean grudging to others what one cannot enjoy himself; "wolf in sheep's clothing" to mean a villain pretending innocence; the "lion's share" to mean all of something; the "lion and the mouse" to suggest that little friends may prove great friends.

The PARABLE (from a Greek word that means comparison) is an extended simile or metaphor, a simple story that might be true (unlike the fable) from which a moral or spiritual lesson can be learned. Some parables, especially those of Jesus in the New Testament, have been condensed into phrases—the good Samaritan and the prodigal son.

APOSTROPHE is speaking *to* inanimate objects as if they were human and personal or to absent persons as if they were present.

Thou hast taught me, Silent River,
Many a lesson, deep and long.—LONGFELLOW.
Hence, loathed Melancholy!—JOHN MILTON.
O death, where is thy sting?   O grave,
where is thy victory?   —ST. PAUL.

VISION represents absent or remote things as present. It is, therefore, a modified form of apostrophe. Note the following:

Is this a dagger, which I see before me,
The handle toward my hand?—SHAKESPEARE.

METONYMY is the use of a sign for the thing meant, the use of one name for another which it suggests. Thus, when you read

The pulpit is a great power,

you know that *pulpit* is used as a sign for the man in the pulpit and his sermon. In like manner you say

The press is powerful.
The pen is mightier than the sword.
The bottle stole his wits away.
His soft heart was better than his soft head.

SYNECDOCHE is that form of metonymy that states a part for a whole, or a whole for a part. In the Lord's Prayer,

Give us this day our daily *bread*

means all food and not just the one kind. In the following examples *hands* mean men and *head* means the whole animal:

Twenty hands are employed in the factory.
He had one hundred head of cattle in the drove.

ANTITHESIS is the suggestion by words and their arrangement of a contrast between ideas.

Man proposes; God disposes.
Deeds show what we are; words, what we should be.

CLIMAX (from a Greek word meaning ladder) is the arrangement of phrases or details of subject matter so that they are increasingly important or striking. The following, from Cicero's oration against Verres, illustrates:

It is an outrage to *bind* a Roman citizen; to *scourge* him is an atrocious crime; to *put him to death* is almost parricide; but to *crucify* him—what shall I call it?

The opposite of this figure is ANTICLIMAX, an arrangement of items in which the last is least important or striking.

And thou Dalhousie, the great god of war,
Lieutenant colonel to the Earl of Mar.
  —POPE.

APHORISM (originally, a definition), is the condensation of great thought within the range of a brief and memorable expression. *Maxim, adage, apothegm, precept, proverb, dictum, saw* are other terms for a brief, pithy saying.

Be not the first by whom the new is tried,
Nor yet the last to lay the old aside.
  —ALEXANDER POPE.

EPIGRAM, like aphorism, is the name given to any pointed and condensed saying. In its Greek original it meant an inscription for a monument or statue. Inscriptions must be brief and should be pointed. Epigrammatic expression has come to connote wit and brilliance especially in verse. It is best illustrated and defined by the famous Roman poet Martial, author of many epigrams:

Three things must epigrams, like bees,
  have all—
A sting, and honey, and a body small.

EUPHEMISM (from the Greek meaning speaking well) is using a pleasant or agreeable word instead of the natural and disagreeable one. The Romans said *Vixit*, he has lived, instead of *Mortuus est*, he died. We speak of passing on—rather than say dying.

INTERROGATION is a question to which no answer is expected or required. (A rhetorical question, it is called.) The answer is implied.

Who hath believed our report? and to whom is the arm of the Lord revealed?
  —ISAIAH 53:1.
Who is here so base that would be a bondman? . . .
Who is here so rude that would not be a Roman?   —SHAKESPEARE.
What! Gentleman, was I not to foresee? or, foreseeing was I not to endeavor to save you from all these multiplied mischiefs and disgraces? Was I an Irishman on that day that

I boldly withstood our pride? or on that day that I hung down my head, and wept in shame in silence over the humiliation of Great Britain? I became unpopular in England for the one, and in Ireland for the other. What then? What obligation lay on me to be popular?   —EDMUND BURKE.

HYPERBOLE (from a Greek word meaning overshooting) is deliberate exaggeration used for the purpose of producing some startling or alarming effect. All figures of speech are to some extent hyperbolical, and hyperbole makes use freely of other figures to accomplish its arresting effects. Such everyday exaggerations as *starving to death, dressed to kill, a perfectly lovely book* and *mad as a hornet* are hyperbole.

We were in our own sight as grasshoppers, and so we were in their sight. . . . The children of the east lay along the valley like locusts for multitude; and their camels were without number, and as the sand which is upon the seashore for multitude.
  —OLD TESTAMENT.

The opposite figure is *understatement*, which the old rhetoricians called *meiosis* or *litotes*. Paul called himself "a citizen of no mean city," another way of saying "a famous city."

IRONY (from a Greek word meaning dissimulation) implies the opposite of what it expresses. A remarkable series of ironical interrogations is to be found in the last chapter of the book of Job in the Old Testament:

"Where wast thou when I laid the foundations of the earth? . . . Canst thou bind the sweet influence of the Pleiades, or loose the bands of Orion? . . . Canst thou draw out leviathan with an hook?"
No doubt but ye are the people, and wisdom shall die with you.   —JOB.

There are several methods of heightening the effect of speech or writing that depend less on the pictures or figures they convey to the mind's eye than on the word sound.

ONOMATOPOEIA is *suiting the sound to the sense*. Such words as *bang, clang, jingle, tingle, ugh* are onomatopoeic words. In Tennyson's "The Passing of Arthur" these words sound like what they describe:

His own thought drove him like a goad.
Dry clash'd his harness in the icy caves
And barren chasms, and all to left and right
The bare black cliff clang'd round him, as
  he based
His feet on juts of slippery crag that rang
Sharp-smitten with the dint of armed heels.

ALLITERATION is the trick of using several words that begin with the same sound or sounds. It was as necessary as meter to early English poetry and is frequent in our everyday phrases like kith and kin, friend or foe, fish, flesh or fowl, mind and matter, tried and true. Shakespeare in *The Tempest* begins a lovely song:

Full fathom five thy father lies.

ASSONANCE is the repetition of similar vowel sounds in the last syllable or the accented syllable of several words. It differs from rhyme because the whole syllable is not identical—the vowel sounds are the same but the consonants are different. "Baby Mary is lazy" is an example of assonance: the vowel sounds in three words are the same.

Rhyme is the repetition of identical sounds at the end of words. It is common in everyday phrases like *near and dear, high and dry*; and it is a characteristic of most European poetry, marking the end of the verse or metrical scheme.

Composition is putting together individual units so as to form a unified and effective whole. It is the essential operation in all forms of art—in painting, music and architecture—as well as speech and writing. Remember this; it will help you when you speak or write. The most important aid to effectiveness is arrangement—arrangement of ideas, arrangement of sentences and arrangement of words in sentences. You may know all the words in the dictionary and all the rules of grammar and still not be able to write well if you do not compose well. The dictionary can hardly be called a composition, but it is useful and effective because it is carefully arranged in alphabetical order. Good writing is writing that says what the writer wants to say in such a way that the reader will understand it, believe it, enjoy it and, when the writer so desires, act in accordance with its suggestions. This is what we mean by effective writing: it produces an effect upon the reader, it gets results. Results in any field of action are best achieved by order. In driving a nail, the force of the blow is not nearly so important as the combination of holding the nail straight and firmly at the point where it is to be driven, holding the hammer at the proper balance and delivering the blows accurately and rhythmically. This principle holds for oral as well as for written composition. Most of us speak more than we write, but writing is the main topic here. Compared with speech, writing is more complex, more premeditated and more entirely dependent upon words and composition.

The Tools of the Writer.—The tools of the writer are words and sentences. Words must be articulated into sentences before they will convey connected ideas. There must be a subject and something said about it—a predicate—to every sentence. Both these elements may be qualified, and the predicate may contain an object; but a sentence must contain a subject and a predicate. Even the imperative, "Listen!" unmistakably implies the subject, *you*. The forms of words and the relationships between them in sentences are governed by the rules of grammar, and those rules that are most frequently operative and most frequently violated will be discussed presently.

Choice of Words.—Words should be simple, precise, concrete and should conform to good usage and the idiom of the language. The choice of words will give clarity and forcefulness or obscurity and lack of color to your style. Each word should be considered not only for itself but for the associations it has come to have in people's minds. Should you wish to describe the tropics, first acquire a suitable vocabulary—words that will create for your reader a mosaic of warmth and brilliance, with a background of the luxuriant tropical flora, heavy exotic fragrances, the constellations that distinguish its night skies from ours and the subtle charms of its

people. To contrast this, compile a word list that you would find adequate to picture a cold, forbidding, cruel climate where summer is brief and nature unproductive, and where the people reflect these conditions in their lives and emotional reactions. Remember that every descriptive adjective has its opposite; study both of them.

FOR SIMPLICITY.—When one writes there is a tendency to choose words not generally used in speech. Avoid it. Write, "I live [not *dwell*] in Springfield." Either word conveys the meaning, but the former is natural and alive, the latter artificial and stiff. This does not mean that you should not use long or unusual words; but when a common word suits your meaning just as well, use it. Do not strain to avoid repetition by substituting words like *bovine* for cow, *tome* for book, *aperture* for window. Ordinarily a word should call attention not to itself but to what it means.

FOR PRECISION.—Precision or discrimination between words of like sound or related meaning can be acquired by scrupulous attention to definition and usage. The writer should train himself to recognize readily the differences between: obtain and attain; secure and procure; survive and recover; apt, likely and liable; imaginary and imaginative; poetry and verse; fact and truth; democracy and republic; human and humane; effective, effectual and efficient; grief and grievance; act, action and activity; last and latest; education, schooling and culture; accurate, correct, exact and precise; start and begin; politic and political. Constant study of the dictionary, especially what it says about synonyms, or words of nearly the same meaning, is the best training.

One of the worst enemies to precision is the lazy use of a familiar general word for specialized meanings that it only vaguely suggests. Many slovenly writers use the word *have* to denote all the meanings accurately expressed by own, hold, keep, buy, inherit, acquire and display. The same is true of the words *be, do* and *go*. This blunder is due partly to the writer's insensitiveness to fine shades of meaning or to his careless use of words. Many people read with the same lack of alertness. Such people, properly speaking, can neither read nor write well.

FOR CONCRETENESS.—A word is concrete when it suggests an image, appeals to the senses. Whenever possible, give the preference to concrete words. Our common words are more accurate than those less used because they are more closely connected with life. *Home* conveys many images; *domicile* calls up few. The specific word is more concrete, more picturesque than the general, as *strode* or *strutted* than walked. Use by preference the common names of things and the more specialized verbs of action.

IDIOMS.—Every language has its idioms—peculiar forms that are in a way

the meat and kernel of it, yet often illogical, capricious and not amenable to rules or principles. No one knows English who does not know its idioms; yet few suggestions can be given as to how they can be learned. They must be acquired by close attention, comparison and careful study of prepositions. We indicate here a few idiomatic expressions by way of illustration. In English we greet one another with "How are you?" or "How do you do?"; in French, *"Comment vous portez-vous?"* ("How do you carry yourself?"); in German one says, *"Wie geht's?"* ("How goes it?") or *"Wie befinden Sie sich?"* ("How do you find yourself?"); in Arabic, *"Salām 'alaikum"* ("The peace be on you").

Much of our idiom centers about prepositions, as: The cars stop at [not *on*] Adams Street. The window is in [not *on*] the west wall. We shall have the privilege of hearing [not *to hear*] a noted speaker. We go into the room and move about in it. We have confidence in and confide in a person, but confide a secret to him, because we have a high regard for him on account of our long intimacy with him. A single verb in combination with various prepositions takes on different meanings, as in: The party broke up. The car broke down. The burglar broke into the safe while the sergeant was breaking in the new recruit, whose wife had just broken out with the measles. The girl broke off her engagement. The executive put off his departure, put up with the delay and finally put over the deal. The man makes out a check and his wife makes up her mind. There are many other types of idioms, for instance, we say, seems to be or looks as if [not *looks to be*]. You may be called down for your mistakes; called for to go on a motor trip; called up on the telephone; called in for consultation; called on by a visitor or for assistance; and called to a bedside. The verb live takes many prepositions, as: He lives in a city, at a hotel, on his income, by his work, up to certain standards, with his family, within his means, out his days and to an advanced age.

The Sentence as Composition.—The sentence is the unit of composition. You never set out merely to write a sentence; you wish to say something about something; so you must know what your material is; that is, you know what you want to express, but you have not yet composed it. The first thing you must do is decide upon a subject. This seems simple, but a great many incorrect sentences result from the writer's choosing the wrong subject, or not sticking to the one he has chosen. In an expression such as, "On preparing to leave, the ax could not be found," grammar calls the first phrase a *dangling participle;* but the real trouble was not with the writer's grammar but with his thought. He started out with a person in his mind as the subject of his sentence, someone who was preparing to leave. Then, after he had passed the first phrase, he thought about something else, the ax. What he had in his mind was something like this: "We prepared to leave. The ax could not be found." The two ideas were so closely related by the fact that they happened at the same time, that he thought they should be expressed in one statement. In order, however, to construct the sentence correctly, he must decide whether *we* or *ax* is the subject, and then stick to it. He may write either: "On preparing to leave, we could not find the ax," or "The ax could not be found when we prepared to leave." The first statement probably is nearer what he wanted to say, but both sentences are correct, consistent and intelligible compositions.

THE FOLGER SHAKESPEARE LIBRARY

LIBRARIES have been in existence since the time of the Egyptian pharaohs, 1200 B.C.

When there are many elements to be included in one sentence, your problem is to decide which is the main idea and how the rest are related to it. Take, for instance, the following series of short sentences: "We came to a path. It led off the wagon road. It led through the woods. This path apparently was not much used. It was a narrow path." These statements are all clear and they are all correct, but they are not composed. In order to make a sentence of them one has to decide which is the most important statement and what relation the others bear to it. Suppose we write it: "We came to a narrow path, apparently not much used, that led off the wagon road and through the woods." Four of the sentences are reduced to modifiers, one becomes an adjective, one a participial phrase, one a relative clause and one an adverbial phrase. The result is a unified impression made up of five distinct elements. The problem of composing a sentence is chiefly the problem of determining in your mind in what relationship the elements stand to each other.

The word that causes the most trouble in sentence composition is *and*. Remember, *and* expresses simple addition; it is only a verbal plus sign. Do not rely on it to express time, place, purpose and result; for these relationships we have *when, where, in order that* and *consequently*. The chances are that you will write correct sentences if you keep your mind on the

fact that such a sentence makes just one statement to which every element in the sentence must be accurately related.

Begin with the subject. Such a beginning will keep you out of many difficulties. Do not be afraid to write a simple, direct statement. What it lacks in variety, it generally gains in clearness and emphasis. More sentences are ineffective because they try to say too much than because they say too little.

One form of the error of writing too much in one sentence calls for special attention because it occurs so frequently. It is generally called the *comma blunder*. The name makes it seem an error in punctuation, but the punctuation is only the mechanism by which the error is shown. Like most mistakes in sentence structure, it is the result of not thinking. The comma blunder is the error of writing two complete sentences in one and separating them by a comma. It would be even worse without the comma. The greatest stumbling block comes when the second statement begins with a personal pronoun (*he, they, it*) or a conjunctive adverb (*then, therefore*), or when there is a close relation of cause and effect, or a contrast, between the two statements. The following sentences are correctly punctuated: "Come on, laddie. It's time to go home." "Tom wasn't afraid. He was simply waiting for the right moment." "You'd better not try that bridge. It isn't safe." "He would not take the crown; therefore 'tis certain he was not ambitious." "Be sure you're right; then go ahead." In writing dialogue be specially careful to avoid the comma blunder. The only exception to the rule here stated is the case of the series form, in which short statements are sometimes separated merely by the comma; e.g., "I have fought a good fight, I have finished my course, I have kept the faith."

AGREEMENT BETWEEN SUBJECT AND VERB.—Grammatical correctness requires that a verb agree with its subject in number; that is, both must be singular or both plural. This rule is generally known and observed, but certain circumstances frequently pro-

duce confusion. The writer is sometimes misled when the verb comes before the subject. Notice the following: "Here were [not *was*] the banking facilities of the colonies." "Coupled with the demand for the teaching of patriotism have [not *has*] come suggestions as to what course such instruction should take." "There exist [not *exists*] in many localities certain superstitions not found elsewhere." Any question in your mind about the number of the verb in such sentences is easily answered by recasting the sentence to begin with the subject. Subjects joined by *and* commonly require a plural verb. "There are [not *there is* or *there's*] my friend Barton and his wife coming toward us."

A plural noun coming between the subject and the verb sometimes creates confusion. "The sound of his steps was gradually lost." "The size of the plates varies with the current capacity of the battery." A collective noun is to be construed as plural when its parts are thought of separately. "The crowd were throwing up their hats and shouting with excitement." "The crowd was headed by a sailor."

AGREEMENT BETWEEN PRONOUN AND ANTECEDENT.—Pronouns have no meaning by themselves. Whatever meaning they have is reflected upon them by their antecedents. Consequently each must agree with its antecedent in number. "The criminal is an enemy of society, and society must constantly fight against him [not *them*]." The indefinite pronouns, *each, everybody, anyone, one* are singular. "Everybody must have plenty of time if he is [not *they are*] to do good work."

The pronoun takes its case from its own office in the sentence, irrespective of the case of its antecedents. If it is the subject, it must be nominative; if it is the object of verb or preposition, it must be objective. "He saw the boys who are going to the circus." "The boys whom he saw are going to the circus." Here we may remind you that the pronoun must always refer definitely to its antecedent. This means that it must be furnished with an antecedent. In the sentence, "There is no use writing to John; he will not answer it," there is no antecedent for *it*. The word *letter*, implied by *writing*, was in the mind of the writer, but it is not expressed, so the sentence is incorrect. "He invited me to join him in a bear hunt, which I readily accepted." Here the antecedent of *which* is the noun implied in the verb, *invited;* but, to make matters worse, *hunt* affords a grammatical antecedent that reduces the sentence to nonsense. All good writing is grammatical. If you do not feel that you have mastered grammar, study its essentials; then put them into practice. Knowing the rules of grammar is of no value until you have become so used to writing and speaking grammatically that you never think of the rules. The good sentence is much more than grammatical—it is clear and forceful.

PUNCTUATION.—Punctuation is a mechanical means for assuring the clarity of the written sentence. The marks aid the eye by separating words that would cause confusion if read in close connection. When you speak, you punctuate with your voice. In the written sentence, the vocal stops are indicated by punctuation, the common marks of which are the comma, the semicolon and the period. They are all marks of separation. For the ordinary minor separations between words, phrases and closely related clauses, we use the comma. When the parts to be separated are more nearly self-sufficient units, we use the semicolon. The period, of course, usually marks the end of a complete statement. The other punctuation marks are used for special purposes that can be easily understood. Punctuation is of no importance for its own sake. You use it only to make sure that you convey your true meaning to the reader. It is particularly necessary that it be indicated, because people read much more rapidly than they listen, and always tend to read a word in close connection with what immediately precedes. Consider the sentence: "They left, strangely moved by what they had seen." The comma after *left* prevents giving the impression, "They left strangely." If that is what you want to convey, however, you place the comma after *strangely* to be sure of making that meaning clear.

PARAGRAPH.—The way to develop your ideas in writing can best be shown here by discussing the function of the paragraph. The paragraph is a device that permits the writer to develop an idea through a series of relatively short, closely related sentences, and at the same time by its physical form enforces on the reader the unity of the group. Remember that the paragraph is not a vehicle for stating an idea. That is the function of the sentence. The paragraph affords the means for developing the idea. It is, therefore, an invitation to do what most beginners do not do, to give the idea room. Do not try to say everything in one sentence. If you do, you will write a crammed, involved, weak sentence, and you will choke your idea. State your topic in a sentence. Then explain it; restate it, perhaps in different terms or from another point of view. Justify it, amplify it with evidence or illustration; and finally point its connection with what has gone before or what is to come next. This will give the separate sections of your composition sufficient body to impress themselves upon the reader, and will keep you from writing a series of disjointed statements that are not really a composition.

Whenever you find yourself writing a series of one- or two-sentence paragraphs, you have before you visual evidence that you are writing disconnectedly. What probably is taking place is this: you are not perceiving the relationship between your topics, and you are therefore not composing your material. If every item that demands a sentence appears to you to be a topic, then every one of them demands that it be developed and your essay must be many times longer. In a composition a sentence that does not itself demand development must belong to the development of some other topic, or it does not belong in the com-

position. A paragraph of less than three sentences generally has no unity of idea.

Three varieties of the short, one-sentence paragraph are permissible: First, in writing dialogue, whatever is said by a single speaker at one time, together with identifying or brief explanatory remarks by the writer, is put into a paragraph by itself. This practice is not at present consistently followed, but it is a great convenience to the reader. Second, when the point is of such supreme importance that you want to drive it into the reader's mind, you can emphasize it visually by printing it separately. This device is useful only for short, direct sentences and must be used sparingly. Third, between larger sections of the composition use a short transition paragraph to point the connection between what has gone before and what is to follow. This transition paragraph does not connect the two single paragraphs between which it stands but the larger groups of paragraphs, one before and one after the transition.

The connection between paragraphs should be logical. It is frequently desirable to express it by means of such words as *moreover, besides, notwithstanding* or *as a result* at the beginning of the succeeding paragraph. The particular usefulness of such words is that they point the direction in which the reader's thought is to turn. A more subtle and firmer coherence may be achieved by concluding one paragraph with the idea that you intend to consider and develop in the next.

The order of paragraphs is determined in great part by the logical sequence of ideas, but it can be managed to advantage by constructing your outline with an eye to the climax. The development of the subject should be so started that by following the logical sequence the most important, most conclusive, most impressive idea will be the last to be presented. The reverse order would frequently satisfy the demands of logic just as well, but it would not be emphatic; the composition would not make so vigorous an impression.

The Principal Forms of Writing.—All that has been said applies to all types of writing. A few special applications of these points to certain special forms may be cited. It is traditional to divide writing into exposition, description, narration and argument. In actual practice we use the different forms together. The object of the first three is to tell, that of argument is to convince.

EXPOSITION.—The term exposition includes all forms of writing that convey information—history, biography, travel, all scientific writing, most essays and letters—in fact, practically all writing that is not creative is expository. Exposition in writing has to do with the point of view and purpose of the writer. Since his object is to inform, the first essential of expository writing is clearness. All that has been said, therefore, about arrangement of material applies with particular force to exposition. Closely allied to order and of equal importance is

proportion. Give your most important facts or ideas more space and elaboration than the others. If every stage in a process or every move in a journey is treated as if it were equally important, nothing will stand out, and the reader's impression of the whole is likely to be jumbled.

Many beginners in exposition do not write clearly because they lack full knowledge of the subject and rely more on the reader's knowledge than on the clearness of their own writing. This attitude is fatal. When you set out to explain a subject to anyone, you must assume that you know more about it than he does. Do not patronize your reader, but don't forget that for the moment you are telling him. If you are writing a report for a teacher, your writing will suffer unless, for the purposes of the report, you and the teacher exchange places. If the reader is to have confidence in the author, the author must first have confidence in himself.

A popular variety of exposition is the familiar essay, the type in which the author, no matter what his subject, really writes about himself, his own impressions, reactions and ideas. A composition on radiators will tell what they are, how they are made and how they work. In a familiar essay on radiators you may tell something about your liking for them on a cold morning, your exasperation with them when you move the furniture, your interpretation of their moods when they gurgle and hiss. In the familiar essay no one can anticipate what the writer will say. It follows, therefore, that a familiar essay will be interesting only if the author has an interesting mind. Do not think that because the style of the familiar essay is chatty and the material digressive that it needs no plan. It needs a very definite plan, but the plan must never show.

DESCRIPTION.—Description is the form of writing that appeals to the senses. Most descriptions are addressed to the sense of sight, although hearing is often called upon, and the other senses to a lesser extent. The first important thing is to choose your point of view. If you are to take your reader to the back of a house, do not start by describing the front of it. When you have chosen your point of view, stick to it. Never change it without saying so. Give your reader a general picture first, and then proceed to the details. If you give him the details first, he will seldom be able to put them together.

In undertaking any kind of writing, never forget that you know more about what you mean to say than your reader does, and that what seems perfectly clear to you, may not be so to him. Above all, in writing description, use a concrete vocabulary—words that vivify the reader's imagination and cause him to see, hear, smell, touch or taste according to your descriptions. It does not suffice to say a scene is beautiful; you must present to the reader the sense impressions that made you conscious of its beauty so that he too will feel it. What a word suggests, the image it brings to mind, its connotations—always important—are particularly so in description. Words suggest much more than their precise meaning. Purple, for instance, may suggest royalty, power, wealth, or, in various contexts, evening, death, distance. As a writer, say all that you can to give the reader the right suggestion and to prevent wrong impressions. Finally, be accurate; do not describe what you do not see, but present accurately what you do see, as you see it.

NARRATION.—Material presented as a sequence of events in time is narration. The outline, therefore, is inherent in the material. Events must follow each other as they actually did. You do not have to start at the beginning, but if you don't, you must relate the events that led up to your starting point as soon as they are necessary to the understanding of what happened afterwards. (This is the cutback method of motion pictures.)

Narration must almost always be supplemented by description. As events do not happen in a vacuum your reader will always make up a scene for them if you do not give him one. Never let him see your events happening in the wrong scene. In writing description and narration it is well to remember that the reader's imagination always runs ahead of you, and that you must keep it from going the wrong way. You can accomplish this by choosing and emphasizing the most significant details.

One of the most important elements in narration is proportion. All the events in a series are not of equal importance, so you must choose those that seem to you to be the most important, and treat them more fully than the rest. Relate less important events to an important one by making them lead up to it and away from it.

ARGUMENT.—The object of argument is to convince. Conviction is brought about by the logical presentation of evidence, and the outline is, therefore, of first importance. The outline should be actually a brief of the composition, so that by reading the outline one can grasp the whole argument. The outline should start with the proposition to be proved, and every successive point should be expressly related to the preceding by some such word as *for, hence, therefore.* The outline should read something like the demonstration of a proposition in geometry. Most written argument is of the informal variety in which there is no clear line between exposition and argument.

All exposition of ideas and all criticism is really argument. Ideas and judgments must be supported by evidence if they are to be impressive. You can write on the devastation of war from facts; but if you write on the futility of war, you must marshal your facts so as to prove the idea that you have derived from them. The evidence consists of facts, and the presentation of them is exposition; the argument consists in the arrangement of those facts and their application to the idea. Do not omit the evidence; assertions without substantiating facts do not convince. Use only evidence that is relevant to the subject. To write a good argument you must always have more knowledge than

you can use. Learn to discard all material that is not directly applicable to the point you intend to make. Do not try to make too many points. Decide on one, or, at most, a few that seem to you to be fundamental to the truth of your proposition and establish them. Argument is of special importance in public speaking.

Relation Between Forms of Writing.— Narration, description and exposition are combined in almost all creative writing; the dominant method determines to a considerable extent the form of writing that results. Thus fic-

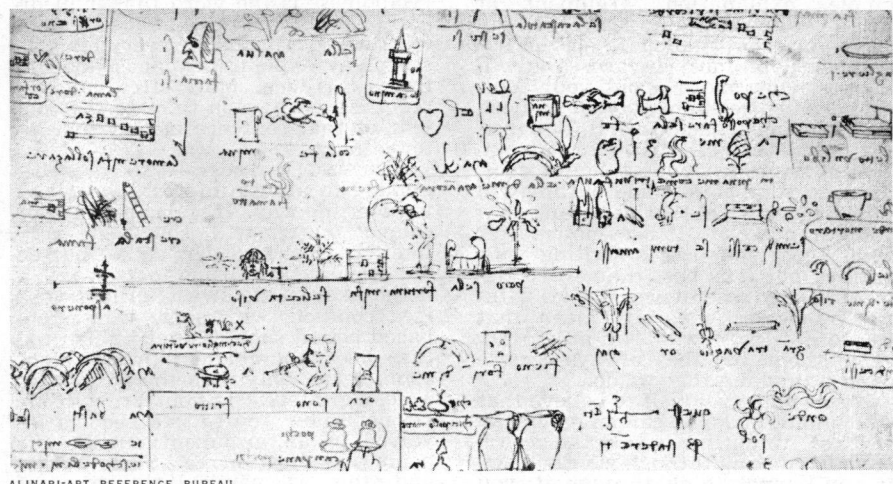

ALINARI-ART REFERENCE BUREAU

FIFTEENTH-CENTURY PICTOGRAPH, drawn by Leonardo da Vinci, appears almost doodle-like.

tion is primarily narration; essays and articles are primarily expository, although an account of a journey or other experience may be mainly descriptive. Much more important than the individual forms is the appreciation of the aim and object of your composition. Use the most effective means of attaining that object. Remember that the special forms almost never appear separately. Narration and description are often the most effective methods of exposition, and all three forms are used in argument. Do not let yourself be hemmed in by forms and formulas. The more persistently you keep your mind on what you want to say and why you want to say it, the better you will write.

Creative and Informative Writing.— Though writing takes many forms, they all group themselves into two varieties—creative and informative. Creative writing includes drama, novel, story, essay and poetry. Informative writing includes articles, reports, lectures, sermons, criticisms, debates and most letters. The fundamental difference between the two varieties is that creative writing aims to present its matter as happening as an experience; whereas informative writing aims to tell the reader something about its subject or to convince him of the writer's opinion. Stephen Vincent Benét's treatment of the battle of Gettysburg in *John Brown's Body* is creative; the same subject matter in a history textbook is informative. The fundamental principles of good writing are common to both varieties. By far the greater part of our writing, however, is in-

formative; therefore we shall treat these fundamental principles chiefly as they relate to informative writing.

Writing the Composition.— In writing, the problems that involve the composition as a whole are: (1) how to begin, (2) how to develop the several phases of the matter clearly and emphatically and (3) how to stop. Your outline is the fundamental guide in solving these problems, but some particular advice may be of use. We shall not stress the formal terms, *introduction* and *conclusion,* as we want to avoid the implication that every com-

position must have a structurally independent introduction and conclusion. That is not necessary.

The characteristics of good writing are correctness, fluency and coherence. Of these, coherence is the only characteristic that applies to the composition as a whole. Since the starting point of writing is neither the words nor the sentences, but the subject matter, which implies the whole composition, we shall first consider the coherence of the composition as a whole, beginning with the subject.

THE SUBJECT.—The first step in organizing your composition is determining its subject. Do not confuse *subject* with *topic.* Filling stations, for example, may be taken as a topic; but before you can make it a subject you must decide what you will say about filling stations. You can make your subject "How To Make a Filling Station Pay," "Filling Station Architecture" or "The Filling Station as a Social Institution." Choosing a subject is often only narrowing a topic by deciding how you will treat it. This narrowing is governed by the time and space at your command, but these conditions really affect chiefly the fullness with which you may treat your subject. Narrow your topic so that you may focus your attention on what you want to say and what impressions you want your reader to get. When you have done this, you are still not ready to write until you have made your outline.

OUTLINES.—Making an outline is the process of deciding what you have to say about your subject. The best way to start is to make a sentence of which the subject is your topic and the predicate, a summation of your ideas about the topic, as: "Filling stations can be made to pay by honest dealing, careful attention to details and constant courtesy not overdone." The way to do this is to think through your material or ideas until you have discovered just what you want your reader to be impressed with. Remember, if you cannot write a sentence about your topic, you cannot write a composition about it. When you have made such a sentence, decide how you will develop each point in it by example, explanation, argument or whatever device seems best. This will show you what material you can use and what you must discard. You will always know more about your topic than will be relevant to your subject, and you must decide what is irrelevant, and be willing to leave it out. Do not try to say everything at once. Stick to your point. The outline will tell you what that point is and how you can make it. It does not matter what form you use in writing your outline, but it is best that every element in it be a sentence. Topics without predicates generally mean that we do not know what we are to say about them; but they always deceive us into thinking that we do.

Never allow yourself to believe that you cannot make or cannot follow an outline. An outline is only the record of your thinking through your subject. If you cannot think through it, you cannot write about it. It is the thinking that is hard, not the writing. You cannot write until you know what you are going to say, and making the outline is the process of deciding what to say. The next thing to do is to say it, nothing more and nothing less. You are now ready to start to write with good assurance that your thought, at least, will be coherent.

How To Begin.—Obviously, the place to begin is at the beginning. The inexperienced writer is afraid to begin simply and directly. Apparently he wants to back into his subject or to creep up on it through tedious and indirect byways. Many compositions are improved by omitting the first paragraph.

Tell your reader what you wish to say, so that he will understand your object and be interested in how you are to accomplish it. No one is interested in puzzling over involved statements. In all your writing remember that your reader is not a mind reader; that what is perfectly clear to you after you have thought long enough upon a subject to write about it, is utterly unknown to him. He does not know, for instance, what your title means to you until you have told him, and if you do not tell him quickly, he will lose interest and stop reading. He must know in a general way, but clearly, the point you intend to make, if he is to understand the elements in its development and to remember them clearly enough to be left with a vigorous impression at the end. It is hard enough to "put Humpty Dumpty together again" if you saw him before his fall; if you never saw him whole, it is practically impossible. All this does not mean that you should begin

bluntly, but even a blunt beginning is ever so much better than a hesitating or a foggy one.

It is not necessary to begin with the theme sentence that stands at the beginning of your outline. It is often a cumbersome, unwieldy sentence, and serviceable to you only because it sums up your thought. The content of that sentence, however, must be expressed at the beginning of your composition. Sometimes it will be simple and compact enough to use almost as it stands. Lytton Strachey begins his essay on Gibbon with the sentence: "Happiness is the word that immediately rises to the mind at the thought of Edward Gibbon." Everything in the essay explains, expands and enforces this idea. More often you will require a paragraph to state the content of that sentence clearly and interestingly.

Arousing Interest.—Use your beginning to arouse interest, as well as to point the way. If you can link your subject matter with something very familiar to the reader, do so; but do not allow your allusion to grow into a little essay of its own. Perhaps your idea conflicts with some well-established belief, such as that human nature does not change; present that conflict, but only with the purpose of arousing interest in your proposition. Do not allow yourself to become involved in an argument outside the point you must make. Sometimes— and this is particularly true of speeches—your best beginning will be an anecdote or an experience that dramatizes your point. Such a story should be short, vivid and directly to

the point, not dragged in as in the ordinary after-dinner speech. There are many ways of beginning, but always the purpose is: first, to tell the reader what you intend to do; second, to arouse his interest in how you are to do it. The amount of introductory material that you can use is limited sharply by the amount of space at your command. Obviously you do not want to take nearly as much space to state your point as you do to explain, develop and enforce it.

How To End.—The chief difficulty about the end of a composition is recognizing it. Many writers, and particularly many speakers, seem not to know when they have said all they intended to say. When you have covered your material and made your point, stop. Do not worry it; do not ruin your climax with repetitions, apologies or irrelevant rhetoric. Particularly, if you have come to an effective and obvious stopping place, do not think that you must write a conclusion. The end of your composition should enforce the whole idea, but it will often do this without a formal conclusion. In an argument it is well to sum up briefly the evidence by which you have supported your contention; but even then, as always, your conclusion should be brief. The arrangement of your material, which you decided upon before you ever started to write, will show you when you have come to the end. Compositions are ruined more often at the beginning and the end than at other points—simply because people are not willing to begin at the beginning and stop when they are through.

IMPORTANCE OF CORRECT ENGLISH

An extensive knowledge of the exact meanings of English words accompanies outstanding success in this country more often than any other single characteristic. It seems to be true that a large vocabulary is typical of successful individuals.

—Johnson O'Connor,
in *The Atlantic Monthly.*

Experts at Stevens Institute recently studied the characteristics of a large group of successful Americans. What had they in common that would explain their common success? The answer was: a large vocabulary, a gift of using words accurately and forcibly. Big business executives have this faculty to a greater degree than college professors!

Language makes our complicated civilization possible, and the more the student knows about language the better he will be fitted to win for himself a high place in life. Language is always useful, in all forms of work and play. The person who has a mind well stocked with words, who can readily choose the right word to express his meaning and who is gifted with the ability to use language that unfolds beautiful pictures and striking sentiments is admired and respected wherever he goes. The possession of a large and accurate vocabulary makes literature more enjoyable, a hobby more fascinating, friendship

more interesting and all of life more satisfying, for it gives a man the power to understand what he reads and hears and to express more accurately and forcefully what he himself thinks.

Many people are profoundly unconscious of the vital need of words and of the continual reliance upon them to carry on even the business of life, to say nothing of its intellectual pleasures. They are content with a pitifully scanty list of words, seldom expressing exactly what they mean. Too often we hear speech filled with trite phrases and coarse, inappropriate slang, speech in which the same terms are used to express sharply contrasting ideas, shallow and surging feelings. Swell, lousy, awful, fierce and lovely are for some the stock of adjectives drawn upon to describe even the deepest emotion and the loftiest aspiration.

Language a Tool.—Words are merely the names for ideas, feelings and things; tools by which to express oneself to others. But how often some opportunity is lost, some great experience withheld, some wrong inflicted because the right tool was not used. To have power with words, one must know how and when to use them and how to pronounce them correctly.

Every day brings new experiences that test your ability to understand, to organize and to communicate to others your reactions. Without words you are helpless. Language, then, should be considered a tool, highly complicated and very efficient when correctly used. It can become hard, shining, sharp steel—or it can be soft, dull lead. To keep it sharp and efficient it must never be carelessly used or neglected.

So important is this power with words that it makes those who possess it distinguished and outstanding among their fellows. A man is known by his vocabulary and the use he

the same, yet what a distance lies between them! Think of the dictionary not as a dull mechanical thing but as one of the greatest achievements of mankind, a whole living, throbbing language imprisoned in a single book! When rightly used the dictionary may be fascinating, exciting, even inspiring. You need not be a slave to it. Often the context of a passage will indicate the meaning of a new word and even give a better understanding of its shade of meaning than the dictionary; but to pronounce this word correctly and make it a part of your active vocabulary, you will find the dictionary an invaluable aid.

gether into one. As a result the grammar was greatly simplified, inflections and declensions were dropped and in many cases there were two words of the same meaning—a plain Germanic word and a fancy Latin word for the same thing, as pig and pork, calf and veal. Gradually these words have come to have slightly different meanings, pig and calf referring to the living animals, pork and veal to their flesh, respectively.

Through the ages English has been continually enriched by the addition of new words, some invented to supply a particular technical need, such as *rayon;* others borrowed from foreign languages—*chauffeur, pajamas, seersucker.* The histories of the following words, even as they are given in an unabridged dictionary, are highly interesting: *artesian, bootlegger, calico, cereal, derrick, fad, meander, panic, shrapnel, sofa, tweed, vaudeville, zeppelin.*

A knowledge of such origins helps in the choice of a particularly applicable word and in an understanding of the two sorts of meanings inherent in many words—the one definitely expressed and the other implied or suggested. The first is the *denoted* meaning and is actual, factual, precise; the second is *connoted* and is figurative and picturesque. Some words have both kinds of meaning; some have only a denoted meaning. *Residence* has not the figurative, connotative and emotional value of *home. Country* has the definite meaning of a certain section of territory but also all the implications of patriotism, love and enthusiasm suggested by the phrase "my country." Likewise *fatherland* means infinitely more than *nation; village,* more than *town;* and *love,* more than *affection.*

Good Usage.—Involving as it does an understanding of the constant evolution of language, caused by changing customs and interests, good usage cannot be memorized from a dictionary, grammar or even a book on the subject. A few rules may serve as guideposts, but good usage cannot be learned from a few sentences. For best results look up a word in an unabridged dictionary and examine the quotations given there to see how the great masters of English have used the word.

Except in realistic dialect avoid certain classes of words; they include: *localisms*—I reckon [suppose], sunup [sunrise], tuckered [tired] out, right smart of [large amount of], some [very] chilly; *vulgarisms*—ain't [am not], might of [have] been, hadn't ought [ought not], must of [have], most [almost] everybody; *improprieties*—leave us be [let us alone], the balance [rest] of the morning, an invite [invitation], real [really] pleasant; *slang terms*—except in rare, colorful instances; *colloquialisms*—anyhow [at any rate], quite [rather] warm, right away [at once], handy [skilful], a nice [pleasant] time; *pretentious and affected terms*—fistic encounter [fist fight], tonsorial parlor [barber shop], culinary department [kitchen]; also *foreign terms*—de trop [superfluous], cuisine [cookery], sub rosa [very con-

METROPOLITAN MUSEUM OF ART

LEAF FROM A MANUSCRIPT of Dioscorides, thirteenth century, gives a recipe for medicine.

makes of it. Keats, for example, is world-famous because his word images defined his own magical thinking and highly developed sense impression. Similarly in prose, a practical, simple, utilitarian style defines Franklin in the same manner that a graceful, fanciful and intriguing style points to Stevenson.

A vocabulary should be large enough to be adapted to any occasion and to any hearer or reader. An amusing story by O. Henry well illustrates this point. A little girl in a newspaper office asked the literary editor to tell her the story of Jack, the Giant Killer. He told the story but after he had finished she asked again if he would please now tell her the story of Jack. The sports editor also tried to tell the story, but still she could not understand. Then the man who knew all about railroads recited the nursery tale in the language of railway transportation; but no one in the newspaper office could tell the story in a way that would interest and reach a child.

How To Use the Dictionary.—When trying to find the exact word to express fully the thought in mind, turn to the dictionary and see how many words are given there to express the varied shades of meaning suggested by the main idea. English, because it has inherited words from both the Germanic and Romance tongues, is particularly rich in them and therefore great care is necessary in selecting just the right word. *Home* for instance is Germanic in origin and *domicile* Latin or Romance and while in fact they mean

For those interested in language itself—how it came to be, how meanings changed, why one word has several meanings and many words mean almost the same thing; why the spelling is as it is and how it is affected by pronunciation, why new words are added and others become obsolete—for these people the dictionary needs no recommendation. The origin of a word gives a valuable clue to its meaning and to its imagery or picture-making quality. The science that treats of root words and original meanings is called *etymology* and it can be intensely interesting. English boasts a particularly rich heritage. A few English words are of Celtic origin, contributed by the people inhabiting Britain before the coming of the Romans. A few others, such as *camp* and *street* and *mile,* were left by the Romans themselves. When the Angles and the Saxons overran the land, they incorporated into their own language these Celtic and Latin words. The Danish invasion added still other words—*by* (which meant town and is now found as a suffix in town names) and perhaps the adjective *same.* When the Normans conquered England in 1066, the English language was principally Germanic with only the few Celtic words and the few Latin words that had been left by Caesar's soldiers and by the Latin-speaking missionaries and priests. The Normans brought with them their French tongue that actually was only a Latin dialect. Neither Anglo-Saxon nor French was able to absorb the other and the two became welded to-

fidentially], *nil admirari* [no enthusiasms], or *Zeitgeist* [spirit of the age]. Except when one is writing for a special group of readers, difficult technical terms like *tort, metabolism* and *isothermic* are out of place and may not be understood.

Words in Use.—Words are of little value unless used with exactness in well-made sentences giving form to a complete idea or thought. In speech, attention must be paid to correct pronunciation so that a single mispronounced word will not detract from the thought. It is a joy to listen to a speaker whose well-constructed sentences move easily from thought to thought or to read a passage that is fluent and clear. No author or speaker is at his best until he has gained complete mastery of his technique, a complete knowledge of the uses of words.

Literature, which is the printed or "frozen" language, is much more than a succession of words; but the words themselves must be completely understood before the meaning of the whole can be grasped. An academic course entirely devoted to the study of Shakespeare's use of words does not destroy appreciation of his poetical qualities, great dramatic skill and amazing knowledge of human nature but gives a truer understanding and enjoyment not only of Shakespeare's plays but of English literature as a whole.

In oratory, debate and every other type of speech-making, a particular effort must be made for clarity and simplicity of sentence structure, because the listener must understand at once or not at all. He cannot re-read or stop to figure out eccentricities of style. A speaker should choose his words with care, keeping always in mind what he wants to say and to whom he is to say it. Words in themselves are important, but it is the use a man makes of them that distinguishes him.

How To Correct Errors.—Correct speech is not a trifle to be easily and quickly acquired. Facility and accuracy come only at the price of constant attention and care. Never be satisfied with communicating thought in a crude approximation of your real meaning, followed by "Oh, you know what I mean!" when you cannot find the words for what you wish to say. A determined attempt to refrain from this form of mental laziness is the best insurance against slovenly speech.

In general the errors made by most people of average intelligence are few and readily corrected. Reading the masterpieces of literature, studying the words and their organization into sentences, as well as the thought, is excellent practice. Give conscious daily attention not only to your own speech but to the speech of others. A man's speech is judged by the worst he does—not by the best. If you wish to use words with correctness and effectiveness on occasion, you must always do so.

A list of words and phrases frequently misused is given below. Study and practice a bothersome word in its correct sense again and again until it is firmly fixed in mind. It will be a study rich in rewards, for language is a storehouse of history and knowledge that offers to the treasure hunter a fortune more fabulous than that of Midas.

WORDS AND PHRASES OFTEN MISUSED

Ability, Capacity. Ability is the power of doing; capacity the faculty of receiving. The ability is in me to do him good. Men's capacities have never been measured.

Abortive means premature, not brought to completion. A plan or an effort but not an act may be abortive.

About should not be used instead of almost. The day is almost [not *about*] gone.

Above, an adverb or preposition, should not be used as an adjective. Say, "The foregoing [not *above*] statement is true"; or "The statement that appears above is true."

Accept, Except. Accept means receive; except means exclude.

Accidently is not a word; the correct form is accidentally.

Accompanied by, Accompanied with. A man is accompanied by his dog; his remark may be accompanied with a grimace.

Ad. Avoid using this abbreviation for advertisement in formal writing and speaking.

Adapted to, for, from. A play is adapted for children; adapted to the taste of children; and may be adapted from a story for children.

Addicted to, Subject to. Addicted to means strongly disposed to; said of a habit or indulgence. Do not confuse with the phrase, subject to, which means exposed to some agency. A man may be addicted to opium, but subject to attacks of rheumatism.

Administer should not be used in the sense of deal. We deal blows; we administer medicine, oaths of office, affairs of state and the like.

Affect, Effect. Affect means influence or pretend; effect means bring about; as: He affected intoxication and affected the audience strongly. I shall effect a reform.

Aggravate means to make worse or to increase in intensity. Say, "The climate aggravates the disease." "His conduct annoys [not *aggravates*] me."

Agree with, Agree to. We agree with a person but agree to a bargain.

Ain't is an indiscriminate contraction for are not, am not and is not. It should not be used except in writing dialect.

Allow is frequently misused for think. Say, "I think [not *allow*] that I shall go to town."

All-around is not recognized by good usage; all-round is the correct expression.

All the, as in all the farther, all the higher, all the faster and similar expressions, should not be used for as far as. Say, "This is as far as [not *all the farther*] I can go." All the, with an adverb, means by that amount, just so much; as: Climbing the hill was all the more difficult because the snow was deep.

Allusion, Illusion. Allusion means a reference; illusion means a deceptive appearance; as a Biblical allusion; an optical illusion.

Alone, Only. That is alone which is unaccompanied; that is only of which there is no other. "He suffered alone" means that no one was with him. "Only he suffered" means that no other person suffered.

Alongside means by the side of, close to, near to. Do not use the preposition, of, after alongside. The ship came alongside [not *alongside of*] the wharf.

Already, All ready. Already means by this time or beforehand; all ready means wholly ready; as: I have already invited him. Dinner is all ready. We are all ready for dinner.

Alright is not a word; use the two words, *all right.*

Alternative should not be used when you refer to more than two things, as in a series. The expression, "He had this alternative left to him," presents a choice between two possibilities.

Altogether, All together. Altogether means wholly, entirely; all together means collectively, in a group; as: He is altogether honest. The king sent the people all together into exile.

Amateur should not be used to mean one who is new or unskilled at a business, a novice. An amateur may be skilled in something he likes but does not pursue as a business; as: He is an amateur photographer.

Anxious means concerned or worried, but not eager. To say, "I am anxious for your safety," is correct; but say, "I am eager [not *anxious*] to hear this concert."

Anybody, Anyone, Anything are singular forms and should always be referred to by singular pronouns, as: Anybody can do as he pleases. Anyone is at his best here.

Anybody else's, Anybody's else. Usage favors the first form, which is correct according to analogy of similar cases that throw the *'s* to the last word of a unified expression, generally nouns in apposition.

Anyplace is not a word; use the two words, *any place.*

Appreciate means to rate at its true value. In such an expression as, "I appreciate your services highly," the adverb, highly, is superfluous, not needed.

Apt, Likely, Liable. Apt means fit; likely means probable; liable suggests unpleasant probability; as: She expressed herself in apt and gracious words. It is likely that we cannot go. If he exposes himself to the weather, he is liable to contract a cold.

As—as, so—as. The first form is correct in affirmative, and the second in negative, propositions; as: We are as wise as our teachers. I am not so young as I used to be.

As I take it is a colloquial expression. Say instead, "As I understand it," or "As it seems to me."

As though is often used incorrectly for as if. Say, "He walked as if he were lame." If the ellipsis is supplied it is easy to see why this is correct—He walked as (he would walk) if [not *though*] he were lame.

Audience is not correct when you mean spectators. An audience listens; spectators see what occurs; as: The preacher had a good audience. Many spectators were at the ball game.

Auto is an abbreviation not desirable in formal writing.

Avocation, Vocation. One's regular work is his vocation; his hobby is his avocation; as: His vocation was teaching; his avocation, collecting antiques.

Avoid is often used incorrectly for prevent. Say, "He will receive no increase in pay if I can prevent [not *avoid*] it."

Aware of, Conscious of. We are aware of a fact, but conscious of our feelings.

Awful, Awfully should not be used as intensives or for supposed force; awful means that which inspires awe, as: The awful mysteries of the world unseen.

Bad, Badly. Badly should not be used for very much or for bad. Say, "I need money very much [not *badly*]"; "I feel bad [not *badly*]."

Balance means the excess of one thing over another and should not be used to mean remainder or what is left. It is correct to say, "He has a large balance (excess of credits over debits) in the bank." "We ate what was left [not *the balance*] of the cake."

Bank on, Take stock in are colloquial phrases and should not be used in the sense of rely upon, trust in, receive as trustworthy or confidently expect. Say, "I rely upon [not *bank on*] your co-operation." "I trust in [not *take stock in*] the new plan."

Because should not be used for the fact that. Say, "The fact that [not *because*] he is absent is no reason why we should not proceed."

Been to is incorrect. Say, "I have been in [not *to*] New York," or "I went to New York." You go to but cannot be to a place.

Begin, Commence, Inaugurate, Initiate vary in meaning; as: We begin the day with breakfast; we commence important work; we inaugurate a campaign; we initiate a policy.

Beside, Besides. Beside means by, near; besides means in addition to, moreover; as: The tree stands beside the house. I have more besides this. She was tardy; besides, she was insolent.

Between is used only of two persons or things; it should not be confused with among, which is used of more than two; as: Between you and me it is understood; among all our friends it is an open secret.

Blame it on is a vulgarism used incorrectly to mean accuse or suspect. Say, "He accuses, suspects or blames [not *blames it on*] me."

Both alike is redundant (that is, has an unnecessary word). In such expressions as: They are both alike; the two boys both have blue eyes, the word *both* should be omitted.

Bran new is often used incorrectly for brand new.

Bring, Fetch, Take. Bring means convey to this point, but is often confused with take; fetch means go and bring; take, remove from here or elsewhere to another place; as: Bring me your books; take these to your teacher. Fetch the racquets from the house.

Bust, Busted are vulgar terms for burst. Say, "The balloon burst." "The bank failed."

But what is incorrectly used to mean that. "I know nothing but what you told me," is correct; but say, "I do not doubt that [not *but what*] he will succeed."

Calculate is often vulgarly used for think or suppose. To calculate means to arrive at or reckon by a mathematical process; as: We calculate costs or the distance from earth to moon. We think that it will rain.

Caliber means the diameter of a body, especially of the hollow inside a cylinder. Figuratively it means capacity of mind. Say, "He has a mind of great caliber"; but "His work is of high order [not *caliber*]."

Can, May are two forms often misused. Can suggests power or ability; may, permission. "Can I take your place?" means "Am I able to do it?" "May I take your place?" requests permission.

Cannot help but is a confusion of two phrases, can but and cannot help. Say, "I can but believe you" or "I cannot help believing you"; never "I cannot help but believe you."

Case, Instance. We note the case (circumstances) of Mr. Jones; we refer to a special instance (example) of need in his experience.

Caused by should be used only to refer definitely to a noun. Say, "His disappointment was caused by the lateness of the train." It is incorrect to say, "He was disappointed, caused by the lateness of the train." The noun, disappointment, should be used instead of the verb, disappointed. Then the word *caused* will have a definite reference.

Censor, Censure have different meanings; to censor is to remove anything objectionable from written, printed or photographed material; to censure is to criticize harshly.

Character, Reputation. One's character is what he really is; one's reputation is what people think and say of him. To have a good character and a poor reputation, or vice versa, is possible but not likely.

Charge, meaning to accuse, takes the preposition, with; as: They charged him with [not *of*] many crimes.

Claim means to demand, as one's due. Say, "I claim my right." "He asserts [not *claims*] that he is your brother."

Clerk is not a verb. Say, "John is a clerk [not John *clerks*] for Smith & Co."

Compare to, Compare with vary in meaning. We compare a strong man to an oak; we compare one city with another.

Complected, Complexioned are dissimilar in meaning. Complected refers to complex weaving; complexioned to the type of complexion, as, light complexioned.

Congregate together is a redundant expression, as the words mean the same thing. In such expressions as: "A large crowd congregated together," the word *together* should be omitted.

Considerable is not an adverb. Say, "He has improved considerably [not *considerable*]."

Continual, Continuous have similar but different meanings; continual means frequently repeated; continuous means uninterrupted, without break as to time and space and is the stronger word. Thus we may say that the flow of a stream is continuous; that the clanging of a bell is continual; that the continual showers drenched the ground.

Convict, Convince. Convict is always used of something wrong, and refers to an outer condition. Say, "The man was convicted of the crime." Convince refers to inner judgment and may be used of either right or wrong. Say, "I am convinced that you are right and that he is wrong."

Correspond to, Correspond with. One act or quality corresponds to another. We correspond with another when we exchange letters with him.

Could of is an illiterate form arising from slovenly pronunciation. The correct expression is could have; so also with may have must have, would have [not *may of, must of, would of*].

Council, Counsel. A council is an assembly or body of people gathered for consultation; counsel means advice, usually given by a counselor (attorney); or, as a verb, to give advice.

Couple means a pair or mates; as: The young couple is living on the hill. A couple of hours, a couple of loaves and other such expressions are incorrect.

Credible, Creditable. Credible means worthy of belief; as, "Dr. Cook's story is not credible." Creditable means worthy; as, "He made a creditable address."

Cute is used as slang; choose a word in good usage such as pretty, vivacious, lively, amusing, dainty, piquant, engaging or some other word of more definite meaning than cute.

Data is the plural of datum, which is seldom used. Compare stratum, strata; erratum, errata.

Definite, Definitive differ widely in meaning. Definite means specific; definitive means final; as: A definite (specific) answer was given, but it was not definitive (final).

Demean is often inaccurately used for bemean (to lower), but means to behave oneself; as: He demeaned himself properly.

Depot, Station are regarded in America as interchangeable; but in England a depot is a place where goods or stores are kept; and the place where a railway train stops for passengers is called a station.

Die of. Patients die of [not *with* or *from*] a disease.

Differ from, with. One thing differs from another in appearance; a person differs with another in opinion.

Different from is preferred to different than. Than is a conjunction; the idea of separation implied by different calls for the preposition rather than a word of comparison.

Directly should not be used to mean as soon as. Say, "We left directly (meaning immediately) after they came"; but not "Directly they came we left."

Disinterested, Uninterested. Disinterested means impartial; uninterested means lacking interest.

Disremember is provincial for forget and should not be used.

Donate as a verb is not approved by all authorities; give and present are better words to use.

Done is a gross error when used as the past tense of do. Say, "I did [never *done*] it."

Done, Finished. These words do not mean the same. Say, "The job was well done for the house is now finished." Done means performed; finished means completed.

Don't is the contraction of do not; never use it instead of does not, for which the contraction is doesn't. Avoid using contractions in formal writing.

Don't think. Say, "I think it will not rain" [not "I *don't think* it will rain]."

Double negatives in English are commonly used but are gross errors. Say, "I didn't know anything [not *nothing*] about it." "I have [not *haven't*] never been there."

Drownded is not a word—say drowned.

Due, Owing. Due means what ought to be paid; as: "The note is due next month." Owing means the same as on account of; as: "It was owing to his daring that the insurrection was checked."

Each is singular in number and should be used with a singular noun and verb. Say, "Each comes in his [not *their*] turn."

Each other, One another. The first phrase refers to only two; the second, to more than two.

E'er, e'en, ne'er, o'er and simliar contractions are legitimate in verse but should not be used in prose.

Elegant means refined, in good taste. Avoid it as a much misused and overused word.

Emigrant, Immigrant are often confused. Emigrants are people going out of a country; immigrants are people coming into a country.

Endorse or **Indorse.** Say, "Endorse or indorse a note" [not *endorse on the back of*], as the word endorse means to write upon the back of. Endorse is the spelling now more common in American usage.

Equally as well. The word *as* is unnecessary. Say, "Equally well."

Etc., an abbreviation for the Latin *et cetera,* means: and other (things). As *et* means and, the phrase and etc. is a repetition and incorrect. Do not write ect.; the correct abbreviation is etc.; but do not use it in formal writing.

Every takes a verb in the singular number; as: Every man was at his post.

Everyone, Everybody, Everything are words of singular number and should always be referred to by singular pronouns; as: Everyone should mind his own business. Everybody has his troubles. Everything is in its place.

Evidence, Testimony, Proof. Evidence is anything that tends to convince; testimony is evidence given by witnesses; proof is whatever establishes the truth of a proposition.

Except, Unless. Except should not be used for unless. Say, "Unless [not *except*] I am delayed, I shall arrive at three."

Existing truths should always be expressed in the present tense. Say, "Galileo taught that the world is [not *was*] round."

Expect refers only to the future and should not be used to mean think or suppose. Say, "I think [not *expect*] I was there at three o'clock." "I suppose [not *expect*] you had a pleasant time yesterday."

Fail is not correctly used unless there is an effort to succeed. He failed to come means that he tried to come but could not—not that he did not come.

Few and **a few** differ in meaning. To say, "Few persons like Mr. Jones," means that he is generally disliked; but the statement, "A few persons like him," means that he has some friends.

Fine should be used sparingly as an adjective and never as an adverb. Choose a more exact and less common word.

Firstly is not the approved form; first is preferred as both adjective and adverb.

First-rate may be correctly used as an adjective, as: He has a first-rate place. The expression, "He did first-rate," is incorrect.

Fix. Be sure that you intend to convey the idea of fastening firmly when you use the word *fix;* it should not be used to mean repair, arrange or set up. Say, "He stopped to repair [not *fix*] the machine"; but "The built-in furniture was fixed to the wall."

Former, Latter, unless followed by a noun (as, the former ruler or the latter member), are avoided in formal English and should never be used except to refer to one of *two.*

Funny means humorous, mirthful and should not be used in the colloquial sense to describe something strange or curious.

Get means to obtain by voluntary effort; it does not signify mere possession. Say, "I have not a cent [not I have not *got* a cent]."

Get over is often incorrectly used for survive, recover or refute. Say, "He recovered from [not *got over*] the disease." "He refuted [not *got over*] the statement."

Get to go is a common expression in some parts of America but should be avoided. Say, "I was unable to go," or "I was prevented from going [not I did not *get to go*]."

Give in the passive must be used carefully. Say "He received [not *was given*] a present." It is all right to say "The present was given."

Go and has a legitimate and effective use, as in the phrase, "Go thou and do likewise"; but it should not be used when only one action is meant. Say, "He ran [not *went and ran*] away."

Good deal, Great deal are correct expressions, as: I have walked a great deal. The boy liked play a good deal better than school.

Good, Well. Good should not be used as an adverb. Say, "You sang well [not *good*]." "Did you sleep well [not *good*] last night?" Note that *well* is an adjective in the sense of healthy.

Guess expresses conjecture; it should not be used for think, suppose or expect. Say, "I was to guess in which hand he held the money"; but "I think [not *guess*] I shall go."

Had better, Had best, Had rather are grammatical and fully approved by good usage. Had better is preferable to would better; but one may use had best or would best, had rather or would rather with equal correctness. Say, "You had better not stay long." "They had best (or would best) attempt no violence." "I had rather (or would rather) go than stay."

Had of is illiterate. Say, "I wish I had [not *had of*] known about it."

Had ought is incorrect; no form of the verb to have can be correctly used as an auxiliary with ought. Use should or ought not. Say,

"He should not [not *hadn't ought to*] have gone."

Hain't is a dialect vulgarism; there is no such contraction for have not or has not.

Hanged, Hung. Hanged is the correst past tense and past participle of hang, meaning put to death by hanging. Say, "He was hanged on the gallows." Hung is the correct past tense for other meanings of the verb hang; as: The pictures were hung.

Healthy, Healthful are not interchangeable. A man in good health is healthy; a good climate is healthful.

Help should not be followed by the word *but* when used in the sense of avoid; it should be followed by a gerund. Say, "I cannot help regretting [not *help but regret*] the change."

How should not be used for what or for the phrase, What did you say?

Human should not be used as a noun. Say, "The house was not fit for human beings [not *humans*] to occupy."

Hygienic, Sanitary. Both words mean pertaining to health. Use hygienic when the condition is a matter of personal habits or rules; use sanitary when the condition is a matter of surroundings (as water or food supply or sewage disposal) or the relations of numbers of people.

If I were. This subjunctive form should be used in all cases in which the conditions are contrary to fact. Say, "If I were you (which I am not), I should go. "If I were a man (which I am not), I should practice law." Use the indicative in cases of uncertainty; as: If I was (meaning uncertainty) in town that day, I did not see you."

Imply, Infer. We imply a meaning in what we say; we infer a meaning from another's remark; as: My words implied confidence in him. I infer from what you say that you are pleased.

In, Into. Use in to signify resting in a place; use into to signify motion toward a place; as: He was standing with his hands in his pockets. I put my hands into my pockets. I came in an automobile. The stranger walked into the room.

Inaugurate means to induct into office or to make a ceremonious beginning, but should not be used in speaking of the simpler things of life or to mean commence or begin.

In back of is a vulgarism, though the similar expression, in front of, is approved. Say, "She sat behind [not *in back of*] me."

Infinitive, Split. The cleft or split infinitive (that is, having an adverb between its two parts) is avoided by careful writers. Say, "He was in a position to observe accurately [not *to accurately observe*]."

Ingenious, Ingenuous. A person is ingenious if he is clever, resourceful; he is ingenuous if he is open and candid.

Initiate suggests ceremonious form and should not be used instead of the word *begin.* Say, "The candidates were initiated into the lodge."

Inside of is an Americanism for the word *within* in time expressions. Say, "It will disappear within [not *inside of*] a week."

Instants, Instance. Instants means moments of time; instance means an example.

It's is the contraction of it is, and should not be written for the possessive, its.

Kind of a. The *a* is superfluous.

Later, Latter. Later means more late; latter means the second in a series of two. Do not use it to refer to the third or fourth of a series; say *last.*

Lead, Led. Led is the past tense, and lead is the present tense of the verb to lead.

Learn, Teach are often misused. To learn is to receive instruction; to teach is to give instruction. Say, "Will you teach [not *learn*] me my lesson?"

Leave, Let. Leave means to cause to remain, or to abandon; let means to permit, and requires the objective case. Say, "Leave your books here." "Leave the place at once." "Let him and me [not *he and I*] go."

Lend, Loan. Lend is a verb; loan a noun; as, I lend a man a dollar, and he receives the loan.

Less, Fewer. Less has to do with amount or quantity; fewer refers to the number of things or persons; as: He had less money and fewer clothes than he needed. Fewer people than usual attended the meeting.

Lie, Lay are often used incorrectly. To lie is neuter (intransitive) and designates a state; to lay is active (transitive) and denotes an action upon an object; it means cause to lie; as: A thing lies on the table. Someone lays it on the table. He lies buried with his fathers. We laid him in the tomb. In the same manner we say, "A thing lies by us until we bring it into use." "We lay it by for some future purpose."

Some confusion may arise from the fact that the word lay appears in both verbs—as the past tense of the intransitive verb, lie (principal parts: lie, lay, lain), and as the present tense of the transitive verb, lay (principal parts: lay, laid, laid), as illustrated by these sentences:

The book now lies on the table.	I now lay the book on the table.
Yesterday it lay on the table.	I laid it there last night.
It has lain there often before.	I have laid it there daily for some time.

Like, As. Like has a prepositional use; as is a conjunction. Say, "It looks as if [not *like*] it was caused by fire." "My brother looks like me." "He acted as if he were insane." "Do it as I do."

Literally. Do not use literally to mean figuratively. Say, "I was figuratively [not *literally*] tickled to death."

Locate should not be used to mean settle; it is used transitively to mean fix or place in a position; as: He located a claim. They settled in Virginia.

Lose, Loose. Lose means to cease having; loose, as a verb, means to set free; and as an adjective, free, not bound.

Lose out should not be used in formal speech or writing; omit out.

Lot, Lots are too frequently used for a great many, a great deal or much. Say, "He had a great deal [not *lot*] of money left to him." "She looks much [not a *lot*] like her brother. The word *lots* means distinct parts or portions; as: He divided his land into lots.

Lunch is an authorized form as both noun and verb.

Mad should not be used for angry.

Majority, Plurality. In a loose sense, majority means the greater part; more strictly, it means the number by which votes cast for one candidate or measure exceed those cast by the opposition. A plurality is the excess of votes received by one candidate over his closest competitor. In an election A receives 500 votes; B, 400 votes; and C, 300 votes. A has a plurality of 100 but no majority.

Might of is a vulgarism for might have.

Monstrous means abnormal or deformed and should not be used to mean large or immense. Say, "It was a monstrous creature." "The crowd was enormous."

Most, Almost should not be used interchangeably. Say, "Most of my friends are artists." "Almost [not *most*] all members were present."

Much should not be used for very. Say, "My work is very [not *much*] different this year." "She was much [not *very*] pleased."

Mutual, Common. We may have friends in common, but the best modern usage forbids the expression, mutual friends. We may have mutual (reciprocal) plans or feelings, such as hatreds or admirations.

My being is the correct form; the possessive case is required with the gerund. Say, "He did not know of my [not *me*] being there." "There is little chance of his [not *him*] winning the game."

Myself should not be used for I. Say, "John and I [not *myself*] are friends."

Near should not be used for nearly. Say, "He was not nearly [not *near*] to unselfish as his brother."

Neglect, Negligence. Neglect is a distinct act; negligence is a habit.

Neither—nor, Not—or. Say, "Neither the man whom his associates had suspected nor [not *or*] the one whom the police had arrested was the criminal." "She could not paint a good picture or [not *nor*] play the violin well."

Nice is a generally misused word; it means delicate, discriminating, fastidious; as: the works of a watch show nice construction. A man may be nice in his manners. The word should not be used to mean agreeable or charming; to say, "I had a nice time," is colloquial.

Nicely should not be used to mean well. Say, "The sick man is doing well [not *nicely*]."

Not as I know of is incorrect. Say, "Not that I know of."

Notorious, Famous. The first implies an undesirable quality; the second, something desirable or worthy. Say, "He was a notorious brigand." "She was famous for her charities."

Noways is incorrectly used for nowise. Say. "He was nowise [not *noways*] to blame."

Nowhere near is a vulgar expression for not nearly.

Nowheres is the vulgar form for nowhere.

O, Oh. Of these interjections, O is used with a noun in direct address and is not separated from the noun by punctuation; Oh, more commonly used, is followed by a comma or an exclamation point; as: Hear, O king, what thy servants would say. Oh, dear!

Observance, Observation. Observance means the practice of observing, as a custom; observation means any act of seeing or noting.

Of should not be used for have; the correct forms are: should have, may have, ought to have.

Off of. In most cases of is superfluous. Say, "The man fell off [not *off of*] the roof."

O.K. means all right, but is a hackneyed expression.

Only is often misplaced; it should immediately precede the word or expression that it limits. Say, "I have only [not *only have*] three dollars." "She sang only [not *only sang*] for us." "She only sang" would mean she did nothing else but sing.

Onto is colloquial. Say, "I get on [not *onto*] a horse"; but "They passed on to (two words) the next gallery."

Orate is an unauthorized form commonly used to mean to give an oration.

Over should not be used in the sense of more than. Say, "I have more than [not *over*] a hundred dollars." "The stick is more than [not *over*] a yard long."

Over with is a crude expression for over; omit with. Say, "Their troubles were over [not *over with*]."

Pants. Trousers is the approved term in correct usage. Pants (from pantaloons) has found colloquial and commercial acceptance.

Part, Portion. A part of a thing is any single section; a portion is an allotted part.

Partake does not apply to eating a meal alone, as the word means to take or share with another.

Partially means with partiality; also it is sometimes used in the sense of partly; as: I have only partially examined the paper.

Participles are not correctly used with conjunctions. Use the complete verb not the participle. Say: "When it is found [not *when found*], make a note of it."

Party applies only to a group of people, not to one person. If you mean an individual, say, "The person [not *party*] you sent to me arrived."

Patron means one who shows consideration or favor. A charity ball or the arts may have patrons, but the word is incorrectly substituted for customer.

Pellmell means mixed or mingled together, therefore the term cannot properly be applied to an individual. To say, "He rushed pellmell out of the house" is obviously wrong.

Per should be used only with Latin nouns, as *per diem, per annum.* With English nouns use *a*, as a day, a year or a pound. The only exception is in formulas and scientific phrases, like "revolutions per minute."

Phenomena is the plural of phenomenon. Say, "It was an interesting phenomenon [not *phenomena*]."

Phone is colloquial and should not be employed in formal writing. Use the complete word *telephone.*

Pled, a colloquial form, should not be used for pleaded. Say, "He pleaded for pardon."

Plenty, a noun, is not in good use as an adjective or adverb. "He had plenty of [not *plenty*] resources." "He had resources in plenty [not *resources plenty*]."

Posted should not be used in the sense of informed. Say, "He is a well-informed [not *well-posted*] man." "If I had been better informed [not *posted*], I could have passed the test."

Practical means related to actual use as opposed to the theoretical or ideal. Do not confuse with practicable, which means capable of being put into practice. A practical scheme (that is, valuable or sensible) may not be practicable until a better opportunity presents itself.

Presume means dare or presuppose and should not be used to mean think or believe. Say, "I may presume too much"; but "I think [not *presume*] he is right."

Preventive is the correct form [not *preventative*].

Principal, Principle. Principal as an adjective means chief or leading; as a noun, a sum of money or the chief official of a school; principle, always a noun, means element, general truth, uprightness; as: The principal of the school is a man of the highest principles; he teaches the principles of physics.

Privilege, Right. A privilege is a special advantage granted or conceded; a right is one's due; as: We grant many privileges, but we claim our rights.

Proof, Evidence. In a law court, proof is evidence sufficient to establish a fact; evidence is whatever is brought forward in an attempt to establish as a fact what has been asserted; as: The evidence against the prisoner was extensive, but hardly proof of guilt. In ordinary speech, the word *proof* is sometimes loosely used as a synonym for evidence.

Propose, Purpose. Propose means to put forward for discussion or consideration; purpose means intend; as: I purpose going to town to propose a plan to my business partner.

Proposition means a thing proposed; as: His proposition was accepted. Do not use loosely, as in the sentence: A berth in a sleeping car is a good proposition during a railway journey at night.

Proved, Proven. Scotch law has a verdict, "not proven." The word *proved* is correct in any other use.

Provided, Providing. Say, "I shall vote for him provided [not *providing*] he is a candidate."

Quite is used in the sense of fully, completely; as: I am quite satisfied; but do not say, "There was quite a crowd," or "I have quite a few friends."

Raise is often misused to mean rear or bring up. We raise chickens, but we rear children.

Rarely ever is a crude expression for rarely or hardly ever.

Real should not be used adverbially in the sense of very. Say, "I am really (or very) [not *real*] tired."

Reckon is provincial for think. Say, "I think or believe [not *reckon*] he will come soon."

Recommend should not be used as a noun; recommendation is the proper word. Say, "The teacher gave him a good recommendation [not *recommend*]."

Relatives, Relations. Say, "My mother and other relatives [not *relations*] are visiting me." "Friendly relations with neighbor nations should be cultivated."

Replace means restore to its place and should not be used in the sense of take the place of.

Respectful, Respectable, Respective differ greatly. He was respectful to his aunt, a respectable old woman, though their respective social positions (position belonging to each) were widely separated. Yours respectfully [not *respectively*] is correct as the complimentary closing of a letter.

Retire should be avoided in the sense of going to bed.

Reverend, as a title should not be used without the words *the* and *Mr., Dr.* or *Father.* The correct form is: The Reverend Mr. (Dr. or Father) Brown [not *Reverend Brown*]. This rule also applies to the title, Right Reverend.

Rise, Raise. Rise is an intransitive verb; raise is a transitive verb. I rise to go home. I raise vegetables. I raise the stone from the ground. Both words are used as nouns: raise only in the sense of an increase in pay as: He gave his servant a raise.

Same is no longer used as a pronoun except in legal documents. Say, "He saw her drop the purse and restored it [not *same* or *the same*] to her."

Scarcely should not be used with a negative.

Seldom ever is crude for seldom or hardly ever.

Set, Sit, like lie and lay, are often confused in their use. To set is both transitive and intransitive; to sit is intransitive. I set the hen, but she sits on her eggs, and is correctly called a sitting hen, though often incorrectly spoken of as a setting hen. The verbs are correctly used as follows: My dress sits well. We shall sit up, that is, not go to bed. Congress sits. We set down figures, but we sit down on the ground. We set a post, set glass, set milk, set the sails, set a broken bone, set a clock, set a price, set jewels, set an example. The sun sets, one sets out to go places, the current sets to the north; one sets forth or sets off; winter sets in.

Shall, Will are perhaps more commonly misused than are any other words in English. The rules with regard to the use of these words are: In declarative sentences, shall is used in the first person and will in the second and third persons to express simple futurity; as: I shall come. You will come. He will come. In questions, however, shall is used rather than will in the second person to indicate simple futurity; as: Shall you come? In the first and third person, will is the correct word; as: Will I come? Will he come? To say, "Shall I come?" would be to

ask permission to come. "Shall he come?" would be a request that he be allowed to come. In other cases, shall and will express purpose or determination on the part of the speaker—will in the first person and shall in the second and third persons.

Shape should not be used loosely to mean manner or condition. Say, "They executed the maneuvers expertly or in an expert manner [not *in good shape*]." "He is in good condition and thoroughly prepared [not *in good shape*] for the debate."

Should, Would in general follow the rules for shall and will. In clauses expressing a condition, should is used in all three persons. If I should try, I should succeed. If he should come, he would meet you. (Should here expresses a condition.) Should is also used in all three persons to express a sense of duty. He or I should come home early. Should here expresses duty.) Would is sometimes used to express a customary action; as: He would come up to the window to look out.

Show up is a vulgarism when used intransitively in the sense of appear, attend, come or be present; and when used transitively in the sense of show or expose.

Sight, usually with of, is colloquial and crude for many, much, a great deal; as: A great many [not a *sight of*] strawberries were shipped.

So is much used in a manner that is loose, vague and often unnecessary. As an intensive, so has been called the feminine demonstrative; as: I was so surprised. Say, "I was much surprised," or, "I was surprised." As a connective, the frequent use of so is the mark of a beginner.

Some should not be used as an adverb. Say, "She was somewhat [not *some*] better the next day." "He did some studying [not *studied some*] that night."

Somewheres is crude for somewhere; never add the *s.*

Speciality is an erroneous spelling of the word *specialty.*

Species, Specie. Species has the same form for both singular and plural and means a particular sort or kind of plant or animal, as: He discovered a new species of sunflower. Specie means money in coins. The exchange was in specie.

Splendid means brilliant and should not be used to refer to what is only ordinarily good or commonplace.

Stationary, Stationery. Stationary is an adjective meaning fixed; stationery is a noun meaning writing materials.

Statue, Stature, Statute. Statue means a carved or molded figure; stature means height; statute means a law.

Stimulant, Stimulus, Stimulation. Stimulant is a concrete element or force to rouse us; stimulus is any general influence with the same purpose; stimulation is the effect produced.

Stop is wrongly used for stay. We stop at the roadside; we stay with a friend or at a hotel.

Such is: (1) To be completed by that, rather than by so that, when a result clause follows; as: There was such a crowd that [not *so that*] he did not find his friends. (2) To be completed by as (rather than by that, who or which) when a relative clause follows; as: I shall accept such arrangements as [not *that*] may be made. He called upon such soldiers as [not *that*] would volunteer for this service to step forward.

Sunday should not be used as a verb. Say, "He spent Sunday [not *he Sundayed*] at home."

Superior than is not in good use; superior to is preferred.

Sure is frequently misused for surely. Say, "He will surely [not *sure*] be here."

Suspicion is not a verb, though so used in dialect. Use suspect instead; as, I suspect [not *suspicion*] him of misrepresenting things.

Swell used as an adjective is a vulgarism that should be avoided.

Take is a colloquialism when used for study. Say, "I studied [not *took*] Spanish and chemistry."

Take and is often unnecessary, sometimes crude or redundant. Say, "He sharpened [not *took and sharpened*] the ax."

Tend, in the sense to look after, takes a direct object without the preposition to. Attend, however, is followed by to. The grocer's assistant tends [not *tends to*] the shop. I shall attend to your wants in a moment.

That for So. Say, "He was so [not *that*] independent, he could not tolerate interference."

That there is incorrect for that. "I want that [not *that there*] box of berries."

Them should not be used as an adjective pronoun. Say, "Those [not *them*] boys are here."

Then is not an adjective. Say, "Then the President [not *the then President*] was Mr. Taft."

Thence is not used with the preposition, from, as it means from that place. Say, "He departed thence at noon."

These kind, Those sort violate agreement or concord; kind and sort are singular nouns and should be modified by singular adjectives. Say, "This kind or that sort is what I prefer."

This here is incorrect; omit the word *here.*

Those. Do not carelessly omit a relative clause after those. Faulty: He is one of those talebearers. Correct: He is one of those talebearers whom everybody dislikes.

Through is often misused in the sense of finished. Say, "I have finished [not *am through with*] my breakfast."

Till should not be carelessly misused for when. Say, "I had scarcely strapped on my skates when [not *till*] Henry fell through an air hole."

Transpire means to leak out, to become known; it should not be used to mean happen. To say, "It transpires that the couple had been married for a year" is correct.

Try and should not be used for try to. Say, "Try to come [not *try and come*]."

Two first, Two last are incorrect. Say, "The first two and the last two sentences were long."

Unique means the only one of its kind. We cannot correctly say, then, that something is "very unique."

Up. Do not use needlessly after such verbs as end, rest and settle.

Used to is the correct form [not *use to* or *usen't to*]. Say, "I used to live there." "You used to travel."

Verbal is misused for oral. He would not write her a note, but sent her an oral [not *verbal*] message. Verbal means in words; therefore both a note and an oral message are verbal.

Very should be accompanied by much when used with the past participle. He was very much [not *very*] pleased with his reception.

Wait on is a vulgarism for wait for. Say, "If I am not there, do not wait for [not *wait on*] me."

Want, Need. Want as a verb expresses both the desire for a thing and the fact that the thing is lacking; need expresses the necessity for a thing. A man may want an automobile, though he may not need one.

Want to should not be used in the sense of should or had better. You should [not *want to*] keep in good physical condition."

Wa'n't should not be used as a contraction for was not or were not except in writing dialect.

Ways is often incorrectly used for way. Say, "I walked a long way [not *ways*] with her."

When should not be used for that in such a sentence as: It was in the afternoon that [not *when*] the races began.

Where should not be used for that in such a sentence as: I see in the paper that [not *where*] our team lost the game.

Which should not be used for who or that in referring to persons. Say, "The friends who [not *which*] had loved him in his boyhood were still faithful to him."

While is often incorrectly used for although or and. Say, "Although [not *while*] I believe you are honest, I cannot vote for you." While means during the time that; as: while I was musing, the fire burned low.

Who. Do not use who in the objective case. Say, "Whom [not *who*] do you want to see?"

Win out is colloquial and should not be used in formal writing or speaking.

Without, Unless. Without is a preposition and should not be used to take the place of the connective, unless. Say, "I shall not go unless [not *without*] my father consents"; or "I shall not go without my father's consent."

Worse should not be used for more. Say, "I fear one thing more [not *worse*] than any other—fire.

Worst kind, Worst way are vulgarisms used in the sense of very much.

Would have should not be used for had in if clauses. Say, "If you had [not *would have*] spoken boldly, he would have granted your request."

Would of is a vulgarism for would have.

You was is incorrect. Use you were for both singular and plural.

Yourself is intensive or reflexive; do not use when the personal pronoun will suffice.

PUBLIC SPEAKING AND DEBATE

Differences between Spoken and Written Style.

—Though the writer and the public speaker have much in common, the processes of writing and speaking are quite different in nature. A good writing style may not be an effective speaking style. Spoken composition and written composition differ chiefly in the following respects:

(1) In speaking, the meaning must be instantly understood. Thought is carried through the ear, not through the eye as in writing. The hearer, therefore, must get the speaker's thought at the moment of utterance or not at all. There is no second chance. Because a speaker must make his thoughts readily and immediately understood, step by step, he must pay particular attention to such elements of composition as clearness, simplicity, conciseness, concreteness, comparison, restatement and illustration.

(2) In speaking, language is aided by voice and action. Meanings are conveyed not by words alone (as in writing) but also by the inflections of the speaker's voice and by expressive gestures.

(3) In speech composition organizing the material is more definitely in the foreground than in writing: main points are more obvious; connective words and phrases are more apparent.

(4) A speaking style demands the frequent use of the elements of personal address. The public speaker has a specific audience, the writer has not. Usually, a writer is impersonal, a speaker personal. Because a definite audience is present on an actual occasion, the speaker must adjust and adapt his discussion of a subject to the personal interests, desires, beliefs, motives and wants of that audience. To do this necessitates the frequent use of *we, our, us, you, your*.

(5) Spoken style requires greater sentence variety than written style. Sufficient variety in sentence length and form will make it easier for the hearer to follow the speaker's thought. Without variety there will be monotony, and monotony creates listlessness, disinterest, sleepiness and boredom. Sentences that are extremely long, complicated or involved should be avoided because an audience will not follow the thought to the end. Theodore Roosevelt and William Howard Taft were masters of the short sentence. Besides varying the length of sentences, a speaker should mingle declarative, imperative, exclamatory and interrogative sentences. Many a speaker's style suffers from a continuous use of declarative sentences. Direct questions add pointedness. A study of the speeches of Abraham Lincoln reveals a most effective use of questions. Variety and interest will be increased also by using balanced, periodic and, occasionally, loose sentences.

Fundamentals of the Speech Process.

—The spoken word holds an increasingly important place in our public and private life because it is man's most-used medium of expression and communication. Private speaking and public speaking have the same purposes of communication between fellow beings. A realization that public speaking is an enlargement and extension of the processes used in private speaking is an invaluable aid to one learning how to speak in public. It is like enlarging a picture. In the enlargement every detail has a little more significance; yet it is the same picture.

The speaker engaged in this process of communication in public is concerned with five fundamental factors. They are within him. They are his potential power. He cannot escape their use. These five essentials are: thought, emotion, language, voice,

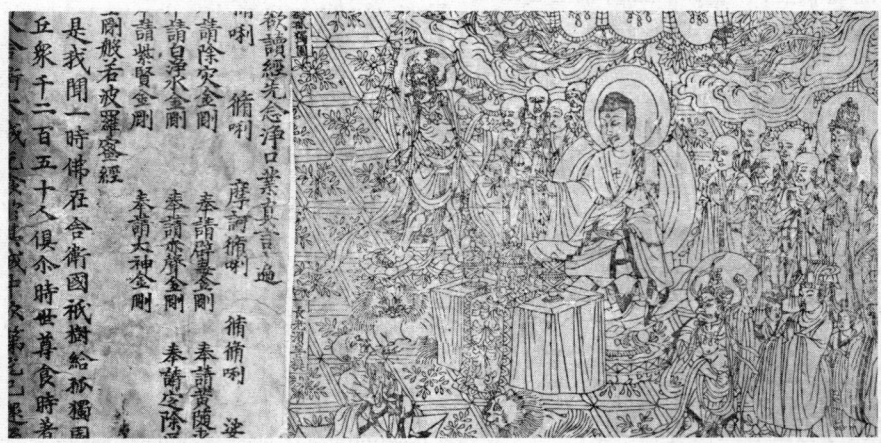

BRITISH MUSEUM PHOTOGRAPHIC SERVICE

DIAMOND SUTRA, Chinese version of Buddha's teachings, is oldest printed book (868 A.D.).

gestures. First of all a speaker is a thinker, a mind. Then he is an emotional being who can feel as well as think. While thinking of the reasons for peace, he can feel the horrors of war. He can likewise create these responses in his hearers because all human beings are fashioned after the same pattern of intellectual and emotional behavior. Language furnishes the symbols with which to shape and mold thoughts and emotions. Words become the speaker's tools. Here it is well to remember that simplicity in language is more to be desired than ornamentation. The speaker's voice and body should function as servants of mind and emotion. Through the medium of language they are constantly carrying messages from the speaker to his audience. Speaking effectively in public, then, becomes largely a matter of co-ordinating and developing these five fundamental factors. Successful speaking demands that they work together for good.

Lack of confidence on the part of a public speaker may be due to a lack of proper co-ordination of his powers. The five forces may not be working well, singly or collectively. The result is timidity, inhibitions, fear, stage fright, repressions. Repression enslaves a speaker, expression gives him freedom. A speaker who himself freezes up will never thaw out his audience.

Confidence can be built up in these specific ways: (1) By thinking positively, not negatively. Thinking "I can" instead of "I cannot." (2) By being thoroughly prepared to speak. (3) By thinking more of the subject, less of oneself. (4) By developing a keen sense of communication. (5) By controlling, not eliminating, nervousness.

Adjustment to the Speech Situation.

—The first factor to consider in a speech situation is the nature of the occasion that demands the speech. An unvarying rule of all speaking is that it must be carefully planned and adjusted to fit the occasion. Whether it be the high school assembly program on Friday, the pulpit on Sunday, the service club on Monday, the parent-teachers meeting on Tuesday, or the monthly meeting of the Community Welfare League on Wednesday—in every case the same vital question is pertinent—will the speech meet the requirements of the occasion? One must consider such things as, how the group has come together, the time limits of the meeting, who the other speakers on the program are, the formality or informality of the occasion.

The second factor is the audience. The presence of the audience is the reason for the speech. Audiences, therefore, must be analyzed. Consideration should be given to such matters as audience size, age, interest, prejudices, sex, fixed beliefs, impelling motives, social levels, occupations and wants. A speaker must ask: Will my audience be a mixed group with general interests or will it be a special group with concerted interests? Will it be conservative or radical? What will be its probable attitude toward me and my subject? Audience attitudes may be classified as interested, indifferent, opposed, hostile.

Building the Speech.

—The five essential steps involved in speech construction are: the purpose, the method, the material, the structure, the style.

Purpose.—Determining the exact purpose is a matter of first importance. Purposeless speaking will be ineffective because it will win no definite response. To secure a response from an audience is the general purpose of all public speaking. In fact, we are justified in classifying public speaking as a useful art because it can be used to attain definite ends. The definite purposes, or ends, are five in number: (1) to inform, (2) to stimulate, (3) to entertain, (4) to secure belief, (5) to induce action.

Method.—There are four methods of presenting a speech: the extemporaneous, the impromptu, the memory, the manuscript. By extemporaneous speaking, we mean that the exact wording of the thought and all the details of delivery are left to the time of speaking, though the general content may have been carefully prepared. To be free from papers and notes will aid directness and fluency. Impromptu speaking is on the spur of the moment without any special preparation either for content or form. The memory method means writing out the speech in full, fixing it in the mind and speaking it exactly as written. It is little used. In using the manuscript method, the speaker reads his speech. This method is not desirable except on very formal occasions, or when exact scientific reports are required, or in radio broadcasting, when a very definite effect must be produced and timing is of the utmost importance.

Material.—In all speaking, there is a what and a how. What is said constitutes the material, the content, the subject matter. The main kinds of material are: facts, examples, statistics, cases, illustrations, ideas, testimony. These materials must be handled in such a way that through analysis and reasoning the components become well mixed and amalgamated. Speech materials may be secured by thinking, reading, conversing, observing, reflecting, interviewing, traveling and reasoning.

To be interesting, a speaker must use interesting material and present it in an interesting manner. The attention of the hearer cannot be ignored. How can attention be captured? By interest. What things are interesting? A public speaker will have little difficulty in creating interest in his hearers if he will judiciously draw upon these interest factors in selecting his material: concreteness, activity, novelty, curiosity, suspense, humor, conflict, imagery. If these elements are woven into substantial material drawn from adequate sources and if the whole is brought well within the experiences of members of the audience, interest will not lag.

Structure.—The structure of the speech means its framework. A well-organized speech has three divisions: introduction, body, conclusion. An outline is essential in order to give a speech correct structure. An outline is the plan—it is the blueprint. It serves as a guide during preparation and delivery. It insures orderly and systematic arrangement of material. It determines the inclusion and exclusion of material. A carefully thought-out plan, systematically arranged on paper and then firmly fixed in the mind, is an insurance policy against chaos and confusion. The principal kinds of outline are: (1) topical—a selective arrangement of points; (2)

chronological—a time-order arrangement; (3) logical—dependent on reasoning. In any outline a few main heads well developed, built up with specific points, enlarged upon with illustrations will be far more effective than the mere enumeration of a large number of main or subheads.

Style.—Style is the manner of expression. It is the manner in which words are used to give form to thought. Style clothes the thought that the outline surveys. Style involves such principles as clearness, coherence, unity, emphasis, economy, figures of speech, rhythm and climax.

Mastery of these principles depends largely upon the speaker's command of words. For the discriminating thinker, words are priceless tools. To insure a flexible speaking style, improve the vocabulary. Of the four vocabularies—reading, writing, hearing and speaking—the speaking vocabulary usually is the most meager, yet it is the one most needed.

The speaking vocabulary can be enlarged in these specific ways: (1) by alertness and vocal responsiveness to environment; (2) by intelligent reading aloud; (3) by conversing with people of education and culture; (4) by gaining a knowledge of other languages; (5) by practice in writing; (6) by reading good literature; (7) by deliberate use of a dictionary.

Delivery of a Speech.—Effective delivery begins with mental attitude and mental processes. The speaker's mental attitude must be one of sureness and confidence in himself and in his ability to interest an audience in his subject. There is no place for inferiority complexes; no place for apologies. The mental process must show power of concentration. The mental relationship between speaker and audience must be based on the idea of genuine communication, which implies having business to transact with the audience—an exchange of ideas. A communicative speaker looks his audience in the eye. He talks directly to and with it and not at, over, under or away from it. Communicative speaking will have the natural, earnest, direct manner of the best conversation—heightened and amplified as circumstances may require. It should be true and sincere, not artificial, exhibitory or bombastic.

The voice does more than carry the speaker's message: it reflects his personality. The sound of the voice constantly creates favorable or unfavorable impressions on the listener. The speaking voice should be distinct, pleasing in tone quality, varied in emphasis, well modulated, capable of responsive changes in force, rate and pitch; it should be expressive in revealing relative thought values and shadings of emotion; it should have resonance and rhythm. To insure correct articulation in uttering words, there must be precision in the use of the several articulators—lips, teeth, tongue and palate. Four aids to articulation are: relaxed throat, loose jaw, nimble tongue and flexible lips.

Controlled bodily actions convey intended and desirable meanings. Uncontrolled bodily actions convey unintended and undesirable meanings. As

an agent of delivery, a speaker's body will convey thought and emotion through poise, posture, gesture, facial expression and movement. At all times, speaking is enlivened and made more forceful by expressive action properly motivated and co-ordinated.

Types of Public Address.—A speech of *introduction* (that is, introducing another speaker) should be formal or informal according to the exact nature of the occasion. The subject matter may be pertinent personal facts about the person being introduced. It should not be too personal and never exaggerated. Reference should be made to the cause the person represents, his field of activity, his outstanding achievements. A speech of introduction should be courteous, gracious and personally considerate. It should bring together in a brief, fitting and sympathetic manner the audience and the person introduced.

The *eulogy* is an address in praise of an individual—living or dead; for example, at a memorial service, a birthday or other anniversary. It should be an appreciative and understanding appraisal of the person's character and achievements.

Dedication addresses are delivered when public buildings are completed, when historic events are commemorated, when statues or monuments are unveiled. In this type of speech, the ambitions, loyalties, sacrifices, sentiments and ideals of the group play an important part. The speaker voices the thought of the group and the mood of the occasion. In selecting material he can be guided by these points: What causes lie behind the dedication? To what is the object being dedicated? In what significant ways can the past, present and future, as they relate themselves to the object dedicated, be linked together?

The *after-dinner* speech is a type universally used. There are two kinds—serious and humorous. The five steps in speech composition given in the section, "Building the Speech," should take care of the serious type. The humorous after-dinner speech, intended purely for enjoyment, is somewhat more difficult to prepare and present. Humor is so elusive and so individual that rules avail little. Suggestions may help. Be brief, spontaneous, imaginative, original, ingenious, light in touch, sparkling if possible and, above all, amusing.

The *lecture* is the longest form of public address. In its preparation the speaker can use in fullest measure the five-point plan of speech building. Particular attention should be given to renewing and sustaining interest during the last half of the address. The lecturer will appeal to such impelling motives as security, happiness, self-preservation, altruism, power, affection, sentiment, pride, property rights, duty, opportunity and social welfare. The lectures of Wendell Phillips, Henry W. Grady, Theodore Roosevelt, Woodrow Wilson and Elihu Root are well worth studying for their fine points of speech composition.

Group Discussion.—The growth of group discussion is proof that speaking is for the many rather than the few. Most significant among the forms of group discussion are: (1) parliamentary, (2) round-table, (3) panel, (4) town-meeting, (5) open forum. Any of these forms may be used by social, educational, business, religious, literary or political groups in a free discussion of questions of common interest to the members of the group. To function well, such meetings should be presided over by a competent chairman who will keep the discussion within bounds and see to it that all members are given a fair hearing.

The five main values found in group discussion are: (1) It provides an adequate outlet for exchange of ideas

The brief is a survey of the argument. It is a logical outline in amplified form giving the complete plan of the case for one side of the proposition. The following rules for brief making are important: (1) The brief should have three divisions—introduction, discussion and conclusion. (2) Every point in the brief should be a complete statement. (3) The relation of main and subordinate points should be indicated by proper symbols. (4) The introduction should be analytical, not argumentative. (5) The logical connections between points may be shown with such words as *for* or *because.*

the question. The speakers who support the proposition (defined above) constitute the affirmative side. The speakers who attack the proposition constitute the negative side. Each speaker is permitted a certain definite length of time for the presentation of his subject. After both the affirmative and negative sides have presented their prepared speeches, each side has an opportunity for rebuttal, or opportunity to answer, challenge and, if possible, overthrow the arguments presented by the other side. Since prior to the debate the speakers on one side have not seen the addresses prepared by the other side, rebuttals must be largely extemporaneous, for they should be directed specifically against the arguments presented by the opposing side. A certain amount of material in rebuttal, however, can be prepared in advance from the speaker's general knowledge of the proposition. In most debates, each speaker is given an opportunity for rebuttal, although in some instances only one rebuttal is permitted for each side.

Affirmative Case.—The first affirmative speaker should fully analyze the proposition and then establish at least one of the main issues. The second affirmative speaker should do three things: (1) refute one or more points presented by the first negative speaker; (2) briefly restate what was proved by his teammate; (3) prove the remaining issue or issues. Because of the rule that no entirely new point may be presented in the rebuttal speeches, the last affirmative speaker must complete the affirmative case. An affirmative case should show: (1) what is wrong with the present situation; (2) that the affirmative proposal is the right remedy.

Negative Case.—In preparing to meet an affirmative case, a negative team may choose any one of these courses: (1) defend the present system; (2) propose changes in it; (3) offer a counter plan different from that of the affirmative. Preceding or during the main argument each negative speaker should devote some time to refutation in attacking the arguments of opponents.

Teamwork.—On both sides close teamwork is necessary to insure consistency and accurate adaptation. In the interests of clearness, emphasis and convincingness, it is well for the last speaker on each side, in both the main arguments and the rebuttals, to summarize the case up to that point. The last affirmative speaker should review the essentials of the entire debate using comparison and contrast to show points of weakness and of strength.

Time Limits.—In interscholastic debating the main speeches usually are ten minutes in length and the rebuttals five. Class debates on simple propositions may be limited to seven-minute main arguments and three-minute rebuttals; or the main speeches may be eight minutes, with one five-minute rebuttal on each side. Usually the order of speaking in rebuttal is reversed, the negative opening the discussion and the affirmative closing it.

ASSOCIATED PRESS

TELEVISION DEBATES were part of the 1960 campaign between Kennedy and Nixon.

because all the members may participate. (2) It is democratic, in that majority and minority beliefs are given a hearing. (3) It develops a sense of consideration for the opinions and viewpoints of others. (4) It leads to intelligent action by bringing out points of weakness and of strength. (5) It quickens the responsibilities of citizenship.

Debating.—Debate is the presentation of each side of a controversial question by opposing speakers under definite rules of procedure. The debater uses exposition only slightly, advancing his case by means of *argument,* the process of influencing the beliefs and actions of others by means of conviction and persuasion—conviction by appeal to reason; persuasion by appeal to emotion.

A *proposition* (an assertion that must be supported or overthrown) is necessary in debating. A mere topic, such as Socialized Medicine, cannot be debated; but one can debate the complete statement, "Resolved, That a plan of socialized medicine should be adopted in the United States." The proposition should be simple, clear, brief, complete, timely, evenly balanced. It should be stated affirmatively.

Analysis means discovering the meaning, approaches, boundaries and issues of the proposition. Five steps are usually involved: (1) cause for discussion, (2) history of the question, (3) definition of terms, (4) exclusion of irrelevant material, (5) finding and stating the main issues.

Proof is the sufficient reason for accepting or rejecting the truth or falsity of the proposition. The purpose of debate is to prove or disprove the proposition. To prove a thing requires evidence. Evidence, then, is all the materials used for proof. This evidence may be found in facts, examples, cases, incidents, analogies, statistics or testimony. To be sound, all evidence must be in the form of accepted truths. Accuracy demands that exact *sources* of evidence be given. The debater deals with the evidence by means of a reasoning process. Reasoning connects the links in the chain of evidence so that justifiable conclusions can be drawn. Most proof is not complete, only approximate. Consequently, a debater should try to establish a reasonable probability. Instead of saying, "We have proved beyond the possibility of a doubt," say, "From this evidence it is reasonable to conclude."

Refutation is the attempt to answer and overthrow the opposing argument. It should be direct, clear, forceful, convincing and extemporaneous. Points should be brought to a focus quickly, argued with brevity, concluded logically. Refutation in rebuttal must be adapted with great care to the argument of the opposition exactly as it was presented. It should have the flexibility, the give and take that characterizes the most effective debating.

Formal Debating.—In formal debating there are usually two (sometimes three) speakers on each side of

THE STUDY OF FOREIGN LANGUAGES

Enrolment in Foreign Languages.—The chief foreign languages studied in the United States are modern French, German and Spanish and ancient Latin. Italian is taught in a few large cities, and Swedish and Norwegian are found on some school programs in Minnesota and North Dakota. A large proportion of boys and girls in New England and in the Middle Atlantic States study French or German; Spanish is strongest in the southwestern states, in California and in the Northwest. Latin has a large proportion of the foreign-language enrolment in the South and in the Middle Atlantic, North Central and West Central States. In general, modern languages have a higher percentage of enrolment in the larger cities, whereas Latin is the language usually taught in the smaller schools that offer only one foreign language. The students of ancient langues, such as Greek, in public and private schools are few in number.

Why Do American Boys and Girls Study Foreign Languages?—The main reasons are: college entrance requirements and school curricula; wishes of parents and a social tradition; the general belief that foreign-language study helps to improve the knowledge of English and to promote accuracy; and the natural curiosity of many pupils about foreign languages and the desire to know what they are like.

Students who intend to become doctors or lawyers realize that Latin will be useful in their professional studies. Many boys and girls feel that a modern language may be of service in business, or in professional work and in travel. They may wish to read the work of French and German investigators in the natural and social sciences who are producing books and articles of value; also the many great literary works produced in France, Italy, Germany and Spain that are not translated into English. The large Spanish-speaking population of Mexico and of Central America and South America makes a knowledge of Spanish commercially valuable to business and professional men and women in the United States.

The Value of Foreign-Language Study.—Various attempts have been made to measure the usefulness and the good effects of foreign-language study. Most school and college graduates consider foreign languages of service in a variety of ways. It has been shown in several cases that foreign-language students surpass nonforeign-language students in progress in English, in knowledge and understanding of foreign countries and in their general culture. In a group of travelers, those who have learned at least one foreign language have a better background historically and culturally and usually take a keener interest and greater pleasure in the varied aspects of life abroad, even in countries whose languages are strange to them. The background that produces this effect may be acquired in other ways, but foreign-language study seems to be the most direct avenue of approach.

It should not be forgotten that the values to be gained from foreign-language study vary with the mastery of the language. The most that can be expected from average American students of a modern language is: first, ability to read those works of fiction, drama, history and the social and natural sciences, that are not unusually difficult in vocabulary, style and thought; second, ability to understand the foreign language in short sentences spoken slowly and simply; third, ability to write the language intelligibly, if not correctly, in simple, short sentences dealing with familiar topics; fourth, ability to speak intelligibly in short sentences, leaving a good deal to the listener to supply; fifth, an enlarged vocabulary in English and a better understanding of language structure; and, sixth, increased desire to learn more about the foreign country and what the country and its people mean in the world today.

The ability to read a foreign language will always be greater than the ability to write, speak or understand it by ear. This is the case also in English. All these abilities tend to disappear with disuse. We often meet persons abroad who once lived in the United States or in England but have almost forgotten their English because they have not used it. Here at home are many thousands who passed through grammar school and learned to read English but have read so little that they are almost illiterate now. During enlistment and draft for the World War it came out clearly that many thousands of young men called for service had never really learned to read their native language in school or had largely lost their ability to read through lack of practice. Consequently, even if foreign-language students attain in school the abilities listed above, they cannot expect to retain those powers unless they exercise them. Reading a modern language is the easiest and readiest form of practice. Reading helps us to increase our vocabulary and our knowledge of the foreign country and its contribution to civilization. That much is a real gain, even if we make no progress in understanding the spoken language or in speaking or writing it.

Suppose a boy or girl asks the question, "What marketable value will I get from the study of a modern language carried to the point you have indicated?" One can answer immediately that aside from teaching and a few other specialized jobs, a student should not expect a job on the strength of his foreign-language equipment. Neither will his knowledge of history, English or mathematics give him a place on a pay roll. He may become a successful lawyer, doctor, journalist, banker, merchant or farmer without knowing anything about the French partitive, the inverted word order in German or the position of object pronouns in Spanish. Likewise, in few such occupations would he use quadratic equations, his knowledge of *Macbeth,* of the American Revolution, of geography or physics. Very rarely do any of these subjects operate directly in practical affairs. Few business houses employ people solely because of their knowledge of a foreign language. There are not enough places in the Department of State, nor as foreign newspaper correspondents, nor as representatives of American firms abroad to absorb many foreign-language experts yearly; but professional men—architects, engineers, journalists, librarians, musicians, artists, doctors, teachers and specialists—all need firsthand contact with the intellectual and artistic output of two foreign countries at least. In a leading university, of nearly 600 candidates for higher degrees in one calendar year, 38 per cent failed the reading test in French that all candidates must pass. Not long ago the deans of seventy-nine medical schools in the United States and Canada expressed distress that so few of their students could read French and German. Similarly, heads of international banking houses regret that so few young men whom they engage can read and understand financial reports and economic discussions written in foreign languages.

Furthermore, we should remember that language is one of the most remarkable and complex forms of human behavior. It is at the same time the most wonderfully flexible and the most definitely fixed of instruments, both for our own thinking and for the expression of thought to others. As one authority puts it: "The division of labor and, with it, the whole working of human society depends upon language." Although in childhood we spend a long period to develop skill in using speech for communication, and then in learning to read, we rarely think of our own language as being the most wonderful and precious instrument that we possess. We do not think about its structure, its kinship with other languages, its origin, how it has developed and is developing with every passing moment. We take it for granted, as during many centuries men took for granted the outer world and the human body. We discuss vigorously questions of correct and incorrect English, such as "ain't," "it's me," "who did you see?" We rarely go farther.

The best way to acquire a fresh outlook on English is to study a foreign language, ancient or modern, which gives us a basis of comparison and invites attention to the way our language is made, to the ways in which its sounds are produced, to the different forms words have according to their relations to one another and to the way and the order in which they come together to express meaning. We learn then that certain words and expressions that can hardly be translated into English are characteristic of a given people, like the French *savoir faire, savoir vivre* and *goût,* the German *Gemütlichkeit,* the Spanish *caballero, hidalgo, simpático* and *mañana por la mañana y mañana será otro día.* The Frenchman's "*Donnez-vous la peine de vous asseoir*" ("Take the trouble to sit down"), and the Spaniard's welcome to his home, which he assures you is "*Su casa de V.*" ("Your house") indicate a civilization founded on more ceremony than ours. They give us a clue to certain aspects of French and Spanish character and a suggestion of the way we should conduct ourselves when in those countries. Even a little reflection on the way kindred words behave in two or more languages of the same group—English cent (hundredth part), French *cent* (hundred) and Spanish *ciento* (hundred); English mansion, French *maison* (house); English alumnus, Spanish *alumno* (pupil); English hound, German *Hund* (dog)—opens our eyes to possibilities that a one-language person is likely to ignore. These examples are drawn from the modern languages, but when we recall that the first three are all derived from the Latin, it is clear that the study of that language provides as rich or even richer material for such comparisons.

Foreign-language study forms habits of close observation and attention to details and gives an opportunity to exercise powers of inference—that is, divining the meaning of the unfamiliar words or phrases in a sentence by our knowledge of the familiar words. The reader may go astray now and then, but he may do that in reading his native tongue, or in studying mathematics or any other subject that involves reasoning. Reading a foreign language provides an excellent opportunity to use our powers of inference and thus to exercise our intelligence.

Foreign-language study has a number of values if the content of the course and the teaching procedure are suitable: First, it calls the student's attention to language, to the way sounds are made, to the way words are put together in order to express meaning, to words themselves—their meanings, their formation and their relationships to words in other languages. Second, it provides practice in assembling words as one would the parts of a machine, and in fitting them together in accordance with certain rules. Doing this calls not only for much care in following directions but for painstaking accuracy. Even a small oversight or modification may quite alter or even spoil the result. Third, it provides one of the best ways of enlarging the vocabulary, improving the powers of expression and increasing the power to read and understand English. Fourth, it brings forcibly to the attention many of the most characteristic features of another country and another civilization, stimulates interest, provokes curiosity and therefore contributes to a broader outlook. The student is encouraged in his desire to travel and to observe understandingly the life of other peoples. Fifth, it opens up to the student who really attains the aims of the course an avenue that can lead

Voici un gorille.
Vwah-see uhng goh-ree.
Here is a gorilla

Il a de longs bras.
Eel ah duh lohng brah.
He has long arms.

FRENCH language book. This page exemplifies one of the methods used to teach a foreign language. First, there is a picture that must be identified from information about it below. This is written in the language. The second line spells out each word phonetically for pronunciation. The third line gives the English translation.

him directly to literature and writings in all possible fields of interest and of knowledge. It also brings him to a point where he can readily increase his oral ability to the degree where it will be useful for speaking and writing. Many students acquire all these values—except oral ability—without residence in a foreign country. Sixth, it allows the student to take advantage of any necessity or opportunity in his profession or business to utilize this knowledge of a foreign language. Seventh, it enables a student more easily and successfully to take up a second or third language later, even though the new language may belong to a different family from those which he has already learned. In the United States, we have always turned toward Europe in our educational and intellectual affairs, and toward the languages of western Europe that are nearest our own in structure and in vocabulary; but if circumstances lead a foreign-language student to look across the Pacific and to deal in person with the peoples there, he will find that experience with a western European language, ancient or modern, has given him a highly useful running start in pursuing the study of an Oriental language.

The Choice of a Foreign Language.—What foreign languages are most advantageous to American boys and girls? If only one ancient language is

on the student's program, **Latin** comes first. If it is skilfully taught, the study of this highly inflected language —the declensions of nouns and adjectives, the conjugations of its verbs, the uses of its cases and tense forms and moods, the patterns into which the sentence structure falls—is an experience unequaled for precision and definiteness. When we remember that nearly half the ten thousand commonest words used in English speech and writing come from the Latin, we see what light this study throws on the origin and meaning of English words. Latin teaching is being reorganized and today, even in a second-year course, the easy Latin that pupils read helps them to form an idea what Roman civilization was like in its family relationships, its government, its religion and in its organization of a world conquered for glory, for power, for trade. Thus they get a concept of an imperialism like that which agitates the world today. Later, when they read Cicero and Livy, they become aware also of the sources of English and French style down into the 19th century and of the background to the speeches used by Musolini in exhorting the Italians. It is commonplace to call Latin a dead language, but like most of the great dead, its ghost still walks the western world. Only those who have studied the language know that the mighty spirit still lives and still speaks today, although in accents that Cicero, Caesar and Vergil would not have understood. If Latin were to disappear from our schools, this voice would still speak on, even though no ear were tuned to catch it. The people of the western world would have cut themselves off from a great segment of their past, like a man forgetting his youth and ignorantly disregarding forces and conditions that made him and his forefathers what they were.

The study of **Greek,** never as widespread as Latin, has lost ground in American secondary schools. Other subjects have crowded it from the course of study, especially as there has been an increase in the secondary school enrolment of students not preparing for college; but Greek, almost a model language in its structure, has much to interest ambitious young people. Greek literature is rich and varied in history, philosophy, the drama and lyric and epic poetry. From Greek even more than from Latin is drawn the terminology of modern natural sciences. The study of Greek makes for an educated man's understanding of English, besides offering an educational experience that exercises the pupils' best powers of memory, inference and attention to detail. Even more than in Latin, the parts of a sentence in Greek are bound together according to definite patterns indicated by the cases of its nouns and the tenses and moods of its verbs. The student of Greek gets all the training values of an experience with a highly inflected language, that is, one in which the relations of the words to one another are indicated by their endings.

Of modern languages, the student must usually choose among French,

German and Spanish. For many years only French and German were taught in our schools. Spanish began to gain ground at the time of the Spanish-American War in 1898, when we became really aware of the vast Spanish-speaking regions south of our borders. Our bordering Mexico and the considerable Spanish-speaking population of our southwestern states give the Spanish language certain practical advantages. Although there are many French-speaking citizens in Louisiana, and the French of Quebec are not far away, these centers have not influenced language study so much as have the Spanish centers. Enough German-speaking centers still exist in various parts of the country to give German, as it were, a home market; and this is even more obviously true of Italian in view of the large Italian population in cities like New York, Chicago and San Francisco; but the Italian immigrant groups were not of the type to bring with them to America so high a degree of culture nor so much interest in education as the class of immigrants from Germany. For the same reason the Spanish-speaking population in our West and Southwest would not have given a strong impetus to the study of Spanish had it not been based on the tremendous commercial importance of the Latin-American countries south of the Rio Grande.

Unquestionably French and German have certain advantages over the other modern languages for most American students. Both countries, like Spain, have produced great literatures. In addition, both have made important contributions to art, music, philosophy, the natural sciences, education, government and to commerce in all its forms. A reading knowledge of these two languages is required of candidates for higher degrees (M.A., Ph.D.), in high-grade American universities, because technical writings (science, engineering, etc.) in French and German are usually not translated into English, so that the specialist in almost any field must have a reading knowledge of both languages. The writings of other European scientists—Russian, say, or Scandinavian—are usually published in French or German versions. As a spoken language, French is more widespread than any other except English. The traveler who speaks English and some French will find someone to whom he can make his wants known in almost any hotel, store, train, steamboat or trolley car in Europe.

French, Italian and Spanish all belong to the Romance group of languages, in which Portuguese and Rumanian also are included. These languages developed from the Latin spoken by Roman soldiers and Roman colonists in these countries and adopted by the original inhabitants during the centuries they were subjects of the far-reaching Roman Empire. Therefore these languages resemble one another in many respects, although they sound very little alike when spoken. They have also many points of resemblance to English, not in structure but in vocabulary, because English and these languages owe a common debt to Latin, and because English has had close contacts with these languages through many centuries. German is nearer to English in structure than the Romance languages, and nearer also in a certain element of the vocabulary (for example: *Haus,* house; *Hund,* dog; *Mann,* man; *Buch,* book; *Hand,* hand; *Weib,* woman; *Maus,* mouse), but when we get away from such simple words, which we call the Anglo-Saxon element in English, the German vocabulary is less like the English than is Latin, French, Italian or Spanish. Furthermore, since German sentences are longer and more complex than English, and German word order is different from ours, we find German more difficult to learn than a Romance language. But an American will learn more quickly to pronounce German intelligibly than French, because our vocal organs when we speak our own language behave more nearly like those of a German than like the vocal organs of speakers in Romance countries.

In the Romance languages, the articles, nouns and adjectives do not change for the different cases; that is, when subject or object or to express possession. The verbs, however, have a much more elaborate set of endings for the different tenses than in English. Learning the verb forms and how to use them is the big task in these languages. German, on the contrary, has a full set of declensions, or changes of form, for articles, pronouns, adjectives and nouns; but German verbs are more like English verbs and demand less study than verbs in the Romance languages.

The German language as a whole, however, calls for more study of forms than the others, consequently, some people think it is more difficult for the beginner than French or Spanish. Others consider this an advantage, not just because study of the language is more difficult, but because it gives to the student a kind of experience and training that the Romance languages do not give. They think also that this experience and training is especially valuable for those who do not study Latin. In view of the close relationship between German and English, students of German can form a much better idea of what the English language was before the Norman conquest of England in the 11th century, for after 1066 the influence of the French spoken by the Normans gradually brought about important changes in the language used in England at that time, especially in introducing in the sentence the word order and much of the vocabulary of the Norman French.

The Age for Beginning.—Teachers often discuss the question, "At what age should foreign-language study begin?" It is probable that in most cases the freshman or sophomore year in high school is early enough to begin Latin or Greek. The very nature of the languages and the way in which they are usually taught seem to demand at least this degree of maturity on the part of the student. The increased rate of progress in knowledge and in understanding is enough to make up for what an earlier beginning would contribute. However, the revision of the Latin course of study made in a number of recently published textbooks enables pupils to begin earlier. This is an advantage, for in these subjects, as in most others, much depends on the choice of material and the way in which it is presented.

In the case of modern languages, the situation is different, especially if speaking ability is the main object. It is true that in most cases where pupils are tested by written examinations, high school pupils rank higher than pupils who begin in junior high school. They read better, make fewer mistakes in writing and have a larger vocabulary and a better knowledge of grammar. On the other hand, oral work prospers more with younger students because they are less interested in subject matter and are amused and entertained by the sort of play involved in oral practice on a new language. The difficulty is, however, that early beginning in public junior high schools usually involves an early dropping of the language in the high school years. Though the average beginner in junior high school studies the language a year longer than if he began in high school, he learns less because he is not able in the earlier years to acquire a real power to do much with the language except commit phrases to memory and get a good accent.

Beginning a modern language in junior high school—or earlier—has great advantages if the language is continued at least two years in high school. Otherwise, it is better to wait until the high school period is reached, even if we suppose that attainment in speech will suffer by the delay. This supposition is based on reasoning rather than upon observed facts. The real point is this: At what stage in the child's school life can he best spare enough time for language study to make it worth while? School authorities at present do not seem to know what to do with the junior high school program. They call it an exploratory period, and the exploring frequently seems to be just pottering with various subjects and doing very little with any of them. Now if foreign-language study in junior high school were open to all students with an I.Q. score of 90–100 and above and were then carried on for at least two years in the next school stage, the results would be beneficial to the junior high school program and to the student, for he would have spent his time on a genuine subject matter of universal interest and importance in itself and in its bearing on other things. The adoption of such a plan would call for a revision of the subject matter of the modern-language course, with less emphasis in the earlier period on grammar and more on reading, pronunciation, hearing and speaking. Naturally the speaking exercises should be planned with care, certain topics in grammar that now are prominent in the course of study from the beginning should not appear until later in a course that has been carefully revised in accordance with this theory.

Length of Period for Foreign-Language Study.—How long must foreign-language study continue in order that the results may be clear gain in terms of attainment in the language?

If speaking means expressing one's opinions, relating an incident, explaining a situation, understanding a Frenchman or a German when he is conversing at normal speed, then to speak a language is the most difficult to attain of all langauge abilities, as every student of the subject knows. Persons often live for years in a foreign country, hire taxis, ride on streetcars, do shopping, order meals, travel on trains and read newspapers, but never become fluent enough to carry on a connected conversation at normal speed.

Except in the case of mature students who learn more quickly and cover much more ground than the usual class, two years is the minimum period for a modern or an ancient language, and three years is more than a half better than two. Especially if speaking ability is an aim, the student cannot in a shorter time fix good habits of pronunciation and of handling sentence patterns; and he cannot acquire sufficient control of vocabulary, idiomatic expressions and changes in word forms. Indeed, it may be said positively that only able and industrious students can make real progress in these particular respects in as short a period as two high-school years. Furthermore, except in college, a two-year period rarely permits enough reading to produce ready reading ability, which in turn is necessary in order that the student may attain even a superficial impression of literature. The skill and the knowledge acquired with so much labor soon fades away with lack of use. Many students enter college after two or three years' study of a foreign language but do not continue the subject. They thus abandon the language at the time when their previous efforts would pay them the largest dividends.

In two high-school years a fairly good and reasonably industrious pupil can acquire a reading vocabulary of 2,000 to 3,000 words frequently used in books and a speech vocabulary of 500 to 600 words, if the content of a modern language course is properly chosen and skilfully taught. He can learn to pronounce intelligibly, to recognize all the important forms of common articles, adjectives, pronouns, nouns and verbs, and to understand immediately how they contribute to the meaning of a given sentence. Having done this, he should be able to read a suitable text at the rate of 125 to 200 words a minute. He should understand slow and simple speech, and himself be able to use a small group of more or less fixed expressions. Such attainment is the maximum that he can expect in two years, and is above what the average pupil usually attains.

In a succeeding year or two he can push his reading ability to a point closer to what it is in English, get acquainted with more mature literary words, learn more about the country and its people, extend the vocabulary he uses in speech and in writing, im-

LOOK MAGAZINE

LEARNING A LANGUAGE is easier for a child because of his ability to imitate. Language laboratories are becoming prevalent in teaching languages. Each child uses earphones to hear tapes and a microphone so the instructor can listen to his pronunciation.

prove his pronunciation and in general reach a point where his knowledge of the language becomes a part of himself.

With Latin and Greek the situation is different. This is partly because forms and sentence structure are more complex; partly because the Latin and Greek authors usually read in school do not produce the varied kinds of simple and entertaining story material that are plentiful in the modern languages and partly because the subject matter taught in these languages is more remote from the young people of the present day. Julius Caesar's account of the war in Gaul, Cicero's speeches in the Roman senate and Xenophon's account of the retreat of his army in Asia Minor contain no love stories, no humorous incidents, no accounts of children's adventures or of the kinds of situations with which we are familiar. A revision of the Latin course of study,

however, has resulted in supplying much easy and interesting reading material, even in the first two years, which places this subject more nearly on a par with the modern languages. The whole range of Latin literature has been skimmed to find material suitable for young people. Thus the pupil gets a truer picture of the Romans and finds them in many respects as human and as varied in their interests and characters as if they were living today.

Few students of Latin and Greek reach the point of reading Caesar and Cicero, Vergil and Horace, Juvenal, Xenophon and Homer in the way they can read Victor Hugo and Molière in French, Goethe and Schiller in German, Cervantes and Alarcón in Spanish, or Manzoni and Verga in Italian. In three years, however, they can learn the forms of the ancient languages, can recognize them and use them in simple sentences, can read many pages of the simpler texts now made available in most recent textbooks, and can learn a great deal about the origin and meanings of English words and about the civilization and history of Greece and Rome and their meaning for the world today. Further than this they can hardly expect to go in the high-school period unless they continue the subject for the full four years.

The First Foreign Language.—The question is often asked: In the case of a pupil who will study an ancient and a modern language, which should he begin first? In many schools it is the practice to permit pupils to study a modern language only after one or two years of Latin. Teachers of modern languages are always glad to have Latin students in their classes, because Latin training assures better progress in a second language, especially a language that has developed from Latin. The Latin student is familiar with grammatical terms and their meanings and has had practice in analyzing sentences into their parts. A student who has successfully completed a period of Latin study and wants to go into another foreign language usually has what is called linguistic ability and has also a taste for this kind of subject.

A commonsense analysis of the situation points to choosing a modern language as the first foreign language. As we have seen, a pupil can learn in a short time to make a wider use of a Romance language or of German than of Latin or Greek. In the case of younger pupils with little interest in grammatical analysis, a modern language can be taught more informally, utilizing play activities, especially those that lead to speaking practice. A pupil can more quickly reach the point of reading a modern language with some ease and thus get the satisfaction of having definitely accomplished something. Furthermore, the experience gained in studying a modern language is valuable preparation for the study of an ancient language, and a modern language begun in junior high school can be carried on long enough to be beneficial and still leave enough time for three years of Latin or Greek in high school.

CLASSIFICATION OF LANGUAGES

The languages of the world are classified either by their form or their family relation as morphological or genealogical.

Morphological.—Comparison of the outward forms (morphology) of languages, show that there are six types:

1. *Root-Isolating,* Chinese and Siamese-Burmese, the words of which have only one syllable and no inflection whatever; they may be used both as nouns and as verbs. Word order alone indicates the value of the various parts of a sentence.

2. *Stem-Isolating,* groups that include the Austronesian or Malayo-Polynesian languages. They are without inflection, number or gender, and various types of verbs are formed by means of prefixes, infixes and suffixes.

3. *Co-ordinating,* forms that embrace the Ancient Egyptian of the hieroglyphic texts; modern Egyptian, called Coptic, and the Bantu group of more than 100 languages spoken in central and South Africa. The modifying words (like our prefixes and suffixes) remain separated from the modified word just as in English the article *the* is separated from the noun to which it belongs.

4. *Agglutinative,* the Turco-Mongol-Tungus, Finno-Ugric and Dravidian of southern and central India which have inflectional elements attached to the word stem without loss of identity, as shown by the Hungarian word, *ember* (man), *ember-ek* (men), *ember-nek* (to the man), *Magyar-ember* (a Hungarian).

5. *Inflectional,* the Hamito-Semitic and Indo-European, having word stems and suffixes or prefixes fused to such a degree that it is often difficult to analyze the word.

6. *Polysynthetic* or *Incorporating,* early Mexican and Eskimo, in which subject, object and verb of a sentence are embodied in one compact form so that the entire sentence appears as one long word.

Genealogical.—More popular at present is the genealogical classification based on the principle of family relationship (mother, daughter and sister languages). Latin is the mother language of all the modern Romance tongues (Italian, French, Spanish, Portuguese, Rumanian and others) because they developed from it. English is a member of the larger Germanic or Teutonic family of languages. It includes also German, Dutch, Swedish, Danish, Norwegian and other branches, all grandchildren of the same dead language of which we have no written documents. It was still spoken about 2,000 years ago when the ancestors of the English people had not yet left the Continent. Their Primitive Germanic speech was a sister language of Latin and Greek (and others), and their mother language is called Primitive Indo-European or Primitive Indo-Germanic, names for this whole family. The name *Aryan,* formerly used for this group, is now applied to the Indo-Iranian division only.

The Indo-European languages have been more thoroughly studied than any other group because the peoples speaking them are among the foremost of ancient and modern history. The scientific method developed for the study of the Indo-European languages has been applied to other languages. Attempts have been made even to build up a complete genealogical tree for all the languages of the world to trace them back to the original language of mankind. It is possible that all languages come from one and the same original language, but we have no means to prove this.

Primitive Indo-European speech that was current between 3000 and 1500 B.C. was already many thousand years removed from the original language of mankind which, according to conservative estimates, must have existed 30,000 to 50,000 years ago. Primitive Indo-European had at least one sister language, of which we have recently found records —the Hittite, an ancient language of Asia Minor, known to us from cuneiform inscriptions that begin around 1900 B.C. Though we have no written records of Primitive Indo-European, by using our knowledge of its sister language, Hittite, we are now able to reconstruct the common parent of Primitive Indo-European and Hittite. The names Indo-Hittite and Primitive Indo-Hittite have been introduced for this hypothetical language.

Of present-day language families that border upon Indo-European, some may be distantly related. The Hamito-Semitic and the Finno-Ugric languages show a slight resemblance to Indo-European. Some scholars believe in the original unity of the Indo-European and Finno-Ugric, of the Indo-European and Hamito-Semitic or of all three families; but other authorities are opposed to such theories. Recently kinship of Indo-European and Korean has been asserted, but not very convincingly. Linguistic relationship does not imply racial kinship (blood relationship), since languages can be transferred from one race to another. The American Negroes did not change their race when they dropped their original African language and accepted an Indo-European tongue. Race and language are two independent concepts.

I. THE INDO-EUROPEAN LANGUAGES

Indo-European languages are divided into two groups—Eastern and Western—with differences typified by the words *centum* and *satem* meaning hundred. The original Western or primitive Indo-European had a guttural *k* sound in the word, but in the Eastern languages this became a sibilant *s*—*satem* in Avestan. In the Western languages the *k* sound was kept—Latin *centum* (pronounced *kentum*), for example. Tocharian, an extinct *centum* language in Chinese Turkestan, is the only exception to this division. Though it is farthest east of all these languages, it belongs to the *centum* group of the West. It probably was introduced into Chinese Turkestan by emigrants from the West.

INDO-IRANIAN or ARYAN. Spoken by people who occupy the great plateau of Iran (Persia) and the valleys of the Euphrates and the Tigris.

Indic or *Sanskrit.* Old Indic included Vedic Sanskrit (a collection of hymns of which the oldest part is called Rig-Veda, which forms the basic part of the scriptures of the Brahman religion) and Classical Sanskrit (100 B. C.–800 A. D.). Middle Indic (or Prakrit) from 300 B. C. on grew out of Old Indic. Pali, the language of the Buddhist scriptures, was a literary form of Middle Indic and as such sterile and without offspring. Modern Indic languages comprise a total of more than 230,000,000 speakers. Among them are Marathi, 19,000,000; Hindi, 63,000,000; Bihari, 36,000,000; Bengali, 50,000,000; and Gypsy, the language of the Gypsies, an emigrant offshoot of a northwestern Indic dialect.

Iranian. Avesta (Old Bactrian) contains as its sole known literature the sacred books of the Zoroastrian (Parsi) religion. Old Persian contains the rock inscriptions of King Darius the Great and his successors. Modern Persian, a standard language of high prestige, is spoken by perhaps 8,000,000 people.

ARMENIAN. Spoken today by nearly 4,000,000 people in Asia Minor; the oldest written records in Armenian date from the 5th century A. D.

THRACO-PHRYGIAN. Thracian is known from a single inscription (*c.* 400 B. C.) found in the western part of the Balkan Peninsula. Phrygian, in Asia Minor, is known from one set of inscriptions dated as early as the 8th century B. C. and from another set from the first centuries of our era.

ILLYRIAN. These languages were spoken round the Adriatic in ancient times and are now known to us only from scant inscriptions or proper names. Albanese, the only modern survival, has been recorded only since the 17th century and is spoken (mainly in Albania) by about 1,500,000.

SLAVIC. The earliest literary documents of this group are translations in Old Church Slavic (or Old Bulgarian) of the second half of the 9th century. The manuscripts are in two scripts—Glagolitic, the older, and Cyrillic, the younger, both derived from the Greek alphabet.

West Slavic. Lechic, a hypothetical language without written records, is the source of Kasubian, Polish and Polabian. Kasubian is spoken by about 100,000 people in the Polish Corridor near Danzig. Although closely related to Polish, Kasubian is itself a distinct tongue. Polish, recorded since the 14th century, is spoken by nearly 21,000,000 people, more than a million of them living in the United States. Polabian died out in the 18th century. Wendish (or Sorbian, Lusatian) survives as a speech island of some 30,000 persons in Upper Saxony. Bohemian (or Czechoslovak), includes Czech, a language with a rich literature of five centuries, and Slovak, with a literature begun only in the 20th century. The two dialects are spoken by about 11,000,000 people. The oldest records date from the 13th century.

South Slavic. Slovene (or Slovenian) is spoken by about 1.5 million people, mainly in northwestern Yugoslavia and was first recorded in the 11th century. Serbo-Croatian is spoken by about 8,500,000 in Yugoslavia.

I. INDO-EUROPEAN

Primitive Indo-European						
Satem Languages	INDO-IRANIAN (ARYAN)	Indic (Sanskrit)	Old Indic / Vedic Sanskrit / Classical Sanskrit	Middle Indic (or Prakrit) / Pali	Marathi / Hindi / Bihari / Bengali / Gypsy
		Iranian	Avesta / Old Persian	Modern Persian	
	ARMENIAN				
	THRACO-PHRYGIAN	Thracian / Phrygian			
	ILLYRIAN	Albanese			
	SLAVIC	West	Lechic / Wendish / Bohemian	Kasubian / Polish / Polabian / Czech / Slovak
		South	Slovene / Serbo-Croatian / Bulgarian	
		East	White Russian / Ukranian / Russian	
	BALTIC	Old Prussian / Lithuanian / Lettish		
	TOCHARIAN			
Centum Languages	GREEK			
	ITALIC	Oscan and / Umbrian / Sabellian / Latin	Romance languages	Portuguese / Spanish / Catalan / Provençal / French / Italian / Ladin / Rumanian
	LIGURIAN			
	CELTIC	Gallic / Gaelic / Britannic	Irish / Scottish / Manx / Cornish / Welsh / Breton
	GERMANIC	North	Old Norse	Swedish / Danish / Norwegian / Icelandic / Low German → Dutch, Afrikaans
		East	Gothic	
		West	German / Anglo-Frisian	High German / Frisian / Anglo-Saxon / Middle English / Modern English

The Orthodox Serbs use Cyrillic, and the Roman Catholic Croats employ Latin characters. Bulgarian is spoken by some 5,000,000. The earliest texts (10th and 11th centuries) are termed Old Bulgarian or Old Church Slavic.

East Slavic. White Russian is spoken by 6,500,000 people around Minsk. Ukrainian (or Ruthenian, Little Russian) is spoken by about 34,000,000 people in southern Russia, Poland, Czechoslovakia and Rumania. Russian (or Great Russian) is spoken by some 80,000,000 people in European Russia and Siberia and has been recorded since the 12th century.

BALTIC. The Baltic group is so closely akin to Slavic that the two are frequently classed together as Balto-Slavic. In the Baltic group are: Old Prussian, spoken in East Prussia and West Prussia until the second half of the 17th century; Lithuanian,

spoken by about 2,700,000 people, 400,000 of them in the United States, with written records dating from the 16th century; Lettish, spoken in Latvia by about 1,500,000 people, with written records since the 16th century.

TOCHARIAN. A language of Central Asia known from manuscript fragments of the 6th century A. D. found in Chinese Turkestan.

GREEK. Our own civilization owes much to the Greek language, since it was the means of transmitting to us the high civilization of the ancient Greeks. It comprises the ancient and modern Greek literary languages and dialects. The ancient Greek dialects are known from many inscriptions, beginning in the 7th century B. C.; from fragments of writing on papyrus beginning in the 4th century B. C. and from a copious literature, whose oldest compositions, the Homeric poems

II. HAMITO-SEMITIC

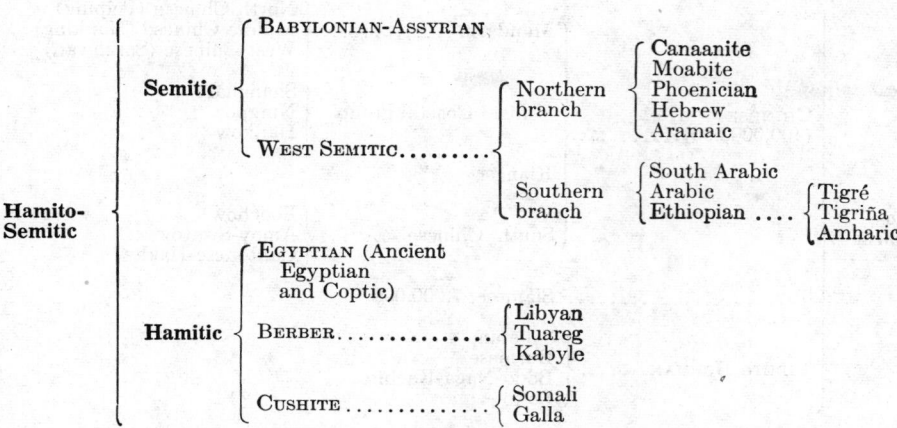

Some of the Semitic peoples (Hebrews, Phoenicians, Assyrians and Arabs) have played very prominent parts in the world's religious and commercial history and have made great literary contributions (the Bible and the Koran).

III. FINNO-UGRIC

(Figures indicate the number speaking the language.)

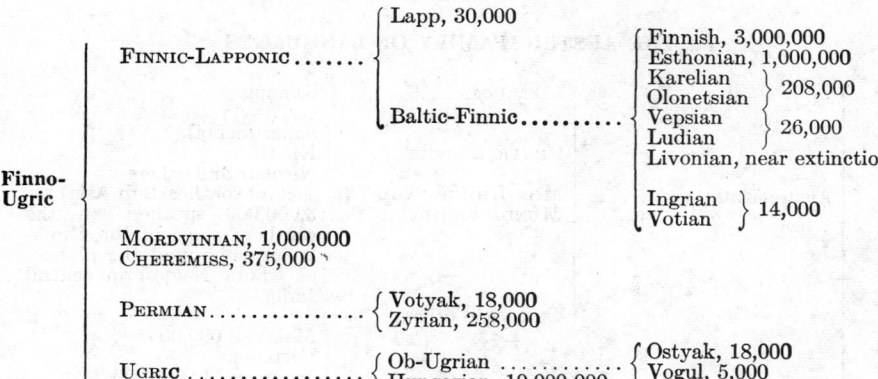

Some investigators believe that the Samoyede family of languages, spoken by some 180,000 persons east of the Ostyak area along the Yenisei River, Siberia, is related to Finno-Ugric. Others go even farther and believe that Finno-Ugric and Samoyede are related to Turko-Tatar (or Altaic), Mongolian and the Tunguse-Manchu languages, forming together with them the Ural-Altaic family.

(*Iliad* and *Odyssey*), are at least 2,700 years old. Today Greek is spoken by some 7,000,000 persons, mainly in Greece.

ITALIC. This family includes the ancient Latin, Sabellian, Umbrian and Oscan. Latin in time entirely absorbed the other three. Umbrian and Oscan were two closely related dialects of ancient Italy. Oscan is preserved in over 200 inscriptions ranging from 300 to 90 B. C. Umbrian was spoken in the district that is still called Umbria. Latin, the ancient dialect of the city of Rome, became the language of the Roman Republic and Empire and at its height was used throughout much of western Europe and the Mediterranean basin. In spite of the breakup of the Roman Empire, Latin continued to be the language of the literary and scholarly classes for many centuries. It is still the official language of the Roman Catholic Church.

From a type of Latin spoken by the masses and called Vulgar Latin came the Romance languages: Portuguese, spoken by 36,000,000 people chiefly in Portugal and Brazil, and connected with Spanish through Galician, as a written language dates from the end of the 12th century. Spanish is spoken by about 65,000,000 people living in Spain, Central America and South America (except in Brazil) as well as by some 100,000 Jews expelled by the Inquisition and scattered over the former Turkish Empire (Judaeo-Spanish). The literary language is based on the Castilian dialect and has a very important literature. Catalan, closely akin to Provençal, is spoken by 4,000,000 people in Catalonia and French Roussillon, with Barcelona and Perpignan as their respective centers. Provençal, spoken in southern France, takes its name from the region of its origin, Provence, originally a Roman province.

It forms a natural connection between French and Italian and is perhaps more closely allied with Italian than with French. From its word for *yes,* it is frequently termed the *langue d'oc,* as French is called the *langue d'oil* (Modern French, *oui*) and Italian the *lingua de si.* Provençal was definitely established as early as the 9th century. It was the language of the troubadours early in the 10th and 11th centuries. Today Provençal is represented by numerous patois.

French is spoken by about 45,000,-000 people in France, Belgium, Switzerland and eastern Canada. It has had three stages of development: Old French (842–*c.* 1300) its earliest text, the Oaths of Strasbourg; Middle French (*c.* 1300–1550) and Modern French (after 1500, especially after 1636). Modern French has a rich literature and has been the diplomatic language of the world since the 16th century. Its world-wide importance reached its climax in the 18th century. Since that time it has lost something of its former prestige, and its place has been taken by English.

Italian in its literary form has developed from the old Tuscan dialect that gained its literary pre-eminence through the writings of Dante, Petrarch and Boccaccio in the 14th century. Although literary Italian is read and spoken by all educated people in Italy, there still remain numerous dialects throughout the peninsula, and natives of southern Italy do not readily understand the dialect of northern Italy. Italian is spoken in various dialects by 41,000,000 people in Italy, Corsica, Malta, southern Switzerland, northern Africa, a small region in southeastern France, in Argentina and the United States of America. Ladin (or Raetian, Raeto-Romanic), spoken by some 44,000 people in the Swiss canton of Graubünden and by 500,000 people living south and southeast toward Frioul, appeared first as a literary language in the 16th century. Rumanian is spoken by 14,000,000 people in Rumania; its origin dates in the second century of our era when the Emperor Trajan conquered Dacia and colonized it with Romans.

LIGURIAN. This ancient widespread linguistic family centering in northern Italy round the present Riviera is very little known, but it was undoubtedly the most important language of central and southwestern Europe before the expansion of Celtic and Italic.

CELTIC. History and evidence of place names show that Celtic was in earlier times spoken over a large part of Europe, including what is now Bohemia, Austria, southern Germany, Switzerland, northern Italy and France. It was superseded in these regions by Latin as a result of Roman conquests and by Germanic languages as a result of the great migrations in the early centuries of our era. Gallic (or Gaulish) was the language of ancient Gaul. We have a few scant inscriptions dating from *c.* 100 B. C. Gaelic or Goidelic: Irish is known from a manuscript literature beginning in the 8th century of our era; a few inscriptions on stone

(Ogham) are perhaps much earlier. It is now spoken by some 400,000 people. Scottish (or Scotch Gaelic), an offshoot of Irish, is spoken by some 150,000 people. Manx is spoken on the Isle of Man as a home language, besides English, by a few hundred people. Of Britannic, Brythonic or British, Cornish has been dead since 1800; its earliest records date from the 9th century; Welsh (or Cymric) is spoken in Wales by about 1,000,000 people; Breton (or Armorican) is spoken in Brittany, France, brought there from Britain, perhaps as early as the 4th century.

GERMANIC. Primitive Germanic, spoken between 1000 B. C. and 200 A.D., represents on the whole that branch of the Indo-European group that remained longest in or near the original territory of the Indo-Europeans. Though at the earliest stage it did not as yet differ much from Primitive Indo-European, about 500 B.C. it underwent radical changes that brought about its definite Germanic characteristics. The most important change in the sound structure of the language is known as the Germanic consonant shift or Grimm's law.

As a result of this change we find, for instance, that the consonants *f th h* that are used in the English language are modern developments of the Indo-European consonants *p t k,* while the modern English consonants *p t k* go back to Indo-European *b d g.*

Indo-European: *p t k   b d g*
English: *f th h   p t k (c)*

The Indo-European form of these consonants is preserved in Greek and Latin. Thus, *p* and *t* in Latin *pater* appear as *f* and *th* in English *father;* *c* (= *k*) in Latin *cornu* or *cor* appears as *h* in *horn* and *heart; t* in Latin *tres* appears as *th* in *three; d* in Latin *duo* or *decem* appears as *t* in *two* and *ten; g* in Latin *gelidus* or *gens* or *genu* appears as *k* (*c*) in *cold, kin* and *knee,* respectively. (There are more particulars to Grimm's law not mentioned here and there are also exceptions to the rule given here.)

North Germanic or Scandinavian. The oldest records of this branch are the Runic inscriptions, some of which date as far back as the 4th century A. D. The language of the oldest period (before 1050) was Old Norse. The bulk of the very valuable and extensive Old Norse literature was composed during the 10th and 11th centuries, chiefly in Iceland. During the 9th and 10th centuries great numbers of Danes and Norwegians settled in northern England and greatly influenced the formation of the English language. Old Norse is divided into East Norse (Swedish and Danish) and West Norse (Norwegian and Icelandic). Today Scandinavian languages are spoken by some 15,000,000. The present-day standard languages are Icelandic, Danish, Dano-Norwegian, Norwegian Landsmaal and Swedish. Iceland was settled by Norwegians a thousand years ago and its language, spoken by some 100,000 people, has come to differ markedly from the other Scandinavian languages.

East Germanic, the language of the

IV. INDO-CHINESE OR SINO-TIBETAN

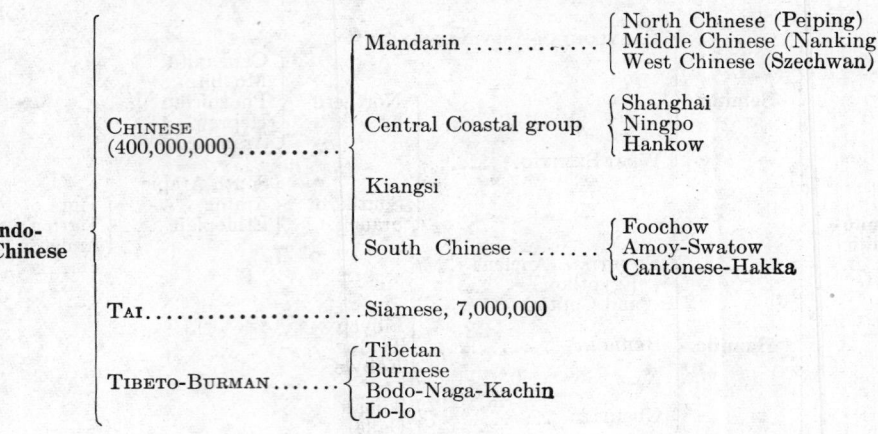

V. DRAVIDIAN

The Dravidian family of southern India and Ceylon includes, besides many lesser languages, Tamil (18,000,000), Malayalam (6,000,000), Kanarese (10,000,000), Telugu (24,000,000) and Brahui (174,000), far off from the rest in the mountains of Baluchistan. In the cultivated dialects the influence of Sanskrit is very noticeable owing to geographical proximity.

VI. THE AUSTRIC FAMILY OF LANGUAGES

Austric

- **Austroasiatic**
  - MALACCA . . . . Semang
  - CENTRAL GROUP . . . . . . { Sakai (Senoi) / Khasi / Nicobar and others }
  - MON-KHMER FAMILY (in parts of southeastern Asia)
  - MUNDA FAMILY . . . . 3,000,000 speakers on the southern slope of the Himalayas and round the plateau of Chota Nagpur in central India
  - CHAM and others

- **Austronesian (or Malayo-Polynesian)** . . . . .
  - INDONESIAN (OR MALAYAN) . . . . . . { Malay, 3,000,000 / Formosan / Javanese, 20,000,000 / Sundanese, 6,500,000 / Maduran, 3,000,000 / Balinese, 1,000,000 / Visaya, 2,750,000 } Philippine languages / Tagalog, 1,500,000 and others / Malagasy, 3,000,000 (in Madagascar) }
  - MELANESIAN . . . . { Solomon Islands / Fiji Islands / Gilbert Islands / Marshall Islands }
  - MICRONESIAN . . . . { Caroline Islands / Marianas / Island of Yap }
  - POLYNESIAN . . . . { Maori / Samoan / Tahitian / Hawaiian / Easter Island }

Goths, Vandals and Burgundians, has long been extinct. East Germanic settlers seem to have preserved their language in the Crimea and elsewhere on the Black Sea until the 18th century. Gothic was spoken in the various Gothic kingdoms on the Baltic Sea, the Black Sea, the Adriatic and the Mediterranean. Almost the only source of our knowledge of the language is found in the fragments of a Bible translation made in the 4th century by Ulfilas (*c.* 311–381), bishop of the Visigoths. Since Gothic is the oldest Germanic language known its study is of great importance to anyone interested in the history of the English language. The inflectional forms occurring in Gothic are much closer to the original Germanic forms than are those used in Old English. Gothic, therefore, is very useful in

UNITED NATIONS

BOLIVIAN children study outdoors while awaiting completion of a new school building. Formal schooling and technical education are part of the assistance offered by UNESCO and the International Labour Organization to help underdeveloped countries advance.

tracing the history of English words and forms.

West Germanic. After the breakup of the Primitive Germanic unity, the western tribes still remained together for some time, forming the area of West Germanic dialects. Later these developed into two major divisions—German and Anglo-Frisian.

German has developed through three periods—Old High German (750–1100), Middle High German (1100–1450) and New High German (after 1450). There are many German dialects: (1) High German, subdivided into Upper German (Alemannian and Bavarian) and Middle German (East Franconian, Rhenish Franconian and Middle Franconian); (2) Low German (Low Franconian, Low Saxon and Plattdeutsch). In the Netherlands a Low Franconian dialect is the literary and official language known to us as Dutch. The language of the Dutch colonists in South Africa became independent and is now called Afrikaans. Flemish is the Low Franconian spoken in the northern half of Belgium. The total number of people speaking Dutch or Flemish is about 13,000,000. Yiddish (Judaeo-German), the language spoken by many of the Jews in eastern Europe and by some of their descendants in other parts of the world (about 10,-000,000), is based on an East Franconian dialect of the Middle Ages. The modern literary German originated in the 14th century. At that time the imperial chancery and many of the lesser courts in Germany adopted German in place of Latin as the official language. Naturally in the intercourse between the imperial and other courts the imperial dialect was adopted.

The so-called imperial dialect was that used by the local court of the emperors, who at that time were living at Prague. So a High German dialect became the *Kanzleisprache*, chancery speech or official language of Germany. Through the work of Luther this language was given its greatest impetus toward widespread usage. In his translation of the Bible he used the language of the Saxon chancery. Gradually one part of Germany after another adopted this as the written language. The German language is spoken by about 90,-000,000 people in Germany, Switzerland, Austria, Italy, Czechoslovakia, Rumania, Russia, Poland, Lithuania, Latvia, Luxembourg, Alsace-Lorraine, the United States, Brazil and Argentina.

Anglo-Frisian was spoken by the Anglians, Saxons, and Frisians who invaded the British Isles in the 5th century and introduced there the language that became English. Frisian, however, is still spoken by some 350,-000 persons on the coast and coastal islands along the North Sea. English has had three periods of development Old English or Anglo-Saxon (after 675–c. 1100), Middle English (1100–1500) and Modern English (after 1500). Its first records date from the 7th century. Old English had four main dialects: Northumbrian, Mercian, West Saxon and Kentish. In the course of centuries English has absorbed a multitude of Scandinavian, Norman-French and cosmopolitan words; but in its structure it is to this day quite as purely West Germanic as it was in Old English times. It is spoken by about 170,000,000 people in the British Isles, the United States, Canada, Australia, New Zealand, South Africa and all the dependencies of England, such as India and Egypt. English is the commercial language of a large part of the world today and its influence in this field is steadily growing. If we count the important factor of foreigners speaking English, it is the most widespread of languages. Local dialects are of small extent and for the most part they are mutually intelligible.

VII. OTHER FAMILIES

Papuan, on New Guinea and adjacent islands.

The Australian language.

The Hyperborean family of languages in the extreme northeastern corner of Asia.

The Sudan languages (455 in all) spoken by the Negro population (some 50,000,000) of central Africa, little known and not all belonging to the same family; best known among them: Wolof and Ful in Senegal and French Sudan, Hausa in the central region, Nubian in the east (round Khartoum).

The vast Bantu family of languages (more than 100) spoken by 50,000,000 people south of the African Sudan: Luganda, Swahili, Kafir, Zulu, Subiya and Herero.

Southwestern Africa has two unrelated linguistic areas: the Bushman, with some 50,000 speakers, and the Hottentot, which is spoken by some 250,000.

The Caucasian languages in the Caucasus region.

Japanese (with 56,000,000), Korean (with 17,000,000), Basque (only surviving form of ancient Iberian) in the Pyrenees Mountains and Etruscan (extinct for 2,500 years) in Italy are so far unclassified.

VIII. NATIVE AMERICAN LANGUAGES

ESKIMO. The language spoken from Greenland over Baffinland and Alaska to the Aleutian Islands and the east coast of Siberia.

AMERICAN INDIAN. In Central America and South America about 15,000,000 Indians speak a number of languages whose relationships are unknown. More than 20 independent families have been set up for Mexico and Central America and about 80 for South America. The Mayan family in Yucatan was the bearer of an ancient civilization. The Arawak and Carib families prevailed once in the West Indies. Quichuan was the language of the Inca civilization.

In North America the territory north of Mexico was inhabited, before the coming of the white man, by nearly 1,500,000 Indians. In this same territory today the number of speakers of Indian languages is some 250,-000, and their languages are tentatively grouped in 24 to 50 entirely unrelated families. Many have already died out. A few of the largest families are:

Algonquian: in eastern and central Canada (Micmac, Montagnais, Cree); in New England (Penobscot, Massachusetts, Natick, Narraganset, Mohican, Delaware); around the Great Lakes (Ojibwa, Potawatami, Menominee, Sack, Fox, Kickapoo, Peoria, Illinois, Miami); and in the western United States (Blackfoot, Cheyenne, Arapaho).

Athapascan: in northwestern Canada, in California (Hupa, Mattole); with a large area in the Southwest (Apache, Navaho).

Iroquoian (surrounded by Algonquian): Huron (or Wyandot); languages of the Iroquois type (Mohawk, Oneida, Onondaga, Cayuga, Seneca, Tuscarora); Cherokee.

Muskhogean: Choctaw, Chickasaw, Creek, Seminole.

The Siouan family: Dakota, Teton, Ogalala, Assiniboin, Kansa, Omaha, Osage, Iowa, Missouri, Winnebago, Mandan, Crow.

The Uto-Aztecan family:

Uto-Aztecan

PIMAN (east of the Gulf of California)

SHOSHONEAN (southern California and eastward) .... { Ute, Paiute, Shoshoni, Comanche, Hopi }

THE NAHUATLAN FAMILY (in Mexico) .... { Aztec }

Artificial Auxiliary Languages.—There have been more than 40 attempts to create a universal language that might serve as a means of communication for all peoples of the earth. This artificial language is not to replace existing tongues but to be a secondary language useful as a means of ready communication between people with different native tongues. Within each country the mother tongue with its great historical and literary tradition will continue to be the principal language. Most early attempts to construct such a language were based not on an existing language but upon the inventor's personal method of classifying ideas and creating words for them. An example of this type of auxiliary language is Ro, invented in 1904 in the United States by the Reverend P. Foster. The most successful creations, however, have been based on one or more existing languages.

Volapük, invented in 1879 by Father Schleyer of Baden, Germany, and based on English, was very popular for a time. Even more successful was the creation of Esperanto in 1887 by

Ludwig Zamenhof of Warsaw. Both Volapük and Esperanto were too complicated for their stated purpose. Other attempts that followed include: Ido (1907), a modified form of Esperanto; Esperanto II; Latino sine flexione (Latin without endings); Occidental and Novial. To be of any use, a constructed language must be easier to learn than the existing natural languages of world importance—English, French, German, Spanish, Russian. This goal can be reached by simplifying the grammatical structure. In vocabulary Latin roots are advantageous because they are fundamental in all the Latin languages of Europe (Italian, French, Spanish, Portuguese, Rumanian) and they are found also in the technical vocabularies of English and most other European languages. Of all constructed languages Novial (New International Auxiliary Language), invented in 1923 by the Danish linguist Professor Otto Jespersen, seems to be the one best suited for its purpose. Its grammar is simplified to the utmost with almost no inflection. The vocabulary is taken from the languages of western Europe. To stimulate public interest in favor of a constructed language, the International Auxiliary Language Association (Iala) was founded in 1924, with headquarters in New York and a European office at The Hague, Netherlands. Activity has been focused on the attempt to choose from the various proposed languages the one easiest to learn, most accurate and most efficient.

DICTIONARY OF ABBREVIATIONS

A., a. Adjective
a, @. (Lat. *ad.*) To; at
A. A. A. S. American Association for the Advancement of Science
A. A. G. Assistant Adjutant General
A1 First Rate (at Lloyd's)
A. B. (Lat. *Artium Baccalaureus.*) Bachelor of Arts
Abbr., Abbrev. Abbreviated, Abbreviation
Abp. Archbishop
A. C. (Lat. *Ante Christum.*) Before Christ
Acad. Academy
Acc., acc. Accusative
Acc., Acct. Account
A. D. (Lat. *Anno Domini.*) In the year of our Lord
Ad., advt. Advertisement
A. D. C. Aide-de-camp
Adj. Adjective
Adj. Adjutant
Adj. Gen. Adjutant General
Ad lib., Ad libit. (Lat. *ad libitum*), At pleasure
Adm. Admiral; Admiralty
Admr. Administrator
Admx. Administratrix
Adv. Adverb
Æ., Æt. (Lat. *Ætatis.*) Of age, aged
A. G., Adjt. Gen. Adjutant General
Ag. (Lat. *argentum.*) Silver
Agr., Agric. Agriculture, Agricultural
Agt. Agent
A. L. of H. American Legion of Honor
Al. Aluminum
Ala. Alabama
Alas. Ter. Alaska Territory
A. M. (Lat. *Artium Magister.*) Master of Arts
A. M. (Lat. *ante meridiem.*) Before noon
Am., Amer. America, American
Amer. Phil. Soc. American Philosophical Society
Amt. Amount
An. (Lat. *anno.*) In the year

Anat. Anatomy, anatomical
Anon. Anonymous
Ans. Answer
A. P. Associated Press
App. Appendix
Approx. Approximate, approximately
Apr. April
Aq. (Lat. *aqua.*) Water
A. R. A. Associate of the Royal Academy
Arab. Arabic, Arabian
Arch. Architecture
Archeol. Archeology
Arith. Arithmetic, arithmetical
Ariz. Arizona
Ark. Arkansas
Arr. Arrive, arrives, arrived, arrival
Art. Article
Assn. Association
Assoc. associate
Asst. Assistant
A. S. S. U. American Sunday School Union
Assyr. Assyrian
Astrol. Astrology
Astron. Astronomy, astronomical
Atty. Attorney
Atty. Gen. Attorney General
Aug. Augustus; August
Avoir. Avoirdupois
b. Born
B. A. Bachelor of Arts
Bal. Balance
Bap., Bapt. Baptist
Bar. Barrel; Barometer
Bart., Bt. Baronet
Bat., Batt. Battalion
Bbl., bbls. Barrel, barrels
B. C. Before Christ
B. C. L. (Lat. *Baccalaureus Civilis Legis.*) Bachelor of Civil Law
Bdls. Bundles
Berks. Berkshire
Bib. Bible, biblical
Biog. Biography, biographical
Biol. Biology, biological

B. LL. (Lat. *Baccalaureus Legum.*) Bachelor of Laws
B. M., B. Mus. (Lat. *Baccalaureus Musicæ.*) Bachelor of Music
Boh. Bohemian, *or* Czech
Bot. Botany, botanical
Bp. Bishop
Br., Bro. Brother
Brig. Brigade
Brig. Gen. Brigadier General
Brit. Britain
B. S. Bachelor of Science
B. Sc. (Lat. *Baccalaureus Scientiæ.*) Bachelor of Science
Bt. Baronet
B. T. U. British Thermal Unit
Bucks. Buckinghamshire
Bush. Bushel
B. V. M. Blessed Virgin Mary
Bvt. Brevet
bx., bxs. Box, boxes
C. Cent, cents; Centigrade; Consul; Centime, centimes
Calif. California; Calendar
Cam., Camb. Cambridge
Cantab. (Lat. *Cantabrigiensis.*) Of Cambridge
Caps. Capitals
Capt. Captain
Card. Cardinal
Cath. Catharine; Catholic
Cav. Cavalry
C. B. Companion of the Bath
C. E. Civil Engineer
Cent. (Lat. *centum.*) A hundred; Centigrade
Centig. Centigrade
Cf. (Lat. *confer.*) Compare
c. ft. Cubic feet
C. G. Coast Guard; Consul General
C. G. S. Centimeter, Gram, Second
C. H. Courthouse
Ch. Church; Chapter
Chap. Chapter
Chem. Chemistry, Chemical
Chron. Chronicle; Chronology

C. I. Order of the Crown of India
C. I. E. Companion of the Order of the Indian Empire
Civ. Civil
Cl. Chlorine
Clk. Clerk
cm. Centimeter
C. M. G. Companion of the Order of St. Michael and St. George
Co. Company; County, Cobalt
C. O. D. Cash on delivery; Collect (*payment*) on delivery
Col. Colonel; Colossians; Column
Coll. College; Collection; Colleague
Colo. Colorado
Com. Commander; Commerce; Commissioner; Committee; Commodore; Common
Commdr. Commander
Commsr. Commissioner
Comp. Compare, comparative; Compound, compounded
Con., contra (Lat.) Against
Cong. Congregation, Congregational, Congregationalist; Congress
Conj. Conjunction
Conn. Connecticut
Cor. Corinthians
Corn. Cornwall, Cornish
Corp. Corporal; Corporation
Cos. Cosine
C. P. A. Certified Public Accountant
Cr. Credit, creditor
Cres. Crescendo
C. S. A. Confederate States of America
C. S. I. Companion of the Star of India
csks. Casks
ct. (Lat. *centum.*) A hundred
Ct. Court
Ct., Conn. Connecticut
Cu. (Lat. *cuprum.*) Copper
cub., cu. ft. Cubic, cubic foot
cwt. A hundredweight; Hundredweights
d. (Lat. *denarius, denarii.*) A penny, pence
d. Died

Dan. Danish
Dat. Dative
D. C. District of Columbia
D. C. L. Doctor of Civil (*or* Canon) Law
D. D. (Lat. *Divinitatis Doctor.*) Doctor of Divinity
D. D. S. Doctor of Dental Surgery
Dec. December; Declination
decim. Decimeter
Def. Definition
Deft. Defendant
Deg. Degree, degrees
Del. Delaware
Del. (Lat. *delineavit.*) He (*or* she) drew it
D. Eng. Doctor of Engineering
Dep., Dept. Department
Deut. Deuteronomy
Dict. Dictionary; Dictator
Dis., Disct. Discount
Dist. District
Dist. Atty. District Attorney
Div. Divide, dividend, division, divisof
D. Lit., D. Litt. Doctor of Literature
D. M., D. Mus. Doctor of Music
D. O. Doctor of Osteopathy; Doctor of Optics
do. (Ital. *ditto.*) The same
doz. Dozen
Dpt. Deponent
Dr. Debtor; Doctor; Dram, drams
D. Sc. Doctor of Science
Du., Dut. Dutch
Duo. 12mo. Duodecimo (12 leaves to a sheet)
D. V. (Lat. *Deo volente*). God willing
D. V. S. Doctor of Veterinary Surgery
dwt. (Lat. *denarius*, and English *weight*.) Pennyweight, pennyweights
E. East, eastern; English; Edinburgh
ea. Each
Eben. Ebenezer
E. C. Established Church
Eccl., Eccles. Ecclesiastes; Ecclesiastical
Econ. Economy
Ed. Editor; Edition
E. E. Electrical Engineer
E. E. M. P. Envoy Extraordinary and Minister Plenipotentiary
e. g. (Lat. *exempli gratia*.) For example
E. I. East Indies, East Indian
Elec., Elect. Electric, electricity
Emp. Emperor, empress
E. N. E. East-northeast
Eng. England, English
Eng., Engin. Engineer, engineering
Eng. Dept. Department of Engineers
Eph. Ephesians; Ephraim
Epiph. Epiphany
Epis. Episcopal
E. S. E. East-southeast
Esq., Esqr. Esquire
et al. (Lat. *et alibi.*) And elsewhere
et al. (Lat. *et alii*, or *aliæ, alia.*) And others
etc., &c. (Lat. *et cæteri, cæteræ* or *cætera.*) And others, and so forth
Ethnol. Ethnology, ethnological
et seq. sq. or *sqq.* (Lat. *et sequentes* or *et sequentia.*) And the following
Etym. or *Etymol.* Etymology
Exec. Executor
Execx. Executrix
Exod. Exodus
Ez. Ezra
Ezek. Ezekiel
E. & O. E. Errors and omissions excepted
F. Fellow; Folio; Fahrenheit
f. Farthing, farthings
f., fem. Feminine
f. Franc, francs
Fahr. Fahrenheit
F. C. S. Fellow of the Chemical Society
Feb. February
Fec. (Lat. *fecit.*) He (*or* She) did it
Fem. Feminine
Feud. Feudal
F. F. V. First Families of Virginia
F. G. S. Fellow of the Geological Society
F. I. C. Fellow of the Chemical Institute
Fig. Figure, figures; figurative, figuratively
Fl. Flemish; Florin, florins; Flourished
Flu. Florida
F. M. Field Marshal
Fo., Fol. Folio
F. O. B. Free on board
For. Foreign
Fr. France, French; Francis; Franes
F. R. A. S. Fellow of the Royal Astronomical (*or* Asiatic) Society
F. R. C. P. Fellow of the Royal College of Physicians
F. R. C. S. Fellow of the Royal College of Surgeons
F. R. G. S. Fellow of the Royal Geographical Society
F. R. H. S. Fellow of the Royal Horticultural Society
F. R. H. S. or *F. R. Hist. S.* Fellow of the Royal Historical Society
Fri. Friday

F. R. M. S. Fellow of the Royal Microscopical Society
F. R. S. Fellow of the Royal Society
Ft. Fort; Foot, feet
F. Z. S. Fellow of the Zoölogical Society
F. & A. M. Free and Accepted Masons
Ga. Georgia
G. A. General Assembly
Gal. Galatians
gal. Gallon, gallons
G. A. R. Grand Army of the Republic
G. B. Great Britain
G. C. B. Grand Cross of the Bath
G. C. M. G. Grand Cross SS. Michael and George
G. C. S. I. Grand Commander of the Star of India
Gen. General
Gen. Genesis; Genitive
Gend. Gender
Genit. Genitive
Gent. Gentleman, gentlemen
Geo. George; Georgia
Geog. Geography, geographical
Geol. Geology, geological
Geom. Geometry, geometrical
Ger., Germ. German
Gi. Gill, gills
G. M. Grand Master
G. O. P. Grand Old Party (Republican)
Gov. Governor
Gov. Gen. Governor General
Govt. Government
G. P. O. General Post Office
gr. Grain, grains; Gross
Gr. Greek
Gram. Grammar, grammatical
gtt. (Lat. *gutta* or *guttæ*.) Drop *or* drops
H. Hour, hours; Hydrogen
Hants. Hampshire
H. B. M. His (*or* Her) Brittanic Majesty
Heb., Hebr. Hebrew, Hebrews
H. H. His (*or* Her) Highness; His Holiness (the Pope)
Hhd. Hogshead, hogsheads
H. I. H. His (*or* Her) Imperial Highness
Hind. Hindu, Hindustan, Hindustani
Hist. History, historical
H. J., H. J. S. (Lat. *his jacet, hic jacet sepultus.*) Here lies, Here lies buried
H. M. His (*or* Her) Majesty
H. M. S. His (*or* Her) Majesty's Service, Ship, *or* Steamer
Hon., Honble. Honorable
Hos. Hosea
H. P. Half-pay; High-Priest; Horse power
H. R. H. His (*or* Her) Royal Highness
Hund. Hundred, hundreds
Ia. Iowa
Ib., Ibid. (Lat. *ibidem.*) In the same place
Icel. Iceland, Icelandic
Id. (Lat. *idem.*) The same
Ida. Idaho
i. e. (Lat. *id est.*) That is
I. H. S. (Lat. *Iesus* [or *Jesus*] *Hominum Salvator.*) Jesus the Savior of Men
Ill. Illinois
Imp., Imperf. Imperfect
Imper. Imperative
in. Inch, inches
Incog. (Ital. *incognito, incognita.*) Unknown
Ind. India, Indian; Indiana
Indic. Indicative
Inf., Infin. Infinitive
Ins., Insur. Insurance
Insp. Inspector
Insp. Gen. Inspector General
Inst. Instant; the present month; Institute, institution
Int. Interest
Interj. Interjection
Intrans. Intransitive
Int. Rev. Internal Revenue
Introd. Introduction
I. O. O. F. Independent Order of Oddfellows
I. O. R. M. Improved Order of Red Men
I. O. U. I owe you
i. q. (Lat. *idem quod.*) The same as
Ir. Ireland, Irish
Is., Isa. Isaiah
Isl. Island
It., Ital. Italic; Italy; Italian
Jan. January
J. C. D. (Lat. *Juris Civilis Doctor.*) Doctor of Civil Law
Jer. Jeremiah
J. G. W. Junior Grand Warden
Jon., Jona. Jonathan
Josh. Joshua
J. P. Justice of the Peace
*Jr. Juror; Junior
Judg. Judges
Jul. July; Julius; Julian
Jun. June
Jun., Junr. Junior
K. King; Knight
Kan., Kans. Kansas
K. B. Knight of the Bath
K. B. King's Bench

K. C. King's Counsel; Knights of Columbus
K. C. B. Knight Commander of the Bath
K. C. M. G. Knight Commander of St. Michael and St. George
Ken., Ky. Kentucky
K. G. Knight of the Garter
K. G. C. Knight of the Grand Cross
Ki. Kings
kilom., kilo. Kilometer
K. of P. Knights of Pythias
K. P. Knight of St. Patrick
Ks. Kansas
K. T. Knight of the Thistle; Knight Templar
Ky. Kentucky
L. Latin; Lake; Lord; Lady
L., l., £. (Lat. *libra.*) Pound, pounds (sterling)
L., lb., ℔ (Lat. *libra.*) Pound, pounds (weight)
La. Louisiana
Lam. Lamentations
Lat. Latin; Latitude
lb. Pound, pounds (weight)
l. c. Lower case (in printing)
l. c., loc. cit. (Lat. *loco citato.*) In the place before cited
Lev. Leviticus
L. H. D. (Lat. *Litterarum Humanorum Doctor.*) Doctor of Humanities
L. I. Long Island
Lib. (Lat. *liber.*) Book
Lieut. Lieutenant
Lieut. Col. Lieutenant Colonel
Lieut. Gen. Lieutenant General
Lieut. Gov. Lieutenant Governor
Linn. Linnæus, Linne, Linnean
Liq. Liquor, liquid
Lit. Literally; Literature, literary
Lit. D. or Litt. D. (Lat. *Literarum Doctor.*) Doctor of Literature
LL. B. (Lat. *Legum Baccalaureus.*) Bachelor of Laws
LL.D. (Lat. *Legum Doctor.*) Doctor of Laws
Lon., Long. Longitude
l. s. d. (Lat. *libra, solidi, denarii.*) Pounds, shillings, pence
Lt. Lieutenant
m. Married; Masculine; Meter, meters; Mile, miles; Minute, minutes
M. Monday; Morning; Monsieur
M. (Lat. *mille.*) Thousand
M. (Lat. *meridies.*) Meridian, Noon
M. A. Master of Arts
Mac., Macc. Maccabees
Maj. Major
Maj. Gen. Major General
Manuf. Manufactures, manufacturing
Mar. March; Maritime
Marq. Marquis
Mas., Masc. Masculine
Mass. Massachusetts
Math. Mathematics, mathematical
Matt. Matthew
M. B. (Lat. *Medicinæ Baccalaureus.*) Bachelor of Medicine
M. C. Member of Congress; Master of Ceremonies
Mch. March
M. D. (Lat. *Medicinæ Doctor.*) Doctor of Medicine
Md. Maryland
Mdse. Merchandise
M. E. Mining Engineer; Mechanical Engineer
M. E. Methodist Episcopal
Me. Maine
Mech. Mechanics mechanical
Med. Medicine, medical; Medieval
M. E. S. Methodist Episcopal South
Messrs. (Fr. *messieurs.*) Gentlemen
Mex. Mexico
Mfd., Mfs. Manufactured, manufactures
Mfg. Manufacturing
M. F. H. Master of Foxhounds
Mich. Michigan
Min. Mineralogy, mineralogical; Minute, minutes
Minn. Minnesota
Miss. Mississippi
Mlle. (Fr. *mademoiselle.*) Miss
MM. (Fr. *messieurs.*) Gentlemen
mm. Millimeters
Mme. (Fr. *madame.*) Madam
Mo. Missouri; Month
mo. Month
Mon. Monday
Mont. Montana
M. P. Member of Parliament
M. P. P. Member of the Provincial Parliament
Mr. Master, Mister
Mrs. Mistress (when abbreviated pronounced mis'sis)
MS. Manuscript
MSS. Manuscripts
MT., Mts. Mount, mountains
Mus. Museum; Music, musical
Mus. B. (Lat. *Musicæ Baccalaureus.*) Bachelor of Music

Mus. D., Mus. Doc., Mus. Doct. (Lat. *Musicæ Doctor.*) Doctor of Music
N. Noon; North; Noun; Number; New; Neuter
N. A. North America, North American
N. B. New Brunswick; North Britain (*i. e.* Scotland)
N. B. (Lat. *Nota bene.*) Note well, Take notice
N. C. North Carolina
N. D., N. Dak. North Dakota
N. E. New England; Northeast
Neb. Nebraska
Neh. Nehemiah
Nem. con. (Lat. *nemine contradicente.*) No one contradicting, unanimously
Neth. Netherlands
Neut. Neuter
Nev. Nevada
New Test., N. T. New Testament
N. F. Newfoundland
N. H. New Hampshire
N. J. New Jersey
N. M. New Mexico
N. N. E. North-northeast
N. N. W. North-northwest
No. (Lat. *numero.*) Number
nol. pros. (*nolle prosequi.*) To be unwilling to proceed
Nom. Nominative
Non seq. (Lat. *non sequitur.*) It does not follow (as a consequence)
Nos. Numbers
Nov. November
N. P. Notary Public
N. S. New style (since 1752); Nova Scotia
N. T. New Testament
Num., Numb. Numbers
N. W. Northwest
N. W. T. Northwest Territory
N. Y. New York
N. Z. New Zealand
O. Ohio; Old
ob. (Lat. *obiit.*) He (*or* she) died
Ob., Obad. Obadiah
obit. (Lat. *obitur.*) He (*or* she) died
Obj. Objective
Obs. Obsolete
Oct. October
Oct., 8vo. Octavo
O. F. Odd Fellows
O. H. M. S. On Her Majesty's Service
O. K. "All correct"
Okl. Oklahoma
Old Test., O. T. Old Testament
O. M. Old Measurement
O. M. I. Oblate of Mary Immaculate
O. R. C. Officers' Reserve Corps
Oreg. or *Ore.* Oregon
O. S. Old Style (previous to 1752)
O. S. B. Order of St. Benedict
O. S. F. Order of St. Francis
O. T. Old Testament
O. U. A. M. Order of United American Mechanics
Oxon. (Lat. *Oxonia, Oxoniensis.*) Oxford; of Oxford
oz. Ounce
P. Page; Participle; Past; Pole; Port
Pa. Pennsylvania
Part. Participle
Pathol. Pathology
P. C. Police Constable; Privy Council, Privy Councilor
P. D. Police Department
Pd. Paid
P. E. Protestant Episcopal
P. E. I. Prince Edward Island
Penn. or *Penna.* Pennsylvania
Per., Pers. Persia; Persian; Personal
Per cent, per ct. (Lat. *per centum.*) By the hundred
Perf. Perfect
Phar., Pharm. Pharmacy
Ph. B. (Lat. *Philosophiæ Baccalaureus.*) Bachelor of Philosophy
Ph. D. (Lat. *Philosophiæ Doctor.*) Doctor of Philosophy
Ph. G. Graduate in pharmacy
Phil. Philip; Philippians; Philosophy, philosophical
Phys. Physics, physical; Physiology, physiological
Physiol. Physiology, physiological
Pinx., Pxt. (Lat. *pinxit.*) He (*or* she) painted it
Pk. Peck
Pl. Place; Plate; Plural
Plup., Plupf. Pluperfect
Plur. Plural
P. M. (Lat. *post meridiem.*) Afternoon
P. M. Past Master; Postmaster
P. M. G. Postmaster General
P. O. Postoffice
Pop. Population
Port. Portugal, Portuguese
Poss. Possessive
pp. Pages
p.p. Past (*or* perfect) participle
P. P. Parish priest
P. P. C. (Fr. *pour prendre congé.*) To take leave. [*T. T. L.*]
p. pr. Present participle

Pr. Present; Priest; Prince
P. R. Prize Ring
prep. Preposition
Pres. President; Present
Prof. Professor
Pron. Pronoun; Pronounced, pronunciation
Pro tem. (Lat. *pro tempore.*) For the time being
Prov. Proverbs, proverbial, proverbially; Provincial, provincially; Provost
Prox. (Lat. *proximo.*) Next, *or* of the next month
P. S. (Lat. *post scriptum.*) Postscript
Ps., Psa. Psalm, psalms
Psychol. Psychology
Pt. Part; Payment; Point; Port; Pint
pwt. Pennyweight
Q. E. D. (Lat. *quod erat demonstrandum.*) Which was to be proved
Q. E. F. (Lat. *quod erat faciendum.*) Which was to be done
Q. M. Quartermaster
Q. M. Gen. Quartermaster General
qt. Quart
q. v. (Lat. *quod vide.*) Which see
R. Railway; Réaumur; River
R. (Lat. *recipe.*) Take
R. A. Royal Academy, Royal Academician; Rear Admiral; Royal Arch; Royal Artillery
R. C. Roman Catholic
R. E. Royal Engineers; Royal Exchange
R. E. Reformed Episcopal
Réaum. Réaumur
Recd. Received
Recpt. Receipt
Ref. Ch. Reformed Church
Reg., Regt. Regiment, regimental
Rep., Repub. Republic; Republican
Rev. Revelation; Reverend
R. F. D. Rural free delivery
Rhet. Rhetoric, rhetorical
R. I. Rhode Island
R. I. P. (Lat. *requiescat in pace.*) May he (*or* she) rest in peace
Riv. River
R. M. Royal Mail; Royal Marines
R. M. S. Royal Mail Steamer; Royal Mail Service
R. N. Royal Navy
R. N. R. Royal Naval Reserve
Rom. Roman, Romans
R. O. T. C. Reserve Officers' Training Corps
R. R. Railroad
R. S. V. P. (Fr. *répondez s'il vous plaît.*) Answer, if you please; Please reply

Rt. Right
Rt. Hon. Right Honorable
Rt. Rev. Right Reverend
R. V. Revised Version
Ry. Railway
S. Saint; Saturday; Section; Shilling; Sign; Signor; Solo; Soprano; South; Sun; Sunday; Sabbath
s. Second, seconds; See; Singular; Son; Succeeded
S. A. South Africa; South America
Sab. Sabbath
Sam., Saml. Samuel
S. A. S. (Lat. *Societatis Antiquarierum Socius.*) Fellow of the Society of Antiquaries
Sat. Saturday
S. C. South Carolina
S. caps., Sm. caps. Small capitals (*in printing*)
Sc. B. (Lat. *Scientiæ Baccalaureus.*) Bachelor of Science
Sc. D. (Lat. *Scientiæ Doctor.*) Doctor of Science
Sc. M. Master of Science
Scrip., Script. Scripture, scriptural
Sculp., Sc. (Lat. *sculpsit.*) He (*or* she) engraved it
S. D., S. Dak. South Dakota
S. E. Southeast
Sec. Second
Sec., Sect. Section
Sec., Secy. Secretary
Sen. Senate, senator
Sen. Doc. Senate Document
Sep., Sept. September
Seq. (Lat. *sequentes, sequentia.*) The following or the next
Serg., Sergt. Sergeant
Sh., S. Shilling, shillings
Sing. Singular
S. J. Society of Jesus
Soc. Society
S. of Sol. Song of Solomon
s. p. (Lat. *sine prole.*) Without issue
S. P. C. A. Society for the Prevention of Cruelty to Animals
S. P. C. C. Society for the Prevention of Cruelty to Children
sp. gr., s. g. Specific gravity
S. P. Q. R. (Lat. *Senatus Populusque Romanus.*) The Senate and People of Rome
sq. Square; *sq. ft.* Square foot, feet; *sq. in.* Square inch, inches; *sq. m.* Square mile, miles; *sq. yd.* Square yard; *sq. rd.* Square rod
Sr. Senior; sir
SS. Saints

SS. (Lat. *scilicet*), namely; (Lat. *semis*), half
S. S. Sunday School
S. S. E. South-southeast
S. S. W. South-southwest
St. Saint; Stone; Strait; Street
S. T. D. (Lat. *Sacræ Theologiæ Doctor.*) Doctor of Divinity
Str. Steamer, steam vessel
Subj. Subjunctive
Suff. Suffix
Sun., Sund. Sunday
Sup. Superior; Superlative; Supplement; Supine; Superfine
Supt. Superintendent
Surg. Surgeon, Surgery
Sur. Gen. Surgeon General
S. W. Southwest
Syn. Synonym, synonymous
T. Tenor; Ton; Tun; Tuesday
Tenn. Tennessee
Ter. Territory
Tex. Texas
Thess. Thessalonians
Thurs. Thursday
Tim. Timothy
T. N. T. Trinitrotoluene (high explosive)
Topog. Topography, topographical
Tp. Township
Tr. Translation, translator, translated; Transpose; Treasurer; Trustee
Trans. Transaction; Translation, translator, translated
Treas. Treasurer
Trig., Trigon. Trigonometry, trigonometrical
Tu., Tues. Tuesday
U. Utah
U. K. United Kingdom
Ult. (Lat. *ultimo.*) Last; Of the last month
Univ. University
U. P. United Press
U. S. United States
U. S. A. United States of America; United States Army
U. S. M. United States Mail; United States Marine
U. S. M. A. United States Military Academy
U. S. N. United States Navy
U. S. N. A. United States Naval Academy
U. S. S. United States Senate; United States Ship *or* Steamer
Ut. Utah
Ux. (Lat. *uxor.*) Wife
V. Verb

V., vs. (Lat. *versus.*) Against
V. (Lat. *Vide.*) See
Va. Virginia
v. aux. Verb auxiliary
V. C. Vice-Chancellor; Victoria Cross
v. def. Verb defective
v. i. Verb intransitive
Vice-Pres. Vice-President
v. imp. Verb impersonal
v. irr. Verb irregular
Vis., Visc. Viscount
Viz. (Lat. *videlicet.*) Namely; to wit
v. n. Verb neuter
Voc. Vocative
Vol. Volume
Vols. Volumes
V.-P. Vice-President
v. r. Verb reflexive
V. Rev. Very Reverend
Vs. (Lat. *versus.*) Against
V. S. Veterinary Surgeon
v. t. Verb transitive
Vt. Vermont
W. Wednesday; Week; Welsh; West, western
Wash. Washington
w. c. Water closet
W. C. T. U. Women's Christian Temperance Union
Wed. Wednesday
w. f. Wrong font (*in printing*)
W. I. West Indies
Wis., Wisc. Wisconsin
Wk. Week
W. Lon. West Longitude
Wm. William
W. N. W. West-northwest
W. S. W. West-southwest
Wt. Weight
W. Va. West Virginia
Wyo. Wyoming
X. Christ
x. An unknown quantity
Xmas. Christmas
Y., Yr. Year
Yd. Yard
Yds. Yards
Y. M. C. A. Young Men's Christian Association
Y. M. H. A. Young Men's Hebrew Association
Yr. Their; Year; Younger; Your
Yrs. Years; Yours
Y. W. C. A. Young Women's Christian Association
Zach. Zachary
Zech. Zechariah
Zeph. Zephaniah
Zool. Zoology, zoological

BIBLIOGRAPHY

HISTORY AND GENERAL ASPECTS

BODMER, FREDERICK. *The Loom of Language.* W. W. Norton & Co., Inc., 1943.

DIAMOND, ARTHUR S. *The History and Origin of Language.* Philosophical Library Inc., 1959.

ERNST, MARGARET and THURBER, JAMES. *In a Word.* Channel Press, Inc., 1962.

HAYAKAWA, S. I. *Language, Meaning and Maturity.* Harper & Bros., 1954.

LAIRD, CHARLTON. *The Miracle of Language.* The World Publishing Co., 1953.

PEI, MARIO. *All About Language.* J. B. Lippincott Co., 1954.

PEI, MARIO. *The Story of English.* J. B. Lippincott Co., 1953.

PEI, MARIO. *The Story of Language.* J. B. Lippincott Co., 1949.

PIONEER SCHOOLHOUSE of early America.

GRAMMAR AND USAGE

BECKOFF, SAMUEL and GRUBER, EDWARD E. *Good English with Ease.* Arco Publishing Co., Inc., 1963.

BERNSTEIN, THEODORE M. *More Language That Needs Watching.* Channel Press, Inc., 1962.

HANDSCHIN, CHARLES H. *Modern Language Teaching.* Harcourt, Brace & World, Inc., 1962.

HODGES, JOHN G. *Harbrace College Handbook* (5th ed.). Harcourt, Brace & World, Inc., 1962.

HOOK, MATHEWS. *Modern American Grammar and Usage.* The Ronald Press Co., 1956.

MCLEAN, MARGARET. *Good American Speech.* E. P. Dutton & Co., Inc., 1953.

A Manual of Style, (11th rev. ed.). The University of Chicago Press, 1949.

WENTWORTH, HAROLD and FLEXNER, S. B. (eds.). *A Dictionary of American Slang.* The Crowell Collier Publishing Co., 1960.

General aspects of
   literature   1343
Literature of power   1347
History of literature   1350
Dictionary of literary
   allusions   1393
Mythology, legend and
   folklore   1421
Books, persons and places
   of the Bible   1450
Weights, measures and
   distances of the Bible   1460
Dictionary of sobriquets
   and pseudonyms   1461
Great libraries   1463
Parallel outlines of
   world literature   1463
Graded reading list   1483

THE NEW YORK PUBLIC LIBRARY

VOLUME SEVENTEEN

LITERATURE

Literature

INTRODUCTION

A good many people nowadays have come to look on literature as the caviar and olives of the dinner of life. That is too bad, for literature is still the bread and butter and the roast of the feast. It was so in the days before there were any books at all, and it is so today when there are hosts of them. Literature is an essential part of life, as necessary as salt. Men can get along without swift vehicles to ride in, without good clothing and comfortable houses. They can even go without commerce and agriculture, without security and peace. But they must have poetry. If there are no books to store it up for them, there will rise up men who can create it orally, without writing, and other men who can carry it in their heads, in memory, and hand it on to the generations to come. The two works of Homer, the Iliad and the Odyssey, were so carried hundreds of years in men's memories and recited by rhapsodists at the ancient Greek banquets. The Homeric tales of heroes and gods in rhythmed lines were the best part of the feast, better than the roasted oxen and the fiery wine. They did the listeners who heard them more good than their food, made them stronger of body and more enduring of spirit, better fighters and better rulers of the people.

Poetry Built a Glorious Greece.—For here is a mystery, and one of the major ones of all human life since the dawn of history: the actions of life put into beautiful rhythm and beautiful words can create new life and poets can prepare people for great battles in war and the far greater battles in peace better than great kings and commanders and makers of law. Poetry is itself a law of life, and one of the major ones. It can build a nation.

It built Greece. First, there was a handful of shepherd kings clinging to a thin-soiled, rocky peninsula. Their life was hard and full of trouble. They had no unity and no security. Their chief calling was war. And one day a man among them—tradition says he was blind, and maybe that was the reason he had time to do it—took one of the petty wars they waged and made it over in his mind. His name was Homer. He took a tenth-rate town with low walls and built its walls up so they brushed on the stars. He took a beautiful captive that town had inside it, and he made her face over into the loveliest face that ever was on earth, "the face that launched a thousand ships." He took the wild and wilful gods that had come into men's minds from the powers of vegetation and the sun and moon, and he made them into more magnificent men than those that walked on the everyday earth. And the men who fought that war he made taller and handsomer and braver than any Greek king ever had been. He put all these people he had created into a long story of violence and bloodshed and battle. And the song that poet had made of the Trojan War was remembered and repeated after him. Greek warriors heard it and they went out inches taller for having heard it and fought ten times as well. And they built up their houses and towns higher and whiter and lovelier as the years went by. That old war fought in Homeric music created shining cities, codes of law, better citizens, new poetry, plays that held Greek citizens spellbound for centuries and made them more merciful men. That war fought by a poet had life in it, as real war never does, being full of death. It made men feel good about life. It made them feel good about suffering, even, and blind chance and bad luck, the oldest and youngest enemies of man. By building men like gods moving to the music of hexameter lines, Homer built actual men into godlike men of valor and justice and patience. And the greatest civilization the world has known, the Greek, flowered in law and poetry and art and architecture beside the Mediterranean, to become the teacher of all later European nations.

The Troy of history was a dirty little town of Asia Minor, full of quarrelsome and small people living in mean and dark and inconvenient houses. But the Troy of poetry is a city of topless walls, of splendid men and women doing splendid deeds of strength and tenderness, a shining city that has actually built better cities over the face of the earth. The geographic Troy is not the real one. The Troy of literature is the real one. That is what literature means.

Poetry Ennobled the Cruel North.—It was the same story among our Germanic ancestors. Before they had any written laws or written books, when they were still half-savage clans fighting all their lives in the forests and by the bleak North Sea, they had their epics, Beowulf, the later Nibelungen cycle of stories, the long Norse sagas. These long tales told of men's bravery in the face of bitter weather, forest darkness and fear and sudden death. And these songs, older than history, older than all science, older than the Christian religion, kept these northern races alive, kept them strong and trained them to become the stout ancestors of the northern European nations of today. Their real leaders were cruel; they stole and lied and butchered. But these leaders in their songs were noble men, they loved the right, loved their warriors as a father loves his children, and died gloriously for their people. Beowulf got his death slaying the dragon that molested the folk.

Poetry once again improved upon life.

Come forward a thousand years more, and in the Borderland between England and Scotland you will find another race of men who lived by fighting and raiding and slaughter. Suffering and sudden death were always in their midst. They had no books, no sufficient laws, no economic security. Their houses were hovels. But though they did without things to eat and wear, they could not do without literature.

They had a whole bagful of ballads, narrative songs of battle and love, songs made up orally by unknown poets, and they handed them on by word of mouth for generations. In these songs, they found the solace and beauty that life could never give them. The men and women in them were handsomer and braver than they were, they did shining acts of pure heroism and devotion, they loved like kings and queens. Things came by mystic threes and sevens, birds talked, harps played by themselves, fairies danced before green hills, roses came up out of lovers' graves and twined together, the youngest children in a family had all the good luck. The horses were covered with silver and gold and tinkling bells. The sails of their ships were silk and the masts beaten gold. And literature once again kept dull and drab life going.

Jump another five hundred years, and in the Appalachian Mountains among the descendants of the men of Daniel Boone you will find American people doing without books, save the Bible, doing without towns and courthouses and schools, but not doing without poetry. They had kept the Border ballads, and sang them to make life worth living. And the ballads actually made them over into men who lived like Robin Hood and the Douglas and Lord Percy of the songs. And Maine lumberjacks and Western cowboys put up with hard food and hard lodging; but they had to have their songs in which men whom poets had made taught them how to work and ride like Cavaliers.

This, then, is the salt of life, literature. Men have cherished and preserved it since the morning of civilization. It is older than history, than science, than law, than most religions, even. Life cannot get on without it. It is more necessary than geography, chemistry, physics or economics. For it corrects life. It improves upon it. It corrects its mistakes, rejects, selects and rearranges. It takes the inconsequential, haphazard and disappointing experience and makes a design of it, with a beginning, a middle and an end. It gives living a purpose and a point. It is art, in brief. It takes inferior and dull men and makes them over into Falstaff and Don Quixote.

Dick Whittington of the story is a better boy than the real one who became Lord Mayor of London. Literature takes savage outlaws and makes them over into Robin Hood and Achilles.

Life is full of anticlimax and lost motion. Literature never is. It improves the material on which it feeds —experience. The best definition of literature is this: Literature says the best that can be said about life. This definition will fit Shakespeare's plays as well as the story of Cinderella. For Shakespeare in his tragedies shows how men may shine the brighter in the face of hate and disaster. Violence and bloodshed, even, can be builders of life. War can be noble when set to the music of singing words. Sorrow can be a pleasure and give delight in a song or story. Tears can teach us in a poem.

For literature does not exist for its own sake. It exists to improve us, to give us fuller and better lives. It adds new strings to the harp of the human heart, like music and art. It is oratory. It exhorts to do something with our living. A poem of Wordsworth entreats us to fit ourselves into the pageant of the seasons and the winds and the stars. Robert Frost urges us to look at stone walls and birch trees closely, to see the astounding loveliness that is there that can make us feel better about ourselves. Every good novel or play ought to make us love human nature more. For the poet or novelist has taken pains to select the best and most striking of the human actions and thoughts and shape them to a pattern of courage, loyalty, or mercy or love.

The forms of literature are many, but the end of them all is one and the same: to make life endurable and worshipful and better.

The First Poetry Was Oral.—Poetry came first, for poetry was closest to singing and easiest to remember. It existed orally for hundreds of years in the form of the epic. It was always accompanied by music, usually of stringed or impact instruments. All epics are more or less alike, whether they are Hindu or Greek or Nordic. The Ramayana and Mahabharata of India tell of deeds of national importance done by great and strong heroes aided by the gods, just as the Homeric epics do. The theme is war. And the wars are fought for the good of the hero's people. Beowulf sought to rid the world of monsters of the Northland just as Odysseus sought to destroy Mediterranean ones. The beast Grendel and Circe who changed men into beasts were villains of the same blood. Epics were the only literature the human race possessed for many years.

Later on, poetry turned to private subjects, as culture advanced, to love especially, to friendship, merrymaking and drinking, and to farewells at the edge of the grave. Poetry became lyric. It was still accompanied by music—of the lyre; hence its name. This fact of music should never be forgotten. It accounts for Campion's and Herrick's grace and simplicity of wording as it does for Sappho's clarity and simplicity in her Greek line.

Our ancestors in Europe sang a good deal of their lyric poetry until quite modern times.

The forms of the Greek lyric poem became very varied. Aeschylus and Sophocles and Euripides invented most intricate ones in their plays. The varieties in metre and stanza of Sappho, Alcaeus and Anacreon were inherited by the Roman Horace and Catullus. The hexameter line, the six-foot line distinguished by its dactyl foot—so named because it was like the human finger with a long joint and two short ones—was combined with a line of iambic and spondaic feet—a short and a long syllable, and two long ones, respectively—in the elegiac form so much used by the Roman poet Ovid.

When Rome fell and the dark came over Europe, poetry did not die out. The Christian church, which had followed the Roman roads and legions

ODYSSEUS AND THE SIRENS

over a continent, developed most elaborate hymns. Rhyme, the most notable device in most modern poetry, was developed by the medieval church. These old hymns are tissues of lovely, intricate double rhyming and of fresh figures of speech. The recurring sound patterns alone make them pleasing even to one who cannot understand the Latin:

> Dies irae, dies illa,
> Solvet saeclum in favilla,
> Teste David cum Sibylla.

These church hymns are the ancestors of modern lyric poetry. They set the troubadours of France off, set the wandering medieval university students off, on their songs of love and spring and woman's beauty, until all France and Germany and England rang with songs of sheer joy in living. Then the Renaissance came and the recovery of the lyric poets of Greece and Rome, Anacreon, Pindar and Horace. And the ancient forms and new ones covered western Europe with poetry. The Italians developed the sonnet, especially Petrarch in his poems to Laura, and this lyric form, usually devoted to the theme of the passion of love, became the universal form it still is to this day. The Elizabethans were particularly in love with it. Shakespeare's sonnets to his Dark Lady are among the best. Sir Philip

Sidney wrote exquisite ones, on his Stella:

> With how sad steps, O Moon, thou climb'st the skies!
> How silently, and with how wan a face!
> What! may it be that even in heavenly place
> That busy archer his sharp arrows tries?
> Sure, if that long-with-love-acquainted eyes
> Can judge of love, thou feel'st a lover's case:
> I read it in thy looks; thy languish'd grace
> To me, that feel the like, thy state descries.
> Then, even of fellowship, O Moon, tell me,
> Is constant love deem'd there but want of wit?
> Are beauties there as proud as here they be?
> Do they above love to be loved, and yet
> Those lovers scorn whom that love doth possess?
> Do they call 'virtue' there—ungratefulness?

The sonnet is the most intimate of all modern lyric forms and the most intricate. It has fourteen lines, and these lines have an involved rhyme scheme and a linking of each turn of the thought. Milton and Wordsworth have written some of their finest poetry in the sonnet.

The Greeks gave the later Europeans a song of triumph, used first by Pindar for the celebration of victory in chariot racing, the ode, a lyric with a combination of short and long, slow lines. It was a favorite with Renaissance poets. Milton used it even in celebration of the birth of the Christ Child:

> No war or battle's sound
> Was heard the world around,
>   The idle spear and shield were high up hung;
> The hookèd chariot stood
> Unstain'd with hostile blood,
>   The trumpet spake not to the armed throng,
> And kings sate still with awful eye,
>   As if they surely knew their sovran Lord was by.

The ancient classical epic, even, was revived by Ariosto and Tasso, and John Milton in *Paradise Lost* celebrated the whole epic history of the Christian religion, the creation and fall of man, in this old form.

Later Gardens of Poetry.—The old Greek and the old Germanic epics were seedbeds for whole later gardens of poetry. They scattered the seeds of an ideal of heroic conduct over the world of western Europe, and new songs came up where these seeds fell; lovers sprang up like the ancient princes, and women replaced battles as the burden of the poets' songs. But there was another source of poetry greater even than the ancient pagan epics. It was a book of the Near East. It was a summary of thousands of years of living and singing under the bright stars of Palestine and Arabia, among lonely deserts where rocks and cedars, springs of sweet water and the grazing sheep were the precious jewels of life. It was an epic of the discovery, behind the figure of the primitive patriarch who loved all his descendants like sons and daughters, of a single loving God. It was the poem of that ancient Hebrew religion, and it was a magnificent poem of a new religion that had flowered from the old—a religion in which Jehovah had become a human Redeemer.

As Christianity spread out of Palestine along the Mediterranean and northward through the forests, it took this hymn of life with it. And the hymn was worked into the very stones and bones of the northern Germanic nations. Other religions have their source books, but none of them has so eloquent a Scripture as the Bible. The Bible was at the roots of the medieval hymns, at the roots of all the best writing of the Middle Ages. The Hebrew of the Old Testament is as beautiful poetry as Homer; the Greek New Testament and the Latin Vulgate of St. Jerome are splendid in rhythm and imagery, too. But probably of all the translations of this greatest inspirer of European civilization, the English is the finest. It is the finest because the minds of the English "Secretaries of the Holy Ghost" were the minds of great poets, and Wycliffe and Coverdale and Tyndale lived the rhythms and imagery of the poetry they translated into English.

> If I take the wings of the morning, and
> dwell in the uttermost parts of the sea; even
> there shall Thy hand lead me, and Thy right
> hand shall hold me.

Most of the English poets, from Langland on, have learned much of the art of poetry from the Bible. The verse of the English Scriptures is a kind of free verse; it has stanzas, but there is no regular length to the lines; yet the rightness of the fall of the words within a phrase, the sweep and cadence of the sentences lift it to the level of the greatest poetry of all. Surely, the first great makers of blank verse, Marlowe and Shakespeare, learned from the Bible. Milton in *Paradise Lost* and *Samson Agonistes* echoes in his figures and phrases the eloquence of the Psalms and Proverbs. William Blake found his chief literary model in the sentences of Job and other books of the Scriptures. The mystical poets have used Revelation and Daniel for a source. Wordsworth and later English poets have followed the biblical rhythms. And that greatest poet America has yet produced, Walt Whitman, has modeled on the Bible, not only the rhythmic phrases of his symphonies of American occupations and scenery, but also the very grandeur and vigor of his hymn in praise of the glory and oneness of all life. Without the Bible, English poetry would not be the rich and stately harmony that it is.

One of the happiest of all the Greek inventions was the pastoral poem.

The Greeks, whose civilization was built upon sheep herding, as was that of the ancient Hebrews, discovered the beauty of sheep and the beauty of simple living among plain country people. It was like a glimpse of the Golden Age men had always dreamed of—men and maidens dancing and making love and tending their flocks in a colorful rustic setting. It was a dream come true. Theocritus began the pastoral poetry with his Idylls. The Roman Vergil carried it on in his Eclogues, widening his interest to the life of all country people and their art of living humbly and well. After the pastoral had been discovered by the Italians of the Renaissance, it spread like a wildfire over the rest of Europe. Spencer introduced it into England in his *Shepheardes Calender,* and it became a popular English form. Even cold England was full of Corydons and Amaryllises,

> Dancing in the chequer'd shade.

The simple life was the one that makes men happiest.

> And the milkmaid singeth blithe,
> And the mower whets his scythe,
> And every shepherd tells his tale
> Under the hawthorn in the dale.

And this song of the simple life, borrowed from the Greeks, spread out into songs of praise of the rightness of country living and the serenity and beauty of country things in the later poetry of nature, such as that of Wordsworth and Robert Frost.

So the garden of lyric poetry has grown richer and richer. The Middle Ages gave us the ballad, the lyric that tells a story; the ballade, the lyric that is a letter; and other French forms like the rondel, with its returning rhymes, and the rondeau, with its two rhymes only, a good example of which is "In Flanders Fields." Then there was the couplet, both four-footed and five, developed especially by Chaucer, the father of English poetry, which leads the mind on by a constant connection of lovely sounds at the end of all the lines.

One of the most famous of all lyric forms is the Renaissance blank verse of the English. It is iambic pentameter and it has no rhyme at all. This is the "mighty line" that Marlowe developed in his tragedies and handed on to Shakespeare to use in his. It is full of a rhythm as right as rain or the beat of a man's heart. It is as though the actors who speak it were men tall as gods:

> Have I not made blind Homer sing to me
> Of Alexander's love and Oenon's death?
> And hath not he that built the walls of
>   Thebes
> With ravishing sound of his melodious harp,
> Made music with my Mephistophilis?

It is finer speaking than men ever do. On the edge of the grave, the great Elizabethan heroes of literature speak like princes:

> *O lente, lente currite, noctis equi!*
> The stars move still, time runs, the clock
>   will strike.
> The devil will come, and Faustus must be
>   damned.

The lyric poet may sing in the rare words and the high-sounding phrases. Or he may tell us to make the most of life in the easiest and commonest phrases:

> Gather ye rosebuds while ye may,
>   Old time is still a-flying,
> And this same flower that smiles today
>   Tomorrow will be dying.

The range in the lyric is all the way from the simplest statement of the beauty of life in the ballads, such as,

> She has kissed him by the candlelight
>   And the charcoal burning red.

to the most elaborate fancy of Keats,

> Where the nightingale doth sing
> Not a senseless, tranced thing,
> But a divine melodious truth;
> Philosophic numbers smooth;
> Tales and golden histories
> Of heaven and its mysteries.

The Poet Seeks the Secret Beauty.—But always, in all of it, there is an improvement on life itself, lovelier fields than ever shone in any sunlight, more picturesque people, brighter birds, taller trees and a mysterious voice speaking in everything. The landscape of Milton's ";L'Allegro" is like one seen through a jewel. Things are seen to swim in a translucent radiance, as those landscapes our grandmothers used to look at through the glass bead at the end of an ivory pencil. Mowers and milkmaids are just where the poet wants them, and they do the right things at the right time, as mowers and milkmaids seldom do in real life. When a poet wishes to have a rooster crow, to wake up his hero, the rooster is right there ready —not *a* rooster but *the* rooster—and he does not have to explain him,

> Then up and crew the red, red cock,
>   And up and crew the gray.

The poet does not have to tell how that bird that announces the morning came to be there. He simply reaches out and puts him there. The poet is not bound by any laws of time or space. If he is writing of the birth of the Saviour, he puts into his song every lovely thing he can find, from the world's ends. A ship is a beautiful thing. He will have that. Three ships are more beautiful than one. So he puts in three. And he has all three of them sail right up to Bethlehem, though that town, in geography, has no seacoast. It does not matter to the poet. He brings the sea up to the town. Bells are splendid things, too, so he puts them in, a thousand years before they are invented. And he makes an archangel the pilot, and John, the Disciple, not born yet, a grownup sailor!

> I saw three ships a-sailing there,
>   —A-sailing there, a-sailing there,
> Jesu, Mary and Joseph they bare
>   On Christ's Sunday at morn.
>
> Joseph did whistle and Mary did sing,
>   —Mary did sing, Mary did sing,
> And all the bells on earth did ring
>   For joy our Lord was born.
>
> O they sailed in to Bethlehem!
>   —To Bethlehem, to Bethlehem!
> Saint Michael was the steresman,
>   Saint John sate in the horn.

Poetry is after the secret beauty in the heart of things, and the poet is bound by the law of his being to use finer words and figures of speech than he uses in conversation on the Mondays and Tuesdays and Wednesdays of life. He is telling of

>   a sense sublime,
> Of something far more deeply interfused,
> Whose dwelling is the light of setting suns,
> And the round ocean and the living air,
> And the blue sky, and in the mind of man.

The poet is looking for the light on the road to Damascus, and he goes out to look for it with a passion deeper than any he ever experiences even in the best moments of living.

Poets have sought, too, as civilization has grown more complex, to compose symphonies on the laws of being and the relation of man to the infinite. One such symphony the ancient Mediterranean world saw in the Roman Lucretius's exposition of the evolutionary philosophy of Epicurus, *De Rerum Natura.* In it, though the poet makes man an ephemeral accident of flowing atoms, his description of the miracle of man's ascent to civilization and of the lovely dance of light through the universe turns his pessimism into a noble hymn. Once again, more than a thousand years later, another inhabitant of the Italian peninsula summed up the genius of his era. Dante, in his *Divine Comedy,* explored the three estates of the medieval universe and charted the progress of man's soul, in a fierce dream of fear and loneliness and loveliness, led by the law of love up to the feet of God. And, finally, a modern German poet, Goethe, in his *Faust,* the history of the progress of another soul, codified the romantic modern faith in rich experience as the proper road to salvation. In this philosophic poetry, as in the epic and the lyric, the search is for the ideal above the actual movement of life.

The Birth of Prose.—Prose literature, too, is in the nature of an improvement on life. Prose came into being as oratory, in Greece and elsewhere. The speech to rouse men to good action led very quickly to the celebration of past actions in well-composed sentences. And so history began. It came to be the major form of literature in the latter days of Greece, in the hands of Thucydides and Plutarch. It flourished all through Roman times. Livy, Tacitus and Suetonius wrote of the greatness of Rome. Letters and treatises on science also were features of Latin literature.

But it was left to modern times to develop prose as a literary medium as universal and as vital as poetry. With the Renaissance came the Italian novella, as written by Boccaccio, the story of love and adventure told in prose. The pastoral was put into prose, too, as in Sidney's *Arcadia.* And tales of travel and adventure sprang up in this medium, such as *Don Quixote* by Cervantes. In fact, the prose tale soon took over the whole material of the ancient epic. Defoe and Swift developed the narrative of travel, the memoir and historical type of story. Richardson, Fielding, Smollett, Sterne and Goldsmith all brought in the elements of everyday living and the color of contemporary events. These 18th-century men really established the novel form, as we know it today, the most universal of all modern mediums. The hero of the novel, unlike the ancient epic figure, came more and more to be the average man, the man from middleclass or lowly life, or even the scapegrace, the footloose, or, as the Knight of la Mancha, the humorous figure. Perhaps the princes of all the scapegraces are those Renaissance French heroes, those bundles of lustiness who poked coarse fun at the church and learning and men's bodies, the characters of François Rabelais.

Laughter in Literature.—This new element of humor, in fact, entirely unknown in the old verse narratives, whether the epic or the romantic tales of knights in the Middle Ages, came to be one of the most characteristic

FROM THE ELLESMERE MANUSCRIPT

WIFE OF BATH from the *Canterbury Tales.*

features of the new novel form. The ancients had laughter in their literature, in plays like those of the Greek Aristophanes and the Roman Plautus, but their laughter was at the expense of mankind and not in defense of it. Laughter is perhaps the greatest modern literary discovery. The modern comic spirit, as presented in the philosophy of George Meredith, deals with the art of making people feel good about life rather than impatient with it. The greatest celebrator of this essence of the comic in human nature probably is the 17th-century French playwright, Molière. He made men smile, and glow in the midst of their smiling, at their absurd seriousness in love and manners and morals. But comedy in the new novel form, as it developed, has rather tended to drain the life out of comedy as a play.

New Heroes and Heroines.—This turning of the novel to ordinary people and events probably is the most significant feature of literature in modern times. Literature has grown steadily democratic, as democracies have risen in different leading countries and as the reading public has steadily grown, thanks to the spread of schools for all and the rise of newspapers. The old kings and princes of the epics and romances were replaced by the new heroes and heroines of the 18th-century novel; a practical middle-class Englishman, Robinson Crusoe; a ship's doctor, Lemuel Gulliver; a servant girl, Pamela; a happy-golucky and good-natured foundling, Tom Jones; and the lovable, modest vicar of Wakefield.

In the 19th century, Dickens put all the lowly men, women and children of the great city of London and the English countryside into his novels. Hawthorne wrote of domestic tragedies in the lives of obscure descendants of the Puritans, making morality into romance. Melville wrote of common sailors. And the great Russians, Turgenev, Tolstoy and Dostoevski, made obscure and common Russians citizens of the whole world. The appeal of the novel became as wide as life. Harriet Beecher Stowe helped bring on the American Civil War with her story of a southern slave, Uncle Tom. The Russian novelists aroused the sympathies of nations for the oppressed people of their country, and their books probably did more than any other thing to bring about the Russian Revolution and the overthrow of czardom.

Today the novel is just as vital a part of life. The novelists are entering the innermost rooms of the human mind by the light of modern psychology. And yet the epic breadth is still often found in this form. Willa Cather has written a whole New World symphony in covering the different kinds of North Americans, those of the Middle West, those of the hot Southwest and those in cold Canada. Her three greatest books are *My Antonia, Death Comes for the Archbishop,* and *Shadows on the Rock.* Thomas Mann, the German novelist, in his *Magic Mountain* has written a symphony of mysterious and amazing life that goes on quietly under cover of life, in silence. And always the characters and happenings of the novel, though growing closer and closer to everyday life, are better or worse, clearer and more single than the things that are done every day and the people who do them. For, in spite of realism, literature is still literature, not life. It is better than mere living. If it were not, then there would be no need for it.

A distinctly modern offshoot of the novel is found in the short story. The form is a testimony to our desire for a pattern or design that we so often miss in actual life. Hawthorne and Poe and O. Henry perfected this type of brief narrative in which the characters are few but sharply etched and the background is often more important than the characters themselves. Poe's *Fall of the House of Usher* and Hawthorne's *Great Stone Face* are as artistic as any poem could be. The short stories of today are full of sharp tragedy and comedy and local color, and they go well with our energetic and rapid living and hunger for excitement. The short story is the most thoroughly American literary form.

The Widening Vistas of Prose.—The prose treatise of the old Greeks and Romans has grown enormously in range and appeal. The growth began in the 17th century. Religion, philosophy, science, even insanity and angling for trout were treated in books full of splendidly rhythmic sentences decorated with rich illustrations and figures of speech. Burton's *Anatomy of Melancholy,* Sir Thomas

Browne's *Religio Medici* and Walton's *The Compleat Angler* are classics read today because, though they treat subjects scientifically, they are full of imagination and emotion. With the coming of the periodical and the newspaper, the treatise has turned into the brief article. Though much of the rich rhythm and color of the older treatise has gone, the article is one of the most vital features of our life in the present.

Another prose form that the Greeks and Romans originated has been vastly developed in modern times, the biography. Beginning as brief sketches of types of people, patterned on the classical Theophrastus, the 17th-century biography grew in the hands of Izaak Walton and Clarendon and Aubrey, and culminated in such works as Boswell's magnificent study of the great Doctor Johnson in all his moments and moods, big and little, and the 19th-century *Life of Scott* by Lockhart. Biography today is even more literary than in the past, for Strachey, Maurois and the other biographers have not only turned away from the idea that a life of a man should be all state papers, in two volumes and with an epitaph but they have attempted to explain the personality of a man as well as his actions. They, too, have used the modern psychology to illuminate figures of the past. Emil Ludwig's biography of Napoleon, Strachey's of Queen Victoria and Maurois's *Ariel*, the life of Shelley, are peaks in this new range of modern biography.

The same trend toward everyday living seen in the novel has gone on in the play. The tragedies of the kings and the high-born of the ancient Greeks and of Marlowe and Shakespeare in Elizabethan England have been replaced by the tragedies written about obscure or average men and women by Ibsen and Eugene O'Neill. Prose, nearer always to the language used every day, has replaced poetry in most modern plays. But the modern tragedy, like the ancient, still proves that man is a creature both pathetic and noble. However obscure his beginnings, as Lincoln's in Drinkwater's play, he has a kind of kingliness in him.

Modern Europe has produced an entirely new prose type in the personal essay. This is a short and often whimsical treatment of familiar subjects of common interest. The Frenchman Montaigne began this attempt to say something both brief and wise about life. Bacon followed Montaigne. Addison and Steele did their best writing in this medium, in the *Tatler* and *Spectator* papers producing Sir Roger de Coverley, Will Honeycomb and their friends. Johnson and Goldsmith carried on in their footsteps. But it was left to the 19th century and Hazlitt, Hunt and especially Charles Lamb to bring the personal essay to something well-nigh perfection. In the *Essays of Elia,* Lamb has made all humanity feel good about old china, roast pork, chimney-sweepers, puns and children that might have been born. Americans also have made men glow with the essay. Washington Irving, Oliver Wendell Holmes in his breakfast-table philosophy, and today's great lover of all that is human, Christopher Morley, as well as the wise and witty Agnes Repplier, have made the form their own.

A Life Beyond Life.—Literature, thanks to periodicals, public libraries and the schools and colleges, has come to mean more and more to more people today than at any time before in the world's history. There are more books and more and more readers. This is a proof, if any last one were needed, that people find in the people made of ink and paper a life beyond life, a romance and wholeness that they miss in life when they live it themselves. For literature is something like religion. Indeed, it has replaced some religions, as it did in ancient Greece. It is a pattern in which human beings may come nigh to perfection. We can worship humor, without any of its awkwardness in real life, in Don Quixote's running at windmills and in Tom Sawyer's getting his friends to pay for the privilege of whitewashing his aunt's fence. A Huckleberry Finn is a major blessing in a book. That is where he belongs. In life he is often a major calamity. Lady Macbeth's place is in a play, not in the house next door. We can sympathize with her on the stage, and so can grow gentler for her very ungentleness. These people are too dark or too bright to live in the common light of day. They are people who can look and act like gods. It is in literature that we look for them. They are the stuff that dreams and literature are made of.

LITERATURE OF POWER

Books of power do not necessarily have in them the element of beauty. Yet it is worth while from time to time to speak in awe and reverence of the power of books.

There are, of course, strong books and weak books, beautiful books and ugly books. Here are some brief observations concerning a few books that, regardless of artistic merit, have had a powerful effect upon the Western and especially the American world of affairs.

Some years ago a gentleman addressing the New York Library Association listed fifteen books as having had a more decisive effect on human history than Creasy's fifteen decisive battles. In his list he undertook to set off the *Iliad* against the Battle of Marathon, Shakespeare against the defeat of the Spanish Armada and Darwin's *Origin of Species* against the Battle of Waterloo. Such suggestions are stimulating but in no way accurate.

In some ways certain books are more powerful by far than any battle, for they have given direction to the human spirit throughout the ages. They have changed human institutions and some of them have caused the shedding of much blood. Many of these books have broken up old disciplines and have offered new freedoms, which in turn have resulted in new disciplines that later on offered a shining mark for a revolutionary new book.

The Bible.—Undoubtedly, the most powerful book of all the ages is the Bible. It has caused the shedding of millions of gallons of blood and has soothed hundreds of millions of aching hearts. The fiery example of insurgent prophets shouting "Thus saith the Lord" has caused many a man to battle for social justice with superhuman strength. The humble example of the long-suffering Christ has caused many millions to live calmly and hopefully in the most difficult circumstances. The vigor of a Saint Paul has given extraordinary energy to many thousands of evangelists.

Yes, here is a book that has proved itself more potent by far than any decisive battle or army or empire. Reinforcing the Bible with great power in producing a Christian discipline are such books as Saint Augustine's *City of God* and Thomas a Kempis's *Imitation of Christ*. In this last we find the individual human soul striving desperately to discipline itself by continuous meditation into what was conceived to be the Christian mold. Thomas Aquinas, the great Dominican scholastic, in his *Summa* assembled the most powerful logical presentation of the Christian doctrine that has ever been put together in one book. The *Summa* today not only has a most powerful effect in the Catholic Church but also in neo-scholasticism, which is having something of a revival outside of the Catholic Church.

It seems that all powerful systems of thought inevitably set up their oppositions, and so we find the careful scholasticism of the Middle Ages provoking many books to make fun of the detailed reasoning of the scholars and the corruption of the clergy. Of these the most influential perhaps was Erasmus's book *The Praise of Folly*.

Breaking the Chains of the Middle Ages.—Many were the books in the 16th century that endeavored to break the old molds. Don Quixote laughed chivalry out of court. Translations of the Bible into native tongues freed the spirit of theological inquiry.

John Milton in England wrote his *Areopagitica* in defense of free speech, and ever since that time English-speaking people have had a tolerance for freedom of expression that cannot be found elsewhere in the world. The Protestants who reached out for a new freedom found it necessary to impose on themselves a new individualistic discipline. To this end Calvin wrote his *Institutes* and John Bunyan his *Pilgrim's Progress.*

The books that really launched the spirit of the Middle Ages out into the field of matter more effectively than any others were Francis Bacon's *Novum Organum* and Copernicus's book on the revolutions of heavenly bodies. These two books coming shortly after the discovery of America aroused the imaginations of men in a new direction. From such books and Newton's *Principia* have sprung the scientists whose devotion to truth is as pure and lofty as that of any priest.

Books That Gave Men Freedom.—With the rise of the scientists also came the rise of the humanists who, like Rousseau, Thomas Paine and Voltaire, wrote their books on the rights of man. Paine and Voltaire had in them a streak of sarcasm, bitterness, satire and humor that stirred men's minds. Thomas Paine's pamphlet *Common Sense* probably did more to arouse the Americans to revolt against England than any other book. He was a stirring orator. Hamilton and James Madison were builders. The *Federalist* essays they wrote were a determining force in bringing about the ratification of the Constitution.

A New Social Philosophy.—In the late 18th and early 19th centuries the doctrine of individualism and competition was set forth in a really powerful way for the first time. The economists and the rising manufacturers rebelled against the limitations of mercantilism, and their views were expressed by Adam Smith in his *Wealth of Nations,* by Ricardo and by John Stuart Mill. Darwin in his *Origin of Species* and Herbert Spencer in his *Social Statics* both expounded the doctrine of natural selection and survival of the fittest. Thus the groundwork was laid for Nietzsche's *Zarathustra* and the violence of the modern German approach based on the doctrine of the superiority of certain germ plasms.

The forces that Darwin, Adam Smith and John Stuart Mill let loose in the biological and economic worlds, combined with those originated by Hegel in the philosophic world, produced in the mind of Karl Marx one of the most powerful books of the 19th century, *Das Kapital.* Whether we like it or not, everyone in the world today is different because of *Das Kapital.* Without *Das Kapital* there would have been neither the communist nor the fascist experiments. More than any other book of the 19th century, all of us today are living under the shadow of *Das Kapital.*

Of all the American religious books of the 19th century it seems probable that *The Book of Mormon* was the most powerful. It reached perhaps only 1 per cent of the people of the United States, but it affected this 1 per cent so powerfully and lastingly that all the people of the United States have been affected especially by its contribution to opening up one of our great frontiers.

The same may also be said for *Science and Health* and perhaps for

several other books of this type, even though the great majority of Americans have been affected by them only indirectly.

20TH-CENTURY BOOKS OF POWER

The 20th century has produced books of power not only in science and politics but also in philosophy and literature. However, this being an age of specialization, we often find that the influential ideas contained in these books have first been propounded in theses and papers for experts. The magazine articles and the works of interpretation have then followed.

There have been few books written in the 20th century which have had the social impact of Darwin's *Origin of Species.* Among these later works should be included; Thorstein Veblen's *The Theory of the Leisure Class* and Sir James George Frazer's *The Golden Bough.*

Science.—The greatest scientific work of the 20th century has been in physics. Einstein's work on relativity is perhaps best summed up in *The Meaning of Relativity,* which shows how finite are man's conceptions of the Universe. Sir James Jean's *The Growth of Physical Science* (1947) completed the picture of the physical world so clearly outlined by Arthur Stanley Edington in *The Nature of the Physical World* (1933). Einstein and Leopold Infeld's *The Evolution of Physics* and Alfred North Whitehead's *Science and the Modern World* brilliantly helped to correlate the world of ideas and the world of phenomena, enabling us to see more clearly how radically 20th-Century science has affected Western culture.

In the field of biology and sociology, Hans Zinsser's *Rats, Lice and History* is a fascinating and sometimes terrifying account of the inter-relation of insects, disease and social evolution. Fairfield Osborn's *Our Plundered Planet* (1948) showed the necessity for intelligent planning and conservation, if life is to continue without disaster on the earth.

Psychology made great strides in the 20th century. A pioneer in American writing in this field was William James. He was followed by the Austrian Sigmund Freud and the Swiss Carl Jung. Freud's *A General Introduction to Psychoanalysis* (1935) and Jung's *Modern Man in Search of a Soul* (1933) are books which have had a great social influence, suggesting reasons for conduct not previously understood or accepted.

Anthropology, Sociology, Economics.—Working hand in hand with the psychologists, the anthropologists and the sociologists have carried their researches further into the lives and habits of both primitive and civilized peoples. The books of Bronislaw Malinowski and Margaret Mead on South Pacific tribes have added significant knowledge in this field. Lewis Mumford's *The Culture of Cities* (1938) examined intelligently the past, present and hoped-for future of the city-unit.

Startling in its effect was Dr. Alfred C. Kinsey's *Sexual Behavior in the Human Male* (1948) detailing statistically the sex habits of a representative cross-section of American males.

In economics, R. H. Tawney's *Religion and the Rise of Capitalism* (1926)

probed into the conditions which led to the linking of two such opposing concepts as the acquisition of capital and the teachings of Christ. James Burnham's *The Managerial Revolution* laid bare the silent revolution which has taken place in capitalist society.

Politics, History.—One of the most powerful books of the 20th century which might come under the head of both politics and history was Adolf Hitler's *Mein Kampf.* It traced the rise of Germany and embodied the vague mysticism and Nietzschean philosophy of National Socialism. It is one of the few books that can be said to equal in political influence the earlier *Das Kapital* of Karl Marx. Many of the modern novelists have based their books on the ideas propounded in these two works.

Charles A. Beard's *The Rise of American Civilization* and Frederick J. Turner's *The Frontier in American History* were two books in the field of American history revealing the changes which have led to America's paramount importance in the world.

In world history, Oswald Spengler's *Decline of the West* (1918–22) and Arnold Toynbee's *A Study of History* (1934–40) are monumental. Spengler attempted to show how cultures have followed a path of growth and decline and concluded that Western culture had passed its peak. Toynbee's work, more scholarly in approach, enquired into the causes of the rise and decline of civilizations.

Philosophy, Literature, Languages.—Henri Bergson's *Creative Evolution* (1907) had great influence on artistic as well as philosophical and aesthetic thought. A cross-current, emerging shortly after World War I, was provided by T. E. Hulme's *Speculations,* which considered philosophical thought and social trends since the Renaissance and stated the case for the new conservatism.

Jean-Paul Sartre's *Existentialism* (1947) was a book emerging partly from the disillusionment of a Europe devastated by World War II and partly from a conviction that 20th-Century philosophy was not practical enough.

In literature, at the beginning of the 20th century, the novels of H. G. Wells had a great effect on the popular thought of an increasingly scientific age. *Things to Come* embodied the idea of a scientific Utopia. Few American novels have had such a social impact as Upton Sinclair's *The Jungle,* a book which led to reforms in food production. Lincoln Steffens' *Autobiography* also was a powerful book. No book can be said to have had greater effect on world literature than James Joyce's epic *Ulysses,* a novel which, following Joyce's theory of *aesthetic statis,* maps the actions and inner thoughts of a set of characters during a day in Dublin. Joyce was the founder of the "stream of consciousness" technique.

There are probably few books of poetry which could be classed under the heading of books of power, but T. S. Eliot's *The Waste Land* (1922) is an exception. The title of his long poem was used as the description of the post-World War I generation.

In the field of language, Hayakawa's pioneer work *Language in Action* led

LITERATURE OF POWER

THE INFLUENCE OF REVOLUTIONARY IDEAS in the twentieth century has been felt in events that have altered the course of history.

SOVFOTO

EUROPEAN
THE FRIGHTENING FORCE OF EMOTIONALISM is reflected in Hitler's Germany (*upper left*), where Nietzsche's "Superman Theory," celebrating the power and heroic force of the select individual, became a basic creed. *Mein Kampf* embodied Hitler's philosophy and foreshadowed the rise of Nazism. The force of Karl Marx's *Das Kapital* was felt throughout the world. Lenin attempted to carry out Marx's program in Russia (*upper right*) to end capitalism as well as absolutism. The theories in Marx's dialectical interpretation of history found fertile soil in the political and economic discontent of the era, to which Communism seemed a practical solution.

WIDE WORLD
THE SCOPES TRIAL (*lower left*), and **THE ATOM BOMB** (*lower right*), reflect the impact of scientific discoveries upon men's thoughts. Darwin's theory of evolution, expounded in *Origin of the Species*, led to the Scopes Trial. Einstein's Theory of Relativity, published in 1916, led to $E=mc^2$, the basis of the atom bomb.

MONKMEYER PRESS

to the founding at the University of Chicago of a School of Semantics, for the study of the meaning of words.

Future Books of Power.—The dominating note of the 20th century has been one of uncertainty in the face of constant new discoveries and of the receding of the comfortable certainties. Einstein's work on relativity and the practical application of nuclear fission has overshadowed all other thought, the seeming impossibility of regulating international affairs peaceably has led to a feverishness which has been re-

flected in the books of the period. However, just as life has gone on in cities under constant air bombardment, so men of genius and perception have produced books of power in science, in psychology, in philosophy, in history and politics which have shown confidence in the spirit of man.

The stage is now set for some of the most powerful books that the world has ever seen. Humanity everywhere is hungry for both a new freedom and a new discipline. The books that played their part in producing modern

capitalism, fascism and communism do not have in them sufficient food for the human soul.

Humanity is infinitely more decent than the infamous acts of the last generation or so would indicate. Modern science and modern technology both tell the story of one world. They tell the need of integrating, synthesizing and co-ordinating knowledge on a higher plane. Such integration is necessary to prevent modern civilization from committing suicide by losing control of its own inventions.

HISTORY OF LITERATURE

GREEK LITERATURE

In the story of Western culture the literature of the ancient Greeks holds a unique place. To begin with, its forms and standards vitally affected the literature of the Romans, and through the Romans they had an influence on the whole modern world. Some literatures—for example, that of India—though containing much of value have somehow been isolated from the general course of what to us is world-literature. Not so with that of the ancient Greeks; for it first helped to determine the literary forms of Latin, which for over a thousand years was the language of culture; and later, when Greek literature came to be known directly to western Europe, it was a prime factor in that mental awakening called the Renaissance. Hence, even had Greek literature lacked a decided intrinsic value, it would have been and still would be important.

But it also commands attention because of its quality. In epic, lyric and dramatic poetry, in historical, rhetor-

ical and philosophic prose, the ancient Greeks set a pattern of excellence. Of their best work, only a relatively small amount is left, and the high repute of their writing depends upon the outstanding character of these scant remains. Their language was an instrument that served them well, with its large vocabulary, its flexible structure, its adaptability to delicate shadings and fine distinctions. Ease in compounding words lent richness to its prose; a combination of long and short syllables gave to its poetry a varied music.

Ancient Greek literature at its best has a simplicity akin to that of ancient Greek architecture. Its prose is economical and concise, without flamboyance or "purple patches." Its poetry lacks idle ornament and has a directness quite unlike the naïveté of the folk song—a directness based on the conscious omission of nonessentials. Neither prose nor verse has anything of the bizarre or *précieux.* Greek literary forms were native to the Greeks themselves, not deriving in any but minor particulars from foreign models. Greek critical sense developed them. The Ionian, Aeolian

and Dorian tribes each contributed its share.

For the sake of convenience, ancient Greek literature may be divided into three periods:

1. *The Early Period,* from remote antiquity to about 475 B.C.

2. *The Attic Period,* from about 475 B.C. to 300 B.C.

3. *The Period of Decline,* from 300 B.C. to 529 A.D.

The first of these three is marked by epic, elegiac, iambic and lyric poetry, and the beginnings of a literary prose; the second, by poetic drama, both tragic and comic, and by historical, oratorical and philosophic prose. The third may be subdivided into (*a*) the Alexandrian period and (*b*) the Graeco-Roman period. The literature of the decline has small value.

THE EARLY PERIOD

Homer and Epic Poetry.—Among the Greeks poetry reached a high degree of artistic finish long before prose did. Of course there was a workaday prose—the kind that Molière's Jourdain was surprised to discover he had been speaking all his life. But literary prose was quite a different thing. The Greek literature extant begins with the *Iliad* and the *Odyssey,* which date from the 9th or 8th century B.C. But before these there were poems of which we can know but little—"songs of the seasons" and hymns, connected with religion; ballads of warfare, chanted by minstrels in the houses of chiefs. It was ancient tradition that the *Iliad,* which tells of the wrath of Achilles, an episode in the famous siege of Troy, and the *Odyssey,* which tells of the wanderings of Odysseus after that siege and of his home-coming, were written by a blind poet named Homer, from the Greek coast of Asia Minor. For a long time, beginning at the end of the 18th century, the *Iliad* was the storm center of the so-called Homeric controversy; some critics asserted that it was first written down in the time of Peisistratus (560–527 B.C.) and was a composite of numerous short poems by various authors. Critical opinion now seems to lean toward the view that the style of the *Iliad* is that of a great creative poet, indebted to tradition for his meter, for certain formulaic language and for episodes in the

SEVENTEENTH-CENTURY WOODCUT

THE ODYSSEY: Polyphemus attempts to wreck Odysseus' ship by hurling rocks and boulders.

story. Certain interpolations have been made by editors, but in the main the *Iliad,* as well as the *Odyssey,* implies a single author; although some believe that the same author did not write both. Both are representatives of epic poetry. To the Greeks an epic meant a heroic narrative in hexameter verse. We know that by the 6th century B.C. a recitation of these poems was an established feature of the Panathenaea (held every four years), when they were delivered in a kind of recitative by a rhapsodist who had dispensed with the harp accompaniment of the earlier minstrel and held a laurel branch as a symbol of inspiration. For the Greeks, Homer was *the poet.* The simplicity, the pathos and the nobility of these poems have been an unceasing challenge to translators. The version of the *Odyssey* by T. E. Shaw (Lawrence of Arabia), published in 1932, was the 28th English rendering.

To various shorter poems of much later date (*The Battle of the Frogs and the Mice; Jack-of-All-Trades;* the *Homeric Hymns*) Homer's name was anciently attached. After Homer's time, several Ionian poets, forming what is called the "Cyclic" school, wrote poems intended to be supplementary to the *Iliad* and the *Odyssey.*

Hesiod (8th century B.C.) of Boeotia gave a new slant to the *epos* in his *Works and Days,* the earliest example we have of what we should call didactic poetry. Written for his brother Perses, who he thought was in need of advice about farm management, this is a sort of Countryman's Year. Hesiod has been termed the first European poet to write of Nature for its own sake. It was he who introduced into literature the "five ages of man" and Pandora's box. Attributed to him was the *Theogony,* an attempt to reduce to a system the fugitive legends of gods and goddesses. For a long time in Greece the epic in the style of the *Iliad* and the *Odyssey* and didactic poetry that gathered up lore and tradition in the manner of Hesiod were all-sufficient. But as oligarchies succeeded to monarchies, and democracies to oligarchies, individuals began to voice their thoughts and feelings; and they did so in two new verse forms suited to their needs, the Elegiac and the Iambic.

Elegiac and Iambic Meters.—An elegy was often but by no means always a lament for the dead. It might deal with almost any reflective theme that moved the poet to direct expression (Gray's *Elegy* is an English example). The elegiac meter was formed by following a hexameter with a pentameter (a verse of five feet, a hexameter with its last foot lopped away), making an elegiac distich or couplet. A musical accompaniment was furnished by the flute. Coleridge's version of Schiller gives in English an impression of this distich:

In the hexameter rises the fountain's silvery column,
In the pentameter aye falling in melody back.

Iambic meter was based on the *iambus,* a foot or measure consisting of two syllables, of which the first was short and the second long Iambic

verse was with the ancient Greeks the next most popular after the epic hexameter. Iambics are also well suited to the English language and are the basis of English heroic verse. These two Ionian forms occupy a place between the Ionian epic and the lyric of the Aeolians and the Dorians. Among the noteworthy elegists were Tyrtaeus and Callinus, warlike in their themes; Archilochus, sometimes martial, sometimes mourning for the dead; Mimnermus of Colophon; Solon, the lawgiver and patriot, who was likewise a pioneer of Athenian letters; Xenophanes; Phocylides and Theognis, who were chiefly devoted to gnomic sayings—in other words, proverbial philosophy. Best known in modern times is undoubtedly Simonides of Ceos, who was employed by the Greek states to write epitaphs for those who fell in the battles of his time. The inscriptions were called *epigrams,* and natural limitations forced conciseness upon the author. Hence arose a literary type—a brief lyric, epigrammatic in style though not intended for an inscription. Perhaps the most famed of Simonides' epigrams was that "On the Spartans Who Fell at Thermopylae":

Stranger, unto the men of Sparta tell
That here, obedient to their laws, we fell.
      —G. B. Grundy

Of the lyricist Timocreon he wrote: "Having eaten much and drunk much, and having said much evil of other men, here I lie, Timocreon the Rhodian." Iambic verse was written by Archilochus, Hipponax and Simonides of Amorgus, all of whom are satirists. Fables, narratives in which animals are made the vehicles of wisdom, were frequently written in iambics, although Aesop, to whom so many of them were attributed, was regarded merely as an ingenious storyteller who had put nothing down in writing, either verse or prose.

Lyric Poetry.—Elegiac poetry now tended toward a specific use in the epigram, and iambics were in time to find their place chiefly in the drama. Personal expression was to reach its ultimate form in lyric poetry—although that term was not known to the Greeks, who called it *melic* poetry. On the technical side, Greek lyric poetry has two distinguishing marks. It is *strophic*—that is, it is written not in successive lines of the same metrical arrangement but in stanzas. (As is the case in English verse, the stanza may vary from the common four-line structure to one of considerable intricacy and length.) It is *logaoedic*—that is, it is written not in successive feet (or measures) of the same metrical length but in some one of various combinations of common and triple time (dactylic and trochaic rhythms). To this second rule there are exceptions, but in the main it is true. In the chanting of lyric poetry the instrument used to accompany the voice was the lyre, to which Terpander had added three strings, giving it thus the compass of an octave. Aeolians and Dorians had each a part in the development of the lyric; and long afterward the grammarians of Alexandria fixed upon a list of nine great lyrists, whose work extended

over almost precisely two centuries (from the middle of the 7th century B.C. to the middle of the 5th). These were: Alcman, Alcaeus, Sappho, Stesichorus, Ibycus, Anacreon, Simonides, Pindar and Bacchylides.

Of the work of the first seven we have only fragments. A papyrus discovered in Egypt by natives in 1896 has, through the efforts of scholars, restored to us a number of complete poems by Bacchylides; and we have a moderately large collection of Pindar's odes. Alcman (Doric for Alcmaeon), Stesichorus, Ibycus, Simonides, Pindar and Bacchylides wrote their lyrics in the manner of the Dorian school; that is, these poems belonged to a form intended for chanting not by one voice but by a chorus. And in them the personal character of the lyric in its strict sense had been for the most part lost because of their public use. For they were written either for public worship or for other important occasions

WILLIAM CAXTON'S FABLES OF AESOP

AESOP, the Greek fabulist, *c.* 620–560 B.C.

of public assembly. Pindar's 44 *epinicia* (odes of victory), in honor of victors in the Isthmian, Nemean, Olympic and Pythian games, are made difficult for modern readers by their wealth of local allusion and their detailed treatment of obscure mythology. They are metrically skillful, and in selected portions we may appreciate their vigor, bold imagery and lofty tone. Ibycus is known in modern literature through Schiller's ballad *Die Kraniche von Ibykus,* which retells the story of how the cranes avenged his murder.

Alcaeus, Sappho, Anacreon.—In general, however, less interest has been shown in modern times in the Dorian than in the Aeolian school of lyric poetry. The chief representatives of the Aeolian school were Alcaeus, Sappho and Anacreon.

Alcaeus of Mitylene was forced by the active part he had taken in civil strife to spend a part of his life in exile but later was allowed to return. His poems included hymns to the gods; partisan songs; love songs, of which the imitation by Horace (*Odes* III, 12) gives an idea, and convivial songs, of which Horace also has imitations in *Odes* I, 9, 18, 37. Their metrical finish was noteworthy. It was Alcaeus who introduced into literature the figure of the "ship of state," which has been doing duty ever since.

The other leader of the Aeolian school, Sappho, was so highly esteemed that temples were built in her honor, her head was struck upon coins and she was known as the *Tenth Muse.* "Sappho," said Strabo, "is a kind of miracle; for within the memory of man there has not, so far as we know, arisen any woman worthy even to be mentioned along with Sappho in the matter of poetry." Greek critics held that she excelled all others in lyric poetry in fine and consistent

GREEK INFORMATION CENTER

THEATRE OF DODONI, where the plays of the great Greek dramatists were produced. On the right and toward the foreground are the tiered stone benches for the audience. On the left are the orchestra, proscenium or backgound, and stage. The action of the play took place on the stage and in the half circle below—an ancient theater-in-the-round.

balance between finish of style and a personal expression of feeling. Among the moderns, J. W. Mackail, professor of poetry at Oxford, has written: "The sole woman of any age or country who gained and still holds an unchallenged place in the first rank of the world's poets, she is also one of the few poets of whom it may be said with confidence that they hold of none and borrow of none, and that their poetry is, in some unique way, an immediate inspiration." Of her nine books of lyrics only broken fragments remain. She is supposed to have invented the Sapphic stanza.

Of Anacreon we have only two complete poems, besides a few remains. His bent was more toward social enjoyment as was evidenced in his festive songs. In connection with this Anacreontic tradition, it may be of interest to note the American national

air *The Star-Spangled Banner* is actually used at third hand; for it was taken from the older song *Adams and Liberty,* which had borrowed it from Samuel Arnold's English drinking song *To Anacreon in Heaven.*

THE ATTIC PERIOD

A new form of Greek poetry now arose, with elements taken from that which had preceded. Its home was Attica. It would be impossible here to explain how this new form, *dramatic* poetry, had its origin. It may only be said that it was a development of a choral hymn (*dithyramb*) honoring the god Dionysus and sung about an altar. Originally the leader of the chorus might take the part of a messenger or even of Dionysus himself and tell an adventure to the chorus, which in turn responded. Next, dialogue was introduced between the leader of the chorus and a selected member of the chorus, who was called by a name that became the usual word for "actor" (*hypocrites*). Aeschylus (525–456 B.C.) brought in a second actor, making the dialogue entirely independent of the chorus, and thus was the real founder of *tragedy.* Forthwith the choral song became secondary to the dialogue. Soon the theater of Dionysus below the Acropolis in Athens was begun—drama's first established home in Greece.

Aeschylus.—As an indication of the amount of Greek literature that has been lost to us, it may be stated that of some eighty works by Aeschylus, only seven are extant: *Agamemnon, The Choephorae* (*Libation-Bearers*), *The Eumenides* (*Furies*), these constituted a trilogy; *Prometheus Bound, The Suppliants, The Seven against Thebes* and *The Persians.* Of these, the *Prometheus,* the second member of a trilogy of which the first and third parts have been lost, is generally ac-

counted the most impressive; *Agamemnon,* the most varied and most richly poetical. Aeschylus is distinguished for elevated phraseology, noble austerity of treatment and a background of profoundly moral sentiment. Of *Prometheus* it has been said: "No work of a similar lofty character certainly has ever been so extensively popular." (J. S. Blackie)

Sophocles.—Sophocles (496–406 B.C.) enlarged the scope of dramatic action by introducing a third actor; and in the design of his plots, the charm of his style, his insight into character and a certain ideal beauty, he has been considered the artist par excellence of the ancient Greek drama. With him, drama became more dramatic and less lyric than it had been with Aeschylus. It is a striking fact that of his 123 dramatic works, only seven remain. These are: *Ajax, Electra, Oedipus Tyrannus, Antigone,* the *Trachiniae* (*The Maidens of Trachis*), *Philoctetes* and *Oedipus at Colonus.* Sophocles succeeds in being more human than Aeschylus. His sufferers move to pity, his martyrs command admiration. To him, it was well with them because their wills were strong, and because there was a higher morality and a diviner justice than appeared in the old traditions of the gods. The *Oedipus Tyrannus* was named by Aristotle in his *Poetics* as an ideal play, and our modern critics have been practically agreed in awarding it the supreme place in Greek tragedy. In his case, as in that of Aeschylus, we must remember that we have only the text of the plays. The music is gone and, lacking musical accompaniment, the meters suffer in modern ears; and even the text bears the marks of ignorance in transcription, and it belongs to a world that even the learned can only imperfectly apprehend. Yet these plays have not lost their power. To modern poets they have spoken as they did to Matthew Arnold, who, as he listened to the full tide on Dover Beach, reflected,

Sophocles long ago
Heard it on the Aegean. . . .

Euripides.—Euripides (*c.* 480–406 B.C.) deprived Greek tragedy of much of its ideal character, bringing it closer to everyday life. In his hands it approached in some ways nearer to the modern world, often sacrificing dignity for human interest or even amusement. He had a skeptical attitude toward the myths and traditions which his predecessors took as they received them. He was often picturesque, often expert in pathos. Of his 92 dramas, we have 18, including the *Phoenissae, Medea, Hippolytus,* the *Bacchae* and *Iphigenia among the Taurians.* Elizabeth Barrett Browning called him—

Our Euripedes, the Human,
    With his droppings of warm tears,
And his touches of things common
    Till they rose to touch the spheres.

Greek Comedy and Aristophanes.—The Attic Greeks first wrought the drama into an art form. They were the first to develop not only tragedy but *comedy,* which sprang originally, like tragedy, from the worship of Dionysus, but from its merrymaking side—an expression of joy over the return of spring after winter's gloom. Greek comedy has been divided into the Old, the Middle and the New. To the Old comedy belonged Cratinus, Crates, Pherecrates, Eupolis, Phrynichus and, chief of them all, Aristophanes (c. 450–c. 385 B.C.). Works are extant of none of these save Aristophanes, and of the 44 works commonly attributed to him, only 11 remain. These are placed by scholars in three groups: (a) The *Acharnians, Knights, Clouds, Wasps,* and *Peace;* (b) the *Birds, Lysistrata, Thesmophoriazusae* and *Frogs;* (c) the *Ecclesiazusae* and the *Plutus.* This grouping is to indicate the decreasing employment of political and personal satire. At his freest, Aristophanes made unsparing attack upon the gods, Athenian institutions, the politicians, the philosophers and others. In the *Clouds,* the most read and most frequently edited of his works, he poked fun at Socrates. Representatives of the Middle comedy were Antiphanes, Anaxandrides and Alexis. They mark a transition toward other interests, and find subjects of ridicule in the Pythagoreans, the Platonic academy, the rhetoricians, the orators. With Menander (342–291 B.C.) we reach the leading dramatist of the New comedy. He wrote about 105 comedies, and we have fragments of seven. His works resembled what is in modern times called the "comedy of manners," were produced as late as Plutarch's time (c. 46–c. 120) and were imitated by the Roman writers Terence and Plautus. St. Paul quotes Menander when he says that evil communications corrupt good manners.

Greek tragedy, though intended for performance before crowds in the open air and therefore in a sense "popular," was not written down to the intelligence of the lowest common denominator. It was no idle pastime, even for Athenians, but demanded close attention and mental focus; and through such discipline the Greeks, though doubtless great talkers, became also good listeners and critics. The Old comedy, in spite of its carnival boisterousness, served, in a time when there was neither daily nor periodical press and when pamphleteering was unknown as a medium of public criticism.

LITERARY PROSE

Herodotus.—A Greek prose literature really began with Herodotus (c. 484–c. 425 B.C.). Before him there had been Ionian prose writers called *logographoi,* as distinguished from the makers of verse. These prose writers compiled early myths or described the geography and the peoples of foreign lands. Their work was no more literature than were the old Saxon chronicles. Herodotus seems to have been the first Greek to whom it occurred that it might be possible to make facts interesting. His travels in various countries were extensive for that age and were undertaken in a spirit of inquiry. The central theme of his *History,* which is written with a sense of unity, is the struggle between Asia and Greece—the rise and fall of Persia; and this is constantly referred to as a divine arrangement by which

overweening power and arrogance and riches meet their Nemesis. In his traveller's tales he sometimes repeats the inventions of dragomans, but moderns have often had occasion to confirm the truth of his statements.

Thucydides.—It has been said about historical writing that if Herodotus was the first artist, Thucydides (c. 455–c. 400 B.C.) was the first thinker. His subject was the Peloponnesian War, of which he was a contemporary; and his idea was that this would have value beyond that of a reasonably accurate story of important events: It would have continuing significance on the general theory that history is likely to repeat itself. He leaves divine agency to Herodotus and is concerned with human affairs. Into the mouths of his characters he put speeches that in substance were supposed to be approximately faithful but in style were his own. It was said that the orator Demosthenes studied Thucydides so carefully that he copied out this history eight times.

Xenophon.—Another historian is Xenophon (c. 434–c. 355 B.C.), who is probably at his best in his *Anabasis* (or *Retreat of the Ten Thousand*), in which he tells the story of Greek mercenaries who, marching to help a pretender seize the Persian throne, are compelled by the pretender's death to make their way home as best they may. This reveals his knack at writing lively narrative with a convincing air of reality. So, too, does the *Memorabilia,* recollections of Socrates, whom he had listened to and admired—abounding in superficial detail but without philosophic content. The *Hellenica,* designed as a continuation of Thucydides' history, is lacking in the organic unity found in both Thucydides and Herodotus. Xenophon's *Cryopaedeia* (*The Education of Cyrus the Elder*) is more romance than history.

Oratory.—Oratory had in Greece a decided influence on the structure of literary prose; hence attention must be given to it in any survey of Greek literature. Even in Homer, eloquence was regarded as essential to a hero: Achilles was trained to be a "speaker of words." In the Attic period any citizen who desired to take a part in Athenian affairs or even to plead in his own defense in a court of law found a study of public speaking rather necessary. Antiphon and Andocides were leading representatives of the earliest school of Attic oratory. Lysias undertook to provide speeches for those who had to plead in the courts and did not wish to rely on their own skill. He therefore dispensed with much of the rhetorical technique that had been in vogue and used the simpler language of common life, though with an art that concealed art. Simplicity, clarity and smoothness made him in his own day the pattern of the "conversational" style. In antiquity, 425 of his speeches were known; we have 34 attributed to him—not all complete. Isocrates (436–338 B.C.) established a flourishing school of oratory. His style of prose, midway between that of the earliest school and that of Lysias, was favored in Greece from the second

half of the 4th century B.C. Studied at Rhodes, it became the model for the Roman Cicero and thus helped to mold the oratory of modern speakers down at least to the middle of the 19th century. Demosthenes (383–322 B.C.) was considered the foremost orator of Greece. His name became familiar in connection with stories of how he overcame natural disadvantages—strengthening his voice by declaiming against the roar of the ocean and correcting his utterance by speaking with pebbles in his mouth. The most famous of his speeches were the twelve *Philippics* denouncing King Philip of Macedonia. The word *philippic* has passed into English speech as synonymous with invective. "Philip," cried Demosthenes, "a man who not only is no Greek, and no way akin to the Greeks, but is not even a barbarian from a respectable country—no, a pestilent fellow of Macedon, a country from which we never get even a decent slave." It is only natural that in modern times Demosthenes should have been appreciated less as a stylist than as an effective, if not profound, orator.

Philosophy.—Philosophic prose is represented by Plato (427–347 B.C.) and Aristotle (384–322 B.C.). As a prose stylist Plato received in Greek literature a place similar to that which as a philosopher he occupied among Greek thinkers. In longer passages of interpretation he achieves a poetical quality that employs the finest shadings of the language; in the ordinary give and take of his *Dialogues* he is dramatic, satirical and shrewd. All of his writings have the dialogue form except the *Apologia,* Socrates' address to his judges. It was a natural form for him to use, because it imitated the actual manner of Socrates' discussions with his pupils. The *Republic,* "the first of all Utopian books," is the younger Plato's envisioning of a city-state in which life should be conducted on a new and better plan. Cicero's *De Republica* is patterned after it. In it, as in the lifelike delineation of persons whose views he wished to defend or combat, Plato showed high literary gifts. Aristotle is of interest to literature through his *Poetics,* which is the pioneer extant work of literary criticism, although of its two books the first, dealing with tragic and epic poetry, alone remains. The first two of the three books of his *Rhetoric* treat of language and style.

THE PERIOD OF DECLINE

When the empire of Alexander had broken up into separate monarchies, the externals of the old Greek life persisted but civilization was not the same. It was not Greek but what has been styled Hellenistic—Hellenic in outward form but not Hellenic in spirit. Egypt fell to the share of Ptolemy, one of Alexander's generals, and its new capital, Alexandria, became the center of the Hellenistic world. The Museum founded there was really the first university in the world, and even more important was the great library there established. The scholars of Alexandria attended painstakingly to the preservation and copying of manuscripts of Greek literature.

Greek was the language of educated persons to such an extent that many of the Jews in Egypt were no longer able to understand Hebrew, and so the Septuagint version of the Old Testament was undertaken. Among the Alexandrian poets were: Callimachus (c. 310–c. 240 B.C.), who was connected with the library; Apollonius Rhodius (c. 295–c. 215 B.C.), author of the epic *Argonautica;* Theocritus (c. 310–c. 245 B.C.), a pastoral or bucolic poet whose *Idylls* showed a fresh and true sense of natural beauty and were imitated by Vergil in the *Bucolics* and the *Georgics*. From him the customary affectedness of the Alexandrian school is largely absent. Bion and Moschus were other pastoral poets often mentioned with Theocritus.

After the conquest of Greece by the Romans, Greek literature found a welcome in Rome. Educated Romans commonly spoke and wrote Greek. Such men as Cicero, for example, were familiar with Greek books. Among those who wrote in Greek during this Greco-Roman period were: Polybius, author of a universal history glorifying Roman power; Diodorus Siculus, whose *Historical Library* was a history of the world down to Caesar's Gallic war; Lucian, whose satirical *Dialogues* have more of the old Greek manner than have any other works of his time; Josephus (*Jewish Archaeology*); Plutarch, whose *Lives* of noted Greeks and Romans have been universally popular; the Stoic philosopher Epictetus; the Emperor Marcus Aurelius, who during his campaigns wrote a volume of reflections on the conduct of life; and the two Neo-Platonists Plotinus and Iamblichus. As for poetry, the best of it that has survived may be found in that collection of short pieces known as the *Greek Anthology*.

The Greek Anthology.— This *Anthology* has come to be regarded as one of the most valuable relics of ancient literature. It is made up of short pieces, mostly in the elegiac couplet, written by a host of authors, many unknown, over a period of 17 centuries (c. 700 B.C. to 1000 A.D.). *Epigram* originally meant inscription, but the term was later extended to include brief lyrics of epigrammatic form. To the Greeks an epigram was not what it is with us —a sententious expression, prose or verse, with a "sting" at the close. Always in poetic measure, it aimed at economy of means and felicity of style but not at striking ideas or surprise endings.

The pieces in the *Anthology* bear to the massive examples of Greek literature much the same relation that the engraved gems, smaller bas-reliefs and figurines bear to Greek sculpture. They deal in simple, vivid fashion with the joys, sorrows, changes, humors and pathos of everyday life. Many are epitaphs or memorials. They include examples of satire, as:

All hail, seven pupils of Aristides the rhetorician, four walls and three benches.
—Unknown (J. W. Mackail, trans.)

Patriotism:

If the best merit be to lose life well,
To us beyond all else that fortune came:
In war, to give Greece liberty, we fell,
Heirs of all time's imperishable fame.
—Simonides, on the Athenian dead at Plataea (W. G. Headlam, trans.)

Love:

On the stars, thou gazest, my Star; would I were heaven to look at thee with many eyes.
—Plato (J. W. Mackail, trans.)

Philosophic content:

I care not for the lands with pastures deep,
Nor wealth of gold with jealous eyes I see;
Nor, having what's enough, I more would reap.
Too much of anything's too much for me.
—Alpheus (G. B. Grundy, trans.)

the Romans appear to have done without a literature. But even in remote times they had their formulaic prayers and chants for public worship; these were metrical, for in an age when writing was known to but a few, meter was an aid to memory. To judge by traces remaining in their proverbs and magical runes, they employed both alliteration and rhyme. That old Italian metric was accented like the English; Latin poetry was afterward quantitative, like the Greek. A verse of high antiquity has been preserved—called by later poets the *Saturnian,* a term indicating something like our "antediluvian." The Saturnian has been likened by Macaulay to the English measure of

"The queen| was in| her par|lor,|| eat- ing| bread and| honey."

There were mourning-chants and *fescennine* verses full of ridicule and rough humor. But no artistic literary use was ever made of these various ancient motives.

It is only in the oldest remains of the Roman law that we can get any insight into the independent Roman mind as it was before Greek works became known to it. The first Roman book was really a code of laws engraved on 12 tablets. The first Roman personality that we may term literary was Appius Claudius Caecus, who translated from the Greek a collection of maxims (*sententiae*) into the old Saturnian verse. He wrote also what may be called the first Latin work in prose—a speech, the pioneer specimen of Roman oratory as a branch of literature.

Livius Andronicus.—Appius Claudius was, however, an isolated figure, and it is only with L. Livius Andronicus (active 240–207 B.C.) that we reach the real beginning of Latin literature.

Livius Andronicus had a school in Rome and for use in the study of the Latin language he translated the *Odyssey* (already a textbook in Greek schools) from Greek into Latin. He did not employ the hexameter measure of the original. Latin had too many long syllables and Greek hexameter too many shorts to make such a transfer easy for an inexperienced versifier. So Livius fell back on the Saturnian jog trot that Appius Claudius had previously tried, and his version, though Cicero likened it to primitive attempts at sculpture, was a favorite text as late as the Augustan period. During the First Punic War the Romans had got acquainted with Greek drama in Sicily. Livius translated and adapted Greek plays, following as well as he could the Greek iambics and trochaics; and these plays were so well received that drama (*ludi scaenici*) became a feature of the Roman games. Gnaeus Naevius (active 235–204 B.C.) also adapted Greek tragedy and comedy, but with greater originality. In tragedy he introduced the *fabula praetextata,* for which he drew upon the legendary or contemporary history of Rome, and in which characters wore the *toga practexta,* the garb of Roman magistrates. Comedy (*fabula palliata,* from the Greek *pallium* or mantle worn by the actors) was his prefer-

LATIN LITERATURE

In a strict sense, according to some authorities, there is not and never was a Roman literature. According to others, the ancient literature we know as Latin was a characteristic expression of Rome. To deny originality to the Romans would be a mistake. In statecraft and jurisprudence they were decidedly original. In practically all other fields they had a way of fitting to their own uses the achievements of others. Indeed, the Greek Posidonius (c. 135–45 B.C.) thought that this aptitude was one of the determining causes of their political growth.

This assimilative gift was nowhere else more clearly in evidence than in the case of their written language. The very characters they used were borrowed from the Greeks of Cumae, the oldest Greek colony in Italy. The developed Latin alphabet became the alphabet of all Romance and Germanic languages. When a Latin literature arose, its forms were in the main directly copied from Greek originals. As the poet Horace said (*Epistles,* II.1,156–157), Greece, though conquered, had been conqueror too. In the epic (Ennius, Vergil), in tragedy (Livius Andronicus, Pacuvius, Ac-

cius), in comedy (Plautus, Terence), in history (Sallust), Latin writers followed Greek patterns. Such authors as Lucretius, Cicero, Vergil and Horace were heavily indebted to the Greeks. Latin metric copied the Greek; and as for vocabulary, Horace admitted that

"New words, if from a Grecian source, Aptly applied, are welcomed as of course."

Nevertheless, as time passed, the Romans did imprint their own character on their literature, sometimes to a marked degree. Satire, as an independent poetic style, they claimed for their own. If Terence, Sallust and Propertius were apish, Plautus, Tacitus and Lucretius were more strongly individual. The Horace of the *Epistles* was more original than the Horace of the *Odes;* and the letter writer Cicero was less derived than Cicero, the adapter of Greek philosophy. The Romans contributed their own notions and turns of speech. Though they did not quite attain Greek flexibility and grace, they had clearness, dignity and force.

But Roman literature was not an organic development. For 1,500 years

ence; and he might have been in a fair way to transplant the Old comedy of Athens to the Roman stage, but his pointed allusions to men and affairs were displeasing to the governing class and he was first imprisoned, then exiled. As an exile he wrote in Saturnian rhythm an epic on the First Punic War, in which he had served.

Plautus.—A bent toward a national literature was shown also by T. Maccius Plautus (active 204–184 B.C.). Twenty of his plays, all that Roman critics thought genuine, have survived, making him the first Roman writer whose works we have in anything like their original extent and form. Plautus came up to Rome from an Umbrian village and, like Shakespeare, was for a time employed around the theatre. His comedies held the Roman stage until the time of Diocletian and were widely popular. They give us a good idea of what the *fabulae palliatae* really were like. Plautus followed the Attic New comedy but was careful to avoid the displeasure of the authorities. He used what may strike us as a very artificial convention. The life he pictured was quite remote from that of Rome. Scenes and characters were Greek, and the characters were derived from what already were stock figures of Greek playwrights. At the same time there were constant allusions to Roman localities, manners and laws; and mingled with borrowed words is the colloquial speech of the author's own place and day. The best of Plautus' works, though lacking art, have comic vigor, lively dialogue (sometimes interlarded with puns) and amusing episode. St. Jerome, after weeping for his sins, turned to Plautus for relief; and the early Renaissance discovered in the Plautine drama a treasure-trove of material. Among the titles are *Aulularia, Captivi, Menaechmi, Miles Gloriosus, Rudens and Trinummus.*

Quintus Ennius.—Plautus traveled but a short way in the direction marked by Naevius; and Quintus Ennius (239–169 B.C.) decided for all time the victory of Greek influence in Latin literature. He was a Calabrian from Magna Graecia, a section of Italy in which were important Greek colonies and where Greek became perfectly familiar to him. A veteran of the Second Punic War, he settled in Rome in 204 B.C., taught Greek and Latin and devoted his best energies to the spread of Greek culture. He was perhaps the most learned man in Rome at that time. The comedies he wrote were of slight value, but the few hundred lines remaining of at least 25 tragedies have led scholars to ascribe to him in this field both eloquence and pathos. More significant was his *Annales,* in which he attempted a national epic on the Homeric pattern but covered altogether too much territory and so failed of an artistic result. He broke from the Saturnian meter and yoked Latin to the Greek dactylic hexameter, which from that time definitely replaced the other. It was rough going, but the poem (of which we have about 600 lines) had a kind of austere dignity and helped to establish rules of good usage for Latin pronunciation.

Cato.—Latin prose is usually said to have begun with M. Porcius Cato 234–149 B.C.), the very same exclusive bigot that ended every one of his speeches before the senate with *Delenda est Carthago* ("Carthage must be destroyed"). He long fought any Greek cultural influence and not until his old age did he learn the Greek language. It was then he began work upon his *Origines* (Origins), in which he traced the early history of the Romans and other Italian tribes and then sketchily brought events down to his own time. It was pointed out by contemporaries that the author made some display of his knowledge of Greek etymologies and sought to connect Rome historically with Greece. Cato also published speeches, and these were highly praised by Cicero, whose own style was utterly different. Only his *De Re Rustica* (On Agriculture), a treatise on farming, has reached us, and that not exactly as he wrote it.

Terence, Caecilius and others.—Caecilius Statius (c. 195–168) translated Menander straight, without trying to insert material of his own or from other comedies. Of Caecilius we have only fragments. Of Terence (P. Terentius Afer, d. 159 B.C.) we have all that the ancients had—six comedies, four of which are derived from Menander. The *Andria* (produced in 166 B.C.), his first play, was as characteristic as any of the later ones, which include the *Phormio* (162) and the *Adelphi* (160). Terence was inferior to Plautus in comic power but superior in plot construction, logical character development and smoothness of dialogue. Less popular with the theatregoing public, he was more highly esteemed by fastidious readers. The life he depicted was strictly Greek with none of Plautus's excursions into Roman manners or local touches. His method is rather that of what the moderns term sentimental comedy, never profound but ordinarily urbane. During the Middle Ages he was read and was taught in schools. In modern times, writers on drama studied his technique, as did Lessing, for example, in the *Hamburgische Dramaturgie.*

Contemporary with Terence was Marcus Pacuvius (c. 220–130 B.C.), a writer of tragedies, some from the Greek, others in the style of the *fabulae praetextatae* that Naevius had invented. The epithet *doctus* (learned) was applied to him, and he was praised for his elevated tone. Somewhat later was Lucius Accius (170–c. 85 B.C.), with whom the young Cicero frequently talked. Accius was sometimes inclined toward post-Euripidean tragedy, maintained upon the contemporary Greek stage; sometimes he used older material already presented by Ennius; but experts seem to agree that he left tragedy no further advanced. Despite the attention then paid in Rome to rhetoric, philology, criticism and literary history—Accius himself wrote in verse on such things—Latin tragedy had in form remained far behind Latin comedy. It was not with tragedy that the Romans were to achieve notable things in serious verse.

Of the 30 books of the *Satires* of

Gaius Lucilius (c. 180–102) there remain only something like 1,000 fragments, mostly couplets or isolated lines. In the opinion of scholars, the loss is much to be regretted. For here was the work of the founder of what has been considered the most truly original and distinctive expression of Latin literature. Written chiefly in hexameters, these satires (the word *satura,* according to the grammarians, meant originally a mixture or medley) were outpourings on this and that: on a trip to Sicily (model for Horace's well-known trip to Brundisium); on poets, and especially dramatic poets; on Roman society, the state, the author's political opponents. Carelessly done, loquacious, unpoetical, they suited a certain old-fashioned Roman taste.

Annalists such as L. Calpurnius Piso went ahead with their compilations, but there was an example of something better in L. Caelius Antipater's account of the Second Punic War. Cornelius Sulla and other public men wrote memoirs. L. Aelius Stilo, a teacher of Cicero, issued studies in philology, and Mucius Scaevola explored the mazes of the law. Only in oratory, however, did Latin prose really flourish at this time. Since Cato's day, oratory had developed greatly. Public men studied it, with Greeks at first for teachers and with Greek exercises. Afterwards Latin schools were opened. At the time of the revolution of the Gracchi, political speeches were revised and used as pamphlets in the factional war. Among the writers of oratorical prose in this era were Gaius Laelius, P. Scipio Aemilianus, Gaius Gracchus, Marcus Antonius and Lucius Crassus. If more had endured of this prose than scattered fragments, we should be able to traverse the development from Cato to M. Tullius Cicero (106–43 B.C.).

Cicero.—To enter here into the much-discussed personal history of Cicero (so large a part of which is also part of the history of Rome) would be as unnecessary as it is impossible. In the chaos that ended the Roman republic he was, if not always consistent, a figure essentially nobler than those about him: a man who sought to avert the evil day and who deserved better of his country than to have his severed head and hands nailed up in the Forum. We can but wish that this humane scholar might have fallen on a less brawling age. Cicero's position in both Latin and general literature has been firmly established. As a prose stylist, he brought Latin to a point it never surpassed. He enriched its straitened vocabulary and coined for it many words, chiefly by translating them from Greek or by copying Greek forms. He took its cramped phrases and made them full, easy, even rhythmical. Its churlish obscurity he transformed into an abundant clearness. He showed that it might have not simply blunt vigor but also an air of good manners. More than this, he invented a prose that is still so readily discernible in living speech that it has been termed the language of civilized mankind.

First of all, Cicero was an advocate, a pleader. That fact led to his political career, and it is a reason for considering his speeches before his other writings. As a rule, these speeches were delivered, if they were judicial, before a jury in a court of inquiry (*quaesitio*); if political, before the senate or the people. Later, they were written out by Cicero from his notes. A few were issued without having been delivered at all. His invective in the tradition of Demosthenes (he had studied Greek eloquence at Athens and Rhodes) was sometimes highwrought but not too much so for Roman liking. In private life he was thought a great wit, but his fondness for joking in public was criticised, just as modern politicians have been criticised for the same thing; and even his pathos was scorned by his adversaries. Leaning in his own views toward the skeptical New Academy, Cicero wrote transcriptions of the Greek speculative philosophy; These were dialogues, in which the followers of various schools expounded their beliefs. In the same fashion he treated of moral and political philosophy, but with illustrations from Roman life and history. These works furnished handbooks for the Romans on the various subjects, and they have continued to be read for their charm of style. In numerous books on rhetoric, Cicero deals with the education of an orator; the subject matter, form and delivery of speeches, the history of Roman oratory and the character of an ideal public speaker. We have some 800 letters of Cicero (a few are *to* him), and the collection gives us a portrait of the man himself and our chief source for the history of the period.

Fifty-eight of Cicero's orations have survived in complete, revised form, and there are fragments of 17 others. Of these the *Pro A. Licinio Archia* (61 B.C.) in defense of an old Greek poet's claim to Roman citizenship is doubtless the most pleasing, though the four *In Catilinam* (63 B.C.) made more noise. The dialogue *De Senectute* (Old Age) has probably been the most read of all the Ciceronian writings. Other works in philosophy were the *Hortensius,* which directed Augustine's thoughts to the serious life, the *De Officiis* (Duties), and the *De Republica,* containing the famous Scipio's Dream, paraphrased by Chaucer in the *Parliament of Foules.*

Varro, Caesar and Sallust.—M. Terentius Varro (116–27 B.C.), a contemporary prose writer, evidently did not profit much by Cicero's labors. Of his works we have a small part of a crabbed treatise *De Lingua Latina* (The Latin Language) and the *De Re Rustica* (Agriculture). Augustine drew upon Varro's *Antiquitates* (Antiquities) for the *City of God.*

While he was crossing the Alps Julius Caesar (100–44 B.C.) wrote a study of the Latin language and dedicated it to Cicero. This, with other writings of his, has been lost. We have his account of the Civil War (to the beginning of the war at Alexandria) and his *Commentarii* (Notes or Memoranda) on the Gallic War, written to persuade the Romans that the conquest of Gaul was a necessary defensive measure. Calculated simplicity of language and an appearance of utmost candor make of this in one sense a work of art, although from its cloak of reserve the vanity of the man at times peers out.

C. Sallustius Crispus (86–36 B.C.) broke away in his *Catilina* and in *Iugurtha,* an account of the Jugurthine War, from the cut and dried style of the annalists and sought to be another Thucydides. Like some English-writing historians and biographers of our own day, he put into the mouths of historical persons words for which he had no record whatever and to those persons ascribed motives and notions for which he had no evidence. Cicero's style may have been somewhat lavish; Quintilian remarks (X,1,106) that not a word could be added to a Ciceronian period, but he also says (IV,2,45, and elsewhere) that Sallust's tightness and abruptness make him difficult for the general reader.

Lucretius.—In a letter written in 55 B.C., Cicero mentions a poem *De Rerum Natura* (The Nature of Things), published not long before. T. Lucretius Carus (98–55 B.C.), a student of Epicurus, wrote in hexameters this interpretation of the Epicurean system, which he hoped thus to make more intelligible and attractive, and through which he believed men might be freed from superstitious dread. It was a heroic task. As poetry the work is extremely uneven, keeping through long passages at a prosy dead-level, then suddenly rising to full-voiced beauty of description, like Wordsworth's, or to some burst of insight. Vocabulary and style are considerably archaized, and the influence of Ennius is seen. In modern times, Lucretius has been hailed as a scientist and compared to Leonardo da Vinci or Sir Isaac Newton. Henry F. Osborn (*Men of the Old Stone Age,* 1916) quotes freely from Lucretius regarding primitive man. It is safe to say that, with all its defects, this is the greatest of didactic poems. Familiar words of Lucretius are: "What is food to one man may be fierce poison to others," and "Continual dropping wears away a stone."

Catullus.—Quite a different sort of poet was Valerius Catullus (87–c. 54 B.C.), a provincial from Verona, town of the Montagues and Capulets. In his way, he was learned enough. He had studied the Alexandrian Greeks, especially Callimachus; he knew Greek mythology; he could attempt the rare and difficult galliambic meter. Better, however, than his translations and copies of Greek originals are the lyrics, full of naturalness and with a "clearness as of the terrible crystal," whatever their theme or mood. Contemptuous, rueful, tender or gay, always he has that forthright simplicity. Of the moderns, Burns has been compared to him, and in insolent satire there is a strong resemblance; but Heine is far nearer to being a counterpart. There are poems to Clodia, graceless specimen of a moneyed aristocracy; and to his country home on Lake Garda; verses of occasion, and generous expressions of sympathy; 10 faultless lines at his brother's grave—one of the best-known pieces of Latin literature; cameolike squibs; outbreaks of high disdain toward the powers-that-be.

Here are Catullus's lines at the tomb of his brother.

Multas per gentis et multa per aequora
  uectus
    aduenio has miseras, frater, ad inferias:
ut te postremo donarem munere mortis
    et mutam nequiquam alloquerer
    cinerem.
quandoquidem fortuna mihi tete abstulit ipsum,
    heu miser indigne frater adempte,
    mihi,
nunc tamen interea haec prisco quae
    more parentum
    tradita sunt tristi munere ad inferias,
accipe fraterno multum manantia
    fletu,
    atque in perpetuum, frater, aue
    atque uale.

These Latin verses have been translated for the VOLUME LIBRARY as follows:

Through many lands and over many a
  sea,
    Brother, I come fulfilling grievous
    trust,
The final tribute thus to render thee
    And call in vain upon thy speechless
    dust,
Since fate has claimed thee undeservedly
And death has torn asunder thee and
  me.
So now the gifts our fathers brought
  of yore,
    Memorials of those beloved when
    living,
    These, drenched with tears, I give to
    thee; and giving,
I bid thee hail—farewell—for evermore!

Vergil.—We pass now from the Ciceronian to the Augustan age and to other outstanding names in Latin poetry—first of which is that of Vergil (P. Vergilius Maro, 70–19 B.C.), who might be called the poet laureate of the new emperor. Vergil was from near Mantua and hence like Catullus a provincial. He studied Epicurean philosophy and first became known in Rome through his *Bucolics* (or *Eclogues*), 10 pastorals of no great length—echoes, often paraphrases, of Theocritus and the Alexandrian school in general. Shepherds with Greek names inhabit now Lombardy, now Sicily and Arcadia; their songs or contests are mingled with thinly disguised references to Roman politics and Vergil's contemporaries. The hexameter is used with a variety and delicacy new to Latin. One of the *Eclogues* (the fourth, addressed to Pollio) made a great impression in Christian times because, with imagery often surprisingly like that of Hebrew writers, it proclaimed a golden age akin to that of Messianic prophecy. Pope's *Messiah* is a sacred eclogue in the style of Vergil.

Vergil was introduced at court; Maecenas, minister of Augustus, became his patron. It is said that

NEW YORK PUBLIC LIBRARY

OVID'S METAMORPHOSES: story of Actaeon. Actaeon, the grandson of Cadmus, loved to hunt. One day, after partaking of his favorite sport, he lost his way and came upon Diana bathing with her nymphs in a pool (left). The goddess, blushing and angry, cast water at Actaeon, transforming him into a stag. He fled, the only human thing left to him being his mind. His own hounds, pursued him until they caught him and tore him apart (*right*). His companions encouraged the slaughter, not realizing it was Actaeon, and he died, Diana having successfully avenged herself.

Maecenas gave Vergil the idea of the *Georgica* (Georgics), an agricultural poem in four books, often regarded as his most original and inventive work. In it he drew from no particular author, although here and there the influence appears of Hesiod, Theocritus, Ennius and Lucretius. It is didactic, evidently intended to glorify the labors of country life and promote Italian agriculture. But it presents sympathetically the pleasures and rewards of country life and extols the character of the old yeomanry; and in its incidental descriptions and passages it succeeds in being as entertaining as any poem of such nature and range may hope to be. The versification is skilful and melodius. To the *Georgics* Vergil had devoted seven years; to his next work, *The Aeneid,* he gave the remainder of his life. This is a kind of Latin *Odyssey,* telling of the wanderings of Aeneas after the fall of Troy, and how eventually he reached Italy and established a new realm. Of the 12 books, the first 6 are the most interesting, and the sixth shows the poet more independent of Homer than elsewhere and at the top of his artistry. In versification, indeed, one turning from the Vergilian hexameter to that of the Homeric poems is likely to feel the technical superiority of Vergil, whom Tennyson called "Wielder of the stateliest measure ever moulded by the lips of man." There is, too, a fusion of philosophy with narrative, of pathos with conflict, that gives Vergil a charm all his own. Uncompleted lines mark the fact that Vergil did not live to revise this epic. The guide of Dante in the lower world, Vergil was for the Middle Ages the poet of poets. In popular tradition he became a magician, the center of strange lore.

Horace.—With Vergil's name that of his friend and coworker Horace (Quintus Horatius Flaccus, 65–8 B.C.) is naturally associated. Horace wrote *Satires,* which according to our later usage, were not satirical (they were even less so than those of Lucilius had been) but rather *causeries* on a variety of topics, with the hexameter treated somewhat informally; and *Epistles,* lifelike pictures of Roman society and seasoned comment on Roman life, mingled with practical maxims on human conduct. Even better known are his *Carmina* (Odes), in which he displays a facility in Greek lyric meters not equalled in Latin literature. These *Carmina* include some *vers de société,* probably no more heartfelt than its countless imitations have been; but most of them reveal courtesy, good humor, kindliness and a certain mellow sagacity, the combination of which has made Horace a favorite in modern times as well as in his own day. He does not scale any idealistic heights but within his limits he is good company. No other Latin poet has been more translated, copied and alluded to in English literature.

Elegiac Poets; Ovid.—The elegy, a personal form without social implications, was in vogue during the later portion of Augustus's reign. The representatives of this elegiac school were Albius Tibullus and Sextus Propertius. Quintilian thought Tibullus especially correct and elegant, though he admits that some chose Propertius (X, 1, 93). In Tibullus there is, to be sure, delicacy and refinement; but these are certainly not the strong points of Propertius, who, though decidedly more original than Tibullus, is often pedantically heavy and obscure. Not so Ovid (Publius Ovidius Naso, 43 B.C.–17 A.D.), whose facile readability appealed to many who found Lucretius, Vergil or Horace too arduous. As late as Elizabeth's more or less spacious days, Ovid was greatly admired by English readers. The best of him is contained in the *Epistolae Heroidum* (Epistles of Heroines) and the *Metamorphoses,* but even at his best his surface brilliance cannot hide his shallowness.

Livy, Seneca and Other Prose Writers.—Best of Augustan prose writers is the historian Livy (Titus Livius, 59 B.C.–17 A.D.), whose *Annales* covered the history of Rome from the founding of the city to 9 B.C. Of its 142 books, 35 have been preserved. As a historian he was, even judged by the standards of his day, remarkably lacking in anything like scholarship, but his style has been called by one modern writer, H. A. J. Munro, the finest prose ever written.

With the Claudian period we enter that later time when Latin Literature became to so large an extent mere rhetorical exercise. Gatherings were held for the purpose of hearing authors read extracts from their books. Lucius Annaeus Seneca (3–65 A.D.), for a while preceptor of Nero, and last great representative of Stoic philosophy is important. He was a writer of great interest to the early Christians. His *Moral Essays* (On Providence, On Tranquility of Mind, On Happy Life and others) are full of substance. The prose departs from the periodic structure of Cicero's, being more broken and direct. The *Satiricon* of Petronius (T. Petronius Arbiter) is a curious medley of a book, best known for the episode of "Trimalchio's Dinner." It has been a leading source of knowledge of the *sermo plebeius,* or common speech, of Rome. The *Pharsalia* of Lucan (M. Annaeus Lucanus, 39–65 A.D.) is an epic on the war between Pompey and Caesar; in spots it is rhetorically effective but not to be mentioned with *The Aeneid.* Aulus Persius (34–62 A.D.) wrote satires, full of borrowings from Horace, in a style that has been likened to what the later Carlyle's might have been, had Carlyle written in verse; but marked by Stoic earnestness. Pliny the Elder (23–79 A.D.), who died in the eruption of Vesuvius, compiled a *Natural History* almost wanting in literary value but crammed with miscellaneous information.

Quintilian (*c.* 35–95 A.D.) in his *Institutio Oratoria* (The Training of the Orator) embodies much sensible literary criticism in readable form. In its tenth book it has a survey of Greek and Roman authors. It was Martial (M. Valerius Martialis, d. 102 A.D. ?) who gave to the *epigram* its present connotation of pointed wit; the Greek epigram was more inclusive. His highly-polished lines dealt crisply with the surface life of his own day.

Tacitus, Juvenal, Pliny the Younger and Others.—One of the leading historians of all time was Cornelius Tacitus (c. 55–116), whose *Agricola* and *Germania* are studies, respectively, of the life of his father-in-law and of the geography of Germany and the life and customs of its tribes. His *Historiae* and *Annales* have come down in very incomplete form but we have enough of them to know that for strength and dramatic vividness (especially in the Annales) few historians in any language are his equals. Juvenal (Decimus Junius Juvenalis, c. 55–c. 130 A.D.) in nis satires is a savage moralist comparable to Dean Swift. Samuel Johnson's *London*, which first made him known as a man of letters, and his *Vanity of Human Wishes*, are both imitations of Juvenal. The letters of Pliny the Younger (Plinius Caecilius Secundus, 62–113 A.D.) show us a different side of Roman life, taking us among gentlefolk of culture and good taste. Those sent by Pliny, when he was governor of Bithynia, to the Emperor Trajan, give us an understanding of Rome's provincial administration. One of them (with the emperor's rescript) throws light on Rome's attitude toward the early Christians and its treatment of them.

This review of classical Latin literature closes with Suetonius (Gaius Suetonius Tranquillus, c. 75–c. 150 A.D.), whose *Lives of the Caesars* abound in biographical detail supplementary to the work of Tacitus and all sorts of unedifying gossip; and Aulus Gellius (second half of the 2d century), whose *Attic Nights* is a booklover's melange of antiquarian lore, grammatical discussions and literary chitchat.

ENGLISH LITERATURE

The great periods of English literature are practically the same as the major eras of English national expansion and development; both have the same continuity of growth and the extent of the influence of English literature may be measured by the far-flung reaches of the nation and of the language itself. In that influence we see those alert and vital characteristics that have made the Anglo-Saxon a symbol of culture and progress and given him the enterprise to carry his colonies and intellectual gifts to the ends of the earth.

In the beginning of this wide span of English literature, the first impetus to learning and the pursuit of letters was given by King Alfred the Great, who ruled from 871 to 901. After the lapse of several centuries the works of Chaucer represent a period of marked social reform in the reign of Richard II (1377–98). Another whirl of the wheel of time and the great dramas of Shakespeare are the literary expression of the cultural and political influences of the Renaissance felt throughout the civilized world during the reign of Queen Elizabeth (1558–1603). Milton very clearly typifies the reaction of the period of reform that swept England under the Commonwealth (1649–60); and Dryden, Addison and Steele represent the era of criticism and comment, influenced by French thought, that followed the Restoration of Charles II (1660–85).

Less than a hundred years afterwards, the spirit of Romanticism dominated English literary expression during the reigns of the four Georges (1714–1830), especially in the poetry of the Lake School and in Scott's novels. The distinguished Victorian authors—Tennyson, the Brownings, Thackeray, Carlyle, Ruskin and many others—show the trend of the social, political and ecclesiastical life of that reign (1837–1901), which, however, held the seeds that were to be sown and come to flower in the sharply contrasting manners and thought of the 20th century, with its brilliant and varied writers from Wells and Shaw to Maugham and Masefield.

Broad Survey.—For convenience in considering English literature, it may be roughly divided into four broad periods: Anglo-Saxon or Old English, 450–1100; Middle English, 1100–1550; Modern English, 1550–1900; and 20th Century. These periods may be subdivided into others for the sake of emphasizing the developments of certain special periods, such as the Norman Conquest and the Renaissance.

Britain has been the home of several races, all Indo-European, each contributing something to the English language. The Celts or Britons, who were in Britain when the island first became known to the civilized world through Caesar's Roman invasion (55 B.C.), are traceable through fewer than a hundred words in the language; they include those ending with *don*, from Celtic *dun*, a fortress, as in *London*. The Celts' descendants still inhabit Scotland, Wales, Ireland and parts of England. The Romans left ruins that still supply mute testimony of their occupation—roads, villas and baths; a few of their words were retained, notably *chester* (found as part of many names of places), from the Latin word *castra*, or camp. Then came the Teutonic invasion by Angles, Saxons and Jutes; and from Anglo-Saxon speech the English language developed its sturdy root and branch upon which Norman speech was subsequently grafted.

Anglo-Saxon or Old English Period, 450–1100.—As these adventurers from the Continent were without the art of writing and had no literature, they depended instead upon their minstrels' songs, which passed from generation to generation as unwritten legends; but as a written language was gradually developed, these minstrels' works were written and preserved. They were rudely metrical and highly poetical.

Many of these old song manuscripts are in the British Museum, London, among them *The Fight of Finnsburg*, *Doer's Lament*, *Widsith* and *Beowulf*, the most notable of this early verse. *Beowulf*, an epic poem more than 3,000 lines long, contains episodes of dramatic interest expressed with force and beauty in rhythmical and alliterative language, simple and yet powerful in its use of images and figures of speech. The following lines (slightly modernized), describing the abode of Grendel and his mother, are typical:

> They dwell in a wilderness by wolves haunted,
> Where the fen-path winds in windy headlands
> And the mountain waterfall is mist-shrouded.

Christian poetry by Caedmon and Cynewulf, the rustic authors, was the next contribution to early English literature. Caedmon, an unlettered herdsman in a monastery, had a strange dream, in which a voice commanded him to sing "the beginning of created things." He at once began to recite in verse form the story of creation, the history of Israel and the coming of Christ. He told his strange story to the abbess, who declared that "heavenly grace had been bestowed on him," and that night in the great hall had him repeat word for word what he had chanted by command from the strange voice. Caedmon died about 680, and his poem was the first attempt to put the story of the Bible in language that the common people of England could understand.

Cynewulf, the first English poet who wrote on separate religious subjects, is the author of *Christ*, a devotional, allegorical poem; *Elene*, a story of finding the true cross; *Juliana*, a saint's legend; and *Judith*, the Bible story of the killing of Holofernes.

The Venerable Bede wrote in priest's Latin the *Ecclesiastical History of Britain*. King Alfred was the force behind the scholars who translated from Latin Bede's *History* and Boethius's *On The Consolation of Philosophy* into the everyday English, or Anglo-Saxon, of the period. Alfred established schools so that the youth could learn to "read the new English tongue perfectly," and he has been called the "Father of English Prose" because he encouraged the use of everyday English and because he collected the *Anglo-Saxon Chronicles*, histories that had been written in different parts of the country at different times. The great part of these Chronicles as we now have them tells the story of England before Alfred's own time. Later continuations carried it on to 1154.

The Norman Conquest, 1066.—The Norsemen, kinsmen of the Danes who were harassing England, had settled in the northern part of France, which was called Normandy after them. They quickly adapted themselves to the language and civilization of northern France and began to make themselves felt as a great power. Under Duke William late in the 11th century they looked around for new lands to conquer and found England the least powerful and most unprotected prey.

William therefore crossed the English Channel and after defeating King Harold of England on the field of Hastings (1066) was hailed William the Conqueror. Norman French became the official language of the government that the Conqueror established in England—the feudal system that was so characteristic of western Europe at the time replacing the Saxon barons and bishops with Norman lords and churchmen. French customs prevailed at court; scholars still wrote in Latin and spoke French with the nobility, but the old-fashioned Anglo-Saxon customs and language were retained by the unlettered.

In time, however, a common speech was developed and gradually a new language emerged. It opened the way to a new expression in native literature that reflected the influence of the culture, spirit and interests of the Continent—the literature of chivalry and romance suggested by the stories and poems sung by the French minstrels; it dealt with adventurous deeds, heroic episodes and enchanting scenes. Mysticism and the supernatural supplied the background and musical accompaniment was used to arouse the listeners. The new forms must have seemed strange to the plain, simple Saxon, whose interests lay with the homely things of toil, his battle with the elements, domestic life and religious worship.

These prose and lyrical romances brought from France centered about three subjects—the exploits of King Arthur and the Knights of the Round Table, Emperor Charlemagne and his peers and the legends of Alexander the Great and Troy and Aeneas.

Though Celtic in origin, the legend of King Arthur has a British background and the first record of this great and chivalrous king is credited to Geoffrey of Monmouth. His *History of the Kings of Britain* (1147) was translated into French verse by Wace, a Norman, and retranslated into English by a monk named Layamon, who called his work *The Brut.*

Middle English, 1100–1550.—This period was one of transition from old to new: the disturbing effects of the Norman Conquest pass away with the establishment of a permanent form of English speech and nationality as Norman and Saxon speech and interests are knit together. The era was marked by the Hundred Years' War between England and France, notable for the English victories of Crécy, Poitiers and Agincourt; the romantic career of Joan of Arc in France; the development of the English parliamentary system that checked the abuses against which the peasants (led by Wat Tyler) revolted, and which brought together the gentleman, the burgess and the villein or tenant—all having an influence upon the writers of the day.

GEOFFREY CHAUCER (1340–1400).—If he was not the Father of English Poetry, Chaucer was the first to employ the iambic pentameter that became the standard form of English heroic verse, and his works definitely established the combined grammatical forms, diction and sentence structure of the French and Saxon tongues into the fundamentals of the English language. Chaucer was the first English story teller; his work combines narrative skill with clever characterization and portrays with wit and understanding of human nature the interests common to all men. Though Chaucer was of humble birth, his native talents gained recognition at the court of Edward III, where he became valet to the king and married the queen's lady-in-waiting. His position led to several diplomatic trips to France and Italy, where his keen observation and studious bent seized upon rich material for his literary works. In addition to being a courtier, diplomat and traveler, Chaucer became a scholar, and his wide sympathies gave sanity and justice to his ideas and opinions.

The works of Chaucer fall into three periods that reflect the various influences of his foreign travels, residence and study, as well as his knowledge of native English types. Chief among his translations from the French (1369–80) are: *Roman de la rose,* a French allegory in which a lady is represented as a rosebud; her lover desires to pluck the rose but is thwarted by various figures symbolizing the opposition of her parents, envy, her modesty, riches and the like; and *Death of Blaunche, the Duchess,* which commemorates the death of the wife of John of Gaunt, Chaucer's first patron. Other stories derived from the French are *Life of Saint Cecyle, Story of Constance, Twelve Tragedies* and *Complaint of Mars.* During his period of Italian influence (1380–85) Chaucer wrote *Troilus and Criseyde,* a story of the fall of Troy; and *Parlement of*

𝕮 The noble and amerous aūcyent hystory of Troylus and Creſyde / in the tyme of the ſiege of Troye. Cōpyled by Geffraye Chaucer.

Troylus.

Creſyde

NEW YORK PUBLIC LIBRARY

CHAUCER. An excerpt from Caxton's Edition of *Troilus and Criseyde* published at Westminster around 1484. The title of the picture is written in Middle English, the form of speech used from 1100–1550. Geoffrey Chaucer is also the author of the *Canterbury Tales.*

Foules, an amusing allegory of a parliament of birds hearing cases in which notable personages are caricatured. Chaucer's *Hous of Fame* was similarly inspired; his *Legende of Goode Women,* about women famous for constancy, was never finished.

In Chaucer's English period (1380–85) his great masterpiece, *Canterbury Tales,* was produced; it has to do with a motley group of Londoners on their annual pilgrimage to the shrine of St. Thomas à Becket at Canterbury. The *Prologue* introduces the characters and tells of their stopping overnight at the Tabard Inn in Southwark on the south side of the Thames, London. In the evening the host, Harry Bailey, suggests that they beguile the journey the next day with stories, the teller of the best story to receive a supper at the end of the journey. Twenty-four tales were told by the pilgrims—a doctor, lawyer, tradesman, monk, nun, priest, country parson, sailor, miller, carpenter, yeoman, an Oxford scholar, a summoner, cook, knight, squire, prioress, farmer, friar, plowman and the lusty Wife of Bath. The stories are equally varied, ranging from serious homilies and poetic romances to ribald adventures. The *Canterbury Tales* gives Chaucer a high place in literature as a realist who cleverly depicts the foibles and virtues of mankind with wit, pathos and profound human philoscphy.

Works by Chaucer's two contemporaries, Lydgate and Hoccleve, show them as imitators, but both were prolific in the use of various verse forms of the day and wrote with charm and poetic insight.

John Gower's *Confessio Amantis* ("Confession of a Lover," 1385–93), was the first allegory in romantic verse in the English language. The ballad form of verse was attempted first by Scottish writers, among them John Barbour, who wrote of episodes in the life of the great hero, Robert Bruce. Two other Scottish poets of this period were James I, who wrote a collection of love poems, *The King's Quair,* and Gavin Douglas (c. 1474–1522), whose translation of Vergil's *Aeneid* was the first complete version made in Britain.

Church worship remained largely pagan in character, the clergy preyed upon the poor and spiritual life was at a low ebb. John Wycliffe so felt the oppression of these conditions that he took steps to bring about social and religious reforms. His followers, the Lollards, prefigured the Protestants of the Reformation. Wycliffe's translation of the Bible in 1384 was the first made in the English language. To William Langland is attributed the 14th-century allegorical poem, *Piers Plowman,* attacking the evils of the day and urging that society can be reformed only if each man will do his duty in his own sphere of life—the peasant at his plow, the knight defending his country, the priest leading his flock by word and deed and the king ruling with justice.

An event of surpassing importance in this period was the introduction of the printing press into England (1476) by William Caxton, a silk merchant of Bruges. He was a lover of litera-

ture and was quick to foresee the enormous impetus the printing press would give to the creation and spread of books. His first book printed in the English language was the *Recuyell* (summary) *of the Historyes of Troye* (1474 or 1475), which he himself translated from the French. He printed the works of Chaucer and Gower and Sir Thomas Malory's *Morte d'Arthur* (1485), which is the great English version of the story of Arthur, Guinevere and Lancelot.

The Renaissance, c. 1525–80.—The Renaissance, or New Birth, that had commenced earlier on the Continent began in England about 1525 and served as a transition between the Middle and Modern periods of English literature. It is called the *Renaissance* because the medieval spirit had largely disappeared and was replaced by a revival of interest in classical literature. Printing was extended, America had been discovered and the globe circumnavigated, and increased trade and various inventions had opened up new interests for man. Scholars began to translate with new zeal the classics of Greek and Latin; the poets Dante, Petrarch and Boccaccio were widely read; grammars and dictionaries appeared; the universities gave increased attention to philosophy, art, science, history. The period well represents a new birth in learning, and its local activities in art and literature gave England a new joy in living, new appreciation of art and the enjoyment of the beautiful in life as stimulated by the great Italian Renaissance that had given the world Petrarch and Michelangelo.

There was a keen rivalry for eminence in writing ballads and inventing new verse forms and the storytelling art that had been introduced by Chaucer was cultivated by other writers. Religious reformation also swept England and there were successive translations of the Bible, notably that by William Tyndale (d. 1536); and from medieval church pageantry, a mighty literary art sprang up—the drama. All in all, this astonishing period may be called the beginning of modern civilization. It was during these years that our own New England and Virginia were settled and they, too, felt this vital influence. Livelier imaginations stirred men to braver deeds and fresher philosophies of living, to more beautiful concepts of intellectual and emotional experiences, to greater achievements in the realms of literature, science, invention and commerce.

In addition to experiments in newer verse forms, the Renaissance in England brought the use of blank verse, or unrhymed iambic pentameter, by Wyatt and Surrey, who translated Vergil's *Aeneid* and also introduced the Italian sonnet into English literature (c. 1575). In Latin, Sir Thomas More wrote *Utopia* (1516), describing a Nowhere, the ideal community of his hopes and dreams. Sir Thomas North translated Plutarch's *Lives of the Noble Grecians and Romans* (1579), which became a source book for the dramatists. Sir Walter Raleigh led the minor Elizabethan poets and wrote *The History of the World*

(1614); John Lyly and his *Euphues, or the Anatomy of Wit* (1579) led the same poets to invent manifold ways of saying the same thing. Sir Philip Sidney published his best-known book, *Arcadia* (1590), a novel in highly ornate prose freely interspersed with verse. Contemporary with him was the great Edmund Spenser (c. 1552–99), whose love of beauty, sound and color in language are evident in his *The Shepheardes Calender* (1579) and *The Faerie Queene* (1590–96), landmarks in the creation of English poetry. *The Faerie Queene* is a long, allegorical treatment of chivalry, love, morality and the supernatural. Through it runs a constant strain of beautiful imagery, presented in a unique nine-line stanza afterwards called *Spenserian.*

English Drama, 1580–1642.—The English theater owes its origin to the church. As all services were read in Latin, the priests conceived the idea of enacting some of the simpler stories of the Bible so that all might understand them. These simple plays took two forms; *miracle* plays or episodes from the Bible that had either an actual miracle or dramatic content like *Noah's Flood* and *The Second Shepherd's Play;* and *morality* plays in which abstract ideas such as Truth, Righteousness, Mercy and Peace were personified, their dialogue representing the triumph of right over wrong. The best-known morality play is *Everyman,* a profound and stirring play of Dutch origin that is presented even today.

In time the church gave the plays outside the church instead of inside, and various guilds took them up, so that certain plays became identified with different towns, especially Coventry, York and Chester. These plays were presented on vans that moved from one village green to another. To give variety, another type of entertainment was introduced, the *interlude,* corresponding somewhat to present-day vaudeville. This form met with such success that it was developed into a longer play structure. Among the early comedies were *Ralph Roister Doister* (1551) by Nicholas Udall; *Gammer Gurton's Needle* (1556) by William Stevenson; *The Arraignment of Paris* by George Peele; and *The Honorable History of Friar Bacon and Friar Bungay* (1592) by Robert Greene. Various plays were written around the Robin Hood theme. In contrast, a number of writers essayed tragedy, such as *Cambyses* by Preston (1537–98), and *Gorboduc* (1562) by Sackville and Norton. Those with historical background are *James the Fourth* by Robert Greene, and *The Spanish Tragedy* by Thomas Kyd (c. 1558–94). Ideas in Christopher Marlowe's plays, *Dr. Faustus* (c. 1588), which had a revival in New York in 1937, and his *Jew of Malta* (c. 1592), were sufficiently impressive to be used by later and more important men, including Shakespeare, with whom Marlowe is thought to have collaborated and whom he greatly influenced by the beauty of his verse and the power of his imagination. "Before Marlowe," said Swinburne, "there was neither genuine blank verse nor a

NEW YORK PUBLIC LIBRARY

THE GLOBE THEATRE was built in 1598 in Southwark on the Bankside, across the Thames from London, and could accommodate about 1,200 theatergoers. Fire destroyed it in 1613.

genuine tragedy in our language." All this experimentation in the dramatic form led the way to the great work of Shakespeare and his immediate contemporaries.

William Shakespeare (1564–1616).—We know very little about the life of this greatest figure in English literature, but we do know that Shakespeare was born in Stratford, April 23, and died there on the anniversary of his birth. He was the son of humble but highly respected parents and received his formal education in the Stratford village grammar school, then ran away to London. Perhaps he had watched the London players who went out to entertain Queen Elizabeth at Kenilworth Castle near by, and wished to attach himself to the London theater. He succeeded in this, first by doing menial tasks; next, he held scripts; then by suggesting revisions he won the privilege of taking small parts; and finally he wrote the plays. He married Ann Hathaway in 1582 and became influential in London by developing the Lord Chamberlain's Dramatic Company, which later became the King's Company.

Shakespeare had an interest in the Globe and Blackfriars theaters and lived and worked in the atmosphere of the theater. It is not recorded that he ever traveled, but he amassed a great store of learning by reading translations from the French and Italian classics and poring over contemporary books of all sorts; his principal sources include *Chronicles of England, Scotland and Ireland* (1578) by Holinshed, and the translation of Plutarch by North. He associated with both high and low in the teeming life of London; he enjoyed many triumphs and suffered numerous losses; though he became wealthy through real estate holdings, he suffered from the ca-

prices of writers and the frailty of friends.

The entire span of Shakespeare's plays reflects his personal experience as well as profound insight into human nature. He was the epitome of that vital period in English history we call Elizabethan. His early plays are rich in comedy, and the style is gay, fanciful, brimming with figures of speech and poetic allusions. They represent a life of youthful enthusiasm, flushed with prosperity and public applause. Then follow the tragedies, somber in style, philosophic in treatment, reflecting the sorrows and troubles of a career turbulent with the storm and stress of life. The final group, embracing historical plays and comedies, reflects the poet's period of retirement, and the style shows full maturity of thought. The following outline presents the probable periods and the types of various groups:

1590–94.—
    Comedies: *Love's Labour's Lost, Comedy of Errors, The Two Gentlemen of Verona*
    Histories: *Henry VI, Richard III, King John*
    Tragedies: *Titus Andronicus*
1594–1600.—
    Comedies: *A Midsummer Night's Dream, The Merchant of Venice, The Taming of the Shrew, Merry Wives of Windsor, Much Ado About Nothing, As You Like It, Twelfth Night*
    Histories: *Richard II, Henry IV, Henry V*
    Tragedies: *Romeo and Juliet, Julius Caesar*
1601–09.—
    Comedies: *Troilus and Cressida, All's Well That Ends Well, Measure for Measure, Pericles*
    Tragedies: *Hamlet, Othello, King Lear, Macbeth, Timon of Ath-*

ens, *Antony and Cleopatra, Coriolanus*
1610–13.—
    Comedies: *Cymbeline, The Winter's Tale, The Tempest, The Two Noble Kinsmen*
    Histories: *Henry VIII*

The plays record a great range of poetic thought, pungent philosophy and the consummate dramatic quality of Shakespeare's master mind; they present many scenes of great imaginative power, virile characterization and surpassing beauty and indicate deep moral insight. The characters Shakespeare created, such as Portia, Hamlet, Lear, Lady Macbeth, Iago, Rosalind, Beatrice and Benedict, Viola, Falstaff, Henry V, Brutus, Cordelia, Prospero and Ariel, are very real and cleverly drawn and rank with the fictitious personages of all time. Shakespeare wrote two narrative poems that alone would have given him high rank as a poet—*Venus and Adonis* (1593) and *The Rape of Lucrece* (1594). His more personal *Sonnets* (1609) carry on the best traditions of the Italian school as well as introduce new rhyming schemes. His lasting influence upon the English language and literature is considered second only to that of the Bible, and has been great also in many foreign countries, including Japan.

Shakespeare's influence stimulated contemporary playwrighting and held the drama in a dominant position. Beaumont (1584–1618) and Fletcher (1579–1625) wrote a sensational tragedy, *The Maid's Tragedy,* and an amusing comedy, *The Knight of the Burning Pestle.* Only Shakespeare surpassed them in the rich power of fancy. Philip Massinger's *A New Way To Pay Old Debts* (1625) is a realistic portrayal of greed, and John Webster's *The Duchess of Malfi* (c. 1616) ranks as the best post-Shakespearian tragedy. Webster's plays were full of terror. The greatest scholar (who was also a dramatist) of the Elizabethan period, however, was Ben Jonson. He wrote *Every Man in His Humour* (1598) in which Shakespeare, who was Jonson's intimate friend, is one of the characters; and all Jonson's plays are filled with the characteristically Elizabethan idea of humors, strongly marked types of erratic personality. Jonson wrote also the incomparable lyric, "To Celia" ("Drink To Me Only with Thine Eyes"). In his dedication in the First Folio edition of Shakespeare's plays, Jonson wrote, "He was not of an age, but for all time."

SIR FRANCIS BACON (1561–1626).—Well born and educated at Cambridge, Bacon was the most outstanding contemporary of Shakespeare. Bacon became a barrister, traveled abroad, was knighted by James I, became Lord High Chancellor and was made a peer. Such a distinguished career had its temptations and Bacon was convicted of bribery and the betrayal of justice, deprived of office, fined and banished from London. Whatever his political faults and offenses, this stigma has not blinded the world to the evidences of his great mind. Bacon was a scientist—maybe the first of modern scientists—scholar, philosopher and prolific writer; most of his works he composed in Latin as well as in English. His *Novum Organum* (1620) and *The Advancement of Learning* (1623) are two parts of an uncompleted work, an exposition of pure scientific reasoning of a new type; *The New Atlantis* (1627) projects a scientific and philosophical idealism—another Utopia—but his more widely known *Essays* (1597), brief, expressive, filled with the wisdom of a mind broad, deep and full, established his place in English literature.

King James Bible (1611).—The last great literary product of the Elizabethan era was the King James version of the Holy Bible, begun in 1604 and completed in 1611 by 54 scholars who revised and compared previous versions, especially the Bishops' Bible of 1568, the Geneva Bible of 1560 and others back to the Tyndale Bible (1525–34) and the Wycliffe Bible (1382 and 1397). On the life of the 17th century, on the thought of the 18th century and even on the style of the 19th century there is no influence to compare with this authorized version of the English Bible. Authors as unlike as Ruskin, Kipling and Lord Dunsany are profoundly influenced by its phrases, its imagery and its rhythms. It was not merely a precursor of the Puritan period of the early 17th century, but like the poetry of Shakespeare and Milton and the prose of Bunyan it was a symbol of a new unity in English speech and letters.

The Puritan Age, 1616–60.—The Elizabethan era with its stormy, adventurous, versatile exponents was the bright, almost gorgeous, flowering of the bold spirit of the Renaissance—man's passionate interest in this world. It was followed by a splendid preoccupation—on the part of at least one English group, the Puritans, the followers of Cromwell—with man's relation to God. It was a period of political controversy and the great Civil War, which ended with the execution of Charles I in 1649 and the ten-year Protectorate under Oliver Cromwell. The theaters had been closed in 1642. In 1660 the kingdom was restored and England's Puritan period was over. Its literature was not distinctively political or Puritan. It could boast of noble prose. The philosophical *Religio Medici* (1643) and *Hydriotophia* or *Urn-Burial* (1658) by Sir Thomas Browne were read in translations on the Continent and are still prized by those who love majestic phrase and quaint grandeur. Jeremy Taylor (1613–67), a great preacher, was on the King's side in the Civil War and was repeatedly imprisoned for his loyalty to the Stuart cause; but he is the foremost literary representative of the pulpit in this whole period, the author of the pious books, *Holy Living* (1650) and *Holy Dying* (1651), a pleader for toleration and the master of musical, powerful, picturesque prose. Izaak Walton's *Compleat Angler* (1653) and his biographies of eminent clergymen who were also famous fishermen were written in an easier simpler style than English literature had known before. A few lovely lyrics were written by

Edmund Waller (1606–87), notably "Go, Lovely Rose"; and Robert Herrick (1591–1674), a country parson, is famous for the charm of his countless brief lyrics and tiny epigrams published in *Hesperides and Noble Numbers* (1648). The metaphysical poets, Herbert, Donne and Cowley wrote abundantly in mystical strain. Donne, who influenced the prose writers and both the Cavalier and the metaphysical poets of his own time, is reflected also in such 20th-century poetry as that of the American, T. S. Eliot, and others, who aroused an interest in Donne's poetry by numerous critical studies and commentaries on his work.

JOHN MILTON (1608–74).—The son of a London law stationer of means, Milton was educated at Cambridge and sent abroad on a "grand tour." He returned to England to use his pen, if not his sword, in the cause of the Civil War and accepted the post of Secretary to Cromwell. His career, something like that of Bacon, was political, diplomatic, studious and literary. As with Shakespeare's works, Milton's too, fall into distinct periods:

BEFORE THE COMMONWEALTH, 1606–40.—*L'Allegro* and *Il Penseroso* are companion studies, respectively, of a man in a social, and then in a meditative, mood. They are marked by fine descriptive passages and abound in imagery. *Lycidas* ranks with the finest elegies written; in form it is like a Greek pastoral. *Comus* is a masque, or play of allegorical ideas and phrases, set to music, written to celebrate the inauguration of the Earl of Bridgewater as Lord Deputy of Wales.

THE COMMONWEALTH, 1640-60.—Milton's political, educational and ecclesiastical pamphlets were cogent utterances, expressing ideas on divorce, politics and freedom of speech far ahead of his time. *Areopagitica* is considered the most famous. His *Sonnets* (only 20 in English) expressed ideas other than those of love and sentiment: far better than his pamphlets they express his thoughts on political questions. Wordsworth called the sonnet in Milton's hand "a trumpet; whence he blew soul-animating strains—alas, too few!"

RETIREMENT, 1660–74.—During this period Milton wrote *Paradise Lost* and *Paradise Regained,* magnificent epics telling the story of the creation of the world, the loss of Eden and its recapture through the Coming of Christ. The descriptions are brilliant, the conceptions inspiring, and the language luxuriant. *Samson Agonistes,* the story of Samson, is in the form of a Greek tragedy and abounds in many scenes of dramatic fervor and poetic beauty but is not comparable to his greatest work, *Paradise Lost.*

Milton is the typical literary figure of Cromwell's time, engrossed in politics and in religion, but a lover of beauty and music and a creator of music and beauty—quite different from the common and mistaken notion of the character of Cromwell's followers.

The passing of Milton, long blind and solitary, came after the close of the era that had given rise to much of his independent thought and ex-

pression, and the literature of the succeeding period had already begun to take on the color and tone of the Restoration.

The Age of Criticism, 1660–1784.—The Restoration of Charles II to the throne, although marked by reopening the theaters and greater freedom in social life, did not mean a return to the Elizabethan mode of thought but an experimentation with the French style and form of literary expression. Charles II, returning from France, had brought something of the court of Louis XIV, with Versailles as its center of wit, science and literature, where Corneille and Racine in tragedy, Molière in comedy and Boileau-Despréaux in criticism were men of the hour. The French style, therefore, was the model to emulate; so the plays of Congreve, Otway, Wycherley and Farquhar savor of French smartness; but soon the neoclassicism of the time gave evidence of a different English quality.

JOHN DRYDEN (1631–1700).—Born in Northamptonshire and educated at Westminster and Cambridge, Dryden sought a literary career in London. He is best known for his political satire in biblical manner, *Absalom and Achitophel* (1681), attacking the earl of Shaftesbury for his attempt to make the duke of Monmouth heir apparent to the throne. In *The Hind and the Panther* (1687), two years after the Catholic James came to the throne Dryden defended the Roman Catholic faith to which he had become converted. His satires are brilliant with well-defined rhythm and incisive picturizations. His "Alexander's Feast" and "St. Cecilia's Day" are Pindaric odes with remarkable metrical beauty. In his prose essays he set a mark for clarity and polish worthy of present-day emulation. Dryden was made Poet Laureate in 1670. His later years were devoted to translating the classics (Vergil, Juvenal and many others). Before he became a satirist he wrote dozens of plays, both comedies and tragedies —*Marriage à la Mode* (1672) and *The Conquest of Granada* (1669–70). Shakespeare's *Antony and Cleopatra* supplied the subject for Dryden's *All for Love* (1678), an attempt to rewrite Shakespeare and make him observe the rules of dramatic unity!

This period of rationalization followed fixed rules for composition, analysis and more or less artificiality of phrasing that resulted in the creation of fixed types in the writing pattern. It produced other writers worthy of note who do not come under the rule of academic composition—notably Samuel Pepys (1633–1703), whose only publication during his lifetime was *Memoirs Relating to the State of the Royal Navy* (1690), but whose reputation rests on his *Diary* (covering the years 1660 to 1669 and not published till 1825), with its lively, chatty intimacy, much imitated in our own time. Samuel Butler's *Hudibras* (1663-64–78) amused the public by its ridicule of the Puritans. John Bunyan's *Pilgrim's Progress* (1678–84) remains an unsurpassed allegory, describing in simple clear English the adventure of redemption, an expression of the soul of English Protestantism in the period of Cromwell and the generation after.

ALEXANDER POPE (1688–1744).—The time of Pope is often referred to as the Augustan Age because its writers were fond of comparing themselves to Vergil, Cicero and Horace, who wrote during the reign of Augustus in Rome. It was marked by the development of the two-party system in England—the Whigs and the Tories—the growth of British colonies in America, a friendly rivalry with France in the arts and the encouragement of civil and religious liberty. The literature of the period was not imaginative nor sentimental but adhered to the theory that life should be appraised by reason, using the great classics as models. The style, therefore, was cold and formal. One innovation that contributed to discussion and the communication of ideas was the coffee-house that quickly became a London institution where men gathered to enjoy talking about literature, politics and what not. Pamphlets and periodicals began to flourish.

Alexander Pope, afflicted with a frail body and a sensitive spirit, was the outstanding writer of the early part of this period. His writings were caustic and brilliant. He was primarily a satirist and a moralist. His verse, employing rhymed couplets, is fluent and witty but not passionate or profound. He set forth his ideas on style in his *Essay on Criticism* (1711); he caricatured the follies of society in his amusing, if exaggerated, *The Rape of the Lock* (1714); he lashed back at his critics and contemporaries in *The Dunciad* (1728); he translated the *Iliad* (1715) in "correct" verse; and he gave to English literature a masterpiece in his *Essay on Man* (1733–34). Pope is the author of many such aphorisms as:

A little learning is a dangerous thing,
Drink deep, or taste not the Pierian spring.

Be not the first by whom the new is tried,
Nor yet the last to lay the old aside.

JONATHAN SWIFT (1667–1740).—Born in Ireland and educated at Trinity College, Dublin, Swift worked his way from poverty to literary and political eminence fighting a morose spirit, many disappointments and a persistent pessimism. Although the author was an ordained clergyman in the Church of England, Swift's *Tale of a Tub* (1704) is a satire on sectarian beliefs. His *Battle of the Books* (1704) pictures a controversy between the claims of classic and modern literature. *Gulliver's Travels* (1726), though it was written to satirize the vices and follies of mankind, became a classic enjoyed for its imaginative quality. The *Journal to Stella* is an intimate record addressed to Esther Johnson, 14 years younger than himself, to whom he gave his affection and confidences; it relates Swift's own doings and contemporary public events and reveals his less gloomy moods.

DANIEL DEFOE (1660–1731).—The son of a London butcher named Foe, Daniel disliked the name and modified it to Defoe, which he distinguished by becoming an innovator of literary forms. A radical pamphleteer, he was frequently imprisoned, and various ironical contributions from his pen were inspired behind bars or in the pillory. Thus it was that he founded the first critical *Review* (1704–13) and became the forerunner of Addison, Steele and many successors; and created and established the novel, with its realistic portrayal of the manners and customs of the time. Defoe's first story, *Robinson Crusoe* (1719), is the best known. He published many other works, among them *Captain Singleton* (1720), *Moll Flanders* (1722), still an outstanding novel, and *The Journal of the Plague Year;* both the last two are imaginative, but *The Journal* is so convincing that it has often been considered purely historical.

JOSEPH ADDISON (1672–1719), RICHARD STEELE (1672–1729).—These two writers represent the essay, a most readable and charming form of prose. Their lives and literary careers were interwoven. Addison's birth and education offset the emotionalism and engaging human qualities of the more humbly reared Steele, an Irishman. Steele founded, wrote and published that varied and attractive journal, *The Tatler* (1709–11), and its sequel, *The Spectator* (1711–12), on both of which Addison collaborated. Accounts of the affairs of that worthy fictitious country gentleman, Sir Roger de Coverley, created by both Addison and Steele, captivate the present-day reader just as they did readers in those far-off days. Earlier, Steele had tried his hand also at plays, of which *The Conscious Lovers* (1722) was the best. Addison's tragedy, *Cato* (1713), was successful then—but is not now. He is better known today for his famous hymn, "The Spacious Firmament on High" and as a contributor to *The Spectator*.

Poetry of the period was written by: Matthew Prior, the first to write light and witty *vers de société;* Edward Young, whose *Complaint, or Night Thoughts* (1742–44) expressed religious Romanticism in blank verse; James Thomson, whose *Seasons* (1730) was utilized as a setting for a Haydn oratorio, and whose *The Castle of Indolence* (1748) ranked high for its Spenserian stanza; and John Gay, who wrote the first English comic opera, *The Beggar's Opera* (1728), which is still played.

The Age of Johnson, 1744–84.—Samuel Johnson, born in 1709 the son of a poor bookseller in Lichfield, was forced to leave his studies at Oxford by his poverty. He tried to teach school, but his group of boys, headed by David Garrick, the future actor, did little but mimic his grotesque mannerisms. This handicapped man then went to London and became a literary hack; he first gained attention by his poem, *London* (1738), which gave him considerable prestige. *The Vanity of Human Wishes* (1749) is considered his best poem. Dr. Johnson was the literary arbiter and autocrat of his day. Recognizing the popularity of Addison and Steele in their periodical essays, he started another series, *The Rambler* (1750-52) and *The Idler* (1758-60), not so sparkling in style or so colorful in characterization as their predecessors. To secure funds to defray the expenses of his mother's funeral, Johnson wrote in the incredibly brief time of one week, *Rasselas, Prince of Abyssinia* (1759), a pedantic novel. From 1747 to 1755 Johnson was busy on his *Dictionary of the English Language.* Another monumental work by Johnson is *The Lives of the Poets* (1781), which passed judgment on a century of English poetry.

Johnson was at his best in conversation, notably at The Club, among whose members were Sir Joshua Reynolds, Garrick, the actor, Bishop Percy, the collector of ballads, Adam Smith, the political economist, Boswell, Fox, Burke and Gibbon. Johnson outshone them all, though he was often rude, blunt and dogmatic. He expressed his prejudices freely, and his intolerance of radicals, medievalists, atheists and the Scottish was pronounced. He was a Tory, a devout churchman and a classicist. He thought that a serious literature should be preserved in Latin, and even his own daily speech showed a preference for Latinized derivatives. Lord Macaulay's estimate of Johnson concludes, "He was both a great and a good man."

In his group at The Club and at the famous eating house, The Cheshire Cheese, on Fleet Street, was James Boswell, who made notations of everything Johnson said, plied him with hypothetical questions and followed him like a shadow. The result was Boswell's *The Life of Samuel Johnson, LL. D.* (1791), remarkable not only for its exhaustive record of Johnson's ways and words but as a portrayal of the personages, manners and thought of the day. It is one of the great biographies of all literature.

The impetus given to fiction at this time came from Richardson and Fielding. Samuel Richardson (1689–1761) wrote in letter form, *Pamela, or Virtue Rewarded* (1740) and *Clarissa Harlowe* (1744–48), both excellent examples of skill in depicting social intrigue. Henry Fielding (1707–54) made his first success with *Joseph Andrews* (1743), burlesquing Richardson's *Pamela;* his masterpiece, *Tom Jones* (1748), is remarkable for characterization, plot, style and humor. Laurence Sterne's *Tristram Shandy* (1759) and *Sentimental Journey* (1768) and Tobias Smollett's *The Adventures of Roderick Random* (1748), *The Adventures of Peregrine Pickle* (1751) and *The Expedition of Humphrey Clinker* (1771) excel in realism.

OLIVER GOLDSMITH (1728–74), poet, novelist and dramatist, whom Garrick called "Noll" and said he "wrote like an angel but talked like poor Poll," contributed to fiction *The Vicar of Wakefield* (1765), which Johnson sold for him to pay his landlady. Goldsmith was another of those lovable Irishmen whose writings so enliven English literature. In his appealing poem, *The Deserted Village* (1770), he vividly depicts the scenes of his home; in his drama *She Stoops to Conquer* (1773), he established the comedy form still employed—plot structure, suspense, climax, humor and characterization. . . . Richard Brinsley Sheridan (1751–1816) followed the dramatic initiative of Goldsmith in two delightful plays, *The Rivals* (1775) and *The School for Scandal* (1777); and in his day was famous as an orator in Parliament. . . . Fannie Burney's *Evelina* (1778), first in the field of fiction delineating family life, won the praise of contemporary men of letters such as Johnson and Scott.

The Johnson period produced two great historians: the Scottish David Hume (1711–76), the first to consider social and literary, as well as political, aspects in his *History of England* (1754–62); and Edward Gibbon (1737–94), whose *History of the Decline and Fall of the Roman Empire* is an exhaustive and discriminating work. . . . Adam Smith's *Wealth of Nations* (1776) established political economy as a science and is still its cornerstone. . . . Edmund Burke (1729–97) was a contemporary statesman of literary quality among whose many papers and speeches the one entitled "On Conciliation with America" stands out as a model of argument, polished in style, noble in sentiment. He was the chief British friend of America in her struggle for freedom. . . . Sir William Blackstone (1723–80) wrote the famous *Commentaries on the Laws of England*.

The Elegy Written in a Country Churchyard (1750) by Thomas Gray (1716–71) attained the rank of a classic, not only in elegiac verse but in its lofty utterance in such lines as, "The paths of glory lead but to the grave"; "Far from the madding crowd's ignoble strife"; and "Full many a gem of purest ray serene." His contemporary, William Collins (1721–59), wrote the ode, "To Evening," and the oft-quoted "Ode Written in 1746," beginning, "How sleep the brave who sink to rest." His style was simpler and less affected than that of most poets of the period.

Transition from Classicism, Late 18th Century.—Early evidences of break with classicism were expressed by James Macpherson (1736–96) in *Fragments of Ancient Poetry* (1761) and *Temora* (1763), purporting to be translations from the Gaelic of Ossian but created by Macpherson himself. In similarly conceived verses, the much discussed Rowley Poems by Thomas Chatterton (1752–70), the unfortunate but precocious boy who won posthumous fame for his poems, *The Bristowe Tragedie* and *Aella*, which he had pretended were copied from old church manuscripts; in Bishop Percy's *Reliques of Ancient English Poetry* (1765). . . . Horace Walpole's ghost romance, *The Castle of Otranto* (1765), with mystery scenes laid in his own Gothic castle, stimulated a revival in the arts and was the first romantic novel and the precursor of the modern mystery story.

The poetry of this period represents many writers who exemplified the love of man and nature, and held less formal and more liberal concepts than their predecessors. To consider in turn those best known: William Cowper (1731–1800), in *The Task* (1785), wrote a blank-verse poem in six books, a charming description of rural scenes with a note of "enthusiasm of

humanity"; he is known also for famous hymns, the humorous poem, "John Gilpin," and the heroic ballad, "The Royal George." . . . George Crabbe's *The Village* (1781), in heroic verse, presents the scene of the laboring class with directness and realism. . . . William Blake, artist and poet, mystic and symbolist almost to the point of insanity, escaped from classicism completely in his lyrics, *Songs of Innocence* (1789) and *Songs of Experience* (1794), which he illustrated with strange, powerful drawings.

Robert Burns (1759–96).—This simple uneducated Scottish peasant did more than any other poet of his time to break the hold of convention on literature and arouse the world to a new appreciation of nature and the common qualities in man. Through poverty his life was hard, though he was eventually acclaimed in fashionable circles. His verse is simple, exuberant, melodic and genuine. His best-known poems are "The Cotter's Saturday Night," "Tam O'Shanter," "To a Mouse," "To a Mountain Daisy," "The Jolly Beggars," and many lyrics that are still sung—"Flow Gently Sweet Afton," "Bonnie Doon," "Auld

WILLIAM WORDSWORTH

Lang Syne" (1788) and many others. Some of his songs were rewritten—with a transforming magic—from old Scotch poems. He died before he was thirty-eight.

The Age of Romanticism, 1800–32.—Romanticism in a literary sense meant a turning from classicism and the revival of medieval thought; an interest in nature and mythology; a return to old ballads and to Spenser and Shakespeare as models. It followed the lure of the beautiful, strange and picturesque in all countries. Cowper, Blake and Burns at home had prepared the way. In Europe the works of Schiller and Goethe in Germany and of Rousseau in France had set examples for the English Romanticists.

William Wordsworth (1770–1850), Samuel Taylor Coleridge (1772–1834).

—Their joint *Lyrical Ballads* (1798) stirred England both by their theories of a new poetry and by their revolutionary character. The book has been called "the most important event in English poetry since Milton." They created The Lake School of poets, as they and other poets lived for the most part in the Lake District of England. Wordsworth attended Cambridge University, traveled on the Continent, became interested in the French Revolution and returned to England to become a Conservative. He then retired to his favorite district to give the world the creations of his philosophic and poetic mind. His poetry had three main liberalizing tendencies—revulsion against artificial poetic diction; a treatment of human nature with truth and appreciation of its inherent goodness; and investing nature with a philosophic content that approaches pantheism. Among his shorter lyrics are "The Solitary Reaper," "I Wandered Lonely as a Cloud," "To the Daisy" and "She Was a Phantom of Delight." His greatest work, "Intimations of Immortality from Recollections of Early Childhood," an ode, shows high imaginative vision. His sonnets are singularly beautiful and fine, and he was the first to write sonnet sequences or series. His longer poems, *The Prelude* and *The Excursion*, seem dull to most readers and in all his poems except the very shortest and best there are dull lines. But he is a great poet.

Coleridge was the chief exponent of Romanticism and of the poetic principles espoused by Wordsworth and differed from him principally in a love of the supernatural and romantic. Coleridge was even more carried away by the dream of a new society and thought of founding, with Southey, a community of poets and philosophers in America. He and Southey married sisters and the necessity of earning their living became of paramount importance. Coleridge spent some time in Germany, learned the language and became imbued with German philosophy. He is best known by the highly imaginative and haunting, "The Ancient Mariner," "Kubla Khan" (1797), which presents a vivid picture of the Mongol dynasty in China, and "Christabel," another supernatural narrative that represents good and evil in conflict. Coleridge was a great literary critic as well as a fine poet. . . . Robert Southey (1774–1843), friend and brother-in-law of Coleridge, left ample evidence of his talent in 109 volumes. He was a master of prose but is remembered for a few short poems, "Inchcape Rock," "The Battle of Blenheim," and "The Cataract of Lodore," with sound imitating sense comparable to Poe's "The Bells."

Sir Walter Scott (1771–1832).—Born in Edinburgh of a prominent family, Scott early became a great student of Scottish life, scenery, legends and ballads. He was an indefatigable worker, soon acquired literary skill and fluency and became a leader in the Romantic school in both poetry and prose. Soon affluent, Scott built his home, Abbotsford, on the Tweed River, where he lived surrounded by his friends, but kept assiduous hours at his desk. His longer narrative poems, *The Lay of the Last Minstrel* (1805), *Marmion* (1808), and *The Lady of the Lake* (1810) are still read and enjoyed because of their flowing couplets and dramatic episodes. Scott's novels are discussed below with those of his contemporaries in fiction.

GEORGE GORDON, LORD BYRON (1788–1824).—Byron was temperamental and extremely sensitive, a poet of high-strung feeling, stubborn convictions and oversentimentality. His life was stormy, bitter, restless. He was master of a wide range of poetry—lyric, satiric, descriptive, narrative and dramatic. Among the best-known lyrics are "She Walks in Beauty," "When We Two Parted," "Maid of Athens" and "Fare Thee Well." His longer works include: *English Bards and Scotch Reviewers* (1809), a diatribe against his critics; *Childe Harold's Pilgrimage* (1812–18), picturing his travels on the Continent; *The Giaour* (1813), the story of a Moslem slave; *The Corsair* (1814), about piracy in the Greek archipelago; *Manfred,* suggested by *Faust; Cain,* the biblical story; and *Don Juan* (1819–24), Byron's masterpiece, an epic

SIR WALTER SCOTT

satire and brilliant exposé of social corruption, British cant and the poet's own passionate life. To many, Byron is best known by his poem, *The Prisoner of Chillon* (written 1817), depicting the imprisonment of François de Bonivard in the Castle of Chillon for his political views.

PERCY BYSSHE SHELLEY (1792–1822).—Highly intellectual and ethereal in his poetic concepts, Shelley was also very independent of spirit. He was university bred, but was expelled for writing the tract, *The Necessity of Atheism* (1811). He lived in Switzerland, but subsequently removed to Italy, where he was drowned in the Bay of Spezia. His works cover a wide range. His lyrics include: "Ode To the West Wind," "Adonais" (in memory of Keats), "To a Skylark," "The Cloud," "Hymn To Intellectual Beauty." Among his longer poems are *Queen*

Mab (1813), *The Revolt of Islam* (1817–18), *The Cenci* (1819), an Italian tragedy, and *Prometheus Unbound* (1820). Shelley's great prose work, *The Defence of Poetry* (1821), an essay in the field of criticism, is still studied.

In 1816 Shelley married Mary Godwin (1797–1851), the daughter of William Godwin and Mary Wollstonecraft. She wrote *Frankenstein* (1818), a unique novel describing a monstrous mechanical contrivance that wrought havoc for its maker. The book gave her fame.

JOHN KEATS (1795–1821).—Keats was of humble parentage and had been apprenticed to a surgeon; but a volume of Spenser's *The Faerie Queene* fell into his hands and thereafter those "realms of gold" possessed him. He gave up surgery for poetry, and the world is indebted to him for *Endymion* (1818), with its oft-quoted line, "A thing of beauty is a joy forever," *The Eve of St. Agnes and Other Poems* (1820) and such shorter poems as "On First Looking into Chapman's Homer," "Ode To a Nightingale," "Ode on a Grecian Urn," "To Autumn," "La Belle Dame sans Merci." His odes have been called "too perfect for criticism." The same could be said of his sonnets. Keats was a victim of tuberculosis and his life was a bright light that burned out quickly; he died before he was twenty-six and lies buried near the ashes of Shelley in the Protestant Cemetery in Rome.

THOMAS MOORE (1779–1852).—Born in Dublin, Moore wrote many hymns and songs that have long been favorites, notably, "Come, Ye Disconsolate," "Oft in the Stilly Night," "The Harp That Once through Tara's Halls," "Believe Me, If All Those Endearing Young Charms" and "'Tis the Last Rose of Summer." *Lalla Rookh* (1817), an Oriental romance, is the best known of Moore's longer poems; he also wrote in prose, notably a biography of his friend, Lord Byron.

Among the minor poets of the period are Thomas Campbell (1777–1844), who wrote "Ye Mariners of England"; Mrs. Hemans (1793–1835), author of *Songs of the Affections;* and Thomas Hood (1799–1845), who wrote comic verse of great worth and the serious poems, "Bridge of Sighs" and "The Song of the Shirt," which show his sympathy with the sad state of factory workers.

The prose writers of the Romantic Period were equally prolific. Periodical literature was coming into its own in *The Edinburgh Review, Blackwood's Edinburgh Magazine* and *The Quarterly Review.* Most of the essayists found their way to fame through these publications. Prose style became a matter not of rules but of personality. Coleridge left an admirable body of prose criticism in his commentary on the plays of Shakespeare. . . . Charles Lamb's *Essays of Elia* (1823) still attracts readers, and the *Tales from Shakespeare* (1807), on which he and his sister, Mary Lamb, collaborated, delights children of all ages. Lamb was witty, romantic and whimsical; his style is fluent and engaging. His friend, William Hazlitt, essayist of taste and distinction, wrote

LORD BYRON

Characters of Shakespeare Plays (1817), *Lectures on the English Poets* (1818) and *The Spirit of the Age* (1825). *Imaginary Conversations* (1824–46), by Walter Savage Landor, gives in dialogue form interesting light on people of historical days. He wrote many short poems with marvelous finish and beauty, brief lyrics and epigrams in the manner of the Greek poets.

THOMAS DE QUINCEY (1785–1859).—A precocious child who ran away from home, De Quincey later met Coleridge and Wordsworth and became established with them at Grasmere in the Lake District, and there began the literary work that made him famous. His *Confessions of an Opium Eater* (1821) gave evidence that he was at his best in the world of fancy, a master of atmosphere and of rhythmic prose. . . . Leigh Hunt (1784–1859) became a journalist and for years edited *The Examiner,* a radical weekly that gained considerable popularity but occasioned Hunt's imprisonment for two years. Though a poet of poets, as shown by his narratives *The Story of Rimini* and *Hero and Leander* and by "Abou ben Adhem" and the famous rondeau, "Jenny Kissed Me," he was also a novelist, dramatist and (best of all) essayist.

Of the fiction in this Romantic Period, Scott's novels are foremost. To pay off a debt incurred from a publishing venture with the House of Ballantyne, Scott wrote one novel after another. No man worked harder. Up at five in the morning, he worked until midafternoon, then took a long walk accompanied by his faithful dogs, or entertained friends. He allowed nothing to disturb this routine. In consequence, he wore himself out, but not before he had given the world masterpieces of romantic fiction. Among Scott's historical novels are such Scottish, English and Continental titles as *Waverley* (1814), *Old Mortality* (1817), *The Legend of Montrose* (1819), *Ivanhoe* (1819), *The Monastery* (1820), *The Abbott* (1820), *Kenilworth* (1821), *The Fortunes of Nigel* (1822), *Quentin Durward* (1823) and *The Talisman* (1825). Other novels include *Guy Mannering* (1815), *The Antiquary* (1816), *The Black Dwarf* (1817), *Rob Roy* (1817), *The Heart of Midlothian* (1818) and *The Bride of Lammermoor* (1819). Scott is one of the world's great masters of narration.

Among Scott's noteworthy contemporaries were: Ann Radcliffe, whose *The Mysteries of Udolpho* (1794) expresses a Gothic element in fiction; the Scottish Jane Porter, who wrote *Thaddeus of Warsaw* (1803) and *The Scottish Chiefs* (1810); William Godwin, author of the novel with a purpose, *The Adventures of Caleb Williams* (1794); Maria Edgeworth, creator of books for children; Mary Mitford, author of *Our Village* (1823); and Jane Austen (1775–1817), a clergyman's daughter whose youth was spent at his vicarage, Steventon, in Hampshire. There she wrote but did not then publish her most famous novel, *Pride and Prejudice* (1813). *Sense and Sensibility* (1811) was the second story written but the first published and, like the others, appeared without her name. *Mansfield Park* (1814) and *Emma* (1816) appeared while Miss Austen still lived; *Persuasion* (1818) and *Northanger Abbey* were published after her death. Her great gifts were delineation, creating living characters and satirizing commonplace social happenings.

The Victorian Era, 183?–81.—The Reform Act had reorganized Parliament and had given the people wider representation in the House of Commons; trade unions were permitted, religious tolerance advanced, municipal reform and better housing were effected; the age of machinery arrived, trade and commerce grew, emigration was encouraged and science found new methods to search for truth. In literature the Victorian era rivaled the Elizabethan or the time of Queen Anne.

THOMAS CARLYLE (1795–1881).—In many ways Carlyle was the most important literary figure of this period, largely because he was an earnest, gloomy prophet with a picturesque style and a peculiar personality. The son of a Scottish mason, Carlyle was intended for the ministry but on graduation from Edinburgh University he turned his attention to teaching and writing. He lived at Craigenputtock, a lonely farmhouse that he had inherited, and at a London home in Chelsea. Carlyle's greatest works are *Sartor Resartus* (1833–34), glorifying the gospel of work; his dramatic and powerful *The French Revolution* (1837); *Heroes and Hero Worship* (1840), essays on great men; *Past and Present* (1843); *Oliver Cromwell's Speeches and Letters* (1845); the *History of Frederick the Great* (1858–65) and *Reminiscences,* which contains the paper on his great attachment to his brilliant and self-sacrificing wife, Jane Welsh, to whose devotion his success is partly attributable, for she gave up her own potential literary career to become his companion and incentive. Carlyle was greatly influenced by German philosophy and even by German style. He hated sham and thought most new ideas in politics and social science were shams. Today

much of his work seems reactionary and bitterly pessimistic.

THOMAS BABINGTON, LORD MACAULAY (1800–59).—After a precocious childhood, Macaulay first came to literary fame by his brilliant essay on Milton in the *Edinburgh Review,* followed by similar sketches of Byron, Addison, Pitt, Warren Hastings, Bunyan, Doctor Johnson, Goldsmith and many others. Macaulay's *History of England* (1848–55) is one of the most interesting histories ever written—maybe because it is so partisan. Its sale in America once rivaled that of the Bible. The *Lays of Ancient Rome* (1842), historic and heroic ballads, is his most popular work. Macaulay was a statesman, an orator and a great administrator in India.

JOHN RUSKIN (1819–1900).—Ruskin early developed art appreciation under his father's tutelage and the fine arts became his chief interest. *Modern Painters* (1843–60) is an authoritative treatise still much used; his *Seven Lamps of Architecture* (1849) and *The Stones of Venice* (1851–53) evidence his attention to economics and social reform. Other works are *Unto This Last* (1862), *Time and Tide* (1867), *Ethics of the Dust* (1866), *Sesame and Lilies* (1865), *The Crown of Wild Olives* (1866) and *Fors Clavigera* (1871–84). He wrote also *The King of the Golden River* (1851), a delightful fairy story for children, and *Praeterita* (1885–89), an autobiography. Ruskin was a stylist who wrote with wit and imagination; he was a reformer and an artist, among the first to rebel against Victorian restrictions. His production was voluminous but masterly, each work distinctive and significant.

MATTHEW ARNOLD (1822–88).—The son of Thomas Arnold, a famous master of Rugby, Matthew continued to be closely identified with education. For thirty-five years he was Inspector of Schools and during 1857–67 was professor of poetry at Oxford, of which he was a graduate. He published a number of volumes of poetry. Famous single poems are: "Thyrsis," a pastoral elegy; "Sohrab and Rustum," an episode from the Persian epic of Firdausi; the sonnet on Shakespeare and the melodious poem, "The Forsaken Merman." *Culture* and *sweetness* and *light* were watchwords with Arnold. He hated Philistinism—a term he coined for modern conventionalism and deafness to new ideas, especially spiritual and esthetic ideas. He wrote *Culture and Anarchy* (1869), *Literature and Dogma* (1873) and many essays.

JOHN HENRY NEWMAN (1801–90).—An Anglican churchman and one of the founders of the Oxford Movement in the Church of England, Newman later joined the Roman Catholic Church and was made a cardinal (1879) by Pope Leo XIII. He wrote the famous hymn, "Lead, Kindly Light," and in clear precise prose wrote *The Idea of a University Defined* (1873), the matchless *Apologia pro Vita Sua* (1865), justifying his religious beliefs, and *The Grammar of Assent* (1870).

Other prose writers of the time include: John Stuart Mill, who wrote

Principles of Political Economy (1848) and various expository works; John Richard Green, author of *A Short History of the English People* (1874), and James Anthony Froude, who also wrote on English history and is the author of *Short Studies on Great Subjects* (1867–82), biographical sketches of English notables; Walter Pater, essayist and critic who was almost poetic in his rhythmical phrasing in *Marius the Epicurean* (1885), *Imaginary Portraits* (1887), *Appreciations* (1889) and *Greek Studies* (1895); and Andrew Lang, the many-sided genius of *Letters to Dead Authors* (1886), various translations, biographical sketches, some folklore and various fairy books.

Three notable figures in science contributed works in support of highly revolutionizing theories during this period: Charles Darwin (1809–82), in his *The Origin of Species* (1859), reconstructed the biological world through the doctrine of evolution; John Tyndall (1820–93), in *Heat Considered as a Mode of Motion* (1863), presented something new in physics; and Thomas Henry Huxley (1825–95), in *Evidence as to Man's Place in Nature* (1863), *Lay Sermons* (1870) and *Essays on Evolution and Ethics* (1893), strengthened the idea of evolution. . . . Herbert Spencer (1820–1903) was the outstanding philosopher of the day and one of the first writers on sociology. His best-known works are *Social Statics* (1851); *Principles of Psychology* (1855); *Education: Intellectual, Moral, Physical* (1861); *First Principles* (1862); and *Principles of Ethics* (1879).

What the historical romance was to the Middle Ages, what the drama was to the Elizabethans, the novel was to the Victorian Era—not only the chief form of literary expression but a medium for influencing public opinion in society, politics and even in theology. The novel with a purpose flourished; but so did pride in craftsmanship and writing for sheer entertainment.

CHARLES DICKENS (1812–70).—Dickens' childhood was unhappy and miserable. When he was seventeen he learned stenography and obtained work as a reporter. His early menial work and later contacts as a police court reporter gave him live material to write about and two lecture trips to America added to it. His style, range of subjects and characters drawn firsthand from the streets and haunts of London made him an outstanding novelist of the time.

Sketches by Boz (1836), his first work, gave but small indication of what his future would develop, but its success encouraged the author to publish his first novel, *Pickwick Papers* (1837), which brought him immediate and lasting fame. *David Copperfield* (1850) portrays scenes of his own boyhood, and *Nicholas Nickleby* depicts his school life. *Oliver Twist* recalls Dickens' experiences among the poor of London; *Little Dorrit* (1858) reveals the prison life to which his father was subjected; and *Bleak House* (1853) delineates his life in a law office. *Martin Chuzzlewit* crystallizes Dickens' unflattering impressions of America and Americans; and *Dom-*

FROM A DRAWING BY GEORGE CRUIKSHANK

CHARLES DICKENS: "OLIVER TWIST." Oliver, an orphan in the workhouse, asks for more food.

bey and Son (1848), *The Old Curiosity Shop* (1840), *Hard Times* (1854), *Great Expectations* (1861) and *Our Mutual Friend* (1864) give firsthand observations Dickens made at different periods of his life.

A Tale of Two Cities (1859) is a stirring novel of the French Revolution with scenes laid in England and France. *A Christmas Carol, The Chimes* and *The Cricket on the Hearth* have become yuletide classics. Cockney traits in many of his characters will always amuse Dickens' readers. The people of his books are remembered and treasured though they are too eccentric to be real.

WILLIAM MAKEPEACE THACKERAY (1811–63).—Born in Calcutta, India, educated at Charterhouse and Cambridge, Thackeray traveled widely and was at home with the aristocracy of any country. After studying law he became editor of the *National Standard* in 1833, but the following year was off to Paris to study art. Continuing to contribute to newspapers, however, when necessity arose he earned his living with his pen. His first real success came with the serial

publication of *Luck of Barry Lyndon* (1844). Among his most eminent works that appeared in the succeeding score of years are *Vanity Fair* (1848), *Pendennis* (1850), somewhat autobiographical, *Henry Esmond* (1852), *The Newcomes* (1855) and *The Virginians* (1858). His characterization is vivid. In his great assemblage of sharply drawn characters, Major Pendennis, Henry Esmond, Colonel Newcome, Barry Lyndon and the incomparable Becky Sharp stand out. Thackeray's style is restrained but graphic and somewhat cynical; he detested sham, affectation and snobbery. He wrote also criticism and light verse—*The English Humorists of the Eighteenth Century* (1853) and *Miscellanies in Prose and Verse* (1855).

Among Victorian novelists who are now known chiefly by one or more successful and outstanding works though they were more widely read in their day, are: Edward George Bulwer-Lytton (1803–73), whose exciting and dramatic *Last Days of Pompeii, Eugene Aram,* and the plays, *Richelieu* and *The Lady of Lyons,* are representative; Charles Reade (1814–84), who

championed ill-treated prisoners in *It Is Never Too Late To Mend* (1856) and wrote *Peg Woffington* (1853), a story of the 18th century, and *The Cloister and the Hearth* (1861), a far better story of the 15th century; Anthony Trollope (1815–82), who habitually wrote just so many words an hour and gave his formula for doing so, and whose stories of English clerical life, *The Warden* (1855), *Barchester Towers* (1857), *The Last Chronicle of Barset* (1867) and many others are the best of their class; and Wilkie Collins (1824–89), whose thrilling mystery stories, *The Woman in White* (1860) and *The Moonstone* (1868) have never been without readers.

Other authors who are now remembered for a single book are: Richard Doddridge Blackmore (1825–1900), for his stirring romance, *Lorna Doone* (1869); Dinah Mulock (1827–87), for *John Halifax, Gentleman* (1857), the story of a self-made man; and Samuel Butler (1835–1902), biologist and opponent of Darwin, for his partly autobiographical novel, published after his death, the bitter and powerful story entitled *The Way of All Flesh* (1903). The late 19th century found a reading public diverted with two inimitable stories by Lewis Carroll (pen name of Charles Lutwidge Dodgson, 1832–97), *Alice's Adventures in Wonderland* (1865) and *Through the Looking-Glass and What Alice Found There* (1872), written for children but charged with shrewd comment upon manners that delights their elders and a wit surprising in the teacher of mathematics who wrote these books.

THE BRONTË SISTERS: CHARLOTTE (1816–55); EMILY (1818–48); and ANNE (1820–49).—Daughters of a poor curate at Haworth, England, motherless after 1821, they were educated at a school for clergymen's daughters and at Roe Head and in Brussels. Charlotte later taught in two of these schools and was twice a governess. Emily also taught but was too frail to live away from home. As the three sisters at first published their poems jointly under the pen names of Currer, Ellis and Acton Bell and then used these names individually for their novels (Currer Bell—Charlotte; Ellis Bell—Emily; Acton Bell—Anne), the public did not know who they were until 1848. Emily wrote one story, *Wuthering Heights* (1847); Anne wrote two, *Agnes Grey* (1847) and *Tenant of Wildfell Hall* (1848), not so good as her sisters' work. Charlotte's *Jane Eyre* (1847), lately dramatized, contributed something new and living to the Victorian novel and achieved the greatest success; it made her famous as Currer Bell! Then over her own name she wrote *Shirley* (1849), a portrait of Emily, and *Villette* (1853). No family in English literature was so talented or wrote so much in a half-dozen years.

CHARLES KINGSLEY (1819–75).—A clergyman, friend of Carlyle and Mill and champion of the working class, for which he advocated and promoted improved sanitation and other benefits, Kingsley wrote several novels with a purpose—notably *Alton Locke* (1849) and *Yeast* (1849); the historical novels *Hypatia* (1853) and *Westward*

Ho! (1855)—the scenes of the first are laid in Alexandria, Egypt, in the 5th century; the second is a story of Elizabethan sea dogs on the Spanish Main —and the children's books, *The Heroes* (1856), a book of Greek myths; *Waterbabies* (1863) and a popularized natural history, *Madam How and Lady Why* (1869).

GEORGE ELIOT (pen name of Mary Anne Evans; 1819–80).—As Dickens and Thackeray treated low and high society, respectively, George Eliot gave the world masterpieces about the life of the English middle class. Born on a farm near Coventry, she strove to educate herself by studying languages and reading widely to match the intellectual progress of her brother. She went to London to help edit the *Westminster Review,* and from that time, through the stimulus of George Henry Lewes, whom she later married, to write fiction.

She was a moralist and a keen psychologist with extraordinary powers of character analysis, and the fault of being overserious. After her first book, *Scenes from Clerical Life* (1857), she wrote *Adam Bede* (1859), *The Mill on the Floss* (1860) and *Silas Marner* (1861). The second period of her writing was less successful: in *Romola* (1862–63), a Florentine novel, *Felix Holt* (1866), *Middlemarch* (1872) and *Daniel Deronda* (1876), she entered new fields that she did not know so well—history and politics. One of her poems, "O Might I Join the Choir Invisible" still lives.

GEORGE MEREDITH (1828–1909).—The son of a tailor, educated in Germany, Meredith was first a journalist and then a publisher's reader. He is best known as an intellectual psychological novelist, but some critics think him a great poet, too. His novels include *The Ordeal of Richard Feverel* (1859), *Beauchamp's Career* (1876), *The Egoist* (1879), *Diana of the Crossways* (1885) and *The Amazing Marriage* (1895). His finest poems were in *Modern Love* (1862). In both prose and verse his style is difficult. His works never became popular but they have been greatly admired by a few.

THOMAS HARDY (1840–1928).—A native of Dorsetshire, England, the locality his novels picture so vividly, Hardy was an architect's apprentice before he became a writer of pessimistic fiction. Among his great novels are *Far From the Madding Crowd* (1874), *The Return of the Native* (1878), *Tess of the D'Urbervilles* (1891) and *Jude the Obscure* (1895). He afterwards devoted himself chiefly to verse, which he preferred: *The Dynasts* (1904–8), his crowning work, a dramatic poem on England during the Napoleonic Wars; and the lyric volumes, *Satires of Circumstance* (1914) and *Winter Words* (1928). Hardy also wrote many short stories, of which "The Three Strangers" ranks among the best in English.

ROBERT LOUIS STEVENSON (1850–94). —Though belonging to the late Victorian era, Stevenson prefigured the 20th-century writers in facility, technique, style and his engrossing interest in his craft. Born in Edinburgh, Scotland, he studied law at the university there, was admitted to the bar in 1875 but did not practice. His delicate health led him to travel instead and he soon began contributing to the *Cornhill Magazine* essays that later appeared in book form as *Familiar Studies of Men and Books* (1882). Among his early stories in the same publication were "A Lodging for a Night" and "New Arabian Nights." He wrote verse of many sorts—the oft-quoted "Requiem" that Sidney Homer set to music; *A Child's Garden of Verses* (1885); and the varied lyrics of *Underwoods* (1887). He is best known for his stories of adventure: *Treasure Island* (1882), *Kidnapped* (1886), *The Master of Ballantrae* (1889) and *The Ebb Tide* (1894). *Doctor Jekyll and Mr. Hyde* (1886) is probably the most popular of all stories of the horror of good and bad in a single man. Besides he wrote several volumes of essays and travels and some of the best letters that an author's friends ever received. No author of his time had so varied a literary appeal or so picturesque and attractive a personality.

Contemporary with Stevenson were George Gissing (1857–1903), William Ernest Henley (1849–1903) and Oscar Wilde (1856–1900). Gissing's realistic *New Grub Street* and *The Whirlpool* are representative of his style and interest. Henley, critic, poet and playwright, wrote *A Book of Verse* (1880) and with Stevenson three plays. He is most famous for his poem, "Invictus," with the lines:

> My head is bloody, but unbow'd . . .
> I am the master of my fate,
> I am the captain of my soul.

ELIZABETH BARRETT BROWNING, an outstanding figure in English literature.

Wilde, Irisn wit, esthete, iconoclast, holds an uncertain niche in literature and the literary worth of his productions is constantly challenged. His plays, *Lady Windermere's Fan* (1892), *A Woman of No Importance* (1893) and *The Importance of Being Earnest* (1895), are witty, ironic, smart. His *Ballad of Reading Gaol* (1898) and *De Profundis* (1905) are probably the most read of his works.

Victorian poetry attained great distinction largely because of its un-Victorian range and depth of subject matter. Of the poetic forms previously created, the sonnet, for example, could scarcely be improved upon; narrative verse also had developed its pattern; and lyric poets had established various rhythms and definite stanza forms; but with the tremendous impetus given to philosophic and scientific thought, poets began to demand a freedom that later on was to break all restraint, both as to form and content.

ALFRED TENNYSON (1809–92).—Conventionally educated and early inclined to poetry, Tennyson published his first volume of poems when only twenty-one. The book was not well received, but nine years later, his second volume brought him instant recognition. For the next 50 years he was a popular favorite. On the death of Wordsworth he was made Poet Laureate. He touched divers subjects and employed many poetic forms. His *Poems* (1842), included "Ulysses" and "Locksley Hall," themes to which he gave deep poetic beauty. Among the longer poems are *The Princess* (1847), a semidramatic story of woman's claim to intellectual parity with man, in which some of the choicest songs in the English language occur—"Sweet and Low," "Tears, Idle Tears," and "Ask Me No More." Tennyson's *Idylls of the King* (1854) retells the Arthurian legends; *In Memoriam* (1850) is a profound inquiry into the meaning of life and death. His lyrics and his figures of speech, alliteration and rhythm are at their height in *Maud and Other Poems* (1855) and *Enoch Arden* (1864).

ELIZABETH BARRETT BROWNING (1806–61).—A wealthy merchant's daughter, Elizabeth Barrett was educated as few women of her time had the good fortune to be, and her superior talents turned her training in the Greek and Latin classics to excellent use, for she became the most important woman in English poetry. She possessed strong emotions and significant ideas, as well as the independence of thought and action to use them effectively. Her verse attracted the poet Browning, and, outwitting her protesting and selfish father (who enjoyed her society and wished her to remain at home), Browning married her in 1846 (the story of which was dramatized and adapted to the screen under the title, *The Barretts of Wimpole Street).* The Brownings lived happily in Florence, Italy, and her *Casa Guidi Windows,* written there, shows her as Browning's equal as a poet. In *Aurora Leigh* (1856), which she considered her highest achievement, she expresses all the passion of an intense and sensitive soul. Her *Sonnets from the Portuguese* are the love lyrics addressed to Browning during their courtship. The sadness of some phases of her life and the seriousness with which she regarded her work are reflected in the tenor of her verse.

ROBERT BROWNING (1812–89).—Well educated by private tutors, Browning studied both art and music, then chose poetry as his field of expression; both his esthetic sense and feeling for rhythm are evident in all he wrote. His work shows fine dramatic power and imagery, subtlety of thought and dominant sympathy for man. His longer narrative poems (like *Sordello* and *The Ring and the Book*) are often difficult reading. He tried too hard for brevity and force; but he was a master in both the short lyric and the longer more philosophical poems—a remarkable range. He had a particular gift of characterization and a rough vigorous power that presents a strong contrast with Tennyson's sweetness and calm. Among his single poems the best-known are: "The Pied Piper of Hamelin," "Pippa Passes," "How They Brought the Good News from Ghent to Aix."

Contemporary with the Brownings were the artists and poets Dante Gabriel Rossetti and William Morris, called Pre-Raphaelites because they strove to revive the ideals of Italian painters before Raphael. Rossetti (1828–82) was of Italian descent and primarily a poet of mystic passion and exquisite workmanship. His *Ballads and Sonnets* (1881), and the individual poems, "Sister Helen," "The White Ship," "The King's Tragedy," "The House of Life" (a sonnet sequence), were painter's verse, rich in color and music. His best-known work, "The Blessed Damozel" (1848), he wrote

NEW YORK PUBLIC LIBRARY
DANTE GABRIEL ROSSETTI

before he was twenty. . . . William Morris (1834–96), designer, printer, Socialist and poet, wrote *The Life and Death of Jason* (1867), *The Earthly Paradise* (1868) and *Sigurd the Volsung* (1877), narrative epics colored by his knowledge of Norse poetry. . . . Algernon Charles Swinburne (1837–1909) stands out strikingly in this group, by which he was strongly influenced, as a poet whose verse has the quality of sensuous, haunting beauty with a wealth of imagery; his verse resembles Byron's. Among his most distinguished works are *Atalanta in Calydon* (1865), *Poems and Ballads* (1866), *Songs before Sunrise* (1871) and *Lyonesse* (1881); he wrote also many love lyrics and ballads and critical essays in passionate prose. His

favorite subjects were revolt, the sea, children, cats. . . . Edward FitzGerald (1809–83) is best known for his exquisite translation, *The Rubáiyát of Omar Khayyam* (1859–68); Francis Thompson (1859–1907), for "The Hound of Heaven" and other mystic verse; Edward Robert Bulwer-Lytton (pen name, Owen Meredith, 1831–91), for *Lucile;* William Sharp (pen name, Fiona Macleod, 1855–1905), for "From the Hills of Dream" (1896) and his leadership in the Celtic revival; and Henry Austin Dobson (1840–1921), for his many bright and graceful lyrics and rondeaus.

SIR WILLIAM SCHWENK GILBERT (1836–1911).—Playwright and poet, Gilbert became world-famous for his work in collaboration with Arthur Sullivan in the popular and humorous light operas, *H.M.S. Pinafore* (1878), *The Pirates of Penzance* (1880) and *The Mikado* (1885), of which he wrote the librettos. After a break with Sullivan, Gilbert's work lost in quality and charm.

The Twentieth Century.—Literary production in England by the 20th century embraced fields of thought and styles of expression that are unexcelled. Its amazing stimulation and growth were due to many causes, foremost of which was doubtless the gradual development of literary forms built up through the years from the days of Chaucer. Public opinion and individual reactions, however, had been remolded by national and international events: The Berlin Congress in 1878 had reshaped political thought; the assassination of the Czar of Russia had sounded an ominous warning; Gladstone's conversion to home rule for Ireland in 1895, Livingstone's and Stanley's work in Africa, the Boer War, 1899–1902, and England's building up colonial empires in Africa and India had very marked effects on English thought and literary expression. Improved rail and water transportation and the invention of the telegraph and telephone helped to eliminate time and space and brought the world's nations closer together; general education, social reforms, labor organizations and, more than all, the increased output of books, magazines and newspapers that quickly disseminated new ideas made writing specialized and literature complex. Ibsen in Norway and Tolstoy in Russia had wielded strong influence. The writers of English fiction had acquired a new style, greater subtlety, more acute insight into human nature and problems and a genuine sympathy with human frailty and suffering.

One group of writers was well established before the close of the 19th century but their work extended into the 20th century. Henry James (1843–1916), the American expatriate, wrote in a painful, elaborate style many psychological, intellectual novels contrasting English and American manners and customs. Among his earlier works are *A Passionate Pilgrim and Other Tales* (1875), *Daisy Miller* (1878) and *The Portrait of a Lady* (1881). Later novels are *What Maisie Knew* (1897), *The Wings of a Dove* (1902) and *The Ambassadors* (1903). Much autobiographical ma-

terial appears in his *A Small Boy and Others* (1913) and *Notes of a Son and a Brother* (1914). . . . Sir Edmund Gosse (1849–1928), biographer, critic and poet, for 10 years librarian of the House of Lords, wrote biographies of Congreve, Donne, Swinburne and Ibsen, many critical essays and the autobiographical *Father and Son*. . . . Henry Arthur Jones (1851–1929), playwright and letter writer, won his first success with *The Silver King* (1882); the subsequent *Liars* and *Mrs. Dane's Defense* enhanced his reputation. . . . Mrs. Humphry Ward (1851–1920) was well known by her *Robert Elsmere* (1888) and *David Grieve* (1892) before her *Eleanor*

CHARLES SCRIBNER & SONS
SIR JAMES BARRIE

(1900), *The Marriage of William Ashe* (1905) and *The War and Elizabeth* (1918) and other novels.

Also of this group are George Moore (1852–1933), novelist of the modern Irish movement (sponsored by Yeats and Lady Gregory) who studied art in Paris, wrote poetry—*Pagan Poems* (1872) and *Flowers of Passion* (1878) —and then attempted to reform English fiction on French models. *The Mummer's Wife* (1885), *Esther Waters* (1894) and *Evelyn Inness* (1898) were the first of his strikingly new novels. *The Brook Kerith* (1916) treats the life of Christ in familiar everyday fashion. Even more typical of the man and his style are *Confessions of a Young Man* (1888) and *Hail and Farewell* (1911–14).

JAMES M. BARRIE (1860–1937).—Of Scottish birth and education, Barrie became both novelist and playwright. He contributed to late Victorian literature *Auld Licht Idylls* (1888); the well-known and loved *The Little Minister* (1891); *Sentimental Tommy* (1896); and to the succeeding period the highly successful plays, *The Admirable Crichton* (1902), *Peter Pan* (1904), *What Every Woman Knows* (1908) and *Dear Brutus* (1917).

GEORGE BERNARD SHAW (1856–1950). —No younger figure of 20th-century English literature has ever succeeded in thrusting aside this older and irrepressible but brilliant Irish Socialist, novelist, playwright and critic. He wrote several novels long ago and many books on socialism. His clever, witty dramas delighted English readers and American playgoers long before they were permitted on the English stage in the early 1900's. Prominent among Shaw's early plays are *Arms and the Man* (1894), *Mrs. Warren's Profession* (first played in 1902) and *Candida* (1897). For Ellen Terry he wrote *Captain Brassbound's Conversion* (1900). His plays, *Man and Superman* (1903), *Back to Methuselah* (1921) and *Saint Joan* (1923), and his elaborate, expository prefaces to the plays made him a much-talked-of man. He received the Nobel Prize in 1925. He was the most original and controversial literary figure of the day and his keen sense of the comic, his caustic wit and consuming desire to upset traditional views in all phases of thought and living have kept him in the public mind for a full half century.

JOSEPH CONRAD (1857–1924).—This foreign-born writer is noted for his command of clear, fluent English, a language he learned late in life. The son of a Polish writer, he was bred to the sea and wrote only after retiring from it. His fascinating stories include *Almayer's Folly* (1895), *The Nigger of the Narcissus* (1897), *Lord Jim* (1900), *The Rescue* (1920) and *The Rover* (1923)—all stories of the sea, but with the adventure of character and psychology, not of episode.

SIR ARTHUR CONAN DOYLE (1859–1930).—A young doctor who wrote to occupy his spare time when his early practice was small, Doyle in 1887 became popular overnight with *A Study in Scarlet,* a detective story with Sherlock Holmes, a new type of mystery solver. He wrote book after book about Holmes, and a successful play starred William Gillette as Holmes. Later a series of the Sherlock Holmes episodes were put on the air. Doyle wrote several excellent historical romances: *Micah Clarke* (1888) about Monmouth's Rebellion; *The White Company* (1891), a story of mercenaries in the 14th century; and *The Exploits of Brigadier Gerard* (1896), about the Napoleonic Wars. He was a British Government propagandist in the Boer War and the First World War and lectured and wrote on spiritualism.

HERBERT GEORGE WELLS (1866-1946).—Sociologist, novelist, historian, the son of a professional cricketer and a lady's maid, Wells gained his education in the Royal College of Science and the University of London through scholarships and was graduated with honors. His early stories dealt largely with scientific speculation in the manner of Jules Verne, as in *The Stolen Bacillus*. He next wrote several novels of a prophetic type—*Anticipations* (1901), *In the Days of the Comet* (1906) and *The War in the Air* (1908), many incidents of which subsequently took place. Following these came a series concerned with portraying contemporary life, including *Ann Veronica* (1909) and *The Passionate Friends* (1913). His stirring story of World War I, *Mr. Britling Sees It*

Through (1918) aroused wide interest. Two years later he published both *Russia in the Shadows* and his monumental *Outline of History,* followed by the *Science of Life* (1929) with J. S. Huxley; the last two works have been more widely read than others of the same type. Well's *Experiment in Autobiography* (1934) is a frank revelation of his life. Many of his books have found great favor in the United States, where he has traveled and lectured.

JOHN GALSWORTHY (1867–1933).—Outstanding in both fiction and the drama, Galsworthy became world-

ERIC SCHAAL

H. G. WELLS

famous for his series of novels, *The Forsyte Saga,* the entertaining history of an engaging family, distinguished in style and revealing deep human insight and fine characterization. Galsworthy's plays have been translated into various languages. *Strife* (1909) and *Loyalties* (1922) put him in the first rank of playwrights. His *Caravan* is a collection of short stories. The Order of Merit was bestowed on him in 1929 and in 1932 the Nobel Prize.

Among other 20th-century writers are: Gilbert Keith Chesterton (1874–1936) who won distinction for his fine critical work, novels, stories, plays and ability as an illustrator. His amazing versatility ranged from discussions of the Roman Catholic Church, to which he became an ardent convert, through well-considered essays on men and things, to novels, poems, whimsicalities and detective stories. He wrote *The Man Who Was Thursday, The Ballad of the White Horse* (1911), *New and Collected Poems* (1929), *Come To Think of It* (1930) and the Father Brown detective stories. . . . Arnold Bennett (1867–1931), prolific critic and novelist, wrote *How to Live on Twenty-four Hours a Day* (1907), *The Old Wives' Tale* (1908), a great novel, *The Card* (1911) and other stories of the Five Towns in northern England. . . .

May Sinclair is best known by her *The Divine Fire* (1904), her first novel.

Twentieth-century English poetry, though not voluminous, has definite distinction in both the older and the newer phases. Among its earlier poets, Alfred Edward Housman (1859–1936), wrote only two small volumes, *A Shropshire Lad* (1896) and *Last Poems* (1922), simple, stark verse of a young man's disillusionment. . . . Maurice Hewlitt (1861–1923), poet and novelist, wrote narrative poems, *The Song of The Plow* (1916) and *The Village Wife's Lament* (1918), and English and Italian historical fiction, *The Forest Lovers* (1897), *Richard Yea-and-Nay* (1900) and *The Fool Errant* (1905).

Few 20th-century writers have enjoyed such world popularity as Rudyard Kipling (1865–1936), whose verse and fiction have universal appeal and great variety of subject. He was born and reared in India, and much of his work is colored by his life there and by British imperialism; it includes *Kim, Plain Tales from the Hills, The Jungle Book, The Just So Stories, Barrack-Room Ballads* and *Departmental Ditties*. His famous "Recessional," "Danny Deever" and other poems set to music are popular songs. Kipling received the Nobel Prize in 1907. . . . Alfred Noyes (1880–1958), poet, dramatist and fiction writer, lectured and taught in America as professor of English literature at Princeton University. His verse includes the trilogy on scientific discovery: *The Watchers of the Sky, The Book of Earth* and *The Last Voyage* (1922–30), *A Tale of Old Japan,* set to music as a cantata by Coleridge-Taylor, many ballads and the striking poem "The Victory Ball." His other work embraces essays, plays, a novel, short stories and biographies of William Morris (1908) and Voltaire (1936).

Irish poets who contributed verse of deep poetic beauty, sometimes mystic, often tragic, include: William Butler Yeats (1865–1939). who received the Nobel Prize in 1923, was one of the founders of the Abbey Theatre, Dublin; wrote for it *Kathleen ni Houlihan* (1902), *The Green Helmet* (1910) and other plays in prose and verse; and also wrote several volumes of poetry, including *Responsibilities* (1914), *The Wild Swans of Coole* (1917) and *The Tower* (1927). . . . George William Russell (1867–1935), painter, poet and leader of the co-operative movement who signed himself Æ, wrote the tragedy, *Deirdre* (1907). . . . John Millington Synge (1871–1909), artist, director of the Abbey Theatre, wrote various Abbey Theatre plays including *The Playboy of the Western World* (1907) which was mobbed by patriotic Irishmen who disliked its picture of Irish character. . . . Padraic Colum (1881–), poet and dramatist, resident in America after 1914 and exponent of the modern Irish literary movement, wrote in verse *Wild Earth* and *Creatures,* edited the *Anthology of Irish Verse* (1921) and wrote the novel, *Castle Conquer,* and the *Myths of the World.*

Two notable English poets of this epoch are Masefield and Brooke. John Masefield (1878–1965), whose lyrics and narrative poems include *Salt-Water Ballads* (1902), *The Everlasting Mercy* (1911), *The Widow in the Bye Street* and *Sonnets and Poems,* is the author also of plays, novels, two stories for boys (*Jim Davis* and *Sard Harker*) and two remarkable studies of Shakespeare. Masefield was made Poet Laureate in 1930. . . . Rupert Brooke (1887–1915) poet, world traveler, was a victim of blood poisoning while serving in the 1st World War. In his two small volumes of verse, *Poems* (1911) and *1914 and Other Poems* (1915) are gems like "Grantchester," "The Great Lover," "The Soldier" and "The Dead."

Contemporary prose writers whose names are everywhere familiar include: Hilaire Belloc (1870-1953), French by birth, who studied at Oxford and became a naturalized English citizen in 1902. He has been called the foremost Catholic scholar outside the clergy. Belloc wrote on war, politics, history, literature—and books to make children behave better. His works include *Robespierre* (1901), *The Path to Rome* (1902), *Marie Antoinette* (1910), *Europe and the Faith* (1920), *Joan of Arc* (1920), *Napoleon* (1932), *Essays of a Catholic Layman in England* (1931) and biographies of William the Conqueror, Charles I, Cromwell and Milton. . . . William Somerset Maugham (1874–1965), novelist, playwright and short-story writer, won fame with his novels *Of Human Bondage* (1916) and *The Moon and Sixpence* (1919), a story based on Gauguin's life. "Miss Thompson," a story of the South Seas in *The Trembling of a Leaf* (1921), was dramatized as *Rain.* Other popular Maugham plays include *Our Betters* (1923) and *The Constant Wife* (1927). His novel, *Cakes and Ale* (1930), gained much interest for its thinly veiled portraits of literary personages. . . . Sir Philip Gibbs (1877–1962), famous news correspondent during the 1st World War, wrote in the cause of world peace several novels and historical volumes including *Now It Can Be Told, The Cross of Peace, European Journey.*

The Imagist School.—Promoted by postwar poets, the Imagist School experimented in forms but wrote mostly in the unrhymed so-called free verse (French, *vers libre*). The Imagist asserts the right of full freedom in the choice of subject, language and treatment and makes bold use of direct, unrestrained diction and imagery. He is free from all vagueness and mysticism—an unrestraint not always of beauty but oftener of harsher reality. The movement soon extended to the drama and was as eagerly embraced by prose writers following the lead of Joyce.

Of the Imagist poets, Wilfred Wilson Gibson (1878–1962) is the earliest; his *Daily Bread* (1910) and *Highland Dawn* (1932) show the development that came through various intervening volumes concerned with the underprivileged and those lacking expression. . . . Siegfried Sassoon (1886–) in his *Counterattack* (1918) presents a graphic interpretation of the futility and brutishness of war. . . . Richard Aldington (1892–1962) led the Imagist poets with *Images Old and New* (1915). He later published other volumes of verse, and among novels, *The Colonel's Daughter* (1931). In 1913 he married the American, Hilda Doolittle (pen name, H. D.), who also became one of the leading Imagists and wrote *Hymen* (1921) and *Red Roses for Bronze* (1931).

James Joyce (1882–1941), Irish novelist and poet, wrote *Chamber Music* (1907), *Dubliners* (1914), the autobiographical *A Portrait of the Artist as a Young Man* (1916) and a play, *Exiles* (1918), before his unconventional novel *Ulysses* (1922) introduced the custom of writing everything that comes into the stream of consciousness.

Other Contemporaries.—John Cowper Powys (1872–1963), critic, novelist and short-story writer, is the author of *Visions and Revisions; Wolf Solent,* for which, perhaps, he is best known; and *Autobiography* (1934). He spent some time in America. One brother, Theodore Francis Powys (1875–1953), a stark realist, wrote *Black Bryony.* Another brother, Llewellyn Powys (1884–1939), traveled in America and contributed his impressions in *The Verdict of Bridgegoose;* and also visited Palestine and wrote *A Pagan's Pilgrimage;* Alyse Gregory Powys, his American wife, wrote *She Shall Have Music,* a novel.

Among leading contemporary dramatists are: Harley Granville-Barker (1877–1946), who produced various Shaw plays and became widely known in America for his striking stage settings; he wrote the plays *Waste* and *Madras House;* Rudolf Besier (1878–1942), who collaborated with Wells on *Kipps* (1912) and with Walpole on *Robin's Father* (1918), wrote *Secrets* (1922) and *The Barretts of Wimpole Street* (1931). The versatile, brilliant and suave Noel Coward—playwright, actor, composer, director—also is a favorite in America for his *Design for Living, Play Parade* and the tremendously stirring *Cavalcade.*

The novelist and critic, Virginia Woolf (1882-1941), cofounder with her husband, Leonard Woolf, of the Hogarth Press, used the stream-of-consciousness method in much of her work. Her novels include *Mrs. Dalloway* (1925) and *The Waves* (1931); her books of criticism are *The Common Reader* (1925) and *The Second Common Reader* (1932). She wrote a biography of Mrs. Browning's spaniel, *Flush* (1933). . . . Hugh Seymore Walpole (1884–1941), novelist and biographer, achieved early success, though not with his first work—two novels written while at Cambridge. His war service in Russia provided material for *The Dark Forest* (1916) and *The Secret City* (1919).

David Herbert Lawrence (1885-1930) wrote *Sons and Lovers.*

No woman in recent English literature became so well known as Katherine Mansfield (pen name of Kathleen Beauchamp, 1890–1923). One of her short stories, "The Fly," has been ranked with the world's best fifteen. One of her important works was her *Journal,* 1914–22. Aldous Huxley (1894–1963), novelist, poet, essayist and biographer, is best known for his *Point Counter Point* (1928).

Recent English Literature.—A remarkable sign of the increasing understanding between England and America has been the popularity of the younger British novelists in the United States. Graham Greene (1904–), became known in America with his *Heart of the Matter* (1948). Evelyn Arthur St. John Waugh (1903–1966) is the best known English satirist. The sardonic *The Loved One* introduced him to a wide American public. Rebecca West (Cecily Fairfield) (1892–), departed from literary tradition in *The Return of the Soldier, The Thinking Reed.* Victoria Sackville-West (1892–1962), poet, novelist, is known for the dignified prose of *The Edwardians, Gray Wethers, The Devil at Westease, The Easter Party.* Elizabeth Dorothea Cole Bowen (1899–), sensitive Anglo-Irish novelist, published *Encounters* (1923); *To the North* (1932), *Death of the Heart* (1938) and *The Heat of the Day* (1949) followed. George Orwell (1903–1950) was a political satirist and allegorist known best for his *Animal Farm* (1945) and *Nineteen Eighty Four* (1949), a prophetic novel. Joyce Cary (1888–1957) published his first novel, *Aissa Saved* (1932) and became known widely with *The Horse's Mouth* (1944). Herbert Ernest Bates (1905–) and Victor Sawdon Pritchett (1900–) are accounted the best short story writers since Katherine Mansfield. Bates' best work is probably *The Black Boxer* (1932) and Pritchett's *It May Never Happen* (1945).

Poetry during the 1930's included writings by W. H. Auden (1907–), S. H. Spender (1909–), F. L. MacNeice (1907–1963) and Cecil Day Lewis (1904–). They wrote of the Machines; in politics they were radical. Auden's latest work is *For the Time Being* (1945); Spender's best later work is *Ruins and Visions* (1942). MacNiece in *Springboard* (1944) is at his mature best. Day Lewis passed from propaganda to philosophical excellence in *Word Over All* (1943). Acclaimed as the best poet of World War II, the Welshman, Dylan Thomas (1914–1954), shows skilled craftsmanship in *Deaths and Entrances* (1945). Craftsmanship with greater freedom characterize recent British literature.

AMERICAN LITERATURE

American literature today is a sturdy adolescent, capable at last of standing on its own feet and filled with new ideas and aspirations. At first it was only natural that the forms in which American thought found expression should be derived from England. English speech, English writing and English culture dominated. English Puritanism had a tremendous influence not only upon the early writers but also upon the general tone of American thought and action. The effects of English romanticism were seen in early fiction and in the poetry of Poe. Nevertheless, all the while, America was breeding a literature of her own, born out of the storm and stress of creating a nation, of reconstructing it after a devastating Civil War and of opening up a vast virginal West where a new native culture could develop.

American literature, so closely allied with the political growth of the country, may be divided into the following periods: the Colonial Period, 1607–1750; the Revolution, Period of Controversy, 1750–1815; the Period of Romanticism, Democracy and the Civil War, 1815–65; the Period of Reconstruction and Growth, 1865–1900; Twentieth Century Literature, 1900–.

Colonial Period, 1607–1750.—To create a great literature, any country must have a folklore and a highly developed nationality and civilization. Colonial America had neither. Traditions come only after generations of men have lived, fought and died. Literature is written only if romantic deeds and scenes rich in historic background exist. Culture is bred only when a nation is orderly, at peace and devoted to the arts. Our New England pioneers, struggling with hostile Indians and an unfriendly soil and climate, had little time to write. The business of making a living engrossed their time and effort.

The few books that were written were largely concerned with descriptions of life in the New World. Shortly after the landing of the Pilgrims in 1620, William Bradford, second governor of Plymouth Colony, wrote *The History of Plimouth Plantation,* a detailed and dramatic account of the colonists' impression of this "weather-beaten face," of fights with the Indians, sicknesses, labors with the soil, social and religious customs, trade and the struggle to educate their youth. Another substantial and valuable history was Governor John Winthrop's *The History of New England.* Samuel Sewall, one of the judges who pronounced death upon the people of Salem who were accused of witchcraft, recorded that survival of medievalism in his *Diary,* written tersely and with real pictorial value.

In the South conditions were even less favorable for book printing because the people were not congregated in towns nor bound together by such strong religious interests as in New England. Captain John Smith wrote *The Generall Historie of Virginia* (1624) and also an account of his personal adventures. William Byrd's *The History of the Dividing Line* is a record of his commission to establish the boundary between Virginia and North Carolina.

Theology engrossed the attention of the New England colonists and permeated their literature. An exception was Anne Dudley Bradstreet, whose work, though conventional, captured something of the Elizabethan flavor. *The Day of Doom* by Michael Wigglesworth is a direful and fiery picture of Judgment Day. Quotations from it were used in *The New England Primer,* a textbook of couplets attempting to teach theology and the alphabet at the same time. The *Bay Psalm Book* proves that the Puritans were not averse to music if it was set to religious verse.

The two great theologians of the period were Cotton Mather and Jonathan Edwards. Both represent New England Calvinism in its severest form. Both were powerful preachers and writers, absolutely relentless in their insistence that the wrath of God and the doom of eternal punishment descends on those who sin. Mather's

THE FRANKLIN INSTITUTE

BENJAMIN FRANKLIN, an American author, inventor, philosopher, and statesman.

The Ecclesiastical History of New England is not a mere church history but a running commentary on life, sin, death and rules of conduct. Edwards' treatises are more intellectual, restrained and logical. The first president of Princeton College, he is known as an educator as well as a theologian and philosopher.

Revolution or Period of Controversy, 1750–1815.—The events that led to the Revolutionary War turned the attention of the American people from the contemplation of an afterlife to consideration of their immediate future. The exciting business of breaking away from English rule and setting up an American government brought forth patriotic verse, impassioned oratory and many political documents.

Poetry was written not by idle observers but by men active in politics, education or diplomacy. The Hartford Wits were a group of young men attempting to write good *English* literature. Later almost all took an active part in the Revolution and wrote such patriotic poems as "The Conquest of Canaan" by Timothy Dwight, which pictured the young nation as a slumbering giant; and "The Columbiad" by Joel Barlow. Francis Hopkinson's "Battle of the Kegs" is a fine satirical poem at the expense of the British. John Trumbull's "Ode to Sleep" marked the advent of lyrical poetry, which flowered later in the work of Philip Freneau, whose "Eu-

taw Springs," "To a Honey Bee," "The Wild Honeysuckle" and "The Indian Burying Ground" are lyrics of real skill and charm. Frank Moore has made an excellent collection of these poems, entitled *Songs and Ballads of the American Revolution.*

The struggle for independence, the Revolutionary War and the drafting of the Declaration of Independence and of the Constitution developed a group of orators not excelled in the English Parliament for clarity of thought and conviction. Among the statesmen who made American history and contributed vital examples of oratory were: Thomas Paine, the much misunderstood liberal, whose vigorous political pamphlets, *Rights of Man* and *Common Sense,* contributed much to the forces that brought about a break between the colonies and the mother country; James Otis, whose speech against the writs of assistance inflamed the colonists against taxation without representation; Patrick Henry, whose "Give me liberty or give me death" rang across the sea; George Washington in his *Farewell Address;* John Adams, John Randolph, Benjamin Franklin and Thomas Jefferson, author of the immortal *Declaration of Independence.* In prose exposition, Alexander Hamilton, James Madison and John Jay collaborated on *The Federalist,* a collection of essays explaining the proposed Federal Constitution and advocating its adoption, a first attempt in the literature of political science.

In nonpolitical prose the work of BENJAMIN FRANKLIN (1706–90) is outstanding. Franklin rose by his own efforts from poverty to wealth, from obscurity to world-wide honor. He was scientist, inventor, editor, diplomat, philosopher and writer. He was our representative in England before the Revolution and in France during the war. *Poor Richard's Almanack* is a storehouse of his wit, wisdom and practical information. Franklin's *Autobiography* is a clearly written account of his earlier life, particularly interesting when read in conjunction with some of his excellent letters. His literary contemporaries included John Woolman, the Quaker preacher whose *Journal* is still read in England as well as in America for its piety and purity of style; Charles Brockden Brown, our first internationally known novelist, and St. John de Crèvecœur, farmer and adventurer. Brown's novels show the influence of English Romanticism in their preoccupation with the strange and mysterious; they also contain a hint of psychological analysis, foreshadowing the work of Poe and Hawthorne. His style is stilted but his descriptions are vivid and his characterizations convincing. He also contributed to the early literary magazines that generally took their material from English sources. Crèvecœur's *Letters from an American Farmer,* written in an easy flowing style, are interesting and accurate observations on rural life.

Period of Romanticism, Democracy and the Civil War, 1815–65.—This period was marked by increased literary output and the establishment of fixed schools in fiction, poetry and philoso-

CHARLES PHELPS CUSHING

RALPH WALDO EMERSON

phy—all against a background of lingering deference to European culture. Politically the period was one of struggle to make unity and democracy out of a hard-won national independence. The virile life of the vast West created the necessity for new standards of living and new modes of thought. Towns springing up in isolated sections were bound together by improved transportation and growing industries; but at the same time dialects, social backgrounds and traditions began to differentiate the New Englander, the Southerner and the Westerner. Such economic questions as the tariff, money, banking and, most of all, slavery, became part of political discussion and legislation. Much of this discussion crept into literature; but quite apart from economics and politics, literature was now for the first time extensively cultivated for its own sake.

WASHINGTON IRVING (1783–1859), a genial and versatile author, traveler and diplomat, was American by birth, education and affection for American scenes and institutions, but much of his work was in the English manner. He did, however, give to the world the first evidence of a native American literary folklore in his *Sketch Book* stories, *Rip Van Winkle* and *The Legend of Sleepy Hollow*. He had previously contributed to the engaging *Salmagundi Papers* and written the delightfully humorous *Knickerbocker's History of New York*. Besides the two famous legends of the Hudson, the *Sketch Book* contains discerning and charming essays on places visited abroad. Irving used the sketch—short and concentrated—in an attempt at originality and so became a godfather of the short story, which was to become the most distinctive contribution of American literature.

JAMES FENIMORE COOPER (1789–1851) invested American scenes and characters with the glow of romantic adventure. He introduced to a reading public that included all of Europe the American woodsman, the American

Indian and the American sailor—romantic, adventurous figures of the New World and of his own time, capable of rivaling and replacing Scott's heroes of the Middle Ages. Like Scott, Cooper is remembered for his vivid imagination, his story-telling ability, his sense of scenic and dramatic values and the heroes he created.

The Southerner, William Gilmore Simms, wrote adventurous historical tales somewhat in the Cooper manner, of which the best known is *The Yemassee*, a story of Indian warfare in Carolina. Very different from Cooper's sea stories, however, are those of Herman Melville, whose *Moby Dick* is not only stirring and gripping but at the same time a mystic allegory of the pursuit of an ideal. Because of its underlying philosophy and symbolism it has been called the first great American novel and is still much read. Another sea story, historically important for its accuracy and the interest it aroused in California, is Richard Henry Dana's *Two Years Before the Mast,* an exciting account of his personal experiences.

New England now became the center of American culture. Emerson, Thoreau, Bronson Alcott and Margaret Fuller wrote philosophy and critical essays; Hawthorne, novels and short stories; Longfellow, Whittier, Lowell and Holmes, poetry. Somewhat outside the New England tradition was William Cullen Bryant, poet and journalist in New York. Still farther removed were Sidney Lanier, poet of the South, Edgar Allan Poe and Walt Whitman, whose work carries over into the next period.

RALPH WALDO EMERSON (1803–82) was the most profound thinker America had yet seen. Scholar, teacher, minister, traveler, lecturer, poet and essayist, he appealed to all who would seek truth for its own sake, forsake tradition and blaze new trails. He was the leader of an idealistic philosophy, termed *Transcendentalism,* which particularly emphasized the power and force of the individual and the essential unity of nature. His philosophy was not consistent but possessed ecstasy, optimism and tremendous enthusiasm, as expressed in such essays as *Self-Reliance, Heroism, Love, Friendship* and *Compensation.* Emerson's *The American Scholar* urges a national self-consciousness and the abandonment of servile adherence to European standards and forms. With Hawthorne, Thoreau and others, Emerson was interested in Brook Farm, a New England attempt at communal living that was unsuccessful. His poetry, largely philosophical, was strongly influenced by his study of Hindu, Persian and ancient Greek literature. Emerson was hailed in England by Carlyle and others as a great prophet and his influence reaches to the present day.

Associated with Emerson at Concord was the eccentric yet clear-headed philosopher, HENRY DAVID THOREAU (1817–62). He, too, was a strong individualist and cried out against the financial and political demands of society. He retired to the shores of Walden Pond, there to build a hut with his own hands and to raise

his own food—not to escape from civilization but to find it. He did not believe in government and his philosophy of passive resistance—an Oriental rather than an American idea—has had a tremendous influence upon the thought of the world. In *Walden* he shows us not only the philosopher but the pure naturalist, keenly interested in the ways of nature and of animal life.

BRONSON ALCOTT was another Concord sage, though his "Orphic Sayings" were never articulate enough to provide substantially for his family of "Marmee, Meg, Jo, Beth and Amy," described by his gifted daughter, Louisa May, in *Little Women, Little Men* and other universally loved novels. He was greatly interested in new methods of education and in the establishment of another communal settlement, Fruitlands.

MARGARET FULLER was one of the first American women to take an active interest in literature and philosophy. She was extremely well educated and a brilliant conversationalist. For two years she edited the *Dial,* a magazine devoted to the philosophical and poetical expressions of Transcendentalism, and contributed much of its content. Through her translations she introduced German thought and philosophy to America.

NATHANIEL HAWTHORNE (1804-64) reflected New England surroundings just as Irving represented urban New York and Cooper rural New York. Hawthorne's early life in Salem made him conscious of 17th-century New England in such of its practices as Salem witchcraft; and his later life in Concord brought him in touch with the metaphysics of Emerson, Thoreau and Bronson Alcott, though he never entirely accepted them. He gave literary prestige to the short story and firmly established it as an artistic medium, finding a ready market in the periodicals that were yearly increasing in number. Through all his tales runs the thread of some moral law. His characters are largely symbolic of ideas, but his settings are realistic

A. DEVANEY, INC.

WALDEN POND

and in the mood he wishes to create. Some of his stories are fantastic; some, pure allegory; others, like *The Great Stone Face*, show great simplicity and fine technique; still others, such as *A Rill from a Town Pump*, are wholly engaging. Hawthorne's novels also reflect his interest in the mental and the mystic. His most significant works, *The Scarlet Letter* and *The House of the Seven Gables* are fine studies of Puritan psychology.

By all estimates, HENRY WADSWORTH LONGFELLOW (1807–82), scholar, teacher and traveler, was the most popular poet of his day, in England almost as much as in America. His poetry has a European flavor and a scholastic background. His popular narrative poems, *Evangeline, The Courtship of Miles Standish* and *Hiawatha*, are American in content but not in feeling. His sonnets, which required concentration of thought and form, are far better poetry than his lyrics and narratives.

JAMES RUSSELL LOWELL (1819–91), like Longfellow, was pre-eminently a scholar. He was much interested in politics and was for many years American Minister to England. His opposition to the Mexican War and the institution of slavery was expressed through the medium of a typical Yankee talking to all and sundry in the famous *Biglow Papers* in both verse and prose. Included in this collection is the delightful poem "Courtin'." *A Fable for Critics* is a collection of racy light verse characterizing his literary contemporaries. Of particular importance is his use of dialect, and the poems in which this is present are much fresher and more original than his formal compositions.

OLIVER WENDELL HOLMES (1809–94) a Bostonian who was distinctly democratic in his sympathies, studied law and medicine and became a great physician and teacher of anatomy. His poetry is memorable particularly for its humor and patriotic feeling, as in "The Height of the Ridiculous," "The Deacon's Masterpiece" and "Old Ironsides." He also wrote the inspiringly beautiful "The Chambered Nautilus" and several noble hymns. A genial, shrewd and apposite commentator, he wrote in prose *The Autocrat of the Breakfast Table*, an unrivaled collection of chatty, diverting comments on life and affairs. His novels were less successful but show a doctor's concern with psychological aspects.

Of this group of New England poets, JOHN GREENLEAF WHITTIER (1807–92) was the most American in his choice of subjects and style of writing. He took an extremely active part in the Abolitionist movement and no single American poem is so full of righteous scorn as Whittier's "Ichabod," an attack on Daniel Webster for his speech on the seventh of March supporting the Compromise of 1850. Among his lyrics and narratives are "The Barefoot Boy," "The Shoemakers," "The Huskers," "Corn Song," "Maud Muller," "Skipper Ireson's Ride," "Barbara Frietchie" and the New England idyl, "Snow-Bound," all American in subject and tone and all contributing to an American treasury of tradition and folklore.

WILLIAM CULLEN BRYANT (1794–1878) was born in New England but departed from its tenets in his emphasis on nature. "Thanatopsis," written when the author was seventeen, is a melancholy poem about death with no Christian hope in it—a pantheist's or nature-lover's religion. He was influenced by such British poets as Gray, Coleridge and Young in choosing as his theme fundamental concepts and the beauty of nature. He wrote, with an austere and dignified touch appropriate to the "High Priest" of Nature, such poems as "Forest Hymn," "The Evening Wind" and "To a Waterfowl," which is comparable in style and spirit to Shelley's "Skylark." He was noted also as a scholar, politician and influential journalist.

EDGAR ALLAN POE (1809–49) was a solitary and brilliant figure in American literature. Born and educated in the South, he had none of the Puritanic qualities of the New England writers. With Hawthorne he contributed much to the development of the American short story, particularly to the detective and mystery story, with *The Gold Bug, The Purloined Letter* and others. He was a critic of considerable ability and in his review of Hawthorne's *Twice-Told Tales* did much to clarify and define the properties of a short story. Perhaps more than any other writer he sounded the possibilities of the morbid—a characteristic that is Latin rather than Anglo-Saxon, Continental rather than American—and his influence in Europe, particularly in France, was tremendous. Horror, despair, the gruesome, the uncanny, the supernatural are all present in his stories and to a lesser extent in his poetry. His poetry, more subjective and revealing than his prose, shows spiritual aspirations, melancholic insight and surcharged emotion. Outstanding poems are "Lenore," "Eulalie," "The Bells," "Annabel Lee" and "The Raven." No one but Coleridge at his best or Swinburne now and then wrote such magically metrical lines with such mysteriously singing sounds.

In the South were Sidney Lanier and Stephen Foster. Lanier was a master of melody who knew poetic form as only a musician can. His "The Marshes of Glynn" and "Song of the Chattahoochee" are marked examples of rhythmic beauty. Foster perpetuated American folklore in such songs as "Oh, Susannah," "Old Black Joe," "Swanee River" and "Camptown Races," for which he wrote both words and music.

On the background of this full flowering of literary excellence fell the sinister shadow of a Civil War. The questions provoked by slavery, state rights and the rapid westward expansion produced oratory unrivalled in any nation. John C. Calhoun, Henry Clay, Edward Everett and Daniel Webster argued brilliantly and forcefully on the explosive questions confronting the nation. Harriet Beecher Stowe's *Uncle Tom's Cabin*, a violently partisan and prejudiced story, helped to fan the abolitionist flames. Such stirring songs as "Maryland, My Maryland" by James Ryder Randall and "The Battle Hymn of the Republic" by Julia Ward Howe became popular.

In this period came the classics of American historical writing: George Bancroft's *History of the United States*, William H. Prescott's *History of the Conquest of Mexico* and *The Conquest of Peru*, John L. Motley's *The Rise of the Dutch Republic* and Francis Parkman's *The Oregon Trail*. LINCOLN's *Gettysburg Address* stands alone in all literature for simplicity, diction, perfection of pattern and cogent utterance.

Period of Reconstruction and Growth, 1865–1900.—The Civil War had caused a new American self-consciousness. This was expressed most fully and most perfectly by WALT WHITMAN (1819–92). Many found him coarse, crude and impossible, but a few (among them Emerson) recognized his greatness and his significance for American literature. Discarding all the conventions of poetic form, subject matter and elegance in the choice of words, he captured in his strong rhythms the very beat and essence of American life, its passion for liberty, its faith in man and democracy. His genius, as expressed in his single volume of poetry, *Leaves of Grass*, won wide acclaim in Europe before it was wholeheartedly acknowledged here. At the same time in New England Emily Dickinson also was breaking away from tradition and expressing in new poetic forms the otherwise hidden fire that was in her. Since she did not allow most of her work to be published until after her death, it was not influential until early in the next century when it gave impetus to the American Imagist movement. The popular and conventional poets of the period were Eugene Field with his "Little Boy Blue" and other poems for children; and James Whitcomb Riley with his enchanting folk poems of the Mid-West.

In prose the most significant development was that of local color or regional fiction, in both the short story and the novel. From the Far West came the saga of the mining camp, the scouts, the adventurers, the gold seekers. Bret Harte's short stories, *The Luck of Roaring Camp* and *The Outcasts of Poker Flat* rudely interrupted the genteel literary tradition of the East. Short stories describing local conditions and characters poured in from all over the country. Joel Chandler Harris delighted children and made a real contribution to the folklore of the American people with his Uncle Remus stories. George W. Cable wrote *Old Creole Days*, containing stories of Louisiana. Sarah Orne Jewett described old folks in old New England towns. Alice French (Octave Thanet) wrote of the changing frontier. The magazines that were becoming cheaper and more numerous supplied an eager market for these stories.

The novel was both regional and romantic. Edward Eggleston in *The Hoosier Schoolmaster* and other stories of early Indiana and Hamlin Garland in *Main Travelled Roads* and his autobiographical *Son of the Middle Border* wrote with great realism. Helen Hunt Jackson in *Ramona* told a story of the Pacific coast Indians; Thomas Nelson Page gave evidence of great literary skill in his novels of Virginia, *In Old Virginia* and *Red Rock;* and James Lane Allen wrote *A Kentucky Cardinal*. In these and in Owen Wister's *The Virginian* and in Jack London's *The Call of the Wild,* the romantic tendency of the earlier part of the century is still evident. It is still more vividly present in such historical novels as Lew Wallace's *Ben Hur, a Tale of the Christ,* Mary Johnston's *To Have and to Hold* and her other stories of early Virginia, in *Hugh Wynne,* a story of the Revolution by S. Weir Mitchell, physician, and in *Janice Meredith* by Paul Leicester Ford, historian.

MARK TWAIN MEMORIAL

MARK TWAIN

Head and shoulders above all these in style and in breadth of understanding and interest was SAMUEL CLEMENS (pen name, Mark Twain), 1835–1910. Born and reared in the Midwest, familiar with the far West and for many years a resident of the East his knowledge of America in the Gilded Age of expansion and enterprise was both intimate and complete. His short stories, novels and essays are filled with humor that is sometimes satirical, but always human and wholly delightful. His use of dialect is judicious and expert. *Tom Sawyer* and *Huckleberry Finn* are beloved stories of American youth. *The Prince and the Pauper* and *A Connecticut Yankee in King Arthur's Court* are combinations of vivid imagination, uproarious humor and good common sense. The best of his writings are frankly and completely American with no trace of European imitation.

Important in the development of the novel were WILLIAM DEAN HOWELLS and HENRY JAMES. Both achieved a more finished style in combination with a truer, less romantic realism than any American writer before them. Both showed great interest in manners and significant details and thus foreshadowed the psychological novel. Henry James was more cosmopolitan than American and finally became an English subject, conceiving

America as provincial, with no artistic insight and no understanding of culture as it was exemplified in Europe. Howells showed an acute awareness of those problems inherent in the unparalleled expansion of industry that in the first decade of the next century were to become almost the sole consideration of American literature. In *The Rise of Silas Lapham,* Howells pictures a typical American businessman of the time—good-hearted but uncouth and uneducated—and thus brings up the problem of social manners and culture in relation to money and its possession. Other novels that heralded the growing interest in social problems were *The Bread-Winners* by John Hay, an unsympathetic treatment of a labor strike, and Edward Bellamy's *Looking Backward,* an imaginative comparison between the world as he knew it in 1887 and as it might be in 2000. Henry Adams in *Mont-Saint-Michel and Chartres* and *The Education of Henry Adams* attempted to evolve a philosophy of education and unity out of the constantly changing complexities of his time. William James, brother of Henry James and the leading American philosopher of the period, accepted this myriad reality with delight and paid less attention to unities and abstractions.

During this period there was evidence of a new movement in the novel, one, however, that would not reach its height until the second and third decades of the twentieth century. This intensified realism with a strong dash of psychology was first evident in the two short novels by Stephen Crane —*Maggie: A Girl of the Streets* and *The Red Badge of Courage*—and in the first novels by Frank Norris— *McTeague* and *Vandover and the Brute,* two unpleasantly realistic stories of character degeneration.

Twentieth-Century Literature.—The twentieth century produced literature in quantities never before equaled. To satisfy a constantly enlarging reading public and to provide entertainment for newly acquired leisure, more newspapers, magazines and books were printed than ever before. Literature entered upon a period of great originality and varied experimentation. The American tradition and spirit needed to be more fully defined and expressed. Writers and critics followed Emerson's fifty-year-old admonitions and dared to attempt and acknowledge an American language and literature distinct from that of the British Isles. Local-color stories placed increasing emphasis on the underlying American psychology and tradition of the different localities. Young writers who had journeyed to Europe in search of inspiration and a cultural background were forced to return to America for a fresh outlook and new enthusiasm.

Boisterously, America entered upon the era of trusts and big business, of fortunes quickly won and lost, of growing labor organization. As a result American literature was for a time almost wholly interested in social problems, in industry, money and labor. It was literature with the definite purpose of criticizing and correcting abuses in a country advancing so

rapidly in material production and prosperity that it took no time to think or to form a philosophy.

The Novel.—The social consciousness of novelists, which was to characterize the literature of the twentieth century, was apparent as early as 1903, when Frank Norris wrote about gambling on the wheat market in *The Pit*. This was followed in 1906 by Upton Sinclair's *The Jungle,* a denunciation of the meat-packing industry. Theodore Dreiser and James Farrell also contributed Chicago studies with *The Financier* and *Studs Lonigan,* respectively. Midwestern values were criticized in the novels of Sinclair Lewis, particularly in *Babbitt* and *Main Street;* the emphasis here was not on corruption, but on the pettiness and intellectual stagnation of the growing middle class.

The Lost Generation of the Twenties broke away from the old accepted forms in literature and founded their own literary group in Paris. This group of disillusioned ex-patriates included F. Scott Fitzgerald, Ernest Hemingway, Ezra Pound, T. S. Eliot, Gertrude Stein, James Joyce, Wyndham Lewis, and John Dos Passos. In the novels of Fitzgerald—*The Great Gatsby* and *Tender Is The Night*— and in Hemingway's *The Sun Also Rises,* the frenetic pace of the era was captured. Several innovations in the genrê were introduced by Joyce's *Ulysses* and Dos Passos' unique trilogy, *U.S.A.*

The Thirties were years of ideals and didacticism; one of the better novels was Hemingway's Spanish Civil War study, *For Whom The Bell Tolls*. At home, awareness of society continued and the literature of exposure increased; Steinbeck's *The Grapes of Wrath,* Caldwell's *Tobacco Road,* and Huxley's *Brave New World* were novels of Concern. The South and the inhabitants of Yoknapatawpha County were at once warmly and critically dealt with by William Faulkner; his novels include *The Sound And The Fury, Absolom, Absolom!,* and *Go Down, Moses.*

Contemporary literature also portrays local color, ethnic groups, and America's self-consciousness. Bernard Malamud writes of the Jewish community, James Baldwin's books, for example, *Nobody Knows My Name,* and those of Ralph Ellison portray the Negro in America. J. D. Salinger, spokesman for the younger generation, writes of the Glass family; he achieved recognition with *Catcher In The Rye.*

Significantly, the best sellers of the 1950's and 1960's were socio-psychological studies, fictional as well as non-fictional, thus carrying the era of social criticism to its height. Among these were Drury's *Advise And Consent* and Lederer's *The Ugly American,* both political exposés, Harper Lee's *To Kill a Mockingbird,* concerned with a southern community, and sociological studies such as Vance Packard's *The Hidden Persuaders* and *The Status Seekers.*

The Short Story.—Among American short story writers of distinction are O. Henry (pseudonym for William Sydney Porter), an acknowledged master of style, and Ring Lardner, noted for his story "Haircut" and his book *How To Write Short Stories.* Many of the major novelists of the era also contributed to the refinement of this genrê; notable among these are Fitzgerald, portrayer of the jazz age, and Hemingway, whose direct, masculine style considerably influenced the younger writers.

Among female writers, Katherine Ann Porter achieved distinction with "Flowering Judas"; Shirley Jackson gained recognition with her variously interpreted "The Lottery"; and Dorothy Parker, witty and satirical, wrote the humorous and much anthologized "The Waltz."

In contemporary letters a group of young writers has infused fresh insight into the short story form. Malamud and Philip Roth combine warmth with humor in their semi-ethnic stories. John Updike's *Pigeon Feathers* proves him a master craftsman.

Poetry.—In poetry the twentieth century brought more freedom in form and subject matter. The realism and the sociological interests so prominent in the novel were apparent in poetry also. Edwin Markham in *The Man with the Hoe* cried out against the slave makers of the centuries. Edgar Lee Masters in *Spoon River Anthology* gave brief epitaphs on men, real and fancied, of a small midwestern town. Edwin Arlington Robinson put into poetry with a philosophic tinge discerning observations on the American character. A more vigorous and original realism is found in the poetry of Vachel Lindsay and Carl Sandburg. Lindsay, a twentieth-century minstrel, tramped the country singing his songs wherever opportunity arose. In them, mostly in ballad style, he marvelously captured the gay throbbing heart of a new land and a new people. Carl Sandburg, singing of the bold and vigorous energy of the Western plains and cities, found poetry in machines and in dirty wind-swept cities, in high-flung girders and in factory workers. The poetry of Robert Frost, without the hurried rhythm of Sandburg and Lindsay, told of simple New England commonplaces and achieved strength from the positive truth of Frost's observation and recording.

More sophisticated and self-conscious poetry was written first by the Imagists and later by T. S. Eliot and Ezra Pound. The Imagists, represented by Amy Lowell, John Gould Fletcher and others, attempted concentration of thought and expression and the elimination of "sweet nothings." This school, influenced by the Oriental forms of China and Japan, forgot cosmic themes and abstractions and attempted to give clear and brief impressions of little things; they experimented in forms, but wrote mostly in unrhymed free verse (French, *vers libre*). Thomas Stearns Eliot, who became an English citizen in 1927, and Ezra Pound (also then resident in England) were greatly fascinated by the myriad connotations of words. Their poetry presupposes a great deal of literary knowledge and imagination in their readers. In addition to being scholarly, Eliot's is strongly rhythmic and highly stimulating. *The*

WIDE WORLD

EDWARD ALBEE, emerging theatrical voice.

Wasteland (1922), with its strong note of disillusion and despair, is generally read as an indictment of modern society. The source notes that Eliot appended to the poem have influenced contemporary literary criticism as much as the poem itself has changed poetic tastes. Eliot is also famed for his plays, *The Cocktail Party* in particular; for the technical control of the metaphysical *Four Quartets;* and for his essays on literary criticism, *The Sacred Wood.*

Pound is best known for his enigmatic, unfinished *Cantos,* which incorporate Ovidian and Dantesque themes within a musical pattern. Eliot cited them as "an inexhaustible reference book of verse forms."

Another master craftsman of the era was Wallace Stevens (1879–1955). His poetry, taken as a whole, proffers an entire poetic treatise on the aesthetics of poetry itself; for him, "poetry is the subject of the poem." Precise, and at times ironical, Stevens uses the basic concept of the interworkings of reality and imagination. His volumes include *Harmonium, Ideas of Order,* and *The Auroras of Autumn;* his notable poems are *The Man With the Blue Guitar* and *Notes Toward A Supreme Fiction.*

A return to more conventional forms was made by Robinson Jeffers, Conrad Aiken, William Rose Benet, Stephen Vincent Benet and Edna St. Vincent Millay. Stephen Vincent Benet's *John Brown's Body,* a long narrative poem of the Civil War, is remarkably well sustained. It has been very widely read. Innovations in American poetry again became the vogue with the typographical and structural eccentricities of e. e. cummings' singular verse.

In clever, rollicking verse that often contains a bite, such rhymsters as Arthur Guiterman, Dorothy Parker and Ogden Nash have made fun of modern manners.

Modern poetry is characterized by anti-formalism, as represented by the Beat Movement and its spokesmen, Jack Kerouac and Allen Ginsberg. Replacing this unacademic group is the equally untraditional poetry of Lawrence Ferlinghetti, whose poems are collected in *Pictures of the Gone World* (1955) and *A Coney Island of the Mind* (1958). He has also written several plays, or "happenings," issued under the title of *Unfair Arguments With Existence.*

Theater.—The three most prominent names in the list of American playwrights are Eugene O'Neill, Tennessee Williams, and Arthur Miller. O'Neill was a prolific author whose sense of the tragic and concern with the psychological made his work powerful, his plays timeless. Among his many works are *Desire Under the Elms* (1924), *Mourning Becomes Electra* (1931), *Ah, Wilderness!* (1933), *The Iceman Cometh* (1946), and his greatest play, *Long Day's Journey Into Night* (1941). Tennessee Williams' successes include *The Glass Menagerie* (1945), *A Streetcar Named Desire* (1947), and *Cat On A Hot Tin Roof* (1955). Miller's social vision was exemplified in the prize-winning *Death of a Salesman* (1949).

Among the other authors of the 1930's and 1940's, several are particularly significant: Thorton Wilder, author of *Our Town* (1938) and *The Skin of Our Teeth* (1942), and William Saroyan, who wrote *The Time of Your Life* (1939).

The American musical comedy has also contributed to the fame of Broadway; the talent of a select group of composers and lyricists have partially changed the theater from tragic to light and entertaining. Increased sophistication and refinement have added to the quality of this form. Outstanding examples include the never-fail efforts of Rodgers and Hammerstein, including such hits as *South Pacific, Carousel, Oklahoma!, The King and I,* and *The Sound of Music;* Lerner and Loewe's *My Fair Lady* and *Camelot;* Cole Porter's *Kiss Me Kate;* and Leonard Bernstein's *Wonderful Town* and *West Side Story.*

Another type of drama has arisen and is being produced in off-Broadway theaters, and on college campuses, by amateurs and intellectuals. This avant-garde drama, which is both experimental and form-shattering, has been heavily influenced by Continental authors: Luigi Pirandello, Bertolt Brecht, Jean Cocteau, Jean Genêt, Eugene Ionesco, and Samuel Beckett. This so-called Theater of the Absurd movement, however, has developed its own uniquely American playwrights, with their own innovating features and their distinctively American idiom. The Absurd, with its emphasis on character interrelationships and its questioning of the ultimate meaning of existence, has introduced more innovations into drama than has any previous school.

Within this type of play, the traditional, Aristotelian plot progression is surplanted by an almost surrealistic and outwardly incoherent series of events; seemingly rambling, raving dialogue has replaced traditional repartee. The action and verbal exchange, which to the uninitiated seems meaningless, is symbolical. The isolation and alienation of the individual, as a basic issue, is seen by these play-wrights as a syndrome of society's sickness. Thus, dialogue purposely does not communicate to the audience and characters often do not seem to reach each other; the surrealistic surfaces resemble the senselessness of life, the static situations symbolize the paralysis of its lonely inhabitants.

While Continental authors write of the anguish and despair of universal man, American playwrights tend to treat contemporary situations with a mocking humor that is often meant to shock. Edward Albee, for example, deals with racial discrimination in *The Death of Bessie Smith;* this is one facet of the society that he censures in *The Zoo Story, The American Dream,* and *Who's Afraid of Virginia Woolf?*.

Other American representatives of this movement are Arthur Kopit, author of *Oh Dad, Poor Dad, Mama's Hung You in the Closet and I'm Feelin' So Sad;* Jack Gelber, who wrote *The Connection,* a play similar in theme to Beckett's *Waiting For Godot,* and *The Apple;* and Jack Richardson, author of *The Prodigal.*

Significant dramatists of the late 1950's and early 1960's also include LeRoi Jones, author of *Dutchman;* James Baldwin, who wrote *Blues For Mr. Charlie;* and Lorraine Hansberry, who won the New York Critics Award in 1958 for *A Raisin in the Sun.* In 1964, she completed *The Sign in Sidney Brustein's Window.*

Literary Criticism.—This field is steadily growing in importance and includes a number of outstanding writers:

Brooks, Van Wyck. *America's Coming-of-Age* 1915; *The Flowering of New England* 1936; *New England: Indian Summer* 1945; Parrington, Vernon L., *Main Currents in American Thought* 1930; **Commager, Henry Steele,** *The American Mind* 1950; Matthiessen, F. O., *The American Renaissance;* Mumford, Lewis, *The Golden Day* 1926; Hicks, Granville, *The Great Tradition* 1935; Lowes, John L., *The Road to Xanadu* 1927; Wilson, Edmund, *Axel's Castle* 1931; Kazan, Alfred, *On Native Grounds* 1942.

Modern Biography.—In the last few years, American writers have turned more and more to the writing of biography. Carl Sandburg described the Life of *Abraham Lincoln* in six volumes; Ray Stannard Baker wrote *Woodrow Wilson;* A. J. Beveridge, *John Marshall;* Douglas S. Freeman, *Robert E. Lee* and *The Life of George Washington;* Alpheus T. Mason wrote *Brandeis.*

There has been an increasing tendency to stress the background more than the purely personal aspects of the subject. This has been particularly noticeable in such books as Arthur M. Schlesinger, Jr.'s *The Age of Jackson,* Ferris Greenslet's *The Lowells and Their Seven Worlds,* and *Paul Revere and the World He Lived In* by Esther Forbes.

There are also some popular biographies which employ some of the techniques of fiction without sacrificing sound scholarship. Among these are, *Yankee from Olympus* by Catherine Drinker Bowman, and *Abigail Adams* by Janet Whitney.

Many of our distinguished Americans have written notable autobiographies: Jane Addams, *Twenty Years at Hull House; The Autobiography of William Allen White;* Henry Stimson *On Active Service;* James M. Cox, *Journey Through My Years; The*

Memoirs of Cordell Hull; Dwight D. Eisenhower, *Crusade in Europe;* the *Autobiography of Lincoln Steffens;* and *The Education of Henry Adams.*

Some other notable autobiographies by Americans of foreign birth are; *The Making of an American* by Jacob Riis, *The Americanization of Edward Bok* by Edward Bok, and *From Immigrant to Inventor* by Michail Pupin.

The New Approach to Science and History.—There is a definite trend toward the writing of history with more attention paid to the literary qualities of the writing, Therefore the new histories are interesting as well as scholarly. The following books have done much to further this new trend in history books. Claude Bower's, *Jefferson and Hamilton* and *The Tragic Era;* Mark Sullivan's, *Our Times; The Great American Bandwagon* by Charles Wertz; *The Mind In the Making* by James Harvey Robinson; *The Rise of American Civilization* by Charles and Mary Beard; *Postscript to Yesterday* and *Not so Long Ago* by Lloyd Morris; Bernard DeVoto's *Year of Decision* and *Across the Wide Missouri;* and Carl Van Doren's *The Great Rehearsal* and *Secret History of the Revolution.* Most of these books consider history from several angles, not only government and politics but also the forces of economics, personalities and culture, literature, art, and science. They are frankly interpretations as well as factual recording, and

to this they owe much of their interest.

Many of our writers on science can qualify as men of letters since their books are so well written. The following books have taken a permanent place in the field of literature as well as factual accounts: William Beebe, *Half Mile Down;* Raymond J. Ditmar, *High Jungle* and *Snakes of the World;* Edwin W. Teale, *Days Without Time* and *Dune Boy;* David G. Fairchild, *Garden Islands of the Great East* and *The World Grows Round my Door;* Willem Van-Loon's fascinating and colorful book *The Story of Mankind;* Clyde Kuckholm's *Mirror for Man* and Hans Zinsser's *Rats, Lice and History.*

American literature has explored every corner of life. For instance, there are books about psychology: H. Alfred Korzybski's *Science and Sanity;* books on etiquette, Arthur M. Schlesinger, Sr.'s *Learning How To Behave;* books on book collecting, Alfred E. Newton's *Amenities of Book Collecting* books about typography, Douglas McMurtrie's *The Golden Book;* about journalism, George Seldes's *You Can't Print That!;* about everyday business, Jesse Rainsford Sprague's *The Making of a Merchant*—all characterized by sound, vital writing as well as by accurate knowledge. All indicate the enormously varied literature that has grown up outside the regular furrows in an attempt to keep the reader abreast of the doer.

FRENCH LITERATURE

After ancient Gaul, conquered by Caesar (57–52 B.C.), became a Roman province, the Gauls gradually adopted the language of their conquerors and modified it into a popular or vulgar Latin that had two forms: the *langue d'oil* in the north and the *langue d'oc* in the south. The Franks and other Germanic tribes that invaded Gaul in the 4th and 5th centuries exerted little influence on the language of the Gallo-Romans but gave their name to the country—France. French, a dialect of the *langue d'oil,* gradually became the national language as the kings extended their rule from Paris over the entire country.

The Middle Ages.—Medieval French literature is astonishing for its richness and variety. It reflected a colorful and active society characterized in religion by the great scholastic theology of the mystic Bernard de Clairvaux (1091-1153) and the rationalist Pierre Abélard (1079-1142). The Provençal literature of the south reached a high point in the 11th and 12th centuries when the influence of its songs and cult of courtly love spread to Spain, Portugal and Italy. From the 11th to the 13th century, epics sung by wandering minstrels reigned supreme in nothern France. One type, the *chansons de geste,* centered mainly around Charlemagne and old French history and featured heroic deeds, both historical and fanciful. The Arthurian cycle, composed of stories about King Arthur and his knights, emphasized Christian and chivalric ideals of courage, loyalty, love and charity. The epics of antiquity told of the fabulous

deeds of Alexander, Aeneas and other heroes of classical antiquity. Most famous of the *chansons de geste* is *La Chanson de Roland,* written in the early 12th century, a story of Charlemagne and his legendary nephew Roland, fighting for Christianity against the Moors of Spain. Chrestien de Troyes (*c.* 1140–*c.* 91) was the principal author of the Arthurian romances and his *Chevalier au Lyon, Tristan* and *Percivale* were widely read and translated by the German poets Wolfram von Eschenbach and Gottfried von Strassburg. The *lais* of Marie de France (12th century) are short love poems with the same subject matter. The most famous, the *Lay of the Honeysuckle,* is a story of Sir Tristram.

In the 12th and 13th centuries the lower classes and the nobility as well delighted in disrespectful and mocking poetry, particularly in the gay and witty though often coarse verse tales known as *fabliaux* and in the satirical animal epic *Le Roman de Renart* ("History of Reynard the Fox") and its successors.

From the 13th to the 15th century French drama was either religious or comical. Miracles, relating some wonderful deeds of saints or martyrs, and mysteries, taken from scriptural incidents and usually from the life of Christ, formed the serious drama, though comic scenes were generally inserted in the most religious plays. The *Jeu de la feuillée* and the *Jeu de Robin et Marion* by Adam de la Halle (13th century) are perhaps the earliest examples of the farce and the comic opera. Later came moralities filled with allegory, the satirical and generally political *soties,* which were plays with allegorical characters, and above all the farces. Of these short plays, without much plot and dependent on surprise and ridicule for laughter, the best known is *L'Avocat* (or *Maître*) *Pierre Patelin* written about 1465, a play about a lawsuit against a shepherd. In it occurs the famous phrase, *"Revenons à nos moutons,"* now a proverb for "Get back to the subject."

The first important prose works were historical chronicles. Geoffroi de Villehardouin (c. 1160–c. 1213), a practical chevalier, wrote about the Fourth Crusade. Jean de Joinville (c. 1224–1317), frank, brave and loyal, wrote an interesting account of the life of St. Louis. Jean Froissart (c. 1337–c. 1410), poet and historian, wrote about the Hundred Years' War. Philippe de Comines (c. 1445–c. 1509), a sceptical and ambitious diplomat, described Charles the Bold and Louis XI from firsthand acquaintance.

The 15th century brought the end of chivalry and feudalism, the sudden use of prose for all literary forms, the growth of a middle class (*bourgeois*) and the infiltration of bourgeois ideals and emotions into literature. These trends are well illustrated in the prose novel *Le Petit Jehan de Saintré* by Antoine de la Salle (1398–1461). This romance, though chivalrous in form, is filled with the bourgeois spirit and shows the end of the idealization of women and the growing importance of money.

The end of the medieval period, like the beginning, produced some splendid poetry—lyric now instead of epic. Charles d'Orléans (1391–1465), a captive in England for 25 years, wrote graceful and sincere little poems lacking great force or purpose. François Villon (1431–c. 63), a great poet and a carefree vagabond whose life was rich with adventure and romance, shows in his poetry a robust love of life, the medieval fear of death and a vivid realism and interest in man. Villon was one of the most romantic personalities of all time and his poetry is a perfect reflection of the man. His ballade with the refrain "Où sont les neiges d'antan?" ("Where are the snows of yesteryear?") is famous. Villon's works are full of underworld slang—and of bold poetry.

Effect of the Renaissance, 16th Century. —The coming of the Renaissance or revival in literature and in the arts was hastened by the wars of Francis I in Italy (putting the French in contact with Italian, and through it with Roman and Greek, civilization), by the invention of printing—the first book left French presses in 1470— and by the growth of the cities and the middle class. The Renaissance was accompanied by the Protestant Reformation in religion. Francis I and his sister Margaret of Navarre, herself an able poet, greatly encouraged artists and men of letters. Through study of the ancient classics, men regained faith in themselves and their abilities and a new love of nature and of living.

The outstanding poet of the first part of the century was Clément Marot (1495–1549). His verse is light, harmonious and sometimes ironical but rarely as forceful as that of Pierre de Ronsard (1524–85) who, as head of the literary society, the *Pléiade,* and author of the epic poem *La Franciade,* was considered the greatest poet of his time. The Pléiade also included Joachim du Bellay (1524–60), Remi Belleau (1528–77), Jean Antoine de Baïf (1532–89), Étienne Jodelle (1532–73), Claude Joseph Dorat (1734–80) and Pontus de Thiard (1521–1605). Their purpose was to bring order out of the current language confusion, and their manifesto was the *Deffense et illustration de la langue française* by du Bellay, which set forth these objectives: to enrich the language, set up poetic standards, cultivate classic forms such as the sonnet and the ode, emphasize the need of work as well as genius and imitate the ancient Greeks and Romans. Du Bellay contributed some lovely sonnets; Ronsard, sonnets, odes and epics; Jodelle, *Cléopâtre,* the first tragedy modeled after the classical with a regular plan, acts and scenes, the unities of time, place and action, a chorus and character study. Robert Garnier (1534–90) continued along the same line. Religious dramas disappeared after 1548 when the Parliament of Paris forbade the representation of mysteries because they had assumed too great freedom.

In prose Jacques Amyot (1513–93), linguist and scholar, made an excellent translation of Plutarch, the basis of the first English versions. The very essence of the Renaissance lies in the work of François Rabelais (c. 1490–1553). His five-volume masterpiece, concerned with the activities of the giant Gargantua and his son Pantagruel, is an uproarious satire filled with strong constructive advice in educational, social and political affairs. The book presents Rabelais's deep interest in nature and man, Renaissance freedom and at times coarseness of thought and expression and an extraordinary richness and variety of language—for Rabelais invented or combined words to suit his pleasure.

The Swiss John Calvin (1509–64), a moving force in the Reformation, put his stern and implacable doctrines in a firm, vigorous and concise style. His influence on prose literature as well as on religious thought was enormous. The religious struggle (1560–98) between the Catholics and the Protestants brought fanaticism on both sides and disillusionment from the first high hopes of the Renaissance. Ronsard wrote martial odes; Agrippa d'Aubigné (1552–1630) upheld the rights of the Calvinists in the satirical poem *Les Tragiques* and his memoirs. The *Satire Ménippée* appeared in 1594; it is remarkable political satire directed against the Holy League that had been formed to combat the Huguenots.

Michel de Montaigne (1533–92) was the great original thinker of the end of the century. In his essays he made a keen though sceptical study of the human mind and heart. He stressed importance of the individual and is still read not only for his polished style but for a philosophy that inspired man to try to understand himself. His ideas on the education of children are still significant. Montaigne's essays were translated into English as early as 1603. His motto was one of doubt, *"Que sais-je?"* ("What do I know?").

Writing memoirs became fashionable; of particular interest are those of François de la Noue (1531–91), a Huguenot soldier nicknamed *Bras de Fer* or Iron Arm; Blaise de Montluc (1503–77), a military governor; Agrippa d'Aubigné; Pierre de Bourdeilles de Brantome (c. 1535–1614), historian; Margaret of Valois (1553–1615), wife of Henry IV; Sully, the great minister; du Bellay, critic and poet.

The Classical Age.—The first part of the 17th century was a period of reform and reorganization—in society, religion, language and literature. Paris became famous for its *salons* soon to be imitated all over Europe. Most famous and productive was the salon of Mme de Rambouillet (1588–1665). All sorts of people congregated there —nobles, fine ladies, princes and princesses, bourgeois authors and artists —and they had a very definite purpose: to refine the language and make it suitable for polite society; to master it as a literary and conversational medium; to give mutual encouragement and criticism. Later this movement was carried too far, especially in the provincial salons outside Paris, and resulted in the *précieux* (fantastic, strained) literature, so elegant and filled with such pretentious phrases that it became ridiculous and fair prey for Molière's wit. On the whole the influence of the salons was beneficial and produced a remarkably varied literature—sonnets, letters, word portraits, madrigals and almost every other type of lyric poetry, besides the pastoral romances showing Italian influence. The novels of Mlle de Scudéry (1607–1701) are impossibly long and filled with heroic and incredible adventures. The *Astrée* by Honoré d'Urfé (1568–1625) is a long account of an idealized pastoral community on the banks of a lovely river. Its people are cultured shepherds and shepherdesses, given to involved amorous and literary discussion. The style is rich and ornate but clear.

Inevitable reaction and satire were supplied by the realistic novels of Paul Scarron (1610–60) and Antoine Furetière (1619–88). The coarseness and crudity of their style well illustrates the debt French literature owes to the salons. More formal and exact reform was brought about by François de Malherbe (1555–1628), a disciple of Ronsard, who defined the different forms of literature and gave rules for their execution. His own poetry is eloquent and correct but a little cold. The founding of the French Academy (the most famous cultural society in the world) by Cardinal Richelieu in 1635 marked the beginning of the great age of French classicism.

Outside the main literary streams but influential was the reform within Catholicism itself, particularly the Jansenist movement that soon incurred the hatred of the Jesuits and emphasized the necessity of divine grace because men cannot be masters of their emotions. Blaise Pascal (1623–62), a mathematical wizard when still very young, later became a Jansenist and in his *Lettres écrites à un provincial* ("Provincial Letters") and *Pensées* ("Thoughts") he did most to strengthen and make immortal their cause. The polished perfection of his irony and the beauty of his style are highly important in the development of French literature. In his emphasis on the insignificance of man and the limitations of his reasoning powers he was directly opposed to another great mathematician, René Descartes (1596–1650) and his followers, known as Cartesians. Starting from the famous phrase *Je pense, donc je suis* ("I think; therefore I am"), Descartes came to the conclusion that a man is no more than his thought and that a man's reason is necessarily truth—notions that greatly affected French literature especially in the 18th century.

In 1661 Louis XIV started his personal rule. At his court in Paris and later at Versailles he gathered about him poets, orators, dramatists, artists and musicians and almost the entire nobility of France. Under his benevolence French classicism, based on the theories and plays of classical Greek and Rome but national in interpretation and universal in truth, reached its greatest glory. The French interpretation of the three unities, as perfected in this century, had a tremendous and often stifling influence upon the drama not only of France but also of Germany and Spain. The great French dramatists themselves—Corneille, Racine and Molière—did not always attain the ideal—that the action of the play be confined to 24 hours, that there be little or no change of scene, and that the plot be continuous and single. Pierre Corneille (1606–84) founded classical poetic tragedy with the *Cid* (1636), which, although it was criticized by the Academy for not perfectly obeying the three unities, has these characteristic traits—exclusion of the comic, forceful psychological analysis, clarity and nobility of style and a logical and simple plot whose climax results from the characters' own thoughts and actions. *Horace* (1639 or '40), *Cinna* (1640) and *Polyeucte* (1643) followed, all showing the triumph of will power over emotion. Corneille's comedy *Le Menteur* (1643) is witty and amusing, but his other tragedies do not measure up to the four just mentioned.

Jean Baptiste Racine (1639–99) brought French tragedy to its fullest perfection. His characters are more human and lovable than Corneille's and his poetry more harmonious. His first great tragedy *Andromaque* appeared in 1667 and was followed in 1668 by his only comedy *Les Plaideurs*. The historical plays *Brittannicus* (1669), *Bérénice* (1670), *Bajazet* (1672) and *Mithridate* (1673) are based on Roman, Near Eastern and Persian history. His *Iphigénie* (1674) and *Phèdre* (1677) have subjects from Greek tragedy, particularly Eu-

ripides. Racine became more and more interested in the Jansenist movement and after 12 years of dramatic inactivity wrote the two religious plays *Esther* (1689) and *Athalie* (1691).

Molière (real name, Jean Baptiste Poquelin; 1622–73) is perhaps the greatest comic dramatist in the history of the world. His portrayals of men and women and their faults and virtues are as true and applicable today as they were nearly three centuries ago. Some of his plays, like *Tartuffe*, the study of a religious hypocrite, and *Le Misanthrope* come very close to tragedy but it was Molière's genius to see and emphasize the ridiculous, using laughter as a corrective. An actor himself, Molière was for 12 years the director of a troupe of strolling comedians. His *Les Précieuses ridicules*, making fun of the elegant affectations of the time, was played in Paris in 1659 and won for him the favor and support of Louis XIV. His greatest plays in verse are *Tartuffe* (1664), *Le Misanthrope* (1666) and *Les Femmes savantes* (1672), which last criticises pedantry by showing the hilarious results of a smattering of education. In prose his greatest works are *L'École des femmes* (1662), *Le Festin de Pierre* based on the Spanish character, Don Juan (1665), *L'Avare* (1668), *Le Bourgeois gentilhomme* (1670) and *Le Malade imaginaire* ("The Imaginary Invalid," 1673). He died immediately after playing the title role in this final play. Molière was an accurate observer, a master of his art and rich in common sense.

Jean de la Fontaine (1621–95) in his poetic *Contes* and *Fables* is unique and perfect. Like Molière he had a grand sense of humor but a touch of

NEW YORK PUBLIC LIBRARY

JEAN RACINE, from an engraving by J. Daulle Gr. du Roy, made in 1762.

bitterness and scepticism. The *Fables* have become children's classics, though only an adult can derive full enjoyment and meaning from these enchanting tales so perfectly expressed.

French classicism is not entirely dependent upon poetry for its glory. The short novel *La Princesse de Clèves* by Marie Madeleine de Lafayette (1634–92) is a charming analysis of a woman's heart, the first in French literature to consider true love rather than its fanciful idealization. It is truly classic in brevity, clarity and unity of action. The letters of Mme de Sévigné (1626–96) are models of prose composition and give an accurate and human picture of the court of Louis XIV and other aspects of 17th-century society. The *Sentences et Maximes Morales* of La Rochefoucauld (1613–80) are striking in their originality, conciseness and wit; bitter and pessimistic in their satire. The Cardinal de Retz (1614–79) led an exciting and dangerous life as an enemy of Mazarin and because he was ambitious in his own behalf. His memoirs reveal a lively and interesting though complicated style. Jean de La Bruyère (1645–96), a Parisian bourgeois and tutor of the duke of Bourbon, in his *Caractères* (1688) wrote brief, often satirical, character sketches of prominent types, describing in a few chosen phrases an entire personality. The charming fairy stories of Charles Perrault (1628–1703) are still children's classics.

Magnificent sermons and funeral orations were delivered by Bossuet (1627–1704), who dared put into them scathing criticism of the nobles and their customs and at times even of the king. For his pupil, the young heir to the throne, he wrote the remarkable *Discours sur l'histoire universelle*. Fénelon (1651–1715), also a religious orator, wrote for his pupil, the duke of Burgundy, the educational and utopian novel *Télémaque* (1699). Fléchier (1632–1710), Bourdaloue (1632–1704), Mascaron (1634–1703) and Massillon (1663–1742) also helped to make religious oratory a significant manifestation of the century.

Nicolas Boileau-Despréaux (1636–1711) formulated the classical ideal—literature should be natural, reasonable, truthful—in *L'Art Poétique* (1674), but his own short poems and the longer mock-heroic poem *Le Lutrin* (1674) are of doubtful value.

From 1685 to 1715 came repeated signs of the breakup of the classical ideal. The French version of the Italian quarrel between the ancients and the moderns raged bitterly, headed by Boileau and Perrault, respectively. Fénelon had severely criticized the absolute monarchy that had done so much to make classicism possible. La Bruyère, Saint-Simon (1675–1755) and Le Sage (1668–1747) were ruthless in their attacks on the contemporary top-heavy setup of society with almost the entire nobility dependent on the monarchy for support. The memoirs of the duke de Saint-Simon, particularly concerned with the final years and the death of Louis XIV, are among the best in a literature rich in memoirs. In the interests of free thought and the broader spread of knowledge, Pierre Bayle (1647–1706) compiled his dictionary, a forerunner of the 18th-century encyclopedias, and Bernard de Fontenelle (1657–1757) started the task of making science fashionable. When Louis XIV died in 1715, French had become an almost universal language, and French dress, manners and art were imitated in every corner of the civilized world.

The Age of Enlightenment, 1715–89.— French literature of the 18th century, compared with the preceding high eloquence and nobility of thought and poetry, was sensible, sceptical and scientific. The philosophy of Descartes gained ascendancy over that of Pascal. The salons were more formally literary. The influence of the Englishmen Newton, Locke and Richardson was strong, and toward the close of the period German literature with its philosophical and historical overtones began to make itself felt in France.

Though they did not want it, the philosophers and historians of the 18th century made the Revolution possible. The two greatest men of the century—Voltaire and Rousseau—present an amazing contrast in personality and thought. François Marie Arouet de Voltaire (1694–1778) had a long and eventful life, part of it spent in prison and part in exile in England. His writings, with a few brilliant exceptions—*Zadig, Candide,* the tragedies *Zaïre* and *Mérope,* parts of his *Dictionnaire philosophique* and some of his *lettres philosophiques*—are seldom read today; but Voltaire's prestige and influence in 18th-century France was enormous. He was considered then a great dramatist and a great poet, worthy successor of the French Classic writers; but he is remembered today for sharp satire, impassioned pleas for political, literary and religious freedom, his bitter fight against all forms of fanaticism, his belief in science and reason, his introduction of English scientific thought and his magnificent attempts to bring these matters to the attention of the whole French people. His histories, particularly *Siècle de Louis XIV,* attained immense popular success that has to some extent survived. His prose is clear, trenchant and witty.

If Voltaire was the fullest and most perfect expression of his own century, Jean Jacques Rousseau (1712–78) was the parent of the future. In the *Contrat Social* (1762) he gives his theory of government—that in the long ago men banded together and of their own free will delegated authority to one of their number to act as representative of the state; therefore the monarchy is not of divine origin but a gift of the people. In *Émile, ou De l'Éducation* (1762), a long treatise novel, he introduces revolutionary ideas of education—succinctly that a child should be truly the child of nature, should grow and learn from the inside and not have learning plastered upon him from the outside. Though some of Rousseau's ideas were exaggerated and impracticable, his work marks the beginning of modern educational methods.

That the whole trend of the century was toward popular enlightenment and the spread of knowledge is evident in the success of the encyclopedists, led by Denis Diderot (1713–84) and d'Alembert (1717–83), whose works plainly prove their desire to reform church and state. Charles de Montesquieu (1689–1755) wanted to make actual laws (not ideal ones—in contrast to Rousseau) understandable to the people in his *Esprit des Lois* ("Spirit of the Laws"). His *Lettres persanes* are admirable and witty comments on contemporary morals and politics. The *Natural History* of Georges de Buffon (1707–88), in accordance with the spirit of the times, is both scientific and literary.

Eighteenth-century drama was far behind that of the preceding century. Voltaire essayed tragedy and many of his plays won immediate popular success. Diderot has been called a miniature Racine. Comedy was more successful in the hands of Marivaux (1688–1763), author of the charming *Jeu de l'Amour et du Hasard* ("Game of Love and Chance"), and in those of Beaumarchais (1732–99), who created the amazing servant, Figaro, in *Le Barbier de Séville* and *Le Mariage de Figaro,* plays influential as propaganda for the Revolution. The work of the only great lyric poet of the period, André de Chénier (1762–94), shows a renewal of interest in Greek antiquity—a movement evident also in painting and sculpture.

In contrast to drama and poetry, the novel showed definite improvement. *Gil Blas* by Alain René Le Sage (1668–1747), though long and episodic, is a dramatic and effective satire whose hero resembles the Spanish picaro, a clever rogue forced to live by his wits and not too particular about his methods. The novels of Marivaux, especially *La Vie de Marianne* (1731–40; in eleven parts), like his plays are first of all entertaining and they also have an elaborate analysis of sentiment. From his name a French noun *marivaudage* has been formed to mean artificially witty and sentimental. *Manon Lescaut* by the Abbé Prévost (1697–1763) is something new in French literature as it succeeds in successfully combining the portrayal of strong passion with full recognition and analysis of actual problems and necessities of everyday life. Signs of a new age became apparent in Rousseau's long novel *Julie, ou la Nouvelle Héloïse* (1760) and in the short *Paul et Virginie* by Bernardin de Saint-Pierre (1737–1814). Rousseau imitated the English novelist Richardson by composing a novel entirely of letters, but he was entirely original in his real love for nature and in his belief that primitive man was good and had been corrupted only through his contact with society. This love of nature and passion for the primitive coupled with his belief in the importance of personal ideas and emotions (as seen in his autobiographical *Confessions*) made him the father of the coming romantic movement. *Paul et Virginie* emphasizes the goodness of nature and of those who grow up with it and adds a new note—interest in the exotic.

Literature during the Revolution and the First Empire was largely confined to oratory (Mirabeau, Danton, Napoleon) and militant journalism (Camille Desmoulins). In 1792 Rouget de Lisle (1760–1836) wrote *La Marseillaise,* the stirring song that became the French national anthem.

Romanticism, 1800–1850.—French romanticism was the result of many influences—a new France created by the Revolution and the Empire, greater knowledge of foreign lands and peoples, the personal influence of Rousseau, contact with German, English, medieval and Oriental literatures and rebellion against the impersonal and regulated art of the 17th century and the rationalism of the 18th century. Its effect on French literature was that of a strong tonic, though its truest representatives were the sentimental *enfants du siècle* (children of the century), who felt themselves lost in a new world. François René de Chateaubriand (1768–1848) in creative writing and Mme de Staël (1766–1817) in criticism and theory were the predecessors of the great romantic heyday (1820–50). Chateaubriand opened up a new road in his beautiful and almost poetic descriptions of nature, in his attempt to replace reason by faith and in his oversentimental unhappiness and discontent with himself and the world. His principal works are *Le Génie du christianisme* (1802), with its delightful American episodes published separately, *Atala* (1801) and *René* (1802), *Les Martyrs* (1809), *Les Natchez* (1826), also laid in America, and *Mémoires d'Outre-tombe* ("Memories from beyond the Grave," 1849–50), personal recollections.

Mme de Staël in her two most famous critical essays *De la Littérature* (1800) and *De l'Allemagne* (1813) called the attention of French writers and thinkers to German Literature, which had reached a high point under the leadership of Goethe and Schiller. Mme de Staël's own novels are now little read, but her theories opened up new vistas.

With romanticism lyric poetry flourished as it had not since the Middle Ages—in *Méditations* and *Harmonies* by Alphonse de Lamartine (1790–1869), poems filled with a soft melancholy and a love of nature and its solitudes; in *Les Nuits* ("Nights") by Alfred de Musset (1810–57), spontaneous, sincere, passionate; in the collected *Poems* (1837) by Alfred de Vigny (1799–1863), bitter, symbolical, stoically unhappy; and in the many volumes of superb poetry by Victor Marie Hugo (1802–85), whose figure dominated the century in every type of creative writing. All these poets escaped from the restraints of old rules of versification and gave free rein to their personal inspiration, giving fresh and beautiful color to French poetry. Lamartine, Vigny and Hugo also wrote ambitious epics that are often symbolically and eloquently beautiful—Lamartine's *Chute d'un ange,* Vigny's *Le cor* and *Moïse,* Hugo's *La Légende des siècles.* Pierre Jean de Béranger (1780–1857) was a popular and prolific song writer.

The drama also broke its classical

bonds, following the theories of Stendhal (real name, Henri Beyle; 1783–1842) in his *Racine et Shakespeare* (1823) and of Hugo in the preface to his play *Cromwell* (1827). Hugo's dramas show his abilities as a poet rather than as a dramatist, for in his desire to escape from the classical he neglects characterization and inner motivation for rich décor and physical action. Vigny's *Chatterton* (1835) has a romantic hero but is classic in its psychological analysis. Musset, the most vivacious of the *enfants,* is unique for his wholly delightful short comedies. The plays of Alexandre Dumas (1802–70) are lacking in finesse but rich in action and color.

Adolphe (1815) by Benjamin Constant (1767–1830) and *Obermann* (1804) by Étienne de Sénancour (1770–1846) are highly subjective novels in which the authors give their own feelings of love and futility searching analysis. Influenced by Walter Scott and by the general renewed interest

GUSTAVE FLAUBERT

in French history, Vigny wrote a historical novel *Cinq-Mars* (1826), and Hugo the unforgettable *Notre Dame de Paris* (1831).

Vigny also wrote the fine prose sketches *Servitude et grandeur militaires;* Lamartine wrote *Confidences* and the short tale *Graziella;* and Musset contributed *La Confession d'un enfant du siècle* (1835). Alexandre Dumas won the hearts of youth with his thrilling *The Three Musketeers* (1844) and *The Count of Monte-Cristo* (1844). George Sand (Mme Dudevant; 1804–76) after experimenting with other types turned to stories of peasant life, which under her romantic hand became poeticized and lovely. Charles Nodier (1780–1844) and Gérard de Nerval (1808–55) specialized in fantastic and symbolic tales.

Interest in history brought new methods of historical writing. Augustin Thierry (1795–1856) went back whenever possible to original sources and was perhaps the first to do real research. Jules Michelet (1798–1874) brought life and interest to history in his "resurrections of the past."

François Guizot (1787–1874) contributed the exact and philosophical *History of Civilization in Europe* (1828). Henri de Tocqueville (1805–59) visited America and his interesting study of democracy *De La Démocratie en Amérique* (1835–9) resulted. Lamennais (1782–1854) and Lacordaire (1802–61) tried to make catholicism more human and democratic. Edgar Quinet (1803–75), scholar, poet and prophet, also Michelet and Hugo were filled with high hopes for a new age of freedom, equality and happiness for all. Both Quinet and Hugo spent many years in exile for their liberal politics.

On the fringe of the romantic movement is the poetry of Théophile Gautier (1811–72) and the prose of Stendhal, Mérimée and Balzac. Gautier was more interested in form and precision of wording than the romantics. Stendhal, born in Grenoble, Switzerland, from choice spent many years in northern Italy. His two novels, *Le Rouge et le Noir* ("Red and Black," 1830) and *La Chartreuse de Parme* (1839), written in a clear and analytical style, are fast-moving and accurate in characterization. Prosper Mérimée (1803–70), sophisticated and accomplished, is remembered for his short stories, particularly *Carmen,* the basis of Bizet's opera of that title, and *Colomba,* a story of Corsican honor; all are moving and colorful in their well-written perfection. Honoré de Balzac (1799–1850) takes his place with Hugo and Flaubert as one of the great novelists of the century. His ambitious scheme for a *Comédie humaine* (his title for his combined works) to cover all the aspects of contemporary French life was almost carried out. His novels are filled with strong three-dimensional life and his people seem actual acquaintances that are met time and again in the various novels. His portrayals of provincial and middle or lower-class Parisian life are best: *Eugénie Grandet, Le Père Goriot, La Cousine Bette.*

Realism and Naturalism, 1850–90.—The Revolution of 1848 and the overthrow of the Second Republic in 1852 brought despair to the utopian hopes of the romantics and ushered in a new generation of authors. Auguste Comte (1798–1857) built a constructive philosophy out of natural science and introduced a new science considered most important of all—sociology. In the *Histoire des origines du Christianisme,* including the *Vie de Jésus,* Ernest Renan (1823–92) showed the effect of a combined religious and scientific training. He sought to explain religion logically without detracting from its spiritual qualities. Hippolyte Taine (1828–93) gave impetus to the naturalist movement in literature by his definition of man as a mass of sensations and impressions capable only of putting together and explaining the single natural facts of his experience. In his *L'Histoire de la littérature anglaise* (1864) he made man a product solely of his race, time and environment.

Everywhere science was praised and practiced—Darwin was widely discussed; Claude Bernard (1813–78)

in physiology and Louis Pasteur (1822–95) in bacteriology made great strides forward in the fight against disease. In criticism Sainte-Beuve (1804–69) was master; his study of Port-Royal, home of the Jansenist movement, and his essays, *Causeries du lundi,* show his interest in personalities and in the relation of literature to social facts; they also reveal a keen discernment and a finished style. The fruits of all this philosophical and scientific activity were evident in poetry, drama, the novel and the short story.

The Parnassian school in poetry, so called from Mount Parnassus, legendary home of Apollo and the Muses, emphasized precision in form and vocabulary, restraint and accuracy in detail and analysis rather than confession of emotion. Illustrative of these ideals is the poetry of Leconte de Lisle (1818–94), José Maria de Heredia (1842–1905) and Sully Prudhomme (1839–1907). The genius of Charles Baudelaire (1821–67) was not fully recognized before his death. Influenced strongly by Edgar Allan Poe, Baudelaire in turn had an enormous influence upon modern poetry. His *Les Fleurs du mal* (1857; "Flowers of Evil") was beautifully translated by George Dillon and Edna St. Vincent Millay in 1936.

The theater showed a growing tendency to portray reality without any softening or idealization—in the comedies of bourgeois life by Émile Augier (1820–89) and in the social drama, still somewhat romantic in the plays of Alexandre Dumas, Fils (*La Dame aux camélias* ("Camille"); but bitterly realistic in those of Henri Becque (1837–99). Of less importance are A. E. Scribe (1791–1861) said to have created modern vaudeville, and Victorien Sardou (1831–1908), remembered for *Madame Sans Gene* (1893). Eugène Labiche (1815–88) leavened his fantasies with bits of good sense and is still beloved for *Le Voyage de M. Perrichon* (1860). The operas of Jacques Offenbach (1819–80) with librettos by Henri Meilhac (1831–97) and Ludovic Halévy (1834–1908) were original expressions of the Second Empire (1852–70).

In the novel Gustave Flaubert (1821–80) firmly established realism in *Madame Bovary* (1856) and *L'Education sentimentale* (1869), where he attempts and achieves accurate reproduction of what might really have happened, attaining a remarkable compromise between art and truth. His style is clear and precise, for each word was chosen with the greatest care. That Flaubert had another, more romantic, side is evident in *La Tentation de Saint Antoine* and *Salammbô* (a story of ancient Carthage), filled with the richness of his vocabulary and imagination.

Realism soon concentrated on the unpleasant and depressing sides of life and became what is called *naturalism.* Guy de Maupassant (1850–93), a disciple of Flaubert, brought to his short stories complete objectivity, sincere observation, exactitude in description and a never-failing knowledge of the possibilities and limitations of his medium. He is the master short-story writer of French literature. Alphonse Daudet (1840-97) in his novels attacking contemporary society was more spontaneous and personal. His delightful series on *Tartarin de Tarascon* shows that laughter had not disappeared from French letters. Jules (1830-70) and Edmond Goncourt (1822-96) carried naturalism to its logical end, attempting to construct novels entirely from firsthand observation or experience. They also aroused interest in 18th-century France and in Japanese culture.

Emile Zola (1840-1902), the most important naturalist, wrote a series of twenty novels, tracing a family through five generations. The most famous of these is *Germinal*. Joris Karl Huysmans (1848-1907), was influenced by Zola; his tormented tone and concern with the supernatural are personal, however. His works reflect nineteenth-century intellectual life.

Standing in sharp contrast to the theories and practice of the realists was still the figure of Victor Hugo. Two volumes of poetry *Les Contemplations* (1856) and *Les Châtiments* (1853) contain some of the loveliest lyrics in the French language and *Les Miserables* (1862) is the crowning achievement of the romantic novel. Hugo, a popular but not a profound philosopher and thinker, was a complete master of language. His death in 1885 was an occasion of national sorrow. He was greatly influenced by English thought, and Swinburne and other English revolutionaries adored him.

Modern Movements.—The discouragement and disillusionment that followed the Franco-Prussian War of 1870-71 and a decline in material prosperity brought a new type of literature and an almost complete abandonment of the old realism based upon worship of science. Foreign influences were strong—Freud, Wagner, Nietzsche, Tolstoy and Dostoevski all left their imprints upon French literature. There was a revival of music and of conversation in salons reminiscent of the 17th century. The influence of Pascal emphasizing human life and faith finally replaced that of Descartes. Henri Bergson (1859-1941), who received the Nobel Prize in 1927, denied that science was all-powerful. He emphasized intuition and belief and gave art a new purpose, the expression of intuition and instinct. Bergson's influence was great and particularly noticeable in the revival of Catholicism, featured by many dramatic conversions. Literary and dramatic criticism flourished in the hands of Francisque Sarcey (1828-99), Ferdinand Brunetière (1849-1906), Jules Lemaitre (1853-1914), Gustave Lanson (1857-1934) and Julien Benda (1867-1956).

In poetry the symbolists—Stéphane Mallarmé (1842-98), Paul Verlaine (1844-96), Jean Arthur Rimbaud (1854-91)—abandoned conventional syntax and meters for more personal expression. Their poetry is essentially vague, fluid, musical, often abstract and filled with veiled symbols. Their successors are Émile Verhaeren (1855-1916), Henri de Régnier (1864-1936), the Comtesse de Noailles (1876-1933), Paul Claudel (1868-1955) and Paul Valéry (1871-1945). Claudel, an ardent Catholic and essentially mystic, sought a hidden reality. Valéry's poetry is purely intellectual; he seems to sit apart from a physical world and set himself word problems in space. In 1920 the dadaist movement denied everything because it felt incapable of solving anything. It was essentially an outgrowth of World War I and could not last long. Poets turned again to symbolism and Catholicism, and, as with Jean Cocteau (1891-1963), to a new classicism.

Drama turned from its preoccupation with bourgeois life and customs to the poetic fancies of Edmond Rostand (1868-1918), beloved for *Cyrano*

PHILIPPE HALSMAN

ANDRÉ GIDE

de Bergerac, L'Aiglon and *Chantecler;* and of Maurice Maeterlinck (1862-1949), Belgian poet and philosopher and winner of the Nobel Prize in 1911. Claudel wrote mystic and symbolic plays like *L'annonce faite à Marie* ("Tidings Brought to Mary," 1912). François de Curel (1854-1928) in *Terre inhumaine* and Eugène Brieux (1858-1932) in *La Robe rouge* (1900) and *Maternité* (1904) contributed to the drama of ideas. Georges de Porto-Riche (1849-1930) and Henri René Lenormand (1882-1951) investigated psychological motives and effects. Jean Giraudoux (1882-1944) wrote witty and striking fantasy in *Amphitryon 38* (1929) and *La Guerre de Troie n'aura pas lieu* ("The Trojan War Shall not Take Place," 1935).

The novel was the most important literary form in both quantity and quality. Subject matter divides roughly into interest in customs—Parisian, provincial and foreign—and interest in psychology and analysis. Form varies from the soft fluidity of Pierre Loti and the musical sensitiveness of Proust to the exotic brilliance of Giraudoux, and the classical restraint and clarity of Gide.

Pierre Loti (real name, Julien Viaud; 1850-1923), a naval officer, wrote naturally and easily of the far corners of France and the world, putting into his style and his books an elusive melancholy, an inescapable feeling of the passing of time and the instability of all earthly things. The Tharaud brothers, Pierre Benoît, Paul Morand and others write of little-known places and people, describing them carefully but with enthusiasm. Pierre MacOrlan and Giraudoux pass swiftly from the land of reality to that of fantasy and back again. The poor and often ugly sides of life are forcefully scrawled in the work of André Chamson, Pierre Hamp and Henri Barbusse, whose books on the war are brutal in their very truth. Charles Péguy (born a peasant) was at once an ardent Catholic and an ardent socialist and filled his writing with force and purpose. Paul Bourget, Maurice Barrès and Edouard Estaunié evidence the continuation of the tradition of careful analysis and discussion.

François Mauriac and André Maurois (best known in America for his biography of Shelley, *Ariel*, 1923), and the American-born Julien Green are interested in emotions, feelings and thoughts rather than external or physical action. Mauriac tries sincerely to portray the essential evil at the heart of man, evil that only true religion can overcome. Sidonie Gabrielle Colette, in a rich and concentrated prose, analyzes her own thoughts and feelings. The prose of Francis Jammes is highly poetical and filled with subtle music. His subject matter and characters are treated with sympathy and understanding. Master in analysis and presentation of the unconscious and subconscious whims of the mind was Marcel Proust (1871-1922) in the novels making up his *A la recherche du temps perdu* "Remembrance of Things Past"). His prose is intricate, beautiful and unique in all literature.

Anatole France (real name, Jacques Anatole Thibault; 1844-1924), sceptical and mocking, was the literary giant of the early 20th century. He pointed out the inconsistencies and failures of government and religion, brought high-flown ideals crashing to earth. In 1921 he received the Nobel Prize.

Romain Rolland (1866-1940), pacifist and idealist, is known for his *Jean Christophe* series. Jules Romains (1885–   ), in his series entitled *Les Hommes de bonne volonte (Men of Good Will)*, produced silhouettes of the soul of Paris. Other significant novelists include André Gide (1869-1951), 1947 Nobel Prize winner; art critic André Malraux; Antoine de Saint-Exupery; and Francoise Sagan.

The most important movement in French letters since World War II revolves around Existentialism, the main representative of which is Jean-Paul Sartre. Sartre's *L'etre et le néant (Being and Nothingness)*, contains the philosophical beliefs embodied in his novels, particularly in *La Nausée (Nausea)*, and his plays: *Les Mouches (The Flies)* and *Huis clos (No Exit)*. Simone de Beauvoir shares Sartre's views and has written the ethical counterpart to his ontological work, *The Ethics of Ambiguity*, as well as several novels. Albert Camus, who disavowed the label of "existentialist," has nevertheless contributed significantly with *L'Etranger (The Stranger)*, *La Peste (The Plague)*, and *Le Mythe de Sisiphe (The Myth of Sisyphis)*.

French drama is represented by the innovating figures of Jean Genet, Giraudoux, Cocteau, Paul Claudel and Samuel Beckett.

GERMAN LITERATURE

Old High German Period, to 1100.—Before 800 the most famous evidence of early Teutonic speech is the Bible translations in Gothic made by Ulfilas (c. 311–381), bishop of the Goths. Poetry and song were present but were not written. Out of the *Völkerwanderung* (migration of peoples) in the 5th century came a whole series of epics, filled with mythological characters and superb heroes. The oldest saga of which there are written records (c. 800) is the *Hildebrandslied* ("Lay of Hildebrand"). Encouraged by Charlemagne, the monasteries produced Christian poetry in German as well as in Latin. The *Heliand* ("Saviour") and the *Gospel Book* of Otfried (c. 810–c. 880) were versions of the life of Christ; the *Gospel Book* was the first in which rhyme appears. Also from the monasteries came the Wessobrunn Prayer; *Muspilli*, a description of Judgment Day; and the *Ludwigslied*, a historical ballad. Other works from the cloisters and courts though written in Latin are German in thought and feeling: the *Waltharilied*, a short epic by Ekkehard of St. Gall; the moralizing dramas of Roswitha (c. 932–1002), a nun of Gandersheim, written to replace the pagan plays of Terence; the *Ruodlieb*, oldest chivalric romance in Germany; and *Ecbasis Captivi* ("The Flight of the Captive"), the first animal epic, featuring the fox, wolf, bear and other creatures, a type of literature popular throughout the Middle Ages and forerunner of the famous French *Roman de Renart* and the fables of La Fontaine.

Middle High German Period, 1100–1350.—In the 12th and 13th centuries contemporary with the powerful Hohenstaufen emperors came the first great period of German literature. Chivalry was at its height—characterized by tournaments, idealization of women, a new concept of love (*Minne*) and all the adventurous ideas brought back by the crusaders. The poet priests and monks were rivaled by wandering lay musicians who produced *König Rother* (c.1160), the *Alexanderlied* (c. 1130) and *Herzog Ernst* (c. 1180). New epics grew up—about Dietrich von Bern (Theodoric the Great) and Charlemagne, and about mythical heroes like Gudrun, Siegfried and Percival. To folk poetry belong the greatest of them all, the *Nibelungenlied* (c. 1200), a masterful mixture of old hero stories, both pagan and Christian; and the *Gudrunlied*, which combines a number of Scandinavian legends and probably belongs to the same cycle as *Beowulf*, presenting a graphic picture of the life of the early vikings.

In the court poetry the influence of French epics and French ideals of chivalry is evident. *Der arme Heinrich* by Hartmann von Aue (c. 1170–c. 1210) is the finest in style. Wolfram von Eschenbach (1170–1220) wrote *Parzival*, a mystical epic of Percival, count of the Grail. Gottfried von Strassburg wrote *Tristan*, the lovely and tragic story of Tristan and Isolde that has been treated time and again in German, French and English literature. In the *Minnesang* (lyric poetry) Walther von der Vogelweide (c. 1170–c. 1228) was master, the best German lyricist before Goethe and the first national poet, singing of church and emperor, of winter and spring and of beautiful women. Legends based on the superstitions and beliefs of the Middle Ages sprang up—legends of the saints, of a Wandering Jew, of a Dr. Faustus.

Transition Period, the Reformation and the Renaissance, 1350–1700.—With the growth of towns and the middle class, the old heroic and chivalric epics were out of touch with the times. Parodies, elaborate allegories and satires became popular; but the form of literature that was to be the favorite of the people for centuries was the *Volksbucher*, prose versions of the old tales.

Drama emerged slowly from its religious connections. In the latter part of the 15th and early 16th centuries the *Minnesang* became the *Meistergesang* (song of the masters), poetry that was taught in schools and written according to strict rules in contrast to the freedom of rhythm and thought that characterized the *Minnesang*. Hans Sachs (1494–1576), a Nürnberg cobbler, the greatest and most prolific of the Meistersinger, is celebrated in Wagner's opera of the same name; but the true vitality of the age lay in the folk poetry that included songs on every subject—war, love, spring—also hymns and fanciful ballads. In prose the animal fables and epics and short humorous anecdotes found high favor. Best and most telling of the humorous satires is the *Narrenschiff* ("Ship of Fools") by Sebastian Brant (1457–1521). In the same century universities were founded in Prague, Vienna, Heidelberg, Erfurt.

The atmosphere that made the Reformation possible resulted mostly from the activities of the mystics and the humanists. Meister Eckhart (c. 1260–1327) proclaimed the mystical relations of the soul to God and the necessity of individual interpretation of religion. Although most of their writings were in Latin, the humanists were influential because they, too, emphasized the value of the individual. Martin Luther (1483–1546), joining the fervor of mysticism with the learning of humanism, posted his theses against indulgences on the door of the Castle Church of Wittenberg in 1517, inaugurating the Reformation. The movement thus started by Luther inspired much written argument and satire. Luther himself did most to give form and unity to the German language in his translation of the Bible, a work whose influence on the German literature and language is comparable to the influence of the King James Bible upon English. His hymns, too, won world-wide recognition and are still widely sung in Protestant churches. Ulrich von Hutten (1488–1523), a knight of Franconia, and Philipp Melanchthon (1497–1560), both humanists, turned their learning to the service of the Reformation. Thomas Murner (1475–1537), a Franciscan monk of Strasbourg, attacked Luther in his bitter satire *On The Great Lutheran Fool* (1522). Johann Fischart, a satirist almost Murner's equal in power, defended the Reformation and achieved fame through his German version of Rabelais' satire on French manners and customs. Toward the end of the 16th century English comedians introduced English plays into Germany, giving the theater there a fresh impulse. The national spirit hardly had time to assert itself before it was swept away by the Latin imitations of the Renaissance and the disaster of the Thirty Years' War.

The most important influence of the period that followed was Martin Opitz (1597–1639), a Silesian whose *Buch von der deutschen Poeterey* ("Book of German Poetry," 1624) formulated rules observed with little variation for a hundred years and did for the German language what Ronsard and the Pléiade had done for French. Literary societies were formed to purify and regulate the language. Paulus Gerhardt (1607–76), a great preacher and hymn writer, escaped from this tightening influence and like Luther modeled his hymns on the popular ballads. Andreas Gryphius (1616–64), the best German dramatist of the 17th century, was strongly influenced, particularly in his tragedies, by Seneca and the stiff Dutch plays of Hooft and Vondel. His comedy, *Herr Peter Squentz*, reminiscent of *A Midsummer Night's Dream*, is fresher and more interesting than are his tragedies.

In the novel, French and Spanish influences were strong. Comparable to the Spanish *Lazarillo de Tormes* and the later French *Gil Blas* was *Der abenteurliche Simplicissimus* ("Adventurous Booby," 1669) by H. J. Christoffel von Grimmelshausen (c. 1620–76), dealing with the turbulent time of the Thirty Years' War. Near the end of the Renaissance, Gottfried Wilhelm Leibnitz (1646–1716), the first great German philosopher, foreshadowed the great period that was to come.

Die Blütezeit (Flowering Age, 1700–1832).—After the devastation of the Thirty Years' War had in some measure been forgotten, a new feeling of nationalism and unity was inspired by common pride in Frederick the Great. In literature the struggle between those who emphasized form and adherence to rules after the manner of the French 17th-century writers and those who insisted upon the importance of content and poetic inspiration ushered in the new age.

Johann Christoph Gottsched (1700–66) in his *Kritische Dichtkunst* ("Critical Art of Poesy," 1730) attempted to set up new standards based on French classicism that was itself an attempt to imitate Greek models. The Swiss poets J. J. Bodmer and J. J. Breitinger emphasized instead English models and medieval German poetry. With the appearance of the epic *Der Messias* ("The Messiah") by F. G. Klopstock (1724–1803), German literature definitely found itself. Klopstock's epic and his *Odes* show the strong influence of Milton and of Macpherson's *Poems of Ossian* and effectively introduce again into German literature feeling, melody and the love of nature and of country. Albrecht von Haller (1708–77) in *Die Alpen* (1734) and E. C. von Kleist (1777–1811) in *Der Frühling* (1749) followed his example. J. J. Winckelmann (1717–68) in *History of Ancient Art* (1764) gave impetus to a new classical movement based upon Greek rather than French art.

GOTTHOLD EPHRAIM LESSING (1729–81) in *Hamburgische Dramaturgie* (1767–8) counseled the switch of attention from the French stage to Shakespeare and German folk drama and himself furnished models for a new German drama—particularly *Minna von Barnhelm* (1767), a new ideal of domestic comedy; *Emilia Galotti* (1772), a new type of national tragedy; and *Nathan der Weise* (1779), an imperishable evangel of brotherhood and religious toleration. He established the use of the iambic pentameter in poetic drama and in *Laokoon* (1766) introduced a new method of art criticism.

IMMANUEL KANT (1724–1804) superbly carried on the philosophic tradition started by Leibnitz. In his *Critique of Pure Reason* (1781) Kant substituted critical philosophy for the old dogmatic metaphysics; the *Critique of Practical Reason* (1788) demands obedience to the moral law; and the *Critique of Judgment* (1790) lays the foundations of modern esthetics. Kant was the inspiration of the transcendentalist movement that so strikingly influenced the group of New England writers led by Ralph Waldo Emerson.

J. G. VON HERDER (1744–1803) was the theorist and apostle of the literary revolution known as the *Sturm und Drang* (storm and stress), whose followers threw aside literary fetters and emphasized the freedom and sacredness of the individual. Attracted to the subject by Rousseau, Herder aroused interest in primitive man and his evolution and recognized and encouraged the best national elements of German literature.

JOHANN WOLFGANG VON GOETHE (1749–1832) and JOHANN CHRISTOPH FRIEDRICH VON SCHILLER (1759–1805) are to German literature what Shakespeare and Milton are to English, Molière to French, Cervantes to Spanish and Dante to Italian. While studying at Strasbourg, Goethe became acquainted with Herder, who interested him in English literature (particu-

larly in Shakespeare) and in the Middle Ages. In the next few years (1772–5) Goethe produced unexcelled examples of the *Sturm und Drang,* including: *Götz von Berlichingen,* a play depicting the struggle of a medieval knight against the new order; *Die Leiden des jungen Werthers* ("Sorrows of Young Werther"), a short novel of disillusionment whose

G. E. LESSING

influence in Germany and France was phenomenal; the *Urfaust,* the first draft of his classic poem, and many perfect lyrics. Schiller wrote dramas filled with symbolism and high ideals. Among these dramas are: *Die Räuber* (1781), *Kabale und Liebe* ("Intrigue and Love," 1784) and *Don Carlos* (1787), composed in iambic blank verse and hinting a departure from the ideals of the *Sturm und Drang.*

In 1775 Goethe was invited to Weimar, and, in the years that followed, this little town became the center of German culture. Herder, C. M. Wieland (tutor of the young heir, Karl August) and later Schiller went there to live. Wieland's interest in medieval Germany was revived by Goethe and Herder, and as a result he wrote *Oberon* (1780), his well-known verse romance. Goethe was soon entrusted with much of the government of the little state and though he wrote very little he became interested in practical affairs and in the arts and sciences, all of which proved useful to him later. On a visit to Italy his understanding and appreciation of Greek classical art deepened and crystallized. *Egmont* (1788) is in the nature of a transition drama; *Iphigenie auf Tauris* (1787) and *Torquato Tasso* (1790) are purely classical. *Wilhelm Meisters Lehrjahre* ("Wilhelm Meister's Apprenticeship"), his greatest novel, also appeared at this time.

While Goethe was governing Weimar, Schiller had become deeply interested in history and in Kant's philosophy; and in 1794, when Goethe and Schiller became close friends, each was able to contribute to the

development of the other. Both wrote masterful ballads. Schiller, urged on by Goethe, turned again with greater surety and power to poetic drama, producing the trilogy *Wallenstein* (1799), *Maria Stuart* (1801), *Die Jungfrau von Orleans* (1802), *Die Braut von Messina* (1803), using a Greek chorus, and *Wilhelm Tell* (1804). Goethe wrote the beautiful pastoral *Hermann und Dorothea* (1798), and once more turned to *Faust,* of which the first part was concluded (1808) only three years after Schiller's death.

The new century brought a new version of *Sturm und Drang* called romanticism, an international phenomenon emphasizing not only the rights of the individual, but patriotism and interest in the Middle Ages. Its philosophers were J. G. Fichte (1762–1814) and F. W. J. von Schelling (1775–1854). A. W. von Schlegel, theorist and critic, contributed a superb translation of Shakespeare. His brother Friedrich von Schlegel wrote the best novel of the romantic school, *Lucinde,* dealing with the limitations of conventional society. Jean Paul Friedrich Richter's novels were highly popular at the time but not of much permanent value. The work of Ludwig Tieck (1773–1853) shows the close connection between the *Sturm und Drang* and romanticism. Heinrich von Kleist and F. L. Zacharias Werner were the best of the poet dramatists. Johann Ludwig Uhland wrote popular ballads, patriotic poems and treatises on German legends. J. von Eichendorf (1788–1857) is remembered for his masterful lyric poems *Wanderlieder* and a gay, picaresque novel *Aus dem Leben eines Taugenichts* ("The Life of a Good-for-nothing"). Goethe alone succeeded in combining classicism and romanticism—in *Dichtung und Wahrheit,* the story of his life, in numerous shorter poems and in *Faust,* the long dramatic poem of a soul that gained redemption through ceaseless striving.

From Goethe to Nietzsche (1832–1900). —The influence of the philosophy of G. W. F. Hegel (1770–1831) now began to replace that of the romantic thinkers, although romantic influence was still felt in the universities, which became productive in philology, history, science and law. The group known as "Young Germany," including Heinrich Heine, Karl F. Gutzkow, Heinrich Laube and others, was formed for political as well as literary reasons. Heine's *Die Harzreise* ("Travels in the Harz Mountains," 1826) and *Buch der Lieder* (1827) still show the romantic influence. Laube gained wide fame as manager of the *Burgtheater* in Vienna. Some of the best prose produced by this group is found in the *Briefe aus Paris* ("Letters from Paris," 1830–33) by Ludwig Börne. Outside this circle the influence of Walter Scott's work resulted in many historical novels, but they were of little lasting value. Besides tragedies, K. L. Immermann wrote *Münchhausen* (1838–9), a novel distinguished for its description of Westphalian peasant life. A. von Platen Hallermund, belonging neither to the romanticists nor to Young Germany, proved himself a master of the sonnet in his

Sonette aus Venedig (1825). Franz Grillparzer (1791–1872), the greatest Austrian dramatist, combined in his plays *Sappho* and *King Ottokar's Rise and Fall* something of both romanticism and classicism. His *Der Traum, ein Leben* has been called an Austrian *Faust.*

The influence of Arthur Schopenhauer (1788–1860) and his philosophic pessimism was quickly felt and as the century progressed that influence gathered increasing force and became evident in the work of Germany's outstanding poetess Annette von Droste-Hülshoff (1797–1848), in the poetry of the Austrian Nikolaus Lenau (1802–50), and in the changing subject matter of the novel and the drama. Social and political problems were treated by Friedrich Spielhagen (1829–1911) and by Gustave Freytag (1816–95). Freytag's comedy *Die Journalisten* (1852) is one of the best in modern German; and his novel *Soll und Haben* ("Debit and Credit," 1855) sets forth the virtues of the German merchant class as contrasted with those of the nobility.

Friedrich Hebbel (1813–63) introduced psychological motives and understanding into the drama; and Otto Ludwig in *Der Erbförster* ("Hereditary Forester," 1850) foreshadows later realism. The provincial novel that had its fling in all the civilized countries of the world was well represented in Germany by Berthold Auerbach, poet of the Swabian Black Forest; by Fritz Reuter, a Meklenburg poet, writing in the Low German of the North; by Theodor Storm in his novels of north Germany; by the Swiss poet and novelist Gottfried Keller (whose romantic and autobiographical novel *Der grüne Heinrich* [1854–5] is in the same tradition as Goethe's *Wilhelm Meister*); and by Paul Heyse, long the central figure of the Munich school of poets, in his short stories portraying Italian peasant life. Another manifestation of the same trend was the popular interest in American life and people aroused by the novels of James Fenimore Cooper.

A brilliant interlude in this pessimistic atmosphere and in the shadow of the coming realism was the establishment of a national theater at Bayreuth by Richard Wagner (1813–83). Wagner's music dramas, *Tristan und Isolde, Die Meistersinger von Nürnberg, Der Ring des Nibelungen* and *Parsifal* have never been equaled in the perfect unity of their music and story.

Das Kapital (1867–94) by Karl Marx (1818–83) became a profound influence the world over. Historical science—especially in the work of L. von Ranke (1795–1886)—and literary criticism took on new importance. Schopenhauer's influence was fading and the rout was complete with the advent of Friedrich Wilhelm Nietzsche (1844–1900), who proclaimed once more the power and heroic force of the individual. *Also sprach Zarathustra* ("Thus Spake Zarathustra," 1883–91), his greatest book in prose (he also wrote admirable lyrics), left an indelible impression on the literature and spirit of his time.

ealism and Reaction.—The influence of French and Russian realism, though

ARTHUR SCHOPENHAUER

mild, is noticeable in the work of Wilhelm Raabe (1831–1910); in that of the Austrian Marie von Ebner-Eschenbach (1830–1916); and in a stronger form in the novels and plays of Hermann Sudermann, especially *Frau Sorge* (1887); in the early work of Gerhart Hauptmann (1862–1946), notably the play, *Die Weber* ("The Weavers," 1892); and with a different slant in the plays of Frank Wedekind (1864–1918). Naturalism or intensified realism is evident in Hauptmann's *Fuhrmann Henschel* (1898); in Max Mell's short novel *Barbara Naderer* (1914); and in the poetry of Arno Holz (1863–1929). Almost at once a new movement was evident—authors no longer attempted photographic portrayal of what they saw but gave their subject a personal interpretation, still, however, without any ethical suggestion. Beauty of form and of content was all-important. In poetry Stefan George (1868–1933) attempted to imprison pure sense impressions. *Buddenbrooks* (1901) by Thomas Mann (1875–1955) is a family history and pure realism in the beginning but evolves toward an impressionistic outlook. In his monumental novel *Der Zauberberg* ("The Magic Mountain," 1925) he abandons realism for philo-

sophical speculation. Hauptmann's work reproduced to an amazing extent the changing ideas of his time, which grew more and more symbolic and subjective, becoming a search for true reality beyond the evident reality. Rainer Maria Rilke (1875–1926) in poetry, Franz Werfel (1890–1945) in the play *Das Reich Gottes in Bohmen,* Georg Kaiser (1878–1945) in *Gas* (1918–20) and Ernst Toller (1893–1939) all succeeded in expressing this literary philosophy in dramatic form.

The 20th century is characterized by an enormous amount of experimentation in respect to both form and content. Stefan Zweig (1881–1942) and Emil Ludwig (1881–1948) have written brilliant if not always accurate historical biographies. Jakob Wassermann (1873–1934) emphasized the psychological in such stories as *Caspar Hauser* and *Aufruhr um den Junker Ernst.* The plays of the Austrian Arthur Schnitzler (1862–1931), which show a doctor's interest in the pathological, are at the same time an accurate reflection of Viennese life. Erich Maria Remarque's (1898–) *All Quiet on the Western Front* is starkly realistic.

Franz Kafka (1883–1924), Austrian novelist and short story writer, exerted a strong influence on French authors: Gide, Camus and Sartre. His work, which often depicts anguish, despair, and guilt, is symbolical and has been variously interpreted by different schools of critics. Much of Kafka's work was never completed and a great deal of it published posthumously, including his two most important novels, *Der Prozess* (The Trial) and *Das Schloss* (The Castle). Stories published during his lifetime include "Das Urteil" ("The Judgement") and "Die Verwandlung" ("The Metamorphosis").

Bertolt Brecht (1898–1956) began the "epic theater" movement and contributed a unique theory of theater; this theory emphasized that a psychological distance should be maintained between audience and actor in order that the artificiality of the stage be kept in mind. Brecht's well-known plays include *The Threepenny Opera, Mother Courage, The Caucasian Chalk Circle,* and *The Good Woman of Sezuan.*

ITALIAN LITERATURE

The Latin language dominated Italy long after it had disappeared from the secular life of the rest of Europe. In Italy alone lay schools existed throughout the Middle Ages. In the 11th and 12th centuries wandering minstrels brought songs and stories in the Provençal dialect from southern France; a little later Arthurian romances and tales of antiquity composed in French invaded Italy and stirred Italian poets to emulation. At first they, too, wrote in the popular language of Provence or of France, but finally in the 13th century a few translations and original writings appeared in Italian, the popular everyday language of Italy. The Italian dialects were descended from Latin much as French and Provençal were

descended from Latin. These dialects differed considerably in the various parts of Italy and many centuries passed before Italy attained a single language even for literary use. Lyric poetry flourished in such cities as Venice, Turin, Ferrara and Mantua and in the so-called Sicilian school under the patronage of Frederick II (1194–1250). The subjects were chivalric adventures and the poems were called *Chansons de Geste* (from the French). Many were written in the Tuscan dialect, perhaps the purest descendant of the Latin language and the dialect that gradually became the literary language of all Italy—partly through the political and cultural importance of Florence.

Guido Cavalcanti (d. 1300), a friend

of Dante, was a Florentine poet, mystic and scholar as evidenced in his *Donna mi prega,* a poem on the meaning of love. Cino da Pistoja 1270–1336), too, made love his subject. Brunetto Latini (*c.* 1212–94) reflected the popular interest in allegory in *Tesoretto.* Prose boasted, besides numerous translations, a collection of tales by Francesco Barberini (1264–1348) and the *Composizione del mondo* by Ristoro d'Arezzo (13th century), a discussion of astronomy and geography, which shows surprisingly original observation. The religious revival of the 13th century was most perfectly personified by St. Francis of Assisi (1182–1226), whose exalted piety and love of nature found expression in the religious hymn *Cantico del Sole.* The beautiful stories that grew up about his life became known as the *Little Flowers of Saint Francis.*

Dante, Petrarch, Boccaccio.—The three great writers whose works determined for all time the integrity and fame of the Italian language and literature are Dante Alighieri (1265–1321) in epic poetry, Francesco Petrarch (1304–74) in lyric poetry, particularly the sonnet, and Giovanni Boccaccio (1313–75) in fiction.

Dante was born in Florence and first saw Beatrice Portinari, whom he later glorified as the ideal of womanhood, at the age of nine. He studied at various universities, was a friend of Guido Cavalcanti and a pupil of Brunetto Latini. He was banished from his native city in 1302 and died in exile in Ravenna. Dante's glory springs from the *Vita nuova* ("New Life"), written partly in prose and partly in verse and giving an account of the poet's ethereal love for Beatrice; from the *Convivio* ("Banquet," *c.* 1307), written after the death of Beatrice when the poet sought consolation in philosophy; and most of all from the *Divina Commedia* ("Divine Comedy"), a great epic divided into three parts—Inferno, Purgatorio and Paradiso. Through the first and second of these realms the poet wanders with Vergil (typifying reason) as his guide; through the third the glorified Beatrice conducts him. Into this magnificent work Dante puts his comments on contemporary people and events and his blame or praise of historical characters. It is one of the world's great poems.

Petrarch foreshadowed the Renaissance in his enthusiastic search for original Latin manuscripts and in his masterful imitations and translations of them. Nevertheless, it is not the Latin works of Petrarch but the Italian lyrics that are treasured as a world heritage. What Beatrice was to Dante, Laura was to Petrarch. He composed many sonnets and songs in her honor and these he divided into two groups—*To Laura in Life* and *To Laura in Death.* The series of six allegorical poems called *I trionfi* ("Triumphs") have Laura as their theme but were undoubtedly inspired by Dante's *Divine Comedy.*

Boccaccio developed Italian prose as Dante and Petrarch had developed Italian verse. As a lecturer on Dante, whose biography he wrote, and a friend of Petrarch, Boccaccio was familiar with the best literary traditions of his time, but in contrast to the two great poets his portrayal of women was realistic rather than ideal. His greatest work, the *Decameron,* is a collection of 100 prose stories, ten stories for each of ten days, told by a mixed group who went in 1348 to a villa outside Florence to escape the plague. Boccaccio was a master in the art of story-telling and his book became both the storehouse and the model for many a future writer, especially Chaucer and Shakespeare.

The end of the 14th century and the beginning of the 15th century was on the whole a period of preparation for the glory of the Renaissance. Latin scholars were busy and a new philosophy of living taken from the ancients upset medieval religious ideals and practices.

Leon Battista Alberti (1404–72), though remarkably proficient in Latin and Greek, wrote also in Italian. He was extremely versatile and did good work in painting, music and architecture.

The Role of Literature in the Italian Renaissance.—The interest aroused by Petrarch in the classic Greek and Latin writers had not died, and the work of collecting, translating and studying the old masters assumed tremendous proportions in the 15th century. Academies were founded at Florence, Naples and Rome to carry on the work. In general men of letters were both scholars and creative writers, often artists and statesmen besides. The great literary patron of the age, a poet and scholar in his own right, was Lorenzo de' Medici or Lorenzo the Magnificent (1449–92), prince of Florence. He drew about him at his court a great group of writers, scholars and artists. Perhaps the most brilliant scholar of the age was Angelo Poliziano (1454–94), called Politian in English. His lyric tragedy *Orfeo* and his narrative poem *La Giostra* are brilliant in style and conception; he was the first to use the octave stanza with any success.

Niccolo Machiavelli (1469–1527) wrote numerous books including *Mandragola,* a good comedy of character, and a *History of Florence,* but he is best-known for his realistic studies of political theory *The Prince* and *Discourses on Livy. The Prince* has aptly been called a manual for despots. In it Machiavelli expounds a theory of the nonmoral character of the state and urges that expediency alone be the criterion by which the actions of rulers be judged. Machiavelli's cynical penetration into human character and his profound analysis of the forces that control politics make his work particularly significant today when the nonmoral diplomacy of fascism and *Machtpolitik* is dominant throughout Europe. As Machiavelli outlined the duties of a prince, Baldassare Castiglione (1478–1529) described those of the perfect gentlemen or courtier in the *Libro del Cortegiano.* This courtier is described as extremely versatile and willing to use all his talents in the service of his prince.

Another great historian was Francesco Guicciardini (1483–1540). His account of the period following the death of Lorenzo de' Medici shows great skill in observation and recording. Artists like Benvenuto Cellini (1500–71), Leonarda da Vinci (1452–1519) and Michelangelo (1475–1564) contributed to literature as well as to art—Cellini wrote a famous autobiography; Leonardo wrote on arts and science; and Michangelo's sonnets are famous. Giorgio Vasari (1511–74) left a record of the great creative geniuses of his time in his *Lives of Eminent Artists.* The martyred Dominican preacher, Girolamo Savonarola (1452–98) in his fiery sermons and pamphlets tried to arouse the people against the excesses and pagan spirit of the times. The tales of Matteo Bandello (1480–1562) were later used as source material by English Elizabethan dramatists. Il Lasca (Antonio Grazzini; 1503–84) is remembered for his tales and prose comedies.

Poetry was many-sided and brilliant. Luigi Pulci (1432–84) in *Morgante Maggiore* and Matteo Boiardo (1434–94) in *Orlando innamorato* took material from the old chivalric legends and injected it with satire, humor and 16th-century digressions. Pastoral poetry with its idealized pictures of a simple and calm life attracted many writers, particularly Jacopo Sannazaro (1458–1530) who produced a masterpiece in *Arcadia* (1504). Lyric poetry for the most part followed in the path of Petrarch, and women like Vittoria Colonna (1490–1547) as well as men like the Cardinal Pietro Bembo (1470–1547) tried their hand at it. The first wild excitement of the escape from the rigid theology of the Middle Ages brought a weakening of faith and lowered ideals of morality. This attitude of doubt and ridicule is well expressed in the mock-heroic poetry (called Bernesque) of Francesco Berni (1497–1536) and his followers—a style imitated in the 19th century by Lord Byron.

The greatest writers of the period were Ludovico Ariosto (1474–1533) and Torquato Tasso (1544–95). Ariosto continued Boiardo's *Orlando inamorato,* the story of Roland and Charlemagne, in *Orlando furioso* (1516), a vast romantic poem of nearly 40,000 lines, rich in invention and description and full of dreamlike chivalry and adventure—the work of a master craftsman completely absorbed in his creation and oblivious to the world about him. Torquato Tasso lived in an age of reverence for ancient scholars, and in his great epic *Gerusalemme liberata* ("Jerusalem Delivered") he attempted to follow the rules of Aristotle. His theme is the capture of Jerusalem by the crusaders under Godfrey of Bouillon in the 11th century, and the epic is elevated in tone, dignified and melodious in language and of thrilling interest. Tasso also wrote the beautiful pastoral poem *Aminta* (1572). Tasso was never quite able to adjust his genius to the practical world, even as he could not perfectly succeed in his attempt to combine classic rules with Ariosto's wealth of imagination.

Italian drama now became important for the first time, though most of it even in this century closely followed Latin models. Machiavelli's comedy *Mandragola* and some comedies by Ariosto and Tasso were worthy of their genius, although each did his best work in other fields. The poetic pastoral drama *Pastor fido* (1590) by Giovanni Battista Guarini (1538–1612) is an excellent picture of an Italian society becoming decadent and artificial in its manners and customs. The comedies of Pietro Aretino (1492–1556) are bold and often abusive in their satire.

The 17th and 18th Centuries.—The immediate period after Tasso was one of increasing decadence, for the vitality and élan of the Renaissance had worn itself out and new inspiration was lacking. Giordano Bruno (1548–1600), Tommaso Campanella (1568–1639) and Galileo Galilei (1564–1642) were tortured or imprisoned for their philosophical and scientific beliefs. The poetry of the Seicentisti (16 hundreds), headed by Giambattista Marini (1569–1625) was overdecorated and complex. A profusion of words partly concealed the lack of ideas, particularly in the poetry of Gabriello Chiabrera (1552–1637). Late in the century the Academy of Arcadia was founded in protest against Marinism, but it succeeded only in introducing a new refinement and delicacy of form. The work of Claudio Monteverde (1567–1643) and Pietro Francesco Cavalli (c. 1602–1676) established the lyric drama or opera as a magnificent popular spectacle and a high form of artistic expression.

Secchia Rapita ("The Rape of the Bucket"), a mock heroic poem by Alessandro Tassoni (1565–1635), is strongly satirical and provides the model for Boileau's *Le Lutrin* and Pope's *Rape of the Lock*. Salvator Rosa (1615–73), musician, painter and poet, criticized the artificiality and overelegance of his time.

In the 18th century Giovanni Battista Vico (1668–1744) studied the historical progress of man; Ludovico Muratori (1672–1750) and Scipione di Maffei (1675–1755) collected and commented upon the original sources of Italian history and recommended that writers turn again to the ancients—but with caution. Giuseppe Parini (1729–99), disgusted with the elegant frivolities and foolish ways in which the nobility wasted time, wrote *Il Giorno* ("The Day"), criticizing these practices severely by seeming to praise them.

In drama Italy had now produced great quantity if not quality. Drama took two forms—rude popular plays and artificial plays written by men of culture for other men of culture. In popular drama the early commedia dell' arte was performed by actors trained to improvise lines and actions from a written plot. This form was defended by Carlo Gozzi (1720–1806) who wrote some delightful fairy-tale comedies. The musical dramas of Pietro Trapassi Metastasio (1698–1782) are far above the ordinary opera text in both plot and poetry. The true drama of the century is seen in the comedies of Carlo Goldoni (1707–93) and in the tragedies of Vittorio Alfieri (1749–1803). Alfieri, who symbolizes the growing Italian desire for freedom of thought and political independence, created modern Italian tragedy on classical models. He observed the Greek unities, introduced only a few characters and had very little action, often picturing the triumph of popular liberty and the downfall of a tyrant. Goldoni replaced the old commedia dell' arte and its fixed types with plays that owe much to the influence of Molière. He is remarkable for his power of characterization and his skill in creating plot interest, though he wrote so rapidly that the form is rough. The end of the century was characterized by a great burst of patriotism, interest in the classics and the *purismo* movement, an attempt to purify the language by eliminating the many gallicisms that had crept in. This interest in language revived the quarrel for supremacy between the dialects of Tuscany and Lombardy.

Modern Italian Literature.—The drama in the 19th century owed much to Ugo Foscolo (1778–1827) and to Alessandro Manzoni (1785–1873); but the fervid patriot Foscolo was greater in his poem *I Sepolcri* ("Sepulchers," 1807) and in the *Lettere di Jacopo Ortis;* and Manzoni became famous for his historical and realistic novel *I Promessi Sposi* ("The Betrothed," 1825). Vincenzo Monti (1754–1828) also wrote for the theater, but his poems best reflect his changing political ideals. His translation of the *Iliad* is remarkably good.

The greatest Italian poet of the early 19th century and one of the best prose writers was Giacomo Leopardi (1798–1837), pessimistic and deeply and truly melancholy. A romantic poet of the period was Silvio Pellico (1789–1854), who is better known, however, for the thrilling story of his imprisonment for liberal political beliefs—*Le mie prigioni* (1832). The romantic movement in Italy was not as it was in France an abandonment of the classics but a fresh understanding of them. Even in the work of Manzoni, the acknowledged head of the romantic movement, realism is prominent.

After 1821 the movement for political independence and unity, called the Risorgimento, was dominant in all forms of Italian life. In poetry G. Giusti (1809–50) made use of satire, and Aleardo Aleardi (1812–78) was a melodious but sentimental patriot. More lasting work was done in the novel—by Massimo T. d'Azeglio (1798–1866), statesman and painter besides, and by Francesco Guerrazzi (1804–73); both used historical subjects to portray their political theories. Vincenzo Gioberti (1801–52) and Giuseppe Mazzini (1805–72) wrote political and philosophical treatises, fired by the ideal of a united and independent Italy. Gioberti first urged rule by the pope and later by a monarch; but Mazzini, idealist and republican to the core, could be content only with a true democracy. Both were at various times exiled and imprisoned for their beliefs. The best literary expression of the time was that of Giosuè Carducci (1835–1907) whose various volumes of poetry show deep sincerity, delight in the classics and belief in the new ideals of individual freedom. They won for him a Nobel prize in 1906.

EDWARD ROONEY

SIX CHARACTERS in search of an author.

In Italy as in the rest of Europe the novel and the short story became increasingly important and showed such realistic tendencies as interest in localities and in dialect. Of this type were the novels of Giovanni Verga (1840–1922), who is best known in America for his tale *Cavalleria Rusticana*, the libretto of the opera by Pietro Mascagni (1863-1945); of Luigi Capuana (1839–1915); of the Neapolitan Matilde Serao (1856–1927); and of the Sardinian Grazia Deledda (1875–1936), winner of the Nobel prize in 1926. The novels of Antonio Fogazzaro (1842–1911) have a larger background.

The poetry of Giovanni Pascoli (1855–1912) is a record of fleeting impressions. Giuseppe Giacosa (1847–1906) was both poet and dramatist. In literary criticism Francesco de Sanctis (1817–83) had introduced a new philosophy regarding literature as a reflection of social and moral conditions. His work was carried on by Benedetto Croce (1866–1952) who has greatly influenced younger writers. Pasquale Villari (1827–1917) and other great teachers contributed scholarly research in the history of literature and of government. Edmondo de Amicis (1846–1908) won fame for his travel stories and for the novel *Il Cuore*, translated as "An Italian Schoolboy's Journal."

The two great names of modern Italian literature are Gabriele d'Annunzio (1863–1938) and Luigi Pirandello (1867–1936). Giuseppe Chiarini (1833–1908), poet and critic, early recognized the value of d'Annunzio's poetry. In the course of his active and prolific life d'Annunzio wrote novels, dramas, short stories and poetry. His writing shows the influence of the great Russian novelists

PORTUGUESE TOURIST AND INFORMATION OFFICE

LUÍS DE CAMÕES

and of the German philosopher Nietzsche. His plays are noted for their brilliance of color, movement and sound. Pirandello, too, was versatile; for he wrote poetry, novels, short stories and finally the plays that brought him world fame and a Nobel prize in 1934. His theme is the unstable and changing quality of life and truth, the denial of any sound and solid reality. Man for him is a thousand things, but never what he thinks he is. The viewpoint is ably portrayed in *Cosi è se vi pare* ("Right You Are If You Think You Are," 1918) and in *Sei personaggi in cerca d'autore* ("Six Characters in Search of an Author," 1921).

Among early 20th century novelists were Alfredo Pansini (1863–1939), gently ironical, and Italo Sevevo (1861–1928), one of the most original European novelists of his day.

In the years between 1910 and 1922, when Fascism came to power, the best writers published in two magazines; *La Voce*, edited in Florence by Giuseppe Prezzolini and *La Ronda*, edited in Rome by Vincenzo Cardarelli and others. To the movement of La Voce, besides writers like Giovanni Papini (1881–1956) and Ardengo Soffici (1879–1964), belonged Renato Serra (1884–1916) killed in the first World War. Other noted writers of the period were Giovanni Boine (1887–1917) and the poets Dino Campana (1882–1932), Clemente Rebora (1885–1947) and Arturo Onofri (1885–1928) who started symbolism in Italian poetry.

The three major representatives of contemporary Italian poetry are Eugenio Montale (1896–   ), author of *Ossi di Seppia* (1925), *Le Occasioni* (1938) and *Finisterre* (1945); Giuseppe Ungaretti (1888–   ); and Salvatore Quasimodo (1901–   ).

In fiction Riccardo Bacchelli (1891–   ) wrote *Il Mulino del Po* which had great success in Italy and is translated into English. Aldo Palazzeschi (1885–   ) and Massimo Bontempelli (1878–1960) both have established solid

reputations. Ignazio Silone, who went into exile during the fascist regime, is the author of *Fontamra* (1930), *Bread and Wine* (1937) and *The Seed Under the Snow* (1940).

A list of the best Italian contemporary writers would be very long. Among the most important are Alberto Moravia (1907–   ), whose novel *The Woman of Rome* had a remarkable success in America; Carlo Levi, author of *Christ Has Stopped at Eboli*, and Elio Vittorini, author of *In Cicily*.

PORTUGUESE LITERATURE

Portugal is rich in lyric and satiric poetry, in histories of conquest, and in tales of exploration.

The first lyric poets in the early 13th century were influenced by the Provençal literature of southern France. Poet kings gathered many singers at court. Their *cancioneiros* ("song books") frequently followed native folkways, whereas most of the court poetry collected later in the *Cancioneiro Geral* (1516) was superficial. In the 14th century, prose was first used in genealogies and religious stories, but Fernão Lopes (c. 1380–c. 1450) gave it fluency in royal chronicles as colorful as those of the Frenchman Froissart. There may have been a Portuguese version of the famous novel of chivalry *Amadís de Gaula*, antedating the Spanish text. Gil Vicente (c. 1465–c. 1536) created genuinely national plays with charming lyrics, in Portuguese and Spanish, a theatre at the same time worldly and devout, popular and aristocratic, mediaeval and humanistic. He was at his height in the *Barcas*, three mystery plays of the "Ferries to Hell, Purgatory, and Heaven" (1517–19).

The Golden Age.—In the 16th century, stimulated by the Italian Renaissance, Portugal boasted an exquisite pastoral literature. A Portuguese, Jorge de Montemór, wrote the great Spanish pastoral *Diana*, including Portuguese verse. Sá de Miranda introduced the sonnet and other literary forms directly from Italy. António Ferreira wrote a classic tragedy on a national legend, Inês de Castro's love and murder (c. 1558). Jorge Ferreira de Vasconcelos composed prose plays reminiscent of the Spanish *Celestina* on Portuguese subjects. Humanism flourished briefly until the Inquisition, established in 1536, rendered it suspect. Damião de Góis befriended Erasmus; Francisco Sanches wrote on the experimental method; Francisco de Olanda discussed aesthetics with Michelangelo.

Romances of chivalry were popular. Morais' *Palmeirim de Inglaterra* (c. 1544) won praise even from Cervantes. The glory of the age, however, lay in its histories and the national epic *Os Lusiadas* ("The Sons of Lusus," i.e. the Portuguese, 1572), the great poem about the Age of Discoveries written by Luis de Camoëns (c. 1524–80), famous also for his melancholy love poetry. The now dramatic, now lyric narrative of *Os Lusíadas* celebrates the Portuguese nation, her kings, Vasco da Gama, and their discovery of the sea route to India.

Historians had a wealth of material, for the Portuguese were then sailing the seven seas, to Morocco, Ethiopia, the East Indies, Brazil, the Far East. Outstanding are the ambitious *Décadas da Ásia*, begun by João de Barros in 1552, who, with Camoëns, gave classic beauty to the Portuguese language. Two of the many travel books are unusual, the *História trágico-marítima*, 12 moving accounts of shipwrecks, and the *Peregrinação*, in which the reformed pirate Fernão Mendes Pinto (c. 1509–83), unjustly called *Prince of Liars*, told of fabulous adventures in the Orient.

Gradual Decline.—During the 17th century, Portugal remained closely linked to Spain. Quevedo's friend Francisco Manuel de Melo (1611–66) composed subtle Portuguese and Spanish verse, witty dialogue, urbane letters, a bachelor's guide for married couples, and a remarkable history of the Catalan Rebellion. Religious poetry and prose flourished. The sermons of António Vieira (1608–97), the edifying tales of Manuel Bernardes, and Luís de Sousa's monastic histories served as models of style. The passionately sincere "Love Letters of a Portuguese Nun" (Mariana Alcoforado) became world famous through a French version.

Early in the 18th century, Portuguese literature fell low, under the sway of French and Italian influences. New academies and Arcadian societies were founded to purify and regulate literature. Pastoral poetry was rampant. The only successful attempts at drama were marionette plays which poked fun at Italian opera. But Francisco Xavier de Oliveira still delights readers with his "Letters" written in Vienna.

Romanticism and Realism.—The poet Almeida Garrett (1799–1854) set out to restore national literature. His blank verse poem *Camões* (1825) was followed by historical dramas such as *Frei Luís de Sousa* (1844). Alexandre Herculano (1810–77) contributed historical fiction inspired by Chateaubriand and Walter Scott. Quental (1842–91) recorded his tragic search for a philosophy in odes and sonnets of haunting beauty. Social protest, against monarchy and church, was vehemently voiced by Guerra Junqueiro (1850–1923). In close touch with French symbolism, poetry became refined and suggestive with Eugénio de Castro (1869–1944).

The novel of manners developed about 1840. Camilo Castelo Branco (1825–90) portrayed national types and passions, often sarcastically. His *Amor de Perdicão* ("Doomed Love") has remained popular. Eca de Queiroz (1845–1900), a keener, more ironic observer, created unforgettable middle-class characters, as in *Os Maias* ("The Maias").

After 1900 the Romantic tradition was revived. Many turned from scepticism to Catholic mysticism and from cosmopolitanism to nationalism. The morbidly self-centered *Só* ("Alone") by António Nobre (1867–1900) announced this trend in poetry. Experimenting with psychology, Fernando Pessoa (1888–1935) assumed different names and personalities to express his complex nature. Women writers became prominent, among them Florbela Espanca (1894–1930).

Much recent fiction describes the daily lives of ordinary Portuguese—fishermen, farmers, shepherds, miners. Aquilino Ribeiro (1885–   ) stands out with tales from the Beira region. The literary essay flourishes with Fidelino de Figueiredo (1888–   ).

RUSSIAN LITERATURE

The early Russian literature of the 11th century was almost entirely translations from Greek religious writing. Secular literature was largely confined to historical chronicles. Only fragments of traditionary tales in rhythmic verse, somewhat similar to English, Spanish and Scandinavian ballads, have survived from this period. One great epic, *The Discourse of the Campaign of Igor,* is marked by great vigor and rich imagery. A wealth of oral folk literature, not extensively published until the 19th century, is best known for its *byliny,* unrhymed narrative poems about legendary or historical characters.

Influences from the West.—After 1650 the influence of the West replaced that of Greece and Byzantium, particularly under the helping hand of Peter the Great; but Russian literature did not become important in itself until the middle of the 18th century with the widespread interest of the upper classes in French manners and culture. The new era begins with Antiokh Cantemir (1708–44), who imitated Horace and Boileau, and with Mikhail Lomonosov (1711–65), a versatile critic and scientist, an influential literary theorist and a writer of magnificent odes. Another great poet whose work though it is in a classic mold throbs with strong life was Gabriel Derzhavin (1743–1816). In the theater French influence was predominant, particularly in the plays of Aleksandr Sumarokov (1718–77). The popular literature of the day shows a rude and ready and often delightful realism, reaching a high point in the comedies of Denis Fon-Vizin (1744–92) and in the *Fables* (1809) of Ivan Krylov (1768–1844). Aleksandr Griboyedov (1795–1829) in his comedy *Göre ot Uma* ("Woe from Wit," 1825) took a first step in the direction of a social problem play.

The political and social revolt inherent in the French Age of Enlightenment (18th century) also awoke echoes in Russia. Satirical journals edited by Nikolay Novikov (1744–1818) were strong enough to provoke the wrath of Catherine II. The strongest influence in the new reform of the Russian language was that of Nikolai Karamzin (1766–1826), who abandoned many old words, introduced new ones and showed a tendency to soften the roughness of the preceding age. His theories are strongly reminiscent of Rousseau.

Between Karamzin and Pushkin was Vasili Zhukovski (1783–1852), famous for his excellent translations into Russian of ancient and modern poets. Idol of Russian literature is Aleksandr Pushkin (1799–1837), whose poetry and prose are rare in their combination of beauty and strength. His historical drama *Boris Godunov* became world famous and the verse-novel *Evgeni Onegin* (1823–31) had a great influence on later Russian writers. Pushkin was head of a group of poets, nominally romantic, but more practical and sure of their medium than many contemporary European romantics. The philosopher of the group was Evgeni Baratynski (1800–44).

Beginning of Social Criticism.—As the century progressed intellectual agitation for the freedom of the serfs and for other liberal reforms increased. One group, the Slavophils, demanded that Russia find in her native history and customs the answers to her problems; the other upheld the necessity and value of introducing western methods. Foremost among the advocates of western influence was the critic Vissarion Byelinski (1810–48). The historian Sergyey Solovev (1820–79) presented a convincing case for westernization in his extensive history of Russia. Mikhail Katkov (1818–87), journalist and editor, though in his youth an advocate of the same ideas later became an ardent and influential Slavophil.

Eloquent and romantic in its expression of revolt against the contemporary society, though sometimes bombastic, is the poetry of Mikhail Lermontov (1814–41). His novel *A Hero of Our Times* (1840) is prophetic—in its analysis of character and situation—of prose masterpieces to follow. More perfect in form and execution is the poetry of Feodor Tyutchev (1803–73), who has been called second only to Pushkin. The folk songs of Aleksyey Koltsov (1808–42) are popular and vital though the work of a single artist and not of a people.

The Masterpieces of Russian Literature.—The middle of the century brought the beginning of the great age of Russian prose literature—when the novels of Turgenev, Dostoevski and Tolstoy became an original and worthy part of world literature. The inaugurator of this golden age was Nikolay Gogol (1809–52) who combined romantic exaggeration with interest in the sordid and mean sides of life. By his work he called attention to the evils of Russian society, to social problems badly in need of solution, to people and places who had not before been thought worthy of consideration.

Ivan Goncharov (1812–91) in *Oblomov* (1858) wrote a magnificent character study of an intellectual. Aleksyey Pisemski (1820–81) described with force and conviction the illiterate classes. Ivan Turgenev (1818–83) in *A Sportsman's Sketches* (1847–52) took the peasant as his subject. Sergei Aksakov (1791–1859) described in animated detail life in East Russia (*A Family Chronicle,* 1856) and his own childhood (*Years of Childhood,* 1858). A little later Mikhail Saltykov (1826–89) in *The Golovlev Family* (1876) exposed the abusive practices of the country squires. These Russian problem novels, particularly those of Turgenev, differ

BETTMANN ARCHIVE

SCENE from Nikolai Gogol's *The Inspector General,* from an 1863 lithograph by P. M. Boklewskiy, illustrating the line "You arch cheat you . . . you want to sue me!"

from the American problem novels of the early 20th century in their deeper psychological understanding, wider application and perfection of style. These universal qualities are present to an even greater degree in the work of Lev (Leo) Tolstoy (1828–1910) and Feodor Dostoevski (1821–81). Tolstoy's great novels *Anna Karenina, War and Peace* and *Resurrection* picture the ever-changing kaleidoscope of life without sacrifice of individual characterization. The tragic but never depressing novels of Dostoevski, *The Idiot, Crime and Punishment* and *The Brothers Karamazov* stand alone in all literature for their portrayal of the human soul.

Drama, too, became more vigorous and more concerned with the realities of everyday life—in the work of Alexsandr Ostrovsky (1823–86) and in Pisemski's *A Hard Lot* (1858). In the work of Ivan Nikitin (1824–61) and then more perfectly and completely in that of Nikolay Nekrasov (1821–77), poetry became realistic and went to peasant life for its inspiration. Aleksyey Tolstoy (1817–75) contributed at the same time some delightful nonsense poetry and blank verse.

Early Twentieth-Century Literature.—The short stories of Vladimir Korolenko (1853–1921) show a sense of humor and narrative ability, but prose in general declined until it received fresh impetus through the short stories of Anton Chekhov (1860–1904) and the novels of Maxim Gorky (1868–1936). Chekhov's work is pervaded by a sense of sorrow and disillusionment but also by a spirit of sympathy and understanding. *The Cherry Orchard* is the most famous of his plays. Gorky was a revolutionist, volatile, irrepressible and virile, and his books express the man. Alexander Kuprin (1870–1938) was more conventional in his stories of army life. Leonid Andreev (1871–1919) and Mikhail Artsibashev (1878–1927) looked at life and found it wanting in higher values and ideals. Andreev is best known in America for the play *He Who Gets Slapped*. Ivan Bunin (1870–1953), received the Nobel Prize in 1933. In *The Village* and *Sukhodol* he returned to the study of provincial Russian life to show vividly the state of affairs that led to the Revolution.

Foreign trends away from realism and toward expression of the poet's own ego together with the influence of the philosophical and mystical poetry of Vladimir Solovev (1853–1900) resulted in the work of the Russian symbolist poets. Dmitri Merezhkovski (1866–1941), once famed as a religious philosopher, probably made his most valuable contribution to Russian literature by sponsoring western ideas.

Among the symbolists whose work combines native Russian realism with phantasy and symbolism, were Feodor Sologub (1863–1927) and Alexander Blok (1880–1921). Sologub's novel *The Little Demon* (1907) is famous.

Post-Revolutionary Literature.—This period (1918–23) was dominated by poets like Mayakovsky and Esenin and by prose writers like Zamaytin, Pilnyak and Babel who portrayed the storm and stress of the Revolution. The impact of the Revolution is the subject of many fine Russian novels including Fedin's *Cities and Years*, Leonov's *The Thief*, and Kaverin's *The Artist Unknown*. Pasternak, Tikhonov and Bagritsky wrote excellent poetry.

Between 1929 and 1934 Russian literature was much used for propagandizing the Five-Year Plan. After 1932 its scope was again broadened, but all Soviet writers were pledged to Socialist realism. To the historical novel, 1924–28, were added patriotic novels. Tynyanov's novels dealing with literary figures, Alexey N. Tolstoy's *Peter the First* and Sergeyev-Tsensky's *The Ordeal of Sevastopol* were important examples. The political oratory and philosophy of Nikolay Lenin (1870–1924) and Leon Trotsky (1877–1940), who on Lenin's death became a rival of Stalin, are also important.

Boris Pasternak (1890–1960), one of Russia's best poets, was awarded (but declined) the Nobel Prize for his novel *Doctor Zhivago*, published in the United States in 1958. Due to the postwar government control of the arts, the book was refused publication in the U.S.S.R.

A brilliant contemporary poet is Yevgeny Yevtushenko. His poem "Babiy Yar" is one example of the author's sensitive response to people.

Current novelists are emigré Nabokov, author of *Lolita*, and Solzhenitsyn, who wrote *One Day in the Life of Ivan Denisovich.*

CANADIAN LITERATURE

Canada has not yet produced a literature distinctly her own. Moreover, the most thickly populated part of Canada is stubbornly bilingual. Neither the French nor the English will yield to the other and as a result there are French and English Canadian literature with little cross-fertilization. In both, individual rather than schools or movements are important. English Canadian literature has been influenced by both Great Britain and the United States; and French Canadian by the literary fashions of France. Very little has been undertaken in drama. Among short stories, Marjorie Picktall's book, *Angel's Shoes* (1922) was exceptional.

History and the Essay.—In English are the highly interesting journals or first-hand accounts of such men as Henry Hudson who discovered what is now called Hudson Bay in the search for a passage across North America; George Vancouver, who adventured on the west coast; Alexander Mackenzie, who first crossed overland to the Pacific; Simon Fraser, who went down the river that now bears his name; and

Davis Thompson, who explored the Columbia River Valley. Scholarly and extensive in scope are *Canada and Its Provinces* (1914 *et seq.*), edited by A. G. Doughty and Adam Shortt, and *Chronicles of Canada* (1914 *et seq.*) edited by G. M. Wrong and H. H. Langton. *The Makers of Canada* contains substantial biographies of Canadian explorers, fur-traders and statesmen. J. B. Brebner's *North Atlantic Triangle*, completed in 1945 in 25 volumes is a series on the *Relations of Canada and the United States*. Two stimulating histories of Canada are D. G. Creighton's *Dominion of the North* (1944) and A. R. M. Lower's *Colony to Nation* (1946). Other nonfiction Canadian works include Richard Finnie's *Canada Moves North* (1942), Bruce Hutchison's *Unknown Country* (1942) and J. M. Gibbon's *Canadian Mosaic* (1938).

Stephen Leacock will be remembered not so much for his sober writings in history and economics, but for his *Nonsense Novels, Literary Lapses* and *Sunshine Sketches of a Little Town.*

Literary criticism has not progressed far in Canada. Substantial work has, however, been done in the development of Canadian literature by Archibald MacMechan, E. K. Brown, A. J. M. Smith, Camille Roy and others.

Poetry.—Canada's best-known English poet was Bliss Carman, whose poems portray the lure of the open road and a singing love of nature. Archibald Lampman also put a musical quality into his praise of nature. The poetry of William Wilfred Campbell shows his deep patriotic and imperialistic sympathies and that of George Frederick Cameron is remarkable for its technical perfection. W. H. Drummond, brought into close contact as a physician with the small farmers of French origin, the *habitants,* captured in his poetry the engaging dialect, the joys and sorrows of this class. Robert W. Service wrote popular ballads of the Yukon and the Far West, *Songs of a Sourdough* (1907). John McCrae won wide acclaim for his poem of World War I, *In Flanders Fields.* With World War I concluded, Canadian poetry in English was ready to turn from patriotic themes, but showed little inclination to return to the contemplation of the granite north. At this critical juncture a Newfoundland-born Toronto professor, Edward J. Pratt, sounded a new note from the elemental forces of the gray relentless seas off his fog-girt island homeland. In 1923 appeared his *Newfoundland Verse.* By the mid-century Pratt had become Canada's most distinguished poet. His use of words and of verse forms to achieve a harmony between form and substance was notable. But the full effect of his influence on the more restrained Canadian poets could not be easily estimated.

The Novel.—Canadian novels have been mainly historical and regional. Among the first was John Richardson's *Wacousta* (1832), a fictional account of Pontiac's Conspiracy of 1763 set in the Detroit area. Thomas Chandler Haliburton in the guise of Sam Slick, a Yankee clockmaker, amusingly caricatured both New Englanders and his fellow Nova Scotians in sketches (1837–44) filled with excellent characterizations but weak in plot structure. In the second half of the 19th century, historical novels were written by William Kirby (*The Golden Dog, a Legend of Quebec*) *and by* Gilbert Parker (*The Seats of the Mighty* and *When Valmond Came to Pontiac*). Charles W. Gordon (Ralph Connor) described the life of the miner and the lumberman on the Canadian frontier. Lucy M. Montgomery described life on Prince Edward Island in the charming *Anne of Green Gables;* and Frederick W. Wallace wrote of Nova Scotia and its clipper ships and fishermen. Ernest Thompson Seton's stories of wild life are loved by all children. Martha Ostenso wrote of prairie life in the Middle West and Mazo de la Roche described a Canadian family in her *Jalna* series. Hugh MacLennan's *Barometer Rising* is a tale centering on Halifax, Nova Scotia. His *Two Solitudes* is bilingual Montreal. The scene of Gwethalyn Graham's *Earth and High Heaven,* is also laid in Montreal. As Canada's maturing literacy and the opening of the Canadian West coincided in time, it was natural that pioneering on the prairies should be the theme of many novels of varying degrees of excellence. Among the best of western fiction writers have been Frederick Philip Grove, Frederick Niven, Nellie L. McClung, Robert J. C. Stead, Laura G. Salverson, Sinclair Ross and William O. Mitchell.

French Contributions.—Like the English, the French have excelled in history and political biography. Exciting journals were left by Jacques Cartier, Samuel de Champlain and Rene de la Salle. Francois-Xavier Garneau's *L'Histoire du Canada,* (1845–52) although somewhat prejudiced is still highly regarded, as is the work of Antoine Gerin-Lajoie who contributed *Dix ans d'Histoire du Canada, 1840–50.* Raymond Casgrain described single historical events or episodes, such as *Montcalm et Levis* (1891), and Benjamin Sulte wrote a more detailed *L'Histoire des Canadiens-Francais* (1884). A more scientific approach was used by

Thomas Chapais in his *Cours d'Histoire du Canada* (1923) and further research has gone into the more recent *Histoire du Canada* of Jean Bruchesi.

Etienne Parent, editor of *Le Canadien,* the first French Canadian newspaper, made it a successful and revealing expression of French Canada. With Octave Cremazie, a poet whose verse is strongly patriotic, and the historian Garneau, Parent founded *Les Soirees Canadiennes,* a periodical designed to preserve the folklore and popular songs of French Canada. Not until about 1860 in Quebec was a conscious effort made by a group of writers toward improvement in literary technique. The group was headed by Casgrain but the most famous member was Louis Frechette, whose work was crowned by the French Academy. *Les Fleurs boreales* (Flowers of the Far North) and *Les Oiseaux de neige* (Birds of Snow) contain the best examples of his lyric poetry. His epic *La Legende d'un Peuple* (1887) celebrates the history of the French Canadians.

New World and much of the Old. Spanish ships sailed round the world, and Spain became supreme in learning, literature and political power, challenged occasionally only by English ships and English men of letters. Cervantes, Lope de Vega and Calderón de la Barca took Spanish literature to new heights and gave it world-wide importance.

MIGUEL DE CERVANTES SAAVEDRA (1547–1616), greatest genius of Spanish literature, was Shakespeare's contemporary. The story of his life is more exciting than fiction, a tale of military service, slavery in Africa, captivity and poverty in his native land. His works consist of the pastoral romance *La Galatea,* numerous plays and masterful dramatic interludes, 12 tales, a posthumous novel and the immortal *Don Quixote* (1605–15). Cervantes intended *Don Quixote* as a chivalric romance that would make ridiculous the already involved and exaggerated novels of adventure so popular at the time and thus put a stop to them. Instead he brought them long-lasting fame, for his two protagonists Don Quixote and Sancho Panza became so real that they bore Cervantes away with them and shaped the story to suit themselves. Don Quixote, the idealist, the optimist, comes to know and finally to accept reality through his friendship with Sancho Panza, servant extraordinary; while Sancho, hard-headed, practical and wholly unimaginative in the beginning, eventually gains something of his master's ability to make life good and true and beautiful. Don Quixote and Sancho have laughed themselves into the hearts of men the world over.

Other noteworthy fiction is found in the picaresque novels or tales about rogues: *Historia de la Vida del Buscón* (1626) by Francisco Gómez de Quevedo y Villegas and *El Diablo cojuelo* (1641) by Luis Vélez de Guevara, presenting a series of animated portraits of 17th-century Spanish life with all its good and bad aspects faithfully reproduced. The *Vida del Buscón* is in the same tradition as *Lazarillo* but is more bitter in its criticism of society and more sophisticated in style.

The poetry of the 16th century, outside the drama, was of two kinds— that which followed the Italian tradition and that which clung to the old Castilian models. Most poets attempted both kinds. In the 17th century Luis de Góngora y Argote (1561–1627) gave his name to a new style that heralded the coming decadence—an artificially involved and overdecorated prose and poetry that made use of double meanings and other literary tricks.

The most inclusive and popular manifestation of the Golden Age was its drama, which was as much of and for the people as for the royal court. Dramatists of the 15th century had taken definite steps to disengage the drama from religious miracle plays and pageants, as shown particularly through the work of the Portuguese Gil Vicente (c. 1470–c. 1536), who wrote various plays in Spanish; also that of Bartolomé de Torres Naharro;

SPANISH LITERATURE

The Latin language was early carried to the Spanish Peninsula and several well-known Latin writers were Spaniards: Seneca, Lucan, Martial, Quintilian and the Christian poet Prudentius. The present Spanish or Castilian language is descended from Latin. Besides Castilian, Catalan in the east and Basque in the north are still vigorous and well exemplified in fine literatures.

The Middle Ages.—The *Cantar de mio Cid* (12th century) is an epic celebrating the mighty achievements of the first national hero of Spain, Ruy Díaz de Bivar (1040–99), known as the Cid. The poem depicts in rugged simplicity and vividness the life and manners of that turbulent age when the Christians of northern Spain were fighting to regain territory lost to the Moors.

That wandering minstrels sang songs and ballads here as in France and Germany is recorded in the 13th-century *Crónica general,* prepared under the direction of Alfonso the Wise (1221–84). Very few such songs remain, except in the *romances,* which were popular tales set to music and conserved by the common people. These *romances* played an important role in the development of Spanish literature.

Spain was the gateway through which the learning of the East passed on to western Europe and this Oriental influence is evident in *Conde Lucanor* by Juan Manuel (1282–c. 1349), a collection of prose tales, fables and anecdotes usually pointing a moral but doing so in a wholly charming manner. The *Libro de buen amor* ("Book of True Love"), by Juan Ruiz (c. 1283–1350), archpriest of Hita, is a perfectly frank account of his love affairs, very well told and showing his remarkable ability in creating characters.

Influence of Dante and the Renaissance. —In the 15th century under the influence of Dante, much moralizing poetry was written; it was without

much value in itself but evidenced the attempt to escape from the crudeness of everyday life and to refine the language. The ideal of the century was Iñigo López de Mendoza, Marquis de Santillana (1398–1458), who combined to a remarkable degree the diverse abilities of soldier, statesman, author, scholar, critic, collector and translator. The chivalric romance was represented by *Amadis de Gaula,* partly written in the 15th century by Garci Rodriguez de Montalvo, who seems to be the first known writer about the adventures of Amadis, although the stories were popular in all northwestern Europe long before this time. In 1499 *La Celestina,* a novel in dialogue, was printed and immediately won well-deserved popularity. This story of a go-between in affairs of the heart is a vivid and honest account of life toward the close of the Middle Ages. Its heroine Celestina is universal in appeal because of her frankness, wit and good nature and as a true product of Spanish society at that time.

The Renaissance brought the development of two types of fiction—the pastoral romance from Italy and the picaresque novel; also an interest in classical and in old Spanish poetry; the beginnings of a secular drama; and the first grammars and vocabularies. One of the first pastorals to appear in Spain was *Diana* by Jorge de Montemayor (1520–61). He had a host of followers, among them Cervantes in *La Galatea* and Lope de Vega in *Arcadia.* Fresher, more vital and much more typically Spanish is the first great picaresque novel, *Vida de Lazarillo de Tormes* (1554), introducing the picaro, a fascinating rogue obliged to live by his wits. In contrast to other Renaissance fiction this book is written in almost conversational style. In its honest presentation of facts it is a remarkable social criticism.

El Siglo de Oro or Golden Age, 1550–1650. —Spaniards governed most of the

both made use of the humor of character and dialect. The first real impetus toward a popular drama came with the plays and skits by Lope de Rueda (c. 1510–c. 1565), credited with founding the theater in Spain.

Like Shakespearean drama in England, this Spanish drama did not bother with the narrow rules of Greek tragedy and was content with unity of action or character. In the plays (1583) of Juan de la Cueva (c. 1550–c. 1610) use is made of the old Spanish *romances*.

Lope de Vega Carpio (1562–1635), known simply as Lope to all Spaniards, realized the full significance and possibilities of the *romances* in Spanish drama. His astounding productivity has probably never been equaled in the annals of literature. Leading an extremely active life as soldier and statesman, even going with the Armada to England, he still managed to write some 2,200 plays in addition to numerous epics, lyrics and tales. For this reason his work is more brilliant in its entirety than in single parts. In the wide range covered by his plays, Lope captured the whole psychology, feeling and life of the Spanish people. His aim was not perfection of form or plot but emotion and interest. His characters are representative of the Spanish masses yet they are men rather than symbols.

Pedro Calderón de la Barca (1600–81) wrote plays different both in form and in spirit. Calderón, unlike many of his literary contemporaries, led a tranquil life, devoting his energies to literature and religion. This is evident in his choice of subjects, many of them religious and allegorical, and in the philosophic undertone in all his plays. This and the sonorous and beautiful though somewhat rhetorical poetry in which he wrote made him popular throughout Europe, especially in Germany. His theme is most often honor, though love and jealousy also play important parts. Calderón's characters, in contrast to those of Lope, are symbols rather than individuals.

Other dramatists, whose work resembles Lope's rather than Calderón's are: Guillén de Castro y Bellvis (1567–1631) whose *Mocedades del Cid* ("Youth of the Cid") inspired Corneille's tragedy; Tirso de Molina (real name, Gabriel Téllez; 1571–1648) who in *El Burlador de Sevilla* created the character of Don Juan; Juan Ruiz de Alarcón y Mendoza (c. 1580–1639, Spanish-Mexican poet whose *La Verdad sospechosa* ("Suspicious Truth") is a comedy based upon character rather than on situation or dialogue; and Francisco de Rojas-Zorilla (1607–c. 48) whose *Del rey abajo ninguno* ("None beneath the King") is a fine illustration of the intricacies of codes of honor.

History and philosophy also flourished. A great wealth of historical material resulted from Spain's extensive conquests and extension of power in Europe. The philosophers were busy studying the ancients, producing social satires or experiencing the depths of religious mysticism. Among those of the last type were Santa Teresa (1515–82) and St. John of the Cross.

The Period of French Influence.—After the death of Philip II in 1598, Spanish power, wealth and prestige declined. French influence in Spain became more and more marked until in 1700, with the accession to the Spanish throne of Philip V, grandson of Louis XIV of France, French domination was complete in literature and in government. The Spanish Royal Academy, modeled on the French Academy, was founded and its members began work upon a Castilian grammar. Almost alone is the work of Ramón de la Cruz, whose theatrical sketches are amusing reflections of the Spanish lower and middle classes.

Early in the 19th century Spain succeeded in throwing off the French yoke in government but not in literature. The victory over Napoleon was followed by a long succession of civil wars that were not conducive to a rebirth of literary activity. Perhaps best of the early 19th-century dramas is *The Maidens' Consent* and other work of Leandro Fernández de Moratín (1760–1828), a follower and translator of Molière. The romantic movement was represented by the Duke of Rivas (1791–1865), José Zorrilla y Moral (1817–93) José de Espronceda (1808–42) and the early plays of José Échegaray (1832–1916); but romanticism was fundamentally unsuited to the Spanish temperament and did not prove as fruitful as the contemporary movements in France, Germany and England.

After 1850 some evidence of new national feeling and a departure from French imitation was seen in the poetry of Gaspar Nuñez de Arce (1834–1903), Salvador Rueda (1857–1933), Vicente Medina (1866–1936) and Rosalía de Castro, whose work is mostly in the Galician dialect; but the real vitality of the period lay in its novels. The international movement toward realism and interest in local customs found expression in the work of Fernán Caballero (1797–1877), Pedro Antonia de Alarcón (1833–91) and José Maria de Pereda (1833–1906). Juan Valera y Alcala Galiano (1824–1905) tempered his realism with idealism and poked fun at contemporary society. Emilia Pardo Bazán (1852–1921) and Armando Palacio Valdés (1853–1938) intensify realism into naturalism. Of a different sort is the work of Benito Pérez Galdós (1843–1920), whose *Episodios nacionales* are vigorous and swiftly moving historical novels. For a time Galdós was attracted by French naturalism, but he finally turned to contemporary psychological problems and was particularly successful in writing about life in Madrid. José Échegaray (c. 1832–1916) handled social problems in his later plays and received the Nobel Prize in 1904.

The 20th Century.—With the Spanish-American War in 1898 came a more conscious effort to create a purely Spanish literature. José Martínez Ruiz (pen name, Azorín; 1874–   ) brought a finely chiseled style to his critical interpretations of Spanish life and literature. Pío Baroja (1872–1956) wrote refreshing novels characteristically Basque in their individuality of judgment and style. The novels of

Ramón Pérez de Ayala (1880–1962), which are often studies in psychology, are exciting and attention holding. Gabriel Miro is unique in his delicate tracery of feeling and exquisite choice of words. Marcelino Menéndez y Pelayo and Ramón Menéndez Pidal did invaluable work in research on old Spanish poetry and prose. In philosophy and criticism the outstanding figure is Miguel de Unamuno (1864–1936), whose mysticism and fine understanding are known in translations throughout the world. More practical in his criticism of current phenomena is José Ortega y Gasset (1883–1955). The work of Vicente Blasco Ibáñez, especially *The Four Horsemen of the Apocalypse*, is of cosmopolitan rather than Spanish importance.

LOPE DE VEGA

The plays of Jacinto Benavente (1866–1954), who received the Nobel Prize, 1922, show the wide range of his interests and complete mastery of his medium. The Alvarez Quintero brothers (Serafín and Joaquín) are famous for their comedies of manners. Facility in composition and understanding of psychology are evident in the plays of G. Martinez Sierra (1881–1947) and his wife. Most typically Spanish are numerous short plays set to music, survivals of the old interludes formerly given between the acts of longer plays.

Eduardo Marquina (1879–1946) is Spain's modern cultivator of the poetic historical drama. One of the outstanding younger dramatists is the teacher-playwright Alejandro Casona (1903–   ), author of *Nuestra Natacha* (1936) and *Dama del alba* (1944). Ramon Sender (1902–   ), is noteworthy among the younger novelists.

Stemming from *modernismo* and the influence of Ruben Dario (1867–1916) contemporary Spanish poetry may be called neo-gongorism. Nevertheless, many of Spain's finest literary efforts have been made in poetry. Frederico Garcia Lorca (1899–1936), a poet was also a distinguished dramatist.

LATIN-AMERICAN LITERATURE

The Spanish and Portuguese colonies in the New World produced no novels and few dramatic conceptions of note. Imaginative literature found its characteristic expression in epic, lyric and satirical poetry. *La araucana* by Alonso de Ercilla (1533–94) set the pattern for epic poetry and inspired numerous imitators in Spanish America. In Brazil, José Basílio da Gama (1740–95), working in the Camonean tradition, was the author of *O Uraguai*, a patriotic epic in which the Indian figures prominently. Lyric poetry reached magnificent heights in the sonnets of the Mexican nun, Sor Juana Inés de la Cruz (1651–95). Her Brazilian contemporary, Gregórió de Matos Guerra (1633–96), surpassed all other colonial poets in the satiric genre.

The Independence period in Spanish America witnessed the transition from neo-classicism to romanticism in poetry and the birth of the first true novel— *El Periquillo Sarniento* by the Mexican journalist Joaqúin de Lizardi (1776–1827). The romantic flowering coincided with the growth of nationalism, and while dependent largely on European models, included such outstanding poets as the Argentinian Esteban Echeverría (1805–51), the Mexican Ignacio Rodríguez Galván (1816–42) and the Brazilians Antônio Gonçalves Dias (1823–64) and Antônio de Castro Alves (1847–71). Romanticism in the novel is best exemplified by Jorge Isaacs' (1837–95) *María*, a sentimental tale set in the Cauca Valley of Colombia, and, in Brazil, *O Guarani* by José Martiniano de Alencar (1829–77), a novel which beautifully illustrates the romantic tendency to idealize the Indian.

The Parnasso-Symbolist movement in European literature was called Modernism in Spanish America. Beginning around 1880 with the publication of *Azul* by Rubén Darío (1867–1916), a Nicaraguan who became the period's most representative literary figure, Modernism numbered among its adherents such fine poets as José Martí (1853–95) of Cuba; Manuel Gutiérrez Nájera (1859–95) of Mexico; José Asuncíon Silva (1865–96) of Colombia; and José Santos Chocano (1875–1934) of Peru. On the whole, the Modernist movement in Spanish America constitutes that region's most valuable gift to world literature. Although its most significant expression is found in poetry, Modernism left its imprint on the novel and the essay, especially on the carefully wrought prose of José Enrique Rodo (1872–1917) in Uruguay and Enrique Larreta (1875–   ) in Argentina. In Brazil the objectivity and preoccupation with form in the French Parnassians were brilliantly reflected in the poetry of Olavo Bilac (1865–1918). The outstanding Brazilian symbolist was João da Cruz E Sousa (1862–98).

Figures in recent Latin American poetry are Gabriela Mistral (1889-1957) of Chile; Juana de Ibarbourou (1895–   ) of Uruguay; Pablo Neruda (1904–   ) of Chile; and Nicolas Guillén (1907–   ) of Cuba. The latter was the most talented member of the *poesía negra* school which in the 1930s found many adherents in Cuba, Puerto Rico, Venezuela and Brazil.

The dominant tendency in the postromantic novel in Latin America was in the direction of realism. In Brazil the best exponents were Joaquim Machado de Assis (1830–1908), and Júlio Robeiro (1845–90). *Os Sertões* by Eclides da Cunha (1866–1909), a profound and sympathetic interpreter of life in the Brazilian hinterlands, must be mentioned. The two most distinguished novelists in Brazil in recent years were José Lins do Rêgo (1901–   ) and Jorge Amado (1912–   ) whose works reflect the deep concern with social problems that is also characteristic of the contemporary novel in Spanish America.

Latin American literature boasts of only one dramatist of major stature— Florencio Sánchez (1875–1910) of Uruguay, who displayed a powerful and original talent in his scenes of lower class existence. The greatest Spanish American short story writer, from Uruguay, was Horacio Quiroga (1878–1937).

For the English reader there are Pedro Henríquez-Ureña, *Literary Currents in Hispanic America*, 1946, and Samuel Putnam, *Marvelous Journey*.

DICTIONARY OF LITERARY ALLUSIONS

Abbot, The, a novel by Sir Walter Scott (published 1820), a stirring tale dealing with the imprisonment of Mary Stuart, Queen of Scots, in Lochleven Castle and her escape. The abbot is Father Ambrose (Edward Glendinning), abbot of Kennaquhair. This novel is a sequel to *The Monastery*.

Abottsford, the estate of Sir Walter Scott, near Melrose on the banks of the River Tweed in Scotland. He purchased it in 1812 and lived there, 1824–32. Several rooms are now kept open for sightseers, among them the library and Scott's workroom, both lined with thousands of books.

Abou Ben Adhem, a short poem by Leigh Hunt. In a dream Abou Ben Adhem saw an angel writing in a book the names of all those who loved the Lord, and he asked if his name were there. Upon being told that it was not Abou said, "Write me as one who loves his fellow men." The next night he dreamed again; the angel once more opened the book, "And lo, Ben Adhem's name led all the rest."

acrostic, any piece of writing, but usually verse, in which sets of letters taken in a certain order spell a word or words. Sometimes a series, composed of the first letter in each line, spells the word or words; sometimes the final letter of each line is used; occasionally letters from the middle of the lines are chosen. If only one set of letters spells a word, the verse is a simple acrostic. If the verse contains more than one hidden series, it is called a double acrostic. The 119th Psalm (in Hebrew) is the most famous acrostic in world literature.

The word *violet* is formed by the first letter from each line of the following verse, reading downward:

Vying with the arbutus for modesty and grace,
Innocent as gleeful smiles on happy childhood's face—
Other flowers demand our love and entrance to our thought—
Love seeks her in her hiding place and spends itself unsought.
Early springtime blossom in your modest garb of blue,
Think not that summer's gorgeous bloom can steal our love from you.

Adam Bede, a novel by George Eliot, published in 1859. It tells of the love of Adam Bede, a carpenter, for Hetty Sorrel, a pretty dairymaid, who does not love him and is betrayed by Arthur Donnithorne, the local squire. Bede marries Dinah Morris, a Methodist preacher, who befriends Hetty. *Adam Bede* is often regarded as the best of the author's works. Dickens said that reading it marked an epoch in his life.

Admirable Crichton (Krī'tun), any paragon of all-round excellence; a name applied to James Crichton (1560–85), a Scottish prodigy of learning and swordplay, who became famous in France and Italy, confounding older scholars by his brilliance. James M. Barrie wrote a play with this title, published 1902. A butler, named Crichton, on a world tour with the three daughters of a British nobleman, is shipwrecked on a desert island, becomes the natural leader of the group, falls in love with Lady Mary, one of the daughters, and becomes engaged to her. But when they are rescued by a passing ship, though Lady Mary rebels against going back to the old conventions, Crichton insists that things must be as they were before the shipwreck. On the island, he says, there has been "as little equality" as there is in England!

Adonais, a poem by Percy Bysshe Shelley (published 1821), an elegy on the death of John Keats. It mourns the death of Keats, condemns the critics whose reviews were thought to have hastened his death and ends on a joyous note, hailing Keats into the company of the immortals.

Aeneid, The, an epic poem in Latin hexameters by Vergil. It tells the story of the flight of Aeneas from Troy after it was captured by the Greeks and of his adventures on land and sea and in the underworld until he came to the river Tiber, where he founded the Roman state.

Aesop's Fables, a collection of very short stories in which animal characters behave and speak like human beings, showing the weaknesses and foibles of human nature. Each fable ends with a moral. They are attributed to Aesop, a deformed Phrygian slave who lived about 620–560 B.C. He was freed by his master and is said to have won fame for his wisdom at the court of Croesus, king of Lydia. There is a legend that Aesop saved the throne for Peisistratus, king of Athens, by telling his fable of *King Log and King Stork* to the discontented mob that was threatening to dethrone him.

Aesop's Fables are the stories that everyone knows. *The Ant and the Grasshopper, The Fox and the Grapes, The Dog and the Bone, The Lion and the Mouse, King Log and King Stork* are familiar to every child.

Probably Aesop never put his fables in writing. The stories themselves are centuries older than Aesop and of Oriental origin. Babrius in the 1st century B.C. put them into Greek verse and Phaedrus in the 1st century A.D. translated them into Latin. In the 14th century, Maximus Planudes, a monk, collected 144 fables, and from these all the later collections known as Aesop's have been taken. La Fontaine translated them charmingly into French verse in the 17th century.

Ah, Wilderness!, a play by Eugene O'Neill, produced and published in 1933. The scene of the action is "a large small-town in Connecticut," and the story is that of the youthful romantic awakening of Richard Miller. A phrase from the Rubáiyát supplies the title.

Alexandrian Age, the period of learning and literary activity in Egypt from 306 B.C. to 30 B.C., when Alexandria, Egypt, was the cultural center of the world. The great Alexandrian Library, containing the largest collection of manuscripts (700,000, it is said) of ancient times, was founded during the reign of Ptolemy Soter of Egypt about 275 B.C. and enlarged by his successors.

The Alexandrian period was distinguished by great scientists and mathematicians—Euclid, Archimedes, Diophantus—and the last of the Greek poets, Callimachus, Theocritus and Apollonius Rhodius.

Alice's Adventures in Wonderland, a whimsical, mock-serious story for children by Lewis Carroll, published 1865. Lewis Carroll was the pen name of Charles L. Dodgson, a mathematician of Oxford University, England. The book was illustrated by Sir John Tenniel. Alice dreams that she follows an entrancing White Rabbit down a rabbit hole and finds herself in a strange land where she meets the Mad Hatter and the March Hare, poor Bill (the lizard), the Duchess, the Cheshire Cat and its grin, the terrifying Queen of Hearts and many other strange personages. *Through the Looking Glass,* published 1871, is a sequel in which Alice dreams again. This time she steps through a looking glass into a chessboard country, where the kings and queens and knights of chess come to life. Humpty Dumpty, Tweedledum and Tweedledee, and the Walrus and the Carpenter are the most famous characters in this fantasy. In both books there are many parodies of famous poems.

allegory, a story with a literal meaning that suggests a deeper figurative meaning. The characters often personify ideas or qualities, a type of person or even a nation. The actions symbolize other more significant actions. An allegory is far more than a metaphor; it calls for greater length of figurative expression and a more sustained imagination on the part of both author and reader. Fables and parables are simple allegories with but one idea or moral to be put over. The long allegory can be narration or description, poetry or drama.

John Bunyan's *Pilgrim's Progress* is the most famous allegory in English—the story of Christian's trials and troubles as he seeks the Celestial City. Maeterlinck's *Blue Bird* is an allegorical fantasy about happiness with the lesson that happiness is not far away but here at home and to be found in acts of kindness.

NEW YORK PUBLIC LIBRARY

ALICE AND CARDS from *Alice in Wonderland.* A drawing by Sir John Tenniel.

alliteration, the beginning of two or more consecutive words, or words near together, with the same letter or sound. Fire and flame, time and tide, spick and span are instances of alliteration in everyday phrases.

Alliteration was the base of ancient German and Old English versification, in which each line broke into two halves with most of the accented syllables beginning with the same sound. A line from the Old English lay *The Battle of Brunanburh* illustrates this rule:

We'rene wi'code ‖ wa'est ofer Pan'-
tum.
(The warriors went west over the
river Pantum).

In all English poetry there is considerable use of alliteration—for example:

"*F*ull *f*athom *f*ive thy *f*ather lies"
a line from a song in Shakespeare's *Tempest;* and
"Where Alph the sacred *r*iver *r*an

Through caverns *m*easureless to *m*an
Down to a *s*unless *s*ea."
  (From Coleridge's *Kubla Khan.*)

ana, a collection of the sayings of a famous person or a collection of anecdotes concerning him. This was the original meaning of the suffix, as in Johnsoniana, material about Johnson. The term has been extended to include a collection of bits of information on any subject. Americana, for instance, means the collected information about America. The suffix has developed into a separate word.

Anabasis, Xenophon's history of the 10,000 Greek mercenaries who marched with Cyrus the Younger against his brother Artaxerxes II, king of Persia, in 401 B.C. It is a stirring account of the march inland (Anabasis, going upcountry) and of the retreat (in Greek, Katabasis, march to the coast, going down) from Persia through Armenia to the Black Sea. Xenophon, the author, accompanied the expedition.

Anacreontics, short poems in praise of wine and women in the style made famous by the Greek poet Anacreon (*c.* 563–478 B.C.) and his imitators. The verse form is usually a line of seven syllables, the first, third, fifth and last being accented. Several English poets wrote this sort of verse, among them Abraham Cowley and John Phillips in the 17th century and Tom Moore at the beginning of the 19th.

anacrusis (Greek, upbeat, unstressed), an unaccented syllable beginning a line of verse that normally begins with an accented syllable; or an extra unaccented syllable at the beginning of a line that normally begins with an unaccented syllable. The word To beginning the second line of the following quotation is an example of anacrusis:

"Is' it time" they rise and cry
"To le'ad our hosts again?"
  (From Margaret Widdemer's *The Old Kings.*)

The new interpretation of English meter would not explain this syllable as an extra sound but would say that for variety the unaccented and the accented syllable had the same time together as an accented syllable usually has—an eighth note plus a dotted quarter to equal a half note. Or even more simply, *to lead* is pronounced as a single syllable *t'lead.*

anapest, in versification, a metrical foot containing three syllables: two unaccented syllables followed by one accented syllable.

I am mon'/ arch of all' / I sur /vey'.
  (From William Cowper's *Verses Supposed to be Written by Alexander Selkirk.*)

Ancient Mariner, The Rime of the, a poem by Samuel Taylor Coleridge, first published in 1798 in the *Lyrical Ballads* of Wordsworth and Coleridge. It is a narrative poem in simple ballad form with a somewhat allegorical idea. The teller of the story on a voyage in the south polar seas had shot an albatross, a bird the sailors considered a sign of good fortune. The dead albatross was hung on the Mariner's neck, and a curse killed the crew and left him in fear and terror. The curse vanishes and the bird falls from his neck when he blesses the beauty of the strange sea creatures. The moral is

He prayeth best who loveth best
All things both great and small.

Anglo-Saxon Chronicle, a history of England down to 1154 A.D., the first prose work in Old English. The chronicle of England to the year 892 was collected from different local sources by order of Alfred the Great, who himself may have dictated the parts relating to his own time. The work was continued under Edward; and there is a full account of the Danish wars up to 924. The sections dealing with the years 925–75 contain the famous lay on the Battle of Brunanburh and several other poems, but the main narrative is in prose.

Anna Karenina, a novel by Leo Tolstoy, translated from Russian into English in 1886. This is one of the world's greatest novels. Wedded to a selfish husband much older than herself, Anna Karenina falls in love with Count Vronsky, a brilliant young officer, and sacrifices her position, home and child for him. When he tires of her, she commits suicide.

anthology, literally, a collection of flowers, hence a collection of beautiful or representative passages from literature. Florilegium, the Latin equivalent for the Greek anthology, was used in the same sense.

The most famous was *The Greek Anthology,* a collection of 4,500 short Greek poems begun by Meleager about 60 B.C. continued by Philippus of Thessalonica, who first applied the word *anthologia* to the collection, and continued and enlarged by various other poets and sophists until about 1320 A.D.

Of the modern anthologies, Palgrave's *Golden Treasury of Songs and Lyrics* (1861 and 1896) is one of the most famous. Sir Arthur Quiller Couch compiled the Oxford Books of English Verse, Ballads, Victorian Verse and English Prose; and Bliss Carman compiled the *Oxford Book of American Verse.* Mark Van Doren has compiled a big anthology of world poetry.

aphorism, a short sentence stating some truth or bit of human wisdom so pithily and vividly that it sticks in the memory. "He is a fool that cannot conceal his wisdom" is an aphorism from *Poor Richard's Almanack.*

Arabian Nights' Entertainments, a collection of about 250 stories of Oriental origin, known also as *The Thousand and One Nights* or *A Thousand Nights and A Night.* They were written in Arabic but the stories themselves are the popular stories of Arabian, Indian and Persian folklore. They were first translated into French by Antoine Galland in 1704–17. Edward William Lane made an abridged translation from the Arabic into English in 1840. The complete translation (1885–88) by Sir Richard Burton is the most famous of all.

The stories are told each night by Scheherazade, who marries a sultan who had been killing his newly married wives each morning after the

NEW YORK PUBLIC LIBRARY

ARTHURIAN LEGEND "The Lady of the Lake." Pen drawing by Aubrey Beardsley.

wedding. Scheherazade stops her narrative at the most exciting point so that the sultan spares her life until the next night. On the thousand-and-first night he decides she is too good and clever to be put to death and that he cannot live without her.

Many famous stories are contained in the *Arabian Nights.* Among the most widely known are those of the Porter of Bagdad, Aladdin, Ali Baba and the Forty Thieves and the Voyages of Sindbad the Sailor.

archaism, the use of old-fashioned or outmoded words or expressions in speech or writing. *Albeit* is an archaism, meaning even so, although. Others are: *haply,* by chance; *meseems,* it seems to me; *prithee,* I pray you, *wight,* a living person, *yclept,* named or called. Such words give an ancient effect especially in poetry.

Arden, an ancient forest in Warwickshire, England, famous in song and story. Most of the scenes in Shakespeare's *As You Like It* take place in Arden.

Ariel, in *The Tempest* by Shakespeare, a spirit of the air who had been bewitched and imprisoned in a pine tree on a lonely island. Prospero, shipwrecked on the island, discovered Ariel, released him and employed him to help work his own magic spells.

Artful Dodger, a youthful character in Dicken's novel *Oliver Twist,* so named because of his skill in dodging the police.

Arthurian Legend, all the material concerning Arthur of Britain in folklore, legend and romance. The historical Arthur has been placed in the 6th century and coupled with the battle of Badon (518) by Nennius in his *History of the Britons,* written in Latin in the 8th century, and by the *Annales Cambriae,* an ancient Welsh

chronicle in Latin, written in the 10th century.

Arthur appears as a mythical hero of superhuman prowess in the *Black Book of Carmarthen,* a 12th century manuscript of ancient Welsh poetry, and as fairy king and warrior slaying monsters and surrounded by superhuman knights in the *Red Book of Hergest,* a 14th century Welsh manuscript containing the *Mabinogion* and five stories about Arthur. Two of these are of Celtic origin and very ancient: *Kilhwch and Olwen* and the *Dream of Rhonabwy.*

Geoffrey of Monmouth in his *History of the Kings of Britain,* written in Latin (12th century), produced the Arthur of romance, son of Uther Pendragon, husband of Guinevere, conqueror of western Europe, who fell in the battle of Camlan after killing his traitorous nephew Modred. Wace, the Norman-French poet, added the Round Table to the story. Layamon translated Wace into English in his *Brut* and added a wealth of color and incident and fairy detail.

Stories of Arthur and his knights were spread all over Europe as early as the 11th century by wandering British bards. There are 12th century carvings of Arthurian scenes on the door of the Modena cathedral.

The great cycle of written Arthurian romance in Europe, however, developed after the 12th century. Chrestien de Troyes wrote an *Erec,* an *Yvain* and the great story of Perceval, the *Story of the Grail.* Wolfram von Eschenbach's *Parzival* is the source of Wagner's. Robert de Boron contributed a *Merlin,* a *Perceval* and *Joseph of Arimathea,* which developed later into the vast *Story of the Holy Grail.* Numerous manuscripts of unknown authorship exist dealing with all this material. Later came a prose *Lancelot,* a *Quest of Galahad,* a *Morte d'Arthur,* followed by a 14th-century verse *Morte d'Arthur* in England and by Sir Thomas Malory's long English prose *Morte d'Arthur* in the 15th century, which was the source for all later writers. Tennyson in *Idylls of the King,* William Morris in *Defense of Guinevere,* E. A. Robinson in his *Lancelot* and his *Tristram,* have drawn for the most part on Malory. The story of Tristram and Iseult was not linked with Arthur until rather late.

As You Like It, a comedy by Shakespeare, first produced about 1599, published in 1623. Duke Frederick's niece Rosalind, disguised as a boy, and Frederick's daughter Celia, dressed as a rustic lass, flee to the forest of Arden and there they meet Orlando who had fallen in love with Rosalind and is now living with her banished father, the rightful duke. Rosalind, as the boy Ganymede, prays Orlando to make love to her "as if she were his Rosalind." Oliver comes to the forest in pursuit of his brother Orlando and is saved by him from a lion, and the two become reconciled. Oliver falls in love with Celia. Touchstone, the court jester, loves Audrey, a simple country maid. The play ends with four weddings under a tree in the forest, and Frederick returns the dukedom to his brother.

The melancholy Jacques and the jester Touchstone are minor characters.

Athos, Porthos and Aramis, "the three musketeers" of Louis XIII of France, in Alexandre Dumas's romance.

Aucassin and Nicolette, a French romance written in the 12th century, translated and adapted into English by Andrew Lang, Swinburne, Laurence Housman and others. It is the love story of Aucassin, son of the Count of Beaucaire, and Nicolette, a Saracen captive maiden. They are separated by the count but after many adventures they are happily reunited.

Augustan Age, the reign (27 B.C.–14 A.D.) of Augustus Caesar, when Latin literature reached its highest development and greatest purity under the patronage of Augustus and his minister Maecenas. The great writers of the period were Vergil, Horace, Ovid and Livy.

The reign of Queen Anne (1702–14) is called the Augustan Age of English Literature, a period marked by Steele, Swift, Pope and Addison.

In France the term is applied to the reign of Louis XIV (1643–1715) when Corneille, Racine and Molière wrote their brilliant plays.

Auld Lang Syne (old long since, old time's sake), a poem written by Robert Burns in 1788, from what he could remember of an old man's singing. The refrain was familiar throughout Scotland long before Burns used it. The song is included in a collection of old Scottish songs compiled by James Johnson, 1787–1803.

Auld Reekie (old smoky), an epithet of Edinburgh, Scotland, on account of its smoky chimneys.

Aurora Leigh, a novel in blank verse by Elizabeth Barrett Browning, published in 1856. Aurora Leigh loves her cousin Romney Leigh but will not marry him because he wants her only to help him in his philanthropic schemes. When he loses his fortune and his sight, they finally understand each other. Many literary and socialistic theories are described in the poem.

autobiography, the life history of a person written by himself. *The Confessions of St. Augustine* (late 4th and early 5th centuries) is probably the world's greatest spiritual autobiography. Cellini's *Autobiography of Benvenuto Cellini* is a vivid picture of the Italian Renaissance and some of its outstanding personages, as well as of the great artist. Rousseau's *Confessions* published in 1782 was the first great introspective (inward-looking) autobiography. Among the most famous modern autobiographies are: Benjamin Franklin's *Autobiography* (1868), Leo Tolstoy's *Confessions* (1882), George Moore's *Memoirs of My Dead Life* (1906) and *Hail and Farewell* (1911–14), Henry Adams's *The Education of Henry Adams* (1906), Edward Bok's *Americanization of Edward Bok* (1920), Mark Twain's *Autobiography* (1922) and the *Autobiography of Lincoln Steffens* (1931).

Autocrat of the Breakfast Table, a series of essays by Oliver Wendell Holmes, published in the *Atlantic Monthly* in 1857–8. The essays are conversations around a boardinghouse breakfast table. The Autocrat comments on art, science, travel and philosophy, with occasional remarks by the Landlady, the Young Man Called John, the Schoolmistress, the Old Gentleman Opposite, the Poor Relation and others. *The Wonderful One-Horse Shay, The Chambered Nautilus, The Old Man Dreams* and other poems by Holmes are in *The Autocrat.*

Avon, Swan of, an epithet given to Shakespeare by Ben Jonson.

Bab Ballads, light verse, written and illustrated by Sir William S. Gilbert, collected in book form 1869–73. The ballads are humorous and satirical, and many of them are songs in the Gilbert and Sullivan operas; for instance, *Patience, Iolanthe, Ruddigore.*

Babbitt, a novel by Sinclair Lewis, published in 1922. The hero is a small-town businessman, George F. Babbitt, who rebels against the materialism of Zenith, his home town, but has to renounce his ideals. Babbitt has come to mean the typical American businessman.

ballad, a short narrative poem in simple stanza form and of unknown folk authorship. Ballads deal with folk legends and heroes and events. The grim and tragic stories bear testimony to their primitive origin, for the true ballads were handed down orally from generation to generation. There were no written ballads before the 15th century, but the ballads themselves are centuries older.

The typical ballad stanza is the simplest of verse forms. It has four lines, of which the first and third are unrhymed and have four accents each; the second and fourth are rhymed and contain three accents each. (Fourteen accents in the four lines.) Occasionally ballads are found in rhymed couplets each couplet having seven accents. But the stanza form of *Sir Patrick Spens* illustrates the typical ballad stanza:

The king' sits in' Dumfer'ling toun'
Drink'ing the blood'-red wine';
"O where' will I' get guid' sailor'
To sail' this ship' of mine' ?"

Probably no ballad was ever composed by a group. An individual made up the song, and the group adopted it. Soldier marching songs, cowboy songs and seamen's chanties of later times originated in the same way.

Francis J. Child, a Harvard professor, collected the *English and Scottish Popular Ballads* (1882–98). Some of the best known of these are *Sir Patrick Spens, The Twa Corbies* (The Two Crows), *Edward, Edward, The Twa Sisters* with its refrain of "Binnorie, O Binnorie," *Barbara Allen* and the tragic *Lord Randal.*

American ballads are of two kinds: those descended from the old Scottish or English ballads, which immigrated with the early settlers, and those that have sprung up spontaneously among the various folk types in America. These are the hillbilly songs of the southern mountaineers, cowboy ballads and songs of the cattle trails, of logging camps and lumberjacks and miners. The popular and widespread *Frankie and Johnny* ballad is of Negro or barroom origin.

Sir Walter Scott and W. E. Aytoun wrote ballad romances on themes from Scottish and Border history.

Lord Macaulay in the *Lays of Ancient Rome* (1842) attempted to reproduce historical legends of early Rome—"Horatius" is the best known, and in "Ivry" and "Naseby" he applied the same method to French and English history.

Later ballads are not historical but nearly always fictional. John Davidson's *Ballad of Hell,* Oscar Wilde's *Ballad of Reading Gaol* and Keats's *La Belle Dame Sans Merci* are modern art ballads.

Banquo, in Shakespeare's *Macbeth,* a thane of Scotland and a general in the army of Duncan, king of Scotland. To thwart a prophecy that Banquo would beget kings, Macbeth, who had already murdered Duncan and seized the throne, murdered Banquo and was thereafter tormented by Banquo's ghost.

NEW YORK PUBLIC LIBRARY

BALLAD "The Dragon of Wantley."

Barbara Frietchie, a poem by John Greenleaf Whittier recounting an incident supposed to have occurred at Frederick, Maryland, during the Civil War. Barbara was a patriotic old woman who refused to lower the Union flag from her home when the Confederates under General Jackson entered the town, and he would not permit his troops to molest her.

Barkis, in *David Copperfield* by Charles Dickens, the stage driver who married Peggotty, the faithful old nurse of David Copperfield. Barkis is famous for his repeated proposal of marriage, "Barkis is willin'."

Barmecide Feast, in the *Arabian Nights,* the story of the beggar Shacabac, who was invited to a feast by one of the Barmecides, a wealthy Persian family. The host enjoyed a hearty meal, but only empty dishes were placed before the hungry beggar. But he praised the food, declared that the wine had gone to his head and he attacked his host. Then he got a fine dinner. So *Barmecide feast* means an imaginary banquet or imaginary plenty.

Barrack-Room Ballads, a collection of poems by Rudyard Kipling, published in 1892, portraying the life and spirit of the common British soldier stationed in India. Many of the poems— *Danny Deever, Gunga Din, Boots, The Road to Mandalay,* for instance— have been set to music.

Barretts of Wimpole Street, The, a play by Rudolf Besier (1931), the love story of Robert Browning and Elizabeth Barrett. Katharine Cornell played Elizabeth on the stage. In the movie version Norma Shearer was Elizabeth and Charles Laughton was her narrow, selfish father.

Battle Hymn of the Republic, a poem by Julia Ward Howe, published in the *Atlantic Monthly* in 1862 and sung to the tune of "John Brown's Body." It was a favorite with Union soldiers in the Civil War.

Becky Sharp, the heroine of Thackeray's *Vanity Fair.* Spirited, clever, selfish, unscrupulous, she charmed many lovers, made a good marriage, won her way to the social position she craved, lost her husband by her intrigues and was brought low again at last, notorious and disreputable. She is portrayed in sharp contrast to Amelia Smedley, a pretty, spiritless, unintelligent girl, whose eventual happy marriage was engineered by Becky Sharp.

belles-lettres (French for fine or beautiful literature), artistic, esthetic or imaginative literature, literature as art, contrasted with practical, informational or scientific writings. Short poems, fiction, drama and, especially, light essays of appreciation are considered belles-lettres.

Ben Hur: A Tale of the Christ, a romance by Lew Wallace, published in 1880. Judah Ben Hur, a wealthy young Jew, is condemned to the Roman galleys, but after many exciting adventures, including the famous chariot race, again becomes a power in his land. He meets Jesus of Nazareth and becomes one of his followers. The book is full of excitement and romance, and its historical and religious setting made the story popular on the stage and in the movies.

Beowulf, an Old English (Anglo-Saxon) epic poem. The story consists of five episodes: (1) Beowulf with a small band of followers goes to aid Hrothgar, king of the Danes, and kills Grendel, a monster that is ravaging the land. (2) Grendel's mother seeks to avenge her son, but Beowulf follows her to her underwater lair and kills her. (3) Beowulf returns home loaded with gifts and rewards to recount his adventures, and on the death of Hygelac becomes king of the Geats. (4) In his old age Beowulf loses his life in combat with a firedragon that is devastating his kingdom. (5) His people, grieving, place his body on a great funeral pyre and bury the dragon's treasure with his ashes. The poem shows a spirit of self-sacrifice and nobility unusual in primitive compositions. The customs and ideals of the people revealed in the narrative give us a good idea of primitive Germanic civilization in the early 6th century. The only manuscript of the poem was written about 1000 A.D.

bibliography, a list of books and articles on a special subject or a certain author. For instance, a complete bibliography of Sir Walter Scott includes the titles of everything that Scott wrote with dates of publication, all editions and formats, and every book about Scott or any of his works and all magazine articles and monographs about him.

In a more general sense bibliog-

raphy is the serious study or descriptive history of all manuscripts and books and their making, including references to authors and editions, the materials used in their make-up and the dates and styles of their printing.

Biglow Papers, The, political satires by James Russell Lowell. The first series (1846–48) opposed the Mexican War; and the second (1862–66) took the Northern and abolitionist side in the Civil War. The principal character is Hosea Biglow, whose New England dialect gives the poems in *Biglow Papers* a quaint, homespun character. Contrasted with this simple homespun style are the long learned prefaces and footnotes by the Rev. Homer Wilbur, full of pedantry and classical allusions.

biography, the written history of the life of a person. Modern biography tries to record the development of a personality, to portray individuals as they really were.

Even in early times there was a certain variety in biography but it was mostly written for political or moral purposes in Greek and Roman times and much later.

In the 4th century B.C. Xenophon wrote a defense of his master Socrates that is called *Memorabilia*—a title something like *memoirs* as it is used today. In the 1st century A.D. Plutarch wrote his *Parallel Lives*, comparing the careers of a score of Romans with the same number of Greeks, pair by pair, and countless later writers (Shakespeare among them) drew on this work for facts and characterization. In Latin: Cornelius Nepos (1st century B.C.) wrote brief lives of illustrious men in a simple clear style; Tacitus, the great historian, wrote a life of his father-in-law Agricola that is a classic; and Suetonius's *Twelve Caesars* (written about 120 A.D.) is gossipy and full of scandal. These are samples of what is called "antique biography," written to emphasize certain moral qualities or to teach a political lesson.

Biography in English begins in the 16th century with William Roper's *Life of Sir Thomas More* and George Cavendish's *Life of Cardinal Wolsey.* In the 17th century Izaak Walton wrote the *Lives* of Donne, Hooker, Herbert and others that are the forerunners of modern personal biography. James Boswell's *Life of Samuel Johnson* (1791) is interesting, personal, detailed and minute. Johnson's own *Life of Cowley* was written, he said, because in a former biography "all was confused and enlarged through a mist of panegyric."

In modern biography Lytton Strachey in *Eminent Victorians* (1918) and *Queen Victoria* (1921) stands out as a portrayer of human beings in whole truth, regardless of popular tradition. Gamaliel Bradford's *American Portraits* (1920) were the first of many spiritual portraits that he called *psychographs.*

Other outstanding modern biographies are: André Maurois's *Ariel* (1923), the life of Shelley, and one of Disraeli (1927); Hervey Allen's *Israfel* (1926), a life of Edgar Allan Poe; Carl Sandburg's *Abraham Lincoln,*

The Prairie Years (1926); and Catherine Carswell's *Life of Robert Burns* (1930).

Black Beauty, the autobiography of a horse, by Anna Sewell, published in 1877. Black Beauty, a finely bred horse, crippled by a drunken groom, is sold to a livery stable, becomes a workhorse, is finally sold into good hands and ends his days in peace. It was the first popular book on kindness to animals and had a huge sale.

blank verse, any verse without rhyme; usually iambic pentameter, the most common metrical form in English dramatic and epic poetry. Iambic pentameter has five metrical feet to a line, each foot having one unaccented syllable followed by one accented syllable. It was first used by Henry Howard, Earl of Surrey, in his translations from the *Aeneid* in the 16th century. The first English drama written in blank verse was Sackeville and Norton's tragedy *Gorboduc* in 1562. Then Christopher Marlowe used it in his tragedy *Tamburlaine* in 1589. Shakespeare adopted and perfected it. No one since has written more beautiful, vigorous or moving blank verse than Shakespeare or more majestic than Milton in *Paradise Lost.* These lines from Tennyson's *Morte D'Arthur* in *The Idylls of the King* illustrate the flow of blank verse:

> "So like a shatter'd column lay the king;
> Not like that Arthur who, with lance in rest,
> From spur to plume a star of tournament,
> Shot thro' the lists at Camelot, and charged
> Before the eyes of ladies and of kings."

Bleak House, a novel by Charles Dickens published serially, 1852–53. It satirizes the injustice of delay in the Court of Chancery. The case of Jarndyce and Jarndyce in which the fortunes of Richard Carstone and his cousin Ada Clare are at stake, in the courts so long that it has eaten up in costs the whole fortune involved, suddenly comes to an end. Among the minor characters: Mrs. Jellyby is devoted to foreign missions but neglectful of her own family; Mr. Chadband is a pious hypocrite; the irresponsible Harold Skimpole is a parody on the poet and critic Leigh Hunt; and Boythorn is patterned on another poet, Walter Savage Landor.

Blithedale Romance, The, a novel by Nathaniel Hawthorne, published in 1852. The scene is the Brook Farm Institute, an experiment in community living.

Bluebird, The, a dramatic fantasy by Maurice Maeterlinck (1909). The allegory of the pursuit of the Blue Bird means that happiness is close at hand in acts of kindness and cannot be held like a possession but must be forever sought and won anew.

Bottom, Nick, the weaver in Shakespeare's *Midsummer Night's Dream.* During a rehearsal for *Pyramus and Thisbe* Puck puts an ass's head on Bottom, and then the fairy queen awakes and falls in love with him be-

NEW YORK PUBLIC LIBRARY

"CARMEN," an opera by Georges Bizet, was performed for the first time in 1875.

cause Oberon has put love drops on her eyes.

Bounty, Mutiny on the, the first of three novels by Charles B. Nordhoff and James H. Hall, published in 1932. It tells the story of the mutiny of the crew of H. M. S. *Bounty* against the cruelty of their commander, William Bligh. They were bound for the West Indies from Tahiti with a cargo of breadfruit trees. On April 28, 1789, they seized William Bligh and set him adrift in an open boat with 18 men who had refused to mutiny. *Men Against the Sea* (1933) tells of the heroic 4,000–mile voyage of Bligh's men in the open boat and their arrival in Batavia. *Pitcairn Island* (1934) is the story of the 25 mutinous members of the crew who sailed the *Bounty* back to Tahiti. Eight of them, under the leadership of Fletcher Christian, embarked again with a number of Tahitians and landed on Pitcairn Island where they founded a colony. This part of the story was celebrated by Byron in his poem *The Island.* Sir John Barrow's *The Mutiny and Piratical Seizure of H. M. S. Bounty,* published in 1831, was the first written narrative of the whole story. The three splendid, stirring novels of Nordhoff and Hall, for all their art, were written with strict adherence to the actual records.

Brobdingnag, in *Gulliver's Travels* by Jonathan Swift, the second strange country visited by Gulliver. Brobdingnag was inhabited by people of gigantic stature and all aspects of life were on the same scale.

Brook Farm Institute (1841–47), an unsuccessful attempt to found an ideal community in New England where all the members should labor with their hands and share their intellectual life. Hawthorne's *Blithedale Romance* is a realistic picture of this community.

caesura (literally cutting), the pause or break in the middle of a line of verse: indicated by double verticals, ‖. In Greek and Latin poetry the caesura occurs without regard to any pause in the sense of the line. The caesura in the first line of Vergil's *Aeneid*

　Arma virumque cano ‖ Trojae qui primus ab oris

is a masculine caesura, as it follows the accent. A feminine caesura is one that follows an unstressed syllable. In English verse, both old and modern, the caesura comes about the middle of a line and usually where the sense causes a natural rhetorical pause. Examples of the caesura:

　Werene wicode ‖ waest ofer Pantum.

(From *The Battle of Brunanburh* in the *Anglo-Saxon Chronicle.*)

　I will speak out aloude ‖ I care not who heare it.

(From Udall's *Ralph Roister Doister.*)

　Hanging so light ‖ and hanging so high
　On the topmost twig ‖ that looks up at the sky.

(From Coleridge's *Christabel.*)

Caliban, in Shakespeare's *Tempest,* son of the witch Sycorax and a slave to Prospero. He was a deformed crude creature meant to typify a primitive savage. Robert Browning's poem "Caliban upon Setebos" is the savage's idea of God.

Call of the Wild, The, a story of the Alaska gold fields by Jack London, published in 1903. Buck, the dog, was stolen as a pup from his home, shipped to Alaska and trained as a sled dog. When his master John Thornton was murdered, Buck ran away into the forest to live with the wolves.

Canterbury Tales, The, a collection of 23 stories written in verse by Geoffrey Chaucer, English poet of the 14th century. The Prologue describes 31 typical medieval folk of different social stations, who agree to entertain themselves on their pilgrimage to Canterbury by telling stories as they ride. Some of the stories are coarse, some refined, some humorous, some

NEW YORK PUBLIC LIBRARY
GULLIVER IN BROBDINGNAG

tragic. Typical of the language are these lines from the Prologue:

　For him was lever have at his beddes heed
　Twenty bokes, clad in blak or reed.

The most widely known of the tales are the Knight's, the Clerk's and the Nun's.

Captains Courageous, a romance by Rudyard Kipling, published in 1897. Harvey Cheyne, the spoiled son of an American millionaire, fell overboard while crossing the Atlantic and was picked up on the Grand Banks by a fisherman in a dory from the schooner *We're Here.* Disko Troop, the old schooner captain, put Harvey to work, and the discipline of the hardy life and the fine spirit of the fishermen worked Harvey's salvation. He returned home a changed boy, healthy and with new ideals.

Carmen, a novel by Prosper Merimée, published in 1847, the basis of the opera *Carmen* by Bizet. Carmen, a beautiful Spanish gypsy girl, ensnares Don José, a cavalry corporal, while he is taking her to prison. He helps her escape, kills her husband, begs her to run off to America with him, kills her when she refuses and then gives himself up to the law. In the opera version Don José kills Carmen in tragic jealousy over her infatuation for a bullfighter.

Carton, Sidney, the hero of Dickens's *Tale of Two Cities,* a dissipated and unprincipled man, takes the place of a condemned prisoner, Charles Darnay, to whom he bears a striking resemblance. This saves Darnay and secures the happiness of Darnay's beautiful wife, with whom Carton is in love.

Casabianca, a poem by Mrs. Felicia Hemans. Casabianca was a 10-year-old boy whose father was in command of the frigate *Orient* during the Battle of Abukir (1792). He blew up his ship to prevent its being captured by the English. The child refused to leave his father and went down with the ship. The poem opens with the well-known line,

　The boy stood on the burning deck.

Castle Rackrent, a novel by Maria Edgeworth, published in 1801. It recounts the follies of an Irish family through several generations. The story lacks plot but has humor and depicts character well.

chanson de geste, literally, a song of great deeds; any epic poem in Old French, written in the 11th to the 15th centuries by poets called *trouvères* in northern France and *troubadours* in southern France, and spread by wandering minstrels called *jongleurs.* They depict the life of chivalry, especially the Emperor Charlemagne, his various wars and the heroic deeds of his paladins. The oldest, most famous and finest is the *Chanson de Roland.* Others are *Ogier the Dane, The Pilgrimage to Jerusalem, Bertha Greatfoot* and *Huon de Bordeaux.*

Chanson de Roland (The Song of Roland), an Old French *chanson de geste.* It recounts the fight of Roland, the most famous of Carlemagne's paladins, against the Saracens. Roland's army was treacherously ambushed at the pass of Roncesvalles in 778. There Roland and his companions fought until every man was killed, and at last, fatally wounded, Roland sounded his horn for help. The call was heard by Charlemagne 30 leagues away. He came and destroyed the Saracens.

Charge of the Light Brigade, a poem by Alfred Tennyson immortalizing an incident of the Battle of Balaklava in the Crimean War. An error in transmitting orders sent a brigade of 673 English cavalrymen on a charge against Russian guns that could result only in their slaughter.

Cheshire Cat, in an old English phrase, "Grin like a Cheshire cat," a simile for a broad, toothy smile. Nobody knows the origin of the comparison. In Lewis Carroll's *Alice in Wonderland* the Cheshire Cat talks to Alice, then vanishes—first, absolutely and immediately; and then by degrees until there is no cat left—just the grin!

Child's Garden of Verses, A, a collection of poems for children by Robert Louis Stevenson, published in 1885. It contains the simple and charming *Where Go the Boats, My Shadow, The Lamplighter, The Unseen Playmate* and the famous dedication to Alison Cunningham, his childhood nurse.

Chillon, a famous castle on the shores of Lake Geneva, Switzerland. It was the prison of Count Bonivard, who defended Switzerland against the Duke of Savoy in the 16th century. The Duke imprisoned Bonivard in one of its dungeons in 1530 for six years. This historic incident is the theme of Byron's *The Prisoner of Chillon.*

Christmas Carol, A, a story of Christmas by Charles Dickens, published in 1843. Old Scrooge, a "clutching, covetous old sinner" and Tiny Tim, the crippled child of Bob Cratchit, Scrooge's clerk, are two of the main characters. It is the story of Scrooge's regeneration: how the spirit of Christmas changed him from an unfeeling money-lover to the kind and benevolent human being who sent a turkey to the Cratchit family and made their Christmas full and merry.

Cid, The (the lord, from a Moorish word), the great national hero of Spain of the 11th century. He is immortalized in the 12th century *Poem of the Cid,* in a 13th century Spanish chronicle and in scores of ballads. Corneille's most famous drama, *The Cid,* celebrates the legend of the hero.

classicism, the principles and qualities of Greek and Roman literature, especially when used as a standard for later works. The principles of classicism are pure and correct language, simple but elegant style, clearness, balance and orderliness of thought and expression. In an unfavorable sense, classicism means too great conventionality, a sacrificing of ease or spirit to the form of the writing; and it is contrasted with romanticism or naturalism.

classics, literary productions of surpassing excellence. They represent the highest standards in literature. Specifically, the classics are the works of the ancient Greek and Roman writers. In general the classics are those works that have stood the test

A CHRISTMAS CAROL. "In came little Bob, the father with . . . his threadbare clothes darned up and brushed, to look seasonable; and Tiny Tim upon his shoulder. Alas for Tiny Tim, he bore a little crutch and had his limbs supported by an iron frame."

of time and remain beloved and valuable through all times, whether their style is classic or romantic.

Cloister and the Hearth, The, a historical novel by Charles Reade, published in 1861. It portrays the wanderings through Holland, Germany, France and Italy of Gerard, father of the distinguished Dutch scholar Erasmus, and thus gives a vivid picture of Europe in the 15th century.

comedy, a play written in an entertaining manner and having a happy ending. It contains light, clever dialogue and amusing situations. Sometimes the term is applied in a literary sense to any composition that treats life truly and seriously but does not leave the reader with a sense of tragedy.

Compleat Angler, The, a discussion of fishing by Izaak Walton, first published in 1653. It is written in dialogue form and contains advice on angling, songs and personal reflections. The full title is *The Compleat Angler, or the Contemplative Man's Recreation.*

Comus, a masque by John Milton presented in 1634 at Ludlow Castle, for the Earl of Bridgewater. The triumph of virtue over evil is the theme. Virtue is embodied in the Lady, who is lost in the wood and lured to the home of the enchanter Comus, a son of Circe. She refuses to drink his potion and is rescued by the Attendant Spirit with the aid of Sabrina, the water nymph.

Confessions of an English Opium Eater, Thomas De Quincey's account of his own experience, published in 1822. It tells how much opium he could take in a day, what the effects were, how various trivial events of his life, glorified and distorted by the influence of the drug, became the material of his dreams, and how in fear of death he gradually reduced his dosage and almost overcame the habit. This book, first published without his name, brought De Quincey a ready market for his writings and assured his literary success.

Cotter's Saturday Night, a poem by Robert Burns, written in 1785, picturing the Scottish laborer's family gathered around the hearth to rest and worship.

Count of Monte Cristo, The, a novel by Alexandre Dumas, the elder, published 1841–5. Edward Dantès is unjustly imprisoned for 20 years through the false accusations of two rivals and the corruption of a magistrate. In prison he learns the secret hiding place of an enormous treasure on the Island of Monte Cristo. He escapes from his dungeon, finds the treasure and establishes himself as Count of Monte Cristo. Then he spends years seeking out his false accusers to satisfy his revenge against them.

couplet, two consecutive rhyming verses. The most usual type is the heroic couplet, 10 syllables to a line, in iambic pentameter.

> A perfect judge will read each work of wit
> With the same spirit that its author writ.
> (From Alexander Pope's *Essay on Criticism*.)

Courtship of Miles Standish, The, a poem by Henry W. Longfellow, published in 1858, portraying life in Plymouth Colony. Miles Standish, captain of Plymouth, sends young John Alden to Priscilla Mullins to ask her hand in his behalf. Priscilla, guessing Alden's own feelings, says, "Why don't you speak for yourself, John?" and they are married.

Coverley, Sir Roger de, a courtly old gentleman of Worcestshire, presented by both Addison and Steele in many of the *Spectator* papers. He was named for his great–grandfather who was said to have invented the old country dance called the Sir Roger de Coverley. Addison described him as "a gentleman that is very singular in his behavior, but his singularities proceed from his good sense."

Crane, Ichabod, a Yankee schoolmaster in Washington Irving's *Legend of Sleepy Hollow* in *The Sketch Book*. He was in love with beautiful Katrina Van Tassell, but he was terrified out of the neighborhood by his rival, Brom Bones, who pursued him one night disguised as the Headless Horseman.

Cranford, a novel by Mrs. Gaskell, first published serially, 1851–53. It describes the life of gentility in a little Cheshire village in the 19th century. Miss Matty Jenkyns and her sister Deborah, Miss Betty Barker, Miss Pole, Miss Forrester and others are described with sympathetic humor. *Cranford* is one of the most charming novels ever written.

Crawley, Rawdon, in Thackeray's *Vanity Fair,* the good-hearted gambling young cavalry officer whom Becky Sharp secretly married. He was the son of Sir Pitt Crawley and was disinherited by his aunt when his marriage was discovered. He was devoted to Becky and left her only after her intrigue with Lord Steyne.

Cricket on the Hearth, The, a Christmas story by Charles Dickens, published in 1846. A singing contest between a cricket on Dot Peerybingle's hearth and a kettle hanging on the crane give the title to the story. The singing contest is won by the cricket, and two love stories end happily. Edward Plummer returns from South America just in time to prevent his old sweetheart, May Fielding, from marrying an ill-natured old man, Tackleton, and dispels the suspicions Tackleton has wrought between the happy Dot and John Peerybingle.

Crisis, The, a novel by Winston Churchill, American fiction writer, published in 1901. It tells the story of a Northern officer and a Southern girl during the Civil War. The scenes are laid in and near St. Louis, Mo., and Lincoln, Sherman and Grant are introduced.

criticism, the art of judging and pointing out the perfections and imperfections of works of art. Appreciation is as much a part of criticism as is flaw detection. The true critic must have knowledge, taste, sympathy and no personal prejudices.

The chief objects of literary criticism are (1) to judge, (2) to interpret, (3) to give personal impressions of books. Matthew Arnold defines criticism as "a disinterested endeavor to learn and propagate the best that is known and thought in the world."

Crossing, The, a historical novel by Winston Churchill, detailing the adventures of a young man during the westward movement of settlers across the Alleghenies into Kentucky and Tennessee from the coastal colonies during the Revolutionary War. George Rogers Clark is the hero.

cycle, all the poems, romances and narratives dealing with a certain hero, his followers and deeds. For instance, all the prose and verse romances that have built up the legend of King Arthur and his Knights of the Round Table constitute the Arthurian cycle. The series centering around Charlemagne and his paladins is called the Charlemagne cycle. The Nibelungenlied is another cycle.

Cyrano de Bergerac, a play by Edmond Rostand, written in 1898. Cyrano, a poet and soldier with a large ugly nose, falls in love with Roxanne but she loves Christian, a member of Cyrano's company. Cyrano, knowing his suit is hopeless, gives himself to the service of the lovers, writes marvelous poems and letters to Roxanne in Christian's name and even woos her one night in the dark. And Roxanne falls in love anew with "the soul" of her lover. Christian is killed in war; Roxanne retires to a convent. Years later Cyrano is injured and dies attended by Roxanne, who too late learns who her real lover was.

dactyl, a metrical foot of three syllables: one accented syllable followed by two unaccented syllables.

The first five feet of each of the following lines are dactyls:

> Still' stands the | for'est pri|me'val;
> but | where' are the | hearts' that
> be|neath' it
> Leaped' like the | roe' when he |
> hears' in the | wood'land the |
> voice' of the | hunts'man?
> (From Longfellow's *Evangeline*.)

In classical meter the dactyl consists of a long followed by two short syllables regardless of accent. The name comes from the Greek word for finger—three syllables like the finger's three joints.

Daisy Miller, a short novel by Henry James, published in 1878. An American girl from Schenectady is traveling in Europe with her mother. Without realizing the difference between European and small-town conventions, the mother allows her daughter the same freedom she had at home. The book reveals how the integrity of a self-respecting American girl was misjudged in the light of a more ancient, artificial code.

d'Artagnan, in *The Three Musketeers* by Alexandre Dumas, a gentleman of Gascony who joins the king's musketeers and becomes the stanch friend of the three comrades Athos, Porthos and Aramis.

David Copperfield, a novel by Charles Dickens, published in 1849–50. It tells the story of the hero David, his sad childhood and bitter experiences as

NEW YORK PUBLIC LIBRARY

ICHABOD CRANE, the principal character of Washington Irving's "The Legend of Sleepy Hollow," which was published in 1819 in his well-known *Sketch Book*.

schoolboy and apprentice, the new home found for him by his aunt Betsy Trotwood, the loss of his child-wife Dora, his success as an author and his later business prosperity and second marriage to Agnes Wickfield. David's nurse Peggotty and her husband Barkis, Little Em'ly, his tyrannical stepfather Mr. Murdstone, his landlord Mr. Micawber, Uriah Heep, Mr. Dick and other characters are famous examples of Dickens's ability in characterization. *David Copperfield* was Dickens's own favorite among his works and is known to be autobiographical.

David Balfour, a novel by Robert Louis Stevenson, published in 1893 and at first entitled *Catriona*. It is a sequel to *Kidnapped*. It tells how David tried and failed to free James Stewart, falsely accused of the murder of Colin Campbell, how Alan

Breck escaped from Scotland to Europe, and how David loved and married Catriona Drummond.

David Harum, a novel by Edward Noyes Westcott, published in 1899. David Harum was a country banker, shrewd, humorous and keen at driving a bargain, especially in horse trades. His dry wit and everyday philosophizings were widely quoted for many years.

Decameron, The, a collection of 100 tales by Boccaccio, an Italian novelist and poet of the 14th century. A group of ladies and gentlemen isolated themselves on a country estate to escape the plague then raging in Florence. Each member of the group told one story a day for ten days. (*Decameron* is Greek for ten days.) Boccaccio revealed himself in these tales as one of the greatest storytellers of all time; these famous tales are the source of many stories used by countless later writers, including Chaucer and Shakespeare.

Decline and Fall of the Roman Empire, a monumental history of Rome from the time of Trajan to the fall of Constantinople in 1453, by Edward Gibbon, published in 6 volumes in 1776–83. It is a moving panorama of the events of the world through about 13 centuries, when barbarism was conquering civilization. Gibbon spent many years in research in every capital of Europe, and so exhaustively did he pursue his theme that the *Decline and Fall* is considered one of the greatest historical works in the English language. It is learned, full of detail, somewhat prejudiced by Gibbon's antipathy to Christianity and his distrust of all noble motives. His book is still a first-class authority.

Desdemona, the heroine of Shakespeare's *Othello,* the beautiful young wife of Othello, the Moor, whom he strangled in a fit of jealousy.

Deserted Village, The, a poem by Oliver Goldsmith, published in 1770. It describes Auburn, Goldsmith's native village in Ireland, which was depopulated to make part of the large private estate of a noble. The village parson and the schoolmaster are sympathetically portrayed. The poem praises the charm and virtue of rural life in contrast with commerce and wealth and its results.

Dhu, Roderick, in Scott's *Lady of the Lake,* a Highland chieftain and outlaw, cousin of Ellen Douglas and a suitor for her hand in marriage.

Diana of the Crossways, a novel by George Meredith, published in 1885. Diana, the heroine, is continually coming to the crossways; that is, she is always having to choose which of two difficult paths to take. Her difficulties are those of love, marriage, divorce and money matters. Diana has wit, beauty and a capacity for loyalty. Her betrayal of a state secret to a newspaper is an incident the historical probability of which has caused much discussion. That her character was modeled upon that of Mrs. Norton, granddaughter of Richard Brinsley Sheridan, is now denied.

dimeter, a verse having two metrical feet.

> This doth' remain'
> To ease' my pain'.
> —George Peele

Divine Comedy, The, the great poetical work of Dante, written in the 14th century. The work is in three parts, describing the world beyond life: the Inferno (Hell), Purgatorio (Purgatory) and Paradiso (Heaven).

The poem presents Dante as a traveler through Hell and Purgatory under the guidance of the old poet Vergil. Hell seemed to him a pit of descending circles to which the various classes of sinners were assigned. And here Dante recognized and spoke with many old friends and famous personages of history and legend. Purgatory seemed a rising mountain within whose circles sinners were classified according to their repentance. Paradise was a world of light, reached only by repentance and purification. His own redemption Dante attributes to the influence and inspiration of his beloved and ideal Beatrice, who stands beside him at last in Paradise.

The poem is an allegory of the progress of the Christian soul, a record of Dante's own spiritual struggle and a learned discourse embracing most of the philosophical and scientific knowledge of the day.

Dixie, a patriotic song composed by Daniel D. Emmett in 1859. Dixie or Dixie Land means the South or the southern states collectively. It was adopted as a war song by the Confederate states during the Civil War and has since lived on as a favorite in all parts of the United States.

Doll's House, A, a play by Henrik Ibsen, published in 1879. Nora, the heroine, is a woman of restricted education who has been carefully protected and brought up without knowledge of the world. The result is that she is only a pretty, though devoted, doll in the house of her husband. She makes tragic mistakes and finally, at the end of the play, leaves the house to learn for herself the wisdom women need. The play is a protest against undue restriction of woman's sphere.

Dombey and Son, a novel by Charles Dickens, published in 1847–48. Mr. Dombey neglects his gentle daughter Florence, but takes great pride in Paul, his son. His pride is shattered by misfortunes. Mrs. Dombey, a second wife, humiliates him by deserting him; Paul dies while he is still a little boy; Mr. Dombey's business fails. Meanwhile Florence, who has gained the friendship of some plain seafaring people, marries one of them, Walter Gay. Her good fortune and faithfulness relieve Mr. Dombey's old age. Among the minor characters are Cap'n Cuttle, Solomon Gills and Susan Nipper, Florence's servant.

Donatello, in Hawthorne's *Marble Faun,* a young Italian count who bears a marked resemblance to the famous statue of a faun by Praxiteles. His character is that of a carefree pagan until he falls in love with Miriam and murders a man for her sake. Then he develops into a conscience-stricken member of civilized society and gives himself up to justice.

Don Juan, a character famous in literature as the type of licentious adventurer. The legend developed around the name of Don Juan Tenorio of Seville and was first used in Spanish

drama in the late 16th century. After seducing the daughter of the governor of Seville, Don Juan killed her father in a duel. Later he jestingly invited the statue of the dead man to a banquet, whereupon the statue grabbed him and delivered him to the devil. Mozart's opera *Don Giovanni* was founded on this story. Byron's poem *Don Juan* follows neither the legend nor the character type. Byron's Don Juan is altogether charming though unprincipled, and his adventures carry him to Greece, Turkey, Russia and England.

Don Quixote de la Mancha, a famous satirical romance by Cervantes, published in two parts, 1605 and 1615. The two chief characters are Don Quixote, a poor country gentleman crazed by reading stories of chivalry, and Sancho Panza, an ignorant but shrewd country fellow, his servant. The pair go adventuring and Don Quixote's insane attempt to conduct himself always as a knight leads them into many ridiculous situations. To his disordered mind windmills are giants and hotel wenches are beautiful princesses. After long wanderings the odd pair return to the village from which they set out and Don Quixote regains his sanity. The book was a burlesque on the chivalric romances and sentiments of the preceding age. But it was also far more; it was a searching discourse on life itself, and is still considered universally applicable.

Dr. Jekyll and Mr. Hyde, The Strange Case of, a novel by Robert Louis Stevenson, published in 1886. Dr. Jekyll, a London physician of good reputation, has discovered a drug that will change him from a kindly, sane man to a hideous person of cruel and criminal instincts. This wholly evil self he calls Mr. Hyde. The story portrays the struggle between good and evil in human nature. Eventually Mr. Hyde takes complete possession of the good doctor and commits a murder. The drug loses its power of restoring the better self, and in despair the poor man commits suicide.

drama (from a Greek word meaning action), a form of literary composition in prose or verse in which a story representing life and character is presented in dialogue and action, and is intended to be given by actors on a stage. Drama has developed into several different types: tragedy, comedy, melodrama, opera, burlesque, farce.

Duncan, in Shakespeare's *Macbeth,* the king of Scotland who was murdered by Macbeth.

East Lynne, a novel by Mrs. Henry Wood, published in 1861. It was made into a remarkably successful stage play, a melodrama, and in 1932 was shown as a moving picture. It is typical of the popular novel of the period.

Lady Isabel Vane, orphaned and bankrupt, was loved by two men, one noble, the other totally unworthy. She married the finer man, but later ran off with the other. Conscience-stricken, however, she left him and returned in disguise to her old home. Her husband had married again, and she hired herself out as nurse to her own children. Her husband recognized her and forgave her on her deathbed.

eclogue, a short pastoral poem, especially one by Vergil. The word originally meant selection, but Vergil's pastorals (*Bucolia*) were published as *Eclogae*, and the word got a special meaning.

Eddas, two ancient works in Old Norse or Icelandic. The first, the Poetic or Elder Edda, erroneously attributed to Saemund the Wise, was compiled between the 10th and 13th centuries, and is a collection of Old Norse poems explaining the creation of the world and celebrating old Norse gods and heroes—the main source of our knowledge of Norse mythology. The second or Prose Edda was written by Snorri Sturluson, an Icelandic historian and statesman of the early 13th century. Its subject matter is Norse mythology of the versification of the skalds, the ancient Icelandic poets.

Education of Henry Adams, The, the autobiography of Henry Adams, privately printed in 1906 and published in 1918. It is written in the third person and so seems remote and objective. All the political and literary ideas of his environment Henry Adams found worthless as a preparation for life; his years at Harvard seemed to him wasted; his courses in European universities never told him what to do in a present world. He was schooled in Washington Civil War politics; he was secretary to his father who was Minister to England; he became a teacher of history at Harvard and editor of the *North American Review,* but he abandoned everything to become a full-time writer and "watcher of the times."

Egoist, The, a novel by George Meredith, published in 1879. The story centers in Sir Willoughby Patterne and his self-centered search for a woman sufficiently perfect to become his wife. There is little action but much analysis of the hero's conceitedness as revealed in his ungenerous treatment of Laetitia Dale, who had long been fond of him and who finally accepted him.

elegy, any short poem of lament, deeply meditative or pathetic in tone. The outstanding example of this type is Gray's *Elegy Written in a Country Churchyard.* Elegy in the modern sense has become restricted to a lament for the dead. Among the greatest elegies of this type in the English language are Milton's *Lycidas,* Shelley's *Adonais* on the death of Keats and Matthew Arnold's *Thyrsis* on the death of Clough.

Elegy Written in a Country Churchyard, a reflective poem by Thomas Gray, published in 1751. The churchyard mentioned is Stoke-Poges in Buckinghamshire, England. The poem reflects upon fleeting fame and inevitable death. It is full of famous phrases.

Elizabethan Age, the period roughly covered by the life of Queen Elizabeth in England (1558–1603) and the years directly following marked great literary output and brilliant achievement, especially in poetry and drama. Shakespeare is the brightest name of the age; yet even his fame does not

obscure such great writers as Edmund Spenser, Sir Philip Sidney, Michael Drayton, Christopher Marlowe, George Chapman, Francis Bacon, Thomas Dekker, Ben Jonson, John Donne, Beaumont and Fletcher, Robert Herrick and many others.

Emma, a novel by Jane Austen, published in 1816. It tells how a clever, self-sufficient girl intent on marrying off her protegée develops into an appreciative woman finally aware of her own failings.

Emperor Jones, The, a one-act play (in eight scenes) by Eugene O'Neill, produced in 1920 and published in 1921. Its action takes place on a West Indian island "as yet not self-determined by White Marines." The leading character is a Negro, a former Pullman porter who arrived as a stowaway and in 2 years became emperor. He was strikingly impersonated by the Negro actor Charles Gilpin.

Enoch Arden, a narrative poem by Alfred Tennyson, published in 1864. Through the accident of shipwreck Enoch Arden does not reach home for 10 years. His wife, long faithful, is finally convinced that he is dead, marries again and once more has a happy home. When Enoch returns, he sees through a window his wife and children and the new husband in a happy scene. He realizes that no good can come from revealing himself. His wife is blameless, and he would not cause her sorrow. He therefore resolves to live alone and unknown until his death.

epic, a long narrative poem celebrating the deeds of the heroes of history or legend. The ancient Greek *Iliad* and *Odyssey* of Homer typify the ancient epic. Vergil's *Aeneid* is the most famous of ancient Roman epics. Out of Iceland came the great epic fragments of the *Elder Edda;* but the Old English *Beowulf* stands out as the most perfect and important epic in all Teutonic literature, although the German *Hildebrand* and *Nibelungenlied* are equally famous. *The Song of Roland* is the greatest epic of France; the *Poem of the Cid* is Spain's. There have been no great modern epics since Milton's great *Paradise Lost,* which is often ranked with the *Iliad* and *Odyssey.*

epigram, originally, an inscription (usually in verse) on a monument; hence, a short poem expressing one pointed thought, often satirical and usually ending with a witticism or a surprise. The greatest of classical writers of epigrams were the Roman poets Martial and Catullus. Coleridge wrote:

What is an Epigram? a dwarfish whole,
It's body brevity, and wit its soul.

Any thought tersely and pointedly expressed in prose or verse, usually in one sentence, which sometimes seems contradictory, may be called an epigram. "Where ignorance is bliss, 'tis folly to be wise" is an epigram of this type.

epithalamium, among the ancient Greeks, a wedding poem, originally sung in chorus at the door of the bridal chamber. Theocritus wrote a marriage song of Helen, and Catullus

composed an epithalamium of great beauty. Edmund Spenser's *Epithalamium* on the occasion of his own marriage (1595) is the most famous in English literature. John Donne wrote several fine poems of this type.

Erehwon, a satirical Utopian novel by Samuel Butler, published in 1872. The title is the reverse spelling of Nowhere—and Nowhere is the literal translation of Utopia. In the strange country of Erehwon disease is a crime and moral ills are matters of concern to be cured. The book is a satire on hypocrisy, the church, parental tyranny and the unintelligence of society in general. In Erehwon machinery had become so highly developed that the people had abolished it, lest it "take charge of life" and destroy mankind.

Erin, the ancient name of Ireland.

essay, a literary composition on any subject, usually in prose. There are three kinds of essay: the formal, polished essay on a specific subject, the purely technical and scientific exposition and the personal essay. The finest of the personal type are the *Essays* of Montaigne in French and the *Essays of Elia* by Charles Lamb in English.

The essay was invented by Montaigne in 1571. He chose the word *essais* to designate his writings as attempts, trials or experiments. The first of Montaigne's *Essays* came out in 1580, the fifth in 1588. They were first translated into English by John Florio in 1603. They were a new kind of writing, dealing with any subject or idea that came to the author's mind. They were brief or rambling, full of interruptions and personal moods and opinions on life and men, formless yet bound together by the personality of the author.

Francis Bacon was the first of the English essayists. He put out a volume of ten essays in 1597; the 1625 volume contained 58 including *Greatness of Kingdoms, Truth, Death, Friendship, Gardens, Reading.* They are personal opinions and reflections, brief and with more literary form than Montaigne's. Abraham Cowley is called the father of the English essay. His *Discourses by Way of Essays* (1668) contains the famous "Of Myself," a perfect example of the personal essay. The *Tatler* and *Spectator* papers (1709–14) of Addison and Steele and the *Essays of Elia* (1820–23) by Charles Lamb are delightful examples of the personal essay. Macaulay's essays (1843–44), dealing with literary and historical topics, and Matthew Arnold's *Essays in Criticism* (1865 and 1888) are polished, impersonal and formal, attacking Philistinism and preaching sweetness and light. Ruskin's essays on economic and social reform and on the appreciation of art are beautiful, picturesque prose. *Sesame and Lilies* (1865) is his best-known collection. Late in the century came the essays of Robert Louis Stevenson, notably *Virginibus Puerisque* (1881) and *Familiar Studies of Men and Books* (1882).

Ralph Waldo Emerson's *Essays* of 1841 and 1844 on such subjects as *Self-Reliance, Compensation, The*

NEW YORK PUBLIC LIBRARY

FAUST, the sixteenth-century conjurer in German legend, is the subject of literature, opera, and art, such as this engraving, made from a drawing by Friedrich A. M. Retzsch, 1834.

Over-Soul, Fate and *Power* are New England transcendental sermons—with no trace of the whimsy of the personal essay. Max Beerbohm, Hilaire Belloc and G. K. Chesterton are prominent among 20th century essayists.

Essay on Man, an essay in rhymed couplets by Alexander Pope, published in 1732–34. It attempts to explain the nature of man, his place in the universe and his relation to mankind and to God. The style is epigrammatic, and many phrases and couplets are famous quotations.

Essays of Elia, a collection of essays by Charles Lamb, published in 1820–23. These are semi-autobiographical essays full of humor and pathos and personal whimsy, easy and brilliant in style. The range of reminiscence and fancy is indicated by some of the titles: *Christ's Hospital, South-Sea House, Old China, Poor Relations, Dissertation upon Roast Pig, Dream Children.* Lamb took the name Elia from an Italian clerk in the South-Sea House of London, where Lamb worked.

Evangeline, a narrative poem by Henry Wadsworth Longfellow, published in 1847, one of the few long poems in English composed in hexameters (the verse of the *Iliad* and the *Aeneid*). The scene is first laid in Grand Pré, Acadia (Nova Scotia), from which the French settlers were expelled by the British in 1755. They were widely scattered through the English and French settlements to the south. Evangeline became separated from Gabriel, her lover, who was sent to one of the French settlements on the lower Mississippi River in Louisiana. In her search for him she finally reached his Louisiana farm only to learn that he had moved west. After many years of quest Evangeline be-

came a sister of mercy, and in an almshouse she found her Gabriel, ill and dying.

Eve of Saint Agnes, The, a poem by John Keats, written in 1819. Madeline believed in the old legend that a maid would dream of her lover on St. Agnes's Eve. An old servant secretly admitted Madeline's lover to her chamber, although he was a foe of her kinsmen. She dreamed of him and woke to find him beside her. The pair escaped together from the castle unseen by the drunken revelers of the night's feast.

Faerie Queene, a long poem by Edmund Spenser, of which Books 1-3 were published in 1590 and Books 4-6 in 1596. There are only six complete books, though Spenser planned to write twelve. The Faerie Queene, Gloriana, symbolizes glory and Queen Elizabeth. Her 12 knights symbolize abstract virtues and at times specific subjects. The Red Cross knight symbolizes holiness and the Anglican Church. Other knights represent temperance, chastity, friendship, justice, courtesy, constancy and so on. The poem has some passages of rare beauty but is dull reading on the whole, with many allusions meaningless to modern readers.

Fagin, in *Oliver Twist* by Charles Dickens, an unscrupulous old Jew who employs pickpockets and thieves and teaches boys to become adept in his profession. The name is used of any thief or trainer of thieves.

Falstaff, Sir John, a famous character in Shakespeare's Henry IV. He is a fat old knight, a jesting, bragging drinker with enough shrewd wit to get out of all his scrapes. Dr. Johnson said that Falstaff "makes himself necessary to the prince by perpetual gaiety and by unfailing power of exciting laughter."

farce, a dramatic work intended only to

be funny and excite laughter. The word comes from the Latin *farcire,* to stuff. In medieval France the actors used to stuff comic byplay and sentences into the religious dramas to lighten the text. The modern farce is purely a light comic drama of highly improbable plot or characterization, sometimes satirical but usually only laugh-provoking.

Farewell Address, George Washington's, George Washington's farewell message to the American people, issued Sept. 17, 1796, during the last days of his presidency. Alexander Hamilton wrote the first draft, but Washington reshaped it and it is spoken of as Washington's own. It is still quoted and revered as embodying the basic fundamentals and ideals of Americanism. A famous passage follows:

> Be Americans. Let there be no sectionalism, no North, South, East or West; you are all dependent one on another, and should be one in union . . . . . . Beware of the baneful effects of party spirit and of the ruin to which its extremes must lead. Do not encourage party spirit, but use every effort to mitigate and assuage it. Keep the departments of government separate, promote education, cherish the public credit, avoid debt. Observe justice and good faith toward all nations; have neither passionate hatreds nor passionate attachments to any; and be independent politically of all. In one word, be a nation; be Americans and be true to yourselves.

Fathers and Sons, a Russian novel by Ivan S. Turgenev, published in 1862. It is a story of the struggle between old and new political and social forces in Russia, as represented by the sons and fathers. Turgenev called the young hero of his novel a *nihilist,* meaning only that he rebelled against all and any authority. Its widespread use as a political term started with this book. The novel portrays the state of society and the mind of the people that later upset old Russia.

Faust, in German legend, a 16th-century conjurer who sold his soul to the devil in return for a certain number of years of happiness and knowledge and power. He appeared in numerous ballads, sermons and Faust books from 1543 on. In 1587 the *History of Dr. Johann Fausten* was published by Johann Spies, which was translated into many languages and appeared in English as *The History of the Damnable Life and Death of Dr. John Faustus.* On this translation Christopher Marlowe based his famous drama *The Tragicall History of Doctor Faustus,* first acted in 1588 and published in 1604. He presents Faustus as a man appealing and human in his zest for the fulness of life and in his remorse when the devil gets him in the end.

Goethe's great drama *Faust* was published in two parts, one in 1808, the second in 1832. It symbolizes the search of the human soul for lasting satisfaction. Faust makes a bargain with Mephistopheles (the devil) to become his if Mephistopheles can give him just once joy so great that to the passing moment he will cry "Oh, stay, thou art so fair." The drama reveals the accumulation of bitterness and discontent that nothing but earthly pleasures brings to the human mind. When at last Faust would hold one moment fast and does cry, "Stay, thou art so fair," it is because he has lost himself in a great and selfless deed. This vitiates the bargain, since the devil had not given him this satisfaction. Thus the soul of Faust is saved.

fiction, all imaginative literature in narrative or drama form. The term embraces drama, short stories, novels and romances. The term is often used as a synonym for novel. Even in historical novels the plot is imaginative and the detail is not historically accurate. Many narrative and dramatic poems are fiction, but the term usually refers to prose.

foot, in versification, a unit of meter. A foot consists of a group of two or three syllables of which one is accented. The principal feet used in English poetry are:

iambus, unaccented plus accented,
trochee, accented plus unaccented,
dactyl, accented plus two unaccented,
anapest, two unaccented plus one accented.

THE METROPOLITAN MUSEUM OF ART
HAMLET AND HORATIO

Forsyte Saga, The, a trilogy of novels by John Galsworthy: *The Man of Property* (1906), *In Chancery* (1920) and *To Let* (1922). The Forsytes were an upper middle-class English family. Their story is traced from 1886 through the late Victorian age into the first 20 years of the 20th century. It is a story of the possessive instinct, embodied in Soames Forsyte, the man of property. He was determined to have what he wanted from life and to exercise his power over his possessions: his property and investments, his wife. The destructive influence of possessiveness on the lives of others, reaching far into the next generation is revealed, and how it turned upon Soames himself to strip him of all he sought. The state took over his investments and his wife became a free personality. *The Forsyte Saga* is the most important of Galsworthy's works. The story was continued in another trilogy called *The Modern Comedy* (1929); and the Forsyte family appears in several other stories by Galsworthy.

Four Horsemen of the Apocalypse, a novel by Vicente Blasco Ibáñez, published in Spanish in 1916 and in English in 1918. It is a World War story up to the Battle of the Marne. A wealthy don from Argentina has moved to Paris; his family has relatives who are Germans, and thus French and German psychology during these stirring times is vividly contrasted. The Four Horsemen are War, Famine, Pestilence and Death. The story culminates in the old man's joy that his son Julio has enlisted with France at last and in the boy's death in the trenches.

Frankenstein, a romance by Mary Wollstonecraft Shelley, wife of the poet, published in 1818. Frankenstein, a young medical student, has discovered the principle of life, constructs a being in the likeness of a man out of bones he has collected and endows it with life. The monster thus created is lonely and unhappy; his frightful appearance creates fear and loathing in all who meet him; and he demands that Frankenstein create a companion for him. When Frankenstein refuses, the monster turns upon his creator with hatred and pursues him to his death. The monster is never seen again.

free verse, verse that is rhythmical without formal meter, stanza or rhyme. The French term *vers libre,* meaning free verse, was adopted by a modern school of poets in Europe and America who sought to liberate poetry from conventions and rules that hamper the scope of poetry. Cadence is the term used for a new kind of internal rhythm in poetry following the rhythms of natural human speech, yet aiming also at variety and balance. Cadence accomplishes a kind of metrical regularity by the use of one constantly recurring line form or a constantly recurring strophe—like a refrain. The influence of the King James version of the Bible had something to do with free verse—a metrical English based on an Oriental poetry form without meter and rhyme but with parallelism and powerful figures of speech.

Walt Whitman's *Leaves of Grass,* is an early and influential example of free verse. Other exponents of the school are Amy Lowell, Carl Sandburg, Ezra Pound and T. S. Eliot.

Gallegher and Other Stories, a volume of short stories by Richard Harding Davis published in 1891. Gallegher in the title story is a quick-witted boy in a newspaper office who turns amateur detective and has many thrilling adventures.

Gettysburg Address, the short address delivered by Abraham Lincoln at the dedication of the Gettysburg National Cemetery, November 19, 1863. The orator of the day was Edward Everett, who spoke for more than an hour. Lincoln intended to say little, and his speech was only 267 words long. Brief, eloquent, moving, unforgettable, it is one of the supreme pieces of American literature. The whole address follows:

"Fourscore and seven years ago, our fathers brought forth on this continent a new nation, conceived in lib-

erty, and dedicated to the proposition that all men are created equal. Now we are engaged in a great civil war, testing whether that nation, or any nation so conceived and so dedicated, can long endure. We are met on a great battlefield of that war. We have come to dedicate a portion of that field as a final resting-place for those who here gave their lives that that nation might live. It is altogether fitting and proper that we should do this. But in a larger sense we cannot dedicate, we cannot consecrate, we cannot hallow this ground. The brave men, living and dead, who struggled here, have consecrated it far above our poor power to add or detract. The world will little note, nor long remember, what we say here, but it can never forget what they did here. It is for us, the living, rather to be dedicated here to the unfinished work which they who fought here have thus far so nobly advanced. It is rather for us to be here dedicated to the great task remaining before us,— that from these honored dead we take increased devotion to that cause for which they gave the last full measure of devotion,—that we here highly resolve that these dead shall not have died in vain,—that this nation, under God, shall have a new birth of freedom,—and that government of the people, by the people, for the people, shall not perish from the earth."

Gilbert and Sullivan operas, a series of comic operas—a remarkable collaboration. The lyrics were by Sir William S. Gilbert and the music by Sir Arthur Sullivan. They were sometimes called the *Savoy operas* because after 1882 they were produced at the Savoy Theatre in London. Many of them are satires on current topics or social customs of the day. They are absurdly whimsical with fantastic rhymes and remarkable patter in the recitatives and songs. Some of the verse had been published separately in *Bab Ballads* (1869 and 1873). The music is light and charming with an occasional suggestion of Sullivan's church-music style. The titles are: *Trial by Jury* (1875), *The Sorcerer* (1877), *H.M.S. Pinafore* (1878), *The Pirates of Penzance* (1879), *Patience* (1881), *Iolanthe* (1882), *Princess Ida* (1884), *The Mikado* (1885), *Ruddigore* (1887), *The Yeomen of the Guard* (1888), *The Gondoliers* (1889), *Utopia, Limited* (1893) and *The Grand Duke* (1896).

Gog and Magog, two huge wooden statues in the Guildhall, London, said to represent two old giants of Albion, or ancient Britain. British legend says that after their race was destroyed by Brute and his followers, Gog and Magog were taken to London to be porters of the palace gate. Geoffrey of Monmouth mentions a giant Goemagot who was killed by Corineus; and the two statues are said to represent Goemagot and Corineus. In William H. Ainsworth's great historical novel *The Tower of London,* two gigantic brothers, porters in the service of Mary Tudor, Queen of England, are named Gog and Magog.

Gold Bug, The, a short story by Edgar Allan Poe, published in 1843. Two men living in a rude house on Sullivan's Island, off shore from Charleston, S. C., discover an old parchment covered with mysterious figures and signs. It is a cipher, which, when solved, leads them to great treasure buried by the old pirate, Captain Kidd.

golden age, any period of great progress and high attainment in the civilization, literature or art of any country. In England the golden age is unanimously considered the Elizabethan age (*c.* 1550–1630).

Golden Ass, a collection of stories in 11 books by Apuleius, written in the 2nd century A.D. It is written in the form of an autobiography by one Lucius, who by mistaken enchantment was changed into an ass. The poor beast had to wander far and wide in search of the charm that would restore him to human shape, and in his wanderings encountered many strange people and adventures. The famous story of *Cupid and Psyche* is in this book. The stories comprise a masterly medley of humor, fantasy and realism.

Goneril and **Regan,** in Shakespeare's tragedy *King Lear* the two elder daughters of the king.

Great Expectations, a novel by Charles Dickens, published in 1861. Pip, a village boy who longed for riches and social station, suddenly received from an unknown source wealth and the chance for an education. In his pride he turns his back on his humble friend Joe Gargery, the blacksmith. But Pip's benefactor turned out to be an escaped convict to whom he had once smuggled food when a small boy, and the old man's touching gratitude and love humbled Pip. The convict was captured, his wealth taken by the state, and Pip's "great expectations" vanished into thin air. After years of hard work he married Estella, his childhood love, whose arrogance had also been humbled by the years.

Green Mansions, a romance by W. H. Hudson, published in 1916. It is a story of the South American tropical forest and the beautiful bird-girl, Rima, who is loved by Mr. Abel. After an idyllic courtship, Rima decides to return to civilization with Abel and find her mother's people. But the discovery that they have been destroyed overwhelms her, and she flees back to her beloved forest. She is captured by the superstitious savages, who think she is an evil spirit, and is burned to death. Abel returns home to live with the memory of his love. No description of the book can convey its magical charm.

Grimm's Fairy Tales, a collection of folk tales (collected 1812–15) by the brothers Jakob and Wilhelm Grimm of Germany. They were translated and published in English in 1823 as *German Popular Stories.* The collection contains the loved and familiar stories of *Hansel and Gretel, Cinderella, Faithful John, The Goose Girl, Tom Thumb, The Frog Prince, Snow White* and many others.

Grundy, Mrs., a person constantly referred to in Thomas Morton's comedy *Speed the Plough.* The other characters when discussing their possible actions, always ask, "What will Mrs. Grundy say?" Fear of the unfavorable opinion of the old lady, who never appears, deters them from following many wholesome natural inclinations. She personified the conventional public opinion that is dreaded by most people.

Gulliver's Travels, a satire by Jonathan Swift, published in 1726. In four parts it tells of the hero's voyages to imaginary lands: Book I, to the island of Lilliput, the land of the pygmies; Book II, to Brobdingnag, the land of the giants; Book III, to various countries, chief of which is Laputa, the home of eccentric scholars; and Book IV, to the country of the Houyhnhnms, a land where horses with an intelligence superior to that of mankind, carry on an ideal government. The first book is a satire on English politics and ecclesiastical controversies. Book II is an indictment of civilized government and human institutions in general. Book III reveals the deceptions of great learning. Book IV is the peak of all satires on human nature and its follies, vices and weaknesses. Its simple style and remarkable imagination have made it a children's story book now that the satire is forgotten.

Hamlet, a tragedy by William Shakespeare, first published in 1603. Hamlet, Prince of Denmark, urged to seek vengeance by the ghost of his murdered father, defers action and indulges in bitter and melancholy indecision. He discovers the truth of the murder by a court play, breaks his engagement with Ophelia, kills her father by mistake instead of his uncle, the king, and is sent to England by the king to be put to death. But he is captured by pirates and returned to Denmark. There he finds that Ophelia, mad with grief, had drowned herself. Hamlet is killed by a poisoned sword in a fencing match with Laertes, Ophelia's brother, but stabs the king before he dies and thus at the last moment avenges his father.

Hard Times, a novel by Charles Dickens, published in 1854. It satirizes extreme reliance upon statistics and a mechanical understanding of human relations. Its best known characters are Thomas Gradgrind, who worships statistics, and Josiah Bounderby, a conceited, self-made man who holds in contempt the humble life from which he came. Mr. Gradgrind is finally awakened to the worthlessness of his material ideals by the misery of his daughter, Louisa. But Mr. Bounderby to the very end can see no flaw in himself.

Heep, Uriah, a character in Charles Dickens's *David Copperfield,* a very 'umble person whom the reader despises for his abject attitudes. His hypocrisy is exceeded only by his treachery and his diabolical cunning.

Henry IV and **Henry V,** two historical plays by William Shakespeare. *Henry IV* was produced about 1597, *Henry V,* in 1599. Both plays deal with the character of Henry V. In *Henry IV,* part 1, the gay life of young Prince Hal is described; in part 2 his reflections upon his manner of life are given; and in *Henry V* the patriotism and wisdom of his character as king are set before us. The action of *Henry V* covers the years from 1414–20, including a treacherous plot upon the king's life by three of his nobles, a campaign in France, the battle of Agincourt and the king's courtship of the French princess, Katherine. The play is remarkable for its patriotic passages and its delineation of typical soldiers, some, like Fluellen the Welshman, Macmorris the Irishman and Jamy the Scot, from different parts of Henry's kingdom; others, like Pistol, Nym and Bardolph, from the scum of the army.

Henry Esmond, a novel in the first person by William Makepiece Thackeray, published in 1852. It is the story of Esmond's life, of his love for Lady Castlewood and his courtship of the beautiful Beatrix Esmond, of his military career, of his part in bringing the Pretender to England when Queen Anne was dying, of the failure of his political hopes, of his disillusionment in Beatrix and finally of his marriage to Lady Castlewood, Beatrix's mother, and their emigration to America. *The Virginians* is a sequel to *Henry Esmond.*

heptameter, a line of poetry containing seven metrical feet. Example: Oh, East is East, and West is West, and never the twain shall meet.—Rudyard Kipling.

hexameter, a line of poetry containing six metrical feet. Example:

> And looking o'er the hedge, before me I espied
> A snow-white mountain lamb with a maiden at its side.
> (From Wordsworth's *The Pet Lamb.*)

Dactylic hexameter is the meter of Greek and Latin epic poetry—the *Iliad, Odyssey* and *Aeneid.* In English it has been imitated in Longfellow's *Evangeline.*

Hiawatha, a poem by Henry Wadsworth Longfellow, published in 1855, written in an eight-syllabled trochaic verse imitated from the Finnish epic *Kalevala.* It embodies many legends and traditions and much of the culture of the North American Indians in the life of Hiawatha, son of Wenonah "and the West Wind, Mudjekeewis." He is reared by his grandmother, "daughter of the moon, Nokomis," marries Minnehaha and becomes the culture hero of his people. He teaches them the culture of maize (Indian corn), picture writing and many other things. With the coming of the white priest he departs for the islands of the blest,

> To the kingdom of Pomenal,
> To the land of the Hereafter.

House of the Seven Gables, a novel by Nathaniel Hawthorne, published in 1851. The story is laid in old Puritan Salem. Poor old Hepzibah Pyncheon who lives in the house of seven gables has had to open a shop because of her poverty. Her old brother Clifford arrives home, his mind weakened by 30 years of unjust imprisonment. Judge Pyncheon, his cousin, who engineered Clifford's arrest, continues to persecute the old man, threatening now to confine him in an asylum. But the malicious judge dies of apoplexy in time for old Hepzibah and Clifford to have a few years of peace.

Huckleberry Finn, The Adventures of, a chronicle of boy life on the Mississippi by Mark Twain (S. L. Clemens), pub-

THE NEW ENGLAND COUNCIL

THE HOUSE OF THE SEVEN GABLES in Salem, Massachusetts. It was built in 1669 by John Turner and is said to have inspired Nathaniel Hawthorne's novel. After several generations, it fell into the hands of Miss Susan Ingersoll, who was Hawthorne's cousin.

lished in 1884. It is a sequel to *Tom Sawyer*. Huck and his pal, Tom Sawyer, run away from home and adventure down the Mississippi River on a raft. Until their final return up the river, thrilling, funny and pathetic incidents succeed one another in rapid succession. Besides telling a purely entrancing boy's story, the book is a remarkable picture of the great river, the life along its banks and the old social order of those days and its problems.

Hypatia, a historical romance by Charles Kingsley, published serially in 1851 and in book form in 1853. The scene is Alexandria in the 5th century A.D. The Roman order is passing. Christianity in both its fanatic and its finer aspects is contrasted with Greek philosophy made sane and new and beautiful through the personality of the lovely, learned Hypatia. Hypatia was finally torn to pieces and burned by a mob of fanatic Christians who were fearful of her influence. Hypatia was a real person, a Neoplatonic philosopher and daughter of the geometrician and astronomer, Theon. She was seized in her lecture room in March 415 by a mob of Christians, tortured and burned to death.

iambus or **iamb,** a metrical foot of two syllables, of which the second is accented. Example:

And I' | awoke' | and found' | me here'.
(From *La Belle Dame Sans Merci* by John Keats.)

idealism, the imaginative or subjective treatment of the subject matter in literature, contrasted with the true-

to-life or photographically realistic treatment. The idealistic writer or artist tries to depict human nature as it might be or ought to be instead of as it is. Idealism is the opposite of realism.

idyl or **idyll,** originally, a little picture or description in prose or verse of pastoral or rustic life. Idyls are usually short poems and take their name especially from the *Idyls* of the Greek pastoral poet Theocritus of the 3rd century B.C. His *Idyls* were imitated by Vergil and other Roman poets, and they are the type from which the modern definition of the word is taken. Wordsworth's *Michael* and Burns's *Cotter's Saturday Night* are true modern idyls. Sometimes *idyl* is used of longer poems, especially if they are sentimental; Tennyson's *Idylls of the King* is the best example in recent literature. The idyl cannot be considered a literary form—the term is not sharply defined.

Idylls of the King, a group of 12 connected narrative poems in blank verse by Alfred Tennyson, published between 1859 and 1885. They tell the story of King Arthur and his knights. Tennyson took his material largely from Malory's *Morte d'Arthur,* but drew also on Layamon's *Brut,* Geoffrey of Monmouth's *History of the Kings of Britain* and Lady Charlotte Guest's translations from the Welsh. His own addition was that Arthur symbolized the perfect knight and king and that his ideal kingdom was undermined by disillusionment and deceit. The *Idylls* are: *The Coming of Arthur, Gareth and Lynette, The Marriage of Geraint, Geraint and*

Enid, Balin and Balan, Merlin and Vivien, Lancelot and Elaine, The Holy Grail, Pelleas and Etarre, The Last Tournament, Guinevere and *The Passing of Arthur.*

Iliad, The, an ancient Greek epic poem attributed to Homer and classed as one of the greatest masterpieces of the world's literature. It tells the story of the 10 years' siege of Troy by Greek armies which sought to bring Helen, the most beautiful of mortal women, back to Sparta, whence she had been carried away by Paris, a Trojan prince. The epic tells of the pitched battles, of individual combats, of the great Greek warrior, Achilles, sulking in his tent, of the fight between Achilles and Hector, during which Hector is slain.

Il Penseroso, a poem by John Milton written in 1632. The word means the pensive or melancholy man. The poem is a companion piece to *L'Allegro* and describes the pleasures of meditative life.

impressionism, the treatment of scenes, characters and emotional reactions in the simplest manner possible, without elaboration of detail or explanation, but as directly as actual impressions are experienced. The term as applied to literature is borrowed from painting and specifically from a school of French painters in the 1860s—Monet, Manet, Renoir, Pissarro, Degas and others—who tried to paint things as they appeared rather than as the artists knew they were. So in painting, impressionism is the recreation of the instant sense impression, of what was true to the artist in the fleeting moment, without detail or reference to permanent fact. In music, it is a kind of description through the creation of moods.

In Memoriam, a series of poems by Alfred Tennyson, published in 1850, but written at intervals from 1833 to 1850. They were inspired by grief for the death of his intimate friend Arthur H. Hallam, who died in 1833, and they record the varying moods and thoughts of Tennyson's sorrow, overwhelming grief and sense of loss gradually deepening into spiritual communion and greater love. The title is Latin and means a memorial.

Innocents Abroad, a book by Mark Twain, published in 1869, telling the experiences of a group of Americans traveling through Europe, Egypt and the Holy Land. Their hard-headed valuation of everything on its own merits makes the book uproariously funny and at the same time a subtle criticism.

Intimations of Immortality from Recollections of Early Childhood, a poem by William Wordsworth, published in 1807. It is an argument for immortality based on childhood memories of pre-existence, which fade year by year yet persist through adult life as intuitions or *intimations.* "Our birth is but a sleep and a forgetting." The human soul comes from afar

" . . . trailing clouds of glory do we come
From God who is our home:
Heaven lies about us in our infancy!
Shades of the prison-house begin to close
Upon the growing boy."

John Gilpin's spouse said to her dear,
 "Though wedded we have been
These twice ten tedious years, yet we
 No holiday have seen.

"To-morrow is our wedding-day,

NEW YORK PUBLIC LIBRARY

THE DIVERTING HISTORY OF JOHN GILPIN, an example of the raucous humor often exhibited by Cowper despite his insanity.

Wordsworth laments that with manhood the vision fades "into the light of common day" but rejoices that nothing can wholly abolish or destroy that strange innate memory.

Ivanhoe, a novel by Sir Walter Scott, published in 1819. Its scene is laid in England in the 12th century, a period of adjustment between the Normans and the Saxons. The Saxon hero, Wilfred of Ivanhoe, a retainer of Richard Coeur de Lion, has been disinherited by his father because he loves his father's ward, Rowena. His successive adventures as a victor in a brilliant Norman tournament, wounded prisoner in Front-de-Boeuf's burning castle and champion of his noble Jewish benefactress Rebecca in her trial for witchcraft end with his marriage to Rowena. Among the characters are Cedric, Athlestane and Rowena, Gurth the swineherd and Wamba the jester, Isaac and Rebecca, Locksley or Robinhood and his band of outlaws, the Norman nobles, De Bracy, Front-de-Boeuf and Bois Guilbert, Prince John and King Richard himself.

Jabberwock, an imaginery monster in *Through the Looking Glass* by Lewis Carroll, the subject of a famous poem "Jabberwocky" found by Alice in a Looking-Glass book. The poem contains many imaginative coined words, and the first two lines are famous:
 'Twas brillig and the slithy toves
 Did gyre and gimble in the wabe.

Jane Eyre, a novel by Charlotte Brontë, published in 1847. It tells the story of the orphan Jane and her unhappy childhood; her life as a governess; her strange wooing by Mr. Rochester, the father of her pupil, a man with a mysterious past; her discovery that he had an insane wife whom he kept under guard in a room of his house;

the burning of the house, the blinding of Rochester in an attempt to rescue his wife from the flames and his subsequent marriage to Jane. The novel describes Lowood, the charitable school where the Brontë sisters actually spent several wretched years. A plain heroine gifted with wit and character and a fascinating, unhappy hero not drawn in the gallant mode made the book famous at once, and its appeal has continued to the present day.

Jerusalem Delivereu (*Gerusalemme Liberato*), an Italian epic poem, story of the First Crusade, written by Torquato Tasso late in the 16th century. Tasso's revision was published in 1593. It was first translated into English in 1594. The most famous translation is by Edward Fairfax (1600) entitled *Godfrey of Bulloigne*. The poem is in 20 cantos and relates the capture of Jerusalem from the infidels by Godfrey of Bouillon and his crusading army at the end of the 11th century. Three sets of lovers augment the story. Rinaldo, Prince of Este, plays the heroic role in the capture of the city, though he lived 100 years later.

John Gilpin, The Diverting History of, a poem by William Cowper, published in *The Task* in 1785. He wrote it one night in 1782 after his sister told him the story to drive away his melancholy. After 20 years of married life John Gilpin and his wife agreed to take a holiday. The family set out for a nearby town tavern in a chaise, with John Gilpin astride a borrowed horse. As soon as the horse began to

trot, Gilpin lost control of it, dashed hatless, wigless and capeless through Edmonton and on to Ware, 10 miles beyond, where he turned the horse around but could not stop until he got back home.

John Halifax, Gentleman, a novel by Dinah Mulock, published in 1857. John Halifax, an orphan at the age of 11, becomes "one of nature's noblemen," rich and famous.

Joseph Andrews, a novel by Henry Fielding, published in 1742. It tells the story of a virtuous servingman, Joseph Andrews. The book was begun as a parody on Richardson's Pamela, the story of a virtuous long-suffering maidservant. Fielding makes his hero, Joseph Andrews, the brother of Pamela. Its most famous character is Parson Adams, a lovable country clergyman.

Julius Caesar, a tragedy by William Shakespeare, produced about 1599 and first printed in 1623. It deals with the assassination of Caesar and the battle of Philippi. Caesar, at the height of his power in 44 B.C., is warned to beware the ides of March, but proceeds to the Senate house, where he is stabbed by the conspirators. The mob hears Brutus deliver a speech justifying the murder of Caesar, but it turns to Antony when he appeals to Caesar's love for them and reads his will. Civil war follows, and Antony and Octavius finally defeat Brutus and Cassius at Philippi.

Because Shakespeare chose to make Brutus the hero of his play, he was forced to overemphasize the ambition of Caesar.

THE METROPOLITAN MUSEUM OF ART

ASSASSINATION OF JULIUS CAESAR. Caesar is in argument with his Senate:
 Caesar: . . . I was constant Cimber should be banished . . .
 Casca: Speak, hands, for me!   (They stab Caesar.)
 Caesar: *Et tu, Brute!* Then fall, Caesar!   (Dies.)   —Act III, Scene 1.

Brutus is the real hero of the play. He loves Caesar and joins the conspiracy only after he is convinced that Rome must be rid of Caesar. Even Antony believes in Brutus's integrity of purpose when he says:

"He only in a general honest thought
And common good to all, made one of them."

Jungle Books, two collections of animal stories by Rudyard Kipling, published in 1894 and 1895. The scenes are laid in the jungles of India. Most of the stories are about the boy Mowgli who was lost from his native village and reared by a she-wolf along with her own cubs. His education by the beasts of the jungle, his troubles and adventures and his final unwilling return to his own kind form the subject matter of a series of entrancing tales. Other stories in the collection have to do with the fabulous white seal of northern waters, little Tomai of the elephants and others. Kipling endows the animals with speech, yet they retain all their own characteristics and never become unnatural personifications.

Justice, a tragedy by John Galsworthy, published in 1910. The love of William Falder for the wife of a man who mistreats her causes him to forge a check to get money to give her release from her husband. He is caught, tried, sentenced to imprisonment. After his release he is arrested again for a failure to report to the authorities. In despair he kills himself. The play was a powerful criticism of certain prison conditions then existing in England.

Kalevala (literally, from the land of Kaleva), the mythological songs and poems of Finland, heard from the peasantry and collected by Zacharias Topelius in 1822 and again by Elias Lönnrot in 1835. Lönnrot enlarged his collection to 22,793 lines for the second book in 1849. The poems are fundamentally lyric, of mythical and heroic subject matter, and date back to very ancient times. The collection is named for the three sons of Kaleva, a Finnish giant: Wainamoinen, god of music and inventor of the harp, Ilmarinen, the smith, and the hero Lemininkainen. Their adventures warring in the far north make up most of the story. There are some sections of great lyrical beauty, such as the description of the creation of the world. An English translation by W. M. Crawford appeared in 1887, and the powerful meter used by Lönnrot had been adapted to English in Longfellow's *Hiawatha* (1855).

Kenilworth, an historical romance by Sir Walter Scott, published in 1819. Its scenes are laid in Elizabethan England. Queen Elizabeth is the central character, surrounded by the famous men of her day, Lord Burleigh, Edmund Spenser, Sir Walter Raleigh and the Earls of Surrey and Leicester. Leicester is the favorite of the queen; rumors of a marriage are in the air, Leicester, however, is secretly married to Amy Robsart, whom he keeps hidden and guarded. The complications arising from this state of affairs come to a head at the great pageant in honor of the queen at Leicester's castle at Kenilworth, with the result that Amy is murdered by Leicester's unscrupulous confidant and follower, Richard Varney. When Leicester confesses his marriage, Elizabeth, feeling duped both as queen and woman, is enraged and disgraces him.

Kidnapped, a novel by Robert Louis Stevenson, published in 1886. The hero of the book, David Balfour, is sent to sea by a treacherous and cruel uncle. There he meets Alan Breck, a spirited and hardfighting Jacobite. They have wonderful adventures on sea and in the Highlands.

Kim, a novel of India by Rudyard Kipling, published in 1901. An Irish orphan, Kim (Kimball O'Hara) grew up in the native quarter of Lahore and became unofficially attached to the British Secret Service in India. Kim fell in with an old Buddhist lama of Tibet whom he accompanied through India in search of the river of Immortality. Eventually members of his father's old Irish regiment found Kim and he was adopted by them and sent to school.

King Lear, a tragedy by William Shakespeare, produced in 1606 and published in 1608. The plot deals with the ingratitude of King Lear's daughters, Goneril and Regan, between whom he has divided his kingdom, and the fidelity of his daughter Cordelia, whom he has disinherited because, despising hypocrisy, she would not protest that she loved him more than her duty. The ungrateful daughters rob the old king of his power, prejudice him against Cordelia and deprive him of all but the bare necessities of life. Their cruelty drives him out into a violent storm one night with a few faithful friends, and in grief he goes insane. Cordelia, however, comes to his aid with an army. Then follows in rapid succession the violent deaths of Goneril, Regan, Cordelia and King Lear.

Koran or **Qurân,** the sacred book of the Mohammedan religion, written in Arabic. It contains the recitations or revelations of Mohammed, delivered orally by him and taken down by scribes or memorized by some of his followers. The final authorized version was put together (660 A.D.) by Zaydibn Thabit, Mohammed's secretary, at the order of the Caliph Uthman. The Koran is probably the most influential book in all human history except the Bible.

Kubla Khan, a poem by Samuel Taylor Coleridge, published in 1816. The subtitle is *A Vision in a Dream.* Coleridge fell asleep over a book of voyages describing strange lands and awoke realizing that he had composed a poem in his sleep. He began at once to write it down but he was interrupted before he finished and could not recapture the vision to complete the poem. The existing fragment, however, about 55 lines, presents the vision of the magical place where Kubla Khan ordered his palace to be built.

It was a miracle of rare device,
A sunny pleasure-dome with caves of ice!

Lady of the Lake, a narrative poem in six cantos by Sir Walter Scott, published in 1810. Ellen, daughter of the outlawed Lord James of Douglas, lives with her father in hiding with Roderick Dhu, a Highland chief, near Lake Katrine. The king (possibly James V) visits them disguised as Fitz-James and falls in love with her, but Ellen loves Malcolm Graeme. Roderick is wounded in a fight with the king. Ellen secures her father's pardon and marries Malcolm. The poem contains several of Scott's finest short lyrics.

Lady or the Tiger, The, a short story by Frank R. Stockton, published in 1882. A princess of a barbaric kingdom secretly loved a young man. When the king learned of this, he condemned her lover to face the wild beasts in the arena, but on the tearful supplication of the princess consented to give him one chance for his life. He was to be placed alone in the arena, facing two doors. Behind one would be a beautiful woman; behind the other, a tiger. If he chose the one concealing the lady, he must marry her; if he chose the one concealing the tiger, he would be devoured. The princess, who had discovered which door concealed the lady and which the tiger, gave her lover a signal which door to choose, but the story does not tell which door it was!

Lady Windermere's Fan, a play by Oscar Wilde, produced in 1892. Lady Windermere decides to leave her husband because he is in love with another woman. She does not know that the other woman is her own mother whom she had not seen since she was a child. The mother finds Lady Windermere's letter of farewell and seeks her out in the rooms of her lover, Lord Darlington. Lord Windermere finds his wife's fan in Darlington's room, and the mother takes the blame for its being there, saying that she herself picked up the fan by mistake. Lord Windermere is then reconciled with his wife.

Lake poets, the three English poets, Coleridge, Wordsworth and Southey, so called because they lived in England's Lake District, a hilly lake region in Cumberland, Westmoreland and Lancashire. The term *Lake school* was first applied to them in ridicule in an article in the *Edinburgh Review* in 1817.

L'Allegro, a short poem by John Milton written in 1632. *L'Allegro* is Italian for the cheerful one. The poem is an idyl in praise of the delights of life in country and town. It is a companion piece to *Il Penseroso.*

Last Days of Pompeii, The, a novel by Bulwer-Lytton, published in 1834. It tells a thrilling story of the ancient city of Pompeii before it was buried by the great eruption of Vesuvius in 79 A.D. It describes gladiatorial contests, banquets, the baths and other scenes from ancient Roman life.

Last of the Mohicans, The, a novel by James Fenimore Cooper, published in 1826. The subject of this story is the French and Indian War in northern New York. The hero is Uncas, a noble young Indian. The other principal character is Natty Bumppo, nicknamed Hawkeye, a woodsman whose knowledge of the forest and of Indian character is complete and whose skill with the rifle is unmatched. Indian treachery, bloody fighting, heroic rescues and hairbreadth escapes follow one another in rapid succession. This is one of the *Leatherstocking Tales.*

Lays of Ancient Rome, a collection of narrative poems by Thomas Babington Macaulay, published in 1842. The series contains the famous *Horatius,* describing the valiant defense of the bridge into Rome by Horatius Cocles against the Tuscans. In the edition of 1848 ballads dealing with French and English history were added.

Leatherstocking Tales, novels of early frontier life by James Fenimore Cooper, all having the same hero, Leatherstocking or Natty Bumppo. The series contains: *The Pioneers* (1823), *The Last of the Mohicans* (1826), *The Prairie* (1827), *The Pathfinder* (1840) and *The Deerslayer* (1841). These books were popular throughout Europe and were translated into the principal languages.

Legend of Sleepy Hollow, The, a short story by Washington Irving, published in *The Sketch Book* in 1820. It narrates the midnight adventures of Ichabod Crane—an ungainly schoolmaster of timorous heart—with a spectral, headless horseman whom he encountered while he was riding home from a party at the home of Katrina Van Tassel, to whom he was paying suit. After his wild race with the headless horseman Ichabod disappeared from the community. Katrina soon afterwards married Brom Bones, a daredevil horseman, who "looked exceedingly knowing" whenever the story of Ichabod was mentioned.

Les Miserables, a novel by Victor Hugo, published in 1862. The title means the wretched ones. Jean Valjean, the hero, is an ex-convict; for stealing a loaf of bread he had been sentenced to the galleys. The generous sympathy of a bishop who befriends him after he is released changes Valjean's whole life and character. He is hounded by Javert, a detective, and when his notoriety as an ex-convict threatens the happiness of Cosette (daughter of a woman Valjean had befriended), the noble Valjean disappears. Cosette and her lover Marius, learning of Valjean's self-sacrifice, search for him and find him as he is dying.

Life of Samuel Johnson, a biography of Samuel Johnson by James Boswell, published in 1791, perhaps the most famous biography in the English language. Boswell began to make notes and collect material for the *Life* when he first met Dr. Johnson in 1763 and set to work at once after Johnson's death in 1784. Boswell's own fame rests almost entirely on this biography of his friend; Johnson's fame is rooted deeply in this book, since his conversations are of more note than his writings.

Life on the Mississippi, an autobiographical story by Mark Twain, published in 1883, picturing his life as a pilot up and down the great river before the Civil War.

limerick, a five-line jingle, usually nonsensical. The meter is anapestic. The 1st, 2d and 5th lines each contain 3 feet and rhyme with one another. Lines 3 and 4 each contain 2 feet and rhyme with each other. The name is thought to come from an old custom of singing extempore nonsense verses at parties to which the chorus was always the same: "Will you come up to Limerick?" Often the limerick has a place name in the first line. Example:

> There was a young lady from Niger
> Who smiled as she rode on a tiger;
> They came back from the ride
> With the lady inside,
> And the smile on the face of the tiger.

Edward Lear's *Book of Nonsense* (1848) contains many limericks.

Little Men, a story for and about boys by Louisa May Alcott, published in 1871. It pictures life in the small boys' school conducted by the Jo of *Little Women* and her husband. *Little Men* is a sequel to *Little Women.* It was followed by *Jo's Boys.*

Little Minister, The, a novel by Sir James M. Barrie, published in 1891, and a play, produced in 1897, with Maude Adams taking the part of Babbie. The little minister, Gavin Dishart, falls in love with the fascinating but mysterious Babbie in Thrums, a village of stern, orthodox Scottish weavers.

JO in *Little Women,* written by Louisa May Alcott. This is possibly the most popular girls' book ever written in English.

Little Women, a story for girls by Louisa M. Alcott, published in 1868. It is about four New England girls, Jo, Meg, Beth and Amy March and was written largely from Miss Alcott's own experiences.

Lochinvar, the hero of a ballad in Scott's *Marmion.* Young Lochinvar loves a lass who is betrothed against her will to a man described in the poem as a laggard. While dancing with her just before the wedding ceremony, Lochinvar asks the girl to flee with him, and she is very willing. Before the outraged bridegroom or her father can stop them the two escape on the horse that Lochinvar had waiting.

Looking Backward, a romance by Edward Bellamy, published in 1888. It is a fantastic story describing the strange experiences and impressions of a Bostonian, Julian West, who goes into a sleep in 1887, awakens in the year 2000 and sees great changes in economic and social conditions.

Lorna Doone, a romance by Richard D. Blackmore, published in 1869. The scene is Exmoor, a county in southwestern England. The time is during the reign of Charles II and James II. The brutal Judge Jeffreys figures in the story. Lorna Doone is the daughter of a family of aristocratic robbers and smugglers. The hero, John Ridd, has many exciting adventures among the outlaws and at last becomes the protector of Lorna against her own kin.

Lycidas, a poem by John Milton, written in 1637. It is an elegy, in which he laments the death of his friend, Edward King.

lyric poetry, the most emotional and musical of the three divisions of poetry, the others being dramatic and epic or narrative poetry. A lyric always expresses emotion, the personal hopes and joys, sorrows and fantasies of the author. It is always comparatively short because great emotion cannot long be sustained. It is usually composed of several stanzas. But sonnets are lyrics, as are also odes, hymns, elegies and the like.

The word *lyric* comes from the Greek *lyra,* an ancient musical instrument of the harp type; and lyrics were originally intended to be sung to the accompaniment of the lyre. They are not now written with that particular intention. Most modern lyrics are written only as confessions of inner experience, meant to be read.

Macbeth, a tragedy by William Shakespeare, first printed in 1623. Macbeth and Banquo, warriors in the army of Duncan, King of Scotland, on their way home from a victory, met three weird sisters. The witches prophesied that Macbeth would first become thane of Cawdor and then king of Scotland and that Banquo would beget kings. The immediate fulfilment of the first prophesy fired the ambition of Macbeth and Lady Macbeth to the point of murdering Duncan. Duncan's two sons fled and Macbeth took the throne. To forestall the prophecy concerning Banquo, Macbeth murdered him also. But Banquo's ghost began to haunt Macbeth. Suspicion began to waken against him, and Lady Macbeth betrayed herself in sleep-walking delirium. Macduff, thane of Fife, took the field against him with strong forces.

Again, in terror of mind, Macbeth consulted the three witches. They told him to beware of Macduff, but that he would not be overthrown till Birnam Wood moved to Dunsinane. This strange prophecy was literally fulfilled. Macduff marched on Macbeth and as the army passed through

Birnam Wood, each man cut off a bough of a tree. Thus Macduff approached Dunsinane in the guise of Birnam Wood. Macbeth was killed and Malcolm, the son of Duncan, became king of Scotland.

Mahabharata, the great Bharata story (*maha* means great), one of the two great epic poems of India (the other being the *Ramayana*). It describes the conflict between two families (descendants of Bharata) for a kingdom in northern India, the Pandavas, five strong brothers and their 100 cousins, the Kauravas. After taking the kingdom the Pandavas abdicated in remorse and went off seeking Indra's heaven. These events are supposed to have happened in the 12th century B.C. The poem as we now have it was probably written 900 or 1,000 years later, in the 2d century. Social and ethical questions, scientific facts, the philosophy and morality of ancient India are described with the story of the family feud. It includes the great sacred lay, the *Bhagavad-Gita*, the summary of Hindu philosophy.

Main Street, a novel by Sinclair Lewis, published in 1920. It portrays the prosaic, humdrum life of a small Minnesota town.

Malaprop, Mrs., the pompous old aunt of Lydia Languish in Sheridan's comedy, *The Rivals.* She uses words so incorrectly that her name has become proverbial for such mistakes as the following: "Headstrong as an allegory on the banks of the Nile"; "precipitate one down the prejudice." The name is from the French phrase *mal à propos,* inappropriate. *Malapropism* means this incorrect use of words or a word or phrase inappropriately used.

Man and Superman, a comedy by George Bernard Shaw, published in 1903. The leading male character is John Tanner, a social revolutionist, utterly opposed to society's conventions and above all determined not to be enmeshed in love and marriage. But Ann Whitefield changes all that. The play is a lively satire on "the tragicomic love chase of the man by the woman."

Man Without a Country, The, a short story by Edward Everett Hale, published in 1863. It is about a captain in the navy on trial for some misdemeanor, who said he hoped he might never hear the name of the United States again. For punishment he was compelled to live forever on board a ship, never touching a port. He died broken-hearted and a fervent patriot. Walter Damrosch wrote an opera on this theme, produced at the Metropolitan Opera House in New York in the 1937–38 season.

Marble Faun, The, a novel by Nathaniel Hawthorne, published in 1860. It is the story of four artists in Modern Rome. Donatello is a young Italian count who bears a close resemblance to the famous statue of a faun by Praxiteles. His character is that of an innocent carefree pagan until he falls in love with Miriam and murders a man who has been persecuting her. Then he develops into a conscience-stricken member of civilized society and gives himself up to justice.

Marjorie Daw, a story by Thomas Bailey Aldrich, published in 1867; it is written in a series of letters. Marjorie Daw is an imaginary girl created for the pleasure of an invalid, John Flemming, by his friend Edward Delaney.

Marmion, a poem by Sir Walter Scott, published in 1808. It paints the manners of feudal times in the heroic style. The poem opens in August, 1513, and ends with the Battle of Flodden Field about a month later. There are six cantos, describing the clangor of arms, troops on the march, drawbridge, portcullis and the other appurtenances of a medieval castle, the intrigues of guilty love and the brutality of medieval punishment. The poems ends on the battlefield and its deeds of valor.

mask or **masque,** an ancient form of drama in which the actors wore enlarged figures of heads to identify the characters and magnify the voices. Dance, dumb show and costume were emphasized over plot or character portrayal. The characters were usually mythological or allegorical. Masks were extremely popular in England in the 16th and 17th centuries and found their greatest exponent in Ben Jonson. One of Jonson's masks, *Pleasure Reconciled to Virtue,* suggested to John Milton the idea for his mask *Comus.*

Meistersinger, a German word meaning mastersingers, applied to societies or guilds of workingmen in Germany from the 14th to the 16th century. They organized to differentiate themselves from the wandering minstrels and devoted themselves to the cultivation of music and poetry. They were pedantic and artificial, especially in their later period. Hans Sachs, author of many meistersongs and plays, figures in Wagner's opera *The Meistersinger of Nürnberg,* which is an answer to Wagner's critics, likening them to the narrow hidebound musicians of the olden times.

melodrama, originally a play with some music and singing and a highly sensational plot. Now a melodrama is any play with striking, exaggerated incidents and violent emotion. *East Lynne* is a typical melodrama.

Merchant of Venice, The, a comedy by William Shakespeare, printed in 1600. Bassanio borrows money from his friend Antonio, the merchant of Venice, in order to court Portia, a rich heiress of Belmont. Antonio, in turn, has borrowed 3,000 ducats from Shylock, the Jewish moneylender, and has promised to forfeit a pound of his flesh if he does not repay it. Antonio's payment is deferred when his ships are delayed by storms, and Shylock demands the pound of flesh nearest Antonio's heart. Portia, disguised as a lawyer, frees Antonio and disgraces Shylock through a legal quibble: he may have the flesh but can shed no blood in taking it. Shylock's goods are declared forfeit for plotting against a citizen of Venice.

meter, systematic rhythm in poetry; the arrangement of syllables in a poem so that each line contains a certain number of accented syllables of metrical feet. The various meters, named for the number of feet in a line, are:

monometer, dimeter, trimeter, tetrameter, pentameter, hexameter, heptameter, octameter.

Midsummer Night's Dream, a comedy by William Shakespeare, printed in 1600. The scenes are laid chiefly in a wood near Athens in the legendary days of King Theseus. The king's courtiers mingle incongruously in the play with the fairies and a group of clownish artisans. The plot is concerned with two pairs of lovers whose tangled affairs are finally straightened out by fairy intervention. The dignified court scenes, the clumsy attempts of the artisans to present a play, the pranks of Puck and the songs and dances of the fairies combine to make a very novel and delightful play. Almost as famous as the play is Felix Mendelssohn's music for it.

Mill on the Floss, The, a novel by George Eliot, published in 1860. The author portrays in a powerful manner the characters of Maggie Tulliver and her brother Tom, children of the miller, and Maggie's unhappy love affairs and misunderstandings with her brother. The book ends with the flood of the Floss and the death of Maggie and Tom, drowned together and reconciled at last.

minnesinger, one of the lyric poets, singers and musicians of Germany who flourished 1150–1350. The word literally means a singer of love songs (from *minne,* love and *singers,* to sing). The minnesinger was usually of noble birth and the songs had to do with courtly love, the worship by a knight of some woman, often far above him in rank. The rules were rigid: the lady's name could not be mentioned or even indicated. The minnesingers wrote both words and music to their songs, which were sung in the courts before knights and ladies. Contests were often held. As the minnesong developed the subject matter enlarged; there were not only songs of courtly love but songs on political and religious themes, crusading songs, fables turned to lays and sacred hymns. The greatest of the minnesingers was Walther von der Vogelweide in the early 13th century.

miracle plays, medieval short dramatic pieces representing Biblical scenes or especially, saints' lives, given at first in the church as a serious part of the service and later outside the church in market places, courtyards and at fairs. Famous examples are *Abraham and Isaac* and *The Harrowing of Hell.* the actors were members of the local handicrafts, the guilds or trades-unions. The surviving Miracles are known by the towns in which they were produced: York, Wakefield, Coventry, Chester. In England these plays were called *mysteries,* especially those dealing with the birth, death or resurrection of Christ. Sometimes robust humor and a sense of the comic were introduced into the religious stories, and the plays were finally forbidden inside the church.

Modern Comedy, The, a series of three novels by John Galsworthy, published in 1929. It is a sequel to the *Forsyte Saga* and includes *The White Monkey* (1924), *The Silver Spoon* (1926) and *Swan Song* (1928).

Monsieur Beaucaire, a novel by Booth Tarkington, published in 1900. The scenes are laid in and near Bath, England, in the 18th century. The hero is ostensibly a French barber, in love with an English lady. In all his difficulties he gives such a good account of himself that he is suspected of being more than a barber, and when the denouement comes he is discovered to be Philippe of Valois. His presence in England and his disguise are accounted for by the fact that he fled from France to escape an undesirable marriage with a princess who had been chosen for him.

Moonstone, The, a novel by Wilkie Collins, published in 1868. The story tells of a strange diamond stolen from the forehead of an Indian idol, cursed by its Brahmin custodians in order to destroy all its unrightful possessors, bequeathed to an English girl and finally restored to its place after being instrumental in mystery and murder. It was one of the first great mystery stories in English.

morality plays, medieval dramatic poems of the 15th century, developed from the miracle plays. The characters are abstractions, personifications of Sin, Hate, Pride, Folly, Lust and the like. The best-known, most imaginative and poetic, is *Everyman,* which has been successfully produced on the modern stage. It is didactic in purpose but genuinely human, representing symbolically the whole life of Man. Other typical moralities are Lindsay's *Satyre of the Three Estaits* and Skelton's *Magnificence.*

Morte d'Arthur, a long, prose narrative embodying the whole Arthurian legend, translated from the French into English and marvelously woven together and expanded by Sir Thomas Malory about 1470. It was printed by Caxton in 1485. It recounts the reign of Arthur from the glorious beginning to the ruin of the Round Table, the quest of the Holy Grail, Lancelot's failure to find it because of his sin, Gawain's failure because of his weariness and Galahad's success because of his purity. Tennyson's *Idylls of the King* is based chiefly on Malory's narrative.

Mother Goose's Tales and Mother Goose's Melodies, a collection of nursery rhymes and stories published in England in 1760 by John Newbery, the first publisher of children's books. It includes the familiar *Baa, Baa, Black Sheep, Little Boy Blue, Patty Cake, Patty Cake* and countless others. Mother Goose herself is a mysterious, untraceable figure who probably comes out of French folklore. The title was taken from Charles Perrault's *Tales of My Mother Goose,* which were first translated into English in 1729. But the later English Mother Goose collections contain many rhymes and stories out of English tradition as well as French, such as *Puss in Boots* and *As I Was Going to St. Ives.*

Munchausen, Baron, a great boaster and teller of tall tales in which he is the central figure. The original character is supposed to have been taken from real life, a German officer, Karl Friedrich Hieronymus von Munchausen (1720–97), who told great stories of his campaigns with a Russian army against the Turks. The Munchausen tales were written by Rudolph Eric Raspe (1737–94), a German living in England. His book was published in English in 1785 and translated into German in 1787 by the poet Gottfried Bürger.

Nicholas Nickleby, a novel by Charles Dickens, published first in serial form in 1838–39. It attacked the cheap, uninspected private schools of Yorkshire and advocated the establishment of national schools. The story is a record of the adventures of young Nicholas Nickleby when he started out in the world. Wackford Squeers, head of Dotheboys Hall, in which Nicholas was for a time employed as a teacher, was one of those whom Dickens referred to as forming "the worthy cornerstone of a structure which, for absurdity and magnificent high-handed *laissez-aller* neglect, has rarely been exceeded in the world."

Nigger of the Narcissus, The: A Tale of the Sea, a story by Joseph Conrad, published serially in the *New Review,* issued in book form in 1897. It appeared in the United States in that year as *The Children of the Sea: A Tale of the Forecastle.* It has to do with the voyage of an East Indiaman homeward from Bombay. Always in the background is the vast changing panorama of the sea. The characters are members of a queerly-assorted crew, among whom is the Nigger, the giant James Wait. "Mr. Conrad," said James Payn, "has, in this book, introduced us to the British merchant seaman, as Rudyard Kipling introduced us to the British soldier." The preface is a noteworthy essay setting forth the author's *credo* as a man of letters.

Notre-Dame de Paris, a romance by Victor Hugo, issued in 1831. The time is at the close of the reign of Louis XI, that able but unscrupulous monarch who likewise appears in Théodore de Banville's play *Gringoire* and in Sir Walter Scott's *Quentin Durward.* The scene is 15th-century Paris, and the action is centered in the great cathedral that looks out over the medieval city. In a manner that is sometimes fanciful to the point of wild extravagance, the characters are caught up in the toils of fate.

novel, a fictional narrative in prose, longer than the short story or novelette; commonly applied to a story in which plot and characters are kept within the possible limits of real life and do not stray away into the domain of the fantastic or the marvelous. Joseph Conrad defined the novel as "a conviction of our fellowmen's existence strong enough to take upon itself a form of imagined life clearer than reality."

octameter, a verse having eight measures or metrical feet.

ode, in ancient usage, a lyric poem designed to be chanted or sung; in modern usage, a sustained lyric having a dignified subject and written in an elevated tone.

Odyssey, The, a Greek epic poem commonly attributed to Homer and regarded as of later date than the *Iliad.* It pictures the adventures of Odysseus (Ulysses) during 10 years of wandering after the Trojan War as he seeks to return to his native island of Ithaca. He escapes many dangers and finally appears as a beggar in his own house, which he finds overrun by a group of insolent suitors of his faithful wife Penelope. He slays the suitors and is welcomed to his own again.

Old Curiosity Shop, The, a novel by Charles Dickens, the first serial to appear in his periodical *Master Humphrey's Clock,* which he established in 1840. As a matter of fact, the shop has little to do with the story except to provide a title and a setting; for Little Nell and her aged grandfather, who keeps it, flee from it to a series of hardships and adventures. Bret Harte's poem "Dickens in Camp" tells of a reading from this story beside a campfire in the "dim Sierras."

Oliver Twist, a novel by Charles Dickens, published in 1837-38, and named from its leading character, a workhouse orphan who runs away to London. After experiences in the underworld he is befriended by a Mrs. Maylie and eventually adopted by Mr. Brownlow. Two of the book's characters, Fagin and Bill Sikes, are among the best-known figures in English literature. Said the author: "I wished to show, in little Oliver, the principle of Good surviving through every adverse circumstance, and triumphing at last."

Ordeal of Richard Feverel, The, one of the major novels of George Meredith, published in 1859. It is the story of a young man reared according to a "system" that quite overlooked human nature. Richard marries Lucy, a farmer's daughter, but in spite of this idyllic episode he comes to grief, and the book, though it has comedy passages, closes tragically. The *Ordeal* has been highly praised as a character study. The original version is preferred to the revision by the author for his authorized edition of 1897.

Origin of Species, The, a scientific work by Charles Darwin, published in 1859. In it he records the results of years of scientific observation in all parts of the world and expounds what is known as his theory of evolution—and especially the idea of natural selection. (The full title is *On the Origin of Species by Means of Natural Selection.*) This epoch-making book aroused controversy of which echoes still persist.

Othello, a tragedy by Shakespeare, produced in 1604, printed in a quarto edition in 1622 and in a folio edition in 1623. Its plot was taken from a story by Giovanni Giraldi. Othello, a Moor in the Venetian service, deceived by the lies and insinuations of the villain Iago, becomes enraged at his wife Desdemona and smothers her. The play is ranked with *Hamlet, King Lear* and *Macbeth.* Othello, "one not easily jealous, but being wrought, perplexed in the extreme," has been portrayed by many eminent actors, of whom perhaps the greatest in the rôle was Tommaso Salvini. Operas by Rossini (1816) and by Verdi (1887) were based on Shakespeare's work.

Outline of History, The, a world-history by H. G. Wells (with the advice and editorial help of Ernest Barker, Sir H. H. Johnston, Sir E. Ray Lankester and Prof. Gilbert Murray), published in the U. S. in 1920. It is described by the author as "an attempt to tell, truly and clearly, in one continuous narrative, the whole story of life and mankind so far as it is known today." Readable in style, it was written primarily to justify Wells' contention that *"history as one whole is amenable to a more broad and comprehensive handling than is the history of special nations and periods, a broader handling that will bring it within the normal limitations of time and energy set to the reading and education of an ordinary citizen."*

Pamela, or Virtue Rewarded, the first of the novels of Samuel Richardson; published in 1740. Told in the form of letters (a characteristic of all Richardson's fiction), the story describes how Pamela Andrews, an upright serving-maid, when pursued by Mr. B——, indignantly evades him, but eventually consents to become his wife. The picture of 18th-century English society is hardly flattering. Henry Fielding's *The Adventures of Joseph Andrews and His Friend Abraham Adams* (1742) was begun as a satire on *Pamela* but outgrew the author's original intention. Critics view *Pamela* as the beginning of the modern analytic novel in English. Unlike the Pamela of Sidney (*Arcadia*) or of Pope (*Epistle to Mrs. Blount*), Richardson's heroine accented her name on the first syllable.

SATAN IN "PARADISE LOST," illustrating the line "Now Night her course begins."

Paradise Lost, an epic poem in blank verse by John Milton, published in 1667. Its purpose is "to justify the ways of God to man." First, the poem relates how some of the angels revolted against God and were cast out of Heaven into Hell to punish their rebellion. They decide to revenge themselves upon the Almighty by invading the earth and leading man to sin. Satan, chief of the fallen angels, corrupts Adam and Eve, the first human beings, and brings about their ex-

pulsion from the Garden of Eden. This expulsion is the "loss of Paradise," which gives the poem its title. *Paradise Lost* is regarded as the greatest epic in the English language.

Paradise Regained, a blank-verse epic poem in four books by John Milton, published in 1671. Its subject is the Redemption. When he returned to Milton the manuscript of *Paradise Lost,* the young Quaker Thomas Elwood remarked: "Thou hast said much here of Paradise Lost, but what hast thou to say of Paradise Found?" After this query, says Elwood, Milton "made no answer, but sat some time in a muse." The poem was a favorite with Milton and admittedly has many beauties, but it was never so well known as its great predecessor.

parody, a literary form in which a serious composition (especially a poem) or the general manner of a serious author is imitated in phraseology and style by means of a travesty dealing with a comically dissimilar theme or one remote from the characteristic subjects of the author in question. Owen Seaman said that parodies might range from "the lowest, a mere verbal echo" to the highest, which was to be looked upon as "pure criticism." Bret Harte's *Condensed Novels* (1867) are remarkable parodies in prose.

Patterne, Sir Willoughby, the leading character of George Meredith's novel *The Egoist* (1879). He is a person utterly lacking in a sense of humor, and is pilloried for his blind smugness and monumental conceit.

Paul et Virginie (Paul and Virginia), a short romantic novel by Jacques Henri Bernardin de Saint-Pierre, published in 1789. Its scene is laid chiefly in the island of Mauritius (a French possession from 1715 to 1810) in the Indian Ocean. The book was an example of the 18th-century "return to nature" in European literature. It quickly passed through numerous French editions and was translated into many other languages. Napoleon is said to have taken a copy of it with him on his Italian campaign.

Peer Gynt, a metrical drama by Henrik Ibsen, published in 1867. It has been stated that Ibsen intended it to be a satire on what he deemed failings of his fellow-countrymen. Peer Gynt is, however, not a mere symbol but a human individual who, after a life of aimless wandering, returns home to discover meaning in life through the agency of Solveig, the drama's heroine. Richard Mansfield produced this work on the American stage in 1907. The musical suite based upon it by Edvard Grieg is well known.

Pendennis, a novel by W. M. Thackeray, published in 1850. It is a character study of Arthur Pendennis, a well-meaning but spoiled and rather unheroic young man, and traces his career first at the university and afterward as a writer and would-be man-of-the-world in London. Only after he has been jilted by the flirtatious Blanche Amory does he awake to a real sense of values. The plot is simpler than in Thackeray's other novels, and the book introduces the figure of Major Pendennis, Arthur's uncle, a convincingly drawn type of

elderly dandy. Like some others of Thackeray's novels it was illustrated by the author himself.

Penrod, a story by Booth Tarkington, published in 1914. It is an intimate study of a boy's contacts and his relations with his elders and with other children. The scene is a small town of the Middle West.

pentameter, a verse having five measures or metrical feet. In English poetry, blank verse and the heroic couplet are traditionally in iambic pentameter.

Pepys' Diary, a record in cipher by Samuel Pepys, translated and first published in 1825. It is a "gossipy chronicle" of his daily doings and gives his impressions of men and events between the years 1660 and 1669. No other book throws such a true light on the manners and customs of the period of the Restoration.

Peter Ibbetson, a romance by George Du Maurier, published in 1891, the first novel of this distinguished English artist. Material world and dream world are so blended that the reader can scarcely distinguish between them. Peter spends his childhood happily in the French country near Paris, where his favorite playmate is the little girl Mimsey Saraskier. His parents die and his coarse and brutal uncle takes him to England, where he attends school and becomes an architect. He falls in love with Mary, the unhappily married Duchess of Towers, whom he discovers to be the Mimsey of the old days. Enraged by infamous lies told by the uncle about Peter's mother, Peter attacks the fellow and, rather by accident than intentionally, kills him. Peter's death-sentence is commuted to imprisonment for life. He and Mary meet again only when he is "dreaming true," though thinking of himself as awake, and then he treads "the old obliterated ways as in a waking dream." Deems Taylor wrote an opera with the same title and plot.

Peter Pan, the central character in Sir James Barrie's fairy play of the same name, an elflike little personage who refuses to "grow up." Joyous and lighthearted little Peter so captivates audiences that the play is regularly repeated in London at Christmas time, and in honor of a literary creation that has brightened a serious world a statue of Peter has been placed in Kensington Gardens. Maude Adams found in *Peter Pan* one of her greatest stage successes.

Père Goriot, Le, a novel (published in 1835) by Balzac; in its style one of the most brilliant of his many works. It is in effect a prose version of Shakespeare's *King Lear.* Goriot is a retired French merchant; the Countess de Restaud and the Baroness de Nucingen take the places of Regan and Goneril, but there is no representative of Cordelia. The book is merciless in its characterizations.

Pickwick Papers, The (more correctly *The Posthumous Papers of the Pickwick Club*), a story by Charles Dickens, issued in parts in 1836–37. It is made up of a series of incidents in the adventurous travels of Samuel Pickwick, Esq., founder and president of the Pickwick Club, and his three cronies, Augustus Snodgrass, Tracy Tupman and Nathaniel Winkle. It introduces a host of other characters, including Alfred Jingle, an eccentric strolling actor; Sam Weller, Pickwick's valet; and the landlady, Mrs. Bardell, whose suit against Pickwick for breach of promise provides one of the most amusing episodes of the book. The *Pickwick Papers* brought fame to Dickens, then only twenty-four. Says F. T. Marzials: "Everybody laughed over it. Everybody talked about it. Everybody felt, confusedly perhaps, but very surely, that a new and vital force had arisen in English literature."

Piers Plowman, The Vision of, an English satirical and allegorical poem of the 14th century; ascribed, from internal evidence, to William Langland (or Longland). It was first printed in 1550. Piers did not have the vision; it was a vision about him. The full title is *The Vision of William concerning Piers the Plowman, together with Vita de Do-Wel, Do-Bet et Do-Best, secundum Wit et Resoun.* The author on a May morning falls asleep upon the Malvern hills and has a dream about the humanity of his day. This poem, which is written in several dialects (with the Midland dialect most favored), throws considerable light on contemporary institutions, both religious and social. W. W. Skeat edited the text in 1887.

Pilgrim's Progress, The, an allegory by the English preacher John Bunyan, of which the first part was issued in 1678. It describes the adventures of its hero, Christian, on his way from the City of Destruction to the Celestial City. He fights with Apollyon, looks on Vanity Fair, passes the castle of Giant Despair and, after these and many other trials, attains to the Delectable Mountains and crosses the Black River to the Shining Gate. It is now supposed that this famous book was written by Bunyan in 1675, while he was a prisoner in the old jail on Bedford bridge. An eighth edition, the last with the author's improvements, appeared in 1682. *The Pilgrim's Progress* with its plain, direct Anglo-Saxon style was welcomed by the common people and was as popular in New England as in the author's own country. A "musical miracle play" by the American composer Edgar Kelley is based on it. A second part by Bunyan (1684), little known, tells of a similar journey by Christiana, Christian's wife.

Pit and the Pendulum, The, a short story by Poe in which one who had been a prisoner of the Inquisition describes the kinds of torture to which he was subjected in the dungeons of Toledo, from which he was rescued in the nick of time by the arrival of a French army.

Plain Tales from the Hills, a collection of short stories of life in India by Rudyard Kipling, published in 1888, when he was 23 and on the staff of the *Lahore Civil and Military Gazette.* It marked the arrival of a distinctive talent and introduced that remarkable trio Mulvaney, Ortheris and Learoyd, privates in B Company of a line regiment, whose adventures were later recounted in their own volume, *Soldiers Three.*

The Anatomy of Man's Body as govern'd by the Twelve Conftellations.
♈ The Head and Face.
♊ Arms
♉ Neck
♌ Heart
♋ Breaft
♎ Reins
♍ Bowels
♐ Thighs
♏ Secrets
♒ Legs
♑ Knees
♓ The Feet.
To know where the Sign is.
Firft Find the Day of the Month, and againft the Day you have the Sign or Place of the Moon in the 6th Column. Then finding the Sign here, it fhews the Part of the Body it governs.
The Names and Characters of the Seven Planets.
☉ Sol, ♄ Saturn, ♃ Jupiter, ♂ Mars, ♀ Venus, ☿ Mercury, ☽ Luna, ☊ Dragons Head and ☋ Tail.
The Five Afpects.
☌ Conjunction, ☍ Oppofition, ✱ Sextile.
△ Trine, □ Quartile.

POOR RICHARD'S ALMANACK. A page from the famous almanac published 1732–1757. Not wishing to appear as both author and publisher, Benjamin Franklin borrowed a pen name from an English almanac by Richard Saunders. *Poor Richard* contained weather information, proverbs, and humor.

Poet Laureate, a title held through letters-patent from the English Crown by the official poet of the British court. The only duty now laid upon one thus chosen is to commemorate in poetry any national event deemed by him worthy of a literary tribute. The honorarium is an annual payment of £72 plus an allowance of £27 "in lieu of a butt of sack"—the butt itself having formerly been given. Bernard Andreas, Edmund Spenser, Samuel Daniel, Ben Jonson and Sir William Davenant all had some kind of recognition as court poets. The official laureateship began with the appointment of John Dryden and following is the list of laureates from that time:

Name	*Born*	*Ap't.*	*Died*
John Dryden	1631	1668	1700
Thomas Shadwell	1642	1689	1692
Nahum Tate	1652	1692	1715
Nicholas Rowe	1674	1715	1718
Rev. Laurence Eusden	1688	1718	1730
Colley Cibber	1671	1730	1757
William Whitehead	1715	1758	1785
Thomas Warton	1728	1785	1790
Henry James Pye	1745	1790	1813
Robert Southey	1774	1813	1843
William Wordsworth	1770	1843	1850
Alfred, Lord Tennyson	1809	1850	1892
Alfred Austin	1835	1896	1913
Robert Bridges	1844	1913	1930
John Masefield	**1875**	**1931**	——

poetry, that form of literature which seeks to express action, feeling or thought in an imaginative form with the aid of rhythmical (and usually metrical) language more heightened than that of prose.

Poor Richard's Almanac, a series of almanacs by Benjamin Franklin published regularly from 1732 to 1757. Many of the best-known American proverbs are from this source; among them is, "Honesty is the best policy." The *Almanac* did much in establishing habits of common sense among the colonists. It was treasured year after year in the new land where reading was scarce, and the homely truths of *Poor Richard* found ready lodgment in the hearts of thrifty souls.

Portia, (*a*) in Shakespeare's *Julius Caesar,* the wife of Marcus Brutus. Grieving that Octavius and Antony have "made themselves so strong," in Brutus's absence she swallows live coals and dies; (*b*) the principal female character in Shakespeare's *The Merchant of Venice,* a "rich heiress," living at her country seat of Belmont, near Venice. By the terms of her father's will her suitors are compelled to choose from three caskets (gold, silver, lead). One of these contains her portrait, and he that chooses it is to be her husband. Bassanio, choosing the lead one, is successful. In the courtroom scene Portia appears as special defense council for Antonio, Bassanio's friend. The part was a favorite one with Ellen Terry and other well-known actresses.

Pride and Prejudice, the first novel by Jane Austen, written in 1796 (when she was 21) and published in 1813. The scene is laid in the English countryside; and though the plot is slight, the intimate drawing of the book's middle-class characters is done with humor and charm. Prejudice is repre-

BETTMANN ARCHIVE

JOHN BUNYAN'S *Pilgrim's Progress.* A dramatic interpretation of the hero, Christian, in battle with the demon Apollyon.

sented by Elizabeth Bennet; Pride, by Mr. Darcy, her wealthy suitor.

Prince and the Pauper, The, a romance by Mark Twain (S. L. Clemens), published in 1881. The plot hinges on the close resemblance between Tom Canty, a poor street boy, and the young prince who later became Edward VI of England. By a clever device the two are made to change places—the prince to wander with Sir Miles Hendon, a disinherited knight; Tom to undergo numerous difficulties because he is ignorant of court etiquette and of the whereabouts of the Great Seal. On the morning of Tom's coronation in the Abbey, the prince reappears, forbids the ceremony, with Tom's aid identifies himself and is duly made king. He rewards Tom and Sir Miles and reigns the more justly and wisely for his experience of humbler life.

Princess, The, a narrative poem by Tennyson, published in 1847; with the subtitle "A Medley." It has to do with an imaginary princess who establishes a university in which women are to learn how to be independent of men. The lyric interludes (such as "Sweet and low," "The splendor falls on castle walls," "Ask me no more") and the incidental song "Tears, idle tears" are among the finest things in Tennyson's works. Sir W. S. Gilbert's *The Princess* was styled by him "a respectful parody" of Tennyson's "exquisite poem."

Prometheus Bound, a drama by Aeschylus, of uncertain date; the only surviving member of a trilogy. In it Prometheus, now bound to the rock by order of Zeus, expresses his defiance and, his will still unbroken, disappears in earthquake and whirlwind.

Prometheus Unbound, a lyrical drama by Shelley, issued in 1820. It was suggested by the title of a lost drama of Aeschylus, in which Prometheus was unchained from the rock to which Zeus had confined him in punishment. Prometheus, in Shelley's hands, is not the god who invoked his own torture by bringing fire to men but represents mankind thirsting after liberty and gifts of the spirit, yet condemned to torture.

prose, any style of language that is not verse, whether it be ordinary, everyday speech or writing or constructively and artistically managed.

proverb, a brief saying presenting in epigrammatic form a bit of traditional wisdom.

Puck of Pook's Hill, a volume of stories by Rudyard Kipling, published in 1906. The children Una and Dan, in a meadow, acting what they remembered of *Midsummer Night's Dream* (with Una as Titania and Dan as Puck, Bottom and all three fairies), encountered Puck himself. Through his kind offices they had glimpses of English history in the making and learned that England "is not any common Earth."

Punch and Judy, a puppet show in which the leading characters are Punch, a humpbacked, hook-nosed fellow who does outrageous and tragic things with the utmost nonchalance, and his wife Judy, whom he beats to death. The origin of Punch is to be found in the

clown of the old Neapolitan comedy, and the name is simply an abbreviation of the Italian Punchinello.

Purple Land, The, by W. H. Hudson, a book of adventures in South America. Perhaps in this book, even more than in *Far Away and Long Ago, Green Mansions* and *Birds and Man,* other books dealing with South America, Hudson displays his powers of description and character analysis and his knowledge of ornithological life. "Without apparent effort"—to quote John Galsworthy—"he takes you with him into a rare, free, natural world, and always you are refreshed, stimulated, enlarged, by going there."

Pygmalion, a play by Bernard Shaw, dated by him 1912. Prof. Henry Higgins, student of phonetics and author of *Higgins's Universal Alphabet,* takes from the London streets Eliza Doolittle, a flower girl who utters "depressing and disgusting sounds," and by his intensive training so alters her speech and manner that at a garden party she is able to pass as a duchess. She falls in love with him and he realizes that she has become a necessary part of his life; so one does not need to take too seriously Higgins's observation that Eliza, his friend Pickering and he "will be three old bachelors together." In the U. S. the piece was first presented in New York on October 12, 1914. It is a modern variation of the old myth of Pygmalion's statue of a beautiful girl that came to life when he admired it so warmly.

Quality Street, a play by Sir James Barrie. Quality Street is a little English country town where, in the period of the Napoleonic Wars, the maiden sisters Phoebe and Susan Throssel keep a dame school. After 10 years of absence at the front, Valentine Brown, with a captain's commission but without his left hand, returns to make to Miss Phoebe (with various amusing contretemps) the avowal she had hoped for long ago. The play's first presentation in the United States was in New York on November 11, 1901, with Maude Adams in the role of Phoebe.

quatrain, a four-line stanza with any of the following schemes of rhyming: *a, a, b, b; a, b, a, b; a, a, b, a; a, b, b, a; a, b, c, b.*

Quentin Durward, a novel by Sir Walter Scott, issued in 1823. It gains its title from the name of a brave young Scotsman who takes service in the Scottish Guards of the French King Louis XI. The king selects him to conduct two vassals of Duke Charles of Burgundy, Isabelle of Croye and her aunt, to the bishop of Liège; the royal scheme is to have William de la Marck, a notorious outlaw, waylay Quentin's party, seize Isabelle and marry her. Quentin succeeds in delivering Isabelle to the bishop, but William attacks the castle of Liège and murders the bishop, Quentin and Isabelle escape, and Isabelle returns to Burgundy. Duke Charles eventually awards her hand to Quentin. This book had a great European success, particularly in France.

Quo Vadis (Latin for "Whither Goest Thou?"), the most popular work of

the Polish novelist Henryk Sienkiewicz, published in the United States in an English translation in 1896. It is a story of life in Rome in the days of Nero and draws strong, sometimes melodramatic, contrasts between the dying civilization of Rome and the new faith of Christianity, just coming into prominence. The title is derived from an ancient legend that relates how Peter, fleeing from Rome, met Jesus on the Appian Way and cried, "Lord, whither goest Thou?" (*Domine, quo vadis?*); to which the answer was, "To Rome, to be crucified again." Whereupon Peter turned back to encounter martyrdom.

Ramayana, an epic poem of India, probably dating from about the beginning of the Christian Era. Its 24,000 stanzas are attributed to a poet called Valmiki. They relate the deeds of Rama, a mythological hero.

Rambler, The, a periodical in the manner of the *Spectator* of Addison and Steele, published in London by Dr. Samuel Johnson. It was issued on Tuesdays and Saturdays from March 20, 1750, to March 14, 1752. All the numbers were written entirely by Johnson except five; and of these, one was by Samuel Richardson, author of *Pamela.*

Ramona, a novel by Helen Hunt Jackson (writing under the pseudonym H. H.), published in 1885. It exposes the treatment received by the American Indians at the hands of the whites and appeals for justice. The same theme had occupied the author in her historical work *A Century of Dishonor* (1881). The scene is southern California in the last days of Mexican rule, when the American *gringos* are beginning to settle in the country. Ramona, a half-breed (Scottish and Indian), elopes with Alessandro, a young Indian of fine character, and the story is the story of their progressive misfortunes through the greed and covetousness of the newcomers. It is filled with local color. Californians took to pointing out for visitors the *hacienda* in which Ramona lived, the chapel in which she prayed and other imaginary spots, but they disregarded the book's real significance.

Rasselas, a romance by Samuel Johnson, published in 1759. It recounts the adventures of Rasselas, an imaginary prince of Abyssinia. According to national custom, the royal family was confined in the Happy Valley between towering mountains. Rasselas, curious as to what the outside world contained, escaped with his sister Nekayah and the poet Imlac, and the three wandered far, in the endeavor to find what place or condition could offer most happiness in life. They finally decided there were objections to almost every supposedly desirable and attractive situation, and determined to return. The name Rasselas or Rasalas means head of the lion in Arabic and is the name of a star in the constellation *Leo.*

Raven, The, a poem by Edgar A. Poe, published in 1845 in his volume *The Raven and Other Poems.* It was widely quoted and reprinted and discussed, became part of the repertory of every elocutionist and to the popular mind was better known than anything else Poe wrote, whether in verse or prose.

realism, in literature, the doctrine and practice of the realists of representing persons and things with alleged scientific faithfulness and in unsparing detail, no attempt being made to modify or to select; opposed to the idealism of the romantic school.

Rebecca, in Scott's *Ivanhoe,* the daughter of Isaac of York. Her charity in nursing the sick, devotion to her old father, bravery and dignity before a court of unjust accusers, determined resistance to the advances of Brian de Bois-Guilbert and generous renunciation of any possible claims upon Ivanhoe, the man she loves, make her a memorable character.

Rebecca of Sunnybrook Farm, a story by Kate Douglas Wiggin, published in 1903. Rebecca goes to live in a distant village with two maiden aunts. The elder of these is austere and dominating; the younger possesses milder attributes but is helpless before her older sister. Rebecca meets with a cold reception and only her buoyant spirit enables her to bear the indignities put upon her. It is her task to wear down the old lady's resistance to good impulses, but with the professional and friendly aid of a young country doctor the miracle is accomplished.

Red Badge of Courage, The, a story by Stephen Crane, published in 1895, when the author was about 24. It is a study of a man's feelings in battle, written by one who had never been in a battle. Henry Fleming, a raw country boy, enlists at the outset of the Civil War. The book describes his mental states as he waits for action, his panic under fire and the development of a new frame of mind in one who had been "an animal, blistered and sweating in the heat and pain of war."

Renaissance, the period of transition from medieval to modern times, distinguished by the revival of letters and of art.

Rescue, The: A Romance of the Shallows, a novel by Joseph Conrad, published in 1920. The shallows are those of the sea that "foams and murmurs on the shores of the thousand islands, big and little, which make up the Malay Archipelago." An atmosphere of exotic lagoons and wooded shores, "far east and still mysterious," surrounds this book. Captain Lingard (King Tom) of the brig *Lightning,* Captain Jörgenson, late of the bark *Wild Rose,* Mrs. Travers, d'Alcacer, and native folk such as Wasub and Immada and Belarab are among the characters involved in a tangle of adventure. This is the story that, when it was seven-eighths done, Conrad laid aside for 20 years until he devised an ending that satisfied him.

Return of the Native, The, the sixth novel of Thomas Hardy, published in 1878. The time is "between 1840 and 1850;" the scene is Egdon Heath in Hardy's Wessex country. The "native" is Clym Yeobright, who has been a jeweler in Paris but wishes to lead a broader and less selfish life, returns to the village in which he was born and there plans to open a school and improve local conditions. His philanthropic schemes are interrupted when he falls in love with Eustacia Vye, an exotic creature, "the raw material of a divinity," with whom he leads a troubled existence. Eustacia drowns herself, and Clym, his sight impaired, finds his vocation as an itinerant open-air preacher and lecturer. A group of Hardy's rural characters lends flavor to the story.

Rewards and Fairies, a group of stories by Rudyard Kipling, published in 1910. Una and David renew their acquaintance with Puck, begun in *Puck of Pook's Hill,* and learn more about past days in England. In this volume appeared the much-quoted poem "*If—.*"

rhyme, a correspondence in sound between two or more syllables or groups of syllables; usually taken to refer to

ROBINSON CRUSOE by Daniel Defoe: "I was exceedingly surprised with the print of a man's naked foot on the shore. . . ."

end-rhyme, the correspondence between the final feet of two or more lines. A *leonine rhyme* occurs when there is a correspondence between the syllables at the first natural break or pause in a line and those at the end of the line (also called an *internal rhyme.* Sometimes the word is spelled *rime.*

rhythm, in prosody, the cadence of verse, dependent upon a succession of long and short syllables.

Ring and the Book, The, a dramatic poem by Robert Browning, the longest of his works, originally published in four volumes in 1868–69. One day the poet had bought in Florence for eight pence an old book giving the court records of a murder trial in seventeenth-century Rome. The events of the tragedy are rehearsed in the poem six times from different points of view by as many different persons; outside opinions and criticisms are offered; the condemned man has his last words. The whole is divided, with the poet's prologue and epilogue, into 12 books—a remarkable constructive effort, rich in philosophic wisdom.

Rip Van Winkle, a short story by Washington Irving that appeared in his *Sketch Book of Geoffrey Crayon,* (published in seven parts, 1819–20). Rip, a good-natured, likable ne'er-do-well, on a hunting excursion falls in with a dwarf who leads him into the fastnesses of the Catskills. The dwarf proves to be a member of a band of little men. Rip drinks the liquor they proffer and falls asleep. He wakes 20 years later to find himself an old man with a long white beard. Having made his way back to the village he discovers that his wife is dead, that many changes have taken place and that a republic has been declared. Joseph Jefferson's best-known part was that of Rip in a play adapted from Irving's story by Dion Boucicault and somewhat altered by the actor himself.

Rivals, The, a comedy by Richard Brinsley Butler Sheridan, produced in 1775, when its author was 24. The rivals are Captain Absolute (*alias* Ensign Beverley) and Bob Acres, contenders for the hand of Lydia Languish. Acres sends a challenge to the unknown Ensign Beverley, but when he reaches the field of honor and discovers that Beverley is none other than his good friend Absolute, he declines to fire. Styled a coward, he declares, "I don't mind the word 'coward;' 'coward' may be said in a joke; but if he called me 'poltroon'—." He abandons all claims to Lydia's favor, and she is forthwith married to Absolute, whom she had known as Beverley and with whom she had been intending to elope.

Robinson Crusoe, a children's classic, by Daniel Defoe, published in 1719. It is one of the most famous stories for boys ever written. Early in the story Robinson Crusoe, sole survivor from a wreck, crawls upon the beach of a deserted island, with only his native wits and the gifts of fortune to save him from starvation. He first rescues from the wrecked vessel tools and provisions which will be of use to him; next he organizes his time and energy, builds a home, plants crops and tames wild creatures. At last Crusoe sees the print of a human foot on the sand of his shore one day. The footprint is that of a savage whom Crusoe names Friday and adopts as a servant. The island is invaded by savages and later by European sailors. All Crusoe's resourcefulness is needed to save his life, but he eventually masters the situation and sails back to England in prosperity. The secret of the book's success lies chiefly in two features: (1) the minute details which make it seem like a record of actual experience, and (2) the ingenuity of Crusoe in fighting a battle for life, alone, under primitive conditions. Crusoe is supposed to have had an original in the Scottish sailor Alexander Selkirk (1676–1721), who at his own request was put ashore on the island of Juan Fernandez off the coast of Chile in 1704 and lived there alone until 1709. Defoe places Crusoe's island somewhere "upon the coast of Guiana, or the north part of Brazil."

Rochester, Edward Fairfax, a character in Charlotte Brontë's *Jane Eyre;* the owner of Thornfield Hall, where Jane becomes a governess. His is a strange, paradoxical nature, but Jane's eventual marriage to him turns out most happily for both.

romance, in prose fiction, a form distinguished from the novel or tale in that it adheres less closely to verisimilitude and freely idealizes.

romantic movement, in modern literature, a marked tendency at the close of the 18th century and the beginning of the 19th to revert to medieval standards of free idealism and to employ even the most fantastic and extravagant methods; opposed, in this sense, to classicism.

Romeo and Juliet, a tragedy by Shakespeare; printed surreptitiously in 1597, issued in corrected form in 1599. "A pair of star-cross'd lovers" between whose families lies an ancient grudge supply the main plot. The scene is Verona, except the first portion of the fifth act, which is at Mantua. The story had filtered down from Italian and French sources. Shakespeare found it in Arthur Brooke's poem *The Tragicall History of Romeus and Juliet* (1562) and in a prose version *The Palace of Pleasure* (1566–67) by William Painter. This play of young love, "the first bewildered, stammering interview of the heart," gives us the mingled grace and brutality of medieval manners. Among its characters is Mercutio, kinsman to the prince of Verona and gallant gentleman, who as he dies exclaims, "A plague o' both your houses!" The dramatic fifth symphony (1839) of Berlioz found inspiration here, as did Gounod's opera *Roméo et Juliette* (1867).

Romola, a novel by George Eliot, published serially in the *Cornhill Magazine* in 1862–63 and in book form in 1863. It is a story of Florentine life at the close of the 15th century. In its crowded pages appears Savonarola, the great religious and social reformer. In spite, however, of the amount of historical detail that the author wrought into the book, interest centers not in Florentine history but in the moral degradation of one of the characters—Tito Melema—a Greek who wanders into the city one morning, a shipwrecked and friendless stranger, but establishes himself in the favor of influential persons, marries Romola and becomes a man of importance. His rise is accompanied by a gradual deterioration, until at the end of the story he is utterly unscrupulous, all through seeking his own interest and taking the easiest way, whether right or wrong. In tracing Tito's debasement through his own actions, George Eliot is illustrating her own saying: "Our deeds determine us as much as we determine our deeds."

Rosalind, a character in Shakespeare's *As You Like It;* daughter of the banished duke and in love with Orlando. She dresses as a boy and goes to the forest of Arden. Mischievous when she teases Orlando about his love and always witty, gay and vivacious, she is,

as Professor Dowden says, "a figure which quickens and restores our spirit as music does."

Rowena, The Lady, in Scott's *Ivanhoe,* the ward of Cedric the Saxon; in love with Wilfred of Ivanhoe, to whom she is married in York minster in the presence of King Richard.

Rubáiyát, The (Quatrains), verses by Omar Khayyám, a Persian philosopher and poet belonging to the second half of the 11th century A.D. and the first quarter of the 12th. The verses record melancholy reflections upon life in vivid and simple figures, likening existence to a day's rest in a journey, or man to a clay pot. The prevailing reflection is that since life is brief and the future uncertain, one should enjoy the present with feast and song. The English poet Edward FitzGerald published in 1859 a translation of these quatrains into English verse of commanding beauty. Liza Lehmann's song cycle *In a Persian Garden* is based on selections from the FitzGerald version.

saga, strictly, a Scandinavian hero story or myth; by extension, any legend or record of ancient history.

satire, in modern literature, any composition, whether in verse or prose, in which ridicule is employed against human beings and their ways.

Scarlet Letter, The, a novel by Nathaniel Hawthorne, published in 1850. Its scene is laid in 17th-century Boston. The heroine is Hester Prynne, who re-

fuses to name the father of her child Pearl. She is forced to stand on the pillory and to wear a scarlet letter A (for adulteress) on the bosom of her dress. Taking up her home on the verge of the wilderness, she devotes her life to deeds of mercy, while Pearl grows up a lonely, elfin creature. At last, after a powerful sermon, the father, the Rev. Arthur Dimmesdale, publicly declares his guilt and dies in Hester's arms. The lofty atmosphere of this book and its pure style made it a 19th-century classic.

Scottish Chiefs, The, a romance by Jane Porter, published in 1810. It centers around the martial exploits of Sir William Wallace, the Scottish national hero, and Robert Bruce is also introduced. It begins in 1296 with the murder of Wallace's wife by English soldiers.

Sense and Sensibility, a novel by Jane Austen, written in 1797–98, later revised and published in 1811. Here, as in her other books, she paints with incomparable fidelity on—to use her own words—a "little bit (two inches wide) of ivory," the middle-class English life she knew. The story reveals how easily sentiment may decline into sentimentality, and is rather a character study than an out-and-out romance like *Pride and Prejudice.* It has its share of what Scott referred to as "the exquisite touch which renders commonplace things and characters interesting."

THE "RUBÁIYÁT OF OMAR KHAYYÁM," Persian poet, is a tribute to love, wine, and fatalism. Edward Fitzgerald's English translation, 1859, refined the Persian's quatrains.

Sentimental Journey Through France and Italy, A, fanciful sketches of continental wanderings, part of what was intended to be a longer work, by Laurence Sterne; published in two volumes in 1768 just before his death. While he was looking at the Bastille, the tourist heard a voice, "I can't get out!" It proved to be the voice of a caged starling, but the tourist, imagining a prisoner who had been confined 30 years, wept bitterly. At a place near Crécy he wept over a dead ass. On other occasions he wept freely. "God tempers the wind to the shorn lamb," often attributed to the Bible, occurs in this book.

Sentimental Tommy, a novel by Sir James Barrie, published in 1895. Tommy is Thomas Sandys, a young Scot with a real literary gift but a tendency to dramatize his life (himself as hero) and a lack of emotional stability. He lives in a world of poses and illusion and conscious pretense and has done so ever since he was a lad and proclaimed that the Auld Licht kirk of Thrums was bigger and lovelier than St. Paul's. The book has humor of a rather grim sort, and the other characters are drawn with much truth. *Tommy and Grizel* (1900) continues the record of Tommy's fortunes.

Sesame and Lilies, the collective title of a group of three lectures by John Ruskin. Of these the first two, *Of Kings' Treasuries* and *Of Queens' Gardens,* were issued together in 1865 (the second having first appeared as a pamphlet in 1864); the third, *The Mystery of Life and Its Arts,* delivered in Dublin in 1868, was later added and a long preface, dated 1871, was written for the three. The theme of the first is the use and value of good books; of the second, the right education of girls; of the third, some of Ruskin's ideals for the conduct of life.

sestet, (*a*) the second portion (the last six lines) of a sonnet; (*b*) any stanza of six verses.

She Stoops To Conquer, a comedy by Oliver Goldsmith, first produced in 1773. It is said to have been founded on an incident in the author's own life. In the play, Marlow, a bashful young man, is on his way to the estate of Hardcastle, whose daughter has been named to him as a desirable wife. Tony Lumpkin, the squire's stepson, directs Marlow to the Hardcastle home, saying that it is an inn at which he may remain overnight. On arriving there, Marlow treats Hardcastle as a landlord and the daughter, the girl whom he had actually come to court, as a barmaid. But she is so favorably impressed with him that she allows him to believe her, though not a barmaid, a poor relation. Thus "she stoops to conquer" and gains a husband.

Sherlock Holmes, the clever detective of Baker Street, hero of Sir Conan Doyle's *A Study in Scarlet, The Sign of Four, Adventures of Sherlock Holmes, Memoirs of Sherlock Holmes, The Return of Sherlock Holmes, The Hound of the Baskervilles, The Valley of Fear, His Last Bow* and *The Case Book of Sherlock Holmes.* The quick-witted, resourceful, nonchalant Holmes and his slow-minded foil Doctor Watson make an effective pair. The character of Holmes, according to Doyle himself, was in part drawn from Dr. Joseph Bell of the Edinburgh Infirmary, who had some of the deductive gifts that Holmes displayed in so superlative a degree. William Gillette, who long played the leading role in his own drama *Sherlock Holmes,* strikingly realized Holmes in person and manner.

Shropshire Lad, A, a book of poems by Alfred Edward Housman, published in 1896. It is a series of lyrics, 63 in number, having both an outward and an inner unity because their background is the region of Wenlock Edge and the Severn and "the wild green hills of Wyre," and because they are direct personal expressions with a local center there but universal in their significance. Simple in their verse forms and their phrases, with not one overwritten line yet never commonplace, they brought a new speech into English poetry; and this was admitted even by those who did not wholly enjoy Stoic philosophy.

Shylock, the Jewish moneylender in Shakespeare's *The Merchant of Venice.* He may be viewed as an "inexorable dog" who hates all Christians and plots against their lives, loves his money and oppresses his young daughter Jessica; or he may be pitied because he belongs to an abused race and stands alone in the play, opposed to all the other characters and deserted even by his daughter. Some actors to whom the role of Shylock has been assigned have portrayed him in the first-named light; but Sir Henry Irving, perhaps the greatest interpreter of the part, made his audiences more friendly toward the old man against whom the entire populace had turned.

Sigurd the Volsung and the Fall of the Niblungs, The Story of, an epic poem by the versatile William Morris, published in 1877. William Sharp once wrote: "The breath of the North blows across these billowy lines as the polar wind across the green waves of the North Sea. The noise of waters, the splashing of oars, the whirling of swords, the conflict of battle, cries and heroic summons to death, re-echo in the ears."

Silas Marner, a novel by George Eliot, published in 1861. "In the old days there were angels who came and took men by the hand and led them away from the city of destruction. We see no white-winged angels now. But yet men are led away from threatening destruction; a hand is put into theirs; ... and the hand may be a little child's". This is the theme of the novel, which shows the redemption of Marner, a miserly weaver, by his love for a little child. He has been robbed of his hoard of gold, but is recompensed by finding Eppie upon his threshold. Eppie turns out to be the unacknowledged daughter of Godfrey Cass, the village squire, by an unfortunate first marriage.

skald, a minstrel of the ancient Scandinavians who composed and sang or recited poetry in honor of heroes and their deeds.

Sketch Book of Geoffrey Crayon, Gent., The, collection of sketches and tales by Washington Irving, published in seven parts in 1819–20. Famous among the stories in the volume are "Rip Van Winkle" and "The Legend of Sleepy Hollow" (the account of Ichabod Crane, Katrina Van Tassel and the headless horseman).

Sohrab and Rustum, a narrative poem in blank verse by Matthew Arnold, called by him "an episode." It appeared in his first series of *Poems* in 1853 with "The Scholar-Gipsy" and other notable verse. "Sohrab and Rustum" tells how the Persian warrior Rustum (Rustam) unwittingly engages in personal combat with his natural son Sohrab, challenger for Rustum's Tartar foes, and mortally wounds him before learning of their relationship. The story comes from the Persian epic the *Shahnamah* (Book of Kings).

sonnet, a poem of 14 lines (customarily in iambic pentameter) arranged in accordance with a prescribed rhyming scheme. There are two leading forms, the Italian (or Petrarchan) and the Shakespearean (or Elizabethan).

Sonnets from the Portuguese, a sonnet sequence by Elizabeth Barrett Browning, published in 1850. It had been printed (but not published) in 1847 as Sonnets by E.B.B. The sonnets are the artistic expression—"the very notes and chronicle," Edmond Gosse called them—of her betrothal to Robert Browning, who declared them to be "the finest sonnets written in any language since Shakespeare's." The present title was suggested by Browning for the edition of 1850 because Mrs. Browning, whose looks were Latin rather than English, had been dubbed by certain intimate friends "The Portuguese."

Spectator, The, an English periodical that succeeded Richard Steele's *Tatler.* From March 1, 1711, to December 6, 1712, it was issued daily (Sundays excepted) by Addison and Steele; from June 18 to December 20, 1714, three times a week by Addison alone. The first series comprised 555 numbers, of which 236 were by Steele, 274 by Addison, the others by various friends. (Pope's *Messiah* was originally written for it.) It gained a certain unity through the idea of an imaginary club and through the presence of the Spectator himself—observer, critic, philosophical teacher. It contained stories and character sketches (including the Sir Roger de Coverley papers); essays on fashion, manners, morals, religion; critiques of literature and the drama. So popular was the work that it could be found upon every breakfast table and in every coffeehouse. Its effects upon English thinking and English manners were decided.

spondee, a metrical foot consisting either of (*a*), in Latin and Greek verse, two long syllables, or (*b*), in English verse, two accented syllables.

Spoon River Anthology, a book of verse by Edgar Lee Masters, issued in book form in 1915. It originally appeared from week to week in *Reedy's Mirror* in 1914–15. Its plan was novel. A succession of the departed inhabitants of an Illinois small town speak from the quiet in which "all, all are sleeping on the hill," and thus they draw vignette portraits of themselves and their former neighbors. Among these voices is introduced that of Anne Rutledge in what is the best and most quoted expression of the series.

Stalky & Co., a story by Rudyard Kipling, published in 1899. It has to do with student life in England and is based on the author's own experiences at the United Services College, Westward Ho, North Devon. Stalky & Co. were Stalky, McTurk and Beetle, "the resourceful three," companions for 7 years. Beetle, editor of the college paper, who enters journalism, is Kipling himself.

stanza, a group of lines of verse arranged in accordance with a definite scheme. It is often, but incorrectly, called a verse.

Strange Interlude, a play by Eugene O'Neill, produced and published in 1928. It received the Pulitzer prize for 1927–28. It aroused discussion through use of a technical device by which the drifting thoughts of the characters break through the regular dialogue and find utterance in an adaptation of an old-time soliloquy.

stream of consciousness, a phrase employed in describing a method by which in fiction writing the author, instead of epitomizing or briefly suggesting a character's thoughts, unwinds them in a jumbled and seemingly endless continuum.

Tale of Two Cities, A, a novel by Charles Dickens, first published serially in *All the Year Round* from April to November, 1859. The two cities are London and Paris, the time is just before and during the French Revolution. Dr. Charles Darnay, nephew of a heartless French marquis, hastens to Paris to aid an old family servant. His wife Lucie and his father-in-law Dr. Manette follow him. Soon they and two friends, the solicitor Jarvis Lorry and the bohemian Sidney Carton, who has long loved Lucie Manette, find themselves caught in the maelstrom of the Terror. Darnay is sentenced to death as an aristocrat, but Carton by a stratagem takes his place in prison and dies by the guillotine. The scene of the execution, with the knitting women calmly numbering the numerous victims as time and again the knife falls, is justly famous.

Tales of a Wayside Inn, a group of narrative poems by Henry W. Longfellow. The first part appeared in 1863; the second, in 1872 (as one of the *Three Books of Song*); the third, in 1873 (as the chief part of *Aftermath*). The arrangement is under the fiction of a company of storytellers at the Red-Horse Tavern in Sudbury, Mass. Probably the most famous of the stories is the landlord's tale, *Paul Revere's Ride*. The inn still stands, a memorial to the poet.

Talisman, The, a novel by Sir Walter Scott, published in 1825. It tells a story of the Third Crusade. Palestine, during an interlude in the fighting, is the scene of its action. Two noble adversaries, Richard the Lion-hearted and Saladin meet when the sultan, in the guise of a physician, attends the king. The plot has to do with the soldierly exploits and the courtship of the Prince of Scotland, disguised as Sir Kenneth of the Couchant Leopard, who wins the hand of Lady Edith Plantagenet. The love story is in Scott's best romantic vein. The romantic effect is heightened by descriptions of the splendor of the armies, of a great sandstorm on the desert and of marvelous feats of swordsmanship.

Tam O'Shanter, a famous poem by Robert Burns, first published in the Edinburgh edition of 1793. It tells in Burns's best vein of the uncanny experiences of

> honest Tam o'shanter
> As he frae Ayre ae night did canter

on a market night, after tarrying overlong by a tavern ingle. Pursued by warlocks and witches and knowing they dare not cross a stream, he urged his mare Maggie across Doon brig, but one witch managed to seize Maggie by the tail, leaving "scarce a stump."

Tanglewood Tales, a collection of stories by Nathaniel Hawthorne, published in 1853. It is a "second Wonder-Book" and continues the series of versions of old Greek myths begun in *A Wonder-Book* (1851). The six stories tell of Theseus and the Minotaur; the Pygmies that battled with the cranes; Circe's palace, where the companions of Odysseus were changed to swine; Ceres and Proserpine; the dragon's teeth and the voyage of Jason and his Argonauts.

Tatler, The, a periodical founded by Sir Richard Steele and edited and published by him in London from 1709 to 1711 under the pseudonym "Isaac Bickerstaff, astrologer." This name he borrowed from Dean Swift, who had assumed it in a controversy with one Partridge, an almanac maker. Of the *Tatler* papers, Steele and Addison together wrote 34; Addison, 41; Steele, the remainder of the 271 numbers. The *Tatler,* issued three times a week, contained political and social news in addition to the essay.

Tempest, The, a romantic drama by Shakespeare, first performed in 1611, first printed in the folio of 1623. It was thus among his last plays. The scene is laid on an enchanted island, apparently Bermuda. The chief character, Prospero, a magician, is a model of magnanimity. Caliban, deformed aborigine with something of human intelligence but no moral sense, contrasts most sharply with Ariel, a sprite who serves Prospero. The plot opens with a tempest, caused by Prospero's magic. This tempest brings to the island Prospero's brother Antonio, who had usurped the throne. After a day of marvels Prospero regains his dukedom, and all sail away to Italy. There are some beautiful songs in the play. Robert Johnson in 1612 wrote music for "Full fathom five" and "Where the bee sucks," and Henry Purcell wrote music for an opera on the same theme produced in 1756 by David Garrick.

Tess of the D'Urbervilles; a Pure Woman, a novel by Thomas Hardy, first published in 1891. Tess Durbeyfield, a beautiful English village girl is a lineal descendant of the aristocratic d'Urbervilles. Alec, a son of that family, pursues Tess and by accident, through no fault of hers, she becomes his victim. A child is born, whom she names Sorrow, but he soon dies. Some years later Angel Clare marries Tess, but he leaves her when on the wedding day she tells him of her past. He experiences a change of heart and tries again to win her love, but Alec seeks to claim her and prevent any reconciliation. Tess kills him, and she and Clare flee, hoping to reach a port whence they may escape. They are overtaken at Stonehenge, and Tess is hanged.

tetrameter, a verse having four measures or metrical feet.

Thanatopsis (A Vision of Death), a reflective poem by William Cullen Bryant, written when he was only 18, published in the *North American Review* in 1817. Its theme is consolation upon thought of death. It has sometimes been asserted that with *Thanatopsis* American poetry had its real beginning.

Three Musketeers, The (*Les Trois Mousquetaires*), also sometimes called *The Three Guardsmen*, a romance by Alexandre Dumas the Elder, published in 1844. It is the first part of a trilogy of which the other two parts are *Twenty Years After* and *The Vicomte de Bragelonne*. These three stories cover the period from 1625 to 1665 and deal with the adventurous career of d'Artagnan, who comes from Gascony to Paris to seek his fortune with a raw-boned horse, a box of magic salve and three crowns in money. In *The Three Musketeers* he manages on his first day to get himself into duels with Athos, Porthos and Aramis, the most dangerous members of the musketeer crops of Louis XIII. He wins the friendship of all and thenceforth the four share both good and evil fortune amid stirring events in the days of Richelieu.

To Have and To Hold, a novel by Mary Johnston, published in 1900. It is a historical romance dealing with life in colonial Virginia in the early 17th century. The hero is Ralph Percy, an English gentleman, who chooses a wife from "indentured" servingmaids newly arrived from England. She turns out to be Jocelyn Leigh, the king's ward, who has fled in disguise to avoid marriage with Lord Carnal. Carnal traces and follows her, his endeavors to seize her and get rid of Ralph Percy provide many adventures, but eventually all ends well.

Tom Brown's School Days, a story by Thomas Hughes (by An Old Boy, says the title page), published in 1857. It has been termed the best story of school life ever written and relates the experiences of the hero at Rugby, including his acquaintance with the famous headmaster Dr. Thomas Arnold. Cricket, football, fagging and bullying and poaching receive much attention. The character of Arthur, one of the boys, is based on that of Arthur Stanley (later dean of Westminster) as he was in student days. *Tom Brown at Oxford* (1861), a sequel, takes the hero to college.

Tom Jones (properly, *The History of*

TAR-BABY AND BR'ER FOX from *Uncle Remus*, a story taken from Negro folklore.

Tom Jones, a Foundling), a novel by Henry Fielding, published in 1749. The hero, Tom Jones, is a foundling who grows up into an impulsive, frank and generous boy. He loves Sophia Western, daughter of the local squire, but has a rival, Blifil, a malicious hypocrite. Tom gets into various escapades, is disinherited, has several discreditable adventures with women; but through all his wanderings remains frank, well-intentioned, and kind of heart. At the end of the story he is discovered to be the rightful heir to a fortune. He reforms, marries Sophia and launches upon a virtuous and happy career.

Tom Sawyer, The Adventures of, a story by Mark Twain (Samuel L. Clemens), published in 1875. It is the first of three works of fiction by him dealing with the Mississippi River and the folk of the Mississippi Valley. (The other two are its sequel, *The Adventures of Huckleberry Finn,* and *Pudd'nhead Wilson.*) With spontaneous humor and a wealth of picturesque and authentic detail, veracious character drawing and racy wisdom, the author describes the vanished life of the old steamboating days he knew so well.

Tommy and Grizel, a novel by Sir James Barrie, published in 1900. It continues the study of "Sentimental Tommy," Thomas Sandys, the gifted young Scot whose ever-shifting moods and fondness for make-believe in which he is cast as hero render him an object of constant thought by the patient Grizel, who long endures his flirtations with other women. Finally his affair with Lady Pippinworth nearly breaks Grizel's heart but she nevertheless enters into a hasty marriage with him—and the result is that proverbially ascribed to hasty marriages.

tragedy, that form of dramatic composition in which a theme of solemn or pathetic character is set forth in action usually proceeding to a fatal outcome and in language of an elevated quality, whether verse or prose.

Treasure Island, a story by Robert Louis Stevenson, published in 1883. The hero is Jim Hawkins, a boy whose father keeps a seaside tavern. At the tavern lives a terrible old seaman who guards the secret of the burial place of pirate treasure. A murderous gang is after this secret, but the old man dies without revealing it, and the map of Treasure Island passes into the possession of Hawkins. Friends of his proceed to fit a vessel to seek the treasure, but their purpose leaks out, and some of the pirate gang enlist in the crew. Mutiny on board ship, cold-blooded murders, strategy and fighting, on sea and ashore, form the material of the remaining story, until the treasure is found. The book has all the best features of a good pirate yarn, including a diabolical villain, Long John Silver, the one-legged cook. It is one of the most captivating yarns ever written.

Trilby, a novel by George Du Maurier, published in 1894. It is a story of life in the Latin Quarter of Paris. Trilby O'Ferrall is a laundress and artist's model and the comrade of three artist friends—Taffy, the Laird and Little Billee, who are all more or less in love with her. Svengali, a repulsive bohemian musician, acquires hypnotic control over her and by this means develops her voice; and she wins fame as a singer while he makes a fortune. When he suddenly dies, her power leaves her. The book, like Du Maurier's other two novels, was illustrated by himself.

trimeter, a verse having three measures or metrical feet.

triolet, an eight-line stanza with two rhymes, the 1st line repeated as the 4th and 7th and the 2d line is repeated as the 8th line.

triplet, a group of three lines of verse rhyming together.

trochee, a measure or metrical foot consisting (*a*) in the classical languages of a long syllable followed by a short; (*b*) in English of an accented syllable followed by an unaccented.

Troilus and Cressida, a tragedy by Shakespeare, produced about 1600, printed (twice) separately in 1609 and in the folio of 1623. Like Chaucer's *Troilus and Cressida,* it is derived not from classic myth but from later romancers. The plot is slight. The scene is Troy and the Greek camp before it. In spite of fine passages, the piece has not been highly ranked among Shakespeare's works nor has it held the stage. It contains the line: "One touch of nature makes the whole world kin."

troubadour, one of a group of lyric poets that arose in Provence, in southern France, towards the close of the 11th century.

trouvère, one of a class of poets of northern France who wrote narrative poetry during a period extending from the 11th century to the 14th.

Twelfth Night, or, What You Will, a comedy by Shakespeare, printed in 1623. The name is derived from the old custom of devoting the twelfth night after Christmas to sports and games. The scene is a city in Illyria and the neighboring seacoast. The poet satirizes the conceited and lan-

guishing Malvolio, at the same time winning our admiration for the wholehearted and faithful Viola. The humor runs from vulgar but droll scenes showing Sir Andrew Aguecheek and Sir Toby Belch in their cups to those of refined comedy with witty dialogue, in which Viola has the leading part. The plot is one of mistaken identity in which four lovers are involved in ludicrous situations.

Twice-Told Tales, two collections of stories by Hawthorne, first published, as he says, "in Magazines and Annuals, extending over a period of ten or twelve years," later assembled in book form in 1837 and 1842. They include such pieces as "The Gentle Boy," "The Great Carbuncle," "A Rill from the Town Pump" and "Legends of the Province House."

Two Years before the Mast, a narrative of sea life by Richard Henry Dana, published in 1840. Forced by eyetrouble to give up his studies, Dana shipped as a foremast hand in the brig *Pilgrim* on a voyage around the Horn to California. He returned in the ship *Alert.* The book gives the hardships and adventures of the common seaman of that time. William Cullen Bryant termed it "equal to *Robinson Crusoe.*"

Typhoon, a volume of four short stories by Joseph Conrad, published in 1902. Like *Youth,* these were written in the period following *The Nigger of the "Narcissus"* and preceding *Nostromo.* Besides the title story, the other three are "Amy Foster," "Falk: A Reminiscence" and "To-morrow." An American edition is called *Falk and Other Stories.* Captain MacWhirr in *Typhoon* has by many been placed among the most interesting examples of Conrad's character drawing.

Uncle Remus, an old Negro, the creation of Joel Chandler Harris, who uses him in *Uncle Remus: His Songs and His Sayings* (1880) and *Nights with Uncle Remus* (1883) as narrator of plantation folklore. Uncle Remus usually tells his stories to a little boy, who listens with consuming interest and asks questions with enthusiasm. The animals, such as Br'er Fox, Br'er 'Possum and Br'er Rabbit, talk and reveal their natural characteristics, somewhat in the style of the animal fables of Aesop. The stories were in great part collected by Harris from legends and tales handed down through generations of Negroes. Some of the stories evidently came from Africa.

Uncle Tom's Cabin, a novel by Harriet Beecher Stowe, published serially in the *National Era* in 1851–52 and in book form in 1852. Judged by its influence upon human life, it must be rated one of the great books of all time. It was read very widely at the time of its publication and had a considerable effect in winning freedom for the negro race in America.

The story depicts the horrors of slavery by tracing the history of Uncle Tom, a faithful old slave, who is sold because of his master's loss of fortune. First he goes to a kind master and has a happy life; but after a few years he has the misfortune to be sold once more, this time to a cruel master, Simon Legree, who tyrannizes over him and finally, in a burst of wrath, has him so severely flogged that he dies from his wounds. Famous passages in the book describe the escape of Eliza, a fugitive slave, from the bloodhounds; the death of Little Eva, daughter of one of Tom's masters; and a slave auction.

In dramatic form, *Uncle Tom's Cabin* was long a favorite of the American theater.

Utopia, a political romance by Sir Thomas More, published in Latin in 1516, and in English translation in 1551 and 1683. Utopia (meaning *no place*) is a country supposed to have been visited by Raphael Hythloday, lately returned from America, whither he had gone as a companion of Amerigo Vespuccio. In Utopia the life is communistic. None is in need, none desires more than he can use. The happiness of the community is above that of the individual. All except the aged or sick must work, but the hours of work are made as few as possible. Education is general, war is detested, laws are scarcely necessary. The pictures painted were in amazing contrast to the conditions of life then current in England, and the volume created endless discussion. From this book, *utopian* came to be applied to any scheme that men desired to characterize as impossible or too idealistic.

Vanity Fair, a novel by William Makepeace Thackeray, first published in 1847–48. The setting is the fashionable world of England at the beginning of the 19th century. In its subtitle this novel is called a story "without a hero." The complete title, accordingly, informs the reader that the world will be depicted as a mart like that in *Pilgrim's Progress,* where only baubles and trinkets are for sale and all at high prices, a place where no man is really heroic, no man without his folly. Becky Sharp, a clever adventuress, is the leading character. Although she had disreputable parents, she succeeds through her own efforts in getting well married, in living lavishly by evading creditors and in winning her way into smart society. At last her husband, Rawdon Crawley, catches her in a compromising situation with Lord Steyne, an old rake, unmasks her and leaves her. Thereafter she sinks into a cheap, vagrant life, trying more or less in vain to seem respectable. The more admirable characters in the book are Amelia Sedley, sweet-natured but weak, and Dobbin, faithful and honest though a bit dull.

Vedas, the ancient Brahmanical sacred books of India, written in Sanskrit. They are designated in four groups, as the Rig-Veda (hymns), Yajur-Veda (liturgy), Sama-Veda (liturgy) and Atharva-Veda (hymns and thoughts). The first-named is the oldest. Reference is made to these usually as the Four Vedas. They were not written at the same time, it is known, but were composed by many hands, probably between the years 2000 and 1500 B.C., and therefore represent the slow development of religious thought in India. *Veda* signifies knowledge or science.

verse, in general, metrical composition as differentiated from prose; specifically, one metrical line composed of a number of feet. *Verse* is often, but incorrectly, used for *stanza.*

vers libre (literally, "free verse"), a term originating in France and used to describe the method of modern French poets who deliberately infringed upon the rules of conventional French prosody.

Vicar of Wakefield, The, a novel by Oliver Goldsmith, published in 1766. The hero of this book is Doctor Primrose, a benevolent, lovable country clergyman. The story tells of the misfortunes which fall upon the Vicar's family, of the follies of Moses, a blundering son, of the worldliness of the mother and daughters, of the family's loss of property and of the elopement of Olivia, one of the daughters, with a philandering squire of the neighborhood. Throughout the troubles that beset him the Vicar maintains a steadfast, hopeful composure. At the end misfortune gives way to prosperity and happiness. The character of the Vicar—a smiling Job—is the great feature of the work. He has been called one of the highest compliments ever paid to human nature.

Victorian Age, the historic period of Queen Victoria, during whose reign (beginning in 1837) many important literary personages appeared in England. Among these were Landor, Carlyle, Newman, Matthew Arnold, Tennyson, George Eliot, Trollope, William Morris, Thackeray, Dickens, Macaulay, Bulwer-Lytton, Disraeli, the Brontës, Froude, Kingsley, Ruskin and the Brownings.

Viola, the heroine of Shakespeare's *Twelfth Night.* Disguised as a page (under the name of Cesario), she enters the service of Orsino, Duke of Illyria, the man she loves. To him she is loyal, even when he bids her help him to woo Olivia.

Virginian, The, a novel by Owen Wister, published in 1902. It is a story of life in the western United States, with authentic local color; abounding in humorous episodes but also possessing in Trampas a first-class villain who makes plenty of trouble.

Virginians, The, a novel by W. M. Thackeray, published in 1859, a sequel to *Henry Esmond.* The young George Washington and Braddock's campaign come into the story of Henry Esmond's grandsons. The scene is first Virginia and then London. Beatrix Esmond reappears as the Baroness Bernstein, much older but no wiser or better than in *Henry Esmond.*

Virginibus Puerisque and Other Papers, a volume of essays by Robert Louis Stevenson, published in 1881. Here we have not Stevenson the story-teller but Stevenson the persuasive moralist. *Virginibus puerisque* is a Latin tag from Horace and means "for girls and boys."

Vision of Sir Launfal, The, a poem by James Russell Lowell, published in 1845. In the old English legends Sir Launfal was one of King Arthur's Knights of the Round Table. In this poem on the night before he was set out on a noble quest he dreamed that though he could win fame and glory in the field and satisfy his debt to the poor by almsgiving, yet the best service he could render mankind was at his own gate, giving himself with his alms.

Walden or Life in the Woods, a work by Henry D. Thoreau, published in 1854. It gives an account of an experiment in simple living. Thoreau tells how he went to live on the shore of Walden Pond, near Concord, Mass. He built a hut with his own hands; he raised beans and other vegetables for his food. By simplifying his life, he was able to support himself with a few hours' labor each day, and to have the major part of his time for reading, walking, writing and the observation of birds, beasts and flowers. He wrote the book not with the idea of arguing that all men should live as hermits in the woods, but as an illustration of the fact that luxury is not essential to high-mindedness and quiet happiness.

Water Babies, The, a fairy tale by the Rev. Charles Kingsley, published in 1863. This has been termed "one of the few perfect fairy stories in the language." It has been said of it that "Even its moralities cannot wither it, nor its educational intention stale its infinite variety."

Waverley novels, The, the collective title given to the historical romances of Sir Walter Scott, the name being used because *Waverley,* published anonymously in 1814, was the first of the series. The others until 1827 appeared as "by the author of *Waverley,*" and then Scott's authorship was revealed.

Way of All Flesh, The, a novel by Samuel Butler (1835–1902). He began it about 1872 and until 1884 "was engaged upon it intermittently." It was posthumously issued in 1903, with two missing chapters (the fourth and fifth) supplied by R. A. Streatfield "in a form which I believe does not differ materially from that which he finally adopted." The story has to do with passages in the lives of members

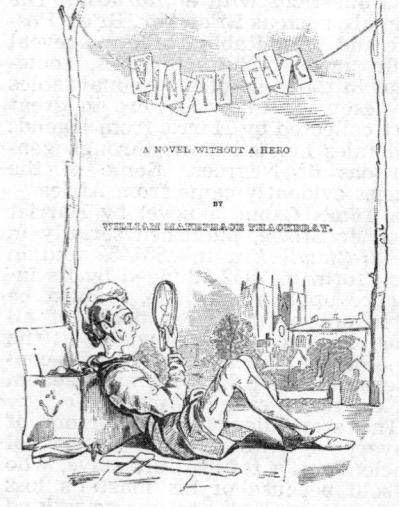

A NOVEL WITHOUT A HERO

BY

WILLIAM MAKEPEACE THACKERAY.

NEW YORK:
HARPER AND BROTHERS.
NEW YORK PUBLIC LIBRARY

DRAWING BY THACKERY for the first page of his satirical novel, *Vanity Fair.*

of the Pontifex family from the year 1807 but is principally concerned with Ernest Pontifex, born in 1835. The main part of the book takes him down to 1867 but the last chapter is supposed to be added as a kind of postscript in 1882. Bernard Shaw termed this novel an extraordinary study of English life, acknowledged his own indebtedness to it, decried the neglect of it and added, "Really, the English do not deserve to have great men."

Wee Willie Winkie and Other Stories, a collection of short stories by Rudyard Kipling, published in 1888; originally one of a series of paper-bound "railway" volumes issued in India, where Kipling began his career. Here may be found the earliest examples of Kipling's stories dealing with children, a type of his work that "exhibits a very winning aspect of the author."

Weller, Sam, in Dickens' *Pickwick Papers,* the cockney boots at the White Hart and afterward valet to Mr. Pickwick, to whom he is wholeheartedly devoted. He is a shrewd, merry, imperturbable and sometimes impudent fellow whose mother wit is unfailing.

Wessex Tales, seven stories by Thomas Hardy, first gathered and issued under that title in two volumes in 1888. They are: The Three Strangers, A Tradition of Eighteen Hundred and Four, The Melancholy Hussar, The Withered Arm, Fellow-Townsmen, Interlopers at the Knap and The Distracted Preacher.

Westward Ho!, a novel by Charles Kingsley, published in 1855. The story tells the adventures of Sir Amyas Leigh, a sailor in the days of Queen Elizabeth. His first voyage was around the world with Sir Francis Drake. Afterward he went to South America to find Rose Salterne, an English girl who had married a Spaniard. After some fighting he and his men have to abandon their ship and strike inland.

For many months the men tramp over the continent, fighting, accumulating gold and rescuing a white girl from the Indians. They return to England at last taking Ayanacora, the white girl, with them. Amyas goes out again soon afterwards to fight against the Spanish Armada and loses his eyesight from being struck by lightning just after the fight is won. He then returns home and marries Ayanacora. The book gives a good picture of the seafaring of the period. Famous persons introduced include Sir Walter Raleigh, Sir Richard Grenville and Edmund Spenser.

Wonder Book, A, a collection of stories by Nathaniel Hawthorne, designed primarily for young folks and published in 1851. In it he retells a half dozen of the old Greek myths: those of King Midas, the Gorgon's head, Pandora's box, the apples of the Hesperides, Philemon and Baucis (who entertained Zeus and Hermes) and the Chimaera (that fire-breathing monster slain by Bellerophon). The series was continued in *Tanglewood Tales.*

Wuthering Heights, the one novel by Emily Brontë, published in 1847, when she was 28. The scene is the moorland of the West Riding of Yorkshire; the time, the early years of the 19th century. The leading character is Heathcliffe, "a man's shape animated by demon life," one of the most wholeheartedly inhuman creatures ever presented in fiction. Though there are bits of humor in the broad Yorkshire of the eccentric old servant Joseph, yet over most of the book, as Charlotte Brontë wrote, "there broods 'a horror of great darkness'," a fierceness of mood that is unrelieved until the few lines of the closing paragraph are reached. Much of the story is supposed to be told by Nelly Dean, an old housekeeper.

Yahoo, in Swift's Gulliver's Travels, part four, one of an imagined race of brutes in human form. They are subject to the Houyhnhnms (pronounced *Whin-hims*), a community of horses possessing intelligence and reason but free from the conflicts of human existence.

Youth: A Narrative; and Two Other Stories, a volume of three long novelettes by Joseph Conrad, published in 1902. The "two other stories" are "Heart of Darkness" and "The End of the Tether." The first American edition was dated 1903. *Youth* is based on a voyage made by Conrad to the East after he had gone to England and obtained a mate's certificate. "Heart of Darkness" he described as part of the "spoil I brought out from the centre of Africa, where, really, I had no sort of business." From it was derived John Powell's *Rhapsodie Nègre.* It has been ranked among the greatest short stories in English.

MYTHOLOGY, LEGEND, AND FOLKLORE

Myth.—A myth is a story. It is supposed to be true, but no one can remember or find out its beginning. All we are sure of is that the myths come out of the far, far past of humanity, and man made them himself to answer the questions that have troubled his heart since time began. How did the world come to be? And what is man? Where does the wind come from? Whose awful wrath can fell a tree with lightning? Whose voice roars in the storm? The sun, the moon, the stars, all the marvels of the universe have made men wonder. Flowers grow; fire burns; people are born and die. "Why?" says the mind of man. "How?" "Who?"

And because men cannot bear to live with these questions unanswered, every people in the world has its own myths, explaining the facts of nature or how some ancient custom came to be, where man got his dear beliefs and how he learned to live his life. Thus myths really belong to the religious rites and faiths of all the people in the world. And the word *myth* usually implies a story connected with some religion.

There are five kinds of myths. The *culture myth* is a story about a god or animal or a race-hero who gave some priceless gift to humanity, like fire or medicine or music. The story of Prometheus, how he created man and later stole fire from heaven and gave it to him for his use and comfort, is a culture myth. *Nature myths* are built around some fact of nature. They personify the elements and all natural phenomena. There are stories of a sun god in every land; everywhere the moon has its deity. Nymphs and dryads inhabit pools and forests. Hyacinths sprang from the blood of a beautiful youth of that name. The four seasons, the seas and rivers have their gods and goddesses. There is no end to them. The third kind of myth tells of the birth and genealogy of the gods and goddesses. The fourth kind explains the *reason* why certain rites and customs began and are cherished.

There is still another kind of myth, the *hero-myth,* which reveals better than any other kind how myths begin and how they grow. Take Beowulf, for instance. Without doubt there was a Beowulf, young and valiant hero of the Geats in Sweden. The names of the kings and many of the warriors with whom he associated are historical names. Without doubt Beowulf was an extraordinary fighter; he was a marvellous swimmer; he was afraid of nothing. In many retellings it was easy for the story of a brave and bloody fight to take on color and elaboration until the hero became a hero of superhuman strength performing supernatural deeds. Not only was he strong and fearless, but he delivered the Danes from the dread marsh-stalker Grendel, who devoured 30 men in a night. Not only could Beowulf swim and dive, but he killed Grendel's mother, the water-demon, in an under-water fight. In stories of this kind it is an easy step from supernatural deeds to supernatural parentage. No mere human being could perform such feats; the man must be the son of a god. How else account for the unbelievable?

The hero-myths in the world are uncountable. And man is still making them. Witness the strange tales that have grown up around the name of T. E. Lawrence, Lawrence of Arabia. These stories are far more than the inevitable legends that follow the name of a hero. They have already begun to take on a supernatural phase, both in Arabia and in England.

Folklore.—No definite line can be drawn between myth and folklore. No one can say exactly where one leaves off and the other begins, except that folklore is ages older. A people have to become fairly civilized before they formulate a definite mythology. But folklore has existed since the most primitive times; it exists today among all primitive peoples and also among the rural and unlettered classes of all highly civilized nations.

Folklore represents the growth of the human mind. It is the spiritual history of the race. Everything that man has learned or done with his hands, everything he has discarded or held fast, everything he has feared or loved or hoped can be found in folklore. There are folk songs and ballads, folk dances, folk customs, folk superstitions and beliefs, folk tales, riddles, rimes and proverbs. All these things represent the way of life and the spirit of a people, their wisdom and their attitudes, the things they believe now and the things they have believed and passed through. The most profitless superstitions and fears exist in folklore side by side with some of the deepest truths of humanity.

Folklore contains in its proverbs all the wisdom the human mind and heart has gathered through the centuries. They are the sum total of human experience. The proverbs of every land come down out of the remote past. "Where there's a will there's a way." "A soft answer turneth away wrath." "He that conquers himself conquers an enemy." These are samples of folk wisdom. "One swallow does not make a summer" has been said for 2000 years. "Time and tide wait for no man." "Hope deferred maketh the heart sick." These are lessons learned.

But it is the folk tale that gives us the fullest picture of the human race with all its strange, devious ways and beliefs, its fears and bravados and its dreams. Probably not half the folk tales in the world have been unearthed and written down. It takes scholars like the German brothers Jacob and Wilhelm Grimm to collect and retell and make immortal the folk tales of a nation. But a wealth of human story has been tapped. There are thousands of folk tales in print today. And there is no literature anywhere more charming and more revealing.

Cinderella is probably the most beloved folk tale in the world. People everywhere love to think that the oppressed will suddenly be given love and riches. And that is the gist of the story in all its versions: a little household drudge, neglected and cruelly treated, is suddenly transformed into the exquisite, beautiful girl whom the prince loves and seeks and marries—to the chagrin of her tormentors, of course. The Cinderella story exists among the folk of all nations in both hemispheres. There are 345 known variants from Alaska to the Cape of Good Hope.

Legend.—A legend is a popular story rooted in history, but which has been elaborated beyond the point of verification. There is little doubt that Robin Hood was a real person, but the stories which have grown up around his name are legends. Charlemagne, king of the Franks, is no legend, but the songs and stories celebrating his grandeur and the exploits of his paladins are among the most famous legends in the world. Alfred is one of the greatest kings in English history, but no one can verify the legend that he sat with troubled mind and forgot to turn the loaves by the fire in the old woman's hut. The story of William Tell is a legend. So is the story of Bruce and the spider.

Fable.—A fable is pure fiction that often embodies supernatural events or circumstances. It is a moral story with a lesson to put over and differs from allegory by its brevity. But the characteristic of most fables is the fact that the characters are beasts who talk and act like human beings. For this reason fables are often called bestiaries.

Many fables are satires. All the weaknesses and pettinesses of human nature are bestowed upon the beasts and held up and mocked for all to feel ashamed of. Everybody knows about the fox who could not reach the luscious grapes and therefore decided they were sour! "Sour grapes" is a familiar jibe at those ungenerous souls who belittle what they cannot have.

Fables, like folk tales and legends, are an ancient form of story. There are no bona fide modern ones. The most ancient are the fables of India collected in the Sanskrit *Panchatantra.* The most famous are the Greek fables of Aesop, which were so widely translated as to be the source of nearly all the fables in Europe. Aesop's *Fables* contain the stories of the fox and the grapes, the hare and the tortoise, the lion and the mouse, and all the others that every child knows best.

Dictionary of Myth, Folklore, Legend and Fable[1]

Abdiel (ab' di el), in Milton's *Paradise Lost,* the only one of Satan's angels who would not join the revolt against heaven.

Achates (a kā' tēz), in Vergil's *Aeneid,* a Trojan, faithful friend of Aeneas. After the fall of Troy he followed Aeneas through all his wanderings and hardships with such fidelity that his name has become the synonym for a loyal friend.

Acheron (ak' ēr on), in Greek mythology, the River of Woe, one of the four rivers of Hades. In the *Odyssey* it was the principal or boundary river of Hades over which Charon ferried the souls of the dead on their journey from the upper to the lower world. It also is used to mean the region of Hades itself.

Achilles (a kil' ēz), the hero of the *Iliad,* son of Peleus, king of Thessaly, and Thetis, a sea goddess. He was the bravest of the Greeks in the Trojan War. When he was born, Thetis plunged him in the Styx, to make his body invulnerable, but she forgot the heel by which she held him. To save him from death in the Trojan War, she sent him to the court of King Lycomedes, where he was dressed as a girl and played with the princesses. But Troy could not be taken, and Odysseus, in the guise of a merchant, went to find him out. Jewels and arms he laid out for sale before the beautiful girls. The one who chose arms he knew was Achilles; and the youth gladly went off with him to war. A young slave girl named Briseis fell to the lot of Achilles one day in a division of booty among the warriors. And when Agamemnon stole her away, Achilles refused to fight again. But death of his friend Patroclus roused him. He went out to slay Hector who had slain his friend. Three times around the walls of Troy he dragged the body of Hector, the great Trojan hero. Achilles was killed by Paris, who shot him in the heel with an arrow.

Actaeon (ak tē' on), in Greek mythology, a famous hunter who offended Artemis. One story is that he came upon her bathing, another that he boasted of being a better hunter than she. For punishment she changed him into a stag, and he was killed by his own dogs.

Admetus (ad mē' tus), a king of Thessaly whom Apollo served nine years as a shepherd. He was the husband of Alcestis.

Adonis (a dō' nis; a don' is), in Greek mythology, a beautiful youth beloved by Aphrodite. When he was killed by a wild boar, the grief of the goddess moved Persephone, Queen of Hades, to allow him to spend six months of the year on earth and six in the underworld. His death and return symbolize winter and summer, and his worship embodied a midsummer festival. Shakespeare's poem, *Venus and Adonis,* tells the love story of the youth and goddess.

Aegir (â'gir; ē'gir), in Teutonic mythology, the god of the sea.

aegis (ē'jis), the symbolic shield of Zeus and Athene.

Aegisthus (ē jis' thus), the youth whom Agamemnon left to guard his kingdom while he was off to the Trojan War. Aegisthus fell in love with Clytemnestra, Agamemnon's wife, who returned his passion. Together they murdered Agamemnon on his return and planned to do away with his son Orestes also. But Orestes was saved by his sister Electra. She encouraged him to avenge their father's death by killing the faithless pair, Aegisthus and Clytemnestra. This story has been made immortal by three Greek tragedians: Aeschylus in his great poetic trilogy, the *Oresteia;* Sophocles in his *Electra;* and Euripides in two tragedies, *Electra* and *Orestes.*

Aeneas (ē nē'as), the son of Anchises and Aphrodite, and one of the heroes of the Trojan War. He married Creusa, daughter of Priam, king of Troy. When Troy was taken and in flames, Aeneas departed bearing his old father on his shoulders and leading his little son Ascanius by the hand. Creusa followed them but was lost. The wanderings of Aeneas from this point on are celebrated in Vergil's great Latin epic the *Aeneid.* With a fleet of 20 ships he sailed from Troy

[1] The scheme of pronunciation used here is explained in detail at the beginning of the dictionary in the VOLUME LIBRARY. The general plan is given below:

HECTOR AND AJAX IN COMBAT ON THE FIELDS OF TROY. In Homer's *Iliad*, one episode relates that Ajax, who after Achilles was the greatest Greek hero, challenged Hector, the hero of Troy, to battle. Hector, son of Priam, was slain by Achilles.

seeking a new home. He was shipwrecked on the coast of Africa, where Dido, queen of Carthage, begged him to remain. She fell deeply in love with him and took her own life in grief when the gods commanded him to take up his travels again. After seven years of adventure and hardship, Aeneas came to the river Tiber. Here he married Lavinia, daughter of Latinus, king of Latium, and founded the city of Lavinium. Aeneas is the legendary ancestor of the city of Rome, for his son founded Alba Longa where Romulus and Remus were born and which was superseded by Rome itself.

Aeolus (ē′ ō lus), in Greek and Roman mythology, the god of the winds. He lived on an island where he kept his four sons, the winds, in a cave. One day Odysseus in his wanderings came to this place, and the kindly Aeolus gave him the four winds tied up in a leather bag, with a command to the fair winds to blow the wanderers home. But one night while Odysseus slept, his sailors decided they too must share the treasure in the mysterious leather bag. They untied the string; the fierce winds rushed out and drove the ships back to Aeolus. He was so disgusted at this stupidity that he would not help them further.

The story of Aeolus is a *culture myth.* He is supposed to have taught men how to sail ships and read the signs of the winds and weather.

Aesculapius (es kū lā′ pi us), the Roman god of medicine. See *Asclepius.*

Aesir (ā′ sir; ē′ sir), in Teutonic mythology the collective name of the gods. There were 13 of them: Odin or Woden and his wife Frigga. Balder, the god of light; Tyr (war); Thor or Donar, the thunder-god, symbolizing strength; Braji (poetry); Forseti (justice); Loki (fire or evil); Vali; Vitharr; Hermod; Hoenir, the strong; Hoder,

the blind; and Heimdall, the watcher. Their abode was Asgard.

afreet (af′ rēt; a frēt′), in Arabian mythology, an evil spirit or demon; a jinni. It is also spelled afrite.

Agamemnon (ag a mem′ non), king of Mycenae, husband of Clytemnestra and brother of Menelaus, king of Sparta, whose wife Helen had been carried off to Troy. Agamemnon was the leader of the Greeks in the Trojan War. When Troy fell, Priam's daughter the prophetess Cassandra fell to his lot and he took her home with him. She foretold his death at the hands of Clytemnestra and her lover, and was herself killed by Clytemnestra. *Agamemnon* is the title of the first of the three great dramatic poems in the Orestes trilogy by Aeschylus.

Aganippe (ag a nip′ ē), in Greek mythology, a fountain near Mount Helicon. Its waters were supposed to give poetic inspiration, and therefore the fountain was sacred to the Muses.

Ajax (ā′ jaks), one of the Greek heroes of the Trojan War. On the death of Achilles, Ajax and Odysseus were rivals for the arms of the dead hero. They fell to Odysseus, and Ajax, maddened by jealousy, killed himself. This is one story. Another is found in Sophocles's tragedy *Ajax,* which tells how Ajax, blinded with insane disappointment, mistook a flock of sheep for the sons of Atreus and slew them all. When his reason returned, he was so ashamed of his deed that he killed himself with his sword.

Ajax the Less, one of the Greek heroes in the siege of Troy. Except for Achilles, none was swifter than he. He was skilled with the spear, but he was a great boaster. On his way home he was shipwrecked, but Poseidon cast him on a great rock. Instead of giving thanks, he bragged that he had saved himself. So Posei-

don split the rock, and Ajax the Less was drowned.

Aladdin (a lad′ in), in the *Arabian Nights,* the son of a poor tailor who finds a magic lamp and ring. Two jinni, servants of the lamp and ring, come to do the bidding of the new owner. Aladdin gains great wealth, marries the Sultan's daughter and builds a marvelous palace.

Alberich (äl′ bēr ik), in Teutonic folklore, the king of the elves. In the German *Nibelungenlied* he is the dwarf who guards the treasure of the Nibelungs. In Wagner's opera *The Rhinegold* Alberich is king of the Nibelungs. He steals the gold of the Rhine Maidens from the bottom of the Rhine and from it makes a magic ring. When it is stolen from him, he puts a curse upon it that brings disaster to all its unrightful owners.

Albion (al′ bi un), the ancient, poetic name for England.

Alcestis (al ses′ tis), in Greek mythology, the wife of Admetus. Apollo had secured the promise of the gods that Admetus need never die, but on condition that when his death-day came, another should offer to die in his place. Alcestis willingly gave her life for her husband. But the grief of Admetus was so great that Hercules brought her back from the lower world. Her story is the subject of Euripides's play *Alcestis* (which is translated in Robert Browning's *Balaustion's Adventure*), and Chaucer included her in his *Legend of Good Women.*

Alcmene (alk mē′ nē), the mother of Hercules.

Alecto (a lek′ tō), one of the Furies.

Alectryon (a lek′ tri on), in Greek mythology, a youth whom Ares set to watch for the dawn. But the boy fell asleep and did not call him. For punishment Ares changed him into a cock, doomed forever to wake and crow at sunrise.

Ali Baba (ä′ lē bä′ bä), in the *Arabian Nights,* a poor woodcutter who one day overheard the magic word by which the Forty Thieves entered their treasure cave. "Open Sesame" said Ali Baba, too, when the thieves were gone; and he entered, loaded his donkey with gold and went home. His brother also went to the cave. But he forgot the word, could not get out and was found and killed by the thieves. At last the robber captain discovered who it was still knew their secret. He hid his men in leather jars that he brought to Ali Baba's house. They intended to jump out and kill him while he slept. But Morgiana, the little servant girl, killed them all with boiling oil.

Allan-a-Dale (al′ an a dāl′), in English legendary ballads, the youngest of Robin Hood's companions. He is aided by the famous outlaw to save his sweetheart from marrying an aged knight. Allan-a-Dale is Robin Hood's minstrel in Scott's *Ivanhoe.*

Allhallows (ôl hal′ ōz), All Saints' Day, Nov. 1. Allhallows' eve (Hallowe'en), Oct. 31, was the last day of the year in the old Celtic calendar. It was the night when witches and spirits were abroad and was called the Night of Samhain, the Night of Death. The death of the old year was celebrated with rejoicing in the store of fruits and other foods laid up for the coming winter. Hallowe'en bonfires are still lighted in the hills of Scotland. It is celebrated in nearly all countries with festivity and the observance (mock or genuine) of many folk superstitions.

Amalthea (am al thē′ a), the nurse of Zeus (Jupiter), who fed him goat's milk from the horn of a goat. This horn became the horn of plenty or *cornucopia.* In some stories the goat was named Amalthea.

Amazons (am′a zonz), a race of warlike women who lived in Pontus near the Euxine Sea. No men were allowed to live among them, and all the boys who were born were either killed or sent to a neighboring country to live with their fathers. In Vergil's *Aeneid,* the Amazons fought against the Greeks in the Trojan War, and their queen was killed by Achilles. One of the Twelve Labors of Hercules was to steal the girdle of their queen Hippolyte.

Amphion (am fī′ on), in Greek mythology, a son of Zeus. He built the walls of Thebes by the sound of a lyre that Hermes had given him. The stones fell into their places with the enchantment of the music.

Anchises (an kī′sēz), the father of Aeneas.

Androclus (an′drō klus) or **Androcles** (-klēz), in Roman legend a runaway slave who hid in a lion's cave in Africa. Without fear he pulled a painful thorn from the lion's paw. In later years, Androclus was captured and thrown to the lions in the arena. But instead of attacking him, one old lion fawned upon him and caressed him. And Androclus and his lion were set free. Bernard Shaw wrote a play based on this story, *Androcles and the Lion.*

Andromache (an drom′ a ke), the wife of Hector. After the capture of Troy and the death of Hector, the Greeks threw her little son Astyanax from the walls of the city, and she was taken captive by Neoptolemus, son of Achilles. Later Andromache became the wife of Helenus, brother of Hector. She is the subject of a tragedy by Racine, based on the *Andromache* by Euripedes.

Andromeda (an drom′ē da), a princess of Ethiopia, whose mother boasted that she was more beautiful than the daughters of Poseidon. In wrath Poseidon sent a sea monster to lay waste the land. Andromeda was chained to a rock in the sea as a sacrifice to be devoured by the creature. Perseus, flying home from his victory over the gorgon Medusa, saw the beautiful maiden and saved her life. He had with him the head of Medusa and one look at it turned the monster into stone. Andromeda was then married to Perseus. Corneille used her story in a French tragedy.

Andvari (än′ dwä rē), in Norse mythology, a dwarf who was robbed of his treasure and his magic ring by Loki. He could change himself into a fish, and it was while he was a pike that Loki caught him and got the ring.

Antaeus (an tē′ us), one of the giant sons of Poseidon and Gaea (Earth). He could not be beaten as long as he touched the ground, for he received new strength from his mother, Earth. Hercules discovered the secret of his strength and lifted the giant into the air and strangled him.

Antigone (an tig′ō nē), in Greek legend, a daughter of Oedipus, king of Thebes, who guided her blind father in his exile. Her two brothers Eteocles and Polynices killed each other in a struggle for the throne. Their uncle Creon, new king of Thebes, forbade the burial of Polynices. But Antigone buried his body by night. For this Creon ordered her to be buried alive. But Antigone took her own life before it could be done. Sophocles's tragedy *Antigone* tells her story.

Anubis (a nū′ bis), in Egyptian religion, the god who leads the dead to the lower world. He is usually represented as a human figure with the head of a jackal.

Aphrodite (af rō dī′ tē), in Greek mythology, the goddess of love and beauty and fruitfulness. Hesiod says she was born of the foam of the sea; but in the *Iliad* she is the daughter of Zeus and Dione. In the *Odyssey* Hephaestus was her husband, and Ares her lover. She was the mother of Eros and of Aeneas by Anchises. She is identified with the Semitic Goddess of love and fertility Astarte (Ishtar) and with the Roman goddess Venus.

Apis (ā′ pis), in ancient Egyptian religion, the sacred bull worshipped as the incarnation of Osiris.

Apollo (a pol′ ō), the god of youth and manly beauty, son of Zeus and Leto; also called Phoebus. He was the god of poetry and music, and the grasshopper was sacred to him as the symbol of song. Orpheus was his son. He was also god of healing and could avert disease or evil. Asclepius, god of medicine, was his son. In Homer, Apollo is the god of prophecy; his oracles were unerring and were honored everywhere. The one at Delphi was the most famous. Apollo was later identified with Helios, the sun god; and Artemis, his twin, was goddess of the moon. The Romans took over the worship of Apollo from the Greeks.

Apollyon (a pol′yun), the destroying angel; the angel of the bottomless pit. In Bunyan's *Pilgrim's Progress,* he was vanquished by Christian when he stood is his way.

Arachne (a rak′nē), a Lydian maiden of great skill as a weaver. So beautiful and perfect was her work that she challenged Athene to a contest. Athene accepted and the two sat down to weave. When Athene looked upon Arachne's web she saw that the girl had woven in the stories of the loves of the gods—Leda and the swan, Europa and the bull, Danae in her tower and the stars falling on it. The work was beautiful, but Athene ripped it into shreds to punish the maiden for her impiety and for daring to challenge her. Then Arachne was in despair and went and hung herself. But Athene changed her into a spider, hanging by a thread from her own web and forever spinning. Arachne means spider.

Arcadia (är kā′di a), an inland plateau of central Greece, shut in by mountains. The ancient inhabitants were shepherds and simple mountain folk. It is celebrated in the literature of many languages as a place of pastoral pleasure and contentment and rest, and has come to symbolize the ideal country of lost or unattainable happiness.

Ares (ā′rēz; âr′ēz), the Greek god of war and battle, son of Zeus and Hera. In Homer's *Odyssey,* Ares was the lover of Aphrodite, whose husband Hephaestus caught him in a net and held him up to be laughed at by the gods. The Romans later identified Ares with their war-god Mars.

Arethusa (ar ē thū′za), a nymph who was loved by the river-god Alpheus. To help her escape, Artemis changed her into a spring, which ran under land and sea to the island of Ortygia. One of the stories says that Alpheus followed her. The upper part of the river Alpheus really does flow underground.

Argonauts (är′ gō nôts), the band of adventurers who sailed with Jason in the ship *Argo* to Colchis to find the Golden Fleece. When Jason demanded his kingdom back from his uncle Pelias, the usurper, Pelias agreed to give it up if Jason would bring back the Golden Fleece. Some time before this his two cousins Helle and Phrixos had been driven from home by the enmity of their stepmother Ino. But their own mother Nephele sent Phrixos a winged ram with a golden fleece on which he and his sister Helle escaped over the sea. Helle fell off and was drowned in the strait that bears her name, the Hellespont; but Phrixos arrived safely, sacrificed the ram, and hung the Golden Fleece in the grove of Ares on the farther shore of Colchis. Here it was guarded by a never-sleeping dragon.

Jason sailed with his companions in the *Argo* and after many adventures they came to Colchis. Aeetes, king of Colchis, would not give up the fleece. He demanded first that Jason yoke his fire-snorting bulls, plow the field of Ares and sow it with the dragon's teeth, from which he expected armed men to rise and kill Jason. But Aeetes's daughter Medea, the enchantress, fell in love with Jason and helped him perform his tasks. Jason took the fleece and sailed home again on the *Argo.* He took Medea with him as his wife, and with her help, he and the Argonauts escaped from the pursuing wrath of Aeetes.

Argus (är′gus), in Greek mythology, a monster with a hundred eyes, which Hera set to watch Io, of whom she was jealous. Zeus, deeply in love with Io, had changed her into a cow but did not succeed in keeping Hera from finding her out. Zeus ordered Hermes to kill the monster. So Hermes played upon the lyre until all the hundred eyes were closed, then he cut off the monster's head. Hera put the eyes of Argus in the tail of the peacock, her sacred bird.

Argus, in the *Odyssey,* the faithful dog of Odysseus, who recognized his master when he returned from 20 years of wandering.

Ariadne (ar i ad'nē), the daughter of Minos, king of Crete. She fell in love with Theseus, an Athenean youth, sent as a sacrifice to be devoured by the Minotaur. Before he entered the labyrinth, she gave him a clue of thread with which to find his way out. Theseus slew the Minotaur and returned to her, following the thread. She fled with him away from Crete, but he abandoned her on the island of Naxos. One story says she died of grief, another that Dionysus found her sleeping there and made her his wife.

Ariel (är'i el), in Shakespeare's *Tempest,* the airy spirit who served the magician Prospero; in Milton's *Paradise Lost,* one of the rebel angels.

Artemis (är'tē mis), in Greek mythology, goddess of the hunt, of nature and of chastity. The oldest conception of Artemis was as a harvest goddess. When Oenus of Calydon did not present her with a harvest offering, she sent the terrible Calydonian boar to ravage his fields. She was goddess of nature, especially wild nature. Her festivals were celebrated with all kinds of animals and fruits. The bear especially was associated with her. The hind was sacred to her. She was also protectress of women and children and goddess of childbirth.

In Homer, Artemis was the daughter of Zeus and Leto and the twin of Apollo. The idea of Artemis as goddess of chastity did not appear until she became the counterpart of Apollo. She was never worshiped as goddess of the moon, though naturally she became identified with the moon-goddess Selene when Apollo became identified with the sun-god Helios. The Romans took over the worship of Artemis and identified her with their own Diana.

Arthur (är'thẽr), a legendary king of Britain of the 6th century. Arthur was an historical Celtic general who warred against the Saxons, a traditional folk hero-king, a fairy king, and the point of departure for a great cycle of medieval romance in prose and verse, Celtic, French, German, English.

Nennius, in his *History of the Britons* in Latin (8th century), mentions 12 battles in which Arthur led the Britons (Celts) against the Saxons. At the battle of Badon "960 men fell in one day . . . and no one overthrew them but Arthur alone, and in all the battles he came out victorious." William of Malmesbury in his *Deeds of the Kings of England* in Latin (1125) mentions Arthur twice and deplores the "wild stories" that had even then grown up around his name.

Geoffrey of Monmouth's *History of the Kings of Britain* also in Latin (1147) gives the framework of the story on which all the later elaborations were hung. In the 400 years between Nennius and Geoffrey the folk-mind had been busy with the legend, and there were more stories in the land than Geoffrey could tell. Geoffrey may have used some Celtic sources now unknown.

Arthur was the son of Uther Pendragon, king of Britain, and Igraine of Cornwall. The elves brought gifts to his cradle: long life and virtue. Very young he became king of Britain, conquered the Scots and the Saxons; Ireland and Iceland, and kingdoms on the continent. He married Guinevere and held his court at Caerleon on Usk. He went to war against the Emperor of Rome and left Modred, his nephew, to guard his kingdom and his wife. Rome was about to fall when Arthur heard that Modred had taken the throne and Guinevere. He hurried home to punish Modred, killed him in the battle of Camlan and was himself mortally wounded. He was taken to Avalon to be healed, and Guinevere entered a nunnery.

To the incident of Arthur's death Celtic folklore adds that some day he will wake and deliver his people from the English. The king asleep in the mountain who will some day rise and retake his kingdom is one of the beloved themes of folk lore, and Arthur still sleeps in many a mountain in Wales. In fact the belief and the hope were so strong that Arthur would come to deliver the Celts (or Britons) of Wales and Cornwall from English rule, that Henry II was prompted to discover a tomb for Arthur—*not* in a mountain but at Glastonbury, with which Avalon was later identified.

The Norman-French poet Wace also added to the story the idea that Arthur would return from Avalon to save his kingdom, along with many other new details, including the Round Table. Wace's poem is the source of Layamon's English *Brut* (13th century), which transformed Arthur from a Celtic to an English king, that the people might have a folk hero to rally to and rival their Norman conquerors. Layamon added for the first time most of the fairy material: the three fairy queens who attended his birth and death, the sword Excalibur given to Arthur by the Lady of the Lake, his magic spear, the fairy boat in which he sailed to Avalon attended by three queens, one of them his fairy sister, Morgan Le Fay.

The Arthur of the romances (developed from the 12th century on by Chrestien de Troyes, Robert de Boron, Wolfram von Eschenbach and others, is only a lay figure. His court of splendor is the background of the romances, his marvelous knights, their loves and adventures and their quest of the Holy Grail are the subject matter. Guinevere and Lancelot, Gawain, Perceval (Parsifal), Elaine of Astolat, Sir Galahad, Merlin, Vivian, Tristan and Iseult—these are the people whose stories word for word remain the most vividly human and realistic and moving stories in the world. And these are the stories Sir Thomas Malory retold and blended in his famous prose *Morte d'Arthur* (1470), the source of all later Arthurian material. Wagner's operas *Parsifal* and *Tristan and Isolde,* Tennyson's *Idylls of the King,* William Morris's *Defense of Guenevere,* Edwin A. Robinson's *Tristram* are some of the modern handlings of the narratives.

Ascanius (as kā'ni us), the son of Aeneas.

Asclepius (as klē'pi us), the Greek god of medicine (Roman Aesculapius). He was educated by the centaur Chiron, who taught him the art of medicine and how to heal with herbs. When he learned to bring the dead to life, Zeus killed him. Many temples were raised in ancient Greece for his worship; and those who slept in the temple dreamed what to do to be cured.

Asgard (as'gärd), in Norse mythology, the abode of the gods. It could be reached only by the rainbow bridge, Bifrost.

Astarte (as tär'tē), the Semitic goddess of love and fertility; the same as the Babylonian Ishtar, identified by the Greeks with Aphrodite, and as the moon-goddess with Selene and Artemis. In the Old Testament she is called Ashtaroth.

Astyanax (as tī'a naks), in Greek mythology, the son of Hector and Andromache, slain by the Greeks.

Atalanta (at a lan' ta), in Greek mythology, a beautiful maiden who challenged all that came to woo her to a foot race. Death was the penalty of defeat. She would marry only the youth who could outrun her. All who dared to race with her were defeated and put to death, until Hippomenes came. One by one he threw in her path three golden apples that

NEW YORK PUBLIC LIBRARY

ATHENA

Aphrodite had given him. While Atalanta turned aside to pick them up, Hippomenes won the race and Atalanta for his wife. Another story says that Atalanta took part in the hunt for the Calydonian boar and was the first to wound the beast. Swinburne's poetic drama *Atalanta in Calydon* treats of this incident.

Ate (ā'tē), a daughter of Zeus, goddess of discord and strife.

Athena (a thē'na) or Athene (-nē), in Greek mythology, the goddess of wisdom, industry and war; also called Pallas Athena. She was the daughter of Zeus and Metis and was born full grown and fully armed from the brain of Zeus. She quarreled with Poseidon over naming the capital of Attica. The gods decided to name the city for whichever one gave mankind the most useful gift. Poseidon split the ground with his trident and produced the horse; Athena's spear struck the bare rock and produced the olive. To her was given the reward, and the city was named Athens.

In Homer's *Iliad* she is goddess of counsel and law, of war, of cities and of women's arts, spinning and weaving. Later she became a goddess of peace and industry and took on certain aspects of the earth-goddess of agriculture. The Romans identified Athena with their goddess Minerva.

Atlantis (at lan'tis), a fabled island in the Atlantic Ocean, west of the Pillars of Hercules. Plato and Pliny both mention it. Plato said it was larger than Asia Minor and Libya and described it as an ideal state. According to the story it was a powerful empire 9000 years before Solon was born and its people overran the kingdoms of the Mediterranean. An earthquake sank it into the sea and shoals still mark the place. Renaissance geographers tried to identify it with the Canary Islands, America, etc. There has always been much scientific speculation as to the actual existence of the Lost Continent. Sir Francis Bacon's *The New Atlantis* is a political treatise on an ideal state.

ROCKEFELLER CENTER, INC.

A MODERN ATLAS. Lee Lawrie's 45-foot statue stands on Fifth Avenue, New York.

Atlas (at'las), one of the Titans. In the *Odyssey* he is the one who "keeps the tall pillars which hold heaven and earth apart." His name was given to a mountain ridge in northwest Africa, and Ovid tells the story of a king of that region named Atlas, who refused a welcome to Perseus. In return Perseus showed him the Gorgon's head and Atlas was turned to stone, a high rocky mountain, doomed forever to support the heavens (or the world) on his shoulders.

Atli (at'lē), in Norse legend, a terrible king whose story and personality are based on the historical Attila, king of the Huns. Atli married Gudrun, by whom he was murdered to avenge the death of Sigurd. In the German *Nibelungenlied,* Atli is called Etzel.

Atropos (at'rō pos), the eldest of the three Fates in Greek mythology, whose shears cut the thread of human life.

Augean (ô jē'an) **Stables,** in Greek mythology, the stables of Augeas, King of Elis, in which he kept thousands of oxen. The stables had never been cleaned. One of the Twelve Labors of Hercules was to clean them. He did it in one day by turning the course of the river Alpheus through them. Augeas had promised Hercules one-tenth of the herd for the job. When he refused to pay, Hercules killed him.

Aurora (ô rō'ra), the Roman goddess of the dawn, corresponding to the Greek Eos.

Auster (ôs'ter), the south wind, also called Notus.

Avalon (av'a lon), in Celtic mythology, the kingdom of the dead. Its name, Isle of Apples, was symbolic of joy. To magic Avalon Arthur was borne to be healed, and Avalon was later identified with Glastonbury in Somerset as Arthur's burial place.

Avernus (a vûr'nus), a small lake in Italy within the crater of an extinct volcano, believed by the ancients to be the entrance to the infernal regions because of the foul smelling vapors that rose from it.

ba (bä), in Egyptian religion, the immortal soul, pictured as a bird with a human head.

Baal (bā'al) or **Bel** (bāl), ancient Semitic god of fertility, bestower of the gifts of nature. The word means literally lord or god and there were many Baals, belonging to different tribes and places, as the Tyrian Baal, Babylonian Baal, etc. His cults developed into an orgiastic form of nature worship.

Bacchus (bak'us), the Greek god of wine. See *Dionysus.*

Balder (bôl'dẽr), in Teutonic mythology, the god of light, son of Odin and Frigga. Frigga exacted a vow from all creation never to harm Balder. Iron, stone, fire, water, trees, beasts and birds all promised. But Frigga forgot to ask the mistletoe. The other gods used to amuse themselves by hurling things at Balder. Arrows, stones, spears or battleaxes could not injure him. But Loki, the mischief maker, cut off a twig of the mistletoe and made a dart of it. "Here" he said to the blind Hoder, "you too may do as the others do." And he directed the aim of Hoder. Balder was pierced by the mistletoe dart and fell dead. Hermod rode straight to the underworld to pray Hela (death) to restore Balder to the grieving gods. Hela agreed to let Balder return to life if all things in the world would weep for him. If one thing did not weep, Balder could not return. Hermod went back with his message. All things on earth wept. But Loki, disguised as an old hag, would not weep. Matthew Arnold's "Balder Dead" tells the story of Hermod's journey to the underworld and Loki's refusal to weep.

Balmung (bäl'moong), in the *Nibelungenlied,* Siegfried's sword; called Nothung in Wagner's operas.

Balor (bal'ôr), in Celtic mythology, king of the Fomors (sea giants). He had one evil eye that destroyed anything it looked upon. His eye was put out and Balor was killed by Lugh, the sun god, in the battle of Moitura between the Fomors and the Tuatha de Danann (the Irish gods).

banshee (bän'shē), in Gaelic folklore, a female spirit whose wailing warns certain families that one of them is about to die. In Gaelic, *bean* (pronounced bän) means woman; *sid* (pronounced shē) means fairy or spirit.

basilisk (bas'i lisk), a reptile of ancient fable, dragon, lizard or serpent, hatched from a cock's egg by a serpent. It was fatal to come within range of its breath or its look.

Baucis and **Philemon** (bô'sis; fi lē'mon), in Greek and Roman mythology, an aged woman and her husband, very poor, who lived in Phrygia. Zeus and Hermes, travelling in disguise, were welcomed and fed in the cottage of the old pair; and not until the pitcher returned to the table many times miraculously filled did Baucis and Philemon realize they were entertaining gods. Their humble cottage was changed into a temple. Their prayer to die together that neither might be left alone was granted, and they were changed into trees that grew at the gate of the temple.

Bedivere (bed'i vẽr), one of the knights of the Round Table, sole survivor with his brother and King Arthur of the battle against Modred in which Arthur was mortally wounded. It was Bedivere who threw the sword Excalibur back into the lake and carried Arthur to the ship that bore him off to Avalon.

Beelzebub (bē el'zē bub), a god of the ancient Philistine city of Ekron; literally, god of flies. Beelzebub probably was a deity who could disperse flies and thus prevent plagues and diseases. In the New Testament he is called a prince of demons. In Milton's *Paradise Lost* he is one of the fallen angels, next in rank below Satan.

Belial (bē'li al; bēl'yal), personification of evil; the devil. The word seems to mean worthless. In the New Testament, Satan is called Belial. In Milton's *Paradise Lost* Belial is one of fallen angels.

Bellerophon (be lẽr'ō fon), son of Glaucus, king of Corinth. He committed murder, and fled to Proetus, king of Argos, for protection. Antæa, Proetus's wife, fell in love with Bellerophon, and when he rejected her advances, she accused him to the king. Proetus sent him to Iobates, king of Lycia, with a secret message asking that he be put to death. Iobates sent him to kill the terrible Chimaera, sure he would meet his death. But Bellerophon killed the Chimaera with the aid of the winged horse Pegasus. After other trials, in which he was successful, Iobates saw his worth and gave him his daughter in marriage. Hawthorne tells this story in his *Wonder Book*.

Bellona (be lō'na), the Roman goddess of war.

Beowulf (bā' ō woolf), mythical, semi-historical warrior hero of the Anglo-Saxon epic poem *Beowulf*, who delivered Hrothgar, king of the Danes, and his people from the monster Grendel. For twelve years Grendel had walked into Hrothgar's great mead hall named Heorot and devoured sometimes 30 warriors in one night. With 14 companions came Beowulf across the sea. He was the nephew of Higelac, king of the Geats. Single-handed he wrestled with the grim stalker from the marshes and tore off his arm. Grendel fled to his den to die. The next night his mother, the water-hog, came to avenge her son and seized on Aeschere, Hrothgar's counsellor. Beowulf followed her to the bottom of the sea. It was a terrible underwater fight; but Beowulf killed her and cut off the head of Grendel who was lying nearby. He swam ashore with nothing left but the hilt of the sword in one hand and the head of Grendel in the other. He returned to his own people, laden with rich gifts.

Years later Beowulf became king of the Geats and ruled for 50 years. In the fiftieth year a fearful dragon began to burn and lay waste the land, and no one dared to approach it. The old king himself, with eleven companions, went out to destroy it. At sight of the fire-breathing monster his companions fled, save Wiglaf who thought only of Beowulf. Beowulf fought without fear, but his sword broke and the dragon sank his poison-fangs in the old king's neck. Then Wiglaf wounded the monster and

BLUEBEARD

Beowulf killed it, but he had received his own death wound. Then he commanded that his barrow be built on the high sea cliff, and here his body was burned with the treasure from the dragon's hill.

Bifrost (bēf'rost), in Norse mythology, the rainbow bridge over which the gods passed between earth and heaven.

Bladud (blā'dud; blăd'ud), legendary king of Britain, father of King Lear.

Blarney (blär'ni) **Stone,** an inscribed stone in Blarney Castle, near Cork, Ireland. There is an old belief that those who kiss the Blarney Stone will thereafter possess "a cajoling tongue and the art of flattery or of telling lies without shame."

Bluebeard (bloo'bērd), a rich old man with an ugly blue beard who murdered his wives one after the other and hid them in a locked room. The story is built around the forbidden door (or forbidden chest) motif, one of the world-wide motifs of folklore, in which curiosity is inevitably punished. But the story is familiar to modern readers largely through the French *Stories of Times Past* of Charles Perrault, first translated into English in 1729.

Old Bluebeard married one young wife after another, and they mysteriously disappeared. Fatima was the name of the seventh. She did not want to marry him but at last consented. Soon after the wedding Bluebeard went off on a journey, leaving with Fatima all the keys of the castle. She could unlock all the treasure; she could go into all the rooms but one. One mysterious door he commanded her not to unlock. But after she had seen all the treasure and all the rooms, Fatima wanted to know what was in this last room. She unlocked the door and discovered the bodies of Bluebeard's dead wives. Overcome with terror, she dropped the key, which became stained with blood. She could not wash it off, though she scrubbed and scrubbed. Bluebeard came back, saw the spot on the key and condemned Fatima to death for her disobedience. But Fatima's brothers arrived just in time to save their sister, and they speedily put an end to Bluebeard.

bogle (bō'gl; bog'l), in Scotland and northern England a goblin or ghost. It is also spelled bogey, bogie, bogy.

Boreas (bō'rē as), in Greek mythology, the *north wind;* called *Aquilo* in Roman mythology.

Bors (bôrs) **Sir,** one of the knights of the Round Table who sought the Holy Grail.

Bragi (brä'gē), in Teutonic mythology, the god of poetry, one of the sons of Odin and Frigga.

Brahma (brä'ma), the chief god of Hindu mythology, the supreme soul or divine reality of the universe. In later Hinduism he became personified as the creator in the great Hindu triad, with Vishnu, the preserver, and Siva, the destroyer.

Bran (bran), in Celtic mythology, god of the underworld, son of the sea god Lir. As a mythical king of Britain he commanded his people to bury his head in the White Mountain London with the face toward France. While

it lay there, he said, no enemies could land on the island. When Arthur dug it up, the Saxon invaders came.

Briareus (brī âr'ē us), in Greek mythology, a giant with 100 hands.

Bronze Age, in classical mythology, the third era of the world, in which warfare prevailed. It followed the Silver Age.

brownie (broun'ī), a friendly goblin of Scotch folklore who performed the household tasks or farm chores at night.

Bruce and the Spider, a Scotch legend that tells how Robert the Bruce, weary and discouraged and in hiding, took new heart to drive the English out of Scotland. He was crowned King of Scotland in 1306 but he was driven from his throne by the English. He took refuge on the isle of Rathlin off the coast of Ireland. One day he was watching a spider mending her web. She would slip down and hang from the beam by her thread and climb laboriously up again. She would slip down and climb up, slip down and climb up, but she never ceased to labor. Thus Bruce learned patience and perseverance and courage. With a small band of followers he sailed back to Scotland to rout the usurpers. It took seven years. Bruce himself led the Scots in the great battle of Bannockburn (1314), which was the end of the English in Scotland.

THE METROPOLITAN MUSEUM

BRAHMA. One concept of the Hindu religion is the belief that the soul of man joins with Brahma when it experiences salvation. In this union, it achieves ultimate reality, for Brahma's nature is that of an absolute, impersonal, transcendent force.

Brunhild[1] (broon'hilt), in the *Nibelungenlied,* Queen of Iceland, overcome by Siegfried in trials of strength and given as wife to Gunther. Siegfried, to tame her, stole her ring and girdle and gave them to his own wife Kriemhild. Brunhild in hate persuaded Hagen, Gunther's retainer, to kill Siegfried.

In Wagner's operas of the *Ring of*

[1] Spelled: Brynhild in the *Volsunga Saga;* Brunhild in the *Nibelungenlied;* Brunnehilde in Wagner's *Ring of the Nibelungs.*

the Nibelungs, Brunnehilde is a daughter of Wotan and youngest of the Valkyrie. She disobeyed her father by trying to aid Siegmund in his fight with Hunding and was condemned to become a mortal woman and sleep within a magic ring of fire until a hero worthy of her should penetrate it and find her. Brunnehilde slept on her mountain until Siegfried, Siegmund's son, grew up and went through the fire and woke her. Their love was perfect until in his adventures a magic drink was given him that caused him to forget Brunnehilde, wed Gudrune and promise Brunnehilde to Gunther. In despair Brunnehilde reproached him, but the magic held him, and he did not love her. Later at a banquet Siegfried drank another magic potion, suddenly remembered Brunnehilde, called her name and was killed by Hagen. Brunnehilde rode into the flames of his funeral pyre and died with him.

In the *Volsunga Saga,* Brynhild was beloved by Sigurd, who forgot her to marry Gudrun. She was wed to Gunnar but brought about Sigurd's death in order to die with him.

Brut (brōōt) or **Brutus,** legendary first king of Britain (great-grandson of Aeneas) who founded New Troy (London). He was the ancestor of Bladud, Lud, King Cole, Vortigern and Arthur. His story is told in Geoffrey of Monmouth's *History of the Kings of Britain,* Wace's *Brut* and Layamon's *Brut.*

Cacus (kā'kus), a giant son of Vulcan. He stole the cattle of Geryon as Hercules was driving them home and dragged them backwards into his cave so that their tracks would seem to be leaving it. But Hercules heard their lowing, found them and killed Cacus.

Cadmus (kad'mus), in Greek mythology, son of Agenor, king of Phoenicia. In the search for his sister Europa, whom Zeus had carried off, he slew a dragon and sowed its teeth across a plain, from which armed men sprang up. They fought among themselves until only five were left. With these five Cadmus founded Thebes. He is said to have given the letters of the alphabet to Greece.

Caduceus (ka dū'sē us), a winged staff entwined by two serpents. As the staff of Hermes, herald of the gods, it became the symbol of heralds— and later of physicians.

Calliope (ka lī'ō pē) the Greek Muse of epic poetry.

Callisto (ka lis'tō), a nymph beloved by Zeus. Hera in jealousy turned her into a bear. She was about to be killed by her son Arcus when Zeus suddenly raised them both into the heavens, as the constellations, the Great and Little Bear, which never set.

Calydonian (kal i dō'ni an) **Boar,** in Greek mythology, the terrible boar sent by Artemis to ravage the fields of Calydon, as a punishment to Oenus for failing to honor her with a harvest offering.

Calypso (ka lip' sō), in the *Odyssey* a sea nymph, ruler of the island Ogygia, who found Odysseus shipwrecked on her coast. She offered him immortal-

ity if he would stay with her, but he would not. She kept him seven years and then allowed him to depart.

Camelot (kam'e lot), the seat of Arthur's court. It has been variously identified by tradition with Winchester, Queen's Camel in Somerset, Caerleon on the river Usk and Camelford in Cornwall.

Canute (ka nūt') or **Cnut** (k'nōōt'), Danish king of England (1017–35) and of Denmark. English legend says that to rebuke the flattery of those around him, Canute sat down by the edge of the sea and commanded the rising tide to come no farther. But the tide rolled in and the waves broke over Canute. Then he exhorted those who called him great to witness that he could not stay by his command "so much as this small portion of water."

Carbonek (kör'bō nek), the castle where Galahad, Perceval and Bors found the Holy Grail.

Cassandra (ka san'dra), a daughter of Priam, king of Troy. When she was young, she was left asleep in the temple of Apollo and her ears were purified by serpents so that she could understand the voices of nature. Apollo gave her the gift of prophecy; but, when she refused his love, he ordained that no one should believe her prophecies. She warned the Trojans to send Helen home to Greece; she warned them against the Wooden Horse; but nobody would heed her words. Upon the capture of Troy she fell to the lot of Agamemnon, returned to Greece with him and was killed by Clytemnestra.

Cassiopeia (kas i ō pē'ya), in Greek mythology, the boastful mother of Andromeda.

Castor and Pollux (kas'tēr; pol'uks), twin brothers, called the Dioscuri, that is, sons of Zeus. They took part in the voyage of the Argonauts and thus became the patrons of sailors and navigation. Castor was famous for his skill in managing horses, and Pollux for his boxing. The gods rewarded their fidelity to each other by placing them together in the heavens. Their constellation is called Gemini, the Twins.

cat of Losanne, a monster cat killed by King Arthur.

Cecrops (sē'krops), the first king of Attica and founder of Athens, which was originally called Cecropia.

Centaurs (sen'tōrs), a race of the mountains of Thessaly, half horse, half man. The famous battle of the Centaurs with the Lapithæ arose from a quarrel at the marriage feast of Hippodamia and Pirithous, king of the Lapithæ. The Centaurs were driven out of the country.

Cerberus (sẽr'bẽr us), the three-headed dog that guarded the entrance to Hades. He prevented the living from entering the lower world and the dead from leaving. Those of the upper world who got by him had to lull him to sleep with music or pacify him with a cake.

Ceres (sē'rēz), the Roman goddess of growing things, especially of food plants and agriculture; mother of Proserpine. The Romans very early superimposed on her worship that of the Greek Demeter.

changeling (chānj'ling), in British folklore, a child of the fairies or elves left in place of a stolen human baby. This superstition is especially prevalent in the Scottish Highlands, where, to this day, a new-born child is carefully watched till the day of its baptism. After that it cannot be stolen by the fairies. A deformed, sickly or idiot child is often thought to be a changeling and cruelly treated.

Chanticleer (chan'ti klēr), the name (meaning sing clear) of the cock in *Reynard the Fox* and other medieval beast fables. Chanticleer figures in Chaucer's *Nun's Priest's Tale.* He is the hero of Edmond Rostand's drama *Chanticleer.*

Chaos (kā'os), the formless void that existed before the creation of the world. Chaos and Love united, and from the union the gods, men and all things were born. Chaos was the mother of Erebus and Night.

Charis (kā'ris), in Homer's *Iliad,* the wife of Hephaestus. Later the name was applied to any one of the three Graces or Charites.

Charlemagne (shär' lē mān), king of the Franks (768–814); emperor of the West (800–814), son of Pepin. Charlemagne, his splendid court and his 12 peers or paladins (like the British Arthur and his knights) are the center of a vast cycle of romance and legend. These romances are called *Chansons de gestes* or songs of heroic deeds, and the *Song of Roland* is the best known to modern readers.

Charlemagne figures as a warrior, a strong and just ruler and champion of Christianity. Roland and Oliver, Turpin, Ogier the Dane, William of Toulouse and Ganelon the traitor are the paladins best known to us. The various romances (or *chansons*) celebrate the wars against the Saxons, wars in Italy and in Spain, wars with Charlemagne's own vassals and against the Saracens, his pilgrimage to Jerusalem, his innocent wife Blanchefleur, falsely accused, and (the high peak of the cycle) the defeat of his rear guard at Roncesvaux, Aug. 15, 778.

Charon (kā'ron; kâr'on), in Greek mythology the boatman who ferried the souls of the dead across the river Styx or Acheron. The fare was a small coin called an obol; and it was the custom to place one in the mouth of a dead person to pay his way to Hades.

Charybdis (ka rib'dis), in Greek mythology a greedy and thieving woman who stole the oxen of Hercules and as punishment was turned into a terrible gulf and whirlpool by Zeus. She was placed opposite the monster Scylla in the strait between Italy and Sicily. There she remained a menace to mariners and sucked down several of the ships of Odysseus. "Between Scylla and Charybdis" means between two dangers, one of which can hardly be avoided.

Children of Ler or Lir (lâr), in Celtic mythology and legend, one of the "three sorrows of story telling." Ler was the Celtic sea god. He had three beautiful children whom Aeife (ē'fà), their jealous stepmother, changed into swans. For 900 years they wandered on the lakes of Ireland until St. Patrick came and drove away the old gods. Then the three swan-children of Ler were restored to human form and converted to Christianity. But they were so old that they died almost immediately.

Chimaera (ki mē′ra), in Greek mythology a female monster with a lion's head, goat's body and dragon's tail, perpetually vomiting flame. It was killed by Bellerophon with the help of the winged horse Pegasus.

Chiron (kī′ron), in Greek mythology, a wise centaur, skilled in medicine, who taught Asclepius the art of herbal healing. Many of the heroes of Greece were his pupils. He was accidentally wounded by Hercules and placed in the heavens by Zeus as the constellation Sagittarius.

Cinderella (sin der el′a), in world folklore, a little household drudge, cruelly treated, who attained wealth and married a prince with the aid of a supernatural guardian. The story is probably of Oriental origin and exists in more than 300 variants from

NEW YORK PUBLIC LIBRARY

CINDERELLA. When her sisters were ready to go to the palace ball, "Cinderella followed them to the coach and after it had whirled them away, sat down and cried."

Alaska to South Africa. But the most familiar version is from the French of Charles Perrault, first translated into English about 1729. Cinderella was a young girl, hated and mistreated by her stepmother for being more beautiful than her own two ugly daughters. Kept in rags and overworked, she was not allowed to go to the king's ball. But her fairy guardian saw to it that she got there. She outshone everyone else and the prince fell in love with her. But each night at midnight she had to run home and he never found out who she was. On the third night she lost one little glass slipper by which in the end the prince identified her and they were married.

Circe (sûr′sē), in the *Odyssey*, a sorceress who lured travelers to her island of Æaea and turned them into beasts with magic herbs. When Odysseus landed there, his comrades were changed into swine. Circe could not

harm Odysseus, for he was protected by the herb *moly,* which Hermes had given him. He compelled her to restore his companions to human form and dwelt with her there for a year.

Clio (klī′ō), the Greek Muse of history.

Clotho (klō′thō), in Greek mythology, the youngest of the three Fates. She presided over the birth of human beings.

Clytemnestra (klī tem nes′tra), in Greek legend, a sister of Castor, Pollux and Helen of Troy. She was the wife of Agamemnon and mother of Orestes, Iphigenia and Electra. When Agamemnon returned from the Trojan War, she murdered him with the help of her lover Aegisthus. She was killed by her son Orestes, to avenge the murder of his father.

Clytie (klī′tē), in Greek mythology, a sea nymph, the emblem of constancy. She loved the sun god Apollo, and when he left her, she was turned into a sunflower, which now every day turns its face to the sun.

cockatrice (kok′a tris). Same as *basilisk.*

Cole, King. See *King Cole.*

Conchobor (kong′kō wur or kon′oor), king of Ulster, uncle of Cuchulain.

Creusa (krē ū′sa), (1) a princess of Corinth and wife of Jason, whom Medea killed with the gift of a poisoned robe; (2) daughter of Priam, king of Troy, and wife of Aeneas.

crocodile tears, insincere tears. In ancient fable crocodiles were said to weep while they devoured their prey.

Crœsus (krē′sus), a 6th-century king of Lydia, considered the richest man in the world. He boasted of his happiness, and Solon rebuked him saying that Crœsus knew not his end. Just as he was about to be burned alive by Cyrus, his conqueror, he called on Solon's name. Cyrus was touched by his story and set him free.

Cronus (krō′nus), in Greek mythology, son of Uranus (heaven) and Gaea (earth). His wife was Rhea. He was warned that a child of his own would overthrow him, so he swallowed his children as soon as they were born, first Hestia, then Demeter, Hera, Hades and Poseidon. But Rhea saved the infant Zeus by giving Cronus a swaddled stone to swallow. When Zeus grew up, he made Cronus give up his brothers and sisters, rebelled against him and dethroned him.

Cuchulain (kōō chul′ in′), the hero of the Ulster cycle of old Irish mythology and legend. He was the son of Lug (Lōō), the sungod, and nephew of Conchobor, king of Ulster, and is believed to have lived in the 1st century A.D. When he was seven years old, he performed amazing feats. At the age of 12 he guarded the possessions of Culain, the smith of Ulster, to make up to him for having killed his hound; and he thereby received his name: Cu (hound) + Culain (of Culain). He married Emer, the daughter of a druid. He saved Ulster single-handed against the forces of Connaught in the War for the Brown Bull or the Cattle Raid of Cuailnge (Cooley). He was killed by magic in a last battle at the age of 27. Lady Augusta Gregory's *Cuchulain of Muirthemne* is the finest modern reworking of the legends.

Cupid (kū′pid), in Roman mythology, the god of love, son of Venus. He is pictured as a winged, naked boy with bow and arrows. A dart from his bow would create love in the breast of whatever god or mortal it wounded. The story of Cupid and Psyche begins with his wounding himself with one of his own arrows.

Cybele (sib′e lē) or **Cybebe** (si bē′bē), the great nature goddess of ancient Anatolia; identified by the Greeks with Rhea.

Cyclopes (sī′klō pēz), a race of one-eyed giants, who dwelt in Sicily. The word is Greek for round-eyed; Cyclops is the singular form. In the *Odyssey,* they were huge man-eating shepherds. They labored for Hephaestus under Mount Etna, helping to forge the thunderbolts of Zeus.

Daedalus (ded′a lus), a skilled Athenian inventor. The Greek word means craftsman. In jealousy he killed his nephew, a too-apt pupil, and fled with his son Icarus to Crete. There he built the labyrinth for King Minos, and later he and his son were shut up in the labyrinth for an offense to Minos. Daedalus made wings for them both of feathers and wax, whereby they escaped. But Icarus flew too near the sun; the wax of his wings melted, and he fell into the sea, thereafter named the Icarian Sea. Daedalus reached Sicily.

Damocles (dam′ō klēz), a flattering attendant of Dionysius, tyrant of Syracuse in the 4th century B.C. Dionysius grew weary of having his own happiness extolled and invited Damocles to taste of a ruler's happiness. At the banquet Damocles looked up and saw a sword above his head hanging by a single hair.

Damon (dā′mon), in Greek legend, the true friend of Pythias. Pythias, condemned to death by the tyrant Dionysius of Syracuse, asked leave to go home to arrange his affairs. Damon offered his own life as pledge for his friend's return. Pythias returned just in time to save Damon from being put to death in his place. Dionysius was so impressed with their devotion that he pardoned Pythias.

Danae (dan′ā ē), in Greek mythology, a daughter of Acrisius, king of Argos. To prevent the fulfilment of an old prophecy that he would die at the hand of her son, Acrisius shut her up in a brazen tower. But Zeus fell in love with her and visited her there concealed in a shower of gold. Perseus was their son. Acrisius set the mother and child adrift in a boat and they were carried to the island of Seriphos.

Danaides (da nā′i dēz), the fifty daughters of Danaus, king of Argos. He had been warned that he would die at the hands of his sons-in-law and commanded his daughters to kill their husbands on their wedding night. They all obeyed but one. The other 49 were sent to Hades to dip water in a sieve forever.

Danu (thán′ōō; dán′ōō), in Celtic mythology, the mother of all the gods.

Daphne (daf′nē), in Greek mythology, a river nymph who was pursued by Apollo. As she fled she prayed the gods to allow her to escape, and she was changed to a laurel tree.

Deianira (dē ya nĭ′ra), the beautiful wife of Hercules, whom he won by feats of strength. In their travels they came to a river that Hercules forded with ease, but Deianira he gave to the centaur Nessus to carry over. Nessus was so won by her beauty that he tried to run off with her. Hercules shot a poisoned arrow after him that gave him a mortal wound. Nessus, dying, told Deianira that his blood-stained robe was a charm to hold the love of her husband. Deianira believed him and years later, when she thought she had cause, sent Hercules the centaur's garment. When it touched his flesh it burned and clung to him. Dying and in agony he hurried home, ascended his funeral pyre and lit the torch. Deianira in grief for what she had mistakenly done hung herself.

Deirdre (dâr′drē), heroine of an old Irish legend, one of the "three sorrows of story telling." When Deirdre was born a druid prophesied that she would bring death to heroes. But because of her great beauty, Conchobor, king of Ulster, marked her for his wife and had her brought up in secret. By accident she met Naoise one of the three sons of Usnech (ōosh′nĕch) in the forest, loved him and fled with him and his brothers to Scotland. Years later Conchobor sent them a message of pardon and called them home. In spite of Deirdre's warning not to go, they returned to Ireland. The three sons of Usnech were at once most treacherously slain and Deirdre killed herself in grief. This is most beautifully told in Lady Augusta Gregory's *Cuchulain of Muirthemne.* William Butler Yeats used the story for his play *Deirdre.* James Stevens wrote a novel *Deirdre.* The unfinished poetic drama *Deirdre of the Sorrows* by John Millington Synge is the finest rehandling of the material.

Delphi (del′fī), a town in ancient Greece near the foot of Mt. Parnassus, famed for the temple and oracle of Apollo. From a cleft in the ground inside the temple came forth sulphurous vapors that were supposed to inspire the priestesses.

Demeter (dē mē′tēr), the Greek goddess of agriculture, fertility and marriage. She was the mother of Persephone, whom Pluto carried off to the underworld. The grief of Demeter moved Zeus to allow Persephone to return to her mother for half of the year and remain the other half with Pluto. This symbolizes the sowing of seed (while Persephone is underground) and the growth of grain (when she returns to the upper world.) The Romans identified Demeter with Ceres.

Deucalion and Pyrrha (dū kā′ li ŏn; pir′a), King and Queen of Thessaly, sole human survivors of the Deluge. One story says they took refuge on the peak of Mt. Parnassus, another that they were nine days in a ship which landed there. They were told by an oracle to cast the bones of their mother behind them to repeople the world. Their mother they understood to be the earth. So they cast stones behind them, and the stones became men and women.

deva (dā′va), in Persian folklore a malignant spirit or demon.

Devil (dev′l), the personification of evil in all folklore and in all formal religions. He has many names and many shapes. In ancient Babylon he was a dragon named Tiamet, in Egypt a serpent called Apap. The Hindus call him Siva. He is the Satan of the Hebrew and Christian religions, referred to at times also as Abaddon or Beelzebub. He was the serpent who tempted Eve and is considered the enemy, tempter and deceiver of mankind. This devil figures as Lucifer in Milton's *Paradise Lost.*

In the Old Testament book of Job, Satan "presents himself before the Lord" and insists that Job's piety depended on his health and wealth. Satan is allowed to tempt Job by taking both health and wealth from him. This notion of Satan seems to explain the words devil and diabolic, for in Greek *diabolus* means the accuser or slanderer.

In the folklore of all uncivilized peoples, calamity, disease, death, everything the primitive mind could not understand or explain, was the work of the devil and his servants.

In the Middle Ages he came into his own. One had only to look out the window to see him pass in the form of a cat, a black dog, a goat or a fiddler who danced men and women to their ruin. Sometimes he was a toad to be placated with a saucer of milk lest he harm the household. Stories, beliefs and personal encounters abounded. Martin Luther threw an ink bottle at him.

But the elegant gentleman devil with horns and pointed ears, long black cloak and tail and cloven hoof is a fairly late development. His is the outgrowth of the medieval story of a man who sold his soul to the devil in exchange for power. This devil is the Mephistopheles of Marlowe's *Doctor Faustus,* Goethe's *Faust* and Gounod's opera, *Faust.*

Diana (dī an′a), Roman goddess of forests and protectress of women in childbirth. She was a very ancient Italian goddess whose priest, the king of the woods, became priest only by killing his predecessor in single combat. Diana (Artemis) of Ephesus was goddess of fruitfulness, the great mother. The Greeks took over the worship of the Greek Artemis and identified it with their own Diana cults. In later literature Diana became goddess of the chase and of the moon.

Diarmait (dēr′mat), in the Fenian cycle of old Irish legend and romance, hero of the romance *The Pursuit of Diarmait and Grainne.* Diarmait was the nephew of Finn MacCumal. Grainne, Finn's chosen wife, fell in love with Diarmait and the two fled together. After long and fruitless search Finn finally caused the death of Diarmait.

Dido (dī′do), a princess of Tyre, queen and founder of Carthage. Her husband was murdered by her brother for his wealth; but Dido fled from Tyre with the treasure. She landed in Africa and bargained for as much land as the hide of a bull would cover. She had it cut into thin strips and with them enclosed enough ground to erect her citadel. A neighboring king named Iarbas coveted the city, demanded her hand in marriage and threatened war should she refuse. Rather than marry him she built her funeral pyre and killed herself. In Vergil's *Aeneid* Dido is a contemporary of the wandering Aeneas, and it is for the love of him and in grief at his leaving her that she takes her own life. She is also called Elissa.

Diomedes (dī ō mē′dēz), in Greek mythology, a tyrant of Thrace, who fed his mares on human flesh, was overcome by Hercules and fed to his own horses. Another Diomedes was a Greek hero in the Trojan War. He entered Troy and helped Odysseus steal the sacred Palladium, without which the Trojans felt unable to defend themselves.

Dione (dī ō′nē), in the *Iliad,* the mother of Aphrodite by Zeus; in Hesiod, a daughter of Oceanus.

Dionysus (dī ō nī′sus), in Greek mythology, god of nature and all growing things, especially of the grape and wine. He is also called Bacchus. He was the son of Zeus and Semele and was brought up in secret by the nymphs to save him from the jealous malice of Hera. When he grew up, he travelled through the world teaching men the arts of civilization, especially the cultivation of the grape. The wild, orgiastic aspects of his cult were strongly resisted in many places. Many stories depict the sad fate of those who opposed him; those who favored him received the gift of the vine, that is, the making and use of wine. The satyrs were his companions and he himself often took on the form of panther, tiger or goat.

Dioscuri (dī′os kū′rī). See *Castor and Pollux.*

Dis (dis), the god of the under world in Roman mythology, identified with the Greek Pluto.

dragon (drag′un), a fabulous monster, pictured as a winged fire-breathing serpent or lizard: in Teutonic mythology called a *fire-drake.* It had one head or many heads, legs or no legs; but everywhere it was essentially a snake. And everywhere it was a bringer of destruction, a guardian of treasure, kidnapper of maidens fair and demander of sacrifices (usually human) for the use of benefits, such as bridges and castles. Many a hero in the myths and folk tales of the world has killed his dragon: Hercules, Thor, Apollo and Perseus, Siegfried, Sigurd, Beowulf, Arthur, Tristram, St. George. In Christian legend the dragon is the symbol of Satan, overcome by the archangel Michael. Many saints are pictured standing upon a dragon, in symbolism of their having conquered evil.

dryads (drī′adz), the wood nymphs of Greek mythology. They lived and died with the trees in which they dwelt.

dwarfs (dwôrfs), in Teutonic mythology, small supernatural beings who dwelt in the bowels of the earth, little old brown men with long white beards and child stature. They were sometimes helpful, more often malicious, and possessed great knowledge and cunning. They were master metal workers and forged the weapons of the gods. They made Thor's hammer and the great chain which held the wolf Fenrir.

Echo (ek'ō), in Greek mythology, a mountain nymph whose incessant talking so annoyed Hera that she deprived her of the power of speech. She could speak only when she was spoken to; and then could only repeat the last words said to her. Another story says that she pined away for love of Narcissus until only her voice was left.

Elaine (ē lān'), in Arthurian legend: (1) The fair maid of Astolat who died for love of Lancelot. (2) The mother of Galahad by Lancelot, daughter of King Pelles.

Electra (ē lek'trä) the daughter of Agamemnon and Clytemnestra who inspired her brother Orestes to avenge their father's murder by killing Clytemnestra and her lover Aegisthus. She married Pylades.

elf (elf), in Teutonic mythology, a superhuman being inferior in power only to the gods. There were two kinds, the elves of light, who dwelt in Alfheim and were friendly to mankind, and the elves of night, the earth-dwelling dwarfs. In more modern literature an elf is a sprite or a fairy.

Elysium (ē lizh'i um), the Elysian Plain or the Elysian Fields, in Greek mythology the abode of the good after death, situated in the West, something like the islands of the Blessed. In Vergil's *Aeneid* the abode of the blessed is a part of the underworld but it has its sun and stars.

Emer (āv'ēr), in the Ulster cycle the most beautiful and learned young girl in Ireland, wife of Cuchulain.

Endymion (en dim'i on), in Greek mythology, a beautiful shepherd boy with whom Selene fell in love while he lay sleeping. She bestowed on him eternal sleep that she might forever watch him. Keats's poem *Endymion* is based on this story.

Eos (ē'os), the Greek goddess of the dawn; same as the Roman Aurora. Every morning she rose in the east from the couch of her husband Tithonus to announce the rising sun.

Erato (er'a tō), the Greek Muse of love poetry.

Erebus (er'ē bus), in Greek mythology, the region of darkness that is the entrance to Hades. Vergil calls it a part of the lower world.

Erinyes (ē rin'i ēz), in Greek mythology the three avenging spirits of Furies who torment wrong-doers. A later conception of them is as snaky-locked women driving their victims to madness.

Eris (ē'ris; er'is), the Greek goddess of discord. She was not invited to the wedding of Peleus and Thetis, and in spite threw a golden apple among the guests, marked "To the fairest." Hera, Athene and Aphrodite each claimed it and appealed to Zeus to decide. He sent them to young Paris, a shepherd on Mt. Ida. Each one made a great promise to win his favor, but when Aphrodite promised him the fairest of all women for wife, to her he gave the prize. Thus Eris with her apple caused even greater strife, for when Paris beheld

Helen, the wife of Menelaus, he fell in love with her and carried her off to Troy. And from this elopement arose the Trojan War.

erlking (ûrl'king'), in Teutonic folklore, the king of the elves, especially inimical to children. In later German legend, his home was the Black Forest. Goethe wrote a poem on this subject, set to music by Schubert and translated into English by Sir Walter Scott.

Eros (ē'ros; er'os), the Greek God of love; same as the Roman Cupid.

Eteocles (ē tē'ō clēz), in Greek legend, the son of Oedipus and brother of Polynices. He usurped the throne of Thebes which he was supposed to hold in alternate years with his brother. Polynices marched against him to reclaim his right, accompanied by seven heroes. In this war, called the Seven Against Thebes, the two brothers killed each other in single combat. Aeschylus wrote a tragedy on this story.

Etzel (et'sel), in German legend the name given to Attila, king of the Huns; called Atli in Norse legend.

Eumaeus (ū mē'us), the swineherd of Odysseus who helped him to slay the suitors of Penelope.

Eumenides (ū men'i dēz), in Greek mythology, a name meaning "the kindly ones," a propitiatory name for the Furies.

Euphrosyne (ū fros'i nē), one of the Graces.

Europa (ū rō'pa), in Greek mythology, a daughter of Agenor, king of Phoenicia, with whom Zeus fell in love. He took on the shape of a beautiful bull and mingled with the cattle of Agenor. Europa noticed and caressed him. When she climbed upon his back, he plunged into the sea and swam off with her to Crete. She became the mother of Minos, Sarpedon and Rhadamanthus.

Eurus (ū'rus), the east wind.

Eurydice (ū rid'i sē), the wife of Orpheus.

Eurystheus (ū ris'thūs), the king of Mycenae who imposed on Hercules the Twelve Labors.

Euterpe (ū tûr'pē), the Greek Muse of music.

evil eye, in folk superstition, an eye having the power to work harm with its glance. Fear of the abnormal is at the root of this belief. Fear of an ugly, deformed eye was extended to eyes in which no flaw was visible. In Latin countries a blue eye is thought to have strange powers; in the north a black eye is feared. In Ireland the shamrock is a charm against its malice. In some places, spitting will avert its influence.

Excalibur (eks kal'i bēr), the sword of King Arthur; also called Caliburn. The ancient Celtic story is that Arthur drew it out of a rock from which no one else could budge it. In Malory's *Morte d'Arthur* it was given to him by the Lady of the Lake. When Arthur died, he bade Sir Bedivere hurl it into the lake. A hand rose from the water to receive it and vanished.

Fafnir (fäv'nir), in Norse mythology, the dragon who guarded the treasure of the dwarf Andvari. He was killed by Sigurd.

fairies (fâr'iz), in world folklore from earliest times to the present day a race of supernatural beings possessed of magic powers. They resemble men and women usually, though many have the power to assume strange or animal shapes. The stories of classic Greek and Roman writers about such beings were the formal expression of

A CHILD has the rare experience of seeing a fairy, magical inhabitant of the woods.

a still older folk belief. Homer's human warriors wooed many a fairy love (nymph, nereid, siren). And all the fairy-wife, demon-lover stories of India and Europe, even the animal-bride stories of the North American Indians, are variants of the same most ancient motif.

The folklore of all peoples has its fairies. Persian folklore has its beautiful, kindly peris and malignant devas; the Arabs and Moors, their genii or jinns; Egyptian lore, its seven hathors who appeared at the birth of a child to predict its future. In Italy fairies were called *fata,* and their home was supposed to be in the Himalayas. All supernatural, magical beings are called fées in Charles Perrault's presentations of French folktales. Germany is full of kobolds, dwarfs, elves and nixes (water sprites). Scandinavian story contributes nisses and trolls to the other Germanic conceptions. The woods and mountains and caves of England too are full of fairies, pixies, sprites, pucks and elves. Goblins are the household spirits there, akin to the Scotch brownies. Kelpies too inhabit the waters of Scotland.

But the Irish fairies have colored all other modern fairy lore. These fairy folk were the *sid* (shē) who lived in the raths (earth mounds) or fairy hills of Ireland; and belief in their presence is far from dead. They were of human stature and very beautiful. They had their kings and cities, their armies and musicians. Music especially was their gift. They had great herds and wonderful horses. And they appeared to men often in the shape of animals, but seldom in their own shapes.

The tiny, dainty fairies of Shakespeare's *Midsummer Night's Dream* have nothing in common with the fairies of folklore. But they have given rise to a whole cult of flowery juvenile literature.

Fata Morgana (fä'tä môr gä'n*a*), (1) in Arthurian legend the fairy Morgan or Morgan le Fay, Arthur's sister and wife of King Uriens; (2) a mirage said to resemble a distant towered city, seen at the strait of Messina between Sicily and Calabria, so called because said to be the work of the fairy Morgan.

Fates (fāts), in classical mythology the female spirits that presided over human destiny. The Greeks called them Moirai. They were the daughters of Zeus, three sisters: Clotho, who spun out the thread of human life; Lachesis, who measured its length, and Atropos, the inflexible one, who cut it. Aeschylus attributed to the Fates power over men and gods alike. The Romans called them Parcae. In Teutonic mythology, they were the Norns, or the Weird Sisters.

Fatima (fä'tē m*a*), the seventh and last wife of Bluebeard.

THE THREE FATES

faun (fôn), in Roman mythology, a lesser rural god, half-man, half-goat. Sometimes fauns are pictured with human bodies, pointed ears, small horns and a goat's tail. Hawthorne's novel *The Marble Faun* is a character study of a young man of innocent, pagan temperament who resembles the marble Faun of Praxiteles.

Faunus (fô'nus), a Roman nature god, protector of animals and herds; identified with the Greek god Pan.

Faust (foust), in German legend a learned man who sold his soul to the devil in exchange for a certain number of years of fulfilled desire and power. There *was* an obscure Dr. Faust of the 16th century, a quack and conjurer, believed to be in league with the devil. Even the dog who followed him was thought to be the devil himself. Marlowe's great drama *Doctor Faustus* follows the legend and gives the man to the devil in the end. Goethe's *Faust*, however, portrays a spiritual development utterly lacking in the original. The mind of Faust found no ultimate fulfilment in what the Devil could give him. In human service he forgot self and his soul was saved.

Fenrir (fen'rir), in Norse mythology, a monster son of Loki; also called the Fenris-wolf. The gods kept him bound with the magic chain Gleipnir. He escaped on the judgment day, swallowed Odin and was killed by Vitharr.

Finn or **Fionn MacCumal** (fin mak kōōl), the hero of the Fenian cycle of old Irish legend and romance, believed to have lived in the 3rd century. He was the father of the bard Oisin and the leader of a band of warriors and hunters of marvelous strength and achievement, which he organized for King Cormac (*c*.250 A.D.). Finn himself was noted for generosity and wisdom. The deeds of these heroes, the Fianna, who wandered through Ireland protecting it against invaders, make up the subject matter of the cycle. The most famous of the Fenian stories is of the search for Diarmait, Finn's trusted nephew, who eloped with Grainne, Finn's promised wife. Lady Augusta Gregory's *Gods and Fighting Men* tells all these tales. Finn is the original of Fingal in Macpherson's forged Ossianic poems. James Stephens's *Irish Fairy Tales* is a charming presentation of the subject matter.

Flora (flō'ra), the Roman goddess of flowers. Her festival, the Floralia, was celebrated on April 28.

Flying Dutchman, a phantom ship whose captain for his blasphemy was doomed to sail the seas and make no port till the day of judgment. Sailors believe that it haunts the waters off the Cape of Good Hope, and to see it in time of storm means disaster. Marryat's *Phantom Ship* is based on this legend; so is Wagner's opera *The Flying Dutchman.*

Fomors (fō'wôrz), in Celtic mythology, the sea-giants who were older than the gods. They were vanquished at the battle of Moitura by the Tuatha de Danann, the ancient Irish gods.

Forseti (fôr'se tē), in Teutonic mythology, one of the sons of Odin, probably a personification of justice.

Fortuna (fôr tū'n*a*), the Roman goddess of fortune in Roman mythology and (under the name Fors Fortuna) of chance.

Fountain of Youth, in medieval legend a magic fountain in Asia in which Alexander the Great and his army bathed and were suddenly restored to youth and strength. The Indians of the West Indies believed there was such a fountain on an island named Bimini. While he was seeking this island, Ponce de Leon discovered Florida in 1513.

Frey (frā) or **Freyr** (frār), the Norse god of fertility, crops and peace. He was one of the Vanir and brother of Freya. His marriage with Gerth (or Gerda), the frozen earth, symbolized the coming of spring.

Freya (frā'a) or **Freyja** (frā'ya), the beautiful Norse goddess of love and night; often called the Venus of the North. She was one of the Vanir, sister of Frey. She was forever being promised to one giant or another in exchange for some favor. In Wagner's opera, *The Rhinegold,* Alberich's cursed magic ring was offered to the giants as a substitute for Freya.

Friar Rush (frī'ẽr rush), in German folklore, the devil in friars' garb, who entered a monastery to seduce the monks.

Friar Tuck (frī'ẽr tuk), the fat outlaw friar who was Robin Hood's confessor. Scott's *Ivanhoe* presents him as the jovial, fighting friar.

Frigga (frig'ga), wife of Odin, queen of the heavens and goddess of marriage. With Odin she ruled heaven and earth. She was often confused with the Norse goddess Freya. Friday is Frigga's day.

Furies (fū'rēz). See *Erinyes; Eumenides.*

Gabriel (gā'bri el), in Jewish and Christian legend, one of the seven archangels. He is the announcer of God's messages to men. In Milton's *Paradise Lost* he is "chief of the angelic guards."

Gaea (jē'a) or **Ge** (jē), the earth goddess, wife of Uranus and mother of the Titans; identified with the Roman Tellus.

Galahad (gal'a had), the chaste and perfect knight who achieved the quest of the Holy Grail. He was the son of Sir Lancelot and Elaine, the daughter of Pelles.

Galatea (gal a tē'a), in Greek mythology, (1) sea nymph beloved by Polyphemus, the Cyclops. She herself loved Acis, a shepherd boy, whom the jealous giant crushed under a rock. Acis was transformed into a river, which gushed from beneath the rock. (2) The name of the beautiful statue carved by Pygmalion, with which he fell in love. His ardor and prayers brought her to life.

Ganelon (gà n lôn'), in the Charlemagne romances, the count of Mayence, the sly and treacherous knight who plotted against all the others and brought about the defeat of the rearguard in the pass of Roncevaux.

Ganymede (gan'i mēd), a Phrygian shepherd boy, so beautiful that Zeus sent an eagle to bring him to Mt. Olympus to become cup-bearer to the gods.

Gareth (gar'eth), a knight of the Round Table, nephew of King Arthur and brother of Gawain.

Garm (gärm), in Norse mythology, the watchdog of Hel.

Gawain (gä'win), a knight of the Round Table, nephew of King Arthur. He went to Rome (later versions say to Brittany) in pursuit of Sir Lancelot with Arthur and was killed immediately upon their return to Britain to recover the kingdom from Modred. Gawain, the perfect knight, brave, courteous and pure, was hero of the 14th-century poem, *Gawain and the Green Knight.*

Gemini (jem'i nī). The twins; see *Castor and Pollux*.

genius (jēn'yus), in ancient Roman belief, the guardian spirit of a person, family, nation or place. Each person at birth was believed to be attended by a spirit that presided over his character and destiny. In Eastern religions two spirits were believed to be at war for a man's soul. Everyone was accompanied by a good and evil genius, which were responsible for his good and evil thoughts, deeds and fortunes. The later guardian angel idea is a variant of the same belief. The plural of genius in this sense is genii.

Geryon (jē'ri on), in Greek mythology, a three-headed, three-bodied monster, possessor of many oxen. Hercules killed him and stole away the oxen.

ghost (gōst), in folk belief since the beginning of time, a spirit or demon, an apparition, a specter. A ghost is usually believed to be the disembodied spirit of a dead person, inhabiting an unseen world but able to appear to certain people or at certain times in bodily semblance. The shades of clas-

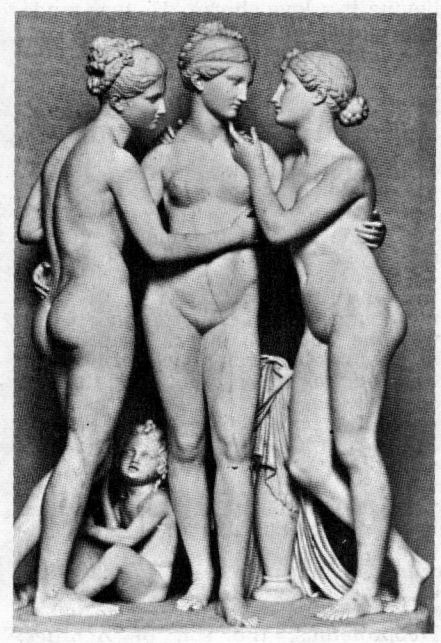

THE THREE GRACES, Alglaia, Euphrosyne, and Thalia. An example of Greek sculpture.

sical mythology are identical with ghosts. Ghostlore is the same the world over. Ghosts guard treasure or they haunt their former neighborhoods in penance for a crime. Sometimes their survivors by a favor can give them peace. A poor ghost will wander on a road for centuries until some fearless and merciful passer-by says "God bless you." But it is dangerous to speak to them or answer them, still more dangerous to touch them. They can pass through material barriers at will, and often are seen by animals when they are invisible to the human eye. Dogs howl or cower when they pass. At cockcrow they must vanish and return to their unseen world.

ghoul (gōol), in Eastern folklore an evil spirit of revolting and terrifying habits. It is believed to open graves and feed on corpses.

giants (jī'ants), in Greek and Roman, Teutonic and Celtic folklore, monstrous, manlike beings of superhuman strength and powers, but ungodlike characteristics. They preceded the gods, who overthrew them. The Greek mythological giants were the sons of Gaea (earth) and Uranus (heaven) or of Gaea and Tartarus (hell).

The giants warred against the Olympian gods and were conquered and confined. Briareus, the hundred-handed, Enceladus, who covered nine acres lying down, and the fire-breathing Typhon were all buried alive under Mt. Aetna. The giants of Teutonic mythology were the Gotunns who fought against the gods on the Judgment Day. In Celtic mythology, the gods vanquished the Fomors or sea giants.

Glaucus (glô'kus), a Greek fisherman who was changed to a sea-god by a magic herb and fell in love with the water-nymph Scylla. To punish Glaucus for his fidelity to the indifferent Scylla, Circe transformed her into the fearful monster who devoured mariners.

Gleipnir (glāp'nir), in Norse mythology the magic chain made by the dwarfs, which held Fenrir until the Judgment Day. The chain was made of the sound of a cat's footstep, the beards of women, stone roots, the breath of fish and bird spit. It looked like a silken string, but it held the monster until the appointed time.

gnome (nōm), a fabulous, diminutive being supposed to dwell within the earth and guard mines and quarries. Late Germanic folklore has confused gnomes with dwarfs and elves.

goblin (gob'lin), an ugly, grotesque little spirit, evil or mischievous.

Godiva (gō dī'va), in English legend, the wife of Leofric, Earl of Mercia in the 11th century. When Leofric put a heavy tax on the townspeople, Godiva pleaded with him to lighten it. He laughed and promised to do so if she would ride naked through the streets at noon. Immediately she sent word through the town of the condition on which the people would be freed of their hard burden. She told the people to stay at home and close their shutters. With grateful hearts the people did so, all except one ungallant fellow, henceforth called Peeping Tom, who was struck blind. Leofric also kept his promise.

Golden Age, in classical mythology the first era of the world when truth and innocence and ideal happiness prevailed. There was no law, nor need for any; there were no weapons, no wars. It occurred during the reign of Saturn, the oldest Italian god of agriculture and civilization.

Golden Fleece, the fleece of the winged ram on which Phrixos escaped from Thebes to Colchis. In the grove of Ares on the shores of Colchis Phrixos hung the Golden Fleece. It was claimed by King Aeetes and guarded by a dragon. Jason came seeking it and with the help of Medea's enchantments secured it and escaped.

Gordian knot (gôr'di an not), a knot tied by Gordius, King of Phrygia, so intricate and complicated that no one could untie it. An oracle prophesied that whoever should master it would rule all Asia. Alexander the Great cut it with one stroke of his sword. To "cut the Gordian knot" means to solve any problem with bold, unconventional action.

Gorgons (gôr'gunz), in Greek mythology, three snaky-haired sisters, horrible monsters with brazen, scaly bodies and long tusks. One look at them would turn the beholder to stone. Of the three, Medusa, the most famous, was slain by Perseus.

Graces (grās'ez), three beautiful daughters of Zeus, called *Charites* in Greek and *Gratiae* in Latin. They were Aglaia (Brilliance), Euphrosyne (Joy) and Thalia (Bloom). They accompanied the Muses and often Aphrodite, Eros or Dionysus.

Grail. See *Holy Grail*.

Grendel (gren'del), in the Old English epic poem *Beowulf*, the man-eating monster from whom Beowulf delivered the Danes.

griffin (grif'in), a fabulous monster with a lion's body, and wings and head of an eagle, believed by the Greeks to guard the gold of Scythia.

Gudrun (good'rōōn), in the *Volsunga Saga,* sister of Gunnar. She turned the love of Sigurd from Brynhild to herself by a magic drink. After his death she was married to Atli.

Guinevere (gwin'e vēr), in Arthurian legend, the wife of King Arthur, beloved by Lancelot. After the love of Guinevere and Lancelot was betrayed to the king, Guinevere entered a nunnery. William Morris's "Defense of Guenevere" and Tennyson's poem "Guinevere" in his *Idylls of the King* treat the old story.

Gunnar (gōōn'när), in the *Volsunga Saga* the king of the Niblungs to whom Sigurd married Brynhild. Gunnar was the brother of Gudrun.

Gunther (goon'tēr), in the *Nibelungenlied* a prince of Burgundy for whom Siegfried won Brunhild as wife. Gunther was the brother of Kriemhild.

Hades (hā'dēz), in Greek mythology: (1) The God of the lower world, in later myth called Pluto; (2) the dim and gloomy lower world, abode of the dead. It was surrounded by four rivers: the Styx, over which Charon ferried the shades of those duly buried; the Acheron or river of woe; Phlegethon, the river of fire; Cocytus, the stream of lamentation; and, in later myth, Lethe, the waters of forgetfulness. Cerberus guarded the entrance. Tartarus was the section in which the wicked suffered torment. The land of the blessed where Aeneas meets the dead heros of Troy in the sixth book of the Aeneid is a part of the underworld.

Hagen (hä'gen) (1), in the *Nibelungenlied* Gunther's grim uncle who killed Siegfried; (2) in Wagner's *Ring of the Nibelungs* the son of Alberich, who killed Siegfried in an effort to obtain the magic ring of the Nibelungs.

Hallowe'en (hal ō ēn'), the evening of October 31. See *Allhallows*.

Harpies (här'pēz), in classical mythology three ugly, foul winged monsters with the faces of women and bodies of vultures. The word *Harpy* comes from a Greek word which means to snatch; the Harpies were believed to snatch the souls of the dead, plunder travelers of their goods and carry off or defile the food of offenders.

Hebe (hē′bē), in Greek mythology, a daughter of Zeus and Hera, and goddess of youth. She served as cupbearer to the gods until Hercules was received among them, when she was given to him in marriage and Ganymede succeeded to her office.

Hecate (hek′a tē), in Greek mythology goddess of the morn and night, of the earth and the underworld. She was represented in triple form with three heads, six arms and holding a torch. In later literature she was the goddess of magic and sorcery, presided over crossroads and was visible to dogs who howled at sight of her.

Hector (hek′tēr), in the *Iliad,* the son of King Priam and Hecuba of Troy, the bravest of the Trojan heroes in the Trojan War. He married Andromache. When Hector killed Patroclus, the friend of Achilles, Achilles arose from his tent, slew Hector and dragged his body at his chariot wheels three times around the walls of Troy and into the camp of the Greeks.

Hecuba (hek′ū ba), the wife of King Priam of Troy and mother of Hector, Paris and Cassandra. When Troy was taken, she fell to the lot of Odysseus and was taken to Greece. She figures in two plays by Euripides, *The Trojan Women* and *Hecuba.*

Heimdall (hām′däl), the watchman of the Norse gods who guarded the bridge Bifrost to keep the giants from getting into Asgard, the abode of the gods. He himself was one of the Vanir. His senses were so keen that he could hear the wool grow on a sheep's back; he could hear the grass grow; he could see a hundred leagues in any direction as well by night as by day. He and Loki killed each other at the end of the world.

Hel (hel) or **Hela** (hel′a), in North mythology, the goddess of the underworld or death. She was the daughter of Loki. Odin cast her into Niflheim to thwart her evil doings. Here she ruled over nine worlds, to which she allotted the dead. All those who died of sickness or old age were sent to her, but those who died in battle were sent to Valhalla.

Helen of Troy, the most beautiful of all women, the daughter of Zeus and Leda. She had many suitors whom she bound by oath to protect her and take up her cause at any time. She married Menelaus, King of Sparta, from whose side she was seduced by Paris. Paris won her with the help of Aphrodite who had promised him the fairest of all women for his wife. The pair fled to Troy together, whereupon Menelaus summoned the Greek heroes, Helen's old suitors, to make war on Troy and win Helen back. After the fall of Troy and the death of Paris, Helen returned to Sparta with Menelaus.

Helios (hē′li os), the Greek sun-god, later identified with Apollo. He was the father of Phaethon. Daily he drove his chariot drawn by four horses across the sky.

Helle. See *Argonauts.*

Hellen (hel′en), son of Deucalion and Pyrrha, mythical ancestor of the Hellenes or Greeks.

Hephaestus (hē fes′tus), in Greek mythology, the god of fire, master smith of the gods and patron of mortal metalworkers. He was the son of Zeus and Hera. For taking his mother's part in a quarrel Zeus hurled him out of Olympus; and forever after he limped having hurt his leg in the fall. In the *Iliad,* his wife is Charis; in the *Odyssey,* Aphrodite. His forges were believed to be under the volcanoes. He made Pandora, the first woman, and he fashioned the armor of Achilles. He was identified with the Roman Vulcan.

Hera (hē′ra), the sister and wife of Zeus and queen of the gods. She was the mother of Ares, Hebe and Hephaestus. She was the goddess of women and marriage and the protectress of wives. Story after story pictures her as a jealous wife working out her resentment on the other loves of Zeus and their children. She became identified with the Roman Juno.

Heracles (her′a klēz), the Greek form of Hercules.

Hercules (hûr′kū lēz), the most celebrated of the Greek heroes, of miraculous strength and prowess. He was the son of Zeus and Alcmene. Hera's jealousy was so great that she sent two huge serpents to destroy the baby, but he seized and crushed them

NEW YORK PUBLIC LIBRARY

THE ABDUCTION OF HELEN OF TROY

in his cradle. In obedience to an oracle he became the servant of Eurystheus, King of Argos, who imposed on him twelve almost impossible tasks, which he successfully performed. The Twelve Labors of Hercules are:

(1) He killed the terrible Nemean lion and brought its skin to Eurystheus.

(2) He killed the monstrous nine-headed Hydra which had been ravaging Argos.

(3) He cleaned the Augean stables in one day.

(4) He captured the swift golden-horned stag of Arcadia.

(5) He brought back the wild boar of Erymanthus to Eurystheus.

(6) He killed the terrible flesh-eating birds of Stymphalus.

(7) He captured the fierce bull of Crete.

(8) He took the mares of Diomedes which ate human flesh.

(9) He stole the girdle of Hippolyte, Queen of the Amazons.

(10) He killed the monster Geryon and stole his cattle.

(11) He secured some of the golden apples from the gardens of the Hesperides.

(12) He grabbed Cerberus, the watchdog of Hades, and dragged him into the upper world.

There are innumerable stories recounting the feats of Hercules. He married Deianira, in a fit of insanity killed his friend Iphitus and was bound as a slave to Omphale who set him to women's work. He died from the poison of the cloak of Nessus which Deianira sent him, believing it a love charm. He was made immortal, was forgiven by Hera and was married in heaven to Hebe.

Hercules, Pillars of, two headlands opposite each other at the Strait of Gibraltar, supposed to have been raised up by Hercules in his travels to find the cattle of Geryon. They were Calpe (Gibraltar, in Europe) and Abila (Sierra Bullones in Africa).

Hermes (hûr′mēz), the son of Zeus and Maia, messenger and herald of the gods. He conducted the dead to Hades. He was the god of science and invention and invented the lyre by fastening strings across a tortoise shell. He was the guardian of travelers, roads and commerce, was gifted with trickery and was the protector of thieves. He stole the cattle of Admetus from under the nose of Apollo and tricked away Aphrodite's girdle. He is represented wearing a winged cap and winged sandals and carrying the winged caduceus. He was identified by the Romans with their god Mercury.

Hermione (hûr mī′ō nē), the daughter of Menelaus and Helen, betrothed to Orestes. She was first married to Neoptolemus, the son of Achilles, whom Orestes killed to regain his bride.

Hero (hē′rō), a beautiful priestess of Aphrodite in the temple at Sestos on the European side of the Hellespont. She was dearly beloved by Leander, a youth on the opposite shore who used to swim across to her every night. One night in a storm he was drowned, and Hero in despair threw herself into the waters and perished also.

Hesperides (hes per′i dēz), the daughters of Hesperus, the Evening Star. They were beautiful nymphs appointed to guard the golden apples given by Gaea to Hera on her wedding day. The wonderful garden of the Hesperides beyond the sea was guarded by a dragon that never slept. To secure some of the golden apples was one of the Twelve Labors of Hercules. He succeeded with the help of Atlas, according to one story; by killing the dragon, according to another.

Hestia (hes'ti a), in Greek mythology, goddess of the hearth and home; identified with Vesta by the Romans.

Hippolyte (hi pol'i tē), Queen of the Amazons. To steal her girdle was one of the Twelve Labors of Hercules. He gave her in marriage to Theseus.

THE METROPOLITAN MUSEUM OF ART

SACRIFICE OF IPHIGENIA, a painting by Giovanni Francesco Romanelli, 1610–1662.

Hippolytus (hi pol'i tus), son of Theseus and Hippolyte. His stepmother, Phaedra, fell in love with him and hanged herself in shame and despair when he repulsed her. She had accused Hippolytus to Theseus of trying to seduce her. Hippolytus fled from his father's wrath to the shore, where his horses took fright at the sea monster sent by Zeus to destroy him. Hippolytus was dashed to death among the rocks. Euripides' *Hippolytus* is based on this version of the story.

Hippomenes (hi pom'e nēz), the youth who won Atalanta in the foot race.

hobgoblin (hob'gob lin), a mischievous imp; a name given to Puck or Robin Goodfellow.

Holger (hol'gēr). Danish national hero. See *Ogier*.

Holy Grail, the platter or cup used by Christ at the last supper, in which Joseph of Arimathea miraculously preserved the blood from the wounds of Christ. The word *grail* seems to be derived from *cratalis,* cuplike). Joseph brought it to Britain where it was guarded for generations. It fed or healed those who saw it, but vanished at the approach of an impure person. It disappeared when its keepers became sinful, and thereafter became the quest of many and many a knight. It could be found only by the chaste and perfect knight. Only Perceval, Bors and Galahad were worthy to achieve the quest. In late Arthurian legend Galahad became the one perfect and successful quester; and it is through Tennyson's *Idylls of the King,* following Malory's *Morte d'Arthur,* that we are familiar with Galahad in the leading role. In the older Grail cycle, however, two romances name Gawain as the quester and winner;

seven name Perceval; and only one, Galahad.

Long before there was a story of Christ's cup or platter, in many parts of the world there were legends and myths about the search for a talisman or charm that would bring health to a sick king and his people.

Horus (hō'rus), the Egyptian god of the sun and day, son of Osiris and Isis.

Humpty Dumpty (hum'ti dump'ti), the egg of the famous nursery rhyme and riddle. The name is applied to any person or thing that cannot be mended, once it is broken.

Hyacinthus (hī'a sin'thus), a beautiful youth whom Apollo and Zephyrus both loved. Hyacinthus loved Apollo. One day while they were playing at quoits together, Zephyrus, in jealousy, turned the quoit as it left Apollo's hand, so that it struck and killed Hyacinthus. Apollo caused a flower to grow from his blood and named it Hyacinth.

Hyades (hī'a dēz), seven nymphs, daughters of Atlas, who killed themselves by weeping for the death of their brother Hyas. Zeus raised them to a constellation in the heavens—a sign of rainy weather.

Hydra (hī'dra), in Greek mythology, the nine-headed monster slain by Hercules as one of his Twelve Labors. Every time a head was cut off two more grew in its place. With the help of Iolaus, Hercules burnt the necks with a torch as soon as the heads were off, and buried the ninth, the immortal head, under a rock.

Hymen (hī'men), the Greek god of marriage.

Hyperion (hī pēr'i on), a Titan, father of Helios the sun, Eos the dawn, and Selene the moon. In late myth the name was given to Apollo—so Hyperion is a proverb of manly beauty.

Hypermnestra (hī pērm nes' tra), the only one of the fifty Danaides who disobeyed her father's command to kill her husband.

Iapetus (i ap'ē tus), one of the Titans, father of Prometheus and Atlas and grandfather of Deucalion, and thus the forefather of humanity. He may be the same as Japhet, son of Noah, ancestor of western nations.

Icarus (īk'a rus), the son of Daedalus.

ichor (ī'kôr), in classical mythology the fluid that ran through the veins of the gods instead of blood.

Ida, Mt. (ī'da), a celebrated mountain in N. W. Asia Minor, overlooking ancient Troy, from whose top the gods watched the Trojan War. From the slopes of Mt. Ida the eagle stole Ganymede; and there to Paris, tending his flocks, came the three goddesses, Hera, Athena and Aphrodite, for his judgment on their beauty. There was another Mt. Ida in Crete where the infant Zeus was concealed and brought up.

Idomeneus (ī dom'e nūs), a king of Crete who fought with the Greeks against Troy. While he was returning home, his ship was overtaken by a great storm, and Idomeneus vowed, if he was delivered, to sacrifice to Poseidon the first object he saw on landing. This was his own son, but Idomeneus kept his vow. He was banished from Crete by his subjects for this cruel act.

Igdrasil. See *Yggdrasil*.

Igraine (ē grān'), the mother of King Arthur.

Ilium (il'i um), the Greek name for the city of Troy.

Indra (in'dra), the good and greatest god of Vedic mythology, god of the air, giver of rains, enemy of the powers of evil. In later Hinduism he became subordinate to Brahma, Vishnu and Siva.

Io (ī'ō), a maiden beloved by Zeus, whom he changed into a cow to conceal her from the jealous Hera. Hermes killed the monster Argus, whom Hera set to watch her rival. Thereafter Hera sent a gadfly to torment Io. It drove her far and wide over the face of the earth. When she reached the banks of the Nile, she was restored to her human shape.

Iphigenia (if i jē nī'a), in Greek legend, a daughter of Agamemnon and Clytemnestra. Her father offered her as a sacrifice to Artemis at Aulis to procure favorable winds on the voyage to Troy. But Artemis pitied her, snatched her away from the knife and the people beheld a goat in her place. Artemis carried her to Tauris and made her a priestess in her temple. Iphigenia was required to sacrifice all strangers who came to Tauris. She was about to sacrifice her own brother Orestes and his companion Pylades, when she recognized them. The three escaped together, stealing away the statue of the goddess with them. Aeschylus used her story in his great Agamemnon trilogy. She is the subject of Euripides' *Iphigenia in Tauris.* Racine and Goethe also based dramas on her story.

Iris (ī'ris), the goddess of the rainbow, on which she traveled back and forth from heaven to earth as the messenger of Zeus and Hera.

Iron Age, in classical mythology, the last age of the world, following the Bronze Age. Iron was discovered; weapons were made; gold was coveted; violence and bloodshed followed. Truth and honor gave way to fraud and crime. Selfishness and love of gain completed the ruin of the world and the gods fled.

Iseult (ī sōolt') or **Isolde** (i sōld'; in German, ē zol' da), the king of Ireland's daughter, wife of King Mark of Cornwall and the true love of Tristram. She cured Tristram of his wounds in Ireland, and he so praised her beauty to King Mark on his return, that Mark sent him back to ask for the hand of Iseult on his behalf. On the ship returning to Cornwall the pair unwittingly drank of a magic love potion which bound them in love forever. Iseult was married to Mark, but nothing could break her love for Tristram. In time the lovers were discovered to the king, and Tristram was stabbed by King Mark. Another version says that Tristram left the court and went to Brittany where he married Iseult of the White Hands. When he lay dying of incurable wounds, he sent for Iseult of Ireland to come and heal him. The ship that was to bring her was to hoist white sails if Iseult were on board. When it appeared with white sails flying, Iseult of the White Hands, jealous and brokenhearted, told him the sails were black. Tristram died in grief and Iseult of Ireland died upon his breast. In Wagner's opera, *Tristan and Isolde,* there is no second Isolde.

Ishtar (ish'tär), the Babylonian goddess of love and fruitfulness; the earth-mother. See *Astarte.*

Isis (ī'sis), the great Egyptian nature-goddess and goddess of motherhood, wife and sister of Osiris. She was represented with the head of a cow.

Ithunn (ē'thōōn), in Teutonic mythology, the wife of Bragi. She kept in a box the apples of youth which the gods tasted whenever they felt old age creeping on.

Ithaca (ith'a ka), the island kingdom of Odysseus and Penelope in the Ionian Sea.

Ixion (iks ī'on), in Greek mythology, a king of the Lapithae in Thessaly. He refused to pay his father-in-law the stipulated wedding price, whereupon the old man stole some of Ixion's horses. Ixion invited him to feast and caused him to fall into a burning pit. For this deed his own people avoided him and denied him all human companionship. Zeus pitied him and took him to heaven, where he fell in love with Hera and bragged of seducing her. For this ingratitude Zeus consigned him to Tartarus to be bound to a wheel forever revolving.

Jack and Jill, two children of a famous old nursery rhyme. The rhyme is perhaps based on the ancient Norse myth of two children who were compelled by their father to draw and carry water all day. The moon pitied and rescued them, and the marks on the moon were believed to represent the two children with their pail.

Jack and the Beanstalk, the title of a famous nursery tale based on a world myth. Jack and his mother were so poor that they had to sell their cow. Jack set out for market and sold the cow to a butcher for a handful of beans. His mother was so angry she threw the beans out the window. One of them took root and overnight grew into the sky. Jack promptly climbed the vine and came to a wide, strange country where a fairy sent him to the house of a giant. There by trickery he stole a red hen (that laid golden eggs) and bags of diamonds and gold. When the giant discovered him, Jack fled home down the beanstalk with the giant in chase. Jack reached the ground and quickly chopped down the vine. The giant fell and was killed, and Jack and his mother lived in plenty ever after. This story is known among the North American Indians and South African natives. The beanstalk is something like Yggdrasil, the old Teutonic world tree, which connected heaven and earth.

Jack the Giant Killer, the title and the hero of an old English nursery tale based on a British story first translated by Geoffrey of Monmouth. Jack was a farmer boy of Arthurian times. He killed the giant of Cornwall by tricking him into a deep pit. With the help of a cloak that made him invisible, boots of marvelous speed and a magic sword, he killed all the giants in the land.

Jamshid (jam shēd'), in Persian mythology the king of the peris. For boasting

that he was immortal he was condemned to take on human shape. He became a splendid and powerful king of Persia and reigned for 700 years. But again he grew arrogant and boastful, was doomed to wretched wanderings and was finally killed by the usurper of his throne. In Firdausi's *Shah Namah* Jamshid is a culture hero who taught mankind the arts of medicine, metalworking and navigation.

Janus (jā'nus), the early Italian god of doorways, gates and entrances and the patron of all beginnings. He may have been a king of ancient Latium whose stronghold was on the Janiculum (the door hill) across the Tiber from the Seven Hills of Rome. Janus is represented with two heads facing in opposite directions, evidently symbolizing the two faces of a door. In the Forum a double tower gate dedicated to him was never closed except in time of peace. He was supposed to stand there guarding the state in wartime and giving luck to the outgoing armies. The first hour of each day was sacred to him as the patron of all beginnings; so were the first day of each month and the first month of the year. January is named for him.

BETTMANN ARCHIVE

JASON, reaching for the lamb with the Golden Fleece. In the foreground, at Jason's feet, is the guardian never-sleeping dragon who was slain by the hero after being lulled with a preparation supplied by his wife Medea, in her efforts to aid Jason.

Jason (jā'sun), a prince of Iolcus in Thessaly, who recovered the Golden Fleece. The throne of Iolcus was usurped by Pelias, his uncle, who agreed to give it up to Jason if he would bring back the Golden Fleece from Colchis. This Jason did with the help of Medea, daughter of the king of Colchis. He married Medea, but later forsook her to marry Glauce

(or Creusa). Medea caused the death of her rival with a poisoned robe and murdered the children of Jason. Jason died of grief.

jinn (jin), plural of jinni.

jinni (ji nē'), in Arabian folklore a demon inhabiting wild and desolate places and representing the hostile elements. In Mohammedan literature jinn are supernatural beings, both good and evil, constituted of fire and able to assume all manner of shapes. They are subject to control by the possessor of a magic ring, lamp or other object.

Jocasta (jō kas'ta), the mother and wife of Oedipus.

John Henry, in American folklore, the famous Negro steel driver, buried in Big Ben Tunnel, West Virginia, with his 12-pound hammer in his hand. In some versions of the story the hammer weighed 40 pounds. John Henry was the most powerful and fastest of the Negro gang at work on the tunnel through the Alleghenies. So fast did he work that a boy had to stand by with a pail of cold water to keep his hammer cool. He was never seen without the hammer in his hand; he named it Lucy after his sweetheart. His boss bragged to a steam drill salesman that he needed no such modern contraption, because for power and speed one of his workmen could beat a steam drill any day. A bet was laid and John Henry rose to the boast. He picked his spot, beat the steam drill down through the rock and died with his hammer in his hand.

Johnny Appleseed, the popular name of John Chapman (1775–1847), American frontier hero, who wandered for 40 years through Ohio, Indiana and Illinois tending apple orchards he had previously planted and teaching frontier settlers how to start and cherish apple trees. In his youth he owned a nursery in western Pennsylvania where he sold or gave away apple tree saplings. He salvaged seeds from cider presses, dried and collected them by thousands in little bags which he gave away to the families of covered wagon trains traveling westward. He paddled down the Ohio with two canoe loads of these little bags, planting orchards in promising spots or giving seeds away to solitary settlers. He went as far as Marietta, Ohio, now the center of one of the finest apple regions in the United States. Johnny Appleseed has become one of the few great American culture heroes; and a wealth of story has grown up around this ragged, solitary roamer, bringing forth fruit in the wilderness: tales of amazing woodcraft, amazing physical endurance, immunity to snakebite, charming wild beasts and healing the sick in lonely places.

Jormungand (yôr'moon gänd), in Norse mythology, a huge sea serpent, the second child of Loki; also called the Midgard Serpent. Odin cast her into the ocean which surrounds the world. There she grew and grew until she encircled the whole earth with her tail in her mouth. She killed Thor and was killed by him at the end of the world.

Joseph of Arimathea (jō'sef, är i ma thē'a), the rich councilor who gave burial to the body of Christ. In British legend he came to Britain teaching

Christianity and founded the monastery at Glastonbury. He was believed to have brought the Holy Grail to Britain.

Jotunn (yŏ'toon), a giant of Norse mythology. Jotunnheim (yō' toon hām) was the abode of the giants on the edge of the world.

Jove (jōv), a variant of Jupiter, the principal god of Roman mythology.

Juggernaut (jug'ẽr nôt), in Hindu mythology, one of the names of Krishna, the eighth incarnation of Vishnu. The name means lord of the world. His idol is at Puri in Orissa, British India. At the time of the famous Juggernaut festival the image is placed in a huge, towering car and dragged in procession by thousands of pilgrims from the temple to what is known as his country house. The distance is only about a mile but the trip takes several days through the crowded streets. The reports that hundreds of devotees throw themselves under the car to be crushed to death are false. An occasional fanatic thus destroys himself, but self-destruction is contrary to the ideas of Vishnu worship.

Juno (jōō'nō), an ancient Italian pre-Roman goddess representing the female principle of life. As her cult developed, she became the savior of women in all their trials, goddess of marriage and childbirth and protectress of female slaves. In Roman mythology, Juno was the wife of Jupiter, goddess of the sky and queen of the gods. Like him she was the deity of the state. Later she became identified with the Greek Hera.

Jupiter (jōō'pi tẽr), the elemental sky god of ancient Italian and Roman mythology. His name apparently means sky father. Jove is a shorter form. He sent light and heat, rain and thunderbolts and was worshipped from the tops of hills. He was the husband of Juno and became the state deity of Rome. He was connected with oaths, treaties, duty and all matters of conscience. Later the Romans identified him with the Greek Zeus.

Kama (kä'ma), in Vedic mythology the desire of the mind or the creator who fulfils desire. In later Hinduism Kama is the god of love, like Cupid. He is represented as riding on a parrot, with bow and arrows, each arrow tipped with a flower.

Kay, Sir (kā), the boastful, ill-humored seneschal of King Arthur.

kelpie (kel'pi), in Scotch folklore a spirit of the water, said to haunt lakes and streams and especially fords and crossings. It may take on various shapes but usually appears in the shape of a horse. It is seen only by those about to drown; for it comes as a warning of death by water.

King Arthur. See *Arthur.*

King Cole or **Coel** (kōl), a legendary king of Britain of the 3rd century. He is mentioned in Geoffrey of Monmouth's *History of the Kings of Britain,* is the subject of John Masefield's poem *King Cole* and is the "merry old soul" of the nursery rhyme.

King Lear (lēr), a legendary king of Britain who undertook to divide his kingdom among his three daughters according to the measure of their love for him. He divided it between the two elder, for the youngest daughter Cordelia said she loved him no more than her duty in one version, no more than salt in another. She was turned off penniless and married the king of France. Lear was driven mad with grief by the neglect and heartlessness of his two elder daughters. But Cordelia re-entered England with her husband at the head of an army and restored the kingdom to Lear. Legend says that he ruled again for three years, and Cordelia after him for five, until the sons of her sisters took her throne and her life. Shakespeare's tragedy *King Lear* ends with the defeat of Cordelia's army.

King Log and King Stork, in Aesop's fable two kings sent to the frogs by Jupiter. When the frogs prayed for a king, Jupiter sent them King Log. They were impressed at first but lost respect for him when they found they could hop upon his back. When they complained to Jupiter of his inactivity, he sent them King Stork, who kept them hopping and devoured them.

Klingsor (kling'zōr), in the Grail legends the magician who set snares and seductions in the way of the questing knights. He was finally overcome by Parsifal.

Knecht Ruprecht (knecht rōō'precht), in German folklore a spirit overseer of children, who appears to them sometime before Christmas. He promises rewards to the good and threatens the bad with a whip. It is a German village custom for one villager to masquerade as Knecht Ruprecht on Christmas Eve and pass from house to house delivering the gifts previously conveyed to him in secret by the parents.

Knight of the Swan, in German legend Lohengrin; in French legend Helias, the grandfather of Godfrey de Bouillon. In Icelandic saga the knight of the swan was named Helis.

kobold (kō'bold), in German folklore a household spirit, often performing services and favors but of a mischievous disposition; and sometimes a gnomish underground spirit inhabiting caves or mines.

Kriemhild (krēm'hilt), in the *Nibelungenlied* a princess of Burgundy, the wife of Siegfried. The hoard of the Nibelungs was her marriage portion. After Siegfried was slain by Hagen, Kriemhild married Etzel, King of the Huns. She lured her brothers to Etzel's court and caused them to be slain to avenge the death of Siegfried. She killed Hagen with Siegfried's sword.

Krishna (krish'na), a Hindu god, the warrior incarnation of Vishnu. He was the brave, clever and invincible warrior who saved mankind from all tyrants. The *Bhagavad-Gita* is the Song of Bhagwan, The Blessed One, that is, Krishna. He cast out fear with the doctrine that Brahma (spirit) pervades all things and therefore men could not really die. Emerson summarized this teaching of Krishna in his short poem *Brahma.*

Kriss Kringle (kris kring'gl), the personification of the German spirit of Christmas; St. Nicholas or Santa Claus. The name derived from *Chriskindl,* meaning the little Christ child.

Kundry (koon'dri), in the Grail legends a beautiful enchantress who helped Klingsor seduce the questing knights. In Wagner's opera *Parsifal,* her spells were broken and she was finally redeemed by Parsifal.

labyrinth (lab'i rinth), in Greek mythology the great maze in Crete built by Daedalus for King Minos to confine the Minotaur.

Lachesis (lak'e sis), the second of the three Fates in Greek mythology, the one who determined the length of the thread of human life spun by Clotho.

Ladon (lā'don), in Greek mythology the dragon that guarded the golden apples in the garden of the Hesperides. He was killed by Hercules.

Lady of the Lake, the lady beloved by Merlin, the enchanter; also known as Vivian and Nimue. To get rid of the doting Merlin she shut him up forever in a bush by magic that he himself had taught her. She stole away the infant Lancelot, reared him in her fairy kingdom and later brought him to Arthur's court. In Malory's *Morte d' Arthur* she gave Arthur the sword Excalibur. Sometimes identified with Morgan le Fay, she was one of the three fairy queens on the ship that bore Arthur to Avalon.

Laertes (lā ûr'tēz), father of Odysseus.

Lancelot (làn'se lot) or **Lancelot of the Lake,** the most famous knight of the Round Table. Secretly he loved Guinevere, Arthur's queen, and she loved him. Lancelot went in disguise to tilt in a three-day tournament, was wounded, was carried to the castle of Astolat and was nursed by the fair maid Elaine, who fell in love with him and died for love of him. The guilty love between Lancelot and Guinevere was finally revealed to the king. Lancelot escaped with the queen to his own castle, where he was besieged by Arthur and Gawain. He gave up the queen to Arthur and fled to Brittany, where Arthur and Gawain pursued him. In the king's absence Modred endeavored to seize Arthur's throne and queen. Arthur hastened home to fight for his own, and in the last battle he and Modred killed each other. Lancelot came hurrying to Arthur's side to help his king. But he was too late, Arthur was dead. Guinevere entered a nunnery, and Lancelot went into a monastery. He lived penitent for six years and died shortly after the death of Guinevere. In Malory's *Morte d' Arthur* Lancelot was one of the knights who sought the Holy Grail. He was allowed to behold it but for his sins could not achieve the quest.

The story of Lancelot's love for Guinevere was developed only in late Arthurian romance, not before the 12th century. In the older version of the Lancelot story, Lancelot was the son of Ban de Benoic, who died of sorrow on being driven from his kingdom. His wife laid the infant Lancelot on the bank of a lake while she stooped to comfort the dying king. The Lady of the Lake snatched him away and brought him up among her maidens. At the age of 15 he returned to the mortal world to have many adventures. He won a three-day tournament, rescued a princess from the castle of the dead and married her, regained his father's throne and died an aged man.

Laocoön (lā ok'ō on), a priest of Apollo in Troy, who warned the Trojans not to accept the Wooden Horse from the Greeks. While he was offering a sacrifice to Poseidon, he had a vision of his two sons being attacked by two

THE METROPOLITAN MUSEUM OF ART

MEDEA. A marble sculpture, dated 1868, of Jason's first wife. Medea aided Jason in the capture of the Golden Fleece.

serpents from the sea. He rushed out to save them, but the serpents crushed him and his sons. The Trojans interpreted this as Athena's punishment to Laocoon for suspecting the Wooden Horse. Vergil tells the story in the *Aeneid*. It is the subject of a famous statuary group in the Vatican. In 1766 Lessing wrote an essay on art entitled *Laokoon*.

Laomedon (lā om'ē don), the king for whom the walls of Troy were built by Apollo and Poseidon. Laomedon refused to pay the two gods when the work was done. In vengeance they sent a sea monster to ravage the land. To appease the gods Laomedon chained his daughter Hesione to a rock for the monster to devour. Hercules offered to rescue the maiden and kill the monster for the price of six horses. But when the deed was accomplished, Laomedon refused to give him the horses, and Hercules killed Laomedon.

Lapithæ (lap'i thē), a people of Thessaly, best known for their battle with the centaurs and the story of their ill-fated king, Ixion.

lares (lā'rēz), in Roman religion originally tutelary spirits presiding over the fields and homes, later regarded as ancestral spirits. The *lar familiaris* was the guardian of the family; *lares compitales* presided over crossroads; *lares praestites* were the guardian spirits of the city.

Latinus (la tī'nus), the legendary king of ancient Latium, ancestor of the Latins. In Vergil's *Aeneid* he was the king of Latium who welcomed Aeneas at the mouth of the river Tiber, and father of the Lavinia whom Aeneas married.

Launcelot. See *Lancelot*.

Leander (lē an'dĕr), see *Hero*.

Leda (lē'da), the mother of Castor and Pollux and Helen of Troy. Zeus saw her bathing in a river and took the shape of a swan in order to make love to her.

Lemnos (lem'nos), an island in the Aegean Sea, sacred to Hephaestos, who was believed to have landed there when Zeus hurled him out of Olympus. At one time all the women on the island killed all the men. The Argonauts found only women inhabiting the island when they touched them.

leprechaun (lep'rē *chon*), in Irish folklore a fairy shoemaker. Human beings see him at times in the shape of an old man. It is believed that when he is caught he will lead one to hidden treasure.

Lethe (lē'thē), one of the rivers of Hades. To drink of its waters brought forgetfulness of the past to the souls of the dead. The word means oblivion.

Leto (lē'tō), the mother of Apollo and Artemis. Hesiod says she was Zeus's first wife. Later myth counts her as one of his many loves. Hera was so jealous of her that she sent a python to torment her. Zeus gave her the floating island of Delos and anchored it to the bottom of the sea so that she might live in peace; and here Apollo and Artemis were born. The Roman name for Leto is Latona.

Lilith (lil'ith), in Jewish folklore a female demon of the night; a vampire. She was especially malignant towards children. In medieval Rabbinical literature Lilith was Adam's first wife, displaced by Eve on whom she worked vengeance by threatening her children. Her spirit became more and more evil. In Goethe's *Faust* Lilith figures as a witch in the Walpurgis Night scene.

Lir or **Ler** (lēr), in Celtic mythology the god of the sea, one of the Tuatha de Danann. The name is spelled Llyr in the Welsh, Cornish and Breton versions. In British legend Lir was a king of Britain, the father of Bran and the mythical founder of Leicester, Lircestre. Shakespeare's *King Lear* is based on this legend.

Little John, one of the devoted companions of Robin Hood, second only to him in skill with the bow and arrow. He was dubbed Little John for his great height. He is a character in Scott's *Ivanhoe*.

Little Red Riding Hood, in European folklore a little girl who went to visit her grandmother and was eaten by the wolf who had crept into the grandmother's bed. In the German version the child escaped. The story is known in English translations from the French Charles Perrault and the German of the Grimm brothers.

Llyr. See *Lir*.

Lohengrin (lō'en grin), a knight of the Grail, son of Parsifal, who was called to the aid of Elsa, princess of Brabant. He was borne from the castle of the Grail to Antwerp in a boat drawn

by a swan. He defeated Count Telramund, Elsa's accuser, and married Elsa on condition that she never ask his name. Years later she broke the promise, and he had to tell it. The swan boat appeared again on the Rhine, and Lohengrin departed, leaving behind him his sword, horn and ring. This is the story followed by Wagner in his opera, *Lohengrin*. In very old French legend the same story is built around the knight Helias, who was one of seven children turned into swans by a cruel grandmother.

Loki (lō'kē), in Norse mythology one of the Aesir, the god of evil and fire, the mischief-maker. Hel, Jormungand and Fenrir were his offspring. He tricked the blind god Hoder into killing Balder and refused to weep to ensure Balder's release from Hel, goddess of death.

Lorelei (lō're lī), in German legend a beautiful siren whose song lured boatmen to their death. She haunted a certain rock in the Rhine, which today bears her name.

Lot (lot), the husband of Arthur's sister Morgan. He was king of Orkney and Lothian and father of Gareth and Gawain. Geoffrey of Monmouth called him king of Norway.

Lotophagi (lō tof'a jī), the Lotus Eaters, in the *Odyssey* a race of people visited by Odysseus in his wanderings. They ate only the fruit of the lotus, which caused forgetfulness of home and a state of dazed langor and contentment. Those of Odysseus' crew who tasted the lotus while they were ashore had to be bound and dragged home. Tennyson's poem *The Lotus-Eaters* describes the experience.

Lucifer (lū'si fĕr), in Semitic mythology the morning star, which fell from heaven. The name was given to Satan, the fallen archangel. In Milton's *Paradise Lost* Lucifer is the fallen rebel. Lucifer is a Latin word meaning light-bearer or morning star; it is used in Isaiah 14:12 of the "son of the morning . . . fallen from heaven."

Lug or **Lugh** (loo*ch*), in Celtic mythology god of the sun and light and fires, one of the Tuatha de Danann. He was the father of Cuchulain.

Luna (lū'na), the ancient Italian moon-goddess, later merged with the Diana of Roman mythology.

Maia (mā'ya), one of the Pleiades, the seven daughters of Atlas. She was the mother of Hermes by Zeus. A Roman goddess Maia, wife of Vulcan, gave her name to the month of May.

Maid Marian, the lady of English folk May Day games and morris dances in which Robin Hood also figures. The late Robin Hood ballads and legends adopted her as his companion and sweetheart in Sherwood Forest. She was identified with Matilda Fitzwater.

Mammon (mam'un), in the New Testament the personification of wealth and greed; from an Aramaic word meaning wealth.

Manannan (mon'an an), the Celtic sea-god, son of Lir, for whom the Isle of Man was named; sometimes called Manawyddon.

manes (mā'nēz), in Roman mythology the gods of the lower world and the shades of the dead. Gods and shades alike were considered divine. Ancestral or parental spirits were worshiped with offerings of garlands, food and wine.

manito (man′i tō) or **manitou** (man′i-tōō), among the Algonquian Indians of North America the great pervading spirit and force of all nature, having both good and evil attributes.

Manu (ma′nōō), in Hindu mythology the ancestor of mankind. During the world flood he was saved by Vishnu in his incarnation as the fish Matsya.

Mark (märk), in Arthurian legend the king of Cornwall, Tristram's uncle and the husband of Iseult.

Mars (märz) in Roman mythology the god of war. He became identified with the Greek Ares. March is his month.

May Day, the first day of May, celebrated with festival and merrymaking in England and all over Europe since medieval times: since 1899 observed as an international Labor Day. The medieval English May Day was observed by all classes from humblest villager to the royal court. Everyone was up before the sun to go "a-maying" or "to bring in the May." They went out to the forests and returned laden with flowers and branches of trees. One tall, straight tree was brought in, stripped of its branches, painted, decorated with streamers and flowers and set up as the center of all the games, plays and dancing for the rest of the day. Most of the May Day dramas were of a merry, comic nature. The most famous of the English May Day plays presented the characters of the Robin Hood ballads, centering around Maid Marian and Robin Hood. Maypoles were forbidden by the English Puritans as heathenish in 1644; but they came into their own again with the Restoration.

The emotional basis of May Day in all countries is the high spirit of spring, joy in the renewal of life and the creative urge in the plant and animal world. The old Roman Floralia (April 28–May 3), a festival in honor of Flora, a fertility goddess, was celebrated in colorful costume with dances and plays. And the Floralia probably goes back to a still more ancient festival of the Latin goddess Maia, who was worshiped as a source of life.

Medea (mē dē′a), a famous enchantress, daughter of the king of Colchis. She fell in love with Jason when he came seeking the Golden Fleece and used her magic to help him secure it. She made sure their escape to Greece by casting the body of her brother in the way of her pursuing father. She restored Jason's father to youth and health but refused to do the same for Pelias, the usurping uncle, after she had induced his daughters to boil his body in a caldron. For this she and Jason were forced to flee to Corinth, where they lived happily for a number of years until Jason deserted her and married Creusa (or Glauce). Medea murdered the children of Jason and killed her rival with a poisoned robe. Euripides wrote a tragedy centered on Medea.

Medusa (mē dū′sa), in Greek mythology the most famous of the three Gorgons. She was beheaded by Perseus, who escaped being turned to stone by looking at her in the mirror of a shield given to him by Athena. Perseus presented her head to Athena when he returned the shield.

Meleager (mel ē ā′jěr), in Greek mythology the son of Oeneus, king of Aetolia in Calydonia. When he was born, the Fates declared he would live until the brand on the hearth was burned away. His mother quickly snatched it, put out the fire and hid the brand. Meleager lived to join the Argonauts and kill the Calydonian boar. He presented its head to Atalanta because she was the first to wound it. This infuriated his two uncles, who wanted the prize for themselves, and in the quarrel which followed Meleager killed them both. When Meleager's mother was told that her son had killed her two brothers, in a flash of resentment she hurled the fateful brand into the fire. As it burned, Meleager died.

Melpomene (mel pom′e nē), the Greek tragic Muse.

Melusina (mel ū sē′na), in French folklore and romance the fairy guardian of the house of Lusignan. She was the daughter of the fairy Pressina. For wrongs done her mother she shut her father up in a mountain. For this he condemned her to take on the shape of a fish (or serpent) from the waist down every Saturday. She could be freed from this enchantment only by marrying a man who would promise never to see her on Saturdays. Count Raymond of Poitiers loved her dearly and willingly made the promise. She brought him wealth and power and built him the castle of Lusignan. But in time his jealousy and curiosity overcame his faith, and he spied on her. He saw his beautiful wife take on her mermaid form and she was doomed to leave him, returning only as a wailing ghost to warn descendants of the family of death or disaster.

Memnon (mem′non), a king of the Ethiopians, nephew of Priam of Troy. He was killed by Achilles in the Trojan War, and the grief of his mother Eos moved Zeus to grant him immortality.

Menelaus (men e lā′us), a king of Sparta, brother of Agamemnon and husband of Helen of Troy.

Mentor (men′tôr), the faithful friend and counselor to whom Odysseus entrusted his household and the education of his son Telemachus when he left for the Trojan War.

Mephistopheles (mef i stof′e lēz), in medieval European demonology one of the seven lords of hell, a development of an ancient Semitic conception of evil, coming through the Chaldeans, Babylonians and Jews. He was the devil to whom Faust sold his soul in exchange for aid and power. In the numerous Faust legends Mephistopheles was a combination of the Christian devil, the kobolds of German folklore and the most ancient powers of darkness and destruction.

Mercury (mûr′kū ri), the ancient Italian god of commerce; identified by the Romans with the Greek Hermes about 495 B.C.

Merlin (mûr′lin), the great magician and seer who aided Arthur in many marvelous ways. He put sleep on the huge knight in the pass who nearly killed Arthur. At one time when Arthur was opposed by eleven kings and one duke, Merlin caused all the tents of the enemies to fall down, and in the panic which followed Arthur conquered his foes. By his help too, Arthur won Guinevere for wife. Merlin made the Round Table and led Arthur to the sword that he took from the marvelous hand and arm that rose out of the lake.

Merlin fell fatally in love with Vivian, the fairy Lady of the Lake, who beguiled him into teaching her the charms and spells whereby she "detained him forever more" in a tower that he himself could not unmake. Thus Merlin was lost to the world forever. Arthur sent knights to search for him, but he was never found. Only Gawain heard his voice coming from a smoke in the forest, charging him to tell Arthur the time had come for the quest of the Holy Grail.

The more ancient Merlin of the Britains was a boy of no mortal father, who revealed to Vortigern the reason why the foundations of his citadel fell down time after time as soon as they reached a certain stage. It was built over a den of dragons, Merlin said, and their perpetual fighting shook the earth. Vortigern ordered workmen to dig and see. Two huge dragons were disclosed, one pure white, one red. The white one killed the red and then disappeared. From this Merlin prophesied that Vortigern would be slain by his enemies. This happened, and Uther Pendragon, the father of Arthur, took the throne. Merlin remained his counselor and Arthur's after him until he was lost to the world by Vivian's spell.

DANISH NATIONAL TRAVEL OFFICE

THE LITTLE MERMAID, a memorial to the story by Hans Christian Andersen, stands in the busy harbor of Copenhagen.

mermaid (mûr′mād), in Teutonic folklore and that of the British Isles a being of the sea or lakes with the body of a beautiful woman but the tail, fins and scales of a fish below the waist. Fairy tales are full of these wonderful beings. They had the power of prophesy and were able to grant temporary superhuman gifts to mortals. They fell in love with human beings sometimes and either came to live on earth in human form until some spell was broken or lured their loves to dwell with them in a realm below the waves. Stories of mermaids and mermen abound in the folklore of nearly all seaboard peoples; and the nereids or sea nymphs, the tritons and sirens of classical mythology personified the same idea. Hans Christian Andersen's lovely story *The Little Mermaid* tells how a mermaid in love with a prince longed for and strove to win a human soul. Matthew Arnold's poem *The Forsaken Merman* pictures the loneliness of a merman and his children whose human mother left them to return to human ways.

Midas (mī'das), the King of Phrygia to whom Dionysus granted that all he touched would turn to gold. He soon tired of the gift when he discovered that the bread he would eat and the wine he would drink turned to hard and solid gold as soon as he touched it. In fear he prayed for the golden touch to be removed from him; and Dionysus bade him wash in the river Pactolus. He did so and was cured, but the sands of the river were turned to gold.

When Midas said he preferred Pan's music to Apollo's, Apollo punished him by giving him ass's ears. Midas kept them covered so that no one but his barber knew the shameful secret. The barber, unable to keep it to himself, dug a little hole in the ground and whispered into it, "King Midas has ass's ears." Reeds grew in that place and forever after whispered when the wind blew, "King Midas has ass's ears."

Midgard (mid'gärd), in Norse mythology the middle earth, halfway between heaven and hell, the abode of mankind. It was surrounded by the great ocean, where lived Jormungand, the Midgard Serpent, who encircled the world.

Mimir (mē'mēr), in Norse mythology the giant who lived beside the root of the world tree, Yggdrasil. Here he drank from the spring which flowed from the root of the tree. And the waters gave him wisdom and all knowledge of the past and the future.

Minerva (mi nûr'va), an old Italian goddess of wisdom, patroness of all the handcrafts and arts. She was the daughter of Jupiter and one of the triad, with him and Juno, worshiped as guardians of the state. She became identified with Greek Athena.

Minos (mī'nos), the son of Zeus and Europa and king of Crete. He was the founder of the Cretan laws and so great was his justice that after death he was made a judge in Hades. Another story makes him the tyrant who exacted yearly tribute from the Athenians of seven youths and seven maidens to feed the monster Minotaur. Minos kept the Minotaur in the labyrinth built for him by Daedalus. He shut Daedalus up in the labyrinth for some offense and when he escaped pursued him to Sicily. There Minos was killed by the daughter of King Cocalus, who poured boiling water in his bath.

Minotaur (min'ō tôr), a monster of Crete, half human, half bull. It was the son of Pasiphae (wife of King Minos) and a white bull which Poseidon had sent to Minos. The bull was so beautiful that Minos spared its life instead of sacrificing it to the god. To imprison this monster, Daedalus built the labyrinth; to feed it, Minos demanded a yearly tribute of Athenian youths and maidens. It was finally killed by Theseus with the help of Ariadne.

Mithras (mith'ras), the Persian god of light who fought on the side of truth

THE METROPOLITAN MUSEUM OF ART

MIDAS BATHING IN THE RIVER PACTOLUS
to rid himself of the golden touch. From a painting by Nicolas Poussin, 1594–1665.

in the eternal struggle between the powers of good and evil, light and darkness.

Mnemosyne (ne mos'i nē), one of the Titans, the goddess of memory. She was the mother of the nine Muses by Zeus.

Modred (mō'dred), a knight of the Round Table, nephew of King Arthur. He seized the kingdom and the queen in Arthur's absence. Modred was killed by Arthur but he gave the king his mortal wound.

Moira (moi'ra), in Greek mythology the fate of a person; later, any one of the three Fates. The plural is Moirai (moi'rī); in Latin, Parcae.

Moloch (mō'lok), an ancient Semitic god to whom living children were sacrificed. In Milton's *Paradise Lost*, Moloch was one of the fallen angels.

Momus (mō'mus), in Greek mythology the personification of mockery and ridicule. He jeered at gods and men alike.

Morgan le Fay (môr'gān lē fā), the fairy (fay means fairy) sister of King Arthur and wife of King Uriens of Gore, whom she tried to kill in his sleep. She schemed for the death of Arthur also, but he killed the traitor who came to do her bidding. She was one of the three queens in the fairy boat which bore the wounded Arthur

away to Avalon. In the Charlemagne legends she was the enchantress Morgana who lived in a lake.

Morpheus (môr' fē us), god of dreams. He is often depicted as a chubby child wearing wings.

Mouse Tower, a strong toll tower on the river Rhine known as the *Mauseturm.* During the great famine in 970 A.D. Hatto, archbishop of Mainz, is said to have shut up the poor in a barn and burnt them to save grain for the rich. Suddenly set upon by hordes of mice he fled across the Rhine and took refuge in the big toll tower. But the mice pursued him by thousands, swam the river and ate him alive in the tower.

Muse (mūz), any one of the nine daughters of Zeus and Mnemosyne, goddesses of the arts and sciences. They were: Clio (history), Euterpe (music), Thalia (comedy and pastoral poetry), Melpomene (tragedy), Terpsichore (dancing and choruses), Erato (lyric and love poetry), Polyhymnia (sacred song), Urania (astronomy) and Calliope (epic poetry).

Myrmidons (mûr'mi donz), soldiers from Thessaly who fought under Achilles in the Trojan War. When a plague wiped out all the inhabitants of the island Aegina, the king prayed Zeus to repeople his kingdom with citizens as numerous as the ants that marched about their business in a nearby oak. The prayer was granted and all the ants rose up to human form. The old king named them Myrmidons, the Greek word meaning ants.

naiads (nā'adz), in Greek and Roman mythology the water nymphs or lesser goddesses of springs and fountains, rivers, brooks and lakes.

Narcissus (när sis'us), a beautiful youth for whose love Echo died. He fell in love with his own reflection in a pool, pined away with longing for the unattainable image and was changed into the flower that bears his name. Narcissism means self-admiration.

Nausicaa (nô sik'ā a), in the *Odyssey* the daughter of Alcinous, King of the Phaeacians. She found the shipwrecked Odysseus on the shore, clothed him and took him to her father, who entertained him royally and provided him with a ship to return home.

Nectar (nek'tēr), in Greek mythology the drink of the gods.

Nemean lion (nē mē'an li'un), in Greek mythology the terrible lion which devoured the herds and ravaged the valley of Nemea. It was killed by Hercules as one of his Twelve Labors.

Nemesis (nem'ē sis), the Greek goddess of vengeance and retribution. Especially did her punishments overtake the proud and arrogant.

Neptune (nep'tūn), an ancient Italian god of fresh water streams and springs. He was worshiped and importuned in midsummer in time of heat and drought. About 399 B.C. the Romans identified him with the Greek sea-god Poseidon.

nereids (nē rē'idz), mermaid daughters of Nereus, a wise old god of the sea. There were said to be fifty daughters in all; Thetis, the mother of Achilles, was the most famous.

Nessus (nes'us), in Greek mythology the centaur who tried to run off with

Deianira, the wife of Hercules, and was shot by him with a poisoned arrow. The dying centaur told Deianira that his blood was a love charm. Years later she steeped her husband's robe in this blood to hold his love, but the garment poisoned him.

Nestor (nes'tôr), in the *Iliad* an aged counselor of the Greeks at the time of the Trojan War. So great was his wisdom and eloquence in extreme old age that any very wise old man is now called a Nestor.

Nibelungs (nē'be loongz), a race of dwarfs in Norway who owned and guarded the treasure of jewels and gold and the magic ring later won by Siegfried. In the *Nibelungenlied*, they are the kings of Burgundy who secured the hoard. The secret of its hiding place was lost when they were all killed.

Niflheim (niv'l hām), in Norse mythology the world of mist and cold and darkness where Hel reigned. It was divided into nine regions to which she allotted the souls of all the dead except those who died in battle. Yggdrasil, the world tree, was rooted in Niflheim.

Nimue (nim'oo a). See *Lady of the Lake.*

Niobe (nī'ō bē), in Greek mythology the proud mother of ten sons and ten daughters, whose pride was most cruelly punished. She bragged of her children to Leto, the mother of only two, Apollo and Artemis. To punish her, Apollo killed all her sons and Artemis killed all the girls. Niobe's grief was so great that in pity the gods changed her into stone. The spring which flows from the rock bears witness that Niobe still weeps.

nix (niks), in Teutonic mythology a water spirit, sometimes seen in human form, sometimes part fish, part human. The female water sprite is a nixie or nixy.

Norns (nôrnz), three goddesses, the fates of Teutonic mythology, who presided over the destiny of gods and men. They lived by the spring of fate at the root of Yggdrasil. Their names were Urth, Verthandi and Skuld (past, present and future).

Notus (nō'tus), the south wind: also called Auster.

nymphs (nimfs), in classical mythology the spirits of mountains, forests, trees and streams, the ocean and little springs. They were beautiful goddesses, often marrying human beings. The nymphs of the ocean were the oceanids. The nereids were sea nymphs, especially of the Mediterranean Sea. The nymphs of rivers, lakes and springs were naiads. Mountain nymphs were called oreads. Dryads were the nymphs of forests, groves and trees.

Nyx (niks), the ancient goddess of night in Greek mythology, a daughter of Chaos: same as Nox, the Roman goddess of night.

Oberon (ō'bĕr on), in medieval folklore, the king of the fairies or elves. He is the Alberich (Auberich, Auberon) of German and French medieval romance, or his son. In *Huon de Bordeaux* he is king of the fairies. The Oberon of Shakespeare's *Midsummer Night's Dream* is a dainty, diminutive being, quite unlike the powerful Alberich of folklore.

oceanids (ō sē'a nidz), the ocean nymphs, daughters of Oceanus, who personified the great river which encircled the earth, and fathered the 3,000 rivers of the world.

Odin (ō'din), the supreme god of Norse mythology, husband of Frigga and father of Balder, Thor, Bragi, Hoder, Tyr, Vali, Vidar, Hermod and others of the Aesir. He was the god of war and reserved the glories of Valhalla for heroes slain in battle. Odin was god of wisdom and to become so, paid Mimir one eye for a drink from the spring of knowledge (Mimir's well) at the foot of Yggdrasil. Two ravens attended him, Hugin and Munin (thought and memory). He is the Woden of Teutonic mythology. Wednesday is Woden's day.

Odysseus (ō dis'ūs), in the *Iliad* and *Odyssey* a king of Ithaca and one of the foremost of the Greek chiefs in the Trojan War. He was one of the suitors of Helen of Troy but married Penelope, whom he was so loath to leave when he was called to rescue Helen from the Trojans that he feigned madness to avoid the obligation of going to war. His ruse was discovered; he had to go to Troy; and he distinguished himself in valor and wisdom during the years of the siege of Troy. On the death of Achilles the arms of that hero were awarded to Odysseus.

The *Odyssey* describes the ten years of wandering and hardship he encountered on his voyage home from the war. He touched upon the shores of the Lotus Eaters in Africa. He escaped death from the one-eyed Cyclops Polyphemus only by his own courageous trickery in blinding the giant and concealing himself beneath one of the Cyclops's sheep as they crowded out of the cave. He remained one year with Circe, the enchantress, and seven years with the ocean nymph Calypso on her island. He braved the dangers of Scylla and Charybdis, heard the sirens sing while he was bound to the mast and thus escaped them. He was shipwrecked on the shores of Phæacia and there cared for by Nausicaa and her father, who gave him ships to continue his voyage home.

At last he reached Ithaca to find his wife surrounded by a host of unworthy suitors, each coveting the kingdom. With the aid of his son Telemachus and his faithful herdsman Eumæus he slew them all and reigned another good sixteen years. Telegonus, his son by Circe, came seeking his father, and unwittingly killed him in a quarrel before he knew who he was. Odysseus was called Ulysses by the Romans.

Oedipus (ed'i pus), the son of Laius and Jocasta, King and Queen of Thebes. Having been warned that he would die by the hand of his son, Laius thought to destroy the newborn child and hung him by his heels on a tree in the forest. From this incident probably he was named Oedipus (Greek, swell foot). A passing herdsman found the infant and saved his life; and Oedipus was adopted and reared by the king of Corinth. In his young manhood he was told by the oracle at Delphi that he was destined to kill his father and wed his own mother. Horrified he fled from Corinth, met Laius

in his wanderings and killed him in a quarrel.

Finally Oedipus came to Thebes where the sphinx was daily devouring the inhabitants. This winged, woman-headed monster was wont to ask one riddle a day of whom she chanced to meet and to devour the hapless one who could not answer it. Oedipus answered instantly the famous question put to him, and the monster killed herself. Creon, the king, had promised the kingdom and his sister Jocasta for wife to whomever should free the city of this peril. Thus Oedipus unknowingly married his own mother and by her had two sons Eteocles and Polynices and two daughters Antigone and Ismene. When the truth of their relationship was revealed to them, Jocasta hanged herself, and Oedipus put out his own eyes and went into exile to Colonus in Attica, followed and cared for by his faithful daughter Antigone. This story is the basis of Sophocles's famous trilogy, *Oedipus Tyrannus, Oedipus Coloneus* and *Antigone.*

Oenone (ē nō'nē), the mountain nymph in Mount Ida who loved Paris and lived happily with him there until he deserted her for Helen of Troy. She prophesied the fall of Troy and bade Paris come to her for care and healing when wounded. He received a mortal wound when the city was taken and had himself borne to Oenone. She refused to heal him, but quickly repented and hurried after him, only to find him dead. In grief she killed herself.

Ogier (ō jiēr') or **Olger** (ōl'ger) **the Dane** one of Charlemagne's knights. When he was 100 years old, this great warrior was carried away to Avalon where Morgan le Fay restored his youth. Every 200 years he is sent back to France to defend the right. Holger Danske is the Danes' name for their national hero.

ogre (ō'gĕr), in European folklore and fairy tales an awful, flesh-eating giant.

Oisin (u shēn'), a warrior and bard of 3d century Ireland, the son of Finn Mac Cumal. There are legends of his conversations with St. Patrick after 432 A.D. His great age is explained by the story that he spent some 200 years with Niam (nēv), daughter of the sea-god Manannan, in the fairyland of youth. *The Wanderings of Oisin,* by William Butler Yeats, uses this material. Oisin is the Ossian of James Macpherson's Ossianic poems; but the matter and spirit of the legends were completely altered by Macpherson.

Old Man of the Sea, in the *Arabian Nights* an old man who induced Sindbad the Sailor to carry him on his back across a stream of water. But he was not the weak and helpless creature he seemed. He twined his arms and legs around Sindbad's body and would not get off. Sindbad was forced to live with this unlovely burden until he finally got the old man drunk, dislodged him and killed him.

Oliver (ol'i vēr), one of the paladins of Charlemagne. He was the true friend and companion of Roland and his equal in arms but more prudent. Three times Oliver urged Roland to sound the horn for help at the Battle of Roncevaux, but Roland would not do so until it was too late.

Olympus (ō lim'pus), a mountain in Macedonia, the abode of the great gods.

Omphale (om'fa lē), the Queen of Lydia whom Hercules served as a slave for three years to expiate a murder. He weaved and spun at her side in woman's garb.

Ops (ops), an ancient Italian goddess of fertility and agriculture; in later Roman mythology she was identified with the Greek Rhea. The Latin word means wealth or resources.

oracle (or'a kl), in classical mythology a place set aside where men might go to question or consult the gods in regard to the future and the conduct of human affairs. The answer was given through the voice of a priest or priestess, often in terms so symbolical that it had to be interpreted. The oracle of Apollo at Delphi was the most famous among the Greeks.

oreads (ōr'ē adz), in Greek mythology nymphs of the mountains.

Orestes (ō res'tēz), in Greek legend son of Agamemnon and Clytemnestra, who avenged the murder of his father by slaying the murderess, his mother and her lover Aegisthus. To cleanse himself of the murder, he was told to bring the statue of Artemis from Tauris to Greece. Having arrived in Tauris, Orestes and his friend Pylades were to be sacrificed, as were all strangers, to Artemis. Iphigenia, the priestess assigned to perform the sacrifice, recognized her brother Orestes and saved his life. The three escaped together in the night, bearing the statue of Artemis with them. To regain his betrothed Hermione, who was married to Neoptolemus, Orestes killed his rival. He became king of his father's kingdom of Mycenae.

Orion (ō rī'on), a young and beautiful hunter, beloved by Eos and slain in jealousy by Artemis. Another story says that Artemis herself loved him and was tricked into shooting him by Apollo. After his death he became a constellation in the heavens.

Ormazd (ôr'mazd) or **Ahura Mazda** (ä hoo'ra maz'da), the supreme god of Persian religion, creator of the world and man. He was the principle of good in the eternal struggle against the powers of evil. The name means wise lord.

Orpheus (ôr'fūs), in Greek mythology a poet and musician of Thrace, son of Apollo and the muse Calliope. He received from Apollo the lyre on which he played so marvelously that he charmed the wild beasts and could make the trees and rocks move and the rivers stand still. When Eurydice, his wife, died from a serpent bite, Orpheus followed her to Hades and begged to be allowed to bring her back. Pluto was so moved by his music that he consented, but on condition that Eurydice follow behind and Orpheus never look back. Orpheus promised; but just as they were leaving the world of gloom, he gave one backward look to see if she was really there. Eurydice vanished again to the realm of the dead, and Orpheus, inconsolable, returned home and vowed never more to associate with women. In revenge the Thracian women tore him to pieces and threw his head in the river Hebrus.

Osiris (ō sī'ris), ancient Egyptian god and judge of the dead. He was the brother and husband of Isis and father of Horus. As ruler of Egypt he taught civilization to his subjects. He was killed by his brother Set (Typhon) but was avenged by Isis and Horus, who defeated Set and set up the worship of Osiris all over Egypt.

Ossa (os'a), a mountain in Thessaly. In the Greek myth the giants piled Ossa upon Pelion (a neighboring peak) in an attempt to take Olympus in their war against the gods.

paladins (pal'a dinz), the twelve peers of Charlemagne, inmates of his palace and his companions at arms. The word *paladin* meant palace dweller first and then warrior. The most famous of the twelve were Roland and Oliver, Ganelon the traitor, Ferumbras and Ogier the Dane.

Pales (pā'lez), the guardian god (female or male) of shepherds and their flocks, herdsmen and cattle. The festival of Parilia or Palilia was celebrated April 21, the day Rome was founded.

Palladium (pa lā'di um), in Greek mythology the famous statue of Pallas Athena, believed to have fallen from heaven during the building of Troy. It was a prized possession, for no harm could befall the city that contained it. Odysseus with the help of Diomedes carried it off before the fall of Troy.

Pallas (pal'as), an epithet of Athena; perhaps it meant brandisher or shaker, for Athena carried a spear.

Pan (pan), in Greek mythology the god of nature, forests and fields and wild life and the patron of flocks and shepherds; associated especially with the pastures of Arcadia. He is represented in human shape with the legs and horns of a goat. He invented the panpipe or shepherd's pipe, a musical instrument made of reeds, which he named syrinx for the beautiful nymph whom he loved and who fled, leaving him "nought but a lovely sighing of the wind." Pan was feared by lonely travelers in the woods, and the mysterious fear that comes from no known cause is called a *panic* fear.

Pandarus (pan'da rus), a son of Lycaon, who aided the Trojans in their war with the Greeks. He broke the truce that had been agreed on by the contending armies. He was later killed by Diomedes.

Pandora (pan dō'ra), in Greek mythology the first woman, created by Hephæstus at the command of Zeus, to punish mankind for the possession of fire, which Prometheus stole from heaven. Each god gave her a gift: Aphrodite gave her beauty, Hermes a subtle tongue and Zeus a closed box, which he told her to give to her husband but never to open. Zeus intended her for a wife for Prometheus, but he would not have her. His brother Epimetheus, however, was less suspicious of a gift from the gods and married her. In time Pandora gave way to curiosity and opened the forbidden box. All the evils of humanity were thus let loose in the world. Hope alone remained to lighten the heart of man.

Parcae (pär'sē), in Roman mythology the three Fates.

Paris (par'is), a son of Priam, king of Troy. When he was born, Hecuba, his mother, dreamed that she gave birth to a flame that burned Troy; whereupon Priam cast the infant out to die on Mount Ida. He was saved and reared by the shepherds of the mountain, and there he lived happily with the nymph Oenone, until he was sought out to judge who was the fairest of the three goddesses, Aphrodite, Hera and Athena. Paris gave the prize, the golden apple of Eris or Discord, to Aphrodite, who promised him the most beautiful woman in the world for his wife. She kept the promise by helping him win and carry off to Troy Helen, the wife of Menelaus of Sparta. Thus Paris fulfilled the prophetic dream and caused the Trojan War and the destruction of Troy. He was killed by an arrow shot by Philoctetes the day the city was taken.

Parnassus (pär nas'us), a mountain in Greece near Delphi, sacred to the Muses of Greek mythology and to Apollo.

Parsifal (pär'si fäl), in Wagner's opera *Parsifal,* the knight who found the sacred spear that alone could heal Amfortas of his wound. Amfortas, king of the Grail castle and the stainless knights who were keepers of the Holy Grail, had been seduced by Kundry, the enchantress sent by the wicked Klingsor to persecute the knights of the Grail. Through her wiles, Amfortas lost the spear and received a fatal wound from Klingsor. Parsifal, the innocent youth reared in simplicity, came to the castle and proved to be the "stainless fool" destined to recover the sacred spear and heal the king. Kundry's charms beset him, but he resisted her and thus broke the power of Klingsor. Parsifal redeemed Kundry and eventually replaced Amfortas as the guardian of the Holy Grail. Parzival and Percival are other forms of the name.

Paul Bunyan (pôl bun'yan), the hero of lumber-camp folklore of the American Northwest. He was a huge lumberjack "mightiest of loggers," performing amazing and impossible feats. Paul Bunyan was born in Maine, turned up in Michigan, walked out to Oregon because the trains were so slow in the old days. The Colorado Canyon is the scratch in the ground where he dragged his pick behind him, carelesslike, on his way.

Paul Bunyan was the greatest logger that ever swung an ax. Two cuts were all he ever made for one tree. Often he made one cut on the forward swing of his ax and cut the tree behind him on the backward swing. He never felled them as he went along but waited until he had cut a whole section; then with one push the whole section would go down. He invented the grindstone. Before that the woodsmen had to sharpen their axes by rolling a rock down hill and running along beside it.

His most prized possession and companion was Babe, the Blue Ox, whose breadth between the horns was 42 ax handles plus a plug of Star tobacco. He had a huge appetite for hot cakes, with a second preference for baled hay. But no one could fool him into eating shredded wheat, even if it was baled. Paul peeled his logs by hitching the ox to one end of a log and holding onto the bark at the other. When Babe pulled, the log came out slick and clean. But how Paul and Babe straightened the road into camp is the most famous of the tall tales. The road was 22 miles long and so crooked it crossed itself eleven times and had three S curves. First Paul told funny stories to the blue ox to get him in a good humor, then he hitched him to one end of the road and pulled the whole thing straight. He found then it was only 8 miles long, so he rolled up the other 14 miles and sold them to Chicago for a boulevard—Michigan Boulevard, named for the state it came from.

The stories of Paul Bunyan are living myths, told, retold and added to year after year. He still swings his ax in the northwest forests, and the only reason he is never seen is because he is too swift for the eye to catch.

Pax (paks), the personification of peace in Roman mythology.

Pecos Bill (pā′kōs bil), the hero of cowboy folklore of the American West. He was born in eastern Texas. When his parents migrated westward, Bill fell out of the wagon as they were crossing the Pecos River. He was a year old then and lived with the coyotes until he was ten. In fact he thought he was a coyote himself, "just a coyote with a bad case of mange." One day a cowboy came along and asked him why he wore no clothes, and this was the first inkling Bill had that he was a human being. After talking to the cowboy Bill decided he would like to take up human ways, so he mounted one of the cowboy's horses and the pair headed for civilization. The horse carried him 11 miles and then collapsed; so Bill put the exhausted creature across his shoulders and carried him in. And that's how he arrived at his first camp.

Pecos Bill became the greatest cow hand of the West. He rode a huge horse that he fed on dynamite and nitroglycerine. No other man could ride him, but Bill could ride anything from a catamount to a cyclone. The only way a cyclone could throw him was to rain out from under him. He invented the lariat and taught the cowboys to rope cattle. He invented the six-shooter and all the best "cuss" words in the language. He wrote all the cowboy ballads and taught them to the cowboys of the West. He even directed all the first wild West movies, but that was on the side. One of the deeds he is loved for most was saving the cattle country from a Pacific tidal wave. When Bill heard it was coming, he hastily threw up a few breastworks —now called the Rocky Mountains.

Bill married a squaw named Slue Foot Sue. He loved her because she was such a fine rider. And it was she who named his famous horse the Widow-Maker. Sue had a sharp tongue at times, and one day Bill, in a fit of aggravation, slung her up into the sky. But he sent her farther than he meant to; in fact, he sent her so far that he realized she would starve to death before she came down. So being a merciful man, he shot her to put her out of her misery.

After this Bill was so lonely that he rode away and took to drinking nitro-

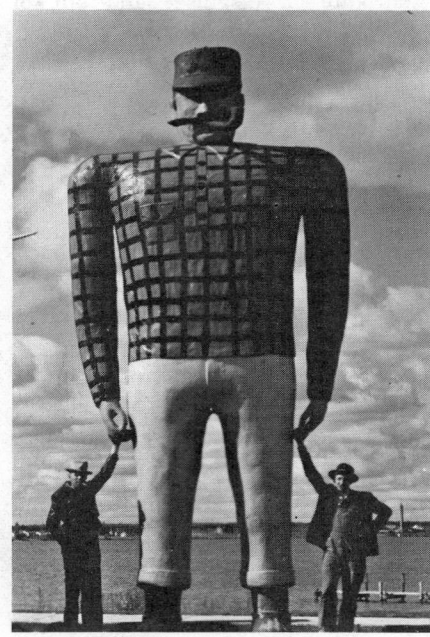

BEMIDJI, MINNESOTA, DAILY PIONEER

PAUL BUNYAN. A statue of the huge lumberjack, the "mightiest of loggers."

glycerine. This pepped him up considerably until he got used to it. Then someone told him that fish hooks would add strength to his drink, and he got in the habit of taking one with each drink. One night, feeling extra low, he swallowed a handful. They struck together inside him, and that one little spark was the end of Pecos Bill. The place where they picked up the pieces is to this day called the Burned Lands.

Pegasus (peg′a sus), the winged horse born from the blood of Medusa at the moment Perseus cut off her head. Athena gave him to the Muses, and his name today symbolizes flights of poetic fancy. When Bellerophon was sent to destroy the chimaera, Athena gave him the golden bridle by which alone a mortal could tame Pegasus. At the sight of the bridle the beautiful horse came gladly to Bellerophon's hand. He allowed himself to be mounted and unflinchingly braved the fire-breathing chimaera in the fight until Bellerophon killed it.

Peleus (pē′lūs), a king of Thessaly who married Thetis, the sea nymph, and became the father of Achilles. At their wedding Eris threw the golden apple among the guests that led to the judgment of Paris, the abduction of Helen and the Trojan War.

Pelias (pē′li as), the uncle of Jason, who usurped the throne of Iolchos. He sent Jason to search for the Golden Fleece. His daughters boiled him in a cauldron expecting Medea to restore him to youth and strength, but she refused to do so.

Pelion (pē′li on), a mountain in Thessaly. The giants piled Ossa, another mountain, on top of it, in trying to take Olympus from the gods.

Pelops (pē′lops), a son of Tantalus. His father once invited the gods to a feast and served to them the cut up body of his son. They recognized it as the flesh of Pelops, however, refused to eat it and restored him to life.

penates (pē nā′tēz), the Roman household gods who presided over the material welfare of the family. The pantry was sacred to them. Their worship was related to that of Vesta and the lares, but they differed from the lares in being gods instead of the deified spirits of family ancestors.

Penelope (pē nel′ō pē), the wife of Odysseus. Although she received no word from her husband after the Trojan War, she believed that he would surely return. Year after year she held off the horde of suitors who surrounded her, coveting the kingdom. She would make her decision, she said, when she had finished weaving a winding sheet for her father-in-law Laertes. She unraveled each night the work she had done in the day. Penelope's Web is still an epithet given to any never-finished task. After 20 years Odysseus returned to her and destroyed the suitors.

Percivale or **Perceval** (pûr′si val), a knight of the Round Table and one of the seekers of the Holy Grail. He caught a glimpse of it along with Galahad and Bors. The original Perceval stories, however, are more deeply rooted in folklore, and in these he was the son of a widow, brought up in ignorance of his noble lineage and reared in the forest to save him from the knowledge and dangers of chivalry. One day he met a company of knights and in admiration of them determined to seek knighthood. He attracted much attention at Arthur's court with his beauty and innocence and eventually became one of the finest of knights. These legends do not link him up with the quest of the Grail. He first appears as a Grail hero in Chrétien de Troyes's *Perceval;* but he is the perfect knight who achieves the quest in seven later Grail romances. He is the hero of Wolfram von Eschenbach's *Parzival.* For the version of the story in Wagner's opera, see *Parsifal.*

peri (pē′ri), in Persian mythology a superhuman being, originally considered the offspring of fallen angels and thought to be of evil influence. Later, peris were regarded as beautiful and kindly fairies.

Persephone (pêr sef′ō nē), the daughter of Zeus and Demeter. She was carried off by Pluto to be his wife and queen of Hades. The grief-stricken prayers of Demeter moved Zeus to let Persephone return to life, but only if she had eaten nothing since her arrival in the lower world. It was discovered that she had eaten a small piece of pomegranate and was therefore in bondage to Hades. She was allowed to spend half of the year with her mother but was compelled to return to Pluto for the other half. Her return to life symbolizes the growth of grain; her sojourn in the lower world, the planting of seed. The Romans called her Proserpine.

Perseus (pûr'sūs), the son of Zeus and Danae. The boat in which Danae and her child were set afloat came safely to the island of Seriphos where Polydectes was king. He fell in love with Danae, and in later years, wishing to be rid of Perseus, assigned him to bring back the head of the Gorgon Medusa. But the gods were on the side of the youth. Athena gave him her shield bright as a mirror so that he could approach the Gorgon without looking on her face, for all who gazed upon Medusa were instantly turned to stone. From Pluto he received the helmet which made him invisible. Hermes loaned him his winged sandals. Thus equipped Perseus was able to come upon Medusa while she slept and cut off her head.

Flying home he sought a night's rest with Atlas on the western edge of the world. Atlas, however, had been warned that a son of Zeus would steal the fruit of his gardens and refused him, whereupon Perseus turned the Gorgon's head toward him and left Atlas turned to stone. Continuing his journey, from above Ethiopia he saw a beautiful maiden chained to a rock in the sea. This was Andromeda, sacrificed to the sea monster sent by Poseidon to punish Cassiopeia's pride in her daughter. Perseus killed the beast and received Andromeda for his wife. Her uncle Phineus came to the wedding feast to take her from Perseus. But Perseus with the Gorgon's head turned him and his attacking band to stone and returned to Seriphos with his wife. He arrived in time to save his mother from the mistreatment of Polydectes. Again with Medusa's head he petrified the king and his court. After this he returned the gifts of the gods and gave to Athena the head of Medusa on her shield. Later in a game of quoits he accidentally killed an old man, one of the onlookers, who turned out to be Acrisius, his grandfather. Thus he fulfilled the prophecy that Danae's father would be killed by Danae's son. He refused the throne of Argos to which he fell heir by this mishap, but exchanged it for another kingdom where he founded the city of Mycenae.

Phaedra (fē'dra), the wife of Theseus, who fell in love with her stepson, Hippolytus, and to punish him for his indifference, accused him to his father of trying to seduce her. The wrath of Theseus caused the death of Hippolytus, and Phaedra killed herself in grief and remorse. Racine based his tragedy *Phèdre* on this.

Phaethon (fā'e thon), the son of Helios, the sun-god. He begged to be allowed to drive his father's great four-horse chariot across the sky. Helios reluctantly consented, doubting his strength. The boy soon lost control of the fiery horses; the chariot dipped too near the earth and scorched it, and the whole world would have been burned had not Zeus killed Phaethon with a thunderbolt. He fell into the river Po, where his sisters wept on the bank until they were changed into poplars.

Phaon (fa'on), a boatman of Mitylene, for whose love Sappho is said to have leaped from the Leucadian rock. Phaon is famous as the old and ugly boatman who would take no pay for ferrying an old and ugly hag over to Asia. The ugly hag proved to be Aphrodite in disguise; and out of gratitude she gave him youth and beauty.

Philemon. See *Baucis and Philemon.*

Phlegethon (fleg'ē thon), the river of fire in Hades.

Phoebe (fē'bē), name for Artemis.

Phoebus (fē'bus), a name for Apollo, apparently meaning shining.

phoenix (fē'niks), a fabulous bird, the Egyptian sun-god. It was large, very beautiful, always male and there were never two in the world at once. It was believed to live for 500 years. At the end of that time it built a nest in which it burned itself alive. From the ashes rose the new, young phoenix, who flew with the burned nest and ashes of his forebear to Egypt and deposited them on the altar of the sun-god.

Pied Piper of Hamelin, a gaily clad piper who rid the small town of Hamelin in Brunswick of a plague of rats. The town was overrun with them, and the people were in desperate plight. The piper offered to rid the town of the rats, and the mayor promised him 1,000 guilders if he could do so. Up and down the streets he played his pipe and the rats came in hordes and followed him. He led them to the river Weser, and they all plunged in and were drowned. But when the piper claimed his reward, the mayor and the town council would give him only 50 guilders. So up and down the streets he piped again, and this time the children came running. Joyously they followed the merry music, and the piper led them away to a door in a hill which closed behind them. And none of them were ever seen again. Robert Browning's poem has made this story famous.

pixy, pixie (pik'si), in English folklore a fairy or sprite who mischievously leads people astray.

Pleiades (plē'ya dēz), The seven daughters of Atlas: Alcyone, Celaeno, Electra, Maia, Merope, Sterope, Taygeta. They were raised to a constellation in the heavens after their death. Merope shines dimmer than the others, out of shame for having married a mortal.

Pluto (plōō'tō), in Greek mythology the god of the lower world: also called Hades. By the Romans he was called Dis. When the three sons of Cronus and Rhea cast lots for their kingdoms, to Zeus fell the heavens, to Poseidon the sea, and to Pluto the lower world. He was a stern god, without softness or pity. The music of Orpheus seeking Eurydice was the only thing ever known to have moved him. Persephone was his wife; Cerberus, his watchdog.

Plutus (plōō'tus), in Greek mythology the god of wealth. He was the son of Demeter and was thought to be blind because he bestowed wealth indiscriminately without consideration of merit.

Pluvius (plōō'vi us), an epithet of Jupiter. It means sender of rain.

Polyhymnia (pol i him'ni a), the Greek muse of sacred poetry and memory.

Polynices (pol i nī'sez), a son of Oedipus. See *Eteocles.*

Polyphemus (pol i fē'mus), a Cyclops, a gigantic shepherd in whose cave Odysseus and twelve of his companions were shut up when they had been shipwrecked on the coast of Sicily. He devoured the men at the rate of two a day. Odysseus escaped only by getting the giant drunk, blinding his one eye with a burning torch and concealing himself beneath one of the sheep as the flocks left the cave to graze. Polyphemus loved the sea nymph Galatea. She spurned him for a shepherd boy named Acis, whom Polyphemus crushed under a huge rock.

NEW YORK PUBLIC LIBRARY

REYNARD THE FOX was first known as a character in Aesop's prose fables but was later reborn through the pen of the French satirist La Fontaine, who wrote in simple verse.

Polyxena (pō lik'sē na), the daughter of Priam and Hecuba of Troy, beloved by Achilles. Achilles was shot in the heel by Paris while suing for her hand. His shade appeared demanding her of the Greeks after the fall of Troy; and she was slain on his tomb.

Pomona (pō mō na), an ancient Italian goddess of fruit trees, beloved by Vertumnus.

Poseidon (pō sī'don), the Greek god of the sea and all waters. He was a son of Cronus and Rhea and brother to Zeus and Pluto. He lived in a golden palace below the sea and was the creator of storms or fine weather. He created the first horse and was worshiped as a god of horses. Wherever his trident struck the earth, either a horse or a spring sprang forth. Poseidon was on the side of the Greeks in the Trojan War because Laomedon of Troy had refused to pay him for building the walls of that city. The Romans identified him with their Neptune.

Priam (prī'am), the last of the Trojan kings. He had fifty sons and twelve daughters, among them Cassandra, Hector, Paris and Polyxena. He was killed by Neoptolemus, the son of Achilles, when Troy was taken.

Prometheus (prō mē'thūs), a son of the Titan Iapetus and a brother of Atlas and Epimetheus. In some stories Prometheus was the creator of mankind; and in all stories, the great culture hero, founder of civilization. He stole fire from heaven in a hollow fennel stalk and gave it to man, teaching him its many uses: how to melt up ores, to fashion tools, weapons and agricultural implements, to keep warm and to coin money. To punish him Zeus chained him to a rock on Mount Caucasus, where a vulture fed perpetually on his liver. It was renewed each night, only to be devoured anew each day. Zeus would gladly have freed him for the knowledge of the one secret that Prometheus withheld, for Prometheus was a prophet and knew by what means Zeus would be dethroned. (The name may mean forethought.) As Prometheus would not tell, he was doomed to bear his torment until some immortal was willing to die in his place. Chiron, the wise centaur, consented to do this; Hercules killed the vulture; and thus Prometheus was freed. Aeschylus celebrated the story in his tragedy *Prometheus Bound*. Shelley's poetic drama *Prometheus Unbound* tells the story of his liberation.

Proserpina (pro sûr'pi na) or in English **Proserpine** (pros'ur pīn). See *Persephone*.

Proteus (prō tūs), a lesser Greek sea-god, tender of the flocks of Poseidon. He had great wisdom and could foretell the future. But he would not answer questions unless compelled to. When he was seized he would rapidly change from one terrifying shape to another—so protean means rapidly changing. But if his questioner held him fast, he would at last resume his own form and give the true answers.

Psyche (sī'kē), the youngest of a Greek king's three daughters, so beautiful that the people's mouths were full of her praises and the altars of Aphro-dite herself became neglected. In jealousy Aphrodite told her son Eros (or Cupid) to inspire Psyche with love for the lowest of mortals. But at sight of her, the boy fell in love himself. He visited her only by night and warned her never to try to learn his name or to behold him. Their happiness might have continued, but Psyche could not resist the taunts of her sisters that her lover must be some hideous monster. And one night she brought a lamp so that she might see him while he slept. So great was her joy at his beauty that her hand shook and a drop of burning oil fell on his shoulder. He awoke and departed in reproach and anger.

Left alone, Psyche wandered through the world seeking her lost love. Aphrodite imposed on her many difficult and impossible tasks, which she performed only with the help of the gods. The last was to bring from Hades some of the beauty of Persephone in a box that she was forbidden to open. She opened it, of course, hoping to make herself more beautiful for her lover. But the box contained only a deep and senseless sleep, which took possession of her and from which she was saved only by Cupid himself. At last in answer to Cupid's prayers, Zeus gave her immortality and the lovers were reunited forever.

In Greek the word *psyche* means soul. And the story of Cupid and Psyche is often considered an allegory of the soul in search of love, taught by suffering and attaining true happiness at last.

puck (puk), in English folklore a hob-goblin, usually of evil intent. In medieval times he became merely a mischievous fairy, often called Robin Goodfellow. The Puck of Shakespeare's *Midsummer Night's Dream* was a mischievous fairy, a servant of Oberon.

Pygmalion (pig mā'li on), a king of Cyprus and a famous sculptor. He fell in love with the statue of a beautiful maiden that he had carved; and Aphrodite heard his prayers and gave the statue life. The statue was named Galatea. *Pygmalion and Galatea* is the title of a comedy by W. S. Gilbert. William Morris's poem *Earthly Paradise* also tells the story, and G. B. Shaw wrote a drama *Pygmalion*.

Pyramus (pir'a mus) and **Thisbe** (thiz' bē), a pair of lovers in ancient Babylon whose parents would not consent to their marriage. They plighted their troth through a chink in the high wall which separated the two houses. One night they agreed to run away and planned to meet outside the walls of the city beneath a mulberry tree. Thisbe arrived first. Terrified by a lion, she ran and hid in a cave. But she dropped her veil, which the lion trampled and smeared with his blood-stained jaws. When Pyramus arrived and saw the veil, he thought Thisbe was dead and killed himself with his sword. When Thisbe ran out of the cave and saw Pyramus dying, she fell upon his sword and died with him. Forever after the mulberry tree bore only red fruit. This tragic story is grotesquely played by Bottom and others in Shakespeare's *Midsummer Night's Dream*.

Pyrrha (pir'a). See *Deucalion*.

Pythias (pith'i as). See *Damon*.

Python (pi' thon), in Greek mythology the great serpent born from the mud and slime which covered the earth after the Great Deluge. It lay in a cave on Mount Parnassus, and there Apollo killed it.

Ra (rä) or **Re** (rā), the supreme god of Egyptian mythology, the god of the sun.

Ragnarok (rag'na rok), in Norse mythology the end of the world and all the gods. It was the day of the great battle between the Aesir and the powers of Hel and Loki. Odin was killed by the wolf Fenrir, who in turn was slain by Vitharr, Odin's son. Thor and the Midgard Serpent fought to the death. Tyr and Garm, the watchdog of Hel, destroyed each other. Loki and Heimdall fought until both were killed. Surt, the chief of the giants, killed Frey. The sun and the earth fell into the sea, and the sky was consumed by fire. But Balder returned from the realm of the dead. Two mortals named Lif and Lifthrasir (Life and the Desire of Life) survived to repeople the world; and a new and happier era was born.

Rahu (rä'hoo), in Hindu mythology the demon dragon who followed the sun and moon about the sky. Whenever he caught one of them he swallowed it and caused an eclipse.

Remus. See *Romulus*.

Reynard the Fox (ren'ērd), the hero of a series of beast fables or bestiaries widespread through France, Germany, Holland and England in the Middle Ages. The most ancient redaction known was written in Latin in Flanders about 940. Scholars (especially the Grimm brothers) testify that the fables are rooted in very ancient Teutonic true animal folklore— that is, the animals did not originally typify men. The Reynard fables, however, were satires or parodies on chivalry, the government and the nobles, the church, monks and nuns. The characters are: Reynard the fox, Bruin the bear, Noble the lion, Baldwin the ass, Tibert the cat, Isengrim the wolf, Grimbert the badger, Chanticleer the cock, Partlet the hen and various others. In all the versions Reynard typifies all that is shrewd and crafty in man or society. He is self-seeking and thoroughly unscrupulous, brought to judgment but escaping his just deserts by his foxiness.

Rhadamanthus (rad a man'thus), a son of Zeus and Europa. So great was the justice of his own life that after death he was made one of the judges in Hades, along with Minos, his brother.

Rhea (re'a), a Titan, daughter of Uranus (heaven) and Gaea (earth), sister and wife of Cronus and mother of the gods. She was also known as Cybele.

Rhinegold or **Rheingold** (rīn'gōld), the cursed treasure of the Nibelungs.

Robin Goodfellow. See *Puck*.

Robin Hood, the romantic outlaw of English ballad and legend who lived with his merry men in Sherwood Forest, robbing the rich to help the poor. He was a yeoman and the idol and ideal of the common people; a hunter and an archer of marvelous skill, fearless and free, merry, lusty, generous and chivalrous and swift to right injustice. His true story is an unsolved riddle, but there is now little doubt that there was a Robin Hood. Perhaps he was one of the earls of Huntingdon, born at Locksley in Nottinghamshire in the 12th century. He figures as Locksley in Scott's *Ivanhoe*.

roc (rok), in Arabian folklore a bird of prodigious size and strength. It fed its young on full-grown elephants. In the *Arabian Nights* a roc that bore Sindbad the sailor out of the Valley of Diamonds.

Roland (rō'land), the nephew of Charlemagne and the most famous of his paladins. The *Chanson de Roland* celebrates his friendship with Oliver, whom he met first as an adversary in battle. The two were so equal in arms that neither could defeat the other, and in mutual admiration they became brothers and companions. From this story comes the phrase "a Roland for an Oliver" meaning worth for worth. In 778 in Charlemagne's expedition into Spain against the Saracens, Roland distinguished himself as a champion of Christianity. When the army was returning through the Pyrenees, Ganelon, the traitor, had Roland put in charge of the rear guard. In the pass at Roncevaux they were set upon by a horde of Saracens and were outnumbered and destroyed. The main army was already far in advance, but not beyond the sound of Roland's magic horn, called Olivant. Three times Oliver begged him to sound the horn for help; but Roland wanted the glory of the fight for themselves and would not blow the call for relief until it was too late, and they were slain. But at last when Charlemagne heard Olivant calling and hastened back to find his favorite warriors dead, he fell with wrath upon the Saracen army and destroyed it to a man. Ganelon was examined and discovered in his treacherous scheme and put to death.

Romulus (rom'ū lus), the legendary founder and first king of Rome. He was the son of Mars and Ilia and the twin of Remus. The two infants were cast into the river Tiber by Amulius, Ilia's uncle, who had usurped her father's throne. The twins were found and suckled by a she-wolf and fostered by wild hill shepherds. In later years they found their grandfather and restored him to his throne after they had killed Amulius. They decided to found a new city on the spot where the she-wolf had found them; and Romulus, of whom it was foretold that he would be the first king, laid the first stones. When Remus laughed and leaped over them, Romulus in anger killed him for his ridicule.

Round Table, the great table of King Arthur around which all the knights could sit in equality without dispute of precedence or honor. The most ancient Celtic stories ascribe marvelous powers to it: It could seat 1,600 knights, yet Arthur could fold it up and carry it with him. Later legend says Merlin made it for Uther Pendragon, Arthur's father, and that Arthur continued the order of knights already established round it. A still later story says that Merlin made it for Arthur with thirteen seats, and that in the thirteenth, the Siege Perilous, no man could sit and live except the one knight destined to achieve the quest of the Holy Grail. There is a huge round table fixed in the hall of Winchester Castle (Camelot) with 25 seats, and local legend holds that this was the famous board of the Arthurian legend.

St. George, the patron saint of England. He was a Roman soldier beheaded by Diocletian in 303 for adhering to Christianity. He was adopted as the patron saint of England by Edward III after the crusades. The legend of his slaying a dragon probably symbolizes the conquest of evil, as it does in many paintings of saints.

St. Nicholas (nik'ō las), the patron saint of Russia, and of children, sailors and thieves. He was a bishop of Myra in Asia Minor in the 4th century. As the guardian of children and bestower of gifts at Christmas time, his name has become Santa Claus.

Santa Claus (san'ta klôz). See *St. Nicholas*.

Satan (sā'tan). See *Devil*.

Saturn (sat'ẽrn), an ancient Italian god of seedtime and agriculture. His reign of peace and happiness was called the Golden Age.

satyr (sat'ẽr), in Greek mythology a minor woodland god, having human form but the tail and ears of a horse. Roman mythology depicted satyrs as faunlike, with the horns and legs of a goat. They were companions of Dionysus, ever gay and making merry.

THE METROPOLITAN MUSEUM OF ART

ST. GEORGE AND THE DRAGON, from a woodcut by Albrecht Dürer, 1471–1528. The origin of St. George's connection with the dragon is obscure but might stem from Greek mythology, in which the dragon always symbolized the powers of evil, chaos, and death.

Scylla (sil'a), a nymph who was turned into a monster and became a perilous rock in the strait between Italy and Sicily, opposite the whirlpool Charybdis. She was loved by the sea-god Glaucus, who implored the enchantress Circe for a charm to melt her indifference. But Circe herself fell in love with Glaucus and in jealousy poisoned the bath of Scylla with herbs. The maiden was terrified in the pool to find herself suddenly surrounded by barking and gaping jaws. She tried to run, only to discover the monsters were part of herself. In despair she hurled herself into the sea and forever after was avoided as a danger to ships and sailors.

Selene (sē lē'nē), the Greek goddess of the moon, like Luna in Roman mythology. She was the daughter of Hyperion, sister of Helios the sun and Eos the dawn. She was loved by Pan, but herself loved the shepherd boy Endymion, to whom she gave the gifts of perpetual youth and perpetual sleep. In later mythology she became identified with Artemis (Roman, Diana).

Semele (sem'e lē), a daughter of Cadmus, beloved by Zeus, by whom she became the mother of Dionysus. Zeus had promised to grant whatever she might ask, but when Semele asked to behold him in the glory in which he appeared before the gods, he warned her not to persist in the perilous wish. She insisted, however, and was consumed by his lightning; but Zeus saved the infant Dionysus.

Set (set), the Egyptian god of evil, called Typhon by the Greeks. He killed his brother Osiris.

Seven Against Thebes. See *Eteocles.*

Seven Sleepers of Ephesus (ef'e sus), seven Christian youths of Ephesus in Asia Minor. In 250 A.D. Decius, Emperor of Rome, ordered all Christians to renounce their faith or be put to death. The seven youths fled from the torturers and hid in a cave in the mountains. But they were followed, and Decius ordered them to be walled up alive. A miraculous sleep fell upon them from which they were awakened about 200 years later by a shepherd who found the cave and rolled away the rocks from the entrance. One of the seven went into the town to buy food. He attracted attention by his ancient style of dress or his ancient money and was taken before a magistrate and questioned. He told his story and led the people to the cave where his companions were found alive and young. When the Emperor Theodosius II heard the story, he came to the cave to see with his own eyes. The youths told him they were a sign to him to believe in the resurrection, and again they fell into a sleep to last until the Judgment Day.

sibyls (sib'ilz), inspired prophetesses of classical mythology. Of ten sibyls the Cumaean, the Delphian and the Erythraean were the most famous. Apollo fell in love with the Cumaean sibyl and offered to grant any wish she might name. She asked to live as many years as there were grains of sand in her hand, but forgot to ask for youth to last the years. When Aeneas came to her for guidance to find his father in the lower world, she was already 700 years old. More and more shriveled she grew with the centuries until only her prophetic voice remained. At one time she went to Tarquin Superbus, a legendary king of Rome, and offered him nine prophetic books for a certain price. He refused to buy them, whereupon the sibyl burned three and offered him the remaining six for the same price. Again he refused. She burned three more. Then Tarquin was afraid they would all be destroyed and he paid the whole price for the remaining three. These Sibylline Books contained prophetic sayings written by the sibyl. They were kept in the temple of Jupiter at Rome and consulted in times of national danger. They were lost when the Capitol burned, 82 B.C.

sid or **sidhe** (shē), the fairyfolk of Ireland.

Siege Perilous, the seat at Arthur's Round Table in which it was perilous for any knight to sit except the one destined to achieve the quest of the Holy Grail. When Galahad, son of Lancelot, arrived at Arthur's court, the people marveled to see him take his place unharmed in the Siege Perilous.

Siegfried (sēg'frēd), in the *Nibelungenlied* the hero who won the treasure of the Nibelungs, the magic sword Balmung and a cap that made him invisible. He helped Gunther win Brünnhilde, queen of Iceland, for wife; and he himself married Kriemhild, the sister of Gunther. Siegfried was killed by Hagen for the sake of the Rhine gold treasure.

In Wagner's operas *The Valkyrie* and *Siegfried,* Siegfried was the son of Siegmund. He broke through the magic fire where Brünnehilde slept on her mountain and won her but drank a magic drink and forgot her to marry Gudrune. He gave Brünnehilde to Gunther. Siegfried was killed by Hagen who coveted the magic ring of the Nibelungs, which Siegfried wore. Brünnehilde had helped to plot this slaying in order to die with him on his funeral pyre.

Sigurd (zē'goort), in the *Volsunga Saga* the hero who killed the dragon Fafnir, loved and won Brynhild, forgot her by a magic drink and married Gudrun, giving Brynhild for bride to Gunnar. He was killed by Gunnar's brother and Brynhild killed herself to join him. Sigurd in the Norse myths corresponds to Siegfried in the *Nibelungenlied.*

Silver Age, in classical mythology the second age of the world, following the perfect Golden Age and preceding the Bronze Age. Zeus ruled during the Silver Age and divided the year into seasons. Then men first knew cold and heat and learned to plow and toil for livelihood. They lost the innocence and unmixed happiness of the Golden Age. They took on pride, and their reverence for the gods grew so dim that Zeus destroyed the whole race.

Sindbad the Sailor (sind'bad), in Arabian folklore and especially in the *Arabian Nights* a young man of Bagdad who lost his wealth and set out on a series of voyages. He had many marvelous adventures. He built a fire on a floating island that turned out to be a whale. He barely escaped from cannibals in one land and came to another where his companions were driven mad from eating the native food. These adventures are like Odysseus' escape from the Cyclops and his visit to the Lotus Eaters. Sindbad married in a strange land and was buried alive with his dead wife but escaped at last from the caverns of the dead. The most famous of his adventures are those with the roc and the Old Man of the Sea.

sirens (sī'renz), in Greek mythology a group of sea nymphs whose singing was so sweet that sailors, hearing it, leapt into the sea and were drowned. Homer says there were two sirens; later writers mention three. Odysseus, being warned against them by Circe, plugged the ears of his sailors with wax and had himself lashed to the mast with orders to his men not to unloose him no matter how desperate his signals. Thus Odysseus and his companions sailed safely by. The Argonauts escaped them only because Orpheus was on board and played the sweeter and more magical music. After these failures, the sirens drowned themselves.

Sirius (sir'i us), in Greek mythology the dog of the hunter Orion, set in the heavens as a star, and called the Dog Star.

Sisyphus (sis'i fus), in Greek mythology a wily king of Corinth, husband of Merope. His punishment in Hades was to roll a huge rock to the top of a hill. Just before he reached the top, it would roll down again, and Sisyphus would have to begin his labors anew.

Siva (sē'va) or **Shiva** (shē'va), the third god of the supreme Hindu triad, the destroyer. He personified not only the powers of destruction but the regeneration and restoration also, which according to Hindu philosophy, always follow after destruction. He was god of the arts: letters, music and especially dancing. His images often represent the cosmic dancer.

Sleipnir (slāp'nēr), in Norse mythology Odin's swift eight-legged horse that could outrun the wind.

sphinx (sfingks), in Greek mythology a winged, woman-headed monster who preyed upon the citizens of Thebes. (The strange word seems to mean strangler). She devoured them at the rate of one a day. She would ask a riddle of anyone she met and devour him if he could not answer it. An oracle foretold that if once the riddle were answered, the spell would be broken and the sphinx would kill herself. Oedipus in his wanderings came to Thebes and was stopped. "What creature walks on four legs in the morning, two at noon and three in the evening?" the sphinx asked. "Man," said Oedipus, explaining that a babe creeps, a grown man walks upright and the aged totter on a stick. The sphinx at once dashed her head against a stone and died, and Oedipus received the reward offered by the king.

The Greek sphinx had nothing to do with the Egyptian statues called by the same name.

Styx (stiks), the principal river of Hades, believed to encircle the lower world seven times. Over this river Charon ferried the souls of the dead. It was held in such terror and reverence that even the gods swore their irrevocable oaths by its name.

Syrinx (sir'ingks), in Greek mythology a water nymph of Arcadia who fled from the love of Pan. She was transformed into the reeds from which he fashioned the panpipe, which he named for her.

Tannhäuser (tän' hoi zēr), in German legend a knight and minnesinger of the 13th century whose wanderings led him to the Venusberg, a mountain in Germany. There he beheld a beautiful woman who lured him into a cave. It was Venus, and for seven years he lived with her in her enchanted land of pleasure within the mountain. At length he repented, left the court of pleasure and made a pilgrimage to Rome to seek forgiveness of his sins. But Pope Urban told him that he could no more be forgiven than the dead staff in his hand could put out leaves. In despair Tannhäuser turned away, forgetting his staff, and returned to the Venusberg. In a few days the dry staff miraculously bloomed, and the Pope sent messengers far and wide seeking Tannhäuser with a message of forgiveness. But he was never found.

Tantalus (tan'ta lus), a son of Zeus and father of Pelops. For his offenses against the gods, he was condemned after death to stand in water up to his chin. Whenever in his great thirst he tried to drink, the waters would rush away. Luscious fruits hung low over his head, but whenever he reached for them they were suddenly withdrawn. From the story of Tantalus comes the word *tantalize*.

Tartarus (tär'ta rus), in Greek mythology the lowest and deepest of the regions of Hades, reserved for the torments of the wicked.

Telemachus (te lem'a kus), the son of Odysseus and Penelope; he went in search of his father, who did not return from the Trojan War. He did not find him, but returned to Ithaca in time to help Odysseus and Eumaeus destroy the suitors who surrounded Penelope.

Themis (thē'mis), an ancient Greek goddess often identified with Gaea, earth. She was the mother of Prometheus. Hesiod calls her a daughter of Uranus and Gaea and mother of the Fates. She personified justice, and her name is Greek for justice, order, right.

Theseus (thē'sūs), a son of Aegeus, King of Athens. He was brought up in the house of his mother in Troezen and when of age went to seek his father. On the way he had many adventures, of which the most famous was his slaying Procrustes, who had only one bed and used to fit all guests to it by cutting them or stretching them to its length. Aegeus was at that time married to Medea, who tried to persuade her husband to poison the stranger when he appeared at his court. But Aegeus recognized his son by the sword at his side and proclaimed him the heir to his throne. Theseus volunteered to free Athens from the yearly tribute of youths and maidens it paid to the Cretan Minotaur. With the help of Ariadne, by whose clue he threaded the labyrinth, Theseus killed the Minotaur and won and carried off Ariadne. He had promised his father that the ship, which put out for Crete under the black sails of mourning, should return under white sails if he had been successful. But he forgot his promise, and when the old king, watching for his son from a high cliff, saw the black sails returning from the sea, he hurled himself down in grief from the cliff and was killed.

Then Theseus, King of Athens, went against the Amazons and married their Queen Hippolyte by whom he had a son Hippolytus. After her death he married Phaedra. His friendship with Pirithous, a king of the Lapithae, is one of the most famous friendships of story. Theseus helped him in the battle of the Lapithae with the centaurs at the time of his marriage to Hippodamia, and when she died, followed his friend to Hades to help him carry off Persephone. But they were caught by Pluto and chained to a rock. Hercules eventually came and freed Theseus but Pirithous had to remain in the lower world. Theseus was killed by Lycomedes, King of Scyros, who pushed him into the sea.

Thetis (thē'tis), one of the nereids, the wife of Peleus and mother of Achilles.

Thisbe. See *Pyramus.*

Thor (thôr), in Norse mythology, the god of thunder, a son of Odin. He was the god of strength and a defender in time of war, a friend of humanity but a stern enemy of the giants. The sound of thunder was from the rolling wheels of his chariot; the thunderbolt was his hammer, which always returned to his hand after being hurled. Thor and the Midgard Serpent killed each other at Rognarok, the last day of the world. Thursday is Thor's day.

Thoth (thôth; tōt), the Egyptian god of wisdom and magic, who invented letters and numbers and was the scribe of the gods.

Titans (tī'tanz), the children of Uranus and Gaea. The sons were Oceanus, Cocus, Crius, Hyperion, Iapetus and Cronus. The daughters were Thea, Rhea, Themis, Mnemosyne, Phoebe and Tethys. The children of Cronus and Rhea were Zeus and the Olympian gods. Cronus dethroned Uranus, and Zeus dethroned Cronus. In this struggle the Titans fought against the gods, were defeated and confined under Tartarus.

Tithonus (ti thō'nus), a son of Laomedon, the founder of Troy. Eos fell in love with him and used her influence with the gods to make him immortal, but she forgot to ask for eternal youth. When he grew old and ugly, she changed him into a grasshopper.

Tom Thumb, in English ballad and legend the inch-high son of a plowman in the time of King Arthur. Once he was swallowed by a cow and once by a giant. He rode in a horse's ear, hid in a cheese and escaped pursuit through a keyhole. He fell into the sea and was swallowed by a fish, which was caught and taken to King Arthur's cook. The cook saved his life, and he was presented to the king and knighted. He was killed in the end by a spider.

Tristram (tris'tram). See *Iseult.*

Triton (trī'ton), a merman of Greek mythology, son of Poseidor, usually represented as blowing on a conch shell to raise or calm the waves.

Trojan War (trō'jan), in Greek legend the war in which Agamemnon, brother of Menelaus, led the Greeks against Troy to recover the beautiful Helen, whom Paris had carried off. They besieged the city for ten years and finally entered it by the ruse of the Wooden Horse. This is the war celebrated in the *Iliad;* in Greek the city was called Ilium.

troll (trōl), in Teutonic folklore a supernatural being, either gigantic or dwarfed and misshapen, conceived of as malignant and to be avoided.

Troy. See *Trojan War.*

Tuatha de Danann (thōō a ha dā dà'nan), the ancient Irish gods, literally the people of Danu. They invaded Ireland in clouds of mist and defeated the Fomors in the great battle of Moitura. When they were defeated by the Milesians, the Tuatha de Danann went to the fairy land of youth and became the *sid,* the fairyfolk of Ireland.

Typhon (tī'fon), in Greek mythology the hundred-headed fire-breathing giant, son of Tartarus and Gaea. He was thought to be the creator of dangerous winds. He made war against the gods, was struck down by the thunderbolt of Zeus and confined under Mount Aetna, whose volcanic eruptions were long thought to indicate Typhon's struggles for freedom.

Tyr (tür), in Norse mythology, the war-god, a son of Odin; in Teutonic mythology, called Tiu (tē' ōō).

Ulysses (ū lis'ēz), the Latin form of Odysseus.

Uranus (ū'ra nus), in Greek mythology the personification of the sky or heaven, wedded to Gaea, earth, and father of the Cyclops, Furies and Titans. He was dethroned by his son Cronus.

Uther (ū'thĕr), a legendary king of Britain and father of King Arthur. See *Merlin.*

Valhalla (val hal'a), the great hall of Odin in Asgard, where the souls of heroes slain in battle were received with rejoicing and honor. The word means hall of the slain. There they fought and hewed each other to pieces for the glory of eternal battle and were forever restored to partake of eternal feasting and merrymaking.

Valkyries (val kir'ēz), in Norse mythology the war maidens, messengers of Odin. They rode through the air above the scene of battle, selecting the warriors worthy to be slain and carrying them to Valhalla. The name probably meant choosers of the slain.

vampire (vam'pīr), in European folklore the ghost or risen body of a dead person who returns at night to suck the blood of the living.

Vanir (vä'nir), a race of Teutonic gods more ancient than the Aesir. They were gods of the air, and among them were Njorth, Frey and Freya, who were later counted among the Aesir.

Venus (vē'nus), an ancient Roman goddess of beauty, thought especially to preside over the beauty of nature and gardens. She was not a goddess of love until she became identified with the Greek Aphrodite.

Vesta (ves'ta), the Roman virgin goddess of the fire and hearth, not only for the home but for the state. The fire in her temple was never allowed to go out and was tended by a group of six virgins, chosen for their beauty and lineage. They were sworn to thirty years of vigilance and chastity, and were buried alive if they broke their vows. Vesta was identified with the Greek Hestia.

Vishnu (vish'nōo), the second god of the supreme Hindu triad, the preserver. The name means the worker, the active one. He dwelt on earth in nine incarnations or avatars, of which the most famous were as Matsya, the fish that saved Manu from the deluge; Krishna, the warrior who saved mankind from tyrants; Rama, who killed the giant Ravan, enemy to gods and men. It is believed that his tenth incarnation is still to come. This will be Kalki, who will save humanity from the present age of wickedness.

Vivian (viv'i an), in Arthurian legend, the lady love of Merlin. See *Lady of the Lake.*

THE METROPOLITAN MUSEUM OF ART

VENUS AND ADONIS, a black chalk heightened with white by François-Andre Vincent.

Vulcan (vul'kan), in Roman mythology, the god of fire and metal working; identified with the Greek Hephaestus.

Walpurgis Night (väl poor'gis), in German folklore the eve of May 1st (May Day), when the devil and the witches were believed to hold a riotous festival on the Brocken peak in the Harz Mountains. Goethe's *Faust* has a famous scene describing Walpurgis Night.

Wandering Jew, in medieval legend a Jew who mocked and laughed at Jesus on his way to the cross. He was condemned to wander on the face of the earth until the second coming of Christ. The legend is the subject of a poem by Goethe and a novel by Eugene Sue.

Wayland (wā'land) **the Smith,** the supernatural blacksmith of Teutonic and English legend; the Volundr of the Norse Eddas and the Wieland of German epic. He forged the famous magic sword Mimung with which Hoder killed Balder. He is a character in Scott's *Kenilworth.*

werewolf (wēr'woolf), in very ancient and almost world-wide folklore a human being turned wolf in form and nature. The change took place by enchantment imposed from without or by the will and power of the person himself because he desired to eat human flesh. He would prey upon his victims in wolf form by night and assume human shape again by day. In countries like India where the Tiger, instead of the wolf, is the natural enemy of man, the were-animal is a tiger. In South America it is the jaguar.

William Tell, a legendary Swiss patriot about the 14th century. He would not do obeisance to the cap of Gessler, an Austrian governor, which had been elevated on a pole for the people to honor. He was arrested and ordered to shoot at an apple placed on the head of his own son. This he did with such true marksmanship that the boy was unhurt. Then with unbelievable swiftness he drew a second arrow and shot Gessler. Thus the people were encouraged to rise against the Austrians. This story is the subject of a tragedy by Schiller and of an opera by Rossini.

witch (wich), a human being with magical knowledge and powers; a sorcerer or sorceress. Belief in witches and wizards and their power to work spells goes back to the most primitive beginnings of all races. In medieval times witches were believed to be in league with the devil, and people suspected of witchcraft were hunted down and put to death in Europe and America well into the 18th century.

Witches were supposed to be able to foretell future events with the help of various animals known as their "familiars." They cast spells and charms, both good and evil, by means of magic words and motions and the use of symbolic objects.

Woden (wō'dn), the Anglo Saxon (Old English) form of the Norse name Odin.

Wooden Horse of Troy, the great image of a horse offered as a gift by the Greeks to the Trojans, the trick by which they entered Troy. Outside the walls of the city they built a horse hollow and huge enough to hold an army. They filled it with warriors and then departed as if to embark

for Greece. One of their number, Sinon, gave himself up to the Trojans and then urged Priam to accept the gift, assuring him it was left in ex-

WOODEN HORSE OF THE TROJAN WAR, a ruse by which the Greeks entered Troy.

change for the Palladium, which Odysseus had stolen from its place in the city. Then the Trojans dragged the monstrous gift inside the walls. Sinon at night released the Greek warriors, who took and burned the city.

Yggdrasil (ig'dra sil), in Norse mythology, an ash tree, the great world tree binding together heaven and earth and hell. It was rooted in hell, where a dragon forever gnawed at the roots. Its trunk supported the world and the top of it reached beyond heaven. It was the tree of life; and it was the tree of knowledge, for Mimir's well of wisdom sprang from its roots. It was the tree of fate, for beneath it sat the Norns presiding over human destiny. An eagle sat in the top and the squirrel Ratatook ran up and down it, carrying strife.

Zephyrus (zef'i rus), in Greek mythology, the personification of the west wind; called Favonius in Latin.

Zeus (zūs), the supreme god of Greek mythology; identified with the Roman Jupiter. Zeus was the youngest son of Cronus and Rhea. Rhea saved him from being devoured by his father and gave him into the keeping of her priests on Mount Ida in Crete. With the sound of their cymbals they drowned the baby's crying and prevented Cronus from discovering him. When he was grown, he overthrew his father and established the Olympian gods, his brothers and sisters, who had been swallowed at birth by Cronus. He married his sister Hera and had many human loves. Zeus was primarily king of the gods and heaven, the sky-god and especially the thunder-god. The thunderbolt was his weapon, and he was worshiped on mountain tops. His worship later took on moral and social aspects and eventually embodied legal and political ideas as well. Zeus was god and protector of the state. He was god of personal and public oaths; murder was abhorrent to him. In his final religious and spiritual aspect, he was regarded as father and creator of the world and men.

Introduction.—The Protestant Bible is a collection of 66 books. With these Roman Catholics include 8 other books, e.g. Ecclesiasticus, Wisdom of Solomon, Judith, Maccabees. When the early Christians were deciding whether a book should be included in the Canon, that is, whether it should be included with the books of the Old Testament that they regarded as the inspired Word of God, or whether it should be regarded as profitable for reading but not inspired and therefore placed in the Apocrypha, they determined the matter by certain tests. These were: whether the book was written in Hebrew; whether it dated back at least as far as the time of Nehemiah; and whether it was mentioned in the New Testament. The books of the Apocrypha are those that did not qualify in one or another of these tests.

The first thirty-nine books of the Protestant Bible compose the *Old Testament,* while the *New Testament* consists of the remaining twenty-seven books and carries the record on from the birth of Christ to about the end of the first century A.D. The material in the Bible was composed at different times during a period of more than a thousand years. The Old Testament was written almost wholly in Hebrew, the New Testament wholly in Greek. The Authorized or King James Version of the Bible in English was completed in 1611. The Revised Version, made during 1881–85, is based upon the King James Version, but is a more accurate translation.

In looking up any name in the following list, if the student does not at once realize the relation of what is said to the general course of events, he should turn to the brief sketch of the history, which is given under the heading *Israel,* because the name Israel more than any other stands for the great tradition of which the Bible is the incomparable and monumental record. The purpose of the individual entries, which are arranged in alphabetical order, is to state the most familiar associations concerned with each name, without reference to any religious lesson to be derived, or to the opinions of scholars regarding authorship and other such questions.

Reference and Abbreviations.—A reference is to the chapter in which occurs the first important mention of the name. When the number of a verse is added, it follows a colon. Thus, "II Kings 6:8" means the eighth verse of the sixth chapter of Second Kings. The abbreviations used are the familiar ones, such as: O.T. for Old Testament; N.T. for New Testament; Gen. for Genesis; Ex. for Exodius; Dt. for Deuteronomy; Sam. for Samuel; chap. for chapter; *c.* for *circa* (Latin for "about").

Aaron, brother of Moses, the first high priest and ancestor of the priests and high priests of Israel. He was spokesman for Moses in appealing to Paraoh (Ex. 7). In the wilderness, when Moses was on Mount Sinai, Aaron set up a golden calf for the people to worship (Ex. 32). He died on Mount Hor (Num. 20).

Abel, a shepherd, second son of Adam and Eve. God accepted his sacrifice but not that of his brother Cain, at which Cain grew angry and killed Abel (Gen. 4).

Abigail, wife of Nabal and later of David (I Sam. 25).

Abner, a general of King Saul and later of David (I Sam. 17).

Abraham or Abram (meaning exalted father or "father of a multitude"), founder of the Hebrew race and the first patriarch; he was born in Ur, a city in Chaldea. Divinely called to be the founder of a new nation, he migrated to Canaan and was exceedingly prosperous.

Absalom, son of David, rebelled against his father but was defeated in battle. When he tried to escape, "Absalom was riding upon his mule, and the mule went under the thick bows of a great oak, and his head caught hold of the oak, and he was taken up between heaven and earth; and the mule that was under him went on" (II Sam. 18:9). He was found and killed.

Acrostics in the Bible lose their distinctive form by translation. There were 22 letters in the Hebrew alphabet. The 119th Psalm has 176 verses, 22 groups of eight verses, each of the eight beginning with the same letter of the alphabet. Proverbs 31:10–31, is 22 verses on the ideal woman, each verse beginning with a letter of the Hebrew alphabet in order. The whole book of Lamentations is a series of acrostics—each chapter has 22 verses, one for each letter of the alphabet; but the third chapter has 66 verses, three for each of the 22 letters.

Acts of the Apostles, the fifth Book of the N.T., gives an account of what happened to the disciples of Jesus after His death. It was written by Luke as a sequel to his Gospel. The first 12 chapters trace the history of the Church in Palestine from Pentecost to the death of Herod, with Peter as the central character. The remainder of the book deals chiefly with the work of Paul. His conversion (chap. 9) is the most graphic and significant of the events narrated.

Adam, the first man; the name means "the man." The biblical narrative says God made Adam out of the dust of the earth, placed him in the Garden of Eden and gave him dominion over all the rest of the animal creation. When he disobeyed God's command not to eat of the fruit (usually spoken of as an apple) of the tree of the knowledge of good and evil, he was driven out of the Garden of Eden and forced to get his food by his own labor. This is called the Fall of Man, and Adam's sin is supposed to have been the origin of all later sin (Gen. 2). Figuratively the name Adam is used to mean original sin or unregenerate nature. The "Old Adam" is contrasted by St. Paul with the "new Adam," man redeemed.

Ahab, a king of Israel (876–855 B.C.), one of the most wicked of the kings. His wife Jezebel, a Phoenician princess, wished to induce the Israelites to worship Baal. At her encouragement, Ahab took Naboth's vineyard from him, and Naboth was stoned to death. For this, Elijah prophesied that Ahab would die and "in the place where dogs licked the blood of Naboth shall dogs lick thy blood, even thine." The deaths of Ahab and Jezebel were in accord with Elijah's predictions (I Kings 17).

Ahasuerus, king of Persia in the Book of Esther.

NEW YORK PUBLIC LIBRARY

THE SACRIFICE OF ABRAHAM. "God tempted Abraham, and said to him . . . Take thy only begotten son Isaac whom you love and go into the land of vision: and there thou shalt offer him for an holocaust . . . And they came to the place which God had shown him . . . And he put forth his hand . . . to sacrifice his son. And behold, an angel of the Lord . . . said to him: Lay not thy hand upon the boy . . . Now I know that thou fearest God, since you have not withheld your only son from Him." Genesis 22:2–12.

BRITISH MUSEUM

THE TOWER OF BABEL was begun when "the earth was of one tongue . . . And they said: Come, let us make a city and a tower, the top whereof may reach to heaven . . . (But the) Lord scattered them . . . And therefore the name thereof was called Babel, because there the language of the whole earth was confounded." Genesis 11:1–9.

Ahithophel, counsellor of Absalom in his conspiracy against David (II Sam. 15).

Amos, the first prophet whose writings have come down to us, was a shepherd at Tekoa, in Judah. About the year 750 B.C., he went to Samaria, the capital of the northern kingdom of Israel, and proclaimed the coming destruction of that kingdom. During a long period of peace and prosperity, Israel had become corrupt, and Amos told the people that God would bring the Assyrians down upon them as a punishment for their sins. He preached the doctrine of righteousness with tremendous force, and was highly indignant at the heartless treatment of the poor amid the luxury and vice he saw all about him. The Book of Amos shows a loftier conception of God than had ever been expressed before.

Ananias, a member of the early Church who sold a piece of property and pretended that he gave the whole amount he received to the Church, while in reality he kept back a part of it. His wife Sapphira shared in the deceit. Peter denounced Ananias, who "fell down and gave up the ghost." His name has been given to liars (Acts 5).

Andrew, brother of Peter, was sent to Jesus by John the Baptist and was the first one called to be a disciple (Mark 13). Tradition says he brought the Gospel to Scythia, which lay north of the Black and Caspian seas, and he has therefore become the patron saint of Russia and Scotland.

Apocalypse, from a Greek word meaning revelation, uncovering, disclosing; is a variant title for the Book of Revelation.

Apocalyptic Literature, the Book of Revelation and other works not accepted in the Biblical canon that reveal the future and promise the coming of a Messiah and a heavenly kingdom. There are apocalyptic passages in the book of Isaiah.

Apocrypha, from a Greek word meaning hidden, secret, spurious, applied to books of uncertain authorship and authority. Famous Apocrypha are the third and fourth Books of Esdras, the Book of Henoch, the Acts of Paul and Thecla.

Apollyon, the angel of the bottomless pit (Rev. 9:11); the name is Greek and means destroying or the destroyer.

Apollos, Paul's friend and fellow worker, "an eloquent man, and mighty in the scriptures" (Acts 18).

Ararat, the mountain on which Noah's ark rested after the Flood (Gen. 8).

Armageddon, the place of the final conflict between the forces of good and evil (Rev. 16:16).

Artaxerxes, the name of two kings of Persia: Artaxerxes I., who ruled from 465 to 425 B.C. and who stopped the rebuilding of Jerusalem (Ezra 4); and Artaxerxes II., king from 405 to 361 B.C., who sent Ezra back to Jerusalem (Ezra 7) and allowed Nehemiah to rebuild the city (Neh. 2).

Assyria, the great empire of which Nineveh was the capital. The Assyrians conquered the northern kingdom of Israel, destroyed Samaria in 722 B.C. and took the people into captivity. Under Sennacherib in 701 B.C., they invaded and devastated the southern kingdom of Judah but failed to take Jerusalem. With the fall of Nineveh in 612 B.C., Assyria passed under the control of the Medes and Persians.

Baal, primarily the god of agriculture, worshipped by the people of Canaan when the Israelites settled among them. Baalim is the Hebrew plural meaning many Baals. Each separate region had its own god Baal, supposed to care for the growth and ripening of the crops and fruit of that region. The word means lord, owner, prince.

Babel, Tower of, begun in prehistoric times by some unknown king but left unfinished, the tower was intended to reach up to heaven; but the work was interrupted through the confusion that arose when God caused the workers to speak in different languages (Gen. 11). The Tower of Babel (that is, of Babylon) was afterwards completed by Nebuchadnezzar and was 325 feet high. Its ruins served for centuries as a brick quarry, but only a great hole where the foundation stood now remains.

Babylon, the capital of the Babylonian Empire. The Babylonians succeeded the Assyrians in their supremacy over Asia after the fall of Nineveh in 612 B.C.; so when Jerusalem was destroyed in 586 B.C., the Jews were carried in captivity to Babylon. In 538 B.C., Babylon was taken by Cyrus the Great, and his Persian Empire succeeded to the position of supremacy. Figuratively the name of the city stands for luxury, wickedness and a place of captivity.

Balaam, a heathen soothsayer in the early days of the conquest of Canaan by the Israelites. He was summoned by Balak, king of the Moabites, and told to curse the Israelites. The ass on which he rode saw an angel in the way and refused to go on. Balaam was therefore led to bless the Israelites instead of cursing them (Num. 22).

Barabbas, a robber and murderer who was released instead of Jesus (Mark 15).

Barnabas, a good-hearted Jew with Greek culture who was associated with Paul in his ministry. He was sent to Antioch and later went with Paul to Jerusalem (Acts 11).

Bartholomew, one of the Twelve Apostles (Matt. 10).

Baruch, friend and secretary of Jeremiah, who dictated his prophesies to Baruch, who read them to the people. The prophesies aroused the wrath of King Jehoiakim, who had Baruch arrested and the roll burned; but Baruch rewrote it. With Jeremiah, he was taken to Egypt. I and II Baruch are Books in the Apocrypha, addressed to the Exiles, to whom they were intended to give encouragement and comfort.

Bath-sheba, wife of Uriah, and afterwards of David, and the mother of Solomon (II Sam. 11).

Beelzebub, a god of the Philistines (II Kings 1). In the N.T. a prince of demons (Matt. 12:24). The name seems to mean Lord of the Flies.

Beersheba, a residence of the patriarchs on the extreme southern boundary of the territory held by the twelve tribes of Israel. As Dan was at the extreme north, the saying "from Dan to Beersheba" indicated the entire extent of the territory (Gen. 21; Judg. 20).

Bel and the Dragon, one of the stories in the Apocryphal part of the Book of Daniel. Bel was an earth god, like Baal.

Belshazzar, the last king of Babylonia, according to the famous account of the handwriting on the wall (Dan. 5).

Benjamin, the youngest and favorite son of Jacob. The tribe of Benjamin united with that of Judah to form the kingdom of Judah after the death of Solomon.

Bethany, a town near Jerusalem, where Jesus came on His last journey. It is given as the scene of His ascension (Luke 24).

Bethel, the place where Jacob had his dream (Gen. 28). After the division of the kingdom, it was the most important shrine of the northern kingdom. The word means house of God.

Bethlehem, the birthplace of Jesus, five miles southwest of Jerusalem.

Boaz. See *Ruth.*

Caiaphas, the high priest before whom Jesus was tried (John 18).

Cain, the oldest son of Adam and Eve, and the first Biblical murderer. After murdering his brother Abel, Cain became a fugitive and vagabond, and a mark was put on him so no one should kill him (Gen. 4).

Calvary. See *Golgotha.*

Cana in Galilee, the place where Jesus performed the miracle of turning water into wine (John 2).

Canaan, the original name of Palestine. The Canaanites were conquered by the Israelites and probably afterwards intermarried with them.

Canticles, another name for *The Song of Songs;* from Latin *canticulum,* little song.

Capernaum, a city of Galilee, where Jesus took up His residence after He left Nazareth (Matt. 4).

Carmel, Mount, a promontory in the northwest part of Palestine, overlooking the Mediterranean. It was closely associated with the lives of Elijah and Elisha, was regarded with veneration, and was famous for its beauty and fertility.

Chaldea, the seacoast region south of Babylonia. The Chaldean kings became kings of Babylonia *c.* 626 B.C., and the names *Babylonian* and *Chaldean,* as used in the Bible, mean very much the same thing. The greatest king was Nebuchadnezzar.

Christ. See *Jesus.*

Chronicles. The book of I and II Chronicles give the history of the children of Israel from a priestly point of view (*c.* 300–200 B.C.), the story of the Chosen Nation reconstituted as the Jewish Church. The Chronicles cover the whole story from Adam to the end of the Exile (538 B.C.), condensing the early material but repeating at length, with interpolations, much of what we find in the four books comprising Samuel and Kings. The new material in Ezra and Nehemiah is a continuation of the same narrative.

Colossians, Epistle of Paul to the, emphasizes how adequate the mission and teaching of Jesus is to the Church and the world. The worship of angels is especially attacked. Colossae was a city in Phrygia on the main route from Palestine to the East.

Corinthians, Epistles to the. Paul lived in Corinth for 18 months, apparently because it offered special opportunities for carrying on his work among the Gentiles. Both epistles were written by Paul in 55 or 56 A.D. In I Corinthians, he rebukes the Church for having factions and disputes; then he writes of marriage as being wise and honorable; then of regard for others' opinions even though one may not agree with them (as in the case of eating meat offered to idols); then of matters regarding public worship. The 13th chapter is the famous one about faith, hope and charity (that is, love). The later chapters of II Corinthians indicate that many people in the Church were hostile to Paul, over which Paul showed his grief.

Cornelius, in Acts 10 "a devout man and one that feared God." He and his household were baptized and admitted to church membership though they did not conform to all the regular requirements. Peter was blamed for this but vindicated himself on the basis of visions he beheld.

Cyrus, king of Persia (538–529 B.C.), captured Babylon in 538 B.C. and permitted the Jews who had been held in captivity to return to Jerusalem (Ezra 1).

Dagon, a god of the Philistines (Judg. 16). The Hebrew word means little fish. He was a fish god.

Damascus, the capital of Syria. It was taken by the Assyrians in 732 B.C. The name is often used to stand for the whole country of Syria. It was on his journey to Damascus that Paul had his vision and was converted (Acts 9).

Dan, son of Jacob and ancestor of one of the Twelve Tribes. The tribe's position was in the extreme north of the territory. So "Dan to Beersheba" means from one end to the other.

Daniel, the hero of the Book of Daniel, a devout Jew who lived in Babylon and was capable of interpreting dreams. He interpreted Nebuchadnezzar's dream of the image made of gold, silver, brass and iron, with feet of clay (chap. 2). His friends Shadrach, Meschach and Abednego were cast into the fiery furnace because they would not worship the image the king had set up, but they came out uninjured (chap. 3). Daniel explained the meaning of the handwriting on the wall at Belshazzar's banquet (chap. 5), and in the lions' den remained unharmed (chap. 6). The rest of the Book (chaps. 7–12) relates a series of four visions Daniel saw that are concerned with the history of the empires from the time of Nebuchadnezzar to the triumph of the Maccabees in 165 B.C.

JOHN M. PRICE, JR.

DAVID. This magnificent stone statue was carved by Michelangelo and stands in the Academy of Fine Arts in Florence, Italy.

David, king of Israel, lived about 1000 B.C. The youngest son of Jesse, he grew up on a farm near Bethlehem. In his youth he was a shepherd, and because of his delight in music he learned to play the harp. Called to the court of King Saul, he played to the troubled king to quiet him. He soon became popular, and one of the most famous of all friendships grew up between him and the king's son Jonathan. While he was still a youth, he had his famous fight with the Philistine giant Goliath, whom he killed with a stone from a sling. This made him immensely popular. He married Saul's daughter Michal, but Saul soon became jealous of David's growing power and popularity and sought to kill him. David escaped and became leader of a wild and lawless band of men. On one occasion he saved Saul's life. After Saul's death David became king. He conquered the stronghold of Jerusalem and made it the seat of his government. Here he brought the Ark of the Covenant and so made Jerusalem the religious as well as the political center of Israel. The early years of his reign were filled with wars of conquest.

His love for Bath-sheba led him to give command that her husband Uriah should be placed in "the forefront of the hottest battle" and then be deserted. Uriah was accordingly killed, and David married Bath-sheba, for which he was sternly rebuked by the prophet Nathan. When his son Absalom rose in rebellion and was defeated and killed, David was overcome with grief. Though so much of David's life was occupied with wars, he was able to organize his government, to develop a sense of loyalty in his people and to unite them in their religious attitude. David was brave, generous, kindly and just, but he had many human weaknesses. David was famous as a poet. His lament at the death of Saul and Jonathan (II Sam. 1) is one of the most moving poems in the world's literature. Many Psalms are attributed to him. The gospels of Matthew and Luke both trace the descent of Jesus from King David, and O.T. prophecies of the Messiah say that he is to come from the house of David.

Dead Sea, referred to as the Salt Sea (Gen. 14) and by other names elsewhere in the Bible, but not by its present name. It is nearly 50 miles long by 10 wide. The consistency of the water makes it possible for one to sit up in it without sinking.

Deborah, a prophetess and judge of Israel. With Barak she caused the defeat of the Philistines in the Battle of Kishon, and celebrated the victory in one of the finest and most stirring songs ever written (Judg. 5).

Delilah, the Philistine woman whom Samson loved and who by betraying him caused his loss of strength and his capture by his enemies (Judg. 16).

Deuteronomy, the fifth book of the O.T.; the word means second law. The main portion of the Book consists of the farewell of Moses to Israel in which he gave out and explained the laws that were to govern the people and told what would befall them if they disobeyed. Deuteronomy ends with an account of the death of Moses. When it was found and read to the people in 621 B.C., it produced a great reform. It had tremendous influence on the prophets and historians who wrote after that time.

Diana, the Latin name of a Greek goddess who had a great temple at Ephesus so vast and magnificent that it was included among the Seven Wonders of the World. When Paul came to Ephesus to preach a new religion, the Ephesians tried to silence him by shouting "Great is Diana of the Ephesians" (Acts 19:21–41).

Ecclesiastes, a Book of the O.T.; so called from its nameless author who calls himself the preacher—Koheleth in Hebrew, Ecclesiastes in Greek. It is one of the Wisdom books. The author at first identifies himself with

King Solomon, but he soon drops this idea and continues simply as Koheleth, the preacher. He says that in nature and in human affairs there is endless repetition and weariness, that all is vanity or emptiness. Therefore, he says, "Eat, drink and be merry." Many bits of wisdom of a more religious tone are thought to have been added by later writers.

Ecclesiasticus, the most remarkable Wisdom books of Apocrypha. It contains good advice on many subjects. It is supposed to be the wisdom of Jesus (Joshua), son of Sirach.

Eden, a luxuriant and ideal garden where Adam and Eve were placed and where everything they could want was provided (Gen. 2). Many people have sought to discover from the description where it was located. The only clue is that it contained a river which divided into four rivers, one of which was the Euphrates. This does not correspond to any place that can now be identified.

Egypt, at the time when the Israelites had their independent kingdom, was the powerful kingdom on the south, and was the rival for world supremacy of Assyria, the great empire to the northeast. After the Israelites under the leadership of Moses escaped from their bondage in Egypt and founded a strong kingdom, the Egyptians realized that this new state could be of great value to them in their conflict with the Assyrians; Isaiah, however, distrusted their offers of friendship. After many reversals of fortune in the struggle between Egypt and the northern empires, Cambyses, son of Cyrus, brought Egypt under Persian dominion in 525 B.C. It regained independence in 414 B.C., but later was brought under Greek control.

Eli, the high priest of the sanctuary at Shiloh in Samuel's childhood (I Sam. 1).

Elijah, the great prophet of the northern kingdom in the time of King Ahab. He prophesied the drought that would result from Ahab's sins, and then went to the brook Cherith, where he was fed by the ravens (I Kings 17). Next, at Zidon, he performed the miracle of keeping full the widow's cruse of oil and jar of meal, no matter how much was taken out, and restored her son to life. After ending the drought, Elijah retired to Mount Horeb, where he heard the "still small voice" in which God spoke after the earthquake and fire (I Kings 19). His last conflict with Ahab was when he denounced him for taking Naboth's vineyard. According to the Scriptural account, Elijah did not die but was taken up to heaven in a chariot of fire (II Kings 2). He was fearless and uncompromising but often despondent. His great accomplishment was in leading the people away from idolatry. In the N.T., it is said that he appeared with Moses at the transfiguration of Christ (Matt. 17).

Elisha, recipient of Elijah's mantle when the chariot of fire appeared, thereafter became Elijah's successor as a prophet and performed many miracles, the most famous being the curing of Naaman, the leper (I Kings 19). He was very patriotic.

Enoch, the father of Methuselah, and supposed not to have died but to have been "translated." The Biblical account (Gen. 5:24) substitutes for the usual "and he died" the strange statement, "And Enoch walked with God: and he was not: for God took him." A very important noncanonical Hebrew apocalyptic work, written at least in part during the second century B.C., is known as the Book of Enoch. It tells the story of the fall of the angels and predicts the coming of the Son of Man.

Ephesians, Epistle to the, the fifth of Paul's epistles and apparently addressed to Christians living in Asia Minor; it seems to have been a circular letter, to be read in various churches in turn and not merely in the church at Ephesus. It consists largely of moral reflections and exhortations, especially urging unity between Jews and Gentiles. Its best-known passage is the comparison of the Christian to the soldier with the whole armor of God, the breast-plate of righteousness and helmet of salvation (chap. 6:10–17).

Ephraim, son of Joseph and ancestor of one of the strongest tribes in the northern kingdom, the strength and central position of which led to the frequent use of the name for the whole kingdom.

Esau, the first-born of the twin sons of Isaac and Rebekah, is represented as a hairy man (Esau is Hebrew for hairy), a hunter and a man of the field. He sold his birthright to his twin brother Jacob for a mess of pottage; and Jacob, pretending to be Esau, deceived their dying father Isaac into giving him the blessing intended for Esau. Esau afterwards forgave Jacob.

Esther. The Book of Esther relates how a Jewish maiden named Esther became the queen of the monarch Ahasuerus (Xerxes), and was able, with the help of her cousin Mordecai, to save her people from the destruction planned for them by Haman, the king's favorite counselor; and of how Haman was hanged on the gallows he had prepared for Mordecai.

Euphrates, a great river in Babylonia.

Eve, wife of Adam, made from Adam's rib (Gen. 2). She was beguiled by the Serpent to eat the fruit of the forbidden tree.

Exodus, the second Book of the O.T., named from the Greek word meaning escape or way out, tells of the escape of the Israelites from Egypt under Moses, of their life in the wilderness and their constitutional history. The Ten Commandments are given in chap. 20.

Ezekiel, one of the Jews carried into captivity to Babylon in 597 B.C. Here he became the religious leader of the exiles and prophesied the destruction of Jerusalem; after this took place in 586 B.C., he prophesied its rebuilding and future greatness. The most admired of his narrated visions is that of the Valley of Dry Bones (Ezek. 37).

Ezra and Nehemiah, originally one Book, consisting of personal memoirs incorporated in a later chronicle and forming a continuation of I and II Chronicles. Ezra and Nehemiah were among the descendants of the Jews who remained in Babylon when Cyrus permitted those who wished to do so to return to Jerusalem. Discouraging reports of how things were going in Judea reached the Babylonian Jews, and both Ezra and Nehemiah, though not at the same time, received permission to return from the Persian monarch Artaxerxes. Nehemiah, the king's cupbearer, acted as governor and rebuilt the walls of Jerusalem. Ezra returned with about 1,500 Babylonian Jews and was the religious leader of the people. He calls himself the priest and the scribe. After his return a great assembly was called, and he read the book of the law of Moses to the people "from early morning until midday," and "gave the sense, so that they understood the reading" (Neh. 8:3, 8). This brought on a great reform. Ezra bitterly opposed intermarriage of the Jews with people of surrounding nations.

Gabriel (Hebrew, man of God), the archangel, announced to Zacharias that he would be the father of John the Baptist and to Mary that she was to be the mother of Jesus (Luke 1).

Gad, son of Joseph and ancestor of one of the Twelve Tribes.

Galatians, Epistle to the, addressed to the people of Galatia, a Roman province in Asia Minor settled by the Gauls, or Celts, c. 300 B.C. The epistle was written by Paul on receipt of disturbing news as to the pride and jealousy that had developed in the churches and the growing disbelief and hostility to Paul under the guidance of false teachers. Paul writes frankly of his own life and mission and follows with a careful analysis of the principles of Christian faith and the need of being free from the Jewish law.

Galilee, the upper portion of Palestine. The Sea of Galilee, closely associated with the ministry of Jesus and His disciples, is the largest fresh-water lake in the country—13 miles long by 8 miles wide. It is a clear, bright-blue body of water, and the surrounding hills make a beautiful landscape.

Gath, one of the principal cities of the Philistines, of which David sang in his lament when Saul and Jonathan died, "Tell it not in Gath" (II Sam. 1:20).

Gaza, an important Philistine city. The story of Samson's carrying off the gates of the city (Judg. 16:3) now gives it its chief fame.

Genesis, the first Book of the O.T. (a Greek word meaning beginning), describes the creation of the world and of man, and carries the Biblical narrative down to the death of Joseph.

Gethsemane, a garden, probably on the slope of the Mount of Olives, where Jesus often went with His disciples (Mark 14).

Gideon, one of the judges of Israel, called Jerubbaal (Let Baal plead) because Gideon cast down the altar of Baal (Ju. 6). Against the Midianites he led an army of 32,000 men and by two tests reduced their number to 300 picked men. Armed with trumpets and lamps in pitchers the 300 threw the Midianites in panic by blowing the trumpets and breaking the pitchers. *Gideon's Band* is a proverb for picked men. The *Gideons* are an organization of American commercial travelers, founded in 1899, to place copies of the Bible in hotel guest rooms and Pullman cars.

Gilead, the name given to a large but not clearly defined section of Palestine east of the Jordan. It is a hilly region of beautiful scenery and was noted for its rich balsam—Balm of Gilead—that was used for the treatment of wounds; the phrase is now a figurative expression meaning anything that will sooth pain.

Gilgal, a place near Jericho where Joshua and his followers first encamped after crossing the Jordan. From that time on it was a religious and military center. Afterward it became one of the chief shrines of the northern kingdom (Josh. 5; Amos 4:4).

Gog and Magog are names (Ezek. 38) and (Rev. 20) of a prince and a land, respectively, opposed to God and His people.

Golgotha, or Calvary (Hebrew and Latin words meaning place of a skull), the scene of the Crucifixion (Matt. 27:33; Luke 23:33). The hill supposed to be the actual site of Calvary is now an Arabian cemetery. Looking across at it from the Mount of Olives, one sees a formation that is curiously like a skull. This may have given the place the name Golgotha.

Goliath, the Philistine giant whom David fought and slew (I Sam. 17).

Gomorrah. See *Sodom.*

Goshen, the northeastern part of Egypt, where the Israelites lived before their escape.

Great Sea, biblical name for the Mediterranean.

Habakkuk, a minor prophet who wrote of the devastations caused by the Chaldeans, asking why God permitted such things to be and praying and prophesying that the spoiler would be despoiled and that "the earth shall be filled with the knowledge of the glory of Jehovah, as the waters cover the sea" (Hab. 2:14).

Hagar, handmaiden of Sarah and mother of Ishmael (Gen. 16).

Haggai, a prophet who urged the rebuilding of the Temple after the Israelites returned from the Exile. The Book of Haggai dates from 520 B.C.

Ham, one of the sons of Noah and supposedly the ancestor of the Egyptians and of other peoples of North Africa (Gen. 10).

Haman. See *Esther.*

Hannah, mother of Samuel (I Sam. 1).

Hebrews, Epistle to the, primarily an argument in favor of Christianity as the final and true religion, rather a sermon on faith than a letter. It is not certain that Paul wrote it, and the precise group to whom it was addressed is not known.

Hebron, a frequently mentioned city near Jerusalem, where David had his seat of government before he moved it to Jerusalem (II Sam. 5). Absalom made it the headquarters for his rebellion (II Sam. 15:10).

Hermon, Mount, a beautiful, snow-capped mountain, 9,200 feet high, about 50 miles north by northeast of the sea of Galilee. It appealed strongly to the poetic imagination of the people, is often referred to in the Psalms and was believed by some to be the Mount of Transfiguration (Mark 9:2).

Herod the Great became king of Judea (subject to Rome) in 39 B.C. He rebuilt the Temple at Jerusalem and made it one of the finest buildings of antiquity. He also rebuilt Samaria and other cities. Though cruel, he kept his country at peace. He caused his wife Mariamne to be put to death on account of his jealousy, and this has made him a tragic figure in modern literature. He is the Herod of the "slaughter of the Innocents" (Matt. 2); and as he died in 4 B.C., it has been suggested that our calendar is incorrect and that the Christian era should begin at that date. At his death, the kingdom was divided among his three sons, of whom Herod Antipas is the Herod usually referred to in the Gospels. It was he who imprisoned John the Baptist and had him beheaded (Mark 6), and to him Pilate sent Jesus (Luke 23).

Herodias, wife of Herod Antipas. See *John the Baptist.*

Hezekiah, king of Judah (720–692 B.C.), joined the neighboring countries to resist the Assyrians, which led to the invasion of the country, the plundering of many of the cities and almost to the capture of Jerusalem. He was devout and carried out many religious reforms, but was wavering and unwise in his political policy (II Kings 18).

Hilkiah, high priest in the reign of Josiah, who discovered in the Temple the Book of the Law (II Kings 22).

Hiram, king of Tyre, who aided Solomon in the building of the Temple (I Kings 5).

Holy Ghost or Holy Spirit, the Third Person of the Trinity.

Holy Land, a name given to Palestine because of its religious associations.

Horeb. See *Sinai.*

Hosea (785–725 B.C.), one of the minor prophets and the book he wrote. After Amos prophesied the destruction of the northern kingdom, Hosea saw the same catastrophe approaching and called the people to repent. He believed that if they repented, God would forgive and spare them. He spoke of the love of God for His people as like that of a husband and a father. Hosea is the most tender of all the prophets.

Isaac, son of Abraham and Sarah. The story of how Rebekah came to be Isaac's wife gives a delightful glimpse of old customs (Gen. 24). He lived long and prospered and seems to have had a quiet and uneventful life.

Isaiah (750–695 B.C.) not only very great as a prophet and poet but was the leading statesman of his time. He opposed joining the league against Assyria (Is. 7) and thus may have kept Jerusalem from sharing the fate of Damascus and Samaria. He bitterly opposed seeking aid from the Egyptians, whom he did not trust. His faith that God would save Jerusalem led him to advise Hezekiah not to surrender the city to Sennacherib when he was besieging it in 701 B.C., and this postponed the downfall of Judah for over a century. Beginning with the 40th chapter, the Book of Isaiah is a prophecy in exalted poetry that is so appropriate to the time when Cyrus was about to permit the exiles to return to Jerusalem that most scholars have no doubt in giving it this date. Much of it has been taken by Christians to refer to the coming of Jesus.

Ishmael, son of Abraham and Hagar, and ancestor of the Ishmaelites, by which term perhaps the Arabians are meant (Gen. 21). Ishmaelite is proverbial for an outcast.

Israel, a name given to Jacob after he wrestled with the angel (Gen. 32:28); the Hebrew word seems to mean contender with God. The Children of Israel were the sons of Jacob and their descendants. The name Israel was applied to the Twelve Tribes until the division of the kingdom after Solomon's death; from then on it was applied to the northern kingdom and the southern kingdom was called Judah. The Israelites are supposedly of Arabian stock, and in Genesis there are many references that indicate their kinship with other Arabian peoples. According to the Biblical account, they came down to Egypt in a time of famine and remained there for a long period as a subject race. Then, under the leadership of Moses, they made their great Exodus—their *going out*—and wandered in the wilderness of the Arabian Peninsula until they were able to gain a foothold in Canaan. There they established themselves under the leadership of Joshua but were for many years at war with other nations and clans who occupied this fertile region. For a time they were subdued by the Philistines, but they broke away and became an independent nation under their first king, Saul. Under their next king, David, they became the strongest state between Egypt on the south and Syria on the north; and under the third and last king of the united nation, Solomon, they were at last peaceful and rich.

When Solomon died, ten tribes under Jeroboam established an independent northern kingdom, while the two tribes of Judah and Benjamin remained loyal to Rehoboam, son of Solomon, and formed the southern kingdom of Judah. The northern kingdom fell, and its capital, Samaria, was captured and destroyed by the Assyrians in 722 B.C. and the people carried into captivity. They are called the Lost Tribes, because nothing more is known of them. They probably intermarried with other peoples and lost their racial and religious identity. The Jews of the present time are descended from the two tribes of the southern kingdom. This kingdom passed under the control of the Babylonian Empire when it became supreme. When the Jews of the southern kingdom were carried into captivity in 597 B.C., and more of them when Jerusalem was taken and destroyed in 586 B.C., they went to Babylon. There they remained till 538 B.C., when Cyrus the Persian took Babylon and permitted the Jews to return.

After the exile, Judea, as it was then called, remained subject to Persia until 333 B.C., when it passed with other Persian dominions into the hands of Alexander the Great, and it remained under Greek control until 142 B.C., when it again became in-

dependent under the Maccabees. Later quarrels led to calling in the Roman general Pompey who entered Jerusalem in 63 B.C. Judea then became a Roman province, which it continued to be in N.T. times. The two chief facts to have in mind regarding the history of Israel are (1) that as a buffer state between Egypt and the northern empires in their struggle for world supremacy, it was bound to lose its independence; and (2) that the Jews of the southern kingdom were able to keep themselves an unmixed race and remain true to their religion when those of the northern kingdom did not, because the Babylonians kept their captives together and the Assyrians had scattered their captives; and because, during the extra century and more that Jerusalem stood after Samaria fell, the Jews formulated their religion and rose to a higher conception of God under the guidance of their great prophets, especially Isaiah and Jeremiah.

Jacob, the younger of the twin sons of Isaac and Rebekah. With his mother's help, he tricked Isaac into giving him the blessing that was intended for Esau (Gen. 27). Jacob fled to escape Esau's rage. At Bethel, he saw the vision of the angels and the ladder (Gen. 28). He served his Uncle Laban seven years to win Rachel for his wife, and then Laban said he must first take the older daughter Leah; so Jacob served seven more years for Rachel. Then with his two wives he returned. In his old age he went with his family to Egypt where the Children of Israel grew up in bondage.

Jael, heroine of a war in the time of the Judges (Ju. 4 and 5). When Sisera, leader of the Canaanites against Israel, was fleeing for his life, she offered him hospitality and while he slept killed him by driving a nail in his temple.

James, son of Zebedee, brother of John and one of the Twelve Apostles. He was killed by Herod (Acts 12:2). Tradition says that he went as a missionary to Spain, hence he became the patron saint of that country. (The Spanish for St. James is Santiago.) St. James the Less may be the same as James, son of Alphaeus, another of the Twelve Apostles, who probably wrote the Epistle of James. This Epistle is composed almost wholly of exhortations and warnings bearing upon practical religious living.

Japheth, third son of Noah (Gen. 10:1). His descendants were supposedly people of Indo-European stock.

Jehu, king of Israel (c. 842–814 B.C.), revolted against the house of Ahab and murdered the kings of both Israel and Judah. It was said of him, "For he driveth furiously" (II Kings 9:20), and so to "drive like Jehu" has become a proverbial expression.

Jehovah, meaning "I am," the name by which God revealed Himself to Moses (Ex. 3). Only the consonants JHVH were used in the Hebrew as the holy name was not to be spoken, and scholars say that the correct pronunciation may be Yahweh.

Jephthah, judge of Israel, vowed to sacrifice the first of his household to

meet him if he returned victorious from the coming battle. He was victorious, and the first one to meet him was his own daughter (Judg. 11).

Jeremiah, among the greatest prophets, began to prophesy in 626 B.C., when the Scythians were devastating Judah; he considered this God's punishment and called the people to reform. In 605 he wrote a stirring poem occasioned by the Battle of Carchemish, calling more urgently for reform. For his unpopular teachings, which were regarded as unpatriotic, he suffered great indignities and persecutions. After the destruction of Jerusalem in 586 B.C., Jeremiah was taken to Egypt, where, tradition says, he was put to death. As a poet, he is intense and impassioned. What makes him one of the most significant figures of all time is the personal and spiritual interpretation that he gave to the Jewish religion in place of the more national outlook of his predecessors.

Two books of the O.T. are attributed to him: Jeremiah, a prophecy of the captivity with autobiographical details; and Lamentations, five poems on the sufferings of his people. In popular speech Jeremiah means one who wails or laments, and a jeremiad is a sorrowful story.

Jericho, the first city of importance captured by the Israelites in their conquest of Canaan. According to the Biblical account, its walls fell down as a result of the Israelites' marching around the city and blowing their trumpets (Josh. 6).

Jeroboam, first king of the northern kingdom (c. 937–915 B.C.). He led the revolt of the Ten Tribes against Rehoboam, son of Solomon (I Kings 11). Jeroboam II (c. 781–740 B.C.) was the king under whom the northern kingdom became prosperous but corrupt.

Jerusalem, the greatest and most sacred city of Palestine. It was captured by David, made resplendent by Solomon and in 586 B.C. destroyed by Nebuchadnezzar. After the Exile it was gradually rebuilt but was destroyed again by Antiochus Epiphanes in 168 B.C. Rebuilt again and beautified by Herod the Great, the sacred city was completely destroyed by Titus in 70 A.D. In 136 A.D., Jerusalem was restored by Hadrian. The Arabs captured Jerusalem in the 7th century and made it the holy place of the Mohammedans. The Crusaders took it in 1099, but it was in the hands of the Turks from 1517 to 1919. In World War I the ancient city was occupied by the Allies. At the present time, Jerusalem is divided between Jordan and Israel.

Jesse, father of *David* (I Sam. 16).

Jesus, called Christ or the Christ, a Greek translation of the Hebrew Messiah, meaning Anointed. The Hebrew form of the name Jesus was Joshua, which meant the Lord is deliverance or salvation. The story of His life is told in the Four Gospels.

Jethro, father-in-law of Moses (Ex. 3).

Jezebel. See *Ahab.*

Joab, nephew of David and commander of his armies. A faithful but cruel soldier (II Sam. 14).

Job, the patriarch, who suffered many misfortunes but was restored to health and prosperity in greater measure than before, because he had stood the test patiently and unquestioningly. In the Book of Job, O.T., he debates this problem of evil, why God sends suffering, with his three friends, Eliphaz, Bildad and Zophar, who maintain that he must have sinned greatly to be afflicted as he is. When these three are silenced, a younger man, Elihu, takes up the argument. Then God answers Job out of the whirlwind. The poetic quality and dramatic power of the Book of Job have hardly been surpassed.

Joel, one of the minor prophets, tells of a great locust plague in terms that suggest an invading army; its poetry is magnificent. The date of the prophecy is uncertain.

John, the "beloved Apostle," is given as the author of the Fourth Gospel, three Epistles and Revelation. The Gospel According to St. John differs from that of Matthew, Mark and Luke in being not so much a biography of Jesus as a beautiful interpretation of His life and significance to the world with special stress on the idea that the Christ is the Word of God made flesh. The first Epistle, a friendly and persuasive talk about the Christian faith and the Christian life, is one of the most beautiful and most loved books in the N.T. The other two epistles are the shortest books in the Bible, each consisting of but one very short chapter.

John the Baptist, cousin and forerunner of Jesus, called the people to repent and prepare for the Messiah. He baptized his followers in the Jordan, and Jesus came to him and was baptized (Mark 3). He is called the Baptist because he baptized Jesus and many others. When Herod Antipas married Herodias, his brother's wife, John denounced him, saying that the marriage was not lawful. At this, Herodias was extremely angry and sought to have him killed. Her daughter Salome danced before King Herod and pleased him so much that he offered her anything she would ask. Herodias told her to ask for the head of John the Baptist, and the king reluctantly granted the request. Figuratively the phrase John the Baptist means any forerunner of a great man or movement, especially if the forerunner is greatly overshadowed by what he announces.

Jonah, a prophet who did not want to obey God's command to go to Nineveh and prophesy its destruction and so started in the opposite direction and took a boat for Tarshish. When a storm arose, Jonah said it was on his account and had the sailors throw him into the sea. The Book of Jonah says that the Lord prepared a great fish (it is spoken of as a whale only in a reference in Matt. 12:40), which swallowed Jonah, and in it he remained for three days. He prayed to God, and God heard him. After his release, Jonah went to Nineveh, made his prophecy and sat outside the city to see if it would be destroyed. But the people of Nineveh repented and God spared them, at which Jonah was angry. God rebuked him for pettiness.

Jonathan, son of Saul and friend of David (I Sam. 18).

Joppa, a seaport in Palestine.

Jordan, the famous river of Palestine. By crossing it, the Israelites began their real conquest of Canaan. The baptism of Jesus and the association of the river with so much of the history of Israel has made it the most sacred of all streams to Christian people.

Joseph, the youngest son of Jacob, until the birth of Benjamin, and his favorite. His brothers were jealous of him, and they sold him to a band of Midianites who took him to Egypt. Here he interpreted Pharaoh's dream as meaning that seven years of plenty would be followed by seven years of famine, and thus the Egyptians were prepared when the famine came. Joseph rose to great power and influence, and when the famine came and his brothers arrived to buy food it was to him that they had to appeal. They did not recognize him, but after a series of tests Joseph revealed himself and became reconciled to them. Then he had his whole family come and settle in Egypt (Gen. 37–50).

Joseph, husband of the Virgin Mary.

Joseph of Arimathaea, a rich man who received and buried the body of Jesus in his own sepulcher (Mark 15:43).

Joshua, the successor of Moses as leader of the Israelites and their commander in the conquest of Canaan. The O.T. Book of Joshua gives an account of this conquest.

Josiah, king of Judah (638–609 B.C.). When the Book of the Law was discovered in the Temple and read to him, he instituted a great reform. He was killed in the Battle of Megiddo attempting to resist an invasion of the Egyptians (II Kings 21).

Jotham, the youngest of the 70 sons of Gideon and the only one who escaped when his brother Abimelech killed all the others and set himself up as King. Jotham opposed this in his Fable of the Trees, in which a bramble was selected to be their king (Ju. 9).

Judah, son of Jacob and ancestor of the tribe that united with that of Benjamin to form the southern kingdom. (For the history of Judah, see *Israel*.)

Judas, one of the Twelve Disciples, named only in Mark 3:18, possibly called Thaddaeus and Labbaeus in other places. The name is a Greek form of Judah.

Judas Iscariot, the Apostle who betrayed Jesus and then hanged himself (Matt. 26). Iscariot seems to mean the man who came from Kerioth, a village in Palestine.

Judas Maccabaeus. See *Maccabees*.

Jude, Epistle of, written by Judas, brother of James; does not say to whom the letter is addressed; it was evidently to people among whom false teachings and false practices had grown up.

Judea, a name given to Palestine after the Exile.

Judges, The Book of, received that name because it deals chiefly with the men who judged Israel; they were the rulers of the people for four centuries before the establishment of the kingdom. The Book begins with the story of the death of Joshua and closes with records of the time of Samuel.

Judith, the heroine of the Apocryphal Book of Judith; she was a beautiful Jewish widow of the city of Bethulia when it was beseiged by Holofernes, a general of Nebuchadnezzar. She went to his tent, and when he was in a drunken sleep cut off his head. The Jews were inspired by his death to defeat their enemies and free their city.

Kings, I and II, historical books that continue the narrative in I and II Samuel. They begin with recounting the death of David and appointment of Solomon as his successor and end with the taking of Jerusalem and the carrying of the Jews in captivity to Babylon.

Laban, uncle of Jacob and father of Jacob's wives, Leah and Rachel.

Lamentations, a book of poetic laments over the fall of Jerusalem and consequent sufferings of the Jews, authorship of which is assigned to Jeremiah.

Lazarus, brother of Mary and Martha, raised from the dead by Jesus (John II). In His parable of the rich man and the beggar, Jesus gives this name to the beggar (Luke 16).

Leah, Jacob's wife.

Lebanon, a mountain range in Syria that extends about 100 miles, parallel to the Mediterranean. The famous cedars of Lebanon were used by Solomon in building the Temple (I Kings 5). A few groves still remain.

Levi, son of Jacob and ancestor of the tribe that had no territory of its own but supplied the priests and the priests' helpers, called Levites, for the other tribes (Josh. 18:7).

Leviticus, the third Book of the O.T., the laws and ordinances to govern the priests and people in their religious observances. The word means having to do with the Levites.

Lot, kinsman of Abraham, settled in the plain of Jordan. When Sodom and Gomorrah were to be destroyed, he was warned by an angel to fly from that region with his household and not to look back. Lot's wife did look back and was turned to a pillar of salt (Gen. 13 and 19).

Luke, a Gentile, probably a Greek (as the name is Greek, not Hebrew), a physician, a friend and co-worker with Paul and author of the Third Gospel and of the Acts of the Apostles. Both are addressed to Theophilus, apparently a man of rank who was not familiar with the situation. The Gospel according to St. Luke is like Matthew's Gospel because both have material that is not in Mark.

Maccabees, Jewish patriots of the 2d century, B.C., notably Judas, called Maccabeus, which apparently means the hammer. He was one of five sons of Mattathias, a priest, who led a Jewish revolt against the Syrians under Antiochus Epiphanes (ruled 175–164 B.C.) when the Syrians desecrated the Temple. Maccabeus succeeded in retaking the Temple, which he purified and rededicated. He was included among the Nine Worthies listed in the Middle Ages. When killed in 161 B.C., his brother Jonathan continued his successes, and his brother Simon won independence for the nation in 142 B.C. The apocryphal books, I and II Maccabees, give a clear and interesting account of these wars.

Magdalene, or Mary of Magdala, the woman from whom Jesus cast out seven demons (Luke 8). She is usually identified with the sinner who anointed His feet (Luke 7).

Malachi, the last Book in the O.T.; the Hebrew word means messenger, and nothing else is known of the prophet who wrote it. It deals chiefly with the need of keeping the law and with the coming judgment that will separate the wicked from the righteous.

Manasseh (1) first-born son of Joseph and ancestor of one of the twelve tribes called by his name; (2) a King of Judah (II Kings 21).

Mark, John Mark (or Marcus), author of the Second Gospel. His mother was named Mary and he worked with Paul. Very little is known about him. His Gospel is the shortest and is generally believed to be the earliest written of the Four.

Martha, the practical sister of Mary, the loving one (Luke 10:38–42).

Mary, Among several of this name in the Gospel narrative are included: Mary Magdalene (see *Magdalene*); Mary, the sister of Martha (see *Martha*); Mary, mother of James and Joseph, was one of those who witnessed the Crucifixion (Mark 15:40); the Virgin Mary, mother of Jesus, a descendant of the House of David espoused to Joseph at the time of the Annunciation (Luke 1:26-38) and honored in the Catholic Churches; with the Infant Jesus, she has been the subject of many of the world's greatest paintings.

Matthew, one of the Twelve Apostles and author of the First Gospel, was a publican (tax gatherer or customs officer) when Jesus called him (Matt. 9:9). The Gospel According to Matthew begins with the genealogy of Jesus and His nativity (chap. 1), which is followed by an account of the slaughter of the innocents, the visit of the Three Wise Men and the flight into Egypt (chap. 2); the work of John the Baptist and baptism of Jesus (chap. 3); the temptations in the wilderness and the calling of the first four Apostles (chap. 4); the Sermon on the Mount (chaps. 5–7), including the Lord's Prayer (chap. 6:9–13); Christ's healing of the sick, quieting of the waters and casting out devils (chap. 8); His teachings, with various parables and miracles (chaps. 9–16); the Transfiguration, prophesy of the Passion and later ministry (chaps. 17–20); His triumphal entry into Jerusalem and His work following that (chaps. 21–25); the conspiracy against Him, the Last Supper, His betrayal by Judas and Peter's denial (chap. 26); His appearance before Pilate, the mockery and crown of thorns, the crucifixion and burial (chap. 27); the announcement of the Resurrection by the angel and the appearance of Jesus to His disciples with His last words to them (chap. 28).

Matthias, chosen to take the place of Judas among the Twelve Apostles (Acts 1:26).

Medes, the people of Media, a country between the Caspian Sea and Persia, extending from Assyria on the west to the great desert on the east. The Medes took Nineveh in 612 B.C. but were subdued by the Persians under Cyrus in 550 B.C. The Medes and Persians are associated in the Book of Daniel.

Melchizedek, a priest and king who bestowed a blessing on Abraham (Gen. 14:18). The combination of priest and king is an ideal twice referred to (Pss. 110; Heb. 7).

Melita, an island in the Mediterranean Sea where Paul was shipwrecked (Acts 27).

Messiah (Hebrew, the anointed) or **Messias** (Greek form of the Hebrew word), the Lord's anointed, a title both of the Kings of Israel, especially Saul and David, and of the expected savior of Israel prophesied throughout the O.T. (Is. 9:1–6, 11:1, 40:1–11, 61:1) and usually connected with the line of King David. The Messianic prophecy of the O.T. contains the most exalted imagery and the fondest hopes of the great prophets—a common heritage of the pious Jew and the Christian believer. The Gospel of Matthew points out the different ways that Jesus fulfilled these prophecies. Jesus' title, the Christ, is a Greek translation of the Hebrew *Messiah.*

Methuselah, grandfather of Noah, reputedly the oldest man, said to have lived to be 969 years old (Gen. 5:27).

Micah, a contemporary of Isaiah who prophesied that the coming destruction of Samaria and Jerusalem, to take place on account of the sins of the people, would be followed by an age of deliverance and restoration.

Michael, the archangel, guardian of the nation of Israel (Dan. 10:13, 21); leader of the heavenly forces in casting out the dragon (Rev. 12:7).

Michal, youngest daughter of Saul and wife of David (I Sam. 18), whose life she saved (I Sam. 19).

METROPOLITAN MUSEUM OF ART

SAINT MICHAEL AND HIS ANGELS battling the demons of Satan is one of a series of fifteen woodcuts by Albrecht Dürer, that depict scenes from the Apocalypse. Apocalypse is the Greek name for the Book of Revelation, the last book of the New Testament.

Midianites, an Arabian people sometimes identified with the Ishmaelites. A band of them carried Joseph to Egypt (Gen. 27). Moses found refuge with them and married the daughter of their priest Jethro (Ex. 2). They appear later as a hostile people against whom Gideon fought (Judg. 7).

Miriam, a prophetess, sister of Moses and Aaron, led the people in a celebration after crossing the Red Sea (Ex. 15:20). With Aaron, she rebelled against the authority of Moses; she became leprous thereafter but was healed at Moses' intercession (Num. 12).

Mizpah (meaning watch tower) is a name applied to several places. When Jacob made his covenant with Laban, he gave the name to a heap of stones set up as a witness and said, "The Lord watch between me and thee, when we are absent from one another" (Gen. 31:49), and in this sense the word is still used.

Moab, a region near the Dead Sea. The Moabites were said to be descended from Lot. They were conquered by David but broke away after the death of Solomon and were later among the most bitterly hated of the peoples that surrounded Judah.

Mordecai, cousin of Esther.

NASH FROM MONKMEYER

MOSES, from a statue by Michelangelo in the church of San Pietro in Vincoli, Rome.

Moses, the great leader of the Israelites in their escape from Egypt and in their wanderings until they reached the Promised Land of Canaan and began its conquest. When the Egyptians were killing every male child to prevent the Israelites from becoming too powerful, the mother of the new-born Moses hid him in an ark of bulrushes on the brink of the river Nile in order to save him. Here he was found and adopted by Pharaoh's daughter. When he was grown, he killed an Egyptian for smiting a Hebrew, and fled to the land of Midian, where he married Zipporah, daughter of Jethro, a priest (Ex. 2). In a burning bush that was not consumed by the fire, God told him to deliver his people (Ex. 3). With his brother

Aaron he appealed to Pharaoh to release the Israelites, and ten plagues were sent to induce Pharaoh to agree.

With each plague Pharaoh agreed, but he afterwards refused. Finally, by killing the first-born of the Egyptians, though no Israelites died (the origin of the Passover), Moses gained consent, and the Israelites crossed the Red Sea, the waters of which divided for them to pass (Ex. 14). On Mount Sinai Moses received the Ten Commandments (Ex. 20). He continued as leader and lawgiver of the people, in spite of much murmuring and discontent. He brought water from a rock (Num. 20) and made a brazen serpent by which people were healed (Num. 21). He died on Mount Nebo, overlooking the "Promised Land" into which he was not permitted to go (Dt. 34). He became the great hero of the people throughout their later history and stands today as one of the most commanding figures of all time. The first five books of the Bible, called the Pentateuch, were attributed to him. In Numbers 12:3 it is said, "Now the man Moses was very meek, above all the men which were upon the face of the earth." This accounts for the expression "as meek as Moses." But on many occasions he showed himself far from meek.

Mount of Olives, a hill near Jerusalem. It was here that Jesus often went with His disciples (Matt. 26:30).

Naaman. See *Elijah.*

Naboth. See *Ahab.*

Nahum, one of the minor prophets. The Book of Nahum is an exultant chant of magnificent poetry written in anticipation of the fall of Nineveh.

Naomi. See *Ruth.*

Nathan, the prophet who rebuked David (II Sam. 12).

Nathanael, called by Jesus "an Israelite, indeed, in whom is no guile!" (John 1:47.)

Nazareth, a city in Galilee, the home of Jesus in his childhood and youth.

Nebo, the mountain from which Moses viewed the Promised Land (Dt. 34).

Nebuchadnezzar (or, more correctly, Nebuchadrezzar), Chaldean king of Babylonia (605–562 B.C.). He defeated the Egyptians at the battle of Carchemish in 605 B.C. and thus established his supremacy in western Asia. Soon thereafter he went to Palestine and received submission from King Jehoiakim. But misled by Egypt and in spite of Jeremiah's protests, Judah revolted against Nebuchadnezzar, who took Jerusalem and carried the leading Jewish families to Babylon in 597 B.C. This is sometimes called the First Captivity. The Second Captivity came in 586 B.C., when Zedekiah, vassal king appointed by Nebuchadnezzar, rebelled and thus brought about the destruction of Jerusalem and the taking to Babylon of nearly all the Jews who were left. Nebuchadnezzar was really a great ruler, constructive and just.

Nehemiah. See *Ezra.*

Nicodemus, a Pharisee and ruler of the Jews who came to Jesus by night and received answers to his questions (John 3). He assisted Joseph of Arimathaea in preparing the body of Jesus for burial (John 19:39).

Nile, the great river of Egypt.

Nimrod, the "mighty hunter" who built Nineveh (Gen. 10).

Nineveh, capital of Assyria, the city of Jonah's mission.

Noah, the hero of the flood story (Gen. 6–10).

Numbers, the fourth Book of the O.T. (so named because it contains a census of the people), records various incidents concerning the Israelites during their wanderings in the wilderness.

Obadiah, a minor prophet who wrote of the doom of Edom, which he attributed to the way the Edomites treated the Israelites when Jerusalem was taken.

Ophir, a place famous for its fine gold (I Kings 9:28; 10:11; Job 28:16).

Palestine, previously called Canaan, the country occupied by the Israelites. It lies between the Mediterranean Sea and the Arabian Desert and was the inevitable route for travelers in time of peace and for armies in time of war between Egypt and the empires of the North. The northern part is very fertile and beautiful.

Patmos, the island where John had the vision of which he wrote (Rev. 1:9).

Paul, originally Saul, was born in Tarsus, a city in the southeastern part of Asia Minor. He went to Jerusalem to be educated as a Rabbi. Christianity first appeared to him as a menace to his own religion as a Jew, and he persecuted Christians, even taking part in the martyrdom of Stephen (Acts 22:19). On the road to Damascus he had the vision that caused his conversion (Acts 9). His various journeys and missionary work are related in the Book of Acts and are frequently referred to in the Epistles. Paul encountered much hostility and was twice imprisoned; he spent two years in Rome, and according to tradition was put to death during a persecution of the Christians by Nero, *c.* 64 A.D. His great work was in interpreting and systematising the Christian religion and extending it to the Gentiles, thus laying the foundation of the world religion that it has since become.

Pentateuch, Greek for five books, the first five books of the O.T., called the Five Books of Moses or the Law of Moses: Genesis, Exodus, Leviticus, Numbers and Deuteronomy.

Persia, the empire that succeeded Babylonia to supremacy in Asia. Cyrus took Babylon in 538 B.C., and permitted the Jews to return to Jerusalem, thus ending the Exile. Of the Persian monarchs, the Bible names Cyrus (Isa. 45), Darius I (Hag. 1), Xerxes ("Ahasuerus"; Esther 1) and Artaxerxes 1 (Ezra 7; Neh. 2). The Persian empire passed into Greek control with the conquest by Alexander the Great in 333 B.C.

Peter, Simon, a citizen of Capernaum, where he was a fisherman, was one of the earliest to become a disciple of Jesus and one of the first to be chosen as an Apostle. His impulsiveness and occasional lapses from complete faith appear in his failing to walk on the water (Matt. 14:28–31), his cutting off the ear of the high priest's servant (John 18:10) and his denial that he knew Jesus (Mark 14:62–72). Peter was the first to whom Jesus revealed Himself after His death. He took a leading part in the early history of the Church and is the central character of the first part of the Book of Acts. Later in life he went to Rome, where, according to tradition, he was the first bishop of the Roman Church, founder of the line of Popes and suffered martyrdom. The First Epistle of Peter was written to give encouragement to persecuted Christians in Asia Minor, and is hopeful in tone; the Second Epistle is mainly concerned with the second coming of Christ.

Pharaoh, the title of the king of Egypt. The pharaoh from whom the Israelites fled was probably Ramses II (1292–25 B.C.). Pharaoh Necho II (609–593 B.C.) defeated Josiah at Megiddo in 609 B.C. but was defeated at Carchemish by Nebuchadnezzar in 605 B.C.

Philemon, Epistle to, a short, personal letter from Paul asking Philemon to take back a runaway slave and promising to make good whatever loss the slave had caused him.

Philip, one of the Twelve Apostles (Mark 3:18).

Phillippians, Epistle to the, written by Paul during one of his imprisonments; he had gone to Philippi in answer to the call to "come over to Macedonia and help us" (Acts 16:9), and the letter is based on this personal acquaintance. It expresses his love, joy and peace, and, unlike most of the epistles, attacks no error either of doctrine or of practice.

Philistines, when the Israelites gained a foothold in Canaan, the Philistines were a people in possession of the seacoast and most of the territory between them and Egypt. The Israelites were at first conquered by the Philistines but broke away under Saul and gained control over them under David. After this they were generally at peace and often in alliance.

Pilate, the Roman procurator of Judea, seemed desirous of freeing Jesus when He was brought before him, and asked, "What evil hath he done?" When the Jews insisted that Jesus should be crucified, he washed his hands, saying, "I am innocent of the blood of this just person" (Matt. 27).

Poetry of the Bible does not have the form we are accustomed to in verse. There is no rhyme and nothing just like our idea of meter. One element in Hebrew poetry was parallelism—the same idea repeated in different forms; opposite ideas placed in striking nearness; or a combination of both these rhetorical devices as in these lines in the 27th Psalm:

   (a) The Lord is my light and my salvation,
      (b) Whom shall I fear?
   (a) The Lord is the strength of my life:
      (b) Of whom shall I be afraid?

Repetition like our refrains and choruses is common: "for his mercy endureth forever," in Psalm 136; "Why art thou cast down, O my soul," in Psalms 42 and 43. The great poetry books of the Bible are the Psalms, Lamentations and Song of Songs.

Potiphar, an officer of Pharoah whose wife tempted Joseph and who was led by her false story of what happened to cast him into prison (Gen. 39).

Prophecy in the Bible does not mean prediction, foretelling, but rather speaking in behalf of another—as in Ex. 7:1 when God tells Moses: "Aaron thy brother shall be thy prophet." The prophet is usually God's mouthpiece. The earlier prophets—Elijah and Elisha—were men of action, reformers. The later prophets—Amos, Isaiah and Jeremiah, notably—were also great writers, true poets. Their books are contributions to the literature of the world.

Proverbs, a book of maxims and longer poems of wisdom, many of which have been attributed to Solomon.

Psalms, a book of lyrical religious poems, attributed to David. The Psalter or Book of Psalms was used as a hymn book in the Second Temple. Hebrew poetry is based on parallelism of thought and expressions, instead of upon meter and rhyme, as in English poetry. The Psalms express both personal and national feeling, and often rise to heights of exaltation and beauty that have made them the most revered and loved of all poetry.

Queen of Sheba, Arabian queen who visited Solomon (I Kings 10).

Rachel. See *Jacob*.

Rahab, a woman of Jericho who aided the spies of Joshua. (Josh. 2.)

Rebekah. See *Isaac*.

Red Sea, the body of water that separates Egypt and Arabia. When its waters parted for them to pass, the Israelites escaped from bondage (Ex. 14).

Rehoboam, son of Solomon and king of Judah (937–920 B.C.). He told those who asked him to reduce the taxes they had paid under Solomon that instead of doing so he would greatly increase them. This led to the revolt of the 10 northern tribes under Jeroboam and left only two tribes to form Rehoboam's kingdom of Judah (I Kings 12).

Reuben, son of Jacob and ancestor of one of the tribes.

Revelation, also called the *Apocalypse* (which is Greek for revelation), the last Book in the N.T.; it was written by St. John the Divine on the Island of Patmos and addressed to the churches of Asia to encourage them in their faith. The highly figurative language makes it difficult to interpret. It is concerned with Satan's attempt to destroy the Church, the great judgment and the final overthrow of Satan, who is to be cast into the bottomless pit while the Church lives on as the Bride of the Lamb.

Romans, Epistle to the, the first of Paul's epistles, deals mainly with the idea that only righteousness is acceptable to God, and that one can be made righteous, can be justified, by faith through Christ's sacrifice.

Ruth, a charming idyll that tells of the devotion of a Moabite woman Ruth to her Israelitish mother-in-law Naomi and of Ruth's second marriage to Boaz, a wealthy Jew. The story ends with the statement that David was descended from Ruth and Boaz, which has been regarded as an argument in favor of intermarriage.

Salome, the daughter of Herodias whose dancing resulted in the execution of John the Baptist.

Samaria, the capital of the northern kingdom, was destroyed by the Assyrians in 722 B.C. In N.T. times, Samaria was one of the three main divisions of Palestine, between Judea on the south and Galilee on the north.

Samson, the strong man of the Bible. The story of his adventures recounts his slaying a thousand Philistines with the jawbone of an ass, his carrying off the city gates of Gaza, his confiding to Delilah that his strength lay in his long hair—which led her to shear it while he slept, so that he was captured by the Philistines, was blinded and forced to grind in the prison house. When he recovered his strength, he pulled down the pillars of the house, in which there were great crowds of people, thus killing more Philistines in his death than he had in all his life before. He is included among the judges of Israel (Judg. 13–16).

Samuel, an early prophet and the official judge or leader of Israel before the establishment of the monarchy. Even when he was a child under the care of the priest Eli he heard the voice of God and foretold the destruction of Eli's house. By divine command he anointed Saul to be king; and when Saul proved unworthy, David was anointed by Samuel. The Books I and II Samuel deal chiefly with the lives of Samuel, Saul and David.

Sarah, sometimes called Sarai, wife of Abraham (Gen. 12).

Sargon, King of Assyria (722–705 B.C.), who took Samaria in 722 B.C.

Satan, the Devil, called in Revelation "the old serpent" and hence identified with the tempter of Eve. In Job he is a cynical and skeptical being who has special jurisdiction on the earth. Matthew represents him as tempting Jesus (chap. 4); and Peter, as walking about like a roaring lion "seeking whom he may devour" (I Pet. 5:8). The ordinary conception of Satan today is based largely on Milton's *Paradise Lost*.

Saul, the first king of Israel, is represented as brave and patriotic but given to brooding and to fits of violent jealousy. For his life in connection with David, see *David*. Saul freed his people from the Philistines but fell in battle while fighting against them at Mount Gilboa.

Saul of Tarsus, the name of Paul before his conversion (Acts 9).

Sennacherib, king of Assyria (705–681 B.C.). In 1701 he invaded Palestine and laid waste many cities but failed to take Jerusalem. Supposedly, while besieging that city, a plague broke out in his army, forcing him to withdraw. This is the usual explanation given of II Kings 19, where it is said that the angel of the Lord smote 185,000 in a single night.

Septuagint (from the Latin word *septuaginta*, meaning 70), the Greek version of the O.T., supposed to have been made in Alexandria by 70 scholars in the 3rd century B.C. It is the version used in the N.T. for quotations from the prophets and the Psalms. This version is often referred to by the Roman numeral LXX, a short way of writing Septuagint.

Seth, third son of Adam (Gen. 4:25).

Shem, oldest son of Noah (Gen. 5:32), regarded as the ancestor of the Jews and other Semitic peoples.

Shiloh, the place where the Tabernacle was set up (Josh. 18:1) and the Ark of the Covenant remained when not carried into battle (I Sam. 4:3). Here the Lord revealed Himself to Samuel (I Sam. 3:21). The place is frequently mentioned elsewhere in the Bible.

Silas, a companion and friend of Paul, who was also a prophet (Acts 15:32).

Simeon, son of Jacob and ancestor of one of the tribes.

Simon, name of nine men referred to in the N.T.: (1) Simon Peter; (2) the Canaanite, one of the Twelve Apostles; (3) a brother of Jesus (Matt. 13:55); (4) a leper in Bethany (Mark 14:3); (5) the man who carried the Cross on the way to Calvary (Mark 15:21); (6) a Pharisee in whose house Jesus commended the woman who anointed His feet with ointment (Luke 7:36–50); (7) the father of Judas Iscariot (John 6:71); (8) a tanner at Joppa with whom Peter lodged (Acts 9:43); and (9) Simon Magnus (Acts 8:9–24).

Sinai, Mount, also called Horeb, the peak on which Moses talked with God and received the Ten Commandments, it is in the southern part of the Sinai peninsula (Ex. 3:1 and 19:11).

Sodom and Gomorrah, cities, usually described as having been near the Dead Sea, destroyed because of their wickedness (Gen. 19).

Solomon, son of David and last king of the Jews as a united nation. He became king in 971 B.C., and during his reign he greatly extended his dominion by peaceful alliances, which were often sealed by marriage. Thus he is credited with 700 wives and 300 concubines (I Kings 11:3), but many scholars regard this as a manner of indicating a large or perfect number, 7 and 3 often being used in this sense. He built a gorgeous palace for himself, and many people, including the Queen of Sheba, were dazzled by his magnificence. Solomon in all his glory is still famous. In building the Temple of Jerusalem, he gave the Jews an inspiration that long outlasted the Temple itself; but he himself was led astray by his wives to worship other gods. He was credited not only with great riches but with great wisdom, and much of the Book of Proverbs was attributed to him. The account of his reign is given in I Kings.

Song of Songs, called in the Authorized Version *The Song of Solomon,* also often called *Canticles,* now is usually regarded as a group of marriage songs written probably in the 3d century B.C. Many religious interpretations have been given it from time to time, and many attempts have been made to reconstruct the story suggested by the poems. One of these is that Solomon took into his harem a young woman about to be married to a simple country youth, and that she escaped and returned to her lover. The poetry is rich and fervid.

Stephen, the first Christian martyr, anticipated Paul in asserting the universal scope of Christianity (Acts 6).

Susanna, the heroine of an apocryphal addition to the Book of Daniel, represented as the wife of a rich Jew of Babylon. Two men grossly slandered her because she resisted them. By examining her accusers separately, Daniel discovered their falsity and had them punished, and Susanna's name was cleared.

Syria, the country north of Palestine, of which Damascus was the capital. It was conquered by Assyria, and Damascus was destroyed in 732 B.C. After the death of Alexander the Great, Syria was one of the four great divisions of the Greek Empire.

Tarsus, birthplace of Paul in southeastern Asia Minor.

Thaddaeus, one of the Twelve Disciples, apparently sometimes called Judas (not Iscariot) and sometimes Lebbaeus.

Thessalonians, Epistles to the, two letters written by Paul to the Church at Thessalonica, a city in Macedonia. They show his affection for his converts and his indignation at those who are hindering the spread of Christianity.

Thomas, the "doubting Apostle," refused to believe in the Resurrection until he had seen and touched Jesus with his hand (John 20:24–29).

Tigris, a great river in Babylonia that joins the Euphrates.

Timothy, Paul's disciple and fellow worker, whom he calls "my own son in the faith" (I Tim. 1:2), and "my dearly beloved son" (II Tim. 1:2). Paul's two epistles to him, I and II Timothy, N.T., are filled with friendly advice about carrying on their work.

Titus, Epistle to, a letter of advice from Paul to one of his assistants.

Tobit, an apocryphal book that tells the story of a good man named Tobit who lost his eyesight but had it restored. The central part of the story is concerned with the journey of Tobit's son Tobias and his marriage to a woman whose seven previous husbands had all been killed by an evil spirit. The angel Raphael is sent to banish the evil spirit and to cure the blindness of Tobit.

Vulgate (from the Latin *vulgata,* meaning in popular, everyday speech), the Latin translation of the Bible begun in the 5th century A.D. by St. Jerome, based on earlier Latin translations from the Greek version (Septuagint) of the O.T. In 1546 it was declared the standard for Roman Catholic church services. The Douay Bible, the English version for Roman Catholics, published in 1582–1610, was made from the Vulgate.

Wisdom Literature, a name applied to several books of the Bible, all philosophy in the form of observation. Sometimes the philosophy is in brief proverbs as in the Book of Proverbs, sometimes in essays as in Ecclesiastes. James and John are Wisdom epistles and some scholars call Matthew's gospel a Wisdom gospel.

Wisdom of Solomon, a book of the O.T. Apocrypha, not proverbs but rather discourses on Wisdom as the governing power of the world and its salvation.

Zacchaeus, a publican "little of stature" who climbed a tree to see Jesus as He passed (Luke 19).

Zechariah, one of the minor prophets, who, with Haggai, urged the rebuilding of the Temple after the Jews returned from the Exile. His prophecy is given in the form of visions. Only the first eight chapters of the Book of Zechariah are usually assigned to him.

Zephaniah, a minor prophet. The occasion of his prophecy was the invasion of the Scythians in 626 B.C., who caused terrible destruction and desolation wherever they went. Zephaniah asserts that the great Day of Jehovah had come upon His people as a result of their sins.

WEIGHTS, MEASURES AND DISTANCES OF THE BIBLE

Dry Measure

1 *log*	=	0.46 quart (early), 0.51 quart (later)
1 *choenix*	=	2 logs
1 *cab*	=	2 choenices
1 *ephah*	=	18 cabs
1 *omer*	=	1/10 ephah
1 *seah*	=	1/3 ephah
1 *homer* (kor)	=	10 ephahs

Liquid Measure

1 *log*	=	0.54 quart (early), 0.59 quart (later)
1 *hin*	=	12 logs
1 *bath*	=	6 hins
1 *kor*	=	10 baths

Weights and Coins

1 *gerah*	=	11.2 grams troy
1 *bekah*	=	10 gerahs
1 *shekel*	=	2 bekahs
1 *mina* (maneh)	=	50 shekels
1 *talent* (kikkar)	=	60 minas

Long Measure

1 *digit*	=	0.75 inch
1 *palm*	=	4 digits
1 *span*	=	3 palms
1 *cubit*	=	2 spans

1 *fathom*	=	4 cubits
1 *reed*	=	1.5 fathoms
1 *furlong*	=	60 reeds
1 *mile*	=	8 furlongs

Day and Night (Ancient)

Morning till about 10 A. M.
Heat of day till about 2 P. M.
Cool of day till about 6 P. M.
First watch till midnight
Middle watch till 3 A. M.
Morning watch till 6 A. M.

Day and Night (New Testament)

Third hour: 6 to 9 A. M.
Sixth hour: 9 to 12 midday
Ninth hour: 12 to 3 P. M.
Twelfth hour: 3 to 6 P. M.
First watch, evening: 6 to 9 P. M.
Second watch, midnight: 9 to 12 P. M.
Third watch, cockcrow: 12 to 3 A. M.
Fourth watch: 3 to 6 A. M.

Approximate Modern Equivalents

Bath, a liquid measure, 9.8 gallons, later 10.7 gallons.

Bekah (split), a weight, about 112 grams troy or half a shekel.

Cab (hollow), a dry measure, 1.86 quarts, later 2.04 quarts.

Choenix, a dry measure, about 0.98 quart.

Cool of day, from 2 to 6 P. M.

Cubit (originally the length of the forearm from the elbow to the tip of the fingers), a long measure, 17.58 inches.

Day, Ancient: morning till about 10 A.M.; heat of day till about 2 P. M.; cool of day till about 6 P.M.

Day, New Testament: third hour, 6 to 9 A. M.; sixth hour, 9 to 12 midday; ninth hour, 12 to 3 P. M.; twelfth hour, 3 to 6 P. M.

Day's journey, 24 miles.

Digit (the width of a finger), 0.75 inch.

Ephah (measure of corn), a dry measure, 1.05 bushels, later 1.15 bushels.

Fathom (spread of arms), a long measure, about 6 feet.

Furlong (length of a furrow), a long measure, 220 yards, ⅛ mile.

Gerah (a bean), a small weight, 11.2 grams troy.

Heat of day, from 10 A. M. to 2 P. M.

Hin, a liquid measure, 1.62 gallons, later 1.78 gallons.

Homer, a dry measure, 10.48 bushels, later 11.49 bushels.

Hour, see *Day.*

Kikkar, see *Talent.*

Kor (round vessel), a dry measure, see *Homer;* also a liquid measure, 97.5 gallons, later 107.0 gallons.

Log, a liquid measure, 0.54 quart, later 0.59 quart; also a dry measure, 0.46 quart, later 0.51 quart.

Mile (thousand paces), a long measure, 8 furlongs.

Mina or maneh, a varying weight and money unit, in Palestine usually 50 shekels.

Morning, from 6 A. M. to 10 A. M.

Omer, a dry measure, 0.42 peck, later 0.46 peck.

Palm (width of the hand), a long measure, 3 or 4 inches.

Reed, a long measure, 10.25 feet; or 6 cubits, 8.79 feet.

Sabbath-day's journey, 2,000 cubits.

Seah (grain), a dry measure, 1.40 pecks, later 1.53 pecks.

Shekel (weight), a weight or a coin of this weight; the ordinary gold shekel of about 252⅔ grains would now be worth about $20.00; the silver shekel of about 224½ grains, about $0.72½.

Span (extended hand), a long measure, about 9 inches.

Talent or kikkar (round mass of metal), a weight and a sum of money; the ordinary gold talent, weighing about 108 lbs., would now be worth about $60,000; a silver talent, weighing about 96 lbs., about $2,000.

Watch, a measure of time through the night. Ancient: first watch till midnight, middle watch till 3 A. M., morning watch till 6 A. M.; New Testament: first watch, evening, 6 to 9 P. M.; second watch, midnight, 9 to 12 P. M.; third watch, cockcrow, 12 to 3 A. M.; fourth watch, morning, 3 to 6 A. M.

DICTIONARY OF SOBRIQUETS AND PSEUDONYMS

Abe (Honest Abe, Old Abe), Abraham Lincoln.

Achitophel, the name given by Dryden in his vigorous political satire *Absalom and Achitophel* to Anthony Ashley Cooper, first Earl of Shaftesbury. This was in allusion to the Biblical Ahithophel (*Hebr.* 1, "brother of folly"), the politician whose activities and fate are described in II Sam., 15-17. In Dryden's work, Charles II is David, and James, Duke of Monmouth, is Absalom.

Adams, Stephen, Michael Maybrick

Adeler, Max, Charles Heber Clark

Adirondack Murray, Rev. William H. H. Murray, whose *Camp Life in the Adirondack Mountains* (1868) first called attention to the Adirondacks as a resort.

Admirable Doctor, The, Roger Bacon

Adonais, the name given by Shelley (in an elegy of that title, published in 1821) to John Keats.

Aeon, Henry Timrod

Agate, Whitelaw Reid

Aglaius, Henry Timrod

Alcon, R., Emily Brontë

Alexander the Corrector, Alexander Cruden, author of a *Concordance of the Holy Scriptures,* who assumed this title because he felt himself divinely appointed to correct British morals.

Anacreon Moore, a name sometimes given to Thomas Moore, who published (1801) a translation of the odes of Anacreon.

Angelic Doctor, The, Thomas Aquinas

Angell, Norman, Ralph Norman Angell Lane

Anstey, F., T. Anstey Guthrie

Apostle of the Indians, Rev. John Eliot

Appleseed, Johnny, John Chapman, who carried from the cider mills of Pennsylvania great quantities of apple seeds to plant them in pioneer Ohio and thus provide orchards for the settlers.

Arp, Bill, Charles Henry Smith

Astrophel (Greek, "star-lover"), the name assumed by Sir Philip Sidney in *Astrophel and Stella,* a cycle of 110 sonnets. "Stella" was Penelope Devereux, sister of the second earl of Essex. Spenser wrote the elegy *Astrophel* in memory of Sidney.

Attic Bee, Plato; Sophocles

Attic Muse, Xenophon

Austrian Hyena, The, Julius Jakob von Haynau, an Austrian general notorious for his cruelty.

Autocrat of the Breakfast-Table, The, a pen name of Dr. Oliver Wendell Holmes; first used by him in articles for the *New England Magazine* of November 1831 and February 1832; revived when he undertook to "shake the same bough again" in a series of 12 papers for the *Atlantic Monthly,* beginning in its first number—that for November 1857. These papers were issued in book form in 1858 and in a new and revised edition (with notes) in 1882.

Ayrshire Bard, The, Robert Burns

Baldy Smith, Gen. William Farrar Smith, a Union officer in the Civil War.

Bard of Avon, The, Shakespeare

Bard of Rydal Mount, The, William Wordsworth.

Bassetto, Corno di, George Bernard Shaw

Beau Brummell, George Bryan Brummell

Beau Nash, Richard Nash, less often styled "King of Bath."

Bell, Acton, Anne Brontë

Bell, Currer, Charlotte Brontë

Bell, Ellis, Emily Brontë

Bell, Lilian, Mrs. Arthur Hoyt Bogue

Bell-the-Cat, Archibald Douglas, fifth Earl of Angus. A meeting of Scottish nobles to overthrow the earl of Mar, favorite of James III, was likened by Earl Gray to the meeting of the mice to hang a bell on the cat's neck. "Who," said he, "will bell the cat?" "I," answered Douglas, "am he that will bell the cat."

Bentzon, Th., Marie Thérèse Blanc

Bettine, Elisabeth Brentano (wife of Ludwig Achim von Arnim). The name was used by her in correspondence with Goethe.

Bickerstaff, Isaac, Esq., Astrologer, the name used by Steele as editor of *The Tatler.* It had previously been employed by Dean Swift in an amusing controversy with one Partridge, an almanac maker.

Biglow, Hosea, James Russell Lowell, as author of *The Biglow Papers.*

Billings, Josh, Henry Wheeler Shaw

Bion, Robert Southey

Birmingham, George A., Rev. James Owen Hannay

Black Jack, Gen. J. A. Logan; Gen. J. J. Pershing

Blacksmith, The Learned, Elihu Burritt, for his linguistic acquirements.

Blind, Mathilde, Mathilde Cohen

Blind Tom, Thomas Wiggins, a negro pianist

Bluff Hal, Henry VIII of England

Bly, Nellie, Elizabeth Cochrane. She made a famous trip around the world.

Bowers, B. M., Mrs. Bertha M. Sinclair-Cowan

Boz, Charles Dickens; used by him for his *Sketches by Boz.* It was derived from Moses, a nickname for Dickens's brother Augustus. Moses, "being facetiously pronounced through the nose, became Bōses, and being shortened, Bōz." By the public the name has been generally pronounced Bōz.

Bozzy, a nickname bestowed on James Boswell by Dr. Samuel Johnson.

Breitmann, Hans, Charles Godfrey Leland

Brick Pomeroy, Marcus Mills Pomeroy

Briscoe, Margaret Sutton, Mrs. A. J. Hopkins

Buffalo Bill, William F. Cody

Buntline, Ned, Edward Zane Judson

Burlington Hawkeye Man, The, Robert J. (Bob) Burdette

Calumet, Francis Hopkinson

Carleton, Will, Frederick Orrin Bartlett

Carmen Sylva, the pen-name of Elizabeth, Queen of Rumania.

Carroll, Lewis, Rev. Charles Lutwidge Dodgson

Carter, Nick, J. Russell Coryell

Caryll, Ivan, John Carl

Caskoden, Edward, Charles Major

Castlemon, Harry, Charles A. Fosdick

Catholicus, Cardinal Newman

Cato, Alexander Hamilton

Cavendish, Henry Jones

Chapman, Maristan, John Stanton Higham

Chapman and Mary Hamilton Chapman

Chinese Gordon, Charles George Gordon, an English soldier who commanded (1863) a Chinese force against the Taiping rebels and was adviser (1880) to the Chinese government. Later, when in Egypt, he was known as Gordon Pasha.

Citizen King, The (*Le Roi Citoyen*), Louis Philippe, King of the French, 1830-48.

Cleishbotham, Jedediah, the assumed compiler of *Tales of My Landlord,* by Sir Walter Scott.

Close, Upton, Josef W. Hall

Clutterbuck, Capt. Cuthbert, the assumed editor of *The Abbot, The Fortunes of Nigel* and *The Monastery,* by Sir Walter Scott.

Connor, Ralph, Rev. Charles W. Gordon. It is said that the name was intended to be Cannor—*Can* for Canada, *Nor* for Northwest—but was altered by an editor.

Conrad, Joseph, Teodor Josef Konrad Korzeniovski

Conway, Hugh, Frederick John Fargus

Coolidge, Susan, Sarah C. Woolsey

Corelli, Marie, Mary Mackay

Corn-law Rhymer, Ebenezer Elliott

Cornwall, Barry, Bryan W. Procter

Craddock, Charles Egbert, Mary N. Murfree

Crayon, Geoffrey, Gent., Washington Irving, as the author of *The Sketch-Book.*

Crib, Tom, Thomas Moore

Crichton, The Admirable, a name given to James Crichton, a versatile young Scottish scholar and swordsman, distinguished as linguist and Latin poet, who at 21 successfully disputed with the learned professors of the University of Padua. The name was used by Sir James Barrie as the title of a play—the Crichton being in this case Lord Loame's butler, who, when Lord Loame's yacht *Bluebell* was wrecked, became leader of the survivors on their desert island in the Pacific.

Crinkle, Nym, Andrew C. Wheeler

Croaker and Co., the style under which Fitz-Greene Halleck and Joseph Rodman Drake wrote for *The Evening Post* of New York (1819) the series of poems, chiefly humorous, known as "the Croaker pieces," dealing with the politics of the time.

Crosby, Fanny J., Frances Jane Van Alstyne (Mrs. Alexander Van Alstyne)

D'Ache, Caran, Emmanuel Poiré

Dale, Alan, Alfred J. Cohen

Danbury News Man, The, James M. Bailey

Danby, Frank, Mrs. Julia Frankau

Deaf Smith and soldier, Erastus Smith, Texas pioneer.

Democritus Junior, the name under which Robert Burton published his *Anatomy of Melancholy.*

Dinesen, Isak, Baroness von Blixen-Finecke

Dizzy, a popular name for Benjamin Disraeli, Earl of Beaconsfield.

Doesticks, Q. K. Philander, Mortimer M. Thompson

Dooley, Mr. (Martin), Finley Peter Dunne, American journalist, who came thus to be known from the name of his character, an Irish-American saloonkeeper of the Archey road, Chicago, whose pungent and searching remarks on current topics appeared weekly in American newspapers and later were collected into volumes.

Downing, Maj. Jack, Seba Smith, who under this name wrote a series of letters for the Portland (Me.) *Daily Courier* and another for the *National Intelligencer* of Washington, D. C.

Drapier, M. B., the signature used by Dean Swift for a series of letters published by him in 1724 and known as "Drapier's letters." These urged the Irish people not to accept the copper halfpence coined by one William Wood, to whom George I had granted a patent. Profits accruing through the difference between the nominal and real value of the coin were to be divided between Wood and the duchess of Kendal, the king's mistress, whose influence had obtained the privilege. A reward was offered for the discovery of the author of the letters, and the patent was eventually cancelled.

Droch, Robert Bridges, American critic and editor.

WALT WHITMAN, "The Good Gray Poet."

Duchess, The, Mrs. Margaret Hungerford

Duncan, Sara Jeanette, Mrs. Everard Cotes

Elia, the name used by Charles Lamb in contributing to the *London Magazine* a series of essays. It had been the real name of a clerk in the South Sea House, where Lamb also was employed in 1780-92.

Eliot, George, the name adopted by Mary Ann (Evans) Lewes (later Mrs. John Walter Cross) when she began to write for *Blackwood's.* She chose George because it was her first husband's Christian name, Eliot because it was "a good, mouth-filling, easily pronounced word."

Ettrick Shepherd, The, a name often given to James Hogg, Scottish poet.

Expounder of the Constitution, an epithet popularly applied to Daniel Webster, who, especially in his second reply to Hayne and his reply to Calhoun ("The Constitution is not a compact between sovereign states"), did so much to clarify and define opinion against nullification.

Fancy, One of the, Thomas Moore

Father Abraham, Abraham Lincoln

Father of His Country, The, Cicero; Washington

Father of History, The, Herodotus

Father of Medicine, The, Hippocrates

Fern, Fanny, Mrs. Sara (Willis) Parton

Fighting Bob, Rear-Admiral Robley D. Evans

Flynt, Josiah, Josiah Flynt Willard

Forester, Frank, Henry William Herbert

Fort, Paul, Frank R. Stockton

Fra Elbertus, Elbert Hubbard

France, Anatole, Jacques Anatole Thibault

Fritz, Der alte (Old Fritz, Old Fred), Frederick II of Prussia

Gath, George Alfred Townsend

Gay, Joseph, John Durant Breval

Gentleman with a Duster, A, Harold Begbie

Good Gray Poet, The, an epithet applied to Walt Whitman, originally by the American author William D. O'Connor in a pamphlet of that title (1866). It was derived from Whitman's appearance at that time—"the flowing hair and fleecy beard, both very gray, and tempering with a look of age the youthful aspect of one who is but forty-five."

Gordon, Julien, Mrs. Julia Grinnell Cruger

Gorki, Maxim, Alexi Maximovitch Pyeshkov

Grace Darling of America, The, Ida Lewis

Graduate of Oxford, A, the name under which John Ruskin published his *Modern Painters.*

Grand, Mme. Sarah, Mrs. Frances E. McFall

Gray, Maxwell, Mary G. Tuttiett

Grayson, David, Ray Stannard Baker

Great Commoner, The, William Pitt

Great Elector, The, Frederick William, Elector of Brandenburg

Green, Anna Katharine, Mrs. Charles Rohlfs

Greenwood, Grace, Mrs. Sara Jane Lippincott

Grile, Dod, the name under which Ambrose Bierce published his *Fables of Zambi the Parsee* in *Fun.*

Gulliver, Lemuel, Dean Swift

Gyp, Comtesse de Martel de Janville

Hall, Holworthy, Harold Everett Porter

Hamilton, Gail, Mary Abigail Dodge

Hans Pfaal, Edgar A. Poe

Harland, Marion, Mrs. Mary V. Terhune

Hawthorne, Alice, Septimus Winner

Hay, Ian, John Hay Beith

Hegan, Alice Caldwell, Mrs. Cale Young Rice

H. H., Helen Hunt Jackson

Hobbes, John Oliver, Mrs. Pearl (Richards) Craigie

Hodge, Toby, Charles McIlvaine

Hoosier Poet, The, James Whitcomb Riley

Hope, Anthony, Anthony Hope Hawkins

Howadji, George William Curtis

Idiot, The, John Kendrick Bangs

Incorruptible, The, Maximilien Robespierre

Ingoldsby, Thomas, Esq., the name under which the Rev. Richard H. Barham published his satirical *Ingoldsby Legends.*

Iron Duke, The, Arthur Wellesley, Duke of Wellington.

Ironquill, Eugene F. Ware

Iron, Ralph, the name under which Olive Schreiner (Mrs. S. C. Cronwright) at the age of 20 published her *The Story of an African Farm.*

Ironside, Edmund (Eadmund) II, King of the West Saxons.

Jean Jacques, Jean Jacques Rousseau

Jim Crow Rice, Thomas D. Rice

Johnson, Benjamin F., of Boone, James Whitcomb Riley

Josiah Allen's Wife (Samantha Allen), Marietta Holley

J. P. Mowbray, Andrew C. Wheeler

J. S. of Dale, Frederick J. Stimson

June, Jenny, Jane Cunningham Croly (Mrs. D. G. Croly)

Kane, Saul, Siegfried Sassoon

Kata Phusin (Greek, "according to Nature"), the pseudonym under which John Ruskin published his *The Poetry of Architecture* in the *Architectural Magazine* of London.

Kerr, Orpheus C., Robert Henry Newell

King-maker, The, an epithet popularly applied to Richard Nevil, Earl of Warwick.

Kirke, Edmund, James Roberts Gilmore

Kit, Prof. John Wilson. It is a diminutive of Christopher, Wilson's regular pseudonym being Christopher North.

Knickerbocker, Diedrich, the name under which Washington Irving published his *A History of New York from the Beginning of the World to the End of the Dutch Dynasty* (2 vols., 1809), a burlesque that satirized top-lofty antiquarians and poked good-natured fun at the burghers.

Last of the Tribunes, The, Cola di Rienzi, for a time head of the municipality of Rome, with the title of tribune of the people.

Last of the Troubadours, The, Jacques Jasmin, Provençal poet (also sometimes called *The Barber-Poet*).

Laughing Philosopher, The, Democritus of Abdera, who was said to laugh at mankind's follies.

Lee, Vernon, Violet Paget

Leslie, Frank, Henry Carter (founder of *Frank Leslie's Illustrated Newspaper*).

Leviathan of Literature, The, a sobriquet of Dr. Samuel Johnson, from the rotund, imposing, sometimes unwieldy style of his prose. Leslie Stephen refers to him as "this literary Behemoth."

Liberator, The, a title of Simon Bolivar, officially conferred on him by New Granada (now Colombia), Peru and Venezuela.

Light-Horse Harry, Henry Lee, commander of "Lee's legion" in the Revolutionary war.

Lion of the North, The, a name given to Gustavus Adolphus of Sweden.

Little Corporal, The, Napoleon Bonaparte

Little Giant, The, Stephen A. Douglas

Little Mac, Gen. George B. McClellan

Littlepage, Cornelius, the name under which James Fenimore Cooper published *Satanstoe.*

Little Phil, Gen. Philip H. Sheridan

Lothrop, Amy, Anna Bartlett Warner, sister of Susan Warner.

Loti, Pierre, Louis M. J. Viaud

Lucky Baldwin, Elias J. Baldwin

Luska, Sidney, Henry Harland

Lyell, Edna, Ada Ellen Bayly

Maartens, Maarten, Joost M. H. Van der Poorten-Schwarz

M'Connachie, the name given by Sir James Barrie (in his rectorial address *Courage*) to "the unruly half of myself: the writing half."

Maclaren, Ian, Rev. John Watson

Macleod, Fiona, William Sharp

Mad Anthony, Gen. Anthony Wayne

Madman of the North, The, a nickname of Charles XII of Sweden.

Maid of Orléans, The, Joan of Arc, who was thus called because she raised the siege of Orléans by the English.

Maitland, Thomas, Robert Buchanan

Malet, Lucas, Mary St. Leger (Kingsley) Harrison (Mrs. William Harrison).

Man of Destiny, The, a grandiose epithet sometimes applied to Napoleon Bonaparte, whose vast egotism caused him to view himself as predestined to be a new Caesar. Nevertheless, said Victor Hugo, "God was bored by him."

Mansfield, Katherine, Kathleen Murry (Mrs. Middleton Murry)

Mantuan Swan, The, Vergil, a native of Mantua

Market Gardener, R. D. Blackmore, who was thus known among the people of Dartmoor.

Marlitt, E., Henriette Eugénie John

Marschall Vorwärts (Marshal Forward), a nickname of Gebhard von Blücher.

Martin, George Madden, Mrs. Attwood R. Martin

Marvel, Ik, Donald G. Mitchell

Maurois, André, Émile Herzog

May, Sophie, Rebecca Sophia Clarke

McManus, Blanche, Mrs. Francis M. Mansfield

Meredith, Owen, Edward Bulwer Lytton, first Earl of Lytton.

Merriam, Florence A., Florence Merriam Bailey (Mrs. Vernon Bailey).

Merriman, Henry Seton, Hugh Stowell Scott

Merry Monarch, The, Charles II of England

Mill-boy of the Slashes, The, Henry Clay (with reference to his early life and surroundings in Hanover county, Virginia).

Miller, Joaquin, Cincinnatus Heine Miller

Miller, Olive Thorne, Mrs. Harriet Mann Miller

Monk Lewis, Matthew Gregory Lewis (from his best-known work, *Ambrosio, or the Monk*).

Morning Star of the Reformation, The, John Wycliffe

Mother Ann, the name given by her followers to Ann Lee, founder of the Society of Shakers.

Mühlbach, Luise, Klara Müller Mundt (Frau Theodor Mundt).

Mulock, Miss, Mrs. George L. Craik, Jr. (Dinah Maria Mulock).

Nasby, Petroleum V., David Ross Locke

Nesbit, E., Mrs. Edith Nesbit Bland

North, Christopher, Prof. John Wilson

Novalis, Friedrich von Hardenberg

Nye, Bill, Edgar Wilson Nye

O. Henry, William S. Porter

Oldboy, Felix, John Flavel Mines

Old Buck, James Buchanan

Old Buena Vista, Zachary Taylor (also sometimes called *Old Zach*).

Old Bullion, Thomas Hart Benton (on account of his arguments in favor of "hard money").

Old Fuss-and-Feathers, Gen. Winfield Scott

Old Hickory, Andrew Jackson

Old Noll, Oliver Cromwell

Old Public Functionary, An, an epithet applied to himself by James Buchanan.

Old Rough-and-Ready, Zachary Taylor

Old Rowley, a nickname of Charles II of England, said to have been taken from the name of his favorite race horse, commemorated in the "Rowley mile" of the Newmarket course.

Old Sleuth, Harlan P. Halsey

Oldstyle, Jonathan, the name under which Washington Irving wrote squibs for the *Morning Chronicle.*

O'Neill, Rose Cecil, Mrs. Harry Leon Wilson

Optic, Oliver, Rev. William T. Adams

Orczy, Baroness, Mrs. Montagu Barstow

O'Reilly, Private Miles, Charles G. Halpin

O'Rell, Max, Paul Blouet

Orinda, The Matchless, the name bestowed by contemporaries upon Katharine Philips (Mrs. James Philips), English poet, who used Orinda as her signature.

Ouida, Louise de la Ramée (said to have been from the childish pronunciation of Louise by a younger sister).

Oxenham, John, William Arthur Dunkerley

Pansy, Isabella Macdonald Alden

Parley, Peter, Samuel G. Goodrich

Partington, Mrs., Benjamin P. Shillaber

Pathfinder (of the Rocky Mountains), The, John Charles Frémont
Peacemaker, The, Henry Clay
Pennsylvania Farmer, A, John Dickinson
Perkins, Eli, Melville D. Landon
Perry, Edgar A., Edgar Allan Poe
Phoenix, John, George H. Derby
Pindar, Peter, John Wolcott
Plon-Plon, Prince Napoleon Joseph Charles Paul Bonaparte (1822-91); said to have been a euphemism for *Craint-Plomb* (Bullet-fearer), alluding to his supposed cowardice in the Crimean War.
Plumed Knight, The, an epithet bestowed on James G. Blaine by Robert G. Ingersoll in a speech at Cincinnati in 1876.
Poet-Naturalist, The, Henry D. Thoreau
Poor Richard (Richard Saunders), a nickname of Benjamin Franklin, from his *Poor Richard's Almanac* (1732-57).
Porte Crayon, Col. David H. Strother
Pretender, The Young, Charles Edward Louis Philip Casimir Stuart
Prout, Father, Francis Mahony
Q, Sir Arthur Quiller-Couch
Quad, M., C. B. Lewis
Quaker Poet, The, John G. Whittier
Queen, Ellery, Frederick Denny and Manfred Lee
Quinn, Dan, Alfred Henry Lewis
Rail-Splitter, The, Abraham Lincoln
Reid, Christian, Frances C. Tiernan
Riddell, John, Corey Ford
Rives, Amélie, Princess Amélie Troubetskoi
Rock of Chickamauga, The, Gen. George H. Thomas
Rohmer, Sax, Arthur Sarsfield Ward
Sage of Monticello, The, a name given to Thomas Jefferson from his country estate of Monticello (Italian, "little mount") in Albemarle County, Virginia, not far from Charlottesville.
Sailor King, The, William IV of England
Saki, Hector H. Munro
Sand, George, Baroness Dudevant (Armandine Dupin, whose first writing was done in collaboration with Jules Sandeau, with the signature Jules Sand. One St. George's day Sandeau urged her to write independently, and from that time she used the pen name George Sand.
Saunders, Marshall, Margaret M. Saunders
Saunders, Richard, Benjamin Franklin, as the editor of *Poor Richard's Almanac.*

Schreiner, Olive, Mrs. S. C. Cronwright
Scourge of God, The, Attila the Hun
Seraphic Doctor, The, Bonaventura (Giovanni di Fidenza)
Sidney, Margaret, Harriett Mulford Lothrop (Mrs. Daniel Lothrop)
Single-speech Hamilton, William Gerard Hamilton, whose maiden speech in Parliament was his only one of consequence.
Sinjohn, John, the name under which John Galsworthy published his first three books —*Jocelyn, Villa Rubein* and *A Man of Devon.*
Slick, Sam, the name of a character in the works of T. C. Haliburton, who adopted it as a pseudonym.
Squibob, John P., George H. Derby
Stella, the name given to Esther Johnson by Jonathan Swift.
Stendhal, Marie Henri Beyle
Stern, Daniel, Marie de Flavigny, Comtesse d'Agoult.
Stirling, Arthur, Upton Sinclair
Stockley, Cynthia, Mrs. H. E. Pelham-Browne
Stonewall Jackson, the name by which Gen. Thomas J. Jackson of the Confederate Army was universally known from the time of the Civil War. It arose through the words of Gen. Bernard E. Bee, who, to encourage his brigade of South Carolinians at the first battle of Bull Run, cried out, "Look at Jackson—there he stands like a stone wall!"
Stretton, Hesba, Sarah Smith
Subtle Doctor, The, the Duns Scotus
Sunset Cox, Samuel S. Cox, from an article by him in the *Ohio Statesman.*
Swan of Lichfield, The, Anna Seward
Swedish Nightingale, The, Jenny Lind (Mme. Otto Goldschmidt)
Teufelsdröckh, Herr, the imaginary author of the *Life and Opinions of Herr Teufelsdröckh,* of which Carlyle's *Sartor Resartus* purported to be an adaptation. Teufelsdröckh (literally, "Devil's dirt") was a popular German name for asafoetida, and Carlyle remarked: "I sometimes think the book *will* prove a kind of medicinal *asafoetida* for the pudding stomach of England."
Thanet, Octave, Alice French
Thumb, Tom, Charles S. Stratton
Tippecanoe, William Henry Harrison, from his victory of Tippecanoe in 1811.
Titcomb, Timothy, J. G. Holland
Titmarsh, Michael Angelo, the name used by Thackeray for several years as a signature

to tales, sketches and essays contributed by him to *Fraser's Magazine.*
Traprock, Walter, George S. Chappell
Trask, Katrina, Kate Nichols Trask (Mrs. Spencer Trask)
Twain, Mark, the pen-name of Samuel L. Clemens, by which he was better known than by his real name. It was derived from the call of the leadsman, "Mark twain!" (that is, the depth is two fathoms) on Mississippi steamboats when Clemens was a pilot.
Uncle Remus, the imaginary narrator of the folklore stories of Joel Chandler Harris.
Unconditional Surrender Grant, Gen. U. S. Grant
Vandegrift, Margaret, Margaret Thomas Janvier
Van Dine, S. S., Willard Huntington Wright, who used this pen name for his detective fiction.
Virgin Queen, The, Queen Elizabeth of England
Voltaire, a name assumed in 1718 by François Marie Arouet.
Wagstaff, Simon, the pseudonym used by Dean Swift in publishing his *Polite Conversation.*
Ward, Artemus, Charles Farrar Browne
Warden, Florence, Mrs. Florence A. P. James
Wash, Redbarn, an anagrammatic pen name of Bernard Shaw.
Watanna, Onoto, Winifred Reeve
Weale, Putnam, Bertram Lenox Simpson
West, Rebecca, the pen name of Cecily Fairfield, taken directly from the name of a character in Ibsen's *Rosmersholm.*
Wetherell, Elizabeth, Susan Warner
Widow Bedott, The, Frances M. Whitcher
William the Testy, Willem Kieft, third governor of New Netherlands
Wilson, J. Arbuthnot, (Charles) Grant (Blairfindie) Allen
Winfield, Arthur M., Edward Stratemeyer
Winter, John Strange, Mrs. H. E. V. Stannard
Wizard of Menlo Park, The, Thomas A. Edison
Wizard of the North, The, an epithet applied to Sir Walter Scott in tribute to the charm of his writings.
Yorick, the pen name under which the Rev. Laurence Sterne published his *A Sentimental Journey.*
Zadkiel, William Lilly; Lieut. Richard J. Morrison

GREAT LIBRARIES

AMERICAN		NUMBER OF VOLUMES	EUROPEAN		NUMBER OF VOLUMES
LIBRARY	CITY		LIBRARY	CITY	
Library of Congress	Washington	8,500,000	Lenin State Library	Moscow	11,000,000
Harvard University	Cambridge	5,250,000	National Public Library	Leningrad	6,000,000
New York Public Library	New York	5,000,000	British Museum	London	5,000,000
Yale University	New Haven	3,800,000	National Library	Paris	5,000,000
Cleveland Public Library	Cleveland	2,300,000	State Library	Munich	2,000,000
University of Illinois	Urbana, Ill.	2,250,000	National Library	Vienna	1,600,000
Chicago Public Library	Chicago	2,200,000	State Library	Berlin	1,500,000
Los Angeles Public Library	Los Angeles	1,900,000	National Library	Madrid	1,500,000
Boston Public Library	Boston	1,800,000	National Library	Naples	1,330,000
University of Chicago	Chicago	1,750,000	Universal & Regional Library	Strasbourg	1,300,000
Cincinnati Public Library	Cincinnati	1,700,000	Bodlian	Oxford	1,260,000
Philadelphia Public Library	Philadelphia	1,600,000	Cambridge University	Cambridge, Eng.	1,250,000

PARALLEL OUTLINES OF WORLD LITERATURE

In., Indian; Per., Persian; Arab., Arabian; Dan., Danish; Swed., Swedish; Ic., Icelandic; Nor., Norwegian; Sp., Spanish; It., Italian; Port., Portuguese; Russ., Russian.

TABLE I. FROM THE BEGINNING TO THE BIRTH OF CHRIST

DATE	EGYPTIAN	BABYLONIAN AND ASSYRIAN	HEBREW	INDIAN AND PERSIAN	CHINESE	HISTORICAL EVENTS
B.C.	*Moral Precepts* of Ptah-hotep. Hieroglyphic records on tombs.	**King Sargon.** — *Tablets.*—Semitic kings in Babylonia.				B.C.
3000 to 2000	*Book of the Dead*—A collection of prayers, mythical in character, dealing with the future of the soul. *Song of the Yarper*—A funeral drinking song.	**Hammurabi** (c. 2100). —*Code.*			*The Five Classics* form the oldest known Chinese literature. They are: 1. *Book of Changes,* philosophy.	2700. Chaldean literature. 2234. Astronomical observation in Babylonia.
2000 to 1000	*Pentaur*—An epic prose poem of battle. *Papyrus Ebers* (c. 1550)—A medical treatise. *Amarna letters*—Clay archives of two kings.		*Oldest Songs of the Old Testament.* — The Song of Deborah. Many of the psalms.	*The Four Vedas* are the oldest Indian literature. Written from B.C. 1500 to 500, they are the sacred books of the Hindus. The *Rig-Veda* is the oldest.	2. *Book of History,* before 650 B.C. 3. *Book of Rites.* 4. *Spring and Autumn,* by Confucius. 5. *Book of Poetry.*	2000. Chaldean rule over Syria. Mycenaean civilization.
	CLASSIC GREEK				**Lao-tse.** — T h e founder of Taoism.	
1000 to 500	**Homer.** — *Iliad* and *Odyssey* — Epic poems containing the story of the siege of Troy and the wanderings of Ulysses. The greatest classic epics. **Hesiod.**—Epic poems; *Theogony; Shield of Heracles; Works and Days.*	668-608. Golden Age of Assyrian literature.	*Joel, Amos, Hosea*— Minor prophets. *Psalms* — Sacred poems. *Isaiah*—greatest of Hebrew prophets. *Jeremiah*—The book of lament.	*The Zend-Avesta,* the bible of Zoroastrianism, is the oldest Persian literature known. The *Puranas* are second in point of age.	**Confucius.** — The most famous of all the sages of China. His doctrines were ethical and political.	776. First Olympiad. 753. Founding of Rome.

TABLE I. FROM THE BEGINNING TO THE BIRTH OF CHRIST—Concluded

Date	Classic Greek	Hebrew	Indian and Persian	Chinese	Historical Events
1000 to 500 B.C. Cont.	**Alcaeus.**—Originated meters in his varied lyrics. **Sappho.**—Leader of the Aeolian lyric poets, noted for her graceful style. **Anacreon.**—A lyric poet who sang of wine, love and good companions. **Alcman.**—Founder of the Dorian lyric school. **Ibycus.**—Early lyric poet. **Xenophanes.**—Poet and founder of Eleatic philosophy.	*Songs of Solomon*—Hebrew pastoral poems.	*Ramayana* (In.)—The second great epic of the early Hindu religion. *Brahmanas* (In.)—Writings to interpret the Vedas.	*The Four Books* rank next to the classics as masterpieces of early Chinese literature. Best of these is the Book of **Mencius,** second in rank among the Chinese sages.	B.C. 586. Babylonian captivity. 492. Persian war. 490. Marathon; age of Pericles.
500 to 400	**Pindar.**—*Triumphal Odes*—The great Dorian lyric poet. **Simonides** and **Bacchylides.** Masters of the choral ode. **Thucydides** and **Herodotus** developed the writing of history into an art. **Aeschylus.**—*Orestia*. **Sophocles.**—*Oedipus Rex*. **Euripides.**—*Bacchae, Alcestis*. These three Athenians produced the best tragic dramas of classic Greek. **Aristophanes.**—*Lysistrata, Frogs*—Master of classic Greek comedy; known for his unbridled satires.	*Job*—A drama of the soul. *Ruth*—An idyl of Jewish life in the period of the judges.	*Upanishads* (In.)—Speculations on the nature of the world and man. *The Vedangas* (In.)—Treatises on science and philosophy.		431–404. Peloponnesian War.
400 to 300	**Plato.**—*Republic*—Athenian teacher and philosopher, the master of prose dialogues. **Demosthenes, Aeschines, Isocrates, Lysias, Antiphon** and **Isaeus** were the great orators of the Golden Age of Greece. **Aristotle,** critic, teacher and philosopher, developed logic and the scientific method. **Xenophon.**—*Anabasis*.	*Malachi*—A minor prophet. *Daniel*—The apocalyptic prophet. *Chronicles* and *Ezra*.	**Panini's** *Sanskrit Grammar*.		390. Gauls sack Rome. 336–323. Alexander the Great.

Date	Alexandrine Greek	Latin			Historical Events
300 to 200	**Theocritus.**—The creator of bucolic poetry in Greek. **Callimachus.**—A minor poet, but a master of mechanical style. **Eratosthenes.**—Leading science writer of his era. *Septuagint version of Scriptures*—A translation by Greek scholars of the Hebrew Scriptures. **Apollonius.**—Scholar who wrote minor epics.	**Livius Andronicus.**—Translator; introduced Greek literature to Rome. **Plautus.**—*Comedies*—Dramas full of broad coarse wit; a model for later dramatists. **Ennius.**—*Annales*—The father of Latin poetry. **Cato the Censor.**—*De Re Rustica*—Father of Latin prose, opposed the Greek influence.			264–241. First Punic War. 218–201. Second Punic War.
200 to 100	**Bion.**—A bucolic poet, noted for sharp comments and exaggerated style. **Moschus.**—Wrote elegant bucolic idyls. **Polybius.**—Detailed, accurate but prosy history.	**Terence.**—Six *Comedies*, adapted from the Greek, marked by broad humor. **Lucilius.**—*Satires*—Daring in language and in subject. **Cicero.**—*Letters, Orations*—The master of rhythmical Latin prose. **Caesar.**—*Commentaries*—Accurate history in clear, concise prose. **Lucretius.**—*On the Nature of Things*—Original Epicurean philosophy. **Catullus.**—Great Latin love *lyrics*, adapted from the Greek.			146. Greece becomes a Roman province. 60–44. Career of Julius Caesar.
100 B.C. to A.D.	The *Anthology* compiled. It contains epigrams from most of the Greek classic poets.	**Sallust.**—*Histories, Catiline Conspiracy, Letters*—A pedantic stylist. **Varro.**—*On Farming*—The most learned man of his time. **Vergil.**—*Bucolics*, idyls of rural life; *Georgics*, formal didactic poems; *Aeneid*, the great epic of Latin literature. **Horace.**—*Odes, Satires, Letters*—The most polished of all Latin lyric writers. From his time Latin poetry declined in quality. **Nepos.**—*Biographies*—Sympathetic treatment, elegant style.			27. Augustus, emperor. 4. Birth of Jesus.

TABLE II. FROM JESUS TO MOHAMMED, 1–600 A. D.

Date	Latin		Greek		Historical Events
A.D. to 100	**Livy** (59 B.C.–17 A.D.).—*History of Rome*—Fine style in colloquial Latin. **Ovid** (43 B.C.–18 A.D.).—*Metamorphoses, Heroides*, etc.—A court poet who wrote much that is beautiful and much that is indecent. **Seneca** (3 B.C.–65 A.D.).—*Tragedies, Essays, Satires*—A Stoic philosopher who created a florid rhetorical style. **Pliny the Elder** (23–79).—*Natural History*—A large work drawn from the writings of other men. **Lucan** (39–65).—*Pharsalia*—A pedantic epic of Roman life. **Petronius** (d. 66).—*Satyricon*—A brilliant picture of the vulgar life of his era.		**Josephus, Flavius** (37–95).—*History of the Jewish War, Jewish Antiquities*—Detailed history written in Greek by a Jew. **Plutarch** (46–125).—*Lives of Greeks and Romans*—A master in sketching character. **Epictetus** (?60–100).—*Discourses*—A Stoic philosopher of profound learning, summed up in pungent maxims. **Dion Chrysostomus** (50–117).—*Orations* famous for beauty of style.		70. Destruction of Jerusalem. 79. Destruction of Pompeii and Herculaneum.
100 to 200	**Martial** (39–104).—*Epigrams*—Original, witty, sometimes vulgar short poems. **Quintilian** (40–118).—*Rhetoric*—Practical education in pleasing style. **Juvenal** (65–140).—*Satires*—Vigorous poems picturing the vices of his era. **Tacitus** (55–117).—*Germania, Histories,* etc.—A terse, vigorous historical writer. **Pliny the Younger** (62–113).—*Epistles*—Best records of his age. **Suetonius** (70–140).—*Lives of the Caesars*—History dry in style but scandalous in content. **Apuleius** (c. 150?).—*Golden Ass*—A satirical romance which was a model for many centuries.	EARLY CHRISTIAN *New Testament* — Mostly written before 100 A.D. and assembled and edited by Greek scholars. **Justin Martyr** (100–165).—*Apologies*—A defender of Christianity. **Tertullian** (160–250).—The father of Christian Latin literature, who influenced all European theology.	**Marcus Aurelius** (121–180).—*Meditations*—Stoic philosopher-emperor. **Lucian** (125–180).—*Dialogues*—A bold satirist, fertile in invention and racy in humor. **Appian** (c. 150).—*Roman History*—Original in method and accurate. **Galen** (130–200).—Prolific writer on medical subjects, long an authority. **Ptolemy, Claudius** (c. 127–150).—*Almagest*—Fixed all astronomical thought for twelve centuries.	ORIENTAL *Talmud,* the code of Jewish laws and social customs, was compiled in the Second Century.	117–138. Trajan. 161–180. Marcus Aurelius.
200 to 400	**Ausonius** (310–390).—A nature poet. **Claudian** (c. 365–408).—*Rape of Proserpine*—The last of the classic Latin poets. A master of language and meter.	**Athanasius** (293–373).—Prolific theological writer, fixing Greek creed. **Ulfilas** (311–381). — *Gothic Bible*—The earliest literary work in German. **Ambrose** (333–397).—*Hymns, Sermons*. **Jerome** (331–420).—*Vulgate Bible*—Father of the Western (Roman) Church. **Chryscstom** (347–407).—*Sermons, Letters*—Scholar and keen observer.	**Plotinus** (204–270).—*Enneads*—A Neoplatonic philosopher. **Longinus** (213–273).—A critic and scholar. *Daphnis and Chloe*—This pastoral romance is the best of Greek romances because of graceful style and natural feeling. *Hero and Leander*—A short love epic.	**Kalidasa** (In.). — *Dramas, Lyrics*—Revived the poetic art in Sanskrit.	225. New Persian empire; Zoroastrianism revived. 325. Council at Nicaea. 395. Division of the Roman Empire. 410. Alaric sacks Rome.

TABLE II FROM JESUS TO MOHAMMED, 1-600 A. D.—Concluded

500 to 600	**Boethius** (470–525). — *Consolations of Philosophy, Translations.*—Almost the last classical Latin prose writer. He ends the Roman period of literature.	**Prudentius** (c. 348–405).— The greatest early Latin *Hymns*. **St. Augustine** (354–430).— *Confessions*—Greatest of the Latin fathers. **Fortunatus, Venantius** (c. 530–600). — *Hymns; The Royal Banners Forward Go* is still in use. **Gregory the Great** (540–604). —*Letters, Dialogues*—As a pontiff he was the great organizer of the services of the Roman Church.	*Moallakat* (Arab.)—A collection of seven odes by as many authors, the finest pre-Moslem Arabic verse.	449. Saxons invade Britain. 455. Vandals sack Rome. 571. Birth of Mohammed. 590. Gregory becomes pope.

TABLE III. FROM MOHAMMED TO DANTE, 600-1300

DATE	ENGLISH	GERMAN	SCANDINAVIAN		ARABIAN, PERSIAN		HISTORICAL EVENTS
600 to 700	*Beowulf*—An epic poem of great antiquity, in spoken form long before this era and brought to England by the Saxons. **Caedmon** (675?).—*Paraphrase of Scripture.* **Bede** (673–735).—*Ecclesiastical History, Scientific and theological treatises*—A summary of learning by the greatest scholar of his age.	This is the period of the infiltration of Roman civilization and Roman ideas. *Lay of Hildebrand* in the old Germanic alliterative verse. Authors are unknown. The *Lay of Hildebrand* is an example of the rough, uncouth ballad out of which the German epic was constructed.	400–1000. *Hundreds of Runic Inscriptions*—Very brief. Some in verse. Important for history, language, art. *Skalds* and the *Elder Edda*, composed between 800 and 1200, are alliterative poems recounting the Norse mythology.		*The Koran*, the sacred book of Islam, collected shortly after Mohammed's death. Many odes and lyrics in Arabic. In the latter half of this century Arabia enjoyed a glorious reputation in science and literature under the patronage of **Haroun-al-Raschid.**		622. Flight of Mohammed from Mecca, the Hegira. 711. The Arabs enter Spain.
700 to 800	**Alcuin** (735–804).—Latin *Grammar* — Orthodox theological treatises. **Cynewulf** (c. 750–825).—Serious religious *poems.*		FRENCH	SCANDINAVIAN	**Abu Hanifah** (702–772).—*Code of Laws*—Still in force in many parts of the Ottoman Empire.		751. Pepin the Short, king of Franks. 800. Charlemagne crowned emperor of the West.
800 to 900	**Alfred the Great** (c. 849–901).— *Translations* of theological and philosophical classics.	**Otfried** (c. 800–870).—*Gospel Book*—A rhymed version of the life of Christ, theology rather than poetry. The oldest German writer whose name is known. *Heliand* (c. 830)—An alliterative epic of the life of Christ.	*Song of Roland.* The greatest of the old French epics relating the adventures of Roland, a nephew of the Emperor Charlemagne.				866. Schism between Greek and Roman churches.
900 to 1000		**Ekkehard.**—*Lay of Walther of Aquitaine* (c. 930)—A short epic in Latin hexameters. **Hroswitha** (c. 940–1000).—*Dramas*—A nun who wrote six dramas in Latin in the Christian spirit of her time to take the place of the pagan plays of Terence. **Notker III** (950–1022).—*Translations*—A forerunner of the Renaissance. He translated into German Boethius's *Consolations of philosophy*, the *Psalter*; Aristotle's *Categories*, etc. *Nibelungenlied* (12th or 13th Century)—This long epic, strong on characterization, is the Iliad of German.			**Rudagi** (d. 954), (Pers.). — *Divan* —Graceful, fluent lyrics. The first great poet of Mohammedan Persia. **Firdausi** (c. 940–1025), (Pers.).—*Book of Kings*—One of the foremost poets of all literature. A great epic dealing with the Persian monarchs. **Avicenna** (980–1037), (Arab.).— *Medicine, Philosophy*—Philosophical and scientific works. His work was a textbook for European scholars throughout the Middle Ages.		962. Holy Roman Empire set up. 1066. Normans conquer England.
1000 to 1100	**William of Malmesbury** (1095–1142).—*History of Kings of England.*			**Ari Thorgilsson** (c. 1050).— *Histories.*	**Hariri** (c. 1054–1122), (Arab.).— *Makamat*—Moral and satirical rhymed picaresque prose.		1096. First Crusade. 1163. Notre Dame of Paris founded.
1100 to 1200	**Geoffrey of Monmouth** (c. 1100–1154).—A largely legendary *History of English Kings.*	**Wolfram von Eschenbach** (c. 1170–1220). — *Parzifal* — The great epic of chivalry. A story of the search for the Holy Grail. **Walther von der Vogelweide** (c. 1170–c. 1227).—Greatest lyric poet of medieval Germany. **Gottfried von Strassburg** (c. 1200).—*Tristan and Isolde*—His great court epic is naturalistic, breathing the spirit of passion. **Berthold von Regensburg** (1247–1272).—*Sermons*—The greatest German preacher of the middle ages. **Meister Eckhart** (1260–1327).—*Sermons*—The first of the mystics.	**Villehardouin** (1150–1212). *Conquest of Constantinople*—A valuable, vivid and reliable history. **Jean, Sire de Joinville** (1224–1317). —*Life of St. Louis*—A chronicle of his times. **Marie de France.**—*Lays* and *Fables* of charming theme and elegant style. *Aucassin et Nicolette* — An excellent example of the chantefable of the twelfth century. **Lorris and Meung.**—Joint authors of the *Romance of the Rose*, a long allegorical poem on the "Art of Loving."	**Snorri Sturluson** (Ic.), (1178–1241). — *Heimskringla*—History of kings of Norway. *Edda.* Scientific handbook on Norse mythology. **Saxo Grammaticus** (Dan.), (1200).— *History of Denmark* — Father of Danish history.	SPANISH *Poem of the Cid* —Great narrative poem on the national hero.	ARABIAN, PERSIAN **Omar Khayyám** (1071–1123) (Pers.).— *Quatrains*—philosophic and meditative stanzas. **Averroes** (1126–1198), (Arab.).— *Science, Philosophy*—Important works which widely influenced western European thought. **Sadi** (Pers.) (c. 1184–1291) *Rose-Garden, Lyrics, Odes.*	1206. Franciscan order founded. 1215. Magna Charta signed. 1248. Cathedral at Cologne begun.
1200 to 1300	**Roger Bacon** (1214–1294).—*Natural Science, Philosophy*—A man in advance of his age, the leading scholar of the era and a writer on diverse topics.						1295. Marco Polo returned to Venice.

TABLE IV. FROM DANTE TO THE PREREFORMATION PERIOD, 1300–1600

Date	English	German	French	Persian	Italian, Spanish, Portuguese	Scandinavian	Historical Events
1300 to 1400	*Piers the Plowman*—Unrhymed alliterative verse, satirical, praises the simple life. **John Wycliffe** (1324–1384).—*Translation of Vulgate Bible into English.* **John Gower** (c. 1325–1408).—Love *Poems* and allegories in Latin and English. **Geoffrey Chaucer** (1340–1400).—*Canterbury Tales, Short Poems*—A scholar, a poet of chivalry and a witty narrator of stories in verse. *Miracle Plays*—Religious allegories of great popularity in the 14th and 15th centuries.	**Tauler** (1300–1361)—*Sermons*—A great evangelist and mystic preacher. **Thomas à Kempis** (1380–1471).—*Imitation of Christ*—A simple devotional book in Latin, long popular.	**Sir John Mandeville** (c. 1370). — *Travels*—A compilation, partly imaginative, translated into many languages. **Jean Froissart** (1337–1410). —*Chronicles*—A vivid but imaginative account of the age of chivalry. **Charles of Orleans** (1391–1468). — *Poems* — Art takes the place of thought and form nears perfection.	**Hafiz** (c. 1375), (Pers.)—*Poems*—Lyrics of vehement style.	**Dante Alighieri** (It.), (1265–1321).—*Divine Comedy*—Great epic, written in the first person. He fixed the character of Italian poetry and influenced the literature of all medieval Europe. **Juan Ruiz** (Sp.), (c. 1325).—*Book of True Love*, a collection of picaresque medieval poems. **Francesco Petrarch** (It.), (1304–1374).—*Sonnets and Songs*—Lyrics of distinctive finished style and fine odes. The forerunner of the Renaissance. **Giovanni Boccaccio** (It.), (1313–1375). — *Decameron*—A series of tales in prose which give a humorous but vivid picture of his age; a forerunner of the short story. **Iñigo López de Mendoza** (Sp.), (1398–1458).—*Sonnets*—The first in Spain to compose sonnets.	**St. Birgitta** (Swed.), (1303–1373).—*Revelations* — Mystical conversations.	1309. Popes in Avignon. 1386. University of Heidelburg founded. 1414–18. Council of Constance. 1431. Joan of Arc burned. 1455. Gutenberg *Bible*, first European printed book. 1453. Fall of Constantinople.
1400 to 1500	**Sir Thomas Malory** (c. 1469).—*Morte d'Arthur*—Worked over a large part of the Arthurian legends in prose. **Sir Thomas More** (1478–1535).—*Utopia*—In Latin; a studied plan for an ideal state.	**Sebastian Brant** (1457–1521).—*The Ship of Fools*—An effective didactic satirical poem. **Erasmus of Rotterdam** (1467–1536).—*Colloquies* — Best thoughts of a cultured scholar and accurate translator.	**François Villon** (1431–aft. 1463).—*Ballads* — The most remarkable poet of the fifteenth century. His *lyrics* are among the masterpieces of French poetry.		**Matteo M. Boiardo** (It.), (1430–1494).—*Orlando Inamorato*—A long epic poem. **Lorenzo de' Medici** (1449–1492).—A patron of art and literature; wrote sonnets and love poems. **Girolamo Savonarola** (It.), (1452–1498). — *Sermons, Poems*—Political and theological writings.	**Christian Pedersen** (Dan.), (1480–1554) — *Translation of Luther's Bible* (1550)—Father of modern Danish literary language.	1477. First book printed in England. 1492. Discovery of America.
1500 to 1600	**William Tyndale** (1484–1536). — *Translation of Bible*—On his translation of the Scriptures later versions are founded. **Hugh Latimer** (1485–1555).—Vivid *Sermons* picturing the abuses of the Catholics. *Ralph Roister Doister*—The first dramatic comedy in English. **John Haywood** (1497–1578).—His *Interludes* were forerunners of comic drama. **Sir Thomas Wyatt** (1503–1542).—*Sonnets, Lyrics*—Made Italian literature a new force in England. **Henry Howard** (earl of Surrey), (1517–1547).—*Translation of the Aeneid, Songs, Sonnets*—Introduced Italian forms and blank verse. **John Foxe** (1517–1587).—*Book of Martyrs*—His book had great influence in strengthening the reformers. **Thomas Sackville** (1536–1608).—*Mirror for Magistrates*. A poet of force and imagination. Worked in collaboration with others on the first English tragedy, *Gorboduc*. **Edmund Spenser** (1552–1599).—*Faërie Queene, Shepherd's Calendar*. Great in the melodious verse and refined style of the romantic allegory, the ode and the sonnet. **Sir Walter Raleigh** (1552–1618).—*History of the World*. **Richard Hooker** (1553–1600).—*Ecclesiastical Polity*, a plan of church government expounded in dignified prose. **John Lyly** (1554–1606).—*Euphues*, a romance which set the style for the novel; he also wrote the first English prose comedies. **Sir Philip Sidney** (1554–1586).—*Arcadia*, a pastoral romance, and typical Elizabethan love *Sonnets*. **Francis Bacon** (1561–1626).—*Essays, Philosophy*—Beautiful and acute style; the father of modern scientific reasoning. **Christopher Marlowe** (1564–1593).—*Dramas* — Most important of Shakespeare's predecessors. He made blank verse an English dramatic vehicle. **William Shakespeare** (1564–1616).—*Dramas* (37 plays), *Sonnets*—A "timeless genius"; best of English writers, distinguished for wit, characterization, plot, philosophy, rhythm, variety and psychological acuteness.	**Thomas Murner** (1475–1537).—Coarse violent *Satires*, especially attacking Luther. **Martin Luther** (1483–1546).—*Translation of the Bible, Treatises, Hymns*—Inaugurator of the Reformation. **Ulrich von Hutten** (1488–1523).—*Poems, Songs* — Humanist; good Latin verse. **Hans Sachs** (1494–1576).—*Shrove Tuesday Plays, Proverb Poems* — Prolific mastersinger. **Philipp Melanchthon** (1497–1560). — *Treatises, Textbooks* — Colleague of Luther. *Till Eulenspiegel* (15th Century)—A large collection of witty, popular anecdotes, the hero of which was the prince of rogues, Till Eulenspiegel. **Johann Fischart** (1550–1590).—The master of German satire in the later sixteenth century. Achieved fame by *The Fortunate Ship of Zürich*.	**Philippe de Commines** (1445–1509).—*Memoirs*—Give accounts of the reigns of Louis XI and Charles VIII. **Margaret of Navarre** (1492–1542).—*Heptameron*, a collection of tales picturing the life of her times. **François Rabelais** (c. 1494–1553).—*Philosophy, Satire* — Scholar, philosopher, satirist and innovator. Rabelais left to posterity the *Life of Gargantua and Pantagruel*, a criticism of contemporary life in the form of a satirical history of civilization. **Clément Marot** (1495–1544). — *Poems* — Excelled in the lighter forms of poetry, such as the rondeau and the ballad, in the older forms. **John Calvin** (1509–1564).—His *Institutes of the Christian Religion* is a statement of the doctrine of the Reformation and shows his remarkable scholarship. **Jacques Amyot** (1513–1593). — *Translations From the Greek*. These translations stand as a model of the best French of the sixteenth century. **Pierre de Ronsard** (1524–1585). — *Sonnets, Odes*, etc.—As a poet of love and nature he enjoyed in his time great celebrity. **Étienne Jodelle** (1532–1573).—His *Cléopâtre*, a tragedy, and *Eugène*, a comedy, mark the beginning of these forms of the modern French drama. **Michel E. de Montaigne** (1533–1592). — Philosophic *Essays* in an easy style, read to this day.		**Politian** (It.), (1454–1494).—*Orfeo*, a drama; lyrics; translations of the classics. **Jacopo Sannazaro** (It.), (1458–1530).—*Arcadia*, a prose romance; lyrics and sonnets. **Niccolò Machiavelli** (It.), (1469–1527).—*History, The Prince*—Profound, unscrupulous thinker, master of polished prose. **Pietro Bembo** (It.), (1470–1547).—His lyrics, formal in style, became a standard pattern. **Ludovico Ariosto** (It.), (1474–1533).—*Orlando Furioso*—A romantic poem of chivalry. **Francesco Guicciardini** (It.), (1483–1540). — *Recollections; History of Italy*. **Gil Vicente** (Port.), (c. 1470–1536).—*Dramas*—Founder of the Portuguese drama. **Bartolome de Las Casas** (Sp.), (1474–1566). — Missionary in America; wrote *History of Spanish conquest*. **Michelangelo** (It.), (1475–1564)—*Sonnets*. **Vittoria Colonna** (It.), (1490–1547). — *Poems* — Sonnets on the death of her husband. **Juan Boscán** (Sp.), (1493–1543).—*Poems* — Introduced Italian verse forms into Spain. **Benvenuto Cellini** (It.), (1500–1571). — *Autobiography*—A remarkable picture of his times. **Garcilaso de la Vega** (Sp.), (1503–1536). — *Poems* — Refined but lacking in originality. **Hurtado de Mendoza** (Sp.), (1503–1575).—*War of Granada*, a history. A picaresque novel, *El Lazarillo de Tormes*, perhaps by him, set the example for this type of literature. **Giorgio Vasari** (It.), (1512–1574).—*Lives of Celebrated Artists*—A gossipy book about artists. **Luís de Camoëns** (Port.), (1524–1579). — *Lusiad, Poems*—Greatest poet of Portugal. *Lusiad* a celebrated historical epic. **Ponce de León** (Sp.), (1528–1591).—*Religious poems*; translations. **Ercilla** (Sp.), (1533–1595).—*Araucana*—An epic poem.	*Morality and Mystery Plays* (Dan.), (1500–1600)—Same origin and fate as in other countries. **Tycho Brahe** (Dan.), (1546–1601).—*Rudolphine Tables*—A landmark in early astronomy.	1509–1547. Henry VIII, king of England. 1517. Luther begins Protestant Revolt. 1531. Collège de France. 1555. Religious Peace of Augsburg. 1572. Massacre of St. Bartholomew. 1581. Independence of Netherlands. 1588. Defeat of the Spanish armada.

TABLE IV. DANTE TO THE PREREFORMATION PERIOD—Concluded

Date	English	German	French	Italian, Spanish, Portuguese	Scandinavian	Historical Events
1500 to 1600 *Cont.*				**Fernando Herrera** (Sp.), (1534–1597).—*Lyrics* and *Odes.* **Torquato Tasso** (It.), (1544–1595).—*Jerusalem Delivered*—A great epic on the Crusades. **Miguel de Cervantes Saavedra** (Sp.), (1547–1616). — *Don Quixote*—The great masterpiece of Spanish literature, a romance of humor, pathos and philosophy. **Pietro Sarpi** (It.), (1552–1623).—*History of Council of Trent* — Philosophical and historical.		1571. Battle of Lepanto.

TABLE V. SEVENTEENTH CENTURY, 1600-1700

English	German	French	Scandinavian	Italian, Spanish, Portuguese	American	Historical Events
Richard Hakluyt (1552–1616).—Detailed and varied *Travels,* marked by tireless enthusiasm. **George Chapman** (1559–1634). — The master translator of *Homer;* mediocre dramas. **Thomas Dekker** (c. 1570–1641). — Realistic, coarse, humorous *Dramas.* **John Donne** (1572–1631). — Sensuous, satirical *Lyrics;* complex metaphysical poems. **Ben Jonson** (1574–1637). —*Dramas, Lyrics*—A scholar and man of letters. **John Fletcher** (1579–1625); **Francis Beaumont** (1584–1616). — Collaborated in *Dramas* of advanced technique but coarse language. **Robert Burton** (1577–1640). — *Anatomy of Melancholy*—Full of out-of-the-way learning and quotations. **John Webster** (1580–1625). — *Tragedies* of exceptional ferocity. **Philip Massinger** (1583–1640), **John Ford** (1586–1639) and **James Shirley** (1596–1666).— These were the leading writers of the *Drama* in Puritan days; mediocre in quality, it is coarse, sometimes witty. **Robert Herrick** (1591–1674).—*Poems*—Lyrics of charming quality and ingenious construction. **Izaak Walton** (1593–1683).—*The Compleat Angler*—A dialogue extolling outdoor life in superb prose. **Sir Thomas Browne** (1605–1682).—*Philosophy, Theology*—A scholar, master of beautiful prose. **Edmund Waller** (1606–1687).—Many graceful *Lyrics;* favored the heroic couplet. **Thomas Fuller** (1608–1661). — *Worthies of England.* **John Milton** (1608–1674). —*Areopagitica, L'Allegro, Il Penseroso, Comus, Paradise Lost, Paradise Regained,* etc. —A poet, grave, learned, of mental dignity and gifted with musical power.	**Jacob Ayrer** (1605). —*Dramas*—He popularized the operetta. **Hugo Grotius** (Dutch), (1583–1645). — *Law, Philosophy, Translations*—Famous scholar and statesman. **Jacob Boehme** (1573–1624). — *Treatises* — The founder of the mystical theosophy of the century. **Georg Weckherlin** (1584–1653). — *Odes* and *Songs*—A minor poet. **Joost van den Vondel** (Dutch), (1587–1679). —Dramatist and poet, greatest figure of Dutch literature. *Gysbrecht van Aemstel, Lucifer.* **Friedrich von Spee** (1591–1635). — Catholic religious *lyrics.* **Martin Opitz** (1597–1639). — *Criticism, Translations, Poems*— Translated from the classics and set up fixed principles of poetic art. **J. M. Moscherosch** (1601–1669). — Satirical *Novels, Poems.* **Friedrich von Logau** (1605–1655). — 3000 German *Epigrams.* **Paul Gerhardt** (1607–1676). — *Hymns* and *Mystical Poems.*	*L'Avocat Patelin*—A masterpiece of the comic play and of the Gallic wit. **François de Malherbe** (1555–1628). — *Poems*—In his odes, songs and sonnets he developed a new technique and a refined vocabulary. **Isaac Casaubon** (1559–1614).—Critic and scholar. **St. François de Sales** (1567–1622). — *Religious Works*—Preacher and writer of religious works whose influence was great. **Racan** (1589–1670). — *Pastoral Poems.* **Guez de Balzac** (1594–1654).—*Letters* which greatly influenced French prose style. **René Descartes** (1596–1650).—The founder of the Cartesian school of *Philosophy,* he also wrote on *Science.* **Vincent Voiture** (1598–1648).—Witty *Letters* and ephemeral verse. **Pierre Corneille** (1606–1684).—*Tragedy, Comedy*—Called the "Father of French tragedy." Of his works four are ranked among the masterpieces of literature: *Le Cid, Horace, Cinna* and *Polyeucte.* **Mlle. de Scudéry** (1607–1701).—Voluminous *Novels* which contain allusions to the events of her day. **Paul Scarron** (1610–1660). — *Comic Plays, Poems*—Author of a number of witty, burlesque poems. His widow became the famous Madame de Maintenon.	**Magnus Olafsson** (Ic.), (1573–1636). — *Dictionary* — First Icelandic dictionary. **Georg Stiernhielm** (Swed.), (1598–1672). — *Poems* — Introduces new period in literature. Earliest Swedish sonnets.	**Lope de Vega** (Sp.), (1562–1635). — *Dramas, Lyrics*—Dramas of unusual number, variety and power. **Galileo Galilei** (It.), (1564–1642). — *Scientific*—Physical and astronomical discussions. **Tassoni** (It.), (1565–1638).—*Rape of the Bucket*—A mock heroic poem. **Tommaso Campanella** (It.), (1568–1639).—Philosophical works; he proposed a communistic Utopia. **Claudio Monteverdi** (It.), (1567–1643).—His *Orfeo* was the first opera of the modern type. **Giovanni Basili** (It.), (1575–1632).— Recorded many charming folk stories. **Gomez de Quevedo** (Sp.), (1580–1645). — *Satires, Novel* —Remarkable wit; versatile in technique. **Calderón de la Barca** (Sp.), (1600–1681). — *Dramas* in fine flowing verse; his death ended the finest age of Spanish literature. **Pietro Cavalli** (It.), (1602–1676). — Many *Operas,* bettering their form. **Antonio de Solis** (Sp.), (1610–1686). — *Conquest of Mexico;* dramatic poems.		1598. Edict of Nantes. 1600. Giordano Bruno burned. 1602. English East India Company. 1603. England and Scotland united under James I. 1607. Jamestown, Va., founded. 1610. Galileo discovered Satellites of Jupiter. 1618–1648. Thirty Years' War. 1620. Voyage of *Mayflower.* 1628. Gustavus Adolphus killed at battle of Lützen.

American column entries:

John Smith (1580–1631).— *A True Relation of Virginia* —A recital of his adventures.

William Bradford (1588–1657). — *History of Plymouth Plantation.*

John Winthrop (1590–1649.) — *History of New England*—A personal narrative.

TABLE V. SEVENTEENTH CENTURY—Continued

ENGLISH	GERMAN	FRENCH	SCANDINAVIAN	ITALIAN, SPANISH, PORTUGUESE	AMERICAN	HISTORICAL EVENTS
Samuel Butler (1612–1680).— *Hudibras*—A witty anti-Puritan satire in verse. **Jeremy Taylor** (1613–1667).—*Holy Living*, etc.—Theological prose of rare poetic beauty. **Richard Baxter** (1615–1691).—*Saint's Everlasting Rest*, a Puritan theological treatise. **Richard Lovelace** (1618–1658).—Artificial *Lyrics.* **Abraham Cowley** (1618–1687).— Love poems and elegies. **John Evelyn** (1620–1706).—*Diary* of a country gentleman. **Andrew Marvell** (1621–1678).—*Lyrics* of country life. **Henry Vaughan** (1622–1695). — Sacred and secular poems.	**Andreas Gryphius** (1616–1664).—*Dramas*, especially comedies, and minor poems. **Philip von Zesen** (1619–1689).—Talented adventure *Novels.* **Christoffel von Grimnelshausen** (1624–1676).—*Satires; Simplicissimus*, the great rogue novel of German literature. **Angelus Silesius** (1624–1677).—Mystical pastoral *Poems.*	**François de la Rochefoucauld** (1613–1680).—*Maxims, Memoirs*—His maxims, full of bold paradoxes, give him a lasting reputation. *Port Royal Textbooks*—Produced from 1620 to 1700, these treatises on Grammar and Logic influenced French literature for a century. **Jean de la Fontaine** (1621–1695). —His *Contes*, inspired by Boccaccio, are full of wit, while his *Fables*, in lightly satirical and highly melodious verse, are a distinct contribution to literature. **Molière** (**Jean B. Poquelin**), (1622–1673). — *Comedies; Le Misanthrope*, etc.—The greatest writer of comedies of his time. He has not been equaled in France, and seldom in any country. **Blaise Pascal** (1623–1662).— *Philosophy, Mathematics* — A thinker and a philosopher. His *Pensées* (Thoughts), and his *Letters* remain as models of French literature. **Mme. de Sévigné** (1626–1696).— *Letters*—Her charming familiar letters written to her daughter give interesting information on the court life of her time. **Jacques Bossuet** (1627–1704).— *Sermons*, etc.—The greatest orator of his time. In his funeral orations especially he reached magnificent oratorical style. **Charles Perrault** (1628–1703).— *Stories for Children*—His stories are known all over the world and have immortalized his name.			**Anne Bradstreet** (1613–1672).— *The Tenth Muse*—An affected didactic poem. She was the first woman writer in America.	1635. French Academy founded. 1642. English civil war. 1648. Peace of Westphalia. 1653-58. Cromwell, Lord Protector of England.
John Bunyan (1628–1688).—*Pilgrim's Progress* is the best known allegory in English; it is distinguished for simple passages of natural beauty **John Dryden** (1631–1700).—*Absalom and Achitophel* contains clever heroic couplets; he also wrote *Tragedies*, fine *Odes*, and political *Satires.* **John Locke** (1632–1704).— *Essay on Human Understanding, Thoughts on Education*, etc.—A sound, practical thinker, whose works illustrate common sense. **Samuel Pepys** (1633–1703). — *Diary* — His *Diary*, not intended to be public, throws light on the life and habits of a capable businessman of the eighteenth century.	**Benedict Spinoza** (Dutch), (1632–167). — *Ethics* — He developed a pantheistic philosophy.				**Michael Wigglesworth** (1631–1705). — *The Day of Doom*—A Calvinistic poem on the day of judgment.	1660. Restoration of the Stuarts. 1664. New Amsterdam surrenders to English. 1666. Great fire of London.
George Etheridge (1635–1691) and **William Wycherley** (1640–1715) excelled in the coarse, witty comedy of the day. **Sir Isaac Newton** (1642–1727).—*Principia*, etc. —A great mathematician, he laid the foundation of our understanding of the mechanical structure of the universe.	**Caspar von Lohenstein** (1635–1683).—*Dramas, Novels*—Represents the decline of German Renaissance. Reveled in themes of blood, incest and cruelty. **Christian Weise** (1642–1708).—Comic, simple *Plays, Novels* of the immediate scene. **G. W. Leibnitz** (1646–1716). — *Philosophic Writings* — The first great scientific German philosopher of the modern type.	**Louis Bourdaloue** (1632–1704).— *Sermons*—A severe and austere Jesuit preacher. **Mme. de Lafayette** (1634–1693). —Her *Princesse de Clèves* was the first modern novel of character. **Nicolas Boileau-Despréaux** (1636–1711). — *Epistles, Art, Poétique, Satires*—An artist and critic who steadied and gave direction to his contemporaries. **Malebranche** (1638–1715). — A Cartesian philosopher and able stylist. **Jean Racine** (1639–1699).—*Tragedy*—Brought the French classic tragedy to its perfection. He excels in the portrayal of feminine love and the imperfections of human nature. **Jean de La Bruyère** (1645–1696). —A moralist who in his *Charactères* satirized his surroundings. **Pierre Bayle** (1647–1706).—*Critical and Historical Dictionary.* A mine of erudition presented with skepticism and humor.	**Thormod Torfaeus** (Ic.), (1636–1719). — *History of Norway*—A revolutionizing history. **Lars Johansson** (Swed.), (1638–1674). — *Lyrics* — Drinking songs, songs of love, casual poems.	**Vincenzo da Filicaja** (It.) (1642–1707).— *Lyrics* — Odes and sonnets in lofty style.		1685. Edict of Nantes revoked.

TABLE V. SEVENTEENTH CENTURY—Concluded

English	German	French	Scandinavian	Italian, Spanish, Portuguese	American	Historical Events
Thomas Otway (1652–1685). — *Venice Preserved* and *The Orphan*; outstanding tragedies of the Restoration Period; deeply emotional.	**Christian Thomasius** (1655–1728). — Delivered the first of university lectures ever given in the German tongue.	**François de la Motte Fénelon** (1651–1715).—*Télémaque*, etc.—Was not equaled in his century for the charm of his style. **Jean François Regnard** (1655–1709).—*Comedies in Verse*—His comedies, especially *Le Joueur*, show a decided talent for the gay intrigue.	**Gunno Dahlstjerna** (Swed.), (1661–1709).—*Elegies* and patriotic *Ballads* in affected style.		**Samuel Sewall** (1652–1730).—*Diaries* of the judge in the Salem witchcraft trials.	1688. English Revolution.

TABLE VI. EIGHTEENTH CENTURY, 1700-1800

English	German	French	American	Italian, Spanish Scandinavian	Historical Events
Daniel Defoe (1661–1731).—*Robinson Crusoe, Moll Flanders* — Superbly told stories; simple English. **Richard Bentley** (1662–1742).—Classical scholar and critic. **Jonathan Swift** (1667–1745).—*Tale of a Tub, Gulliver's Travels*—Unequaled as a satirist and writer of allegories in simple, idiomatic English. **William Congreve** (1670–1729).—*Dramas*—*The Old Bachelor*, other poetic comedies, much admired in his day. **Joseph Addison** (1672–1719). — *Essays* — Originator of the social essay, marked by kindly, gentlemanlike humor in the urbane style. **Sir Richard Steele** (1672–1729). — *Essays* — Established the *Tatler*. A collaborator with Addison. **George Farquhar** (1678–1707).—*The Beaux Stratagem*—Master of brilliantly witty comedies of coarse tone. **Edward Young** (1683–1755). —Somber *Poems* of splendid melody. **Bishop Berkeley** (1684–1753). — Idealist *Philosophy* — A very acute Irish thinker. **John Gay** (1685–1732).—*Dramas, Fables*—His *Beggar's Opera* was the hit of his day. **Alexander Pope** (1688–1744). —*Poems*—The model poet of the English classical era, master of the couplet, but wanting in emotion. **Samuel Richardson** (1689–1761). — *Novels*; *Clarissa Harlowe, Pamela, Sir Chas. Grandison* — Popularized the long sentimental moral novel, and excelled in drawing feminine character. **Henry Carey** (1690–1743).—*Sally in Our Alley*, other light verse. **Bishop Butler** (1692–1752). —*Natural and Revealed Religion*—The orthodox moralist of his day, ponderous in style and commonplace in method. **Earl of Chesterfield** (1694–1773). — *Letters*, admired for finished style and shrewd wit. **George Sale** (1697–1736).—A minor writer; his translation of *The Koran* was long classic. **James Thomson** (1700–1748).—*The Seasons*, etc.—A delicate feeling for the quieter aspects of nature, harmoniously expressed. **Henry Fielding** (1707–1754).—*Tom Jones, Amelia*, etc.—The first English realistic novelist. Depicts life broadly and faithfully.	**Heinrich von Ziegler** (1663–1696).—Minor *Poems*; a pioneer in the *Historical Novel*. **Christian von Wolff** (1679–1754). — *Philosophical Writings* — The modern scholastic who popularized philosophy and brought rationalism to bear upon theology. **J. C. Guenther** (1695–1723). —*Lyrics*—A lyric poet of personal feeling, modeling his lyrics upon the ballad. **J. Bodmer** (Swiss), (1698–1783).—*Criticisms, Translations*. **J. C. Gottsched** (1700–1766). —*Dramas, Criticisms*—He sought to reform the German drama on the model of the French, but was the victim of acid literary quarrels. **Friedrich von Hagedorn** (1708–1754). — *Lyrics, Fables*—Essentially a social poet. He gave the dominant tone to the German lyric for twenty-five years.	**Jean Massillon** (1663–1742).—*Orations*—One of the great French preachers. **Alain René Le Sage** (1668–1747). —Wrote *Comedies*—*Gil Blas*, a satirical novel, was one of the first to depict truly the manners of society. **Duc de Saint Simon** (1675–1755). — *Court Memoirs*—An original writer. **Philippe Destouches** (1680–1754). — *Comedies in Verse*—His *Le Glorieux* is an excellent comedy of manners. **Montesquieu** (1689–1755).—*The Spirit of Laws*—A scholar who satirized his age. **Alexis Piron** (1689–1773). —Witty short *Poems*, *Epigrams*, minor poetic *Comedies*. **Voltaire (François Marie Arouet)** (1694–1778).—*History, Letters, Philosophy, Poems, Dramas*, etc.—The greatest literary genius of the eighteenth century. Poet, historian, political and satirical writer, philosopher, writer of tragedies, he greatly influenced the thought of his era. **Abbé Prevost** (1697–1763). — *Manon Lescaut*, a classic psychological study of passion.	**Cotton Mather** (1663–1728).—Many wordy *Sermons*, painfully didactic. **William Byrd** (1674–1744).—*The Dividing Line and other tracts*—Full of fresh humorous observations on life. **Robert Beverly** (1675–1722).—*History of Virginia* — A straightforward narrative. **Jonathan Edwards** (1703–1758).—*Sermons, Freedom of the Will*—A metaphysician and Calvinist teacher. **Benjamin Franklin** (1706–1790).—*Poor Richard's Almanack, Autobiography*—Wise and sagacious utterances of an avowed utilitarian.	**G. Battista Vico** (It.), (1668–1744).—*Scienza Nuova*—Metaphysical and scientific. **Scipione Maffei** (It.), (1675–1755).—*Dramas*—His *Merope* is the first classic Italian tragedy. **Ludvig Holberg** (Dan.), (1684–1754). — *Comedies, Historical Works, Philosophy, Comic Poetry*—Founder of Danish drama. **Emanuel Swedenborg** (Swed.), (1688–1772).— *Philosophy* — Prominent scientist. Founder of a mystic religious sect. **Pietro Metastasio** (It.), (1698–1782). — *Musical Dramas* — Lyric smoothness of melody frequently weakens his thought.	1697. Peace of Ryswick. 1701. War of Spanish Succession begins. 1704. Boston *News Letter* established. 1710. St. Paul's Cathedral, London, completed. 1714. War of Spanish Succession ends. 1715. Louis XIV dies. 1720. South Sea and Mississippi speculative bubbles. 1727. George II, king of England. 1734. University of Göttingen founded.

TABLE VI. EIGHTEENTH CENTURY, 1700-1800—Continued

English	German, Swiss	French	Scandinavian	Italian, Russian American	Historical Events
Samuel Johnson (1709-1784). — *Dictionary, Rasselas, Lives of the Poets, Vanity of Human Wishes*—A man great in eighteenth century learning and letters. The critical authority of his day. **David Hume** (1711-1776).—*History of England*—The first learned historian of England. An empirical philosopher. **Laurence Sterne** (1713-1768). —*Tristram Shandy, Sentimental Journey*—A writer in whom affectation becomes an art.	**Albrecht von Haller** (1708-1777). — *Science* — Great Swiss anatomist and physiologist. **C. F. Gellert** (1715-1769).—*Novels, Letters, Fables, Poems*—A great stylist in verse, he produced the pioneer German social novel. **Ewald von Kleist** (1715-1759). — *Nature Poetry, War Odes*—A spirit of melancholy unites with his passionate love for nature.	**Comte de Buffon** (1707-1788).—*Natural History*—A great naturalist and a writer whose style still serves as a model. **Louis Gresset** (1709-1777).—*Poems, Comedies* of manners. **Jean Jacques Rousseau** (1712-1778). — *Confessions, Philosophy*—A writer of world-wide influence, he led the shift from classicism to romanticism in European literature. **Denis Diderot** (1713-1784).—*Fiction, Encyclopedie* (Ed.)—One of the most powerful exponents of the ideas and philosophy of the eighteenth century. **Étienne de Condillac** (1715-1780). — *Metaphysics, Treatise on Sensations.*	**Karl von Linné** (Swed.), (1707-1778).—*Botany, Travels*—Founder of science of botany. **Olof von Dalin** (Swed.), (1708-1763).— *Journalism, History, Comedy, Tragedy, Poems.*	**Carlo Goldoni** (It.), (1707-1793). — *Comedies* — Animated character comedy, mostly in prose. **Mikhail Lomonosov** (Russ.), (1711-1765). — *Lyrics* — Scholar and poet. Put Russian folk songs in durable metrical verse.	1740. Reign of Frederick the Great begins.
Thomas Gray (1716-1771).— *Elegy in a Country Churchyard*, etc.—A scholar-poet. Production limited but of fine workmanship. **Horace Walpole** (1717-1797). —*Letters*, among the best in English, witty and of unbounded range. He pioneered in the *Novel* of Terror. **Gilbert White** (1720-1793).— *Natural History of Selborn*, a classic of minute observation and graceful style. **Tobias Smollett** (1721-1771). —*Humphrey Clinker, Roderick Random*, etc.—Picaresque tales inclined to vulgarity. **Sir William Blackstone** (1723-1780). — *Commentaries on the Laws of England* —The classic legal textbook for a century. **Adam Smith** (1723-1790).— *Wealth of Nations*—The first great modern economist. **Oliver Goldsmith** (1728-1774).—*Vicar of Wakefield, Essays, Deserted Village, She Stoops to Conquer*, etc. —A true and graceful touch both in prose and poetry. **Edmund Burke** (1729-1797). —*Essays, Orations*—Prose, sometimes musical and poetical, and, at the same time, with a statesman's grasp of principle. **Thomas Percy** (1729-1811). —*Reliques*, an admirable collection of ancient ballads. **William Cowper** (1731-1800). —*The Task, John Gilpin*, etc.—Divests poetry of the affectations of Pope. Writes on simple themes.	**F. G. Klopstock** (1724-1803). —Epic *Messiah*, *Lyrics, Odes*—The first great German poet of the eighteenth century. **G. E. Lessing** (1729-1781).— *Criticisms, Plays*—The greatest critic of Germany. He developed a new type of national German tragedy. **Solomon Gessner** (Swiss), (1730-1788).—*Idyls, Pastorals*—His *Idyls* attained great popularity. **C. M. Wieland** (1733-1813). —*Oberon, Novels*—A master of brilliant witty comedy who greatly advanced German style. **Immanuel Kant** (1724-1804). —*Critical Philosophy*—The greatest German philosopher. Substituted critical philosophy for the old dogmatic metaphysics, demanded obedience to the moral law, laid the foundations of modern æsthetics. He was the founder of the transcendental philosophy.			**Carlo Gozzi** (1722-1806).— Italian *Fable* dramas. **Guiseppe Parini** (It.), (1729-1799), *Poems, Odes*—His *Giorno* is one of the masterpieces of dignified style in Italian poetry. **Girolamo Tiraboschi** (It.), (1731-1794). — *Literary History*—A valuable history of Italian literature.	1745. Jacobite rising in Scotland. 1756-1763. Seven Years' War.
James Macpherson (1736-1796).—A Scottish poet who excelled in rhythmical tales of Gaelic heroes. **Edward Gibbon** (1737-1794). —*Decline and Fall of the Roman Empire*—A painstaking and learned historian. **James Boswell** (1740-1795). —*Life of Samuel Johnson*— Shows the true reporter's instinct for the point of a story. The book is one of the most delightful biographies ever written. **William Paley** (1743-1805). —*Evidences of Christianity, Natural Theology.* **Hannah More** (1745-1833). —*Coelebs in Search of a Wife*, a novel, *Sacred Dramas.* **Jeremy Bentham** (1748-1832). — *Philosophy, Essays*—Great critic of legislation and government.	The next century was the Golden Age of German literature. **J. G. von Herder** (1744-1803).—*Criticisms, History* —The chief factor in the literary revolution known as "storm and stress." His work in history sets forth the evolution of human institutions.	**Augustin de Beaumarchais** (1732-1799). — *Comedies* — Celebrated especially for his two witty, spirited and well constructed plays, *Le Barbier de Séville* and *Le Mariage de Figaro.* **Bernardin de St. Pierre** (1737-1814). — *Paul and Virginia.* This popular prose idyl brings into French literature the taste for Nature as it is.	**Karl Mikael Bellman** (Swed.), (1740-1795). —*Songs, Lyrics*—Bubbling joy of life in ballads, odes and drinking songs.	**AMERICAN** **George Washington** (1732-1799).—*Farewell Address, State Papers*, etc.—Broadly patriotic and well-considered. **Patrick Henry** (1736-1799). —*Speeches, Letters*, etc.— Eloquent, ardent patriotism. **Thomas Paine** (1737-1809). — *The Crisis, Common Sense, Rights of Man, Age of Reason*, etc.—A talented and widely read political pamphleteer.	1763. *Georgia Gazette* established at Savannah. 1772. Partition of Poland. 1776. American independence declared.

TABLE VI. EIGHTEENTH CENTURY—Concluded

English	German	French	Scandinavian	Italian	Historical Events
Richard B. Sheridan (1751–1816).—*The Rivals, School for Scandal, Speeches*, etc.—Writer of witty dialogue and constructor of telling stage situations. **George Crabbe** (1754–1832).—*Tales in Verse*, other realistic narrative poems. **William Blake** (1757–1827).—*Songs of Innocence, Songs of Experience*—A master of the simple lyric, he illustrated his works by admirable tinted engravings. **Robert Burns** (1759–1796).—Scottish poet. *Poems*—Lyrics, songs and satires in Scottish dialect, marked by music, pathos and wit. The national poet of Scotland.	**Johann Wolfgang von Goethe** (1749–1832). — *Dramas, Lyrics, Elegies, Sonnets, Epigrams* — The greatest German poet. A universal genius. Before 1800 he had mastered ballad poetry, sung finished odes, lived his story of *Werther*, and created a new German classicism in *Iphigenie, Tasso*, and *Hermann and Dorothea*. His life poem, *Faust*, typifies the philosophical struggle of the poet's own life. **Friedrich von Schiller** (1759–1805). — *Dramas, Lyrics, History*—Reflects the ideal yearnings of his time. Aimed to lead men to consecrate their gifts to *the good, the beautiful and the true*. He is the best-loved poet among the Germans. **August von Kotzebue** (1761–1819).—*Plays*—A prolific writer, very popular in his day.	**Comte Mirabeau** (1749–1791).—*Orations*—The greatest orator of the French Revolution. **Claude Rouget de Lisle** (1760–1836).—*Marseillaise* — The immortal national hymn of France. **André Chénier** (1762–1794). — *Lyrics* — A model in purity of form and passion in style, following the old classic pattern.	**Edv. Storm** (Nor., 1749–1794).—*Heroic Ballads*. **Johan Henrik Kellgren** (Swed.), (1751–1795).—*Journalism, Poems*—Lyric and satiric poetry. A scholar and critic, he led the revival of Swedish literature.	**Vittorio Alfieri** (It.), (1749–1803). — *Classical Tragedies*.	1786. Swedish Academy founded. 1789. Beginning of French Revolution. 1792. French Republic declared. 1796. Washington issues his "Farewell Address." 1799. Death of Washington. Napoleon, First Consul in France.

TABLE VII. EARLY NINETEENTH CENTURY, 1800-1875

English	American	French	German, Scandinavian	Other Countries	Historical Events
	Thomas Jefferson (1743–1826).—*Notes in Virginia, Declaration of Independence, Letters*. **John Marshall** (1755–1835).—*Life of Washington, Decisions*, etc. **Alexander Hamilton** (1757–1804).—*Contributions to the Federalist*—Keen and ingenious political articles.				1804. Napoleonic code adopted in France.
			J. G. Fichte (1762–1814).—*Philosophic Writings, Orations*—The philosopher of the German Romantic school and the exponent of the philosophy of individualism. **Jean Paul Friedrich Richter** (1763–1825).—*Novels, Esthetics*—Guilty of crude style and bad construction, his books have fine imaginative passages.		1805. Battles of Austerlitz and Trafalgar. 1806. Battle of Jena. Napoleon controls Germany. 1806–07. Berlin and Milan Decrees establishing the Continental System. 1807. Battle of Friedland. Peace of Tilsit.
Maria Edgeworth (1767–1849). — *Popular Tales* — Stories of middle-class domestic life.	**Alexander Wilson** (1766–1813).—*American Ornithology* — Pioneer investigations.	**Mme. de Staël** (1766–1817).—*L'Allemagne, Delphine, Corinne*, etc.—Shrewd political ideas; a leader in the Romantic school in French letters. **Benjamin Constant** (1767–1830).—A skeptic in *Politics, Religion*. **Jean François Michaud** (1767–1839).—*History of the Crusades*, etc.—Advanced the technique of biographical writing. **François de Chateaubriand** (1768–1848). — *René, Genius of Christianity, Atala*, etc.—A talented and versatile writer, he had great influence on the literature of the first half of the nineteenth century. **Baron de Cuvier** (1769–1832).—His *Animal Kingdom* is the pioneer work in zoological classification.	**Alexander von Humboldt** (1769–1859).—*Science, Travels*. **A. W. von Schlegel** (1767–1845). — *Art Criticism, Translations* — The great critic of the Romantic school. **Zacharias Werner** (1768–1823).—*Plays, Sonnets*—A great dramatist of the Romantic school. **Friedrich Schleiermacher** (1768–1834). — *Addresses, Criticisms* — An eloquent preacher of the Romantic school. **Ernst Moritz Arndt** (1769–1860).—*Warsongs, Lyrics*. **Friedrich Hölderlin** (1770–1843).—*Hyperion*, minor *Lyrics*. **G. W. F. Hegel** (1770–1831).—*Philosophy*—The philosopher of collectivism and of evolution in history.	**Carlo G. Botta** (It.), (1766–1837).—*Histories*. **Ivan Krylov** (Russ.), (1768–1844).—Popular witty *Fables*.	
William Wordsworth (1770–1850). — *The Excursion, Poems*—Nature poems, descriptive poems and many fine sonnets. He revived simple verse forms and expressed feeling for nature.					1807. Fulton's steamboat on the Hudson.

TABLE VII. EARLY NINETEENTH CENTURY—Continued

English	American	French	German, Scandinavian	Other Countries	Historical Events
James Hogg (1770–1835).— *Pastorals, Shepherd's Calendar*—A minor Scottish lyricist. **Sir Walter Scott** (1771–1832). —*Novels, Lady of the Lake, Poems.*— Developed the English historical novel with great success. A master of natural wholesome narrative poetry. **Sydney Smith** (1771–1845).— *Sermons, Essays*—The witty divine. Master of the expository style. **James Montgomery** (1771–1854).— *Hymns.* **Samuel T. Coleridge** (1772–1834).—*Essays, Rhyme of Ancient Mariner, Translation,* etc.—A man of remarkable gifts, intellectual and poetic; a keen critic; a natural master of verbal melody.	**Charles Brockden Brown** (1771–1810). — His *Wieland,* wierd and uneven, was the first American novel. **William Wirt** (1772–1834).— *Life of Patrick Henry, Letters of a British Spy.*	**Charles Fourier** (1772–1839). — *Socialism* — An economist of advanced ideas.	**Heinrich Zschokke** (1771–1848). — *Novels* — Prolific historical novelist. **Novalis (Friedrich von Hardenberg)** (1772–1801). — *Novels, Lyrics, Criticism*— The sentimental poet of the Romantic school. His *Hymns to the Night* are spirituals of enduring quality. **Friedrich von Schlegel** (1772–1829).—*Criticism; Novels* —A minor poet, he was a leading novelist of the German Romantic school. **Franz Mikael Franzén** (Swed.), (1772–1847).— *Poems, Hymns*—Exquisite lyric poems. **Ludwig Tieck** (1773–1853).— Fantastic *Novels, Lyrics*— His *Puss in Boots* is an enduring satirical drama.		1808. Napoleon interferes in Spain. Beginning of Peninsular War. 1809. Austrians defeated at Wagram. Peace of Schönbrunn.
Robert Southey (1774–1843). —*Biographies of Nelson, Wesley,* etc., *Poems*—A minor poet with an even rhythmical prose style. **Charles Lamb** (1775–1834).— *Essays of Elia,* etc.—A quaint and delicate essayist, blending humor and pathos. **Walter Savage Landor** (1775–1864).—*Imaginary Conversations, Count Julian, Heroic Idyls,* etc.—Classic scholar and remarkable stylist. **Jane Austen** (1775–1817).— *Novels; Pride and Prejudice, Emma,* etc.—Her novels depicting upper middle-class life are delightfully realistic and full of quiet humor. **Thomas Campbell** (1777–1844).—*Pleasures of Hope, Lyrics,* etc.—His lyrics have much vigor and verve. **Henry Hallam** (1777–1859). — *Europe During the Middle Ages, Constitutional History of England*— Strong, vigorous, historical writing from a standpoint now antiquated. **William Hazlitt** (1778–1830). — *Table Talk, English Poets,* etc.—Critical essays in simple vigorous style. **Thomas Moore** (1779–1852). —*Biographies, Lalla Rookh, Irish Melodies,* etc. —Sentimental songs of remarkable melody.				Jean Charles Sismondi (It.), (1773–1842).— *Histories.*	1810–12. Napoleon at zenith of power.
	James Kirk Paulding (1779–1860). — *Novels* —Pioneer in the American historical novel. **Francis Scott Key** (1780–1843).—*Poems, Star Spangled Banner,* etc.—The chief poem is a national song of patriotic ardor. **William E. Channing** (1780–1842).—*Addresses, Sermons* —A popular orator. **John James Audubon** (1780–1851).—*Birds of America* —A pioneer in American scientific writing. **Daniel Webster** (1782–1852). —*Orations.* **Thomas Hart Benton** (1782–1858). — *Thirty Years' View*—Memoirs of a politician.	**Pierre de Béranger** (1780–1857). —*Lyrics*—His rhythmical patriotic songs were very popular in his day.	**F. N. J. Schelling** (1775–1854).—*Philosophy*—A disciple of Spinoza, taught the identity of spirit and nature. **Ernst Theodor Hoffmann** (1776–1822). — Fantastic Romantic *Novels* on supernatural themes. **Heinrich von Kleist** (1777–1811).—Historical *Dramas,* minor *Novels.* **F. de la Motte Fouqué** (1777–1843).—*Tales, Lyrics*—A Romanticist, popularly known for his charming *Undine.* **Clemens Brentano** (1778–1843).—*Novels,* collector of German *Ballads.* **Achim von Arnim** (1781–1831).—Romanticist *Novels, Poems.* **Adelbert von Chamisso** (1781–1838). — *Peter Schlemihl, Poems*—A later Romantic lyricist. **Esaias Tegnér** (Swed.), (1782–1846).—Popular lyrical *Poems, Frithiofs Saga.*		1812. Napoleon invades Russia. Grande Armée destroyed. 1812. War between U. S. and Great Britain. 1813. Battle of Leipzig.
Leigh Hunt (1784–1859).— *Essays, Sketches, Memoirs, Poems*—A minor poet. A *littérateur* of appreciation rather than of creative power.		**Henri Beyle** (Stendhal), (1783–1842). — *Novels* — His novels *Le Rouge et le Noir* and *La Chartreuse de Parme* mark the beginning of the analytical psychological novel.	**Erik Gustaf Geijer** (Swed.), (1783–1847). — *History, Philosophy, Poems.*		1814. Napoleon abdicates.

TABLE VII. EARLY NINETEENTH CENTURY—Continued

English	American	French	German, Scandinavian	Other Countries	Historical Events
Thomas De Quincey (1785–1859).—*Confessions of an Opium Eater*, etc.—A scholar and prolific but uneven writer, he produced some passages of superb color.	**Washington Irving** (1783–1859). — *Knickerbocker's History of New York, Sketch Book*, etc.—Humorous tales, characterized by delicate sentiment and grace. He was the first American writer to be recognized in Europe.	**François Guizot** (1787–1874).—Philosophical *Histories*.	**Jacob Grimm** (1785–1863).—*Fairy Tales, Dictionary*—With his brother Wilhelm, founder of modern German philology and compiler of the great German dictionary; known in literature for his large collection of *Fairy Tales*. **Ludwig Börne** (1786–1837).—*Letters from Paris*—A Jew from the Frankfort ghetto. Famous for his *Letters*, written as a protest against narrowing social limitations. **Wilhelm Grimm** (1786–1859). — *Critical Writings* — See Jacob Grimm mentioned above. **A. Justinus Kerner** (1786–1862).—*Lyrics, Soothsayer of Prevost*—Lyric poet and Romantic mystic. **Ludwig Uhland** (1787–1862). — *Criticism, Ballads* — Poet of Romantic type. He wrote enduring ballads and patriotic songs. **J. von Eichendorff** (1788–1857).—*Lyrics, Life of a Good-for-Nothing*—A poet of nature, one of the best lyricists of the German Romantic school. **Arthur Schopenhauer** (1788–1860). — *Philosophy* — The philosopher of pessimism. **Friedrich Rückert** (1788–1866).—*Sonnets in Armor, Poems*—Poet of the war of Liberation.	**Alessandro Manzoni** (1785–1873).—*Novel, Dramas*—*The Betrothed*, an unsurpassed Italian novel.	1815. Napoleon defeated at Waterloo. 1819. Steamship *Savannah* crosses Atlantic. 1821. Greek war of independence against Turkey.
Lord Byron (1788–1824).—*Poems* — Vigorous, eloquent, sardonic, iconoclastic, he was above all a subjective poet, approaching genius when his emotions were aroused.	**James Fenimore Cooper** (1789–1851).—*Leather Stocking Tales, The Spy*, etc.—He put the American Indian in literature. The pioneer in American frontier fiction and sea stories, able in plot and action but stilted in characterization. **Jared Sparks** (1789–1866).—Pioneer *American Biographies*.		**B. S. Ingemann** (Dan.), (1789–1862). — *Novels, Lyrics, Hymns*—Romantic idealization of Middle Ages.	**Silvio Pellico,** (1789–1854).— Italian dramatist, poet, novelist.	
	Fitz-Greene Halleck (1790–1867). — Spirited, sometimes graceful *Poems, Marco Bozzaris*, etc.	**Alphonse de Lamartine** (1790–1869).—*Poems, History of the Girondists*, etc.— An early but outstanding poet of the Romantic school, showing fine harmony and high ideals.			1823. Monroe Doctrine declared.
Percy B. Shelley (1792–1822).—*Queen Mab, Adonais, The Sky Lark*, etc. all evincing impulsive emotion and a remarkable gift of lyrical melody. **Frederick Marryat** (1792–1848).—*Peter Simple, Jacob Faithful*, etc.—Boys' stories, usually of the sea. **Felicia Hemans** (1793–1835).—*Lyrics*—A minor poet of grace, sweetness and tenderness.	**George Ticknor** (1791–1871). — *History of Spanish Literature*—Scholarly and authentic. **John Howard Payne** (1792–1852).—*Home Sweet Home* an enduring lyric; *Dramas*.	**Eugène Scribe** (1791–1861).—Gay, light popular *Comedies*. **Victor Cousin** (1792–1867).—*Philosophy, Metaphysics*—The chief Eclectic philosopher.	**Theodor Körner** (1791–1813).—*Lyre and Sword*, a collection of patriotic lyrics. **Franz Grillparzer** (1791–1872).—*Dramas, Lyrics*—The greatest Austrian dramatist. *Waves of the Sea and of Love* is a great modern love tragedy.		1810–26. South American Revolution.
	Samuel G. Goodrich (1793–1860).—*Peter Parley Books* — Popular introductions with a flavor of fiction. **William Cullen Bryant** (1794–1878).—*Translations, Letters, Poems: Thanatopsis*, etc. — First distinguished American poet, successful in simple rhythms.	**Casimir Delavigne** (1793–1843). — Minor *Dramas, Elegies*.	**Karl J. L. Almqvist** (Swed.), (1793–1866).—*Book of the Thorn Rose*; mystical *Novels, Essays, Poems*. **Wilhelm Müller** (1794–1827).—*Lyrics*—Master of the popular lyric. Poet of the German people.		1824. National gallery in London opened.
John Keats (1795–1821).—*Endymion, Hyperion*, etc.—A master of romance and subtle pathos in finished melody. **Thomas Arnold** (1795–1842).—*Roman History, Sermons, Essays*—A historian of the old school. **Thomas Carlyle** (1795–1881).—*French Revolution, Cromwell, Sartor Resartus, Essays*, etc.—A prose poet, a historian of insight and industry, impatient of shams.	**Joseph Rodman Drake** (1795–1820).—*The Culprit Fay*—Cleverly executed, but ingeniously fanciful. **John Pendleton Kennedy** (1795–1870). — *Swallow Barn, Horse Shoe Robinson*, etc. — Old-fashioned but interesting pictures of Southern life.	**Augustin Thierry** (1795–1856).—*History of France*, etc.—Historian of the Romantic school.			1825. Erie Canal opened.

TABLE VII. EARLY NINETEENTH CENTURY—Continued

English	American	French	German, Scandinavian	Other Countries	Historical Events
	William H. Prescott (1796–1859).—*Conquest of Peru, Ferdinand and Isabella,* etc.—Histories remarkable for distinctive clear style, based on earnest research. Thomas C. Haliburton (Canadian), (1796–1865). — *Sam Slick* — Humorous with the raciness of the soil.		August von Platen (1796–1835).—*Venetian Sonnets, Poems, Stories.* K. L. Immermann (1796–1840). — *Novels* — A late Romantic writer.		
Samuel Lover (1797–1868).—Irish *Songs* and *Stories.*	Hugh Swinton Legaré (1797–1843).—Stilted *Addresses, Articles, Letters.*	Louis Adolphe Thiers (1797–1877).—Realistic *History of the French Revolution, the Empire,* etc.	Heinrich Heine (1797–1856).—*Lyrics, Short Stories*—The greatest lyric poet after Goethe, strongly imbued with Romanticism. Best known as the author of *The Journey to the Harz Mountains* (1826), and the *Book of Songs* (1827). Henrik Hertz (Dan.), (1797–1870). — *Dramas, Epics, Satires*—Most original in his lyric poetry.		
Thomas Hood (1798–1845). — *Poems* — A humorous poet of the first rank: some pathetic verses of high quality.		Auguste Comte (1798–1857).—Influential founder of *Positive Philosophy.* Jules Michelet (1798–1874). — *History of France*—Gave a new conception of history.	Wilhelm Häring (W. Alexis), (1798–1871). — *Patriotic Novels.* August Hoffmann von Fallersleben (1798–1874).—Many musical *Lyrics;* his *Deutschland Über Alles* became a national hymn.	Giacomo Leopardi (It.), (1798–1837).—An outstanding critic whose pessimistic poems exhibit fine artistic skill.	1828. First passenger railway in U. S.
	Amos Bronson Alcott (1799–1888). — *Concord Days, Table Talks, Sonnets and Canzonets*—A leader of the Transcendentalist philosophy.	Honoré de Balzac (1799–1850).—*Novels*—The author of the *Comédie Humaine,* a collection of novels which embraces the whole of society. Balzac is considered as the chief of the "realistic school," although there is idealism in his novels. Alfred de Vigny (1799–1863).—*Cinq Mars,* etc.—One of the poets of the Romantic school.		Aleksandr Pushkin (Russ., 1799–1837). — *Poems, Stories, Novels, Dramas* —A great poet. Romantic at first. Later emphasized national feeling in Russian literature.	1829. Andrew Jackson, President of the U. S. Stephenson's locomotive *Rocket.*
Thomas B. Macaulay (1800–1859).—*Essays, History of England, Lays of Ancient Rome*—Far from impartial, he makes history alive and readable. Cardinal Newman (1801–1890).—*Apologia pro Vita sua* —An able orthodox theological propagandist.	George Bancroft (1800–1891). — *History of the United States*—Faithfully prepared and honestly presented. The first successful detailed American history.		C. D. Grabbe (1801–1836).—Pessimistic but ably characterized *Dramas.* Fredrika Bremer (Swed.), (1801–1865). — *Novels* —Describes family life of middle classes realistically.	Manuel Breton de los Herreros (Sp.), (1800–1873). — *Dramas*—Gives a good picture of Spanish social life.	1830. Revolution in France.
Harriet Martineau (1802–1876). — Didactic *Stories, Tracts*—A woman of sound scholarship and liberal ideas.	Horace Bushnell (1802–1876).—Didactic *Tracts.*	Victor Hugo (1802–1885).—*Novels, Lyrics*—A leader of the Romantic school. His poetry, epic and lyric, is rarely surpassed. His great novel, *Les Miserables,* ranks equally high in prose. Alexandre Dumas (*père*), (1803–1870). — *Novels, Dramas*—The author of a large number of popular novels based upon historical and remarkable for their easy style and the tireless action of their romantic characters. Among his important plays *Henry III.* was a milestone in the development of the French Romantic drama.	Wilhelm Hauff (1802–1827) —*Lichtenstein, Man in the Moon, Short Stories*—An able writer of historical novels. Nikolaus Lenau (Austrian), (1802–1850).—His gloomy *Lyrics* were among the greatest in artistic skill of his age.		1832. Reform Bill in England.
Sir Edward Bulwer Lytton (1803–1873).—*Last Days of Pompeii, Last of the Barons,* etc.—A versatile and successful *littérateur.* George Borrow (1803–1881). —*Travels, Romances* of Gypsy life.	Ralph Waldo Emerson (1803–1882). — *Conduct of Life, Representative Men, Essays, Poems*—The prophet of American culture. Coalesces oriental ideas and occidental individualism. Jacob Abbott (1803–1879).—*Rollo Books*—Popular favorites of unsophisticated youth.				1833. Slavery outlawed in British Empire.
		Prosper Mérimée (1803–1870).—*Stories, Novels*—His tender romantic stories are still popular.			
Benjamin Disraeli (1804–1881). — *Lothair, Vivian Grey,* etc.—Artificial society novels.	Nathaniel Hawthorne (1804–1864).—*Twice Told Tales, Scarlet Letter, Marble Faun,* etc.—Wrote with poetic spirit in charming style of the glories and trials of early New England and fanciful allegorical romances.	Eugène Sue (1804–1857).—*Mysteries of Paris, Wandering Jew,* etc.—His popular novels, in which imagination plays the principal part, were enjoyed in his time. C. A. de Sainte-Beuve (1804–1869).—*Criticisms,* etc.—Is the master of criticism of his period. George Sand (Mme. Dudevant), (1804–1876). — *Novels*—Her literary career was divided between romantic novels and philosophical novels.	Eduard Mörike (1804–1875). — *Lyrics, Stories* — The great lyric poet of Swabia. Johan Ludvig Runeberg (Finland), (1804–1877).—*Poems, Dramas.*		
		Alexis de Tocqueville (1805–1859).—*Political Science, Histories*—In *Democracy in America* the institutions and customs of the country are keenly observed.	Hans Christian Andersen (Dan.), (1805–1875).—*Fairy Tales, Novels, Dramas, Poems*—Used language of the people and of childhood. Next to Bible, his *Fairy Tales* have been translated into the most foreign languages.		1835. Texas proclaimed independent.

TABLE VII. EARLY NINETEENTH CENTURY—Continued

English	American	French	German, Scandinavian	Other Countries	Historical Events
Elizabeth Barrett Browning (1806–1861).—*Aurora Leigh, Poems*—A pleasing lyrical gift and warm, human sympathy made her a favorite poetess in the Victorian era. **John Stuart Mill** (1806–1873).—*Political Economy*—Of thorough intellectual honesty and diamond-clear intellect, he furthered the cause of political justice and personal freedom. **Edward FitzGerald** (1809–1883).—A minor poet, remembered for his superb *Translation* of Omar Khayyám. **Charles Darwin** (1809–1882).—*Origin of Species, Descent of Man*—Lucid and attractive in style and an unflinching lover of truth, he completely changed the direction of biological science. **Alfred Tennyson** (1809–1892). — *In Memoriam, Idylls of the King, Poems*—The national poet of the late nineteenth century; a painstaking artist and master of verbal melody.	**Nathaniel P. Willis** (1806–1867). — *Poems, Sketches, Editorials*, etc. **William Gilmore Simms** (1806–1870).—*Poems, Novels, Biography*, etc.—Versatile, original and artistic writer whose frontier tales were the outstanding Southern novels of his time. **Henry W. Longfellow** (1807–1882).—*Outre Mer, Hyperion, Poems, Hiawatha*, etc.—Popular in appeal and simple in form, his work is conventional but important because it introduced much European culture to American readers. **John G. Whittier** (1807–1892).—*Editorials, Household Poems* — Melodious but uneven verse; a poet with a cause, Abolition. **Edgar Allan Poe** (1809–1849).—*Tales, Poems: Raven, Annabel Lee*, etc.—Creator of the modern short story form, inventor of the "detective story," an acute critic and an unsurpassed lyricist, he was one of the foremost literary figures produced in America. **Oliver Wendell Holmes** (1809–1894).—*Autocrat of the Breakfast Table, Novels, Poems*—Clever, witty, versatile and skilful both in verse and prose.		**Heinrich Laube** (1806–1884). — *Novels, Plays* — Witty, but seldom a delicate poet. His chief works are novels or dramas of radical spirit. **Jonas Hallgrimsson** (Ic.), (1807–1845).—*Island Gunnarsholmi*—Popular patriotic songs.	**Aleksyey Koltsov** (Russ.), (1808–1842). — *Lyrics* of deep feeling. **Nikolay Gogol** (Russ.), (1809–1852).—*Plays, Tales, Novels*—The greatest of Russian satirists, and the first widely acclaimed Russian novelist.	1837. Victoria crowned queen. 1839. Daguerre's perfected photographic process. Belgium independent of Netherlands. Neutrality guaranteed.
Elizabeth Gaskell (1810–1865).—*Cranford, Mary Barton*, etc.—One of the first to make economic problems the basis of a story.	**Margaret Fuller (Ossoli)** (1810–1850).—*Summer on the Lakes, Papers on Literature and Art*—A minor Transcendentalist. **Theodore Parker** (1810–1860). —Liberal theological thinker. Courageous abolitionist.	**Alfred de Musset** (1810–1857). — *Tales, Poems, Dramas*—Some of his tragic love poems — *Les Nuits, le Souvenir*, etc. — are among the most beautiful in French literature. His comedies blend dream and reality. **Henri Martin** (1810–1883).—A standard *History of France*.	**Fritz Reuter** (1810–1874).—Dialect *Poems, Novels*—A born storyteller, with broad realistic humor. **H. Ferdinand Freiligrath** (1810–1876). — *Poems, Translations*.		1840–42. Opium War in China. 1842. Webster-Ashburton Treaty.
William M. Thackeray (1811–1863).—*Vanity Fair, The Newcomes, Henry Esmond*—Sentimentalist, satirist and humorist, but with great powers of characterization, especially of the everyday social elements. **Charles Dickens** (1812–1870). —*Novels: David Copperfield, Oliver Twist, Christmas Carol*, etc.—A broad humorist, unsurpassed in power of characterization, whose social novels revolutionized the conditions of life for the underprivileged in England. **Robert Browning** (1812–1889).—*Dramatic Lyrics, Poems, The Ring and the Book* — A psychological poet capable of obscure thought but incapable of barbarous melody. **Charles Reade** (1814–1884). —*Peg Woffington, Cloister and Hearth*, etc.—A popular novelist with a vigorous style. **Anthony Trollope** (1815–1882).—*Barchester Towers*, etc.—Admirably realistic presentation of English society, political and ecclesiastical. **Charlotte Brontë** (1816–1855).—*Jane Eyre, The Professor*, etc. — Novels based on narrow experience but remarkable for characterization and ornate style. **Emily Brontë** (1818–1848).—*Wuthering Heights*, a novel of limited scope but peculiar style. **James Anthony Froude** (1818–1894).—*History of England*—A brilliant prose writer, makes history interesting and suggestive.	**Harriet Beecher Stowe** (1811–1896). — *Uncle Tom's Cabin*, etc.—The outstanding American propaganda novel, far-reaching in its influence. **John Lothrop Motley** (1814–1877). — *Dutch Republic, United Netherlands*—A rapid, easy style in presenting results of research. **Richard Henry Dana** (1815–1882).—*Two Years Before the Mast*—One of the earliest American sea tales. **Samuel A. Allibone** (1816–1889).—*Literature and Authors*, etc.—Laborious and valuable bibliography. **Henry D. Thoreau** (1817–1862). — *Walden, Excursions*—Redolent of nature love, and cultured scholarship.	**Théophile Gautier** (1811–1872).—*Criticism, Novels, Poems*—Poet and prose writer who regarded beauty of style as more important than emotion or theme. **Victor Duruy** (1811–1894).—*History of Rome*. **Eugène Labiche** (1815–1888).—*Comedies*—A master in the art of writing light comedies. **Leconte de Lisle** (1818–1894).—Pessimistic *Poems*—One of the great poets of the century. He was the head of the group called the Parnassians, who sought above all technical perfection in poetry.	**Berthold Auerbach** (1812–1882). — *Novels*, naïve *Short Stories*—The poet of the Black Forest. **Friedrich Hebbel** (1813–1863). — *Dramas* — The chief German dramatist of the period. A great innovator. **Otto Ludwig** (1813–1865).—*Dramas, Novels*—Master of detail painting in his novels. **J. Moe** (Nor.), (1813–1882). —*Poems*—Lyrics. **Richard Wagner** (1813–1883). —*Operas*—Creator of the music-drama. Insisted that German drama must be national and so drew for themes on older Germanic myths. **Emanuel Geibel** (1815–1884). —*Poems, Voices of the Time*—Successful writer of popular songs. **Gustav Freytag** (1816–1895). — *Novels, Dramas* — His *Ancestors* is a cycle of modern German novels. **Theodor Storm** (1817–1888). —*Lyrics, Novels*—Masterful writer of the novel of reminiscence. The lyric note is prominent in his prose. **Theodor Mommsen** (1817–1903). — Foremost scholar and historian of Roman antiquity.	**Alexander Hertzen** (Russ.), (1812–1870). — *Journalism*. **Mikhail Lermontov** (Russ.), (1814–1841). — *Poems, Novels* — Powerful prose. **José de Espronceda** (Sp.), (1816–1842).—*Lyric Poetry*. **Aleksyey Tolstoy** (Russ.), (1817–1875). — Artistic historical *Dramas*. **Ivan Turgenev** (Russ.), (1818–1883). — *Stories, Novels* — Great prose artist. His social novels are pessimistic in tone.	1844. Electrical telegraph between Baltimore and Washington. 1845–6. Famine in Ireland. 1846–48. United States at war with Mexico.

TABLE VII. EARLY NINETEENTH CENTURY—Continued

English	American	French	German, Scandinavian	Other Countries	Historical Events
George Eliot (1819–1880).—*Silas Marner, Spanish Gypsy, Poems*. The first great English woman novelist. A realist with insight, wit and skill in characterization. **Charles Kingsley** (1819–1875).—*Hypatia, Westward Ho! Poems*—His novels, though at times too sentimental, are vigorous and wholesome. **John Ruskin** (1819–1900).—*Stones of Venice, Modern Painters*, etc.—A great stylist.	**Herman Melville** (1819–1891).—*Moby Dick, Typee*, etc.—His adventure novels of the South Seas marked a definite advance toward maturity in American letters. **James Russell Lowell** (1819–1891).—*Among My Books, My Study Windows, Biglow Papers, Poems: Sir Launfal*, etc. — Keen, sparkling, scholarly and artistic. **Walt Whitman** (1819–1892).—*Poems: Leaves of Grass, My Captain*, etc.—Unique for his period both in style and subject matter, he led in the departure from European patterns. **Julia Ward Howe** (1819–1910).—*Social and Philosophical Papers, Battle Hymn of the Republic.*		**Gottfried Keller** (1819–1890).—*Novels, Short Stories*—Master of the short story. Strong independence of spirit reflected in this Swiss poet. **Theodor Fontane** (1819–1898). — An outstanding dramatic *Critic* who wrote minor poems and novels.		1848. Napoleon declared President in France. Revolutionary movement sweeps Europe. 1849. Gold rush to California.
John Tyndall (1820–1893).—*Scientific Papers.* **Herbert Spencer** (1820–1903).—*First Principles*, etc.—A deep thinker but ponderous in style.	**Margaret J. Preston** (1820–1897).—*Beechenbrook, Cartoons, Colonial Ballads.*	**Émile Augier** (1820–1889).—*Dramas*—One of the masters of the modern French drama. **Gustave Flaubert** (1821–1880).—*Novels*—Torn between Realism and Romanticism, he wrote outstanding examples of each form, *Madame Bovary* of one, *Salammbô* of the other. **Octave Feuillet** (1821–1890).—Minor society *Novels, Dramas.* **Charles Baudelaire** (1821–1867).—*Flowers of Evil*—His lyrics show unmatched metrical skill, but his subjects are often vulgar.		**Feodor Dostoevski** (Russ.), (1821–1881). — *Novels* — Great power of psychological analysis is shown in his tragic *Crime and Punishment* and *The Brothers Karamazov.* **Nikolay Nekrasov** (Russ.), (1821–1888). — *Lyrics* — Rare lyric power.	1850. Compromise on slavery issue in United States.
Matthew Arnold (1822–1888). — Distinguished literary *Essays and Criticisms, Sohrab and Rustum, Poems*— As a poet inclined to pessimism; weak in melody.	**Thomas Buchanan Read** (1822–1872).—*Poems: Drifting, Sheridan's Ride*, etc. **Edward Everett Hale** (1822–1909).—*The Man Without a Country* was one of the outstanding early American short stories. **Donald G. Mitchell** (1822–1909). — Graceful meditative essays, *Dream Life, Reveries of a Bachelor.*	**Henri Murger** (1822–1861).—*Novels*—His *Scenes of Bohemian Life* depicts the life of a class of students. **Edmond de Goncourt** (1822–1896). — *Novels* — He and his brother Jules de Goncourt were among the first Impressionists. They are the apostles of "modernism." **Émile Erckmann** (1822–1899).—*Novels* of local color.			1852. Napoleon declared Emperor after coup d'état.
Thomas Hughes (1823–1896).—*Tom Brown at Oxford*, etc.—Advanced the character of juvenile literature. **Wilkie Collins** (1824–1889).—His *Woman in White* and *Moonstone* were pioneers in the modern detective *Novel.* **Thomas Henry Huxley** (1825–1895).—*Man's Place in Nature*, etc.—A master of scientific exposition. **Richard Blackmore** (1825–1900). — *Novels: Lorna Doone*, etc.—Infused an element of romance into the novel.	**Francis Parkman** (1823–1893). — *Oregon Trail, Montcalm and Wolfe*, etc.—Romantic, picturesque and lifelike historical works. **George W. Curtis** (1824–1892).—*Potiphar Papers, Prue and I*, etc. **Bayard Taylor** (1825–1878).—*Northern Travel, Greece and Russia, Poems of the Orient, Translation of Faust*—Too good at many things to be best at any.	**J. Ernest Renan** (1823–1892).—*Life of Jesus*, etc.—Critic and historian but above all an artist. **Alexandre Dumas** (*fils*) (1824–1895).—*Novels, Dramas*—His *Dame aux Camélias* was an outstanding novel and drama of the era. His wit and concise style developed the modern comedies of manners.	**Conrad Ferdinand Meyer** (Swiss), (1825–1898). — *Short Stories, Novels*—One of the best historical novelists of the century.	**Sándor Petöfi** (Hung.), (1823–1849). — *Lyrics, Translations*—One of the great lyric poets of the nineteenth century. Full of the passion, melancholy and humor of the Hungarian. **Juan Valera** (Sp.), (1824–1905). — *Pepita Jiménez*, other popular *Novels*, in elegant prose.	1853–56. Crimean War.
Dinah Maria Mulock (1826–1887).—*John Halifax* and other *Novels, Poems.*	**Stephen Collins Foster** (1826–1864).—*Old Folks at Home, My Old Kentucky Home*, etc.—A master in the popular folk lyric.		**J. V. von Scheffel** (1826–1886).—*Epics* and *Historical Novels*—*Ekkehard* was an outstanding success.	**Mikhail Saltykov** (Russ.), (1826–1889). — *Satiric Tales.*	
Walter Bagehot (1826–1877).—Profound *Treatises* on Economics and Finance.	**Lew Wallace** (1827–1905).—*Ben Hur*, one of the most popular novels ever written, and minor books.	**Francisque Sarcey** (1827–1899).—*Criticism*—A recognized authority on the drama.			
Dante Gabriel Rossetti (1828–1882).—*Poems: The Blessed Damozel*, etc.—A highly imaginative poet, a master of color. **George Meredith** (1828–1909).—*Diana of the Crossways*, etc.—Psychological novels of extraordinary power.		**H. A. Taine** (1828–1893).—*History of Literature*, etc.—*Origins of Contemporary France* shows his genius as a critic and as historian. **Jules Verne** (1828–1905).—*Twenty Thousand Leagues Under the Sea, Around the World in Eighty Days*, etc.—His novels pioneer in the field of extravagant fiction based on scientific ideas.	**Victor Rydberg** (Swed.), (1828–1895). — *Philosophy, History, Novels, Poems*—Scholar, poet, and philosopher. **Henrik Ibsen** (Nor.), (1828–1906).—*Dramas, Poems*—A leading dramatic genius of the nineteenth century. In sharp satire and vivid dialogue he attacked social problems.	**Leo Tolstoy** (Russ.), (1828–1910).—*Novels, Essays, Criticisms* — Powerful pessimistic and realistic novels, as *Anna Karenina.*	
	Henry Timrod (1829–1867).—Minor *Poems.* **Chas. Dudley Warner** (1829–1900).—*My Summer in a Garden, Little Journey*, etc.—Charming travel essays.		**Friedrich Spielhagen** (1829–1911).—*Novels* — The novelist of German social conditions.		1857–8. Sepoy mutiny in India.

TABLE VII. EARLY NINETEENTH CENTURY—Continued

English	American	French	German, Scandinavian	Other Countries	Historical Events
Christina Rossetti (1830–1894).—A Victorian poet whose careful, sincere work was agreeable to her times.	**John Esten Cooke** (1830–1886).—*Novels: Survey of Eagle's Nest*, etc. **Emily Dickinson** (1830–1886).—*Lyrics* of delicate mystical charm.	**Jules de Goncourt** (1830–1870).—*Novels*—See Edmond de Goncourt (1822–1896).	**Paul Heyse** (1830–1914).—*Novels, Short Stories, Poems*—A Nobel Prize winner.		1861–65. Civil War in the United States.
Edward Lord Lytton (Owen Meredith), (1831–1891).—*Biography of Bulwer Lytton, Lucile*, etc.—Fluent writer of light verse.	**Paul Hamilton Hayne** (1831–1886).—*Sonnets, Legends, Lyrics.*	**Victorien Sardou** (1831–1908). — *Dramas* — Clever comedies and social satires.			
Edwin Arnold (1832–1904).—*Light of Asia, Poems*—Journalist and prolific minor poet. **Lewis Carroll** (Charles L. Dodgson) (1832–1898).—*Alice in Wonderland, Through the Looking Glass*, etc.—World-famous classic fantasies, written for children, loved by adults.	**Horatio Alger** (1832–1899).—A prolific and very popular producer of didactic success stories for boys. **Louisa May Alcott** (1832–1888).—*Little Women, Little Men*—Stories of childhood with lasting popular appeal. **Petroleum V. Nasby** (David R. Locke) (1833–1888).—Satiric propaganda *Letters.* **Edmund C. Stedman** (1833–1908). — *Victorian Poets, Poets of America*, etc.—Poet and critic.	**Henri Meilhac** (1831–1897), **Ludovic Halévy** (1834–1908). — *Comedies* — They collaborated to create the "operetta."	**Björnstjerne Björnson** (Nor.), (1832–1910). — *Novels, Dramas, Poems*—Leading novelist and poet of Norway in his day. **Jonas Lie** (Nor.), (1833–1908).—*Stories, Dramas*—Sketches of Nature and popular life in the north of Norway.	**José de Pereda** (Sp.), (1833–1906).—*Bucolic Novels* in simple dialect. **José Echegaray** (Sp.), (1833–1916).—*Dramas* — Most prominent representative of the modern Spanish dramatists.	1866. Prussia defeats Austria in Seven Weeks' War.
William Morris (1834–1896).—*Essays on Art*, etc., *Poems*—Prolific narrative poet whose epics, based on medieval legends, were exceptional. **George du Maurier** (1834–1896). — *Peter Ibbetson, Trilby*—Artist and poet. *Peter Ibbetson* is a fanciful romance of dream life. *Trilby*, a masterful study of character.	**Chas. Farrar Browne** (Artemus Ward) (1834–1867).—*Artemus Ward, His Book*, etc.—Humorous in exaggeration. **Frank R. Stockton** (1834–1902). — *Rudder Grange, The Lady or the Tiger*—Ingenious in plot, straightforward in style. **Moses Coit Tyler** (1835–1900).—*History of American Literature.* **Samuel L. Clemens** (Mark Twain) (1835–1910).—*Innocents Abroad, Huckleberry Finn*, etc.—Thoroughly representative of American humor and a master of folklore.	**Édouard Pailleron** (1834–1899).—Graceful light *Comedies.*	**Heinrich von Treitschke** (1834–1896).—His *Histories* are distorted by his extreme patriotism. **Felix Dahn** (1834–1912).—Historian and historical novelist.	**Giosué Carducci** (It.), (1836–1907).—*Poems*—Lyrics of liberty.	1867. Second Reform Bill in England.
William Gilbert (1836–1911).—Collaborated with Sullivan to produce ingenious, popular comic operas which have never been surpassed. **John Richard Green** (1837–1883).—*History of the English People*—Clear and simple style. **Algernon Chas. Swinburne** (1837–1909). — *Poems*—A poet of remarkable musical power, master of headlong but involved prose. **John Morley** (1838–1923).—*Criticisms, English Men of Letters*, (Ed.)—A critic and a thinker of force and scope.	**Thomas Bailey Aldrich** (1836–1907).—Minor *Novels* and light *Verse.* **William Dean Howells** (1837–1920).—*Venetian Life, Rise of Silas Lapham*, etc.—Realistic and entertainingly descriptive novels. **John Burroughs** (1837–1921).—*Wake Robin, Winter Sunshine*—A critic and essayist and unsurpassed writer on Nature. **John Muir** (1838–1914).—*Travels* and nature study in melodious prose. **F. Hopkinson Smith** (1838–1915). — Minor *Novels*, good Southern color. **Mary Mapes Dodge** (1838–1905).—*Hans Brinker*—In high favor with children. **Thomas R. Lounsbury** (1838–1915).—*Life of Cooper, Studies in Chaucer* etc.	**Henri Becque** (1837–1899).—*Dramas*—A pioneer in the naturalistic drama.	**Georg Ebers** (1837–1898).—*Egyptology, Novels*—Wrote novels dealing with Egyptian life.		1868. President Johnson impeached.
William De Morgan (1839–1917).—Popular *Novels.* **Walter H. Pater** (1839–1894).—*Marius the Epicurean*, etc.—A wonderfully finished prose style, which sometimes diverts attention from the thought. **John Addington Symonds** (1840–1893).—*Translations, Criticism*—A scholar in poetic technique. **Henry Austin Dobson** (1840–1921).—*Vignettes in Rhyme, Proverbs in Porcelain*—Pictured eighteenth century social and literary life in charming light verses. **Thomas Hardy** (1840–1928).—*Novels: Tess of d' Urbervilles*, etc.—Novels of English country life. His books possess at once wit, realism and simplicity of style. **Robert W. Buchanan** (1841–1901).—*Alone in London, Poems*—A minor poet and dramatist.	**Francis Bret Harte** (1839–1902).—*Luck of Roaring Camp, Gabriel Convoy, Poems*—Frontier tales of international fame. **Joaquin Miller** (1841–1913).—*Songs of the Sierras*—Verse of unorthodox form but filled with the beauty of his subject.	**Sully-Prudhomme** (1839–1907).—*Poems*—One of the great poets of the nineteenth century. A leader in the Parnassian school. **Alphonse Daudet** (1840–1897).—*Novels* in superb prose, blending pathos and humor and descriptive power. **Émile Zola** (1840–1902).—*Novels*—Called the head of the naturalistic school.	**Ludwig Anzengruber** (1839–1889). — *Dramas, Prose Tales, Poems*—Highly endowed Austrian dramatist. A pioneer of realism.	**Giovanni Verga** (It.), (1840–1922). — *Novels*—Tales of Sicilian peasantry marked by accurate characterization in simple style.	1869. Transcontinental railroad completed in United States. 1870–71 Franco-Prussian War. 1871. France a republic.

TABLE VII. EARLY NINETEENTH CENTURY—Concluded

English	American	French	German, Scandinavian	Other Countries	Historical Events
	Ambrose Bierce (1842–1914). —*Verse, Short Stories*—An eccentric writer of unusual wit and sarcasm. **Sidney Lanier** (1842–1881).—*Marshes of Glynn, Tiger-Lilies, Poems*—Artistic and exceptionally musical minor verse. **John Fiske** (1842–1901). —*Myths and Myth-Makers*, scholarly *Histories*. **William James** (1842–1910). —A leader in Pragmatic *Philosophy* and a pioneer in analytical *Psychology*. **Henry James** (1843–1916).— *Daisy Miller, Portrait of a Lady*, etc.—Unique and exaggerated style. **George W. Cable** (1844–1925). —*Old Creole Days*, etc.— *Novels* admired for fine local color.	**Stéphane Mallarmé** (1842–1828).—Founder of the Decadent school of French *Poetry*. **Albert Sorel** (1842–1906).— His history of *Europe and the French Revolution* is much esteemed. **François Coppée** (1842–1908). — *Poems, Dramas* — Excelled in pictures of real life and the study of interiors. **José de Heredia** (1842–1905). —His *Poems* are on a small scale but perfect in form. **Paul Verlaine** (1844–1896).— *Poems*—A unique poet, leader of the Symbolists; he developed new rhythmic ideas. **Anatole France** (1844–1924). — *Novels* of admirable ironic style and plot, critical of the life of his time.	**Karl Robert Eduard Hartmann** (1842–1906).—*Philosophy, Criticism*. **Georg Brandes** (Dan.), (1842–1917).—*Literary Essays*—A piercing literary critic. **Peter Rosegger** (Austrian), (1843–1918). — *Novels* of peasant life. **Friedrich Nietzsche** (1844–1900).—*Philosophy, Criticisms*—Prophet of individualism. His greatest work, *Thus Spake Zarathustra*, left an indelible impression on the literature of his time. **Detlev von Liliencron** (1844–1910). — *Epics, Poems* — The chief lyric poet of the epoch.		1871. Unification of Germany and Italy. 1873. Financial panic. 1876. Centennial Exposition, Philadelphia. Electoral commission awards presidency to Hayes.
William Henley (1849–1903). —*Invictus* and other short poems of great power. **Edmund Gosse** (1849–1928). — *Criticism* and minor *Poems*.					

TABLE VIII. MODERN LITERATURE

English	American	French	German, Scandinavian	Other Countries	Historical Events
	Arthur S. Hardy (1847–1930). —*Novels*.	**Frédéric Masson** (1847–1923). — *Histories* — His best known work is on Napoleon. **Émile Faguet** (1847–1916).— A *Critic* of great scholarship. **Ferdinand Brunetière** (1849–1906).—*Criticism*. **Jean Richepin** (1849–1926). —*Dramas*.	**Ernst von Wildenbruch** (German), (1845–1909).—*Dramas, Short Stories, Poems*—A great historical dramatist.	**Antonio Fogazzaro** (It.), (1842–1911). —*Poetry, Novels*. **Benito Pérez Galdós** (Sp.), (1845–1920). —*Novels, Dramas* —Depicts political and religious life. **Henryk Sienkiewicz** (Polish), (1846–1916). — *Novels*—Historical. **Edmondo de Amicis** (It.), (1846–1908). —*Travels, Novels* —*Cuore* is best known for brilliant descriptive passages.	1878. Congress of Berlin.
Robert Louis Stevenson (1850–1894).—*Poems, Essays, Stories*—A great stylist. **Henry Arthur Jones** (1851–1929). — Able social *Dramas*. **George Moore** (1852–1933). — *Novels*, minor *Poems*—A leader in the revival of Irish letters.	**Joel Chandler Harris** (1848–1908). — Southern Negro and animal tales. **James Lane Allen** (1849–1925). — *Novels*. **Sara Orne Jewett** (1849–1909).— *Novels, Short Stories* of New England scenes and characters. **Charles Egbert Craddock** (Mary N. Murfree) (1850–1922). — *Novels* of the Southern Appalachians. **Eugene Field** (1850–1895).— *Poems* of childhood—*With Trumpet and Drum*. **Edwin Markham** (1852–1940). —*Man with the Hoe*, other realistic poems. **Henry van Dyke** (1852–1933).—*Essays, Poems*. **Mary E. Wilkins Freeman** (1852–1930). — Realistic, severe *Stories* of rural New England.	**Guy de Maupassant** (1850–1893).—A master of the *Short Story*. **Pierre Loti** (pseud. of Louis M. J. Viaud), (1850–1923). —*Novels, Travels*. High descriptive talent; sought perfection of style. **Paul Bourget** (1852–1935).— *Novels*—A keen analyst.	**August Strindberg** (Swed.), (1849–1912). — *Realistic Novels, Dramas, Lyrics*. **Ellen Key** (Swed.), (1849–1926)—Sociological writings.	**Giuseppe Giacosa** (It.), (1847–1906). —*Dramatic Poetry*, including libretti for Puccini's operas.	1881. American Federation of Labor organized.
Arthur Wing Pinero (1855–1934). — Many popular *Dramas*. **George Bernard Shaw** (1856–1950).—*Essays, Plays*—A critic and writer of high rank. **Oscar Wilde** (1856–1900).— Melodious *Poems* and *Dramas* of great wit and humor. **John Davidson** (1857–1909). —*Lyrics* and *Ballads* of Scotland. **Joseph Conrad** (1857–1924). —Of Polish birth. A novelist whose sea stories take first rank. **George Gissing** (1857–1903). — *New Grub Street*, other *Novels* of the very poor.	**James Whitcomb Riley** (1853–1916). — *Poems* of *Childhood*. **Thomas Nelson Page** (1853–1922). — *Novels* — *In Ole Virginia*. Adept in Negro dialect and characterization. **Francis Marion Crawford** (1854–1909). — *Novels* — Best known for his *Saracinesca* series. **William Drummond** (Canadian), (1854–1907).— *Poems* of the French habitant. **Thorstein Veblen** (1857–1929). — *Economics* — A leader of unorthodox viewpoint. **Gertrude Atherton** (1857–1948). — *Novels* — Many of them historical. **Margaretta W. Deland** (1857–1919).—*Novels*—New England life.	**Jules Lemaître** (1853–1914). —*Dramas, Criticism*. **Paul Hervieu** (1857–1915).— *Dramas, Novels*.	**Hermann Sudermann** (German) (1857–1928). — *Plays, Novels*—His greatest novel was *Dame Care*. **Henrik Pontoppidan** (Dan.), (1857–1943). — *Novels* — Great writer of ironic prose.	**Armando Palacio Valdés** (Sp.), (1853–1938). — *Realistic Novels*. **Vsevolod Garshin** (Russ.), (1855–1888).— *The Red Flower*, other *Short Stories* of horror and madness. **Matilde Serao** (Sp.), (1856–1927). — *Novels*—Popular in style.	1883. Triple Alliance, Germany, Austria, Italy. 1886. Haymarket riots in Chicago. 1887. Queen Victoria's Jubilee.

TABLE VIII. MODERN LITERATURE—Continued

English	American	French	German, Scandinavian	Other Countries	Historical Events
William Watson (1858–1935). —Long thoughtful *Poems* in traditional form.	**Agnes Repplier** (1855–1950). — *Essays* remarkable for light ironic touch.	**Eugène Brieux** (1858–1932). —*Dramas* dealing with social problems.	**Selma Lagerlöf** (Swed.), (1858–1940).—*Novels, Short Stories* of great charm. The first woman writer to win a Nobel Prize.		
A. Conan Doyle (1859–1930). —Popular *Novels*. His *Sherlock Holmes* is the outstanding character of detective fiction.		**Henri Bergson** (1859-1941). —*Philosophy, Essays.* A leading exponent of the idea of creative evolution.	**Karl von Heidenstam** (Swed.), (1859–1940). — *Novels, Poems.*		
Francis Thompson (1859–1907). — Minor *Poems*, mystical in theme.					
A. E. Housman (1859–1936). —His *Shropshire Lad* and other lyrics of the countryside are marked by distinctive direct language.					
Sir James M. Barrie (1860–1937). — *Novels, Plays—Little Minister* and other tales of Scottish peasantry. He was a master of whimsy.	**Hamlin Garland** (1860–1940). — *Novels* — His realistic *Middle Border* series is most popular.	**René Doumic** (1860–1937).—*Criticism*—History of French literature.	**Knut Hamsun** (Nor.), (1860–1952).—*Novels*—Depicts life of the laborer with masterly psychological analysis and keen description.	**Anton Chekhov** (Russ.), (1860–1904). — *Dramas, Short Stories.*	1892. Homestead steel strike.
	Charles W. Gordon (Ralph Connor, pseud.), (1860–1937).—A Canadian writer of life in western Canada.		**Gustaf Froding** (Swed.), (1860–1911).—*Lyrics.*		
Sir Rabindranath Tagore (In.), (1861–1941)—*Poems, Essays, Stories.*	**Louise Guiney** (1861–1920). —A minor poet of polished but traditional style.				
	Bliss Carman (Canadian), (1861–1921).—*Poetry.*				
	Emily Pauline Johnson (Canadian), (1862–1913).—*Poetry.*	**Maurice Maeterlinck** (Belgian), (1862–1949).—*Plays* —Many mystical plays, *The Blue Bird* being one of the most popular.	**Gerhart Hauptmann** (German), (1862–1946).—Master of naturalism in social *Dramas—The Sunken Bell.*		
	Sir Horatio Gilbert Parker (Canadian), (1862–1919). —*Historical novels.*	**Marcel Prévost** (1862-1941). —*Novels* of brilliant style but morbid plot.	**Arthur Schnitzler** (Austrian), (1862–1931).—Witty light *Plays.*		
	William S. Porter (O. Henry), (1862–1910). — Master of the short story with surprise ending—*The Four Million.*	**Maurice Barrès** (1862–1923). —*Novels.*			
	Edith Wharton (1862–1937). —*Novels—House of Mirth.*				
	John Fox, Jr. (1863–1919).— *Novels*, largely of the southern mountains.		**Arno Holz** (German), (1863–1929).—*Criticism*—A minor poet, he founded the German Naturalist school.	**G. d'Annunzio** (It.), (1863–1938).—*Novels, Plays, Poetry.* Eccentric in purpose, but consistent in rich rhetorical skill and beauty of expression.	1893. World's Columbian Exposition, Chicago.
	George Santayana (1863–1952). — *Philosophy, Poems, Novel.*		**Oskar Levertin** (Swed.), (1862–1906). — *Short Stories, Essays, Poems*—A great literary critic.		
			Richard Dehmel (German), (1863–1920). — Minor *Poems.*		
			Hermann Bahr (Austrian), (1863–1934). — *Criticism;* Viennese comedies.		
			Gustav Frenssen (German), (1863–1945). — *Jorn Uhl*, other novels of the countryside.		1894. Pullman strike forcibly put down. Coxey leads army of unemployed to Washington. Captain Dreyfus convicted in France.
Israel Zangwill (1864-1926). — *Novels, Dramas, Essays* — Depicts Jewish life.	**Richard Hovey** (1864–1900). —*Stein Song* and other romantic *Lyrics.*		**Frank Wedekind** (German), (1864–1918). — *Novels, Plays.*		
William Butler Yeats (Irish), (1865–1939). — *Poetry, Dramas* — Irish settings.	**Clyde Fitch** (1865–1907).— *Society Plays.*		**Sven Hedin** (Swed.), (1865–1952).—*Travels.*		
Rudyard Kipling (1865-1936). — *Stories, Novels, Poems*—Best known for tales of the English in India — *Soldiers, Three, Jungle Book.*	**Meredith Nicholson** (1866–1947). — *Novels* of the day.	**Romain Rolland** (1866–1943). —*Novels—Jean Christophe.*		**Jacinto Benavente** (Sp.), (1866–1954). —*Psychological Dramas.*	
Herbert G. Wells (1866–1946).—*Novels, History.*				**Vicente Blasco Ibáñez** (Sp.), (1867–1928). — *Novels—Four Horsemen of the Apocalypse.*	
Arnold Bennett (1867–1931). — *Novels* of the common people of his time.					
John Galsworthy (1867–1933).—*Novels, Drama;* realistic studies of social problems.					
George Russell (Æ, pseud.), (Irish), (1867–1935). — Melodious mystical *Lyrics.* A leader of the Irish revival.	**Stephen Leacock** (Canadian), (1869–1944). — *Humor, Short Stories.*	**Edmond Rostand** (1868–1918).—*Dramas*—His *Cyrano de Bergerac* began a revival of romantic drama.	**Stefan George** (German), (1868–1933).—A symbolist poet; melodious *Lyrics.*	**Maxim Gorki** (Russ.), (1868–1936). — *Novels* — Depicts labor's struggles.	1898. Spanish-American War.
Stephen Phillips (1868-1915). — *Poems* — Tragedies in blank verse.	**William Vaughan Moody** (1869-1910). — *Poems, Dramas—Great Divide.*	**Francis Jammes** (1868-1938). —A mystic poet of the Decadent school.			
	Edgar Lee Masters (1869–1950).—Iconoclastic *Biography;* realistic, epigrammatic verse.	**André Gide** (1869–1951).— Psychological *Novels.*	**Martin Andersen Nexo** (Dan.), (1869–1954).—*Novels.*		1899–1901 South African War.
	Edwin Arlington Robinson (1869–1935).—*Poetry.*				
	Booth Tarkington (1869–1946).—*Novels, Plays*—Depicts modern American youth.			**Miguel de Unamuno** (Spain) (1864–1937).—*Novels.*	
	Frank Norris (1870-1902). —Epic *Novels* of great power.				1900. Boxer uprising in China.

TABLE VII. MODERN LITERATURE—Continued

ENGLISH	AMERICAN	FRENCH	GERMAN, SCANDINAVIAN	OTHER COUNTRIES	HISTORICAL EVENTS
	Mary Johnston (1870–1936): Romantic *Historical Novels* with Southern settings.		Ricarda Huch (German), (1864–1947).— *Novels.*		
	Ray Stannard Baker (1870–1946). — *Biography;*		Hjalmar Gullberg (1867–).—Poet.		
John Millington Synge (Irish), (1871–1909).— *Plays* of Irish life.	Theodore Dreiser (1871–1945).—Pessimistic Realistic; *Novels.* Stephen Crane (1871–1900). —*The Red Badge of Courage,* other novels and short stories of action.	Marcel Proust (1871–1922). —Psychological *Novels.* Henri Barbusse (1871–1935). —Bitter realistic *Short Stories.*		Leonid N. Andreyev (Russian), (1871–1919).—*Short Stories, Plays.*	
	Norman Duncan (Canadian); (1871–1916).—Tales of Labrador Life. Paul Dunbar (1872–1906):— The first accepted Negro poet.	Paul Valery (1871–1945).— *Novels, Poetry.* His appeal is to the mind; not the heart. Paul Fort (1872–1960).—*Free Verse.*			
Gilbert K. Chesterton (1874–1936). — *Essays, Criticism, Satire.*	Robert W. Service (Canadian); (1874–1958). — *Poems* —Yukon Life. Amy Lowell (1874–1925).— *Poems*—Critic of her day. Ellen Glasgow (1874–1945). —Realistic social *Novels* of the South.		Johan Bojer (Nor.); (1872–1959). — *Novels*—Depicts man's struggle for life by the sea. Jacob Wassermann (Austrian), (1873–1934). — *Novels.*		
W. Somerset Maugham (1874–1965).—*Novels, The Razor's Edge.*	Zona Gale (1874–1938). — *Short Stories;* realistic satirical *Novels.* Gertrude Stein (1874–1946). —Experimental *Prose.*		Johannes V. Jensen (Danish), (1873–1950).—*Novelist, Short Stories.*		
Winston Churchill (1874–1965). History—*Their Finest Hour.*	Robert Frost (1875-1963).— *Poems*—Depicts country life.				1903. First successful airplane flight.
John Masefield (1875–1965).—*Poems, Plays.*	Willa Sibert Cather (1876–1950).—*Novels*—Life in the Middle West in early days.	Henry Bernstein (1876–1953).—*Dramas.*	Rainer Maria Rilke (Ger.), (1875–1926).—Lyric *Poet.* Thomas Mann (German); (1875–1955). — *Novels*— *Joseph and His Brethren.*	Grazia Deledda (It.), (1875–1936).— *Novels.*	1904–05. Russo-Japanese War.
	Sherwood Anderson (1876–1941)—Many *Novels.* Jack London (1876–1916). —*Stories*—Adventures on land and sea.	Comtesse de Noailles (1876–1933).—*Poetry.*			1906. San Francisco earthquake and fire.
	Lloyd C. Douglas (1877–1951).—*Novel, The Robe,* charming *Essays.*		Georg Kaiser (German), (1878–1945). — Impressionistic *Dramas.*		
Lord Dunsany (Irish), (1878–1957). — *Dramas*— Irish life and legend.	Carl Sandburg (1878–). —*Poems, Novels.* Rachel Crothers (1878–1958).—Clever social comedy—*Dramas.*				
E. M. Forster 1879–). Novels—*Passage to India.*					1911. Standard Oil trust ordered dissolved.
Alfred Noyes (1880–1958).— *Poems.* Virginia Woolf (1882–1941). —*Novels* in the "stream of consciousness" technique.	Nicholas Vachel Lindsay (1879–1958). — *Novels.* James Branch Cabell (1879–1958). — *Novels*— The Devils Own Dear Son. Jurgen.		Emil Ludwig (German), (1881–1948).—*Biographies.* Sigrid Undset (Nor.); (1882–1949).—*Novels.*	Franz Kafka (Austrian). (1883–1924). *Psychological Novels.*	1912–13. Balkan Wars.
John Drinkwater (1882–1937): — *Plays, Abraham Lincoln.* James Joyce (1882–1941).— Symbolistic *Novels*— *Ulysses, Finnegans Wake.*			Lothrop Stoddard (1883–1950).—"*Into the Darkness: Nazi Germany Today.*"		1914. World War I began.
D. H. Lawrence (1885–1930). —*Novels, Plays.*	Sara Teasdale (1884–1933).— Musical *Lyrics.* Ezra Pound (1885–).— *Poems, Translations.* Sinclair Lewis (1885–1951). *Novels* — Depicts American small-town life: *Main Street* being his best known story.	Andre Maurois (psued. of Emile Herzog); (1885–). — *Novels, Biography.* Francois Mauriac (1885–).—Psychological *Novels*—Harsh realism.	Lion Feuchtwanger (German), (1884–1958). — *Dramas, Novels.* Fritz von Unruh (German), (1885–). — Expressionistic *Dramas.*		1915. *Lusitania* torpedoed.
	Carl Van Doren (1885–1950). — *Novels, Biographies.* Joyce Kilmer (1886–1918—). —*Poems.* Hilda Doolittle (H. D.), (1886–1961). — An Imagist poet.	Jules Romains (pseud. of Louis Farigoule); (1885–). — *Novels, Poems, Plays.*			1917. United States joins Allies.
Rupert Brooke (1887–1915). —A minor poet.					
	T. S. Eliot (1888–1965).— *Critic, Experimental Poetry, Drama,* Cocktail Party. Maxwell Anderson (1888–1959).—*Drama.*	Paul Morand (1888–).— *Novels, Poems*—Impressionistic in style.			1918. World War I ended.
	Eugene O'Neill (1888–1953). —*Dramas*—Depicts the sordid side of life: *Anna Christie.*			Gabriela Mistral (Chile), (1889–1957). —*Poet.*	1920. League of Nations.
Noel Coward (1889–).— Versatile comedy; *Dramas.*	Hervey Allen (1889–1949). *Anthony Adverse.* Christopher Morley (1890–1957). *Essays, Poems, Novels.* Edgar Guest (1881–1959). *Poems.*		Frank Thiess (German); (1890–). — Mystic rural *Novels.*	Laura Goodman Salverson (1890–), (Can.).— *Autobiography.*	1922. Irish Free State.
Katherine Mansfield (1890–1923).—*The Fly,* other distinguished short stories. Angela Thirkill (1890–1961). —Novelist—Life in Cathedral Towns.	Louis Bromfield (1896–1956). *Novels—Early Autumn, Mrs. Parkington, The Rains Came.* Sidney Howard (1891–1939). —*Drama.*	Jean Cocteau (1891–1963). —*Novelist, Drama, Critic.*	Franz Werfel (German), (1890–1945). — *Novels, Plays,* —The Goat Song, Song of Bernadette.	Karel M. Capek (Czechoslovak), (1890–1938). — *Plays* — Modernistic, *R. U. R.*	
Richard Aldington (1892–1962).—*Poems, Novels.*	Edna St. Vincent Millay (1892–1950).—*Poems.* Pearl S. Buck (1892–). —Stories of Chinese Life.		Ernst Toller (German), (1893–1939).—Expressionist *Dramas.*	Lajos Zilahy (Hungarian), (1891–). — *Novels, The Dukays.*	
Rebecca West (Cecily Fairfield) (1892–1962). Journalist, essayist, novelist, critic. *The Thinking Reed, Henry James, The Fountain Overflows.*	John Marquand (1893–1960).—*Satirical Novels. Point of No Return.* Laurence Stallings (1894–).—*Drama.* John Dos Passos (1896–).—*Manhattan Transfer, The Grand Design.*	Andre Malraux (1895–). —*Novels.*		Arthur S. Bourinot 1894–), (Can.) —*Verse.*	

TABLE VIII. MODERN LITERATURE—Concluded

ENGLISH	AMERICAN	FRENCH	GERMAN, SCANDINAVIAN	OTHER COUNTRIES	HISTORICAL EVENTS
	William Faulkner (1897–1962).—Bitter *Novels, Intruder in the Dust.* Thornton Wilder (1897–).—*Bridge of San Luis Rey, Our Town.* Ernest Hemingway (1898–1962).—*Novels of disillusionment.* Stephen Vincent Benet (1898–1943). — *Short Stories, Poems, John Brown's Body.*	Heinz Pol, *"Suicide of a democracy."* Jean Paul Sartre—*Novels, Drama, Existentialist. Red Gloves, Respectful Prostitute, Nausea.*	Erich Maria Remarque (German), (1898–).—*Novels—All Quiet on the Western Front.*	Freda Utley (1898–). —	1929. Financial depression in the United States begins.
Cecil Scott Forester (1899–1966).—*Novels, Captain Hornblower.* Nevil Shute (1889–1961).—*Novels.* Elizabeth Bowen (1899–).—*Novels—The Heat of the Day.*	Thomas Wolfe (1900–1938).—*Stirring Novels.* Margaret Mitchell (1900–1949).—*Novel, Gone With The Wind.* John Gunther (1901–).—*History, Novels, Death Be Not Proud.*			Franklin D. Mc-Dowell (Can.). *Historical Novel.*	1937–38. Wars in Spain and in China. 1939–45. Allies Win World War II.
Evelyn Waugh (1903–1966).—*Novels — Brideshead Revisited.*	John Steinbeck (1902–).—*Novels, Grapes of Wrath, The Wayward Bus.* Countee Cullen (1903–1946).—*Negro poet.* James Gould Cozzens (1903–).—*Novels, Guard of Honor, By Love Possessed.* F. L. Schuman (1904–).—*Night Over Europe.*	Maurice Herzog.—*Personal narrative—Annapurna.* J. Y. Cousteau. — *Personal narrative — The Silent World.*		Alan Paton (So. Africa) (1903–). *Novels, Cry The Beloved Country.*	1948. Beginning of cold war with Russia.
Hope Muntz (1907–).—*Novels—Golden Warrier.* R. C. Hutchinson (1907–).—*Novels—The Elephant and the Castle.*		Jacques Maritain. — *Artist-philosopher—Creative Intuition in Art and Poetry.*	Par Lagerkvist (1891–).—*Novels, Drama—Barabbas.* Halmut Gollwitzer (German).—*Unwilling Journey.*	Mikhail Sholokhov (Rus.), (1905–). — *Quiet Flows the Don.*	1950. Atomic research continues. 1952. War in Korea. U. N. troops fight Communists.
Richard Llewellyn—*Novels*	Willian Saroyan (1908–). — *Novel, Drama — Adventures of Wesley Jackson.* Ben Ames Williams *"House Divided."* A. B. Guthrie — *Historical Novels—The Way West.* John Hersey—*Novels, Hiroshima, The Wall.*	Jean Giono. — *Novel — The Horseman on the Roof.*	Franz von Papen (German) —*Memoirs.* Bertolt Brecht (1898–1956).—*Drama—Mother Courage, The Caucasian Chalk Circle, Threepenny Opera, Mahagonny.*	Nikos Kazantzakis (1885–) (Grecian.) — *Novel — Zorba the Greek.*	
Joyce Cary (1888–1957).—*Novels—Prisoner of Grace.* Victoria Sackville-West (1892–1962). — *Novels — The Edwardians, Easter Party.*				Alexandra Tolstoy. (Russian) — *Biography of Tolstoy: A Life of my Father.*	
Gwendolen Raverat.—*Reminiscences—Period Piece.*	Will Durant.—*History—The Story of Civilization.*			Ignazio Silone. (Italian)—*Novel—A Handful of Blackberries.*	1956. Unrest in Israel, Cyprus, and Far East.
	Tennessee Williams. — *Drama — The Glass Menagerie, American Blues, Cat on a Hot Tin Roof, Sweet Bird of Youth.*	Vercors—*Novels—Le silence de la mer.*		Boris Pasternak. —*Novels, poems—Dr. Zhivago.* Salvatore Quasimodo.—*Poems.*	1960. Exploration of Space.
Ernest Jones. — *Biography of Sigmund Freud.*	J. D. Salinger—*Nine Stories, The Catcher in the Rye, Franny and Zooey.* Lillian Hellman—*Drama—The Children's Hour, The Little Foxes, Toys in the Attic.* Carson McCullers—*Novels—The Heart Is a Lonely Hunter, The Member of the Wedding.*	Simone de Beauvoir (1908–). — *Novels — L'Invitee, The Mandarins, The Second Sex.* Albert Camus (1913–1960). —*Novels, Philosophy—La Peste, L'Etranger, Le Tombeau, The Myth of Sisyphus.*		Vladimir Nabokov *Novels, poems Lolita.*	
Dylan Thomas (1914–1953). —*Poetry—Adventures in the Skin Trade, Quite Early One Morning, Under Milkwood.* Wystan Hugh Auden (1907–).—*Poetry—Another Time, The Age of Anxiety, Homage to Clio.* John Osborne (1929).—*Drama—The Entertainer, Look Back in Anger, Luther.* Harold Pinter (1930).—*Drama — The Birthday Party, The Caretaker, The Dumbwaiter.* Samuel Beckett (Irish, 1906–). — *Drama — Waiting for Godot, Endgame, Krapp's Last Tape, Molloy.*	William Carlos Williams (1883–1963). — *Poetry — The Broken Span, The Desert Music, Journey to Love, Paterson.* Wallace Stevens (1879–1955) —*Poetry—Transport to Summer, The Auroras of Autumn, Harmonium, Ideas of Order.* Mary McCarthy (1912–) —*Novels—Memories of a Catholic Girlhood, The Group, The Groves of Academe.* Saul Bellow, (1915–)—*Novels—The Adventures of Augie March, Henderson the Rain King, Herzog.* James Baldwin (1924–).—*Novels—Go Tell It on the Mountain, Notes of a Native Son, The Fire Next Time.* Edward Albee (1928–).—*Drama—The Zoo Story, The Death of Bessie Smith, The American Dream, Who's Afraid of Virginia Woolf?*	Eugene Ionesco (1912–). — *Drama — Rhinoceros, Les Chaises, La Jeune Fille a Marier, Amedee.* Jean Genet (1909–).—*Drama—The Blacks, The Balcony, The Maids, Deathwatch.*		Yevgeny Yevtushenko (Russian, 1933–). — *Poetry — The Prospectors of the Future, Third Snow, Longbow and Lyre.*	1963. Pres. John F. Kennedy assassinated. 1965. War in Vietnam, space flights continue.

BOOKS can open up the world of nature, telling of the daily wanderings of an insect through the grass, the bright cobwebs woven by the spider, and the life of the deer and squirrel in forest and field.

HELEN BUTTFIELD

NATIONAL FILM BOARD OF CANADA

A. DEVANEY, INC.

NATIONAL FILM BOARD OF CANADA

GRADED READING LIST

ELEMENTARY GRADE LEVEL

School grade for which each book is suitable is shown in parentheses. K means kindergarten; PS, preschool.

ADVENTURE AND MYSTERY

BOWERS, GWENDOLYN. *Brother to Galahad.* Henry Z. Walck, Inc., 1963. (4–8)

ENRIGHT, ELIZABETH. *Gone-Away Lake.* Harcourt, Brace & World, Inc., 1957. (4–6)

LANIER, SIDNEY (ed.). *The Boy's King Arthur.* Charles Scribner's Sons, 1917. (6–8)

MUIR, LYNETTE. *The Unicorn Window.* Abelard-Schuman Ltd., 1961. (3–7)

NEAVLES, JANET. *The Mystery of the Pharaoh's Treasure.* J. B. Lippincott Co., 1963. (2–6)

NORTON, ANDRÉ. *Scarface.* Harcourt, Brace & World, Inc., 1948. (4–6)

PYLE, HOWARD. *Some Merry Adventures of Robin Hood.* Charles Scribner's Sons, 1954. (5 up)

PYLE, HOWARD. *The Story of Sir Launcelot and His Companions.* Charles Scribner's Sons. (5–9)

SENDAK, MAURICE. *Where the Wild Things Are.* Harper & Bros., 1963. (K–3)

SERRAILLIER, IAN. *The Way of Danger (The Story of Theseus).* Henry Z. Walck, Inc., 1963. (2–6)

TOWNSEND, J. DAVID. *The Cats Stand Accused.* Houghton Mifflin Co., 1961 (3–6).

WARBURG, SANDOR STODDARD (ed.). *St. George and the Dragon,* by Spenser. Houghton Mifflin Co., 1963. (4–6)

AMERICA

BAKELESS, KATHERINE and JOHN. *Spies of the Revolution.* J. B. Lippincott Co., 1962. (5–7)

BAKER, BETTY. *The Shaman's Last Raid.* Harper & Bros., 1963. (4–6)

BRINK, CAROL R. *Caddie Woodlawn.* The Macmillan Co., 1935. (4–6)

FARQUHAR, MARGARET C. *Colonial Life in America: A Book to Begin On.* Holt, Rinehart & Winston, Inc., 1962. (K–2)

HOLLAND, JANICE. *They Built a City: The Story of Washington, D.C.* Charles Scribner's Sons, 1953. (5–7)

LAND, MYRICK and BARBARA. *The Changing South: New Riches for the Land of Cotton* (Challenge Books). Coward-McCann, Inc., 1958. (5–9)

LAWSON, DON. *Young People in the White House.* Abelard-Schuman Ltd., 1961. (3–7)

MIERS, EARL S. *The Rainbow Book of American History.* The World Publishing Co., 1955. (4–6)

PHELAN, MARY KAY. *The White House: A Book to Begin On.* Holt, Rinehart & Winston, Inc., 1962. (K–2)

REYNOLDS, QUENTIN. *Custer's Last Stand* (Landmark Books). Random House, Inc., 1951. (5–9)

VAN RENSSELAER, ALEXANDER. *The Picture History of America.* Doubleday & Co., Inc., 1961. (4–6)

NEW YORK PUBLIC LIBRARY

ANIMALS from the first English encyclopedia, by Bartholomew Anglicus, 1494.

ANIMALS

ANCHARSVARD, KARIN. *Bonifacius and Little Bonnie.* Translated by C. M. Ancharsvard and K. H. Beales. Abelard-Schuman Ltd., 1963. (1–4)

ATWATER, RICHARD and FLORENCE. *Mr. Popper's Penguins.* Little, Brown & Co., 1938. (4–6)

BATES, H. D. *Achilles the Donkey.* Franklin Watts, Inc., 1963. (K–2).

BLUM, LISA-MARIE. *The Mysterious Merry-Go-Round.* Abelard-Schuman Ltd., 1962. (1–4)

DE BOIS, WILLIAM PÈNE. *Lion.* The Viking Press, Inc., 1956. (1–3)

BOND, MICHAEL. *A Bear Called Paddington.* Houghton Mifflin Co., 1960. (1–4)

BORTEN, HELEN. *Copycat.* Abelard-Schuman Ltd., 1963. (K–3)

BRUNHOFF, JEAN DE. *Babar and Father Christmas.* Random House, Inc., 1933. (PS)

BRUNHOFF, JEAN DE. *The Story of Babar, the Little Elephant.* Random House, Inc., 1933. (PS)

BRUNHOFF, JEAN DE. *The Travels of Babar.* Random House, 1933. (PS)

CRAIG, M. JEAN. *The Dragon in the Clock Box.* W. W. Norton & Co., Inc., 1962. (PS–K)

DAUGHERTY, JAMES. *Andy and the Lion.* The Viking Press, Inc., 1938. (1–4)

ELMER, IRENE. *Benjamin.* Abingdon Press, 1961. (1–3)

EZO. *My Son-In-Law the Hippopotamus.* Abelard-Schuman Ltd., 1962. (3–7)

FARLEY, WALTER. *Black Stallion.* Random House, Inc., 1941. (5–8)

GRAHAME, KENNETH. *The Reluctant Dragon.* Holiday House, 1953. (1–4)

HENRY, MARGUERITE. *Born to Trot.* Rand McNally & Co., 1950. (5–8)

HENRY, MARGUERITE. *King of the Wind.* Rand McNally, 1958. (5–8)

HENRY, MARGUERITE. *Misty of Chincoteague.* Rand McNally & Co., 1947. (5–8)

HOLL, ADELAIDE. *Lisette.* Lothrop, Lee & Shepard Co., Inc., 1962. (2–4)

HOLLANDER, JOHN. *Various Owls.* W. W. Norton & Co., Inc., 1963. (K–3)

JOHNSON, CROCKETT. *The Lion's Own Story.* Harper & Bros., 1963. (K–1)

KING, RUTH. *Nana, the Parlor Boarder.* Abelard-Schuman Ltd., 1954. (PS–1)

KNIGHT, ERIC. *Lassie, Come Home.* Holt, Rinehart & Winston, Inc., 1940. (4–6)

LEAR, EDWARD. *The Owl and the Pussycat.* Doubleday & Co., Inc., 1962. (PS–3)

LLOYD, NORRIS. *The Desperate Dragons.* Hasting House Publishers, Inc., 1962. (1–4)

MANNHEIM, GRETE. *Farm Animals.* Alfred A. Knopf, Inc., 1964. (K–2)

MEMLING, CARL. *Seals for Sale.* Abelard-Schuman Ltd., 1963. (K–3)

PACK, ROBERT. *How to Catch a Crocodile.* Alfred A. Knopf, Inc., 1964. (K–3)

PARADIS, MARJORIE. *Mr. De Luca's Horse.* Atheneum, 1962. (4–7)

POTTER, BEATRIX. *The Tale of Peter Rabbit.* Frederick Warne & Co., Ltd., 1903. (K–2)

POTTER, MIRIAM. *Goofy Mrs. Goose.* J. B. Lippincott Co., 1963. (K–3)

PRIESTLEY, LEE. *Rocket Mouse.* Abelard-Schuman Ltd., 1961. (1–4)

SALTEN, FELIX. *Bambi: A Life in the Woods.* Grosset & Dunlap, Inc., 1926. (5 up)

SCHLEIN, MIRIAM. *The Bumblebee's Secret.* Abelard-Schuman Ltd., 1958. (K–3)

SEWELL, ANNA. *Black Beauty.* The World Publishing Co. (4–6)

U.S. NAVY

PENGUIN CHICKS being fed in Antarctica.

SLOBODKIN, LOUIS. *The Late Cuckoo.* The Vanguard Press, Inc., 1962. (K–3)

SMITH, DODIE. *The Hundred and One Dalmatians.* The Viking Press, Inc., 1957. (4–8)

SURANY, ANICO. *The Golden Frog.* G. P. Putnam's Sons, 1963. (1–3)

TODARO, JOHN and ELLEN, BARBARA. *Phillip the Flower-Eating Phoenix.* Abelard-Schuman, 1961. (K–3)

TRESSELT, ALVIN and WHEATON, WILBUR. *An Elephant Is Not a Cat.* Parents' Magazine, 1962. (2–4)

BIOGRAPHY

BEARD, CHARLES A. *The Presidents in American History.* Julian Messner, Inc., 1961. (5–7)

COLVER, ANNE. *Thomas Jefferson: Author of Independence* (edited by Mary Austin). Garrard Publishing Co., 1963. (2–5)

COY, HAROLD. *The First Book of Presidents.* Franklin Watts, Inc., 1960. (1–4)

DAUGHERTY, JAMES. *Daniel Boone.* The Viking Press, Inc., 1939. (4–6).

LATHAM, JEAN L. *Drake: The Man They Called A Pirate.* Harper & Bros., 1960. (5–7)

LAWSON, ROBERT. *Ben And Me.* Little, Brown & Co., 1939. (5–8)

McNEER, MAY. *America's Abraham Lincoln.* Houghton Mifflin Co., 1957. (4 up)

NORTH, STERLING. *Mark Twain and the River.* Houghton Mifflin Co., 1961. (5–7)

PACE, MILDRED M. *Clara Barton.* Charles Scribner's Sons, 1941. (4–6)

HELEN BUTTFIELD

A SEAL'S WAY of sunbathing in the water.

AN ELEPHANT, the largest and most powerful land animal, has its own portable shower.

TREZ, DENISE and ALAIN. *The Little Knight's Dragon.* The World Publishing Co., 1963. (K–3)

WEIR, ROSEMARY. *Albert the Dragon.* Abelard-Schuman, 1961. (1–4)

WHITE, E. B. *Stuart Little.* Harper & Bros., 1945. (4–6)

BEGINNING BOOKS

ALEXANDER, ANNE. *I Want to Whistle.* Abelard-Schuman Ltd., 1958. (K–3)

BONSALL, CROSBY N. *Who's a Pest?* Harper & Bros., 1962. (1–2)

COLE, WILLIAM. *Frances Face-maker: A Going to Bed Book.* The World Publishing Co., 1963. (PS–2)

FALLS, C. B. (illustrator). *A B C Book.* Doubleday & Co., Inc., 1957. (PS–1)

GUILFOILE, ELIZABETH. *Nobody Listens to Andrew.* Follett, 1957. (1–3)

MUNARI, BRUNO (illustrator). *Bruno Munari's A B C.* The World Publishing Co., 1960. (PS–1)

PHELAN, MARY KAY. *The Circus: A Book to Begin On.* Holt, Rinehart & Winston, Inc., 1963. (K–2)

SEUSS, DR. *500 Hats of Bartholomew Cubbins.* The Vanguard Press, Inc., 1938. (K–3)

SEUSS, DR. *Hop on Pop.* Random House, Inc., 1963. (1–2)

D'AULAIRE, INGRI and EDGAR P. *Abraham Lincoln.* Doubleday & Co., Inc., 1957. (2–5)

DAVIDSON, MARY R. *Buffalo Bill: Wild West Showman* (edited by Mary C. Austin). Garrard Publishing Co., 1963. (2–5)

DESMOND, ALICE C. *Martha Washington.* Dodd, Mead & Co., 1942. (5–8)

EBERLE, IRMENGARDE. *Edward Jenner and Smallpox Vaccination.* Franklin Watts, Inc., 1962. (5–7)

EPSTEIN, SAM and BERYL. *George Washington Carver: Negro Scientist* (Discovery Books, edited by Mary C. Austin). Garrard Publishing Co., 1963. (2–5)

GRAVES, CHARLES P. *Annie Oakley: The Shooting Star* (edited by Mary C. Austin). Garrard Publishing Co., 1963. (2–5)

GUTHRIDGE, SUE. *Tom Edison: Boy Inventor.* The Bobbs-Merrill Co., Inc., 1947. (3–5)

HAMMONTREE, MARIE. *Will and Charles Mayo: Boy Doctors.* The Bobbs-Merrill Co., Inc., 1954. (3–5)

JOHNSTON, JOHANNA. *Thomas Jefferson: His Many Talents.* Dodd, Mead & Co., 1961. (5–6)

JUDSON, CLARA I. *City Neighbor: The Story of Jane Addams.* Charles Scribner's Sons, 1951. (5–7)

PARLIN, JOHN. *Amelia Earhart: Pioneer in the Sky* (Discovery Books, edited by Mary C. Austin). Garrard Publishing Co., 1963. (2–5)

SHEPHARD, ESTHER. *Paul Bunyan.* Harcourt, Brace & World, Inc., 1941. (4–6)

SPERRY, ARMSTRONG. *Voyages of Christopher Columbus* (Landmark Books). Random House, Inc., 1950. (6–8)

STEINBERG, ALFRED. *Woodrow Wilson.* G. P. Putnam's Sons, 1961. (6–8).

STEVENSON, AUGUSTA. *Booker T. Washington: Ambitious Boy.* The Bobbs-Merrill Co., Inc. (4–6)

STEVENSON, AUGUSTA. *Buffalo Bill: Boy of the Plains.* The Bobbs-Merrill Co., Inc. (3–5)

TALLANT, ROBERT. *The Pirate Lafitte and the Battle of New Orleans* (Landmark Books). Random House, Inc., 1951. (5–7)

TREGASKIS, RICHARD. *John F. Kennedy and PT-109* (Landmark Books). Random House, 1962. (5–7)

FINE ARTS

BALET, JAN. *What Makes an Orchestra?* Henry Z. Walck, 1951. (4–6)

BORTEN, HELEN. *Do You See What I See?* Abelard-Schuman Ltd., 1959. (K–3)

BORTEN, HELEN. *A Picture Has a Special Look.* Abelard-Schuman Ltd., 1961. (2–5)

BUCHANAN, FANNIE and LICKENBILL, CHARLES L. *How Man Made Music.* Follett Publishing Co., 1963. (4–7)

BULLA, CLYDE ROBERT. *Stories of Favorite Operas.* Thomas Y. Crowell Co., 1959. (4 up)

KING, ANN. *Full of Wonder.* The World Publishing Co., 1959. (K–6)

MOORE, LAMONT. *The First Book of Architecture.* Franklin Watts, Inc., 1961. (5–8)

LANGUAGE AND COMMUNICATION

ASIMOV, ISAAC. *Words from the Myths.* Houghton Mifflin Co., 1961. (5 up)

COURTIS, STUART A. and WATTERS, GARNETTE. *Illustrated Golden Dictionary for Young Readers.* Golden Press, Inc., 1956. (4–6)

LAIRD, HELEN and CHARLTON. *The Tree of Language.* The World Publishing Co., 1957. (4–6)

SOKOL, CAMILLE. *Dis-Moi.* Holt, Rinehart & Winston, Inc., 1963. (1–3)

SCHLEIN, MIRIAM. *Laurie's New Brother.* Abelard-Schuman Ltd., 1961. (PS–1)

SHORTALL, LEONARD. *Sam's First Fish.* William Morrow & Co., Inc., 1962. (1–2)

UNGERER, TOMI. *Snail, Where Are You?* Illustrated by the author. Harper and Row, 1962. (K–3)

WILLIAMS, JAY and LUBELL, WINIFRED. *I Wish I Had Another Name.* Atheneum Publishers, 1962. (K–4)

YASHIMA, TARO. *Umbrella.* The Viking Press, Inc., 1958. (PS–1)

NEW YORK PUBLIC LIBRARY

EARLY EXPLORERS of the Arctic region used Eskimo techniques in hunting walruses. Note the kayak (canoe) moving toward the animals.

NORMAN, GERTRUDE. *The First Book of Music.* Franklin Watts, Inc., 1954. (3–5)

YOUNG, MARY. *Singing Windows.* Abingdon Press, 1962. (5–8)

GEOGRAPHY

DESMOND, ALICE C. *Your Flag and Mine.* The Macmillan Co., 1960. (5–7)

EPSTEIN, SAM and BERYL. *The First Book of Maps and Globes.* Franklin Watts, Inc., 1959. (4 up)

HILLYER, VIRGIL M. and HUEY, EDWARD. *A Child's Geography of the World.* Appleton-Century-Crofts, 1951. (4–8)

HINE, AL and ALCORN, JOHN. *Where in the World Do You Live?* Harcourt, Brace & World, Inc., 1962. (K–3)

HISTORY

FRIEDMAN, ESTELLE. *Digging into Yesterday.* G. P. Putnam's Sons, 1958. (5 up)

KIRTLAND, G. B. *One Day in Elizabethan England.* Harcourt, Brace & World, Inc., 1962. (3–5)

RICH, LOUISE D. *The First Book of the Vikings.* The Viking Press, Inc., (6 up)

HOME AND FAMILY

ANGLUND, JOAN WALSH. *A Friend Is Someone Who Likes You.* Harcourt, Brace & World, Inc., 1958. (PS–1)

ANGLUND, JOAN WALSH. *Love Is a Special Way of Feeling.* Harcourt, Brace & World, Inc., 1960. (PS–1)

APELL, CLARA and MOREY. *Now I have a Daddy Haircut!* Dodd, Mead & Co., 1962. (PS up)

AYARS, JAMES STERLING. *Happy Birthday, Mom.* Abelard-Schuman Ltd., 1963. (1–4)

BEIM, LORRAINE and JERROLD. *Two Is a Team.* Harcourt, Brace & World, Inc., 1945. (3–5)

BURTON, VIRGINIA L. *The Little House.* Houghton Mifflin Co., 1942. (1–3)

CLARK, MARGERY. *The Poppy Seed Cakes.* Doubleday & Co., Inc., 1924. (1–3)

DUNCAN, LOIS. *Silly Mother.* The Dial Press, Inc., 1962. (K–2)

LOVELACE, MAUD. *Betsy-Tacy.* The Crowell-Collier Publishing Co., 1940. (3–4)

RAND, ANN and PAUL. *I Know a Lot of Things.* Harcourt, Brace & World, Inc., 1956. (PS)

REYHER, BECKY. *My Mother Is the Most Beautiful Woman in the World.* Lothrop, Lee & Shepard Co., Inc. (2–5)

LIFE IN DIFFERENT COUNTRIES

ARNOTT, KATHLEEN. *African Myths and Legends.* Henry Z. Walck, Inc., 1963. (2–6)

BERRY, ERICK. *Eating and Cooking Around the World: Fingers Before Forks.* The John Day Co., Inc., 1963. (4–7)

BISHOP, CLAIRE H. *Five Chinese Brothers.* Coward-McCann, Inc., 1938. (1–3)

CARPENTER, FRANCES. *African Wonder Tales.* Doubleday & Co., Inc., 1963. (4–6)

COPELAND, FRANCES. *Land Between: The Middle East.* Abelard-Schuman Ltd., 1958. (3–7)

EVANS, EVA KNOX. *Why We Live Where We Live.* Little, Brown & Co., 1953. (4–7)

FERGUSON, CHARLES W. *Getting to Know the U.S.A.* Coward-McCann, Inc., 1963. (5 up)

FLACK, MARJORIE. *The Story About Ping.* The Viking Press, Inc., 1933. (PS–3)

GRIFFIN, ELLA. *Continent in a Hurry: The Challenge of Africa Today* (Challenge Books). Coward-McCann, Inc., 1962. (5–9)

HUME, LOTTA. *Favorite Children's Stories from China and Tibet.* Charles E. Tuttle Co., 1963. (3–6)

HELEN BUTTFIELD

PEOPLE IN OTHER LANDS and the legends and customs of other times come to life in books.

KAYE, GERALDINE. *Great Day in Ghana: Kwasi Goes to Town.* Abelard-Schuman Ltd., 1962. (1–4)

KIRN, ANN. *Two Pesos for Catalina.* Rand McNally & Co. (PS–3)

LUM, PETER. *Great Day in China: The Holiday Moon.* Abelard-Schuman Ltd., 1963. (1–4)

RIWKIN-BRICK, ANNA and LINDGREN, ASTRID. *Marko Lives in Yugoslavia.* The Macmillan Co., 1963. (1–3)

SUTHERLAND, EFUA. *Playtime in Africa.* Atheneum, 1962. (2–5)

MYTHS AND TALES

ANDERSEN, HANS CHRISTIAN. *Fairy Tales.* The World Publishing Co. (4–6)

GRIMM BROTHERS. *Tales from Grimm.* Translated by Wanda Gág. Coward-McCann, Inc. (4–6)

HAZELTINE, ALICE I. (compiler). *Hero Tales from Many Lands.* Abingdon Press, 1961. (5–7)

HOMER. *Children's Homer.* The Macmillan Co., 1962. (5–7)

JACOBS, JOSEPH (ed.). *Fables of Aesop.* The Macmillan Co., 1950. (4–6)

LAMB, CHARLES and MARY. *Tales from Shakespeare.* The Crowell-Collier Publishing Co., 1942. (4–8)

LANG, ANDREW (ed.). *Arabian Nights.* David McKay, 1946. (4 up)

MARTIGNONI, MARGARET (ed.). *The Illustrated Treasury of Children's Literature.* Grosset & Dunlap, Inc., 1955. (K–7)

WHITE, ANNE TERRY. *The Golden Treasury of Myths and Legends.* Golden Press, Inc., 1959. (5 up)

NUMBERS

ADLER, IRVING. *The Giant Golden Book of Mathematics: Exploring the World of Numbers and Space.* Golden Press, Inc., 1960. (5 up)

FISHER, MARGERY M. *One and One.* The Dial Press, Inc., 1963. (PS–2)

MYLLER, ROLF. *How Big Is a Foot?* Atheneum Publishers, 1962. (K–2)

TUDOR, TASHA. *1 is One.* Henry Z. Walck, Inc., 1956. (K–2)

OLD FAVORITES

ALCOTT, LOUISA MAY. *Jo's Boys.* Little, Brown & Co., 1867. (4 up)

ALCOTT, LOUISA MAY. *Little Men.* Little, Brown & Co., 1867. (4 up)

ALCOTT, LOUISA MAY. *Little Women.* Little, Brown & Co., 1867. (4 up)

ALIKI. *The Story of Johnny Appleseed.* Prentice-Hall, 1963. (1–2)

ANDERSEN, HANS CHRISTIAN. *The Emperor's New Clothes.* Harcourt, Brace & World, Inc., 1959. (4–6)

BANNERMAN, HELEN. *The Story of Little Black Sambo.* J. B. Lippincott Co., 1923. (K–2)

BARRIE, JAMES M. *Peter Pan.* Charles Scribner's Sons, 1950. (4–6)

BAUM, L. FRANK. *Wizard of Oz.* Grosset & Dunlap, Inc., Publishers. (4 up)

BROWN, MARCIA (il.). *Cinderella.* Scribner's, 1955. (1–3)

BROWN, MARCIA. *Puss in Boots.* Charles Scribner's Sons, 1952. (1–3)

BURNETT, FRANCES HODGSON. *The Little Princess.* J. B. Lippincott Co., 1963. (4–6)

BURNETT, FRANCES HODGSON. *The Secret Garden.* J. B. Lippincott Co. (4–6)

CARROLL, LEWIS. *Alice's Adventures in Wonderland* and *Through the Looking Glass.* The Macmillan Co., 1956. (4–6)

COLLODI, C. *Adventures of Pinocchio.* The Macmillan Co., 1953. (3–6)

COONEY, BARBARA. *Chanticleer and the Fox.* The Crowell-Collier Publishing Co., 1958. (1–4)

DODGE, MARY MAPES. *Hans Brinker, or the Silver Skates.* Charles Scribner's Sons, 1915. (5–8)

ESTES, ELEANOR. *The Middle Moffat.* Harcourt, Brace & World, Inc., 1942. (4–6)

ESTES, ELEANOR. *The Moffats.* Harcourt, Brace & World, Inc., 1941. (4–6)

GRAHAME, KENNETH. *Wind in the Willows.* Charles Scribner's Sons, 1933. (5 up)

HARRIS, JOEL CHANDLER. *Uncle Remus: His Songs and His Sayings.* Meredith Publishing Co., 1962. (3–6)

HAYWOOD, CAROLYN. *"B" is for Betsy.* Harcourt, Brace & World, Inc., 1939. (3–4)

KIPLING, RUDYARD. *Jungle Book.* Doubleday & Co., Inc., 1932. (4–7)

LANGSTAFF, JOHN and ROJANKOVSKY, FEDOR. *Frog Went A-Courtin'.* Harcourt, Brace & World, Inc., 1962. (PS–3)

LOFTING, HUGH. *The Voyages of Doctor Doolittle.* J. B. Lippincott Co., 1922. (3–6)

McGINLEY, PHYLLIS. *The Plain Princess.* J. B. Lippincott Co., 1945. (3–5)

MILNE, A. A. *The House at Pooh Corner.* E. P. Dutton & Co., Inc., 1961. (PS–3)

MILNE, A. A. *Winnie-the-Pooh.* E. P. Dutton & Co., Inc., 1961. (PS–3)

REED, PHILIP (il.). *Mother Goose and Nursery Rhymes.* Atheneum Publishers, 1963. (PS–2)

REED, PHILIP (il.). *The Seven Voyages of Sinbad the Sailor.* Atheneum Publishers, 1962. (4–6)

RICE, ALICE HEGAN. *Mrs. Wiggs of the Cabbage Patch.* Meredith Publishing Co., 1963. (3–6)

SPYRI, JOHANNA H. *Heidi.* The Macmillan Co., 1963. (4–6)

TAYLOR, SIDNEY. *All-of-a-kind Family.* Follett Publishing Co., 1951. (3–6)

THURBER, JAMES. *Many Moons.* Harcourt, Brace & World, 1944. (4–5)

TRAVERS, P. L. *Mary Poppins.* Harcourt, Brace & World, Inc., 1934. (4–7)

TWAIN, MARK. *Adventures of Huckleberry Finn.* Harper & Bros., 1931. (5 up)

TWAIN, MARK. *Adventures of Tom Sawyer.* Harper, 1932. (5 up)

TWAIN, MARK. *The Prince and the Pauper.* Harper, 1931. (5 up)

WIGGIN, KATE DOUGLAS. *Rebecca of Sunnybrook Farm.* Houghton Mifflin Co., 1888. (4–7)

WYSS, JOHANN D. *Swiss Family Robinson.* Grosset & Dunlap, Inc., 1913. (5–8)

POETRY

ALDIS, DOROTHY. *All Together: A Child's Treasury of Verse.* G. P. Putnam's Sons, 1952. (1–3)

FROST, ROBERT. *The Road Not Taken.* Holt, Rinehart & Winston, Inc., 1951. (5 up)

FROST, ROBERT. *You Come Too.* Holt, Rinehart & Winston, Inc., 1959. (5 up)

LONGFELLOW, HENRY WADSWORTH. *Paul Revere's Ride.* The Crowell-Collier Publishing Co., 1963. (3 up)

MILNE, A. A. *Now We Are Six.* E. P. Dutton & Co., Inc., 1927. (PS–6)

MILNE, A. A. *When We Were Very Young.* E. P. Dutton & Co., Inc., 1924. (PS–6)

MILNE, A. A. *The World of Christopher Robin.* E. P. Dutton & Co., Inc., 1958. (PS–6)

STEVENSON, ROBERT LOUIS. *A Child's Garden of Verses.* Charles Scribner's Sons, 1905. (1–4)

RELIGION

DOUGHERTY, KATHERINE. *A Street of Churches.* Abingdon Press, 1962. (K–3)

PYNE, MABLE. *The Story of Religion.* Houghton Mifflin Co., 1954. (4–7)

SOURDEL, DOMINIQUE. *Islam.* Walker & Co., 1963. (2–6)

SCIENCE

ALEXANDER, ARTHUR. *The Hidden You: Psychology in Your Life.* Prentice-Hall, Inc., 1962. (4–6)

ALLEN, GERTRUDE. *Everyday Insects.* Houghton Mifflin, 1963. (K–3)

ARNOLD, OREN. *Marvels of the Sea and Shore.* Abelard-Schuman Ltd., 1963. (3–7)

BEELER, NELSON F. and BRANLEY, FRANKLYN M. *Experiments with a Microscope.* Crowell-Collier Publishing Co., 1957. (5–7)

BEHN, HARRY. *All Kinds of Time.* Harcourt, Brace & World, Inc., 1950. (1–3)

CARONA, PHILIP B. *Things That Measure.* Prentice-Hall, Inc., 1962. (3–5)

CONGER, MARION. *Who Has Seen the Wind?* Abingdon, 1959. (K–1)

COOPER, ELIZABETH K. *Science in Your Own Back Yard.* Harcourt, Brace & World, Inc., 1958. (5–8)

CROSBY, PHOEBE. *Junior Science Book of Rock Collecting.* Edited by Nancy Larrick. Garrard, 1963. (2–5)

FERAVOLO, ROCCO V. *Junior Science Book of Magnets.* Edited by Nancy Larrick. Garrard Publishing Co., 1963. (2–5)

FERAVOLO, ROCCO V. *Junior Science Book of Weather Experiments.* Edited by Nancy Larrick. Garrard Publishing Co., 1963. (2–5)

FISHER, AILEEN. *I Like Weather.* Thomas Y. Crowell Co., 1963. (K–2)

FLETCHER, HELEN J. *For Junior Doctors Only.* The Bobbs-Merrill Co., Inc., 1961. (5–6)

FOLLETT, ROBERT J. R. *Your Wonderful Body.* Follett Publishing Co., 1963. (1 up)

FREEMAN, IRA M. *All About the Wonders of Chemistry.* Random House, Inc., 1954. (5–6)

GOLDSTEIN, RHODA. *Tools of the Scientist.* Prentice-Hall, 1963. (5–6)

KEEN, MARTIN. *The How and Why Wonder Book of the Human Body.* Grosset & Dunlap, Inc., Publishers, 1961. (4–7)

KRAUSS, RUTH. *The Growing Story.* Harper & Bros., 1947. (PS–2)

LARRICK, NANCY. *See for Yourself.* E. P. Dutton, Inc., 1952. (1–3)

LEWIS, ALFRED. *The New World of Plastics.* Dodd, Mead & Co., 1963. (2–6)

McNAUGHT, HARRY. *The Golden Book of Science.* Golden Press, Inc., 1963. (5–9)

MORGAN, ALFRED POWELL. *First Chemistry Book for Boys and Girls.* Scribner's, 1950. (5–7)

PEATTIE, DONALD CULROSS. *The Rainbow Book of Nature.* The World Publishing Co., 1957. (4–6)

SANDERSON, IVAN T. *The Continent We Live On.* Random House, Inc., 1962. (5–7)

SELSAM, MILLICENT. *A Time for Sleep.* W. R. Scott. (3–6)

SMITH, FRANCES C. *The First Book of Conservation.* Franklin Watts, Inc., 1954. (4–7)

STAMBLER, IRWIN. *Space Ship: The Story of the X-15.* G. P. Putnam's Sons, 1961. (5–7)

SULLIVAN, GAVIN. *Pioneer Germ Fighters.* Atheneum Publishers, 1962. (5–9)

TEE-VAN, HELEN DAMROSCH. *The Trees Around Us.* The Dial Press, Inc., 1960. (1–4)

WOLFE, LOUIS. *Probing the Atmosphere: The Story of Meteorology.* G. P. Putnam's Sons, 1961. (6–8)

WYLER, ROSE and AMES, GERALD. *The Golden Book of Biology: A Child's Introduction to the Science of Life.* Golden Press, Inc., 1961. (4–8)

STORIES ABOUT BOYS

BERQUIST, GRACE. *The Boy Who Couldn't Roar.* Abingdon Press, 1960. (1–3)

BESKOW, ELSA. *Pelle's New Suit.* Harper & Bros., 1929. (PS–3)

BROWN, MARCIA. *Dick Whittington and His Cat.* Charles Scribner's Sons, 1950. (K–4)

BURTON, VIRGINIA. *Mike Mulligan and His Steam Shovel.* Houghton Mifflin Co., 1939. (1–3)

CARLSON, NATALIE S. *Alphonse, That Bearded One.* Harcourt, Brace & World, Inc., 1954. (3–5)

GARRETT, HELEN. *Angelo the Naughty One.* The Viking Press, Inc., 1944. (K–3)

GRAMATKY, HARDY. *Hercules.* G. P. Putnam's Sons, 1940. (K–3)

JOHNSON, CROCKETT. *Harold and the Purple Crayon.* Harper & Bros., 1958. (PS–2)

JUSTUS, MAY. *New Boy in School.* Hastings House Publishers, Inc., 1962. (4–6)

AMERICAN MUSEUM OF NATURAL HISTORY

THE TRAPDOOR SPIDER (*above*) lives alone in a silk-lined tunnel under the ground, closing the door firmly behind him with a plug of dirt. The female lays her eggs in a silken cocoon, for which she shows great maternal concern. Some wasps, such as the *Polistes* (*right*), are more sociable creatures; they build a communal nest out of paper that they manufacture by chewing wood to a pulp. As cells are made, the queen lays eggs in them; these become larvae.

U.S. DEPARTMENT OF AGRICULTURE

HELEN BUTTFIELD

AN OLD MAN with a bird's-nest beard stands in the doorway of his junk shop in Istanbul.

LEXAU, JOAN. *Olaf Is Late.* The Dial Press, Inc., 1963. (K–2)

McCLOSKEY, ROBERT. *Homer Price.* The Viking Press, Inc., 1943. (3–6)

OLSEN, IB SPANG. *The Boy in the Moon.* Abingdon Press, 1963. (K–3)

STORIES ABOUT GIRLS

ANDERSON, NEIL. *Freckle Face.* Thomas Y. Crowell Co., 1957. (K–3)

BEMELMANS, LUDWIG. *Madeline.* The Viking Press, Inc. (K–3)

BEMELMANS, LUDWIG. *Madeline's Rescue.* The Viking Press, Inc., 1953. (K–3)

BOTHWELL, JEAN. *Omen for a Princess.* Abelard-Schuman Ltd., 1963. (5 up)

BUCKLEY, HELEN. *Where Did Josie Go?* Lothrop, Lee & Shepard Co., Inc., 1962. (PS–1)

CAUDILL, REBECCA. *The Best-loved Doll.* Holt, Rinehart & Winston, Inc., 1962. (K–3)

COOMBS, PATRICIA. *Dorrie's Magic.* Lothrop, Lee & Shepard Co., Inc., 1962. (1–4)

FIELD, RACHEL. *Hitty: Her First Hundred Years.* The Macmillan Co., 1929. (4–6)

FRANÇOISE. *Minou.* Charles Scribner's Sons, 1962. (PS–2)

HUNT, MABEL L. *Little Girl with Seven Names.* J. B. Lippincott Co., 1936. (3–4)

LEXAU, JOAN. *Millicent's Ghost.* The Dial Press, Inc., 1962. (PS–2)

JUNIOR AND SENIOR HIGH SCHOOL

School grade for which each book is recommended is shown in parentheses.

ADVENTURE AND TRAVEL

DEFOE, DANIEL. *Robinson Crusoe.* Scribner's, 1958. (7–9)

FORESTER, C. S. *Captain Horatio Hornblower.* Little, Brown & Co., 1939. (9 up)

GILSON, CHARLES. *The Clash of Fleets: The Story of Ten Great Sea Battles.* Abelard-Schuman Ltd., 1963. (7 up)

HEYERDAHL, THOR. *Kon-Tiki.* Rand McNally & Co., 1950. (7 up)

LINDBERGH, CHARLES A. *Spirit of St. Louis.* Charles Scribner's Sons, 1956. (9 up)

LONDON, JACK. *Jack London Stories.* The Platt & Munk Co., Inc., 1960. (7–9)

NORDHOFF, CHARLES and HALL, JAMES N. *Mutiny on the Bounty.* Little, Brown & Co., 1932. (9 up)

RAU, SANTHA RAMA. *My Russian Journey.* Harper & Bros., 1959. (9 up)

SKINNER, CORNELIA OTIS and KIMBROUGH, EMILY. *Our Hearts Were Young and Gay.* Dodd, Mead & Co., 1942. (9 up)

STEVENSON, ROBERT LOUIS. *Kidnapped.* Scribner's, 1886. (7 up)

STEVENSON, ROBERT LOUIS. *Treasure Island.* Charles Scribner's Sons, 1886. (7 up)

STEINBECK, JOHN. *Travels with Charley.* The Viking Press, Inc., 1962. (9 up)

THOMPSON, ESTELLE. *A Twig Is Bent.* Abelard-Schuman, 1962. (9–12)

VERNE, JULES. *Around the World in Eighty Days.* Dodd, Mead & Co., 1872. (7 up)

VERNE, JULES. *Twenty Thousand Leagues Under the Sea.* Charles Scribner's Sons, 1869. (7 up)

WELLS, H. G. *Seven Science Fiction Novels.* Dover Publications, Inc., 1950. (9 up)

WOUK, HERMAN. *Caine Mutiny.* Doubleday & Co., Inc., 1951. (11–12)

AMERICA

BENARY-ISBERT, MARGOT. *The Long Way Home.* Harcourt, Brace & World, Inc., 1959. (6–9)

CATTON, BRUCE. *The Battle of Gettysburg* (Junior Library). American Heritage, 1963. (9 up)

CATTON, BRUCE. *This Hallowed Ground.* Doubleday & Co., Inc., 1962. (7 up)

COOPER, JAMES FENIMORE. *Last of the Mohicans.* Charles Scribner's Sons. (8 up)

COOPER, JAMES FENIMORE. *The Leatherstocking Saga.* Pantheon Books, Inc., 1954. (8 up)

DICK, TRELLA LAMSON. *The Island on the Border: A Civil War Story.* Abelard-Schuman, 1963. (5–10)

FERBER, EDNA. *Cimarron.* Grosset & Dunlap, Inc., Publishers. (11 up).

FOLEY, RAE. *Famous American Spies.* Dodd, Mead & Co., 1962. (6–8)

FORBES, ESTHER. *Johnny Tremain: A Novel for Old & Young.* Houghton Mifflin Co., 1943. (7–9)

JACKSON, SHIRLEY. *The Witchcraft of Salem Village* (Landmark Books). Random House, Inc., 1956. (5–9)

JAMES, WILL. *Will James' Book of Cowboy Stories.* Charles Scribner's Sons, 1951. (7–9)

JANEWAY, ELIZABETH. *The Early Days of Automobiles* (Landmark Books). Random House, Inc., 1956. (5–9)

LANCASTER, BRUCE and PLUMB, J. H. *The Revolution* (American Heritage Books). American Heritage Publishing Co., Inc., 1957. (9 up)

LAWSON, DON. *The United States in World War I; The Story of General John J. Pershing and the American Expeditionary Forces.* Abelard-Schuman, 1963. (7–12)

LAWSON, DON. *The United States in World War II: Crusade for Freedom.* Abelard-Schuman Ltd., 1963. (7–12)

LAWSON, TED W. *Thirty Seconds over Tokyo* (Landmark Books). Random House, Inc., 1953. (5–9)

LORD, WALTER. *The Good Years: From 1900 to the First World War.* Harper & Bros., 1960. (10 up)

MARSHALL, S. L. A. *World War I* (American Heritage Books). American Heritage Publishing Co., Inc., 1964. (9 up)

MITCHELL, MARGARET. *Gone with the Wind.* The Macmillan Co., 1961. (11–12)

RICHTER, CONRAD. *The Light in the Forest.* Alfred A. Knopf, Inc., 1953. (9 up)

ROBERTS, KENNETH. *Northwest Passage.* Doubleday & Co., Inc., 1959. (11 up)

SCHAEFER, JACK W. *Shane.* Houghton Mifflin Co., 1954. (7 up)

SCHECHTER, BETTY. *The Peaceable Revolution.* Houghton Mifflin Co., 1963. (7–12)

SETON, ANYA. *The Winthrop Woman.* Houghton Mifflin Co., 1958. (9 up)

TUCHMAN, BARBARA. *The Guns of August.* The Macmillan Co., 1962. (9 up)

WHITE, THEODORE H. *The Making of the President, 1960.* Atheneum Publishers, 1961. (10 up)

WISTER, OWEN. *The Virginian.* Grosset & Dunlap, Inc. (9 up)

ANCIENT WORLD

COSTAIN, THOMAS B. *The Silver Chalice.* Doubleday & Co., Inc., 1952. (11 up)

DAVIS, W. S. *A Day in Old Rome.* Biblo & Tannen Booksellers & Publishers, Inc., 1963. (10–12)

DOUGLAS, LLOYD. *The Robe.* Houghton Mifflin Co., 1942. (9 up)

HAMILTON, EDITH. *The Greek Way.* W. W. Norton & Co., Inc., 1949. (11 up)

PFEIFFER, JOHN E. and COON, CARLETON S. (consultant). *The Search for Early Man* (Horizon Caravel Books). American Heritage Publishing Co., Inc., 1963. (9 up)

RUGOFF, MILTON and GOODRICH, L. CARRINGTON (consultant). *Marco Polo's Adventures in China* (Horizon Caravel Books). American Heritage Publishing Co., Inc., 1964. (9 up)

WELLS, R. F. *On Land & Sea with Caesar.* Biblo & Tannen Booksellers & Publishers, Inc., 1963. (10–12)

NEW YORK PUBLIC LIBRARY

FANTASTIC FLYING MACHINE, designed in the United States in the nineteenth century.

ANIMALS

ADAMSON, JOY. *Born Free.* Pantheon Books, Inc., 1960. (9 up)

BAGNOLD, ENID. *National Velvet.* William Morrow, 1949. (7 up)

FARLEY, WALTER. *Man O'War.* Random House, Inc., 1962. (7 up)

LONDON, JACK. *Call of the Wild.* The Macmillan Co., 1903. (6–9)

NEVILE, EMILY CHENEY. *It's Like This, Cat.* Harper & Row, 1963. (7–9)

RAWLINGS, MARJORIE K. *The Yearling.* Scribner's, 1939. (7–9)

TERHUNE, ALBERT PAYSON. *Lad: A Dog.* E. P. Dutton, 1959. (6–9)

ART

CHENEY, SHELDON W. *Story of Modern Art.* The Viking Press, Inc., 1958. (9 up)

CRAVEN, THOMAS. *The Rainbow Book of Art.* The World Publishing Co., 1956. (7–9)

HOLME, BRYAN (ed.). *Pictures to Live With.* The Viking Press, Inc., 1959. (7 up)

MUNRO, ELEANOR C. *The Golden Encyclopedia of Art: Painting, Sculpture, Architecture, and Ornament, from Prehistoric Times to the Twentieth Century.* Golden Press, Inc., 1961. (9 up)

RUSKIN, ARIANE. *The Pantheon Story of Art for Young People.* Pantheon Books, Inc., 1964. (7–9)

TAYLOR, FRANCIS H. *Fifty Centuries of Art.* Harper Bros., 1960. (9 up)

BIOGRAPHY

ANDRIST, RALPH K. and SCHLESINGER, ARTHUR M., JR. (consultant). *Andrew Jackson, Soldier and Statesman* (Junior Library). American Heritage, 1963. (10 up)

BAKER, RACHEL. *Chaim Weizmann: Builder of a Nation.* Julian Messner, Inc., 1950. (7–9)

COMMAGER, HENRY S. *America's Robert E. Lee.* Houghton Mifflin Co., 1951. (7–9)

DONOVAN, FRANK R. and BELL, WHITFIELD J. *The Many Worlds of Benjamin Franklin* (Junior Library). American Heritage Publishing Co., Inc., 1964. (9 up)

FRANK, ANNE. *Anne Frank: Diary of a Young Girl.* Doubleday & Co., Inc., 1952. (9 up)

JENKINS, ELIZABETH. *Elizabeth the Great.* Coward-McCann, Inc., 1959. (9–12)

KELLER, HELEN A. *The Story of My Life.* Doubleday, 1954. (7–9)

KIELTY, BERNARDINE. *Marie Antoinette.* Random House, 1955. (7–9)

NOBLE, IRIS. *Clarence Darrow: Defense Attorney.* Julian Messner, Inc., 1958. (7–9)

NOBLE, IRIS. *Egypt's Queen: Cleopatra.* Julian Messner, Inc., 1963. (7–9)

NOBLE, IRIS. *Joseph Pulitzer.* Julian Messner, Inc., 1957. (7–9)

ROOSEVELT, ELEANOR. *This I Remember.* Harper & Bros., 1949. (9 up)

SHIPPEN, KATHERINE B. *Leif Eriksson.* Harper & Bros., 1951. (7–9)

STONE, IRVING. *The President's Lady.* Doubleday & Co., Inc., 1941. (9 up)

VANCE, MARGUERITE. *Scotland's Queen: The Story of Mary Stuart.* E. P. Dutton & Co., Inc., 1962. (7 up)

STORIES FOR YOUNG PEOPLE

BENSON, SALLY. *Junior Miss.* Doubleday & Co., Inc. (7 up)

CATHER, WILLA. *My Antonia.* Houghton Mifflin Co., 1918. (9 up)

CAVANNA, BETTY. *A Time for Tenderness.* William Morrow & Co., Inc., 1962. (8–10)

Luftreise des Herrn Blanchards zu Nürmberg, Anno. 1787.

NEW YORK PUBLIC LIBRARY

THE POSSIBILITY OF FLYING is one theme that has always made man's imagination soar.

DALY, MAUREEN. *Seventeenth Summer.* Dodd, Mead, 1948. (7 up)

DU JARDIN, ROSAMOND. *Boy Trouble.* J. B. Lippincott Co., 1953. (7 up)

FORBES, KATHRYN. *Mama's Bank Account.* Harcourt, Brace & World, Inc., 1943. (8 up)

GLASGOW, ELLEN. *Vein of Iron.* Harcourt, Brace & World, Inc., 1935. (9 up)

HOLT, VICTORIA. *Mistress of Mellyn.* Doubleday & Co., Inc., 1960. (9 up)

LOVELACE, MAUD H. *Betsy and the Great World.* The Crowell-Collier Publishing Co., 1952. (7–9)

MEANS, FLORENCE C. *Reach For A Star.* Houghton Mifflin Co., 1957. (7–12)

MORLEY, CHRISTOPHER. *Parnassus on Wheels.* Lippincott, 1955. (9 up)

PENNOYER, SARA. *Maggie in Fashion.* Dodd, Mead & Co., 1961. (8–10)

STOLZ, MARY. *Ready or Not.* Harper & Bros., 1953. (9–11)

STOLZ, MARY. *The Sea Gulls Woke Me.* Harper & Bros., 1951. (9–11)

THANE, ELSWYTH. *Dawn's Early Light.* Duell, Sloan & Pearce, Inc., (9 up)

WHITNEY, PHYLLIS. *The Highest Dream.* David McKay Co., Inc., 1956. (7–9)

HISTORY

DONOVAN, FRANK R. and KENDRICK, THOMAS D. (consultant). *The Vikings* (Horizon Caravel Books). American Heritage Publishing Co., Inc., 1964. (9 up)

GUNTHER, JOHN. *Inside Europe Today.* Harper & Bros., 1962. (10 up)

HEROLD, J. CHRISTOPHER. *The Age of Napoleon* (Horizon Books). American Heritage Publishing Co., Inc., 1963. (9 up)

HERSEY, JOHN. *Hiroshima.* Alfred A. Knopf, Inc., 1946. (9 up)

MOSCOW, HENRY and BLACK, CYRIL E. (consultant). *Russia Under the Czars* (Horizon Caravel Books). American Heritage Publishing Co., Inc., 1962. (7–10)

REYNOLDS, ROBERT L. and MACARTHUR, DOUGLAS, II (consultant). *Commodore Perry and Japan* (Junior Library). American Heritage Publishing Co., Inc., 1963. (9 up)

SELINKO, ANNEMARIE. *Desirée.* William Morrow & Co., Inc., 1953. (9 up)

SHIRER, WILLIAM L. *The Rise and Fall of the Third Reich.* Simon & Schuster, Inc., 1960. (9 up)

VARBLE, RACHEL M. *Three Against London.* Doubleday & Co., Inc. (7–8)

WILLIAMS, JAY and LIGHTBODY, CHARLES WAYLAND (consultant). *Joan of Arc* (Horizon Caravel Books). American Heritage Publishing Co., Inc., 1963. (9 up)

MUSIC AND DANCE

BERNSTEIN, LEONARD. *The Joy of Music.* Simon & Schuster, Inc., 1959. (9 up)

COMMINS, DOROTHY B. *All About the Symphony and What It Plays.* Random House, Inc., 1961. (7–10)

CROSS, MILTON. *The New Milton Cross' Complete Stories of the Great Operas* (rev. ed.). Edited by Karl Kohrs. Doubleday & Co., Inc., 1955. (9 up)

DE MILLE, AGNES. *The Book of the Dance.* Golden Press, Inc., 1963. (7 up)

LEWIS, RICHARD. *In Praise of Music.* Orion Press, 1964. (9–12)

POSELL, ELSA. *American Composers.* Houghton Mifflin Co., 1963. (7 up)

SAMACHSON, DOROTHY and JOSEPH. *The Fabulous World of the Opera.* Rand McNally & Co., 1962. (8 up)

MYSTERY AND SUSPENSE

DOYLE, ARTHUR CONAN. *Adventures of Sherlock Holmes.* Harper & Bros., 1892. (9 up)

DU MAURIER, DAPHNE. *Rebecca.* Doubleday & Co., Inc. (11 up)

MONTAGUE, EWEN. *Man Who Never Was.* J. B. Lippincott Co., 1954. (9 up)

ORCZY, EMMUSKA. *Scarlet Pimpernel.* G. P. Putnam's Sons, 1905. (9 up)

POE, EDGAR ALLAN. *Gold-bug and Other Tales and Poems.* The Macmillan Co., 1953. (7 up)

RINEHART, MARY ROBERT. *Mary Roberts Rinehart's Mystery Book.* Holt, Rinehart & Winston, Inc., 1947. (9 up)

STEVENSON, ROBERT LOUIS. *Dr. Jekyll and Mr. Hyde, and Other Stories.* Coward-McCann, Inc. (9 up)

STEWART, MARY. *The Moon-spinners.* William Morrow & Co., Inc., 1963. (9 up)

STEWART, MARY. *Nine Coaches Waiting.* William Morrow & Co., Inc., 1959. (9 up)

MYTHOLOGY AND FOLKLORE

BULFINCH, THOMAS. *Mythology.* Crowell-Collier Co. (9 up)

HAMILTON, EDITH. *Mythology.* Little, Brown & Co., 1942. (7 up)

PICARD, BARBARA LEONIE. *The Iliad of Homer.* Henry Z. Walck, Inc., 1960. (7–9)

SAINT-EXUPÉRY, ANTOINE DE. *The Little Prince.* Harcourt, Brace & World, Inc., 1943. (7 up)

SUTCLIFF, ROSEMARY. *Beowulf.* E. P. Dutton & Co., Inc., 1962. (7–12)

TAYLOR, N. B. *The Aeneid of Virgil.* Henry Z. Walck, Inc., 1961. (7–9)

CLASSICS—OLD AND NEW

AUSTEN, JANE. *Pride and Prejudice.* Dodd, Mead & Co., 1813. (9 up)

BENÊT, STEPHEN VINCENT. *The Devil and Daniel Webster.* Holt, Rinehart & Winston, Inc., 1937. (9 up)

BLACKMORE, RICHARD D. *Lorna Doone.* Dodd, Mead & Co., 1943. (7 up)

BRONTË, CHARLOTTE. *Jane Eyre.* Dodd, Mead & Co. (7 up)

BRONTË, EMILY. *Wuthering Heights.* Dodd, Mead & Co., 1847. (7 up)

CHUTE, MARCHETTE. *Stories from Shakespeare.* The World Publishing Co., 1956. (7–9)

CONRAD, JOSEPH. *Lord Jim.* Doubleday & Co., Inc. (11 up)

CRANE, STEPHEN. *The Red Badge of Courage.* Appleton-Century-Crofts. (7 up)

DANA, RICHARD HENRY. *Two Years Before the Mast.* Dodd, Mead & Co. (9 up)

DICKENS, CHARLES. *David Copperfield.* Dodd, Mead & Co., 1850. (7 up)

DICKENS, CHARLES. *Great Expectations.* Dodd, Mead & Co. (7 up)

DICKENS, CHARLES. *Oliver Twist.* Dodd, Mead & Co. (7 up)

DUMAS, ALEXANDRE. *Count of Monte Cristo.* Dodd, Mead & Co. (7 up)

DUMAS, ALEXANDER. *Three Musketeers.* Dodd, Mead & Co., 1844. (7 up)

ELIOT, GEORGE. *Silas Marner.* Dodd, Mead & Co. (9 up)

GALSWORTHY, JOHN. *The Forsyte Saga.* Charles Scribner's Sons, 1933. (11 up)

GILBRETH, FRANK B., JR. *Cheaper by the Dozen.* The Crowell-Collier Publishing Co., 1963. (7 up)

HAWTHORNE, NATHANIEL. *The House of Seven Gables.* Dodd, Mead & Co. (9 up)

HAWTHORNE, NATHANIEL. *The Scarlet Letter.* Dodd, Mead & Co. (9 up)

HEMINGWAY, ERNEST. *The Old Man and the Sea.* Charles Scribner's Sons, 1952. (11 up)

HERSEY, JOHN R. *A Bell for Adano.* Alfred A. Knopf, Inc., 1944. (9 up)

HIEATT, A. K. and CONSTANCE. *The Canterbury Tales.* Golden Press, Inc., 1961. (7 up)

HILTON, JAMES. *Good-bye, Mr. Chips.* Little, Brown & Co., 1934. (9 up)

HILTON, JAMES. *Lost Horizon.* William Morrow & Co., Inc., 1936. (9 up)

HUGO, VICTOR. *The Hunchback of Notre Dame.* Dodd, Mead & Co.

HUGO, VICTOR. *Les Misérables.* Dodd, Mead & Co. (9 up)

HULME, KATHRYN. *The Nun's Story.* Little, Brown & Co., 1956. (11 up)

KIPLING, RUDYARD. *Captains Courageous.* Doubleday & Co., Inc., 1953. (7 up)

KIPLING, RUDYARD. *Kim.* Doubleday & Co., Inc., 1899. (7–9)

KIPLING, RUDYARD. *Kipling Stories.* The Platt & Munk Co., Inc., 1960. (7–9)

LEE, HARPER. *To Kill a Mockingbird.* J. B. Lippincott Co., 1960. (10 up)

LLEWELLYN, RICHARD. *How Green Was My Valley.* The Macmillan Co., 1940. (11 up)

MARQUAND, JOHN P. *The Late George Apley.* Little, Brown & Co., 1937. (11 up)

MAUGHAM, W. SOMERSET. *Of Human Bondage.* Doubleday & Co., Inc. (11 up)

MELVILLE, HERMAN. *Moby Dick.* Dodd, Mead & Co., 1851. (9 up)

SAINT EXUPÉRY, ANTOINE DE. *Wind, Sand and Stars.* Harcourt, Brace & World, Inc., 1939. (9 up)

SMITH, BETTY. *A Tree Grows in Brooklyn.* Harper & Bros. (9 up)

SCOTT, WALTER. *Ivanhoe.* Dodd, Mead & Co. (9 up)

SWIFT, JONATHAN. *Gulliver's Travels.* Grosset & Dunlap, Inc., Publishers, (7–9)

TARKINGTON, BOOTH. *Penrod.* Doubleday & Co., Inc., 1931. (7–9)

THACKERAY, WILLIAM. *Vanity Fair.* Dodd, Mead & Co. (9 up)

TOLSTOY, LEO. *Anna Karenina.* Translated by Constance Garnett. The Modern Library, Inc. (10 up)

TWAIN, MARK. *A Connecticut Yankee in King Arthur's Court.* Harper & Bros., 1899. (9 up)

WALLACE, LEW. *Ben Hur.* Dodd, Mead & Co. (9 up)

WILDER, THORNTON. *Bridge of San Luis Rey.* Grosset & Dunlap, Inc., Publishers. (10 up)

WOLFE, THOMAS. *Look Homeward, Angel.* Scribner's. (9 up)

WRIGHT, LOUIS B. (consultant) and the editors of *Horizon. Shakespeare's England* (Horizon Caravel Books). American Heritage Publishing Co., Inc., 1964. (9 up)

OTHER LANDS

ASIMOV, ISAAC and BOYD, WILLIAM C. *Races and People.* Abelard-Schuman Ltd., 1955. (7–12)

BUCK, PEARL. *The Good Earth.* The John Day Co., Inc., 1949. (9 up)

DENNIS, LLOYD and FIELD, JOHN S. *Land of Promise.* Abelard-Schuman Ltd., 1962. (7–12)

LANDON, MARGARET. *Anna and the King of Siam.* The John Day Co., Inc., 1947. (7 up)

LAVOLLE, L. N. *The Key to the Desert.* Translated by Hugh Shelley. Abelard-Schuman Ltd., 1963. (7–12)

LEDERER, WILLIAM J. and BURDICK, EUGENE. *The Ugly American.* W. W. Norton & Co., Inc., 1958. (9 up)

LEVIN, MEYER. *The Story of Israel for Young People.* Random House, 1964. (9 up)

MEAD, MARGARET. *People and Places.* The World Publishing Co., 1959. (7 up)

MICHENER, JAMES A. *Bridges at Toko-Ri.* Random House, 1953. (9–12)

PATON, ALAN. *Cry, The Beloved Country.* Charles Scribner's Sons, 1948. (11 up)

REMARQUE, ERICH MARIA. *All Quiet on the Western Front.* Little, Brown & Co., 1929. (9 up)

URIS, LEON. *Exodus.* Doubleday & Co., Inc., 1958. (10 up)

POETRY

BROWNING, ELIZABETH BARRETT. *Sonnets from the Portuguese.* Peter Pauper Press. (9 up)

LEWIS, RICHARD. *The Moment of Wonder.* Dial Press, 1964. (9–12)

SANDBURG, CARL. *The People, Yes.* Harcourt, Brace & World, Inc., 1936. (9 up)

WHITMAN, WALT. *Leaves of Grass.* The Modern Library, Inc. (9 up)

SCIENCE

ASIMOV, ISAAC. *Inside the Atom.* Abelard-Schuman Ltd., 1961. (7 up)

ASIMOV, ISAAC. *The Kingdom of the Sun* (rev. ed.). Abelard-Schuman Ltd., 1963. (7–12)

ASIMOV, ISAAC. *Realm of Measure.* Houghton Mifflin Co., 1960. (7 up)

SUSAN WEILEY

OPERA, an art form that intimately fuses music and drama, produces a strong emotional impact. The scene is from a 1965 Metropolitan Opera production of Verdi's *Il Trovatore.*

HOKUSAI. "GREAT WAVE." FOGG ART MUSEUM

THE STRENGTH OF THE SEA, captured in a Japanese print as in Carson's *The Sea Around Us.*

ASIMOV, ISAAC. *The World of Carbon.* Abelard-Schuman, 1958. (9 up)

BRUCKNER, KARL. *The Golden Pharaoh.* Pantheon Books, Inc., 1959. (7 up)

CARSON, RACHEL. *The Sea Around Us.* Oxford University Press, Inc., 1961. (10 up)

CARSON, RACHEL. *Silent Spring.* Houghton Mifflin Co., 1962. (9 up)

COUSTEAU, JACQUES YVES and DUMAS, FRÉDÉRIC. *Silent World.* Harper & Bros., 1953. (7 up)

DUBOS, RENÉ. *The Unseen World.* Oxford University Press, Inc., 1962. (9 up)

GLEMSER, BERNARD. *All About Biology.* Random House, 1964. (7–9)

LEERBURGER, BENEDICT A., JR. *Josiah W. Gibbs: American Theoretical Physicist* (Immortals of Science series). Franklin Watts, Inc., 1963. (8–12)

RAVIELLI, ANTHONY. *Wonders of the Human Body.* The Viking Press, Inc., 1954. (6–9)

RIEDMAN, SARAH R. *Your Blood and You: The Story of Circulation* (rev. ed.). Abelard-Schuman Ltd., 1963. (7–12)

RIEDMAN, SARAH R. and GUSTAFSON, ELTON. *Portraits of Nobel Laureates in Medicine and Physiology.* Abelard-Schuman, 1963. (7–12)

SEABORG, GLENN T. and VALENS, EVANS G. *Elements of the Universe.* E. P. Dutton & Co., Inc., 1958. (9 up)

WRIGHT, HELEN and RAPAPORT, SAMUEL. *The Amazing World of Medicine.* Harper & Bros., 1961. (7 up)

SOCIAL COMMENTARY

BURDICK, EUGENE and WHEELER, HARVEY. *Fail-Safe.* McGraw-Hill, Inc., 1962. (9 up)

GOLDING, WILLIAM. *Lord of the Flies.* Coward-McCann, Inc., 1962. (9 up)

LEWIS, SINCLAIR. *Arrowsmith.* Harcourt, Brace & World, Inc. (11 up)

LEWIS, SINCLAIR. *Main Street.* Harcourt, Brace & World, Inc. (9 up)

ORWELL, GEORGE. *Animal Farm.* Harcourt, Brace & World, Inc., 1954. (10 up)

ORWELL, GEORGE. *Nineteen Eighty-four.* Harcourt, Brace & World, Inc., 1949. (10 up)

PACKARD, VANCE. *The Status Seekers.* David McKay, 1959. (9 up)

THOREAU, HENRY DAVID. *Walden.* Dodd, Mead & Co. (10 up)

ADULT BOOKS

REFERENCE BOOKS

BARTLETT, JOHN (comp.). *Familiar Quotations: A Collection of Passages, Phrases and Proverbs Traced to Their Sources in Ancient and Modern Literature.* Little, Brown & Co., 1955.

GRIGSON, GEOFFREY (ed.). *The Concise Encyclopedia of Modern World Literature.* Hawthorne Books, 1963.

HART, JAMES D. (ed.). *Oxford Companion to American Literature.* Oxford University Press, 1956.

HARVEY, PAUL (ed.). *Oxford Companion to English Literature.* Oxford University Press, Inc., 1946.

HERZBERG, MAX J. (ed.). *The Reader's Encyclopedia of American Literature.* Thomas Y. Crowell Company, 1962.

KUNITZ, STANLEY J. and HAYCRAFT, HOWARD. *Twentieth Century Authors: A Biographical Dictionary of Modern Literature.* The H. W. Wilson Co., 1955.

MAGILL, FRANK N. with McGREENE, IAN P. (eds.). *Masterpieces of Christian Literature in Summary Form.* Harper & Row, Publishers, 1963.

MAGILL, FRANK (ed.). *Masterpieces of World Literature in Digest Form* (3rd ed.). Harper & Bros., 1960.

SPENDER, STEPHEN and HALL, DONALD (eds.). *The Concise Encyclopedia of English and American Poets and Poetry.* Hawthorn Books, Inc., 1963.

STEINBERG, SIEGFRIED (ed.). *Cassell's Encyclopedia of World Literature* 2 vols. Funk & Wagnalls, 1954.

THRALL, WILLIAM FLINT. *A Handbook to Literature.* The Odyssey Press, Inc., 1960.

GENERAL CRITICISM

ALLOTT, MIRIAM (comp.). *Novelists on the Novel.* Columbia University Press, 1959.

BOWRA, C. M. *Heroic Poetry.* St. Martin's Press, Inc., 1952.

BROOKS, CLEANTH (ed.). *Tragic Themes in Western Literature.* Yale University Press, 1960.

CAMPBELL, JOSEPH. *The Hero With a Thousand Faces.* Bollingen Foundation, 1962.

DAICHES, DAVID. *The Novel and the Modern World.* The University of Chicago Press, 1960.

ELLIOTT, ROBERT C. *The Power of Satire: Magic, Ritual, Art.* Princeton University Press, 1960.

EMPSON, WILLIAM. *Seven Types of Ambiguity.* The World Publishing Co., 1963.

FEINBERG, LEONARD. *The Satirist.* Iowa State University Press, 1963.

HAVIGHURST, WALTER. *Masters of the Modern Short Story.* Harcourt, Brace & World, Inc., 1962.

HEROLD, J. CHRISTOPHER. *The Age of Napoleon.* Harper & Row, Publishers, 1963.

HUGHES, H. STUART. *History as Art and as Science.* Harper & Row, Publishers, 1964.

JAMES, HENRY. *The Art of the Novel.*

HELEN BUTTFIELD

POETRY OF NATURE: a Thorean theme.

Edited by R. P. Blackman. Charles Scribner's Sons, 1934.

LUBBOCK, PERCY. *The Craft of Fiction.* Charles Scribner's Sons, 1921.

LUKACS, GEORG. *The Historical Novel.* Basic Books, Inc., 1963.

MACY, JOHN A. *Story of the World's Literature.* Liveright Publishing Corp., 1950.

PRIESTLEY, JOHN BOYNTON. *Literature and Western Man.* Harper & Bros., 1960.

SCHOLES, ROBERT. *Approaches to the Novel.* Chandler Publishing Company, 1961.

STANFORD, W. B. *The Ulysses Theme.* The Macmillan Co., 1955.

THOMPSON, STITH. *The Folktale.* Holt, Rinehart & Winston, Inc., 1960.

WATT, IAN. *The Rise of the Novel.* University of California Press, 1957.

WELLEK, R. *History of Modern Criticism, 1750–1950.* 3 vols. Yale University Press, 1955.

WIMSATT, WILLIAM K. and BROOKS, CLEANTH. *Literary Criticism: A Short History.* Alfred A. Knopf, Inc., 1957.

POETRY ANTHOLOGIES

UNTERMEYER, LOUIS. *Modern American Poetry and Modern British Poetry: Combined New and Enlarged Edition.* Harcourt, Brace & World, Inc., 1962.

VAN DOREN, MARK. *An Anthology of World Poetry.* Harcourt, Brace & World, Inc., 1964.

AFRICAN LITERATURE

HUGHES, LANGSTON (ed.). *An African Treasury.* Crown Publishers, Inc., 1960.

AMERICAN LITERATURE

History and Criticism

ALDRIDGE, JOHN W. *After the Lost Generation.* McGraw-Hill, Inc., 1951.

ALLEN, GAY W. *The Solitary Singer: A Critical Biography of Walt Whitman.* The Macmillan Co., 1955.

ANDERSON, CHARLES ROBERTS. *Emily Dickinson's Poetry.* Holt, Rinehart & Winston, Inc., 1960.

BEACH, JOSEPH WARREN. *Obsessive Images.* University of Minnesota Press, 1960.

BROWER, REUBEN A. *The Poetry of Robert Frost: Constellations of Intention.* Oxford University Press, Inc., 1963.

CARGILL, OSCAR. *The Novels of Henry James.* The Macmillan Co., 1961.

COWLEY, MALCOLM. *After the Genteel Tradition: American Writers Since 1910.* W. W. Norton, 1937.

DAVIDSON, EDWARD. *Poe: A Critical Study.* Harvard University Press, 1957.

DORSON, RICHARD M. *American Folklore.* University of Chicago Press, 1954.

GWYNN, FREDERICK L. and BLOTNER, JOSEPH L. *The Fiction of J. D. Salinger.* University of Pittsburgh Press, Inc., 1963.

HEDLAND, LAURENCE. *The Expense of Vision: Essays on the Craft of Henry James.* Princeton University Press, 1964.

HOFFMAN, FREDERICK J. *The Twenties: American Writing in the Postwar Decade.* The Viking Press, Inc., 1955.

HOWARD, LEON. *Literature and the American Tradition.* Doubleday & Co., Inc., 1960.

HOWE, IRVING. *William Faulkner: A Critical Study.* Random House, Inc., 1952.

HUBBELL, J. B. *The South in American Literature, 1607–1900.* Duke University Press, 1954.

JONES, H. M. *Guide to American Literature and Its Backgrounds Since 1890* (rev. ed.). Harvard University Press, 1959.

LEISY, ERNEST. *The American Historical Novel.* University of Oklahoma Press, 1950.

LISCA, PETER. *The Wide World of John Steinbeck.* Rutgers University Press, 1958.

LONGLEY, JOHN LEWIS, JR. *The Tragic Mask—A Study of Faulkner's Heroes.* University of North Carolina Press, 1963.

LYDE, MARILYN JONES. *Edith Wharton: Convention and Morality in the Work of a Novelist.* University of Oklahoma Press, 1959.

MATTHIESSEN, F. O. *American Renaissance: Art and Expression in the Age of Emerson and Whitman.* Oxford University Press, 1941.

MAXWELL, D. E. S. *American Fiction: The Intellectual Background.* Columbia University Press, 1963.

MILLER, PERRY (ed.). *The Golden Age of American Literature.* George Braziller, Inc., 1963.

MUMFORD, LEWIS. *Herman Melville: A Study of His Life and Vision.* Harcourt, Brace & World, Inc., 1963.

PARRINGTON, V. L., JR. *American Dreams: A Study of American Utopias.* Little, Brown & Co., 1947.

PARRINGTON, V. L., JR. (ed.). *The Connecticut Wits.* Harcourt, Brace & World, Inc., 1926.

PARRINGTON, V. L., JR. *Main Currents in American Thought.* Harcourt, Brace & World, Inc., 1935.

PATTEE, F. L. *Development of the American Short Story.* Harper & Bros., 1923.

PRITCHARD, JOHN D. *Criticism in America.* University of Oklahoma Press, 1956.

QUINN, A. H. and others. *The Literature of the American People: An Historical and Critical Survey.* Appleton-Century-Crofts, 1951.

SPILLER, ROBERT E. *The Cycle of American Literature: An Essay in Historical Criticism.* The Macmillan Co., 1955.

SPILLER, ROBERT E. and others. *Literary History of the United States.* 4 vols. The Macmillan Co., 1948.

STEVENSON, ELIZABETH. *Henry Adams.* The Macmillan Co., 1955.

STEWART, RANDALL. *Nathaniel Hawthorne.* Yale University Press, 1948.

THORP, W. *American Writing in the Twentieth Century.* Harvard University Press, 1962.

WAGENKNECHT, EDWARD. *Calvacade of the American Novel: From the Birth of the Nation to the Middle of the Twentieth Century.* Holt, Rinehart & Winston, Inc., 1952.

WAGENKNECHT, EDWARD. *Mark Twain: The Man and His Work.* University of Oklahoma Press, 1961.

WAGGONER, H. H. *Hawthorne: A Critical Study.* Harvard University Press, 1955.

WHICHER, STEPHEN. *Freedom and Fate: An Inner Life of Ralph Waldo Emerson.* University of Pennsylvania Press, 1953.

Poetry

MASTERS, EDGAR LEE. *Spoon River Anthology.* The Macmillan Co., 1963.

MATTHIESSEN, F. (ed.). *Oxford Book of American Verse.* Oxford University Press, Inc., 1964.

SANDBURG, CARL. *Complete Poems.* Harcourt, Brace & World, Inc., 1951.

WHITMAN, WALT. *Leaves of Grass.* Random House, Inc., 1964.

WILLIAMS, WILLIAM CARLOS. *Selected Poems.* New Directions, 1963.

Prose

ADAMS, HENRY. *Mont-Saint-Michel and Chartres.* Houghton Mifflin Co., 1936.

CLARK, WALTER VAN TILBURGH. *The Oxbow Incident.* Random House, Inc., 1964.

DANA, RICHARD H. *Two Years Before the Mast* (Great Illustrated Classics). Dodd, Mead & Company, 1961.

DOS PASSOS, JOHN. *U.S.A.* Houghton Mifflin Co., 1963.

DREISER, THEODORE. *An American Tragedy.* The World Publishing Co., 1963.

DREISER, THEODORE. *Sister Carrie.* Modern Library, 1963.

EMERSON, RALPH WALDO. *Emerson Reader.* Edited by Alfred Kazin and Daniel Aaron. Dell Books, 1955.

FAULKNER, WILLIAM. *Light in August.* Random House, Inc., 1964.

FAULKNER, WILLIAM. *The Sound and the Fury* and *As I Lay Dying.* The Modern Library, Inc., 1946.

HAWTHORNE, NATHANIEL. *The House of Seven Gables.* E. P. Dutton & Co., 1963.

HAWTHORNE, NATHANIEL. *The Scarlet Letter.* Edited by Kenneth S. Lynn. Harcourt, Brace & World, Inc., 1961.

HEMINGWAY, ERNEST. *A Farewell to Arms.* Charles Scribner's Sons, 1962.

HEMINGWAY, ERNEST. *The Old Man and the Sea.* Charles Scribner's Sons, 1962.

HENRY, O. *The Best Short Stories.* Random House, Inc., 1964.

JAMES, HENRY. *The Ambassadors.* Edited by Leon Edel. Houghton Mifflin Co., 1960.

JAMES, HENRY. *Portrait of a Lady.* Random House, Inc., 1964.

LARDNER, RING. *The Best Short Stories of Ring Lardner.* Charles Scribner's Sons, 1962.

LEWIS, SINCLAIR. *Babbitt* (Harbrace Modern Classic). Harcourt, Brace & World, 1962.

LEWIS, SINCLAIR. *Main Street* (Harbrace Modern Classic). Harcourt, Brace & World, Inc., 1962.

MELVILLE, HERMAN. *Moby Dick.* Random House, Inc., 1964.

O'HARA, JOHN. *49 Stories.* Random House, Inc., 1964.

POE, EDGAR ALLAN. *Complete Tales and Poems.* The Modern Library, Inc., 1963.

PORTER, KATHERINE ANNE. *Pale Horse, Pale Rider.* Random House, Inc., 1964.

SALINGER, J. D. *Catcher in the Rye.* Little, Brown & Co., 1951.

SALINGER, J. D. *Nine Stories.* Random House, Inc., 1964.

STEINBECK, JOHN. *Of Mice and Men.* The Viking Press, Inc., 1963.

STOWE, HARRIET BEECHER. *Uncle Tom's Cabin.* Random House, Inc., 1964.

THOREAU, HENRY DAVID. *Walden.* Edited by Edwin Way Teale. Dodd, Mead & Co., 1955.

TWAIN, MARK. *Complete Short Stories of Mark Twain.* Edited by Charles Neider. Doubleday & Co., 1957.

TWAIN, MARK. *A Connecticut Yankee in King Arthur's Court* (Great Illustrated Classics). Dodd, Mead & Co., 1961.

WARREN, ROBERT PENN. *All The King's Men.* Harcourt, Brace & World, Inc., 1947.

WHARTON, EDITH. *Ethan Frome.* Charles Scribner's Sons, 1962.

NEW YORK PUBLIC LIBRARY

OPULENT CAMEL of the exotic Near East.

ARABIC LITERATURE

ARNOLD, THOMAS and GUILLAUME, ALFRED (eds.). *The Legacy of Islam.* Oxford University Press, 1931.

CLASSICAL LITERATURE

History and Criticism

BALDRY, HAROLD CAPARNE. *Greek Literature for the Modern Reader.* Cambridge University Press, 1951.

BULFINCH, THOMAS. *Mythology* (rev. ed.). Thomas Y. Crowell, 1962.

FINLEY, MOSES I. *The World of Odysseus.* The Viking Press, Inc., 1954.

HADAS, MOSES. *A History of Greek Literature.* Columbia University Press, 1963.

HAMILTON, EDITH. *The Great Age of Greek Literature.* W. W. Norton Co., Inc., 1942.

HAMILTON, EDITH. *The Greek Way.* W. W. Norton & Co., Inc., 1930.

JAEGER, WERNER. *Paideia: Ideals of Greek Culture.* 3 vols. Oxford University Press, Inc., 1939.

OWEN, E. F. *The Story of the Iliad.* Oxford University Press, Inc., 1947.

SYMONDS, JOHN A. *Studies of the Greek Poets.* Macmillan, 1950.

Poetry

HOMER. *The Iliad.* Translated by Richmond Lattimore. The University of Chicago Press, 1951.

HOMER. *The Odyssey.* Translated by Robert Fitzgerald. Doubleday & Co., Inc., 1961.

EAST EUROPEAN LITERATURE

HASEK, JAROSLAV. *The Good Soldier Schweik.* Doubleday, 1930.

KRIDL, MANFRED. *Survey of Polish Literature and Culture.* Columbia University Press, 1957.

ENGLISH LITERATURE

History and Criticism

ALLEN, WALTER E. *The English Novel: A Short Critical History.* E. P. Dutton & Co., Inc., 1955.

ALVAREZ, ALFRED. *Stewards of Excellence.* Scribner's, 1958.

AUDEN, W. H. and PERSON, N. H. (eds.). *Poets of the English Language.* 5 vols. Viking Press, 1950.

BAUGH, A. C. and others. *A Literary History of England.* Appleton-Century-Crofts, 1948.

BELL, INGLIS and BAIRD, DONALD. *The English Novel, 1578–1956.* Alan Swallow, Publisher, 1959.

BERNBAUM, ERNEST. *Guide Through the Romantic Movement.* The Ronald Press Co., 1949.

BRODERN, ARTHUR G. *The Art of Beowulf.* University of California Press, 1959.

BROOKS, CLEANTH. *The Well-Wrought Urn.* Harcourt, Brace & World, 1956.

BROOKS, CLEANTH and WARREN, ROBERT PENN. *Understanding Poetry.* Holt, Rinehart & Winston, 1960.

BUSH, DOUGLAS. *English Poetry.* Methuen & Co., Ltd., 1952.

CECIL, DAVID. *Hardy the Novelist.* The Bobbs-Merrill Co., Inc., 1943.

CHAMBERS, E. K. *English Literature at the Close of the Middle Ages.* Oxford University Press, Inc., 1945.

CHAMBERS, R. W. *Beowulf: An Introduction to the Study of the Poem* (3rd ed.). Cambridge University Press, 1959.

COULTON, G. G. *Chaucer and His England.* Barnes & Noble, 1963.

DAICHES, DAVID. *A Critical History of English Literature.* 2 vols. The Ronald Press Co., 1961.

DAICHES, DAVID. *The Present Age in British Literature.* Indiana University Press, 1958.

DOBREE, BONAMY. *English Literature in the Early Eighteenth Century, 1700–1740.* Oxford University Press, 1959.

EVANS, B. IFOR. *Tradition and Romanticism.* Longmans, Green & Co., Ltd., 1940.

FRENCH, R. D. *A Chaucer Handbook.* Appleton-Century-Crofts, 1947.

GEORGE, A. G. *T. S. Eliot: His Mind and Art.* Taplinger, 1963.

HANSON, LAURENCE and ELIZABETH. *The Four Brontës.* Oxford University Press, Inc., 1949.

HILLYER, ROBERT SILLIMAN. *In Pursuit of Poetry.* McGraw-Hill, Inc., 1960.

HOWES, ALAN B. *Yorick and the Critics.* Yale University Press, 1958.

KETTLE, ARNOLD. *Introduction to the English Novel.* 2 vols. Longmans, Green & Co., Ltd., 1951.

KNAPP, LEWIS M. *Tobias Smollett: Doctor of Men and Manners.* Princeton University Press, 1949.

LOOMIS, LAURA HIBBERD. *Adventures in the Middle Ages.* Burt Franklin, Publisher, 1962.

LOOMIS, ROGER S. (ed.). *Arthurian Literature in the Middle Ages.* Oxford University Press, Inc., 1959.

LOOMIS, ROGER S. *Introduction to Medieval Literature, Chiefly in England.* Columbia University Press, 1939.

LOOMIS, ROGER S. and LAURA H. (eds.). *Medieval Romances.* The Modern Library, Inc., 1957.

McCONKEY, JAMES. *The Novels of E. M. Forster.* Cornell University Press, 1957.

McCUTCHEON, R. P. *Eighteenth-Century English Literature.* Oxford University Press, 1949.

McKILLOP, ALAN D. *Samuel Richardson, Printer and Novelist.* The Shoe String Press, Inc., 1960.

PEARSON, HESKETH. *Johnson and Boswell.* Harper & Bros., 1958.

PEARSON, WALTER. *Walter Scott: His Life and Personality.* Harper, 1954.

QUINTANA, RICARDO. *The Mind and Art of Jonathan Swift* (2nd ed.). Oxford University Press, Inc., 1953.

RICKERT, EDITH. *Chaucer's World.* Edited by C. C. Olson and M. M. Crow. Columbia University Press, 1948.

STEVENSON, LIONEL. *The Ordeal of George Meredith.* Charles Scribner's Sons, 1953.

TAYLOR, H. T. *Thought and Expression in the Sixteenth Century.* 2 vols. The Macmillan Co., 1930.

TILLYARD, EUSTACE M. W. *The Elizabethan World Picture.* Random House, Inc., 1962.

TINDALL, WILLIAM Y. *Forces in Modern British Literature, 1885–1946.* Alfred A. Knopf, Inc., 1947.

VINAVER, EUGENE. *Sir Thomas Malory.* Oxford University Press, 1929.

WAGENKNECHT, EDWARD C. *Cavalcade of the English Novel from Elizabeth to George VI.* Holt, Rinehart & Winston, Inc., 1954.

WEDGWOOD, C. V. *Seventeenth-Century English Literature.* Oxford University Press, Inc., 1950.

WILLIAMSON, GEORGE. *The Donne Tradition.* Harvard University Press, 1930.

Poetry

BROWNING, ROBERT. *Poems and Plays.* Random House, Inc., 1964.

CHAUCER, GEOFFREY. *Complete Poetical Works in Modern English.* The Macmillan Co., 1964.

ELIOT, T. S. *The Complete Poems and Plays, 1909–1950.* Harcourt, Brace & World, Inc., 1962.

KEATS, JOHN and SHELLEY, PERCY BYSSHE. *Complete Poetical Works.* Random House, Inc., 1964.

QUILLER-COUCH, ARTHUR (ed.). *Oxford Book of English Verse.* Oxford University Press, Inc., 1964.

Prose

ADDISON, JOSEPH, and STEELE, RICHARD. *The Spectator.* Edited by Gregory Smith. 4 vols. E. P. Dutton & Co., Inc., 1934.

ARNOLD, MATTHEW. *The Portable Matthew Arnold.* Edited by Lionel Trilling. The Viking Press, Inc., 1949.

AUSTEN, JANE. *The Complete Novels.* The Modern Library, Inc., 1933.

BENNETT, ARNOLD. *The Old Wives' Tale.* The Modern Library, Inc., 1931.

BOSWELL, JAMES. *The Life of Samuel Johnson.* Oxford University Press, Inc., 1953.

BRONTË, CHARLOTTE. *Jane Eyre.* Edited by Joe Lee Davis. Holt, Rinehart & Winston, 1950.

BRONTË, EMILY. *Wuthering Heights.* Edited by Mark Schorer. Holt, Rinehart & Winston, Inc., 1950.

BUNYAN, JOHN. *The Pilgrim's Progress.* Edited by Louis L. Martz. Holt, Rinehart & Winston, Inc., 1955.

BUTLER, SAMUEL. *The Way of All Flesh.* Edited by Royal A. Gettmann. Holt, Rinehart & Winston, Inc., 1948.

CARLYLE, THOMAS. *The French Revolution.* 2 vols. E. P. Dutton & Co., Inc., 1932.

CARROLL, LEWIS. *Complete Works.* The Modern Library, Inc., 1936.

CHESTERTON, G. K. *The Man Who Was Chesterton.* Edited by R. Y. Bond. Dodd, Mead & Co., 1937.

CONRAD, JOSEPH. *Lord Jim.* The Modern Library, Inc., 1931.

DEFOE, DANIEL. *The Fortunes and Misfortunes of the Famous Moll Flanders.* Edited by Godfrey Davies. Holt, Rinehart & Winston, Inc., 1949.

DEFOE, DANIEL. *Robinson Crusoe.* E. P. Dutton & Co., Inc., 1931.

DICKENS, CHARLES. *Bleak House.* E. P. Dutton & Co., Inc., 1932.

DICKENS, CHARLES. *David Copperfield.* Edited by Earle Davis. Holt, Rinehart & Winston, Inc., 1948.

DOUGLAS, NORMAN. *South Wind.* The Modern Library, Inc., 1925.

DOYLE, ARTHUR CONAN. *The Adventures and Memoirs of Sherlock Holmes.* The Modern Library, Inc., 1946.

DURRELL, LAWRENCE. *The Alexandrian Quartet.* E. P. Dutton & Co., Inc., 1957–60.

ELIOT, GEORGE. *Middlemarch.* Grove Press, 1950.

FIELDING, HENRY. *The History of Tom Jones, A Foundling.* 2 vols. E. P. Dutton & Co., Inc., 1932.

FORSTER, E. M. *A Passage to India.* Harcourt, Brace & World, Inc., 1949.

GALSWORTHY, JOHN. *The Forsyte Saga.* Charles Scribner's Sons, 1934.

GIBBON, EDWARD. *The Portable Gibbon.* Edited by Dero A. Saunders. The Viking Press, Inc., 1952.

GOLDSMITH, OLIVER. *The Vicar of Wakefield.* Edited by F. W. Hiller. The Modern Library, Inc., 1953.

GREENE, GRAHAM. *The Power and the Glory.* Viking Press, 1946.

HARDY, THOMAS. *The Mayor of Cas-* terbridge. Edited by Harvey C. Webster. Holt, Rinehart & Winston, Inc., 1948.

HARDY, THOMAS. *The Return of the Native.* Edited by Albert J. Guerard. Holt, Rinehart & Winston, Inc., 1950.

HAZLITT, WILLIAM. *Selected Essays.* Edited by George Sampson. Cambridge University Press, 1917.

HUXLEY, ALDOUS. *Brave New World.* Harper & Bros., 1950.

HUXLEY, ALDOUS. *Point Counter Point.* The Modern Library, Inc., 1930.

KIPLING, RUDYARD. *Kim.* The Modern Library, Inc., 1950.

LAWRENCE, D. H. *Sons and Lovers.* The Modern Library, Inc., 1923.

MANSFIELD, KATHERINE. *The Garden Party and Other Stories.* The Modern Library, Inc., 1922.

MAUGHAM, W. SOMERSET. *Of Human Bondage.* Doubleday, 1942.

MEREDITH, GEORGE. *The Ordeal of Richard Feverel.* The Modern Library, Inc., 1927.

SCOTT, WALTER. *The Heart of Midlothian.* Edited by David Daiches. Holt, Rinehart & Winston, Inc., 1948.

SCOTT, WALTER. *Quentin Durward, Ivanhoe, and Kenilworth.* The Modern Library, Inc., 1933.

SMOLLETT, TOBIAS. *The Expedition of Humphrey Clinker.* Edited by R. G. Davis. Holt, Rinehart & Winston, Inc., 1950.

SNOW, CHARLES PERCY. *The Conscience of the Rich.* Charles Scribner's Sons, 1958.

STERNE, LAWRENCE. *The Life and Opinions of Tristram Shandy, Gentleman.* Edited by James A. Work. The Odyssey Press, Inc., 1940.

SWIFT, JONATHAN. *Gulliver's Travels, A Tale of a Tub, and The Battle of the Books.* Edited by W. A. Eddy. Oxford University Press, Inc., 1929.

SWIFT, JONATHAN. *The Portable Swift.* Edited by Carl Van Doren. The Viking Press, Inc., 1949.

THACKERAY, WILLIAM MAKEPEACE. *The History of Henry Esmond, Esq.*

NEW YORK PUBLIC LIBRARY

EXPLORERS AND OCEAN VOYAGERS have been subjects of many novels and adventure stories.

Harper Bros.

ORWELL, GEORGE. *A Collection of Essays.* Doubleday & Co., Inc., 1954.

ORWELL, GEORGE. *Nineteen Eighty-four.* Edited by Richard H. Rovere. Harcourt, Brace & World, Inc., 1956.

PEPYS, SAMUEL. *Diary, 1660–1669.* Edited by Lord Braybrooke. 2 vols. E. P. Dutton & Co., Inc., 1934.

READE, CHARLES. *The Cloister and the Hearth.* Pocket Books, Inc., 1960.

RICHARDSON, SAMUEL. *Pamela, or Virtue Rewarded.* 2 vols. E. P. Dutton & Co., Inc., 1933.

RUSKIN, JOHN. *Selections and Essays.* Charles Scribner's Sons, 1918.

SANDS, D. B. (ed.). *The History of Reynard the Fox: Translated and Printed by William Caxton in 1481.* Harvard University Press, 1960.

THACKERAY, WILLIAM MAKEPEACE. *Pendennis.* 2 vols. E. P. Dutton and Company, Inc.

THACKERAY, WILLIAM MAKEPEACE. *Vanity Fair.* Edited by John W. Dobbs. Holt, Rinehart & Winston, Inc., 1955.

TROLLOPE, ANTHONY. *Barchester Towers.* Edited by Bradford A. Booth. Holt, Rinehart & Winston, Inc., 1949.

VERNE, JULES. *Journey to the Center of the Earth.* Longmans Green, 1959.

WAUGH, EVELYN. *A Handful of Dust.* New Directions, 1945.

WELLS, H. G. *Tono Bungay.* The Modern Library, Inc., 1931.

WILDE, OSCAR. *The Portable Oscar Wilde.* Edited by Richard Addington. The Viking Press, Inc., 1948.

FRENCH LITERATURE

History and Criticism

BARKER, RICHARD HINDRY. *Marcel Proust.* Criterion Books, Inc., 1958.

BRÉE, GERMAINE and GUITON, MARGARET. *The Age of Fiction: The French Novel from Gide to Camus.* Rutgers University Press, 1957.

BRÉE, GERMAINE. *Camus.* Rutgers University Press, 1959.

BRERETON, GEOFFREY. *A Short History of French Literature from the Middle Ages to the Present Day.* Penguin Books, Inc., 1955.

FROHOCK, WILLIAM M. *André Malraux and the Tragic Imagination.* Stanford University Press, 1952.

GILMAN, M. *The Idea of Poetry in France: From Hordar de la Motte to Baudelaire.* Harvard University Press, 1958.

GREEN, FREDERICK C. *French Novelists, Manners, and Ideas from the Renaissance to the Revolution.* Appleton-Century-Crofts, 1929.

GUTHRIE, RAMON and DILLER, GEORGE E. *French Literature and Thought Since the Revolution.* Harcourt, Brace & World, Inc., 1962.

HARVEY, PAUL. *The Oxford Companion to French Literature.* Oxford University Press, Inc., 1959.

HASTINGS, HESTER. *Man and Beast in French Thought of the 18th Century.* The Johns Hopkins Press, 1962.

HEMMINGS, F. W. *Emile Zola.* Oxford University Press, Inc., 1953.

PEYRE, HENRI. *The Contemporary French Novel.* Oxford University Press, Inc., 1955.

ROGERS, SAMUEL. *Balzac and the Novel.* University of Wisconsin Press, 1953.

SAINTSBURY, GEORGE. *French Literature and Its Masters.* Alfred A. Knopf, Inc., 1946.

THODY, PHILIP. *Jean-Paul Sartre.* The Macmillan Co., 1960.

Poetry

APOLLINAIRE, GUILLAUME. *Selected Writings.* Translated by Roger Shattuck. New Directions, 1950.

BAUDELAIRE, CHARLES. *Flowers of Evil.* Translated by Geoffrey Wagner. New Directions, 1946.

MALLARMÉ, STÉPHANE. *Poems.* Translated by Roger Fry. New Directions, 1950.

RIMBAUD, ARTHUR. *Prose Poems from the Illuminations: A Season in Hell.* 2 vols. New Directions, 1946.

Song of Roland. Translated by Frederick Luquiens. The Macmillan Co., 1952.

VERLAINE, PAUL. *Selected Poems.* Translated by C. F. MacIntyre. University of California Press, 1948.

VILLON, FRANCOIS. *Poems.* Liveright Publishing Corp., 1927.

Prose

BALZAC, HONORÉ DE. *Old Goriot.* E. P. Dutton & Co., Inc., 1935.

CAMUS, ALBERT. *The Plague.* Alfred A. Knopf, Inc., 1948.

CAMUS, ALBERT. *The Stranger.* Random House, Inc., 1964.

COLETTE. *Chéri, and the Last of Chéri.* Farrar, Straus & Co., 1953.

DUMAS, ALEXANDER, PÈRE. *The Three Musketeers.* Modern Library, 1925.

FLAUBERT, GUSTAVE. *Madame Bovary.* Translated by Francis Steegmuller. Random House, Inc., 1957.

FRANCE, ANATOLE. *The Crime of Sylvestre Bonnard.* Dodd, Mead & Co., 1931.

GENET, JEAN. *Our Lady of the Flowers.* Grove Press, Inc., 1963.

GIDE, ANDRÉ. *The Counterfeiters.* The Modern Library, Inc., 1931.

HUGO, VICTOR. *Les Misérables.* The Modern Library, Inc., 1925.

MALRAUX, ANDRÉ. *Man's Fate.* The Modern Library, Inc., 1931.

MAUPASSANT, GUY DE. *The Portable Maupassant.* Edited by Lewis Galantière. Viking, 1947.

MAURIAC, FRANÇOIS. *River of Life.* Farrar, Straus & Co., 1957.

MAUROIS, ANDRÉ. *Olympio: The Life of Victor Hugo.* Harper & Bros., 1956.

MONTAIGNE, MICHEL E. DE. *Essays.* The Modern Library, Inc., 1933.

PASCAL, BLAISE. *Pensées and the Provincial Letters.* The Modern Library, Inc., 1941.

PRÉVOST, ABBÉ. *Manon Lescaut.* E. P. Dutton & Co., Inc., 1929.

PROUST, MARCEL. *Remembrance of Things Past.* 2 vols. Random House, Inc., 1934.

RABELAIS, FRANÇOIS. *The Portable Rabelais.* Edited by Samuel Putnam. The Viking Press, Inc., 1946.

ROUSSEAU, JEAN-JACQUES. *Confessions.* The Modern Library, Inc., 1945.

SARTRE, JEAN-PAUL. *The Age of Reason.* Alfred A. Knopf, Inc., 1947.

STENDHAL, M. DE. *The Red and the Black.* The Modern Library, 1929.

VALÉRY, PAUL. *Selected Writings.* New Directions, 1950.

VOLTAIRE, FRANÇOIS MARIE AROUET DE. *The Portable Voltaire.* The Viking Press, Inc., 1949.

ZOLA, EMILE. *Germinal.* The Macmillan Co., 1959.

ZOLA, EMILE. *Nana.* Doubleday & Co., Inc., 1963.

GERMAN LITERATURE

History and Criticism

GRAY, RONALD D. *Kafka's Castle.* Cambridge University Press, 1956.

HATFIELD, HENRY C. *Thomas Mann.* New Directions, 1951.

LANGE, VICTOR (ed.). *Great German Short Novels and Stories.* The Modern Library, Inc., 1952.

ROSE, ERNEST. *A History of German Literature.* New York University Press, 1960.

CHARLES PHELPS CUSHING

VICTOR HUGO (1802–1885), author of *Les Misérables; The Hunchback of Notre Dame.*

SOKEL, WALTER H. *The Writer in Extremis: Expressionism in Twentieth-Century German Literature.* Stanford University Press, 1959.

WITTE, WILLIAM. *Schiller.* The Macmillan Co., 1949.

WOOD, FRANK H. *Rainer Maria Rilke: The Ring of Forms.* University of Minnesota Press, 1958.

Poetry

FORSTER, LEONARD W. (ed.). *The Penguin Book of German Verse.* Penguin Books, Inc., 1958.

Prose

KAFKA, FRANZ. *The Trial.* Alfred A. Knopf, Inc., 1937.

HOFFMANN, E. T. A. *Tales of Hoffmann.* A. A. Wyn, Inc., 1946.

MANN, THOMAS. *Death in Venice and Other Stories.* Random House, 1964.

MANN, THOMAS. *The Magic Mountain.* Alfred A. Knopf, Inc., 1953.

REMARQUE, ERICH MARIA. *All Quiet on the Western Front.* Little, Brown & Co., 1929.

SCHILLER, FRIEDRICH. *On the Aesthetic Education of Man.* Yale, 1954.

INDIAN LITERATURE

GARRATT, GEOFFREY T. (ed.) *The Legacy of India.* Oxford University Press, 1937.

IRISH LITERATURE

History and Criticism

DILLON, MYLES. *Early Irish Literature.* The University of Chicago Press, 1948.

ELLMANN, RICHARD. *James Joyce.* Oxford University Press, Inc., 1959.

ELLMANN, RICHARD. *Yeats: The Man and the Masks.* The Macmillan Co., 1948.

Poetry

YEATS, WILLIAM BUTLER. *Collected Poems.* The Macmillan Co., 1963.

Prose

JOYCE, JAMES. *A Portrait of the Artist as a Young Man.* The Viking Press, Inc., 1956.

JOYCE, JAMES. *Ulysses.* The Viking Press, Inc., 1948.

ITALIAN LITERATURE

History and Criticism

BURCKHARDT, JACOB. *The Renaissance.* The Modern Library, Inc., 1954.

DE SANCTIS, FRANCESCO. *History of Italian Literature.* 2 vols. Basic Books, Inc., 1960.

STAMBLER, BERNARD. *Dante's Other World.* New York University, 1957.

Poetry

ALIGHIERI, DANTE. *The Portable Dante.* Edited by Paolo Milano. The Viking Press, Inc., 1947.

KAY, GEORGE (ed.). *The Penguin Book of Italian Verse.* Penguin Books, Inc., 1958.

PETRARCH. *Sonnets and Songs.* Translated by Anna Maria Armi. Pantheon Books, Inc., 1946.

Prose

BOCCACCIO, GIOVANNI. *The Decameron.* Translated by Frances Winwar. The Modern Library, Inc., 1955.

CELLINI, BENVENUTO. *Autobiography.* Translated by J. A. Symonds. The Modern Library, Inc., 1927.

D'ANNUNZIO, GABRIELE. *The Daughter of Ioris.* Little, Brown & Co., 1907.

MANZONI, ALESSANDRO. *The Betrothed.* Translated by Archibald Colquihoun. Dutton, 1951.

MORAVIA, ALBERTO. *The Woman of Rome.* Translated by Lydia Holland. Farrar, Straus & Co., 1949.

PETOELLO, DECIO (ed.). *Italian Short Stories from the Thirteenth to the Twentieth Centuries.* Dutton, 1932.

JEWISH LITERATURE

BROWNE, LEWIS. *The Wisdom of Israel: An Anthology.* Random House, Inc., 1945.

HAEKIN, ABRAHAM. *Zion in Jewish Literature.* Herzl Press, 1961.

WAXMAN, MEYER. *A History of Jewish Literature from the Close of the Bible to Our Own Days.* Thomas Yoseloff, Publishers, 1960.

ORIENTAL LITERATURE

HIGHTOWER, J. R. *Topics in Chinese Literature: Outlines & Bibliographies.* Harvard University Press, 1950.

HSIA, C. T. *A History of Modern Chinese Fiction.* Yale University Press, 1961.

KEENE, DONALD. *Japanese Literature: An Introduction for Western Readers.* Grove Press, 1955.

PERSIAN LITERATURE

ARBERRY, A. J. (ed.). *The Legacy of Persia.* Oxford University Press, 1953.

KHAYYÁM, OMAR. *The Rubaiyat.* Translated by Edward Fitzgerald. Thomas Y. Crowell Company, 1950.

RUSSIAN LITERATURE

History and Criticism

BERDYAEV, NICHOLAS. *Dostoevsky.* Meridian Books, 1963.

GIDE, ANDRÉ. *Dostoevsky.* New Directions, 1963.

MUCHNICK, HELEN. *An Introduction to Russian Literature.* Doubleday & Co., Inc., 1947.

SLONIM, MARC. *An Outline of Russian Literature.* Oxford University Press, 1958.

SOKOLOV, Y. M. *Russian Folklore.* The Macmillan Co., 1952.

STRURC, GLEB. *Soviet Russian Literature, 1917–1950.* University of Oklahoma Press, 1951.

Poetry

YARMOLINSKY, ABRAHAM (ed.). *A Treasury of Russian Verse.* The Macmillan Co., 1949.

Prose

CHEKHOV, ANTON. *Short Stories.* The Modern Library, Inc., 1932.

DOSTOEVSKY, FYODOR. *The Brothers Karamozov.* The Modern Library, Inc., 1932.

DOSTOEVSKY, FYODOR. *Crime and Punishment.* Random House, 1964.

GOGOL, NIKOLAI. *The Collected Tales and Plays of Nikolai Gogol.* Pantheon Books, Inc., 1964.

PASTERNAK, BORIS. *Dr. Zhivago.* Pantheon Books, Inc., 1958.

SHOLOKHOV, MIKHAIL. *The Silent Don.* 2 vols. Alfred A. Knopf, Inc., 1959.

TOLSTOY, LEO. *Anna Karenina.* Penguin Books, Inc., 1950.

TOLSTOY, LEO. *War and Peace.* The Modern Library, Inc., 1931.

TURGENEV, IVAN. *Fathers and Sons.* Holt, Rinehart & Winston, Inc., 1949.

YARMOLINSKY, ABRAHAM (ed.). *A Treasury of Great Russian Short Stories.* The Macmillan Co., 1944.

SCANDINAVIAN LITERATURE

BREDSDOFF, ELIAR and others. *Introduction to Scandinavian Literature.* Cambridge University Press, 1951.

EINARSSON, STEFAN. *A History of Icelandic Literature.* The Johns Hopkins Press, 1957.

GUSTAFSON, ALRIK. *A History of Swedish Literature.* University of Minnesota Press, 1961.

SPANISH LITERATURE

History and Criticism

BRENAN, GERALD. *The Literature of the Spanish People.* Cambridge University Press, 1953.

CASTRO, AMERICO. *The Structure of Spanish History.* Princeton, 1954.

PEERS, E. ALLISON (ed.). *Critical Anthology of Spanish Verse.* University of California Press, 1949.

TREND, J. B. *The Civilization of Spain.* Oxford University Press, Inc., 1944.

Prose

CERVANTES, MIGUEL DE. *Don Quixote.* Translated by Samuel Putnam. 2 vols. The Viking Press, Inc., 1949.

GIRONELLO, JOSÉ MARIA. *The Cypresses Believe in God.* Alfred A. Knopf, Inc., 1955.

METROPOLITAN MUSEUM OF ART

"MAJAS ON A BALCONY": Francisco Goya.

WELSH LITERATURE

PARRY, THOMAS. *A History of Welsh Literature*. Translated by H. I. Bell. Oxford University Press, Inc., 1955.

THOMAS, DYLAN. *Quite Early One Morning*. New Directions, 1963.

THOMAS, DYLAN. *Under Milk Wood*. New Directions, 1963.

THEATER

General Reference Books

CHENEY, SHELDON. *The Theatre: Three Thousand Years of Drama, Acting and Stagecraft*. Longmans, Green & Co., Ltd., 1959.

GRANVILLE-BARKER, H. *The Study of the Drama*. The Macmillan Co., 1934.

HARTNOLL, PHYLLIS. *The Oxford Companion to the Theater*. Oxford University Press, Inc., 1957.

KERR, WALTER. *The Theater in Spite of Itself*. Simon and Schuster, Inc., 1963.

KITTS, HUMPHREY D. F. *Form and Meaning in Drama*. Barnes & Noble, Inc., 1956.

MELCHINGER, SIEGFRIED. *Encyclopedia of Modern Drama*. Edited by Henry Popkin and translated by George Wellworth. Horizon, 1963.

NICOLL, ALLARDYCE. *The Development of the Theater: A Study of Theatrical Art from the Beginnings to the Present Day* (4th ed. rev.). Harcourt, Brace & World, Inc., 1962.

NICOLL, ALLARDYCE. *The World of Harlequin*. Cambridge University Press, 1963.

History and Criticism

ATKINS, STUART P. *Goethe's Faust: A Literary Analysis*. Harvard University Press, 1958.

BALL, ROBERT H. and PARROTT, M. *A Short View of Elizabethan Drama*. Charles Scribner's Sons, 1943.

BIEBER, MARGARETE. *The History of the Greek and Roman Theater*. Princeton University Press, 1961.

BOAS, FREDERICK S. *An Introduction to Stuart Drama*. Oxford University Press, Inc., 1936.

BRADLEY, A. C. *Shakespearean Tragedy*. The Macmillan Co., 1932.

BROOKE, C. F. TUCKER. *The Tudor Drama*. Houghton Mifflin Co., 1911.

BROOKE, C. F. TUCKER and PARADISE, N. B. *English Drama, 1580–1642*. D. C. Heath & Co., 1933.

BROUSSARD, LOUIS. *American Drama: Contemporary Allegory from O'Neill to Tennessee Williams*. University of Oklahoma Press, 1962.

CHAMBERS, EDMUND K. *The Elizabethan Stage*. 4 vols. Oxford University Press, Inc., 1923.

CHAMBERS, EDMUND K. *The Medieval Stage*. 2 vols. Oxford University Press, Inc., 1921.

CHUTE, MARCHETTE. *Introduction to Shakespeare*. E. P. Dutton & Co., Inc., 1951.

CHUTE, MARCHETTE. *Shakespeare of London*. E. P. Dutton & Co., Inc., 1949.

DUCKWORTH, GEORGE E. *The Nature of Roman Comedy*. Princeton University Press, 1952.

ELLIS-FERMOR, UNA. *Shakespeare the Dramatist*. Edited by Kenneth Muir. Barnes & Noble, Inc., 1961.

FLICKINGER, ROY C. *The Greek Theater and Its Drama*. The University of Chicago Press, 1960.

GASSNER, JOHN. *Masters of the Drama*. Dover Publications, Inc., 1954.

GELB, ARTHUR and BARBARA. *O'Neill: A Biography*. Harper & Bros., 1962.

GORCHAKOV, N. A. *The Theater in Soviet Russia*. Columbia University Press, 1957.

GUICHARNAUD, JACQUES and BECKELMAN, JUNE. *Modern French Theater From Giraudoux to Beckett*. Yale University Press, 1961.

HEWITT, BARNARD W. *Theater U.S.A., 1668–1957*. McGraw-Hill, Inc., 1959

HUGHES, GLEN. *A History of the American Theater, 1700–1950*. Samuel French, Inc., 1951.

KNIGHT, G. WILSON. *The Imperial Theme* (3rd ed.). Barnes & Noble, Inc., 1961.

KRAUSE, DAVID. *Sean O'Casey: The Man and His Work*. The Macmillan Co., 1962.

KRUTCH, JOSEPH WOOD. *The American Drama Since 1918: An Informal History*. George Braziller, 1957.

KRUTCH, JOSEPH WOOD. *Comedy and Conscience After the Restoration*. Columbia University Press, 1949.

MILLER, JORDAN YALE. *American Dramatic Literature*. McGraw-Hill, Inc., 1961.

NETHERCOT, ARTHUR. *Men and Supermen: The Shavian Portrait Gallery*. Harvard University Press, 1954.

NICOLL, ALLARDYCE. *British Drama: An Historical Survey From the Beginnings to the Present Time* (5th ed.). Barnes & Noble, 1963.

NICOLL, ALLARDYCE. *Shakespeare: An Introduction*. Oxford University Press, Inc., 1953.

PRICE, JULIA. *The Off-Broadway Theater*. Scarecrow Press, Inc., 1962.

REYNOLDS, ERNEST. *Modern English Drama: A Survey of the Theatre from 1900*. George G. Harrap & Co., Ltd., 1949.

RIDLER, ANNE. *Shakespeare Criticism 1935–1960*. Oxford University Press, Inc., 1963.

STOCKFORD, MARTHA HALE. *Shakespeare, Sophocles: Dramatic Themes and Modes*. College and University Press, 1963.

STOLL, ELMER EDGAR. *Art and Artifice in Shakespeare*. Barnes & Noble, Inc., 1962.

VARNEKE, B. V. *History of the Russian Theater*. Macmillan, 1951.

WILLETT, JOHN. *The Theater of Bertolt Brecht*. New Directions, 1959.

Playwrights

ADAMS, JOSEPH QUINCY (ed.). *Chief Pre-Shakespearean Dramas*. Houghton Mifflin Co., 1924.

ARISTOPHANES. *Five Comedies*. Translated by Benjamin Bickley Rogers and edited by Andrew Chiappe. Doubleday & Co., Inc., 1955.

BRECHT, BERTOLT. *Seven Plays*. Edited by Eric Bentley. Grove Press, 1961.

CAWLEY, A. C. (ed.). *Everyman and Medieval Miracle Plays*. E. P. Dutton & Co., Inc., 1959.

CHEKHOV, ANTON. *Plays*. The Modern Library, Inc., 1930.

GOETHE, JOHANN WOLFGANG VON. *Faust*. Modern Library, 1930.

GORKY, MAXIM. *Seven Plays*. Yale University Press, 1945.

GRENE, DAVID and LATTIMORE, RICHMOND (eds.). *Complete Greek Tragedies*. 9 vols. The University of Chicago Press.

IBSEN, HENRIK. *Eleven Plays*. The Modern Library, Inc., 1935.

LANDIS, PAUL N. (ed.). *Six Plays by Corneille and Racine*. The Modern Library, Inc., 1931.

MOLIÈRE, JEAN BAPTISTE. *Comedies*. 2 vols. E. P. Dutton, 1929.

NOYES, GEORGE R. (ed.). *Masterpieces of the Russian Drama*. Appleton-Century-Crofts, 1933.

O'NEILL, EUGENE. *Plays*. 3 vols. Random House, Inc.

PIRANDELLO, LUIGI. *Naked Masks: Five Plays by Luigi Pirandello*. Edited by Eric Bentley. E. P. Dutton & Co., 1952.

ROBINSON, LENNOX (ed.). *The Irish Theater*. The Macmillan Co., 1939.

SHAKESPEARE, WILLIAM. *The Complete Works of Shakespeare*. Edited by George Lyman Kittredge. Ginn & Co., 1936.

STRINDBERG, AUGUST. *Six Plays*. Translated by Elizabeth Sprugge. Doubleday & Co., Inc., 1955.

METROPOLITAN MUSEUM OF ART

INDIAN MINIATURE showing ladies of the court is an illustration of a tune, or *ragini*.

History of mathematics 1501
Arithmetic 1508
Algebra 1532
Geometry 1556
Trigonometry 1581
Calculus 1594
Advanced mathematics 1596
Mathematics glossary 1601
Bibliography 1608

VOLUME EIGHTEEN

MATHEMATICS

JOHN NASO

WEIGHTS AND MEASURES

	Unit	Abbreviation	Units of Same System	Metric/U.S. Equivalent
Length				
U.S.	mile	mi	5,280 feet, 320 rods, 1,760 yards	1.609 kilometers
	furlong	fur	0.125 mile, 40 rods, 660 feet	201.2 meters
	rod	rd	5.50 yards, 16.5 feet	5.029 meters
	yard	yd	3 feet, 36 inches	0.914 meter
	foot	ft or '	12 inches, 0.333 yard	30.480 centimeters
	inch	in or "	0.083 foot, 0.027 yard	2.540 centimeters
Metric	myriameter	mym	10,000 meters	6.2 miles
	kilometer	km	1,000 meters	0.62 mile
	hectometer	hm	100 meters	109.36 yards
	decameter	dkm	10 meters	32.81 feet
	meter	m	0.001 kilometer	39.37 inches
	decimeter	dm	0.1 meter	3.94 inches
	centimeter	cm	0 01 meter	0.39 inch
	millimeter	mm	0.001 meter	0.04 inch
Area				
U.S.	square mile	sq mi or m²	640 acres, 102,400 square rods	2.590 square kilometers
	acre	a or ac	4,840 square yards, 43,560 square feet	4,047 square meters
	square rod	sq rd or rd²	30.25 square yards, 0.006 acre	25.293 square meters
	square yard	sq yd or yd²	1,296 square inches, 9 square feet	0.836 square meter
	square foot	sq ft or ft²	144 square inches, 0.111 square yard	0.093 square meter
	square inch	sq in or in²	0.007 square foot	6.451 square centimeters
Metric	square kilometer	sq km or km²	1,000,000 square meters	0.3861 square mile
	hectare	ha	10,000 square meters	2.47 acres
	are	a	100 square meters	119.60 square yards
	centare	ca	1 square meter	10.76 square feet
	square centimeter	sq cm or cm²	0.0001 square meter	0.155 square inch
	square millimeter	sq mm or mm²	0.01 square centimeter	0.002 square inch
Volume				
U.S.	cubic yard	cu yd or yd³	27 cubic feet, 46,656 cubic inches	0.765 cubic meter
	cubic foot	cu ft or ft³	1,728 cubic inches, 0.0370 cubic yard	0.028 cubic meter
	cubic inch	cu in or in³	0.00058 cubic foot, 0.000021 cubic yard	16.387 cubic centimeters
Metric	decastere	dks	10 cubic meters	13.10 cubic yards
	stere	s	1 cubic meter	1.31 cubic yards
	decistere	ds	0.10 cubic meter	3.53 cubic feet
	cubic centimeter	cu cm or cm³ or cc	0.000001 cubic meter	0.061 cubic inch
	cubic millimeter	cu mm or mm³	0.001 cubic centimeter	0.0001 cubic inch
Weight				
Avoirdupois	short ton		20 short hundredweight, 2,000 pounds	0.907 metric ton
	long ton		20 long hundredweight, 2,240 pounds	1.016 metric tons
	short hundredweight	cwt	100 pounds, 0.05 short ton	45.359 kilograms
	long hundredweight	cwt	112 pounds, 0.05 long ton	50.802 kilograms
	pound	lb or lb av or #	16 ounces, 7,000 grains	0.453 kilogram
	ounce	oz or oz av	16 drams, 437.5 grains	28.349 grams
	dram	dr or dr av	27.343 grains, 0.0625 ounce	1.771 grams
	grain	gr	0.036 dram, 0.002285 ounce	0.648 gram
Troy	pound	lb t	12 ounces, 240 pennyweight, 5,760 grains	0.373 kilogram
	ounce	oz t	20 pennyweight, 48 grains	31.103 grams
	pennyweight	dwt or pwt	24 grains, 0.05 ounce	1.555 grams
	grain	gr	0.042 pennyweight, 0.002083 ounce	0.0648 gram
Apothecaries'	pound	lb ap	12 ounces, 5,760 grains	0.373 kilogram
	ounce	oz ap or ℥	8 drams, 480 grains	31.103 grams
	dram	dr ap or ʒ	3 scruples, 60 grains	3.887 grams
	scruple	s ap or ℈	20 grains, 0.333 dram	1.295 grams
	grain	gr	0.05 scruple, 0.002083 ounce, 0.0166 dram	0.0648 gram
Metric	metric ton	MT or t	1,000,000 grams	1.1 short tons
	quintal	q	100,000 grams	220.46 pounds
	kilogram	kg	1,000 grams	2.2046 pounds
	hectogram	hg	100 grams	3.527 ounces
	decagram	dkg	10 grams	0.353 ounce
	gram	g or gm	0.001 kilogram	0.035 ounce
	decigram	dg	0.10 gram	1.543 grains
	centigram	cg	0.01 gram	0.154 grain
	milligram	mg	0.001 gram	0.015 grain
Capacity				
U.S. Liquid Measure	gallon	gal	4 quarts (231 cubic inches)	3.785 liters
	quart	qt	2 pints (57.75 cubic inches)	0.946 liter
	pint	pt	4 gills (28.875 cubic inches)	0.473 liter
	gill	gi	4 fluidounces (7.218 cubic inches)	118.291 milliliters
	fluidounce	fl oz or fl℥	8 fluidrams (1.804 cubic inches)	29.573 milliliters
	fluidram	fl dr or fl ʒ	60 minims (0.225 cubic inch)	3.696 milliliters
	minim	min or m̃	1/60 fluidram (0.003759 cubic inch)	0.061610 milliliter
U.S. Dry Measure	bushel	bu	4 pecks (2,150.42 cubic inches)	35.238 liters
	peck	pk	8 quarts (537.605 cubic inches)	8.809 liters
	quart	qt	2 pints (67.200 cubic inches)	1.101 liters
	pint	pt	1/2 quart (33.600 cubic inches)	0.550 liter
British Imperial	bushel	bu	4 pecks (2,219.36 cubic inches)	0.036 cubic meter
	peck	pk	2 gallons (554.84 cubic inches)	0.0009 cubic meter
	gallon	gal	4 quarts (277.420 cubic inches)	4.545 liters
	quart	qt	2 pints (69.355 cubic inches)	1.136 liters
	pint	pt	4 gills (34.678 cubic inches)	568.26 cubic centimeters
	gill	gi	5 fluidounces (8.669 cubic inches)	142.066 cubic centimeters
	fluidounce	fl oz or fl℥	8 fluidrams (1.7339 cubic inches)	28.416 cubic centimeters
	fluidram	fl dr or fl ʒ	50 minims (0.216734 cubic inch)	3.5516 cubic centimeters
	minim	min or m̃	1/60 fluidram (0.003612 cubic inch)	0.059194 cubic centimeter
Metric	kiloliter	kl	1,000 liters	1.31 cubic yards
	hectoliter	hl	100 liters	3.53 cubic feet
	decaliter	dkl	10 liters	0.35 cubic foot
	liter	l	0.001 kiloliter	61.02 cubic inches
	deciliter	dl	0.10 liter	6.1 cubic inches
	centiliter	cl	0.01 liter	0.6 cubic inch
	milliliter	ml	0.001 liter	0.06 cubic inch

Mathematics

HISTORY

The Origins of Mathematics.—When prehistoric man found a way to answer the questions "how much?" and "how many?" he laid the foundations of mathematics.

Stones from the Paleolithic period, with notches and geometric designs carved on them, indicate that a low level of mathematical thinking existed in the early part of the Stone Age. In the fifth and fourth millennia B.C., large groups of people inhabiting the fertile regions on the banks of long, navigable rivers—the Nile in Egypt, the Euphrates and Tigris in Mesopotamia, the Indus in Pakistan, the Ganges in India, and the Hwang Ho (Yellow River) in China—developed a utilitarian form of mathematics that made it possible for them to keep pace with their advances in engineering, agriculture, and trade. At this time the notches formerly used in recording a count were replaced by symbols (*numerals*), and calendars were devised to let the farmer know when to plant, to harvest, and to expect heavy rains. A crude geometry used to survey land also existed in this period.

Egyptian Contributions.—Although all these river civilizations can claim great antiquity for their achievements in mathematics, only the Egyptians and Mesopotamians left tangible evidence of a systematic development of the subject prior to 1100 B.C. From the Egypt of 3500 B.C., for example, there is a royal mace inscribed with a record of the amount of loot seized by the king in a great battle. There are drawings on the walls of Egyptian temples and pyramids indicating that a method of taxation involving extensive bookkeeping was in use as long ago as 3000 B.C. Several papyri dealing with pharmacology prove that a system of weights and measures as sophisticated as any in use up to the nineteenth century was well established 5,000 years ago among the people of the Nile valley.

Knowledge of Egyptian mathematics is derived mainly from a study of 110 problems and their solutions, which are to be found in two well-preserved papyri—the *Moscow Papyrus*, written about 1850 B.C., and the *Rhind (Ahmes)*

Papyrus, which was copied in 1650 B.C. by Ahmes from an older manuscript. These papyri, in a cursive writing called *hieratic*, show that the Egyptians had complete mastery of the fundamental operations of arithmetic (addition, subtraction, multiplication, and division) for both whole numbers and fractions; that they could solve simple equations; and that their interest in mathematics was not confined to its utilitarian aspects, as had been the case in an earlier day—problems of a recreational nature such as puzzles were beginning to appear. The geometry mentioned in these papyri was of a strictly mensurational type, limited to finding areas and volumes of the common geometric figures and solids. The solutions to these measurement problems were probably based on good guesses backed up by observation of sample figures. As a result, some formulae are indicative of great ingenuity on the part of their discoverers, while others fall so far short of the correct result that they bear witness to the lack of the power to generalize and to a complete absence of a deductive basis. Thus, Egyptian mathematics might be classed as trial and error rather than as a true science.

Babylonian Contributions.—Although the failure to develop a deductive system of geometry also characterized the efforts of the Babylonians, they towered over their Egyptian neighbors in the other branches of mathematics, algebra and the theory of numbers. These talented people wrote by pressing a stylus on a tablet of wet clay. Since the clay was later fired to harden it, many thousands of these tablets, most of them dating from 2000 B.C. to 200 B.C., have been preserved. Recent studies of these tablets indicate that the pre-eminence of the Babylonians in mathematics was due in no small part to their ability to represent whole or fractional numbers of any size by using a place system of numeration with the base 60, called a *sexagesimal system*. Their system was used in the same manner in which we use the base 10, with one exception—the Babylonians did not have a symbol for zero. Late in their history they employed a punctuation mark, the period, to indicate the absence of a symbol between two other symbols in a numeral. Since this mark was never used alone or at the end of a numeral to indicate the

absence of units (ones) in the number, it cannot be called a "zero." Moreover, the Babylonians did not have a counterpart of the decimal point, a symbol that serves to separate the whole number from the fraction. With all its shortcomings, however, the Babylonian system of writing fractions was so superior to other methods that European mathematicians and astronomers used it until the late sixteenth century, when the decimal fraction was invented. The base 60, moreover, has survived a span of more than 4,000 years, for it is still used in the ordinary units for telling time and measuring angles (60 seconds = 1 minute; 60 minutes = 1 degree or 1 hour). In the solution of equations and sets of equations, of both first and second degrees, the Babylonians had no peers among the ancient peoples. They also had a knowledge of number theory, such as the method of finding sets of three whole numbers that can be measures of the sides of a right triangle.

Greek Mathematics.—While observation and intuition, fortified by a certain amount of reasoning, play a role in the mathematical invention, the major discoveries in the subject have been made through a formal system of deductive thinking. Such a system was completely foreign to the methods of the Egyptians and Babylonians. It is this formalization of deductive thinking, which has given rise to present-day *axiomatics*, that must be considered the foremost Greek contribution to mathematics. In the hands of the Greeks, the method consisted of the adoption of a list of geometrical statements (*postulates* or *axioms*) that were considered so self-evident as to be acceptable without proof, followed by logical deduction of a whole body of statements, each of which was based on a postulate or on some previously proved statements. Moreover, an attempt was made to define all terms used. Although the Greek concept of a deductive science has undergone a significant revision in modern times, the Greeks provided the world with the first example of a procedure that is now characteristic of all branches of mathematics.

The Greeks also were the first to mention mathematicians by name and to take pride in their exploits. Thales of Miletus (c. 640–546 B.C.), who is credited with the invention of (*demonstrative*) *geometry*, was the earliest

NEW YORK PUBLIC LIBRARY

THE "ELEMENTS" by Euclid was written about 300 B.C. This book has had more editions and translations than any other on mathematics. Shown is a page in Latin printed in 1482.

and so on *ad infinitum*. Movement is therefore impossible, claimed Zeno, since the moving body would have to traverse an infinite number of segments in finite time.

Another problem of this period that left its mark on mathematics is that of "squaring the circle"; that is, constructing a square equal in area to a particular circle. The proof that this construction cannot be made with the two instruments—the unmarked straight edge and the compasses to which geometricians of the Greek school were limited—had to wait until 1882 and the work of the German mathematician Ferdinand Lindemann. In the centuries that intervened between the framing of the problem and Lindemann's work, attempts to solve the problem yielded many new branches of mathematics and revealed the nature of number.

With the founding of Alexandria (named for Alexander the Great) in 332 B.C., the center of mathematical studies moved from Athens back to Egypt. The first of the Hellenistic (Alexandrian) mathematicians of note was Euclid, who wrote the *Elements*, a book on geometry that has gone through more editions and translations than any other on mathematics. It might be said that with Euclid the Greek development of axiomatics reached its zenith. Until the mid-twentieth century, the *Elements* was studied in simplified and abridged versions by secondary-school children the world over. Geometry that employs the axioms set forth by Euclid is called Euclidean geometry.

Although Euclid is the most widely known of the Hellenistic mathematicians, greatest (perhaps of all antiquity) was Archimedes (c. 287–212 B.C.), who lived in the Greek colony of Sicily after a period of schooling in Alexandria. Archimedes devised a way of representing large numbers with a few symbols, in order, as he said in his *Sand-Reckoner*, to be able to represent the number of grains of sand in a volume equal to that of the earth, a volume that he had correctly calculated by using as diameter a measure obtained by Eratosthenes (c. 275–195 B.C.). Besides finding a formula for the volume of the sphere, Archimedes discovered the formula for its surface area and for areas of figures bounded by various curves, such as parabolas and spirals. His method foreshadowed the invention of the integral calculus 18 centuries later. However, Archimedes' discoveries in the realm of physics (such as the lever, the pulley, and the screw) overshadow his less utilitarian work in mathematics, and he is better known as the world's first mechanical engineer than as an outstanding mathematician.

A contemporary of Archimedes, Apollonius of Perga (fl. 247–205 B.C.) carried almost to completion the study by geometric means of the sections of a right circular cone made by cutting the

mathematician whose name has come down to us. Thales set up a list of postulates for geometry and, on the basis of these, proved about a half-dozen *theorems*, one of which gives a set of conditions under which two triangles are congruent.

The work begun by Thales was carried forward by Pythagoras (c. 582–507 B.C.), who organized geometry into a deductive science and proved many theorems. The most famous of these theorems, which states that the sum of the squares of the sides of a right triangle equals the square of the hypotenuse, bears his name. Pythagoras founded a secret society that had for one of its tenets the belief that "number" is the basis of all creation. A member of the group, or possibly Pythagoras himself, made one of the most far-reaching discoveries in the history of mathematics—the recognition of the existence of segments of lines with measures that could not be represented by whole

numbers or quotients of whole numbers —the *irrationals*. (In the decimal system, irrational numbers are represented by the nonrepeating, infinite decimals.) Pythagoras is also credited with the discovery of the mathematical laws of harmony, which deal with a certain progression of numbers. Because of their connection with music, the system is called "harmonic."

In the two centuries following Pythagoras, the Greek school made notable contributions to the philosophical aspects of mathematics. Among the problems that engaged mathematicians of the period were the paradoxes of Zeno of Elea (c. 475 B.C.). One of the simplest of these is the argument that it is impossible for a moving body to reach its destination, because before the body in motion can traverse an entire distance, it must reach the halfway mark; and before getting to the halfway mark, it must get to the quarter mark, the eighth, the sixteenth,

cone at varying angles. He subjected the sections (ellipse, hyperbola, parabola), which had been known to mathematicians since about 335 B.C., to detailed analysis. Apollonius discussed the basic properties of asymptotes, chords, axes, tangents, and so on, for these curves and thereby paved the way for their application to modern mechanics and astronomy. The significance of the work of Apollonius in this field was not realized until the development of projective geometry, which did not occur until the seventeenth century.

Archimedes and Apollonius were the last of the great theoretical mathematicians until the Renaissance. With the exception of the work of these two—and even some of their work was motivated by the possibility of application—beginning in the third century B.C., practical arithmetic and astronomy provided the impetus for all the major advances in mathematics until the sixteenth century. Thus, the Alexandrian school of mathematics became a partner of the budding science of astronomy, and from it came the opposing concepts of the motion of the earth in relation to the sun—the *heliocentric theory* of Aristarchus of Samos (third century B.C.), the Copernicus of antiquity—and the *geocentric theory* of Apollonius of Perga, which had the support of most of the ancient astronomers who considered the topic. The greatest of these astronomers, Hipparchus (fl. 130 B.C.), the father of trigonometry, adopted the geocentric theory, as did Claudius Ptolemy (fl. 150 A.D.), whose *Almagest* became the astronomical Bible of medieval and Renaissance Europe.

Alexandria also fathered the beginning of algebra as a subject studied without recourse to geometry, through the works of Diophantus (third century B.C.). He invented a symbolism that was to be a transition between the primitive algebra (called *rhetorical algebra*), in which the statement of problems is given solely in words, and that of modern times, which is completely symbolic. The symbolism invented by Diophantus is called "syncopated" because it used the first letters of words to replace the words. Diophantus also made a systematic study of equations in which the number of quantitative conditions put on the unknowns is smaller than the number of unknowns. Diophantus showed how to solve these if a qualitative condition, such as "the answer must be a whole number," is placed on the variables; this type of solution comes under the heading of *Diophantine analysis*.

The Middle Ages.—Beginning with the fall of Rome, 476 A.D., mathematics entered a stagnation that lasted nearly 800 years. During this sterile era, very little work of consequence can be attributed to European mathematicians. One of the few exceptions during this period was Anicius Manlius Severinus Boethius (c. 480–c. 524), who managed to reconstruct a fragment of Euclid's geometry and some of the Greek theory of numbers. However, between 400 and 1200, the development of mathematics advanced mainly through the efforts of the Hindus and the Arabs, who have contributed some of the most important of mathematical concepts.

Hindu Influence.—After the burning of the library of Alexandria by the Arabs in 642 A.D. the center of mathematical activity moved to Persia (Iran and Afghanistan) and to India, countries that had previously benefited by an influx of scholars from Egypt, Mesopotamia, and Greece during the decline of Roman power in the East. With the advantages gained by their invention of zero and a positional decimal system of numeration (the Hindu-Arabic system we use today), the Indians managed to surpass all their predecessors in the development of methods of calculation (*algorithms*) and in the solution of algebraic problems. They devised a formula for solving quadratic (second-degree) equations, and managed to solve some cubic (third-degree) equations. They gave rules for simplifying complicated radicals, for operating with zero and with negative numbers, and discovered "imaginary" numbers (numbers involving $\sqrt{-1}$). Their algebra was rhetorical.

Arab Influence.—When they conquered Persia and culturally penetrated India, the Arabs became acquainted with the mathematics of the vanquished people and adapted it to the mathematics they had found in Alexandria. The great importance of the Arab school of mathe-

matics stems from the fact that their scholars translated the Greek works into Arabic, thus preserving the manuscripts that they had not destroyed. Moreover, they added to this store of Greek mathematics the arithmetic and algebra that had been developed in India. The only fields in which they made major contributions of their own were astronomy and spherical trigonometry. From the ninth century to the twelfth century, the Arab universities in Spain attracted European mathematicians, among whom were Gerbert, who later became Pope Sylvester II (d. 1003), and Adelard of Bath (c. 1120), who made a translation into Latin of an Arabic version of Euclid's *Elements* and commented on an arithmetic prepared from earlier works by Al-Khowarizmi (fl. 820). A corruption of the latter's name resulted in the word *algorism* (an efficient written method of calculation), while the Arabic word *al-jabr*, in the title of his work on the subject, accounts for the word "algebra."

Revival of European Mathematics.—The meager writings of Boethius constituted the only source of mathematical knowledge in the medieval church schools until the appearance in Ireland, England, and continental Europe of translations of Arabic works. The first book by a European explaining the Hindu-Arabic numerals, and methods of computing with them, that was more than a translation of an Arabic source was *Liber Abaci* ("Book of the Abacus") written in 1202 by Leonardo da Pisa, also known by his self-given nickname of Fibonacci ("Son of a Simpleton").

NEW YORK PUBLIC LIBRARY

THE ABACUS, an early form of the digital computer, was used to perform mathematical computations prior to the Christian Era. This sixteenth-century woodcut shows two men calculating sums on their abaci while a scribe records their answers.

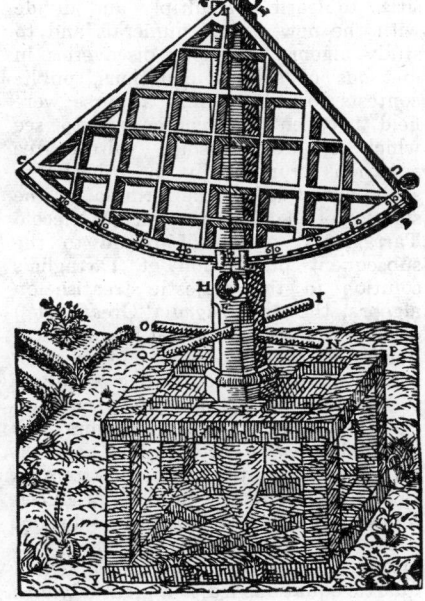

NEW YORK PUBLIC LIBRARY

PRE-GALILEAN ASTRONOMY relied on such nontelescopic instruments as this quadrant reproduced from Tycho Brahe's *Astronomiae Instauratae Mechanica*, published in 1598. Despite the crudeness of these instruments, astronomers were quite accurate.

BETTMANN ARCHIVE

GOTTFRIED WILHELM VON LEIBNIZ, noted for development of differential calculus.

The Fibonacci sequence 1, 1, 2, 3, 5, 8, . . ., in which each term (after the first two) is the sum of the two preceding terms, made its first appearance in this book. Mathematicians have connected this sequence with the "divine proportion" or "golden section," a proportion for line segments that is pleasing to the eye, prized by artists of the Renaissance. The advent of Fibonacci marked the beginning of three and a half centuries of Italian domination in the field of mathematics. Students from all over the Western world flocked to Italian universities to learn to multiply and divide with the new Arabic numerals and to study algebra. To spur discoveries in methods of solving equations, public contests for honors and a purse were held between two contenders to see which one could solve third-degree equations proposed by the other. One such contest led to the formula for the solution of all cubic equations by Niccolò Tartaglia (c. 1500–1557) and to the subsequent publication of Tartaglia's solution in the majestic treatise on algebra, the *Ars Magna* ("Great Art") of Jerome Cardan in 1545. It was a student of Cardan, Lodovico Ferrari, who solved the general fourth-degree (quartic) equation. For the three centuries that followed, activity in algebra was directed toward solving the general fifth-degree (quintic) equation. Attempts to unravel this knotty problem produced much new mathematics, but no solution.

The interest in algebra that was aroused by the solution of the cubic and quartic equations led to a great advance in the development of symbolic notation. This intermittent but agelong struggle started with the use by the Egyptians of the word "heap" for the unknown and hieroglyphs of legs walking left or right to represent addition and subtraction, respectively. By the middle of the eighteenth century, all the symbols of classical algebra had been invented, with mathematicians of many European countries taking part in the development. The question of notation, however, still occupies mathematicians.

Seventeenth-Century Developments.— Although every development in mathematics has its impact, some are so revolutionary that they alter the subject's course of development. One such advance came in 1637, when the French mathematician René Descartes published his *Discourse on Method.* In his essay on geometry, Descartes made use of a pair of numbers to locate a point in reference to a pair of conveniently drawn intersecting lines. This correspondence between number and point made it possible to study geometric relations by means of equations. The union of algebra and geometry in this manner is known as *analytic geometry,* and was a necessary step toward the invention of the calculus.

Most inventions in mathematics have been preceded by an extended period of preparation and by a particular need for the innovation. This was the case in the formulation of the *integral calculus,* which had its beginnings in Archimedes' great work on quadrature (finding areas bounded by curves). When Johannes Kepler (1571–1630) tried to explain his observations on the motion of the earth in relation to the sun, he made use of the conic sections invented in one form by the Greek mathematician Menaechmus (c. 350 B.C.) and in another form by Apollonius of Perga. Kepler also made use of a crude type of calculus to formulate one of his laws on planetary motion. It remained for Sir Isaac Newton (1642–1727) and Gottfried Wilhelm von Leibniz (1646–1716) to invent a *differential calculus*

BETTMANN ARCHIVE

BLAISE PASCAL, French mathematician, developed a theory of projective geometry.

and to discover that the processes of differentiation and integration are related operations. Although Leibniz published his results before Newton and used a notation superior to that of the English mathematician, the fact that the two had met and had exchanged correspondence led to one of the most bitter priority quarrels in the annals of science. Today both are granted credit for independent discovery.

The great astronomical developments that followed the use of the telescope by Galileo Galilei (1564–1642) in making celestial observations required quick methods of calculation. The invention of *logarithms* by John Napier in 1614 filled this need and gave great impetus to the development of *trigonometry.*

ERIC POLLITZER

PROJECTIVE GEOMETRY was one of the scientific principles utilized by Renaissance artists as they brought realism into painting. The dotted lines in this seventeenth-century woodcut illustrate the perspective the artists used to achieve a three-dimensional effect.

Moreover, the application of mathematics to the art of gambling, which had small beginnings among Italian algebraists in the fifteenth and sixteenth centuries, came to the mathematical foreground with the formulation of the laws of probability in the work of the French mathematician Pierre de Fermat (1601–1665) and Blaise Pascal (1623–1662) in 1653. The latter was also responsible for the first mechanical adding machine based on the use of gears. This device followed closely the invention of the slide rule by William Oughtred (1574–1660) in 1632.

The seventeenth century, which provided the setting for the invention of logarithms, analytic (coordinate) geometry, the theory of probability, and the calculus, also witnessed another important development—the invention by Gérard Desargues (1593–1662) and Blaise Pascal of *projective geometry*, which treats of geometric relations that remain invariant under central projection, a subject related to perspective.

Eighteenth-Century Developments.—During the seventeenth and eighteenth centuries, the attention of mathematicians was focused on the extension of the scope of probability of the calculus to physics and astronomy. The eighteenth century can be called the century of the great analysts, as those who have made signal contributions to the calculus are known. The Swiss mathematician Leonhard Euler (1707–1783) was the most prolific of these. The years he spent in Russia at the invitation of Catherine the Great laid the foundation for the excellence of Russian mathematicians in modern times. He and Joseph Louis Lagrange (1736–1813) invented the *calculus of variations*, a subject of great importance in applied mathematics.

BETTMANN ARCHIVE

KARL FRIEDRICH GAUSS, important European mathematician, gave new insight to the understanding of circular measurement.

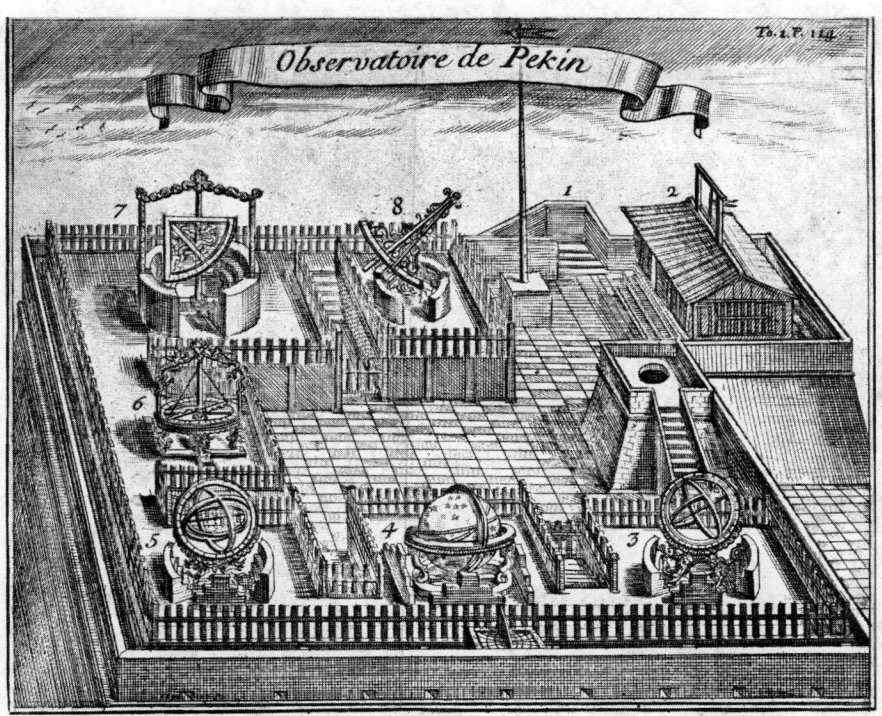

NEW YORK PUBLIC LIBRARY

CHINESE OBSERVATORY at Peking was equipped with a large number of surprisingly accurate astronomical instruments, including the equatorial armillary (3), celestial sphere (4), zodiacal armillary (5), azimuth indicator (6), quadrant (7), and sextant (8). These instruments were indicative of a correspondingly high degree of mathematical sophistication.

■ **CHINESE CONTRIBUTIONS.**—The eighteenth century also witnessed the introduction into Europe, via the returning Jesuit missionaries, of Chinese mathematics. Although little is known of the early development of Chinese mathematics, because their early writings—written on perishable substances such as bark and bamboo—have not survived, it has been ascertained that the Chinese had developed a body of mathematical knowledge that was already ancient in 1100 B.C. In the years following the Arab conquest of Alexandria, many scholars moved eastward into India, which had trade and diplomatic relations with China. It is therefore assumed by historians that a very limited exchange of mathematical knowledge did take place between Europeans and Chinese and may have been responsible for the Chinese influence on the development in Europe of such areas as *determinants* (square arrays of numbers that are related to the coefficients of the unknowns in a set of equations that can be used to solve the equations) and of a set of numbers giving the coefficients of the expansion of a binomial raised to any positive integral power (the *Pascal triangle of numbers*).

It is definitely known, moreover, that Jesuit missionaries to China brought back to Europe, as early as the seventeenth century, knowledge of an equivalent of the *binary system* of numeration. This place system of numeration, which

requires only two symbols—0 and 1—was resurrected by mathematicians building the first electronic computers; the "0" was indicative of the absence of a current and the "1" of the presence of a current. In the more recently developed computers, the binary system has been replaced by other methods of registering a number.

Rise of Non-Euclidean Geometry.—One of the topics that was intensively investigated during the eighteenth century was Euclid's *parallel postulate*, the modern equivalent of which is the statement that through a point outside a straight line, one, and only one, straight line may be drawn parallel to the given line. Mathematicians over the centuries had tried to prove this statement; that is, to derive this statement as a consequence of the other postulates and definitions of Euclid. In 1733, a book giving the results of an investigation into the consequences of denying this postulate and of substituting for it two postulates, each contradicting Euclid's, was published by an Italian Jesuit, Girolamo Saccheri (1667–1733). The two types of geometry that stemmed from the postulates that Saccheri substituted for Euclid's were so strange that even a hundred years after the publication of Saccheri's work, when Europe's most renowned mathematician discovered one of the two geometries of Saccheri, he was too timid to make

INTERNATIONAL BUSINESS MACHINES CORPORATION

MÖBIUS STRIP, discovered by A. F. Möbius in 1858, is a topological curiosity that has only one surface and only one edge. For this reason, when pushed completely around the strip along its track, the arrow will return to its starting point but will be inverted.

public his investigations. The mathematician in question was Karl Friedrich Gauss (1777–1855), the founder of the modern German school of mathematics, who is today credited with having been the first mathematician of note to have reached the conclusion that Euclid's *parallel postulate* was independent of the other postulates of Euclid, and to have recognized that it is possible to create another type of geometry that is as valid as that of Euclid. Gauss coined the word "non-Euclidean" to describe the new geometry. The name most widely associated with the discovery of the non-Euclidean geometry of the type studied by Gauss, however, is that of Nikolai I. Lobachevsky (1793–1856), whose first publication on the subject appeared in 1829. The Hungarian János Bolyai (1802–1860) is also given credit for the independent discovery of a non-Euclidean geometry, although his work did not make its appearance until 1832 and resembled that of Gauss and Lobachevsky. In 1854 a student of Gauss, Georg Riemann (1826–1866), lectured at Göttingen University on another type of non-Euclidean geometry—the *elliptic geometry* that was first mentioned in Saccheri's work.

The importance to mathematics of

the discovery of non-Euclidean geometries lies in the fact that it freed mathematics from the notion that a postulate, or axiom, had to meet with acceptance because it was a "self-evident" truth; that is, that it was consistent with our experience in the physical world. With the advent of the non-Euclidean geometries and the subsequent change in the concept of the function of a set of postulates, it became possible to develop mathematical systems entirely divorced from what we consider to be reality. Mathematics became abstract—it could no longer be conceived of as a subject that expounds absolute truths, but instead had to be thought of as one that draws necessary inferences from a set of postulates that may or may not be true.

Modern Mathematics.—While geometry was undergoing profound changes of aspect in the early part of the nineteenth century, the study of algebra was also being subjected to sweeping revision. The problem that sparked the revolution in algebra concerned the search for a solution to the equation of fifth degree, a search that had been going on in mathematical circles for the three centuries following Lodovico Ferrari's solution of the fourth-degree equation.

Two young men were involved, and both were tragic figures in that they died without having enjoyed the public acclaim their work earned for them. Niels Henrik Abel (1802–1829), who died of tuberculosis caused by deprivation, proved the impossibility of solving the general equation of fifth degree in terms of radicals. This brought to an abrupt close the three-century-old search for a solution to the general quintic. (Unknown to Abel, however, the theorem had been proved inadequate by Paolo Ruffini [1765–1822] some 25 years earlier. It is now called the Abel-Ruffini theorem.) Evariste Galois (1811–1832), the other young genius, spent the night before a fatal duel writing a memoir on his theory of groups as they applied to the problem of solving algebraic equations. Although he had been anticipated by both Lagrange and Ruffini in this work, Galois was the first mathematician to show the structure of the *transformation group* associated with the roots of an algebraic equation and to point the way to the development of an abstract algebra. Today the Galois theory of equations has been superseded by more powerful methods, but his was the work that initiated a new school of mathematics—one in which the study of both algebra and geometry became a matter of studying transformation groups.

■ **STATISTICS.**—The study of *statistics* emerged as a separate discipline when mathematicians began to apply the theory of probability to fields other than gambling. Abraham De Moivre (1667–1754), known for his contributions to the theory of complex numbers, investigated the distributions of errors in a large collection of data and came upon a bell-shaped curve, now known as the *normal curve*. The first applications of statistics were related to astronomical data, and it was in this area that major contributions were made to the theory by several members of the Bernoulli family (seventeenth-eighteenth centuries), Pierre Simon de Laplace (1749–1827), Adrien Marie Legendre (1752–1833), Karl Friedrich Gauss, and a host of other mathematicians. The application of statistics to the analysis of social problems began with Adolphe Quetelet (1796–1874), a Belgian mathematician and astronomer who conceived of studying the incidence of various types of crime in a given population. This type of application was furthered by the work of Sir Francis Galton (1822–1911), who widened the scope of statistics to many fields, including education. The use of statistics in solving problems related to business and manufacturing is comparatively new, having received great impetus during World War II. It should be noted that the Russians have been active in this area and have made important contributions.

■ **TOPOLOGY.**—One of the subjects that has been largely responsible for changing the whole aspect of mathematics is *topology*. Generally classified as a branch of geometry, topology is concerned with the transformations that can be applied to a surface by twisting, stretching, and bending—but not cutting or breaking into—the surface. It is also applied to the study of nets of lines connecting points and to a variety of problems involving the location of geometric entities without regard to size. Although conceived originally as an oddity for mathematical recreation (and called *analysis situs* by the first to mention it, Gottfried Wilhelm von Leibniz), it has at the present time many applications to such diverse studies as economics and electrical circuitry. A pure mathematician now studies it by algebraic means.

■ **BOOLEAN ALGEBRA.**—When Leibniz searched for a "universal characteristic" that would make it possible to study logic from the point of view of the form of a statement divorced from the meaning of the words used in framing it, he anticipated the modern development of *symbolic logic*, which had its real beginnings about 1850 in the work of the Englishman George Boole (1815–1864). In his books *Symbolic Logic* and *Investigation into the Laws of Thought*, Boole used algebraic symbolism and the operations of arithmetic, as well as the symbols 0 and 1, to indicate "falsity" or "truth" of a statement. He also used the concept of classes of entities, the finite sets of modern mathematics. The modern Boolean algebra is an outgrowth of this effort and has become one of the tools of applied mathematics.

■ **TRANSFINITE NUMBERS.**—Whereas Boole developed an algebra of finite sets, the German mathematician Georg Cantor (1845–1918) dared attack the problem of formulating an algebra of infinite sets, the measures of which are called *transfinite numbers*. This work met with fierce denunciation by many prominent contemporaries, and it has only recently come to be fully appreciated as one of the most original and useful concepts of modern mathematics, forming the foundation of function theory and topology.

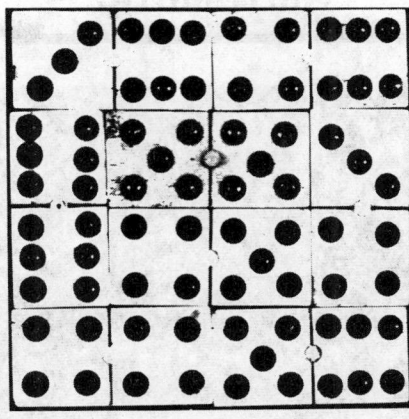

INTERNATIONAL BUSINESS MACHINES CORPORATION

MAGIC SQUARES are arrays of numbers whose columns, rows, and diagonals yield the same sum upon addition. The square on the left, whose sum is 19, is composed of dominoes. The array on the right, which was devised by the German painter Albrecht Dürer in 1514, uses each of the consecutive numbers from 1 to 16 only once and has a sum of 34.

■ **MATHEMATICAL ANALYSIS.**—Based on the work of Joseph Louis Lagrange, *mathematical analysis* began its development during the first third of the nineteenth century. Among the pioneers in mathematical analysis, besides Lagrange, were Sir William Rowan Hamilton (1805–1865) and Karl Gustav Jacobi (1804–1851), who formulated some of the basic equations of *analytical dynamics*, which has proved to be of great value to engineers and physicists. In the late nineteenth century, the American physicist Josiah Willard Gibbs (1839–1903) was attracted to the work of Hamilton, as well as to that of Hermann Gunther Grassmann, who had made formidable contributions to *geometric algebra*. By modifying their theories and combining them with his own, Gibbs formulated *vector analysis*, one of the physicist's most powerful mathematical tools.

Modern Mathematical Progress.—The theory of sets was evolved by Cantor at a time when mathematicians were occupied with the foundations of the subject. Since most of mathematics depends on (or grows out of) arithmetic, the first concern was with a definition of number that, together with certain postulates, could be used to evolve the whole body of mathematics. Advances in arithmetization were made by the German mathematician Karl T. Weierstrass (1815–1897), Georg Cantor, and Richard Dedekind (1831–1916), and the French mathematician Charles Meray (1835–1911). The work was carried forward by Giuseppe Peano (1858–1932) who, in collaboration with a large group of mathematicians, undertook to rewrite the whole system of mathematics in symbolic form. In the course of this work the group, publishing under the name of Peano, invented many of the symbols now used in set theory and logic. Peano's system of postulates makes it possible to derive the entire arithmetic of numbers from a small number of statements.

Another group of mathematicians is rewriting the whole body of mathematics in the rigor available to mathematicians in the mid-1960's. This group, which is composed of a varying number of France's best mathematicians (with a few nationals of other countries), writes under the name of the nonexistent "General Nicholas Bourbaki." They have produced about three dozen volumes on mathematics that have been used as resource materials by other writers and present the ultimate in the axiomatization of mathematics. It is this group that was instrumental in causing the revision of the curricula and methods of teaching mathematics that has recently been under way in most countries of the world.

The theory of sets left two questions that have only recently been answered. At the International Congress of Mathematicians in 1900, the German mathematician David Hilbert (1862–1943) gave an address in the course of which he suggested 15 problems that required solution. Among these problems was that of determining whether or not there was a transfinite number between that of the measure of Cantor's smallest transfinite, which corresponds to the size of the set of counting numbers, and the larger one, which corresponds to the size of the set of rational numbers. Professor Paul Cohen of Stanford University proved that the existence of an in-between number could neither be proved nor disproved.

The outcome of Cohen's work is that the theory of sets is placed in exactly the same position in which geometry found itself when the non-Euclidean geometries were proved to have the same degree of validity as that of Euclid. It is quite possible, therefore, that his work may have as profound an impact on the development of mathematics as the invention of the non-Euclidean geometry had more than a century ago.

—Linda Allegri

INTERNATIONAL BUSINESS MACHINES CORPORATION

CUBE OF LIGHTS visually illustrates the answer when any number from one to eight is multiplied, squared, or cubed by lighting the appropriate number of bulbs.

ARITHMETIC

FLAGS, SYMBOLIZING ENEMY PLANES shot down, were used by pilots. This is an example of one-to-one correspondence, or *equivalent sets.*

Numbers.—The study of arithmetic is concerned with the notion of number and the fundamental concepts and relations that pertain to the use of numbers. As is often the case, the basic terms are not easily definable, if, indeed, they can be defined at all without circular reasoning. Although the sense of quantity is undoubtedly as old as historical man, records of the earliest development of numbers are lost. Man could probably keep "count" long before he had developed a written language. Records do indicate, however, that work with a system of numbers dates back to approximately 3500 B.C.

A number is a complete abstraction—something that cannot be seen. In order to better understand the nature of number, the concept of *set* is introduced. Basically, the term "set" is also undefined, although it does have several synonyms. A set may be thought of as a collection, a class, an aggregate, or an ensemble of anything whatsoever that one might wish to include in it. The items, objects, people, numbers, or ideas that may be used in constructing a particular set are referred to as the *members* or *elements* of the given set. Ordinarily, the elements that belong to a given set are identified by certain distinguishing characteristics. Thus, it is always possible to ascertain which elements belong to a given set and which elements do not. The set containing no elements is referred to as the *null,* or *empty, set.* A few common illustrations of the set concept are: a set of dishes, a herd of sheep, a class of students, a collection of stamps, a set of numbers. Since sets can be created mentally, there is no end to the kinds or quantity of sets that can be defined. Man's mental processes are continually organizing data

into sets, for sets enable him to understand the nature of number. The two sets below include as elements only those markings (which have no particular meaning) seen within the closed curves.

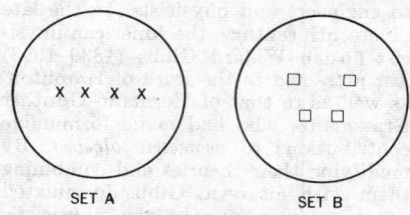

Each of these sets has different elements, yet one's mind is immediately aware of a property that is common to both of them. That property can be demonstrated in the diagram below.

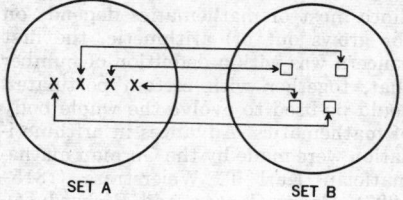

When the elements from set A are paired with the elements of set B, there are no elements left over in either set. Thus, each element of set A is said to correspond to one, and only one, element of set B, and each element of set B corresponds to one, and only one, element of set A. This pairing, or matching, of elements in two (or more) sets is called a *one-to-one correspondence.*

All of the sets whose elements can be placed in a one-to-one correspondence with each other are said to be *equivalent sets,* regardless of what the individual

elements in each set may be. All equivalent sets are said to possess the same *cardinal* property. This property of sets answers the question "how many?" and is one of the fundamental aspects of the number concept. Equivalent sets are said to have the same cardinal number.

It is common practice to use capital letters to denote particular sets, and to enclose within a pair of braces the elements or statements describing the elements of the set. For example, to indicate the set of letters that constitute the English alphabet, one could use either: set $A = \{a,b,c,d,e,f,g,h,i,j,k,l,m,n,o,p,q,r,s,t,u,v,w,x,y,z\}$, or set $A = \{$all the letters of the English alphabet$\}$. To express the number associated with the set of letters from the English alphabet, one could write $n(A) = 26$. If set $A = \{\square\square\square\}$, then $n(A) = 3$; if set $A = \{1,2,3,4\}$, then $n(A) = 4$. In general, if A represents a particular set, then $n(A)$ is a number. However, it should be noted that a number is not the same as a set.

It is conjectured that, prior to the development of a number vocabulary, ancient man used bags of stones, notches in a stick, and similar devices to keep track of how many animals he had in a given year. For example, for each sheep or goat in a herd he would have one, and only one, stone. He had thus established a one-to-one correspondence between the elements in his herd and the elements in his bag of stones. During recent wars, airplane crews painted a picture on their planes for each enemy plane they destroyed. The familiar practice of making penciled tally marks when keeping a count of certain quantities of items is still another illustration of the use of the basic one-to-one correspondence idea, which is similar to the techniques used by primitive man.

■ **MODEL COLLECTIONS.**—An extension of the one-to-one correspondence concept occurred with the development of model collections that served to represent the cardinality (the "how many") of certain sets. For example, the set of wings on birds was used to symbolize the concept of "twoness"; the legs on certain animals, "fourness"; the fingers on a man's hand, "fiveness"; and so on. The names of these model collections could then be used to express the same information that had previously required the use of bags of stones or notches in a stick. The words for the model collections eventually underwent changes; they eventually lost their concrete and descriptive origins and became abstract words. Vestiges of these model collections are still apparent in some of the number-words of various cultures that exist today.

A second aspect of the concept of number can be illustrated in the following manner. In any racing competition there may be many contestants who begin; however, the final results are indicated by the order in which the contestants finish, that is, first, second, third, and so on. Here the concept of number tells the order of events. This is called the *ordinal* property of numbers. Common illustrations include house numbers, telephone numbers, and license numbers.

The process of counting could not be developed until the model collections had been arranged in a definite, ordered sequence. The very essence of counting implies that it must be possible to establish a natural progression of increasing magnitude among the model collections; that is, the model collections that are used to denote cardinality cannot be used in counting until they have been ordered (arranged) so that it is possible to move from one model to its successor that has one more member in it. Names and symbols can now be assigned to the cardinal numbers of these sets. To count a set of objects involves

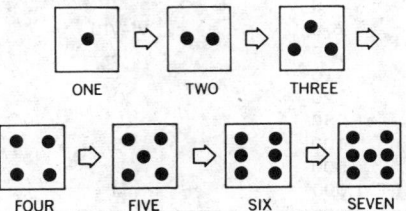

assigning to every element in the set a name from the ordered model collection beginning with the smallest and continuing until the last element in the set to be counted has been assigned a name from the model collection. The last name to be assigned is the ordinal number of the set. By this matching, two questions can be answered: "how many?" and "which one?" These questions correspond to the terms "cardinal" and "ordinal," respectively. The property of immediate succession that all counting numbers have is basic to the scientific process.

Systems of Numeration.—Knowledge of the historical development of a set of symbols (model collections) and of a language for conveying number sense is largely a matter of extrapolation and conjecture. The dates of man's earliest attempts at symbolization are lost. However, it is known from various artifacts that the Egyptians by 3500 B.C., and the Greeks and Chinese at about the same time, had used the tally mark (either a simple horizontal or vertical stroke) to refer to their beginning numbers. As the quantity of strokes increased, other symbols were introduced to summarize collections of the simple strokes. The various sets of symbols that were the inventions of men and have differed between cultures are called the *numerals* or *number symbols*. These numerals are the pictorial representations that man uses to refer to numbers which are complete abstractions. A set of numerals and the rules for their usage constitute a *numeration system*.

The set of symbols used today in the Western world is called *Hindu-Arabic* because it was probably first developed by the Hindus by 250 B.C.; it was later transported to Europe by the Arab traders. The earliest set of Hindu symbols did not contain the symbol zero; this was not introduced until about 600 A.D. Similarly, the general appearance of some of the original symbols has undergone modifications. Until the invention of the printing press in the fifteenth century, standardization of all written material was difficult.

■ **EGYPTIAN.**—In studying systems of numeration, there are certain underlying principles that are evident. For example, an *additive principle* is involved in the systems where different symbols are used to indicate collections of other symbols. Thus, to find the number that is being represented by a set of symbols (numerals), the individual numbers represented are simply added. An early illustration of this principle is the ancient Egyptian hieroglyphic system of numeration. (See the accompanying chart.) Note that considerable repetition of basic symbols was necessary in order to

WIDE WORLD

ORDINAL PROPERTY of numbers can be illustrated by a race. This aspect of number tells the order of events, or how the runners finish.

Egyptian System of Numeration

Modern Hindu-Arabic Numerals	Egyptian Numerals	
1	ǀ	a simple stroke
2-9	ǁǀ-ǀǀǀǀǀ	series of simple strokes
10	∩	a heel bone
20	∩∩	two heel bones
55	∩∩∩∩∩ǀǀǀǀǀ	five heel bones and five simple strokes
100	𓍢	a coiled rope
1000	𓆼	a lotus flower
1,000,000	𓁨	a man in astonishment

Roman System of Numeration

Modern Hindu-Arabic Numerals	Roman Numerals
1	I
2-3	II–III
4	IV
5	V
6-8	VI–VIII
9	IX
10	X
20	XX
50	L
100	C
500	D
1,000	M

Babylonian System of Numeration

Modern Hindu-Arabic Numerals	Babylonian Numerals	
1	𒁹	
2-9	𒁹𒁹-𒁹𒁹𒁹	
10	⟨	
60	𒁹	
600	⟨	
3602	⟨𒁹𒁹	(early)
3602	⟨𒁹𒁹𒁹	(later; use of a symbol for the empty place)

Greek System of Numeration

Modern Hindu-Arabic Numerals	Greek Symbol	Greek Name
1	A	alpha
2	B	beta
3	Γ	gamma
4	Δ	delta
5	E	epsilon
6	F	digamma
7	Z	zeta
8	H	eta
9	Θ	theta
10	I	iota
20	K	kappa
30	Λ	lambda
40	M	mu
50	N	nu
60	Ξ	xi
70	O	omicron
80	Π	pi
90	Ϙ	koppa
100	P	rho
200	Σ	sigma
300	T	tau
400	Υ	upsilon
500	Φ	phi
600	X	chi
700	Ψ	psi
800	Ω	omega
900	λ	sampi

represent large numbers. Also, the Egyptian system did not consider as important the order or position in which the symbol occurred in the representation of a particular number. Thus, a number such as 13 could be represented either as ǀǀǀ ∩ or ∩ ǀǀǀ. It is interesting to see that their system was based on ten, but that they did not have a symbol for zero and they did not use place value. Despite these limitations in their system of numeration, they did build the great pyramids between 3000 and 2000 B.C., which certainly required considerable mathematical sophistication.

■ ROMAN.—The Romans, whose influence was at its peak at about 100 A.D., had developed a system of numeration that was also essentially additive at first. However, later developments introduced both *subtractive* and *multiplicative principles*. The Romans used an *abacus* to perform their computations and then recorded the results using the Roman numerals. Subtraction was later introduced and was used when a smaller number preceded a larger one; the two quantities were considered together and the smaller was subtracted from the larger.

To express the number nine, the Romans used IX, which meant subtracting the quantity one from the quantity ten. This technique is believed to have been introduced in order to save space in writing or printing and therefore was probably a relatively recent innovation to the system. To represent large numbers, the Roman system used a bar over particular numerals. One bar meant that the symbol underneath was to be multiplied by one thousand. For example: $\overline{XXIV}$ represented the quantity 20,004. Using two bars above a numeral meant that the symbols underneath were to be multiplied by one million. Thus $\overline{\overline{XXIV}}$ represented 20,000,004. Whereas the Egyptian numeration system was a simple additive system, the Romans employed some subtraction and multiplication. The Romans also made some use of place value based on ten; that is, L = 5 × 10, C = 10 × 10, D = 5 × 10 × 10, and M = 10 × 10 × 10. While addition and subtraction may be performed quite easily in the Roman system, multiplication and division are difficult.

■ BABYLONIAN.—From ancient Babylonian (about 3000 B.C.) recordings on cuneiform tablets (cuneiform was the written language of the Sumerians, or Babylonians) there are indications that they were the first to use the principle of position, or place value. They performed their writing on soft pieces of clay with a stylus; the clay tablets were left to dry in the sun or were baked to form hard tablets that have been preserved to the present time. The oldest of these tablets, dated at about 3000 B.C., is from the city of Ur. The recognition and subsequent use of place value has been referred to as a most important step in the development of an efficient numeration system.

The Babylonians used an essential base of sixty; and since they wrote with a stylus on their clay tablets, the symbol for unity (one) appears as a wedge, 𒁹. This wedge symbol was used to indicate one, sixty, sixty-sixties, or higher multiples of sixty, depending upon its position within the numerical representation. To denote the quantity ten, they put two wedge marks together at a slight angle to each other, ⟨. In some of the records it appears that they may have used different-size wedges to distinguish between one and sixty. Their early use of place value consisted primarily of leaving a vacant space between wedges. Later, they put two double wedges together to represent zero. Some examples of their numeration are shown in the accompanying chart.

Today units of time are used that reflect the Babylonian base sixty (*sexagesimal*): sixty seconds in a minute, sixty minutes in an hour. Angle measurements also reflect the base sixty. Babylonian astronomers kept very accurate records of sun and moon eclipses. These and other records that have been well preserved on clay tablets have provided a complete legacy of Babylonian mathematical and scientific accomplishments.

■ GREEK.—The Greeks, whose civilization lasted roughly from 600 B.C. to 400 A.D., used a very simple system of numeration. It was based on ten, but neither had a symbol for zero nor used place value. They used letters from their alphabet to represent numbers. (See the accompanying chart.)

The Greeks made many contributions to the area of mathematics, in particular the area of proofs. Their greatest work was in geometry; they even did their algebra problems geometrically whenever possible because their numeration system was poorly developed.

■ HINDU-ARABIC.—The numeration system that is presently used in the United States and most other countries is basically Hindu in origin. However, through the 2,000 years since its first known usage, it has undergone several major modifications. The earliest Hindu numbers were called Brahmi numbers and did not have a symbol for zero nor did they make use of place value. By 500 A.D., the Indian symbols did include a zero and made use of place value. It was the Arab traders of this period that brought the system from India to Europe, and thus today it is referred to as the *Hindu-Arabic numeration system*. It is called a *base*, or *scale*, *ten* (*decimal*) *system*, because it uses only ten basic symbols or digits: 0, 1, 2, 3, 4, 5, 6, 7, 8, 9. These basic symbols are said to have face value. In addition to their face value, the location of a particular digit in a number representation is significant. This gives the digits positional, or place, value (similar to the technique introduced earlier by the Babylonians) in addition to their face value. Finally, the system uses the additive principle. Consider the Hindu-Arabic numeral, 5,965. This expresses the number five thousand nine hundred and sixty-five. The representation may be rewritten in the following form to illustrate the positional and additive principles: $5,000 + 900 + 60 + 5$. By using powers of ten (exponential representation) this can be written in the form: $(5 \cdot 10^3) + (9 \cdot 10^2) + (6 \cdot 10^1) + (5 \cdot 10^0)$. Note that $10^0 = 1$. In this system of numeration, place value is in terms of powers of ten. The English language has definite words to describe some of these, as shown below.

Words Used to Describe Powers of Ten in U.S.*

Word	Numeral	Power of Ten
Units	1	10^0
Tens	10	10^1
Hundreds	100	10^2
Thousands	1,000	10^3
Ten thousands	10,000	10^4
Hundred thousands	100,000	10^5
Millions	1,000,000	10^6
Ten millions	10,000,000	10^7
Hundred millions	100,000,000	10^8
Billions	1,000,000,000	10^9
Ten billions	10,000,000,000	10^{10}
Hundred billions	100,000,000,000	10^{11}
Trillions	1,000,000,000,000	10^{12}

* In the United States and France, the system shown in this table is used to name the powers of ten; in England and Germany, a slightly different system is used.

In a system of numeration (such as the Hindu-Arabic) that makes use of a definite base and possesses the important symbol zero, uses positional notation, and is additive, any whole number can be represented by the general expression:

$$N = a_n x^n + a_{n-1} x^{n-1} + \ldots + a_2 x^2 + a_1 x^1 + a_0 x^0,$$

where x represents the particular base and a represents the respective coefficient. For example, in the Hindu-Arabic decimal system, the numeral 5,965 has 10 as its base, or x, value, and the coefficients are 5, 9, 6, and 5, reading from right to left.

$$N = 5,965$$
$$= (5 \cdot 1000) + (9 \cdot 100) + (6 \cdot 10) + (5)$$
$$= (5 \cdot 10^3) + (9 \cdot 10^2) + (6 \cdot 10^1) + (5 \cdot 10^0)$$

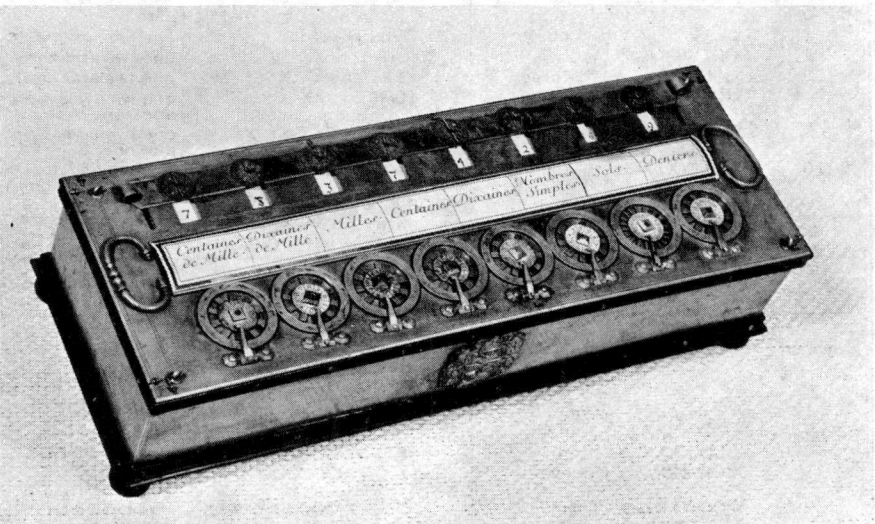

MATHEMATICAL CALCULATING DEVICES have existed for millennia. The clay tablet (*above*) was used in Babylon about 1600 B.C. The Roman abacus (*center*) dates back more than two thousand years and is not unlike the abacus used by the Chinese. The calculator (*below*), developed by Blaise Pascal in 1647, led the way to the computer of today.

■ **QUINARY SYSTEM.**—The use of other base values has received extensive consideration during recent years. For example, consider a system of numeration that has all the properties of the Hindu-Arabic, but which, instead of having ten different digits, has only five digits, 0, 1, 2, 3, 4. This would constitute a *base*, or *scale, five (quinary) system.* Having reached the number represented by 4, and thereby exhausting the individual digits, "fiveness" would be represented by the numeral 10, "sixness" by 11, "sevenness" by 12, and so on.

Note that the numerals 10, 11, and 12 are not read as ten, eleven, and twelve. They are read as either one-zero (one collection of five and no ones), one-one (one collection of five and one), one-two (one collection of five and two) or as five, six, and seven, respectively. Whereas our base ten system is referred to as a *decimal system* because it has ten different digits, the base five system is called a *quinary system*. In base ten, there is a *decimal* point to indicate the separation of a whole number and a fraction, whereas in base five this separation point would be called the *quinary* point. The accompanying table shows a comparison of base ten and base five in terms of the symbols, basic collections, and possible word names.

■ **BINARY SYSTEM.**—Another base that has found extensive usage in recent years is the *binary*, or *base two, system.* This is the simplest significant base that can be used. It has only two symbols and again it is convenient to use the symbols from base ten, 0 and 1. Records indicate that Thomas Harriot used a binary system during the early seventeenth century. Later in the same century, Gottfried Wilhelm Leibniz attempted to use the binary system for a religious purpose. He had hoped to convince the Chinese emperor that God (whose symbol was unity, or one) created everything from the void, which was, of course, represented by the zero. However, until the recent development of electronic data processing and computers, usage of base two was negligible. The reason that base two has become so vital to computers is that there are many electrical components, such as switches, relays, magnetic particles, and electronic tubes, that are capable of only two different positions, "On" and "Off." To represent the number one, a switch or relay may be closed so that electrical current will flow; to represent zero, the switch or relay may be open so that no current will flow.

In the binary system, the place values are in multiples of two. Thus, the numeral (1 or 0) in the rightmost place represents either 1 or 0, the next place represents the two's place, the next the four's, etc. For example, 110101 may be written in base two as follows:

$$(1 \cdot 2^5) + (1 \cdot 2^4) + (0 \cdot 2^3) + (1 \cdot 2^2) + (0 \cdot 2^1) + (1 \cdot 2^0)$$

The accompanying table compares base ten and base two in terms of their symbolization, basic collections, and possible word names.

■ **DUODECIMAL SYSTEM.**—Another base that has received considerable attention recently is the *duodecimal*, or *base twelve, system.* The utilization of this base necessitates the introduction of two new symbols; often *t* and *e* are used to represent the concept of "tenness" and "elevenness." Thus, a complete set of digits for base twelve is: 0, 1, 2, 3, 4, 5, 6, 7, 8, 9, *t*, and *e*. Twelve is represented by 10 (one-zero). The advantages of this base are to be found in the area of division. Whereas the base ten has only 2 and 5 as factors, a base of twelve has 2, 3, 4, and 6. This provides a considerable advantage in computations that involve fractions. Many products are handled in lots, or collections, of twelve. For example, eggs are sold by the dozen, or dozen-dozen (gross). In 1944, the Duodecimal Society of America was founded and has served as the center of activity for those persons interested in the promotion of this base. The accompanying table compares base ten and base twelve in terms of symbolization, basic collections, and possible word names.

To summarize the discussion of numeration systems, the accompanying table compares the four bases which have been presented.

In order to perform the basic operations of arithmetic (addition, subtraction, multiplication, and division) in the various bases, the basic addition and multiplication facts must be known. The following tables present this information, which will be referred to in the next section.

Comparison of Base Ten with Base Five

Symbol	Base Ten Collections	Names	Symbol	Base Five Collections	Names
0		zero	0	X	zero
1	X	one	1	X	one
2	XX	two	2	XX	two
3	XXX	three	3	XXX	three
4	XXXX	four	4	XXXX	four
5	XXXXX	five	10	XXXXX	one five and zero
6	XXXXXX	six	11	XXXXX X	one five and one
7	XXXXXXX	seven	12	XXXXX XX	one five and two
8	XXXXXXXX	eight	13	XXXXX XXX	one five and three
9	XXXXXXXXX	nine	14	XXXXX XXXX	one five and four
10	XXXXXXXXXX	ten	20	XXXXX XXXXX	two fives and zero
11	XXXXXXXXXX X	eleven	21	XXXXX XXXXX X	two fives and one
25	XXXXXXXXXX XXXXXXXXXX XXXXX	twenty-five	100	XXXXX XXXXX XXXX XXXXX XXXXX	one five-fives, zero fives and zero
43	XXXXXXXXXX XXXXXXXXXX XXXXXXXXXX XXXXXXXXXX XXX	forty-three	133	XXXXX XXXXX XXXX XXXXX XXXX XXXX XXXXX XXXXX XXX	one five-fives three fives and three $(1 \cdot 5^2 + 3 \cdot 5^1 + 3 \cdot 5^0)$

Comparison of Base Ten with Base Two

Symbol	Base Ten Collections	Names	Symbol	Base Two Collections	Names
0		zero	0		zero
1	X	one	1	X	one
2	XX	two	10	XX	one two and zero
3	XXX	three	11	XX X	one two and one
4	XXXX	four	100	XX XX	one two-twos and zero
5	XXXXX	five	101	XX XX X	one two-twos and one
10	XXXXXXXXXX	ten	1010	XX XX XX XX XX	(names become very cumbersome)
16	XXXXXXXXXX XXXXXX	sixteen	10000	XX XX XX XX XX XX XX XX	

Comparison of Base Ten with Base Twelve

Symbol	Base Ten Collections	Names	Symbol	Base Twelve Collections	Names
0		zero	0		zero
1	X	one	1	X	one
9	XXXXXXXXX	nine	9	XXXXXXXXX	nine
10	XXXXXXXXXX	ten	t	XXXXXXXXXX	ten
11	XXXXXXXXXX X	eleven	e	XXXXXXXXXX	eleven
12	XXXXXXXXXX XX	twelve	10	XXXXXXXXXXXX	one twelve and zero
18	XXXXXXXXXX XXXXXXXX	eighteen	16	XXXXXXXXXXXX XXXXXX	one twelve and six
24	XXXXXXXXXX XXXXXXXXXX XXXX	twenty-four	20	XXXXXXXXXXXX XXXXXXXXXXXX	two twelves and no ones

Addition Facts

Base Ten

+	0	1	2	3	4	5	6	7	8	9	10
0	0	1	2	3	4	5	6	7	8	9	10
1	1	2	3	4	5	6	7	8	9	10	11
2	2	3	4	5	6	7	8	9	10	11	12
3	3	4	5	6	7	8	9	10	11	12	13
4	4	5	6	7	8	9	10	11	12	13	14
5	5	6	7	8	9	10	11	12	13	14	15
6	6	7	8	9	10	11	12	13	14	15	16
7	7	8	9	10	11	12	13	14	15	16	17
8	8	9	10	11	12	13	14	15	16	17	18
9	9	10	11	12	13	14	15	16	17	18	19
10	10	11	12	13	14	15	16	17	18	19	20

Base Twelve

+	0	1	2	3	4	5	6	7	8	9	t	e	10
0	0	1	2	3	4	5	6	7	8	9	t	e	10
1	1	2	3	4	5	6	7	8	9	t	e	10	11
2	2	3	4	5	6	7	8	9	t	e	10	11	12
3	3	4	5	6	7	8	9	t	e	10	11	12	13
4	4	5	6	7	8	9	t	e	10	11	12	13	14
5	5	6	7	8	9	t	e	10	11	12	13	14	15
6	6	7	8	9	t	e	10	11	12	13	14	15	16
7	7	8	9	t	e	10	11	12	13	14	15	16	17
8	8	9	t	e	10	11	12	13	14	15	16	17	18
9	9	t	e	10	11	12	13	14	15	16	17	18	19
t	t	e	10	11	12	13	14	15	16	17	18	19	1t
e	e	10	11	12	13	14	15	16	17	18	19	1t	1e
10	10	11	12	13	14	15	16	17	18	19	1t	1e	20

Base Five

+	0	1	2	3	4	10
0	0	1	2	3	4	10
1	1	2	3	4	10	11
2	2	3	4	10	11	12
3	3	4	10	11	12	13
4	4	10	11	12	13	14
10	10	11	12	13	14	20

Base Two

+	0	1
0	0	1
1	1	10

Multiplication Facts

Base Ten

×	0	1	2	3	4	5	6	7	8	9	10
0	0	0	0	0	0	0	0	0	0	0	0
1	0	1	2	3	4	5	6	7	8	9	10
2	0	2	4	6	8	10	12	14	16	18	20
3	0	3	6	9	12	15	18	21	24	27	30
4	0	4	8	12	16	20	24	28	32	36	40
5	0	5	10	15	20	25	30	35	40	45	50
6	0	6	12	18	24	30	36	42	48	54	60
7	0	7	14	21	28	35	42	49	56	63	70
8	0	8	16	24	32	40	48	56	64	72	80
9	0	9	18	27	36	45	54	63	72	81	90
10	0	10	20	30	40	50	60	70	80	90	100

Base Twelve

×	0	1	2	3	4	5	6	7	8	9	t	e	10
0	0	0	0	0	0	0	0	0	0	0	0	0	0
1	0	1	2	3	4	5	6	7	8	9	t	e	10
2	0	2	4	6	8	t	10	12	14	16	18	1t	20
3	0	3	6	9	10	13	16	19	20	23	26	29	30
4	0	4	8	10	14	18	20	24	28	30	34	38	40
5	0	5	t	13	18	21	26	2e	34	39	42	47	50
6	0	6	10	16	20	26	30	36	40	46	50	56	60
7	0	7	12	19	24	2e	36	41	48	53	5t	65	70
8	0	8	14	20	28	34	40	48	54	60	68	74	80
9	0	9	16	23	30	39	46	53	60	69	76	83	90
t	0	t	18	26	34	42	50	5t	68	76	84	92	t0
e	0	e	1t	29	38	47	56	65	74	83	92	t1	e0
10	0	10	20	30	40	50	60	70	80	90	t0	e0	100

Base Five

×	0	1	2	3	4	10
0	0	0	0	0	0	0
1	0	1	2	3	4	10
2	0	2	4	11	13	20
3	0	3	11	14	22	30
4	0	4	13	22	31	40
10	0	10	20	30	40	100

Base Two

×	0	1
0	0	0
1	0	1

■ **CONVERSIONS.**—Numerals written in various bases (that is, numeration systems that employ the same general principles as the Hindu-Arabic system) can be converted to base ten notation.

Examples:

Change 324_{five} to base ten notation.

$$= (3 \times five \times five) + (2 \times five) + 4$$
$$= (3 \times 25) + (10) + 4$$
$$= 75 + 10 + 4$$
$$= 89_{ten}$$

Change 1101_{two} to base ten notation.

$$= (1 \times two \times two \times two) + (1 \times two \times two) + (0 \times 2) + 1$$
$$= (1 \times 2 \times 2 \times 2) + (1 \times 2 \times 2) + (0 \times 2) + 1$$
$$= 8 + 4 + 0 + 1$$
$$= 13_{ten}$$

Change $2e5_{twelve}$ to base ten notation.

$$= (2 \times twelve \times twelve) + (e \times twelve) + 5$$
$$= (2 \times 12 \times 12) + (11 \times 12) + 5$$
$$= 288 + 132 + 5$$
$$= 425_{ten}$$

To change numbers written in base ten numerals to other base numerals we again make use of the fact that the size (or quantity) of the base collections has to be altered. Whether the collections are larger or smaller than ten will depend upon whether the new base is larger or smaller than ten.

Example:

Change 97_{ten} to base five notation. In base five the values of the places are one, five, five $\times$ five, five $\times$ five $\times$ five, and so on. In base ten these place values

Comparison of the Four Bases Presented

Base Ten (Decimal)	Base Five (Quinary)	Base Two (Binary)	Base Twelve (Duodecimal)
1	1	1	1
2	2	10	2
3	3	11	3
4	4	100	4
5	10	101	5
6	11	110	6
7	12	111	7
8	13	1000	8
9	14	1001	9
10	20	1010	t
11	21	1011	e
12	22	1100	10
50	200	110010	42
100	400	1101100	84
1000	13000	1111101000	6e4

are 1, 5, 25, and 125. Thus 97_{ten}

$$= 75 + 20 + 2$$
$$= (3 \times 25) + (4 \times 5) + 2$$
$$= (3 \times five \times five) + (4 \times five) + 2.$$

This last expression is written as 342 in base five, since it represents three collections of five-fives, four collections of five, plus two ones. The following procedure of a step by step breakdown into multiples of five is equivalent to repeated division by five.

5)97		
19	with a remainder of 2	This indicates there are 19 fives and 2 ones.
5)19		
3	with a remainder of 4	This indicates there are 3 five-fives and 4 fives.
5)3		
0	with a remainder of 3	This indicates there are no collections of five × five × five; however, there are 3 five-fives.

INTERNATIONAL BUSINESS MACHINES CORPORATION

ELECTRONIC COMPUTERS rely almost entirely upon the binary system because electronic tubes and transistors are capable of only two different positions: "On" and "Off."

By writing the remainders in the reverse order of the repeated division, the correct result of 342 is obtained. Therefore, $97_{ten} = 342_{five}$.

Example:

Change 475_{ten} to base two notation using the repeated division procedure as shown above.

$2)\dfrac{475}{237}$	with a remainder of 1
$2)\dfrac{237}{118}$	with a remainder of 1
$2)\dfrac{118}{59}$	with a remainder of 0
$2)\dfrac{59}{29}$	with a remainder of 1
$2)\dfrac{29}{14}$	with a remainder of 1
$2)\dfrac{14}{7}$	with a remainder of 0
$2)\dfrac{7}{3}$	with a remainder of 1
$2)\dfrac{3}{1}$	with a remainder of 1
$2)\dfrac{1}{0}$	with a remainder of 1

By writing the remainders in the reverse order of the repeated division as in the previous example, the result $475_{ten} = 111011011_{two}$ is obtained.

Example:

Change 1862_{ten} to base twelve notation using the repeated division procedure as shown above.

$12)\dfrac{1862}{155}$	with a remainder of 2
$12)\dfrac{155}{12}$	with a remainder of e
$12)\dfrac{12}{1}$	with a remainder of 0
$12)\dfrac{1}{0}$	with a remainder of 1

By writing the remainders in the reverse order of the repeated division as in the previous examples, the result $1862_{ten} = 10e2_{twelve}$ is obtained.

■ **OPERATIONS.**—To perform the operation of addition in base ten, one has had to learn the 100 fundamental addition facts or combinations. To add in base five, the 25 fundamental combinations must be known; in base twelve there are 144, while in base two there are only 4 basic combinations. The tables previously given illustrate what the fundamental facts are for each of the bases mentioned.

The following example is given in order to review the steps that are taken in adding, or finding the sum of, two numbers in base ten.

Example:

Find the sum of 28_{ten} and 45_{ten}.

$$\begin{array}{r} 2 \text{ tens} + 8 \text{ ones} \\ + 4 \text{ tens} + 5 \text{ ones} \\ \hline 6 \text{ tens} + 13 \text{ ones} \\ = 7 \text{ tens} + 3 \text{ ones} \\ = 73_{ten} \end{array}$$

The same general procedure is used to find the sum of two numbers in other bases. The following examples illustrate this for the bases five, twelve, and two.

Examples:

Find the sum of 22_{five} and 14_{five}.

$$\begin{array}{r} 2 \text{ fives} + 2 \text{ ones} \\ + 1 \text{ five} + 4 \text{ ones} \\ \hline 3 \text{ fives} + 11 \text{ ones*} \\ = 4 \text{ fives} + 1 \text{ one} \\ = 41_{five} \end{array}$$

(*Note: $2 + 4 = 11$ in base five.)

Find the sum of 36_{twelve} and 75_{twelve}.

$$\begin{array}{r} 3 \text{ twelves} + 6 \text{ ones} \\ + 7 \text{ twelves} + 5 \text{ ones} \\ \hline t \text{ twelves} + e \text{ ones*} \\ = te_{twelve} \end{array}$$

(*Note: $3 + 7 = t$ and $6 + 5 = e$ in base twelve.)

Find the sum of 101_{two} and 011_{two}.

$$\begin{array}{r} 1(\text{two} \times \text{two}) + 0(\text{two}) + 1 \text{ one} \\ + 0(\text{two} \times \text{two}) + 1(\text{two}) + 1 \text{ one} \\ \hline 1(\text{two} \times \text{two}) + 1(\text{two}) + 10 \text{ one} \\ = 1(\text{two} \times \text{two}) + 10(\text{two}) + 0 \text{ one} \\ = 10(\text{two} \times \text{two}) + 0(\text{two}) + 0 \text{ one} \\ = 1000_{two} \end{array}$$

To perform the operation of subtraction (inverse operation of addition) the fundamental combinations in the addition table must again be referred to. To find the difference of two numbers, that is, $a - b$, a number c must be found which, when added to b, will equal a.

For example, in base ten $8 - 3 = 5$ since $8 = 3 + 5$. The following examples are given to show the steps performed in subtraction.

Examples:

Find the difference of 861_{ten} minus 284_{ten}.

$$\begin{array}{r} 8 \text{ hundreds} + 6 \text{ tens} + 1 \text{ one} \\ - 2 \text{ hundreds} + 8 \text{ tens} + 4 \text{ ones} \\ \hline \end{array}$$

$$\begin{array}{r} 7 \text{ hundreds} + 15 \text{ tens} + 11 \text{ ones} \\ = - 2 \text{ hundreds} + 8 \text{ tens} + 4 \text{ ones} \\ \hline 5 \text{ hundreds} + 7 \text{ tens} + 7 \text{ ones} \\ = 577_{ten} \end{array}$$

(Check: $861 - 284 = 577$ since $861 = 284 + 577$ in base ten.)

Find the difference of 321_{five} minus 142_{five}.

$$\begin{array}{r} 3 \text{ five-fives} + 2 \text{ fives} + 1 \text{ one} \\ - 1 \text{ five-fives} + 4 \text{ fives} + 2 \text{ ones} \\ \hline \end{array}$$

$$\begin{array}{r} 2 \text{ five-fives} + 11 \text{ fives} + 11 \text{ ones} \\ = - 1 \text{ five-fives} + 4 \text{ fives} + 2 \text{ ones} \\ \hline 1 \text{ five-fives} + 2 \text{ fives} + 4 \text{ ones} \\ = 124_{five} \end{array}$$

(Check: $321 - 142 = 124$ since $321 = 142 + 124$ in base five.)

Find the difference of $4e2_{twelve}$ minus 212_{twelve}.

$$\begin{array}{r} 4 \text{ twelve-twelves} + e \text{ twelves} + 2 \text{ ones} \\ - 2 \text{ twelve-twelves} + 1 \text{ twelve} + 2 \text{ ones} \\ \hline 2 \text{ twelve-twelves} + t \text{ twelves} + 0 \text{ ones} \end{array}$$

(Check: $4e2 - 212 = 2t0$ since $4e2 = 212 + 2t0$ in base twelve.)

To multiply and divide in the various bases, the fundamental multiplication facts for each base are necessary. The operation of multiplication can be performed by either a horizontal or a vertical procedure.

Examples:

Multiply 4563_{ten} by 18_{ten} using the horizontal procedure.

$$\begin{aligned} &= 18(4 \text{ thousands} + 5 \text{ hundreds} + 6 \text{ tens} \\ &\quad + 3 \text{ ones}) \\ &= (18 \times 4) \times 10^3 + (18 \times 5) \times 10^2 \\ &\quad + (18 \times 6) \times 10^1 + (18 \times 3) \\ &= (72 \times 10^3) + (90 \times 10^2) + (108 \times 10^1) + 54 \\ &= 82134_{ten} \end{aligned}$$

Multiply 4563_{ten} by 18_{ten} using the vertical procedure.

$$\begin{array}{r} 4563_{ten} \\ \times 18_{ten} \\ \hline 36504 \\ 4563 \\ \hline 82134_{ten} \end{array}$$

These procedures are equally applicable to multiplication in other bases, but the vertical procedure is more frequently used.

Examples:

Multiply 34_{five} by 4_{five}.

$$\begin{array}{r} 34_{five} \\ \times 4_{five} \\ \hline 301_{five} \end{array}$$

(Note: $4 \times 4 = 31$ in base five. Write the 1 and carry 3 fives. The second step involves multiplying 4×3, which equals 22 in base five, and then adding the carry of 3; $22 + 3 = 30$ in base five.)

Multiply 243_{five} by 24_{five}.

$$\begin{array}{r} 243_{five} \\ \times 24_{five} \\ \hline 2132 \\ 1041 \\ \hline 13042_{five} \end{array}$$

Multiply 39_{twelve} by 8_{twelve}.

$$\begin{array}{r} 39_{twelve} \\ \times 8_{twelve} \\ \hline 260_{twelve} \end{array}$$

(Note: $8 \times 9 = 60$ in base twelve. Write the 0 and carry 6 twelves. The second step involves multiplying 8×3, which equals 20 in base twelve, and then adding the carry of 6; $20 + 6 = 26$ in base twelve.)

Multiply 11011_{two} by 111_{two}.

$$\begin{array}{r} 11011_{two} \\ \times 111_{two} \\ \hline 11011 \\ 11011 \\ 11011 \\ \hline 10111101_{two} \end{array}$$

(Note: In this base, multiplication is very easy; the only problem is in adding the various products.)

To perform the operation of division (inverse operation of multiplication), the facts from the multiplication table are used. In dividing we are "undoing" multiplication. In base ten, for example, $8 \times 6 = 48$, while $48 \div 8 = 6$. This can be stated in a general way which holds true for all bases: If $a = b \times c$, then $a \div b = c$ and $a \div c = b$. There are several forms used in performing the operation of division, which are discussed more fully in the section on operations on whole numbers. For the purpose here, the more commonly used method, as illustrated for the base ten below, will be employed.

Example:

Divide 6270_{ten} by 38_{ten}.

$$
\begin{array}{r}
165_{ten} \\
38_{ten})\overline{6270_{teu}} \\
38 \\
\hline
247 \\
228 \\
\hline
190 \\
190 \\
\hline
\text{(no remainder)}
\end{array}
$$

(Note: It is assumed that the reader is familiar with this procedure. If not, see the section on division of whole numbers, page 1091.)

In this example there was no remainder after the last step. In practice, however, there frequently is a remainder that may be expressed as a fraction or a whole number of units; or further steps may be taken in the division process to express the remainder as a decimal fraction.

Example:

Divide 422_{ten} by 4_{five}.

$$
\begin{array}{r}
103_{five} \\
4_{five})\overline{422_{five}} \\
4 \\
\hline
22 \\
22
\end{array}
$$

Divide 434_{five} by 23_{five}.

$$
\begin{array}{r}
14_{five} \\
23_{five})\overline{434_{five}} \\
23 \\
\hline
204 \\
202 \\
\hline
2 \quad \text{(with a remainder of 2)}
\end{array}
$$

Divide 11_{two} by 10_{two}.

$$
\begin{array}{r}
1_{two} \\
10_{two})\overline{11_{two}} \\
10 \\
\hline
1 \quad \text{(with a remainder of 1)}
\end{array}
$$

Divide 11101_{two} by 101_{two}.

$$
\begin{array}{r}
101_{two} \\
101_{two})\overline{11101_{two}} \\
101 \\
\hline
1001 \\
101 \\
\hline
100 \quad \text{(with a remainder of 100)}
\end{array}
$$

Divide $e3_{twelve}$ by 5_{twelve}.

$$
\begin{array}{r}
23_{twelve} \\
5_{twelve})\overline{e3_{twelve}} \\
t \\
\hline
13 \\
13
\end{array}
$$

Divide $9et_{twelve}$ by $5e_{twelve}$.

$$
\begin{array}{r}
18_{twelve} \\
5e_{twelve})\overline{9et_{twelve}} \\
5e \\
\hline
40t \\
3e4 \\
\hline
16 \quad \text{(with a remainder of 16)}
\end{array}
$$

The operation of division is relatively more difficult than the other operations since it involves addition, subtraction, and multiplication.

It is possible to use fractions in these other bases, even though their appearance is somewhat confusing at first. For example, in base ten, one-half is indi-

cated by the symbol $\frac{1}{2}$. Since base two has no symbol 2, one-half would be expressed as $\frac{1}{10}$two. The fraction eleven-twelfths from base ten ($\frac{11}{12}$) would be $\frac{e}{10}$ in base twelve. If it is desired to express these fractions as decimal fractions, the need for naming the decimal point must be recognized, since it by name refers to the decimal, or base ten, system. For base five, the term *quinary point* could be used, for base two, the *binary point*, and for base twelve, the *duodecimal point*.

It should be noted that after having performed any one of the four operations in a base other than ten, it is always possible to check the work by converting the numbers involved into base ten and then reperforming the operation.

The study of the growth and development of numeration systems closely parallels the growth and scientific accomplishments of civilizations. This study also permits a better understanding and appreciation of the present base ten system. The fact that base ten is used does not necessarily mean that it is the best of all possible numeration systems. It has been said that, had Cleopatra's nose been an inch longer, the course of history might have been different. So too, the course of numeration systems might have been appreciably different had man been born with more or less than ten fingers. It is important to realize, however, that without an efficient numeration system advances in other areas of knowledge would be greatly impeded, if not made impossible at some points. It can also be speculated that if man had a better system (whatever that might be), his civilization would now be further advanced.

The Whole Numbers.—In the previous section the set of natural numbers was defined. For instance, the natural number 2 is the number of the set $A = \{a, b\}$ and is also the number of any set which may be placed in one-to-one correspondence with the set A. The set of all such numbers is $N = \{1, 2, 3, 4, 5, 6, \ldots\}$. The set of *whole numbers* will be thought of as the natural numbers together with the number zero. Zero (0) is defined as the number of an empty set, that is, a set with no elements. An example of an empty set would be the set of all living men over 12 feet tall. For convenience, the set of whole numbers will be denoted by the capital letter $W = \{0, 1, 2, 3, 4, 5, 6, 7, \ldots\}$.

In studying the system of whole numbers, we shall be interested in the usual operations on whole numbers and the laws which govern the behavior of whole numbers with respect to these operations. Let us consider what is meant by the term *operation*. By an operation on the whole numbers we mean any process which associates a single unique whole number with one, two, three, or more whole numbers. For example, the operation which associates 1 with 1, 4 with 2, 9 with 3, 16 with 4, and so on, is called

the *squaring* operation. Since this operation associates a single element of W with a single element of W it is called a *unary* operation. Most of the usual operations with whole numbers are *binary* operations, since they associate a single unique element of W with a *pair* of elements of W. Addition associates the single element 5 with the pair of elements (2, 3) and multiplication associates the element 6 with the pair (2, 3). As an example of a *ternary* operation, consider the operation of taking the maximum of three whole numbers. Under this operation max $(2, 4, 7) = 7$.

Basic Operations.—The operations of addition, multiplication, subtraction, and division are commonly called the four fundamental operations of arithmetic. Of these operations, addition and multiplication are basic, since subtraction and division may be defined from them. In the operation of addition, two whole numbers are associated with a third whole number called the *sum*. Each of the two given numbers is called an *addend*. In the operation of multiplication, two whole numbers are associated with a third whole number called the *product*. Each of the two given whole numbers is called a *factor*. Thus, (a, b, c elements of W) $a + b = c$ is written for addition and $a \times b = c$, or $a \cdot b = c$, or $ab = c$ for multiplication.

■ **ADDITION.**—The operation of addition is very closely allied with the counting process and the experience of combining sets of objects. For example, suppose that there are two separate bookshelves and it is desired to determine the total number of books on them. There are two alternatives: the two collections of books can be mentally combined into one set and the total number of books can be added; or, the number of books on each shelf can be counted and then "added" to find the total number of books. It is in the comparison of these two techniques that the germ of the meaning of addition is found.

Now consider the problem of finding the sum of 3 and 4 ($3 + 4$), assuming no previous knowledge of such sums. To determine the sum, choose any set A which has 3 elements and any other set B which has no elements in common with A and contains 4 elements. For example, let $A = \{r, s, t\}$ and $B = \{a, b, c, d\}$. As in the bookshelf example, the total number of letters of the alphabet that are in the two sets can be found by combining them into a single set and counting. Combining two sets into a single set in this way is called taking their union and is denoted by the symbol $A \cup B$. (In general the union of two sets is the set which contains all elements that belong to either of them.) Here $A \cup B = \{r, s, t, a, b, c, d\}$ and the number of elements in $A \cup B$ is 7, by counting. It is on this basis that it can be concluded that $3 + 4 = 7$.

Of course it is not necessary or practical to carry out such an involved procedure in every situation that requires addition. Rather, it is used as an illustration of the basic meaning of the operation from which the definition and further properties are deduced. Any process which leads to the sum of two whole numbers in the above sense will be called an addition.

■ **DEFINITION.**—The definition of addition of whole numbers can now be easily framed in terms of the above example and the language of sets. If m and w are any two whole numbers, and A and B are two sets with no elements in common such that $n(A) = m$ and $n(B) = w$, then $m + w = n(A) + n(B) = n(A \cup B)$. Note that the restriction that A and B have no elements in common is a necessary one. If the two sets were to have elements in common, these would be counted only once in the union of the two sets, whereas they would be counted once in each of the individual sets. This is made clear if one considers the set A to be members of the Rotary Club in a given community and B to be the members of the Chamber of Commerce in the same community. Presumably, there will be some overlap in the membership of these two organizations. It is clear that the total number of persons in the two organizations is not the sum of the numbers of persons in each organization.

On the basis of this definition there are several important and readily apparent properties possessed by the operation of addition with whole numbers: (1) For any two whole numbers m and w there is always a whole number v associated with them as their sum; this is called the *closure property of addition* for whole numbers. (2) For any two whole numbers m and w the sum is the same regardless of the order in which taken, that is, $m + w = w + m$; this principle is called the *commutative law of addition*. (3) For any three whole numbers m, w, and v, $m + w + v = (m + w) + v = m + (w + v)$. Since the definition of addition is as a binary operation it does not directly provide a technique for adding more than two whole numbers. The law just stated, called the *associative law of addition*, gives a technique for adding three whole numbers in two different ways. By this law $2 + 3 + 5 = (2 + 3) + 5 = 5 + 5 = 10$, or $2 + 3 + 5 = 2 + (3 + 5) = 2 + 8 = 10$. In practice, the *associative* and *commutative* laws allow the addition of whole numbers in any order or grouping. (4) The whole number zero (0) has the special property that when added to any whole number the result is that same whole number. Thus $m + 0 = m$ for any whole number m. 0 is called the *identity* element for the operation of addition. No other whole number has this property. This property of zero, though seemingly trivial, will be seen to be very important.

■ **MULTIPLICATION.**—There are at least two possible alternative interpretations for the operation of multiplication. The first of these is essentially in terms of the operation of addition. For example, $3 \cdot 4$

may be thought of as finding the total number of elements in three sets of 4 elements each, or $4 + 4 + 4$. Using the *associative law of addition*, $4 + 4 + 4 = 8 + 4 = 12$. One difficulty with the above process is that from this interpretation it is not readily evident that $3 \cdot 4 = 4 \cdot 3$. In this case it would appear that $3 \cdot 4 = 4 + 4 + 4$ and $4 \cdot 3 = 3 + 3 + 3 + 3$. These two results are entirely different in form, and in the general case would not appear alike at all. However, returning to the original example of three sets of four elements, a reasonable interpretation can be worked out. Place the three sets of four elements each in an array where the elements of each set appear in a row.

a	b	c	d
e	f	g	h
i	j	k	l

From this it is apparent that the elements in each column make up four sets of three elements each and that the total number of elements in each case must be the same. The fact that the elements of three sets are displayed in a rectangular array suggests that it may be possible to arrive at the definition of multiplication directly from notions about sets and counting, as was done with addition. First, suppose that there are two sets A and B such that $n(A) = 3$ and $n(B) = 4$. To establish an operation or process on these sets that will yield a set containing a number of elements equal to $3 \cdot 4$, or 12, which is completely general. As model sets let $A = \{a, d, f\}$ and $B = \{w, r, t, y\}$. Let an array of the elements in B appear as follows.

y	y	y
t	t	t
r	r	r
w	w	w
a	d	f

For each element of the set A, the elements of B will be written in a column over that element. Then, to determine $3 \cdot 4$, the number of squares in the array containing an element of B are counted and this is seen to be 12. As a further

refinement of this procedure, one might construct an array as shown below. Here

y	x	x	x
t	x	x	x
r	x	x	x
w	x	x	x
	a	d	f

instead of actually inserting the letters w, r, t, y in each square of the columns, the positions are identified by placing the letters in a reference column at the left, just as the elements of A appear at the bottom of the array. Note also that the symbol x appearing in each square actually identifies a pair of letters, one each from set A and set B, in that order. As a further refinement of this process, construct a *lattice* of points as shown.

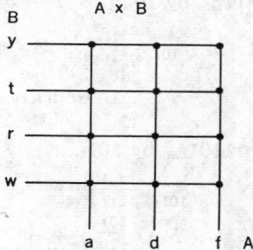

Each point of the lattice represents a pairing of an element of the set A with an element of the set B, for example, the points in the first column represent the pairs (a, w), (a, r), (a, t), (a, y). From the lattice, the product $3 \cdot 4$ may be determined by counting the total number of points in the lattice or by counting the number of elements in each column and then adding. Since there are 4 elements in each column, $3 \cdot 4 = 4 + 4 + 4 = 12$ and the two interpretations of multiplication are related. The process illustrated of forming ordered pairs of elements from two sets, A and B, where the first element of each pair is selected from A and the second from B, is called taking the *set product*, and is written $A \times B$. These set products clearly give a model for defining the operation of multiplication of whole numbers in set language.

■ **DEFINITION.**—If r and s are two whole numbers and if A and B are two sets such that $n(A) = r$ and $n(B) = s$, then

Steps	Justification
$21 + 65 = (20 + 1) + (60 + 5)$	Hindu-Arabic system of numeration.
$\quad = (2 \cdot 10^1 + 1 \cdot 10^0) + (6 \cdot 10^1 + 5 \cdot 10^0)$	Hindu-Arabic system of numeration.
$\quad = 2 \cdot 10^1 + (1 \cdot 10^0 + 6 \cdot 10^1) + 5 \cdot 10^0$	Associative law for addition.
$\quad = 2 \cdot 10^1 + (6 \cdot 10^1 + 1 \cdot 10^0) + 5 \cdot 10^0$	Commutative law for addition.
$\quad = (2 \cdot 10^1 + 6 \cdot 10^1) + (1 \cdot 10^0 + 5 \cdot 10^0)$	Associative law for addition.
$\quad = (2 + 6) \cdot 10^1 + (1 + 5) \cdot 10^0$	Distributive law.
$\quad = 8 \cdot 10^1 + 6 \cdot 10^0$	Basic addition facts.
$\quad = 80 + 6$	Hindu-Arabic system of numeration.
$\quad = 86$	Hindu-Arabic system of numeration.

$r \cdot s = n(A) \cdot n(B) = n(A \times B)$. In terms of this definition and the previous illustration, it is evident that $4 \cdot 3 = n(B \times A)$. The lattice for $B \times A$ as constructed clearly indicates that the

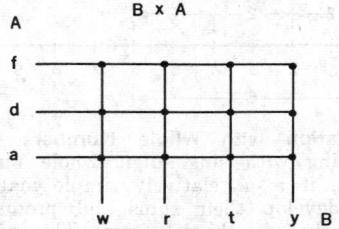

number of elements in $B \times A$ is the same as the number of elements in $A \times B$. In general, a one-to-one correspondence could be set up by associating the ordered pair (y, x) of $B \times A$ with the ordered pair (x, y) of $A \times B$. Thus, from this definition, it follows that $3 \cdot 4 = 4 \cdot 3$ and generally $r \cdot s = s \cdot r$. On the basis of this definition, the operation of multiplication with whole numbers is seen to possess many properties analogous to those of addition:

(1) *Closure property:* for any two whole numbers r and s, there is a third whole number such that $r \cdot s = t$.

(2) *Commutative law:* for any two whole numbers r and s, $r \cdot s = s \cdot r$.

(3) *Associative law:* for any three whole numbers r, s, and t, $r \cdot s \cdot t = (r \cdot s) \cdot t = r \cdot (s \cdot t)$. Since multiplication, like addition, is a binary operation, this law gives a means of multiplying three whole numbers in two different ways. This law can be illustrated as follows: $2 \cdot 3 \cdot 5 = (2 \cdot 3) \cdot 5 = 6 \cdot 5 = 30$, or $2 \cdot 3 \cdot 5 = 2 \cdot (3 \cdot 5) = 2 \cdot 15 = 30$.

(4) *Identity element:* the whole number 1 has the property that if a is any whole number $a \cdot 1 = a$. No other whole number has this property, which is a very important one in carrying out the operations of arithmetic.

(5) The number zero (0) plays a special role in multiplication in that for any whole number a, $a \cdot 0 = 0$.

Each of the principles previously discussed has referred to addition and multiplication as an individual process. In much of the work with the operations of arithmetic, the relationship of the two operations is the primary concern. This relationship is called the *distributive law*, which is stated as follows: for any three whole numbers a, b, and c, $a \cdot (b + c) = (a \cdot b) + (a \cdot c)$. By this law, the product $3(4 + 7)$ may be calculated in two different ways: $3(4 + 7) = 3 \cdot 11 = 33$ or $3(4 + 7) = (3 \cdot 4) + (3 \cdot 7) = 12 + 21 = 33$. The *distributive law* follows as a consequence of the definitions of addition and multiplication.

Inverse Operations.—The two operations of subtraction and division may be defined in terms of set language, but may also be defined in terms of the operations of addition and multiplication. Both approaches are useful and will be illustrated in the following paragraphs.

■ SUBTRACTION.—Suppose that two whole numbers u and v are given and it is desired to determine what the difference of v and u, or $v - u$, is. The process of determining the whole number associated with v and u, $v - u$, is called subtraction. The whole number v is called the *minuend*, and the whole number u, the *subtrahend*.

As a specific example, let $u = 4$ and $v = 7$. Then take as model sets $A = \{a, d, s, f\}$ and $B = \{z, x, c, b, j, g, h\}$. Clearly $n(A) = 4$ and $n(B) = 7$. The operation of subtraction can then be thought of as placing the set A in one-to-one correspondence with some subset of B and then counting the number of elements in the remaining subset of B. Placing A in one-to-one correspondence with $\{x, b, j, h\}$ the remaining subset of B is $\{z, c, g\}$ and its number is 3. Therefore, it can be concluded that $7 - 4 = 3$. This is equivalent to the "take away" interpretation of subtraction.

A clear restriction on this operation is that u is less than or equal to v. In general, given two whole numbers u and v, u may be less than v, v may be less than u, or u may be equal to v. Therefore, it is not always possible to subtract two whole numbers. The operation of subtraction must be carried out in a *specific order*. The fact that $7 - 4 = 3$ does not tell anything about the difference $4 - 7$, which does not exist in the set of whole numbers. In order for such differences to exist the scope of the number system must be expanded.

A desirable alternative to the preceding interpretation of the operation of subtraction relates subtraction to the operation of addition. In the discussion of the meaning of subtraction, note that it was necessary to partition the set B into two sets with no elements in common so that the sum of the numbers of these two sets is $n(B)$, or 7. The definition of subtraction in terms of addition is then that the difference of two whole numbers v and u is a whole number w (if it exists) such that the sum of u and w is v. In the example $7 - 4 = 3$ since $4 + 3 = 7$. This relationship of addition and subtraction is called *inverse*, or subtraction is the *inverse operation* to addition. This is equivalent to the "additive" interpretation of subtraction.

The properties of subtraction are much more restricted than those of addition. It is evident from the discussion above that the whole numbers are not closed under the operation of subtraction and that subtraction does not obey a commutative law. The operation also does not have an associative law. With respect to the whole number 0 and any whole number a, $a - a = 0$, $a - 0 = a$, but $0 - a$ is not defined unless $a = 0$. These properties follow from the definition of subtraction and properties of addition since $a = a + 0$, $a = 0 + a$ and $0 = 0 + 0$. The *distributive law* can be extended to subtraction in a restricted sense. For example, $3(7 - 4) = 3 \cdot 3 = 9$ or $3(7 - 4) = 21 - 12 = 9$. In general, $a \cdot (b - c) = (a \cdot b) - (a \cdot c)$ provided c is less than or equal to b.

■ DIVISION.—In the operation of division one is given two whole numbers, m and n, and asked to associate them with a third whole number, p, called the *quotient* of m and n; this is written $m \div n = p$, $m/n = p$, or $n)\overline{m}$. In this operation, m is called the *dividend* and n the *divisor*. The operation of division may be interpreted in more than one way. For instance, 12 divided by 4 may be thought of as partitioning a set of 12 elements into 4 equal sets and then counting the number of elements in each set as the quotient. The operation can also be thought of as partitioning the 12 elements into distinct sets each of which contains 4 elements and then counting the number of such sets as the quotient. Division can also be thought of in terms of repeated subtraction. That is, subtract 4 from 12, then subtract 4 from the difference and continue until the difference is 0. The number of times 4 has been subtracted before reaching this difference of 0 is the quotient of 12 and 4.

All of these interpretations are mathematically similar in that the quotient is a number such that when it is multiplied by the divisor the product is the dividend. In the example, $3 \cdot 4 = 12$ in each case. Division is thus related to multiplication as an inverse operation. The definition of division in terms of multiplication is then that the quotient of two whole numbers m and n is a whole number p (if it exists) such that

Justification of the Process of Multiplication

Steps	Justification
$34 \times 5 = (30 + 4)(5)$	Hindu-Arabic system of numeration.
$= (3 \cdot 10^1 + 4 \cdot 10^0)(5 \cdot 10^0)$	Hindu-Arabic system of numeration.
$= (3 \cdot 10^1 \times 5 \cdot 10^0) + (4 \cdot 10^0 \times 5 \cdot 10^0)$	Distributive law.
$= 3(10^1 \times 5)10^0 + 4(10^0 \times 5)10^0$	Associative law for multiplication.
$= 3(5 \cdot 10^1)10^0 + 4(5 \cdot 10^0)10^0$	Commutative law for multiplication.
$= (3 \times 5)(10^1 \times 10^0) + (4 \times 5)(10^0 \times 10^0)$	Associative law for multiplication.
$= (3 \times 5)(10^1) + (4 \times 5)(10^0)$	Law of exponents.
$= 15 \cdot 10^1 + 20 \cdot 10^0$	Basic multiplication facts.
$= (1 \cdot 10^1 + 5 \cdot 10^0)10^1 + (2 \cdot 10^1 + 0 \cdot 10^0)10^0$	Hindu-Arabic system of numeration.
$= (1 \cdot 10^1 \cdot 10^1 + 5 \cdot 10^0 \cdot 10^1) + (2 \cdot 10^1 \cdot 10^0 + 0 \cdot 10^0 \cdot 10^0)$	Distributive law.
$= 1(10^1 \cdot 10^1) + 5(10^0 \cdot 10^1) + 2(10^1 \cdot 10^0) + 0(10^0 \cdot 10^0)$	Associative law for multiplication.
$= 1 \cdot 10^2 + 5 \cdot 10^1 + 2 \cdot 10^1 + 0 \cdot 10^0$	Law of exponents.
$= 1 \cdot 10^2 + (5 + 2)10^1 + 0 \cdot 10^0$	Distributive law.
$= 1 \cdot 10^2 + 7 \cdot 10^1 + 0 \cdot 10^0$	Basic addition facts.
$= 100 + 70 + 0$	Hindu-Arabic system of numeration.
$= 170$	Hindu-Arabic system of numeration.

the product of n and p is m, that is, $m = n \cdot p$.

Consideration of the conditions under which the quotient of two whole numbers exists leads to some interesting properties of the division operation: (1) The quotient of a nonzero number and zero must be *undefined*. As an example consider $6 \div 0$. Suppose that quotient is some whole number, k. Then by definition $0 \cdot k = 6$. But this is impossible since $0 \cdot k = 0$. Thus, there is no whole number which is the quotient of 6 and 0. (2) The quotient of 0 and 0 is *indeterminate*. Suppose $0 \div 0 = t$. Then $0 = 0 \cdot t = 0$ and the definition is satisfied. But suppose also that $0 \div 0 = v$, where $v \neq t$. Here again, $0 = 0 \cdot v = 0$ and the definition is again satisfied. Therefore, $0 \div 0$ may be any whole number whatsoever and is said to be *indeterminate*. On the basis of (1) and (2), *0 is ruled out as a divisor*. Hence, in succeeding examples the *divisor will always be nonzero*. (3) $a \div 1 = a$, since $a = 1 \cdot a$. (4) $a \div a = 1$, since $a \cdot 1 = a$. (5) $0 \div c = 0$, since $c \cdot 0 = 0$. (6) In general, $a \div b$ exists if and only if b is a factor of a. This means that there is a whole number c such that $b \cdot c = a$. Then by definition, c is the quotient of a and b. If b is not a factor of a, as in $13 \div 4$, the quotient does not exist in the set of whole numbers. For such quotients to exist, it is necessary to extend the scope of the number system.

The whole numbers do not have closure for the operation of division but quotients when they exist are *unique*. Furthermore, neither the *commutative* nor the *associative laws* hold for division. There is a restricted distributive law for division with respect to addition and subtraction. If a, b, and c are whole numbers and $c \neq 0$, $(a + b) \div c = (a \div c) + (b \div c)$, provided that c is a factor of both a and b. Under the same restrictions, and $a > b$, $(a - b) \div c = (a \div c) - (b \div c)$.

Examples:

$$(12 + 9) \div 3 = 4 + 3 = 7$$
$$(12 - 9) \div 3 = 4 - 3 = 1$$

The Number Line.—By marking an initial point on a straight line as 0 and establishing a certain length as a unit distance, it is possible to establish a correspondence between the whole numbers and a set of points on a line. Using this geometric representation of the whole numbers, the four operations of addition, subtraction, multiplication, and division can be illustrated.

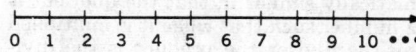

To add two whole numbers, for example, 3 and 4, on the number line, mark off 3 units on the number line from 0 to 3, and then mark off 4 units from 3. The terminal point is found to be 7. Thus $3 + 4 = 7$.

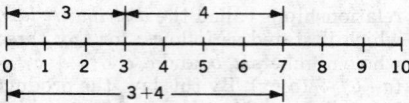

In like fashion 4 and 3 are added and the result is again 7; $3 + 4 = 4 + 3 = 7$.

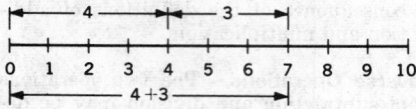

To multiply two whole numbers, say 2 and 3, the additive interpretation is used and 3 units and 3 units are added, again obtaining $2 \cdot 3 = 6$. Again, $3 \cdot 2 = 6$ by a similar process, as illustrated.

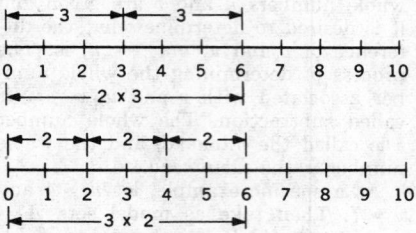

Subtraction on the number line may be thought of in two ways. To find the difference $8 - 3$, mark off 8 units from 0 to the right and then mark off 3 units from 8 to the left, arriving at 5 as the result. This is the "take away" interpretation of subtraction.

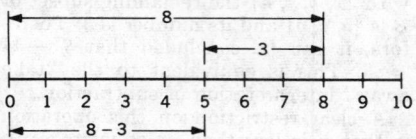

The second illustration is in terms of the definition of the operation of subtraction. Here 3 units are marked off to the right of 0 and 8 units to the right of zero and then count the number of units from 3 to 8; that is, we find the number which, when added to 3, yields 8 as the sum. This is the "additive" interpretation of subtraction.

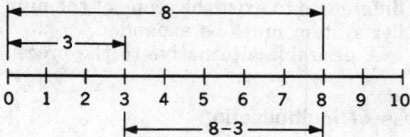

The operation of division can also be carried out in two ways on the number line. To find $6 \div 3$, for example, mark off 6 units to the right of 0 and then divide this segment into distinct segments of 3 units each. Finding that there are two such segments, it is concluded that $6 \div 3 = 2$.

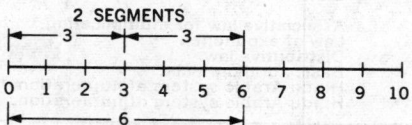

In the second interpretation, divide the segment from 0 to 6 into 3 equal segments. The number of units in each segment is 2. Again, $6 \div 3 = 2$.

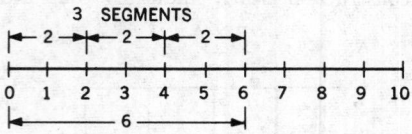

Calculation with Whole Numbers.—In dealing with single-digit whole numbers, it is a relatively simple matter to develop their sums and products directly from the definitions. This information for the digits 0 to 9 is usually collected in the addition and multiplication tables. From these tables, using the definitions of subtraction and division, it is possible to obtain many differences and quotients. The difference $9 - 4$ would be found by identifying the number which, when added to 4, gives 9 as a sum, or by completing the sentence $4 + \square = 9$. The quotient $6 \div 3$ would be found in a similar manner by completing the sentence $3 \times \square = 6$.

To find sums and products for numbers having a multiple-digit numeral, such as 288 and 24, and to find differences and quotients, these elementary methods do not suffice. The definitions guarantee that $288 + 24$, $288 \cdot 24$, $288 - 24$ and $288 \div 24$ all exist but do not give any practical technique for finding their numerical representation. In order to calculate efficiently with whole numbers, it is necessary to develop systematic processes that consist of a series of easy steps for finding the numeral representing such sums, products, differences, and quotients. To be efficient, these processes should make each step in the process as automatic as possible and should require as little writing as possible. Such processes for carrying out the operations of arithmetic are called *algorithms*.

Historically there have been many different algorithms used in calculations with the operations of arithmetic. The algorithms presently used are the result of centuries of refinement. Each of these algorithms compresses a large number of concepts into a relatively short process. These algorithms make it possible for elementary school children today to perform calculations that were exceedingly difficult if not impossible for scholars of a few centuries ago.

■ **ADDITION.**—This is the way the addition of 34 and 23 appears using the customary algorithm for addition:

$$\begin{array}{r} 34 \\ +23 \\ \hline 57 \end{array}$$

The numbers to be added are arranged in a vertical fashion so that the units digits fall in a column. This automatically ensures that the other digits will fall in the proper place-value position. The columns are then added individually and, if no column totals more than 9, these column totals yield the digits of the sum. To show how this process is derived from the basic properties of whole numbers, represent the sum as $34 + 23$. Then, using the numerals in expanded form and the commutative and associative laws for addition: $34 + 23 = (30 + 4) + (20 + 3) = (30 + 20) + (4 + 3) = 50 + 7 = 57$. Adding 30 and 20 strictly in terms of the fundamental combinations is accomplished by writing $30 + 20 = 3 \cdot 10 + 2 \cdot 10 = (3 + 2) \cdot 10 = 5 \cdot 10$ (by the distributive law) $= 50$. This notion operates generally whenever digits are added in a given place-value column. Now consider the following addition:

$$\begin{array}{r} 326 \\ 275 \\ 142 \\ \hline 743 \end{array}$$

Here addition of the digits in the units column results in a number greater than 9, in this case 13 units. Ten units are changed to 1 ten and shifted to the tens column. Again, adding ten digits in the tens column results in 14 tens. Changing 10 tens to 1 hundred and shifting it to the hundreds column, the digits in the hundreds column are added, and the final result thus obtained. Further insight into this process is obtained by writing each numeral in expanded form:

$$(300 + 20 + 6) + (200 + 70 + 5)$$
$$+ (100 + 40 + 2)$$
$$= (300 + 200 + 100) + (20 + 70 + 40) + (6 + 5 + 2).$$

This rearrangement is accomplished through repeated applications of the commutative and associative laws and is identical with the column arrangement of digits by place value. Adding the quantities in each parentheses $600 + 130 + 13$ is obtained. Each of these additions involves the basic combinations and the distributive law. To complete the process:

$$600 + (100 + 30) + (10 + 3)$$
$$= (600 + 100) + (30 + 10) + 3$$
$$= 700 + 40 + 3 = 743.$$

This latter process is equivalent to what is called "carrying" in arithmetic.

In performing such additions the columns may be added up or down. Often the columns are added one way and then added the other way as a check on the calculation. Although the present algorithm adds the units column first, the reason is purely one of economy in writing. However, it is possible to begin with the column farthest to the left:

$$\begin{array}{r} 457 \\ 391 \\ 729 \\ \hline 1400 \\ 160 \\ 17 \\ \hline 1577 \end{array} \qquad \begin{array}{r} 457 \\ 391 \\ 729 \\ \hline 1467 \\ 57 \\ \hline 1577 \end{array}$$

The second method given is one of a number of ancient algorithms known as scratch methods. These originated from the practice of performing calculations on a slate or dust board. Rather than scratching out the digit as was done above, the corrected digits would be wiped out and replaced. The advent of printing and pen-and-pencil work made this process impractical. Theoretically, there are some real advantages in the method, since the digits that make the least difference in the answer are added last, when the mind may have fatigued and error is more likely.

■ **MULTIPLICATION.**—The operation of multiplication involves more steps and is slightly more complex than the operation of addition. The process of multiplication will first be illustrated with several examples and then the reasoning that lies behind it will be examined.

Example:

$$3 \times 72$$

To carry out such multiplications, the two numerals are first arranged vertically with the place values aligned as in addition. The digit 3 of the multiplier then multiplies in turn each digit of the multiplicand from right to left, the products being obtained from the basic multiplication table and written in order from right to left below the line.

$$\begin{array}{r} 72 \\ \times 3 \\ \hline 216 \end{array}$$

In this case, $3 \times 2 = 6$ and $3 \times 7 = 21$, the digits 21 being written to the left of 6 in the product.

Example:

$$6 \times 247$$

Again, the factors are arranged in vertical order with the place values aligned. In this example, however, when multiplying 6×7, the product is 42, a two-digit numeral. Therefore, do not write 42 below the line, but just the 2 in the units place, and hold the 4. Multiply 6×4, obtaining 24. Now add the 4 as a carry to 24, obtaining 28. Again, write only the 8 below the line and to the left of 2, holding the 2 as a carry to the next place. Then take the product of 6 and 2, which is 12, and, after adding the carry, 2, write the sum 14 to the left of 8 and 2, obtaining the product, 1482.

$$\begin{array}{r} 247 \\ \times 6 \\ \hline 1482 \end{array}$$

Example:

$$47 \times 597$$

Proceeding as before, write the two factors in vertical order with place values aligned. In this example there are two digits in the multiplier.

$$\begin{array}{r} 597 \\ \times 47 \\ \hline 4179 \\ 23880 \\ \hline 28059 \end{array}$$

The multiplication is carried out in two steps. First step, using 7, the units digit of 47, is precisely as in the preceding example. This product is called a partial product. Then obtain a second partial product by multiplying the second digit, 4: 4×597. Since 4 really represents 40, or 4 tens, the units digit in this partial product is 0. Otherwise, this partial product is obtained in the same way as was the first. Finally, the two partial products are added to obtain the result, 28,059. In practice, the 0 at the right of the second partial product is not written. If the multiplier in examples similar to this one contains more than two digits, the process is continued until as many partial products as digits in the multiplier have been obtained.

Example:

$$30 \times 342$$

This is a special case where the units digit of the multiplier is zero.

$$\begin{array}{r} 342 \\ \times 30 \\ \hline 000 \\ 10260 \\ \hline 10260 \end{array} \qquad \begin{array}{r} 342 \\ \times 30 \\ \hline 10260 \end{array}$$

In the first process, follow through the example as before. The second process is a convenient shortcut that may also be extended to multipliers ending in any number of zeros. Note that this is a special case of multiplication by 10, 100, 1000, etc., for $10 \times 36 = 360$, $100 \times 36 = 3600$, $1000 \times 36 = 36,000$, etc.

Example:

$$206 \times 3152$$

This example illustrates the handling of a zero digit in the multiplier when it is not a terminal digit.

$$\begin{array}{r} 3152 \\ \times 206 \\ \hline 18912 \\ 00000 \\ 630400 \\ \hline 649312 \end{array} \qquad \begin{array}{r} 3152 \\ \times 206 \\ \hline 18912 \\ 63040 \\ \hline 649312 \end{array}$$

The example on the left has been worked out completely, as in preceding examples; the example on the right appears in the abbreviated form commonly used.

The rationale behind these processes in multiplication lies mainly in the use of the distributive law. For instance, in multiplying 3×72, first write 72 in expanded form as $70 + 2$. Then $3 \cdot (70 + 2)$ is $3 \cdot 70 + 3 \cdot 2$, by the distributive law, and $3 \cdot 70 + 3 \cdot 2 = 210 + 6 = 216$. In similar fashion, $6 \cdot (247) = 6 \cdot (200 + 40 + 7) = 6 \cdot 200 + 6 \cdot 40 + 6 \cdot 7 = 1200 + 240 + 42 = 1200 + 282 = 1482$. Where the multiplier has more than a single digit, the process can still be explained in terms of the distributive law. For the product 47×597, first write the multiplier in expanded form, obtaining $(40 + 7) \cdot 597$. Then, using the distributive law once again, this equals $(40 \cdot 597) + (7 \cdot 597)$. Now, expanding 597 gives $40 \cdot (500 + 90 + 7) + 7 \cdot (500 + 90 + 7)$. To arrange this in the usual order of the algorithm, use the commutative law of addition to write $7 \cdot (500 + 90 + 7) + 40 \cdot (500 + 90 + 7)$. Again, using the distributive law, this then becomes $(7 \cdot 500 + 7 \cdot 90 + 7 \cdot 7) + (40 \cdot 500 + 40 \cdot 90 + 40 \cdot 7)$. Carrying out these operations gives $(3500 + 630 + 49) + (20{,}000 + 3600 + 280) = (3500 + 679) + (20{,}000 + 3880) = 4179 + 23{,}880$. These last two numbers are the partial products which are added to obtain the product, 28,059.

As with addition, the multiplication process can be carried out from left to right, and scratch methods were used in the past. First two methods illustrated below are left-to-right methods.

```
  637        637        28
× 24          24       516
 12         1274       4748
  6         2548      12624
 14        15288       6377
 24                      63
 12                   15288
 28
15288
```

In the first method, the digit 2 is first used as a multiplier, place values arranged in order from left to right. Then 4 is used as a multiplier, place values again in order from left to right but shifted one place to the right. This method can be used letting the multiplier digits occur in any order if the place values are properly accounted for. By using a little mental arithmetic for carries, the process can be further condensed. In the second method the multiplier digits are used from left to right but the digits of the multiplicand are in the usual order.

The third method is the ancient scratch method. The multiplicand is first placed underneath the multiplier so that the units digit falls under the first digit of the multiplier. The digit 2 is then used to multiply each digit of 637 from left to right, carries taken care of by scratching out a previously written digit and writing the corrected digit above it. The multiplicand is then shifted one place to the right and multiplied by 4, repeating the previous steps. The product then appears around the top of the work.

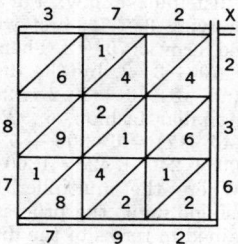

Another ancient algorithm for multiplication, which is very easy to use, is the *lattice*, or *grating, method*. To illustrate $236 \cdot 372$: in this method a grating having as many columns as the multiplicand and as many rows as the multiplier is set up. The digits of the two factors are then arranged as shown. Diagonal lines are drawn from upper right to lower left. The numbers in each row represent the digital products, the first digit of a two-digit product being placed above the diagonal. Then, the digits in each diagonal path are summed up to obtain the product, 87,792.

■ **SUBTRACTION.**—There are several algorithms presently in use for the operation of subtraction. These may be classified in terms of the way that the numerals are transformed when digital differences do not exist. Consider $379 - 36$, usually written in vertical form:

$$
\begin{array}{r}
379 \\
- \; 36 \\
\hline
343
\end{array}
$$

The two numerals are placed so that the units digits lie in a column thus aligning place values. Then each digit is subtracted from the one above ($9 - 6 = 3$, $7 - 3 = 4$, and $3 - 0 = 3$). By definition these would be found by completing the sentence $6 + \square = 9$, $3 + \square = 7$, and $0 + \square = 3$. It is quite common, however, for the take-away combinations to be taught as distinct from sums previously learned. In this case the subtraction of the digits would be carried out as: 9 take away 6 is 3, and so on. The second basic procedure in subtraction is illustrated in the difference $263 - 137$. Here, if the digits are aligned in the proper way, as below, it is found that the difference $3 - 7$ in the units column does not exist. Thus, some transformation in the structure of the numeral must be made in order to apply the same procedure as before. The two usual ones are illustrated:

```
 263       25¹3
-137      - 13 7
          ─────
           12 6

 263       26¹3
-137      - 14 7
          ─────
           12 6
```

In the first example, ten is borrowed from the tens place of 263, reducing the tens digit to 5. The 10 is then added to the 3 in the units place making a total of 13 units. Then $13 - 7 = 6$, $5 - 3 = 2$, $2 - 1 = 1$ and the subtraction is complete. In the second example, 10 is added to the 3 in the units place, making a total of 13 units and 1 is added to the tens place of 137, making this number 147. Then $13 - 7 = 6$, $6 - 4 = 2$ and $2 - 1 = 1$, completing the subtraction. To further illustrate these two processes, each numeral is written in expanded form.

$$
\begin{aligned}
263 &= 200 + 60 + 3 \\
&= 200 + (50 + 10) + 3 = 200 + 50 + 13 \\
137 &= 100 + 30 + 7 \qquad = 100 + 30 + 7 \\
&\qquad\qquad\qquad\qquad \overline{\;= 100 + 20 + 6 = 126}
\end{aligned}
$$

Here the use of the numeration system and the associative law of addition enables the exchange of place values so that the 7 may be subtracted from 13, eliminating the need to perform the impossible subtraction $3 - 7$.

$$
\begin{aligned}
263 &= (200 + 60 + 3) + 10 = 200 + 60 + 13 \\
137 &= (100 + 30 + 7) + 10 = 100 + 40 + 7 \\
&\qquad\qquad\qquad\qquad\quad \overline{\;100 + 20 + 6} \\
&\qquad\qquad\qquad\qquad = 126
\end{aligned}
$$

Here the principle operating is what might be called "compensation." Add 10 to the 3 in the units place to obtain a number from which 7 may be subtracted and then add ten to the subtrahend to compensate for this change in the minuend. This 10 cannot be added to the 7 in the units place here, for it would again give an impossible subtraction. Therefore, add it to the 30 in the tens place, leaving the 7 in the units place undisturbed. Since 40 is less than 60, the subtraction can be completed.

The two processes illustrated apply not only when the digital differences do not exist in the units column, but also when such differences fail to exist in any place-value column. An example is given using each method.

$$
\begin{array}{r}
53004 \\
- \; 14765 \\
\hline
38239
\end{array}
$$

$$
\begin{aligned}
53004 &= 50000 + 3000 + 000 + 00 + 4 \\
&= 50000 + 2000 + 1000 + 00 + 4 \\
&= 50000 + 2000 + 900 + 100 + 4 \\
&= 50000 + 2000 + 900 + 90 + 14 \\
&= 40000 + 12000 + 900 + 90 + 14
\end{aligned}
$$

Then,

$$
\begin{array}{r}
40000 + 12000 + 900 + 90 + 14 \\
- \; 10000 + \; 4000 + 700 + 60 + \; 5 \\
\hline
30000 + \; 8000 + 200 + 30 + \; 9 = 38239
\end{array}
$$

or,

```
   4 2 9 9
  5¹3¹0¹0¹4
 -1 4 7 6 5
 ──────────
  3 8 2 3 9
```

Using the first process, it is necessary to make many exchanges in place value to arrive at a form in which the subtraction may finally be completed. This example also indicates what is done when an exchange cannot be made with the place value immediately at the left. To obtain a 10 to add to 4 in the units place, it was necessary to exchange 10 hundreds for 1 thousand, then 10 tens for 1 hundred, and finally 10 units for one ten. It was also necessary to exchange 10 thousands for 1 ten-thousand. The problem as it might appear with all place-value exchanges indicated is also given above. Usually these exchanges are done mentally so that the result would appear as in the initial statement of the problem. Another approach is:

$$
\begin{array}{r}
50000 + 13000 + 1000 + 100 + 14 \\
20000 + \; 5000 + \; 800 + \; 70 + \; 5 \\
\hline
30000 + \; 8000 + \; 200 + \; 30 + \; 9 = 38239
\end{array}
$$

or

```
  5¹3¹0¹0¹4
  2 5 8 7
  1 4 7 6 5
 ──────────
  3 8 2 3 9
```

In this process, we have added 10, 100, 1000, and 10,000 to the minuend in the units, tens, hundreds, and thousands places and compensated by adding the same amounts to the subtrahend, but in the corresponding place-value columns. The problem as it might appear with the changes indicated in the two numerals is given above. Here, again, the changes are made mentally so that such a subtraction would actually appear as in the original problem. The principles in operation in the first process illustrated are the principles of the system of numeration and the laws governing the operation of addition and subtraction. The second process involves a rule of law, not previously discussed, relating to the operation of subtraction: if the difference $a - b$ of any two whole numbers exists and is equal to c, then for any whole number d, the difference $(a + d) - (b + d)$ exists and is also equal to c. To establish this principle, we note that if $a - b = c$ then by definition $a = b + c$. Adding d to both sides of this equality $(a + d) = (b + d) + c$ is then obtained. Therefore, $(a + d) - (b + d) = c$ by definition. Thus the steps used in the second process are justified in terms of the basic properties of whole numbers.

■ **DIVISION.**—The division algorithm is perhaps the most difficult of the algorithms for the four fundamental operations with whole numbers. For students it is often the least understood; it is apt to be performed in a mechanical way and with little understanding. Thus, it is also the operation that is the most subject to error on the student's part. Although division, as previously indicated, is defined only for the case in which the divisor is an exact factor of the dividend (that is, even division), we can make certain statements about pairs of whole numbers, m and n, even though m is not an even divisor of n. For instance, given the pair of whole numbers, 63 and 5, we can express 63 in terms of the largest multiple of 5 which is less than 63, or $60 = 12 \cdot 5$, and the excess, or 3: $63 = 12 \cdot 5 + 3$. Here 12 is called the quotient and 3 the remainder. The whole numbers have the property that, given any pair of them, a quotient and remainder can be found as above, provided that the second number given is not zero. Thus, the pair 27, 7 yields 3 as a quotient and 6 as a remainder, since $27 = 7 \cdot 3 + 6$. Note that the remainder is a number less than the second number of the pair of numbers given. This relation is a basic property of the whole numbers, usually stated as follows: If m and n are two whole numbers, and $n \neq 0$, there is a unique pair of whole numbers, q and r, such that $m = n \cdot q + r$ and r is less than n. The process by which the numbers q and r are actually determined is the familiar process of long (or short) division. Either of these, since they are basically the same, can be referred to as the *division algorithm*. In this context it is usual to call the number n the *divisor*, the number m the *dividend*, the number q the *quotient*, and the number r the *remainder*. Using this terminology, the *basic division relation* given above may be restated as *dividend = divisor × quotient + remainder*, where the remainder is less than the divisor and the divisor is nonzero.

With this information, the usual division algorithm used to find the numbers q and r, that is, a quotient and remainder for a given dividend and divisor, will be considered. In the examples given, the steps necessary to find the result will be noted, deferring detailed explanation of the process at present.

Example:

$$838 \div 3.$$

It is customary to arrange the work in the form 3)838. (1) In the stepwise procedure only the first digit, 8, of the dividend is considered at first and one must find the highest multiple of 3 contained in 8, which is 2. Since 8 is in the hundreds place of the dividend, 2 is in the hundreds place of the quotient. To indicate this, the 2 is usually written directly above the eight, as shown below. Then the product $2 \cdot 3 = 6$ is written below the 8 and subtracted from it, giving a difference of 2. (2) The next step then is to bring down (adjoin) the tens digit of the dividend, 3, to 2, yielding 23. Next consider the highest multiple of the divisor, 3, contained in 23, which is 7; 7 is thus written in the tens place of the quotient and the product $7 \cdot 3 = 21$ is written below 23 and subtracted from it, yielding a difference of 2. (3) Then the units digit of the dividend, 8, is adjoined to this, yielding 28. Since the highest multiple of 3 contained in 28 is 9, the final digit of the quotient is 9. Multiplying 9 times 3 and subtracting the result, 27, from 28, the difference is 1. Since 1 is less than 3, the process is complete giving the quotient as 279 and the remainder as 1. The result is checked by verifying that $838 = 3 \cdot 279 + 1$ as it does to satisfy the basic division relation.

$$
\begin{array}{ll}
(1) \quad 3\overline{)838} & \\
\qquad \underline{6} & \\
\qquad 2 &
\end{array}
\qquad
\begin{array}{ll}
(2) \quad 3\overline{)838} & \\
\qquad \underline{6} & \\
\qquad 23 & \\
\qquad \underline{21} & \\
\qquad 2 &
\end{array}
\qquad
\begin{array}{ll}
(3) \quad 3\overline{)838} & \\
\qquad \underline{6} & \\
\qquad 23 & \\
\qquad \underline{21} & \\
\qquad 28 & \\
\qquad \underline{27} & \\
\qquad 1 &
\end{array}
$$

If there are more digits in the dividend, the process is simply repeated in the same way until all the digits are exhausted and the final remainder is less than the divisor.

Example:

$$2457 \div 5.$$

In the preceding example the divisor was contained in the first digit of the dividend. In this example this is no longer true. Therefore, in the first step of the process it is necessary to consider not just the first digit of the dividend but the first two digits, 24. Then the highest multiple of 5 contained in 24 is 4, which is then the first digit of the quotient. This digit is not written over the 2 of the dividend, but over the 4 in the hundreds place. Otherwise the division is carried out exactly as in the first example. Note that in the second step the difference obtained is zero. Thus, when the units digit is adjoined, it becomes 07, which is the same as the single digit 7.

$$
\begin{array}{l}
\quad\ 491 \\
5\overline{)2457} \\
\underline{20} \\
\ \ 45 \\
\ \ \underline{45} \\
\ \ \ 07 \\
\ \ \ \ \underline{5} \\
\ \ \ \ \ 2
\end{array}
$$

Example:

$$3219 \div 8.$$

$$
\begin{array}{ll}
(1) \quad 8\overline{)3219} \\
\quad\ \ \ \ 402 \\
\quad\ \ \ \underline{32} \\
\quad\ \ \ \ 01 \\
\quad\ \ \ \ \ \underline{0} \\
\quad\ \ \ \ \ 19 \\
\quad\ \ \ \ \ \underline{16} \\
\quad\ \ \ \ \ \ 3
\end{array}
\qquad
\begin{array}{ll}
(2) \quad 8\overline{)3219} \\
\quad\ \ \ \ 402 \\
\quad\ \ \ \underline{32} \\
\quad\ \ \ \ 019 \\
\quad\ \ \ \ \underline{16} \\
\quad\ \ \ \ \ 3
\end{array}
$$

This example is given to illustrate the handling of a situation such as occurs in the second step where the divisor, 8, is not contained properly in 1. Thus the highest multiple of 8 that is less than or equal to 1 is 0, since $0 \cdot 8 = 0$. We therefore write 0 as the second digit of the quotient, subtract 0 from 1, and continue as before. This step is sometimes abbreviated as shown in (2).

Example:

$$2345 \div 9.$$

$$
\begin{array}{ll}
(1) \quad 9\overline{)2345} \\
\quad\ \ \ \ 260 \\
\quad\ \ \ \underline{18} \\
\quad\ \ \ \ 54 \\
\quad\ \ \ \ \underline{54} \\
\quad\ \ \ \ \ 05 \\
\quad\ \ \ \ \ \ \underline{0} \\
\quad\ \ \ \ \ \ 5
\end{array}
\qquad
\begin{array}{ll}
(2) \quad 9\overline{)2345} \\
\quad\ \ \ \ 260 \\
\quad\ \ \ \underline{18} \\
\quad\ \ \ \ 54 \\
\quad\ \ \ \ \underline{54} \\
\quad\ \ \ \ \ 05 \\
\quad\ \ \ \ \ \ 5
\end{array}
$$

This example illustrates the occurrence of the same type of situation as in the final step of the division in the previous example, where the final digit of the quotient is 0 and the remainder is 5. The abbreviated form is shown in (2).

Example:

Each of the preceding examples may be carried out by what is known as *short division*, where the work is performed as shown below. The intermediate steps are done mentally. (R denotes the remainder.)

$$
\begin{array}{ll}
3\overline{)8^2 3^2 8} & 5\overline{)24^4 57} \\
\ \ 2\ 7\ 9 R1 & \ \ 4\ 91 R2 \\
\\
8\overline{)3219} & 9\overline{)23^5 45} \\
\ \ 402 R3 & \ \ 2\ 60 R5
\end{array}
$$

The preceding section has outlined the basic processes involved in the division algorithm. The extension of these processes to more complex examples will now be illustrated.

Example:

$$475 \div 13.$$

$$
\begin{array}{r}
36 \\
13\overline{)475} \\
39 \\
\hline
85 \\
78 \\
\hline
7
\end{array}
$$

Since the divisor contains two digits we must take at least two digits of the dividend for the first step of the division. In this case the number formed by the first two digits of the dividend contains 13 and the highest multiple of 13 contained in 47 is 3. Thus the first digit of the quotient is 3. This digit will be in the tens place of the quotient, since the 7 of 47 is in the tens place of the dividend. Subtracting $3 \cdot 13 = 39$ from 47 the difference is 8. Adjoining the last digit of the dividend gives 85. Since the largest multiple of 13 contained in 85 is 6, the last digit of the quotient is 6. Subtracting $6 \cdot 13 = 78$ from 85, the difference is 7. Since 7 is less than the divisor, 13, the process is complete, yielding a quotient of 36 and a remainder of 7.

Example:

$$2351 \div 46.$$

$$
\begin{array}{r}
51 \\
46\overline{)2351} \\
230 \\
\hline
51 \\
46 \\
\hline
5
\end{array}
$$

In the event that the number formed by the first two digits of the dividend does not contain the divisor we take the number formed by the first three digits of the divisor in the first step of the process and place the first digit of the quotient accordingly. Otherwise the process is completed in the same way.

If the divisor contains more than two digits the procedures shown for two-digit divisors apply.

Example:

$$
\begin{array}{r}
557 \\
416\overline{)231745} \\
2080 \\
\hline
2374 \\
2080 \\
\hline
2945 \\
2912 \\
\hline
33
\end{array}
$$

The first step entails taking at least the number formed by the first three digits in the dividend. Since this number, 231, does not contain the divisor, add an additional digit to obtain 2317. Then obtain the largest multiple of 416 contained in 2317. By trial, this is seen to be 5. Then $5 \cdot 416 = 2080$ is subtracted from 2317 and the process continued as before. The first digit, 5, of the quotient is

the same place value as the 7 of 2317 is in the dividend.

In general, then, in dividing a multiple-digit number, the process is initiated by taking the number formed by the successive digits of the dividend, either as many digits or one more digit than contained in the divisor. The highest multiple of the divisor contained in this number is the first digit of the quotient. The place value of this digit in the quotient is the same as the place value of the last digit used in the dividend. The process is then completed as in previous examples.

In the examples given so far, the process of finding the highest multiple of the divisor contained in a given number was found by simple trial. In some cases this may involve several trials before the highest such multiple is found. In the following examples, a simple procedure for estimating quotient digits or obtaining trial quotient digits is given.

Example:

$$10,769 \div 423.$$

$$
\begin{array}{r}
25 \\
423\overline{)10769} \\
846 \\
\hline
2309 \\
2115 \\
\hline
194
\end{array}
$$

According to the rule, the number formed by the first three digits of the dividend must be considered first. Since 423 is not contained in 107, it is necessary to take 1076. The procedure to be illustrated for obtaining trial quotient digits is sometimes called the one-step rule. This involves taking just the first digit, 4, of the divisor, and obtaining the highest multiple of 4 contained in the number formed by the first two digits of the dividend, 10. This number is 2. Then try 2 as the highest multiple of 423 contained in 1076. Since $2 \cdot 423 = 846$, the choice is correct. Therefore, the first digit of the quotient is 2. Continuing the process, the highest multiple of 423 contained in 2309 must be found next. Again, take 4 and the number formed by the first two digits of 2309, or 23. The highest multiple of 4 contained in 23 is 5; $5 \cdot 423 = 2115$ which is less than 2309. Hence, the second quotient digit is 5. Subtracting, a remainder of 194 is obtained and the process is complete.

In the above example the estimated quotient digit turned out to be the correct quotient digit in each step. This, however, is not always the case.

Example:

$$9627 \div 36.$$

$$
\begin{array}{r}
267 \\
36\overline{)9627} \\
72 \\
\hline
242 \\
216 \\
\hline
267 \\
252 \\
\hline
15
\end{array}
$$

Since 36 is contained in the number formed by the first two digits of the dividend, the first quotient digit can be placed in the same place value as the 6 of 9627. To estimate this quotient digit, use only the first digit, 3, of 36 and the first digit, 9, of the dividend. This yields a trial quotient digit of 3. Since $3 \cdot 36 = 108$, this is too large. But $2 \cdot 36 = 72$. Hence, the first quotient digit is 2. Continuing, the next step is to find the highest multiple of 36 contained in 242. It is seen that the highest multiple of 3 contained in 24 is 8, but $8 \cdot 36 = 288$, which is too large. Reducing the digit to 7, $7 \cdot 36 = 52$ which is still too large. Reducing again, $6 \cdot 36 = 216$. The second quotient digit is then 6. In the final step, it is necessary to find the highest multiple of 36 contained in 267. The one-step rule gives 8 as a trial quotient digit, but it is known from the previous step that this has to be reduced to 7. Thus the final quotient of 267 and a remainder of 15 is obtained.

In this second example, the one-step rule did not give the correct quotient digit in any step, whereas in the first example it yielded the correct quotient digit every time. In general, the rule will give the correct quotient digit about 65 per cent of the time. Fortunately, whenever the quotient digit is incorrect it is invariably too large. For this reason, it is known that whenever the product of the trial quotient digit and the divisor is less than the dividend, the quotient digit is correct. The one-step rule may be made more useful if it is observed that divisors such as 38, 176, and 567 are actually closer to 40, 200, and 600 than they are to 30, 100, and 500 and that, therefore, with such divisors the one-step rule is apt to yield too high a quotient digit.

To gain an understanding of the reasoning involved in the division algorithm, it is necessary to examine the processes used more closely. The processes previously illustrated represent a considerable refinement of properties associated with the basic division relation.

Let us examine a typical division by a single-digit divisor, as illustrated in a previous example: 838 divided by 3, or $3\overline{)838}$. First, rewrite the dividend in expanded form, so that the problem is then written $3\overline{)800 + 30 + 8}$. The first step in the algorithm, finding the largest multiple of 3 contained in 8, is then seen to actually represent finding the largest multiple of 3 in terms of 100's contained in 800, which is 200. Multiplying $200 \cdot 3$ and subtracting the product from 800 the difference is 200.

$$
\begin{array}{r}
200 \\
3\overline{)800 + 30 + 8} \\
600 \\
\hline
200 + 30 = 230
\end{array}
$$

Adding the 30 to this leaves a remainder of $230 + 8$, or 23 tens and 8 units. The next step in the algorithm is to find the largest multiple of 3 in terms of tens. This will be 7 tens, or 70. Multiplying

$70 \cdot 3$ and subtracting the product from

$$\begin{array}{r} 200 + 70 \\ 3)\overline{800 + 30 + 8} \\ 600 \\ \hline 200 + 30 = 230 \\ 210 \\ \hline 20 + 8 = 28 \end{array}$$

230 the difference is 20. Adding 8 to this the remainder is 28. In the final step, the

$$\begin{array}{r} 200 + 70 + 9 = 279 \\ 3)\overline{800 + 30 + 8} \\ 600 \\ \hline 200 + 30 = 230 \\ 210 \\ \hline 20 + 8 = 28 \\ 27 \\ \hline 1 \end{array}$$

largest multiple of 3 in terms of units contained in 28, which is 9, is found. Multiplying $9 \cdot 3$ and subtracting the product from 28 a final remainder of 1 is obtained. This process may be summarized in a more familiar form:

$$\begin{array}{r} 9 \\ 70 \\ 200 \\ 3)\overline{838} \\ 600 \\ \hline 238 \\ 210 \\ \hline 28 \\ 27 \\ \hline 1 \end{array}$$

One of the greatest difficulties with the process of division previously illustrated is that it is imperative that the quotient digits be correct at each step of the process. A method for finding the quotient and remainder for two given numbers which avoids this difficulty has seen increasing acceptance in recent years. This process is illustrated below.

To find the quotient and remainder for 475 divided by 27, for example, the numbers are set up as $27)\overline{475}$. The work is then carried out as displayed. In step

$$\begin{array}{r|ll} 27)475 & 8 & (1) \\ 216 & & \\ \hline 259 & 7 & (2) \\ 189 & & \\ \hline 70 & 2 & (3) \\ 54 & & \\ \hline 16 & 0 & (4) \\ \hline & 17 & (5) \end{array}$$

(1) it is estimated that $8 \cdot 27$ is contained in 475. 8 is thus written in the first line at the right and $8 \cdot 27 = 216$ is subtracted from 475. (2) Since the remainder 259 is larger than 27, the process is repeated. This time it is estimated that $7 \cdot 27$ is contained in 259 and 7 is written on a line to the right of 259; $7 \cdot 27 = 189$ is then subtracted from 259. Since the remainder, 70, is larger than 27, the process is again repeated. This time the estimate that $2 \cdot 27$ is contained in 70 is made and 2 is written on a line at the right of 70 (3). Subtracting $2 \cdot 27 = 54$ from 70, the remainder is 16, which

is less than 27. Write a 0 on the line at the right (4) to indicate this and then total the multiples of 27 contained in 475. This total is 17 (5) and thus the quotient is 17 and the remainder is 16. This process will work no matter what multiples of 27 are used at each step, except that they must not be greater than the number involved; for example, in the first step, 20 could not be used since $20 \cdot 27 = 540$, which is larger than 475. Below two other solutions to the problem are given, using this method.

$$\begin{array}{r|l} 27)475 & 8 \\ 216 & \\ \hline 259 & 8 \\ 216 & \\ \hline 43 & \\ 27 & 1 \\ \hline 16 & 0 \\ \hline & 17 \end{array} \qquad \begin{array}{r|l} 27)475 & 10 \\ 270 & \\ \hline 205 & 7 \\ 189 & \\ \hline 16 & 0 \\ \hline & 17 \end{array}$$

In the second solution above, the steps are identical with those in the usual algorithm for long division. The advantages of this alternate method of performing long division lie in its clarity and its direct relation to the fundamental processes involved. The usual method still remains probably the most efficient for the skilled calculator.

Prime and Composite Numbers.—The entire set of whole numbers can be separated into two categories called the primes and composites. A *prime* number is any whole number, with the exception of one, that is divisible only by one and itself. One is not usually considered to be a prime number. Numbers that are not prime are called *composite* numbers. For example, 5 is a prime number, since only 1 and 5 are the divisors, or factors, of 5; whereas 6 is a composite number, since it has the factors 2 and 3 in addition to 1 and 6. More specifically, if three whole numbers, a, b, and c, are related in the following manner, $ab = c$, then both a and b are referred to as the divisors or *factors* of c. The number c is called a multiple of the numbers a and b. When c can be expressed as a product of a and b, ab, where both a and b are greater than 1, then c is called a composite number. This may be observed from the two examples given above: $5 \cdot 1 = 5$ (prime); $2 \cdot 3 = 6$ (composite).

The *fundamental theorem of arithmetic* (also called the *unique factorization theorem*) states that every composite number is capable of being factored uniquely (that is, one and only one way, except for the order) into a product of prime numbers. Note the following examples:

$$30 = 2 \cdot 3 \cdot 5$$
$$252 = 2^2 \cdot 3^2 \cdot 7$$
$$646 = 2 \cdot 17 \cdot 19$$

Thus, every whole number greater than 1 is either a prime or is expressible as a product of primes.

Mathematicians have devoted considerable effort to investigate the nature of prime numbers. Euclid presented a proof that there is an infinitude of prime

numbers, thus simultaneously demonstrating that there is no largest prime. Although others have reached the same conclusion in different manners, no one has found a technique or formula which will produce all of the prime numbers. Given a particular large number (odd number, since all even numbers with the exception of 2 are obviously composite), it is usually not easy to determine whether it is a prime or composite number. Tables have been made which list prime numbers up to a certain value; however, to extend these tables becomes a formidable task. The task of finding and determining which numbers are primes has been greatly eased by the use of high-speed electronic computers, even though these efforts are limited. An early technique for determining all prime numbers less than a given number is credited to the Greek scholar, Eratosthenes (276–194 B.C.) and is called the "Sieve of Eratosthenes." This method may be illustrated as follows: To find all of the prime numbers less than 100, begin by writing down all of the numbers up to 100. To begin the sieve cross out all of the numbers that contain 2 as a

Sieve of Eratosthenes

1	2	3	~~4~~	5	~~6~~	7	~~8~~	~~9~~	~~10~~
11	~~12~~	13	~~14~~	~~15~~	~~16~~	17	~~18~~	19	~~20~~
~~21~~	~~22~~	23	~~24~~	~~25~~	~~26~~	~~27~~	~~28~~	29	~~30~~
31	~~32~~	~~33~~	~~34~~	~~35~~	~~36~~	37	~~38~~	~~39~~	~~40~~
41	~~42~~	43	~~44~~	~~45~~	~~46~~	47	~~48~~	~~49~~	~~50~~
~~51~~	~~52~~	53	~~54~~	~~55~~	~~56~~	~~57~~	~~58~~	59	~~60~~
61	~~62~~	~~63~~	~~64~~	~~65~~	~~66~~	67	~~68~~	~~69~~	~~70~~
71	~~72~~	73	~~74~~	~~75~~	~~76~~	~~77~~	~~78~~	79	~~80~~
~~81~~	~~82~~	83	~~84~~	~~85~~	~~86~~	~~87~~	~~88~~	89	~~90~~
~~91~~	~~92~~	~~93~~	~~94~~	~~95~~	96	97	~~98~~	~~99~~	~~100~~

factor, with the exception of 2. This then removes all of the even numbers greater than 2 which are obviously not primes. The next step is to cross out all of the numbers that contain 3 as a factor, with the exception of 3. This will remove numbers such as 9, 15, and 21. The next number to consider is 4—however, it has already been crossed out since it contained 2 as a factor. The next number to consider is 5. Again cross out the numbers above 5 which contain 5 as a factor. This includes such numbers as 25, 35, 40. Continue this general procedure of moving up from one number to the next until all numbers have been crossed out which contain the smaller numbers as factors. The accompanying table indicates the final result of this procedure. The numbers that are not crossed out are the prime numbers less than 100. It is to be observed that in this example it was only necessary to cross out multiples of prime numbers less than the square root of 100, namely 2, 3, 5, and 7. In finding all of the primes less than

1,000, it is necessary to consider only primes less than $\sqrt{1,000}$, or the primes up to and including 31. To determine whether a given number is prime or composite without going through the sieve completely, simply try one prime after another until all of the primes up to the square root of the number under consideration have been tried. For example, to determine if the number 161 is prime or composite, first find the $\sqrt{161}$, which is 12 plus a fraction. If the number 161 is composite it must have as a divisor one of the following primes: 2, 3, 5, 7, 11. These are the only divisors that need to be tried. Since 7 divides 161 ($7 \cdot 23$), the number is composite. This technique can of course be extended to any number desirable and since it is very mechanical, it is easily adaptable to devices such as punched cards. Computers can be programmed to determine primes quite easily.

In looking at the prime numbers up to 100—2, 3, 5, 7, 11, 13, 17, 19, 23, 29, 31, 37, 41, 43, 47, 53, 59, 61, 67, 71, 73, 79, 83, 89, 97—no pattern is easily discernible. The primes do not seem to occur at regular intervals; in fact they are very erratically distributed. This apparent lack of pattern continues as larger numbers are investigated and is the reason that no formula or technique has been developed for determining what numbers are prime.

There have been many attempts made at finding a formula; one of these is $n^2 - n + 41$, where n is any whole number. It is interesting to note that when n is 1, 2, 3, . . . the expression will give primes—for a while. When $n = 1$, the answer is 41, which is prime; when $n = 2$, it is 43, which is the next prime, etc. But when $n = 41$, the answer is $41^2 - 41 + 41$, which is obviously not prime, since 41^2 is a composite number.

When large-scale distributions of primes are considered, the following values appear. The first five entries are the result of actual counts, while the last two are the result of calculations.

Number of Primes

up to	is
1,000	168
10,000	1,229
100,000	9,592
1,000,000	78,498
10,000,000	664,579
100,000,000	5,761,455
1,000,000,000	50,847,478

Advanced number theory seems to indicate that this pattern has meaning in terms of the ultimate distribution of primes. Until 1951, the largest known prime number was $2^{127} - 1$, which is written out as 170,141,183,460,469,231, 731,687,303,715,884,105,727. In 1951, with the help of electronic computers, a much larger prime was determined. This number is $180 \times (2^{127} - 1)^2 + 1$.

One of the many unsolved problems involving prime numbers is called "Gold-

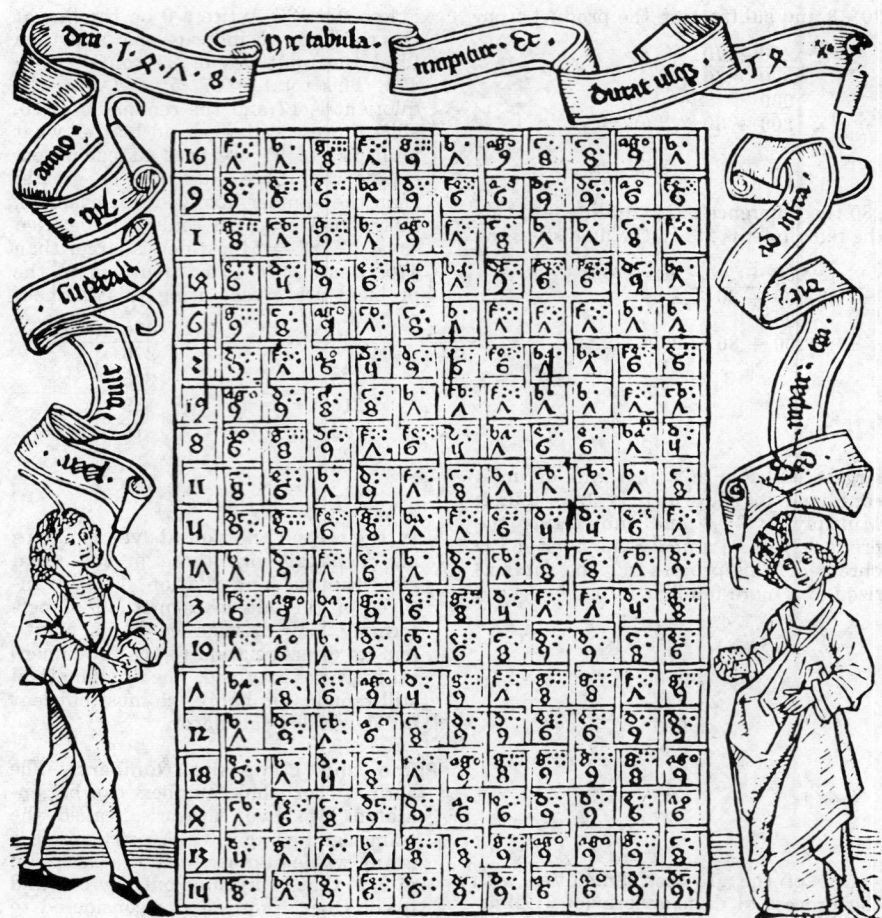

BETTMANN ARCHIVE

THIS MEDIEVAL CALENDAR with mystic figures relied upon both astronomy and mathematics.

bach's conjecture." C. Goldbach (1690–1764) noted that every even number can be written as the sum of two primes, that is, it worked for all the even numbers he tested. However this conjecture has never been proven, nor have any cases been found where it is not true.

There are some prime numbers that differ from each other by only 2, such as 3 and 5, 5 and 7, 11 and 13, 17 and 19, 29 and 31, 41 and 43, . . . , 10,006,427 and 10,006,429 . . . Such pairs of prime numbers are called prime twins and these, too, seem to occur less frequently as the numbers get larger. However it is believed that there is an infinite number of these, though again no proof of this conjecture has been found.

■ **PERFECT NUMBERS.**—The ancient Greeks had developed an extensive belief in what we today call numerology. They were intrigued with numbers such as 6 and 28, since these numbers are equal to the sum of their proper divisors. That is, the proper divisors of 6 are 1, 2, and 3. Adding $1 + 2 + 3$ gives 6. The number 28 has as proper divisors 1, 2, 4, 7, and 14. The sum of these is 28. Numbers which possess this characteristic were called the *perfect numbers*. These perfect numbers are indeed scarce; 6 and 28 are the first two, while the fifth one is

33,550,336. Even though Euclid found an expression which will find all of the perfect numbers, there are still only 17 known perfect numbers, even with the help of high-speed computers. It is not known how many there are, nor have any odd perfect numbers been found.

■ **NUMEROLOGY.**—These same Greeks that found the first perfect numbers also developed other mystic meanings for certain numbers. They considered 1 as the source of all other numbers. Since even numbers are divisible by 2, they are considered to be weak and therefore feminine. The odd numbers were considered to be strong and masculine. The number 5 was used to represent marriage, since it is the sum, or union, of 2 and 3, male and female. Death was represented by the number 8, while 9 represented immortality.

The Greeks also used the number 7 extensively in their culture; for example, the seven wise men, the seven wonders of the world, and the seven liberal arts that constituted the curriculum in their schools. The number 7 is still very much in vogue; it is seen in the seven days in a week and citizens' vote upon reaching 21, which is equal to 3 times 7. There are many other examples that reflect ancient numerology.

■ **GEOMETRY.**—Another interesting classification of numbers is based on the geometric figures that can be made by using objects to represent numbers. These figurate numbers are called rectangular, triangular, or square numbers.

The rectangular numbers may be illustrated in the following manner:

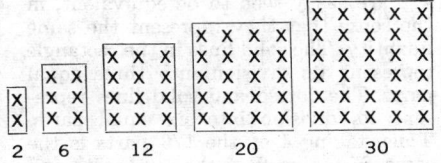

These numbers may also be represented in this manner:

$$1 + 1 = 2$$
$$1 + 1 + 2 + 2 = 6$$
$$1 + 1 + 2 + 2 + 3 + 3 = 12$$
$$1 + 1 + 2 + 2 + 3 + 3 + 4 + 4 = 20$$
$$1 + 1 + 2 + 2 + 3 + 3 + 4 + 4 + 5 + 5 = 30$$

The triangular numbers may be illustrated in this manner:

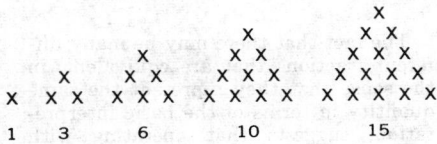

These numbers are represented in the following manner:

$$1$$
$$1 + 2 = 3$$
$$1 + 2 + 3 = 6$$
$$1 + 2 + 3 + 4 = 10$$
$$1 + 2 + 3 + 4 + 5 = 15$$

The square numbers are illustrated by making square configurations:

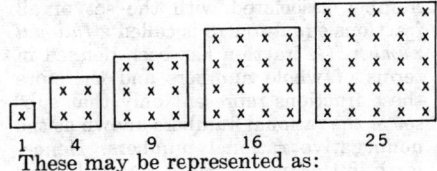

These may be represented as:

$$1$$
$$1 + 3 = 4$$
$$1 + 3 + 5 = 9$$
$$1 + 3 + 5 + 7 = 16$$
$$1 + 3 + 5 + 7 + 9 = 25$$

There are many other possible configurations that can be made to represent various kinds of numbers. It is interesting to note that cubes can be represented by three-dimensional arrangements of objects.

Greatest Common Factor.—The problem of finding the factorization of a whole number is important to the arithmetic of fractions. Specifically, in order to "reduce" a particular fraction it is necessary to make use of the *greatest common factor* (also called the *greatest common divisor*) of the numerator and the denominator. Consider the factors or divisors of the two numbers 48 and 36.

The number 48 has the factors: 1, 2, 3, 4, 6, 8, 12, 16, 24, 48.

The number 36 has the factors: 1, 2, 3, 4, 6, 9, 12, 18, 36.

Note that these two numbers have the following factors (divisors) in common: 1, 2, 3, 4, 6, 12. Since 12 is the largest of these, it is called the greatest common factor (g.c.f.) of 48 and 36.

Additional illustrations are:

$$(14, 21) \text{ g.c.f.} = 7$$
$$(3, 12) \text{ g.c.f.} = 3$$

It is always possible to find the g.c.f. after the numbers have been factored into all possible factors. A simple visual inspection is all that is necessary to select the one that is the largest among the factors that are common. (Two numbers which have no factors in common other than 1, such as 5 and 19, are said to be *relatively prime* to each other.)

A second method for finding the g.c.f. of two numbers involves the use of the division algorithm and is called the *Euclidean Algorithm* after Euclid, who is credited with having developed it. To understand its use, first observe that the g.c.f. of any two numbers must divide the difference between the two numbers. Note the examples above. In each case the difference between the two numbers is divisible by the g.c.f. Using this fact, it is possible to perform repeated division until the g.c.f. is found. The rule for carrying out this procedure is as follows: Divide the larger of the two numbers by the smaller. Then divide the divisor by the remainder from the first division. Continue dividing the last divisor by the last remainder until there is no remainder except zero. The last divisor prior to attaining the zero remainder is the g.c.f. of the two numbers. When this number turns out to be one, then the numbers are relatively prime. Note the process in the following examples.

Example:

Find the g.c.f. of the numbers in the box below by using the Euclidean Algorithm.

The steps in *C* may be rewritten in the following fashion:

$$1832 = (5 \times 362) + 22$$
$$362 = (16 \times 22) + 10$$
$$22 = (2 \times 10) + 2$$
$$10 = (5 \times 2) + 0$$

$$1832 - (5 \times 362) = 22$$
$$362 - (16 \times 22) = 10$$
$$22 - (2 \times 10) = 2$$

It is possible to find the greatest common factor (divisor) of more than two numbers by simply considering the numbers in pairs. For example if there are three numbers, a, b, and c, the first step is to find the g.c.f. of a and b. The second step involves finding the g.c.f. of the g.c.f. of a and b and the number c. As an illustration consider finding the g.c.f. of (30, 168, 231).

First step: Find the g.c.f. of (30, 168).

```
       5
   30)168
      150  1
      18)30
         18  1
         12)18
            12  2
            6)12
               12  g.c.f. = 6
```

Second step: Find the g.c.f. of (6, 231).

```
         38
      6)231
        228  2
        3)6
           6  g.c.f. = 3
```

The g.c.f. of (30, 168, 231) is therefore 3.

Least Common Multiple.—Another term that is used in conjunction with the arithmetic of fractions is the *least common multiple* (*l.c.m.*). The least common multiple of two numbers is the smallest number which is a multiple of both of them. For example, the least common multiple of 5 and 6 is 30, while the least common multiple of 21 and 30 is 210. Observe that if the two numbers are relatively prime, then the l.c.m. is their

A. (36, 48)

```
           1
       36)48
          36  3
          12)36
             36
              0
```

(Since 12 is the last divisor used to obtain the zero remainder, it is the g.c.f. of 36 and 48. This checks with the previous method.)

B. (5, 19)

```
          3
       5)19
         15  1
         4)5
           4  4
           1)4
             4
             0
```

(Since the last divisor here is 1, the two numbers are relatively prime.)

C. (362, 1832)

```
            5
      362)1832
          1810  16
          22)362
             352  2
             10)22
                20  5
                2)10
                  10
                   0
```

product. The least common multiple and the greatest common factor are related in the following manner. The least common multiple is equal to the product of the two numbers under consideration divided by the greatest common factor of the two numbers, as shown below.

$$\text{l.c.m.} = \frac{21 \times 30}{\text{g.c.f.}}$$

Since the g.c.f. of (21, 30) is 3, the product of 21×30 is divided by 3.

$$\text{l.c.m.} = \frac{21 \times 30}{3} = \frac{630}{3} = 210$$

The least common multiple can also be found by inspecting the prime factorization of the two numbers. Again using the above example,

$$21 = 3 \times 7$$

The least common multiple must have factors 2, 3, 5, and 7, producing 210.

$$30 = 2 \times 3 \times 5$$

The greatest common factor (divisor) and the least common multiple are used primarily in the arithmetic operations involving the rational numbers (commonly called the fractions).

Fractions.—The numbers that are usually referred to as the fractions are represented by symbols such as 2/3, 8/6, 7/1, 5/6, etc. Such symbols may have several possible interpretations. Consider, for instance, 2/3. This may be interpreted as dividing a quantity into three equal parts and then taking *two* of them to represent 2/3. Or, 2/3 may be thought of as the result of dividing two whole quantities into three equal parts.

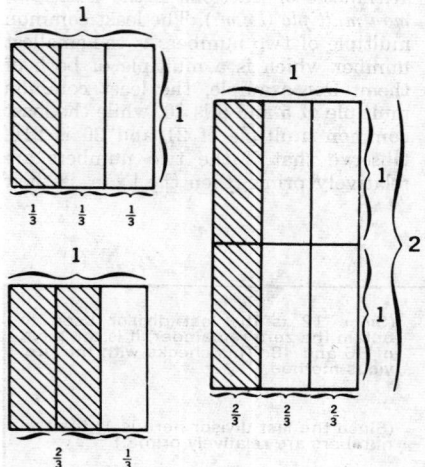

The accompanying diagrams represent these processes geometrically. In this sense, 2/3 is thought of as 2 times 1/3 in the first instance and as 1/3 times 2 in the second. Also, 2/3 may be thought of as $2 \div 3$. That is, $2 \div 3 = 2/3 = k$, where k is a number such that $2 = 3k$, satisfying the definition of division. Still yet another interpretation of the symbol is that of ratio, which is sometimes writ-

ten 2 : 3. This interpretation results from comparing sets, or magnitudes. If set A has 2 elements and set B has 3 elements, then the ratio of the number of elements in A to the number of elements in B is written as 2/3.

All of these interpretations are important and have had a long development historically. Since all are identical mathematically, the following may be chosen as the basic interpretations of the symbol a/b: (1) Interpret a/b as dividing a whole quantity into "b" parts and then taking "a" of them, or (2) interpret a/b as taking "a" whole quantities and dividing the aggregate into "b" equal parts, then taking one of these equal parts.

In each interpretation of fractions the essential meaning is conveyed in terms of a pair of whole numbers. Furthermore, the pair is ordered since 2/3 is distinct from 3/2 in any of the interpretations. These considerations allow us to state the following definition: A fraction is an ordered pair of whole numbers a and b, usually written in the form a/b or $\frac{a}{b}$, where b is not 0. In the usual terminology, a is the *numerator* and b is the *denominator* of the given fraction. In the case that a is less than b, a/b is a proper fraction, for example, 5/8. In the case that a is greater than or equal to b, a/b is called an improper fraction, for example, 9/5. This does not imply that there is anything wrong with writing such a fraction, but the words "proper" and "improper" merely distinguish two particular types of fractions.

Since by the basic interpretation, the fraction 3/1 would mean beginning with three whole quantities, dividing the aggregate into one equal part, and then taking one of these parts, it is evident that $3/1 = 3$ or, in general, $n/1 = n$. Also, the two diagrams below illustrate the geometric interpretation of the improper fraction 4/3. In the smaller diagram, a unit area has been divided into thirds and a fourth third has been added. In the larger diagram, one third of each of four unit areas has been shaded. In both diagrams, the total shaded area is *4 thirds*. From these, it is again evident that $4/3 = 1 + 1/3$. Hence, we should always interpret such symbols as $2\frac{3}{4}$, $5\frac{3}{5}$, and $7\frac{5}{8}$ as a short way of writing $2 + 3/4$, $5 + 3/5$, and $7 + 5/8$.

In similar fashion, 4/4, 3/3, and, in general, n/n (n is any nonzero whole number) are all equal to 1. This is illus-

trated by the accompanying diagram.

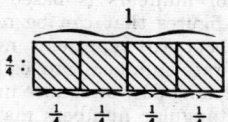

■ **EQUALITY.**—The two fractions 2/3 and 4/6 are easily seen to be equivalent, in the sense that they represent the same quantity. The solid lines in the rectangle represent its division into three equal parts. The dotted and solid lines represent its division into six equal parts. Thus, taking 4 of the 1/6 parts is the same as taking 2 of the 1/3 parts and hence it agrees that $2/3 = 4/6$.

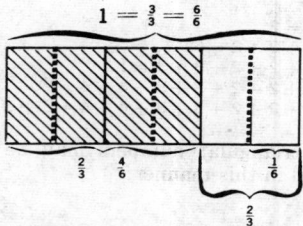

The fact that there may be many different fractions that are equivalent, in the sense that they represent the same quantity in terms of the basic interpretation, suggests that operating with fractions may not be quite the same as operating with whole numbers. For instance, the fraction 2/3 is one member of a set containing an unlimited number of fractions equivalent to it: $2/3 = 4/6 = 6/9 = 8/12 = 10/15 = \ldots$ However, the fact that all of these fractions represent the same quantity suggests that there may be only *one number* involved here which has many representations, or names, as a fraction. This single number associated with the set of all fractions equal to 2/3 is called a *rational number*. (A fraction has been defined in terms of whole numbers and therefore these fractions represent only that subset of the rational numbers known as the nonnegative rational numbers. Henceforth in this article, when rational numbers are spoken of they will mean a nonnegative rational number.) Since the same is true for any fraction a/b, any particular fraction is a name for a unique rational number, but there may be many fractions which name the same rational number. With the agreement that all fractions equivalent to a given fraction are merely names for the same number, rules can be developed for operating with them just as with whole numbers.

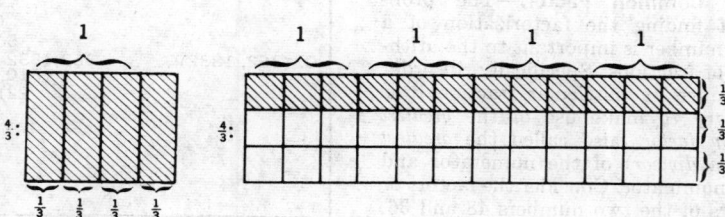

A simple test for equivalence of fractions may be formulated as follows: If a/b and c/d are fractions then $a/b = c/d$ if, and only if, $ad = bc$. To see that the test really works, consider the example given above, 2/3 and 4/6. Here $a = 2$, $b = 3$, $c = 4$ and $d = 6$; $a \cdot d = 2 \cdot 6 = 12$, and $b \cdot c = 3 \cdot 4 = 12$, verifying that $2/3 = 4/6$. If the problem of determining whether or not the fractions 6/9 and 8/12 are equivalent by the basic interpretation were considered, it would be found to be a considerable task; but by the rule given it is easy, since $6 \cdot 12 = 8 \cdot 9 = 72$. It is important to note that a, b, and c are whole numbers and $b \neq 0$, $c \neq 0$; then $ac/bc = a/b$ follows, using the above basic rule for equivalence of fractions, since $(ac)b = (bc)a$. The latter equality holds, since the properties of whole numbers assures us that the product of three whole numbers is the same regardless of the order or grouping used in the multiplication. Thus, using this principle, $6/9 = (2 \cdot 3)/(3 \cdot 3) = 2/3$ and $8/12 = (2 \cdot 4)/(3 \cdot 4) = 2/3$, verifying again that $6/9 = 8/12$. This latter principle is the basic rule for changing a given fraction to an equivalent fraction, which is another name for the same unique rational number.

■ **ADDITION.**—The addition of whole numbers was defined in terms of properties of sets. A similar approach will be used to motivate the definition for addition of fractions. Consider $3/12 + 5/12$.

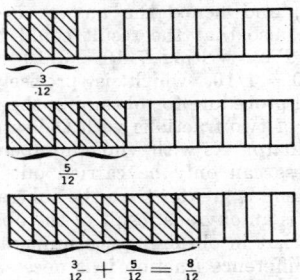

$$\underbrace{\qquad}_{\frac{3}{12}}$$

$$\underbrace{\qquad}_{\frac{5}{12}}$$

$$\frac{3}{12} + \frac{5}{12} = \frac{8}{12}$$

Thus, the sum must be 8/12, and it is evident that whenever two fractions have the same whole number in the denominator the sum is found by taking the sum of the whole numbers in their numerators as the numerator of the sum and the *common denominator* as the denominator of the sum. Hence, for two fractions, a/b and c/b, the definition is that $a/b + c/b = (a + c)/b$. However, this definition does not immediately show how to add two fractions which do not have the same whole number as a denominator. To see how to proceed, consider $1/4 + 2/3$. These two fractions do not have the same denominator, but by the rule developed for changing a fraction to an equivalent fraction the denominator of 2/3, or 3, may be used to change 1/4 to $(1 \cdot 3)/(4 \cdot 3) = 3/12$ and the denominator of 1/4, or 4, to change 2/3 to $(2 \cdot 4)/(3 \cdot 4) = 8/12$. The fractions then become $1/4 + 2/3 = 3/12 + 8/12 = 11/12$. On this basis any two fractions may be added regardless of whether or not they have the same denominator. Thus, in general,

$$a/b + c/d = ad/bd + bc/bd$$
$$= (ad + bc)/bd$$

for any two fractions a/b and c/d. It should be noted that this process is not the simplest possible one in that the denominator bd may be larger than is absolutely necessary for the two fractions involved. It is true, nevertheless, that this denominator will produce the desired sum, but perhaps not in what is usually called the simplified, or reduced, form. For example, if 3/8 and 5/12 are added by the above rule the sum is

$$(3 \cdot 12) + (8 \cdot 5)/(8 \cdot 12) = 76/96.$$

The reduced or simplest form of any fraction is a fraction equivalent to the given fraction such that the numerator and denominator have no factor in common. Thus, since

$$76/96 = (19 \cdot 4)/(24 \cdot 4),$$

it is not the simplest form but is equivalent to 19/24, which is in simplest form.

In practice the addition of fractions is carried out by means of the rule which applies to fractions having the same denominator. When the two fractions to be added do not have the same denominator, the notion of the *least common denominator* is used to obtain two equivalent fractions having the same denominator. Consider the example $3/8 + 5/12$ again. These two fractions must be changed to equivalent fractions having the same denominator. Certainly both fractions may be changed to fractions with a denominator $8 \cdot 12$, or 96, as shown above. But is this the smallest number that will serve as a common denominator? What is desired, of course, is to change each fraction to one having a denominator which is the smallest whole-number multiple of each given denominator. Thus, it is desired to change each denominator to a number which is the *least common multiple* of the given denominators. In this case the least common multiple of 8 and 12 is 24. This number is then referred to as the *least common denominator* of the two given fractions. Then the fractions may be changed to $(3 \cdot 3)/(8 \cdot 3) = 9/24$, $(5 \cdot 2)/(12 \cdot 2) = 10/24$. Then the sum is 19/24, as before. Note that the result is now in simplest, or reduced, form.

In some cases it is not readily evident what the least common denominator of two given fractions would be by inspection. In this case the techniques used for finding the least common multiple of two whole numbers may be helpful. Consider $13/36 + 28/45$. To find the least common multiple of 36 and 45, write each in factored form: $36 = 2 \cdot 2 \cdot 3 \cdot 3$, and $45 = 3 \cdot 3 \cdot 5$; then write the product of all prime factors that appear in either 36 or 45, repeating each of these as a factor the greatest number of times it is repeated in either 36 or 45. This gives the product $2 \cdot 2 \cdot 3 \cdot 3 \cdot 5$, or 180—the least common multiple of 36 and 45 and the least common de-

nominator of the given fractions. When the numbers are written in factored form it is easy to see what multiples of 36 and 45 must be taken in changing the two fractions to ones having denominator $2 \cdot 2 \cdot 3 \cdot 3 \cdot 5 = 180$. The denominator 36 would have to be multiplied by 5, and 45 would have to be multiplied by $2 \cdot 2$. These multiples could also be found by dividing 180 by 36 and by 45. Thus it follows that

$$13/36 + 28/45 = (13 \cdot 5)/(36 \cdot 5)$$
$$+ (28 \cdot 4)/(45 \cdot 4)$$
$$= 65/180 + 112/180 = 177/180$$

Several special cases in the addition of fractions arise when considering improper fractions, addition of whole number and fractions, and the treatment of symbols such as 4-2/3. The following examples illustrate procedures for dealing with these special cases.

Example:

$$5\text{-}3/4 = 5 + 3/4$$
$$= 5/1 + 3/4$$
$$= 20/4 + 3/4$$
$$= 23/4$$

Example:

$$2\text{-}3/8 + 3\text{-}7/8 = (2 + 3/8) + (3 + 7/8)$$
$$= (2 + 3) + (3/8 + 7/8)$$
$$= 5 + 10/8$$
$$= 5 + (8/8 + 2/8)$$
$$= 5 + (1 + 2/8)$$
$$= 6 + 2/8$$
$$= 6 + 1/4$$
$$= 6\text{-}1/4$$

The addition in this example can also be carried out by converting 2-3/8 to 19/8 and 3-7/8 to 31/8 as follows:

$$2\text{-}3/8 + 3\text{-}7/8 = 19/8 + 31/8$$
$$= 50/8$$
$$= 48/8 + 2/8$$
$$= 6 + 2/8$$
$$= 6 + 1/4$$
$$= 6\text{-}1/4$$

The addition can be further altered by converting 50/8 to 25/4 and then continuing as above.

The question also arises in connection with the above as to which of the symbols, 5-3/4 or 23/4, is preferable, since they both represent the same number. There is no absolute answer to this question. In the mathematical sense, 23/4 is possibly the preferred form because of the consistency of symbolism, but one would certainly not go to a store and ask for 23/4 yards of material. The preferable symbol would then be the one that is most appropriate to the situation. In any case, to work successfully with fractions, the meaning of both symbols must be understood.

■ **MULTIPLICATION.**—To illustrate the operation of multiplication of fractions, consider the following series of examples; base the conclusions on the initial interpretations given to the symbol a/b, where a and b are whole numbers, and b is not zero.

Example:

$$3 \times \frac{2}{5}$$

Interpreting multiplication by a whole number as continued addition (as was illustrated with multiplication of a whole number by a whole number) this result would be $2/5 + 2/5 + 2/5 = 6/5$. Also, $2/5$ could be interpreted as $2 \times 1/5$. Then $3 \times (2 \times 1/5) = (3 \times 2) \times 1/5 = 6 \times 1/5 = 6/5$. This has the geometric interpretation shown below.

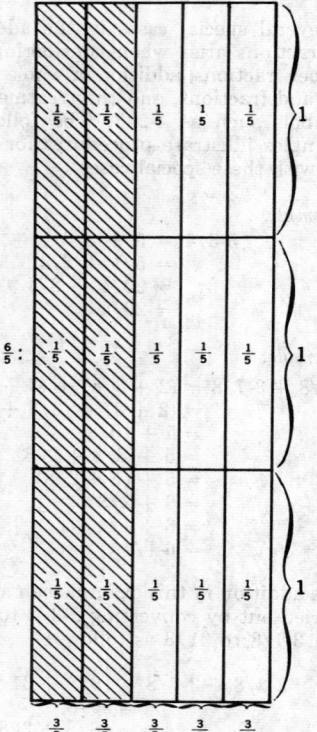

Example:

$$\frac{2}{5} \times 3$$

Here $2/5$ is interpreted as $2 \times 1/5$ again and then $2 \times 1/5 \times 3 = 3 \times 1/5 \times 2 = 2 \times 3/5$. Geometrically, this may be thought of as dividing the aggregate of three whole quantities into five equal parts and then taking two of them.

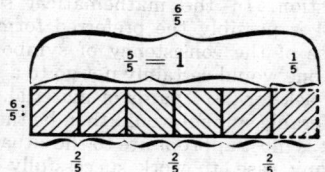

Example:

$$\frac{2}{3} \times \frac{3}{4}$$

In terms of the basic interpretation of symbols, this may be interpreted as 2 units of $3/4$ divided into three equal parts, or as dividing $3/4$ into three equal

parts and then taking two of them. In either case $2/3 \times 3/4$ will be $2/4 = 1/2$. The result is illustrated geometrically.

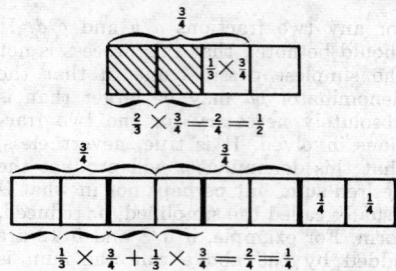

Example:

$$\frac{2}{5} \times \frac{3}{4}$$

This could be interpreted as dividing $3/4$ into five equal parts and then taking two of them. To divide $3/4$ into five equal parts, it is easier if $3/4$ is first changed to $(3 \cdot 5)/(4 \cdot 5) = 15/20$. Then, if $15/20$ is divided into five equal parts, each equal part will be $3/20$ and then taking two of them gives the result $6/20$, or $3/10$.

In each of these examples it is easily verifiable that the same result could be obtained by writing each factor in fractional form and multiplying the whole numbers that appear respectively in the numerators and denominators to obtain the fraction that represents the product. Thus, $3 \times 2/5 = 3/1 \times 2/5 = 6/5$, $2/3 \times 3/4 = 6/12$, and $2/5 \times 3/4 = 6/20 = 3/10$. With the suggestion of these examples, multiplication can be defined as follows: If a/b and c/d are fractions, then $a/b \times c/d = ac/bd$.

The examples below illustrate several general procedures that are helpful in carrying out the multiplication of fractions in varying situations.

Example:

$$\frac{12}{17} \times \frac{2}{3} = \frac{12 \cdot 2}{17 \cdot 3} = \frac{4 \cdot 3 \cdot 2}{17 \cdot 3}$$
$$= \frac{(4 \cdot 2) \cdot 3}{17 \cdot 3} = \frac{8}{17}$$

Here it is shown that in multiplying fractions it is helpful to try to identify common factors in the numerator and denominator before carrying out the actual multiplication, using the rule $ac/bc = a/b$ to obtain the simplest form of the product.

Example:

$$12 \times \frac{11}{24} = \frac{12}{1} \times \frac{11}{24} = \frac{12 \cdot 11}{12 \cdot 2} = \frac{11}{2}$$

Example:

$$6 \times 3\frac{4}{7} = 6\left(3 + \frac{4}{7}\right) = (6 \cdot 3) + \left(6 \cdot \frac{4}{7}\right)$$
$$= 18 + \frac{24}{7} = 18 + \left(3 + \frac{3}{7}\right)$$
$$= (18 + 3) + \frac{3}{7} = 21 + \frac{3}{7} = 21\frac{3}{7}$$

Alternatively, since $3\text{-}4/7 = 25/7$, $6 \times 25/7 = 6/1 \times 25/7 = 150/7 = 21\text{-}3/7$.

Example:

$$2\frac{2}{3} \times 3\frac{5}{8} = \left(2 + \frac{2}{3}\right) \times \left(3 + \frac{5}{8}\right)$$
$$= 2\left(3 + \frac{5}{8}\right) + \frac{2}{3}\left(3 + \frac{5}{8}\right)$$
$$= 6 + \left(2 \times \frac{5}{8}\right) + \left(\frac{2}{3} \times 3\right) \times \left(\frac{2}{3} \times \frac{5}{8}\right)$$
$$= 6 + \frac{5}{4} + 2 + \frac{5}{12}$$
$$= 6 + 2 + \left(\frac{15}{12} + \frac{5}{12}\right)$$
$$= 8 + \frac{20}{12} = 8 + 1 + \frac{2}{3} = 9 + \frac{2}{3} = 9\frac{2}{3}$$

Since $2\text{-}2/3 = 8/3$, and $3\text{-}5/8 = 29/8$, the product may also be found by finding $8/3 \times 29/8 = (8 \cdot 29)/(3 \cdot 8) = (29 \cdot 8)/(3 \cdot 8) = 29/3 = 9\text{-}2/3$. Usually in cases such as the two previous examples, it is easier to change the symbols to fractional form before carrying out the multiplication.

Note that in the above examples it was necessary to assume commutative laws and associative laws for multiplication and addition and also that the distributive law holds for fractions.

■ **SUBTRACTION.**—The operation of subtraction for fractions is defined in a way that is analogous to the definition of subtraction of whole numbers. That is, the difference of two fractions, a/b and c/d, is e/f if, and only if, e/f is a fraction such that $a/b = c/d + e/f$. Thus to find $7/10 - 3/10$, note that $3/10 + 4/10 = 7/10$, and hence the answer is $4/10$. Note also that the result could be obtained by writing $7/10 - 3/10 = (7 - 3)/10 = 4/10$, which is precisely the usual procedure for obtaining the difference of two fractions with the same denominator. As with whole numbers, this process can only be carried out if the minuend is greater than the subtrahend. This is an obvious result of the observation that in obtaining the numerator of the difference fraction it is necessary to find the difference of two whole numbers.

The question then arises as to how one determines which of two given fractions is the greater. This question did not arise with the whole numbers, since the system of numeration renders the result immediately. Of course, if the two fractions have the same denominator, as in the example, then the result follows from the fact that $7 > 4$. But what about $7/12$ and $11/20$? One procedure would be to change both fractions so that they have the same denominator. The most direct way to do this is to write $7/12 = (7 \cdot 20)/(12 \cdot 20) = 140/240$, and $11/20 = (11 \cdot 12)/(20 \cdot 12) = 132/240$. It then is immediately evident that $7/12$ is greater than $11/20$. Thus, for any two fractions a/b and c/d, the first would be changed to ad/bd and the second to bc/bd; the first is greater than the second if, and only if, ad is greater than bc.

In the same way, if a/b and c/d are any two fractions, the first may be changed to ad/bd and the second to bc/bd; their difference will then be the fraction $(ad - bc)/bd$, provided $ad > bc$.

This is similar to the general rule for the addition of fractions.

In subtraction, as in addition, the least common multiple of denominators (*least common denominator*) is used to make the process as efficient as possible. Also, similar comments apply where symbols such as 3-5/8 appear.

Example:

$$\frac{11}{21} - \frac{3}{7} = \frac{11}{7 \cdot 3} - \frac{3}{7} = \frac{11}{7 \cdot 3} - \frac{3 \cdot 3}{7 \cdot 3}$$
$$= \frac{(11 - 9)}{21} = \frac{2}{21}$$

Example:

$$7\frac{3}{8} - 2\frac{5}{12} = \left(7 + \frac{3}{8}\right) - \left(2 + \frac{5}{12}\right)$$
$$= (7 - 2) + \left(\frac{3}{8} - \frac{5}{12}\right)$$

But $3 \cdot 12$ is less than $8 \cdot 5$. Hence, the last subtraction cannot be performed. Therefore, it is necessary to go back and change $7 + 3/8$ to $6 + (1 + 3/8) = 6 + 11/8$. This gives $(6 - 2) + (11/8 - 5/12)$. However, $6 - 2 = 4$ and the least common multiple of 8 and 12 is 24. Then $11/8 - 5/12 = (11 \cdot 3)/(8 \cdot 3) - (5 \cdot 2)/(12 \cdot 2) = 33/24 - 10/24 = (33 - 10)/24 = 23/24$. Therefore, the difference is $4 + 23/24 = 4\text{-}23/24$. The problem might also be carried out by changing 7-3/8 to 59/8 and 2-5/12 to 29/12, then subtracting.

■ **DIVISION.**—As has been seen, the operations of addition and subtraction are quite readily explained in terms of the basic interpretations. Multiplication is a little more difficult, but is fairly easily understood in terms of these interpretations. Division, however, seems to be more difficult, and an attempt to provide an adequate rationale will start with the most elementary considerations.

Division of a whole number by a fraction: It seems reasonable to interpret the symbol $3 \div 1/4$ as asking the question: how many 1/4ths are contained in 3? Since there are four 1/4ths in 1, there must be three times as many, or 12, in 3. Thus the result of the division is 12. Note that $12 = 3 \times 4/1$. Again, what is $3 \div 2/3$? First the question, how many 2/3rds are contained in 1, must be answered. Now $1 = 2/3 + 1/3$ and 1/3 is 1/2 of 2/3. Hence the number of 2/3rds in 1 is 1-1/2. The number of 2/3rds in 3 is then $3 \times 1\text{-}1/2 = 4\text{-}1/2$. Note that $4\text{-}1/2 = 9/2 = 3 \times 3/2$.

Division of a fraction by a whole number: Here it is necessary to give a slightly different interpretation of the operation of division, namely, that of dividing 1/4 into three equal parts. Thus, 1/4 is changed to the equivalent fraction 3/12. Taking 1/3 of 3/12, the result of the division is then 1/12. Again, note that $1/12 = 1/4 \times 1/3$.

Division of a fraction by a fraction: The symbol $2/3 \div 3/5$ may be regarded as asking: How many 3/5 in 2/3? And again, it is first necessary to find how many units of 3/5 are contained in 1.

Since $1 = 5/5 = 3/5 + 2/5$, there is one unit of 3/5 in 1 with 2/5 remaining. But $2/3 \times 3/5 = 2/5$. Hence, there are 1-2/3 units of 3/5 in 1. Therefore, there will be 2/3 as many in 2/3. Now $2/3 \times 1\text{-}2/3 = 2/3 \times 5/3 = 10/9 = 1\text{-}1/9$, which is $2/3 \times 5/3$.

In every case it is evident that the final result could have been obtained by means of the usual rule for division, which is to invert the divisor and multiply. However, the arguments used are not complete and perhaps not sufficient to justify this rule for division. A fresh look at the operation of division from the standpoint of the properties of fractions themselves is therefore in order.

First note that any fraction of the form a/a, where a is not zero, has the identity property for multiplication. That is, for any given fraction c/d,

$$c/d \times a/a = ca/da = c/d.$$

Thus 2/2 has this property, as does any fraction equivalent to it. Recalling the earlier discussion, 1/1, 2/2, 3/3, and all fractions of this form are names for the same rational number. It is customary to give this rational number the name 1, since it behaves as an identity for multiplication. Thus, it is seen that any fraction, which is a particular name for some rational number, multiplied by any fraction of the form a/a, yields a fraction which is a name for the same rational number.

Also, it is easily seen that for any nonzero fraction, say 2/3, there is a fraction formed by inverting the given fraction, 3/2, which has the property that $2/3 \times 3/2 = 6/6 = 1$, the identity for multiplication. It must be remembered that 3/2 is not the only fraction which has this property in relation to 2/3, since any fraction equivalent to 3/2 has the same property. But if the fraction 2/3 is interpreted as naming a particular *rational number*, then there is only *one* rational number, whether it be named by 3/2 or by some equivalent, that yields 1 as a product. This rational number is called the *inverse*, or *reciprocal*, of the given rational number. Therefore, the rational number named by 3/2 is called the *inverse* of the rational number named by 2/3. In this sense every fraction $a/b \neq 0$ has an inverse, b/a.

It is now possible to frame a definition of division of fractions similar to that framed for division of whole numbers (note: reference is made to the symbols as fractions with the understanding that they be thought of as a name for a rational number): The quotient of a/b and c/d is e/f if, and only if, $a/b = c/d \times e/f$. For example, $2/3 \div 3/5 = 10/9$, since $2/3 = 3/5 \times 10/9$.

Now let us look once again at the usual rule for division, that $a/b \div c/d = a/b \times d/c$. Or, stated in words, to divide two fractions, invert the divisor and multiply. For example, consider $3/4 \div 5/7$. Let x/y name the quotient. Then, by the definition of division, it must follow that $3/4 = 5/7 \times x/y$. Now

if these two expressions are equal they will certainly remain equal if they are both multiplied by the 7/5, which is the inverse of 5/7. Thus $7/5 \times 3/4 = 7/5 \times 5/7 \times x/y = 1 \times x/y = x/y$. Hence, the quotient x/y is $7/5 \times 3/4 = 3/4 \times 7/5$, justifying the usual rule on the basis of the definition of division and the existence of inverses. (Note that the associative law and the commutative law for multiplication are assumed.)

Another procedure for performing the operation of division with fractions is illustrated below.

$$6/7 \div 2/3 = (6/7 \times 21) \div (2/3 \times 21)$$
$$= 18 \div 14 = 18/14 = 9/7$$

This procedure is based on the principle that the quotient remains unchanged when the dividend and divisor are multiplied by the same or equal fractions. In the illustration, the multiplier used is the least common denominator of the fractions involved in the division. Also, the interpretation of the fractional symbol as representing an indicated division is utilized; that is, $a/b = a \div b$. Further utilization of this idea would enable the solution to be written as follows:

$$\frac{6/7}{2/3} = \frac{6/7 \times 21}{2/3 \times 21} = 18/14 = 9/7$$

In still another variation on this theme, the reciprocal of the divisor, 3/2, is used as a multiplier and the result is obtained as follows:

$$\frac{6/7}{2/3} = \frac{6/7 \times 3/2}{2/3 \times 3/2} = \frac{6/7 \times 3/2}{1}$$
$$= 6/7 \times 3/2 = 18/14 = 9/7$$

Neither of these procedures involves learning the rule given for division usually stated, yet each gives the required result.

In concluding the section on fractions, note once more that a fraction names a particular number, called a rational number, but that there may be many fractions which name the same rational number. A given rational number is usually named by a fraction in its reduced, or simplest, form.

The set of rational numbers has many properties analogous to the whole numbers plus some additional ones. This set obeys the commutative and associative laws of addition and multiplication. It is closed for the operations of addition and multiplication and also for division. This means that given any two rational numbers, their sum, product, and quotient are also rational numbers. The set contains identity elements for addition and multiplication, the rational numbers named by 0/1 and 1/1. It has been seen that each rational number, a/b, has a multiplicative inverse, b/a, such that $a/b \times b/a = 1$. The distributive law of multiplication with respect to addition also holds, that is,

$$a/b \times (c/d + e/f)$$
$$= (a/b \times c/d) + (a/b \times e/f).$$

The rational numbers have an additional property that distinguishes them from the whole numbers. This is that the rational numbers are said to constitute a *dense* set. This means that between any two rational numbers, no matter how close together, there still remains another rational number. In fact, between any two rational numbers there are an unlimited number of rational numbers. If the rational numbers are interpreted as points on a line, this

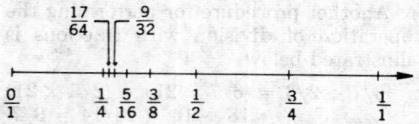

DENSE SET OF RATIONAL NUMBERS

means that the points representing rational numbers are closely packed together. The property of denseness makes a rational number completely adequate for all practical measurement purposes, whereas the whole numbers are adequate only for counting purposes. This is illustrated in practice when rulers of increasing precision are obtained simply by increasing the number of subdivisions in the unit of measure.

Ratio, Proportion, and Per Cent.—Many everyday problems involve the comparison of two numbers. Some examples are: the number of games a team wins compared with the total number of games played; the circumference of a circle compared to its diameter ($c/d = \pi$); the number of boys compared to the number of girls in a class; and, from trigonometry, there are the comparisons of the measures of the sides of a right triangle. Comparisons may be done in two ways. One may compare by subtraction or by division. Comparison by division is referred to as a *ratio* and is expressed as a/b (or $a : b$), where a and b are natural numbers. Notice that they look like the rational numbers—indeed the rational numbers derived their name from ratios. Ratios imply a quotient. To illustrate: suppose that Kathy is 3 years old and Anne is 5 years old. The ratio of Kathy's age to Anne's age is 3/5; that is, Kathy is three-fifths as old as Anne. Records indicate that about 2000 years ago the Greeks made extensive use of ratios in comparing lengths of line segments, sizes of angles, and areas of regions.

Proportion is a statement that shows that two ratios are equal. Thus, if the ratios a/b and c/d represent the same comparison they may be set equal to each other as: $a/b = c/d$. The values a, b, c, and d are called the four members of the proportion. One of the useful facts about proportions is that if $a/b = c/d$, then $ad = bc$, as proven below.

Proof:

Given $a/b = c/d$. Multiply both numbers by bd:

$$(bd)(a/b) = (bd)(c/d)$$

Simplify by dividing both the numera-

tor and denominator by b on the left and by d on the right side of the equality, with the result:

$$ad = bc.$$

The importance of this is that if any three members of a proportion are known, the fourth can always be found. For example, what number bears the same ratio to 20 as 3 does to 4? The ratio x to 20 is equal to the ratio 3 to 4.

$$x/20 = 3/4$$
$$4x = 60$$
$$x = 15$$

A recipe calls for 6 eggs to make 24 cookies. How many eggs are necessary to make 36 cookies? Again a proportion:

$$6/24 = x/36$$
$$24x = 216$$
$$x = 9$$

When comparing denominative quantities by division, the values must be expressed in common units. Thus 6 inches to 2 feet would give a ratio 1/2:2 which is equal to 1/4 when both are expressed in feet. If inches are used, 6/24 is obtained, which is also equal to 1/4. The ratio itself is a pure number and has no units attached to it.

Per cent is closely related to the concept of ratio. The term "per cent" is derived from the Latin *per centum*, which means "by the hundred." Thus, 5 per cent means 5 out of one hundred. As a ratio, this would be written 5/100. The per cent symbol, %, was introduced as early as the fifteenth century, although it was not used extensively until recently. Today the meaning of per cent is somewhat broader than was the original interpretation. For example, expressions such as 700%, 5000%, and so on, are often used. Per cent is viewed as a ratio a/b where b is always 100. The three ways in which a per cent may be expressed are: $a/100$, $0.01 \times a$, and $a\%$.

Examples:

An investment of $5000.00 yields an annual return of $200.00. What is the per cent of return?

$$\frac{200}{5000} = \frac{x}{100}$$
$$5000x = 20000$$
$$x = 4\%$$

A bank pays interest at the rate of 5 per cent per year. How much interest will an investment of $250.00 yield annually?

$$\frac{5}{100} = \frac{x}{250}$$
$$x = \$12.50$$

How many dollars should be invested at 6 per cent to yield an annual income of $300.00?

$$\frac{6}{100} = \frac{300}{x}$$
$$x = \$5,000$$

In general this can be formulated as: $i/100 = p/b$, where $i/100$ is the rate of interest, p is the percentage of return, and b is the base, or amount invested.

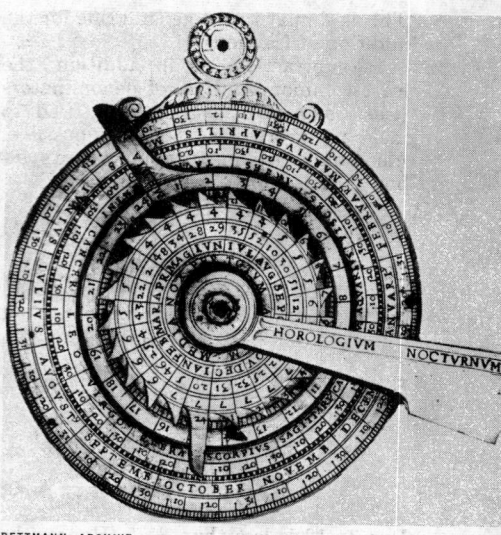

BETTMANN ARCHIVE

CIRCULAR ITALIAN CALENDAR, used during the sixteenth century, was designed to be used in the evening as well as daytime.

Number Congruence.—The concept of number congruence and the symbolism related to this idea were introduced by Karl Friedrich Gauss (1777–1855). To illustrate the concept of number congruence, look at the face of a watch or clock. If it is 10 P.M. now, what time will it be in 7 hours? The problem is to add 10 and 7 on the face of a clock. As is seen, one gets 5 as the answer rather than 17. The reason for getting 5 o'clock is that the common clock repeats itself every 12 hours. The odometers in automobiles repeat every 100,000 miles. The days of the months repeat in approximately 30-day cycles. The days of the year repeat in 365¼ days. There are many additional examples, among them such common devices as gas meters, water meters, and electric meters.

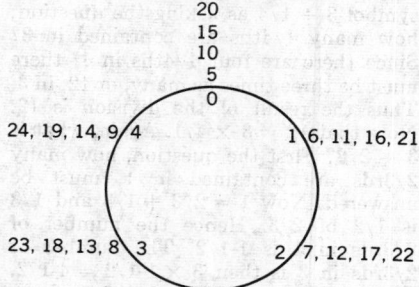

Suppose one were to look at the face of a clock that has only 5 positions on it. With a little reflection, it will be seen that these basic positions are the remainders one can obtain when dividing any whole number by 5. In this example, one can say that all the whole numbers that have the same remainder when divided by 5 are congruent to each other. Thus 1, 6, 11, 16, . . . belong to the same set; that is, they are congruent because they each have a remainder of 1 when divided by 5. The numbers 4, 9, 14, 19, . . . each have 4 as a remainder when divided

BETTMANN ARCHIVE

TRAVEL DESKCLOCK with a sun motif on the cover was made in Sweden in 1760. Early timepieces such as these contained a rather complex system of gears powered by a central mainspring. Most of these clocks had to be wound and adjusted at least once a day.

BETTMANN ARCHIVE

CALENDAR sculptured in clay was used about 3,500 years ago in Crete. Agricultural symbols often represented time periods.

by 5 and these are called congruent.

Thus, *two whole numbers "a" and "b,"* *which have the same remainder when divided by a number "m,"* are said to be *congruent in modulo "m."* The number m is called the modulus, which is the Latin term meaning "little measure." The symbolization of this expression is: $a = b$ mod m (mod is used as an abbreviation for modulo) if, and only if, $a - b = k \cdot m$, where k is an integer. This statement is read: a is congruent to b in modulo m if, and only if, the difference between a and b can be expressed as a multiple of m. Another way of saying this is that the difference between a and b is exactly divisible by m. Using modulo 5, it is seen that the numbers 22 and 7 are congruent since $22 - 7 = 3 \cdot 5$. However, 31 and 8 are not congruent in modulo 5, for $31 - 8$ cannot be expressed as a multiple of 5. Associated with each modulus is a table of addition and multiplication facts. For modulo 5 the following facts are presented.

Modulo 5

+	0	1	2	3	4		×	0	1	2	3	4
0	0	1	2	3	4		0	0	0	0	0	0
1	1	2	3	4	0		1	0	1	2	3	4
2	2	3	4	0	1		2	0	2	4	1	3
3	3	4	0	1	2		3	0	3	1	4	2
4	4	0	1	2	3		4	0	4	3	2	1

For modulo 2, it is seen that there would be two sets of congruent numbers, the even and the odd. The addition and multiplication facts for modulo 2 are presented below:

Modulo 2

+	0	1		×	0	1
0	0	1		0	0	0
1	1	0		1	0	1

The common clock is thus modulo 12.

Shortcuts.—As man learned more about the numbers he had created and their uses he began to find timesaving techniques for doing ordinary calculations. Most of these techniques can very simply be explained in terms of the basic structure of the base ten numeration system. For example, the use of exponents has made it possible to multiply and divide very large and very small numbers easily, for example, $10^{15} \times 10^5 = 10^{20}$, and $10^{-16}/10^5 = 10^{-21}$. Some of the powers of 10 are shown below.

$$1000 = 10 \cdot 10 \cdot 10 = 10^3$$
$$100 = 10 \cdot 10 = 10^2$$
$$10 = 10 = 10^1$$
$$1 = \frac{10}{10} = 10^0$$
$$.10 = \frac{1}{10} = 10^{-1}$$
$$.01 = \frac{1}{100} = 10^{-2}$$
$$.001 = \frac{1}{1000} = 10^{-3}$$

More specialized techniques have also been devised; for example, to multiply a number by 5, divide the number by 2 and multiply by 10, for example, $46 \times 5 = 46/2 \times 10 = 230$. To multiply a number by 25, divide the number by 4 and multiply by 100; for example, $84 \times 25 = 84/4 \times 100 = 2100$.

Notice that both of these techniques depend on the number being multiplied also being divisible by 2 and 4, respectively. If this is not the case, then very little time is saved by using this technique.

To multiply a number by 11 is very simple. Notice the usual procedure:

$$\begin{array}{r} 3542 \\ \times\ 11 \\ \hline 3542 \\ 3542 \\ \hline 38962 \end{array}$$

Careful examination of this process re-

veals it can be performed as follows:

$$3\ 5\ 4\ 2$$
$$3\ 8\ 9\ 6\ 2$$

Begin by writing down 2.
Then add $4 + 2 = 6$.
Then add $5 + 4 = 9$.
Then add $3 + 5 = 8$.
Finally write down 3.

There are many rules for testing divisibility of numbers. Some of the common ones are:

Divisibility by 2: For a number to be divisible by 2 it must end in 0, 2, 4, 6, or 8.

Divisibility by 3: A number is divisible by 3 only if 3 divides the sum of the digits in the number; for example, 435 is divisible by 3, because $4 + 3 + 5 = 12$, which is divisible by 3.

Divisibility by 4: If the last two digits of a number form a number that is divisible by 4 then the entire number is divisible by 4; for example, 2536 is divisible by 4, since 36 is divisible by 4.

Divisibility by 5: Only numbers ending in 0 or 5 are divisible by 5.

Divisibility by 6: Only numbers divisible both by 2 and by 3 are divisible by 6, for example, 156.

Divisibility by 7: A number is divisible by 7 if the difference between twice the units digit and the number formed by the remaining digits is exactly divisible by 7, for example, 161, since $16 - 2 = 14$ which is divisible by 7.

Divisibility by 8: If 8 divides the number formed by the last three digits, then 8 divides the number; for example, 5144 is divisible by 8 since 144 is.

Divisibility by 9: A number is divisible by 9 if the sum of the digits is divisible by 9; for example, 3987 is divisible by 9, since $3 + 9 + 8 + 7 = 27$, a number which is divisible by 9. This fact, which was used rather extensively in the past in checking the results of basic operations, is called "casting out nines."

—H. Laverne Thomas and Viggo P. Hansen

ALGEBRA

Scope.—Algebra is the study of numbers and the relations among them. It is more generalized than arithmetic, since it deals with symbols that can represent many different numbers. However, these symbols are manipulated by the same four basic operations—addition, subtraction, multiplication, and division—as are numbers. Indeed, algebra might be thought of as generalized arithmetic.

Types of Numbers.—The natural numbers (counting numbers, such as 1, 2, 3, . . .) behave well in addition and multiplication. The addition of two natural numbers results in a sum that is also a natural number, and the same holds true for the result of the multiplication of two natural numbers. But subtraction and division raise problems that are solved only by expanding the system of natural numbers.

Consider the expression $a - b$. If a and b are both natural numbers, and if a is larger than b, there is no problem; the result is a natural number. But if b is larger than a, no natural number can express the result. Hence, *negative numbers* were added to the "vocabulary" of numbers. (The expanded system, which includes negative whole numbers and also the number 0, is called the *integers*.) Negative numbers make subtraction possible for all numbers. For example, $6 - 8$ is said to be negative 2, written as -2. Positive numbers are written with a plus sign. (Numbers without signs are assumed to be positive.)

Division, however, presents a problem that even the integers cannot always handle. Sometimes division of two integers results in another integer ($6 \div 3 = 2$), but often it does not ($2 \div 3$ and $5 \div 2$ cannot be expressed as integers). Hence, fractions were included, producing the system of *rational numbers*. Fractions make division of one number by any other number (except zero) always possible. Other extensions of the number system will be discussed.

Number Line.—The positive numbers, negative numbers, and fractions are shown on a number line in Figure 1.

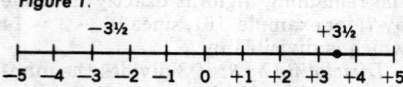

Figure 1.

Beginning at a fixed point on the line designated as 0, the positive whole numbers are marked off in order at points that lie at equal intervals to the right of 0; the negative numbers are similarly marked off at points to the left of 0. Fractions are marked off at points between the whole numbers. Thus $-3\frac{1}{2}$ lies midway between -3 and -4. Every number, positive or negative, is thus assigned to one, and only one, point on the number line.

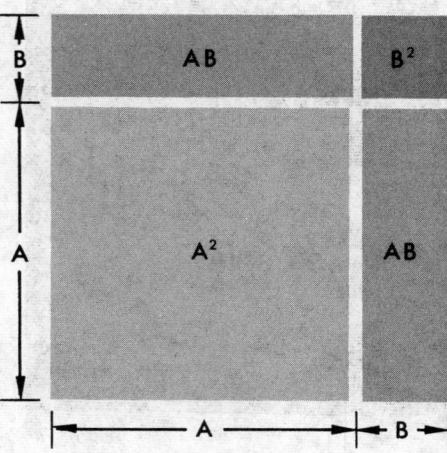

ALGEBRAIC EXPANSION was one of the many mathematical principles first understood by the Greeks over two thousand years ago. Although they lacked the algebraic shorthand with which to express such problems, they knew how to solve them geometrically. The diagram above illustrates the principle of *squaring*, in which a square of a known area is increased proportionately on all sides. If the original area, A^2, whose sides are A feet long, is increased on each side by the length B, the area of the resulting square can be determined by adding the areas of the small rectangles (AB, AB, and B^2) to the area of the original square (A^2). Expressed algebraically, this would read: $2AB + B^2 + A^2$. The Greeks, however, did not formulate algebra as a branch of mathematics distinct from geometry until much later. Diophantus (c. 275) was the first to devise an algebraic symbolism to express such concepts without geometry.

Basic Postulates.—Algebra, like all branches of mathematics, is a postulational system. Certain basic statements are assumed to be true about numbers and the relations among them; other truths are then evolved by logical reasoning. The basic statements that are assumed to be true are called *postulates*, or *axioms*.

The basic postulates about the operations of addition and multiplication on the numbers of arithmetic are assumed to hold true for the expanded system of positive and negative numbers and fractions of algebra. These postulates make it possible to determine the meaning of addition, subtraction, multiplication, and division on the signed numbers of algebra, for they govern the ways numbers can be combined.

The *commutative postulate for addition* states that if two numbers are added, they may be added in any order without affecting the result. That is, $a + b = b + a$ if a and b represent any of the signed numbers of algebra.

The *associative postulate for addition* states that if three numbers are to be added, any two may be added first and their sum then added to the third without affecting the result. That is, $(a + b) + c = a + (b + c)$. (Parentheses are used as a symbol of grouping; the parentheses around $a + b$ in the statement above signify that the sum of a and b is to be treated as a whole.)

The *commutative postulate for multiplication* states that if two numbers are to be multiplied, they may be multiplied in either order without affecting the result; that is, ab is equal to ba. (In algebra the multiplication of two letters, or of a letter and a number, is indicated by writing them adjacent to each other without a sign between: xy means "x times y," and $5c$ means "5 times c.")

The *associative postulate for multiplication* states that if three numbers are to be multiplied, any two may be multiplied first and their product then multiplied by the third without affecting the result: $(ab)c$ is equal to $a(bc)$.

The *distributive postulate* states that if the sum of two numbers is to be multiplied by a third number, the result will be the same if the sum is taken first and then multiplied, or if each of the two numbers is multiplied by the third number and the two resulting products are then added; that is, $a(b + c)$ is equal to $ab + ac$.

Operations.—Each of the fundamental operations of arithmetic can be performed on the signed numbers in such a way that the five basic postulates above will be true.

■ ADDITION.—The expression $(+3) + (+2)$ means positive 3 plus positive 2. This may be done on the number line. A positive number is added by moving to the right (starting at 0) a number of spaces equivalent to this number's distance; a negative number is added by a similar movement to the left. Thus, to add $+2$ to $+3$, start at $+3$ and move two spaces to the right, arriving at $+5$ (Fig. 2). Therefore, $(+3) + (+2) = +5$.

Similarly, $(+3) + (-2) = +1$; move two spaces to the left from $+3$ to add -2 to it. Reversing the order does not

Figure 2.

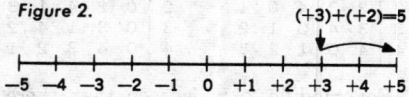

change the result; thus $(-2) + (+3)$ also gives $+1$ under the procedure used to interpret addition. These examples illustrate that the commutative postulate for addition holds true.

The number line should be used to add groups of three signed numbers, using various orders of addition, to show that this procedure also satisfies the associative postulate for addition.

It is possible, of course, to add signed numbers without using the number line.

To do so requires use of the concept of the absolute value of a number. The *absolute value* of a number is its magnitude without regard to sign. The absolute value of both +2.3 and −2.3 is 2.3; the absolute value of −5 is 5.

Thus, there are two principles for adding signed numbers that will give the same results as were obtained by the use of the number line:

(1) The sum of two numbers that have the same sign is the sum of their absolute values with the common sign written in front of it.

Examples:

$$(+) \frac{\begin{array}{r} +3 \\ +2 \end{array}}{+5} \qquad (+) \frac{\begin{array}{r} -4 \\ -5 \end{array}}{-9} \qquad (+) \frac{\begin{array}{r} +2\frac{1}{2} \\ +3\frac{1}{4} \end{array}}{+5\frac{3}{4}}$$

(2) The sum of two numbers that have different signs is the difference of their absolute values with the sign of the number having the larger absolute value written in front of it.

Examples:

$$(+) \frac{\begin{array}{r} +3 \\ -2 \end{array}}{+1} \quad (+) \frac{\begin{array}{r} -2 \\ +3 \end{array}}{+1} \quad (+) \frac{\begin{array}{r} -8 \\ +5 \end{array}}{-3} \quad (+) \frac{\begin{array}{r} -9 \\ +9 \end{array}}{0}$$

■ **SUBTRACTION.**—Subtraction is the inverse operation to addition. This means that it is possible to subtract +3 from +8 by asking what must be added to +3 to get +8. On the number line, one must move five spaces to the right (+5) to get from +3 to +8. Therefore if +3 is subtracted from +8, the result is +5.

Similarly, one must move three spaces to the left to get from +7 to +4, and therefore (+4) − (+7) = −3. Again, (−5) − (−3) = +2, since one must move two spaces to the right to get from −5 to −3. Finally, (+4) − (−7) = +11, for going from −7 to +4 is a move of eleven spaces to the right.

To be able to subtract signed numbers without referring to the number line requires the concept of an additive inverse.

The *additive inverse* of a number is the number with the same absolute value but opposite sign. Thus, the additive inverse of +3 is −3, and that of −8 is +8.

Rewriting the subtraction examples above:

$$(-) \frac{\begin{array}{r} +8 \\ +3 \end{array}}{+5} \quad (-) \frac{\begin{array}{r} +4 \\ +7 \end{array}}{-3} \quad (-) \frac{\begin{array}{r} -3 \\ -5 \end{array}}{+2} \quad (-) \frac{\begin{array}{r} +4 \\ -7 \end{array}}{+11}$$

and comparing them with the following addition examples:

$$(+) \frac{\begin{array}{r} +8 \\ -3 \end{array}}{+5} \quad (+) \frac{\begin{array}{r} +4 \\ -7 \end{array}}{-3} \quad (+) \frac{\begin{array}{r} -3 \\ +5 \end{array}}{+2} \quad (+) \frac{\begin{array}{r} +4 \\ +7 \end{array}}{+11}$$

a principle for subtracting signed numbers is evident: A number may be subtracted from another number by adding its additive inverse to the other number. Thus,

$$(-) \frac{\begin{array}{r} -7 \\ +5 \end{array}}{}$$

becomes

$$(+) \frac{\begin{array}{r} -7 \\ -5 \end{array}}{-12}$$

(since −5 is the additive inverse of +5). Similarly:

$$(-) \frac{\begin{array}{r} -3 \\ -4 \end{array}}{+1} \quad (-) \frac{\begin{array}{r} -7 \\ +5 \end{array}}{-12} \quad (-) \frac{\begin{array}{r} +8 \\ -3 \end{array}}{+11} \quad (-) \frac{\begin{array}{r} -3 \\ -3 \end{array}}{0}$$

In algebra, the plus sign and the minus sign are used in more than one way. A minus sign may indicate the operation of subtraction, as in (+3) − (+5), or it may indicate a negative

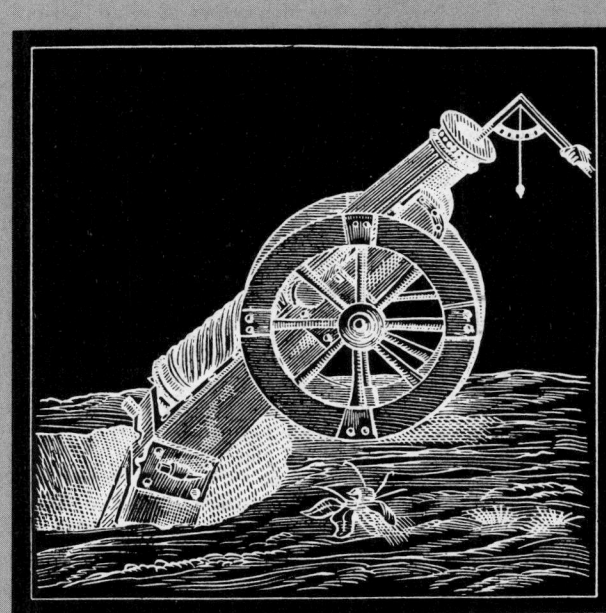

ITALIAN ALGEBRAISTS of the sixteenth century matched wits in many problem-solving contests, but the most brilliant feat of all was Niccolò Tartaglia's solution of cubic equations. Between bouts of pure mathematics, Tartaglia (1500–1557) solved such military problems as the angle of a cannon's trajectory (*above*). Jerome Cardan (1501–1576) stole his cubic solution, added his own solution of quartic equations, and published both in 1545 in his *Ars Magna*, covering all known algebra.

number, as in −3. The plus sign is similarly used to indicate addition and also to indicate a positive number. Confusion may arise as to which meaning of the minus sign is intended in an expression such as 5 − 3. It is customary to think of this expression as meaning "positive 5 combined with (added to) negative 3," which is equal to positive 2. This way of interpreting the sign is convenient for handling expressions involving more than two terms. Thus, 4 − 6 + 3 + 2 means "positive 4 combined with negative 6, then combined with positive 3, and then with positive 2"; the result is positive 3. Try combining 7 − 11 − 9 + 3 in this manner. It is advantageous to make use of the associative postulate by adding all positive numbers and all negative numbers first, then combining the two results (answer is −10).

■ **MULTIPLICATION.**—The expression $(+3)(+4)$ represents the product of positive 3 and positive 4 and is evaluated as $+12$ since the positive numbers are the counterparts of the natural numbers of arithmetic. Similarly, $(+3)(−4)$ can be interpreted as the sum of three negative fours $(−4 −4 −4)$ and, hence, is equal to −12. Also, $(−3)(+4)$ can be changed to $(+4)(−3)$ by the commutative postulate for multiplication and is, therefore, also −12 by an interpretation similar to that of the previous example. On the other hand, $(−3)(−4)$ cannot be assigned a value using an interpretation of multiplication as repeated addition, as was done in the previous examples, because both factors are negative. However, it has already been shown that $(−3)(+2)$ is −6. But $(−3)(+2)$ is the same as $(−3)(6 − 4)$ and therefore $(−3)(6 − 4)$ must equal −6. By the distributive postulate, $(−3)(6 − 4) = −18 + (−3)$ $(−4)$. In order to make this last result, $−18 + (−3)(−4)$, equal −6, the expression $(−3)(−4)$ must be equal to $+12$.

Rewriting the examples above, we obtain:

$$\begin{array}{cccc} +3 & +3 & -3 & -3 \\ (\times)\underline{+4} & (\times)\underline{-4} & (\times)\underline{+4} & (\times)\underline{-4} \\ +12 & -12 & -12 & +12 \end{array}$$

Thus, the principles for multiplying signed numbers are:

(1) The product of two numbers having the same sign is the product of their absolute values with a positive sign written in front of it.

(2) The product of two numbers having different signs is the product of their absolute values with a negative sign in front of it.

Examples:

$$\begin{array}{l} (−5)\,(−6) = +30 \\ (−7)\,(+2) = −14 \\ (+9)\,(−3) = −27 \\ (+8\tfrac{1}{2})(+2) = +17 \end{array}$$

■ **DIVISION.**—Division is the inverse operation to multiplication. The *multiplicative inverse* of a number is the number which when multiplied by it gives a product of 1. Thus, $\tfrac{1}{3}$ is the multiplicative inverse of 3, since $3 \times \tfrac{1}{3} = 1$, and $\tfrac{2}{5}$ is the multiplicative inverse of $\tfrac{5}{2}$. The multiplicative inverse of a number is also called its *reciprocal.*

It must be kept in mind that each division example may be transformed into a multiplication example by changing the divisor to its multiplicative inverse and then multiplying by it. For example, the division example $8 \div 2$ is the same as the multiplication example $8 \times \tfrac{1}{2}$, since $\tfrac{1}{2}$ is the multiplicative inverse of 2.

Since any division example can be changed into a multiplication example, the method of obtaining the sign of the answer in division (quotient) must be the same as that used in multiplication. Therefore, these principles for the division of signed numbers logically follow:

(1) The quotient of two numbers having the same sign is the quotient of their absolute values with a positive sign written before it.

(2) The quotient of two numbers having different signs is the quotient of their absolute values with a negative sign written before it.

Examples:

$$\begin{array}{l} (+12) \div (+3) = +4 \\ (−18) \div (−2) = +9 \\ (−27) \div (+3) = −9 \\ (+15) \div (−30) = −\tfrac{1}{2} \end{array}$$

Use of Letters.—It has already been pointed out that algebra achieves a generalization not possible in arithmetic, because in algebra letters are employed to represent unspecified numbers. Each letter represents any one of a certain set of numbers called the *domain* or *replacement set* for that letter. Suppose that in the expression $b + 7$ the domain of b is the set $\{1, 2, 3, 4, 5\}$. Then b may be replaced by 1, 2, 3, 4, or 5. Hence, b is termed a *variable,* and its possible replacements are 1, 2, 3, 4, or 5.

In contrast to a variable, a number such as 75, which has one fixed value, is called a *constant.* If b is replaced by 1, the expression $b + 7$ equals 8; if b is 2, the expression equals 9, and so on. To take another example, suppose that the domain of x in the expression

$$\frac{x + 3}{2}$$

is the set $\{−2, −1, 0, 1, 2\}$. If the variable x is replaced by −2, the expression equals $\tfrac{1}{2}$; if by −1, the expression equals 1, and so on. If no domain is specified for a particular letter, the domain is considered to be the largest possible set of numbers for that letter. (At this point, the largest possible set of numbers can be thought of as including all positive and negative integers and fractions, and zero.)

Evaluating Expressions.—An algebraic expression is a number expressed by means of letters and numbers connected by signs of operation, for example, $5a + 3b^2 − \tfrac{1}{2}bc$. To *evaluate* an algebraic expression means to find the number it represents. This is done by replacing the variables in the expression by the numbers they represent.

Example:

To evaluate $2a + 3b$ when $a = 4$ and $b = −2$ means to replace a by 4 and b by −2. After substitution, the expression yields $2(4) + 3(−2)$, or $8 − 6$, which is 2.

It has already been noted that writing two letters or a number and a letter adjacent to one another without any sign between them implies that they are to be multiplied together. Thus xy means x is to be multiplied by y and $3x$ means x is to be multiplied by 3.

When a number represented by a symbol is to be multiplied by itself, it is customary to write x^2 instead of xx. Similarly, x^3 stands for xxx, y^7 stands for the product of seven y's, and 3^2 means $3(3)$, or 9. When a number is multiplied by itself, the product is called a *power* of that number. Thus, x^2 is called the second power of x, or x squared; x^3 is the third power of x, or x cubed; x^4 is the fourth power of x; x^5 is the fifth power of x, and so on. The number that is multiplied by itself is the *base,* and the superscript, which indicates the power, is called the *exponent.* Thus, in the example $5^2 = 25$, 5 is the base, 2 is the exponent, and 25 is the second power of 5, or 5 squared.

If s represents the number of inches in the side of a square, s^2 represents the number of square inches in its area; if $s = 9$, $s^2 = 81$. If e represents the number of inches in the edge of a cube, e^3 represents the number of cubic inches in its volume; if $e = 2$, $e^3 = 8$, that is, $2 \times 2 \times 2$.

An exponent applies only to the base that precedes it. Thus, xy^2 means xyy and $2x^3y$ means $2xxxy$. If two or more bases are to be raised to the same power, they are placed in parentheses and the superscript is placed outside. Thus, $a(bc)^2$ means $a(bc)(bc)$, or ab^2c^2.

Examples:

To evaluate $8a^2$ when $a = −3$, replace a by −3:

$$8(−3)^2 = 8(9) = 72$$

To evaluate $−2a^3b$ when $a = −1$ and $b = 3$, replace a by −1 and b by 3:

$$−2(−1)^3(3) = −2(−1)(3) = 6$$

To evaluate $5x(yz)^2$ when $x = −2$, $y = 4$, and $z = 2$, replace x by −2, y by 4, and z by 2:

$$\begin{array}{l} 5(−2)(4 \times 2)^2 \\ 5(−2)(8)^2 \\ 5(−2)(64) \\ −640 \end{array}$$

Order of Operations.—The commutative and associative postulates for addition imply that the order in which numbers are added does not affect the result. Thus, $2 + 3$ is the same as $3 + 2$, and $2 + (3 + 5)$ is the same as $(2 + 3) + 5$. Similarly, the order in which numbers are multiplied does not affect the result according to the commutative and associative postulates for multiplication. Subtraction and division, however, are not commutative: $5 - 2$ is not the same as $2 - 5$, and $8 \div 2$ is different from $2 \div 8$. Furthermore, when more than one operation is involved in evaluating an expression, the order in which the operations are performed does affect the result. In evaluating $3a^2$ when $a = 5$, if 5 is squared first ($5^2 = 25$) and then multiplied by 3, the result is 75; but if 3 is multiplied by 5 first ($3 \times 5 = 15$) and the result is then squared, the final result is 225. Similarly, in evaluating $a + 2b$ when $a = 5$ and $b = 6$, if 5 is added to 2 first ($5 + 2 = 7$) and the answer is then multiplied by 6, the result is 42; but if 6 is first multiplied by 2 ($6 \times 2 = 12$) and the answer is then added to 5, the result is 17.

To prevent such ambiguities in evaluating expressions, the following order is always used in performing operations:

(1) Operations included within signs of grouping, such as parentheses or fraction lines, are performed first.

(2) Numbers are then raised to powers.

(3) Multiplications and divisions are performed next.

(4) Additions and subtractions are performed last.

Following this order in evaluating $3a^2$ when $a = 5$, the power (25) is obtained first and then multiplied by 3, producing the correct result, 75. In evaluating $a + 2b$ when $a = 5$ and $b = 6$, the multiplication of 2 by 6 is performed before adding the 5, producing the correct result, 17.

Example:

To evaluate $2\pi r(r + h) + 3h$, when $\pi = 22/7$, $r = 7$, and $h = 2$, substitute the numbers for the letters:

$$2\left(\frac{22}{7}\right)(7)(7 + 2) + 3(2);$$

perform the operations in parentheses first:

$$2\left(\frac{22}{7}\right)(7)(9) + 3(2);$$

multiplications and divisions next:

$$396 + 6;$$

and add and subtract last:

$$402.$$

Parts of Algebraic Expressions.—The quantities added together algebraically in an expression are called the *terms* of the expression. Thus, in $2a^2 - 3bc + 5c$, there are three terms: $2a^2$, $-3bc$, and $+5c$. Terms can be recognized by the fact that they are separated from one another by plus or minus signs.

An expression containing only one term is called a *monomial*. Thus, $-17x^3y$ is a monomial. An expression containing two terms, such as $2a + 3$, is called a *binomial*. An expression containing three terms, such as $y^2 - 3 + 4x$, is called a *trinomial*. Any expression having more than one term is called a *polynomial*. For example, $4z - 7$ and $7a + 15b^2c - 36a^2 + 17c$ are polynomials.

The numbers that are multiplied together to form an expression are called the *factors* of the expression. The factors of the term $7x^2y$ are 7, x^2, y, $7x$, $7x^2$, xy, x^2y, $7y$, and so on. (These may be considered as exact divisors of elements contained in the expression.)

The numerical factor of a term is called the *numerical coefficient* of that term. In $-7x^2y$, -7 is the numerical coefficient. In c^3d^2, the numerical coefficient is not explicitly written but is understood to be 1.

The factors of a term that consist of letters form the *literal factor* of the term. In $-7x^2y$, x^2y is the literal factor.

Like terms are terms that have the same literal factors. Thus, $5x^2y$, $-3x^2y$, and $+\frac{1}{2}x^2y$ are like terms.

Unlike terms are terms that do not have the same literal factors. Thus, $-2a$, $5b$, 5, $7x^2$, $6x$, $2x^2y$, and $2xy^2$ are unlike terms. Note that literal factors are unlike unless both the letters and the exponents associated with each of them are exactly the same.

Operations on Monomials.—Since algebraic expressions represent numbers, the question arises as to how the operations of addition, subtraction, multiplication, and division can be performed on them. This question will be examined first with respect to monomials.

■ **COMBINING TERMS.**—Like terms may be combined by making use of the postulates for operations on numbers. To combine $-3xy$ and $+5xy$, the commutative postulate for multiplication permits changing them to $xy(-3)$ and $xy(+5)$. By the distributive postulate, this sum is the same as $xy(-3 + 5)$ or $xy(+2)$, and is equal to $2xy$. Comparing this result with the two original terms shows that like terms may be combined by combining their numerical coefficients and multiplying the result by their common literal factor. To add $+7d$ and $-9d$, we combine their numerical coefficients ($+7 - 9 = -2$) and multiply this by the common literal factor, getting $-2d$.

Examples:

		$+7x^2y$		$-4c^2$
$+3a$		$-2x^2y$		$+7c^2$
(+) $-7a$		(+) $-3x^2y$		(+) $-2c^2$
$-4a$		$+2x^2y$		c^2

Combining like terms in effect makes it possible to add or subtract any like terms.

■ **MULTIPLYING MONOMIALS.**—To multiply $+13a$ by $-2b$, the indicated product $(+13a)(-2b)$ may be rewritten as $(+13)(-2)(ab)$ by the application of the commutative and associative postulates for multiplication. Hence, the product is $-26ab$.

Comparing the last result with the original factors shows that a short way to get the product of two monomials is to multiply their coefficients and then to multiply this product by the product of their literal factors. Thus, $(-3x^2)(-2y)$ would be $+6x^2y$.

Sometimes the two monomials to be multiplied contain powers of the same base, as in the case of $(3a^2)(5a^4)$. Since $(3a^2)(5a^4)$ means $(3aa)(5aaaa)$, which is $15aaaaaa$, or $15a^6$, it can be seen that powers of the same base can be multiplied by adding the exponents. Thus, $(x^3)(x^4) = x^7$.

Examples:

$$(+2a^3b^2)(-7a^2b^7) = -14a^5b^9$$
$$c^3(5c^2d) = 5c^5d$$
$$3xy^3(-4x^2y^2) = -12x^3y^5$$
$$2a(3b^2)(-5b) = -30ab^3$$

In the last example above, the literal factor b in the last parentheses is understood to have the exponent 1. The literal factor b^3 in the result is obtained by adding the exponent 1 to the exponent 2 of b^2 to produce the exponent 3 in the product b^3.

Repeated multiplication of monomials may occur when raising a monomial to a power. Thus, $(-2x^2)^4$ means $(-2x^2)(-2x^2)(-2x^2)(-2x^2)$, or $16x^8$.

■ **DIVIDING MONOMIALS.**—Since division is the inverse operation to multiplication, to divide $+16a^5$ by $-2a^3$ means to find the expression which when multiplied by $-2a^3$ will give $+16a^5$. This expression is $-8a^2$. Division of monomials is thus accomplished by dividing the numerical coefficients and multiplying this result by the result obtained by dividing the literal factors. Literal factors with the same base are divided by keeping that base and subtracting the exponents.

Examples:

$$(+6x^5) \div (-2x^2) = -3x^3$$
$$\frac{-12x^3y^2}{4xy^2} = -3x^2$$
$$\frac{-14ab^3c}{-2ab} = 7b^2c$$

Operations on Polynomials.—The same operations that were shown to be workable with monomials can also be worked with polynomials.

■ **ADDING POLYNOMIALS.**—Since the like terms can be combined, two or more polynomials can be added by arranging them so that their like terms are in vertical columns; the like terms in each column can then be combined.

Example:

To add the polynomials $3x^2 - 2xy + 4y^2$, $5y^2 - x^2$, and $-5xy + 3x^2 + 3$, ar-

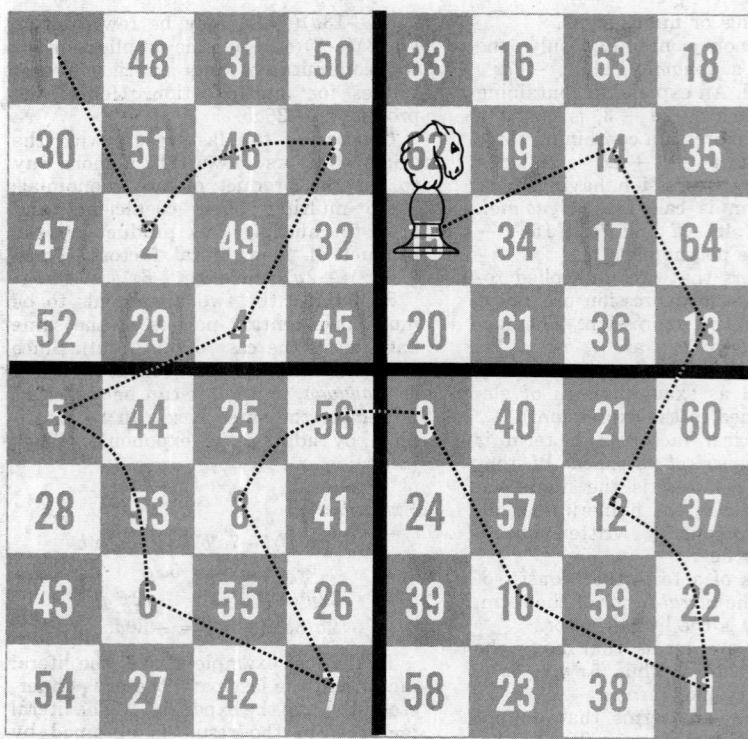

SCRIPTA MATHEMATICA

IN THIS MAGIC SQUARE devised by Leonhard Euler (1707–1783) each horizontal or vertical row totals 260, while half of each row totals 130. Its most fascinating feature is that a chess knight starting from box 1 and moving in its pattern of two squares up and one over will land on all 64 boxes in numerical sequence.

range like terms in vertical columns and add:

$$3x^2 - 2xy + 4y^2$$
$$-x^2 \qquad + 5y^2$$
$$3x^2 - 5xy \qquad + 3$$
$$\overline{5x^2 - 7xy + 9y^2 + 3}$$

■ **SUBTRACTING POLYNOMIALS.**—It was shown that subtracting a quantity is equivalent to adding the additive inverse of that quantity. Thus, polynomials may be subtracted by arranging them so that like terms are in vertical columns, changing the signs of the terms in the polynomial to be subtracted (thus obtaining its additive inverse), and then combining like terms.

Example:

To subtract $-5b + 2a + 4c$ from $3a + 7b$, arrange like terms in columns, write the additive inverse of the polynomial to be subtracted, then combine like terms:

$$3a + 7b$$
$$\underline{-2a + 5b - 4c}$$
$$a + 12b - 4c$$

■ **MULTIPLYING POLYNOMIALS.**—To multiply a polynomial, such as $2x(3x^2 - y + 5)$, the distributive postulate requires that each term of the polynomial be multiplied, in turn, by the monomial. The product is the sum of all the resulting terms.

Examples:

The expression is then multiplied:

$$2x(3x^2 - y + 5)$$
$$6x^3 - 2xy + 10x$$

Another illustration:

$$-2a^2(2 + 4ab + 7b^2)$$
$$-4a^2 - 8a^3b - 14a^2b^2$$

If an expression involves a set of parentheses preceded by a plus sign, the parentheses may be removed by multiplying the polynomial enclosed within it by $+1$. Thus, $2 + (x - 5y)$ becomes $2 + x - 5y$.

To remove a set of parentheses preceded by a minus sign, multiply the enclosed polynomial by -1. Thus, $5 - (2a + 3b - 7c)$ becomes $5 - 2a - 3b + 7c$.

Suppose it is desired to multiply $3x - 5y$ by $2x + 3y$. By the distributive postulate, $(3x - 5y)(2x + 3y)$ equals $(3x - 5y)(2x) + (3x - 5y)(3y)$. Using the commutative postulate, this becomes $2x(3x - 5y) + 3y(3x - 5y)$, and a second application of the distributive postulate shows it to be equivalent to $2x(3x) + 2x(-5y) + 3y(3x) + 3y(-5y)$. Thus, the multiplication of two polynomials has been reduced to a series of multiplications of pairs of monomials: $6x^2 - 10xy + 9xy - 15y^2$. By combining the two like terms, $6x^2 - xy - 15y^2$ is the final product. In other words, two polynomials are multiplied by each other by multiplying each term of the first polynomial by each term of the second and adding the resulting terms.

In practice, this operation is carried out by arranging the two polynomials to be multiplied in such a way that one is under the other as in multiplication in arithmetic. Partial products are obtained by multiplying the first polynomial by each term of the second much

as the top number is multiplied by each digit of the lower one in multiplication in arithmetic. Finally, the partial products are added.

Example:

To multiply $3x - 5y$ by $2x + 3y$, multiply each term of $3x - 5y$ by $2x$, and each term of $3x - 5y$ by $3y$. Then place like terms in columns and add:

$$3x - 5y$$
$$2x + 3y$$
$$\overline{6x^2 - 10xy}$$
$$\underline{+ 9xy - 15y^2}$$
$$6x^2 - xy - 15y^2$$

Similarly,

$$2a - 5$$
$$6a + 7$$
$$\overline{12a^2 - 30a}$$
$$\underline{+ 14a - 35}$$
$$12a^2 - 16a - 35$$

■ **DIVIDING POLYNOMIALS.**—Since the operation of dividing a polynomial by a monomial is the inverse of multiplying, the division operation may be accomplished by dividing each term of the polynomial, in turn, by the monomial and writing the quotient as the sum of the resulting terms.

Example:

To divide $5x^3 - 10x^2 + 15x$ by $5x$, divide each term of the numerator by $5x$:

$$x^2 - 2x + 3.$$

Factoring.—The *factors* of an expression are the expressions that when multiplied together give the original expression. Thus, 6 and 2 are factors of 12; so are 4 and 3. In the expression, $3x^2 + 6x$, the factors are $3x$ and $(x + 2)$, because $3x(x + 2) = 3x^2 + 6x$.

To *factor* an expression means to express it as the product of two or more quantities. Thus, $3x^2 + 6x$ is factored when it is written as $3x(x + 2)$. In factoring, it is agreed that only integers are to be used as coefficients and that the factors are not to include the original expression and 1.

If an expression cannot be written as the product of any factors other than itself and 1, the expression is said to be *prime*.

Highest Common Factors.—Factoring and multiplication are opposite processes. The expression $2a(x - 3y)$ is changed to $2ax - 6ay$ by multiplication; the expression $2ax - 6ay$ is changed back to $2a(x - 3y)$ by factoring. Whenever a polynomial is multiplied by a monomial, an expression results that can be factored back into a polynomial multiplied by the monomial. The monomial is called a *common factor* because it is a factor of each term of the polynomial. It is customary to factor in such a way as to get the largest such common monomial factor, and hence this type of factor is known as the *highest common monomial factor*. The highest common monomial factor has as its coefficient the largest integer that will divide into every term of the polynomial; its literal factor consists of the highest power of each literal factor that will divide into every term of the polynomial.

To factor $2x^3 - 8x^2y + 6x^2$, note that 2 is the largest integer that will divide into every term of the polynomial, and x^2 is the highest power of x that will divide into every term. Since y will not divide into every term, it is not in the common factor. The highest common monomial factor is therefore $2x^2$. The other factor is obtained by dividing $2x^2$ into the polynomial. Thus, $2x^3 - 8x^2y + 6x^2$ can be factored into $2x^2(x - 4y + 3)$. Note that multiplication should produce the original expression again and therefore will serve as a check on factoring.

For example, $24a^2b^3 - 18a^2b^4$ factors into $6a^2b^3(4 - 3b)$; $\pi R^2 - \pi r^2$ factors into $\pi(R^2 - r^2)$; and $2x^2y - 3xy - 5y^2$ factors into $y(2x^2 - 3x - 5y)$.

Multiplying Binomials.—As explained earlier, two polynomials such as $5a - 3b$ and $2a - 4b$ may be multiplied by a method similar to that used for multiplying large numbers in arithmetic:

$$\begin{array}{r} 5a - 3b \\ 2a - 4b \\ \hline 10a^2 - 6ab \\ -20ab + 12b^2 \\ \hline 10a^2 - 26ab + 12b^2 \end{array}$$

However, when both polynomials are binomials, as is the case here, it is pos-

sible to write down the product almost at sight.

Note that the first term of the answer $10a^2$ is the product of the first terms of the two binomials $(5a)(2a)$. The last term of the answer $12b^2$ is the product of the last term of the two binomials $(-3b)(-4b)$. The middle term is the sum of the two cross products, $(5a)(-4b) + (2a)(-3b)$, or $(-20ab) + (-6ab)$, or $-26ab$.

The entire work for the multiplication can be conveniently arranged in the following manner:

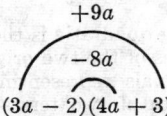

$$(5a - 3b)(2a - 4b)$$
$$10a^2 - 26ab + 12b^2$$

The inner and outer cross products are generally listed as shown before they are combined algebraically to give the middle term.

Examples:

Multiply $(2x - 1)(3x + 2)$ at sight.

$$(2x - 1)(3x + 2)$$
$$6x^2 + x - 2$$

Multiply $(x + 7)^2$, which is the same as $(x + 7)(x + 7)$.

$$(x + 7)(x + 7)$$
$$x^2 + 14x + 49$$

The product in each of these examples is a trinomial which is quadratic; that is, the variable appears to the second power and to no higher power. Such a trinomial is called a *quadratic trinomial*.

Factoring Quadratic Trinomials.—A quadratic trinomial is an expression of the form $ax^2 + bx + c$ where x stands for some variable and a, b, and c are constants not equal to ($\neq$) 0. Since such an expression results when two binomials are multiplied, factoring such a quadratic trinomial should result in two binomial factors.

To factor a quadratic trinomial, such as $5x^2 + 28x - 12$, look for two binomial factors such that the product of their first terms is $5x^2$: $(5x \quad)(x \quad)$. The product of the last terms of the binomials must be -12; but -12 has many factors: 2 and -6, -2 and 6, 3 and -4, -3 and 4, 12 and -1, and -12 and 1. The factors to select for the last term of the binomial must be such that the resulting cross products combine algebraically to give $28x$, the middle term of the quadratic trinomial. By trial and error it can be determined that 6 and -2 will do this provided

-2 is placed in the same binomial factor with $5x$ and 6 placed with x:

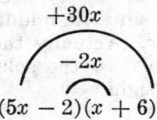

$$(5x - 2)(x + 6)$$

It may happen that the first term of the quadratic trinomial has more than one possible set of factors, as occurred in the previous example with the last term. If this is the case, the correct factors can only be determined by trial and error, making sure that the combination of the cross products of the binomials gives the correct middle term. Thus, in factoring $12a^2 + a - 6$, $12a^2$ has several pairs of factors and so does -6. The correct factors are

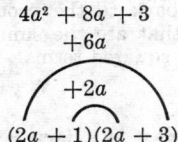

$$(3a - 2)(4a + 3)$$

Any other combination will not result in a product equivalent to the original expression.

If the terms of a quadratic trinomial are not in descending order of exponents, it is necessary to arrange them in this order before factoring.

Example:

To factor $4a^2 + 3 + 8a$, rearrange in descending order of exponents and factor as follows:

$$\begin{array}{c} 4a^2 + 8a + 3 \\ (2a + 1)(2a + 3) \end{array}$$

If the squared term of a quadratic trinomial is negative and the constant is positive, it is more convenient to arrange the terms in ascending order of exponents although it is possible to factor if they are arranged in descending order.

Example:

To factor $56 - b^2 - b$, rearrange in ascending order of exponents and factor as follows:

$$\begin{array}{c} 56 - b - b^2 \\ (8 + b)(7 - b) \end{array}$$

Sometimes a quadratic trinomial has two equal factors: $x^2 - 6x + 9$ factors as $(x - 3)(x - 3)$. This may also be written as $(x - 3)^2$.

Not all quadratic trinomials are factorable into the type of factors specified. For example, $x^2 + 4x + 2$ cannot be factored to give two factors with coefficients that are integers. The first term, x^2, requires that x be the first term of each binomial. The last term, 2, can be written only as the product of 2 and 1. But $(x + 2)(x + 1)$ does not equal $x^2 + 4x + 2$, since its middle term is $3x$ instead of $4x$. (Actually the factors involve decimals, so the solution cannot be found by sight.)

Product of Sum and Difference.—If the binomials $(x + 3)$ and $(x - 3)$, which represent the sum and difference of the same two terms x and 3, are multiplied together, a quadratic without a middle term results because the cross products add to zero:

$$
\begin{array}{c}
\overbrace{}^{-3x} \\
\underbrace{}_{+3x} \\
(x + 3)(x - 3) \\
x^2 - 9
\end{array}
$$

The resulting quadratic is the difference of the squares of the two original terms. When binomials representing the sum and difference of two terms are multiplied, the product is always the difference of their squares.

Examples:

$$(x - 5)(x + 5) = x^2 - 25$$
$$(2x + 3y)(2x - 3y) = 4x^2 - 9y^2$$
$$(2 - x)(2 + x) = 4 - x^2$$

Since multiplication of the sum and difference of two terms will produce an expression that is the difference of their squares, factoring an expression that is the difference of two squares should change it back to the product of two binomials that are the sum and difference of the squared terms.

Examples:

The term $x^2 - 9$ factors as $(x + 3)$ $(x - 3)$; $4y^2 - 1$ factors as $(2y - 1)$ $(2y + 1)$; $49a^2 - 36b^2$ factors as $(7a - 6b)(7a + 6b)$.

Complete Factoring.—In factoring an expression, the highest common monomial factor should be removed first. The resulting factor may be a factorable quadratic trinomial or a difference of two squares. If it is one of these, it may be replaced by two binomial factors by factoring again. In other words, factoring should be continued until *prime factors* (factors that cannot be factored further) are obtained.

In factoring $12x^2 + 14x - 10$, the highest common monomial factor is 2, giving $2(6x^2 + 7x - 5)$. But $6x^2 + 7x - 5$ is also factorable, giving

$$
\begin{array}{c}
\overbrace{}^{-3x} \\
\underbrace{}_{+10x} \\
2(3x + 5)(2x - 1)
\end{array}
$$

Examples:

To factor $4a^3 + 48a - 28a^2$, rearrange in descending order of exponents, factor the highest common monomial, and then factor the quadratic trinomial as follows:

$$
\begin{array}{c}
4a^3 - 28a^2 + 48a \\
4a(a^2 - 7a + 12) \\
\overbrace{}^{-3a} \\
\underbrace{}_{-4a} \\
4a(a - 4)(a - 3)
\end{array}
$$

To factor $x - 25x^3$, factor the highest common monomial and then factor the difference of two squares:

$$x(1 - 25x^2)$$
$$x(1 - 5x)(1 + 5x)$$

When a difference of two squares is factored, it is possible for one of the factors to be another difference of two squares.

To factor $16x^4 - y^4$, factor as a difference of two squares and then factor $4x^2 - y^2$:

$$(4x^2 - y^2)(4x^2 + y^2)$$
$$(2x - y)(2x + y)(4x^2 + y^2)$$

Fractions.—In arithmetic, fractions are reduced to lowest terms by making use of the principle that the numerator and denominator of a fraction may be divided by any nonzero quantity without changing the value of the fraction. This principle is a consequence of the fact that when the numerator and denominator are divided by the same nonzero quantity, a, the fraction is really divided by a/a, or 1, and hence remains the same. Using this principle, $\frac{6}{8}$ is reduced to the equivalent fraction $\frac{3}{4}$ by dividing both numerator and denominator by 2. The quantity by which the numerator and denominator are divided (in this case 2) must be a factor of both.

Algebraic fractions are reduced by making use of the same principle as is used in arithmetic. The value of any algebraic fraction is unchanged if the numerator and denominator are both divided by the same nonzero quantity; in order to divide, the quantity must be a factor of both numerator and denominator.

Example:

To reduce

$$\frac{-4xy^3}{10xy^2}$$

to lowest terms, divide numerator and denominator by $2xy^2$. The answer is

$$\frac{-2y}{5}.$$

Division by zero is undefined, but the above solution need not be qualified by adding that $x \neq 0$ and $y \neq 0$. The original fraction contains x and y as factors of its denominator, hence it may be assumed they do not equal zero.

If the numerator or denominator of an algebraic fraction is a polynomial, it is usually necessary to factor it before reducing to determine what factors may be divided into both numerator and denominator.

Example:

To reduce

$$\frac{3x - 6}{9x - 18},$$

factor numerator and denominator,

$$\frac{3(x - 2)}{9(x - 2)},$$

and divide both numerator and denominator by 3 and $(x - 2)$. The answer is $\frac{1}{3}$. Notice that x cannot equal 2, since this would result in division by 0; but $x \neq 2$, because the original fraction would be undefined if it did.

Example:

To reduce

$$\frac{x^2 + 2x}{x^2 - 3x - 10},$$

factor numerator and denominator:

$$\frac{x(x + 2)}{(x - 5)(x + 2)};$$

and divide numerator and denominator by $(x + 2)$:

$$\frac{x}{x - 5}.$$

Signs of Fractions.—Every fraction may be considered to have three signs: the sign of the numerator, the sign of the denominator, and the sign of the whole fraction. All three are shown in the fraction

$$+\frac{-a}{+b}.$$

Consider the effect of these signs on the value of a fraction:

The fraction $+(+4/+2)$ has the value $+2$, because it may be interpreted as the positive value of the result of dividing $+4$ by $+2$.

The fraction $+(-4/-2)$ also has the value $+2$, because it means the positive value of the result of dividing -4 by -2.

The fraction $-(-4/+2)$ has the value $+2$, because it means the negative value (additive inverse) of the result of dividing -4 by $+2$.

The fraction $-(+4/-2)$ has the value $+2$, because it means the negative value (additive inverse) of the result of dividing $+4$ by -2.

Each of the four fractions above can be obtained from any one of the other three by changing exactly two signs, and all four have the value $+2$. These fractions illustrate the principle that any two of the signs of a fraction may be changed without changing the value of the fraction.

It is sometimes necessary to employ the above principle to change the signs of a fraction in order to facilitate reducing the fraction or performing other operations with it.

Accordingly, in attempting to reduce the expression

$$\frac{25 - 5x}{x^2 - 25},$$

factoring produces the form

$$\frac{5(5 - x)}{(x - 5)(x + 5)}.$$

In this form, there is no common factor to divide both numerator and denominator. By changing two signs, such as the signs of the fraction and of its numerator, this fraction becomes

$$-\frac{5(x - 5)}{(x - 5)(x + 5)},$$

which reduces to

$$-\frac{5}{x + 5}.$$

It should be emphasized at this point that in a case such as

$$\frac{3(x + 2)}{2(2 + x)},$$

it is not necessary to make any sign changes in order to reduce to $\frac{3}{2}$, since $x + 2$ and $2 + x$ are the same except for the fact that their terms happen to be written down in different orders; they are equal by the commutative postulate for addition.

■ **MULTIPLICATION.**—In arithmetic, fractions are multiplied by multiplying their numerators together to form the numerator of the product and multiplying their denominators together to form the denominator of the product. For example,

$$\frac{2}{5} \cdot \frac{3}{7} = \frac{6}{35}.$$

Algebraic fractions are multiplied in exactly the same way. As in arithmetic, *like factors* in the numerator and denominator may be "canceled," that is, divided out by applying the principle that the numerator and denominator may be divided by the same nonzero number without changing the value of the fraction. (The dot [·] between the fractions is used to denote multiplication since the usual times sign [×] might be confused with x.)

Example:

To multiply

$$\frac{10x^2y}{3} \cdot \frac{2y}{5x},$$

divide numerator and denominator by $5x$, with the result:

$$\frac{2xy}{3} \cdot \frac{2y}{1};$$

and multiply numerators together and denominators together for the answer:

$$\frac{4xy^2}{3}.$$

If an integral expression is to be multiplied by a fraction, it is helpful to think of it as having the denominator 1.

Example:

To multiply

$$2x \cdot \frac{3y}{x^2},$$

write $2x$ with the denominator 1:

$$\frac{2x}{1} \cdot \frac{3y}{x^2};$$

divide numerator and denominator by x:

$$\frac{2}{1} \cdot \frac{3y}{x};$$

and multiply numerators together and denominators together with the result:

$$\frac{6y}{x}.$$

If in fractions to be multiplied, the numerator or denominator or both are polynomials, it is advisable to factor them first. This makes it easy to reduce by dividing numerator and denominator by the factors that appear in both.

Example:

To multiply

$$\frac{x^2 - 16}{x} \cdot \frac{2x}{3x - 12},$$

factor:

$$\frac{(x - 4)(x + 4)}{x} \cdot \frac{2x}{3(x - 4)};$$

divide numerator and denominator by x and by $(x - 4)$:

$$\frac{x + 4}{1} \cdot \frac{2}{3};$$

and multiply numerators together and denominators together:

$$\frac{2(x + 4)}{3}.$$

■ **DIVISION.**—In arithmetic, the division example $\frac{3}{4} \div \frac{7}{8}$ is performed by changing the divisor to its multiplicative inverse and then multiplying. Thus $\frac{3}{4} \div \frac{7}{8}$ becomes $\frac{3}{4} \cdot \frac{8}{7}$, or $\frac{6}{7}$. The multiplicative inverse, or reciprocal, of a number is formed by inverting the number. Thus, the multiplicative inverse, or reciprocal, of $\frac{4}{3}$ is $\frac{3}{4}$; and $\frac{3}{1}$ is the multiplicative inverse, or reciprocal, of $\frac{1}{3}$.

Algebraic fractions can also be divided by multiplying by the multiplicative inverse, or reciprocal, of the fraction that is the divisor.

Example:

To divide

$$\frac{3x^3}{6} \div \frac{x^2}{9},$$

change to multiplication by replacing the divisor with its multiplicative inverse:

$$\frac{3x^3}{6} \cdot \frac{9}{x^2};$$

divide numerator and denominator by 3 and by x^2:

$$\frac{x}{2} \cdot \frac{9}{1};$$

and multiply numerators together and denominators together:

$$\frac{9x}{2}.$$

Numerators and denominators that are polynomials should be factored to make it possible to reduce the answer.

Example:

To divide

$$\frac{x^2 - 4x - 21}{3x + 6} \div \frac{x - 3}{x + 2},$$

factor and change to multiplication by replacing the divisor with its multiplicative inverse:

$$\frac{(x - 7)(x + 3)}{3(x + 2)} \cdot \frac{x + 2}{x - 3};$$

divide numerator and denominator by $(x + 2)$:

$$\frac{(x - 7)(x + 3)}{3} \cdot \frac{1}{x - 3};$$

and write the products of numerators and denominators to give the respective numerator and denominator of the answer:

$$\frac{(x - 7)(x + 3)}{3(x - 3)}.$$

■ **ADDITION AND SUBTRACTION.**—In arithmetic, if fractions have the same denominator, they are added or subtracted by adding or subtracting their numerators and placing the result over their common denominator. Thus, $\frac{2}{5} + \frac{1}{5} = \frac{3}{5}$.

Algebraic fractions that have the same denominator are added and subtracted (combined) in the same way.

Example:

To combine

$$\frac{2}{x - 2} + \frac{1}{x - 2} - \frac{5x}{x - 2},$$

add and subtract the numerators and place the sum over the common denominator:

$$\frac{2 + 1 - 5x}{x - 2};$$

and combine like terms:

$$\frac{3 - 5x}{x - 2}.$$

In arithmetic, when fractions do not have the same denominators, they must first be changed to equivalent fractions having the same denominators before they can be added or subtracted. Such equivalent fractions are obtained by multiplying the numerator and denominator of each fraction by some nonzero number so selected that the multiplication will produce the common denominator in each. To add $\frac{1}{3}$ and $\frac{2}{7}$, $\frac{1}{3}$ is first changed to $\frac{7}{21}$ by multiplying its numerator and denominator by 7. In thus employing the principle that the value of a fraction is unchanged if its numerator and denominator are both multiplied by the same nonzero number, in effect the fraction is multiplied by 1. The second fraction, $\frac{2}{7}$, is changed to the equivalent fraction, $\frac{6}{21}$, by multiplying both its numerator and denominator by 3. In their new equivalent forms, $\frac{7}{21}$ and $\frac{6}{21}$ can be added to give $\frac{13}{21}$. The combination of the fractions was made possible by obtaining a common denominator (21 in this case) that was divisible by each of the original denominators.

Algebraic fractions can also be added or subtracted by converting them to equivalent fractions with a common denominator that is divisible by each of the original denominators.

Example:

To combine

$$\frac{5}{2x^2y} - \frac{2}{3xy} + \frac{4}{x^2},$$

the common denominator must be divisible by $2x^2y$, $3xy$, and x^2. The lowest common denominator is $6x^2y$. Note that each literal factor appears in the lowest common denominator raised to the highest power to which it appears in any individual denominator. The denominator of the first fraction, $2x^2y$, must be multiplied by 3 to convert it to the common denominator, $6x^2y$. Therefore, its numerator, 5, must also be multiplied by 3 to keep the value of the fraction unchanged. In a similar manner, the second fraction must be multiplied by $2x/2x$, and the third by $6y/6y$. The example then becomes

$$\frac{5(3)}{2x^2y(3)} - \frac{2(2x)}{3xy(2x)} + \frac{4(6y)}{x^2(6y)};$$

and after multiplying:

$$\frac{15}{6x^2y} - \frac{4x}{6x^2y} + \frac{24y}{6x^2y};$$

and combining the numerators over the common denominator, we obtain

$$\frac{15 - 4x + 24y}{6x^2y}.$$

It is sometimes necessary to change two of the signs in one fraction to convert it to a form with the same denominator as another.

Example:

To combine

$$\frac{2}{x - 2} + \frac{3}{2 - x},$$

change the sign of the second fraction and the sign of its denominator:

$$\frac{2}{x - 2} - \frac{3}{-2 + x} \quad \text{or} \quad \frac{2}{x - 2} - \frac{3}{x - 2};$$

combine the numerators over the common denominator:

$$\frac{2 - 3}{x - 2}$$

and combine like terms:

$$\frac{-1}{x - 2}.$$

This answer may also be written as

$$\frac{1}{2 - x}$$

by changing the signs of the numerator

and denominator; this form has the advantage of having fewer minus signs.

In combining fractions with polynomial denominators, it is necessary to factor the denominators in order to discover the lowest common denominator.

Example:

To combine

$$\frac{3}{y^2 + 7y + 10} - \frac{2}{y^2 - 25},$$

first factor the denominators:

$$\frac{3}{(y + 5)(y + 2)} - \frac{2}{(y + 5)(y - 5)}.$$

Since the lowest common denominator must be divisible by each of the original denominators, it must contain as factors all the factors in any one of the original denominators. In this case the lowest common denominator is $(y + 5)$ $(y - 5)(y + 2)$.

Next change each fraction to an equivalent fraction with the common denominator:

$$\frac{3(y - 5)}{(y + 5)(y + 2)(y - 5)} -$$
$$\frac{2(y + 2)}{(y + 5)(y - 5)(y + 2)};$$

multiply in the numerators:

$$\frac{3y - 15}{(y + 5)(y + 2)(y - 5)} -$$
$$\frac{2y + 4}{(y + 5)(y - 5)(y + 2)};$$

and combine the numerators over the common denominator:

$$\frac{3y - 15 - (2y + 4)}{(y + 5)(y - 5)(y + 2)}.$$

Note how the parentheses preceded by the minus sign are used to ensure that the second fraction is subtracted from the first. To complete the operation, remove the parentheses:

$$\frac{3y - 15 - 2y - 4}{(y + 5)(y - 5)(y + 2)};$$

and combine like terms:

$$\frac{y - 19}{(y + 5)(y - 5)(y + 2)}.$$

Sentences.—In algebra, statements such as $2 + 3 = 5$ are called *sentences*. This particular type of sentence is called an *equation*, since it states that two quantities are equal. Other types of sentences such as $8 - 11 \neq 5$ are called *inequalities*, because they state that two quantities are unequal; the sign $\neq$ is read "is not equal to." The expression $8 > 5$ is also an inequality which states that 8 is greater than 5. The symbol $>$ is read "is greater than" and the symbol $<$ is read "is less than." It should be noted that the larger end of the symbols $>$ and $<$ faces the larger number. Thus, $-3 < -1$ is an inequality stating that -3 is less than -1.

All of the sentences above, both equations and inequalities, are true state-

ments. The expressions on each side of the equals or inequality signs are called the sides or members of the equation or inequality. In true sentences, both members actually bear the relation to each other which is expressed by the sign connecting them.

Sentences may also be false. For example, $-8 + 5 = 5$, $-13 > -2$, $8 < 2$, and $4 + 3 \neq 7$ are all false statements, because their members are not related in the manner expressed by the sign connecting them.

■ **OPEN SENTENCES.**—Some sentences contain variables denoted by letter symbols. Such sentences may be either true or false, depending on the value assigned to the variable; hence they are called *open sentences*. For example, $x + 3 = 7$ is true if, and only if, $x = 4$; $y + 2 > 5$ if and only if $y > 3$. Some open sentences are combinations of equations and inequalities. For example, $x + 2 \geqq 5$ states that the number x added to 2 is either greater than or equal to 5 (this will be true if, and only if, $x \geqq 3$).

■ **SOLVING OPEN SENTENCES.**—Solving an open sentence is the process of finding the numbers in the domain of the variable that make the sentence true. The set of numbers that make an open sentence true is called the *solution set* of the sentence. The numbers that form the solution set of an equation are also known as the *roots* or *solutions* of the equation. In the equation $x + 2 = 8$ the solution set is $\{6\}$. This solution set has only one element; thus the equation has only one root, 6. In contrast to this, the open sentence $2x + 3 = x + x + 3$ is an equation whose solution set consists of all possible values of x. This equation has an infinite number of roots if the domain of x is infinite. On the other hand, the sentence $x - 3 = x$ will not be true for any replacement for x. This equation has no root; its solution set is the empty set, which can be written as θ. The solution set for the inequality $x + 3 > 7$ consists of all numbers greater than 4; there are an infinite number of replacements for the variable that will make this inequality true if the domain of x includes all the positive integers and fractions greater than 4.

Set Notation.—One method of indicating a set is by enclosing the members in braces. Thus, $\{2, 3, 5\}$ stands for the set consisting of 2, 3, and 5. However, since it is impossible to list all the members of a solution set that has an infinite number of members, mathematicians also use another notation for showing sets that is especially suitable in such a case: $\{x \mid x > 4\}$ is read "the set of all values of x such that x is greater than 4." This notation, called the *set-builder notation*, may also be used for sets that are not infinite. Thus, $\{x \mid -2 < x \leqq 5$, x is an integer$\}$ is read "the set of x such that x is greater than -2 and less than or equal to 5 and x is an integer," and is the same as the set $\{-1, 0, 1, 2, 3, 4, 5\}$.

Checking Solutions.—The process of showing that a number is a member of the solution set of an equation or inequality is called *checking* the solution. An equation is checked by replacing the variable with the number that is the supposed root, and showing that the resulting values of both members of the equation are equal, that is, showing that the expressions on both sides of the equals sign are the same. To check that -10 is a root of $2x + 3 = x - 7$, replace x by -10 and evaluate both members of the equation. The check would appear as follows:

$$2x + 3 = x - 7$$
$$2(-10) + 3 \overset{?}{=} -10 - 7$$
$$-20 + 3 \overset{?}{=} -10 - 7$$
$$-17 = -17$$

A solution to an inequality may similarly be checked by replacing the variable with the number being checked and seeing whether the resulting values of both members make the sentence true. To check $-1\frac{1}{3}$ as a solution for $x - 3 < 7$, replace x by $-1\frac{1}{3}$:

$$x - 3 < 7$$
$$-1\tfrac{1}{3} - 3 \overset{?}{<} 7$$
$$-4\tfrac{1}{3} < 7$$

Equivalent Expressions.—Two equations or two inequalities that have the same solution set are said to be *equivalent*. The equations $x + 3 = 5$ and $2x + 7 = 11$ are equivalent equations; both have $\{2\}$ as their solution set, as may be seen by checking $x = 2$ in each of them. However, $x + 3 = 5$ and $x + 3 = 6$ are not equivalent equations; the solution set of the first is $\{2\}$, but the solution set of the second is $\{3\}$. The inequalities $x + 3 > 5$ and $x > 2$ are equivalent, since the solution set for both consists of all numbers greater than 2, that is, the solution set of both is $\{x \mid x > 2\}$.

The concept of equivalent equations is important in solving or finding the solution set of an equation. It is very obvious that the solution set of the simple equation $x = 3$ is $\{3\}$, but it is not so easy to discover that the solution set of the more complicated equation $5x - 7 = 2x + 2$ is also $\{3\}$. However, both equations are equivalent, since 3 is the only root of each. In algebra, solving equations consists of changing complicated equations into equivalent equations that are simpler in the sense that their solution sets are more obvious.

Solving First-Degree Equations.—*First-degree equations* are equations whose variables are raised to the first power but no higher. Thus, $2x + 3 = 5x - 7$ is a first-degree equation, but $x^2 + x + 3 = 0$ is not, because the variable appears to the second power. First-degree equations are also called *linear equations* because they can be represented as straight lines; the section on the graphs of equations makes this clear.

As stated above, the method for solving first-degree equations consists of transforming them into equivalent equations in which the variable is alone on one side and a number is alone on the other. The four postulates that follow make it possible to solve various forms of first-degree equations. (Actually these postulates apply to an equation of any degree, but they are used here to solve only first-degree equations.)

■ **FIRST POSTULATE.**—If the same number is added to both members of an equation, an equivalent equation results.

This postulate makes it possible to get the variable alone on one side of an equation by removing a number that was subtracted from it originally.

Example:

To solve $x - 5 = 2$, add 5 to each member:

$$\begin{array}{rr} x - 5 = & 2 \\ +5 & +5 \\ \hline x = & 7 \end{array}$$

Check:

$$x - 5 = 2$$
$$7 - 5 \overset{?}{=} 2$$
$$2 = 2$$

Since the variable represents a number, this postulate may be used to add an expression containing the variable to each member of the equation. Thus, it is possible to remove a negative term containing the variable from the side of the equation on which this term is not wanted.

Example:

To solve $-x = 7 - 2x$, add $2x$ to each member:

$$\begin{array}{rr} -x = & 7 - 2x \\ +2x & +2x \\ \hline x = & 7 \end{array}$$

Check:

$$-x = 7 - 2x$$
$$-7 \overset{?}{=} 7 - 2(7)$$
$$-7 \overset{?}{=} 7 - 14$$
$$-7 = -7$$

In order to have a simple equation with an obvious solution set, it is not necessary to have the variable on the left side of the equation; it is sufficient that the variable be alone on one side and that the other side consist of a single number. If it is convenient, the variable may appear on the right side.

Example:

To solve $13 = x - 5$, add 5 to each member:

$$\begin{array}{rr} 13 = & x - 5 \\ +5 = & +5 \\ \hline 18 = & x \end{array}$$

Check:

$$13 = x - 5$$
$$13 \overset{?}{=} 18 - 5$$
$$13 = 13$$

■ **SECOND POSTULATE.**—If the same number is subtracted from both members of an equation, an equivalent equation results.

This postulate makes it possible to get the variable alone on one side of the equation by removing any number that was added to it originally. It can also be used to remove a term containing the variable from a side of the equation on which it is not wanted.

Example:

To solve $x + 5 = 9$, subtract 5 from each member:

$$\begin{array}{rr} x + 5 = & 9 \\ -5 & -5 \\ \hline x = & 4 \end{array}$$

Check:

$$x + 5 = 9$$
$$4 + 5 \overset{?}{=} 9$$
$$9 = 9$$

Example:

To solve $x + 7 = 2$, subtract 7 from each member:

$$\begin{array}{rr} x + 7 = & 2 \\ -7 & -7 \\ \hline x = & -5 \end{array}$$

Check:

$$x + 7 = 2$$
$$-5 + 7 \overset{?}{=} 2$$
$$2 = 2$$

The number subtracted from both members of an equation may be represented by an expression containing the variable.

Example:

To solve $3x = 2x - 8$, subtract $2x$ from each member:

$$\begin{array}{rr} 3x = & 2x - 8 \\ -2x & -2x \\ \hline x = & -8 \end{array}$$

Check:

$$3x = 2x - 8$$
$$3(-8) \overset{?}{=} 2(-8) - 8$$
$$-24 \overset{?}{=} -16 - 8$$
$$-24 = -24$$

The first two postulates for solving equations, in effect, permit removing a term from one side of an equation and transferring it to the other side with its sign changed. If 6 is added to both members of $x - 6 = 5$, the -6 term disappears from the left member and appears as $+6$ on the right side of the equation. If 4 is subtracted from both members of the equation $x + 4 = 12$, the $+4$ term disappears from the left member and appears as -4 on the right side of the equation.

The situation illustrated in the two examples above makes it possible to write the result of adding or subtracting the same quantity from both members of an equation without actually showing the intermediate step of adding or subtracting. Thus, $x - 7 = 5$ becomes $x = 5 + 7$, by adding 7 to both members. To solve, combine like terms:

$$x = 12.$$

Similarly,

$$x + 15 = 2$$

becomes

$$x = 2 - 15$$

by subtracting 15 from both members. Therefore,

$$x = -13.$$

The short-cut method for adding or subtracting the same quantity from both members of an equation by moving a term from one side to the other and changing its sign is called *transposition*.

■ **THIRD POSTULATE.**—If both members of an equation are multiplied by the same nonzero number, an equivalent equation results.

This postulate makes it possible to get a variable alone by removing a number by which the variable was originally divided. The reason for requiring a nonzero multiplier is that if both members of an equation are multiplied by 0, the result is always $0 = 0$. Since $0 = 0$ no matter what x is, the resulting equation is not truly equivalent to the original.

Example:

To solve $x/5 = 7$, multiply both members by 5:

$$5\left(\frac{x}{5}\right) = 5(7)$$
$$x = 35$$

Check:

$$\frac{x}{5} = 7$$
$$\frac{35}{5} \stackrel{?}{=} 7$$
$$7 = 7$$

Example:

To solve $-\frac{3}{4}x = 12$, multiply both members by $-\frac{4}{3}$:

$$-\frac{4}{3}\left(-\frac{3}{4}x\right) = -\frac{4}{3}(12)$$
$$x = -16$$

Check:

$$-\frac{3}{4}x = 12$$
$$-\frac{3}{4}(-16) \stackrel{?}{=} 12$$
$$12 = 12$$

■ **FOURTH POSTULATE.**—If both members of an equation are divided by the same nonzero number, an equivalent equation results.

This postulate makes it possible to get a variable alone by removing the number by which it was multiplied originally (that is, its numerical coefficient).

Example:

To solve $4x = 12$, divide both mem-

bers of the equation by 4:

$$\frac{4x}{4} = \frac{12}{4}$$
$$x = 3$$

Check:

$$4x = 12$$
$$4(3) \stackrel{?}{=} 12$$
$$12 = 12$$

Example:

To solve $18 = -2x$, divide both members by -2:

$$\frac{18}{-2} = \frac{-2x}{-2}$$
$$-9 = x$$

Check:

$$18 = -2x$$
$$18 \stackrel{?}{=} -2(-9)$$
$$18 = 18$$

It is frequently necessary to employ more than one of the postulates to find the solution of an equation.

Example:

Consider the equation $3y + 9 = 15$. In order to get the variable alone on one side of the equation it is necessary to remove both the 9 which was added to it and the coefficient 3 which was multiplied by it. To solve, subtract 9 from both members:

$$\begin{array}{r} 3y + 9 = 15 \\ -9 \quad -9 \\ \hline 3y \quad = 6 \end{array}$$

and divide both members by 3:

$$\frac{3y}{3} = \frac{6}{3}$$
$$y = 2$$

Check:

$$3y + 9 = 15$$
$$3(2) + 9 \stackrel{?}{=} 15$$
$$6 + 9 \stackrel{?}{=} 15$$
$$15 = 15$$

Example:

To solve $y + 16 = 3y + 2$, subtract y and 2 from both members:

$$\begin{array}{r} y + 16 = 3y + 2 \\ -y - 2 = -y - 2 \\ \hline 14 = 2y \end{array}$$

and divide both members by 2:

$$7 = y.$$

Check:

$$y + 16 = 3y + 2$$
$$7 + 16 \stackrel{?}{=} 3(7) + 2$$
$$7 + 16 \stackrel{?}{=} 21 + 2$$
$$23 = 23$$

Note that the check of the solution to an equation must always be made by substituting the value being checked in the *original* equation. If an error has been made at any point in the solution, the equations appearing after the error will not be equivalent to the original

equation, and the fact that a solution checks in one of these later equations will not guarantee that it is also a root of the original.

If an equation contains several like terms, it is advisable to combine them before using the postulates that transform the equation into a simpler equivalent equation.

Example:

To solve $14x + 35 - 6x - 48 = 5 + 2$, combine like terms so that $8x - 13 = 7$, and add 13 to both members:

$$\begin{array}{r} 8x - 13 = \quad 7 \\ + 13 \quad + 13 \\ \hline 8x \quad = \quad 20 \end{array}$$

and divide both members of the equation by 8:

$$\frac{8x}{8} = \frac{20}{8}$$
$$x = 2\frac{1}{2}$$

Check:

$$14x + 35 - 6x - 48 = 5 + 2$$
$$14\left(2\frac{1}{2}\right) + 35 - 6\left(2\frac{1}{2}\right) - 48 \stackrel{?}{=} 5 + 2$$
$$35 + 35 - 15 - 48 \stackrel{?}{=} 5 + 2$$
$$7 = 7$$

Example:

To solve $8x + 5 - 2x = 7 + 2x - 10$, combine like terms:

$$6x + 5 = 2x - 3;$$

subtract $2x$ and 5 from both members by the method of transposition:

$$6x - 2x = -3 - 5;$$

combine like terms:

$$4x = -8$$

and divide both members by 4:

$$\frac{4x}{4} = \frac{-8}{4}$$
$$x = -2$$

Check:

$$8x + 5 - 2x = 7 + 2x - 10$$
$$8(-2) + 5 - 2(-2) \stackrel{?}{=} 7 + 2(-2) - 10$$
$$-16 + 5 + 4 \stackrel{?}{=} 7 - 4 - 10$$
$$-7 = -7$$

If an equation contains parentheses, they should be removed before proceeding with the rest of the solution.

Example:

To solve $2 - 5(x - 3) = 1 + (x - 8)$, remove parentheses:

$$2 - 5x + 15 = 1 + x - 8;$$

combine like terms:

$$17 - 5x = x - 7;$$

add 7 and $5x$ to both members by transposing:

$$17 + 7 = x + 5x;$$

combine like terms:

$$24 = 6x;$$

and divide both members of the equation by 6:

$$\frac{24}{6} = \frac{6x}{6}$$
$$4 = x$$

Check:

$$2 - 5(x - 3) \overset{?}{=} 1 + (x - 8)$$
$$2 - 5(4 - 3) \overset{?}{=} 1 + (4 - 8)$$
$$2 - 5(1) \overset{?}{=} 1 + (-4)$$
$$2 - 5 \overset{?}{=} 1 - 4$$
$$-3 = -3$$

Solving Problems.—One of the important applications of algebra is solving problems through the use of equations.

Consider this problem: If a certain number is subtracted from 40, the result is the same as 1 more than twice the number.

The problem is solved by choosing a variable x to represent the number to be found. Then $40 - x$ is the result when the number is subtracted from 40, and $2x + 1$ represents 1 more than twice the number. The statement of the problem is an open sentence which, when translated into algebraic symbols, is the equation $40 - x = 2x + 1$.

To solve the problem add x and subtract 1 from both members:

$$40 - 1 = 2x + x;$$

combine like terms:

$$39 = 3x;$$

and divide both members by 3:

$$13 = x.$$

As a check of the solution to a problem, the supposed answer must satisfy the conditions prescribed by the problem. Substitution in the equation would not constitute a satisfactory check for the solution to a problem, since the problem may have been translated incorrectly in writing the equation. Checking the conditions of the problem solved here, if the number is 13, then subtracting it from 40 would give 27. One more than twice 13 is also 27, thus showing that the answer is correct.

Sometimes the identification and representation of the quantities involved in a problem are more subtle than in the previous one. Consider this problem: Find three consecutive odd integers whose sum is 249. Begin by choosing n to represent the first odd integer. Consideration of two consecutive odd integers (such as 7 and 9) will show that the second integer is 2 more than the first. Therefore, $n + 2$ will represent the second odd integer. Adding another 2 will produce the third odd integer, $n + 4$. It is customary to list and identify the variable and any other quantities that must be represented in terms of it in order to write the equation.

In this problem let n equal the first odd integer; $n + 2$, the second consecutive odd integer; and $n + 4$, the third consecutive odd integer.

The problem states that the sum of the three consecutive odd integers is 249. Translating this into an algebraic equation gives

$$n + (n + 2) + (n + 4) = 249.$$

To solve the problem, remove parentheses:

$$n + n + 2 + n + 4 = 249;$$

combine like terms:

$$3n + 6 = 249;$$

subtract 6 from both members:

$$3n = 249 - 6$$
$$3n = 243$$

and divide both members by 3:

$$n = 81$$
$$n + 2 = 83$$
$$n + 4 = 85$$

Check:

Inspection shows that the answers are three consecutive odd integers. And since $81 + 83 + 85 = 249$, the answers are correct.

Sometimes it is helpful to represent the information in a problem by using a tabular form.

Example:

How many pounds of candy worth 63 cents per pound should be mixed with candy worth 81 cents per pound to produce a mixture of 60 pounds to sell at 75 cents per pound?

Let x be the number of pounds of 63-cent candy to be used. The remainder of the 60-pound mixture, $60 - x$, must be taken from the 81-cent candy. All of the quantities used in the problem are shown in the following table:

Price per Pound (cents)	Weight (pounds)	Total Value (cents)
63	x	$63x$
81	$60 - x$	$81(60 - x)$
75	60	$75(60)$

The equation in this problem cannot be obtained by a direct translation of any explicit statement in the problem. However, it is implied that the sum of the values of the two ingredients must equal the value of the mixture. Writing this relationship in algebraic symbols:

$$63x + 81(60 - x) = 75(60).$$

Solution:

$$63x + 4860 - 81x = 4500$$
$$63x - 81x = 4500 - 4860$$
$$-18x = -360$$
$$x = 20$$

Thus, the amount of 60-cent candy required is 20 pounds.

Check:

$$60 - 20 = 40 \text{ lb. of } 81\cancel{c} \text{ candy}$$

20 lb. at 63¢	$12.60
40 lb. at 81¢	$32.40
60 lb. at 75¢	$45.00

In some problems, such as those involving uniform motion, it may be help-

ful to draw a diagram in order to discover what the equation is.

Example:

A boat left port traveling at 30 miles per hour. Four hours later a helicopter was sent after the boat from the same port traveling at 90 miles per hour over the same course. How long will it take the helicopter to catch the boat?

Draw a diagram to represent the distances traveled by the boat and by the helicopter (Fig. 3). It is evident that

Figure 3.

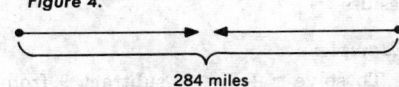

these distances are equal, since both started from the same point and ended at the same point. Therefore, expressions are needed for the distances traveled by each; these are obtained by multiplying the rate of each by the time of travel.

Letting x equal the number of hours for the helicopter to catch the boat, and noting that the boat will therefore travel $4 + x$ hours before being intercepted, the data for the problem can be represented as follows:

	Rate (miles per hour)	$\times$ Time (hours)	$=$ Distance (miles)
Boat	30	$4 + x$	$30(4 + x)$
Helicopter	90	x	$90x$

Solution:

$$30(4 + x) = 90x$$
$$120 + 30x = 90x$$
$$120 = 90x - 30x$$
$$120 = 60x$$
$$2 = x$$

Thus, the helicopter would overtake the boat in 2 hours.

Check:

In 2 hours the helicopter would go 90×2, or 180 miles. The boat would travel $4 + 2$, or 6 hours, and in 6 hours, it would go 30×6, or 180 miles, and the helicopter would overtake the boat at this point.

A second example will show the importance of drawing a distance diagram to get the equation.

Example:

Two trains are scheduled to leave stations 284 miles apart and travel toward each other at 33 mph and 38 mph, respectively. How long will it take them to reach the point where they are supposed to pass each other?

Figure 4.

284 miles

Drawing the diagram to show the distances traveled by the two trains up to the point where they meet, it is evident that the sum of the distances moved is equal to the 284 miles between the two stations (Fig. 4).

Letting x equal the time each train travels until they meet, the facts are:

	Rate (miles per hour)	×	Time (hours)	=	Distance (miles)
First train	33		x		$33x$
Second train	38		x		$38x$

Solution:

$$33x + 38x = 284$$
$$71x = 284$$
$$x = 4$$

Thus, the trains will meet in 4 hours.

Check:

In 4 hours the first train will travel 33×4, or 132 miles; in 4 hours the second train will travel 38×4, or 152 miles, and $132 + 152 = 284$ miles.

Solving Inequalities.—Just as first-degree equations are solved by transforming them into equivalent equations, so inequalities are solved by transforming them into inequalities in which it is easy to see the solution set.

The inequality $13x - 5 > 6 + 2x$ and the inequality $x > 1$ are equivalent, for in both the solution set consists of all values of the variable x that are greater than 1; that is, the solution set is $\{x \mid x > 1\}$. In the second inequality it is easy to see what the solution set is; in the first it is not (the reader should try substituting a value of x greater than 1, say 2, to satisfy himself that it actually makes the first sentence true).

To find the solution set of a complicated inequality, it is transformed into a simpler but equivalent inequality by using four postulates similar to those used in solving equations.

■ **FIRST POSTULATE.**—If the same number is added to both members of an inequality, an equivalent inequality results.

Example:

To solve $x - 10 < 28$, add 10 to each member:

$$\begin{array}{rr} x - 10 < & 28 \\ +10 & +10 \\ \hline x < & 38 \end{array}$$

Example:

To solve $-x < 4 - 2x$, add $2x$ to each member:

$$\begin{array}{rr} -x < & 4 - 2x \\ +2x & +2x \\ \hline x < & 4 \end{array}$$

■ **SECOND POSTULATE.**—If the same number is subtracted from both members of an inequality, an equivalent inequality results.

Example:

To solve $x + 9 < 2$, subtract 9 from each member of the inequality, thus yielding an equivalent inequality:

$$\begin{array}{rr} x + 9 < & 2 \\ -9 & -9 \\ \hline x < & -7 \end{array}$$

Example:

To solve $7x > 6x + 3$, subtract $6x$ from each member:

$$\begin{array}{rr} 7x > & 6x + 3 \\ -6x & -6x \\ \hline x > & 3 \end{array}$$

■ **THIRD POSTULATE.**—If both members of an inequality are multiplied by the same positive number, an equivalent inequality results; if both members of an inequality are multiplied by the same negative number and the direction of the inequality is reversed, an equivalent inequality results.

The need for making a distinction between what happens when inequalities are multiplied by positive numbers and what happens when they are multiplied by negative numbers will be clear if an example is considered. Suppose we take the true sentence $5 > 3$. Multiply both members by positive 2 and the result is

$$+2(5) > +2(3)$$
$$10 > 6$$

Take the original true sentence but multiply both members by negative 2 and reverse the direction of the inequality:

$$5 > 3$$
$$-2(5) < -2(3)$$

Then the true sentence results:

$$-10 < -6.$$

The application of the third postulate to the solution of an inequality requiring a positive multiplier will be illustrated first in solving

$$\frac{x}{4} > 5.$$

Multiply both members by positive 4:

$$4\left(\frac{x}{4}\right) > 4(5)$$
$$x > 20$$

An application of the third postulate to the solution of an inequality requiring a negative multiplier is shown next in solving

$$\frac{x}{-2} < 7.$$

Multiply both members by negative 2 and reverse the direction of the inequality:

$$-2\left(\frac{x}{-2}\right) > -2(7)$$
$$x > -14$$

Example:

To solve $5 < x/4$, multiply both members by positive 4:

$$4(5) < 4\left(\frac{x}{4}\right)$$
$$20 < x$$

The answer to this inequality can also be written as $x > 20$.

Example:

To solve $x/-8 > 1/2$, multiply both members by -8 and reverse the direction of the inequality:

$$-8\left(\frac{x}{-8}\right) < -8\left(\frac{1}{2}\right)$$
$$x < -4$$

■ **FOURTH POSTULATE.**—If both members of an inequality are divided by the same positive number, an equivalent inequality results; if both members of an inequality are divided by the same negative number and the direction of the inequality is reversed, an equivalent inequality results.

The need to distinguish between what happens when the members of an inequality are divided by a positive number and when they are divided by a negative number is similar to the reasoning for the third postulate.

Example:

To solve the inequality $3x > 1/2$, divide both members by $+3$:

$$\frac{3x}{3} > \frac{1}{2} \div 3$$
$$x > \frac{1}{6}$$

Example:

To solve the inequality $26 < -2x$, divide both members by -2 and reverse the direction of the inequality:

$$\frac{26}{-2} > \frac{-2x}{-2}$$
$$-13 > x$$

This answer can also be written as $x < -13$.

More than one of the postulates for transforming an inequality into a simpler equivalent inequality may have to be used to discover the solution set.

Example:

To solve $x - 2 > 3x + 6$, add 2 to, and subtract $3x$ from, each member of the inequality (using transposition method):

$$x - 3x > 6 + 2;$$

combine like terms:

$$-2x > 8;$$

divide both members by -2, and reverse the direction of the inequality:

$$x < -4.$$

Quadratic Equations.—A *quadratic equation* is an equation in which the variable appears raised to the second power and to no higher power than the second. Thus, a quadratic equation is also called a *second-degree equation*. Any quadratic equation can be put in the form $ax^2 + bx + c = 0$ where $a \neq 0$. In this form, x stands for the variable, and a, b, and c stand for the coefficients. Note that b and c may be 0 but that a cannot be 0, since the equation would then have no term with the second power of the variable. The equations $x^2 + 2x - 8 = 0$, $3x^2 - 2 = 5x$, $7 - x^2 = 3$, $-3x^2 = 22$, and $x^2 + x = 0$ are all quadratic, but not $2x + 3 = 4$ or $x^3 - 3x^2 + 2 = 0$.

A quadratic equation such as $x^2 + 2x - 8 = 0$ cannot be solved solely by the four postulates for first-degree equations. These postulates provide no means for disposing of the x^2 term so that an equivalent equation with a single x on one side and a single number on the other can be obtained.

■ **SOLUTION BY FACTORING.**—The quadratic equation $x^2 + 2x - 8 = 0$ is in a form that suggests factoring the left member: $(x + 4)(x - 2) = 0$. In factored form, the equation represents a situation in which the product of two numbers is equal to zero: $(\quad)(\quad) = 0$. The product of two numbers can be zero if, and only if, one or both of the two numbers is zero. Thus, if $(x + 4)(x - 2) = 0$, either the factor $x + 4$ must equal 0, or the factor $x - 2$ must equal 0, or both must equal 0.

Thus, if the first factor, $x + 4$, equals 0, we have a first-degree equation $x + 4 = 0$, whose solution is $x = -4$. Setting the second factor, $x - 2$, equal to 0 gives another first-degree equation, $x - 2 = 0$, whose solution is $x = 2$. It happens that in this case both factors cannot equal 0 at the same time. Thus the solution set of the original quadratic equation is $\{-4, 2\}$. Both of these roots may be checked by substitution, one at a time, in the quadratic equation.

The complete solution and check for $x^2 + 2x - 8 = 0$ would be as follows:

$$x^2 + 2x - 8 = 0;$$

factor:

$$(x + 4)(x - 2) = 0;$$

set each factor equal to 0:

$$x + 4 = 0 \qquad x - 2 = 0$$

and solve the resulting first-degree equations:

$$x = -4 \qquad x = +2$$

Check:

$$\text{For } x = -4:$$
$$x^2 + 2x - 8 = 0$$
$$(-4)^2 + 2(-4) - 8 \overset{?}{=} 0$$
$$16 - 8 - 8 \overset{?}{=} 0$$
$$0 = 0$$

$$\text{For } x = 2:$$
$$x^2 + 2x - 8 = 0$$
$$(2)^2 + 2(2) - 8 \overset{?}{=} 0$$
$$4 + 4 - 8 \overset{?}{=} 0$$
$$0 = 0$$

It is extremely important to realize that the procedure for solving quadratic equations by factoring hinges on the fact that the product of the factors must be zero. If the product of two factors is anything but zero, it is impossible to reach any conclusion concerning the value of the individual factors. For example, if the product of two factors is

$+12$, one factor may be $+6$ and the other $+2$; one may be -6 and the other -2; or they may be 4 and 3, 12 and 1, 24 and $\frac{1}{2}$, 36 and $\frac{1}{3}$, or 18 and $\frac{2}{3}$, and so on. For this reason, all the nonzero terms of a quadratic equation must be brought together on one side of the equation with a single zero on the other side before one can proceed to the solution of the equation through factoring.

Example:

To solve $2x^2 + 5x = 3$, subtract 3 from both members:

$$2x^2 + 5x - 3 = 0;$$

factor:

$$(2x - 1)(x + 3) = 0;$$

set each factor equal to 0:

$$2x - 1 = 0 \qquad x + 3 = 0$$

and solve the resulting first-degree equations:

$$2x = 1$$
$$x = \frac{1}{2} \qquad x = -3$$

Check:

$$\text{For } x = \frac{1}{2}:$$
$$2x^2 + 5x = 3$$
$$2\left(\frac{1}{2}\right)^2 + 5\left(\frac{1}{2}\right) \overset{?}{=} 3$$
$$\frac{1}{2} + \frac{5}{2} \overset{?}{=} 3$$
$$3 = 3$$

$$\text{For } x = -3:$$
$$2x^2 + 5x = 3$$
$$2(-3)^2 + 5(-3) \overset{?}{=} 3$$
$$2(9) + 5(-3) \overset{?}{=} 3$$
$$18 - 15 \overset{?}{=} 3$$
$$3 = 3$$

The procedure for solving a quadratic equation by factoring may make use of any one of the types of factoring. It may be necessary, for example, to factor the difference of two squares in order to solve.

Example:

To solve $x^2 = 64$, subtract 64 from both members:

$$x^2 - 64 = 0;$$

factor:

$$(x - 8)(x + 8) = 0;$$

set each factor equal to 0:

$$x - 8 = 0 \qquad x + 8 = 0$$

and solve these two equations:

$$x = 8 \qquad x = -8$$

Check:

$$\text{For } x = 8: \quad \text{For } x = -8:$$
$$x^2 = 64 \qquad x^2 = 64$$
$$(8)^2 \overset{?}{=} 64 \quad (-8)^2 \overset{?}{=} 64$$
$$64 = 64 \qquad 64 = 64$$

It may be necessary to take out the highest common monomial factor.

Example:

To solve $2y^2 - y = 0$, factor:

$$y(2y - 1) = 0;$$

set each factor equal to 0:

$$y = 0 \qquad 2y - 1 = 0$$

and solve:

$$2y = 1$$
$$y = 0 \qquad y = \frac{1}{2}$$

Check:

$$\text{For } y = 0: \qquad \text{For } y = \frac{1}{2}:$$
$$2y^2 - y = 0 \qquad 2y^2 - y = 0$$
$$2(0)^2 - 0 \overset{?}{=} 0 \qquad 2\left(\frac{1}{2}\right)^2 - \frac{1}{2} \overset{?}{=} 0$$
$$0 - 0 \overset{?}{=} 0 \qquad 2\left(\frac{1}{4}\right) - \frac{1}{2} \overset{?}{=} 0$$
$$0 = 0 \qquad \frac{1}{2} - \frac{1}{2} \overset{?}{=} 0$$
$$0 = 0$$

An equation of this type is often incorrectly solved because of a misapplication of one of the postulates concerning equivalent equations. It would be incorrect to change the equation $2y^2 - y = 0$ to $2y - 1 = 0$ by dividing both members by y. The postulate governing division of both members of an equation by a number states that an equivalent equation is produced only when the division is by a nonzero number. The variable y may possibly equal 0, hence it cannot be used as a divisor. The equation $2y - 1 = 0$ is not equivalent to the original equation, $2y^2 - y = 0$, because $2y - 1 = 0$ has only one root, $\frac{1}{2}$, while $2y^2 - y = 0$ has two roots, 0 and $\frac{1}{2}$. In general, one may not divide by an expression containing the variable without considering the possibility that the expression may equal zero for some value or values of the variable. Note, on the other hand, that in the equation $2y - 2 = 0$, it is perfectly correct to divide both members by 2, yielding the equivalent equation $y - 1 = 0$; in this case, the division is by a nonzero number as required by the postulate. The equations $2y - 2 = 0$ and $y - 1 = 0$ are equivalent; both have the root 1 as their only solution.

It is sometimes advantageous to divide both members of a quadratic equation by a nonzero number even before factoring in order to simplify the solution of the equation.

Example:

To solve $15x^2 + 30 = 45x$, subtract $45x$ from each member:

$$15x^2 - 45x + 30 = 0;$$

divide both members by 15:

$$x^2 - 3x + 2 = 0;$$

factor:

$$(x - 2)(x - 1) = 0;$$

set each factor equal to 0:

$$x - 2 = 0 \qquad x - 1 = 0$$

and solve these two equations:

$$x = 2 \qquad x = 1$$

Check:

For $x = 2$:   For $x = 1$:
$$15x^2 + 30 = 45x \qquad 15x^2 + 30 = 45x$$
$$15(2)^2 + 30 \qquad 15(1)^2 + 30$$
$$\overset{?}{=} 45(2) \qquad \overset{?}{=} 45(1)$$
$$15(4) + 30 \qquad 15(1) + 30$$
$$\overset{?}{=} 45(2) \qquad \overset{?}{=} 45(1)$$
$$60 + 30 \overset{?}{=} 90 \qquad 15 + 30 \overset{?}{=} 45$$
$$90 = 90 \qquad 45 = 45$$

In all of the quadratic equations solved so far, two roots have been obtained. It is true, in general, that quadratic equations have two roots. These roots, however, may be equal to each other.

Example:

To solve $x^2 = 6x - 9$, subtract $6x$ from each member and add 9 to each member:

$$x^2 - 6x + 9 = 0;$$

factor:

$$(x - 3)(x - 3) = 0;$$

and set each factor equal to 0:

$$x - 3 = 0 \qquad x - 3 = 0$$
$$x = 3 \qquad x = 3$$

Check:

For $x = 3$:
$$x^2 = 6x - 9$$
$$(3)^2 \overset{?}{=} 6(3) - 9$$
$$9 \overset{?}{=} 18 - 9$$
$$9 = 9$$

The quadratic equation in the above example is considered to have two roots, although both roots are 3. Mathematicians prefer to establish general statements which have as few exceptions as possible. In higher mathematics, it is shown that an equation of the nth degree, where n is a positive integer whose members are polynomials, has exactly n roots, although some or all of these roots may be equal. Thus, a first-degree equation has exactly one root, a second-degree equation has exactly two roots; a third-degree equation has exactly three roots, and so on. When the graphs of second-degree equations are studied, other reasons also appear for considering them to have two roots, even though these roots may be equal.

■ **INCOMPLETE QUADRATIC EQUATIONS.**—Any quadratic equation can be put in the form $ax^2 + bx + c = 0$, where $a \neq 0$. When $b = 0$, the equation is a special case of the quadratic of the form $ax^2 + c = 0$ and is known as an *incomplete quadratic equation*. For example, $6x^2 - 24 = 0$ is an incomplete quadratic equation. It may be solved by dividing both members by 6 to yield $x^2 - 4 = 0$. This can be factored into $(x - 2)(x + 2) = 0$; when each factor is set equal to 0, two roots, $+2$ and -2, are obtained.

However, $6x^2 - 24 = 0$, like other incomplete quadratic equations, can also

be solved by a method that depends on transforming it into a form in which the square of the variable is equal to a number: $6x^2 = 24$, $x^2 = 4$, so $x = +2$ or $x = -2$. Finding the number whose square is the given number is called finding the square root of the given number. The square root of 4 was found to be $+2$ or -2. The equation $x^2 = 4$ was really solved by taking the square root of both members and assuming that the square roots of equal quantities are equal. To solve $x^2 = 36$, the square roots of both members can be taken, obtaining $x = +6$ and $x = -6$ (this result is usually written in the shorter form, $x = \pm 6$).

The method for solving an incomplete quadratic equation without factoring is illustrated below.

Example:

To solve $3x^2 - 75 = 0$, divide both members by 3:

$$x^2 - 25 = 0;$$

add 25 to both members:

$$x^2 = 25;$$

and take the square roots of both members:

$$x = \pm 5.$$

Check:

For $x = +5$:   For $x = -5$:
$$3x^2 - 75 \overset{?}{=} 0 \qquad 3x^2 - 75 \overset{?}{=} 0$$
$$3(5)^2 - 75 \overset{?}{=} 0 \qquad 3(-5)^2 - 75 \overset{?}{=} 0$$
$$3(25) - 75 \overset{?}{=} 0 \qquad 3(25) - 75 \overset{?}{=} 0$$
$$75 - 75 \overset{?}{=} 0 \qquad 75 - 75 \overset{?}{=} 0$$
$$0 = 0 \qquad 0 = 0$$

Square Roots.—In solving $x^2 = 4$, it was pointed out that this open sentence speaks of a number whose square is 4. A number whose square is a given number is said to be a *square root* of the given number. In other words, the square root of a number is one of the two equal factors of the number.

Every perfect square has two square roots which are opposite in sign. The positive one is called the *principal square root* of the number. By conventional notation the symbol $\sqrt{}$ (called a *radical sign*) is used to stand for the principal square root only. Thus $\sqrt{25} = 5$, $\sqrt{100} = 10$, $\sqrt{36} = 6$. Note that $\sqrt{2}(\sqrt{2}) = 2$. The negative square root is denoted by placing a minus sign before the radical sign: $-\sqrt{9} = -3$.

In the examples considered so far, only the square roots of perfect squares have been mentioned. The question may arise as to whether there is a solution to the equation $x^2 = 3$. Certainly there is no integer or fraction whose square is 3. In order to make it possible to take the square root of any positive number, the number system must be extended by inventing new numbers that are the square roots of *nonsquare* positive numbers. This is analogous to the extensions of the number system that were made earlier to make other operations possible in gen-

eral. The present extension makes it possible to take the square root of any positive number. The reason for limiting the square root to positive numbers in the present extension of the number system is that the product of two equal numbers of the kinds which have so far been used will always be a positive number, whether the numbers being multiplied are both positive or both negative. Therefore, the square root of a negative number would have to be a number possessing different properties from the numbers used up to this point. However, another extension of the number system is made later to provide numbers that are the square roots of negative numbers, called *imaginary numbers*.

■ **IRRATIONAL NUMBERS.**—The integers and fractions used so far can all be expressed as ratios of two integers. Thus, $\frac{1}{2}$ is the ratio $1 : 2$, 3 is $3 : 1$, $2\frac{1}{3}$ is $7 : 3$, and so on. The set of integers and fractions is therefore called the set of *rational numbers* because of their relation to ratios.

The square roots of nonsquare numbers, however, cannot be expressed as the ratio of two integers; therefore, they are included in the set of numbers called the irrational numbers. An *irrational number* is one that cannot be expressed as the ratio of two integers. Thus $\sqrt{3}$ is irrational, but $\sqrt{4}$ is rational, since $\sqrt{4} = 2$.

Square roots of nonsquare numbers are not the only irrational numbers; for example, π is irrational. Just as the square root of a number is one of its two equal factors, so the *cube root* is one of its three equal factors; and the cube roots of noncube numbers are also irrational. The expression $\sqrt[3]{8}$ represents the principal cube root of 8, which is 2. Therefore $\sqrt[3]{8}$ is rational, but $\sqrt[3]{9}$ is irrational. The small 3 used with the radical sign to indicate the cube root is called the *index* of the radical; when no index is shown, it is understood to be 2, as in $\sqrt{3}$. Note also that it is possible to have a cube root of a negative number: $\sqrt[3]{-27}$ is -3.

When rational numbers are expressed as decimal fractions, the decimal fractions either terminate or continue indefinitely, repeating a certain sequence of digits. For example, $5\frac{1}{2} = 5.5$ and $\frac{1}{4} = 0.25$ both terminate, but $\frac{1}{3} = 0.33333$ ... and $\frac{1}{7} = 0.142857142857$ ... do not —they continue onward (the three dots at the end indicate a continuing repetition of the pattern of digits). Irrational numbers, when expressed as decimal fractions, neither terminate nor repeat a pattern. For example, $\sqrt{2}$ is approximately equal to 1.41421, but its exact value cannot be represented as a finite decimal. Although there is no exact decimal representation for an irrational number, there is a precise location on the number line for every irrational number. For example, $\sqrt{2}$, since it is approximately 1.41421, is located between 1 and 2 (Fig. 5). Its precise position can be found by marking off a distance to the right of the zero point that is exactly equal to $\sqrt{2}$ units. This

Figure 5.

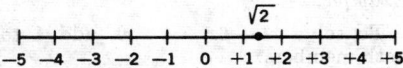

exact length can be found as the hypotenuse of a right triangle whose legs are each 1 unit. If such a triangle is constructed using the same distance to represent a unit as is used on the number line (Fig. 6), the hypotenuse will be $\sqrt{2}$, since the square of the hypotenuse must equal the sum of the squares of the legs by the Pythagorean theorem: (hypotenuse)$^2 = 1^2 + 1^2 = 2$.

Figure 6.

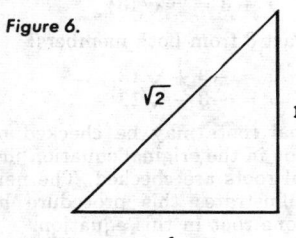

The rational and irrational numbers together form the set of numbers called the *real numbers*. Mathematicians have shown that every point on the number line represents a real number, and that every real number represents a point on the number line.

■ **COMPUTING SQUARE ROOTS.**—The square root of a number, even if it is a perfect square, may not be obvious by inspection. The process of finding a square root in such a case will be illustrated with the square root of 6.76: The digits are first grouped in pairs beginning at the decimal point and pairing in both directions:

$$\sqrt{6.76}$$

The largest square less than or equal to the first pair (4 in this case) is written below it and its square root, 2, is placed above the pair in the answer:

$$\begin{array}{r} 2 \\ \hline \sqrt{6.76} \\ 4 \end{array}$$

Subtraction is performed as in long division and the next pair, 76, is brought down:

$$\begin{array}{r} 2 \\ \hline \sqrt{6.76} \\ 4 \\ \hline 2\,76 \end{array}$$

The answer, 2, is doubled and used as a trial divisor:

$$\begin{array}{r} 2. \\ \hline \sqrt{6.76} \\ 4 \\ \hline 4\,|\,2\,76 \end{array}$$

A digit, in this case 6, is placed above the next pair in the answer and also written at the right end of the trial divisor, the digit being chosen in such a way that the product of the divisor and

itself will be as large as possible without exceeding the remainder, 276:

$$\begin{array}{r} 2.\,6 \\ \hline \sqrt{6.76} \\ 4 \\ \hline 46\,|\,2\,76 \\ 2\,76 \end{array}$$

Continue this until all number pairs have been brought down and used.

In the example above, 2.6 is the square root of 6.76, and this may be checked by multiplying 2.6 by 2.6 to show that the product is 6.76.

■ **APPROXIMATING IRRATIONALS.**—The approximate decimal values of square roots of numbers that are not perfect squares may be calculated by the same process as that used to get the square root of perfect square numbers.

Suppose it is desired to find the square root of 19 to the nearest tenth. Pairs of zeros are added after the decimal point, enough pairs being added to calculate one more decimal place than required in the answer.

$$\begin{array}{r} 4.\,3\,5\,+ \\ \hline \sqrt{19.00\,00} \\ 16 \\ \hline 83\,|\,3\,00 \\ 2\,49 \\ \hline 865\,|\,51\,00 \\ 43\,25 \end{array}$$

The answer to the nearest tenth is 4.4 since 4.35+ is more than the halfway point (4.35) between 4.3 and 4.4. Had the calculated answer been 4.34 or less, the answer to the nearest tenth would have been given as 4.3.

Operations on Radicals.—Irrational numbers involving radical signs, such as $2\sqrt{5}$, are called *radicals*. Since they are numbers, it can be assumed that the results of adding, subtracting, multiplying, and dividing them must be consistent with the postulates that have been assumed to govern these operations on the other sets of numbers, such as the integers and fractions.

■ **MULTIPLICATION.**—Suppose it is desired to multiply two radicals with the same index, such as $\sqrt{25}$ and $\sqrt{4}$. The product, $(\sqrt{25})(\sqrt{4})$, is the same as $(5)(2)$, the answer to which is 10. The same answer would result if the numbers under the radical sign, called the *radicands*, were multiplied together to form the radicand of the product: $(\sqrt{25})(\sqrt{4}) = \sqrt{100}$, which is 10. If the radicands are not perfect squares as they are in the above example, consideration of their decimal approximations will show that this is a suitable procedure for producing their product, provided they have the same index. Thus, $(\sqrt{3})(\sqrt{7}) = \sqrt{21}$ and $(\sqrt[3]{4})(\sqrt[3]{5}) = \sqrt[3]{20}$.

If the radicals to be multiplied have numerical coefficients, for example, $2\sqrt{5}$ and $3\sqrt{6}$, they may be multiplied by multiplying the coefficients and making this product the coefficient of the answer. By the commutative and associative postulates for multiplication, $(2\sqrt{5})$

$(3\sqrt{6})$ is the same as $(2)(3)(\sqrt{5})(\sqrt{6})$, or $6\sqrt{30}$.

Multiplication of radicals of the same index is thus performed by multiplying their coefficients to form the coefficient of the answer and multiplying their radicands to produce the radicand of the answer.

Examples:

$$(-4\sqrt{5})(3\sqrt{7}) = -12\sqrt{35}$$
$$(3\sqrt{2})(\sqrt{5}) = 3\sqrt{10}$$

■ **DIVISION.**—Since division is the inverse of multiplication, solving $21\sqrt{18} \div 3\sqrt{6}$ is equivalent to asking the question, "By what number must $3\sqrt{6}$ be multiplied to give $21\sqrt{18}$?" The answer, $7\sqrt{3}$, shows that division of radicals of the same index may be performed by dividing their coefficients to form the coefficient of the answer and dividing their radicands to form the radicand of the answer.

Examples:

$$36\sqrt{75} \div 9\sqrt{3} = 4\sqrt{25}$$
$$\frac{28\sqrt{30}}{7\sqrt{10}} = 4\sqrt{3}$$

■ **SIMPLIFICATION.**—Since $(\sqrt{4})(\sqrt{3}) = \sqrt{12}$, in turn $\sqrt{12}$ can be transformed into $(\sqrt{4})(\sqrt{3})$. But $\sqrt{4} = 2$, and therefore $\sqrt{12} = 2\sqrt{3}$. The form $2\sqrt{3}$ is considered simpler than $\sqrt{12}$ because its radicand is a smaller number. Radicals that are square roots are simplified by "removing" any factors that are perfect squares in order to make the radicand as small as possible. When $\sqrt{18}$ is broken up into $(\sqrt{9})(\sqrt{2})$ and then written as $3\sqrt{2}$, the perfect square, 9, is, in effect, "removed" from the radicand.

Examples:

$$\sqrt{50} = (\sqrt{25})(\sqrt{2}) = 5\sqrt{2}$$
$$\sqrt{27} = (\sqrt{9})(\sqrt{3}) = 3\sqrt{3}$$
$$3\sqrt{12} = 3(\sqrt{4})(\sqrt{3}) = (3)(2)\sqrt{3}$$
$$= 6\sqrt{3}$$

It is customary to simplify radicals before listing them as final answers. In multiplying $3\sqrt{6}$ by $2\sqrt{15}$, $6\sqrt{90}$ is first obtained. Upon simplifying, this becomes $(6\sqrt{9})(\sqrt{10})$, or $(6)(3)\sqrt{10}$; hence, $18\sqrt{10}$.

It is not necessary to remove the largest perfect square factor in simplifying a radical as long as the process is continued until there are no more perfect square factors to be removed. Thus, in simplifying $\sqrt{72}$, if one had noticed that $\sqrt{72} = (\sqrt{36})(\sqrt{2})$, one would have obtained $6\sqrt{2}$ by removing the 36. Yet one might have written $\sqrt{72}$ as $(\sqrt{9})(\sqrt{8})$ instead, and gotten $3\sqrt{8}$, which, in turn, is $(3\sqrt{4})(\sqrt{2})$, or $(3)(2)\sqrt{2}$, and finally $6\sqrt{2}$.

■ **ADDITION AND SUBTRACTION.**—Just as $5x - 3x + 7x$ can be combined into one term, $9x$, by the application of the distributive postulate, so the same postulate requires that $5\sqrt{3} - 3\sqrt{3} + 7\sqrt{3}$ become $9\sqrt{3}$ when combined. Just as

$2x + 3y$ cannot be combined into one term, neither can $2\sqrt{5} + 3\sqrt{7}$ be combined. Radicands must be the same in order to combine radicals. But $5\sqrt[3]{7} + 2\sqrt{7}$ cannot be combined into one term although both radicands are the same, for in order to combine radicals their indices must be the same as well as their radicands. Radicals having the same index and same radicand may be combined by algebraically combining their coefficients and writing the sum before their common radical factor.

Examples:

$$7\sqrt{2} - 4\sqrt{2} + 9\sqrt{2} = 12\sqrt{2}$$
$$8\sqrt{7} - 18\sqrt{7} = -10\sqrt{7}$$
$$9\sqrt[3]{5} - 8\sqrt[3]{5} = \sqrt[3]{5}$$

Radicals cannot be combined into a single term if their radicands differ, but it is sometimes possible to change a radicand by simplifying it to make it the same as that in another radical to which it is to be added.

Example:

To combine $7\sqrt{50} - 4\sqrt{98}$, simplify as follows:

$$(7)(\sqrt{25})(\sqrt{2}) - (4)(\sqrt{49})(\sqrt{2})$$
$$(7)(5)\sqrt{2} - (4)(7)\sqrt{2}$$
$$35\sqrt{2} - 28\sqrt{2}$$
$$7\sqrt{2}$$

Imaginary Numbers.—The extension of the number system to include irrational numbers makes it possible to have a square root for every positive number in the number system. However, the rational and irrational numbers do not include the square roots of negative numbers. In fact, the property of multiplication that makes the product of two positive numbers a positive number and the product of two negative numbers also a positive number makes it impossible to get a negative number by squaring any of the real numbers.

To compute the square roots of negative numbers, the number system is extended to include another class of numbers whose squares are negative. The symbol i is used for the number which is $\sqrt{-1}$. The number i is called an *imaginary number*. This symbol, i, was chosen to represent this number because it is the initial letter of the word "imaginary."

Notice that $i^2 = -1$. Since $\sqrt{-4}$ can be simplified as $(\sqrt{4})(\sqrt{-1})$, or $2\sqrt{-1}$, $\sqrt{-4}$ is $2i$; $\sqrt{-49}$ would be $7i$, and so on. It is possible to simplify $\sqrt{-3}$ as $(\sqrt{3})(\sqrt{-1})$; therefore, $\sqrt{-3}$ is $i\sqrt{3}$. If $2i$ is squared, it equals $4i^2$, which in turn is $4(-1)$, or -4.

If $-3i$ is squared, $(-3i)^2$, it equals $9i^2$, which, in turn, is $9(-1)$, or -9. The square of an imaginary number is a negative real number.

Complex Numbers.—The imaginary numbers, when combined with the real numbers, form an extended number system called the *complex number system.*

Complex numbers include all the real numbers, such as the rational numbers 5 and $\frac{2}{3}$; all the irrational numbers, such as $\sqrt{2}$ or $\sqrt[3]{73}$; all the imaginary numbers, such as $-2i$ and $i\sqrt{5}$; and combinations of both real and imaginary terms, such as $2 - 3i$ or $\sqrt{2} + 7i$. The complex numbers obey the commutative and associative postulates for addition and multiplication and the distributive postulate. But most important, any first-degree or second-degree equation whose coefficients are complex numbers will have solutions which are also complex numbers.

Completing the Square.—Since factoring is restricted to the use of integral coefficients, a quadratic equation whose roots are irrational cannot be solved by factoring. A method for solving a quadratic equation, called *completing the square*, does permit solutions whether the roots are rational or irrational.

The method of completing the square requires transforming the equation into a form in which the square root of both members can be taken, as in the method for solving an incomplete quadratic equation. In order to take the square root, a perfect-square trinomial is needed on the side containing the variable. Therefore, a method is required for getting a perfect square there. Examination of quadratic trinomials that are perfect squares, such as $x^2 + 6x + 9$ which is $(x + 3)^2$, or $x^2 - 8x + 16$ which is $(x - 4)^2$, shows that the constant term (9 in the first example) must be the square of one-half the middle term's coefficient (in the first example, one-half of 6 is 3). In the method of solving a quadratic equation by completing the square this fact is used to create, or "complete," a perfect square on one side.

Example:

To solve $x^2 + 4x - 21 = 0$, add 21 to both members:

$$x^2 + 4x = 21;$$

complete the square by adding to both members the number found by taking one-half of 4 and squaring it ($4 \div 2 = 2$ and $2^2 = 4$):

$$x^2 + 4x + 4 = 21 + 4;$$

factor:

$$(x + 2)^2 = 25;$$

take the square root of both members:

$$x + 2 = \pm 5;$$

and subtract 2 from both members:

$$x = \pm 5 - 2,$$

combine, and solve:

$$x = 3 \qquad x = -7$$

This example illustrates the use of the method of completing the square in an equation whose roots are rational. This equation could have been solved by factoring. The next example illustrates the use of the method for an equation whose

roots are irrational and which, therefore, cannot be solved by factoring.

Example:

To solve $x^2 + 6x - 4 = 0$, add 4 to both members:

$$x^2 + 6x = 4;$$

complete the square by taking one-half of 6, squaring it, and adding the result to both members:

$$x^2 + 6x + 9 = 4 + 9;$$

factor:

$$(x + 3)^2 = 13;$$

take the square root of both members:

$$x + 3 = \pm\sqrt{13};$$

and subtract 3 from both members:

$$x = -3 + \sqrt{13}$$
$$x = -3 - \sqrt{13}$$

Irrational roots may be checked by substitution in the original equation just as rational roots are checked. The next example illustrates this procedure by checking one root in this equation.

Check:

For $x = -3 + \sqrt{13}$:

$$x^2 + 6x - 4 = 0$$
$$(-3 + \sqrt{13})^2 + 6(-3 + \sqrt{13}) - 4 \stackrel{?}{=} 0$$
$$9 - 6\sqrt{13} + 13 - 18 + 6\sqrt{13} - 4 \stackrel{?}{=} 0$$
$$0 = 0$$

Quadratic Formula.—Any quadratic equation in one variable may be put into the form $ax^2 + bx + c = 0$ where a, b, and c stand for the coefficients of x^2, x, and the constant term, respectively, and $a \neq 0$. By solving the equation $ax^2 + bx + c = 0$, which stands for any quadratic equation, mathematicians evolved a formula that gives the roots of any quadratic equation when the particular values of a, b, and c for that equation are substituted in it. The method of completing the square was used to solve $ax^2 + bx + c = 0$. Starting with $ax^2 + bx + c = 0$, divide both members by a:

$$x^2 + \frac{b}{a}x + \frac{c}{a} = 0;$$

subtract c/a from both members:

$$x^2 + \frac{b}{a}x = -\frac{c}{a};$$

complete the square (one-half of b/a is $b/2a$, and squaring gives $b^2/4a^2$):

$$x^2 + \frac{b}{a}x + \frac{b^2}{4a^2} = -\frac{c}{a} + \frac{b^2}{4a^2};$$

factor:

$$\left(x + \frac{b}{2a}\right)^2 = \frac{-4ac + b^2}{4a^2};$$

take the square root of both members:

$$x + \frac{b}{2a} = \frac{\pm\sqrt{b^2 - 4ac}}{2a};$$

and subtract $b/2a$ from both members:

$$x = \frac{-b \pm \sqrt{b^2 - 4ac}}{2a}.$$

Since $ax^2 + bx + c = 0$ represents any quadratic equation, its solution,

$$x = \frac{-b \pm \sqrt{b^2 - 4ac}}{2a},$$

is a formula for the roots of any quadratic equation.

The use of the formula is illustrated below in solving a quadratic equation that has rational roots.

Example:

To solve $x^2 = 10 - 3x$, put the equation in $ax^2 + bx + c = 0$ form:

$$x^2 + 3x - 10 = 0;$$

identify a, b, and c:

$$a = 1 \quad b = 3 \quad c = -10$$

use the formula:

$$x = \frac{-b \pm \sqrt{b^2 - 4ac}}{2a};$$

substitute values of a, b, and c:

$$x = \frac{-3 \pm \sqrt{9 - 4(1)(-10)}}{2(1)};$$

and simplify:

$$x = \frac{-3 \pm \sqrt{9 + 40}}{2}$$

$$x = \frac{-3 \pm \sqrt{49}}{2}$$

$$x = \frac{-3 \pm 7}{2}$$

$$x = 2 \quad x = -5$$

The use of the quadratic formula to obtain irrational roots is shown next.

Example:

To solve $4x^2 - 3x = 2$, put the equation in the $ax^2 + bx + c = 0$ form:

$$4x^2 - 3x - 2 = 0;$$

identify a, b, and c:

$$a = 4 \quad b = -3 \quad c = -2$$

use the formula:

$$x = \frac{-b \pm \sqrt{b^2 - 4ac}}{2a};$$

substitute:

$$x = \frac{3 \pm \sqrt{(-3)^2 - 4(4)(-2)}}{2(4)};$$

and simplify:

$$x = \frac{3 \pm \sqrt{9 + 32}}{8},$$

$$x = \frac{3 \pm \sqrt{41}}{8},$$

$$x = \frac{3 + \sqrt{41}}{8} \quad x = \frac{3 - \sqrt{41}}{8}$$

■ **SOLVING PROBLEMS.**—Some problems result in quadratic equations.

Example:

The length of a rectangular plot of ground exceeds three times its width by 1 foot. Its area is 52 square feet. Find its length and width.

Let x equal the number of feet in width, $3x + 1$ the length. As the area of a rectangle is width times length, $x(3x + 1)$, the area is $x(3x + 1) = 52$. Remove parentheses:

$$3x^2 + x = 52;$$

subtract 52 from both members:

$$3x^2 + x - 52 = 0;$$

factor:

$$(3x + 13)(x - 4) = 0;$$

set each factor equal to 0:

$$3x + 13 = 0 \qquad x - 4 = 0$$

and solve:

$$3x = -13$$
$$x = \frac{-13}{3} \qquad x = 4$$

The root $-13/3$ must be rejected as an answer to the problem, since the domain of the variable, x, must be restricted to positive numbers if it is to represent the number of feet in the width of a rectangle. If $x = 4$, $3x + 1 = 13$. Thus the plot is 4 feet wide and 13 feet long.

Check:

For length:	For area:
4	13
$\times$ 3	$\times$ 4
12	52
+ 1	
13	

Some problems may result in roots that are not rational.

Example:

A man has 30 feet of fencing to enclose a rectangular area of 40 square feet. Find the length and width of the rectangle to the nearest tenth of a foot.

Let x equal the number of feet in the length of the rectangle. Since 30 represents two lengths plus two widths, one length plus one width is 15 feet. Therefore, $15 - x$ is the number of feet in the width. Area is length times width:

$$x(15 - x) = 40$$
$$15x - x^2 = 40$$

Add x^2 and subtract $15x$ from both members:

$$0 = x^2 - 15x + 40.$$

The right member of this equation is not factorable. However, it may be solved by using the formula

$$x = \frac{-b \pm \sqrt{b^2 - 4ac}}{2a}.$$

Identify a, b, and c:

$$a = 1 \quad b = -15 \quad c = 40$$

substitute:

$$x = \frac{15 \pm \sqrt{225 - 4(1)(40)}}{2(1)}$$

$$x = \frac{15 \pm \sqrt{225 - 160}}{2}$$

$$x = \frac{15 \pm \sqrt{65}}{2}$$

and to get the answer to the nearest tenth, calculate $\sqrt{65}$ to the hundredths place:

$$
\begin{array}{r}
8.\ 0\ 6+ \\
\sqrt{65.00\ 00} \\
64 \\
\hline
\end{array}
$$

$$
\begin{array}{r|l}
160 & 1\ 00 \\
& 0 \\
1606 & 1\ 00\ 00 \\
& 96\ 36 \\
\end{array}
$$

The hundredths place in the approximate square root of 65 is kept through the rest of the calculation and the rounding off to the nearest tenth is done last.

$$x = \frac{15 \pm 8.06}{2}$$

$$x = \frac{23.06}{2} \qquad x = \frac{6.94}{2}$$

$$x = 11.53 \qquad x = 3.47$$

$$x = 11.5 \qquad x = 3.5$$

The length could not be 3.5 feet because it would then be smaller than the width of the rectangle. Therefore, the length is 11.5 ft.

If $x = 11.5$, $15 - x = 3.5$. The rectangle is 11.5 feet long and 3.5 feet wide.

A check of these answers above will not produce the exact area specified in the problem. But since the dimensions are approximate, their product will approximate the area:

$$
\begin{array}{r}
11.5 \\
\times\ 3.5 \\
\hline
575 \\
345 \\
\hline
40.25 \\
\end{array}
$$

(The exact area is 40.)

Sentences in Two Variables.—The open sentence $2x + y = 7$ contains two variables, x and y, each of which may be regarded as having a set of possible replacements or a domain. The open sentence will be true or false when a pair of numbers—one for x and one for y—is substituted in the equation. Thus, if $x = 2$ and $y = 3$, the sentence is true. It is also true if $x = 3$ and $y = 1$, if $x = 5$ and $y = -3$, or if $x = 2\frac{1}{2}$ and $y = 2$. There are an infinite number of pairs of values of x and y that will make the sentence true. However, not all pairs of values of x and y make it true. If $x = 2$ and $y = 1$, for example, the sentence will be false.

When an open sentence contains two variables, a solution consists of a pair of numbers—one number for each variable. Furthermore, the pair of numbers causes the sentence to be true only if the numbers are substituted for the correct variables. That is, the pair $x = 2$ and $y = 3$ makes $2x + y = 7$ a true sentence, but $x = 3$ and $y = 2$ does not. The pair of numbers in which $x = 2$ and $y = 3$ is represented by the notation $(2,3)$, with the number representing x listed before that representing y (note that they are in alphabetical order). Such number pairs as $(2,3)$ are said to be *ordered pairs*, since any pair is different from the pair consisting of the same numbers with their order reversed. That is, $(-5, 2)$ represents the ordered pair in which $x = -5$ and $y = 2$, whereas $(2, -5)$ represents the ordered pair in which $x = 2$ and $y = -5$.

The solution set of an open sentence in two variables is a set of ordered pairs of numbers. Thus, in $2x + y = 7$, some of the ordered pairs in the solution set are $(2,3)$, $(1,5)$, $(5,-3)$, $(2\frac{1}{2},2)$.

Example:

Some of the ordered pairs in the solution set of $3x - 2y = 8$ are:

$$(2, -1), (3, \tfrac{1}{2}), (4, 2), (0, -4).$$

Finding Number Pairs.—A good way to obtain some of the ordered pairs included in the solution set of an equation in two variables is to solve the equation for one variable in terms of the other. Then, by substituting arbitrarily selected values for the other variable, the corresponding values of the one solved for can be discovered. Thus, to get some of the ordered pairs in the solution set for $3x + y = 5$, transform the equation into $y = -3x + 5$ by subtracting $3x$ from each member. In this form, y is expressed in terms of x. Arbitrarily picking a value of x, say $x = 2$, gives $y = -3(2) + 5$, or $y = -1$, as the corresponding y value that will make the sentence true. If $x = 3$, $y = -3(3) + 5$, or $y = -4$. Therefore, $(3, -4)$ is another ordered pair in the solution set of $3x + y = 5$. For convenience, the ordered pairs are often arranged in a table:

x	2	3	4	5
y	-1	-4	-7	-10

A more difficult example might involve more than one step in solving for one variable in terms of the other. To get ordered pairs for the solution set of $5x - 2y = 3$, add $2y - 3$ to each member:

$$5x - 3 = 2y;$$

and divide both members by 2:

$$\frac{5x - 3}{2} = y.$$

The equation is now transformed so that it is solved for y in terms of x. Substituting arbitrarily selected values of x, the corresponding values of y are:

x	0	1	2	-7
y	$-\frac{3}{2}$	1	$\frac{7}{2}$	-19

Solution Sets for Inequalities.—A procedure similar to that for obtaining ordered number pairs in the solution set of an equation in two variables is useful for getting the same information for an inequality in two variables. The inequality is transformed so that one of the variables alone constitutes one member and the other member is an expression in terms of the other variable. This form permits discovery of possible values of the first variable when arbitrary values of the second are substituted for it.

Consider the inequality $2x - y > 5$. Subtracting $2x$ from each member gives $-y > -2x + 5$; dividing by -1 and reversing the direction of the inequality gives $y < 2x - 5$. If a value is now chosen for x, say $x = 1$, y can be any number less than $2(1) - 5$ that is less than -3, for instance, $-3\frac{1}{2}$. Thus the ordered pair $(1, -3\frac{1}{2})$ is in the solution set; so are $(1, -4)$, $(1, -10)$, and so on.

Simultaneous Equations.—Suppose two equations, for example, $x + y = 1$ and $2x + y = 9$, involve the same two variables, each variable having the same domain in both equations. Such equations are said to be *simultaneous* and the pair of equations is called a *system of equations*.

A certain set of ordered pairs will constitute the solution set of the first equation and another set of ordered pairs will constitute the solution set of the second equation. In the example considered here, the table

x	0	1	5	8
y	1	0	-4	-7

shows a small part of the solution set of $x + y = 1$, and the table

x	0	1	5	8
y	9	7	-1	-7

shows a small part of the solution set of $2x + y = 9$. It will be noted that the ordered pairs in the two solution sets differ in general, but that one pair, $(8, -7)$, is in both sets.

If the respective members of the two equations are added:

$$
\begin{aligned}
x + y &= 1 \\
2x + y &= 9 \\
\hline
3x + 2y &= 10
\end{aligned}
$$

a new equation is obtained. This new equation, also in two variables, has a solution set that consists of ordered pairs of numbers, and among them is the pair $(8, -7)$, which was in the solution sets of both of the two equations that were added. The reason for this will be apparent if each equation is thought of as being transformed so that its right member is zero. The first equation will then be in the form $A = 0$, where A stands for all the terms in the left member. The second equation will be in the form $B = 0$. If these are added, the sum will be in the form $A + B = 0$. Replacing x and y by any ordered pair from the solution set of the first equation will make A zero, and replacing x and y by any ordered number pair from the second equation will make B zero. The ordered number pair that makes both A and B zero will also make $A + B$ zero. Furthermore, any solution of the first equation that is not a solution of the second will make A zero but not B, and therefore will not make $A + B$ zero; that is, it will not be a solution to $A + B = 0$. Consequently, the only number pairs from the solution sets of two equations being added that will be in the solution sets of the resulting equation are those

number pairs that are in the solution sets of both.

Adding two equations thus gives an equation that has their common solution in its own solution set. If, before adding two equations, the members of either or both are multiplied by nonzero constants, their common solutions will also be solutions of the resulting equation. For if the constants used to multiply each are m and n, respectively, then the resulting equation will take the form $mA + nB = 0$. Whenever A and B are zero, mA and nB also will be zero and so will their sum. Whenever either A or B is not zero, mA or nB will not be zero and neither will their sum.

■ **SOLVING BY ADDITION.**—Solving a pair of simultaneous equations means finding their common solutions, that is, the ordered number pairs that make both of them true.

The principle of the preceding section can be used to find the common solution of two simultaneous equations. This is done by adding them in such a way as to eliminate one of the variables.

Example:

To solve the system

$$
\begin{aligned}
3x + y &= 5 \\
x - y &= 7 \\
\hline
4x &= 12 \\
x &= 3
\end{aligned}
$$

substitute this value of x in either of the two original equations (in this case the second, $x - y$, is easier to use):

$$
\begin{aligned}
3 - y &= 7 \\
-y &= 7 - 3 \\
y &= -4
\end{aligned}
$$

The common solution is $x = 3$, $y = -4$, or the number pair $(3, -4)$.

To check this solution, the number pair must be substituted in *both* original equations, since the fact that it checks in one does not guarantee that it will also check in the other.

Check:

$3x + y = 5$	$x - y = 7$
$3(3) - 4 \overset{?}{=} 5$	$3 - (-4) \overset{?}{=} 7$
$9 - 4 \overset{?}{=} 5$	$3 + 4 \overset{?}{=} 7$
$5 = 5$	$7 = 7$

The method of solving simultaneous equations by addition depends on eliminating one of the variables through adding. Adding two equations will eliminate one variable when the coefficients of that variable are additive inverses of one another, that is, are equal in absolute value but opposite in sign, as in the above equations ($+y$ and $-y$).

Example:

In the system

$$
\begin{aligned}
2a + b &= 3 \\
2a - 3b &= -41
\end{aligned}
$$

neither variable has coefficients that are additive inverses of each other in the two equations. However, this situation can be achieved by multiplying both members of the second equation by -1. The preceding section has shown that such a procedure will not affect the fact that the common solution will be a solution of the equation formed by adding.

Multiply the second equation by -1 and add:

$$\begin{aligned} 2a + b &= 3 \\ -2a + 3b &= 41 \\ \hline 4b &= 44 \end{aligned}$$

divide both members by 4:

$$b = 11;$$

and substitute 11 for b in the first equation and solve for a:

$$\begin{aligned} 2a + 11 &= 3 \\ 2a &= 3 - 11 \\ 2a &= -8 \\ a &= -4 \\ \end{aligned}$$
$$a = -4 \qquad b = 11$$

Check:

$$\begin{array}{ll} 2a + b = 3 & 2a - 3b = -41 \\ 2(-4) + 11 \overset{?}{=} 3 & 2(-4) - 3(11) \overset{?}{=} -41 \\ -8 + 11 \overset{?}{=} 3 & -8 - 33 \overset{?}{=} -41 \\ 3 = 3 & -41 = -41 \end{array}$$

In the system

$$\begin{aligned} 3x + 4y &= 18 \\ 5x - y &= 7 \end{aligned}$$

adding will not eliminate either variable. However, if the second equation is first multiplied by 4, adding will eliminate y, since its coefficients will then be additive inverses of each other: $+4y$ and $-4y$.

Multiply both members of the second equation by 4 and add:

$$\begin{aligned} 3x + 4y &= 18 \\ 20x - 4y &= 28 \\ \hline 23x &= 46 \end{aligned}$$

divide both members by 23:

$$x = 2;$$

substitute 2 for x in the second equation and solve for y:

$$\begin{aligned} 5x - y &= 7 \\ 5(2) - y &= 7 \\ 10 - y &= 7 \\ -y &= 7 - 10 \\ -y &= -3 \\ y &= 3 \\ \end{aligned}$$
$$x = 2 \qquad y = 3$$

Check:

$$\begin{array}{ll} 3x + 4y = 18 & 5x - y = 7 \\ 3(2) + 4(3) \overset{?}{=} 18 & 5(2) - 3 \overset{?}{=} 7 \\ 6 + 12 \overset{?}{=} 18 & 10 - 3 \overset{?}{=} 7 \\ 18 = 18 & 7 = 7 \end{array}$$

At times it is convenient to multiply both equations in a system by different nonzero constants in order to get the coefficient of one variable to be the additive inverse of the other.

Example:

Solve:

$$\begin{aligned} 2x - 3y &= 2 \\ 5x + 4y &= 51 \end{aligned}$$

This system will be solved by first multiplying the first equation by 4 and

the second by 3 to make it possible to eliminate y by adding. The first equation might have been multiplied by 5 and the second by -2 to cause the elimination of x by adding. Multiply the first equation by 4, the second by 3, then add:

$$\begin{aligned} 8x - 12y &= 8 \\ 15x + 12y &= 153 \\ \hline 23x &= 161 \end{aligned}$$

divide both members by 23:

$$x = 7;$$

substitute 7 for x in the first equation and solve for y:

$$\begin{aligned} 2x - 3y &= 2 \\ 2(7) - 3y &= 2 \\ 14 - 3y &= 2 \\ -3y &= 2 - 14 \\ -3y &= -12 \\ y &= 4 \\ \end{aligned}$$
$$x = 7 \qquad y = 4$$

Check:

$$\begin{array}{ll} 2x - 3y = 2 & 5x + 4y = 51 \\ 2(7) - 3(4) \overset{?}{=} 2 & 5(7) + 4(4) \overset{?}{=} 51 \\ 14 - 12 \overset{?}{=} 2 & 35 + 16 \overset{?}{=} 51 \\ 2 = 2 & 51 = 51 \end{array}$$

Before adding the equations in a system, the equations should first be transformed so that the terms containing the variables are on one side of the equation and the constant terms are on the other side.

Example:

To solve

$$\begin{aligned} 5x &= 5 - 2y \\ 3y &= 15 - 9x \end{aligned}$$

change the equations:

$$\begin{aligned} 5x + 2y &= 5 \\ 9x + 3y &= 15 \end{aligned}$$

multiply the first equation by -3, the second by 2, then add:

$$\begin{aligned} -15x - 6y &= -15 \\ 18x + 6y &= 30 \\ \hline 3x &= 15 \end{aligned}$$

divide both members by 3:

$$x = 5;$$

substitute 5 for x in the second equation and solve for y:

$$\begin{aligned} 3y &= 15 - 9x \\ 3y &= 15 - 9(5) \\ 3y &= 15 - 45 \\ 3y &= -30 \\ y &= -10 \\ \end{aligned}$$
$$x = 5 \qquad y = -10$$

Check:

$$\begin{array}{ll} 5x = 5 - 2y & 3y = 15 - 9x \\ 5(5) \overset{?}{=} & 3(-10) \overset{?}{=} \\ 5 - 2(-10) & 15 - 9(5) \\ 25 \overset{?}{=} 5 + 20 & -30 \overset{?}{=} 15 - 45 \\ 25 = 25 & -30 = -30 \end{array}$$

■ **SOLVING BY SUBSTITUTION.**—In the system

$$\begin{aligned} x + 3y &= 9 \\ 4x + 5y &= 22 \end{aligned}$$

it is very easy to transform the first equation in order to have one variable—x in this case—expressed in terms of the other:

$$x = 9 - 3y.$$

If this expression for x is substituted for x in the other equation, the resulting equation will contain only the variable y and will have in its solution set the ordered number pairs common to the solution sets of both original equations. Substituting $9 - 3y$ for x in $4x + 5y = 22$ gives

$$4(9 - 3y) + 5y = 22.$$

To solve the problem remove parentheses and combine like terms:

$$\begin{aligned} 36 - 12y + 5y &= 22 \\ 36 - 7y &= 22 \end{aligned}$$

subtract 36 from both members:

$$\begin{aligned} -7y &= 22 - 36 \\ -7y &= -14 \end{aligned}$$

divide both members by -7:

$$y = 2;$$

and substitute 2 for y and solve for x as follows:

$$\begin{aligned} x &= 9 - 3y \\ x &= 9 - 3(2) \\ x &= 3 \\ \end{aligned}$$
$$x = 3 \qquad y = 2$$

Check:

$$\begin{array}{ll} x + 3y = 9 & 4x + 5y = 22 \\ 3 + 3(2) \overset{?}{=} 9 & 4(3) + 5(2) \overset{?}{=} 22 \\ 3 + 6 \overset{?}{=} 9 & 12 + 10 \overset{?}{=} 22 \\ 9 = 9 & 22 = 22 \end{array}$$

This method of solving a system of simultaneous equations is known as the *method of substitution*, because one variable was eliminated by substituting for it an expression in terms of the other variable.

The method of substitution may be used on any pair of simultaneous first-degree equations, but it is particularly convenient to use when one of the equations is in a form that expresses one variable in terms of the other.

Example:

Thus, in the system

$$\begin{aligned} a - 14 &= 2b \\ b &= 4a \end{aligned}$$

the second equation gives b in terms of a. Substituting this expression for b in the first equation gives

$$\begin{aligned} a - 14 &= 2(4a) \\ a - 14 &= 8a \end{aligned}$$

To solve the problem, subtract a from each member and combine like terms:

$$\begin{aligned} -14 &= 8a - a \\ -14 &= 7a \end{aligned}$$

divide both members by 7:

$$-2 = a;$$

and substitute -2 for a and solve for b:

$$b = 4a$$
$$b = 4(-2)$$
$$b = -8$$
$$a = -2 \qquad b = -8$$

Check:

$$
\begin{array}{ll}
a - 14 = 2b & b = 4a \\
-2 - 14 \overset{?}{=} 2(-8) & -8 \overset{?}{=} 4(-2) \\
-2 - 14 \overset{?}{=} -16 & -8 = -8 \\
-16 = -16 &
\end{array}
$$

If one of the variables appears with a coefficient of 1 in one of the equations in a system, this equation can be easily transformed so that it is solved for this variable in terms of the other. This, then, is the same situation as existed in the last illustration. Therefore, the method of substitution is convenient to use whenever one of the variables appears with a coefficient of 1 in one of the equations.

Example:

Solve:

$$6x - 4y = 2$$
$$y - 4x = -3$$

In the second equation, the coefficient of y is 1. Solving this equation for y gives

$$y = 4x - 3.$$

Substitute $4x - 3$ for y in the first equation:

$$6x - 4(4x - 3) = 2;$$

remove parentheses and combine like terms:

$$6x - 16x + 12 = 2$$
$$-10x + 12 = 2$$

subtract 12 from both members and combine like terms:

$$-10x = 2 - 12$$
$$-10x = -10$$

divide by -10:

$$x = 1;$$

and substitute 1 for x and solve for y:

$$y = 4x - 3$$
$$y = 4(1) - 3$$
$$y = 1$$
$$x = 1 \qquad y = 1$$

Check:

$$
\begin{array}{ll}
6x - 4y = 2 & y - 4x = -3 \\
6(1) - 4(1) \overset{?}{=} 2 & 1 - 4(1) \overset{?}{=} -3 \\
6 - 4 \overset{?}{=} 2 & 1 - 4 \overset{?}{=} -3 \\
2 = 2 & -3 = -3
\end{array}
$$

The next example illustrates an application of the method of substitution in a case in which no variable has a coefficient of 1. This will show that the method of substitution is applicable even in this situation, although elimination by addition is probably easier to use.

Example:

In the system

$$2x - 3y = 2$$
$$5x + 4y = 51$$

solve the first equation for x in terms of y:

$$2x = 2 + 3y$$
$$x = \frac{2 + 3y}{2}$$

substitute for x in the second equation:

$$5\left(\frac{2 + 3y}{2}\right) + 4y = 51;$$

remove parentheses:

$$\frac{10 + 15y}{2} + 4y = 51;$$

multiply by 2 and combine like terms:

$$10 + 15y + 8y = 102$$
$$10 + 23y = 102$$

subtract 10 from both members and combine like terms:

$$23y = 102 - 10$$
$$23y = 92$$

divide by 23:

$$y = 4;$$

and substitute 4 for y and solve for x:

$$x = \frac{2 + 3y}{2}$$
$$x = \frac{2 + 3(4)}{2}$$
$$x = \frac{2 + 12}{2}$$
$$x = 7$$
$$x = 7 \qquad y = 4$$

Check:

$$
\begin{array}{ll}
2x - 3y = 2 & 5x + 4y = 51 \\
2(7) - 3(4) \overset{?}{=} 2 & 5(7) + 4(4) \overset{?}{=} 51 \\
14 - 12 \overset{?}{=} 2 & 35 + 16 \overset{?}{=} 51 \\
2 = 2 & 51 = 51
\end{array}
$$

Simultaneous Equation Problems.— When problems involve two unknown quantities it is often convenient to represent each of them by a separate variable. To solve the problem, values of the two variables must then be found. If one equation is written to express a relationship between these two variables, it will have an infinite number of pairs in its solution set. If a second equation expressing another relationship between the same two variables can be written, it will also have an infinite number of pairs in its solution set. However, the common solution, or solutions, to the two equations will give answers for the variables that satisfy the relationships between them expressed in both equations. The number of such common solutions is generally small. In fact, all of the simultaneous equations (all of which were first degree) solved so far have had only one common solution. The question of the possible number of common solutions will be discussed in detail in the section on graphs.

Example:

A motorist paid \$3.23 for 10 gallons of gasoline and 1 quart of oil. At the same time, another motorist paid \$3.31 for 8 gallons of the same grade of gasoline and 3 quarts of the same type of oil. Find the price of 1 gallon of gasoline and 1 quart of oil.

Let x represent the price in cents of 1 gallon of gasoline and y represent the price in cents of 1 quart of oil.

Since the cost of an item is obtained by multiplying the price per unit by the number of units bought, the purchase of the first motorist gives the equation

$$10x + y = 323;$$

that of the second motorist:

$$8x + 3y = 331.$$

(Note that \$3.23 is 323 cents; expressing the equation in cents avoids decimals.)

It is convenient to solve the system of equations above by using the method of substitution, since the first equation can be solved for y in terms of x by transforming it into

$$y = 323 - 10x.$$

Substitute for y in the second equation:

$$8x + 3y = 331$$
$$8x + 3(323 - 10x) = 331$$

remove parentheses and combine like terms:

$$8x + 969 - 30x = 331$$
$$-22x + 969 = 331$$

subtract 969 from both members and combine like terms:

$$-22x = 331 - 969$$
$$-22x = -638$$

divide by -22:

$$x = 29;$$

and substitute 29 for x and solve for y:

$$y = 323 - 10x$$
$$y = 323 - 10(29)$$
$$y = 323 - 290$$
$$y = 33$$
$$x = 29 \qquad y = 33$$
$$\text{Gas}: 29\cancel{c} \text{ gal.} \qquad \text{Oil}: 33\cancel{c} \text{ gal.}$$

Check:

First motorist's purchase:

$$
\begin{array}{l}
\text{Gas}: 10 \text{ gal. at } 29\cancel{c} = \$2.90 \\
\text{Oil}: 1 \text{ qt. at } 33\cancel{c} = \underline{.33} \\
\phantom{\text{Oil}: 1 \text{ qt. at } 33} \$3.23
\end{array}
$$

Second motorist's purchase:

$$
\begin{array}{l}
\text{Gas}: 8 \text{ gal. at } 29\cancel{c} = \$2.32 \\
\text{Oil}: 3 \text{ qt. at } 33\cancel{c} = \underline{.99} \\
\phantom{\text{Oil}: 3 \text{ qt. at } 33} \$3.31
\end{array}
$$

The use of two variables and two simultaneous equations is particularly valuable in solving problems involving aircraft flying with or against the wind or ships sailing with or against the current.

Example:

A plane can travel 1,080 miles in 6 hours when flying with the wind but it takes 5 hours to go only 600 miles when flying against the wind. Find the speed of the plane in still air and the speed of the wind.

If we let x equal the speed of the plane

in miles per hour when flying in still air and y equal the speed of the wind in miles per hour, then the speed of the plane flying with the wind will be $x + y$, and speed of the plane flying against the wind will be $x - y$.

	Rate (miles per hour)	$\times$	Time (hours)	$=$	Distance (miles)
With wind	$x + y$		6		$6(x + y)$
Against wind	$x - y$		5		$5(x - y)$

The equation representing the flight with the wind is

$$6(x + y) = 1,080;$$

and the flight against the wind:

$$5(x - y) = 600.$$

Removing parentheses gives the system:

$$6x + 6y = 1,080$$
$$5x - 5y = 600$$

It is convenient to solve this system by dividing both members of the first equation by 6 and both members of the second equation by 5 and then adding:

$$x + y = 180$$
$$\underline{x - y = 120}$$
$$2x = 300$$

Then divide both members by 2:

$$x = 150;$$

substitute 150 for x and solve for y:

$$x + y = 180$$
$$150 + y = 180$$

subtract 150 from both members:

$$y = 30$$

$x = 150$	$y = 30$
Plane : 150 mph	Wind : 30 mph

Check:

The plane's speed with the wind is $150 + 30$, or 180 mph. In 6 hours it will go 6×180, or 1,080 miles. The plane's speed against the wind is $150 - 30$, or 120 mph. In 5 hours it will go 5×120, or 600 miles.

Graphs.—It was pointed out previously that the real numbers may be represented on a number line. A fixed point on this line is chosen to represent zero, and the positive numbers are arranged to the right of the zero point at points appropriately spaced according to the scale used. The negative numbers are similarly arranged at points to the left.

■ **ONE VARIABLE.**—Consider the equation $x + 5 = 7$. It has one solution, 2, which may be pictured as a darkened point on the number line as in Figure 7.

Figure 7.

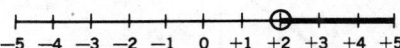

This illustration represents the solution set of $x + 5 = 7$ pictorially, and the darkened point on the number line is therefore called the *graph* of the solution set of $x + 5 = 7$.

For the inequality $x + 5 > 7$, if the domain of x is all the real numbers, the solution set consists of all the real numbers greater than 2. This solution set can be pictured on the number line as a darkened line beginning at 2 and extending indefinitely to the right, a circle around 2 being used to indicate that 2 itself is not included in the solution set (Fig. 8). Note, however, that

Figure 8.

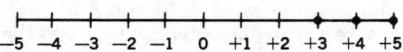

the solution set contains numbers on the darkened line that are very close to 2, for example, 2.00001. The darkened line without the point 2 is the graph of the solution set of $x + 5 > 7$.

The solution set of any sentence consists of all those numbers *in the domain of the variable* that make the sentence true. If the inequality $x + 5 > 7$, whose graph was considered in the previous example, is again examined, but if the domain of the variable x is now the set of integers instead of the set of all real numbers, a different graph will result. The solution set with the new domain will consist of integers only, and the graph will appear as a series of discrete points, as shown in Figure 9.

Figure 9.

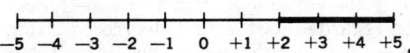

The graph of the open sentence $x + 5 \geq 7$ is a combination of the graph of the equation $x + 5 = 7$ and the graph of the inequality $x + 5 > 7$. If the domain of x is the set of all real numbers, the graph of $x + 5 \geq 7$ is a line (Fig. 10). There is no circle at 2, since 2 is a member of the solution set.

Figure 10.

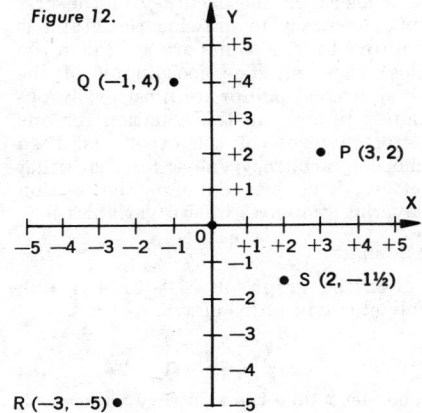

The quadratic equation $x^2 - 2x - 3 = 0$ has two roots, 3 and -1, which are obtained after factoring it into the form $(x - 3)(x + 1) = 0$ and setting each factor equal to 0. The graph of the solution set of this equation appears as two points on the number line (Fig. 11).

Figure 11.

■ **TWO VARIABLES.**—The solution sets of sentences in two variables consist of ordered number pairs. These cannot be pictured on the number line, since the number line can show only numbers, and not number pairs.

In order to picture, or graph, ordered number pairs, they are represented by points on a plane, such as the surface of a page of this book, instead of by points along a line. Each point of a plane representing a number pair is located with reference to two axes perpendicular

to each other, as in Figure 13. The horizontal axis—the x axis—is a number line used to locate the first number in a number pair. The vertical axis—the y axis—is another number line that is used to locate the second number in the number pair. The two axes, or number lines, intersect at their zero points, and this point of intersection, therefore, represents the point $(0,0)$, which is called the *origin*. To locate a point representing some number pair, such as $(3,2)$, count three units along the x axis to the right of the origin (this is the positive direction for x), and then up two units in a direction parallel to the y axis (the positive direction for y). In Figure 12, P is the point $(3,2)$.

Negative values of x are counted off along the x axis to the left of the origin and negative values of y are counted off in the descending direction parallel to the y axis. Q in Figure 12 is the point $(-1,4)$, while R is the point $(-3,-5)$, and S is the point $(2,-1\frac{1}{2})$.

The procedure for locating a point that represents an ordered number pair is similar to the method of locating a street corner by giving the number of the avenue and the number of the street which intersect there. It may also be compared to the method a navigator uses for locating a position by giving the longitude and latitude of that position.

Every ordered number pair represents one, and only one, point in the plane, and every point in the plane has one, and only one, ordered number pair corresponding to it. The pair of numbers that corresponds to a point is known as the *coordinates* of the point. Thus, $(3,2)$ are the coordinates of P in Figure 12. The x coordinate is called the *abscissa* of the point; the y coordinate is its *ordinate*. Hence, the abscissa of P is 3 and the ordinate is 2.

The method of setting up a correspondence between ordered number pairs and the points in a plane which is explained here is known as the *rectangular coordinate system* (because the axes are at right angles to each other). It is also called the *Cartesian coordinate system* in honor of the French mathematician René Descartes (1596–1650), who invented it. Other coordinate systems are used in more advanced mathematics.

Figure 12.

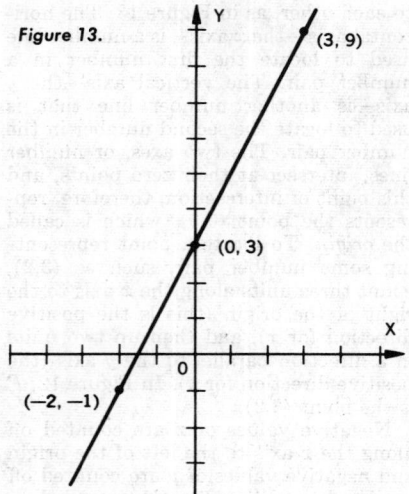

Figure 13.

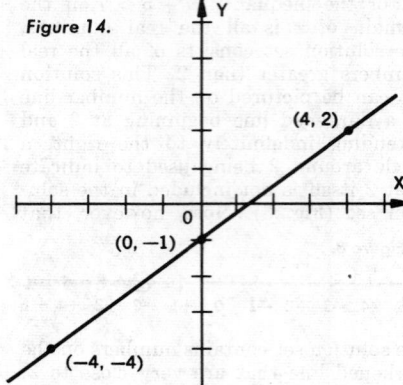

Figure 14.

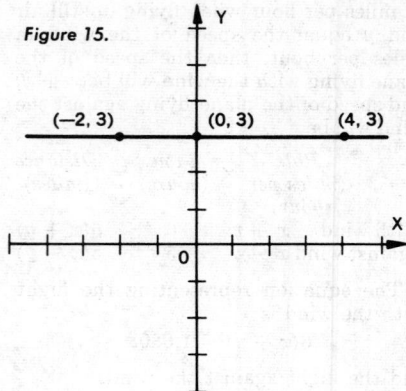

Figure 15.

Graphing First-Degree Equations.—
The solution set of the equation $y = 2x + 3$ is a set of ordered pairs. Some of them are shown in the following table:

x	-2	0	3
y	-1	3	9

If the points corresponding to these number pairs are located on a rectangular coordinate system they will lie in a straight line (Fig. 13).

In advanced mathematics it is proved that the points representing the solution set of any first-degree equation in two variables must lie in a straight line. Furthermore, all the points along the line will represent the ordered number pairs in the solution set. The graph of the solution set of $y = 2x + 3$ is the line (Fig. 13) that passes through the three points whose coordinates are shown in the table. The graph includes all the points on the line—each representing an ordered pair in the solution set. The graph is usually referred to as the graph of the equation $y = 2x + 3$. Notice that if any point whatsoever is now taken on the line, for example, $(\frac{1}{2}, 4)$, its coordinates will make the open sentence true: $4 = 2(\frac{1}{2}) + 3$.

To draw the graph of a first-degree equation, it is customary to plot at least three points on the Cartesian coordinate system; two points will enable the line to be drawn, and the third point serves as a check on the accuracy of the first two. Accuracy in drawing the graph is improved if the points are not taken too close together. The coordinates of the three needed points are most easily obtained by solving the equation for one letter in terms of the other and then choosing arbitrary values for that other letter. (This was done in the section covering sentences in two variables.)

Example:

For the graph of $4y - 3x + 4 = 0$, solve for y in terms of x:

$$4y = 3x - 4$$
$$y = \tfrac{3}{4}x - 1$$

Then let x take the arbitrary values -4,

0, and 4. The corresponding values for y are:

x	-4	0	4
y	-4	-1	2

Plotting these points and drawing the straight line determined by them gives the graph of this equation (Fig. 14).

A first-degree equation in one variable, such as $y = 3$, can be regarded as a first-degree equation in two variables by considering the missing variable to have a coefficient of 0. The equation $y = 3$ could be thought of as $y + 0x = 3$. The solution set of $y = 3$ will then consist of ordered number pairs (the second number will always be 3) and the graph of $y = 3$ can be represented on the Cartesian coordinate system. Some of the ordered pairs in the solution set of $y = 3$ are:

x	-2	0	4
y	3	3	3

What this really means is that $y = 3$ no matter what value x assumes; hence the graph is a line parallel to the x axis and three units above it, as in Figure 15.

A first-degree equation that contains only the variable x, such as $x = -2$, may be regarded as the first-degree equation $x + 0y = -2$. Since in this form it has two variables, its solution set will consist of ordered number pairs, some of which are shown in the following table:

x	-2	-2	-2
y	3	0	-2

Here $x = -2$ no matter what value y assumes, hence the graph of $x = -2$ is a line parallel to the y axis and two units to the left of it, as shown in Figure 16.

Inequalities in Two Variables.—To draw the graph of the inequality $y > 2x + 3$, note that this open sentence requires the y value of each ordered pair in its solution set to be larger than the corresponding y in the equation $y = 2x + 3$. The graph of the inequality $y > 2x + 3$, therefore, consists of all points in the plane above the line that represents the graph of $y = 2x + 3$. These points are shown in the shaded half-plane above the line in Figure 17. The shaded area is referred to as a half-plane since it extends indefinitely upward and to the left.

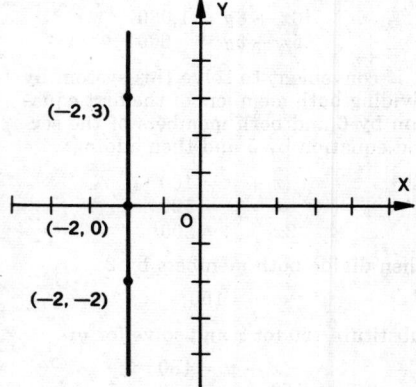

Figure 16.

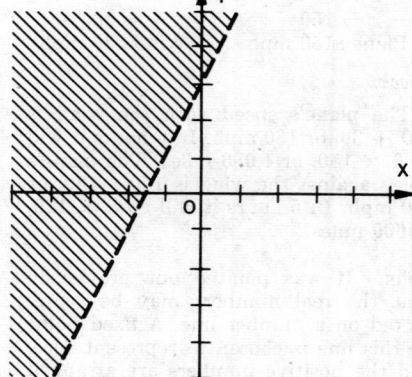

Figure 17.

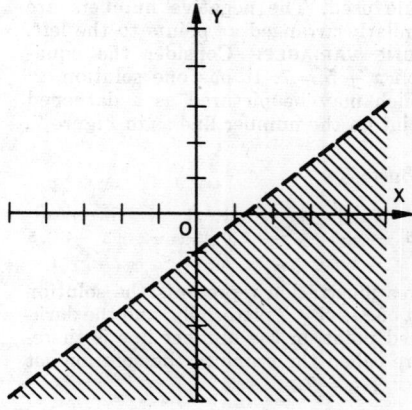

Figure 18.

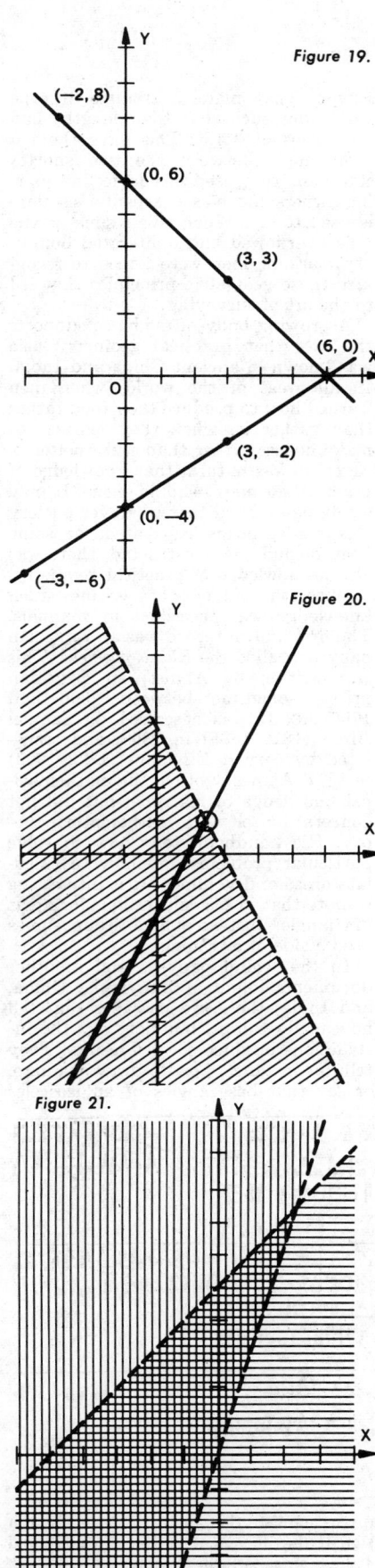

Figure 19.

(−2, 8)
(0, 6)
(3, 3)
(6, 0)
O
(3, −2)
(0, −4)
(−3, −6)

Figure 20.

Figure 21.

However, the line representing $y = 2x + 3$ is not included in the graph of $y > 2x + 3$. If the open sentence had been $y \geqq 2x + 3$, the solution set would consist of the shaded portion including the line that forms its lower boundary.

To obtain the graph of the solution set for the inequality $y < \frac{3}{4}x - 1$, draw the graph of $y = \frac{3}{4}x - 1$. This graph has already been worked out in the preceding section. The graph of $y < \frac{3}{4}x - 1$ consists of all points in the plane below the line representing $y = \frac{3}{4}x - 1$ and not including it. This is the shaded portion in Figure 18.

Graphing Two Variables.—The graph of an equation in two variables shows the points whose coordinates are the solutions to the equation. If the graphs of two such equations are drawn on the same axes, then their common solution can be obtained by reading the coordinates of any points where the graphs intersect. This is illustrated on two first-degree equations in two variables.

Example:

To solve graphically the system

$$3y = 2x - 12$$
$$x + y = 6$$

solve each equation for y:

$$y = \frac{2x - 12}{3}$$
$$y = 6 - x$$

For $y = \dfrac{2x - 12}{3}$:

x	−3	0	3	6
y	−6	−4	−2	0

For $y = 6 - x$:

x	−2	0	3	6
y	8	6	3	0

Both graphs are plotted on the same axes in Figure 19. The common solution is read off the graph as the point (6,0) where the two graphs intersect. Thus the common solution is $x = 6$ and $y = 0$.

Check:

$$3y = 2x - 12 \qquad x + y = 6$$
$$3(0) \overset{?}{=} 2(6) - 12 \qquad 6 + 0 \overset{?}{=} 6$$
$$0 \overset{?}{=} 12 - 12 \qquad 6 = 6$$
$$0 = 0$$

The last example helps to explain why there is generally one common solution to two simultaneous first-degree equations. A first-degree equation has a graph that is a straight line. If two straight lines intersect at all, they intersect in exactly one point. Of course, two straight lines may not intersect. If a graphic solution of $y = 2x + 3$ and $y = 2x - 2$ is attempted, it will be discovered that they are parallel lines and their common solution is, therefore, the empty set. The reader should attempt to solve this system by one of the two algebraic methods developed earlier to see that these procedures will not give a common solution either.

In addition to the possibility that the

graphs of two equations may not meet at all, there is also the possibility that two graphs may coincide, so that all the solutions of one are solutions of the other. The equations $y = 3x - 1$ and $2y = 6x - 2$ have the same graph and all the number pairs that make one true are also solutions to the other. The reader should notice that one of the postulates concerning transforming equations indicates that these two equations must be equivalent and, therefore, must have the same solutions.

In the discussion so far, only first-degree equations have been considered, and first-degree equations have graphs that are straight lines. Equations of a higher degree than first have graphs that are curved lines. The graphs of such equations may intersect at more than one point even when the graphs do not coincide. For example, two circles can intersect at two points. As a result, there is usually more than one common solution for a system of equations if at least one of them is of a higher degree than the first.

Graphing Equalities and Inequalities. —A system consisting of an inequality and an equality may also be solved graphically.

Example:

Solve graphically the system

$$y < 4 - 2x$$
$$y = 2x - 2$$

The graph of $y < 4 - 2x$ consists of all points below the line representing $y = 4 - 2x$ (the shaded part in Figure 20). The line representing $y = 2x - 2$ lies partly within this shaded portion and partly outside of it. The darkened lower part of the line, which is within the shaded portion, represents the common solution set of the inequality and the equality. Note that the encircled point $(1\frac{1}{2}, 1)$ is not one of the number pairs in the common solution, because the shaded solution set does not include the dotted line that forms its boundary.

The graphic method may be used to get the solution set of a system of inequalities.

Example:

Show graphically the solution set of

$$y > 3x$$
$$y < x + 5$$

The graph of the first sentence consists of all points above the line $y = 3x$, as shown by vertical cross-hatching in Figure 21. The graph of the second sentence consists of all points below the line $y = x + 5$, shown by horizontal cross-hatching on the graph. The common solutions to the two inequalities are represented by all points within the area covered by both horizontal and vertical cross-hatching.

—Lester W. Schlumpf

GEOMETRY

EGYPTIAN STATE TOURIST ADMINISTRATION

STONE ARCHES at Egypt's Temple of Deir el-Bahri reveal an early knowledge of geometry.

SECTION ONE

Practical Geometry.—Geometry has its origins in antiquity. Archeological discoveries show that ancient peoples were very much aware of geometric shapes and relations. The designs on early Egyptian pottery, 4000–3500 B.C., use groups of parallel lines, and ancient pottery from all parts of the world uses concentric circles, squares, rectangles, and triangles.

Daily problems of farmers and artisans of long ago motivated the search for methods to measure lengths, areas, and volumes. Astronomers learned how to measure the size of an angle. Both ancient Babylonians and Egyptians used a knowledge of practical geometry in their irrigation and construction projects.

Thus, it must have been recognized early in man's development that the shortest distance between two points is along a straight line between those points.

Early use of the plumb line indicates a knowledge of some of the properties of right angles and perpendiculars to planes. Similarly, the use of circular

shapes such as wheels in ancient Babylonia clearly indicates a knowledge of some of the properties of circles.

A famous example of a geometric proposition was used by the rope-stretchers (*harpedonaptae*) of ancient

Egypt. They made a triangle of rope with sides such that their lengths had the ratios of 3:4:5. This gave them a right angle between the two shorter sides; and they used this device in squaring corners, much as a carpenter's square is used today. When rivers such as the Nile overflowed and obliterated boundary markers, men were forced to recognize those geometric principles that led to the art of surveying.

A growing body of evidence supports the fact that practical geometry also was known in ancient China and India. In all areas of the world, when men learned how to produce their food rather than gather it, when they learned to make houses rather than seek shelter in caves, it was natural that knowledge of practical geometry should ensue. It may safely be asserted that wherever pottery was made, farms cultivated, or some form of building constructed, there was also a knowledge of practical geometry.

With the advent of writing, such knowledge was inscribed in manuals. The first known record was an Egyptian papyrus, called the *Rhind papyrus*. This was written by Ahmes, an Egyptian priest, sometime between 2000 and 1700 B.C. It was described by Samuel Birch (1813–1885) in 1868, and translated by August Eisenlohr (1832–1902) in 1877. Ahmes wrote of the mathematical knowledge of his time, but did not concern himself with mathematical theory. His handbook tells how to solve particular problems and how to calculate areas and volumes. It is interesting to note that in his calculations for areas of triangles, instead of an altitude Ahmes used a side of a triangle.

In the Rhind papyrus and in other documents found in Babylonia, China, and India, there are passages that tell how to do things, but not why the instructions produce correct results. They tell, for instance, how to draw a square, or say that base angles of an isosceles

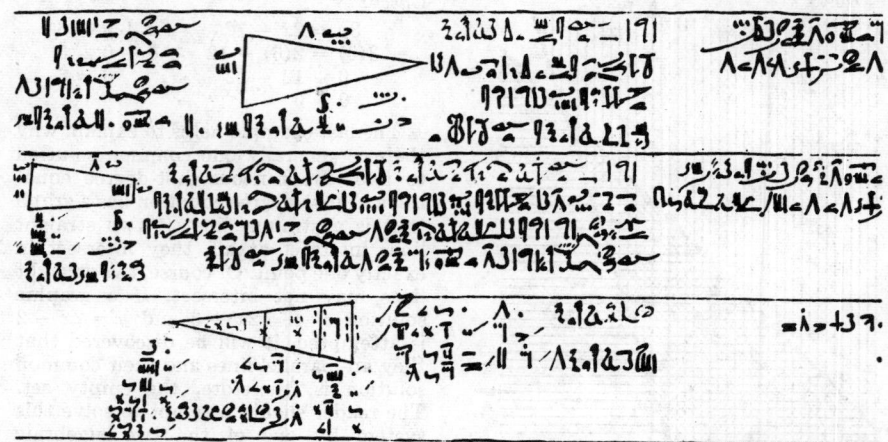

PREBIBLICAL MATHEMATICS written on Rhind papyrus indicate that the early Near Eastern civilizations were familiar with fractions. Translated, the document reads: "What equal areas should be taken from 5 fields if the sum of these areas is to be 3 setat?"

ENGELHARD, MONKMEYER

GREEK ARCHITECTURE, with its logic and balance, represents, in stone, the characteristics of early Greek philosopher-mathematicians.

triangle have equal measures, but no effort is made to explain why the figure will be a square, or why in a triangle the equality of the measures of the two base angles follows logically from the equality of the lengths of the two sides opposite these angles. There were no known attempts to demonstrate logical geometric relations before 600 B.C.

The geometry that is taught today in the elementary grades is *practical geometry*, sometimes called *informal geometry*. Students learn it by drawing figures with rulers, and by measuring with rulers and protractors. The facts they learn usually are not logically related to each other. Generally in the tenth grade, these logical relations are studied as *theoretical geometry*, sometimes called *formal geometry*.

SECTION TWO

Theoretical Geometry.—As far as is known, Thales (c. 640–546 B.C.), a Greek philosopher of Miletus, was the first to use logic in geometry. His travels took him to Babylon and Egypt, and there he increased his knowledge of practical geometry. There are no primary sources of the development of

early Greek mathematics, only references in documents dating from the fourth century B.C. But it is safe to say that Thales and his successors were not content to know that a proposition about geometric figures was true; they wanted to know why it was true.

The essential characteristic of this school of thinking is the use of logic, that is, the demonstration that one statement follows inevitably from another statement or group of other statements. The impulse to demonstrate such a relation is not motivated by utility, but by the desire to understand. It is the difference between knowing how to do something (the *know-how*), and knowing why it succeeds (the *know-why*).

From 600 B.C. to 300 B.C., there was a veritable explosion of geometric discovery that can be accounted for by the *method of logic*, or, as it is sometimes called, the *method of deduction*. This method produced understanding and insight, which in turn led to new discoveries. Thales found a deductive proof for about six geometric facts, and his success inspired others to follow his example. A partial list of famous Greek mathematicians who followed Thales includes Pythagoras (c. 582–507 B.C.), Anax-

agoras (c. 500–428 B.C.), Hippocrates (c. 460–c. 377 B.C.), Democritus (c. 460–357 B.C.), and Eudoxus of Cnidus (fl. 300 B.C.).

The deductive method is vital in the study of formal geometry as well as in all mathematics and theoretical science. It is illustrated by the following example.

Suppose it is known from practical geometry that the sum of the measures of the three angles of any triangle is 180°. It would then follow that in a right triangle there are two angles whose measures have the sum of 90°. The proof might be:

Let the measures of the angles of the right triangle be A, B, and C, with $C = 90°$. It then follows that:

(1) $\quad A + B + C = 180°$
(2) $\qquad\qquad C = 90°$
(3) $\qquad\quad A + B = 90°$

The first statement is assumed to be true through a knowledge of practical geometry. The second statement is true because it is characteristic of all right triangles. The third statement, which is the desired conclusion, follows from a knowledge of *number facts*. (This number fact will be discussed later along with other number principles.)

About 300 B.C., Euclid (fl. 300 B.C.) made a compilation of the geometry that was known at the time. His most famous work is the thirteen-book *Stoicheia* ("Elements"). The organization of Euclid's geometry follows the form that is known today as a *postulational system*. Euclid selected a few geometric facts as a basis and demonstrated how all the others could be deduced from them as logical consequences flowing from these few.

The impact of the *Elements* on the development of mathematics, science, and philosophy cannot be overrated. It demonstrated how a large body of knowledge could be organized in such a manner that it is a coherent structure rather than a collection of unrelated facts. As such, it serves as a model for scientists even to this day.

Mathematicians scrutinized the *Elements* for imperfections, and these finally were corrected by David Hilbert (1862–1943). The *Elements* also stimulated the discovery of new geometric facts. Mathematicians devised alternate postulational systems that began with different assumptions. This was particularly true of Nikolai Lobachevsky (1793–1856), János Bolyai (1802–1860), Karl Gauss (1777–1855), and Bernhard Riemann (1826–1866).

The origin and development of theoretical geometry is rooted in the fact that Thales' logical demonstrations worked with relations or properties of geometric figures rather than with the figures themselves. In the example of a logical proof concerning a right triangle, such a triangle was not drawn, nor were the sizes of its angles examined. Three statements or propositions were employed: (1) about the sum of the measures of the three angles of any triangle; (2) about a characteristic property of all right triangles; (3) about a property of numbers.

Consider some properties of such a simple object as a line. Perhaps it is a taut string or a line drawn with ruler and pencil. The four properties of a physical line are: (1) It can be seen. (2) It has a beginning and an end. (3) It consists of molecules that have spaces between them; therefore it is discontinuous. (4) It has a measurable width, even if it is necessary to use a microscope to determine this.

On the other hand, mathematicians think of a line in geometry as having the following properties: (1) It cannot be seen. (2) It has neither beginning nor end. (3) It is continuous, made up of points that have no space between them. (4) It has no width.

In other words, the mathematician's line is an abstraction. It is not the same as the carpenter's line or the draftsman's line. Similarly, mathematical points and planes are abstractions, not to be confused with physical dots and physical flat surfaces. One is prompted to ask why the mathematician has conceived of a line that differs from a physical line.

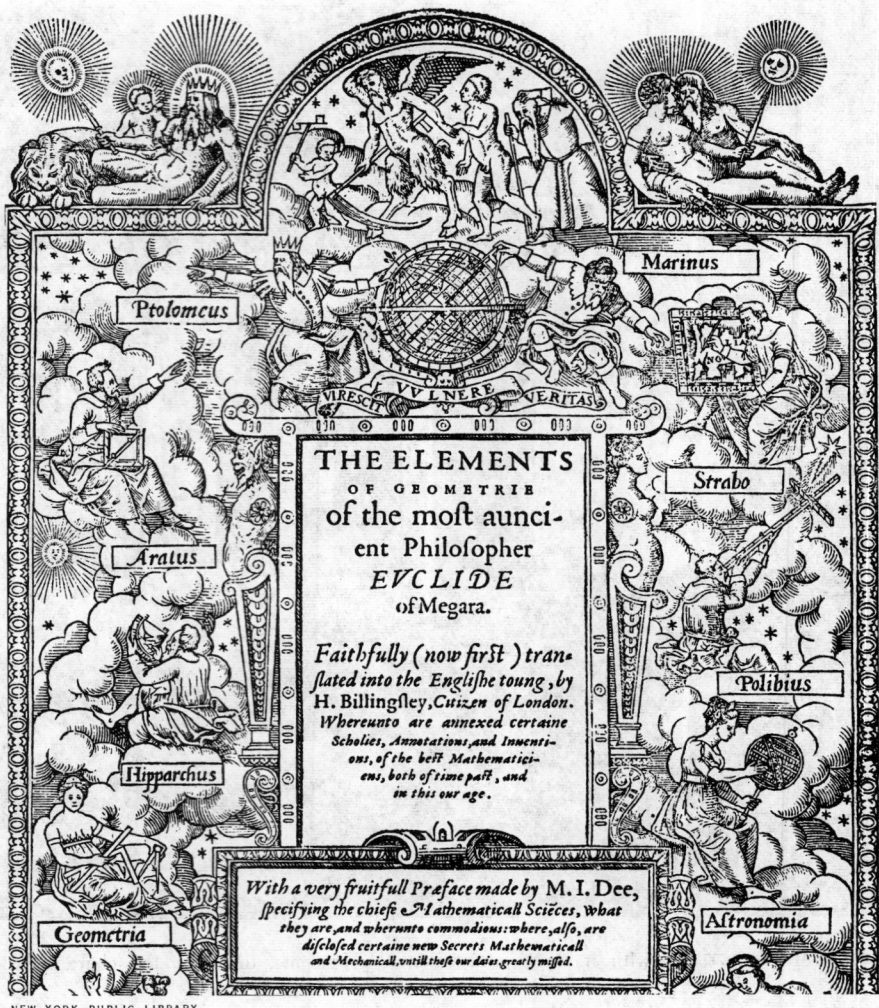

NEW YORK PUBLIC LIBRARY

THE ELEMENTS, a book written by Euclid about 300 B.C., has influenced all mathematics.

The answer lies in the simplicity that ensues when he constructs logical proofs. One might then ask whether the logical consequences bear any resemblance to the facts that are true of physical lines. This is answered only by finding the logical consequences and then noting how well they conform to reality. The success of postulational thinking lies in such continual verifications. Then one might ask why geometry books have diagrams, since these are physical objects. The diagrams serve to suggest (not to prove) relations among geometric abstractions.

We might say that practical geometry studies physical geometric objects and results in a list of assorted facts. On the other hand, theoretical geometries study geometric abstractions and result in a list of propositions that are organized as a *postulational system*.

There are four steps in constructing a postulational system. The first is to list the concepts or terms that are to be *primitive*, or undefined. It is impossible to define all terms of the system because any definition of a term contains other terms. In the case of the first definition, these other terms thus are undefined.

This procedure is not the method of a dictionary, which attempts to define all terms and therefore must indulge in some circular definitions.

There are four initial, undefined terms: "set," "point," "line," and "plane." Also accepted as undefined are such common words of daily discourse as "and," "or," "of," and "all." The first definition is that of *space*, which is defined as the set of all points. Other definitions are postponed until the "betweenness" relation has been established. One might ask how objects with no definitions can be discussed. This is partly remedied in the next step.

The second step in constructing a postulational system is to list all the statements about the undefined terms for which no proof is offered. This helps to identify what the undefined terms represent. These statements are called *axioms*, *postulates*, or *assumptions*. Euclid seemed to reserve the term "postulate" for those statements that apply to geometric objects, and the term "axiom" for all other statements. Many contemporary mathematicians call all assumptions "postulates." We cannot tell whether postulates are true until a meaning is given to each of their undefined terms. When a meaning is assigned to each undefined term and each postulate then becomes true, a model of the postulational system is formed. In that case, the postulates are *consistent*. A postulational system may have more than one model if more than one meaning can be given to undefined terms. Mathematicians find it convenient to start with a few postulates, but this is not a logical necessity.

The third step is to decide on the rules of logic by means of which new statements are deduced from the postulates. Generally the classical Aristotelian logic, in which a statement is either true or false, is used.

The fourth step is to use the postulates and the rules of logic to deduce new statements. These are called *theorems*. A *corollary* is a theorem that is an immediate logical consequence of another theorem. A *lemma* is a theorem whose only importance is to prepare the way for another theorem that is considered significant in the system. This fourth step occupies practically all of the student's effort and time.

The choice of postulates in a system is a mathematician's prerogative. This became clear in the early part of the nineteenth century, when non-Euclidean geometries were created in which at least one of the postulates differed from one in Euclid's set. Since then, a variety of geometries have been created. A brief account of some of these geometries appears later.

A postulational system is therefore a system of propositions based on a set of undefined terms; definitions using these terms or already defined terms; a set of postulates; a set of rules of logic; and, using these as a basis, the theorems that can be deduced from them.

SECTION THREE

Principles of Logic.—The following are principles of logic often used in geometry.

1. A *proposition* is a statement capable of being true or false.

Notation. Propositions are denoted by *p, q, r,* etc.

Example. p: Some living trees grow leaves. *q:* The earth is flat.

2. A *conjunction* of two or more propositions uses the connective "and." It is also a proposition. A conjunction is true if, and only if, each of its component propositions is true.

Example. In the above example, "*p* and *q*" is false because "*q*" is false.

3. A *disjunction* of two propositions uses the connective "or." It is also a proposition. A disjunction is true if either or both parts are true.

Example. In the example above, "*p* or *q*" is true because "*p*" is true.

4. The *negation* of "*p*" is "*p* is false," or "not *p*."

Example. The negation of "it is rain-

ing" is the statement "it is not raining."

5. An *implication* has the form "*p* implies *q*," or "if *p* then *q*." The proposition following "if" is called the *antecedent*, or *hypothesis*. The proposition following "then" is called the *consequent*, or *conclusion*. An implication is considered true if the antecedent is false or the consequent is true.

6. The implication "if *p* then *q*" may be expressed, "the fact that *p* is true is a *sufficient condition* that *q* is true" or "the fact that *q* is true is a *necessary condition* that *p* is true."

7. The proposition "*p* is a *necessary* and *sufficient* condition for *q*" means, "if *p* then *q* and if *q* then *p*." In this case, *p* and *q* are *equivalent conditions* and must agree in their true values. This may also be stated, "*q* is true if, and only if, *p* is true."

8. The *converse* of "if *p* then *q*" is "if *q* then *p*." The converse of a true implication need not be true.

9. The *inverse* of "if *p* then *q*" is "if not *p* then not *q*." The inverse of a true implication need not be true.

10. The *contrapositive* of "if *p* then *q*" is "if not *q* then not *p*." The contrapositive of a true implication is necessarily true.

Comment. The converse of the inverse of an implication is the contrapositive of the implication.

11. "If *p* implies *q* and *q* implies *r*, then *p* implies *r*" is called the *law of syllogism*. Most proofs in geometry follow this pattern. They consist in showing that *a* implies *b*, that *b* implies *c* . . . , and finally that *r* implies *s*. The conclusion is that *a* implies *s*. It is sometimes known as the *direct method*.

12. The truth of "if *p* then *q*" does not guarantee that *q* is true. It also must be known that *p* is true. The principle "if *p* is true and if *p* implies *q*, then *q* is

true" is called the *rule of detachment*, or *modus ponens*.

13. In the *indirect method* used to prove "if *p* then *q*," "*p* and not *q*" is assumed, and by reasoning with these propositions, postulates, and theorems, it is deduced either that *p* is false or that some postulate or theorem already accepted as true is false.

14. A *definition* has the "if, and only if" meaning.

Example. The definition "a right triangle is a triangle one of whose angles is a right angle" yields the following two propositions: (1) If a triangle is a right triangle, one of its angles is a right angle. (2) If one of the angles of a triangle is a right angle, it is a right triangle. The definition may also be stated: A triangle is a right triangle if, and only if, one of its angles is a right angle.

The purpose of a definition is to replace a larger set of words with a smaller set.

SECTION FOUR

Basic Number Principles.—Properties of points and point sets, such as lines and planes, can be examined by relating them to properties of numbers. Following are the basic principles and properties of real numbers that are used in elementary algebra.

Definition of Equality.—In the equality *a* = *b*, the symbol = means that *a* and *b* are names of the same object. In this article the object may be a number, a point, or a set of points.

Properties of Number Equalities.—In the following sentences, *a, b,* and *c* are real numbers.

Substitution Principle. In any equal-

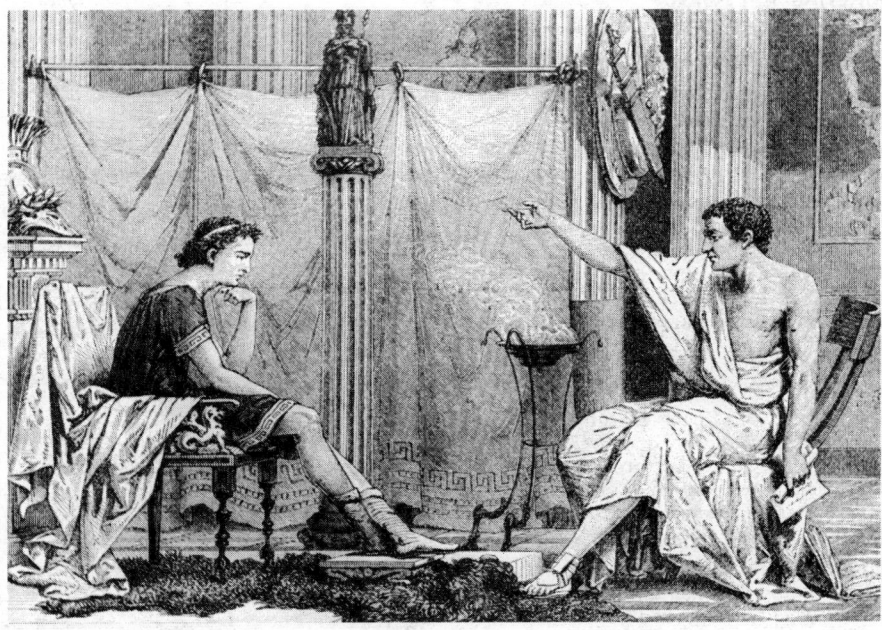

BETTMANN ARCHIVE
ARISTOTLE, Greek philosopher and logician, taught Alexander the Great of Macedon.

ity, one name of an object may be replaced by another.

Reflexive Property. For any a, $a = a$.

Symmetric Property. If $a = b$, then $b = a$.

Transitive Property. If $a = b$ and $b = c$, then $a = c$.

Addition Property. If $a = b$, then $a + c = b + c$.

Multiplication Property. If $a = b$, then $ac = bc$. Also, if $ac = bc$ and $c \neq 0$, then $a = b$.

Properties of Order (Inequalities).—If a and b are distinct numbers, then either $a > b$ (read a is greater than b) or $b > a$, but not both.

Transitive Property. If $a > b$ and $b > c$, then $a > c$.

Addition Property. If $a > b$, then $a + c > b + c$.

Multiplication Properties. If $c > 0$ and $a > b$, then $ac > bc$. If $0 > c$ and $a > b$, then $bc > ac$.

The statement $a > b$ may also be written $b < a$ (b is less than a). The order properties may be rephrased by using $<$ in place of $>$, except for the multiplication properties.

The statement $a < b$ and $b < c$ may be abbreviated as $a < b < c$. A number x that is between a and b may be referred to by writing either $a < x < b$, or $b < x < a$, depending on the respective values of a and b.

It is now possible to develop a postulational system that is a revision of Euclid's geometry. The choice of postulates is guided by the contributions of several groups who have made valuable suggestions concerning the revision of school geometry, particularly the *School Mathematics Study Group.*

SECTION FIVE

INCIDENCE RELATIONS

Postulate 1.—Space contains at least two *distinct points.* Points generally are identified by capital letters.

Postulate 2.—Every line is a set of points and contains at least two points.

Postulate 3.—If P and Q are two distinct points, there is exactly one line that contains them.

Notation. The symbol $\overleftrightarrow{PQ}$ is used to denote the *unique line* that contains P and Q. P and Q *determine* one *line.* Lower-case letters are used to name a line.

Postulate 4.—No line contains all points of space.

■ THEOREM 5-1.–Space contains at least three points that are not in one line.

Proof. Postulate 1 states that space contains at least two points that may be called A and B, respectively. By Postulate 3, they determine $\overleftrightarrow{AB}$. Postulate 4 supplies a third point not in $\overleftrightarrow{AB}$, Q.E.D. (*quod erat demonstrandum,* meaning "which was to be proved").

■ THEOREM 5-2.–Two distinct lines cannot intersect in more than one point.

Proof. Let the two lines be r and s. If r and s intersect in two distinct points, A and B, then by Postulate 3, $\overleftrightarrow{AB} = s$ and $\overleftrightarrow{AB} = r$. Therefore, $r = s$. But this contradicts the information that r and s are distinct. Thus it must be concluded that r and s cannot intersect in two points, Q.E.D.

Definition. If three or more points are contained in one line, they are *collinear* (lie on or pass through the line). If three points are not in one line, they are *noncollinear.*

Postulate 5.—Every plane is a set of points and contains at least three noncollinear points.

Postulate 6.—If P, Q, and R are three distinct noncollinear points, then there is exactly one plane that contains them.

Notation. A plane is named by listing three noncollinear points of the plane, for example, plane PQR.

■ THEOREM 5-3.–Space contains at least one plane.

Proof. Theorem 5-1 supplies three noncollinear points, and Postulate 6 states that there is one plane that contains them, Q.E.D.

Comment. Some aspects of geometry are confined to one plane. When limited to one plane, the subject is called *plane geometry.*

Postulate 7.—No plane contains all points of space.

Notation. A *set* is denoted by { }. For instance, the set consisting of the pair A,B is written {A,B}.

■ THEOREM 5-4.–Space contains at least two distinct planes.

Proof. Theorem 5-3 supplies one plane, which contains three noncollinear points, A, B, and C. Postulate 7 supplies a fourth point, D, not in plane ABC. The sets {D,A,B} and {D,A,C} cannot both contain collinear points since, if they did, $\overleftrightarrow{DA}$ would contain B and C and therefore A, B, C would be collinear. But this would contradict the given information that they are not collinear. Therefore, either {D,A,B} or {D,A,C} determines a plane different from plane ABC, which does not contain D. Finally, this plane is a set of points, and, by Postulate 5, it is in space, Q.E.D.

Postulate 8.—If two distinct points of a line belong to a plane, then every point of the line belongs to that plane.

Postulate 9.—If two distinct planes intersect, then their intersection is a line.

Comment. Postulates 8 and 9 express for theoretical geometry what is felt intuitively for physical flat surfaces. The study of properties of point sets in more than one plane is called *solid geometry.*

Pl 2. **FIGURES DE LA GÉOMÉTRIE** *Page 7 et suis.*

EIGHTEENTH-CENTURY FRENCH TEXTBOOK concentrated entirely on the geometry of Euclid.

NEW YORK PUBLIC LIBRARY

SECTION SIX

Distances and Coordinates.—Practical geometry uses a ruler to measure how far one dot is from another. Theoretical geometry uses an "abstract ruler." The notion of a correspondence helps in creating this tool. A *correspondence* is a matching scheme by which each member of one set is associated with a unique member of a second set. In Postulate 10 two sets are used. The first consists of pairs of points in space; the second consists of the positive numbers.

Postulate 10.—If A and B are distinct points, there exists a correspondence that associates with each pair of distinct points in space a *unique positive number*, such that the number assigned to the pair $\{A,B\}$ is one.

Definition. The pair $\{A,B\}$ in Postulate 1 is a *unit pair*. The number associated with a pair of distinct points is the distance between them relative to $\{A,B\}$. In Postulate 1 it is stated that any pair of points may be used as a unit pair, and that the distance between two points relative to this unit pair is a positive number.

Definition. The distance between a point and itself relative to any unit pair is zero.

Notation. The distance between a point P and a point Q relative to a given unit pair is written PQ. The phrase "relative to a unit pair" corresponds in the physical world or practical geometry to a linear unit of measure, such as an inch, mile, or meter.

Postulate 11.—Let $\{A,B\}$ and $\{C,D\}$ be two unit pairs. Then for every pair of distinct points P and Q in space,

$$\frac{PQ \text{ (relative to } \{A,B\})}{PQ \text{ (relative to } \{C,D\})}$$

is a *constant*.

An interpretation of this postulate may take the following form. If any distance is measured in inches and also in feet, the quotient of the two measures is constant. In this case the quotient is 12, since there are always 12 inches in every foot.

Definition. A *one-to-one correspondence* between two sets is a correspondence that matches every member of the first set with a unique member of the second set, and also matches every member of the second set with a unique member of the first set.

Definition. Let $\{A,B\}$ be any unit pair and let l be any line. A coordinate system on l relative to $\{A,B\}$ is a one-to-one correspondence between the set of points on l and the set of all real numbers if for any two points of l, P and Q, associated respectively with numbers p and q, and $p > q$, then PQ (relative to $\{A,B\}$) $= p - q$. The point on l that is associated with zero is the *origin*, and the point on l associated with 1 is the *unit point*. The number that a coordinate system on a line associates with a point is the *coordinate* of that point in the coordinate system.

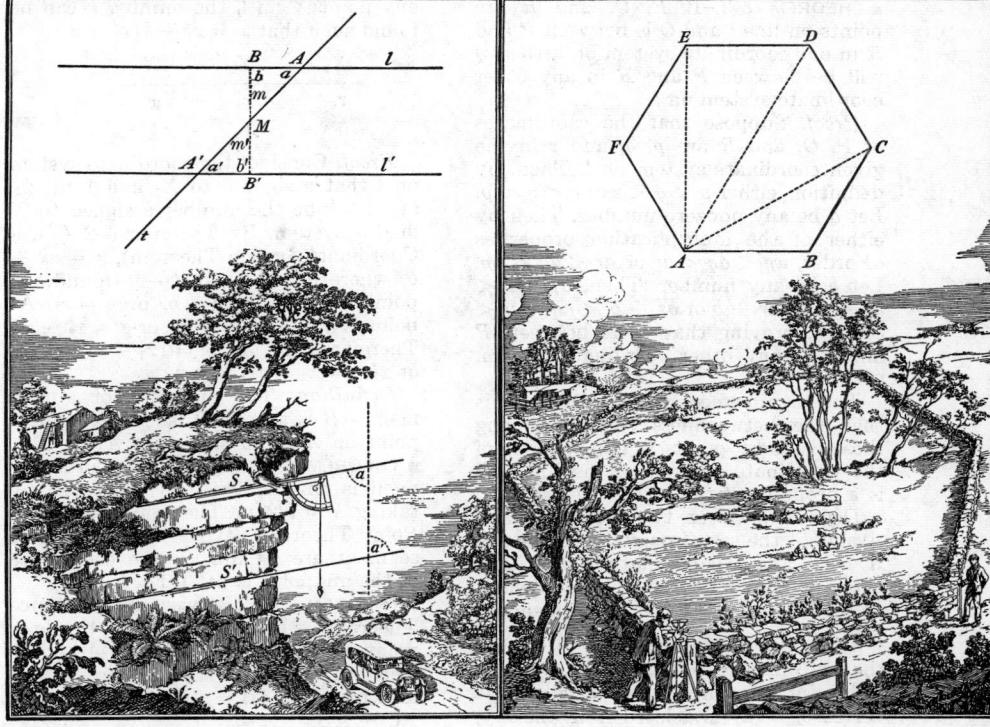

NEW YORK PUBLIC LIBRARY

EARLY TWENTIETH-CENTURY TEXTBOOKS in America taught mathematics by presenting practical problems. The problems illustrated above involve the use of trigonometry and geometry in the measurement of distances in various practical applications.

Postulate 12 (Ruler Postulate).—If $\{A,B\}$ is a unit pair and l is any line, and if P and Q are any two distinct points on l, then there is a unique coordinate system on l relative to $\{A,B\}$, such that its origin is P and the coordinate of Q is positive.

Comment. This postulate implies that a line contains as many points as there are real numbers.

■ **THEOREM 6-1** (Origin and Unit-Point Theorem).—If P and Q are any two distinct points, then there is a unique coordinate system on $\overleftrightarrow{PQ}$ relative to $\{P,Q\}$, such that P is the origin and Q is the unit point of the system. The proof of this theorem follows directly from Postulate 12 (Ruler Postulate) by taking $\{A,B\} = \{P,Q\}$.

■ **THEOREM 6-2** (Two-Coordinate-System Theorem).—Let a line, l, and two coordinate systems on l be given. Then there exist two numbers, a and b $(a \neq 0)$, such that for any point on l with coordinate x in one system and y in the other, $y = ax + b$.

Proof. Let distinct points P and Q on l have coordinates x_1 and x_2 in the first coordinate system, and y_1 and y_2 in the second coordinate system. Let X be any other point of l with coordinate x in the first coordinate system and y in the second.

P	Q	X	
x_1	x_2	x	l
y_1	y_2	y	

A number of cases need to be considered.

To begin with, it may be assumed (without loss of generality) that $x_1 < x_2 < x$. There are six possible inequalities for the y coordinates. Postulate 11 says that if $y_1 < y_2 < y$, then

$$\frac{x - x_2}{y - y_2} = \frac{x - x_1}{y - y_1} = \frac{x_2 - x_1}{y_2 - y_1}.$$

The equality of any two of the three fractions and $x_1 \neq x_2$ imply that

$$y = \frac{y_2 - y_1}{x_2 - x_1},$$
$$x = \frac{x_1 y_2 - x_2 y_1}{x_2 - x_1}.$$

Let $a = (y_2 - y_1)/(x_2 - x_1)$ and $b = (x_1 y_2 - x_2 y_1)/(x_2 - x_1)$, and the theorem for the case $y_1 < y_2 < y$, is proved.

If $y_1 < y < y_2$, then

$$\frac{x - x_2}{y_2 - y} = \frac{x_2 - x_1}{y - y_1} = \frac{x_2 - x_1}{y_2 - y_1}.$$

These equations lead to the result $x = x_2$, which contradicts the assumption $x_2 < x$.

In all the cases to be considered, the outcome, therefore, will be either $y = ax + b$, or a contradiction, such as $x = x_2$, $x = x_1$, or $y = y_1$.

Finally, it is verified that if $x = x_1$, then $y = y_1$; and if $x = x_2$, then $y = y_2$. Therefore, X can be any point on the line l.

Definition. Let P, Q, and R be points on line l and let there be a coordinate system on l that gives P, Q, and R coordinates p, q, and r, respectively. Q is between P and R if, and only if, q is between p and r.

■ THEOREM 6-3.–If P, Q, and R are points on line l and Q is between P and R in one coordinate system on l, then Q will be between P and R in any other coordinate system on l.

Proof. Suppose that the coordinates of P, Q, and R are p, q, and r in the given coordinate system on l. Then, by definition, either $p < q < r$ or $r < q < p$. Let a be any nonzero number. Then by either of the multiplication properties of order, $ap < aq < ar$ or $ar < aq < ap$. Let b be any number. Then, $ap + b < aq + b < ar + b$ or $ar + b < aq + b < ap + b$, proving that Q is between P and R in any other coordinate system, Q.E.D.

The significance of this theorem is that the betweenness relation among these collinear points is independent of the coordinate system on the line and is a property of the points themselves.

Definition. Given two distinct points A and B, the set of points consisting of A, B, X, and Y (such that for all X, X is between A and B, and B is between A and Y) is the ray AB and is denoted $\overrightarrow{AB}$. All other points of $\overleftrightarrow{AB}$ and A form the ray opposite $\overrightarrow{AB}$. A is the *vertex* or *end point* of each of these rays. If the vertex of a ray is deleted from the ray, what is left is a half line with end point A. Rays that have the same vertex are *concurrent rays*.

Definition. The set of points consisting of A, B, and all points between A and B is *segment* AB and is denoted $\overline{AB}$. A and B are the *end points* of $\overline{AB}$ and all its other points are *interior points*.

The length of a segment joining two points is the distance between the two points.

Two segments are congruent to each other if they have the same length. "$\overline{AB}$ is congruent to $\overline{CD}$" is abbreviated as follows: $\overline{AB} \cong \overline{CD}$.

The following are easily proved properties of congruence of line segments.

Reflexive property. For all $\overline{AB}$, $\overline{AB} \cong \overline{AB}$.

Symmetric property. If $\overline{AB} \cong \overline{CD}$, then $\overline{CD} \cong \overline{AB}$.

Transitive property. If $\overline{AB} \cong \overline{CD}$ and $\overline{CD} \cong \overline{EF}$, then $\overline{AB} \cong \overline{EF}$.

■ THEOREM 6-4 (Point-Plotting Theorem).— Given a unit pair $\{A,B\}$, point P, and positive number p, then on any ray with vertex P there is a unique point R such that $PR = p$.

Proof. Let $\overrightarrow{PS}$ be any ray. By Theorem 6-1, there is a unique coordinate system on $\overleftrightarrow{PS}$ such that P is the origin and S is the unit point. By Postulate 11,

$$\frac{PS \text{ (relative to } \{P,S\})}{PS \text{ (relative to } \{A,B\})} = k.$$

In this coordinate system kp determines point R such that PR (relative to $\{A,B\}$) $= p$, Q.E.D.

■ THEOREM 6-5 (Two-Point Theorem).— In a given coordinate system on line l, let x_1 and x_2 be the respective coordinates of given distinct points x_1 and x_2 on l. Then if x is the coordinate of

any point X on l, the number k can be found such that $x = x_1 + k(x_2 - x_1)$.

X_1	X_2	X	
x_1	x_2	x	l
0	1	k	

Proof. Consider the coordinate system on l that assigns 0 to X_1 and 1 to X_2, and let k be the number assigned to X in this system. By Theorem 6–2 (Two-Coordinate-System Theorem), $x = ak + b$, where a and b are to be found. At point X_1, $x_1 = a \cdot 0 + b$, or $b = x_1$. At point X_2, $x_2 = a \cdot 1 + x_1$, or $a = x_2 - x_1$. Therefore, at X, $x = (x_2 - x_1)k + x_1$, or $x_1 + k(x_2 - x_1)$, Q.E.D.

Definition. The midpoint of a segment $\overline{AB}$ is a point X such that it is a point on $\overline{AB}$ and such that $\overline{AX} \cong \overline{XB}$.

■ THEOREM 6-6.–The midpoint of a segment is unique. This can be proved by taking $k = l/2$ in Theorem 6-5 (Two-Point Theorem). If the endpoints of a segment are x_1 and x_2, the coordinate of the midpoint is $(x_1 + x_2)/2$.

■ THEOREM 6-7 (Betweenness-Distance Theorem).—Let A, B, and C be three points such that B is between A and C. Then $AB + BC = AC$ for any given unit pair. Or, $AB = AC - BC$ or $BC = AC - AB$.

Proof. By Postulate 12 (Ruler Postulate), take the coordinate system with A as the origin and to C assign a positive number, c. Let the number assigned to B be b. Then $0 < b < c$. Since $AB = b$, $BC = c - b$, and $AC = c$, it follows that $AB + BC = AC$. However, no reference was made to a specific unit pair, so the proof applies to any unit pair, Q.E.D.

Comment. This theorem served as part of the basis for David Hilbert's (1862–1943) development of *betweenness relations for points*.

SECTION SEVEN

Angles.—To prepare for a study of angles, *separation principles* must be considered.

Definition. A set containing more than one point is a *convex set* if, and only if, the segment joining any two of its points contains only points of the set.

Example. A segment is a convex set, but the set consisting of one exterior point of a segment and the segment is not.

■ THEOREM 7-1.—The intersection of any two convex sets is a convex set.

Proof. The intersection of any two sets contains only elements that belong to both sets. Consider any two points, A and B, in the intersection. Because A and B are members of both convex sets, $\overline{AB}$ also belongs to both and hence is contained in the intersection, Q.E.D.

Postulate 13 (Plane-Separation Postulate).—For any plane and any line in that plane, the points of the plane that are not contained in the line form two sets, each of which is convex; and every segment that joins a point of one set to a point of the other intersects the given line.

Definition. Each of the convex sets in Postulate 13 is a *half plane*. The line separates the plane into two opposite half planes, and is the *edge of each half plane*. If a half plane has edge l and contains point P, it is the *P side of l*.

■ THEOREM 7-2.–If a ray intersects a line only in its end point, then the interior of the ray is contained in one of the half planes whose edge is the given line.

Postulate 14.—For any plane, the points of space that do not lie in that plane form two convex sets such that every segment that joins a point of one set to a point of the other set intersects the given plane.

Definition. An *angle* is the set of points contained in two concurrent, noncollinear rays. (Two collinear rays form either a *zero angle* or a *straight angle*, neither of which is included in this definition. They are omitted in order to simplify the mathematical notion of the interior of an angle.) The rays are the *sides of the angle*, and the common vertex of the rays is the *vertex of the angle*.

Notation. The angle formed by $\overrightarrow{VA}$ and $\overrightarrow{VB}$ is named $\angle AVB$. The vertex of the angle appears in the middle. If it is not ambiguous, the angle may also be called $\angle V$.

Comment. $\angle AVB = \angle BVA$ because they consist of the same set of points and hence name the same subject.

Comment. To some extent, the method of constructing a measure for abstract (mathematical) angles is similar to that of constructing a measure for the distance between two points.

Postulate 15.—There exists a correspondence that associates each angle in space with a unique number between 0 and 180.

Definition. The number in Postulate 15 is the *measure of the angle*.

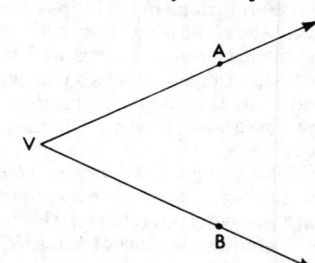

Notation. The measure of $\angle ABC$ is denoted: $m \angle ABC$.

Definition. Let V be any point in a plane. A *ray coordinate system* in that plane, relative to V, is the one-to-one correspondence between all the rays in the plane with vertex V, and the set of all numbers x such that $0 < x < 360$ with the following properties: If numbers r and s correspond to $\overrightarrow{VR}$ and $\overrightarrow{VS}$ in the plane, and if $r > s$ then, $m \angle RVS = r - s$, if $r - s < 180$. $m \angle RVS = 360 - (r - s)$, if $r - s > 180$. $\overrightarrow{VR}$ and $\overrightarrow{VS}$ are opposite rays if, and only if, $r - s = 180$.

Postulate 16 (Protractor Postulate).—If $\overrightarrow{VA}$ and $\overrightarrow{VS}$ are noncollinear rays in a plane, then there is a unique ray coordinate system in the plane relative to V such that $\overrightarrow{VA}$ corresponds to zero, and every ray in the B side of $\overleftrightarrow{VA}$ corresponds to a number less than 180.

■ **THEOREM 7–3** (Angle Construction Theorem).—Given a half plane with edge $\overleftrightarrow{VA}$ and a number r, such that $0 < r < 180$, there is then a unique ray $\overrightarrow{VR}$ such that $\overrightarrow{VR}$ is in the given half plane and $m\angle AVR = r$.

Definition. Given three concurrent rays in a plane—$\overrightarrow{VA}$, $\overrightarrow{VB}$, and $\overrightarrow{VC}$—$\overrightarrow{VB}$ is said to be *between* $\overrightarrow{VA}$ and $\overrightarrow{VC}$ if, and only if, there is a ray coordinate system in the plane relative to V, such that the respective ray coordinates, 0, b, and c of $\overrightarrow{VA}$, $\overrightarrow{VB}$, and $\overrightarrow{VC}$, are such that $b < c$.

■ **THEOREM 7–4** (Betweenness-Angles Theorem).—If $\overrightarrow{VB}$ is between $\overrightarrow{VA}$ and $\overrightarrow{VC}$, then $m\angle AVB + m\angle BVC = m\angle AVC$. This may also be expressed: $m\angle AVC - m\angle AVB = m\angle BVC$.

Definition. A ray is the *midray of an angle* if the ray is between the sides of the angle and forms with them two angles of equal measure.

■ **THEOREM 7–5.**—Every angle has a unique midray.

Definition. The midray of an angle bisects the angle and is called the *angle bisector.*

The *interior of an angle* may be described in any one of the following ways:

(1) The interior of $\angle AVB$ is the set of rays between $\overrightarrow{VA}$ and $\overrightarrow{VB}$ if V is deleted from the set. This is set R.

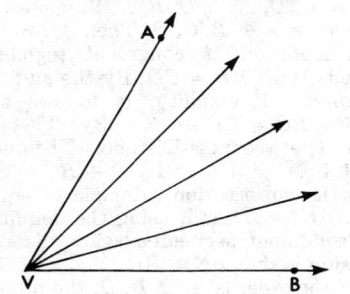

(2) The interior of $\angle AVB$ is the intersection of two half planes: the A side of $\overleftrightarrow{VB}$ and the B side of $\overleftrightarrow{VA}$. This is set I.

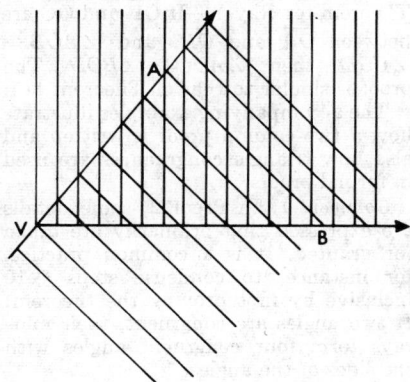

(3) The set of interior points of all segments that have one end point in $\overrightarrow{VA}$ and the other in $\overrightarrow{VB}$, with V deleted from this set, is set S.

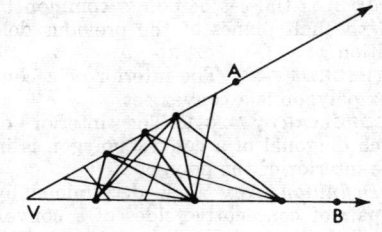

Postulate 17.—Sets R and I described above are equal and contain set S.

■ **THEOREM 7–6.**—The interior of any angle is a convex set.

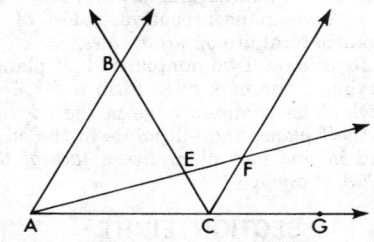

■ **THEOREM 7–7.**—Let A, B, C, E, F, and G be *coplanar points* such that A, B, and C are noncollinear, E is between B and C, $\overrightarrow{EF}$ and $\overrightarrow{EA}$ are opposite rays, and $\overrightarrow{CA}$ and $\overrightarrow{CG}$ are opposite rays. Then $\overrightarrow{CF}$ is between $\overrightarrow{CB}$ and $\overrightarrow{CG}$.

Comment. The proof depends upon establishing that F is on the B side of $\overleftrightarrow{CG}$ and also on the G side of $\overleftrightarrow{BC}$, and is therefore an interior point of $\angle BCG$. Then $\overrightarrow{CF}$ is between $\overrightarrow{CB}$ and $\overrightarrow{CG}$.

Definition. The *exterior of an angle* is the set of all points in the plane of the angle that are contained neither in the angle nor in its interior.

Definition. The two angles formed by three concurrent rays, two of which are opposite rays, are a *linear pair of angles*.

■ **THEOREM 7–8.**—The sum of the measures of the angles in a linear pair is 180.

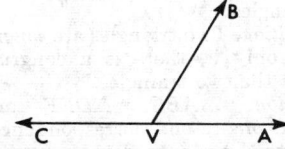

Proof. Suppose the opposite rays are $\overrightarrow{VA}$ and $\overrightarrow{VC}$, and the third ray is $\overrightarrow{VB}$. By Postulate 16 (Protractor Postulate), there is a ray-coordinate system in which $\overrightarrow{VA}$ corresponds to 0, $\overrightarrow{VC}$ corresponds to 180, and $\overrightarrow{VB}$ corresponds to a number, b, between 0 and 180. Therefore, $m\angle AVB = b$, $m\angle BVC = 180 - b$, and $m\angle AVB + m\angle BVC = 180$, Q.E.D.

■ **COROLLARY 7–8–1.**—If $\overrightarrow{OA}$ and $\overrightarrow{OB}$ are opposite rays, and $\overrightarrow{OC}$ and $\overrightarrow{OD}$ are in the same half plane with edge $\overleftrightarrow{AB}$ such that $\overrightarrow{OC}$ is between $\overrightarrow{OD}$ and $\overrightarrow{OA}$, then $m\angle AOC + m\angle COD + m\angle DOB = 180$.

Definition. Two coplanar angles are a pair of *adjacent angles* if, and only if, they have one side in common and their interiors have no points in common.

Comment. A *linear pair* of angles is also a pair of adjacent angles.

■ **THEOREM 7–9.**—If the sum of the measures of two adjacent angles is 180, they are a linear pair of angles.

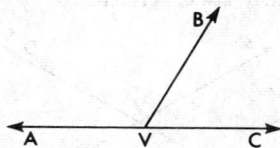

Proof. Let the two adjacent angles be $\angle AVB$ and $\angle BVC$. By Postulate 16 (Protractor Postulate), there is a ray coordinate system that assigns 0 to $\overrightarrow{VB}$, a to $\overrightarrow{VA}$ and c to $\overrightarrow{VC}$. Since $\overrightarrow{VB}$ intersects $\overleftrightarrow{AC}$, A and C are in opposite half planes with edge $\overleftrightarrow{VB}$; either a or c is less than 180, and the other is more than 180. If $a < 180$, then $m\angle BVA = a$, and $m\angle BVC = 360 - c$. By hypothesis, $a + 360 - c = 180$, or $c - a = 180$. Therefore, $\overrightarrow{VA}$ and $\overrightarrow{VC}$ are opposite rays, Q.E.D.

Definitions. An angle whose measure is 90 is a *right angle.* An angle whose measure is less than 90 is an *acute angle.* An angle whose measure is greater than 90 is an *obtuse angle.*

■ **THEOREM 7–10.**—If the measures of two angles in a linear pair are equal, then each angle is a right angle.

Definition. The lines determined by two rays that are sides of a right angle are *perpendicular.* If two rays or two segments determine perpendicular lines, they are *perpendicular rays*, or *perpendicular segments.*

Notation. $\overleftrightarrow{AB}$ is perpendicular to $\overleftrightarrow{BC}$ is written: $\overleftrightarrow{AB} \perp \overleftrightarrow{CD}$.

Definition. Two angles that have the same measure are *congruent* to each other.

Notation. $\angle ABC$ is congruent to $\angle DEF$ is written: $\angle ABC \cong \angle DEF$.

The properties of congruence of angles are as follows:

Reflexive property. For all $\angle A$, $\angle A \cong \angle A$.

Symmetric property. If $\angle A \cong \angle B$, then $\angle B \cong \angle A$.

Transitive property. If $\angle A \cong \angle B$ and $\angle B \cong \angle C$, then $\angle A \cong \angle C$.

■ **THEOREM 7–11.**—If two angles are right angles, they are congruent to each other.

Definitions. If the sum of the measures of two angles is 180, they are a pair of *supplementary angles*, and each is said to be the *supplement* of the other. If the sum of the measures of two angles is 90, they are a pair of *complementary angles*, and each is said to be the *complement* of the other.

■ **THEOREM 7–12.**—The two angles in a linear pair are supplementary angles.

■ **THEOREM 7–13.**—If two angles are congruent and supplementary, then each is a right angle.

■ **THEOREM 7–14.**—Supplements of congruent angles are congruent to each other.

■ THEOREM 7–15.—Complements of congruent angles are congruent to each other.

Definition. If the sides of two angles form two pairs of opposite rays, they are a pair of *vertical angles.*

■ THEOREM 7–16.–If two angles are vertical, they are congruent.

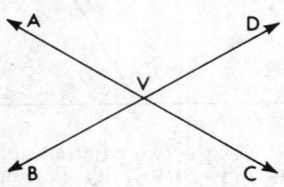

Proof. Let the angles be $\angle AVB$ and $\angle DVC$, with opposite rays $\vec{VA}$ and $\vec{VC}$, and $\vec{VB}$ and $\vec{VD}$. Since $\angle BVA$ and $\angle AVD$ are a linear pair, they are supplementary. In like manner $\angle AVD$ and $\angle DVC$ are supplementary. Therefore, $\angle BVA$ and $\angle DVC$ are congruent, Q.E.D.

Comment. If two lines intersect, they form two pairs of vertical angles.

■ THEOREM 7–17.–If two intersecting lines are perpendicular, they form four right angles.

■ THEOREM 7–18.–Given a line in a plane and a point on the line, then there is one, and only one, line in the plane perpendicular to the given line containing the given point.

Comment. The proof of this theorem depends on Theorem 7–3 (Angle-Construction Theorem) and Theorem 7–17.

Definition. If three points are noncollinear, the set of points in the three segments determined by them is a *triangle.* Each of the three given points is a *vertex of the triangle,* and each segment is a *side of the triangle.*

Notation. If the three given points are A, B, and C, the triangle is denoted $\triangle ABC$; the sides are denoted $\overline{AB}$, $\overline{BC}$, $\overline{CA}$.

Definition. In $\triangle ABC$, $\angle ABC$, $\angle BCA$, and $\angle CAB$ are angles of $\triangle ABC$. A side of a triangle and the angle whose vertex is not a point of that side are *opposite* each other.

Definition. The set of points common to the interiors of the three angles of a triangle is the *interior of the triangle.*

■ THEOREM 7–19.–The interior of a triangle is a convex set.

Definition. Let A, B, C, and D be given coplanar points such that no three are collinear and $\overline{AB}$, $\overline{BC}$, $\overline{CD}$, and $\overline{DA}$ do not intersect each other in interior points. The set of points contained in the four segments is a *quadrilateral;* each of the given points is a *vertex of the quadrilateral;* each segment is a *side of the quadrilateral;* and a segment joining two nonconsecutive vertices is a *diagonal of the quadrilateral.*

Notation. The quadrilateral defined above is denoted, quadrilateral $ABCD$.

Definition. A *polygon* is a convex poly-

gon if, and only if, each side lies in the edge of a half plane that contains the rest of the polygon.

Definition. The *interior of a convex polygon* is the set of points common to all the half planes of the previous definition.

■ THEOREM 7–20.–The interior of a convex polygon is a convex set.

● COROLLARY 7–20–1.–The interior of each diagonal of a convex polygon is in the interior of the polygon.

Definition. Any angle determined by a pair of consecutive sides of a convex polygon is an *angle of the polygon.* Two angles having consecutive vertices of the polygon are *consecutive angles of the polygon.*

Definition. Two nonconsecutive angles of a quadrilateral are *opposite angles.* Two nonconsecutive sides of a quadrilateral are *opposite sides.*

Definition. Two nonplanar half planes having a common edge form a *dihedral angle.* The common edge is the *edge of the half plane,* and all points in the edge and in one half plane are a *face of the dihedral angle.*

SECTION EIGHT

Congruences.—In the physical world, two objects are congruent if they have the same shape and size. The congruence of two physical objects can sometimes be demonstrated by noting how corresponding parts fit each other.

In theoretical geometry there is also a concern with one-to-one correspondences, and congruence between two triangles is considered to be a property of a correspondence between their vertices.

Definition. If the vertices of $\triangle ABC$ and the vertices of $\triangle DEF$ are made to correspond A to D, B to E, and C to F, then the *corresponding parts* of the triangles are, in pairs, $\angle A$ and $\angle D$, $\angle B$ and $\angle E$, $\angle C$ and $\angle F$, $\overline{AB}$ and $\overline{DE}$, $\overline{BC}$ and $\overline{EF}$, and $\overline{CA}$ and $\overline{FD}$.

Definition. A one-to-one correspondence between the vertices of two triangles, in which corresponding parts are congruent, is a *congruence* between the two triangles.

Definition. Two triangles are *congruent* if, and only if, there is a congruence between the two triangles.

Notation. $\triangle ABC \cong \triangle DEF$ means that the one-to-one correspondence, A to D, B to E, and C to F, is a congruence.

Properties of Triangle Congruence.—These are consequences of the definition of congruent triangles:

Reflexive property. For all $\triangle ABC$, $\triangle ABC \cong \triangle ABC$.

Symmetric property. If $\triangle ABC \cong \triangle DEF$, then $\triangle DEF \cong \triangle ABC$.

Transitive property. If $\triangle ABC \cong \triangle DEF$ and $\triangle DEF \cong \triangle GHI$, then $\triangle ABC \cong \triangle GHI$.

Definition. An angle of a triangle is said to be *included* between the two sides of the triangle that are contained in the rays of the angle. A side of a triangle is said to be *included* between

two angles of the triangle if its end points are vertices of the angles.

Notation. "Two sides and their included angle of a triangle" is abbreviated S.A.S. "Two angles and their included side" is abbreviated A.S.A. "The three sides of a triangle" is abbreviated S.S.S. "The three angles of a triangle" is abbreviated A.A.A.

Postulate 18 (S.A.S. Postulate).—Given a one-to-one correspondence between the vertices of two triangles (not necessarily distinct), if two sides and the included angle of one triangle are congruent to the corresponding parts of the other triangle, then the correspondence is a congruence.

Postulate 19 (A.S.A. Postulate).—Given a one-to-one correspondence between the vertices of two triangles (not necessarily distinct), if two angles and the included side of one triangle are congruent to the corresponding parts of the other triangle, then the correspondence is a congruence.

Postulate 20 (S.S.S. Postulate).—Given a one-to-one correspondence between the vertices of two triangles (not necessarily distinct), if the three sides of one triangle are congruent to the three sides of the other triangle, then the correspondence is a congruence.

Comment. Postulates 19 and 20 can be deduced as a logical sequence from Postulate 18 and previous postulates. Some schools postulate them.

■ THEOREM 8–1 (Betweenness-Addition Theorem for Points).—If points B and C are between A and D, and if $\overline{AB} \cong \overline{CD}$, then $\overline{AC} \cong \overline{BD}$.

Proof. The order of points might be A, B, C, D, or A, C, B, D. Suppose that the order is A, B, C, D. Then $\overline{AB} \cong \overline{CD}$, by definition of congruent segments, implies that $\overline{AB} = \overline{CD}$. By the addition property of equality, it follows that $\overline{AB} + \overline{BC} = \overline{CD} + \overline{BC}$. By Theorem 6–7 (Betweenness-Distance Theorem), $\overline{AB} + \overline{BC} = \overline{AC}$, and $\overline{CD} + \overline{BC} = \overline{BD}$. By the substitution principle of equality, $\overline{AC} = \overline{BD}$ and, using the definition of congruent segments, again the conclusion is that $\overline{AC} \cong \overline{BD}$.

If the order is A, C, B, D, the proof is the same, with the modification that $\overline{AB} - \overline{BC} = \overline{CD} - \overline{BD}$; but all reasons remain unchanged.

■ THEOREM 8–2 (Betweenness-Addition Theorem for Rays).—If $\vec{OB}$ and $\vec{OC}$ are between $\vec{OA}$ and $\vec{OD}$, and $\angle AOB \cong \angle COD$, then $\angle AOC \cong \angle BOD$. The proof is similar to that of Theorem 8–1.

The accompanying examples illustrate how a two-column proof is written and also how triangle congruences are used in formal proofs.

Comment 1. In Proof 2, some details are expressed that ordinarily are taken for granted. It is a common practice, for instance, to condense steps 7–10 inclusive by first proving the theorem: If two angles are congruent, their midrays form four congruent angles with the sides of the angles.

Two-Column Proofs

Proof 1.

Hypothesis: *P, Q, R, S* are collinear in that order, with $PQ \cong RS$. *A* and *B* are on opposite sides of *PS*. $PA \cong SB$ and $RA \cong QB$.
Conclusion:
$\angle PAR \cong \angle SBQ$.

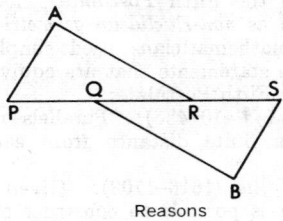

Statements

1. *Q* and *R* are between *P* and *S*.
2. $PQ \cong RS$.
3. $PR \cong QS$.
4. $PA \cong SB$ and $RA \cong QB$.
5. $\triangle PAR \cong \triangle SBQ$.
6. $\angle PAR \cong \angle SBQ$, Q.E.D.

Reasons

Hypothesis.
Hypothesis.
Betweenness-Addition Theorem for points.
Hypothesis.
S.S.S. Postulate.
Definition of congruent triangles.

Proof 2.

Hypothesis: *A, B, C, D* are collinear points, in that order. *E* is not in *AD*. *F* is between *E* and *B*, and *G* is between *E* and *C*, such that *CF* is the midray of $\angle ECB$, and *BG* is the midray of $\angle EBC$. $\angle ABE \cong \angle DCE$. Conclusion: $CF \cong BG$.

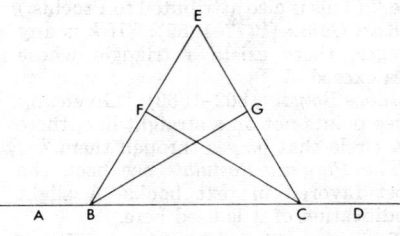

Statements

1. *A, B, C, D* are collinear, in that order.
2. $\angle ABE$ and $\angle EBC$ are a linear pair. Also, $\angle DCE$ and $\angle ECB$ are a linear pair.
3. $\angle EBC$ is the supplement of $\angle ABE$; $\angle ECB$ is the supplement of $\angle DCE$.
4. $\angle ABE \cong \angle DEC$.
5. $\angle EBC \cong \angle ECB$.
6. $BC \cong CB$.
7. *CF* is the midray of $\angle ECB$; *BG* is the midray of $\angle EBC$.
8. $m\angle FCB = \frac{1}{2}m\angle ECB$; $m\angle GBC = \frac{1}{2}m\angle EBC$.
9. $m\angle FCB = m\angle GBC$.
10. $\angle FCB \cong \angle GBC$.
11. $\triangle FBC \cong \triangle GCB$.
12. $CF \cong BG$, Q.E.D.

Reasons

Hypothesis.
Definition of a linear pair.

If two angles form a linear pair, they are supplementary.
Hypothesis.
If two angles are congruent, their supplements are congruent.
Reflexive property of congruence of segments.
Hypothesis.

Definition of a midray.

Multiplication property of equality of numbers.
If two angles have equal measures, they are congruent.
A.S.A. Postulate.
If two triangles are congruent, their corresponding parts are congruent.

Proof 3.

Hypothesis: In $\triangle ABC$, $AB \cong AC$.
Conclusion: $\angle B \cong \angle C$.

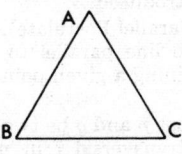

Statements

1. $AB \cong AC$.
2. $BC \cong CB$.
3. $CA \cong BA$.
4. $\triangle ABC \cong \triangle ACB$.
5. $\angle B \cong \angle C$, Q.E.D.

Reasons

Hypothesis.
Reflexive property of congruence.
Symmetric property of congruence.
S.S.S. Postulate.
If triangles are congruent, corresponding parts are congruent.

Comment 2. It is possible to read this proof without referring to the figure, if it is kept in mind that *A* corresponds with *D*, *B* with *C*, *F* with *G*, and *E* with itself. The beginning student of geometry will find this a valuable exercise.

Definition. A triangle is called *isosceles* if two of its sides are congruent. In an isosceles triangle, the congruent sides are *arms* (or *legs*); the third side is the *base*. The angle included between the arms is the *vertex angle*. The angles that include the base are the *base angles*.

■ THEOREM 8–3.–If a triangle is isosceles, then its base angles are congruent.

Proof. Let the triangle be $\triangle ABC$, with $\overline{AB} \cong \overline{AC}$. Considering $\triangle ABC$ and $\triangle ACB$, refer to Proof 3.

Definition. A triangle is *equilateral* if its three sides are congruent to each other. A triangle is *equiangular* if its three angles are congruent to each other.

■ COROLLARY 8–3–1.–If a triangle is equilateral, it is equiangular.

■ THEOREM 8–4 (Converse of Theorem 8–3).–If two angles of a triangle are congruent, then the sides opposite these angles are congruent.

Comment. The proof of this theorem is similar to that of Theorem 8–3.

■ COROLLARY 8–4–1.–If a triangle is equiangular, then it is equilateral.

Example. How Theorem 8–3 and Theorem 8–4 can be used.

To Prove. If in $\triangle ABC$, $\overline{AB} \cong \overline{AC}$, *E* is between *A* and *B*, *F* is between *A* and *C*, $\overrightarrow{CE}$ is the midray of $\angle ACB$, $\overrightarrow{BF}$ is the midray of $\angle ABC$, and *CE* and *BF* intersect in *G*, then $\overline{CG} \cong \overline{BG}$.

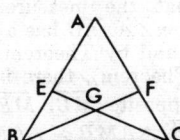

Proof. By Theorem 8–3 and the hypothesis that $\overline{AB} \cong \overline{AC}$, it follows that $\angle ACB \cong \angle ABC$. From the hypothesis that $\overrightarrow{CE}$ is the midray of $\angle ACB$ and that $\overrightarrow{BF}$ is the midray of $\angle ABC$, and from the multiplication property of equality, it follows that $\angle ECB \cong \angle FCB$. By Theorem 8–4, it follows that $\overline{BG} \cong \overline{CG}$, Q.E.D.

Comment. Little attention was given to the statement that if $\angle ACB \cong \angle ABC$, then $m\angle ACB = m\angle ABC$; also, if $m\angle ECB = m\angle FBC$, then $\angle ECB \cong \angle FBC$. Both of these follow from the definition of congruent angles. It is common practice to make this kind of omission.

Definition. A *median of a triangle* is a segment whose end points are a vertex of the triangle and the midpoint of the opposite side.

■ THEOREM 8–5.–The median to the base of an isosceles triangle bisects the vertex angle and is perpendicular to the base.

Proof. If in $\triangle ABC$, $\overline{AB} = \overline{AC}$, and *D* is the midpoint of $\overline{BC}$, it follows from Postulate 20 (S.S.S. Postulate) that $\triangle ADB \cong \triangle ADC$. This leads to the conclusion that $\angle BAD \cong \angle CAD$, Q.E.D. It also follows that $\angle ADB \cong \angle ADC$.

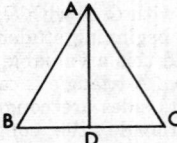

Since the latter pair of angles is a linear pair, they are right angles and $\overline{AD} \perp \overline{BC}$, Q.E.D.

■ THEOREM 8-6.—The bisector of the vertex angle of an isosceles triangle bisects the base and is perpendicular to the base.

Definitions. Each angle of a triangle is an *interior angle of the triangle.* An angle that forms a linear pair with an interior angle of a triangle is an *exterior angle of the triangle.* Each exterior angle is *adjacent* to the interior angle with which it forms a linear pair, and *remote* to the other interior angles of the triangle.

■ THEOREM 8-7.—The measure of an exterior angle is greater than the measure of either of its remote interior angles.

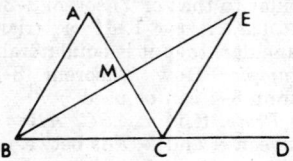

Proof. Let the triangle be $\triangle ABC$. Consider one case in which it is to be proved that the measure of exterior $\angle ACD > m\angle A$. $\overline{AC}$ has a unique midpoint, M, and by Theorem 6-4 (Point-Plotting Theorem), there is a point on the ray opposite $\overrightarrow{MB}$, $\overrightarrow{ME}$, such that $\overrightarrow{ME} = \overrightarrow{MB}$. $\triangle AMB \cong \triangle CME$ (S.A.S.). By Theorem 7-7, $\overrightarrow{CE}$ is between $\overrightarrow{CA}$ and $\overrightarrow{CD}$. This implies that $m\angle ACD > m\angle ACE$. Since $m\angle ACE = m\angle A$, $m\angle ACD > m\angle A$. Other cases are similarly proved, Q.E.D.

■ THEOREM 8-8.—Given a line and a point not on the line, then there is only one line that contains the point and is perpendicular to the given line.

Proof. If there were two perpendiculars, there would be a contradiction of Theorem 8-7, Q.E.D.

SECTION NINE

Parallel Lines.—A formal treatment of parallel lines requires a postulate concerning their existence. Euclid used one known today as the *Fifth Postulate,* or *Euclid's Parallel Postulate:*

"If a straight line falling on two straight lines makes the interior angles on the same side less than two right angles, the two straight lines, if produced indefinitely, meet on that side on which are the angles less than two right angles."

The complexity of this statement suggested to many mathematicians that it

could be shown to be a logical consequence of Euclid's other postulates. This effort, over many centuries, led to the discovery of geometries that were based on postulates, one of which was contradictory to the Fifth Postulate. These are known as *non-Euclidean geometries.*

Other mathematicians used simpler alternative statements that are equivalent to the Fifth Postulate:

Proclus (c. 410–485): "Parallels remain at a finite distance from each other."

John Wallis (1616–1703): "Given a triangle, it is possible to construct another triangle similar to it."

Adrien Legendre (1752–c. 1833): "The sum of the three angles of a triangle is two right angles."

John Playfair (1748–1819): "Through a given point, not on a given line, only one parallel can be drawn to the given line." (This is also attributed to Proclus.)

Karl Gauss (1777–1855): "If k is any integer, there exists a triangle whose area exceeds k."

János Bolyai (1802–1860): "Given any three points not on a straight line, there is a circle that passes through them."

The *Playfair Postulate* has been the most favored in text books. A slight modification of it is used here.

Definition. Two lines are *parallel* if they are coplanar and do not intersect.

Notation. The statement "$\overleftrightarrow{AB}$ is parallel to $\overleftrightarrow{CD}$" is abbreviated $\overleftrightarrow{AB} \parallel \overleftrightarrow{CD}$.

Definition. Given two distinct coplanar lines, a line that intersects them in two distinct points is a *transversal* of the two lines.

■ THEOREM 9-1.—If a transversal is a perpendicular to each of two lines, then the lines are parallel.

Proof. Let the lines be p and q; the transversal, s. If p and q are not parallel, they meet at a point from which two perpendiculars to s exist. This contradicts Theorem 8-8, Q.E.D.

Comment. The significance of this theorem lies in the conclusion that through a given point not on a line, there exists at least one line containing the point and parallel to the line. But it does not permit the conclusion that this parallel is unique. To accomplish this, a postulate is introduced.

Postulate 21 (Parallel Postulate).—There is at most one line parallel to a given line and containing a given point not on the given line.

Definition. Let p and q be two distinct lines cut by transversal t in points P and Q, respectively. Let A and B be points of p and q, respectively, in opposite half planes having edge t. Then $\angle APQ$ and $\angle BQP$ are a *pair of alternate interior angles.*

If two angles are a pair of alternate interior angles, then each of these angles and the vertical angle of the other are a *pair of corresponding angles.*

Let p and q be two distinct lines cut by a transversal t in points P and Q, respectively. Let C and B be points of

KARL FRIEDRICH GAUSS, German mathematician, founded the modern theory of numbers and also worked in geometry.

p and q, respectively, in the same half plane with edge t. Then $\angle CPQ$ and $\angle BQP$ are a *pair of consecutive interior angles.*

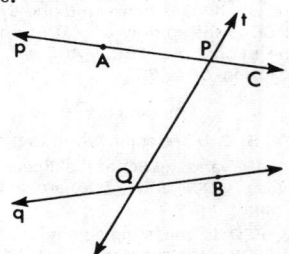

■ THEOREM 9-2.—If a transversal of two coplanar lines forms a pair of congruent alternate interior angles, then the lines are parallel.

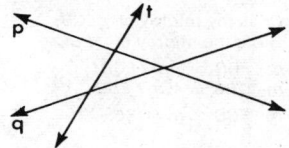

Proof. Let the lines be p and q and the transversal t. Using the indirect method of proof, start with the assumption that p and q intersect, thus determining a triangle with t. But by Theorem 8-7, this implies that the alternate interior angles have unequal measures. Therefore, $p \parallel q$, Q.E.D.

■ COROLLARY 9-2-1.—If a transversal of two coplanar lines forms a pair of congruent corresponding angles, then the lines are parallel.

■ COROLLARY 9-2-2.—If a transversal of two coplanar lines forms a pair of consecutive interior angles that are supplementary, then the lines are parallel.

■ THEOREM 9-3.—If two lines are parallel, then any transversal of these two lines forms a *pair of congruent alternate interior angles.*

Proof. Let the parallel lines be p and q, and let the transversal t intersect p and q in P and Q, respectively. Take A

NEW YORK PUBLIC LIBRARY
EARLY EUROPEAN MATHEMATICIANS. John Wallis (1616–1703) (*left*), English geometry professor, laid the groundwork for calculus. Adrien Legendre (1752–c. 1833) (*center*) contributed to the theory of ellipsoids. John Playfair (1748–1819) (*right*) wrote *Elements of Geometry*.

and *B* on opposite sides of *t* so that $\angle APQ$ and $\angle BQP$ are a pair of alternate interior angles. By Postulate 16

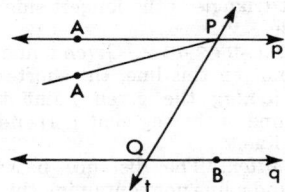

(Protractor Postulate), there is a point *A′* on the *A* side of *t* such that $m \angle A'PQ = m \angle BQP$. Then $\overrightarrow{PA'} \parallel q$, by Theorem 9–2. But Postulate 21 (Parallel Postulate) states that there is at most one parallel to *q* containing *P*. Therefore $\overrightarrow{PA'} = \overrightarrow{PA}$, and $m \angle APQ = m \angle A'PQ = m \angle BQP$, Q.E.D.

■ COROLLARY 9–3–1.–If two lines are parallel, then any transversal of these lines forms with them a *pair of congruent corresponding angles*.

■ COROLLARY 9–3–2.–If two lines are parallel, then any transversal of these lines forms with them a *pair of consecutive interior angles* that are supplementary.

■ COROLLARY 9–3–3.–If two lines are parallel, any transversal of these lines that is perpendicular to one is perpendicular to the others.

■ THEOREM 9–4.–If each of two coplanar lines is parallel to the same third line, then they are parallel to each other.

Proof. If the two coplanar lines intersect, there will be two intersecting lines parallel to the third line—a contradiction of Postulate 21 (Parallel Postulate). Therefore, they do not intersect and, being coplanar, they are parallel, Q.E.D.

Comment. This theorem includes a case of three lines not in one plane.

Comment. The relationship of parallelism for lines in a plane has the symmetric and transitive properties. If the definition of parallel lines were to include the case of a line being parallel to itself, the relationship would have the reflexive property as well.

■ COROLLARY 9–4–1.–If a line that is coplanar with two parallel lines intersects one, it also intersects the other.

■ COROLLARY 9–4–2.–Given two sets of parallel lines in a plane such that a line of one set is perpendicular to a line of the second set, then every line in one set is perpendicular to every line in the second set.

Definition. Two segments are *parallel segments* if, and only if, they lie in parallel lines.

Definition. A quadrilateral is a *parallelogram* if each of its sides is parallel to the side opposite it.

Notation. Parallelogram *ABCD* is written: $\square ABCD$.

Comment. In $\square ABCD$, $\overline{AB} \parallel \overline{CD}$, $\overline{BC} \parallel \overline{DA}$.

■ THEOREM 9–5.–In any parallelogram, each side is congruent to the side opposite it.

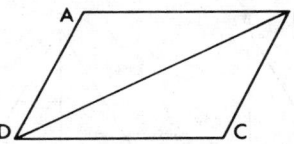

Proof. By Theorem 9–3, $\angle ABD \cong \angle CDB$, $\angle ADB \cong \angle CBD$. Since $\overline{BD} \cong \overline{DB}$, $\triangle ABD \cong \triangle CDB$, leading to the conclusion that $\overline{AB} \cong \overline{CD}$, and $\overline{AD} \cong \overline{CB}$, Q.E.D.

■ COROLLARY 9–5–1.–The diagonal of a parallelogram forms two congruent triangles with the sides of the parallelogram.

■ COROLLARY 9–5–2.–In any parallelogram, each angle is congruent to its opposite and supplementary to its adjacent angle.

■ COROLLARY 9–5–3.–Given two parallel lines, then segments that have their end points in the given lines and are perpendicular to them have the same length.

Definition. The length of any segment in Collary 9–5–3 is the distance between the two parallel lines.

Comment. Corollary 9–5–3 is sometimes phrased, "Parallel lines are everywhere equidistant."

■ THEOREM 9–6 (Converse of Theorem 9–5).–If each side of a quadrilateral is congruent to the side opposite it, then the quadrilateral is a parallelogram.

Proof. Let the quadrilateral be *ABCD*. Then by Postulate 20 (S.S.S. Postulate) $\triangle ABD \cong \triangle CDB$, $\angle ABD \cong \angle CDB$, and $\overline{AB} \parallel \overline{CD}$. Similarly, $\overline{AD} \parallel \overline{CB}$, Q.E.D.

Comment. Theorems 9–5 and 9–6 can be stated as one theorem as follows: A quadrilateral is a parallelogram if, and only if, each side is congruent to the side opposite.

■ COROLLARY 9–6–1.–If each angle of a quadrilateral is congruent to its opposite angle, then the quadrilateral is a parallelogram.

■ THEOREM 9–7.–If two sides of a quadrilateral are parallel and congruent, then the quadrilateral is a parallelogram.

■ THEOREM 9–8.–The diagonals of a quadrilateral bisect each other if, and only if, the quadrilateral is a parallelogram.

Comment. If the quadrilateral is *ABCD*, then two statements are to be proved: If *ABCD* is a parallelogram, $\overline{AC}$ and $\overline{BD}$ bisect each other. If $\overline{AC}$ and $\overline{BD}$ bisect each other, then *ABCD* is a parallelogram.

Definition. A parallelogram is a *rhombus* if, and only if, it is equilateral.

■ THEOREM 9–9.–A parallelogram is a rhombus if, and only if, each diagonal bisects one of its angles.

■ THEOREM 9–10.–A parallelogram is a rhombus if, and only if, its diagonals are perpendicular to each other.

Definition. A parallelogram is a *rectangle* if, and only if, one of its angles is a right angle.

■ THEOREM 9–11.–A parallelogram is a rectangle if, and only if, it is equiangular.

■ THEOREM 9–12.–A parallelogram is a rectangle if, and only if, its diagonals are congruent.

Definition. A parallelogram is a *square*

if, and only if, it is a rhombus and a rectangle.

Comment. The square has all the properties of rectangles and rhombuses.

Definition. A quadrilateral is a *trapezoid* if, and only if, exactly two of its sides are parallel. The sides that are parallel are its *bases*, and the nonparallel sides are its *arms* (or *legs*). The angles containing a base are a *pair of base angles*.

Definition. A trapezoid is an *isosceles trapezoid* if, and only if, its arms are congruent.

■ THEOREM 9–13.–A trapezoid is an isosceles trapezoid if, and only if, a pair of base angles are congruent.

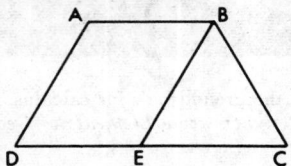

Proof. Let $ABCD$ be the trapezoid with $\overline{AB} \parallel \overline{CD}$. Let E be a point in $\overleftrightarrow{DC}$, such that $\overline{BE} \parallel \overline{AD}$. Then $\overline{AD} \cong \overline{BE}$. If $\overline{AD} \cong \overline{BC}$, then $\overline{BE} \cong \overline{BC}$ and $\angle C \cong \angle BEC \cong \angle D$. If $\angle C \cong \angle D$, then $\angle BEC \cong \angle C$ and $\overline{BC} \cong \overline{BE} \cong \overline{AD}$, Q.E.D.

■ THEOREM 9–14.—A trapezoid is an isosceles trapezoid if, and only if, its diagonals are congruent.

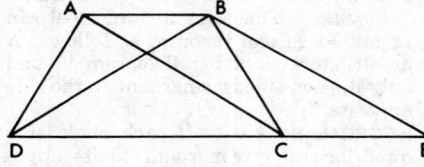

Proof. Let $ABCD$ be the trapezoid with $\overline{AB} \parallel \overline{CD}$. Let E be in $\overleftrightarrow{DC}$ such that $\overline{BE} \parallel \overline{AC}$. Then $\overline{AC} \cong \overline{BE}$. If $\overline{AC} \cong \overline{BD}$, then $\overline{BD} \cong \overline{BE}$, $\angle BDE \cong \angle BED \cong \angle ACD$, $\triangle ACD \cong \triangle BDC$ (S.A.S.), and $\overline{AD} \cong \overline{BC}$. If $\overline{AD} \cong \overline{BC}$, $\angle ADC \cong \angle BCD$, $\triangle ADC \cong \triangle BCD$, and $\overline{AC} \cong \overline{BD}$, Q.E.D.

■ THEOREM 9–15.—The sum of the measures of the angles of a triangle is 180.

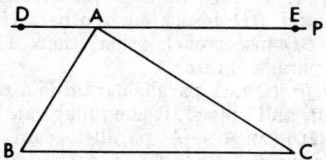

Proof. Let the vertices of the triangle be A, B, and C. There is a unique line p, containing A and parallel to $\overleftrightarrow{BC}$. Let D be a point on p such that D and C are on opposite sides of $\overleftrightarrow{AB}$. Let E be a point on p such that E and B are on opposite sides of $\overleftrightarrow{AC}$. By Corollary 7–8–1, $m\angle DAB + m\angle BAC + m\angle CAE = 180$. By Theorem 9–3, $m\angle DAB = m\angle ABC$, and $m\angle EAC = m\angle ACB$. By the substitution principle, $m\angle ABC + m\angle BAC + m\angle ACB = 180$, Q.E.D.

Comment. In the geometry developed by Nikolai Lobachevsky, this sum is less than 180; in the geometry developed by Bernhard Riemann, it is greater than 180.

■ COROLLARY 9–15–1.–The measure of an exterior angle of a triangle is equal to the sum of the measures of the remote interior angles.

■ COROLLARY 9–15–2.–Given a correspondence between the vertices of two triangles, if two pairs of corresponding angles are congruent, then the third pair of corresponding angles is congruent.

■ COROLLARY 9–15–3.–(S.A.A. Theorem.) Given a correspondence between the vertices of two triangles, if two angles and a side opposite one of them in one triangle are congruent to the corresponding parts of the second triangle, then the correspondence is a congruence.

■ COROLLARY 9–15–4.–The sum of the measures of the angles of a quadrilateral is 360.

Comment. If $ABCD$ is the quadrilateral, then the convexity of the quadrilateral permits the conclusion that $\overrightarrow{AC}$ is between $\overrightarrow{AB}$ and $\overrightarrow{AD}$. This allows the conclusion that $m\angle BAC + m\angle CAD = m\angle BAD$, a key step in the proof of this theorem.

Definition. If one of the angles of a triangle is a right angle, the triangle is a *right triangle*. The side opposite the right angle is the *hypotenuse of the right triangle*. Each of the other two sides is a *leg of the right triangle*.

■ COROLLARY 9–15–5.–The angles of a right triangle that are opposite the legs are complementary.

■ THEOREM 9–16 (Hypotenuse-Leg Theorem).—Given a correspondence between the vertices of two right triangles in which the vertices of the two right angles correspond, if the hypotenuse and leg of one triangle are congruent to the corresponding parts of the other triangle, then the correspondence is a congruence.

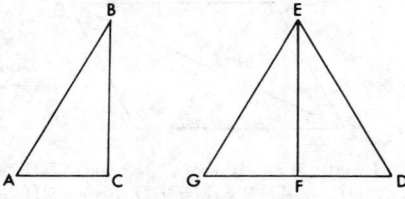

Proof. Let the triangles be $\triangle ABC$ and $\triangle DEF$, with $\angle C$ and $\angle F$ as the right angles. Let $\overline{AB} \cong \overline{DE}$ and $\overline{BC} \cong \overline{EF}$. On the ray opposite $\overrightarrow{FD}$, there is a point G such that $\overline{FG} \cong \overline{CA}$. $\triangle ABC \cong \triangle GEF$ (S.A.S.) and hence, $\angle A \cong \angle G$. But $\overline{GE} \cong \overline{AB} \cong \overline{DE}$. Therefore, $\angle D \cong \angle G \cong \angle A$, and by Corollary 9–15–3 (S.A.A. Theorem), $\triangle ABC \cong \triangle DEF$, Q.E.D.

Definition. If the members of $\{x,y\}$ and $\{x',y'\}$ are numbers such that x corresponds to x', y corresponds to y', and $x > y$, then the numbers of $\{x,y\}$ are unequal in the same order as the corresponding numbers of $\{x',y'\}$ if, and only if, $x' > y'$.

■ THEOREM 9–17.–If the length of two sides of a triangle are unequal, then the measures of the angles opposite these sides are *unequal in the same order*.

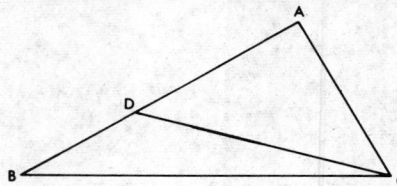

Proof. Let the triangle be $\triangle ABC$ with $\overline{AB} > \overline{AC}$. Then by Theorem 6–4 (Point-Plotting Theorem), there is a point D between A and B such that $\overline{AD} = \overline{AC}$. Therefore, $\overrightarrow{CD}$ is between $\overrightarrow{CA}$ and $\overrightarrow{CB}$ and $m\angle ACB > m\angle ACD = m\angle ADC$. But $m\angle ADC > \angle B$. Therefore, by the transitive property of order, $m\angle ACB > m\angle ABC$.

■ THEOREM 9–18.–If the measures of two angles of a triangle are unequal, the lengths of the sides opposite these angles are unequal in the same order.

■ COROLLARY 9–18–1.–The hypotenuse of a right triangle is the longest side of the triangle.

■ COROLLARY 9–18–2.–Given a line and a point not on this line, the shortest segment joining the given point to the given line is the segment perpendicular to the line.

Definition. The distance between a point and a line not containing this point is the length of the perpendicular segment joining the point to the line. The distance between a line and a point on the line is defined as zero.

■ COROLLARY 9–18–3.–If $\overline{AB}$ is the longest side of $\triangle ABC$, then the perpendicular segment joining C to $\overleftrightarrow{AB}$ intersects $\overline{AB}$ between A and B.

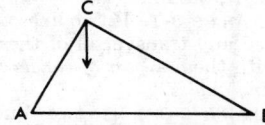

Proof. Let the perpendicular segment from C to $\overleftrightarrow{AB}$ be $\overline{CD}$. If $D = A$, then $\overline{CB} > \overline{AB}$. If $D = B$, then $\overline{CA} > \overline{AB}$. If D is in ray opposite $\overrightarrow{AB}$, then $\overline{CB} > \overline{BD} > \overline{BA}$. If D is in the ray opposite $\overrightarrow{BA}$, then $\overline{AC} > \overline{AD} > \overline{AB}$. Therefore, D is between A and B, Q.E.D.

■ THEOREM 9–19.–The set of points equally distant from the sides of an angle is the midray of the angle.

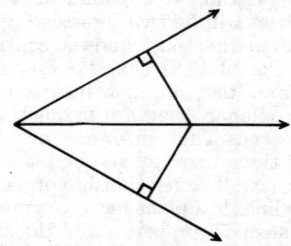

Comment. The proof of this theorem requires two parts: to show that every point on the midray is equally distant from the sides (S.A.A.); to show that if a point is equally distant from the sides, it is on the midray (Hypotenuse-Leg Theorem).

■ THEOREM 9-20.–The set of points in a plane, equally distant from two given points in the plane, is the perpendicular in the plane to the segment joining the given points and containing its midpoint.

■ THEOREM 9-21 (Triangle-Inequality Theorem).—The sum of the lengths of two sides of a triangle is greater than the length of the third side.

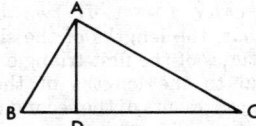

Proof. Let the triangle be $\triangle ABC$, with $\overline{BC}$ the longest side. Then by Corollary 9–18–3, the perpendicular from A to $\overleftrightarrow{BC}$ intersects it in D, between B and C. $\overline{AB} > \overline{BD}$ and $\overline{AC} > \overline{DC}$. Therefore, $\overline{AB} + \overline{AC} > \overline{BD} + \overline{DC} = \overline{BC}$. If $\overline{BC} = \overline{AB} > \overline{AC}$, then $\overline{AB} + \overline{AC} > \overline{BC}$. The proof is obvious, if $\overline{BC}$ is not the longest side, Q.E.D.

SECTION TEN

Similarity.—A formal treatment of similarity is suggested by a knowledge of the practical geometry of objects that have the same shape. Instances of such objects are models, architect's plans, and maps. As with congruences, similarities are based on one-to-one correspondences. In these correspondences, corresponding angles have equal measures and corresponding lengths are proportional. Since a formal treatment of congruent angles already has been presented, it is now time for a formal treatment of proportionality.

Definitions. Suppose the numbers in $\{p,q,r, \ldots\}$ have a one-to-one correspondence with the numbers in $\{a,b, c, \ldots\}$, p corresponding to a, q to b, r to c, and so on, where there are at least two numbers in each set and where the dots $(\ldots)$ indicate there may be any amount of numbers. The numbers p, $q,r, \ldots$ are proportional to the numbers $a,b,c, \ldots$ if, and only if, there is a nonzero number k such that $p = ka$, $q = kb$, $r = kc, \ldots$. The number k is the *constant of proportionality.*

Notation. $\bar{\text{p}}$ is used to mean "are proportional to." An ordered set of numbers is indicated by writing them in parentheses. Thus, $(3,6,5) \bar{\text{p}} (6,12,10)$ means that $3 = k \cdot 6$, $6 = k \cdot 12$, $5 = k \cdot 10$. It is obvious that the constant in this proportionality is $\frac{1}{2}$.

Properties of Proportionality

Reflexive property. $(a,b,c, \ldots) \bar{\text{p}} (a,b,c, \ldots)$. In this case, $k = 1$.

Symmetric property. If $(p,q,r, \ldots) \bar{\text{p}} (a,b,c, \ldots)$, then $(a,b,c, \ldots) \bar{\text{p}} (p,q, r, \ldots)$. If in the first-mentioned proportionality the constant of proportionality is k, it is $\frac{1}{2}k$ in the second.

Transitive property. If $(a,b,c, \ldots) \bar{\text{p}} (d,e,f, \ldots)$ and $(d,e,f, \ldots) \bar{\text{p}} (h,i,k, \ldots)$, then $(a,b,c, \ldots) \bar{\text{p}} (h,i,k, \ldots)$.

Addition property. If $(a,b,c, \ldots) \bar{\text{p}} (r,s,t, \ldots)$, then $(a + b + c + \ldots, a,b,c, \ldots) \bar{\text{p}} (r + s + t + \ldots, r,s,t, \ldots)$. This is true because $a = kr$, $b = ks$, $c = kt, \ldots$, and $(a + b + c + \ldots) = k(r + s + t + \ldots)$.

Examples. Since $(10,15,25) \bar{\text{p}} (2,3,5)$, then by the addition property of proportionality $(50,10,15,25) \bar{\text{p}} (10,2,3,5)$.

Given: $(a,b,7) \bar{\text{p}} (4,8,3)$. To find: a, b: $7 = 3k$; therefore $k = \frac{7}{3}$. Hence, $a = \frac{7}{3} \cdot 4 = {}^{28}\!/_3$ and $b = \frac{7}{3} \cdot 8 = {}^{56}\!/_3$. Given: $(a,b,c) \bar{\text{p}} (d,e,f)$. To write a proportionality starting with (b,c,a), (d,e,f) must be rewritten to maintain the one-to-one correspondence. Hence, $(b,c,a) \bar{\text{p}} (e,f,d)$.

Definition. A proportionality is a *proportion* if, and only if, each of its sets of numbers consist of two numbers.

Properties of Proportions.—Given that a, b, c, and d are positive numbers, then:

Inversion property. If $(a,b) \bar{\text{p}} (c,d)$, then $(b,a) \bar{\text{p}} (d,c)$.

Alternation property. If $(a,b) \bar{\text{p}} (c,d)$, then $(a,c) \bar{\text{p}} (b,d)$.

Product property. $(a,b) \bar{\text{p}} (c,d)$ if, and only if, $ad = bc$.

Comment. $(a,b) \bar{\text{p}} (c,d)$ is also written $a : b = c : d$ or $a/b = c/d$.

Example. Given: $(4,9) \bar{\text{p}} (x,2)$. To find x, use the product property to write $9x = 8$, and $x = \frac{8}{9}$. By the inversion property, $(9,4) \bar{\text{p}} (2,x)$. By the alternation property, $(4,x) \bar{\text{p}} (9,2)$. By the addition property, $(13,4) \bar{\text{p}} (x + 2,x)$ or $(13,9) \bar{\text{p}} (x + 2,2)$.

Definition. A one-to-one correspondence between the vertices of two triangles (not necessarily distinct) such that corresponding angles are congruent and corresponding sides are proportional, is called a *similarity*, and the two triangles are said to be *similar* to one another.

Notation. The statement $\triangle ABC$ is similar to $\triangle DEF$ is abbreviated: $\triangle ABC \sim \triangle DEF$.

Comment. The definition may be generalized for the one-to-one correspondence between two convex polygons having the same number of sides.

In any similarity there are three conditions to be satisfied: (1) There is a correspondence between all the vertices of one polygon with all the vertices of a second polygon. For this correspondence: (2) Corresponding angles are congruent. (3) Corresponding sides are proportional.

Notation. Given $\triangle ABC$, the length of the side opposite A is designated by a; the length of the side opposite B, by b; and so on. In general, the lower-case letter designates the length of the side opposite the vertex with the corresponding capital letter. Thus, if $\triangle ABC \sim \triangle DEF$, it follows that $(a,b,c) \bar{\text{p}} (d,e,f)$.

Definition. If $\triangle ABC \sim \triangle DEF$, the *proportionality constant of the similarity* is k, the proportionality constant in the proportionality $(a,b,c) \bar{\text{p}} (d,e,f)$.

AN ARCHITECT'S MODEL illustrates one-to-one correspondence, or *similarity*. In these correspondences, angles have equal measures and corresponding lengths are proportional.

Comment. Given $\triangle ABC \sim \triangle DEF$, then $\triangle ABC \cong \triangle DEF$ if, and only if, $k = 1$. From this fact it is obvious that a congruence between two triangles is a special case of similarity.

■ THEOREM 10–1.—The similarity relation between convex polygons is reflexive, symmetric, and transitive.

Comment. The proof follows directly from the corresponding properties of the congruence relation between angles and the proportionality relations between two sets of numbers.

Postulate 22 (Proportional-Segments Postulate).—If a line is parallel to one side of a triangle and intersects the other two sides in interior points, then the measures of one of those sides and the two segments into which it is cut are proportional to the measures of the corresponding segments in the other side.

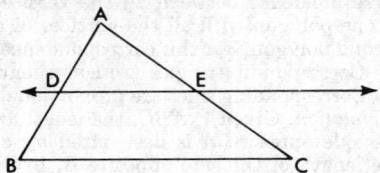

Comment. Postulate 22 is sometimes stated more briefly as follows. If a line is parallel to one side of a triangle, it divides the other two sides proportionally. In terms of the diagram, if $l \parallel \overline{BC}$ and l cuts $\overline{AB}$ in D, between A and B, and cuts $\overline{AC}$ in E, between A and C, then $(\overline{AB}, \overline{AD}, \overline{DB}) \; \bar{\text{p}} \; (\overline{AC}, \overline{AE}, \overline{EC})$.

■ THEOREM 10–2.—Given three coplanar parallel lines and two transversals, then the corresponding segments on the transversals are proportional.

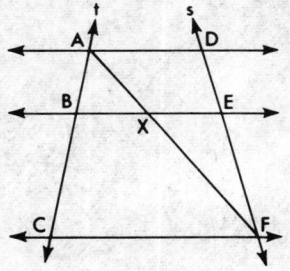

Proof. In the diagram above, let $\overleftrightarrow{AD} \parallel \overleftrightarrow{BE} \parallel \overleftrightarrow{CF}$, where A, B, and C are in transversal t and D, E, and F are in transversal s. By Corollary 9–4–1, $\overleftrightarrow{AF}$ intersects $\overleftrightarrow{BE}$ in X. Then by Postulate 22, $(\overline{AB}, \overline{BC}) \; \bar{\text{p}} \; (\overline{AX}, \overline{XF}) \; \bar{\text{p}} \; (\overline{DE}, \overline{EF})$. Therefore, by the transitive property of a proportionality, $(\overline{AB}, \overline{BC}) \; \bar{\text{p}} \; (\overline{DE}, \overline{EF})$, Q.E.D.

■ THEOREM 10–3.—If a triangle and a positive number k are given, there is a triangle that is similar to the given triangle with proportionality constant k.

Proof. Let the given triangle be $\triangle ABC$. If $k < 1$, there is a point D in $\overline{AB}$ such that $\overline{AD} = kc$. The parallel to $\overline{BC}$ containing D cuts $\overline{AC}$ in E, such that $\overline{AE} = kb$. Also, there is a point F in $\overline{AB}$ such that $\overline{BF} = kc$. The parallel to

$\overline{AC}$ containing F cuts $\overline{BC}$ in G, such that $\overline{BG} = ka$. $\triangle ADE \cong \triangle FBG$ (A.S.A.). Therefore, $DE = ka$. $\triangle ADE \sim \triangle ABC$ because corresponding angles are congruent and corresponding sides are proportional, with k as the proportionality constant.

If $k = 1$, then the given triangle is congruent to itself and hence similar.

If $k > 1$, a similar proof can be constructed with D in $\overrightarrow{AB}$ and F in $\overrightarrow{BA}$ such that $\overline{AD} = \overline{BF} = kc$, Q.E.D.

■ THEOREM 10–4 (S.S.S. Similarity Theorem).—A correspondence between two triangles for which corresponding sides are proportional is a similarity.

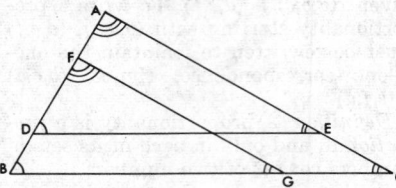

Proof. Let the triangles be $\triangle ABC$ and $\triangle A'B'C'$, with A corresponding to A', B to B', and C to C'. Then $(a,b,c) \; \bar{\text{p}} \; (a',b',c')$, with the proportionality factor k. There exists $\triangle A''B''C''$, similar to $\triangle ABC$, with the proportionality factor k, by Theorem 10–2. Its sides have lengths ka, kb, and kc, and hence $\triangle A''B''C'' \cong \triangle A'B'C'$. Therefore, by the transitivity property of similarities, $\triangle ABC \sim \triangle A'B'C'$, Q.E.D.

■ THEOREM 10–5 (S.A.S. Similarity Theorem).—If for a correspondence between two triangles, two sides of one triangle are proportional to the corresponding sides of the other and the included angles are congruent, then the correspondence is a similarity.

Proof. Let the triangles be $\triangle ABC$ and $\triangle A'B'C'$, with $(a,b) \; \bar{\text{p}} \; (a',b')$ and $\angle C = \angle C'$. There is a $\triangle A''B''C''$ similar to $\triangle ABC$ with proportionality factor $k = a''/a = b''/b$. Therefore, $a'' = ka = a'$, $b'' = kb = b'$. Moreover, $\angle C'' = \angle C = \angle C'$. Therefore, $\triangle A''B''C'' \cong \triangle A'B'C'$ (S.A.S.), and $\triangle ABC \sim \triangle A'B'C'$, Q.E.D.

■ COROLLARY 10–5–1.—If a line divides two sides of a triangle into proportional segments, it is parallel to the third side.

■ COROLLARY 10–5–2.—The line that bisects one side of a triangle and is parallel to a second side bisects the third side.

■ COROLLARY 10–5–3.—The segment that joins the midpoints of two sides of a triangle is parallel to the third side and is half as long as the third side.

■ THEOREM 10–6 (A.A. Similarity Theorem).— If for a given correspondence between two triangles, two angles of one triangle are congruent to the corresponding angles of the other, then the correspondence is a similarity.

Proof. In $\triangle ABC$ and $\triangle A'B'C'$, let $\angle A \cong \angle A'$, and $\angle B \cong \angle B'$. Take k such that $c' = kc$, and consider $\triangle A''B''C'' \sim \triangle ABC$ with the proportionality constant k. Then $c'' = kc$ and $c' = c''$. Also $\angle A'' \cong \angle A \cong \angle A'$

and $\angle B'' \cong \angle B \cong \angle B'$. Therefore, $\triangle A'B'C' \cong \triangle A''B''C''$ and $\triangle A'B'C' \sim \triangle ABC$, Q.E.D.

Definition. Given a point not in a line, the intersection of the perpendicular to the line containing the given point is called the *projection of the point on the line.* Given a point in a line, its *projection on that line* is defined to be the point itself.

Definition. The segment that joins a vertex of a triangle to the projection of the vertex on the line of the opposite side is called the *altitude of the triangle from that vertex.*

■ COROLLARY 10–6–1.—If two triangles are similar, the lengths of the sides and the altitudes of the first triangle are proportional to the lengths of the corresponding segments of the second triangle.

Definition. The *projection of a segment on a line* is the set of projections of all the points in the segment on the line.

Comment. As here defined, an altitude, or a projection of a segment on a line, is a set of points. The phrases "length of an altitude" or "length of the projection of a segment on a line" are often abbreviated to "altitude" or "projection of a segment on a line," respectively, for convenience. The context indicates which meaning is intended.

■ THEOREM 10–7.—In any right triangle, the altitude to the hypotenuse separates the triangle into two similar triangles, each similar to the original right triangle.

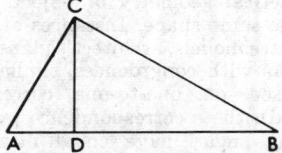

Proof. Since the hypotenuse $\overline{AB}$ is the longest side, the projection of C on $\overline{AB}$, D, is between A and B. $\triangle CAD \sim \triangle BAC$, and $\triangle BCD \sim \triangle BAC$ (A.A. Similarity Theorem 10–6). By the transitive property, $\triangle CAD \sim \triangle BCD$, Q.E.D.

■ COROLLARY 10–7–1.—The square of the altitude to the hypotenuse of a right triangle is equal to the product of the projection of the legs on the hypotenuse.

■ COROLLARY 10–7–2.—The square of the length of either leg of a right triangle is equal to the product of the projection of that leg on the hypotenuse and the length of the hypotenuse.

■ THEOREM 10–8 (Pythagorean Theorem).—In any right triangle, the square of the length of the hypotenuse is equal to the sum of the squares of the lengths of the two legs.

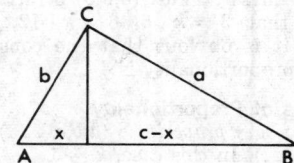

Proof. Let the triangle be $\triangle ABC$, with $\angle C$ the right angle. Let the projection of $\overline{AC}$ on $\overline{AB}$ be x and the projection of $\overline{CB}$ on $\overline{AB}$ be $c - x$. By Corollary $10-7-2$, $b^2 = cx$, and $a^2 = c(c - x)$, or $c^2 - cx$. By the addition property of equality, $a^2 + b^2 = c^2$, Q.E.D.

Comment. The Pythagorean Theorem is probably the most famous of all mathematical theorems, and was known to the ancient Egyptians and Indians. However, Pythagoras was the first to prove it formally. A key principle in surveying and construction, the theorem is likewise important in scientific and mathematical studies. It has more formal proofs than any other theorem. (One of these proofs was discovered by President James A. Garfield.)

■ THEOREM 10-9 (Converse of the Pythagorean Theorem).—If the square of the length of one side of a triangle is equal to the sum of the squares of the lengths of the other two sides, then the triangle is a right triangle with the first side as hypotenuse.

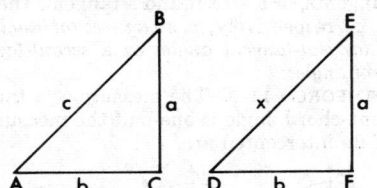

Proof. Let the triangle be $\triangle ABC$, with $c^2 = a^2 + b^2$. There is a right triangle, DEF, such that $\overline{DF} = b$ (Ruler Postulate), $\angle F$ is a right angle (Protractor Postulate) and $\overline{FE} = a$ (Point Plotting Theorem). If $\overline{DE} = x$, then by the Pythagorean Theorem, $x^2 = a^2 + b^2$. Since x and c are positive numbers, $x = c$, and $\triangle ABC \cong \triangle DEF$. Therefore, $\angle C$ is a right angle, Q.E.D.

Comment. Because it is convenient, the Pythagorean Theorem and its converse often are abbreviated, "the square of a side" instead of "the square of the length of a side." If this convenience is used, the Pythagorean Theorem and its converse may be stated: A triangle is a right triangle if, and only if, the square of one side is equal to the sum of the squares of the other two sides.

Comment. Certain families of similar right triangles occur frequently in engineering and mathematical problems, and are listed below.

3, 4, 5 triangles. These include all triangles whose sides have lengths $3k$, $4k$, $5k$, where k is any positive number. They are right triangles, since $(3k)^2 + (4k)^2 = (5k)^2$ for any k.

Example. If the lengths of the legs of a right triangle are 12 inches and 16 inches, the hypotenuse must be 25 inches long ($k = 3$).

5, 12, 13 triangles. These include all triangles whose lengths are $5k$, $12k$, $13k$.

Example. If the hypotenuse of a triangle is $13 \cdot 4$ inches long and one leg is $12 \cdot 4$ inches long, the other leg must be $5 \cdot 4$ inches long.

Right isosceles triangles. In this case, (a,b,c) p̄ $(1,1,\sqrt{2})$ and each acute angle measures 45.

Example. If the hypotenuse of a right isosceles triangle is 20 feet long, and the length of each leg is represented by x, then $(x,x,20)$ p̄ $(1,1,\sqrt{2})$; the constant of proportionality is $20/\sqrt{2}$ and $x = 20/\sqrt{2}$.

30, 60, 90 triangles. In these triangles, if $m\angle A = 30$, $m\angle B = 60$, $m\angle C = 90$, then (a,b,c) p̄ $(1,\sqrt{3},2)$.

Example. If $b = 12$ inches, then $(a,12,c)$ p̄ $(1,\sqrt{3},2)$; the constant of proportionality is $12/\sqrt{3}$ and $a = 12/\sqrt{3}$, $c = 24/\sqrt{3}$.

SECTION ELEVEN

Circles.—A *circle* is the set of all points in a given plane whose distances from a given point in the plane are a given number. The given point is the *center of the circle.* The given number is the *radius of the circle.* A *chord of a circle* is a segment that joins two points of the circle. A *diameter of a circle* is a chord that contains the center. A *radius* (plural, *radii*) *of a circle* is also defined as the segment that joins the center to any of its points. (The context will suggest whether a radius is a number or a set of points.) The *end point* of a radius that is a point of the circle is its *outer end.*

Definition. Circles with congruent radii are *congruent circles.*

■ THEOREM 11-1.—The radii of a circle or of congruent circles are congruent.

■ THEOREM 11-2.—The diameters of a circle or of congruent circles are congruent.

Definition. The *interior* of a circle is the set of all points in the plane of the circle whose distances from the center are less than its radius. The *exterior of a circle* is the set of all points in the plane of the circle whose distances from the center of the circle are greater than its radius.

Comment. "The inside of a circle" is frequently used to mean "the interior of a circle." A point is *on* or *in* a circle if it is a point of the circle.

Definition. A *tangent to a circle* is a line in the plane of the circle that intersects the circle in exactly one point. This point is the *point of tangency,* or the *point of contact.* The circle and the line are *tangent* at this point.

Definition. A *secant to a circle* is a line in the plane of the circle that intersects the circle in exactly two distinct points.

■ THEOREM 11-3.—Given: a line and a circle in the same plane. If the projection of the center of the circle on this line is: (a) outside the circle, then the line is outside the circle; (b) on the circle, then the line is a tangent to the circle; (c) inside the circle, then the line is a secant to the circle.

Proof. Let the center be C, the line l, the projection of C on l, P, and radius r:

(a) If P is outside the circle, $\overline{CP} > r$. Since $\overline{CP}$ is the shortest distance from C to l, all points of C are exterior points.

(b) If P is on C, then $\overline{CP} = r$. $\overline{CP}$ is the shortest distance from C to l, and therefore all other points of l are ex-

terior points. Hence, l is a tangent.

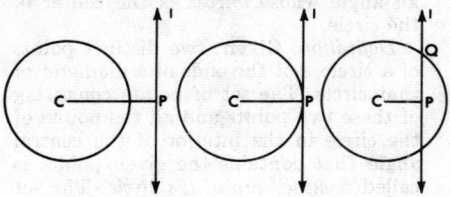

(c) If P is an interior point, then $\overline{CP} < r$. If Q is a point on l and also on the circle, then $(\overline{CP})^2 + (\overline{PQ})^2 = r^2$, or $(\overline{PQ})^2 = r^2 - (\overline{CP})^2$. Since $r > \overline{CP}$, and r and $\overline{CP}$ are positive numbers, $r^2 > (\overline{CP})^2$ and $r^2 - (\overline{CP})^2 > 0$. Therefore, $\overline{PQ}$ exists and is equal to $\sqrt{r^2 - (\overline{CP})^2}$. By Theorem 6-4 (Point-Plotting Theorem), Q can be found in either of the two rays contained in l with endpoint P. Therefore, there are two points that are on l and also on the circle. Hence, l is a secant, Q.E.D.

■ COROLLARY 11-3-1.—Given a circle and a coplanar line, the line is a tangent to the circle if, and only if, it is perpendicular to the radius of the circle at the outer end of the radius.

■ COROLLARY 11-3-2.—A diameter of a circle bisects a nondiameter chord of a circle if, and only if, it is perpendicular to the chord.

■ COROLLARY 11-3-3.—In the plane of a circle, the perpendicular bisector of a chord contains the center of the circle.

■ COROLLARY 11-3-4.—If a line in the plane of a circle contains an interior point, it intersects the circle in exactly two points.

■ THEOREM 11-4.—Chords of congruent circles are congruent if, and only if, their distances from the center are the same.

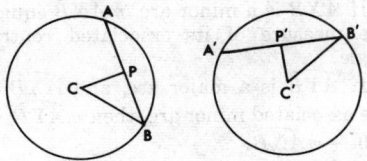

Proof. Let two circles have centers C and C', and let the chords be $\overline{AB}$ and $\overline{A'B'}$ in the respective circles. Let the projection of C on $\overline{AB}$ be P, and that of C' on $\overline{A'B'}$ be P'. By Theorem 10-8 (Pythagorean Theorem), $(\overline{CB})^2 = (\overline{CP})^2 + (\overline{PB})^2$ and $(\overline{C'B'})^2 = (\overline{C'P'})^2 + (\overline{P'B'})^2$. Since $\overline{CB} = \overline{C'B'}$, $(\overline{CP})^2 + (\overline{PB})^2 = (\overline{C'P'})^2 + (\overline{P'B'})^2$. It follows that $\overline{PB} = \overline{P'B'}$ if, and only if, $\overline{CP} = \overline{C'P'}$. By Corollary 11-3-2, $\overline{PB} = \frac{1}{2}\overline{AB}$ and $\overline{P'B'} = \frac{1}{2}\overline{A'B'}$. Therefore, $\overline{AB} \cong \overline{A'B'}$ if, and only if, $\overline{CP} = \overline{C'P'}$.

Definition. Two circles are *tangent* if, and only if, they are coplanar and tangent to the same line at the same point. Tangent circles are *internally tangent* if their centers lie on the same side of the common tangent, and *externally tangent* if their centers are on opposite sides of their common tangent.

■ THEOREM 11-5.—If two circles are tangent, then their centers are collinear with the point of contact.

Definition. A *central angle of a circle* is an angle whose vertex is the center of the circle.

Definition. Given: two distinct points of a circle, not the ends of a diameter of that circle. The set of points consisting of these two points and all the points of the circle in the interior of the central angle that contains the given points is called a *minor arc of the circle*. The set consisting of the two points and all the points of the circle in the exterior of the central angle is a *major arc of the circle*. If the two points are ends of a diameter of the circle, then the set of points consisting of the two points and all points of the circle on the same side of the diameter is a *semicircle*. The two given points in a minor arc, a major arc, or a semicircle are the *end points of the arc*.

Notation. An arc whose end points are A and B is denoted by $\overset{\frown}{AB}$. Since there are two arcs of a circle with these endpoints, ambiguity can be avoided by using a third point of the arc, such as

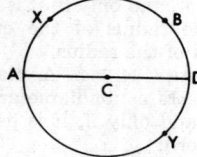

X and then designating the arc $\overset{\frown}{AXB}$. In the illustration $\overset{\frown}{AXB}$ is a minor arc and $\overset{\frown}{AYB}$ is a major arc. $\overset{\frown}{ABD}$ or $\overset{\frown}{AYD}$ is a diameter if $\overline{AD}$ contains C, the center of the circle.

Definition. If $\overset{\frown}{AXB}$ is any arc, then its *degree measure*, designated $m\overset{\frown}{AXB}$, is defined as follows:

If $\overset{\frown}{AXB}$ is a minor arc, $m\overset{\frown}{AXB}$ equals the measure of its associated central angle.

If $\overset{\frown}{AYB}$ is a major arc, and $\overset{\frown}{AXB}$ is the associated minor arc, then $m\overset{\frown}{AYB} = 360 - m\overset{\frown}{AXB}$.

If $\overline{AB}$ is a diameter then $m\overset{\frown}{AB} = 180$.

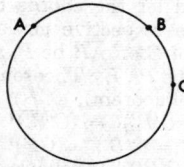

Postulate 23.—If $\overset{\frown}{AB}$ and $\overset{\frown}{BC}$ of a circle have only B in common and if the set of all points in $\overset{\frown}{AB}$ and $\overset{\frown}{BC}$ is an arc, $\overset{\frown}{AC}$, then $m\overset{\frown}{AB} + m\overset{\frown}{BC} = m\overset{\frown}{AC}$.

Comment. This postulate can be proved easily if $\overset{\frown}{AC}$ is a minor arc or a semicircle. If $\overset{\frown}{AC}$ is a major arc, the proof is difficult. In this article it is taken as a postulate.

Definition. An angle is *inscribed in an arc* if the angle contains the two end points of the arc and the vertex is a point of the arc, but not an end point. $\angle ABC$ is inscribed in a major arc,

$\angle DEF$ is inscribed in a semicircle, and $\angle GHK$ is inscribed in a minor arc.

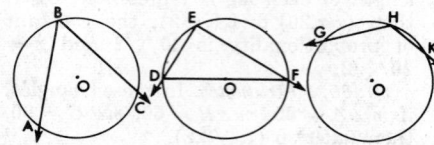

Definition. An angle *intercepts an arc* if each side of the angle contains one of the end points of the arc, and except for its end points, the arc is in the interior of the angle, as shown below.

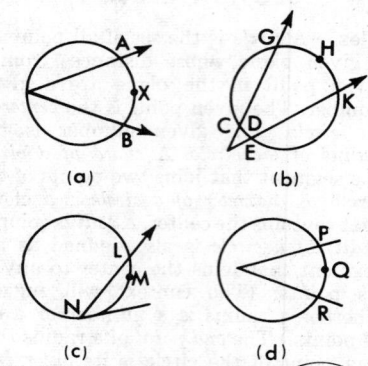

(a) (b)

(c) (d)

In (a) the angle intercepts $\overset{\frown}{AXB}$; in (b) the angle intercepts $\overset{\frown}{CDE}$ and $\overset{\frown}{GHK}$; in (c) the angle intercepts $\overset{\frown}{LMN}$; and in (d) the angle intercepts $\overset{\frown}{PQR}$.

■ **THEOREM 11-6.**–The measure of an inscribed angle is half the measure of the intercepted arc.

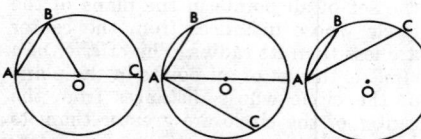

Proof. Let the inscribed angle be $\angle BAC$ intercepting $\overset{\frown}{BC}$. Let O be the center of the circle. Consider three cases:

(1) If O is on one side of $\angle A$, say in $\overrightarrow{BC}$, then $\overline{BO} \cong \overline{AO}$ and by Corollary 9-15-1, $m\angle BOC = 2m\angle A$. By the definition of an arc measure, $m\angle BOC = m\overset{\frown}{BC}$. Therefore, $2m\angle A = m\overset{\frown}{BC}$ and by the multiplication property of equality, $m\angle A = \frac{1}{2}m\overset{\frown}{BC}$.

(2) If O is an interior point of $\angle BAC$, then $\overrightarrow{AO}$ is between $\overrightarrow{AB}$ and $\overrightarrow{AC}$. Therefore $m\angle BAC = m\angle BAD + m\angle DAC$. But by example (1), $m\angle BAD = \frac{1}{2}m\overset{\frown}{BD}$, $m\angle DAC = \frac{1}{2}m\overset{\frown}{DC}$. By postulate 23 $m\overset{\frown}{BD} + m\overset{\frown}{DC} = m\overset{\frown}{BC}$. Therefore, $m\angle BAC = \frac{1}{2}m\overset{\frown}{BC}$.

(3) If O is an exterior point of $\angle BAC$, a proof similar to that of example (2) can be written by considering $\overrightarrow{AC}$ to be between $\overrightarrow{AB}$ and $\overrightarrow{AO}$, Q.E.D.

■ **COROLLARY 11-6-1.**–An angle inscribed in a semicircle is a right angle.

■ **COROLLARY 11-6-2.**–Angles inscribed in the same arc are congruent.

Definition. In congruent circles (not necessarily distinct) two arcs are con-

gruent if they have the same degree measure.

■ **COROLLARY 11-6-3.**–Congruent angles inscribed in congruent circles intercept congruent arcs.

■ **THEOREM 11-7.**–In congruent circles, if two chords, not diameters, are congruent, then the associated minor arcs are congruent and the associated major arcs are congruent.

Comment. The proof can be based on Postulate 20 (S.S.S. Postulate) and the definition of the degree measure of an arc.

■ **THEOREM 11-8.**–In congruent circles, if two arcs are congruent, then the associated chords are congruent.

Definition. If the vertex of an angle is on a circle, and one side is contained in a tangent and its other side contains a chord, the angle is a *tangent-chord angle*.

Definition. If the vertex of an angle is an exterior point of a circle and its sides are contained in two secants, or two tangents, or a secant and a tangent, then it is, respectively, a *secant-secant angle*, a *tangent-tangent angle*, or a *secant-tangent angle*.

■ **THEOREM 11-9.**–The measure of a tangent-chord angle is one-half the measure of its intercepted arc.

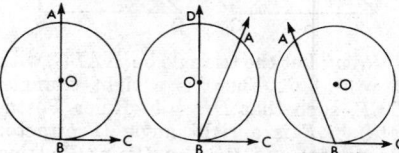

Proof. Let the angle be $\angle ABC$ with $\overrightarrow{BC}$ contained in tangent $\overleftrightarrow{BC}$ at B, and let O be the center of the circle. If O is in $\overrightarrow{BA}$, then $\overline{AB} \perp \overleftrightarrow{BC}$ and $m\angle ABC = 90$ or one-half the measure of a semicircle. If O is an exterior point of $\angle ABC$, and $\overline{BD}$ is a diameter, then $\overrightarrow{BA}$ is between $\overrightarrow{BD}$ and $\overrightarrow{BC}$ or $m\angle ABC = m\angle DBC - m\angle DBA = 90 - \frac{1}{2}\overset{\frown}{DA} = \frac{1}{2}\overset{\frown}{AB}$. A similar proof can be given if O is an interior point of $\angle ABC$, Q.E.D.

■ **THEOREM 11-10.**–If the vertex of an angle is an interior point of a circle and its sides are contained in two secants, then its measure is one-half the sum of its intercepted arc and the intercepted arc of its vertical angle.

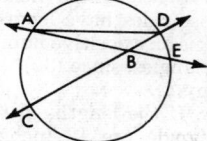

Proof. If $\angle ABC$ is the angle and the secants cut the circle in A, D, E, and C, then $m\angle ABC = m\angle BDA + m\angle BAD = \frac{1}{2}(m\overset{\frown}{AC} + m\overset{\frown}{DE})$, Q.E.D.

■ **THEOREM 11-11.**–The measure of a secant-secant angle, or a tangent-tangent angle, or a secant-tangent angle is one-half the difference of the intercepted arcs.

Example. Suppose as shown, $m\overset{\frown}{DA} =$

100, $\overline{DE} \parallel \overline{AB}$, $\overleftrightarrow{AB}$ is a tangent at A, and $\widehat{EF} \cong \widehat{FA}$. Then $\angle E \cong \angle A$,

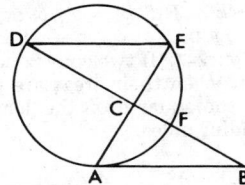

$m \angle E = 50 = m \angle A$, and $m\widehat{EFA} = 100$. $m\widehat{FA} = 50$, $m \angle B = \frac{1}{2}(100 - 50) = 25$, $m \angle DCA = \frac{1}{2}(100 + 50) = 75$.

Comment. The above angle measure theorems may be remembered by noting that when the vertex of the angle is on the circle (inscribed angle or tangent-chord angle), its measure is one-half the *measure* of the intercepted arc; when it is an interior point, its measure is one-half the *sum* of the measures of the intercepted arcs; when it is an exterior point, one-half the *difference* of the intercepted arcs.

Definition. If $\overleftrightarrow{AB}$ is a tangent to a circle at B, then $\overline{AB}$ is a *tangent segment* from A to the circle.

■ THEOREM 11-12.—The two tangent segments from an exterior point to a circle are congruent.

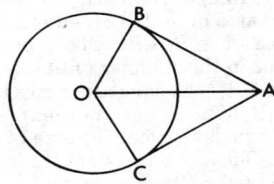

Proof. Let A be the exterior point, $\overline{AB}$ and $\overline{AC}$ the tangent segments, and O the center of the circle. Then $\triangle OBA \cong \triangle OCA$ by Theorem 9-16 (Hypotenuse-Leg Theorem), and $\overline{AB} \cong \overline{AC}$, Q.E.D.

■ COROLLARY 11-12-1.—The line containing an exterior point and the center of a circle bisects the tangent-tangent angle whose vertex is the exterior point.

Definition. If secant $\overleftrightarrow{CD}$ intersects a circle in A and B such that A is between C and B, then $\overline{CB}$ is the *secant segment* from C to the circle, and $\overline{CA}$ is its *external secant segment* from C to the circle.

■ THEOREM 11-13.—Given an exterior point of a circle, the product of the lengths of any secant segment from the point to the circle and its external secant segment is a constant.

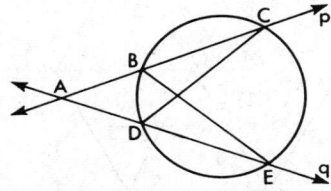

Proof. Let the given point be A and let p and q be any two secants containing A and intersecting the circle as shown. Then by Theorem 10-6 (A.A. Similarity Theorem) for similar tri-

angles, $\triangle ADC \sim \triangle ABE$. It follows that $(\overline{AC}, \overline{AD})\ \bar{p}\ (\overline{AE}, \overline{AB})$, and by the product property of proportionality, that $\overline{AC} \cdot \overline{AB} = \overline{AE} \cdot \overline{AD}$. Since p and q are any secants containing A, the proof is complete, Q.E.D.

■ THEOREM 11-14.—Given an exterior point of a circle, and a tangent segment and a secant segment from this point, the product of the lengths of the secant segment and its external secant segment is equal to the square of the length of the tangent segment.

Definition. The square of the length of a tangent segment from a point to a circle is the *power of the point* with respect to the circle.

■ THEOREM 11-15.—If two chords of a circle intersect, the product of the lengths of the segments of one is equal to the product of the lengths of the segments of the other.

Comment. The proof depends on showing that a pair of triangles are similar, as was done for Theorem 11-13.

Comment. For any circle, given an interior point of the circle and any chord containing this point, the product of the lengths of the chord's segments is a constant.

SECTION TWELVE

Areas.—Like the length of a segment, the measure of an angle, and the degree measure of an arc, area is also a measure and therefore a number. First, the mathematical object to which this kind of measure is applied must be defined.

Definition. A *triangular region* is the set of all points of a triangle and its interior. A *polygonal region* consists of a finite number of coplanar triangular regions. Examples are shown in the following diagram.

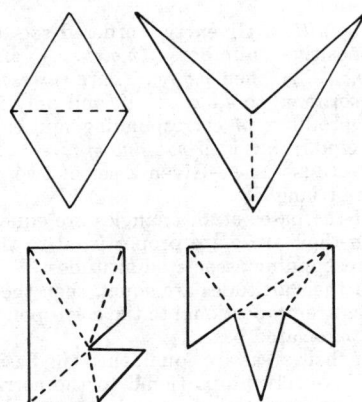

Definition. If a polygonal region consists of a convex polygon and its interior, then the polygon is the *boundary of the polygonal region* and the interior of the polygon is the *interior of the polygonal region.*

Comment. A convex polygon can be considered as a combination of triangular regions in more than one way, as shown below.

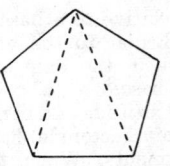
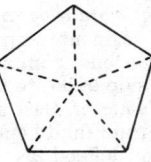

Postulate 24.—If S is any given polygonal region, there is a correspondence that associates to each polygonal region in space a unique positive number, such that the number assigned to S is 1.

Definition. The given polygonal region in this postulate is the *unit area* and, relative to this unit area, the number that is associated with a polygonal region is its *area.*

Comment. Postulate 24 does not tell what the area of a polygonal region is, except that of the unit area. For this information, more postulates are needed.

Postulate 25.—Given a polygonal region R and also given that it consists of two polygonal regions R_1 and R_2 such that R_1 and R_2 have in common only a finite number of segments, then relative to a given unit area, the area of R is the sum of the areas of R_1 and R_2.

Examples. This postulate is illustrated below. Figure (d) shows two triangular regions that have a triangular region in common; therefore Postulate 25 does not apply.

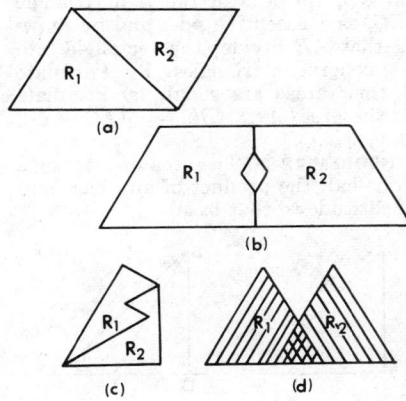

Postulate 26.—If two triangles are congruent, then their triangular regions have the same area relative to any given unit area.

Comment. It is often convenient to abbreviate "area of polygonal region" as "area of a polygon." However, the strict interpretation of "area of a polygon" would refer to the area of the points in a set of line segments, which is not a polygonal region.

Definition. Given a unit pair for measuring distances, a unit area is a *unit square* if, and only if, the unit area is bounded by a square such that the measure of a side of the square is one.

Postulate 27.—Given a unit pair for measuring distances, the area of a rectangle relative to a unit square is the product of the measures of any two consecutive sides.

Definition. Any side of a parallelogram is a *base of the parallelogram.* An *altitude of the parallelogram* relative to a base is the segment perpendicular to the base whose end points are in the base and the side opposite the base.

Comment. Base and altitude of a parallelogram (and hence of a rectangle) have been defined as segments. When the context makes it clear, "the length of the base" sometimes is abbreviated to "base;" "altitude" is treated similarly. Using these abbreviations, Postulate 27 states that the area of a rectangle is the product of a base and the related altitude. If the area, base, and related altitude of a rectangle are denoted by A, b, and h, respectively, then $A = bh$. The area of a square A, each of whose sides has length S, is then given by $A = s^2$.

■ THEOREM 12-1.—The area of a right triangle is one-half the product of the lengths of two legs.

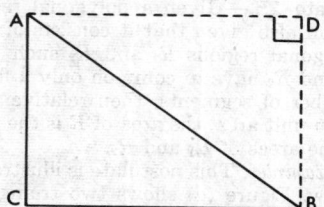

Proof. This theorem can be proved by considering the rectangle having $\overline{AC}$ and $\overline{CB}$, the legs of the right triangle ABC, as consecutive sides and by showing that $\overline{AB}$ divides the rectangle into two congruent triangles. By Postulate 26, their areas are equal; by Postulate 27, the area of $\triangle ABC = \frac{1}{2}(\overline{AC} \cdot \overline{CB})$, Q.E.D.

■ THEOREM 12-2.—The area of a triangle is one-half the product of any base and the altitude to that base.

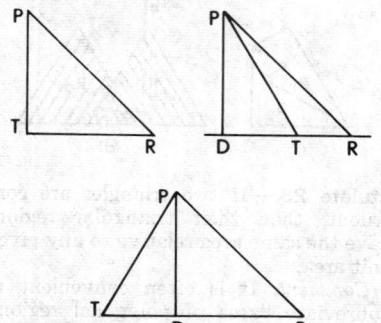

Proof. Let the triangle be $\triangle PTR$ and let the projection of P on $\overleftrightarrow{TR}$ be D. Let $\overleftrightarrow{TR} = b$, $\overrightarrow{PD} = a$, and A equal the area of $\triangle PTR$. If $D = T$ or $D = R$, then by Theorem 12-1, $A = \frac{1}{2}ab$. If D is between T and R, then $A = $ area of $\triangle TPD + $ area $\triangle DPR = \frac{1}{2}a \cdot TD + \frac{1}{2}a \cdot DR = \frac{1}{2}ab$. If T is between D and R, then the area of $\triangle DPR = $ area of $\triangle DPT + A$, and $A = \frac{1}{2}a(\overline{DR} - \overline{TR}) = \frac{1}{2}ab$. If R is between T and D, a similar proof follows, Q.E.D.

■ COROLLARY 12-2-1.—The area of an equilateral triangle whose side has length s is $(s^2\sqrt{3})/4$.

■ COROLLARY 12-2-2.—The area of a rhombus is one-half the product of the lengths of the diagonals.

■ THEOREM 12-3.—The area of a parallelogram is the product of a base and the associated altitude.

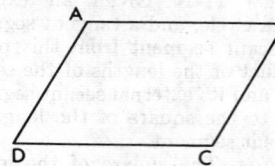

Proof. If $ABCD$ is a parallelogram with base $\overline{DC}$ and associated altitude h, then the area of $\triangle ADC = \frac{1}{2}\overline{DC} \cdot h$. Since $\triangle ADC \cong \triangle CBA$, and the area of $ABCD = $ area of $\triangle ADC + $ area of $\triangle ACB$, it follows that the area of $ABCD = DC \cdot h$, Q.E.D.

■ THEOREM 12-4.—The area of a trapezoid is one-half the product of its altitude and the sum of its bases.

Definition. The *median of a trapezoid* is the segment that joins the midpoints of its two nonparallel sides.

■ COROLLARY 12-4-1.—The area of a trapezoid is equal to the product of its altitude and the length of its median.

Summary of area formulas

Rectangle	$A = bh$
Square	$A = s^2$
Triangle	$A = \frac{1}{2}bh$
Parallelogram	$A = bh$
Equilateral triangle	$A = \dfrac{s^2\sqrt{3}}{4}$
Rhombus	$A = \frac{1}{2}d \cdot d'$
Trapezoid	$\begin{cases} A = \dfrac{h}{2}(b + b') \\ A = hm \end{cases}$

Definition. Given two ordered sets of n positive numbers $(p,q,r, \ldots)$ and $(a,b,c, \ldots)$, then $p,q,r, \ldots$ are *inversely proportional* to $a,b,c, \ldots$ if, and only if, the products of corresponding numbers are equal; that is, if $pa = qb = rc = \ldots$.

■ THEOREM 12-5.—Given a set of two or more triangles:

If the bases of all triangles are equal, then their areas are proportional to the corresponding associated altitudes.

If their altitudes are equal, then their areas are proportional to the corresponding associated bases.

If their areas are equal, then the bases are inversely proportional to the corresponding associated altitudes.

Comment. A theorem similar to Theorem 12-5 may be written about parallelograms.

■ THEOREM 12-6.—If two triangles are similar, then their areas are proportional to the squares of the lengths of the corresponding sides.

Proof. Let A and A' represent the areas of these triangles. Let b represent the length of one side of the first triangle and a represent the altitude to that side. Let b and a' represent the lengths of the

corresponding segments in the second triangle. Then $(b',a') = \bar{p} (b,a)$, $b' = kb$, and $a' = ka$. It follows that $A' = \frac{1}{2}b'a' = \frac{1}{2}k^2b \cdot a = k^2A$. But $k^2 = b'^2/b^2$ or (A,A') $\bar{p} (b^2, b'^2)$, Q.E.D.

■ THEOREM 12-7.—If two convex polygons are similar, then their areas are proportional to the squares of the lengths of corresponding sides.

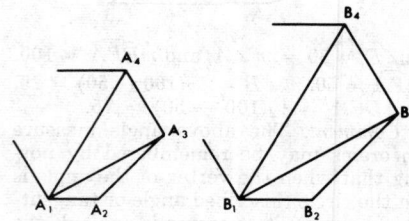

Proof. Since there is a one-to-one correspondence between the vertices of the two polygons, they have an equal number of vertices. Let the polygons be $A_1A_2A_3A_4 \ldots A_n$ and $B_1B_2B_3B_4 \ldots B_n$. By Theorem 10-5 (S.A.S. Similarity Theorem), $\triangle A_1A_2A_3 \sim \triangle B_1B_2B_3$. Since $\overrightarrow{A_3A_1}$ is between $\overrightarrow{A_3A_2}$ and $\overrightarrow{A_3A_4}$, it follows that $\angle A_4A_3A_1 = \angle A_4A_3A_2 - \angle A_1A_3A_2$. A similar conclusion follows for $\angle B_4B_3B_1$. Thus, $\triangle A_1A_3A_4 \sim \triangle B_1B_3B_4$ also can be proved by the S.A.S. Triangle Similarity Theorem as can the area of $\triangle A_1A_2A_3$ equals k^2 times the area of $\triangle B_1B_3B_4$. The process may continue in this manner until it is proved that $\triangle A_1A_{n-1}A_n$ equals k^2 times the area of $\triangle B_1B_{n-1}B_n$. Hence, the area of $A_1A_2A_3 \ldots A_n$ equals k^2 times the area of $B_1B_2B_3 \ldots B_n$. This is equivalent to the conclusion of the theorem, Q.E.D.

Definition. The *perimeter of a polygon* is the sum of the lengths of its sides.

■ COROLLARY 12-7-2.—If two convex polygons are similar, their perimeters are proportional to the lengths of corresponding sides or corresponding diagonals.

SECTION THIRTEEN

Regular Polygons and Circles.—A convex polygon is *regular* if its sides are congruent and its angles are congruent.

■ THEOREM 13-1.—The bisectors of the interior angles of a regular polygon meet at a point.

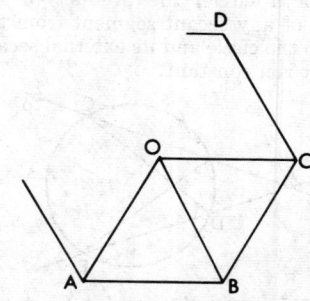

Proof. Let the polygon be $ABCD \ldots$, with $\angle A \cong \angle B \cong \angle C \ldots$ and $\overline{AB} \cong \overline{BC} \cong \overline{CD} \ldots$. Let the bisectors of $\angle A$ and $\angle B$ meet at O. Then, since $\frac{1}{2}m \angle A = $

½m ∠ B, $\overline{OA} = \overline{OB}$. It can be proved that △OAB ≅ △OBC ($\overline{OA} = \overline{OB}$, ∠OAB ≅ ∠OBC, $\overline{AB} ≅ \overline{BC}$); hence, m ∠OAB = m ∠OCB = ½m ∠ B = ½m ∠ C. Therefore, the bisector of ∠ C contains O. Similarly, the bisectors of ∠ D . . . meet in O, Q.E.D.

Definition. The *center of a regular polygon* is the point of intersection of the midrays of the angles of the polygon. The triangle formed by any two consecutive vertices of a regular polygon and its center is a *central triangle of the polygon.*

■ COROLLARY 13-1-1.–The central triangles of a regular polygon are isosceles, and are congruent to each other.

Definition. A *radius of a regular polygon* is the segment from a vertex to its center.

■ COROLLARY 13-1-2.–The radii of a regular polygon are congruent.

Definition. An *apothegm of a regular polygon* is the segment that joins the center to its projection on a side.

■ COROLLARY 13-1-3.–The apothegms of a regular polygon are congruent.

■ THEOREM 13-2.–The sum of the measures of the interior angles of a convex polygon having n sides is $(n - 2) \cdot 180$.

Proof. Let the polygon be $ABCD \ldots N$, and let O be any interior point. Then the sum of the measures of the angles in △OAB, △OBC, . . . is $n \cdot 180$. But the sum of the measures of the angles whose vertex is O, is $2 \cdot 180$. Since $\overrightarrow{BO}$ is between $\overrightarrow{BA}$ and $\overrightarrow{BC}$, m ∠ABO + m ∠OBC = m ∠ABC.

Similar conclusions can be made of m ∠BCD, m ∠CED . . . . Thus, the sum of the measures of the interior angles of the polygon is $n \cdot 180 - 2 \cdot 180 = (n - 2) \cdot 180$, Q.E.D.

■ COROLLARY 13-2-1.–The measure of each interior angle of a regular polygon having n sides is $(n - 2)/n \cdot 180$.

■ COROLLARY 13-2-2.–The measure of each exterior angle of a regular polygon having n sides is $360/n$.

Comment. Each exterior angle forms a linear pair with its adjacent interior angle.

■ COROLLARY 13-2-3.–The sum of the measures of the exterior angles of a polygon, one at each vertex, is 360.

■ COROLLARY 13-2-4.–The measure of each central angle of a regular polygon of n sides is $360/n$.

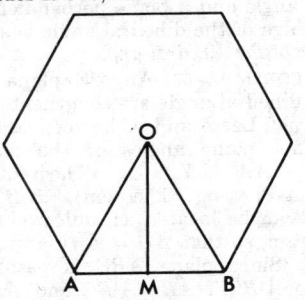

Example 1. Suppose a polygon, as shown, is a regular hexagon with each side having length 10. m ∠AOB = 60, $\overline{AM} = 5$, m ∠AOM = 30, m ∠MAO =

60. $(\overline{AM}, \overline{MO}, \overline{OA})$ p̄ $(1, \sqrt{3}, 2)$. Therefore, $\overline{MO} = 5\sqrt{3}$, $\overline{OA} = 10$.

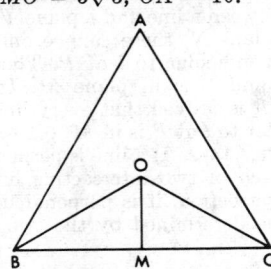

Example 2. Suppose ABC is an equilateral triangle with radius 12. m ∠BOM = 60, $(\overline{OM}, \overline{MB}, \overline{BO})$ p̄ $(1, \sqrt{3}, 2)$. Therefore, $k = 6$, $\overline{OM} = 6$ and $\overline{MB} = 6\sqrt{3}$.

■ THEOREM 13-3.–If two regular polygons have the same number of sides, they are similar.

Proof. Since they are equilateral, the sides of one are proportional to the sides of the other. That the corresponding angles are congruent can be seen from Corollary 13-2-1. Therefore, the polygons are similar, Q.E.D.

■ COROLLARY 13-3-1.–If two regular polygons have the same number of sides: (a) their perimeters are proportional to the lengths of the sides or radii or apothems; (b) their areas are proportional to the squares of the lengths of the sides or radii or apothegms.

■ THEOREM 13-4.–The area of a regular polygon is one-half the product of an apothegm and the perimeter ($A = ½ap$).

■ COROLLARY 13-4-1.–If s is the length of each side of a regular polygon having n sides and a is the length of an apothegm, then its area is $½ans$.

A rigorous treatment of the circumference of a circle or the area of a circular region depends upon the *theory of limits* and is usually studied in the calculus. Lacking a knowledge of this theory, a plausible treatment is presented here.

■ THEOREM 13-5.–If a circle is divided into n congruent, nonoverlapping arcs, and their end points are joined successively by chords, a regular polygon is formed.

Proof. The chords are congruent and the angles of the polygon are inscribed in congruent arcs, Q.E.D.

Definition. A polygon whose vertices are on a circle is an *inscribed polygon.*

Comment. Let P_n represent the perimeter of a regular polygon inscribed in a given circle and having n sides. Consider the sequence of numbers $p_3, p_4, p_5, \ldots$ for a given circle. It can be shown that this sequence of numbers is increasing; that it is limited even though it is increasing; that by taking n large enough, P_n can be made to be as close to this limit as desired. This limit is defined as the circumference of the circle. This is denoted by $P_n \to C$ (P_n approaches C).

Definition. The *circumference of a circle* is the limit of the perimeters of the inscribed regular polygon.

■ THEOREM 13-6.–The quotient of the circumference of a circle divided by its diameter, or $C ½ 2r$, is the same for all circles.

Proof. (Not rigorous.) Given a circle with center O and radius r and another circle with radius O' and radius r', consider the regular n-gons inscribed in each.

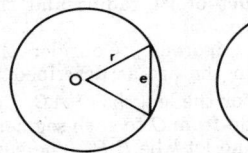

Let e and e' be the lengths of their respective sides. Then (e, e') p̄ (r, r') and (ne, ne') p̄ $(2r, 2r')$ or (p, p') p̄ $(2r, 2r')$. As n increases, $p \to C$, and $p' \to C'$. Therefore, it is plausible that (C, C') p̄ $(2r, 2r') \cdot C/2r$ is a constant of proportionality, Q.E.D.

Comment. $C/2r$ is denoted by π.

■ COROLLARY 13-6-1.–C equals $2\pi r$.

■ COROLLARY 13-6-2.–Circumferences of circles are proportional to their radii.

If A_n represents the area of an inscribed regular polygon, it is possible for a given circle, to write the sequence of numbers $A_3, A_4, A_5 \ldots$. Again it can be proved that A_n approaches a limit.

Definition. A *circular region* consists of all the points in a circle and in its interior.

Definition. The *area of a circular region* is the limit of the areas of the inscribed regular polygons. It is convenient to write "area of a circle" for "area of a circular region."

■ THEOREM 13-7.–The area of a circle with radius r is πr^2.

Proof. (Not rigorous.) Consider A_n the area of the inscribed regular polygon having n sides ($An = ½ap$). As n increases, $An \to A$, the area of the circle; $a \to r$; and $p \to C$. It is plausible that $A = ½r \cdot C = ½r \cdot 2\pi r$ or $A = \pi r^2$, Q.E.D.

■ COROLLARY 13-7-1.–The area of a circle is proportional to the square of its radius (or diameter).

Definition. If $\widehat{AB}$ is an arc of a circle with center O, and $P_1, P_2, P_3 \ldots P_{n-1}$ are distinct points of $\widehat{AB}$ such that m ∠AOP₁ ≅ ∠P₁OP₂ ≅ . . . ≅ ∠Pₙ₋₁OB, then the length of $\widehat{AB}$ is the limit of $AP_1 + P_1P_2 + \ldots P_{n-1}B$ as n is taken larger and larger.

Notation. The length of $\widehat{AB}$ is designated $l\widehat{AB}$.

Comment. The degree measure of $\widehat{AB}$ is not to be confused with $l\widehat{AB}$.

Postulate 28.—The lengths of arcs in congruent circles are proportional to their degree measures.

Comment. If $\widehat{AB}$ is a semicircle of a circle with radius r, then $m\widehat{AB} = 180$, but $l\widehat{AB} = \pi r$. It is clear that $(l\widehat{AB}, \pi r)$ p̄ $(m\widehat{AB}, 180)$ and that $k = \pi r/180$.

■ THEOREM 13-8.–An arc of degree measure q contained in a circle with radius r has length $L = (\pi r/180) \cdot q$.

Proof. By Postulate 28, $(L, \pi r)$ p̄ $(q, 180)$. Therefore, $L = (\pi r/180) \cdot q$, Q.E.D.

Definition. If $\overparen{AB}$ is an arc of a circle with center O and radius r, then all the points of the circle that are in the interior of $\angle AOB$ and the points in $\overline{OA}$ and $\overline{OB}$ are a *sector*. The *arc of the sector* is $\overparen{AB}$, and the *radius of the sector* is r.

■ THEOREM 13–9.–The area of a sector is half the product of its radius and the length of its arc.

Proof. (Not rigorous.) Consider the set of points in the arc as described in the definition for the lengths of $\overparen{AB}$. Let h be the altitude from O to each segment such as $\overline{P_2P_3}$, and let b be $\overline{P_2P_3}$. The sum of the areas of $\triangle AOP$, $\triangle P_1OP_2, \ldots$ $\triangle P_{n-1}OB = n \cdot \frac{1}{2}h \cdot b$ or $\frac{1}{2}h \cdot nb$. But $np \to l\overparen{AB}$ and $h \to r$. Therefore, the area of the sector is $\frac{1}{2}(r \cdot \frac{1}{2}l\overparen{AB})$, Q.E.D.

■ COROLLARY 13–8–1.–The area of a sector of radius r and arc degree measure q is $(\pi r^2/360) \cdot q$.

SECTION FOURTEEN

Parallelism and Perpendicularity

Theorem 5–3 states that space contains at least two planes. This assertion rests primarily on the assumptions that a line contains at least two points and that a plane is determined by three noncollinear points. However, Postulate 12 (Ruler Postulate) states that every line contains as many points as there are real numbers. This implies the existence of a limitless number of planes. In this section there will be an investigation of some relations among these planes and the general relations among points, lines, and planes.

Comment. It can be shown that a unique plane is determined by any of the following: (a) three noncollinear points; (b) two intersecting lines; (c) a line and a point not contained in the line; or, (d) two parallel lines.

Definition. A line and a plane are *perpendicular to each other* if, and only if, they intersect and every line in the plane that contains the point of intersection is perpendicular to the given line.

Postulate 29.—There exists exactly one plane that contains a given point and is perpendicular to a given line.

Comment. The given point may or may not be in the given line.

■ THEOREM 14–1.–The plane that is perpendicular to a given line at a given point in the line contains every line that is perpendicular to the given line at that point.

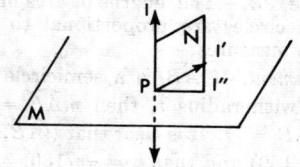

Proof. Let l be the given line, P the given point, and M the plane that is perpendicular to l at P. If $l' \perp M$ at P, then l and l' intersect and determine a

plane, N, that intersects plane M in a line, l''. By the definition of perpendicularity between a line and a plane, $l'' \perp l$. But in plane N, there can be only one line perpendicular to l at P. Therefore $l'' = l'$, and l' is in plane M. In this manner it is proved that every line perpendicular to l at P is in M, Q.E.D.

■ THEOREM 14–2.–If a line is perpendicular to each of two intersecting lines at their intersection, it is perpendicular to the plane determined by the two lines.

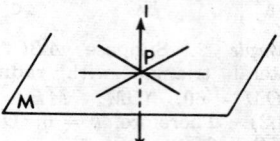

The above figure shows only three of the lines in plane M that contain P. Line l, which is perpendicular to each of these three (and all others in M containing P), is perpendicular to plane M and plane M is perpendicular to line l.

■ THEOREM 14–3.–There is exactly one line that is perpendicular to a given plane at a point in the plane.

Definitions. A line and a plane are *parallel to each other* if, and only if, they have no point in common. Two planes are *parallel to each other* if, and only if, they have no point in common.

■ THEOREM 14–4.–If a plane intersects one of two parallel lines in a point, then it also intersects the other in a point.

Proof. Let the plane be M and the lines be l_1 and l_2, and let M and l_1 intersect in P only. Since $l_1 \parallel l_2$, they determine a plane, N, that is necessarily distinct from M. But M and N have P in common. Hence, they intersect in a line, q, that is distinct from l_1. Therefore, q must intersect l_2 in exactly one point, Q.E.D.

■ COROLLARY 14–4–1.–If a plane is parallel to one of two parallel planes, it is also parallel to the other.

■ THEOREM 14–5.–If a plane intersects each of two parallel planes, the intersections are parallel lines.

Proof. Let the intersections be p and q. If they were to intersect, then the planes that are given parallel would also intersect. Therefore, p and q do not meet, and since they are coplanar, they are parallel, Q.E.D.

■ THEOREM 14–6.–If a line intersects one of two parallel planes, it intersects the other.

■ COROLLARY 14–6–1.–If a line is parallel to one of two parallel planes, it is parallel to the other.

■ THEOREM 14–7.–If two distinct planes are perpendicular to the same line, they are parallel.

Proof. If they meet, then they will form a triangle with two right angles, Q.E.D.

■ THEOREM 14–8.–If a line is perpendicular to one of two parallel planes, it is perpendicular to the other as well.

Postulate 30.—If two lines are perpendicular to the same plane, they are parallel.

Comment. This proposition can be proved. Because the proof is difficult for beginning geometry students, some schools prefer to postulate it.

■ THEOREM 14–9.–If a plane is perpendicular to one of two parallel lines, it is perpendicular to the other also.

■ THEOREM 14–10.–If two lines are each parallel to a third line, they are parallel to each other.

Proof. A plane is considered perpendicular to one of these lines, and it is shown that each line is perpendicular to it. By Postulate 30, the lines are parallel, Q.E.D.

Comment. This theorem extends a similar theorem for two coplanar lines to two lines not necessarily coplanar.

■ THEOREM 14–11.–Given a plane and a point not in the plane, there is exactly one line that contains the point and is perpendicular to the plane.

Comment. This theorem extends Theorem 14–3.

■ THEOREM 14–12.–There is exactly one plane parallel to a given plane and containing a given point not in the given plane.

■ THEOREM 14–13.–If two planes are parallel to a third plane, they are parallel to each other.

Definition. Given a plane and a point not in the plane, the *projection of the point on the plane* is the intersection of the line containing the point and the perpendicular to the plane.

■ THEOREM 14–14.–The shortest segment between a plane and a point not in the plane is the segment that joins the point to its projection on the plane.

Definition. The *distance between a point and a plane* that does not contain the point is the length of the segment that joins the point to its projection on the plane.

■ THEOREM 14–15.–If two planes are parallel, then all points in one plane have the same distance to the other plane.

■ COROLLARY 14–15–1.–If a line is parallel to a plane, then all the points in the line have the same distance to the plane.

■ THEOREM 14–16.–The set of all points that are equidistant from the end points of a given segment is the plane that contains the midpoint of the segment and is perpendicular to the line determined by the segment.

Definition. The intersection of a dihedral angle and a plane perpendicular to the edge of the dihedral angle is a *plane angle of the dihedral angle.*

■ THEOREM 14–17.–Any two plane angles of a dihedral angle are congruent.

Proof. Let A and A' be vertices of two distinct plane angles of the dihedral $\angle X - AA' - Y$. By Theorem 6–4 (Point-Plotting Theorem), B, B' and C, C' can be located as indicated in the diagram, so that $\overline{AB} = \overline{A'B'}$ and $\overline{AC} = \overline{A'C'}$. Since plane ABC is parallel to plane $A'B'C'$, $\overline{AB} \parallel \overline{A'B'}$, and $ABB'A'$ is a parallelogram. Similarly, $ACC'A'$ is a parallelogram. Hence, $\overline{BB'} \parallel \overline{AA'}$, $\overline{BB'} = \overline{AA'}$, $\overline{CC'} \parallel \overline{AA'}$, $\overline{CC'} = \overline{AA'}$. By the transitivity properties of parallelism and equality, $\overline{BB'} \parallel \overline{CC'}$ and $\overline{BB'} = \overline{CC'}$. Hence, $BB'C'C$ is a parallelogram and

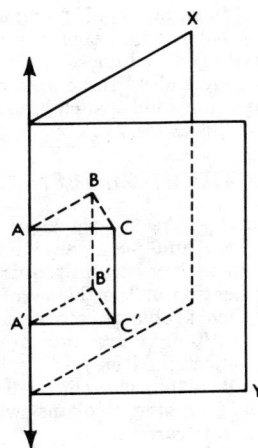

$\overline{CB} \cong \overline{C'B'}$. Therefore, $\triangle ABC \cong \triangle A'B'C'$ (S.S.S.) and $\angle A \cong \angle A'$, Q.E.D.

Definitions. The *measure of a dihedral angle* is the measure of any of its plane angles. A *right dihedral angle* is a dihedral angle whose measure is 90. The planes determined by the faces of a right dihedral angle are *perpendicular to each other.*

■ THEOREM 14–18.—If a line is perpendicular to a plane, then any plane containing this line is perpendicular to the given plane.

■ THEOREM 14–19.—If two planes are perpendicular, then any line in one plane that is perpendicular to their line of intersection is perpendicular to the other plane.

■ THEOREM 14–20.—If two planes are perpendicular, then any line perpendicular to one at a point on their intersection is contained in the other.

■ THEOREM 14–21.—If each of two intersecting planes is perpendicular to a third plane, then their line of intersection is perpendicular to this plane.

Proof. Let the intersection of the two planes intersect the third plane at P. The line perpendicular to the third plane at P must lie in each of the two intersecting planes by Theorem 14–20. It must therefore be the line of intersection of these two planes, Q.E.D.

SECTION FIFTEEN

Polyhedrons.—A *polyhedron* is the set of all the points in a finite number of polygonal regions, each of which is bounded by a convex polygon such that the interiors of no two polygons have points in common, and such that each side of each polygon is also a side of exactly one of the other polygons. Each vertex of each polygon is a *vertex of the polyhedron.* Each side of each polygon is an *edge of the polyhedron.* Each of the polygonal regions is a *face of the polyhedron.*

A polyhedron is named according to the number of faces that it contains.

Polyhedrons	
Faces	Name
4	tetrahedron
5	pentahedron
6	hexahedron
8	octahedron
10	decahedron
12	dodecahedron
20	icosahedron

Definition. If a plane and a polyhedron intersect, the intersection is a *section of the polyhedron.*

Definition. A polyhedron is a *convex polyhedron* if every section that contains at least three noncollinear points is either a convex polygon or a face of the polyhedron.

Definition. A *regular polyhedron* is a convex polyhedron, all of whose faces are bounded by regular polygons having the same number of sides, and such that all vertices of the polyhedron belong to the same number of faces.

Comment 1. There are exactly five types of regular polyhedrons, as shown below. They are called the *Platonic figures,* or *Platonic solids.*

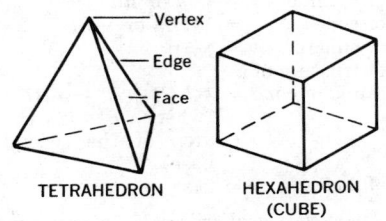

TETRAHEDRON   HEXAHEDRON (CUBE)

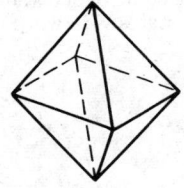

OCTAHEDRON

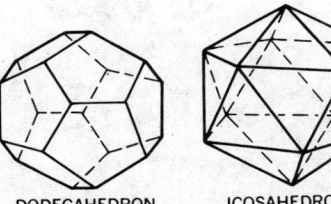

DODECAHEDRON   ICOSAHEDRON

Comment 2. It is easily proved that the faces of a regular polyhedron are congruent. This property is often used as part of the definition of a regular polygon.

Definitions. Given: a convex polygon and a point not in the plane of the polygon. The set of all rays, each of which has the given point as end point and a point of the polygon, is called a *polyhedral angle.* The given point is the *vertex of the polyhedral angle,* and each ray containing a vertex of the polygon is an *edge of the polyhedral angle.* An angle with the given point as vertex and

containing two consecutive vertices of the polygon is a *face angle of the polyhedral angle.* A *face of a polyhedral angle* is the set of points in a face angle and its interior. A polyhedral angle having three faces is a *trihedral angle.*

■ THEOREM 15–1.—The sum of the measures of any two face angles of a trihedral angle is greater than the measure of the third face of the angle.

■ THEOREM 15–2.—The sum of the measures of all the face angles of a polyhedral angle is less than 360.

Example. If two face angles of a trihedral angle have measures 70 and 120, and x represents the measure of the third face angle, then: by Theorem 15–1, $x + 70 > 120$; by Theorem 15–2, $x + 70 + 120 < 360$.

These imply that $x > 50$ and $x < 170$; that is, x is between 50 and 170.

Comment. Using Theorems 15–1 and 15–2, and the definition of a regular polyhedron, it can be proved that there are exactly five types of regular polyhedrons.

Definition. A *prism* is a polyhedron such that two of its faces are bounded by congruent polygons in parallel planes, and each of the remaining faces is bounded by a parallelogram with two sides in the congruent polygons. The faces bounded by the congruent polygons are *bases.* Prisms are classified according to their bases. One with a triangular-region base is a *triangular prism;* one with a rectangular-region base is a *rectangular prism;* and so on.

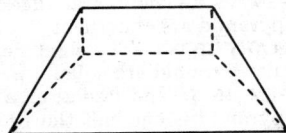

Definitions. A *parallelepiped* is a prism whose base is bounded by a parallelogram. A *rectangular parallelepiped* is a parallelepiped each of whose faces is bounded by a rectangle. A *cube* is a parallelepiped each of whose faces is bounded by a square.

The faces of a prism that are not the bases are *lateral faces.* The *lateral surface of a prism* is the set of all points in the lateral faces. The intersection of two lateral faces is a *lateral edge of the prism.* A prism is a *right prism* if, and only if, a lateral edge is perpendicular to a base.

A *right section of a prism* is the intersection of the prism with a plane that is perpendicular to and intersects the interior of every lateral edge of the prism. The *altitude of a prism* is a segment whose end points are in the planes that contain the bases of the prism and is perpendicular to these planes.

The *lateral area of a prism* is the sum of the areas of all the lateral faces of the prism.

■ THEOREM 15–3.—The lateral area of a prism is equal to the product of the length of a lateral edge and the perimeter of a right section.

■ COROLLARY 15–3–1.—The lateral area of a right prism is the product of the length of a lateral edge and the perimeter of a base.

Definition. A *pyramid* is a convex polyhedron that is contained in a polyhedral angle, except for one of its faces, which is its *base*. The *vertex of the pyramid* is the vertex of the polyhedral angle.

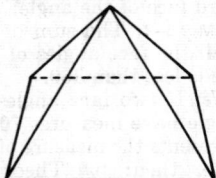

The segment that joins the vertex to its projection on the plane of the base is the *altitude of the pyramid.*

Like prisms, pyramids are classified according to the boundary of the base.

Definitions. A pyramid is a *regular pyramid* if, and only if, its base is bounded by a regular polygon and one end point of the altitude is the center of the base. A *slant height of a pyramid* is the distance between its vertex and an edge in its base.

Definition. The *lateral faces of a pyramid* are the faces that are contained in its polyhedral angle. The *lateral edges of a pyramid* are those of its edges that have the vertex of the pyramid as one end point.

Definition. The *lateral area of a pyramid* is the sum of the areas of its lateral faces.

■ THEOREM 15–4.—The lateral edges of a regular pyramid are congruent.

■ COROLLARY 15–5–1.—The slant heights of a regular pyramid are equal.

■ THEOREM 15–5.—The lateral area of a regular pyramid is one-half the product of a slant height and the perimeter of the base.

■ THEOREM 15–6.—Every polygon section of a pyramid, made by a plane parallel to that of its base, is similar to the boundary of the base. The distances from the vertex to the planes of the intersection and the base are proportional to the corresponding sides of these similar polygons, and the areas of the polygonal regions are proportional to the squares of these distances.

Definition. A *frustum of a pyramid* is a polyhedron whose edges consist of those of the base of the pyramid, the intersection of the pyramid by a plane parallel to that of the base, and the segments contained in the edges of the pyramid between corresponding vertices of the base and the section. The section and its interior is also a *base of the frustum.*

■ THEOREM 15–7.—The lateral faces of a frustum of a regular pyramid are congruent isosceles trapezoids.

■ THEOREM 15–8.—The lateral area of a frustum of a regular pyramid is one-half the product of the height of a lateral face and the sum of the perimeters of the bases: $L = \frac{1}{2}h(p + p')$.

By the method of limits similar to that described for polygons and circles, a cylinder and a cone may be defined.

In a right circular cylinder with base radius r and height h:

$$\text{lateral area} = 2\pi rh,$$
$$\text{total area} = 2\pi rh + 2r^2.$$

In a right circular cone with base radius r, height h, and slant height s:

$$\text{lateral area} = \pi rs,$$
$$\text{total area} = \pi rs + \pi r^2.$$

The area of a sphere with radius r is $4\pi r^2$.

The commonly used volumes are listed below for reference:

B = area of base
h = height
s = slant height
r = radius of the base of a right circular cylinder or cone, or radius of a sphere
V = volume
A = area
V of right prism = Bh
V of pyramid = $\frac{1}{3}Bh$
V of cylinder = πr^2h or Bh
V of cone = $\frac{1}{3}\pi r^2h$ or $\frac{1}{3}Bh$
V of sphere = $\frac{4}{3}\pi r^3$
V of frustum of a pyramid or cone = $\frac{1}{3}h(B + B' + \sqrt{BB'})$ (where B' is the area of the second base)
A of zone = $2\pi rh$

Comment. Cavalieri's principle may be used to prove some of the above volume formulas. It states: If two polyhedrons have their bases in parallel planes and if any intersections with these polyhedrons made by a plane parallel to the bases are boundaries of polygonal regions with equal areas, then the polyhedrons have equal volumes.

The principle also can be used to treat other types of solids, such as spheres, cylinders, and cones.

SECTION SIXTEEN

Constructions.—The drawing with straightedge and compass only of figures that satisfy certain requirements is an application of the theory of geometry. In such problems, abstract points and sets of points are interpreted as physical objects. After finding how to make the drawing, one shows how the theory of geometry explains why the construction is correct.

The word "construct" is used here to indicate a drawing operation employing only a straightedge and one or more compasses.

It is assumed that:

(1) Compasses can be used to draw a circle, or part of a circle, given its center and either its radius or a point in the circle.

(2) The straightedge can be used to draw a line segment that contains one or more given points.

(3) The circles and line segments so drawn are the physical counterparts of mathematical circles, lines, or line segments.

In each of the construction problems that follow, the construction and the related theory that explains why the con-

EGYPTIAN STATE TOURIST ADMINISTRATION

THE PYRAMIDS at Giza, Egypt, were constructed over a period of centuries by people who exhibited an amazingly accurate knowledge of both mathematics and engineering.

struction yields the desired results are indicated.

1. Given a ray $\overrightarrow{AB}$ and a segment $\overline{CD}$, construct a point E on $\overrightarrow{AB}$ such that $\overline{AE} \cong \overline{CD}$.

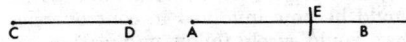

Construction. With $\overline{CD}$ as radius and A as center, draw the arc of the circle that intersects $\overrightarrow{AB}$. The intersection E is the desired point.

Related Theory. Since A is inside the circle, $\overline{AE}$ is a secant and hence cuts the circle in two points, one of them in $\overrightarrow{AB}$. In addition, the radii of a circle are congruent.

2. Given $\overrightarrow{AB}$ and $\overline{CD}$, construct E in $\overrightarrow{AB}$ such that $\overline{AE} = 2 \cdot CD$.

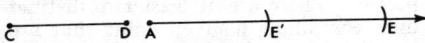

Construction. Locate E' such that $\overline{AE'} = \overline{CD}$, and then in $\overrightarrow{E'B}$ locate E such that $\overline{E'E} = \overline{CD}$ (it is assumed that E is between A and B). Thus $\overline{AE} = 2 \cdot CD$.

Related Theory. Theorem 6–4 (Point-Plotting Theorem).

Comment. This construction can be extended to find F such that $\overline{AF} = m \cdot CD$, where m is any positive integer.

3. Given $\overline{AB}$, construct its midpoint.

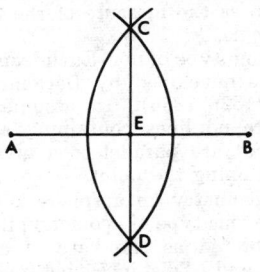

Construction. The arcs shown are drawn with A and B as centers, and with a radius that is greater than half of $\overline{AB} \cdot \overline{CD}$ intersects $\overline{AB}$ in E, the desired midpoint.

Related Theory. $\triangle ACD \cong \triangle BCD$ (S.S.S.). Therefore, $\overline{CE}$ is the midray of $\angle ACB$. Since $\triangle ACB$ is an isosceles triangle with $\overline{AC} \cong \overline{BC}$, then $\overline{CE}$ bisects $\overline{AB}$. (Theorem 9–20 may be used for an alternate proof.)

4. Given $\overline{AB}$, construct the perpendicular to $\overline{AB}$ at its midpoint.

Construction. Use Construction 3.

Related Proof. The bisector of the vertex angle of an isosceles triangle is perpendicular to the base and bisects the base.

5. Given $\angle ABC$, construct its midray.

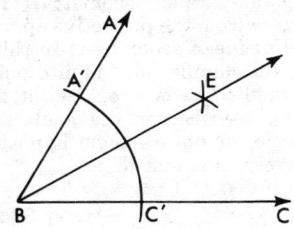

Construction. With B as center and any radius, draw an arc intersecting $\overrightarrow{BA}$ and $\overrightarrow{BC}$ in A' and C', respectively. With A' and C' as centers and a radius greater than half of $A'C'$, draw arcs intersecting in E. Then BE is the desired midray.

Related Theory. $\triangle BA'E \cong \triangle BC'E$ (S.S.S.); therefore, $\angle A'BE \cong \angle C'BE$.

6. Given line l and P in l, construct the perpendicular to l at P.

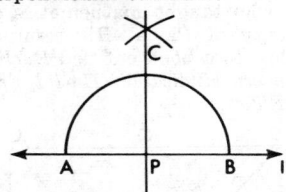

Construction. With P as center and any radius, draw an arc intersecting l in A and B. Then use Construction 4 on $\overline{AB}$, locating C. $\overleftrightarrow{CP}$ is the desired line.

Related Theory. $\triangle ACP \cong \triangle BCP$ (S.S.S.). Then $\angle APC \cong \angle BPC$. Since these angles are a linear pair, each is a right angle.

7. Given line l and P not in l, construct the perpendicular to l containing P.

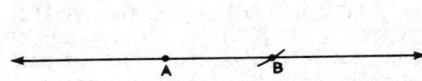

Construction. Take point A in l. If $\overline{PA} \perp l$, the desired construction is completed. If $\overline{PA}$ is not perpendicular to l, then with P as center, and $\overline{PA}$ as radius, draw an arc. Since $\overline{PA}$ is greater than the shortest distance from P to l, this circle intersects l in a second point, B. Complete the construction using Construction 3 on $\overline{AB}$.

Related Theory. If $\overrightarrow{PA}$ is not perpendicular to l, then Theorem 11–3 states that l and the circle with P as center and $\overline{PA}$ as radius will intersect in two points.

8. Given $\angle ABC$, $\overrightarrow{DE}$ and a half plane H with edge $\overrightarrow{DE}$, construct $\overrightarrow{DF}$ in H, such that $\angle ABC \cong \angle EDF$.

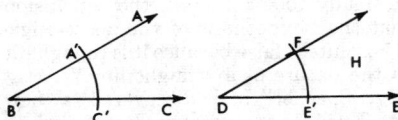

Construction. Construct congruent circles with B and D as centers and any radius, thus locating C' on $\overrightarrow{BC}$, A' on $\overrightarrow{BA}$ and E' on $\overrightarrow{DE}$. With E' as center and $\overline{A'C'}$ as radius, draw an arc in H intersecting the circle with D as center, thus locating F. Then $\overrightarrow{DF}$ is the desired ray.

Related Theory. Since $\overline{E'F}$ and $\overline{A'C'}$ are congruent chords in congruent circles, $\triangle A'BC' \cong \triangle FDE'$ (S.S.S.) and $\angle ABC \cong \angle EDF$.

9. Given line l and point P not in l, construct the line parallel to l, containing P.

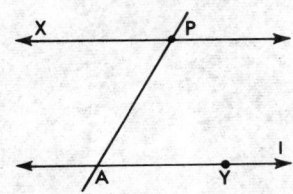

Construction. Choose any point in l, A, and use Construction 8 to make $\angle XPA \cong \angle YAP$, where Y is in l and X and Y are in opposite half planes having $\overrightarrow{AP}$ as edge.

Related Theorem. Theorem 9–2.

10. Given three segments with lengths a, b, c, respectively, construct a fourth segment with length d such that $(a,b) \bar{\mathrm{p}} (c,d)$.

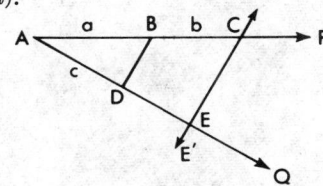

Construction. With any point A as endpoint, draw two distinct rays, $\overrightarrow{AP}$ and $\overrightarrow{AQ}$. With radius a and center A, locate B on $\overrightarrow{AP}$ such that $\overline{AB} = a$. Then with center B and radius b, locate C on $\overrightarrow{BP}$ such that $\overline{BC} = b$. (It is assumed that B is between A and P.) With center A and radius c, locate D on $\overrightarrow{AQ}$ such that $\overline{AD} = c$. Use Construction 9 to construct $\overleftrightarrow{CE'} \parallel \overleftrightarrow{BD}$. Let $\overleftrightarrow{CE'}$ intersect $\overrightarrow{AQ}$ in E. Then $\overline{DE} = d$.

Related Theory. Postulate 22 (Proportional-Segments Postulate).

11. Given $\overline{AB}$, and two positive numbers, a and b, locate a point C in $\overline{AB}$ such that $(\overline{AC}, \overline{CB}) \bar{\mathrm{p}} (a,b)$.

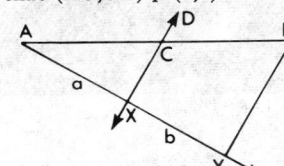

Construction. Draw any ray $\overrightarrow{AP}$ not collinear with $\overline{AB}$. On $\overrightarrow{AP}$ locate X and Y, with X between A and Y such that $\overline{AX} = a$, and $\overline{XY} = b$. Apply Construction 9 to draw $\overleftrightarrow{XD} \parallel \overleftrightarrow{YB}$. Then $\overleftrightarrow{XD}$ intersects $\overline{AB}$ in the desired point C.

Related Theory. Theorem 6–4 (Point-Plotting Theorem) and Postulate 22 (Proportional-Segments Postulate).

SECTION SEVENTEEN

Some Non-Euclidean Geometries.—Euclid's formulation of his parallel postulate is quite complex, as can be seen by referring to the discussion of parallel lines. On the other hand, his other postulates are stated simply. This contrast suggested to many that the parallel postu-

FAMOUS GEOMETRICIANS. (*Top to bottom*) Nikolai Lobachevsky (1793–1856), Bernhard Riemann (1826–1866), Jules Henri Poincaré (1854–1912), and Arthur Cayley (1821–1895).

late could be deduced from Euclid's other postulates, but all attempts to do this failed. Some mathematicians hoped to show that the parallel postulate is a logical consequence of the other postulates by showing that if a contradictory of the parallel postulate is assumed, a contradiction within the postulational system could eventually be deduced. Such an attempt was made by the Italian priest, Girolamo Saccheri (1667–1733), who taught mathematics at the University of Pavia. His results were published in a book entitled *Euclides ob omni naevo vindicatus* (*Euclid Freed of Every Flaw*).

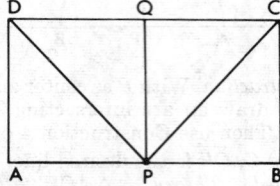

Saccheri studied what is known today as the *Saccheri quadrilateral*. He considered two congruent segments, perpendicular to $\overline{AB}$ at A and B, respectively, on the same side of $\overleftrightarrow{AB}$. If P and Q are midpoints of $\overline{AB}$ and $\overline{DC}$, respectively, then $\triangle ADP \cong \triangle BCP$ (S.A.S.), $\angle ADP \cong \angle BCP$, and $\overline{DP} \cong \overline{CP}$. Also, $\triangle DPQ \cong \triangle CPQ$ (S.S.S.). $\angle PDQ \cong \angle PCQ$ and $\angle ADC \cong \angle BCD$. If the last pair of angles are called the *summit angles* of the Saccheri quadrilateral, three possibilities may be considered: (1) The summit angles are both right angles. (2) The summit angles are both acute angles. (3) The summit angles are both obtuse angles.

Saccheri called these the *right-angle hypothesis*, the *acute-angle hypothesis*, and the *obtuse-angle hypothesis*. He was able to show that the parallel postulate is a consequence of the right-angle hypothesis and (using the infinitude of a straight line) that the obtuse-angle hypothesis produces a contradiction of another postulate. But when he assumed the acute-angle hypothesis, he obtained many seemingly strange results. None of them contradicted theorems that do not depend on the parallel postulate, so he finally took refuge in the conclusion that the "hypothesis of the acute-angle is absolutely false because it is repugnant to the nature of a straight line." Actually, Saccheri had discovered a new non-Euclidean geometry, but failed to realize the importance of the discovery.

It was not until the early nineteenth century that Karl Gauss (1777–1855) stated: "The assumption that the acute sum (of a triangle) is less than 180° leads to a curious geometry, quite different from ours (the Euclidean) but thoroughly consistent, which I have developed to my entire satisfaction. The theorems of this geometry appear to be paradoxical, and, to the uninitiated, absurd, but calm, steady reflection reveals that they contain nothing at all impossible."

Gauss was the greatest mathematician of his time, if not of all time. He started a study of parallels while still in his twenties, and kept up the study for more than thirty years. But he did not publish his results; he was fearful that he would become involved in controversies that would surely follow publication.

The first mathematician to publish a non-Euclidean geometry was the Russian, Nikolai Lobachevsky (1793–1856), a professor at the University of Kazan. The second mathematician (who was not aware of the work of Lobachevsky) was János Bolyai (1802–1860) who wrote a 26-page appendix for his father's two-volume treatise on geometry, which was published in 1832–1833.

Gauss, Lobachevsky, and Bolyai assumed a statement that might be expressed: There are at least two distinct lines containing a given point that are parallel to a given line not containing the given point.

The geometry in which this postulate holds is *hyperbolic geometry*. Some of the theorems in this geometry are as follows: (1) There are an infinite number of lines, containing a given point, that are parallel to a given line not containing the point. (2) The angle sum of any triangle is not constant and is less than 180. (3) The difference between 180 and the angle sum of a triangle can be taken as the measure of the area of the triangle.

A second type of non-Euclidean geometry was developed by Bernhard Riemann (1826–1866). It assumes that there are no lines containing a given point that are parallel to a given line not containing the point.

The geometry on a sphere is an example of this type of geometry, if "line" is interpreted as the "arc of a great circle" and "distance between two points" as "the length of the arc of the great circle." In such a geometry, the following theorems can be proved: (1) The angle sum of any triangle is greater than 180 and less than 540. (2) The excess of the angle sum of a triangle over 180 can be taken as a measure of the area of the triangle. (3) Two lines meet in two points.

There are also other geometries in which the "no parallel" postulate is used. Among them is *elliptic geometry*, in which the first two of the above theorems are valid, but in which two lines meet in exactly one point. The German mathematician Felix Klein (1849–1925) suggested the term "hyperbolic" for the two-parallel geometry, "parabolic" for the one-parallel geometry, and "elliptic" for the no-parallel geometry. These terms arose from the projective approach to non-Euclidean geometries. In this approach, the number of "infinite points" on a straight line is two, one, or none, according to whether the acute-angle, right-angle, or obtuse-angle hypothesis, respectively, is assumed.

—Harry Sitomer

TRIGONOMETRY

Analytic Trigonometry.—The word "trigonometry" literally means "measurement of triangles." For a long time, this classical aspect of trigonometry overshadowed the subject, with impressive applications to such fields as surveying, navigation, and astronomy. However, after the seventeenth century, the development of calculus revealed applications of trigonometry to such phenomena as heat flow, mechanical oscillations, and electronics, which had nothing to do with triangles or angles. The *analytic* rather than the *geometric* aspects of trigonometry became an important tool for mathematicians, physicists, engineers, and other scientists.

Coordinate Systems.—An idea that lies at the very root of many other branches of contemporary mathematics, from elementary plane geometry to advanced mathematical analysis, is the assumption that a *one-to-one correspondence* can be established between the points of any straight line and the members of the ordinary system of numbers—the so-called *real numbers*. Such a one-to-one correspondence is depicted in Figure 1. It is called a *coordinate system* on the line *L*.

The basic idea of a coordinate system is that once a unit length is defined on any line *L* by choosing "zero" and "one" as distinct points, then to each point *P* of that given line *L* there is associated a *unique* real number *r*, the coordinate of *P*. Conversely, to each real number (coordinate) *r*, there corresponds a unique point *P* on line *L*. The point *O*, which corresponds to the coordinate zero, is called the *origin* of the coordinate system. Positive coordinates correspond to points of *L* that are on one side of the origin (*positive side* of line *L*), while negative coordinates correspond to points of *L* on the other side of the origin (*negative side*). The natural order of the coordinates yields a corresponding arrangement of the points of line *L*. The *natural order* is defined as follows: Given any pair of real numbers, *a* and *b*, only one of three relationships is true—*a* is less than *b* ($a < b$), *a* is equal to *b* ($a = b$), or *a* is greater than *b* ($a > b$). The common convention for the arrangement of points of a line is that the coordinates are in an increasing order from left to right, as shown in Figure 1.

The great advantage of this correspondence of points with numbers is that one has available all properties of the real number system when studying geometrical properties of points and lines.

The idea of a coordinate system is readily extended to the points of any plane by choosing two intersecting lines, *X* and *Y*, in this plane and setting up a coordinate system on each of these lines, using the point of intersection *O* as a common origin for these coordinate systems. The lines *X* and *Y* are usually chosen perpendicular to each other, and are called the *X-axis* and *Y-axis*, respectively. The same scale is usually chosen on both axes, especially for the purpose of defining distance. (*Oblique axes*, or axes with different scales, are also possible and useful for certain purposes; however, they will not be discussed in this article.)

As shown in Figure 2, perpendiculars *PQ* and *PR* are drawn from any point *P* to the *X*-axis and the *Y*-axis, respectively. On the *X*-axis there is a unique coordinate *x* corresponding to *Q* and, similarly, on the *Y*-axis there is a unique coordinate *y* corresponding to *R*. Any point *P* of the plane now corresponds to a unique *ordered pair* of numbers (*x*, *y*). The value of *x*, the first coordinate, is called the *abscissa* of point *P*. The value of *y*, the second coordinate, is called the *ordinate* of point *P*.

An important formula from elementary coordinate geometry must be used now. It is the *distance formula*, which expresses the distance between any two points in the plane. By letting the coordinates of these points be x_1, y_1 and x_2, y_2, and applying the Pythagorean theorem to a diagram such as Figure 3, we obtain

$$d = \sqrt{(x_2 - x_1)^2 + (y_2 - y_1)^2}.$$

Unit Circle.—An important case of this distance formula arises when one considers the distance of any point (*x*, *y*) from the origin, whose coordinates are, of course, (*O*, *O*). Denoting this distance by *r* (Fig. 4), we obtain

$$r = \sqrt{x^2 + y^2}.$$

If the distance *r* is held fixed, while the point (*x*, *y*) is permitted to vary, the *locus* of point (*x*, *y*)—that is, the set of all points (*x*, *y*) with a fixed distance from the origin—is clearly a circle of radius *r*. This circle is completely specified by this equation for each fixed positive value of *r*. An equivalent equation is

$$x^2 + y^2 = r^2,$$

provided it is understood that the value of *r* is a fixed number greater than or equal to ($\geq$) zero; if $r = 1$, the preceding equation becomes a *unit circle* (Fig. 5), and the equation obtained is

$$x^2 + y^2 = 1.$$

The study of trigonometry in this article will be based upon the unit circle.

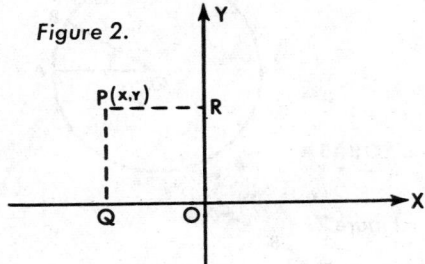

Figure 2.

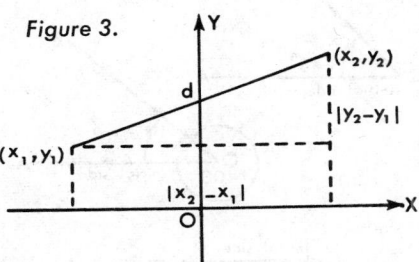

Figure 3.

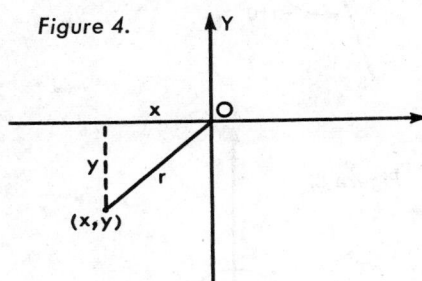

Figure 4.

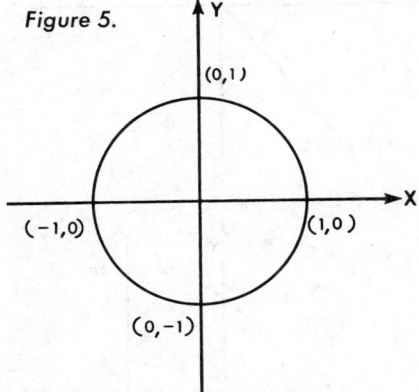

Figure 5.

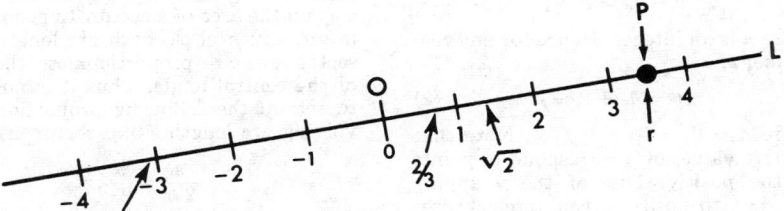

NUMBER LINE is basic to every branch of mathematics, for it establishes the relationship among the elements of the number system that is being used. The close-packed number line shown here contains both the rational and irrational and the positive and negative numbers.

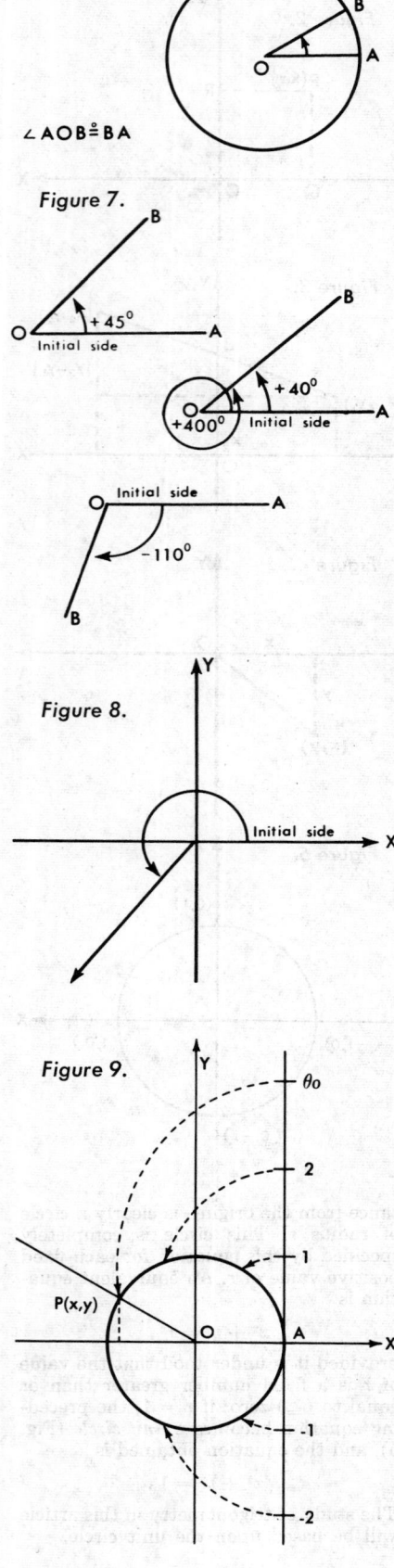

Figure 6.

$\angle AOB \overset{\circ}{=} BA$

Figure 7.

$+45^\circ$
Initial side
A
B

$+40^\circ$
$+400^\circ$
Initial side
A
B

Initial side
A
-110°
B

Figure 8.

Y
Initial side
X

Figure 9.

Circular Measure.—The circumference of a circle is divided into 360 equal parts, called *arc degrees*. Also, the number of angle degrees in a central angle equals the number of arc degrees in the intercepted arc, as shown in Figure 6.

In trigonometry, both the amount of rotation and the direction of rotation are important. Thus, an angle can be defined as *positive* if the rotation is counterclockwise, and as *negative* if the rotation is clockwise. The angle may have any magnitude, depending on the amount and direction of the rotation, as shown in Figure 7.

When an angle has its *vertex* at the origin and its *initial side* along the positive X-axis, it is said to be in the *standard position*, as shown in Figure 8.

It is useful in trigonometry to extend the method of measuring angles by introducing *circular measure*. Instead of associating a unique number of degrees with each given angle, in circular measure an *entire set* of real numbers is associated with the angle. Each number in this set measures an amount of rotation from the initial side to the terminal side. The amounts of rotation are expressed precisely in the following way: At point A in Figure 9, a line is drawn tangent to the unit circle, and the coordinate system is assigned to this line as it was assigned to the Y-axis, but starting at point A.

This new line is "wrapped around" the circle as indicated by the dotted arcs in Figure 9; each point of the line will fall upon a definite point of the circle. However, each time the line wraps around the circle, a new point of the line will fall onto the same place as a previous point. Therefore, each point P on the circle will correspond to an infinite number of points of the wrapping line, each new point arising after one complete rotation. These points are therefore spaced along the wrapping line at intervals of 2π, because that is the circumference of the unit circle.

Suppose θ_0 is the coordinate of the first point on the positive side of the wrapping line, which corresponds to point P_1 on the circle. Then

$$0 \leqq \theta_0 < 2\pi . \qquad (1)$$

If θ is the coordinate of any other point on the wrapping line that corresponds to the same point P on the circle, then θ must differ from θ_0 by an integral multiple of 2π; that is,

$$\theta - \theta_0 = 2n\pi ,$$

where n is an integer. Hence for any real number θ,

$$\theta = \theta_0 + 2n\pi , \qquad (2)$$

where $n = 0, \pm 1, \pm 2, \dots$. Note that positive values of n correspond to points on the positive side of the wrapping line; i.e., to positive (counterclockwise) rotations. Negative values of n correspond to points on the negative side of the wrapping line; i.e., to negative (clockwise) rotations.

The smallest counterclockwise rotation that corresponds to any specific point P on the unit circle is expressed by the value θ_0. All rotations that yield this (same) point P are represented by the set of all values of θ in equation (2) for a given θ_0. It is this set of real numbers that is associated with $\angle AOP$ in Figure 9. This special value θ_0 is often referred to as the *circular residue* of θ.

Although there are many possible values associated with a given angle (in standard position), it should be observed that a real number θ determines a unique point P on the unit circle and hence a unique angle in standard position. Each angle in standard position has many circular measures, but each circular measure determines a unique angle in standard position. For the purposes of this discussion, an angle of circular measure will be referred to as $\angle \theta$.

The relationship between circular measure and degree measure for angles is easily seen in the table below, where a circular measure of 2π corresponds to one complete rotation of the wrapping line (360° in degree measure).

Degree Measure		Circular Measure
360°	....	2π
180°	....	π
90°	....	$\dfrac{\pi}{2}$
60°	....	$\dfrac{\pi}{3}$
45°	....	$\dfrac{\pi}{4}$
$\dfrac{180°}{\pi}$	....	1
1°	....	$\dfrac{\pi}{180}$
$\dfrac{180°}{\pi}\theta$	....	θ
d°	....	$\dfrac{\pi d}{180}$

An angle of circular measure 1 is often called an angle of 1 *radian*. For this reason, circular measure is often called *radian measure*.

From Figure 9 it is clear that an angle of 1 radian intercepts an arc of unit length on a unit circle. It will be seen that an angle of 1 radian is equal to an angle of $180°/\pi$—about 57.3° in degree measure.

Arc Length and Sector Area.—One advantage of circular measure over degree measure is that the former yields simpler formulas for the length of an arc of a circle and the area of a sector. In geometry, in any given circle both arc length and sector area are proportional to the size of the central angle. Thus it is possible to set up the following proportions involving arc length s and sector area A:

$$\frac{s}{2\pi r} = \frac{\theta}{2\pi} , \qquad (3)$$

$$\frac{A}{r^2} = \frac{\theta}{2\pi} , \qquad (4)$$

where r is the length of the radius and the central angle θ is expressed in circu-

Figure 10.

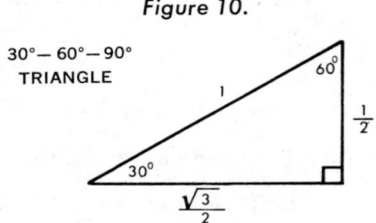

30° – 60° – 90°
TRIANGLE

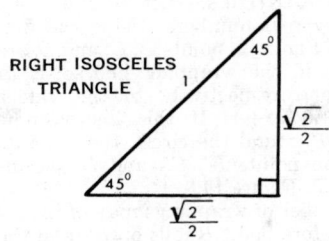

RIGHT ISOSCELES
TRIANGLE

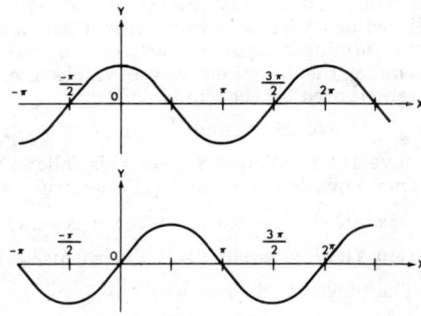

Figure 11.

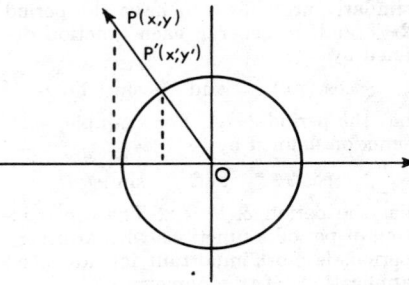

Figure 12.

lar measure. From this it follows that

$$s = r\theta \text{ (arc length)} , \qquad (5)$$

$$A = \tfrac{1}{2}r^2\theta \text{ (sector area)} . \qquad (6)$$

These formulas are most useful in advanced mathematics.

Sine and Cosine Functions.—Take any real number θ. Corresponding to the value θ, there is a unique point P on the unit circle. The point P has a unique pair of coordinates (x, y) and determines a unique $\angle AOP$ in standard position (which will also be called $\angle\theta$). The values of the coordinates x and y, which are determined in this manner from the given real number θ, are called the *cosine of θ* and the *sine of θ*, respectively. They are abbreviated as follows:

$$\cos \theta = x \qquad \text{and} \qquad \sin \theta = y . \quad (7)$$

Since

$$x^2 + y^2 = 1 ,$$

we obtain

$$(\cos \theta)^2 + (\sin \theta)^2 = 1 ,$$

for all real θ. This is generally written:

$$\cos^2 \theta + \sin^2 \theta = 1 , \qquad (8)$$

for all real θ. However, to each real number θ, there corresponds a unique value of $\cos \theta$ as well as a unique value of $\sin \theta$. Thus, *sine* and *cosine* may properly be referred to as *functions*. The *domain* of each of these functions (the values that θ may assume) consists of all the real numbers. The *range* of each of these functions (the values that $\cos \theta$ or $\sin \theta$ may assume) consists of all the real numbers from -1 to $+1$, inclusive.

The determination of the values of $\cos \theta$ and $\sin \theta$ for every real value of θ requires higher mathematical techniques. However, these values can be tabulated for a large number of particular values of θ, corresponding to special angles such as 30°, 45°, 60°, and 90°, which are readily handled by the methods of elementary plane geometry. In this connection, consider the special right triangles in Figure 10. Using these special triangles and simple coordinate geometry, the accompanying table is constructed.

A more extensive table, listing approximate values of these functions, is included at the end of this article.

The graphs of the cosine and the sine functions can easily be plotted with the aid of the accompanying table. In plotting these graphs, the values of θ are found along the X-axis; the values of cos

Values of Cos θ and Sin θ

θ (Degree Measure)	θ (Circular Measure)	Cos θ	Sin θ
0°	0	1	0
30°	$\frac{\pi}{6}$	$\frac{\sqrt{3}}{2}$	$\frac{1}{2}$
45°	$\frac{\pi}{4}$	$\frac{\sqrt{2}}{2}$	$\frac{\sqrt{2}}{2}$
60°	$\frac{\pi}{3}$	$\frac{1}{2}$	$\frac{\sqrt{3}}{2}$
90°	$\frac{\pi}{2}$	0	1
120°	$\frac{2\pi}{3}$	$-\frac{1}{2}$	$\frac{\sqrt{3}}{2}$
135°	$\frac{3\pi}{4}$	$-\frac{\sqrt{2}}{2}$	$\frac{\sqrt{2}}{2}$
150°	$\frac{5\pi}{6}$	$-\frac{\sqrt{3}}{2}$	$\frac{1}{2}$
180°	π	-1	0
210°	$\frac{7\pi}{6}$	$-\frac{\sqrt{3}}{2}$	$-\frac{1}{2}$
225°	$\frac{5\pi}{4}$	$-\frac{\sqrt{2}}{2}$	$-\frac{\sqrt{2}}{2}$
240°	$\frac{4\pi}{3}$	$-\frac{1}{2}$	$-\frac{\sqrt{3}}{2}$
270°	$\frac{3\pi}{2}$	0	-1
300°	$\frac{5\pi}{3}$	$\frac{1}{2}$	$-\frac{\sqrt{3}}{2}$
315°	$\frac{7\pi}{4}$	$\frac{\sqrt{2}}{2}$	$-\frac{\sqrt{2}}{2}$
330°	$\frac{11\pi}{6}$	$\frac{\sqrt{3}}{2}$	$-\frac{1}{2}$
360°	2π	1	0

θ (or $\sin \theta$) are then found along the Y-axis.

Considering Figure 9 once again, observe that the coordinates of point P are by definition $\cos \theta$, $\sin \theta$, because point P is located on a unit circle. Suppose point P is located on the terminal ray of $\angle \theta$ at a distance $OP = r$ from its vertex, as shown in Figure 12.

Let P' be the point where the terminal ray OP intersects the unit circle; i.e., $OP' = 1$. If the coordinates of P are (x, y) while those of P' are (x', y'), then (by similar triangles):

$$\frac{x}{x'} = \frac{y}{y'} = \frac{OP}{OP'} = \frac{r}{1} .$$

Hence,

$$x = rx' \qquad \text{and} \qquad y = ry' .$$

However since P' is on the unit circle,

$$x' = r \cos \theta \qquad \text{and} \qquad y' = r \sin \theta .$$

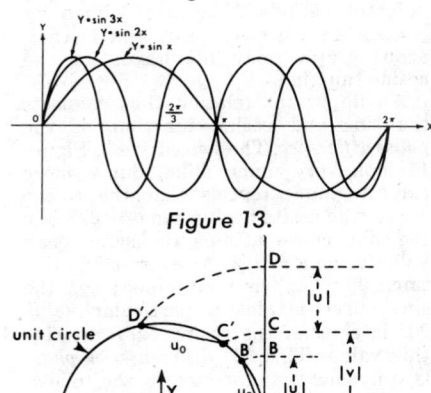

Figure 13.

Figure 14.

Hence,

$$x = r \cos \theta \qquad \text{and} \qquad y = r \sin \theta . \quad (9)$$

This holds true for any point P' (x', y').

■ **ANALYTIC PROPERTIES.**—From the definition of the sine and cosine functions, it follows that they each possess the important property of *periodicity*. This means that they each repeat the values they assume over certain specified intervals. The smallest interval over which sine and cosine exhibit this repetition is an interval of length, 2π. These functions are therefore called periodic functions with period 2π. The periodicity is conveniently expressed as follows:

$$\cos (\theta + 2\pi) = \cos \theta , \qquad (10)$$

$$\sin (\theta + 2\pi) = \sin \theta , \qquad (11)$$

for all real θ. The periodicity is also apparent in the graphs of Figure 11.

One can readily construct periodic functions with a period other than 2π by forming *composite functions*. For example, the functions whose values are represented by the expressions

$$\cos 2\theta \quad \text{and} \quad \sin 2\theta$$

have the smaller period π. This follows from equations (10) and (11) because

$$\cos 2(\theta + \pi) = \cos (2\theta + 2\pi) = \cos 2\theta,$$

$$\sin 2(\theta + \pi) = \sin (2\theta + 2\pi) = \sin 2\theta.$$

The functions defined by

$$\cos 3\theta \quad \text{and} \quad \sin 3\theta$$

similarly are shown to have the period $2\pi/3$ and, in general, each function defined by

$$\cos (A\theta) \quad \text{and} \quad \sin (A\theta)$$

has the period $2\pi/A$. For example, each function defined by

$$\cos \pi\theta \quad \text{and} \quad \sin \pi\theta$$

has the period $2\pi/\pi = 2$. The construction of periodic functions with arbitrary periods is most important for advanced applications of trigonometry.

Figure 13 depicts sine graphs having different periods. They are defined by $y = \sin Ax$, since $A = 1, 2,$ and 3. Analogous graphs may be drawn for the cosine function.

An important relation that connects the sine and cosine functions is the *phase difference*. The two curves in Figure 11 look very much alike, but a more careful glance reveals that the cosine curve reaches its peak when $\theta = 0$, while the sine curve attains the same peak value when $\theta = \pi/2$. At every stage this same 90° "lag" is maintained; i.e., the sine curve attains a particular value 90° later than the cosine curve attains this value. This 90° *difference in phase* is conveniently expressed in the following purely analytic form:

$$\sin \left(\theta + \frac{\pi}{2}\right) = \cos \theta, \quad \textbf{(12)}$$

for all real θ.

This relation can be derived purely analytically from an even more general relation connecting the cosine and sine functions. However, before proceeding with this task, note that all the relations mentioned thus far have an important quality: they are true for all real values of θ. For example, equation (8) asserts that

$$\cos^2 \theta + \sin^2 \theta = 1,$$

for all real θ. Whenever an equation containing a variable is true for all permissible values of this variable (such as θ), the equation is called an *identity*. (The permissible values will usually be clear from the context.)

The identity

$$\cos^2 \theta + \sin^2 \theta = 1$$

follows directly from the definitions of the cosine and sine functions. It will be used here to define many important identities.

■ **BASIC IDENTITIES.**—Let u and v be arbitrary real numbers. Using the diagram of Figure 9, points B, C, and D are marked on the wrapping line so as to correspond respectively to the values u, v, and $u + v$. If this line is now wrapped around the circle, these points fall upon points B', C', and D', as indicated in Figure 14.

A number of wrappings may of course occur before point B falls on B', and the same is true for the points C' and D'. In all cases, however, the length of arc AB' will certainly be the *circular residue* of AB, namely u_0. Hence, chord AB' and chord $C'D'$ have the same length. This length can be determined by applying the distance formula in equation (1) to the pairs of points A, B' and C', D'. By definition, the coordinates of these points are:

$$
\begin{aligned}
A: &\quad (1, 0) \\
B': &\quad (\cos u, \sin u) \\
C': &\quad (\cos v, \sin v) \\
D': &\quad \cos (u + v), \sin (u + v).
\end{aligned}
$$

Applying the distance formula to the equality

$$(AB')^2 = (C'D')^2,$$

we obtain

$$(\cos u - 1)^2 + (\sin u)^2 = [\cos (u + v) - \cos u]^2 + [\sin (u + v) - \sin v]^2.$$

The left side of the above equation then becomes

$$\cos^2 u - 2 \cos u + 1 + \sin^2 u.$$

Because

$$\cos^2 u + \sin^2 u = 1,$$

this reduces to

$$2 - 2 \cos u.$$

Similarly, the right side of this equation reduces to

$$2 - 2[\cos (u + v) \cos v + \sin (u + v) \sin v].$$

Equating these two expressions yields the following fundamental identity:

$$\cos u = \cos (u + v) \cos v + \sin (u + v) \sin v, \quad \textbf{(13)}$$

for all real values of u and v.

From this identity further important identities can be obtained. First, since equation (13) holds true for all real values of u and v, then if w is any real number, u may be replaced by $w - v$:

$$\cos (w - v) = \cos w \cos v + \sin w \sin v, \quad \textbf{(14)}$$

for all real values of w and v.

If $w = 0$, equation (13) becomes

$$\cos (-v) = \cos 0 \cos v + \sin 0 \sin v.$$

But $\cos 0 = 1$ and $\sin 0 = 0$. Hence,

$$\cos (-v) = \cos v, \quad \textbf{(15)}$$

for all real values of v.

Equation (14) shows that cosine is an *even function*. A function f is called an even function only if $f(-x) = f(x)$ for all permissible values of x.

Returning to equation (14), substitute $w = \pi/2$:

$$\cos \left(\frac{\pi}{2} - v\right) = \cos \frac{\pi}{2} \cos v + \sin \frac{\pi}{2} \sin v.$$

But $\cos \pi/2 = 0$ and $\sin \pi/2 = 1$. Hence,

$$\cos \left(\frac{\pi}{2} - v\right) = \sin v, \quad \textbf{(16)}$$

for all real values of v.

Replacing v by $(\pi/2 - u)$ in equation (16) yields the following identity as an immediate corollary:

$$\sin \left(\frac{\pi}{2} - u\right) = \cos u, \quad \textbf{(17)}$$

for all real values of u.

Equations (16) and (17) exhibit the important relationship of *complementarity*. Whenever $u + v = \pi/2$, u and v are *complementary*. Either of these values is then the *complement* of the other. Identities (16) and (17) may now be expressed verbally as follows:

The sine of a real number is the cosine of its complement.

The cosine of a real number is the sine of its complement.

Identities (15) and (16) together yield a derivation of the "90° phase difference" property mentioned previously. In equation (16), let $v = \theta + \pi/2$, where θ may be any real number. This gives

$$\cos (-\theta) = \sin \left(\theta + \frac{\pi}{2}\right).$$

But, by equation (15), $\cos (-\theta) = \cos \theta$. Hence,

$$\sin \left(\theta + \frac{\pi}{2}\right) = \cos \theta.$$

for all real θ. This completes the derivation of equation (12).

Return to equation (14) and substitute $v = -(\pi/2)$:

$$\cos \left(w + \frac{\pi}{2}\right) = \cos w \cos \left(-\frac{\pi}{2}\right) + \sin w \sin \left(-\frac{\pi}{2}\right).$$

But from equation (15) $\cos -(\pi/2) = \cos \pi/2 = 0$, and from equation (16), letting $v = \pi$,

$$\sin \left(-\frac{\pi}{2}\right) = \cos \pi = -1.$$

Hence,

$$\cos \left(w + \frac{\pi}{2}\right) = -\sin w, \quad \textbf{(18)}$$

for all real w. In this formula, replace w by $-v$:

$$\cos \left(\frac{\pi}{2} - v\right) = -\sin (-v),$$

and make use of equation (16); thus,

$$\sin (-v) = -\sin v, \quad \textbf{(19)}$$

for all real v. Equation (19) shows that sine is an *odd function*. A function f is called an odd function only if $f(-x) = -f(x)$ for all permissible values of x.

Identities (15) and (19) make it unnecessary to tabulate sines and cosines of negative numbers. For example, to determine the value of $\sin(-\pi/3)$ and $\cos(-\pi/3)$, proceed as follows:

$$\sin\left(-\frac{\pi}{3}\right) = -\sin\frac{\pi}{3} = -\frac{\sqrt{3}}{2},$$
$$\cos\left(-\frac{\pi}{3}\right) = \cos\frac{\pi}{3} = +\frac{1}{2}.$$

With periodicity of sine and cosine, it is unnecessary to tabulate their values outside of the interval $(0, 2\pi)$. Identities (12) and (18) further cut this down to the interval $(0, \pi/2)$. Thus, trigonometry tables need actually be computed only for numbers from 0 to $\pi/4$ (0° to 45° in degree measure).

From equation (14) another very important identity may be obtained by replacing v by $(-v)$:

$$\cos(w + v) = $$
$$\cos w \cos(-v) + \sin w \sin(-v).$$

Using equations (15) and (19),

$$\cos(w + v) = $$
$$\cos w \cos v - \sin w \sin v, \quad \textbf{(20)}$$

for all real values of w and v.

There are also formulas for $\sin(w + v)$ and $\sin(w - v)$. Using equation (20) replace w by $w + \pi/2$:

$$\cos\left(w + \frac{\pi}{2} + v\right) = $$
$$\cos\left(w + \frac{\pi}{2}\right)\cos v - \sin\left(w + \frac{\pi}{2}\right)\sin v.$$

Using equations (18) and (12) we have

$$-\sin(w + v) = $$
$$-\sin w \cos v - \cos w \sin v,$$
$$\sin(w + v) = $$
$$\sin w \cos v + \cos w \sin v, \quad \textbf{(21)}$$

for all real values of w and v.

Replacing v by $-v$ in equation (20) and using equations (14) and (18), we obtain

$$\sin(w - v) = $$
$$\sin w \cos v - \cos w \sin v, \quad \textbf{(22)}$$

for all real values of w and v.

Special cases of identities (22) and (14) are

$$\sin(\pi - v) = \sin v, \quad \textbf{(23)}$$
$$\cos(\pi - v) = -\cos v, \quad \textbf{(24)}$$

for all real v.

The last two identities exhibit the *supplementarity* relationship. Whenever $u + v = \pi$, u and v are supplementary. Either of these values is then the *supplement* of the other. Identities (23) and (24) may thus be expressed verbally:

The sine of a real number is the sine of its supplement.

The cosine of a real number is the negative of the cosine of its supplement.

Double- and Half-Argument Identities.—

In identities (20) and (21), let $w = v = \theta$, where θ may be any real number. Thus,

$$\cos 2\theta = \cos^2\theta - \sin^2\theta, \quad \textbf{(25)}$$
$$\sin 2\theta = 2\sin\theta\cos\theta, \quad \textbf{(26)}$$

for all real θ. Identity (24) can be expressed in two other useful ways by using the basic identity (8):

$$\cos^2\theta + \sin^2\theta = 1.$$

From this we obtain

$$\cos^2\theta = 1 - \sin^2\theta,$$
$$\sin^2\theta = 1 - \cos^2\theta.$$

Substituting each of these in turn into equation (24), we obtain

$$\cos 2\theta = 1 - 2\sin^2\theta, \quad \textbf{(27)}$$
$$\cos 2\theta = 2\cos^2\theta - 1, \quad \textbf{(28)}$$

for all real θ. Formulas (25) through (28) are known as the *double-argument* formulas. (They are also called the *double-angle* formulas when θ is interpreted as the measure of an angle.)

Solving equation (27) for $\sin^2\theta$, we obtain

$$\sin^2\theta = \frac{1 - \cos 2\theta}{2},$$

for all real θ. As a result, therefore, we obtain

$$\sin\theta = \pm\sqrt{\frac{1 - \cos 2\theta}{2}}.$$

However, the ambiguity of sign requires some further discussion. By definition, the values of $\sin\theta$ are positive whenever the circular residue θ_0 is between 0 and π; the values of $\sin\theta$ are negative whenever the circular residue θ_0 is between π and 2π. Hence, to be precise,

$$\sin\theta = \sqrt{\frac{1 - \cos 2\theta}{2}},$$

whenever $0 \leqq \theta_0 \leqq \pi$, and

$$\sin\theta = -\sqrt{\frac{1 - \cos 2\theta}{2}}, \quad \textbf{(29)}$$

whenever $\pi < \theta_0 < 2\pi$.

These formulas are also useful when considered as *half-argument* rather than double-argument formulas. This is done by letting $\phi = 2\theta$; that is, $\theta = \phi/2$. Then equation (29) becomes

$$\sin\frac{\phi}{2} = \sqrt{\frac{1 - \cos\phi}{2}},$$

whenever $0 \leqq (\phi/2)_0 \leqq \pi$, and

$$\sin\frac{\phi}{2} = -\sqrt{\frac{1 - \cos\phi}{2}}, \quad \textbf{(30)}$$

whenever $\pi \leqq (\phi/2)_0 \leqq 2\pi$.

Similarly, by solving equation (28) for $\cos\theta$ and replacing θ by $\phi/2$ we obtain

$$\cos\frac{\phi}{2} = \sqrt{\frac{1 + \cos\phi}{2}},$$

whenever $0 \leqq (\phi/2)_0 \leqq \pi/2$, or $3\pi/2 \leqq (\phi/2)_0 \leqq 2\pi$, and

$$\cos\frac{\phi}{2} = -\sqrt{\frac{1 - \cos\phi}{2}}, \quad \textbf{(31)}$$

whenever $\pi/2 \leqq (\phi/2)_0 \leqq 3\pi/2$.

By way of an application, use these formulas to determine the values of $\sin 15°$ and $\cos 15°$ ($\sin\pi/12$ and $\cos\pi/12$). Letting $\phi = 30°$ ($\phi = \pi/6$), $\phi/2 = 15°$.

Since $(\phi/2)_0 = \pi/12$, use the first formula in each case:

$$\sin 15° = \sin\frac{\pi}{12} = \sqrt{\frac{1 - \frac{\sqrt{3}}{2}}{2}},$$

$$\cos 15° = \cos\frac{\pi}{12} = \sqrt{\frac{1 + \frac{\sqrt{3}}{2}}{2}}.$$

These expressions simplify to

$$\sin 15° = \frac{1}{2}\sqrt{2 - \sqrt{3}},$$

$$\cos 15° = \frac{1}{2}\sqrt{2 + \sqrt{3}}.$$

Equivalent expressions are

$$\sin 15° = \frac{\sqrt{6} - \sqrt{2}}{4},$$

$$\cos 15° = \frac{\sqrt{6} + \sqrt{2}}{4},$$

because

$$\left(\frac{\sqrt{6} \pm \sqrt{2}}{2}\right)^2 = \frac{6 \pm 2\sqrt{12} + 2}{4} = $$
$$\frac{8 \pm 4\sqrt{3}}{4} = 2 \pm \sqrt{3}.$$

Hence,

$$\sqrt{2 \pm \sqrt{3}} = \frac{\sqrt{6} \pm \sqrt{2}}{2}.$$

Sum and Difference Formulas.—

From equations (14), (20), (21), and (22), it is possible to obtain further identities, useful in more advanced work:

$$\sin(w + v) + \sin(w - v) = $$
$$2\sin w \cos v,$$
$$\sin(w + v) - \sin(w - v) = $$
$$2\cos w \sin v,$$
$$\cos(w + v) + \cos(w - v) = $$
$$2\cos w \cos v, \quad \textbf{(32)}$$
$$\cos(w + v) - \cos(w - v) = $$
$$-2\sin w \sin v,$$

for all real values of w and v.

If $w + v = r$ and $w - v = s$, these identities can be rewritten as follows:

$$\sin r + \sin s = $$
$$2\sin\frac{r + s}{2}\cos\frac{r - s}{2},$$
$$\sin r - \sin s = $$
$$2\cos\frac{r + s}{2}\sin\frac{r - s}{2},$$
$$\cos r + \cos s = \quad \textbf{(33)}$$
$$2\cos\frac{r + s}{2}\cos\frac{r - s}{2},$$
$$\cos r - \cos s = $$
$$-2\sin\frac{r + s}{2}\sin\frac{r - s}{2},$$

for all real values of r and s.

Tangent and Cotangent Functions.—

The functions tangent and cotangent are abbreviated and defined as

$$\tan\theta = \frac{\sin\theta}{\cos\theta} \quad \textbf{(34)}$$

provided $\cos\theta \neq 0$,

$$\cot\theta = \frac{\cos\theta}{\sin\theta} \quad \textbf{(35)}$$

provided $\sin\theta \neq 0$.

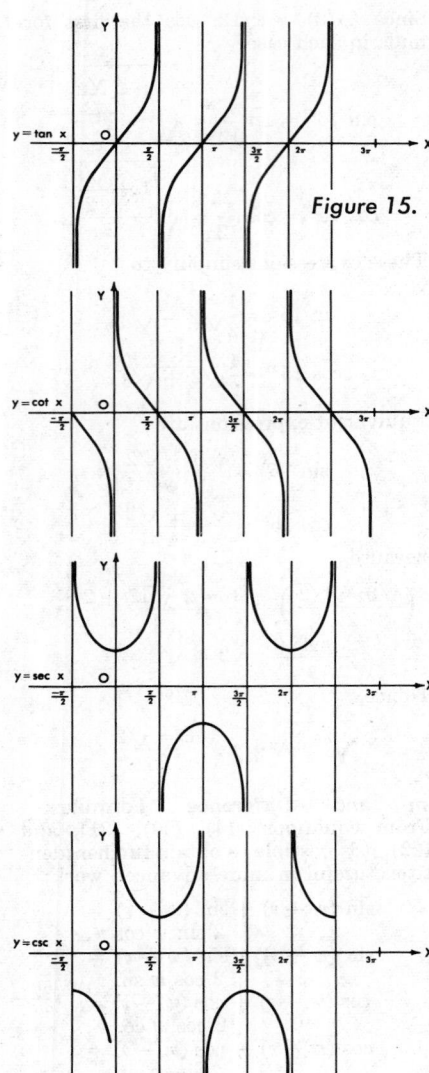

Figure 15.

Secant and Cosecant Functions.—The functions secant and cosecant are abbreviated and defined as follows:

$$\sec \theta = \frac{1}{\cos \theta} \qquad (36)$$

provided $\cos \theta \neq 0$,

$$\csc \theta = \frac{1}{\sin \theta} \qquad (37)$$

provided $\sin \theta \neq 0$.

Observe that all the functions tangent, cotangent, secant, and cosecant are not defined for certain real values of θ. The tangent and secant are undefined whenever θ_0 (the circular residue of θ) is either $\pi/2$ or $3\pi/2$. The cotangent and cosecant are undefined whenever θ_0 is either 0 or π. For all other values of θ, these functions have well-defined values given by equations (34) through (37). Values of the tangent function are found in the accompanying table. See graphs of these functions in Figure 15.

Further Basic Identities.—Important new identities, readily derived from equations (34) through (37) and the earlier identities, are listed below. The

reader should verify these identities. (The proofs for most of them are fairly easy.) Note that these equations are true for all *permissible* values of θ, u, v, w, etc.

$$\tan \theta = \frac{1}{\cot \theta}, \quad \cot \theta = \frac{1}{\tan \theta} \qquad (38)$$

$$\tan^2 \theta + 1 = \sec^2 \theta \qquad (39)$$

$$\cot^2 \theta + 1 = \csc^2 \theta \qquad (40)$$

$$\tan (v + w) = \frac{\tan v + \tan w}{1 - \tan v \tan w} \qquad (41)$$

$$\tan (v - w) = \frac{\tan v - \tan w}{1 + \tan v \tan w} \qquad (42)$$

$$\tan 2\theta = \frac{2 \tan \theta}{1 - \tan^2 \theta} \qquad (43)$$

$$\tan \frac{\theta}{2} = \sqrt{\frac{1 - \cos \theta}{1 + \cos \theta}}$$

whenever $0 \leq (\theta/2)_0 < \pi/2$, or $\pi \leq (\theta/2)_0 < 3\pi/2$, and

$$\tan \frac{\theta}{2} = -\sqrt{\frac{1 - \cos \theta}{1 + \cos \theta}}, \qquad (44)$$

whenever $\pi/2 < (\theta/2)_0 \leq \pi$, or $3\pi/2 < (\theta/2)_0 \leq 2\pi$.

$$\tan \frac{\theta}{2} = \frac{1 - \cos \theta}{\sin \theta} \qquad (45)$$

provided $\sin \theta \neq 0$.

Inverses of Functions.—If real numbers u and v are so related that

$$u = \sin v, \qquad (46)$$

then every real number is a possible value of v; but not every real number is a possible value of u. In fact, the values of u are confined to the interval from -1 to $+1$, inclusive. This fact has already been expressed in the statement that sine is a function whose domain consists of all real numbers, but whose range consists of all real numbers from -1 to $+1$, inclusive. If the values of v are plotted on a graph along the X-axis and the corresponding values of u (i.e., of $\sin v$) are located on the Y-axis, then the sine curve of Figure 11 is obtained.

Now reverse the graphing procedure and locate the values of u along the X-axis and the corresponding values of v along the Y-axis (Fig. 16).

Plotting the graph in this way amounts to interpreting equation (46) as follows: For each real value u in the interval from -1 to $+1$, inclusive, there are various real values v (infinitely many, in fact) such that $u = \sin v$. Stated differently, v is a real number *whose sine is u.* It has become customary to designate the set of all real numbers whose sine is u by either of the following expressions: $\sin^{-1} u$ (read: "inverse sine of u"), or arc sin u (read: "arc sine u"). The first of these expressions will be used. Equation (46) is therefore seen to be completely equivalent to the sentence, *v is a member of the inverse sine of u.* This may be abbreviated:

$$v \mathrel{\text{E}} \sin^{-1} u . \qquad (47)$$

(*Note*: Many textbooks still use the incorrect notation "$v = \sin^{-1} u$," when they really mean "$v \sin^{-1} u$.")

Figure 16.

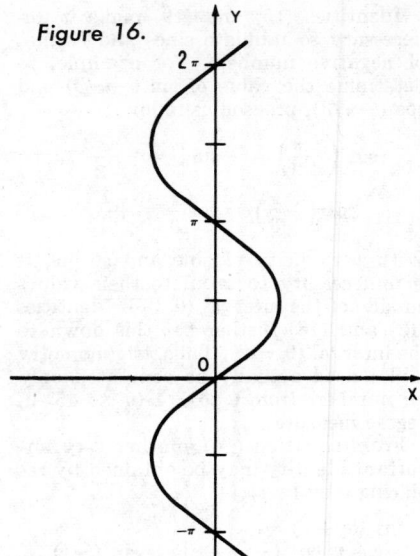

As an example, observe that

$$\sin^{-1} 1 = \left\{ \frac{\pi}{2}, \frac{-3\pi}{2}, \frac{5\pi}{2}, \frac{-7\pi}{2}, \ldots \right\}.$$

Hence, the equations

$$\sin \frac{\pi}{2} = 1, \quad \sin \left(\frac{-3\pi}{2} \right) = 1, \ldots$$

may be expressed in "inverse notation" as follows:

$$\frac{\pi}{2} \, \epsilon \, (\sin^{-1} 1), \quad \frac{-3\pi}{2} \, \epsilon \, (\sin^{-1} 1), \ldots$$

The inverse sine is not a function according to the modern use of this term, because $\sin^{-1} u$ is not a unique real number for each permissible value of u. The inverse sine is an example of a *relation*. (Relations are more general than functions. In fact, a function is a "single-valued relation.")

Although $\sin^{-1}$ is not a function, it can be used to define a function by imposing appropriate restrictions on its range; i.e., on the values it may assume. A restriction that is usually adopted is one that confines the values of $\sin^{-1} u$ to the interval from $-\pi/2$ to $+\pi/2$, inclusive. For each permissible value of u (from -1 to $+1$, inclusive) there is only one member in the set $\sin^{-1} u$ that meets this restriction. This value is called the *principal value* of $\sin^{-1} u$. This principal value is denoted $\mathrm{Sin}^{-1} u$ (read: "principal inverse Sine of u"). Observe that for each value of u in the interval -1 to $+1$, inclusive, there is a unique value $\mathrm{Sin}^{-1} u$, with the properties

$$\mathrm{Sin}^{-1} u \, \epsilon \, \sin^{-1} u ,$$
$$-\frac{\pi}{2} \leq \mathrm{Sin}^{-1} u \leq \frac{\pi}{2} . \qquad (48)$$

Examples are

$$\mathrm{Sin}^{-1} 0 = 0 ,$$
$$\mathrm{Sin}^{-1} 1 = \frac{\pi}{2} ,$$
$$\mathrm{Sin}^{-1} (-1) = -\frac{\pi}{2} ,$$
$$\mathrm{Sin}^{-1} \left(-\frac{1}{2} \right) = -\frac{\pi}{3} .$$

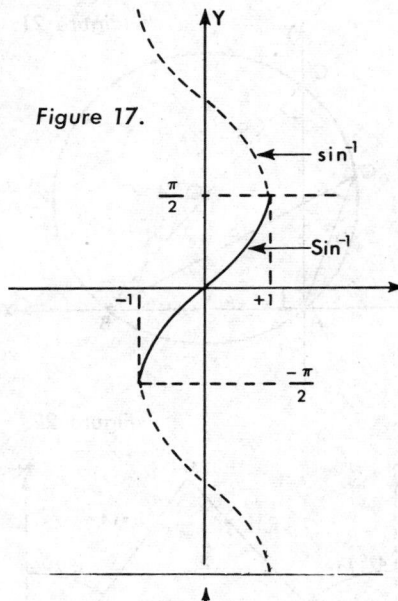

Figure 17.

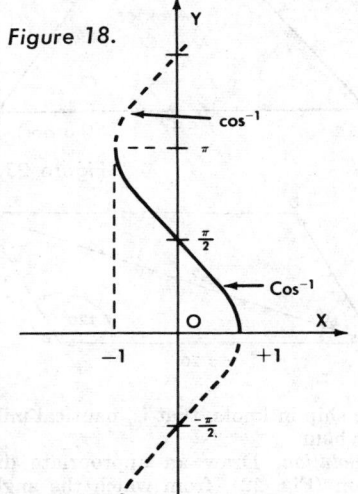

Figure 18.

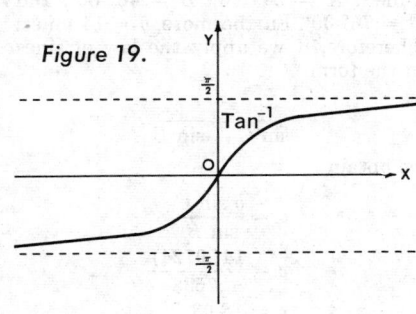

Figure 19.

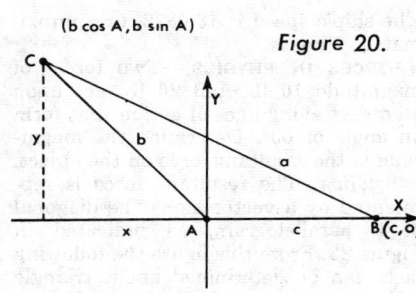

Figure 20.

The principal inverse sine is therefore a function in the modern sense of the term. Its graph is actually a portion of the graph of the inverse sine relation, as shown in Figure 17.

In a completely analogous manner, one may define inverse relations for each of the other five trigonometric functions. Thus the equation

$$u = \cos v \qquad (49)$$

is written equivalently as

$$v \in \cos^{-1} u \qquad (50)$$

where $\cos^{-1} v = \{$real numbers whose cosine is $v\}$.

The *principal inverse cosine* is defined by

$$\text{Cos}^{-1} u \in \cos^{-1} u$$

and   (51)

$$0 \leqq \text{Cos}^{-1} u \leqq \pi .$$

Its graph is depicted in Figure 18.

The equation

$$u = \tan v \qquad (52)$$

is equivalent to the sentence

$$v \in \tan^{-1} u \qquad (53)$$

where $\tan^{-1} u = \{$real numbers whose tangent is $u\}$.

The *principal inverse tangent* is defined by

$$\text{Tan}^{-1} u \in \tan^{-1} u$$

and   (54)

$$\frac{-\pi}{2} \leqq \text{Tan}^{-1} u \leqq \frac{\pi}{2} .$$

Its graph is given in Figure 19.

The principal values of the remaining three trigonometric functions may conveniently be defined in terms of the three that have already been defined:

$$\text{Cot}^{-1} u = \text{Tan}^{-1} \left(\frac{1}{u} \right), \qquad (55)$$

$$\text{Sec}^{-1} u = \text{Cos}^{-1} \left(\frac{1}{u} \right), \qquad (56)$$

$$\text{Csc}^{-1} u = \text{Sin}^{-1} \left(\frac{1}{u} \right), \qquad (57)$$

for all permissible values of u.

The inverse relations and inverse functions of trigonometry play an important role in calculus and more advanced analysis.

Laws of Cosines and Sines.—Most of the applications of the trigonometric functions to geometry stem from two important laws—the *law of cosines* and the *law of sines*.

■ **LAW OF COSINES.**—Consider any triangle ABC and designate the measures of its sides and angles in the conventional way by a, b, c and A, B, C, respectively. Let a rectangular coordinate system be chosen so that angle A is in standard position, as indicated in Figure 20. Relative to this set of axes, the coordinates of point C are ($b \cos A$, $b \sin A$). Applying the distance formula to side BC, we find that

$$a^2 = (b \cos A - c)^2 + (b \sin A - 0)^2$$
$$= b^2 \cos^2 A - 2bc \cos A + c^2 + b^2 \sin^2 A$$
$$= b^2 (\cos^2 A + \sin^2 A) + c^2 - 2bc \cos A$$
$$\therefore a^2 = b^2 + c^2 - 2bc \cos A , \qquad (58)$$

for any triangle ABC.

A completely analogous argument, with either angle B or angle C in standard position, establishes the following:

$$b^2 = c^2 + a^2 - 2ac \cos B , \qquad (59)$$

$$c^2 = a^2 + b^2 - 2ab \cos C , \qquad (60)$$

for any triangle ABC.

Each of the formulas (58), (59), and (60) is referred to as the *law of cosines*. This law is clearly a generalization of the Pythagorean theorem, and is applicable to all triangles, not just to right triangles.

■ **LAW OF SINES.**—This law can be derived directly from the law of cosines in a purely algebraic fashion. Although there are simpler derivations based upon purely geometrical arguments, it is useful to give the purely analytic proof that follows. Solving equation (58) for $\cos A$:

$$\cos A = \frac{b^2 + c^2 - a^2}{2bc} .$$

From this, it follows that

$$\sin^2 A = 1 - \cos^2 A$$
$$= 1 - \frac{(b^2 + c^2 - a^2)^2}{4b^2c^2}$$
$$= \frac{4b^2c^2 - (b^2 + c^2 - a^2)^2}{4b^2c^2} .$$

This may be written

$$4b^2c^2 \sin^2 A$$
$$= [2bc + (b^2 + c^2 - a^2)]$$
$$\quad [2bc - (b^2 + c^2 - a^2)]$$
$$= [(b^2 + 2bc + c^2) - a^2]$$
$$\quad [a^2 - (b^2 - 2bc - c^2)]$$
$$= [(b + c)^2 - a^2][a^2 - (b - c)^2]$$
$$= (b + c + a)(b + c - a)$$
$$\quad (a - b + c)(a + b - c) .$$

Now if s is the *semi-perimeter* of triangle ABC, that is,

$$s = \frac{a + b + c}{2} ,$$

then

$$2s = a + b + c ,$$
$$2(s - a) = b + c - a ,$$
$$2(s - b) = a - b + c ,$$
$$2(s - c) = a + b - c .$$

Hence,

$$4b^2c^2 \sin^2 A =$$
$$2s \cdot 2(s - a) \cdot 2(s - b) \cdot 2(s - c) ,$$

or

$$b^2c^2 \sin^2 A = 4s(s - a)(s - b)(s - c) ;$$

if

$$K = \sqrt{s(s - a)(s - b)(s - c)}, \qquad (61)$$

this becomes

$$b^2c^2 \sin^2 A = 4K^2 .$$

Solving for $\sin A$, and noting that $\sin A > 0$ because $0 < A < \pi$, we then obtain

$$\sin A = \frac{2K}{bc} . \qquad (62)$$

In exactly the same manner it can be proved that

$$\sin B = \frac{2K}{ac}, \qquad (63)$$

$$\sin C = \frac{2K}{ab}. \qquad (64)$$

Further, if we apply equations (62), (63), and (64) it is then possible to obtain the following:

$$\frac{\sin A}{a} = \frac{\sin B}{b} = \frac{\sin C}{c} = \frac{2K}{abc}. \qquad (65)$$

This is the *law of sines*.

The geometrical significance of K is evident if equation (62) is written in the following form:

$$K = \frac{1}{2}bc \sin A = \frac{1}{2}c(b \sin A).$$

Referring to Figure 20, it can be seen that this is the same as

$$K = \frac{1}{2}cy,$$

so K is actually the area of triangle ABC.

We have thus succeeded not only in deriving the law of sines from the law of cosines, but we have also obtained incidentally a famous formula (*Heron's formula*) for the area of a triangle, namely

$$K = \sqrt{s(s-a)(s-b)(s-c)}.$$

Another interesting geometric result involving K is obtained by circumscribing a circle around triangle ABC of Figure 20, as indicated in Figure 21. This circle must intersect the Y-axis at another point C', and since angle BAC' is a right angle, the segment joining B to C' is a diameter of the circle. Its length is therefore $2R$, where R is the radius of the circumscribed circle. Furthermore, the inscribed angles C and C' have the same measure because they intercept the same arc AB. Applying the law of sines to triangle ABC', we obtain

$$\frac{\sin C'}{c} = \frac{\sin \angle BAC}{2R} = \frac{\sin \frac{\pi}{2}}{2R} = \frac{1}{2R}.$$

But since $C = C'$, this gives

$$\frac{\sin C}{c} = \frac{1}{2R}. \qquad (66)$$

From this we may obtain two interesting results. Inverting both sides, we see that the common value of the ratios $a/\sin A$, $b/\sin B$, and $c/\sin C$ is actually the length of the diameter of the circumscribed circle, namely $2R$. Furthermore, in applying equations (65) and (66) we see that the following result is obtained:

$$\frac{1}{2R} = \frac{2K}{abc},$$

$$\therefore R = \frac{abc}{4K}. \qquad (67)$$

This expresses the radius of the circumscribed circle in terms of the three sides of triangle ABC and its area K.

Two other classical formulas that are derivable from the laws of sines and cosines are

$$\frac{a-b}{a+b} = \frac{\tan \frac{1}{2}(A-B)}{\tan \frac{1}{2}(A+B)}, \qquad (68)$$

$$\cos \frac{1}{2}A = \sqrt{\frac{s(s-a)}{bc}}. \qquad (69)$$

Equation (68) is called the *law of tangents* and equation (69) is known as the *cosine of the half angle* formula. Both are useful in computations involving triangles.

De Moivre's Theorem.—A fundamental interweaving of trigonometry with the theory of complex numbers is seen to be incorporated in the principle that has come to be known as *De Moivre's theorem*, as follows:

$$\begin{aligned}(\cos \theta + i \sin \theta)^2 \\ = \cos^2 \theta + (2 \sin \theta \cos \theta)i \\ + i^2 \sin^2 \theta \\ = (\cos^2 \theta - \sin^2 \theta) \\ + i(2 \sin \theta \cos \theta);\end{aligned}$$

that is,

$$\begin{aligned}(\cos \theta + i \sin \theta)^2 \\ = \cos 2\theta + i \sin 2\theta.\end{aligned}$$

Then, multiplying both sides again by the expression

$$(\cos \theta + i \sin \theta),$$

the equation may be expressed in the following manner:

$$\begin{aligned}(\cos \theta + i \sin \theta)^3 \\ = \cos 2\theta \cos \theta - \sin 2\theta \\ + i(\sin 2\theta \cos \theta + \cos 2\theta \sin 2\theta) \\ = \cos(2\theta + \theta) + i \sin(2\theta + \theta).\end{aligned}$$

Therefore,

$$\begin{aligned}(\cos \theta + i \sin \theta)^3 \\ = \cos 3\theta + i \sin 3\theta.\end{aligned}$$

The general rule is apparent and can be readily proved by the method of mathematical induction. For example, if n is a positive integer and θ is any real number, then the equation will read as follows:

$$\begin{aligned}(\cos \theta + i \sin \theta)^n \\ = \cos n\theta + i \sin n\theta.\end{aligned} \qquad (70)$$

As a matter of fact, this formula can be shown to be true when n is a negative integer or even a fraction, provided a suitable interpretation is given to the fractional power of a complex number when it appears on the left side of equation (70).

Sample Applications.—Following are a few sample applications of the above trigonometrical principles.

■ **NAVIGATION.**—A lighthouse is located 14 nautical miles from a harbor and its bearing from the harbor is 35° 20′ west of north. A ship sails due west from the harbor for two hours and then observes the bearing of the lighthouse is 41° 10′ east of north. Determine the speed of

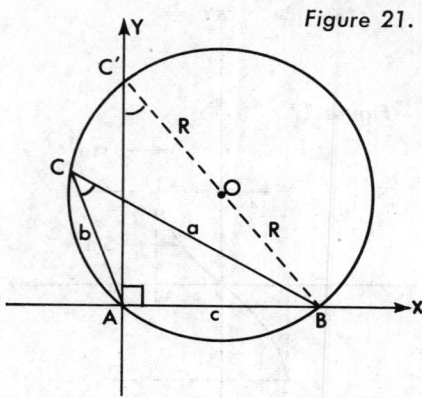

Figure 21.

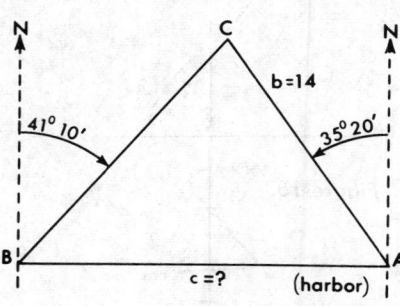

Figure 22.

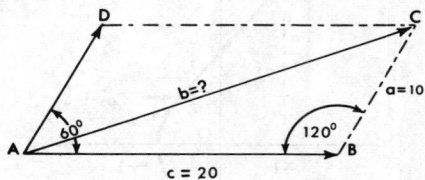

Figure 23.

the ship in knots, that is, nautical miles per hour.

Solution. Draw an appropriate diagram (Fig. 22), from which the angles of triangle ABC can be readily determined: $A = 54° 40′$, $B = 48° 50′$, and $C = 76° 30′$. Furthermore, $b = 14$ miles. Therefore, if we apply the law of sines in the form

$$\frac{c}{\sin C} = \frac{b}{\sin B},$$

we obtain

$$c = \frac{b \sin C}{\sin B}$$

$$c \approx \frac{14(.9724)}{.7528}$$

$$c \approx 18.08.$$

The ship's speed is 18.08/2, or approximately 9 knots.

■ **FORCES IN PHYSICS.**—Two forces of magnitude 10 lb. and 20 lb. act upon an object along lines of action that form an angle of 60°. Determine the magnitude of the resultant force on the object.

Solution. The resultant force is represented by a vector along the diagonal of a parallelogram, as indicated in Figure 23. From this figure the following facts can be determined about triangle ABC: $a = 10$, $c = 20$, $B = 120°$. Hence, using the law of cosines in the form

$$b^2 = a^2 + c^2 - 2ac \cos B,$$

we obtain

$$\begin{aligned} b^2 &= 100 + 400 - 2(10)(20)(-.5000) \\ &= 500 + 200 \\ &= 700 \end{aligned}$$

$$\therefore b = \sqrt{700} \approx 26.5.$$

The magnitude of the resultant force is therefore approximately 26.5 lb.

■ **ALTERNATING CURRENT.**—A 60-cycle alternating current has a peak voltage of 100 volts. Determine the drop in voltage .01 second after it reaches its peak.

Solution. The voltage at any time (t seconds) after reaching its peak may be represented by

$$E = 100 \cos 120\pi t,$$

because the period of $\cos 120\pi t$ is $2\pi/120\pi$, or 1/60 second. When $t = 0$, this yields the peak voltage

$$E_0 = 100 \cos 0 = 100 \text{ volts}.$$

When $t = .01$ this yields the new voltage

$$\begin{aligned} E_{.01} &= 100 \cos 1.2\pi \\ &= 100 \cos 216° \\ &= -100 \cos 36° \\ &\approx -100 \ (.5878) \\ E_{.01} &\approx -59 \text{ volts}. \end{aligned}$$

Note. The voltage has already reversed itself by this time (.01 second after peak). The drop from peak voltage is thus given by

$$E_0 - E_{.01} \approx 100 - (-59) = 159 \text{ volts}.$$

—A. M. Glicksman

Values of Trigonometric Functions (Using Degree Measure)

Angle	Sin	Cos	Tan	Angle	Sin	Cos	Tan
1°	.0175	.9998	.0175	46°	.7193	.6947	1.0355
2°	.0349	.9994	.0349	47°	.7314	.6820	1.0724
3°	.0523	.9986	.0524	48°	.7431	.6691	1.1106
4°	.0698	.9976	.0699	49°	.7547	.6561	1.1504
5°	.0872	.9962	.0875	50°	.7660	.6428	1.1918
6°	.1045	.9945	.1051	51°	.7771	.6293	1.2349
7°	.1219	.9925	.1228	52°	.7880	.6157	1.2799
8°	.1392	.9903	.1405	53°	.7986	.6018	1.3279
9°	.1564	.9877	.1584	54°	.8090	.5878	1.3764
10°	.1736	.9848	.1763	55°	.8192	.5736	1.4281
11°	.1908	.9816	.1944	56°	.8290	.5592	1.4826
12°	.2079	.9781	.2126	57°	.8387	.5446	1.5399
13°	.2250	.9744	.2309	58°	.8480	.5299	1.6003
14°	.2419	.9703	.2493	59°	.8572	.5150	1.6643
15°	.2588	.9659	.2679	60°	.8660	.5000	1.7321
16°	.2756	.9613	.2867	61°	.8746	.4848	1.8040
17°	.2924	.9563	.3057	62°	.8829	.4695	1.8807
18°	.3090	.9511	.3249	63°	.8910	.4540	1.9626
19°	.3256	.9455	.3443	64°	.8988	.4384	2.0503
20°	.3420	.9397	.3640	65°	.9063	.4226	2.1445
21°	.3584	.9336	.3839	66°	.9135	.4067	2.2460
22°	.3746	.9272	.4040	67°	.9205	.3907	2.3559
23°	.3907	.9205	.4245	68°	.9272	.3746	2.4751
24°	.4067	.9135	.4452	69°	.9336	.3584	2.6051
25°	.4226	.9063	.4663	70°	.9397	.3420	2.7475
26°	.4384	.8988	.4877	71°	.9455	.3256	2.9042
27°	.4540	.8910	.5095	72°	.9511	.3090	3.0777
28°	.4695	.8829	.5317	73°	.9563	.2924	3.2709
29°	.4848	.8746	.5543	74°	.9613	.2756	3.4874
30°	.5000	.8660	.5774	75°	.9659	.2588	3.7321
31°	.5150	.8572	.6009	76°	.9703	.2419	4.0108
32°	.5299	.8480	.6249	77°	.9744	.2250	4.3315
33°	.5446	.8387	.6494	78°	.9781	.2079	4.7046
34°	.5592	.8290	.6745	79°	.9816	.1908	5.1446
35°	.5736	.8192	.7002	80°	.9848	.1736	5.6713
36°	.5878	.8090	.7265	81°	.9877	.1564	6.3138
37°	.6018	.7986	.7536	82°	.9903	.1392	7.1154
38°	.6157	.7880	.7813	83°	.9925	.1219	8.1443
39°	.6293	.7771	.8098	84°	.9945	.1045	9.5144
40°	.6428	.7660	.8391	85°	.9962	.0872	11.4301
41°	.6561	.7547	.8693	86°	.9976	.0698	14.3007
42°	.6691	.7431	.9004	87°	.9986	.0523	19.0811
43°	.6820	.7314	.9325	88°	.9994	.0349	28.6363
44°	.6947	.7193	.9657	89°	.9998	.0175	57.2900
45°	.7071	.7071	1.0000	90°	1.0000	.0000	

Values of Sin x and Cos x (Using Circular Measure: for $0 \le x \le 1.57$)

x	Sin x	Cos x	x	Sin x	Cos x	x	Sin x	Cos x	x	Sin x	Cos x
.00	.0000	1.0000	.40	.3894	.9211	.80	.7174	.6967	1.20	.9320	.3624
.01	.0100	1.0000	.41	.3986	.9171	.81	.7243	.6895	1.21	.9356	.3530
.02	.0200	.9998	.42	.4078	.9131	.82	.7311	.6822	1.22	.9391	.3436
.03	.0300	.9996	.43	.4169	.9090	.83	.7379	.6749	1.23	.9425	.3342
.04	.0400	.9992	.44	.4259	.9048	.84	.7446	.6675	1.24	.9458	.3248
.05	.0500	.9988	.45	.4350	.9004	.85	.7513	.6600	1.25	.9490	.3153
.06	.0600	.9982	.46	.4439	.8961	.86	.7578	.6524	1.26	.9521	.3058
.07	.0699	.9976	.47	.4529	.8916	.87	.7643	.6448	1.27	.9551	.2963
.08	.0799	.9968	.48	.4618	.8870	.88	.7707	.6372	1.28	.9580	.2867
.09	.0899	.9960	.49	.4706	.8823	.89	.7771	.6294	1.29	.9608	.2771
.10	.0998	.9950	.50	.4794	.8776	.90	.7833	.6216	1.30	.9636	.2675
.11	.1098	.9940	.51	.4882	.8727	.91	.7895	.6137	1.31	.9662	.2579
.12	.1197	.9928	.52	.4969	.8678	.92	.7956	.6058	1.32	.9687	.2482
.13	.1296	.9916	.53	.5055	.8628	.93	.8016	.5978	1.33	.9711	.2385
.14	.1395	.9902	.54	.5141	.8577	.94	.8076	.5898	1.34	.9735	.2288
.15	.1494	.9888	.55	.5227	.8525	.95	.8134	.5817	1.35	.9757	.2190
.16	.1593	.9872	.56	.5312	.8473	.96	.8192	.5735	1.36	.9779	.2092
.17	.1692	.9856	.57	.5396	.8419	.97	.8249	.5653	1.37	.9799	.1994
.18	.1790	.9838	.58	.5480	.8365	.98	.8305	.5570	1.38	.9819	.1896
.19	.1889	.9820	.59	.5564	.8309	.99	.8360	.5487	1.39	.9837	.1798
.20	.1987	.9801	.60	.5646	.8253	1.00	.8415	.5403	1.40	.9854	.1700
.21	.2085	.9780	.61	.5729	.8196	1.01	.8468	.5319	1.41	.9871	.1601
.22	.2182	.9759	.62	.5810	.8139	1.02	.8521	.5234	1.42	.9887	.1502
.23	.2280	.9737	.63	.5891	.8080	1.03	.8573	.5148	1.43	.9901	.1403
.24	.2377	.9713	.64	.5972	.8021	1.04	.8624	.5062	1.44	.9915	.1304
.25	.2474	.9689	.65	.6052	.7961	1.05	.8674	.4976	1.45	.9927	.1205
.26	.2571	.9664	.66	.6131	.7900	1.06	.8724	.4889	1.46	.9939	.1106
.27	.2667	.9638	.67	.6210	.7838	1.07	.8772	.4801	1.47	.9949	.1006
.28	.2764	.9611	.68	.6288	.7776	1.08	.8820	.4713	1.48	.9959	.0907
.29	.2860	.9582	.69	.6365	.7712	1.09	.8866	.4625	1.49	.9967	.0807
.30	.2955	.9553	.70	.6442	.7648	1.10	.8912	.4536	1.50	.9975	.0707
.31	.3051	.9523	.71	.6518	.7584	1.11	.8957	.4447	1.51	.9982	.0608
.32	.3146	.9492	.72	.6594	.7518	1.12	.9001	.4357	1.52	.9987	.0508
.33	.3240	.9460	.73	.6669	.7452	1.13	.9044	.4267	1.53	.9992	.0408
.34	.3335	.9428	.74	.6743	.7385	1.14	.9086	.4176	1.54	.9995	.0308
.35	.3429	.9394	.75	.6816	.7317	1.15	.9128	.4085	1.55	.9998	.0208
.36	.3523	.9359	.76	.6889	.7248	1.16	.9168	.3993	1.56	.9999	.0108
.37	.3616	.9323	.77	.6961	.7179	1.17	.9208	.3902	1.57	1.0000	.0008
.38	.3709	.9287	.78	.7033	.7109	1.18	.9246	.3809			
.39	.3802	.9249	.79	.7104	.7038	1.19	.9284	.3717			

ANALYTIC GEOMETRY

Introduction.—Historically, geometry began as the study of the measurement and properties of geometric figures. The intuitive findings of the Egyptians and Babylonians were organized into a mathematical science by Euclid around 300 B.C., and for centuries geometry developed through Euclid's "axiomatic method." The growth of arithmetic and algebra paralleled the development of geometry. In the seventeenth century, mathematicians began to employ numerical and algebraic techniques in the study of geometric figures. This method, now called *analytic geometry*, was systematized by René Descartes (1596–1650). Later it was found that the methods of geometry likewise could be applied to problems in algebra.

Coordinate Systems.—The central fact that allows analytic geometry to serve as a link between algebra and geometry is that sets of numbers (or sets of sets of numbers) can be put into a one-to-one correspondence with a set of points—a correspondence called a *coordinate system*. Simplest coordinate system is the correspondence between the set of real numbers and the points on a line.

On a line of infinite extent, below, choose a point P. Label this point 0.

$$-5 \quad -4 \quad -3 \quad -2 \quad -1 \quad 0 \quad +1 \quad +2 \quad +3 \quad +4 \quad +5$$

Choose points at equal distances in both directions on the line; label those to the right 1, 2, 3, . . . and those to the left -1, -2, -3, ... It is a basic assumption of mathematics that all of the points on the line will be in a one-to-one correspondence with the set of real numbers.

We can now describe any set of points

BETTMANN ARCHIVE

RENÉ DESCARTES, French philosopher and mathematician, greatly influenced geometry.

on the line by means of *open sentences* (equations, inequalities, and similar relationships). Indicating the point or points suggested by an open sentence is called *graphing the open sentence*.

Examples:

(1) $x = 2$

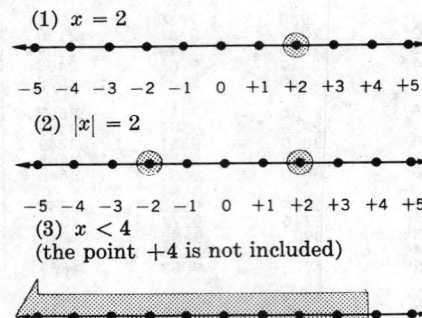

(2) $|x| = 2$

(3) $x < 4$
(the point $+4$ is not included)

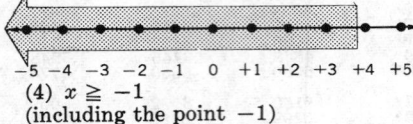

(4) $x \geqq -1$
(including the point -1)

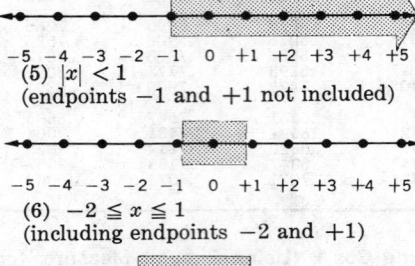

(5) $|x| < 1$
(endpoints -1 and $+1$ not included)

(6) $-2 \leqq x \leqq 1$
(including endpoints -2 and $+1$)

(The sign $<$ means "is less than"; $>$ means "is greater than"; $\leqq$ means "is less than or equal to"; $\geqq$ means "is greater than or equal to." The sign $|\ |$ indicates the absolute value of a number, that is, $|x| = x$ if $x > 0$, $|x| = -x$ if $x < 0$, and $|0| = 0$.)

The geometric figure designated by (4) is a *ray*; that by (5) is an *interval open at both ends*; that by (6) is a *segment*. It can be seen in these examples that geometric figures can be designated by algebraic open sentences. The basic idea of analytic geometry is to examine these geometric figures by studying the corresponding open sentences.

Coordinates in a Plane.—If two of the number lines described in the preceding section are drawn so that they are perpendicular to each other and intersect at their zero points, they form a set of *axes* for a plane coordinate system. The location of any point in the plane is given by an *ordered pair of numbers*. The first number in the pair designates the distance (in the positive or negative direction) from the vertical axis, which is called the Y *axis*; the second number designates the distance from the hori-

zontal axis, which is called the X *axis*. The two numbers in the ordered pair are called the *coordinates* of the point they designate. The first number is the x coordinate, or *abscissa*; the second is the y coordinate, or *ordinate*. Below are some points and their coordinates:

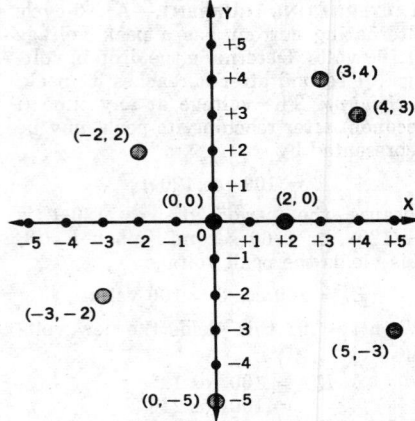

It is clear that there is only one point designated by a given pair of coordinates and that there is only one pair of coordinates corresponding to any given point. As in the case of the coordinate system on a line, open sentences involving the variables x and y may be used to designate sets of points in the plane.

Open Sentences and Their Graphs.—Sets of points can be described by statements, open sentences in two variables, and functional notation.

Examples:

(1) Find the set of points (x, y), such that y has the value of the largest whole number that is less than or equal to x. Thus y will always be a whole number, while x need not be. The ordered pairs $(3\frac{1}{4}, 3)$, $(2.3, 2)$, $(0, 0)$, $(-2, -2)$, and so on, belong to this set. The graph of the set is:

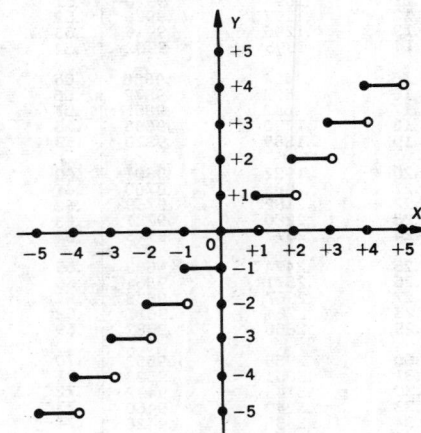

(The solid dots on the graph indicate points included in the segment; hollow dots, points not in the segment.)

(2) To every x, where x is **a real number**, associate its **absolute value**. The graph is:

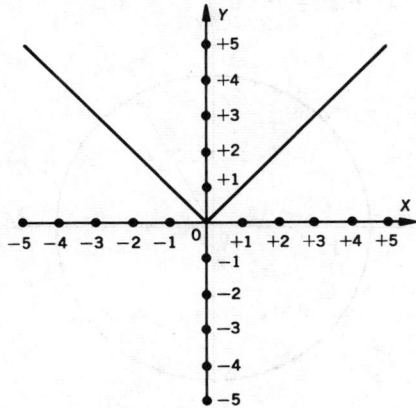

(3) The solution set of an equation or inequality may also be graphed. The *solution set* is the set of numbers that make the open sentence true. The solution sets for the following open sentences are:

(a) $y = x$, a straight line.
(b) $y^2 = x$, a parabola passing through the origin.
(c) $y = x^2 + 1$, a parabola displaced from the origin.
(d) $x^2 + y^2 \leqq 25$, a circle.

(a) $y = x$

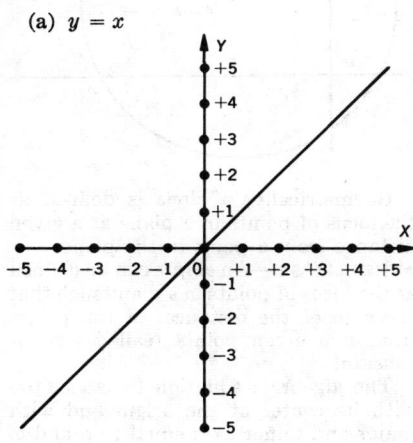

(b) $y^2 = x$

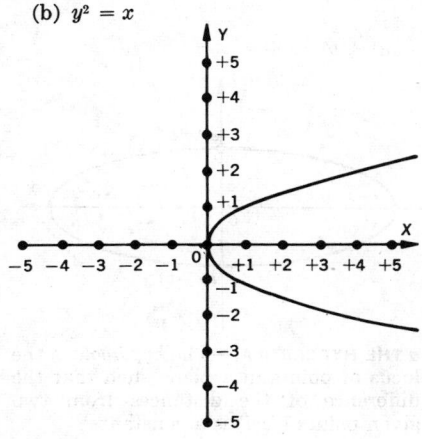

(c) $y = x^2 + 1$

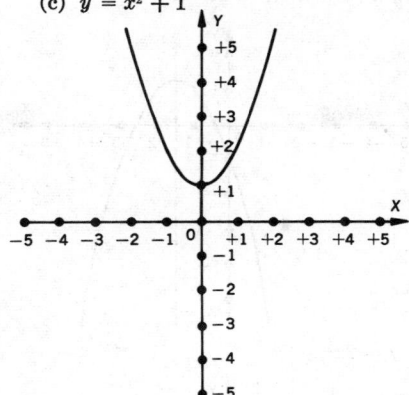

(d) $x^2 + y^2 \leqq 25$

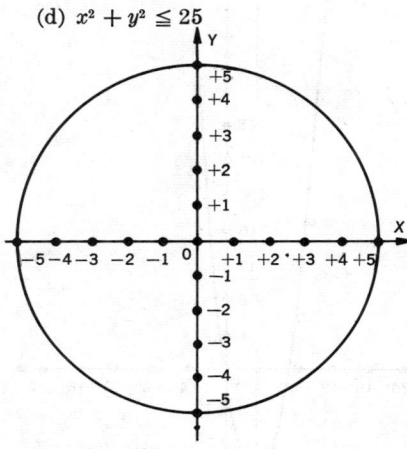

Linear Functions.—Certain subsets of points in a plane form patterns that have the shape of common geometric figures, such as a straight line, circle, ellipse, or cycloid. These figures correspond to certain specific types of equations. In analytic geometry equations of the form

$$Ax + By = C$$

(where A, B, and C are real numbers) have solution sets that form a straight line when graphed. Such equations as $3x - y = 5$ and $y = 2x + 7$ are of this type. It is also true that every straight line can be represented by an equation of this general form. Hence such equations are known as *linear equations*.

Slope-Intercept Form.—Any linear equation can be put into the form

$$y = mx + b.$$

By inspection we see that the number pair $(0, b)$ is a member of the solution set for this equation. The number b shows the graph's distance from the X axis when $x = 0$. Since $x = 0$ on the Y axis, b indicates the point at which the graph crosses this axis. For this reason, b is called the *y intercept of the line.*

Further inspection shows that the number m determines how much of a change there will be in the value of y for every change of one unit in the value of x. For example, if $m = 2$, y will increase by two units whenever x increases by one unit; if $m = -\frac{1}{2}$, y will decrease

by one-half unit whenever x increases by one unit. In terms of the graph of the equation $y = mx + b$, m shows how much of a change there will be in the y direction for each change of one unit in the x direction; that is, it indicates what the *slope* of the line will be.

If (x_1, y_1) and (x_2, y_2) are two points on the line, then

$$y_1 = mx_1 + b,$$
$$y_2 = mx_2 + b.$$

Subtracting equations to eliminate b,

$$y_2 - y_1 = m(x_2 - x_1);$$

$$m = \frac{y_2 - y_1}{x_2 - x_1},$$

which is the slope of the line. Note that this expression is not defined if $x_2 = x_1$, since this would make the denominator equal 0. It follows that vertical lines, for which $x_2 = x_1$, do not have slopes. The equations $x = 0$, $x = -7$, and $x = 2$ are

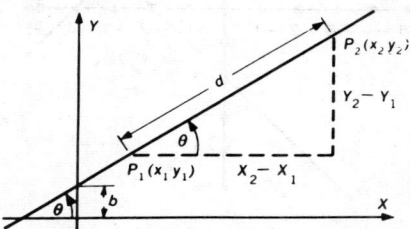

of this type. The diagram above shows that the slope m represents the tangent of the angle the line makes with the positive direction of the X axis. The angle, θ, is the *inclination of the line.* Note that if a linear equation is put into the form $y = mx + b$, it can be determined by inspection where the graph will cross the Y axis and what its slope will be. For this reason it is called the *slope-intercept form.* When an equation is in this form, it is simple to construct its graph by finding the intercept and constructing the slope.

If two lines are parallel, they have equal slopes. The converse is also true. Therefore, two lines with slopes m_1 and m_2 are parallel if, and only if, $m_1 = m_2$. (Two vertical lines that have no slopes are, of course, parallel.) By deduction it can be seen that two lines will be perpendicular if, and only if, $m_1m_2 = -1$. (Here, again, neither line may be vertical; that is, neither m_1 nor m_2 may equal zero.)

The diagram above also suggests a method by which the midpoint of the line P_1P_2 can be found. Consideration of the properties of similar triangles shows that the midpoint will be

$$\left(\frac{x_1 + x_2}{2}, \quad \frac{y_1 + y_2}{2} \right).$$

With the help of the Pythagorean theorem, the diagram can be used to develop a method of finding the distance d between two points on a line:

$$d^2 = (P_1P_2)^2 = (x_2 - x_1)^2 + (y_2 - y_1)^2;$$
$$d = \sqrt{(x_2 - x_1)^2 + (y_2 - y_1)^2}.$$

This is known as the *distance formula.*

Simultaneous Equations.—It is clear that a very simple application of the geometry of straight lines leads to a technique for solving simultaneous linear equations. For example, consider the two equations

$$x + y = 4 \quad \text{and} \quad x - y = 2.$$

The graphs of the solution sets of these equations are shown in the diagram below. The coordinates of the point of intersection of the two lines clearly constitute the *intersection* of the solution sets of the two equations.

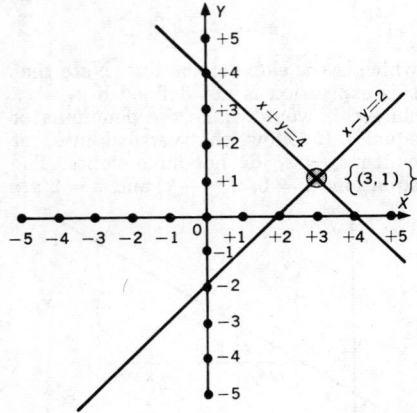

Quadratic Functions.—Consider an equation of the form

$$y = ax^2 + bx + c.$$

The set of ordered pairs of numbers (x, y) that satisfy such an equation—that is, constitute the solution set of such an equation—is the *quadratic function:*

$$f(x) \rightarrow ax^2 + bx + c.$$

The graphs of all such functions take the form of a *parabola.*

Examples:

$$y = x^2 - 2x + 1$$

$$y = x^2 + 1$$

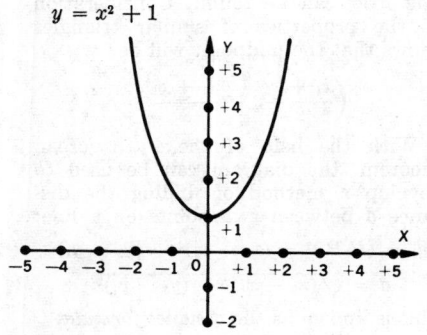

$$y = -x^2 + 3x - 1$$

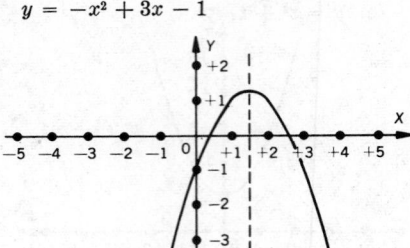

$$y = 2x^2 + 7x$$

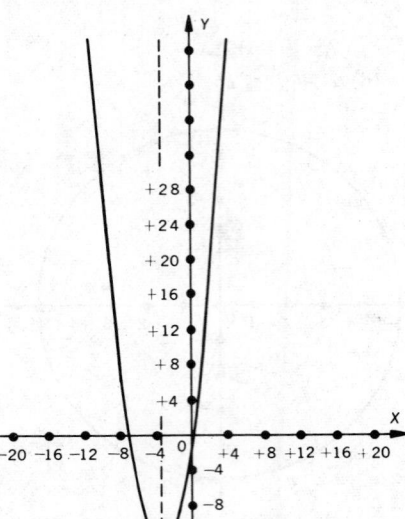

Again, the geometric properties of these figures can be studied by examining the corresponding equations. For example, each of the parabolas is symmetric about a line whose equation is given by $x = -(b/2a)$. In the examples above this yields: $x = 1$, $x = 0$, $x = 3/2$, and $x = -(7/4)$. The parabolas also have *maximum* and *minimum* points. The coordinates of these are given by $[-(b/2a), (4ac - b^2)/4a]$. In the examples, these work out to $(1, 0), (0, 1), (3/2, 5/4)$, and $[-(7/4), -(49/8)]$. The sign of c determines the direction in which the parabola opens. If the sign is positive, the opening is up or to the right; if it is negative, the opening is down or to the left.

Conic Sections.—Just as the graphs of all linear equations prove to be straight lines, so all quadratic equations yield graphs that have a family resemblance.

Consider a conic surface consisting of two infinitely extending cones placed tip to tip. Planes intersecting such a surface can produce circles, parabolas, ellipses, and hyperbolas. (In special cases the intersections can also produce a point, a line, or two intersecting lines.) These figures are known as *conic sections.* They are the graphs of various possible types of quadratic equations.

■ **THE CIRCLE.**—The equation of a *circle* with its center at the origin and radius r is

$$x^2 + y^2 = r^2.$$

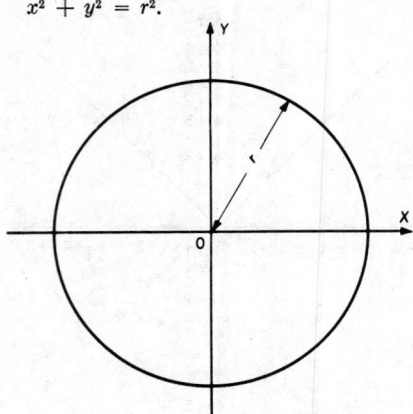

The equation of a circle with its center at point (a, b) and radius r is

$$(x - a)^2 + (y - b)^2 = r^2.$$

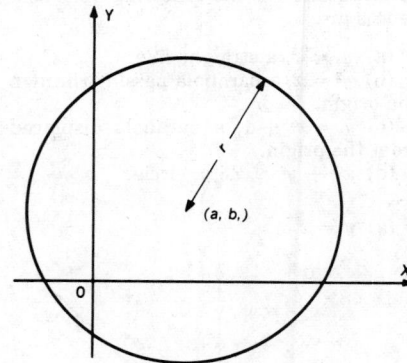

Geometrically, a *circle* is defined as the locus of points in a plane at a given distance from a point in the plane.

■ **THE ELLIPSE.**—An *ellipse* can be defined as the locus of points in a plane such that the sum of the distances of the points from two given points (called *foci*) is constant.

The algebraic equation for an ellipse with its center at the origin and with major and minor axes equal to a and b, respectively, is

$$\frac{x^2}{a^2} + \frac{y^2}{b^2} = 1.$$

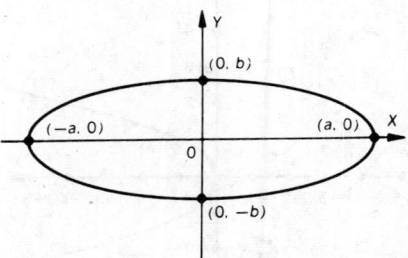

■ **THE HYPERBOLA.**—The *hyperbola* is the locus of points in a plane such that the difference of the distances from two given points (*foci*) is a constant.

The equation for a hyperbola with its center at the origin is

$$\frac{x^2}{a^2} - \frac{y^2}{b^2} = 1.$$

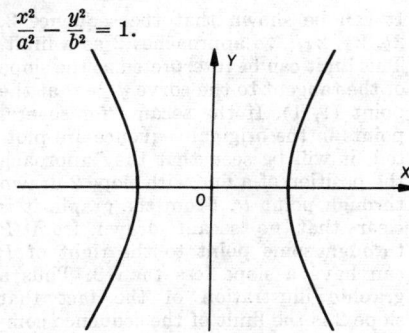

■ **THE PARABOLA.**—It has already been seen that the parabola is the graph of the quadratic equation $y = ax^2 + bx + c$. Geometrically, the *parabola* is defined as the locus of points in a plane equally distant from a given point (*focus*) and a given line (*directrix*). The equation of a parabola that has its vertex at the origin and its focus at $(p, 0)$ is

$$y^2 = 4px.$$

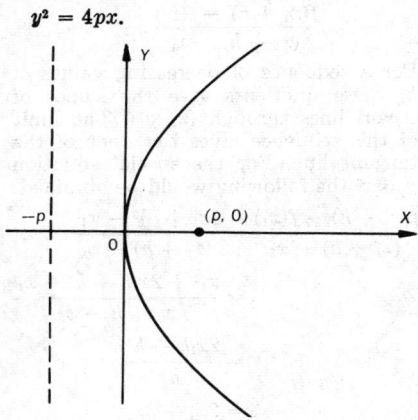

In this case the equation of the directrix is $x = -p$.

Other Coordinate Systems.—The coordinate system used here for the plane is known as the *rectangular* (or *Cartesian*, in honor of Descartes) *coordinate system*. There are several others. Rectangular coordinates can be extended to three-dimensional space by adding a third axis perpendicular to the two used so far. Points, then, are located by ordered sets of triple numbers (x, y, z) which give the point's distance from three mutually perpendicular planes. The graphs of equations in three variables form three-dimensional geometric figures, such as the sphere.

■ **POLAR COORDINATES.**—Points in a plane can be designated by *polar coordinates* as well as by rectangular coordinates. Select a ray AB in the plane. Choose some point P in the plane (assuming for sake of illustration that it does not lie on AB). Draw a line from A to P. Clearly, the location of P may be described in terms of the length of AP and the angle PAB. (For simplicity,

the length of AB is called r, and $\angle PAB$ is called θ.) Thus the point P can be located in terms of an ordered pair of numbers (r, θ). As can be seen from the drawing (with the help of trigonometry), polar coordinates and rectangular coordinates are related as follows:

$$y = r \sin \theta,$$
$$x = r \cos \theta,$$

where (x, y) are the rectangular coordinates of P.

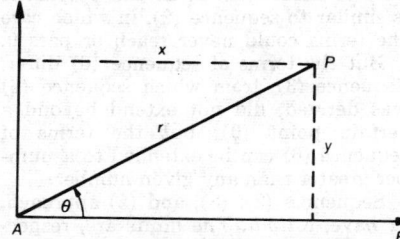

Descriptions of loci that give coordinates of points in terms of other variables are called *parametric equations*.

Equations of Some Loci

Trigonometric Functions

$y = \sin x$

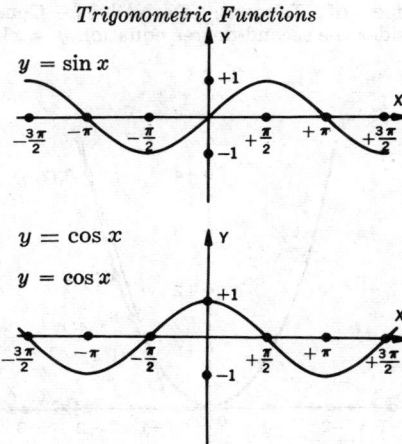

$y = \cos x$

$y = \cos x$

Exponential and Logarithmic Functions

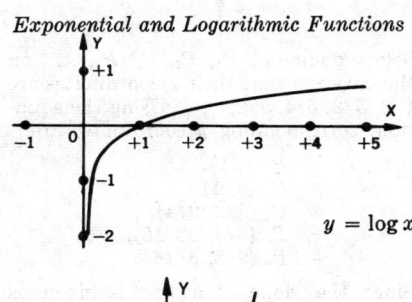

$y = \log x$

$y = e^x$

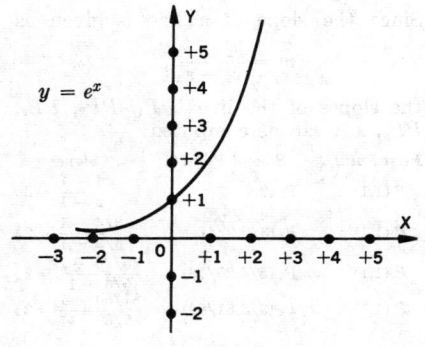

Spirals
$r = e^{a\theta}$ (logarithmic spiral)

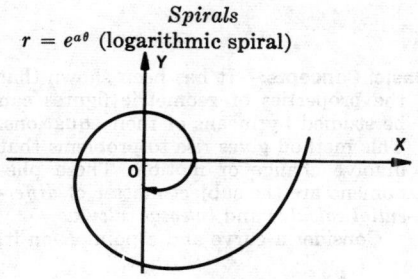

$r = a\theta$ (spiral of Archimedes)

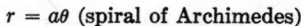
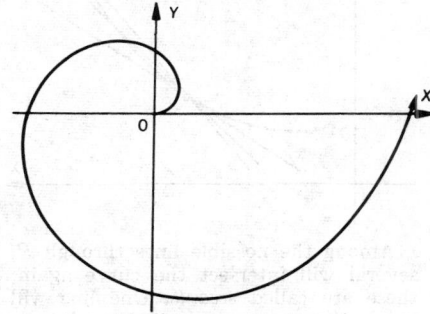

Cycloid
(Path of point on circumference of circle as circle rolls along straight line.)

$$x = a(\theta - \sin \theta)$$
$$y = a(1 - \cos \theta)$$

or

$$x = a \cos^{-1}\left(\frac{a-y}{a}\right) \pm \sqrt{2ay - y^2}$$

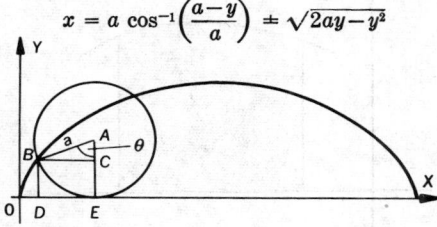

Four-leafed Rose
$r = \sin 2\theta$

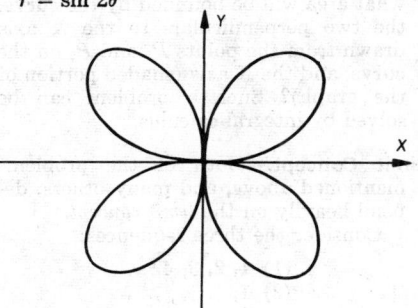

Lemniscate
$r = a^2 \cos 2\theta$

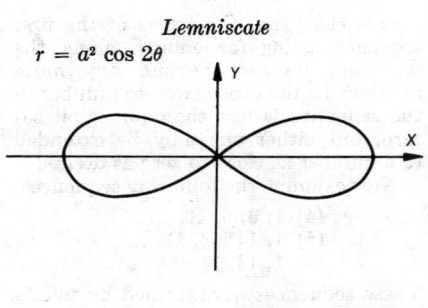

—Julius H. Hlavaty

CALCULUS

Basic Concepts.

Basic Concepts.—It has been shown that the properties of geometric figures can be studied by means of their equations. This method gives rise to problems that involve change or motion. These phenomena are the subject matter of *differential calculus* and *integral calculus*.

Consider a curve and a point P on it.

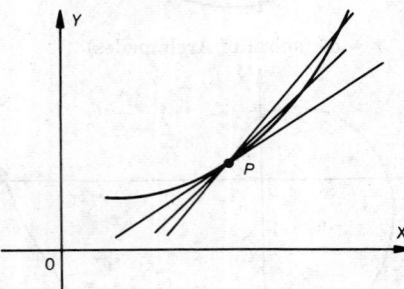

Among the possible lines through P, several will intersect the curve again; these are called *secants*. One line will touch the curve only at the point P; this is the *tangent* to the curve at P. The slope of this tangent can be determined by differential calculus.

Take a curve with points P_1 and P_2.

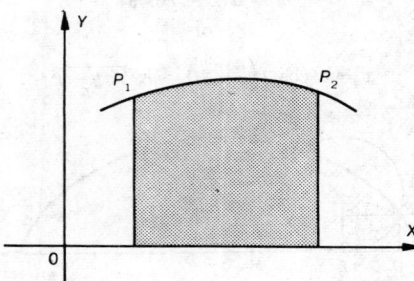

If the equation of the curve is known, what area will be bounded by the curve, the two perpendiculars to the X axis drawn from the points P_1 and P_2 on the curve, and the X axis (shaded portion of the graph)? Such a problem can be solved by integral calculus.

Limit Concept.

Limit Concept.—Both of the problems mentioned above, and many others, depend heavily on the *limit concept*.

Consider the three sequences:

(1) 1, 2, 3, 4, . . .
(2) $1, \frac{1}{2}, \frac{1}{4}, \frac{1}{8}, \ldots$
(3) $1, \frac{1}{2}, \frac{1}{3}, \frac{1}{4}, \ldots$

It is clear that the terms of the first sequence, going far enough along the sequence, increase beyond any finite number. In the other two, no number in the sequence is less than (or equal to) zero, but either one may be extended to a number as close to zero as desired.

Now examine the following sequences:

(4) 1, 3, 6, 10, . . .
(5) $1, 1\frac{1}{2}, 1\frac{3}{4}, 1\frac{7}{8}, \ldots$
(6) $1, 1\frac{1}{2}, 1\frac{5}{8}, 2\frac{1}{12}, \ldots$

These sequences were formed by taking the first term, the sum of the first two terms, the sum of the first three terms, and so on, of sequences (1), (2), and (3), respectively.

The terms of sequence (4) increase beyond any given number. In this respect, sequence (4) is similar to sequence (1) from which it was derived.

The terms of sequence (5) can never be 2 or more than 2. In this respect it is similar to sequence (2), in which case the terms could never reach or pass 0.

But the terms of sequence (6) differ. Sequence (3), from which sequence (6) was derived, did not extend beyond a certain point (0); but the terms of sequence (6) can be extended to a number greater than any given number.

Sequences (2), (3), and (5) approach, or have, a *limit*. The limits are, respectively, 0, 0, and 2. The other sequences have no limit. Hence a sequence has a limit if, and only if, no matter how many terms are taken, a number (*limit*) cannot be reached or surpassed.

Slope of Tangent, Derivatives.

Slope of Tangent, Derivatives.—Consider the second-degree equation $y = x^2$.

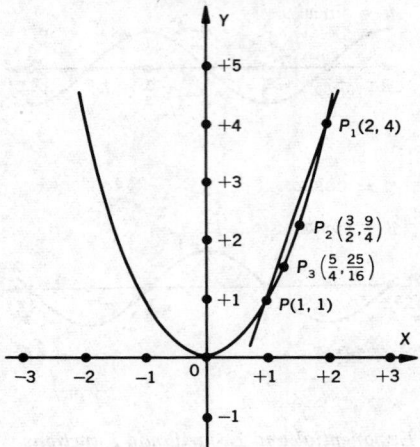

Select points $P, P_1, P_2, P_3, P_4, \ldots$ on the curve so that their x coordinates are 1, 2, 3/2, 5/4, 9/8, ... Using the equation, corresponding y coordinates are

P (1, 1),
P_1 (2, 4),
P_2 (3/2, 9/4),
P_3 (5/4, 25/16),
P_4 (9/8, 81/64).

Since the slope of a line is given as

$$m = \frac{y_2 - y_1}{x_2 - x_1},$$

the slopes of the lines $PP_1, PP_2, PP_3, PP_4, \ldots$ can be computed:

First Point	Second Point	Slope
P (1,1)	P_1 (2,4)	$\frac{4-1}{2-1} = 3$
P (1,1)	P_2 (3/2,9/4)	$\frac{9/4-1}{3/2-1} = 2\frac{1}{2}$
P (1,1)	P_3 (5/4,25/16)	$\frac{25/16-1}{5/4-1} = 2\frac{1}{4}$
P (1,1)	P_4 (9/8,81/64)	$\frac{81/64-1}{9/8-1} = 2\frac{1}{8}$

It can be shown that the sequence 3, $2\frac{1}{2}, 2\frac{1}{4}, 2\frac{1}{8}, \ldots$ approaches 2 as a limit. This limit can be interpreted as the slope of the tangent to the curve $y = x^2$ at the point (1, 1). If the secants for several points in the original sequence are plotted, it will be seen that they approach the position of a line with slope 2 drawn through point P. From the graph, it is clear that no secant drawn from P through some point to the right of P can have a slope less than 2. Thus a graphic illustration of the fact that slope 2 is the limit of the sequence comprising the slopes of the secants is produced.

A more general description can be obtained for this example. Let $y = f(x)$. [The expression $f(x)$, which is read "f of x," simply means "some function of x." In the previous example, $f(x) = x^2$.] Choose a point (x_1, y_1), that is, $[x_1, f(x_1)]$ and a point $[x_1 + h, f(x_1 + h)]$, where $x_1 + h$ is the abscissa of some point near (x_1, y_1). Now consider the quotient

$$\frac{f(x_1 + h) - f(x_1)}{(x_1 + h) - x_1}.$$

For a sequence of decreasing values of h, these quotients give the slopes of secant lines through (x_1, y_1). The limit of this sequence gives the slope of the tangent line. For the special equation $y = x^2$ the following would be obtained:

$$\frac{f(x_1 + h) - f(x_1)}{(x_1 + h) - x_1} = \frac{(x_1 + h)^2 - x_1^2}{(x_1 + h) - x_1}$$
$$= \frac{x_1^2 + 2x_1 h + h^2 - x_1^2}{x_1 + h - x_1}$$
$$= \frac{2x_1 h + h^2}{h}$$
$$= 2x_1 + h.$$

Intuitively, it is clear that the limit would be $2x_1$ (for h can be made as small as necessary). This limit, $2x$ (where we now wish to consider the x coordinate of *any* point on the curve), is called the *derivative* of x^2. The process of finding derivatives is called *differentiation*.

The derivative of a function $f(x)$ is designated by a variety of symbols in the literature. For example, if $y = f(x)$, the derivative of y with respect to x can be stated as

$$y' = \frac{dy}{dx} = D_x y =$$
$$\lim_{h \to 0} \frac{f(x + h) - f(x)}{(x + h) - h} = f'(x).$$

Formulas of Differentiation.

Formulas of Differentiation.—The differentiation of $y = x^2$ that was shown is a special case of a general formula. If $y = x^n$,

$$\frac{dy}{dx} = nx^{n-1}.$$

Complete formulas for differentiating various expressions can be found in textbooks on calculus. Following are some of the more common such formulas:

$$\frac{d(C)}{dx} = 0 \qquad (C = \text{constant})$$

If $u = f(x)$ and $v = g(x)$:

$$\frac{d(Cu)}{dx} = C\frac{du}{dx},$$

$$\frac{d}{dx}(u + v + \ldots) = \frac{du}{dx} + \frac{dv}{dx} + \ldots,$$

$$\frac{d}{dx}(uv) = u\frac{dv}{dx} + v\frac{du}{dx},$$

$$\frac{d}{dx}\left(\frac{u}{v}\right) = \frac{v\frac{du}{dx} - u\frac{dv}{dx}}{v^2},$$

$$\frac{d}{dx}(u^n) = nu^{n-1}\frac{du}{dx},$$

$$\frac{d}{dx}(\sin x) = \cos x,$$

$$\frac{d}{dx}(\cos x) = -\sin x,$$

$$\frac{d}{dx}(\ln u) = \frac{1}{u}\frac{du}{dx} \qquad (\text{natural log}),$$

$$\frac{d}{dx}(e^u) = e^u\frac{du}{dx}.$$

The Definite Integral.—Consider the equation $y = x^2$, the graph of which is shown below. Take two points on the curve P_1 (1, 1) and P_2 (2, 4). The problem is to find the area of the shaded portion—

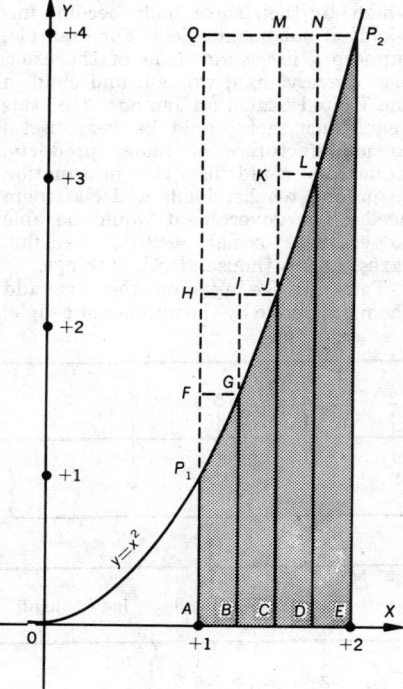

the area bounded by the curve, the X axis, and the two perpendiculars P_1A and P_2E.

P_1A is extended to Q, and QP_2 is drawn; a rectangle is formed the area of which gives a very rough approximation of the shaded area. If this rectangle is divided in half by drawing CM, and lines MP_2 and HJ are added, a better approximation can be had by taking the area of rectangles $AHJC$ and CMP_2E.

Determining a Curve Area Algebraically

Rectangle Approximation	Base	Height	Area
(1) AEP_2Q	AE = 1	$EP_2 = 4$	4
(2) $AHJC$	AC = 1/2	CJ = 9/4	9/8
$+CMP_2E$	CE = 1/2	$EP_2 = 4$	2
			3 1/8
(3) $ABGF$	AB = 1/4	BG = 25/16	25/64
$+BCJI$	BC = 1/4	CJ = 9/4	9/16
$+CDLM$	CD = 1/4	DL = 49/16	49/64
$+DEP_2N$	DE = 1/4	$EP_2 = 4$	1
			2 23/32

Dividing these two rectangles in half, as shown in the illustration, and repeating the process, the approximation can be improved further. At this point it becomes evident that better and better approximations are produced by repeating this procedure until the actual area under the curve is approached as a limit. The above table on determining a curve area serves to illustrate, algebraically, what is occurring.

It can be shown that the sequence 4, $3\frac{1}{8}$, $2\frac{23}{32}$, ... approaches $2\frac{1}{3}$ as a limit. This means that if the units of measure on the two axes are 1 inch each, the area bounded by the curve, the X axis, and the perpendiculars drawn at $x = 1$ and $x = 2$ would be $2\frac{1}{3}$ square inches.

The process of finding the limit of this sequence is called *integration*, and the number $2\frac{1}{3}$ is called the *definite integral* of $y = x^2$ from $x = 1$ to $x = 2$.

The Indefinite Integral.—The process of finding the *indefinite integral* is the fundamental theorem of integral calculus. It develops that there is a remarkable relationship between differentiation and integration. In regard to the function $f(x)$, the process of finding a function $F(x)$ such that $f(x)$ is the derivative of $F(x)$, or $F'(x) = f(x)$, is called *integration*. $F(x)$ is called an *integral* of $f(x)$, or an *antiderivative* of $f(x)$. The symbol for integration is $\int$ and is written

$$F(x) = \int f(x),$$

although the more customary form is

$$F(x) = \int f(x)dx.$$

For example,

$$\int x^2 dx = \tfrac{1}{3}x^3,$$

since the formula for differentiation shows that

$$\frac{d}{dx}(\tfrac{1}{3}x^3) = 3 \cdot \tfrac{1}{3} \cdot x^2 = x^2.$$

Note that $\tfrac{1}{3}x^3 + 5$ and $\tfrac{1}{3}x^3 + C$ (where C is any constant) are also integrals of x^2, for

$$\frac{d}{dx}(\tfrac{1}{3}x^3 + 5) = \frac{d}{dx}(\tfrac{1}{3}x^3) + \frac{d}{dx}(5)$$
$$= x^2 + 0 = x^2.$$

In general, if $F(x)$ is an integral of $f(x)$, so is $F(x) + C$. For this reason, $\int f(x)dx$ is called the *indefinite integral* of $f(x)$.

The connection between the definite integral and the indefinite integral is illustrated by the following. It develops that if $F(x)$ is an indefinite integral of $f(x)$, then the definite integral of $f(x)$ from $x = a$ to $x = b$ is given by

$$\int_a^b f(x)dx = F(b) - F(a).$$

For the special case in the previous problem the shaded area is

$$\int_1^2 x^2\, dx.$$

Following the general formula

$$\int f(x)dx = \tfrac{1}{3}x^3 = F(x),$$
$$F(2) = 8/3 \qquad F(1) = 1/3.$$

The shaded area is

$$\frac{8}{3} - \frac{1}{3} = \frac{7}{3} = 2\frac{1}{3}.$$

The techniques of integration depend on using tables of differentiation because of the relationship between these two branches of calculus.

Applications.—The problem used to introduce differential calculus—finding the slope of the tangent to a given curve at a given point—is related to the problem of having two variables change their values, when the object is to find the *rate* of change of one with respect to the other. This is exactly the situation in problems of velocity of a moving body where the variables are time and distance. Calculus also relates to the inverse physical problem, for example, when the velocity of a moving body is known, to find the law that describes its motion. Calculus is a basic tool in modern science and engineering, because it supplies a language for expressing physical laws in precise mathematical terms and provides a technique for studying the consequences of these laws.

Derivatives are used in problems of instantaneous rates of change, velocities, and accelerations. Differentiation is used in solving problems of maxima and minima, in the study of related rates of change, and in tracing simple and complex curves.

Integral calculus may be applied to the study of complicated regions, moments of inertia, hydrostatic pressure, work, distance, acceleration, and volume.

—Julius H. Hlavaty

ADVANCED MATHEMATICS

Logarithms.—The simplest arithmetical operation is addition. Next in complexity would probably be subtraction, then multiplication, and last, division. It would be convenient, then, if one could find the product of two numbers by addition rather than by the use of traditional multiplication techniques.

Though it seems impossible, John Napier (1550–1617), a Scottish inventor, discovered a solution which utilizes the peculiar properties of the powers of numbers. To multiply numbers raised to powers, their exponents are added:

$$3^1 \times 3^2 = 3^{1+2} = 3^3$$
$$3 \times 9 = 27 = 3^3$$

The two base numbers (the 3's in this example) must be the same. But with that as the only requirement, Napier had a tool to do exactly what he wanted: a method of multiplying by simple addition. An English geometry professor, Henry Briggs (1561–1630), helped him set up the system. For convenience they chose the number 10 as the base rather than 3. Then they made a table of powers. Just a small part of the table is shown below. The full table is given at the end of this article.

$$1 = 10^{0.0000} \qquad 6 = 10^{0.7782}$$
$$2 = 10^{0.3010} \qquad 7 = 10^{0.8451}$$
$$3 = 10^{0.4771} \qquad 8 = 10^{0.9031}$$
$$4 = 10^{0.6021} \qquad 9 = 10^{0.9542}$$
$$5 = 10^{0.6990} \qquad 10 = 10^{1.0000}$$

Now, to multiply two numbers, say 2×4, translate them first into their powers of 10, or

$$2 \times 4 = 10^{0.3010} \times 10^{0.6021}.$$

Add the exponents,

$$10^{0.3010} \times 10^{0.6021} = 10^{0.9031},$$

and reconvert to the numerical form:

$$8 = 10^{0.9031}.$$

For convenience, it is possible to eliminate the constant writing of the exponents, which Napier called *logarithms* (abbreviated *log*). Thus the logarithm of 2 is 0.3010. The operation can be stated: *To find the product of two numbers add their logarithms.*

There is no special magic about the base number 10. Any positive number except 1 can serve as base. Today two bases are popular. Natural logarithms use base 2.71828.... Common logarithms use the base 10. Briggs and Napier chose 10 for a very practical reason. Note that

$$5 = 10^{0.6990} \ (\log \ 5 = 0.6990)$$
$$50 = 10^{1.6990} \ (\log \ 50 = 1.6990)$$
$$500 = 10^{2.6990} \ (\log 500 = 2.6990).$$

The *mantissa* (the four characteristic numbers to the right of the decimal point in the logarithms) is the same whenever the same significant figures appear in the original number. The convenience of 10 as a base therefore comes from the fact that only one table of logarithms for 1,000 numbers (three significant figures) is needed. It doesn't matter if the number to be multiplied is actually in the billions; if there are no more than three significant figures, the one table will serve.

For example, multiply 455 by 81.1. To find the mantissa of 455, look for 45 in the left column of the table and check across the row to the column headed 5 at the top. This gives the mantissa, or 6580. Since 455 lies between 100 and 1,000, its logarithm lies between 2 and 3, or 2 plus a decimal fraction, hence 2.6580. (In other words, the number added in front of the mantissa is equal to the number of places to the right of the first digit before the decimal point.) Find the logarithm of 81.1; then add both logarithms:

$$\log 4.55 = 0.6580, \log 455 \ = 2.6580$$
$$\log 8.11 = 0.9090, \log 81.1 = \underline{1.9090}$$
$$\text{sum} = \overline{4.5670}$$

Look up 0.5670 in the body of the table and read up and across to find 369 as its *antilogarithm* (the number whose logarithm was found). Then take care of the number 4 preceding the decimal point by counting off 4 decimal places in the antilogarithm from the right of the first digit, adding zeros as necessary. The answer is 36,900.

To divide, reverse the process and subtract logs; to solve $36,900 \div 455$,

$$\log 36,900 = 4.5670$$
$$\log \quad 455 = 2.6580$$
$$\text{difference} = \overline{1.9090}$$
$$\text{antilog } 1.9090 = 81.1.$$

Slide Rule.—The slide rule is merely a mechanical tool for adding logarithms in exactly the way described above. Instead of adding numbers, however, it adds lengths. Take two rulers and place them side by side. By placing the 0 of the upper scale on the 2 of the lower scale, mark off a 2-inch length. Now, to add 3 inches to the 2 inches, read opposite the 3 on the upper scale and find a 5 on the lower scale: $2 + 3 = 5$.

Now suppose instead of equal lengths, positions are marked according to the logarithmic proportions given in the short list above. By adding log 2 and log 3 log 6 is found. The two numbers have been multiplied by adding their logarithms. For simplicity most slide rules are not marked with the mantissas as shown here, but simply with the numbers whose logarithms their lengths represent. Also, decimal points are omitted in slide rules (these must be calculated). Thus, the above setting could just as well represent $20 \times 300 = 6,000$ or $2.0 \times 0.3 = 0.6$.

By subtracting logarithmic lengths, division may be performed. This slide rule has been set: $9 \div 3 = 3$.

Statistics.—Statistics is the name given to the study of large sets of numbers which, by their sheer bulk, become unwieldy if not meaningless. For example, suppose a list were made of the exact age of every man, woman, and child in the United States on January 1 of this year. Such facts could be very useful to manufacturers of many products. Educators could use the information to predict teacher loads and classroom needs. The government would be able to estimate social security benefits, taxes, and a thousand other things.

Take all the ages on the list, add them up, divide by the number of people,

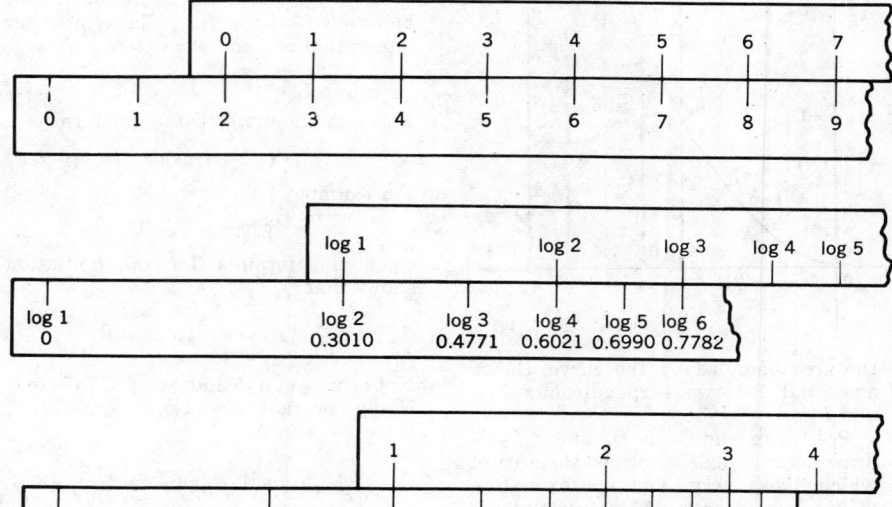

SLIDE RULE is a mechanical tool for adding or subtracting logarithms of numbers.

and an average (statisticians call it a *mean*) is obtained. The mean is significant because it may, for some purposes, represent the whole group. Thus the average weight of the American man has been increasing over the past hundred years, so it can be said that Americans are getting heavier. But there are dangers in giving too much importance to the mean. The mean annual income of U.S. citizens in the year 1960 was $6,900. What does this mean? There are many people who earn less than this and there are people who earn much more. Further, the few people who earn high incomes have an effect which distorts the mean. In this case, it makes more sense to list the incomes of all the people in increasing amounts and then count off from the bottom or from the top until you have gone exactly halfway through this list. The individual at this position earns more than what half the total population does and less than the other half. His income is the *median*, and for the United States in 1960 the median income was $5,600 per year, or a good deal less than the mean. For that reason, perhaps it is more representative.

■ **PROBABILITY.**—Statisticians have discovered an interesting thing about large sets of numbers. Certain kinds of data take very regular distributions. Suppose we were to divide a group of 899 men by weight. A typical count might be:

>   130 to 139 lb.—   2 men
>   140 to 149 lb.— 30 men
>   150 to 159 lb.— 140 men
>   160 to 169 lb.— 275 men
>   170 to 179 lb.— 270 men
>   180 to 189 lb.— 145 men
>   190 to 199 lb.— 32 men
>   200 to 209 lb.—   5 men

These numbers may be plotted in a graph with weight along the horizontal axis and numbers of men along the vertical axis. Note that the plot is symmetrical about the centerline, which in this case is the mean (170 lb.). This characteristic curve occurs so frequently that it is called a *normal* or *probability curve*. The essential shape is always the same. It is best described by the distance from the centerline to the inflection point (where the curve changes from concave to convex), and this distance is always called *sigma* (Greek σ).

It turns out that almost two-thirds of all the things measured (899 men in this example) fall between the two inflection points of any normal curve (between 159 lb. and 181 lb., above).

The probability curve has many interesting and important applications, but only two will be considered here. The first is what the statistician calls a *sample*, and his problem arises in this way: He would like to know whether the distribution of weights in the example above really represents the weights of all male adults in the United States. If it is a good representation,

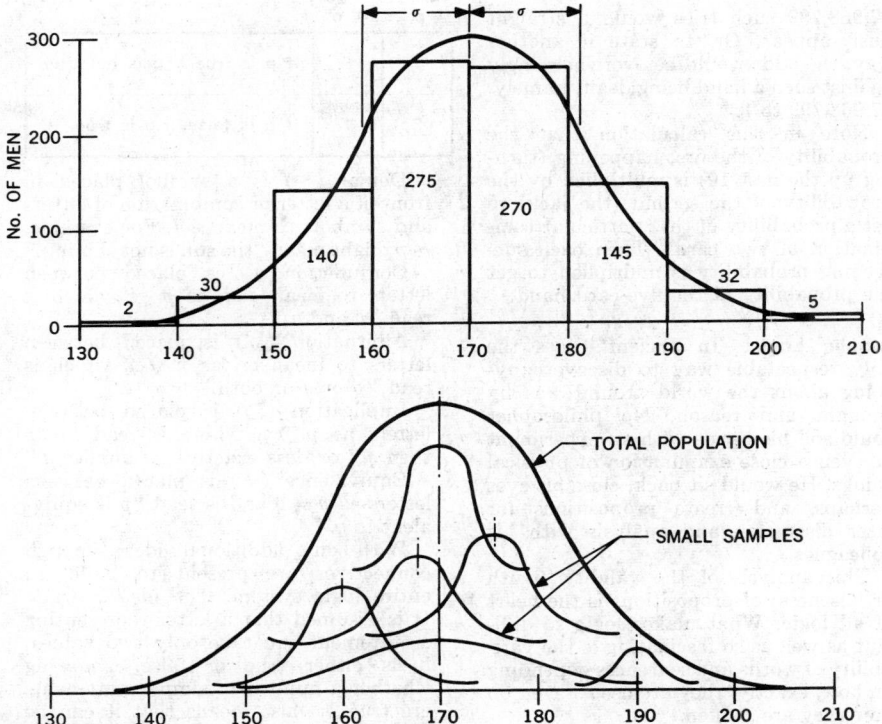

PROBABILITY CURVE illustrates graphically how a random group of 899 men could be represented by weight. The lower curve is a breakdown of several random samples.

then his job is substantially reduced, since there are over fifty million men he would need to weigh if the limited group were untrustworthy.

Imagine for a moment all the many such limited groups that could be chosen out of the total population of male adults. Some groups would be small, but quite representative of the total; others would be less representative.

Once again, almost two-thirds of the groups would have means that were within one sigma of the mean of the total population. So we could say that any group chosen at random has a two-out-of-three chance of having its mean within one sigma (11 lb.) of the mean of all groups. If these odds are not satisfactory they can be improved by widening the "tolerance." For example, 99.7 per cent of all groups would have means between three sigmas below and three sigmas above the mean of the total population. Thus, it is 99.7 per cent certain that the mean of the sample is within 33 lb. of the average for the whole population.

This calculation is called a finding of the *confidence level* (odds) for any particular range, and the procedures here are exactly the same in principle as those used to figure the odds in any probability calculation.

Probability always starts by finding out how many ways a thing can possibly happen: the number of groups in the discussion above, the number of ways two dice can fall, the number of card hands that can be held. Then how many

particular combinations are possible must be determined: the number of ways a seven can be thrown, or the number of royal flushes that can be turned in order from the first five cards at the top of a deck.

There are many rules for figuring out such combinations, but rules never substitute for simple common sense. Consider a pair of dice. Each has six sides. The first die can fall in any of six ways. For each way the first die falls, the second can fall in any of six ways. This makes a total of 36 possible throws—6 × 6. Now, how many ways can a seven be thrown? Just six: 1–6, 2–5, 3–4, 4–3, 5–2, 6–1. Therefore, what are the odds of throwing a seven? Six out of 36.

What are the odds of throwing a five? This makes four possibilities out of the 36 (1–4, 2–3, 3–2, 4–1). Therefore, it is more likely that a seven will be thrown than a five: 6 out of 36 to 4 out of 36, or 6 to 4.

The straight flush calculation is even simpler. The first card must be a 10. There are only four 10's so the odds are 4 out of 52. The second card must be a jack of the same suit as the 10. Only one card will do and only 51 cards remain. The odds are 1 out of 51 that you will draw the right jack. The same holds true for the other three cards needed:

$$\frac{4}{52} \times \frac{1}{51} \times \frac{1}{50} \times \frac{1}{49} \times \frac{1}{48} = \frac{4}{311,875,200}$$

Thus, if five cards were drawn an indefinite number of times, only once in

77,968,799 such tries would a straight flush appear. Or, to state it another way, the odds would be overwhelmingly against such a hand being dealt, namely, 77,968,799 to 1.

Note in this calculation that the probability of the first happening (turning up the first 10) is multiplied by the probability of the second (the jack) to get a probability of that particular combination of two cards. Then each succeeding probability is multiplied to get the probability of the five-card hand.

Symbolic Logic.—In ancient times the only respectable way to discover anything about the world around was by thought and reason. No philosopher could soil his hands with an experiment or even a close examination of physical things. He would sit back, close his eyes perhaps, and create propositions for later discussion and analysis with his colleagues.

This analysis of the validity (truth or falseness) of propositions is the heart of all logic. What makes logic so difficult as well as so fascinating is the variability of words and sentences depending on how, exactly, they are used—even on how they are spoken.

In the eighteenth century, when great political as well as industrial revolutions were stimulating the minds of men, several mathematicians wondered whether the clear-cut and precise techniques of mathematics might not be of assistance in logic. They were concerned with the need for a technique of logical analysis, not the content of the propositions, just as algebra is concerned with the correct relationships of the variables x, y, and so forth, not that these are heights in feet, or quantities of water in gallons, or some other measurable thing.

Logic had always been presented in words and sentences whose exact meanings had to be defined carefully. Wouldn't it be simpler if words were left out completely, were switched to symbols—perhaps like those used in mathematics—which could be defined exactly and then manipulated to discover new relationships? The answer is yes; there is such a simple and very powerful tool.

In the most widely used system (obviously many sets of symbols and rules of manipulation are possible) single alphabet letters represent single propositions or sentences. The letters p, q, r, and so on might mean "It is raining," or "All men are mortal," or "My aunt's half brother has a twisted ankle." They are much like the variables in algebra and, as in that branch of mathematics, symbolic logic is not concerned with what propositions they actually represent.

Words and sentences in language are related by certain connectives. The symbols in the new logic must be similarly related. The following is a basic set of connectives.

p	$\sim p$	
T	F	If p is true, p is not true.
F	T	If p is false, p is true.

Denial ($\sim$) is a symbol placed in front of a letter or combination of letters and symbols to mean *not*. For example, $\sim p$ might mean "the sun is not shining."

Conjunction ($\cdot$) is placed between letters to mean *and*, as $p \cdot q$, which is read "p and q."

Alternation ($\vee$) is placed between letters to mean *or*, as $p \vee q$, which is read "p or q or both."

Implication ($\supset$) is placed between letters as $p \supset q$, which is read "if p then q," or, less exactly, "p implies q."

Equivalence ($=$) is placed between letters as $p = q$ and is read "p is equivalent to q."

With one additional idea, enough connectives are present to build an entire logic system. The idea is *truth*. It is assumed that a letter representing a statement can take only two values; it is either true or false. Knowing whether a number of simple statements are true or false means that it can be discovered whether and when a complex combination of these statements is true or false.

Analyses of truth are rather easily made with a *truth table*, a simple mechanical method of considering all possibilities. For example, the following tables clarify the meanings of the symbols defined above.

p	q	$p \cdot q$	$p \vee q$	$p \supset q$	$p = q$
T	T	T	T	T	T
T	F	F	T	F	F
F	T	F	T	T	F
F	F	F	F	T	T

$$\sim\{[p \cdot (\sim q)] \vee [(p \vee r) \supset q]\}$$

p	q	r	$\sim q$	$p \cdot (\sim q)$	$p \vee r$	$(p \vee r) \supset q$	$\sim\{[p \cdot (\sim q)] \vee [(p \vee r) \supset q]\}$
T	T	T	F	F	T	T	F
T	T	F	F	F	T	T	F
T	F	T	T	T	T	F	F
T	F	F	T	T	T	F	F
F	T	T	F	F	T	T	F
F	T	F	F	F	F	T	F
F	F	T	T	F	T	F	T
F	F	F	T	F	F	T	F

The first table shows: only when p and q are both true does $p \cdot q$ become true; if either p or q is true then $p \vee q$ is true; the statement $p \supset q$ is false only when the implication fails (that is, when p is true even though q is false); and $p = q$ is true whenever p and q are both false or both true.

Now this set of values can be applied to much more complex statements. Consider this one: "It never happens that either my wineglass is full and I am not thirsty or else I am thirsty if either my wineglass is full or the wine is sour."

Let p represent "My wineglass is full"; q represent "I am thirsty"; and r represent "The wine is sour." In symbolic form the sentence is:

$$\sim\{[p \cdot (\sim q)] \vee [(p \vee r) \supset q]\}$$

The second truth table then sets up all possible combinations of truth and falseness for the three propositions.

The results are rather surprising. The only time the statement is true is when the wineglass is not full, I am not thirsty, and the wine is sour. Or, to think about it in another way, if the statement as a whole is true it can be deduced that the wineglass is not full, I am not thirsty, and the wine is sour.

All this may seem like an interesting exercise which common sense could have performed more quickly. But many practical applications have been made, applications as far apart as can be imagined. The first is in the design of complex electrical control systems. Here the electrical engineer substitutes 1 and 0, or ON and OFF, for true and false. He then substitutes his electric switches for the p, q, and r propositions and sets them up so that for any particular combination of switch settings the entire circuit will be ON or OFF as he needs.

Suppose, in the previous example, instead of a wineglass and thirst you had three switches, p, q, and r, and the only time a certain light was to be ON was when there was no sun (p is 0), the window is covered (q is 0), and someone is in the room (r is 1). The engineer could make a circuit like the symbolic proposition written in the table above and have his answer.

Another application of symbolic logic is for the analysis of the significance of statements in legal documents, in treaties, in newspaper reports, or in propaganda. In English, the statements would be quite confusing, but transformed into symbols and manipulated in these mechanical ways (sometimes by computers) the truth suddenly becomes apparent.

A TRUTH TABLE is a graphical method of evaluating all possible variables. This table evaluates the many combinations of p, q, and r, as discussed in the text. Symbolic logic is the mathematician's way of converting concepts into a form that can be analyzed numerically. Computers can be programmed to handle such concepts.

Topology.—At first glance, topology seems to be simply an extension of plane and solid geometry—an extension that goes beyond the lines and angles of these studies and concerns itself with shape. However, the applications of the theorems of topology are by no means limited to physical objects. They have been applied in logic, philosophy, and even in the strategies of war.

Topology really began with the discovery by René Descartes (1596–1650) in 1640 and Leonhard Euler (1707–1783) in 1752 that a simple polyhedron—a solid made up of plane figures such as triangles, rectangles, and so on—with no through-holes has a consistent relationship between the number of vertices, edges, and faces:

$$\text{vertices} - \text{edges} + \text{faces} = 2 .$$

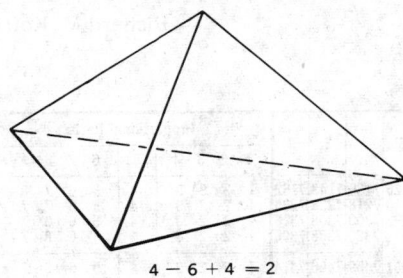

$4 - 6 + 4 = 2$

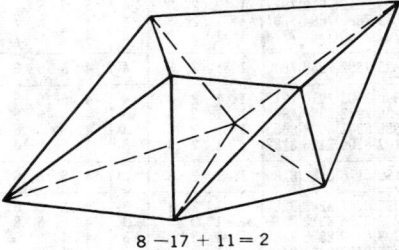

$8 - 17 + 11 = 2$

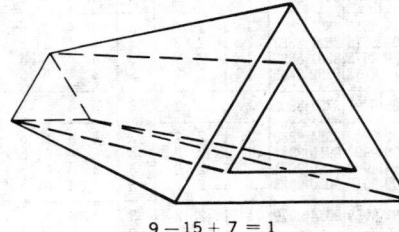

$9 - 15 + 7 = 1$

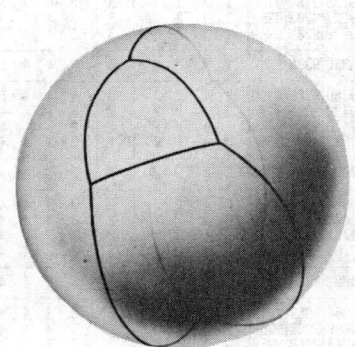

$5 - 8 + 5 = 2$

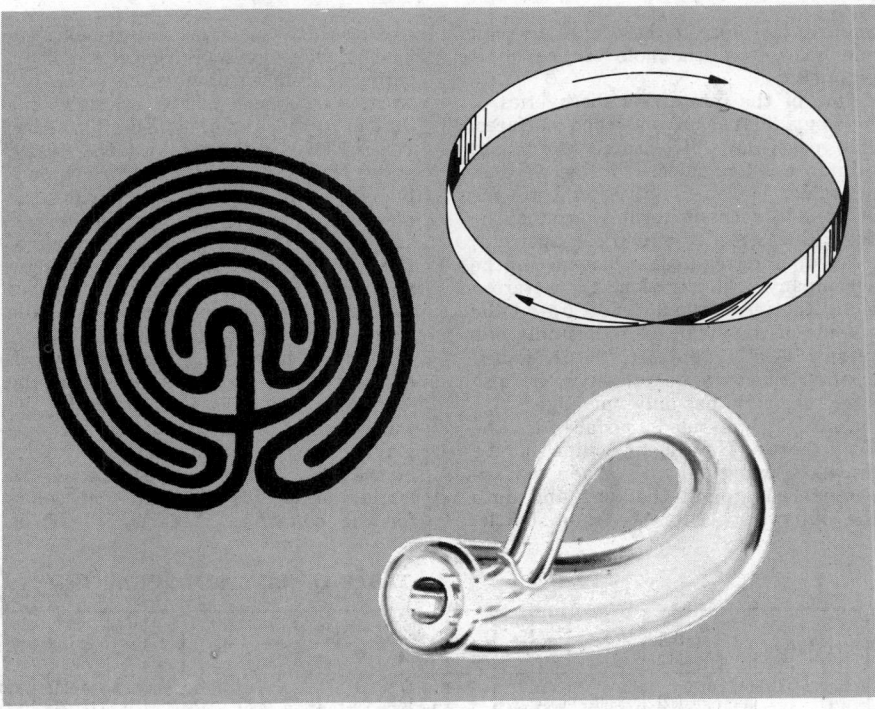

TOPOLOGICAL FIGURES attempt to give dimension to concepts that, in many cases, are only theoretical. The maze (*left*) and the Möbius strip (*right*) are both closed curves. The Klein bottle (*lower right*) is a one-sided figure; it has neither inside nor outside.

Note that the illustration with a hole in it does not follow Descartes's formula because the polyhedron is not simple. However, the formula will apply to all simple polyhedrons and even to solids with curved faces and edges or even to a sphere with areas marked off by curved arcs and vertices indicated by the intersections of these arcs.

This wide applicability suggests that the formula is really independent of the exact dimensions or angles and concerns itself only with shape. Thus, it was the first truly topological formula.

How can this shape, characteristic, or property be precisely defined? First, the topologist looks at any solid or plane figure as an aggregate of an infinite number of points. The body shape is defined by those points which happen to lie on its boundaries (the *perimeter* of a plane figure, the *surface* of a solid). He says that two figures are topologically similar when a point can always be found in the one which will correspond to one, and only one, point in the other.

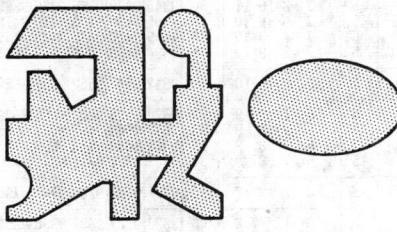

Further, the distance between any two points in the one body will reduce or increase as the distance between the cor-responding points in the other is reduced or increased.

Following these rules, solids of quite different shape would have the same topological properties. However, if a hole were punched in the rubber triangle it would change the topological properties because a circle that encloses the hole would not now be able to reduce in size to a point as its corresponding circle can in the unpierced triangle.

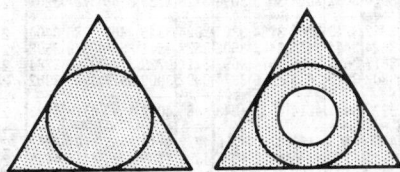

The solid triangle is said to be *simply connected* because any encircling line (starting with the outer boundary) can be reduced in size to a point within the triangle. The triangle with the hole does not permit this. The outer perimeter would have to shrink across the hole to reduce to a point. This figure is said to be *multiply connected*.

It should be noted here that any multiply connected figure may be made into a simply connected figure by making

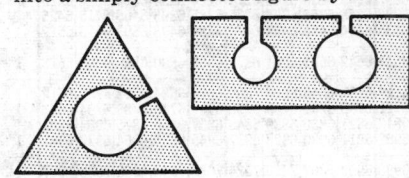

one cut (or more if there is more than one hole) from the hole to the outer perimeter.

One of the interesting discoveries of topology is that of one-sided surfaces. The page on which these words are printed has two sides. If a line were on one side, it could not extend to the other side without turning around the edge. But consider a loop of paper cut, twisted, and reglued as shown in the accompanying illustration. A line started along the inside would wind up on the outside of the strip, for it has only one surface. A. F. Möbius (1790–1868) discovered this strange property; he also noted the strip has only one edge.

Another one-sided surface is the Klein bottle. Here again a line can be drawn starting on the inside surface and traced around the loop and onto the outer surface of the same bottle.

These are some of the peculiarities that topology considers. Sometimes these subjects seem so obvious as to be unworthy of mention. For example, the *Jordan curve theorem*, named after Marie Ennemond Camille Jordan (1838–1922), states that any closed curve drawn on a plane without crossing itself divides the plane into two domains, an inside and an outside. Oddly enough the proof of this seemingly obvious statement is by no means simple. Jordan's own proof was in error and only recently have simple proofs been demonstrated.

Another interesting problem which has not yet been solved is called the *four-color map*. It is well known by the experience of a thousand years of mapmaking that any map of the countries of the world, or of any portion of the world, needs only four different colors for the countries. That is, it can be printed so that no two countries having the same color have boundaries of any finite length in common. But is this always so? It is suspected, of course, that it is, but so far the proof has been made that five colors are always sufficient. No one has yet demonstrated that this can be achieved with four.

Thus far only geometrical figures have been considered, but obviously the "points" that make up the plane or solid figure do not have to be points in space. They could be members of a group (or *class*, to use a logician's term) and in that way something about the general relationships of groups of people or things might be discovered. This is why topology has become the mathematician's mathematics, the philosopher's logic, and the mapmaker's amusement.

—Richard M. Koff

TABLE OF COMMON LOGARITHMS

	0	1	2	3	4	5	6	7	8	9	Proportional Parts								
											1	2	3	4	5	6	7	8	9
10	0000	0043	0086	0128	0170						4	9	13	17	21	25	30	34	38
						0212	0253	0294	0334	0374	4	8	12	16	20	24	28	32	37
11	0414	0453	0492	0531	0569						4	8	12	15	19	23	27	31	35
						0607	0645	0682	0719	0755	4	7	11	15	19	22	26	30	33
12	0792	0828	0864	0899	0934	0969					3	7	11	14	18	21	25	28	32
							1004	1038	1072	1106	3	7	10	14	17	20	24	27	31
13	1139	1173	1206	1239	1271						3	7	10	13	16	20	23	26	30
						1303	1335	1367	1399	1430	3	7	10	12	16	19	22	25	29
14	1461	1492	1523	1553							3	6	9	12	15	18	21	24	28
					1584	1614	1644	1673	1703	1732	3	6	9	12	15	17	20	23	26
15	1761	1790	1818	1847	1875	1903					3	6	9	11	14	17	20	23	26
							1931	1959	1987	2014	3	5	8	11	14	16	19	22	25
16	2041	2068	2095	2122	2148						3	5	8	11	14	16	19	22	24
						2175	2201	2227	2253	2279	3	5	8	10	13	15	18	21	23
17	2304	2330	2355	2380	2405	2430					3	5	8	10	13	15	18	20	23
							2455	2480	2504	2529	2	5	7	10	12	15	17	19	22
18	2553	2577	2601	2625	2648						2	5	7	9	12	14	16	19	21
						2672	2695	2718	2742	2765	2	5	7	9	11	14	16	18	21
19	2788	2810	2833	2856	2878						2	4	7	9	11	13	16	18	20
						2900	2923	2945	2967	2989	2	4	6	8	11	13	15	17	19
20	3010	3032	3054	3075	3096	3118	3139	3160	3181	3201	2	4	6	8	11	13	15	17	19
21	3222	3243	3263	3284	3304	3324	3345	3365	3385	3404	2	4	6	8	10	12	14	16	18
22	3424	3444	3464	3483	3502	3522	3541	3560	3579	3598	2	4	6	8	10	12	14	15	17
23	3617	3636	3655	3674	3692	3711	3729	3747	3766	3784	2	4	6	7	9	11	13	15	17
24	3802	3820	3838	3856	3874	3892	3909	3927	3945	3962	2	4	5	7	9	11	12	14	16
25	3979	3997	4014	4031	4048	4065	4082	4099	4116	4133	2	3	5	7	9	10	12	14	15
26	4150	4166	4183	4200	4216	4232	4249	4265	4281	4298	2	3	5	7	8	10	11	13	15
27	4314	4330	4346	4362	4378	4393	4409	4425	4440	4456	2	3	5	6	8	9	11	13	14
28	4472	4487	4502	4518	4533	4548	4564	4579	4594	4609	2	3	5	6	8	9	11	12	14
29	4624	4639	4654	4669	4683	4698	4713	4728	4742	4757	1	3	4	6	7	9	10	12	13
30	4771	4786	4800	4814	4829	4843	4857	4871	4886	4900	1	3	4	6	7	9	10	11	13
31	4914	4928	4942	4955	4969	4983	4997	5011	5024	5038	1	3	4	6	7	8	10	11	12
32	5051	5065	5079	5092	5105	5119	5132	5145	5159	5172	1	3	4	5	7	8	9	11	12
33	5185	5198	5211	5224	5237	5250	5263	5276	5289	5302	1	3	4	5	6	8	9	10	12
34	5315	5328	5340	5353	5366	6378	5391	5403	5416	5428	1	3	4	5	6	8	9	10	11
35	5441	5453	5465	5478	5490	5502	5514	5527	5539	5551	1	2	4	5	6	7	9	10	11
36	5563	5575	5587	5599	5611	5623	5635	5647	5658	5670	1	2	4	5	6	7	8	10	11
37	5682	5694	5705	5717	5729	5740	5752	5763	5775	5786	1	2	3	5	6	7	8	9	10
38	5798	5809	5821	5832	5843	5855	5866	5877	5888	5899	1	2	3	5	6	7	8	9	10
39	5911	5922	5933	5944	5955	5966	5977	5988	5999	6010	1	2	3	4	5	7	8	9	10
40	6021	6031	6042	6053	6064	6075	6085	6096	6107	6117	1	2	3	4	5	6	8	9	10
41	6128	6138	6149	6160	6170	6180	6191	6201	6212	6222	1	2	3	4	5	6	7	8	9
42	6232	6243	6253	6263	6274	6284	6294	6304	6314	6325	1	2	3	4	5	6	7	8	9
43	6335	6345	6355	6365	6375	6385	6395	6405	6415	6425	1	2	3	4	5	6	7	8	9
44	6435	6444	6454	6464	6474	6484	6493	6503	6513	6522	1	2	3	4	5	6	7	8	9
45	6532	6542	6551	6561	6571	6580	6590	6599	6609	6618	1	2	3	4	5	6	7	8	9
46	6628	6637	6646	6656	6665	6675	6684	6693	6702	6712	1	2	3	4	5	6	7	7	8
47	6721	6730	6739	6749	6758	6767	6776	6785	6794	6803	1	2	3	4	5	5	6	7	8
48	6812	6821	6830	6839	6848	6857	6866	6875	6884	6893	1	2	3	4	4	5	6	7	8
49	6902	6911	6920	6928	6937	6946	6955	6964	6972	6981	1	2	3	4	4	5	6	7	8
50	6990	6998	7007	7016	7024	7033	7042	7050	7059	7067	1	2	3	3	4	5	6	7	8

	0	1	2	3	4	5	6	7	8	9	Proportional Parts								
											1	2	3	4	5	6	7	8	9
51	7076	7084	7093	7101	7110	7118	7126	7135	7143	7152	1	2	3	3	4	5	6	7	8
52	7160	7168	7177	7185	7193	7202	7210	7218	7226	7235	1	2	2	3	4	5	6	7	7
53	7243	7251	7259	7267	7275	7284	7292	7300	7308	7316	1	2	2	3	4	5	6	6	7
54	7324	7332	7340	7348	7356	7364	7372	7380	7388	7396	1	2	2	3	4	5	6	6	7
55	7404	7412	7419	7427	7435	7443	7451	7459	7466	7474	1	2	2	3	4	5	5	6	7
56	7482	7490	7497	7505	7513	7520	7528	7536	7543	7551	1	2	2	3	4	5	5	6	7
57	7559	7566	7574	7582	7589	7597	7604	7612	7619	7627	1	2	2	3	4	5	5	6	7
58	7634	7642	7649	7657	7664	7672	7679	7686	7694	7701	1	1	2	3	4	4	5	6	7
59	7709	7716	7723	7731	7738	7745	7752	7760	7767	7774	1	1	2	3	4	4	5	6	7
60	7782	7789	7796	7803	7810	7818	7825	7832	7839	7846	1	1	2	3	4	4	5	6	6
61	7853	7860	7868	7875	7882	7889	7896	7903	7910	7917	1	1	2	3	4	4	5	6	6
62	7924	7931	7938	7945	7952	7959	7966	7973	7980	7987	1	1	2	3	3	4	5	6	6
63	7993	8000	8007	8014	8021	8028	8035	8041	8048	8055	1	1	2	3	3	4	5	5	6
64	8062	8069	8075	8082	8089	8096	8102	8109	8116	8122	1	1	2	3	3	4	5	5	6
65	8129	8136	8142	8149	8156	8162	8169	8176	8182	8189	1	1	2	3	3	4	5	5	6
66	8195	8202	8209	8215	8222	8228	8335	8241	8248	8254	1	1	2	3	3	4	5	5	6
67	8261	8267	8274	8280	8287	8293	8299	8306	8312	8319	1	1	2	3	3	4	5	5	6
68	8325	8331	8338	8344	8351	8357	8363	8370	8376	8382	1	1	2	3	3	4	4	5	6
69	8388	8395	8401	8407	8414	8420	8426	8432	8439	8445	1	1	2	2	3	4	4	5	6
70	8451	8457	8463	8470	8476	8482	8488	8494	8500	8506	1	1	2	2	3	4	4	5	6
71	8513	8519	8525	8531	8537	8543	8549	8555	8561	8567	1	1	2	2	3	4	4	5	5
72	8573	8579	8585	8591	8597	8603	8609	8615	8621	8627	1	1	2	2	3	4	4	5	5
73	8633	8639	8645	8651	8657	8663	8669	8675	8681	8686	1	1	2	2	3	4	4	5	5
74	8692	8698	8704	8710	8716	8722	8727	8733	8739	8745	1	1	2	2	3	4	4	5	5
75	8751	8756	8762	8768	8774	8779	8785	8791	8797	8802	1	1	2	2	3	3	4	5	5
76	8808	8814	8820	8825	8831	8837	8842	8848	8854	8859	1	1	2	2	3	3	4	5	5
77	8865	8871	8876	8882	8887	8893	8899	8904	8910	8915	1	1	2	2	3	3	4	4	5
78	8921	8927	8932	8938	8943	8949	8954	8960	8965	8971	1	1	2	2	3	3	4	4	5
79	8976	8982	8987	8993	8998	9004	9009	9015	9020	9025	1	1	2	2	3	3	4	4	5
80	9031	9036	9042	9047	9053	9058	9063	9069	9074	9079	1	1	2	2	3	3	4	4	5
81	9085	9090	9096	9101	9106	9112	9117	9122	9128	9133	1	1	2	2	3	3	4	4	5
82	9138	9143	9149	9154	9159	9165	9170	9175	9180	9186	1	1	2	2	3	3	4	4	5
83	9191	9196	9201	9206	9212	9217	9222	9227	9232	9238	1	1	2	2	3	3	4	4	5
84	9243	9248	9253	9258	9263	9269	9274	9279	9284	9289	1	1	2	2	3	3	4	4	5
85	9294	9299	9304	9309	9315	9320	9325	9330	9335	9340	1	1	2	2	3	3	4	4	5
86	9345	9350	9355	9360	9365	9370	9375	9380	9385	9390	1	1	2	2	3	3	4	4	5
87	9395	9400	9405	9410	9415	9420	9425	9430	9435	9440	0	1	1	2	2	3	3	4	4
88	9445	9450	9455	9460	9465	9469	9474	9479	9484	9489	0	1	1	2	2	3	3	4	4
89	9494	9499	9504	9509	9513	9518	9523	9528	9533	9538	0	1	1	2	2	3	3	4	4
90	9542	9547	9552	9557	9562	9566	9571	9576	9581	9586	0	1	1	2	2	3	3	4	4
91	9590	9595	9600	9605	9609	9614	9619	9624	9628	9633	0	1	1	2	2	3	3	4	4
92	9638	9643	9647	9652	9657	9661	9666	9671	9675	9680	0	1	1	2	2	3	3	4	4
93	9685	9689	9694	9699	9703	9708	9713	9717	9722	9727	0	1	1	2	2	3	3	4	4
94	9731	9736	9741	9745	9750	9754	9759	9763	9768	9773	0	1	1	2	2	3	3	4	4
95	9777	9782	9786	9791	9795	9800	9805	9809	9814	9818	0	1	1	2	2	3	3	4	4
96	9823	9827	9832	9836	9841	9845	9850	9854	9859	9863	0	1	1	2	2	3	3	4	4
97	9868	9872	9877	9881	9886	9890	9894	9899	9903	9908	0	1	1	2	2	3	3	4	4
98	9912	9917	9921	9926	9930	9934	9939	9943	9948	9952	0	1	1	2	2	3	3	4	4
99	9956	9961	9965	9969	9974	9978	9983	9987	9991	9996	0	1	1	2	2	3	3	3	4

MATHEMATICS GLOSSARY

Abscissa.—See *Cartesian coordinates.*

Absolute value (numerical value).—In geometry, the distance of a point from the zero point on an ordinary number scale, regardless of its direction. Hence, the absolute value of 3 is 3; of −7, 7; and of zero, 0. The absolute value of *a* is denoted by |*a*|; hence, |3| = 3, |−7| = 7, and |0| = 0.

Abstract mathematics (pure mathematics).—Those branches of modern mathematics, such as topology, that have no meaning in terms of "real" or "specific" interpretations. Unlike applied mathematics, which has meaning in terms of physical experiences, these branches are studied solely as a means of extending knowledge.

Addition.—One of the fundamental operations of arithmetic. The combination of two numbers, *x* and *y*, by addition is denoted by $x + y$; the result of the combination is the *sum* of the numbers.

Algebra.—The branch of mathematics that involves the investigation of the properties of numbers by means of literal symbols, or variables, such as *a*, *b*, *x*, and *y*, instead of constants, such as 1, 2, and 100. Since algebraists can work in generalities rather than with specific instances, the scope of their work is not as limited as that of arithmeticians. Typical algebraic problems are the solving of equations and the summation of series.

Algebraic equation.—See *Equation.*

Algorithm (algorism).—Any method of computation whose procedure has been standardized in the form of rules. Familiar examples of algorithms are the processes of long division and of checking addition by "casting out nines."

Alternating series.—See *Series.*

Analysis.—The branch of higher mathematics that deals with the solution of complex physical problems. A powerful tool used by physicists and engineers, analysis grew out of the calculus and was extensively developed by Joseph Louis Lagrange (1736–1813), Karl G. J. Jacobi (1804–1851), and Sir William Rowan Hamilton (1805–1865).

Analytic geometry (coordinate geometry).—The branch of mathematics that involves the application of algebraic methods to geometric figures and systems. Developed primarily by René Descartes (1596–1650), it involves the use of coordinate systems that relate the point, which is the fundamental element of geometry, to the number, which is the fundamental element of algebra.

Angle.—The inclination of one line, or ray, to another, measured in *degrees* or *radians*. The lines are called the *sides* of the angle; their common point, the *vertex* of the angle. An angle is represented by the symbol ∠, and ∠*ABC* designates an angle with sides *AB* and *BC* and vertex *B*. The *interior angle* is

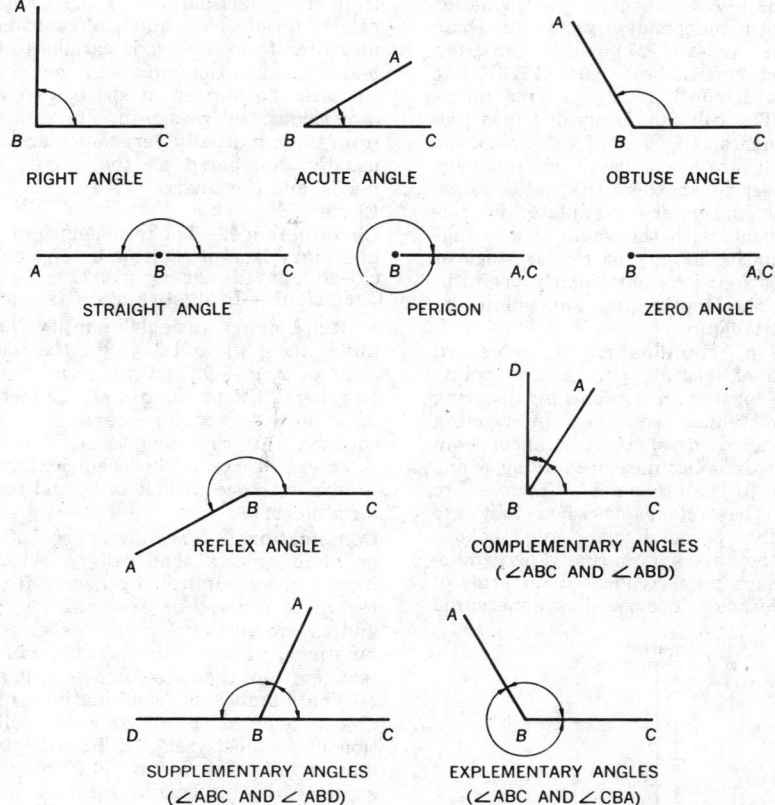

RIGHT ANGLE   ACUTE ANGLE   OBTUSE ANGLE

STRAIGHT ANGLE   PERIGON   ZERO ANGLE

REFLEX ANGLE   COMPLEMENTARY ANGLES
(∠ABC AND ∠ABD)

SUPPLEMENTARY ANGLES   EXPLEMENTARY ANGLES
(∠ABC AND ∠ABD)   (∠ABC AND ∠CBA)

the smaller of the angles formed by the intersection of the two lines, and the *exterior angle* is the larger angle formed. A *right angle* is one of 90°, or $\pi/2$ radians. An *acute angle* is one of between 0° and 90°, and an *obtuse angle* is one of between 90° and 180°. A *reflex angle* is one between 180° and 360°. A *straight angle* is one of 180°, or π radians; hence, a straight angle is one in which the sides form a straight line. An angle of 360°, or 2π radians, is a *perigon*, while one of 0° is a *zero angle;* in both of these, the sides of the angle coincide. An *oblique angle* is one that is not a multiple of 90°. Two angles are *complementary* if their sum is 90°; each is called the *complement* of the other. Two angles are *supplementary* if their sum is 180°; each is called the *supplement* of the other. Two angles are *explementary,* or *conjugate,* if their sum is 360°; each is called the *explement,* or *conjugate,* of the other. In solid geometry, a *dihedral angle* is formed by the intersection of two planes.

Antilogarithm.—See *Logarithm.*

Applied mathematics.—Those branches of mathematics, such as analysis, that deal with physical, biological, and sociological experiences. While applied mathematics, in its present sense, deals only with mathematical operations, such as computer programming, in its broadest sense it is one of the principal tools of the engineer, the physicist, and the social scientist.

Area.—The two-dimensional measure of the region enclosed within the boundaries of any plane geometric figure.

Arithmetic.—The art of calculation using positive real numbers. Four fundamental operations—addition, division, multiplication, and subtraction—form the basis of all arithmetical calculations.

Arithmetic progression.—See *Progression.*

Arithmetic series.—See *Series.*

Axiom (postulate).—A self-evident proposition that is accepted without further proof; axioms are the basic propositions by which all other propositions of the theory are proved. Although the terms "axiom" and "postulate" were used to differentiate between "common notions" (axioms) and "geometric properties" (postulates) by Euclid, the terms are generally considered synonymous in modern usage.

Axis.—Any one of several lines, usually imaginary, that have importance in a particular connotation. An *axis of symmetry* divides a figure into two mirror images. An *axis of rotation* is the line about which an object turns. An *axis of revolution* is the line about which a plane figure is rotated to generate a surface of revolution.

Binary number system.—See *Number system.*

Binomial.—A polynomial that is the sum of two terms, such as $3x^2 + 2y$, or $ax^3 − bx$.

Boolean algebra.—An algebraic notation used in logic, devised by George Boole (1815–1864). While some of the rules of Boolean algebra resemble those of ordinary algebra, others are quite different.

Calculus.—A branch of mathematics developed independently by Sir Isaac Newton (1642–1727) and Gottfried Wilhelm von Leibniz (1646–1716) that deals with continuously varying quantities. The calculus is divided into two subbranches. *Differential calculus* deals with the rate of change of one quantity in respect to another. *Integral calculus*, which is the inverse of differential calculus, deals with the value of a changing quantity at any particular stage of its variation; it is particularly useful in finding the length, area, and volume of geometric figures.

Cartesian coordinates.—A standard method of locating points. The points can be located in a plane by denoting their distances from two intersecting lines called *axes*, the distance from either axis being measured along a line parallel to the other axis. The axes are said to be *rectangular* when they are mutually perpendicular and *oblique* when they are not mutually perpendicular. Each point is located in terms of its *coordinates*. The coordinate measured

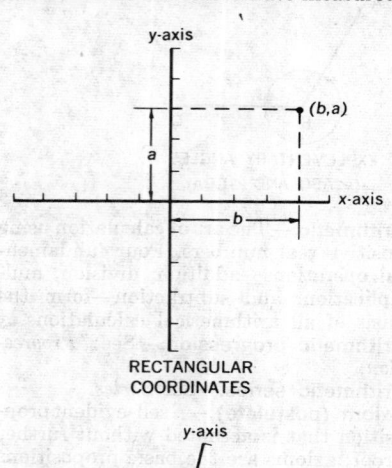

RECTANGULAR
COORDINATES

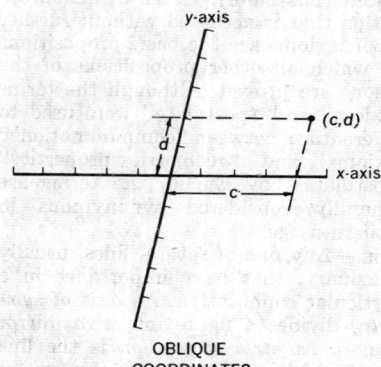

OBLIQUE
COORDINATES

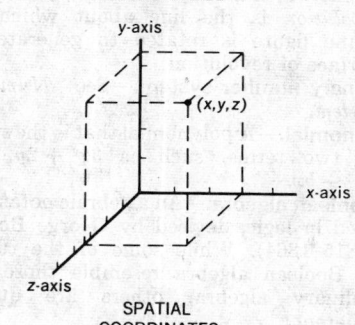

SPATIAL
COORDINATES

from the *y*-axis parallel to the *x*-axis is called the *abscissa*, and the coordinate measured from the *x*-axis parallel to the *y*-axis is called the *ordinate*. A point can similarly be located in space, or three dimensions, by measuring its distance from three mutually perpendicular axes, usually designated as the *x*-axis, the *y*-axis, and the *z*-axis.

Circle.—See *Conic.*

Circumference.—The total length of the boundary line of a circle or any other closed curvilinear figure. $C = 2\pi r$.

Coefficient.—In algebra, a constant term written before a variable quantity. Thus in $3x$, $3(x + y)$, and $3xy$, 3 is the coefficient of x, $x + y$, and xy, respectively. In general, the product of all the factors of a term except for one term is the coefficient of that one term. Thus, in $-3axyz$, $-3axy$ is the coefficient of z, $-3axz$ is the coefficient of y, and so on for all terms.

Combinations.—The different sets of one or more objects that can be selected from a given number of objects without regard to order. For example, x,y, y,z, and x,z are all the possible sets, or combinations, of two objects that can be selected from the three objects x, y, and z. The number of combinations of n objects selected r at a time is any collection of r objects selected from a given number of objects, n. This may be expressed by the general formula

$$\frac{n!}{(n-r)!\,r!}$$

In the example, $n = 3$ (x, y, z) and $r = 2$; substituting in the formula, $3!/(3-2)!\,2!$ or $(3 \times 2 \times 1)/(2 \times 1) = 3$.

Common denominator.—Of two or more fractions, an integer or polynomial that is an exact multiple of each denominator. For example, the common denominator of $\frac{1}{2}$, $\frac{1}{4}$, and $\frac{1}{5}$ is 20, 40, 60 and so on. The smallest common denominator (in the above example, 20) is called the *least*, or *lowest*, *common denominator*.

Common factor (common divisor).—Of two or more integers or polynomials, an integer or polynomial that is a divisor of each. For example, common factors of 12 and 24 are 2, 3, 4, 6, and 12. The greatest common divisor (in the above example, 12) is called the *highest common factor.*

Common logarithm.—See *Logarithm.*

Complementary angle.—See *Angle.*

Concurrent.—In geometry, two or more lines or planes having one point in common.

Cone.—In solid geometry, a figure whose base is a circle, ellipse, or convex curve and whose sides taper up to a *vertex*, or *apex*. If the base is a circle, the figure is called a *circular cone;* if the base is an ellipse, the figure is called an *elliptic cone;* and if the base is a convex curve, the figure is called a *convex cone.* If the axis (the line from the center of the base to the vertex) is perpendicular to the base, the cone is a *right cone;* in any other configuration, it is an *oblique cone.* The *frustrum of a cone* is the figure that

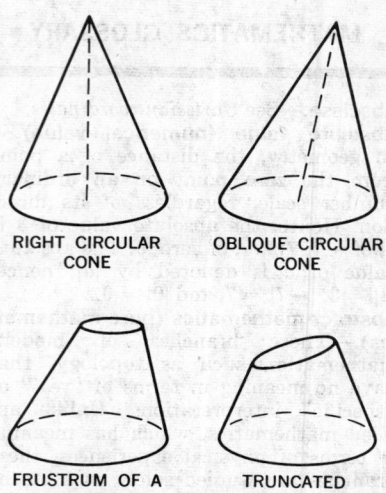

RIGHT CIRCULAR
CONE

OBLIQUE CIRCULAR
CONE

FRUSTRUM OF A
CONE

TRUNCATED
CONE

results when a cone is cut by a plane parallel to the base, and a *truncated cone* is the figure that results when a cone is cut by a plane not parallel to the base.

Congruent.—In geometry, figures that coincide when superimposed upon one another. Examples of congruent figures are line segments of equal length and angles of equal measure.

Conic (conic section).—The intersection of a circular conical surface by a plane. The shape of the section depends upon the position of the cutting plane. If the cutting plane is perpendicular to the axis, the section is a *circle.* If the plane is not parallel but does not cut the base, the section is an *ellipse.* If the plane is not parallel and does cut the base, the section is a *parabola.* If the plane cuts both *nappe* of the cone, the section is a *hyperbola.* Conics are sometimes defined in terms of their *eccentricity*, which is the ratio of the distances from a fixed point to a fixed line of

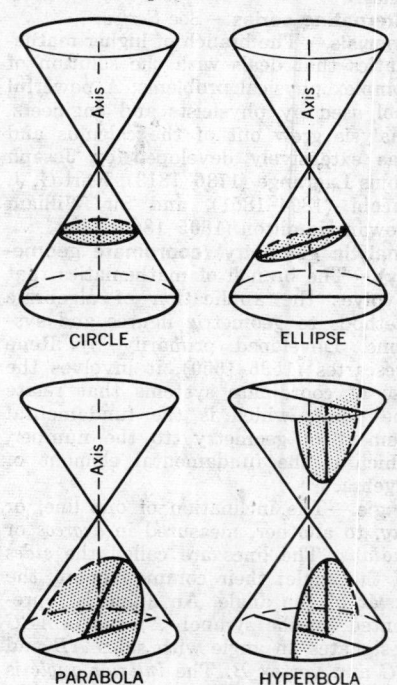

CIRCLE

ELLIPSE

PARABOLA

HYPERBOLA

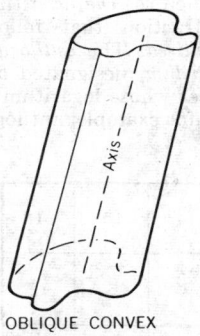

OBLIQUE CONVEX
CYLINDER

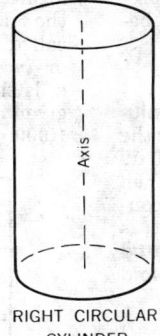

RIGHT CIRCULAR
CYLINDER

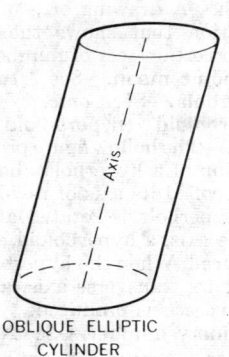

OBLIQUE ELLIPTIC
CYLINDER

any point on the conic. If the eccentricity equals 0, the conic is a circle; if the eccentricity is less than 1, the conic is an ellipse; if the eccentricity equals 1, the conic is a parabola; and if the eccentricity is greater than 1, the conic is a hyperbola.

Consistent equation.—See *Equation.*

Constant.—Any quantity, such as 2 or π, whose value does not change, or is regarded as fixed, during any sequence of mathematical operations. A constant number is sometimes called an *absolute number.*

Curve.—A line that can be described in terms of an equation; hence, a straight line is a special case of a curve. An *arc* is any segment of a curve between two of its points.

Cylinder.—In solid geometry, a figure of constant cross section whose base is either a circle, an ellipse, or a convex curve. If the base is a circle, the cylinder is a *circular cylinder;* if the base is an ellipse, the cylinder is an *elliptic cylinder;* and if the base is a convex curve, the cylinder is a *convex cylinder.* If the axis (a line joining the centers of the two bases) is perpendicular to the bases, the cylinder is a *right cylinder;* in any other configuration, it is an *oblique cylinder.*

Decimal number system.—See *Number system.*

Denominator.—See *Fraction.*

Differential calculus.—See *Calculus.*

Diaphantine analysis.—A method of finding the solutions of certain algebraic equations in two or more variables, provided the solutions are restricted to integers.

Discriminant.—In algebra, an expression used in determining whether or not the roots of an equation are real or imaginary. For a quadratic equation, $ax^2 + bx + c = 0$, the discriminant is $b^2 - 4ac$: if the discriminant equals zero, the two roots are equal; if the discriminant is negative, the roots are imaginary; and if the discriminant is positive, the roots are real.

Division.—One of the fundamental operations of arithmetic. Basically, division is the determination of how many times one number or quantity is contained in another; thus, it is the inverse operation to multiplication. When one number or quantity, the *dividend*, is divided by another, the *divisor*, the result is called their *quotient.* For example, the quotient

x/y of two numbers x and y is the number z (so that $x = yz$), provided that y does not equal zero.

Duodecimal number system.—See *Number system.*

e—The base of hyperbolic or natural logarithms. The value of e, to ten places, is 2.7182818284 . . .; it is a nonrepeating decimal. The term, which ranks with pi (π) in its importance to mathematics, was introduced by the Swiss mathematician Leonhard Euler (1707–1783).

Ellipse.—See *Conic.*

Ellipsoid (ellipsoid of revolution).—The hollow figure whose plane sections are all either ellipses or circles. An ellipsoid is produced by rotating an ellipse about one of its axes: when formed by rotation about the longer, or major, axis of the ellipse, the ellipsoid is *prolate;* when formed by rotation about the shorter, or minor, axis of the ellipse, the ellipsoid is *oblate.* An ellipsoid is sometimes called a *spheroid.*

Equality.—The state of being identical. Equality is expressed by the sign " $=$." The statement "$1 + 1 = 2$" means that "$1 + 1$" and "2" are different terms for the same quantity. A *continued equality* is three or more quantities set equal by means of two or more equality signs: $x = y = z$. An *inequality,* expressed by the sign " $\neq$," denotes two quantities that are not identical: $1 + 1 \neq 3$.

Equation.—A mathematical statement of equality between two quantities. There are two types of equations, *identities* and *conditional equations,* although the latter are usually referred to simply as equations. An equation is an identity when it is always true for any values of the variables within it; for example, $a(a - b)(a + b) = a^3 + ab^2$. An equation is conditional if it is valid for only certain values of the variables in the equation; for example, $x + y = 3$ is valid when $x = 2$ and $y = 1$ (and for some other values), but is invalid when $x = 5$ and $y = 3$. An *algebraic equation* is one in which each side is an algebraic expression. A *linear equation* is an algebraic equation of the first degree, such as $y = mx + b$. A *binomial equation* is one that has the form $x^n - a = 0$. A *quadratic equation* is one of the second degree, such as $ax^2 + bx + c = y$. A *reciprocal equation* is one in which the variables can be replaced by their reciprocals without changing the value

of the equation; for example, if in $x + 1 = 0$ the x is replaced by its reciprocal $1/x$, when the resulting equation is simplified it becomes $1 + x = 0$, which is identical to the original equation. When two or more equations involving two or more unknowns can be solved for one or more values of the unknowns that are common to all equations, the equations are called *consistent.* In order to test the equations for consistency, they must be *simultaneous;* that is, they must represent curves with points that are in conjunction.

Equilateral.—In geometry, having all sides equal. The word is usually used as an adjective to describe a polygon with sides of equal length.

Equilateral triangle.—See *Triangle.*

Even number.—See *Number.*

Exponent.—A term in which a number is placed to the right of and above a symbol. For example, in the expression x^a, x is called the *base* and a the *power.* (It should be noted that some mathematicians use "power" in the same sense that they use "exponent.") When the exponent is a positive integer, the power is a symbol for repeated multiplication; that is, $5^2 = 5 \times 5$ and $5^4 = 5 \times 5 \times 5 \times 5$. When the power is a negative integer, it indicates that the value of the term is the reciprocal of the repeated multiplications, or $x^{-n} = 1/x^n$; for example, $5^{-2} = 1/(5 \times 5) = 1/25$. When the power is 0, regardless of the base, the value of the term is 1. The five laws of exponents are summarized in the table at the end of the article on advanced mathematics.

The *degree* of a term is the power, or sum of the powers. For example, x^2 is of the second degree, $2x^5$ is of the fifth degree, and $2xy^2z^3$ is of the sixth degree. The degree of an equation is that of the highest-degree term in that equation; hence, $3x^3 + 2xy + y = 0$ is a third-degree equation.

Exponential series.—See *Series.*

Factorial.—For a positive integer n, the product of all the positive integers equal to or less than n, denoted by $n!$ (read "n factorial"); hence, $n! = 1 \times 2 \times 3 \times \ldots \times (n - 1) \times n$. For example, $6! = 1 \times 2 \times 3 \times 4 \times 5 \times 6 = 720$. By convention, $0!$ has been given the value 1.

Fermat number.—A whole number of the form $F_n = 2^{2n} + 1$, where $n = 0$, 1, 2, 3, and so on. The equation was devised by Pierre de Fermat (1601–1665) to compute prime numbers. However, Leonhard Euler (1707–1783) showed the $F_5 = 2^{2 \cdot 5} + 1 = 4,294,967,297$ is factorable into $(641)(6,700,417)$ and, therefore, that all Fermat numbers are not necessarily prime.

Fibonacci sequence (Fibonacci numbers).—An unending sequence of integers proposed by Leonardo da Pisa, or Leonardo Fibonacci (thirteenth century), formed according to the rule that each integer (except the first two) is the sum of the preceding two. The first 14 numbers of the sequence are: 1, 1, 2, 3, 5, 8, 13, 21, 34, 55, 89, 144, 233, 377.

Formula.—A fixed rule, general principle, or standard form stated in mathematical terms. For example, the area of a triangle is given by the formula $A = \frac{1}{2}bh$, where b is the length of the base and h is the height of the altitude.

Fraction.—The indicated quotient of two quantities, a/b, where a is called the *numerator* and b is called the *denominator*. A *simple fraction* (sometimes called a *common* or *vulgar fraction*) is one in which both the numerator and the denominator are integers. A *unit fraction* is a simple fraction in which the numerator is unity. A *complex fraction* is one in which the numerator or the denominator, or both, are simple fractions. A *proper fraction* is one in which the numerator is smaller than the denominator. An *improper fraction* is one in which the numerator is equal to or greater than the denominator.

Function.—A relationship of the object or objects of one set with each object in another set. For example, the expression $y = x^2 + x + 2$ defines y as a function of x. If the function $y = x^2 + x + 2$ is denoted by $y = f(x)$, then the value of y when $x = 3$ is $f(3) = 3^2 + 3 + 2 = 14$.

Geometric construction.—In Euclidean geometry, any construction that is made by using only an unmarked straightedge and a compass. A geometric construction is limited to the drawing of straight lines, arcs, and circles.

Geometric mean.—See *Mean*.

Geometric progression.—See *Progression*.

Geometric series.—See *Series*.

Geometry.—The branch of mathematics that deals with the shape and size of objects and the nature of space. *Plane geometry* deals with the properties and relations of plane figures, such as angles, polygons, and conics. *Solid geometry* deals with the properties and relations of three-dimensional figures, such as spheres, polyhedrons, and planes. These geometries were developed by Euclid (c. 300 B.C.) in his 13-volume book *Elements*, and are therefore referred to as *Euclidean geometries*. *Non-Euclidean geometries* differ in that they consider Euclid's "parallel postulate"—that only one parallel can be drawn to a given line through a point outside that line—to be invalid, thus changing the nature of the space in which the geometries are discussed.

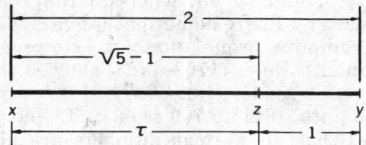

Golden section (golden ratio).—A division of a line segment xy by a point z so that the two parts of the segment are in the ratio $\tau:1$, where r is the positive root of the expression $x^2 - x - 1 = 0$; that is, $(\sqrt{5} + 1)/2$. This division of a line is very pleasing to the eye and is frequently used by artists; the ratio also has applications in musical theory.

Graph.—A drawing or geometric representation that shows the relation between certain sets of numbers.

Harmonic mean.—See *Mean*.

Hyperbola.—See *Conic*.

Hyperboloid (hyperboloid of revolution).—The hollow figure produced by the rotation of a hyperbola about one of its axes, called its axis of revolution. When the hyperbola is rotated about its conjugate axis, a hyperboloid of *one sheet* is produced. When the hyperbola is rotated about its transverse axis, a hyperboloid of *two sheets* is produced.

Imaginary number.—See *Number*.

Integer.—Any of the numbers . . . , -2, -1, 0, $+1$, $+2$, ... *Positive integers* are $+1$, $+2$, and so on; *negative integers* are -1, -2, and so on.

Integral calculus.—See *Calculus*.

Intercept.—See *Cartesian coordinates*.

Inverse operation.—The operation that, when performed following a given operation, would cancel the effect of the given operation. Thus, subtraction is the inverse operation to addition, and division is the inverse operation to multiplication.

Inverse trigonometric functions.—See *Trigonometric functions*.

Irrational number.—See *Number*.

Isosceles.—In geometry, having two equal sides. The word is usually used as an adjective to describe a polygon.

Isosceles triangle.—See *Triangle*.

Lemma.—A theorem that is proved for use in the proof of another theorem.

Line (straight line).—A special case of a curve. In Euclidean geometry, the concept of "line" is one of an unswerving path. In Cartesian coordinates, a line has the equation $y = mx + b$, where m is the slope and b is the y-intercept. A *ray* is either of the two portions into which a line is divided by a single point on the line.

Linear equation.—See *Equation*.

Logarithm.—A mathematical device by means of which numerical computation may be facilitated. The logarithm of a number, N, to a given base, x, is the index of the power, a, to which that base must be raised to produce the number; hence, $x^a = N$. For example, since $10^3 = 1,000$, 3 is the logarithm of 1,000 to the base 10, written $\log_{10} = 1,000 = 3$. Logarithms that use 10 as a base are called *common*, or *Briggsian logarithms*, after Henry Briggs (1561–1630), who introduced them. Logarithms that use e (2.71828 . . .) as a base are called *natural*, or *Napierian logarithms*, after John Napier (1550–1617), who introduced them. Natural logarithms may be converted to common logarithms by multiplying the natural logarithm by 0.434294, a factor called the *modulus of common logarithms*; common logarithms may be converted to natural logarithms by multiplying the common logarithm by 2.302585, a factor called the *modulus of natural logarithms*. Thus, $\log_{10}N = 0.434294\ \log_e N$, and $\log_e N = 2.302585\ \log_{10}N$. The integer preceding the decimal point of the logarithm is called the *characteristic*, and the decimal fraction that follows is called the *mantissa*. The *antilogarithm*, or *inverse logarithm*, designated antilog a, is the number whose logarithm is the given number; for example, antilog$_{10}$3 = 1,000.

4	14	15	1
9	7	6	12
5	11	10	8
16	2	3	13

4 x 4 SQUARE

17	24	1	8	15
23	5	7	14	16
4	6	13	20	22
10	12	19	21	3
11	18	25	2	9

5 x 5 SQUARE

Magic square.—A square array of integers in which the sum of the integers in each column, each diagonal, and each row is the same. The *order* of the square is the number of integers in the columns and rows; thus, a 4×4 square is of the order four, and 5×5 square is of the order five.

Mantissa.—See *Logarithm*.

Mathematical signs and symbols.—Letters, marks, and abbreviations representing operations, quantities, or relations used in mathematical expressions, equations, and formulas. Some of the most common signs and symbols are shown in the table on the next page.

Mathematics.—The systematic study of arrangement, number, quantity, and shape. Mathematics is generally described in terms of abstract, or pure, mathematics and applied mathematics. The study of mathematics is usually divided into three major branches: algebra, analysis, and geometry.

Mean (average).—The "central quantity" of a set of quantities. There are three types of means: the *arithmetic mean* (usually referred to as the *mean* or *average*), m; the *geometric mean*, g; and the *harmonic mean*, h. For two numbers, x and y, $m = (x + y)/2$; $g = \sqrt{xy}$; and $1/h = (\frac{1}{2})(1/x + 1/y)$. If x and y are positive, the harmonic mean is less than the geometric mean, which is less than the arithmetic mean. For example, if

Selected Mathematical Signs and Symbols

Symbol	Meaning
$+$	plus; positive
$-$	minus; negative
$\pm$	plus or minus
$\mp$	minus or plus
$\times$ or $\cdot$	multiplied by; times
$/$ or $\div$	divided by
$>$	is greater than
$<$	is less than
$\equiv$	is identical to
$=$	is equal to
$\geqq$ or $\geq$	is greater than or equal to
$\leqq$ or $\leq$	is less than or equal to
$\neq$	is not equal to
$\approx$ or $\doteqdot$	is approximately equal to
$\sim$	is similar to; equivalent
$\cong$	is congruent to; congruent
$\parallel$	is parallel to; parallel
$\perp$	is perpendicular to; perpendicular
$:$	is to; the ratio of
$\therefore$	therefore; hence
$\because$	because; since
$\angle$ or $\measuredangle$	angle
$\llcorner$ or $\llcorner$	right angle
$\propto$	varies directly as
∞	infinity
a^n	reciprocal $(1/a^n)$
$\|a\|$	absolute value (of a)
ϵ	is a member of the set of
$\%$	per cent
$f(a)$ or $g(a)$	function of f (or of g) at a
$\log$ or $\log_{10}$	common logarithm; logarithm to the base 10
$\ln$ or $\log_e$	natural logarithm; logarithm to the base e
antilog	antilogarithm
$\sqrt{}$	root of
i	$\sqrt{-1}$
$\triangle$	triangle
$\square$	parallelogram
$\square$	square
$\bigcirc$ or $\odot$	circle
Q.E.D.	which was to be proved
$\doteqdot$	is measured by
Σ	summation
$\int$	integral
Π	product
a'	a prime
dy/dx or $f'(x)$	the derivative of y with respect to x
$\delta u/\delta x$ or u_x	the partial derivative of u with respect to x

$x = 7$ and $y = 28$, then $h = 11.2$, $g = 14.0$, and $m = 17.5$. For n numbers, $x_1, x_2, \ldots x_n$, the three means may be found by the following formulas:

$$\frac{1}{h} = \left(\frac{1}{n}\right)\left(\frac{1}{x_1} + \frac{1}{x_2} + \ldots + \frac{1}{x_n}\right)$$

$$g = \sqrt[n]{x_1 x_2 \ldots x_n}$$

$$m = \frac{1}{n}\left(x_1 + x_2 + \ldots + x_n\right)$$

Median.—In statistics, of an odd number of increasing numerical values, the middle value; of an even number of increasing numerical values, the arithmetic mean of the two middle values. For example, the median of 15, 20, 50, 60, 133 is 50; of 15, 20, 50, 60, 133, 134 is 55.

Mixed number.—In arithmetic, the sum of an integer and a fraction, such as $3 + \frac{1}{2}$, or $3\frac{1}{2}$; in algebra, the sum of a polynomial and a rational algebraic fraction, such as $3x + 3 + 1/(x - 1)$.

Multiplication.—One of the fundamental operations of arithmetic. Basically, multiplication is the determination of the value of a specified number of repeated additions of the same quantity or integer; thus, $m \times n = m + m + \ldots + m$ (m added to m $n - 1$ times). In $m \times n$, which may also be written $(m)(n)$, $m \cdot n$, or mn, $= p$, m is the *multiplicand*, n is the *multiplier*, and p is the *product*.

Natural logarithm.—See *Logarithm*.

Nomograph (nomogram or alignment chart).—A graphic method of computation in which three lines or curves, usually parallel to one another, are graduated in such a way that a straight-edge cutting across them will give the related values of three variables. For example, a nomograph can be constructed, as in the accompanying illustration, in which one scale represents the distance in miles traveled by an automobile, a second scale represents the number of gallons of gasoline used by the automobile, and the third scale represents the number of miles per gallon.

Number.—In general terminology, a positive integer. A *rational number* is either an integer or a fraction of the form a/b, where a and b are both integers but do not equal zero. An *irrational number*, such as e, π, or $\sqrt{2}$, is a number that is not expressible as an integer or a fraction composed of integers. *Real numbers* include all rational and irrational numbers. *Imaginary numbers* include all complex numbers of the form $a + bi$ (where $i = \sqrt{-1}$), a and b are real numbers, and $b \neq 0$. An *even number* is any integer divisible by 2, and an *odd number* is any number that is not so divisible.

Number system.—A method of numeration and the rules for arithmetic computation with the notations thus devised. The most familiar of the number systems is the *decimal number system*. This system uses place values and the base, or *radix*, 10; for example, 3502.16 is the notation for $3 \times 10^3 + 5 \times 10^2 + 0 \times 10^1 + 2 \times 10^0 + 1 \times 10^{-1} + 6 \times 10^{-2}$. The *binary number system*, which is also known as the *dyadic number system*, also uses place values, but the base number is 2 rather than 10. Only 2 digits, 0 and 1, are required, and these are called *bits* (from *bi*nary dig*its*). The *octonary number system* is also a place-value system and has a radix of 8, while the *duodecimal number system*, which is another place-value system, has a radix of 12.

Numerator.—See *Fraction*.

Oblique.—An adjective meaning "slanted," that is, neither parallel nor perpendicular. An *oblique angle* is any angle that is not a multiple of 90°, an *oblique line* is one that is neither parallel nor perpendicular to another line, and an *oblique triangle* is one that does not contain a right angle.

Obtuse angle.—See *Angle*.

Octonary number system.—See *Number system*.

Odd number.—See *Number*.

Ordinate.—See *Cartesian coordinates*.

Parabola.—See *Conic*.

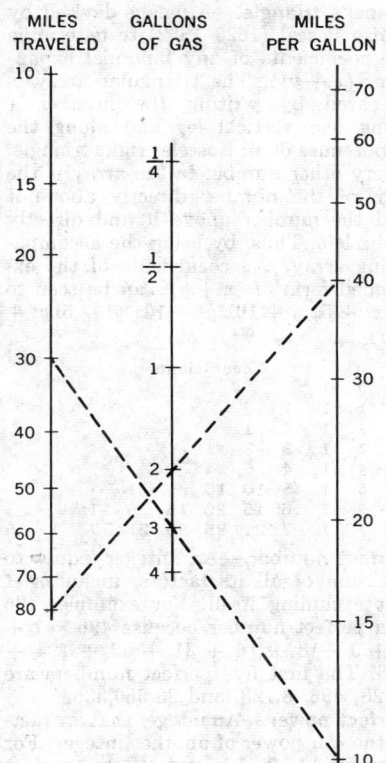

Paraboloid (paraboloid of revolution).—The hollow figure produced by the rotation of a parabola about its axis. An *elliptic paraboloid* is one whose plane sections parallel to the axis of revolution yield parabolas, and whose plane sections perpendicular to these parabolas yield ellipses. A *hyperbolic paraboloid* is one whose plane sections yield hyperbolas and parabolas.

Parallelogram.—A quadrilateral in which the opposite sides are parallel. A *rhombus* is a parallelogram in which all four sides are equal in length; a *square* is a parallelogram in which all four sides are of equal length and in which adjacent sides are perpendicular; and a *rectangle* is a parallelogram in which the adjacent sides are perpendicular and are of different lengths.

Parameter.—An *arbitrary constant* (a variable representing an unspecified constant) in a mathematical expression or formula that distinguishes one member of a group from the others.

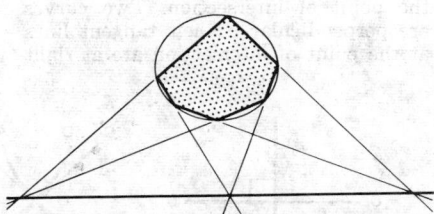

Pascal's theorem.—A proof by Blaise Pascal (1623–1662), showing that when a hexagon is inscribed in a conic, the three points of intersection of the three pairs of opposite sides lie on a straight line.

Pascal's triangle.—A means devised by Blaise Pascal (1623–1662) to determine the coefficients of any binomial expansion, $(x + y)^n$. The triangular array is prepared by writing the number 1 along one vertical leg and along the hypotenuse of an isosceles right triangle. Every other number in the array is the sum of the number directly above it and the number above it and directly to its left. Thus, by using the accompanying array, the coefficients of the expanded form of $(x + y)^5$ can be seen to be $x^5 + 5x^4y + 10x^3y^2 + 10x^2y^3 + 5xy^4 + y^5$.

n	coefficients						
0	1						
1	1	1					
2	1	2	1				
3	1	3	3	1			
4	1	4	6	4	1		
5	1	5	10	10	5	1	
6	1	6	15	20	15	6	1
7	1	7	21	35	35	21	7	1

Perfect number.—An integer equal to the sum of all its factors, including 1 but excluding itself. For example, 496 is a perfect number because $496 = 1 + 2 + 4 + 8 + 16 + 31 + 62 + 124 + 248$. The first five perfect numbers are 6, 28, 496, 8,128, and 33,550,336.

Perfect power.—An integer that is exactly the nth power of another integer. For example, 4, 9, 16, and 25 are perfect squares (2^2, 3^2, 4^2, and 5^2, respectively); and 8, 27, 64, and 125 are perfect cubes (2^3, 3^3, 4^3, and 5^3, respectively).

Permutation.—The different arrangements or sequences that can be made of all or part of a given number of objects. All possible permutations of x, y, and z are:

x	x,y	y,x	x,y,z	z,x,y
y	y,z	z,y	x,z,y	z,y,x
z	x,z	z,x	y,x,z	y,z,x

A permutation of n objects taken r at a time, denoted by $_nP_r$, is equal to $n!/(n - r)!$ Thus, in the first column (above), $_3P_1 = 3!/2! = 3$; in the next two columns, $_3P_2 = 3!/1! = 6$. A permutation of n objects taken all at a time is equal to $n!$ Thus, in the last two columns, $3! = 6$.

Perpendicular.—Intersecting at right angles. If two lines in a plane intersect at right angles, each is called a perpendicular, or *normal*, to the other. A line is perpendicular to a curve if it is perpendicular to a tangent to the curve at the point of intersection. Two curves are perpendicular if their tangent lines at the point of intersection are at right

angles. A line is perpendicular to a plane if it is perpendicular to every line in the plane that passes through the point of intersection.

Pi (π).—The ratio of the circumference of a circle to its diameter. The value of π, to ten places, is $3.1415926535\ldots$; it is a nonrepeating decimal. A rational approximation of π that is adequate for most calculations is 22/7; a more accurate approximation is 355/113. π ranks with e in importance to mathematics.

Plane geometry.—See *Geometry*.

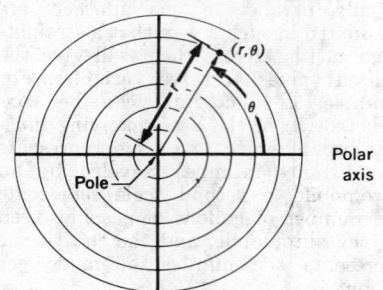

Polar coordinates.—A standard method of locating points. The points can be located in a plane by finding their distances from a fixed point and the angles that the lines from this point to the given points make with a fixed line, which is called the *polar axis*. The line from the fixed point, which is called the *pole*, to a given point is called a *radius vector* and is designated by the letter r; the angle of rotation from the polar axis to the radius vector is designated by the Greek letter *theta*, θ. The polar coordinates of a point are thus written (r, θ).

Polygon.—A plane figure in which n points, called *vertices*, are connected by n lines, called *sides*, which may or may not cut across one another. A polygon is named according to its number of sides: one of three sides is a *triangle*; of four sides, a *quadrilateral*; of five sides, a *pentagon*; of six sides, a *hexagon*; of seven sides, a *heptagon*; of eight sides, an *octagon*; of nine sides, a *nonagon*; of ten sides, a *decagon*; of twelve sides, a *dodecagon*; and of n sides, an *n-gon*. A polygon is *convex* if a line drawn through any one side does not cut across the polygon; it is *concave* if a line drawn through any one side cuts across the figure. A polygon is *equiangular* if all its angles are equal and *equilateral* if all its sides are of equal length. A *regular polygon* is one that is both equiangular and equilateral.

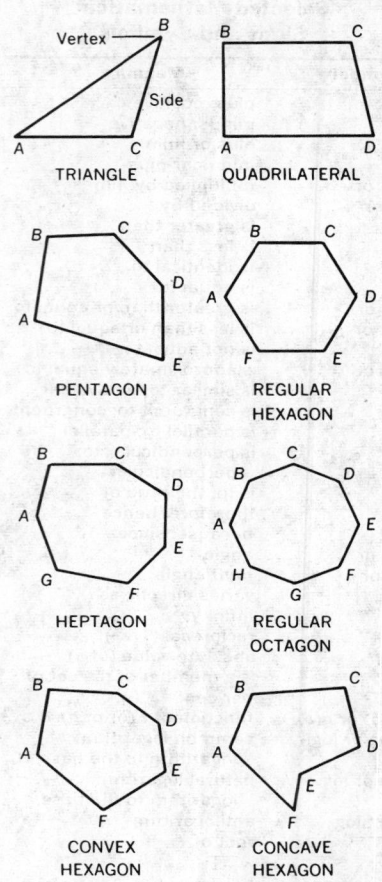

Polyhedron.—A three-dimensional figure bounded by plane surfaces, called *faces*, that are all polygons. A polyhedron is named according to its number of faces: one of four faces is a *tetrahedron;* of five faces, a *pentahedron;* of six faces, a *hexahedron;* of seven faces, a *heptahedron;* of eight faces, an *octahedron;* of nine faces, a *nonahedron;* of ten faces, a *decahedron;* of twelve faces, a *dodecahedron;* and of twenty faces, an *icosahedron*. A polyhedron is *convex* if a plane containing any one of its faces does not pass through the figure; it is *concave* if the plane cuts through the figure. A *regular polyhedron* is one whose faces are all congruent polygons and all of whose polyhedral angles are congruent. There are only five regular polyhedrons: a tetrahedron, a hexahedron (or cube), an octahedron, a dodecahedron, and an icosahedron.

Postulate.—See *Axiom*.

Power.—See *Exponent*.

Prime number.—A positive integer divisible only by itself and by unity. The first ten prime numbers are 2, 3, 5, 7, 11, 13, 17, 19, 23, and 29 (1 is usually excluded). There is no limit to the number of prime numbers, but no one has yet been able to devise a general formula by which the prime numbers may be determined.

Probability.—The likelihood, or chance, of any event taking place. For example, there are two possible results when a

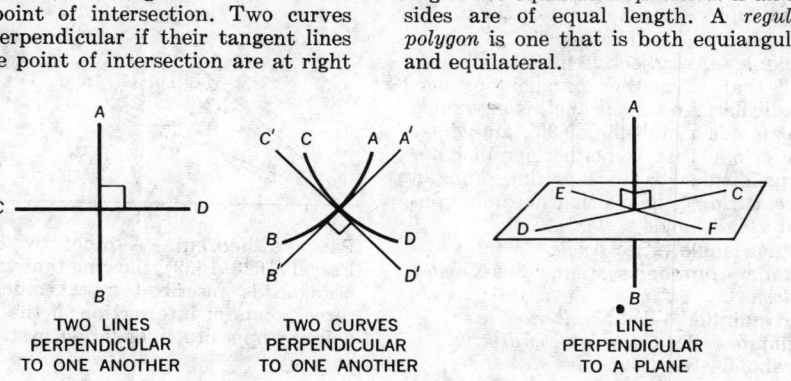

TWO LINES PERPENDICULAR TO ONE ANOTHER   TWO CURVES PERPENDICULAR TO ONE ANOTHER   LINE PERPENDICULAR TO A PLANE

coin is tossed—heads and tails; hence, the likelihood of tossing a head (or of tossing a tail) is one in two, and the probability is 1/2.

Progression.—A sequence of terms that has a first number but no fixed last number, and in which each term is related to every other term by a fixed law. An *arithmetic progression* is a sequence in which each term, except the first, is equal to the preceding term plus a constant; for example, $1, 3, 5, 7, 9, \ldots$. A *geometric progression* is a sequence in which the ratio of each term, except the first, to the preceding one is the same throughout the sequence; for example, $1, 4, 16, 64, 256, \ldots$. A *harmonic progression* is one in which the reciprocals of the terms form an arithmetic progression, for example, $1, \frac{1}{3}, \frac{1}{5}, \frac{1}{7}, \frac{1}{9}, \ldots$.

Projective geometry.—The study of those properties of plane geometric figures that do not change upon being projected.

Pythagorean theorem.—The relationship of the lengths of the sides of a right triangle, first introduced by the Greek mathematician Pythagoras (died c. 497 B.C.). The theorem states that the sum of the squares of the lengths of the legs, a and b, of a right triangle equals the square of the length of the hypotenuse, c; $a^2 + b^2 = c^2$. Any three positive integers that satisfy this equation are called *Pythagorean numbers*.

Quadratic equation.—See *Equation*.

Quadrilateral.—See *Polygon*.

Radical.—In algebra, the indicated root to be extracted from a quantity, such as $\sqrt{x}$ or $\sqrt[3]{5}$. The *index*, or root to be extracted, is written over the radical sign; for example, $\sqrt[2]{x}$, $\sqrt[3]{x}$, $\sqrt[4]{x}$, $\sqrt[n]{x}$ denote that the square root, cube root, fourth root, and nth root of x are to be extracted. The quantity under the radical sign (in the above examples, x) is called the *radicand*.

Radix.—See *Number system*.

Ratio.—The relative magnitudes of two numbers or quantities. The ratio of m to n is written m/n or $m{:}n$. The equality of two ratios is called a *proportion;* for example, $m{:}n = o{:}p$ (read "m is to n as o is to p").

Rational number.—See *Number*.

Real number.—See *Number*.

Regular polygon.—See *Polygon*.

Regular polyhedron.—See *Polyhedron*.

Right triangle.—See *Triangle*.

Right angle.—See *Angle, Perpendicular·*

Scalene triangle.—See *Triangle*.

Sequence.—A set of numbers arranged in the same order as are the positive integers. Thus, $1, 2, 3, 4 \ldots n$ and $1/x$, $1/2x^2$, $1/3x^3$, $1/4x^4 \ldots 1/nx^n$ are typical sequences. If a sequence continues after the last written term, it is an *infinite sequence;* if the sequence terminates at a finite number, it is a *finite sequence*.

Series.—An expression that indicates the sum of the terms of either a finite sequence (a *finite series*) or an infinite sequence (an *infinite series*). An *alternating series* is an infinite series whose terms are alternately positive and negative,

for example, $1 - \frac{1}{2} + \frac{1}{3} - \frac{1}{4} + \ldots + (-1)^n - \frac{1}{n} + \ldots$. An *arithmetic series* is the expression indicating the sum of the terms in an arithmetic progression, for example, $1 + 3 + 5 + \ldots + n + \ldots$. An *exponential series* is an expansion of the exponential function e^x, where $e = 2.71828$; $e^x = x/1! + x^2/2! + x^3/3! + \ldots + x^n/n! + \ldots$. A *geometric series* is the expression indicating the sum of the terms in a geometric progression, for example, $1 + \frac{1}{2} + \frac{1}{4} + \frac{1}{8} + \ldots + 1/2^{n-1} + \ldots$. A *harmonic series* is the expression indicating the sum of a harmonic progression, for example, $1 + \frac{1}{2} + \frac{1}{3} + \frac{1}{4} + \ldots + 1/n + \ldots$.

Set (class).—A collection of particular things, such as a set of points or a set of numbers. The individual items within a set are the *elements* or *members;* each element is said to belong to the set.

Simultaneous equation.—See *Equation*.

Solid geometry.—See *Geometry*.

Statistics.—The branch of mathematics that deals with the methods of obtaining and analyzing quantitative data through the use of probability theory. Statistics finds application in both physical sciences, such as physics, and social sciences, such as economics.

Subtraction.—A fundamental operation of arithmetic. Basically, subtraction is the inverse operation to addition. The difference $m - n$ is the number a such that $m + a = n$. In $m - n = a$, m is called the *minuend*, n is called the *subtrahend*, and a is called the *remainder*.

Supplementary angle.—See *Angle*.

Theorem.—A general conclusion, proved through the use of axioms and/or lemmas, of a mathematical theory.

Topology.—The branch of modern geometry that deals with the changes undergone by three-dimensional figures as they are pulled, stretched, bent, twisted, or otherwise distorted without tearing or breaking them and without causing the loss of identity of the points contained within them. One of the fields of abstract, or pure, mathematics, topology has little practical application.

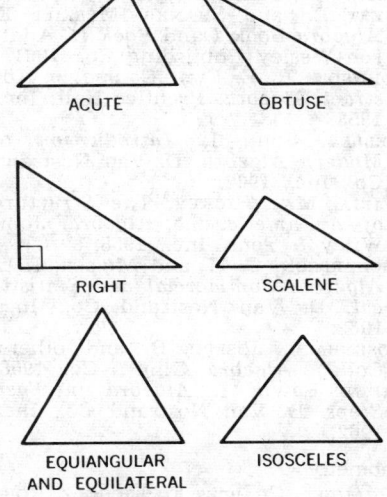

ACUTE   OBTUSE

RIGHT   SCALENE

EQUIANGULAR   ISOSCELES
AND EQUILATERAL
(REGULAR)

Triangle.—A three-sided polygon formed by joining three points, called *vertices*, that do not fall in a straight line, by three straight lines, called *sides*. A triangle is *acute* if all the interior angles are less than 90°, *obtuse* if one angle is greater than 90°, *right* if one angle is exactly 90°, *oblique* if no angle is 90°, and *equiangular* if all of the angles are equal (60°). A triangle is *scalene* if none of its sides are of equal length, *isosceles* if two of its sides are of equal length, and *equilateral* if all of its sides are of equal length.

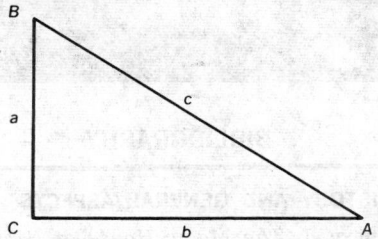

Trigonometric functions.—The six ratios of the sides of a right triangle. The functions are called *sine, cosine, tangent, cotangent, secant,* and *cosecant,* and are abbreviated as *sin, cos, tan, cot* (or *ctn*), *sec,* and *csc,* respectively. The ratios may be defined in relation to the accompanying diagram as follows:

$$\sin A = \frac{\text{opposite side}}{\text{hypotenuse}} = \frac{a}{c} = \frac{1}{\csc A}$$

$$\cos A = \frac{\text{adjacent side}}{\text{hypotenuse}} = \frac{b}{c} = \frac{1}{\sec A}$$

$$\tan A = \frac{\text{opposite side}}{\text{adjacent side}} = \frac{a}{b} = \frac{1}{\cot A}$$

$$\cot A = \frac{\text{adjacent side}}{\text{opposite side}} = \frac{b}{a} = \frac{1}{\tan A}$$

$$\sec A = \frac{\text{hypotenuse}}{\text{adjacent side}} = \frac{c}{b} = \frac{1}{\cos A}$$

$$\csc A = \frac{\text{hypotenuse}}{\text{opposite side}} = \frac{c}{a} = \frac{1}{\sin A}$$

The *inverse trigonometric functions*, or *antitrigonometric functions*, are denoted by $\sin^{-1}$, $\cos^{-1}$, $\tan^{-1}$, $\cot^{-1}$, and so on, or by *arc sin, arc cos, arc tan, arc cot,* and so on. The relationship between the trigonometric and inverse trigonometric functions may be shown as follows:

Function	Inverse Function
$\sin 30° = \frac{1}{2}$	$\sin^{-1} \frac{1}{2} = 30°$
$\cos 30° = \sqrt{3}/2$	arc cos $\sqrt{3}/2 = 30°$
$\tan 60° = \sqrt{3}$	$\tan^{-1} \sqrt{3} = 60°$
$\cot 45° = 1$	arc cot $1 = 45°$
$\sec 60° = 2$	$\sec^{-1} 2 = 60°$
$\csc 30° = 2$	arc csc $2 = 30°$

Variable.—An arbitrary symbol, such as $a, b, c \ldots x, y,$ or z, that can represent any one of a set of numbers, quantities, or other entities. The set is called the *range* of the variable, and any element within the set is called a *value* of the variable.

Volume.—The three-dimensional measure of the region enclosed within the boundaries of any solid geometric figure.

Zero.—The integer denoting the absence of any elements in the set under consideration. The introduction of the concept of "zero" by the Hindus made possible the extent of the science of mathematics that is studied today.

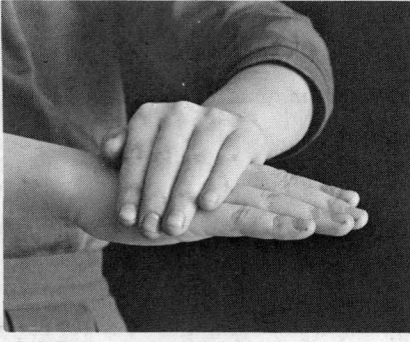

INTERNATIONAL BUSINESS MACHINES, INC.

THE PROBABILITY of an event's occurring can be calculated. For example, when a coin is tossed, it can fall as either heads or tails; the probability of tossing heads is 50–50.

BIBLIOGRAPHY

HISTORY AND GENERAL ASPECTS

ADLER, I. *The Magic House of Numbers.* New American Library of World Literature, Inc., 1957.

BAKST, AARON. *Mathematics: Its Magic and Mastery.* D. Van Nostrand Co., Inc., 1952.

EVES, H. *An Introduction to the History of Mathematics.* Holt, Rinehart & Winston, Inc., 1953.

FEHR, H. F. and SOBEL, M. A. *Mathematics for Everybody.* Pocket Books, Inc., 1963.

FELIX, L. *The Modern Aspect of Mathematics.* Translated by J. H. Hlavaty and F. H. Hlavaty. Basic Books, Inc., 1960.

HEIMER, RALPH T. and NEWMAN, MIRIAM. *The New Mathematics for Parents.* Holt, Rinehart and Winston, Inc., 1954.

HOGBEN, L. T. *Mathematics for the Millions* (3rd ed.). W. W. Norton & Co., Inc., 1951.

JOHNSON, DONOVAN A. and GLENN, WILLIAM H. *Exploring Mathematics on Your Own.* Webster Publishing Co., 1960.

KASNER, EDWARD and NEWMAN, JAMES. *Mathematics and the Imagination.* Simon and Schuster, Inc., 1963.

KRAMER, E. E. *The Mainstream of Mathematics.* Fawcett Publications, Inc., 1961.

LAND, FRANK. *The Language of Mathematics.* Doubleday & Co., Inc., 1963.

MOTT-SMITH, GEOFFREY. *Mathematical Puzzles for Beginners and Enthusiasts.* Dover Publications, Inc., 1955.

MUIR, J. *Of Men and Numbers.* Dell Books, 1961.

NEWMAN, JAMES (ed.). *The World of Mathematics.* 4 vols. Simon and Schuster, Inc., 1963.

REID, CONSTANCE. *A Long Way from Euclid.* Thomas Y. Crowell Co., 1963.

SAWYER, W. W. *Prelude to Mathematics.* Penguin Books, Inc., 1955.

SMITH, D. E. *History of Mathematics.* 2 vols. Dover Publications, Inc., 1923.

TURNBULL, HERBERT. *The Great Mathematicians.* New York University Press, 1961.

ELEMENTARY MATHEMATICS

ALLENDOERFER, C. B. and OAKLEY, C. O. *Principles of Mathematics.* McGraw-Hill Book Co., Inc., 1955.

COOLEY, H. R. and others. *Introduction to Mathematics.* Houghton Mifflin Co., 1949.

RICHARDSON, M. *Fundamentals of Mathematics.* The Macmillan Co., 1958.

Arithmetic

BANKS, J. HOUSTON. *Learning and Teaching Arithmetic.* Allyn and Bacon, Inc., 1959.

BENDICK, JEANNE. *How Much and How Many?* McGraw-Hill, Inc., 1947.

BRUMFIEL, CHARLES F.; EICHOLZ, ROBERT E.; and SHANKS, MERRILL E. *Fundamental Concepts of Elementary Mathematics.* Addison-Wesley Publishing Co., Inc., 1962.

LAY, L. CLARK. *Arithmetic: An Introduction to Mathematics.* The Macmillan Co., 1961.

MUELLER, F. J. *Arithmetic: Its Structure and Concepts.* Prentice-Hall, Inc., 1955.

Algebra

ASIMOV, ISAAC. *Realm of Algebra.* Houghton Mifflin Co., 1961.

BIRKHOFF, G. and MACLANE, S. *A Survey of Modern Algebra.* The Macmillan Co., 1953.

BRUMFIEL, CHARLES F.; EICHOLZ, ROBERT E.; and SHANKS, MERRILL E. *Algebra Book I and Book II.* Addison-Wesley Publishing Co., 1961.

JOHNSON, R. E. *First Course in Abstract Algebra.* Prentice-Hall, Inc., 1953.

KELLEY, JOHN L. *Introduction to Modern Algebra.* D. Van Nostrand Co., Inc., 1962.

MARIA, MAY HICKEY. *The Structure of Arithmetic and Algebra.* John Wiley & Sons, Inc., 1958.

RICHARDSON, C. H. and MILLER, I. L. *Algebra: Commercial and Statistical.* D. Van Nostrand Co., Inc., 1962.

ROSENBACH, JOSEPH B. and others. *College Algebra.* Ginn & Co., 1958.

STEIN, EDWIN I. *Algebra in Easy Steps.* D. Van Nostrand Co., Inc., 1962.

Geometry

BRUMFIEL, CHARLES F.; EICHOLZ, ROBERT E.; and SHANKS, MERRILL E. *Geometry.* Addison-Wesley Publishing Co., Inc., 1960.

MOISE, EDWIN and DOWNS, FLOYD L. *Geometry.* Addison-Wesley Publishing Co., Inc., 1963.

SKOLNICK, D. *Dynamic Solid Geometry.* D. Van Nostrand Co., Inc., 1952.

SMITH, ROLLAND R.; ULRICH, JAMES F.; and CLARK, JOHN R. *Plane Geometry.* Harcourt, Brace & World, Inc., 1956.

SMITH, ROLLAND R., and ULRICH, JAMES F. *Solid Geometry.* Harcourt, Brace & World, Inc., 1957.

INTERMEDIATE MATHEMATICS

Trigonometry

FISHER, ROBERT C. and ZIEBUR, ALLEN D. *Integrated Algebra and Trigonometry.* Prentice-Hall, Inc., 1958.

SMITH, ROLLAND R., and HANSON, PAUL P. *Trigonometry.* Harcourt, Brace & World, Inc., 1957.

HIGHER MATHEMATICS

Analytic Geometry and Calculus

FISHER, ROBERT C. and ZIEBUR, ALLEN D. *Calculus and Analytic Geometry.* Prentice-Hall, Inc., 1961.

SAWYER, W. W. *What is Calculus About?* Random House, New Mathematical Library, 1961.

SMITH, E. S. and others. *Analytic Geometry.* John Wiley & Sons, Inc., 1954.

THOMAS, GEORGE B. *Elements of Calculus and Analytic Geometry.* Addison-Wesley Publishing Co., Inc., 1959.

WELLS, VOLNEY H. *Elementary Calculus.* D. Van Nostrand Co., Inc., 1941.

Miscellaneous

BOEHM, GEORGE A. W. and the editors of *Fortune* (eds.). *The New World of Math.* The Dial Press, Inc., 1959.

KELLEY, JOHN L. *An Introduction to Modern Algebra.* D. Van Nostrand Co., Inc., 1962.

LANGER, SUZANNE. *An Introduction to Symbolic Logic.* Dover Publications, Inc., 1962.

MOSTELLER, FREDERICK; ROURKE, ROBERT E. K.; THOMAS, GEORGE B. *Probability and Statistics.* Addison-Wesley Publishing Co., Inc., 1961.

WEAVER, WARREN. *Lady Luck: The Theory of Probability.* Doubleday & Co., Inc., 1963.

VOLUME NINETEEN

PHILOSOPHY & RELIGION

Philosophy 1611
Religion 1621
Bibliography 1634

THE METROPOLITAN MUSEUM OF ART

Philosophy and Religion

PHILOSOPHY

What Is Philosophy?—The history of philosophy is the history of man's curiosity. We seek knowledge not only of what we see but also of what is beyond the limits of our senses. Thales (early sixth century B.C.) is considered the first philosopher because he attempted to explain the whole of nature by what he thought was the basic matter of the cosmos —water. It is quite likely, however, that the first philosopher was the first man. Man looks at something and declares it beautiful, sees an act and says it is good, finds a puzzle and solves it—if only for the pure joy of finding a solution. Thus, in a sense philosophy contains the natural history of the human mind. Today men who pursue the vast horizons of philosophy are the ones referred to as philosophers, although all men philosophize a bit at times.

The early Greeks gave us the word "philosophy." It means, literally, "love of wisdom," from *philein,* 'to love,' and *sophia,* 'wisdom.' Men who put knowledge in order, who make a system of the many areas of man's endeavor, explaining his mind and his actions, are the lovers of wisdom, the philosophers whose thoughts are the substance of the history of Western philosophy.

■**METAPHYSICS.**—The broadest and most speculative field of philosophy is *metaphysics.* It is the study of that which is beyond the world of natural experience—the supernatural. Metaphysics' is concerned with the nature of being as such, rather than with the nature of specific beings. A system of metaphysics attempts to give us knowledge about the ultimate nature of the universe—its origin and structure (*cosmology*) and its creation (*cosmogony*).

NEW YORK PUBLIC LIBRARY

THE COSMOLOGICAL TALE of the Flood, inscribed on a clay tablet in Babylonian cuneiform, is one of man's attempts to explain a natural event in supernatural terms.

■**EPISTEMOLOGY.**—Philosophers must proceed by certain methods when they examine the world and attempt to make a systematic explanation of its many natures. It is necessary to decide, before any comprehensive system can be constructed, exactly what knowledge is, what sort of things can be known, how anything can be known, and how this knowledge can be used. The field of philosophy concerned with this is called *epistemology,* coming from the Greek for "theory of knowledge." Some philosophers believe that knowledge is what we learn through our five senses; others believe that it is what we know by faith, or by intuition, or by a combination of these. Philosophical systems have differing characteristics, depending on which body of knowledge is adopted.

■**LOGIC.**—Logic as a method of thinking is applicable to practically all areas of philosophy. It is the field in which philosophers set forth the rules for valid reasoning. In Western philosophy the principal characteristic of valid reasoning or argumentation is that no part of an argument may contradict another part—a thing cannot be both A and not A. Reasoning must, by following certain rules first worked out by Aristotle, be consistent and coherent as well as noncontradictory.

Formal logic does not deal with the content of statements, but only with the form in which statements must be expressed in order for a valid conclusion to be drawn. It thus applies to all statements, philosophical and otherwise. There are philosophers who ignore the traditional rules of logic, but they are few and appear mainly in Oriental philosophy, where logic follows somewhat different rules.

Beginning with a mathematical revolution in the late nineteenth century, different ways of expressing logical statements and the relationships between them were added to traditional Aristotelian logic. Modern logic expresses statements by symbols, thus getting closer to the form and further from the content of the statement. This is referred to as *symbolic logic.*

■**AXIOLOGY.**—Axiology is the study of values—ethical, social, political, religious, and esthetic or artistic. Truth is a matter of what is; value is concerned with what ought to be. Investigations of what ought to be are grouped under a division of philosophy called *axiology,* derived from the Greek for "theory of values."

Ethics is concerned with what "the good" is. When we say that an act, or an event, or a statement is good, what do we mean? How can we apply the term "good," which implies a judgment of value? To say that something is good could mean that it contains some quality which makes it good, or it could simply mean that whatever its qualities are, we approve of it, like it, or derive pleasure from it. The question thus arises of whether goodness is a quality which something possesses like its color or size, or whether goodness is determined by our reaction or opinion.

Social philosophy and *political philosophy* are similar to ethics. However, these fields attempt to answer questions about the good in relation to society as well as to individuals.

Perhaps the most controversial questions of value are those in the field of *esthetics.* What is an artist? How does he create a work of art? What is an aesthetic response? What is a work of art? What is "beauty"? Why is art important to man? Society and the standards which it sets can often answer questions of value in the fields of ethics and politics, but not in art. Questions of esthetic value are more personal, more individual. Confusion has been compounded by statements to the effect that esthetic questions are really ethical, social, or religious in nature. In reality, judgments in esthetics should attempt to explain the nature of art in specifically artistic terms.

Philosophy and Other Studies

■**LITERATURE.**—The essence of literature is its ability to project human experience onto the written page. Embodied in the literary work are the author's judgments and values, the approach to life which proceeds from his philosophical principles. It would not be difficult to define the philosophy of a particular age if only the literature of the times remained. In Alexander Pope's eighteenth-century *Essay on Man* there is as valid an expression of Augustan thought as in the writings of the Earl of

NEW YORK PUBLIC LIBRARY

EARLY THOUGHT combined natural science, religion, cosmology, and philosophy. This Hindu world-picture envisions the universe supported on the back of a giant tortoise.

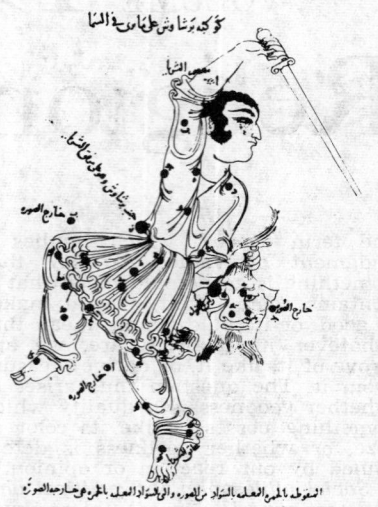

NEW YORK PUBLIC LIBRARY

ASTRONOMICAL SCIENCE, astrological speculation, and myth combine in this Arabic depiction of the constellation Perseus.

METROPOLITAN MUSEUM OF ART

THE STRUGGLE BETWEEN GOOD AND EVIL is an eternal preoccupation of both philosophy and religion. The hero-god Krishna of Hindu mythology, exemplifying the spirit of good, vanquishes the demon Kaliya in a symbol of man's search for transcendent ethical values.

Shaftesbury or John Locke, the acknowledged philosophers of that age. Too, Wordsworth's *Prelude* epitomizes the romantic viewpoint of the early nineteenth century and Camus's *L'Etranger* inspires an awareness of the absurd which lies at the core of modern existentialist thought.

■ **SCIENCE.**—The relationship between philosophy and science has been especially clear since the seventeenth century, when Descartes and Newton espoused ideas which gave rise to the "mechanistic" theory of the universe. Through most of the next two centuries philosophy became the slave of science and limited itself to the boundaries set by scientific discovery. There was, for example, an acceptance of the duality of mind and matter, as well as an insistence on regarding the world as something that could be explained mathematically.

It was not until the advent of William James and the pragmatists that modern philosophy freed itself from the limitations of science and came into its own, professing for the first time the *theory of organism*. Man was looked upon not as a combination of two opposites, mind and matter, but as a single organism with both mental and physical functions. Since then philosophy and science have become invaluable allies, due largely to the reevaluation of scientific methods by such people as Bertrand Russell and Albert Einstein.

■ **RELIGION.**—The relationship between religion and philosophy is perhaps the most understandable one because religion expresses a philosophical belief concerning the nature of the universe. As early as Neoplatonism we can detect the delineation of strong religious feeling which often turned into mysticism or an overwhelming desire for divine redemption. Within the tradition of Western Christianity religion has produced a Thomas

Aquinas, who attempted to reconcile Aristotelianism with Christianity and believed that there could be no valid philosophical viewpoint incompatible with Christian theology.

The rise of Protestantism, while it threatened the Scholastic viewpoint, still determined to put philosophy at the service of religion. Martin Luther, definitely anti-Scholastic, was nevertheless a profoundly spiritual man vitally concerned with religion and determined to interpret philosophical principles in the light of faith. Even today, when many are hardly committed to any traditional code of belief, there is a strong attempt to find the philosophical basis for a belief in something higher than oneself.

History of Western Philosophy

■ **MILESIAN SCHOOL.**—Greek philosophy had its formal start at Miletus in the early part of the sixth century B.C. Thales, about whom very little is known, was the first philosopher of the Milesian school, which included Anaximander and Anaximenes. It is not Thales' only surviving philosophical statement—that the primary cause of everything is to be found in water —which makes him important today; it is the fact that he made one of the first attempts to explain the world in naturalistic terms.

More is known about Anaximander. Greek science at that time was not so much concerned with objects of direct experience, such as water, as it was with pairs of opposing qualities, such as wetness and dryness, hardness and softness. Anaximander abandoned the search for a single element and postulated a boundless "something" out of which all the pairs of opposites could be derived. With

NEW YORK PUBLIC LIBRARY

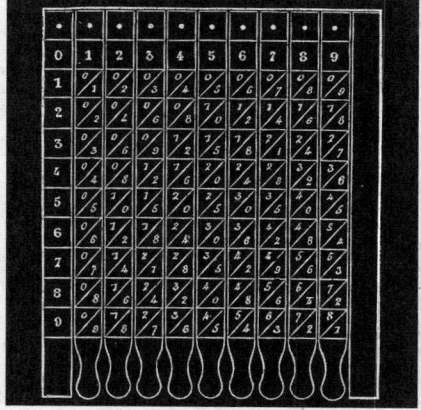

PYTHAGORAS AND HIS FOLLOWERS believed that the basic structure of the universe was mathematical and discoverable. Creators of the multiplication table (*right*), they found relationships between numbers in music, science, and art. The notes from Pythagoras' lyre (*left*) were produced by a mathematical ratio between the lengths of the strings.

this system he felt he could account for the existence of all things.

For Anaximenes the "boundless" was too indeterminate. He chose air as the ultimate element, change as the ultimate process of air. The world was a breathing organism.

■**PYTHAGORAS.**—The pursuit of the primary cause, or the essence of being, along natural or physical lines led to a development in the field of mathematical speculation. Pythagoras (570–c. 496 B.C.) put forth a mathematical theory, but it is not in true scientific form. He gives a special mystical place to numbers; things, in fact, *are* numbers. The essence of being is not to be found in matter, but in form. Number is what gives form, is what limits the Unlimited. Every type of life is included; everything is explained in terms of numbers. Justice, for instance, is a square number; the number seven represents opportunity. It is not difficult to understand how such concepts became part of religious and political movements as well as of philosophical schools of thought.

■**HERACLITUS.**—Heraclitus (c. 544–484 B.C.) is called the "Weeping Philosopher" because of the aura of gloom created by his philosophical outlook. He was the first to inquire in detail into the nature of something which was self-evident to earlier philosophers—change. How is it possible to reconcile change and permanence? Nothing ever is; everything is constantly becoming. Understandably Heraclitus chose fire as ultimate matter—literal fire—because it best embodies the principle of change. Fire is in a constant state of flux, and this, according to Heraclitus, is true of everything. Even the unity which Heraclitus allows to fire and to all things is changing; but to prevent chaos, the process of change is rhythmical. Everything is passing into something else through a rhythmical alternation—contrast and strife between opposites. A thing is what it is, relative to change. Good and evil are relative to this same change, and knowledge is the perception of the unity of the opposites within the process of change.

■**ELEATICS.**—Xenophanes (c. 570–475 B.C.), founder of the school at Elea, examined the world as a poet and a mystic. He proposed that "the One," or one good, is the source of all that is; and that this One is the eternal and unchanging natural world. This belief is not so much *monotheistic* (suggesting one god who rules over all things) as it is *pantheistic* (recognizing that one ruling principle is found in the forces of nature).

Following Xenophanes, Parmenides (c. 540–470 B.C.) took the ideas of permanence and "the One" and made them into a coherent system of thought. And it was Parmenides who turned philosophy from strictly metaphysical speculation to the concrete examination of ideas and concepts. There is no such thing as change for Parmenides; only "the One" exists—immovable, immutable, indivisible. The most important thing about the universe is its completeness, its finality; multiplicity and variety are not to be considered.

Zeno and Melissus were also philosophers of the Eleatic school. Zeno is best remembered for his arguments against motion. He demonstrated that the idea of permanence is more acceptable to common sense than is the notion of change. For an object to travel from one point to another, it must first cover half of the distance, then half of the half, and so on until it has passed an infinite number of halfway points. But this cannot be done even in an infinite amount of time. Therefore, if an object keeps traveling halfway to its destination, it will never arrive. According to this argument, motion is impossible. These thoughts brought philosophical investigations to a logical impasse. But the Pluralists were able to provide a solution.

■**PLURALISTS.**—The first of the Pluralists was Empedocles (c. 492–432 B.C.), who tried to explain change in terms of a single element composed of various independent units. The parts of the One move; change is actually an alteration in composition of the dif-

fering parts of the substance. Empedocles thought he could thus explain how the four elementary substances—earth, air, fire, and water—combine and change to make the natural world. Pairs of opposites still persist; they provide the force to move the four elements together and apart. Love, for instance, moves things together; hate moves them apart. Knowledge is possible, according to Empedocles, because we are made of the same things as the objects of knowledge. We recognize like by like.

Anaxagoras (c. 500–428 B.C.) believed that four elements were too few to explain the diversity of the universe. The primary matter, for Anaxagoras, consists of "seeds" which, in essence at least, contain all the properties of the finished products which they become through the movement of "the Mind." The Mind, the only self-moved cause, is the architect which builds a universe with the seeds. This is the first concept of the rational power of the mind.

Leucippus, another fifth century B.C. Greek philosopher, was the first to bring pluralism to the brink of *atomism.* He stated that all particles of matter are identical in nature, differing only in shape, size, and position. He also discredited outside causes of movement, such as love or mind, and said the particles' ability to move was part of their own nature.

Democritus (c. 460–370 B.C.), who ranks with Plato and Aristotle in the comprehensiveness of his system, brought the atomic theory of matter to its first bloom. Democritus' theory of reality consists of atoms moving in a void, reaching souls as knowledge and senses as impressions.

■**EARLY MORALISTS.**—Even during the early development of scientific thought there was some effort to establish ethical systems. A certain amount of ethical curiosity had always been alive among the Greeks, as is shown in the writings of Homer, Herodotus, and Thucydides. Changing governments and social ferment heightened the philosophers' interest in matters of duty and moral obligation. At first

HELEN BUTTFIELD

METROPOLITAN MUSEUM OF ART

EGYPTIAN HIEROGLYPHICS gave form to mythopoetic concepts of the universe in symbolic picture-writing. Pre-Socratic Greek philosophy moved toward a more unified and naturalistic explanation of the nature of things. The unending spirals in the frieze (*above*) suggest the Heraclitean flux; the discrete particles parallel the atoms of Democritus.

ATHENS NATIONAL MUSEUM

IN THE PLATONIC WORLD, beauty of particular human forms reminds man of a higher reality, the Idea of Beauty itself. Plato's ideal was a hierarchical, rigidly structured society where the virtue of each man related to his particular class and he was trained accordingly.

this was most evident among the *Sophist* school of philosophy, prominent during the middle of the fifth century B.C.

The Sophists began as teachers with rather special pupils. Able young men who wished to enter public service had to be well trained and educated—especially in oratory and rhetoric. The Sophists taught these gentle arts of persuasion, and many of their opinions were thus carried to the public via their students. Among the best known of the Sophists were Hippias of Elis, Prodicus of Ceos, Gorgias, and Protagoras —whose philosophy was summed up by the statement, "Man is the measure of all things."

Socrates took the Sophist tradition out of its individualistic setting in an attempt to achieve a universally valid system of thought. His chief concern was the examination of the moral life. His influence later extended to the *Cyrenaics* and *Cynics*, who were concerned with these questions but found the good life in the pleasure of the individual's own senses, not in knowledge or society. Aristippus and Theodorus were the major Cyrenaics; Antisthenes and Diogenes were the important Cynics. The Cynics were systematically antisocial and advocated a very simple, retiring life. It was Diogenes who, it is said, walked about with a lantern day and night, looking for an honest man.

■ **SOCRATES AND PLATO.**—Plato (427–347 B.C.) represents one of the high points of Greek philosophy. Although it is not easy to determine how much of his work was influenced by Socrates (c. 470–399 B.C.), it appears that the early dialogues show a stronger Socratic influence than do the later ones. Plato's dialogues present a rather idealized view of Socrates when they are compared with two other contemporary accounts of the philosopher, given by Aristophanes and Xenophon. Socrates left no writings of his own; he was a teacher, or as he said of himself, an intellectual midwife assisting in the birth of ideas.

This is consistent with the famous Socratic method of teaching, whereby the teacher ostensibly imparts no knowledge but forces the student, during rigorous questioning, to recall the knowledge with which he was born. This is closely related to Socratic irony, in which the teacher proclaims he has no knowledge when, in fact, he is a wise man. Socrates is said to have had many mystical experiences, especially with his *daimon,* or demon, who is supposed to have told him when he was about to do something wrong. Socrates was condemned to death by the citizens of Athens for being irreligious and also because the Athenians felt he was a corrupting influence on their youth.

Plato shared Socrates' otherworldly or spiritualistic view of life. He separated the world of the senses and the world of the intellect in a much more formal manner than it ever had been done before. What our senses tell us of this world belongs to a low order of reality—a world of opinion. Reality in the truest sense is the world of Ideas, or Forms, which Plato discovered by gradually freeing himself from the hold of the senses. Platonic love, for instance, is love between souls, not between physical beings. This theory of reality is also a theory of knowledge. Plato opposes what the senses tell us to the truths which the intellect discovers. However, his separation of the worlds of senses and ideas is not complete. The world of the senses participates in the world of ideas. There is, for example, the idea of tableness, in which every table participates and to which it owes its sensible existence. Plato never explains exactly what this participation means or how it works.

Plato's ethical and political philosophies are also related to his theories of reality and knowledge. Man's greatest happiness lies in contemplation of the highest Ideas, ultimately the Idea of the Good. The philosopher is the man who can do this, and ideally he is also the man best suited

to be the head of the state. These men, whose chief virtue is wisdom, would be the philosopher kings in Plato's state. Below them would be the guardian class, whose chief virtue is courage and whose souls are spirited and warlike, fitting them to defend the state. The lowest class would be the workers or artisans, who are subject to their passions and whose chief virtue must be temperance.

Art was to have its place in Plato's society, but only as a type of propaganda serving to bring out the best and most rational qualities of the citizens. Any artistic expression was to be carefully censored. All beautiful things would be included in the Form or Idea of Beauty, one of the highest of the Ideas.

Plato's academy was located in Athens. The students strolled through the city or sat under the trees, discussing philosophy and mathematics. A man who perhaps was one of Plato's pupils became one of the most comprehensive philosophers of all times, bringing his mind to bear on every field of knowledge known to his age. He was Aristotle, the last of the great Greek thinkers.

■ **ARISTOTLE.**—Aristotle left Athens and traveled through the Aegean. He then returned to Macedonia and became the tutor of King Philip of Macedon's son Alexander, who later was known as Alexander the Great.

Aristotle was born in Macedon, a port in northern Greece. At the age of eighteen he was sent to Athens and may have studied at Plato's academy for over 20 years. While he was in Athens, Aristotle in 335 B.C. founded his own philosophical school, the Lyceum, where he lectured while walking through the halls and gardens, a habit which gave rise to the name "peripatetic" or walk-about philosophy. He was forced to leave shortly before his death in 332 B.C. because of anti-Macedonian feelings in Athens. He died in Euboea.

Aristotle's students are to a great extent responsible for preserving his work, foremost of which is, perhaps, his comprehensive work on logic. This work was the first of its scope and order, and it is yet to be surpassed. It delineated the form in which valid arguments should be presented. Logic was, according to Aristotle, the basic method to be used in the pursuit of all knowledge.

Aristotle divided the science of knowledge into three realms: (1) theoretical or objective knowledge; (2) knowledge concerned with conduct; (3) productive knowledge which guided the arts. All three divisions were based on principles of logic. Aristotle maintained that knowledge is gained by the discovery of four basic factors, often referred to as *causes*. There are four necessary questions which must be answered: What is it? (formal cause); Out of what is it made? (material cause); By what is it made? (efficient cause); Why is it made? (final cause). Every object in the world of the senses is therefore a union of form and matter, structure and material. Real being, then, is not in another world, as Plato believed, but in this world. This is one of the major differences between Plato and Aristotle. For Plato the Ideas were abstract, existing outside the world; Aristotle thought that Ideas are independent of objects. However, matter is not wholly independent of either. Matter is a potentiality until it is actualized by form. Change, then, is potential being changing into actual being—a process of becoming.

The highest happiness for man, according to Aristotle, is found in the perfection of the rational mind. All other functions of the mind are subordinated to theoretical contemplation—one part moral, the other intellectual. One important part of Aristotle's thoughts on moral virtue is the emphasis on the "Golden Mean," a balance between extremes. For instance, courage is the mean between rashness and cowardice.

METROPOLITAN MUSEUM OF ART

THE GREEK IDEAL of the balance between extremes, the Golden Mean, is embodied in these caryatids from the Erechtheum, as it also is in Aristotle's philosophic writings.

■**LATER ETHICAL PERIOD.**—Aristotle was the last of the great systematic philosophers to appear for many centuries. Later Greek and Roman philosophers were more concerned with the social and ethical questions of their times.

Epicurus of Samos (342–270 B.C.) combined the hedonism of the Cyrenaics—the followers of Aristippus of Cyrene—with the atomism of Democritus. *Hedonism* is a philosophical theory which supports the idea that pleasure is the chief good in life; atomism is the theory that the universe is composed of small, indivisible particles. *Epicureanism*, which combines the two, prescribes a life free of pain—one of wisely selected pleasures. Deeply opposed to the Epicureans were the Stoics. The founder of Stoicism was Zeno, and among its later followers were Seneca, Epictetus, and Marcus Aurelius, the emperor. Zeno started from the premises of *Cynicism*, a branch of the Socratic school of philosophy, which maintained that virtue is the only good and disclaimed everything else —riches, honors, freedom, and pleasure. The Stoics went beyond this negative philosophy, adopting the Cynics' ideals of virtue, endurance, and self-sufficiency, but added a concept of reality as an organic whole. Man is part of nature, not opposed to it; but he must evaluate nature and regulate his own conduct according to rational principles which may demand that he give up his life if he cannot live as he should.

Parallel to these movements was the school of the *Skeptics*, founded by Pyrrho of Elis (360–270 B.C.), a contemporary of Aristotle. He was a practical thinker concerned about the lack of agreement among philosophers. All philosophical thought seemed inconclusive. He, like Arcesilaus, Carneades, Aenesidemus, and Sextus Empiricus, questioned the results of philosophy and concluded that mankind must be satisfied with one ultimate condition—that of ignorance on all questions.

Science, Eclecticism, and Neoplatonism. —In Alexandria in northern Egypt, growing commercial demands led to the development of mathematics. It was in the latter half of the fourth century B.C. that Euclid developed a geometry which was to last, unquestioned and unelaborated, until the nineteenth century. At the same time, in Rome, speculative thought was piecing together the heritage of its past. This phase of philosophy, of a strictly practical nature, was perhaps best characterized by Cicero, the second-century-B.C. Roman philosopher and statesman, and by a tendency to popularize the past.

By 200 B.C. the influence of Alexandria had waned, and Hellenistic and Jewish thought had become dominant. Philo, a man of great scholarly ability, attempted to reconcile Judaic teaching and Greek philosophy. As a Neoplatonist he interpreted Hebrew scriptures as allegories, in an attempt to bring the spirit of man's soul closer to the concept of one God. Thus the philosophical past

NORTH CAROLINA MUSEUM OF ART

MEDIEVAL PHILOSOPHY in the West was dominated by the image of Jesus Christ.

began to join the coming Christian movement.

Growth of Christian Philosophy.—The later ethical period in philosophy was followed by a religious period characterized by Christian principles, predominantly those expressed by Thomas Aquinas. This movement began partly as a reaction against the logical subtleties and formalities of the later Stoics, but it was more than reaction. Christianity preached the equality of men under one omnipotent God, an afterlife, and the great significance of the face-to-face contact which had taken place between man and God. As such, it was a fast-spreading, popular, and influential philosophical movement.

■**THOMAS AQUINAS.**—After the fall of Rome the Christian Church was the strongest remaining institution which stood for law and order. The survival of the conceptualism of Greece, the Roman ideas of law and government, and the Teutonic sense of morality was possible because they became part of the dogma and ideals of the Church. *Scholasticism*, a philosophical movement which began about 900 A.D., was a natural outgrowth of these characteristics. It was a philosophy of absolute and unquestioned dogma, following a set of rules attempting to show that the articles of faith were consistent and rational. Scholasticism had a small body of ideas with which to work, but it contributed a great deal to the basic structure of the Church.

The early development of Christianity was deeply influenced by Platonic thought. Philosophers of the times questioned the reality of universal concepts and explored the nature of particular objects. These questions were argued by such religious scholars as Erigena, Anselm, and Abelard. The beginning of the twelfth century saw a revival of Aristotelian thought within the Church. This was accomplished mostly through the study of Arabs who had preserved the works of Aristotle. The Crusaders brought Aristotle to the Church, and Thomas Aquinas (1224–1274) made him "the Philosopher."

Aquinas tried to unite philosophy and revelation—reason and faith. Again such questions as the reality of universals, the primacy of God's knowledge, and the nature of His will became important. In volume after volume of theological discourse Aquinas deals with very complex questions concerning the dogma of the Church, morality, art, and knowledge. For answers to these questions he referred to two sources of authority: Aristotle and the Church.

Modern Philosophy.—Men such as William of Occam and Roger Bacon were among the first to consider the challenge of science to philosophy. They learned that Aristotle could be interpreted and applied just as easily by the naturalistic philosopher as by the theologian and that the use of scientific methods in the pursuit of knowledge could be a tremendous asset to the philosopher. These men moved philosophy closer to mathematics and empirical observation.

The Renaissance added a new humanism to the search for knowledge, which exalted human life to the realms of the beautiful and the majestic. The idealization of humanity and of this world encouraged the scientific spirit of knowledge to separate further from the concerns of the Church. It was a period of revolt against authority of every kind.

■**FRANCIS BACON.**—It was Francis Bacon (1561–1626) who first interpreted philosophy as an endeavor completely divorced from theology, which aims at improving the condition of man by uncovering the secrets of nature. According to Bacon, the principal method of philosophy is *induction*—the formation of general statements of knowledge from the observation of particular facts. He wanted to clear away the popular misconceptions which man held about

ETTORE NALDONI

AQUINAS IN PHILOSOPHY and Giotto in painting sum up the faith of the Middle Ages and anticipate Renaissance naturalism.

himself and his universe and to replace these opinions with knowledge gained through experience.

■**THOMAS HOBBES.**—The English philosopher Thomas Hobbes (1588–1679) concentrated on the *deductive* side of philosophical methodology, where conclusions are derived by reasoning. Today Hobbes holds a prominent place in the history of philosophical thought because of his early speculations on the nature of society. Hobbes began his philosophy with the reduction of all causes to motion, all reality to matter, and all knowledge to deduction and mathematics. Later he applied this method of thinking to a study of society.

Hobbes believed that man formed a society out of egotistic desires to fulfill certain basic appetites. Without society, men would be in a constant state of war—a life "solitary, poor, nasty, brutish, and short." Man can

gain more by peaceful living in a society; thus he freely submits his will to the will of the state, which in turn becomes the arbiter of right and wrong.

■**RENÉ DESCARTES.**—The flowering of modern philosophy is thought to have begun with René Descartes, the French philosopher born to a well-to-do family in 1596. Descartes was exposed early to the best education available, yet he felt that he knew nothing; he doubted the adequacy of learning. He began to clear his mind in an attempt to find what knowledge could not be doubted. Using intuition and deduction, Descartes finally arrived at the first necessary truth—his own existence. Doubt must have a doubter. "I think, therefore I am," observed Descartes.

Having thus proved the existence of the self, Descartes proceeded to prove the existence of God. Every cause has as much reality as its effect. The effect which Descartes considers is the existence of the *idea* of a perfect God. Since man is imperfect and all things around him are imperfect, he can not formulate the idea of such a perfect being as God. The only cause great enough to produce the idea of such a being is God himself.

In this way Descartes proved the existence of mind and of God—but what about matter? First it is necessary to be clear and distinct. By using geometry, according to Descartes the clearest and most distinct of the sciences, he discovered the essence of matter in extension and motion. The mind and the body, for Descartes, are two separate entities acting upon one another. Several difficulties arise from this attitude. How do such different things act upon each other? Where do they interact? Many philosophers tried to answer these.

■**BENEDICT SPINOZA.**—In one respect Benedict (Baruch) Spinoza (1632–1677) was like Descartes—geometry was his model. Spinoza wrote his major work, the *Ethics*, in the form of a study of geometry, with definitions, axioms, postulates, and corollaries. This work went beyond ethics for Spinoza. It included all knowledge—metaphysical and religious, as well as ethical. Philosophy was the ordering of all knowledge. Spinoza's central idea is the unity of all things, even of mind and matter. Finite things, he believed, are unreal. There is only one substance, God, who has two known attributes: thought and extension. This is all we can say of the deity; beyond that, God is an abstraction, for all is God and God is all. Our salvation from the finite nature of things lies in freeing ourselves from the bondage of emotions by indulging in the freedom of an intuitive knowledge of God. This, said Spinoza, leads us to a state of blessedness.

■**GOTTFRIED WILHELM VON LEIBNITZ.**—Gottfried Leibnitz (1646–1716) rejected Spinoza's idea of unity. Substance for him was composed of separate, indivisible, autonomous units. He also rejected the notion of the passivity of matter which can be derived from Descartes's theory of matter as extended substance. For Leibnitz reality is activity. He substitutes

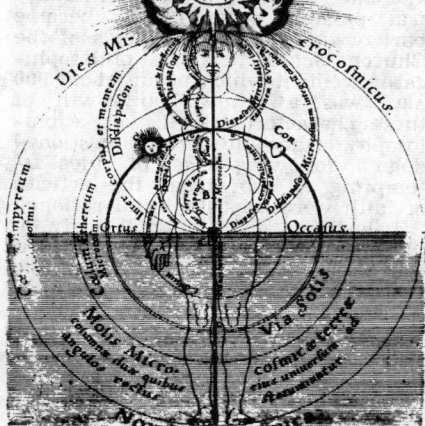

NEW YORK PUBLIC LIBRARY

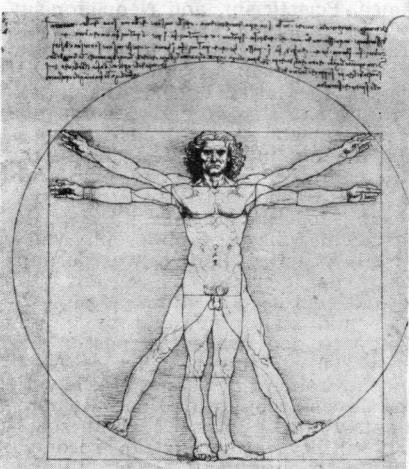

ALINARI-ART REFERENCE BUREAU

MEDIEVAL MAN was the focus of cosmic forces, subject to the will and grace of God, judged and measured by divine rule. Leonardo's Renaissance man (*right*) measured his own universe, subjecting nature to avid scrutiny and ordering the world on a more human scale.

the power of resistance for the fact of extension, making substance no longer passive but active. Substance thus is individual units in action.

Descartes' problem was how mind and matter could interact; Spinoza made mind and matter attributes of the same substance, which thus was both extended and unextended at the same time—a contradiction. In order to avoid the problems confronted by both Descartes and Spinoza, Leibnitz made in matter centers of force; he called these *monads* and gave them degrees of importance, the highest being souls or spirits. Unity in the world is the result of preestablished harmony. The monads, not influenced by one another, are moving in a harmony preexistent in the mind of God. This is how mind and body work together, how moral purpose is attainable, and how knowledge enters the mind.

The thought of Descartes, Spinoza, and Leibnitz places great importance on, and gives great rationality to, the mind or spirit—the rational element of man. Their systems are all variations of *rationalism* and are characterized by an emphatic concern with metaphysics. The period in philosophy which follows them is characterized by an emphasis on epistemology, the study of the nature and validity of knowledge, and on observation rather than on thought alone.

Early British Empiricism

■JOHN LOCKE.—John Locke (1632–1704) founded the tradition of empiricism in Britain. In addition to his famous works on liberty and the state, Locke gave to philosophy what may be its most broadly applicable field—epistemology. Locke dealt with epistemology as it relates to practical knowledge, rather than limiting it to the dogmatic consequences of metaphysics. He proposed that man is born with a *tabula rasa,* or blank slate. This is to say that man has no innate ideas; experience writes all of what he knows on an empty page. Man gets all of his knowledge from sensation and reflection. Objects have primary qualities—the qualities which cannot be separated from the object itself; they also have powers to produce sensations, but these are secondary qualities not contained in the object itself. These sets of qualities are the source of our knowledge.

■GEORGE BERKELEY.—Locke's theories did not pretend to offer any metaphysical subtleties; they were clarifications of everyday thoughts and commonsense beliefs. George Berkeley (1685–1753), bishop of Cloyne, took another approach to philosophy. Not only are secondary qualities in the mind, said Berkeley, but so are primary qualities. As a matter of fact, everything that is, is in the mind. To be is to be perceived. This raises the question of whether or not something continues to exist when there is no one to perceive it. In order to give continuity to the world, Berkeley maintained that when no one was perceiving an object, God was. He thus left the world intact. According to Berkeley, God is also the cause of our own ideas; we exist in His mind.

■DAVID HUME.—David Hume (1711–1776) developed the thought of Locke and Berkeley one step further. Berkeley had taken primary qualities—those which cannot be separated from the essence of an object—out of their objects and had put them in the mind. Hume denied the existence of a continuous or identifiable self; he said that we have no impression from which the idea of self could come. Hume felt that all ideas arise in the mind as the result of vivid, direct sensory stimuli, called impressions. While Berkeley maintained that we cannot know material substance, Hume went further and denied Berkeley's claim that we can know spiritual or any other kind of substance.

Hume criticized the idea of causality. We have, he said, no impression of cause, but merely one of contiguity and succession. We do not receive an impression of cause as such; the only impression which we can receive is that of certain things following each other in certain ways. There is no impression of necessary connection. Maintaining such a connection is merely a habit of mind. Hume analyzed nearly all common beliefs in this manner, even those in the fields of ethics and religion. Because of this he is a famous skeptic in modern philosophy. His influence is still felt.

■ENLIGHTENMENT AND KANT.—The literature and philosophy of the eighteenth century was characterized by dependence on reason. Emphasis was placed on man's freedom as a rational being, and the old enthusiasms and dogmas of the past were rejected. No idea was accepted without rigorous examination—reason was the ultimate judge. As a result, that side of life connected with feeling or emotion received almost no attention. This was the age of Voltaire and the *Encyclopedists* (advocates of deism and scientific rationalism), the *Deists* and the English moralists, the early *materialists,* Rousseau, Lessing, and Herder. This was the *Age of Enlightenment.* The man who has been called the greatest philosopher of this age, and one of the greatest critical minds of all ages, is Immanuel Kant (1724–1804).

CITY ART MUSEUM, ST. LOUIS

METROPOLITAN MUSEUM OF ART

METROPOLITAN MUSEUM OF ART

THE MATERIALIST-IDEALIST controversy has haunted philosophy since the seventeenth century. Do things exist in themselves, independent of the observer, or do they exist only insofar as they are perceived? Zurbarán's *Still Life* (*top*) presents an externally real world of Lockean primary qualities belonging to things in themselves. In Vermeer's *Young Woman with a Water Jug* (detail, *left*) objects are revealed by light, existing, as Berkeley believed, because they are perceived. Later with Monet, only sense impressions remain and the façade of *Rouen Cathedral* (*right*) dissolves in a shimmer of colored light.

Kant never left the German province where he was born. As a physicist and astronomer he read Hume's work and was, in his own words, awakened from his "dogmatic slumbers." Taking ideas from both Leibnitz and Locke—the active and the passive mind—Kant created a philosophical system which did not end in the skepticism of Hume. According to Kant, there is a part of the world which we cannot know—the *noumenon,* which is beyond the senses, beyond reason. But the world which we do know—the phenomenal world—is open to both our senses and our reason. The various categories of the mind, through the media of time and space, receive sensations and make them intelligible—they arrange them according to the invariable structure of the mind. Reality is made up by the mind's structure.

The basic ethical principle for Kant is duty; his ethical theories are based on the fact that man has free will

NEW YORK PUBLIC LIBRARY

IMMANUEL KANT found reality dependent upon the structuring of the human mind and phenomena intelligible only insofar as their order accords to human reason.

and can choose to act in accordance with this principle. Thus the highest good is to act from a sense of duty. The central rule of Kant's ethical doctrine is called the categorical imperative and states that every individual ought to act so that the principle governing his action can be made into a universal law, binding for all men. The place of Kantian thought in philosophy is of the greatest importance. Much of later philosophy is a reaction either for or against one or another of Kant's ideas.

■**GEORG WILHELM FRIEDRICH HEGEL.**—The philosophy of Hegel (1770–1831) is obscure; it admits of such wide interpretation, and is based on such subtleties of logic, that it cannot be justly treated outside of a lengthy book. However, it is possible to give

a brief outline of the path which his thought takes. Hegel's major starting point is a sense of history—no other philosopher has ever expressed this so thoroughly. He maintains that history, or human experience, is a progressive expression and embodiment of reason. This absolute idealism of Hegel led him to the belief that experience *is* reason—"what is rational is actual, and what is actual is rational." Man has freedom to the extent to which he is conscious of himself as a rational being—this is freedom of spirit. And the highest calling of man is to act in accordance with what Hegel calls the absolute idea, the world spirit which unfolds itself through history.

History advances by means of a dialectic; this is also the way man's reasoning process works. An idea is taken (thesis); its opposite is considered (antithesis); a synthesis is created from the two, which in turn becomes the thesis for another series. Hegel discusses art, religion, and philosophy as means of bringing about the final synthesis in which the world spirit will be completely realized. Ideally philosophy brings everything to completion; it is the world spirit in conversation with itself—the self-thinking idea. The first important reaction against Hegel is found in one of his contemporaries, Schopenhauer.

■**ARTHUR SCHOPENHAUER.**—Because of the place which Schopenhauer (1788–1860) occupies in the school of philosophy known as *idealism,* he can be said to share in the beginnings of contemporary existentialism with Kierkegaard and Nietzsche. Idealism has been the largest tradition in Western philosophy since Plato. It includes all philosophies which find reality, or at least the most important reality, in ideas, mind, spirit, or reason. These are philosophies which deny or degrade matter and the whole range of man's emotional life.

For Schopenhauer reality is the Will. Reason cannot tell us about reality; only intuition can. Intuition leads us not only to think but also to act. Will not only leads us; it drives us. We are, in Schopenhauer's pessimistic view, driven by want, by desire, by Will—by a will to live and to go on suffering. Salvation lies in denying the Will through art, and through the extinction of consciousness in a final state of Nirvana.

Idealism by no means died with Hegel. It had such brilliant advocates as Johann Herbart, Samuel Taylor Coleridge, Friedrich Schelling, T. H. Green, F. H. Bradley, Bernard Bosanquet, and Benedetto Croce. During the years in which Hegel and Schopenhauer were teaching on the Continent, another movement known as *utilitarianism* began in Britain.

■**UTILITARIANISM.**—Utilitarianism is an ethical position which, in the words of Jeremy Bentham (1748–1832), advocates "the greatest good to the greatest number." In developing his "hedonic calculus" Bentham attempted to set forth a way in which a careful measure of the greatest good could be taken. John Stuart Mill (1806–1873) modified Bentham's position by objecting to a mere quantity of pleas-

ure. For man it is the quality of the pleasure which counts: better a dissatisfied man than a satisfied pig.

Contemporary Philosophy

■**DIALECTICAL MATERIALISM.**—A very large segment of today's world lives under what purports to be Karl Marx's philosophy. The ends and the creeds of this contemporary school of thought do indeed use the tenets of Marx's dialectical materialism, but the forms of government and the means used are often far from anything Marx intended. Karl Marx (1818–1883) had a sense of history as conscious as that of Hegel, from whom he took the dialectical interpretation of history—history proceeding by a dialogue between opposite forces, opposing interests. According to Marx, history takes a predetermined course independent of, and uninfluenced by, man's actions. It begins with a primi-

ALINARI-ART REFERENCE BUREAU

RATIONALISM permeated the eighteenth century. Goya's etching, *The Sleep of Reason Produces Monsters,* pictures the terrors that swarm when reason abdicates.

tive kind of *communism* in an agricultural society which has within it, as does every stage of history, the seeds of its own destruction. History progresses through feudalism and capitalism to a sophisticated industrial community of a classless society. This is a purely economic interpretation of history, materialistic as well as deterministic. It was made much broader and more practical by Frederick Engels and Vladimir Lenin.

■**LOGICAL POSITIVISM.**—In the late nineteenth century a revolution in science blossomed after centuries of dependence on the ideas of the past. Theories and methods began to break away from the ideas of Newton and Euclid. Science was reevaluated, and it became clear that philosophy was to have the task of clarifying the meaning of the statements of the new, as well as of the old, science. At the

University of Vienna a group of young men known as the Vienna Circle set out to find a method of clarification which would be valid for any statement which made sense. They were led by Moritz Schlick, Rudolf Carnap, and Otto Neurath; and they took their inspiration from the brilliant earlier positivism of Ernst Mach.

This philosophical movement spread to England and the United States through the work of Ludwig Wittgenstein, A. J. Ayer, and others; here it became known as *logical empiricism*. Its main tenet became known as the *verifiability theory*. Ayer formulated the rule that a statement, in order to be true or false, must be empirically verifiable—it must be open to proof by experiment or observation. Wittgenstein stressed the point that the role of philosophy is

ments. William James (1842–1910) applied the same criterion to all areas of human endeavor. The name "pragmatism" was introduced by Peirce, who used it in reference to his own work in an attempt to distinguish it from the work of James.

The thought of John Dewey (1859–1952) took its own direction—that of *instrumentalism*, where ideas are the instruments of action, and the usefulness of an idea determines its truth. Dewey applied himself to an examination of every part of human life, calling for a fresh approach to every problem. For Dewey, all was moving and changing. Static, dogmatic, or traditional answers would not do for new problems—for any problem. We choose among solutions, and only with the success or failure of our solutions are we able to test the validity of the ideas behind them.

win's work on the theory of evolution opened man's biological life to philosophical scrutiny. The most comprehensive of the philosophers in this tradition was Henri Bergson (1859–1941), who based his philosophy on the principles of duration and of the life force (his famous *élan vital*). Intuition was for Bergson a combination of the objectivity of science and the directness of artistic experience; through it we understand duration.

Before Darwin's time Herbert Spencer maintained in his philosophy that the principle of development is the key to human understanding and to life. The work of Darwin had a great influence on Spencer's work, especially in his naturalistic ethics.

■**EXISTENTIALISM.**—Modern existentialism is a movement which stands against the general trend of Western philosophy. This approach to philo-

METROPOLITAN MUSEUM OF ART

SOCIAL PHILOSOPHY of the 1800's was infused with class consciousness and a sense of history. Daumier's *Third Class Carriage* evokes Marx's concern for the poor.

PHILADELPHIA MUSEUM OF ART

ANALYTIC CUBISM'S involvement with the basic structure of painting parallels the absorption of logical positivism with language analysis, the meaning of statements. Picasso's *Nude Female* (*above*) accepts the "real" as a structure of variable relationships and multiple appearances. Klee's *Letter Ghost* (*below*) is an image whose multiple meanings resemble Wittgenstein's experiments with language games.

PHILLIPS GALLERY, WASHINGTON, D.C.

THE CREATIVE VITALITY that animates Matisse's *Interior* expresses the *élan vital* of Bergson, who found in direct experience of life itself a meaning lost in analysis.

to clarify language, not to give knowledge. He thus introduced the idea of language games which explore the various ways in which we convey different ideas and emotions.

Associated with linguistic analysis and the revolution in science is the rise of *symbolic logic*. Bertrand Russell and Alfred North Whitehead presented what was perhaps the most profound and monumental work since Newton, the *Principia Mathematica,* opening the field of symbolic logic.

■**PRAGMATISM.**—*Pragmatism* forms the American expression of the increased interest in science and practical affairs. Essentially this is the work of three men—Charles Sanders Peirce, William James, and John Dewey, whose thought differs slightly from the other two. Peirce (1839–1914) first expressed the idea that a statement is true or false according to its results; he intended this as a test for the validity of scientific state-

MUSEUM OF MODERN ART

Philosophy and Evolution.—Developments in the field of biology had a fresh impact on philosophy in the late nineteenth century. Charles Dar-

sophic thought has been developing for over a century. Western philosophy has traditionally been concerned with the ascendancy of spirit, mind, or reason—the intellect. Matter and emotions usually have occupied only a minor place in the history of thought, if they have been left any place at all. Existentialism is an attempt to say something philosophically meaningful about man's life and the way he lives, his emotions and the world as he meets it. The existence and the nature of consciousness, the meaning of the world, rather than the truth or falsity of it, are the main interests of the existential philosopher. The most unusual thing about the existentialists is that they differ so widely among themselves. They are not really a school of philosophy; they are a group of philosophers who share common problems but have no common answers.

Soren Kierkegaard (1813–1855) and

MUSEUM OF MODERN ART

ANXIETY, by Edvard Munch demonstrates the idea of existentialists that man without God despairs of life. Van Gogh's *Starry Night* shows the Christian Existentialist notion of the struggle of man's will in a universe of a remote God.

LOOK MAGAZINE: MUSEUM OF MODERN ART

Friedrich Nietzsche (1844–1900) are the fathers of modern existentialism. Kierkegaard as a Christian existentialist was concerned mainly with man's relationship to God and the despair which man feels when he is conscious of himself and his position before God. He believed that truth is subjective and that no system of philosophy can encompass a human life. He accused Hegel's philosophical system of building a beautiful house while man lives in the barn—as all men must.

Nietzsche was almost wholly interested in man's relationship to man. His thought centers around man's will to power—the most important human reality—and how it can be best expressed. "God is dead," says Nietzsche. "Modern man has killed him, and now man must accept the responsibility of being thrown back on himself for answers to the questions of life."

Martin Heidegger (1889–   ) deals with the questions of existentialism in a more technical manner. Heidegger, a contemporary German philosopher, has taken the age-old question of the being of things and has made it his task to explore the *being* of human life. His philosophy is highly abstruse and technical in its vocabulary, but many other philosophers have profited much from his theories.

The foremost of these philosophers is Jean-Paul Sartre. In his philosophical works, as well as in his literary works, Sartre has shed light on the questions of consciousness, choice, and freedom.

The existential movement is highly concerned with ethical problems. One of its most highly respected moralists was Albert Camus (1913–1960), who denied being either a philosopher or an existentialist. This is perhaps true, except that it could be said of him that he was the first of a new kind of philosopher, the nonsystematic philosopher who sought not only philosophical but also literary expression and achieved both with equal success. He consistently illuminated the beauty and value of a life without a transcendant meaning, creation without a creator.

■**PHENOMENOLOGY.**—*Phenomenology* in its modern form was started by Edmund Husserl, who influenced both Heidegger and Sartre. It is a very technical philosophy which attempts a description of subjective feelings without trying, as psychology does, to formulate causal laws. Husserl maintained that both formal and material universal truths were observable. Much of his work had to do with the nature of consciousness.

PHILOSOPHY GLOSSARY

Absolute.—Without conditions or qualifications. In metaphysics, without any external relationships; a simple entity.

Absolutism.—Opposed to relativism. In metaphysics it is the theory of reality as absolute. In axiology it is the theory that values are objectively real and uniform.

Agnosticism.—The theory that knowledge is impossible. In theology, the theory that God is unknowable.

Antinomy.—Conflict between two equally acceptable but contradictory principles.

Atomism.—Any theory which says that reality is composed of plural, separate, and irreducible elements.

Categorical.—Unconditional. Opposite of hypothetical.

Contingent.—Whatever can be thought of as existing or not. Not logically necessary, but verifiable by experience.

Deduction.—Inference from one or more propositions to a conclusion logically implied by, and made necessary by, the propositions. Validity of the argument is more important in deductive reasoning than is the truth of the propositions.

Deism.—Belief that God is totally other than the world, transcends it completely. Contrasts to immanence.

Determinism. — Theory that every event is totally conditioned by a cause which precedes it.

Dialectic.—In Hegel this is the process of reason which indicates the structure of reality. A dialogue between two opposite viewpoints.

Empiricism. — The theory that all knowledge comes from, and can be verified only by, the senses. Opposed to rationalism and intuitionism.

Hedonism.—Psychological hedonism states that man seeks pleasure; ethical hedonism, that he ought to seek pleasure.

Induction.—The process by which a general statement of knowledge is arrived at by observation of many individual events.

Innate ideas.—Ideas which are said to be in the mind before, or independent of, experience.

Intuition.—Direct, immediate apprehension of an object.

Mysticism.—The theory that the nature of reality is totally or partially inaccessible to either the senses or the intellect.

Nominalism.—Theory that universals are merely names or words and that particulars are real.

Occam's razor (*law of parsimony*).— Theory that any explanation is better if it is as simple as possible.

Realism.—Plato's theory that universals are real, particulars less real. Also the theory that something will still exist if all consciousness disappears entirely.

Teleology.—Study of the ends or purposes of events.

—Charles J. Jones

BIBLIOGRAPHY

CORNFORD, FRANCIS MACDONALD. *Before and After Socrates.* Cambridge University Press, 1932.

CURTIS, STANLEY JAMES. *A Short History of Western Philosophy in the Middle Ages.* The Newman Press, 1950.

FRANKEL, CHARLES. *The Golden Age of American Philosophy.* George Braziller, Inc., 1960.

MILLER, HUGH. *An Historical Introduction to Modern Philosophy.* The Macmillan Co., 1947.

RELIGION

Definition.—Religion may be defined in terms of worship, belief, feeling, moral behavior, personal or social values, or attitudes and relationships; it may be defined in relation to individuals, or societies, or cultures, or institutions. Almost all definitions include what people do in the way of religious behavior, what they believe about God and man and the God-man relationship, and why they act and believe as they do. Not only the actions, attitudes, and relationships which involve religious behavior, but also the underlying motivations and commitments for such behavior must be included in any general understanding of religion. In other words, both the means used, such as prayer, sacrifice, ritual, or moral obedience, and the end served, such as the divine will, man's ultimate destiny, or the quest for a relationship to God, are part of what religion means.

Another way of responding to the question, "What is religion?", is to identify its major characteristics or qualities. Religion is a continuing human phenomenon. Its traces are found wherever one dips into human history, as anthropologists have shown and historians have supported. Religious questions and patterns of behavior, such as the symbolism reflecting man's self-awareness, his quest to know the meaning of his existence, and his concern to relate himself to an unlimited and undying absolute, are found in the dim prehistoric past, in ancient civilizations along the Yangtze, the Nile, and the Euphrates, and in both old and new cultures today, East and West.

Still another major characteristic is suggested by the fact that religion is expressed through and supported by institutions. These institutions provide entrance into a given religion, and they are essential to an effective expression of that religion in society. Institutions set the conditions for religious behavior and belief; they often

METROPOLITAN MUSEUM OF ART

STONE FIGURE, carved about 2500 B.C. and used in many of the primitive religious rites.

have authority with regard to the interpretation of sacred writings; and they provide tangible modes of expression for the intimate and ultimate meanings of man's life and worship. Institutions—churches, temples, synagogues—are the educational centers by which the religious heritage is transmitted, and from them come the missionary endeavors by which the religion expands and extends itself.

In addition to these anthropological, sociological, and historical approaches, there are others which are attributed to the psychologists, the philosophers, and the theologians. For example, religion may be seen as the most decisive and fundamental of human concerns; a religious crisis often discloses the most basic commitments or attitudes of a person or of a people. Thus the saint, the prophet, and the religious leader are figures worthy of special study from the psychological point of view. Philosophical investigation critically attends to the meaning and truth of religious claims and relates these tenets to experience as a whole. When the claims, beliefs, and values which are held in one religion conflict with those of another, the question of their truth is examined by the philosopher or the theologian. Religious convictions and activities are the expression of a people's view of the meaning of existence. Thus scholars of religion deal with the most intimate and ultimate concerns of men and of cultures.

Religion in Various Cultures

■**PRIMITIVE RELIGION.**—Attempts have been made to fit all primitive religions into one precise formula, to discover a common origin, and to trace a single line of evolutionary development for all religions. Scholars, however, have been forced to abandon these attempts. Primitive peoples fall into a multiplicity of distinct groups; the historical relations among these groups are much too complex to enable the scientist to give a general description of primitive religion. Yet two generalizations about primitive peoples are reasonably well established by cultural anthropologists: (1) the apparently simple and uncomplicated social structures and practices of the primitives appear under closer scrutiny to be very complex and delicately balanced; (2) there is a definite continuity between the basic needs and activities of primitive peoples and those of civilized man. The apparently limitless variations in customs, institutions, mythologies, beliefs, and ways of thought are in large measure variations on certain common themes of human liv-

HARRISON FORMAN

ON BALI, an island of Indonesia, the traditions of generations are still maintained. The Balinese, known throughout the world for their musical and artistic skills and high level of culture, here perform the Ketchak, a ritualistic dance believed to exorcise the evil spirits.

ing; they are reflections of universal human needs. Religion is one of man's basic needs; it is a recurrent theme throughout the history of mankind.

Earlier anthropologists such as Emile Durkheim called attention to the *we-consciousness* of primitive peoples, the power of group relationships. This has proved to be a helpful contribution, but his claim that *totemism*—the identification of cosmic power with the power of the group—is the basic form of all primitive religious life is not valid. Sir James George Frazer studied certain practices identified with totemism, such as dances, sacrifices, and other rituals. He concluded that either of two fairly distinct aims may have been present: the bending of cosmic and social powers to the will of the individual or group, or the bending of the will of the individual or group to the powers which they consider as superior. The first of these activities he called *magic;* the second he thought to be more distinctively religious.

Magic often involves the primitive tendency to believe that things which are alike or similar are actually identical. The image of the enemy may thus be destroyed in the belief that the enemy himself will be affected. Or it may involve an assumption that a certain sequence of events, not necessarily causally connected, will recur if the first act of the sequence is repeated—the medicine man performs a certain act, an event occurs; it is felt that a repetition of this magical formula will produce the same event which followed its performance the first time. If a magical instrument is involved, it may be used as a fetish for good or ill. Once regulations for the control of the fetish are established, those not trained in its use regard it as taboo—not to be handled. In Frazer's view, sacrifice is the key to the difference between magic and religion. Sacrifice involves the personal attitude of the participant. In its more highly developed forms, sacrifice relates to the will or attitude of the worshipper; it is not simply designed to persuade the deity.

The belief in spirits, and the activities associated with this belief, are as universal in primitive societies as totemic or magical practices. Primitive peoples live in a world of intangible spirits which serves, as did the Greek gods, to "naturalize man and humanize nature." This effort to bridge the gap between the animate and the inanimate by attributing conscious life to nature or natural objects is called *animism.* Primitive peoples thus live in several worlds at once—notably, this normal world and the "other world." Animism is thought to be the source of many things which continue in religious practice and belief today. These beliefs in their refined form, along with the religious literature and the patterns of worship which developed in particular religions, are thought to indicate a line of direct connection between primitive and later more highly developed religions. Students of religion should, however, be on guard against the *genetic fallacy,* in

which the conclusion is quickly drawn that, because religious behavior is reflected in crude animistic patterns, all religion therefore is nothing but an emotional expression of a prescientific fear of nature. Because of the perils of such reductionism, the efforts of anthropologists to identify religious belief and behavior must be supplemented by the work of religious historians, by whom the whole range of development is examined.

In the historical study of religion, it is often possible to see clearly delineated stages. As a result of this approach, religions have been classified as polytheistic, pantheistic, and monotheistic. Animism may be an early form of *polytheism,* which refers to belief in a plurality of gods or divine beings. The efforts of primitive man to overcome the distance between the gods and the world could have produced *pantheism*—where everything in nature is God. The religious position which stands in sharp contrast to pantheism is *monotheism,* which recognizes one and only one God—distinct from and transcendent over the world. It is no longer assumed that these represent clearly defined stages in the history of religion as a whole. However, these three positions, taken with respect to the nature of deity, enable philosophers and theologians to distinguish between what they call lower and higher forms of religion.

Religion in Egypt and Babylonia.—There is evidence that centuries before the curtain of history rose in ancient Egypt (about 3400 B.C.), the valley and delta of the Nile were made up of a number of independent states, each with a separate government and individual divine guardians. Gradually an amalgamation of these units took place, culminating in the establishment of a single empire containing both lower and upper Egypt. Development in religion closely paralleled political events—local guardians or gods either were joined with those of neighboring states (thus the hyphenated names of deities) or they were completely subdued by the other gods. The supreme gods in the two kingdoms—*Set* in upper Egypt and *Horus* in lower Egypt—were both eventually defeated. When Memphis was the capital of the empire, the god *Ptah* was supreme; when Thebes was capital, *Amon* was the chief god.

Priests brought order out of the confusion of reigning deities, thus giving rise to legends which group them by families. The best known triad was that of *Osiris, Isis,* and *Horus.* Legend indicates that Set was the brother of Osiris and slew him, disposing of the body in the Nile, which carried it to the sea, and finally to Phoenicia. Isis, heartbroken over her husband's death, found the body and returned it to Egypt. The body was discovered by Set, who in anger tore it limb from limb and scattered the pieces abroad. Isis resumed her sorrowful quest, giving a separate burial to each part of the body as she found it. This is the reason why there are so many burial places of Osiris. To

avenge his father's death, Horus, by then grown to manhood, attacked Set and after a long battle defeated and bound him and delivered him to Isis; she set him free. Other versions tell of Osiris' restoration to life, his rule of the underworld, and even his place in the Isis cult of the Roman world.

The natural powers were also identified as deities, especially the sky, the sun, the moon, and the Nile. They were often represented in animal form; Horus, for example, as sky-god and later as sun-god, was shown as a falcon. The worship of the sun-god *Ra,* who was thought to be the supreme god, prevailed for a time. In the brief period of the reign of Amenhotep IV, *Aton,* the solar disc, was acknowledged as the one and only god. This was the beginning of monotheism. In line with this innovation, the pharaoh changed his name to Ikhnaton, and ordered the name of the rival god Amon obliterated from monuments and temples. The reform soon lost its power, and the return to the worship of Amon was initiated by the famous Tutankhamen, whose richly stored tomb was found intact in 1922. The subsequent history of Egyptian religion is often said to be one of slow decay.

A prominent feature of Egyptian religion is its emphasis on the life after death and particularly on the immortality of the pharaoh. Tomb inscriptions testify to a belief in a joyful afterlife—beyond the river, in the land beyond the setting sun. As a result of this emphasis, the Egyptians carefully preserved the pharaoh's corpse through their highly developed art of embalming; they practiced elaborate security measures to protect the body from molestation. They also provided the tomb with tools, food, and furnishings to serve the pharaoh in his next life, and with statues and painted images of slaves and companions. In time, ethical considerations were linked with the belief in an afterlife—Egyptians felt that the manner in which a man lived determined his future destiny. Elaborate inscriptions and papyrus rolls found in the tombs and coffins were concerned with the afterlife. These writings are known as the *Book of the Dead,* and constitute the primary sacred literature of ancient Egypt.

■**BABYLONIA.**—The religion which emerged in the region between the Tigris and Euphrates rivers is similar to the religion of the Nile. Babylonia had many temples, tombs, and monuments which have yielded rich findings for archaeologists and historians. Political and religious developments were closely related, and there was the same tendency in Babylonia as was seen in Egypt, to group gods in triads. The sun and moon occupied high positions among the gods, and a fairly well developed ethical system, reinforced by religion and magic, resulted. Among the differences between Egyptian and Babylonian religion, we should note that Babylonia did not concern itself with animal worship, and neither was there any attempt at monotheism nor any elaboration on the afterlife. The triad best known in Babylonian religion was composed of *Sin*—the moon-god, *Shamash*—the sun-god, and *Ishtar*—the goddess of fertility. Shamash was the supreme judge of the world, or as Hammurabi (Babylonian king, 2067–2025 B.C.) claimed, "the guide of the gods as well as the ruler of men." It was supposedly from Shamash that the king received the remarkable law code known by his name. Since Hammurabi also brought about the unity of Babylonia, *Marduk*, the god of his capital, became the supreme god, thus requiring a revision of legends and sacred texts.

The upper regions of Assyria underwent a similar religious development under the sway of the chief god *Assur*, who was named after the capital city. Associated with Assur were the Babylonian gods, Shamash and Ishtar. Ishtar, however, was not the goddess of fertility, but of war, thus serving Assyria's warring interests. Students familiar with these ancient developments in Egypt, Babylonia, and Assyria often see striking parallels to the Old Testament—their epics contain similar stories of creation and flood; religious movements were intimately affected by political developments; religion, ethics, and the afterlife were interrelated; and the gods were either grouped by threes or there was some approach toward monotheism.

Religion in Ancient China.—The Orient contains a breadth and inclusiveness of religious and philosophical thought. The religions of China are Confucianism, Taoism, and Buddhism; however only the first two are native to China. These religions overlap at many points; the same person may be Confucian, Taoist, and Buddhist at the same time in different areas of his life. There are many common practices among these religions, the most common of all being ancestor worship. Also, all three cults view religion as primarily ethical.

■**CONFUCIANISM.**—Confucianism stands for the belief that those who seek to live the "good life" and hope to find salvation through good behavior must base their moral code upon an acceptable view of the world. Confucius (551?–479 B.C.) did not found a religion along these lines, he merely gathered up certain elements from past religious beliefs and formulated them. He did stamp them with his own personality and his own emphases, but he was mainly concerned with passing on a religious heritage which he believed essential to his time. This heritage expressed a strong sense of man's dependence on the earth, society, and the universe. Confucius' literary studies of the past led him to believe that the virtues inherent in the religious heritage needed to be recovered for the sake of political strength and social stability. He believed that only such a return to the ancient past could save his people from the chaos which threatened from invasions and increasing rebellion and internal discontent. He also proposed political reforms so that peace and harmony might be achieved. Throughout his lifetime,

METROPOLITAN MUSEUM OF ART
ANCESTOR WORSHIP in the Orient.

Confucius was a teacher. Late in life he edited his classics, which with later additions make up the basic religious literature—the *Book of History*, the *Book of Poetry*, the *Book of Changes*, the *Book of Rites*, and the *Spring and Autumn Annals*.

Confucius' disciples collected his sayings, continued to disseminate his ideas, and produced a number of additional books. His greatest pupil, Mencius (372–289 B.C.), did much to popularize his teachings; largely as a result of his work, the teachings of Confucius once again became contemporary issues. Confucian thought contains at least four emphases: (1) the motivation of ethical behavior, (2) the importance of duty, (3) basic social relations, and (4) ancestor worship. Ethical behavior is motivated both by linguistic clarity, which Confucius called "the rectification of names," and by an attitude of mutuality or compassion. To develop responsibility and peace, he asserted that men should know the key meaning of terms, especially of nouns. The emperor should really know what "emperor" means, the father should know what it means to be a "father." Ethical behavior is motivated not only by dependable communication, but also by *Jen*, an attitude which involves doing what is mutually beneficial to the self and to others, while refraining from that which is harmful both to the self and to others. Some have seen this as the negative version of the Golden Rule—what you do not want done to yourself, do not do to others.

Emphasis upon duty is related to Jen, since to do what is of mutual benefit, rather than mutual harm, to yourself and others is to act from a sense of duty. Behavior, however, must proceed from *Li*—a sense of propriety, sensitivity, and discretion. When relations are governed by duties, kindness prevails, the good life is lived as an art, and there is har-

mony, balance, and order in all of life. The good man also appreciates culture, for he lives with dignity and a fine measure of ceremony. This is applied to the five basic social relations of (1) emperor to subject, (2) father to son, (3) husband to wife, (4) elder brother to younger brothers, and (5) elders in general to juniors in general. Li for the emperor means sensitivity to the needs of subjects and behavior appropriate to and exemplary for them; Li for subjects means grateful emulation of the emperor and obedience to him. Of all relations, Confucius treated most fully the relation of father to son and son to father. Filial piety thus became the cornerstone in the foundation of all social relations.

Religious practices, being part of traditional rites and ceremonies, were encouraged by Confucius. Confucians celebrate social unity, thus reminding men of their dependence upon their heritage, while adding to the harmony of their lives. The popular rituals of Confucianism surround ancestor worship—an extension of filial piety. Nothing is more important than having a son to carry on the ancestral rites, to perform the elaborate ceremonies connected with burial, to keep the ancestral tablet, and, at times, to preserve the ancestral temples. Very little of this ritual emphasizes the soul and its immortality, or the afterlife, and almost no stress is given to the gods. Confucius himself is remembered as a sage and he is praised as such in liturgies used in official ceremonies. His contribution was in the field of ethics, where he held that human nature is naturally good, that the will is free, that conduct derives from attitudes, and that virtue has its own reward.

■**TAOISM.**—The other religion natural to China, Taoism, had its beginnings in the work of Lao-tse, a contemporary of Confucius. He retired from his work as keeper of the archives at the imperial court and wrote down his teachings in a book called the *Tao Teh King*. This book states what the Tao or the Way is for the four powers of the universe: man takes his law from the earth, the earth takes its law from heaven, heaven takes its law from Tao; the law is spontaneous for Tao. To know the law or the Way is to be enlightened, and to submit to it is inactivity—since most of the world's ills result from action. The sacred literature of Taoism includes the *Tao Teh King* and the commentary prepared by Lao-tse's disciple, Chuang-tse. Modern Taoism has become exceedingly superstitious and ritualistic. Its chief contribution to religion as a whole is to be found in the emphasis which Taoists place on the deification of Lao-tse and other men, systems of magic and ceremony, and the reinforcing of devotional and traditional practices.

Religion in India
■**HINDUISM.**—Hinduism is a broad term used to describe a vast range of rites, codes, myths, and philosophies which have accumulated in a long history of religion in India. It finds its unity

LOOK MAGAZINE

THE GANGES, the sacred river of India, draws pilgrims for the annual bathing festivals.

in ethnic factors and, more recently, in national emphases. It is the product of a long period of development, which includes the early Vedic, the Brahmanic or philosophical, the devotional or theistic, and the sectarian stages. Two thousand years of ferment, assimilation, and structuring have gradually produced the cultural phenomenon known as Hinduism. Out of many internal and external conflicts, numerous legends and epics were created which now make up the body of Hindu literature. Among these are "The Adventures of Rama" (*Ramayana*) and "The Great Bharata War" (*Mahabharata*). Epics and folk tales include magic ritual guides, hymns, and prayers, along with theological speculation. The more important ones were handed down orally and eventually took on the status of classics; these were called Vedas—they are the world's oldest religious literature.

Our knowledge of the Vedic period is derived chiefly from the Rig-Veda, a collection of hymns and prayers to the gods. It reflects a vigorous and hardy Aryan people, living off the soil. Theirs was a religion concerned with flocks, pasturelands, and plentiful milk and butter. So highly esteemed were agrarian products that heaven was pictured as a lush meadowland with pools of butter. The people were life-loving; they wished to have long and abundant lives; and salvation was achieved in this world. The deified objects of worship were humanized powers of nature—the sky, the sun, the moon, storms, wind, and others. Thirty-three principal gods were divided into three main groups —gods of the sky, gods of the atmosphere, and gods of the earth. Of all these, *Indra*, an atmosphere-god, was ranked first; about one-fourth of all hymns are in his honor. He was the storm-god, as well as the war-god. The great ethical god of the Vedas was *Varuna*, who possessed the ability to see even the hidden sins men commit; his was the power to forgive. Closely associated with Varuna was the god *Mitra*, who, as *Mithra*, became a highly important figure in

later *Zoroastrianism* (a Persian religion founded by the seventh-century-B.C. prophet Zoroaster). Both Varuna and Mitra were associated with the sun; sacrifices to them were made at special times or particular seasons of the year. Simplicity governed worship at the early stages but more complex ritualism developed quickly.

Since religious rites were the accepted way of relating the individual and the society to nature, the power of the priests who controlled nature steadily increased. Moreover, sharp social distinctions apparently developed at an early stage between the lighter-skinned Aryans and the darker Dravidians, the latter group being forced to the bottom of the social and occupational scale. Thus, both economic elements and color gave rise to castes. (The Hindu word for caste is *varna*, meaning color.) Additional distinctions arose from vocational considerations. Rulers, warriors, priests, farmers, and artisans were set apart by special duties with distinct privileges assigned to each caste. Eventually the Brahmans, or priests, gained the upper hand, since the religious aspects of social stability were the most fundamental. The priestly position was made secure when voluminous detailed descriptions of the rites and ceremonies were written down in Brahmanas. These writings date from about 700 B.C.; the Brahmans were required to read and follow them. This caused another distinction to be made—between the literate and the illiterate; the educated controlled the uneducated.

Philosophical concepts underwent important changes as a result of the shift from the Vedic view of this-worldly salvation to two new emphases: (1) belief in the transmigration and reincarnation of souls (*samsara*), and (2) belief in an inexorable law of cause and effect which operates upon and determines the direction of successive reincarnations (*karma*). Hinduism in this Brahmanic period interpreted life as if it were a wheel of unceasing rebirth. The goal of religion and philosophy

was to discover ways of release from the revolving cycles. The Hindus no longer desired a long life; the problem now was finding a means for escape from life. Linked with the concept of rebirth was the law of *karma*, holding simply that "as ye sow, so shall ye reap." What you are and what you can become depend on what you have been and have done, either in this life or some other. This impersonal law makes no exceptions, and the task of religion is to neutralize the law, to satisfy its demands, and to offer sacrifices. In time the decline of the old Vedic gods was effected, and the search for other explanations of the universe began. This led to the formulation of the great philosophies of India, with their characteristic explanation of the universe as one single whole, and their strong pantheistic tendencies.

Through most of Hindu history, *samsara*, *karma*, and caste have been three facets of a single world view. Also, the way of knowledge, the way of devotion, and the way of works have been linked by the very nature of reality. Within a single lifetime, the search for salvation may proceed through all three ways, resulting in a final stage in which the individual lives as a *Sannyasin*, or holy man. In this stage he leaves his hermitage and mingles in the world, but not as one of the world. Extreme disregard of all fleshly requirements joins with rigorous physical and mental discipline through *yoga* to free man from the wheel of life and the demands of this world. The final goal is then achieved—beyond good and evil and all finite things; this is *samadhi*. The true character of all life and suffering would be seen, for they are not real but *maya*—that illusory power which causes us to believe in the phenomenal world. When this condition is achieved, meditation can proceed without regard for physical needs. Thus the ideal of self-salvation and retirement from active life is realized.

In addition to the Vedic, Brahmanic, and Upanishadic literature, the most beloved and influential classic of Hinduism is the Bhagavad-Gita, which extols the way of devotion—a personal communion with a personal god—as a valid way to salvation. Caste obligations are the most important in this quest for salvation, but what is done in accordance with the way of works out of a sense of duty must continue to be related to the way of knowledge; hence the way of devotion is related to both the ways of knowledge and of works. This identification is the source of the doctrine of nonviolence (*ahimsa*), which the Hindu nationalist leader, Mahatma Gandhi (1869–1948), used as an organized method of social conflict and resolution. Classical Hindu ways of work and devotion are still very much alive in contemporary India, and they serve religious ends as well as purposes of political and social reform.

■**BUDDHISM.**—Between the eighth and the fourth century B.C., additional philosophical writings were added to the total body of Hindu scripture. These writings, in the form of dia-

UNITED NATIONS

GOVERNMENT OF INDIA TOURIST OFFICE

INFORMATION SERVICE OF INDIA

RELIGIONS OF INDIA. This Hindu temple (*above right*) in Bhubneshwar dates from the 800s AD. For Sikhs, the most sacred shrine is the Golden Temple (*above left*) in Amritsar. A center for Muslims is the Jama Masjid *(below right)* in Delhi, the largest mosque in India. This Jain temple (*below left*) is located in Amravati, in southeastern India.

INFORMATION SERVICE OF INDIA

UNITED NATIONS

BUDDHISM. The "Wall of the Buddhas" (*above*) is near the ancient city of Bamian, in Afghanistan. It contains cave dwellings and two colossal statues of the Buddha. The famous statue of the reclining Buddha (*below*) is located in the Himalayas, in Katmandu, Nepal.

UNITED NATIONS

logues and monologues, are called *Upanishads*. They direct thought to the higher forms of knowledge in which the ultimate One, Brahman, is the source and totality of all being. To know this truth is to be saved. This was the way of truth of Gautama (563–483 B.C.), the Indian philosopher and founder of Buddhism.

Gautama, who came to be called Gautama Buddha, immersed himself in the philosophical classics and the practices of self-mortification, while he conducted a passionate search for what is called his "enlightenment." Holding to basic doctrines of *samsara* and *karma*, and adhering to the Hindu version of man's religious problem, he taught the *Fourfold Noble Truths* which are central to Buddhism. The first of these truths asserts that all is sorrow, or *dukkha;* the second, that sorrow springs from desire or craving; the third, that desire may be eliminated; and the fourth, that desire may be eliminated and sorrow overcome by following the middle path—the *Eightfold Noble Path.* This path is marked by (1) right belief, (2) right aspiration, (3) right speech, (4) right conduct, (5) right livelihood, (6) right effort, (7) right mindfulness (frame of mind), and (8) right rapture. The state of deliverance to which the path leads is *Nirvana*—a state of bliss or nothingness, supreme wisdom, the indescribable. What separated Buddha's teachings most sharply from Hinduism was his belief in the universality of the Way; no caste distinctions were recognized by him, whether based on tradition, color, vocation, or social status. This inspired a geographically and spiritually universal faith. With the help of a monastic order and missionary purpose, Buddhism soon spread beyond India to Ceylon, Burma, China, and Japan, as well as to Southeast Asia. Many variations mark the different types of Buddhism in these lands. The sharpest distinction is between southern, or *Hinayana,* Buddhism and northern, or *Mahayana,* Buddhism. Devotional practices as well as the roles of priests are markedly different in these two schools. Although it began as a reform move-

MONKMEYER PRESS PHOTO SERVICE

BUDDHA in bronze, cast in medieval Japan.

ment within Hinduism, Buddhism developed widely divergent views as to the goal of religion and its attainment. It grew strong in distant lands, but in India it was reabsorbed into Hinduism and has practically disappeared from the land of its origin.

Mahayana Buddhism had its greatest impact in Japan, which it reached via China and Korea in the twelfth and thirteenth centuries. One development is known as *Zen.*

There is no point at which the essence of Zen approaches the forms and aims of traditional Western religions. Zen has no sacred scripture whose word is law and no rigid doctrine or dogma. There is no saviour and no promise of eternal rewards. The essence of Zen may be summed up:

> A special transmission outside the Scriptures;
> No dependence upon words and letters;
> Direct pointing to the soul of man;
> Seeing into one's own nature and the attainment of Buddahood.

To the Western mind, Zen may be validly thought of as a way of life rather than as a religion. Its goal is the attainment of *satori,* a final state of illumination which releases man from the bondage of dualism. No longer is there a concern for intellectual explanations of birth, death, and ultimate purpose. *Satori* brings about an intuitive understanding of one's self; as a result, man is able to live a contented life.

Religion in Persia.—The plateau of Iran —an arid, windswept land where, for early inhabitants, life was at its best a severe struggle, and where the elements seem to be in perpetual conflict—provided the home for a people closely akin to the Aryan invaders of India among whom Hinduism developed. These peoples were also related to the early settlers of Greece and Rome. There were many striking similarities among these geographically separated peoples, in both language and religion. A luxuriant polytheism of nature deities, a vast priesthood, and a ritualized form of religion were all to be found on this plateau. However, with the work of the prophet Zoroaster, or Zarathustra, religion was reformed. He introduced innovations which resulted in the formation of Zoroastrianism. Zoroaster is thought to have lived in the seventh century B.C., around the time of Buddha, Lao-tse, Confucius, and Jeremiah. The little that is known about him is available in the *Gathas.* (These ancient poems have been included in the Zoroastrian scriptures, the *Avesta.*) According to tradition, Zoroaster, after spending many years in meditation in desert places, finally received his revelation from *Ahura Mazda,* the Zoroastrian god, and became a prophet.

Three emphases are found in Zoroaster's teaching. He rejected polytheism in favor of one god—Ahura Mazda, later known as *Ormuzd.* He declared that God was good, and that evil resulted from the spirit of evil— *Angra Mainyu,* who was the antith-

esis of Ahura Mazda. Conflict between the two forces is the major motif; it is reflected in the many lesser conflicts between light and darkness, truth and falsehood, right and wrong. His final emphasis is upon a day of judgments, when the good are rewarded by Ahura Mazda, and the evil suffer the torments of hell. It was Zoroaster's policy to try first to convert princes and then the people; he was successful in the conversion of King Vishtasp, and thus his religion became the religion of the age. His reforms included a high estimation of daily tasks and their faithful performance; all of this was thought to aid the triumph of good over evil.

In time, however, the old gods reappeared and Zoroaster was included among them. Mithra assumed a place of particular prominence; angels and devils held important places; and belief in the future life was centered upon a doctrine of the resurrection of the body before the final judgment. Extreme ritualism was introduced by a priestly caste, probably the Magi (priests of ancient Persia or Media), and purity of ritual worship was of the highest importance. The ethical emphasis was not entirely lost, and the modern descendants of Zoroastrianism, the Parsis of India, are a progressive, well-educated, and healthy leaven in that society, where they exercise an influence out of proportion to their numerical strength. Even though there are those Parsis who wish to initiate reforms and use a modern language for worship instead of the Avestan language, there is also a conservative group which holds to the ancient heritage.

Religion in Japan.—Japan, like China, has more than one religion; however, it has only one which is native, and that is *Shinto*—"The Way of the Gods." The other primary religions are Buddhism and Christianity. The beginnings of Shinto lie in the far-distant past, in nature worship and in the deification of individuals, such as emperors and war heroes. The festivals of Shinto deal with the changing seasons. The most notable of these is the food offering which is meant to be performed by a newly crowned *mikado,* or emperor; in the eleventh month after his accession, the emperor himself is to offer the food to the gods. Another less elaborate festival is known as the *new tasting,* when the first rice of the new harvest is eaten. Other festivals have to do with the planting season, prayers for rain, and daily meals. Simple, unadorned temples are characteristic of Shinto, and both the priesthood and the ethical code are equally unpretentious. Magic and ethics seem to be intermixed without discrimination, thus indicating an undeveloped religion. A prevalent feature of Shinto is the purification rituals used to wash away evil.

In ancient legends the story is told of the creation of the Japanese islands by two gods, *Izanagi* and *Izanami;* they were supposedly the progenitors of numerous gods, of the emperors, and of all Japanese people. Belief in the divine descent of the emperors is the basis of Shinto on a state level and there is fierce loyalty associated with it. According to some scholars, recent developments have brought about a more spiritualistic, idealistic, and even ethical religion. Although Shinto is native to Japan it has a relatively small ceremonial following. Buddhism, existing alongside Shinto, is sometimes not readily distinguishable from it, but it has had favorable development in Japan since its arrival in the sixth century. Buddhism gained its strength through institutions—temples, schools, hospitals, and also through developments in the arts and sciences. Although Buddhism came to Japan from China and Korea, the Japanese soon adapted all of Buddhism to their own ways of life and thought. In the nineteenth century, Shinto revived and threatened Buddhism's supremacy in Japan. But the inadequacies of Shintoism and recent political changes have reversed this tendency. Now Japan is a nation of three religious movements—Buddhism, Shinto, and Christianity; the latter is a small minority faith practiced predominantly among the educated groups.

Religion in Greece and Rome.—Primitive religions worshipping the powers of nature were carried by successive waves of invasion into the Grecian peninsula. These were added to the relatively civilized developments of early Minoan culture. Early Greek religion represents a fusion of these two streams. In spite of the fact that ancient Greece was composed of isolated communities which existed in small pockets scattered throughout the valleys and plains, a universally accepted pattern of religious belief gradually emerged. *Zeus,* the supreme deity, was viewed anthropomorphically. He was thought to dwell on Mount Olympus, from which he ruled the world. The other gods carried out different functions under Zeus's general direction. Yet each of these gods retained a separate identity; the pantheon is filled with representatives of almost all the natural forces, all phases of human life, and all aspects of Greek civilization. Major figures include *Hera,* the wife of Zeus and goddess of marriage; *Poseidon,* god of the sea; *Athena,* goddess of civilization; *Artemis,* goddess of the moon; *Ares,* god of war; *Apollo,* god of the sun and of the oracle at Delphi; *Aphrodite,* the goddess of love; *Demeter,* goddess of fertility; and endless others.

In the sixth century, the older religion, so strongly connected to this world through its nature deities, was challenged by a religion which claimed to transcend the world. This new religious movement, known as *Orphism,* was more individualistic, more highly ritualistic than the old religion, and carried a zealous missionary message of salvation. It was one of a group of mystery religions which flourished in the later period of Grecian history. The most important of its mysteries centered about the goddess *Demeter.* Its rites were performed at the city Eleusis, where it was part of the state religion.

The philosophical preoccupation for which Greece is most noted also left its mark on religious tradition. Not all of the philosophers of Greece were concerned with religion, but most of them accepted the concept of ethical monotheism. The poets and dramatists, who had a more direct access to the people than the philosophers did, emphasized the unity of the moral order of the world and its divine rule under Zeus. Although it is no longer a living religion, the influence of Olympian religion on literature and art, with the influence of the mystery religions and the philosophers upon Christianity, is still such as to make Greek religion a living force in the world.

■ **ROMAN RELIGION.**—There are many similarities between the Greeks and the Romans with respect to religion; the most striking difference between the two lies in the fact that the Romans did not think of the gods as persons while the Greeks did. A more animistic view prevailed, even though Jupiter could be identified with Zeus. The basic concerns were apparently different and nature spirits were not individualized. Early Romans had many gods who were divided into categories according to function. However, they had no temples, no religious images, and no special priests. As the state developed, changes took place in religion—some of the household gods then became gods of the state. *Janus,* keeper of the city gate; *Vesta,* caretaker of the sacred fire; the *Penates,* guardians of the economy; and *Mars,* the god of war, were all originally household deities. In most cases the priests were merely public officials, responsible for carrying out the proper religious observances.

As the Roman world came into contact with other civilizations, many changes occurred, especially in regard to the number of gods admitted to the pantheon. Most of these were Greek, with Latinized names—Aphrodite thus became Venus; Hera became Juno; Ares was known as Mars; Artemis as Diana, and so on. Finally, as Rome extended its rule, its pantheon became the pantheon of the world. It was Roman policy to be tolerant toward the gods of all religions and hospitable toward their worship, as long as it did not interfere with the state.

Among the new religions which thus penetrated the Roman world were the oriental cults, offering a well-defined plan of salvation and the future life—a topic of very little interest in Roman religion. The Isis cult, with its story of the resurrection of Osiris, brought the message of immortality; the Mithraic cult was of equal power. Throughout the empire, either Christianity or some similar religion was practiced, but not in Rome itself. There the old worship was carried forward, including worship of the emperor, and his deification upon death. However, Roman religion yielded rapidly to the sweeping power of Christianity. During the reign of Constantine, it became the state-acknowledged religion. Nevertheless some of the old religions and

mystery cults left indelible impressions on this new religion, which in less than a century had grown from a small sect within Judaism to the official religion of Rome.

Judaism

■ **HISTORICAL JUDAISM.**—About 2000 B.C., a Semitic tribal chieftain, known to later generations as Abraham, left the land of his birth and led a group of wandering tent-dwellers on a westward migration. For the Jewish people, the whole of history is seen in religious terms; Israel is considered the "seed of Abraham," and he is known as the first of the patriarchs. The stories of the patriarchs (Abraham, Isaac, and Jacob), and the tales of Jacob's twelve sons (most notably Joseph) indicate a tribal unity and social organization like that of similar nomadic groups throughout the Middle East. Many of the religious customs of Judaism are also typically nomadic and can be associated with animistic religious patterns. However, one striking difference is found in the Hebrew concept of covenant—the sense of personal relation between the Jewish people and their God, which is based on the decision or the choice of God and involves obligations for men and promises of blessing from Yahweh, or God. This covenant relationship is central to the long course of Israel's life and worship. Trusting obedience and divine commitment bind the people of faith to their God, who is known as the Lord of history.

The prophets of Israel, who epitomized its faith, proclaimed a transcendent God who at the same time is active in the world—He is encountered as divine will in history and in society. This God has a purpose for His world and for its peoples; this is indicated not only in the promises of the covenant which bind God and man together in a correlative manner, but it is also shown in the requirements of brotherhood among all men, in the high value placed on time and on history, and in the very intention of creation itself, as in the creation narratives. From the relatively tiny land of Israel have sprung three of the world's greatest religious traditions—Judaism, Christianity, and Islam. Hebrew religious life and thought have thus influenced the cultures of most of the world. The record of Israel's faith is to be found in the Hebrew scriptures (known as the Old Testament in the Bible).

Around 1300 B.C., Moses led Abraham's descendants, the Hebrews, out of their Egyptian slavery to the threshold of the promised land—Canaan. From the events of Moses' lifetime, the Hebrew faith was born. The *Exodus* from Egypt and the giving of the law at Mount Sinai stand at the center of the Hebrew view of history; this was the crucial disclosure of God's will for human life, and all interpretation ultimately comes back to these events. God's revelation of Himself to Moses was a specific historical crisis. The divine command and Moses' response set the note of historical destiny and determined the ethical concepts which are basic not

ARNOLD EAGLE

THE TORAH, from the Hebrew "law" or "teaching," refers to the first five Books of Moses.

only to divine deliverance but also to human destiny. The Ten Commandments which God gave to Moses dictate the terms of Israel's service to God and they also contain rules covering moral, social, and cultic duties. Of central importance is the emphasis which the law places upon monotheism—the service of the one and only creator, God, is the whole meaning of Israel's existence.

After the time of Moses, the people underwent a period of intertribal strife; however, through the work of judges, kings, and prophets, they finally became a nation—a unified kingdom. Prophetic religion arose when Israel's national existence was declining and was threatened; yet it stands in dramatic continuity with the whole of Israel's history. The prophets called the people of Israel to a renewed awareness of the covenant relationship and of the obedience which was expected of them. The prophets—Elijah, Ezekiel, Amos, Hosea, Isaiah, Micah, Jeremiah, and others—worked under the command of God to reform and purify Israel's understanding of their God and of what was required of them in the service of God. Some of the high points in the literature of Israel are the writings of these prophets.

The prophetic writings and the careers of the prophets cover the period from the middle of the eighth century B.C. through the Babylonian Exile (imposed by the Chaldean king Nebuchadnezzar in 586 B.C. after his conquest of Judea) and well into the post-Exilic period, when some of the dreams for a restoration of the community of Israel in the homeland were being fulfilled. The intense preoccupation of the prophets with God as sovereign, creator, and Lord of history persisted throughout, linked with a sense of the divine judgment, and the ultimate hope of the fulfillment of God's purposes. Prophetic thought was also marked by a certain skepticism toward ritual, which the prophets felt had degenerated into empty

formality. Along with the decline of Israel's fortunes, the repeated invasions which she was undergoing, and the forced exile of her strongest citizens, there persisted the undisturbed hope of an eventual kingdom of happiness and prosperity. The coming of a Messiah was to prepare the way for this new kingdom; the Messiah was to bring about either an earthly kingdom or an otherworldly kingdom at the end of history—this was the hope which nourished the people's faith, and it is still an aspect of contemporary Judaism and Christianity, for the Christians feel that the Messiah has already come in the person of Jesus Christ.

■POST-EXILIC PERIOD.—After 538 B.C., small groups of Jews returned from Babylonia to reoccupy Jerusalem and the surrounding country. A new temple was built and the gathering and editing of the documents of Israel's history and faith was advanced under the general supervision of a group of priestly scholars. For priestly religion, sacrifice was of great importance and the keeping of the laws was most emphasized; thus the major writings from this period deal with the details of religious observances (the purification rituals most particularly) and with the details of the law formulated in the *Torah.* Through the giving of the Torah, or Law, God had spoken to his people and set them apart for a special task.

In this post-Exilic community, many different patterns of thought and faith appeared; the priestly and legal traditions of thought persisted; there was the strong devotional aspect of Judaism; and in literature, two distinct traditions emerged—the Wisdom literature (such as Ecclesiastes, Proverbs, and Job) and the apocalyptic idea of history building to a climax: a great calamity was to come in the near future which would serve as preparation for the dawn of a new age. This was a desperate way of saying what Israel's prophets had said all along—that even amid crisis

God is the ruler of history.

Between 63 B.C. and 132 A.D., when Palestine was a Roman province, conflicting schools of thought arose among the Jews. The divergent views which they held were of importance in the shaping of later Judaism. Among these groups the *Pharisees* were most concerned with the faith of the fathers; they held strictly to the Scriptures as the norm for judging all of human life. They did, however, add interpretations to provide for the contemporary situation. The *Sadducees,* by contrast, were a more accommodating party and enjoyed the favor of the ruling powers, while the *Essenes* lived under strict religious discipline in monastic communities. The *Zealots* were the more nationalistic and rebellious group; they were more radical than the *Herodians,* a party among the Jews which favored home-rule. Political fortunes also greatly affected the religion of this post-Biblical period, and increasing attention was given to the fulfillment of the Apocalypse. The war which began in 67 A.D. culminated in the siege of Jerusalem and the destruction of the post-Exilic temple (70 A.D.). As the Jews scattered and wandered from land to land, they took their faith with them, their Law, and their ways. These Jews, as well as those already scattered around the world, are known as the *Jews of the Dispersion* (the Diaspora). It was among these people that the Judaism of the modern period developed—religious rituals were elaborated; the synagogue took on a role of increasing importance; their Scriptures were translated into Greek and many other languages, and the Jewish philosophical traditions were further developed. This was also the period of formation for the *Talmud,* the authoritative body of Jewish tradition. The Talmud is composed of *Mishnah* and *Gemara.* The *Mishnah,* which was formulated during the second century A.D., is the codification of the oral law of Judaism; it is a body of legal-religious decisions which develop the thought of the Mosaic Law. The *Gemara,* supplementary material which comments on the *Mishnah,* was outlined during the fourth century A.D. with additions made during the sixth century. Within the religious life, the Torah was interpreted in the temple, in the synagogues, and in schools; oral interpretation was provided by the rabbis, among whom the names of Shammai and Hillel stand out.

Whether in Dispersion or in the homeland, Judaism involves a concrete way of life. Characteristic of Judaism are: (1) the observance of the Sabbath, (2) loyalty to the dietary laws, (3) circumcision, (4) synagogue attendance, (5) *Bar-Mitzvah*—a ceremony to incorporate boys of the age of thirteen into the religious group, (6) the keeping of holy days and festivals, such as *Passover*—the commemoration of the Exodus; *Shabuoth* (the Feast of Tabernacles)—involving the building of huts in memory of the forty years of wandering in the desert; *Rosh Hashanah* (New Year); and *Yom Kippur* (Day of Atonement)—a day of repentance.

GERARD DAVID, MUSÉE COMMUNALE, BRUGES

THE BAPTISM of Christ by John the Baptist marked the start of Christ's public life.

DIRK BOUTS, ST. PETERS, LOUVAIN

THE LAST SUPPER with the apostles took place on the evening before Christ's death.

For the faithful Jew, religion is what it has been for the fathers, not contemplation or speculation, but the concrete performance of what is required within an ongoing covenant between God and His people.

Christianity.—Christianity first began as part of Judaism and many of its basic ideas are essentially in accord with the Hebraic tradition. The Hebrew Scriptures are the Old Testament of the Christian Bible; for the earliest Christians, the Scriptures were exactly what they were for the Jews of the time. It was the Messianic hope of Israel which was believed to have been fulfilled in Jesus Christ; He was acclaimed by His earliest followers "the Anointed One" in whom the new age of the Kingdom of God had begun. Not much is known of the early life of Jesus except the little which is contained in the Gospels. These books, standing at the beginning of the New Testament, tell of His birth and of several incidents related to the prophecy of His coming; also they provide a few glimpses of His youth. However, what stands out most in the Gospel accounts are these things: that the coming of Christ was prepared for by a prophet—John the Baptist; that His birth was an astonishing and unique event; that He was born and grew up in humble surroundings; and that the Gospel authors believed Him to stand in the Messianic tradition and in the line of King David whose reign served as its model.

Jesus' baptism, which was performed by John the Baptist, marked the beginning of His public life and ministry. A time of retreat in the wilderness, where He turned back temptation, confirmed his special vocation. His public career involved preaching the imminent coming of the new kingdom, calling for repentance and obedience to God, and performing miracles of healing and exorcism

(driving out evil spirits). Jesus also surrounded Himself with a group of twelve disciples, and gave them intensive teaching in preparation for the events which would mark the climax of His life and the beginning of their ministry.

The Gospels tend to imply that the high point of Jesus' relationship with the disciples comes with their confession of His Messiahship: "Thou art the Christ, the Son of the living God" (Matt. 16:16). (The term "Christ" [*Christos*] is the Greek translation of the Hebrew word "Messiah.") Because of the likelihood that this claim would be regarded as blasphemous by the leaders of Judaism and as subversive by the Roman authorities, Jesus enjoined secrecy upon His disciples. Although Jesus was deeply influenced by various elements in the Hebrew prophetic tradition concerning the Messiah, His view was not altogether consonant with the expectations of His contemporaries. He therefore redefined and altered its meaning for His followers, discussed with them His unavoidable death and assured them of His continued presence in the Spirit.

The last days of Jesus' life, His death, and His resurrection form nearly half of the Gospels. This last week was filled with many incidents which showed His authority, in its spiritual and nonpolitical nature, and the way in which it conflicted with that of both the Romans and the Jews. After the decisive turning point in His ministry, when He was acknowledged to be the Messiah, Jesus started for Jerusalem, timing His arrival to coincide with the Passover festival. His entrance into Jerusalem amid popular demonstrations carried clear messianic implications—yet instead of riding on a war horse, Jesus came as a man of peace on the back of a donkey. On Thursday of the last week, the disciples secretly ar-

ranged for a room where they might share the Passover meal with their Master. The bread and wine of the traditional Passover meal were reinterpreted by Jesus as His own body and blood, through which a new covenant was made between God and men. After the meal and a time of private prayer in the Garden of Gethsemane, a crowd, sent by the Jewish authorities and directed by the traitorous disciple Judas, took Jesus prisoner. He was tried on charges of blasphemy, which carried the death penalty. Because Roman permission was necessary, there was a further trial the next morning before the governor, Pontius Pilate, which resulted in the actual sentence on a charge of sedition. Thus the short earthly life of Jesus was ended by His crucifixion that same day.

■**EARLY CHURCH.**—The teachings of Jesus emphasize the love of God and the reality of His Kingdom. Faith is said to be an integral part of the good life, and both nature and history are seen not only as the products of God's creative activity but also as the spheres of His continuing care. The strong moral dimension present in Jesus' teachings led to a summary of the Law and of the prophets which held love above all other things—the love of God and of man. Jesus taught the unity of precept and practice—indeed His life was the embodiment of what He taught. After His death and resurrection, the disciples, remembering His teachings, established the Church. It was born of the faith that Jesus' death was not the end but the beginning of His rule as the Lord of Life; the Spirit (or Holy Ghost) was given to the Church to carry on in Jesus' place. Early chapters of the Book of the Acts of the Apostles, found in the New Testament of the Bible, contain a record of the early history of the Church. This is a vivid account of the gift of the Spirit to the Church and of the apostles' preaching concerning Jesus as Messiah and resurrected Lord. It is followed by accounts of the early spread of Christianity in a missionary movement. (St. Paul, or Paul of Tarsus, is one of the leading figures in this movement.) Most of those who believed in Jesus as Messiah were faithful Jews who kept the law and worshipped in the temple; yet they went out to proclaim the "good news"—the Gospel. Wherever they found groups of believers they instructed them in the practice of the Last Supper—the breaking of bread and the prayers which are a perpetual memorial of Jesus' sacrifice.

Such a history is incomplete without special mention of Saint Peter. The most prominent of the twelve apostles, Peter received Christ's call while fishing in the Sea of Galilee. Christ entered the boat, addressed the multitude, and then turned to Peter and his brother Andrew, saying: "Come follow me, and I will make you fishers of men" (Matt. 4:18-22). At once they "left their nets and their father" to follow Him. The Bible also makes it clear that Peter was present at almost all of the climactic moments of Christ's human life. He was a witness to Christ's transfiguration, and was also with Him at Gethsemane and at the Last Supper. Luke (24-34) also tells us that after the Resurrection, it was to Peter that Christ made one of His first appearances. Finally and most significantly, it was to Peter that Christ entrusted His priestly power. "And I say to thee, thou art Peter, and upon this rock I will build my Church, and the gates of hell shall not prevail against it. And I will give thee the keys of the kingdom of heaven; and whatever thou shalt bind upon earth shall be bound also in heaven, and whatever thou shalt loose on earth shall be loosed in heaven" (Matt. 16:13).

A new source of difficulty for the early Christian community arose over the admittance of the non-Jews, or *Gentiles,* in the Mediterranean world to the Church. Not all of the Jewish Christians were completely committed to everything in the Torah; when Gentiles were added to their number and the strength of their influence increased, the break between the Church and Judaism could no longer be avoided. Central to this period was Paul of Tarsus, who, being well-schooled in Judaism and a devout Pharisee, was at first an avowed enemy of the Church. However, because of a strange revelatory experience while traveling on the road to Damascus, he was converted to Christianity, becoming its foremost missionary, advocate, and interpreter. He is as much the hero of the second part of Acts as Peter is of the first.

Paul dedicated himself to establishing the Church beyond Jerusalem and Palestine, especially in the Gentile cities along the Mediterranean coast. His interpretations of the Christian faith, found in the letters which he wrote to his missionary churches, comprise a major part of the New Testament writings. Paul felt that life "in Christ" meant freedom from the burdens of the Law (Christ had already fulfilled its basic demands); yet he also felt that the new Christian life brought about a regeneration and moral renewal which fulfilled the Law. The difference is that for Paul, the keeping of the Law is the product of man's satisfactory relation to God and not the means of achieving it. This view was rooted in his own experience; on the basis of it, he advocated that Gentiles should not have to complete the requirements of Jewish law before being baptized into the Church.

■ **CHURCH AND STATE.**—Because of the Church's contact with Hellenism and with Greek philosophy, early Christian writers made an effort to translate the Gospel into terms current in the Mediterranean world. Christianity was probably viewed not only as an illicit movement, but also as merely one of the many oriental mystery cults which flooded the Roman Empire at the time. Many aspects of the new religion were determined by the fact that its environment was chiefly hostile, superstitious, and philosophically oriented. The Christians' refusal to worship Caesar—if "Christ is Lord" then it could not also be that "Caesar is Lord"—led to persecutions, martyr-

doms, and increased conflict between the Church and the Empire. Although Christians were willing to believe in the good of the Empire, to follow its laws, and to claim citizenship in it, the Church was not granted the status of a recognized religion until the early part of the fourth century. It did gain tolerance, and soon after that the Emperor Constantine made Christianity the official state religion. Even though the fear of further persecution had ended, there were still the perils of compromise and weakened convictions to be faced. Whether the Church conquered the Empire or the Empire conquered the Church is still an unanswered question.

There were two basic problems confronting the Church in the ensuing period: the need to provide for the organization of the Church, and the need to state the exact nature and meaning of the Christian faith, especially in relation to other religions and philosophies. A body of Christian thought and teaching was finally developed, some of which was related to classical Greek culture—this is the basis of the Church's educational policies. There was also a systematic theological statement which was meant to serve as the norm of right belief. The earliest statements of Christian faith were the *creeds* formulated by the Church—among these is the *Apostles' Creed* (a statement of faith by the Roman Church, the original form written in Greek and dating from some time before 250 A.D.). These creeds are a reflection of the controversies of the time, and are to a great extent responses to prevailing heresies. Among the major creeds are those formulated by the *Council of Nicaea* (325 A.D.) and the *Council of Chalcedon* (451 A.D.) It was the question of authority in religious practices and in interpretation

Religions of the World

Christians	850,000,000
Roman Catholics	475,000,000
Greek Orthodox	150,000,000
Protestants	225,000,000
Lutherans	70,000,000
Presbyterians	41,000,000
Baptists	40,000,000
Episcopalians	30,000,000
Methodists	12,000,000
Mormons	2,210,000
Disciples of Christ	2,100,000
Congregationalists	2,000,000
Latter Day Saints	1,240,000
Jehovah's Witnesses	625,000
Mennonites	300,000
Christian Scientists	269,000
Moravians	265,000
Unitarians	128,000
Society of Friends	108,000
Others	23,000,000
Moslems	350,000,000
Buddhists	350,000,000
Hindus	300,000,000
Confucianists	300,000,000
Taoists	50,000,000
Shintoists	25,000,000
Jews	12,000,000
Zoroastrianists	1,000,000

Source: Landis, Benson Y., *World Religion,* E. P. Dutton & Co., 1964

of the faith which led to the problem of Church organization. Resident bishops gradually began to supplant traveling evangelists, and the ministry became a full-time occupation—one which set the clergy apart from the laity by ordination and by the taking of vows. By the middle of the fifth century, the authority of the bishop of Rome was, if not uncontested, at least widely recognized and highly respected. The early simplicity of Christian worship was greatly elaborated and the patterns followed in worship were more and more frequently those set by the Church of Rome.

With the division of the Empire into eastern and western segments, the cultural, theological, and liturgical differences within the Church increased. This culminated, in the eleventh century, in the formal separation of the Eastern or Orthodox churches from those of the West. Until the Protestant Reformation in the sixteenth century, it was the Church of Rome—the Holy Catholic Church—which served as the unchallenged religious authority in the West and the principal formative influence in Western civilization. Within this church developed the doctrine, organization, and practice which have become modern Christianity. Among its permanent contributions must be included art and architecture, the preservation and transmission of literature, and the formulation of a philosophical and theological thought which managed to relate, and often harmonize, knowledge based on faith with objective or rational knowledge. Although Christian thinkers have held many different positions on the problem of faith and knowledge, it may be said that most views are either in line with or informed by the views of Augustine, Anselm, Abelard, or Thomas Aquinas. In the thought of these Christian scholars we find much that is basic to the rich and broad heritage of Christian belief.

■ **PROTESTANT REFORMATION.**—Although the historic faith of Christendom can claim wide acceptance, there is great diversity within Christianity on questions of doctrine, authority, social relations, the ministry, and the liturgy. Cultural and political factors often enhance these controversies. There is a wide gap separating the Eastern and Western churches, and an even wider one separating their thought from the ideas of the Reformation. The complex historical movement known as the *Protestant Reformation* was related to the Renaissance, to the rise of modern nationalism, and to the shift from feudalism to an urban, middle-class society. Yet it also had distinctly religious and philosophical sources. What has been called "the Protestant principle" is as old as the prophetic tradition. It holds that all human life stands under the judgment of God; thus, nothing human or man-made can properly be considered equal with God or given the allegiance which belongs to God alone. On this basis, opposition to the power (and the decadence) of the Roman papacy became a central issue in the Protestant movement. The deep and

LUTHER, leader of the German Reformation.

ANTI-LUTHER cartoon, sixteenth century.

intense conviction of the sovereignty of God was linked with an equally firm belief that human salvation results not from man's works but from the grace of God. The Reformation rested entirely on the authority of the Bible, which was believed to be the sole source of Christian faith. Because of the central place which the Bible occupied in Protestant thought, it was translated into the languages of the people. It was printed, distributed, and subjected to extensive critical study—causing the Protestant movement to spread rapidly in Europe and to add force to the people's demands for religious liberty. Although many prepared the way for the Reformation, Martin Luther and John Calvin were its spearheads on the Continent. They left upon it the imprint of their own experiences, scholarship, and theological emphases, thus giving rise to the two major streams of Continental Protestantism called Lutheranism and Calvinism.

The English Reformation included national and political, as well as religious, factors. A deep-seated national tradition, embracing all aspects of culture, and reinforced by the strength of the Protestant movement within the Church, eventually led England to break with Rome. The resulting Anglican tradition assumed its distinctive form through the preparation of *The Book of Common Prayer,* the development of an episcopal form of government, the adoption of the "Thirty-nine Articles," the acceptance of Richard Hooker's writing, and the translation of the Bible into Elizabethan English (the King James Version). There were extreme groups who wanted to "purify" religious observances and church government to an even more radical degree. These were the *Puritans,* who played an important role not only in English history but also in that of the New World. Other extremists formed sects which dissociated themselves from the Church, refused all compromise with the world, and renounced the

world or forsook the Church entirely, in the interest of exclusivism. These groups include the *Waldensians, Anabaptists, Mennonites,* and the *Quakers,* along with various forms of *Pietism* and *Separatism.* Not only have these groups been important to the strength and expansion of the Christian movement in general, but they have also influenced the churches themselves—in the rise of *Methodism* and *Congregationalism,* for example.

■**COUNTER-REFORMATION.**—The Counter-Reformation, the Catholic response to the Reformation, began within the Church as an attempt to deal with the very corruptions and distortions against which Protestants had protested; however, it also included the attempt to reassert traditional Roman Catholicism by all available means. While a number of monastic orders had arisen within the Church in earlier centuries, the Counter-Reformation was the source of a new order—the Society of Jesus (also known as the *Jesuits*). Its military founder, Ignatius Loyola (1491–1556), was of great significance in the revitalization of the clergy, in the extension of education, and in the expansion of missionary endeavors in the Far East and the New World.

The Council of Trent (1545–1563) instituted theological reforms which resulted in the Inquisition and the Index (a list of books forbidden to Catholics by ecclesiastical authority) in Spain, Italy, and France. It was not until the Vatican Council of 1870, during the time of Pope Pius IX, that the doctrine of papal infallibility was formally proclaimed by the Church. Still more recent developments include further refinement of the Roman Catholic position on the church-state relationship (this has important implications in the area of public education), the place of the Virgin Mary as the mother of Christ, and the doctrine of her Assumption, as well as the emphasis upon the seven sacraments as guideposts of worship. Only two sacraments are considered essen-

tial in Protestant churches; these are Baptism and the Lord's Supper, or Holy Eucharist; the additional five in Roman Catholicism are confirmation, penance, matrimony, holy orders (ordination), and extreme unction (preparation for death).

Christianity has been severely challenged by movements in the modern world—political, cultural, philosophical, and religious or pseudo-religious. Industrialization, urbanization, and nationalism are some of the major forces which have called for changes and revisions within traditional Christianity. The rise of science offered ideas conflicting with traditional Christian belief, especially where literal interpretation of the Scriptures was concerned, and brought about tensions which have preoccupied religious thinkers for more than a century. Emotional reactions to the challenges of science, along with the excessive fervor of some evangelical and revivalist movements, have often only served to aggravate the split between theology and rational thought, and between the church and other cultural and educational institutions. However, it may also be noted that a number of significant responses to these challenges have appeared in recent Christian thought and life. There has been a growing quest for unity in the ecumenical movement which aims both at a revitalization of the churches and at a closer identification among them. In recent years the ecumenical movement has grown beyond Protestant and Eastern Orthodox circles to include, and gain new impetus from, the Roman Catholic Church itself. There has been a theological renaissance, bringing fresh viewpoints and a more intensive study of Biblical sources and doctrines, of the traditional formulations of Christian faith, and of the basic nature of religious thought and language. Along with a quest for unity and for common criteria of authority, there has also been evidence of a new willingness on the part of the church to enter more deeply into the life of the world, in order to effect necessary social changes and to affirm the sacred and inherently Christian status of secularized culture.

Religion in the Arab World

■**ISLAM.**—At the same time that Christianity reached its height in the West (at the beginning of the fourth century), the lot of the Jew worsened. The tolerance which the Roman Empire had afforded Judaism gave way to suspicion, discrimination, and persecution. It was during this period that the Arabian civilization and Islam burst upon the world with the work of the prophet Mohammed, who was critical of both Christians and Jews. He deplored the strife and the low cultural level and standard of living among his fellow Arabs. His religious visions were in the form of oracles addressed to his fellow citizens of Mecca. Mohammed was forced to flee from Mecca to Medina—this is the event known by the Moslems as the *Hegira,* and is now marked as the beginning of their calendar (corresponding with 622 A.D.). Mohammed

ARABIAN AMERICAN OIL COMPANY

ARABIAN AMERICAN OIL COMPANY

ISLAM. The holy cities of Mecca (*right*) and Medina (*above*) are visited by many thousands of pilgrims each year (below).

SAUDI ARABIAN PUBLIC RELATIONS BUREAU

was successful in Medina as a religious, political, and military leader, and he eventually led his armies to victory over Mecca. After his death in 632 A.D., Mohammed's followers took up his religious and military conquests and did not rest until Islam spread from India to Spain.

The term "Moslem" means one who "submits"—to the sovereign will of Allah. Rigorous monotheism, proclaimed through a succession of prophets including Abraham, Moses, and Jesus and leading to Mohammed, and taught in the sacred writings of the *Koran*, is the essential basis of Islamic religion.

Among other essential aspects of Islam is a vivid belief in the Last Judgment, along with the requirements of prayer five times daily, attendance at religious services in a mosque, giving alms for care of the poor, fasting during the daytime in the holy month of Ramadan, and, if possible, making a pilgrimage to Mecca sometime during one's lifetime. The Islamic ethical code involves strict prohibitions on gambling and drinking. Mohammedan men are permitted to marry a number of women and also to divorce any of them with some degree of facility. Islam has a strict theism similar to that of Christianity and Judaism. Along with this it has a missionary movement whose zeal for converts has, at times, driven it to extreme militarism and conversion by force. Yet there have been long periods when Islam was tolerant of Jews and Christians. Since the defeat of the Moors in Spain and France, in the late fifteenth century, Islam has not been a strong influence in the West. However, expansions throughout southeast Asia and in Africa have made it an institution of much more than religious interest to the Arab peoples. One of the most important features

GRAPHIC HOUSE

A MOSLEM, shoeless, faces Mecca in prayer.

of modern Islam is that it always lowers all racial barriers; all the faithful are brethren and the spread of Islam in the name of peace, brotherhood, and temperance is now considerable. Not only is it an important living religion and an integral part of pan-Arabic nationalism, but it can also claim for itself something of the status of a world religion.

Religion Today.—It is true that the modern age has been moving away from traditional religion; yet it is still a living social force whose influence should not be underestimated. Religion is of very real importance in the lives of individuals, families, and societies. It is of significance and influence in the arts and in literature, and it contributes to man's personal views and to all types of human relationships. Religion is also of interest in the continuing movement of nationalism and in the international or intercultural aspects of modern human life.

The relationship of religion to nationalism has become one of the most vexing problems of the age. Many of the traditional religions are set in sharp conflict with the ideologies of modern history; the story of the church-war (*Kirchenkampf*) with German Nazism is well known, and the current struggle of the church with Communism is part of what has so often been called "the battle for the minds of men." Modern ideologies often serve the same function as religion—they are faiths which men live by, and as such they are inescapably in conflict with religion. Some theologians not only make the distinction between ideology and faith but also between religion and faith.

In the contemporary world, the insecurities and tensions between East and West, manifested in a prolonged Cold War, have given heightened meaning to national sovereignty and integrity. Religion has therefore been used to help define a nation's distinctive culture, to provide focus for national unity, and to establish a well-defined and secure value system. In this way religion has been an important factor in the recent history of India. America often claims religious foundations for the principle of democracy—yet the very claim of freedom requires that the nations claiming it give freedom in worship and religious practice. Thus modern nations are frequently called upon to support both positive religious feeling and neutrality with respect to religion.

The most basic religious issues, whatever the formal relationship of church and state may be, are generally ethical. It is assumed that strong religious foundations in a society support higher levels of behavior and aspiration than would otherwise exist. Therefore, however central and important theology may be to the church, much of religion is ultimately devoted not to speculation and meditation, but rather to action. Religion in the modern world must be a response to the basic questions of man's nature and destiny, his freedom and his relationships with others,

UNITED PRESS INTERNATIONAL

POPE JOHN XXIII opened the Ecumenical Council in Vatican City, Rome, in 1962.

his creaturely dependence, and his creativity in philosophy, art, science, and morality. It is when religion touches on man, his work, and his personal life that it becomes most significant. When questions concerning God are raised in an existing religious context, God is the object—or subject—not of abstract speculation, but of intimate and ultimate concern to men. It is then that moral reasoning can become informed by Carl Michalson's warning and challenge: "God is God, and man is man; this is the very structure of reality."

—J. Edward Dirks

BIBLIOGRAPHY

The Coming of Christ (Cowles/Doubleday Book). Cowles Magazines and Broadcasting, Inc., 1963.

An Encyclopedia of Religion. The Philosophical Library, Inc., 1945.

FINKELSTEIN, LOUIS (ed.). *The Jews: Their History, Culture and Religion* (3rd ed.). 2 vols. Harper & Bros., 1960.

GARD, RICHARD A. (ed.). *Buddhism* (*Great Religions of Modern Man* series, edited by Richard A. Gard). George Braziller, Inc., 1963.

LANDIS, BENSON Y. *World Religions.* E. P. Dutton & Co., Inc., 1957.

ROPS, HENRI DANIEL (ed.). *Twentieth-Century Encyclopedia of Catholicism.* Hawthorn Books, Inc., 1958–64.

WATTS, ALAN W. *The Way of Zen.* Pantheon Books, Inc., 1957.

WHITEHEAD, ALFRED N. *Religion in the Making.* The Macmillan Co., 1956.

WILLIAMS, JOHN ALDEN (ed.). *Islam* (*Great Religions of Modern Man* series, edited by Richard A. Gard). George Braziller, Inc., 1963.

VOLUME TWENTY

PLANTS

Plant life 1637
Plants 1648
Bibliography 1700

THE NEW YORK PUBLIC LIBRARY

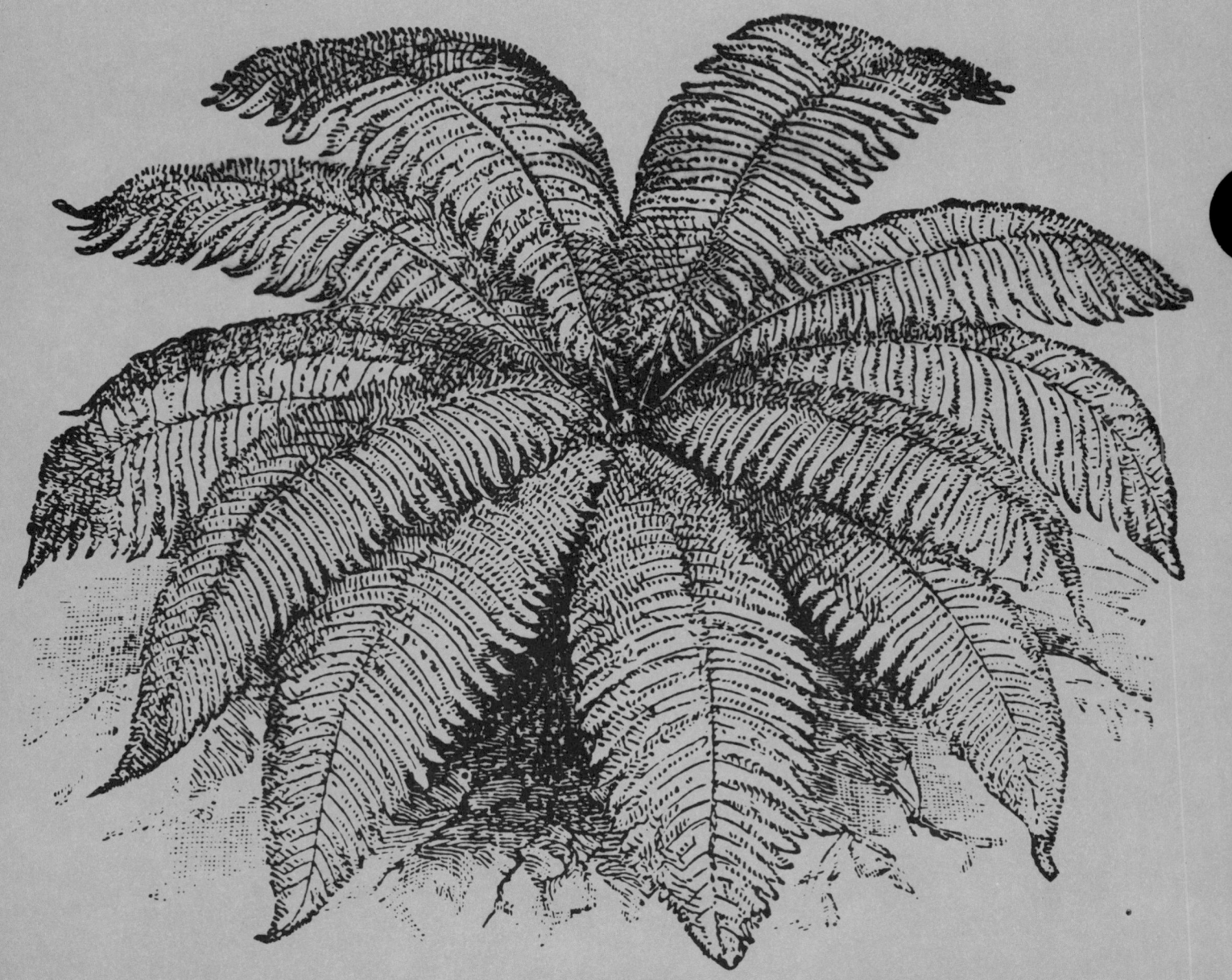

TODEA SUPERBA.

Plants

PLANT LIFE

All living organisms on earth are either animals or plants. The main characteristics that distinguish plants are ability to manufacture their own food from raw materials through the process of photosynthesis; general presence of chlorophyll; fixed location in their environment; and cellulose in their body structure.

These differentiating qualities are quite obvious in the higher forms of plant life. The acacia tree, for example, could hardly be confused with the giraffe that browses on its leaves. In the lower forms, however, the differences are not so clear: the molds and fungi, lacking in chlorophyll, cannot manufacture their own food and therefore must live parasitically on other plants; some plants ingest and devour insects; the algae, diatoms, bacteria, and many seaweeds move about freely and often vigorously in water, soil, and air; the slime molds are totally lacking in the characteristic plant building materials, cellulose. Yet all of these are plants.

In the very lowest orders the distinctions between plants and animals cannot be made at all, and in the realm of microbiology, plants and animals are considered as a single group of living organisms. This provides still more evidence of the common ancestry of plant and animal life.

Plants are literally vital to all animal life on earth. Without plants there would be no oxygen; without grass the grazing animals—and man —could not survive. Plants make up the staple food of mankind throughout the world, and only with great difficulty can man adapt himself to land where they do not thrive.

Even in the arctic wastes the chain of life depends on the simplest plants. The caribou and reindeers feed on lichens, a simple combination of algae and fungi; the seal, whose body furnishes the Eskimo with almost all the necessities of life, feeds on fish that feed on other fish, which in turn are all dependent on the simple protozoan plankton—floating sea plants.

BOTANY

The branch of biology dealing with all aspects of plant life is called *botany*. It includes the study of structure, activities, distribution, origin, classification, and uses of plants.

METROPOLITAN MUSEUM OF ART: THE CLOISTERS

NATURAL SCIENCE in the Middle Ages was studied with a naive naturalism that often wandered into the fantastic. The unicorn in this fourteenth-century tapestry is a product of the imagination; the plants are not. Most have been identified by genus and species.

Botany also touches on many other areas of study, some of which are *taxonomy*, or *plant systematics*, the grouping of related forms in a systematic order; *morphology*, the description of physical forms; *anatomy*, the phase of morphology dealing with structure; *histology*, the study of tissues; *physiology*, dealing with the processes, activities, and phenomena incidental to and characteristic of living matter; *cytology*, the study of the structure and physiology of individual cells; *pathology*, the description and investigation of the causes and control of diseases; *genetics*, the study of inheritance and breeding; *ecology*, the relationship of living organisms to their environment; and *paleobotany*, the study of fossilized plants and the evolution of plants.

In addition, there are several botanic specialities dealing with particular groups of plants. Some of these are *microbiology*, the study of microscopic forms of life; *bacteriology*, the study of bacteria; and such other branches of botany as *algology*, *mycology*, and *lichenology*, dealing with algae, fungi, and lichens, respectively.

Other related fields, once considered parts of botany but now regarded as practical sciences are *agronomy*, dealing with field-crop production; *horticulture*, dealing with greenhouse, garden, and orchard plants; and *forestry*, dealing with trees and forests.

HISTORY. The first studies of plants were primarily concerned with their magical and medicinal values; and the early stages of botany are more closely allied to myth, magic, and poetry than to the scientific method. Yet such contemporary drugs as digitalis, quinine, paregoric, and morphine had their origins in medicinal plants that for centuries have been man's pharmacological storehouse.

The first actual botanist was Theophrastus (c. 372–c. 287 BC), a pupil of Aristotle. He described and categorized plants, dividing them arbitrarily into *trees, bushes,* and *herbs.* In the first century AD Dioscorides and Pliny the Elder described many plants, stressing medical uses.

It was not until the 1500s that botany, and especially the classification of plants, became systematized. The invention of printing made possible the publication of the first *herbals,* books describing wild and cultivated plants and illustrated with woodcuts. One of the best of these herbals was written by Otto Brunfels (1488–1534), a German botanist.

Contemporary with Brunfels were Hieronymus Bock, author of *Materia Medica,* and Leonhard Fuchs (1501–1566), who wrote a glossary of technical terms, the first terminology of botany. Up to this point, attempts at systematic classification were crude at best; and the main concern of botanists was still with the medicinal virtues of plants.

Taxonomy. The need to distinguish useful plants led gradually to greater accuracy of description and eventually to an interest in *taxonomy,* the organization of the myriad plant forms in a scheme demonstrating their interrelationships.

The Italian botanist Andrea Cesalpino (1519–1603) made the first formal attempt at a methodical classification of plants. In his *De Plantis* (1583), he divided the 1,520 plants then known into 15 classes, basing his divisions on the character of the fruit. John Ray (1627–1705), an English naturalist, developed a system of natural affinities. He separated the flowering from the flowerless plants, calling them *dicotyledons* (having two seed leaves) and *monocotyledons*

NEW YORK PUBLIC LIBRARY

LINNAEUS, naturalist, physician, and philosopher, founded systematic botany.

(having one seed leaf), respectively. The same names are used today.

Linnaeus. Karl von Linné (1707–1778), the Swedish botanist who is also known by his Latin name Carolus Linnaeus, founded a system of nomenclature that was based on the characteristics of stamens and pistils; since these are the reproductive organs of the flower, the system is often called the *sexual system.* It was essentially an artificial arrangement, as Linnaeus himself knew; he considered it only a temporary method, to be used until a natural system of classification was developed.

Linnaeus also contributed much to *nomenclature,* or the naming of plants; and his *binomial method,* with one name for the *genus* and a second, qualifying word for the *species,* is universally accepted.

DARWIN was often caricatured and his ideas mocked by an angry and sceptical public.

A notable advance was made by Antoine de Jussieu (1748–1836), professor of botany at the Jardin des Plantes in Paris. The necessity for logical arrangement of the plants caused him to devote considerable time to the problem, and in his *Genera Plantarum* (1789) he outlined a plan that included the best features of Ray's and Linnaeus' systems. It was based on a close study of plant organs, made use of Linnaeus' simple definitions, and showed in general the natural relationships of plants, thus forming the basis for the natural classification predicted by Linnaeus.

Augustin de Candolle (1778–1841) showed that the natural affinities of plants must be found by a study of morphology, not of physiology.

Darwin. The most important influence on taxonomy was Darwin's theory of evolution and the origin of species by natural selection, published in 1859. "Natural" came to mean related by descent, and any classification scheme became a cross section of the course of evolution. This relationship of systematics and evolution, together with the identification and classification of new species, is the main concern of taxonomists now.

CLASSIFICATION OF PLANTS. The ordering of the more than 350,000 known forms of plants into groups of related organisms is the task of taxonomy. In the taxonomic system, every living plant form has its place in relationship to all other forms, both living and extinct.

Plants that seem to be related because of similarities in form and structure are assigned to a definite group; and smaller groups, based on some common characteristics, are formed within larger divisions. Some organisms do not fit well into any group, or perhaps they fit indifferently into several groups, for during the course of evolution all types and degrees of diversity have developed.

Nature is not concerned with the maintenance of groups, and organisms may be shifted from one group to another as taxonomic knowledge increases. The purpose of classification is to present a natural system of relationships; ideally, it aims not to create an artificial ordering but to discover the order inherent in the working of natural forces. Thus, a truly natural system of classification is also an evolutionary system, reflecting in its organization progressive differentiation of plant forms.

Logic of Classification. The logic of the taxonomic system is that of describing the order and connection of the various forms in terms of their relative similarity or, stated conversely, in terms of their progressive differentiation. Starting from the most general or inclusive group, all living organisms belong to the *Organisma;* this expresses the similarities between all animals and plants and their differences from all nonliving forms.

The next step in differentiation is that between plants and animals: all plants belong to the kingdom *Planta,* whose members share some of the properties of animals and are differentiated from them in other commonly shared properties. Differentiation continues in this fashion, with each group sharing certain characteristics with the preceding group, yet also differing from it in other characteristics.

In each case the succeeding group is a function of the preceding one and branches from it like a limb on a tree. Each limb in turn has smaller branches, and these branches give rise to even smaller ones. When a particular group has been so closely defined that there can be found no further characteristics to differentiate its members, the system is closed.

Every property of every plant in the series has a place in the system at some level. Thus, every member of the last group in each series can be placed in relation to every other plant, and organism, in the world.

As just described, the taxonomic system represents a progression from overall similarity to greater and greater differentiation, or *heterogeneity.* Viewed from the other direction, that is starting from the most differentiated unit, the same system presents a picture of greater and greater similarity, or *homogeneity.*

In order to find the position of a particular plant—for example, a white oak tree (*Quercus alba*)—in the whole taxonomic system, it is necessary to start with the particular and proceed through the more and more general groups. From this standpoint, the units of classification are ranged in order of increasing inclusiveness, from the most differentiated to the most undifferentiated.

The basic unit is the *species,* in this case *alba* (the white oak); the next step is the *genus* (plural *genera*), which for the oak is *Quercus.* (In some cases there are also types or *varieties* of species, but these are generally artificial and are not maintained in nature.) A group of closely related genera is a *family;* the oaks belong to the family *Fagaceae,* together with the chestnuts and beeches.

Families are in turn grouped in *orders,* and the *Fagaceae* belong to the order *Fagales,* which includes two other families, the birch and the beech. Groups of related orders are called *classes,* in this case the *Dicotyledoneae,* a large class of 47 orders that includes most flowering trees and many flowering plants.

The class *Dicotyledoneae,* together with the *Monocotyledoneae,* forms the important subdivision *Angiospermae,* to which belong all flowering trees and plants. The largest group within the plant kingdom is the *phylum,* and the oak is a member of the seed-bearing *Spermatophyta.*

The divisions into orders, classes, and phyla, and the groupings of the phyla into subkingdoms, has not been conclusively determined; and a number of systems are current. Many botanists hold that the *Thallophyta* as formerly constituted and the *Pteridophyta* do not represent true natural groupings; some have designated two main subkingdoms as *Thallophyta* and *Embryophyta.* Other systems propose a phylum *Tracheophyta,* which groups together all of the vascular plants.

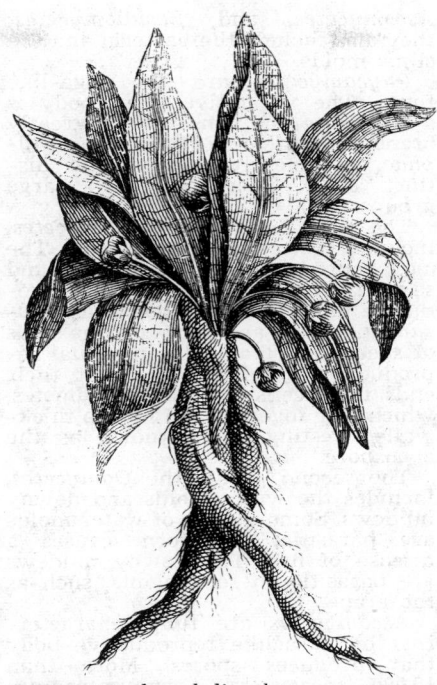

MANDRAKE, long believed to possess magical powers and credited with human attributes, was thought to shriek if uprooted.

The classification given above, although not the most recent or the most accurate in terms of evolutionary relationships, is still common.

Kingdom Planta

Phylum Thallophyta (simple plants without roots, stems, leaves; usually one-celled reproductive organs).
  Subdivision **Algae** (containing chlorophyll, e.g., pond scums, seaweeds).
  Subdivision **Fungi** (lacking Chlorophyll, e.g., molds, mushrooms).
Phylum Bryophyta (simple plants without roots, stems, leaves; many-celled reproductive organs).
  Class **Hepaticae** (live worts)
  Class **Musci** (mosses)
Phylum Pteridophyta (complex plants with true roots, stems, and leaves, and possessing vascular tissue, but lacking seeds).
  Class **Filicineae** (ferns)
  Class **Equisetineae** (horsetails)
  Class **Lycopodineae** (club mosses)
Phylum Spermatophyta (complex plants with true roots, stems, and leaves, vascular tissue, and bearing seeds).
  Subdivision **Gymnospermae** ("naked seed" plants, bearing cones, e.g., pines, spruce).
  Subdivision **Angiospermae** ("covered seed" plants or true flowering plants; e.g., grasses, maples, roses, orchids).
  Class **Monocotyledoneae** (embryo bearing one cotyledon and flower parts typically in 3's; e.g., tulips, orchids).
  Class **Dicotyledoneae** (embryo bearing two cotyledons and flower parts in 4's or 5's; e.g., roses, beans).

LIVING PLANTS

THALLOPHYTES. The phylum *Thallophyta* consists of plants possessing neither true roots, stems, nor leaves. They may be unicellular or multicellular; each type may be found in various forms.

Two divisions are recognized, algae and fungi. Algae are usually "independent," possess chlorophyll, and are able to manufacture their own food. Fungi do not possess chlorophyll and are dependent upon an outside source of carbon-furnishing food, such as the carbohydrates.

Algae. The oldest and simplest of all green plants, the *algae* range from simple unicellular organisms to complex, multicellular colonies. They vary in size from diatoms only a fraction of an inch in diameter to seaweeds 150 to 200 feet long. Although primarily water plants, algae grow all over the globe, from the ice and snow of the Arctic regions to the backs of certain turtles living in tropical regions.

While many species are attached, others constitute much of the floating life of aquatic habitats. The smaller forms especially are an important source of food for aquatic animal life. Reproduction may be effected by simple *fission* (splitting off) or by non-sexual spores that may be motile or nonmotile.

Except for the flowering plants, the algae are the most numerous and widespread of all green plants; but they are a heterogeneous group whose exact interrelationships are not known. They include over 50,000 known species, grouped under different systems in various phyla. Some of the most important types are the following:

Green algae, the *Chlorophyceae,* are those algae in which chlorophyll is conspicuous. They are more numerous than all others combined and include about 10,000 species. The more primitive forms are unicellular, and some possess whiplike motile organs (cilia) in the active state.

Reproduction is primarily by simple fission—a parent cell becoming quiescent and dividing in two. Since death of the parent cell does not occur, any cell may be immortal. Sexual reproduction also occurs when two motile cells (or gametes) fuse to form a new cell.

The simple green algae are of special interest as steps in the chain of evolution. *Euglena,* a single-celled form with one whiplike cilia, may stand at the diverging point of plants and animals. Other green algae may be ancestors of the higher plants.

Filamentous forms of the green algae are numerous; these are the typical pond scums. Green algae of various types also occur in the sea, from the many one-celled forms that constitute large parts of plankton to such complex seaweeds as *Ulva,* the sea lettuce, which consists of colonies of cells forming broad ribbons or leaflike structures.

Diatoms are peculiar unicellular algae whose cell walls are impregnated with silica and fitted together in a boxlike shape. The hard, glasslike walls persist after the death of the cells and settle to the ocean floor, forming large deposits of *diatomaceous earth,* an exceptionally fine abrasive. Much petroleum is also of diatom origin.

Blue-green algae, the *Myxophyceae,* owe their common name to the occurrence of a blue pigment along with the chlorophyll. They may occur as single cells, but colony-forming species are more common. A gelatinous sheath or extensive jelly may enclose the colony, and in stagnant water the blue-green algae may give off a disagreeable odor. There are simple algae, apparently with less organization of the cell than any other algal group. Reproduction is by simple fission.

Brown algae, the *Phaeophyceae,* show great structural complexity and include the largest of all algal forms. They are almost exclusively marine, and include common rockweed and seaweeds. Species of *Laminaria,* or kelp, occur in deeper, colder waters. On the Pacific coast a giant kelp *Nereocystis,* often grows to exceed one hundred feet in a season. Many species break loose and float with the ocean current, often in great quantities; the Sargasso Sea is named after one algae genus, *Sargassum.* Chlorophyll is present in these algae, but is masked by the occurrence of another, golden-brown pigment in the plastid.

Reproduction in the brown algae is by spores or, often, by gamete production. The common rockweeds, *Fucus,* reproduce only by sexual gametes, and their life cycle resembles that of the flowering plants. The brown algae are used for food, especially in the Orient, and supply iodine and considerable fertilizer.

Red algae, the *Rhodophyceae,* are generally red and typically marine. They may be filamentous, massive, and highly differentiated; or they may be membranous. They often frequent deep waters, and in regions of plentiful sunshine have been found at depths exceeding three hundred feet.

FUNGI. The second great division of the thallophytes, the *fungi,* are commonly filamentous in the vegetative condition and are distinguishable from the algae primarily by the absence of chlorophyll.

Practically speaking, fungi occur wherever organic matter exists, since one or more species may inhabit any dead or non-living material and many species attack living tissues, especially those of seed plants. The chief classes of fungi are *Phycomycetes,*

Ascomycetes, and *Basidiomycetes;* they also include the bacteria and the slime molds.

Phycomycetes are the alga-like fungi. The vegetative plant body is a *mycelium* and consists of a greatly branched system of threads, or *hyphae,* not clearly divided into distinct cells. There are two large groups.

The first group, the *zygomycetes,* includes the common bread mold. The mold reproduces both nonsexually and sexually. Nonsexual spores are produced in structures known as *sporangia,* which are borne at the ends of specialized filaments; in sexual reproduction, hyphae cut off at their ends form cells that act as gametes, which fuse together and form a thick-walled resting spore known as the *zygospore.*

The second group, the *Oomycetes,* includes the water molds and downy mildews. Some species of water molds are parasitic; one form causes a disease of fish. The downy mildews are parasitic on seed plants, such as the grape.

Ascomycetes are fungi characterized by a saclike reproductive body that produces spores. More than 10,000 species of ascomycetes are known, and they occur in many different situations.

The *saprophytic* species (those inhabiting dead material) are found abundantly upon decaying vegetation and in or on the soil. The blue and green molds of foods, such as *penicillium,* from which the drug penicillin is made, belong to this group. It also includes a few families of fungi with large and fleshy fruit bodies, such as the edible morels and truffles. Another useful group is that of the *yeasts.*

Parasitic species are likewise numerous, and cause such plant diseases as apple scab and rose mildew.

Basidiomycetes are a class of fungi that comprises orders and families varying in both structure and habitat, but the different subclasses are

all related through the possession of *basidia* (club-shaped cells) that typically bear four spores. *Rusts* and *smuts* constitute the main parasitic groups; other divisions include the vast majority of the fleshy or woody fungi, such as mushrooms. Smut fungi are most recognizable during the spore stage.

Some rust fungi exhibit an exceedingly complicated life history. The black-stem rust of wheat has one stage on the wheat and related plants and another on the barberry. The apple rust passes from the apple to the red cedar and from the red cedar back to the apple. On the host plant the fungi are ordinarily characterized by the occurrence of rusty spots; these are the beds of the fungal spores.

Woods and fields yield hundreds of fungi variously known as mushrooms, toadstools, and puffballs. They grow in the soil or on decaying logs and vegetation, and a considerable number cause heartwood or sapwood decay of trees. Among fleshy forms there are both edible and poisonous species. They vary in texture from soft, spongy forms to hard, woodlike growths; in size, they range from the microscopic to two feet across.

Bacteria. Among the fungi there are usually included the smallest plants known, the *bacteria,* or *schizomycetes.* They seem, however, to constitute an independent group, perhaps related to some of the lower algae. They are so small that they are visible to the unaided eye only when growing in colonies of many hundreds or thousands. If they were arranged end to end, it would require about 500 of these bacteria of average size to reach across the head of a pin.

Under favorable conditions, bacteria reproduce by fission at an astonishingly rapid rate. Some also produce spores at the rate of a single spore per cell; these enable them to survive hostile conditions.

Bacteria are universally found in air, water, and soil, as well as on and within all living bodies. They have harmful effects as producers of disease in plants, animals, and man, but they are also beneficial as agents of the decay that return nutrients to the soil, and as the *nitrogen bacteria* that are vital in completing the cycle of this important element. Bacteria are also the agents of many useful fermentation processes. They are used commercially in the dairy industry, in wine-making, and in the curing of tobacco.

Slime Molds. *Myxomycetes,* or *slime molds,* are organisms sometime classed as plants and sometimes classed as animals. They form a slimy mass of naked protoplasm in decaying matter in moist, warm places.

The multinucleate protoplasm moves in amoeboid fashion and can ingest solid food, a characteristic that links the slime molds closely to the animal world.

Lichens. A *lichen* consists of a fungus and an algae growing together in a *symbiotic,* or mutually helpful, relationship to form a dual colony so closely associated that the colonial composite acts as one. To a degree the fungus is parasitic upon the alga and

BETTMANN ARCHIVE

BENEATH THE FOREST FLOOR, the mushroom plant extends a network of filaments. The familiar cap, with its spore-producing gills, makes up the "fruit," or reproductive body.

NATIONAL COAL ASSOCIATION

HELEN BUTTFIELD

FERNS have survived almost unchanged from the time 350 million years ago when they left their imprint (*left*) fossilized in the earth.

holds it captive, but the alga is thus enabled to grow in many places where it could not otherwise exist. Within the lichen, the alga multiplies vegetatively; the fungus has its characteristic spore reproduction.

Lichens commonly grow on trunks and branches of trees, on rocks, and on soil. Some are flat and leafy, and some are mosslike. Reindeer moss, really a lichen, is typical of the mosslike group. Lichens are often gray-green and are very resistant to extremes of cold and drought. In the Arctic, they sustain the vast reindeer herds.

MOSSES AND MOSSLIKE PLANTS.
Members of the class *Bryophyta*, mosses and mosslike plants, constitute a considerable group of green plants higher in the scale of development than the algae, but less complex than seed plants. In some classifications

they are considered the lowest members of the subkingdom *Embryophyta*, plants that form embryos. However, they lack the vascular tissues characteristic of the higher forms.

Mosses. Small, green, flowerless plants, the mosses grow erect but are usually no more than one to two inches high. They occur commonly in moist environments as miniature velvety or feathery growths carpeting the ground, growing on rocks, on the trunks of trees, and even in ponds or running water. The parts of the mosses usually visible look like those of higher plants; they have a stemlike axis with numerous leaves. But there is no true stem or root, such as characterize seed plants.

The mosses are among the most primitive of plants and have persisted almost unchanged since they arose about 300 million years ago. Because

they have given rise to no other forms, the mosses are considered a terminal evolutionary group.

Liverworts. Primitive land and fresh-water plants, the liverworts are closely related to the mosses. Their growth pattern is flat and branching, and they resemble some seaweeds in appearance. They are the simplest land plants surviving, and may have evolved from certain algae.

FERNS AND FERN ALLIES. The *ferns*, together with a few related families of the class *Pteridophyta*, are the remnants of a once flourishing form of plant life that dominated the earth's vegetation for years. Geologically one of the oldest groups, the ferns originated in the Paleozoic era, 350 million years ago. Giant *tree ferns* once covered the earth, and the energy they gathered from the sun and stored in their tissues is preserved in the earth's great coal deposits.

Ferns are characterized by large, divided, feather-like leaves, or *fronds*, which usually uncurl from the tip. They have short stems that often grow underground. Unlike the mosses, they have true roots. Ferns, like the higher plants, have vascular tissues that transport nutrients and water from the roots to the leaves.

Ferns are abundant on the moist, shaded, forest floor and along streams; some species, however, thrive on rocky cliffs or slopes. Geographically, these plants range from the Arctic to the equatorial jungles and rain forests, where tree ferns often reach heights of forty feet.

Alternation of Generations. Reproduction in the ferns is marked by a distinct *alternation of generations*, which involves two different forms: the first is the familiar fern plant, which has a root, stem, and leaves; the second is a thin, flat, heart-shaped plant called the *prothallium*. Prothallia produce male and female sex organs in which gametes are developed. A male gamete fuses with an egg, and

HELEN BUTTFIELD

LICHENS, as enduring as the stone they cover, are among the most primitive land plants.

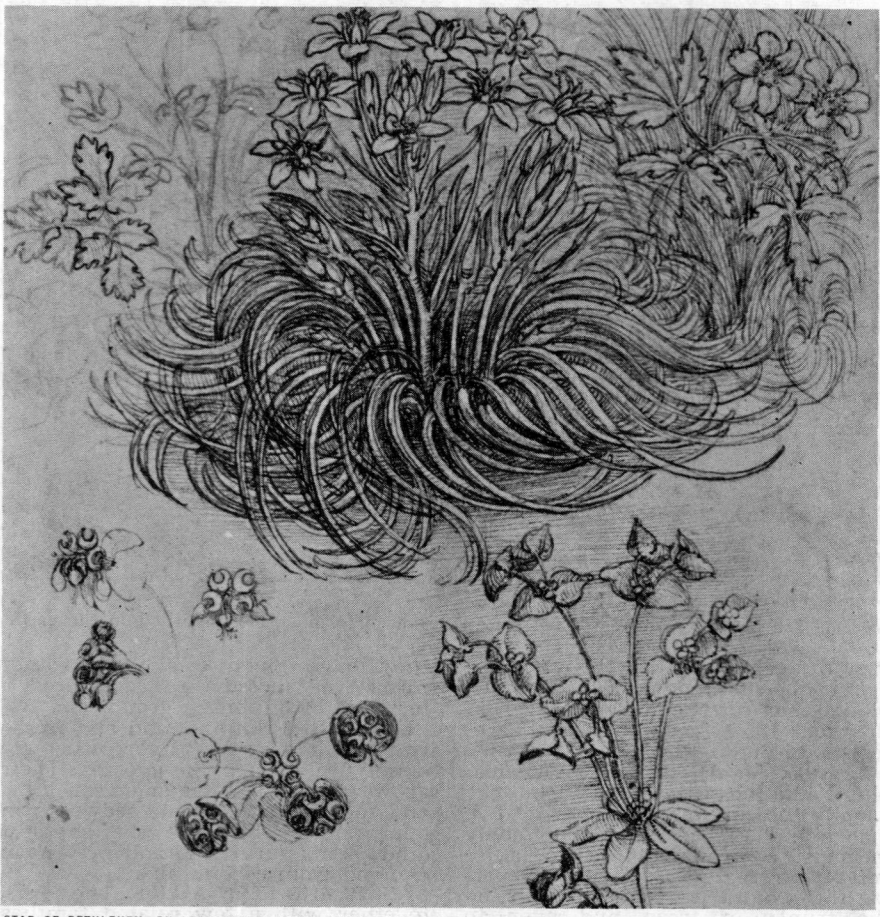

STAR OF BETHLEHEM, BY LEONARDO DA VINCI; ALINARI-ART REFERENCE BUREAU

THE FLOWERING PLANTS are the highest evolutionary form in the plant kingdom and the flower itself is the most effective means of reproduction evolved by any of the plants.

from the fertilized egg develops the fern plant with its roots, stem, and leaves.

On the underside of the fern's leaves there are small spore cases, or *sporangia,* which are often distributed as dots, rows, or larger masses. In these spore cases, large numbers of single-celled spores are produced; when they germinate, they give rise to the prothallia. Thus, the prothallia are *gametophytes* producing gametes, and the leafy fern is a *sporophyte* producing spores.

Club Mosses. Also called *ground pines, club mosses* are rarely more than three feet high. These relatives of the fern are neither mosses nor pines; they are small evergreen plants that have simple leaves resembling pine or hemlock needles. Sometimes they grow upright, but often they trail on the ground, where they propagate by means of *runners,* or elongations of the root stock that send up new sprouts. They also reproduce spores.

Horsetails. Only twenty-five living species of *horsetails* are known, and all of these belong to a single genus. Many extinct forms, however, have been found in fossils. Horsetails are the only surviving representatives of a group containing members that grew to over ninety feet.

Horsetails are composed of underground stems that send up tall, verti-cal, jointed stalks and of branches covered with scalelike leaves. These plants are also called *scouring rushes,* a name derived from the rough texture imparted by the silica they contain.

Cycads and the Ginkgo. The *cycads* are plants that resemble tree ferns in general appearance, but reproduce by means of seeds. Few in number today, they are the remains of a once dominant group which flourished in the great fern forests of the Permian age.

The *ginkgo,* also called the maiden-hair tree, has fan-shaped leaflets, similar in form to those of the maidenhair fern. This leaf-form is found on no other flowering plant and the ginkgo represents a missing link between ferns and flowering plants.

SEED PLANTS. The *spermatophyta,* or seed plants, the highest division in the plant kingdom, contains all plants that reproduce by means of seeds. It includes all living trees and flowering plants. Seed plants form the dominant part of the vegetation of the earth today and thus can be considered the highest, or most successful, plant form.

Seed plants embrace two major divisions: the *gymnosperms,* or "naked seed" plants, in which the seeds lie exposed and unprotected on the cone scales, and the *angiosperms* or "enclosed seed" plants in which the seeds are borne inside a jar-shaped swelling, the ovary, located at the base of the flower pistil.

Gymnosperms. Familiar examples of gymnosperms are the pines, spruces, and other evergreen trees or shrubs with conelike fruits, known as the *Coniferae.* This group forms the great coniferous forests of the temperate zones and includes the largest plants on earth, the giant redwoods.

Vascular or woody tissues reach a high state of development in the stems and roots of conifers. The leaves of mature pines are called *needles;* they are retained for more than a year, giving rise to the name *evergreen.* These needles are highly specialized in structure and are adapted to resist extremes of cold and dryness. Morphologically they are grouped in *fascicles* (clusters) of two, three, or five needles, depending upon the species.

In the conifers the spore-bearing leaves or scales (*sporophylls*) do not constitute a flower. As the scales of the seed-bearing cones separate, the winged seeds may be seen, a pair under each scale.

In the pine, the embryo plant within the seed is surrounded by a considerable food-storage layer, called the *endosperm,* and the whole is enclosed by the seed coat, or *integument.*

Maturity of the seed is accompanied by a certain amount of drying out and by a period of inactivity, or *dormancy.* The seed remains dormant until it absorbs water, and *germination,* or sprouting, ensues. The young seedling, free of the seed coat, consists of root; bud, or *plumule;* and a whorl of long, green seed leaves, or cotyledons.

Angiosperms. The angiosperms, or true *flowering plants,* include the great majority of the familiar flowers and weeds, as well as all the trees and shrubs except the gymnosperms. The angiosperms have seeds and a complex tissue system in which vascular or woody elements attain a further advanced state of differentiation, and they exhibit the highest evolutionary development through the production of flowers.

The angiosperms, which include more than half the known plants— about 200,000 species—are subdivided into two groups. In the *monocotyledons* the young seedling bears a single seed leaf, or *cotyledon. Dicotyledons* bear two seed leaves, sometimes thickened, that provide reserves of organic food. Another characteristic of dicotyledons is apparent in the mature plant: the *venation,* or vein system, of the monocotyledons is parallel, as in corn; in dicotyledons it is netted, or *reticulate,* as in the rose.

There are other characteristics, of both floral parts and inner structure, that are generally distinctive of the two groups, such as the three-part flower structure of the monocotyledons, as opposed to the four or five parts that are found in dicotyledons.

Monocotyledons include such families as the grasses (*Gramineae*) which furnish the cereal grains, pasture grasses, and ornamental grasses;

tropical palms (*Palmaceae*), including the date and coconut palms; lilies and related plants (*Liliaceae*); bananas and plantains (*Musaceae*); and the highly prized orchids (*Orchidaceae*), famous both for the delicacy and variety of their waxlike flowers and for the remarkable modification in floral parts, the latter having come about in adjustment to insect pollination.

The orchids and the grasses show extreme differences in floral anatomy. The orchid flower's extreme complexity represents a high point in evolutionary development; the grass flower, also an advanced form, shows a high degree of reduction of parts, consisting of a pistil with ovary, style, and two feathery stigmas, and three stamens enclosed in scalelike leaves, or *bracts*.

Dicotyledons are nearly five times as numerous as monocotyledons; they are also regarded as geologically the older group. They have attained far greater diversity in form and have advanced to higher types of development.

Among families exhibiting less complex types of floral structure are the willows and the poplars (*Salicaceae*), which have simple flowers in spikelike branches called *catkins*. Related to the willows are other families without showy floral parts, such as the walnut-hickory family (*Juglandoceae*) and elms (*Ulmaceae*).

In a varied group of families that includes the pinks, sweet Williams,

AMERICAN MUSEUM OF NATURAL HISTORY

DECIMATED by the caddis fly, these leaf skeletons reveal the supporting venation.

carnations (*Caryophyllaceae*), water lilies (*Nymphaeceae*), buttercups, columbines, peonies, and clematis (*Ranunculaceae*), there are many wild and garden plants. All of these have distinct petals (are *polypetalous*), and the carpels are either separate or united.

The rose family (*Rosaceae*) and the pulse family (*Leguminosae*) are closely related, and together they constitute a very considerable part of the separate-petal series of families. As a whole, the rose family is rather heterogeneous; its members include the blackberries, roses, and cherries.

In the pulse family there are several thousand species, among which are the lupines, clovers, beans, peas, and acacias. Generally the *corolla* (floral leaf) is *papilionaceous* (butterfly-like); the fruit is characteristically a pod or legume.

Among the families of dicotyledons in which the petals are united are the mints (*Labiatae*), fragrant herbs, and shrubs with flowers that are commonly two-lipped. The nightshade family (*Solanaceae*) includes the potato, tomato, eggplant, tobacco, and petunia; the flowers are prevailingly rotate, and the fruit is a *berry* (as in tomato) or a capsule (as in Jimson weed). Melons are the fruit of certain members of the gourd family (*Cucurbitaceae*).

Botanists generally agree in placing the composite family (*Compositae*) at the pinnacle of development in the plant kingdom. This is the family of sunflowers and goldenrods, asters and thistles, chrysanthemums and dahlias. It also includes lettuce, globe artichoke, and salsify. It is a huge family with perhaps 12,000 species, nearly all of which are annuals or perennial herbs; the woody members are not trees.

The outstanding characteristic of the composite family is the compact head of many flowers—some with ray flowers (as in sunflowers) and some without (as in thistles). The fruits are hard and one-seeded (*achenes*), and are often provided with a feathery appendage, or *pappus* (as in dandelions), that helps wind distribution of the seeds.

PLANT STRUCTURE

From the smallest bacteria, 1/50,000 of an inch long, to the largest angiosperm, 372 feet tall, plants are made up of *cells*, the basic units of life. The study of cell structure and function is called *cytology*.

CELLS. A typical plant cell is enclosed by the *cell wall*, which is composed primarily of cellulose and nonliving substances and gives support and form to the cell and the whole plant. The enclosed *protoplasm* is a viscous, transparent, living matter composed of water, proteins, sugars, fats, acids, and salts.

Protoplasm is differentiated into two aspects. The dark, usually round *nucleus* controls the chemical activities of the cell and bears the *chromosomes*, carriers of hereditary traits. Surrounding the nucleus is the *cytoplasm*, in which are the structures

that carry on the physiological cell functions: the *plastids*, including chlorophyll-bearing *chloroplasts* that are capable of photosynthesis; the *chromoplasts*, containing red and yellow coloring; the *leucoplasts*, which build sugar into starch grains; *mitochondria*, which produce chemical regulators; *vacuoles*, liquid-filled spaces that serve as storage areas; starch grains and crystals.

TISSUES. In all multicellular plants the individual cells are organized into *tissue*. *Histology* is the study of these groups of structurally similar cells that are organized to perform physiological functions.

Embryonic Tissue. *Meristem*, or young tissue, consists of thin-walled, active cells rich in protoplasm. They are able to divide by cell division and thus to continue the growth of the organ. All other tissues are derived from meristem by differentiation or modification. *Cambium*, the layer of active growth and cell formation in stems and roots of dicotyledons, is a form of meristem.

Permanent Tissue. The new cells produced by division and differentiation of the meristematic cells become the permanent tissue of the plant. As these cells mature, they no longer reproduce by cell division but expand in size. The cell walls stretch and, in many instances, thicken; the cytoplasm thins out and the major portion of the cell interior is taken up by the enlarged vacuole. Further modifications in shape and structure occur as the cell takes its place within one of the various types of permanent tissue.

There are two kinds of permanent tissues: *simple tissues,* in which each tissue is composed of similar cells; and *complex tissues,* in which different types of cells work together as a unit to perform certain physiological functions. Most plant parts are composed of simple tissues. However, the *xylem* and *phloem,* the vital carriers of water and food, are complex tissues consisting of parenchyma, fibrous, sieve, and vascular tissues.

Parenchyma, or soft tissue, consists of mature, thin-walled, usually short cells that have attained their growth, such as the tissue of ripened fruits and the green tissue of leaves.

Collenchyma tissue consists of long cells with thick angles. In many stems it occurs as a strengthening tissue just beneath the epidermis.

Sclerenchyma, or stone tissue, consists of thick-walled usually short cells, so tightly packed that they form a hard mass, as in nutshells and the "stones" of many fruits.

Fibrous and bast tissue consists of thick-walled, elongated cells so tightly packed together that they make up wood fibers (fibrous tissue) and bark (bast tissue) of the stems of most higher plants. Bast fibers are used in ropemaking and linen making.

Sieve tissue consists of elongated, usually large cells, more or less united into tubes and having only slightly thickened walls. The name derives from the perforation of the transverse partitions between the cells in a sievelike pattern; through these perforations the protoplasm connects from cell to cell. Sieve tissue occurs primarily in the young bark and is important in conveying organic food.

Vascular tissue is also tubular, but the continuity of the cavity is usually more complete than in sieve tissue. When they are young, these tubes contain protoplasm; but eventually they contain water or air. Vascular tissue occurs in the woody parts of stems and leaves.

Epidermal tissue, a single layer of cubical cells, constitutes the outer layers of leaves, young stems, and roots.

ANATOMY OF SEED PLANTS

Although the lower plants have developed quite complicated forms and structures and have adapted very successfully to a wide range of environments, the most highly differentiated and evolved structures are found in the angiosperms.

The bodies of typical seed plants are composed of four kinds of parts: *roots, stems, leaves,* and *flowers* (which in turn produce *fruit* and *seeds*). The first three structures are found also in the mosses, ferns, liverworts, and other lower forms; but flowers and their accessory products are exclusive to seed plants.

ROOTS. All living organisms, including the plants, are descended from forms which originated in the sea; and no cells, animal or vegetable, can exist without access to that most important element, water.

In the higher plants, the *root* is the vital link between the plant and its lost aquatic environment. Through its roots a plant absorbs the water that makes up most of its tissues and that it uses to carry on its life processes, as well as some oxygen and most of the mineral nutrients it requires.

Root Structure. All roots are covered at the growing tip with a *root cap*

which protects the sensitive tip and serves as a boring point to push into the soil. Behind the root caps, the sides of the roots are covered with many fine *root hairs,* made up of single cells, which penetrate the soil and increase the roots' absorption.

Root Systems. The slender, branching roots of grasses, corn, and wheat are *diffuse systems* spreading over wide but relatively shallow areas. *Tap-root systems,* such as those of the carrot and beet, are made up of a single primary root that probes deeply into the soil and often is thickened to serve in food storage.

Specialized Roots. Adaptations to particular needs are the *aerial roots* of ivy and other *epiphytes* (plants that grow on other plants but are not parasitic); *prop roots* of corn and fig trees, which act as buttresses; *adventitious roots,* which drop down from the stem to lend additional support to many tropical trees; and the *aerating roots* of the cypress and mangrove, which grow above water to obtain oxygen.

STEMS. The *stem* is the part of the plant that supports the leaves and reproductive organs and supplies them with water and mineral nutrients absorbed by the roots. It also serves to carry food back down to roots and other parts for storage.

Most stems grow above the ground (*aerial stems*), but some grow below the surface (*subterranean stems*). Aerial stems are either *herbaceous* or *woody,* an important feature distinguishing groups of plants. All gymnosperms have woody stems, while those of angiosperms can be either woody or herbaceous.

It is generally believed that woody stems are the more primitive and that herbaceous stems have evolved from them. Herbaceous stems are soft and green, covered by an epidermis; they grow in length but little in diameter

and are chiefly *annual* (confined to a single growing season). Woody stems are hard and are covered with a tough layer of bark. They grow considerably in diameter and are chiefly *perennial* (surviving through many growing seasons).

Woody Stems. Internally, *woody stems* are made up of two kinds of tissue, the outer *bark* and the inner *wood;* these are separated by a single layer of cells, the growing *cambium* layer. As the cambium cells divide the outer portions become differentiated into a layer of cells called *phloem,* and the inner cells form the *xylem.*

Phloem cells transport food, and the xylem cells conduct moisture throughout the plant. This formation of new cells causes a thickening in the diameter of the stem, and it is thus that the trunks of trees continue to increase in girth. The cells produced in the summer are larger and therefore lighter in color; the winter cells are smaller and appear darker.

This color differential creates the *annual rings* marking a year's growth. As a tree grows, the inner layers become clogged and loaded with tannins, resins, and gums. These make up the hard, dark *heartwood,* while the outer, more active layers constitute the *sapwood.*

Herbaceous Stems. Herbaceous stems resemble young woody stems in structure except that the xylem and phloem are arranged in clusters called *vascular bundles,* which are either scattered throughout the stem (monocotyledons) or arranged in a circle (dicotyledons). Herbaceous stems are chiefly annual, and growth is primarily in the length, not the diameter.

Buds. Buds are the growing ends of the stems of both woody and herbaceous plants and are the immature forms of leaves and flowers. *Terminal buds* provide growth at the tip of a stem or twig; *lateral buds* or *axillary buds* form side branches as well as leaves and flowers.

In annuals and tropical woody plants, the buds grow continuously; but in woody plants of temperate climates they become dormant when the plant slows its metabolism during the winter.

Subterranean Stems. *Rhizomes* are horizontal stems growing on or beneath the ground; they serve for storage of food and for reproduction. They are perennial and send up new shoots each year. *Tubers* are the enlarged tips of rhizomes; highly specialized for the storage of food, they are also, as with the potato, important means of propagation.

Bulbs, such as those of the onion and tulip, and *corms,* such as those of the gladiolus and crocus, are enlarged stem buds with overlapping leaves. They serve for storage and reproduction and as a means of carrying the dormant plant through seasons unfavorable to growth.

LEAVES. Leaves are the plant structures specialized primarily for the manufacture of food through photosynthesis. Thus, most leaves are constructed so as to provide the greatest possible surface area and are ar-

HELEN BUTTFIELD

POWERFUL ROOTS anchor the beech tree firmly in the ground while, deep in the soil, their growing tips spread out, searching for the moisture that nourishes the crown.

ranged so as to expose this surface to the maximum amount of sunlight.

Leaf Form. Most leaves consist of a slender stalk, or *petiole,* and a broad, expanded blade, or *lamina.* From the apex of the petiole, *veins* extend into the blade. Veins serve for mechanical support, for the transport of raw materials through the leaf, and for carrying away the products elaborated by the green cells.

Leaves vary in size from a fraction of an inch up to 60 feet, as in the palm tree. In shape they range from the long, thin blades of grass to the circular leaves of the nasturtium and water lily; there are many irregular forms also, as in the maples and oaks.

The *venation* (arrrangement of the vein) is characteristic for different kinds of plants: *net* venation in dicotyledons and *parallel* venation in monocotyledons. In *pinnate* net venation, the petiole extends as a main vein or midrib through the center of the leaf, lateral veins extending off it on each side to give a featherlike appearance; this is found in the apple and elm. In *palmate* net venation, several larger veins radiate from the apex of the petiole, as in the maple.

The leaf blade may be simple, as in the apple, or compound, consisting of *leaflets.* The leaflets may have the pinnate arrangement, as in the pea and tree of heaven; or the leaf may be palmately compound, the leaflets arranged at the end of the petiole like the fingers on a hand.

The leaves of grasses are specially modified in that, instead of a distinct petiole, the basal part of the petiole is a sheath that closely surrounds the stem. At the base of the blade there is a special growing zone, so that grass leaves continue to increase in length for long periods.

Leaves may undergo many modifications. *Bud scales* are greatly reduced leaves that overlap and protect the delicate bud tissues during cold and drought. The thick, fleshy leaves of sedum and other succulent plants store quantities of water.

Some barberry leaves are modified into *spines;* and in the pea, some of the leaflets are modified into *tendrils* that assist the plant in climbing. Very curious modifications occur in the insectivorous plants, such as the pitcher plants and Venus's flytraps; the latter's leaves are modified to attract and capture the insects that are digested by these plants.

Longevity. The leaves of most of the temperate zone plants do not continue to grow as do the grasses; they live for a single season and then fall. Such plants are *deciduous,* as opposed to the evergreens, which retain their leaves for a longer period—normally not for more than four years.

The falling of the leaves is the result of chemical changes in which the substance *auxin* plays a considerable part. In autumn, a special layer of cells, called the *abscission layer,* forms at the base of the petiole; these cells block the flow of water and nutrients. As a result, the chlorophyll decomposes, resulting in the yellow and orange pigments typical of autumn foliage. The red colors are new pigments that develop within the

HELEN BUTTFIELD

THE WINGED SEED of the Jeffrey Pine and the feathery seed of the dandelion are two examples of highly efficient seed dispersal; these need merely the air and the wind.

cells. Meanwhile, the middle cells of the abscission layers disintegrate and the leaf breaks off and falls, leaving a *leaf scar* on the stem.

Leaf Arrangement. Leaves usually are arranged on the stem in one of three ways: *spiral,* or *alternate,* one leaf at a node, the leaves forming a continuous ascending spiral on the stem, as in the apple or elm; *opposite,* two leaves that usually are directly opposite each other, as in the maple; *whorled,* three or more leaves at the same node, as in the lily.

Buds are regularly found in the *axils* of the leaves and, under favorable conditions, will grow into branches bearing leaves or flowers.

Internal Structure. In a cross section of a leaf blade, different types of tissues and cells are observed.

Epidermis.—The *upper epidermis* and *lower epidermis* each consists of a single layer of cells that covers the entire leaf surface, protecting the tissues within from mechanical injury and drying out. The epidermis, particularly the upper one, is usually covered with a waxy *cuticle,* which further prevents loss of water.

The epidermal cells are longer and wider than they are deep and, as viewed from the surface, have wavy cell outlines. Among the epidermal cells are special crescent-shaped *guard cells,* which contain chloroplasts. Between the guard cells are openings called *stomata* (singular, *stoma*). The size of these openings is regulated by the movements of the guard cells. It is through the stomata that the gaseous exchange takes place between the interior of the leaf and the air. Water vapor escapes and carbon dioxide enters for the process of photosynthesis; oxygen escapes as a product of photosynthesis or enters in connection with respiration.

Mesophyll.—Between the upper and lower epidermis there are specialized chlorophyll-bearing cells. Beneath the upper epidermis, long, narrow cells are arranged in a palisade fashion, and between these and the lower epidermis are more or less rounded or irregularly shaped cells arranged to form a loose, spongy tissue, with abundant air chambers between. These cells are largely concerned with carbohydrate manufacture.

Vascular bundles.—These are the veins of the leaves, as seen from the surface; the larger ones branch into smaller bundles, which may end in a single cell.

FLOWERS. From the standpoint of the continuation of the species, which is the only *natural* purpose, the flower and its resulting fruit and seed are the most important structures of the plant. It is for the flower's support that the entire plant is designed. The flower is the reproductive organ of the higher plants; its function is to produce the seed containing the male and female gametes that will unite in sexual reproduction and produce the new generation.

Flower Parts. The basic flower parts can be divided into four sets of structures. The outer set of parts (green in some plants) is the *calyx,* the individual leaves of which are the *sepals.* Next there is a set of showy leaves known as the *corolla,* the individual parts of which are *petals;* these are brightly colored and often secrete an aromatic and sweet substance (*nectar*) that attracts insects. Within the petals are a group of small sporophylls, the *stamens.* A stamen consists of a slender stalk (*filament*) with a pollen-bearing *anther* at its tip.

The central and last structure constitutes a united set, termed a *pistil,* that is made up of several parts, or *carpels.* Each group of carpels has an enlarged basal *ovule sac,* a terminal *stigma,* and a connecting shank known as the *style.* In the ovule sac there are differentiated ovules within which the egg gametes are produced.

The sepals and petals are known as *accessory parts* because they are not directly concerned with reproduction. The *essential parts* are the stamens (male parts) and the pistils (female parts).

Pollination. The development of the seed is preceded by the process of *pollination. Pollen* is produced on certain specialized structures and carried by the wind or by insects to the female structures. *Self-pollination* is the transfer of pollen within a single flower or from one flower to another on the same plant; *cross pollination* is the transfer of pollen from one plant to the female structures of another plant. There the pollen germinates, giving rise in a short time to male gametes that fuse with the female gamete. The latter develops into the embryo plant that, surrounded by protective structures, becomes the seed.

SEEDS AND FRUITS. The *seed* develops from the ovule and consists of the young embryo plant with its surrounding nutritive and protective tissues. The seeds are enclosed in the ovary during their development; the fully developed ovary with its adjacent parts constitutes the *fruit*.

Seeds. The seed consists of a *seed coat*, usually tough and partly impervious to the water that is necessary for germination; an *embryo*, the miniature plant that develops from the fertilized egg, or *zygote*; and the *endosperm*, or food-storage tissue that nourishes the germinating plant or seedling.

Effective seed dispersal is vital to the angiosperms because the parent plant is not mobile; seeds must be widely scattered to provide optimum conditions for germination and growth. Most of the striking characteristics of seeds and fruits are adaptations that aid dispersal: by wind, as in the wings of the maple seed and plumes of the dandelion; by spines and burrs that adhere to animals, as in the cockleburs; by floating, as in the coconut; or by the fleshy fruits of such plants as apples and cherries, which are eaten by animals and thus have their seeds distributed.

Fruits. There are several different kinds of fruits.

Fleshy fruits.—Soft and pulpy at maturity, *fleshy fruits* include the *berries* (grape, tomato, orange, squash); the *drupes* (cherry, peach, olive); and the *pomes* (pear, apple).

Dry fruits—Dry and hard at maturity, dry fruits fall into two types. Those that split open at maturity are the *dehiscent* fruits and include *follicle* (milkweed); *legume* (pea); and *capsule* (iris, lily). Fruits not splitting open are *indehiscent: achene* (buckwheat, sunflower); *caryopsis*, or grain (cereals); *samara*, or winged (maple, ash, elm); and *nut* (oak, chestnut).

Structural differences.—Fruits are called *simple* when they develop from a single or a compound ovary within the flower. If there are several separate carpels in the flower, an *aggregate* fruit is formed; in the raspberry there is an aggregation of many drupes. A *multiple* fruit arises when the fruits developed from separate flowers remain united, as in the mulberry and pineapple.

PLANT PHYSIOLOGY

ABSORPTION OF WATER AND NUTRIENTS. Active living plants contain a high percentage of water, and every growing plant must in some way be in contact with a water supply. While the seaweeds and floating algae are surrounded by water, the land plants have had to develop specialized structures, the roots, to penetrate the soil in search of moisture.

In such complex plants the cell walls are in close contact; and thus, although the leaf cells may be many feet from the absorbing roots, the distribution of water is so perfect that there is indirect water contact with the soil through long chains of tissue cells.

Each cell takes its water from some other cell or conducting vessel nearer the constant supply. Unless a plant contains a quantity of dead tissue, as in trees or shrubs, the water content is usually 75 percent to 80 percent of its weight.

Chemical Nutrients. Plants contain the chemical elements carbon, hydrogen, oxygen, nitrogen, phosphorus, sulfur, potassium, calcium, magnesium, and iron. Carbon, hydrogen, and oxygen enter into the composition of the carbohydrates as starch, cellulose, and dextrins. Proteins contain these same three elements, plus nitrogen, and minute traces of phosphorus and sulfur. In addition to these ten elements, minute traces of copper, manganese, boron, and zinc have been found to be necessary for plant growth.

Carbon, in the form of carbon dioxide, and oxygen are obtained mainly from the air; the other elements, usually in the form of nitrates, phosphates, and sulfates, are obtained in solution from the soil.

Absorption and Conduction. All the elements except carbon and oxygen, as well as the vital water molecules in which these elements are dissolved, must somehow be absorbed by the roots and carried, sometimes hundreds of feet, upward through the stem or trunk to the leaves. This task, which is actually an extraordinary and complex chemical and physical process, begins in the single-celled root hairs.

The walls of the root-hair cells are made up of *semipermeable membranes* that permit the passage of liquids from a less dense to a more dense solution, a process known as *osmosis*. Since the protoplasm inside the cells is of greater density than the water outside, the root cells absorb water; the cells become *turgid* from the increasing water content, and *root pressure* then forces the water up into the stem. However, this force is not strong enough to raise water more than a few inches off the ground.

The force that moves the nutrient-laden water up to the leaves is actually a form of suction and results from the plant's loss of water vapor through its leaves *(transpiration)*. Thus, the actual force that draws the water upward is the great absorptive capacity of the dry, waterless air surrounding the plant.

Transpiration. The water and mineral nutrients absorbed by the roots are conducted through the xylem to the leaves, where they are utilized in food production. A large proportion of water absorbed is there transpired through millions of small pores, or *stomata*, on the leaf surfaces, which open or close according to the water pressure in surrounding cells.

PHOTOSYNTHESIS. *Photosynthesis* is the unique process of green plants in which they manufacture not only their own food, but also the food for all higher organisms. The raw materials are carbon dioxide from the air and water from the soil; the energy for the process is obtained from sunlight.

Photosynthesis takes place in the chlorophyll-bearing part of the living cells. Since most green cells are found in the leaf, the latter is the principal site of photosynthesis. The chief product synthesized is sugar; oxygen is given off.

Leaves are thin, broad, expanded structures and thus expose a large surface for the absorption of sunlight. The carbon dioxide necessary for photosynthesis enters the leaf through the same pores that function in transpiration, the stomata. The number of stomata varies greatly in different plants. Sometimes they are confined to one surface of the leaf; in other cases they are found on both.

FOOD STORAGE AND DIGESTION. The sugar manufactured in the leaves and other green portions of the plant may be stored temporarily in the form of starch. Most of it is soon transported to other parts of the plant, where it is utilized for building up the plant tissues. Some of it is used in the synthesis of proteins, which are manufactured in any living plant cell; the nitrogen for the proteins is derived from salts absorbed through the roots.

The legumes, such as peas and clover, are able to utilize the free nitrogen of the air through the presence of certain bacteria, called *nitrogen-fixing bacteria,* that develop characteristic nodules on the roots of these plants.

Much of the organic material manufactured during the growing season is stored as carbohydrates, fats, and proteins in the seeds and fruits, tuber, and roots. Upon the return of growing conditions, the plant utilizes this stored material; but, before it can do this, it must change it from an insoluble form to a soluble form for transportation. This is the process of *digestion* and is carried out by means of enzymes.

RESPIRATION. The plant must have a supply of energy in order to carry on the various life processes. This energy

HELEN BUTTFIELD

SUNLIGHT AND AIR surround the growing, green leaf. Within the leaf, the mysterious processes of life are carried on; these include: respiration, transpiration, and the chemical transformations of photosynthesis.

HELEN BUTTFIELD

PUSHING UP through the dead leaves in the forest, the young mayapple will break free, expanding in a delicate umbrella. Tendrils uncoiling toward the light exemplify every plant's constant growth.

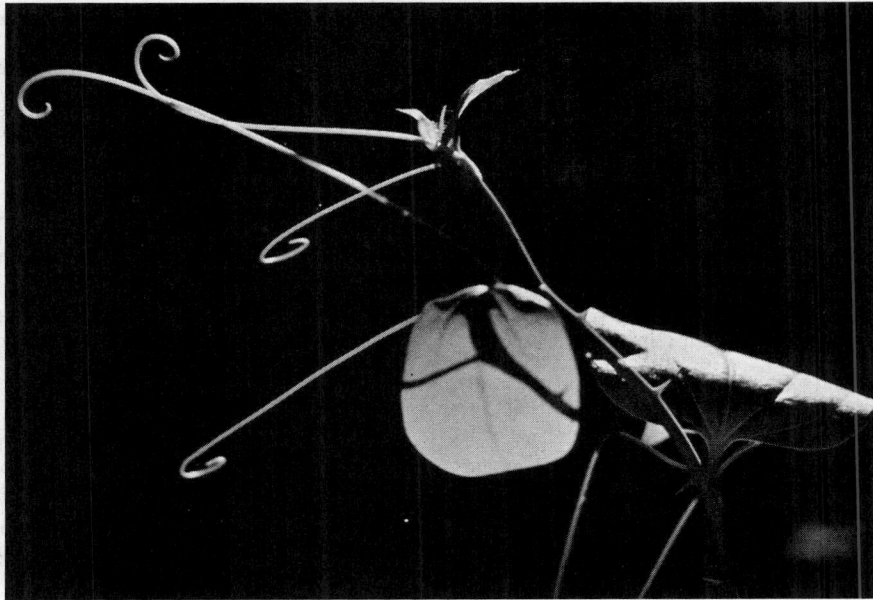

comes from the breaking down of the complex organic compounds within the cell; most of these breakdowns are associated with *respiration.*

It is a common mistake to confuse photosynthesis and respiration. Respiration is the same in green plants, nongreen plants, and animals. The chief end product of respiration is carbon dioxide, but one of the end products of photosynthesis is oxygen.

ASSIMILATION. The final conversion of carbohydrates, fats, and proteins into living material (protoplasm) is called *assimilation,* a process whose inner working still eludes the scientists' grasp. Very little is known except that assimilation can take place only where life already exists.

Since assimilation is the process by which living, organic protoplasm is created out of nonliving, inorganic materials, the problem of its mechanics is very close to the mystery of life itself.

STIMULUS AND RESPONSE. One of the basic characteristics of living matter is a property known as *irritability.* It is this that enables living protoplasm to be stimulated by outside forces and to respond to them, either positively or negatively. Without this capacity to respond to outside stimuli, no organism could live and grow. Although plants are less sensitive than animals in some respects, there are many stimuli to which they respond quickly and intensely.

Tropisms. In general, the most important stimulus to almost all plants is light, and their response to it is called *phototropism.* If a sunflower seedling, for example, is illuminated from one side, the stem will bend and the plant grow toward the source of light. This bending is the result of the concentration of auxin, a growth-stimulating hormone, on the side of the stem away from the light. Since the cells on that side grow more rapidly they force the stem to bend gradually toward the light. *Mimosa pudica* and certain other legumes close their

leaves when they are placed in darkness and expand them when moved to the light.

Another important though invisible force is the pull of the earth itself. If a seedling is laid horizontally in the dark, the stem will grow upward and the root will bend and grow downward; both growths are in response to the influence of gravity and are, respectively, negative and positive forms of *geotropism.* Roots are also sensitive to the closeness of water and will grow toward it; this is known as *hydrotropism.*

Other Motions. Movements called *turgor movements* are responses of certain plants to light, temperature, and touch, and are usually more rapid than the tropisms. The leaves of clover fold up at night in *sleep movements;* the leaves of the mimosa will fold and droop on being touched; and the specialized leaves of the Venus's flytrap are extremely sensitive to contact, closing to entrap any insect that lights on them.

Photoperiodism. A recent development in physiology is the discovery of *photoperiodism,* the effect of the daily duration of light exposure on reproductive activity. Some plants are *short-day* plants that require brief periods of light in order to reach the flowering stage; others are *long-day* plants and flower only when they are exposed to long periods of light.

PLANT GROWTH. Growth is a familiar characteristic of all living organisms and a vital one for plants, for, unlike animals, when plants cease to grow, they will soon die. Growth is closely related to movement, which is obvious in the slow upward growth of the young seedling, less apparent in the steady spiraling motion made by growing shoots and even by roots.

Germination. Within each seed is a dormant embryo plant, conceived and nurtured on the parent plant, then dispersed and arrested in its growth until it finds the conditions necessary to renew its activity. Primary among these conditions are warmth and wa-

ter, although other factors will also affect the chances of germination. Most seeds are able to withstand fairly long periods of inactivity before germinating—some up to 2,000 years, as in the case of certain lotus seeds.

When water permeates the hard seed coat, it permeates the cells, expanding their length up to one hundred times. The root of the sprouting plant emerges, the cells growing actively at the tip. Behind the tip, the cells elongate rapidly, continually increasing the length of the root.

As soon as the cells in any zone cease elongating, root hairs develop to establish the vital connection with the soil and water. The same elongation takes place in the stem until the young seedling is formed. Further growth requires new cells produced by cell division, which takes place in the *meristematic zone* at the tip of both stem and root.

Growth Regulation. The hormone *auxin,* present in the growing tips, has been shown to control growth in the young stem and root. This growth is precisely regulated, for each plant has a certain pattern that it must follow. Buds are formed and the leaves set out at exact and regular intervals, and modifications of the various parts are controlled to produce the proper structures when and where they are needed.

Growth rate, as well as form, is a function of the specific inheritance of the plant and of the favorableness of the environment. The bamboo grows with great rapidity, the oak and the bristlecone pine with extreme slowness; the maximum relative-growth rate of each is highest with adequate sunlight, warmth, moisture, and soil nutrients.

Every structure, organ, or individual plant has growth characteristics peculiar to itself and different requirements as to growth conditions. Therefore, some plants grow primarily in the spring or in midsummer; some grow in all seasons.

—Helen Buttfield

PLANTS

ABACÁ, an important plant native to the Philippine Islands, cultivated for the long strong fibers in its leaves. Known as Manila hemp, the fibers are 6 to 12 feet in length and are used in better grades of rope and cable because they wear well and do not easily jam or kink in pulleys.

Abacá bears 12 to 20 clusters of leaf stalks, each 15 to 25 feet tall, from which large, undivided leaves rise. It requires a warm, damp climate and deep, rich soil. Attempts to introduce its culture into other tropical islands and into America have largely failed. Family: Banana (Musaceae); genus and species *Musa textilis.*

ACACIA, a large genus consisting of about 500 different kinds of woody shrubs and trees, found mostly in warm climates throughout the world. Acacias have pinnately compound or feather-like leaves, clusters of small, yellow or white flowers, and, usually, long, sharp thorns. Those of Australia are called wattles. An African species yields gum arabic. An Indian species, called cutch, provided the original dye for khaki cloth. Family: Pea (Leguminosae).

ACANTHUS, a genus consisting of about 25 different kinds of handsome, thorny shrubs native to the tropics and subtropics of the Old World. Their leaves are usually broad, shiny, and deeply notched.

Acanthus flowers are in spikes, generally white, purple, or red. They are familiar because they were the models used by the ancient Greeks and Romans for decorative designs on architectural columns. In Christian painting and sculpture the acanthus leaf often symbolizes heaven. Family: Acanthus (Acanthaceae).

ACONITE, any of about 75 different kinds of hardy, perennial herbs found in mountain regions of the North Temperate Zone. They have palmate leaves, ornamental, yellow or purplish-blue flowers, and a dangerous poison in all parts. The uppermost sepal is helmet-like, giving these plants the common name of monkshood.

The European yellow aconite is called wolfsbane; it is cultivated as a garden plant and for medicinal purposes. The drug derived from it can be used in small doses as a sedative for certain respiratory and cardiac ailments. Family: Buttercup (Ranunculaceae); genus *Aconitum.*

AGAVE. See *Century Plant.*

AGERATUM, or flossflower, a genus of about 30 different kinds of tropical American herbs with opposite leaves and flowers in small, tassel-like, clustered heads. *A. mexicana,* the most easily grown as a border plant, is usually blue, but it may be white or rose-colored. Family: Daisy (Compositae).

AGRIMONY, any of about 10 different kinds of coarse, perennial herbs native to temperate regions of Eurasia, North America, Brazil, and South Africa. The pointed and toothed leaflets on the pinnately compound leaves are generally of several sizes on a single leaf. Small, yellow flowers grow in stiff spikes at the top of the 2- to 4-foot stems and develop seeds enclosed in a spiny bur. Family: Rose (Rosaceae).

AKEE, or vegetable brain, a tropical African tree that grows to 40 feet; its fruit, which is straw-colored to magenta, is also called akee. The fruit is about 3 inches long and encloses 3 shiny, spherical seeds to which are attached a corresponding number of spongy, ivory-white arils.

At exactly the correct stage of ripeness, the arils can be cooked to make a delicious vegetable with a nutty flavor. At any other stage, the whole fruit is deadly poisonous. Cultivation of the akee is forbidden in the United States, but it is a favorite food tree in Jamaica and some other Caribbean areas. Family: Soapberry (Sapindaceae); genus and species, *Blighia sapida.*

ALDER, any of about 20 different kinds of small, deciduous trees with toothed leaves and conelike fruits, most of which are native to the North Temperate Zone, although some are found south along the Andes. Alders usually grow in swamps and along the edges of streams.

The alder's wood is soft and unsuited for construction purposes, but has been used for turning and in making charcoal. Yellow, red, and brown dyes are obtained from the wood, and the bark is a source of tannin. Family: Birch (Betulaceae); genus *Alnus.*

ALFALFA, or lucerne, one of the world's leading forage plants for cattle, probably native to southwestern Asia or southeastern Europe, but now grown extensively in the United States. Its roots grow very deep, helping the plant to resist drought.

Alfalfa leaves have a high content of protein, and they can be dried to form an alfalfa meal. The flowers are small, purple, and followed by a twisted pod resembling a snail shell.

BURPEE SEEDS

AMARYLLIS

Family: Pea (Leguminosae); genus and species, *Medicago sativa.*

ALLIGATOR PEAR. See *Avocado.*

ALLSPICE, or Jamaica pepper, or pimento, a small evergreen tree of the West Indies with fragrant, leathery leaves; the spice that is made from its fruits, which are picked unripe and cured by artificial heat, is also called allspice. The flavor seems to combine and suggest those of cinnamon, clove, and nutmeg. Jamaica and Grenada are the most important sources of allspice. Family: Myrtle (Myrtaceae); genus and species, *Pimenta officinalis.*

ALMOND, a small tree native to central Asia, but now cultivated extensively around the Mediterranean and in California for its seeds, which resemble those of a peach and develop similarly inside a stony covering coated with a soft flesh and outer skin. The blossoms of the almond are beautiful, suggesting those of the peach and cherry trees, to which the almond is related.

Bitter almonds are often used for flavoring extracts; at one time they were the chief source of the poison called prussic acid, which is chiefly hydrocyanic acid. Sweet almonds are used in candy and desserts; horticultural varieties are hard-shelled, soft-shelled, and paper-shelled. Family: Rose (Rosaceae); genus and species, *Prunus amygdalus.*

ALOE, a genus consisting of about 200 different kinds of shrubby or treelike perennial plants with succulent leaves in dense rosettes either at the ground or the ends of the branches. They are native chiefly to South Africa, particularly to the Karroo deserts, where local people have learned to use them to make tonics, purgatives, and dyes. Family: Lily (Liliaceae).

ALYSSUM, a genus containing about 100 different kinds of herbs native to Europe and west-central Asia, mostly with fragrant, white or yellow flowers in clusters. Sweet alyssum (*A. maritimum*) is a favorite border plant, bearing white flowers most of the summer; golden alyssum (*A. saxatile*), known also as goldentuft, blooms profusely in early spring. Family: Mustard (Cruciferae).

AMARANTH FAMILY (Amaranthaceae), a group of about 800 different species in 64 genera, chiefly plants of tropical regions. Some are cultivated as decorative plants; others are noxious weeds. See *Cockscomb, Pigweed,* and *Tumbleweed.*

AMARYLLIS, or belladonna lily, a bulbous plant native to South Africa, now cultivated widely outdoors in warm, moist countries and indoors elsewhere for the annual cluster of large, bell-shaped flowers it produces at the top of a tall stalk. The name amaryllis is sometimes given to related plants from tropical America, which produce similar stalks of flowers before any

1648

leaves appear. Family: Amaryllis (Amaryllidaceae); genus and species, *A. belladonna.*

AMARYLLIS FAMILY (Amaryllidaceae), a group of about 1300 different species in 90 genera, many of them highly adapted for survival in arid parts of tropical and subtropical regions. See *Amaryllis, Century Plant, Narcissus, Rose-of-Sharon, Sisal, Snowdrop, Taro,* and *Tuberose.*

ANEMONE, a genus of about 100 different kinds of perennial herbs, mostly from the North Temperate Zone, but some from the Andes. They produce divided leaves from the base of the plant and showy flowers with sepals but no petals.

The delicate, starlike flower of the wood anemone, or windflower (*A. quinquefolia*), is characteristic of early spring in North American forests. The European pasque-flower (*A. pulsatilla*) and American pasque-flower (*A. patens*) bloom before the leaves expand. The blood-red poppy anemone (*A. coronaria*) grows in the open on rocky ground all around the Mediterranean Sea. Family: Buttercup (Ranunculaceae).

ANISE, an aromatic herb of eastern Mediterranean countries, raised for its seeds and the oil that can be obtained from them. The seeds are used for flavoring in condiments, candy, and cheese, and for making a liqueur. The oil is helpful in hiding the unpleasant flavor of medicines and in adding fragrance to soap and some perfumes. The leaves can be used for seasoning and garnishing. Family: Carrot (Umbelliferae); genus and species, *Pimpinella anisum.*

APPLE, any of a large number of different horticultural varieties of fruit trees native to the North Temperate Zone. The greenish-gray, oval leaves grow thickly on the spreading branches, making a pleasant shade tree. In early spring it bears small clusters of beautiful, 5-petalled blossoms that are white, tinged with pink.

The fruits ripen in summer. Each is round, reddish or yellow outside, with a central core that is star-shaped in cross section. Named varieties have been developed according to the flavor of the fruits (from sweet to sour), the color, the keeping and cooking qualities, and the normal range of sizes. Family: Rose (Rosaceae); genus and species, *Pyrus malus.*

APRICOT, a small fruit tree native to central Asia but now grown in mild, temperate climates throughout the world. The oval, orange-colored fruit has a flavor similar to that of the related peach and plum. Apricots require careful handling because they bruise easily. They are used fresh, dried, and canned. Family: Rose (Rosaceae); genus and species, *Prunus armeniaca.*

ARAUCARIA FAMILY (Araucariaceae), a group of 37 different species in 2 genera, all evergreen, coniferous trees and shrubs, mostly of the South Temperate Zone, where they are often the dominant and most valuable native timber trees. The kauri-pine (*Agathis australis*) of New Zealand is important for lumber and also for Manila-copal resin, used in paints and varnishes.

The monkey-puzzle tree (*Araucaria araucana*) of Chile is widely cultivated in warm countries as a curiosity because of its short, stiff leaves, which completely cover the branches. See also *Norfolk Island* pine.

ARBOR VITAE, literally "tree of life," a small or medium-sized, cone-bearing, evergreen tree of eastern North America from Tennessee to Canada, producing small, flat, soft leaves pressed close to the stems and hiding them. Family: Cypress (Cupressaceae); genus and species, *Thuja occidentalis.*

ARBUTUS, or ground laurel, or mayflower, or trailing arbutus, a creeping plant with oval, hairy, evergreen leaves and clusters of fragrant, white

T.H. EVERETT
ARBUTUS

or pink blossoms in early spring. It grows in light, sandy loam, but is becoming extinct or rare in many areas of New England and the eastern United States where it was formerly common because people often tear out the plants when they pick the flowers.

Arbutus is also a genus consisting of about 20 kinds of evergreen shrubs and trees native to western North America (such as the madroño, *A. menziesii,* which yields timber), Central America, and Mediterranean countries. Family: Heath (Ericaceae); genus and species, *Epigaea repens.*

ARNICA, a genus containing about 18 different kinds of perennial herbs, found in temperate and mountainous regions in Eurasia and North America, including mountain tobacco (*A. montana*), which has large, yellow heads of flowers. The roots and leaves of several species yield an extract used in liniments for sprains and bruises. Family: Daisy (Compositae).

ARROWHEAD, any of about 40 different kinds of marsh plants that produce ribbon-shaped leaves under water and arrowhead-shaped leaves in air. A leafless stalk bears whorls of white flowers, each with 3 white petals. American Indians and the Chinese, as well as other people in both hemispheres where arrowhead is native, dig the fleshy, tuberous roots as a source of starchy food. Family: Waterplantain (Alismataceae); genus *Sagittaria.*

ARROWROOT, any of a number of distantly related and unrelated plants with large, tuberous, underground stems from which a nutritious starch similar to sago can be extracted. According to tradition, arrowroot starch is particularly easy to digest, and, therefore, is a good food for infants and invalids.

West Indian arrowroot (*Maranta arundinacea*) is a member of the arrowroot family (Marantaceae); East Indian arrowroot (*Curcuma angustifolia*) is a member of the ginger family (Zingiberaceae); Queensland arrowroot (*Canna edulis*) is a tropical American member of the canna family (Cannaceae); Portland arrowroot, from the European cuckoo-pint (*Arum maculatum*), is a member of the arum family (Araceae); Hawaiian arrowroot, or pia, is from a Polynesian, liliaceous plant (*Tacca pinnatifida*) of family Taccaceae; and Florida arrowroot, or Seminole bread, or coontie, is from a member (*Zamia floridana*) of the cycad family (Cycadaceae).

ARTICHOKE, a herbaceous plant with long, prickly leaves and an upright stem 2 to 3 feet high, bearing heavy heads of white- or violet-colored flowers, each head surrounded by edible, fleshy, green bracts. Native to Mediterranean countries, the artichoke is widely cultivated (particularly in Tunisia and California) as a source of edible bracts, which are cooked as a vegetable. The so-called Jerusalem artichoke (*Helianthus tuberosus*) is a sunflower with edible, tuberous roots. Family: Daisy (Compositae); genus and species, *Cynara scolymus.*

ARUM FAMILY (Araceae), a group of about 1500 species in 105 genera, mostly of tropical regions, including plants of marshes, woodland herbs, climbing shrubs, and perching plants with aerial roots. Although the roots, stems, and leaves vary so greatly, the flowers are clustered on a cylindrical stalk (the spadix) partly surrounded by a prominent and brightly colored, leaflike bract (the spathe). See *Arrowroot, Calla lily, Jack-in-the-pulpit,* and *Skunk cabbage.*

ASH, any of about 65 different kinds of trees 50 to 125 feet high when mature, with opposite leaves that are pinnately compound and flowers that are followed by winged seeds called samaras or ash-keys. Native to north temperate regions, ash trees are valued for shade and as a source of strong, lightweight wood. Several are grown and harvested commercially, the wood used particularly for oars, baseball bats, and tool handles. The inner bark from some yields a dyestuff. The Mediterranean flowering ash (*Fraxinus ornus*) is unusual because of its showy, white petals; most European species and all those native to North America lack petals, making the flowers inconspicuous. Family: Olive (Oleaceae); genus *Fraxinus*.

ASPARAGUS, a large genus of about 300 different kinds of herbaceous plants in which the true leaves are mere scales on the green stems at the places where short, green side-shoots, called phylloclades, arise and serve in photosynthesis. All are native to the Old World particularly Africa.

One kind of asparagus (*A. Officinalis*) is cultivated for its edible young stems; when these are permitted to grow they appear feathery and produce either yellow-green, bell-shaped flowers bearing pollen, or less conspicuous, smaller flowers that mature to red berries containing seeds. Florists raise asparagus-fern (*A. plumosus*) and a related, thorny species they call smilax. (*A. asparagoides*) and use as a hardy decorative material that can be added to floral bouquets. Family: Lily (Liliaceae).

ASPEN. See *Poplar*.

ASPHODEL, any of about 12 different hardy, stemless, herbaceous plants with fleshy roots, long, gray-green leaves, and tall clusters of white or yellow flowers. They are native to warmer parts of Europe and Asia, and figure prominently in Greek mythology because they were regarded as flowers of the dead. The asphodel referred to by Shakespeare and other poets of England and France is believed to have been the related daffodil. Family: Lily (Liliaceae); genus *Asphodelus*.

ASTER, a genus composed of about 600 different kinds of tall, hardy perennials native to North America, where they are particularly abundant, and to Eurasia and Africa. They characteristically bloom in autumn, bearing flowers in starlike heads varying in color from white to pink, violet, and purple. The wild aster of Britain has been hybridized with several kinds form North America to produce the handsome horticultural Michaelmas daisy, which blooms as late as Michaelmas (September 29). Family: Daisy (Compositae).

AVOCADO, or alligator pear, a medium-sized tree of the West Indies and tropical America, with thick, oval, evergreen leaves and clusters of small, greenish flowers. The avocado can be used as a shade tree, or trimmed low in cultivation so that its fruits are easy to pick. The fruit is about the size of a large pear, green or purple outside, with a thick, soft, greenish-yellow, oily pulp around a single, large, central seed.

The pulp is eaten alone or used in salads. The seeds yield a black dye. Oil from the fruit can be used in soaps and in oil lamps. While avocados are taken for granted because they are so

U.S. DEPARTMENT OF THE INTERIOR
AZALEAS

common in the American tropics, they are prized as a delicacy in temperate regions. Family: Laurel (Lauraceae); genus and species, *Persea americana*.

AZALEA, any of a large number of deciduous shrubs in the vast genus *Rhododendron*, native to arctic and north temperate regions, and to tropical mountains as far south as New Guinea and Australia. The leaves are small, smooth-edged, oval, and dull-green; the flowers fragrant, funnel-shaped, and white, yellow, pink, or flame-colored. Many horticultural varieties have been developed, but the wild flame azalea (*R. calendulaceum*) of the Appalachians, and the rhodora (*R. canadense*) are highly esteemed. Family: Heath: (Ericaceae); genus *Rhododendron*.

BABY'S–BREATH, a fine-stemmed, narrow-leaved plant with feathery stalks of tiny pink or white flowers, characteristic of limy soil and native to Eurasia. It is widely cultivated as a perennial in gardens, where it grows to 1 to 3 feet, and is used in decorative bouquets. Family: (Caryophyllaceae); genus and species, *Gypsophila paniculata*.

BACHELOR'S BUTTON. See *Cornflower*.

BALD CYPRESS, a swamp tree of the southeastern United States, that grows in water or waterlogged soil; air reaches its roots through blunt, porous, upward projections called cypress knees. Attaining a height of 150 to 170 feet, the tree sheds all of its needles in autumn and grows new needles in spring. Like the larch, the dawn redwood, and a few other conifers it is deciduous. Its wood is hard and especially valuable for shingles. Family: Bald-cypress (Taxodiaceae); genus and species, *Taxodium distichum*.

BALD CYPRESS FAMILY (Taxodiaceae), a group of about 16 species in 9 genera, all but one native to the North Tem-

perate Zone; the exception is found in Tasmania. All are trees or shrubs with needle-like or scalelike leaves and woody cones. See *Bald-cypress*, *Cedar*, and *Sequoia*.

BALM, an aromatic, perennial herb with lemon-scented, paired leaves, growing 1 to 2 feet high and producing clusters of almost white flowers all summer. Native to Eurasia, it has been adopted as a garden plant and has escaped from cultivation to grow on roadsides and open woodlands. Family: Mint (Labiatae); genus and species, *Melissa officinalis*.

BALM OF GILIAD. See *Poplar*.

BALSA, or corkwood, a small tree of the West Indies, Central America, and northern South America, with palmately compound leaves, white flowers as much as 6 inches across, and the lightest wood known. The wood is used for airplane floats, for such rafts as the *Kon-Tiki*, and for model-making. Family: Bombax (Bombacaceae); genus and species, *Ochroma lagopus*.

BALSAM, or garden balsam, an erect, branching, annual herb 1 to 2½ feet in height, with succulent, pale-green branches, narrow, finely-toothed leaves, and short-stalked flowers in pastel colors ranging from white to deep crimson. Native to humid mountain valleys in northern India, it has been planted widely in gardens of temperate zones. The most popular variety is double-flowered. Family: Jewelweed (Balsaminaceae); genus and species, *Impatiens balsamina*.

BALSAM FIR. See *Fir*.

BAMBOO, any of about 200 different kinds of tall grasses bearing leaves at well-marked joints, between which the strong stems are hollow. They form dense thickets in tropical and subtropical countries, or clamber, vinelike, over trees, forming impenetrable tangles. Tallest is the giant bamboo (*Dendrocalamus giganteus*) of India and Malaysia, which attains a height of 120 feet.

Most widely cultivated is a smaller bamboo (*Bambusa vulgaris*) of Madagascar and tropical Asia, used to build bridges, houses, pipelines, and supports for climbing crops (such as beans and yams), and to make utensils of many kinds. Young bamboo shoots are cut as food for people in various countries; they are also a major part of the diet of gorillas in the Congo. Family: Grass (Gramineae).

BANANA, a tall, treelike, herbaceous plant of the Old World tropics, sometimes growing to more than 30 feet, with leaves 5 to 20 feet long. As each upright stem matures, it forms a terminal cluster of flowers that becomes pendant. As each spathelike bract of the flower bud opens, it exposes about a dozen flowers; the fruits from these ripen as a "hand" of bananas. Thus a single stem of bananas at the harvesting stage supports many hands, with the greener fruit closer to the remains of the bud. Additional stems from the same root system perpetuate the life of the plant after each stem load of fruits matures and the stem dies. Cultivated bananas have no seeds and must be propagated from cuttings of the root system. Bananas are second only to coconuts as commercial products of tropical countries. Family: Banana (Musaceae); genus and species, *Musa sapientum.*

BANANA FAMILY (Musaceae), a group of about 150 species in 5 genera, widely distributed in the tropics. Most are large herbs, often treelike, with broad leaves and a flower cluster that opens between spathelike bracts. It includes the famous traveler's-tree (*Ravenala madagascariensis*) of Madagascar, the decorative bird-of-paradise flowers (*Strelitzia* species) of South Africa, the handsome baliser (one of about 50 species of *Heliconia*), which is the national flower of Trinidad, and the various kinds of bananas. See *Abacá* and *Banana.*

BANEBERRY, any of about 12 different kinds of perennial herbs of the North Temperate Zone, growing 1½ to 2 feet tall, with coarsely toothed, compound leaves. The sepals drop from the small, fuzzy, white flowers as soon as they open. The flower clusters are soon followed by bright-red or waxy-white, poisonous berries on conspicuous red stalks. A Eurasian species (*Actaea spicata*) and 2 in North America (*A. alba* and *A. rubra*) are called herb Christopher. Family: Buttercup (Ranunculaceae); genus *Actaea.*

BANYAN TREE. See *Fig.*

BAOBAB, or cream-of-tartar tree, any of about 10 different kinds of tropical, deciduous trees with enormously thick trunks to 30 feet in diameter. They are native to open savannas of continental Africa, Madagascar, and

UNITED NATIONS
BANANAS

northern Australia. During prolonged dry seasons in Africa, elephants sometimes use their tusks to break through the bark of baobab trees to get at the moist, pulpy interior. The inconspicuous flowers are followed by a gourdlike fruit with a woody shell and a soft, edible, slightly acid pulp. These fruits offer a generous supply of food where monkeys can get at them and are known as monkey bread. Family Bombax (Bombacaceae); genus *Adansonia.*

BARBERRY, any of about 175 different kinds of thorny shrubs native to the North Temperate Zone, particularly Asia and the Andes. Japanese barberry (*Berberis thunbergii*), which has smooth-edged leaves, simple spines, and rather dry, plump, scarlet fruit scattered along its spreading stems, is used as a prickly hedge.

The fruit of the European barberry (*B. vulgaris*), in which many of the leaves are reduced to triple or branching spines, is borne in clusters at the tips of the branches; cultivation of this plant is prohibited in many states where wheat cultivation is important because it is the alternate host for the fungus disease known as wheat rust. A native American barberry (*B. canadensis*), which does not grow in Canada, produces fruit in flat clusters on stiff stems as much as 3 feet tall. Family: Barberry (Berberidaceae).

BARBERRY FAMILY. (Berberidaceae), a group of about 300 species in 10 genera, all perennial herbs and shrubs of the North Temperate Zone. See *Barberry, Mayapple,* and *Oregon grape.*

BARLEY, an annual grass native to Asia but now cultivated throughout the world for its grain. The individual seeds are small, and, like wheat, are produced in heads among stiff, projecting hairs; they contain no gluten and cannot be made into raised bread. Flat bread and porridge can be made of this cereal, however, and these have been customary foods in North Africa and the Near East since at least 5000 BC.

In North America, barley is raised chiefly as a food for stock animals, for use in the manufacture of malt beverages, as a breakfast cereal, and as baby food. Malt is sprouted barley seeds. Family: Grass (Gramineae); genus and species, *Hordeum vulgare.*

BASSWOOD. See *Linden.*

BAYBERRY, or candleberry, or wax myrtle, any of several different kinds of densely branching shrubs with aromatic, leathery foliage, fragrant bark, and small berries that yield wax when boiled in water. The bark is sometimes used in astringents and tonics; the wax is commonly made into candles. Family: Bayberry (Myricaceae); genus *Myrica.*

BAYBERRY FAMILY (Myricaceae), a group of about 40 species in 2 genera, all aromatic shrubs or trees of temperate and subtropical regions. They include sweet fern (*Comptonia aspleni-*

folia) of eastern North America, sweet gale (*Myrica gale*) of bogs in northern and temperate Eurasia and North America, as well as bayberry. See also Bayberry.

BAY–RUM TREE. See *Myrtle.*

BEAN, any of a large number of different erect or climbing plants with small, white, purplish, scarlet, or yellow flowers that are followed by elongated pods containing several somewhat flattened seeds. Usually the leaves are compound, consisting of 3 leaflets. The broad bean (*Vicia faba*) of the Old World is generally dried and ground up with peas and lentils, and made into soup or porridge.

Lima beans (*Phaseolus limensis*) and kidney beans (*P. vulgaris*) are from the New World and are regarded as vegetables; while still in their green, immature pods, they can be cooked as snap beans or string beans. Soybeans (*Glycine soja*), which have long been eaten by Asian peoples, from Manchuria to Japan, are now cultivated extensively as food for livestock and as a source of useful oils. Family: Pea (Leguminosae).

BEAR GRASS, any of a number of different North American, liliaceous plants with grasslike leaves and a conspicuous cluster of flowers borne on a tall, upright stalk. The name is given to several species of *Yucca* in the Gulf States and deserts of the Southwest, to some of the aloe-like sotols (*Dasylirion*) of Texas and Mexico, to camass or quamash (*Camassia*), which grows from edible bulbs in western North America, and to plants (*Xerophyllum tenax*) of western mountainsides that bear batonlike heads of creamy-white, fragrant flowers. Family: Lily (Liliaceae).

BEDSTRAW, any of about 300 different kinds of weak-stemmed, sprawling, flowering herbs found in most temperate regions, all with square stems, leaves in whorls, and clusters of small, white, yellow, or purple flowers.

Those varieties with minute hooks on the stems and leaves show resistance to crushing. This feature, and their pleasant fragrance, have made them favorite materials with which to stuff mattresses. Family: Madder (Rubiaceae); genus *Galium.*

BEECH, any of 10 different kinds of symmetrical, deciduous trees native to temperate parts of the Northern Hemisphere, generally with ash-gray bark that is so smooth that it tempts people to carve their initials into it. In medieval Germany, beechwood boards were inscribed with runes and symbolic charms. Today, the water-resistant, fine-grained wood of beech trees is valued for furniture, flooring, and tool handles because it does not split easily.

Some kinds of beech attain a height of 100 feet, with silky, oval leaves that bear coarse teeth along the sides; the flowers are small with both staminate and pistillate flowers on the same tree. Prickly husks open to drop the beechnuts, which are small, triangular, with a rich, delicate flavor. Beechnuts and acorns from oaks were formerly referred to as the mast, which was important for fattening hogs. In the Southern Hemisphere related trees called Antarctic beech (*Nothofagus* species) form large forests. Family: Beech (Fagaceae); genus *Fagus*.

BEECH FAMILY (Fagaceae), a group of about 600 species in 6 genera, many of them important timber trees. Half of the species are oaks. Equally famous, although far fewer, are the beeches and chestnuts of the North Temperate Zone. South America, New Zealand, Australia, Tasmania, and the East Indies have comparable forests of Antarctic beech trees (*Nothofagus*), including the myrtle tree (*N. cunninghami*) of Australia, which yields valuable timber. See *Beech, Chestnut,* and *Oak.*

BEET, a biennial herb native to northern Europe, where for centuries it has been cultivated for both its luxuriant tops and its straw-yellow, enlarged roots, which develop in the first year of growth. The tops can be cooked as potherbs; a favorite variety is called Swiss chard. A different variety with red instead of yellow roots appeared in the 16th century, and has been propagated widely in Britain and Anglo-America.

Sugar beets, which have a higher than normal concentration of sucrose in the roots, were developed in the late 18th century as a source of refined table sugar. In its second year the beet plant produces a new whorl of leaves and a tall branching stem bearing flower clusters and a large number of small seeds. Family: Goosefoot (Chenopodiaceae); genus and species, *Beta vulgaris.*

BEGONIA, a genus of tropical flowering plants containing more than 800 different kinds, most numerous in northern South America. The individual flowers are often showy, but always either pistillate or staminate, although both types may be included in the same cluster. The ovary bears winglike extensions, which remain conspicuous on the capsule.

Many kinds and horticultural hybrids are also cultivated for their handsome leaves, which may be shiny with wax or fringed with long hairs, and for their flowers. Some have fibrous roots, and others have tuberous or bulbous roots. Family: Begonia (Begoniaceae, which includes four other small genera of similar plants).

BELLADONNA, or deadly nightshade, a coarse herb growing 2 to 5 feet tall from a thick, perennial root, with large, smooth-edged leaves and dull-purple, solitary flowers that are followed by plump berries that range in color from purple to black when ripe. Native to Europe, it has escaped from cultivation in other temperate lands. It is the source of the poisonous alkaloid atropin. Crude extracts of this substance from the roots and stems were formerly used in Europe by actresses who wished to make

T.H. EVERETT

BEGONIA

their eyes appear more attractive by chemically dilating their pupils. The purified extract can be used to relieve pain, particularly in spasms. Family: Potato (Solanaceae); genus and species, *Atropa belladonna.*

BELLADONNA LILY. See *Amaryllis.*

BERGAMOT, a small tree of southern Europe and Asia Minor, with leaves and flowers resembling those of orange trees and small, lemon-yellow fruits shaped and formed like oranges, but yielding a fragrant, essential oil used in the manufacture of perfumes, cosmetics, and liqueurs. Wild bergamot (*Monarda fistulosa,* of the mint family, Labiatae) is an entirely different fragrant herb of North America, bearing terminal clusters of lilac-colored, pink, or white flowers. Family: Rue (Rutaceae); genus and species, *Citrus bergamia.*

BIGONIA FAMILY (Bignoniaceae), a group of about 750 species in 110 genera, chiefly tropical shrubs, trees, or woody creepers (lianas). Included are some of the world's most beautiful flowering trees, such as the species of *Jacaranda* native to Brazil and the West Indies, which have showy, blue or purple flowers, and the African tulipan or flame tree (*Spathodea campanulata*).

The sausage trees (*Kigelia* species) of tropical Africa and Madagascar, which produce elongated, woody fruits on long stalks, and the calabash tree (*Crescentia cujete*) of tropical America, which bears huge, spherical, hard-shelled fruits on its trunk and branches, are among the most unusual. See *Calabash tree, Catalpa,* and *Trumpet creeper.*

BINDWEED, or wild morning-glory, any of several different trailing, herbaceous vines from perennial roots, native to Eurasia but now widespread as weeds on roadsides and vacant land in temperate North America. It clambers on other plants, winding

around them and spreading its spear-shaped leaves and pink to white, bell-shaped flowers in the sun. Family: Morning-glory (Convolvulaceae); genus *Convolvulus.*

BIRCH, any of about 40 different kinds of woody plants of arctic, alpine, and temperate areas of the Northern Hemisphere, with saw-edged leaves that open after pollen has been distributed from long, staminate catkins and caught from the wind by shorter clusters of pistillate flowers. Arctic and alpine birches are often mere shrubs, but in the Temperate Zone the species include many graceful, trees as much as 70 feet tall.

The bark is conspicuously marked with crosswise, narrow slits (lenticels) and may be white, gray, brown, black, or red, according to the species. From canoe, or paper, birch (*Betula papyrifera*) of Canada and the northern United States, Indians cut the bark to make coverings for canoes and wigwams. Today white birch is grown as an ornamental tree.

The aromatic bark of the black birch (*B. lenta*) of eastern North America yields oil for wintergreen. The sap of others can be used instead of maple sap to produce a sweet syrup or the raw material for birch beer. Family: Birch (Betulaceae); genus *Betula.*

BIRCH FAMILY (Betulaceae), a group of about 105 species in 6 genera, all deciduous shrubs and trees with simple leaves and flowers in pendant catkins. See *Alder, Birch, Hazel,* and *Hornbeam.*

BIRTHWORT FAMILY (Aristolochiaceae), a group of about 400 species in 6 genera, 300 of them in *Aristolochia* (including *A. durior*), most of which are tropical, twining shrubs and perennial herbs. Wild ginger (*Asarum canadense*) of eastern North America is a woodland wild flower with a few kidney-shaped leaves shading peculiar, globular, chocolate-brown flowers growing at ground level. See *Dutchman's pipe.*

BITTERSWEET, either of 2 different types of woody vines bearing simple, ovate leaves and small, conspicuous fruits. One, the nightshade (*Solanum dulcamara*) of temperate Eurasia, which has been introduced and become widespread in other parts of the world, bears small clusters of pink or violet flowers, followed by bright-red, poisonous berries. It is a member of the Potato Family (Solanaceae).

The other, known also as wax-work, is a climbing plant (*Celastris scandens* of the eastern United States or *C. orbiculatus* from eastern Asia) with inconspicuous clusters of greenish flowers at the tips of side branches. In autumn, the ivory-colored coverings of the fruits split open and drop off, exposing brilliant scarlet or crimson seeds in a tight, spherical cluster. It is a representative of the Staff-tree Family (Celastraceae).

BITTERROOT, a low-growing, perennial herb of western North America, with starchy, edible roots, small, succulent leaves, and large, pink- or rose-colored flowers close to the ground. The roots were eaten by the Indians and early white colonists. It is the state flower of Montana. Family: Purslane (Portulacaceae); genus and species, *Lewisia rediviva.*

BLACKBERRY, any of 20 or more different kinds of thorny brambles of North America, with stalked leaflets in the compound leaves, and raspberry-like, edible fruits borne in terminal clusters. The canelike, arching stems grow 5 to 6 feet high and usually bear fruit in their second or third year. Family: Rose (Rosaceae); genus *Rubus.*

BLACK-EYED SUSAN, or yellow daisy, a handsome, North American wildflower, 1 to 2 feet tall, bearing a flower head the center of which is composed of numerous tiny, brown flowerets closely packed, surrounded by gay, yellow petals of flowers that have lost their reproductive parts. It thrives in dry fields, blooms from June to September, and is the state flower of Maryland. Family: Daisy (Compositae); genus and species, *Rudbeckia hirta.*

BLACK HAW, or sweethaw, or stagbush, a coarse shrub or small tree growing 15 to 40 feet tall, with spreading branches, oval leaves that turn bright red in autumn, and clusters of white flowers in April or May. Native to eastern North America, it is used as a decorative tree. Family: Honeysuckle (Caprifoliaceae); genus and species, *Viburnum prunifolium.*

BLADDERWORT, any of about 250 different kinds of carnivorous water plants found throughout the world but most varied in South America and the East Indies; they are always found in sluggish streams and ponds.

The submerged leaves, which are finely divided, bear bladder-like traps ⅛ to ¼ inch long, with hinged doors that swing inward suddenly, sucking small animals into the interior where they are held and digested. Bladderwort produces upright stems bearing white or yellow flowers, which are pollinated by flying insects. Family: Bladderwort (Lentibulariaceae); genus *Utricularia.*

BLADDERWORT FAMILY (Lentibulariaceae), a group of about 260 species in 6 genera, mostly carnivorous plants growing in moist places in the North Temperate and South Temperate zones and on mountains of tropical America. See *Bladderwort* and *Butterwort.*

BLEEDING HEART. See *Dutchman's-breeches.*

BLOODROOT. a delicate, herbaceous, perennial flower of woodlands in eastern North America, which produces an upright stem with a single, circular leaf tightly rolled around the single flower bud. The leaf opens in early spring; the flower expands its 8 to 12 white petals and lasts only a day or two. All parts of the plant contain an orange-red juice. Indians formerly gathered the thick, under-ground stems of bloodroot to obtain the juice for use as warpaint and basket dye. Family: Poppy (Papaveraceae); genus and species, *Sanguinaria canadensis.*

BLUEBELL, any of a number of low-growing plants with blue, bell-shaped flowers, particularly the widespread harebell (*Campanula rotundifolia,* of the bellflower family, Campanulaceae) of temperate Eurasia and North America, which bears one flower at the nodding tip of each of its hairlike stems, and has been made famous in poetry and prose as the "bluebell of Scotland." The name bluebell is also given to the European wood hyacinth (*Scilla nonscripta*) and the grape hyacinth (*Muscari botryoides,* both of the lily family, Liliaceae).

In New Zealand the name bluebell is used for some kinds of tuftybells (*Wahlenbergia,* a large genus of the bellflower family). In North America, bluebells may be the Virginian cowslip (*Mertensia virginica,* of the borage family, Boraginaceae), the American brooklime (*Veronica americana,* of the figwort family, Scrophulariaceae), the Jacob's ladder (*Polemonium reptans,* of the phlox family, Polemoniaceae), or the leatherflower (*Clematis crispa,* of the buttercup family, Ranunculaceae).

BLUEBERRY, any of a number of different kinds of shrubby plants of wide distribution, bearing small, bell-shaped, pink or white flowers and blue-black berries, which are usually edible and often confused with those of the related huckleberry. Many horticultural varieties have been developed from the highbush blueberry (*Vaccinium corymbosum*) of dry uplands in eastern North America, which yield large crops of berries with a delicious flavor, highly esteemed when eaten fresh, dried, frozen, or canned. Family: Heath (Ericaceae); genus *Vaccinium.*

T.H. EVERETT

BOUGAINVILLEA

BLUEBONNET. See *Lupine.*

BLUEGRASS, any of several different pasture grasses with a bluish color on the upright stems (culms). In North America, bluegrass is generally either Kentucky bluegrass (or junegrass, or speargrass, *Poa pratensis*), which is native to subarctic meadows and moist slopes in Eurasia and North America but grows well in Kentucky and other regions, or Canada bluegrass (or wiregrass, *P. compressa*), which is native to Eurasia but is now widespread in North America. Unrelated grasses are given the same name in Australia and New Zealand. Family: Grass (Gramineae).

BOMBAX FAMILY (Bombacaceae), a group of about 140 species in 22 genera, all trees of the tropics, often of vast girth or with enormous buttresses. See *Balsa, Baobab,* and *kapok.*

BONESET, any of several different related American herbs with a stout, hairy stem growing 2 to 5 feet tall and bearing wrinkled, saw-edged leaves and clusters of flowers in shaggy heads; the flowers are usually greenish-white or pale pink. The Indians used extracts from the flowers and leaves in treating ague and fevers. Family: Daisy (Compositae); genus *Eupatorium.*

BORAGE, a coarse, hairy, annual or biennial herb native to Europe, where it is cultivated as a source of nectar for bees. It has been introduced and become widespread in many other temperate areas of the world, and is noted for its clear, blue flowers. Family: Borage (Boraginaceae); genus and species, *Borago officinalis.*

BORAGE FAMILY (Boraginaceae), a group of about 2000 species in 100 genera, widely distributed, mostly herbs, commonly with simple, smooth-edged leaves covered with rough, bristly hairs. See *Bluebell, Borage, Forget-me-not,* and *Heliotrope.*

BOSTON IVY, a hardy, deciduous, woody vine native to China and Japan that climbs by means of branching tendrils with expanded, adhesive pads at the tips. Its long-petioled, simple leaves turn red or orange in autumn and usually fall before the petioles do, exposing clusters of dark purple fruits.

Introduced into New England and Canada, the plant provides wall covering in places where English ivy is killed by cold. A close relative in eastern North America is the Virginia creeper (*Parthenocissus quinquefolia*) with compound leaves consisting mostly of 5 leaflets. Family: Grape (Vitaceae); genus and species, *Parthenocissus tricuspidata.*

BOUGAINVILLEA, a genus of South American vines that bear flowers in groups of 3, surrounded by 3 purple or red conspicuous bracts. A Brazilian species (*B. spectabilis*) is cultivated in warm countries as a decorative covering for walls. Family: Four-o'clock (Nyctaginaceae).

BOUNCING BET, or soapwort, an attractive, perennial herb with a sturdy, smooth stem, smooth, oval leaves, and clusters of pink or white flowers. Native to Europe, it has become a roadside weed in North America. Colonial housewives crushed its leaves into water to produce a lather possessing some of the qualities of a soap solution. Family: Pink (Caryophyllaceae); genus and species, *Saponaria officinalis.*

BOX, a popular evergreen shrub native to western and southern Europe, cultivated in many temperate and cool climates as a hedge plant. It grows slowly to a height of 16 feet, producing small, oval leathery leaves so close together that they provide privacy and a screen from the wind. The flowers are inconspicuous. The pale yellow wood is very hard and sometimes used for wood engraving and for making wind instruments. Family: Box (Buxaceae); genus and species, *Buxus sempervirens.*

BOX ELDER. See *Maple.*

BRACKEN, or brake, any of several kinds of tall, coarse ferns growing 2 to 14 feet tall, their fronds divided into 3 branches and bearing spore cases underneath the edges. Found throughout the world, particularly in dry, rocky pastures, these ferns can be dug up to extract a solution used as a bitter beverage or for tanning from their thick, underground stems. Family: Polypody (Polypodiaceae); genus *Pteridium.*

BRAZIL NUT, a tree that grows in moist soil along river banks in northern South America, where it attains a height of 100 to 150 feet, and bears huge, oval, leathery leaves, creamy-white flowers, and large, globular pods containing 18 to 24 wedge-shaped, oily seeds, each in a hard seed coat. The seeds, called brazil nuts, are flavorful and edible, and yield an oil used by watchmakers and artists, as well as by native people for fuel in lamps. Family: Brazil nut (Lecythidaceae); genus and species, *Bertholletia excelsa.*

BRAZIL NUT FAMILY (Lecythidaceae), a group of 315 species in 18 genera, all tropical trees with simple leaves clustered at the ends of the branches. Included is the strange cannonball tree (*Couroupita guianensis*) of northern South America and the West Indies, which bears large rust-colored, woody, seed-filled capsules on short, twisted side branches extending from the main trunk; it is a source of good timber. See also *Brazil nut.*

BREADFRUIT, a tropical tree with thick, oval leaves that are deeply indented around the edge. Native to the South Pacific islands, where it rarely grows to more than 40 feet tall, the breadfruit is valued for its large, spherical, green fruits, each pebbled on the outside and full of a starchy pulp that is edible when baked or fried. A sticky substance that oozes from wounds in the bark can be used as birdlime or to seal the seams of small boats.

Strong bast fibers can be removed from the inner bark and woven into tapa cloth. The wood itself can be used to build houses or canoes. First described by Capt. James Cook, breadfruit was introduced into the West Indies as food for Negro slaves by Capt. William Bligh after an expedition to Tahiti aboard the famous ship *H.M.S. Bounty.* Family: Mulberry (Moraceae); genus and species, *Artocarpus incisa.*

BRIDAL WREATH. See *Spiraea.*

BROCCOLI. See *Mustard.*

BROOM, any of several related plants with long, slender, stiff, green branches, small leaves, and showy, yellow flowers resembling those of a sweet pea. Scotch broom (*Cytisus scoparius*), which is native to Britain and temperate parts of Europe, has been introduced into North America, South Africa, and New Zealand, where it grows well. A medicine made from the foul-tasting twigs and seeds has been used as a diuretic.

Other plants to which the name broom is applied include several kinds of gorse (*Genista* and *Ulex* species) of Europe, western Asia, and north Africa. Family: Pea (Leguminosae).

BROOMCORN, a tall coarse, annual sorghum native to warm parts of Eurasia, but cultivated in America since colonial days. It has escaped from cultivation. It raises jointed stems either 4 to 6 feet tall (dwarf variety) or 10 to 14 feet tall (standard variety), which bear long leaves and terminate in a brushlike cluster of inconspicuous flowers. After the seeds have ripened the long "broom straws" of the flower cluster are gathered and

T.H. EVERETT

BUCKTHORN

used to make brooms and brushes. Family: Grass (Gramineae); genus and species, *Sorghum vulgare technicus.*

BRUSSELS SPROUTS. See *Mustard.*

BUCKEYE. See *Horsechestnut.*

BUCKTHORN, any of about 100 different kinds of woody shrubs, mostly from the North Temperate Zone. They include some that attain a height of 12 feet, with black bark, small, scalloped leaves, tiny 4-petalled, yellowish-green flowers, and blue-black berries which yield a purgative juice and a pigment used by painters. Most buckthorns have thorny branches.

Dried bark of the western North American *Rhamnus purshiana* is called *cascara sagrada* (sacred bark), and is the source of a mild laxative. Family: Buckthorn (Rhamnaceae); genus *Rhamnus.*

BUCKTHORN FAMILY (Rhamnaceae), a widely distributed group of about 550 species in 45 genera, all tree or shrubs with simple leaves and flowers that, strangely, have stamens that are opposite to the petals instead of alternate with them. Several kinds are valued for their fruits, as well as for drugs or ornamental planting. See *Buckthorn* and *Jujube.*

BUCKWHEAT, an annual herb with a slender, jointed stem, 2 to 3 feet tall, bearing heart-shaped leaves and clusters of small, white, pink, or purplish-red flowers. Although the plant is not a grass, the ripened seeds are regarded as a cereal crop.

Cultivated for many centuries in the Orient, buckwheat was introduced into Europe and then into North America where it is grown in the northeastern United States as a food for cattle and poultry, or made into a flour for griddle cakes. Buckwheat honey has a distinctively dark color, and a strong flavor. Family: Buckwheat (Polygonaceae); genus and species, *Fagopyrum sagittatum.*

BUCKWHEAT FAMILY (Polygonaceae), a group of about 800 species in 32 genera, mostly herbs of the North Temperate Zone, but including also some shrubs, climbing vines, and trees. They are encountered as small trees on tropical beaches, for example, the sea grape (*Coccoloba uvifera*), which has edible fruits; or as coral-vine (*Antigonum leptopus*) of Mexico and Central America, which climbs trellises or tall trees and bears a profusion of pink flowers. See *Buckwheat, Dock, Rhubarb,* and *Sheep sorrel.*

BULRUSH, any of about 200 different kinds of grasslike herbs with narrow leaves in 3 rows that provide a sheath for the triangular stem. Widely distributed, they are plants of shallow water or wet soil, particularly characteristic of bogs, marshes, and wet moorland in areas where the climate is cool. The end of the stem bears many flowers in a clublike cluster. The "bulrushes" of which the floating cradle of the infant Moses was made were probably *Iris* because bulrushes do not grow in Egypt, whereas *Iris* leaves are still used for such purposes along the Nile. Family: Sedge (Cyperaceae); genus *Scirpus*.

BUNCHBERRY, a low-growing herb of cool, damp woodlands in northeastern North America, producing 4 to 6 oval leaves above which a slender stalk bears 4 to 6 conspicuous, white bracts resembling petals around the central cluster of inconspicuous green flowers. When ripe, the clustered scarlet berries are edible. Family: Dogwood (Cornaceae); genus and species *Cornus canadensis*.

BURDOCK, a coarse biennial herb native to temperate Eurasia but now widespread as a weed in North America. In its first year it produces broad, wavy-edged leaves, and stores nourishment in a sturdy root. The following year it raises a branched, leafy stem with flowers opening in heads from July until the frost arrives.

Hooked bristles cover the flower heads, which have pink or purplish florets packed tightly together, converting the cluster of ripened seeds into a bur that catches on to clothing or the fur of passing animals. New burdocks grow along paths, fences, and walls where the burs are scratched free or fall. Family: Daisy (Compositae); species chiefly *Arctium lappa*, the great burdock, *A. minus*, the common burdock, and *A. nemorosum*, or hybrids among these.

BURNING BUSH. See *Euonymus*.

BUTTERCUP, or crowfoot, any of about 300 different kinds of wildflowers with tough, green, branching stems 3 to 30 inches tall, bitter juice, small, deeply-cut leaves, and cup-shaped flowers, generally golden-yellow and intensely reflecting. They are found in wet areas of cool and temperate regions, in the Arctic, north temperate, and alpine areas of the Americas and New Zealand. The Mt. Cook lily (*Ranunculus lyalli*) has large, white flowers and is the national flower of New Zealand. Family: Buttercup (Ranunculaceae); genus *Ranunculus*.

BUTTERCUP FAMILY (Ranunculaceae), a group of about 1500 species of herbs, vines, or shrubs in 5 genera, common to both the North Temperate and South Temperate zones. See *Aconite, Anemone, Baneberry, Bluebell, Buttercup, Clematis, Columbine, Hellebore, Hepatica, Larkspur, Marsh marigold, Monkshood, Peony, Wolfsbane,* and *Woodbine*.

BUTTERFLY BUSH, a decorative, tall, branching herb of northwest China, with showy clusters of small, lilac-colored flowers that attract butterflies and other insects. Widely introduced as a garden plant, it thrives in sunny, warm climates. Family: Logania (Loganiaceae): genus and species, *Buddleia alternifolia*.

BUTTERFLY–FLOWER, a tall, herbaceous plant native to Chile but widely introduced into gardens for its lacy, fernlike leaves and varicolored flowers, each of which has small, wing-like petals suggesting those of a butterfly. Family: Potato (Solanaceae); genus and species, *Schizanthus pinnatus*.

BUTTERFLY WEED. See *Milkweed*.

BUTTERNUT. See *Walnut*.

BUTTERWORT, any of about 40 different kinds of small, herbaceous plants that grow in wet soil. They are prevalent in the North and South Temperate zones and the mountains of tropical America.

Thick oblong leaves arise in a rosette close to the ground; first they capture and then they digest insects that alight and are caught on the sticky surface. Small clusters of violet-like flowers, generally blue or purple, are borne on an upright stalk, which is about 4 inches tall. Family: Bladderwort (Lentibulariaceae); genus *Pinguicula*.

BUTTONWOOD. See *Plane-tree family*.

CABBAGE. See *Mustard*.

CACAO, a small tree native to Central America and northern South America, with a thick trunk that grows to 40 feet, spreading branches with a downy covering, leathery, oval leaves that hang downward, and inconspicuous, pink flowers on cushion-like projections from the trunk; the large fruits, 10 to 14 inches long and 5 inches in diameter, are dark purplish-red on the outside, and have 25 to 50 purple seeds embedded in a mucilaginous, pink pulp.

The seeds, or cocoa beans, can be removed by hand, cured by fermentation, and dried. Later they can be ground and processed to make cacao powder and chocolate. Cacao orchards that provide the world with chocolate have always been planted with a cover of taller trees to provide the necessary shade; this is particularly true of tropical Africa. Family: Sterculia (Sterculiaceae); genus and species, *Theobroma cacao*.

CACTUS FAMILY (Cactaceae), a group of about 1700 species in 120 genera, originally from the New World, most with fleshy stems armed with spines and bristles, leaves that drop off without expanding, and large flowers followed by a fleshy berry. Many are cultivated for their unusual form and handsome flowers. Prickly-pear (*Opuntia* species), barrel cactus (*Ferocactus* species), Christmas cactus (*Zygocactus truncatus*) from Brazil, and organ-pipe cactus (*Cereus marginatus*) are among the forms that have attracted widespread attention. See *Night-blooming Cereus* and *Saguaro*.

CALABASH TREE, a small tree native to tropical America, with opposite leaves on its small branches but with flowers extending from the bark of large branches and the trunk. The fruits develop as much as 12 inches in diameter, with a hard rind. Native people clean out the central pulp and seeds, thus creating a woody calabash

U.S. DEPARTMENT OF THE INTERIOR
CACTUS

that can be used to carry liquids or as a drinking utensil. Family: Bignonia (Bignoniaceae); genus and species, *Crescentia cujete*.

CALCEOLARIA, or slipperwort, a genus containing about 200 different kinds of herbaceous, perennial plants native to America from Mexico to Tierra del Fuego, growing 1 to 2 feet tall, bearing oval leaves and usually, yellow flowers with red markings, each flower with a large, saclike, lower lip and a small, erect, upper lip. Family: Figwort (Scrophulariaceae).

CALENDULA. See *Pot marigold*.

CALLA LILY, a cultivated South African herbaceous plant with thick, starchy, horizontal, underground stems and green, upright stems bearing large, white, flower-like spathes around a bright yellow spadix of minute flowers. A golden calla (*Zantedeschia elliottiana*) has white-spotted leaves and a yellow spathe.

The name calla is actually that of the genus of a related but small-flowered water arum (*Calla palustris*), which is native to the bogs and marsh edges of the North Temperate Zone. Family: Arum (Araceae); genus and species, *Zantedeschia aethiopica*.

CALTROP, any of more than 20 different kinds of Eurasian, African, and American perennial herbs and shrubs with opposite, leathery leaves, the inconspicuous flowers of which produce hard fruits with sharp, rigid spines. These fruits, called caltrops, may puncture the tires of bicycles and automobiles as well as wound the feet of man and animal; *Tribulus terrestris*, which is a native weed from the Mediterranean to Tibet that has been introduced and become widepsread elsewhere, is therefore called puncture weed.

In the Middle Ages arms makers used the caltrop fruit as a model for a metal device with 4 sharp spikes equally spaced in radial directions; one of these spikes always pointed upward no matter how the device rested, thus readily maiming a horse or man who stepped on it. Family: Caltrop (Zygophyllaceae); genera *Tribulus* and *Kallstroemia*.

CALTROP FAMILY (Zygophyllaceae), a group of about 250 species in 27 genera, chiefly plants of warm regions, all with opposite leaves. Several kinds are grown as ornamental, and some are useful trees. Bean capers *(Zygophyllum fabago)* of Asia Minor yield buds than can be pickled for use as a condiment. See *Caltrop, Creosote-bush,* and *Lignum vitae.*

CAMELLIA, a genus of Asian shrubs with glossy, pointed, slightly toothed, evergreen leaves and waxy, roselike flowers, 3 to 7 inches in diameter, ranging in color from red to white. Of the 80 different species, many are cultivated widely in temperate areas as house plants.

C. sinensis, native to the area from Japan to India, is raised on plantations to yield young twigs and partly opened leaves that are cured, dried, and later steeped to yield a tea. Tea bushes or tea trees can naturally attain a height of 30 feet, but they are usually pruned to a height of 3 to 5 feet to enable workers to reach more easily the young growth that is to be picked. Family: Tea (Theaceae).

CAMOMILE, or chamomile, any of several related branching herbs with pinnately dissected leaves and solitary, terminal heads of small, daisylike flowers. These plants have long been gathered or cultivated for their aromatic foliage and young stems, which are the source of a drug used to induce perspiration and to inhibit muscular spasms. Some species are grown as decorative garden plants. Family: Daisy (Compositae); genera *Anthemis* and *Matricaria.*

CAMPHOR. See *Cinnamon.*

CANDYTUFT, any of about 30 different kinds of herbaceous, branching, stiff plants with toothed or deeply cut, narrow leaves and showy white or crimson flowers in which the lowest 2 of the 4 petals are larger than the others. The first species introduced as low-growing garden plants were annuals from Candia on the island of Crete; hence the name candytuft. Others that are now widely cultivated are evergreen perennials, produced primarily in Mediterranean countries. Family: Mustard (Cruciferae): genus *Iberis.*

CANNA, a genus of about 60 different kinds of tropical American plants that comprise a separate family. Many are cultivated for their large, sheathing leaves, which are green, bronze, or red, and for their terminal clusters of red, white, or yellow flowers in which the conspicuous parts are 1 to 5, petal-like, modified stamens. The underground stem of *C. edulis,* from Central America, is starchy and edible and known as Queensland arrowroot. Family: Canna (Cannaceae).

CANTALOUPE. See *Melon.*

CANTERBURY BELL. See *Bellflower.*

CAPE JASMINE. See *Gardenia.*

CAPER, any of about 350 different kinds of shrubs and small trees found in warm climates, some climbing by means of tendrils from the axils of the simple leaves. The showy flowers have 4 sepals, 4 petals, and numerous stamens. The flower buds of a Mediterranean species called capers *(Capparis spinosa)* are dried for use as seasoning; the plants are cultivated for this purpose. Family: Caper (Capparidaceae); genus *Capparis.*

CAPER FAMILY (Capparidaceae), a group of about 700 species in 46 genera, all tropical or subtropical herbs, shrubs, or trees. One kind, the Spider-flower *(Cleome spinosa)* of tropical America, is a widespread, cultivated, garden ornament, named for its extraordinarily long, projecting stamens. See also *Caper.*

CARAWAY, an erect, biennial herb with aromatic, pinnately compound leaves, and white or pink flowers in clusters, producing small seeds with a distinctive flavor. The plants are cultivated in many temperate countries.

Plants were introduced from Europe to obtain seeds that are dried and added as flavoring to bread, cheese, candy, soups, and sauces. An oil extracted from the seeds is used in soaps and perfumes. Family: Carrot (Umbelliferae); genus and species, *Carum carvi.*

CARDAMOM, an East Indian herb with elongated, sheathing leaves and a stem growing to 10 feet, topped by a spike of white-striped, purple flowers that are followed by 3-cornered pods containing aromatic, brown, white-lined seeds. Cultivated for its seeds, particularly in Ceylon, India, and Latin America, cardamon is the source of medicinal substances with stimulant and purgative qualities as well as the preferred source of a spice that is added to curries.

The name cardamom (or cardamon or cardamum) is also given to alternate spices from a related plant, *Anomum cardamon,* of Java. Family: Ginger (Zingiberaceae); genus and species, *Elletaria cardamomum.*

CARDINAL FLOWER. See *Lobelia.*

CARNATION. See *Pink.*

CAROB. See *Locust.*

CARROT, or Queen Anne's lace, a biennial, herbaceous plant with finely divided leaves and flat-topped clusters of small white flowers. It is native to Europe but has been introduced and become widespread as a weed all over the world.

A cultivated variety, with a large, edible, yellowish or reddish-orange root from its first year of growth, is valued as a food because of its high content of vitamin A and minerals. Family: Carrot (Umbelliferae); genus and species, *Daucus carota.*

T.H. EVERETT

CAMELLIA

CARROT FAMILY (Umbelliferae), a group of about 2900 species in 125 genera, represented on all continents but most numerous in the North Temperate Zone. Most are biennial or perennial herbs with aromatic leaves, the stalks of which enclose the stems, and with flat-topped clusters of flowers (umbels). See *Anise, Caraway, Carrot, Celery, Dill Fennel, Parsley, Parsnip,* and *Poison hemlock.*

CASCARA SAGRADA. See *Buckthorn.*

CASHEW, a small tree native to the American tropics, with alternate, simple leaves, clusters of 5-part flowers, and distinctive fruits called cashew apples, each with a large, pearlike, fleshy portion below which a hard-shelled seed, called a cashew nut, projects. The cashew apple is edible; the seeds can be made edible by roasting to destroy a poisonous, irritating compound and break the shells. Family: Sumac (Anacardiaceae); genus and species, *Anacardium occidentale.*

CASSAVA, or manioc, or yuca, either of 2 kinds of erect, slender, woody plants of tropical America, with stems growing to 9 feet tall and bearing large leaves that are deeply notched into 3 to 7 long, narrow, spreading lobes. The fleshy underground stems, which may be 3 feet long and 9 inches in diameter, are dug up, purified of any bitter poisonous substances present, and converted into either a flour from which a flat bread can be made or into a pudding known as tapioca.

These foods are produced from cultivated cassava plants; they provide a poor diet but are the principal sources of nutritional calories in many parts of Latin America, tropical Africa, and from Malaya through the East Indies and the South Pacific islands. Family: Spurge, (Euphorbiaceae); genus and species, *Manihot esculenta* (bitter) and *M. palmata* (sweet).

CASTOR–OIL PLANT, or palma Christi, a tropical perennial shrub or small tree of Africa and Asia, which reaches a

BURPEE SEEDS

CARROTS

height of 30 to 40 feet, with palmately compound, bronze-green leaves, small flowers in loose clusters, and spiny capsules that contain poisonous, mottled seeds.

The castor-oil plant grows quickly and produces fruits even in temperate climates, where it is killed by winter frosts and can therefore be cultivated only as an annual. Castor oil can be extracted from the seeds; it is used as a violent laxative and as a fine lubricating oil. Family: Spurge (Euphorbiaceae); genus and species, *Ricinus communis*.

CATALPA, a genus comprised of 10 different trees of East Asia and eastern North America, including the West Indies, several of which have been introduced and become widespread beyond their native areas for their attractive, large, heart-shaped, mostly opposite leaves; their tall, open clusters of 2-lipped, frilled flowers; and their useful wood. They produce drooping, cylindrical pods 6 to 20 inches long for which the trees are often called Indian beans or cigar-trees. Family: Bignonia (Bignoniaceae).

CATNIP, an aromatic, perennial herb native to Eurasia, with an erect, square stem, opposite, pointed, serrate, velvety leaves, and terminal whorls of white, purplish, or blue-tinged flowers. Introduced and widespread in most temperate parts of the world, it was long valued as the basis of a catnip tea used for colic and colds. Cats are attracted by the odor of the fresh or dried aerial parts of the plant. Family: Mint (Labiatae); genus and species, *Nepeta cataria*.

CATTAIL, any of 12 different perennial herbs found in marshes all over the world, with starchy, horizontal stems in water-soaked soil and erect, sword-shaped leaves partially sheathing upright stems that end in club-shaped spikes of minute flowers. The top of the spike consists of staminate flowers which soon drop off, leaving a naked length of stem beyond the clustered, pistillate flowers, which have a furry

appearance. The single genus is in a family by itself. Family: Cattail (Typhaceae); genus *Typha*.

CAULIFLOWER. See *Mustard.*

CEDAR, in the strict sense, any of 4 different kinds of handsome, evergreen, coniferous trees native to Eurasia, where 3 are becoming rare because of the excessive harvesting of the fragrant wood. Only the deodar (*Cedrus deodara*) in its native Himalayan forests is not yet seriously threatened.

The famous cedar of Lebanon (*C. libanotica*) is represented today by a few dwindling forests in Turkey and scattered trees introduced elsewhere. The Cyprus cedar (*C. brevifolia*) is threatened in addition by goats and fires. The Atlantic cedar (*C. atlantica*), which was once widespread in Algeria and Morocco, is now scarce.

All cedars have rather short, sharp needles arranged in spirals on spurlike side branches; they shed their winged seeds when the ovulate cones disintegrate, dropping their scales and leaving only the central supporting stem attached to the branch.

Many unrelated coniferous trees with fragrant wood belonging to genera *Chamaecyparis* (North American), *Juniperus* (North Temperate), *Libocedrus* (Pacific coasts), *Thuja* (North American and East Asian), and *Widdringtonia* (African, in the cypress family, Cupressaceae), and *Cryptomeria* (Japanese, in the baldcypress family, Taxodiaceae), are commonly referred to as cedars. Family: Pine (Pinaceae); genus *Cedrus*.

CELANDINE, a European biennial herb 1 to 2 feet tall, with a sprawling, brittle stem, deeply notched, alternate leaves, and odorless, yellow flowers; its yellow juice, which stains skin and clothing, contains a dangerous poison. Family: Poppy (*Papaveraceae*); genus and species, *Chelidonium majus*.

CELERY, a biennial herb native to Europe but widely cultivated for its fleshy petioles, which are eaten raw or cooked, and for its seeds, which are dried for use as a condiment. It has fibrous roots, a very short stem, and deeply divided leaf blades. When allowed to flower, it produces small blossoms in flat topped clusters. Family: Carrot (Umbelliferae); genus and species, *Apium graveolens*.

CENTURY PLANT, any of about 230 different kinds of succulent-leaved plants of arid and semiarid areas from northern South America to the southern United States. Most have stems that remain very short and produce an ever greater whorl of thick sword-shaped leaves until a critical amount of nourishment has been accumulated. Then, during a month or two of rapid growth, the stem extends upward to a height of as much as 20 feet, displaying a large cluster of fragrant, yellow, tubular flowers. After blooming, the plant develops seeds and sometimes suckers, but the leaves and main stem die. Originally believed to require a century to bloom, cen-

tury plants normally need 20 years or less. Many are cultivated for the strong fibers in their leaves, which include henequen (from *Agave fourcroydes*), sisal (from *A. sisalana* and *A. letonae*), istle (from *A. lophantha* and *A. funkiana*), Mauritius hemp (from *Fourcroya gigantea*), cabuya (from *F. cabuya*), and fique, the fibers of which are used in making Colombian coffee bags (from *F. macrophylla*). Family: Amaryllis (Amaryllidaceae); genera *Agave* and *Fourcroya*.

CHARD. See *Beet.*

CHERIMOYA. See *Custard-apple.*

CHERRY, any of several trees of the North Temperate Zone with small, smooth, oval leaves usually finely toothed around the edge, beautiful clusters of fragrant, white or pinkish flowers, and edible fruits with a soft pulp and a central, armored seed.

Some, such as the black cherry (*Prunus serotina*) of eastern North America, attain a height of 100 feet and are sought after for their hardwood. Others such as the sweet cherry (*P. avium*) of southern Europe and the sour cherry (*P. cerasus*) of Asia, are appreciated for their fruit. Still others, such as the flowering cherry (*P. serrulata*) of Japan, are planted for their spring flowers and attractive foliage; the small and rather tasteless fruits are left for the birds. Family: Rose (Rosaceae); genus *Prunus*.

CHESTNUT, any of 10 different kinds of shrubs and trees of the Northern Hemisphere, bearing alternate leaves that are coarsely serrate and have conspicuously straight side veins. The staminate flowers are borne in cream-colored, loose catkins; the pistillate flowers are small but produce 2 or 3 nuts grouped in a leathery bract, which opens to release them.

Best known is the Spanish or Italian chestnut (*Castanea sativa*) of the Mediterranean region, with large, edible nuts, sold freshly roasted on street corners in many large cities. The American chestnut (*C. dentata*), of the eastern United States and Canada, was formerly important as a timber and nut tree, but it has almost been exterminated by a fungus blight that still prevents it from becoming reestablished. Family: Beech (Fagaceae); genus *Castanea*.

CHICKWEED, any of about 200 different kinds of frail, quick-growing, herbaceous perennials of temperate regions, rarely more than 8 inches tall, with small, oval leaves in pairs at swellings on the slender stems, and with solitary or clustered white flowers bearing 5-notched petals. Both flowers and seeds are produced throughout the spring and summer. Family: Pink (Caryophyllaceae); evenly divided between genera *Stellaria* and *Cerastium*.

CHICORY, or succory, a perennial herb of the Mediterranean region, now cosmopolitan as a weed. The lower leaves are oval, the upper leaves on the stiff, flowering stems are very small and bractlike, and the flower heads are 1½ inches across and composed entirely of strap-shaped florets in varying shades of blue.

In Europe the long, heavy taproots are dug up, dried, and pulverized to make a substitute for coffee or to adulterate the coffee. The blanched lower leaves can be used for salads. A close relative, the endive (*Cichorium endiva*), has frilly, bitter, edible leaves. The endive is cultivated largely for use in salads. Family: Daisy (Compositae); genus and species, *Cichorium intybus*.

CHINABERRY, or bead tree, or pride of India, a fast-growing, spreading tree native to eastern Asia and northern Australia but introduced widely. It has alternate, pinnately compound leaves, large clusters of fragrant, purplish flowers, which are followed by nearly spherical, yellow fruits ½ inch in diameter. The thin pulp soon dries over the armored seed, producing a "bead." Family: Mahogany (Meliaceae); genus and species, *Melia azedarach*.

CHOCOLATE. See *Cacao.*

CHRISTMAS BERRY, a shrub or small tree native to California and used there in place of holly for Christmas decorations. Growing 5 to 25 feet high, the tree has pale, aromatic bark, glossy, serrate, evergreen leaves, loose clusters of white flowers, and bright red berries which are edible, pleasant tasting, and ripen during the coldest part of winter. Family: Rose (Rosaceae); genus and species, *Heteromeles arbutifolia*.

CHRISTMAS ROSE. See *Hellebore.*

CHRYSANTHEMUM, a genus of about 150 different kinds of annual and perennial herbaceous plants of the Northern Hemisphere and Africa, some of which are attractive weeds, and others of which are cultivated for their handsome flowers. All have notched or pinnately divided leaves and flattened flower heads.

The oxe-eye daisy or whiteweed (*C. leucanthemum*) of Eurasia is now almost cosmopolitan in temperate regions. The East Asian species (particularly *C. morifolium*) were cultivated in early times, leading Japan to adopt a stylized chrysanthemum with 16 florets as its national emblem; horticultural varieties include many in which all florets are strap shaped and twisted, the flower heads as much as 10 inches across and in many colors. Family: Daisy (Compositae).

CINCHONA, a genus of perhaps 40 different kinds of trees native to mountain slopes from Peru northward to Costa Rica, with red bark, spreading branches, opposite, ovate leaves, and open clusters of pink flowers. The fruit is a capsule that opens to release its many seeds. Known since about 1630 as a source of an anti-malarial drug, quinine, cinchona trees have been cultivated in India and Java; the latter country is the principal commercial producer of the drug itself, which is extracted from the bark, called Peruvian bark. Family: Madder (Rubiaceae).

CINERARIA, the florist's name for a herbaceous perennial plant from the Canary Islands, with large, ovate leaves, short, branching stem, and large, daisy-like flowers with purple disc florets and white, red, or purple ray florets. *Cineraria* is a genus of South African herbs and low shrubs with thistle-like flowers. Family: Daisy (Compositae); genus and species, *Senecio cruentus*.

CINNAMON, a small evergreen tree native to Ceylon, but cultivated in China, tropical America, Florida, and California for the inner bark of its young shoots and branches, which yields a popular flavoring, cinnamon. The tree itself has large, ovate, paired leaves, loose clusters of malodorous, greenish flowers, and small, fleshy fruits. Oil can be extracted from the fruit and leaves as well as from the bark, but only the light, yellowish-brown bark can be powdered as a spice; the spice has a sweet, warm taste from the aromatic oil it contains.

A closely related tree native to Formosa, Japan, and China (*Cinnamomum camphora*) is now cultivated in California, Texas, and Florida as a shade tree, a windbreak, and a source of gum; it is the principal source of camphor, which is distilled from young shoots or old trees cut into chips. Family: Laurel (Lauraceae); genus and species, *Cinnamomum zeylanicum*.

CITRON, a small evergreen tree with irregular branches, large, oval leaves, and bluish blossoms. It is native to India, China and Southeast Asia but is cultivated chiefly in southern Europe, primarily for its greenish-yellow lemon-shaped fruits, 5 to 6 inches long; the fruit rind is candied and the juice used as a beverage or concentrated to a syrup. An oil extracted from citron leaves is used in making perfume. Family: Rue (Rutaceae); genus and species, *Citrus medica*.

CLEMATIS, a genus containing about 230 different kinds of vines and climbing shrubs with opposite compound leaves the petioles of which are tendril-like and curl around supports. The flowers of all lack petals but have 4 showy sepals and many stamens. Represented on most continents in areas with cool summers, the genus is best known in eastern North America as virgin's-bower, or old-man's-beard (*C. virginiana*), which has feathery plumes attached to the many seeds in each cluster of a flower. Family: Buttercup (Ranunculaceae).

CLOVER, any of about 300 different kinds of herbaceous plants native to temperate and subtropical regions, bearing palmately compound leaves with 3 to 5 leaflets, and round heads of tiny, closely packed, white, pink, or purplish flowers. Bees make some of the most delicious honey known from their nectar. Clovers are valuable forage plants for livestock, and are often grown as part of a rotational sequence for soil improvement. Family: Pea

DURPEE SEEDS

CINERARIA

(Leguminosae); genus *Trifolium*. See also *Sweet clover.*

CLOVE TREE, a tropical evergreen tree with large oval leaves, native to the East Indies, where it grows to a height of 50 feet. It is cultivated near the seacoasts and on tropical islands of South America, the West Indies, and Africa, particularly Zanzibar. It is pruned as a low shrub from which the buds of the clustered, crimson flowers can easily be picked in order to be dried and used as spice cloves. Each tree yields from 5 to 75 pounds of cloves annually.

The spice is used for making candy and clove liqueur, and for flavoring. Oil of cloves, extracted by distillation, is used in medicine, soaps, and perfumes. Family: Myrtle (Myrtaceae); genus and species, *Eugenia aromatica*.

CLUB MOSS, any of about 180 different kinds of creeping herbaceous plants found almost all over the world, with upright stems clad in evergreen and bractlike leaves, bearing spore cases either among the leaves or clustered to form the club-shaped ends of the vertical stems. The spores are carried by wind, and can germinate in moist soil into ½-inch, carrot-shaped plants with sex organs. Fertilized eggs in these develop into the club moss.

Because of a fancied resemblance, various club mosses are known as staghorn evergreen, ground pine, ground fir, and ground cedar. Few grow more than a foot tall, and most live in moist forests. Family: Club moss (Lycopodiaceae); genus *Lycopodium*.

COCA, a small shrub of mountain slopes in Bolivia and Peru, with straight branches growing to a height of 8 feet, bearing small, oval leaves distinctly marked with a transparent area on each side of the midrib; the small, white flowers are followed by small, black berries. The native people have learned to pluck the leaves as soon as each is stiff enough to break when bent, to dry them, and to keep them dry. The product, which resembles tea

UNITED NATIONS

CORN

leaves, is chewed by Indians at work or on long journeys, dulling hunger and fatigue and apparently giving them strength and endurance; or it is marketed as a source of the drug cocaine, which is used as a local anesthetic in surgery. Coca belongs to a genus of about 200 different species native to the American tropics, many of which contain smaller amounts of cocaine. They form a small family. Family: Coca (Erythroxylaceae); genus and species, *Erythroxylum coca.*

COCKSCOMB, a low-growing, herbaceous plant of tropical Asia, widely cultivated in temperate gardens as an annual because, about its long, pointed, green leaves, it produces a monstrous flower head suggesting a rooster's comb. The flower head is sometimes as wide as the plant is tall and consists of crimson, orange, or creamy-white flowers at the ends of multiple stalks that grow in a fan-shaped bundle. Family: Amaranth (Amaranthaceae); genus and species, *Celosia aristata.*

COCOA. See *Cacao.*

COFFEE, any of about 45 different kinds of small trees with paired, oval, shining, evergreen leaves and clusters of fragrant, white flowers from which, after about 7 months, crimson, cherry-like fruits develop, each containing 2 flat seeds known as coffee beans.

Native to Arabia and tropical Africa, particularly Ethiopia and Madagascar, a few species have been intensively cultivated for their beans in Ceylon, Java, and elsewhere in the East Indies, as well as in Brazil, Cuba, Central America, and Colombia. These beans are cured and dried and later ground and brewed to make a mildly stimulating beverage containing caffeine. Family: Madder (Rubiaceae); genus and species, *Coffea arabica.*

COFFEE TREE. See *Kentucky Coffee tree.*

COLUMBINE, any of about 50 different kinds of graceful, perennial herbs of the Northern Hemisphere, with long-stalked palmately compound leaves and large, showy flowers at the end of the branches; each flower has 5 sepals and 5 long-spurred petals that secrete nectar. Family: Buttercup (Ranunculaceae); genus *Aquilegia.*

COREOPSIS, a genus that comprises about 115 different kinds of weak-stemmed herbs ranging from 12 to 15 inches tall, mostly native to North America but found also in Africa and Hawaii. They produce a few narrow leaves and many long-stalked, yellow or pink, daisy-like flowers. Several species are cultivated as ornaments in temperate gardens. The most notable is an annual, *C. calliopis,* the ray florets of which are red, maroon, or yellow.

The name tickseed is given to many species, particularly *C. major* of eastern North America, because the small, flat fruits have tiny hooks that cause them to adhere to fur and clothing. Family: Daisy (Compositae).

CORN, or Indian corn, or maize, an erect, herbaceous, annual grass native to mountainous tropical America, domesticated by the Indians and developed horticulturally into many diverse genetic strains, chiefly for the fruits (called kernels) borne in a tight spiral (the cob) within a sheath of spathe-like leaves (the husk), from the end of which the long, threadlike filaments (the silk) extend. Pollen from a terminal cluster of stamens (the tassel) is carried by the wind, pollinating each of the separate, clustered, pistillate flowers from which the kernels develop.

Various strains of corn grow 2 to 30 feet tall; the chief food varieties are dent, flint, flour, pod, pop, and sweet corn. Corn stalks, with their partly sheathing, elongated, coarse leaves are cut for storage and fermentation in farm silos. They are used to provide winter food for livestock. Family: Grass (Gramineae); genus and species, *Zea mays.*

CORNEL. See *Dogwood.*

CORNFLOWER, or bluebottle, or bachelor's button, a slender annual herb of southern Europe, now common in gardens throughout the temperate zones. It grows 1 to 2 feet tall, with small, grayish leaves and fringed, trumpet-like flower heads containing many blue, pink, or white florets. Family: Daisy (Compositae); genus and species, *Centaurea cyanus.*

COTTON, any of several different cultivated, annual, branching, erect herbs of tropical and subtropical regions, with alternate, 3-lobed leaves, and large, showy, creamy flowers that turn red on the second day after opening. The fruit is a globular capsule, called a boll, filled with fluffy fibers attached to the flattened seeds.

Wild cotton grows more than 15 feet tall, but domesticated species are short to facilitate picking the ripe bolls, from which the fibers are removed for use in making textiles and the seeds for the extraction of a commercial cottonseed oil. Family: Mallow (Malvaceae); genus *Gossypium.*

COTTONWOOD. See *Poplar.*

COWPEA, or black-eyed pea, a sprawling, herbaceous plant native to tropical Asia, now cultivated in warm parts of Europe, North America, and Africa for its edible seeds, which may be eaten fresh or dried for storage and later soaked before cooking.

The plant itself is a twining annual with 3-part leaves and a few purplish flowers; it produces pods growing to 12 inches long, with kidney-shaped seeds, each usually with a black spot around the point of attachment. Family Pea (Leguminosae); genus and species, *Vigna sinensis.*

COWSLIP. See *Marsh marigold* and *Primrose.*

CRABGRASS, a coarse, annual European grass, now almost cosmopolitan on cultivated land and wasteland in temperate regions. It has a creeping stem, rough, hairy leaves 2 to 10 inches long, and radiating spikes of minute, grayish-yellow flowers that produce red or purple seeds. In some parts of Europe crabgrass is raised as forage for livestock. Family: Grass (Gramineae); genus and species, *Digitaria sanguinalis.*

CRANBERRY, either of 2 closely related, slender, creeping, shrubby plants with alternate, leathery, small, evergreen leaves which are dark above and paler below, the edges curving downward. The plants have up to 10 nodding, pink or white, bell-shaped flowers on each branch, followed by red, spherical fruits that float on water. Cranberries grow on boggy or peaty soil, along swamp edges, and on floating bogs.

The small-berried species is found across Eurasia and North America, and at higher elevations in the south; the larger-berried North American species is cultivated in artificial bogs that can be flooded at harvest time. The fruits are used for canning, preserving, and in baking. Family: Heath (Ericaceae); genus and species, *Vaccinium oxycoccus* (small-fruited) and *V. macrocarpon.*

CRAPE MYRTLE, an Oriental shrub or small tree with paired, oval, glossy, green leaves and showy, open clusters of lavender-colored flowers, often called "lilac-of-the-South" in the southeastern United States, where it is commonly planted as an ornament. Family: Loosestrife (Lythraceae); genus and species, *Lagerstroemia indica.*

CREOSOTE BUSH, a tough, perennial shrub of deserts in Mexico and the adjacent United States, growing 3 to 4 feet tall, with gray stems marked with black paired leaflets at the end of each petiole; after a rainfall, it produces yellow flowers.

Few animals will eat the foliage or stems because of the strong, tarry odor, even though the creosote-bush is one of the few types of vegetation that has adopted well to conditions of extreme chronic drought. Family: Caltrop (Zygophyllaceae); genus and species, *Larrea tridentata.*

CRESS, any of several different kinds of small, perennial herbs that grow prostrate or buoyed up by running water, with hot-tasting leaves sought as ingredients for salads, or as a garnish or seasoning. They can be cultivated for home use in tubs or frames that hold water. If allowed to flower, all produce small clusters of white or yellow blossoms, each with 4 petals.

The most common kinds are the European watercress (*Nasturtium officinale*), the garden cress or peppergrass (*Lepidium sativum*) from Mediterranean countries, the wild peppergrass (*L. virginicum*) from North America, which has been introduced into Europe, and the winter cress (*Barbarea verna*), from the North Temperate Zone. Family: Mustard (Cruciferae).

CROCUS, a genus of about 70 different kinds of bulbous, herbaceous plants, most of which are native to the Mediterranean region. They blossom in early spring before extending their narrow, stiff, white-lined, green leaves, a characteristic that makes them attractive as ornaments. A fall-flowering species (*C. vernus*) is harvested in Spain for the stigmas of its blossoms, which yield saffron dye.

The name autumn crocus, or meadow saffron, is given to an unrelated bulbous plant (*Colchicum autumnale* of the lily family, Liliaceae) that produces flowers in autumn after its leaves of the year have shriveled and disappeared; its bulbs and seeds are the source of the poisonous alkaloid colchicine, which is used in medicine and horticulture. Family: Iris (Iridaceae).

CROTON, a genus that comprises about 600 different kinds of tropical shrubs native to the Old World and the New, many of them with handsomely mottled leaves in shades of green, yellow, and dark red, usually with long, terminal spikes of small flowers, the staminate flowers commonly nearer the tip of the same spike than the pistillate ones. An Asian species (*C. tiglium*) yields croton oil, which is a strong purgative. The cascarilla (*C. cascarilla*) of the Bahamas and Florida yields a bark known as Eleuthera bark or cascarilla bark and is used to make a tonic and an incense. Family: Spurge (Euphorbiaceae).

CUBEB. See *Pepper*.

CUCUMBER, a trailing annual, herbaceous plant that probably originated in Asia south of the Himalayas, but is now cultivated throughout the world for its edible fruits. The hairy stem bears 3-lobed leaves and bell-shaped, yellow flowers on short stalks; the green, fleshy, oblong fruit is eaten fresh, cooked, or pickled. A close relative from the West Indies (*Cucumis anguria*) bears prickly, small fruits called gherkins. Family: Gourd (Cucurbitaceae); genus and species, *Cucumis sativus*.

CURRANT, any of a small number of branching, shrubby perennials with smooth stems, round, scalloped leaves, clusters of small, yellowish or purple flowers, and, later, similar clusters of red, black, striped, or white berries. Cultivated in many temperate countries are the Eurasian red currants (*Ribes rubrum* and *R. vulgare*) and Eurasian black currants (*R. nigrum*); they bear edible fruits that can be eaten raw, cooked, or preserved. The fruits of the golden currant (*R. aureum*) of the western United States are regarded as less important than their bright yellow, fragrant blossoms, which are unusual because they are tubular rather than bell-shaped. Family: Saxifrage (Saxifragaceae); genus *Ribes*.

CUSTARD-APPLE, a small, West Indian tree with large, leathery leaves and solitary, nodding flowers bearing 3 sepals and usually 6 petals, as well as numerous stamens and separate pistils. The fleshy fruits of the separate pistils unite as they ripen, often becoming very large.

Introduced into many other parts of the tropics, custard-apples are cultivated for their fruits, which are too soft to ship, and are generally eaten with a spoon. Related trees from the American tropics, yielding different but delicious fruits, include the sweetsop or sugar apple (*Annona squamosa*), the soursop (*A. muricata*), and the cherimoya (*A. cherimolia*), all used in making drinks, ices, jellies, and preserves. Family: Custard-apple (Annonaceae); genus and species, *Annona reticulata*.

CUSTARD-APPLE FAMILY (Annonaceae), a group of about 850 species in 80 genera, chiefly woody plants— shrubs, vines, or trees—with aromatic, simple leaves. See *Custard-apple* and *Papaw*.

CYCAD, any of about 100 different kinds of woody shrubs and trees widely distributed in the tropics and subtropics, with thick, slow-growing stems that have a very large pith, alternate, pinnately compound, leathery, evergreen leaves, and separate staminate and ovulate cones, the seeds often brightly colored and with a fleshy covering.

Many cycads are palmlike, two kinds (*Macrozamia* species) in eastern Australia growing to a height of 60 feet. The "palms" of hotel lobbies in many parts of the world are actually either *Cycas revoluta* of southeastern China and southern Japan or *Dioon edule* of Mexico. The seeds of the latter are starchy and can be ground into an edible meal.

The pith of the sagopalm (*Cycas circinalis*) of the East Indies yields sago starch, which is almost indistinguishable from that of many true palms (family Palmaceae). In Florida, the Seminole Indians dug the heavy, short, underground stems of the native cycads (chiefly *Zamia floridana*), called coonties, as a source of starchy flour. Family: Cycad (Cycadaceae).

CYCLAMEN, a genus of 13 different kinds of herbaceous, perennial plants native to southern Europe and Asia Minor, with leathery, kidney-shaped leaves on long stalks, and nodding flowers with reflexed petal lobes, white, rose, pink, or purple in color. One species (*C. persicum*) is cultivated in greenhouses and homes of northern Europe and North America for its flowers. Family: Primrose (Primulaceae).

CYPRESS, any of 12 different kinds of evergreen, coniferous trees native to warm parts of the Northern Hemisphere. All grow tall, with tiny leaves less than 1/4 inch long, closely pressed to the branchlets, and small cones composed of less than 20 cone scales. None tolerates hard frosts or extended cold weather.

The funeral cypress (*Cupressus funebris*) of China, which grows like a tall, dark green column with branches that hang down and are said to "weep," is planted in cemeteries in many warm countries. Family: Cypress (Cupressaceae); genus *Cupressus*.

CYPRESS FAMILY (Cupressaceae), a group of about 140 species in 15 genera, all shrubs or trees with scalelike or needlelike leaves and mature cones that are dry and woody or fleshy and berry-like. See *Arbor vitae, Cedar, Cypress,* and *Juniper*.

DAFFODIL. See *Narcissus*.

DAHLIA, a genus of perennial plants native to Mexico and Central America, including about 9 different kinds, of which one, *D. pinnata*, is grown widely as an ornamental garden flower. The wild plant grows 2 to 6 feet tall and bears compact heads of red flowers, each with a yellow center.

More than 10,000 horticultural varieties have been developed in every color except blue. Although many of the varieties produce seeds that will germinate, the named kinds are usually grown from the tuberous roots, which have buds at the stem end. Family: Daisy (Compositae).

DAISY, any of a number of different plants that produce flat flower heads surrounded by a radiating row of white petals. The lawn daisy (*Bellis perennis*), a stemless little plant that produces 1-inch flower heads on 2- or 3-inch slender stalks from spring until autumn is widespread in Britain and has been introduced by Europeans into many parts of North America, Asia, and New Zealand. A field full of tall, white daisies usually consists of the ox-eye, marguerite, or whiteweed (*Chrysanthemum leucanthemum*) of Eurasia, which has become a pasture weed in Canada and the United States.

The Shasta daisy, with flower heads up to 4 inches in diameter, is a hybrid developed by Luther Burbank chiefly from the smaller *Chrysanthemum maximum* of the Pyrenees. Daisy-like flowers also open on more than 125 different kinds of daisy-bushes (*Olearia*) in New Zealand, Australia, and New Guinea, where these shrubs often form thickets. Family: Daisy (Compositae).

DAISY FAMILY (Compositae), the largest family of flowering plants, with more than 20,000 species in 950 genera, widely distributed and including shrubs and a few trees as well as herbs. All are easy to recognize by their flower heads, in which many flo-

PLANT TYPES

IRVIN L. OAKES FROM NATIONAL AUDUBON SOCIETY

MOREL MUSHROOM

© WALT DISNEY PRODUCTIONS

AIRPLANT BLOSSOM

ANTHONY MERCICA FROM NATIONAL AUDUBON SOCIETY

BEAR GRASS

EL AL

BARLEY FIELD

EL AL

DWARF BANANA

© WALT DISNEY PRODUCTIONS

HEDGEHOG CACTUS

© WALT DISNEY PRODUCTIONS

BARCO

© WALT DISNEY PRODUCTIONS

PAPAYA

FLOWERS

ZINNIA

LOTUS

CLEOME (CASPER PLANT)

WATER LILY

SINGLE CHRYSANTHEMUM

COSMOS

PETUNIA

FLOWERS

PHOTOS BAUMAN/LOOK

GLADIOLUS

DAHLIA

HELIOTROPE

PHLOX

JAPANESE CHRYSANTHEMUM

ROSES

TREES

WILLIAM HARLOW FROM NATIONAL AUDUBON SOCIETY

TWO CROWN SHAPES OF AMERICAN ELM

ARTHUR W. AMBLER FROM NATIONAL AUDUBON SOCIETY

NORWAY MAPLE

DENNIS BROWN FROM NATIONAL AUDUBON SOCIETY

REDWOOD

RICHARD PARKER FROM NATIONAL AUDUBON SOCIETY

ASPENS

rets are attached side by side to the broad end to the stalk and surrounded by a row of bracts called an involucre. See *Ageratum, Arnica, Artichoke, Aster, Black-eyed Susan, Boneset, Burdock, Camomile, Chicory, Chrysanthemum, Cineraria, Coreopsis, Cornflower, Dahlia, Daisy, Dandelion, Edelweiss, Elecampane, Everlasting, Gaillardia, Golden-glow, Goldenrod, Guayule, Hawkweed, Ironweed, Joe Pye weed, Lettuce, Marigold, Mayweed, Pot-marigold, Ragweed, Safflower, Sagebrush, Salsify, Sunflower, Tarragon, Thistle, Wormwood, Yallow,* and *Zinnia.*

DANDELION, or blowballs, a common weed of lawns introduced from Europe and now kept widespread in the United States by its light-weight fruits, each with a terminal tuft of silky hairs that catches the wind. The bright yellow flowers are borne on tall, hollow stalks that rise from a flat rosette of leaves; the leaves, which are toothed along the edges, have led to the name dandelion (*dents-de-leon,* "lion's teeth").

Europeans commonly gather the leaf rosettes and boil them as potherbs, or collect the flowers and extract their sugar as the basis of dandelion wine. Family: Daisy (Compositae); genus and species, *Taraxacum officinale.*

DASHEEN. See *Taro.*

DEVIL'S–PAINTBRUSH. See *Hawkweed.*

DEWBERRY. See *Blackberry.*

DILL, a biennial herb of southern Europe and North Africa, originally cultivated in Asia Minor, India, and North America for its seeds, but more recently for its immature flower clusters and leaves as well. From all these an extract called dill herb oil can be obtained for use in flavoring. Like caraway and anise extracts, it apparently reduces gas in the human digestive tract. Family: Carrot (Umbelliferae); genus and species, *Anethum graveolens.*

DOCK, any of several coarse weeds of Eurasia, now widespread, each a perennial with a long, stout taproot, broad, ruffled leaves, and a stem 1½ to 3 feet tall, topped by clusters of small, green flowers. They grow on poor, acid soil, where other plants do not find enough nourishment, and provide some food for livestock. In Eurasia the young shoots are used as a vegetable. Mexican tanner's dock (*Rumex hymenosepalus*) yields canaigre, an extract used in tanning hides. Family: Buckwheat (Polygonaceae); genus *Rumex.* See also *Burdock.*

DODDER, any of about 160 different kinds of rootless, leafless, non-green, parasitic vines that grow as annual plants, twining around the stalks of other vegetation. They are native to most temperate and tropical countries. At intervals along the yellow, red, or white, threadlike stems are short suckers that extend into the tissues of the host plant and absorb nourishment.

The pink flowers generally appear in small clusters from July to September, and are followed by capsules of minute, ripe seeds that travel as impurities among seeds of crop plants. Family: Morning-glory (Convolvulaceae); genus *Cuscuta.*

DOGBANE, any of about 25 different kinds of herbaceous perennial plants native to the North Temperate Zone, with paired, simple leaves on branching stems 1 to 4 feet tall, and small clusters of pinkish-white, bell-shaped flowers. Family: Dogbane (Apocynaceae); genus *Apocynum.*

DOGBANE FAMILY (Apocynaceae), a group of about 1300 species in 300 genera, widely distributed but best represented in the tropics. They include trees, shrubs, tropical woody vines, and herbs, all with milky sap and simple, smooth-edged leaves. Some yield drugs, latex, tannins, and other valuable substances, whereas others are valuable chiefly as ornaments. Frangipani or temple tree (*Plumeria rubra*), native to tropical America, is grown for its perfumed, clustered flowers. See *Dogbane, Indian Hemp, Oleander,* and *Periwinkle.*

DOGTOOTH VIOLET, or dog's-tooth-violet, any of several similar and related fawn lilies with a pair of mottled, basal leaves, producing in early spring a nodding, single flower at the top of a slender stalk. The Eurasian dogtooth violet (*Erythronium denscanis*) has a red or purple flower. The eastern North American area has a yellow violet, adder's-tongue (*E. americanum*), and a white one (*E. albidum*). A rosy-pink dogtooth violet (*E. propullans*) is native to Minnesota. Family: Lily (Liliaceae); genus *Erythronium.*

DOGWOOD, any of about 40 different kinds of shrubs and trees with simple leaves, native to the North Temperate Zone and to tropical mountains. Their small but often conspicuous fruits remain after the leaves drop in autumn, providing winter food for birds. The widespread red osier dogwood (*Cornus stolonifera*) forms thickets that may be identified by the many smooth, red stems and, in autumn, white or lead-colored fruits; its flowers are inconspicuous.

The flowering dogwoods, small trees in which the flower clusters are conspicuous because of the 4 to 7 white or colored, petal-like bracts associated with them, include the Cornelian cherry (*C. mas*) of central and southern Europe and western Asia, the western dogwood (*C. nuttallii*) of British Columbia to California, and the eastern dogwood (*C. florida*) of eastern North America, including eastern Mexico. Family: Dogwood (Cornaceae); genus *Cornus.*

DOGWOOD FAMILY (Cornaceae), a group of about 125 species in 18 genera found in temperate areas in the Northern and Southern hemispheres, including the higher slopes of tropical mountains. They are woody undershrubs, shrubs and trees with simple leaves. See *Bunchberry, Dogwood,* and *Tupelo.*

DOUGLAS FIR, a tall, straight tree of western North America, with flattened needles on short stalks and pendant cones 2 to 4 inches long, which are unique because every cone scale is accompanied by a 3-pronged bract that projects half an inch or so beyond the scale. When the leaves drop off the stem is smooth, as in a true fir; the cones, however, remain attached until after the seeds have been dispersed, whereas those of a true fir disintegrate to release the seeds.

Douglas fir grows to a height of 221 feet, and is the leading timber tree in America today, yielding about a quarter of the lumber produced in the United States and Canada. Family: Pine (Pinaceae); genus and species, *Pseudotsuga taxifolia.*

DUTCHMAN'S–BREECHES, a woodland wildflower of northeastern North America, with delicate, green leaves and slender stalks 5 to 10 inches high, bearing rows of small, heart-shaped, spurred, white or pink flowers shaped somewhat like the ballooning breeches once worn by Dutch peasants.

Closely related are the bleeding heart (*Dicentra spectabilis*) of China and Japan, which is cultivated in gardens because of its rosy-red and pink flowers, and the squirrel corn (*D. canadensis*), named for the yellow, tuberous knobs on its buried, horizontal stems. Family: Fumitory (Fumariaceae); genus and species, *Dicentra cucullaria.*

DUTCHMAN'S–PIPE, a woody, climbing vine native to eastern North America, from Pennsylvania to Georgia and Alabama, now widely cultivated for its smooth, heart-shaped leaves and its clusters of showy flowers, each resembling a Dutch pipe. The showy part is the calyx, for petals are lacking. Family: Birthwort (Aristolochiaceae); genus and species, *Aristolchia durior.*

EBONY, any of several related trees of equatorial Africa and tropical Asia, the intensely hard, black, heartwood of which can be given a high polish. India and Ceylon are the principal sources for *Diospyros ebenum*, which attains a height of 100 feet, and has oblong leaves, fragrant, yellow flowers, jet-black bark, and almost white sapwood surrounding the valuable heartwood. Family: Ebony (Ebenaceae); genus *Diospyros.*

EBONY FAMILY (Ebenaceae), a group of 325 species in 5 genera, all shrubs or trees with simple, smooth-edged, leathery leaves. They are most numerous in Southeast Asia but are widely represented in tropical and subtropical regions. See *Ebony* and *Persimmon.*

EDELWEISS, an alpine plant with narrow, wooly, white leaves and flowers with many separate heads, which are clustered so close together that insects can walk from one to the next, obtaining nectar and pollinating the blossoms. Native to high peaks in the European Alps, where it is endangered by excessive picking, it is now cultivated in gardens in many temperate parts of the world. In cultivation it sometimes grows to 6 feet. Family: Daisy (Compositae); genus and species, *Leontopodium alpinum.*

EGGPLANT, a bushy, annual plant native to northeastern India, domesticated and cultivated in warmer parts of Eurasia, North America, Australia, and New Zealand for the pendant, oblong, edible fruits, which may be purple, yellow, or white. The stems are spiny, the leaves large and lobed, and the flowers are violet-colored. Family: Potato (Solanaceae); genus and species, *Solanum melongena.*

ELDER, any of about 20 different kinds of shrubs and trees native to temperate and tropical lands, with pinnately compound leaves and flat clusters of tiny flowers that are followed by juicy fruits, each containing 3 tiny, armored seeds.

The fruits of the European elder (*Sambucus nigra*), native to western Asia and North Africa and to Europe, and of the common American elder (*S. canadensis*) in eastern Canada and the United States are eaten by birds unless they are harvested. The berries are made into elderberry pie or used as the basis of elderberry wine. Family: Honeysuckle (Caprifoliaceae); genus *Sambucus.*

ELECAMPANE, or horseheal, a tall, coarse herb of Eurasia, with large, egg-shaped tubers on the roots, and 4-inch heads of daisy-like flowers bearing golden-yellow petals around the rim and disc florets that change in color from yellow to tan as they mature.

The root tubers yield a medicinal agent rich in the carbohydrate inulin, with a warm, bitter taste and an odor suggestive of that of camphor. Family: Daisy (Compositae); genus and species, *Inula helenium.*

ELEPHANT'S EAR. See *Begonia.*

ELM, any of about 30 different kinds of trees native to the North Temperate Zone and the mountains of tropical Asia, bearing simple leaves that are oblique at the base and winged fruits with the seed at the center. The American elm (*Ulmus americana*) develops a wide-spreading crown, making it a valuable shade tree. It rises to a height of 160 feet with a top 75 feet across; the wood is so cross-grained that it can hardly be split.

The slippery elm (*U. rubra*) of the eastern United States has a mucilaginous inner bark that has been used medicinally. Like the European elm or the English elm (*U. campestris*), and the Chinese elm (*U. parvifolia*), it is a lesser tree but is immune to the fungus infection known as the Dutch elm disease, which is destroying the New England elms. Family: Elm (Ulmaceae); genus *Ulmus.*

ELM FAMILY (Ulmaceae), a group of nearly 160 species in 15 genera, all shrubs or trees with simple leaves that are native to the North Temperate Zone and mountains of tropical Asia. See *Elm* and *Hackberry.*

BURPEE SEEDS

EGGPLANT

ENDIVE. See *Chicory.*

EUCALYPTUS, or gum trees, a genus of tall trees including about 600 different kinds native to Australia, New Guinea, and the adjacent islands. The leaves are usually narrow and pendant, casting little shade. The sepals and petals drop from the flowers as they open, exposing a tuft of stamens that are commonly bright red, gold-tipped, and attractive to pollinating insects. The fruits are hard and dry.

A fast-growing eucalyptus, the Australian bluegum (*E. globulus*), has been introduced in many temperate areas as a windbreak and as a quick source of wood. It grows to a height of 50 feet in about 5 years. Tallest is the gum tree (*E. regnans*) of eastern Australia, which attains a height of 326 feet and a diameter of 25 feet at chest height. Oil of eucalyptus, used medicinally for colds and bronchial infections, is extracted from the young twigs and leaves of several different kinds. Family: Myrtle (Myrtaceae).

EUONYMUS, a genus of shrubs and trees native to the Northern Hemisphere and Australia, with about 100 different species, many of them evergreen. All have spreading branches, pointed, serrate leaves, open clusters of drooping, purple flowers, and seeds covered by bright orange or red arils, which are exposed in autumn when the fruit capsule breaks open.

The European spindle-tree (*E. europaeus*) and the burning-bush or wahoo (*E. atropurpureus*) of eastern North America are often raised as ornamental shrubs or trees partly because their leaves turn a rich purplish-red in autumn before dropping; they grow to 25 feet tall. The winged spindle-tree (*E. alatus*) also displays such rich fall coloring; it is native to eastern Asia and has corky, winglike projections from its branches. Family: Stafftree (Celastraceae).

EUPHORBIA, a large genus of latex-bearing plants native to subtropical and warm, temperate parts of Africa and America. Most have succulent, spiny stems, simple leaves, and tiny flowers in large, nectar-producing glands.

Of the 1600 different kinds, the most widely cultivated are the poinsettia (*E. pulcherrima*) of Mexico and Central America, the flower clusters of which are made conspicuous by an open whorl of adjacent, bright red or white leaves, and the prickly crown-of-thorns (*E. splendens*) of Madagascar, often planted as a hedge; the latter bears a succession of slender stems from its woody branches, holding 2 or 4 scarlet "flowers," each of which is a diminutive cluster.

Africa south of the Sahara has tree euphorbias, which resemble organ-pipe cacti, and have adapted in a similar way to store water in arid highlands. Family: Spurge (Euphorbiaceae).

EVENING PRIMROSE, any of about 100 different kinds of American herbs found from the Arctic to Patagonia. Most bear bright butter-yellow or white flowers that open late in the day and close again permanently the following dawn, often changing to a pink or magenta color as they fade.

Hawkmoths are attracted by scent to serve as pollinators. The seeds have a thin membrane that catches the wind; in this fashion any gust can distribute them widely. The root and upper foliage of some kinds are edible. Family: Evening-primrose (Onagraceae); genus *Oenothera.*

EVENING–PRIMROSE FAMILY (Onagraceae), a group of about 650 species in 20 genera, widely distributed, growing as herbs, shrubs, or trees with simple leaves. See *Evening-primrose, Fireweed, Fuchsia,* and *Godetia.*

EVERLASTING, any of several different kinds of annual plants the dried blossoms of which have a strawlike texture; they retain their color and form and can be displayed as decorations throughout the winter.

The flower heads, cut before they open fully, are often hung upside down to be dried and then dyed in assorted colors. This custom presumably began with the wild immortelle (*Helichrysum orientale*) of Asia and Africa, which is cultivated in southern Europe, but it has also been followed with the Australian *Waitzia* and the North American species of *Anaphalis, Antennaria,* and *Gnaphalium.* Family: Daisy (Compositae).

FENNEL, a stout, aromatic, perennial herb native to Europe, bearing leaves that are divided into threadlike projections from the midrib, flat heads of yellow flowers, and slender seeds about ¼ inch long. The young leaves are sometimes eaten as salad greens, and the seeds used as a relish or as the source of a fragrant oil used in perfumes and soaps. Introduced into North America, it has sometimes become a troublesome pasture weed. Family: Carrot (Umbelliferae); genus and species, *Foeniculum officinale.*

FIG, any of about 800 different kinds of tropical and subtropical shrubs and trees, which have a palatable, milky juice in their alternately arranged leaves and produce a unique, pear-shaped, inverted receptacle enclosing tiny flowers that produce small fruits. The edible part of the fig is the fleshy receptacle, which may be eaten raw, fresh, dried, cooked, or preserved, or may be used as the base from which wine and other alcoholic beverages are made.

The commercial fig is the product of a 20-foot tree (*Ficus carica*) of western Asia, now cultivated in all Mediterranean countries and the United States; its fruits vary in color from white to yellow, purple, and black. The India-rubber plant (*F. elastica*) of India and Java, which was formerly a commercial source of rubber, is now widely cultivated as a house plant with glossy, oblong leaves.

The peepul tree, or botree (*F. religiosa*), which is sacred to Gautama Buddha, is planted outside Buddhist shrines, providing shade, a useful lac, and an extract useful in tanning leather. The banyan tree (*F. benghalensis*) of the East Indies supports its outspread, heavy limbs on strong, adventitious roots that grow down to the soil and become thick; a single tree can extend itself in this way over are usually greenish, purple, or blood-(Moraceae); genus *Ficus*.

FIGWORT, any of about 150 different kinds of coarse herbs native to the North Temperate Zone, found especially in Asia, with a 4-sided stem, mostly opposite leaves, and a loose, terminal cluster of flowers shaped like those of the snapdragon. The flowers are usually greenish, purple, or blood-red. Fleshy knobs on the horizontal, underground stems of some species were once believed to be evidence that the plants could be used to cure fig-warts and scrofula. Family: Figwort (Scrophulariaceae); genus *Scrophularia*.

FIGWORT FAMILY (Scrophulariaceae), a group of about 2600 species in 200 genera, represented on all continents, mostly herbs and low shrubs with simple leaves and bilaterally symmetrical flowers, the 5-part corolla typically 2-lipped. Included are the imperial tree (*Paulownia tomentosa*) of China and Japan, which grows 40 feet tall with large, heart-shaped leaves and clusters of white flowers; the louseworts (*Pedicularis* species), which are partially parasitic on tree roots; and the paintbrush (*Castilleja* species), chiefly of western North America, in which the upper leaves and bracts near the inconspicuous flowers are brightly colored in orange and red. See *Bluebell, Calceolaria, Figwort, Foxglove, Mullein, Snapdragon,* and *Veronica*.

FILBERT. See *Hazel*.

FIR, any of about 40 different kinds of coniferous, evergreen trees native to Eurasia and North America, which release their winged seeds when their upright cones disintegrate. Balsam firs, particularly the North American

BURPEE SEEDS

FORGET–ME–NOT

Abies balsamea, yield a fragrant resin from numerous "blisters" on the trunk that is used in medicine. With the exception of the noble fir (*A. nobilis*) of the northwestern United States and adjacent Canada, the firs are less valuable than the spruces for lumber; young firs are favored as Christmas trees. Family: Pine (Pinaceae); genus *Abies*.

FIREWEED, or great willow herb, a perennial, herbaceous plant of cool, temperate, and arctic-alpine parts of the Northern Hemisphere, where its lightweight, hair-tufted seeds germinate on cleared and burned-over land, leading to a conspicuous stand of stout stems 5 to 7 feet tall; these stems are generously clad in narrow, green leaves shaped like those of the willow, and end in a conspicuous, elongated cluster of magenta or pink flowers. Family: Evening primrose (Onagraceae); genus and species, *Epilobium angustifolium*.

FLAX, a slender, upright, herbaceous plant native to Eurasia, with almost grasslike leaves and few branches. At the tip of each branch it produces a delicate, violet-blue flower with petals that spread about ¾ inch across. The seeds, from which linseed oil is extracted, ripen in globular capsules.

To obtain fibers to be made into linen thread, the plants are harvested when the seeds are not yet fully ripe; at this stage, the fibers in the stems are at their best for removal and working. Weaving linen from flax plants is one of man's oldest technical achievements. Today, most of the fibers are from the Soviet Union and Europe from Poland to France. Family: Flax (Linaceae); genus and species, *Linum usitatissimum*.

FORGET–ME–NOT, or scorpion-grass, any of about 300 different kinds of low herbs of temperate regions, some of which are supposed to have curled clusters of flower buds suggestive of a scorpion's upturned tail, and others to have leaves resembling mouse-ears, thus inspiring the generic name *Myosotis*. The European forget-me-not (*M. scorpioides*) has been widely introduced as a decorative plant for flower borders, where its small, pink buds open into pale blue blossoms; when it escapes from cultivation, it thrives in its normal surroundings—partly shaded banks of shallow streams as well as other wet places. Family: Borage (Boraginaceae).

FORSYTHIA, or goldenbells, a genus with just 4 species of shrubs native to temperate parts of Eurasia, but now widely cultivated for their arching stems on which bright yellow flowers open before the leaves expand in spring. The 4-pointed petals diverge symmetrically from the rim of a bell-like throat. The pointed leaves have saw-teeth along the edges, and are arranged alternately along the stems. Family: Olive (Oleaceae).

FOUR-O'CLOCK, or marvel of Peru, a handsome herb with opposite leaves and clustered, trumpet-shaped flowers that open petal-like sepals with amazing regularity about four o'clock every afternoon, stay open through the night, and close again around sunrise. In its native Peru and in warm parts of the United States, four-o'clock is a perennial, whereas in temperate regions it is cultivated as a garden annual. Family: Four-o'clock (Nyctaginaceae); genus and species, *Mirabilis jalapa*.

FOUR-O'CLOCK FAMILY (Nyctaginaceae), a group of about 250 species in 28 genera, mostly herbs or woody plants of the tropics and subtropics, in which the floral parts seem reversed: the 5, united sepals are petal-like, the petals are absent altogether, and the imitation corolla is backed by green, sepal-like bracts. See *Bougainvillea* and *Four-o'clock*.

FOXGLOVE, any of about 25 different kinds of tall herbs of the Old World from the Canary Islands to central Asia, growing to a height of about 5 feet, with scattered, ovoid leaves and a tall spike of yellow, white, pink, or purple, spotted, tubular flowers that hang like inverted bells. *Digitalis purpurea* from western Europe has been widely introduced as an ornament, and is the principal source of the powerful heart stimulant digitalis. Family: Figwort (Scrophulariaceae); genus *Digitalis*.

FREESIA, a genus composed of 3 different kinds of herbaceous plants native to South Africa that grow from bulbs and produce an upright stem with small leaves and linear clusters of trumpet-shaped, fragrant flowers varying in color from white to cream, yellow, rose, and lavender. They are raised as house plants in many countries. Family: Iris (Iridaceae).

FRITILLARY, or checkered lily, any of about 50 different bulbous herbs of the North Temperate Zone, which produce nodding clusters of bell-

BURPEE SEEDS

GAILLARDIA

shaped flowers the petals of which are checkered or spotted. Among the most handsome species cultivated as an ornament is the crown imperial (*Fritillaria imperialis*) of Iran. Family: Lily (Liliaceae); genus *Fritillaria*.

FUCHSIA, a genus of shrubs and trees, chiefly from Central and South America, with about 75 different species, including 2 in New Zealand. The plants have dark green, paired, oval leaves and funnel-shaped, pendant flowers on slender stalks. The sepals are usually a different color from the petals, providing such striking color contrasts as red and blue, red and cream, or scarlet and green. The plumlike fruits contain red seeds.

Many ornamental fuchsias are found in outdoor gardens of warm regions or grown as house plants in colder climates. They are often of hybrid origin. Family: Evening primrose (Onagraceae).

FUMITORY, a leafy-stemmed, branching, annual plant of Mediterranean countries, now cultivated in the United States and elsewhere in warm temperate parts of the world that escapes from cultivation into waste ground. The dense spikes of small, spurred, irregular, purplish flowers are followed by cylindrical capsules, each with a single seed. The name refers to the odor of the roots when they are first pulled from the soil. Family: Fumitory (Fumariaceae); genus and species, *Fumaria officinalis*.

FUMITORY FAMILY (Fumariaceae), a group of about 425 species in 19 genera, widespread in the North Temperate Zone and in South Africa. All are weak, smooth herbs with a watery sap and bilaterally symmetrical flowers. See *Dutchman's-breeches* and *Fumitory*.

FURZE. See *Gorse*.

GAILLARDIA, or blanket flowers, a genus of stiff, herbaceous wildflowers comprising 12 different kinds native to the western United States, all growing 2 to 3 feet tall, with a few oval, notched leaves and conspicuous flower heads, the red or yellow ray flowers of which form a bright halo around a golden center. Several have been developed by horticulturalists as garden flowers, which are popular because they bloom until late autumn. Some are annuals and others perennials. Family: Daisy (Compositae).

GARDENIA, a genus of about 100 different woody shrubs native to the Old World tropics, with broad, simple, opposite, evergreen leaves, and attractive, regular flowers. The fruits are bright orange and as much as 1½ inches long in cultivated gardenias such as the cape-jasmine (*G. jasminoides*) of China, so named because the first plants brought to England came from the Cape of Good Hope.

Bearing fragrant, white or yellow flowers that have a waxy texture and last a long time, gardenias have become popular greenhouse plants in cool places; in warm regions, such as southeastern United States, they bloom outdoors and are used for decorative hedges. Family: Madder (Rubiaceae).

GARLIC, a strong-smelling, small onion native to southern Eurasia, with spearlike leaves rising from a hard bulb that reproduces itself as it grows, providing additional small bulbs (called cloves) within the tough outer skin. Cultivated for use as a flavoring, garlic has been introduced into many regions and has escaped from cultivation to roadsides and fields.

Along with such related plants as wild garlic (*Allium oleraceum* from Europe and *A. canadense* from eastern North America) and European field-garlic (*A. vineale*), it has become a hazard in pastures because cows tend to eat it, thus spoiling the taste of their milk. Family: Lily (Liliaceae); genus and species, *Allium sativum*.

GENTIAN, any of about 500 different kinds of herbaceous plants of temperate, cool, and especially alpine regions all over the world. They bear single or clustered, showy flowers late in the growing season. Most have deep, purplish-blue flowers, but some (particularly in the Andes) have pink or red, and a few have yellow flowers.

Several kinds are known as closed or bottle gentians because the petals of their deep, tubular corollas never spread; bumblebees force their way into these flowers to get nectar and attend to pollination. Gentian seeds are small, winged, and wind-distributed.

Those of the fringed gentian (*Gentiana crinita*) of moist woodlands from Maine to Minnesota and southward have had so little chance to ripen in recent years because people pick the flowers, that the plant is facing extermination. The flowers are lovely azure, urn-shaped blossoms with fringed edges that turn down. Because it is an annual in the south-

ern parts of its range and a biennial in the northern parts, the fringed gentian depends for survival upon producing seeds from each flower.

The roots of the yellow gentian (*G. lutea*) of southern Europe and Asia Minor yield a drug formerly used as a tonic. Many other gentians produce a dye called gentian violet, which can be extracted and used in treating various skin and respiratory infections. Family: Gentian (Gentianaceae); genus *Gentiana*.

GENTIAN FAMILY (Gentianaceae), a group of about 800 species in 70 genera, widely distributed, some in the Arctic and on high mountains. All have opposite, simple leaves and clusters of regular flowers. The petal tips of the flowers uncurl as the bud opens.

A very different related plant is the water snowflake, or floating heart. Twenty different varieties of this plant grow in shallow ponds and slow-flowing streams, their heart-shaped leaves floating like waterlily pads on the surface; water snowflakes are often cultivated in garden pools and large aquaria. See also *Gentian*.

GERANIUM, a name applied widely and without discrimination to herbaceous plants of two related genera. About 300 of them are known as cranesbills (*Geranium*) from the shape of the fruit, and 250 are known as storksbills (*Pelargonium*).

Cranesbills have 5 similar petals without sepal extended in the form of a hollow spur. The upper 2 petals of storksbills are smaller, larger, or bear different markings, and the sepal behind these is extended into a long, hollow spur that is joined for its whole length to the flower stalk. Cranesbills include the wild geranium (*G. maculatum*) of eastern North American meadows, thickets, and woodlands, and the herb Robert (*G. robertianum*), found on gravelly shores and rocky woodlands of much of North America, Eurasia, and North Africa.

The hardy house plant known as geranium, which survives in poor soil with little attention as long as it gets warmth, sun, and an occasional watering, is a storkbill developed horticulturally, primarily from a South African ancestor; most are aromatic, with stiff stems, luxuriant, round, or nearly heart-shaped leaves, and large heads of red, rose, pink, yellow, or white, irregular blossoms.

The essential oil extracted from leaves and stems of *Pelargonium* is called geranium oil and is used in perfumes. Family: Geranium (Geraniaceae).

GESNERIA FAMILY (Gesneriaceae), a group of about 1200 species in 85 genera, most of them tropical and subtropical herbs with opposite leaves. A number are widely enjoyed as ornamental plants for house or greenhouse. Cape Primrose (*Streptocarpus* species) is native to South Africa and Madagascar.

African-violet (horticultural varieties from 3 species of *Saintpaulia*), native to East Africa, propagates easily from leaves in water. The Brazilian gloxinia (*Sinningia*) is similar in many ways, although with much larger flowers and a need for an annual period of inactivity. See also *Gloxinia*.

GILLYFLOWER. See *Stock* and *Wallflower*.

GINGER, a herbaceous perennial of tropical and subtropical Asia, generally a cultivated species with alternate, narrow, grasslike leaves along an upright, reedy stem rising from a fleshy, underground rhizome (horizontal stem), which also produces slender stalks topped with clusters of flowers.

The cultivated species is no longer found wild; it is believed to have been adapted by early man in tropical Asia. The spice ginger is made from the rhizomes, which may be scrubbed, dried, and then ground, or cooked while fresh and then candied.

In North America, an unrelated perennial herb (*Asarum canadense* and other species of the birthwort family Aristolochiaceae) is called wild ginger; it has an aromatic rhizome that produces 2 kidney-shaped, furry leaves and a bell-shaped flower without petals, which is purple inside and green outside. Family: Ginger (Zingiberaceae); genus *Zingiber,* particularly *Z. officinale*.

GINGER FAMILY (Zingiberaceae), a group of about 1400 species in 47 genera, chiefly tropical, perennial herbs with fleshy, underground stems and 2-ranked leaves or whorls of basal leaves. Several yield valuable spices. Others are outstandingly beautiful, such as the brilliant torchflowers (*Hedychium* species) native to Madagascar and Southeast Asia, and the shellflower (*Alpinia speciosa*) of the East Indies. See *Arrowroot, Cardamom,* and *Ginger*.

GINKGO, or maidenhair tree, an erect, generously branching Oriental tree that attains a height of 60 to 80 feet and bears clusters of fan-shaped leaves on short, woody spurs rising from the main branches. The staminate trees produce stamens in clusters resembling catkins. The ovulate trees form ovules in pairs on short spurs and, later, seeds that appear plumlike, with a fleshy outer covering over an inner stony layer. When ripe, the fleshy covering decomposes, emitting a fetid odor.

Staminate trees are therefore preferred for ornamental planting. They are hardy and grow well in cities, despite soot, exhaust fumes, and pavement reaching to within a few inches of the trunk on all sides. The single species (*Ginkgo biloba*) is a "living fossil," with no wild representatives known. It has been perpetuated by Oriental monks in temple grounds. Fossil ginkgoes have been found in many parts of Eurasia and North America. Family: Ginkgo (Ginkgoaceae).

GINSENG, any of about 6 different kinds of herbaceous, woodland plants of tropical and eastern Asia and temperate North America, growing 1 to 4 feet high, with alternate compound leaves and flat or globular clusters of small, yellow flowers that produce scarlet, fleshy fruits.

The Chinese have long considered the fleshy roots a valuable medicine and pay a high price for those of the Manchurian species (*Panax schinseng*) and a lower price for the kind native to eastern North America (*P. quinquefolius*). Family: Ginseng (Araliaceae); genus *Panax*.

GINSENG FAMILY (Araliaceae), a group of about 800 species in 65 genera, most abundant in tropical America and Southeast Asia, all with 5-part, small flowers in clusters that are flat-topped or spherical. It includes the devil's club (*Echinopanax horridus*), a dangerously spiny shrub native to western North America from California to Alaska, and the rice-paper tree (*Tetrapanax papyrifera*) of Formosa, from which rice-paper is made. See *Ginseng, Ivy,* and *Spikenard*.

GLADIOLUS, a genus of bulbous plants with narrow, linear leaves and spikes of large, stemless, irregular, trumpet-shaped flowers. In addition to the 250 different species native to Africa and southern Europe, many horticultural varieties have been developed. They are propagated by natural division of the bulbous corms and produce large flowers that are white, yellow, pink, rose, purple, or combinations of more than one color. Family: Iris (Iridaceae).

GLOXINIA, a low-growing, tuberous, Brazilian herb with large, thick, hairy, deeply-veined, spreading leaves and large, bell-shaped flowers. Cultivated as a decorative house plant, it has developed horticultural varieties with red, rose, pink, or white flowers, rather than the violet-colored flowers characteristic of the wild plants. Family: Gesneria (Gesneriaceae); genus and species, *Sinningia speciosa*.

T.H. EVERETT
GINKGO

GODETIA, a genus of herbaceous plants native to western North America, with about 25 different species of which one, called summer's darling or farewell-to-spring (*G. amoena*), bearing large, satiny petals ranging in color from white to deep red, is widely cultivated as a garden ornament. Family: Evening primrose (Onagraceae).

GOLDEN BELL. See *Forsythia*.

GOLDEN CHAIN. See *Laburnum*.

GOLDEN GLOW, a coarse, perennial, garden plant developed by horticulturalists from a flower of eastern North America. Golden glow has spherical heads of golden-yellow disc florets 2 to 4 inches across and hardly any, or no ray florets. Family: Daisy (Compositae); genus, species, and named variety, *Rudbeckia lacinata hortensis*.

GOLDENROD, any of about 90 different kinds of perennial herbs, one native to Britain and parts of Europe, one to the Azores, a few found in temperate Asia and South America, and the vast majority in North America where they brighten forest, field, and roadside with feathery sprays of small flowers, usually golden-yellow but sometimes white or greenish in color.

They are flowers of late summer and autumn, some of them growing on rough, hairy stems 7 feet tall that bear many small leaves all the way up. Family: Daisy (Compositae); genus *Solidago*.

GOOSEBERRY, a low-growing, spiny shrub, sometimes 3 feet tall, native to North Africa and much of Europe, producing 3-lobed leaves, small, pale yellow blossoms in loose clusters, and spherical, shiny fruit with minute seeds. Cultivated varieties, with edible green or purple fruit, are raised in cool parts of Europe, North America, South Africa, New Zealand, and Australia. The fruit is eaten raw or used in cooking and in making preserves. Family: Saxifrage (Saxifragaceae); genus and species, *Ribes grossularia*.

GOOSEFOOT FAMILY (Chenopodiaceae), a group of about 1400 species in 102 genera, widely distributed but especially well represented in arid and salty or alkaline areas. They include annual and perennial herbs, shrubs, and some small trees, often with fleshy enlargements on the stems where leaves are attached or where leaves would have been attached had the stem not been leafless.

Glasswort, or samphire (*Salicornia* species), are fleshy, leafless herbs of seacoasts, often changing in color from bright green to brilliant red in autumn. See *Beet, Lamb's-quarters, Pigweed, Saltbrush, Spinach,* and *Tumbleweed*.

GORSE, or furze, or whin, any of about 20 different kinds of spiny, woody shrubs; its green spines are modified leaves. It is native to Europe and North Africa, but has been widely introduced as a soil-binding plant, a hedge, and a source of young growth appealing to sheep and other livestock. It is also grown for the large, yellow, fragrant flowers that precede the conspicuous brown pods. Family: Pea (Leguminosae); genus *Ulex*.

GOURD, a fleshy fruit with a thick, firm, outer part (the rind) surrounding a more fibrous, soft part (the pulp) in which the seeds are embedded; also, the plant that produces such a fruit. Most are members of the gourd family (Cucurbitaceae) and are usually vines native to Africa or warm and temperate parts of the Northern Hemisphere.

Some gourds are raised for their fruits, others as ornaments, and still others to be dried, cleansed of their pulp, and made into drinking vessels, dishes, and musical instruments.

GOURD FAMILY (Cucurbitaceae), a group of about 850 species in 100 genera, mostly tropical and subtropical prostrate or climbing herbs with tendrils that appear along the length of the stems. Many are cultivated for food or for their decorative value. See *Cucumber, Gourd, Melon, Pumpkin, Squash,* and *Vegetable sponge.*

GRAPE, any of about 60 different kinds of woody vines mostly native to temperate parts of the Northern Hemisphere. The spherical fruits are also called grapes. The grape plant or grapevine bears simple, heart-shaped leaves, and climbs by means of tendrils that are highly adapted terminal buds growing out of side branches that lack leaves. The flowers are small, green, and generally hairy; the fruits are small or large, seeded or seedless, tart or sweet, green, red, blue, or greenish-white in color.

Grapes may be eaten raw, dried as raisins, or used in fermentative processes to make many kinds of wine. Until the 1600s, almost the only grape in cultivation was the one that was domesticated in prehistoric times in southern Europe and Asia Minor. Its culture was introduced into America before the value of the American species was recognized.

The principal species used are the European *Vitis vinifera* and the North American *Vitis labrusca*, as well as numerous hybrids and horticultural varieties. Family: Grape (Vitaceae); genus *Vitis*.

GRAPE FAMILY (Vitaceae), a group of about 600 species in 11 genera, native to the tropics, subtropics, and some temperate regions, chiefly climbing shrubs with terminal buds that become tendrils, requiring the stem to continue growth by an apparent bend as the axillary bud extends into a new branch. The flowers are clustered and produce berries.

Among cultivated plants in this family are the trailing begonia (*Cissus discolor*) of Java and the peppervine (*Ampelopsis arborea*) of the southern United States. See *Boston ivy, Grape,* and *Woodbine.*

GRAPEFRUIT, a small tree with large, ovate leaves and fragrant, white flowers, discovered first in the West Indies and probably derived from the

BURPEE SEEDS

GOURDS

pummelo or shaddock (*Citrus grandis*) of Southeast Asia. The fruits of the grapefruit grow in clusters of 5 to 15, and include among the varieties developed by horticulturalists a number of thin-skinned and seedless types differing considerably from the original stock. The fruit is eaten fresh, canned, or made into juice. Family: Rue (Rutaceae); genus and species, *Citrus paradisi*.

GRAPE HYACINTH, any of about 40 different kinds of small, bulbous plants with bladelike leaves and clusters of bell-shaped flowers at the top of upright stems. The clusters suggest bunches of blue, white, or yellow grapes. Native to Mediterranean Europe, they have been introduced widely as plants used in flower borders and rock gardens. Family: Lily (Liliaceae); genus *Muscari*.

GRASS FAMILY (Gramineae), a very large family with about 4500 species in 500 genera, the most widely distributed of vascular plants. Many have the ability to lie dormant during protracted droughts.

They have colonized prairies, plains, savannas, campos, pampas, steppes, and veldts, and are a source of food for grazing animals, a great variety of seed-eating birds, and rodents. They have fibrous roots, typically hollow stems, and parallel-veined leaves. Their flowers are clustered and so specialized that only the stamen and pistil seem to correspond to parts of flowers in other plant families.

See *Bamboo, Barley, Bluegrass, Broom corn, Buckwheat, Corn, Crabgrass, Millet, Pampas grass, Papyrus, Reed, Rice, Rye, Sorghum, Sudan grass, Sugar cane, Timothy,* and *Wheat.*

GROUND IVY, or gill-over-the-ground, a delicate but prolific creeping and trailing plant with a square stem, round or kidney-shaped leaves on short petioles, and clusters of blue or yellow flowers. It is native to Europe

but has been introduced into many parts of the world and has escaped from cultivation to become a weed. Family: Mint (Labiatae); genus and species, *Glechoma hederacea*.

GROUNDNUT. See *Peanut.*

GROUND PINE. See *Clubmoss.*

GUAIACUM. See *Lignum Vitae.*

GUAVA, a small tree with square stems, opposite leaves, fragrant, white flowers with four petals, and mildly acid, yellow fruits about the size of a hen's egg. Native to the West Indies, it is now cultivated extensively in the southern United States, North Africa, Malaya, and China. The pinkish flesh of the fruit is too soft to withstand transportation, but it is eaten raw where grown or made into jams and jellies. Family: Myrtle (Myrtaceae); genus and species, *Psidium guajaba*.

GUAYULE, a branching shrub with luxuriant, silvery leaves, native to the North American southwest, and now cultivated in Texas and Mexico for its latex, which contains solid particles suitable for extraction and manufacture into a valuable rubber.

When about 4 years old the whole plant is pulled up, dried, crushed, and immersed in water. The particles that have been suspended in the cell sap then float to the top and can be skimmed off. Between 150 and 200 million pounds of this material are used annually. Family: Daisy (Compositae); genus and species, *Parthenium argentatum*.

GUNNY. See *Jute.*

GUTTA–PERCHA. See *Rubber.*

GYPSOPHILA. See *Baby's-Breath.*

HACKBERRY, any of about 60 different small trees of the Northern Hemisphere, with elmlike leaves and plumlike fruits. The bark of the most widespread species in eastern North America (*Celtis occidentalis*) is silvery and deeply grooved into a checkered pattern. The wood is soft, easily broken by strong windstorms and accumulations of sleet, but useful for making boxes, baskets, and some kinds of furniture.

Hackberries are often planted as windbreaks and as shade trees in the southern United States. Family: Elm (Ulmaceae); genus *Celtis*.

HAREBELL. See *Bluebell.*

HAWKWEED, any of perhaps 2000 different kinds of herbaceous perennial plants of temperate and cool climates in the Northern Hemisphere, the Andes, and South Africa. Most have hairy, simple leaves in a whorl close to the ground and hairy, upright stalks bearing one or more flower heads. All of the florets in each head bear strap-shaped corollas, which are commonly orange, yellow, or scarlet. Many are noxious weeds that reproduce by seeds and runners. Family: Daisy (Compositae); genus *Hieracium*.

HAWTHORN, any of perhaps 1000 different kinds of woody shrubs and small trees of the North Temperate Zone with alternate leaves that are deeply cut into lobes, prominent spines on the stems, and clusters of pink or white flowers that open in spring. The flowers are followed by small, red, yellow, blue, or black, apple-like fruits called haws. Family: Rose (Rosaceae); genus *Crataegus.*

HAZEL, any of 8 different shrubs and small trees of the North Temperate Zone, with oblong to round leaves that are folded lengthwise in the bud, drooping catkins of staminate flowers, budlike, pistillate flowers with conspicuous red stigmas in early spring, and hard-shelled seeds released from leaflike bracts that develop around the ripening fruit.

The seeds of the European hazel (*Corylus avellana*) are produced commercially by orchards in Italy, Turkey, Spain, and the state of Oregon for sale as filberts. A filbert differs from the hazelnuts of other species in that it is larger but shows no distinctive difference in shape, texture, or taste. Family: Birch (Betulaceae); genus *Corylus.*

HEATH, any of about 500 different tough, branching shrubs and trees of Europe, southwestern Asia, and South Africa, with small, white, pink, or purple, cuplike flowers, and 4-chambered capsules that open to release small seeds. A great many heaths are characteristic of moorlands. The tree heath (*Erica arborea*) of the Mediterranean region grows to a height of 65 feet and furnishes brierwood for briar pipes. Family: Heath (Ericaceae); genus *Erica.*

HEATH FAMILY (Ericaceae), a group of about 1900 species in 70 genera, almost all woody shrubs and trees. The heath constitutes the characteristic vegetation of moors, many mountain slopes and swamps in temperate and subarctic lands, and the higher slopes of tropical mountains. See *Arbutus, Azalea, Blueberry, Cranberry, Heath, Heather, Huckleberry, Madroña, Manzanita, Mountain-laurel, Pipsissewa, Rhododendron,* and *Wintergreen.*

HEATHER, or ling, a low-growing evergreen shrub native to Greenland, Europe, and western Asia but now introduced into eastern North America and covering large areas of moorland. The leaves are minute, overlapping, and in opposite pairs. The small pink, purple, or white flowers generally arise on one side of the stem or its branches, near the tip. The bright color is in the calyx, which overlaps and hides the small corolla.

In true heaths (*Erica*), on the other hand, the calyx is small and the corolla shows the color. Family: Heath Ericaceae); genus and species, *Calluna vulgaris.*

HELIOTROPE, any of about 250 different kinds of herbs, vines, shrubs, and small trees, chiefly native to tropical South America, but found also in warm parts of Eurasia and North America. All have simple leaves and

T.H. EVERETT
HELIOTROPE

funnel-shaped or tubular flowers with flaring petals borne in spikes. Many horticultural varieties of the cherry-pie (*Heliotropium arborescens*), native to Ecuador and Peru, are cultivated for their perfumed flowers. Family: Borage (Boraginaceae); genus *Heliotropium.*

HELLEBORE, any of about 22 different kinds of evergreen plants native to southern Europe, with glossy, palmately compound leaves, and showy, cup-shaped flowers that lack petals but have white, pink, or purple sepals. The powdered roots of some have been used in medicine as a sedative and in agriculture as an insecticide.

A cultivated ornamental plant is the Christmas rose or black hellebore (*Helleborus niger*), which blooms in winter and often pushes its rather stiff, 2-inch flowers through the snow. Each flower has 5, widely spreading, white, petal-like sepals and numerous golden stamens. Family: Buttercup (Ranunculaceae); genus *Helleborus.*

HEMLOCK, any of 12 different coniferous, evergreen trees characteristic of forests in China, Japan, and North America, but not native to Europe or other continents. The needles are flat, with 2 white lines beneath, and are arranged on the 2 sides of drooping branches. Tan colored cones grow on the under-sides of the branches and release winged seeds.

The eastern hemlock (*Tsuga canadensis*) of North America grows well in the shade of hardwood forests and is valuable for the tannins in its bark. Western hemlock (*T. heterophylla*) of the Pacific Northwest is a much larger, stronger tree, rising to about 260 feet, and yielding inportant timber, as well as bark that is rich in tannins. Family: Pine (Pinaceae); genus *Tsuga.* See also *Poison hemlock.*

HEMP, an erect or twining annual plant native to Asia, growing 3 to 18 feet high, with 3 to 7 narrow, toothed leaflets on each of its palmately compound leaves. The inner bark is valu-

able for its tough fibers, which are made into twine, rope, canvas, and sailcloth. Resin extracted from hairs on the stem and leaves contains a mixture of narcotic compounds responsible for the drug effects obtained from smoking the dried unextracted plant materials, known as marijuana, hashish, or charas. Hemp seeds are used for feeding cage birds and as the source of a commercial oil resembling linseed oil. Family: Hemp (Cannabinaceae); genus and species, *Cannabis sativa.*

HEMP FAMILY (Cannabinaceae), a small group of 3 species in 2 genera, often included in the Mulberry family (Moraceae). The genus *Cannabis* has only one species, hemp (*C. indica*). See *Hemp* and *Hop.*

HENEQUEN. See *Century Plant.*

HEPATICA, or liverleaf, a small genus of woodland wildflowers blooming in early spring in the North Temperate Zone. Each plant consists of a basal whorl of 3-lobed leaves on slender, hairy petioles and, in season, a number of white, pink, or lavender flowers with many stamens but no petals, the petal-like sepals providing the color.

There are two species native to eastern North America; one, *H. triloba,* is native to Eurasia but not to the British Isles. Family: Buttercup (Ranunculaceae).

HERB CHRISTOPHER. See *Baneberry.*

HIBISCUS, or rose-mallow, a genus of herbs, shrubs, and small trees native to tropical and subtropical countries, with large, showy flowers. One (*H. rosasinensis*), known as rose-of-China, or shoeblack plant, or shoeflower, has almost become a symbol of the tropics because of its wide cultivation as a decorative hedge plant. Its blossoms collapse permanently at the end of a day. They contain a black dye that makes them suitable for polishing and cleaning black shoes.

More than 1000 horticultural varieties of the hibiscus plant with distinctive names and petals of many colors and forms have been developed.

Among the 200 other species of the genus, the Asian rose-of-Sharon (*H. syriacus*) with 3-lobed leaves and cup-shaped, red flowers is commonly planted as an ornamental shrub; okra, or gumbo, or bandakai (*H. esculentus*), which probably originated in northeastern Africa, is cultivated extensively in tropical West Africa, southeastern United States, Turkey, and India for its edible, partly ripened capsules, which are mucilaginous unless properly cooked. Family: Mallow (Malvaceae).

HICKORY, any of several kinds of trees native to eastern North America and Southeast Asia, with large, shiny, pinnately compound leaves, trunks 60 to 160 feet tall, tough, close-grained wood, and small flowers in separate clusters, the staminate flowers in yellow, tassel-like catkins and the pistillate flowers in stiff spikes. The leathery coverings of the fruits crack open, releasing the armored seeds, which fall to the ground.

Some species are shagbark or shellbark hickories; these shed their old bark in long, flat strips that loosen gradually and curl slightly away from the trunk. Others are more smoothbarked, marked only by deep surface furrows. Most have edible kernels in the seeds. The pecan (*Carya pecan*) grows to a height of 150 feet, and yields the best nuts of any member of the group; a native of the Mississippi Valley, the Southwest, and into Mexico, it is now cultivated in large orchards in Georgia and adjacent states. Family: Walnut (Juglandaceae); genus *Carya*.

HOLLY, any of about 280 different kinds of shrubs and trees with alternate, simple leaves and small clusters of regular flowers that are followed by berry-like fruits containing several nutlets. They are widely distributed, although Europe has only one, *Ilex aquifolium:* a small tree with very hard wood, leathery, glossy, evergreen leaves, and bright red fruits that remain in place until mid-winter. The European holly was used in pagan rituals, and later found a place in Christmas ceremonies.

An American holly (*I. opaca*) with prickly leaves that are only slightly less glossy than those of the European holly is used for Christmas purposes in the New World, although fruits develop only on the pistillate trees when they are near the fruitless staminate trees. Some hollies, such as black alder (*I. verticillata*) of swamps in the eastern United States, are deciduous. Others are appreciated because their prickly leaves contain caffeine and can be brewed into the popular beverage, *yerba maté,* or Paraguay tea (from the South American evergreen shrub *I. paraguariensis*). Family: Holly (Aquifoliaceae); genus *Ilex*.

HOLLYHOCK, a tall, biennial herb with large wrinkled leaves on an erect stem that grows 5 to 6 feet high, producing an ascending progression of saucer-shaped flowers in white, pink, yellow, lavender, and even a violet so dark that it seems black. Native to the Balkans, the plant was brought to western Europe by returning Crusaders and adopted as a stately garden flower. In Egypt its leaves are sometimes cooked as a vegetable. Family: Mallow (Malvaceae); genus and species, *Althaea rosea*.

HONEYDEW MELON. See *Melon*.

HONEY LOCUST. See *Locust*.

HONEYSUCKLE, any of about 180 different kinds of erect or climbing shrubs with opposite, simple leaves and paired flowers that are bilaterally symmetrical and often both fragrant and supplied generously with nectar. Native to the Northern Hemisphere, they include several shrubs that have been introduced widely and cultivated for their flowers and, in some cases, the evergreen cover the climbing species provide over unwanted native vegetation. Family: Honeysuckle (Caprifoliaceae); genus *Lonicera*.

T.H. EVERETT

HONEYSUCKLE

HONEYSUCKLE FAMILY (Caprifoliaceae), a group of about 275 species in 18 genera, chiefly native to the Northern Hemisphere, mostly trees or shrubs, but many climbing vines, all with opposite leaves and clustered flowers. It includes the twinflower (*Linnaea borealis*), found in the far north of both Eurasia and North America. See *Blackhaw, Elder, Honeysuckle, Viburnum,* and *Woodbine*.

HOP, a perennial climbing vine of Eurasia, with rough stems 15 to 20 feet long, coarse, lobed leaves, staminate flowers on some plants and pistillate flowers on others. The pistillate flowers are enclosed by green bracts (the "hops" of brewers) which bear yellow, dustlike grains of a bitter substance used to give flavor and sparkle to beer. Family: Hemp (Cannabinaceae); genus and species, *Humulus lupulus*.

HOREHOUND, a perennial herb with a square stem, opposite, hairy, silvery leaves, and clusters of small, white flowers in the leaf axils. Native to the Mediterranean countries from the Canary Islands to western Asia, it has been cultivated and naturalized elsewhere for an extract used in candies and in syrups designed to treat colds and coughs. Family: Mint (Labiatae); genus and species, *Marrubium vulgare*.

HORNBEAM, any of about 20 different small trees of the North Temperate Zone, with gray bark, hard wood, drooping branches, oval, serrate leaves that turn orange in autumn, and separate clusters of staminate and pistillate flowers in catkins. The small, oneseeded fruits are winged. Family: Birch (Betulaceae); genus *Carpinus*.

HORSE CHESTNUT, a handsome, deciduous tree attaining a height of 60 feet, with opposite, palmately compound leaves. The leaflets are wedge-shaped and toothed along the edges. Pyramidal clusters of creamy flowers are followed by prickly fruits that open to release large, inedible seeds resembling chestnuts.

Native to the Balkans and the Caucasus, the horse chestnut is cultivated widely as an ornamental tree. Relatives from South America and the North Temperate Zone include the buckeyes of California, the north central states, and the southeast. The light wood of these trees is used for paper pulp and the manufacture of artificial limbs. Family: Horse chestnut (Hippocastanaceae); genus and species, *Aesculus hippocastanum*.

HORSERADISH, a perennial herb native to Eurasia, growing to about 2 feet in height, with narrow leaves, clusters of white flowers, and white, fleshy roots that are edible and used as a condiment. The plant is now widely cultivated and used to give flavor to relishes. Family: Mustard (Cruciferae); genus and species, *Armoracia rusticana*.

HORSETAIL, any of about 25 different kinds of perennial rushlike herbs with hollow, jointed stems. They have neither leaves nor flowers and are found throughout the world except in the Australasian region. Most are less than 3 feet tall, but the *Equisetum giganteum* of the West Indies and tropical South America may attain a height of 36 feet.

Several species are native to both Eurasia and North America, such as the scouring rush (*E. hyemale*), the stems of which are so harsh because of the siliceous material they contain that poineers and peasants have used them to scour pots, floors, and other surfaces. All horsetails develop terminal clusters of spore cases. The spores germinate on suitable moist surfaces and grow into small, special plants bearing the sexual reproductive organs. Fertilized eggs from these grow into the familiar herbs. Family: Equisetaceae; genus *Equisetum*.

HUCKLEBERRY, any of about 40 different kinds of shrubs 1 to 6 feet tall, with smooth, oval, leathery leaves, white or pink, bell-shaped flowers, and clusters of glossy, black berries containing 10 minute, hard seeds. Native to the Americas, they are often confused with blueberries (*Vaccinium*), which have somewhat less acid berries and no armor around the seeds. Family: Heath (Ericaceae); genus *Gaylussacia*.

HYACINTH, any of about 30 different kinds of hardy, bulbous herbs native to Mediterranean countries and South Africa. They are cultivated widely for their early spring flowers, which are fragrant, bell-shaped, white, pink, blue, or violet, and grow in tall, compact clusters that precede the stiff, bladelike leaves.

The name is also given to some related plants of other genera, such as the wood hyacinth (*Scilla nonscripta*) of the Old World, and the wild hyacinth (*Camassia scilloides*) of eastern North America. Family: Lily (Liliaceae); genus *Hyacinthus*. See also *Grape Hyacinth*.

HYDRANGEA, a genus containing about 80 different species of woody shrubs native to the North Temperate Zone. They attain a height of 8 to 20 feet, and bear large, paired leaves and round heads composed of globular flowers. The Oriental species (*H. paniculata*) is the most common ornamental species, with flowers ranging from white to pink and blue. The wild hydrangea (*H. arborescens*) of eastern North America attains a height of 10 feet and grows mostly on wet soils rich in lime. Family: Saxifrage (Saxifragaceae).

ICE PLANT, a succulent, low-growing plant of South Africa, with leaves densely covered with small, bladder-shaped hairs that glisten like ice crystals. Grown as a ground cover, rather than for its small white or pink flowers, the plant is cultivated extensively in southern California and elsewhere. It does not tolerate hard frosts.

The juice of the plant can be used as a diuretic and demulcent. In Spain the ashes of its leaves and stems are often added to the mixture used in making glass. Family: Carpetweed (Aizoaceae); genus and species, *Mesembryanthemum Crystallinum*.

INDIAN HEMP, a widespread North American perennial herb with a milky juice in tough stems 2 to 4 feet tall. It has paired, oval leaves, and bell-shaped, white or greenish flowers in terminal clusters. Indians used the fibers of the inner bark for making rope. Family: Dogbane (Apocynaceae); genus and species, *Apocynum cannabinum*.

INDIAN PIPE, a colorless, saprophytic plant of moist woodlands in North America. It lives on dead vegetable matter in the soil with the help of a fungal partner. The upright stems are covered with waxy, white scales, and they terminate at a height of 4 to 10 inches in a nodding, white, cylindrical flower. The stem and flower turn black when picked. As the seeds ripen, the stem straightens, shrivels, and turns blackish-brown, holding an upright capsule. Family: (Pyrolaceae); genus and species, *Monotropa uniflora*.

INDIAN TOBACCO. See *Lobelia.*

INDIAN TURNIP. See *Jack-in-the-pulpit.*

INDIGO, a shrubby plant native to the East Indies. The blue dye obtained by fermenting and oxidizing the juice from the odd-pinnate leaves of this plant is also called indigo. Cultivation of indigo for the dye industry was formerly a major occupation in India and other warm parts of Asia and South America, but operations virtually ceased when cheaper synthetic dyes became available. Family: Pea (Leguminosae); genus and species, *Indigofera tinctoria*.

IRIS, a genus of about 200 different species found in the North Temperate Zone, all with grasslike or sword-shaped leaves, usually growing from a fleshy underground stem. The flow-

ers have 3 showy sepals which turn down (called by horticulturalists "the falls") while 3 similar petals turn up ("the standards"); the 3 branches of the style on the pistil are often petal-like, arching over the stamens.

Many species, hybrids between species, and horticultural varieties are cultivated for their flowers. The Florentine iris (*I. florentina*), with white flowers, is probably the model for the French emblem, the fleur-de-lis ("flower of the lily"). The dried and powdered roots of this and a few other European irises, known as orris root, are used to give an imitation violet fragrance to perfumes, tooth pastes, and other cosmetics. Family: Iris (Iridaceae).

IRIS FAMILY (Iridaceae), a group of about 1500 species in 58 genera, native to all but the coldest regions, mostly herbaceous plants with storage organs in underground stems or roots, and sword-shaped or grasslike leaves rising from the base. Their flowers differ from those of lilies and related families in having only 3 stamens instead of 6. See *Crocus, Freesia, Gladiolus,* and *Iris.*

IRISH MOSS, or carrageen, a soft seaweed growing attached to rocks at moderate depths along North Atlantic coasts, where it is often torn loose and cast ashore in vast quantities by winter storms. Although technically a red alga, it may be green, yellow, purplish, or brown.

When gathered, washed, and dried in the sun, it can be pulverized to make a flourlike material of some food value. Soaked in water, it becomes mucilaginous and is used to give body to soups and desserts such as blancmange, or to medicines such as cough mixtures. Family: Gigartina (Gigartinaceae); genus and species, *Chondrus crispus*.

T.H. EVERETT
JACK–IN–THE–PULPIT

IRONWEED, any of about a dozen North American, rough-stemmed, coarse, herbaceous perennials growing as high as 10 feet, with many alternate, narrow, pointed leaves and clusters of purplish-red or white flowers that resemble thistle heads without prickles. They produce prodigious numbers of seeds, and spread quickly over neglected or overgrazed land, offering little that attracts livestock but providing abundant nectar for honeybees.

Some of their relatives in Africa are valuable timber trees. These are perhaps the largest representatives of the family. Family: Daisy (Compositae); genus *Vernonia*.

IVY, or English ivy, a vigorous climbing plant native to temperate Eurasia, with dark glossy, oval or 5-lobed, evergreen leaves, yellowish flowers, and clusters of black berries. It clings by means of short, aerial roots penetrating small cavities in wood or stone surfaces.

Garlands of ivy were used in ancient Greece to decorate statues of Dionysus or Bacchus, and became a symbol of those establishments where wine was sold by the glass. Later, ivy-clad walls became a mark of institutions of learning. Introduced into the New World, ivy forms an attractive ground cover in the southern United States, but is often killed by winter cold in northern states and Canada.

The name ivy is commonly given to other creeping and climbing plants. Family: Ginseng (Araliaceae); genus and species, *Hedera helix*. See *Boston Ivy, Poison Ivy,* and *Woodbine.*

JACK-IN-THE-PULPIT, or Indian turnip, any of several herbaceous, woodland plants of temperate North America, bearing one or more palmately compound leaves. It has a single flower cluster with a spathe extended into a flaplike hood (the "pulpit") around the central column (the spadix, or "Jack") bearing the tiny staminate and pistillate flowers.

The thick, short, underground stem is made acrid by a sap containing needle-like crystals of poisonous calcium oxalate, which the Indians removed with boiling water to obtain an edible food. Family: Arum (Araceae); genus *Arisaema*.

JAPONICA, or flowering quince, a popular Oriental ornamental shrub. It has spreading spiny branches 3 to 6 feet tall, glossy leaves, scarlet or orange flowers blooming early in the year, and 2-inch, globular, hard fruits rich in pectin and suitable for making into a jelly. Family: Rose (Rosaceae); genus and species, *Chaenomeles lagenaria*.

JASMINE, any of about 200 different erect or climbing shrubs native to all continents except Africa and Australasia. Several are cultivated in warm, temperate, and tropical countries for their attractive and fragrant white or yellow starlike flowers borne on climbing, slender stems among delicate, pinnately compound leaves. The fresh flowers are used to make perfume. Dried flowers are often added to tea in China and Japan.

The name jasmine is often given to the unrelated yellow jessamine (*Gelsemium sempervirens* of the strychnine family, Loganiaceae), an evergreen vine with clustered, golden flowers native to swamps in the southeastern United States. Family: Olive (Oleaceae); genus *Jasminum*.

JEWELWEED, or touch-me-not, or snapweed, any of several herbaceous plants of the North Temperate Zone, with hollow, juicy stems 2 to 5 feet tall, oval leaves, and clusters of pendant, orange flowers shaped like those of the snapdragon but with a spur formed by the extended calyx.

The fruits are explosive capsules that shatter when ripe, scattering the pellet-like seeds over a radius of several feet. Sparkling drops of water often adorn the leaves in the early morning, giving them the name of jewelweed. Family: Jewelweed (Balsaminaceae); genus *Impatiens*.

JIMSON WEED, or thorn-apple, a malodorous and dangerously poisonous coarse annual native to the Asian area between India and the Caspian Sea. It is now almost cosmopolitan as a rank weed growing to 5 feet, with broad leaves toothed around the margin and white, trumpet-shaped flowers that are followed by a prickly, ovoid seed capsule. The sweet-tasting seeds are deadly poisonous; all other parts of the plant are almost equally dangerous. Family: Potato (Solanaceae); genus and species, *Datura stramonium*.

JOE-PYE WEED, a herbaceous perennial of eastern North America with oval, serrate leaves whorled around its thick stems; the stems are 3 to 10 feet tall and bear flat-topped clusters of pink or purple flowers. It was named after Joe Pye, a traveling Indian medicine man of New England, who advertised a tonic made from this plant. Family: Daisy (Compositae); genus and species, *Eupatorium purpureum*.

JONQUIL. See *Narcissus*.

JUDAS TREE. See *Redbud*.

JUJUBE, a shrub or small tree of southern China and the East Indies, attaining a height of 20 to 50 feet, with alternate leaves, hooked spines, and plumlike fruits about the size of olives. These fruits are known as jujubes or Chinese dates. It has been introduced into the southern United States as an ornamental tree, but preserved jujubes are still imported from Mediterranean countries and Japan. Family: Buckthorn (Rhamnaceae); genus and species, *Zizyphus jujuba*.

JUNIPER, any of about 60 different kinds of shrubs and trees native to the North Temperate Zone, with scale-like or needle-like, evergreen leaves and one-seeded, fleshy cones known as juniper berries. Oil of juniper, extracted from these cones, is used medicinally as a diuretic, and commercially in the manufacture of varnish and the flavoring of gin.

Eastern red cedar (*Juniperus virginiana*) provides long-lasting posts, railroad ties, and wood for making lead pencils, but because it is an alternate host for the fungus causing apple rust, some states prohibit the planting of this tree near apple orchards. Western juniper (*J. occidentalis*) grows at moderate altitudes in the mountains of western North America, sometimes reaching the age of 2000 years. Family: Cypress (Cupressaceae); genus *Juniperus*.

JUTE, or gunny, the fiber from the inner bark of either of two East Indian shrubs, which are raised as annuals and grow 6 to 12 feet tall. They are planted so close together that they produce almost no branches. The fiber is used for cheap twine, cording, burlap, bagging, oakum, and strong wrapping paper. Family: Linden (Tiliaceae); genus and species, *Corchorus capsularis* and *C. olitorius*.

KAFIR CORN. See *Sorghum*.

KALE. See *Mustard*.

KAPOK, or silk-cotton tree, a tropical American tree of moderate height, with large, 5-lobed leaves; a heavy, ridged trunk; bark studded with conical, blunt spines; bell-shaped flowers; and pods full of fluffy, silky fibers that can be separated from the seeds.

These fibers are water-resistant, buoyant, elastic, but not useful for spinning. Kapok trees are cultivated extensively in Java, Malaysia, Ceylon, and the Philippine Islands to obtain the fibers. The fibers are used to stuff mattresses, life-preservers, and pillows, and for the manufacture of wallboard, ceiling insulation, and even bathing suits. The oil from kapok seeds is used in foods and soap. Family: Bombax (Bombacaceae); genus and species, *Ceiba pentandra*.

KENTUCKY COFFEE TREE, a deciduous, hardwood tree of the southeastern United States, growing 50 to 100 feet. It has rough, scaly, reddish-gray bark; twice pinnately compound leaves; terminal clusters of white flowers; and pods containing black seeds, which were used by the colonists as a substitute for coffee beans. The hard wood is useful for fence posts. Family: Pea (Leguminosae); genus and species, *Gymnocladus dioica*.

KOHLRABI. See *Mustard*.

KUDZU, a hairy, twining vine native to southeastern Asia. It has luxuriant foliage and clusters of purple flowers. In the United States it has been planted as a decorative porch vine capable of climbing 60 feet or more, and in the southern states, as a soil binder to control erosion on slopes. Family: Pea (Leguminosae); genus and species, *Pueraria lobata*.

KUMQUAT, any of 6 different Asian shrubs 6 to 8 feet tall, with glossy, green, simple leaves, fragrant, white flowers, and fruits the size of an olive resembling miniature oranges. The fruits may be eaten raw or preserved, and are now the basis for the cultivation of kumquats in the southern United States. Family: Rue (Rutaceae); genus *Fortunella*.

LABURNUM, a genus consisting of 3 different kinds of small European and western Asian trees with dark 3-parted leaves and pendant sprays of bright yellow flowers. *L. anagyroides* is cultivated for Easter decorations and as the principal source of the alkaloid cytisine, used in medicine. Golden-chain (*L. vulgare*), is popular in the southern United States for decorative outdoor planting. The wood of all of these trees is used in fine cabinet work. Family: Pea (Leguminosae).

LACQUER TREE, or varnish tree, any of several unrelated trees from which substances can be extracted for the production of lacquer or varnish. Most notable is a small tree of China and Japan, with handsome, pinnately compound leaves that turn orange-red in autumn. A mildly toxic latex can be obtained from these trees by slashing the bark on the trunk or stripping the bark from branches less than an inch in diameter. The viscous latex turns black upon exposure to air.

Chinese workmen who have become immune to its irritating effect upon the skin paint the blackened latex on boxes, trays, and other objects, and later smooth the coating with a stone tool to produce a handsome, high luster. The practice began in prehistoric times and reached the greatest perfection during the Ming dynasty (1364–1644 AD). Family: Sumac (Anacardiaceae); genus and species, *Rhus vernicifera*.

LADY'S SLIPPER, any of about 30 different kinds of perennial, woodland orchids of the North Temperate Zone, with coarse, fibrous roots, broad, pleated leaves that clasp the stem, and mostly solitary, showy flowers atop a tall stalk. The lower lip (labellum) of the corolla resembles the toe part of a shoe or moccasin, inspiring the other common names of shoeflower or moccasin flower.

The lady's slipper flower may be white, pink, purple, yellow, brown, orange, or red, plain or attractively mottled. The large yellow lady's slipper (*Cypripedium pubescens*) is often grown in shady gardens. Family: Orchid (Orchidaceae); genus *Cypripedium*.

LAMB'S-QUARTERS, an annual plant native to western Asia but now cosmopolitan as a weed of roadsides and neglected land, growing as a straight stem to 1 to 9 feet, with narrow, serrate leaves and sprays of greenish-white flowers. In Eurasia the green portions of young plants are sometimes cooked and eaten. Family: Goosefoot (Chenopodiaceae); genus and species, *Chenopodium album*.

LARCH, any of about 10 different kinds of needle-leaved trees of the North Temperate Zone, bearing deciduous needles in clusters of 10 or more, and small cones from which winged seeds are distributed by the wind. All larches produce useful wood.

The European larch (*Larix decidua*) is the source of a yellow resin called Venice turpentine, used in lithography. The American larch (*L. laricina*), known also as the tamarack or hackmatack, grows in cold bogs across the continent from Alaska to New England. Family: Pine (Pinaceae); genus *Larix*.

LARKSPUR, any of about 200 different kinds of herbaceous plants found in the North Temperate Zone, with palmately lobed or divided leaves and an upright, sturdy stem growing to 2 to 7 feet. The stem is topped by a graceful cluster of handsome flowers, each with the top sepal prolonged into a spur that is hollow and surrounds similar extensions from the top 2 petals. The 5 sepals and 2 or 4 petals are all petal-like, in blue, purple, pink, pale yellow, white, or blended colors.

Horticulturists reserve the name larkspur for annuals and use the generic name for perennials. Many wild larkspurs are poisonous to cattle. Family: Buttercup (Ranunculaceae); genus *Delphinium*.

LAUREL, or sweet bay, a handsome tree of Mediterranean countries, with aromatic, glossy, evergreen leaves, yellow flowers, and purple fruits resembling cherries. Wreaths and coronets were made with its leafy branches as a traditional sign or honor for the winners in Greek games.

A similar and related tree, California laurel (*Umbellularia californica*), found in forests of California and Oregon and growing to a height of 80 feet, yields hard wood used a great deal in cabinetry. Family Laurel (Lauraceae); genus and species, *Laurus nobilis*. See *Mountain laurel.*

LAUREL FAMILY (Lauraceae), a group of about 1100 species in 45 genera, chiefly shrubs and trees with aromatic bark, aromatic, smooth-edged leaves, and clustered flowers, native to tropical and subtropical regions.

Some varieties such as the greenhart (*Nectandra rodioei*) of northern South America and the stinkwoods (*Ocotea* species) of South Africa, grow very slowly and produce exceedingly hard, strong wood.

Other varieties, such as the camphor-tree (*Cinnamomum camphora*) native to Formosa, Japan, and south China, and the cassia-bark tree (*C. cassia*) of southern China, rank along with cinnamon as a source of valued extracts and flavorings. See *Avocado, Cinnamon, Laurel, Sassafras,* and *Spicebush.*

LAVENDER, a low-growing, perennial, evergreen shrub of temperate Eurasia, with narrow, grayish-green leaves, and tall spikes of pale lilac-colored flowers. Both leaves and flowers are clad in fine hairs among which are glands containing a fragrant oil.

Fresh flowers are quite often used commercially to make lavender perfumes and other cosmetics; dried leaves and flowers are used in the manufacture of toiletries.

Southern France and Scotland have become centers of the lavender industry, although the plant itself is cultivated extensively as a garden ornament in North America. Family: Mint (Labiatae); genus and species, *Lavandula officinalis*.

LEEK, a slender, bulbous plant native to the Near East but now widely introduced and cultivated for its tasty, slender, cylindrical bulb and soft succulent leaves, which are milder than those of an onion. When it is allowed to mature it produces a cluster of white or pink flowers. Leeks are used commonly in the Old World and the New as a relish, a condiment, and to add flavor to soups. Family: Lily (Liliaceae); genus and species, *Allium porrum*.

LEMON, a low-growing, evergreen tree of Southeast Asia, 10 to 12 feet tall, with glossy, oval leaves and fragrant, white flowers. Its yellow, acid fruit is rich in citric acid and vitamin C. Cultivated for thousands of years in Asia and in warm parts of Europe, it is now grown extensively in subtropical America. The glandular rind of the fruit is frequently candied, preserved, or used in grated form to add a distinctive flavoring to foods. Family: Rue (Rutaceae); genus and species, *Citrus limon*.

LENTIL, an annual branching herb of the Mediterranean region, 6 to 18 inches tall, the pinnately compound leaves ending in climbing tendrils, the blue or white pealike flowers followed by small pods each containing 2 lens-shaped, gray or red seeds. The plant is cultivated extensively in the Old World for its edible seeds, which are made into soups and porridges. Family: Pea (Leguminosae); genus and species, *Lens culinaris*.

LETTUCE, an annual plant probably native to Asia Minor, cultivated for at least 2500 years as the most popular of salad ingredients. Until the Middle Ages, only the loose-leaved variety was known. Left to grow, it produces a stem 2 to 3 feet tall, topped by small clusters of white- or cream-colored flowers in which every floret

BURPEE SEEDS
LEEKS

is strap-shaped. Head lettuce, which was a new horticultural variety in the 1500s, is now generally preferred to leaf lettuce. Another variety is Cos, or romaine lettuce, with spoon-shaped leaves that have a broad midrib; it was first discovered on the Greek island of Kos. Lettuce contains important vitamins and minerals but virtually no food energy. Family: Daisy (Compositae); genus and species, *Lactuca sativa*.

LICORICE, a herbaceous perennial plant native to Europe, with pale green, pinnately compound leaves, a stem about 3 feet tall, and purple flowers resembling those of peas and beans. It is cultivated extensively in southern Europe for its fibrous roots, from which a sweet black extract can be obtained for use in candies, soft drinks, and in flavoring medicines and tobacco.

A related plant, wild licorice (*Glycyrrhiza lepidota*), found widely in the plains and pasturelands between Mexico and central Canada, has sweet-tasting roots that yield their flavor when chewed. Family: Pea (Leguminosae); genus and species, *Glycyrrhiza glabra*.

LIGNUM VITAE, any of 6 different tropical American trees with extremely hard, heavy wood, pinnately compound leaves, blue, 5-petalled flowers, and seeds in capsules. Most grow to 15 to 30 feet and yield a gum (guaiacum) used in the treatment of rheumatic and skin diseases. The wood of the *Guaiacum officinale*, native to Forida, the West Indies, and northern South America, is the hardest and heaviest of commercial woods. Family: Caltrop (Zygophyllaceae); genus *Guaiacum*.

LILAC, any of about 25 different kinds of woody shrubs with thick, oval, paired leaves and clusters of white or purplish, 4-petalled flowers, which usually emit a strong and characteristic pleasant fragrance. Native to temperate Eurasia, lilacs are cultivated extensively in North America; many horticultural varieties have been developed, chiefly from *Syringa vulgaris* of southeastern Europe. Syringa is also the common name of an unrelated, different plant. Family: Olive (Oleaceae); genus *Syringa*. See also *Mock orange.*

LILY, in the strict sense, any of about 60 different kinds of herbaceous, perennial, bulbous plants of the North Temperate Zone, with upright stems, scattered or whorled, narrow, sessile leaves, and large, trumpet-shaped flowers, the 6 petal-like parts of which curve back upon themselves to display the inner surface.

Easter lilies are usually either the white-trumpet lily (or Bermuda lily, *Lilium longiflorum*) of Japan, which blooms in late March and early April, or they are the very similar madonna lily (*L. candidum*) of southern Europe, which flowers from late April through May. Handsome markings on the inner surface of the flower are features of the golden-banded lily (*L. auratum*) of the Orient and of the various tiger lilies with nodding blossoms, such as the Turk's-cap lily (*L. superbum*) of the eastern United States. Family: Lily (Liliaceae).

LILY FAMILY (Liliaceae), a group of more than 4,000 species in about 250 genera, widely distributed, mostly perennial herbs with a storage organ in the shortened stem, horizontal underground stem, or enlargement of the roots. Generally the flowers are regular, with a 6-parted display of petals and petal-like sepals, and a united ovary of 3 parts that ripens to form a capsule or a berry. See *Aloe, Asparagus, Asphodel, Beargrass, Bluebell, Dogtooth violet, Fritillary, Garlic, Grape hyacinth, Hyacinth, Leek, Lily, Lily of the valley, Mariposa lily, Rose of Sharon, Smilax, Solomon's seal, Trillium, Tuilp,* and *Yucca.*

LILY OF THE VALLEY, either of 2 similar, small, perennial herbs of the North Temperate Zone, with freely spreading horizontal stems, scattered, oblong, upright leaves, and slender, one-sided sprays of small, fragrant, nodding, bell-shaped flowers which are followed by red, poisonous berries that contain a few seeds.

The North American species (*Convallaria montana*) is native to woodlands in the southern Appalachians; the European species (*C. majalis*) has been widely introduced and has become naturalized. Family: Lily (Liliaceae); genus *Convallaria*.

LIME, a small evergreen tree native to the East Indies, with glossy, oval, evergreen leaves, fragrant, white flowers, and small, greenish-yellow, acid fruits, the juice of which is used in beverages and for flavoring. Limes are cultivated throughout Mexico, the West Indies, parts of southern Florida, and southern Europe. Family: Rue (Rutaceae); genus and species, *Citrus aurantifolia*.

LINDEN, or basswood, any of 12 different fast-growing trees of the North Temperate Zone, with soft wood, heart-shaped leaves, and fragrant, creamy-white flowers in small clusters at the tip of pendant stalks to which a green, oval bract is attached for much of the length.

Bees obtain a large amount of nectar from basswood flowers, and the wood is often used in the manufacture of beekeeper's supplies, furniture, woodenware, charcoal, and paper pulp. Family: Linden (Tiliaceae); genus *Tilia*.

LINDEN FAMILY (Tiliaceae), a group of about 400 species in 41 genera, mostly tropical shrubs and trees with simple, alternate leaves and clustered regular flowers. The linden tree and jute are chief among those that grow in temperate regions. See *Jute* and *Linden*.

LITCHI, a genus of a single species (*L. chinensis*). It is a handsome evergreen tree with large, pinnately compound leaves, small flowers, and oval or spherical fruits slightly more than an inch in diameter, each with a

BURPEE SEEDS

LILY

leathery skin, a pink pulp, and a central seed. When dried, the skin becomes wrinkled, brown, and brittle; the pulp becomes somewhat like that of a raisin. Cultivated extensively in the Far East since prehistoric times, its origin is uncertain. The tree is rarely raised in the western world. The fruits, dried or preserved and known as litchi nuts (also spelled lychi or leechee), are imported as expensive luxuries. Family: Soapberry (Sapindaceae).

LIVE–FOREVER. See *Orpine*.

LIVE OAK. See *Oak*.

LOBELIA, a genus of about 250 different kinds of herbs, shrubs, and treelike plants widely distributed in tropical and temperate regions. All have tubular flowers with 2 upturned upper petals and 3 lower petals forming a sort of lip.

Several kinds of lobelia with showy blossoms have been cultivated and developed horticulturally as garden plants. These include the shrubby little blue lobelia (*L. erinus*) of South Africa, used as an edging for flower beds in the Northern Hemisphere, and the cardinal flower (*L. cardinalis*) native to meadows and freshwater shores in eastern North America, its stem 2 to 4 feet tall topped by an open cluster of scarlet flowers.

Colonists in the eastern parts of North America found the Indians drying and smoking the leaves of another native kind (*L. inflata*), now known as Indian tobacco. It has large, oval leaves, small, blue flowers, and inflated capsules, and contains at least one alkaloid that is poisonous if taken internally.

In the Old World, lobelias include extraordinary species, such as the tree lobelia (*L. keniensis*) of high, misty mountain slopes in equatorial Africa, which produces leafy stems 10 to 15 feet tall, from which sturdy flower spikes rise another 6 to 8 feet. Family: Lobelia (Lobeliaceae).

LOCOWEED, any of several different kinds of bushy, herbaceous plants of the western United States and adjacent parts of Canada and Mexico. The plants are sometimes eaten by starving livestock. Within a few months, however, the animals develop symptoms of poisoning, such as an inability to drink or eat; these symtoms are usually soon followed by death. This effect has been attributed to at least 8 species of genus *Astragalus* and 3 of *Oxytropis*. Family: Pea (Leguminosae).

LOCUST, any of several different trees with pinnately compound leaves and flowers resembling those of peas. The flowers are followed by seed pods that turn brown and release the seeds. The name was originally given to the carob tree (*Ceratonia siliqua*) of the Mediterranean region, the unripened pods of which are edible and called St. John's bread. Its seeds may have been the original weights of "carats" used by jewelers. Black locust (*Robinia pseudoacacia*), a valuable timber tree of eastern North America which is now planted in many other parts of the world, grows to a height of 80 feet, producing very hard, durable wood and drooping clusters of showy, white flowers. Its branches bear pairs of sharp spines.

The honey locust (*Gleditsia triacanthos*) attains a height of 140 feet, its branches and bark armed with stiff spines that fork repeatedly. Its pods are filled with a sweet natural gum that children like to chew. Family. Pea (Leguminosae).

LOGANBERRY, a hybrid bramble produced from a cross between the western dewberry (*Rubus ursinus*) of California and the widespread red raspberry (*R. idaeus*). It was discovered in 1881 by Judge J. H. Logan and named for him (*R. loganobaccus*). It thrives in the northwestern United States, producing large fruits resembling purplish raspberries; it has not been grown with as much success elsewhere in the United States. Family: Rose (Rosaceae).

LOGANIA FAMILY (Loganiaceae), a group of about 800 species in 32 genera, including herbs, shrubs, climbing vines, and trees, all native to tropical and subtropical regions and most with opposite, simple leaves. It includes the Carolina, yellow jessamine (*Gelsemium sempervirens*), sometimes erroneously called jasmine, which is grown as a porch vine and is the state flower of South Carolina. See *Butterfly bush* and *Nux vomica*.

LOGWOOD, a small Central American tree with peculiarly ribbed bark, thorny branches, pinnately compound leaves, and almost symmetrical, 5-petalled, yellow flowers. Its dark red heartwood yields a valuable dye called haematoxylon, which can be used to dye felt, woolens, and silk a permanent black, purple, blue, or red color. An astringent extract from the wood is also used in medicine. Family: Pea (Leguminosae); genus and species, *Haematoxylon campechianum*.

LOOSESTRIFE FAMILY (Lythraceae), a group of about 475 species in 23 genera, widely distributed but most numerous in tropical America, including herbs, shrubs, and trees with simple, smooth-edged leaves, usually paired or in whorls, and flowers in which sepals, petals, and stamens all arise from the rim of a tubular part.

The henna plant (Lawsonia inermis), a small shrub native to countries from northern Australia to India and East Africa, has shoots and leaves that yield the orange-red dye used for religious purposes and personal adornment.

The 25 kinds of loosestrife (Lythrum) are slender herbs with pink or magenta flowers, often giving their color to great areas of low, wet ground where they grow to 3 feet and bloom in mid-summer. The name loosestrife is also used for yellow-flowered herbs (Lysimachia species of the primrose family, Primulaceae). See also Crape myrtle.

LOQUAT, a small, Oriental, evergreen tree with large, oblong leaves, rust-colored underneath; fragrant, white flowers; and acid, yellow fruits shaped like miniature pears. In cultivation the tree grows to 10 to 12 feet, blossoms in autumn, and produces its fruits in spring. The fruits can be eaten raw, cooked, or preserved. Orchards of loquats have been established in California and the Gulf states. Family: Rose (Rosaceae); genus and species, Eriobotrya japonica.

LOTUS, any of several aquatic plants of the Old World as well as their close relatives in America. The pink-flowered, sacred lotus of China, Tibet, and India (Nelumbo nucifera), like the yellow-flowered lotus (N. lutea) of the West Indies and the eastern United States, usually raises its circular leaves and flowers out of the ponds and quiet streams in which it grows.

The Egyptian lotuses include one with blue flowers (Nymphaea caerulea) and one with white (N. lotus); the latter is the floral emblem of Egypt. In both, the leaves ordinarily float on the water surface and the flowers extend little, if at all, on exposed stalks. The mythical lotus tree, which yielded fruits reputed to cause forgetfulness of all responsibilities, may have been the jujube. Family: Water-lily (Nymphaeaceae). See also Jujube.

LUFFA. See Vegetable sponge.

LUPINE, any of about 100 different kinds of herbaceous plants native to North America and Europe, with palmately compound leaves and tall, upright spikes of pealike flowers. The flowers of the lupine are usually blue, but they may also be white, yellow, red, or purple.

Many lupines contain poisonous substances in their foliage, flowers, and seed pods, causing loss of life to deer and livestock that eat them in times of extreme hunger. The bluebonnet (Lupinus subcarnosus) is the state flower of Texas. Family: Pea (Leguminosae); genus Lupinus.

MADDER, a perennial herb native to Eurasia, with a thick root, a slender stem bearing repeated whorls of leaves, and small clusters of yellow flowers which are followed by fleshy berries. Until 1869, madder was cultivated extensively for the dye alizarin, which could be extracted from its roots. The discovery of a cheap way to synthesize the dye from coal tar put an end to the industry.

When animals eat madder, the coloring becomes concentrated in their bones, claws, and beaks, and these parts of their bodies become orange-red. Madder dye was used to give color to many mummy cloths found in old Egyptian tombs. Family: Madder (Rubiaceae); genus and species, Rubia tinctorium.

MADDER FAMILY (Rubiaceae), a group of more than 5,000 species in 400 genera, chiefly of tropical and subtropical regions, all with smooth-edged, opposite leaves with large stipules, clustered, regular flowers, stamens attached to the petals, and the corolla attached to the ovary.

They include the delicate Eurasian herb (Rubia tinctorium) from which madder dye ("turkey red") was formerly obtained, the low-growing bluets (Houstonia caerulea) of North America, the partridgeberry (Mitchella repens) of North American woodlands, the shrubby buttonbush (Cephalanthus occidentalis), and the many kinds of shrubby gardenias from the Old World, of which the fragrant-flowered ancestor for most cultivated varieties is the Chinese Gardenia jasminoides. See Bedstraw, Cinchona, Coffee, and Madder.

MADROÑA, or madroño, either of two closely related evergreen shrubs or trees of western North America, growing to 125 feet, with smooth, red bark that peels in strips, large, glossy leaves that are white below, edible, orange-red fruits called "madrona apples," and a fine-grained wood that can be made into a superior grade of charcoal which is ideal for use in gunpowder. Family: Heath (Ericaceae); genus and species, Arbutus menziesii (Pacific coast) and A. xalapensis (northwest Mexico).

MAGNOLIA, a genus of about 20 different species of decorative shrubs and trees native to eastern Asia and North America, with aromatic bark, large, fragrant, waxy, white, yellow, or rose-colored flowers as much as 12 inches in diameter, and cone-shaped clusters of fruits. A hybrid between two Chinese species is cultivated in the northern United States and Europe for its flowers, which open in spring before the leaves.

The large-flowered magnolia (M. grandiflora), native to the southern states and the state flower of both Louisiana and Mississippi, is an evergreen tree growing to 70 feet, with handsome, dark green, glossy leaves and lemon-scented, creamy flowers 8 inches or more across. A smaller evergreen, the sweet bay (M. virginiana), is native to swamplands in the southeastern states, which are then known as "bay-lands." Although it attains

a height of only 15 feet, its thick, short trunk is used to make wooden bowls and utensils. Family: Magnolia (Magnoliaceae).

MAGNOLIA FAMILY (Magnoliaceae), a group of about 100 species in 10 genera, all woody shrubs or trees with simple, alternate leaves and, usually, large, showy flowers in which the receptacle is elongated beyond the petals, bearing first a spiral of many stamens and then a spiral of carpels which mature and convert the floral cluster into a large, aggregate fruit. See Magnolia and Tuliptree.

MAHOGANY, any of several related tropical trees that produce a valuable hard, red-brown wood suitable for cabinetmaking. Most highly esteemed is Swietenia mahogani, native to the West Indies and Central America, and cultivated in Florida and India.

Mahogany has compound leaves resembling those of the honey locust, clusters of small flowers, and large, dull brown, pearshaped fruits. African mahogany (Khaya senegalensis), Indian mahogany (Toona ciliata) of India and northern Australia, and Philippine mahogany (T. calantus) are similar. Family: Mahogany (Meliaceae).

MAHOGANY FAMILY (Meliaceae), a group of about 1000 species in 50 genera, chiefly tropical shrubs and trees with compound leaves and clustered, regular flowers. It includes the West Indian cedar (Cedrela odorata), which provides the fragrant wood used in cigar boxes and is supposedly insect-repellent. See Chinaberry and Mahogany.

MAIDENHAIR TREE. See Ginkgo.

MAIZE. See Corn.

MALLOW, any of about 30 different kinds of Eurasian and north African herbs, many of them annuals and biennials. Most have alternate lobed leaves, pink, white, or blue flowers, and flattened fruits commonly called cheeses, which are enclosed in 2 or 3 tough, leaflike bracts rather than the 6 to 9 bracts of the closely related marshmallow and hollyhock.

The high mallow (Malva sylvestris) and round-leaved mallow (M. rotundifolio) have been introduced into North America and other continents, escaping from cultivation to become roadside weeds. Family: Mallow (Malvaceae); genus Malva.

MALLOW FAMILY (Malvaceae), a group of about 1500 species in 82 genera, widely distributed but most numerous in tropical America. Whether they appear as herbs, shrubs, or trees, they have simple, alternate leaves and, in each regular flower, a central column of stamens beyond which the style and stigma protrude. See Cotton, Hibiscus, Hollyhock, Mallow, and Marshmallow.

MANDRAKE, a herbaceous plant of southern Europe and northern Africa, with a thick taproot that is often forked equally, suggesting a human torso with legs. The short stem bears a tight whorl of spreading, ovate leaves, and a single, purplish flower. Many ancient superstitions developed in relation to this plant, including the claim that it shrieked when pulled from the ground.

Dried, powdered mandrake root was used to increase fertility in women and as an emetic, purgative, and mild narcotic throughout Europe and the Orient. The name mandrake is sometimes applied to the American mayapple (*Podophyllum peltatum*). Family: Potato (Solanaceae); genus and species, *Mandragora officinarum*.

MANGEL-WURZEL. See *Beet*.

MANGO, a small tree of the East Indies, growing to 50 feet, with glossy, oval leaves, sprays of yellow flowers, and large, pear-shaped, green fruits with a delicious, yellow pulp around a central, flattened seed. The fruit of the wild mango is smaller and less palatable than that of horticultural varieties now in cultivation in most tropical and subtropical countries. The roasted seeds are occasionally eaten. Family: Sumac (Anacardiaceae); genus and species, *Mangifera indica*.

MANGROVE, any of several different low-growing trees of tropical and subtropical shores, which grow in shallow sea water and form dense thickets. Red mangrove (*Rhizophora mangle*) of tropical America and West Africa has opposite leaves, and multi-branched aerial roots that grow downward from spreading branches.

The seeds germinate while still attached to the parent plant and fall free only after developing a long, dagger-shaped root and a terminal bud from which leaves can quickly spread. Black mangrove (*Avicennia nitida*), an unrelated tree of the vervain family (Verbenaceae), generally grows in water-soaked soil, and gets air to its roots through upright, pencil-sized, leafless stems that grow upward for 4 to 6 inches until exposed.

The white mangrove (*Laguncularia racemosa*) of tropical America and Africa, and button mangrove (*Conocarpus erecta*) of the same regions, are members of the combretum family (Combretaceae); their bark is often harvested as a source of tannin. Family: Mangrove (Rhizophoraceae).

MANILA HEMP. See *Abacá*.

MANIOC. See *Cassava*.

MANZANITA, a stiff, branching, evergreen shrub native to the Pacific coast of North America, where it forms dense thickets or contributes to the harsh chaparral vegetation of arid areas. It produces smooth leaves, white or pink flowers, and brown fruits resembling small apples. The bark is conspicuously reddish or chocolate-brown. Family: Heath (Ericaceae); genus and species, *Arctostaphylos pungens*.

MAPLE, any of about 150 different kinds of trees and shrubs of the Northern Hemisphere and of moun-

BURPEE SEEDS

MARJORAM

tains in Java and Sumatra, all with paired leaves and paired, winged fruits (samaras) commonly known as maple keys. Many are tall trees with palmately lobed, simple leaves on long stalks and valuable hardwood. In early spring they yield a slightly sweet sap that can be boiled to make syrup or maple sugar.

Most valuable are the sugar maple (*Acer saccharum*) of the northeastern United States and adjacent Canada, which attains a height of 120 feet, and the slightly smaller sycamore maple (*A. pseudoplatanus*) of central Europe and Asia Minor. Faster growing and with softer wood are the Norway maple (*A. platanoides*) of Eurasia, and the silver maple (*A. saccharinum*) and red maple (*A. rubrum*) of eastern North America.

Box elder (*A. negundo*) of eastern Canada and the northeastern United States, which, peculiarly, has pinnately compound leaves, is a still weaker tree, growing best in wet woodlands and near streams. The largest assortment of maples is native to Japan. In autumn the foliage of most maples undergoes a spectacular change in color through all shades from yellow and orange to deep red. Family: Maple (Aceraceae); genus *Acer*.

MARGUERITE. See *Daisy*.

MARIGOLD, any of about 20 different kinds of daisy-like, herbaceous plants native to the New World from Argentina to the southern United States, with aromatic, dissected leaves and orange-red flower heads firmly supported by a cluster of green bracts. The two kinds cultivated most widely are the tall, straight-stemmed "African" species (*Tagetes erecta*) and the dwarf "French" marigold (*T. patula*),

both originally from Mexico. The related pot-marigold (*Calendula officinalis*) of Mediterranean Europe, Asia Minor, and North Africa was formerly used for flavoring and raised widely as a potherb. Now it is cultivated as an ornament which produces flowers much of the summer; each flower head is large and orange-gold. Family: Daisy (Compositae); genus *Tagetes*.

MARIPOSA LILY, any of about 40 different kinds of bulbous herbs of western North America, with narrow leaves and tulip-like flowers handsomely marked with colorful spots on white, red, yellow, or lilac petals. A mariposa lily, *Calochortus nuttalii*, is the state flower of Utah. Family: Lily (Liliaceae); genus *Calochortus*.

MARJORAM, any of several related aromatic, perennial herbs native to the Mediterranean coasts. They are widely cultivated and have also escaped from cultivation to grow naturally along roadsides. They have square stems, paired, oval leaves, and either short clusters of purple flowers (*Origanum*, especially *O. vulgare*) or grayish leaves and white flowers (*Majorana hortensis*). Family: Mint (Labiatae).

MARSHMALLOW, an erect perennial herb of temperate Eurasia and North Africa, growing to 4 feet, with oval leaves and delicate, pink flowers. Formerly its roots were gathered and used in the manufacture of a sweet, white confection which is now produced artificially from cane syrup. Family: Mallow (Malvaceae); genus and species, *Althaea officinalis*.

MARSH MARIGOLD, a perennial herb of eastern North America, growing in wet places, producing glossy, kidney-shaped leaves on hollow stalks, and, usually, bright yellow flowers in spring. Young leaves and stems of the marsh marigold are eaten as greens. The whole plant is often called cowslip. Family: Buttercup (Ranunculaceae); genus and species, *Caltha palustris*.

MATÉ. See *Holly*.

MAYAPPLE, an erect perennial herb of eastern North America, with a long, branching root, umbrella-shaped leaves on tall, stout stalks, and solitary, nodding, waxy, white flowers followed by oval, yellow, fleshy fruits.

The fruits are the least poisonous part of the plant. The roots are the most dangerous part because they contain several toxic materials; these poisons have been used in primitive medicine. Mayapple is sometimes known as the American mandrake, or wild jalap. Family: Barberry (Berberidaceae); genus and species, *Podophyllum peltatum*.

MAYFLOWER. See *Arbutus*.

MAYWEED, or dog fennel, a branching perennial herb native to Eurasia and North Africa, now widespread as a weed, with pinnately dissected leaves emitting a strong, unpleasant odor, and yellow-centered, white-rayed flower heads an inch in diameter resembling daisies. The leaves were formerly employed in preparing a tea used in treating colic. The garden camomile (*Anthemis nobilis*) is a closely related plant with a pleasant odor; a tea from its foliage was once used as a blood purifier. Family: Daisy (Compositae); genus and species, *Anthemis cotula*.

MEDLAR, a small, branching tree native to Eurasia and much cultivated in Europe for its globular fruits, which resemble crab apples and have a tart flavor in the freshly-ripened, gritty pulp. When they are killed by the frost and partially decayed, the unpreserved fruits have a better flavor. Family: Rose (Rosaceae); genus and species, *Mespilus germanica*.

MELON, a prostrate vine, or the large, spherical, or egg-shaped fruit, with a thick, fleshy rind and a fibrous, seed-filled center. The term is generally used to describe all horticultural varieties of the muskmelon (*Cucumis melo*) of tropical Asia and Africa, such as cantaloupes, cassaba melons, honeydew and Persian melons, and rock melons, and the varieties of the watermelon (*Citrullus vulgaris*) of tropical Africa, including the citron, or preserving melon. Insects carry pollen from the starlike, yellow, staminate flowers to the similar pistillate flowers on the same hairy prickly stems, partially concealed below large, round leaves.

Cantaloupes have an orange pulp and a hard skin raised in ridges, often in a netlike pattern. Cassaba melons are large, round, and smooth-skinned, with a rich, creamy pulp; they mature late and are often called winter muskmelons. Honeydew melons are oval in shape, ivory to white externally, with thick, green, sweet flesh. Rock melons, or European cantaloupes, are hardly grown in the United States and Canada; they are small, with a tough skin raised in high ridges, and a comparatively shallow, orange-red flesh.

Watermelons, which were cultivated in Egypt in ancient times, have a thick, green or green and white rind surrounding a sweet red pulp, and may weigh 50 pounds or more when mature; the pulp is eaten raw, the rind pickled, and the seeds sometimes enjoyed as if they were thin-shelled nuts. Family: Gourd (Cucurbitaceae).

MESQUITE, any of about 30 different kinds of tropical and subtropical thorny trees and shrubs native to arid regions and most conspicuous in the American Southwest, South America, and Hawaii where, after locally heavy rains, the seeds germinate and send down extremely long roots. The taproots attain a depth of as much as 60 feet, reaching underground supplies of water that other plants have failed to reach. Wherever mesquite grows into unstunted trees 40 to 50 feet tall, there is water within 40 feet of the earth's surface.

The branches bear deciduous, twice pinnately compound leaves, and spikes of odorous, greenish-yellow flowers followed by yellow or brown seed pods. The pods of the common mesquite (*Prosopis juliflora*) are long and straight; those of the screw bean (*P. pubescens*) are twisted into spirals. The seeds are eaten by Indians and Mexicans, and the foliage by livestock. As fodder, mesquite provides an inadequate diet and symptoms of a fatal deficiency develop in cattle that continue to eat virtually no other foods for a few months. Family: Pea (Leguminosae); genus *Prosopis*.

MIGNONETTE, any of about 50 different kinds of small, herbaceous plants native to arid areas around the Mediterranean Sea and Asia. They have small, alternate leaves and spikes of fragrant flowers with tufts of brownish stamens on the upper petals. Beekeepers sometimes plant mignonette as a nectar-producing plant that gives a pleasant flavor to the honey made by their bees.

Two Mediterranean species have become roadside weeds in the New World, one (*Reseda alba*) with white flowers and the other (*R. lutea*) with yellow flowers. Horticulturalists have developed larger, greenish flowers in the common mignonette (*R. odorata*), which has broad leaves and grows very close to the earth, forming a dense blanket over the soil or providing attractive edgings for bower beds. Family: Mignonette (Resedaceae); genus *Reseda*.

MILKWEED, any of about 90 different kinds of perennial herbs native to America and Africa, with erect stems, opposite or whorled leaves, an abundant milky juice that may contain poisonous substances. The clustered, small flowers have 5 petals that turn backward, exposing pairs of pollen masses linked by peculiar fibers that catch onto the legs of insects. Weak insects are often caught, whereas strong bees and butterflies carry the paired masses of sticky pollen and

T.H. EVERETT

MIGNONETTE

often accomplish cross-pollination. A pollinated flower develops into an inflated pod that splits along one side to release flat seeds, each with a tuft of satiny, white hairs that catch the wind.

The common milkweed (*Asclepias syriaca*) of eastern North American fields and roadsides, which was accidentally introduced into Asia Minor and later spread through much of Eurasia, has purple-pink or brownish-pink blossoms. Butterfly weed (*A. tuberosa*) of North America is often cultivated in gardens for its bright orange flowers. Family: Milkweed (Asclepiadaceae); genus *Asclepias*.

MILKWEED FAMILY (Asclepiadaceae), a group of about 1700 species in 100 genera, mostly tropical, perennial herbs or shrubs (including climbing vines), usually with a milky sap, simple, paired, smooth-edged leaves, and clustered flowers. It includes the strange carrion flowers (*Stapelia* species) of South Africa, which resemble cacti in their succulent green stems and reduced leaves. See *Milkweed* and *Waxflower*.

MILKWORT, any of about 500 different kinds of herbaceous and shrubby plants native to Eurasia and Africa, with bitter-tasting, simple leaves and attractive, irregular flowers in which the conspicuous parts are two petal-like sepals; of the five sepals, only these two are red, white, blue, or yellow instead of green.

According to superstition, a decoction made from the leaves of the common milkwort (*polygala vulgaris*) would induce more production of milk in nursing mothers. Seneca snakeroot (*P. senega*) of eastern North America is the source of an irritant drug. Family: Milkwort (Polygalaceae); genus *Polygala*.

MILLET, any of a number of different grasses cultivated in the Orient for more than 5,000 years, and generally regarded as the "poor man's cereal" although the nutritional quality of the grains is higher than that of rice as it is eaten. Common, or proso, millet (*Panicum miliaceum*) is cultivated in the Soviet Union, whereas little millet (*P. miliare*) is the favorite in India; both are members of the huge genus of panic grasses.

Italian millet (*Setaria italica*), grown in the Near East and China, is a foxtail grass. Pearl millet, known also as cattail millet (*Pennisetum glaucum*), is favored in parts of India and in the Sudan. More distantly related grasses include finger millet (*Eleusine coracana*) and broomcorn millet (*Sorghum vulgare technicus*), which are popular in Africa and India.

All millets yield grains that can be used to thicken soups or mixed with wheat to make a bread flour that will rise when baked. In North America and much of Europe millets are cultivated chiefly for poultry feed. Family: Grass (Gramineae).

MIMOSA, a genus of tropical and subtropical trees, shrubs, vines, and herbs containing about 350 species native to America, Africa, and Asia.

All have feathery, pinnately compound leaves, white or pink flowers in fuzzy, globular clusters, and seeds in bivalved pods. The sensitive plant (*M. pudica*), a roadside weed in tropical America, has become famous because its leaflets and leaves fold quickly when touched. Family: Pea (Leguminosae).

MINT, any of about 15 different kinds of aromatic herbs native to the Northern Hemisphere, with square stems, opposite leaves, and clusters of blue, pink, or white flowers. Several are cultivated for the volatile oil that can be extracted from the leaves. It is used to flavor candies and to give a pleasing odor to perfumes and soaps.

Whole, fresh leaves of peppermint (*Mentha piperita*) are often added to beverages or chopped and cooked gently to make a sauce for meat. Spearmint (*M. spicata*) has become most famous as a flavoring for chewing gum. European pennyroyal (*M. pulegium*) and an American substitute, mock pennyroyal (*Hedeoma pulegioides*), are also used to flavor foods. Family: Mint (Labiatae); genus *Mentha*.

MINT FAMILY (Labiatae), a group of about 3200 species in more than 200 genera, widely distributed but most numerous in Mediterranean countries, chiefly herbs with square stems and opposite leaves but sometimes shrubs, climbing vines, or trees. The epidermal cells secrete aromatic oils and the flowers are clustered, usually with a 2-lipped corolla and the 4 stamens of different lengths—2 long and 2 short. See *Balm, Catnip, Ground ivy, Horehound, Lavender, Marjoram, Mint, Oswego tea, Rosemary, Sage, Self-heal,* and *Thyme*.

MISTLETOE, any of more than 1000 different kinds of herbaceous and shrubby parasitic plants, principally of tropical regions, growing at the expense of trees to which the mistletoes are attached by modified roots called haustoria. Most have opposite or whorled, simple leaves on branching stems, small, green or colored flowers, and a sticky covering over the seeds. Birds that pick the small fruits have difficulty swallowing the sticky seeds and scrape them off on tree branches to which the seeds adhere while germinating.

European mistletoe (*Viscum album*) grows on many trees, especially apple, and was used in pagan ceremonies. The magic attributed to the mistletoe is the source of the custom of kissing under the plant at Christmas time. In the New World the plant used for this purpose is the American mistletoe (*Phoradendron flavescens*) of the eastern United States. Family: Mistletoe (Loranthaceae).

MOCK ORANGE, a hardy European shrub that grows to 6 to 12 feet, with brown bark, oval leaves about 4 inches long, and large, sweet-scented, white or cream-colored flowers that open late in spring. Often called a "syringa" because its stems were made into pipe stems, it is not related to the lilac (*Syringa*). The state flower of Idaho, known there only as the syringa, is *Philadelphus lewisii*. Family: Saxifrage (Saxifragaceae); genus and species, *Philadelphus coronarius*.

MONKSHOOD. See *Aconite*.

MORNING GLORY. See *Bindweed*. ....

MORNING-GLORY FAMILY (Convolvulaceae), a group of about 1200 species in 50 genera, chiefly climbing herbs and woody vines of the tropics, but including shrubs and trees, some of which are thorny and adapted for arid conditions. See *Bindweed, Dodder,* and *Sweet potato*.

MOUNTAIN ASH, a small North American tree with pinnately compound leaves, clusters of creamy flowers that produce bunches of orange-scarlet berries, and soft, weak wood. Its flowers and fruits are decorative, and attract bees and fruit-eating birds. Moose and deer often eat the leaves and young twigs. Closely related is the Eurasian rowan (*Sorbus aucuparia*). Neither tree commonly grows taller than 30 feet and both live best in cool climates protected from the wind. Family: (Rosaceae); genus and species, *Sorbus americana*.

MOUNTAIN LAUREL, a small evergreen shrub of eastern North America, with leathery leaves and beautiful clusters of rose-pink flowers. It is the state flower of Pennsylvania. A close relative is sheep laurel or lambkill (*Kalmia angustifolia*), which is poisonous to young sheep. Family: Heath (Ericaceae); genus and species, *Kalmia latifolia*.

MULBERRY, any of about 12 different kinds of small trees native to the North Temperate Zone, which have leaves of many different shapes (oval, notched, and lobed) on the same tree, and clusters of small flowers followed by very sweet fruits. Most favored

BURPEE SEEDS
MORNING GLORY

for eating raw, cooked, or preserved are the black fruits of black mulberry (*Morus nigra*), native to western Asia. Red mulberry (*M. rubra*) of the eastern United States also produces edible fruits as well as wood that is resistant to decay. White mulberry (*M. alba*) of China is raised to provide leaves on which silkworms can feed. Family: Mulberry (Moraceae); genus *Morus*.

MULBERRY FAMILY (Moraceae), a group of about 1000 species in 73 genera, all with a milky juice and alternate, smooth-edged leaves. Most are plants of tropical and subtropical regions and many are important for their edible fruits. It includes the breadfruit (*Artocarpus altilis*), a tall tree with large, deeply lobed leaves and hard, spherical fruits that can be eaten baked, boiled, or fried, and the jackfruit (*A. heterophyllus*); both are from Southeast Asia but are widely cultivated in the tropics.

One of the fast-growing pioneer trees in tropical America is the trumpet tree (*Cecropia peltata*), which harbors fierce, biting ants in hollow spaces reached through small holes in the axils of the leaves. See *Fig, Mulberry, Osage orange,* and *Paper mulberry*.

MULLEIN, any of about 260 different kinds of tall, biennial herbs of the temperate parts of Eurasia, many now introduced and naturalized elsewhere. Best known is the common mullein (*Verbascum thapsus*) which, in its second year, raises an upright stem 2 to 7 feet tall above large, hairy, whorled lower leaves. On this stem a succession of flowers open, each for a single day. The plant is sometimes called flannel leaf or feltweed because of the felty texture of the leaves. Family: Figwort (Scrophulariaceae); genus *Verbascum*.

MUSKMELON. See *Melon*.

MUSTARD, any of several related annual, biennial, and sometimes perennial herbs native to Eurasia, where they have been cultivated for thousands of years as a source of small, round seeds producing a pungent oil. The plants themselves have stiff, branching stems 1 to 6 feet tall, and loose clusters of yellow flowers, each with 4 petals about ½-inch long. Young plants (mustard greens) are cooked as a slightly bitter potherb in some regions.

Black mustard (*Brassica nigra*), a hairy plant with black seeds, is the principal source of the mustard seeds that are dried and pulverized for use as a condiment in Europe, excluding the British Isles, and as the major ingredient of mustard in North America. White mustard (*B. hirta*), a rough plant with less hair and pale gray seeds, is preferred in Britain and many former British colonies for its "hotter" flavor. Small amounts are blended with black mustard powder and starch to make the mixture milder to suit the tastes of inhabitants of the New World. Rape (*B. rapa*) is an annual with leaves that clasp the stems. Now known only in cultivation, rape is raised as a forage crop as well as for its seeds, which yield rape oil (useful as a food, lubricant, and lamp fuel). Its seeds are also used as bird food. The closely related turnip (*B. napus*), like the rutabaga (*B. napobrassica*), stores a great amount of food in a swollen root during its first year of growth, and is cultivated as a root crop for human use and as fodder for livestock.

Chinese cabbage (*B. pekinensis*), sometimes called celery cabbage or pe-tsai, grows in a lettuce-like head of tightly wrapped, edible leaves. The inner leaves are white, crisp, and tasty. It has been raised as a salad green and vegetable in China since the first century AD and has been introduced into the United States.

Ordinary cabbage (*B. oleracea*) has been developed horticulturally from a wild Eurasian cliff plant to include the varieties known as cabbage (*B. oleraceae capitata*), eaten raw, cooked, or slightly fermented and salted as sauerkraut; kale (*B. oleracea acephala*), a headless variety with curly leaves; kohlrabi (*B. oleracea gongolodes*), which has a turnip-like enlargement of the stem just above the ground; Brussels sprouts (*B. oleracea gemmifera*), which has tight edible buds 1 to 2 inches in diameter clustered on the thick stalk; broccoli (*B. oleracea italica*), with narrow, long, erect leaves around a large, round-topped cluster of flower buds; and cauliflower (*B. oleracea botrytis*), which produces an edible head of misformed but delicately flavored, white flower stalks and buds. Family: Mustard (Cruciferae); genus *Brassica*.

MUSTARD FAMILY (Cruciferae), a group of about 2500 species in some 350 genera, mostly native to the North Temperate Zone, particularly to Mediterranean countries. All are herbs with alternate, simple leaves. Flowers with 4 sepals and 4 petals, 4 long stamens and 2 short ones around a pistal mature to become a pod that opens to release its seeds. See *Alyssum, Candytuft, Cress, Horseradish, Mustard, Peppergrass, Radish, Shamrock, Shepherd's purse, Stock,* and *Wallflower.*

MYRTLE, any of about 75 different kinds of tropical and subtropical shrubs and trees with glossy, green leaves and white or faintly pink flowers that are followed by small, black, fleshy berries. The classical myrtle (*Myrtus communis*), from which wreaths were fashioned as crowns for victorious athletes, is a strong-scented ornamental shrub native to the Mediterranean region but now grown as a hedge in the southern United States.

Myrtle wood is fine grained and useful in turning fine gunstocks. An oil extracted from the leaves has medicinal value. Various parts of the plant, all pleasantly strong smelling, are used for perfumes and cosmetics. Family: Myrtle (Myrtaceae); genus *Myrtus.* See also *Crape Myrtle.*

MYRTLE FAMILY (Myrtaceae), a group of about 3000 species in 80 genera, all shrubs or trees of warm climates, most numerous in America and Australia, with leathery, simple leaves

BURPEE SEEDS

NARCISSUS

dotted with glands containing volatile oils, and regular flowers usually in clusters. Among members of this family are many of the tall timber trees of Hawaii, New Zealand, Australia, and the East Indies, including not only members of the huge genus *Eucalyptus,* but also of *Metrosideros, Leptospermum, Melaleuca,* and *Callistemon* (bottlebrush ; for most of these, only local common names have been developed. See *Allspice, Clove tree, Eucalyptus, Guava,* and *Myrtle.*

NARCISSUS, a genus of bulbous Eurasian herbs with slender leaves and white or yellow flowers on tall stalks, each flower with a 6-part perianth opening to display a ruffled disc- or trumpet-shaped crown. Cultivated all over the world as early spring garden flowers, several of the 40 different species have become well known.

The common name narcissus is usually restricted to *N. incomparabilis,* in which the crown is well developed and edged in reddish-orange, while the rest of the flower is white. The poet's narcissus (*N. poeticus*) has a much smaller crown, making the white perianth itself the most conspicuous part of the blossom.

The daffodil (*N. pseudo-narcissus*) bears solitary flowers on each stalk; its yellow fragrant blossom has a prominent crown of the same color. Jonquils (*N. jonquilla*) have clustered, pale yellow, fragrant flowers and crowns that are small and somewhat flattened. The polyanthus narcissus, or Chinese sacred lily (*N. tazetta*) produces a flat-topped cluster of yellow or white flowers with small crowns. Family: Amaryllis (Amaryllidaceae).

NASTURTIUM, a weak-stemmed, clambering herb of South America, now cultivated in gardens on many continents. It has circular leaves with stalks

attached at the center, and with handsome, spurred, irregular flowers. The 5 petals of the flower may be yellow, scarlet, or maroon. All parts of the plant, including the seed capsules, have a pleasant, pungent aroma, which can be used to add flavor to salads. Pickled seed pods are sometimes used as a garnish for meat.

Dwarf horticultural varieties of nasturtium grow only a few feet tall, whereas others climb by sensitive leaf stalks to a height of 20 feet or more. The similar and closely related canary-bird flower (*Tropaeolum peregrinum*) is also cultivated for ornamental purposes. Watercress (genus *Nasturtium* of the mustard family, Cruciferae) is unrelated. Family: Nasturtium (Tropaeolaceae); genus and species, *Tropaeolum majus.*

NECTARINE. See *Peach.*

NETTLE, any of a number of related plants belonging to several genera native to most continents, and notable for the intensely irritating effect of a toxic material contained in stiff glandular hairs on the leaves. These hairs break after penetrating skin and release the irritant, which causes acute but usually temporary itching. Yet the young plants of some species are gathered and cooked as edible greens, and the roots of a few are harvested as a source of a lasting yellow dye.

Many nettles have strong stem fibers, but preparation for textile use is often difficult. Chinagrass, or ramie (*Boemeria nivea*), of Southeast Asia, yields the toughest and silkiest fiber known. Nettletree (*Laportea gigas*) of Australia grows to a height of 90 feet. A close relative, the wood-nettle (*L. canadensis*), is a perennial herb of eastern North America, growing no more than 3 feet tall.

Most famous of the nettles are the cosmopolitan members of genus *Urtica,* of which more than 30 species are known. Some are annuals easy to eradicate by cutting off the tops before their inconspicuous greenish flowers produce seeds, and others annuals that must be dug out or killed with herbicide chemicals. Family: Nettle (Urticaceae).

NIGHT–BLOOMING CEREUS, any of several climbing cactus plants with stems ribbed lengthwise, supporting themselves by means of aerial roots. They open solitary, huge, creamy, fragrant flowers as much as a foot in diameter for an hour or two in late evening, only to close them permanently before dawn. These cacti are native to the southwestern United States, Mexico and Central America, and the West Indies. Horticultural varieties and hybrids have been developed, partly from a spectacular wild species (*Cereus grandiflorus*). Family: Cactus (Cactaceae).

NIGHTSHADE, loosely, any of 1700 different kinds of herbs, shrubs, and trees of tropical and temperate regions classified in genus *Solanum* of the potato family (Solanaceae). Specifically, either the common Eurasian nightshade (*Solanum nigrum*), which is now almost cosmopolitan as a prostrate or erect herb with small clusters of white flowers followed by bunches of poisonous black berries, or the bittersweet (*Solanum dulcamara*).

Enchanter's nightshade, 9 different north temperate and arctic plants growing from underground stems, is unrelated (genus *Circaea* of the evening-primrose family, Onagraceae); it produces paired leaves and short upright clusters of small white or pink flowers which are followed by similar clusters of dry fruits with hooked bristles that travel as burs. See also *Bittersweet*.

NORFOLK ISLAND PINE, an evergreen coniferous tree native to South Pacific islands, now widely introduced in warm climates or grown indoors in tubs for its symmetrical whorls of branches bearing luxuriant, short, needle-like leaves. Family: Araucaria (Araucariaceae); genus and species, *Araucaria excelsa*.

NUTMEG, an evergreen tree native to the Molucca Islands in the East Indies, now cultivated in the West Indies and tropical America. It grows 50 to 60 feet tall and has simple, oval leaves and tiny sprays of bell-like flowers that are either staminate or pistillate.

The flowers produce a peachlike, fleshy fruit of which the central seed is eggshaped and enclosed in a waxy, red membrane. The flesh of the fruit is preserved to be eaten as a candy, or made into a jelly. The membrane, which turns yellow, is dried for sale as the spice mace; the seed is grated or ground as the spice nutmeg. Family: Nutmeg (Myristicaceae); genus and species, *Myristica fragrans*.

NUX VOMICA, a medium-sized tree native to India and Ceylon and cultivated elsewhere in the tropics, with shining, oval leaves, clusters of greenish flowers, and globular, white fruits about the size of an orange. The bark, often called false Angostura bark, yields a bitter tonic. The green seeds embedded in the fruit are the principal source of the poisonous alkaloid strychnine. Family: Logania (Loganiaceae); genus and species, *Strychnos nux-vomica*.

OAK, any of about 300 different kinds of hardwood trees, native to the North Temperate Zone and islands of the South Pacific, with simple leaves and separate staminate and pistillate flowers. The staminate flowers are clustered in pendant, loose catkins; the pistillate flowers are solitary or in small groups close to the stem. The fruits are acorns, borne in a cup.

They mature in one year on members of the white-oak group, which bear round-lobed leaves and include the widespread Eurasian brown oak or English oak (*Quercus robur*), the only oak in Britain, and such American trees as the eastern white oak (*Q. alba*), Californian white oak (*Q. lobata*), post oak (*Q. Stellata*), bur oak (*Q. macrocarpa*), and overcup oak (*Q. lyrata*). The acorns take 2 years to ripen and usually germinate in the third year on members of the red-oak group, which have sharp-pointed lobes on the leaves and include the

American trees known as red oak (*Q. rubra*), black oak (*Q. velutina*), water oak (*Q. nigra*), pin oak (*Q. palustris*), and willow oak (*Q. phellos*). Many of these trees grow to a height of 100 to 170 feet, and produce valuable lumber. They often hold their dead leaves far into the winter, although by then the handsome autumn colors have faded to a dull brown.

In the southeastern United States a valuable evergreen oak (*Q. virginiana*) is known as live oak. A much smaller evergreen oak of Mediterranean countries, growing only about 40 feet tall, is the cork oak (*Q. suber*), from which the light, spongy, bark can be stripped in thick sheets about once every 9 years to be made into the cork products of commerce. Some cork trees are grown in the United States, but the world's major cork supply comes from Portugal and Spain. Family: Beech (*Fagaceae*); genus Quercus.

OAT, an annual grass native to temperate regions of the Old World, cultivated in Eurasia for thousands of years as a forage plant, as a cereal for human use, and as food for horses. The plant grows 3 to 5 feet tall, with thin, narrow, long leaves beyond which the stem continues upward, arching over because of the weight of the many grains, each of which is surrounded by chaffy bracts. Family: Grass (Gramineae); genus and species, *Avena sativa.*

OKRA. See *Hibiscus.*

OLEANDER, a small evergreen shrub or tree 7 to 15 feet tall, with narrow, stiff leaves and sprays of attractive flowers in colors ranging from white to rose. Native to the Orient and southern Europe, the oleander has been cultivated for ornamental purposes for many years in warm parts of both hemispheres, often as a hedge, though all parts of the plant are poisonous if eaten. Family: Dogbane (Apocynaceae); genus and species, *Nerium oleander.*

BURPEE SEEDS

OXALIS

OLIVE, a small evergreen tree native to warm, semiarid areas of Eurasia and North Africa, cultivated for thousands of years and introduced into western North America, South America, and Australia as a source of fruits (olives) and oil. A branch from an olive tree, with its dull, willow-like, gray-green leaves, has long been regarded as a symbol of peace.

Olive flowers are shining-white, clustered, and followed by small, eggshaped, plumlike fruits which turn black as they ripen. Olives are bitter and inedible until treated with lye and given time to ferment under careful control. Olive oil is obtained from pressed, ripe olives. Family: Olive (Oleaceae); genus and species, *Olea europaea.*

OLIVE FAMILY (Oleaceae), a group of about 500 species in 22 genera, all shrubs, climbing vines, or trees of tropical and warm temperate climates with opposite leaves and clusters of regular flowers, usually with just 2 stamens. See *Ash, Forsythia, Jasmine, Lilac, Olive,* and *Privet.*

ONION, a biennial herbaceous plant native to southwestern Asia, but now widely cultivated for the pungent flavor in its succulent leaf bases, which form a bulblike enlargement just below ground level. In its second year an onion plant produces a tall, upright stalk with a cluster of inconspicuous, white flowers from which the seeds may germinate before being shed from the fruits.

Horticultural varieties of large size, or flattened instead of spherical shape, or red instead of white color, or sweeter and less "hot" flavor are raised on every continent and are often known as Bermuda or Spanish onions, although the seed may be imported from the Canary Islands. Closely related are the chive (*Allium schoenoprasum*), the leek (*A. porrum*), and the shallot (*A. ascalonicum*) from Mediterranean countries, cultivated widely as flavoring for salads, stews, and cooked meats. Family: Lily (Liliaceae); genus and species, *Allium cepa.*

ORANGE, any of a number of closely related, small trees native to southern Asia, yielding some of the world's most important fruits. The unpruned trees may grow to 35 feet, with glossy, oval, evergreen leaves on short stalks that bear a narrow wing along each side. The fragrant, white flowers are followed by spherical fruits composed of 10 to 12 fleshy sections surrounding the seeds, enclosed in a tough rind beset with oil glands.

The rind may be dried or candied, or its oil may be removed for separate uses as bitter flavoring. Orange pulp is particularly rich in vitamin C, and is commonly crushed to make a nourishing beverage that can be frozen or concentrated for later use. Whole oranges are made into marmalade. For this use, the sour, or Seville, orange (*Citrus aurantium*) is often preferred; it is native to Malaysia, but much cultivated in Spain. The sweet orange (*C. sinensis*), native to China and Southeast Asia, has been horticulturally developed to produce the seedless navel orange (introduced from Brazil and cultivated extensively in California), and the Washington and Valencia oranges. The Temple orange is believed to be a hybrid between the sweet orange and the mandarin orange or tangerine *(C. reticulata),* a native of the Philippines and Southeast Asia; its rind is removed with special ease, making it a luxury fruit, raised extensively in the Gulf States. Family: Rue (Rutaceae); genus *Citrus.*

ORCHID FAMILY (Orchidaceae), an immense group of about 15,000 different species in 450 genera, often regarded as the most highly developed of all the monocotyledonous plants. Widely distributed, those of all arctic regions and most temperate regions are terrestrial, whereas the majority in tropical regions are perching plants (epiphytes) that perch on forest tree branches and bark. All family members are perennial herbs, the terrestrial ones with thickened roots, the perching ones with aerial roots specialized for absorbing water and with the stem swollen at the base to form a water-storage organ called a pseudobulb. The flowers are bilaterally symmetrical, often very showy, solitary or in clusters, with the lowest (innermost) of the 3 petals generally larger and often extended to form a spur or sac.

The fruit is a capsule containing a large number of exceedingly minute seeds that have almost no store of food and, hence, are dependent upon germinating soon after they ripen.

Ladyslippers (genus *Cypripedium)* of North Temperate woods have showy, solitary flowers, whereas the showy orchis *(Orchis spectabilis)* of eastern North America and many of its relatives produce spikes of smaller blossoms. Of the tropical perching orchids, the American species of genus *Cattleya* are especially favored for corsages because of their large size and handsome colors.

A climbing orchid, with glossy, oval leaves, is the vanilla plant *(Vanilla fragrans)* native to Mexico, and cultivated in the West Indies and Asia for its long, slender fruit capsules, which can be cured and from which the flavoring vanilla can be extracted. Artificial vanilla is now available at lower cost from other plant sources.

OREGON GRAPE, a small shrub native to the Pacific coast of North America, growing to about 5 feet, with spiny, compound leaves and clusters of yellow flowers followed by dark berries resembling grapes. Its flower is the state flower of Oregon. Family: Barberry (Berberidaceae); genus and species, *Mahonia aquifolia.*

ORPINE, or live-forever, an erect, perennial, succulent herb native to Eurasia. It is cultivated in rock gardens around the world for its 1- to 4-inch thick, tooth-edged leaves and its 15-inch fleshy, gray-green stems bearing clustered, white, purple, pink, or yellow flowers. Named live-forever because of the long survival of separated parts of the plant, which take

root if given an opportunity, it was kept on hand during the Middle Ages for its supposed value in promoting the healing of wounds. It is a member of a genus containing about 500 species, known generally as stonecrops, of which *Sedum acre,* with its creeping, succulent, evergreen leaves and yellow, starlike flowers, is widely grown in gardens. Family: Orpine (Crassulaceae); genus and species, *Sedum telephium.*

ORPINE FAMILY (Crassulaceae), a group of about 1300 species in 33 genera, widely distributed but primarily found in arid regions of the Mediterranean, the American Southwest, and south-central Asia. Many are cultivated in rock gardens for their novel, often cactuslike shapes. Jade plant *(Crassula arborescens)* is a treelike member of a large genus.

Cigarette-plant *(Kalanchoe verticillata),* and various kinds of life plants *(Bryophyllum* species) from the Old World tropics produce new small plants with leaves and roots in the notches of their leaves; they drop these smaller leaves to the ground as an asexual mode of reproduction. Other members of the family are known as hen and chickens because of their ability to produce new plants on short runners, thus covering the ground with close-set rosettes of fleshy leaves; live-forever or houseleek *(Sempervivum tectorum)* of southern Europe has this characteristic. See also *Orpine.*

ORRIS ROOT. See *Iris.*

OSAGE ORANGE, or bow wood, a sprawling, thorny tree 30 to 60 feet tall, native to the region between Texas and Missouri, the home of the Osage Indians. It has glossy, green leaves, staminate and pistillate flowers on separate trees, and hard, round, inedible, yellow fruits formed by the joining together of the receptacles, floral parts, and ripened ovaries of several adjacent flowers. The bark yields yellow, tan, orange, gold, and olive-colored dyes, and the wood has the strength and flexibility needed for the construction of bows for archery, tool handles, posts, and woodenware. Family: Mulberry (Moraceae); genus and species, *Maclura pomifera.*

OSIER. See *Willow.*

OSWEGO TEA, or bee balm, a perennial herb native to eastern North America, with a square stem that grows to about 3 feet, opposite, fragrant, pointed leaves, and shaggy clusters of showy, red flowers. A close relative of wider distribution in the United States and Canada is the taller, lavender-flowered, wild bergamot *(Monarda fistulosa).* Family: Mint (Labiatae); genus and species, *Monarda didyma.*

OXALIS, a genus of about 850 different species of small, perennial herbs with delicate stems filled with sour juice, small, clover-like leaves, and solitary or clustered regular flowers with 5 petals that may be pink, lavender, yellow, or white and that generally close at night and in dull weather,

as do the leaflets of the compound leaves. Known generally as wood sorrels, they are widely distributed, but are most numerous in South Africa, on the slopes of the Andes, and in wet parts of Central America and Mexico. Those native to North America and Europe are often marketed in pots as shamrocks at St. Patrick's Day celebrations. Family: Oxalis (Oxalidaceae).

OYSTER PLANT. See *Salsify.*

PALM FAMILY (Palmaceae), a group of about 1500 different species in 200 genera, mostly thick-stemmed, unbranched, evergreen trees topped by a cluster of large, simple, palmate leaves (in fan palms) or pinnately compound leaves (in feather palms).

Palms have enormous economic importance in tropical and warm, temperate climates for almost every part of the tree is useful. Dead leaves are used to thatch the roofs of native houses; strips from fresh leaves are woven into mats, baskets, and wall panels; buds and many kinds of palm fruits are edible and nutritious, or yield raw materials for making sugar, wine, cosmetics, and waxes; whole trunks and strips cut lengthwise from the trunks provide valuable building materials; and fibers from the leaves are made into textiles, clothing, and hats. Door mats in countries far from the tropics are commonly composed of fibers known as coir, made from the husks of coconuts and called coco mats.

Fan palms include the cabbage palm *(Sabal palmetto),* which attains a height of 80 feet on the higher ground of some of the isolated areas in the Florida Everglades, and the prostrate scrub palmetto *(Serenoa repens),* found in neglected pastures from the Carolinas to Texas. The clambering fan palms of the Old World tropics include the *Raphia ruffia* of Madagascar, the extraordinarily long leaves of which are a source of strong raffia fiber, and the sago palms *(Metroxylon rumphii* and *M. laeve)* of the East Indies, the pith of which yields sago starch. The largest known seeds are those of a fan palm, the double coconut *(Lodoicea sechellarum)* of the Seychelles, which in the husks weigh 30 to 40 pounds and take 10 years to ripen.

The coconut palm itself *(Cocos nucifera)* is a feather palm, thriving close to salt water, rising 60 to 100 feet, producing large fruits in clusters with each seed covered by a thick, buoyant husk as well as a hard shell, and containing a layer of nutritious "meat" surrounding a cavity filled with a juice called coconut milk. The dried meat is copra, a principal product of tropical coasts, which is made into soap, coconut oil, and animal food.

Other feather palms of great economic value include the date palm *(Phoenix dactylifera)* of tropical Africa and Asia, which yields edible fruits, date sugar, and structural materials, as well as shade under the equatorial sun; the oil palm *(Elaeis guineensis)* of West Africa, cultivated extensively in the East Indies and tropical America, which yields fruits from which palm oil is extracted for use in soaps, medicines, and industry; and the betel palm (*Areca catechu*) of Southeast Asia, which produces egg-sized fruits that are generally harvested before they ripen. The husk is torn off and the mottled seed boiled, sliced, and dried in the sun for sale as "betel nut." More than 300 million people enjoy chewing betel nut, which is prepared for consumption by wrapping a small piece in a leaf of the betel pepper (*Piper betle*), along with a pellet of lime, and perhaps a pinch of some aromatic spice.

Still another feather palm is the royal palm (*Roystonea regia*) of Florida and Cuba, the smooth, gray, columnar trunks of which are greatly admired along public avenues.

PALMETTO. See *Palm Family.*

PALOVERDE, any of 3 related, small, spiny, desert trees of the North American southwest, with stiff branches, green, smooth bark, delicate, pinnately compound leaves that drop as soon as drought returns after a period of rain, and clusters of small, bright, yellow, 5-petalled flowers. Family: Pea (Leguminosae); genera and species, *Cercidium floridum*, *C. torreyanum*, and *Parkinsonia aculeata*.

PAMPAS GRASS, the common name given to an ornamental, tall, reedlike grass (*Cortaderia argentea*), native to mountainous country in southern Brazil and Argentina. It is cultivated in California for the decorative effect produced by its massed, coarse, basal leaves, its waving, fluffy plumes of flowers, and its 6-to-12-foot-high seeds. A similar grass with the same name (*Gynerium argenteum*) forms natural hedges along water courses in the pampas of southern South America. Family: Grass (Gramineae).

PANSY. See *Violet.*

PAPAW, or pawpaw, any of 8 different kinds of shrubs or small trees native to southeastern and eastern North America, all with large, feather-veined, pointed leaves and solitary flowers where the leaves of the previous year joined the stems.

The dull purple flowers are followed by large, pulpy fruits containing several seeds, each enclosed within a fleshy part called an aril. The pulp of the common papaw (*Asimina triloba*) is sweet and edible in autumn, but all other parts of the tree give off an unpleasant odor when bruised. Family: Custard-apple (Annonaceae); genus *Asimina.*

PAPAYA, a tall, herbaceous plant of tropical America that grows to a height of 25 feet, with a crown of large, palmately lobed leaves on long stalks and clusters of yellow flowers high on the main stem followed by huge, ovoid, melon-like fruits weighing 15 to 20 pounds.

Each papaya fruit contains a thick, orange pulp surrounding a fibrous center filled with spherical black seeds. The ripe pulp has the consistency of muskmelon. Its distinctive, pleasant flavor is greatly appreciated in salads or as a breakfast fruit. An enzyme in papaya leaves is pepsin-like, and is used to tenderize meats. Family: Papaya (Caricaceae); genus *Carica,* particularly *C. papaya.*

PAPER MULBERRY, a small, attractive tree native to Southeast Asia and the Pacific islands, but cultivated in subtropical parts of the United States as well. It has evergreen, ovate leaves that give dense shade, small clusters of flowers followed by mulberry-like fruits, and a fibrous bark that is used throughout the tree's native range to make tapa (bark cloth) for decorative material and clothing. Family: (Moraceae); genus and species, *Broussonetia papyrifera.*

PAPRIKA. See *Pepper, Red.*

PAPYRUS, a long-stemmed, reedlike sedge native to northeastern Africa, growing to 15 feet, the 3-ranked, narrow leaves and triangular stems of which are topped by an umbrella-shaped cluster of minute flowers borne on a radiating array of fine stalks. The ancient Egyptians cut the pith of this marsh plant into long strips, arranged them into layers, and soaked and pressed them to form long sheets and rolls of writing material.

Papyrus is grown in warm parts of Europe and the United States as a decorative plant. Closely related is the umbrella plant (*Cyperus alternifolius*) of Madagascar and the Mascarene Islands, raised as a house plant for its clumps of 3 to 10 stems, 1 to 3 feet tall, which bear whorls of rough, blade-like leaves arranged like the ribs of an umbrella. Clusters of greenish flowers appear at the tops of the stems in winter. Family: Sedge (Cyperaceae); genus and species, *Cyperus papyrus.*

BURPEE SEEDS

PARSLEY

PARSLEY, a low-growing, biennial herb of southern Europe, widely cultivated for its bright green, finely-divided leaves, which are used as a garnish and seasoning, and for the small, hard, paired fruits, which at the end of its second year, ripen from umbrella-like clusters of small, yellowish green flowers.

Parsley seeds can be used as a seasoning, and an oil from the seeds can be used as a medicine. One variety, Harburg parsley, has a thick root eaten as a vegetable. Family: Carrot (Umbelliferae); genus and species, *Petroselinum crispum.*

PARSNIP, a biennial, herbaceous plant that stores food in a thick taproot during its first year and produces a stem 2 to 5 feet tall with many compound leaves and flat-topped clusters of yellow flowers in its second year.

Native to Europe, it is used as a winter fodder for cattle and as a food for man. It is harvested after a killing frost at the end of the first growing season destroys the exposed parts and induces the formation of sugar from the starch in the underground root. Family: Carrot (Umbelliferae); genus and species, *Pastinaca sativa.*

PASQUEFLOWER. See *Anemone.*

PASSIONFLOWER, any of about 400 different kinds of tropical climbing vines, most of them native to western South America. They generally have simple, alternate leaves and a succession of paired flowers along the stem, each flower with a peculiar ring of petal-like parts growing out of the tubular support of the stamens.

The common passionflower (*Passiflora caerulea*) from Brazil, which is widely cultivated in warm countries, has flowers colored blue, purple, and white, followed by peach-sized berries. A delicious beverage can be prepared from the pulp.

A passionflower with 1-inch yellow blossoms (*P. lutea*) and another (*P. incarnata*) with 3-inch, white and purple flowers are native to the southern United States. Brazilian and West Indian species with particularly large fruits are often cultivated and called granadillas. Fruits of *P. quadrangularis,* or giant granadillas, may be 10 inches long. Family: Passionflower (Passifloraceae).

PEA, any of 6 different related kinds of perennial herbs, mostly native to the Mediterranean region, with pinnately compound leaves, some leaflets modified to form tendrils used in climbing, and with characteristic bilaterally symmetrical flowers in which the lowest 2 petals join to form a pouch (keel). The fruits are straight pods containing a single row of spherical seeds.

Garden peas (*Pisum sativum*) have been cultivated for at least 1,000 years in Eurasia as a vegetable and as stock food. Often the whole pea plant is plowed under as "green manure" to enrich the soil. The living roots accomplish a great deal in this respect because they bear nodules in which bacteria use atmospheric nitrogen to produce nitrogenous substances nourishing to the pea plant and others in the same earth. Family: Pea (Leguminosae); genus *Pisum*.

PEA FAMILY (Leguminosae), a huge group with about 13,000 species in some 550 genera, probably the second largest family of plants, including herbs, shrubs, climbing vines, and trees. Many are thorny and most have nodules on their roots containing nitrogen-fixing bacteria. All produce a pod of some kind as the fruit. See *Acacia, Alfalfa, Bean, Broom, Clover, Cowpea, Gorse, Indigo, Kentucky coffee tree, Kudzu, Laburnum, Lentil, Licorice, Locoweed, Logwood, Lupine, Mesquite, Mimosa, Paloverde, Pea, Peanut, Redbud, Sandalwood, Shamrock, Sweet clover, Sweat pea, Tamarind, Tonka bean tree, Tumbleweed, Vetch, Wattle tree, Wisteria,* and *Yellowwood.*

PEACH, a small, many-branched tree easily injured by frost, native to southern China and introduced first in Europe and then the southern United States. Many varieties have been developed and some with more attractive flowers than others, producing larger fruits with special features, for instance, "freestone" instead of "clingstone" flesh.

All have simple leaves, attractive, pink, 5-petalled flowers, and edible fruits with a juicy flesh outside an armored, central seed. Smooth-skinned nectarines differ from most other varieties of peach, which have a downy or velvety covering over the fruit. Family: Rose (Rosaceae); genus and species, *Prunus persica.*

PEANUT, a sprawling, annual, herbaceous plant native to Brazil, with pinnately compound leaves and bright yellow flowers, which give rise to pods on long stalks. The ripening pods bend downward, enter the earth, and mature hidden in the soil. The peanut commonly eaten is not a nut, but the dried seed of this plant.

It has been known in South America since prehistoric times and cultivated in Africa for more than 400 years. In Africa it is known as groundnut or goober. The green parts are made into hay for livestock and the seeds are eaten raw, boiled, roasted, in cakes and candies, or crushed into peanut butter and peanut oil. Family: Pea (Leguminosae); genus and species, *Arachis hypogaea.*

PEAR, a small Eurasian tree with glossy, pointed, wavy-edged leaves, white flowers, and sweet, sometimes gritty, ovoid fruits. Dwarf trees are preferred for cultivation, because the fruits can be harvested easily.

Among the varieties, the Bartlett has a sweet fruit, the Seckel or sugar pear, a small, hard, sweet fruit, and the Kieffer pear, a coarse fruit with less flavor but a firmness that lasts into winter. The closely related sand pear *(Pyrus sinensis)* of China and Japan is often used as a strong root upon which to graft fruit-bearing tops of more desirable kinds of pears. Family: Rose (Rosaceae); genus and species, *Pyrus communis.*

T.H. EVERETT

PEACH

PECAN. See *Hickory.*

PEEPUL, or pipal tree. See *Fig.*

PELARGONIUM. See *Geranium.*

PENNYROYAL. See *Mint.*

PEONY, any of several different kinds of herbaceous perennials with deeply divided leaves on long stalks. All except the wild peony *(Paeonia browni)* of mountains in the Pacific states are native to Eurasia.

About 700 named varieties have been developed from the European common peony *(P. officinalis)* hybridized with the Chinese and Siberian white peony *(P. albiflora)*. These are remarkable for the size of their flowers, the "doubleness" through development of extra petals instead of stamens, and the variety of colors ranging from white to pink to red to magenta.

Tree peonies, which produce an upright, woody stem 3 to 6 feet tall and flowers of a particularly satin-like texture as much as 12 inches across, have been developed from the moutan peony *(P. suffruticosa)* of eastern Asia through hybridization with a closely related species *(P. lutea)*. In colonial times extracts from the roots of common peonies were used as a nerve tonic. Family: Buttercup (Ranunculaceae); genus *Paeonia.*

PEPPER, the most valuable spice in commerce today, produced from the fruits of a climbing, woody vine native to India. It has stems reaching 20 to 30 feet above the ground, ovate leaves, and spikes of inconspicuous flowers followed by yellowish-red, globular berries, each about ¼-inch in diameter, with a single seed (the peppercorn) covered by a thin pulp. Unripe fruits are gathered, dried, and

ground whole to produce black pepper, whereas ripe fruits are dried, peeled, and soaked in water to free the seeds which are ground to make white pepper.

Cultivated in the Orient since ancient times, pepper became so important to the traders of the 1400s that they explored the world, seeking a shorter route to tropical India to obtain the spice. Pepper is still produced in Indonesia, India, and Thailand, as well as in some parts of Africa and tropical America.

A related plant, the betel pepper *(Piper betle)* of the East Indies provides the fresh leaves chewed with dried fragments of betel nut. Another East Indian relative is cubeb *(P. cubeba)*, a woody, climbing shrub the aromatic, bitter berries of which are dried and used in remedies for respiratory ailments. Family: Pepper (Piperaceae); genus *Piper.* See also Palm Family.

PEPPER FAMILY (Piperaceae), a group of about 1400 species in 12 genera, chiefly herbs and shrubs of the tropics with stems jointed or swollen where the leaves arise and with the inside conducting tissue more or less scattered.

The flowers are clustered in spikes and produce small, fleshy fruits with a single, central seed. Most of the species are members of the large genus *Piper* and of the genus *Peperomia,* of which several among the 500 species are cultivated as house plants for their handsome foliage. See also *Pepper.*

PEPPERGRASS, or pepperwort, any of about 130 different kinds of annual herbs widely distributed in temperate regions, with branching stems to 2 feet high, curly, notched leaves, and ascending clusters of small, white flowers. The foliage is edible and has a "hot" taste, which has led to the cultivation of one species *(Lepidium sativum)* from Mediterranean countries as garden cress. It has escaped from cultivation in many regions and become a weed. Family: Mustard (Cruciferae); genus *Lepidium.*

PEPPERIDGE. See *Tupelo.*

PEPPERMINT. See *Mint.*

PEPPER, RED, a woody shrub native to tropical America, perennial in warm climates, but grown as an annual where frost occurs in winter. The leaves are generally pinnately compound; the flowers are small, solitary, and followed by a hollow berry with a thick rind containing many small, flat seeds. Cultivated by the Indians, the plant was discovered by Spanish explorers and introduced into Europe, where the sweet, or bell, pepper was developed horticulturally to be eaten green or ripe (red). Paprika is made from dried, ripe, bell peppers.

Another mild variety is the Spanish sweet pepper, known as pimento. The smaller, "hotter" varieties are used in making chili and tabasco sauce as condiments. Cayenne pepper is made from the dried, ground fruits of the Guinea pepper *(Capsicum annuum)* and the spur pepper (*C. fastigiatum*). Peppers are rich in vitamin C and have a variety of medicinal uses. Family: potato (Solanaceae); genus and species, *Capsicum frutescens*.

PEPPER TREE, an evergreen tree native to America from Mexico to Chile, with graceful, drooping branches bearing pinnately compound leaves, clusters of small, whitish, staminate or pistillate flowers, but not both on the same tree, and bright red or rose-colored firm fruits, each with a central armored seed. It has been introduced into Florida and California, where winters are mild, as an ornamental and hedge tree capable of growing 20 to 50 feet tall. Family: Sumac (Anacariaceae); genus and species, *Schinus molle*.

PERIWINKLE, or running myrtle, a perennial, trailing plant with glossy, dark, paired, evergreen leaves and solitary, purplish-blue flowers. Native to the Old World from western Europe to Asia Minor, it has been widely introduced into temperate lands as a ground cover thriving in shady areas. A tropical relative (*Vinca rosca*) from Madagascar tolerates greater summer heat but is susceptible to winter cold. Family: Dogbane (Apocynaceae); genus and species, *Vinca minor*.

PERSIMMON, any of several different shrubs and small trees, native to the Northern Hemisphere, that grow to 50 feet and produce simple, leathery, smooth-edged leaves, bark splitting into a pattern of squares, and staminate flowers on separate trees from the pistillate flowers.

The flowers are followed by spherical, orange-brown fruits, resembling tomatoes and as much as 3 inches in diameter. The flesh is sour until touched by frost and completely ripe. The cultivated persimmon (*Diospyros kaki*) of Japan comes in seedless as well as seeded varieties; it is grown in the Pacific states as well as in the Orient. The wild persimmon of the southern United States (*D. virginiana*) and the date plum (*D. lotos*) of China also produce edible fruits. Family: (Ebenaceae); genus *Diospyros*.

PE–TSAI, or Chinese cabbage. See *Mustard*.

PETUNIA, a genus of tropical American, herbaceous annuals with weak, hairy, stems 6 to 24 inches tall, smooth, oval leaves, and fragrant, trumpet-shaped, ruffled flowers of white, purple, violet, or mixed colors. Most frequently cultivated as a garden flower in the United States are the Argentinian purple petunia (*P. violacea*), the white petunia (*P. axillaris*), and hybrids between these and other species. Family: Potato (Solanaceae).

PHLOX, a genus of about 50 different kinds of annual and perennial herbs, one species of which is native to northeastern Siberia. The others are native to North America. They produce stiff stems, narrow, stalkless leaves, and clusters of white, pink, red, purple, or mottled flowers in which the corolla is 5-lobed with a slender tube expanded into a flat display.

Many cultivated annual varieties are horticultural forms of the Texan species (*Phlox drummondii*), with red or purple blossoms. Dwarf phlox, chosen as a rock-garden ornament, is generally the moss pink or ground pink (*P. subulata*) of eastern North America; it has tiny tufted leaves and clusters of magenta, pink, or lilac flowers that open early in the spring.

A taller related plant is wild sweet william (*P. maculata*), about 2½ feet tall, with clusters of pink or purple flowers. It is native to stream edges and rich woodland soil in eastern North America. Family: Phlox (Polemoniaceae).

PIGNUT. See *Hickory*.

PIGWEED, any of several related herbaceous plants, chiefly annuals of almost cosmopolitan distribution as weeds, flowering inconspicuously late in the summer, and belonging to genera *Chenopodium* (especially the European *C. lanceolatum* and *C. paganum*), *Cycloloma* ("American winged pigweed") and *Axyris* ("Russian pigweed," of the goosefoot family, Chenopoliaceae), and *Amaranthus* (especially the cosmopolitan *A. hybridus* and *A. retroflexus* of the amaranth family, Amaranthaceae).

PIMENTO, or Pimiento. See *Pepper, Red*.

PIMPERNEL, a low spreading herb native to Europe, with small, oval leaves and solitary, scarlet, white, or blue petals united at the base and closing in dull weather and at night; hence the popular English name "poor man's weatherglass." The many-seeded capsules contain fruits resembling pep-

BURPEE SEEDS

PETUNIA

percorns, which has led to the introduction of this plant along most coasts of the world and in fields a long distance inland. Family: Primrose (Primulaceae); genus and species, *Anagallis arvensis*.

PINE, any of about 90 different kinds of evergreen coniferous trees with needles of two types: one borne singly in spirals around stems, the other in bundles of 2 to 5 enclosed in papery sheaths at the base. The needles, ranging from 1 to 24 inches long, may be retained on the tree from 2 to 8 years according to the species.

Among 5-needle pines, the most valuable for timber are the North American white pine (*Pinus strobus*), found east of the Rockies and as far south as Guatemala; the western white pines (*P. monticola*) of the North American Pacific coast; and the sugar pine (*P. lambertiana*) of California and Oregon, which attains a height of about 250 feet and produces cones 20 inches or more in length.

Three-needle pines include the western yellow pine (*P. ponderosa*) and the longleaf pine (*P. palustris*) of the American southeast, a valuable source of turpentine and resins. Included among the 2-needle pines are the important Scotch pine (*P. sylvestris*) of northern Eurasia, the lodgepole pine (*P. contorta*) of western North America, and the stone pine (*P. pinea*) of Mediterranean countries, which yields edible seeds called pignolias.

Edible pine seeds, known as piñon nuts, were gathered as winter food by American Indians in the southwest, chiefly from the nut pine (*P. edulis*) and the singleleaf pine (*P. monophylla*), which has solitary leaves. Family: Pine (Pinaceae).

PINE FAMILY (Pinaceae), a group of about 210 species in 9 genera, all coniferous trees with winged seeds, yielding more lumber than any other family of plants. See *Cedar, Douglas Fir, Hemlock, Larch,* and *Spruce*.

PINEAPPLE, any of 5 different spiny plants native to tropical America, with a basal rosette of long, stiff, saw-edged, and sharp, pointed leaves among which the stem eventually grows upward to terminate in a cluster of inconspicuous greenish or purple flowers. The ovaries join together as they ripen, forming one multiple fruit from each flower cluster.

Often the stem continues for a short distance between the ovaries and beyond the multiple fruit to bear a short cluster of harsh, stiff, green leaves. *Ananas sativa* has been developed to yield juicy, large, sweet fruits, weighing from 3 to 20 pounds, which are cut from the plant with the terminal tuft of shorter leaves still in place.

About three-quarters of all edible pineapples and pineapple products are raised and produced in the Hawaiian Islands; additional large plantations have been established in Puerto Rico and other parts of the West Indies, and in Malaysia. Wild pineapple, or pinguin (*Bromelia pinguin*), from tropical America forms almost impenetrable tangles along the edges of rain forests and yields a valuable fiber from its leaves. It is sometimes grown in the tropics as a fruitbearing plant or as an ornament. Family: Pineapple (Bromeliaceae); genus *Ananas*.

PINEAPPLE FAMILY (Bromeliaceae), a group of about 1500 species in 65 genera, all but one species native to America. Most are short-stemmed, often with stiff, fleshy leaves in a rosette which holds rain water. Included are the most conspicuous perching plants of the tropical rain forests. They are epiphytes, frequently called "air plants" because they take no nourishment from the tree branches on which they grow. See *Pineapple* and *Spanish moss*.

PINK, any of almost 300 different kinds of low-growing or sprawling perennial herbs native to Eurasia and Africa, with narrow, paired, grasslike leaves and showy, fragrant flowers the 5 petals of which are conspicuously notched or "pinked" at the outer edge. Many are cultivated as garden flowers or have escaped to become widespread on other continents to which they were introduced.
   The garden or grass pink (*Dianthus plumarius*) commonly has flowers almost 2 inches in diameter. The carnation (*D. caryophyllus*) produces solitary blooms of larger size; horticultural varieties are often double in size. Sweet william (*D. barbatus*), with a flat-topped cluster of flowers the petals of which usually have a line of color across, has long been a favorite of English gardeners. Family: Pink (Caryophyllaceae); genus *Dianthus*.

PINK FAMILY (Caryophyllaceae), a group of about 1800 species in 80 genera, all herbs with simple, opposite leaves and flowers with notched ("pinked") petals. See *Baby's-breath, Bouncing Bet, Chickweed,* and *Pink*.

PINK, GROUND. See *Phlox*.

PIPSISSEWA, or prince's pine, a small, perennial herb of dry woodlands in the northern parts of the North Temperate Zone. Its extensive horizontal, creeping, underground stems give rise to short, upright stems bearing thick, glossy, evergreen leaves and loose, terminal clusters of white flowers with waxy, concave petals and expanded filaments on the stamens. Family: (Ericaceae); genus and species, *Chimaphila umbellata*.

PISTACHIO, a tree native to the Mediterranean countries, growing 25 feet tall with compound leaves and producing three leaflets and olive-like fruits containing an edible green seed, much prized for its delicate flavor. A close relative from the same region is the terebinth tree (*Pistacia terebinthus*), which yields Chian turpentine, the only oily resin of this kind not obtained from a conifer. Family: Sumac (Anacardiaceae); genus and species, *Pistacia vera*.

T.H. EVERETT
POINSETTIA

PITCHER PLANT, any of several insectivorous plants with pitcher-like leaves that hold rainwater in which insects drown, are digested, and soluble products absorbed as nitrogenous nourishment for the plant. Native to bogs and swamps in the New World are the members of the pitcher-plant family Sarraceniaceae, including 7 or more (genus Sarracenia) in eastern North America, 1 (genus *Darlingtonia*) in northern California and southern Oregon, and 4 (genus *Heliamphora*) in high mountains of Venezuela and the Guianas.
   In the tropics of Asia and of Australia, particularly in the jungles of Borneo and adjacent parts of the East Indies, are 66 members of the monkeycup family, Nepenthaceae, all in genus *Nepenthes*. These are herbs or climbing shrubs with pitchers at the ends of the leaves or climbing tendrils. An Australian pitcher plant (*Cephalotus follicularis*), found in marshes of Western Australia, is the sole member of family Cephalotaceae; only its lower leaves form insect-catching pitchers.

PLANE–TREE FAMILY (Platanaceae), a group of 8 different kinds of trees in a single genus (*Platanus*), native to the Northern Hemisphere, with massive trunks growing to 170 feet tall; tough wood; broad, deciduous leaves with 3 pointed lobes; leaf stalks concealing the axillary buds; and pendant clusters of minute flowers that mature into spherical heads of small, pyramidal, brown fruits.
   The plane tree (*P. orientalis*), which is native to Eurasia, from the Mediterranean to the Himalayas, is widely planted along city avenues for its pleasant shade. Like the sycamore tree (*P. occidentalis*) of eastern North America and the California sycamore (*P. racemosa*), the plane tree has a thin, brittle bark which scales off in large patches leaving chalky white or yellow areas, as though the tree had been painted for camouflage purposes.

PLANTAIN FAMILY (Plantaginaceae), a group of about 200 species in 3 genera, almost all members of the cosmopolitan genus Plantago and chiefly weeds of temperate areas. They have fibrous roots, rosettes of thick, long leaves, short stems, and spikes of tiny, greenish or white flowers atop slender stalks 8 to 10 inches tall.
   The common broad-leaved plantain (*P. major*) is found in lawns, and its seeds are eaten by birds. The narrow-leaf plantain or buckhorn (*P. lanceolata*) tends to crowd out valuable grasses in meadows and pastures. The name plantain is also given to certain tropical bananas that are cooked before being eaten.

PLUM, one of several related small trees native to Asia, with smooth, oval, saw-edged leaves, close-grained wood frequently used for cabinet work, a bitter sap containing cyanides, clusters of white flowers that open early in the year (sometimes before the leaves), followed by smooth-skinned, fleshy fruits containing a single, smooth, armored seed.
   Damsons, greengages, and prune plums are varieties of the common plum (*Prunus domestica*) which has been grown extensively for its fruit in Europe and North America. Prunes, or dried plums, include certain varieties developed for cultivation in California, or those from a West Indian tree (*P. occidentalis*).
   Also cultivated in the United States are the native American wild plum (*P. americana*), the hardy Canadian black plum (*P. nigra*), and the Japanese plum (*P. salicina*). Family: Rose (Rosaceae); genus *Prunus*.

POINSETTIA, a small tree of tropical America with large, jagged-edged leaves and similar brilliant leaves in irregular whorls near the tips of the branches, radiating from under the strange small flowers; these are borne in cuplike clusters, each with one pistillate and several staminate flowers. Reaching the peak of display before Christmas and lasting well through the holiday season, poinsettias are cultivated for sale as indoor decorations; the cut ends of the stems should be dipped in boiling water or sealed with paraffin or flame to prevent the loss of the milky juice.
   There are a number of related herbaceous plants that are native to the southeastern United States. Among these is painted leaf (*Euphorbia heterophylla*), which has a splash of orange-red across the stalk end of its green leaves, near its terminal clusters of equally inconspicuous flowers. Family: Spurge (Euphorbiaceae); genus and species, *Euphorbia pulcherrima*.

POISON HEMLOCK, an erect, perennial herb native to southern Europe, introduced and well established in eastern North America, Mexico, South America, and elsewhere, and growing to 5 feet tall. Only the lower leaves are long-stalked but all leaves are twice pinnately compound. The small flowers are borne in umbrella-like clusters to 3 inches across followed by paired, small, dry fruits. The thick root might easily be mistaken for a parsnip. All parts of the plant, and especially its seeds, are deadly poisonous. A cupful of poison hemlock juice was a standard dose for suicide or execution of prisoners in ancient Greece. Family: Carrot (Umbelliferae); genus and species, *Conium maculatum*.

POISON IVY, an erect shrub or climbing, woody, perennial vine with deciduous, compound leaves of 3 oval leaflets, the middle one larger than the lateral ones, but all bearing a few small teeth along the sides. Small, greenish flowers in clusters are followed by hard, gray, globular berries.

All of the plant, including the underground horizontal stems and roots, is poisonous, causing the affected skin or stomach lining to swell and blister. Highly susceptible people react from contact with domestic animals that have walked through poison ivy plants in underbrush, or from smoke from fires in which poison ivy plants are burning. The active agent is urushiol, an oily substance.

Similar effects are caused by related poison sumac *(Rhus vernix)*, of eastern North America, and poison oak *(R. diversiloba)*, of California. Family: Sumac (Anacardiaceae); genus and species, *Rhus radicans*.

POKEWEED FAMILY (Phytolaccaceae), a group of about 125 species in 17 genera, chiefly herbs and woody perennials of the American tropics and subtropics. The most familiar of them in the United States and Canada is the pokeweed or pigeonberry *(Phytolacca americana)*. It has a large, poisonous root from which a stout, smooth stem grows upward each spring bearing drooping, large leaves pointed at each end, and short spikes of petal-less flowers, each with 5 white or pinkish, petal-like sepals.

By midsummer, elongated loose clusters of plump, black berries ripen, their enclosed seeds probably distributed by birds that are immune to the poison. All parts of the plant are poisonous, except young shoots under 4 inches long in the spring; these may be cooked and eaten after the root is removed. They taste much like asparagus. Pokeweed is found along roadsides and in wasteland.

POLYPODY FAMILY (Polypodiaceae), a group of more than 7000 species in about 170 genera, most with compound leaves rising from large underground stems. They are the largest family of ferns.

The family includes the fern *(Onoclea sensibilis)* of eastern North America and eastern Asia, the fronds of which are very sensitive to frost; the Christmas fern *(Polystichum acrostichoides)* of North America, which is evergreen; the spleenworts *(Asplenium* species) and the maidenhair ferns *(Adiantum* species) of temperate and tropical regions; and the large staghorn *(Platycerium* species) of Australia, Southeast Asia, and Africa, which is a handsome perching plant often displayed in greenhouses of temperate regions. See *Bracken* and *Walking fern*.

POMEGRANATE, a small tree native to northern India and Afghanistan, cultivated throughout the Orient and in parts of Europe and the United States, with glossy leaves and short-stalked, bell-like, scarlet flowers which are followed by orange-red, fleshy fruits about the size of an orange, with a thick, leathery rind surrounding a delicious, juicy, acid pulp containing many large seeds. The sirupy beverage made from the pulp of pomegranates is called grenadine. Family: Myrtle (Myrtaceae); genus and species, *Punica granatum*.

POMELO. See *Grapefruit*.

POND LILY. See *Water lily*.

POPLAR, any of about 40 different kinds of quick-growing trees native to the North Temperate Zone, with soft wood and thin bark, used commonly for fuel and paper pulp. Their broad, triangular leaves on long flattened stalks flutter in the breeze, and turn golden-yellow in autumn.

Drooping catkins of staminate or ovulate flowers are borne on separate trees and appear in spring before the leaves. The seeds are dropped when ripe and carried by the wind which catches on the cotton-like fibers extending from the seed covering.

These trees were frequently planted along streets and avenues until city planners discovered how quickly the roots invade and clog sewers. The European white poplar *(Populus alba)*, the leaves of which have a feltlike coating of white hairs beneath, the gray poplar *(P. canescens)*, and the columnar Lombardy poplar *(P. nigra italica)* were introduced into America. Native American types include the widespread quaking aspen *(P. tremuloides)*, the balsam poplar *(P. balsamifera)* of Canada, the cottonwood *(P. deltoides)* of eastern states, and the black cottonwood *(P. trichocarpa)* of the Pacific coast from California to Alaska, which attains a height of 225 feet. Family: Willow (Salicaceae); genus *Populus*.

POPPY, any of nearly 200 different kinds of related herbaceous annuals and perennials native to the Northern Hemisphere, South Africa, and Australia, about 100 of them in the large genus *Papaver*. Most have deeply-cleft, hairy leaves, a milky juice, and long stalks supporting hairy, nodding, egg-shaped flower buds from which the green sepals drop off when the 4 to 6 or more thin, white or colorful petals open.

On opening, the flower turns upright, exposing its many stamens and flat-topped crown formed by the union of the stigmas. The crown then becomes the top of the seed capsule. When ripe, the capsule opens 4 to 20 small pores, through which the seeds are shaken free.

The Oriental poppy *(P. orientale)* produces large, orange or scarlet flowers as much as 10 inches in diameter; the Iceland poppy (P. nudicaule), which is native to all the arctic lands, is a dwarf plant with delicate petals to 2 inches across in pastel shades ranging from white to pink,

or yellow. The common European poppy *(P. dubium)* and the opium poppy *(P. somniferum)* of Mediterranean countries are cultivated far beyond their native regions.

The opium poppy is grown for the milky juice that can be collected from the unripe capsules. Although a dangerous narcotic when smoked, it is also a valuable medicine when prepared in various forms such as laudanum, morphine, paregoric, and codeine. All of these are sedatives capable of relieving acute pain, but also habit-forming. The California poppy *(Eschscholtzia californica)* is the state flower of California; it produces silvery foliage and cup-shaped, orange or yellow flowers. Family: Poppy (Papaveraceae).

POPPY FAMILY (Papaveraceae), a group of about 250 species in 28 genera, mostly of the Northern Hemisphere, chiefly herbaceous plants with showy, solitary flowers and a milky or colored sap. See *Bloodroot, Celandine,* and *Poppy.*

PORTULACA. See *Purslane.*

POTATO, a branching, herbaceous plant native to western South America, with pinnately compound leaves on a stem 1 to 2 feet high and small, white or purple flowers that produce bitter, yellow, seed-filled berries. The fibrous roots produce underground stems with fleshy, swollen tips (tubers) that are starchy and edible.

Potato plants are generally propagated from pieces of tubers which have buds ("eyes") that grow into leafy stems. Over 600 varieties have developed. Family: Potato (Solanaceae); genus and species, *Solanum tuberosum*.

POTATO FAMILY (Solanaceae), a group of about 2200 species in 85 genera, principally in tropical and temperate regions of Central and South America. Included are herbs, shrubs, climbing vines, and trees, with clustered flowers distinguished by a 5-parted, wheel- or tubular-shaped corolla.

The very stiff and spiny Kaffir thorn *(Lycium afrum)* of South Africa, used for hedges and as a lion-proof temporary fence around cattle pens is a close relative of the widely cultivated matrimony vine (L. halimifolium), a climbing shrub with purple flowers and orange berries native to Asia. Chinese lantern *(Physalis alkekengi)* and gooseberry tomato *(P. peruviana)* have their fruits concealed within paper-thin bracts resembling Oriental paper lanterns.

See *Belladonna, Butterfly flower, Eggplant, Jimson weed, Mandrake, Nightshade, Pepper (red), Petunia, Potato, Salpiglossus, Tobacco,* and *Tomato.*

POT MARIGOLD, a large annual herb native to Mediterranean countries, with simple, pointed leaves to 5 inches long, the leaf base more or less clasping the stout, straight, somewhat hairy stem. The leaves and terminal flower heads, which have orange-yellow ray petals around a darker center, are cultivated for use as potherbs. Horticulturalists have developed many varieties with larger and more decorative flowers. The dried flowers have been used as a laxative, a healing agent for wounds, and a kidney stimulant. Family: Daisy (Compositae); genus and species, *Calendula officinalis*.

PRIMROSE, any of about 500 different kinds of low-growing perennial herbs native to the Northern Hemisphere, particularly to mountainous or northern regions. The simple leaves are mostly in a basal whorl, above which hairy stalks raise flat-topped clusters of flowers with fringed petals that are white, yellow, rose, red, or lavender.

Many primroses are grown as garden ornaments or house plants, particularly those that bloom early in the spring, such as the Eurasian cowslip (*Primula veris*), the European primrose (*P. vulgaris*) of Mediterranean countries, and the horticultural hybrid known as polyanthus (*P. polyantha* or *P. variabilis*). Family: Primrose (Primulaceae); genus *Primula*.

PRIMROSE FAMILY (Primulaceae), a group of about 800 species in 28 genera, widely distributed but most numerous in the North Temperate Zone. They are almost all perennial herbs with opposite or whorled leaves, and flowers with the 5 petals united and the 5 stamens opposite the petals producing capsules. See *Cyclamen*, *Pimpernel*, *Primrose*, and *Shooting star*.

PRIVET, any of about 50 different kinds of shrubs with dark, oval, small leaves, clusters of fragrant, white flowers at the ends of the branches, followed by black berries. Several kinds tolerate trimming and pruning, even into artistic shapes, and remain evergreen except where the winter weather is severe.

The common privet (*Ligustrum vulgare*) of the Mediterranean region is a favorite in Europe as a hedge plant. "California" privet (*L. ovalifolium*) is native to Japan. Family: Olive (Oleaceae); genus *Ligustrum*.

PRUNE. See *Plum*.

PUMPKIN, a trailing vine native to America, with a prickly stem, dark green, 3- or 4-lobed leaves, large, yellow, bell-shaped flowers, and huge, globular, dull-orange fruits with vertical ribs, the white seeds of which are in a fibrous pulp surrounded by a medium-hard rind.

Cultivated by the Indians as a vegetable, the pumpkin can be eaten boiled, baked, canned, crushed, or used for livestock food. Pumpkins are popular for use on Halloween at which time they are hollowed out and carved as jack-o'-lanterns. A burning candle is placed inside the pumpkin and glows through the translucent rind.

Horticultural varieties of economic value are the summer squash (*Cucurbita pepo condensa*), of many different shapes, and the yellow-flowered gourd (*C. p. ovifera*). Family: Gourd (Cucurbitaceae), genus and species, *Cucurbita pepo*.

PURSLANE, or pussley, a trailing, succulent herb of tropical America, now almost cosmopolitan as a weed except in Mexico, India, China, and France, where it is cultivated and sold as a salad green or potherb.

The smooth, fleshy stem is green, branched, easily broken, and supports successive whorls of fleshy leaves that are rounded at the tip and break readily from the stem. The inconspicuous yellow flowers, ¼ inch across, open for a few hours in early morning, are pollinated by insects, and close permanently, soon to be followed by small seed capsules that shed ductlike, flattened seeds. The seeds survive hard winters, permitting the purslane to grow as an annual in cold climates; it reproduces readily from fragments of stem and leaves.

Closely related succulent plants widely cultivated in rock gradens and flower beds include the garden purslane or rose moss (*Portulaca grandiflora*), native to South America, which opens to the sun large, cup-shaped flowers with rose, red, or orange petals. Family: Purslane (Portulacaceae); genus and species, *Portulaca oleracea*.

PUSSY WILLOW. See *Willow*.

PYROLA FAMILY (Pyrolaceae), a group of 70 species in 10 genera, chiefly of the North Temperate Zone and Arctic, either perennial evergreen herbs or non-green plants nourished by the decay of vegetable matter in the soil. See *Indian pipe*, *Snow plant*, and *Wintergreen*.

QUEEN ANNE'S LACE. See *Carrot*.

QUINCE, a small shrub or tree growing to 15 feet, native to central Asia, with crooked branches bearing downy, oval leaves and white or pink flowers, followed by hard, fragrant, acid, yellow fruits. Widely introduced and cultivated for the fruit, quince trees are hardy and deciduous, their fruits inedible raw but esteemed for making jelly and as a source of pectin for marmalade. The seeds are coated with a

BURPEE SEEDS

RADISHES

mucilaginous substance used in making cosmetics. The related flowering quince (*Chaenomeles lagenaria*), or "japonica," is a cultivated, ornamental shrub from Japan, with spiny branches, handsome rose or orange flowers opening very early in spring, and edible fruits. Family: Rose (Rosaceae); genus and species, *Cydonia oblonga*.

RADISH, a small, herbaceous annual, probably of Asiatic origin, cultivated as a vegetable by the Chinese for over 3000 years, widely adopted for the pungent flavor of its enlarged edible roots, red, white, gray, or black in color, from which coarse, lobed leaves arise in a basal whorl. Late in the summer the stem grows upward, bearing erect clusters of pink, 4-petalled flowers, which are followed by short pods full of black, spherical seeds. Family: Mustard (Cruciferae); genus and species, *Raphanus sativus*.

RAFFIA. See *Palm*.

RAGWEED, any of about 20 different kinds of coarse herbs native to America and Africa, usually with deeply lobed or dissected leaves and inconspicuous, greenish flowers the fine pollen of which is windblown, causing allergic symptoms of "hay fever" in many people. Several species are widespread weeds in grain fields, growing as annuals but with hardy seeds that often live several years before germinating. Family: Daisy (Compositae); genus *Ambrosia*.

RAMIE. See *Nettle*.

RAPE. See *Mustard*.

RASPBERRY, any of several related kinds of thorny shrubs with arching, woody branches bearing toothed, compound leaves, white flowers, and edible red, black, purple, yellow, or white fruits formed as aggregates from many separate pistils on the same finger-shaped receptacle. Unlike blackberries, raspberries are easily separated from the receptacle. They can be eaten raw or cooked, and are preserved. Wild raspberries are commonly called thimble berries.

The most common cultivated kinds are the red raspberry (*Rubus idaeus*) of Eurasian and North American north country, the blackcap raspberry (*R. occidentalis*) of eastern North America, and the decorative, pink-flowered, fragrant, flowering raspberry (*R. odoratus*) of eastern North America. Family: Rose (Rosaceae); genus *Rubus*.

REDBUD, a small tree native to eastern North America, with heart-shaped leaves and clusters of small, pealike, magenta flowers, followed by oblong, flat pods that are winged along the upper edge.

The redbud is cultivated in many parts of the country for its decorative value because its flowers open before the leaves in early spring. The redbud is the American counterpart to the similar Judas tree (*Cercis siliquastrum*) of Mediterranean countries. Family: Pea (Leguminosae); genus and species, *Cercis canadensis*.

REDWOOD. See *Sequoia*.

REED, an almost cosmopolitan grass growing from branching, horizontal, under-ground stems, from which stout, hollow, upright stems rise to 10 or 15 feet, clad in wide, flat leaves to 2 feet long and topped with sprays of rose, lavender, or silvery flowers partly hidden among long bristles.

The horizontal stems growing in swampy or marshy areas catch decaying vegetable matter and sediments and help make new land. Some roofs in Europe are thatched with reeds.

The related giant reed (*Arundo donax*) of southern Europe, which grows in clumps to 15 feet high, has strong stems that are often used for fishing poles and said to be of bamboo; hard, dry, thin pieces from the stem are used in making musical reed instruments. Family: Grass (Gramineae); genus and species, *Phragmites communis*.

RHODODENDRON, a genus of about 850 different kinds of shrubs native to arctic and north temperate regions and to tropical mountains southward through New Guinea to Australia. They have simple leaves, smooth edged or toothed, and showy flowers in clusters from terminal buds. Most of the deciduous species are called azaleas.

Several of the evergreen rhododendrons are cultivated. Some have been horticulturally developed into many varieties. The rosebay, or great laurel rhododendron (*R. maximum*) is the state flower of West Virginia; the western rhododendron (*R. californicum*) is the state flower of Washington. Family: Heath (Ericaceae). See also *Azalea*.

RHUBARB, or Pie plant, a herbaceous perennial native to Central Asia, with thick, horizontal, underground stems from the ends of which coarse, triangular, wrinkled leaves grow on long, green, pink, or red stalks. The leaves and underground stems are poisonous, but the leaf stalks are edible, acid but sweet, and are commonly used in cooking.

A related species (*Rheum officinale*), which is native to China and Tibet, is the source of a root extract used in Oriental medicine for indigestion and diarrhea for over 4000 years. Family: Buckwheat (Polygonaceae); genus and species, *Rheum rhaponticum*.

RICE, an annual grass, probably native to Southeast Asia, usually cultivated in shallow ponds ("paddies") in warm parts of the Orient and the United States, but raised on drier land in Latin America with smaller yields of fruit (grain). Rice grows 2 to 6 feet tall, with narrow leaves and terminal clusters of inconspicuous flowers that produce the fruits.

When ready for harvesting, the water is drained from the paddy, the plants cut, threshed to free the fruits, and the grains polished to remove the seed coats. The product becomes edible when boiled in a little water. About 90 percent of the world's rice is grown in the Orient.

UNITED NATIONS
RUBBER TREE

A related plant, wild rice (*Zizania aquatica*) of the North American marshes, is an important food for water birds. Indians formerly beat out the grains into their canoes as they paddled among the rice plants; now it is a delicacy highly prized in modern cooking. Family: Grass (Gramineae); genus and species, *Oryza sativa*.

ROSE, any of about 150 different species, as well as an immense number of horticultural varieties of erect or climbing shrubs with pinnately compound leaves, the stalks of which are expanded into large, leaflike stipules where they join the stem; to a European the large stipules distinguish a briar (*Rosa*) from a bramble (*Rubus*, raspberries and blackberries), which has small stipules.

Roses usually have thorny stems and bear single or double flowers that are generally fragrant, ranging in color from white to yellow, pink, and many shades of red. The fruits, called hips, are enclosed within a fleshy receptacle and are edible. Rose petals, too, may be candied and eaten.

Roses, particularly the damask rose (*R. damascena*), are cultivated on a large scale in Bulgaria as the source of a rich perfume known as attar of roses, and of a rose oil.

Roses are native to the northern temperate regions and to the tropical mountains; many species, particularly from Eurasia, have been developed to produce flowers of outstanding beauty, such as the named varieties of tea roses (*R. fragrans* and *R. odorata*) of China, the multiflora rose (*M. multiflora*) of China and Japan, the sweetbriar (*R. eglanteria*) of western Asia, the cinnamon rose (*R. cinnamomea*), and the Scotch rose (*R. spinosissima*) from all across Eurasia into the British Isles. Family: Rose (Rosaceae); genus *Rosa*.

ROSE FAMILY (Rosaceae), a large group of about 3200 species in some 115 genera, widely distributed but particularly numerous in the North Temperate Zone. They include herbs, shrubs, and trees with alternate leaves and flowers in which the corolla is attached to the rim of a short tube that bears the numerous stamens.

See *Agrimony, Almond, Apple, Apricot, Blackberry, Cherry, Christmas berry, Hawthorn, Japonica, Loganberry Loquat, Medlar, Mountain ash, Peach, Pear, Plum, Quince, Raspberry, Rose, Serviceberry, Spiraea,* and *Strawberry*.

ROSEMARY, a fragrant shrub with square stems and small, simple, opposite leaves, native to arid coasts of Mediterranean countries, but cultivated in other regions for the pungent, warm taste which the leaves and young stems add to foods and medicines. The small flowers are unusual in having just 2 stamens. They are sometimes gathered to add a distinctive character to perfumes. Family: Mint (Labiatae); genus and species, *Rosmarinus officinalis*.

ROSE OF CHINA. See *Hibiscus*.

ROSE OF SHARON, any of several unrelated plants, including the meadow saffron (*Colchicum autumnale* of the lily family, Liliaceae), narcissus (*Narcissus* of the amaryllis family, Amaryllidaceae), a creeping, succulent plant (*Hypericum calycinum* of the mangosteen family, Guttiferae), and the shrubby Oriental mallow (*Hibiscus syriacus*), which grows 10 to 20 feet tall, with saw-edged, sharp-pointed, oval leaves and wide-open, bell-shaped flowers in a white, purple or rose color, resembling those of hollyhocks. See also *Hibiscus*.

ROWAN. See *Mountain Ash*.

RUBBER PLANT. See *Fig*.

RUBBER TREE, Brazilian or Pará, a tropical forest tree 60 to 100 feet tall, with long-stalked leaves, green flowers in highly specialized clusters partially surrounded by an enlarged receptacle, and with dry capsules full of small seeds.

Amazon Indians long ago learned to cut the bark to collect the milky juice (latex) from the vertical tubes, and to use the latex to make rubber balls for games. Rubber trees are set out in vast plantations, particularly in Southeast Asia and, to a lesser extent, in Africa.

Many other unrelated plants of different plant families also yield latex that can be converted into special kinds of rubber. These include the gutta-percha (*Palaquium gutta*), a Malaysian tree of the sapodilla family (Sapotaceae); the India-rubber plant (*Ficus elastica*), a small tree of India and Java now cutivated indoors for ornamental purposes; the guayule (*Parthenium argentatum*), a low-growing herb native to the southwestern United States, resembling a small sunflower, and a Russian dandelion (*Taraxacum kok-saghyz*), both of the daisy family (Compositae); and various members of the mulberry (Moraceae) and dogbane (Apocynaceae) families.

Family: Spurge (Euphorbiaceae); genus and species, *Hevea brasiliensis*.

RUE, a strongly scented shrub native to southern Europe and Asia Minor, now introduced widely and widespread, with a woody stem 1 to 2 feet high bearing notched, bitter leaves and clusters of yellow flowers. An oil extracted from its leaves was formerly regarded as a valuable medicine.

Meadow rue is unrelated. It includes any of about 10 different herbs (*Thalictrum* species, of the buttercup family, Ranunculaceae) that grow to 7 feet, with dissected leaves and plumelike clusters of flowers in which the white, yellow, or rose-colored sepals are the most conspicuous parts. Family: Rue (Rutaceae); genus and species, *Ruta graveolens*.

RUE FAMILY (Rutaceae), a group of about 1300 species in 140 genera, most abundant in Australia and South Africa, but well represented in other tropical and temperate regions. They include herbs, shrubs, and trees, usually with compound leaves dotted with glandular spots containing an aromatic oil, and with clustered flowers in which the stamens are attached at the base or on the rim of a peculiar, elevated extension of the stalk (receptacle). See *Bergamot, Citron, Grapefruit, Kumquat, Lemon, Lime, Orange,* and *Rue.*

RUSH, any of about 225 different kinds of herbaceous plants native to most countries, with narrow, grasslike leaves on stiff, upright, slender stems rising from a creeping, horizontal, buried stem; inconspicuous flowers are borne atop the tallest stems. Many rushes are marsh plants; the most widespread is the common rush (*Juncus effusus*), which also forms dense stands in wet meadows.

In Japan mats are made from rush stems. In Europe rush stems 3 to 4 feet high are collected to be made into chair seats, baskets, and rope. The pith from the thickest stems could be removed, soaked in tallow, and used for lampwicks or "rush lights." Family: Rush (Juncaceae); genus *Juncus.*

RUTABAGA. See *Mustard.*

RYE, a hardy, annual grass, probably native to southern Europe and Asia Minor, cultivated as a cereal in southeastern Europe for at least 2000 years. It grows 7 to 10 feet tall, with ribbon-like leaves and long, bearded spikes of flowers.

The straw is useful in making hats, paper, packing, and mattress stuffing. The grains can be ground to make flour for black bread, mixed with wheat flour to make a softer rye bread, or used as the base for rye whiskey.

Rye is often sown as a cover crop or grown to be plowed under as a green manure. Wild rye or lyme grass (*Elymus arenarius*) of northern Eurasia and North America is a related plant that grows well on bare sand and is often used to anchor sand dunes or bared soil. Family: Grass (Gramineae); genus and species, *Secale cereale.*

SAFFLOWER, an annual herb native to the East Indies but cultivated extensively in warm parts of North Africa, India, southern Europe, and the United States. It grows 1 to 3 feet tall, with prickly leaves and heads of bright orange, daisy-like flowers. In the Old World it is raised mostly for the pale red dye that can be obtained from the flowers, and which is used for rouge and for coloring silks. An oil used in cooking and in drying paints and varnishes can be extracted from its seeds.

The safflower plant is sometimes called bastard saffron or false saffron because a drug can be obtained from its dried flowers and used medicinally in place of the drug saffron. Family: Daisy (Compositae); genus and species, *Carthamus tinctorius.*

SAFFRON. See *Crocus.*

SAGE, any of about 550 different kinds of herbaceous and shrubby plants native to temperate and tropical countries and to all continents, usually with square stems 1 to 2 feet tall, paired leaves, and clusters of blue, purple, scarlet, pink, or white flowers.

Garden sage (*Salvia officinalis*) is a European perennial that is cultivated widely in the United States as well. Its aromatic leaves are dried and used to flavor sausages, cheeses, and dressings; in addition, a tea, which served as a tonic, was formerly brewed from its leaves. The showy scarlet sage (*S. splendens*), native to Brazil, is a tropical annual with spikes of vivid scarlet, 2-lipped flowers; it is commonly grown as a garden plant. Family: Mint (Labiatae); genus *Salvia.*

SAGEBRUSH, any of several different shrubs of arid areas in the southwestern United States and Mexico, with stiff branches 1 to 12 feet tall, notched, silvery leaves, and sprays of yellow flowers resembling small daisies. The common sagebrush (*Artemisia tridentata*) is the state flower of Nevada. Sagebrush is eaten to a limited extent by cattle and sheep and is used as an emergency fuel. Family: Daisy (Compositae); genus *Artemisia.*

SAGO PALM, any of several different true palms or palmlike cycads from the pith of which an edible starch can be obtained. See *Cycad* and *Palm.*

SAGUARO, a giant tree cactus native to the Arizona-Sonoran desert of the American southwest. Largest of all cacti, it grows to 60 feet, the spiny, fluted, columnar trunk sometimes supporting 1 or more armlike side branches, each of which may be crowned at the tip with waxy white, yellow-centered, night-blooming flowers that produce pear-shaped, edible fruits. Family: Cactus (Cactaceae); genus and species, *Cereus giganteus.*

SALPIGLOSSIS, a genus of branching herbs native to Chile, with branching stems growing to 2 feet, alternate pointed leaves, and large, trumpet-shaped flowers from which a tongue-like stamen protrudes. One of the 5 species (*S. sinuata*) is called painted tongue and is commonly cultivated in gardens of the Temperate Zone for its velvety night-opening flowers of white, yellow, or red, which are often marked with brilliantly colored veins; for these qualities it has sometimes been described as the "orchid of hardy annuals." Family: Potato (Solanaceae).

SALSIFY, or oyster plant, a herbaceous biennial native to southern Europe, with smooth-edged, grasslike leaves and a thickened, edible, tapering taproot that is creamy-white and has an oyster-like flavor when cooked. In its second year the plant produces an upright stem that grows to 3 feet and is topped by large, solitary heads of purple, daisy-like flowers. Family: Daisy (Compositae); genus and species, *Tragopogon porrifolius.*

SALTBUSH, any of several different kinds of herbaceous or woody shrubs adapted for living conditions on alkaline and arid soils, primarily in Australia and the American southwest.

Saltbushes have gray-green leaves with a salty taste, attain a height of as much as 10 feet, and bear clusters of separate staminate and pistillate flowers, in some instances on the same plant. The most widespread American species (*Atriplex argentea*) has been introduced into wasteland as far east as Ohio and westward to the Pacific coast. Family: Goosefoot (Chenopodiaceae); genus *atriplex.*

SALVIA. See *Sage.*

SANDALWOOD, any of a number of unrelated tropical trees with close-grained, fragrant wood, used for incense, boxes, and fine furniture.

Most important of these is white sandalwood (*Santalum album*) of India and Malaysia; its wood is used for funeral pyres, powdered to form, with colored solutions, a paste that is used for caste marks, carved for decorative purposes, or processed to yield a fragrant oil. Red sandalwood (*Lingoum santalinus*, of the pea family, Leguminosae) from the East Indies is less valuable. Family: Sandalwood (Santalaceae); genus, chiefly *Santalum.*

SAPODILLA, or naseberry, a small tree of tropical America that grows to 60 feet and bears stiff, evergreen leaves, white flowers, and reddish-brown berries the size of oranges, with a dark yellow, juicy pulp. On large plantations, particularly in Yucatan, the milky latex from the bark, called chicle, is tapped, collected, and used in makng chewing gum. Family: Sapodilla (Sapotaceae); genus and species, *Achras zapota.*

SAPODILLA FAMILY (Sapotaceae), a group of about 600 species in 40 genera, almost all trees with a milky sap, alternate simple, leathery, smooth-edged leaves, and stamens in 2 or 3 whorls. The outer stamens are modified and become petal-like and sterile. See *Rubber tree, Sapodilla,* and *Sapote.*

SAPOTE, or marmalade plum, or mammee apple, a small West Indian tree with simple leaves and white flowers, producing large, sweet, edible berries containing a single, large seed.

The russet-brown fruit resembling a ripe pear in taste, is a local favorite, but does not ship well. A rich oil can be extracted from the seed to be used in confections. Family: Sapodilla (Sapotaceae); genus and species, *Calocarpum sapota*.

SARSAPARILLA. See *Smilax*.

SASSAFRAS, a shrub or tree native to eastern North America, growing 40 to 100 feet high in southern states, and 3 to 5 feet high in northern states. It has oval or lobed leaves, soft, yellow wood, corky roots, greenish-yellow flowers (the staminate and pistillate flowers on the same plant), and purplish-red berries with red bracts.

The wood is sometimes used for fence posts and small boats. An extract from the aromatic red bark of the roots is used in sassafras tea, and as the flavoring for root beer and other confections. The oil of sassafras, which is also obtained from the roots, is used in medicine and cosmetics. The leaves are sometimes used, along with okra, to flavor soups. Family: Laurel (Lauraceae); genus and species, *Sassafras albidum*.

SAXIFRAGE, any of about 300 different kinds of herbaceous plants native to lands from the highest Arctic to Tierra del Fuego. Many of the plants are alpine, low-growing annuals and perennials, usually with a basal whorl of leaves, and a short, upright stalk bearing a cluster of small flowers.

Some are among the first plants to bloom in the year; others are among those that grow highest on mountain slopes, where they bloom on rocks or in crevices between boulders. Family: Saxifrage (Saxifragaceae); genus *Saxifraga*.

SAXIFRAGE FAMILY (Saxifragaceae), a group of about 1200 species in 80 genera, widely distributed, growing as herbs, shrubs, or small trees with clustered, regular flowers. It includes grass-of-Parnassus (*Parnassia palustris*), a perennial herb of northern and alpine parts of the Northern Hemisphere that bears a single large, white flower from a basal whorl of leaves on each upright 12-inch stalk. See *Gooseberry, Hydrangea, Mock-orange*, and *Saxifrage*.

SCHIZANTHUS. See *Butterfly flower*.

SCREWPINE, any of 180 different kinds of shrubs and small trees native to the Old World, from Africa, through Indonesia, to Australia, with stiff, shiny, sword-shaped leaves in a conspicuous spiral around the branching stems.

The trunk produces a good many stiltlike, prop-roots from above the ground, which sometimes remain after the lowest part of the trunk itself has died and decayed. Clusters of inconspicuous flowers, either staminate or pistillate, develop close to the branches; an aggregate fruit develops from them, on the outer surface of which the pattern of individual ovaries can be traced, much as on a pineapple. Family: Screwpine (Pandanaceae); genus *Pandanus*.

SEDGE, any of perhaps 1000 different kinds of grasslike herbs, chiefly of temperate regions and tropical mountains, with triangular, upright stems that are solid (never hollow like grass stems) and grow from a few inches to a few feet tall with narrow leaves that may be saw-edged and sharp enough to cut human skin.

Small green or brown flowers are borne in bristly spikes, the pistillate flowers in a saclike structure which persists and covers the hard nutlets that contain the seeds. Sedges are found mostly on marsh edges and in wet, poorly drained ground. Family: Sedge (Cyperaceae); genus *Carex*.

SEDGE FAMILY (Cyperaceae), a large group of more than 3000 species in about 85 genera, chiefly marsh plants of temperate and frigid regions, and widely distributed. Cotton-grass (*Eriophorum species*), found in bogs and moorlands of the Northern Hemisphere, shows ball-like, white masses on tall, slender stalks, each ball composed of fine bristles that become hairs as they extend out in radial directions from each pistillate flower.

Sawgrass (*Cladium Jamaicense*) is the most common plant in the Everglades of Florida, and with its sharp-edged leaves makes travel difficult through marshes and swamps in much of the southern United States and West Indies. See *Bulrush, Papyrus*, and *Sedge*.

SEDUM. See *Orpine*.

SELF-HEAL, or heal-all, a low-growing perennial herb native to the Northern Hemisphere, with a subterranean, creeping stem, many upright square stems, opposite leaves, and dense clusters of blue or purple, 2-lipped flowers. At one time it was believed to be useful as a salve for cuts and wounds. Family: Mint (Labiatae); genus and species, *Prunella vulgaris*.

SENECA SNAKEROOT, a perennial herb native to North America east of the Rockies but restricted to higher elevations in the Southeast. It grows to 18 inches, with smooth, pointed, alternate leaves clasping the erect stem at regular intervals, and a terminal cluster of greenish-white flowers; this green color appears in the petal-like sepals as well as the 3 petals. The medicine senegin was formerly extracted from the roots. Family: Milkwort (Polygalaceae); genus and species, *Polygala senega*.

SENSITIVE PLANT. See *Mimosa*.

SEQUOIA, a genus of mammoth, coniferous trees native to the western United States, with ridged, cinnamon-colored bark, short branches, sharp, scalelike needles barely longer than the diameter of the young stems in the big tree (*S. gigantea*) or flat, stiff needles growing to 1 inch in the coastal redwood (*S. sempervirens*).

It is thought that some sequoia trees may range in age from 3000 to 4000 years. The big trees grow at elevations of 5000 to 8500 feet on the west side of the Sierra Nevada in California. The trunks grow to 280 feet in height, 35 feet in diameter, and produce egg-shaped cones 2 to 3¾ inches long.

Coastal redwood trees often attain a height of 369 feet, a diameter of nearly 18 feet at chest height, and have cones ¾ to 1 inch in diameter; they grow in the fog belt of western California and Oregon in groves never more than 30 miles from the Pacific Ocean. Their lightweight, fungus-resistant wood is valuable for the construction of houses and furniture. Family: Bald-cypress (Taxodiaceae).

SERVICEBERRY, or Juneberry, or shadbush, any of about 25 different kinds of shrubs or trees of the temperate Northern Hemisphere, growing to 30 feet, with simple leaves and white or pink flowers in loose clusters opening in early spring, followed by sweet, edible, purple fruits containing up to 10 seeds. Family: Rose (Rosaceae); genus *Amelanchier*.

SESAME, a woody herb native to India but now cultivated throughout the East, growing 2 to 4 feet tall, with lobed leaves and pink or yellow, trumpet-shaped flowers.

An oil is obtained from sesame leaves and seeds for use in cooking, confectionary, soap-making, lighting, medicine, and the manufacture of India ink. Sesame seeds themselves are flat, ivory-colored, and used to garnish baked goods or made into candy. Family: Pedalium (Pedaliaceae); genus and species, *Sesamum indicum*.

SHALLOT. See *Onion*.

SHAMROCK, the floral emblem of Ireland and the common name of several plants that bear 3-part, compound leaves with almost circular leaflets, including clovers (*Trifolium* species), the black medic (*Medicago* species of the pea family, Leguminosae), the wood sorrel (*Oxalis* species of the oxalis family, Oxalidaceae), and the European watercress (*Nasturtium officinale* of the mustard family, Cruciferae).

SHEEP LAUREL. See *Laurel*.

SHEEP SORREL, or field sorrel, or garden sorrel, a small annual or perennial herbaceous plant native to Europe but introduced into America and elsewhere, and widespread as a weed indicative of poor, acid soil. From a subterranean, branching, creeping, tough, horizontal stem, it sends up many erect, vertical stems growing to 1 foot, usually from the middle of a whorl of leaves shaped like arrowheads on long stalks.

The flowers, in a loose, branching cluster atop the stem, are either yellow and staminate or red and pistillate, on separate plants, flowering most of the summer and producing small seeds that drop to the ground and quickly germinate. The leaves have a pleasant, sour taste from the oxalic acid they contain but are poisonous if eaten in quantity. It is unrelated to wood sorrel (*Oxalis*). Family: Buckwheat (Polygonaceae); genus and species, *Rumex acetosella*.

SHEPHERD'S PURSE, a low-growing annual or perennial herb native to Eurasia but now cosmopolitan, with a basal rosette of notched leaves and a slender upright stem growing to 10 inches and bearing small, white flowers and, later, 3-cornered, pouchlike pods that open to release minute seeds. It is one of the most familiar of small weeds. Family: Mustard (Cruciferae); genus and species, *Capsella bursa-pastoris.*

SHOOTING STAR, any of about 30 different kinds of herbaceous perennials native to Eurasia and western North America, with basal, stemless leaves and pink or white flowers on tall stalks, suggesting those of cyclamens. Each blossom possesses stamens that protrude from the folded corolla. Family: Primrose (Primulaceae); genus *Dodocatheon.*

SISAL, a large perennial plant of arid and semiarid regions of tropical America, now cultivated in Florida, the West Indies, Africa, and the Far East, with a basal whorl of succulent, swordlike leaves about 5 feet long and 4 inches wide, containing sturdy fibers useful for making cord, twine, and rope.

At maturity sisal produces a tall, upright stem growing to 12 feet, with clustered, malodorous flowers. Family: Amaryllis (Amaryllidaceae); genus and species, *Agave sisalanx.*

SKUNK CABBAGE, a coarse herb, with broad leaves, growing in wet woodlands in eastern North America and eastern Asia. In very early spring before its leaves unfurl, it produces a number of greenish-yellow flowers on short stalks (spadixes), partly surrounded by purple-streaked, green hoods (spathes). The disagreeable odor of the flowers appears to attract flies, which act as pollen carriers. Family: Arum (Araceae); genus and species, *Symplocarpus foetidus.*

SMILAX, a genus containing about 300 different species of herbs, vines, and climbing shrubs, mostly of tropical and subtropical regions, with net-veined leaves and tendrils that are modified stipules. The prickly greenbrier (*S. rotundifolia*), native to dry woodlands in the eastern parts of North America, is regarded as an obnoxious pest.

Sarsaparilla is an oil extracted from the roots of several different kinds, particularly from *S. officinalis* of Honduras, *S. medica* of Mexico, and *S. ornata* of Jamaica. The "smilax" sold by florists is actually the mature, finely-divided foliage of either the prickly asparagus (*Asparagus asparagoides*) or of the asparagus-fern (*A. plumosus*); these are quite different plants of the same family. Family: Lily (Liliaceae).

SMOKE TREE, either of two shrubs or small trees, with leathery leaves and large clusters of minute flowers on fine stalks with multiple branches; these give the cluster the appearance of a cloud of brownish smoke. The cultivated European smoke-tree (*Cotinus coggygria*) is smaller than the

BURPEE SEEDS
SNAPDRAGON

American species (*C. americanus*), which is also known as chittamwood. In both the European and American species the staminate and pistillate flowers are on separate plants, and the few fruits consist of small, round berries. Family: Sumac (Anacardiaceae); genus *Cotinus.*

SNAPDRAGON, an annual or perennial herb native to the Mediterranean region, cultivated as an ornament and horticulturally developed into many varities popular in gardens of both hemispheres. The plants grow from 8 to 36 inches tall and are topped with handsome spikes of 2-lipped flowers with white, yellow, orange, rose, red, or purple corollas that open when squeezed at the sides and snap shut when released. Family: Figwort (Scrophulariaceae); genus and species, *Antirrhinum majus.*

SNOWDROP, an early-blooming, bulbous herb native to the Mediterranean region but widely cultivated for the small, bell-shaped, white flowers that often push through the late snows of winter, before the long, narrow, grasslike leaves appear. Family: Amaryllis (Amaryllidaceae); genus and species, *Galanthus nivalis.*

SNOW PLANT, a brilliant, red, saprophytic plant of California mountain country, often seen under big trees. It attains a height of 3 to 12 inches and opens waxy-red, bell-like flowers. The plant lacks chlorophyll and derives all of its nourishment from the decay of organic matter; it is a relative of the Indian pipe. Family: Pyrola (Pyrolaceae); genus and species, *Sarcodes sanguinea.*

SOAPBERRY, an evergreen shrub or small tree native to warm countries from Mexico to northern Argentina, with pinnately compound leaves, open clusters of small, white flowers, and globular, ivory-colored berries that blacken in autumn. The berries contain saponins that act like soap in water but may cause severe irritation of human skin.

A related deciduous tree (*Sapindus drummondi*) of the central and southwestern United States attains a height of 50 feet and yields wood used in

making baskets and packsaddle frames. Family: Soapberry (Sapindaceae); genus and species, *Sapindus saponaria.*

SOAPBERRY FAMILY (Sapindaceae), a group of about 1100 species in some 130 genera, mostly tropical shrubs and trees with alternate leaves and clustered flowers. Many provide timber, edible fruits, or serve decorative purposes. See *Akee, Litchi* and *Soapberry.*

SOAPWORT. See *Bouncing bet.*

SOLOMON'S SEAL, any of about 30 different kinds of herbaceous perennials native to the North Temperate Zone, with large, fleshy, subterranean, horizontal stems marked with seal-like scars where the upright, vertical stems of previous years have separated at death. The vertical stems, growing to a height of 8 feet, arch over gracefully, bearing paired, oval leaves at the tip and paired, short stalks with pink or ivory, pendant, bell-like flowers and, later, purplish berries.

An allied genus (*Smilacina*), with about 20 different species native to America, is called false Solomon's seal or plumelily; the flowers and fruits are clustered in a terminal plumelike group. Family: Lily (Liliaceae); genus *Polygonatum.*

SORGHUM, a genus of coarse, tall grasses native to the Old World, found chiefly in tropical and subtropical regions, with 13 different species, of which several have been cultivated and developed horticulturally as important crops. Egyptian millet, or Johnson grass (*S. halepense*), is a valuable forage grass where it has been introduced in the southern United States, but it is a weed of cultivated fields farther north. The Eurasian broom corn or guinea corn (*S. vulgare*) is cultivated as a cereal in the Mediterranean countries.

Specialized varieties include kaoliang (var. *nervosum*, a cereal of China), durra (var. *durra*, a cereal of North Africa), kafir-corn (var. *caffrorum*, a cereal of South Africa), shallu (var. *roxburghii*, a cereal of India), molasses sorghum (var. *saccharatum*, which yields a sweet juice similar to cane juice), and broomcorn (var. *technicus*, in which the stiff stalks that support the flowers and seeds are particularly long and useful in making brooms). Family: Grass (Gramineae).

SORREL. See *Sheep sorrel.*

SOURSOP. See *Custard apple.*

SPANISH MOSS, a feathery, silver-gray, epiphytic plant native to the southern United States, the West Indies, and Central America, with slender, threadlike stems several feet long, bearing short, pointed, scalelike leaves and small, yellow flowers, but no roots. It absorbs moisture and mineral nourishment from water vapor and dust in the air, and can grow equally well on a telephone wire or the outstretched limb of a live oak tree. It is often gathered for use as upholstery packing. Family: Pineapple (Bromeliaceae); genus and species, *Tillandsia usneoides.*

SPEEDWELL. See *Veronica.*

SPICEBUSH, a shrub native to eastern North America, growing to 15 feet, with flexible, aromatic, young branches, alternate leaves tapering at both ends, and small, yellow, fragrant flowers appearing in spring before the leaves. Some leaves are staminate and others are pistillate; they produce oval, red, fleshy, aromatic fruits.

The older wood will burn while still green. The bark and fruit can yield an astringent oil of supposed medical value; this oil is not related to the drug benzoin, which is extracted from Oriental trees of the genus *Styrax* (family Styracaceae). Family: Laurel (Lauraceae); genus and species, *Lindera benzoin.*

SPIKENARD, either of 2 unrelated herbaceous plants with enlarged, underground stems from which a fragrant, medicinal extract can be prepared.

The Old World spikenard (*Nardostachys jatamansi*) of the Far East is a member of the valerian family (Valerianaceae). The New World spikenard (*Aralia racemosa*) of eastern North America is a woodland plant with compound leaves and spherical clusters of minute, greenish flowers followed by purple-black berries; like its close relative, wild sarsaparilla (*A. nudicaulis*), it is a member of the ginseng family (Araliaceae).

SPINACH, a hardy, annual, herbaceous plant native to Asia, introduced into Europe in the 15th century and brought to America by early settlers. It has a thick cluster of oval or arrow-like, dark green leaves rich in iron, vitamins A, B complex, and C, and an upright branching stalk attaining a height of 2 to 3 feet in summer and bearing inconspicuous flowers in a cluster. It is regarded as a table vegetable and is prepared by boiling. Family: Goosefoot (Chenopodiaceae); genus and species, *Spinacia oleracea.*

SPINDLE TREE. See *Euonymus.*

SPIRAEA, a genus consisting of about 80 different species of shrubs native to the North Temperate Zone, found particularly in central and eastern Asia, many of them widely cultivated for their clustered flowers, each of which has 5 small petals of a red, pink, or white color.

Several of the wild species of spiraea found in North America are known as meadow sweet, while one, *S. tomentosa,* commonly found in pastures of eastern Canada and the northeastern states, is called steeplebush or hardhack. Bridal wreath (*S. prunifolia*), with delicate white flowers in clusters on a dense shrub about 10 feet tall, is an Oriental species raised in gardens of the temperate zones. Family: Rose (Rosaceae).

SPRUCE, any of about 45 different kinds of evergreen, coniferous trees native to cool and cold, temperate parts of the Northern Hemisphere,

with needles borne on short, woody projections. These projections remain as roughness on the stem after the needles fall. The needles are angular in cross-section, but can be rolled between thumb and forefinger. The cones, which vary in size from 1 to 10 inches in length according to species, are always pendant.

Spruces yield valuable timber and are the world's most important source of pulp for paper. Norway spruce (*Picea abies*), a timber tree that is a handsome ornament, has been introduced to America from Europe. Sitka spruce (*P. sitchensis*), native to western America from California to Alaska, grows to 300 feet. The principal pulp spruces are eastern American red spruce (*P. rubra*) and black spruce (*P. nigra*). Family: Pine (Pinaceae); genus *Picea.*

SPURGE, any of several hundred different herbaceous and shrubby plants with milky juice, classified in genus *Euphorbia* and related genera, mostly native to warm, temperate, and subtropical regions, varying remarkably from one species to another in manner of growth, form of leaf, and details of flower. A spurge native to the north-central United States, but now widely cultivated as a decorative plant for gardens, is snow-on-the-mountain (*E. marginata*), an erect annual with broad, oval leaves; the uppermost leaves have broad, white edges.

Flowering spurge (*E. corollata*) of the eastern United States has conspicuous, white, round or oval appendages around its inconspicuous flower clusters; the flowers thus acquire a distinctive appearance without giving the impression that they have essentially the same form as the "flowers" of poinsettia (another spurge). Family: Spurge (Euphorbiaceae).

SPURGE FAMILY (Euphorbiaceae), a large group of about 7300 species in 283 genera, commonly cactus-like or heathlike, although many are herbs, shrubs, climbing vines, and trees. See *Cassava, Castor-oil plant, Croton, Euphorbia, Poinsettia, Rubber tree, Spurge, Tallow-tree,* and *Tung tree.*

SQUASH, any of a number of closely related, coarse, prostrate, annual herbs or climbing vines native to tropical America, with large, rough leaves on thick, hollow stems and large, yellow flowers followed by edible fruits of many shapes. Fruits of winter squash (*Cucurbita maxima*) sometimes weigh more than 100 pounds.

Before Europeans arrived, the Indians were cultivating squashes in every section of the United States and depicting squash flowers in their cultural and religious rites. Family: Gourd (Cucurbitaceae); genus *Cucurbita.* See also *Pumpkin.*

SQUIRREL CORN. See *Dutchman's breeches.*

STAFF TREE, a low-growing evergreen tree native to the East Indies, bearing large clusters of small, regular flowers and, later, spherical, fleshy fruits with bright orange appendages attached to the seeds. From the seeds a medicinal

oil called oleum nigrum is obtained. Family: Staff-tree (Celastraceae); genus and species, *Celastrus paniculatus.*

STAFF-TREE FAMILY (Celastraceae), a group of about 500 species in 45 genera, widely distributed, growing as shrubs, climbing vines, and trees, with simple leaves and clustered, small, greenish flowers. They usually have brightly-colored fleshy appendages (arils) attached to the seeds. See *Bittersweet, Euonymus,* and *Staff tree.*

STOCK, or gillyflower, a somewhat woody, erect biennial or perennial plant native to Mediterranean countries, growing 2 feet high, with narrow, blunt leaves. Both stem and leaves are coated with short hairs giving them a grayish, feltlike, or wooly appearance. The attractive flowers in terminal clusters are in pastel shades of yellow, orange, rose, blue or magenta, or white, and are usually fragrant. Many horticultural varieties have been developed for cultivation in gardens. Family: Mustard (Cruciferae); genus and species, *Mathiola incana.*

STONECROP. See *Orpine.*

STRAWBERRY, any of several related plants native to Europe and North America, with very short stems, 3-part, coarse, saw-edged leaves on long stalks, attractive white flowers, and bright red fruits. The fruits are composed of the fleshy, edible receptacle in the surface of which small, hard nutlets with seeds are embedded.

Cultivated berries are larger, softer, and often sweeter than the wild forms. American strawberries and some of the horticultural hybrids cultivated for this favorite fruit reproduce by runners (horizontal, naked stems above ground that produce new plants with roots at the tip). Family: Rose (Rosaceae); genus *Fragaria.*

SUDAN GRASS, a coarse cereal grass native to central Africa, introduced into the central United States as a drought-resistant hay and pasture plant, growing 5 to 9 feet tall with long clusters of tiny blossoms from which small, edible seeds develop. Family: Grass (Gramineae); genus and species, *Sorghum vulgare sudanensis.* See also *Sorghum.*

SUGARCANE, a tall grass, probably native to Southeast Asia, now cultivated throughout the tropics and subtropics for the sweet juice that can be obtained from its upright stems; it is the world's principal source of sugar. The plant grows to 6 to 16 feet, bearing coarse, narrow, grasslike leaves at intervals along its many-jointed stems, and a handsome plume of minute flowers at its summit.

The crop is prepared for harvesting when ripe by burning off the dry leaves and cutting the stems (canes) close to the ground. At the sugar mill the canes are crushed, their juice extracted, and the refuse (bagasse) used for fuel or processed into paper or wallboard. The juice is concentrated to produce molasses and purified to yield crystalline cane sugar.

Major producers of sugar cane are Cuba, India, Java, Hawaii, and countries of tropical America. Family: Grass (Gramineae); genus and species, *Saccharum officinarum.*

SUMAC, any of several shrubs and low trees native to North America and warm parts of Europe, with pinnately compound leaves, a milky juice, 4- or 6-lobed flowers, and clusters of bright red, hairy berries. The staghorn sumac *(Rhus typhina)* of eastern North America is often grown as a decorative plant. It grows to 30 feet, with angular branches; all of its young growth is covered with velvety hairs.

Some sumac plants produce clusters of greenish-yellow, fragrant, staminate flowers, and others, less conspicuous, pistillate flowers that mature into upturned, pyramidal clusters of crimson fruits. Aromatic sumac *(R. aromatica),* or polecat bush, of the central and eastern United States, which grows to 6 feet, is often planted along roadsides.

Related species include the poison sumac *(R. vernix),* which is also known as poison elder and poison dogwood and grows in swamps, and the poison oak *(R. toxicodendron)* of dry, sandy uplands in eastern North America. Like poison ivy *(R. radicans),* they cause a severe irritation of human skin. Family: Sumac (Anacardiaceae); genus *Rhus.* See also *Poison Ivy.*

SUMAC FAMILY (Anacardiaceae), a group of about 600 species in 73 genera, chiefly tropical, growing as shrubs or trees, with a milky sap and resin ducts, the leaves alternate and the flowers in clusters. Many cause inflammation of the skin. See *Cashew, Lacquer tree, Mango, Peppertree, Pistachio, Poison Ivy, Smoke-tree,* and *Sumac.*

SUNDEW, any of about 90 different low-growing, insectivorous plants native to all continents but most numerous and varied in Australia. They have basal rosettes of leaves bearing sticky, glandular hairs and slender, upright stems topped by clusters of small, white flowers. The glandular hairs produce shining droplets of secretion to which insects are attracted, and thus caught, enfolded by movements of the leaf, and digested.

The long-leaved sundew *(Drosera longifolia)* and the round-leaved sundew *(D. rotundifolia),* which has round leaves on narrow stalks, live on poorly drained hillsides and bog margins in cool, temperate, and arctic regions of Eurasia and North America. Family: Sundew (Droseraceae); genus *Drosera.*

SUNDEW FAMILY (Droseraceae), a small group of about 100 species in 5 genera, all insectivorous herbs with highly specialized leaves and small clusters of regular flowers supported by slender, upright stalks. *Aldrovanda vesiculosa,* a floating plant with no roots, native to the Old World from Central Europe to Australia, has whorls of leaves that close on and catch aquatic insects and worms. See *Sundew* and *Venus-flytrap.*

BURPEE SEEDS

SUNFLOWERS

SUNFLOWER, any of about 60 different kinds of herbaceous annuals and perennials native to North America, with large, daisy like flowers distinguished by a flat, central area of seed-producing disc florets surrounded by a handsome display of sterile ray florets, the strap-shaped petals of which are commonly bright yellow.

The common sunflower *(Helianthus annuus)* is native to Texas and Mexico, sacred to the Incas of Peru, and now the state flower of Kansas. It is widely cultivated as an ensilage crop and for its edible seeds, from which a valuable oil can be extracted. Its hairy stem grows 3 to 20 feet high, with coarse, saw-edged leaves and a flower head up to 18 inches in diameter. Sunflower stalks are used as fuel in many parts of eastern Europe and Asia.

The Jerusalem artichoke *(H. tuberosus)* is a sunflower native to central North America and cultivated by Indians for its edible, thick, underground stems, which grow to 4 inches long. It is an attractive garden plant and its roots are nourishing for livestock. Family: Daisy (Compositae); genus *Helianthus.*

SWEET BAY. See *Laurel.*

SWEET CLOVER, an erect tough annual or perennial herb, native to Eurasia but widespread in America. It has a deep, strong taproot, small, 3-part, compound leaves, and many slender spikes of small white or yellow flowers from which bees obtain a nectar that gives a distinctive flavor to honey.

It is grown extensively as hay, known as Bokhara clover, helps anchor the soil, and also enriches it with nitrogenous compounds produced by bacteria in the root nodules. Family: Pea (Leguminosae); genus and species, *Melilotus alba* (white-flowering) and *M. officinalis* (yellow-flowering).

SWEET GUM, a deciduous tree native to wet forests in North and Central America, growing to 150 feet in annually flooded areas of Mississippi, and often cultivated as an ornamental shade tree because of the strange, corky ridges that distinguish its young-

er stems and the gorgeous red or orange color that appears when its large, simple, star-shaped leaves take on their fall coloration. Its flowers lack a corolla and appear on the same plant in tight clusters that are either staminate or pistillate, the latter developing into spherical, burlike masses that drop ½-inch, winged seeds in autumn.

The reddish-brown wood of sweet gum is used instead of mahogany or walnut in furniture, flooring, and veneers. A related Asian species *(Liquidambar orientalis)* and an unrelated tree *(Styrax offiicinalis* of the storax family, Styracaceae) yield an aromatic resin called storax from their bark. Family: Witch hazel (Hamamelidaceae); genus and species, *Liquidambar styraciflua.*

SWEET PEA, a herbaceous annual plant native to Sicily, introduced into northern Europe and then America in the 18th century for its handsome, fragrant butterfly-shaped flowers in white, lavender, blue, peach, pink, or red. The flowers grow in clusters of 3 or 4 on slender, climbing stems. The stems have pinnately compound leaves and twining tendrils, which are formed from modified, terminal leaflets. Family: Pea (Leguminosae); genus and species, *Lathyrus odoratus.*

SWEET POTATO, a perennial, trailing vine native to South America, introduced to Europe by Columbus, now widely cultivated in warm countries for its swollen, starchy, edible roots. It produces heart-shaped leaves and purple flowers. Although it is the original plant to be called a potato, and the "Irish" or white potato was named after it, the horticultural variety of sweet potato with the sweetest flavor is often incorrectly called a yam. Family: Morning-glory (Convolvulaceae); genus and species, *Ipomoea batatas.*

SWEETSOP, or Sugar Apple. See *Custard Apple.*

SWEET WILLIAM. See *Pink.*

SWISS CHARD. See *Beet.*

SYCAMORE. See *Plane-tree Family.*

SYRINGA. See *Lilac* and *Mock Orange.*

TALLOW TREE, a small tree native to China and Formosa, introduced to Europe and America as an ornament with glossy, oval leaves and long clusters of very small flowers, followed by seeds with a waxy covering. The wax has long been valued in China and India as a dressing for cloth, a material that could be made into soap, and a tallow for making candles that give a very clear light. The hardwood is sometimes used for engraving. Family: Spurge (Euphorbiaceae); genus and species, *Sapium sebiferum.*

TAMARACK. See *Larch.*

TAMARIND, an evergreen shade tree native to tropical Africa, but cultivated in India and other tropical countries. It grows to about 80 feet, with pinnately compound leaves bearing many leaflets, and clusters of white, yellow, or pink flowers followed by long, narrow, knotty, brown pods containing a juicy, brown pulp and small seeds. The pulp can be used to make a cooling drink, jellies, and preserves. The leaves yield a mordant used in dyeing cloth. The wood is hard and durable, suitable for cabinetmaking. Family: Pea (Leguminosae); genus and species, *Tamarindus indica*.

TAMARISK, any of about 80 different kinds of shrubs and small trees native to warm and tropical regions of the Old World, introduced also into semi-arid parts of America, many of them tolerating extended drought and salty or alkaline soil. The densely branching stems bear smooth-edged, thick, or scalelike leaves, often suggesting those of heaths, and small, white flowers in slender spikes.

In desert areas, tamarisks provide shelter and break the wind. Along rivers and intermittent streams in arid lands, they absorb a great deal of water, which they lose in transpiration at the expense of other adjacent plants that are less well adapted to desert conditions. Family: Tamarisk (Tamaricaceae); genus *Tamarix*.

TANGERINE. See *Orange.*

TAPIOCA. See *Cassava.*

TARO, a horticultural variety of a perennial herb native to India and Malaysia, cultivated widely as the source of a staple food in much of the world's tropics, particularly in the Orient and the Pacific islands. The plant grows best in wet soil, producing long stalks, large, triangular leaves shaped like arrowheads, inconspicuous flowers resembling miniature calla lillies, and large, starchy, edible, underground stems (corms).

The wild ancestor of taro, dasheen *(Colocasia esculenta),* has sweeter but more slender corms containing less starch. Taro corms can be boiled or dried and ground into a meal; in the Hawaiian Islands the meal is fermented to a paste called poi that is often regarded as the native delicacy.

Florists sometimes offer dasheen or taro leaves, which they call elephant's ear, for decorative purposes. The term elephant's ear is also used to describe cultivated members of a related genus *(Caladium)* and certain unrelated begonias. Family: Arum (Araceae); genus, species, and horticultural variety, *Colocasia esculenta antiquorum.*

TARRAGON, a perennial herb native to Europe, with smooth branches, aromatic, simple leaves, and globular heads of tubular flowers. The foliage, which has a bitter taste, is used to flavor vinegar, pickles, and salads. The flavor is contained in an oil that can be extracted from the plant; the oil is known as tarragon oil or estragon oil. Family: Daisy (Compositae); genus and species, *Artemisia dracunculus.*

TEA, an evergreen shrub or small tree that grows to 30 feet, native to eastern Asia from India to Japan and cultivated extensively in Asia and equatorial Africa. The tree is pruned to 3 to 5 feet tall to facilitate the harvesting of its buds and young shoots. If these are allowed to mature, the shrub bears many leathery, oval, saw-edged leaves with thick veins and fine hairs below, as well as clusters of faintly fragrant, ivory-white or pink flowers, which produce woody fruits containing several seeds resembling hazelnuts.

The cultivated tea plants include many hybrid strains but the method of harvesting is much the same for all. Tea leaves are picked from the same bushes 20 to 30 times a year. The first picking (flush) yields buds and very young leaves, which contribute to the best grades of tea. New buds and leaf shoots induced to grow by the first plucking provide for the next pickings.

The final picking of the year includes the old leaves and completely strips the shrubs, providing the coarsest grade of tea. After the picked buds and leaves have wilted, they are rolled by hand. Those dried with a minimum of fermentation make green tea; those allowed to ferment more extensively before drying make black tea. Family: Tea (Theaceae); genus and species, *Camellia sinensis.*

TEA FAMILY (Theaceae), a group of about 500 species in 30 genera, chiefly of tropical and subtropical regions, growing as trees or shrubs with simple leaves and flowers bearing several whorls of stamens. The franklinia, or lost camellia tree *(Gordonia alatamaha),* is now extinct except in cultivation, although it was discovered in Georgia as recently as 1765; it has large, white flowers suggesting waxy poppies. See *Camellia* and *Tea.*

TEAK, a tall tree native to India and Malaysia, cultivated on huge plantations, with a straight trunk growing to 200 feet, a spreading crown, 4-sided branchlets with a central pith, and leaves attaining 24 inches in length and 12 in width, suggesting those of tobacco. The branches terminate in upturned clusters of small, white flowers.

The timber is fragrant, the heartwood a golden yellow that becomes darker and mottled with seasoning; it ranks with mahogany in value and is used for expensive furniture, homes, temples, and ships. Some teak carvings preserved in Indian temples are more than 2000 years old. In Burma an oil extracted from teak wood is used in medicine and commerce. Family: Vervain (Verbenaceae); genus and species, *Tectona grandis.*

TEASEL, any of 12 different kinds of prickly, stemmed, biennial plants native to Mediterranean countries, East Africa, and across the Caucasus to India. Wild teasel *(Dipsacus sylvestris)* is now a widespread weed, with long leaves that are toothed and prickly on the edges, the stem attaining a height of 5 or more feet and branching near the top to bear cone-shaped clusters of lavender, purple, or blue flowers among stiff bristles, each whole head guarded by about 6 narrow, modified leaves.

A cultivated variety of teasel, called fuller's teasel *(Dipsacus sylvestris fullorum),* has particularly stiff hooked bristles between the flowers in the head. When firm ripe heads are split lengthwise, they can be mounted on long wooden rollers under which new woolen cloth is shifted back and forth during the fulling process; the bristles raise the nap by picking gently at the cloth surface. Family: Teasel (Dipsacaceae); genus *Dipsacus.*

THISTLE, any of several different coarse, prickly, herbaceous plants, many widespread or cosmopolitan as weeds. Most are members of the daisy family (Compositae), with tubular flowers clustered in cylindrical heads, often surrounded by prickly, green bracts. The Scotch thistle *(Onopordum acanthium),* the national emblem of Scotland, falls into this category; it grows to 10 feet, bearing lobed, toothed, prickly, cotton-wooly leaves with a covering of gray hair. It is widespread as a weed.

Russian thistle *(Salsola kali tenuifolia)* is a very different plant. Native to Eurasia but now grown in America, it has short, stiff, prickly leaves on a repeatedly branched stem growing to 4 feet, which dries as a huge, loose, open globe and breaks loose from the root to become a tumbleweed, scattering its seeds as it rolls along in the wind; it is a member of the goosefoot family (Chenopodiaceae).

THORN APPLE. See *Jimson-weed*

THYME, any of about 40 different kinds of low-growing, perennial shrubs native to Eurasia and Africa, most with a square, woody stem 1 to 2 feet high, narrow, aromatic, paired leaves, and clusters of lilac-colored, 2-lipped flowers. The garden thyme *(Thymus vulgaris)* of Mediterranean Europe and North Africa grows straighter than the wild, creeping thyme *(T. serpyllum).*

Thyme is more favored as a source of leaves, as a condiment, or as a source of the essential oil of thyme, which is used medicinally. Wild thyme has been introduced to America and has escaped from cultivation to become a weed. Family: Mint (Labiatae); genus *Thymus.*

TIMOTHY, a perennial grass native to Europe but widely introduced and cultivated as a leading hay crop. It is tolerant of cold weather and withstands drought well; some varieties have bulbous enlargements for food storage in the region where the stems arise from the roots. The minute, purple flowers are borne in an elongated, club-shaped head resembling a miniature cattail head; the purple color is that of the long stamens. Family: Grass (Gramineae); genus and species, *Phleum pratense.*

TOBACCO, a broad-leaved, annual herb native to Central and South America. Long before the coming of the Europeans to the New World, it was cultivated in the Caribbean islands and North America for the leaves, which were smoked in special pipes. The plant grows upright, bearing handsome leaves, a straight stem growing to 6 feet, and attractive white or pink tubular flowers. The leaves are stripped from the stems either before or after the stalks have been cut; they are dried and processed for manufacture into cigars, cigarettes, smoking tobacco, chewing tobacco, or snuff. Today the United States leads in all-purpose tobacco production.

Several related plants with larger flowers are favorites in gardens. They are known generally as nicotine and their flowers open mostly at night. Family: Potato (Solanaceae); genus and species, *Nicotiana tabacum*.

TOMATO, a herbaceous annual plant native to tropical South America, with a straggling, hairy stem, notched, pinnately compound leaves, small clusters of yellow flowers, and spherical, red or yellow berries. Introduced as a curiosity into Europe by Spanish explorers, tomatoes were known as "love apples" and thought to be poisonous.

Only within the last century has the tomato been widely recognized as harmless, edible, delicious, and rich in vitamins, whether eaten raw, cooked, pickled, canned, or crushed into juice. Family: Potato (Solanaceae); genus and species, *Lycopersicon esculentum*.

TONKA BEAN TREE, a tree of tropical South America, growing to 80 feet, with pinnately compound leaves and irregular flowers, producing fleshy pods containing black, fragrant seeds called tonka beans. The beans contain coumarin, a sweet-smelling carbohydrate. They are used in flavoring tobacco and in making artificial vanilla and perfumes. Family: Pea (Leguminosae); genus and species, *Dipteryx odorata*.

TREE OF HEAVEN, a deciduous tree native to China but commonly introduced into urban areas of Europe and North America, escaping from cultivation to become widespread. It grows to 90 feet in height and 40 inches in diameter at chest height, with large, pinnately compound leaves and either ill-smelling, small, greenish, staminate flowers or inconspicuous, pistillate flowers, which produce strange, 2-inch fruits with a seed at the center resembling twisted strips of brown paper.

The tree survives in cities despite polluted air and the paved soil that surrounds it. Family: Quassia (Simaroubaceae); genus and species, *Ailanthus altissima*.

TRILLIUM, a genus of delicate woodland wildflowers, native to North America and eastern Asia, with about 30 different species, all with short, thick, underground, horizontal stems from which they produce upright stems every spring. Each stem has a single whorl of 3 net-veined leaves and a terminal flower with 3 large petals.

In eastern North American woodlands, the most familiar are the large, white trillium (*T. grandiflorum*), the ill-smelling red trillium (*T. erectum*), and the attractive, painted trillium (*T. undulatum*), which has red stripes on its white petals. Family: Lily (Liliaceae).

TRUMPET CREEPER, or trumpet vine, either of two woody vines with bright-green, pinnately compound leaves and

clusters of orange or scarlet, trumpet-shaped flowers. The stout stem clambers with the aid of tendrils over rocks, walls, trellises, trees, and sometimes roofs, occasionally reaching a height of 80 feet. Family: Bignonia (Bignoniaceae); genus and species, *Campsis radicans* (eastern North America) and *C. grandiflora* (native to China, but widely introduced as an ornament).

TUBEROSE, a herbaceous perennial plant native to Mexico, grown widely in gardens and greenhouses in temperate regions of both hemispheres for its long spikes of heavily perfumed, waxy, white, tubular flowers on stalks about 3 feet tall. The name tuberose has nothing to do with tubes or roses; instead, it refers to the tuberous, rather than bulbous, roots from which the narrow leaves and flower stalks grow. Family: Amaryllis (Amaryllidaceae); genus and species, *Polyanthes tuberosa*.

TULIP, any of about 50 different kinds of bulbous, perennial herbs native to north temperate parts of Eurasia, particularly to the steppes of Central Asia. Many kinds are now cultivated, especially in Holland, as the basis of an important horticultural industry. All tulips have sheathed bulbs, broad, tapering leaves, and large, showy, cup-like flowers. The original wild species (*Tulipa gesneriana*) is sometimes called the cottage tulip. The early-blooming, yellow-tipped, red, Van Thol tulips were derived from another wild tulip (*T. suaveolens*) from the vicinity of the Caspian Sea. Family: Lily (Liliaceae); genus *Tulipa*.

TULIP TREE, a handsome, tall, straight, deciduous tree native to the eastern United States, growing to 200 feet, with a cone-shaped top composed of branches bearing broad, simple, lobed leaves and strikingly tulip-like, greenish-yellow flowers. The soft wood, sometimes known as whitewood or canoewood, is still used for wooden-

BURPEE SEEDS

TOMATO

ware and interior finishes; for many years the Indians used the wood to make large canoes. The only close relative is a Chinese tree with similar blossoms. Unrelated tropical trees, such as the African tulipan (*Spathodea campanulata* of the bignonia family, Bignoniaceae), are sometimes called tuliptrees. Family: Magnolia (Magnoliaceae); genus and species, *Liriodendron tulipifera*.

TUMBLEWEED, any of a number of mostly unrelated plants of plains and prairies that break loose from their roots when mature and dry, curl into almost spherical masses, and tumble over and over, scattering their small seeds, as they are blown by the wind.

The native tumbleweed, covering much of North America, is usually *Amaranthus graecizans* of the amaranth family (Amaranthaceae). It might also be a winged pigweed (*Cycloloma*), a bugseed (*Corispermum*), a Russian thistle (*Salsola tragus* of the goosefoot family, Chenopodiaceae), or a member of the pea family (Leguminosae), such as the scurf pea (*Psoralea*) or wild indigo (*Baptisia*).

TUNG TREE, either of two kinds of small, deciduous trees native to China, now cultivated in vast orchards in the southeastern United States for the valuable oil that can be extracted from the seeds. The tree itself grows to 40 feet, flowering in early spring before leafing out. One to several pistillate flowers in the same cluster grow together with many staminate flowers; the apple-shaped fruit matures in early autumn.

Tung oil from the seeds is used in varnishes as a drying agent; it is also used in the manufacture of paints, oilcloth, linoleum, waterproof textiles, electrical insulation, and printing ink. Family: Spurge (Euphorbiaceae); genus and species, *Aleurities fordii* (semitropical) and *A. montana* (more cold-resistant).

TUPELO, or pepperidge, or sour gum, any of different kinds of small, water-loving trees native to India, eastern Asia, and North America, growing to 40 to 60 feet, with drooping lower branches, leathery simple leaves, and clusters of separate staminate and pistillate flowers on the same tree. The fruits are red, blue, or purple. Like the cherry, they have a central seed in a fleshy pulp. Both the cottongum or water tupelo (*Nyssa aquatica*), and the black gum (*N. sylvatica*) produce useful timber, and are often grown in parks for their brilliant red autumn foliage. Family: Dogwood (Cornaceae); genus *Nyssa*.

TURNIP. See *Mustard*.

UMBRELLA PLANT. See *Papyrus*.

VALERIAN, any of about 200 different sun-loving, hardy, perennial herbs of cool and alpine regions in the Northern Hemisphere, with thick, strong-scented roots and underground stems, simple or delicate pinnately compound leaves, and luxuriant clusters of tiny, sweet-smelling, pink, lavender, or white flowers. Common valerian *(Valeriana officinalis)*, often called garden heliotrope, is frequently grown in the New World and the Old as a border plant. Its dried roots and underground stems yield a valuable drug used in nervous disorders. Unrelated plants with blue, cuplike flowers and showy foliage (genus *Polemonium* of the family Polemoniaceae) are often called Greek valerian or Jacob's ladder. Family: Valerian (Valerianaceae); genus *Valeriana*.

VALERIAN FAMILY (Valerianaceae), a group of about 370 species in 10 genera, chiefly of the North Temperate Zone and high elevations in the Andes. Most are herbs, usually with a 5-parted corolla, the calyx often developing later as a bristly appendage to the small dry seed. See *Spikenard* and *Valerian*.

VANILLA. See *Orchid Family*.

VEGETABLE SPONGE, or dishcloth gourd, or Loofah, a tropical vine with large, coarse leaves, yellow, bell-shaped flowers, and a slender fruit, 10 to 40 inches long, with a fibrous skeleton through the pulp. Although the fruit rind is edible, the fibrous portion is commonly saved, washed, and used as a sponge or in the preparation of cloth and hats. Family: Gourd (Cucurbitaceae); genus and species, *Luffa cylindrica*.

VENUS'S–FLYTRAP, a low-growing, insectivorous plant of North and South Carolina, displaying a rosette of shiny, green leaves with winged stalks and bilobed blades. The blades are edged with long, coarse projections and the upper surface of each lobe is armed with 3 sensitive bristles. If these are agitated, as by an insect crawling over them, the 2 lobes of the leaf fold abruptly and the long projections fit together, forming a cage.

Slowly the plant brings the leaf surfaces against the insect, secretes digestive juices, and absorbs the products of digestion. After closing without catching an insect, or after absorption is complete, the leaf blades spread apart, ready to act as a trap again. Mature plants send up a slender, vertical stalk to 7 inches high, with a cluster of white flowers at the top. Family: Sundew (Droseraceae); genus and species, *Dionaea muscipula*.

VERBENA, a genus of herbaceous plants native to temperate and tropical regions of both hemispheres, with about 230 species, bearing opposite leaves and spikes of flowers all through the summer. A few kinds, such as Eurasian vervain *(V. officinalis)*, have been introduced and grown in North America; it has branching, smooth stems and purple flower spikes.

Horticultural verbena hybrids include the sweet-scented verbena (referred to as *V. hybrida*). European moss verbena *(V. erinoides)* is often grown in hanging baskets. A related plant is the lemon verbena *(Lippia citriodora)* native to South America and cultivated in North America and Europe for the lemon fragrance of its leaves and its large pyramidal clusters

BURPEE SEEDS

WALLFLOWER

of flowers, which are smaller than those of true verbenas. Family: Vervain (Verbenaceae).

VERONICA, or speedwell, a genus of about 150 different species of small, herbaceous plants native to the North Temperate Zone, mostly with opposite, simple leaves on creeping or erect stems, and spikes of small, wheel-shaped, blue flowers. All contain large amounts of vitamin C, and some can be cooked as potherbs. One, called American brooklime *(V. americana)* because it grows along stream edges, has been recommended as a preventative for scurvy. Family: Figwort (Scrophulariaceae).

VETCH, any of about 150 different kinds of prostrate and climbing perennial herbs native to the Northern Hemisphere and temperate South America, with pinnately compound leaves often extended at the tip into tendrils, white or purple, pealike blossoms in short or solitary spikes, and a compressed pod from each flower.

The narrow-leaved, common vetch *(Vicia sativa)* of Europe and the British Isles, and the hairy or winter vetch *(V. villosa)* of eastern Europe are among those that have been widely introduced and become widespread in most temperate climates, sometimes planted and plowed under as a green manure, and often harvested as forage for livestock. Family: Pea (Leguminosae); genus *Vicia*.

VIBURNUM, a genus of shrubs and small trees native to temperate and subtropical regions, especially of Asia and North America, with simple leaves and clusters of white or pink flowers followed by fleshy fruits, usually red or black, for which the plants are sometimes called "wild raisins." The Eurasian guelderrose *(V. opulus)*, which has spherical flower clusters instead of flat-topped ones, has been developed into a widely cultivated ornamental shrub, the snowball bush

(V. o. roseum), which must be propagated by cuttings because its large flowers are sterile. Tree viburnums 15 to 30 feet tall include the nannyberry or sweet viburnum *(V. lentago)*, of eastern North America, and the twistwood or wayfaring tree *(V. lantana)*, native to Europe but introduced and widespread in the New World. Family: Honeysuckle (Caprifoliaceae).

VIOLET, any of about 400 small, herbaceous plants native to the North Temperate Zone, mountains in tropical Latin America, and tropical and southern Africa. They grow best in moist places, spreading oval or heart-shaped leaves on long stalks, and raising irregular, 5-petalled flowers on individual, long stalks; one long-spurred petal contains the nectar.

The widely cultivated perennial pansies, with flowers of many colors and patterns resembling human faces, have been developed by horticulturists from the wild European violet *(V. tricolor)* known as heart's-ease. Pansies escape from cultivation into lawns and wild areas, their flowers shrinking in size; the plant is then known as a Johnny-jump-up. A majority of violets have purple flowers; indeed, the flower gives its name to the color purple. Family: Violet (Violaceae); genus *Viola*.

VIRGINIA CREEPER. See *Boston Ivy*.

WAKE–ROBIN. See *Trillium*.

WALKING FERN, or walking leaf, a small fern native to eastern North America, with simple, lance-shaped, leathery, evergreen leaves tapering to slender, elongated tips, which droop down to the earth and take root, starting new plants. The base of each leaf is heart-shaped, and the spore cases are irregularly scattered on both sides of the midrib over the under surface of the blade. Family: Polypody (Polypodiaceae); genus and species, *Camptosorus rhizophyllus*.

WALLFLOWER, or gillyflower, a tall, herbaceous plant native to eastern Mediterranean countries, often cultivated in gardens as an ornament behind the flower bed or on the wall. The wild plant has yellow flowers with 4 petals, but horticultural varieties in many pastel shades have been developed. Family: Mustard (Cruciferae); genus and species, *Cheirinia cheiri*.

WALNUT, any of 15 different kinds of tall timber trees native to the Old World and the New, growing to 70 or 150 feet, with large, pinnately compound leaves; tiny, staminate and pistillate green flowers borne on the same tree; and usually, spherical, hard-shelled seeds enclosed in a leathery or fibrous husk. The commercial nuts, called walnuts, are from the Circassian or Persian walnut tree *(Juglans regia)*, native to western Asia from Iran to India, but much cultivated in England and known there as the English walnut; its seeds are particularly sweet and large, and its hard, gray-brown, mottled wood warps so rarely that it is prized for furniture-making.

The Black walnut (*J. nigra*) of the eastern United States is equally valuable for fine timber, but its seeds have a stronger flavor. Butternut (*J. cinerea*) of the eastern United States is less valuable, with smaller fruits that are oblong, pointed, and contain an oil from which a stain for dyeing homespun woolens was made in colonial days.

The California walnut (*J. californica*) is frequently used in walnut orchards of the western United States as the best root upon which to graft fruit-bearing branches of the Persian walnut; the trees are then called California budded walnuts. Family: Walnut (Juglandaceae); genus *Juglans*.

WALNUT FAMILY (Juglandaceae), a small group of about 60 species in 6 genera, all deciduous shrubs or trees with alternate, pinnately-compound leaves. The staminate flowers grow in catkins and the solitary, pistillate flowers mature into a hard shell around the seed that is enclosed by a leathery or fibrous husk. See *Hickory* and *Walnut*.

WATER CHESTNUT, or horn-nut, or water caltrop, an aquatic herb native to tropical Eurasia, with mottled, oval, floating, feathery, underwater leaves and spongy stalks. The small, white flowers are raised above the water surface, and produce large, horned, or spiny fruits with a thin shell that encloses a sweet, edible seed. In the Orient these seeds are roasted or eaten raw, whereas in Mediterranean countries they are ground into a flour. Family: Water chestnut (Hydrocaryaceae); genus and species, *Trapa natans*.

WATERCRESS. See *Cress*.

WATER LILY, any of several related kinds of aquatic plants native to ponds and shallow, slow-moving streams of many parts of the world. The fleshy stems grow in the bottom sediments of the marshes and produce flat, padlike leaves on long, slender stalks. The leaves float on the water's surface; the shiny green upper surface of the leaf is normally dry while the bottom is wet. Some leaves extend their flowers into the air, while others allow the flowers to float with them on the water's surface.

The yellow pond lily (*Nuphar advena*) of the eastern United States and Canada has almost spherical flowers. The yellow parts are sepals; the petals are tiny and usually overlooked. More fragrant is the white water lily (*Nymphaea odorata*) of the same region, with almost indistinguishable white sepals, and white petals that open widely, displaying the yellow stamens. The giant among water lilies is the *Victoria regia*, with leaves to 6 feet across that are turned up at the edges and prickly beneath; it is native to the Amazon valley and northeastern South America. Family: Waterlily (Nymphaeaceae).

WATER-LILY FAMILY (Nymphaeaceae), a small group of about 90 species in 8 genera, widely distributed in shallow, fresh waters. Aquarium fanciers often provide extra oxygen and food for their fish by cultivating fish grass (*Cabomba* species), native to tropical America, which has brushlike, green stems of finely divided leaves and g r o w s completely submerged; or water shield (*Brasenia schreberi*), which has floating leaves on long stalks that come to the center of the under surface of the leaf. See *Lotus* and *Water lily*.

WATERMELON. See *Melon*.

WATER PLANTAIN, any of 6 different marsh plants of temperate regions, with fleshy stems growing in the bottom sediments of the marshes, and long-stalked leaves differing in shape according to the depth of the water in which they grow. Those that are submerged are generally grasslike; those that emerge from the water into the air are oval or lance-shaped and pointed at the tip; and those on the shore are more heart-shaped.

Submerged plants rarely open their flowers, which are self-pollinating; on the other hand those that grow in the air have small clusters of white or purple flowers that are visited by insects. Family: Water-plantain (Alismataceae); genus *Alisma*.

WATER-PLANTAIN, FAMILY (Alismataceae), a small group of about 75 species in 14 genera, widely distributed, found mostly in wet ground or shallow, fresh water, and most common in the Northern Hemisphere. See *Arrowhead* and *Waterplantain*.

WATTLE TREE, any of several different kinds of low branching trees native to Australia, with pinnately compound leaves and clusters of bright yellow flowers. Young saplings are easily bent and are used for making fences and primitive dwellings. The common wattle (*Acacia longifolia*) is the national flower of Australia. Family: Pea (Leguminosae); genus *Acacia*.

WAX FLOWER, a climbing, evergreen, perennial plant native to southern China, with stiff, cylindrical stems, leathery, shiny, oval leaves, and clusters of pink, fragrant flowers, from which a copious and sweet nectar often drips. Cultivated indoors in temperate climates or outdoors where frost is rare, it is usually propagated by cuttings and requires much water. Family: Milkweed (Asclepiadaceae); genus and species, *Hoya carnosa*.

WAYFARING TREE. See *Viburnum*.

WHEAT, an annual grass native to central Asia and southern Europe, cultivated since prehistoric times for its cereal grains, and now one of the world's chief crops. It has tall, slender stems, ribbonlike leaves, and bearded, terminal clusters of flowers that mature into heads of grain. Wheat contains more gluten than many other cereal grains, and is especially suited for making into bread flour.

Spring wheat, planted in the spring and harvested in early summer, is grown in the northern United States, Canada, and other cold temperate regions. Winter wheat, planted in the fall and harvested late in the following spring, is preferred in warmer regions. Durum wheat has particularly hard, starchy grains, and yields semolina flour, which serves as the basis for most macaroni products. Family: Grass (Gramineae); genus *Triticum*, particularly the species *T. sativum*.

WILLOW, any of about 300 different kinds of fast-growing shrubs and trees with simple, narrow leaves and flowers in catkins; the pistillate flowers mature as loose capsules with numerous hairy seeds. Willows are found throughout t h e w o r l d—as creeping perennials between boulders in the Arctic and on high mountains, and as 100-foot trees along streams and in wet soil in warmer countries.

The young branches of many willows are used in making baskets and wicker furniture. These branches are called osiers. They take their name from a European basket willow (*Salix viminalis*).

One of the largest species is the black willow (*S. nigra*) of eastern North America. Weeping willow (*S. babylonica*), native to China, is popular as an ornamental tree because of its gracefully a r c h i n g, drooping branches. Pussy willows (chiefly the eastern North American *S. discolor* and *S. humilis*) have gray, furry catkins that open in early spring before the leaves appear, generally after dropping their stiff, shiny brown bud scales on the snow. Family: Willow (Salicaceae); genus *Salix*.

WILLOW FAMILY (Salicaceae), a group of about 340 species in two genera, widely distributed, but most numerous in the North Temperate Zone and the Arctic. See *Poplar* and *Willow*.

WINTERGREEN, either of 2 unrelated types of evergreen plants with shiny, leathery leaves; one is native to heaths and northern woodlands in both the Old World and the New, and the other is characteristic of similar places in the eastern part of North America. The original wintergreens, members of genera *Chimaphila* and *Pyrola* of the pyrola family (Pyrolaceae), were so named before the discovery of America, and are known in the New World as "false wintergreens" to distinguish them from "true wintergreen" or checkerberry (*Gaultheria procumbens* of the heath family, Ericaceae).

Wintergreen oil, used medicinally or as a flavoring, can be obtained from the leaves of *Gaultheria* or made synthetically. The leaves, the white, waxy flowers in small clusters, and the brilliant red berries all have the same pleasant flavor.

WISTERIA, or *wistaria*, a genus consisting of 6 species of climbing, woody vines native to eastern Asia and eastern North America, with pinnately compound leaves and handsome clusters of pea-shaped, white or lavender flowers. In horticultural varieties of the Chinese (*W. chinensis*) and

Japanese (*W. floribunda*) wistaria, the flower clusters range from 1 to 5 feet in length, and the pods that follow the flowers are hairy. In the shrubby species native to southeastern United States (*W. frutescens* and *W. macrostachya*), the clusters are smaller and more fragrant, the pods bare. Family: Pea (Leguminosae).

WITCH HAZEL, any of 6 different kinds of shrubs or trees native to eastern Asia and eastern North America, with alternate, simple leaves, and fragrant, yellow flowers with long, twisted, narrow petals that open in late autumn and sometimes again in early spring.

The fertilized ovules, enclosed by the hairy ovary wall, develop in the spring amid a mucilaginous material that becomes compressed as the fruit dries. Eventually the tip of the fruit opens and the brown seeds are shot out explosively for many feet. The astringent extract from the leaves and scaly bark is used in lotions and medicines. Family: Witch hazel (Hamamelidaceae); genus *Hamamelis*.

WITCH-HAZEL FAMILY (Hamamelidaceae), a group of about 100 species in 23 genera, all trees or shrubs with alternate simple leaves, chiefly Asiatic but found also in eastern North America, Africa, and Australia. See *Sweet gum* and *Witch hazel*.

WOLFSBANE. See *Aconite*.

WOODBINE, a common name given to several different, unrelated, climbing plants with tough stems that tend to tie together the bushes and trees upon which they grow.

They include the Virginia creeper (*Parthenocissus quinquefolia*) of the grape family, (Vitaceae); the common woodbine (*Lonicera periclymenum*) and Italian woodbine (*L. caprifolium*) of the honeysuckle family (Caprifoliaceae); and the virgin's-bower (*Clematis virginiana*), native to eastern North America and a member of the buttercup family (Ranunculaceae). See *Boston ivy* and *Clematis*.

WOOD SORREL. See *Oxalis*.

WORMWOOD, a coarse, perennial herb native to southern Europe and central Asia, with hairy, branching stems growing to 3 feet from a thick, subterranean branching stem. The twice or thrice pinnately compound leaves growing low on the stem have long stalks, whereas those higher up have short stalks. Several small heads of yellow flowers develop on each wormwood plant.

Once cultivated in Eurasia and introduced into North America, wormwood is generally regarded as a historically interesting weed, for a dark green, bitter oil extracted from it gave much of the flavor to absinthe and various tonics. Family: Daisy (Compositae); genus and species, *Artemisia absinthium*.

YAM FAMILY (Dioscoreaceae), a group of about 650 different species in 10 genera, mostly plants of warm, temperate, and tropical regions with her-

T.H. EVERETT

WITCH HAZEL

baceous or woody climbing stems, large, net-veined leaves, and clusters of small, inconspicuous flowers followed by a fleshy berry or a dry capsule.

Most useful to man are members of the large genus *Dioscorea*, which have thick, starchy, underground stems or tubers worth cultivating for food. The edible parts of the common white yam (*D. alata*) grow to a length of 8 feet, weigh 30 to 100 pounds, and are made edible by roasting or boiling. In the United States the name yam is sometimes applied incorrectly to some varieties of the unrelated cultivated sweet potato.

YARROW, a milfoil, a herbaceous perennial, native to Europe but now widespread as a weed found on roadsides and in fields, bearing finely-divided leaves that have a pleasant aromatic fragrance and upright stems terminating in a flat-topped cluster of small, white or (rarely) pink flowers.

The name milfoil refers to the thousands of fine divisions on each soft leaf of the yarrow. Family: Daisy (Compositae); genus and species, *Achillea millefolium*.

YELLOWWOOD, a branching tree native to the central and southern United States, from 40 to 60 feet tall, with pinnately compound leaves that turn yellow in autumn. The tree has brittle, yellow wood from which a dye can be extracted, and long sprays of sweet-smelling, white flowers. It is sometimes known as gopherwood. Family: Pea (Leguminosae); genus and species, *Cladastris lutea*.

YEW, any of about 9 different kinds of shrubs and small trees native to the Northern Hemisphere, with evergreen needles more or less borne in 2 ranks along the outstretched branches. The seeds are dry or nutlike, surrounded except at their tips by a soft, fleshy, colorful enlargement of the tip of the flower stalk. English yew (*Taxus baccata*) has tough, flexible wood, and

was formerly important in the construction of bows for archery. Western yew (*T. brevifolia*) of the Pacific coast of North America is a relatively scarce, medium-sized tree with fine-grained wood valuable in cabinet-making and for canoe paddles. Ground-hemlock (*T. canadensis*), a shrub of thickets in east-central North America, is often used decoratively around buildings and for making wreaths.

The foliage, bark, and seeds of all yews contan poisonous substances; English yew, in fact, is regarded as the most poisonous plant in Britain. Cattle will eat yew branches if given an opportunity, and children may be harmed if they swallow yew seeds while sampling the attractive, red, fruitlike covering. Family: Yew (Taxaceae); genus *Taxus*.

YUCA. See *Cassava*.

YUCCA, a genus of perennial plants native to southern North America and Central America, with a woody stem bearing a dense whorl of long, pointed, swordlike leaves, and majestic clusters of waxy, ivory-white flowers with a sticky pollen that is distributed only by certain small moths (*Pronuba yucca*).

A spirelike yucca (*Y. filamentosa*) of the eastern United States is called Adam's needle. A branching species (*Y. brevifolia*) of the southwestern states, which grows to 20 to 30 feet, is known as the Joshua tree. New Mexico has chosen the Spanish bayonet (*Y. gloriosa*) as its state flower. Other species of the genus are known as Spanish dagger, beargrass, and candle-of-God. Family: Lily (Liliaceae).

ZINNIA, a genus of 12 different species of herbaceous plants native to southern North America, with opposite leaves lacking stalks, and handsome, terminal heads of daisy-like flowers. The common cultivated zinnias of gardens are horticultural varieties of the species *Z. elegans*, introduced from Mexico. Family: Daisy (Compositae).

BIBLIOGRAPHY

Bold, Harold Charles. *Morphology of Plants*. Harper & Bros., 1957.

Bold, Harold Charles. *The Plant Kingdom*. Prentice-Hall, Inc., 1960.

Muller, Walter Henry. *Botany: A Functional Approach*. The Macmillan Co., 1963.

Northern, H. T. *Introductory Plant Science*. The Ronald Press Co., 1958.

Schery, Robert W. *Plants for Man*. Prentice-Hall, Inc., 1952.

Selsam, Millicent. *Plants That Move*. William Morrow, Inc., 1962.

Sinnott, Edmond Wape. *Botany: Principles and Problems*. McGraw-Hill, Inc., 1963.

Wilson, Carl Lewis and Walter E. Loomis, *Botany*. Holt, Rinehart & Winston, Inc., 1962.

VOLUME TWENTY ONE

RECREATION

Activities 1703
Associations 1742

ARTHUR FREED

Recreation

ACTIVITIES

Recreation is a basic human need; it is a spontaneous expression of childhood and a necessary relaxation for the well-poised adult. The need for play has long been recognized. One of the most lucid statements of the principles of recreation was set forth by Howard Braucher, Secretary of the National Recreation Association; the following principles are particularly noteworthy:

Every child needs to be exposed to the growth-giving activities that have brought satisfaction through the ages—to climbing, chasing, tumbling; to tramping, swimming, dancing, skating, ball games; to singing, playing musical instruments, dramatizing; to making things with his hands, to working with sticks and stones and sand and water; to building and modeling; to caring for pets; to gardening; to nature; to trying simple scientific experiments; to learning team play, group activity and adventure, comradeship in doing things with others.

Every child needs to discover which activities give him personal satisfaction. In these activities he should be helped to develop the essential skills. Several of these activities should be of such a nature that he can keep them up in adult life.

Every man should have certain forms of recreation which require little space and which can be fitted into small fragments of time.

Every man needs to know well a certain limited number of indoor and outdoor games which he himself likes so that there will never be an occasion when he cannot think of anything to do. . . .

. . . Those recreation activities are most important which most completely command the individual so that he loses himself in them and gives all that he has and is to them. . . .

. . . The happy play of childhood is essential to normal growth. Normal men are most likely to grow from the children who have played well and happily. Normal men more easily continue normal as they keep up childhood habits of play.

The means of recreation given in the following pages include those that are *educative,* training brain and muscle to act quickly and accurately; *recreative,* tending to produce relaxation from care; *corrective,* restoring balance and poise to overwrought bodies; and *hygienic,* stirring the sluggish organs of the body so they will better perform their functions.

Athletics have been popular in the United States since Colonial days, but they received a great impetus in the 1850s, '60s and '70s through the establishment of intercollegiate meets. This interest led to the formation in 1875 of the Intercollegiate Association of Amateur Athletes of America (known as the "I.C.4A.'s"); in 1879 the National Association of Amateur Athletes of America was formed; and

in 1888 the Amateur Athletic Union of the United States. The control of athletic events has since been distributed among many associations: *local* elementary and high *school* groups; *intercollegiate* conferences (particularly the National Collegiate Athletic Association) with a *regional* or *national* range; and the Y.M.C.A. and similar organizations, *national* groups with the Amateur Athletic Union as the major governing body. The major body with *international* scope is the American Olympic Association with 79 member bodies. In 1937 the Amateur Athletic Union and the National Collegiate Athletic Association were allowed six members each on the governing committee of the American Olympic Association.

Members of the A.A.U. and the I.C.4A. are all amateurs, and the two bodies have similar rules defining amateur standing, which differs primarily from professional standing in the professional's acceptance of money for services as a player or coach. The A.A.U. rules on all sports except tennis, golf, rowing, football and outdoor baseball, which have their individual governing bodies. Amateur standing is closely scrutinized in these sports also, but *open* tournaments, as in golf, are often held, in which both amateur and professional entrants may compete. The Olympic games and other international championship meets specify that all contestants be sworn amateurs.

ANGLING

(Intermediate Grades to Adults)

Angling is the art of catching fish with a rod, line and bait as a recreation; it is termed *angling* in contrast to *fishing,* which is a commercial occupation. There are two branches of the sport—angling in fresh water and angling in the sea.

The boy with a crooked stick, a length of twine, a bent pin and an angleworm probably gets as great a thrill from angling as does the older person with elaborate equipment. The latter attends carefully to the selection of his rod, of which there are several approved varieties. The favorite is of steel or of split bamboo, in three pieces, which may be securely joined into one length when in use. Whether of wood, bamboo or steel, the forms do not vary; an inch or more in diameter at the butt, they taper to a point and possess the property of elasticity to a high degree.

Lines are of finely braided silk or twisted linen threads. To protect them against sizable fish, next above the hook is a strand of gut, which the fish cannot sever by biting. The

line is wound upon a reel that is clamped to the handle of the rod through eyelets. The hook is of finely tempered steel; a good hook will not bend but will remain rigid against stress.

To lure different kinds of fish, a variety of bait is recommended. Bass are caught with minnows, small frogs and crawfish; trout are attracted to minnows, grasshoppers and worms. Artificial bait (*flies*) consists of brightly colored pieces of feathers, fur, wool and so on, held together by thread, wax and the like and fastened close to the hook.

After the rod has been used, it should be wiped with a dry rag and gone over again with an oily cloth. If the rod is put away while wet, it may mildew and the glue will be so softened that the rod may soon be ruined.

For the protection of the fish supply in most states there are closed seasons of the year when it is unlawful to fish for one or more varieties. In practically every state angling is declared illegal during the spawning season.

Angling becomes a competitive group sport by means of casting contests for accuracy and distance.

AQUAPLANING

(Senior High School and Adults)

An aquaplane is a narrow raft, light in weight, about 8 feet in length and less than 3 feet in width. Three ropes are attached to the front. One, from 20 to 30 feet in length, is fastened to the stern of a swift motor boat; two short ropes, made secure at the extreme ends of the front, are grasped by the rider to assist in maintaining equilibrium.

The sport of aquaplaning consists of standing erect on the aquaplane, grasping the two ropes firmly for support and riding atop the water at a rapid rate behind the motor boat that furnishes the power. As the rider is quite likely to lose his footing and be pitched headlong into the water, only good swimmers should attempt to ride unless the route is in very shallow water.

ARCHERY

(Late Elementary School to Adults)

Archery is a recreation that consists of shooting at a target with a bow and arrow and at varying distances. It has never lost its vogue throughout the hundreds of years since the bow and arrow were the equipment of medieval armies.

A bow, arrows, quiver, arm guard or bracer and shooting gloves or finger tips are necessary equipment. The

Drawing The Bow

best wooden bows are still made of yew from Italy, Spain and the northwestern United States. Other satisfactory woods are the American Osage orange, tropical lancewood and lemonwood. Jointed steel bows have been used with enthusiasm since 1927.

The English longbow was usually 5 feet long. The practice now is to have it about equal in height to the bowman. Women's bows are from 5 feet to 5 feet 6 inches and have a pull of 18 to 35 pounds. Men's bows are from 5 feet 8 inches to 6 feet with a pull of 36 to 80 pounds; Boy Scout bows have a pull of 15 pounds.

Like fishing rods, bows are made either solid or spliced and are glued. The one-piece, "self" bow has the pleasanter action, but costs more and is more apt to warp or spring out of shape. Very long bows are likely to be spliced in the middle. The wood is rounded on the inside, toward the string and flattened on the other side.

A target arrow is painstakingly made, with a main shaft of Norway pine, cedar or spruce and a piece of hardwood to carry the metallic head. A square notch is cut at the base for the string, and just forward of the notch three feather guides are attached, either by glue, silk winding or a celluloid coating. If these feathers curve, it is important that they all curve in the same direction. Cadmium-plated arrows with feathers affixed by celluloid also are used successfully.

The string of the bow is made of flax or linen, silk-wound to prevent abrasion by the arrow nock and carefully waxed or glued.

Targets for the modern sport or archery, made of solidly pressed straw or of cork, are 4 feet in diameter, with a series of concentric rings 4⅘ inches broad. Each ring has a value that determines the scoring: inner

circle (gold), 9 points; inner ring (red), 7 points; next ring (blue), 5 points; next ring (black), 3 points; outer ring (white), 1 point. The bull's eye is 4 feet from the ground and the target is tipped back at the top.

The course for women is 60 yards long with shooting lines 50, 40 and 30 yards from the target; the field for men is 100 yards in length, with the lines at 80, 60, 50 and 40 yards from the target.

The archer with the largest total score wins a tournament unless there is a tie, when the archer with the largest total score at the longest range would be the winner.

Archery courses may be installed economically in basements, attics or gymnasiums, and there should be a backstop for the target of bales of straw or felt. If the range is to be less than the regulation, the target would be made correspondingly smaller—a 2-foot target is correct for a field of 15 yards.

BADMINTON

(Junior High School to Adults)

Badminton is a comparatively new game in America, but is becoming popular because of its close relationship to tennis. It is an especially desirable game for younger children who like tennis; tennis rackets are too heavy for them, while the badminton racket is very light, and the game is less strenuous.

Badminton can be played indoors or outdoors upon a court with a net whose top is 5 feet from the floor or ground. The doubles court is 20 feet wide by 44 feet long. On each side of the net there is a 6-foot service line and back of that two 13-foot courts, one on either side, and the back boundary line is 2½ feet wide. The singles court is practically the same but does not have a separate back boundary line and is only 17 feet wide.

The racket is similar to that used in tennis but much lighter, and the handle is longer, resembling a squash racket. A shuttle consisting of a weighted cork with a row of feather is used instead of a ball.

The object of the game is to make returns before the shuttle touches the ground. This makes the game interesting and very fast. As the shuttle is struck with a racket it goes swiftly for a short distance and then slows down suddenly. It requires accurate judgment to cope with this change of pace. Scoring is similar to that of volleyball and is easy for a beginner to follow. Badminton is an especially desirable game because it does not require expensive courts and high fence protection. The shuttle never goes far, so that time is not lost in retrieving it.

BASEBALL

(Late Elementary School to Adults)

Baseball is a game played by two opposing teams of nine men each, on a field marked in the form of a square, with a plate called a *base* at each corner. This field is known as a *diamond* and is 82 feet square for boys under 16 years of age and 90

feet square for players over 16. The participants on each side are a pitcher, catcher, first baseman, second baseman, third baseman, shortstop, right fielder, center fielder and left fielder. An umpire is chosen to rule on each play and have full authority to decide any controversy.

The object of the game is to make as many runs as possible, that is, make circuits of the four bases as a result of hits by an individual batter or other members of his team. The members of each team bat in turn according to the manager's schedule.

The opposing team in the field, the *outs,* employ various accepted methods of *putting out* the batters or base runners, so that they may take their turn at bat. The team that makes the larger number of runs wins the game; in case of a tie at the end of the ninth inning, the game is continued until one team scores more runs than its opponent in the same number of innings.

A standard game of baseball consists of nine innings. The captain of the home team chooses whether his men shall bat or take the field for the first half of the first inning, but it has become standard practice for him to allow the visiting team to bat first. After three men of the side first at bat have been put out, the teams exchange places and so alternate throughout the game, each half inning continuing until three men have been put out.

The game begins when the fielders of one side have taken their positions and the first batter has come "up" to the home plate.

The pitcher delivers the ball to the batter, and the batter attempts to hit the ball out of reach of the fielders so that he may run the bases. He is allowed three fair opportunities to hit the ball or three *strikes*. One *strike* is called:

1. Whenever the batter swings at a pitched ball and misses.

2. Whenever the ball is legally thrown by the pitcher over the home plate at a height between the batter's knees and shoulders although the batter does not swing at it. The umpire is the final judge of whether a given pitched ball meets these conditions.

3. Whenever a *foul tip* (that is, a ball just grazed by the bat but not deflected above the batter's head) is caught by the catcher.

4. When the batter, on the first or second strike, hits a *foul* (that is, a ball that settles outside the lines running from the home plate to first and third base). Fouls (other than a foul tip held by the catcher or a foul bunt) may be hit on the third strike without penalty.

5. Whenever the ball is *bunted* (that is, not swung at, but met with the bat and tapped slowly) and a foul results. It makes no difference whether the foul bunt occurs on the first, second or third strike.

If the batter does not swing at a pitched ball and if, in the judgment of the umpire, the ball does not pass fairly over the plate between the batter's knees and shoulders, a *ball* is called. The batter is permitted to take first base if four *balls* are thrown before three *strikes*.

Becoming a Base Runner.—A man at bat, standing at the home base (or home plate), becomes a base runner:

1. If he makes a fair hit (not a foul) by intercepting a pitched ball with his bat and knocking it into *fair* territory within the diamond or within lines that are left and right extensions of the diamond.

2. If the umpire calls *four balls* on the pitcher.

3. If a third strike called by the umpire is not caught and held by the catcher.

4. If the person or clothing of the batter is hit by a pitched ball at which he does not swing and which he makes a reasonable effort to avoid.

5. If the catcher interferes with his attempt to bat.

6. If a fair-hit ball touches the person or clothing of an umpire or base runner before touching a fielder.

Advancing a Base.—A runner may advance from first or any base whenever he can touch the next plate before the ball can intercept him. If two men claim the same base as the result of one hit or pass to base succeeding another, the first runner is forced to advance to the next base. The runner may also advance a base if he is blocked from a base by a fielder who is trying to catch the batted ball or if the umpire calls a balk. A move out of position by the catcher for an intentional base on balls allows the runner to advance a base; also an illegal stop or catch by a fielder permits the runner to advance. He is further entitled to a base if the pitched ball passes the catcher and hits a building or fence within 60 feet.

Putting Out.—A player is declared *out* in any one of 20 cases, the commonest being these:

1. If he bats either a foul or a fair hit that is caught by an opponent before the ball touches the ground. (Except a foul tip caught by the catcher, which counts only as a strike.)

2. If, while he is a batter, three strikes are called on him.

3. If, while he is a base runner, he is touched by a ball in the hands of an opponent, unless some part of the runner's person is in contact with a base to which he is entitled.

4. If he is forced by a fair hit or third strike fumbled by the catcher to advance to any base (usually first base) and the ball is fielded and held by an opposing player in contact with that base before the runner reaches it.

5. If he interferes with a player attempting to field a batted ball.

6. If, while he is running bases, he runs more than 3 feet from the base line to escape being tagged by an opposing fielder with the ball, except to avoid an opponent who is fielding a batted ball. But a player is permitted to overrun first base and may not be touched out while returning.

7. If, after a fair or foul fly ball is caught, the ball is held by a fielder in contact with any base occupied by a base runner at the time the ball is batted before the base runner retouches such base after the catch. A

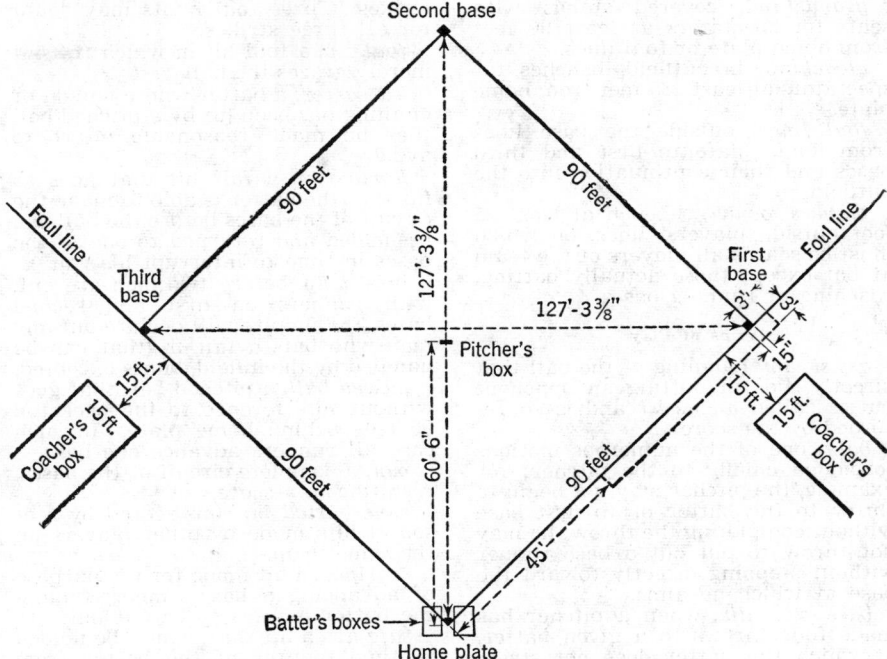

Diagram of a Baseball Diamond

base runner is said to occupy a base up to the instant he touches the next base.

Three *outs* are permitted to each team in each inning. After three players have been put out, the team at bat is retired for that inning, and the fielding team becomes the batting team. Any runners who may be on base at the time the third out is made lose their advanced positions; each inning begins with all of the bases clear.

A run is scored every time a base runner legally touches the home plate before three men are put out, except that a run cannot be scored on the third out if the batter is put out before reaching first base or if the third out is the result of a *force play,* that is, the touching of a base by a fielder with the ball before the base is reached by a base runner forced to advance to it by a fair hit by the batter.

Materials

official ball, Reach or Spalding, cork center, yarn wound, horsehide cover, 9 to 9¼ inches circumference, 5 to 5¼ ounces.

bat, hardwood, round, tapering, diameter not over 2¾ inches, not over 42 inches long.

catcher's or first baseman's glove, any size, shape or weight.

all other gloves, weight not over 10 ounces, size not over 14 inches around palm.

protector, a padded or air-filled shield as breastplates for the bodies of umpire and catcher.

mask, a wire headgear for catcher and umpire stationed behind the bat, especially to protect against foul tips.

leg guard, a lower defensive armor for umpire and catcher.

base, stuffed white canvas bag, 15 inches square, attached by its center

at intersection of base lines for first, second and third bases.

home plate, five-sided white rubber plate. Front 17 inches, side 8½ inches, running along base lines 12 inches each.

pitcher's plate, white rubber, 24×6 inches, located 60 feet 6 inches from the home plate. For boys under 16 the pitcher's box is 50 feet from the home plate.

toe plate, heel plate, spiked to prevent slipping.

Grounds

diamond or infield, a square, 90 feet on a side, within or near which the pitcher, catcher, basemen and shortstop play their defensive game against the batsmen and base runners of the opposing team.

outfield, the clear space beyond first, second and third bases, in which the three fielders work. The outfield should extend at least 235 feet from the home plate.

pitcher's box, a position for the pitcher, in which one or both of the pitcher's feet are touching the pitcher's plate.

catcher's box, a triangular space 10 feet deep, behind the home plate.

batter's box, a rectangle 4 × 6 feet, at right and left of home plate, 6 inches from the plate.

player's lines, enclosed rectangles 50 × 75 feet along base lines each side of home plate, to be kept clear of all players not actually engaged in the game.

coachers' lines, outside the diamond, 15 feet from the foul line and parallel to it, near first and third bases, beyond the players' lines. One coacher may work along this line at first and one at third, but never within the line.

backstop, a large upright frame covered with wire netting, at least 90 feet behind home plate.

grandstand, covered stands with seats for spectators at least 90 feet from home plate or foul lines.

bleachers, in outfield, benches for spectators at least 235 feet from home plate.

foul lines, outside the base lines from home plate to first and third bases and their continuation into the outfield.

players' bench, a bench at least 25 feet outside players' lines, on which must be seated all players of the team at bat except those actually batting, coaching or running bases.

Terms of Play

assist, any handling of the ball that directly aids in putting an opponent out is called *an assist* and is so recorded by the scorer.

balk, one of the numerous motions forbidden chiefly to the pitcher; for example, the pitcher may not begin to throw to the batter or to first base without completing the throw; he may not throw to put out a base runner without stepping directly toward the base at which he aims.

base on balls, when a pitcher has made four throws to a given batter, at which the batter does not strike and which do not pass over any part of the home plate, the batter is entitled to become a base runner at first base.

base runner, a player who has ceased to be a batter and is on his way around the diamond in an attempt to score.

batting order, a regular arrangement of player's names for succession in batting. Batting order cannot be changed during a game, except by the use of substitutes. When a player is succeeded by a substitute, he cannot re-enter the game.

blocked ball, a ball that, while in play, touches any person not in the game. In case of a blocked ball, the players running bases may advance until the ball is again in the pitcher's hands.

bunt, bunt hit, a form of batting in which the ball strikes the bat, which remains horizontal in the batter's hands. A bunted ball is commonly a sacrifice (see below), though a swift runner with a quick getaway may sometimes "beat out" a well-placed bunt, especially if there is indecision among the fielders as to who shall field the bunted ball. A bunted foul counts as a strike, even though it is a third strike.

called game, a game terminated by the umpire because of rain, panic, fire, darkness or any other cause that might endanger or seriously inconvenience players or spectators. Games thus ended before the fifth inning is completed are commonly called *no game;* if five innings have been played, and the game is stopped, the score at the conclusion of the last inning is considered the final score.

caught stealing, the putting out of a base runner who is trying to make a base on the sly.

chance, the opportunity of a fielder to field a ball in such manner as to assist in retiring a base runner.

foul strike, fouls count toward the first two of a batter's three possible strikes. Three foul bunts may count for all three strikes.

foul tip, a foul hit in which the bat merely grazes the ball.

hit batter, a batter whose person or clothing has been hit by a pitched ball that he made reasonable effort to avoid.

home run, a fair hit that goes so far that the batter is able to make the circuit of the bases before the ball can be fielded and returned to one of the bases in time to interrupt his run.

infield fly, before two men are out, with runners on first and second bases, the umpire will declare out any man who bats a fair fly that can be handled by the infield, bunts excepted.

passed ball, a pitched ball that goes without interference to the backstop 90 feet behind home plate. In such case all runners advance one base.

run, a complete circuit of the bases, resulting in a score.

runs batted in, runs scored by reason of hits made by other players on the same team.

sacrifice, a hit made for the purpose of advancing a base runner, though the batter expects to be put out.

safe hit, a hit that cannot be fielded in time to prevent the batter from reaching first base.

shut out, a game in which a team is prevented from making any score.

strike, in general, one of three batting opportunities when the ball is pitched properly over the home plate.

time, temporary suspension of play by the umpire.

wild pitch, a pitched ball so high or wide that it cannot be fielded effectively by the catcher.

double play, triple play, a play in which two or three runners are put out by clever fielding in quick succession.

drawn game, a game with a tie score, called by the umpire after five or more innings.

earned run, scored when a player reaches home base by reason of safe hits, sacrifice hits, stolen bases, bases on balls, wild pitches and balks but not by reason of fielding errors or penalties other than those implied in this list.

error, in general, any misplay in fielding.

extra innings, play that runs beyond the regular nine innings by reason of a tied score.

fair hit, a hit that settles on the foul line or inside the diamond, short of first or third base; a hit that, passing first or third base, bounds on fair territory or first strikes on fair territory.

fly, a ball batted high in fair territory.

forfeited game, a game awarded by the umpire against an offending team by reason of broken rules of play.

foul, foul hit: (1) short of first or third base, a batted ball that settles outside the diamond or would so settle if not interfered with; (2) a batted ball that bounds past first or third base into foul territory; (3) a batted ball that first lands on foul territory beyond first or third base.

The Box Score.—Newspapers publish in compact columns the record of each important baseball game. Below is the score of one of the most famous games in the history of baseball—the final game of the World's Series between the Boston Red Sox (American League) and the New York Giants (National League), at Boston, played October 16, 1912. Several of the greatest players of all time participated—"Christy" Mathewson, pitcher of the famous *fadeaway* drop curve; "Smoky Joe" Wood, speed-ball pitcher; "Tris" Speaker, star outfielder. The game was the eighth of the series (each team had won three games, and one game had been tied), and so great was the popular interest that the hard-fought presidential campaign and the attempted assassination of Theodore Roosevelt in Milwaukee that had occurred a few days earlier were crowded off many front pages to make room for the report. The game ran to 10 innings with the score tied 1 to 1 at the beginning of the 10th. The Giants scored what should have been the winning run in their half of the 10th inning; in the last half of the 10th inning, a pinch hitter, Engle, lifted a fly to center field. Fred Snodgrass, Giant center fielder fumbled the easy catch; and Engle, thus allowed on base, later scored the tying run. The Giant defense became rattled; and Tris Speaker, who should have been put out on an easy foul near first base, drove Engle in with a long single. Snodgrass's error, which was universally blamed for the loss of the game by the Giants, became known as the "$30,000 muff" since this was the amount lost by the Giant players in consequence.

New York (Giants)

	AB.	R.	H.	TB.	PO.	A.	E.
Devore, rf	3	1	1	1	3	1	0
Doyle, 2b	5	0	0	0	1	5	1
Snodgrass, cf	4	0	1	1	4	1	1
Murray, lf	5	1	2	4	3	0	0
Merkel, 1b	5	0	1	1	10	0	0
Herzog, 3b	5	0	2	3	2	1	0
Meyers, c	3	0	0	0	4	1	0
Fletcher, ss	3	0	1	1	2	3	0
Shafer, ss	0	0	0	0	0	0	0
Mathewson, p	4	0	1	1	0	3	0
McCormick*	1	0	0	0	0	0	0
Totals	38	2	9	12	29†	15	2

* Batted for Fletcher in 9th.
† 2 out when winning run scored.

Boston (Red Sox)

	AB.	R.	H.	TB.	PO.	A.	E.
Hooper, rf	5	0	1	1	3	0	0
Yerkes, 2b	4	1	1	1	0	3	0
Speaker, cf	4	0	2	2	2	0	1
Lewis, lf	4	0	0	0	1	0	0
Gardner, 3b	3	0	1	2	1	4	2
Stahl, 1b	4	1	2	3	15	0	1
Wagner, ss	3	0	1	1	3	5	1
Cady, c	4	0	0	0	5	3	0
Bedient, p	2	0	0	0	0	1	0
Wood, p	0	0	0	0	0	0	0
Henriksen*	1	0	1	2	0	0	0
Engle†	1	1	0	0	0	0	0
Totals	35	3	8	11	30	18	5

* Batted for Bedient in 7th.
† Batted for Wood in 10th.

Score by innings:

New York	0	0	1	0	0	0	0	0	0	1—2
Boston	0	0	0	0	0	0	1	0	0	2—3

2 base hits—Murray (2), Herzog, Gardner, Henriksen, Stahl. Sacrifice hit, Meyers. Sacrifice fly, Gardner. Stolen base, Devore. Left on bases, New York 11, Boston 9. Bases on balls, off Bedient 3; off Mathewson 5; off Wood 1. First base on errors, New York 1, Boston 1. Struck out, by Mathewson 4; by Bedient 2; by Wood 2. Time, 2h. 37m. Umpires—At plate O'Laughlin; on bases Rigler; in left field Klein; in right field Evans.

Meaning of Abbreviations.—AB, times at bat; R, runs; H, (safe) hits; TB, total bases made on safe hits (example, a two-base hit and a three-base hit count for five total bases); PO, put-outs; A, assists; E, errors.

In scoring put-outs the player holding the ball at the instant the out is made is credited; thus, the catcher, not the pitcher, is credited with the put-out on a strike-out; the first baseman is credited when the batter is thrown out at first base on a ground hit to the infield. In most scores the total number of put-outs scored by the winning team is 27 (3 in each of 9 innings); the number scored by the losing team is either 24 or 27 depending on whether the winning team took the field first or second in the first inning. If the team entitled to bat second is ahead at the end of the first half of the 9th inning, there is no point in playing the game out, and accordingly only 24 put-outs will ordinarily be made by the winning team. It occasionally happens that an out occurs without a put-out being scored; for example, when a base runner is hit by a batted ball. In such a case the box score usually carries a footnote explaining why the number of put-outs is not 24 or 27.

Times at bat are not counted if the batter receives a base on balls, makes a sacrifice hit or becomes a base runner in consequence of being struck by a pitched ball. It may thus happen that runs may be scored by players whose "times at bat" in the box score is zero.

Batting averages are figured by dividing the number of base hits made by a player by the number of times at bat; in the batting average a home run counts the same as a single or one-base hit. Batting averages are spoken of in terms of the number of hits per thousand times at bat; thus a player who makes 6 hits in 20 times at bat has an average of 6/20 or 300/1000 and is said to bat 300.

BASKETBALL

(Junior High School to Adults)

This most popular of all American indoor games was invented in 1891 by James Naismith, a student at the Springfield, Mass., Y.M.C.A., to fill the need for an active game to bridge the period between fall sports and those of the following spring. It is played on a specially marked court between two opposing teams that endeavour to score the larger number of goals by tossing the ball through the opponents' basket.

Two teams of five men (two forwards, two guards and a center) play for two halves of 20 minutes each, with an intermission of 15 minutes. Women's basketball teams are usually formed of six players with an additional center and observe somewhat different rules of play.

A basketball court is a rectangle with clearly marked sides and end lines with a maximum size 94 feet long and 50 feet wide and a minimum size 74 feet long and 42 feet wide. The court for younger players should be the minimum size.

At the center of each end of the court, a bottomless "basket" of string is suspended 10 feet above the floor from a wire ring 18 inches in diameter, carried by a backboard 4 feet wide and 6 feet long. The ball is an inflated leather bladder 29½ in. minimum to 30 in. maximum in circumference.

Free-throw lines are 24 inches long, directly in front of the baskets, 17 feet from the end lines. Free-throw lines are so marked that no player of either side may come within 3 feet of the ball during its progress from the free-throw line to the basket.

At the center of the court is a circle with a radius of 2 feet. A second concentric circle is drawn with a radius of 6 feet. It is here that the ball is put in play by the referee.

A goal scored from the field in the ordinary course of the game counts two points; a goal secured from the free-throw line as the penalty for a foul committed by opponents counts one point.

Two classes of fouls are distinguished: *Personal fouls* are declared for forbidden roughness in personal contact, for holding a player or blocking his progress. For personal fouls, the penalties range from one free throw to the disqualification of the player for the remainder of the game. Five personal fouls of any sort during a game disqualify the player for the remainder of that game.

Technical fouls are called for other violations of the rules; for example, it is forbidden to *carry* the ball more than one step in any direction; to delay the game, to talk to officials during the game and so on.

To *dribble* is to keep the ball moving, in one player's possession, by throwing, batting, rolling or bounding it on the floor with one hand. A dribble ceases if the ball comes to rest in one or both hands, if it touches both hands at once, or if it touches a second player. The ball may be batted in the air only once during a dribble. A player may throw for goal after dribbling.

The ball is *dead* after a goal is made, or a goal after foul is made; the referee hands the ball to a player of the team against whom the score was made, and from back of the goal line he throws, rolls or bounces it to another player.

A ball becomes dead when it goes out of bounds. The last player who touches it before it leaves the court is held to be the cause of its going out of bounds. The referee commonly designates the nearest opposing player to put the ball in play by throwing, rolling or bounding it to another player in the court.

A ball is *held* when two opposing players have one or both hands on it or when a closely guarded player is held by the referee to be withholding the ball from play. A held ball is dead until put in play by the referee at the spot where held, in the same manner as at the beginning of the game, except that a ball held in either end zone must be thrown out by a member of the defending team.

If the referee is unable to decide who is responsible for a ball going out of bounds, he declares a *jump ball* near the boundary line, two players of his own choosing jumping for it when he tosses it up.

Five charged time-outs may be taken by each team during the game. There is one additional time out allowed for each team for each extra period. More time outs may be taken, but they are counted as technical fouls. It is recommended for younger boys of junior high school age, that the game be divided into four quarters of 6 minutes each, with a 2-minute rest following the first and third quarters and an intermission of 10 minutes between halves.

BOWLING

(Junior High School to Adults)

Bowling is a game played on a long, specially constructed alley; the purpose of the contest is to roll large balls down the alley and knock over as many as possible of the 10 pins at the far end. The alley is very smooth, constructed of boards set on edge, so the balls rolled upon it will move forward as directed without any deviation; it is 42 inches wide and 60 feet long from starting point to the number-one pin. On each side of the alley is a narrow depression to receive balls that are poorly directed and to return them to the player.

The pins are of hardwood and are set at the lower end of the alley in this fashion:

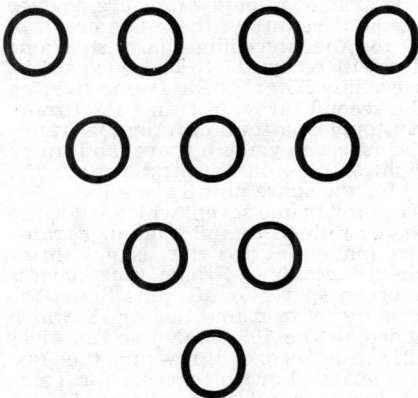

The standard-sized ball is 27 inches in circumference and weighs 16½ pounds; smaller sizes and weights also are available.

A player throws two balls in succession from any distance behind the foul line with the hope of toppling over all 10 pins; if he does it in one throw, he makes a *strike;* if in two throws, a *spare.* If he leaves some pins standing, he is credited with the number of pins downed. If he gets a strike, it counts 10 plus all the pins downed in the next two throws; if he gets a spare, it counts 10 plus the number of pins downed in the next single throw. The score for each two balls constitutes a *frame,* and there are 10 frames to be filled in each game.

When a strike is made, no score is immediately recorded, but a cross is made in the small square set in the corner of the frame, and the result of the frame cannot be put into figures until two more balls are thrown. If a spare is made, a diagonal line is put into the small square, and not until the next ball is rolled can the figure for that frame be added.

The accompanying diagram shows the scores for two players; the system of scoring can be explained from the exhibit of player J.C.B.:

NAME	1	2	3	4	5	6	7	8	9	10	STR.	SP.	TOTAL
J.C.B.	9	26	35	55	72	80	98	106	124	133	1	4	133
E.W.M.	20	38	47	65	84	93	111	130	139	158	1	6	158

In his first two throws only 9 pins were downed. In the second frame he secured a spare, and in the third frame 7 pins on the first ball, which credits him with 17 points to be added to the 9 in the first frame or a total of 26 for the second frame. On his second throw in the third frame 2 more pins are downed, which gives him 9 for that frame, which is added to the 26 of frame two, making 35 to and including frame three. In the fourth frame a strike occurs, and a cross records it. In the fifth frame of two balls, a spare is made, counting 10 to be added to the 10 for the preceding strike, totalling 20, which total is added to the 35 shown in frame three, a grand total of 55 for frame four.

In frame six only 7 pins are downed on the first throw; there is a credit of 10 for the preceding spare, so frame five will record 17 to be added to the preceding 55 or 72 for frame five; on the second throw in frame six 1 more pin topples, a total of 8 for the frame. Frame seven yields a spare; and frame eight, 8 pins on the first throw; the 10 for the spare plus 8 gives 18 for the score for frame seven, which, added to the 80 totaled to and including frame six, makes 98, for the second throw yielded nothing. Frame nine records another spare, or 10, plus 8 for the first throw in frame ten, or 18, which added to the 106 totaled so far gives 124; the second throw in the last frame adds 1 or 9 altogether for frame 10, and this, added to 124 up to and including frame nine, gives 133 for the game. If a strike is made on the tenth frame, two more balls may be thrown; if a spare is made, as in E.M.W.'s score, one more ball may be thrown and the result is added to the score.

Candlepins and Duckpins. There are two interesting variations of the game of bowling (tenpins). One, known as *candlepins*, is played in the same way and with the same sized bowling ball as tenpins, but the candlepins are in the general shape of a candle, long, narrow and nearly straight from bottom to top.

The other variation of bowling is a game called *duckpins*, played with very much smaller pins and balls about the size of croquet balls. The rules, scoring and procedure are as in bowling. This game is especially attractive for women and children since they can get from it practically all the sport of bowling but without the strain of handling a heavy ball.

BOXING
(Junior High School to Adults)

Boxing is a desirable activity in the modern program of physical education when it is conducted on a proper basis. It is a contest of pluck, skill and endurance and under competent instruction develops in the participants a sense of honor, integrity and fair play.

As a sport boxing was in vogue among the early Greek and Roman athletes. In those days the contestants armed their fists with strips of rawhide (the *cestus*), which were often loaded with iron or lead. In England, where the sport became immensely popular, rules were formulated that made its practice less brutal and laid the foundation for the dominance of intelligence over sheer strength.

Modern boxing is a contest of skill in which the contestants strike at each other with the closed fist that is covered with leather gloves stuffed with horsehair. With the use of boxing gloves came the adoption of new rules framed by the marquis of Queensbury. Under newer and better rules boxing has become a leading sport and exercise.

General Suggestions

Position. The left arm and left foot are advanced; the right foot is placed at a right angle to the body for a brace in starting, and the right heel is slightly lifted for quick action. The left side of the body is advanced to a *quarter* position and the boxer crouches slightly. The thumb is safe

Defense Position

only when it is kept outside and close to the clenched fist.

Distance. Do not waste strength making or guarding blows that could not reach their mark. Work in quickly before really attempting to land. Give as little warning as possible. Make the blows rapid with a quick getaway. In gauging distance by extending the arm, work around toward the left, away from the opponent's dangerous

right arm, until there is an opportunity to lead.

Muscles. Keep the muscles active but not strongly contracted, except in the very act of striking or receiving a heavy blow.

Movements. Bend the body forward and back from hips; bend head, neck, shoulders and back quickly, freely in all directions. These movements deceive the enemy as to distance and are useful in guarding, in covering and in launching an attack. This is called *weaving*.

Offense. It is exceedingly important to answer every aimed blow of an opponent by a counter blow, at the same time guarding with the other arm. There are many scientific methods of offense and defense, but the fundamental blows are the *straight left jab* and the *right cross*. The jab is aimed at the opponent's body and face and the right hand is used to guard. Many points may be won by a boxer who has mastered the straight left jab.

Straight Left Jab

Right Cross

The right cross is a more dangerous blow used most successfully in answer to a left jab and is aimed at the head or chin, over the opponent's left arm.

The *straight right* differs from the right cross by going under the opponent's left arm and is aimed at the body or chin.

The *uppercut* is a blow employed at close quarters, directed upward to the pit of the stomach or chin.

A *hook* may be delivered from the side with the hand and with the arm in a curved position. Follow all successful blows with a *rush* and shower blows rapidly whenever possible to do so.

Defense. Give careful attention to defense. The chief means of guarding against attack are blocking, shoving aside a blow, stopping an opponent's blow by a quick counter blow, slipping, ducking and side stepping. Study the signs of a coming blow. The eye of your opponent is the great telltale. Watch it and you may see where he intends to aim his next blow.

To *block* is to receive on the fist or arm a blow meant for the body or head. In the instant of using one hand for blocking, watch for an opening for the other. Put only enough effort in the blocking motion to ward off the force of the blow. The right arm is the main guard. Do not extend it too far in blocking or you will leave an opening.

Coming blows may be shoved aside to the right or left. It is occasionally possible to shove an opponent's right across to your right, or his left to your left, thus turning him partially around, making an opening and perhaps disturbing his balance. The open palm does well in blocking and shoving off blows.

Stops are quick counter blows with the left hand shot out for the head or body in the instant you feel the enemy is going to strike. Stops are good when they beat the other fellow to it and counteract the force of his blow or head it off altogether. While making stops with the left, change the guard of the right to protect both body and face.

A *slip* is a sudden jerk of the head or body to right or left, letting a blow glance by. If the blow is from the opponent's right, slip to your right and vice versa.

A *duck* is a big slip, usually to avoid a swing for the head. Guard the chin while ducking and make a counter blow with the other hand.

A *side step* has three swift movements; retreat one step, spring to right one step and turn to left, facing opponent.

A *feint* is a useful preparation for a lead; it is a short step forward with the left, a rapid blow that you know will not quite land, instant recovery and instantly a longer step, with a real blow. Feinting is commonly done with the left hand. If done with the right, feint for the head and lead for the body or feint low and strike high. Feinting succeeds only when it causes the enemy to raise or lower his guard and leave an opening. Feints are used also to draw leads from the opponent, which, being expected, can be blocked and countered to marked advantage. The feint and the real blow following are almost always by the same hand. A good feinter may succeed in lessening his opponent's confidence.

There are four main types of knockout, and it is well to know about them, possibly for offense and surely for defense. These four blows land (1) on the point of the chin or near it; (2) on the solar plexus or pit of the stomach; (3) over the heart; and (4) on the neck close under the ear. The most painful of these is the stomach blow; the most transient effect is from the blow under the ear.

Skill in boxing can come only through constant practice. A punching bag is indispensable, and so are chest weights used in all possible positions.

Breathing exercises and long runs in the open are good for the *wind,* and some active game like tennis is fine for increasing speed on the feet. Most necessary of all are a wrestling mate and a skilful sparring partner.

CAMPING

Where, When and How.—The best vacation is the one that offers complete change. No matter how well we like our complex modern civilization it is fun to return to the primitive at times —provided we know the essentials of primitive living. It is possible to be very comfortable with minimum equipment if that minimum includes the right things and to be very uncomfortable with maximum equipment if the articles are unwisely chosen. With the right clothing and a knowledge of how, one can live comfortably in the open in all kinds of weather.

Before you start on a camping trip make sure of the laws of the locality or country you plan to visit. Many states have stringent laws regarding campfires and even camping; fishing and hunting laws must be obeyed and licenses procured. Get a map and study it.

The kinds and amounts of equipment depend largely on the kind of camping you plan to do—permanent or movable, cabin, auto trailer or tent —and the kind of transportation. The minimum equipment for an auto-camping trip is far different from that for a hiking trip where the weight is limited to a pack carried on the back or for a canoe trip where portages must be made. The season, too, must be considered. Hunting equipment is needed in the fall; fishing, in the spring and summer. So first decide where, when and how and then make a check list of what.

Check List

Special Equipment

flashlight	notebook
camera	first-aid kit
fishing tackle	maps
gun and ammunition	blanket pins
canteen	toilet articles

Clothing

shirts, blouses (flannel, cotton)	shoes (moccasins, sneakers)
trousers (knickers, slacks, breeches)	pajamas sweaters bathing suit
socks, stockings (wool, cotton)	hat handkerchiefs
coat	

Camping Equipment

tent	waterproof matchbox
blankets	cot
waterproof sheet	air mattress
poncho	muslin bag
lantern	table (folding)
axe or hatchet (sheathed)	chairs (folding)
belt knife or jack-knife	cooking outfit folding water bag
compass	stove
	reflecting baker

Foods

sugar	dehydrated vegetables and soups
salt	egg powder
flour	milk powder
baking powder	evaporated milk
butter	cereals—oatmeal, rice, cornmeal, whole wheat
bacon	
prunes	
apricots	
raisins	

Put everything you think you can possibly need on the list—then choose from it, eliminating what you consider is not necessary. Just before you pack up, check your outfit with the list to make sure you have not left out any essential.

Choosing the Camp Site.—Use care in choosing the camp site. Find an open, level spot for the tent, where the drainage is good; if camping for more than a night, it is important that the sun reach the tent sometime during the day to prevent dampness; as a general rule a camp facing the south or east is preferable. Drinking water is a necessity. If there is a spring nearby the water is probably safe but TAKE NO CHANCES. Carry a bucket of water from the nearest dwelling and, if you have the slightest doubt, boil the water and then aerate it by pouring it from one container to another. It is wise to remember that courtesy pays—it is better to ask permission to camp than to have an irate owner put you off.

Tents.—Until the advent of the trailer camps were divided into two kinds: permanent, for which the cabin and wall tent are the accepted shelters, and the movable variety for which various small tents have been designed. The *wall tent* is shaped much like a house, with a ridge pole and with walls about 4 feet high; it is usually made of canvas or duck, has an extra fly stretched over the roof for added protection from sun and rain and is usually built over or on a wooden platform. Wooden instead of canvas walls make it still more permanent. If it is lined with mosquito netting or bobbinet for excluding insects, it makes a comfortable summer home. If it is not built on a platform or wooden floor, a canvas floor adds much to livability. A generous sod cloth around the bottom helps to keep out vermin and insects. For camping in wooded country it is not necessary to carry tent poles or stakes.

The simplest of the movable or cruising tents is the *dog* tent, which consists merely of a large square or rectangular piece of canvas, balloon silk or other waterproofed material with loops on two sides. It is stretched over a horizontal pole and the loops staked down on either side. Thick boughs may be stuck in the ground at one or both ends for extra protection from wind or rain. If one is caught in the woods without any shelter, a lean-to may be built of boughs by standing poles or large branches diagonally against a horizontal pole and covering them thickly with boughs, arranged so they will shed rain. Throughout the Adirondacks and some parts of the Catskills log lean-tos have been built on many of the trails for the use of campers.

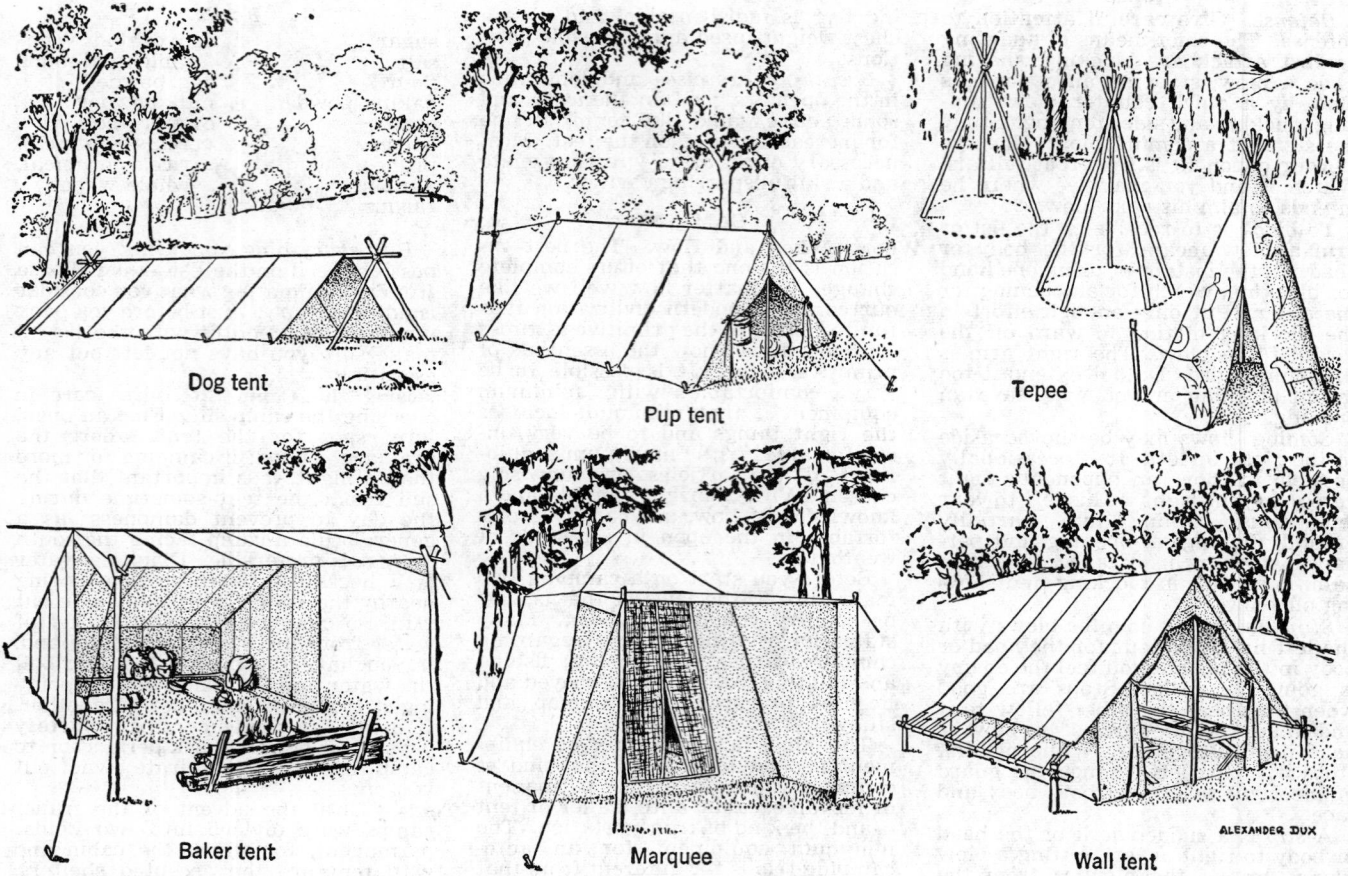

Dog tent

Pup tent

Tepee

Baker tent

Marquee

ALEXANDER DUX

Wall tent

SIX TYPES OF TENTS with varying degrees of simplicity and ease in carrying and setting up. The dog tent requires only a waterproof groundsheet and stakes; the pup tent is supplied with poles, pegs, and ropes and is quite easy to set up. In a countryside where there are pine trees that will supply long, straight poles, the *tepee* can be used; a fire may be built inside. The *marquee* and wall tents are good for long campouts, when moving is unnecessary; while they are very comfortable and spacious, they are heavy to carry.

The *marquee* tent is popular for the semipermanent camp or on the auto-camping trip where weight is not an item, for it has plenty of head room. Shelter tents of various types are available, the A or *wedge-shaped* tent and variations of it being perhaps the most popular. The *baker tent*—so called because it resembles the folding baker—is a favorite cold-weather tent because a campfire built in front of it sends the warmth into the tent. The Indian *tepee* is the only tent in which a fire can be built and it is only suitable in lodge-pole-pine country. Tents with sewed-in ground cloths are a great advantage except that, like canoes, the floor must not be walked on with boots or shoes.

Think about ventilation in choosing your tent—a small window in the back will add much to comfort; and, if you are camping in fly or mosquito season, have it fitted with a bobbinet or netting front. Materials for tents are either water-repellent or waterproofed by a number of processes. Jointed tent poles and metal tent pegs should be carried along unless you are traveling in wooded country. Whatever type of tent you choose, roll it carefully and pack it with poles and stakes in its own bag so that it can be pitched as soon as you reach a camp site, without unpacking the other duffel.

Beds and Bedding.—The hiker or canoe cruiser who must limit the weight of his pack has not much choice in sleeping equipment. He may carry a waterproof-covered sleeping bag with an awning arrangement over the head and sleep in the open—the disadvantage of this is that he cannot do much about it if he gets too warm; the waterproof covering prevents the evaporation of perspiration and causes a clammy feeling. Sleeping bags are best suited to really cold weather. The camper may carry a small tent and woolen blankets—two are enough for any ordinary weather—with a poncho or waterproof sheet. Light, loosely woven woolen blankets are much warmer than hard, tightly woven ones.

Staying rolled in a blanket is not easy to do. It is better to carry a supply of blanket pins and pin the blankets into a bag, leaving the top layer loose so that it may be thrown off if one gets too warm. There must be as many layers under as over the body for much cold comes from the ground; and there must always be a waterproof sheet under the blankets. Camp cots are fine in the permanent camp and may be carried on an automobile trip. Twice as many blankets are needed under one as over if he sleeps on a cot without a mattress, however, as the wind then has a fine chance to chill one. A wind- and waterproof poncho will serve as well.

Air mattresses that roll into compact bundles and are inflated before using make comfortable beds. Too much air makes them hard; a small bicycle pump helps the inflating process. Mattress pads of kapok, wool and cotton also are on the market. A muslin bag or tick, which weighs little and occupies little space, may be stuffed with grass, ferns, hay, boughs or leaves and adds much to the comfort. There is always the bough bed—wonderful if carefully made, awful if not. Balsam, spruce or hemlock boughs are best for the purpose; use only small ones and place logs to form the boundaries so the bed will not spread. Starting at the head, lay a row of boughs across with the tips up, place the second row over these with their tips just a little below the first ones, and so on until the bed is long enough. Use plenty of boughs and lay them carefully so all the butts will be well buried and the tips form a soft, fragrant couch. When you pack up, roll the blankets into a compact bundle of whatever shape best fits the pack and wrap it carefully in the waterproof sheet or poncho, so there will always be a dry bed.

Campfire and Cook Fires.—There is a difference between the two. A campfire can be as large as one wishes or

Campfire   Cooking fire with crane and reflecting baker

Stone fireplace

CAMPFIRES can be built in various ways. For warmth, a large fire throws wide heat; for cooking, a small fire sends heat directly up.

the weather demands; but a cooking fire must be small. *Dry wood and air* are the two necessary ingredients for any fire. Standing dead trees are best; even in rainy weather it is possible to find a few dry, dead branches and twigs on the under sides of trees. Lay the fire carefully, placing small split sticks crisscross in layers, the first two about 6 inches apart, with plenty of dry twigs laid over each layer and some dry tinder placed on the windward side. The wetter or greener the wood, the more kindling material or heat is required to make it burn. Learn the burning qualities of various woods. Oak and hickory will burn fairly well even when green; poplar and balsam will not; pine makes a quick, hot fire. Never throw wood on or at a fire—lay it carefully in place; and *never forget to put out the fire.* Never build a fire where there is danger of its spreading; choose rocks, bare soil the bank of a stream; make a rough fireplace of stones if that is possible or place the fire between two green logs—with their tops flattened off they make a good resting place for pans.

Simple cooking irons or a small grate with folding legs are convenient to hold pots; or a crane may be rigged up and the pots fastened to it with hooks. Be sure to use green wood for the crane so that it will not catch fire. A reflecting baker makes delicious baked things possible. A variety of camp stoves are on the market.

The Cook Kit.—The Boy Scout cook kit is good for an individual outfit. Other excellent kits consisting of cups, plates, bowls, pails, coffeepot, frying pan, knives, forks and spoons, all fitted so that they nest in a compact bag, are available in aluminum or tin, for parties of two, four or more. If you choose an aluminum outfit, be sure to specify that cups and spoons be of tin or enamelware, if you do not want to burn your tongue. If you assemble your own outfit, plan it so that the different articles fit into one another and choose a frying pan that has a hinged handle to fold back when not in use and holes in the handle in which a long, green stick may be put for convenience when cooking.

Camp Lights.—With the exception of the auto camp where the headlights may be utilized, lighting the camp is a problem. Several kinds of lanterns—kerosene, gasoline and electric—are on the market. All have good and bad points. Perhaps the simplest and

most satisfactory of all is the folding candle lantern with a good supply of plumbers' candles (they last longer than ordinary ones).

Foods and Cookery.—Where space and weight are not limited or where one has ready access to stores, canned meats, vegetables, soups and fruits are fine; even if you expect to find fresh food along the trail, it is well to carry a supply. Evaporated milk often proves more satisfactory than fresh. The food list for the canoe cruise deep into the wilderness, however, must be carefully planned. Dried fruits, dessicated vegetables, milk and egg powders must be depended upon. Bacon is the staple meat. Wherever you go, make your emergency supplies ample, for wayside replenishments are not always dependable, the fish do not always bite or the rabbits appear when the hunter wants them.

Pack all dry staples—salt, flour, coffee and tea—in small waterproof bags; push- or screw-top tins are satisfactory for butter and other soft foods. Then pack all the small food bags in a large food pack, placing the articles used least at the bottom. Practice some simple cookery at home before starting out on a trip—learn to make a stew, a chowder, biscuits, muffins and the like.

Personal Kit.—Suitcases and similar luggage are taboo in camp. Clothing and toilet articles must be packed in *duffel bags.* The chief requisites of camp clothing are durability and suitability. Except in the very hottest weather, wool is the most satisfactory material. Hikers will find woolen socks or stockings much more comfortable; canoeists will find that wool makes wet feet much more endurable. Sneakers or moccasins are the only footwear for a canoe. High-heeled shoes are never suitable in outdoor living and besides are dangerous.

First-aid Kit.—Regular packaged first-aid kits are on the market, but you can assemble your own. Gauze, bandages, adhesive tape, absorbent cotton, iodine or other antiseptic, a pair of tweezers, small scissors, ammonia—the small swabs of iodine and ammonia that are used by crushing the ends are a convenient form—vaseline, mosquito lotion and preventive (oil of citronella is good), sunburn lotion and soda. If you have your own pet remedies, obtain them in compact and nonbreakable containers and pack them in a waterproof bag. Before you go to camp, it is a good idea to practice some simple first aid—rescue and

resuscitate someone from simulated drowning. Be sure you know how to treat sunburn, insect bites, small wounds, nose bleed; and practice applying different types of bandages.

Outdoor Hazards.—The three real villains that threaten comfort or even life in the woods are *poison ivy, poison sumac* and *snake bite.* There are only three really poisonous snakes in the United States—the rattlesnake, copperhead and cottonmouth water moccasin. It is well to become familiar with their habits and their habitats. The rattlesnake is found quite generally over the country, although those of the prairie are small and hence not so venomous. The most dangerous is the great diamond rattlesnake of the South. The rattlesnake, if he is awake, warns by rattling before he strikes. The copperhead lives in the mountainous and hilly regions of the eastern and southern United States and west through Kansas, Oklahoma and Texas. It neither gives warning before striking nor tries to get out of the way. The cottonmouth moccasin is found in North Carolina and south and west through Kentucky, southern Illinois, Oklahoma and eastern Texas, usually near water or hanging from trees that overhang the water. All snakes sleep during the day and, if they are stepped on, may strike instantly. It is wise to wear high moccasins or shoes in snake country as the bite is not so venomous through leather or other clothing.

In case of snake bite the first thing to do is to twist a tourniquet, using any piece of cloth available, between the bite and the heart to keep the poison from circulating through the system. Then cut the wound open so that it will bleed freely and suck out the poison, spitting it out. Snake-bite remedies are available; or you can carry along a hypodermic syringe and potassium permanganate to inject near the wound.

Poison ivy takes many forms from the tiny vine in the grass to the large shrub; its leaves vary in color, but it always may be distinguished by the *three leaves to the group,* as contrasted with the five leaves of regular ivy. No one is immune to poison ivy all the time. He who escapes one time may succumb the next, if it happens to be a warm, muggy day or he is not quite at his best physically. Ordinary yellow laundry soap is a good preventive. Wash with it, rubbing vigorously. Baking soda applied promptly often checks the poison.

Weak ammonia water is another remedy; or the druggist will give you a prescription. Poison sumac—not the staghorn, with its big red fruit clusters—is more poisonous than ivy. It is found in low ground and has white berries, and the bushes grow quite large. Remedies are the same as those for poison ivy.

Carrying the Pack.—Comfortable footwear and a well-arranged pack are the two most important requisites to a successful hiking trip. Be sure to have shoes that are long enough and wear two pairs of lightweight wool socks or

TOO HIGH   TOO LOW   JUST RIGHT

Carrying A Pack

stockings to give a cushion for the feet. Never try to carry extra items in the hands; they should be kept free. Be sure that any sharp articles are put in the center or outside the pack so that they will not dig into your back when you walk. The real old timer carries his pack by a tumpline around his forehead; most moderns prefer to use shoulder straps.

Whether packcloth and strap or pack bag, it should be fitted just right to the center of the back. The weight should not come upon the small of the back but high enough so that the neck column helps to hold and steady it. A pack that lies too low on the back will grow heavier and heavier as one travels. The lower end of the pack should not extend much below the middle of the back. Remember when adjusting it that the body inclines forward when walking.

CANOEING

A Word of Warning.—Canoes, although they are the most maligned of water craft, are safe and easily managed if they are used properly. They will ride heavy seas, shoot the wildest rapids, follow the most devious courses—in the hands of experts. The tyro should be careful. No one who cannot swim should enter a canoe or try to paddle one. Even the good swimmer will do well to stick to the canoe if overturned, for it will always float.

When entering a canoe step into the middle—not to the side; and do not try to stand up or change places while afloat. The lower the center of gravity, the better the balance; in rough water it is better to sit in the bottom rather than on seats. In fact the expert does not even have seats in his canoe.

Choosing the Canoe and Paddles.—The choice of a canoe depends on the water on which it is to be used. The deep and wide cruising model is best suited for open water and for carrying heavy loads; the narrow, shallow canoe is satisfactory for small, protected streams; too short a canoe is tippy.

Paddles, like shoes, should fit the user. The bow paddler should choose a paddle about 6 inches shorter than himself; the stern paddler, one whose length equals his own height. Maple paddles are strong; those of spruce are light. In large, open waters a pair of double blades, which fasten together with a ferrule and enable the paddler to stroke first on one side and then the other, will help to move the craft more rapidly, especially if one paddles alone. The middle is the best place to sit and paddle if one is alone in the canoe.

Paddling.—The stern paddler is the captain and pilot and steers the canoe; the bow paddler sets the stroke. It is better to learn to paddle in the bow, with the stern paddler directing. A quick, even stroke, starting the paddle out from the side a little and pulling it straight back, is good. Do not reach too far forward to start; and recover quickly, for the stroke is valueless after it passes the body. The stern paddler adjusts his stroke to that of the bow paddler, but the finish is different, for he must steer the canoe by turning his paddle like a rudder. He does this by turning the near or inside edge of the paddle back with a roll of the wrists while it is alongside the body, not after it has passed. Steering should always be done by turning the paddle rather than by swinging it from one side of the canoe to the other. The Indian sits on his feet in the bottom of the canoe to paddle; modern canoes have built-in seats; a position between these two styles, which many canoeists prefer, is to kneel on the bottom with hips against a thwart.

Care of the Craft.—Never step or sit in a canoe when it is on shore; hold it lengthwise to the dock and free from projections when you embark. If you must get in from a beach, push it off and wade to the floating depth of the canoe. Always wear moccasins or sneakers, never shoes or boots, in the canoe. When it is not in use, turn it upside down in a shady place if possible. Scrape the canoe and give it a new coat of paint or varnish every spring. On a cruise it is well to carry along patches—you may strike a snag.

Canoe Cruising.—When you have learned to paddle, plan a canoe cruise. Whether it be the wilderness nearest you or the one far away, there is no other way to get so close to it. To paddle along a narrow stream where you can watch the life on shore, pick out a suitable camping spot and pitch your tent for the night is great fun though strenuous. Do not put off finding the camping spot until too late in the day—it is amazing how camp sites disappear along toward night. Pack your duffel in compact waterproof packs or bags, arrange it carefully in the center of the canoe, the heaviest pieces in the bottom, and lash each one to the thwarts. Then, if you should tip over, your duffel will not go to the bottom.

To Carry the Canoe.—A canoe is not so heavy, but it is rather unwieldy. The Indian method of portage is practical

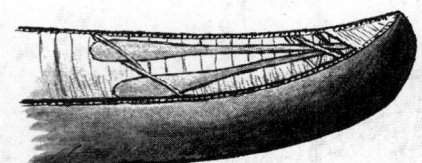

Paddles Arranged For Portage

for one man. Tie one end of a stout string or thong to the middle thwart close to the gunwale. Stretch it taut and tie the other end of it to the opposite gunwale. Slip the two paddle blades, lying flat, under the string and bind the handles on the forward thwart with another string. Spread the blades apart enough to admit the head; then, standing on the left side of the canoe with face to the stern, grasp the gunwale on the far side a little forward of the middle thwart with the left hand and that on the near side with the right; swing the canoe up over the head so that your head goes between the paddles just forward of the middle thwart with the flat sides of the paddles resting on the shoulders. Thus the face is toward the bow and, by tipping it up a little, the trail ahead is visible.

Two-Man Portage

The easiest way for two men to carry a canoe is to swing it upside down so that the bow is on the right shoulder of the front man and the stern on the left shoulder of the rear man.

For Shelter.—Many canoe cruisers use their canoes, turned upside down and propped up at one end, as shelter instead of carrying tents. Some rig up side curtains that fit the sides of the canoe, fastening them to the gunwales with snap fasteners. The only disadvantage of using the canoe as shelter

SHELTER can be made by staking up a canoe and fastening waterproof curtains, cut to fit the curved sides, to the inner edges of the gunwales by loops and pulleys.

is that it cannot be used otherwise at the same time. But, if you have made sure of all supplies before you pitch camp, this will not matter.

Sleeping in the Canoe.—It is fun to sleep in a canoe. Choose a night when you can be fairly sure it will not rain. Remove the center thwarts and spread mattress and blankets in the bottom of the canoe, with a poncho over the top to keep off dampness. Paddle out to a quiet, sheltered spot that is free of any obstructions into which the canoe might bump as it swings with breeze or current and drop anchor (any heavy object securely tied to a rope).

Racing.—A canoe regatta can be held any place where a group of canoes is assembled. To make a race fair the boats must be as nearly alike as possible in length, beam and weight. Contestants also should be grouped as to size or age and as to proficiency with the paddle. Any number of straightaway races may be held—the one-man single-blade, one-man double-blade, two-man single- and double-blade, four men in each and, if war canoes are available, 9- to 15-man races.

Then there are many kinds of stunt races, such as the hand paddle (using the hands for paddles), tilting contests, tug-of-war, in which paddlers in two canoes tied stern to stern with about 4 feet of rope between them try to paddle in opposite directions from a center line; the hurry-scurry race that consists of a 50-yard dash to shore from a given point inland, a 50-yard swim to a canoe anchored outstream and a 50-yard paddle; also a cruising race that consists of loading the camping outfit in the canoe, paddling a certain distance and pitching camp in the shortest possible time. Clever paddlers learn to *flip* their canoes—turn them over, right them and flip the water out by rocking from side to side with a hand on each gunwale. (Always get back in the canoe from the end, never from the side). Flipping races are exciting.

Sailing.—Sailing canoes are of two kinds. The ordinary cruising canoe rigged with a single lateen sail and steered with a paddle held overside is a practical arrangement that can be paddled or sailed as the occupant prefers and often enables the canoe cruiser to rest or to make better time on a fairly large body of water. The decked sailing canoe, a wooden boat with two leg-of-mutton sails and fitted with a centerboard and rudder is a wonderful racing machine, to be sailed only by the expert.

CHECKERS

(Elementary School to Adults)

The game of checkers (called *draughts* in England) has been known in one form or another for 3,500 years. It is played by two players upon a board divided into 64 squares alternately colored red and black, although any two contrasting colors are satisfactory. Each player places his 12 thick red or black disks, called *men,* on the same-colored squares on his side of the board, thus occupying three horizontal rows. All the disks for each player are of one color.

The object of the game is to remove the opponent's men from the board by a series of strategic moves. With the players alternating in their moves, the men are moved diagonally only, one square at a time, unless a move brings a man into the diagonal next to an opponent's man; then it is necessary to *jump* the opponent by moving over his man to the square next beyond and, in the jump, removing from the board the man that was thus exposed. However, a jump cannot be made unless the diagonal square beyond the opponent's man is vacant. By adroit maneuvering a player may lead his opponent into such positions that more than one of his men may be jumped at a time.

Each player moves his men toward the opposite side of the board. If a man successfully passed step by step across the board to the opponent's first row and is moved into an empty space there, that man so advanced becomes a *king,* for he has reached the opposing *king row.* A king is distinguished by being *crowned*—that is, by having another man placed on top, making the king double height. A king has the advantage over an ordinary man in that he may move both forward and backward.

When one player has removed all his opponent's men or has placed his own men in such positions as to block his opponent from making any move without loss of a man, the game is won.

CHESS

(Junior High School to Adults)

Chess is a highly scientific game of great antiquity, played on the same board that is used in checkers. Only two players may participate. Each contestant plays with 16 *men*—a king, a queen, two knights, two bishops, two castles (or rooks) and eight pawns. The opposing sets of men are usually colored black and white or black and red.

In beginning play each player arranges his men in the two horizontal rows of the board nearest him. The queen is placed *on her color;* that is, the player who has the black or darker set of men will place his queen on the dark square that is fourth from one end in the first row. The opposing queens thus face each other across the board. The king occupies the square next to the queen, so the king and queen rest on the two squares that occupy the center of the row. On either side of these two the bishops are placed; next to the bishops are the knights; the castles (rooks) occupy the two corners. The pawns are ranged along all the squares in the second row.

The rules regarding the moving of the men are intricate. The queen may be moved diagonally, straight ahead or straight backward, as far as the route is clear; this is the principal piece on the board, so far as freedom of movement is concerned. The king may move only one square at a time in any direction; his freedom of movement is less than that of any other piece on the board. He is, however,

the object of the defense and attack that is the main feature of the game, and he is therefore the most important piece on the board. A bishop may not leave its color but may be moved diagonally as far as the path is clear. The knight always moves two squares—one straight ahead and one diagonally. Like every other piece in the game the knight cannot move unless there is a vacant square to which it may proceed, or unless the player wishes to capture a man occupying the square to which the piece moves, in which event the captured man is removed from play. The castles may be moved forward or backward in a straight line as far as their path is clear but never diagonally. When a pawn is first moved, it may be set directly ahead two squares or only one square as desired; after it has once been moved, it may thereafter be moved only one square at a time. When the pawn is not capturing a man from the opposition, it moves directly forward; but it moves diagonally when the object of the move is to capture an opposing man.

In moving to capture any man, the moved man goes into the position or square occupied by the piece to be removed. When by strategical moves against the king, the next move would capture him, the player who thus puts his opponent's king in jeopardy says, "Check!" This is a warning that the owner of the hard-pressed king must move that piece if possible to a place of safety where he cannot be captured by the next assault or must interpose another piece. This may be difficult, for the king may move only one square at a time. When the king is eventually trapped and cannot move anywhere without capture by the opponent's next move, the result is *checkmate,* and the game is ended.

The above is but a brief outline of the game. A good book of rules is suggested for careful study by anyone who would become proficient. Chess is the most scientific of all games; it does not depend upon luck or good fortune but rather upon acumen, clear thinking and the ability to look ahead to see the effect of present and future plays. The movements of the men are so intricate that the chessboard becomes a battlefield on which more than a dozen different forces of varying power on each side are marshaled against the enemy.

CRICKET

(Junior High School to Adults)

Cricket is a favorite game in England and many other parts of the British Empire, and its popularity has been increasing in some sections of the United States. Cricket is played by two teams of 11 players on a level field, which should be about 100 yards wide and 150 yards long.

Two *wickets* are placed 22 yards apart; each wicket is a set of three stumps or posts 27 inches high, supporting a loose block of wood called a *bail.* The posts must be too close together to let a ball through them, but must be sensitive enough to make the bail fall off if a pitched ball hits the wicket. The ball varies from 9 to 9¼ inches in circumference and averages 5½ ounces in weight. The bat is flat, 3 feet in length, 4½ to 5 inches wide for the upper 2 feet and with a handle tapered to a thickness comparable to the handle of a baseball bat.

The wicket is the center front of a space 8 feet 8 inches in length called the *bowling crease;* this marks the position of the bowler or pitcher. Four feet in front of and parallel to each wicket is a line marking the batter's position called the *popping crease.* Two batters are up at once, one by each wicket. In each inning all the players come to bat. While one team is at bat, the other is in the field. A bowler or pitcher stands beside each wicket, and each bowler throws in turn at the opposite wicket. His delivery of the ball is not a throw or a pitch; the arm is held straight and not jerked. If he can hit his mark, the bail will fall, and the batter at that wicket will be out (bowled out). It is the batter's business to hit the ball before it strikes the wicket.

All batted balls are fair hits, and each hit requires the two runners to exchange places before the other's wicket. There are four main ways of putting a batter out: (1) if he fails to hit the pitched ball and it strikes the wickets; (2) if he bats a ball that is caught on the fly; (3) if the ball is thrown to the wicket and the bail is knocked off before he has completed his run; (4) if he oversteps the boundaries of the popping crease.

The batsman may make up to 6 runs for each hit if he has time, and since many long hits are made with the flat bat the score often runs into hundreds and the game may go into several days of play.

CROQUET
(Elementary School to Adults)

Croquet is a popular game that is commonly played on lawns, municipal parks and country-club greens. It is simple to set up and the upkeep is not expensive. The court need not be of any exact dimensions, although 30 feet wide by 60 feet long is a common size. Any level, smooth grass plot is excellent. The boundaries can be marked with a white cord.

At each end of the court there is a colored stake or post, carrying stripes of various colors representing the colors of the croquet balls and surmounted by a red top. The balls are made of wood 3¼ inches in diameter and are painted in colors corresponding to those on the stakes. The more expensive balls are of hard rubber; these will outlast the wooden balls and are better in play. There are either nine or ten wire wickets in a court; they are 1 foot above ground, as in the following diagram, W representing the wickets and O the stake:

```
          W     W
O WW  W   W   WW O
          W     W
```

There may be one or two wickets in the center of the court. Wooden mallets are used to drive the balls over the court and through the wickets.

Two or more people may play as opponents or as teams. The ball is started from one end of the court directly in front of the stake and the object of the game is to get the ball through all the wickets and back to the home stake before other players reach home stake. The specified circuit the ball must make passes through the two wickets before the home stake, to the upper right-hand wicket, to the center one, the lower right-hand one, the two lower post wickets and to the lower stake. From the lower stake the ball is driven through the two lower post wickets, to the lower left-hand wicket, to the center one, the upper left-hand one, through the upper post wickets to the home stake again.

Players take turns in playing their balls. When teams are playing, alternate turns are taken by players of the respective teams. If the ball goes through one wicket, it entitles the player to one more stroke; if through two wickets at a time, to two more strokes. No player may hit the same ball twice in succession unless he first drives his own ball through another wicket. A player is permitted to play upon others' balls, giving him additional strokes to go through the wickets. When teams are playing, the game is not won until all the balls of a team have gone through all the wickets and returned to home stake. Each of the players on a team gives his partner every advantage and tries to keep both balls together over the course. When one player has made the complete circuit of the wickets, he may choose to be a *rover* and assist his partner and hinder his opponents before finally striking out by hitting the home stake.

A scientific refinement of croquet is the game called *roque,* played on a smooth, perfectly level court with a border of cement, rubber or wood from which shots may be banked as in billiards. The wickets are smaller, and the mallets usually have shorter handles than in ordinary croquet.

FOOTBALL
(Senior High School to Adults)

Football is a highly technical game governed by exacting rules and to one ignorant of its details may seem an unintelligible series of falls and rushes. College football, sometimes called *American Rugby,* is adapted from English Rugby but differs from it in many ways. College football and English Rugby use an ellipsoidal (oval) ball in contrast to association football, more commonly called *soccer,* in which a spherical ball is employed.

The game is played on a field 160 feet wide and 300 feet long, with *end zones* at each end 30 feet long and the full width of the field. A line divides the field in two equal parts and on each side are 10 white crosslines 5 yards apart. Counting from the center, the 10th crossline at each end of the field is a goal line. The area enclosed by the side lines and the goal lines is the field of play. At the middle of each end zone line stand two goal posts, 18 feet 6 inches apart, with a crossbar 10 feet above the ground.

Two teams of 11 men each play the game. The general object of each team is to advance the ball toward and across the opponent's goal line. This advance is made by throwing the ball, carrying it or kicking it, subject to rules. The team not in possession of the ball attempts to block the advance, either by checking the progress of the player who carries the ball or by getting possession of the ball itself.

A football game is divided into two halves, and each half into two quarters. The quarters are usually 15 minutes long with an intermission of 15 minutes between halves and 1 minute between quarters. The length of the intermissions may be lengthened by mutual agreement of both teams.

At the beginning of the game the opposing captains toss up for choice of goal or kickoff. If the winner of the toss chooses goal, the other side must kick off. At the beginning of the third quarter, the team that lost the initial toss-up has its choice of goal or kickoff. For the second and fourth quarters, the teams exchange goals.

The team that has possession of the ball makes the attack or offensive. For this attack the opening play of the first and third quarters is a kickoff. At kickoff the ball is sent into the opponent's territory by a place kick from the holders' 40-yard line—the line 10 yards from the middle of the field on the attackers' side. If the opponents secure possession of the ball after a kickoff, they become the attacking party. At kickoff the team

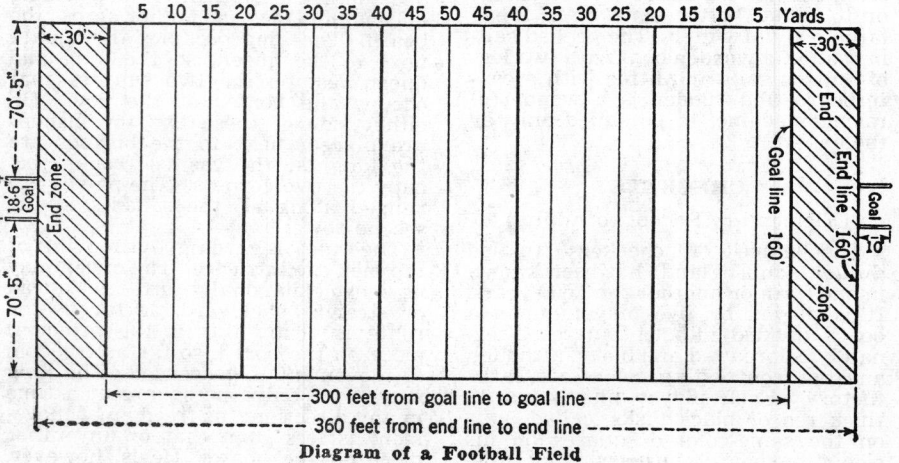

Diagram of a Football Field

Four of America's 20,000,000 anglers
stand enrapt in the classic,
early-morning pursuit of the trout.

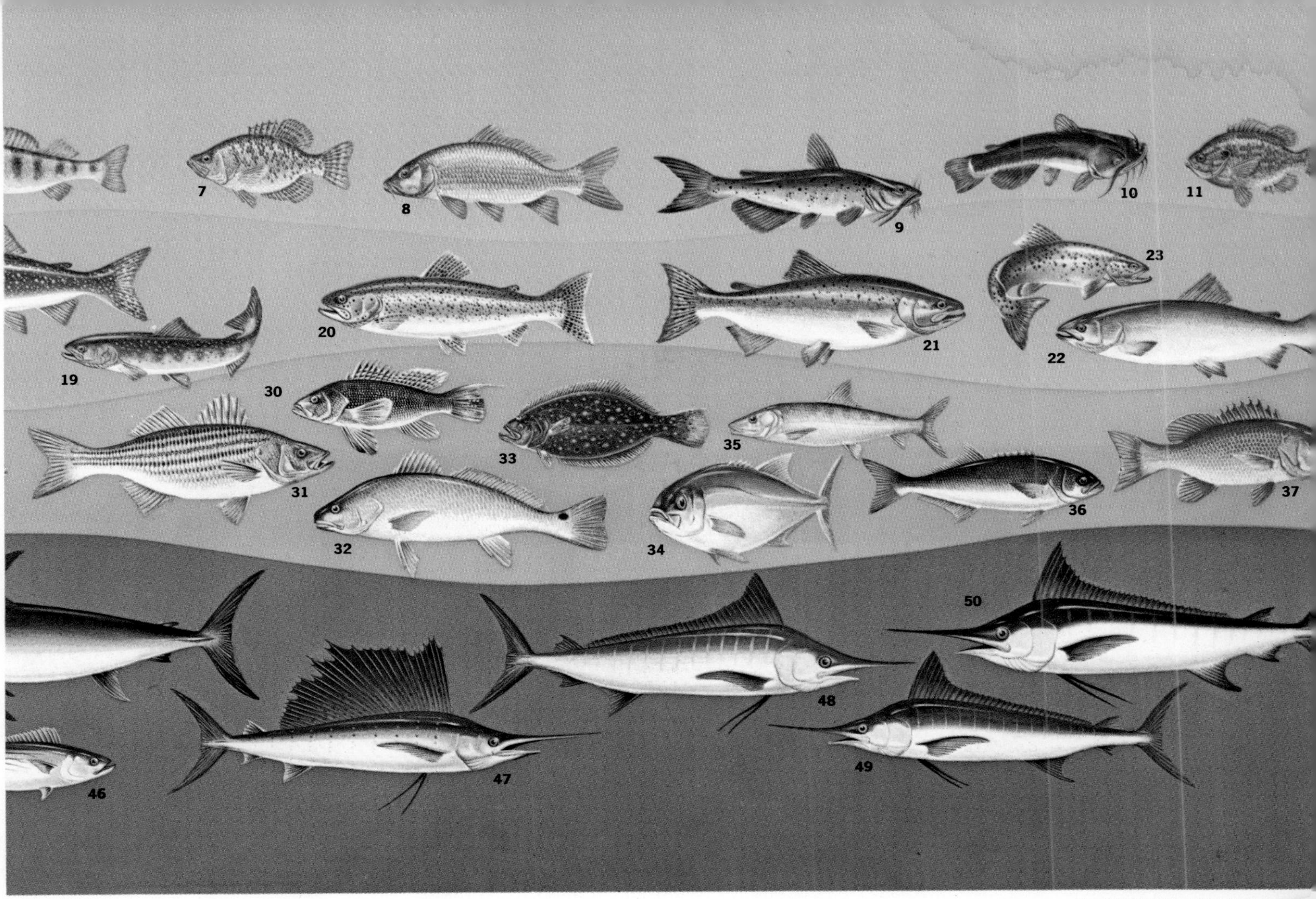
7
8
9
10
11
19
20
21
22
23
30
31
32
33
34
35
36
37
46
47
48
49
50

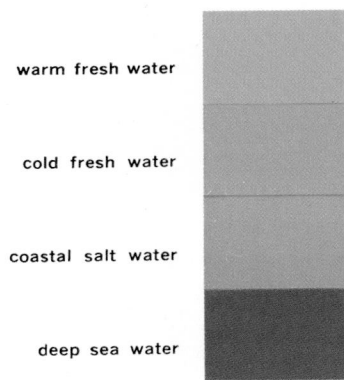

ILLUSTRATION BY HERB WILEN

warm fresh water
cold fresh water
coastal salt water
deep sea water

FISH

1. Bluegill. **2.** Walleyed Pike. **3.** Pickerel. **4.** Largemouth Black Bass. **5.** Smallmouth Black Bass. **6.** Yellow Perch. **7.** Black Crappie. **8.** Carp. **9.** Channel Cat. **10.** Bullhead. **11.** Sunfish. **12.** Muskellunge. **13.** Northern Pike. **14.** Brown Trout. **15.** Brook Trout. **16.** Cutthroat Trout. **17.** Rainbow Trout. **18.** Lake Trout. **19.** Dolly Varden Trout. **20.** Steelhead Trout. **21.** Chinook Salmon. **22.** Atlantic Salmon. **23.** Landlocked Salmon. **24.** Robalo. **25.** King Mackerel. **26.** Black Grouper. **27.** Cobia. **28.** Weakfish. **29.** California White Sea Bass. **30.** Sea Bass. **31.** Striped Bass. **32.** Channel Bass. **33.** Flounder (summer). **34.** Yellowtail. **35.** Bonefish. **36.** Bluefish. **37.** Red Snapper. **38.** Dolphin. **39.** Yellowfin Tuna. **40.** Bluefin Tuna. **41.** Amberjack. **42.** Wahoo. **43.** Tarpon. **44.** Barracuda. **45.** Swordfish. **46.** Bonito. **47.** Sailfish. **48.** Striped Marlin. **49.** White Marlin. **50.** Blue Marlin.

LURES

1. Mouse. **2.** Nitwit Popper. **3.** Popit. **4.** Small Hoppie. **5.** Large Hoppie. **6.** Godart. **7.** Preska Toff. **8.** Brownie Popper. **9.** Hair Frog. **10.** Darter. **11.** Gold Digger. **12.** Jointed Pike. **13.** Babalu. **14.** Preska Perche. **15.** Large Rani. **16.** Female Beaverkill. **17.** Brown Hackle. **18.** Dark Hendrickson. **19.** Royal Wulff. **20.** Muddler Minnow. **21.** Squirrel Tail. **22.** Silver Darter. **23.** Black Ghost. **24.** Jock Scott. **25.** Black Dose Fly. **26.** Blue Quill. **27.** Black Gnat. **28.** Grasshopper. **29.** Black Irresistible. **30.** Ratface Macdougal. **31.** Red and White Bucktail. **32.** Grey Ghost. **33.** Nine Three. **34.** Thunder and Lightning. **35.** Optic Minnow. **36.** Black and White Bucktail. **37.** New England Rose. **38.** Royal Coachman Streamer. **39.** Green Highlander. **40.** Silver Doctor. **41.** Giant Jointed Eel. **42.** Goo Goo Eyes Popper. **43.** Flat Squid. **44.** Chum Spoon. **45.** Gibbs Darter. **46.** Hopkins' Jog. **47.** Record Spoon. **48.** Japanese Feather. **49.** Pet Spoon. **50.** Mirror Lure.

Fifty favorite American fish—and fifty lures most likely to fool them

Weirdly transformed, today's fisherman can invade the fish's own element in search of a day's catch.

THE HUNTER, stalking his quarry, uses a rifle descended from the Kentucky flintlock of American frontier days.

JAMES L. MULLALY

American Guns for game and game birds.

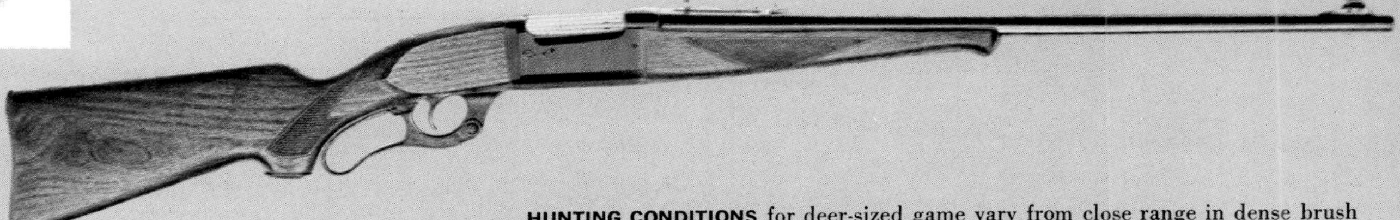

ILLUSTRATIONS BY HERB WILEN

HUNTING CONDITIONS for deer-sized game vary from close range in dense brush and timber, to long range on open plains or across canyons. Lever, pump and automatic loading rifles handle fast for close shooting, and blunt, heavy bullets in medium-power cartridges make good brush buckers. For open shooting, the accurate bolt-action rifle, with pointed bullets in high-velocity cartridges, provides flat trajectory and killing punch at 300 yards or more. The Savage Model 99 (left) is one of many rifles used for deer and similar game.

Big game demands the heaviest gun.

FOR DANGEROUS GAME, a hunter choses the heaviest rifle he can handle, with ammunition that will stop the animal in its tracks. The .338 Magnum cartridge, with 200- and 250-grain bullets, in the Winchester Model 70 Alaskan rifle (left) was designed for the heaviest American animals, and for African and Indian medium-big game, including lion and tiger. Such powerful cartridges as the .300 and .375 Magnums, the .30-06 Springfield, .280 Remington and the .270 Winchester with heavy bullets have brought down bear, moose and elk.

Shotguns come in all varieties.

A RULE OF THUMB for birds is: small shot for small birds; larger shot for larger birds. Number 7½ or 8 shot is good for small birds like quail; number 5 and 6 shot for grouse, pheasant and for ducks over decoys. Use BB, number 2 or 4 shot for geese and turkey. The type of gun is up to the hunter. Some prefer the bolt action; some, the fast-operating pump gun or the autoloader; others rely on the versatile double-barrel shotgun. Shown here are a Browning 12-gauge autoloader (top) and 16-gauge Winchester model 21 double (bottom).

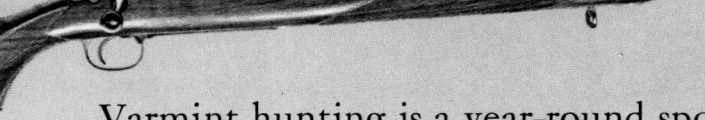

Varmint hunting is a year-round sport.

MOST VARMINTS are small targets and are usually shot in wide-open country where they can see the hunter more easily than he can spot them. Although varmint hunters use almost every caliber and type of gun, the true devotee prefers the superaccurate, bolt-action rifle mounted with a scope sight of six-power or more. He shoots cartridges especially designed for varmints—the .222 and .224 Remington, .220 Swift and .243 Winchester, or larger calibers with lightweight, high-velocity bullets. Rifle shown is Remington Model 724.

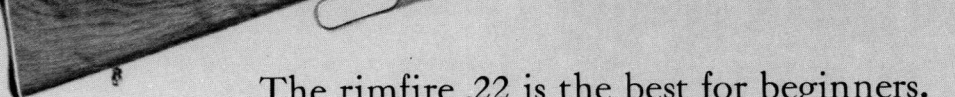

The rimfire .22 is the best for beginners.

SMALL EDIBLE GAME and small pests are bagged in great numbers with the .22 rimfire—most popular rifle in America. Twenty-two's range from cut-down models for youngsters to 16-pound target arms. In bolt, pump, lever and auto-loading action, they are extraordinarily accurate. Hollow-point bullets are recommended for nonedible game; solid-point bullets will save the meat and pelt. The .22, much like a big-bore rifle in design, is an inexpensive gun for all-season shooting. Above is the time-tried Marlin 39-A Mountie.

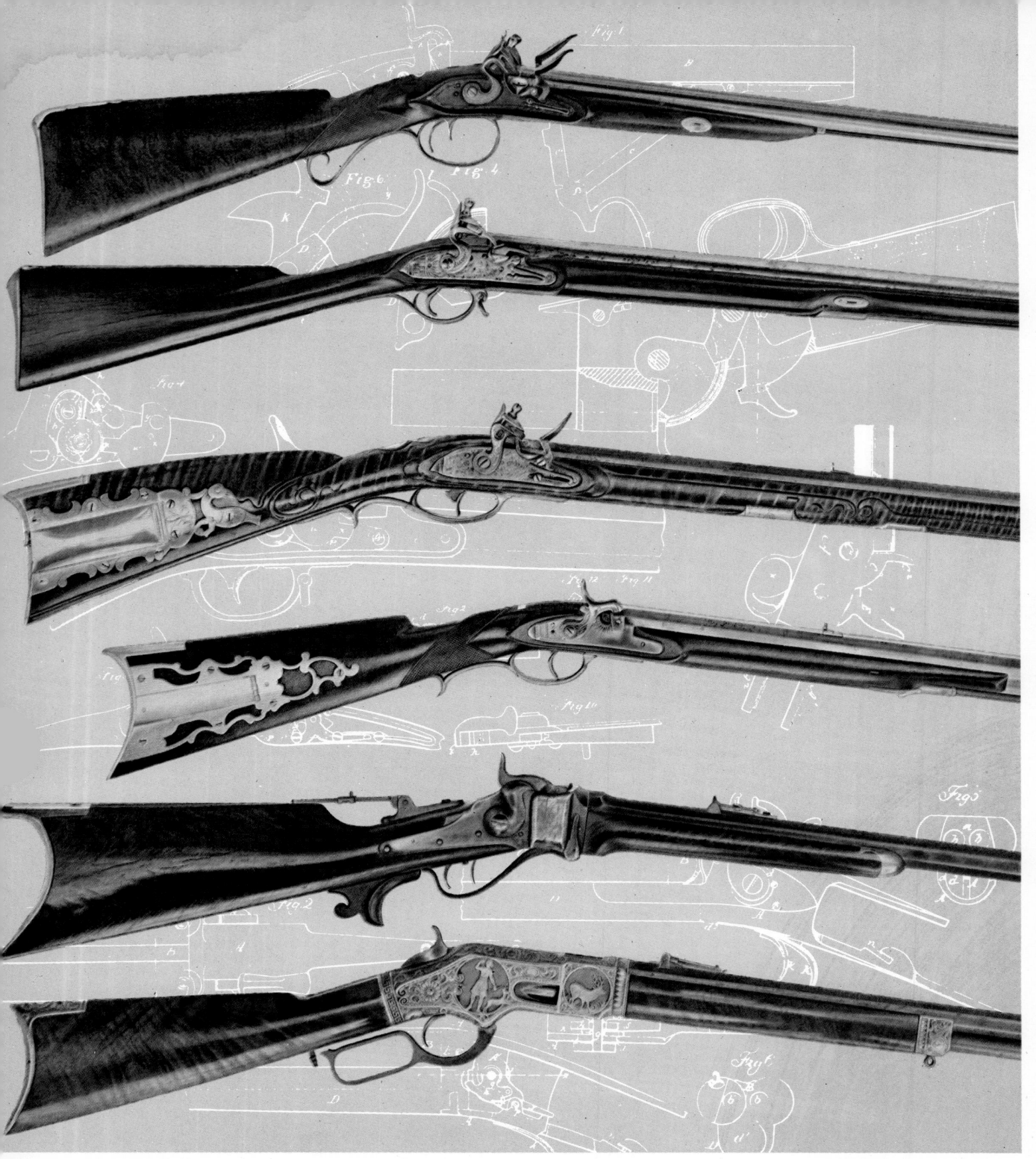

THE RIFLES used by sportsmen today are direct descendants of the Kentucky flintlock, first native-American gun and basic tool of the pioneer. As the frontier moved West, the need for greater mobility and more rapid firing led to the invention of the percussion cap and self-contained cartridge. These collector's items from the Winchester Museum illustrate that development: Top, 18th century double-barreled flint lock shotgun; single-shot fowling piece, converted from flint to caplock in 1828; muzzle-loaded Kentucky flintlock, made from 1728 to 1840; plains rifle, a variation of the Kentucky; Sharps sporting rifle, once used by buffalo hunters; Model 1866 repeating rifle, first to bear the Winchester name.

possessing the ball may not advance beyond the crossline on which the ball lies, nor may the opponents come within 10 yards of that line until the kick is made.

There are four general methods of putting the ball in play: punt, drop kick, place kick and scrimmage. As just explained, a place kick is used to open each half game. After a free catch, any one of the four methods may be used.

Definitions and Chief Rules of Play.—The principal terms used in football are listed alphabetically and defined below.

Down. A down, the name of each new play, occurs when the referee blows his whistle and declares the ball *dead.* When a player carrying the ball is so held that he cannot advance, the ball is *down,* and either the player or the referee may call it so. If the man carrying the ball is so held by an opponent that any part of his body other than his hands or feet touches the ground while he is so held, the ball is down. Other chief instances of downs or dead balls are: after a touchdown, touchback, safety or goal has been made; in general: when the ball goes out of bounds at the side; after an incompleted forward pass; while the penalty for a foul is being enforced and after a fair catch.

If a team having continuous possession of the ball fails to make a 10-yard advance during four consecutive downs, the ball goes to the opponents on the fifth down.

No play may be made while the ball is dead, except as provided by rules for reopening play in the case.

To make a *drop kick,* a player lets the ball fall from his hands and kicks it just as it rebounds from the earth: When a player has an opportunity to catch a ball that is in the air from an opponent's kick, he may signal for a *fair catch* by raising his arm, in which case he must not be interfered with in his attempt at a catch. If he succeeds in catching the ball and takes no more than two steps after catching it, his team is entitled to put the ball back into play by any one of the four methods already mentioned—scrimmage, drop kick, punt or kick from placement.

Forward Pass. The ball may be thrown from a point either on or behind the line of scrimmage, forward for any distance toward the opponents' goal. Gripping the ball is a more satisfactory hold before a pass than is the open-hand throw. Any member of Team A may pass the ball to any other member if the other player is on the end of the line or 1 yard back of the line of scrimmage. Any member of Team B may attempt to catch or bat the ball by bona fide methods even if some roughness is involved and, if he succeeds, may advance with it or call it down in his possession. After a member of Team B has touched the ball, any player of either side may seek to gain possession of it. If a ball passed forward is not caught but strikes the ground either before or after being touched by a player of either side, the pass is incomplete, and the ball is returned to the point from which it was passed. An incomplete

forward pass counts as a down at the spot of the preceding down.

Snapping the Ball is handing or passing it back from its position on the ground with a quick and continuous motion of the hand or hands, the ball actually leaving the hand or hands in this motion. While resting on the ground and prior to the snap the long axis of the ball must be at right angles to the scrimmage line.

A Shift is a simultaneous change of position by two or more offensive players after the ball is ready-for-play in a scrimmage down and before the next snap.

Lateral Pass. A lateral pass may be made at any time during the game, either across the field or backward if desired. It may be intercepted in the air by a member of the other team and advanced; but if the ball strikes the ground or is dropped on a fumble, it is declared dead for the other team but not for the offensive team.

Foul. Certain violations of rules are considered fouls (see *Penalties*).

Free Kick. A punt, drop kick or place kick following a fair catch is called a *free kick.* During this play all players must be inbounds and all of the players on the offensive team, except the holder of the ball, must be behind the ball. Other team must be behind restraining line and at least 5 of them within 5 yds. of that line.

Field Goal. A goal kicked from the field by a drop or placement kick during the regular progress of the play. The ball must go over the crossbar or over one of the goal posts. Score, 3 points.

Hurdling. An attempt by the runner to jump over a player who is still on his feet, or to jump over a player on the scrimmage line within 5 yds. from the spot of the snap, with both feet or knees foremost. A man carrying the ball more than 5 yds. from the point of beginning the play may not attempt to jump over a player who is still on his feet. When he is in the open a player on his knee may be hurdled without a penalty being exacted.

Kickoff. First and third halves are opened by this play. It is a place kick from the 40-yard line of the team possessing the ball.

Offside. A team is offside when a player or any part of his person is beyond the line of scrimmage or his restraining line when the ball leaves the center's hands or on the kickoff.

Out of Bounds. The ball is out of bounds when either the ball or the player carrying it touches the ground on or outside the side line or side line extended. If a ball kicked by a member of Team A goes out of bounds without touching a member of Team B, the ball goes to Team B; but if such a ball touches a member of Team B before going out, it belongs to the team that last secured possession of it. A ball out of bounds must be brought back into the field one-third the width of the field. No player may be out of bounds when the ball is put in play except the kicker and the holder of the ball in a place kick.

Place Kick. A ball kicked while it is resting on the ground, either free, as at kickoff, or supported by an assisting

player.

Punt. A kick in which the ball is struck as it drops from the player's hands and before it touches the ground.

Safety. A safety is made when the ball is declared dead, behind or on the goal line, in the hands of a player defending his own goal, provided that the impetus that sent the ball over the goal line was given by a member of the defending team. Certain other technical cases of fouls, incomplete passes or kicks across the side lines also constitute safeties. A safety made by a player of Team A counts two points for Team B.

Scrimmage, the action of putting the ball in play between closely opposing lines of players. At least seven men of offensive team must be on the scrimmage line when the ball is put in play. There are really two scrimmage lines, separated by the length of the ball as it lies lengthwise on the field. To be in position on the scrimmage line, a player must have two hands or two feet or one hand and the opposite foot, within 12 inches of his team's line. The seven men in the line-up for scrimmage are, each way from the middle: center, right and left guards, right and left tackles and right and left ends. Back of the line, 1 yard or more, are: the quarterback, the right and left halfbacks and the fullback. The ball is put in play by being snapped back on signal from center to a back. The quarterback calls secret signals giving directions to his teammates, including the runner to whom the ball is passed.

Touchback resembles a safety; it occurs when a member of Team B holds the ball behind B's goal line, having been forced behind his goal line by Team A. After a touchback or a safety, the defenders who made the touchback or the safety put the ball in play anywhere on their own 20-yard line.

Touchdown, made when a ball lawfully held by a member of either team is declared down, on, over or behind the opponents' goal line. A touchdown counts 6 points and entitles the team that just scored to add an additional point if successful in kicking the ball over the crossbar of the goal post or in passing or rushing the ball across the goal line.

Penalties.—Losses of 5 to 15 or more yards are imposed according to the nature of the violation of the rules.

Loss of 5 yards: Excess time-out illegally requested or used; illegal delay of the game; failure to complete substitution before play starts; entry of substitute when ball is in play; violation of free kick formation; violation of scrimmage formation; interference with opponents or ball; player in motion less than 5 yards back; player out-of-bounds when ball is snapped; ball not put in play by snap when so specified; putting ball in play before ready-for-play; false start; player on line receiving snap; illegal forward pass (also loss of down if by A); defensive holding; crawling; handing ball forward beyond line; handing ball forward illegally behind the line; intentionally grounding pass (also loss of down).

Loss of 15 yards: Violation of rules during intermission; team not ready to play at scheduled time; illegal return to game; failure to pause one second in shift play; forward pass illegally touched (also loss of down); offensive pass interference (also loss of down); interference with opportunity to catch kick; ineligible receiver down field (also loss of down); interlocked interference; illegal use of hands and arms by offense; striking, kicking, kneeing; meeting with knee, striking with locked hands, etc.; roughing the kicker; piling; hurdling; tripping; tackling out-of-bounds; running into opponent obviously out of play; clipping; side line coaching; persons allowed on field; one representative in case of accident; unsportsmanlike conduct; unnecessary roughness.

Loss of a Down: Ineligible receiver down field (also 15 yards); illegal forward pass by team A; forward pass illegally touched (also 15 yards); intentionally grounding pass (also 5 yards); offensive pass interference (also 15 yards).

Loss of Half Distance to Goal Line: Foul within 1-yard line to prevent play; foul by defensive team behind its own goal line.

Offended Team's Ball at Spot of Foul: Short free kick illegally touched by kicking team; illegally touching free kick after going out-of-bounds; defensive pass interference; scrimmage kick illegally touched by kicking team; illegally batting ball; illegally kicking or kicking at a free ball; other fouls when the ball is free.

Suspension from Game: For illegal return to game; for illegal equipment.

Disqualification: For striking, kneeing and kicking; for roughing the kicker; for any flagrantly unsportsmanlike conduct.

Forfeiture of Game: Refusal of either team to play when ordered; fouls to prevent play.

GOLF
(Junior High School to Adults)

Golf is an outdoor game played on a *course* or *links.* The game probably originated in Holland or Belgium in the early Middle Ages. Very soon afterwards it became popular in Scotland, but it was not until the 19th century that its popularity spread to England and the United States, where it has become a national pastime.

A golf course contains either 9 or 18 *holes.* Each hole consists of a *tee,* a level plot of varying size on which the ball is teed up for the initial shot on each hole; a *fairway* or lawn extending all or most of the way from the tee to the green; and the *green,* generally a roundish plot made of very closely cut grass or in some places of sand. In the green is the hole, about 4¼ inches in diameter and 4 inches deep, into which the ball must go before the next hole can be played.

Clubs of various shapes are used to hit the ball off the tee into the fairway or into the *rough* (the uncut grass surrounding the fairway) and from there to the green and the hole. The position of the hole is marked by a slender pole with a colored flag. The pole is removed from the hole when all the players have reached the green. The fairway may contain natural hazards, such as trees, rocks, small streams or ponds; and artificial ones, such as *bunkers* (mounds of earth) and *traps* (depressions filled with sand).

The distance from the tee to the hole may be anywhere from 60 to 650 yards. Each hole should theoretically be played in *par,* the number of strokes needed to reach the hole from the tee. Par for holes of 250 yards or less is generally 3; for holes of 251 to 445 yards, 4; and of 446 to 600 yards, 5. This may vary somewhat according to the difficulty of the hole; and on each course there is an official par for each hole. When a player makes a hole in one less than par, he gets a *birdie.* If he does it in two strokes less than par, he has an *eagle.* The purpose of the game, therefore, is to hit the ball, without touching it except by the clubs, from tee to hole in as few strokes as possible. The lowest score is the best score.

The clubs used in golf may be classified in three general groups: wooden clubs for long shots; iron clubs for intermediate shots; and the putter for use on the green in actually hitting the ball into the hole.

Golf is usually played in *twosomes* (one player against another) or *foursomes* (partners against partners). Players are usually accompanied by a caddie, who carries the bag of clubs. The player who takes the fewest strokes on the first hole has the *honor;* that is, he starts first on the next hole and so on. After all the players have driven off the tee, the one farthest from the hole shoots next, and play continues in this manner until all the balls are holed. *Colonel Bogey* is an imaginary opponent who makes every hole in a little more than par and so provides competition for a single player. The bogey for each hole is not official.

Golf is usually scored in one of two ways: in *match* play the score is by holes; that is, whoever wins the most holes wins the match; in *medal* play the score is by strokes, and whoever has the fewest number of strokes for the number of holes played wins the match. There are numerous and interesting variations: in *two-ball foursomes* partners alternate shots on the same ball; in a *Nassau match,* one point is given for winning the first 9 holes, one for the second 9 and one for the 18. Women use the same courses as men, though sometimes special tees a few yards closer to the green are provided for their use.

HANDBALL
(Late Elementary School to Adults)

Handball is a game that may be played outdoors but is often played in an indoor gymnasium. There are two main divisions of the game: *Four-wall handball,* an old Irish game played with four walls, front, sides and rear; and *one-wall handball,* the American adaptation of the Irish game, which originated in New York about 1900 and is played against a single wall. The single-wall court is more commonly used and enables camps and outdoor playgrounds to feature the game. Because it is more common and practicable, only the one-wall game will be described.

Dimensions of the One-wall Court. A handball floor is 34 feet long by 20 feet wide. The front wall is 16 feet high. A line called the *short line* is drawn on the floor parallel to the front wall and 16 feet from it. Nine feet farther from the wall, behind the short line, markers are placed to indicate an imaginary line known as the *service line.* If the court is outdoors, 6-foot wire extensions should be built above the wall and on the side lines to stop balls that miss the wall.

The game is played by two to four persons on opposing teams. The object is to secure points by causing the op-

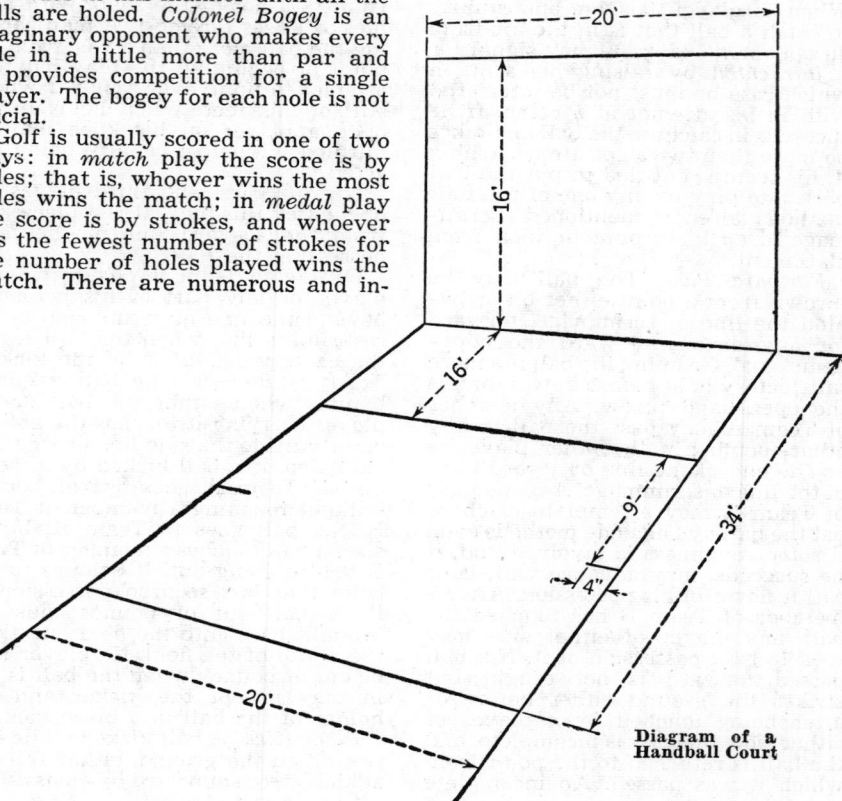

Diagram of a Handball Court

ponent to fail in his effort to hit the wall. In the United States 21 points constitute a game.

The standard handball is a black rubber ball 1 inches in diameter ⅞ and 2 ounces in weight. It may be hit with either hand. The hand is best held as a shallow cup, deepest at the second joint, where the ball strikes. Gloves may be worn.

Each effort to win a point begins with a service from the space between the short line and service line. For this play a ball is dropped to the floor and hit on the first bounce. A player may bounce the ball twice before swinging at it but will be out unless he swings on his third try. A ball served must go to the front wall without striking any other object, must hit the wall above the 4-inch baseboard and in rebounding must first touch the floor beyond the ace line—though it may be made to strike side and back walls on its way to the floor. A served ball that strikes between the front wall and the ace line in its rebound from the front is a *short* ball. A *long* ball, one that strikes the floor behind the back line, may combine with short balls to lose the three attempts at fair service, and the hand-in becomes hand-out. Each fair service cancels whatever shorts and longs the server may have against him.

If a served ball strikes properly behind the ace line, the receiver (an opponent) must return it on the fly or first bound to the front wall above the baseboard. After this first service and return the players alternate in striking the ball until one fails to get it back to the front. Only the served ball must strike behind the ace line in rebounding from the front wall; all returned balls may fall on either side of the ace line as long as they stay within the court. Balls in play may be volleyed before they strike the floor or be hit on first bound.

In general intentional interference, blocking the ball, is a *foul;* unintentional interference by an opposing player is called a *hinder.* Fouls are punished, but a hinder is merely followed by reservice from the same player. It is always a foul, however, to stop a ball on its way to the front wall. It is a foul to strike a ball with both hands or to touch the ball twice in one attempt at batting.

Since only the server can score, fouls by the hand-in forfeit the ball, and fouls by the hand-out score for the server.

The officials of handball are a referee and a scorer.

HOCKEY

(Senior High School to Adults)

Hockey is a stick game of ancient origin passed down the centuries from the Persians to the Greeks, to the Romans and northward to the Britons. It became one of the national games of England and Scotland. In Ireland it was played differently and was called *hurling* or *hurley.* Boys in the United States have a simple game called *shinny* that they play with a curved stick and ball or block of wood and which is based on some of the principles of hockey. There are two

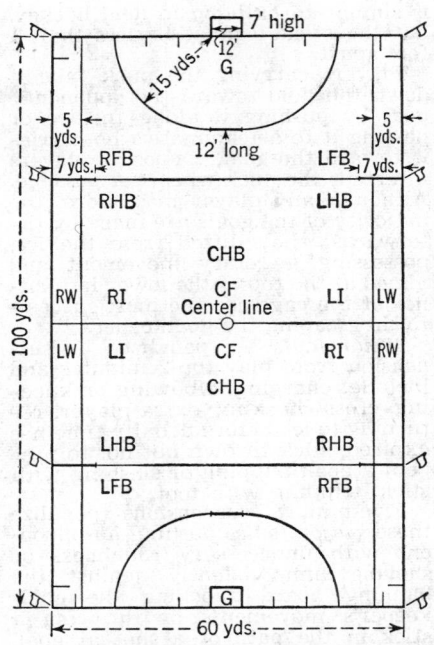
Diagram of a Hockey Field
Positions of players: RFB, right fullback; LFB, left fullback; RHB, right halfback; LHB, left halfback; CHB, center halfback; RW, right wing; RI, right inside; CF, center forward; LI, left inside; LW, left wing; G, goalkeeper

major divisions of this sport—field hockey and ice hockey.

Field Hockey.—The playing field is 90 or 100 yards in length by 50 or 60 yards in width; for secondary schools the size is reduced to 85 yards by 45 yards. There are 5-yard strips along each side. The goal posts are 12 feet apart at the middle of each end with a crossbar at a height of 7 feet. A net is placed back of the goal to catch the ball. Fifteen yards directly in front of each goal line, a 4-yard line is drawn in white; ends of this forward line are connected with the goal line by arcs with the goal posts as centers and a radius of 15 yards. This space is called the *striking circle.* Boundary lines are called *side lines* and *goal lines.* respectively. The field is divided into four 25-yard sections by a *mid-line* and two *quarter lines.*

The game is played by two teams of 11 members each; each eleven has five forwards, three halfbacks, two fullbacks and one goalkeeper, with general positions as shown in the diagram. The players use hooked or bent sticks with blades of ash and handles of cane, often with rubber inserts. The sticks weigh up to 28 ounces. Lighter sticks are used by the forwards and heavier sticks by the backs. The ball is painted white and is the same size as a cricket ball—9 inches in circumference and 5½ ounces in weight. Heavy low-heeled shoes without spikes or cleats are worn.

The object of the game is to pass the ball from player to player until it is driven into the opponents' goal. All shots at goal must be made from within the striking circle. Each goal scores one point.

The forwards are the chief attackers; the halfbacks assist the forwards; fullbacks break up attacks by the

enemy; goalkeepers block shots at goal. Every attacking man is guarded by a corresponding opponent.

Only players *onside* may strike a ball toward the opponents' goal. A player is *offside* when the ball has last been hit or rolled in by a member of his own team behind him, unless at the time the player is in his own half of the field, unless the striker or roller-in is nearer the opponents' goal line, or unless there are three or more opponents between the player and the goal he is attacking. An offside player becomes onside when his teammate who last touched the ball passes him toward the opponents' goal, or when an opponent touches the ball.

It is permissible to stop the ball by using any part of the body, but only the goalkeeper may kick the ball. A ball caught in the hands must be dropped at once to fall perpendicularly.

Back strokes are not permitted. A player may hook sticks with an opponent within striking distance of the ball.

The beginning of a hockey game is an operation known as the *bully,* for which two opposing players stand on the center line, each with the opponents' goal at his left hand and with the ball between them. Each must strike the ground and the opponent's stick three times in succession, after which both are free to strike the ball. During this operation all players of each side must be in their regular team positions.

A bully on the mid-line is also used at the beginning of the second half and after each scoring of a goal. If an attacker drives the ball across the opponents' goal line outside the posts, a bully must be played on the 25-yard line nearer this goal. An intentional foul by the defenders within the 25-yard line calls for a *penalty corner;* an unintentional foul of the same type gains a *corner* (a hit taken within 3 yards of a corner flag); a penalty corner is taken from any point of the goal line not less than 10 yards from the nearer goal post.

When any player causes the ball to go out of bounds at the side, one of his opponents must put the ball back in play by rolling it into the field in any direction. For this purpose only one man may be outside the 5-yard line, and no player may enter the 5-yard line until the roll-in is begun.

It is a foul (1) to hold, strike, push, trip or kick an opponent; (2) to raise the stick above the shoulders; (3) to strike with the back of the stick (4) to strike the ball while offside; (5) to cross between a player and the ball in order to prevent his striking.

Penalty for each of these fouls is one free hit by the opponents, the defenders standing at least 5 yards from the man who makes the free hit.

The game has two halves of 30 minutes each. Halves of 15, 20 or 25 minutes are often used by younger players. The referee is head official and has charge of the ball. An umpire in each half of the field watches the conduct of players and reports certain classes of fouls assigned to him.

Ice Hockey.—Ice hockey was originally called *bandy* and is more popular than field hockey in countries where there is ice in the winter. To most Americans, therefore, *hockey* means *ice hockey*. In its simplest form of driving a ball across a given limit with a stick, ice hockey has been known for at least 5 centuries in northern Europe. The present form of the game has been played in Great Britain for over 65 years; the international rules of play emanated from Canada.

The rink for ice hockey is at least 165 feet long by 60 feet wide and not greater than 250 feet by 110 feet. The rink is surrounded by a board fence called the *banking board*, approximately 40 inches high; the purpose of this board is to permit the *puck* to rebound. The goals, open net- or wire-covered cages 6 feet broad and 4 feet high, are placed at the center of each end line. Sixty feet from each end *zone lines* are drawn across the rink; the remaining center area is called the *center zone*.

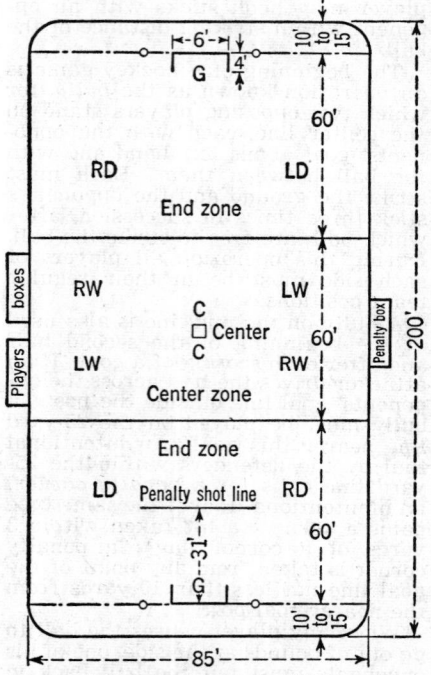

Diagram of a Hockey Rink

Positions of players: G, goalkeeper; RD, right defense; LD, left defense; RW, right wing; LW, left wing; C, center

The players are on skates and carry official ice-hockey sticks. The puck is a flat solid disk of vulcanized rubber 1 inch thick and 3 inches in diameter and the banking boards keep it almost constantly in play, so that ice hockey is one of the fastest and most strenuous of sports. Heavy gloves and shin guards and head guards are necessary equipment to protect from injury during play. The goalkeeper wears heavier guards fully covering his legs and a padded protector for his chest.

Each team has 6 players formed of right and left wing (forwards), center (also a forward), right and left defense and goalkeeper. Both hockey teams endeavor to secure the larger score by shooting the puck into the opponents' goal. Each fair goal counts one point.

The *facing off* that starts the game

is similar to *bullying* in field hockey, but the sticks cannot be less than 1 foot apart.

Players carrying the puck take it down the field toward the opponents' goal by pushing it along the ice or passing it to a teammate who carries it toward the goal. Opposing players intercept the puck whenever possible. Although any player may score, the majority of the goals are made by the forwards; shots lifted from the ice, possessing a rotary movement and aimed at the top of the lower left corner of the cage are the most successful in escaping the goalkeeper.

Minor fouls are penalized by suspension from play for 2 minutes and include: charging, elbowing or kneeing, cross checking, extra player, returning to ice before penalty time has expired, stick thrown but not to prevent a goal, tripping or slashing with stick, tripping with foot.

Five-minute suspensions penalize these *major fouls:* pushing an opponent with unnecessary roughness or shoving him violently against the banking board, blocking the goalkeeper's movements or throwing a stick in the path of a shot at goal. Any extreme or obviously unnecessary roughness may earn suspension from the rest of the game. After his suspension time is up, the player immediately re-enters the rink.

A substitute may replace any player at any time during the game when play is officially stopped by the main official, the referee, or his assistant. A timekeeper, assistant timekeeper, penalty timekeeper and two goal umpires also are used.

The game is played in three 20-minute periods with 10-minute intermissions between periods. In case of a tie overtime is allowed.

HORSESHOE PITCHING

(Late Elementary School to Adults)

Horseshoe pitching is an ancient and popular informal contest and has become a standard event outdoors and at picnics. A less scientific form of the game is called *quoits* and employs a flat, iron ring instead of an open-end horseshoe.

Courts for informal play have iron stakes 30 to 40 feet apart, usually the greater distance unless the players are women or boys. The stakes are in the center of a *pitcher's box* 6 feet square, with a wooden frame 1 inch above the ground. Moist sand or loam is used to fill the pitcher's box to a depth of 6 inches or more. The stakes are 1 inch in diameter and are 8 inches above the surface of the surrounding clay.

Each player is allowed two shoes that may not be more than 7 inches wide and 7½ inches long, or over 2½ pounds in weight. After a toss for the choice of first pitch or follow, the two to four players take turns in pitching, the player with the larger score throwing first. No player may pitch from a step ahead of the line 3 feet in front of each stake that forms the pitcher's box on penalty of forfeiting his score by the pitch.

Any shoe that strikes the ground or frame of the pitcher's box in called a

foul shoe and does not score; if a shoe encircles the stake or peg it is called a *ringer* and scores three. A *leaner,* a shoe that hits the peg without encircling it, counts as the closest shoe to the stake, which always scores one point. If two or more shoes are equal distances from the peg or are ringers, it is a tie and no points are given. A shoe may be moved by the impact of another shoe and both are measured from their new position. A score of 21 or 50, as agreed upon, constitutes a game.

ICEBOATING

(Senior High School to Adults)

An American Sport.—Iceboating, although practiced a little in Holland, the Scandinavian countries, Russia and Great Britain, is distinctly an American sport. Iceboat races were held on the Hudson River in the latter part of the 18th century, and iceboating is a popular winter sport in many parts of Canada and the United States.

The first iceboat was merely a square box with a skate on either side for runners and one in the back for a rudder. The modern boat, which will speed 70 miles an hour, consists of a long, single, wooden beam (usually of bass, pine or butternut) set on a crossbeam at right angles and about two-thirds of the way forward to make a kite-shaped frame. To the crossbeam are attached two runners set into oak frames; a third runner is attached to the lengthwise beam at the rear end for a rudder, which is worked by a tiller, usually made long enough for the steersman to lie in the box and steer with his feet while his hands manipulate the sails.

The passenger box (usually triangular or elliptical) is placed on the beam just ahead of the rudder. The single mast may be either ahead of or at the junction of the beam and crossbar. The mast and spars are usually hollow and are rigged with pliable steel wire. A mainsail and jib rigging are generally used, and the sail area varies from 300 to 600 square feet.

The sailing course for a race is an equilateral triangle, each side 1 mile long. The boats must sail a certain number of times around the course.

Scootering.—A development of the iceboat peculiar to Great South Bay off the south shore of Long Island is the *scooter,* which consists of a duckboat fitted with runners and sails. It originated, so the story goes, with the duck hunters who grew tired of pulling their boats over the ice to open water. At first they equipped their boats with runners only, which made it easier to push the boats. Then someone tried the sail. The modern scooter has standard equipment and is a strong boat 14 feet long with a 5-foot beam, on the bottom of which two long runners are set midway each side of the center, and two shorter ones are placed well out to each side to carry the boat when it heels over. The sail area, mainsail and jib, is 150 square feet, the mainsail stretched far astern on a long boom; the jib (by which the boat is steered) stretched out on the bowsprit. The scooter's great advantage over the iceboat is that it is amphibious and hence well adapted to places where the ice has many open spots.

LACROSSE

(Senior High School to Adults)

Lacrosse is a field game of North American Indian origin that has long been a favorite in Canada and is gaining popularity in the United States and Great Britain. Lacrosse resembles hockey in some respects but has a different-shaped club in which the ball is carried to the goal.

Two teams of 12 players each play on a field that may be 100 to 130 yards long and 70 to 85 yards wide. Most fields allow about 20 yards back of each goal across the width of the field. The goals are set midway at the ends of the playing field in a space 12 feet deep and 18 feet long called the *goal crease* and are formed by two poles 6 feet high and 6 feet apart with a crossbar to which a net is attached. A circle in the exact middle of the field has a diameter of 20 feet.

The rubber sponge ball may be 7¾ to 8 inches in circumference and 4½ to 5 ounces in weight; for camp use the ball is sometimes whittled from softwood. The racket or *crosse* may have a handle of any desired length, but the net-covered oval triangle formed by the bent stick may not be more than 12 inches wide. Rubbersoled shoes are worn.

The purpose of the game is to throw or carry the ball into the opponents' goal. At the start of play each team has a goalkeeper, point, cover point and third-home man in a line up the field directly before their goal, right and left defense, center, right and left attack, and third-, second- and first-home men in front of the opponents' goal.

The play begins with *facing*—a maneuver corresponding to the bully of hockey and the center-jump of basketball. Two players face each other, left hands toward the goal they are to attack and the ball placed between the reverse surfaces of their crosses. On signal, each draws his crosse sharply toward him and is then free to try for the ball. He may bat the ball if he chooses or scoop it up and run with it, but the best of tactics is to begin as promptly as possible a series of short quick passes toward the goal. The Canadians have developed amazing team play, and their pass work is more remarkable than that of the best basketball player considering the tools by which the passing must be done. It is possible to throw the ball 100 yards or more with the crosse, but short throws retaining control of the ball are better in the long run.

Charging is not permitted, but a man may block the progress of an advancing player by standing in his way. When the ball goes out of bounds, the two nearest opposing players must *face* not less than 4 yards from the boundary line.

It is a foul to strike, push, hold or trip an opponent; to throw the crosse; to interfere with a player who has not the ball; to interfere with the goalkeeper before the ball passes into the crease; to touch the ball with the hand. (A goalkeeper may stop the ball with his hands, as in hockey.)

The penalty for a foul is either suspension from 1 minute to 5 minutes or a *free position*. A personal foul earns suspension for the rest of the game. If a free position or throw is to be made, the referee designates a player of the side against which the foul was committed to make such play with the ball as he may choose, no opponent being permitted within 5 yards when his play is made. A free throw cannot be declared within 10 yards of the goal endangered by it.

PING-PONG or TABLE TENNIS

(Junior High School to Adults)

Ping-pong is an indoor table game adapted from lawn tennis; it is played on a standard table with small, hollow celluloid balls and a solid-faced racket or paddle. The racket is of plain wood or surfaced with sandpaper, rubber, leather or cork, and the blade is 5¼ inches wide and 6½ inches long with a handle 5¼ inches long. The standard table is painted dark green, is 30 inches above the floor and is 5 feet wide by 9 feet long. White lines (about ¾ of an inch wide) go lengthwise down the center of the table top and around its outside edges. The net, stretched across the center, is dark green with white binding and is 6¾ inches in height.

Either solid or folding tables may be used; for informal or home use, tables may run as small as 5½ by 3 feet, and the net is adjusted to allow a ¾-inch height for each foot of table length.

Singles or doubles games may be played by two or four persons, and rules similar to those used in tennis apply, except that only one serve (underhand) is permitted, no ball may be volleyed (hit before the bounce), and in singles service may be to either court.

The purpose of the game is to return the serve so that the receiver cannot get it back into his opponent's half of the table. A *fault* in service or failure to make a fair return during play adds one point to the opponent's score. The first player to earn 21 points with a 2-point margin over his opponent is declared the winner. A score of *20-all* requires one player to secure two points in a row to win.

Each player serves five times in succession, then receives five times, and so on until the game is won or the score is 20-all. After 20-all is reached, service changes after each point.

In doubles the serve must be to alternate courts as in tennis, and partners take turns serving; that is, when A and B are playing against C and D, A serves five times, then C, B and D each serve five times. In doubles each player may take one side of the court, or he may alternate shots with his partner. When partners alternate shots, it is a fault if the ball is returned twice in succession by the same player.

An exciting game in which several people can participate is played as follows: All stand around the ping-pong table, with one player at each end holding a racket. After the ball is served, the server drops the racket and starts around to the other end of the table, and the player behind him picks up the racket and makes the next shot, again dropping the racket for the next player. After a player makes three misses, he drops out. As the players become fewer, the game becomes more exciting, and finally only three are left rushing madly around the table. One soon drops out, and the survivors are proclaimed the winners.

POLO

(Adults)

Polo is the ancient predecessor of hockey—the game with stick and ball. Judging by the records and literary references, hockey on foot always derived from the mounted version. Authentic polo originated in Persia more than 2,000 years ago and spread throughout the East. Polo was played for the first time by Europeans in 1863, English cavalry officers forming the first polo club in Calcutta in 1864–65. News of the game spread to England and the first game was played there by army teams in 1869 with improvised mallets and wooden balls about the size of cricket balls. Through the enthusiasm of a visiting American journalist, James Gordon Bennett, the game was introduced to the United States in 1876. The first game between the United States and another nation's team took place in 1886, when an English team won the cup offered by the Westchester Polo Club. In 1921 a committee met in London and drew up rules for polo that have since been adopted universally with minor local changes. Teams from Argentina have played United States teams since 1922, and many expert American players prefer Argentine ponies. The major national governing body for polo is the United States Polo Association, which includes the Intercollegiate Association as a member organization.

Polo fields are 150 to 200 yards wide and about 300 yards long and may be boarded on all sides. Goal posts are 24 feet apart, 250 yards distant from each other and are made of light wood that may break without injury to a player or his mount. The game is played by riders on horseback; its object is to drive a 3-inch white wooden ball, by the stroke of a long, flexiblehandled mallet, between the opponents' goal posts. The usual game is divided into *chukkers* or periods of 7½ or 8 minutes each, with 3-minute intermissions; at the half, a 7-minute rest is allowed. Match play outdoors has 4-man teams with two forwards and two backs, but indoor polo is usually played by 3-man teams. A system of handicaps for less skilled players has done much to widen the popularity of the game.

The requirements of the game are severe, and considerable danger and expense are involved. The major prerequisites are excellent horsemanship, clear and cool headwork and the ability to make controlled shots, forward or backhand, and to meet the flying ball with the head of the mallet.

Fouls are declared for all cases of careless, reckless, dangerous riding, for roughness in personal contact with an opponent or for cruel treatment of the ponies. It is a foul for a dismounted player to strike the ball or for any assistance to be given in the progress of the game by a person who comes on the field for that purpose.

Each foul subtracts one-quarter or one-half point from the score of the offending team. A goal made, directly or indirectly, by means of foul play does not count. Fair goals count one point.

ROWING

(Senior High School to Adults)

Rowing is propelling a boat by oars operated by two or more persons; *sculling* is a similar operation by one person who uses a pair of sculls or short oars approximately 2 feet shorter than those for rowing. A single shell as used for sculling is about 26 feet long, eleven inches wide, with a weight of 28 pounds.

Rowing has been officially recognized as a sport for over a century, although records exist of rowing races in England as far back as 1715. Rowing was used for purely utilitarian purposes in transportation, war and commerce from early days until the Elizabethan age.

Outriggers (steel frames for placing the row-locks well out at the side of the boat) were invented in 1845 by Clasper, a builder at Oxford, and started the rapid development of the long, narrow, light modern racing *shells*. The sliding seat now universally employed in intercollegiate contests was first used by Yale in 1870.

Shells with 6 to 10 oars were used in many historical races but the 8-oared shell has become the common type. An 8-oared shell is about 60 feet long, 2 feet wide, about 9½ inches deep and weighs between 270 and 300 pounds. In an 8-oared shell each man pulls one oar or *sweep*, about 12 feet 3 inches long. Races in a regular rowing regatta are likely to include single and double sculls and sweeps in pairs, fours and eights.

An 8-oared crew is accompanied by a *coxswain*, who sits in the stern facing forward, steers the boat and has the responsibility of setting the speed of the stroke. In spurts a racing crew is likely to finish a short race at about 41 strokes to the minute. Longer courses of 3 miles or more take a steady pace of about 33 and quicken at the finish to 38 or better.

The first oarsman facing the coxswain is the *stroke oar*, who receives the advice of the coxswain and himself sets the stroke that the others must take. Other oarsmen must follow his lead or there can be no hope of winning. Good generalship is required in placing the men to distribute both the weight and the strength to the best advantage. In general the less the rudder has to be used, the more energy can go into the straightaway course, for turning the shell even slightly creates a drag in the water that slows the speed.

Much depends on form. The sliding seat makes it possible to use muscles from neck to toes, but it is no easy matter to bring all the muscles into the smooth co-ordination that means the greatest possible drive and power. Long before the spring season opens, muscles are disciplined by practice on gymnasium rowing machines.

Certain types of stroke have proved advantageous. Best results require that the oar blades should not be deeply plunged during the stroke but should be merely covered by water. To *feather* is to give such a downward flip to the wrist and forearm as to make the oar blade skim along nearly parallel to the surface of the water in the recovery after each stroke. If the oar is spoon-shaped, it is sometimes allowed to touch the water lightly as it swings back, thus sustaining a part of the weight of the oar on the water; but much of this saves the rower at the expense of the pace. Feathering is universal, in order to cut the resistance of the air in the backward thrust of the oar.

Rowing is a favorite intercollegiate contest wherever a water course is available, but it is by no means limited to the colleges and universities. Secondary schools have excellent crews, and they have competed creditably in the great English regatta at Henley. Boat clubs practice the world over, and annual regattas are of national and international interest.

SMALL-BOAT SAILING

One of the very finest of all outdoor sports, sailing a small boat, not only gives a great amount of thorough enjoyment but is highly valuable as training in judgment, quickness of decision, and the development of courage.

A small *cat-rigged* boat is the best kind in which to learn, because its equipment is simple and the comparatively wide *beam* (breadth) that marks the typical catboat makes it safe. Cat-rigged means rigged as a catboat, with only one sail, and with the mast set far forward in the *bow* (forward end). A cat generally has a *centerboard* set in the middle of the boat, which can be raised and lowered and is used in sailing against the wind. The sail may be either triangular or quadrilateral. In either case the lower end of the sail is fastened to a *boom*, a horizontal spar free to swing horizontally with the mast as a pivot. A quadrilateral sail has also a *gaff*, a shorter pole supporting the upper edge of the sail. The gaff also pivots against the mast.

The sail is raised and lowered by means of one *halyard* (rope to hoist sail) in the case of the triangular, two halyards in the case of the quadrilateral sail, because one is needed to adjust the outer end of the gaff. When the boat is under way, the sail is controlled by means of a rope, called the *sheet*, fastened to the boom at its *after* (rear) end.

The boat is steered and controlled by means of *rudder* and *tiller*. The rudder is a square or rectangular flat piece of wood or metal at the stern end under the water; the tiller is a handle that is attached to the top of the rudder and extends into the cockpit or open space where the helmsman sits.

If the catboat is fastened to a moor-

ing and you go aboard to go sailing, *before* you raise the sail, if it is the triangular type, you should do two things: (1) see that the sheet is unfastened from the cleat and neatly coiled so as to run freely; (2) pull your boat up close to the mooring and fasten her there; then raise the sail and, when it is all the way up, fasten the halyard to the *cleat* (wooden or metal device used for holding ropes fast). Coil the halyard neatly and place it *out of the way* where it will not get trampled and snarled. One of the very first things to learn and remember is to *keep ropes coiled and out of the way of your feet*, for in a sudden squall, it is very important to lower the sail quickly or to let the sheet run out fast.

Your boat, with sail up, is *still fastened to the mooring*. In that position she will *swing to the wind* with her sail shaking in the wind, if you follow the above directions. If you did not leave the sheet free and have the boat fastened close to the mooring, every little variation of the wind would fill the sail and start your boat forward, drive her this way and that, perhaps even keel her over dangerously.

Now ready to start sailing *before the wind* or *sailing free*, see once more that the sheet is neatly coiled and free to run; next see that your centerboard is *up*; then go forward and unfasten from the mooring the *painter* (rope from bow to mooring), but *don't yet let go* the mooring; still holding on to it with one hand, throw the painter inside your boat out of the way. Put both hands on the mooring and pull your boat briskly up to and past the mooring, so that she will head *off the wind* (away from the wind) and will have a little headway, then get quickly back to your sheet and tiller. Haul the sheet in smartly and at the same time put your tiller *up* (away from the sail). These motions should be made quickly but *smoothly and evenly—not* jerkily and with a rush. Gradually *pay out* (let run) the sheet as the boat's head falls off until you are headed *before the wind*.

It is important not to pay out the sheet too fast or you will spill the wind from the sail, lose headway and thus lose control of your boat. One of the most important principles of good sailing is *always to have some headway for good control of your boat*.

Having swung your boat off dead before the wind, you may *cleat the sheet fast* (fasten it tight to a cleat) and give your entire attention to steering a straight course. The beginner should *never* cleat the sheet fast *except* when the boat is dead before the wind. In this position the sheet cannot be let out any farther, so it is all right to cleat it. At any other time, it may be dangerous to have the sheet cleated fast, for you cannot then let it run quickly if a heavy puff of wind strikes. Letting it run out spills the wind from the sail and is a safeguard against an upset.

When sailing before the wind, it is well for a beginner to select some object directly ahead—either on shore or in the water, provided the object is stationary—at which he can steer, thus being enabled to judge quickly and easily whether he is *holding a true course* (steering straight). It often seems to a beginner that it would be very easy to steer a straight course right before the wind, but this is not true. The pressure of the wind is constantly tending to head the boat around *into the wind* (toward the wind). This tendency must continually be counteracted with the tiller. Remember that the tiller always should be pulled in the direction opposite to that in which you want your boat to go. In thus counteracting the boat's motion, however, do not swing the bow back too far; when you see that your boat is approaching a straight course again, begin to let up on your tiller pull; and when you are straight on the course, steady the tiller there. To haul your tiller too far up will cause the boat to *jibe*, that is, the boat's stern will shift so as to bring the wind *around the end of the boom*, and the sail will swing across the boat with great speed and force if the wind is heavy and if the sail is not well controlled by the sheet. This may be dangerous if there is much wind and a high sea.

It is important to know how to jibe properly. In the *flying jibe*, the sheet is not trimmed at all, and the sail comes *flying* over with the full force of the wind behind it. The beginner is advised not to experiment with the flying jibe except under expert supervision. The safest way to jibe is to *trim* (adjust the angle of) your sail in close over the boat before you jibe, and then let the sheet run out *through your hands smoothly and rapidly* as the wind gets behind the sail. You should swing your boat *up* or *toward* the wind, *while* you trim your sheet in close. Then when you swing your boat *off* (away from) the wind for the jibe, you have everything well under control.

If you are dead before the wind and want to go back to your starting point *without* jibing, first drop your centerboard. You will need that to sail against the wind; then trim your sheet gradually and keep gradually putting your tiller *down* until your boat is *close on the wind*—that is, headed close into the wind, with the sail *closehauled* (close in along the rail of the boat) and with the *luff* of the sail (the part next to the mast) shaking very little. *On the wind* you must constantly watch that your boat shall neither come into the wind so that the whole sail shakes, nor fall off the wind too far. *Watch the luff of your sail* is the best motto for the novice. When it stops trembling, you are too far off the wind; when it begins to snap and shake strongly, you are too far into the wind.

When the wind is coming over the *starboard* (right) bow, you are on the *starboard tack* (right leg of a boat's course); when the wind is over your *port* (left) bow, you are on the *port tack*. Suppose you are close-hauled on the starboard tack. To *go about* to the port tack, put your tiller *down* with a smooth, rapid motion and your boat will shoot up into the wind with her sail shaking. Keep moving your tiller in the direction in which you started it until the sail swings across the boat

and fills on the port tack. As soon as your sail fills on the new tack, steady the boat with the tiller so that the luff is just shaking a little and then proceed as you did on the starboard tack, always watching the luff.

Sailing with wind abeam means sailing with the wind coming across your boat from either side *amidships* or at a right angle to the hull. *Sailing with wind quartering* is sailing with the wind coming from either side diagonally over the stern. In both cases you have to be on your guard against a strong tendency for the boat to *broach to* (swing into the wind while running free). Remember to watch the luff and also to avoid swinging your tiller too hard and far at a time.

To *make a landing* or *pick up the mooring* is not easy. It is an art in itself. Get an expert to demonstrate for you and then let you experiment.

A beginner should take along an experienced sailor to instruct him and to help him in case of emergency; he also should do his utmost to *carry out the instructions without assistance*. This is the quickest possible way to learn.

You should know how to swim before you try to learn to sail.

You should not take other people sailing until you really know how to sail well! You have no right to take the responsibility of other people's safety until you are qualified to meet any of the emergencies that may and do arise.

SKATING
(All Ages)

Early and Modern Skates.—Bone runners tied to the feet with leather thongs were the skates of the early Norsemen. The next development, supposedly in the 3d century, was the wooden skate with an iron runner that was screwed on to the heel of the shoe and strapped to the toe. Steel runners later replaced the iron ones, then came the all-steel skate. The club skates of the 1890s were of this last type. They were fastened to the shoes by adjustable clamps and were likely to come off at embarrassing moments, often bringing a sole of shoe off too. Although ordinary shoes were worn, they had to have strong, fairly heavy soles for the clamps to get a grip. The skates were all steel, with blades about 3/16 inch thick, resting on the ice at only one point of an arc, thus earning the name of *rockers*. These rockers tended to curves and to pleasing variations of balance, which made for graceful rather than speedy skating.

With the advent of hockey as a popular ice game new types of skates designed for quick stops, speed, lightness and safety were introduced. The skating shoe became a permanent part of the skating outfit, with the plates of the skates riveted to it. One of the most popular of these modern skates is the Norwegian, which has blades of especially hardened steel, from 16½ to 19 inches long, thin and straight, borne on three aluminum tubes, one horizontal, two vertical. For soft ice the width of the blade is about ⅛ inch. It may be narrower for very hard ice.

Skating as a Sport.—In ancient times the Scandinavians, Finns and Dutch were the most proficient skaters because in their countries skating was a means of transportation as well as a sport. In England references to the art of skating appeared as early as the 12th century. European colonists brought the sport to America. In modern times skating has become a popular and well-organized winter sport in practically all the European countries, in Japan and, of course, in Canada and the United States. Contests are held annually in the winter resorts of Europe; skating is always a part of the winter sports contests at Montreal and Lake Placid. Twenty-three nations belong to the International Skating Union. The organizations of each country—the Amateur Skating Association of Canada, the Amateur Skating Union in the United States—are subject to its rulings.

Contests.—There are two general types of modern skating contests. One emphasizes speed; the other, grace and ingenuity. Each has its devotees, and national and international contests are held annually in each branch of the sport.

Figure Skating, although an accomplishment of individual skaters long ago, first became subject to definite contest rules in the 19th century. It has been highly developed in Europe, on both the Continent and the British Isles, where two distinct styles—the Anglo-Swiss, in which the body remains almost upright, the leg that cuts the figure is held straight, and the other leg straight out behind and the arms loosely at the sides; and the Continental, in which the knee of the leg cutting the figure is bent slightly, and the other leg is used in various positions to balance the body.

For Speed. In America speed skating has always been more popular than figure skating. Most of the contests held are for speed. Speed records in short-distance skate racing do not differ greatly from sprinting records on foot—the 100-yard dash on skates is made in approximately 9 seconds. By official agreement the title of champion in international speed contests goes to the winner of three out of four races, the distances being 500, 1,500, 5,000 and 10,000 meters (a meter is slightly in excess of 3 feet).

Ice Hockey. Perhaps America's greatest interest in skating is shown in the popularity of ice hockey. Hockey matches, attended by huge crowds, are held in the skating rinks of most of the large northern cities each season. Many intercollegiate matches are held. The game itself is described in the article on hockey.

The recreational popularity of skating is also great and is quite sure to remain so. Outdoor rinks are a feature of most cities in the snow country. In many large cities indoor skating rinks, where the ice is frozen mechanically, are kept open the greater part of the year.

Ice Games.—There are numerous games besides hockey that may be adapted to skating. Tag, pom-pom-pullaway, ice basketball and baseball, crack the whip, ice shinney and ice shuffleboard are just a few.

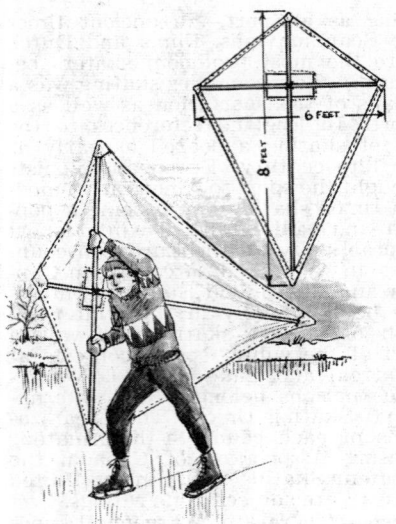

SKATE SAIL of lightweight duck. The edges should be hemmed and corners reinforced. Two spars should be about one inch square glued and lashed with rawhide or fish line.

Skate Sailing.—In broad, open stretches skating with a sail is fine sport. These sails should be absolutely flat and stretched very tight. Spars and rigging should be strong, yet sufficiently light and simple in construction to be handled easily in cold, windy weather. Spruce or lightweight ash are good for spars; bamboo also is light and strong. The spars are better in two sections. The skate sail is kite-shaped and should be about 24 square feet in area for a person weighing around 100 pounds. Small windows or portholes, about 3 by 7 inches, made of celluloid, add much to the safety and are quite necessary for racing.

Stunt-Skating Races.—In addition to straight skating races many stunt races add variety and fun to a tournament—backward races, in which the contestants skate a given distance (not too far) backwards; skateless races, in which the participants go through the motions of skating without skates; a one-skate race, in which each contestant wears a skate on one foot and runs or jumps with the other; the three-legged race, in which various couples compete as they stand side by side with the inside legs tied together at ankle and knee; and tandem races in which the contestants skate in pairs, one behind the other.

Skate jumping is good sport. In this the contestants skate up to a given line and jump. The distance is measured to the nearest spot any part of the body touches. In an *obstacle skating race* a number of obstacles, such as low hurdles to be jumped or tables to be climbed over or crawled under, are placed at regular intervals on the racing track.

SKIING
(All Ages)

Skis, which originated in the Scandinavian countries, were originally, like our American snowshoes, a means of transportation over deep snow. They are still used for this purpose in both Europe and America and have many advantages over the snowshoe in open country but are not practical in forested regions. In recent years skiing has risen to a high place among winter sports in those countries.

The original skis were long, narrow leather-covered snowshoes. Modern ones consist of long, narrow strips of wood—ash, oak, beech, birch, spruce or hickory—pointed and turned up at the toes. Their length depends on the height of the wearer. They should be just long enough so that when stood on end upright the wearer can reach their tops with the tips of his fingers. Their width varies from 3 to 3½ inches at the rear, 2¾ to 3⅛ inches in the middle or narrowest part and 3½ to 5 inches in the broadest part at the front where the bend begins. They are thickest in the middle—from 1 to 1⅜ inches—and taper out to as little as ⅜ inch at the ends. The bottoms are either smooth or have small grooves to prevent snow from caking on them. They are oiled and waxed to a high polish. Skis are attached to the feet by straps, called the *binding*, which fit over the instep and heel. These are attached to the ski about midway, often with a thin plate of brass or zinc under them for a footrest.

Material for Skis.—Hickory or white ash with a straight, even grain running from end to end is the best material for skis. If you wish to make your own, choose the heaviest of these woods you can find, as it is better seasoned.

Ski Sticks.—Good ski sticks (about shoulder high) are necessary to assist progress and balance. A good quality bamboo makes a light, elastic and strong stick. A metal ice peg is fitted to the end of the stick by a ferrule, which adds strength. A few inches above this peg is a ring or disk made of hard rubber, metal or wicker to prevent the stick from sinking too deeply in the snow.

The Art of Skiing.—Taking long, gliding steps, with the heel raised at each movement forward, the skier can glide at a steady, swift pace over the snow on level ground without the skis leaving the surface. To go downhill he must place the feet closely together with one a little ahead of the other, lean the body forward in a crouched position, and, using the sticks as brakes and balancers, slide. The climb uphill may be made by stepping, in which the skier stands with the skis at right angles to the hill and steps up sidewise, or by facing the slope and ascending straight up with the skis turned at an angle in herringbone fashion. In making a turn the body leans slightly in the opposite direction from the turn with the weight on the stationary foot and the knee on that same side bent slightly to maintain the balance. The other leg is raised forward until the rear end of the ski is on the snow, swung clear around and placed parallel to the stationary leg but with the toe pointing in the opposite direction; the stationary foot is then lifted and turned around with the body until it heads in the same direction as the first ski. In making a turn on a hillside the valley foot is always the stationary one.

Skiing On A Level Surface
Knees flexible and relaxed, upper part of body bent forward, skis brought forward by the toes

Uphill By Herringbone
Weight on the left ski while the right is brought forward, and vice versa

Uphill By Side-stepping
Weight on the left ski while the right is brought a step up, and vice versa

Turning On Skis

Downhill Crouch

As a Sport.—Skiing as a sport first began in Norway in 1860; the first American ski club was organized in Minnesota in 1881. Norway, Sweden, Switzerland, Great Britain, Canada and the United States all hold ski tournaments that are governed by the rules of the International Federation of Ski Events and are classified in two general divisions—racing and jumping —and in combinations of the two. In the United States two organizations— the United States Amateur Ski Association and the Eastern United States Ski Association—foster the principal tournaments. In addition all over the northern part of the country numbers of collegiate interscholastic, interclub, state and interstate competitions are held each snow season. The Canadian Amateur Ski Association co-operates with the two United States associations.

Ski Racing.—
Ski Running and Turning. Contestants run on skis from a starting line over a 50-yard level course to a turning line, make a turn and race back to the starting line.

Cross-country Contests. Mark out a course over a given distance (from ½ to 3 or 4 miles according to the ability and endurance of the contestants) uphill, downhill, across level stretches. Contestants start at a given signal, travel by whatever skiing method seems best to them and whoever finishes first wins.

Uphill. An uphill course varying in steepness is laid out. Contestants start at a signal from a given starting line at the bottom, using the climbing method (stepping or herringbone) designated—or a choice may be allowed if preferred.

Barrel Staves versus Regulars. Younger children often make their own skis from barrel staves. Any of the races may be tried with these. Or it may be interesting to have a contest between skiers with regular skis and those with barrel staves.

Skijoring. Teams consisting of two contestants on foot drawing one on skis compete over a course varying in length from 100 to 500 yards. (The term is also used for the ski sport of being towed by a horse.)

Ski Jumping.—Ski jumping has become very popular, both in Europe and America. Great skill and daring have been developed. In 1893 the record

jump, made at Red Wing, Minn., by Torjus Hemmestvelt, was 103 feet. Since then the jumping distances have increased continually. In 1937 the record jump for an American was 245 feet. The world record of 324 feet was held by Sigmond Ruud.

The Take-off.—The take-off for a ski-jumping contest is built into the side of a hill. The jumper starts up the hill some distance above the take-off to acquire speed, leans over as he approaches the take-off and straightening the body, leaps into the air. He must keep the legs close together while in the air, bend his knees and hit the ground with one foot a little ahead of the other, legs yielding to preserve balance and lighten the force of the impact.

Ski Sailing.—On broad open stretches, with a good stiff breeze, skiing with a sail (built like that described for skating) is good sport. The snow must have a layer of soft, firm snow on top; a hard crust is bad for the skis. It is not possible to sail as fast on skis as on skates and one must tack into the wind at broad angles and step around with the sail overhead when changing tacks.

SNOW MODELING

Building a snowman has long been a favorite occupation of childhood; but snow modeling is much more than this. A number of schools and cities conduct regular snow-modeling contests every snow season.

The first step in modeling a figure is to build a foundation block of snow, from 2 to 3 feet square, pour water on it and leave it to freeze. Before it freezes insert sticks (four if you wish to model a 4-legged animal) in it on which to start building the body of the figure. Mold wet snow roughly to the sticks; if they are to form the legs of a body, tie their tops together with wire and either weave strands of the wire across or place sticks across to make a support for the snow that is to form the body. Moisten the snow to a packing consistency and build the body. When the body is roughly molded, insert sticks for the head, tail or arms and mold them roughly with snow.

When the rough figure is shaped, use modeling sticks, spoons and the fingers to shape and smooth it. Then sprinkle with water and leave it to freeze. To color the statue, paint it with water colors.

In contests it is necessary that participants be classified as to age, experience, ability and the like.

SNOWSHOEING

Invented by the Indians of the northern part of America to help them walk on deep snow, snowshoes consist of a single strip of hickory or other tough, pliable wood curved into a more or less oval shape with the ends fastened together at the back, reinforced with one or two crossbars and interwoven, much like a tennis racket, with a webbing of caribou or deerskin thongs. Moccasins or other soft-soled shoes are worn with them.

A small opening is left in the webbing just behind the front crossbar, into which the toe fits when walking.

Leather or woven straps fastened on the crossbar hold them on the feet. Walking on them is quite simple. It is only necessary to lift one shoe a little, carry it over and ahead of the other and put it down so that its narrow rear part fits against the wide curved part of the other shoe. The beginner is inclined to do a straddle walk to avoid stepping on his own feet; this is not necessary and is very fatiguing. Care must be taken in turning, however, not to step with one shoe on the tail of the other and so cause an upset. Experts travel 30 miles or more a day on snowshoes, but it is wise for the beginner not to overdo, for a very painful lameness, called *mal de raquette* by the Canadian voyageurs, may result.

Styles of Snowshoes.—The style of snowshoe varies with the type of country in which it is used. There are four general types. The first two, which are used most in the northern country, particularly by trappers, are long and narrow (about 5 feet by 1 foot in the widest part). The first of these is narrow and sharp at each end, broadens out in the middle and is turned up at the toe; the other turns up in front and has a long, pointed tail. The third kind, which is, perhaps, that most generally used for sports, curves in a fairly broad oval in front, is about 3½ feet long, 16 to 18 inches wide and has a medium length narrow tail. The fourth kind is almost round in shape, with a stumpy tail, and is called the *bear paw.* It is used mostly in heavily wooded sections.

Snowshoeing as a Sport.—The sport of snowshoeing is highly developed in Canada, where many snowshoe clubs hold many competitions. In the United States snowshoe hikes, obstacle races and cross-country races are held in many of the colleges in the snow country. The Dartmouth Outing Club climbs Mt. Washington every winter; the Appalachian Club stages mountain-climbing expeditions, and the Intercollegiate Winter Sports Union makes snowshoe racing a part of their schedule.

SOCCER

(Junior High School to Adults)

The rules of association football, known in the United States as *soccer*, were first published in 1863 at Cambridge University, England. The game has grown steadily in popularity because of its simple rules and the ease with which spectators may follow the movements of the players.

The field is rectangular with a minimum length of 75 yards and width of 65 yards and a maximum of 120 yards by 110 yards. At the middle of each end are goal posts 8 yards apart with a crossbar 8 feet above the field. A mid-line divides the field across, and from the middle of this line a circle with a 10-yard radius is drawn. Flags mark the corners of the field. A penalty kick mark is 12 yards in front of the mid-point of each goal line. A corner kick area is a quadrant drawn from each corner with a radius of 1 yard.

The diagram shows the *goal areas,* 6 yards ahead of both goals and 20

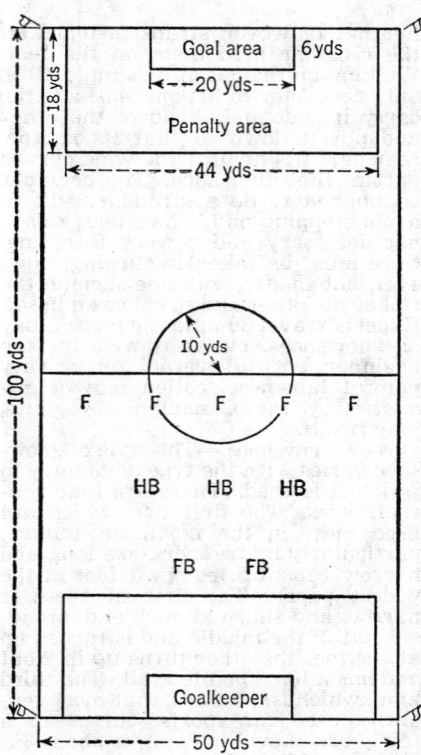

Diagram of a Soccer Field
Positions of players: F, forward; HB, halfback; FB, fullback

yards across, and the *penalty areas,* 18
yards in front of the end line and 44
yards in breadth. A smaller field, 200
feet long and 140 feet wide, is recommended for players on the junior-high-
school levels; the goal areas on such
fields are 30 by 18 feet, and the penalty areas are 108 by 45 feet.

The official soccer ball is round,
smaller than a basketball, not more
than 28 inches nor less than 27 inches
in circumference.

Eleven players form a team and endeavor to score by kicking or knocking the ball between the goal posts
and *under* the opponents' crossbar.
Each goal counts one point. There are
five forwards, the two outside called
the *right* and *left wings,* three halfbacks, two fullbacks who act mainly
as guards and the goalkeeper, with
positions as shown in the diagram.

After the toss for choice of goal or
kickoff, the game begins by a place
kick toward the opponents' goal from
the center of the field. At the kickoff
no member of either team may cross
the mid-line until the ball is kicked,
nor may any opponent approach
within 10 yards of the ball until that
time. After the scoring of goal by
either team, their opponents kick off
at center.

The ball may be advanced only by
kicking or knocking the ball with
other parts of the body than the hands
or arms. Only the goalkeeper may
handle the ball in guarding the goal.
He may carry or dribble it four
steps. The players make long kicks or
keep the ball close to their feet and
dribble it down the field, passing it to
a teammate whenever advisable. The
forwards are the main offensive play-

ers and are blocked mainly by the
halfbacks and backs.

If the ball crosses a side line, a
member of the team that did not drive
it is allowed a *throw-in* by an overhead throw from both hands. The
throw-in may not score a goal.

If the attackers send the ball over
the end line outside the goal posts, a
member of the defending team has a
goal kick from within the goal area,
no opponent being permitted within
10 yards. The ball is in play as soon
as kicked.

If the defenders send the ball over
their own goal line, the attackers
have a free kick (known as a *corner
kick*) from the nearest corner, no opponent to be within 10 yards. A corner
kick may score a goal.

A player is off-side if he is nearer
his opponents' goal line than the ball
at the moment the ball is played unless: he is in his own half of the field,
there are two of his opponents nearer
to their own goal line than he, the
ball last touched an opponent or was
last played by him, or he receives the
ball direct from a kick or throw-in.

If play is suspended for time out,
substitution or injury to a player, it is
resumed by the referee tossing the
ball up at the point where it became
dead. At toss-up, the ball is not in
play until it strikes the ground.

A *foul* may be called for offside
play; for touching the ball with the
hands (except the goalkeeper); for
tripping, kicking, kneeing, pushing,
holding or roughly charging an opponent.

Penalties vary according to location. If the defenders commit personal
fouls within the penalty area, the attackers have a *penalty kick* from the
penalty-kick mark, 12 yards in front
of the goal. For fouls committed by
either party outside the penalty area
and by the attackers within that area,
the offended party is awarded a free
kick at the spot where the foul occurred.

The officials of soccer are one referee and two linesmen. Linesmen are
the referee's assistants, particularly
charged with watching the ball, noting
the cause of its crossing bounds or
goal line and furnishing necessary
measurements of free kicks.

SOFTBALL, PLAYGROUND BASE-
BALL and INDOOR BASEBALL

(Late Elementary School to Adults)

The major sport of baseball has
three popular adaptations: softball,
playground baseball and indoor baseball. In most features—purposes,
scoring and rules—they are so similar
to baseball that only their differences
from the parent game will be noted.

SOFTBALL.—Softball is the favorite
variant of baseball and has features
that make it more suitable for women
and children to play, but skilled athletes enjoy it. Softball differs from
baseball mainly in the following rules:

1. The size of the diamond is 60 feet
square, instead of 90 feet, and the
pitching distance is 43 feet from home
plate rather than 60 feet. The pitching
distance for women is 35 feet.

2. In slow pitch games the size of
the diamond is 45 feet square and the
pitching distance is 35 feet.

3. The standard softball is not so
hard as a baseball and is approximately 12 inches in circumference (instead of 9 inches). A ball with raised
outside seams is not permissible.

4. The standard bat is shorter and
smaller in diameter than a baseball
bat, not more than 34 inches long
nor more than 2⅛ inches in diameter.

5. The pitch in softball must be underhand, unlike the overhand pitch in
baseball; the softball pitch must be
made with the hand below the hip
after a full-arm swing.

6. Bunting is not permissible in softball but is common practice in baseball.

7. Fewer bases are stolen in softball, as base runners are not permitted to leave base until the ball
has reached or passed home plate or
been hit by the batter.

8. The batter is declared to be out
after the third strike, even if the
catcher has not caught the ball.

9. If a pitched ball strikes a batter
who makes an honest effort to avoid
it, it is called *a ball,* but unlike baseball does not entitle the batter to proceed to first base unless the ball happens to be the fourth ball thrown to
the same batter.

10. Softball pitchers watch balks
more carefully; except at the commencement of each inning, any delay
of more than 20 seconds by the pitcher
may be called a ball.

11. A runner is not permitted to
score from third on any pitched ball
that passes him.

12. Shoes with sharp spikes or blunt
spikes longer than ⅜ inch are not allowed; golf cleats were forbidden in
1938.

13. The regular game in softball has
7 innings instead of 9, as in baseball.

PLAYGROUND BASEBALL.—This game
is very similar to softball. As in slow
pitch softball the playground baseball
diamond has base lines 45 feet in length
and a pitcher's box 35 feet from home
plate. The bat may be longer than the
34-inch softball bat and the 12-inch ball
also is used. There are 10 players on
each side, and the additional player is
called a *right* shortstop; 7 innings constitute a game. The game is very
popular.

INDOOR BASEBALL.—Indoor baseball
is played on the smallest of all baseball diamonds, 27 feet square with the
pitcher's box 23 feet from the center
of home base. If the building is sufficiently large to permit it, diamonds
with 35-feet base lines and pitcher's
box 30 feet from home may be used.
Nine innings may be played with
seven to nine players on a team, assigned to their positions by the team
captain. Balls 14 inches in circumference are used on the 35-feet square
diamonds, and on the smaller diamonds 17-inch balls are required.
Shoes with corrugated rubber soles
are worn.

SQUASH RACKETS

(Junior High School to Adults)

Squash rackets is an adaptation of
the old game of rackets that was
played by aristocrats of the Middle
Ages. Modern tennis is a similar but
newer game; squash-racket courts
were first standardized in 1911 by the

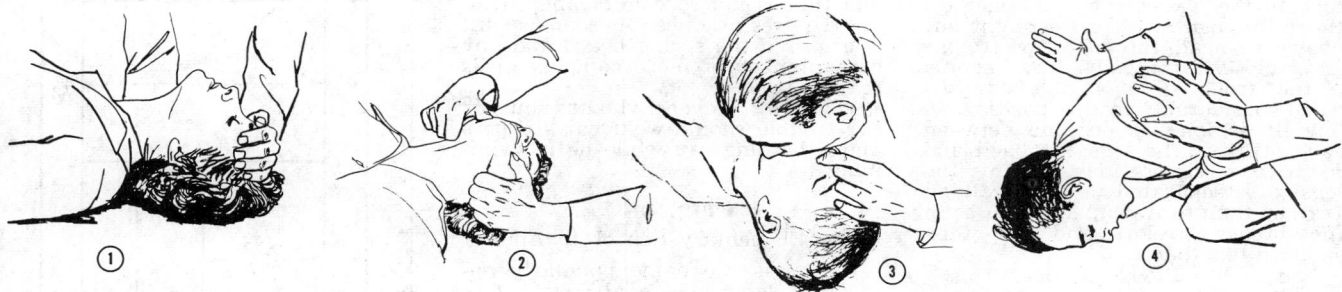

AMERICAN RED CROSS

ARTIFICIAL RESPIRATION (mouth-to-mouth resuscitation). (1) Place victim on back, remove foreign matter from mouth, and tilt head back with chin up. (2) Push or pull jaw into jutting-out position. (3) Place mouth tightly over victim's and at same time pinch nostrils shut. Blow into victim's mouth. (4) If no air exchange, turn victim on side, give blows between shoulders. Repeat.

English Tennis and Rackets Association.

The standard American court (narrower than the English) is 31 or 32 feet long and 18½ feet wide, with a back wall 7 feet high and front and side walls 15 feet high; there are, therefore, five playing surfaces. The back and side walls are painted white and are of wood or composition, and the front wall is of composition. Since light and ventilation are provided from the ceiling, squash courts are best located on upper floors. Entrance to the court is through a door in the rear wall made flush with the playing surface.

A red service line 6½ feet from the floor sets off the top area, within which balls must strike in service. Nearest the floor is a forbidden area, within which no ball may strike without loss to the man who drives it there. The upper part of this forbidden area is commonly covered by the *telltale*—a loose strip of sheet metal 17 inches wide, painted black. Balls that strike here are noted because of their resonant impact. The planking is left bare for 9 inches next to the floor to aid in the recovery of balls.

The back wall is divided across by a line 6½ feet from the floor, below which line lies the playing surface for all balls that are to rebound to the front wall.

The floor is divided lengthwise into equal parts and crosswise by a service line 10 feet from the back wall. Behind this line are the right and left boxes, between which service alternates, and forward are the right and left service courts.

The usual game and official contest are between two players but four persons may play. Official squash rackets have bent ash frames and are unlike tennis rackets only in their longer handles and smaller, circular heads. Official balls are of black rubber.

Play is begun by a service, as in tennis. The choice of serve is determined by spinning rackets. The server stands in either box, tosses up the ball and strikes it as it comes down. He must alternate between the boxes until he loses service. A served ball must hit in the upper rectangle of the front wall, above the service line and must rebound into the opposite court from the one used for service. The ball must be returned by the oppo-

nent on the volley or before second bounce to the front wall above the telltale. Except in service, balls may strike the front wall anywhere above the telltale. In returning a ball to the front either player may use caroms from the floor, rear wall or side walls. After service, a ball coming from the front may similarly carom from any or all playing surfaces, including the floor, but it must be played before it strikes the floor a second time or the point is lost. A player is permitted to aim at but not to strike a ball twice during one effort at return.

A failure to serve correctly is called a *fault*. Two faults or one failure to return a ball in due turn causes the server (*hand-in*) to become receiver (*hand-out*).

A *fly ball*, directly from the racket, is dead if it strikes above a boundary line on any of the four walls, but a bounding ball is not counted as dead in such case.

A *let* is a failure for which the player failing is not responsible under the rules; for example, if a player is interfered with by his opponent, or if a player is hit by an opponent's ball on its way to the front wall, no score can follow as a result of the failure to return. If a ball coming from the front wall strikes a player, no let is allowed.

A player's deliberate interference before a strike is called a *balk* and a free point is given to his opponent.

Only the server can score or make *aces* in squash by the failure of the hand-out to keep the ball properly coming back to the front. The first person to reach a score of 15 points wins the game, provided that whenever the score is tied at 13 or 14, the hand-out sets the game by announcing whether the winner of the next three or next five points shall have the game. A match consists of the best three out of five games.

SWIMMING

Learn to Float.—Floating is much easier in salt water than in fresh, and in deep water than in shallow. First hold on to a rope, dock or someone's hands, submerge the chin, let the body float out until you get the feeling that the water holds you up. Still holding on, take a deep breath, immerse the face, hold the breath as long as possi-

ble and relax. Practice this. Let go with one hand, making all movements slowly; let go with both hands, moving the arms and legs gently. When you find that the body actually floats, you have taken the first important step. Try the same thing on your back. Unless you are absolutely unable to relax or are unusually skinny or bony, you will find that you can lie stretched out on the water for an indefinite time. Wade out in the water until it is waist or even shoulder deep, turn the back to shore, lean backward and let the feet come up, then move the hands and feet slowly and see how quickly you bump the shore.

Learn to Breathe.—Beginners try to keep their chins dry and so make swimming harder; for the more nearly flat the body lies in the water, the better it floats. In all the racing strokes the face is under water more than it is out, so it is necessary to learn to breathe differently. A good general rule is to breathe in through the mouth and out through the nose. The mouth need not be closed under water. One should exhale slowly while the face is submerged and so be ready for a quick intake.

Swimming Strokes

Breast Stroke. A swimming frog illustrates the leg motion of this stroke. The knees are drawn up under the body and well apart, the legs kicked out straight and then brought quickly together. At the same time the hands are drawn up in front of the chest with the palms together and then shot forward (the palms turned outward as they go to push as much water as possible), and the arms sweep around at each side at right angles to the body and then are drawn in to start a new stroke. Snapping the legs together and pushing the water back with the palms propels the body forward. The chin should be kept as low as possible in the water, letting the water wash in and out of the mouth.

Side Stroke. This movement is all done under water with the body on the side (usually the right). The right arm swings out and up and down as the left swings back, down and up, each pushing as much water as possible with the palm on the downward stroke. When the right arm is straight up, the left is straight down. This is the position at the beginning and end of each stroke with the body lying long in the water, the feet together, the right arm stretched straight out above the head, the left arm straight down close to the body. The impetus of the stroke will shoot the body forward considerably in this position, so hold it as long as possible between each stroke. The legs cut back and forth in a scissors kick. In this the legs are separated as in walking (rather than drawn up sidewise as in the breast stroke) and are then snapped together.

The Over-and-Over Stroke. This is a variation of the side stroke and gives greater speed. The right arm is pulled down toward the hips with the palm pushing as much water as possible, turned sidewise, forward and up straight above the head. While the right arm is held at the hips, the left arm is moved in front of the head, is then pulled down past the face, chest and hips, where it is straightened and brought up out of the water to the position in front of the face again. The legs are kicked apart when the left arm is at the shoulder on the downward pull and are drawn back together again when it is back in the starting position.

The Trudgen and Crawl. In both these strokes, which are popular for racing, the swimmer lies in the water face downward, rolling from side to side and twisting the head to bring the mouth up for air. The trudgen, named after an English swimmer, J. Trudgen, who learned it in South America, involves a double, overarm movement, the two arms alternating, and a scissors kick. The Australian crawl, which originated with the natives of the South Sea Islands and became popular in Australia, uses a short, alternating overarm stroke, a sort of downward flip from the elbow, like the motion of good base throwing on a ball diamond, with a similarly alternating thrash of the lower leg. In the true Australian crawl the right arm and the left leg strike together; then the left arm and the right leg. In the American adaptation the arms are used independently of the leg motion and the angle of the leg stroke is narrowed. All of the upper motion of the arms takes place out of the water in both these strokes.

Treading Water. As soon as a swimmer has become confident enough to go over his depth he should learn to tread water. This consists of standing erect and moving the feet as if climbing a steep flight of stairs. The ability to do this gives complete confidence in the water.

Artificial Aids.—If you learn to swim in deep water, water wings, inflated belts and the like are a necessity; in shallow water it is just as well not to use them as they prevent acquiring self-confidence.

Diving.—Every swimmer should be able to dive—at least well enough to get in the water without sliding or falling in. The easiest way to learn is to stand on the side of the pool or a float, lean over until the body is nearly double, lower the head between the outstretched arms—and plunge, entering the water headfirst with the legs straight. The first time you will prob-

ably go flat on the water with a bang and that is not so comfortable. Diving requires practice. As soon as skill is acquired the spring board and any of a number of more complex dives may be tried.

WARNING: Anyone who has sinus or ear trouble should wear ear stoppers and a bathing cap while he is swimming.

TENNIS
(Late Elementary School to Adults)

Tennis is the name popularly applied to *lawn tennis* although it is more correctly used to designate *royal* or *court tennis,* which is played on a limited number of expensive indoor courts.

In 1874 Major Walter Wingfield patented specifications for lawn tennis, adapted from the ancient game of court tennis and with simplified features that were suitable for an outdoor game. Since that date lawn tennis has become the most widely played of all ball games.

The following Code of Rules is the official Code of the International Lawn Tennis Federation, of which the United States Lawn Tennis Association is a member. It is reprinted here through the courtesy of these two organizations.

Lawn Tennis—Singles Game

Rule 1
The *Court* shall be a rectangle 78 feet long and 27 feet wide. It shall be divided across the middle by a net, suspended from a cord or metal cable of a maximum diameter of one-third of an inch, the ends of which shall be attached to, or pass over, the tops of two posts, 3 feet 6 inches high, which shall stand 3 feet outside the court on each side. The height of the net shall be 3 feet at the center, where it shall be held down taut by a strap not more than 2 inches wide. There shall be a band covering the cord or metal cable and the top of the net for not less than 2 inches nor more than 2½ inches in depth on each side. The lines bounding the ends and sides of the court shall respectively be called the *Base Lines* and the *Side Lines*. On each side of the net, at a distance of 21 feet from it and parallel with it, shall be drawn the *Service Lines*. The space on each side of the net between the service line and the side lines shall be divided into two equal parts called the *Service Courts* by the *Center Service Line,* which must be 2 inches in width, drawn half-way between, and parallel with, the side lines. Each base line shall be bisected by an imaginary continuation of the center service line to a line 4 inches in length and 2 inches in width called the *Center Mark,* drawn inside the court and at right angles to and in contact with such base line. All other lines shall be not less than 1 inch nor more than 2 inches in width, except the base lines, which may be 4 inches in width, and all measurements shall be made to the outside of the lines.

Rule 2
The permanent fixtures of the court shall include not only the nets, posts,

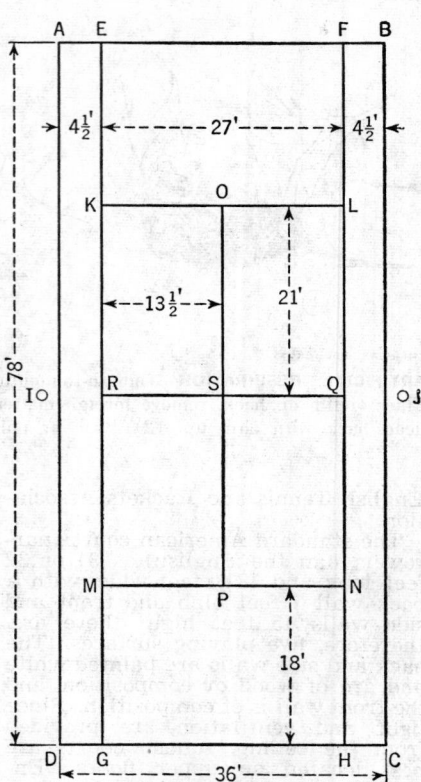

Diagram of a Lawn-Tennis Court
The doubles game is played with the alleys

cord or metal cable, strap and band, but also, where there are any such, the back and side stops, the stands, fixed or movable seats and chairs round the court, and their occupants, all other fixtures around and above the court, and the umpire, foot fault judge and linesmen when in their respective places.

Rule 3
The ball shall have a smooth outer surface, seams in the cover shall be stitchless. The ball shall be more than 2½ inches and less than 2⅝ inches in diameter and more than 2 ounces and less than 2 1/16 ounces in weight. The ball shall have a bound of more than 53 inches and less than 58 inches when dropped 100 inches upon a concrete base, and a deformation of more than .265 of an inch and less than .290 of an inch when subjected to pressure of 18 lb. applied to each end of any diameter. All tests shall be made in accordance with the Regulations in the Appendix hereto.

Rule 4
The players shall stand on opposite sides of the net; the player who first delivers the ball shall be called the *Server,* and the other the *Receiver.*

Rule 5
The choice of sides and the right to be Server or Receiver in the first game shall be decided by toss.

The player winning the toss may choose, or request his opponent to choose:—

(*a*) the right to be Server or Receiver, in which case the other player shall choose the side; or

(b) the side in which case the other player shall choose the right to be Server or Receiver.

Rule 6

The service shall be delivered in the following manner. Immediately before commencing to serve the server shall stand with both feet at rest behind (i.e., further from the net than) the baseline, and within imaginary continuations of the center-mark and side line. The server shall then project the ball by hand into the air in any direction and *before it hits the ground* strike it with his racket, and the delivery shall be deemed to have been completed at the moment of the impact of the racket and the ball. A player with the use of only one arm may utilize his racket for the projection.

Rule 7

The Server shall throughout the delivery of the service—
(a) Not change his position by walking or running.
(b) Maintain contact with the ground.
(c) Keep both feet behind (i.e., further from the net than) the base line.

Rule 8

In delivering the service, the Server shall stand alternately behind the right and left courts, beginning from the right in every game. The ball served shall pass over the net and hit the ground within the service court which is diagonally opposite, or upon any line bounding such court, before the Receiver returns it.

Rule 9

The service is a *Fault* (a) if the Server commit any breach of Rules 6, 7 or 8, (b) if he miss the ball in attempting to strike it, (c) if the ball served touch a permanent fixture (other than the net, strap or band) before it hits the ground.

Rule 10

After a fault (if it be the first fault) the Server shall serve again from behind the same half of the court from which he served that fault, unless it was a fault because he served from behind the wrong half, when he shall be entitled to deliver one service from behind the other half.

A fault may not be claimed after the next service has been delivered.

Rule 11

The Server shall not serve until the Receiver is ready. If the latter attempt to return the service, he shall be deemed ready. If, however, the Receiver signify that he is not ready, he may not claim a fault because the ball does not hit the ground within the limits fixed for the service.

Rule 12

The service is a *Let* (a) if the ball served touch the net, strap or band, provided the same be otherwise good, (b) if a service or fault be delivered when the Receiver is not ready (see Rule 11). In case of a let, the service counts for nothing, and the Server shall serve again, but a let does not annul a previous fault.

Rule 13

At the end of the first game the Receiver shall become Server, and the Server, Receiver; and so on alternately in all the subsequent games of a match. If a player serve out of turn, the player who ought to have served shall serve as soon as the mistake is discovered. All points scored before such discovery shall be reckoned, but a single fault served before such discovery shall not be reckoned. If a game shall have been completed before such discovery, the order of service shall remain as altered.

Rule 14

A ball is in play from the moment at which it is delivered in service (unless a fault or a let), and remains in play till the point is decided.

Rule 15

The Server wins the point (a) if the ball served touch the Receiver or anything which he wears or carries before it hits the ground, (b) if the Receiver otherwise lose the point as provided by Rule 17.

Rule 16

The Receiver wins the point (a) if the Server serve two consecutive faults, (b) if the Server otherwise lose the point as provided by Rule 17.

Rule 17

A player loses the point if—
(a) He fail, before the ball in play has hit the ground twice consecutively, to return it directly over the net [except as provided in Rule 20 (a) or (c)].
(b) He return the ball in play so that it hits the ground, a permanent fixture or other object outside any of the lines which bound his opponent's court [except as provided in Rule 20 (a) and (c)]; or
(c) He volley the ball and fail to make a good return even when standing outside the court; or
(d) He touch or strike the ball in play with his racket more than once in making a stroke; or
(e) He or his racket (in his hand or otherwise) or anything which he wears or carries, touch the net, posts, cord or metal cable, strap or band, or the ground within his opponent's court at any time while the ball is in play; or
(f) He volley the ball before it has passed the net; or
(g) The ball in play touch him or anything that he wears or carries, except his racket in his hand or hands; or
(h) He throw his racket at and hit the ball.

Rule 18

A ball falling on a line is regarded as falling in the court bounded by that line.

Rule 19

If the ball in play touch a permanent fixture (other than the net, posts, cord or metal cable, strap or band) after it has hit the ground, the player who struck it wins the point; if before it hits the ground, his opponent wins the point.

Rule 20

It is a good return—
(a) If the ball touch the net, posts, cord or metal cable, strap or band, provided that it passes over any of them and hits the ground within the court;
(b) If the ball, served or returned, hit the ground within the proper court and rebound or be blown back over the net, and the player whose turn it is to strike reach over the net and play the ball, provided that neither he nor any part of his clothes or racket touch the net, posts, cord or metal cable, strap or band or the ground within his opponent's court, and that the stroke be otherwise good;
(c) If the ball be returned outside the post, either above or below the level of the top of the net, even though it touch the post, provided that it hits the ground within the proper courts;
(d) If a player's racket pass over the net after he has returned the ball, provided the ball pass the net before being played and be properly returned;
(e) If a player succeed in returning the ball, served or in play, which strikes a ball lying in the court.

Rule 21

In case a player is hindered in making a stroke by anything not within his control, except a permanent fixture of the court, the point shall be replayed.

Rule 22

If a player wins his first point, the score is called 15 for that player; on winning his second point, the score is called 30 for that player; on winning his third point, the score is called 40 for that player; and the fourth point won by a player is scored *Game* for that player, except as follows:

If both players have won three points, the score is called *Deuce;* and the next point won by a player is scored *Advantage* for that player. If the same player wins the next point, he wins the game; if the other player wins the next point, the score is again called *Deuce;* and so on, until a player wins two points immediately following the score at deuce, when the game is scored for that player.

Rule 23

The player who first wins six games wins a set, except as follows:

If both players have won five games, the score is called *Games-All*, and the next game won by a player is scored *Advantage Game* for that player. If the same player wins the next game, he wins the *Set;* if the other player wins the next game, the score is again called *Games-All;* and so on until a player wins two games more than his opponent, when the set is scored for that player.

Rule 24

The players shall change sides at the end of the first, third and every subsequent alternate game of each set, and at the end of each set, unless the total number of games in such set be even, in which case the change is not made until the end of the first game of the next set.

Rule 25

The maximum number of sets in a match shall be five or where women take part, three.

Rule 26

Except where otherwise stated, every reference in these Rules to the masculine includes the feminine gender.

Rule 27

In matches where an Umpire is appointed, his decision shall be final; but where a Referee is appointed, an appeal shall lie to him from the decision of an Umpire on a question of law, and in all such cases the decision of the Referee shall be final.

The Referee, in his discretion, may at any time postpone a match on account of darkness or the condition of the ground or the weather. In any case of postponement the previous score and the previous occupancy of courts shall hold good, unless the Referee and the players unanimously agree otherwise.

Rule 28

Play shall be continuous from the first service till the match be concluded; provided that after the third set, or when women take part, the second set, either player is entitled to a rest, which shall not exceed 10 minutes, except that in the countries situated between Latitude 15° North and Latitude 15° South such rest shall not exceed 45 minutes, and provided further that when necessitated by circumstances not within the control of the players, the Umpire may suspend play for such a period as he may consider necessary. If play be suspended and be not resumed until a later day the rest may be taken only after the third set (or when women take part, the second set) of play on such later day, completion of an unfinished set being counted one set. These provisions shall be strictly construed, and play shall never be suspended, delayed or interfered with for the purpose of enabling a player to recover his strength or his wind or to receive instruction or advice. The Umpire shall be the sole judge of such suspension, delay or interference, and after giving due warning he may disqualify the offender.

The Doubles Game

Rule 29

The foregoing rules shall apply to the *Doubles Game* except as follows:

Rule 30

For the doubles game, the court shall be 36 feet in width, *i.e.,* 4½ feet wider on each side than the court for the singles game, and those portions of the singles side lines which lie between the two service lines shall be called the *Service Side Lines.* In other respects the court shall be similar to that described in Rule 1, but the portions of the singles side lines between the base line and the service line on each side of the net may be omitted if desired.

Rule 31

The pair who have to serve in the first game of each set shall decide which partner shall do so, and the opposing pair shall decide similarly for the second game. The partner of the player who served in the first game shall serve in the third; the partner of the player who served in the second game shall serve in the fourth, and so on in the same order in all the subsequent games of a set. The order of service having been decided shall not be altered during the set, but it may be changed at the beginning of a new set.

Rule 32

The pair who have to receive the service in the first game of each set shall decide which partner shall receive the first service and the opposing pair shall decide similarly in the second game of each set. Partners shall receive the service alternately throughout each game and the order of receiving the service having been decided shall not be altered during the set, but it may be changed at the beginning of a new set.

Rule 33

If a partner serve out of his turn, the partner who ought to have served shall serve as soon as the mistake is discovered, but all points scored, and any fault served before such discovery, shall be reckoned. If a game shall have been completed before such discovery, the order of service remains as altered.

Rule 34

If during a game the order of receiving the service is changed by the receivers, it shall remain as altered until the end of the game in which the mistake is discovered, but the partners shall resume their original order of receiving in the next game of that set in which they are receivers of the service.

Rule 35

The service is a fault as provided for by Rule 9, or if the ball served touch the Server's partner or anything which he wears or carries; but if the ball served touch the partner of the Receiver or anything which he wears or carries, before it hits the ground, the Server wins the point.

Rule 36

The ball shall be struck alternately by one or other player of the opposing pairs, and if a player touch the ball in play with his racket in contravention of this Rule, his opponents win the point.

TOBOGGANING

The toboggan, which seems to have originated with the Indians of northeastern America, was used by them to haul their possessions over the trackless snow. It consisted of a strip of bark turned up in front and reinforced by strips of wood along the edges and crosswise. The Eskimos make toboggans from strips of whalebone.

The modern toboggan is made of thin strips of wood (usually maple, hickory or ash) placed side by side and held in place by crosswise cleats. The under sides of the strips are curved slightly and polished. The toboggan is about 18 inches wide and from 6 to 8 feet long. It has no steering apparatus. The rear man must crouch on one knee and stretch the other behind to use as a rudder. Or the single user may lie prone and steer with his toes. For this reason toboggans are not as practical for coasting as sleds or bobs unless a track or slide is built to keep them within bounds.

Uses of the Toboggan.—Toboggans are most used as a means of transportation in places where the climate is dry and cold and there are quantities of soft, fluffy snow. In Alaska dog teams harnessed to toboggans draw heavy loads of supplies great distances, and races with toboggans and dog teams are popular. Winter campers and hunters in the north woods use them to haul equipment and game.

Toboggan Slides.—The easy way to make a toboggan slide is to cut out a track deep enough to control the toboggan on a natural hill or slope that is covered with a thick layer of snow. In places where winter sports are a specialty, a wooden framework is covered with snow. Quebec, Montreal and Lake Placid in America have famous slides. The sport is popular in Switzerland, where it is called *lugeing,* though the real Swiss *luge* is a small sled and not a toboggan.

TRACK AND FIELD EVENTS

Track and field events are unlike games in their emphasis on individual or group contests instead of on cooperation in team play. In track and field events the individual can endeavor without interference to surpass rivals in standardized contests held outdoors on a prepared course or track. *Track events* are divided into walking, running and hurdling races; and *field events* are commonly confined to weight throwing, jumping and vaulting.

Before a meet all contestants report to the clerk of the course on arrival, register, enter for certain events, receive handicaps according to previous records and receive a number for the meet. They are subject to decisions made by the referee and his assistants, the clerk of the course, starter, inspectors, finish judges, timekeepers, scorer, field judges and marshal.

Track events have the following divisions:

Sprinting—100-yard dash, 220-yard dash
Middle-distance races—440-yard run, ½-mile run
Long-distance races—1-mile run, 2-mile run and longer distances
Track-relay race—¼-mile to 4-mile relay
Cross-country race—1½-mile to 7-mile run
Walking race—220-yard to 2-mile walk
Hurdle races—120-yard high hurdle, 220-yard low hurdle, 440-yard intermediate hurdle.

Sprints or Dashes (*Late Elementary School to Adults.*)—Sprints or dashes cover any distance from 40 to 440

ON YOUR MARK   GET SET   PISTOL REPORT   STRIDING   FINISH

yards (¼ mile), according to the age of the runner. Dashes for 4th-grade pupils should be 40 yards for girls and 50 yards for boys and should be lengthened about 10 yards for each grade up to the 8th.

The course is divided into lanes, one for each contestant. These lanes are assigned by lot and should be 3 feet or more in width. Runners who are not handicapped start from *scratch,* a starting line drawn across the track. They usually dig holes about 3 inches deep for the toes of each foot; such holes or their substitute starting blocks aid in establishing a drive at the start. A crouch start is taken when the starter says, "Get ready," or "On your marks," with the front (usually the left) foot 8 to 12 inches behind scratch and the knee of the back (usually the right) leg placed on the ground near the instep of the front foot. Both hands are placed on the starting line in one of the three illustrated positions and the elbows are locked.

At the starter's call, "Get set," the body is moved well forward, with its weight mainly supported by the hands and front leg. When all the runners have been poised for 2 seconds or more, "Go," is shouted by the starter or he fires the pistol as the signal to run.

Short strides are preferable for the first 10 yards but are lengthened thereafter. The rear foot should not be raised too high, the hands should not rise above the chest and the toes should not point out. The best stride is made on the ball of the foot with the knee bent no more than necessary.

Middle-Distance Runs (*Senior High School to Adults.*)—Runs of ¼ mile to ¾ mile are called *middle-distance* runs; they are most frequently run on an oval track. The same arm action is used in these runs as in the sprints but with a more relaxed swing. The stride is long, and the runner may drop his heels a little more than in the sprint. Lanes are sometimes used for ¼-mile runs but are usually discarded for the longer races. Middle-distance runs are likely to begin vigorously, to use a moderate middle pace and to end with a dash. These runs are not recommended for boys or girls under 15 or 16 years of age.

Long-Distance Runs (*Senior High School to Adults.*)—Runs of 1 or 2 miles are the true distance runs and with the ½-mile middle-distance run sometimes employ the erect start instead of the crouch. The erect standing start is assumed with one foot toeing scratch and the other back one pace. The best distance runners put in long, conditioned training before their races and acquire a perception of proper *pacing,* the maintenance of equal speed throughout a run. Training for distance runs should never be begun without a physician's approval.

The marathon is the longest of running races, the usual course being 26 miles 385 yards long. Runs to 90 miles have been staged by British athletes but the marathon is a track event suitable only for mature men of exceptionally good physique, great endurance and long training in distance running. This race should be prohibited to boys under 21 years of age.

Track—Relay Runs (*Junior High School to Adults.*)—Relay races are run by several competing teams over a stated course; each of the usual four members of a group runs an equal distance (except in medley relay races) and passes the stick to another teammate. The standard relay distances for track meets are ¼ mile, ½ mile, 1 mile, 2 miles and 4 miles; in the ¼-mile race, four men run 110 yards each; in the ½ mile, four men run 220 yards each; and so on.

Each competitor in a relay runs a sprint and the same technique is used, except that only the first runner can employ the crouch start. The first runners are started as in dashes; no other runner may start until he has received the *baton* or stick from the teammate who precedes him in the race. The delivery of the baton or any other stated token must occur by passing (not throwing) within a 20-foot space marked off for the purpose. An inspector is stationed at each of these starting points to see that the rules are observed.

Novelty relays, not used in regular track events, are well-liked as amusements in indoor gymnasiums and at picnics and carnivals; they may be run by hopping, jumping, crawling on all fours, rolling or carrying some object, by sack racing or with other diverting variations.

Racing

Cross-Country Competition (*Senior High School to Adults.*)—Runs across country may be from 1½ to 7 miles long although the English national championship and the International race have 10-mile runs. The course is marked by 1-foot-square flags, the blue flag showing that the course runs directly ahead, the white flag directing a turn to the right and the red flag pointing out a turn to the left. The flags are on poles from 2 to 4 feet above the ground.

If teams compete on cross-country runs they usually consist of five men, the four who finish first scoring points for their group—one for first place, two for second and the like—the team with the lowest score winning the event.

Runners of high-school age should not be allowed to overexert nor to run more than a 2-mile cross-country race.

Walking Contests (*Junior High School to Adults.*)—Walking contests are very popular in England and on the Continent but have lost favor in championship events in the United States because it is so difficult to supervise the run, enforce rules and distinguish between a run and a fair walk. Heel-and-toe walking races are conducted differently from running races only in the rule that contestants must walk; the rear toe must not be raised until the forward heel has hit the ground. The knee must be locked, the arms are swung vigorously and because of the resultant jerky motion, the walking race is very fatiguing.

The Hurdles (*Senior High School to Adults.*)—Three types of hurdle races are run: one of 120 yards with high (3½-foot) hurdles, one of 220 yards with low (2½-foot) hurdles and one of 440 yards with intermediate (3-foot) hurdles. The 440-yard hurdle is unusually tiring and is omitted in intercollegiate championship events, although it is still included in A.A.U. meets. For all course lengths, 10 fencelike hurdles divide the course into 11 parts; the 120-yard-hurdle course has 15-yard end sections and 10 yards between the hurdles; the 220-yard and 440-yard courses are divided into 11 equal sections of 20 and 40 yards, respectively.

Hurdling is an adaptation of sprinting, so the same start and rules are used except for *taking the hurdle* by a leap. The object of the race is to clear the obstacles with the least possible interference with sprinting speed. Most runners spring from the same foot before each leap, jump with the chest bent close to the front leg and with the arms spread. The best hurdlers almost graze each bar. If more than two hurdles are knocked down, the runner is disqualified; record runs are never made unless all hurdles remain upright. Courses on indoor tracks vary from 40 to 60 yards with three to five low or high hurdles.

Field events have the following divisions:

JUMPING

Running high jump
Standing high jump
Running broad jump
Standing broad jump
Three standing broad jumps
Running hop, step and jump

WEIGHT THROWING

Shot-put—16-pound shot
Hammer throw—16-pound hammer
Fifty-six-pound weight throw
Javelin throw
Discus throw

VAULTING

Pole vault—for height or distance

Running High Jump (*Late Elementary School to Adults.*)—The high jump is one form of the sport of jumping that has been a favorite from ancient times. Jumping for height requires a landing pit of soft earth or sand, which may vary from 10 to 14 feet in width and 14 to 16 feet in length. The high jumps employ a pair of uprights 12 feet apart, bored for pegs not longer than 3 inches and supporting a light crossbar; the crossbar may be triangular, with each face 1¾ inches wide, or square with rounded edges, 1⅛ inches wide. A light bamboo pole may serve as the crossbar for informal jumping. The running ground is V-shaped, so that contestants can get a 36- to 40-foot approach from either side. In intercollegiate practice a *balk line* is drawn on the ground 3 feet in front of and parallel to the bar; any runner who steps over this line twice in an attempt to jump is judged to have made one trial. The usual take-off varies from 3 to 4½ feet at any point in front of the bar.

The purpose of both the running and the standing high jump is to clear the bar without knocking it off its pegs. The bar is first placed at a height all the runners can clear and raised peg by peg. Displacing the bar or leaving the ground in any attempt is called a *trial*. Three trials are permitted at each height. A contestant may decline to try at any particular height and may come in at a greater height later on, but there may be no return to lower levels, except to break a tie. Each jumper drops out of the contest when he fails to clear the bar.

The major principle of the modern high jump is the *layout*—the moving of the body from a vertical to a horizontal position at the moment of clearing the bar. The *scissors jump,* most commonly employed by the amateur, is least efficient because the jumper does not use the layout and is in a sitting position as he clears the bar. The Sweeney, half Sweeney, short-hook Sweeney and California or western jump are variations of the *roll-over* style and have been instrumental in achieving record jumps. The jumper rolls sidewise over the bar in these jumps but must avoid crossing the bar with his head in advance of either foot, as such a position results in an illegal jump. Record jumps have been within 2 and 3 inches of 7 feet.

Standing High Jump (*Late Elementary School to Adults*).—The rules and technique of the running high jump apply to this jump except that the jumper is not allowed to run or hop before his take-off from a crouching position about 18 inches in front of the bar. He may lift first one foot and then the other or jump from both and hop over the bar with or without a layout. A foot lifted twice or two springs without a try at a jump count as a trial.

Running Broad Jump (*Junior High School to Adults*).—This event requires a running track of cinders or firm earth 4 feet wide and 80 feet long with a mark 20 feet in front of the take-off plank; the runner judges his stride by the manner in which he touches this mark. The take-off plank varies in width, the standard being 8 inches wide and 4 to 6 feet long, but is always sunk broad side up on a level

with the ground. Behind the take-off board the soil is dug out 3 inches deep and 1 foot wide for leverage in springing from the plank. The pit starts 5 feet in front of the take-off plank; it may be from 5 to 8 feet wide, from 20 to 25 feet long, is dug to a depth of about 1 foot and the ground mixed with sand or sawdust to be soft for landing.

Each contestant takes as much run as he pleases—the ordinary run is about six paces—so timing his steps as to bring his jumping foot on the take-off plank for the spring. If the running path is soft or the wind unfavorable, more is lost than gained by long runs. The runner approaches the board at full speed, lands solidly on his jumping leg and without pause makes a crouching spring, flings his arms forward for a lift and while he is still in the air, thrusts his legs and arms forward in order to maintain balance and to make his mark as far as possible from the plank. Some broad jumpers keep the knees well up near the chin and land in a forward-bending crouch. Extending the legs too soon often causes a fall backward. A *hitch kick* or powerful step taken during the time the contestant is in the air is an aid in achieving distance.

Jumps are measured from the forward or unburied edge of the take-off plank to the nearest mark made by the jumper in landing. For this reason he must be careful not to fall backward or even throw a hand back to support himself in landing, for any mark so made will lower his record.

A step over the take-off plank counts as a trial although the jump is not measured. When a large number of competitors is entered, each has three trial jumps, and a convenient number of winners from these trials enters the final competition. In the finals each man again has three jumps, and the best of the three jumps made by each man is his record for the event. Record jumps have exceeded 26 feet.

Standing Broad Jump (*Junior High School to Adults*).—This event uses a regular take-off board, with both feet on the board and the arms upright when the spring is made. Preliminary hops or runs are not permissible. Toes may overhang the edge of the board for starting thrust. If, as sometimes happens, the jump is from a scratch line on the ground, the toes may touch this line but must not overreach it. Three trials are used, as in the running jumps.

Triple standing broad jump is the same as the standing broad jump except that three jumps are made in succession.

Running Hop, Step and Jump (*Junior High School to Adults*).—The start is like that of the running broad jump with one foot on the take-off board. The foot that makes the take-off must make the first landing; the opposite foot at once takes the step; then without a pause both feet register the final jump. The distance is measured from the scratch line or take-off board, as in the other types of jumps for distance.

Shot-put (*Junior High School to Adults*).—Both the shot and hammer

are thrown from a circle that is 7 feet in diameter with a *toe board* 4 inches high around 4 feet of its circumference. Putting the shot has been practiced as a sport in Ireland for more than a century. The shot is a round metal ball weighing 16 pounds for competition between men, 12 pounds for high-school boys and 8 pounds for

INITIAL POSITION for shot-put: right shoulder is dropped to begin shift across circle.

women and junior high-school students.

The contestant must not step across or beyond the toe board in putting the shot or leave his throwing position until the throw is measured. The measurement is made from his position on the circle to the nearest mark made by the shot.

The shot must be *put* overhand, not thrown—that is, it must not be drawn back of the ear in line with the shoulder; at the beginning of the action it usually rests *on* the shoulder, in the hand as near the end of the fingers as strength permits to give leverage. Form is important: (1) a half crouch at the rear of the circle, the weighted shoulder drawn far back and low; (2) a sliding glide forward; (3) a twisting shift of the feet and and an upward lunge of the whole body, while the putting arm straightens, and even the fingers add their push or *flip* at the end, like the kick of the toes in swimming. The putter should avoid a pause between this series of actions, making the put a smooth flow of motion.

Each contestant has three trials. The best of the three is his record for the event. In 1934 the shot was put 57 feet and 1 inch.

Hammer Throw (*Adults*).—The hammer is thrown from the same type of circle that is used for the shot-put. The hammer is a circular metal weight with a flexible wire handle and grips; the entire hammer weighs 16 pounds and is no more than 4 feet in length.

The event has rules similar to those governing the shot-put but the form differs. The hammer may be thrown without a turn but the majority of contestants use from one to three turns. The handle is gripped near the ends of the fingers and the initial position is taken with the back toward the course of the throw. The hammer is swung around the head with the arms straight; after several swings the body is twisted around. After the pivot, a jump is taken to the edge of the circle where the hammer is released. Crossing the legs or dragging the foot at the end of the heave may prevent the thrower from leaving the circle.

All fair throws must fall within a 90-degree sector marked on the ground. As the event is dangerous for spectators, wire screen protectors often are provided or the watchers are kept 200 feet in all directions from the throw. The amateur record was made in 1913—189 ft. 6½ in.

Fifty-Six-Pound Weight Throw (*Adults*).—The 56-pound weight is thrown in A.A.U. events but has been omitted from many intercollegiate meets. The undergraduate intercollegiate meets include a 35-pound-weight-throwing contest in preference to one with the heavier weight. Both weights are thrown for distance from a 7-foot circle.

The 35- and 56-pound weights have a circular metal sphere with a triangular handle having 7¼-inch sides. The weight is thrown like a hammer except that the starting position is taken with the head bent near the knees, the arms between the legs and the hands grasping the weight, which is placed on the ground. The swing to the left can be followed successfully by only one turn. Fouls and measurements for this event are similar to those for the hammer throw.

Javelin Throw (*Senior High School to Adults*).—The javelin throw grew out of the throwing of spears in ancient wars; it was a popular feature of the old Olympic games in Greece and was first popularized as a modern sport in Sweden. The javelin has a wooden shaft with an attached iron or steel point and a whipcord-wound grip at the center of gravity; it must be about 8½ feet long and weigh no less than 1.76 pounds.

The javelin is held by the grip with the thumb extending along the shaft; it is thrown by a full-arm swing from behind a scratch line after as long a run as the contestant requires, although the usual distance is 15 yards. A hop is helpful after the run, with the javelin held parallel to the outflung arms and with the body turned to one side. Both feet should be on the ground when the javelin is cast.

Only those throws are counted in which the point of the javelin strikes the ground first. The distance of the throw is measured from the scratch line or the scratch line extended to the place where the javelin point touches the ground. Each contestant is credited with the best of three trial throws. If a javelin breaks in the air, it is not counted as a trial.

Discus Throw (*Senior High School to Adults*).—Discus throwing was a favorite sport of the Greeks and the modern version uses a similar but freer style. The standard discus is a convex circular wooden object approximately 9 inches in diameter and with a metal rim. It may not weigh less than 4 pounds 6.4 ounces. Throws are made from a circle 8 feet 2½ inches in diameter; to be valid they must fall within a 90-degree sector. Rules governing discus throwing are about the same as those for the shot-put.

There are two styles of throwing the discus—one (the old Greek form), with prescribed motions from a fixed position; the other (the modern free style) conducted much like the shot-put, except that the discus is really slung with a full-arm swing rather than thrown.

Pole Vault (*Senior High School to Adults*).—The pole vault for height has the same purpose as the high jump—to clear a bar without displacing it. The pole vault requires: a runway about 4 feet wide and 100 feet long; uprights at least 12 feet apart and about 20 feet high, notched or pinned for half-inch or one-inch lifts of the crossbar; a landing pit of soft earth with a sawdust top; and a standard pole. The pole is 16 feet long, of female bamboo, wound with electric tape for grip and plugged with wood at the lower end. A 14-foot pole is preferable for beginners. Mid-point in front of the uprights is the *planting-pit,* a hole to receive the pole at the moment of the vault; this pit may be 6 to 9 inches deep, about 24 inches long and 18 inches across the middle of a wide plank sunk between the uprights with a 2-inch projection to stop the end of the pole. Fifteen feet in front of the bar is a *balkline,* which may not be crossed by a contestant without counting against him as a trial.

A vaulter measures the pole against the height of the crossbar, grasps it with his right hand slightly *below* this point and places his left hand 2 to 3 feet *lower* on the pole. He carries the pole with this grip on a rapid sprint up the runway. As he places the end of the pole in the planting-pit, he slides his lower hand up the pole next to the upper hand and by the pull and thrust of both arms swings his body to a horizontal position above the pole with the feet forward. The pole is then shoved back and the vaulter lands in the pit. A good vaulter may clear the bar as high as 15 feet from the ground.

TRACKING

The story of tracks in the snow is an interesting one always, particularly in the woods, for those who learn to read it. Each bird, animal and human being makes a different track, and each track varies according to the mood of the tracked. Br'er Rabbit's larger hind feet are always ahead of his front ones—and if you follow him you can soon tell by the tracks whether he was afraid and in a hurry or taking a leisurely hop. Some animals (the muskrat, raccoon and red squirrel) make tracks that are amazingly like the impress of the human hand in shape.

Recording the Story.—The most common way to get a record of tracks is to photograph them. To do this one must learn to judge lights and shadows on the snow, and even then results are not always good for often the best tracks lie in shadow too deep for the camera. Making plaster-of-Paris casts is a satisfactory and fairly simple process. It requires only plaster of Paris, available at any hardware store and water (carry some along unless you are certain of finding it on the trail) with which to mix it. An average-sized track—fox or dog—will take less than ½ pound of plaster. Have a tin box or can to mix the plaster and water, stirring with a stick to remove all lumps and making the mixture about the consistency of thick cream. Pour it into the track and leave it until it hardens. You will then have a negative of the track. Positives may be made in clay, plaster or plasticene. Shaped into paper weights, book ends and the like, they make decorative ornaments. The best snow is that near the melting point—soft and well packed; tracks in snow that has melted a little and then frozen also make good prints. If it is a dry, cold day so that the snow is soft and powdery, it is well to take along a sprayer of some sort and spray the track gently with water until it is icy.

Tracks in sand or mud also may be preserved with plaster of Paris.

VOLLEYBALL

(Junior High School to Adults)

Volleyball is a widely popular game because it does not require great skill, is not strenuous, has simple equipment and rules and may be played by teams of 6 to 12 persons.

Across the middle of a rectangular court not larger than 30 feet by 60 feet, a net is stretched with the upper edge 8 feet from the floor. For younger boys and girls the court is 25 feet by 50 feet, and the net may be 7½ or even 6½ feet from the floor. The object of each team is to keep the ball beyond the net in the enemy's country and to prevent its striking the ground in home territory.

A standard volley ball is an inch smaller in diameter and much lighter than a basketball, though a basketball will do when the game is played for recreation only. Any tennis net will serve for the net.

Teams in official play have six players, but 12 may play. Women's teams usually have eight players; in all teams the players stand in rows across the court, the server standing outside the lower right-hand corner of the court. The server tosses up the ball and bats it with his hand toward the opponents' court. He may use either or both open hands but must not use doubled fists. No matter how many play, each player must take his turn at serving the ball and must continue to serve until his side is out, by reason of faulty service, foul or failure in returning the ball. To be successful a serve must be hit over the net and into the opponents' court. Men are allowed one attempt at service, but younger players and women are permitted two.

When a team makes a foul or fails in service or return, the referee calls, "Side out"; service passes to the opposing team, and each of the losers moves on one stage in his rotation toward service. Served balls are dead if they touch the net, but returned balls may be recovered from the net.

After service, the ball may be hit by three teammates who *relay* the ball before it is sent over the net. The game for women permits any number of relays if the same player does not hit the ball twice in succession.

The ball is dead or *out of bounds* when it touches the floor, goes out of the court, strikes a player below the hips or when the referee blows his whistle. After the ball is dead, service goes to the opposite team.

Fouls. No player may touch the net or reach over the net to strike a ball. No player may be helped or supported while striking the ball. Players must remain in their own court. Catching or holding the ball is illegal; *dribbling* (touching the ball twice in succession) is prohibited. Players must not delay the game by batting the ball about unnecessarily; they must seek legitimately to advance their score. Stepping into the court during service and serving out of order are illegal plays.

If the serving side makes a foul, the ball goes to the opponents, and an additional penalty of one point may be added to the opponents' score if the foul is for unsportsmanlike conduct or for addressing officials. A foul by the receivers adds a point to the servers' score. Only the servers may score, except for fouls.

The first side to score 15 points by their own service wins the game, providing that they possess two or more points more than their opponents. Otherwise the game continues until one side is two points ahead. The game for women has two 15-minute halves and the winning team has the higher score at the end of play.

The officials are a referee, a scorer and two linesmen. The referee is chief official and works near the middle of the field, with a linesman at each end.

WRESTLING

Wrestling is a sport that consists of a hand-to-hand encounter between two unarmed contestants who attempt to throw each other. It is, no doubt, as old as man, but the rules of the game have changed from age to age. In the old Greek wrestling matches, for instance, no hold below the waistline was permitted. In the Irish collar-and-elbow contests neither man may for an instant let go his hold on his opponent's collar.

In Japan a wrestling match was recorded as early as 23 B.C. and, except for the period from the 12th to the 17th century, wrestling has always been popular there. Japanese wrestlers try to increase their weight as much as possible, instead of reducing as in other countries. Jujitsu, a kind of trick wrestling that probably origi-

nated with the Japanese army, is still practiced there but is not the regular wrestling form.

In England a number of wrestling styles were developed. One of them, the Lancashire or catch-as-catch-can, which is a combination of upright and ground wrestling, is the style used in Great Britain and America today. The Greco-Roman style, which originated in France and has no relation to classic wrestling, is popular on the Continent. It is almost entirely ground wrestling and holds below the hips and tripping are not allowed.

Catch-as-catch-can Wrestling.—In this form of wrestling a fall is secured whenever both shoulders squarely touch the floor at once. Only strangle holds, shutting off an opponent's wind are barred. At least 25 different holds are named and distinguished by professional wrestlers. There is not much value in a mere list of wrestling positions. The moves may, however, be divided into:

The Approach, which should be cautious, the body leaning forward, the arms bent a little at the elbow and out in front with the hands open, fingers together and curved, the feet spread apart with the weight fairly distributed.

The First Hold, in which the opponents first assume the referee's hold, each with his right hand on the other's neck and his left holding the other's right elbow.

To Go Behind.—This is an offensive move to get behind the opponent to throw him to the mat; the leg dive, elbow throw, arm pull and chin lift are the moves used. The defensive move is to try to keep the body bent forward and not to be forced into an upright position.

To Take to Mat.—One way to take the opponent to mat is to drop to the knees behind him, grasp his ankles and push him forward with the head and shoulders. The defensive move is to try to go forward and out of the hold. A second offensive move is to fasten the opponent's left arm between his body and yours, quickly place one or both feet against his and throw him off balance to the left, keeping close as he falls. The defensive move is to keep the arm from being caught and to reach back between your legs and grasp the opponent's leg. A third offensive is to lift the opponent into the air and throw him; the defensive move is to relax, so that it is more difficult to be thrown off balance, and to twist a leg around the opponent's leg, so that he lifts against himself.

To Keep the Advantage.—When the offensive player has his opponent down, he must try to keep him there by holding his elbow with one hand and twining the other arm around his abdomen. Then he can bring one leg inside and twist it around the opponent's. He can also try to keep the man underneath off balance and tire him out by keeping part of his weight on him.

Out from Underneath.—The defensive move, if taken to the mat, is to catch oneself with the hands and knees well spread to keep the balance and then try to get from under. In the *arm roll* the defensive man seizes the wrist of the arm that is around his abdomen,

pulls it and turns his body so that the opponent rolls off. It helps to hook a foot under his thigh and lift with that too. Another move is to *sit out* from under by suddenly throwing the feet out in front and sitting down flat on the floor, pulling the opponent's hands loose, straightening and twisting out of his hold. A move similar to this is a *body twist,* performed by loosening the opponent's fingers from the abdomen, raising up and stepping forward with one leg and turning upward to face the opponent.

Pinning Holds.—Once the opponent is brought to the mat he must be rolled over on his back and then overpowered. Common holds are: the *near half nelson* (arm underneath the opponent's arm and across his back with the hand on his head), combined with the *farther leg* in which your other arm reaches under the opponent and grasps the thigh or knee of his opposite leg from the back and pulls the leg toward you, keeping your body at right angles and chest against his; with the *waist lock* in which the pressure is relaxed to allow the body to turn; and with the *farther arm* in which the arm is twisted around the opponent's opposite wrist from the inside. The defensive for these is to keep the head and neck stiff and use the arm roll, sit out or body twist.

The near leg and *far arm* consists of the under man reaching across and grasping his opponent's far arm from in front and rolling him over by raising his nearer leg, following with the crotch hold and locking the arms when the opponent is rolled off. The defensive move is to try to twist out as the opponent is reaching for the leg.

The jackknife hold consists of a near half nelson with one arm and a crotch hold with the opposite leg, forcing the opponent's head down so that he rolls forward until his shoulders touch the mat. The defensive is to keep the head up and try to get out of the underneath position.

The three-quarter nelson consists of following the near half nelson by clasping hands around the opponent, the second hand crossing under his chest. With it you twist your leg around his and press until his body turns, return to the half nelson and pin him with a crotch hold.

The farther half nelson is the opposite of the near (reach across his back and underneath his farther arm). It may be combined with the side scissors (one leg placed over the opponent's body and locked with the under leg).

The top scissors consists of a straddle on the back of the opponent with the legs wrapped around, the feet crossed and pushed back between his legs so that his arms are forced forward until he lies flat. The defensive move is to keep the elbows in so tight that the opponent cannot get his legs around you.

Wrestling Contests.—The time regulation for amateur matches is 10 minutes; for high-school matches, 8 minutes. A *fall* consists of pinning both shoulders to the floor for 2 seconds by referee's silent count. The *full nelson, hammer lock* and *toe hold* are barred in amateur contests.

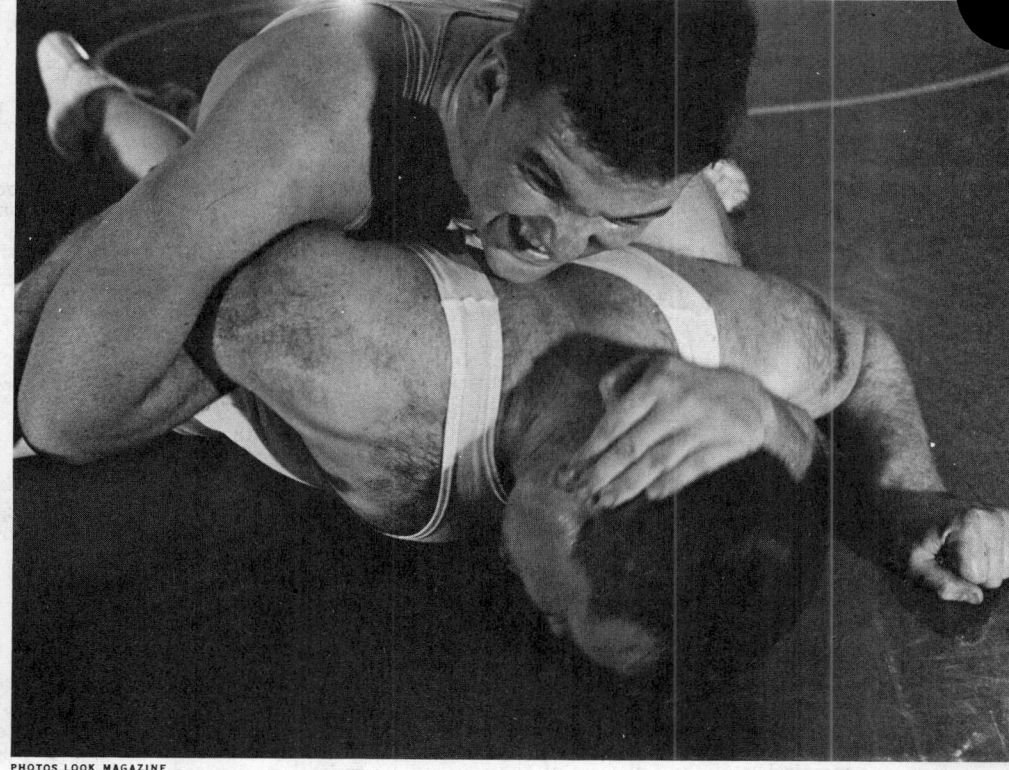

PHOTOS LOOK MAGAZINE

BOYS' CLUBS OF AMERICA

BOYS' CLUBS OF AMERICA, with headquarters in New York, work with youth in many cities.

ASSOCIATIONS

Actors' Equity Association; headquarters, New York; founded 1915. An organization to better the working conditions and protect the legal rights of actors.

Advancement of Colored People, National Association for the; headquarters, New York; founded 1909. An interracial association for the furtherance of the civil rights and promoting the interests of colored people in the United States.

Aeronautic Ass'n of U. S. A., National; founded in 1905 as Aero Club of America; present name adopted in 1922; headquarters, Washington. An association for the advancement of aviation.

Alcoholic Foundation, The; headquarters, New York; founded 1938; associated with Alcoholics Anonymous, a benevolent organization for the reformation of alcoholics with the assistance of former addicts. All relations are strictly confidential.

Amateur Softball Ass'n of America; headquarters, Newark; founded 1933; an association of the followers of the sport.

American Academy of Arts and Letters, see *Arts and Letters.*

American Academy of Political and Social Sciences, see *Political and Social Sciences.*

American Association for the Advancement of Science, see *Science.*

American Association of University Professors, see *University Professors.*

American Association of University Women, see *University Women.*

American Astronomical Society, see *Astronomical Society, American.*

American Automobile Association, see *Automobile Association, American.*

American Bankers Association, see *Bankers Association, American.*

American Bar Association, see *Bar Association, American.*

American Bible Society; headquarters, New York; founded 1816. A religious, nonsectarian organization for encouragement of wider distribution and use of the Bible.

American Civil Liberties Union, see *Civil Liberties Union.*

American College of Surgeons, see *Surgeons.*

American Farm Bureau Federation, see *Farm Bureau Federation, American.*

American Federation of Arts, see *Arts.*

American Federation of Labor; headquarters, Washington; founded 1881. A group of labor unions, organized by trades and industries, which seeks to improve working conditions in industry and to provide relief for the families of members on strike.

American Federation of Musicians, see *Musicians, American Federation.*

American Geographical Society, see *Geographical Society, American.*

American Institute of Architects; headquarters, Washington; founded 1857. A professional group, designed to advance the standards of its members and protect their interests.

American Legion, The; headquarters, Indianapolis, Ind.; founded 1919. An organization of those who served in the armed forces of the United States during its wars. Local posts in hundreds of communities have fraternal meetings and support local educational and social activities; these are grouped in departments by states. The national organization devotes much effort to political activities intended to improve the economic condition of its members. The American Legion Auxiliary is an affiliated organization for the families of Legion members.

American Library Association, see *Library Association, American.*

American Mathematical Society, see *Mathematical Society, American.*

American Medical Association, see *Medical Association, American.*

American Nurses Association, see *Nurses Association, American.*

American Osteopathic Association, see *Osteopathic Association, American.*

American Philosophical Society, see *Philosophical Society, American.*

American Physical Society, see *Physical Society, American.*

American Prison Association; headquarters, New York; founded 1844. A benevolent organization devoted to betterment of prison conditions and the rehabilitation of prisoners.

American Radio Relay League, see *Radio Relay League, American.*

American Red Cross, see *Red Cross, American.*

American Revolution, Daughters of the, National Society; headquarters, Washington; first organized at Washington in 1890, incorporated by Act of Congress in 1896. The membership is restricted to those whose ancestors were in the American army during the Revolution. The society supports patriotic activities of various sorts.

American Society for the Prevention of Cruelty to Animals; headquarters, New York; founded 1866. An organization to provide relief for animals in the cities, to destroy stray animals and to prevent the abuse of horses in harness.

American Sunbathing Association, see *Sunbathing Association, American.*

Animals, American Society for the Prevention of Cruelty to, see *American Society for the Prevention of Cruelty to Animals.*

Architects, American Institute of, see *American Institute of Architects.*

Arts, American Federation of; headquarters, New York, founded 1909. An association of many local and special organizations intended to promote the interests of all branches of pure and commercial art.

Arts and Letters, American Academy of; headquarters, New York; founded 1904. A self-perpetuating group of persons who have attained distinction in literature or the arts.

Astronomical Society, American; headquarters, Madison, Wis.; founded 1897. A professional group, designed to support the activities of its members and advance the science.

Audubon Society, National; headquarters, New York; founded 1905 by George Bird Grinnell and named after John James Audubon, the ornithologist. An endowed association working with all local and special organizations interested in the propagation and preservation of wild life. *Audubon Magazine* is the official magazine.

Authors' League of America; headquarters, New York; founded 1912. A professional group for advancing the standards and guarding the legal rights of its membership.

Automobile Association, American; headquarters, Washington; founded 1902. An association of local clubs working in the interests of automobile owners

Bankers Association, American; headquarters, New York; founded 1875. The principal organization of commercial banks in the United States, designed to advance standards and improve the economic and political position of its membership.

Baptist Youth Fellowship; headquarters, Philadelphia; formed 1941; social and charitable organization with groups in most Baptist churches designed to appeal to the interests of youth.

Bar Association, American; headquarters, Chicago; formed 1878. The professional, advisory, self-regulating organization of the legal profession, designed to maintain the standards and promote the interests of its membership.

Big Brother and Big Sister Federation; headquarters, New York; founded 1917; an affiliation of 47 local organizations throughout the nation engaged in welfare work among the youth of the cities.

Boy Scouts of America; headquarters, New York; founded 1910. Subordinate local troops in all sections seek to develop citizenship and character in boys and stimulate interest in nature and outdoor life.

Boys' Clubs of America; headquarters, New York; founded 1906. A federation of boys' clubs in the various cities, working for

BOY SCOUT learning the art of building a camp fire. Composed of Cub Scouts 8–10, Boy Scouts 11–13, and Explorers 14 years and above, scouting has chapters all over the world. Their motto is "Be Prepared."

entertainment and character advancement among its membership.

Business and Professional Women's Clubs, see *Women's Clubs, National Federation of Business and Professional.*

Chamber of Commerce of the United States; headquarters, Washington; formed 1912. A national organization to study and give information on business matters and to correlate the activities of over 1,300 local business organizations.

Chemical Society, American; headquarters, Washington; founded 1876. A professional organization designed to advance the interests of its members and to make available the results of their work.

Christian Endeavor, International Society of; headquarters, Columbus, Ohio. Dr. Francis E. Clark formed the first Young People's Society of Christian Endeavor in the Congregational Church at Portland, Me., in 1881. The World's Christian Endeavor Union was formed in 1895. It is an interdenominational religious group working for the advancement of the Christian religion among young people.

Churches of Christ in the U. S. A., National Council of; headquarters, New York. A federation of Christian denominations working for the general advancement of their common interests.

Cincinnati, Society of the; headquarters, Washington; founded 1783 with George Washington as president. Originally made up of officers of the American army in the Revolution, membership is hereditary and restricted; its activities are mainly honorary.

Civil Liberties Union, American; headquarters, New York; founded 1920. A group designed to advance the cause of freedom of speech for political and social minorities and to defend by propaganda and legal measures the rights of individuals.

Congress of Industrial Organization; headquarters, Washington; formed 1935. An affiliation of labor organizations grouped by plants and industries instead of by trades; it seeks to protect the rights of its members and better their economic situation.

Crippled Children and Adults, National Society of; headquarters, Chicago; founded 1921. An organization for improving opportunities of treatment and the rehabilitation of the crippled.

Daughters of the American Revolution, National Society, see *American Revolution, Daughters of the, National Society.*

Disabled American Veterans; headquarters, Cincinnati; founded 1920. Composed of wounded and other disabled veterans, the organization seeks to advance their economic condition and to secure adequate care for those in need of aid.

Eagles, Fraternal Order of; headquarters, Kansas City; founded 1898. An organization that provides fellowship and promotes the welfare of its members. The order also engages in benevolent activities.

Eastern Star, Grand Chapter; Order of; headquarters, Washington; founded 1896. A benevolent society restricted in membership to Masons and their families, whose local units participate in community charity work and in social affairs.

Education Association of the United States, National; headquarters, Washington; founded 1857. A group composed of teachers and school executives that seeks to promote educational activities of all kinds and to advance the status of the profession.

Elks, Grand Lodge, Benevolent and Protective Order of; headquarters, Chicago; founded 1868. A fraternal organization, restricted to cities, which provides security for its membership and engages in local charitable activities. The original Elks Club was founded in New York in 1866 as a good-fellowship club by a group of men who took the head of an elk from Barnum's Museum as their emblem. Benevolent aspects were gradually assumed.

Engineers, American Assn. of; 8 So. Michigan Ave., Chicago 3 (1915); M. E. McIver, Sec.

English-Speaking Union; (1920); 19 E. 54 St., New York 22.

Exchange Club, National; headquarters, Toledo; founded 1917. An association, restricted in membership, of local groups of business men working for higher standards and for local programs of civic and community betterment.

Farm Bureau Federation, American; headquarters, Chicago; founded 1919. Com-

DADE THORNTON, NATIONAL AUDUBON SOCIETY

SANCTUARIES for wildlife fall under the auspices of the National Audubon Society. This refuge, which is in Everglades National Park, Florida, is home for many species of wildlife.

posed of farmers and their families, this organization co-ordinates the political activities of local farmer associations and develops programs to advance their common interests.

4-H Clubs, under supervision of the Extension Service in U. S. Department of Agriculture, Washington, with local control by county extension agents; to improve the 4 H's—Head, Hands, Heart and Health. Founded 1907.

Freemasonry, 33d Degree Scottish Rite of: The Mother Supreme Council, organized in Charleston, S. C., in 1801, became the southern Jurisdiction with seat at Washington, D. C., when the Supreme Council for the Northern Jurisdiction was organized in 1813 with seat at Boston. One of the most active and wide-spread of the many Masonic orders, this secret benevolent fraternity works through its local lodges to provide security for its membership and participates in community charitable activities.

Freemasons, The. The Masonic fraternity is the largest, oldest and most widely distributed secret society in the world. Introduced into America by English Masons about 1730, Masons of various rites met in scattered lodges irrespective of their original affiliations, but organizations of the more powerful branches by states and localities soon developed. In addition to the Scottish Rite and Royal Arch Freemasons and the Eastern Star, important Masonic groups include the Grotto, a social fraternity, the Knights Templars, and the Shrine or Nobles of the Mystic Shrine. The total membership of master masons in the United States is about 2,988,000.

Freemasons of the United States, Royal Arch, General Grand Chapter; headquarters, Coldwater, Mich., founded 1797. A Masonic order, this secret benevolent fraternal organization with many local units shares in community charity work and provides security for its members.

Garden Clubs, National Council of State; headquarters, New York; founded 1929. An association for broadening the scope of amateur gardeners.

Geographic Society, National; headquarters, Washington; founded 1888. An organization of world-wide scope, designed to advance and spread geographic knowledge. The membership includes subscribers to the Society's *National Geographic Magazine.*

Geographical Society, American, headquarters, N. Y.; founded 1852. An organization formed to encourage geographical exploration and discovery and to provide a place to obtain accurate information on every part of the globe.

Girl Scouts, Inc.; headquarters, New York; founded 1912. Its local troops in all sections work to advance character and outdoor activities among growing girls and to promote an interest in good citizenship.

Hadassah (Women's Zionist Organization of America); headquarters, New York; founded 1912. An organization to promote the religious and social welfare of its members.

Hibernians in America, Ancient Order of: headquarters, Brooklyn, N. Y.; formed 1836. A semisecret benevolent fraternal order limited in membership to Roman

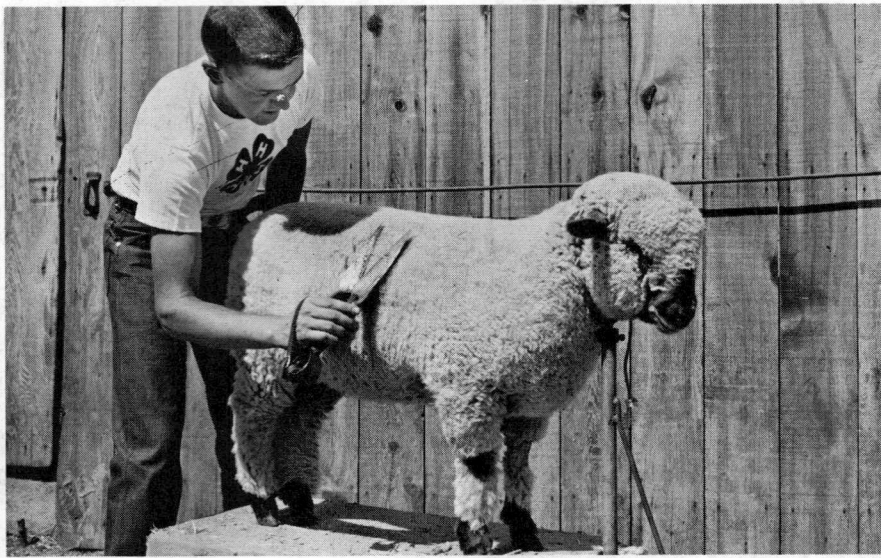

NATIONAL 4-H SERVICE COMMITTEE. INC.

4-H CLUBS are educational programs especially for rural boys and girls. Affiliated with the Department of Agriculture, 4-H is a national system of education in agriculture and home economics, assisted by state and other agencies. The name comes from the symbol of the club, seen on the boy's tee shirt—a four-leaf clover having an H on each leaf, standing for the four aims of the club: the improvement of head, heart, hands, and health. Here a member trims the fleece of a sheep for a 4-H exhibition.

Catholic men of Irish birth or ancestry; Irish immigrants were formerly the special care of this order.

Independent Order of Odd Fellows, Sovereign Grand Lodge, see *Odd Fellows Sovereign Grand Lodge, Independent Order of.*

Izaak Walton League of America; headquarters, Chicago; founded 1922; 20,-000 members. A national organization interested in the preservation of wild life for recreation and sport, particularly fishing, and working to promote co-operation between sportsmen and legal authorities.

Junior Leagues of America, The Association of; headquarters, New York: more than 100 leagues. The Junior League of the N. Y. College Settlement, organized by Miss Mary Harriman in 1900, was the nucleus; in 1920 Mrs. Willard Straight organized the 39 leagues then formed in different cities into a National Association; headquarters were established in New York city in 1926. Essentially a federation of young women of accepted social rank, its local units participate in social and charitable activities.

Kiwanis International; headquarters, Chicago; founded 1915. A union of local organizations of business and professional men, restricted in membership, dedicated to better business standards and social and civic improvement.

Knights of Columbus; headquarters, New Haven; founded 1882. A fraternal and benevolent society of Roman Catholic men, devoted to educational charities and the economic security of its members.

Knights of Pythias; headquarters, Minneapolis; founded 1864. A fraternal benevolent organization with local units in all parts of the nation; it has worked actively to secure economic security for its members and their families.

Knights Templar, see *Freemasons.*

Lawn Tennis Association, United States; headquarters, New York; founded 1881. An association of tennis clubs for the furtherance of their common interests.

Leonard Wood Memorial for the Eradication of Leprosy; headquarters, New York; founded 1927. A society working for the elimination of leprosy in all parts of the world.

Library Association, American; headquarters, Chicago; founded 1876. A professional society for the advancement of the status of its members and the improvement of library service.

Lions International (International Association of Lions Clubs); headquarters, Chicago; organized 1917 in Chicago by Melvin Jones; a non-political and non-sectarian federation composed of business and professional men, whose objectives are to promote fellowship, international understanding, and community service.

Loyal Order of Moose, see *Moose, Loyal Order of.*

Maccabees, The; headquarters, Port Huron, Mich.; founded 1878. A benevolent, secret fraternal society organized in a lodge system with a fixed ritual.

Masons, The, see *Freemasons.*

Mathematical Society, American; headquarters, Providence, R. I.; founded 1888. A professional group devoted to the advancement of knowledge in its special field.

Medical Association, American; headquarters, Chicago; founded 1847. A professional organization, made up of state and local divisions, to which belong most of the physicians of the country. It works to advance the conditions of its members and to promote health and medical knowledge through established channels.

Methodist Youth, National Conference of, formerly the Epworth League. Change made in 1940 when three branches of Church united; program by Youth Dept. Nashville, Tenn.

Moose, Loyal Order of; headquarters, Mooseheart, Ill.; founded 1888. A social benevolent fraternity that promotes the security of its members.

Music Clubs, National Federation of; headquarters, New York; founded 1872. A union of the music clubs of the United States devoted to the furtherance of music appreciation and enjoyment.

Musicians, American Federation of; headquarters, New York; founded 1896. 217,000 members. A labor union working for the economic advancement of members of the profession.

National Congress of Parents and Teachers, see *Parents and Teachers, National Congress of.*

National Education Association of the United States, see *Education Association of the United States, National.*

National Exchange Club, see *Exchange Club, National.*

National Geographic Society, see *Geographic Society, National.*

National Institute of Social Sciences, see *Social Sciences, National Institute of.*

National Research Council, see *Research Council, National.*

National Rifle Association, see *Rifle Association, National.*

National Safety Council, see *Safety Council, National.*

Needlework Guild of America; headquarters, Philadelphia; founded 1885. A federation of local women's units united in charitable and social endeavors.

Newspaper Publishers Association, American; headquarters, New York; founded 1887. An association for maintaining the standards and promoting the service of newspapers.

Nobles of the Mystic Shrine, Ancient Arabic Order of, see *Shrine, Ancient Arabic Order of Nobles of the Mystic.*

Numismatic Society, American; headquarters, New York; founded 1858. An organization for the study and preservation of old coins; to establish their authenticity and maintain the standards of collectors.

Nurses Association, American; headquarters, New York; founded 1896. A professional organization that guards the standards and economic status of its members.

Odd Fellows Sovereign Grand Lodge, Independent Order of; headquarters, Baltimore, Md.; founded 1819. An affiliation of many local lodges of a patriotic, secret, benevolent fraternal order that shares in community charities and provides relief for its membership. The Independent Order of Odd Fellows, Manchester Unity, which was organized in Manchester, England, in 1810, was the first of the Friendly Societies to take definite form.

Olympic Association, United States; as American Olympic Association, incorporated by Act of Congress, Sept. 21, 1950. Headquarters, New York; the American unit of the international sports organization.

Order of Eastern Star, Grand Chapter, see *Eastern Star, Grand Chapter, Order of.*

Order of Elks, Grand Lodge, Benevolent and Protective, see *Elks, Grand Lodge, Benevolent and Protective Order of.*

Order of Owls, see *Owls, Order of.*

Osteopathic Association, American; headquarters, Chicago; founded 1897. The professional organization of practicing osteopaths, it defends their rights and works to promote knowledge in that field.

Owls, Order of; headquarters, Hartford; founded 1904. A benevolent fraternal order with social and protective aims.

Parents and Teachers, National Congress of; headquarters, Chicago; founded in 1897 by Mrs. Theodore W. Birney, as the National Congress of Mothers; developed into the National Congress of Mother and Parent-Teacher Associations in 1908 and changed to the National Congress of Parents and Teachers in 1924. A federation of local units in which parents and teachers work to advance the efficiency of the schools.

Pen Women, National League of American; headquarters, Washington; founded 1897. An association of women writers for their mutual profit and pleasure.

Phi Beta Kappa, headquarters, N. Y.; first chapter founded at William and Mary College, 1776; United Chapters of Phi Beta Kappa, 1883. An organization in which membership is restricted to those of scholarly attainments. Vassar received the first chapter given to a women's college in 1898.

Philatelic Society, American; founded 1886; headquarters, State College, Pennsylvania. An association of stamp collectors for preserving records and assembling data concerning rare stamps.

Philosophical Society, American; headquarters, Philadelphia; founded 1727 by Benjamin Franklin. This, the oldest scientific association in America, has a rigidly restricted membership and works to advance knowledge and encourage its spread.

Physical Society, American; headquarters, New York; founded 1899. A professional organization that supports the diffusion of knowledge in its field and guards the special interests of its members.

Poetry Society of America; headquarters, New York; founded 1910. A professional group for the promotion of the interests of its members and the protection of their work.

Political and Social Sciences, American Academy of; headquarters, Philadelphia; founded 1889. The academy publishes papers and reports to promote political and social science.

Prevention of War, National Council for; headquarters, Washington; founded 1921. An association for considering the causes of war and the methods of eliminating them.

Radio Relay League, American; headquarters, Hartford; formed 1914. A cooperative organization of amateur radio operators that maintains emergency communication channels and works to improve facilities.

Red Cross, American; headquarters, Washington; founded 1881. The central organization of the principal facilities in the country for the relief of disaster

victims, the improvement of hygiene, the succor of the disabled in warfare and the eradication of disease.

Research Council, National; headquarters, Washington, founded 1915. A central body for the direction and stimulation of scientific investigation, particularly for the national good, with membership by invitation.

Rifle Association, National; headquarters, Washington; founded 1871. An organization of sportsmen engaged in the betterment of standards in that field, the conservation of wild life and the promotion of contests of skill.

Rotary International; headquarters, Chicago. A federation of local organization of business and professional men, restricted in membership, which endeavor to promote ethics, fellowship and civic and community ideals. The first Rotary Club was organized in Chicago, Feb. 23, 1905, by a lawyer, Paul P. Harris, and the members met in rotation at different offices. A National Association with 16 clubs was formed in 1910 and an International Association in 1912. The name was changed to Rotary International in 1922, and the federation now includes clubs around the world.

Royal Arcanum; headquarters, Boston; founded 1877. A benevolent fraternity, devoted mainly to the security of its membership.

Safety Council, National; headquarters, Chicago; founded 1913. The national group for the advancement of accident prevention and the elimination of industrial and highway hazards.

Science, American Association for the Advancement of; headquarters, Washington; founded 1848. A professional organization with several affiliated scientific groups, all working to foster knowledge in the sciences.

Shrine, Ancient Arabic Order of Nobles of the Mystic; headquarters, Chicago; founded 1871. A social fraternity with membership restricted to Masons of rank.

Social Sciences, National Institute of; headquarters, New York; founded 1889. A co-ordinating group that supports the diffusion of knowledge in its field.

Society of Cincinnati, see *Cincinnati, Society of the.*

Sons of the American Revolution, National Society, headquarters, Washington; founded 1889. Corresponding to the Daughters of the American Revolution, which it preceded. The members are men whose ancestors fought in the American Army during the Revolution. The Society is interested in the preservation of American history and in the promotion of patriotic activities.

Sons of Union Veterans of the Civil War, see *Union Veterans of the Civil War, Sons of.*

Spanish War Veterans, United; headquarters, Washington; founded 1898. An organization of veterans of the war with Spain, to guard their security and economic status.

Sunbathing Association, American; headquarters, Mays Landing, N. J.; founded 1931. A group that supports propaganda in the cause of nudism.

Surgeons, American College of; headquarters, Chicago; formed 1913. A professional organization that fosters the advancement of knowledge and the economic status of surgeons.

Travelers Aid Association, National; headquarters, New York; founded 1917. An association for assisting travelers, giving information and lending aid when needed.

Union Veterans of the Civil War, Sons of; headquarters, Reading; founded 1881. A patriotic society that supports commemorative activities and guards the interests of surviving veterans; membership is restricted to descendants of Union soldiers.

United Spanish War Veterans, see *Spanish War Veterans, United.*

University Professors, American Association of; headquarters, Washington; founded 1915. A professional organization for the improvement of the status of its members and maintenance of standards.

University Women, American Association of; headquarters, Washington; founded 1882. A federation of local units of university women, with social and civic-betterment objectives.

Veterans of Foreign Wars of the United States; headquarters, Kansas City; founded 1899. A patriotic society with membership limited to those who have served American armies outside the boundaries of the country; it works for the security of its members and the promotion of patriotic activities.

Wildlife Federation, National; headquarters, Washington; founded 1937. An organization for the preservation of the birds, plants and animals of the country.

Women's Clubs, General Federation of; headquarters, Washington. After a preliminary meeting of representatives of women's clubs in New York in 1889 a constitution was adopted in 1890, and a charter was granted by Congress in 1901. Some 15,000 groups in the United States and foreign countries are affiliated. A co-ordinating body to advance the common causes of many local organizations.

Women's Clubs, National Federation of Business and Professional; headquarters, New York; founded 1919. A co-ordinating organization for local units of women in professional and business occupations, with general social and civic-betterment purposes.

Women Voters of the U. S., League of; headquarters, Washington; founded 1920. A non-partisan organization whose object is to interest women in voting and encourage participation in public affairs.

Woodmen of America, Modern; headquarters, Rock Island, Ill.; organized at Lyons, Ia., by Joseph Cullen Root in 1883. A fraternal benevolent society that fosters the security of its members.

Woodmen Circle, Supreme Forest, headquarters, Omaha. A fraternal benevolent society organized in local units whose chief purpose is the security of its members.

Young Men's Christian Associations of the United States; headquarters, New York. The Y.M.C.A. was first organized in England in 1844 by George Williams, and branches were soon formed in France, Holland, Canada, India, Australia and the United States (Boston, 1851). The first World-Conference was held in 1855, and the National Council was founded in 1866. The federation is designed to advance the religious, intellectual, physical and social welfare of young men.

Young Men's Hebrew Association; headquarters, New York; formed 1874. An organization to promote the religious and social welfare of its members.

Young Women's Christian Associations of the United States; headquarters, New York; formed 1906 (first local association founded in Boston in 1866). A federation of clubs designed to promote the physical, intellectual, social, moral and spiritual interest of young women, particularly those without family attachment. A World's Y.W.C.A., formed in 1894, has headquarters in Geneva.

Zionist Organization of America; headquarters, New York; founded 1897. An association for the advancement of Jewish interests, particularly the renationalization of the Jewish race.

Zonta International; headquarters, Chicago; founded 1919. The central organization of local professional clubs for women.

YMCA

YOUNG MEN'S CHRISTIAN ASSOCIATIONS OF THE UNITED STATES. Riding is a popular sport at many of the YMCA's 1,300 summer camps.

History of science	1749
Astronautics	1763
Astronomy	1780
Chemistry	1798
Life science	1839
Physics	1869

VOLUME TWENTY TWO

SCIENCE

CITIES SERVICE COMPANY

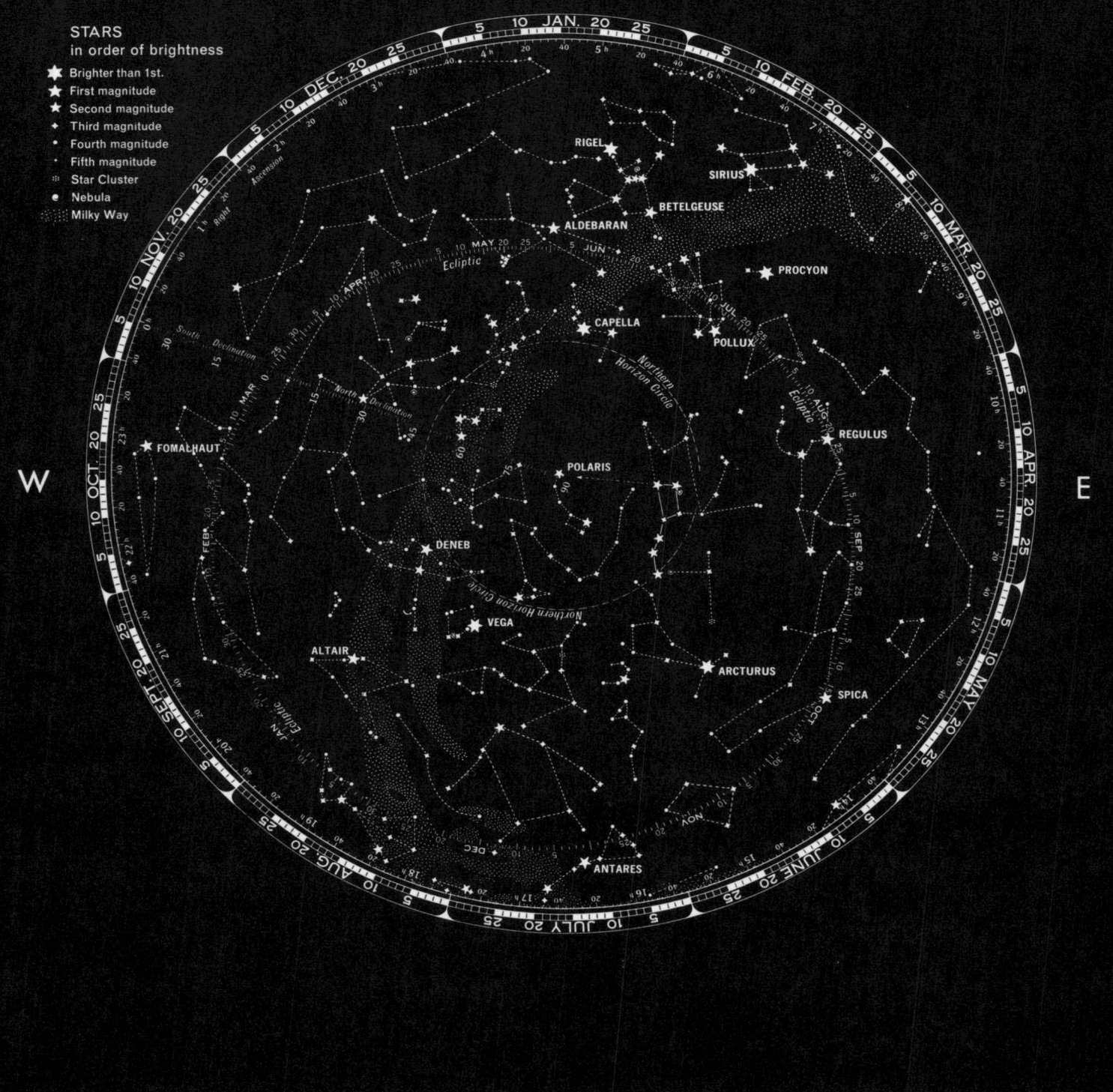

STARS
in order of brightness

★ Brighter than 1st.
★ First magnitude
★ Second magnitude
✦ Third magnitude
• Fourth magnitude
• Fifth magnitude
⁜ Star Cluster
● Nebula
⋯ Milky Way

COPYRIGHTED BY RAND McNALLY & COMPANY. R.L. 64Y33

STAR CHART of the Northern skies can be used by anyone living in North America. The approximate position of any star at any time can be obtained from the chart. Face north and rotate the book until the current date is at the top of the chart. The stars and constellations in the upper two-thirds of the chart are those visible in the sky at about 9 P.M. The star nearly at the center of the chart is Polaris, the North Star. The stars within the Northern Horizon Circle correspond to the stars that rotate counter-clockwise around the North Star, and are always above the horizon for anyone living at 40° North Latitude. The stars to the right of center will be visible in the eastern sky; those to the left of center will be visible in the western sky. Stars close to the upper edges of the chart will be close to the southern horizon. To visualize the positions of the stars directly overhead and in the southern sky, hold the star chart with the current date pointing south. Some stars will appear brighter than others. The Order of Brightness guide in the upper left hand corner will aid in identification. Stars close to the horizon may be obscured by the surface haze.

Science

HISTORY

Definition.—The basic motive behind all scientific investigation—the compelling need to reduce the observable world to comprehensible terms—is as old as mankind. Science, however, is a relatively recent result of this desire to understand, and it would be well to come to some understanding of what science is before attempting to view its history.

Science is surprisingly difficult to define. One definition states that it is an organized body of knowledge. This explanation seems satisfactory until it is realized that by this definition a telephone directory becomes a respectable scientific publication and the *Handbook of Chemistry and Physics* appears worthy of the Nobel Prize. Yet it does contain an important element of truth. It serves to emphasize that science deals with facts—facts arranged in an orderly way, permitting easy access to them.

Another concept of science singles out its ability to predict the future. There is something appealing in the austerity of this definition but there is also something lacking. Bookmakers, after all, stake their livelihoods on the accuracy of their predictions, but few would insist that "bookies" are scientists. And accuracy of prediction, alone, is never sufficient proof of the validity of a theory; an explanation of how and why it works is necessary. It should be noted, however, that in the history of science there have been systems of considerable sophistication (such as the Babylonian lunar theory and Ptolemaic astronomy) which eschewed explanation and relied for their intellectual authority upon their ability to predict certain specific phenomena with a high degree of accuracy.

The greatest part of the history of science is concerned with the explanation of observed facts—explanations of how or why a particular effect or group of effects is produced. For more than 90 per cent of the period during which science has existed, this type of explanation has made up the body of scientific theory. There are, however, various kinds of explanations. There is a world of difference between an explanation of the motion of the moon that relies upon the desires of a moon-goddess and one that appeals to a law of universal attraction. For what follows, it is of the utmost importance to realize pre-

NEW YORK PUBLIC LIBRARY

DETAILED AND ACCURATE OBSERVATIONS are the basis upon which the scientist builds hypotheses about the nature of the universe. Tycho Brahe, a sixteenth-century Danish astronomer, using a great steel quadrant with a radius of over six feet, made the extremely precise measurements from which Kepler later devised his theories of planetary motion.

cisely what this difference is. It is definitely not one that involves either the description of the moon's position or the prediction of its future points in space. In both theories, description and prediction may be exactly the same. Where they do differ is in vulnerability to criticism. The use of a moon-goddess protects the theorist from any and all lunar aberrations.

If the moon suddenly went shooting off at a tangent the priest of the moon-goddess would immediately call attention to the fact that his patroness had an urgent appointment elsewhere and decided to leave. The theory remains intact. The poor Newtonian astronomer is in much worse shape. Should the moon suddenly depart from the neighborhood of the earth,

NEW YORK PUBLIC LIBRARY

PIX. INC.

ECLIPSES were regarded with awe and terror in ancient times; the Chinese, who first recorded a solar eclipse in 2137 B.C., believed it was caused by a dragon swallowing the sun (*top left*). Yet the successful prediction of eclipses was one of the earliest triumphs of scientific investigation. The drawing (*left*) shows the moon moving across the face of the sun during a partial eclipse.

the theory of universal attraction would have to be abandoned unless some other body could be detected whose gravitational force would account for the moon's strange behavior. Thus, the faith placed in scientific conclusions is not the result of the ability of scientific theories to answer all questions, but their ability to withstand the most severe criticism, both theoretical and experimental. If a theory is inherently irrefutable, it may be true but it does not have to be scientific. God's will may always be done, but it is rarely open to human comprehension. The history of science is, in good part, the gradual evolution of theories open to criticism.

One further point in connection with scientific theories is worth mentioning. If we require of them only that they be capable of empirical refutation, then the way is left open for the almost infinite multiplication of *sources* of theory. As long as an idea can be tested by actual experiment, it makes no difference whether the idea came from long years of laboratory work or from a daydream. Experiment, it should be noted, is used here not as an instrument of

discovery but the most powerful critical tool the scientist possesses.

What, then, is science? It certainly contains accurate factual description. Many sciences, such as botany or mineralogy, were nothing but factual description until the nineteenth century. It also is predictive, for if a theory is to be taken seriously, it must give some insight into what we may expect in the future. Above all, it is explanatory, telling us not only what happens, but why. In the essay that follows all three of these elements will be traced, although the most attention will be focused upon the changing status of scientific theories. Two phases will be distinguished. In the first, extending in time from antiquity until the scientific revolution of the seventeenth century, the basic theory was essentially theological and, therefore, not entirely open to empirical refutation. The scientific revolution consisted essentially in the introduction of the principle of refutability, and from that time on, scientific theories have fallen because of the criticisms directed at them. Grasping these threads, the tour through the centuries of the history of science can now begin.

■**BEGINNINGS OF SCIENCE.**—From the remotest antiquity, man has wrestled with his environment in an effort simply to stay alive. Facts and their classification were of obvious importance. The hunting of wild game and the gathering of vegetable foods required this minimal intellectual activity. Certain regularities in nature, too, permitted the prediction of the more obvious aspects of natural phenomena. Explanations were magical and mystical, although it is probable that even this stage was reached only after millennia of intellectual effort.

The discovery of agriculture and the evolution of the social organism of the agrarian village created entirely new conditions of both practical and intellectual life. A new complexity developed in human affairs, the handling of which required specialists. Both in Egypt and Mesopotamia, a priestly caste, engaged in the regulation of social activity, emerged. In order for taxes to be assessed, land to be worked, and the whole complex social machinery kept in smooth working order, various new skills had to be developed. Among these were a method of keeping records and some kind of basic mathematics.

■**EGYPTIAN MATHEMATICS.**—Egyptian mathematics was relatively simple and straightforward and was used primarily for practical computations. Through its use, the Egyptians were able to compute complicated areas and volumes. There is little doubt that they could calculate the volume of a cylinder and the area of a sphere. Their greatest achievement in practical mathematics was the calculation of the volume of the frustum of a pyramid. The Egyptians, however, went beyond such purely practical matters and were able to solve linear and quadratic equations containing one unknown.

■**MESOPOTAMIAN MATHEMATICS.**—Mathematics in Mesopotamia was quite another matter. Earliest mathematical texts date from c. 1600 B.C. Of these, one group, called Table Texts, involved the tabulation of the results of various computations for handy reference. The other, the Problem Texts, were clearly intended for teaching mathematics to Babylonian scribes and presented the learner with exercises with which he could sharpen his skills.

The Table Texts are computations made on the basis of a sexagesimal system in which the basic unit is 60 rather than 10. The Table Texts comprise ordinary multiplication tables, tables of reciprocals, squares, square roots, cubes, and cube roots. With these tables handy, it was possible for the Babylonians to attack and solve quite advanced mathematical problems. A millennium before Pythagoras, they knew the Pythagorean theorem and worked with Pythagorean numbers with facility. They enjoyed numbers for numbers' sake and developed mathematical relationships of great complexity more than a thousand years before these numerical relationships were applicable to any physical process.

The Mesopotamians also created a mathematical astronomy of a very high order. By using approximations, a creditable lunar theory was devised by which the lunar calendar could be adjusted to the solar. The invention of the zodiac (an imaginary belt in the heavens) provided an essential astronomical reference band and, together with the use of mathematics, permitted the creation of a respectable planetary theory. When amalgamated with the Greek tradition, it was to produce an astronomical system not overthrown until the sixteenth century.

Classical Greek Science.—It was in the city of Miletus in Ionia that the first school of Greek scientific speculation emerged. Thales (c. 600 B.C.) is traditionally considered the first natural philosopher of Greece but it should be noted that absolutely nothing is known about him directly. No writings of his have survived, and the account which credits him with the prediction of a solar eclipse in 585 B.C. is suspect. What does seem certain is that the tradition Thales did create with Anaximander (611–547 B.C.) and Anaximenes (c. 570 B.C.) was a radical new departure in the history of thought.

To the Ionians, the god-ridden world of Homer was no fit place for a rational man. The harmony and regularity of the universe belied the capriciousness of the Homeric deities and the Ionians searched for the principle of unity and order behind the seeming diversity of observable reality. They thus initiated a quest that still endures. There must, they felt, be some *thing* that remained essentially itself through all time and whose modifications produced the world of constant flux. To Thales, this thing was water, for water could freeze and become like stone, or vaporize and become like air, and thus take up all the guises of common materials. Anaximenes chose air as his essential substratum. When air is compressed it becomes warm; when it is rarefied it becomes cold. Hence physical process gave rise to physical qualities. For Anaximander, an observable material thing seemed to be a result rather than a cause. The true essence underlying all reality must itself be without qualities but capable of assuming them all. The necessity for the invention of this metaphysical entity—what Anaximander called the "boundless"—was obvious. Water was *essentially* wet. No matter what you did to it, it retained the quality of wetness. Water, therefore, could not enter into substances that were essentially dry. The "boundless," however, suffered from no such difficulties for it could adopt the quality of dryness as easily as it could that of wetness.

All these schemes were but tentative beginnings on the road to science. They could give vague qualitative explanations of events, but they could not stand up under intense critical scrutiny. The most important of the critics of the Ionians was Parmenides of Elea (c. 540–450 B.C.). His point was a simple, but devastating, one. If water, for example, was constantly appearing in different forms, how could a rational man speak of it as water? For something to be and to be known, it must not change; it must exist in and of itself through eternity. Change, Parmenides therefore concluded, is mere illusion. Reality consists in what is unchanging and eternal; the universe, therefore, is really an unchanging sphere. While the logic of Parmenides' position was impeccable, by rejecting the observable world it also rejected any attempt at devising a meaningful explanation of that world.

In the period before Socrates altered the main course of Greek philosophy, two major attempts were made to depict the essential reality behind the observable world. Leucippus (fl. c. 475 B.C.) and Democritus (c. 470–400 B.C.) proposed an atomic theory that could satisfy both Parmenides' conditions of changelessness and the requirements of a hypothesis intended to explain the world of experience. The metaphysical world consisted of atoms, which were described as eternal, unchanging spheres moving through a void. The world of experience resulted from the collision and clumping of atoms and was constantly in flux and changing.

■**PYTHAGOREANISM.**—The name of Pythagoras (c. 550 B.C.) is associated with the other departure from Ionian materialism. Like Thales, Pythagoras the man is shrouded in the mists of tradition and little, if anything, is known about him as a person. Upon his entry into history, we find a man drunk with numbers and filled with the mysterious essences of Eastern religion. He founded an ascetic sect quite foreign to the Greek way of life and placed number mysticism at its very center. The universe, said Pythagoras, was made up essentially of numbers. Relations between things were really relations between numbers. The flux of the world was no more than the flux of number, changing through infinite combinations, but reducible in the last analysis to the unchanging reality of the integer. Algebra, that is, Babylonian algebra, one might insist, was the key which all Greece was seeking.

The Pythagorean theory of numbers was, as such, merely an interesting competitor with the other theories of reality then spreading throughout Greece. It contained one element, however, that set it apart from these and was to give it an extraordinary influence in the history of science. Pythagoras (or his followers, for it is difficult to distinguish between them) did more than assume that relations between physical objects were essentially mathematical: they also proved it. It was the triumph of the Pythagoreans to show that the musical note produced by a stretched string was dependent (all other things being equal), in a simple mathematical way, upon the length of the string. It is by no means obvious that a musical tone and the length of a lyre string should be related by a simple mathematical ratio. Having discovered that this was so, the Pythagoreans were then in a position to create a mathematical musical theory in which they could calculate musical tones from algebraic functions. The full import of this should be clearly seen. The Pythagoreans had been successful in translating physical things into mathematical quantities. They could then operate upon these new functions by mathematical means to derive new physical relations. A tool of hitherto undreamed of power was hereby made available to the natural philosopher. More important than this, however, was the vision of the universe that the Pythagorean system made prevalent. If the cosmos were essentially mathematical, then the main task of the natural philosopher was to seek out the mathematical beauty that was to inspire men for centuries after the Pythagoreans as a sect had vanished.

The Pythagoreans were also responsible for the direction taken by Greek mathematics. Their original inspiration had been algebraic, stemming from Babylonia. By insisting that number was, in some mysterious sense, physical, the Pythagoreans committed themselves to a universe in which all magnitudes could be represented by the ratio of integers. Then, to the horror of the members of the sect, it was found that the diagonal of a unit square was incommensurable. It is impossible to represent $\sqrt{2}$ by the ratio of two integers but it is, of course, possible to represent it by the diagonal of a unit square, that is, geometrically. Hence, the algebraic way was abandoned in favor of the geometric, and geometry was to become uniquely Greek.

■PLATONIC SCIENCE.—The course of physical speculation in Greece was abruptly altered by the advent of Socrates. It was not that Socrates was opposed to the search for a principle of physical reality; he simply felt that if this search did not include man and the moral universe, it was irrelevant to the proper concern of men for their own moral and political condition. Socrates' great disciple, Plato (427–347 B.C.), set himself the task of bringing physics, morality, and politics together into a single system. The glue that was to hold these disparate elements together was a theology from which Plato deduced the basic elements of his philosophy.

Like his predecessors, Plato had to come to grips with the dualistic tension between *being* and *becoming* created by Parmenides. For Parmenides' unchanging sphere, Plato substituted the *Ideas*, those ideal, unchanging forms from which the observable world drew its principles of organization. The principle of change was uniquely the property of brute matter which strove constantly to return to chaos. Form and harmony in the observable world were the result of the influence (or the participation) of the Ideas in matter. To apprehend the Ideas required that the mind, drugged, as it were, by its association with brute matter, be revived by the contemplation of the purest of earthly forms. These, Plato insisted, were the geometrical forms, and mathematics, therefore, was considered to be the most efficacious of all intellectual purges.

Mathematics also provided a key to the system of the world, for Plato took over the Pythagorean belief in the essential mathematical harmony of the world. He also adopted the elements of their cosmology which, with numerous modifications, was to reign supreme until Copernicus.

Plato considered the heavens to be literally divine, and divinity, of course, implied perfection. Ordinarily, one would not expect a perfect thing to change in any way since change would suggest that the body was *not* perfect and was trying to improve itself. The stars did undoubtedly move, hence they were not *quite* perfect. The next best thing to not moving at all was to move in perfect motion. The Pythagoreans had already remarked that circular motion was the only motion which could go on for an eternity without changing. Hence the stars moved in circles. The planets, however, presented a problem. They, too, were almost perfect but they manifestly did not move in circles. Plato, therefore, set his disciples the great astronomical problem of antiquity: How could the motion of the planets be reduced to circular motion in order "to save the phenomena," that is, in order to force the

 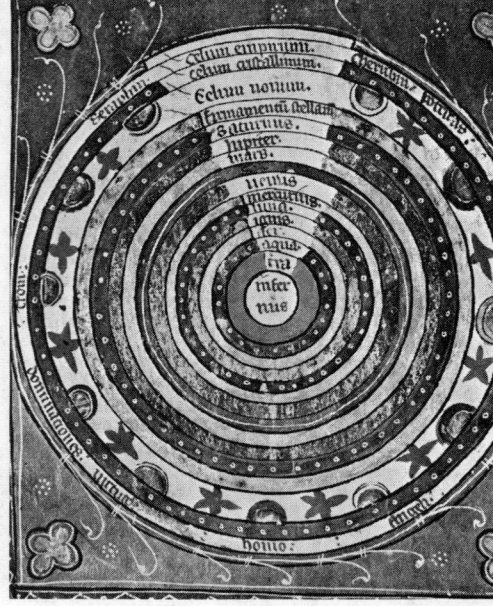

NEW YORK PUBLIC LIBRARY

THROUGH MYTH, MAGIC, AND SCIENCE, men have tried to comprehend the universe and man's relation to it. The Egyptians imagined the world to be a flat disc, above which arched the sky-goddess Nut, her body spangled with stars. In Ptolemy's universe, myth gives way to mathematics, and the earth is enclosed in a finite series of geometric circles.

planetary orbits into those paths dictated for them by philosophy. The solutions were many and ingenious. Eudoxus (409–356 B.C.) suggested a scheme of spheres, one within the other, having a common center but revolving at different speeds around different axes. The resultant of all these motions was that of the planet. Still another solution, to become the mathematical model of Claudius Ptolemy (fl. 140 A.D.), involved the motion of a point upon a circle whose center lay upon another circle. The speed of rotation of the deferent (upon which the center of the first circle lay) and of the epicycle (upon which the point was fixed) could be adjusted arbitrarily so that the resultant motion closely resembled that of any one of the planets.

■ARISTOTELIAN SCIENCE. — Astronomy was one of the few scientific subjects Plato considered worthy of study. Those other subjects which brought man into too close proximity with matter could serve only to degrade the intellect. This viewpoint was vehemently rejected by Aristotle (384–322 B.C.), Plato's student and one of the greatest minds of all time. To Aristotle, there was no sense in Plato's separation of the Ideas from the matter they influenced. Not only did this introduce the clumsy intermediary of the Demiurgos, a kind of cosmic mechanic, who molded matter along the lines of the Ideas, but it seems to require the multiplication of the number of Ideas beyond the realm of probability. What Aristotle did was to unite form and matter within the object. Change was no longer a degradation of form, but a working out of the form inherent in the body undergoing change. Aristotle illustrated his thought by an

appeal to four causes. The *material cause* was the matter of which a body was composed. The *efficient cause* was that cause which accounted for the shaping of the matter. It might be the chisel of a sculptor or an inherent principle, such as that which determined the evolution of an oak tree from an acorn. The *formal cause* was the principle of form which determined the action of the efficient cause. In the case of the sculptor, it would be his idea of what the sculpture should look like; in the case of the acorn, it would be the form of the oak tree inherent in the acorn. The fourth cause, the *final cause*, was the ultimate purpose for which the object was intended. To the artist, it was his concept of beauty which determined the form of the statue, guided his hand, and dictated his choice of material. The final cause was, therefore, the single most important factor in explaining any natural phenomenon. Once one found out the cosmic purpose of some event, the rest followed rather simply.

Aristotle generally accepted the scheme of the universe as depicted by Eudoxus. The Aristotelian universe was divided into two essentially different parts at the sphere of the moon. Above the moon, all was perfect and unchanging as befitted the divine nature of the heavenly bodies. Below the moon, generation and corruption, rectilinear motion and general chaotic change took place. The analysis of sublunar motion was of particular importance for the future of science for it was here that the Aristotelian system was to be mortally wounded. Aristotle distinguished two kinds of local motion: natural and violent. Natural motion was that type of motion brought about by a natural, inherent cause. Thus a stone fell to the ground because its natural place was at the earth, or center of the universe, and, when displaced, it strove to regain its natural place. The other elements, water, air, and fire, would in similar fashion move to their natural places. When a stone was hurled through the air, however, it did not, at once, fall to the ground. Its flight through the air was contrary to its natural tendencies and this was why it was called violent motion. Why, Aristotle asked, did the stone continue to move contrary to its natural tendency when it left the hand and there was nothing there to push it? Obviously, a body could not keep moving when the cause of its motion (the hand) was removed. Something, therefore, must continue pushing it. This "something," Aristotle suggested, was the air which was pushed out in front of the stone and rushed back behind it in order to prevent a vacuum from being formed. The air then continued to push the stone along.

■ **PROGRESS IN MEDICINE.**—The Egyptian and Babylonian civilizations had made little progress in the study of sickness and health as natural occurrences. It was the Greeks, particularly those associated with the school of Hippocrates of Cos (c. 400 B.C.), who first insisted that medicine should be divorced from the supernatural. Disease was not a demonic visitation, but the result of natural causes. What these causes were, whether a disharmony of the four humors, or some hitherto undiscovered disruption of physiological function, was not so easily answered. Nevertheless, a giant step had been made, for by reducing medicine to the circumference of man's reason, the precondition was created for development of a rational medical science.

■ **HELLENISTIC SCIENCE.**—The period of Greek civilization before the conquests of Alexander the Great (356–323 B.C.) produced the overall philosophical framework within which science was to exist for the next millennium and a half. During the Hellenistic period (roughly 330 B.C.–150 A.D.) many details of this picture were filled in. The Museum of Alexandria, founded by the new Greek rulers of Egypt, became the intellectual center of the ancient world. The astronomical works of the later Babylonians, through the extraordinary efforts of Hipparchus (c. 190–120 B.C.) and Claudius Ptolemy, were combined with the Greek astronomical tradition to create a mathematical astronomy of hitherto unattainable precision. The application of Babylonian mathematics to the Greek system of epicycles permitted the calculation of astronomical positions to a degree unsurpassed until the late sixteenth century. The addition of new and precise observational data also contributed to the exactness of Ptolemaic astronomy.

The Museum of Alexandria was also the center of physiological activity. Human dissections were performed and a number of discoveries made. The greatest physiologist of antiquity, Galen of Pergamum (131–201 A.D.), was not, however, a member of the Museum. He was a distinguished physician who utilized the physiological and anatomical discoveries of his predecessors, together with the results of his own dissections of apes and pigs, to formulate a system of physiology of enormous influence. Through the hypothesis of three "spirits," the *natural* (which provided nutrition), the *vital* (which was the principle of vitality or movement), and the *animal* (the basis for sensation and thought), Galen was able to tie the various organs of the body together into a single, harmonious whole. Furthermore, Galen was able to utilize the Aristotelian four causes to advantage and give his physiology the proper philosophical foundation.

Early in the Hellenistic period, physics reached its highest point in antiquity. The works of Archimedes of Syracuse (287–212 B.C.) were the culmination of the mathematical tradition of the Pythagoreans, without the number mysticism of this sect. His work on the lever and on hydrostatics showed that the translation of physical entities into mathematical quantities (that is, length, weight, and density) was even more fruitful than the Pythagoreans had dreamed. Just as important, Archimedes also showed that it was not necessary to be a numerologist to discover the mathematical laws of nature. In 212 B.C. Archimedes was slain by a Roman soldier in the sack of Syracuse. There is something symbolic in this murder, for as Rome cast its pall over the Mediterranean world, the sciences stagnated and died. In spite of their considerable administrative skill and great engineering ability (or perhaps because of them), the Romans took little interest in the theoretical constructions of their Greek subjects. By the end of the Empire, the great Greek achievement was known to but a few and the manuscripts in which almost a thousand years of this sustained, brilliant intellectual effort was recorded, lay moldering, unused, in a few scattered libraries. The march of the barbarians and the sack of Rome provided the proper funeral for the death of ancient science.

Survival of Ancient Science.—The collapse of Rome left behind many handsome ruins which were to inspire the generations that followed. Part of the legacy were the thousands of manuscripts that recorded the heights to which Greek science had ascended and which the Romans, by and large, had ignored. That such precious and delicate remnants of antiquity did not perish in the upheavals that accompanied the dissolution of the Roman Empire is to the eternal credit of the Christian Church, the Byzantines, and the Moslem conquerors.

The early Christians were not profound philosophers. Their religion had enormous appeal to the poor and the oppressed but it could make little headway against the sophistication of the ancient philosophers. In order to demonstrate its superiority to the philosophical systems of antiquity, the philosophers themselves had to be studied. A text concerning Epicurus might literally reek with heresy but if it were to be refuted it had first to be studied. And, in order for it to be studied properly by those competent to refute it, it had to be copied. So it happened that many of the profane writings of antiquity were passed on to future generations by monks writing in their scriptoria.

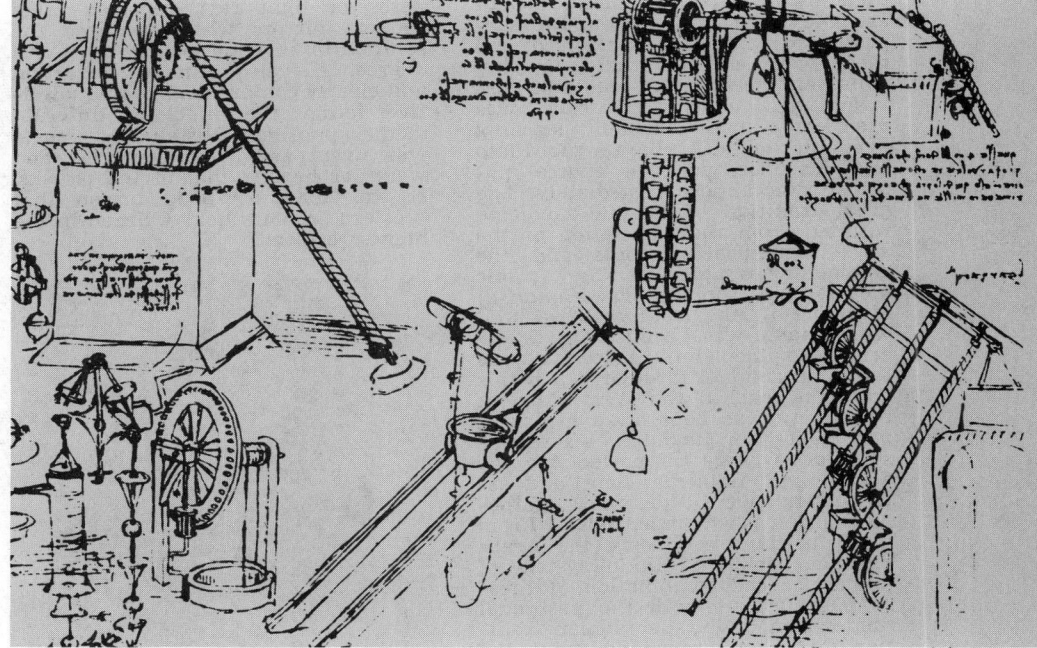

THE GENIUS OF ARCHIMEDES in mathematics and the invention of mechanical contrivances was not equaled until the Renaissance. Leonardo da Vinci used many of Archimedes' ideas, such as the water screw and wheel, in his numerous scientific and engineering drawings.

Senior   Adolphus

NEW YORK PUBLIC LIBRARY

THE ALCHEMISTS' DREAM of transmuting lead into gold was never realized, but their mystic treatises amassed much chemical information and their endless combinations of substances did result in chance discoveries such as gunpowder (*right*), attributed to a German monk.

The most important channel for the transmission of ancient science was the hordes of Islam. Erupting from the Arabian Peninsula in the seventh century, Islam rapidly conquered most of the ancient world. An aura still surrounded the name of Rome and the invaders preserved much of that civilization which they set out to conquer. No doubt the stubborn refusal of Byzantium to bow before them intensified Arabic respect for the higher culture of antiquity. As so often happens, the conquerors were conquered by their own subject peoples. Ancient art, literature, and science far surpassed anything Islam possessed, and these were eagerly studied by her rulers and scholars. A regular translating and copying industry was created to make ancient learning available in the Arabic tongue. Plato and Aristotle were, of course, put into Arabic almost immediately. The great tradition of Islamic medicine resulted from the translation of the ancient medical treatises and the commentaries thereon by Arabic medical philosophers. The *Canon of Medicine* by Ali ibn-Sina (980–1037), whose name was Latinized by Western Schoolmen into Avicenna, was the main channel through which this tradition reached the West. Ancient astronomy was kept alive in Islam, particularly in Baghdad, where observatories were supported by the Caliph and mathematicians and astronomers were honored. Mathematics flourished under Islam. From their far-flung conquests, the Arabs brought back the Hindu system of numerals. The combination of these simple numbers with the positional numeration of the Babylonian tradition made for a most powerful and simple computational system. It also restored an interest in numbers rather than lines, and Islamic algebra did much to restore the mathematical balance between geometry and algebra upset by the Pythagoreans.

The only area in which Islam introduced anything really new into science was in optics. Here the work of Ibn al-Haytham, or Alhazen (965–1038), as he was known to the West, was fundamental. He opposed Euclid and Claudius Ptolemy on the origin of vision, considering sight as the result of something impinging upon the eye, rather than as an effect of something passing from the eye to the object. He investigated problems of reflection, and even dealt with the paths of light rays reflected from convex mirrors which required the solution of an equation of the fourth degree. He also studied refraction and clearly comprehended, in qualitative terms, the effect of different media upon light. His study of lenses was unsurpassed for centuries and went far beyond that of the Greeks. It was for very good reason that Western scholars held Alhazen in the highest esteem.

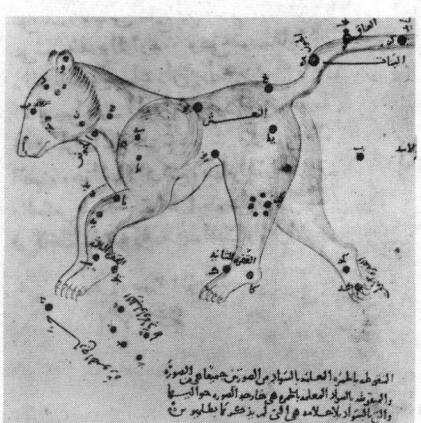

NEW YORK PUBLIC LIBRARY

GREAT BEAR CONSTELLATION, in Arabic.

Beginnings of the New Science.—By the twelfth century the political instability and economic parochialism that had marked European civilization since the fall of Rome were disappearing. Powerful political entities had emerged, and trade, stimulated by the Crusades, was increasing rapidly. The Church, in particular, found itself facing a world in which its traditions seemed out of date. A new confidence filled the air; what yesterday had seemed a rock of faith today revealed itself as a heap of sand. "I believe that I may know" had formed more than one saint's credo in those centuries when knowledge seemed futile in the face of God's displeasure and the uncertainty of events. "I know that I may believe" was Peter Abelard's (1079–1142) proud, almost arrogant, challenge to the past and summons to his own century. It was no coincidence that the twelfth century witnessed the creation of the University of Paris and the first flood of translations of ancient learning.

One of the fascinations of the medieval period lies in the order and dimensions of the dreams medieval man dreamed. Conscious of his fall he built cathedrals that sought divinity in every stone of their architure; while barons revolted time and again against their kings, he had visions of a unified empire that might recapture some of the grandeur that was Rome; conscious of his intellectual inferiority, he zealously collected every scrap of ancient knowledge. Only in his faith did he feel secure and the heir to something antiquity had not possessed.

Medieval science must be viewed in this double context. Men like Roger Bacon aspired for ultimate knowledge and power while, at the same time, they saw knowledge of this world as an aid in the real goal of all knowledge, that of God.

ANDERSON-ART REFERENCE BUREAU

NATURAL HISTORY developed from the fantasy of the Middle Ages into a new realism during the Renaissance. Fabulous beasts, such as the griffin (*left*), disappeared and artists examined the natural world with the scientific curiosity reflected in Dürer's *Rhinoceros*, 1515.

■**ALCHEMY.**—Alchemy began as a more or less rational investigation of the properties of matter and the principles of their interaction. The Aristotelian basis of all existing bodies was a formless *materia prima* whose only property was the ability to take on qualities. If one defined gold as a heavy, yellow metal all that was necessary was to implant the qualities of heaviness and yellowness in a baser metal, say lead or mercury. The qualities themselves were considered to be separate entities which could be abstracted from or added to the *materia prima* if the alchemist knew the correct procedures. The correct procedures, however, were singularly difficult to find and the search for them was what lead alchemy into demonology and all its accompanying nonsense. The philosopher's stone was the magic wand that would accomplish the miracle of transmutation. Its value was enhanced when the idea was introduced from China that the stone or elixir would also provide its discoverer with eternal life.

The theological impetus to science formed two distinct traditions in the twelfth and thirteenth centuries. Neoplatonism, in a somewhat vague form, had survived the Dark Ages and was refreshed and revivified by the twelfth-century Renaissance. Neoplatonic philosophy viewed the material world as the result of a series of divine emanations, gradually becoming degraded in a scale reaching from the Godhead to brute matter. In this system light played a particularly important part. It was itself immaterial, but it existed in the material world, thus bridging the gap between the divine and the mundane.
■**THE FRANCISCANS.**—The Franciscans, whose order was founded in 1210, were fascinated by light and saw in it a nearness to God, hence worthy of study. The work of Alhazen pointed the way. Robert Grosseteste (c. 1175–

1253), although not himself a Franciscan, taught them and was the leading figure in the creation of medieval optics. He did some work on mirrors and lenses but, most importantly, dimly glimpsed the role of experiment in science. It was this aspect that Roger Bacon forcefully called to his contemporary's attention. It is, therefore, a bit surprising to discover that, while there was a great deal of very clever talk and discussion of the role of experiments, very few actual experiments were performed.
■**THE DOMINICANS.**—The Dominican order was founded by Saint Dominic in 1205 specifically to combat heresy. It was largely because of their orthodoxy that they were given the task of examining the flood of translations, especially of Aristotle, that were produced in the twelfth century. The first contact with Aristotle came as a shock to Western Christendom. The greatest philosopher of antiquity was found to contradict Scripture: The world, said Aristotle in flat opposition to *Genesis*, was eternal. Moreover, and this was even more disquieting, he was able to prove it by a logic far superior to anything the West could offer in rebuttal. The Church moved swiftly and forbade the reading of Aristotle until such time as his "errors" could be reconciled with Revelation. It was the Dominicans who performed this invaluable service. Albertus Magnus (1206–1280) was the first great medieval student of Aristotle. He initiated the studies by which Aristotle was made not only acceptable, but fundamental, to the Catholic faith. In his treatment of Aristotle there was none of that uncritical awe which was later to become the fashion. Aristotle, St. Albertus knew, was only human and could err.
■**THOMISM.**—The assimilation of Aristotelian philosophy was completed by Albertus Magnus' great pupil, St.

Thomas Aquinas (1225–1274). With extraordinary skill, St. Thomas was able to work most of Aristotle's system into the fabric of Catholic theology. The result was the monumental *Summa Theologica*, which still stands today as the Catholic Church's most comprehensive and closely reasoned statement of its theology.

The effect of St. Thomas' achievement on science was twofold. In the Thomist system, the duality between matter and spirit which had been a marked feature of earlier theology was banished. The world of nature led by degrees to the realm of God; there were no abysses separating the two. The study of nature, therefore, was by no means a worthless, or even theologically dangerous, occupation as many of the Church fathers had insisted. Instead, it was one of the paths by which it was possible to rise to an apprehension of divinity. Thomism, then, was and is not hostile to science so long as the study of science leads one closer to God.

Thomism was not, however, a scientific system. It was, specifically, a theology, and natural science was clearly subordinate to theological issues. In theory, points of natural science were always open to question, but, in fact, once the *Summa* was accepted as official doctrine it became increasingly difficult to challenge any part of it successfully. The pyramid stood or fell as a whole. To reject one stone, no matter where it came from, was to weaken the entire edifice. Thomism, therefore, was both unfavorable and favorable to the development of science. So long as there was but one church, a rather wide latitude of opinion could be tolerated. When the Church's monopoly of salvation was successfully challenged by the Protestant revolt of the sixteenth century, attitudes hardened, perspectives narrowed, and science suffered.

YERKES OBSERVATORY

NO PICTURE OF THE UNIVERSE could explain observed planetary motion as long as the earth remained unmoving at the center. Copernicus dared to assert that the earth and other planets revolve around the sun.

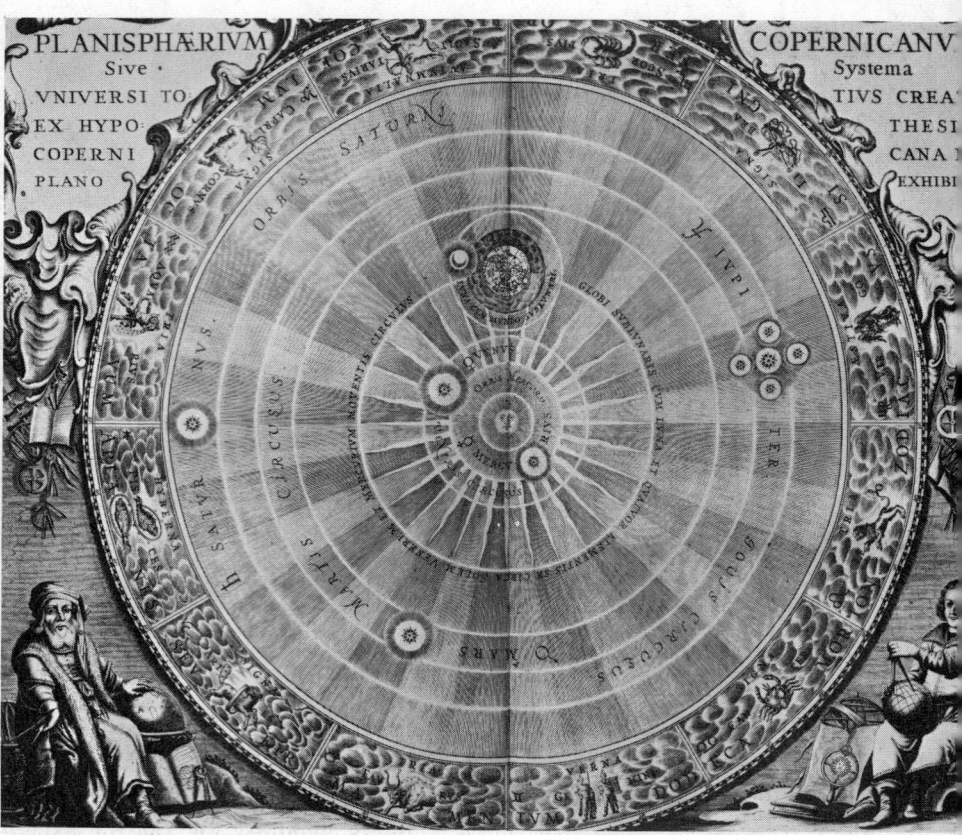

BETTMANN ARCHIVE

Scientific Revolution.—Origins of the seventeenth-century scientific revolution have been disputed by historians for the past two centuries. Some have seen it as the result of the liberation of the European mind by the Protestant Reformation; others have attributed it to the rise of the middle class, with its characteristic curiosity and quantitative penchant. Still a third school prefers to view modern science as a philosophical revolution in which the elements of science were entirely redefined. Finally, there is the view that modern science arose from a technological revolution which, by focusing attention upon the exploitation of nature, stimulated the search for natural laws. There are elements of truth in all these interpretations. While the Protestants were no more friendly or hostile to science than the Catholics, the very proliferation of Protestant sects made it possible for the holders of heterodox views to gain a hearing. The middle class, too, made its contribution. From its ranks came much of the driving force behind the attack on nature, which was provided by the vision of economic reward attendant upon eventual victory.

More important than these factors, however, was the reorientation in philosophy. The Copernican system owed far more to philosophical presuppositions than it did to anything else and classical dynamics was founded by challenging a fundamental tenet of Aristotelian philosophy. The technological innovations of the Renaissance were also to make an important contribution to seventeenth-

century science. By the seventeenth century fairly complicated machinery was in use in a number of industries. They provided the analogy upon which science was to call for two centuries. The universe and its component processes could be likened to a machine and, like a machine, the universe could be understood in terms of the separate operations of its parts. The advantage of this approach over the organic analogy used by Aristotle is obvious. An organism is more than the sum of all its parts and there is always the temptation to call upon occult powers to account for this excess. Machines, on the other hand, are rigidly determined; understand the parts and one understands the machine. There is no room for mystery and the very lack of mystery is an indicator of success. The equations must always balance; mass and energy must be conserved. Such is the mechanical view and it was within this framework that science developed until the end of the nineteenth century.

■**COPERNICAN ASTRONOMY.**—Nikolaus Copernicus' (1473–1543) work, *On the Revolutions of the Heavenly Orbs,* was a strange one, combining the wildest speculations with page after page of tedious calculations. The purpose behind it was a laudable one in the eyes of his contemporaries, but few believed it could be attained. There had been, for over a century, a gradually increasing tension within astronomy. The Aristotelian universe had long been accepted as giving a true *physical* picture, for it could explain *why* the planets and stars

moved. Although Claudius Ptolemy's epic work, the *Almagest,* had been translated in the twelfth century, there were few who could really work with its mathematics until the fifteenth century. The Ptolemaic system, with its deferents and epicycles, provided an excellent *mathematical* model of the universe, for from it *how* the planets moved could be calculated with considerable accuracy. The two systems, however, were incompatible with one another. One or both must be wrong and it was his search for a single model that led Copernicus to suggest moving the earth from its central position. His primary reasons for this revolutionary step were philosophical and aesthetic rather than logical or empirical. As a student in Italy, he had become imbued with the Neoplatonism of the Italian Renaissance and its metaphysics of light. There, too, he had become acquainted with Pythagorean thought and its emphasis upon mathematical harmonies. The emphasis upon light focused his attention on the sun as the source of this pure emanation; the apparent gain in mathematical simplicity which resulted from placing the sun at the center of the planetary system convinced him that this was where the sun really belonged.

Furthermore, a heliocentric approach removed some of the most difficult problems with which astronomy had been wrestling since antiquity. The observed change of brightness in the planets, for example, followed directly from a heliocentric system. So, too, did the deviation of the planets from circular motion. When one realized that the earth also moved around the sun, then the observed paths of the planets were the resultants of the motions of the earth and the planets.

The Copernican system was mathematically equivalent to the Ptolemaic. Indeed, one of the reasons for its slow acceptance was that it was only equivalent, not superior, to it. Physically, the Copernican system was attractive in that it accounted for a number of mysterious phenomena in a most satisfactory way. On one point, however, it remained inferior to the Aristotelian model, at least in the eyes of many of Copernicus' contemporaries: Copernicus could offer no sound reason for planetary motion. It is no exaggeration to say that the scientific revolution consisted in the search for an explanation that would preserve the Copernican arrangement of the heavenly bodies and, at the same time, explain why the planets moved about the sun.

■ CONTRIBUTIONS OF KEPLER.—Johannes Kepler (1571–1630) clearly recognized the necessity of accounting for the earth's annual revolution around the sun. Kepler was a passionate adherent of Copernicus' doctrine because he, too, was impressed by the beauty of a heliocentric universe. Kepler was also a Pythagorean, convinced that mathematical harmonies gave the real clue to physical reality. His entire life was spent in searching for them. He was certain that his greatest discovery was the fact that the five regular Platonic solids—the cube, tetrahedron, octahedron, dodecahedron, and icosahedron—could be inscribed within planetary orbs.

Fortunately for Kepler, he was associated for some time with the greatest observational astronomer of the sixteenth century, Tycho Brahe (1546–1601). Kepler's mathematical

flights of fancy were, therefore, strictly controlled by Brahe's accurate data. It was from these data that Kepler computed the orbit of Mars and found, somewhat to his horror, that it was *not* a circle but an ellipse. Although difficult to fit into the Copernican system, it was fatal to the Aristotelian, for even the cleverest philosopher found it impossible to suggest a reason why planetary souls moved in ellipses. Kepler, however, could at least fumble toward an explanation based upon the power of the sun to hold its numerous family together. Kepler's second law of planetary motion stated that the line drawn from the sun to a planet (the radius vector) sweeps out equal areas in equal times. To put it another way, a planet moves faster when it is nearer to the sun than when it is farther out. His third law stated that the square of the period of revolution of a planet around the sun is proportional to the cube of its mean distance from the sun. For example, if two planetary periods are compared, it is obvious that the one farther out moves more slowly. From these laws, Kepler postulated the existence of some entity, perhaps a force of some kind, emanating from the sun like light, that pushed the planets in their orbits.

■ GALILEO'S WORK.—The same problem of accounting for planetary motion in a heliocentric system also occupied the man who may rightly be called the first of the modern mathematical physicists, Galileo Galilei (1564–1642). Paradoxically, his solution led him to reject Kepler's first law that planets move in ellipses. Like Kepler, Galileo was a Copernican for largely aesthetic reasons. A heliocentric universe was simply neater than a geocentric one. There was not, with Galileo, the number mysticism that marked Kepler's ap-

proach. Galileo's hero was Archimedes, not Pythagoras.

The problem of motion had intrigued Galileo since his youth. He had early become suspicious of Aristotle's whole account of both the *how* and the *why* of motion. While investigating falling bodies he had been led by experiments on inclined planes to the discovery of the law of free fall which he first enunciated in 1604. *Why* a body fell according to the law, however, escaped him for 30 years. His work with inclined planes permitted Galileo to formulate a mental experiment of fundamental importance for the progress of Copernicanism. From it, he deduced that, if there were not resistance to its motion, once put in motion a sphere would move in a circle till eternity. To the anti-Copernican who scornfully asked why the earth should move around the sun, Galileo answered, why shouldn't it? Circular motion had no cause; it simply continued forever. The consequence of this simple mental experiment was revolutionary. To Aristotle, only rest needed no causal explanation; all other motion or change had to be accounted for. Now, a certain kind of motion had achieved the same status as rest. It, too, needed no explanation; it simply was. Motion was as natural as rest—what needed explanation henceforth was not motion but *change* of motion. The static cosmos of the Greeks had been transformed into the dynamic universe of classical mechanics.

The final blow to Aristotelian physics came with Galileo's analysis of uniformly accelerated motion. This problem had been extensively studied in the Middle Ages when it was recognized that Aristotle's explanation was inadequate. Granted that a heavy body wished to return to its natural place, why did it go

NEW YORK PUBLIC LBRARY

INTERNATIONAL BUSINESS MACHINES CORPORATION

MECHANICS AND MATHEMATICS became the dominant image of the seventeenth-century scientific revolution and the means by which the universe could be understood. The wheels of Pascal's algebraic calculator (*left*) reduced the mysterious to precise and measurable mathematical units, while the machines of industry (*right*) turned each new scientific discovery into a technological tool.

AXIOMATA
SIVE
LEGES MOTUS

Lex. I.

Corpus omne perseverare in statu suo quiescendi vel movendi uniformiter in directum, nisi quatenus a viribus impressis cogitur statum illum mutare.

Projectilia perseverant in motibus suis nisi quatenus a resistentia aeris retardantur & vi gravitatis impelluntur deorsum. Trochus, cujus partes cohaerendo perpetuo retrahunt sese a motibus rectilineis, non cessat rotari nisi quatenus ab aere retardatur. Majora autem Planetarum & Cometarum corpora motus suos & progressivos & circulares in spatiis minus resistentibus factos conservant diutius.

Lex. II.

Mutationem motus proportionalem esse vi motrici impressae, & fieri secundum lineam rectam qua vis illa imprimitur.

Si vis aliqua motum quemvis generet, dupla duplum, tripla triplum generabit, sive simul & semel, sive gradatim & successive impressa fuerit. Et hic motus quoniam in eandem semper plagam cum vi generatrice determinatur, si corpus antea movebatur, motui ejus vel conspiranti additur, vel contrario subducitur, vel obliquo oblique adjicitur, & cum eo secundum utriusque determinationem componitur.
Lex. III.

Lex. III.

Actioni contrariam semper & aequalem esse reactionem: sive corporum duorum actiones in se mutuo semper esse aequales & in partes contrarias dirigi.

Quicquid premit vel trahit alterum, tantundem ab eo premitur vel trahitur. Siquis lapidem digito premit, premitur & hujus digitus a lapide. Si equus lapidem funi alligatum trahit, retrahetur etiam & equus aequaliter in lapidem: nam funis utrinque distentus eodem relaxandi se conatu urgebit Equum versus lapidem, ac lapidem versus equum, tantumque impediet progressum unius quantum promovet progressum alterius. Si corpus aliquod in corpus aliud impingens, motum ejus vi sua quomodocunque mutaverit, idem quoque vicissim in motu proprio eandem mutationem in partem contrariam vi alterius (ob aequalitatem pressionis mutuae) subibit. His actionibus aequales fiunt mutationes non velocitatum sed motuum, (scilicet in corporibus non aliunde impeditis:) Mutationes enim velocitatum, in contrarias itidem partes factae, quia motus aequaliter mutantur, sunt corporibus reciproce proportionales.

Corol. I.

Corpus viribus conjunctis diagonalem parallelogrammi eodem tempore describere, quo latera separatis.

Si corpus dato tempore, vi sola M, ferretur ab A ad B, & vi sola N, ab A ad C, compleatur parallelogrammum ABDC, & vi utraque feretur id eodem tempore ab A ad D. Nam quoniam vis N agit secundum lineam AC ipsi B D parallelam, haec vis nihil mutabit velocitatem accedendi ad lineam illam B D a vi altera genitam. Accedet igitur corpus eodem tempore ad lineam B D sive vis N imprimatur, sive non, atque adeo in fine illius temporis reperietur alicubi in linea illa

THE THEORY OF IMPETUS dominated medieval concepts of physics until the time of Galileo. Newton defined new laws of motion in his *Principia Mathematica*; the pages above show the first three laws, which define inertia, force, and the equality of action and reaction.

faster the nearer to earth it came? Increase in speed required, according to Aristotelian ideas, an increase in the cause of the speed. Or, decrease in speed, as when a body was thrown upward, required that the cause somehow exhaust itself. In order to handle this problem medieval philosophers had devised a theory based on the concept of impetus. Impetus was a substantial form added to a thrown body by the action of the thrower; as the body traveled upward, the impetus gradually wore itself out in fighting against the natural tendencies of the body to fall. When the impetus just balanced the gravity, the body came to a brief halt and then began to fall. As it fell, its motion generated impetus (in some mysterious fashion) which increased its impetus, which increased its speed, and so on. The *cause* of motion remained internal as the body moved in a polarized space, that is, toward or away from that point in the universe where it belonged.

Galileo was perfectly aware of this medieval work and, in his youth, was imbued with the ideas of the impetus theory. Its difficulties were obvious: It required that an effect (acceleration) generate its own cause (impetus). Furthermore, the theory implied that impetus, and therefore acceleration, depended upon either the speed of the body at every instant or the distance the body had traveled. Neither alternative could stand the test of experiment. For years, Galileo sought an explanation of his law of free fall and finally, in 1638, in his *Discourses on Two New Sciences,* Galileo announced the key. Acceleration depended upon time, not distance or speed. By thus removing the cause of change of motion from

a spatial to a temporal dimension, Galileo radically altered the definition of space itself. Instead of having qualities (such as a center toward which the earth tended), space was turned into the space of Euclidean geometry. No direction had any priority over any other direction. Space was homogeneous; bodies moved through this space according to simple mathematical laws.

■WORK OF NEWTON.—A new tack was taken by Isaac Newton (1642–1727). From Galileo he learned the principles of the new dynamics. From Kepler he received the idea of force but purified it to rid it of its mystical connotations. With these as a foundation, Newton deduced that a body attracted by another body by a force acting along the line connecting their centers and varying inversely as the distance would travel in an ellipse. However, it was not until his friend Edmund Halley (1656–1742) discovered what he had deduced and nagged him ceaselessly that Newton put his ideas in order. The result was perhaps the most important scientific book ever written, *Principia mathematica philosophiae naturalis (The Mathematical Principles of Natural Philosophy).* Its appearance in 1687 announced the culmination of the scientific revolution.

In a severely mathematical style Newton cautiously laid the groundwork for his three laws of motion in the *Principia.* The first law is the principle of inertia, which defines the steady state of the dynamic universe. The second law defines force in terms of mass and acceleration, thus turning an intangible and vague concept into an experimentally determinable quantity. The third law states the equality of action and re-

action, which is the very basis of statics and plays an essential role in dynamics. From these three laws, all ordinary problems of statics and dynamics could successfully be attacked. Even more important was the application of these laws to one specific problem: planetary motion. Here Newton had to postulate a gravitational force varying inversely as the square of the distance and directly as the product of the masses involved. The result was stunning. The system of the world fell neatly into place. For two centuries the *Principia* was both the boldest manifesto of the scientific revolution and the cornerstone of the new science. It did far more than lay down laws; it provided a vision of physical reality.

If the scientific revolution is properly to be understood, the world of the *Principia* must be compared with that of Aristotle. The difference can most clearly be seen by comparing what was considered to be an adequate explanation in each system. For an Aristotelian, the four causes provided a complete knowledge of an object or an event. The final cause—the purpose—was the key cause but this was often impossible to ascertain. In physics, particularly, processes had no obvious purpose, they must be sought in the mind of God. Physics, therefore, had almost inevitably to become theology and thereby leave the arena of experimental criticism. To the Newtonian an explanation consisted in giving the mathematical laws of action and in providing a physical picture of the process in terms of matter, motion, and force. It has often been said that the scientific revolution banished the question "why?" from science and substituted "how?" for it.

NEW YORK PUBLIC LIBRARY

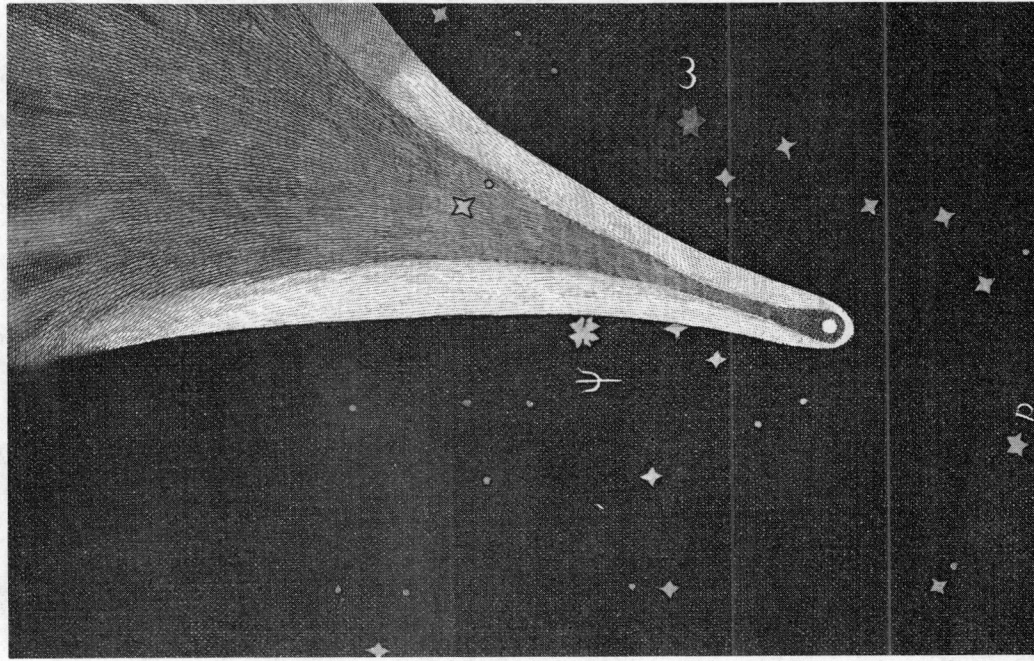

NEWTON'S LAWS OF MOTION became the key to the understanding of celestial mechanics. Herschel's discovery that double stars obey the law of gravitation and the accurate prediction of the cycles of Halley's comet and the comet of 1811 (*right*) substantiated Newton's accuracy.

In the case of an ultimate "why?" this is true, but we should be careful not to eliminate the "why?" on a lesser level. "How?" is answered by a mathematical equation; "why?", in a physical sense, is answered by appealing to the mechanical philosophy. Why certain effects are produced can be answered by applying the Newtonian laws of motion to matter under given, clearly defined conditions. Thus, Newtonian science also answers "why?" but without having recourse to the Deity.

■**MEDICAL PROGRESS.**—There is one last aspect of the scientific revolution that requires mention. The authority of antiquity was finally broken by men of the seventeenth century. The realization that the ancients were often simply factually mistaken liberated science from the dead hand of tradition. This aspect is seen most clearly in the biological sciences where the issues did not involve a radical new picture of the universe.

In 1543, Andreas Vesalius (1514–1564) published his *De corporis humani fabrica (On the Structure of the Human Body),* intended as an atlas of human anatomy. Vesalius' primary concern was an accurate description of the human body, not a new theory of physiology. He was unable to free himself completely from Galen's physiology, but he did point out a number of anatomical errors made by his great predecessor. As anatomical investigation became more and more intensive, further faults were found until, by the early seventeenth century, anatomical knowledge forced a revision of Galenic physiology. This was William Harvey's (1578–1657) great contribution. The anatomical discovery of valves in the veins led Harvey to question the ebb and flow of blood through the veins demanded by Galen's theory. Harvey showed that the blood could only flow in one direction through the veins to the heart. From this, it followed that the blood *must* circulate, even though Harvey could not find the connection he was certain must exist between the veins and the arteries. To Harvey, the court of last resort was not what the ancients had said but what Nature herself showed. This aspect of the scientific revolution took science out of the library and into the laboratory. Ideas need not arise from experiments—they rarely do—but they must somewhere, sometime, meet the acid test of experimental attack.

Newtonian Science.—The scientific revolution led to an ever-increasing pace of scientific discovery and development which would take volumes to detail. All that can be done here is to trace out certain threads to indicate some of the triumphs and failures of the new science.

■**ASTRONOMY.**—Having begun in astronomy, the new science soon revolutionized this study. Newton's laws of motion and principle of gravitation provided the necessary foundation for an understanding of celestial mechanics. The prediction of the return of the great comet now named after Edmund Halley (1656–1742) was the first dramatic triumph of Newtonian theory. The discovery of double stars by Sir William Herschel (1738–1822) and the fact that they, too, obeyed the Newtonian law of gravitation showed that this principle and the other laws expressed in the *Principia* were truly universal.

The apex of Newtonian astronomy was reached with the discovery of Neptune by Urbain Leverrier (1811–1877) and John Couch Adams (1819–1892) in 1846. From small perturbations in the orbit of Uranus, both men, independently of one another, mathematically deduced the existence and location of a new planet. If there were any who doubted the Newtonian synthesis, this discovery converted them. There was, nevertheless, one small astronomical problem that served to perturb a few people. The orbit of Mercury stubbornly refused to obey Newtonian laws. One small planet was not enough, however, to shake confidence in classical dynamics and it was not until Albert Einstein (1879–1955) seriously modified Newtonian mechanics by introducing the theory of relativity that Mercury rejoined the family of planets, moving in accordance with scientific law.

■**PHYSICS.**—The Newtonian synthesis bore its most abundant fruit in areas quite distinct from astronomy. Before Newton, the phenomena of heat, light, electricity, and magnetism were almost total mysteries. The laws of action of light had only been barely glimpsed. The classical treatise on the magnet by William Gilbert (1540–1603) had only lifted a corner of the veil covering this subject. Heat and electricity were almost entirely outside the pale of science.

Newton's work on optics laid a firm foundation for the study of this subject. Considering light to be composed of minute imponderable particles of different sizes (size determined color), Newton treated light as the result of the passage of these particles through space, following the ordinary laws of motion. His *Opticks,* published in 1704, was to be the textbook on light for a century.

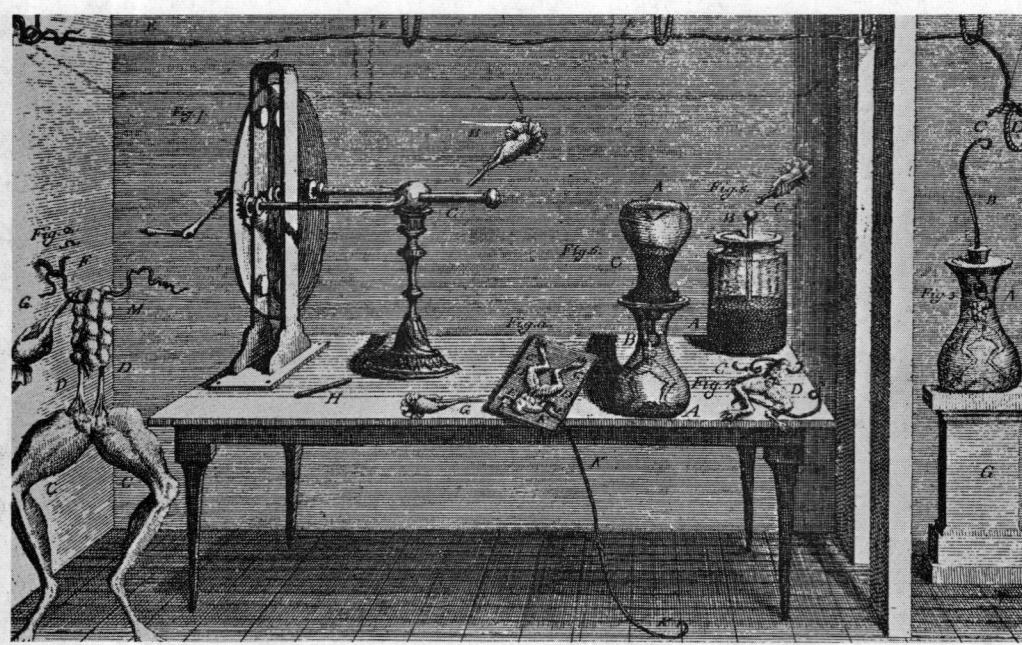

BURNDY LIBRARY

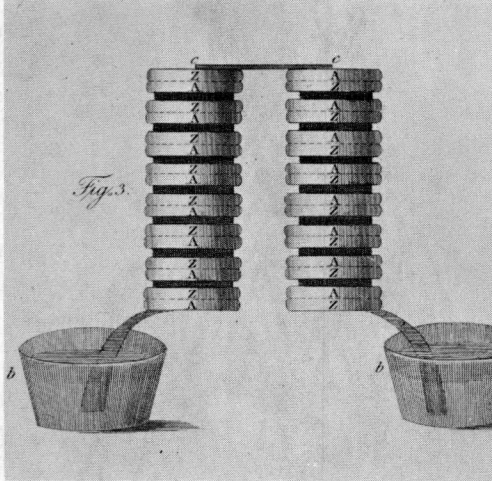

BURNDY LIBRARY

THE FIRST ELECTRIC PILE or battery (*right*), made by Alessandro Volta, had zinc and silver discs separated by brine-soaked paper; it was the result of Galvani's experiments on "animal electricity" in the frog.

Even Newton was puzzled by electricity, magnetism, and heat. While the latter might be considered the result of the "intestine motion of the particles of a body," this did not really help much in understanding heat flow and other thermal phenomena. Similarly, the supposition of electrical and magnetic effluvia permitted one to form a vague mental picture of electrical and magnetic phenomena but did not permit these two areas to be treated in detail. In the eighteenth century, these subjects were to become an integral part of Newtonian science.

The theory of heat profited greatly from the invention of fairly accurate thermometers. The mercury thermometer was introduced about 1715 by Gabriel Daniel Fahrenheit (1686–1736) and the new science of thermometry permitted an objective investigation of events often before beclouded by subjective factors.

The study of heat was greatly advanced by Joseph Black (1728–1799) of Scotland. Black's observations of the slowness with which the winter's snow melted led him to the discovery of latent and specific heats in the 1750's. This discovery, in turn, forced the formulation of a new theory of heat since latent heat, in particular, seemed irreconcilable with a hypothesis of heat as molecular motion. So was introduced what Black called the "matter of heat" and Antoine Laurent Lavoisier (1743–1794) later christened "caloric." Caloric was an imponderable fluid whose particles repelled one another (thus causing the expansion of bodies to which caloric was added) and which could exist in two different ways in matter. When free, the addition of caloric raised the temperature of a body; when combined with matter, the caloric became latent and addition of more caloric caused a change of state but not a change of tempera-

ture. It was this aspect that gave the caloric theory long tenacious life. The famous experiments of Count Rumford (Benjamin Thompson) in the 1790's "proving" that heat *had* to be a mode of motion were ignored for 50 years because latent heat was seemingly inexplicable in this theory.

Electricity and magnetism were also reduced to Newtonian terms of attraction and repulsion in the same century. In the 1780's Charles Augustin de Coulomb (1736–1806) suggested that electricity consisted of two imponderable fluids, positive and negative. Positive particles repelled one another and repulsions adhered to the Newtonian inverse-square law. Similarly, the two magnetic fluids also obeyed this law. The only difference between the electrical and magnetic fluids (and it was an important one) was that the electrical fluids could move between the particles of ponderable matter whereas the magnetic fluids were confined within these particles. When, in 1803, the English chemist John Dalton showed that the particles of ponderable matter were differentiated from one another by specific weights, the system seemed complete. From the largest star to the smallest atom, including even matter so subtle that it had no gravitational attraction for gross matter, the Newtonian laws held. It was this seeming simplicity that led Pierre Simon de Laplace (1749–1827) to suggest that, if one knew the position and momentum of every particle in the universe and could make the necessary computations, the entire future course of the cosmos could be predicted exactly.

■CONVERSION OF FORCES.—At the very time that Laplace was triumphantly declaring the finality of Newtonian science, there were rumblings of an earthquake that would ultimately bring this edifice tumbling down. The German philosopher Immanuel

Kant (1724–1804) had already attacked the very foundations of Newtonian science in the 1780's by denying the existence of matter as something hard and atomic. All we can know about matter, Kant declared, are the forces associated with it. To assume that a force must arise from a material substratum is a metaphysical step that has little justification in experience. Furthermore, it may blind one to the interconnectedness of phenomena and thus really prevent scientific progress. For example, if the imponderable fluids are separate entities, there is no reason to suspect that they can interact or be transmuted into one another. If, on the other hand, they are merely different manifestations of the basic forces of attraction and repulsion, then the conversion of one force into another should cause no surprise.

Kant's suggestions created the school of *Naturphilosophie* in Germany and led to fantastic speculations as well as to some solid scientific achievements. Great impetus was given to the idea of the convertibility of forces with discovery by Alessandro Volta (1745–1827) of the voltaic pile in 1800. In the same year, it was found that an electric current could decompose water. This tied the force of chemical affinity and that of electricity closely together. In 1832, Michael Faraday (1791–1867) showed that the conversion of electrical force into chemical affinity, and vice versa, followed precise laws.

Within fifty years of Volta's discovery, the cycle of the conversion of forces was almost complete. Hans Christian Oersted (1777–1851) showed that electricity could be converted into magnetism in 1820; Michael Faraday revealed the opposite effect in 1831 with his discovery of electromagnetic induction. The conversion of electricity into heat was recognized from the very beginning of electrodynamics; thermoelectricity was discovered by Thomas Johann Seeback (1770–1831) in 1821. The effect of magnetism on light was discovered by Michael Faraday in 1845. He sought in vain for a similar effect due to electricity but this was not discovered until 1875 by John Kerr. The conversion of light into electricity (the photoelectric effect) was discovered in 1879.

■ENERGY.—To a large extent, these conversions were sought by those persons who believed in the unity of the forces of nature. To them, nothing was lost in the conversion of one force into another. What was lacking, however, was a common measure of force. This was supplied in the 1840's in the writings of Hermann Ludwig von Helmholtz (1821–1894), Julius Robert Mayer (1814–1878), and James Prescott Joule (1818–1889). The result was the concept of energy and by 1850 the principle of conservation of energy had been accepted as a fundamental law of nature.

The focus upon force, rather than matter, led to the development of new theories of the ways in which energy could be transmitted. Newtonian physics depended upon two forces: attraction or repulsion acting at a distance and the impact of one body on another. In the early 1800's, Thomas Young (1773–1829) in England and Augustin Fresnel (1788–1827) in France suggested another way in which energy, at least the energy of light, could be transmitted. Light, they argued, could be viewed as wave motion in an ether. Here the energy lay in the medium, not in any particle or mass. This concept was the leading string in the researches of Michael Faraday. He extended it to electricity and magnetism in a series of classical researches. These researches, in turn, were the basis for the mathematical field theory of James Clerk Maxwell (1831–1879). Problems raised by Maxwell's treatment of the field, in turn, led to Albert Einstein's theory of relativity and general field theory in the twentieth century. Pierre de Laplace would have found Einstein's universe quite different from the one he had envisioned in the early 1800's.

■CHEMISTRY.—The development of chemistry in the post-Newtonian period was less dramatic than that of physics. Except for John Dalton's atomic theory, attempts to apply Newtonian principles were not successful. The chemical revolution, associated with the name of Antoine Laurent Lavoisier, was largely a recognition of this fact. Chemical theories of the eighteenth century had all appealed to essentially metaphysical entities, whether these were Epicurean atoms or the even more elusive phlogiston of the German chemists. Lavoisier's revolution consisted in making the elements of chemistry those substances, and only those substances, which were palpable and capable of being fitted, by weight, into a chemical equation. The discovery that combustion was the result of the combination of a ponderable gas, oxygen, with a combustible and not the release of the imponderable, al-

most undetectable, phlogiston provided the dramatic proof of the values of this method. Lavoisier's approach, when added to John Dalton's atomic theory (which provided substances with the basic atomic parameter of weight), created the foundations of analytical chemistry. Throughout the nineteenth century, chemists could be relatively certain that they knew what their retorts were filled with.

The mechanics of chemical reactions were almost totally veiled in mystery throughout most of the nineteenth century. Electrochemistry indicated that electricity played a vital role, but precisely what this role was remained unknown until the twentieth century. Edward Frankland's suggestion in 1852 that elements had a specific combining ratio or valence accorded with experimental fact but could not be explained until the present century. Even the periodic law, enunciated by Dmitri Mendeleev (1834–1907) in 1869, was more an ordering of facts than a mature theory. Explanation of the periodic properties of the elements had to await the development of the modern theory of atomic structure.

The most important contribution to nineteenth-century chemical theory (besides Dalton's) was the concept of the tetravalent carbon atom whose bonds were directed toward the corners of a regular tetrahedron. With this idea, August Kekulé (1829–1896) was able to bring some order

into the chaos of organic chemistry. In the hands of Joseph Achille Le Bel (1847–1930) and Jacobus Henricus van't Hoff (1852–1911) this hypothesis grew into stereochemistry and could relate chemical qualities (in part) to molecular structure.

■BIOLOGY.—The last of the subjects with which the Greeks dealt seriously to develop into a mature scientific discipline was biology. By and large, biological sciences prior to the nineteenth century had dealt with classification and the problems of health and disease. The enormous growth in purely factual knowledge of living forms in the seventeenth century demanded the invention of some classificatory system that would simply permit the student to find descriptions of specimens and recognize what he saw. The most successful taxonomic attempt was that of Carolus Linnaeus (or Karl von Linne, 1707–1778). Although his system of classification of plants was based on the now rejected primacy of the sexual organs, his binomial nomenclature made it possible to classify huge numbers of specimens conveniently. When the doctrine of evolution revealed the genetic basis of classification the Linnaean system was easily adapted.

The problems of health and disease were still posed in terms of classical physiology. Attempts to introduce seventeenth-century atomism into medicine, such as that of Hermann Boerhaave (1668–1738), were ingenious but notably unsuccessful

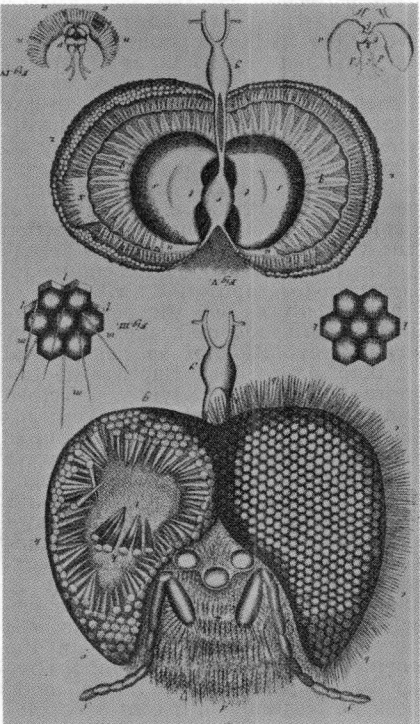

NEW YORK PUBLIC LIBRARY   BURNDY LIBRARY

EXTENDING THE SCOPE of man's vision toward the infinitely far, the telescope revealed new facts that changed the picture of the world. The same principle, applied to the infinitely small, produced the microscope, invented by Galileo and greatly improved by Robert Hooke. With Hooke's compound microscope (*left*), observers such as Jan Swammerdam found new wonders in the previously invisible complexities of the eye of the bee (*right*).

NEW YORK PUBLIC LIBRARY

AMERICAN MUSEUM OF NATURAL HISTORY

cochemical terms. The development of finer techniques of physical and chemical analysis made it increasingly possible to probe down to the very molecular basis of life, and what was discovered was in accordance with the same laws that were found operative in other sciences.

This survey ends with the nineteenth century, for the modern scientific revolution that began with relativity and the quantum theory demands separate treatment. The beginning of the twentieth century also witnessed something quite new in the history of science. Where before there had been a number of different sciences with but few common elements, there now existed a single unifying foundation. The great principles of the conservation of matter and energy apply as well to the living cell as to the exploding atomic nucleus or an ordinary chemical reaction. Living forms are not the only ones considered to evolve; cosmologists today look to the evolution of the universe and its parts. The culmination of thousands of years of intellectual effort which we have traced so briefly in these pages has been the creation of one science with many branches forming a series of separate disciplines. It is this essential unity that is perhaps the greatest achievement of the human mind.

—L. Pearce Williams

CHARLES DARWIN'S theory of organic evolution represents one of the greatest examples of the scientific method; accurate observation and a massive accumulation of data led to the creation of a hypothesis relating the fossilized trilobite (*right*) to man himself.

from the patient's point of view. It was not until Louis Pasteur's (1822–1895) classical work established the germ theory of disease that a truly scientific basis of medicine was created.

Most notable biological achievements of the eighteenth and nineteenth centuries were the theory of evolution through natural selection and the creation of biology as an experimental science. In the eighteenth century, geographical distribution of living creatures and the paleontological record inspired ideas of the gradual evolution of species instead of their fixity. Jean Baptiste de Lamarck (1744–1829) vividly described the constant flux in nature, but his psychological, almost mystical, causes for the transformation of species were unacceptable to the majority of scientists. It was Charles Robert Darwin's (1809–1882) use of the mechanism of natural selection that led to his theory being taken seriously. Unfavorable variations were weeded out by the mechanical operation of the environment. No vital spirits or will power were needed to explain the change of forms over millennia. Given the expanded time scale made possible by nineteenth-century geology, it required no great intellectual effort to visualize evolution by means of natural selection. Armed with this principle, the interconnections of the animate world could begin to be seen. The theory of evolution was the periodic table of biology.

During the nineteenth century, bi-

ology became a full-fledged experimental science. The major obstacle to the achievement of this aim was the strength of the feeling that living matter somehow did not obey the ordinary laws of inorganic matter. The discovery of the circulation of the blood did not remove this feeling. The fact that the blood obeyed the laws of hydrodynamics did not unduly impress the vitalists. The arteries and veins, after all, were pipes and therefore the blood acted like any other fluid going through pipes. What were forever hidden from view, it was felt, were the processes of life, such as digestion or nervous function. This was where the "vital spirits" came in and this principle of life was, by definition, not susceptible to scientific or experimental study.

Assaults on this position were made in the eighteenth century, but it was in the nineteenth century that the full battle began. In the laboratories of such men as Johannes Purkinje (1787–1869), Johannes Müller (1801–(1858), and especially Claude Bernard (1813–1878) the mysteries of living tissue were gradually revealed. There it was shown that living matter, while complicated, was no less subject to scientific analysis than any other. It was possible to formulate hypotheses and then subject them to the same type of experimental test as those applied in physics and chemistry. By the end of the nineteenth century, an overall picture of life was possible in physi-

BIBLIOGRAPHY

ASIMOV, ISAAC. *The Intelligent Man's Guide to Science.* Basic Books, Inc., 1963.

CONANT, JAMES BRYANT. *On Understanding Science: An Historical Approach.* Yale University Press, 1947.

DAMPIER, WILLIAM C. *History of Science.* Cambridge University Press, 1963.

FEUER, LEWIS SAMUEL. *The Scientific Intellectual.* Basic Books, Inc., 1963.

FORBES, ROBERT J. and DIJKSTERHUIS, E. J. *A History of Science and Technology.* 2 vols. Penguin Books, Inc., 1963.

GARDNER, ELDON JOHN. *History of Life Science.* Burgess Publishing Co., 1963.

GILLISPIE, CHARLES COULSTON. *The Edge of Objectivity.* Princeton University Press, 1960.

GOOD, IRVING JOHN and others (eds.). *The Scientist Speculates: An Anthology of Partly Baked Ideas.* Basic Books, Inc., 1963.

HALL, ALFRED RUPERT. *From Galileo to Newton: 1630–1720.* Harper & Row, Publishers, 1963.

NEWMAN, JAMES ROY. *Science and Sensibility.* Simon and Schuster, Inc., 1960.

SARTON, GEORGE. *History of Science and the New Humanism.* George Braziller, Inc., 1956.

SARTON, GEORGE. *The Life of Science: Essays in the History of Civilization.* Abelard-Schuman Ltd., 1948.

TAYLOR, FRANK SHERWOOD. *An Illustrated History of Science.* Frederick A. Praeger, Inc., 1955.

ASTRONAUTICS

Scope.—*Astronautics* encompasses all human activities in space—unmanned satellites circling the earth, space probes sent to another planet, manned space capsules, and the piloted spaceships to come. The word was coined by the French aviation pioneer Robert Esnault-Pelterie as a title for his book *l'Astronautique,* printed in Paris in 1930. It is derived from the Greek roots *aster,* meaning 'star,' and *nautes,* meaning 'sailor.' An astronaut, therefore, is literally a "sailor to the stars." The Russian term *cosmonaut* is derived from the Greek word *kosmos,* which actually means 'well-ordered' but is used to mean the universe—the well-ordered universe as distinct from chaos.

Early History.—Although astronautics has developed as a science only recently, it has a considerable history; the early part consists of philosophical and scientific speculations on the nature of other worlds.

These speculations began well before the birth of Christ. The classical philosophical school of the Pythagoreans believed the moon to be a solid mass, like the earth, and inhabited. While other classical philosophers disagreed with the Pythagoreans on practically every point, they did agree that the moon was a solid body with mountains and valleys.

■LITERARY BACKGROUND.—The first man to devote an entire book to the moon was the Greek biographer Plutarch (c. 46–c. 120). In his work *De facie in orbe lunae* ("On the Face That Can Be Seen in the Orb of the Moon") Plutarch stated that the moon was inhabited, although not by people; he had either "demons" or the souls of the dead in mind. Since the philosophers were in general agreement that the moon was a solid body, and since it did not occur to anyone that a habitable body might not be inhabited, it was only natural to speculate how such a body might be reached. The first speculation known was written forty years after Plutarch's death by the Greek satirist Lucian of Samosata. While Lucian used the opportunity to poke fun at everything in reach of his stylus, he did express a wish to reach the moon.

Some 1,400 years later an English bishop, Francis Godwin, wrote a book in which a number of huge birds, called *gansas,* carry the hero to the moon. In the same year, 1638, another English bishop, John Wilkins, published a serious philosophical discussion on the possibility of life on the moon. Ten years later, Wilkins published a second edition in which he enumerated the possibilities of reaching· the moon.

While these early space-flight fantasies are properly catalogued under the heading of literature rather than science, they did keep the idea of traveling into space—specifically, to the moon—alive. A number of ideas now in the process of being realized first appeared in works of fiction.

■SCIENTIFIC BACKGROUND.—One of the most important contributions in the field of astronautics was made by the German astronomer Johannes Kepler (1571–1630). It is interesting that Kepler had also written a moon-travel fantasy, *Somnium* ("Sleep"), in which Plutarch's "demons" carry astronomers across the bridge of the earth's shadow during a lunar eclipse.

In his work *Astronomia nova* ("The New Astronomy," 1609), Kepler stated that the true shape of the orbit of a planet around the sun is an ellipse and that the position of the sun is not at the center of the ellipse but at one of its two focal points. In this same work, he also stated that a planet moves more rapidly when it is in the section of its orbit that is closer to the sun, and that it moves more slowly when in the section of its orbit that is farthest from the sun. Looking for a mathematical relationship governing this change in orbital velocity, Kepler imagined a line from the sun to the planet that he called the *radius vector.*

He then saw that "the radius vector sweeps over equal areas in equal times." This law permitted the calculation of both past and future positions of a planet once the size of its orbit and its degree of elongation (*eccentricity*) were known. Kepler called the orbit point closest to the sun the *perihelion* (from the Greek words *helios,* meaning 'sun,' and *peri,* meaning in this case 'to go around'). Of course, on each orbit there also was a point where the planet was farthest from the sun; Kepler (using the Greek word *apo,* which means 'to go away' or 'to be away') called this the *aphelion.*

Kepler also coined the term *satellite.* Before his time, the only known satellite was the moon. However, during Kepler's lifetime, Galileo Galilei (1564–1642) discovered the four major moons of Jupiter. Kepler, in a letter to Galileo, suggested a general term for planetary attendants, coining "satellite" from the Greek *satellos,* 'attendant.'

Kepler had shown *how* the planets move. Sir Isaac Newton (1642–1727) showed *why* they move. By introducing the two concepts of *universal gravitation* (any body in the universe attracts every other, although very weakly if the distance is great) and *inertia* (any body remains in its state of rest or of motion unless influenced by an external force), Newton gave astronomers the laws that had escaped scientists for centuries. In explaining how the moon moves around the earth, in his *Mathematical Principles of Natural Philosophy,* Newton even developed the theory of artificial satellites.

In this work, Newton used a diagram showing the earth with a high imaginary mountain that had a horizontally mounted gun on its top. The principle of satellite motion is really quite simple: if the gun first fires its projectile with a certain velocity, and impact on the ground takes place a certain distance from the mountain then a projectile fired with a higher muzzle velocity will have its impact point a greater distance away. Newton explained this by showing that the earth's gravitational pull re-

NEW YORK PUBLIC LIBRARY

JULES VERNE envisioned a moon trip in 1865. Capsules made up the projectile.

BROWN BROTHERS

JOHANNES KEPLER proved that planets travel in an elliptical orbit around the sun.

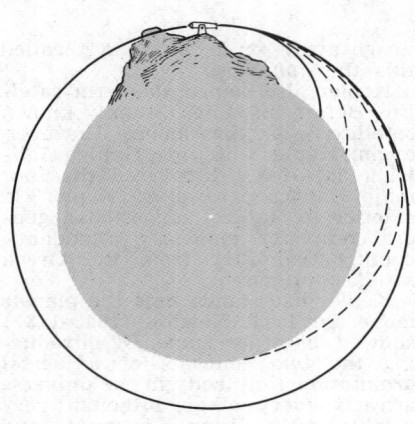

NEWTON'S DIAGRAM showing an earth orbit.

mains constant. The faster projectile will cover a greater horizontal distance per second. The result is that the curvature of the trajectory grows shallower as the muzzle velocity increases. If the velocity of the projectile is great enough, the curvature of its trajectory will become so shallow that it corresponds to the curvature of the ground below. It thus orbits the earth.

However, Kepler and Newton developed only the basic principles of astronautics. Over two centuries of scientific detail had to accumulate before any astronautical applications could come from their work.

It is not known who was the first to calculate the velocity required for an object to stay in orbit around the earth. However, any mathematician could have done it after Karl Friedrich Gauss (1777–1855) had published his work on the calculation of orbits early in the nineteenth century. Whoever performed the calculation first must have jumped to the conclusion that an orbit could never be achieved. If a satellite could be orbited at the earth's surface, it would have to move at the rate of almost 5 miles per second to compensate for the earth's gravitational pull. Even at a point a thousand miles from the earth, the required velocity is 4.4 miles per second.

Early Rocketry.—The name of the inventor of the first rocket is not known. However, it is certain that he was a Chinese, for the first mention of rockets appears in ancient Chinese writings. In a Chinese work, in which the siege of the city of Kai-fung-fu (1232) is described, "arrows of flying fire" are mentioned. The invention of these rockets, similar to those now called *fireworks rockets*, must have taken place sometime between 1200 and 1230. The chronicles of the city of Cologne mention a rocket in 1258, and Arab scientists of the same period referred to rockets by the name of *alsichem alkhatai*, which means "Chinese arrows." For about two centuries rockets were used as weapons of war,

but by 1400 the recently invented guns came into general use and replaced them. However, there was one military target against which rockets still found an application—the large, flammable sails and tarred rigging of ships. For this reason rockets continued to be used as a weapon on the high seas. On land the rocket assumed a far more peaceful role in the mid-sixteenth century; it then became the mainstay of large, often expensive fireworks displays.

Nevertheless, a number of military men and private experimenters questioned whether or not improved rockets could perform military duties in competition with artillery. Yet, in spite of some interesting demonstrations, they failed to convince their respective governments.

■ **CONGREVE ROCKETS.**—One man, the English army captain (later general) William Congreve (1772–1828), did succeed in returning the rocket to the battlefield. Reading about British defeats caused by rocket fire during the Indian campaigns—especially during the two battles of Seringapatam in 1792 and 1799—he decided to investigate the existing fireworks rockets for their possible usefulness. Within two years he had improved the accuracy and range of rockets, primarily by increasing their size. The largest fireworks rockets he had been able to buy in London had had a diameter of 1½ inches and a length of not much more than a foot. The early *Congreve rockets* had a diameter of 3½ inches and a length of 40½ inches. The front of the sheet-iron rocket case held the warhead, which contained an incendiary charge. The maximum range of the Congreve rockets was 3,000 yards—1,000 yards more than the maximum range of the heavy 10-inch mortar then used by the English army. Congreve rockets were used in various battles during the reign of Napoleon. They also were employed when the British bombarded Fort McHenry during the War of 1812 and are referred to in the American national anthem. Congreve rockets were also used when British troops burned the White House. The rockets were not fired into the building, but were wedged between the beams, then ignited.

Rockets were not used to a great extent because there was no production machinery for them; they had to be made individually by hand. Also, the propulsive charge was unreliable: rockets that had been stored for more than six months were likely to explode on ignition or to fly erratically if they worked at all.

Beginnings of Scientific Astronautics.—Although a great many rockets were produced during the nineteenth century, for the most part they were considered toys and were neglected by science. No mathematician sat down to evolve a theory of rocket flight; no physicist took the trouble to investigate the way in which they operated; and no engineer thought of improving them.

When rockets finally were investigated scientifically, it was because Sir Isaac Newton implied that they

would operate in space. His third law stated that reaction is equal (in power) but opposite (in direction) to action, or the actions of two bodies are equal (in power) but point in opposite directions. This law was valid without regard to the surroundings—a rocket would operate whether it was surrounded by water or air, or was in a vacuum. Thus, it could be a means for traveling through space.

This concept occurred independently to several people during the last decade of the nineteenth century. In 1891, an inventor in Berlin, Hermann Ganswindt, lectured on the possibility of space travel and even drew a design for a spaceship.

Another German, mathematics professor Kurt Lasswitz, used his spare time to develop a theory of space travel. He suggested *parking orbits* around the earth from which a spaceship could be placed into an orbit that would intercept the orbit of another planet. He embodied his ideas in a best-selling novel *Auf zwei Planeten* ("On Two Planets"), which he published in 1897. Although Lasswitz even gave examples of how to perform the calculations necessary to attain the proper orbits, his readers thought his book only a very interesting novel; no one believed that he had propounded valid theories.

Another early space prophet was the Russian high school teacher Konstantin Eduardovitch Ziolkovsky (1857–1935). He also began by writing a space-travel story (*On the Moon,* 1893), but then started work on a nonfictional treatise on space travel. It was finished in 1898 but not published until 1903, under the title *Exploration of Planetary Space by Means of Reaction-powered Equipment.* Although outdated, a few observations from this treatise are worth mentioning. Ziolkovsky introduced the Russian word *sputnik* ('travel companion') in the sense of artificial satellite. He also listed possible fuels for the superrockets he advocated. One fuel listed was kerosene, which is used today for

ESTHER C. GODDARD

large rockets in both the Soviet Union and the United States.

The next trio of space-travel prophets, an American and two Germans, came to the fore two decades later. The American was Robert H. Goddard (1882–1945), a professor of physics. In 1914, he obtained two U.S. patents, one mentioning the possibility of using liquid fuels for rocket propulsion, the other dealing mainly with the concept of the step rocket —a smaller rocket carried by a larger one. During World War I, Goddard measured the thrust of various types of propellant powders. He also invented a device for demonstrating that a rocket will work in a vacuum. In addition, he calculated a shot to the moon.

The two German authors were Hermann Oberth (1894–   ), whose book *Die Rakete zu den Planetenräumen* ("The Rocket into Interplanetary Space") was published in 1923, and Walter Hohmann (1880–1944), whose book *Die Erreichbarkeit der Himmelskörper* ("The Attainability of the Heavenly Bodies") was published in 1925. Oberth, like Goddard, mentioned high-altitude research rockets, although he went further than Goddard and predicted piloted rockets capable of orbiting the earth. Hohmann, however, assumed the existence of a rocket-powered spaceship and calculated which orbits would have to be traveled in order to reach the nearer planets; he also calculated the amount of fuel required for each maneuver, the duration of the trips, and the amount of food, water, and oxygen required for the crew. Thus, Hohmann's work might be called the most advanced of the three.

■ **FIRST LIQUID-FUEL ROCKETS.**—Although Goddard wrote about solid fuels, mentioning liquid fuels only casually, and Oberth stressed the use of liquid fuels for rocket propulsion, the first man actually to build a liquid-fuel rocket was Goddard. His first rocket made its flight from a farm near Auburn, Massachusetts, on March 16, 1926. Quoting from Goddard's report,

"The rocket traveled a distance of 184 feet in 2.5 seconds, as timed by stop watch." The Soviet Union's first liquid-fuel rocket, constructed by a group of young enthusiasts led by Anatoli Blagonravov, made its initial test flight during the spring of 1932. Apparently it was erratic, for no details have ever been revealed.

Mass Ratio.—The theory of rocket propulsion, as worked out by Goddard and Oberth, showed, among other things, that it is important for the rocket to keep burning for a long period of time. Fireworks, the only rockets in existence when the theory was developed, had burning times of half a second or less and consequently could not be propelled very high. It was shown by comparatively simple mathematics that if rocket *A* had a burning time of 25 seconds and could reach a certain altitude, rocket *B* would go twice as high if it had enough fuel to burn for another 5 seconds. It became obvious that a rocket should carry as much fuel as possible yet be as light as possible.

If the mass of the fuel carried is designated as M_F, the mass of the rocket itself as M_S, and the payload (a package of scientific instruments, for example) as M_P, the take-off mass of the rocket is $M_F + M_S + M_P$. After all the fuel is consumed, there is a remaining mass of $M_S + M_P$. Oberth called the take-off mass M_o, the remaining mass M_L, and the ratio M_o/M_L the *mass ratio* of the rocket.

Oberth also showed that if the mass ratio is equal to *e* (2.71828 . . . , the basis of natural logarithms) the rocket's velocity will equal its *exhaust velocity,* provided that the rocket is not restricted by either air resistance or a gravitational field. For example, if a rocket of the mass ratio *e* were in orbit around the sun at an appreciable distance from the earth, and if the exhaust velocity of the fuel used were equal to 6,000 feet per second, the rocket, after consuming its fuel, would move 6,000 feet per second faster than its velocity prior to firing.

If the rocket had to overcome air resistance and to climb against the gravitational pull of the earth, the mass ratio would have to be higher to produce the same result. The German V-2 rocket had a take-off weight of 28,200 pounds, which was distributed as follows: $M_F = 19,400$ pounds, $M_P = 2,200$ pounds, and $M_S = 6,600$ pounds. The remaining mass, M_L, therefore was 8,800 pounds, and the mass ratio, M_o/M_L, equaled 3.2. The exhaust velocity at sea level was 6,560 feet per second, but the maximum velocity was 5,575 feet per second, almost 1,000 feet per second less than the exhaust velocity. In space, far from the earth, the velocity would have been about 7,700 feet per second. The difference between this theoretical velocity and the actual velocity—2,125 feet per second—was due to the earth's gravitational pull and to air resistance. If the same rocket could have been built with the structure weighing only half of what it did, the mass ratio would have been about 5 and the theoretical velocity would have been nearly 11,000 feet per second. In reality, however, a mass ratio of 5 is most difficult to realize and could be surpassed only in exceptional cases. Even if a rocket with a mass ratio of 6 could be built, it could not reach orbital velocity with the fuel that is now available.

Staging.—One method of attaining an orbit is the step principle, which was stressed by both Goddard and Oberth. To illustrate the principle, assume that the payload of a rocket is another, smaller rocket. When the fuel supply of the first rocket has been consumed, the second stage is ignited. The second rocket can achieve a velocity that no single rocket using the same fuel could ever attain. To use the example of the V-2 once more, if the payload (warhead) of 2,200 pounds had been a 2,200-pound rocket with the same mass ratio as the first stage, then the final velocity of the second stage would have been twice that of the first stage (actually

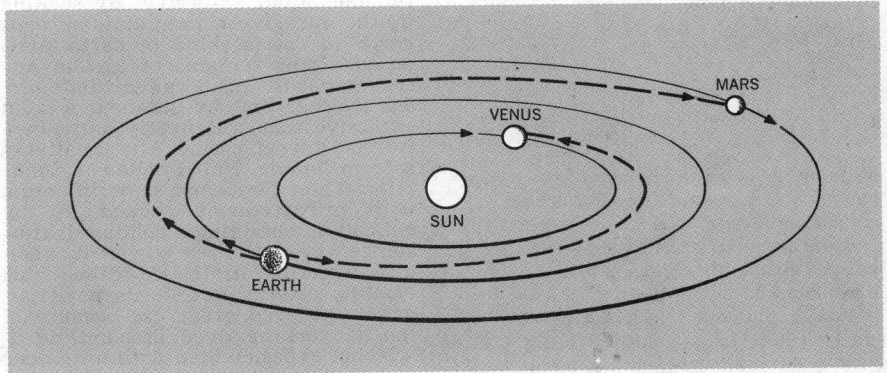

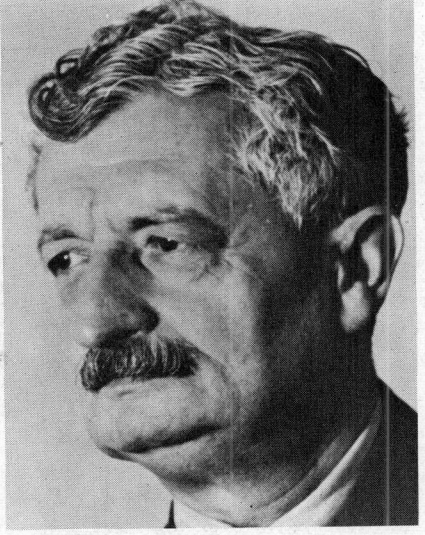

SPACE PIONEERS of the twentieth century used the scientific foundation developed by Newton, Kepler, and Gauss to build the vehicles and perfect a technology to reach into space. Robert Goddard (*left*) developed rocket fuels and flight-tested several successful vehicles; and Hermann Oberth (*right*) calculated the amount of fuel required for a space flight as well as the velocities needed to attain a proper orbit. In 1925, a German, Walter Hohmann, calculated the orbits required to reach the nearest planets. He drew the trajectories (*above*) for journeys to Venus or Mars.

AMERICAN INSTITUTE OF AERONAUTICS AND ASTRONAUTICS

a little more, because the second stage would not be ignited until it attained an altitude of 20 miles, where air resistance is negligible).

The final velocity of the second stage of a two-stage rocket is equal to that of another rocket whose mass ratio is equal to the product of the mass ratios of both stages. That is, if the first stage has a mass ratio of 3 and the upper stage has a mass ratio of 4, then the velocity attained by the upper stage is the same as that which would be attained by a single rocket with a mass ratio of 12. While it is impossible to build a single rocket with a mass ratio of 12, it is entirely feasible to build rockets with mass ratios of 3 and 4. To reach the high velocities necessary to escape the earth, rockets that have two or three stages are needed. Rockets with more than three stages are, as a rule, impractical, although they are sometimes built.

Specific Impulse.—There are two possible yardsticks for measuring the power of a fuel: the theoretical exhaust velocity and the specific impulse. As an example of the former, one could state that ethyl alcohol burned with pure oxygen produces an exhaust velocity of 13,800 feet per second; however, in reality it is impossible for a fuel to reach the theoretical exhaust velocity because there are always losses of some kind. *Specific impulse,* therefore, provides a better yardstick: It measures the amount of thrust (in pounds) produced by burning a unit amount of fuel for one second. To calculate the specific impulse, the thrust of rocket engine, expressed in pounds, is divided by the fuel consumption per second. If a rocket engine produces 80,000 pounds of thrust and consumes 280 pounds of fuel per second, it has a specific impulse of 80,000/280, or 285.7 seconds. If the same rocket engine were designed for a less powerful fuel and had to consume 400 pounds of fuel per second to produce a thrust of 80,000 pounds, the specific impulse would be 200 seconds. The specific impulse of modern rockets is higher than 220 seconds but has reached 300 seconds only in experiments.

Fuel Systems.—There are three basic types of fuel systems: all-liquid, all-solid, and hybrid. In addition, each type has subdivisions.

■LIQUID FUELS.—In a liquid-fuel rocket, the *bipropellant system* is the rule. In this subdivision, the rocket uses two different liquids housed in separate tanks. One of the liquids is the fuel proper; the other, usually liquefied oxygen (called LOX), is the oxidizer. The two most common fuels burned with oxygen are refined kerosene, which is used in the Atlas rocket, and ethyl alcohol, which was used in the V-2, the Viking, and the first stage of the Vanguard rocket. Bipropellant systems using liquid oxygen have the highest specific impulse. Unfortunately, they have a disadvantage in that liquid oxygen has a very low boiling point and therefore evaporates quickly. Thus, once the rocket has been fueled, it must be fired within half an hour.

The most powerful fuel combination of the all-liquid bipropellant systems is hydrogen burned with oxygen. A hydrogen-oxygen rocket, called *Centaur,* was successfully launched late in 1963.

Another variety of the bipropellant system uses RFNA (red fuming nitric acid) as the oxidizer. RFNA is rich in oxygen and does not evaporate easily. However, it is a very corrosive liquid, and special precautions must be taken when handling it. During early experimentation with RFNA, it was discovered that some fuels, when brought in contact with it, spontaneously burst into flame. This type of fuel-oxidizer combination is known as a *hypergolic* fuel. The first hypergolic fuel to be used was a combination of nitric acid and aniline; it was this fuel that powered the small American WAC-Corporal rocket. Unsymmetrical dimethyl hydrazine, which has proved more powerful and reliable than aniline, was used in combination with RFNA in the second stage of the Vanguard rocket.

Hypergolic combinations are advantageous in that they can be left on the launching pad for some time without loss of fuel and are easy to ignite. Many rocket engineers, however, shy away from hypergols, for if a small leak develops somewhere, it can lead to a disastrous fire.

Another liquid-fuel system is the *monopropellant system.* Here, one fuel tank contains a liquid mixture of fuel and oxidizer. A monopropellant needs ignition only when it enters the combustion chamber. The prime danger is that the flame may travel back through the fuel pipes and ignite the fuel supply in the tank, which would then explode. To date, there is no safe monopropellant.

■SOLID PROPELLANTS.—Solid propellants consist of a mixture of fuel and an oxidizer; thus, they are similar to the propulsive charges of the earliest rockets. The first modern solid rocket fuels, known as *double-base powders,* were developed by Alfred Nobel (1833–1896). Nobel began with nitroglycerine, a powerful but highly unreliable liquid explosive. By soaking up the nitroglycerine in *diatomaceous earth* (a special kind of earth composed of the remains of certain microorganisms, also called *diatomite* and *kieselguhr*), he obtained a solid explosive that was nearly as powerful as nitroglycerine but relatively safe to handle. Nobel called it *dynamite.* Then he began experimenting with nitroglycerine soaked up by guncotton, obtaining a gelatinous substance even more powerful than nitroglycerine itself. He called this *blasting gelatin;* despite its power, it never achieved great use because of the dangers involved in handling it.

Nobel experimented with a number of additives to make his blasting gelatin safer to handle and more solid. The resulting explosives received such names as *Ballistite* and *Cordite.* The overall term, *double-base powders,* referred to the fact that both basic ingredients, nitroglycerine and guncotton, are explosives. Virtually all the military bombard-

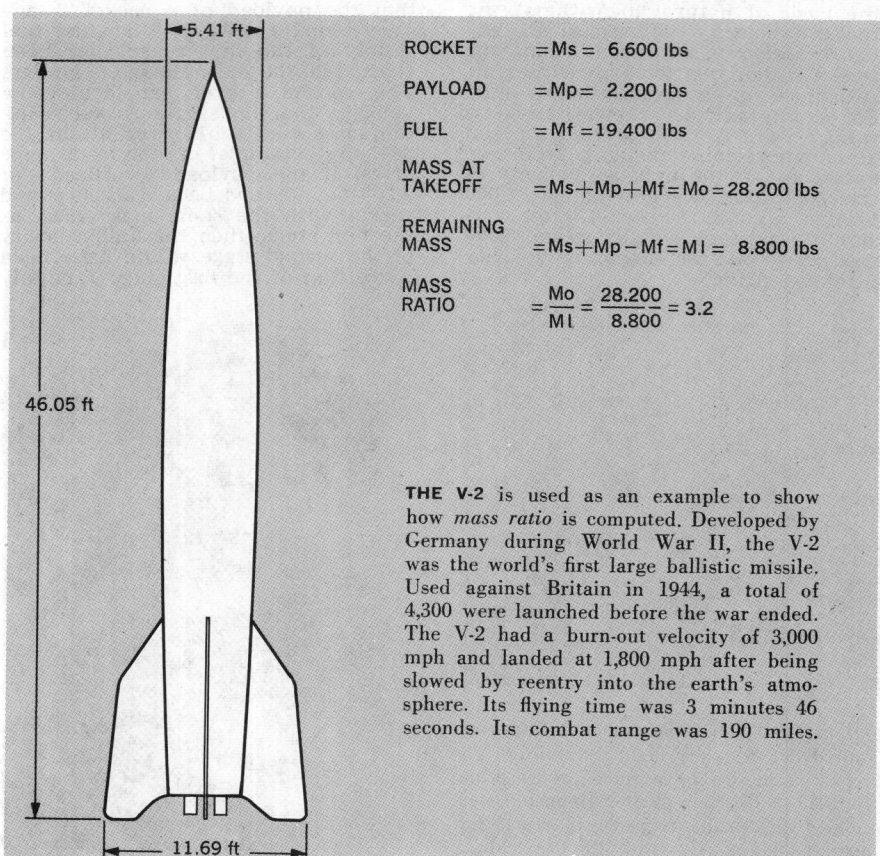

ROCKET	$= Ms =$ 6.600 lbs
PAYLOAD	$= Mp =$ 2.200 lbs
FUEL	$= Mf =$ 19.400 lbs
MASS AT TAKEOFF	$= Ms + Mp + Mf = Mo =$ 28.200 lbs
REMAINING MASS	$= Ms + Mp - Mf = Ml =$ 8.800 lbs
MASS RATIO	$= \dfrac{Mo}{Ml} = \dfrac{28.200}{8.800} = 3.2$

THE V-2 is used as an example to show how *mass ratio* is computed. Developed by Germany during World War II, the V-2 was the world's first large ballistic missile. Used against Britain in 1944, a total of 4,300 were launched before the war ended. The V-2 had a burn-out velocity of 3,000 mph and landed at 1,800 mph after being slowed by reentry into the earth's atmosphere. Its flying time was 3 minutes 46 seconds. Its combat range was 190 miles.

U.S. ARMY   U.S. AIR FORCE   NASA

U.S. MISSILES. The Jupiter (*left*) and the Atlas (*center*) are operational. The Saturn (*right*) will carry a manned capsule to the moon.

ment rockets used by both sides in World War II had some form of Cordite or Ballistite propelling them.

But while the double-base powders performed military functions satisfactorily, it was soon found that they were not ideal rocket propellants. They were sensitive to temperature —on very cold days they would burn more slowly than on warm days—so obviously they could not be used where a high degree of accuracy was required. In addition, it also became clear that double-base grains could not be made very large, and thus would always burn too rapidly.

Double-base powders are still used for comparatively small military rockets, but new solid fuels have been developed for the larger missiles and research rockets. Details of composition and manufacture are, of course, secret; but the main ingredients of these modern solid fuels are synthetic rubber and an oxidizer (for example, ammonium perchlorate) kneaded into the rubber during the manufacturing process. Various additives, such as powdered metals, improve the reliability and sometimes increase the power of this mixture.

There are three main types of modern solid propellants. One is the *suspended grain*, which burns along its whole length; this is used in small military rockets. Because the grain burns along its whole length, one speaks of an *unrestricted burning charge* in these fuels. The other two types of fuels have propelling charges that fit tightly into the casing. They are called *wall-fitting charges*, or *restricted burning charges*. In one

type the charge is just a tightly fitting cylinder of propellant that is ignited at one end and slowly burns until it is completely consumed. This type of construction, which has been nicknamed "cigarette burner," provides a comparatively low thrust for a fairly long time. It is rarely used. The common type of wall-fitting charge has a center hole that runs the length of the charge. Ignition takes place in this center hole; the charge burns from the inside outward.

■**HYBRID SYSTEMS.**—If a wall-fitting charge with a center hole consisted solely of the fuel part of the solid fuel, the fuel could burn only if oxygen were supplied to it. This could be done by blowing gaseous oxygen through the center hole from the front end. Such a system is called a *hybrid system*, and various aspects are now under development.

Atomic Rocket.—The *atomic rocket*, now under development as a part of a larger development project called Project Rover, differs from all other rockets in that no fuel is actually burned. In a normal rocket—whether the propellant is liquid, solid, or hybrid—fuel is burned to produce large quantities of combustion gases. These gases are then expelled through the exhaust nozzle to produce a reaction. In the atomic rocket, heat is supplied by an atomic reactor. Hydrogen gas from a storage tank, where it is stored in liquefied form, is then led through the atomic reactor, where it is heated. When heated, the gas expands and is expelled through the exhaust nozzle; however, the exhaust

stream is unburned hydrogen.

The atomic rocket, when completed, is expected to show a specific impulse of about 325 seconds, which would make it far superior to any rocket that burns fuel. The ultimate goal in the development of atomic rockets is one that does not need liquid hydrogen but can operate on water. If that can be accomplished, a long step forward will have been taken. It is known, for example, that there is water on Mars. If atomic rockets that operate with water are developed, it would only be necessary to provide enough water for the trip to Mars; the water for the return trip could be obtained on Mars. Thus, the weight required of the rocket could be reduced.

Development of Rocket Engines. — In 1930 more than half a dozen groups of researchers were investigating the problems of the liquid-fuel rocket. There were, in the United States, Robert H. Goddard, who was then in New England but was soon to move to New Mexico; and two societies, the Cleveland Rocket Society in Cleveland and the American Rocket Society in New York. Both of these groups failed to accomplish a great deal, mainly for lack of resources. The Cleveland Rocket Society collapsed, but the American Rocket Society has grown into the largest rocket society in the world.

The remaining researchers were in Europe. In France, one of the pioneers of aviation, Robert Esnault-Pelterie, had established a research laboratory to try to build a high-altitude rocket. In Austria, Eugen Sänger, then professor of engineering at the University of Vienna, carried out a long series of rocket-motor tests. In Russia, an organization called GIRD (from the initial letters of the Russian words for "Group for the Investigation of Motion by Reaction") prepared the first Russian liquid-fuel rockets. In Germany the Society for Space Travel (*Verein für Raumschiffahrt*) actively conducted research.

All these researchers had one main problem on their hands: the building of the device that came to be called the rocket motor. In outline, this was a metal container with inlets for the fuel and the oxidizer at one end and an exhaust nozzle at the other. Even though the rocket motor was a completely new device, some knowledge from other fields of engineering could be utilized. The fuel inlets and the injection nozzles already existed and were even being mass-produced for diesel engines; unfortunately, these were the wrong size, but the detail problem had been solved.

It was also known how the exhaust nozzles had to look: they had to be of the so-called *convergent-divergent* type, which means that the nozzle first narrows to a point of smallest cross section (called the *throat*) and then flares out again. This shape is necessary because a gas flowing through a nozzle at a speed less than that of sound will move faster as the nozzle gets narrower. A gas moving at a speed greater than that of sound will slow down in a narrowing nozzle, but a supersonic gas stream will speed up in a flaring nozzle. The design of the rocket's exhaust nozzle therefore had to take these phenomena into consideration. The combustion gases coming from the chamber where the fuel had been burned would move fast, but not as fast as sound. Hence they would speed up as the nozzle narrowed and, if everything was of the right size, they would reach the speed of sound at the throat. They would then enter the flaring section of the nozzle and speed up more, so that they

would leave the nozzle opening (called the *muzzle*) with a speed exceeding that of sound.

The main problem encountered in the construction of the rocket motor, however, was that the heat of burning was much greater than the melting point of any metal that could be used to build the motor. Hence, rocket motors had a tendency to develop two holes while burning: one near the center of the combustion chamber and one near the throat of the nozzle. For short burning times, say up to 1½ seconds, this could be avoided by making the metal quite thick. But for longer burning times, a cooling system of some kind was mandatory. At first a cooling jacket with cold water in it was tried, but the weight of the water was prohibitive. Then it was realized that a cold liquid was available: the fuel from the tank. Therefore, the fuel was no longer injected directly into the rocket, but instead went through the cooling jacket before entering the combustion chamber. The early rocket motors consisted of only a combustion chamber and an exhaust nozzle with a formfitting cooling jacket. As the motors grew larger, however, more than one fuel pipe and one oxygen pipe were needed, and at a later date the fuel pump was attached to the rocket motor. The entire system —rocket motor, piping, pumps, and whatever auxiliary devices are needed—is called the *rocket engine*.

Progress in Germany.—By 1935 the number of research groups had shrunk. The Cleveland Rocket Society and the German Society for Space Travel had ceased to exist, Eugen Sänger was working in the field of aerodynamics, and the American Rocket Society, while still in existence, had stopped experimenting. There were now only one individual experimenter, Robert H. Goddard, and three active groups: a Russian group under Anatoli Blagonravov, a German army group under Captain (later General) Walter Dornberger and Wernher von Braun, and the

small French group around Robert Esnault-Pelterie. Esnault-Pelterie never finished his high-altitude rocket because of the advent of World War II, but the other three had initial successes. In December 1934 the German army group fired two rockets, of a type they called *A-2,* to altitudes of about 6,500 feet. During the summer of 1935 Goddard fired several rockets, one of which went as high as 7,500 feet; and the Russian group made about a dozen shots, of which the highest came close to six miles.

Seven years later the picture had changed again. The Russians had stopped rocket experimentation altogether. Goddard, after a hiatus of a few years, worked on rockets as take-off aid for Navy flying boats. The German army group had progressed to the first large rocket.

After the initial success with the A-2 rockets, the Germans had built a larger rocket called *A-3* and had begun to make sketches for a much bigger one called *A-4.* It then became apparent that work on the A-4 could not be started without more experiments with the A-3. Therefore, before starting the A-4, they still built another type, called the *A-5.* In 1942 the first few A-4's were built. The new rocket was quite troublesome for some time—indeed, there were only two successful shots among the first fourteen. But the two successes proved that the A-4 could be made to work, and a somewhat lighter version of the A-4 became the rocket known as the *V-2.*

Postwar Developments.—Since all of the other nations had dropped out of the race, the field of large rockets was a German monopoly for nearly a decade. The V-2 had been such a long step forward that everybody else's plans had become obsolete. Hence it was only logical that, after the war, the V-2 should become the basis of the programs of other countries. The United States had developed only one medium-size liquid-fuel rocket named the *WAC-Corporal;* the work was done by a California group that owed its existence to Theodore von Kármán. Therefore, the rocket program of the United States began with about 70 V-2 rockets that had been captured in parts. The German research and planning staff, including Dornberger and Von Braun, was also brought to the United States.

The Russians had captured two V-2 rockets in working order—they had been earmarked for troop training— and, of course, the manuals that accompanied them. Contrary to popular impression, the Russians did not capture any of the important rocket scientists; a number of men from the original production line were held in Russia only temporarily. The Russians, therefore, began with a production line for V-2 rockets but proceeded to their own designs.

In the United States, the captured V-2 rockets were used up in a program that combined high-altitude research and the familiarization of American military men and scientists with large rockets. The first United States design, about half the size of

U.S. ARMY

A JUPITER intermediate-range ballistic missile is being assembled on a production line.

the V-2, was a rocket called the *774*, in which a new idea for steering a rocket was tried. Instead of having graphite vanes inserted into the exhaust blast, as the Germans had done, the whole rocket motor of the *774* was suspended on gimbals so that it could be swiveled for balancing and steering. This idea was then incorporated into the Navy's Viking rockets, the first American design to become well known. In the meantime, *Project Bumper* had been carried out, consisting of eight V-2 rockets that had been equipped with second stages consisting of specially adapted WAC-Corporal rockets. On February 24, 1949, the second stage of Bumper 5 rose to an altitude of 250 miles, the first man-made device to climb beyond the atmosphere of the earth.

Since the Viking rockets were a Navy project, the Army asked Wernher von Braun to produce a new but bigger V-2-type rocket. This became known as the *Redstone*, after the Redstone Arsenal near Huntsville, Alabama, where it was developed. A number of Redstone rockets were set aside to test components for the next larger Army rocket, the Jupiter, which was to have a range of 1,500 miles. For this reason the Redstone rockets used in this test program were called *Jupiter-C*, the *C* standing for "components." At the same time the Air Force was developing still another 1,500-mile rocket, the *Thor.* Jupiter and Thor were to be intermediate-range missiles. The intercontinental missiles, *Atlas* and *Titan*, were developed later.

U.S. Space Programs.—When rocket development had reached the Redstone rocket, it became clear to the experts in the field that the experiment that Sir Isaac Newton had been able to perform only on paper could now be carried out in actuality. The Redstone itself did not have a great range, but it could carry a heavy payload. If staging were used, the Redstone could carry the upper stages needed to attain orbital velocity.

In 1954 *Project Orbiter* was formulated. It was to be a joint Army-Navy project, with the Army furnishing the rockets and the Navy supplying everything else. The rocket was to be a Redstone, with clusters of small solid-fuel rockets forming upper stages. The uppermost stage, a single, small, solid-fuel rocket, was to be placed into orbit. Project Orbiter could have put a small artificial satellite into orbit in the spring of 1956. However, in 1955 it was decided to discontinue Project Orbiter and proceed with a new project, *Project Vanguard*. The plan was to put a satellite into orbit in the autumn of 1957.

Vanguard was an entirely new rocket of three stages. The first-stage propellant was a liquid-fuel (alcohol and oxygen) rocket and was based on the experience gained with Project Viking. The second stage was to be a new rocket using hypergolic liquid fuels, and the third stage was to be a new solid-fuel rocket.

In 1956 the Russians announced that they, too, had a satellite project. Since Project Vanguard was already falling behind schedule—there were too many new things to be developed and not enough money had been appropriated for the test—the Army proposed to launch an artificial satellite by means of its new Jupiter-C rocket. However, the Secretary of Defense, Charles Wilson, forbade this.

Because of his order, the first artificial satellite to be orbited was the Russian *Sputnik I*, on October 4, 1957. This was followed by *Sputnik II* on November 3, 1957. At this point Neil McElroy, Wilson's successor as Secretary of Defense, ordered the Army to go ahead with the Jupiter-C program. *Explorer I*, first American satellite to orbit, was launched by a Jupiter-C on February 1, 1958.

Artificial Satellites. — The orbits into which artificial satellites can be and have been placed can be divided into two main categories, stable (permanent) and unstable (temporary). A *stable orbit* is one that is well outside the earth's atmosphere along its entire length. The first satellite to attain such an orbit was Vanguard I. Vanguard I will, therefore, continue to orbit the earth until it is artificially removed from orbit, possibly by a manned spaceship.

An *unstable orbit* is one whose perigee section is inside the earth's atmosphere. The process that takes place in this case is technically known as *orbital decay*, the end product of which is reentry and burn-up of the satellite. An explanation of orbital decay is that the satellite, in passing through the upper atmosphere, loses a little of its momentum because of *atmospheric drag* (the resistance of air molecules to the satellite's motion). Since it has lost momentum, the satellite cannot travel as far away from the earth as it did previously. Hence, the next apogee reached is somewhat closer to the earth than the preceding apogee. With each succeeding orbit, the apogee point slowly approaches the earth, thereby making the orbit more circular. Finally the apogee will be as close as the perigee, which means, of course, that the whole orbit is inside the fringes of the earth's atmosphere. Then the nearly circular orbit becomes a spiral; and when the satellite reaches denser layers of the atmosphere, it will burn up in the heat caused by compression of the air in its path.

The majority of the artificial satellites put into orbit were research satellites that were expected to be useful for only a limited period of time, say six months or less. It was desirable to put these satellites into unstable orbits so that they would not clutter up space when their useful life was over. There were some slipups in the early years of the space age—for example, Vanguard II and Vanguard III unnecessarily assumed stable orbits—but in general the early research satellites were placed into unstable orbits and have since reentered and burned up.

However, some satellites should be in stable orbits, namely those that are called the *working satellites*. The U.S. space program includes several types: satellites to aid navigation, such as *Transit;* satellites to aid weather forecasters, such as *Tiros* and *Nimbus;* and finally, communications satellites, such as *Echo, Telstar, Relay,* and *Syncom.* All these satellites must be in stable orbits to perform their functions.

Of the orbits around the earth, there is one that deserves special mention. A satellite in an orbit 22,300 miles above sea level will need 24 hours to circle the earth once. If this satellite is moving eastward over the equator, it will keep pace with the turning of the earth beneath it. It will, therefore, seem to hang motionless over one point of the equator. This type is a *synchronous* satellite, which means that it is moving "in time with" the turning earth.

A COMMUNICATIONS SATELLITE, such as the Relay (*right*), if put in the orbit shown above, would have an angular velocity identical to that of the earth. Thus, if satellite S_1 were above point A on the earth's surface, it would travel to point S'_1 while point A moved to A'. Three such synchronous satellites could cover the earth's surface, with the exception of a small area at the North and South poles.

NOVOSTI PRESS AGENCY

NASA

NASA

Manned Orbital Flights

Name of Astronaut	Name of Spacecraft	Date of Launching	Apogee (Miles)	Perigee (Miles)	Number of Revolutions	Duration of Flight
Maj. Yuri A. Gagarin	Vostok I	Apr. 12, 1961	187.75	109.5	1	89.1 min.
Cmdr. Alan B. Shepard, Jr.	Freedom 7	May 5, 1961	116.5	—	sub-orbital	15 min.
Capt. Virgil I. Grissom	Liberty Bell 7	July 21, 1961	118.0	—	sub-orbital	15 min.
Maj. Gherman S. Titov	Vostok II	Aug. 6, 1961	160.0	110.3	17½	25 h. 18 min.
Lt. Col. John H. Glenn, Jr.	Friend-ship 7	Feb. 20, 1962	162	92	3	4 h. 56 min.
Lt. Cmdr. M. Scott Carpenter	Aurora 7	May 24, 1962	167.4	99	3	4 h. 50 min.
Maj. Andrian G. Nikolayev	Vostok III	Aug. 11, 1962	156	113	64	94 h. 25 min.
Lt. Col. Pavel R. Popovich	Vostok IV	Aug. 12, 1962	157	112	48	71 h. 3 min.
Cmdr. Walter M. Schirra, Jr.	Sigma 7	Oct. 3, 1962	176	100	5¾	9 h. 14 min.
Maj. L. Gordon Cooper, Jr.	Faith 7	May 15, 1963	165.8	100.2	22	34 h. 20 min.
Lt. Col. Valery Bykovsky	Vostok V	June 14, 1963	140	109	81	119 h. 6 min.
Jr. Lt. Valentina A. Tereshkova	Vostok VI	June 16, 1963	144	112	48	70 h. 50 min.
Konstantin Feoktistov, Lt. Boris B. Yegorov and Col. Vladimir Komarov	Voskhod	Oct. 12, 1964	254	111	16	24 h. 17 min.
Col. Pavel I. Belyayev Lt. Col. Aleksei Leonov	Voskhod II	March 18, 1965	307.5	108	17	26 h. 2 min.
Capt. Virgil Grissom	Gemini 3	March 23, 1965	140	100	3	4 h. 53 min.
Maj. James McDivitt Maj. Edward H. White	Gemini 4	June 3, 1965	182	100	62	97 h. 48 min.
Lt. Col. Gordon Cooper Lt. Cmdr. Charles Conrad	Gemini 5	Aug. 21, 1965	219	100	120	190 h. 56 min.
Cmdr. James A. Lovell Col. Frank Borman	Gemini 7	Dec. 4, 1965	203	100	206	329 h. 30 min. (approx.)
Lt. Col. David R. Scott Neal Armstrong	Gemini 8	March 16, 1966	147	87	7	10 h. 42 min.
Lt. Col. T. P. Stafford Lt. Cmdr. E. A. Cernan	Gemini 9A	June 3, 1966	144	86	44	72 h. 21 min.
Cmdr. John W. Young Maj. Michael Collins	Gemini 10	July 18, 1966	475.64	86.5	43	70 h. 46 min.
Cmdr. Charles Conrad Lt. Cmdr. Richard Gordon	Gemini 11	Sept. 12, 1966	850	100	44	71 h. 17 min.

SPACE TRAVELERS. Yuri Gagarin (*top*), the first man in space, is a Soviet cosmonaut. John Glenn (*bottom*) was the first American to orbit the earth. American astronauts John Young and Michael Collins (*center*) achieved rendezvous and docking missions in Gemini 10.

Manned Flight.—Soon after the first satellites had been successfully orbited, both the Soviet Union and the United States began to think about manned orbits. However, the two countries approached the problem in different ways.

■**U.S. EFFORTS.**—In the United States the preparations began with two suborbital flights to a height of about 120 miles and a distance of about 300 miles. This was followed by Mercury-Atlas IV, a fully functioning Mercury capsule containing a dummy that simulated breathing and perspiring. This was launched on September 13, 1961. The capsule was deorbited by remote control after one orbit and was recovered 161 miles east of Bermuda 109 minutes after take-off. This was followed on November 29, 1961, by Mercury-Atlas V, which carried the chimpanzee Enos. Since the interior of the capsule began growing hot during the second orbit, the test was terminated after two orbits. The capsule was recovered and the animal found to have endured the trip well. Only after all these tests were successfully concluded was a manned orbit attempted. On February 20, 1962, Lt. Col. John H. Glenn became the first American to orbit the earth.

Project Mercury consisted of a total of four orbital flights that occurred after the preliminary orbits with the chimpanzee Enos and the suborbital flights. It came to an end after these four flights—two of three hours each, one of six hours, and one of one day—were made. The next step will be *Project Gemini*, using a two-man capsule. An unmanned Gemini capsule was launched and successfully recovered in 1964.

■**SOVIET EFFORTS.**—The Russians did not perform any manned suborbital flights, but sent large capsules with animals into orbit, beginning with *Sputnik V*. After they had recovered these animal capsules repeatedly, Maj. Yuri Gagarin became the first man in space by completing one orbit on April 12, 1961. The name of his ship was *Vostok* (the Russian word for 'east'); the name was given to the space vehicle because the first Russian sailing vessel to circumnavigate the globe had been named Vostok. The second Vostok went into orbit on August 6, 1961, with Maj. Gherman Stepanovitch Titov aboard; it remained in orbit for 25 hours 18 minutes, and made a total of 17½ circuits of the globe.

Planetary Probes.—Recalling the early books on space travel, it can be said that everything Robert H. Goddard wrote had been turned into reality by —to pick an arbitrary date—January 1, 1963. Likewise, everything Hermann Oberth set down in his work was reality on that date, with the exception of the manned orbiting satellite, the "space station." The orbits Walter Hohmann investigated are still untraveled by man, but they have been traversed by unmanned devices called *planetary probes.*

Going into orbit around the earth, going to the moon, and traveling to another planet are three entirely different problems. Not only are the distances to be coped with growing larger, but there are also several fundamental differences involved. If a rocket is put into an orbit around the earth, the calculations can be made as if the earth were the only body in the universe. The orbit of an artificial satellite is not influenced by the fact that the earth is moving around the sun at the same time. The orbit is not even disturbed by a relatively close body like the moon— it has been calculated that the path of an artificial satellite would differ from reality by only one yard if the moon did not exist, a difference far too small even to be detected.

Similarly, in sending a rocket to the moon, the calculations can be made as if the earth and its moon were the only two bodies in the universe. Both travel around the sun, at the same distance from the sun (compared to the earth's distance of 93,000,000 miles from the sun, the distance of 240,000 miles to the moon

is negligible), and at very nearly the same rate of speed. Hence, in theory, a shot to the moon could be made at any moment. In practice, there are certain periods at which a moon shot is easier to accomplish than at others, but these periods are preferred for one reason only: the problem of guidance is less complicated.

But when it comes to reaching another planet, the problem has to be faced that the various planets move in their orbits with greatly varying velocities. Mercury races around the sun at the rate of nearly 30 miles per second, while Saturn moves at only 6 miles per second.

When Walter Hohmann began his investigations, he first tried to calculate what type of flight path between the orbit of the earth and the orbit of another planet would involve the smallest expenditure of fuel. He found that the flight path that just touched the orbits of the earth and, say, Venus involved the least expenditure of fuel. Hohmann had compared five possible flight paths, which he labeled *A, B, C, D,* and *E.* The one that just touched the two planetary orbits, but did not cross either one of them, happened to be the one he had labeled *A.* Therefore, scientists now refer to it as the *Hohmann-A orbit.* Hohmann calculated the time needed for a ship to travel along the A-orbit from the earth to Venus to be 146 days. In reality, there are minor deviations from this figure, partly because the earth's orbit is slightly elliptical, but mainly because only an approximation of the A-orbit is actually traveled. Since Venus moves at the rate of 21.7 miles per second, and since

its average distance from the sun is 67 million miles, it takes 224.7 earth days to complete one orbit. The earth, with an orbital velocity of 18.5 miles per second, is moving at an average distance of 93 million miles from the sun and needs 365¼ days to complete one orbit. Since the rocket needs 146 days for its trip, a Venus probe must be launched at a time when Venus is 146 days of orbital travel away from the point in its orbit that the rocket will reach. Obviously, one cannot launch a probe to Venus (or to Mars, for that matter) at any time one happens to be ready. There are short periods—of about ten days each—when a launching can be made. Of course, one can aim for the orbit of the other planet at any time; but if the target planet is to be at that point of its orbit, attention must be paid to the *periods of possibility,* which are now referred to as *windows.* The time between two windows is a little less than two years, although it varies for each planet. Therefore, missing one such period means a considerable delay before the next time for launching.

Sending a probe to another planet also differs in method from the simple orbit around the earth or the moon shot. For an orbit around the earth, the only requirement is that the satellite have enough velocity to stay in orbit and that the direction of its movement be parallel to the ground. In the case of a moon shot, the principle is to aim at that point of the sky where the moon will be when the rocket arrives there—the transit time of the Russian moon shot was 35 hours—and the motion of the

MOON PROBE. After launching (1) a corrective maneuver must be made (2) to assure the vehicle's proper attitude. If this adjustment is successful, the probe will be on target (3) to hit the moon. Retro-rockets (4) must decelerate the vehicle to ensure a safe impact (5).

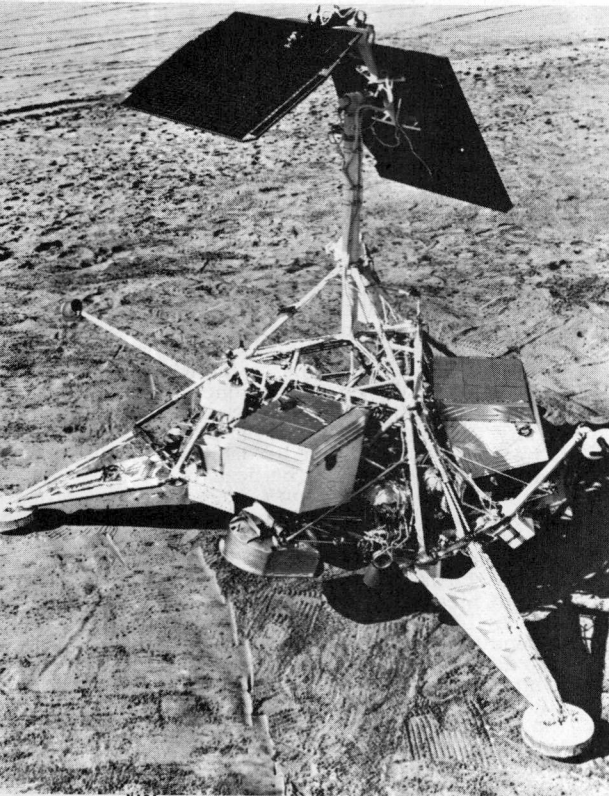

Moon Shots and Planetary Probes

Spacecraft	Date	Weight	Results
Metchtá (Lunik 1)	Jan. 2, 1959	3,245 lb.	Missed moon by 4,600 miles and went into orbit around the sun between orbits of the earth and Mars. Orbital period is 444 days.
Cosmic Rocket II (Lunik II)	Sept. 12, 1959	860 lb.	Hit moon south of mountains called Lunar Apennines. Transit time was 35 hours; impact velocity was about 6,000 mph.
Pioneer V	Mar. 11, 1960	94.8 lb.	Fired into orbit between orbits of Venus and the earth. Orbital period is 311 days.
Sputnik VIII (Russian Venus probes)	Feb. 12, 1961		Fired from orbiting Sputnik VIII. Transmitter failure; instrument capsule in orbit similar to that of Pioneer V.
Ranger III	Jan. 26, 1962	727 lb.	Missed moon and went into orbit around sun; orbit similar to that of Pioneer IV.
Mariner II	Aug. 27, 1962	449 lb.	Passed Venus at a distance of 21,648 miles on December 14, 1962, reporting on conditions on that planet. First successful planetary probe. Now in orbit around sun.
Ranger V	Oct. 18, 1962	730 lb.	Passed 300 miles from the moon. Now in orbit around sun.
Mars I (Russian Mars probe)	Nov. 1, 1962	1,196 lb.	Russian planetary probe which must have passed Mars in June 1963. Radio contact was lost in March 1963. In orbit around sun between the earth and Mars. Orbital period unknown, must exceed 500 days.
Moon IV	Apr. 2, 1963	3,135 lb.	Russian lunar probe, possibly intended for soft landing, missed moon by 5,300 miles.
Ranger VI	Jan. 30, 1964	730 lb.	Perfect shot to the moon, impacted near crater Arago, but cameras failed to work.
Zond I	Apr. 2, 1964	???	Russian probe launched from parking orbit, probably for Venus. In orbit around sun; no data due to transmitter failure.
Ranger VII	July 31, 1964	806.49 lb.	First successful moon shot. Within a distance of from 1,300 miles to 1,000 miles from the moon's surface and within a time span of 16 minutes 40 seconds, 4,316 pictures of the moon were relayed to earth. Crashed into Sea of Clouds.
Mariner IV	Nov. 28, 1964	575 lb.	Passed Mars at a closest distance of 5,400 miles on July 14, 1965, taking 22 pictures of which 17 were useful, showing large impact craters on Mars. Now in orbit around sun.
Zond II	Nov. 30, 1964	???	Russian space probe aimed for Mars, lost electrical power after a few weeks, must have passed Mars within a day of Mariner IV passage. In orbit around sun.
Ranger VIII	Feb. 17, 1965	809 lb.	American lunar probe, took 64.9 hours to reach the moon, crashed into Sea of Tranquillity just north of lunar equator. Transmitted 7,137 excellent pictures.
Ranger IX	Mar. 21, 1965	809 lb.	Took 64.5 hours to reach the moon, impacted in crater Arago, transmitted 5,814 pictures.
Zond III	July 18, 1965	???	In interplanetary orbit, took and transmitted pictures of the moon's far side.
Luna VII	Oct. 4, 1965	3,180 lb.	Russian probe was supposed to land on the moon's surface. Missed target and is now orbiting the sun.
Luna VIII	Dec. 3, 1965	3,414 lb.	Russian probe designed for soft landing, crashed on moon's surface.
Luna IX	Feb. 3, 1966	???	220-pound payload with camera landed on the moon, and took about 9 pictures.
Luna X	April 7, 1966	???	540-pound payload was put into orbit around the moon by Russia.
Surveyor I	May 30, 1966	2,194 lb.	Soft landing on the moon was made on June 2, more than 10,300 pictures were taken in the first lunar day.
Surveyor II	Sept. 2, 1966	2,194 lb.	Crashed on moon as stabilizing rockets failed to fire at midcourse command.

NASA

SURVEYOR I, shown (*top*) in full-scale mock-up, made a soft landing on the moon June 2, 1966, and for over a month sent back thousands of detailed photographs. A composite of two of them (*bottom*) shows an 18-inch rock twelve feet from the spacecraft, whose shadow is at the lower left. Such pictures enabled scientists to find that the dusty, rocky lunar surface is firm enough to support manned landings.

NASA

PICTURES FROM SPACE taken by American astronauts. Major Edward White took a twenty-minute "walk in space" on June 3, 1965 (see also frontispiece). The photograph of the Florida peninsula was taken from the Gemini V spacecraft. Cape Kennedy, in the foreground, can be seen projecting into the Atlantic Ocean. Astronauts Edward White and James McDivitt (*below*) exit from their spacecraft during training exercises held in the Gulf of Mexico.

NASA

NASA

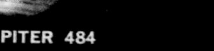

MERCURY 36
VENUS 67
EARTH 93
MARS 142

ASTEROID BELT

JUPITER 484

SATURN 887

DISTANCES OF PLANETS FROM THE SUN IN MILLIONS OF MILES

VAST DISTANCES separate our earth and its neighboring planets revolving in the solar system. The chart above indicates relative sizes of the nine planets and their respective distances from the sun in

millions of miles, ranging from the closest, Mercury, to far-off Pluto. The asteroid belt between Mars and Jupiter is cluttered with cosmic debris, from pebbles to rocks as large as mountains.

PHYSICAL GLOBE © RAND MCNALLY INC. ILLUSTRATION BY HERB WILEN

ORBITAL PHASE

1—Unmanned space observatory

2—Multi-passenger spaceship in orbit

3—Weather satellite system operational

4—Radio-TV relay satellite system operational

5—Meeting of two satellites in space

INITIAL STAGES

OF UNITED STATES

ORBITAL AND

INTERPLANETARY

SPACE PROGRAM

INTERPLANETARY PHASE

1—We crash-land instruments on the moon.
2—Soft landing of lunar instruments achieved.
3—Multi-passenger spaceship circles the moon.
4—First men land on moon's surface and return.
5—Manned spaceship circles Mars and returns.
6—Manned spaceship circles Venus and returns.
7—First men land on Mars and begin exploring.

MOON

URANUS 1,785

NEPTUNE 2,797

PLUTO 3,670

VENUS AND MARS are the next two targets after the moon on our probable space time-table. Besides learning more about the structure of the universe and the laws which govern it, scientists hope to solve one of the biggest unanswered questions: Is there life outside the earth? By 1985 the first men to explore another planet may land on Mars, whose mysterious markings still baffle astronomers.

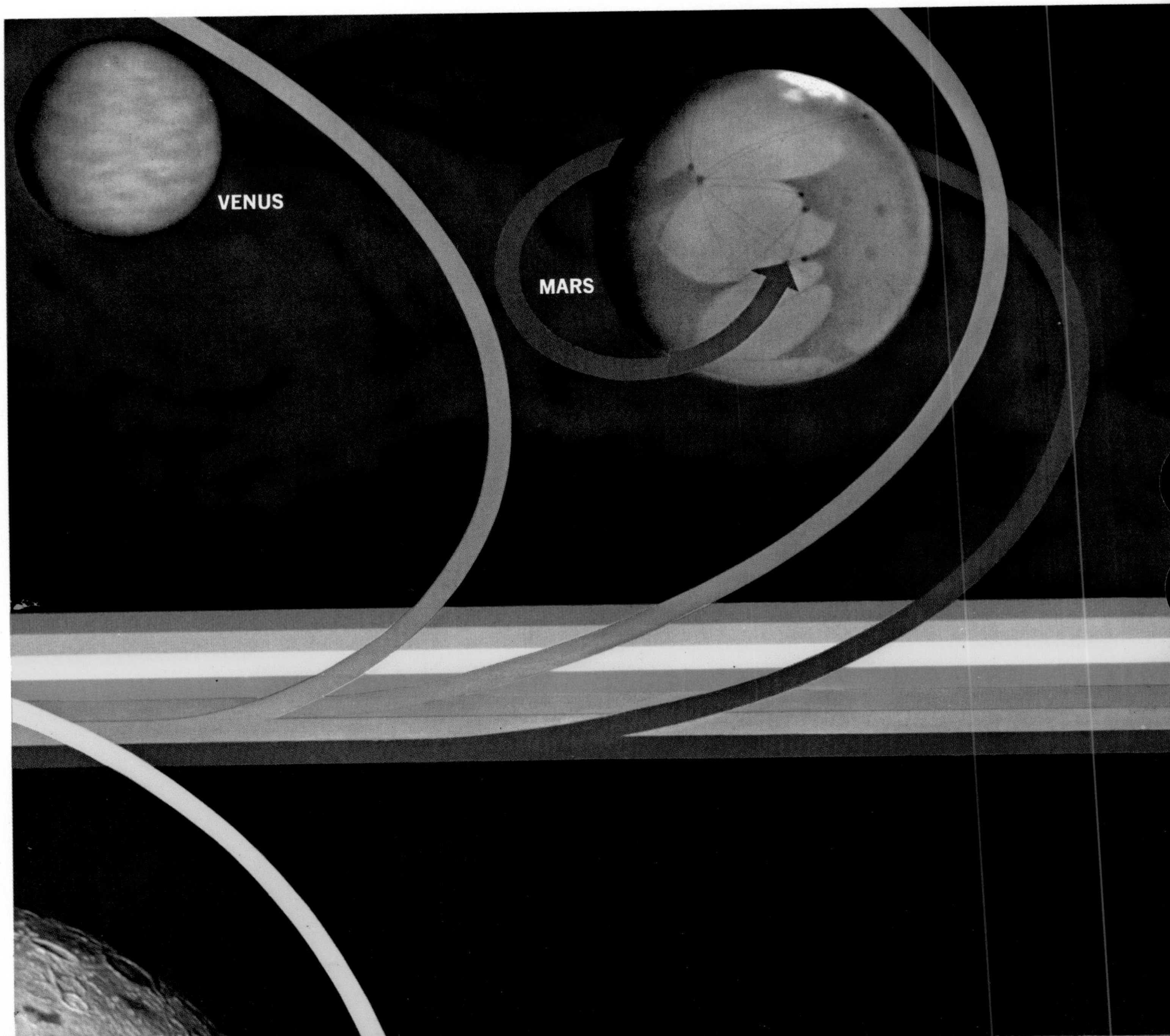

VENUS

MARS

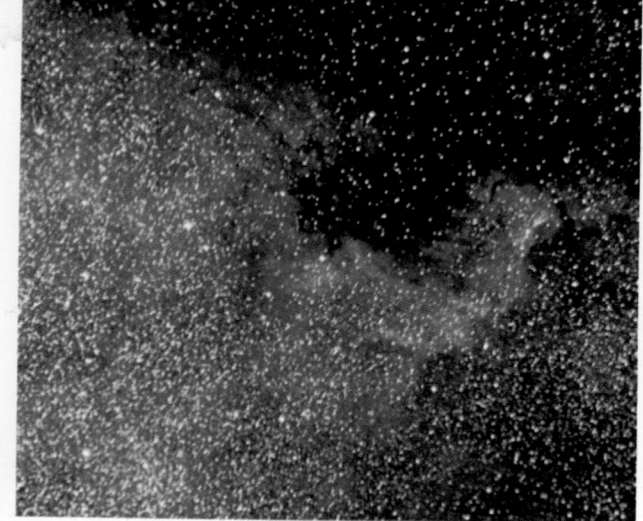

MT. WILSON AND PALOMAR OBSERVATORIES

LICK OBSERVATORY   LICK OBSERVATORY

PLANETS, GALAXYS, AND NEBULA as seen through the telescope. The markings on Saturn (*above left*) and Jupiter (*above right*) can be clearly seen. The Great Nebula in Orion (*below*) and the North American Nebula (*center* and *left*) have been observed for many centuries.

ABOVE & BELOW, MT. WILSON AND PALOMAR OBSERVATORIES

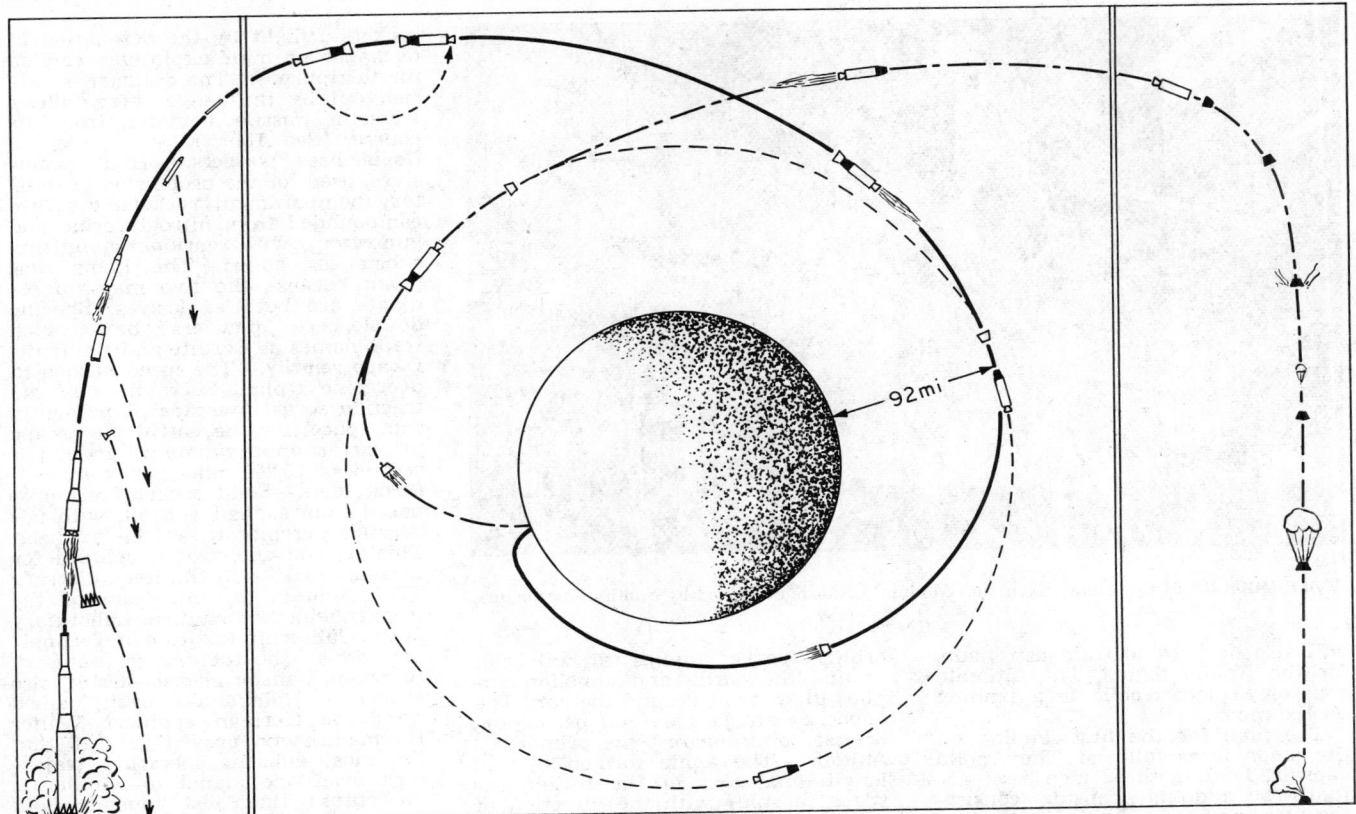

PROJECT APOLLO will send a manned *Gemini* capsule to the moon. After blast-off, the booster stages will separate from the capsule and the space vehicle will reverse its position so that its retro-rockets will be in position to reduce speed upon entering a lunar orbit. Then, 92 miles above the surface of the moon, a Lunar Ex-cursion Module, LEM, will be detached from the main capsule and land on the moon's surface while the parent vehicle remains in orbit. Two astronauts will explore the moon while the third is orbiting. After leaving the moon, LEM will join the parent capsule and return to earth, making a parachute landing.

rocket consists of climbing more or less vertically out of the earth's gravitational field until the gravitational field of the moon becomes more powerful. Then the rocket simply falls into the moon's gravitational field.

The motion of a planetary probe, however, is in the sun's gravitational field. Since, before firing, the rocket is a part of the earth, it moves around the sun in the earth's orbit at the rate of 18½ miles per second. After firing, the rocket has a velocity that is, as seen from the sun, greater or less than 18½ miles per second. If the velocity is greater, the sun will not be able to hold the rocket in the earth's orbit; and the rocket will drift outward in the solar system in the direction of the orbit of Mars. If the rocket's velocity is less than the orbital velocity of the earth, the sun's gravitational pull will make it drift inward in the solar system, in the direction of the orbit of Venus.

The principle of an interplanetary shot is to add the rocket's velocity to the orbital velocity of the earth, or else to subtract the rocket's velocity from the orbital velocity of the earth —just the right amount of velocity, and at just the right time, while a window exists. Whether the rocket's velocity is added or subtracted depends on the time of day. If the rocket is fired vertically, it will add its velocity to the earth's velocity

if the shot is made at dawn. The section of the earth that experiences dawn is its *leading edge;* the section that experiences dusk is the *traveling edge.* Hence, a rocket launched at dawn will move faster than the earth, as seen from the sun, and as a consequence will drift outward in the solar system; the rocket launched at dusk will move more slowly than the earth and will be drawn inward in the solar system.

■**PARKING ORBITS.**—In the foregoing explanation, it has been assumed that the launching is made from the ground. However, it can be done in a different manner, a manner that is preferred by the Russians even though they have suffered quite a number of failures with their planetary probes. This method consists of first putting the rocket, or rather, its upper stages and the payload, into an orbit around the earth. Such an orbit is called a *parking orbit.* The upper stages are then fired by radio command from the ground when their motion has put them in the proper position.

Future Expectations.—The foreseeable future of astronautics consists, in the main, of extending or completing what has already been started. Within a few years, working systems of navigational satellites, of weather observation satellites, and of communications satellites may be achieved.

In addition to these unmanned satellite systems, there will be at least one manned space station in a comparatively low orbit around the earth, probably 350 miles above sea level, so that it will be safely inside the inner Van Allen Belt. The space station will probably be wheel-shaped so that it can be rotated to produce an artificial gravity by centrifugal force, thus making daily routine more convenient for the occupants. The main objective will be scientific research in space.

While a satellite large and heavy enough to serve temporarily as a space station can be put into orbit by the *Saturn I* rocket, the actual space station will have to wait until shuttle rockets for transporting provisions and relief crews have been developed. There will be a need for such shuttle rockets for other purposes, too. For example, it is likely that large communications satellites in synchronous orbits will need occasional inspection and maintenance.

■**PROJECT APOLLO.**—The American space program does not yet contain a space station as one of its goals. Once Project Gemini, which involves a space capsule similar to, but larger than, that of Project Mercury, is completed, *Project Apollo* will begin. The Gemini capsule, built for two men, will serve as a prototype for the still larger capsule of Project Apollo, and

SCALE MOCK-UP of the Lunar Excursion Module, LEM, is evaluated by group of astronauts.

will also be used to train astronauts for the Apollo flights. The ultimate goal of Project Apollo is a landing on the moon.

The plan for the first landing on the moon is as follows: The Apollo capsule, holding three men, will actually be a double capsule, consisting of a main capsule and a landing capsule called a *Lunar Excursion Module,* or *LEM.* The whole Apollo device will first be put into an orbit around the moon. Then the landing capsule, holding two men, will be detached and go in for a landing while the third man remains in orbit around the moon in the main capsule. After the explorers have done their work, they will leave the lunar surface in their landing capsule and return to the main capsule. Then all three astronauts will return to earth in the main capsule, leaving the landing capsule in orbit around the moon. When approaching the earth, the capsule will first go into orbit around the earth. It will then reenter the atmosphere in the usual manner.

ASTRONAUTICAL GLOSSARY

Abort.—A rocket shot that cannot be carried to its conclusion. An abort may be due to a malfunction preventing take-off, or it may be the intentional destruction of the rocket because of its deviation from its trajectory, thereby endangering life or property. (See *Destruct.*)

Acquisition.—A term meaning that a missile or satellite has been "caught" in a radar beam for tracking. Also, the name given to the radar equipment used in tracking.

Airglow.—A very faint luminescence of the night sky, caused by the release of energy stored by molecules of the upper atmosphere during daylight. It can be detected only with very sensitive photographic plates that are exposed for several hours.

Apogee and aphelion.—Both of these terms mean the farthest point of an orbit. Apogee applies to an orbit around the earth, and aphelion applies to an orbit around the sun. The opposites are *perigee* and *perihelion,* orbital points nearest the primary.

Attitude.—The angle formed by the longitudinal axis of the rocket (or space capsule) with the direction of motion. Normally this angle is zero, as is the case when the rocket travels nose first.

Back-up vehicle.—A rocket identical with one being prepared for launching that is held in reserve in case the planned launch goes awry.

Booster.—One or several powerful rocket units that supply a great amount of thrust at take-off. Normally the burning time of a booster is short, sometimes less than thirty seconds. The bottom stage of a multi-stage rocket is sometimes referred to as the booster, but it is more properly called the first stage.

Chemical fuel.—A propellant that depends upon an oxidizer for combustion. Liquid and solid rocket propellants are chemical fuels.

Circum.—A prefix meaning 'around'; a *circumsolar* orbit is an orbit around the sun; a *circumlunar* orbit is an orbit around the moon; and a *circumpolar* orbit is an orbit around the earth that passes over both poles.

Coriolis effect.—Named after its propounder, G. G. Coriolis (1792–1842). This term describes the influence of the earth's rotation on the trajectory of a long-range missile. In the Northern Hemisphere, missiles traveling parallel to the earth's surface are deflected to the right; and in the Southern Hemisphere, to the left.

Countdown.—The countdown is not just the last ten seconds before take-off counted backward, as commonly believed; it is a complete list of all the things to be done—from placing the rocket on the launching pad to firing. A full countdown usually lasts ten hours; the counting of seconds after lift-off is called the *countup.*

Destruct.—A term coined to signify the premeditated destruction of a rocket in flight by the detonation of packages of high explosives carried for this purpose. The destruct is carried out by the range safety officer when a missile deviates from its course. (See *Abort.*)

Double-base powders. — High explosives, used for the propulsion of military bombardment rockets, that are compounded from nitroglycerine and guncotton, with various stabilizing substances added. The name was given because the two main ingredients are both explosives. Specific double-base powders have such trade names as Cordite and Ballistite.

Escape velocity.—The speed needed to overcome a planet's gravitational attraction so as to escape permanently into space; for the earth, the escape velocity is approximately 7 miles per second, or 25,200 miles per hour.

Galcit fuels.—Solid rocket fuels prepared from asphalt and oil, with potassium perchlorate as the oxidizer. This type of fuel was developed for take-off rockets for military aircraft. The name is a contraction of the Guggenheim Aeronautical Laboratory of the California Institute of Technology, where the fuels were prepared.

Hohmann transfer ellipse.—Orbit, also known as *Hohmann-A* orbit, named after the German engineer Walter Hohmann, who proved in 1925 that the most efficient spaceship trajectory from one planet to another is an ellipse that just touches both planetary orbits.

Impact area.—The area where a long-range missile or space capsule is expected to land on return to earth.

Jettison.—To cast off something no longer needed; for example, the heat shield of a manned capsule after reentry has been accomplished.

Launch pad.—Sometimes referred to only as the pad, it is the platform or other supporting structure from which a rocket vehicle is launched.

Life-support system.—In manned spacecraft, the mechanisms and de-

ASTRONAUTS James Lovell and Elliot See are studying pictures of the lunar surface.

vices needed to provide food, to control the composition of the cabin air and the dehumidifying apparatus, and to maintain the temperature at a comfortable level.

Liquid propellants. — Those chemical fuels and their oxidizers that are stored in the liquid state aboard rockets. Typical liquid fuels and their oxidizers are: kerosene and liquid oxygen (LOX); ethyl alcohol and liquid oxygen; aniline and red fuming nitric acid (RFNA); and unsymmetrical dimethyl hydrazine (often called "dimazine") and RFNA. (See *Solid propellants.*)

Missile. — A device whose sole purpose is to reach a target and cause destruction. Missiles are classified by their means of propulsion: *rocket-propelled missiles* are powered by rocket motors; *air-breathing missiles* are powered by internal-combustion engines or turbines. (See *Rocket.*)

Nose cone. — The front, or a covering over the front, of a rocket or satellite. Its purpose is to withstand the heat caused by friction as the projectile passes through the atmosphere.

Orbit. — The path described by a rocket, satellite, spacecraft, or planet as it travels through space. A *geocentric orbit* is one that has the earth at its approximate center; a *heliocentric orbit* is one that has the sun at its approximate center.

Outer space. — That region, extending outward indefinitely, beyond the upper limit of the earth's atmosphere. Outer space is subdivided into four parts: *cislunar space* is the region enclosed by the orbit of the moon; *interplanetary space* is the region between any two planets of the solar system (the earth is, naturally, one of the planets); *interstellar space* is the region between any two stars (the sun is the star nearest to us); and *intergalactic space* is the region between any two galaxies (the Milky Way is the galaxy of which our sun is a member).

Oxidizer. — A chemical element or compound, either oxygen or containing oxygen, that supports the burning of a fuel or propellant. The term is also used when fluorine is used in lieu of oxygen. (See *Galcit fuels, Liquid propellants,* and *Solid propellants.*)

Parking orbit. — A geocentric orbit into which the upper stages of a rocket and its payload (usually a planetary probe) may be placed. The payload may then be launched at the proper moment, by radio command from the ground, from this orbit.

Payload. — The useful cargo, such as a manned capsule, planetary probe, or satellite, carried by a launch vehicle.

Perigee and perihelion. — See *Apogee and aphelion.*

Permanent orbit. — A satellite is in a permanent orbit around the earth when every point of its orbit is so far from the earth that no atmospheric resistance is encountered anywhere along the orbit. Such a satellite will never reenter the atmosphere.

Perturbation. — A minor change in orbit caused by a force other than the sun's gravitational attraction, usually the gravitational influence of another planet. Very light and large satellites, such as Echo, are also perturbed by the sun's radiation pressure.

Primary. — The body that is being orbited by another, smaller body. The primary of a satellite is the planet of which it is a satellite; the primary of a planet is the sun.

Retro-rocket. — Generally, a rocket firing in the direction of movement to reduce the velocity, usually to slow down an object in orbit so it will reenter the earth's atmosphere.

Rocket. — Any vehicle that uses internally stored oxygen (or other oxidizer) instead of atmospheric oxygen for the combustion of its fuel. More specifically, in astronautics, the launch vehicle for a manned capsule, planetary probe, or satellite. (See *Missile.*)

Satellite. — Any body, natural or arti-

ficial, which is in orbit around a planet. The word is derived from the Greek *satellos,* meaning 'attendant.'

Scrub. — Postponement of a rocket shot because of a malfunction detected during the countdown.

Solid propellants. — Those chemical fuels and their oxidizers that are stored in the solid state aboard rockets. Solid propellants combine a synthetic rubber as the fuel, oxidizers, such as ammonium perchlorate, and small amounts of powdered metals, such as aluminum. (See *Liquid propellants.*)

Sustainer engine. — In a rocket with a booster, the sustainer is the rocket engine that keeps burning, to sustain thrust and acceleration, after the booster has ceased to function.

Ullage rockets. — Small rockets, usually solid-fuel units, needed for the operation of large liquid-fuel units in space. After a liquid-fuel rocket has ceased burning, the fuel remaining in the tanks, being weightless, will distribute itself at random inside the tank. The purpose of the ullage rockets is to provide a short push to "shake down" the fuel into the proper place so that the liquid-fuel motors can be started again.

Umbilical cord. — An external cable attached to the rocket, through which electric current is carried to the devices in the rocket; this saves the batteries in the rocket until they are required. The umbilical cord drops off just before lift-off.

Vernier rockets. — Small rockets used to adjust the velocity of a large rocket — for example, an intercontinental missile — to the precise value needed for the particular mission.

Zero G. — Also called *weightlessness* or *free fall.* Weightlessness occurs when a body freely follows the pull of gravity without resisting it, as is the case when a satellite is in orbit.

—Willy Ley

BIBLIOGRAPHY

BERGAUST, ERIK. *The Next 50 Years in Space.* The Macmillan Co., 1964.

CHESTER, MICHAEL. *Rockets and Space Craft of the World.* W. W. Norton & Co., Inc., 1964.

CLARKE, ARTHUR C. *Interplanetary Flight.* Harper & Bros., 1960.

DE LEEUW, HENDRIK. *From Flying Horse to Man in the Moon.* St. Martin's Press, Inc., 1963.

DIAMOND, EDWIN. *The Rise and Fall of the Space Age.* Doubleday and Co., Inc., 1964.

LEVITT, ISRAEL M. and COLE, D. M. *Exploring the Secrets of Space.* Prentice-Hall, Inc., 1963.

LEY, WILLY. *Our Work in Space.* The Macmillan Co., 1963.

LEY, WILLY. *Rockets, Missiles, and Space Travel* (rev. ed.). The Viking Press, Inc., 1957.

THOMAS, SHIRLEY. *Men of Space.* Chilton Co., 1960.

VAN ALLEN, JAMES A. (ed.). *Scientific Uses of Earth Satellites.* The University of Michigan Press, 1956.

WEISER, WILLIAM J. *Space Guidebook.* Coward-McCann, Inc., 1960.

NASA

MANNED ORBITING RESEARCH LABORATORY (MORL) is presently still in the research stage. MORL, with three Gemini spacecraft attached, would be capable of year-long missions.

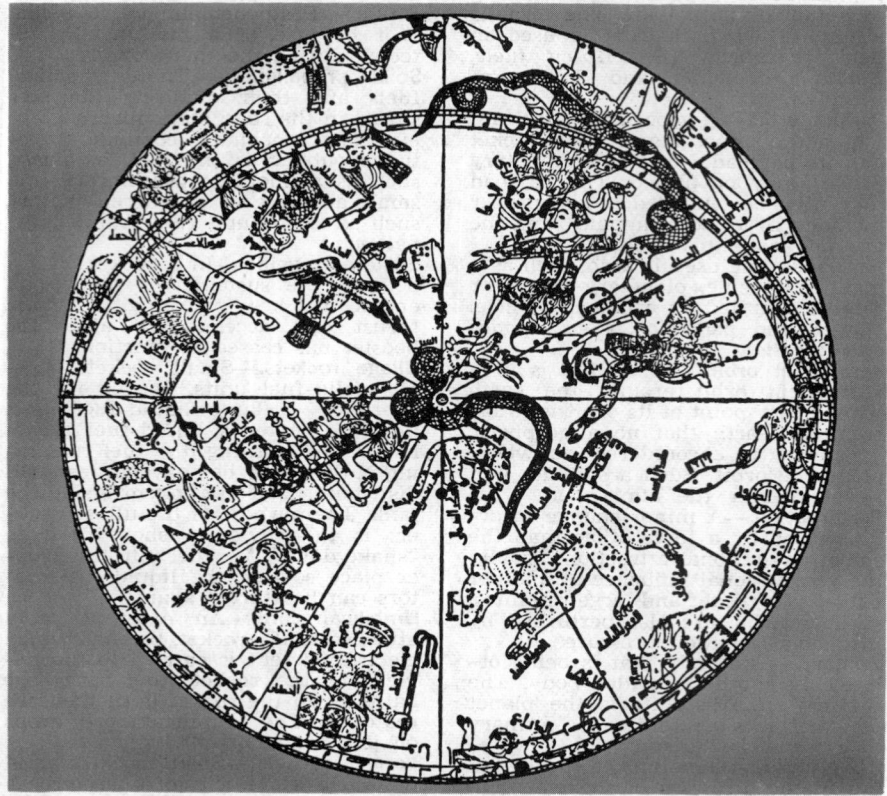

ANCIENT ARABIC celestial sphere showing the constellations of the Northern Hemisphere.

Astronomy is the oldest science. Its name is derived from Greek roots: *astro,* meaning 'star,' and *nomos,* meaning 'law.' Actually, astronomy is the study of all heavenly bodies, their positions, distances, motions, dimensions, composition, and physical condition—our own galaxy, the Milky Way, as well as all other galaxies.

Solar System.—The *solar system* is the total system of the sun. Our solar system is made up of nine principal planets, thirty-one known natural satellites or moons that circle some of the planets, thousands of tiny planetoids or asteroids, millions of comets, innumerable meteoroids, and vast quantities of interplanetary dust and gas. The magnetic and radiation fields around the sun and the planets are also important parts of the system.

The volume of space our solar system occupies can be visualized as a sphere more than ten billion miles across, with the sun at its center. Only minor parts of the system extend to the extreme borders of this sphere. The planets are located relatively close to the sun; they lie in a plane, and all revolve around the sun in the same direction.

■ **SOLAR GRAVITY.**—All material particles in the solar system, from the giant planet Jupiter to those no bigger than a grain of sand, pursue individual *orbits,* or paths around the sun. Our moon revolves around Earth, but it also revolves with Earth around

the sun. Viewed from Earth, the moon's orbit appears as a near circle. Viewed from the sun, the path of the moon would appear much like Earth's but with "wiggles" in it.

Material particles orbit the sun because of the gravitational pull that the sun's large mass exerts over them. This force is continuous and would, theoretically, pull all members of the solar system into the sun if they themselves were not moving. A planet can be visualized as a stone tied to a string; the sun, as a boy swinging the stone in a circle over his head. The pull of the string on the stone keeps the stone from flying off its orbit. If the stone were not moving, however, the same amount of pull would quickly bring the stone to the boy in the same way that a planet, if not moving, would be pulled into the sun.

■ **DISTRIBUTION OF MATTER.**—Two striking features of the solar system that are often overlooked are its isolation in space and its relative emptiness. The system is a near vacuum separated by immense distances from other near vacuums. The sun possesses over 99 per cent of all matter in our solar system. If the remaining 1 per cent were spread evenly over the volume of space represented by the sun's sphere of influence, there would still exist a vacuum far better than can be produced in a laboratory.

■ **DISTANCE RELATIONSHIPS.**—Most matter outside the sun is concentrated in nine relatively dense pellets, the

planets. Relationships in the planetary system can be illustrated as follows. In a 250-foot square representing the space occupied by the solar system, the sun would be represented by a sphere ⅓ inch in diameter at the center of the field. The planets would appear as nine tiny spheres, the largest of which would be ⅟₈₀ inch in diameter; they would be situated in random directions about the sun at distances of approximately 1, 2, 3, 4½, 15, 30, 60, 90, and 120 feet. Earth would be represented by a ¾₁₀₀₀-inch sphere about 3 feet from the sun; Pluto, by a sphere approximately the same size as Earth, but nearly 120 feet away. The star closest to the sun would be a sphere similar in size to the sun placed in another field about 150 miles away. This illustration could be expanded to include planetary spheres surrounding the other star to represent its planetary system, but their existence cannot be definitely proved because they cannot be seen. There are, however, many theoretical reasons supporting belief in the existence of other solar systems.

Dynamics of the Solar System.—In the model described above, the relative distances of the planets from the sun (1, 2, 3, 4½, 15, 30, 60, 90, 120 feet) suggests a regular mathematical series. The arrangement seems to be far too orderly to have happened purely by chance.

■ **BODE'S LAW.**—This orderliness of division was noted years ago; and an empirical relation, known as *Bode's law,* was formulated by Johann Elert Bode (1747–1826). Using this law, it is possible to make a rough estimate of the distances from all known planets (except Neptune) to the sun in terms of Earth's distance from the sun, or *astronomical units* (*A.U.*). (Earth is approximately 93 million miles from the sun; therefore, one astronomical unit is equivalent to 93 million miles.)

The law works in this manner: Set down a series of 4's. Add the number 3 to the second 4; then 6 to the third; 12 to the fourth, and so on, doubling the number added each time. Then divide the sums by 10 to obtain the approximate distance from each planet (except Neptune) to the sun in astronomical units. The accompanying chart of Bode's law clearly illustrates this method.

Here Bode's law holds quite well out to Uranus. If Neptune did not exist, the law would also give the distance from the sun to Pluto fairly well. The 38.8 A.U. distance the law predicts for Neptune is close to Pluto's actual 39.5 A.U. distance.

No theoretical basis for Bode's law has ever been found. It does not follow, as do other relationships, from either the laws of motion or the law of gravitation.

In 1781, when the planet Uranus was discovered in an orbit predicted by Bode's law, a great search was begun for a "missing planet" at 2.8 A.U., between the orbits of Mars and

Bode's Law

Mercury	Venus	Earth	Mars	Asteroids	Jupiter	Saturn	Uranus	Neptune	Pluto
4	4	4	4	4	4	4	4	4	4
+0	+3	+6	+12	+24	+48	+96	+192	+384	+768
4	7	10	16	28	52	100	196	388	772
divided by 10 =									
.4	.7	1.0	1.6	2.8	5.2	10.0	19.6	38.8	77.2
actual distances in astronomical units (A.U.) =									
.4	.7	1.0	1.5	2.8	5.2	9.5	19.2	30.0	39.5

Jupiter. This search resulted in the discovery of not one, but hundreds of tiny planets, or *asteroids,* orbiting in the region. It is believed that these asteroids are the remnants of one or more larger bodies that originally orbited in the region.

■KEPLER'S LAWS.—Although no theoretical explanation appears to exist for Bode's law, there is a physical explanation for the exact relation between the distances and periods of planets discovered by Johannes Kepler (1571–1630) and later elaborated upon by Isaac Newton (1642–1727). The *period* of a planet is the time it takes to make one complete *revolution* around the sun. (*Rotation,* on the other hand, describes the turning of a planet on its axis. One complete revolution of the earth takes approximately 365 days; one rotation, one day.) The accompanying chart lists distance from the sun, diameter, periods, mass, density, and number of satellites of each planet.

Kepler showed that the cube of a planet's distance from the sun in astronomical units is equal to the square of that planet's period ($D^3 = P^2$). For example, Mars is 1.52369 A.U.'s from the sun. This figure cubed is 3.5374. The square root of 3.5374 is 1.8808, which is exactly the period of Mars. Therefore, when either a planet's distance from the sun or its period is known, the other quantity can be found by use of this formula. This law applies not only to the planets, but also to each and every member of the solar system orbiting the sun, even the tiny meteoroids. Since, however, the minor members of the system often travel in highly elliptical orbits, their average distance from the sun must be computed before applying Kepler's law to determine the period. The law can also be used to describe the distance and period relationship of a satellite to its parent, or *primary.*

This distance and period relationship was actually the last of three laws discovered by Kepler, known collectively as *Kepler's three laws of planetary motion.* The first law describes the type, or "shape," orbit that every member of the solar system follows—a curve that looks like an elongated circle, called an *ellipse.* The second law describes the rate at which a planet moves on its elliptical path. In order, the three laws are:

1. The orbit of every planet is an ellipse, with the sun at one focus.

2. The *radius vector* (line connecting the sun and planet) sweeps over equal areas in equal times.

3. The cubes of the mean distances of the planets from the sun are proportional to the squares of their sidereal periods.

■CELESTIAL MECHANICS.—More than a half-century after Kepler discovered his descriptive laws, Isaac Newton proved them to be a natural consequence of the universal law of gravitation and of the laws of motion of material objects.

The law of gravity states:

$$F \backsim \frac{m_1 m_2}{d^2}$$

In other words, every material particle (m_1) attracts any other material particle (m_2) with a force (F) that is proportional ($\backsim$) to the product of the masses ($m_1 m_2$) divided by the square of the distance between them (d^2).

The law of motion of material objects states:

$$F = ma$$

The force (F) necessary to impart a certain acceleration (a) to a mass (m) is the product of mass and acceleration (ma).

It has been stated that as the planets move about the sun, they must be constantly accelerated, or else they would fly off into space. The force producing this acceleration is gravity. The combination of the two equations thus forms the basis for the complex subject of celestial mechanics. *Celestial mechanics* proves

that, under the force of gravity, the planets move in the way described by Kepler's laws—and in no other.

In addition to the sun's gravitational force, every member of the solar system pulls on every other member to varying degrees. Because of this, calculating the exact orbit of the lighter and more easily influenced members, such as comets, is an exacting task. If, for instance, a comet passes fairly close to the giant planet Jupiter, whose gravitational pull can rival the sun's at close range, the comet's orbit will change.

Celestial mechanics also makes possible the precision with which the occurrence of eclipses of the sun and moon can be predicted many years in advance, and is now employed in calculating the orbits of artificial satellites and rockets. In this respect there is no difference between a natural celestial object and one placed in space by man; they act the same.

The solar system, looked at as a sort of clockwork or mechanical device, can be described as a star (the sun) around which the planets course with mathematical precision, and a great host of minor bodies course in a much less regular fashion.

Physical Nature of the Solar System.— Members of the solar system form a family of individuals with widely different physical characteristics—so different, in fact, that one well might wonder whether they really do belong to one physical family. They differ not only in size, but also in chemical composition and density. In spite of these disparities, they do appear to have had a common origin. The variations in size, composition, and density are probably attributable to the manner in which the planets condensed out of the original solar *nebula* (cloud). Although it is not known exactly how the solar system originated, it is commonly held that there was once an extensive gas and dust nebula from which our system evolved. Such clouds have been detected in other regions of space; and it is thought that they may develop into other solar systems, as ours probably did billions of years ago.

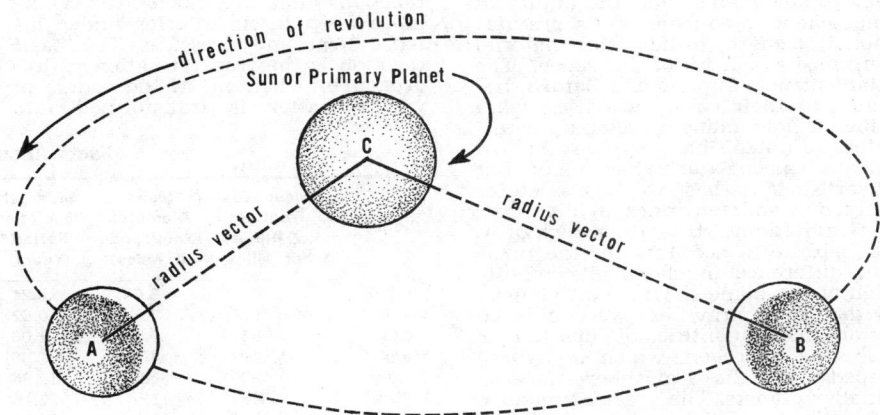

KEPLER'S SECOND LAW states that the radius vector between a body and its primary will pass through equal areas in equal times. Thus, the area of triangle *ABC* is equal to the area formed when the body passes between any other points in its orbit in the same time.

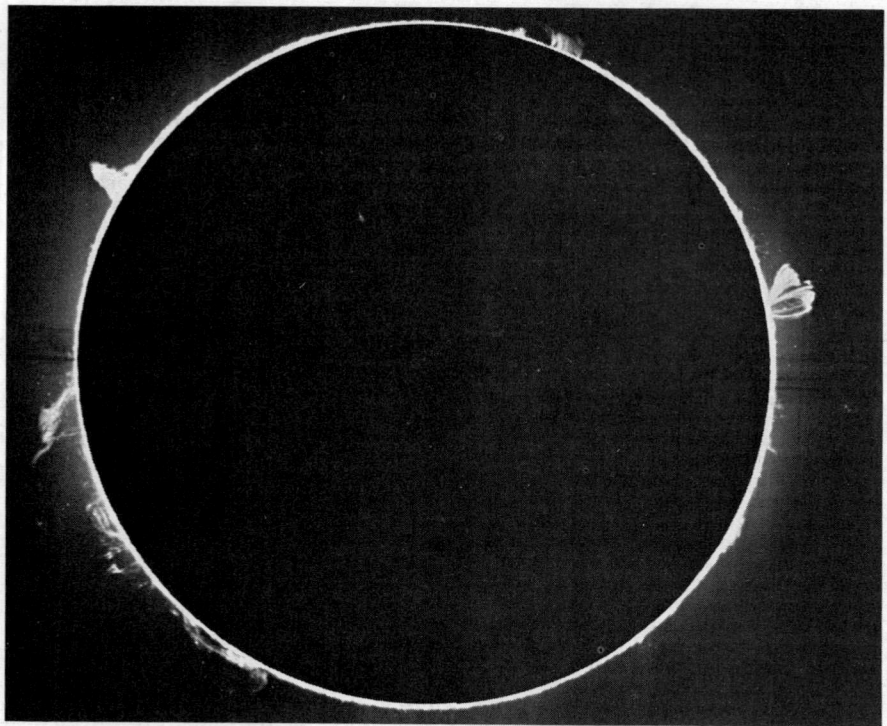

MOUNT WILSON AND PALOMAR OBSERVATORIES

SOLAR PROMINENCES flare out from the sun's surface thousands of miles into space.

radiant energy, ultimately resulting in the sunlight we see and the radiated heat we feel.

The sun is the "powerhouse" of the solar system. Its mighty gravitational power holds the planets on their courses; its radiation warms the solar system; its visible light, reflected from the surfaces and atmospheres of the planets, makes them visible to us. (No planet shines by its own light—only by reflected sunlight.) The sun is the source of energy that originally made life on Earth possible, and the one that constantly sustains it. Our power sources (coal, oil, and the like), food, and even weather conditions can be directly attributed to the sun. We, too, are a form of "canned solar energy."

■**MERCURY.**—Mercury is the planet closest to the sun. It is also the smallest, the hottest, and the fastest-moving of the planets. One-third larger than Earth's moon, but smaller than the two largest moons of Jupiter, Mercury is approximately 3,000 miles in diameter. Its 88-day period of rotation is the same as its period of revolution. Hence, one side of the planet always faces the sun, and the other side always faces away from the sun. The temperature of the sunward side is hot enough to melt lead, while the dark side, heated only by the distant stars, must be close to absolute zero (−459.6° F.). Because of its small size, Mercury has no atmosphere and no satellites. It is a dead planet.

■**VENUS.**—Venus is about 200 miles smaller in diameter than Earth and almost as massive. Because of this similarity in size, Earth and Venus are often considered "twin planets." Like Earth, Venus holds an appreciable atmosphere; but unlike Earth's atmosphere, which is transparent, the atmosphere of Venus is clouded and opaque. Radio waves, however, can "see" through the cloud layer. Signals transmitted from Earth and collected by radio telescopes on Earth and, most recently, by the Mariner spacecraft, indicate the surface temperature of Venus to be about 700° F.

The atmosphere of Venus is rich in carbon dioxide and lacking in free oxygen; only small traces of water vapor have been detected. The surface of the planet therefore must be baked dry, and it may be this condition that causes the Cytherean cloud layer. Continuous "dust storms" ranging over the hot, dry surface may be

The original nebula (see *Origin of the Solar System*) from which our system evolved probably contained much more material than the combined mass of all members of the present solar system. It is suspected that as the central portion condensed and became hot, much of the original nebula literally evaporated into space. The central portion eventually became the sun, and whirlpools of celestial material relatively close to the developing sun formed the planets. Similarly, smaller whirlpools of material in the immediate neighborhood of the planets became satellites or moons. Satellite formation was, therefore, determined by two factors: the existence of whirlpools of celestial material in the immediate area of the developing planet; and the ability of the planet, by virtue of its gravitational strength, to hold this material within its sphere of influence. The giant planets Jupiter and Saturn, because of their strong gravities, were able to hold many developing satellites. Jupiter has twelve known moons, and Saturn has nine; but dwarfish Mars has two tiny satellites only five and ten miles in diameter.

Gravitational strength, or lack of it, probably also accounts for the present difference in chemical composition of the planets. The giant planets, with strong gravities, were able to retain large quantities of such lighter gases as hydrogen, which easily escaped from the atmospheres of the smaller planets. The great abundance of hydrogen in the atmospheres of the giants allowed the formation of many hydrogen compounds not found in the atmospheres of the smaller planets. Location is another factor.

Distance from the sun would determine the amount of light and heat received from the sun and would, in time, affect chemical evolution.

The original mass of a planet, therefore, appears to account for the present differences in chemical make-up of the planets rather than any basic differences in the materials from which they had been formed.

Major Members of the Solar System

■**THE SUN.**—Our central star—the sun —is a glowing sphere of gas about 864,000 miles in diameter with a mass of 332,000 Earths. Its temperature varies from a comparatively cool 10,000° F. at the surface to about 28,000,000° F. near the center.

The sun shines because of nuclear reactions that are constantly taking place deep in its interior under intense heat and pressure. The basic reaction is the transformation of hydrogen into helium, in the course of which matter is transformed into

Facts About the Planets

Planet	Mean Dist. from Sun (Millions of Miles)	Mean Diameter (Thousands of Miles)	Sidereal Revolution Period (Years)	Axial Rotation Period* (At Equator)	Mass (Earth = 1)	Density (Water = 1)	Natural Satellites
Mercury	36	3.0	0.24	88d	0.05	5.2	0
Venus	67	7.6	0.62	10d–30d	0.82	5.1	0
Earth	93	7.9	1.00	23h 56m	1.00	5.5	1
Mars	142	4.1	1.88	24h 37m	0.11	4.0	2
Jupiter	483	86.8	11.86	9h 50m	318.20	1.3	12
Saturn	886	71.5	29.46	10h 14m	95.20	0.7	9
Uranus	1,783	29.4	84.02	10h 49m	14.60	1.6	5
Neptune	2,794	27.0	164.78	15h 48m	17.20	2.2	2
Pluto	3,670	3.6	248.42	6d 9h	0.91	4.0?	0

*Figures given represent days (d), hours (h), and minutes (m).

largely responsible for the clouds that keep us from seeing the surface. Unlike Earth, Venus has no satellites.

■EARTH.—If Earth could be seen from Venus, it might be described as follows: "Earth is a blue-green planet, similar in size to Venus, or about 8,000 miles in diameter. It is noted for its great oceans of water and for its polar ice caps, which remain relatively stable throughout its seasons. Its atmosphere contains oxygen. Earth has one moon, about one-fourth its own size."

■MARS.—With about one-half the diameter and one-tenth the mass of Earth, Mars has a thin, transparent atmosphere that allows direct observation of its surface. The distance separating Mars and Earth ranges from 35 million to 245 million miles. When the small planet is closest, it is usually in a good position for viewing. It is our own atmosphere that hinders a truly clear view of Mars.

It was once considered a strong possibility that life as we know it—even a higher form of life—existed on Mars. This idea was prompted by the observation of markings on the surface of Mars that change with the Martian seasons. Certain areas that are bluish or greenish during the Martian spring turn yellowish and then grayish during the Martian summer and autumn. This led to the belief that at least simple botanical forms that grow here on Earth also grow on Mars. Then some astronomers claimed to have observed a series of fine markings, which they called "canals," on the surface of Mars. Hypothesizing that such a network of canals implied intelligent construction, an impressive case was made for the existence of intelligent life on the planet.

Other scientific evidence, however, is overwhelmingly opposed to this idea. The very rare atmosphere, the low temperature, and the lack of appreciable water vapor—along with the absence of oxygen—all argue against the possibility of any life as we know it in the Martian environment (except perhaps lichens or other simple botanical forms).

Mars rotates completely once every 24 hours 37 minutes, and makes one complete circuit around the sun in 687 days. It has two tiny satellites, about five and ten miles in diameter.

■JUPITER.—The diameter of the planet Jupiter is eleven times that of Earth; its mass, equal to 318 Earths. It is a giant planet, larger and heavier than all the other planets combined. Jupiter has a strong surface gravity (about three times that of Earth), enabling it to hold a deep atmosphere. Because of this many-hundred-mile-deep layer, the solid surface of Jupiter is visually obscured; we see only the outer atmosphere. Jupiter is also the fastest-rotating of the planets; despite its size, it spins very rapidly, making one complete rotation in just under ten hours. It takes Jupiter twelve years to make one complete revolution around the sun.

Jupiter also has the most satellites. The twelve moons that circle the giant create a veritable miniature solar system. Four of these moons are giants—two of them larger than Earth's. These four—Io, Europa, Ganymede, Callesto—were discovered by Galileo in 1610 with the help of a new invention, the telescope.

■SATURN.—The planet Saturn is second only to Jupiter in size, mass, speed of rotation, and number of satellites. Like Jupiter, it possesses an extensive atmosphere of hydrogen compounds, making it impossible for us to see its solid surface with our present astronomical instruments.

Saturn has nine moons, but its most outstanding feature is its system of rings. These three thin concentric rings of tiny celestial particles that encircle the planet are probably the remnants of a crushed moon. What leads to this belief is that the rings lie within a gravitational danger zone known as *Roche's limit,* within which the gravitational grip of the planet is great enough theoretically to crumble a large object. It is thought that a satellite came within the danger zone, was crushed by Saturn's force of gravity, and its remnants circle the planet, forming these rings.

■URANUS AND NEPTUNE.—Just as Earth and Venus are considered the "dwarf twins," the planets Uranus and Neptune are the "giant twins." Only Jupiter and Saturn exceed the two in diameter and mass.

Uranus was the first planet discovered by means of a telescope. Neptune was the first planet discovered as the result of an orbital prediction. Uranus has five satellites; Neptune, two. The "giant twins" are so distant from the heat of the sun that many chemical compounds existing as gases on Earth are frozen solids.

■PLUTO.—The tiny planet Pluto is the most remote and was the last to be discovered (1930). It is out so far in space, in fact, that the sun, viewed from Pluto's surface, would appear as only a very bright star. With a probable diameter of 3,600 miles, Pluto is only slightly larger than Mercury, the smallest and nearest planet to the sun. Even more than Uranus and Neptune, its surface is probably frozen solid and only dimly lit by the distant sun. It has no known satellites. Pluto also has the longest period of revolution of all nine planets—248 years.

The Minor Members

■ASTEROIDS.—Asteroids are small solid bodies found mainly between the orbits of Mars and Jupiter. They are too small to be seen without a telescope, and are thought to be remnants of a collision of larger objects that once orbited in the region they now occupy. Their discovery was the result of a search begun for a "missing planet" predicted by Bode's law (see pages 1308 and 1309).

Since the first asteroid, Ceres, was discovered in 1801, the orbits of more than 1,500 have been computed; many more are known to exist. Some meteorites found on Earth are believed to be closely related to the asteroids.

■COMETS.—Beyond the orbit of Pluto, far out in the distant reaches of the solar system, is believed to be the domain of the *comets*—loose configurations of ice and celestial dust formed from scattered material left at the outer edges of the original solar nebula. In this hinterland of the solar system, the formation of large bodies is impossible. Only loose aggregates of material, held together by their own gravities, can exist.

It is believed that the feeble gravitational forces exerted by the distant stars and planets will occasionally alter a comet's orbit, in effect withdrawing it from the distant storehouse and sending it toward the sun on a highly elliptical orbit. (The periods of comets' revolutions vary widely and can range from three years to millions of years.) As the comet approaches the sun, the icy particles of which it is composed are warmed, causing them to dissociate and move away from the main body, thereby forming the luminous and

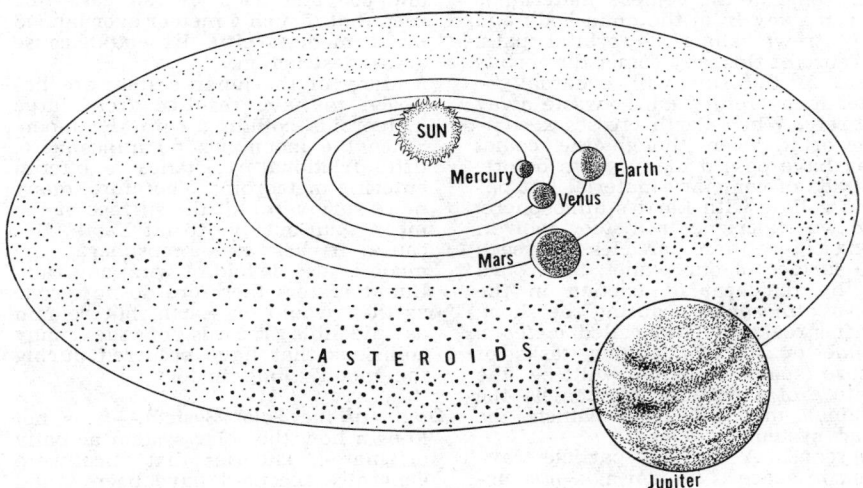

ASTEROID BELT, which is filled with small, solid chunks of rock—almost all of which are too small to be seen without the aid of a telescope—lies between the orbits of Mars and Jupiter. The asteroids, or planetoids, are believed to be the remains of large bodies that once traveled around the sun but were subsequently destroyed in a cosmic disaster.

ARIZONA METEOR CRATER, near Winslow, is about 4,000 feet wide and 600 feet deep.

extensive tail that is regarded as an identifying feature. (The tail shines partly by directly reflected sunlight and partly by reradiated sunlight absorbed by gases in the comet's atmosphere.)

Light also exerts pressure, much too slight to affect more substantial celestial bodies, but strong enough to affect the microscopic particles that make up a comet's tail. This, plus the additional driving force provided by a solar ring of charged particles, explains why comet tails generally point away from the sun. Even when a comet is on its outward journey into space, the tail precedes the comet body—just as smoke from a ship precedes the ship when a strong tail wind is blowing.

With each new approach to the sun, some of the comet's material is driven away from the main body and left strewn along its orbital path. Because of this, any comet that orbits close to the sun will eventually—after many return trips—waste away entirely. When Earth crosses a comet's orbit, even though the comet may have passed many years before, the bits of cometary material left behind collide with Earth's atmosphere, and we experience a meteor shower. Long before these particles can reach the surface of our planet, they burn up by the heat of friction in the upper atmosphere, causing the short, swift streaks of light called *meteors.*

One of the challenging tasks of future space research will be the capture of a portion of a comet—the original material from which the solar system evolved.

■**METEORS.**—A meteoric particle traveling in space is known as a *meteoroid.* The same particle, after it enters Earth's atmosphere and is made luminous by friction with the upper air, is called a *meteor.* Any part of the meteor that reaches Earth's surface is known as a *meteorite.*

Meteors arising from a collision of Earth with the cometary debris are neither large enough nor dense enough to withstand the rough ride through Earth's atmosphere. These exceedingly fragile particles are, therefore, destroyed by friction long before reaching Earth's surface.

The very bright meteors that do sometimes penetrate the atmosphere and survive to hit Earth have a different origin. They are really tiny asteroids composed largely of iron, nickel, combinations of iron and nickel, or stone, and are capable of withstanding the enormous heat of entry. The great pit in Arizona, known as the Arizona Meteor Crater, is the result of just such a prehistoric collision of Earth and a small asteroid. The crater is about 4,000 feet across and 600 feet deep. It can easily be seen that if such a meteor ever landed on a modern city, it would cause great destruction.

Many of the lunar craters are believed to have resulted from large meteoroids colliding with the moon. Since the moon has no atmosphere, little frictional resistance is offered entering meteoroids. Therefore, many more survive to hit the surface of the moon than survive to hit Earth. Because it has no atmosphere, the moon is also devoid of wind and rain. Lunar craters therefore do not erode as they would on Earth, but remain as indelible records of the many collisions that have occurred during the moon's long history.

Origin of the Solar System.—It is not known how the solar system actually originated. Theories that once were generally accepted have been found to possess fatal faults.

Two main divisions of knowledge are presently being applied to the problem of origin. The first is a knowledge of the crucial properties of the solar system, explained in

terms of physical processes; the second, a knowledge of the physics of gases, magnetic fields, and gravitational dynamics. All factors that constitute these two divisions of knowledge must be considered before a coherent theory, explaining how they originated, can be formulated. In short, it is first necessary to know exactly what is to be explained before an adequate theory can be deduced; *what is* must be clearly described before we can attempt to explain *what was.*

■**PROPERTIES OF THE SOLAR SYSTEM.**—The outstanding properties of the solar system as it exists today are:

1. The system is isolated in space.

2. The sun possesses the preponderant mass of the total system (more than 99 per cent).

3. The planets possess the preponderant angular momentum of the system. (The sun rotates slowly in relation to the speed at which the planets rotate.)

4. There are two distinct "solar families" in the system. The first family is made up of the solid, spherical planets that revolve about the sun in circular orbits essentially in one plane, rotating on their axes. The second family is made up of the smaller objects—such as comets and meteoroids—that often are of low density, generally with elongated orbits and a great variety of inclination to the planets' central plane.

5. There are satellite systems around some of the planets, with almost all satellites revolving around their primaries in the same direction as the primaries rotate on their axes.

6. Earth's moon is out of proportion to its primary when compared with other satellites in the solar system, which are small compared with their primaries.

7. Small, dense planets are closest to the sun (Mercury, Venus, Earth, Mars) and farthest from the sun (Pluto), with large, massive planets at intermediate distances. The asteroids occupy the Bode gap between one of the smallest planets (Mars) and the largest planet (Jupiter).

These major properties of the solar system must be considered in relation to the estimated age of the sun (six billion years) and the planets (four and one-half billion years).

■**PAST THEORIES.**—Incomplete consideration of these outstanding properties of the solar system caused some of the early theories to prove inadequate. One of the earliest theories, the *nebular hypothesis,* proposed by Immanuel Kant (1724–1804) and Pierre Simon Laplace (1749–1827), stated that the sun condensed from a primordial gas cloud and that as it shrank in size, it spun faster and faster, throwing off rings of material from its equatorial regions; these rings condensed into the planets. This hypothesis is untenable for two reasons. First, such rings would disperse rather than condense; second, the sun would still be spinning very rapidly, but this is not true.

The later *close-encounter theories* were based on the proposition that the sun once had a close encounter with another star. One explanation following from this was that the encounter caused huge tidal effects on the surface of the sun; these effects pulled long filaments of material from it, and the material later condensed to form the planets.

Another theory based on the close-encounter idea was that the encounter caused quantities of solar material to be ejected, and that this material quickly cooled to form small, solid *planetesimals* that later grew into the planets through slow accretion.

These close-encounter theories are inadequate because they cannot account for the great angular momentum, or "quantity of motion," of the planets. For example, a passing star could not exert a pull strong enough to bring the mass of Uranus and Neptune out to their present distances from the sun and also, at the same time, impart to them the orbital angular momentum they now possess.

■ **PRESENT THEORIES.**—Most current explanations of the origin of the solar system revert to the original nebular hypothesis, but with several very important differences.

One of these theories postulates a large and relatively massive nebula containing much more material than now constitutes the solar system. This nebula is assumed to have possessed a highly turbulent motion, as has been observed in other nebulae in space. As the major portion condensed, it formed a slowly rotating but still dark sun; turbulent eddies in the outer nebula became interlocked gravitationally to form the relatively massive nuclei of the present planets. Lesser eddies around the larger nuclei became the nuclei of the satellites. A preferential direction of revolution and rotation was soon established by the mutual cancellation of nonadditive motions. As the primeval sun condensed, it became hot, heating the embryonic planetary system and evaporating and driving off into space much of the original material of the nebula. New planets were thus freed of their cocoon of primordial material.

Although such a theory overcomes the inadequacies of previous theories, it almost entirely lacks the mathematical precision that is required of a physical explanation. This, however, may be impossible to accomplish because what is being asked is, in effect, a mathematically precise account of an event that occurred billions of years ago under physical conditions that may have been markedly different from those of today.

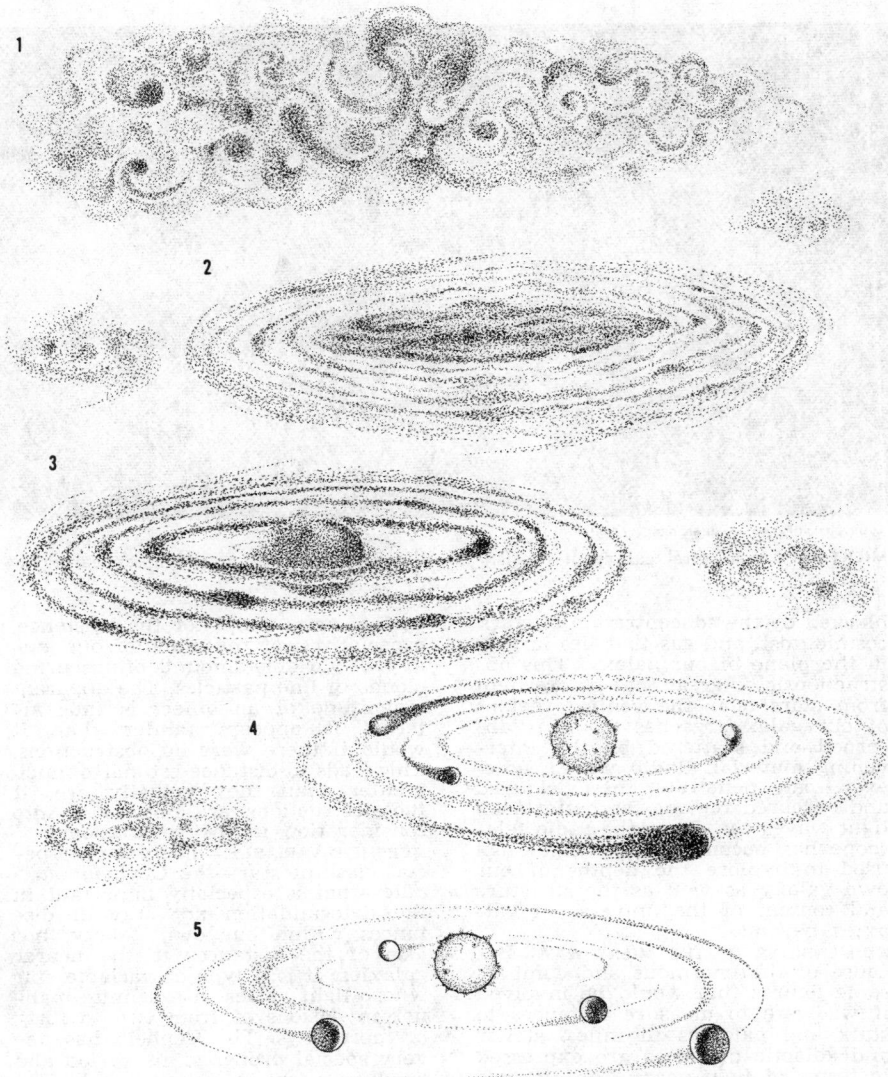

FORMATION OF THE SOLAR SYSTEM theoretically took place when a nebula (1) contracted and began to rotate (2). The major portion of the nebula condensed to form the sun (3), while lesser eddies formed the planets (4), eventually cooling to form the solar system (5).

The Universe of Galaxies.—The sun is but one of a hundred billion stars that make up an isolated system of stars in space. This system is one among millions of other star systems scattered throughout the universe. Each of these huge systems of stars is called a *galaxy*.

■ **MILKY WAY.**—The galaxy to which Earth belongs is called the *Milky Way*. The name describes what we see when we look along the circumference of the galaxy's distant rim. The millions of stars along our line of sight converge, appearing as a milky-white haze.

Our galaxy is a highly flattened, rotating, spiral aggregate of stars, dust, and gas. It has a rim because, unlike some galaxies that are roughly spherical or ellipsoidal in shape, the Milky Way belongs to that large group of galaxies shaped like a watch. Our star—the sun—is located far from the galactic center, near one of the spiral arms (see illustration). Consequently, if we look outward—perpendicular to the page—we see relatively few stars, with many open spaces through which we can peer out toward the realm of the myriad other galaxies. If, however, we look along the plane of the galaxy—along the page—our view of the universe outside our own galaxy is completely

Facts About the Galaxies

Galaxy	Apparent Magnitude	Distance (Millions of Light Years)	Absolute Magnitude
Andromeda (M 31)	+4.3	2.5	—20
M 101	+8.2	12	—20
M 81	+7.9	6.8	—19
Virgo Cluster	...	30	...
Coma Cluster	...	150	...
Hercules Cluster	...	300	...
Bootes Cluster	...	700	...
Hydra Cluster	...	1,100	...

MOUNT WILSON AND PALOMAR OBSERVATORIES

MILKY WAY is a spiral galaxy. It consists of billions of stars, one of which, appearing toward the outer rim of this galaxy, is our sun.

blocked by the concentration of stars, cosmic dust, and gas that lies largely in the plane of our galaxy. This obstruction is so great that before light from stars near the central regions of our galaxy reaches us, it is absorbed and scattered by the intervening material. Radio waves, however, can penetrate these clouded and obscured regions far better than light waves can. Thus the radio telescope has become the principal tool used to explore the depths of our own galaxy as well as the structure and content of the universe of galaxies beyond.

■DIMENSIONS OF THE MILKY WAY.—

Because of the enormous and cumbersome figures that would be involved if we were to measure distances to stars and galaxies in miles, stellar and galactic distances are expressed in terms of *light-years*—the distance light travels in one year. Since light travels at 186,000 miles per second, one light-year is equivalent to about six trillion miles.

Although the term "Milky Way" describes the crowded visible part of our galaxy, it applies to the galaxy as a whole. The length of the Milky Way is nearly 100,000 light-years. Its thickness is variable and difficult to measure accurately. It will suffice to say the galaxy is about five to six times longer than it is thick.

Virtually the only way of estimating distances in the galaxy is by noting the difference between apparent and absolute magnitudes of its various members. The *apparent magnitude* is how bright the member appears to be; the *absolute magnitude* is how bright the member would appear to be from a standard distance of ten *parsecs,* or 32.6 light-years. The absolute magnitudes are assumed from previous knowledge, which generally was determined for similar objects much closer to the sun. Thus the true brightness of blue, giant stars may be regarded as known, no matter where in the galaxy they are found. This is also true of other standard objects. This method of measurement would be nearly

perfect were it not for the existence, especially near the plane of our galaxy, of variable amounts of obscuring clouds of fine particles. The apparent magnitude of an object is thus altered; it appears fainter than it would if there were no obstructions. This leads to distance estimates much greater than they actually are, if the obstructions are not taken into consideration in the calculations.

■CEPHEID VARIABLE.—

There is one special class of star—*the Cepheid variable*—that is especially important in the determination not only of distances within our own galaxy, but also of the distances to the nearer galaxies. It is a type of variable star whose light varies in a definite manner in periods of from two to forty or more days. The Cepheid has one very special property: its period and brightness are closely related. The longer the period of variation, the greater the star's absolute brightness. Consequently one need only observe the time it takes the Cepheid star to pulsate, and one immediately knows its absolute magnitude. It was by means of these "lighthouses in space" that the distance to the Andromeda nebula was determined, finally settling the great controversy among astronomers in the early part of this century as to whether objects such as the Andromeda galaxy were single peculiar stars, relatively close by,

or distant systems of stars. Not until 1924 was mankind presented with the grand picture of a universe of galaxies, rather than a universe of isolated stars.

■POPULATION OF A GALAXY.—

A galaxy contains many varieties of individual members. It is incorrect to consider a galaxy as merely a relatively uniform distribution of stars of assorted spectral classes. The population within a galaxy varies with position in the galaxy, much as the type of population and number of people vary with location within a city.

The study of the structure and composition of the galaxy forms a major branch of astronomy, and a brief survey cannot do the subject justice. Yet a summary can be made. A galaxy is composed of stars in various stages of evolution and of dust and gas not in stellar form.

The nonstellar matter is frequently in turbulent motion and appears to be the principal source of the continuous galactic radio radiation observed with radio telescopes over a wide band of frequencies. One particular frequency received from galactic sources is the famous 21-cm. line that arises from neutral hydrogen. By monitoring it, the extent of hydrogen gas clouds throughout the galaxy and beyond can be observed.

Much of the cosmic dust in the galaxy can be detected only because it

Facts About the Stars

Star	Apparent Magnitude	Distance (Light Years)	Absolute Magnitude	Spectral Class
Sirius	−1.6	8.7	+1.4	Ao
Alpha Centauri	+0.3	4.3	+4.7	Go
Vega	+0.1	27	+0.5	Ao
Capella	+0.2	46	−0.5	Go
Arcturus	+0.2	37	0.0	Ao
Rigel	+0.3	650	−6.0	B8
Altair	+0.9	16	+2.4	A5
Aldebaran	+1.1	16	−0.5	K5
Autares	+1.2	170	−3.0	MO
Deneb	+1.3	540	−5.0	A2
61 Cygni	+5.6	11	+7.9	K5

obstructs the passage of light from stars beyond it. The *Great Rift* and other dark lanes in the Milky Way are caused by clouds of dark obscuring matter lying close to the galactic plane and revolving, with the stars, about the central mass of the galaxy.

When, however, such interstellar matter lies in the vicinity of one or more hot, bright stars, it can reflect their light or fluoresce from their ultraviolet radiation. What would otherwise be dark obscuring matter becomes luminous, thereby furnishing some of the more beautiful spectacles on the celestial sphere. The famous Orion, Trifid, and Lagoon nebulae are examples.

New stars are still forming out of the dust and gas in the galaxies. The newly minted stars and those formed within the last several billion years are known as *Population I* stars. Older stars whose histories go back to the early stages of the galaxy are called, for historical reasons, *Population II* stars.

Because of their greater age, Population II stars differ somewhat in chemical composition from the Population I stars; the latter have a greater concentration of metals than their forerunners. It is thought that metals were formed in the interiors of the "first generation" giant stars and later diffused into galactic space. The metal deficiency in the Population II stars causes the *H–R diagrams,* which will be explained later on, of the two main stellar populations to differ sensibly. Population II red giants attain considerably greater brightness than do Population I giants.

There are many subsystems of stars within our galaxy, notably the open clusters and globular clusters. *Open clusters,* such as the Pleiades and the Hyades, are Population I stars. They represent clusters of several hundred stars apparently formed within one large gas cloud in the recent astronomical past. *Globular clusters* are spherical collections of Population II stars, each cluster having thousands of stars. Several hundred globular clusters are known. They do not exhibit the general flattening of a galaxy, but form a spherical halo around its center. All of the globular clusters are situated closer to the center of our galaxy than is the sun.

The sun itself lies about two-thirds of the way out from the center of the galaxy and slightly out of its central plane, close to one of the main spiral arms of our galaxy.

The Milky Way is considered a giant member of the local group of galaxies that includes the Andromeda, which may be even larger.

■GALAXIES.—Galaxies usually occur in large groups. The *Coma cluster* of galaxies, for instance, contains approximately 10,000 separate galaxies. Generally speaking, such clusters include galaxies of all types. Some clusters, however, favor spiral galaxies; others, the elliptical variety.

Even before the true nature of galaxies was known (in the past they were called nebulae, and were included with the true gaseous nebu-

lae), attempts were made to classify them as to types and forms. The *Hubble classification* predominated for many years and is still of importance because of its simplicity and broad coverage, even though more detailed classifications have since been made.

Galaxies have been found in undiminishing numbers to the limits of modern optical and radio telescopic "sight." The distance to the most remote known galaxy is uncertain, but it may be as much as six billion light-years or more away.

The Expanding Universe.—The spectroscopic analysis of galactic light confirms its stellar nature. The spectra of galaxies conform to what could be expected of the combined light of millions of stars. The speed at which a galaxy moves toward or away from us can, therefore, be determined in the same manner that the radial velocities of the individual stars can be determined, namely, by observation of what is known as the *Doppler shift* of the absorption lines in the spectrum.

A most surprising discovery was made as a result of such measurements. The farther away a galaxy is, the faster it appears to be receding from us. This outstanding observation was recently confirmed by radio telescope observations of distant galaxies that emit strong radio waves. The most distant ones seem to be moving away from us at incredible speeds—up to 90,000 miles per second.

Astronomers quickly realized that even if these observations are correct, it does not necessarily imply that our galaxy is at the center of the universe. If an ordinary classroom were expanding, for example, like a balloon being blown up, then no matter where one was sitting, all other seats in the classroom would appear to be receding—the more distant seats at a greater rate of speed.

If the universe is expanding, there

is still the question of whether this is a real expansion or merely the effect of the geometry of huge distances. In any event, the close correlation of velocity and distance has given us a fine indicator for the determination of the distances to galaxies. Once their spectral speed is determined, their distance also is known.

The speed of recession increases by about 125 kilometers per second for every million parsecs of distance. This "constant" of proportionality is known as the *Hubble parameter.* It is one of the most important proportions in the science of astronomy.

There are two major opposing theories of the expanding universe. One, usually associated with George Gamow (1904–   ), asserts that the universe is evolving and is at present rapidly expanding. The other, associated with the English astronomer Fred Hoyle (1915–   ), holds that the universe is in a "steady state"; that the galaxies disappearing beyond our observational horizon are replaced by new ones formed from spontaneously generated hydrogen. Both theories are unsatisfactory.

Stars.—Stars are large, generally spherical masses of gas that have become self-luminous through nuclear reactions occurring deep within their interiors. The laws of physics show that once a quantity of interstellar gas and dust, great enough to hold itself together by self-gravitation, is gathered together, a star will result. The gas will slowly condense to form a dark, cold, spherical body. As gravitational contraction continues, the temperature and pressure at the center of the gaseous mass will initiate the nuclear reactions that transform hydrogen into helium and eventually into heavier elements.

In this natural process of element formation, some of the mass of the star is continuously transformed into energy, according to the famous re-

MOUNT WILSON AND PALOMAR OBSERVATORIES

PLEIADES, also known as the Seven Sisters and the Little Dipper, are fourth-magnitude stars. The six bright spots are images of stars brighter than the fourth magnitude.

lation of Einstein: $E = mc^2$. This fundamental law states that a mass (m) of one gram is the equivalent of the square of the velocity of light (c^2, or 9×10^{20}) ergs of energy (E). The star maintains its outflow of luminous energy until the fuel supply is exhausted and the star eventually "dies." The laws of physics also show that the type of star that develops—large or small, brilliant or faint, very hot or relatively cool—depends primarily on the amount of material from which it originally condensed. The twinkling points of light we see in the night sky are, in reality, huge atomic energy plants whose powers immeasurably exceed man's relatively feeble attempts to release the energy locked inside the nuclei of atoms.

The stars appear as twinkling points of light for two reasons: their great distance and the instability of our own atmosphere. Their distance makes them appear to us as true points of light rather than disks (as the planets, moon, and sun appear to us), and the unstable atmosphere causes the feeble rays of light from these seeming points to zigzag as they pass through the atmosphere on their way to our eyes. If Earth had no atmosphere, the stars would not seem to twinkle.

There are many different types of stars. They vary greatly in true brightness, size, temperature, and spectral appearance. The sun is in some ways an average star—brighter than many, not as bright as others.

These individual differences can be explained in relatively simple physical terms. It is first important, however, to distinguish the true properties of stars from those apparent properties that result from the distance between us and them.

■**STELLAR DISTANCES.**—The star (other than the sun) closest to us is about

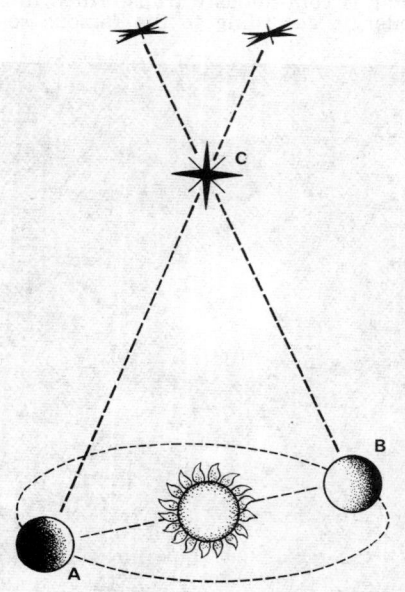

PARALLAX of star at point C is one-half its apparent movement as viewed when Earth is at points A and B in its orbit.

4½ light-years away. It is the closest of the approximately 100 billion other stars in the gigantic complex of stars we call the Milky Way.

The most distant stars in our own galaxy are more than 50,000 light-years away; other galaxies of stars are millions and even billions of light-years away.

■**MEASUREMENT OF DISTANCE.**—The fundamental method of measuring the distance to a star is known as the *trigonometric parallax method*. As Earth moves around the sun, a relatively nearby star will appear to shift its position in the sky relative to more distant stars. By measuring these minute angular shifts, the distance of the star can be determined trigonometrically. One-half the total apparent shift of the star with respect to the background is called the star's *trigonometric parallax*. It also follows that the parallax of a star is the angle subtended at the star by the radius of Earth's orbit.

No star has a parallax of more than one second of arc (approximately the angle subtended by a penny at a distance of 2½ miles). The nearest star, Alpha Centauri, has a parallax of three-quarters of a second of arc. By definition, a parallax of one second corresponds to a distance of one *parsec* (*parallax* of one *second*). The distance of a star in parsecs is thus 1/parallax. One parsec is equal to 3.26 light-years.

The trigonometric method works only for the relatively nearby stars because the distant stars are used as a background reference. The trigonometric shifts of the latter are virtually negligible, and specialized methods must be used to determine their distances and the distances of the extremely remote galaxies.

There are many highly specialized methods that can be used for certain groups of stars, but the more general are based on the fact that *the intensity of light varies inversely as the square of the distance*. In other words, if two stars of the same intrinsic, actual brightness are placed one and two units of distance away from Earth, the more distant star will appear four times fainter than the closer one. If, then, the actual brightness of a star is known, its distance can be derived simply by noting how bright or faint it appears.

■**MAGNITUDES.**—The brightness of a star as it appears to us is expressed technically as its *apparent magnitude*. The scale of stellar magnitudes is logarithmic and takes into account the fact that visual sensation varies logarithmically; that is, the eye senses the ratios of brightness of sources, rather than the arithmetical differences in brightness. For example, a two candlepower light will look proportionately as bright to the eye when compared with a one candlepower light, as will a 100 candlepower light compared with a 50 candlepower light, because the ratio in both cases is 2:1. The difference in magnitude (Δm) between two stars is expressed mathematically as follows:

$$\Delta m = 2.5 \log_{10} \frac{I_1}{I_2}$$

Thus:

Difference in Magnitude (Δm)	Ratio of Brightness
1	2.51
2	6.30
3	15.84
4	39.80
5	100.
10	10,000.
20	100,000,000.

We shall see shortly that the absolute magnitude of a star can be judged fairly accurately from the appearance of its spectrum and, hence, the star's distance can be found.

Distances so determined are called *spectroscopic parallaxes*. This method is an extension of the fundamental, but less accurate, method of trigonometric parallaxes. The latter, however, in addition to methods applicable in special cases to certain groups of stars, serves to establish a range of actual luminosities of stars.

As defined, the absolute magnitudes of stars range from about +20 for the very faintest to −10 for the very brightest. Since every step of five magnitudes corresponds to an advance of 100 in brightness, it can be readily seen that the range in true luminosity of stars is enormous—a total range of thirty magnitudes, or a ratio of 100^6, or 10^{12}—one trillion times.

The truly bright, giant stars can be seen at enormous distances, while the fainter ones must be relatively close to be seen at all. The great majority of stars are fainter than the sun and can be seen only with the aid of a telescope—only when they are in our general part of the galaxy. The stars we see when we glance up at the sky at night are, predominantly, intrinsically bright, faraway stars—beacons far out in space. For every star that can be seen with the naked eye, there are 100 or more closer to us that cannot be seen, even at moderate distances, because they are intrinsically faint.

■**LUMINOSITY AND TEMPERATURE.**—The luminosity of a star depends directly on its size (surface area) and on how brightly each unit area shines (luminosity = surface area × luminosity of unit area). A star can appear bright even though it is relatively faint per square yard. A small, intensely brilliant star will appear as bright as an enormous but faint star.

A star's surface brightness and color depend on its surface temperature. The radiation laws of physics show that the energy flow through the surface of a star varies as the fourth power of the temperature (*Stefan's law*). A star with twice the surface temperature of another will, therefore, emit 16 times as much energy per unit area.

The total luminosity of a star, then, reveals nothing of the star's size unless we also know the star's surface brightness. To find this, the star's temperature must be known.

■**WIEN'S LAW.**—The temperature of a star can be determined fairly accurately by noting its color. Stars behave much like "black bodies," that is, like bodies that obey the laws of

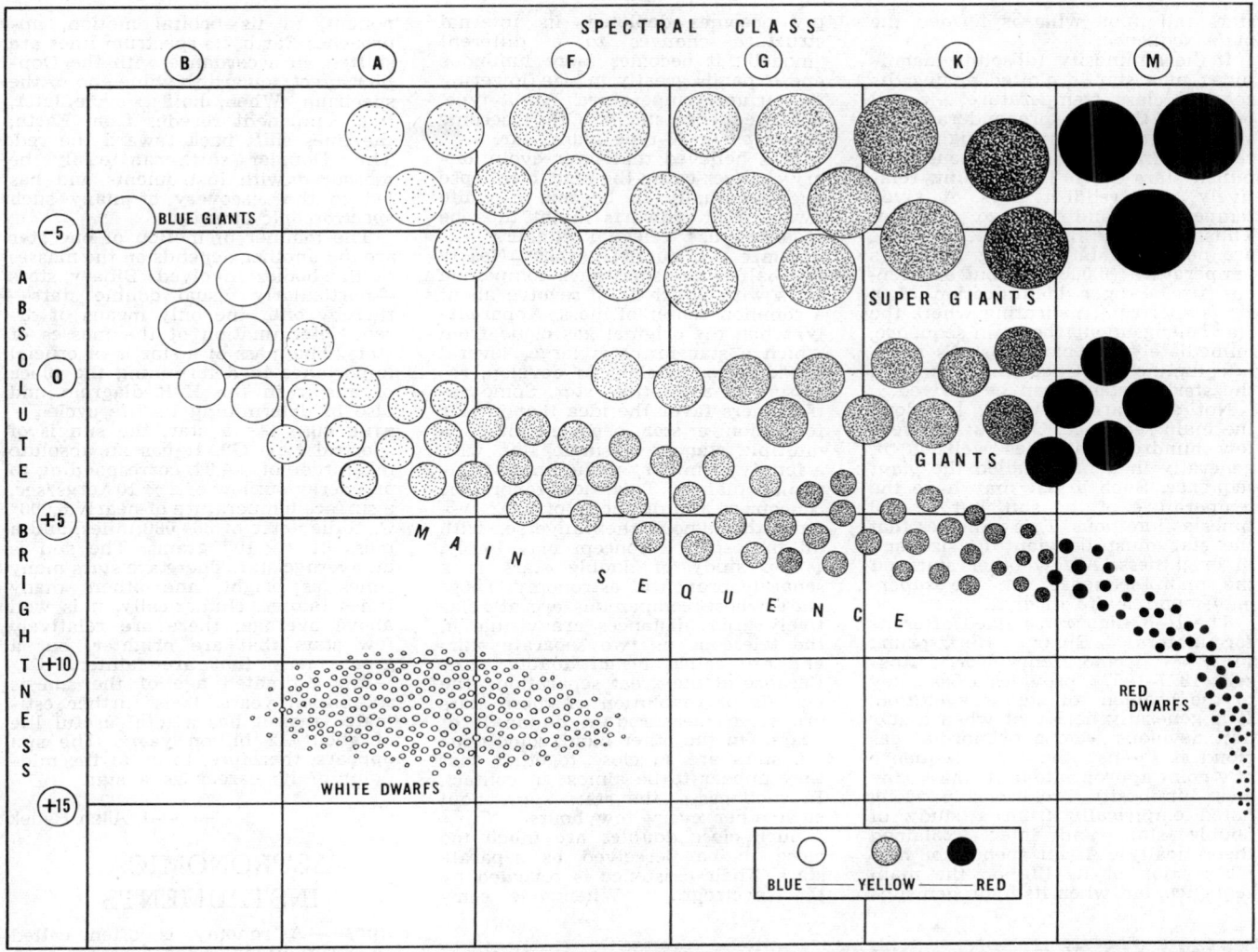

SPECTRAL CLASS

B   A   F   G   K   M

BLUE GIANTS

SUPER GIANTS

GIANTS

MAIN SEQUENCE

WHITE DWARFS

RED DWARFS

BLUE —— YELLOW —— RED

H-R DIAGRAM, which provides a key to stellar evolution, plots the spectral class (based on temperature) of a star against its absolute brightness. The main sequence, which consists of yellow stars bounded by blue giants at one end and red dwarfs at the other, contains most of the known stars. Above the main sequence are the yellow and red giants and supergiants, and below it are the white dwarfs. It is believed that evolutionary changes will cause a star to collapse and eventually to become a white dwarf.

radiation. Of these laws, *Wien's law* states that the most predominant color in the spectrum of a star is a function of the temperature—the hotter the temperature, the bluer the color. Like a piece of metal as it is heated, first it glows a dull red; then, as its temperature rises, it becomes brighter (as stated in Stefan's law), and also becomes, in turn, orange and bright yellow (as in Wien's law). If the metal did not melt and vaporize, it would become green and then blue. Stars of course are completely vaporized but still conform with radiation laws. An orange-yellow star such as Arcturus has a temperature of about 4,500° C.; our yellow sun has a temperature of about 6,000° C.; the bluish star, Rigel, has a surface temperature of some 18,000° C. There is, however, a more accurate method of determining stellar temperatures.

■**STELLAR SPECTRA.**—The surface temperature of a star greatly influences its tenuous atmosphere. Temperature is a direct expression of thermal mo-

tion in the material whose temperature is being measured. It is an index of the energy of motion of atoms and molecules; the higher the temperature, the greater the motion of atoms and molecules.

Such motions "thermally excite" the atoms to various energy states. Again, the higher the temperature, the higher the energy states attained by the atoms of the various chemical elements in the star's atmosphere.

The ability of an atom to absorb energy from the starlight pouring out from the lower levels of a stellar atmosphere (thus producing the *Fraunhofer lines,* or familiar absorption lines, in the spectrum of a star) depends on the particular energy state the atom is in. This, as we have seen, depends on the temperature of the stellar surface. It follows, therefore, that the kind of absorption spectrum a star exhibits depends on both the chemical elements present in its atmosphere and the temperature of the atmosphere.

Thus the spectrum of a star is an

accurate index of temperature. Long before this fact became known, astronomers had classified stellar spectra on an arbitrary scale of *A, B, C, D,* and so on. It soon developed, however, that certain assigned letters were either superfluous or misplaced. The principal standard spectral classes of stars used today follows, with the approximate temperature corresponding to each spectral class listed.

D	50,000° C.	G	5,500° C.
B	20,000° C.	K	4,500° C.
A	10,000° C.	M	3,000° C.
F	7,500° C.		

In use, each major spectral class is further subdivided into decimal parts. The spectral class of the sun is *G2,* a temperature of 6,000° C.

■**H–R DIAGRAM.**—Although it might seem that for a given stellar temperature there might be a large range of sizes (and thus a large range of luminosity) it does not happen that way in nature for one very good reason: the very great majority of stars fall upon what is termed the *main sequence.*

If the luminosity (absolute magnitude) of a star is plotted against its spectral class (temperature), it will be found that the preponderance of stars are on a nearly straight line, running from highly luminous, hot, bluish stars down to the faint, relatively cool, reddish stars. A given temperature and size go together. Thus, along the main sequence there are no other stars having the sun's temperature (6,000° C.) but a different size. Proper identification of a star's spectrum, indicating where the star belongs along the main sequence, immediately reveals the star's absolute luminosity. Once this is known, the star's distance can be derived.

Not all stars, however, lie along the main sequence. One out of every few hundred stars lies well off it, generally in a band called the *giant sequence.* Such a star may have the temperature of the sun, but be 100 times as luminous. This indicates that the star must be giant in size and in brightness. A few other stars off the main sequence are the *supergiants* and *white dwarfs.*

The *H–R diagram,* named after its formulators, Ejnar Hertzsprung (1873–   ) and Henry Norris Russell (1877–1957), provides a basic key to the problem of stellar evolution. It is generally held that when a star first develops from a primordial gas cloud it "joins" the main sequence at a point appropriate to its mass (the mass-luminosity relationship long noted empirically from a study of double stars and later explained theoretically). A star spends the major portion of its life on the main sequence, but when its hydrogen supply becomes depleted, its internal structure changes to a different "model"; it becomes more luminous and expands greatly in size, lowering its surface temperature. An *A*-type, main-sequence star will thus become a *G*-type or *K*-type giant star.

It is believed that later evolutionary changes cause the star to collapse and eventually to become a white dwarf. White dwarfs might thus be regarded as "celestial clinkers."

■**DOUBLE AND MULTIPLE STARS.**—Nearly one-half of the stars have companion stars with which they revolve about a common center of mass. Apparently, when the original gas cloud from which a star forms is large, several condensation nuclei can develop, resulting in a *multiple star.* Some astronomers favor the idea that in star formation a star becomes either a multiple star or a single star with a family of minor, nonluminous companion planets. This view favors the concept of a multiplicity of solar systems throughout the universe, with all that such a concept may imply.

The study of double stars is a separate branch of astronomy. Those stars whose companions are at relatively great distances are visible in the telescope as two separate stars and are called *visual double stars.* Because of the great separations, the periods of revolution of these stars are often measured in hundreds of years. On the other hand, some double stars are so close together that they appear to be almost in contact. In such cases, the stars spin about each other every few hours.

Such *close doubles* are much too close to be perceived as separate stars. Their existence is revealed by the spectrograph. When one component, in its orbital motion, approaches Earth, its spectrum lines are shifted, in accordance with the *Doppler effect,* toward the blue end of the spectrum. When, half a cycle later, this component recedes from Earth, the lines shift back toward the red. This *Doppler shift* can easily be measured with instruments and has led to the discovery of many such *spectroscopic binaries.*

The manner of motion of one star around another depends on the masses of the bodies involved. Binary stars —particularly visual double stars— thereby offer the only means of direct determination of the masses of stars. The mass of a star is of crucial importance in determining the place of a star in the H–R diagram and also in determining its life cycle.

■**THE SUN.**—As a star, the sun is of spectral type *G2.* It has an absolute magnitude of +4.84, corresponding to an energy outflow of 4×10^{33} ergs/sec, a surface temperature of nearly 6,000° C., a diameter of 864,000 miles, and a mass of 2×10^{33} grams. The sun is an average star. There are stars many times as bright, and others many times fainter. Numerically, it is well above average; there are relatively few stars that are brighter, but a great many that are fainter.

The estimated age of the sun is six billion years. It is further estimated that it has a total useful life of about 12 billion years. The sun appears, therefore, to be at the midpoint of its career as a star.

—J. Allen Hynek

ASTRONOMICAL INSTRUMENTS

Purpose.—Astronomy is often called an observational science rather than an experimental science because an astronomer must be satisfied with what he can learn from observing what already exists in the universe and how it behaves; there is no opportunity to experiment with celestial bodies. Therefore, astronomical laboratories are called observatories, and astronomical instruments are almost all observing instruments. These instruments are designed to give as much information as possible about objects that are observed.

Only four things can actually be observed about any celestial body: the present position of the body and how its position changes with time; the features of its surface—these are observable on only a few bodies (no more than half a dozen); the brightness of the body (how much light is received from it); and the color of its light (the amount of light received in wavelengths of energy).

All of this information can be obtained by using the eye alone, but only to a limited extent. The eye, guided by such accurate angle-measuring instruments as quadrants or sextants, can determine the positions of stars to a few minutes of arc. The eye alone can see some features on the moon's surface and can distinguish the brightness of the stars and their colors to a surprising degree.

INTERNATIONAL BUSINESS MACHINES CORPORATION

NINETEENTH-CENTURY TELESCOPE opened additional areas to astronomical research.

But for very accurate measurements of all these things, the human eye is aided in astronomy by an instrument called a *telescope*, supplemented by several different kinds of accessory instruments.

Optical Telescopes.—An *optical telescope* is a device for collecting a large amount of light, greater than the eye alone can collect, and concentrating it onto a small area where it can be observed by the eye, recorded on a photographic film, or measured in some way. There are two basic kinds of telescopes: the refracting (lens-type) telescope, and the reflecting (mirror-type) telescope.

■**REFRACTING TELESCOPES.**—In a *refracting telescope* a large glass lens, shaped in a convex (outward-bulging) curve on each surface, is called the *telescope objective.* When light from a star reaches the lens, it bends slightly as it passes through. Where the light enters the lens at the greatest angle with the surface, it bends most. The curvature of the lens is designed so that all of the light passing through the glass is bent toward a single point behind the lens called the *focal point,* or *focus.* An observer examines the light at the focus through another small lens, called an *eyepiece,* which works very much like a magnifying glass.

■**REFLECTING TELESCOPES.**—In a *reflecting telescope,* the light from a celestial body passes down a tube to the surface of a mirror mounted at the bottom of the tube. The surface of the mirror, which is the objective, is ground to a very precisely curved shape; on large mirrors, the curve is part of a parabola. The curved surface of the mirror reflects the light back up the tube toward a focus, where all the light passes through a single point. Since the focus is directly in the path of the incoming light, it usually cannot be observed directly, so the light is reflected from a secondary mirror inside the tube to bring the focus to a more convenient location. If the secondary mirror reflects the light to one side of the tube, the telescope is a *Newtonian,* after Sir Isaac Newton, the English astronomer who devised this type of instrument about 1670. If the secondary mirror reflects the light back down the tube through a hole in the center of the primary mirror, the telescope is a *Cassegrain,* after the astronomer Guillaume N. Cassegrain, who invented it in 1672. In very large reflecting telescopes, the focus can be seen directly by an observer in a cage inside the tube itself. The observer's cage blocks off a small amount of the light going down the tube toward the primary mirror (as do the secondary mirrors), but this does not interfere with the quality of the telescope in any way.

■**SIZE.**—The largest telescopes are all of the reflecting variety for a number of reasons. It is easier to cast mirrors than large lenses because only the surface of the mirror must be perfect, while all the glass and both surfaces of a lens must be perfect. It is also easier to mount and support a large mirror because it can be

MOUNT WILSON AND PALOMAR OBSERVATORIES

200-INCH HALE TELESCOPE points skyward to photograph a specific portion of the moon.

held by a frame over its entire bottom surface, while a lens must be supported around its edge. For the same size telescope, a reflector is much less expensive than a refractor because the glass of the mirror does not have to be perfect and only one surface has to be ground and polished. The largest reflecting telescopes are the 200-inch Hale telescope at Mt. Palomar, California, the 120-inch telescope of the Lick Observatory, Mt. Hamilton, California, and the 100-inch Hooker telescope at Mt. Wilson, California. The largest lens-type telescope is the 40-inch refractor of the Yerkes Observatory, Williams Bay, Wisconsin. The size of a telescope is always the diameter of the objective lens or mirror, as the case may be.

■**FUNCTIONS.**—A telescope performs four important functions for an astronomer. First, it increases his *pointing accuracy;* that is, the telescope allows him to point more accurately in a required direction and also to measure more accurately the direction in which he is pointing his instrument. Second, a telescope provides *magnifying power;* that is, it makes distant and small objects appear larger than they appear to the naked eye. Third, a telescope provides *light-gathering power;* that is, it makes faint objects appear brighter because it gathers all the light falling on a large objective and concentrates it for the astronomer to see. Fourth, a telescope gives *resolving power;* that is, it enables the astronomer to separate and to see distinctly objects so close together that they appear as one to the naked eye.

The pointing accuracy of a tele-

scope depends somewhat on the focal length of the telescope. The *focal length* is the distance from the objective to the focal point. Long-focus telescopes can be pointed more accurately than short-focus telescopes. More important than focal length, however, are the size and accuracy of the measuring circles built into the telescope mounting and the sturdiness and accuracy of the mounting itself. Specially designed telescopes with rigid and accurate mountings and with large, finely divided measuring circles are used to determine accurately the positions of stars and changes in their positions. These telescopes are usually mounted so that they are free to move only along the meridian, the north-south line in the sky. They are called *meridian telescopes* or *transits.* The accuracy of positions toward which other telescopes are pointed is checked against the positions of certain stars that have been carefully measured by meridian telescopes.

The magnifying power of a telescope depends upon its focal length. When a telescope is pointed at an extended object, such as the sun or moon, the size of the image at the focus depends upon the distance from the lens or mirror to the focus. If the focal length of a telescope is 10 feet, for example, the image of the moon at the focal plane will be about 1 inch across, but it would be about 10 inches across if the focal length of the telescope were 100 feet. If a photographic film were placed at the focus of such a telescope, it would record a picture of the moon one foot in diameter. Telescopes that are designed to observe the surface features of the sun, moon, and planets are therefore always long-focal-length telescopes.

The magnification of a telescope that is used for visual observation depends upon another factor, the focal length of the eyepiece. The *visual magnifying power* of a telescope is the ratio of the focal length of the objective to the focal length of the eyepiece. Visual magnification can be increased in any telescope by using an eyepiece of shorter focal length, thus increasing the ratio governing the magnification. However, there is a practical limit to the magnifying power that can be used with any given telescope, usually about 30 to 40 times the diameter of the objective. For a 4-inch telescope (diameter of objective), the practical limit of magnifying power is therefore about 150. Using an eyepiece of a focal length that gives a magnifying power higher than 150 for such a telescope results in a loss of quality and light in the image.

For use with stars, faint nebulae, and galaxies, the remaining two functions of a telescope, light-gathering power and resolving power, are the more important. The magnifying power of a telescope is of no value in observing stars, since they are essentially point sources of light without any area to be magnified. Stars are so far away that, in spite of their great size, nothing but a point of light can be seen in even the largest telescopes. As a matter of fact, very large telescopes of good quality produce extremely small images of stars—the smaller the better. Thus, stars that are close together can be better resolved into individual images.

The light-gathering power and the resolving power of a telescope both depend upon the size of the objective lens or mirror. The amount of light that a telescope receives varies with the square of the objective's diameter. Thus, a 100-inch telescope, with a diameter 10 times as great, would receive 10 squared (10^2), or 100, times as much light as a 10-inch telescope. Theoretically, this 100-inch telescope could detect objects 100 times fainter than the faintest object detectable in the smaller instrument. This is the real purpose of building exceptionally large telescopes with objective diameters of 100 or 200 inches. Such telescopes are used primarily to observe stars, nebulae, and galaxies that are too faint to be observed by smaller instruments. In so doing, they can observe objects at very great distances, objects that may be as bright as nearby objects, but have been dimmed by the effect of distance. These very large telescopes, therefore, are effective in pushing the limits of the observable universe to ever-greater distances.

Photographic Telescopes.—Large telescopes are seldom used today for visual observations. They are almost always used with one of several accessory devices that record the images they produce or that measure or analyze the light they gather. For recording the appearance or position of stars, nebulae, and galaxies, tele-

scopes are used as photographic instruments. Photographic film holders are placed in the focal plane of the telescope, and the images are recorded on the film. The resulting picture is a permanent record of the field of the sky being examined.

Photographic telescopes have another tremendous advantage. The image seen by the eye represents the light that reaches the eye in a very brief moment. But the image recorded on a film can represent all of the light accumulated over several hours of exposure. Since the intensity of the image on the film continues to build up as long as it is exposed to light, a photograph can record stars or galaxies that could never be observed visually. Throughout the exposure of the film, of course, the telescope must be pointed in precisely the same direction.

■MOUNTING.—Telescopes are mounted in two ways, alt-azimuth and equatorial. In an *alt-azimuth mount*, the telescope is free to move up or down (in altitude) or horizontally around the sky (in azimuth). This type of mounting is usually found only on smaller telescopes. In an *equatorial mount*, the telescope is free to move around an axis parallel to the axis of the earth's rotation. The telescope is first set to a position corresponding to the star's distance above or below the plane of the earth's equator. Then, when the telescope moves around the polar axis, it moves in a path that corresponds to the star's path of motion across the sky. In a photographic telescope, this motion is provided with motors geared to the speed of the earth's rotation, so that the telescope tracks the stars being photographed as they move. Throughout the exposure of the film, the drive of the telescope compensates exactly for the rotation of the earth.

Photometers and Spectrographs.—Two important accessories used with modern telescopes are photometers and

HARVARD COLLEGE OBSERVATORY
RADIO TELESCOPE hears sounds from space.

spectrographs. A *photometer* is similar in principle to a photoelectric cell. When light from a star falls on a tiny photosensitive cell, the cell regulates the amount of electric energy sent to a meter according to the intensity of the star's light. The meter then indicates the brightness of the star. A *spectrograph* is an instrument that produces a photograph of a star's spectrum. The star's light is allowed to pass through a device, such as a prism, which spreads the light out into all of its colors, or its *spectrum*. The spectrum is recorded on film; this allows the spectra of faint objects to be observed. The features of the star's spectrum—the nature and intensity of its dark or bright lines—can then be examined.

Electronic Equipment.—In addition to telescopes and their accessories, astronomers use a variety of other instruments to assist them in analyzing the records provided by their telescopes. They use special instruments to measure the position and intensity of images recorded on film. In today's astronomy, the use of electronic equipment is becoming increasingly important. Electronic image intensifiers have been developed to suppress the background brightness of the sky and to enhance the images of very faint stars and galaxies. Many complex theoretical problems in astronomy, such as the nature of stellar interiors, can be solved only by the use of high-speed electronic computers. And electronic equipment is essential in the radio telescopes that today explore the radio universe.

Radio Telescopes.—The *radio universe* is the radiation that is naturally produced in frequencies of energy called *radio waves*. Celestial bodies produce radio waves just as they produce light waves. *Radio telescopes* are designed to collect and focus these radio waves just as optical telescopes collect and focus light. But since radio waves cannot be seen or recorded on films, they must be handled electronically. They are amplified, and the frequency or intensity is recorded on a meter or chart. In this way, the sky is looked at through a new kind of "light." It has been found that many things look different in this "radio light" and that some things can be observed only with the use of radio telescopes.

Space Techniques.—The next developments in astronomical instruments will be those designed for use in space. Some have already been developed and used, such as the *stratoscope telescopes,* which were flown by balloons to altitudes of more than 80,000 feet, and the *orbiting solar observatories* (OSO satellites) and *orbiting astronomical observatories* (OAO satellites). These projects involve instruments for many purposes, but perhaps most important are those for exploring the sky in ultraviolet energy. This short-wave form of energy is blocked from the earthbound instruments by the atmosphere, but can be observed in space. Astronomers expect that the future exploration of the sky in ultra-violet energy will be as valuable as radio observations have been.

—Thomas D. Nicholson

ASTRONOMY GLOSSARY

Aberration of light. — The apparent change of direction (or bending) of light from a celestial body, causing an apparent change in the position of that body, that results from the motion of the earth in its orbit. By analogy, if a person stands in a rainstorm, and there is no wind, the raindrops will come down on him vertically; hence, he must hold an umbrella directly overhead to keep dry. However, if he begins running, he will have to hold the umbrella so that it points ahead of him, at an angle to the vertical, because the raindrops will seem to be coming at a slant. The faster the person runs, the greater the apparent deviation of the raindrops from the vertical.

The earth travels in its orbit at an average speed of 18½ miles per second. Therefore, in order for a particular star to be seen, a telescope must be aimed at an angle to the vertical, just slightly ahead of the true direction, just as a person running in a rainstorm must hold his umbrella at a slant.

If the earth were traveling along a straight-line path, there would be no way to ascertain the true position of a star. However, since the earth travels in a particular direction at one time of the year and in the opposite direction six months later, all the stars seem to shift slightly in position. The *constant of aberration* is the angular displacement thus observed. It is equal to 20.47 seconds of arc and is the same for all stars. In calculating the true position of a star, it is necessary to take note of this aberrational displacement.

Although all stars show the same total displacement in the course of a year, the amount of displacement on a given observation is not constant, except for a star situated precisely at the ecliptic pole. For the actual aberration to be equal to 20.47 seconds of arc, it is necessary that the earth's direction of motion be exactly perpendicular to the direction of the star. This generally happens only twice a year for a given star. Consider, for example, a star in the plane of the ecliptic. Twice a year the earth will cross the imaginary line passing through the star and the center of the earth's orbit; at each of these crossings the star's aberration will be the maximum, 20.47 seconds. At two other points in its orbit the earth will be moving directly away from the star; at these times aberration will be zero.

Albedo. — The fraction of light reflected from the surface of a celestial body that is not self-luminous. The magnitude of the fraction depends upon the atmosphere and the surface of the body. For example, the moon, which has no atmosphere and a very

rough and broken surface of dark-colored rock, has a low albedo; Venus, on the other hand, whose atmosphere is filled with dense clouds, has a high albedo. The albedo of each of the planets in the solar system, in order of decreasing magnitude, is: Venus, 0.76; Uranus, 0.66; Jupiter, 0.51; Saturn, 0.50; Earth, 0.39; Neptune, 0.26; Pluto, 0.16; Mars, 0.148; Mercury, 0.058—the moon's albedo, at 0.072, is slightly greater than Mercury's.

Altitude.—See *Horizon system.*

Apex of the sun's way.—The point on the celestial system toward which the solar system is moving at a speed of about 12 miles per second. This point, located in the constellation Hercules, is also known as the *solar apex.*

Aphelion.—The point on the orbit of a planet, or any other member of the solar system, that is farthest from the sun. (See *Orbit.*)

Apogee.—The point on the orbit of the moon or any artificial satellite that is farthest from the earth.

Apsides.—The two points in the orbit of a celestial body that are respectively the farthest from and the closest to the attracting primary. Each of the points is called an *apsis* or *apse.* A line drawn between them is called the *line of apsides* and is identical with the orbit's major axis (longest diameter). (See *Orbit.*)

Aries, first point of.—See *Equinox.*

Asteroids.—Small planetary bodies of varying dimensions. The orbits of most of these lie between the orbits of Mars and Jupiter. They are also called *minor planets* or *planetoids.*

Astronomical unit (a.u.).—The mean distance from the earth to the sun, equal to the semimajor axis (one-half the longest diameter) of the earth's orbit. It is the unit of measurement for distances within the solar system. One astronomical unit is equal to 92,887,000 ± 20,000 miles.

Aurora.—An electrical display seen above the earth's poles as arcs, rays, and streamers of green, red, and yellow. It is the result of the discharge of electricity at heights of 50 to 150 miles caused by the action on the rarefied atmospheric gases of high-speed particles (alpha particles and electrons) shot from the sun to the earth. In the Northern Hemisphere the display is called the *aurora borealis, aurora polaris,* or *northern lights;* in the Southern Hemisphere it is called the *aurora australis.*

Azimuth.—See *Horizon system.*

Baily's beads.—A phenomenon, discovered by Francis Baily (1774–1844), in which, during the last seconds before the solar eclipse becomes total, bright spots are seen on the dark edge of the moon. These spots, or beads, are produced by sunlight shining between the mountains on the surface of the moon.

Barnard's star.—A faint star in the constellation Ophiuchus, discovered by Edward Emerson Barnard in 1916, that has the largest proper motion (the angle through which a star appears to move against the background of stars on the celestial sphere) measured to date. Only about 200 stars are known with a proper motion as great as ⅒ that of Barnard's star, and most stars have

a proper motion about ¹⁄₁₀₀ that of Barnard's star. In 1963, it was established that Barnard's star is circled by a planet, called *Barnard's planet.*

Celestial sphere.—An imaginary sphere, of indeterminate radius, around the earth on whose surface all celestial objects, regardless of their real distance, are assumed to be projected. If the plane of the earth's equator were to be extended indefinitely, it would cut the celestial sphere at the *celestial equator.* The celestial equator may be thought of as a great circle passing completely around the celestial sphere, midway between the celestial poles. The *celestial poles* may be found by extending a line through the earth's poles until it touches the celestial sphere. The point on the celestial sphere directly over the head of the observer is the *zenith;* the point directly opposite the zenith, on the opposite side of the celestial sphere, is the *nadir.* The celestial poles are therefore fixed reference points on the celestial sphere while the zenith and nadir vary with the position of the observer. Another great circle on the celestial sphere is the ecliptic, which is the apparent path of the sun among the stars. Because the earth's axis is not perpendicular to its orbit, the ecliptic cuts the celestial equator at an angle of 23½°. This inclination makes the sun seem to rise and set at a slightly different point each morning and evening and to cause the seasons. The points of intersection of the celestial equator with the ecliptic are called *equinoxes.*

Chromosphere.—The inner atmosphere of the sun, extending from 300 to 6,000 miles above the sun's surface, or photosphere, and consisting of permanent gases. The lower part of the chromosphere is called the *reversing layer;* the name is derived from a phenomenon that takes place in this region, in which the dark absorption lines of the solar spectrum are formed by reversal from bright emission lines. *Prominences,* vast flame-like eruptions of gas reaching hundreds of thousands of miles from the sun, arise from the chromosphere.

Circumpolar star.—A star that does not rise and set but is always above the horizon. The angle between the star and the celestial pole must be less than or equal to the observer's latitude; thus, the number of such stars varies with the places of observation on the earth.

Comet.—A member of the solar system having a very small mass and usually forming a long, gaseous tail as it approaches the sun. The tail of a comet always points away from the sun because it is blown away from the sun by the solar winds. The *coma,* or head of the comet, is probably composed of ice and dust.

Conjunction.—See *Planetary configurations.*

Constellation.—A group of stars, not necessarily in the same system, that seems to form the outline of a figure. The names of constellations are usually of mythological origin. Constellations are much used in astrology, but have little significance in astronomy. (See *Zodiac.*)

Copernican system.—See *Heliocentric system.*

Counterglow.—See *Gegenschein.*

Day.—Any one of several divisions of time. It is the period of the earth's rotation about its axis. An *apparent solar day* is the time elapsing between two successive passages of the true sun across the same meridian; it is not of constant length because of the earth's elliptic orbit. A *mean solar day* is the time elapsing between two successive passages of the mean sun across the same meridian; it is of constant length. A *sidereal day* is the time elapsing between two successive passages of the vernal equinox across the same meridian; it is of constant length.

Declination.—See *Equator system.*

Doppler effect.—A phenomenon, explained by Christian Johann Doppler (1803–1853), in which the observed wavelength of the light received from an approaching or receding body is changed. The amount of change depends upon the speed of approach or recession. When a star or galaxy recedes from the earth, its spectral lines are shifted toward the red end of the spectrum—this is called the *red shift.* When a star or galaxy is approaching the earth, its spectral lines shift toward the violet end of the spectrum—this is called the *violet shift.* The Doppler effect is utilized in many fields; here it is used to determine the motion of a celestial body relative to the earth.

Earthlight (*earthshine*).—The sunlight reflected from the earth's surface that produces a faint illumination of the dark side of the moon.

Eclipse.—The obscuring of the light from one celestial body by another. In a *solar eclipse,* the moon moves between the sun and the earth so as to obscure the light of the sun as seen from the earth. In a *lunar eclipse,* the earth moves between the sun and the moon so that the moon is in the earth's shadow.

The region of partial shadow surrounding the dark cone in an eclipse is called the *penumbra.* The dark cone, or region of complete shadow, is called the *umbra.*

It would seem that there would be an eclipse of the moon at every full moon and an eclipse of the sun at every new moon. But this is not the case because the moon's orbit is inclined to the orbit of the earth. If the full moon is not near the ascending or descending node of its orbit, it will be so far from the plane of the ecliptic that it will pass above or below the earth's shadow and will not be eclipsed. If the new moon is not near one of the nodes, its shadow will pass above or below the earth and the sun will not be eclipsed. If the shadow of the earth and the full moon are near enough to one of the nodes so that the moon passes entirely into the shadow, a *total lunar eclipse* results. If only part of the moon enters the shadow, a *partial lunar eclipse* occurs. Most persons have witnessed a lunar eclipse, for the phenomenon can be seen by all the people on the night side of the earth at the same instant. In fact, an eclipse of the moon is visible to

considerably more than a hemisphere because in the four hours that may pass from the time the moon first touches the earth's shadow until it completely leaves it, the earth has turned on its axis 60 degrees. There are between 15 and 16 lunar eclipses in 10 years. The eastern side of the moon becomes darker some time before it actually reaches the shadow; then a "bite" is taken out of the moon's disk, and this "bite" increases in size until the whole moon is darkened. Presently, a small, bright arc emerges on the opposite side and grows until the whole lunar surface is again in sunlight.

If the new moon's cone-shaped shadow does not pass above or below the earth and is long enough to reach it, a *total solar eclipse* occurs. The sun is totally obscured from those parts of the earth that the moon's shadow touches. If the new moon's shadow is in line with, but falls short of reaching, the earth, as it often does, a ring of sunlight shows around the disk of the moon; this is called an *annular eclipse.* A solar eclipse is visible as total only within the narrow shadow path. For some hundreds of miles on either side of the shadow path, the sun may be observed in *partial eclipse.* The shadow travels at high speed, and for any one place on the earth the average duration of total eclipse is three minutes. At any one station a total eclipse of the sun will be visible only once in 300 or 400 years.

Eclipses follow a regular cycle. An eclipse, whether solar or lunar, repeats itself every 6,585 days, or 18 years 11⅓ days. This interval between eclipses is called the *saros.*

Ecliptic.—The apparent path of the sun around the celestial sphere. (See *Celestial sphere.*)

Ephemeris.—A table, published at regular intervals, in which the daily position of the sun, moon, planets, artificial satellites, selected stars, and other data necessary for astronomical and navigational observations have been computed.

Epicycle.—In geocentric or Ptolemaic astronomy, a term used to describe the circular orbit traveled by the sun, the moon, and all the planets other than the earth. The center of the epicycle was on a larger circle, called the *deferent.* The sun, the moon, and the planets revolved in their epicycles, and the epicycles themselves revolved around the earth on the deferent circle. The concept of epicycles was ultimately disproved by Johannes Kepler (1571–1630), when he showed that an ellipse could be substituted for a series of epicycles to explain the motion of each planet around the sun.

Equator system.—A means of fixing the position of a celestial body upon the celestial sphere. The lines of latitude and longitude must be imagined to extend from the earth until they cut the celestial sphere. The equator of the earth will cut the celestial sphere at the *celestial equator.* The parallels of latitude will cut the celestial sphere in great circles, called *parallels of declination,* that are north and south of the celestial equa-

tor and parallel to it. The *declination* of a celestial body is its angular distance north or south of the celestial equator. A star with a declination of 30° north, or +30, as this is generally represented, lies directly above the parallel of latitude that is 30° north of the equator. The meridians of longitude intersect the celestial sphere in great circles, called *hour circles,* extending from pole to pole. The angular distance to one of these hour circles, measured in an easterly direction from the vernal equinox, is the *right ascension.* Thus, a star may have a right ascension of 6 hours 30 minutes, which means it is 97°30′ east of the vernal equinox.

Equinox.—A point of intersection of the celestial equator with the ecliptic. There are two equinoxes: the sun crosses the celestial equator at a point called the *vernal equinox,* or *first point of Aries,* on March 20 or 21 (the first day of spring); the sun crosses the celestial equator at a point called the *autumnal equinox* on September 22 or 23 (the first day of autumn).

Faculae.—Large, bright areas of hot gases, at a higher temperature than the average for the sun's surface, located near the top of the photosphere. They can most easily be seen near sunspots and at the edge of the sun's disk.

Fireball.—See *Meteor.*

Flocculi.—Small, bright or dark markings on the chromosphere of the sun —irregular clouds of gas, usually containing calcium or hydrogen.

Gegenschein. — Sometimes called *counterglow,* a faint illumination of the sky, sometimes seen at night in the ecliptic opposite to the position of the sun. It is produced by the scattering of sunlight by dust particles in space, and is related to the zodiacal light. (See *Zodiacal light.*)

Geocentric system (*Ptolemaic system*). —A system of planetary motion, as described in a treatise by Claudius Ptolemy (second century), in which the sun, moon, and planets revolved around a stationary earth; the fixed stars were supposedly attached to an outer sphere surrounding the earth. It was eventually replaced by the idea of the heliocentric system. (See *Heliocentric system.*)

Harvest moon.—In the Northern Hemisphere, the full moon that occurs each year nearest the date of the autumnal equinox, September 22 or 23. Its remarkable feature is that for several successive nights it rises at much more nearly the same hour than at other times of the year. The phenomenon may be understood by considering that the path of the moon through the stars, roughly the same as the ecliptic, is inclined to the celestial equator; and on the date of the autumnal equinox, the full moon is in the vernal equinox, directly opposite the sun.

Heliocentric system (*Copernican system*).—A system of planetary motion, as described by Nikolaus Copernicus (1473–1543), in which the earth and the other planets move in paths around a fixed sun. This system, which is the basis of the present-day concept of the solar system, superseded the geocentric system of Claudius Ptolemy. (See *Geocentric system*.)

Horizon system.—A means of fixing the position of a celestial body upon the celestial sphere. The observer projects the visible horizon onto the celestial sphere to form a great circle, called the *astronomical horizon*. Starting from the zenith, an arc, called a *vertical circle*, is drawn so that it intersects the astronomical horizon. The *altitude* of a celestial body is the angular distance from the horizon to the celestial body, measured along the vertical circle passing through the celestial body. The *azimuth* is the direction angle of the celestial body, measured in the plane of the astronomical horizon; the zero point of the azimuth is generally taken as being due south and rotating to the right. Thus, in the horizon system, the position of a star could be given as altitude 45°, azimuth 30°.

Hour circle.—See *Equator system*.

Inferior planet.—See *Planetary configurations*.

Latitude.—On the earth, the angle measured along a meridian to any particular point; this is often called *terrestrial latitude. Celestial latitude*, the angular distance of a celestial body above or below the ecliptic, is one coordinate in the ecliptic system for fixing the position of any celestial body on the celestial sphere (the other coordinate is celestial longitude). *Galactic latitude* is the angular distance of a celestial body above or below a great circle chosen to represent the plane of the Milky Way.

Libration (from the Latin *libra,* 'a balance').—An apparent oscillation, or rocking, in the motion of a celestial body as viewed from its primary, similar to the oscillations of a balance scale before it comes to rest. The term is most commonly applied to the motion of the moon. Libration causes slightly different portions of the moon's surface to be visible from the earth at different times of the month, although on the average the moon keeps the same face always turned to the earth. Libration arises from the fact that the axial rotation of the moon is uniform, while the speed of revolution (orbital motion) is variable. The compounding, or resultant, of the two motions gives the moon a small oscillating rotation relative to the earth. The moon's libration makes about 41 per cent of its surface always visible (neglecting its phases), and 18 per cent alternately visible and invisible; thus, about 41 per cent of the moon's surface is never seen from the earth.

Light-year.—A unit of measure of stellar distances. One light-year is equal to the distance light travels in one year: $5,878 \times 10^9$ miles, or $63,290$ astronomical units.

Longitude.—On the earth, the angle measured at the center of the earth between the points at which the meridian through Greenwich, England, and the meridian through any particular location cross the equator; this is often called *terrestrial longitude. Celestial longitude*, the angular distance measured eastward along the ecliptic from the vernal equinox

to the meridian passing through the poles of the ecliptic and a particular celestial body, is one coordinate in the ecliptic system for fixing the position of a celestial body on the celestial sphere (the other coordinate is celestial latitude). *Galactic longitude* is the angular distance measured eastward along a great circle chosen to represent the plane of the Milky Way from a point designated as the galactic center to the meridian passing through the poles of the galaxy and a particular celestial body.

Magellanic clouds.—Two irregular galaxies in the Southern Hemisphere. Known as the *Greater Magellanic Cloud* and *Lesser Magellanic Cloud*, respectively, their names are derived from their sizes and the fact that as seen from the Straits of Magellan they pass not far from the zenith. They are the two nearest galaxies to the Milky Way. The Greater Magellanic Cloud is 30,000 light-years in diameter and 144,000 light-years from the earth; the Lesser Magellanic Cloud is 23,400 light-years in diameter and 164,000 light-years from the earth.

Mean sun.—A fictitious body that moves around the celestial equator at a uniform rate, postulated for convenience in measuring time. Because the earth does not move around the sun at a constant rate, and because the ecliptic is inclined to the celestial equator, the sun appears to travel around the earth at different speeds at different times of the year. By measuring time through the use of a mean, or average, sun instead of the real sun, clocks do not have to be corrected to compensate for changes in the speed of the sun throughout the year.

Meteor.—A class of celestial bodies that are seen as streaks of light in the night sky as they burn because of frictional heating while falling through the earth's atmosphere. They are sometimes called *shooting stars* (although they are not stars) when they are not brighter than the planet Venus, and *fireballs* when they are brighter than Venus. If the meteor does not vaporize completely as it passes through the atmosphere, the portion that survives to strike the earth's surface is called a *meteorite*.

Midnight sun.—The sun when it shines throughout the night in the Arctic or Antarctic regions during the summer months.

Minor planets.—See *Asteroids*.

Month.—Any one of several divisions of time. A *calendar month* is an arbitrary division of the year. An *anomalistic month* is the time elapsing between two successive passages of the moon through perigee in its orbit; it is equal to 27.5455 days. A *sidereal month* is the time elapsing between two successive passages of the moon through a point in its orbit obtained by drawing a line from the center of the sun to a fixed point on the celestial sphere; it is equal to 27.32166 days. A *synodic month* is the time elapsing between two successive passages of the moon through either conjunction or opposition, or the time elapsing while the moon completes going through all of its

phases; it is equal to 29.53059 days. A *tropical month* is the time elapsing between two successive passages of the moon through the ascending node of the ecliptic, equal to 27.32158 days.

Nadir.—The point on the celestial sphere directly below the observer and directly opposite the zenith. (See *Celestial sphere*.)

Nebula.—Any luminous patch seen among the stars. More specifically, a cloud of dust or gas that can be seen because of the absorption, emission, or reflection of light.

Neutron star.—A star composed solely of neutrons packed very closely together. The existence of these stars has been postulated by astrophysicists, and in 1963 the discovery of several through the use of orbiting satellites was claimed, although these claims have not yet been verified. A cubic inch of a neutron star would weigh about one billion tons, its surface temperature would be about 20 million degrees Fahrenheit, and it would emit light only in the X-ray region of the spectrum.

Nodes.—The points on the celestial sphere at which the orbit of any body of the solar system crosses the ecliptic. The term is most commonly applied to the points at which the moon crosses the ecliptic. The *ascending node* is the point at which the body passes from south of the ecliptic to north of it. The *descending node* is the point at which the body passes from north to south. The nodes of an orbit do not remain at the same points on the ecliptic; over long periods of time they move around the ecliptic in the retrograde (west to east) direction. The nodes of the earth's orbit are the vernal and autumnal equinoxes.

Northern lights.—See *Aurora*.

Nova.—A star that flares from obscurity to great brilliance and then sinks slowly back to obscurity. A nova is sometimes called a *new star* or a *temporary star*. A *supernova* is an exceptionally bright nova. A supernova that appeared in Taurus in 1054 was visible in broad daylight for a time, and can now be seen as the Crab nebula. A *recurrent nova* is a star that has increased significantly in brightness more than once. A *permanent nova* is a star that has streams of gas flaring from its surface, as if it were in a continual state of eruption.

Nutation (from the Latin *nutatio*, meaning 'to nod').—A movement of the earth's axis like the nodding of a top, which causes the celestial pole to trace a wavy path as it moves among the stars. Nutation is caused by a variation in the attraction of the sun and moon as their movement alters their positions relative to the earth. (See *Precession*.)

Occultation.—The hiding of one celestial body by another, as eclipse of a star or planet by the moon.

Orbit.—The path traveled by one celestial body as it moves about another under the influence of its gravitational attraction. There are six factors that must be known in order to determine the orbit of a celestial body and the body's position in it: the inclination of the orbit to the plane of the primary, the semi-major axis, the date on which the body passes perihelion, the eccentricity of the orbit, the longitude of perihelion, and the longitude of the ascending node.

Parallax.—The apparent change of position of a celestial body against the celestial sphere when viewed from two different points, called the *ends of the baseline. Geocentric,* or *diurnal, parallax* is the angular distance a celestial body appears to move when the baseline is the diameter of the earth. *Heliocentric,* or *annual, parallax* is the angular distance a celestial body appears to move when the baseline is the diameter of the earth's orbit, or one astronomical unit. *Lunar parallax* is the geocentric parallax of the moon, and *solar parallax* is the geocentric parallax of the sun.

Parsec.—A unit of measure of stellar distance. One parsec equals 1.916×10^{12} miles, 206,205 astronomical units, or 3.26 light-years. It is the distance at which the radius of the earth's orbit subtends an angle of 1 second. Therefore, if a celestial body were exactly 1 parsec from the earth, it would have a parallax of 1 second of arc. The convenience of the parsec as a unit of stellar measurement is that a star's distance in parsecs is equal to the reciprocal of its parallax in seconds of arc.

Perigee.—The point on the orbit of the moon or of any artificial satellite that is closest to the earth.

Perihelion.—The point on the orbit of a planet, or of any other member of the solar system, that is closest to the sun. (See *Orbit.*)

Period.—The time that elapses while a celestial body makes one complete revolution in its orbit. A *sidereal period* is the time that elapses between two successive crossings of a particular line from the sun to a fixed point on the celestial sphere. A *synodic period* is the time that elapses between two successive crossings of a line passing through the center of the earth and of the sun.

Perturbations. — Disturbances caused by the gravitational force of a celestial body that result in the deviation of another celestial body from its regular orbit. An observation of the perturbations caused by a body can help in the calculation of its mass.

Phases of the moon.—The apparent changes seen in the shape of the moon in the course of a month. When the moon is in conjunction—between the earth and the sun—it is called a *new moon.* The next day, a *waxing crescent* appears as the moon begins moving to the east of the sun. A quarter of a lunar month later, the moon is at *first quarter* and is on the meridian, or due south, at sunset; at first quarter, one-half the face of the moon is illuminated. As the moon continues moving eastward, more and more of its face continues to become illuminated, and the phase is called *waxing gibbous.* After another quarter of a lunar month, the entire face of the moon can be seen and it rises at sunset; this is called a *full moon.* As the moon continues moving around the earth, less and

less of its face shows each day, and the phase is called *waning gibbous.* After another quarter of a lunar month the moon is at *last quarter;* once again half the face is illuminated, but now the moon rises about midnight and is due south at sunrise. As the moon continues to move in its eastward path, still less and less of the surface is illuminated each day, and the phase is said to be *waning crescent.* Finally, at the completion of the lunar month, the moon fades from sight and is a *new moon* again.

Photosphere.—The visible surface of the sun; the envelope of gas surrounding the sun.

Planetarium.—Both an instrument for artificially duplicating the appearance of the heavens and the large, specially constructed auditorium in which it is housed. By means of a complex projector, the representation of one half of the celestial sphere may be thrown on the interior of a large, concave hemispherical dome. The instrument may be set to depict the celestial sphere as seen from any terrestrial latitude and for any time; it may be operated to show apparent celestial motions, such as the diurnal motion and the changes due to precession. The moon, sun, and planets are shown by means of special projectors, and their apparently complex motions are faithfully reproduced. Various speeds may be used, so that the diurnal motions of the heavens, and even the annual motions, may be compressed into a few seconds. This acceleration gives a realization of the annual course of the sun among the stars, the planetary orbits, and the intricate apparent motions of the planets in them.

Planetary configurations.—The positions of a planet relative to the earth and some other body, usually the sun. For a *superior planet*—one whose orbit is outside that of the earth—there are four critical positions relative to the sun: *conjunction, opposition, east quadrature,* and *west quadrature.* The planets are shown in color on pages 1298 and 1299. For an *inferior planet*—one whose orbit is inside that of the earth—there is no position of opposition or quadrature. There are, however, two conjunctions: *superior conjunction,* when the sun is between the earth and the planet, and *inferior conjunction,* when the planet is between the earth and the sun. There is a third critical position, called *greatest elongation,* when the planet's angular distance from the sun as observed from the earth is a maximum; this occurs when the line joining the earth and the planet is tangent to the planet's orbit. The term *conjunction* is also used to indicate the time when two superior planets have the same celestial longitude; that is, when they are closest together. Jupiter and Mars, for example, are in conjunction when the plane passing through the earth, Jupiter, and Mars is perpendicular to the ecliptic, or when the three planets are most nearly in a straight line.

Planetoids.—See *Asteroids.*

Pole.—One of the ends of the axis of a sphere. The earth's axis passes through the earth's surface at the

North and South poles and touches the celestial sphere at the north and south celestial poles.

Precession.—The movement of the equinoxes around the ecliptic and the conical motion of the earth's axis. Discovered by Hipparchus (c. 160–125 B.C.) precession was mathematically explained by Isaac Newton as being caused by the unequal attraction of the sun and moon on the earth's equatorial bulge. The equinoxes take about 215,800 years to complete their revolution about the ecliptic in a retrograde (west to east) direction. Because of precession, in the year 15,000 the north celestial pole will no longer be marked by Polaris, but will instead be near the boundary line between the constellations Lyra and Hercules, about halfway between the bright stars Vega and Gamma Draconis. The angular rate of precession is 50.26 seconds.

Prominences.—See *Chromosphere.*

Protoplanet.—Original ball of matter from which a planet was formed.

Ptolemaic system. — See *Geocentric system.*

Quadrature.—See *Planetary configurations.*

Quasar (*quasi-stellar radio source*).— A brightly shining body that resembles a star, but is so distant that it must be hundreds of billions of times brighter than the brightest star. The first quasars were identified early in 1963 by means of the radio waves they emit; since then, about a dozen others have been located, some of which pulsate like variable stars.

Radiant energy.—Electromagnetic radiation, such as heat, light, radio waves, X rays, and gamma rays, given off by the sun and other stars.

Radio star.—A particular region in the Milky Way or the space beyond from which radio waves are emanating. Only a few of these regions have been identified as containing celestial bodies, as the Crab nebula.

Radio telescope.—A device for detecting radio waves coming to the earth from outer space. The usual structure for the device is that of a large parabolic reflector (a bowl shape, like that of a radar antenna) that can be rotated so as to gather radio signals from any section of the heavens, and that focuses the incoming signals on an aerial at its center. The largest radio telescope in the world, located at Jodrell Bank, England, and operated by the University of Manchester, has a parabolic reflector with a 250-foot diameter.

Regression.—The clockwise (west to east) motion of the vernal and autumnal equinoxes.

Retrograde motion.—The apparent motion of a planet from west to east among the stars, caused by a combination of its true motion with that of the earth. It was this retrograde motion that necessitated the postulation of epicycles in the geocentric, or Ptolemaic, system.

Reversing layer.—See *Chromosphere.*

Revolution.—Orbital motion of a planet or satellite about its primary.

Right ascension.—See *Equator system.*

Roche's limit.—The closest point to which a satellite can approach its primary without the tidal effects produced by the planet's gravitational field pulling the satellite apart. Roche's value is 2.44 times the planet's diameter.

Rotation.—The turning of a celestial body on its axis; for example, the turning of the earth on its polar axis.

Saros.—See *Eclipse.*

Scintillation (*twinkling*).—The irregular variation in the brightness of a star, caused by variations in the density of different layers of the earth's atmosphere. As a ray of light passes through the air, it is bent or refracted. The amount of this refraction depends upon the density of the air. Because the air at different levels is at different temperatures, and the successive layers of air are being continuously shifted by winds, the slight distortions of a ray of light are different from instant to instant.

Seasons.—The four divisions of the tropical year that begin when the sun reaches specific points on the ecliptic. *Spring* begins when the sun reaches the vernal equinox and lasts for 92 days 20 hours 12 minutes. *Summer* begins when the sun reaches the summer solstice, and lasts for 93 days 14 hours 24 minutes. *Autumn* begins when the sun reaches the autumnal equinox, and lasts for 89 days 18 hours 42 minutes. *Winter* begins when the sun reaches the winter solstice, and lasts 89 days 30 minutes.

Shooting star.—See *Meteor.*

Solar apex.—See *Apex of the sun's way.*

Solar wind.—A stream of hot gas, caused by the expanding corona of the sun, that travels at speeds of about 999,000 miles per hour. It is composed of hydrogen and is responsible for the outer portions of the Van Allen radiation belts around the earth, for auroras in the earth's atmosphere, and for terrestrial magnetic storms. It also blows the tails of comets away from the sun.

Solstices.—The two points on the ecliptic when the sun is at its maximum distance from the celestial equator. At the summer solstice (for the Northern Hemisphere) the sun's declination is 23½° south of the celestial equator.

Sunspot.—A dark area representing a cool region in the sun's photosphere. Sunspots vary greatly in size and shape, the largest ones covering more than 100,000 miles of the sun's surface. Each spot has a dark center, called the *umbra*, that has a less dark region, called the *penumbra*, around it. Sunspots start as small points, develop rapidly, and last for periods ranging from a few hours to several months. A *sunspot cycle*, which lasts for an average of 11.1 years, is the period during which the number of sunspots builds up from a minimum to a maximum and then returns to a minimum. The time from a maximum to a minimum, about 6.5 years, is longer than the time from a minimum to a maximum—4.6 years.

Superior planet.—See *Planetary configurations.*

Telescope.—An optical instrument for making distant objects appear closer. An astronomical telescope consists of a system of lenses and mirrors that brings the light to a focus, and the image formed at the focus is then magnified. Almost all astronomical telescopes are equipped with cameras so that pictures may be taken to provide permanent records of observations. In a *reflecting telescope,* such as a *Newtonian* or *Cassegrain reflector,* the light gathered by the telescope is reflected from a polished surface or mirror to form an image that is then magnified by an eyepiece. In a *refracting telescope,* which was the first form of the telescope, no mirror is used. A *Schmidt telescope* is a special type of reflecting telescope that records large areas of the sky in one wide-angle photograph.

Terminator.—Line separating the illumined side of a planet or satellite.

Tides.—The alternate rises and falls of the earth's waters, caused by the gravitational attractions of the moon and, to a lesser extent, of the sun.

Time measurement.—A means of determining the extent of the duration of an event or a series of events. Time is measured by the hour angle (15° equaling one hour) of a particular point on the celestial sphere with respect to the observer. *Apparent solar time* is the westward hour angle of the sun measured from the observer's celestial meridian. *Apparent noon* is the moment when the sun is on the observer's celestial meridian. *Mean solar time* is the westward hour angle of the mean sun measured from the observer's celestial meridian. *Sidereal time* is the westward hour angle of the vernal equinox measured from the observer's celestial meridian. *Standard time* is the mean solar time legally adopted by a city or country for the major portion of the year. The meridian of longitude through Greenwich, England, is the *standard meridian,* and each meridian west of Greenwich that is a multiple of 15° has a standard time the same multiple of one hour earlier than that of Greenwich; thus, the meridian 60° west of Greenwich has a standard time 4 hours (4 × 15°) earlier than that of Greenwich. *Universal time* is the mean solar time of the Greenwich meridian. The *equation of time* is the difference at any instant between apparent and mean solar time.

Transit.—The apparent passage of a celestial body across a line on the celestial sphere or across any other celestial body as seen from the earth. A star is in transit when it crosses a celestial meridian. Mercury and Venus are in transit when they pass across the face of the sun. A satellite, such as one of Jupiter's moons, is in transit when it passes across the face of its primary.

Vernal equinox.—See *Equinox.*

Year.—Any one of several divisions of time. A *tropical year* is the time elapsing between two successive passages of the earth through the vernal equinox; it is equal to 365.242196 days, and is the year on which the calendar is based. A *calendar year* has 365 mean solar days. A *leap year* has 366 mean solar days, and is effected by adding an extra day to the calendar year when the year number is divisible by 4, such as 1968; a leap year is necessary to prevent the calendar from falling behind by one full day every fourth year. An *anomalistic year* is the time elapsing between two successive passages of the earth through the point of perihelion in its orbit; it is equal to 365.25964 days. An *ecliptic year* is the time elapsing between two successive passages of the sun through the ascending node of the moon's orbit; it is equal to 346.62003 days. A *sidereal year* is the time elapsing between two successive passages of the earth through a fixed point in its orbit; it is obtained by drawing a line from the center of the sun to a fixed point on the celestial sphere; it is equal to 365.25636 days.

Zenith.—A point on the celestial sphere directly above the observer and directly opposite the nadir. (See *Celestial sphere.*)

Zodiac.—A zone extending about 9° on either side of the ecliptic that contains the orbits of the sun, moon, and all the planets except Pluto. The ancient Greeks divided the zodiac into 12 equal divisions of 30°, called the *signs of the zodiac.* Each of these signs was named for the principal constellation it contained. The vernal equinox was a convenient reference point for dividing the zodiac. Therefore, the Greek astronomer Hipparchus (second century B.C.), who named the signs of the zodiac systematically, laid off 12 segments of 30°, counting eastward from the vernal equinox. He found that the segments coincided with the following 12 constellations:

♈ Aries (Ram)	♎ Libra (Balance)
♉ Taurus (Bull)	♏ Scorpio (Scorpion)
♊ Gemini (Twins)	♐ Sagittarius (Archer)
♋ Cancer (Crab)	♑ Capricornus (Goat)
♌ Leo (Lion)	♒ Aquarius (Water Bearer)
♍ Virgo (Virgin)	♓ Pisces (Fishes)

These 12 constellations gave the names to the 12 signs of the zodiac.

Zodiacal light.—A faint illumination of the evening sky extending along the ecliptic. It is caused by the scattering of sunlight by meteoric dust in the plane of the solar system.

BIBLIOGRAPHY

BAKER, ROBERT HORACE. *Astronomy.* D. Van Nostrand Co., Inc., 1964.

CHAMBERLAIN, JOSEPH MILES. *Planets, Stars and Space.* Creative Educational Society, 1962.

DeGANI, MEIR H. *Astronomy Made Simple.* Doubleday & Co., Inc., 1963.

GAMOW, GEORGE. *The Birth and Death of the Sun.* The Viking Press, Inc., 1964.

HOYLE, FRED. *Frontiers of Astronomy.* Harper & Bros., 1955.

LEY, WILLY. *Watchers of the Skies: An Informal History of Astronomy from Babylon to the Space Age.* The Viking Press, Inc., 1963.

MOORE, PATRICK. *The Picture History of Astronomy.* Grosset & Dunlap, Inc., Publishers, 1962.

CHEMISTRY

History.—The first use of chemistry predates recorded history. When man began tanning hides for clothing, mixing clay to make pottery, and preparing medicines and dyes from plants, roots, and herbs, he employed elementary chemical processes. The development of chemistry as a science, however, came much later. By no stretch of the imagination could the prehistoric tanners, potters, and medicine men be considered scientists. Although they knew how to invoke chemical reactions, their knowledge resulted from the chance experience of trial and error. They did not experiment in the true sense of the word, and made no effort to discover *why* something would happen.

The Greek philosophers were the first to ask, Why? About 2,500 years ago, in the fifth century B.C., Democritus (c. 460–c. 370 B.C.) and Leucippus proposed the idea that everything was made of atoms and that these atoms were indivisible. At about the same time, Empedocles (c. 495–c. 435 B.C.) said that all matter was made of one fundamental substance called *ylem,* or *hyle,* which was the same in all objects. He went on to say that the differences between various bodies was caused by the presence of varying amounts of four elements—earth, air, fire, and water—in each body. Aristotle (384–322 B.C.), who was the most famous scientist of his day, accepted Empedocles' theory and added to it. Because of Aristotle's influence, the theory of Democritus and Leucippus remained obscured for over 2,000 years.

Unfortunately, the Greek philosophers engaged in no experimentation, depending instead upon speculation. They paid little attention to chemical processes, thus limiting the scope of their inquiries. The Egyptian and Phoenician scientists of the same period, on the other hand, developed their chemical technology by experimenting with chemical processes; however, they exhibited little desire to find the underlying principles.

Alchemy.—However, when Aristotle's pupil, Alexander the Great, conquered Egypt about 332 B.C., a merging of the Greek and Egyptian sciences resulted. From these emerged a prescientific chemistry called *alchemy,* whose primary goal was the transmutation of one metal into another. Many of the processes of early metallurgy seemed to support the idea that a *base metal,* such as iron or lead, when treated with an unknown material, would be changed (or transmuted) into silver or gold. The alchemists strove for eighteen centuries to find this unknown material, which they called the *philosopher's stone.* In addition, the alchemists searched for the *elixir of life,* a drink that would supposedly rejuvenate the aged; and a *universal solvent,* which would enable them to dissolve anything on the earth. As far-fetched as the ideas of a philosopher's stone, an elixir of life, and a universal solvent may seem today, many of the

leading men of early science were sure that these were practicable.

Men such as Albertus Magnus (c. 1193–1280) and Roger Bacon (c. 1214–1294) were brilliant alchemists. Through the fourteenth and fifteenth centuries, the alchemists were the sole practitioners of chemistry. By the early sixteenth century, however, alchemy began its death throes, for it was in this period that the school of *iatrochemistry* (medical chemistry) developed. Through the work of such men as Philippus Aureolus Paracelsus (1493–1541), Jan Baptista van Helmont (1577–1644), and Sylvius (1614–1672), the cornerstone of chemical physiology was set in place. During this period, too, the work of such men as Agricola (1494–1555) and Johann Rudolf Glauber (1604–1668) expanded the knowledge of chemical materials and processes.

Founding of Modern Chemistry.—The seventeenth century might well be considered as the begining of scientific chemistry. By this time the work of the iatrochemists and their contemporaries had completely destroyed alchemy. The work of Francis Bacon (1561–1626) in chemistry, Galileo Galilei (1564–1642) in astronomy and physics, William Harvey (1578–1657) in anatomy, and William Gilbert (1540–1603) in physics during the latter part of the sixteenth century had established the superiority of the *scientific method* (inductive reasoning) over the *Aristotelian method* (deductive reasoning). In the Aristotelian method, the scientist would first state a self-evident truth (such as that heavy bodies fall faster than light ones) and then prove it by finding a phenomenon that could be explained by this truth (such as that a pound of lead obviously falls faster than a feather). In the scientific method, the scientist derives a general conclusion from a multi-

BETTMANN ARCHIVE

THE LABORATORY of a medieval alchemist.

tude of observations and experiments (such as dropping a ten-pound lead weight and a five-pound lead weight from the top of a tall building and seeing that they fall at exactly the same speed) and then applies the conclusion to specific cases (such as that a pound of lead and a feather will fall at the same speed in a vacuum).

■**TRUE CHEMISTS.**—Following these pioneers, men like Jean Rey (fl. 1630) and John Mayow (1640–1679) became chemists in the modern sense of the word. However, it is Robert Boyle (1627–1691) who deserves to be called the father of modern chemistry. Boyle was the first to distinguish between elements, compounds, and mixtures. In his book, *The Sceptical Chymist,* published in 1661, he stated the goal of modern chemistry—investigation of the composition and properties of substances, to be explained in terms of elements. In addition, Boyle pioneered chemical analysis and the study of chemical reactions, and established the relationship between the pressure and volume of a fixed amount of gas, a relationship known as Boyle's law.

■**PHLOGISTON THEORY.**—Among the major questions that the seventeenth century chemists tried to answer was what caused combustion. In an effort to explain this, Johann Joachim Becher (1635–1682) and his student Georg Ernst Stahl (1660–1734) developed the theory of *phlogiston.* Phlogiston was a principle and therefore could not be isolated; it could be known only by its effects. According to the phlogiston theory, only those substances that contained phlogiston could burn. When such a substance burned, the phlogiston was thought to escape into the air. It was not until the eighteenth century and the introduction of quantitative chemistry that the phlogiston theory was finally disproved. Phlogiston's importance to chemistry was that it was the first unified chemical theory.

Rise of Quantitative Chemistry.—The next great advance in chemistry was made in the eighteenth century. The industrial revolution began during this period, and chemists were called upon to make their contributions. As a result, the eighteenth century was a period of remarkable growth and discovery. Among the more noteworthy advances were the studies of chemical affinity by Etienne François Geoffroy (1672–1731) and Torbern Olof Bergman (1735–1784); the independent isolation of oxygen by Joseph Priestley (1733–1804) and Karl Wilhelm Scheele (1742–1786); the discovery of hydrogen by Henry Cavendish (1731–1810); and the work of Joseph Black (1728–1799) on heat and temperature.

The greatest chemist of the eighteenth century, however, was Antoine Laurent Lavoisier (1743–1794). Based on the work of his predecessors, Lavoisier devised a method of chemical nomenclature, developed a theory of acid and base formation,

ANTOINE LAURENT LAVOISIER,
FERMIER GÉNÉRAL NÉ A PARIS LE 16 AOUT 1743.

BETTMANN ARCHIVE

ANTOINE LAVOISIER (*left*) proposed the law of conservation of mass. During the French Revolution, he was arrested (*above*) and executed.

and proposed the law of conservation of mass. His greatest contributions, however, were to propose the theory of oxidation and to disprove the phlogiston principle. In 1756, a Russian chemist, Mikhail Lomonosov (1711–1765), had proved that when iron rusted, it gained weight by combining with something in the air. In 1774, Lavoisier repeated Lomonosov's experiment and concluded that the iron had combined with oxygen. By 1778, utilizing his theory of oxidation, Lavoisier was able to explain quantitatively many of the reactions the phlogistonists had either ignored or been unable to explain.

Atomic Hypothesis.—Having been freed from the phlogiston principle by Lavoisier's work, chemistry made great strides forward. John Dalton (1766–1844), an English schoolmaster, conducted a number of experiments on pure and mixed gases. In an effort to explain his results, and influenced by the writings of the early Greek philosophers Democritus and Leucippus, Dalton proposed his atomic hypothesis in 1808. Dalton's hypothesis stated that matter was composed of discrete particles called atoms, and that all atoms of the same element were alike; but that atoms of different elements were different. As part of his hypothesis, Dalton also stated that compounds were formed by the union of atoms of different elements in simple numerical proportions, and that if elements formed more than one kind of compound, the different weights of each compound were in the ratio of small whole numbers (*the law of multiple proportions*).

Progress in the Nineteenth Century.—Stimulated by Dalton's atomic hypothesis, the progress made during the following one hundred years was astounding. More than half of the elements presently known to man were discovered. Jöns Jakob Berzelius (1779–1848) developed a standardized system of chemical symbols and formulas in 1819. Robert Wilhelm Bunsen (1811–1899) and Gustav Robert Kirchhoff (1824–1887) developed the science of chemical spectroscopy. The studies of electrolysis

by Michael Faraday (1791–1867) led to the theories of ionic interactions proposed by Svante August Arrhenius (1859–1927) and Jacobus Hendricus van't Hoff (1852–1911), while the phase rule proposed by Henri Louis Le Châtelier (1850–1936) advanced the field of physical chemistry considerably. Indeed, the number of men who made significant contributions to the development of chemical science during this period is so great it is impossible to list them all here. Nevertheless, two advances were made whose importance necessitates their mention in great detail—the development of organic chemistry and establishment of the periodic system.

■**GROWTH OF ORGANIC CHEMISTRY.**—Between 1810 and 1815, improved methods of analysis led to the development of methods for the analysis of *organic compounds* (compounds of carbon that were thought to be producible only by living organisms). During this period, several classes of organic compounds were recognized. The greatest advance, however, was not made until 1828, when Friedrich Wöhler (1800–1882) converted an inorganic salt (ammonium cyanate, a compound produced by neither plants nor animals) into the organic compound urea. Justus von Liebig (1803–1873) later collaborated with Wöhler to establish the existence of a number of organic groups that remain unaltered through many chemical changes. The next stride forward was made by Friedrich Kekulé (1829–

BETTMANN ARCHIVE

JOHN DALTON, famous English chemist.

1896), who developed the concept that carbon had a fixed combining power, or *valence*. This idea that carbon had the ability to form four "bonds" with other atoms led to the use of structural formulas to represent organic compounds and made the organic chemist's task far simpler.

■**PERIODIC SYSTEM.**—Once John Dalton established his atomic hypothesis, chemists began to search for some relation between the properties of the elements and their atomic weight (the relative weights of the elements when the weight of carbon is arbitrarily set at 12.000). In 1829, Johann Döbereiner (1780–1849) proposed his rule of triads. Döbereiner noted that in several groupings of three elements of similar properties, called *triads*, the central element had an atomic weight that was almost the arithmetical mean of the other two. (For example, if chlorine, bromine, and iodine are grouped, it is found that the atomic weight of chlorine is 35.453, the atomic weight of bromine is 79.909, and the atomic weight of iodine is 126.904; the arithmetical mean of the atomic weights of chlorine and iodine is 81.179, or slightly more than the atomic weight of bromine.) This regularity led to the idea that the triads were but a part of a regular system that included all the elements. However, atomic weights were not put on an accurate basis until 1858, when Stanislao Cannizzaro (1826–1910) developed a new method for their determination, so no significant advances were made through the use of Döbereiner's triads. In 1863, John A. R. Newlands (1837–1898) discovered another means of categorizing the elements. He found that when the elements were listed in order of increasing atomic weight, each succeeding eighth element had similar properties. Since the eighth element was "a kind of repetition of the first, like the eighth note of an octave in music," Newlands called this relation the *law of octaves*. Unfortunately, the system did not work for elements heavier than chlorine, and the law of octaves fell into disuse. However, in 1869, Dmitri I. Mendeleev (1834–1907) published a periodic table based on the law of octaves, in which he had made adjustments for the difficulty presented by the elements heavier than chlorine. This arrangement was so good, and the concept was so clearly developed, that Mendeleev's name has been connected with the periodic table ever since, even though Julius Lothar Meyer (1830–1895) independently made the same discovery one year after Mendeleev.

Chemistry in the Twentieth Century.—

In the twentieth century, the line separating chemistry and physics has blurred to the point where it is now almost indistinguishable. The reason for this is that the chemist has found he can no longer deal solely with the thought of reactions between elements and compounds. He must now do his thinking on the atomic and subatomic scale, and thus his sphere of interest considerably overlaps that of the nuclear physicist. In the early part of the twentieth century, the emphasis was on developing a clear picture of the atom. Great progress in the determination of atomic structure was achieved through the work of Sir Joseph John Thomson (1856–1940), Ernest Rutherford (1871–1937), and Henry G.-J. Moseley (1887–1915). Much effort was concentrated on the study of radioactivity, based upon the discovery of radium by Pierre and Marie Curie in 1898. Sir William Henry Bragg (1862–1942) and his son William Lawrence Bragg (1890–   ) pioneered in the study of crystal structure through the use of X-ray diffraction techniques. As the century progressed, Gilbert Newton Lewis (1875–1946), Irving Langmuir (1881–1957), and Linus Carl Pauling (1901–   ) contributed to the chemist's understanding of chemical bonding. Others, such as Peter Joseph Wilhelm Debye (1884–   ), clarified the mechanism of chemical reactions. In 1940, three radioactive elements that do not occur naturally on earth (promethium, plutonium, neptunium) were synthesized, as have been nine other elements since.

The progress made in chemistry since 1900 could fill several books of this size, and it is impossible to properly evaluate and emphasize the importance of all that has been done within the scope of this article. It is fairly safe to say, however, that the accomplishments of the second half of the twentieth century will probably dwarf those of the first half in the same manner that the contributions of the iatrochemists have dwarfed those of the alchemists.

Branches of Chemistry.—

Prior to the seventeenth century, there were no branches of chemistry. Indeed, prior to that time, there were no chemists —at least not in the sense of a chemist as a man who specializes in the study of chemistry. Until the early 1600's no one specialized in any particular field of science. Instead, men were scientists—they studied and experimented in all fields.

However, as the years passed and the amount of background knowledge an experimenter had to possess increased, men began to specialize. First the biological scientists separated from the physical scientists; then the physical scientists separated to form the branches of chemistry, physics, and geology. Thus, scientists like Robert Boyle (1627–1691), who studied gases, became chemists; those like Isaac Newton (1642–1727), who studied mechanics, became physicists. As the background knowledge an experimenter needed continued to grow, these subdivisions subdivided within themselves. In this way, a number of specialized branches of chemistry came into being before the end of the nineteenth century.

As time passed, it became evident that the sharp boundaries separating one branch of chemistry from another, as well as those separating chemistry from the other branches of science, were practically nonexistent. The branches of chemistry are, therefore, of only limited significance, for they overlap each other and the other branches of science. Indeed, it might be said that the divisions between the sciences are divisions of convenience, and that nature has but small regard for them. Nevertheless, the branches of chemistry are of considerable historical importance and deserve recognition, if only for this reason.

Inorganic chemistry is the study of the properties and reactions of all the elements and their compounds, except most of the compounds of carbon. It is concerned with the occurrence of these elements in nature, methods of obtaining them, and the laboratory techniques, theories, hypotheses, and laws basic to all branches of chemistry.

Organic chemistry is the study of the compounds of carbon, the hydrocarbons, and the fluorocarbons. The majority of compounds found in living organisms, dyes, plastics, petroleum, petroleum products, and many other materials are organic. Thus, there are hundreds of thousands of carbon compounds for the organic chemist to study.

Physical chemistry is the study of the dependence of physical properties of materials upon their chemical composition, and of the physical changes that accompany chemical reactions. Physical chemistry is itself divided into several branches. *Colloid chemistry* is concerned with the behavior of finely divided particles of matter; *surface chemistry*, with the behavior of surfaces; *chemical thermodynamics*, with the role of energy in chemical reactions; *chemical kinetics*, with the speed and mechanism of chemical reactions; *electrochemistry*, with the behavior of chemical substances when treated with an electric current and with the production of electricity by chemical means; and *photochemistry*, with the chemical effects of electromagnetic radiation and with the production of electromagnetic radiation in chemical change.

Analytical chemistry is concerned with the splitting of materials into component parts (or constituents) by chemical methods to determine composition. In *qualitative analysis*, the chemist determines the constituents of the material, irrespective of their amount. In *quantitative analysis*, the chemist must determine the amounts in which the various constituents are present in a material.

Nuclear chemistry is the study of reactions that produce new elements, of the chemical effects produced by high-energy radiation, and of the tracing and behavior of radioactive isotopes.

Biochemistry is the study of the chemical composition and behavior of living organisms and life processes. In many respects it is a combination of organic chemistry, physical chemistry, botany, and zoology.

Geochemistry is concerned with the chemical study of the earth's crust, and the application of chemistry to processes (such as the formation of minerals and the metamorphosis of rocks) within the earth.

Industrial chemistry merges chemistry and chemical engineering. It includes the design, installation, and maintenance of industrial equipment for chemical reactions, the technology and financial practices necessary for collecting raw materials and marketing products, and the development of large-scale, economically feasible industrial processes from research.

—A. D. Levy

BETTMANN ARCHIVE

NEILS BOHR, Danish nuclear chemist, was one of the first to suggest to President Franklin D. Roosevelt that an atomic chain reaction, key to the atomic bomb, was a possibility.

INORGANIC CHEMISTRY

Basic Definitions.—*Chemistry* is the body of knowledge and practices concerned with the properties of atoms, ions, and molecules and with the changes that can be brought about in the arrangement of their electrons. Specifically excluded from chemistry is the study of the changes that occur in the nucleus of the atom. Before atomic structure was understood, chemistry was defined as the study of the properties of substances and of the transformations that substances undergo. *Inorganic chemistry*, one of the primary branches of chemistry, is the study of the specific properties of the atoms of the different elements, the ions and molecules they form (excluding molecules of certain carbon compounds which are the concern of organic chemistry), their occurrence in nature, the methods of obtaining them, their usefulness in our culture, and the laboratory techniques, theories, and laws all chemists must use.

Three concepts basic to all sciences,—and especially relevant to inorganic chemistry—are volume, mass, and energy. The volume of an object is the amount of space it occupies. Mass and energy are more abstract concepts, however. Mass can best be understood in terms of the *law of universal gravitation,* which states that all matter is attracted to all other matter by a force that varies inversely as the square of the distance between them. The closer the bits of matter are to each other, the more strongly they are attracted. The *weight* of an object is a measure of this attraction or force. The weight of an object thus varies with its position relative to other bodies near it, though the actual amount of matter in it is always the same. The word *mass* expresses this unchanging inertial quantity of matter in an object. The concept of *energy* is even more abstract. Many kinds of energy have been distinguished, some of the most familiar being mechanical, chemical, heat, radiant, electrical, nuclear, and kinetic. Each can be converted into any of the other kinds. For example, in an automobile engine the chemical energy of a gasoline and air mixture is converted into the heat energy of the gases produced by the explosion of the mixture; the gases expand and push the piston down, turning the crankshaft and the rear wheels in a transfer of mechanical energy; as the car begins to move, it acquires kinetic energy. Another example is that of the kinetic energy of falling water, which can be transformed through a turbine into mechanical and then into electric energy, which in turn can be changed into heat, radiant, or again to mechanical energy.

Such concepts are useful because they can be expressed quantitatively, that is, in numbers. All the physical properties of materials, such as index of refraction, density, color, conductivity, magnetic strength, tensile strength, coefficient of expansion, heats of fusion and vaporization, compressibility, and many more, are measured by mathematical formulas derived from the basic units of measurement—length, time, and mass, and a fourth unit for electricity. On the other hand, chemical properties cannot be reported quantitatively; they are descriptions of chemical reactions in which one or more substances will participate.

The most important basic principle in science is the law of conservation of matter and of energy, which states that matter can be converted into energy, and vice versa, but the sum of the two before any event is the same as the sum of the two after the event. All experimental evidence supports the principle. It is further assumed, because so far nothing denies it, that all matter and energy obey the identical laws throughout the universe.

Kinetic Molecular Theory.—The basic structure of matter is defined by the *kinetic molecular theory,* which states that all matter consists of ultimate, or finite, particles in constant motion, and that their motion, or kinetic energy, is what we call heat. The greater their heat energy, the faster they move, and thus the greater their kinetic energy. The kinetic energy of an object equals $\frac{1}{2}mv^2$, m being the object's mass and v its speed. The law applies to any atom, ion (electrically charged atom), or molecule (atoms in chemical union); and it applies with qualifications to any subatomic particle, although chemists are interested only in electrons, protons, and neutrons. All these particles are perfectly elastic and lose none of their kinetic energy to friction when they collide, as bulk matter always does. The identification of heat energy with movement of basic particles explains many baffling aspects of nature, including the structure and properties of the three *states,* or *phases,* of matter: gas, liquid, and solid (see also *Properties of Matter,* page 1202).

■**GASES.**—A gas consists of atoms, ions, or molecules moving at random in space. They travel along individual

BETTMANN ARCHIVE

CUNEIFORM TEXT of a Babylonian chemical formula from the seventeenth century B.C.

paths free of the influence of other particles' attraction but, because of collisions with one another, constantly change direction. The volume of the particles themselves is but a minute fraction of the space they can occupy. Since they are perfectly elastic, the sum of the energies of two particles before a collision equals the sum of their energies after the collision, although the energy will be distributed differently between them. At no instant do all the particles in a gas move with the same speed or in the same direction. Therefore, when we speak of the temperature of a gas, we are speaking of the average kinetic energy of all the particles. Slow ones are being speeded up and fast ones are being slowed down by collisions, so that, according to calculations made by the British physicist James Clerk Maxwell (1831–1879), about half of the particles possess speeds within 30 per cent of the average. A few are always traveling very rapidly and a few very slowly, but in any gas or mixture of gases, the kinetic energy of many molecules is close to the average.

The pressure of a gas is understandable in terms of the continual bombardment of the walls of a container by rapidly moving particles. The pressure, which is the same everywhere on every wall of the container, is determined by the number of impacts per unit time and by the force of the impacts. If the gas in a container with a movable top is compressed, the average distance the particles travel between collisions is reduced, and the number of impacts each second on the container walls is increased. Therefore, when a gas is compressed, its pressure increases. If the gas is allowed to expand, there will be fewer impacts per second on the container walls, and the pressure will be less. *Boyle's law*—named for its discoverer, Robert Boyle (1627–1691)—states that a volume (V) of a fixed amount of gas is inversely proportional to the pressure (P), if the temperature (T) is constant. Thus, $V \propto 1/P$ or $V = k/P$ (k is the constant of proportionality) if T is constant.

If the gas in the container is heated from the outside, the kinetic energy of each particle is increased, and the particle will hit with greater impact and greater frequency. Therefore, the pressure of the gas will rise. In order to maintain the original pressure, the gas must be allowed to expand. On the other hand, if the gas is cooled from the outside, the particles will move more slowly, the number of their impacts per unit time will decrease, and the pressure will decrease. In order to exert the same pressure as it did at a higher temperature in a larger space, the gas must be compressed. If this reduction in volume is measured, it is found that for each drop of 1° C. starting at 0° C., the gas will shrink 1/273 of its volume. Theoretically then, at −273° C. the gas will vanish. This means that, since shrinking in volume due to cooling is proportional to the lowering of kinetic energy, at −273° C. all motion of the particles ceases—they will be without any heat energy. This temperature is called *absolute zero*. Thus, on a Kelvin or Rankine thermometer, both of which are calibrated to register absolute temperatures, absolute zero (−273.16° C. or −459.6° F.) is 0°. *Charles's law,* formulated by Jacques Alexandre César Charles (1746–1823), states that the volume of a fixed amount of gas is proportional to the absolute temperature, if the pressure remains the same. Thus $V \propto T_a$ (V is the volume and T_a is the absolute temperature), or $V = kT_a$ (k is the constant of proportionality), when P is constant. Boyle's law and Charles's law can be combined into one equation: $V = 1/P$ (T_a), or $PV = kT_a$.

If different gases are mixed, each will exert the pressure that it would in that space if it were by itself. The statement that the total pressure of several different gases in the same containers equals the sum of their individual pressures is *Dalton's law of partial pressures,* named after its discoverer, John Dalton (1766–1844). *Graham's law,* formulated by Thomas Graham (1805–1869), states that a gas diffuses through small openings at a rate inversely proportional to the square root of its density.

In two containers of equal size, containing the same number of molecules at the same temperature, the pressures will be the same. Therefore, equal volumes of all gases at the same temperature and pressure must contain equal numbers of molecules. This was proved in 1811 by Amadeo Avogadro (1776–1856) and is called *Avogadro's hypothesis*. It provides a method for comparing the masses of different molecules. If a known volume of gas A is weighed and the same volume of gas B is weighed under the same conditions, then the number of A molecules equals the number of B molecules; if the total weight of all the molecules of gas B is four times as great as that of all the molecules of gas A, then each molecule of B weighs four times as much as each molecule of A. Actually, it is not necessary that the volume, the temperature, and the pressure of the gases be the same, because any set of these measurements can be compared to a selected standard of temperature and pressure, which by international agreement is 0° C. and 760 mm. of mercury.

The earth's atmosphere is a mixture of gases whose composition, density, and temperature are constantly changing. Any experiment not sealed from the atmosphere will be affected by it; if the effect is significant, it is necessarily part of the report of that experiment. A gas in a container exerts the same pressure in all directions because of its kinetic energy; the atmosphere, which is not enclosed, does not escape into space because of gravity, which keeps it much more dense at the surface of the earth. The pressure of the atmosphere at a point on the earth's surface is the actual weight of air above that point.

INTERNATIONAL BUSINESS MACHINES CORPORATION

PRECOOLING low-temperature apparatus with liquid nitrogen involves cryogenics.

A common experience with a gas is that it cools as it expands. This phenomenon is called the *Joule-Thomson effect* after its discoverers, James Prescott Joule (1818–1889) and William Thomson (1824–1907). The effect is explained by the fact that there is an attraction between gas molecules during the instant of a collision; this must be overcome as they bounce apart. The energy to overcome the attraction is derived from the molecules' heat. When a gas has a fixed volume, the number of collisions each second does not change, and the speeding up and heating just before each impact takes place equal the cooling just after. If the gas is expanding, the heat lost by molecules working against attraction is not all regained, and the gas cools. The Joule-Thomson effect is the basis of all refrigeration systems.

The gas laws are accurate for an imagined ideal gas whose molecules are considered to be mathematical points. Since real molecules have volume and mass and attract one another when in close proximity, the gas laws are inaccurate for high pressures or low temperatures.

■ **LIQUIDS.**—When a gas is cooled and the average kinetic energy of its molecules is reduced, the molecules will spend more time in each other's vicinity. The forces of attraction between them will make it more difficult for the molecules to bounce apart. Eventually they will lose enough energy, as the cooling is continued, to be unable to bounce apart and will cling together. As the temperature is lowered still further, clusters grow into droplets of liquid. Within the liquid phase the molecules continue to move with the same average kinetic energy that they have in the gas phase at the same tem-

perature, but they cannot escape each other and merely slide about. A liquid maintains its volume at any fixed temperature.

To turn a liquid into a gas, heat must be added to it from the outside. The heat is absorbed by the molecules and increases their kinetic energy; and the increased energy enables them to overcome each other's attraction. Whatever the temperature of the liquid, the vapor directly above it has the same temperature, and all the molecules in both phases have the same average kinetic energy. The energy that a molecule must acquire in order to move from liquid to gas is called its *heat of vaporization*. When a gas molecule gives up its freedom in space and returns to the liquid phase, it gives up to the environment its *heat of condensation,* which is identical to its heat of vaporization. In a closed container partly filled with liquid, fast-moving molecules in the liquid that have absorbed their heat of vaporization through collisions or radiation leave the liquid surface, while slow-moving molecules in the vapor are trapped by the liquid surface when they hit it and give up their heat of condensation. If the temperature is kept constant in the closed container, the exchange of molecules is equal, and the total number of molecules in the gaseous phase does not change. A *dynamic equilibrium* exists between liquid and gas. Any change in temperature changes the kinetic energy of the gas molecules and therefore changes the vapor pressure. If the gas molecules escape from the container, the liquid evaporates; an evaporating liquid is always cooler than its environment because each escaping molecule takes away with it a measure of heat.

In a boiling liquid enough heat is being supplied from outside to cause evaporation throughout the liquid. However, no matter how fast a liquid is boiled (that is, no matter how much heat is applied), its temperature remains constant and is the same as the temperature of its vapor until all the liquid has evaporated. Then more heat will raise the temperature of the vapor.

An average molecule at the surface of a liquid is pulled downward into the liquid by forces of attraction that are greater than the upward attraction exerted by the vapor. This greater attraction of surface molecules pulls drops into a spherical shape. The wetting of surfaces is determined by a complicated set of affinities and repulsions between a liquid and a solid. In a narrow tube the result may be to pull a liquid upward or to depress it, a phenomenon called *capillary action*. Trees lift tons of water from their roots to their foliage, partly by capillary action and partly by osmosis.

A gas can be compressed until its molecules are so close together that they release their heat of condensation and become liquid. Each gas, however, has a *critical temperature* above which it cannot be liquefied by pressure.

■**SOLIDS.**—When a liquid is cooled, a temperature, called the *freezing point*, is reached at which the slowly moving molecules are caught by new forces of attraction, forces stronger still than those of the liquid. The molecules relinquish their freedom of motion entirely and cling together. As cooling is continued, more are trapped, and a crystal begins to form within which the molecules continue to vibrate around one position. Besides their freedom they have lost a specific amount of energy, called their *heat of fusion.*

Under certain conditions, all three phases of some substances, such as water, can thus exist together at the freezing point. Any molecule in this three-phase system can change its condition to solid, liquid, or vapor, according to whether it gains or loses its heat of fusion and its heat of vaporization. It should be noted, however, that the temperatures of the solid, the liquid, and the vapor in a three-phase system, are the same.

Each substance has a distinctive freezing point and boiling point, but all substances lose all heat and kinetic energy at 0° absolute. At temperatures close to this, matter shows bizarre properties that the kinetic molecular theory cannot explain. For example, at cold near 0° Kelvin, helium creeps out of its container, and metals become superconductors of electricity.

When the molecules in a crystal freeze, they arrange themselves to give the crystal one of half a dozen geometric shapes by which the substance can be identified. Solids without crystal shape are called *amorphous.* Some substances have more than one crystal shape, each melting at a different temperature; and these are called *allotropic forms.* Most solids have vapor pressures far smaller than those of their liquids, but a few have such high vapor pressures that they turn directly into a gas, or *sublimate,* without passing through the liquid phase. Solid carbon dioxide (dry ice), iodine, and naphthalene are examples of substances that undergo sublimation.

Atomic Theory.—The kinetic molecular theory does not try to explain the chemical properties of substances or what happens in a chemical reaction. This is accomplished by the *atomic theory* and by knowledge of atomic structure.

All the matter in the universe consists of substances called *elements;* the smallest part of an element that still has all the properties of that element in bulk is called an *atom.* In chemical combination, the atoms of the elements unite to form molecules. A *molecule* is the smallest particle of a compound that shows all the properties of that compound. There are 91 naturally occurring elements and 13 others that have been created by man in nuclear reactors. The universe consists of these hundred-odd elements and of the compounds they form with one another, a number that is almost unlimited, theoretically and in reality. Over a million compounds are known

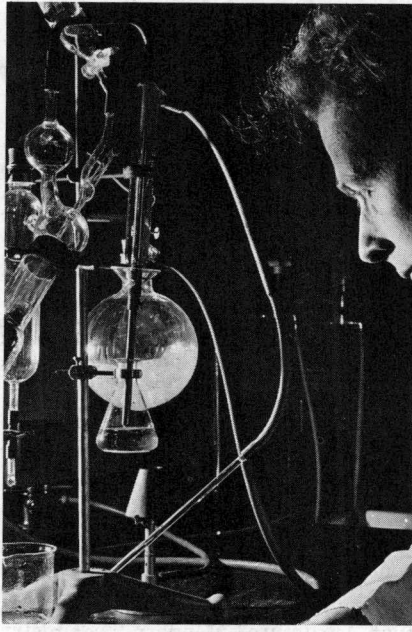

EXPERIMENTAL CHEMIST is determining the nitrogen content in petroleum fractions.

today, a great many of which never existed before they were synthesized in the laboratory.

All the atoms of an element are alike in every way (except in mass: see ISOTOPES) and are unlike the atoms of every other element. All the molecules of a compound are alike in every way; that is, the same kinds of atoms always join together in the same proportion to form the same kind of molecule. The same atoms may also join together in different proportions to form different molecules. For example, carbon atoms may unite with oxygen atoms in three different proportions to form three different compounds: one carbon atom may join with one oxygen atom to form carbon monoxide; one carbon atom may join with two oxygen atoms to form carbon dioxide; three carbon atoms may join with two oxygen atoms to form carbon suboxide. During the process of chemical combination, neither matter nor energy is created or destroyed. However, an energy change is always associated with chemical reactions. Usually heat and/or light will be released to the surroundings or absorbed from it. The quantity of heat and/or light involved is specific for each reaction.

Each element has been assigned a symbol consisting of one or two letters—for example, the symbol for hydrogen is H; for oxygen, O; for carbon, C; for helium, He; for iron, Fe; and for gold, Au. These symbols are used as a form of shorthand by the chemist. To designate a compound, the symbol of each element present in the molecule is written. If more than one atom of any of the elements is present in the molecule, the number of atoms is written as a subscript to the right of the symbol for that element. Thus, the three

compounds of carbon and oxygen named above would be written as CO (carbon monoxide), CO_2 (carbon dioxide), and C_3O_2 (carbon suboxide). If the chemist desires to indicate more than one molecule of the compound, the number of molecules is written to the left of the formula of the compound—for example, 2CO, $3CO_2$, $15C_3O_2$, etc.

Atomic Structure.—The modern concept of *atomic structure* is based upon existence of three subatomic particles: the electron, the proton, and the neutron. The *electron* has a negative electrical charge; the *proton,* a positive electrical charge; and the *neutron,* no electrical charge (that is, it is electrically neutral). Like charges repel one another and unlike charges attract each other; all protons repel all other protons and all electrons repel all other electrons, but any proton and any electron attract each other. The positive charge on the proton exactly equals the negative charge on the electron. The atom as a whole is neutral.

The first structure proposed for the atom was that of a sphere of positive electricity in which electrons were embedded to make it electrically neutral. When experiments proved that the atom, tiny though it is, consists largely of space, the electrons were imagined in positions at some distance from a positive nucleus. However, this could not explain why the electrons were not pulled into the nucleus.

To overcome this and several other serious objections to the model, in 1913 the Danish physicist Niels Bohr (1885–1962) postulated a different kind of electron structure around the nucleus. In the Bohr model of the atom, every atom consists of a nucleus that is positively charged and, at a distance from it, a number of electrons that exactly balance the positive charge and are in continuous motion around the nucleus. The simplest pictorialization is a dot for the nucleus and a circle around it for the path of the electron, but this is an extremely symbolic representation of what really exists. An atom with a radius of 10^{-8} centimeters has a nucleus only a thousandth as large. It is impossible to draw a scale model on a sheet of paper because a visible dot representing the nucleus would have to have a dot representing the electron drawn many yards away. To make representation still more difficult, nearly all the mass of the atom is in the nucleus; each proton and neutron weighs almost 1,800 times as much as an electron, yet the electron can be said to have a volume 2½ times that of a proton.

According to the Bohr model of the atom, the electron travels around the nucleus at speeds in the range of the speed of light. In the pictorial representation of the atom, the direction of movement of the electron can be indicated by an arrow on the circle representing the electron's orbit around the nucleus. Although the direction is constant, the electron orbits in all planes around the nucleus, and sometimes its path is circular, sometimes elliptical, sometimes dumbbell-shaped, and sometimes too complicated to describe. When an electron orbiting the nucleus in a certain way receives more energy from the outside through collision or through absorption of radiation, the electron will move into a different orbit farther from the nucleus. Finally, each electron and each nucleus spins on its own axis; and the atom as a whole also spins about, or vibrates around one spot, according to the kinetic molecular theory.

A reference to physics is necessary to understand why the atom retains its shape when all its parts are moving. If a stone on the end of a string is swung fast enough, it will travel around, or orbit, the person swinging it. This phenomenon is explained by Sir Isaac Newton's first law of motion, which states that a body at rest tends to remain at rest and a body in motion tends to remain in motion in the same direction (that is, along a straight-line path) unless an external force acts upon it. The tendency to remain at rest or in straight-line motion is called *inertia*. Thus the stone, having been placed in motion, tends to fly off in a straight line, at right angles to the string. The inertial pull away from the center of the orbit is called *centrifugal force* (although it is not really a force). The string exerts the continuous external force required to overcome the straight-line motion of the stone and change the stone's path into a circular orbit. The force exerted by the string toward the center of the orbit is called *centripetal force*. In an atom, the electron is attracted to the nucleus because the electron has a negative charge and the nucleus has a positive charge. However, the electron does not fall into the nucleus because the inertial tendency of its motion—its tendency to move away in a straight line—balances the centripetal force of the attraction of the nucleus.

The contemporary model of the atom with all its details is based on information collected by a variety of instruments. Highly heated atoms emit light. If the light is studied in a spectroscope, distinctive lines are found in the spectrum for each element. The lines can be interpreted as specific variations in electron arrangements within the different atoms. In the mass spectrograph, atoms are given an electrical charge and are then lobbed by a magnetic field at a photographic plate; the heavier ones will land at nearer places on the plate than the lighter ones. The point of each atom's impact appears as a spot on the film. By studying the distances traveled by the atoms, the masses of the different atoms can be calculated. X rays projected through a crystal are scattered by the latticework of atomic nuclei in the crystal and, falling on a photographic plate, produce a pattern of dots. From the pattern the three-dimensional lattice of atoms in the crystal can be worked out to give accurate figures for the diameter of the atoms. A system of using electrons as though they were rays of light produces photographs of shadows cast by very large molecular shapes from which a great deal of information about atomic structure can be deduced. Most vital of all sources of information are the various so-called *atom smashers*, the first of which, the *cyclotron,* was built in 1933, and the *nuclear reactors,* or *atomic piles,* the first of which was developed in 1941. In all these, the nuclei of atoms are broken up and the results are recorded and studied. For example, the results may be recorded as streaks and spots on photographic plates, as needles moving across instrument faces, as threads of mist, as scintillations on a screen of fluorescent chemical, as intensity of a glow, or as a rate of clicking in earphones. These and other kinds of sensory observations are made in quantitative terms, and the figures are then translated by formulas into statements of mathematical relationship between different parts of atoms. Such statements are developed into concepts of structure that, though far from fully understood, are nevertheless used in probing further into that structure. Modern chemistry utilizes a great deal of nuclear knowledge to explain chemical activity.

■ **ELECTRONS.** — The most important parts of the atom in chemical reactions are the electrons orbiting around the nucleus. Some of these electrons seem to be imbedded in the nucleus itself, but these do not concern the chemist. The electron reveals two sets of properties, one indicating it is a solid particle and the other that it is a wave. That is, the electron behaves both as a particle and as a wave, a dual nature for which there is no theory. The wave aspect is defined by *quantum mechanics,* which was developed when units of energy were discovered to exist and to have measurable mass. The units were named *quanta,* and a quantum of light is called a *photon.* Electrons orbiting in an atom can absorb and emit photons. Another aspect of the electron is that no fixed position for it in the atom can be ascertained. Instead of saying that an electron orbits at a certain distance from the nucleus, it is more accurate to say that the probability of finding the electron is greatest at a certain distance from the nucleus. In chemistry the most useful concept of an electron is that it is a solid particle whose position can always be stated precisely; the probability and wave aspects of the electron are seldom referred to. Nevertheless, both the physical and chemical properties of the elements are being viewed with increasing freedom as expressions of mathematical relationships based on quantum mechanics. The reason for this recent shift from physical models to mathematical definitions lies in the fact that knowledge of the energy distribution within the atom is far more useful for explaining and predicting chemical reactions than knowledge of the geographical distribution of bits of subatomic matter. However, no single view explains everything that is known.

■ **NUCLEUS.** — Thirty-four different kinds of particles have been isolated and defined in terms of their mass, speed, electrical charge, spin, whether they fit the mathematical definitions for bits of energy or for bits of matter, and how they will react with each other upon collision. Chemistry is primarily concerned with only three of these particles—the electron, the neutron, and the proton. The neutron, which has no electrical charge, weighs slightly more than the proton, which has a positive charge. Their mass is so much greater than that of any of the other particles that the mass of all the others together is considered negligible in chemical computations. Protons and neutrons are joined in the nucleus of the atom with electrons—other than those orbiting outside—and other elementary particles in a manner that is not yet clear. Because of the comparatively great mass of neutrons and protons, the entire mass of the atom is considered as being concentrated in the nucleus. The electron, proton, and neutron can exist singly and can endure, as far as is known, through eternity, while the other bits liberated when the nucleus is broken are considerably less stable. The electrons that exist in the nucleus manifest their presence only upon the rupture of the nucleus, something that never happens in chemical reactions, and so they do not come into chemical discussion. They are referred to as *beta particles* to keep their origin in view.

Thus, the basis of atomic structure is a nucleus containing protons and neutrons surrounded by rapidly moving electrons. Since, as has been stated, the atoms of each element are identical (except for mass) but are different from the atoms of every other element, it stands to reason that this difference between atoms must be one of protons, neutrons, and electrons. There must be at least 104 different combinations, one for each of the 104 known elements. Studies of atomic structure have established that elements can be listed in such a way that an atom of each succeeding element on the list has exactly one proton more than the element preceding it. For example, hydrogen, No. 1 on the list, has one proton; helium, No. 2 on the list, has two

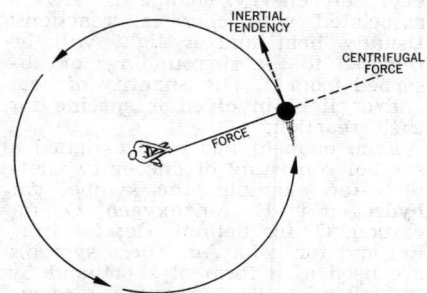

CENTRIPETAL AND CENTRIFUGAL FORCE are opposing actions causing atoms to retain their shape. If a man were to swing a weight, the inertial tendency would be for the weight, like electrons about a nucleus, to move away in a straight line.

TABLE OF ATOMIC WEIGHTS
(Based on Carbon-12)

Name	Symbol	Atomic Number	Atomic Weight	Name	Symbol	Atomic Number	Atomic Weight
Actinium	Ac	89	227	Mercury	Hg	80	200.59
Aluminum	Al	13	26.9815	Molybdenum	Mo	42	95.94
Americium	Am	95	243	Neodymium	Nd	60	144.24
Antimony	Sb	51	121.75	Neon	Ne	10	20.183
Argon	Ar	18	39.948	Neptunium	Np	93	237
Arsenic	As	33	74.9216	Nickel	Ni	28	58.71
Astatine	At	85	210	Niobium	Nb	41	92.906
Barium	Ba	56	137.34	Nitrogen	N	7	14.0067
Berkelium	Bk	97	249	Nobelium	No	102	254
Beryllium	Be	4	9.0122	Osmium	Os	76	190.2
Bismuth	Bi	83	208.980	Oxygen	O	8	15.9994
Boron	B	5	10.811	Palladium	Pd	46	106.4
Bromine	Br	35	79.909	Phosphorus	P	15	30.9738
Cadmium	Cd	48	112.40	Platinum	Pt	78	195.09
Calcium	Ca	20	40.08	Plutonium	Pu	94	242
Californium	Cf	98	251	Polonium	Po	84	210
Carbon	C	6	12.01115	Potassium	K	19	39.102
Cerium	Ce	58	140.12	Praseodymium	Pr	59	140.907
Cesium	Cs	55	132.905	Promethium	Pm	61	147
Chlorine	Cl	17	35.453	Protactinium	Pa	91	231
Chromium	Cr	24	51.996	Radium	Ra	88	226
Cobalt	Co	27	58.9332	Radon	Rn	86	222
Copper	Cu	29	63.54	Rhenium	Re	75	186.2
Curium	Cm	96	247	Rhodium	Rh	45	102.905
Dysprosium	Dy	66	162.50	Rubidium	Rb	37	85.47
Einsteinium	Es	99	254	Ruthenium	Ru	44	101.07
Erbium	Er	68	167.26	Samarium	Sm	62	150.35
Europium	Eu	63	151.96	Scandium	Sc	21	44.956
Fermium	Fm	100	253	Selenium	Se	34	78.96
Fluorine	F	9	18.9984	Silicon	Si	14	28.086
Francium	Fr	87	223	Silver	Ag	47	107.870
Gadolinium	Gd	64	157.25	Sodium	Na	11	22.9898
Gallium	Ga	31	69.72	Strontium	Sr	38	87.62
Germanium	Ge	32	72.59	Sulfur	S	16	32.064
Gold	Au	79	196.967	Tantalum	Ta	73	180.948
Hafnium	Hf	72	178.49	Technetium	Tc	43	99
Helium	He	2	4.0026	Tellurium	Te	52	127.60
Holmium	Ho	67	164.930	Terbium	Tb	65	158.924
Hydrogen	H	1	1.00797	Thallium	Tl	81	204.37
Indium	In	49	114.82	Thorium	Th	90	232.038
Iodine	I	53	126.9044	Thulium	Tm	69	168.934
Iridium	Ir	77	192.2	Tin	Sn	50	118.69
Iron	Fe	26	55.847	Titanium	Ti	22	47.90
Krypton	Kr	36	83.80	Tungsten	W	74	183.85
Lanthanum	La	57	138.91	Uranium	U	92	238.03
Lawrencium	Lw	103	257	Vanadium	V	23	50.942
Lead	Pb	82	207.19	Xenon	Xe	54	131.30
Lithium	Li	3	6.939	Ytterbium	Yb	70	173.04
Lutetium	Lu	71	174.97	Yttrium	Y	39	88.905
Magnesium	Mg	12	24.312	Zinc	Zn	30	65.37
Manganese	Mn	25	54.9380	Zirconium	Zr	40	91.22
Mendelevium	Md	101	256				

protons; lithium, No. 3, has three protons; gold, No. 79, has 79 protons; and lawrencium, No. 103 on the list, has 103 protons. The number of an element on the list is called the *atomic number* of that element. It is usually designated by the letter *Z*, and is the same as the number of its protons. Since an atom is electrically neutral, the number of electrons orbiting the nucleus is equal to the number of protons within the nucleus.

While the number of protons in the nucleus is constant for any element, the number of neutrons in the nucleus does not follow any order and can vary in the atoms of an element. For example, oxygen, which is element No. 8 because each of its atoms contains eight protons, has some atoms with eight neutrons, some with nine neutrons, and some with ten neutrons. Each is called an *isotope* of oxygen; almost every element has a number of isotopes. Neutrons do not affect the properties of an element except its mass. The only atom that has no neutrons is protium, the most prevalent isotope of hydrogen, which is element No. 1 on the list because all of its isotopes have a single proton for a nucleus. An isotope of hydrogen called *deuterium* has one neutron with the single proton; water molecules containing deuterium are called *heavy water*. Another hydrogen isotope, called *tritium,* has two neutrons with the single proton.

Atomic Weight.—The chemist is not interested in the actual weight of a single atom, for he deals in bulk matter that contains millions upon millions of atoms. Nevertheless, he must know how the masses of atoms compare with one another. For this purpose the commonest isotope of carbon, which has six protons and six neutrons, has been selected as the standard of *atomic weight* and has been assigned the value of 12. Until 1963 the standard was oxygen, with an atomic weight of 16, but the change affects the old table of atomic weights only very slightly. On the atomic weight scale, the proton has a relative weight of 1.0073; the neutron, 1.0087; and the electron, 0.0005486. Thus, very few elements have atomic weights that are whole numbers. For many calculations in chemistry and physics, however, protons and neutrons are considered to have relative weights of 1 each, and the electrons a mass of zero. Therefore, the *mass number* of an atom is the sum of its neutrons and protons, each counting as 1. It amounts to a workable approximation of the atomic weight. The mass number of hydrogen's most common isotope, protium, is 1; of deuterium, 2; and of tritium, 3. The mixture of hydrogen isotopes found in nature produces a relative atomic weight of 1.008. The atomic weight of uranium's mixture of isotopes is 238.03, but the mass number of the best-known uranium isotope is 235, the sum of 92 protons and 143 neutrons.

The isotopes of an element are chemically indistinguishable, but they can be separated by methods sensi-

MOLECULAR MODEL shows the orbital relationships of electrons within molecules.

tive to the slight differences among their masses. The mass spectrograph is one device that will separate isotopes. Repeated diffusion of gases through porous clays will concentrate the lighter, faster isotopes. The isotopes of an element are so thoroughly mixed by natural forces that, whatever their source, the percentages are always the same. Tin mined in South America has a mixture of isotopes in the same proportion as tin mined in Asia; and refining and use do not vary this proportion. No matter where a sample of water is taken, from Arctic ice or the smoke of burning coal, for every 5,000 atoms of protium there will be 1 atom of deuterium.

Electron Cloud.—Every atom is electrically neutral; for each proton in the nucleus there must be an electron orbiting outside it. Hydrogen, with its single proton nucleus, has a single orbiting electron; and uranium's 92 protons are neutralized by 92 orbiting electrons. If any free electron comes near any free proton, they will affect each other's travel; and if conditions are right, the electron will go into orbit around the proton to create a hydrogen atom. If a naked nucleus with 26 protons and 30 neutrons plows into a cloud of electrons, and the temperature is not over a few thousand degrees, 26 of the electrons will at once arrange themselves around the nucleus to form an atom of iron.

The electrons are both spinning about the nucleus that attracts them and also adjusting against each other's movements and the forces of repulsion that exist among them. At any time the energy of an electron in an atom can be increased, causing it to change its position. But there is a lowest energy level for each electron in an atom; and in the discussion that follows, all the electrons are considered to be at their lowest level of energy, which is also called their *unexcited state* or *ground state*. Several modes of arrangement for electrons can be imagined, but the evidence shows that they are spaced at different distances from the nucleus, as though on the surfaces of concentric spheres, or *shells*. Outer shells hold more electrons than inner ones, since they have a greater surface over which to distribute them.

The nucleus has a field of forces around it in space and the electrons, with their own fields, occupy specific positions within it, positions determined by the total balance of energies. The total energy of an electron is defined in four ways, called *quantum numbers;* there is a choice in each category, and every electron can be described by these four quantum numbers. No two electrons in an atom can have all four of their quantum numbers the same, but they can have as many as three alike.

According to an electron's total energy, or quantum number, it will occupy a definable energy area in the atom relative to other electrons. The principal quantum number relates to the number of the shell, or sphere, starting with 1 for the shell nearest the nucleus and proceeding outward to shell 7. Shells are also labeled *K, L, M, N, O, P, Q*. The *K* shell or shell 1, is complete when it has two electrons in it. No more can be accommodated at that distance from the nucleus, whether in a helium atom or a lead atom. The *L* shell is complete when it contains eight electrons. The total number of electrons a shell can contain is given by the term $2n^2$, where n is the number of the shell. Thus the *M* shell accommodates a total of 2×3^2, or 18, electrons. The *N* shell has a maximum of 32; the *O* shell could have 50, the *P* shell could have 72, and the *Q* shell, 98. The three outer shells are never completely filled, although in the heavier atoms all of them contain some electrons and the first four are completely filled.

Each shell consists of a band of subshells, lettered from inner to outer *s, p, d, f* into which the electrons of that shell are distributed. Each shell begins with an *s* subshell, and every *s* subshell has a maximum of two electrons; every *p* subshell has a maximum of six electrons; every *d* subshell has room for ten electrons; and those atoms large enough to have *f* subshells occupied fill them with fourteen electrons. Each subshell imposes a different kind of orbit on its resident electrons. In the *s* subshell, both electrons have circular orbits. All *p* subshell orbits are dumbbell-shaped. The *d* and *f* subshell orbits have more complicated shapes.

As the atomic numbers of the elements increase and protons are added to the nucleus, each balancing electron enters the position that requires the least energy to be maintained against the pull of the nucleus and the repulsion of other electrons. For the first twenty elements, the positions are filled in regular manner, each subshell becoming complete before the next one is begun. After calcium (Ca), the twentieth element, the sequence of energy levels does not coincide with the sequence of subshells. The larger shells overlap each other, and new shells are begun before inner ones are completed. The order in which subshells are filled is shown in the accompanying table.

When the *K* shell's *s* subshell is complete in helium (He) with two electrons, the *L* shell, or shell 2, begins outside it with one electron in the 2s subshell, to make lithium (Li). Beryllium (Be), with four protons, adds the fourth electron to the 2s subshell. Boron (B) adds its fifth electron to the 2p subshell. Carbon (C) also adds its sixth electron to the 2p subshell, and so do nitrogen (N), oxygen (O), fluorine (F), and neon (Ne), so that the 2p subshell has its full quota of six electrons and shell 2 is complete. It cannot accommodate any more electrons in its other possible subshells 2d and 2f. A new shell, *M*, or shell 3, begins with its 3s subshell by taking the eleventh electron in sodium (Na) and the twelfth electron in magnesium (Mg). Then the 3p subshell fills until argon (Ar) is reached, which now has eight electrons in shell 3. Theoretically, the 3d subshell should begin to fill. Instead, shell 4, or *N*, begins outside the incomplete shell 3. Two electrons go into shell 4, and with scandium (Sc), the 21st element, the 21st electron finds the position of lowest energy in the incomplete *M* shell's 3d subshell. The 4p subshell completes itself in krypton (Kr) after the 3d subshell fills up. With only eight electrons in the *N*, or 4, shell, which has a total capacity of 32, the *O* shell, or shell 5, begins in rubidium (Rb). After the 5s subshell has two electrons, and the 4d subshell is completed, only after that does the 5p subshell resume filling up. When the *O* shell, shell 5, has eight electrons, the sixth, or *P*, shell is begun.

From the above description, it can be seen that the four following rules are always observed:

(1) The outermost shell can contain no more than eight electrons.

(2) The next-to-the-outermost shell can contain no more than 18 electrons.

(3) An outermost shell can contain no more than two electrons if the next-to-the-outermost has not reached its maximum.

(4) A next-to-the-outermost shell cannot contain more than nine electrons unless the second-from-outermost has reached its maximum.

Thus, a new shell begins whenever an outermost shell has filled its s and p subshells, even though that shell does not have its full quota of electrons and must then complete itself inside the s subshell of the new outermost shell. This phenomenon suggests that the configuration of two electrons in the *K* shell and the first eight electrons in any other shell is an extremely stable one, for it creates a recurring pattern in the electron arrangement. When the elements are listed in the order of increasing atomic number and the distribution of their electrons in the various energy levels is noted, the stability of this electron structure becomes evident. As can be seen from the table of electron distribution, each of the so-called inert gases has this arrangement: helium (He), atomic number 2, has two electrons in the *K* shell; neon (Ne), atomic number 10, has two electrons in the *K* shell and eight in the *L* shell; argon (Ar), atomic number 18, has two electrons in the *K* shell, eight in the *L* shell, and eight in the *M* shell; krypton (Kr), atomic number 36, has two electrons in the *K* shell, eight in the *L* shell, eighteen in the *M* shell, and eight in the *N* shell; xenon (Xe), atomic number 54, has two electrons in the *K* shell, eight in the *L* shell, eighteen in the *M* shell, eighteen in the *N* shell, and eight in the *O* shell; and radon (Rn), atomic

number 86, has two electrons in the *K* shell, eight in the *L* shell, eighteen in the *M* shell, thirty-two in the *N* shell, eighteen in the *O* shell, and eight in the *P* shell.

The Periodic Law.—As a result of the recurring electron pattern, the elements can be grouped in periods beginning with an element that has one electron in a new shell and ending with an element that has eight in that same shell (or, in the case of the *K* shell, only two electrons). These periods can then be placed under one another in such a way that all elements with a single electron in the outermost shell fall under one another, forming a vertical group, those with two electrons in the outermost shell fall under one another, and so on, ending with a vertical group that contains all the elements with eight electrons in the outermost shell. The facts that allow the elements to be grouped in such a way are summed up in the *periodic law*, which states that the atomic structures of the elements are a periodic function of the number of protons in the nucleus. Since the properties of the elements can be explained only by their atomic structures, the properties are also a periodic function of the number of protons in the nucleus. Based on these facts, a periodic chart, or table, of the elements can be worked out.

All modern chemistry functions on principles based upon the periodic law. For example, without it there would be no theoretical justification for saying that metals can be recognized as a group of elements with certain properties in common. Some similarities, such as those of certain metals, were known even to the alchemists, and early in the nineteenth

A Typical Periodic Arrangement

Group I-A	II-A											III-A	IV-A	V-A	VI-A	VII-A	
Alkali Metals	Alkaline Earths	←———————— Transition Metals ————————→										Boron–Aluminum Family	Carbon Family	Nitrogen Family	Chalcogens	Halogens	Inert Gases
1 H																	2 He
3 Li	4 Be	III-B	IV-B	V-B	VI-B	VII-B		VIII-B			I-B	5 B	6 C	7 N	8 O	9 F	10 Ne
							←Platinum Metal Triads→			Coinage Metals	II-B						
11 Na	12 Mg											13 Al	14 Si	15 P	16 S	17 Cl	18 A
19 K	20 Ca	21 Sc	22 Ti	23 V	24 Cr	25 Mn	26 Fe	27 Co	28 Ni	29 Cu	30 Zn	31 Ga	32 Ge	33 As	34 Se	35 Br	36 Kr
37 Rb	38 Sr	39 Y	40 Zr	41 Nb	42 Mo	43 Tc	44 Ru	45 Rh	46 Pd	47 Ag	48 Cd	49 In	50 Sn	51 Sb	52 Te	53 I	54 Xe
55 Cs	56 Ba	57 *La	72 Hf	73 Ta	74 W	75 Re	76 Os	77 Ir	78 Pt	79 Au	80 Hg	81 Tl	82 Pb	83 Bi	84 Po	85 At	86 Rn
87 Fr	88 Ra	89 †Ac															

58 Ce	59 Pr	60 Nd	61 Pm	62 Sm	63 Eu	64 Gd	65 Tb	66 Dy	67 Ho	68 Er	69 Tm	70 Yb	71 Lu
90 Th	91 Pa	92 U	93 Np	94 Pu	95 Am	96 Cm	97 Bk	98 Cf	99 Es	100 Fm	101 Md	102 No	103 Lw

* Lanthanide Series

† Actinide Series →

century chemists began to study these inexplicable groupings with the hope of discovering the cause. In 1869, Dmitri I. Mendeleev announced his periodic law, which stated that the properties of the elements are a periodic function of their atomic weights. He presented the scientific world with the first periodic chart of the 70 or so elements that were then known, arranged in horizontal periods and vertical groups. If his table were brought up to date and rearranged to accommodate new information, it would coincide exactly with the table based on electron structures. In other words, the properties of the elements are a result of the electron structures of the atoms.

The structural reason for the separation into A groups and B groups lies in the fact that the A-group elements are filling their outermost shells, while the B-group elements are filling inner shells and have only a few electrons in the outermost shell. This difference is strikingly reflected in the different properties of the A and B elements.

Large modern wall charts carry a great deal of information in the box devoted to each element: physical properties, such as melting and boiling points, crystal structure, color, density, hardness, conductivity, heat of fusion, solubility; chemical properties, such as heats of reaction and types of compounds formed with oxygen; and radioactive properties, such as half-life and what kind of particle the atom emits. Careful study reveals trends in the properties of a group rather than precise similarities.

Chemical properties cannot be graphed because they are not numerical. In general, the elements of any one group react chemically to form compounds in a way that is very similar. The compounds formed by the elements in any one group have similar properties. There are many exceptions, but the cyclical, or periodic, tendencies are unmistakable.

One of the most revealing graphs is that constructed with the atomic number and the *atomic volume,* which is calculated by dividing the atomic weight of an element by its density, thus obtaining a comparative figure. As the mass of the nucleus increases, it is found that the volume of the whole atom does not always increase—it sometimes shrinks. The largest atomic volumes are found in the group I-A elements; the smallest, in the middle groups. The explanation lies in the force with which the nucleus holds its cloud of electrons. Lithium's (Li) three protons hold two electrons in the K shell and one in the L shell. Beryllium (Be) has four protons and the greater attractive force of this nucleus holds four electrons, held in the same two shells as those of lithium, a little closer to itself. Boron (B) has five protons that draw its five electrons even closer to the nucleus. Carbon (C), although it has six electrons, is almost the same size as boron. Oxygen (O) and fluorine (F), with six and seven electrons in the L shell respectively, are smaller in volume than one would predict.

However, helium (He), which ends the period and completes the eight-electron configuration in the outermost shell, suddenly enlarges. Apparently, in order to get that eighth electron into the L shell, the nucleus of eight protons has to loosen its grip on the electrons and allow a greater distance between them. Sodium (Na), in whose atoms a new shell begins, cannot shrink itself because of that new shell, and is therefore larger than lithium (Li) above it. But magnesium (Mg), with two electrons in the new shell, is smaller than sodium (Na). Again the increasing attractive power of the nucleus pulls the larger number of electrons, in the same period or shell arrangement, closer to itself until the end of the period. The largest atom, franconium (Fr), following the trends outlined above, is found at the bottom of group I-A;

ELECTRONEGATIVITIES
Pauling's Scale

Element		Electronegativity
Potassium	(K)	0.8
Sodium	(Na)	0.9
Lithium	(Li)	1.0
Magnesium	(Mg)	1.2
Silicon	(Si)	1.8
Boron	(B)	2.0
Arsenic	(As)	2.0
Hydrogen	(H)	2.1
Phosphorus	(P)	2.1
Selenium	(Se)	2.4
Carbon	(C)	2.5
Sulfur	(S)	2.5
Iodine	(I)	2.5
Bromine	(Br)	2.8
Nitrogen	(N)	3.0
Chlorine	(Cl)	3.0
Oxygen	(O)	3.5
Fluorine	(F)	4.0

the smallest, except for hydrogen, is boron (B).

The cyclic nature of atomic volume is extremely important when studying the structure of crystals and the formulas of complex compounds. Obviously, a small atom will be arranged in different geometrical positions with a group of considerably larger atoms than it will with a group of atoms its size.

Ionization. — The key group around which the periodic nature of the elements turns is the one numbered 0, called the *inert gases* or *rare gases:* helium (He), neon (Ne), argon (Ar), krypton (Kr), xenon (Xe), and radon (Rn). The energies in these atoms are so firmly balanced that until 1962 (when compounds of xenon were prepared) none of them was known to form any compounds. They will not combine with other elements under ordinary conditions because their eight outermost electrons (two outermost, in the case of helium) mesh to produce a structure that is more stable than that which any other number of outermost electrons can produce. Inert gases will not even cling to each other to form liquids, except at extremely low temperatures.

The arrangement of eight outer-

most electrons is so stable that an element immediately following an inert gas tends to lose its new electron quite readily in order to achieve such a structure. Elements with two or three outermost electrons will also give them up to uncover a stable electron arrangement. An atom that has lost electrons to acquire a stable configuration is no longer electrically neutral because the protons outnumber the remaining electrons; the particle as a whole has a positive electrical charge. In such a state, the atom is called a *positive ion,* or a *cation.*

An element that precedes an inert gas in the same period and has seven, six, or five electrons in its outermost shell tends to seize any free electrons it finds, adding one, two, or three to its outermost shell in order to bring the total to eight. An atom with such an arrangement has more electrons than protons and therefore has a negative charge; it is called a *negative ion* or *anion.*

All atoms, except those of the inert gases, form ions easily. The tendency to lose electrons is called *ionization potential,* and is a measure of the energy required to remove the electrons. The lower the ionization potential, the less energy required to remove the electrons and the more easily ions are formed. As a result, the ionization potential is lowest for the elements in the first few groups of the periodic table, for they lose their few outermost electrons easily. The measure of the tendency to gain electrons is called *electron affinity.* The greater an atom's electron affinity, the more strongly the atom tends to attract electrons in an effort to assume a stable electron structure. Electron affinity is highest for the elements in the groups at the right-hand side of the periodic table because these atoms gain electrons. Both ionization potential and electron affinity are useful concepts, but more useful than either is the concept of *relative electronegativity.* The harder it is to remove an electron from a neutral atom or an ion, the higher the electronegativity of that atom or ion is. Elements with seven outermost electrons have the highest electronegativities, and elements with a single outermost electron have the lowest. Since the term is a relative one, fluorine (F), with the highest affinity for electrons of all the elements, was the standard chosen against which the others were compared; and it was given an electronegativity of 4. The inert gases, which would have even higher electronegativities, were omitted because they do not usually form compounds.

Atoms of elements in groups I-A, II-A, and III-A can lose their few outermost electrons as a result of energy changes due to ordinary electric fields, heat, collisions, radiation, or chemical reactions. Considerably more energy than is available in ordinary laboratory work is required to remove the outer shell when it contains four or more electrons. It can be done in strong electric fields or at very high temperatures, but not in chemical reactions. After the outer shell of an atom has been stripped, electrons can be plucked out of the inner shells one by one, either by increasingly powerful positive fields that will overcome the pull of the nucleus or by intense heat. All the electrons of any atom can be boiled off by temperatures equivalent to those at the surface of the sun, which can be duplicated in special laboratory equipment. The heats estimated for the interiors of stars decompose the nucleus itself into its components.

Valence.—Chemical reactions involve only the loss and gain of electrons in the outer shell and, in some cases, a few electrons in the inner shells of atoms. Such electrons are called *valence electrons,* and the outermost shell is called the *valence shell.* The number of electrons an atom can lose or gain in a chemical reaction is the *electrovalence* of that element. All the elements in group I-A have one valence electron, which is lost in chemical reactions to leave a positive ion with a single positive charge; the electrovalence of such an element is +1. Group II-A elements have an electrovalence of +2, for they can give up two electrons to form an ion with a double positive charge. Similarly, group III-A elements have an electrovalence of +3, for they can give up three electrons. The group IV-A elements have an electron affinity high enough to prevent them from losing their electrons easily in chemical reactions; therefore, their electrovalence varies. The group V-A elements do not lose their five valence electrons, but instead pull three electrons into their valence shell to complete the octet; thus, their electrovalence is −3. The group VI-A elements pull two electrons into their valence shell to complete the octet and have an electrovalence of −2. The group VII-A elements need pull only one electron into their valence shell to complete the octet and have an electrovalence of −1. In A groups, the above rule is almost always observed. In B groups, however, there is fluctuation; and the group number does not necessarily indicate the electrovalence. In addition, the B-group elements often have more than one electrovalence; for example, mercury (Hg), which is in group I-B, has electrovalences of +1 and +2. The ion formed when an atom gives up or gains electrons in its valence shell is written with the electrical charge as a suffix to the symbol of the element. For example, an ion of sodium, which has an electrovalence of +1 and whose ions thus have a single positive charge, is represented as Na^+; magnesium, with an electrovalence of +2, forms the ion Mg^{++}; aluminum, which has an electrovalence of +3, forms the ion Al^{+++}; phosphorus, with an electrovalence of −3, forms the ion P^{---}; the ion of sulfur, electrovalence −2, is S^{--}; chlorine, electrovalence −1, forms Cl^-.

All elements that lose electrons in chemical reaction to become cations are called *metals;* elements that gain electrons to become anions are called *nonmetals.* Metals are on the left side of the table in the first three A groups; nonmetals, on the right in the last five A groups. The inert gases, in group 0, are also classed as nonmetals. In all A groups, only the *s* and *p* subshells of the outermost shell are being filled. The B groups, placed between groups II-A and III-A, contain the *transition metals,* whose *s* and *p* subshells are only partly filled while their *d,* and sometimes *f,* subshells are filling up. They have electrovalences of +1, +2, and +3. A few elements on either side of a dividing line between metals and nonmetals are called *metalloids* because they behave either as metals or as nonmetals, depending on the conditions.

Group I-A elements are called the *alkali metals,* group II-A consists of the *alkaline earth metals,* and the elements of group VII-A are called the *halogens.* Into the place occupied by lanthanum (La), element 57, 14 other elements must be squeezed together because they are completing *f* subshells deep within and are chemically very similar. The grouping is called the *lanthamide series,* or the *rare earth metals,* because when the first few were discovered they were thought to be much less abundant in the earth's crust than they have proved to be. Element 89, actinium (Ac), also has 14 other elements with it in its box, all of them filling *f* subshells. The *actinide series* contains 11 of the 12 man-made elements. (The other man-made element is promethium.) Both of these series are placed at the bottom of the periodic table in order not to stretch the table impractically.

Size of Ions.—Since all atoms lose or gain electrons, it is useful to know how this affects volume of the atom. When lithium (Li) loses its single valence electron, the nucleus—with its now unbalanced positive charge—pulls the remaining electrons much closer to itself. The diameter of the lithium ion, Li^+, is less than a third of the lithium atom's. Beryllium (Be) loses two electrons, and the two extra positive charges in the nucleus pull the remaining electrons into an even smaller volume than Li^+. Boron (B) and carbon (C) do not form ions easily, but oxygen (O) adds two electrons to its valence shell. Its ion, O^{--}, has a diameter more than three times as large as the electrically neutral atom, O. Fluorine (F), which adds a single electron, enlarges even more. In any metal group, the ions are always much smaller than the atoms, although the heavier ions are larger than the lighter ones in the same group. Among the nonmetals, the ions are always much larger than the atoms and they, too, increase in size as they get heavier. The largest ion of all is thus that of radon, Rn^-, at the bottom of group VII-A. The smallest, except for hydrogen, H^+, would be that of boron, B^{+++}.

Chemical Bonding.—An atom does not have any of the properties of its ion except mass number. The two particles are completely different in their chemical and physical behavior. Any ion can be forced—through chemical reaction, electrical fields, radiation, or heat—to accept or relinquish electrons and become a neutral atom again. The energy content of an atom can never be that of its ion, so a shift of electrons always involves an energy change in the particle. Such a shift and energy change always occur in a chemical reaction. Two general kinds of chemical reaction are recognized, resulting in either electrovalent or covalent bonds.

The difference in electron affinity, or in relative electronegativity, between metals and nonmetals is great enough so that if their atoms are brought together under the right conditions the metal loses its lightly held electrons to the much more electronegative nonmetal. Indicating valence electrons as dots around the symbol for an element, the following happens in the reaction between sodium (Na) and chlorine (Cl):

$$Na \rightarrow \cdot \ddot{\underset{..}{Cl}} :$$

The transfer produces two ions, Na^+ and Cl^-. Sodium metal (in the atomic state) in bulk is silvery, lighter than water, and reacts with water to produce hydrogen gas and a powerful, poisonous alkali, sodium hydroxide. Chlorine in bulk is a greenish poisonous gas and a strong bleaching agent. The shift of a single electron between the two atoms liberates a great deal of heat energy, and the resulting ions, clinging together because of their opposite charges, crystallize into a white solid that is ordinary table salt, Na^+Cl^-.

A calcium (Ca) atom can lose its two valence electrons to two chlorine (Cl) atoms, each chlorine atom accepting one electron, in the following manner:

$$\ddot{\underset{..}{Cl}} \cdot \nwarrow \cdot Ca \cdot \nearrow \cdot \ddot{\underset{..}{Cl}} :$$

This reaction produces the compound calcium chloride, $Ca^{++}Cl_2^-$. Magnesium (Mg), which has an electrovalence of +2, and oxygen (O), which has an electrovalence of −2, can transfer electrons in the following manner to form the compound magnesium oxide, $Mg^{++}O^{--}$:

$$Mg: \rightarrow \ddot{\underset{..}{O}} :$$

The shift of electrons from less electronegative to more electronegative atoms is called *electrovalent bonding,* or *ionic bonding,* and it produces one kind of chemical reaction.

Two metals cannot form electrovalent bonds with each other, for while both can donate electrons, neither is sufficiently electronegative to accept them. (Metal atoms do bond together; the mechanism involved is discussed in a later section of this article.) Two nonmetals cannot form electrovalent bonds with each other, either, because neither will give up electrons. However, two nonmetals can share their valence electrons to produce a molecule that has a *covalent bond.* Sharing of electrons, instead of transferring them, is a second kind of mechanism found in chemical combination.

For example, when two chlorine atoms combine to form a chlorine molecule, each shares one of its own electrons with the other; in this manner, both have an outermost shell containing eight electrons, two of which are orbiting around both nuclei. The covalent bond may be pictured as follows:

$$:\overset{..}{Cl}:\overset{..}{Cl}:$$

SODIUM   CHLORINE

CHLORINE   CHLORINE

IONIC BOND
SODIUM CHLORIDE   COVALENT BOND
(TABLE SALT) MOLECULE   CHLORINE GAS MOLECULE

The formula for the molecule is Cl_2. Two oxygen atoms may form a covalent bond between them by sharing two electrons from each atom, a total of four. Thus, four electrons in the diatomic oxygen molecule, which has the formula O_2, are orbiting both nuclei. The covalent bond is:

$$:\overset{..}{O}::\overset{..}{O}:$$

Nitrogen atoms combine into a diatomic molecule with a triple covalent bond, N_2:

$$:N:::N:$$

Hydrogen has only one electron, but this is in the K shell, which is complete with two; therefore, hydrogen atoms combine with a covalent bond to form H_2, which is a molecule of hydrogen gas. Sulfur and oxygen form two kinds of compounds with covalently bonded molecules: sulfur dioxide, SO_2, and sulfur trioxide, SO_3. Carbon dioxide, CO_2; carbon monoxide, CO; carbon tetrachloride, CCl_4; and ammonia, NH_3, are all compounds in whose molecules atoms are covalently bonded.

It is possible for one atom to provide both electrons of a covalent bond with another atom and establish what is called a *coordinate covalent bond*. All covalent bonds are an overlapping of s and p electron orbitals.

If one of the atoms in a covalently bonded molecule has a stronger affinity for electrons than has the other atom, then the shared pair will be held more closely by the stronger nucleus. Such a shared pair will give the molecule an unbalanced configuration of charges, making the more electronegative area of the molecule more negative in character than the other area. The molecule as a whole remains neutral, but one end is negative and the other positive. It is called a *polar molecule*, and the bond is a *polar covalent bond*.

Covalence represents the number of electrons the element shares, and has no positive or negative sign because no ions are produced. Most nonmetals have more than one covalence, being able to share their electrons in several ways. Metalloids have covalence, as well as negative and positive electrovalence. Some transition metals form covalent bonds.

All chemical bonds are electrovalent, covalent, or polar covalent; the latter can be so strongly polar that the molecule has almost an electrovalent configuration, or it can be so little polar that it is almost covalent. The difference in electronegativity between the bonding atoms determines the kind of bond they form.

A distinction must be made between a covalently bonded molecule and the ions of an electrovalent bond. The ions cling together because of their opposite charges, and in the gaseous state the ions of a compound can be considered as a single molecule. In the liquid state the ions are free to move about, and they cling to whatever oppositely charged ion is nearest. A molecule, therefore, cannot exist among ions in the liquid state. In the solid state, each ion is held in its position according to the specific crystal structure of the compound and is surrounded by oppositely charged ions, to each of which it is attracted with equal force. Therefore, in the solid state no molecule exists among ions.

The bonds between atoms in a covalently bonded molecule are far more powerful than any that can exist between ions. When molecules of a covalent compound are liquefied, they continue to be separate entities; whatever attraction exists between the separate molecules, holding them in liquid contact, is very weak compared to the bond between the atoms constituting the molecule. When a covalent compound solidifies, the attraction between molecular surfaces, binding them into the crystal lattice, is still very weak compared to the bond between atoms within such molecules.

Chemical Formulas.—A formula for a compound is a precise representation of the actual number of atoms bonded into a unit molecule, or of ions associated in the simplest combination. In all inorganic formulas, the least electronegative, or most metallic, element is named first, followed by the progressively more electronegative, or less metallic, elements. The last element has an ending formed according to a system that is part of the language of chemistry. Compounds composed of only two elements always have the less metallic element end in *-ide*, whether the compound is electrovalent or covalent. Examples are carbon monoxide, CO; carbon dioxide, CO_2; aluminum bromide, $AlBr_3$; hydrogen oxide (or water), H_2O; and carbon tetrachloride, CCl_4. Formulas for ionic or electrovalent compounds, although they cannot be considered to represent true molecules, are often written as groups of ions, for example, sodium oxide, $Na_2^+O^{--}$, calcium bromide, $Ca^{++}Br_2^-$, and potassium sulfide, $K_2^+S^{--}$. Formulas for compounds with three or more elements use the same sequence, but the endings vary.

Chemical Equations.—A chemical reaction is a shift of electrons in the valence shell of an atom, and the shift is always brought about by a change in the distribution of energies within the atom. All chemical reactions can be represented in the form of a chemical equation. When two atoms of chlorine collide and combine to form covalently bonded chlorine molecules, the equation is:

$$Cl + Cl \rightarrow Cl_2.$$

The plus sign indicates that the masses and energies reacting are added together and also that the two atoms touch under conditions that bring about a shift of electrons. The arrow indicates that the atoms have actually reacted and that their electron configuration has changed; the arrow is also an "equals" sign.

The primary usefulness of a chemical equation lies in the fact that the total number of atoms of each element on one side of the arrow is equal to the total number of atoms of each element on the other side of the arrow. If the total number of atoms is not equal, the equation is said to be *unbalanced;* if the total number of atoms is equal, the equation is said to be *balanced*. A good example of the balancing of a chemical equation is the reaction in which hydrogen (H) and oxygen (O) combine to yield water (H_2O), which could be written:

$$H + O \rightarrow H_2O \text{ (unbalanced)}.$$

However, hydrogen and oxygen both exist as diatomic molecules, so this is somewhat more properly written as:

$$H_2 + O_2 \rightarrow H_2O \text{ (unbalanced)}.$$

The equation is still unbalanced because there are two oxygen atoms on the left side of the arrow but only one on the right side. To balance the number of oxygen atoms, it reads:

$$H_2 + O_2 \rightarrow 2H_2O \text{ (unbalanced)}.$$

Now the number of hydrogen atoms no longer balances, for there are only two on the left but four on the right. Therefore, the equation must be:

$$2H_2 + O_2 \rightarrow 2H_2O \text{ (balanced)}.$$

This equation for the reaction is now balanced, with four hydrogen atoms and two oxygen atoms on each side.

Other equations, however, are much more complex and their equations much more difficult to balance. For example, the unbalanced equation for the reaction between phosphorus (P) and nitric acid (HNO_3) in the presence of water, which yields phosphoric acid (H_3PO_4) and nitric oxide (NO), may be written:

$$P + HNO_3 + H_2O \rightarrow H_3PO_4 + NO$$
$$\text{(unbalanced)}.$$

The balanced equation is:

$$3P + 5HNO_3 + 2H_2O \rightarrow 3H_3PO_4 + 5NO.$$

In addition to the basic method of writing and balancing chemical equations, several conventions are used. Vertical arrows indicate that an element or compound is a gas, as in $H_2\uparrow$ or $CO_2\uparrow$, or an insoluble substance as in $AgCl\downarrow$ or $BaSO_4\downarrow$. The letters *g*, *s*, and *l* as subscripts indicate whether the reactant or product is in the liquid, gaseous, or solid state, for example: $H_{2(g)}$, $H_2O_{(l)}$, or $BaSO_{4(s)}$. The symbol $+E$ or $-E$ may be added to the right-hand side of an equation to show that energy is either gained from or lost to the surroundings during the reaction. An "equals" sign ($=$) or arrows pointed in opposite directions ($\rightleftarrows$) may replace the single arrow ($\rightarrow$) to show that the reaction is in equilibrium or that the reaction can proceed in either direction. The arrow may also have a triangle placed above ($\overset{\triangle}{\rightarrow}$) or below ($\underset{\triangle}{\rightarrow}$) it to show that the reactants must be heated if the reaction is to proceed.

Calculations. — The determination of correct formulas for compounds is one of the most important aspects of chemical research, and many kinds of analytical procedure have been worked out using relative atomic weight figures in the calculations. For example, suppose the formula is wanted for the gas formed when pure carbon burns in oxygen. By calculating the actual weights of carbon and oxygen used up in the reaction, or by breaking up the gas molecules in various ways and calculating the weights of carbon and oxygen obtained, it is found that 27.29 per cent of the compound formed is carbon and 72.71 per cent is oxygen. In round numbers, the atomic weights of oxygen and carbon are 16 and 12, respectively. Dividing the percentage of each element by its atomic weight gives the ratios of the elements in the compound. In this case the ratio is one atom of carbon to two of oxygen. The empirical formula is therefore CO_2, but the actual molecule could be C_2O_4 or C_3O_6 or any other combination of the atoms in the ratio of one to two. Using Avogadro's hypothesis, or any other method for determining relative molecular weights, the gas formed is found to have a molecular weight of 44. Since the molecular weight of the compound CO_2 would be $12 + (2 \times 16)$ or 44, the molecular weight of C_2O_4 would be $(2 \times 12) + (4 \times 16)$ or 88, the molecular weight of C_3O_6 would be $(3 \times 12) + (6 \times 16)$ or 132, etc. Thus, the correct molecular formula is CO_2, carbon dioxide.

In a balanced equation, symbols stand for single atoms and formulas for single molecules. Symbols also represent their relative atomic weights and formulas their relative molecular weights:

$$C + O_2 \rightarrow CO_2$$
$$12 \quad 32 \quad 44$$

As long as these ratios are observed, any weights of carbon and oxygen will combine completely, without leftovers. Thus, 12 grams, 12 pounds, or 12 tons of carbon will need 32 grams, 32 pounds, or 32 tons of oxygen to combine completely and produce 44 grams, 44 pounds, or 44 tons of carbon dioxide. One ton of carbon requires $32/12$ or $2\frac{2}{3}$ tons of oxygen for complete combustion and

will produce $44/12$ or $3\frac{2}{3}$ tons of carbon dioxide. Thus, the equivalent weight of any unknown in a chemical reaction can be calculated. Without this quantitative use of chemical equations, there could be no chemistry in the modern sense. In fact, the equation was developed precisely to handle the quantitative realities of modern chemistry.

The equation is used to calculate volumes of gases as well. A quantity of oxygen that weighs 15.999 grams, a quantity of hydrogen that weighs 1.008 grams, a quantity of sulfur that weighs 32.064 grams, and a quantity of any element that weighs its atomic weight number in grams will all have the same number of atoms, since atomic weights are ratios obtained when the weights of equal numbers of atoms are compared, according to Avogadro's hypothesis. This amount of an element is called its *gram atomic weight*. The same reasoning holds for molecules, and the weight in grams of the molecular weight number is the *gram molecular weight* of a compound. The *gram equivalent weight* of an element is the weight that will displace one gram atomic weight of hydrogen or will combine with half of one gram atomic weight of oxygen. More practically, the gram equivalent weight of an element is its gram atomic weight divided by its *oxidation number*. The number of atoms or molecules in the gram atomic weight or gram molecular weight of any element or compound has been calculated from various experiments. It is called *Avogadro's number*, or a mole, and is represented by the letter *N*. It is 6.024×10^{23} atoms or molecules. When a mole of any substance is vaporized at standard temperature and pressure (STP), it will occupy 22.4 liters, which is called the *gram molecular volume*. Thus, 32 grams of oxygen gas occupy 22.4 liters at STP, and 44 grams of CO_2 gas occupy 22.4 liters. Therefore, 100 grams of carbon would react completely with $22.4/12 \times 100$ liters of oxygen.

When 1 mole, or 12 grams, of carbon is completely burned, the energy produced has been measured as 94,030 calories. From this, the heat produced by burning any amount of carbon can be calculated, using the same method as above.

If there is not enough oxygen present when carbon burns, carbon monoxide is produced. The balanced equation is

$$2C + O_2 \rightarrow 2CO + E_a.$$

If the CO is then burned, the balanced equation for that reaction is

$$2CO + O_2 \rightarrow 2CO_2 + E_b.$$

The sum of $E_a + E_b$, for one mole of carbon, is 94,030 calories. The reaction illustrates the *law of Hess* (Germain Henri Hess, 1802–1850), which states that no matter how many steps a reaction takes for its completion, the sum of the energies produced at each step exactly equals the energy that would be produced if the reaction took place in one step. It is a special case of the law of conservation of matter and energy.

A reaction that produces energy in the form of heat is called *exothermic*, and a reaction that absorbs heat in order to proceed is called *endothermic*. Most reactions take place in a series of steps, and not all of the steps need be exothermic.

Radicals.—Groups of covalently bonded atoms, which function as a single particle but have an electrical charge and therefore are not molecules, are called *radicals*. SO_4^{--}, NO_3^-, NH_4^+, and CO_3^{--} are some common radicals. They participate in many reactions, exactly as ions do; and they form parts of compounds, just as ions do. Since they function as ions, they are often referred to as ions. Radicals, however, cannot be neutralized into molecules with the same composition. There is no such molecule as SO_4, for example, nor one whose formula is NH_4. If radicals are robbed of their electrical charge, they break up into smaller radicals or into molecules, atoms, and ions.

Mechanism of Reactions. — Obviously, not every collision between atoms and molecules results in a reaction. The wood of a match does not burn, though its molecules are incessantly bombarded by millions of oxygen molecules every second, until the temperature has been raised sufficiently by the flaming match head, which has been forced into reacting by the heat of friction. The temperature at which the energy configuration of atoms allows an electron shift into a new configuration of energies is called the *activation level* of energy in the atoms. Below this excited state, no reaction can take place.

Molecules can be excited, or activated, by radiation, electrical fields, collisions, and—by far the most common—heat. Activation levels of energy are thus usually reported as temperatures below which no appreciable reaction can take place. At no time, according to the kinetic molecular theory, do all the molecules in any system have the same kinetic energy; the temperature of a gas, liquid, or solid is only a measure of the average kinetic energy of the molecules. In many cases where no reaction seems to be taking place, a few molecules with very high energy content may be reacting. An example is iron rusting at ordinary temperature. But even when the bulk of a substance has been raised to activation level, all its molecules do not instantly react, partly because some will have lower energies, partly because most molecules have key spots on which they must be hit, and partly because they cannot all collide at the same instant.

In the case of gases whose molecules are moving very rapidly and colliding billions of times a second, a reaction often becomes an explosion because all the molecules have a chance to react within a second or two. When the mixture of reactants includes a solid or a liquid, collisions are restricted to their surfaces. The number of collisions is increased enormously by powdering and vaporizing the reactants or by dissolving them in a common liquid. Increasing the concentration of one or all of the reactants will increase the number of collisions each second. Raising the temperature will increase the number of collisions, their force, and the number of molecules at activation level.

Finally, a great many reactions will not take place to any appreciable extent unless a *catalyst* is present. A *catalyst* is a substance, usually a solid, that participates in a reaction but emerges from it unchanged. Very small amounts are needed. The theory of catalysis is that reacting molecules will combine on the molecular surface of the catalyst to form a complex—sometimes with the catalyst—that then allows the final step of the reaction to take place at a lower activation level. The molecules are twisted, as it were, by the catalyst into configurations that produce the same readiness to react that an elevation of temperature would. Some catalysts, called *negative catalysts,* work in reverse and inhibit, or retard, reactions. However, chemists are primarily interested in catalysts that accelerate reactions.

The *rate of reaction* can be measured by weighing the reactants before the reaction begins, then isolating and weighing them at regular intervals after the reaction has started. The rate is reported as the number of grams reacting per second. It is of prime importance in industry, where the largest yield is wanted in the least amount of time. Industrial research seeks ways to speed up reactions by altering temperatures and concentrations, which include pressure conditions; by new catalysts; by engineering changes in the pattern of flow in and out of reactors; or by changes in the design of equipment.

The actual steps by which reactions take place are being studied with radioactive isotopes having the same chemical properties as the stable atoms; their presence in intermediate compounds can be traced with radiation detectors. Some of the simplest reactions have proved to be very complicated in the order in which they form intermediate molecules. Every formation of a molecule is attended by an energy change, and no theory can yet predict or follow the involved balancing of forces that determine the reaction sequence.

■**REVERSIBLE REACTIONS.**—The study of reactions is complicated because most reactions are reversible; that is, stable atoms and molecules that react under one set of conditions will be re-formed under another set of conditions because there is no reason why the shift of electrons cannot be reversed. In the reversible reaction

$$A + B \rightleftarrows C + D,$$

consider that all the reactants and products are gases and that the reaction takes place in a closed container. At the start of the reaction only A and B are present, and their concentration is measured. A little later some C and D will have formed, and the concentration of A and B will be less. The number of fruitful collisions, and thus the rate of the reaction of $A + B$, will steadily decrease as they are used up. Eventually there will be no A and no B left, and the container will be completely filled with C and D. Let us assume that the configurations of $A + B$ contain more energy than the configurations of $C + D$. Therefore, energy in the form of heat will be produced when the reaction moves to the right. If the temperature of the pure C and D mixture is raised so that the heat, which is the difference of energy content between the two sets of reactants, is provided from the outside, then C and D will absorb that heat and, with this extra energy, their atoms re-form A and B.

Pure cases of reaction in one direction at one temperature and the reverse at another are extremely rare, however, because at all times there are molecules present with greater and lesser energies than the average. As soon as some C and D are formed, a few of them will have kinetic energies and potentials high enough so that they will re-form into A and B when they collide. As the concentration of C and D increases, the number of such fruitful collisions, and thus the rate of the reaction $C + D$, will increase. The rate $A + B$ decreases. At a certain instant the two rates will be equal, and the reaction is said to have reached a *dynamic equilibrium.* However, the two reactions do not stop. $A + B$ continues at the rate set by the particular conditions in the container, and so does $C + D$ at exactly the same rate. If the concentration of A, B, C, or D is changed, or if the temperature is changed, then the rate of reaction of each side of the equation will change until they are the same and dynamic equilibrium is reestablished.

This phenomenon is defined by the *principle of Le Châtelier* (Henri Louis Le Châtelier, 1850–1936): when a system is in equilibrium and one of the factors producing the equilibrium is altered, the system will always react in such a way as to absorb the change and re-establish a new equilibrium with the changed factors.

■**LAW OF MASS ACTION.**—A bracket around a formula or symbol stands for concentration. $[A]$ means the percentage of all the A molecules in a reaction. Of course, instead of counting molecules, the reactants are weighed. The rate of reaction is always directly proportional to the number of collisions, which is directly proportional to the concentration of molecules. The rate of reaction of $A + B$ is expressed as the product of their concentrations, $[A] \times [B]$. The rate of a reaction at any fixed temperature, no matter how much or how little of the reactants are present, is always the same. That is, in any mixture at that temperature the concentrations will be changed by a shift in one or the other direction in order to achieve the same product of concentrations. $[A]$ and $[B]$ will not always be the same, but their product will; and it is expressed mathematically in the equation

$$[A] \times [B] = k_t.$$

At the same temperature t,

$$[C] \times [D] = k_t.$$

At equilibrium the two equations can be combined into

$$\frac{[C] \times [D]}{[A] \times [B]} = K_t.$$

This equation expresses what is called the *law of mass action,* or *law of chemical equilibrium*; K is the equilibrium constant for that reaction at that temperature. In the reversible reaction

$$mA + nB + \cdots \rightleftarrows pC + qD + \cdots$$

$$\frac{[C]^p \ [D]^q}{[A]^m \ [B]^n} = K_t.$$

Any variation in concentration of any reactant produces a shift in the equilibrium that will change the concentration of all the other reactants and reestablish the same constant k_t. Some well-known reversible reactions are:

$$H_2 + I_2 \rightleftarrows 2HI,$$

$$CaCO_3 \rightleftarrows CaO + CO_2$$

(in the production of quicklime from limestone),

$$2SO_2 + O_2 \rightleftarrows 2SO_3$$

(in the manufacture of sulfuric acid),

$$N_2 + 3H_2 \rightleftarrows 2NH_3$$

(in the manufacture of ammonia by the Haber process).

The total removal of one of the participants in a reversible reaction will bring about a completion of the reaction in the direction of the lost participant. In the equation for the equilibrium constant, if one of the concentrations becomes zero, K becomes zero or infinity. A product can be removed easily if it is a gas or an insoluble solid in a solution. When there is more than one gas or there is a mixture of miscible liquids, or a mixture of solids and liquids dissolved in one another, the problem of bringing about a complete reaction is often too difficult or too expensive, and only a percentage of the theoretical yield can be obtained. For instance, in the Haber process all the reactants are gases at reacting temperatures. By raising the temperature, the concentrations are shifted toward the right, and larger yields of ammonia are obtained. But above a certain temperature the decomposition of ammonia into nitrogen and hydrogen proceeds at an accelerated rate, and the yield of ammonia diminishes. Thus, for every reversible reaction there is an optimum temperature that must be determined by experiment, for no theoretical computation is possible. In industry, the problem of obtaining maximum yields is often solved indirectly by having one of the by-products, or an undesired compound, react with something that will carry it away as a gas or precipitate it. However, no matter how complex a set of multiple reactions may be, in a closed system, for each reaction in that mixture, the law of mass action holds, as does the law of conservation of matter and energy.

If a catalyst is added to a reversible reaction, the rates in both directions are equally affected, and thus the same constant is obtained. Of course, if the system is not in equilibrium when the catalyst is added, the catalyst will seem to speed up the rate only in one direction until equilibrium is reached.

■**HEAT OF REACTION.**—One of the most important aspects of chemical reaction is the heat or some other form of energy, such as light, produced. The *heat of reaction* is the primary goal in the burning of fuels. In other reactions the heat is usually wasted, but often it can be utilized to raise the temperature of fresh reactants to activation levels. The accompanying graph suggests the energy changes involved. The energy, in the form of heat, added to $A + B$ to raise them to activation level, is r-q. The same amount of heat is given back after the formation of C and D and is not part of the heat of reaction. The amount q-p is the energy that has been released by the shift of electrons and is always the same, no matter at what temperature the reaction occurs.

In an endothermic process the graph can be reversed. The heat of reaction q-p must be provided, together with the heat to raise $C + D$ to activation level, in order to fix the configuration of atoms in A and B.

■**OXIDATION-REDUCTION REACTIONS.**—The commonest of all reactions is the combination of elements and compounds with oxygen. It is always an exothermic process. When it occurs rapidly enough, the evolution of heat is sufficient to produce light and flames; and the process of oxidation is then called *burning*. Almost every element combines with oxygen, and some form more than one oxide. If the element is a metal, the general reaction can be written:

$$M: + :O: \rightarrow M^{++} :O:^{--}$$

If the element is a nonmetal:

$$:A: + :O: \rightarrow :A: :O:$$

A great many reactions that do not include oxygen can be considered similar to the ones shown above. The meaning of *oxidation* has been expanded to include all reactions in which electrons are actually transferred or in which they can be counted as though they had been transferred. In the reaction between sodium and chlorine,

$$Na \cdot + \cdot Cl : \rightarrow Na : Cl :$$

sodium loses its electron to chlorine and is therefore oxidized. Chlorine, which gained an electron, was the *oxidizing agent*.

Every element is said to be in a *zero oxidation state* when its atom is neutral; this state can be diminished or increased. In the above equation, sodium's oxidation state is raised from 0 to +1, while chlorine's is lowered from 0 to −1 when they react. Every molecule, including the theoretical union of an ionic compound, is neutral; therefore the + and − oxidation states of the elements in the compounds must cancel out to 0. The *oxidation number* of sodium in table salt is +1, and that of chlorine is −1. The sum of the two is zero.

The process opposite to oxidation is called *reduction*. The word is even older than oxidation, and it originally meant the process of liberating a metal from its ore by making the oxygen of the metallic oxide combine with carbon. In the above reaction, chlorine has been reduced, the *reducing agent* being sodium. In other words, in an oxidation-reduction reaction an oxidizing agent is reduced, a reducing agent, oxidized.

Elaborating the concept, *oxidation numbers* replace the concept of valence and are much more useful in tracing electron shifts through different molecular formulas in an equation. The total increase of oxidation numbers must equal the total decrease, while with valence no such mathematical equating is possible. Every element has several oxidation states that become oxidation numbers when their atoms are in a molecule. Since the majority of inorganic reactions are of the oxidation-reduction type, the count of electrons, as though they were really gained or lost whatever the bond, in effect ties the chemical equation directly into the reality of relative electronegativities.

To illustrate this, the reaction between nitric acid (HNO_3) and iodine (I_2) can be used. They form iodic acid (HIO_3), nitrogen dioxide (NO_2), and water (H_2O). The unbalanced equation is

$$HNO_3 + I_2 \rightarrow HIO_3 + NO_2 + H_2O$$
(unbalanced).

The hydrogen atoms do not change their oxidation state, nor do the oxygen atoms. Iodine in the molecular state has an oxidation number of 0. In the HIO_3 molecule, oxygen has a total of −6 and hydrogen has a total of +1. Thus, iodine must have an oxidation number of +5 in order to create a neutral molecule. In HNO_3, nitrogen has an oxidation number of +5 for the same reason, but in NO_2 its oxidation number is only +4. Thus, by scanning the totals, a balanced equation is arrived at:

$$10HNO_3 + I_2 \rightarrow 2HIO_3 + 10NO_2 + 4H_2O$$

Elements, compounds, ions, and radicals are known as either good oxidizing agents or good reducing agents, depending on the energy with which they seize or donate electrons. The general rule follows the shift of electronegativity across the periodic table, nonmetals being good oxidizing agents and metals being good reducing agents. Transition metals vary considerably in this property, acting sometimes as reducing agents and sometimes as oxidizing agents, depending on the other reactant's relative electronegativity. Oxidation-reduction reactions can be expressed in partial electronic equations:

$$2M^0 - 4e^- \rightarrow 2M^{++};$$
$$O^0_2 + 4e^- \rightarrow 2O^{--}.$$

When the two partials are added:

$$2M^0 + O^0_2 \rightarrow 2M^{++}O^{--}.$$

Bonding in Solids.—The only types of bonding discussed have been ionic (or electrovalent), covalent, polar covalent, and coordinate covalent. When an ionic compound solidifies, each cation (+) is surrounded by anions (−), and each anion is surrounded by cations. The alternating lattice of + and − charges in three dimensions is one in which the bond between an ion and any other oppositely charged ion near it is identical; that is, the bonding force of the solid at any point in it is between oppositely charged particles and is therefore equal in all directions. When covalently bonded molecules solidify, the bonds between the molecules are weak compared to the bonds within the molecule and are the result of what are called *van der Waals forces of attraction,* named after Johannes Diderik van der Waals (1837–1923) who first measured them. The nucleus of each molecule weakly attracts the electrons of nearby molecules, and the molecules are pulled into a pattern in the solid such that the forces acting on individual atoms vary considerably in different directions. Polar covalent molecules bond into the solid state with an orientation of their positive and negative ends. When nonmetallic elements solidify, the atoms bond to one another with covalent arrangements of their electrons, sometimes in very complicated fashion, to form interlocking rings or, like carbon atoms in the diamond structure, to form chains. The entire crystal of such an element can be considered a molecule, in a sense, because there is no variation in the energy of the bonds from atom to atom. No unit can be found consisting of only a few atoms bound differently from the way the unit is bound to other units.

■**METALLIC BONDING.**—When metal atoms solidify, there are not enough valence electrons to share in the usual way, and in any case the low electronegativity of metals sheds electrons. The bonding is imagined as one in which nuclei, having lost their freedom of motion due to cooling, attract the clouds of electrons of adjacent nuclei with a force far stronger than that of electrical charges or of weak van der Waals forces. In fact, the forces of attraction are in the range that binds atoms into covalent molecules. They actually pull the inner shells of metal atoms together, squeezing the few valence electrons into the empty spaces among the atoms. These empty spaces exist not merely as physical holes in the structure but as areas where the liberated valence electrons can repose and expend least energy against the complex forces of attraction and repulsion around them.

When pressure is exerted on a crystal, or when it receives a blow, the lattice particles shear or the structure shatters. When a solid metal is hammered or bent, it gives. The atoms are not held rigidly by their electron distribution. Valence electrons are associated with all the adjacent nuclei and belong to no particular one. Thus, when the structure is bent, these relatively free electrons move from one vacant space to another, and the atoms are allowed to slide past one another into new positions. Along the inside of a bend, the atoms are squeezed out by pressure and slide toward the outside of the bend to take up the space that would otherwise be a crack or tear in the metal. When a metal is hammered, the outer atoms are simply pounded down among the others, the free valence electrons taking up new positions. Thus, a solid metal is also an ionic structure, but there are only positive ions with electrons dispersed among them without regard to any particular nucleus.

■CONDUCTIVITY.—The concept of metallic bonding explains electric current as a flow of electrons. If fresh electrons are pressed into one end of a metal wire from a source outside the wire (such as a battery), they will force the nearest valence electrons to shift position. They, in turn, will bump the next layers of free electrons, and the pressure will be passed along to the end of the wire, where the final layer of free electrons will be forced to leave the wire altogether. The speed at which the pressure is transmitted is the speed of an electric current, which is close to the speed of light; and it is conceived of as a wave. The actual movement of the electrons along the wire is a relatively slow affair. If the temperature of a metal is raised, its conductivity becomes less because the atoms are vibrating with greater energy and obstruct flow of the valence electrons.

Electrochemistry.—If a strip of copper is put in water, a few copper (Cu) atoms will be dislodged and will go into solution as cations, Cu^{++}, leaving their valence electrons in the strip and giving it a minute negative charge. The negative charge serves to attract the positive copper ions back to the strip to re-form atoms. However, initially the copper atoms are dislodged to form ions faster than the ions are attracted back to re-form atoms. Therefore, the number of excess electrons on the strip continues to increase and the negative charge slowly grows. When a sufficient number of excess electrons produces a large enough negative charge on the strip, the ions will be attracted back to form atoms at the same rate that atoms are discharged to form ions. Thus, a dynamic equilibrium will exist between the copper ions in solution and the copper atoms of the strip:

$$Cu^0 \rightleftarrows Cu^{++} + 2e.$$

Any strip of metal will allow some of its atoms to dissolve in water, leaving the strip negatively charged. However, the affinity of each metal for its electrons varies, so that the number of excess electrons that build up on a strip varies with the metal. Zinc metal clings to its electrons with less affinity than does copper; therefore, a larger concentration of electrons will build up on a zinc strip before the equilibrium is established. In other words, the zinc strip will build up a higher electric charge than the copper strip.

If a zinc strip is put in water containing Cu^{++} ions, from such a salt as $Cu^{++}SO_4^{--}$, a copper ion hitting the zinc strip will take up two of the excess electrons left by the dissolving zinc ions because copper has greater affinity for electrons than has zinc. The resulting copper atom will stick to the zinc. Whenever a copper ion, Cu^{++}, removes electrons and becomes a neutral atom, Cu^0, another zinc atom, Zn^0, is freed to escape as an ion, Zn^{++}. Copper ions in solution are blue; zinc metal is grey. Gradually the zinc strip becomes coated with reddish copper while the blue of the solution fades. The reaction is a chemical one and can be written as an equation:

$$Zn^0 + Cu^{++} \rightarrow Zn^{++} + Cu^0.$$

According to the convention of oxidation-reduction reactions, when a metal is ionized, it has also been oxidized; when the ion is turned back into the neutral metal, it has been reduced. Thus, copper has been reduced and zinc oxidized in the above reaction, which has been called an electrochemical reaction.

■ELECTROCHEMICAL CELLS.—If a zinc strip and a copper strip are put into the same container of water, the charge on the zinc will become higher than that on the copper, for the oxidation potential of zinc is greater. If the strips are connected by a wire conductor, the difference in charges on them will produce a pressure of electrons from the zinc to the copper. If, at the same time, electrons can be removed or neutralized on the copper strip, electrons will flow from the zinc to the copper through the connecting wire. The neutralizing is done by adding an electrovalent compound, a compound whose ions will act as transporters of electrons to the water. Copper sulfate is suitable for the zinc-copper combination. The copper ions added to the solution by the copper sulfate will be far in excess of the concentration that the copper strip would produce in pure water. The copper ions will therefore deposit on the copper strip in order to bring about the proper dynamic equilibrium between copper atoms and copper ions. As they deposit, using up electrons on the strip, the zinc strip's larger concentration of electrons will flow along the wire toward the copper. This in turn allows more zinc ions to go into solution liberating more electrons. A current of electrons will flow from zinc to copper along the conductor as long as the oxidation-reduction reactions continue at both strips.

The various parts of such a system are put together in what is called a *voltaic cell,* after Alessandro Volta (1745–1827), who first constructed one. There are several variations of voltaic cells, one of the more common being the *Daniell cell,* invented by John F. Daniell in 1836. In the Daniell cell, a zinc electrode is immersed in a zinc sulfate solution and a copper electrode is immersed in a copper sulfate solution. The two solutions may be separated by a porous membrane, or a gravity-type cell may be used in which the less dense zinc sulfate floats on top of the more dense copper sulfate. The ions pass through the porous membrane or through the interface between the two solutions.

Various combinations of electrovalent or ionic compounds in water solution, called *electrolytes,* and of metal strips, called *electrodes,* have been designed for different purposes. Cells can be constructed in which the two solutions contain metal ions that are oxidized and reduced at electrodes made of nonreacting substances, such as carbon. In the familiar dry cell, pastes have been substituted for liquid solutions, and one electrode is nonreactive. Batteries consist of many electrochemical cells arranged in such a way that each one's electromotive force is fed to a single pair of electrodes. In a storage cell, the reaction proceeds until an equilibrium is reached when no more current can flow; by forcing a current from another source through the cell the reactions are reversed and the potentials in the cell are built up again: the cell has been recharged.

■ELECTROMOTIVE SERIES.—The chemical reaction that takes place at each electrode of a voltaic cell is half of the complete reaction that takes place in the cell as a whole. Thus, chemical reaction in each half-cell can be seen as a measure of the oxidation potential for the metal in contact with its own ion. When both half-cells have the same oxidation potential, no current can flow. The *electromotive force,* or voltage, is produced between half-cells of different oxidation potential. The oxidation potential for a half-cell cannot be measured directly, but one can be hooked up to a standard half-cell and comparative figures can be obtained. The standard chosen is hydrogen gas in contact with its ion in a molal solution, and this is given the value of 0. Metals, in contact with their ions in molal solution, can be arranged in order of decreasing oxidation potential. Such a list is called an *electromotive series.* Any metal will take electrons from any metal above it on the list and will replace the ion in solution of any metal below it on the list.

■ELECTROLYTES.—Electrolytes are ionic compounds. In metallic conductors, the electricity is conducted by electrons. In *electrolytic conductors* or *electrolytes,* the current is carried by ions rather than by electrons. Any compound that has one or more ionic bonds can function as an electrolyte. For example, Na^+Cl^-, $Mg^{++}Cl_2^-$, and $Al^{+++}Cl_3^-$, are all electrolytes. Compounds that contain radicals, such as $Na^+NO_3^-$ or $Ca^{++}SO_4^{--}$, are also electrolytes. The radical's atoms are covalently bonded, and the radical is extremely stable. However, it will accept or donate electrons to form ionic compounds and thus can electrolytically conduct electricity.

■ELECTROLYSIS.—If an electrolyte is melted, or fused, in a container and electrodes connected to a source of electrical current are placed into the container, then the cations and positive radicals will move toward the negatively charged electrode, or *cathode,* where they are reduced, while the anions and negatively charged radicals will move toward the positive electrode, or *anode,* where they are oxidized. At the electrodes, also called *poles,* each kind of ion and radical is relieved of its electrical charge. The ions are turned into neutral atoms, and the radicals are broken up into their component atoms. If the electrolyte is table salt, Na^+Cl^-, the Na^+ moves to the negative pole and the Cl^- to the positive pole. The reactions that take place are: $Na^+ + e^- \rightarrow Na^0$ and $Cl^- - e^- \rightarrow Cl^0$ or, more properly, $Cl^- \rightarrow Cl^0 + e^-$. The sodium atoms appear as pure, silvery, solid sodium metal at the cathode, while the chlorine atoms combine into diatomic molecules of greenish-yellow chlorine gas at the anode.

In taking up electrons at the cathode, where the source of the current piles them, sodium allows more electrons to move there. In giving up their electrons at the anode, chlorine ions replenish the source of the current. Thus, a melted electrolyte conducts electricity, though in a completely different way from that of a metal.

An electrolyte dissolved in water also conducts electricity. The radicals and ions move about freely in the water; and when electrodes are introduced, each radical or ion moves to the oppositely charged pole, where it accepts or gives up electrons. However, the neutral metal and nonmetal produced in the water may combine with the water, so that the end products of the electrolysis of a table salt and water solution are chlorine gas and hydrogen gas, never chlorine and sodium metal. A water solution of hydrochloric acid, HCl, on the other hand, results in the decomposition of the water into hydrogen gas and oxygen gas. The explanation makes use of the concept of oxidation-reduction and of relative electronegativities.

Electrolysis is the principle used in *electroplating.* The object to be plated is made the cathode in a solution containing ions of the metal with which the object is to be plated. A current is passed through the solution, the metal ions in the solution are reduced at the cathode, and they bond to the surface of the object.

Solutions.—Most chemical reactions take place in solutions, which are vital to laboratory work as well as industry, partly because of their general use and partly because they facilitate measuring out accurate quantities of reagents. The world can be thought of as being made of pure elements, pure compounds, and mixtures of elements and compounds in any numbers and any proportions. In heterogeneous mixtures, at least one compound is present in the form of particles or droplets large enough to settle out or to be separated by filtration, centrifuging, or mechanical means. Heterogeneous mixtures, in other words, contain "lumps" large enough to be seen through a microscope. Homogeneous mixtures, on the other hand, are uniform throughout; that is, their components are individual molecules, atoms, or ions that cannot be separated by filtration. They are called *solutions.* There are solutions of a gas in a gas, gas in a

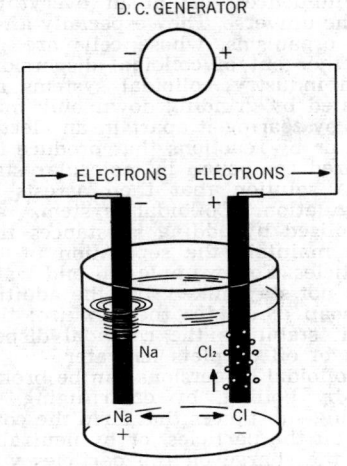

D. C. GENERATOR

ELECTRONS   ELECTRONS

Na   Cl₂

Na   Cl

ELECTROLYSIS of sodium chloride, NaCl, liberates sodium ions at the negative electrode, or *cathode,* and chlorine gas at the positive electrode, or *anode.*

liquid, and gas in a solid; of a liquid in a gas, liquid in a liquid, and liquid in a solid; and of a solid in a gas, solid in a liquid, and solid in a solid. The component present in the smaller amount is called the *solute;* the component present in the larger amount is called the *solvent.* A solvent may have many solutes dissolved in it.

Solutions are defined in several ways: *concentration* is the weight of solute in a certain volume of solvent; *percentage composition* is the weight of solute in relation to the total weight of solute plus solvent. A *molar solution* contains 1 mole (1 gram molecular weight) of solute in 1 liter of solvent. Thus, since calcium carbonate, $CaCO_3$, has a gram molecular weight of 100.06, a molar solution of $CaCO_3$ would contain 100.06 grams of $CaCO_3$ in 1 liter of water (50.03 grams in a half-liter, or 200.12 grams in 2 liters), and a 2.5 molar solution would contain 250.15 grams of $CaCO_3$ in 1 liter of water. A *molal solution* contains one mole of solute in 1,000 grams of solvent. Thus, a molal solution of $CaCO_3$ would contain 100.06 grams of $CaCO_3$ in 1,000 grams of water (or 50.03 grams in 500 grams of water, or 200.12 grams in 2,000 grams of water), and a 2.5 molal solution would contain 250.15 grams of $CaCO_3$ in 1,000 grams of water. A *normal solution* contains one gram equivalent weight of solute in 1 liter of solvent. Thus, a 1 normal solution of $CaCO_3$ contains $100.06 \div 2$ or 50.03 grams of $CaCO_3$ in 1 liter of water (25.015 grams in a half-liter, 100.06 grams in 2 liters), and a 2.5 normal solution contains 125.075 grams of $CaCO_3$ in 1 liter of water.

In the laboratory, to avoid weighing out very small amounts of some commonly used reagent many times a day, a solution of the reagent is made up in large quantities and is standardized; that is, its exact composition is determined by analysis and then computed into molarity, molality, or normality. Liquid-meas-

uring apparatus, such as pipettes and burettes, are calibrated to $\frac{1}{10}$ cc.; and thus, minute quantities of the desired solute for a reaction can be measured accurately and rapidly.

All gases and some liquids, such as alcohol and water, dissolve to an unlimited extent in each other; but usually there is a limit to the amount of solute that a solvent will absorb. The process of dissolving involves the weakening of the bonds between the solute molecules by the solvent molecules. If both are covalent and similar in other ways, they generally dissolve each other because the bonding is similar. Ionic compounds generally do not dissolve well in covalent solvents but will, often to an unlimited extent, in ionic solvents. Often a compound is formed by the solute and solvent molecules, and this compound then disperses through the solvent. When solids break up and dissolve in a liquid, they must take up some heat from their environment, cooling the solution, just as a solid melts only when it has acquired its heat of fusion. If the solute simultaneously forms a compound with the solvent, heat may be generated.

When a solvent has absorbed as much solute as the various forces of attraction and repulsion permit, the solution is called *saturated.* If a solid solute is being stirred into a liquid solvent, at the saturation point the molecules of the undissolved solid will be in dynamic equilibrium with the dissolved molecules. There will also be a constant exchange between the two states, but the actual number of dissolved molecules will not change. The concentration of a substance in a saturated solution is usually expressed as grams of solute per 100 grams of solvent, and is called the *solubility* of the substance. Solubility varies with temperature and generally increases with a rise in temperature. In the case of a gas dissolved in a liquid or solid, additional heat makes the gas molecules move about more actively and escape. Thus, heating decreases the solubility of gases in liquids. However, an increase in pressure usually increases the solubility of a gas.

With care, it is possible to dissolve more solute than a normally saturated solution will contain. The solution is then called *supersaturated,* and any disturbance of this condition will immediately precipitate out the amount of the solute in excess of the saturation limit.

The freezing point of any pure solvent is lowered by the addition of a solute, and its boiling point is raised, to an extent proportional to the concentration. When a mole of any covalent solute is added to 1,000 grams of water, the freezing point is always depressed 1.86° C. and the boiling point is raised 0.513° C. By measuring the freezing point or boiling point of an unknown solution, its molality can be calculated, and from that the molecular weight of the solute can be computed.

This mathematical change in boiling and freezing points can be explained in terms of the kinetic molecular theory, and relates to the actual number of molecules of solute present and to the vapor pressure they exert. Ions released into solution are more numerous than covalent molecules would be for a solution of the same molality. Ordinary salt fills its solvent with twice as many particles as sugar, which is a covalent compound. Thus, the depression of the freezing point and raising of the boiling point with electrovalent solutes is always greater than with covalent solutes. In addition, the change is not constant for all concentrations of electrovalent solutes because of the varying degrees of ionization that take place as the solution is diluted. Alcohol and glycol are familiar solutes added to water to lower its freezing point, especially in engine coolants. Salt would be better and cheaper, but it corrodes metal parts; it is used in ice.

Colloids.—Intermediate between true solutions and heterogeneous mixtures is *colloidal dispersion.* The *dispersion medium,* analogous to a solvent, contains the *disperse phase,* analogous to a solute. The particles of the disperse phase do not settle out, cannot be filtered out, and cannot be seen in a microscope; these are properties of a true solution. However, the particles scatter light in the *Tyndall effect,* show *Brownian movement,* have electrical charges on them without being ionic, and in other ways reveal that they are not molecules but agglomerations of molecules, hundreds or thousands of them gathered in submicroscopic kernels. The kernels are prevented from coagulating or growing because they have all acquired the same kind of electrical charge, so that each is repelled by the others, or because they have each acquired a covering of solvent molecules that act as buffers.

The size of a colloidal particle has been defined as between 1 mμ and 200 mμ in diameter, 1 mμ being one millionth of a millimeter. If the molecule is small, a great many can cling together to form a colloidal particle, but some organic molecules are themselves so large that a single one can be considered a colloidal particle. Since most reactions begin with a mixing of bulk matter, proceed through molecules, and end with bulk matter, the process must pass through the colloidal stage. The properties of this special state of mat-

ter influences just about everything in the universe. They especially affect life organisms, whose cells are put together out of colloidal dispersions.

In industry, colloidal systems are created by grinding down bulk matter, by tearing it apart in an electric arc, or by reactions that produce the desired compound in molecular state in a solution that then arrests its coagulation. Colloidal systems are stabilized by adding substances that will maintain the separation of the particles. For example, oil and water will not stay mixed, but the addition of soap *emulsifies* the mixture; that is, it stabilizes the colloidal dispersion of oil droplets in water.

Colloidal dispersions can be broken up by boiling, by centrifuging, by adding substances that strip the coating off the particles, or by neutralizing the charge on the particles with an electrolyte or in an electrical field. This last method, called *electrophoresis,* is the principle used in Cottrell precipitators. These precipitators are installed in factory chimneys to remove both poisonous and valuable wastes before they are spewed into the atmosphere. The smoke passes through baffles that are electrically, and oppositely, charged. Whatever their charges, particles will stick to the oppositely charged plate, become neutralized, and coagulate rapidly.

Water.—In a vast number of reactions, traces of water must be present to act as a catalyst. Water is the most universal solvent known, and its properties primarily derive from the structure of its molecule. The oxygen atom is covalently bonded to two hydrogen atoms, which are not directly opposite one another but at an angle of 105°. The positive charges of the hydrogen nuclei are concentrated at one side of the molecule, while on the opposite side, the oxygen atom, with its far greater number of electrons, creates a concentration of negative charges. Thus, the water molecule has one end more positively charged than the other negative end. It is a polar molecule and is called a *dipole.* The oxygen end of the dipole, being more negative, repels the oxygen end of all other water molecules but attracts the more positive, or hydrogen, end of all water molecules. This orientation gives water a lower freezing point, a higher boiling point, and a greater heat of

fusion and heat of vaporization than similar compounds whose molecules are not polar. The polar nature of water enables it to dissolve other polar compounds more easily, each water molecule prying into the solid with the appropriate positive or negative end.

When hydrogen is covalently bonded to atoms that have high electronegativity, such as oxygen, nitrogen, and fluorine, the proton tends to link into the electron cloud of other molecules containing such atoms. Although the link is weak, it is substantial enough to measure and is called a *hydrogen bond.*

Acids, Bases, and Salts.—Three groups of compounds—acids, bases, and salts—have been known from antiquity. Most acids taste sour, turn a dye called litmus a red color, react with many metals to produce hydrogen gas, and combine with bases to form salts and water. Most bases taste bitter, have a soapy feel, turn litmus a blue color, and combine with acids to form salts and water. Salts are generally crystalline solids at ordinary temperatures. Thus, there are no naturally occurring bases and acids in the Earth's inorganic crust, but a large percentage of the crust consists of hundreds of different kinds of salts. It is from these salts that many acids and bases are commercially manufactured.

Acid-base reactions have been known from antiquity and are as important in chemistry as oxidation-reduction reactions, though there are relatively far fewer acids and bases than oxidizing agents. In the modern theory of acid-base reactions, water plays a key role. By far the most important property of water is the fact that its molecules react with one another to produce ions. The equation expressing this can be written as follows:

$$H_2O + H_2O \rightleftarrows H_3O^+ + OH^-$$

The cation is called the *hydronium ion,* and the anion is the *hydroxide ion.* If the OH$^-$ is somehow removed or suppressed so that the concentration of H$_3$O$^+$ is in excess, then the solution will have a sour taste, turn litmus blue, react with many metals to produce hydrogen, and combine with bases to form salts. In other words, a solution with a greater concentration of H$_3$O$^+$ than of OH$^-$ will have all the properties of an acid. If the H$_3$O$^+$ is suppressed or eliminated, and the concentration of OH$^-$ is increased, the solution will have all the properties of a base. It will taste bitter, have a soapy feel, turn litmus blue, and combine with acids to produce salts. Thus, the ions into which pure water dissociates are the ions that give aqueous solutions of acids and bases their characteristic properties. In pure water, the concentration of H$_3$O$^+$ always equals the concentration of OH$^-$ and the two ions cancel out each others' properties, so that pure water is neither sour nor bitter and does not affect litmus. However, it can react with either a base or an acid as an acid or a base.

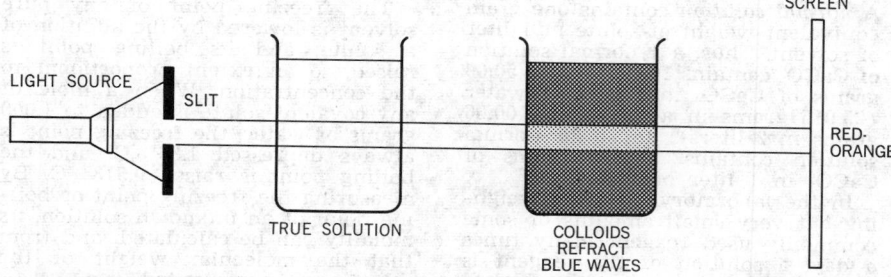

TYNDALL EFFECT can be used to distinguish colloidal suspensions from true solutions. A beam of white light passes through the true solution without change but is refracted when passing through the colloid. Here the particles selectively refract only the blue waves, and the red-orange waves pass through the colloid to illuminate the screen.

Several theories have been used to explain acid-base reactions. One is the *proton transfer theory* (announced independently by Johannes Nicolaus Brønsted and Thomas Martin Lowery in 1923), by which an acid is defined as a substance that has a tendency to lose a proton, and a base as a substance that has a tendency to gain a proton. A proton in any chemical reaction is always the nucleus of a hydrogen atom or is a hydrogen ion, H^+. The strength of an acid is a measure of its tendency to lose a proton, and the strength of a base is a measure of its tendency to take up a proton. It follows that when an acid gives up a proton, it becomes a unit that, in turn, may take up, or accept, a proton to reproduce the acid. It is then possible to write the general equation for an acid as

$$A \rightleftharpoons H^+ + B.$$
Acid   Proton   Base

An acid and a base related in this manner are said to form a *conjugate pair;* the *conjugate acid* is the proton donor and the *conjugate base* is the proton acceptor; the reaction is called protolysis.

To illustrate that an acid or a base may be either a molecule or an ion, these equations should be noted:

Acid   Proton   Base

$$HCl \rightleftharpoons H^+ + Cl^-$$
$$NH_4^+ \rightleftharpoons H^+ + NH_3$$
$$H_2SO_4 \rightleftharpoons H^+ + HSO_4^-$$
$$HSO_4^- \rightleftharpoons H^+ + SO_4^{--}$$

The proton transfer theory is also useful in describing the ionization of water. In the ionization of water, one water molecule acts as an acid and donates a hydrogen ion, or proton, H^+, to the other molecule that, acting as a base, attaches the proton to a pair of available valence electrons.

Since the reaction is reversible, the hydronium ion then acts as an acid and donates a proton to the hydroxide ion acting as a base. No theory explains why, in pure water, some molecules accept and others donate protons.

In pure water the concentration of each ion that is formed is always the same and is very small in quantity, which explains why pure water is such a poor conductor of electricity. Using the law of mass action formula,

$$\frac{(OH^-)(H_3O^+)}{(H_2O)} = K$$

where K is the equilibrium constant. Since the concentration of water molecules is relatively enormous, and therefore constant compared to the slight concentration of ions in it, the equation for the equilibrium constant can be written:

$$(OH^-)(H_3O^+) = K_w.$$

By experiment, K_w has been determined to be 1×10^{-14} at room temperature. The concentration of each ion in pure water is therefore 1×10^{-7}. If the concentration of H_3O^+ is changed, the concentration of OH^- must change proportionately in order to maintain the constant K_w.

A former theory of acid-base reactions, propounded by Svante Arrhenius in 1883, held that the hydrogen ion itself, the H^+, was the acidic particle and that the concentration of H^+ in a solution indicated its strength. A notation was devised in which H^+ was transformed by logarithms into simple numbers and called the *pH factor,* or value. This notation is still the only one in use. The pH of a neutral solution is 7; a pH of less than 7 indicates an acid solution; and a pH of more than 7 indicates a basic, or alkaline, solution. Blood, for example, has a pH value of about 7.2, which is slightly alkaline.

Instead of pH we should write pH_3O, but the change has not been seriously proposed. A strong acid is one that ionizes vigorously and completely even in small amounts of water, thus donating all its protons at a high rate. A weak acid ionizes only slightly in solutions of high concentration, and it must be diluted with large amounts of water before it will yield all its protons. The common strong acids are sulfuric, H_2SO_4; hydrochloric, HCl; and nitric, HNO_3. Among the weak acids are phosphoric, H_3PO_4; carbonic, H_2CO_3; and all the organic acids, such as acetic, $HC_2H_3O_2$, and oxalic, $C_2H_2O_4$. Strong bases produce large concentrations of hydroxide ions in water. They include the hydroxides of the alkali metals, such as sodium hydroxide, NaOH, and of the alkaline earth metals, such as calcium hydroxide, $Ca(OH)_2$. A weak base is ammonium hydroxide, NH_4OH, which must be diluted before it will ionize completely.

Most pure acids are covalently bonded compounds, and it is their aqueous solutions that are used in chemistry. In the mixture produced by the reaction

$$HCl + H_2O \rightleftharpoons H_3O^+ + Cl^-,$$

it is the H_3O^+ that acts as the proton donor when a base is added. Most familiar bases already have a hydroxide ion that they yield in solution, for example, Na^+OH^-. Some substances yield protons to strong bases and accept protons from strong acids; these are called *amphoprotic compounds.* One of these is water.

All acids react with all bases to produce water and a salt. For example:

$$HCl + NaOH \rightleftharpoons Na^+Cl^- + H_2O,$$
$$H_2SO_4 + Ca(OH)_2 \rightleftharpoons Ca^{++}SO_4^{--} + 2H_2O,$$
$$HNO_3 + KOH \rightleftharpoons K^+NO_3^- + H_2O.$$

Salts are always electrovalent compounds composed of those parts of acids and bases, whether radicals or ions, that are neither the hydronium nor the hydroxide ion. Thus NaCl, KNO_3, and $CaSO_4$ are salts.

Pure water is neutral; that is, when an acid and a base are allowed to react in exactly the right proportions, so that equal concentrations of H_3O^+ and of OH^- are produced, the solution will be neutral. In other words, it is neither acidic nor basic and has a pH of 7. The process of adding acid and base together is called *neutralization.* In the laboratory the technique used in performing neutralization reactions is called *titration.* An acid of known concentration, or molality, is measured slowly from a burette into a sample of base of unknown strength; when the mixture has become neutral, the known amount of acid that was used to neutralize the sample enables calculation of the amount of base present in the sample. Similarly, the strength of the basic solution is standardized by titrating it with an acid solution.

When the solution becomes neutral, the *end point* of the reaction has been reached. It is revealed by an *indicator*, which is a dye that has a different color in acid solutions from its hue in basic solutions. A few drops of the indicator, added to the solution being titrated, colors the solution according to its pH value. At the end point, the color changes quite abruptly. There are many indicators, each of which changes color at a specific pH value. Two commonly used indicators are litmus, which is red in acid and blue in base, and phenolthalein, colorless in acid and purple in base. Titration is often carried out with a potentiometer, an electrical apparatus that measures the conductivity of a solution and indicates neutrality faster and more precisely than visual indicators.

Salts of strong acids and strong bases (such as NaCl and KNO_3) ionize in water to form neutral solutions. However, the ions of salts of weak acids and strong bases (such as $NaC_2H_3O_2$ and K_2CO_3) will react with water to form alkaline solutions, while the ions of salts of strong acids and weak bases (such as NH_4Cl and $CaSO_4$) will react with water to form acidic solutions. Any process of reaction with water is called *hydrolysis.*

■BUFFER SOLUTIONS. — Both sodium chloride, NaCl, and ammonium carbonate, $(NH_4)_2CO_3$, have a pH of 7 in water solution. If a small quantity of dilute hydrochloric acid, HCl, is added to the NaCl solution, it becomes strongly acidic, lowering the pH to about 4. When the HCl is added to the $(NH_4)_2CO_3$ solution, its pH is hardly changed. Similarly, the addition of a small quantity of sodium hydroxide, NaOH, would raise the pH of the NaCl solution to about 10, while the pH of the $(NH_4)_2CO_3$ solution would hardly be changed. The ammonium carbonate solution resists a change of pH when an acid or a base is added; this is called a *buffer action.* A *buffer solution* is defined as a solution that is resistant to change of pH upon the addition of an acid or base. Buffer solutions usually consist of a weak acid and its salt (which is the weak acid's conjugate base), or of a weak base and its salt (which is the weak base's conjugate acid). The salt of a weak acid and a weak base, as shown above, also acts as a buffer. The fluids in a living organism maintain their constant pH value because they are buffered solutions.

—Louis Vaczek

ORGANIC CHEMISTRY

Historical Development.—The term "organic" was first associated with chemistry as a convenient classification for substances of plant or animal origin. Although organic substances (alcohols, oils, fats, sugars, and such) had been known for thousands of years, their chemistry received little attention until the eighteenth century. At this time substances or compounds of natural origin were divided arbitrarily into three classes: mineral, vegetable, and animal. It was quickly recognized that compounds obtained from vegetable and animal sources always contained carbon and hydrogen and were more closely related to each other than to compounds of mineral origin. The discovery that in many instances the *same* compound could be isolated from both vegetable and animal sources initiated a reclassification of substances into two groups: those substances produced by living organisms were defined as *organic* and those substances not produced by living organisms were classified as *inorganic*.

This first general definition unfortunately was understood to imply that organic compounds were produced under the influence of a *vital force*. Laboratory synthesis of organic compounds was considered in the realm of fantasy, although inorganic compounds routinely were prepared in the laboratory. This *vitalistic theory* was doomed by the discovery by a German chemist, Friedrich Wöhler (1800–1882), that an organic compound could be produced without the aid of a living organism. In 1828 Wöhler noted that evaporation of an aqueous solution of ammonium cyanate, an inorganic substance, resulted in the formation of urea, an organic compound previously found in animal urine. Stimulated by this observation, nineteenth-century chemists inaugurated a new era in synthetic chemistry by devising methods of forming simple organic compounds from their elements. Today, few organic compounds are considered beyond the scope of laboratory synthesis.

While the terms "inorganic chemistry" and "organic chemistry" apparently have lost their original meanings, the early method of classification remains. All so-called organic compounds contain carbon. This element commands a major branch of chemistry because its compounds far outnumber the known compounds of all of the other elements combined. Thus, *organic chemistry* often is defined as the chemistry of carbon compounds. While not completely accurate (the oxides of carbon, their metal salts, and a few miscellaneous carbon-containing compounds commonly are treated in textbooks of inorganic chemistry), this brief definition adequately distinguishes organic chemistry from other branches of chemistry.

Nature of the Covalent Bond.—The concept of how carbon is linked or bonded to itself and to other atoms is fundamental to understanding organic chemistry. The carbon nucleus contains six positively charged protons that are complemented by six negatively charged electrons distributed in two shells outside the nucleus. The inner shell contains two electrons and does not tend to accept or lose electrons. The outer shell (*valence shell*) contains the remaining four electrons, four fewer than the eight required to fill the second shell. In the periodic table carbon occupies a position between lithium (an electron donor) and fluorine (an electron acceptor). To achieve maximum stability, an atom prefers to take the easiest route to a full valence shell. In the case of lithium, the lone electron in the outer shell tends to be donated to a convenient electron acceptor such as fluorine, which possesses seven electrons in its valence shell. The carbon atom, with four electrons in the outer shell, could acquire a full valence shell either by losing all four of these electrons or by gaining four additional electrons to complete the partially filled shell. However, either process would be energetically unfeasible. This becomes evident when one envisions the state of an atom after one electron is lost. The atom is no longer electrically neutral, but possesses a positive charge. Loss of a second electron is now more difficult because of enhanced attraction by the nucleus. Loss of a third and fourth electron would be even more difficult. By similar reasoning, acquisition of four electrons is prohibited by repulsion of additional incoming electrons through the negative charge established by the first electron accepted.

While carbon does not tend to gain or lose electrons and form a charged ion, it may combine with other elements by "sharing" electrons. Carbon may share its four valence electrons (represented by crosses) with the single valence electrons (represented by dots) of four hydrogen atoms to form the organic compound methane. In effect the carbon atom has attained a full outer shell, and each hydrogen atom has attained a full valence shell by gaining an electron. This sharing of electrons results in a stable molecule. Since there has been no net gain or loss of electrons, methane is electrically neutral. Each electron pair linking hydrogen to carbon constitutes a *covalent bond*.

The ability of carbon to bond in a covalent manner accounts primarily for the distinguishing characteristics of organic compounds. Hydrogen commonly is considered an electron donor, as in hydrogen chloride. In the same sense chlorine is considered an

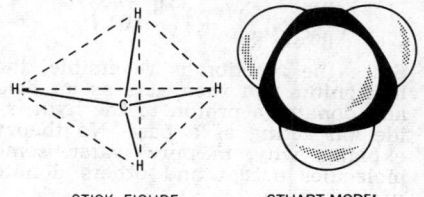

Methane | Hydrogen chloride | Chloroform

electron acceptor, but both hydrogen and chlorine form covalent bonds with carbon to form stable, electrically neutral compounds. In chloroform the outer shells of all atoms involved possess a complete valence shell without actual electron transfer or formation of ionic charge.

Structure of Organic Molecules.—The *structural formula* for methane, the simplest organic compound, usually is drawn as a planar projection in which the carbon atom is surrounded by four hydrogen atoms linked by solid lines, each line representing an electron pair or covalent bond. Further abbreviation is common in the literature of organic chemistry, and the "stick figure" is shortened to CH₄. Application of these conventions

Kekulé Formula | | **Chemical Formula**

$H-C-H$ with H above and below | or | CH_4

Methane

$Cl-C-Cl$ with Cl above and below | or | CCl_4

Carbon tetrachloride

$H-C-C-O-H$ | or | CH_3CH_2OH

Ethyl alcohol

to more complex molecules may be illustrated by the structural formulas for carbon tetrachloride and ethyl alcohol.

Although structural formulas representing organic compounds routinely are depicted as planar, they must be interpreted as three-dimensional entities. Careful investigations

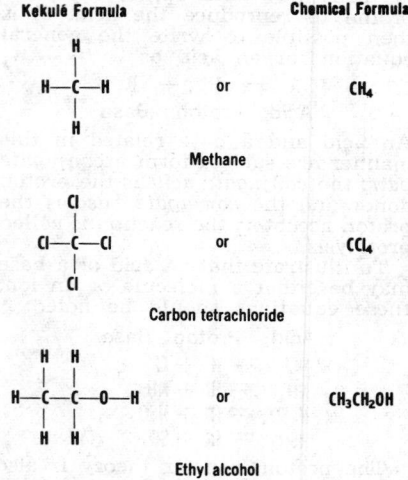

STICK FIGURE | STUART MODEL

have proved that the four covalent bonds of carbon project from the nucleus in such a manner that they are equidistant from each other. Thus, the methane molecule possesses a tetrahedral configuration; that is, the bonds are directed toward the four corners of a regular tetrahedron or pyramid. This three-dimensional concept of the arrangement of bonds about a carbon atom applies not only to methane, but also to the carbon atom in general when it is bonded to four distinct atoms or groups.

While methane may be unambiguously depicted by its molecular formula CH₄, more complex organic compounds require the use of structural formulas. The molecular for-

Organic Compounds

Name	Chemical Formula	Kekulé Formula	Structural Formula
Ethane	C_2H_6		CH_3CH_3
Propane	C_3H_8		$CH_3CH_2CH_3$
Butane	C_4H_{10}		$CH_3CH_2CH_2CH_3$
Isobutane	C_4H_{10}		CH_3CHCH_3 $\quad\quad CH_3$

mula indicates the number of each kind of atom present in the molecule, but does not describe the arrangement. As can be seen from the accompanying table, increasing the length of the carbon chain to four carbons leads to the molecular formula C_4H_{10}, which does not distinguish between two different compounds, butane and isobutane. In organic chemistry there are many cases where a given molecular formula represents two or more compounds that differ in physical and chemical properties. Such compounds, having the same molecular formula but differing in physical and chemical properties, are known as *isomers.* This phenomenon, known as *structural isomerism,* prevails because atoms are arranged in a fixed manner in an organic molecule; and the arrangement differs in each isomer.

Structural isomerism may be manifested when atoms other than carbon and hydrogen are involved. Substitution of a chlorine atom for one of the hydrogen atoms of butane would lead to two possible compounds: 1-chlorobutane and 2-chlorobutane.

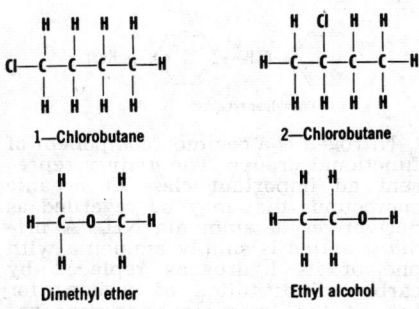

1—Chlorobutane 2—Chlorobutane

Dimethyl ether Ethyl alcohol

(In naming organic compounds, the carbon atoms are numbered consecutively from one end of the chain to the other: in 1-chlorobutane, the chlorine atom is attached to the first carbon; in 2-chlorobutane, to the second carbon atom.) Even though butane contains ten replaceable hydrogen atoms, inspection of the three-dimensional pictures of all ten possible chlorobutanes (C_4H_9Cl) will demonstrate that they are identical to either 1-chlorobutane or 2-chlorobutane. A third type of structural isomerism is evident with the two compounds of the molecular formula C_2H_6O.

An organic compound of two or more carbon atoms linked solely by carbon-carbon single bonds is described as *saturated.* However, carbon may form multiple bonds by sharing more than one pair of electrons with an adjacent carbon atom. Such compounds are said to be *unsaturated. Alkenes,* organic compounds containing one or more carbon-carbon double bonds, may be represented by their simplest member, ethylene. Both

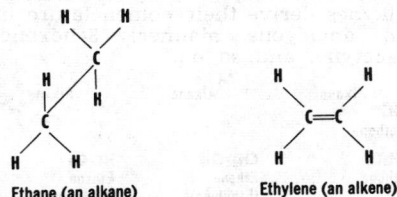

Ethane (an alkane) Ethylene (an alkene)

carbon atoms of ethylene are tetravalent, but are not in the tetrahedral configuration of ethylene's saturated counterpart, ethane. Each carbon shares two of its valence electrons with the other, and the result is a *covalent double bond* in which both carbons and the atoms bonded to them lie in one plane. The carbon-carbon double bond is more reactive than the single bond and will undergo *addition reactions* with such reagents as hydrogen, bromine, and hydrogen bromide.

Alkynes are organic compounds that contain one or more *covalent*

triple bonds. In the simplest member, acetylene, both carbons share six valence electrons and the molecule is linear; that is, both carbons and the two groups bonded with them lie in a straight line. The triple bond is more reactive than the double bond and under appropriate conditions may undergo a *double addition reaction.*

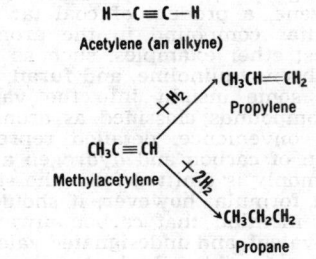

$$H-C \equiv C-H$$

Acetylene (an alkyne)

Many organic compounds contain carbon chains closed into rings. They are known collectively as *alicyclic compounds* and behave chemically as do their open chain derivatives. The simplest member of the series is cyclopropane, a gas used as a surgical anesthetic. Cyclobutene and cyclopentadene are but two of the possible variations on this theme that extends to *bicyclic, tricyclic, tetracyclic,* and *polycyclic* systems. A

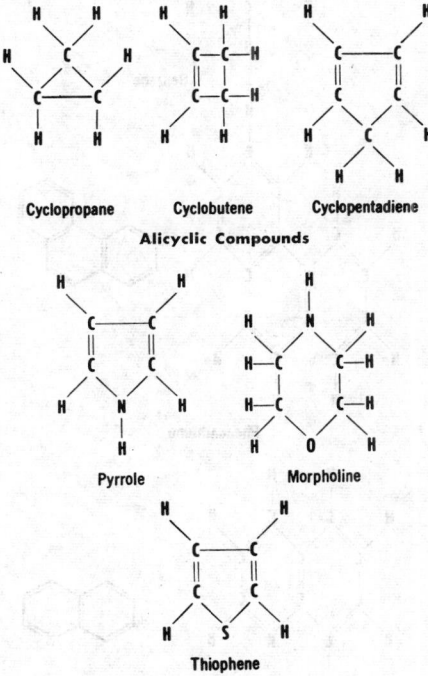

Cyclopropane Cyclobutene Cyclopentadiene

Alicyclic Compounds

Pyrrole Morpholine

Thiophene

Heterocyclic Compounds

major branch of chemistry deals with *heterocyclic compounds:* that is, cyclic derivatives containing atoms other than carbon (pyrrole, morpholine, thiophene, and so on). Thus, the unique bonding nature of carbon provides a vast number of possible structures.

Aliphatic and Aromatic Compounds.— Compounds containing carbon and hydrogen fall into two broad categories:

aliphatic and aromatic. *Aliphatic compounds* were so named because the first members of this class to be studied were natural fats and fatty acids (the Greek word for fat is *aliphos*). *Aromatic compounds* derive their name from the pleasant odor common to many earlier-known representatives. In general, aromatic compounds are cyclic systems containing two or more double bonds. Benzene, a product of coal tar, is a familiar compound in the aromatic series; other examples, such as phenanthrene, quinoline, and furan, provide some insight into the variety of compounds classified as aromatic. For convenience, detailed representation of carbon and hydrogen atoms commonly is omitted from the structural formula; however, it should be kept in mind that carbon always is tetravalent, and undesignated valences represent carbon-hydrogen covalent bonds.

The modern basis for classification of an organic compound as aliphatic or aromatic involves the chemical

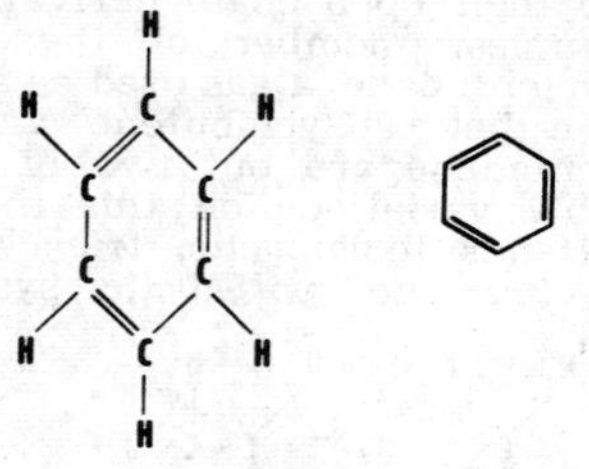

Benzene

Phenanthrene

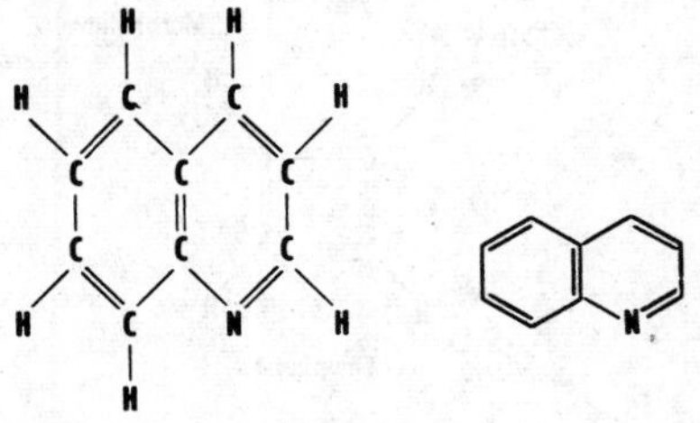

Quinoline

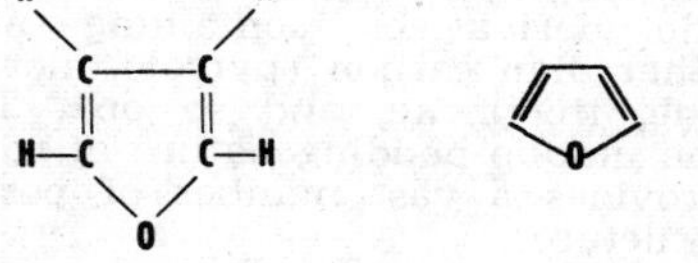

Furan

Aromatic Compounds

properties, that is, the types of reaction, the molecule will undergo. Aromatic compounds, although structurally unsaturated, do not lend themselves to addition reactions as readily as do aliphatic alkenes. Under conditions that transform cyclohexene into cyclohexane by addition of hydrogen, benzene exhibits no tendency to be hydrogenated. When treated with chlorine or bromine, alkenes react by *addition*, whereas aromatic compounds react by *substitution* of a hydrogen atom. The tendency for an unsaturated cyclic compound to undergo substitution rather than addition reactions is a common criterion for assignment to the aromatic classification group.

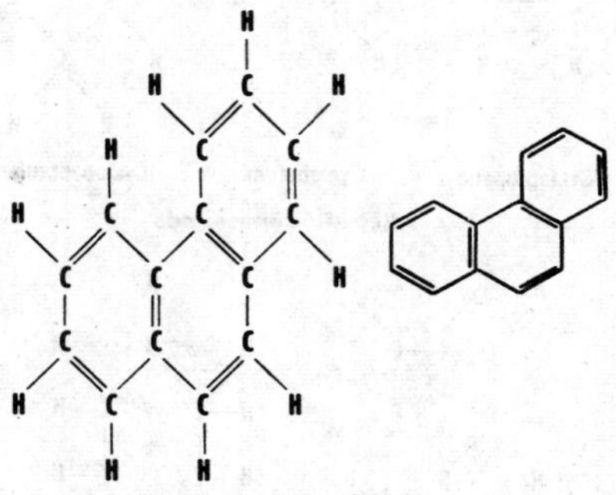

Functional Groups.—An organic compound may also be classified according to the type or types of functional groups present in the molecule. A *functional group* is a portion of a molecule (either one atom or a group of atoms) that passes through a given reaction unchanged, or that reacts independently of the rest of the molecule. In organic reactions, the functional group frequently is the "handle" by which one organic compound is converted to another, either by undergoing a chemical change itself or by its ability to confer special chemical properties on an adjacent carbon atom or atoms.

The carbon-carbon double bond and the carbon-carbon triple bond are examples of functional groups, since their presence confers unique properties on a molecule. Alkenes generally are denoted in the nomenclature of organic chemistry by replacing the suffix *-ane* of the saturated alkanes with the suffix *-ene*. Similarly, the alkynes utilize the suffix *-yne*. Examples are shown in the accompanying table (common names appear in parentheses). The position of the multiple bond is indicated by numbering the carbon chain with the functional group nearest the end of the chain. Alkanes containing more than five carbon atoms are termed hexane (C_6), heptane (C_7), octane (C_8), nonane (C_9), and decane (C_{10}). The corresponding alkenes and alkynes derive their nomenclature in an analogous manner: 3-hexene, 2-octyne, and so on.

Alkane	Alkene	Alkyne
CH_4 Methane	. . .	. . .
CH_3CH_3 Ethane	$CH_2\text{-}CH_2$ Ethene (Ethylene)	$HC\text{-}CH$ Ethyne (Acetylene)
$CH_3CH_2CH_3$ Propane	$CH_2\text{-}CHCH_3$ Propene (Propylene)	$HC\text{-}CCH_3$ Propyne (Methylacetylene)
$CH_3CH_2CH_2CH_3$ Butane	$CH_2\text{-}CHCH_2CH_3$ 1-Butene	$CH_3C\text{-}CCH_3$ 2-Butyne
$CH_3CH_2CH_2CH_2CH_3$ Pentane	$CH_3CH\text{-}CHCH_2CH_3$ 2-Pentene	$HC\text{-}CCH_2\text{-}CH_2CH_3$ 1-Pentyne

The majority of functional groups contain carbon and/or hydrogen in conjunction with other atoms, while others are composed solely of atoms other than carbon and hydrogen. The halogens (fluorine, chlorine, bromine, and iodine) commonly are present in organic compounds. These compounds

are called either *alkyl halides* or *haloalkanes*.

When organic halogen compounds are treated with sodium or potassium hydroxide, they form the corresponding *alcohols* by replacement of the halogen with a *hydroxyl function* (-O-H). Alcohols generally are denoted by the suffix *-ol* or the prefix *hydroxy-*. *Ethers* are obtained by

CH_3CH_2Br

Bromoethane or
ethyl bromide

Dichlorodifluoromethane

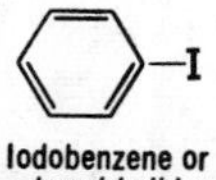

Iodobenzene or
phenyl iodide

Organic Halides

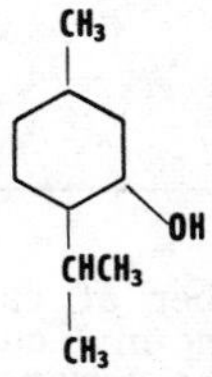

Menthol

$HOCH_2CH_2OH$

1,2—Dihydroxyethane
or ethylene glycol

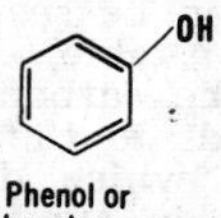

Phenol or
hydroxybenzene

Alcohols

treating two molecules of an alcohol with an acid or by treating the sodium derivative of an alcohol with an alkyl halide. The ethers, characterized by one oxygen bonded to two carbon atoms, may be symmetrical or unsymmetrical, depending upon whether the oxygen-linked groups are the same or different.

$$2CH_3CH_2OH \xrightarrow{\text{acid}} CH_3CH_2OCH_2CH_3 + H_2O$$

Diethyl ether

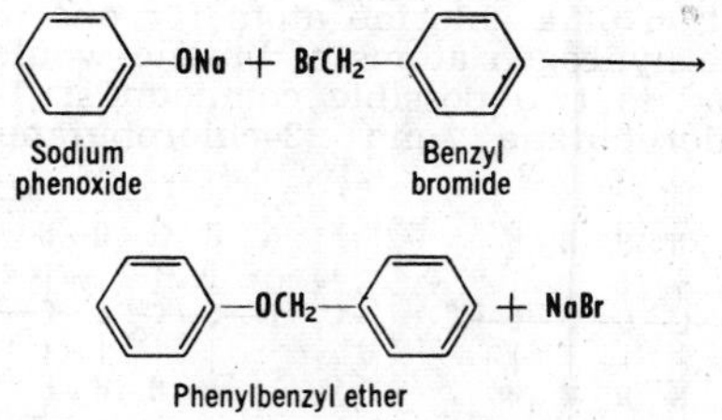

Sodium
phenoxide

Benzyl
bromide

Phenylbenzyl ether

Nitrogen is a common component of functional groups. The *amines* represent an important class of organic compounds that may be regarded as derivatives of ammonia NH_3. A *primary amine* is simply ammonia with one of its hydrogens replaced by carbon. Substitution of carbons for two of the ammonia hydrogens results in a *secondary amine;* a *tertiary amine* is a nitrogen atom completely substituted by carbon. By stepwise oxidation, amines may be converted to *nitroso*-compounds and to *nitro*-

compounds. A well-known explosive, trinitrotoluene (TNT), contains three nitro groups that are bonded in a benzene ring.

In many respects phosphorus behaves like nitrogen in organic reactions. *Phosphines* possess many of the chemical properties of amines. The basic differences between nitrogen and phosphorus—phosphorus is a

CH₃NH₂

Methylamine
(primary amine)

Piperidine
(secondary amine)

Organic Nitrogen Compounds

Aminobenzene
or aniline

Nitrosobenzene

CH₃CH₂PH₂
Ethylphosphine

CH₃PHCH₃
Dimethylphosphine

Triphenylphosphine

Organic Phosphorus Compounds

larger atom and forms stronger bonds with oxygen, carbon, and the halogens—have stimulated a great deal of research in *organophosphorus chemistry* over the past decade.

Carbon is capable of forming multiple bonds with elements other than itself. A variety of functional groups embody this property, among them

Acetaldehyde

Vanillin

Aldehydes

Dimethyl ketone
or acetone

Camphor

Ketones

the *imine group* (>C=N–) and the *thiocarbonyl group* (>C=S), but most important to the organic chemist is the *carbonyl group* (>C=O). Many alcohols may be oxidized by removing two hydrogen atoms to yield a

carbonyl compound. When the carbonyl derivative contains a C–C–H group, it is termed an *aldehyde*; when it contains a C–C–C group, it is known as a *ketone*. Specific examples of aldehydes are acetaldehyde and vanillin. The latter, a flavoring agent found in vanilla, contains three functional groups: an aldehyde, an ether, and an alcohol. Specific examples of ketones are acetone and camphor. Camphor, which imparts the characteristic odor to camphorated oil, is a bicyclic aliphatic ketone.

Formic acid

Acetic acid

Benzoic acid

Nicotinic acid

CH₃CH₂COH + NaOH ⟶ CH₃CH₂CONa + H₂O
Propionic acid   Sodium propionate

Carboxylic Acids

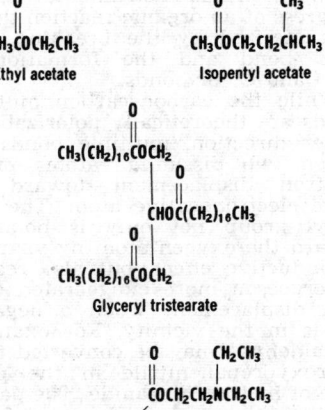

Acetic anhydride

Ethyl acetate

Isopentyl acetate

Glyceryl tristearate

Procaine or Novocaine

Carboxylic Acid Derivatives

The carbon-oxygen double bond is present in the carboxyl group (–C–O–H) of *carboxylic acids*. Carboxylic acids, such as formic acid,

acetic acid (vinegar), benzoic acid, and nicotinic acid (niacin, a vitamin of the B complex), are commonly found in nature. The term "acid" refers to the ability of the O–H bond to react with alkali to form salts. Salts of aliphatic carboxylic acids with long carbon chains are useful as soaps.

Carboxylic acid anhydrides are prepared by strong heating of carboxylic acids alone or in the presence of a dehydrating agent. As the name suggests, acetic anhydride is the product of two molecules of acetic acid less one molecule of water. *Carboxylic acid halides* are the product of replacement of the hydroxyl portion of the carboxyl function by halogen. These reactive compounds are useful in the preparation of other carboxylic acid derivatives, for they react rapidly with alcohols to yield *carboxylic esters* and with ammonia or amines to yield *carboxylic amides*. The odor of specific carboxylic esters may be detected in many common fruits. Animal fats are triple esters of glycerin (1,2,3-trihydroxypropane) with three long-chain (16 or 18 carbons) aliphatic carboxylic acids. Esters are frequently used in medicinal agents, such as aspirin and Novocain.

CH₃C≡N
Acetonitrile

Benzonitrile

CH₃CH₂OCCH₂C≡N
Ethyl cyanoacetate

Nitriles

A *nitrile*, or *organic cyanide*, may be obtained upon dehydration of a carboxylic amide and is characterized by a carbon-nitrogen triple bond. Some examples are acetonitrile, benzonitrile, and ethyl cyanoacetate.

CH₃CH₂CH₂CH₂SH
Butyl mercaptan
(a thioalcohol)

CH₃CH₂SCH₂CH₃
Diethyl sulfide
(a thioether)

CH₃CSH
Thioacetic acid
(a sulfoxide)

Diethyl sulfone

Methanesulfonic acid

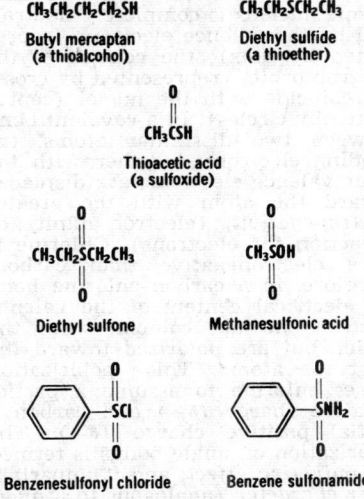

Benzenesulfonyl chloride

Benzene sulfonamide

Organic sulfur compounds

Sulfur is chemically similar to oxygen, and most of the oxygen-bearing functional groups have sulfur-bearing counterparts. The nomenclature follows the same pattern, with the prefix *thio-* incorporated into the chemical name. *Thioalcohols,* or *mercaptans,* are responsible for the unpleasant odor of household gas. Other sulfur-containing functional groups include *thioethers, thioketones,* and *thioacids.* In addition, sulfur can combine with oxygen to form sulfoxides ($-\overset{O}{\underset{}{S}}-$), sulfones ($-\overset{O}{\underset{O}{S}}-$), *sulfinic acids* ($-\overset{O}{\underset{}{S}}-O-H$), and *sulfonic acids* ($-\overset{O}{\underset{O}{S}}-OH$). Sulfonic acids are related to carboxylic acids in that they may be converted to similar

Terramycin

derivatives termed *sulfonyl halides, sulfonic esters,* and *sulfonamides.*

This summary is merely a random sampling of the more common functional groups present in organic molecules. A number of the specific examples demonstrate that more than one group may be present in a given molecule. However, even with the most complex multifunctional molecule, such as Terramycin, it is possible to manipulate a single group selectively without affecting the other groups.

Electron Displacement.—Within a molecule, when a covalent bond links two identical atoms, the two electrons forming the covalent bond may be considered as shared equally by both nuclei. The positive charge of each atomic nucleus is completely neutralized by the valence electrons (represented by dots); the centers of the electron orbits (represented by crosses) coincide with the nuclei (represented by circles). In a covalent bond between two dissimilar atoms, the bonding electrons, together with the other valence electrons, are displaced toward the atom with the greater *electronegativity* (electron affinity, or attraction for electrons). Chlorine is more electronegative than carbon; therefore, in a carbon-chlorine bond the electrical centers of the valence electrons do not coincide with the nuclei, but are *polarized* toward the chlorine atom. This polarization causes chlorine to assume a partial negative charge ($\delta-$) and carbon a partial positive charge ($\delta+$). The polarization of single bonds is termed the *inductive effect,* and it imparts a *polar character* (analogous to a magnet) to the molecule.

Valence electrons may be attracted or repelled by an approaching positive or negative charge. This mode of electron displacement is termed *polarizability* and differs from permanent polarization (inductive effect)

in that electrons will resume their previous positions relative to the nucleus when the charge is withdrawn. The ability to displace valence electrons from their resting position is dependent upon the force by which they are attracted to the nucleus. The greater the nuclear attraction, the more difficult it is for the electrons to be displaced by an oncoming ion. As the distance between the valence electrons and the nucleus of a given atom becomes greater, nuclear attraction of the electrons become weaker. The polarizability of a particular bond determines its ability to be cleaved and thus enter into a chemical reaction, such as substitution of a hydroxyl group for a halogen in the conversion of an alkyl halide to an alcohol.

Multiple bonds are readily polarizable and on this basis are prone to undergo addition reactions. Treatment of an alkene, such as propene, with hydrogen bromide results in the formation of an alkyl bromide. The addition may be considered to proceed in a stepwise fashion, initiated by approach of a positively charged hydrogen ion. As the hydrogen ion nears the double bond, electrons are displaced toward the positive charge (curved arrow). Should the hydrogen ion migrate away from the propene molecule, the electrons would return to their original position. However, the polarizability of the double-bond electrons allows displacement to a degree whereby they enter the sphere of influence of the hydrogen nucleus to form a covalent carbon-hydrogen bond. At this stage the adjacent carbon bears a positive charge, but its electron deficiency is quickly relieved by attraction of a bromide ion that supplies two electrons to form a covalent carbon-bromine bond. Thus, the polarizability of a carbon-carbon double bond is instrumental in the progress of an organic reaction that is characterized by the breaking of a C—C bond and the formation of C—H and C—Br bonds.

While the carbon-carbon multiple bonds are theoretically polarizable in either direction, multiple bonds between two dissimilar atoms prefer electron displacement toward the more electronegative atom. The carbonyl group not only is polarized toward the oxygen atom by virtue of its inductive effect, but also readily undergoes a more exaggerated electron displacement when a negative ion is in the vicinity. For example, acetaldehyde may be converted to 2-hydroxypropanenitrile in the presence of hydrogen cyanide. The partial positive charge on carbon induced by oxygen attracts the negatively charged cyanide ion, whose approach repels the polarizable double-bond electrons. When the negative ion is within bonding distance of the carbonyl carbon, the free electron pair of the cyanide ion is capable of forming a covalent carbon-carbon bond. At this point, the electron pair that previously constituted a carbon-oxygen bond resides solely at the oxygen atom, confirming upon it a negative charge. A nearby hydrogen ion is capable of neutralizing the

charge by utilizing the free electron pair to form a covalent hydrogen-oxygen bond. This type of addition reaction demonstrates the formation of a C—C bond at the expense of a C—O bond and represents one method of extending the carbon chain of an organic molecule.

Nature of Organic Reactions.—Organic reactions differ from inorganic reactions in a number of interesting respects. Whereas inorganic reactions frequently are instantaneous and quantitative, organic reactions tend to proceed at a measurable rate and rarely lead exclusively to a single product. These differences are reasonable when one considers that inorganic reactions, such as the neutralization of hydrogen chloride by sodium hydroxide, involve small, mobile ions that are attracted to each other by virtue of their opposite electric charges. On the other hand, organic compounds commonly are bulky and possess minimal attraction for each other. Reaction usually occurs as a result of random collision of molecules; however, the rate of collision may be increased by accelerating molecular motion through the application of heat. Unfortunately, sensitive organic compounds tend to decompose upon heating and are lost by conversion to degradation products instead of reacting by the desired route. Frequently the reactants may combine in more than one way or may react with the desired product to yield by-products. It is necessary to design experimental conditions—reactants, solvent, catalyst, temperature, time, and other factors—to achieve a selective conversion to the desired product, but the quantitative organic reaction is rare indeed. Degradation products and by-products not only account for the loss of starting materials but also complicate the isolation of the product. Although a variety of elegant purification techniques are available, separation of a useful product from contaminants usually involves a significant, but unavoidable, waste of material.

To be more specific, consider what takes place during an organic reaction: the process of bond cleavage and formation. The conversion of A—B to C—A involves breaking the covalent bond A—B and forming a new covalent bond, C—A. The *mechanism* of the reaction depends upon the manner in

$$C + A-B \rightarrow C-A + B$$

which these bonds are broken. Three courses are possible, and the natures of A, B, and C, in conjunction with the experimental conditions, determine which course is operant in a given reaction.

When each atom of A—B retains one electron of the pair, the reaction mechanism is termed *homolytic fission,* or a *free-radical reaction.* Free radicals are electrically neutral, extremely reactive particles that tend to react by addition to multiple bonds. In general, reactions of this type are induced by heat, light, or compounds that themselves generate free radicals, such as peroxides.

A—B cleavage may proceed with A capturing the electron pair. A *hetero-*

$$A:B \rightarrow A: + B \cdot$$
$$A \cdot + C \rightarrow AC \cdot$$

Homolytic fission

$$A:B \rightarrow A:^{\ominus} + B^{\oplus}$$
$$A:^{\ominus} + C \rightarrow A:C$$
$$B^{\oplus} + :C \rightarrow B:C^{\ominus}$$

Heterolytic fission

lytic fission, or *ionic reaction,* occurs and C is considered an *electrophilic* (electron-seeking) *reagent* that now shares the electron pair that A wrested from B. An electrophilic reagent is an electron-deficient atom or group that prefers to attack a molecule at the point of greatest negative charge. When A is a group in which carbon bears the free electron pair, the group is termed a *carbanion.*

The remaining generalized reaction mechanism involves heterolytic cleavage in which C is a *nucleophilic* (nucleus-seeking) *reagent* possessing an unshared electron pair available for formation of a covalent bond with B. A nucleophilic reagent prefers to attack a center of electron deficiency. A group, such as B, in which a carbon atom bears the positive charge is termed a *carbonium ion.*

For simplicity, the reaction mechanisms have been depicted as stepwise: first bond cleavage, then bond formation. Although this sequence commonly occurs, the two steps may blend into a concerted transition from A—B to C—A in a manner that requires less energy. When methyl iodide reacts with hydroxide ion, the resultant methyl alcohol has been shown to be formed by Mechanism I rather than Mechanism II. As a hydroxide ion approaches methyl iodide from "behind" carbon in a line with the C—I bond, the bond is polarized and stretched to the point where the C—O bond begins to form and the C—I bond begins to break. When both bonds are of equal strength, neither molecule, CH_3I or CH_3OH, exists as a separate entity. In this state, the system can either form CH_3OH or revert to CH_3I. When the three-dimensional concept of the carbon atom is envisioned, it becomes clear that this *concerted displacement* of the iodide ion has inverted the spatial relationship of the bonds about carbon, similar to turning an umbrella inside out.

The task of discussing the vast number of useful organic reactions becomes less overwhelming when one considers them merely as sequences of a few basic transformations, each usually involving a limited portion of a molecule. A particular sequence, or *reaction mechanism,* may be common to a large number of seemingly different reactions and the transformations involved, that is, the breaking and forming of bonds, by nature must be the same, regardless of the process involved. There are three major types of reaction mechanisms: substitution, addition, and elimination.

■**SUBSTITUTION.**—*Nucleophilic substitution* reactions in general involve displacement of a group (B) from an atom (A) by a reagent (C) that possesses an unshared pair of electrons. The attacking nucleophilic reagent may or may not bear a negative charge. Conversion of an alkyl halide to an alcohol affords an excellent example in which the reagent, hydroxide ion, bears a negative charge. Other examples of this important group of reactions include conversion of an alcohol to an alkyl halide and conversion of an alkyl halide to an ether.

Electrophilic substitution may be described as displacement of a group

Nucleophilic Substitution

$$A-B + C^{\oplus} \rightarrow A-C + B^{\oplus}$$

Electrophilic substitution

$$A-B + :C \rightarrow A:C + B$$

Alcohol

Alkyl halide

Alkyl halide

Ether

(B) from an atom (A) by a reagent (C) that is capable of accommodating two additional electrons. Electrophilic reagents commonly bear a positive charge. Aromatic compounds may undergo substitution by displacement of a hydrogen ion from a carbon ring upon attack of a positively charged group. In this manner, an aromatic system may acquire a variety of such substituents as nitro, halogen, sulfonic acid, and carbonyl. The synthesis of sulfanilamide, an antibacterial drug, illustrates the utility of electrophilic aromatic substitution. Acetanilide is treated with chlorosulfonic acid to yield sulfonyl chloride; conversion to the sulfonamide is effected with ammonia; and sulfanilamide is produced upon cleavage of the carboxylic amide group by hydroxide ion.

■**ADDITION.**—*Addition* reactions involve the attack of an electrophilic or nucleophilic reagent upon a multiple bond. Alkenes and alkynes may react with a wide variety of reagents,

such as hydrogen, halogens, and inorganic acids, to yield saturated products. The mechanism of addition was demonstrated by the conversion of propylene to 2-bromopropane. Carbonyl groups react by addition of nucleophilic reagents, such as alcohols, amines, mercaptans, and hydrogen cyanide. The addition of hydrogen cyanide to acetaldehyde, discussed earlier, proceeds via a mechanism common to this general type of addition reaction. Carbanion addition to carbonyl groups is an important method of forming a carbon-carbon bond. A carbanion may arise from a compound containing a particular type of functional group, such as nitrile or carbonyl, that permits cleavage of a neighboring C—H bond by a strong base, such as sodamide $(NaNH_2)$. The highly reactive carbanion may attack a carbonyl group in another molecule to form an intermediate possessing a negatively charged oxygen atom. Two specific examples below demonstrate the manner in which this intermediate may react to yield products retaining most of the atoms present in the original compounds. Carbanion reactions make possible the construction of the carbon skeleton of a molecule, thereby laying the foundation for the synthesis of complex organic compounds.

■**ELIMINATION.**—*Elimination reactions* may be viewed as the reverse of addition reactions; that is, multiple bonds are formed by the loss of two groups from adjacent atoms. Specific examples include conversion of 1,2-dibromopropane to propene or propyne, and conversion of cyclohexanol to cyclohexene or cyclohexanone. Obviously, choice of reaction conditions is of prime importance to the course of elimination.

The three major reaction mechanisms do not include many types of reactions in which the carbon skeleton of a molecule may be built up, torn down, or even rearranged. While only a superficial treatment of organic reactions is practical here, it should be remembered that the fundamental processes of bond cleavage and formation are the same whatever course a particular reaction may follow.

Structure Determination. — Knowledge of the structural formula is essential in dealing with an organic compound. Intelligent research and application of the principles of organic chemistry demand that the chemist have an accurate picture of the molecule under study. The development of modern methods of measuring physical properties has facilitated an understanding of the structure of complex molecules.

In order to determine unambiguously the structure of an organic molecule, the compound must be obtained in a highly pure state. Such purification techniques as solvent extraction, distillation, crystallization, and adsorption are employed. Every organic compound possesses distinct physical properties (boiling point, melting point, refractive index, molecular rotation, and so on, and purification is assumed to be complete when these properties become constant upon repeated application of the above techniques.

The pure compound is first subjected to a variety of physical measurements that provide a great deal of information concerning the structure. Elemental analysis and molecular-weight determination define the molecular formula (the types of atoms present and the number of each). The infrared spectrum allows identification of certain functional groups. Information concerning the distribution of multiple bonds is available from the ultraviolet spectrum. Nuclear-magnetic resonance spectroscopy primarily presents a picture of the hydrogen atoms present in the molecule and their spatial relationship to each other. The mass spectrometer cleaves a molecule in relatively predictable fashion; and the number and weight of each fragment, coupled with information from other physical measurements, provide further insight into the structural formula. X-ray crystallography, which yields a diffraction pattern with crystalline solids, is capable of outlining an accurate three-dimensional picture of the molecule; but at present the calculations involved are too tedious for routine use of this technique.

While in some cases the measurement of physical properties is sufficient to define clearly the structure of an organic compound, the majority of structural problems require a study of chemical properties. The knowledge of characteristic reactions of functional groups allows interpretation of the behavior toward various reagents. Reaction of the molecule with acids, alkalis, oxidizing agents, and other substances often leads to identifiable fragments whose structure and possible mode of formation may further clarify the problem. Analysis of the bits of data concerning the physical and chemical properties makes it possible to assign a structure that distinguishes the compound in question from all other possibilities. Confirmation of the structural proposal usually is effected by total synthesis from compounds of known structure.

Complex Organic Molecules.—Due to the complexity of most organic substances isolated from living organisms, little progress was made in structure determination of natural products prior to the twentieth century. Multifunctional compounds of high molecular weight are present throughout plant and animal tissue. The most ubiquitous fall into two categories: carbohydrates and proteins. In general, these compounds are *polymers,* a series of simple molecules bonded to each other in repeating units.

Carbohydrates are distinguished by their high oxygen content. Simple carbohydrates, such as glucose, are termed *monosaccharides;* these may be linked together as ethers to form *polysaccharides.* Glucose, a source of energy for many plants and animals, is stored by animals as glycogen, a polysaccharide composed of 30,000 or

more glucose units. Plants synthesize two important glucose polysaccharides: starch, their energy reserve, and cellulose, a supporting tissue.

Proteins, which carry out a multitude of functions important to living organisms, are large molecules composed of a sequence of *amino acids* linked by carboxylic amide groups. Approximately twenty amino acids,

Glycine　　　　　Histidine

Methionine

Glycylhistidylmethionine

such as glycine, histidine, and methionine, are common to proteins and may exist in an infinite number of sequences. The glycylhistidylmethionine residue represents a unit typical of those found in proteins. Many familiar substances are natural proteins: fibroin (silk), keratin (hair, skin, and nails), gelatin, insulin, albumin, and globin (the major component of hemoglobin, the oxygen carrier in blood).

Vitamins, while not structurally related to each other, are dietary factors essential to animal growth. The variation in structure is evident

Vitamin B₂

by inspection of the structures of vitamins B₂ (riboflavin), D₂ (calciferol), and nicotinic acid (niacin).

Ergosterol

Vitamin D₂ is obtained by irradiation of ergosterol, a common animal lipid containing the tetracyclic *steroid* ring system. Other naturally occurring

steroids include cholesterol (a widely publicized lipid), testosterone (a male hormone), estradiol (a female hormone), and cortisone (a hormone of the adrenal cortex).

Vitamin D₂

Cortisone

Plants and lower animals are capable of synthesizing complex molecules that are useful to man. Familiar examples in the field of medicine include such alkaloids as morphine (a potent analgesic) and quinine (an antimalarial drug), as well as the antibiotics Terramycin and penicillin. *Macromolecules* (a general term for organic compounds of high molecular weight) produced by plants play an important role in our everyday life. Rubber is a polymer of isoprene ($CH_2=CCH_3-CH=CH_2$); cotton contains 97 to 99 per cent cellulose; and wool is a protein. In recent years organic chemists have been able to prepare synthetic polymers with tensile strength, elasticity, heat stability, and chemical stability that vastly exceed those of natural rubber. These macromolecules are synthesized by joining many small molecules, and contain thousands of repeating units.

Modern methods of polymerization have been responsible to a large degree for our high standard of living. Synthetic fibers and plastics have played no small part in the excellent quality and low cost of consumer goods. Such terms as polyamide, polyester, polyvinyl, and polyacrylate refer to polymers derived from simple organic molecules. A selection of examples includes nylon (a polyamide fiber), Dacron (a polyester fiber noted for its tensile strength and resiliency), Saran (a vinyl polymer useful as a fiber or plastic), Orlon (a fiber, obtained from polyacrylonitrile, known for its resistance to sunlight, weathering, and chemicals), and Lucite (a polyacrylate plastic, useful as an adhesive and protective coating).

Organic Synthesis.—The importance of organic synthesis becomes apparent when one considers that the function of protoplasm, the material that is the basis of life, depends upon the availability of organic substances. Synthesis of the building blocks of life constantly is under way. Although the organic chemist cannot compete with living tissue, he has come a long way since Friedrich Wöhler first discovered that an organic compound could be elaborated from inorganic matter outside a living cell. During the past century man has learned some of the basic principles involved in the construction of carbon-containing substances and has applied this knowledge to duplicate the products of plant and animal chemistry. Delight in his newly discovered ability has prompted him to devote a great deal of effort to the synthesis of natural products readily available to him. Many crowning achievements, such as the syntheses of glucose, morphine, penicillin, and chlorophyll, must be regarded only as academic in view of the fact that these compounds are obtained more economically from nature.

The value of these achievements, however, should not be underestimated. The mere fact that a chemist can produce a complex organic molecule from inorganic sources has demolished the psychological barriers to progress. Nature has provided many useful substances that the chemist has improved through synthesis. The physician has at his disposal drugs that calm agitated patients or induce sleep when natural sleep is impossible. Before the advent of synthetic tranquilizers and sedatives, these results were obtained only with opium, cocaine, or ethyl alcohol. While opium and alcohol still are popular in other areas, synthetic medicinals are used extensively in therapy. Natural fibers are being displaced by more versatile and durable synthetics. Such structural materials as wood and metals are being replaced by plastics.

Biological Chemistry.—The branch of science that deals with the chemistry of all forms of living organisms is termed *biological chemistry*, or *biochemistry*. This relatively recent discipline evolved after organic and physical chemists had developed theories and techniques applicable to biological problems. Only fifty years ago, biochemistry was considered an applied science concerned primarily with problems of the medical and agricultural worlds. Today biochemistry has taken a place among the pure or theoretical sciences, and its primary aim is to investigate the chemical transformations that occur within living cells. The modern term *molecular biology* has been applied to the analysis of the laws that control life on the molecular level.

The chemical constitution of living organisms differs tremendously from one species to another. Within the same organism such various tissues as blood, bone, and muscle are quite different in their chemical makeup. However, a pattern of similarity in the individual cells is evident from tissue to tissue or from species to species. All living cells contain water, inorganic salts, and a myriad of organic compounds. In general, the majority of organic matter falls roughly into three categories: carbohydrate, lipid, and protein. Carbohydrate compounds include monosaccharides and their higher-molecular-weight derivatives. The more common lipids are

fatty acids and their esters (fats), long-chain aliphatic alcohols and their esters (waxes), and steroids. Proteins, which are amino-acid polymers, occupy a central position in the construction and function of living matter. They are intimately related to all phases of activity that constitute life in the cell. Collagen is the main structural protein of connective tissue. Enzymes, the substances that catalyze the chemical reactions of the cell, are primarily protein. Other proteinaceous materials function to transport oxygen (hemoglobin), regulate life processes (insulin and thyroid hormone), and protect the organism from infection (gamma globulin). In fact, the type of protein present in a cell is primarily responsible for the obvious anatomical and functional differences between various kinds of cells and tissues.

Living organisms depend upon energy to function. Animals require an intake of organic material; their diet may consist of carbohydrates, fats, and/or proteins, since all may be used more or less interchangeably for the production of energy. Mammals also depend upon their diet for vitamins, some of which are indispensable portions of certain key enzymes. Plants, on the other hand, obtain their energy from sunlight and require no organic nutrients. Their structural materials are synthesized from carbon dioxide, water, inorganic salts, and a source of nitrogen. Light-catalyzed synthesis of carbohydrates in plants (*photosynthesis*) is not only responsible for supplying the plant with its needs, but also indirectly furnishes animal nutritional requirements. The mere fact that plant and animal organisms utilize the same basic organic compounds denotes a great similarity in cellular chemistry.

Higher animals possess a digestive system that functions to degrade their macromolecular diet into small molecules capable of being assimilated by individual cells. Polysaccharides are converted to monosaccharides, and proteins are digested to their component amino acids. Monosaccharides are utilized for the production of energy, while the amino acids are polymerized within the individual cell to form its characteristic proteins. All living cells function in a state of continual degradation and repair. While the structure of the molecules involved may differ, the patterns of breakdown and synthesis are similar in all living organisms.

The most important monosaccharide in animal organisms is glucose. Glucose commonly is stored in the liver as glycogen and released into the blood stream as needed to nourish body tissues. Muscles also store glucose as glycogen to be utilized when energy is needed. When the muscle oxygen supply is adequate, glucose is oxidized completely to carbon dioxide and water; when it is inadequate, glucose is converted to lactic acid. The process of converting glucose (or its polymer, glycogen) to lactic acid is termed *glycolysis* and occurs *anaerobically* (without the utilization of oxygen). Glycolysis occurs in most animal

tissues and may be represented by the general equation:

$$C_6H_{12}O_6 + 6O_2 + 38ADP + 38P_i \longrightarrow$$
$$6CO_2 + 6H_2O + 38ATP$$

Glucose

The conversion of each glucose molecule to two lactic acid molecules is simultaneous with *phosphorylation* of adenosine diphosphate (ADP) by inorganic phosphate (P_i) to adenosine triphosphate (ATP). Glycolysis actually occurs by a series of nine reactions, each requiring a specific enzyme catalyst. The individual conversions are simple and may involve transfer of hydrogen or phosphate from one molecule to another, but the important feature is the concomitant formation of ATP from ADP. The energy released in the breakdown of glucose is stored as high-energy phosphorus-oxygen bonds in the two molecules of ATP produced. This "stored energy" is available for use by the cell as needed. Cleavage of ATP to ADP and inorganic phosphate allows energy to be released for use in muscle contraction, synthesis of complex molecules, conduction of nerve impulses, and a host of other energy-requiring activities necessary for maintaining life processes.

An important intermediate in the glycolytic pathway, pyruvic acid

$$(CH_3\text{-}\overset{\text{O}}{\overset{\|}{C}}\text{-}\overset{\text{O}}{\overset{\|}{C}}\text{-OH}),$$ may be *aerobically* (by means of oxygen) converted to carbon dioxide and water in a stepwise fashion. This biochemical pathway frequently is termed the *tricarboxylic acid cycle*. Each step in the sequence is catalyzed by a specific enzyme and, as with glycolysis, the energy released is captured by ATP for future use in the tissue. The aerobic phase of glucose metabolism yields a far greater quantity of energy than the anaerobic phase, since the complete oxidation of one molecule of glucose produces 38 molecules of ATP. This simplified picture of carbohydrate metabolism exemplifies the secrets of molecular biology that the biochemist can learn.

Much of the energy released as a result of metabolism is utilized by the organism in synthesizing the materials necessary for life and growth. The nutritive materials consumed by an animal often bear little resemblance to the substances required for normal function. Thus, small molecules are converted to carbohydrates, lipids, and proteins that are native to the particular organism. The uncanny ability of each type of cell to repair itself by reproducing a variety of specialized macromolecules has amazed scientists through the ages. Reproduction by cell division, replication of a complete cell with all its inherent complexities, represents a wonder of nature that was considered beyond the realm of man's intellect. Recently scientists have identified *nucleic acids* as the information-transmitting molecules responsible for the orderly reproduction of proteins, the major cellular constituents. Nucleic acids are macromolecules composed of subunits called *nucleotides*.

IVAN MASSAR, BLACK STAR

CHEMISTRY is concerned with transformation of matter. Within these pipes and distillation towers, chemical reactions are induced to produce high polymers, the basic materials of plastics such as acetate vinyl.

THE BASIC STRUCTURE OF MATTER and the chemical riddle of life itself are subjected to relentless scrutiny. The scientist (*below*), studying cancers produced by urethane in mice thyroids, seeks to learn why cells become malignant. Others search to find (*center, left to right*) what substances change drone larvae into queen wasps; how a simple penicillin mold can destroy bacteria; and what forces inform the crystal patterns of quinidine. Modern chemistry also continues an older search, expressing the amorphous mystery of nature in exact, definable, and communicable symbols; these are more precise than those inherited from the alchemists (*below*).

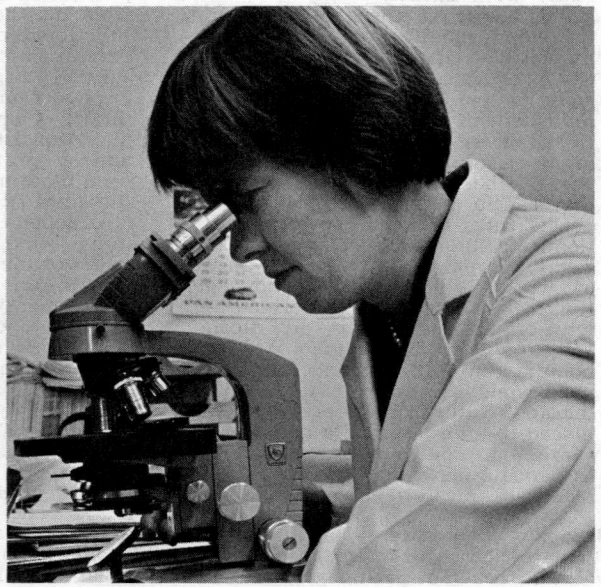

TOM KING, AMERICAN CANCER SOCIETY

U.S. DEPARTMENT OF AGRICULTURE

CHARLES PFIZER AND COMPANY

LOOK MAGAZINE

Nucleotides may be further subdivided into three units: a nitrogenous base (for example, adenine, a component of ATP), a monosaccharide, and a phosphate group. Thus nucleic acids are *polynucleotides* in which the phosphate residues act as bridges in the manner illustrated. All cells contain two types of nucleic acids—ribonucleic acid (RNA) and deoxyribonucleic acid (DNA)—that are differentiated on the basis of whether they contain ribose or deoxyribose as the monosaccharide portion. DNA functions as the storehouse for synthesizing information, while RNA plays a variety of roles in transmitting the information. Even the simplest cell contains thousands of proteins, all recorded in DNA and coordinated and controlled by RNA. DNA determines which protein will be manufactured; RNA picks up the blueprint of DNA's information, collects the individual amino acids needed, arranges them in the proper order, and releases the finished protein after the carboxylic amide linkages are formed. Much of the detail of this process has been uncovered, and research is in progress to determine the role of nucleic acids in memory and learning.

—James Muren

ANALYTICAL CHEMISTRY

Types of Analysis.—*Analytical chemistry* is the branch of chemistry that seeks to determine the composition of matter. It is divided into qualitative analysis and quantitative analysis. When performing a *qualitative analysis,* the chemist seeks to determine what elements or compounds are in a sample. When performing a *quantitative analysis,* he must determine the exact percentage or concentration of the various constituents in the sample. Obviously, a qualitative analysis must be performed before a quantitative analysis can be made. Analytical chemistry is divided into *organic analysis* and *inorganic analysis,* depending on the nature of the sample.

Analysis is also divided according to the size of the sample tested. *Macroanalysis* usually deals with samples weighing from 0.1 to 5 grams. *Microanalysis* deals with samples in the range of 0.001 to 0.01 gram. Microanalysis is not as accurate as macroanalysis, but it is useful in biochemistry, criminal investigation, analysis of paint in valuable paintings, and other situations where the size of the sample is necessarily limited. *Semimicroanalysis* refers to testing done with samples intermediate in size between those characteristic of microanalysis and macroanalysis; *ultramicroanalysis* extends microanalysis to samples smaller than 0.001 gram.

An analysis is said to be *ultimate* if the composition is reported in terms of the elements present; it is *proximate* when larger chemical units, such as molecules, are determined.

Analysis plays an important role in practically all manufacturing proc-esses, controlling the quality of starting materials, intermediates, and finished products. It also is a major part of chemical and medical research.

Methods of Analysis.—The study of the elements has revealed certain characteristic reactions of elements and their compounds. Where other elements do not interfere (or mask these reactions), these reactions provide a shortcut to identifying constituents in a sample. However, because of interference, these characteristic reactions (for example, flame tests and borax bead tests) have limited use.

Analysis of a sample usually takes place in four steps: sampling, preparation for analysis, determination of constituents, and evaluation of results.

■**SAMPLING TECHNIQUES.**—*Sampling* can be as simple as pouring a liquid from a bottle. More often it involves obtaining a representative portion of the material to be studied. For example, how does one find the composition of a boatload of ore? Usually a portion (about a pound) is removed from each ton as it is unloaded, to produce a *gross sample*. This is still too large to work with, so it is crushed, blended, and divided into quarters. The process is repeated until a suitably small sample is obtained. Sampling a single lot of a solid material usually involves collecting a representative portion with a hollow auger that cuts through the various layers. Sampling liquids in several containers of different size is usually done by taking proportionate amounts from each and mixing the liquids.

■**PREPARATION FOR ANALYSIS.**—*Preparation for analysis* consists of putting the sample in aqueous solution. If the sample is water-soluble or already in solution, it is ready for analysis without further treatment. Samples of alloys and minerals insoluble in water can generally be dissolved in an appropriate acid. If no acid can dissolve the sample, the analyst must resort to *fusion,* heating the solid until it melts and then treating it with a suitable reagent (called a *flux*) to make it water-soluble.

■**DETERMINATION.**—*Determination* is the step that identifies and finds the amount of each constituent in a sample. It is usually accomplished by two groups of methods: those depending on a chemical reaction of the constituent and those based on some physical property of the constituent. Chemical methods include titrametric and kinetic. In *titrametric* methods, the analyst determines the amount of a reagent that will react with the sample. In *kinetic* methods, he determines the rate of reaction of the sample with a reagent.

Qualitative analysis of inorganic substances by chemical methods makes use of the fact that most inorganic substances are *ionic;* that is, they are composed of atoms or groups of atoms that have either lost or gained electrons. Atoms or groups that have lost electrons are positively charged and are called *cations;* those that have gained electrons are negatively charged and are called *anions.* There are about 30 common members of each group. Determination consists of treating the sample with a series of reagents to separate it into groups of similar constituents and then further treating these groups until the exact composition is known.

Quantitative analyses of inorganic materials are done by gravimetric or volumetric methods. In *gravimetric analysis* the element or compound is isolated in the form of a definite chemical compound and then weighed. In *volumetric analysis* the amount of reagent needed to react completely with the sample is determined; no isolation of constituents is needed. Volumetric methods are faster but less accurate than gravimetric methods. However, errors can usually be kept within allowable limits by careful calibration of equipment and by the use of controlled experimental conditions.

Most physical methods involve observing the behavior of the sample when it is exposed to some form of energy or to elementary particles of high energy. Classification of these methods is usually based on the type of energy involved.

Methods using some form of electromagnetic energy are called *optical methods* (a somewhat confusing term, since it includes use of short and long wavelengths in addition to those in the normal visual spectrum). Optical methods depend on the fact that under suitable conditions matter can be made to emit, absorb, reflect, or refract the electromagnetic radiation. Typical *emission methods* help identify elements by the characteristic radiation they give off when excited by an electric charge, ultraviolet light, or other intense radiant-energy source. *Spectrophotometry* and *colorimetry* measure the amount of energy absorbed by the sample. *Reflection methods* study the characteristics of energy reflected from the sample—*X-ray diffraction,* for example, studies the interference or reinforcement of reflections from the planes of a crystal. *Refraction methods* make use of the change in the speed of light as it passes through matter—the amount of change being a characteristic of the sample material.

The most widely used *electrical methods* are based on the reaction of materials in solution at electrode surfaces. Current, potential, and time required for a reaction are measured.

Magnetic methods study the behavior of the sample in a magnetic field. The mass spectrograph, for example, studies the movement of charged particles in a magnetic field.

Thermal methods determine the amount of heat generated or absorbed during a chemical reaction. Sometimes the amount of heat gained or lost is noted; other methods note the temperature at which a change occurs.

Analysis of organic samples may be done to determine the elements or compounds present in a sample. To determine the elements present, the sample is decomposed to form inorganic compounds of the constituents; these are then identified and measured by inorganic methods.

Determining compounds present is more difficult. If the sample has a constant boiling or melting point, it probably contains only one compound. The reason for this is that if a sample contains more than one compound, and these compounds have significantly different boiling or melting points, then the component with the lower boiling or melting point will be removed more quickly than the component with the higher boiling or melting point; the boiling or melting point of the sample, instead of being constant, will steadily increase. If only one compound is present in the sample, it can be identified by studying its physical properties and its reactions with various reagents. If the sample has more than one constituent, these must be separated by fractional distillation, extraction, or fractional crystallization. The individual compounds can then be identified.

■**EVALUATION OF RESULTS.**—*Evaluations of results* are usually reported along with the possible amount of error that may be inherent in the method of analysis used. The error is reported in terms of the *relative error* and expressed in parts per thousand, since parts per hundred or percentage error might be confused with the other frequent references to percentage. If an analysis is performed by several chemists, each using different methods, the weighted average of their results is reported as the *most probable value*.

—John Price

PHYSICAL CHEMISTRY

Scope.—*Physical chemistry* is the branch of chemistry that studies the dependence of physical properties on the chemical composition of the different forms of matter and notes the changes these forms undergo. In describing these relationships, three states of matter are considered: gaseous, liquid, and solid.

Gases.—Matter in the gaseous state is distinguished by a tendency to occupy all the space available. This tendency can be counteracted by external forces; for example, the earth's atmosphere is confined within definite limits by the gravitational pull on the gaseous molecules. Gases are particularly susceptible to changes in pressure and temperature.

Robert Boyle in 1622 showed that the volume occupied by gas varies inversely with its pressure if its temperature is kept constant. In 1802 Joseph Louis Gay-Lussac and John Dalton discovered that at constant pressure gases expand when heated and that the change in volume is proportional to the rise in temperature.

Gay-Lussac later discovered that volumes of reacting gases and of their gaseous products can be expressed by simple numerical relationships. Interpretation of these simple volume ratios and of identical behavior of gases toward pressure and temperature is aided by Amadeo Avogadro's hypothesis, which states that equal volumes of different gases at the same temperature and pressure contain the same number of molecules.

The molecules of a gas move about in space at very high velocities. They collide with each other frequently and strike the walls of the containing vessel, creating the pressure exerted by the gas. If the volume of the gas is increased, the number of molecular impacts on a given area is decreased —hence, the pressure drops. The pressure of a gas does not decrease with time, showing that the collisions between molecules are perfectly elastic and that there is no loss of velocity as a result of such collisions.

Liquids.—If the temperature of a gas is brought below a certain value and the pressure is gradually increased, the gas condenses into a *liquid*. Above a *critical temperature*, a gas will not condense into a liquid no matter how much pressure is applied. Substances in the liquid state have greater densities, greater internal friction, greater cohesive pressures, and much smaller compressibilities than they have in the gaseous state. Many of the changes are due to the increase in attractive forces acting between the molecules, which are more closely packed in the liquid state than they are in the gaseous state.

The *vapor pressure* of a pure liquid is the pressure at which the liquid is in equilibrium with its vapor phase. This equilibrium pressure depends only on temperature, not on the relative amounts of liquid and vapor present. The *boiling point* of a liquid is defined as the temperature at which the vapor pressure equals the external pressure.

The *surface tension* of a liquid accounts for the fact that drops of a liquid generally are spherical. A molecule in the bulk of a liquid is usually attracted equally in all directions by surrounding molecules in an area of equal density. But at or near the surface of a liquid, molecules are more strongly attracted by the molecules in the liquid phase than they are by those in the gaseous phase, thus creating an inward force at the interface. This inward force pulls the molecule into a spherical shape.

Different liquids have varying optical properties as a result of differences in their chemical composition. *Refraction*, the change in direction of a homogeneous ray of light when it passes from a medium of one density to a medium of different density, is used to help determine the structure of liquids; different liquids bend a ray of light by different amounts. *Dispersivity*, the difference in refractivity for light of differing wavelengths, also lends itself to the study of structural differences in liquids.

When a beam of polarized light is passed through certain liquids, the plane of polarization is rotated to a new direction. Noting the direction of rotation and the amount of angular displacement helps identify unknown substances. This is important in examining complex organic liquids.

Solids.—When liquids are cooled in such a way as to form regular polyhedral crystals, they are said to have passed into the solid state. For some time it was customary to speak of *amorphous* (uncrystallized) and *crystalline* solids, but analysis has shown that many seemingly amorphous substances are definitely *microcrystalline*, while others are *supercooled liquids* with very high viscosity. The solid state now is generally identified with the crystalline condition; matter in this form resists shearing stresses and has properties that differ in different directions—unlike gases and liquids.

Normal formation of crystals depends on time. Rapid separation of a solid tends to produce granular aggregates whose crystalline structure is difficult to recognize. There is an overlap between the liquid and solid states as far as rigidity is concerned. Highly viscous fluids (such as glass) pass into a fluid condition gradually and continuously when the temperature is raised—unlike crystals, which change properties suddenly at the melting point. On the other hand, most crystals are rigid and fracture when subjected to pressure; but some have such weak forces in the crystal structure that they can be easily distorted and made to flow. Hence, they simulate some of the properties of liquids, yet are solids because they have the optical properties of crystals and possess a definite melting point.

The properties and forms of crystalline solids depend on the arrangement of the atoms or molecules within the crystal. These are no longer free to move from point to point, but occupy a definite mean position in the lattice of the crystal. However, the atoms or molecules do vibrate about this mean position; and if the temperature is raised enough, they will break free of the force holding them in place and move freely, marking the transition to the liquid state.

The onetime supposition that every substance has a unique crystalline form has been disproved by the discovery of *isomorphism* (the tendency of different substances to crystallize in the same form) and *polymorphism* (the existence of the same chemical substance in more than one crystalline form). Sulfur, for example, is polymorphous—it has two interconvertible crystalline forms. Below 96° C. the rhombic form predominates; above 96° C. the stable form is monoclinic sulfur. The temperature at which both forms may exist is known as the *transition temperature*.

—John Price

NUCLEAR CHEMISTRY

Scope.—*Nuclear chemistry* is the branch of chemistry dealing with the effects of radiation and the processes that produce it—fusion, fission, and radioactive decay. Among the important applications of radiation are the tracing of chemical and biological reactions, radiography (X-ray photography), the study of catalysis in chemical reactions, medical therapy, and the supplying of power for orbiting satellites.

■**FISSION REACTIONS.**—The raw material for *fission reactions* is uranium, which has several isotopes. The only significant naturally occurring isotope is that of mass number 235, abbreviated U-235. When an atom of U-235 absorbs a neutron, its nucleus becomes unstable and splits into two *fission fragments*, releasing radiant energy and a number of neutrons. This process is the basis for atomic bombs, nuclear reactors, and the peaceful uses of atomic energy planned under *Project Plowshare*: excavating harbors and canals, creating underground heat supplies for removing oil from shale, and mining.

■**FUSION REACTIONS.**—The *fusion reaction* involves the combination of atoms to produce heavier atoms, such as the combination of two hydrogen atoms to form helium. As is the case with fission, fusion results in a loss of mass, which is converted to energy. Extremely high temperatures are required for fusion; so far, only the explosion of a fission bomb has produced the needed temperature on a large scale. Research is now going on to perfect a controlled fusion reaction. One big problem is to find a vessel to contain the reaction. The heat of a fusion reaction is so intense that it would melt any solid material; therefore, a strong magnetic field called a *magnetic bottle* is used to contain the reaction. Another problem is to keep out impurities that inhibit the reaction; the use of a high vacuum is providing the answer. The third major problem is to obtain the high temperature and particle density required for the reaction; the solution appears to be the introduction of large amounts of energy to produce a current of ionized gas and use of a magnetic field to compress the gas.

When controlled fusion reactions are perfected on a large scale, they will be able to provide energy for the world for many centuries. So far, however, fusion reactions have been accomplished only on a small scale in laboratories.

■**CHAIN REACTIONS.**—Large-scale uses of fission depend on the *chain reaction*. In a chain reaction, the splitting of one nucleus by a neutron liberates other neutrons that can trigger further splitting of other fissionable nuclei. Elements that will produce this effect are known as *fertile materials*; the most important ones are U-235, U-238, and thorium-232. Fertile materials produce fissionable isotopes by neutron irradiation and capture.

The first successful chain reaction was carried out at the University of Chicago on December 2, 1942, under the direction of Enrico Fermi. Fermi used an *atomic pile* made up of uranium cubes (as the fissionable material) embedded in graphite, which would absorb neutrons and thereby control the reaction.

Nuclear Reactors.—In recent years, commercial applications of atomic energy have been growing. The nuclear industry has perfected a cycle of operation consisting of mining uranium and thorium ores, chemical processing, fabrication into fuels and other components of nuclear reactors, reprocessing of spent fuel, and disposal of by-product waste. Nuclear reactors are producing electricity that promises, within a few years, to become competitive in cost with conventional power sources in many areas, and they have proved success-

ful in providing long-lasting power supplies for isolated military installations and ships. The possibility of using nuclear power to provide heat for industrial chemical processes is also being investigated.

Nuclear reactors are usually classified as burners, breeders, or converters, depending on the isotope used as fuel. *Burners* use separated U-235 fuel and find application as research, test, portable, and mobile reactors. *Converters* use natural or partially enriched uranium fuel, producing plutonium as a final product. The reactors at Hanford, Washington, and Savannah River, South Carolina, are converters. *Breeders* are a special type of converter in which more fissionable material is produced than is actually used.

Reactors are also classified by the physical state of the fuel: *heterogeneous*, in which fuel is formed into long rods or thin plates, or *homogeneous*, in which fuel is dispersed in an aqueous, molten-salt, or molten-metal solution or *slurry*; by the neutron energy in the fission-capture process: *fast*, *intermediate*, or *thermal*; and by the coolant used: *gas, pressurized water, boiling water, organic metal*, or *liquid metal*.

Uses of Radioactive Isotopes.—Medical science has made widespread use of radioactive isotopes of various elements in diagnosis and treatment. Some 40 isotopes have been used in diagnosis, relying on the fact that the radioactive isotopes of most elements behave similarly to isotopes that are not radioactive. Radioactive isotopes can easily be traced by a counting device, such as a Geiger counter. Radioactive iodine, for example, is used in studying thyroid conditions and also can be an aid in operations for removal of diseased thyroid glands—before the operation the patient is given a dose of radioactive iodine that settles in the gland; when no excess radiation is left in the area, the surgeon knows the entire organ has been removed.

Other radioisotopes have been used in studying various body functions of humans and animals—as in testing metabolism and in determining the importance of trace elements in the diet. They can also be used to detect various malfunctions and to treat malignancies.

Radioisotope tracers have helped to determine residues of detergents left on food products, to estimate the lean-meat content of animals, and to trace the movement of water. This last process makes use of the fact that the hydrogen in some atoms of rainwater is converted to heavy hydrogen by cosmic-ray bombardment in the atmosphere and by nuclear weapons tests. After twelve years, half of the radioactive hydrogen in the rainwater decays, providing a gauge for measuring the age of underground water.

In addition, the tracing process has helped chemists discover the mechanisms of certain chemical reactions. In some organic reactions, for example, it is difficult to determine which reagent has supplied which atoms in the end product. By selec-

tively "labeling" the reagents with radioisotopes, the chemist can determine the donor of a particular atom or group of atoms by checking the final product for radioactivity. Radiation also has been used to speed up chemical reactions, such as the polymerization of certain plastics, and to vulcanize rubber. Radioactive isotopes are also being investigated as a possible means of preserving foods for long periods of time without refrigeration; in the process, called *irradiation*, the bacteria that cause decay of the food are killed by exposure to radioactivity.

—John Price

BIBLIOGRAPHY

ANDERSON, H. V. *Chemical Calculations*. McGraw-Hill, Inc., 1955.

ANDREWS, DONALD HATCH and KOKES, RICHARD J. *Fundamental Chemistry*. John Wiley & Sons, Inc., 1962.

ASIMOV, ISAAC. *World of Carbon*. Abelard-Schuman Ltd., 1958.

ASIMOV, ISAAC. *World of Nitrogen*. Abelard-Schuman Ltd., 1958.

CLEMENTS, RICHARD. *Modern Chemical Discoveries*. E. P. Dutton & Co., Inc., 1963.

CRAM, DONALD J. and HAMMOND, GEORGE S. *Organic Chemistry*. McGraw-Hill, Inc., 1959.

DUFFY, GEORGE H. *Physical Chemistry*. McGraw-Hill, Inc., 1962.

FARBER, EDUARD. *The Evolution of Chemistry*. The Ronald Press Co., 1952.

FIESER, LOUIS F. and MARY A. *Introduction to Organic Chemistry*. D. C. Heath & Co., 1957.

FRIEDLANDER, GERHART and KENNEDY, JOSEPH W. *Nuclear and Radiochemistry*. John Wiley & Sons, Inc., 1955.

GERO, ALEXANDER. *Textbook of Organic Chemistry*. John Wiley & Sons, Inc., 1963.

GLASSTONE, SAMUEL. *Elements of Physical Chemistry*. D. Van Nostrand Co., Inc., 1960.

MARTIN, ROBERT BRUCE. *Introduction to Biophysical Chemistry*. McGraw-Hill, Inc., 1964.

McCUE, JOHN JOSEPH GERALD and SHERK, KENNETH WAYNE. *The World of Atoms*. The Ronald Press Co., 1963.

NITZ, OTTO WILLIAM JULIUS. *Introductory Chemistry*. D. Van Nostrand Co., Inc., 1961.

PAULING, LINUS. *General Chemistry*. W. H. Freeman & Co., Publishers, 1956.

REICHEN, CHARLES ALBERT. *History of Chemistry*. Hawthorn Books, Inc., 1963.

SWIFT, ERNEST H. *A System of Chemical Analysis for the Common Elements*. W. H. Freeman & Co., Publishers, 1955.

TAYLOR, FRANK SHERWOOD. *The Alchemists, Founders of Modern Chemistry*. Abelard-Schuman Ltd., 1949.

VACZEK, LOUIS. *The Enjoyment of Chemistry*. The Viking Press, Inc., 1964.

TABLE OF ELEMENTS

At. wt., atomic weight; At. no., atomic number; Sp. gr., specific gravity; M.P., melting point °C.; B.P., boiling point °C.; E.R., electrical resistance per centimeter cube in millionths of ohms; C.S., crystal structure: C = cubic, whether body- or face-centered unknown; Cb = cubic, body-centered; Cf = cubic, face-centered; H = hexagonal; T = tetragonal. All temperatures in the text are in degrees Centigrade (°C.).

Element	Occurrence, Preparation, Date of Discovery, and Discoverer	Properties	Chief Compounds and Uses
Actinium (Ac) At. wt. 227 At. no. 89 Valence 3 Sp. gr. 10.1 M.P. 1,050°	From breakdown of uranium. • By bombardment of bismuth. • 1899; Debierne.	Radioactive; half-life ranges from 20 years to 3.7 seconds. It is between calcium and lanthanum.	Used in research.
Aluminum (Al) At. wt. 26.9815 At. no. 13 Valence 3 Sp. gr. 2.6 M.P. 660° E.R. 2.62 C.S. Cf	Cryolite, bauxite, impure emery, ruby, sapphire (Al_2O_3). • Commercially, by electrolysis of Al_2O_3 from bauxite, dissolved in cryolite; water power usual source of electrical energy. • 1825; Oersted.	Silver-white, ductile metal; malleable at 120°; tensile strength (wrought) 16 tons per square inch. Better conductor of electricity, weight for weight, than copper. Acted upon by dilute hydrochloric acid, slowly by sulfuric acid, but not by nitric acid or the acids in foods. Soluble in alkaline hydroxides.	Used for cooking utensils, boatbuilding, airplanes, small articles requiring lightness and strength, and electric leads. The powdered metal is used as a body for paint; its mixture with ferric oxide, called thermite, is used for producing very high temperatures (up to 2,700°).
Americium (Am) At. wt. 243 At. no. 95 Valences 3, 4, 5, 6 Sp. gr. 11.87 M.P. 850°	Bombardment of uranium-238 with very high energy electron volts leads to formation of isotope. • 1944; Seaborg, James, Morgan, Ghiorso.	Radioactive, transuranium element. Alpha activity amounts to 70 billion alpha disintegrations per minute per milligram.	Used in research.
Antimony (Sb) At. wt. 121.75 At. no. 51 Valences 3, 5 Sp. gr. 6.62 M.P. 630.7° B.P. Red heat E.R. 39 C.S. H	Free and as stibnite (Sb_2S_3). • Roasting stibnite gives Sb_2O_4, which is then reduced by heating with carbon. • 1450; Valentine.	White, brittle, crystalline metal. Its alloys expand on solidification, give very sharp castings for type. Does not tarnish, but may be burned in air; unites directly with the halogens.	Constituent of type metal, Britannia metal, Babbitt metal (used for bearings), and other alloys. Oxide (Sb_2O_3) is both basic and acidic. Trichloride, butter of antimony ($SbCl_3$), is easily hydrolyzed. Tartar emetic is used in medicine and dyeing.
Argon (Ar) At. wt. 39.948 At. no. 18 Valence 0 Density 39.9 (oxygen = 32) B.P. −185.7° M.P. −189.2°	Present in the air 0.94 per cent by volume. • To isolate from air, carbon dioxide is removed by soda lime, water by phosphorus pentaoxide, oxygen by red-hot copper, nitrogen by magnesium and calcium; fractional distillation of residue yields argon. • 1894; Rayleigh, Ramsay.	Monatomic gas, identified by its characteristic spectrum seen by examining light emitted when the gas is placed in a vacuum tube at low pressure and sparked. More soluble than nitrogen in water; 100 volumes of water dissolves 4 volumes of argon under ordinary conditions.	Forms no compounds, hence its name, argon, meaning 'inert.'
Arsenic (As) At. wt. 74.9216 At. no. 33 Valences 3, 5 Sp. gr. 5.7 B.P. 450° (sublimes) M.P. 480° (under pressure)	Free as arsenical pyrites ($FeSAs$), orpiment (As_2S_3), and realgar (As_2S_2). • By heating arsenical pyrites ($FeSAs \rightarrow FeS + As$). • 1649; Schröder.	Steel-gray, dull metallic, crystalline element classed as a metalloid because it is between metals and nonmetals. Vapor density corresponds to As_4 at 644°, and to As_2 at 1,700°. Burns in air and unites directly with the halogens, sulfur, and many metals.	Used for hardening lead shot. All compounds are poisonous. White arsenic (As_2O_3) is partly basic, forming a chloride, and partly acidic, forming arsenites. Scheele's green is a dangerous pigment used in wallpaper. Traces of arsenic may be detected by Marsh's test, in which intensely poisonous arsine (AsH_3) is formed.
Astatine (At) At. wt. 210 At. no. 85 Valence 7	By bombardment of bismuth with alpha particles. • 1940; Segré, Corson, MacKenzie.	Synthetic element similar to polonium. All the known isotopes are short-lived.	Used in research.
Barium (Ba) At. wt. 137.34 At. no. 56 Valence 2 Sp. gr. 3.5 M.P. 850°	As barite, or heavy spar ($BaSO_4$) and witherite ($BaCO_3$). • By electrolysis of the fused chloride ($BaCl_2$). • 1808; Davy.	Silver-white, lustrous, malleable metal harder than lead. Like calcium, it reacts slowly with water to give barium hydroxide and hydrogen. The vapors of its compounds impart green color to the Bunsen flame.	Peroxide (BaO_2) is used in manufacture of oxygen and hydrogen peroxide; nitrate and chlorate in pyrotechnics to produce green fires; sulfate as the body for permanent white paint and for filling glazed paper. All its soluble compounds are poisonous.
Berkelium (Bk) At. wt. 249 At. no. 97 Valences 3, 4 M.P. 1,278°	By bombardment of americium with alpha particles. • 1949; Seaborg, Ghiorso, Thompson.	Radioactive, transuranium element.	Used in research.
Beryllium (Be) At. wt. 9.0122 At. no. 4 Valence 2 Sp. gr. 1.8 M.P. 1,350° E.R. 18.5 C.S. H	In beryl [$Be_3Al_2(SiO_3)_6$]. • By electrolysis of the fused double fluoride $BeF_2 \cdot 2KF$. • 1797; Vauquelin.	Hard, white metal that tarnishes when heated in air; soluble in dilute acids when powdered.	Hydroxide [$Be(OH)_2$] is feebly acidic as well as basic, thus resembling the hydroxide of zinc. Emerald is beryl colored green by chromium oxide.
Bismuth (Bi) At. wt. 208.980 At. no. 83 Valences 3, 5 Sp. gr. 9.8 M.P. 271° B.P. c 1,200° E.R. 115 C.S. H	Free and as trioxide (Bi_2O_3) and trisulfide (Bi_2S_3). • Ore is roasted, then heated with charcoal and metallic iron to remove traces of sulfur. • 1450; Valentine.	Exceedingly brittle, crystalline, shiny metal, white with tinge of pink. Expands on solidification. Does not tarnish, and can be burned in air. Dissolves in oxygen acids. Most diamagnetic substance known.	Used for making fusible alloys such as Wood's metal (melting point 60.5°), used in plugs of fire sprinklers, boiler safety valves, and for taking casts. The oxynitrate is used in medicine and as a cosmetic.

TABLE OF ELEMENTS (Continued)

Element	Occurrence, Preparation, Date of Discovery, and Discoverer	Properties	Chief Compounds and Uses
Boron (B) At. wt. 10.811 At. no. 5 Valence 3 Sp. gr. amorphous 2.4 crystalline 2.5 B.P. 2,200°	As boric acid (H_3BO_3), borax ($Na_2B_4O_7 \cdot 10H_2O$), and colemanite ($Ca_2B_6O_{11} \cdot 5H_2O$). • Amorphous, by reducing B_2O_3 with magnesium; impure crystalline, by reducing B_2O_3 with excess aluminum. • 1808; Gay-Lussac, Thénard, Davy.	Amorphous form is a greenish-black powder that burns in air at 700°, forming B_2O_3 and BN. Boron is oxidized by adding hot concentrated nitric acid or sulfuric acid to boric acid.	Compounds are analogous to those of silicon. Borax is used as a flux and, in solution, as a mild alkali because of its hydrolysis. Boric acid is used as a weak antiseptic and preservative.
Bromine (Br) At. wt. 79.909 At. no. 35 Valence 1 Sp. gr. 3.12 M.P. —7° B.P. 58.8°	In sea water, as alkali bromide; in upper layers of salt deposits as sodium and magnesium bromide. • By treatment of brine with sulfuric acid and manganese dioxide, or with chlorine. • 1826; Balard.	Dark-red liquid; smells like chlorine; vapor irritates eyes, throat, and nose. Dissolves in 30 parts of water (bromine water). Combines with most other elements, but less vigorously than chlorine.	Potassium bromide is used in pharmacy; silver bromide, in photography. Bromine is used in preparation of organic dyes and as disinfectant.
Cadmium (Cd) At. wt. 112.40 At. no. 48 Valence 2 Sp. gr. 8.6 M.P. 321.7°	With zinc ores, as carbonate and sulfide. • Comes over in first portions in distillation of impure zinc. • 1817; Stromeyer.	Silver-white metal, more ductile and more malleable than zinc. Burns in air; is attacked by dilute acids.	All compounds are poisonous, little ionized. Sulfide is basis of cadmium yellow; iodide is used in pharmacy; metal as protective plating.
Calcium (Ca) At. wt. 40.08 At. no. 20 Valence 2 Sp. gr. 1.55 M.P. 810° E.R. 4.6 C.S. Cf	As carbonate (Iceland spar, calcite, aragonite, marble, chalk, limestone), sulfate (gypsum), phosphate (apatite), fluoride (fluorspar), complex silicates (feldspars, pyroxines, amphiboles). • By electrolysis of the fused chloride, or heating the iodide with sodium. • 1808; Davy.	White crystalline metal, harder than lead. Can be cut, drawn, rolled, and turned. Reacts with water and burns in air at red heat, forming the oxide (CaO) and the nitride (Ca_3N_2). Unites with hydrogen to form CaH_2, whose reaction with water is source of hydrogen for balloons. Salts color test flame yellowish-red.	Oxide (quicklime) is used for mortar and to remove hair from hides. Hydroxide mixed with sand forms mortar; solution is limewater. Plaster of Paris is less hydrated sulfate; takes up water on setting to form gypsum. Phosphates are fertilizers.
Californium (Cf) At. wt. 251 At. no. 98 Valence 3	By bombardment of curium with helium ions. • 1950; Seaborg, Thompson, Ghiorso, Street.	Radioactive, transuranium element.	Used in research.
Carbon (C) At. wt. 12.01115 At. no. 6 Valences 4, 6 Sp. gr. diamond 3.5 graphite 2.3 amorphous 1.9 M.P. Not realized; volatilizes near 3,500°	Free as diamond and graphite; in combination with hydrogen as petroleum; with oxygen as carbon dioxide; with these and other elements as coal and in plant and animal tissues; as many carbonates. • By dry distillation of wood or coal, yielding charcoal and coke, respectively. • Known in antiquity.	Diamond is crystalline, and is the hardest of minerals; dark-colored bort used for cutting and grinding. Graphite has black metallic luster, is crystalline, and may be scratched by the fingernail. Charcoal is amorphous and can absorb gases and coloring matters. All three forms burn in oxygen to form carbon dioxide.	The carbon compounds form the substance of organic chemistry. Carbon dioxide results from burning coal, coke, wood, oil, or illuminating gases, from fermentation and decay (slow burning), and from exhalation. Carbon monoxide is a deadly gas.
Cerium (Ce) At. wt. 140.12 At. no. 58 Valences 3, 4, 6 Sp. gr. 7.0 M.P. 640° E.R. 78 C.S. C	As silicate in cerite, along with neodymium, praseodymium, and lanthanum; also in monazite sand. • By electrolysis of the fused chloride. • 1803; Berzelius, Klaproth, Hisinger.	Metal with the color and luster of iron; like tin in hardness; very ductile and malleable. Burns in air more easily and more brightly than magnesium. Emits sparks when scratched with steel.	Welsbach incandescent gas mantles contain 1 per cent cerium dioxide (CeO_2). Alloys are used for gas and cigar lighters.
Cesium (Cs) At. wt. 132.905 At. no. 55 Valence 1 Sp. gr. 2.4 M.P. 26.3° B.P. 670°	In certain micas, mineral waters, and the ashes of certain plants. • By heating the hydroxide (CsOH) with magnesium or by electrolysis. • 1860; Bunsen, Kirchhoff.	Silver-white metal resembling rubidium and potassium. The softest of all solid metals; one of the most active metals and the most electropositive. Reacts violently with water. Cesium gives two bright lines in the blue of the spectrum; its name comes from *caesius*, meaning 'sky-blue.'	Used in certain photoelectric cells; in vacuum tubes to eliminate traces of gases.
Chlorine (Cl) At. wt. 35.453 At. no. 17 Valences 1, 7 Sp. gr. (liquid) 1.3 M.P. —101.6° B.P. —33.6°	In sea water as chlorides of the alkalis and alkaline earths; in salt deposits as like compounds. • By electrolysis of alkali chloride, fused or in solution; by the action of manganese dioxide (MnO_2) on hydrochloric acid (HCl). • 1774; Scheele.	Greenish-yellow gas with characteristic odor. Acts violently on respiratory tract. Unites directly with all elements except oxygen, nitrogen, and the argon family. Displaces bromine and iodine from their compounds, substitutes hydrogen in organic compounds.	Gas is used in extracting gold and in preparing bleaching and disinfecting agents. In presence of water it bleaches many coloring matters. Forms chlorides, such as NaCl, KCl, $CaCl_2$; hypochlorites, as solution of $Ca(OCl)_2$; chlorates, as $KClO_3$, used for matches and in pyrotechnics; and perchlorates, as $KClO_4$.
Chromium (Cr) At. wt. 51.996 At. no. 24 Valences 2, 3, 6 Sp. gr. 6.9 M.P. 1,515° E.R. 2.6 C.S. Cb	As chromite [$Fe(CrO_2)_2$]. • By reducing the oxide of chromic acetate (Cr_2O_3) with aluminum filings. • 1797; Vauquelin.	Steel-gray, lustrous, brittle, very hard metal. At high temperatures it burns in air to form green Cr_2O_3. Attacked by dilute sulfuric acid or hydrochloric acid, but not by nitric acid.	Used in alloys of steel and nickel. Chrome green (Cr_2O_3) and chrome yellow ($PbCrO_4$) are pigments. Bichromates (such as $K_2Cr_2O_7$) are used in photo processes, tanning and dyeing, and as oxidizing agents, as in batteries. The metal, like nickel, is used as a protective and decorative plating.
Cobalt (Co) At. wt. 58.9332 At. no. 27 Valences 2, 3 Sp. gr. 8.9 M.P. 1,480° E.R. 9.7 C.S. H (?)	As smaltite ($CoAs_2$) and cobaltite (CoAsS) found with iron and nickel. • By igniting the oxide in hydrogen. • 1735; Brandt.	White, metallic, malleable metal, less tenacious than iron. Turns pinkish on exposure to air. Less active chemically than iron.	Intensely blue silicates are used in coloring porcelain and constitute the pigment smalt.

TABLE OF ELEMENTS (Continued)

Element	Occurrence, Preparation, Date of Discovery, and Discoverer	Properties	Chief Compounds and Uses
Copper (Cu) At. wt. 63.54 At. no. 29 Valences 1, 2 Sp. gr. 8.92 M.P. 1,084.1° E.R. 1.69 C.S. Cf	Free as cuprite, copper glance, chalcopyrite, and malachite. • After removal of iron and sulfur, the oxide is reduced by heating with carbon. It is refined electrolytically. • Known in antiquity.	Red, lustrous, very ductile and malleable metal; high tensile strength (14 tons per square inch); second only to silver in electrical conductivity. In ordinary air it gradually becomes coated with basic carbonate. In absence of air, nitric acid alone among the dilute acids attacks it; in the presence of air, even acids in foodstuffs can dissolve it.	Used for coins, electrical leads, electroplating, roofing, cooking vessels, and for making such alloys as brass, bell and gun metals, German silver, and the bronzes. The soluble compounds are poisonous and are used as agricultural germicides. Blue vitriol is $CuSO_4 \cdot 5H_2O$; the basic acetate is verdigris.
Curium (Cm) At. wt. 247 At. no. 96 Valence 3 Sp. gr. 7 (?)	By bombardment of plutonium-239 with helium ions. • 1944; Seaborg, James, Ghiorso, Morgan.	Radioactive, transuranium element.	Used in research.
Dysprosium (Dy) At. wt. 162.50 At. no. 66 Valence 3 Sp. gr. 8.56 M.P. 1,500°	In monazite, gadolinite, and other rare minerals. • By fractional crystallization of bromates. • 1886; Boisbaudran.	Rare earth. The oxide is dysprosia (Dy_2O_3), found with three other rare earths.	Salts are green or yellow and show characteristic absorption bands. They are the most magnetic of all salts.
Einsteinium (Es) At. wt. 254 At. no. 99 Valence 3	Prepared by intensive neutron irradiation of plutonium-239. • 1954; Thompson, Harvey, Choppin, Seaborg, Ghiorso.	Radioactive, transuranium element.	Used in research.
Erbium (Er) At. wt. 167.26 At. no. 68 Valence 3 Sp. gr. 9.16 M.P. 1,525°	In gadolinite and other rare minerals. • 1843; Mosander.	Rare earth. The oxide erbia (Er_2O_3) is found with holmia, thulia, and dysprosia.	Salts are rose-colored and show characteristic absorption spectra.
Europium (Eu) At. wt. 151.96 At. no. 63 Valences 2, 3 Sp. gr. 5.22 M.P. 11.50°	In monazite and other rare minerals. • 1900; Demarçay.	This element so closely resembles samarium that they are difficult to separate analytically.	Salts are pinkish and show a faint absorption spectrum.
Fermium (Fm) At. wt. 253 At. no. 100 Valence 3	Prepared by intensive neutron irradiation of plutonium-239. • 1955; Thompson, Harvey, Choppin, Seaborg, Ghiorso.	Radioactive, transuranium element.	Used in research.
Fluorine (F) At. wt. 18.9984 At. no. 9 Valence 1 Sp. gr. (liquid) 1.14 at −187° M.P. −223° B.P. −187°	As cryolite (Na_3AlF_6), fluorspar (CaF_2), and very widely elsewhere in small quantities. • By electrolysis of dry hydrogen fluoride at −23°. • 1886; Moissan.	Pale yellowish-green gas that unites with every element except oxygen and the argon family. Rapidly displaces oxygen from water, chlorine from hydrogen chloride; attacks glass.	Hydrogen fluoride is used for etching glass and in silicate analysis. Silver fluoride is soluble and calcium fluoride is insoluble, in contrast with the other halides of these metals.
Francium (Fr) At. wt. 223 At. no. 87 Valence 1	Disintegrates so rapidly that it is almost impossible to obtain in sufficient quantity for weighing. • 1939; Perey.	Synthetic radioactive element; heaviest of the alkali metals.	Used in research.
Gadolinium (Gd) At. wt. 157.25 At. no. 64 Valence 3 Sp. gr. 7.94 (?) M.P. 1,350°	In gadolinite and samarskite. • 1886; Marignac.	Closely resembles terbium in its compounds.	Salts are colorless and show absorption bands only in the ultraviolet.
Gallium (Ga) At. wt. 69.72 At. no. 31 Valence 3 Sp. gr. 5.9 M.P. 30.1°	In iron ores, zinc blende, and bauxite. • By electrolysis of an alkaline solution of its salts secured from zinc. • 1875; Boisbaudran.	Bluish-white, tough metal that can be cut with a knife. Like aluminum, it is soluble in hydrochloric acid and caustic soda, but not in nitric acid.	Forms two chlorides, $GaCl_3$ and $GaCl_2$, that yield very characteristic spark spectra. Alloys with aluminum and cadmium are used for optical mirrors and cathodes.
Germanium (Ge) At. wt. 72.59 At. no. 32 Valences 2, 4 Sp. gr. 5.5 M.P. 985.5°	In the rare mineral argyrodite. • By the reduction of the dioxide (GeO_2) by carbon. • 1886; Winkler.	Grayish-white, brittle, lustrous metal, insoluble in hydrochloric acid. Combines directly with the halogens.	Close relation of this element to carbon and silicon is shown in the compound germanium chloroform. Mendeleev described it before its discovery, calling it ekasilicon. The oxide is used to treat pernicious anemia.
Gold (Au) At. wt. 196.967 At. no. 79 Valences 1, 3 Sp. gr. 19.32 M.P. 1,062.4° Co. E. 14.2	Chiefly free, but also a telluride; many specimens of iron pyrites are auriferous. • From gold-bearing sands by washing away the lighter materials and dissolving the gold from the residue by mercury, which is subsequently separated from the gold by distillation. • Known in antiquity.	Soft, bright-yellow metal, easily scratched by a knife; most ductile and malleable of the metals; excellent conductor of heat and electricity. Chemically, gold is rather inert and is not attacked by the oxygen of the air, by hydrogen sulfide, or by any single acid.	Pure gold is 24-carat gold. Jewelry is made in 18-, 14-, and 9-carat gold. Addition of copper increases hardness and rigidity. Sodium chloraurate is used for toning in photography, and potassium auricyanide is used in electrogilding.

TABLE OF ELEMENTS (Continued)

Element	Occurrence, Preparation, Date of Discovery, and Discoverer	Properties	Chief Compounds and Uses
Hafnium (Hf) At. wt. 178.49 At. no. 72 Valence 4 Sp. gr. 12.1 M.P. 1,700°	Associated with zirconium. • By decomposing the tetraiodide. • 1922; Coster, Hevesy.	Analogous to zirconium.	Similar to zirconium compounds, from which it is separated by fractional crystallization.
Helium (He) At. wt. 4.0026 At. no. 2 Valence 0 Sp. gr. (liquid) 0.15 B.P. —268.7° M.P. below —272°	In the air to the extent of 1 to 2 volumes per million; also occluded in certain minerals. First observed in sun's spectrum. • Neon and helium are boiled off crude argon, and the neon, when cooled, solidifies. • 1895; Ramsay.	Lightest gas except hydrogen, transparent, odorless, and colorless.	Forms no compounds. Used for balloons; not flammable.
Holmium (Ho) At. wt. 164.930 At. no. 67 Valence 3 Sp. gr. 8.76 M.P. 1,500°	Rare earth metal that occurs with, and is separated from, the erbium subgroup of the rare earths. Has never been isolated. • 1878; Soret.	Salts are orange-yellow and similar to those of dysprosium.	Used in research.
Hydrogen (H) At. wt. 1.00797 At. no. 1 Valence 1 Sp. gr. (liquid) 0.07 M.P. —259.1° B.P. —252.7°	In the air to the extent of 1 volume per 20,000 volumes of air; combined, in water (11.19 per cent by weight), natural gas, petroleum, and animal and vegetable bodies. • By treating zinc with hydrochloric or sulfuric acid; by electrolysis. • 1766; Cavendish.	Lightest gas, transparent, odorless, and colorless. Soluble in water (2 volumes in 100 volumes of water under average conditions), in platinum, in palladium (502 volumes in 1 volume of palladium). Burns in air and in chlorine and unites with many other elements.	Its two oxides are water and hydrogen peroxide, the latter used in solution as a bleaching agent. Every acid contains hydrogen as an essential constituent. Its compounds with carbon and other elements number over 100,000.
Indium (In) At. wt. 114.82 At. no. 49 Valences 1, 3 Sp. gr. 7.3 M.P. 156°	In zinc blende (ZnS) in small quantities. • Electrolytically from solutions of its salts. • 1863; Reich, Richter.	White, malleable metal, softer than lead; about as heavy as tin.	Compounds color the nonluminous gas flame blue and show a characteristic indigo blue line in the spectrum—hence its name.
Iodine (I) At. wt. 126.9044 At. no. 53 Valences 1, 5, 7 Sp. gr. 4.95 M.P. 113.5° B.P. 184.3°	In the ocean and certain seaweeds; always in the combined state. • From iodides by displacement of their iodine by chlorine. • 1811; Courtois.	Dark gray, brittle solid with a metallic luster. Vapor is violet, as are its solutions in chloroform and carbon bisulfide. Requires more than 5,000 parts of water for solution. Combines directly with many elements, but is much less active than chlorine or bromine.	Used in pharmacy as an antiseptic and in prescriptions for the treatment of goiter. Potassium iodide and iodoform likewise find application in medicine. The alkyl iodides are much used in synthetic organic chemistry.
Iridium (Ir) At. wt. 192.2 At. no. 77 Valences 3, 4 Sp. gr. 22.42 M.P. 1,950° E.R. 6.0 C.S. Cf	With platinum. • From platinum ores by a complex series of operations. • 1804; Tennant.	White metal, brittle when cold, very hard, and one of the heaviest substances known. Attacked by fused alkalis, but not by aqua regia.	Used for pointing gold pens. Its alloy with 9 parts of platinum is used for standard meter bars because of its unalterability. Used as a black color in china decorations.
Iron (Fe) At. wt. 55.847 At. no. 26 Valences 2, 3 Sp. gr. 7.86 pig 7.03–7.73 M.P. 1,535° wrought 1,600° steel 1,375° gray pig 1,275° white pig 1,075° E.R. 10.0 C.S. Cf, Cb	As magnetic oxide (Fe_3O_4), hematite (Fe_2O_3), limonite ($2Fe_2O_3 \cdot 3H_2O$), siderite (Fe_2CO_3), which are important ores; iron pyrites (FeS_2); in rocks as complex silicates; in plants and animals. • Pig iron is prepared in blast furnace by reduction of the ore by means of carbon monoxide in presence of suitable flux. From pig iron, wrought iron is obtained by puddling, and steel by the Bessemer, open-hearth, or other processes. • Known in antiquity.	White, malleable, ductile, magnetic metal, that is unchanged in dry air, but rusts in water and moist air. Easily attacked by dilute acids, but not by fused alkalis. Cast iron contains 2 to 5 per cent carbon and other impurities, and is hard and brittle. Wrought iron contains less than 0.2 per cent carbon and is softer and tougher, with tensile strength of 22 to 25 tons per square inch. Steel contains from 0.2 to 1.5 per cent carbon, and is permanently magnetic.	The metal is used as a structural material for rails, machinery, tools, etc. Jeweler's rouge and Venetian red consist of the oxide (Fe_2O_3). Rust is chiefly hydrated oxide. Hammer scale and lodestone have the composition Fe_3O_4. Ferric chloride ($FeCl_3$), ferrous iodide (FeI_2), and other iron compounds are used in medicine. Green vitriol ($FeSO_4 \cdot 7H_2O$) is used in making ink and in dyeing.
Krypton (Kr) At. wt. 83.80 At. no. 36 Valence 0 M.P. —169° B.P. —151.8°	In minute quantities in the air. • From crude argon by fractional distillation. • 1898; Ramsay, Travers.	Inert, colorless, and odorless gas resembling, but denser than, argon.	Forms no compounds and is identified by its characteristic spectrum.
Lanthanum (La) At. wt. 138.91 At. no. 57 Valence 3 Sp. gr. 6.15	As lanthanite [$La_2(CO_3)_3 \cdot 8H_2O$]. • By electrolysis of the fused chloride ($LaCl_3$). • 1839; Mosander.	Rare earth; iron-gray metal; tarnishes in air to steel-blue; malleable and ductile. Attacked slowly even by cold water.	When heated in air, it forms a strongly basic oxide (La_2O_3) that is diamagnetic, and a nitride (LaN).
Lawrencium (Lw) At. wt. 257 At. no. 103	By bombardment of californium with boron ions. • 1961; Ghiorso, Sikkeland, Larsh, Latimer.	Radioactive, transuranium element.	Used in research.
Lead (Pb) At. wt. 207.19 At. no. 82 Valences 2, 4 Sp. gr. 11.34 M.P. 327° E.R. 21.9 C.S. Cf	End product of certain radioactive decompositions. As galena (PbS) and in silver ores. • By calcination of partially roasted galena. Purification is effected by Parkes process.	Soft, gray metal; malleable and of low tensile strength, relatively impermeable to X rays. In presence of air, water acts on lead to produce the hydroxide which, being slightly soluble, may cause lead poisoning. When heated in air, lead is oxidized to litharge (PbO) and, under suitable conditions, to minium (Pb_3O_4).	Used for water pipes, roofs and gutters, and storage batteries. For shot it is alloyed with 0.4 per cent arsenic. Type metal contains 20 per cent antimony. Babbitt metal, for bearings, contains over 70 per cent lead. Solder and pewter are alloys of lead and tin. The basic carbonate, white lead, is the basis of most oil paints.

TABLE OF ELEMENTS (Continued)

Element	Occurrence, Preparation, Date of Discovery, and Discoverer	Properties	Chief Compounds and Uses
Lithium (Li) At. wt. 6.939 At. no. 3 Valence 1 Sp. gr. 0.53 M.P. 186° B.P. above 1,400° E.R. 9.3 C.S. C	In amblygonite [$Li(AlF)PO_4$]. • By electrolysis of the fused chloride ($LiCl$). • 1817; Arfvedson.	Lightest metal; silver-white, softer than lead, tarnishes quickly in air, and easily reacts with water. When heated, it unites vigorously with nitrogen.	The carbonate (Li_2CO_3) is used in medicine as a solvent for uric acid, lithium urate being soluble. The salts give a carmine flame coloration.
Lutetium (Lu) At. wt. 174.97 At. no. 71 Valence 3 Sp. gr. 9.849 H.P. 1,700°	In euxenite. • 1907; Urbain, Welsbach.	Like ytterbium but has lower magnetic susceptibility.	Its compounds resemble those of ytterbium.
Magnesium (Mg) At. wt. 24.312 At. no. 12 Valence 2 Sp. gr. 1.74 M.P. 633° B.P. 1,100° E.R. 4.5 C.S. H	As magnesite ($MgCO_3$), dolomite ($MgCO_3 \cdot CaCO_3$), carnallite ($MgCl_2 \cdot KCl \cdot 6H_2O$), and in very many complex silicates. • By electrolysis of dried, fused carnallite. • 1808; Davy, Bussy.	Silver-white, very lightweight metal, ductile when hot, and malleable. It tarnishes in air and reacts slowly with water, rapidly with steam. Burns in air to the oxide (MgO), emitting a very bright light. Unites directly with nitrogen.	Used as a reducing agent. Sulfate, known as Epsom salts, is used in medicine, as are the oxide (magnesia), the carbonates, and the citrate. The bright light emitted when the metal is burned in air is used in photography.
Manganese (Mn) At. wt. 54.9380 At. no. 25 Valences 2, 3, 4, 6, 7 Sp. gr. 7.2 M.P. 1,230° E.R. 5 C.S. CT	As pyrolusite (MnO_2), braunite (Mn_2O_3), hausmannite (Mn_3O_4), and manganese spar ($MnCO_3$). • By heating Mn_3O_4 with aluminum filings. • 1774; Gahn.	Steel-gray, hard, brittle metal with a pinkish tinge. Rusts in moist air and is attacked by dilute acids.	Ferromanganese and spiegeleisen are alloys with iron, used in making steel tougher. With copper it forms the tough, hard manganese bronzes, with tensile strength up to 30 tons per square inch.
Mendelevium (Md) At. wt. 256 At. no. 101 Valence 3	By bombardment of einsteinium-253 with helium ions. • 1955; Thompson, Harvey, Choppin, Ghiorso, Seaborg.	Radioactive, transuranium element.	Used in research.
Mercury (Hg) At. wt. 200.59 At. no. 80 Valence 1, 2 Sp. gr. 13.6 M.P. −38.8° B.P. 356.9° E.R. 95.8	Free and as cinnabar (HgS). • By roasting cinnabar: $HgS + O_2 \rightarrow Hg + SO_2$ • Known in antiquity.	Silver-white, mobile liquid, 20 per cent heavier than lead. Has vapor pressure of 0.0002 millimeter at 0°. Tarnishes slowly in air and is attacked only by nitric among the dilute acids. Vapor is monatomic.	Used in thermometers and barometers. Alloys, some of which are used in dentistry, are called amalgams. Calomel ($HgCl$) is administered internally in medicine; corrosive sublimate ($HgCl_2$) forms a solution with very powerful germicidal properties.
Molybdenum (Mo) At. wt. 95.94 At. no. 42 Valences 3, 4, 5, 6 Sp. gr. 10.2 M.P. 2,110° E.R. 4.8 C.S. Cb	As molybdenite (MoS_2) and wulfenite ($PbMoO_4$). • By reducing the oxides with aluminum powder. • 1782; Hjelm.	White metal as malleable as iron; will not scratch glass. Insoluble in hydrochloric or dilute sulfuric acid.	Ferromolybdenum alloys are used in the manufacture of special steels.
Neodymium (Nd) At. wt. 144.24 At. no. 60 Valences 3, 4 Sp. gr. 6.9 M.P. 840°	With cerium and lanthanum. • By electrolysis of the fused chloride. • 1885; Welsbach.	Rare earth; yellowish metal; tarnishes in air.	Salts are rose-violet; solutions show characteristic spectra.
Neon (Ne) At. wt. 20.183 At. no. 10 Valence 0 B.P. c −243°	Minute quantities in atmosphere. • Neon and helium are boiled out of crude argon and the neon separated from helium by cooling with liquid hydrogen. • 1898; Ramsay, Travers.	Colorless, odorless, transparent, inert gas resembling argon.	Forms no compounds; is recognized by its characteristic spectrum. Used in glow tubes for display signs.
Neptunium (Np) At. wt. 237 At. no. 93 Valences 3, 4, 5, 6 Sp. gr. 20.45 M.P. 640°	Produced in nuclear chain reactions. • 1940; McMillan, Abelson.	Synthetic radioactive element. Emits alpha particles. Half-life is 2,200,000 years.	Oxide is dark brown.
Nickel (Ni) At. wt. 58.71 At. no. 28 Valences 2, 3 Sp. gr. 8.8 M.P. 1,452° E.R. 6.9 C.S. Cf	As nicollite ($NiAs$) and nickel glance ($NiAsS$). • By igniting the oxalate in hydrogen. • 1751; Cronstedt.	White, very hard, lustrous metal; malleable, ductile, and tenacious. Rusts slowly in air and is easily attacked only by nitric acid.	Metal furnishes protective coating when plated on iron. German silver is an alloy of nickel, copper, and zinc. Nickel chromium steel is used for armor. Manganin, containing nickel, copper, and manganese, is used for electrical resistors. It is a catalyst, especially in hydrogenation.

TABLE OF ELEMENTS (Continued)

Element	Occurrence, Preparation, Date of Discovery, and Discoverer	Properties	Chief Compounds and Uses
Niobium (Nb) At. wt. 92.906 At. no. 41 Valences 1, 2, 4, 5 Sp. gr. 12.7 M.P. 1,950°	In the mineral columbite ($FeCb_2O_6$). • By reduction of the dioxide (NbO_2) by paraffin. • 1801; Hatchett.	Light gray, malleable, ductile metal, as hard as wrought iron; not affected by acids, even aqua regia. The hydride (NbH) burns in air.	Compounds occur with those of tantalum, which they closely resemble.
Nitrogen (N) At. wt. 14.0067 At. no. 7 Valences 3, 5 Sp. gr. (liquid) 0.808 M.P. —209.8° B.P. —195.8°	Free nitrogen forms about 80 per cent of the air by volume. Also in Bengal saltpeter (KNO_3), Chile saltpeter ($NaNO_3$). • 1772; Rutherford.	Colorless, odorless, transparent gas, rather inactive chemically. At ordinary temperature and pressure, 100 volumes of water dissolve 1.5 volumes of nitrogen.	Nitrous oxide, or laughing gas, is used by dentists. Nitric acid has many applications in technical chemistry. Ammonia is a very soluble gas. Many nitrogen compounds are used as fertilizers.
Nobelium (No) At. wt. 254 At. no. 102 Valence 3	1957; Fields.	Radioactive, transuranium element.	Used in research.
Osmium (Os) At. wt. 190.2 At. no. 76 Valences 2, 3, 4, 6, 8 Sp. gr. 22.48 M.P. 2,700°	With platinum. • By reducing tetroxide (OsO_4). • 1804; Tennant.	Gray metal, harder than glass; heaviest of the known elements.	Its alloy with iridium is used in tipping gold pens. Osmium tetroxide is used as a microscopic stain for fat.
Oxygen (O) At. wt. 15.9994 At. no. 8 Valence 2 Sp. gr. (liquid) 1.13 M.P. —218.4° B.P. —183°	Free oxygen forms about 20 per cent of the air by volume. Water contains 88.88 per cent oxygen. The rocks of the earth's crust contain about 45 per cent in combination, chiefly as silicates. • In the laboratory, by heating potassium chlorate ($KClO_3$). Commercially, from the air. • 1774; Priestley, Scheele.	Colorless, odorless, tasteless, transparent gas, slightly heavier than air. At ordinary temperature and pressure, 100 volumes of water dissolves 3 volumes of oxygen. Very active chemically, combining directly with all but a few elements to form oxides. Many substances burn more vigorously in oxygen than in air. Liquid oxygen is magnetic.	Gas is sold compressed in mild steel cylinders, and is used for the oxyhydrogen blowpipe, in medicine, and for chemical purposes. Necessary to support animal respiration and ordinary combustion. Enters as a constituent into all oxides, most salts, and many organic compounds.
Palladium (Pd) At. wt. 106.4 At. no. 46 Valences 2, 4 Sp. gr. 12 M.P. c 1,535° E.R. 10.8 C.S. Cf	With platinum and gold in nickel ores. • By a complex series of processes from platinum ores. • 1803; Wollaston.	Silvery, malleable, ductile metal, related to platinum, unlike which, however, it may be attacked by nitric acid. Under suitable conditions it can absorb over 900 volumes of hydrogen.	Since it does not tarnish, it is used for coating silver goods, and by dentists as a substitute for gold. Like platinum, it is used as a catalyst.
Phosphorus (P) At. wt. 30.9738 At. no. 15 Valences 3, 5 Sp. gr. white 1.82 red 2.2 M.P. (white) 44° B.P. 287°	As phosphates, such as apatite [$Ca_5F(PO_4)_3$]; in bones, teeth, and brain; and in seeds of plants. • By reduction of calcium phosphate by carbon with a suitable flux in an electric furnace. • 1669; Brand.	Exists in two allotropic modifications: white phosphorus, which is waxy in consistency, soluble in carbon bisulfide, foul-smelling, and poisonous; and red phosphorus, which is a solid, insoluble in carbon bisulfide, odorless, and not poisonous. White phosphorus has a low ignition temperature, hence its former use in matches.	Red phosphorus is used in the manufacture of matches, as is the compound P_4S_3. In the form of superphosphate of lime, phosphorus is an important artificial fertilizer. The chlorides PCl_5 and PCl_3 are much used in organic chemistry. Compounds are used in medicine.
Platinum (Pt) At. wt. 195.09 At. no. 78 Valences 2, 4 Sp. gr. 21.45 M.P. 1,753° E.R. 10.5 C.S. Cf	Free, alloyed with platinum metals, as nuggets in alluvial sands in the Urals, in California, and elsewhere. • Freed from the metals with which it is alloyed by a complex series of processes. • 1557; Scaliger.	Silvery, tenacious, very heavy, ductile, malleable metal, unaltered in moist air and not attacked by any single common acid. Aqua regia, fused alkalis, alkali nitrates, and cyanides, however, do attack it. Platinum sponge and platinum black are finely divided forms.	Because of its resistance to acids, platinum is used for chemical vessels and electrodes. Since its coefficient of expansion is close to that of glass, platinum wires can be fused through glass without danger of breakage on cooling. The salts are used in photography. The metal is more expensive than gold and is used in jewelry.
Plutonium (Pu) At. wt. 242 At. no. 94 Valences 3, 4, 5, 6 Sp. gr. 19.7 M.P. 640°	Present to a small extent in uranium ores. • Produced in nuclear chain reactions. • 1940; Seaborg, McMillan, Wahl, Kennedy.	Synthetic radioactive element. Emits alpha particles. Half-life is 24,300 years.	Used in atomic bombs and atomic devices.
Polonium (Po) At. wt. 210 At. no. 84 Valences 2, 4 Sp. gr. 9.3 M.P. 254°	With bismuth in uranium minerals. • Metal has been isolated only in minute quantities. • 1898; the Curies.	Radioactive element. Half-life is 136 days.	Compounds resemble those of tellurium.
Potassium (K) At. wt. 39.102 At. no. 19 Valence 1 Sp. gr. 0.86 M.P. 62.5° B.P. 760°	As sylvite (KCl), carnallite ($KCl \cdot MgCl_2 \cdot 6H_2O$); in plant and animal ashes, and in many complex silicates. • By reduction or electrolysis of fused potassium hydroxide (KOH). • 1807; Davy.	Silver-white, lustrous, very lightweight metal, as soft as wax; tarnishes instantly in moist air. Chemically very active, decomposing in the cold and uniting violently with the halogens, sulfur, and oxygen.	Alloy (with sodium) is used in high-temperature thermometers. Bengal saltpeter is the nitrate and is used in pyrotechnics, for gunpowders, and as a preservative. Iodide, KI, is used in pharmacy. With nitrogen and phosphorus, it is one of the three basic fertilizer elements.

TABLE OF ELEMENTS (Continued)

Element	Occurrence, Preparation, Date of Discovery, and Discoverer	Properties	Chief Compounds and Uses
Praseodymium (Pr) At. wt. 140.907 At. no. 59 Valences 3, 4 Sp. gr. 6.5 M.P. 940°	With cerium and lanthanum. ● By electrolysis of the fused chloride. ● 1885; Welsbach.	Rare earth; yellowish metal; remains untarnished in air.	Salts are leek-green, and their solutions have characteristic absorption spectra.
Promethium (Pm) At. wt. 147 At. no. 61 Valence 3	In monazite residues and with the cerium earths, from which its salts are separated. ● 1945; Marinsky, Glendenin, Coryell.	Rare earth metal, produced artificially. Recognized by its X-ray spectrum and its optical absorption spectrum. Radioisotopes have been identified.	Compounds are similar to those of samarium and neodymium.
Protactinium (Pa) At. wt. 231 At. no. 91 Valence 5 Sp. gr. 15.37	In uranium minerals. ● Metal has been isolated; about 130 milligrams may be secured from 1,000 kilograms of uranium. ● 1917; Hahn, Meitner, Soddy, Cranston.	Radioactive element, emitting alpha particles. Its half-life is 12,000 years.	Compounds resemble those of tantalum.
Radium (Ra) At. wt. 226 At. no. 88 Valence 2 Sp. gr. 5 (?) M.P. 700°	In minute quantities in pitchblende and other uranium ores. ● Metal has been isolated; bromide is separated from the barium bromide prepared from pitchblende by fractional crystallization. ● 1898; the Curies, Bémont.	In all of its compounds, the metal has the power of emitting certain radiations. These can pass through materials that are opaque to light, render air a conductor, affect a photographic plate, and cause a zinc-sulfide screen to fluoresce visibly.	Rays from radium compounds (such as $RaBr_2$, $RaCl_2$, $RaCO_3$) act destructively on living tissues.
Radon (Rn) At. wt. 222 At. no. 86 Valence 0 Sp. gr. (liquid) 4.4 M.P. —71°	Admixed with air. ● By passing air through solutions of radium salts. ● 1900; Dorn.	Inert gas of the helium family; radioactive, emitting alpha particles; half-life is 3.83 days.	Forms no compounds. Used in treatment of cancer; enclosed in minute glass vessels the size of a small match head, it is inserted into the tumor.
Rhenium (Re) At. wt. 186.2 At. no. 75 Valences 1, 4, 6, 7 Sp. gr. 20.53 M.P. 3,167°	In molybdenum and platinum ores. ● 1925; Noddack, Tacke, Berg.	Silver-white, hard metal, heavier than gold. Only tungsten is less fusible. Chemical properties are similar to those of manganese.	May be used in electronics when better methods for its purification are developed.
Rhodium (Rh) At. wt. 102.905 At. no. 45 Valences 2, 3, 4 Sp. gr. 12.1 M.P. above 2,000° E.R. 5.1 C.S. Cf	In the ores of platinum. ● By a complex series of processes from platinum ores. ● 1803; Wollaston.	Silvery, malleable, ductile metal; does not tarnish in air; not attacked by aqua regia.	The red chloride ($RhCl_2$) is formed by the action of chlorine on the metal. Rhodium-platinum alloy is used for thermocouples to measure high temperatures.
Rubidium (Rb) At. wt. 85.47 At. no. 37 Valences 1, 3, 5 Sp. gr. 1.53 M.P. 38.5° B.P. 696°	Found with cesium. Salts are associated with those of potassium. ● By heating the hydroxides with magnesium or by the electrolysis of the cyanides or hydroxides. ● 1860; Bunsen, Kirchhoff.	Silver-white metal resembling potassium; reacts vigorously with water.	Compounds show characteristic flame spectra with two red lines.
Ruthenium (Ru) At. wt. 101.07 At. no. 44 Valences 3, 4, 6, 7, 8 Sp. gr. 12.1 M.P. above 2,000°	In the ores of platinum. ● By a complex series of processes from platinum ores. ● 1844; Klaus.	Hard, white, brittle metal, oxidized when heated in air. Scarcely attacked by aqua regia; very infusible. Chemical properties resemble those of osmium.	The following oxides are known: Ru_2O_3, RuO_2, RuO_4, as well as salts corresponding to RuO_3 and Ru_2O_7. Ruthenium red, an ammoniacal compound, dyes silk a beautiful yellow, but its high price limits its usefulness.
Samarium (Sm) At. wt. 150.35 At. no. 62 Valences 2, 3 Sp. gr. c 7.7 M.P. 1,300°–1,400°	In monazite and samarskite. ● By electrolysis of the chloride. ● 1879; Boisbaudran.	Rare earth; whitish-gray metal; tarnishes in air.	Salts are topaz-yellow and are similar to those of lanthanum.
Scandium (Sc) At. wt. 44.956 At. no. 21 Valence 3 Sp. gr. 3.02 M.P. 1,200°	In the minerals euxenite and gadolinite. Existence of this element was predicted by Mendeleev in 1869; he called it ekaboron. ● 1879; Nilson.	This element has not been isolated.	Chloride ($ScCl_3$) shows a characteristic spark spectrum.
Selenium (Se) At. wt. 78.96 At. no. 34 Valences 2, 4, 6 Sp. gr. amorphous 4.26 monoclinic 4.28 hexagonal 4.8 M.P. amorphous 50° monoclinic 170°–180° hexagonal 217° B.P. 690° E.R. 1.2 C.S. THC	Free in some specimens of sulfur and in combination with lead, iron, and other metals, as in pyrites. ● Amorphous, by reducing selenious acid (H_2SeO_3) by sulfur dioxide. With tellurium it is obtained from the anode slime of copper refineries. ● 1817; Berzelius.	Three varieties are known: (1) red amorphous, soluble in carbon bisulfide from which it is deposited as (2) red translucent monoclinic crystals, soluble in carbon bisulfide; (3) bluegray metallic selenium, insoluble in carbon bisulfide. This last form conducts electricity much better when exposed to light; conductivity increases with light intensity.	Selenium cells are used as indicators of intensity of illumination. The compounds strongly resemble those of sulfur. Hydrogen selenide is a foul-smelling, flammable gas. Selenic acid (H_2SeO_4) is a more powerful oxidizer than sulfuric acid and dissolves gold. The oxychloride is a valuable solvent for resins, fish oils, etc.

TABLE OF ELEMENTS (Continued)

Element	Occurrence, Preparation, Date of Discovery, and Discoverer	Properties	Chief Compounds and Uses

Silicon (Si)
At. wt. 28.086
At. no. 14
Valence 4
Sp. gr.
  amorphous 2.35
  crystalline 2.4
M.P. 1,420°
B.P. c 3,500°
	Silicon dioxide (SiO_2) occurs as flint, quartz, quartz sand, etc. Igneous rocks are composed largely of silicates, and silicon constitutes more than 25 per cent of the earth's crust—more than any other element except oxygen.
	• By reducing sand with coke in an electric furnace.
	• 1823; Berzelius.
		Amorphous silicon is a brown powder that burns when heated in air. Crystalline silicon forms black needles. It is less active than the amorphous variety and is attacked only slowly by a mixture of hydrofluoric and nitric acids. It unites with fluorine, however, at ordinary temperatures.	Silicon is used in steelmaking. Silicon steel is more magnetic than iron. Ornamental varieties of quartz find uses as gems, as do several natural silicates. Silicon carbide, or carborundum (SiC), is used as an abrasive. Sodium silicate solution is water glass, used to protect sandstone and to preserve eggs. Common glass is a mixture of sodium and calcium silicates.

Silver (Ag) At. wt. 107.870 At. no. 47 Valence 1 Sp. gr. 10.53 M.P. 961° B.P. 2,050° E.R. 1.62 C.S. Cf	Native, as sulfide (AgS_2) often associated with galena; as chloride (AgCl), etc. • From lead by the Pattinson process or the Parkes process; from the ores by the Mexican and other processes. • Known in antiquity.	White, highly lustrous, tough, very ductile, malleable metal; best conductor of heat and electricity known. Liquid silver dissolves oxygen. It is unaffected by the oxygen of moist air; its tarnishing is caused by the action of hydrogen sulfide. It dissolves in dilute nitric acid and in hot concentrated sulfuric acid.	Used for tableware, ornaments, coins, etc. U.S. sterling silver contains 90 per cent silver, 10 per cent copper. Lunar caustic is silver nitrate. This salt and the halides of silver are used extensively in photography. For electroplating, a bath of potassium argenticyanide is used.
Sodium (Na) At. wt. 22.9898 At. no. 11 Valence 1 Sp. gr. 0.97 M.P. 97.5° B.P. 742° E.R. 4.6 C.S. C	In the sea as chloride (NaCl); in salt deposits as chloride, borate, and nitrate; in many complex silicates in rocks. • By electrolysis of fused sodium hydroxide (NaOH). • 1807; Davy.	Silver-white metal, soft as wax. Immediately tarnishes at ordinary temperatures. Like potassium, it is very active, uniting directly with many other elements and vigorously reacting with cold water.	Used in manufacture of chemicals. Sodium chloride (common salt) is a necessity of life for most animals, and is used in manufacture of hydrochloric acid, chlorine, and sodium compounds. Sodium carbonate, or washing soda, and sodium hydroxide are used for cleaning and for manufacture of soap and chemicals. Sodium bicarbonate is baking soda. The sulfate is known as Glauber's salt; the thiosulfate, by photographers, as "hypo."
Strontium (Sr) At. wt. 87.62 At. no. 38 Valence 2 Sp. gr. 2.55 M.P. 782°	As strontianite ($SrCO_3$) and celestite ($SrSO_4$). • By electrolysis of the fused chloride. • 1790; Crawford.	White metal; harder than sodium, softer than calcium; tarnishes to a yellow tint. Like calcium, it is active enough to react vigorously with cold water.	The nitrate and chlorate are used in fireworks for red color. All volatile compounds color the Bunsen flame red.

Sulfur (S)
At. wt. 32.064
At. no. 16
Valences 2, 3, 4, 6
Sp. gr.
  rhombic 2.07
  monoclinic 1.96
M.P.
  rhombic 112.4°
  monoclinic 119°
B.P. 444.6°
	Native, in combination with most metals as sulfides, and with some metals as sulfates.
	• By melting the free sulfur away from the rocky matrix, and subsequent purification by distillation.
	• Known in antiquity.
		Natural sulfur is rhombic in crystalline form, yellow, brittle, and of vitreous luster. It is a poor conductor of heat and electricity. This and the monoclinic variety are soluble in carbon bisulfide, while amorphous sulfur is not. When heated, sulfur unites directly with most other elements.	Used to prepare sulfur dioxide (SO_2), which is used in making sulfuric acid and sulfites and for bleaching; also for vulcanizing rubber and in manufacture of black gunpowder. Sulfuric acid (H_2SO_4) is to the chemical industry what iron is to engineering.

Tantalum (Ta) At. wt. 180.948 At. no. 73 Valences 2, 4, 5 Sp. gr. 16.6 M.P. 2,996°	In tantalite and many other rare minerals. • By the action of sodium tantalofluoride (Na_2TaF_7). • 1802; Ekeberg.	Hard, silver-white metal; ductile and malleable when hot; of very high tensile strength. The hot metal can absorb 740 volumes of hydrogen. Not attacked by aqua regia.	Used for filaments for electric lamps until tungsten replaced it; in surgical instruments and in rectifiers; and as a substitute for platinum.
Technetium (Tc) At. wt. 99 At. no. 43 Valences 6, 7 Sp. gr. 11.50 M.P. 2,140°	By bombardment of molybdenum with deuterons. • 1937; Perrier, Segré.	The first artificially produced element. Resembles rhenium and manganese.	Used in research.

Tellurium (Te)
At. wt. 127.60
At. no. 52
Valences 2, 4, 6
Sp. gr.
  crystalline 6.3
M.P.
  crystalline 455°
B.P. 1,400°
	Free and as tellurides.
	• By reducing tellurous acid (H_2TeO_3) by means of sulfur dioxide.
	• 1782; Müller.
		Crystalline variety is white, has metallic luster, and conducts heat and electricity. Precipitated variety is black and of lower density. Element is related to sulfur, but is more metallic.	Compounds find few applications; in coloring glass, gives silver a platinum finish. Telluric acid (H_6TeO_6) has basic as well as acidic characteristics, in keeping with the position of the element between the metals and nonmetals.

Terbium (Tb) At. wt. 158.924 At. no. 65 Valence 3 Sp. gr. 8.33 M.P. 1,450°	In gadolinite, samarskite, and other rare minerals. • 1843; Mosander.	Rare earth element.	Salts are almost colorless; oxide is almost black.
Thallium (Tl) At. wt. 204.37 At. no. 81 Valences 1, 3 Sp. gr. 11.86 M.P. 303° E.R. 18.1 C.S. T	In crookesite and in small quantities in many samples of iron pyrites. • Precipitated by zinc from solution obtained by suitable treatment of flue dust from sulfuric acid works. • 1861; Crookes.	Bluish-white, leadlike metal; rather soft and malleable, but of low tensile strength. Decomposes water rapidly at red heat and dissolves in dilute acids.	Forms two sets of salts: thallous and thallic. The salts, used in making optical glass, are poisonous. All the compounds show a characteristic green line in the spectrum.

TABLE OF ELEMENTS (Continued)

Element	Occurrence, Preparation, Date of Discovery, and Discoverer	Properties	Chief Compounds and Uses
Thorium (Th) At. wt. 232.038 At. no. 90 Valence 4 Sp. gr. 11.0 M.P. 1,842° C.S. C	In monazite sand. • By reducing potassium thorium chloride with sodium, or by electrolysis of fused potassium and sodium chlorides. • 1828; Berzelius.	Metal has the color of nickel; can be burned in air. Hydrochloric acid attacks it slowly.	The nitrate $Th(NO_3)_4 \cdot 6H_2O$ is used in making Welsbach incandescent mantles, which consist of 99 per cent thorium dioxide. Very radioactive.
Thulium (Tm) At. wt. 168.934 At. no. 69 Valence 3 Sp. gr. 9.34 M.P. 1,600°	In gadolinite and other yttrium minerals. • 1879; Cleve.	Rare earth element; has never been isolated.	Salts are a pale blue that is destroyed very easily by minute quantities of erbium.
Tin (Sn) At. wt. 118.69 At. no. 50 Valences 2, 4 Sp. gr. 7.3 M.P. 232° E.R. 11.4 C.S. TC	As cassiterite (SnO_2). • After roasting, the ore is reduced by heating with carbon. • Known in antiquity.	Silver-white, rather soft, very malleable, ductile metal; practically unchanged in air. When heated, it may be burned in air. Dilute nitric acid is the only dilute acid that attacks it rapidly. When kept long at temperatures below 0°, ordinary tin changes to a brittle, gray, powdery form.	Much tin is used in coating iron for tinplate. A constituent of Britannia metal, pewter, solder, bronze, etc. Forms two sets of salts: stannous and stannic. Pink salt is used in dyeing. Mosaic gold is essentially stannic sulfide.
Titanium (Ti) At. wt. 47.90 At. no. 22 Valences 2, 3, 4 Sp. gr. 4.5 M.P. below 1,800° C.S. C	As rutile (TiO_2) and ilmenite ($FeTiO_3$). • By reducing the chloride ($TiCl_4$) by means of sodium. • 1791; Gregor.	Hard, brittle metal, resembling polished steel. May be forged at low red heat. Dissolves in dilute sulfuric acid and decomposes in steam at 800°. Unites easily with nitrogen.	Used in alloys, as a white pigment (paint and paper), and as a coloring for ceramics.
Tungsten (W) At. wt. 183.85 At. no. 74 Valences 2, 4, 5, 6 Sp. gr. 19.3 M.P. 3,380° E.R. 5.48 C.S. Cb	As wolframite ($FeWO_4$) and as scheelite ($CaWO_4$). • By reducing tungstic acid (H_2WO_4) by carbon at high temperatures. • 1783; De Elhuyar.	Hard, brittle, gray metal, attacked by chlorine only at 250°, although it can be caused to burn in air. Slowly acted upon by dilute acids and even by water.	Used for filaments of incandescent electric lamps, giving an efficiency of 1.3 watts per candlepower. Tungsten steel has 5 per cent tungsten. Sodium tungstates are used as mordants in dyeing.
Uranium (U) At. wt. 238.03 At. no. 92 Valences 2, 3, 4, 5, 6 Sp. gr. 18.7 M.P. 1,150°	As pitchblende, which contains U_3O_8. • By reducing the oxides with aluminum. • 1789; Klaproth.	White, lustrous metal; tarnishes in air and reacts slowly with cold water. Combines directly with many other elements.	All compounds are radioactive in proportion to their radium content. Glass to which uranium compounds have been added shows a greenish-yellow fluorescence. Used in atom bomb.
Vanadium (V) At. wt. 50.942 At. no. 23 Valences 2, 3, 4, 5 Sp. gr. 5.5 M.P. 1,710° C.S. Cb	In a few rather rare minerals. • By reduction of the dichloride (VCl_2) in hydrogen. • 1830; Sefström.	Silver-white lustrous metal, harder than quartz. Does not tarnish or react with water at ordinary temperatures, but can be burned in oxygen.	Added to steel even in small quantities (0.2 per cent), it increases the tenacity and elastic limit without reducing ductility.
Xenon (Xe) At. wt. 131.30 At. no. 54 Valence 0 Sp. gr. (liquid) 3.52 M.P. —140°	In minute quantities in the air, 1 volume in 170 million. • By fractionation of liquid argon. • 1898; Ramsay, Travers.	Transparent, colorless, odorless gas; very inert like argon. Densest member of the argon family.	Forms no compounds.
Ytterbium (Yb) At. wt. 173.04 At. no. 70 Valence 3 Sp. gr. 7.01 M.P. 1,800°	In gadolinite, euxenite, and other rare minerals. • 1878; Marignac.	Rare earth.	Compounds show a characteristic spark spectrum.
Yttrium (Y) At. wt. 88.905 At. no. 39 Valence 3 Sp. gr. 5.51 M.P. 1,490°	In gadolinite, euxenite, and other rare minerals. • By electrolysis of sodium yttrium chloride. • 1794; Gadolin.	Gray, lustrous metal.	Chloride yields a characteristic, though complex, spectrum.
Zinc (Zn) At. wt. 65.37 At. no. 30 Valence 2 Sp. gr. 7.14 M.P. 419.4° C.S. H	As zinc blende (ZnS), calamine ($ZnCO_3$), zincite (ZnO), etc. • After roasting, the ore is reduced by coal, the metal distilling off. • Known in antiquity.	Bluish-white, lustrous, brittle metal; malleable and ductile at 120°; tarnishes in moist air. Reacts slowly with cold water, and rapidly when heated in steam. Dissolves in dilute acids and sodium hydroxide solution.	Used for roofs, gutters; galvanic batteries. Iron galvanized with zinc, preventing rust. Zinc alloyed with copper to make brass. In paint, zinc oxide is less toxic than lead oxide. Salts used in medicine, chloride and sulfate in antiseptic solutions.
Zirconium (Zr) At. wt. 91.22 At. no. 40 Valence 4 Sp. gr. 6.4 M.P. 1,852°	As zircon ($ZrSiO_4$). • By reducing the oxide (ZrO_2) with carbon in an electric furnace. • 1789; Klaproth.	Hard, gray metal remaining bright in air; oxidizes slowly at white heat. Dissolves in aqua regia and caustic potash solution.	Oxide is contained in some incandescent gas mantles; is used for furnace linings and as a cleansing agent in metallurgy. Increases tensile strength of armor plate. Carbide is an abrasive.

LIFE SCIENCE

ORIGIN OF LIFE

Theories dealing with the origin of life attempt to account for the fact that there are living organisms on a planet that contained no life when it was formed. It is difficult to define what is meant by a "living organism" because there are many characteristics associated with living things. However, there are only two essential characteristics necessary for an organism to undergo evolution—the ability to *reproduce* and the ability to *mutate* (undergo change). Therefore, a *living organism* will be defined as an entity that is (a) capable of making a reasonably accurate copy of itself, and (b) subject to a low rate of mutation, with these mutations transmitted to its progeny.

Spontaneous Generation.—The problem of the origin of life in the modern sense was not considered by the ancient thinkers. They held that life could arise spontaneously from organic matter, as well as by sexual and asexual reproduction. The evidence for this belief was the common observation that insects and small animals arose from decaying meat and rotting grain. Thus life was considered to be originating at that time, the process was apparently a simple one, and there was no difficult problem to consider.

In 1668, Francesco Redi performed an experiment to disprove the theory of spontaneous generation. He placed some meat in a flask and covered the flask with muslin so that flies could not lay their eggs on the meat. No maggots, which are the larval form of flies, developed in the meat as long as the flask remained covered. This demonstration was sufficient to disprove the theory of spontaneous generation for higher organisms, but it did not apply to microorganisms. In 1765, Lazarro Spallanzani conducted similar experiments showing that microorganisms would not appear in various nutrient broths if the

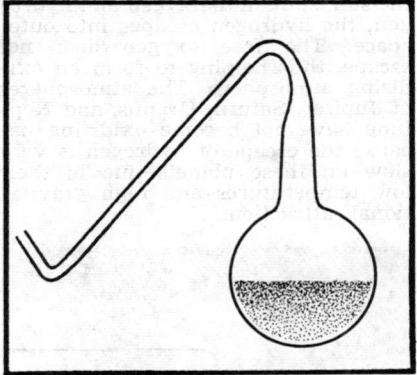

PASTEUR'S apparatus, by which he disproved spontaneous generation of life.

flasks were sealed and boiled. Objections were raised that the boiling had destroyed the "vital force" in both the nutrient broth and the air. This "vital force" was thought to be necessary for the spontaneous generation of life. Spallanzani could show that the broth was still suitable for the growth of organisms by readmitting air to the flasks, but he could not prove that the heating process had left the air in the flasks unchanged.

It was not until 1862 that the theory of spontaneous generation was conclusively disproved by Louis Pasteur. He placed a nutrient broth in a flask that had a long, S-shaped tube attached. This S-shaped tube allowed air to pass freely in and out of the flask. However, all dust, molds, and bacteria were caught on the sides of the curved tube The broth was boiled to kill any microorganisms present, and the flask was then allowed to cool. No microorganisms formed in the cooled broth. Since the air could pass freely in and out of the flask, and the broth subsequently could be

shown capable of growing microorganisms, this experiment showed that no "vital force" in the broth or the air had been destroyed. Pasteur and John Tyndall were able to extend these experiments to show that the "spontaneous generation" of organisms in nutrient broths is due to contamination by atmospheric microorganisms. These experiments were convincing, and no serious case has since been made in favor of the spontaneous generation of living organisms from nutrient broths.

Other Theories.—Charles Darwin's theory of evolution by natural selection simplified the problem of the origin of life. With this theory he could account for the evolution of the most complex plants and animals from the simplest single-celled organisms. Acceptance of his theory means the problem of origin of life is concerned with how this most primitive organism arose on earth.

It has been proposed that life was created by a supernatural event. This proposal, however, is not a scientific hypothesis since, by its very nature, it is not subject to experimental investigation.

In 1903, Savante Arrhenius offered a theory that life developed on earth as a result of a spore or other stable form of life coming to this planet in a meteorite from outer space or driven to the earth by the pressure of sunlight. One form of this theory assumes that life had no origin but, like matter, has always existed. Analysis of long-lived radioactive elements shows that the elements were formed about five billion years ago. If the elements have not always existed, it is difficult to understand how life could have always existed. Another form of this theory assumes that life was formed on another planet. However, most scientists doubt that any known form of life could survive for very long in outer space

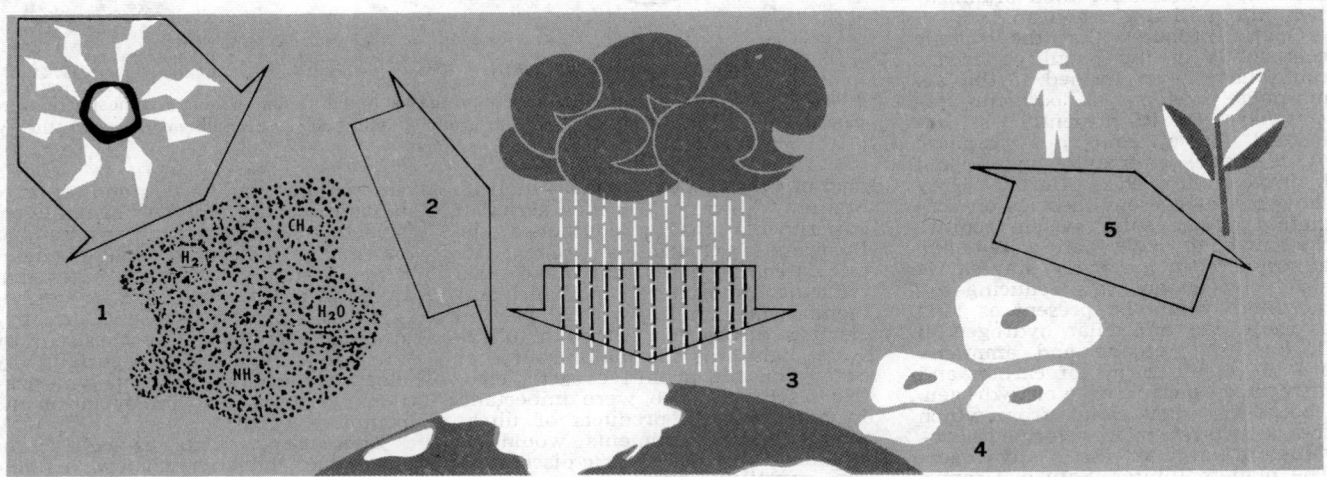

OPARIN'S THEORY maintained that sunlight caused a reaction of the materials in an oxidizing atmosphere (1), which contains hydrogen (H_2), ammonia (NH_3), methane (CH_4), and water (H_2O), to form simple organic compounds. These collected in clouds (2) and were carried to the earth (3) by precipitation. Continued reaction produced life forms (4) and, finally, more advanced life (5).

then fall through the earth's atmosphere without being destroyed. Therefore, although not disproved, this theory is held to be improbable.

It has been proposed that life developed from inorganic matter by a very improbable event—a spectacular accident. Such an organism would have had to live in an inorganic environment, and it would have had to synthesize all of its cellular components from carbon dioxide, water, and other inorganic materials. The chances for this improbable event are much too small for it to have occurred in the five billion years since the earth was formed.

■OPARIN'S THEORY.—The most plausible theory was proposed in 1938 by the Russian biologist, Alexander I. Oparin. He suggested that the first living organism arose spontaneously, not out of inorganic material, but out of the large quantities of organic material that he proposed were present in the oceans of the primitive earth. The simple organic compounds reacted to form structures of greater and greater complexity, until finally something was formed that could be called living. The formation of the first living organism was, then, the product of a series of simple reactions, none highly improbable.

Oparin's hypothesis is not in conflict with the demonstration by Pasteur that spontaneous generation does not take place. Pasteur only showed that spontaneous generation cannot take place at the present time and under present conditions. Such a demonstration does not say anything about spontaneous generation in the past and under different conditions. Two of the conditions necessary for spontaneous generation are that large quantities of organic compounds accumulate and that sufficient time is available for these compounds to organize into a living organism. This implies that spontaneous generation could occur on earth only when there was no life. Wherever there are living organisms, they will devour any organic compounds, thereby preventing their accumulation and reducing the time available for their organization into a living organism.

Oparin proposed that the organic compounds in the primitive oceans could have been formed if the atmosphere was not an *oxidizing atmosphere* as it presently is, but instead was a *reducing atmosphere* of methane, ammonia, water, and hydrogen. In 1952, Harold Urey showed that present theories on formation of the solar system require the earth to have had a reducing atmosphere in its early stages. He also showed that this reducing atmosphere would be present as long as there was molecular hydrogen in it, because methane and ammonia are the stable forms of carbon and nitrogen in the presence of hydrogen. The cosmic dust cloud, from which the solar system was formed, contained a large excess of hydrogen. The planets Jupiter, Saturn, Uranus, and Neptune still have reducing atmospheres. The planets Mercury, Venus, Earth, and Mars have developed oxidizing atmospheres since

they were formed. This results from the fact that a water molecule, when exposed to the ultraviolet light from the sun, splits into oxygen and hydrogen; the hydrogen escapes into outer space. The free oxygen does not escape, thus helping to form an oxidizing atmosphere. The atmospheres of Jupiter, Saturn, Uranus, and Neptune have not become oxidizing because the escape of hydrogen is very slow on these planets due to their low temperatures and high gravitational attraction.

duced hydroxy acids, fatty acids, urea, and a number of other organic compounds.

The amino acids were not produced directly by the electric discharge, but rather by the reaction of smaller molecules produced by it. The smaller molecules included hydrogen cyanide and aldehydes.

In 1961, John Oro showed how hydrogen cyanide could be used to synthesize adenine, one of the purine bases in nucleic acids. He simply allowed a concentrated solution of

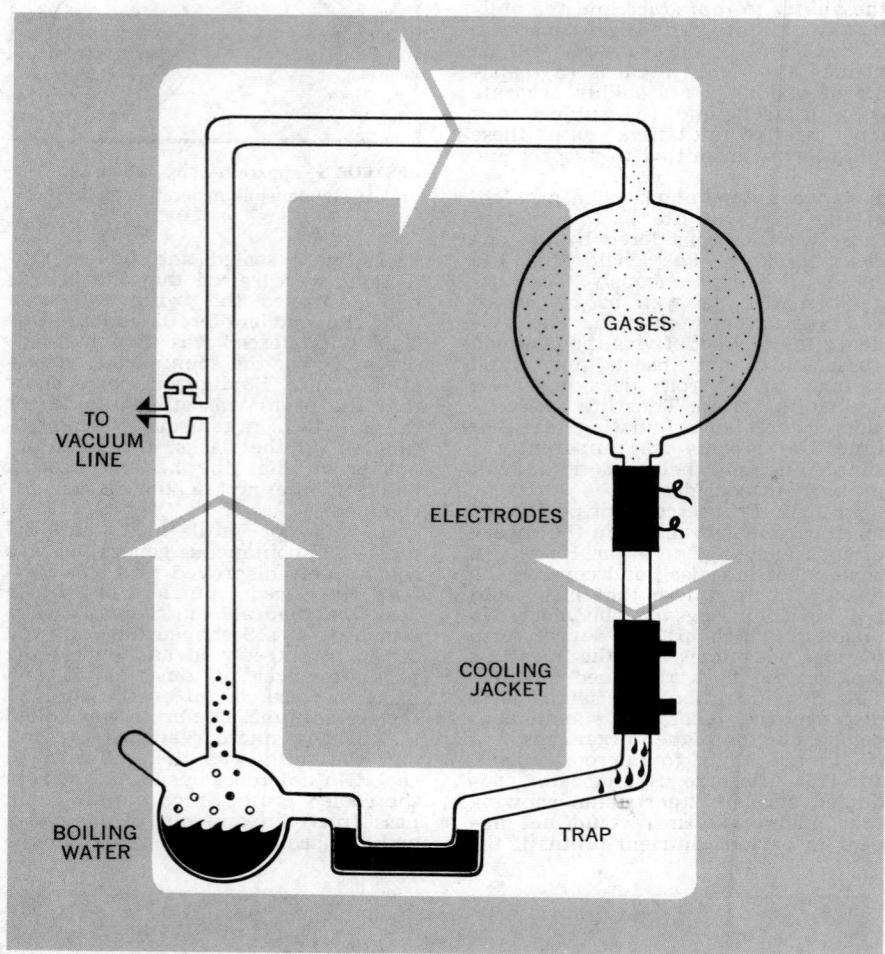

MILLER'S EXPERIMENT, in which the four gases found in an oxidizing atmosphere were passed through an electric discharge to produce amino acids, strengthened Oparin's theory.

Origin of Organic Compounds.—In 1953, Stanley Miller performed a series of experiments that strengthened the theories of Oparin and Urey. He circulated the gases that make up a reducing atmosphere (methane, ammonia, water, and hydrogen) past an electric discharge. Although ultraviolet light was the major source of energy on the primitive earth, electric discharges also were important. In addition, the products of ultraviolet light experiments would be similar to those of electric discharges. The result of Miller's experiments was the production of *amino acids,* the basic building blocks of proteins. In addition to the amino acids, the electric discharge experiments pro-

ammonium cyanide to stand. A large amount of black *polymer* of unknown structure formed, as well as a number of smaller molecules, including adenine. A number of other bases that occur in nucleic acids can be synthesized by similar processes. Since hydrogen cyanide is synthesized by ultraviolet light and especially by electric discharges, such polymerizations were probably important on the primitive earth.

These experiments, as well as related ones, have shown how a number of simple organic compounds may have been synthesized on the primitive earth. This is a small part of the total problem. It is still necessary to understand in more detail how the amino acids, purines, pyrimidine, sugars, and fatty acids were synthesized. An important problem is to show how *peptides,* which are polymers of the amino acids, could have been synthesized under conditions that were present on the primitive earth. The same problem occurs for the synthesis of polymers containing purines, pyrimidines, sugars, and phosphate. These polymers are called *polynucleotides.* There are also the various difficulties of organizing these polymers into structures that are able to perform a primitive "biological" function.

These are difficult problems, but they are all subject to laboratory investigation. In this area of science, what had been thought to be extremely difficult has frequently turned out to be very simple. Therefore, although there are no explanations for these problems at the present time, it is reasonable to believe they eventually will be solved, and with relatively simple answers.

Nature of First Living Organisms.—In present living organisms, reproduction proceeds by duplicating the genes, followed by the synthesis of more enzymes and other cell constituents, and division of the cell into two fragments. The *genes,* which are located in the *chromosomes,* are composed of *deoxyribonucleic acid,* or DNA. Mutations occur when the base composition of the DNA is changed by an imperfect duplication, by ionizing radiation, or by other factors. Since the characteristics required in order to call an organism "living" are the ability to duplicate and the ability to mutate, it has been proposed that the first living organism was simply a strand of DNA, which, with the presence of necessary enzymes, could duplicate.

This organism would be similar to a virus except that it would have the enzymes necessary for its reproduction. A virus consists of DNA—in some viruses, the nucleic acid is *ribonucleic acid* (RNA) instead of DNA—surrounded by a coat of protein. A virus is capable of duplication, but only within another living cell, where the virus makes use of the cell's enzymes and metabolites.

Oparin proposed a different model for the first living organism, a *coacervate particle.* (A coacervate is a type of *colloid*—a substance that consists of very small particles suspended in solution.) These coacervates would accumulate organic material from their environment, grow in size, and then split into two or more fragments. In the course of time, the coacervate particles would develop the ability to form fragments more and more like each other. Later, these coacervate particles would incorporate a genetic apparatus to carry out very accurate duplication.

Our knowledge of present living organisms would speak in favor of the DNA model for the first living organism. DNA carries the biological information for the synthesis of the entire organism. The duplication of DNA appears to be a simpler process than the synthesis of protein

and other cell constituents. DNA can be duplicated outside a living cell in a system containing the DNA to be duplicated, the *monomers* of the DNA, and a single enzyme. A system more complex than this would probably be needed to duplicate a strand of DNA on the primitive earth. A mechanism to accumulate the monomers and to hold the system together would probably be needed in addition to the single polymerizing enzyme. It might also be necessary for the first organism to synthesize this enzyme and perhaps several others. It is reasonable to think that such a system may have developed on the primitive earth.

Evolution of Early Organisms.—The first living organism must have obtained all of its small-molecule *metabolites* from the environment and then used these small molecules to build up polymers. There are many bacteria that obtain their metabolites from their environment. These are called *heterotrophic bacteria.* Many other bacteria and all plants synthesize their cell constituents from carbon dioxide, water, and other minerals; they are called *autotrophic organisms.* The first living organisms must have been heterotrophic organisms; it is necessary to explain how a heterotrophic organism could evolve into an autotrophic one, since the first organisms would have used up the available metabolites.

When the supply of a needed metabolite became exhausted, it must have been necessary for the organism to learn to synthesize this metabolite without which it would not have been able to live and to grow. A mechanism by which heterotrophic organisms could acquire various *biosynthetic pathways,* some of which are very long and complicated, was proposed in 1945 by Norman Horowitz. It has been found that the presence of an enzyme in an organism is often dependent on a single gene. This is known as the "one gene—one enzyme" hypothesis. Suppose that the synthesis of A involves the steps

$$D \xrightarrow{c} C \xrightarrow{b} B \xrightarrow{a} A$$

where *a, b,* and *c* are the enzymes, and A, B, and C are compounds that the organism cannot synthesize. If A becomes exhausted from the environment, then the organism must synthesize A in order to survive. It is extremely unlikely that there would be three simultaneous mutations to give the enzymes *a, b,* and *c;* but a single mutation to give enzyme *a* would not be unlikely. If compounds D, C, and B were in the environment when A was exhausted, an organism with enzyme *a* could survive while the others would die out. Similarly, when compound B was exhausted, enzyme *b* could arise by a single mutation, and organisms without this enzyme would die out. By continuing this process, the various steps of a biosynthetic process could be developed, with the last enzyme in the sequence being the first to develop, and the first enzyme developing last.

■**ENERGY SOURCES.**—Every organism must have a source of energy in order to carry out its metabolic functions. Animals obtain their energy from the oxidation of organic compounds. Plants obtain their energy from sunlight. There are many microorganisms that obtain their energy from simple fermentation reactions. For instance, the lactic acid bacteria obtain energy by fermenting glucose:

$$C_6H_{12}O_6 \longrightarrow 2CH_3CH(OH)COOH + \text{energy}$$
glucose   lactic acid

The energy appears in the biologically useful form of adenosine triphosphate (ATP). Fermentation reactions do not require the use of molecular oxygen, which was absent from the primitive earth. The first organisms could have obtained their energy supply by fermentation until the supply of fermentable compounds in the environment was exhausted. Then it would have been necessary to develop the more complicated process of photosynthesis. *Photosynthesis* is the process whereby the energy in sunlight is used to make ATP and to reduce carbon dioxide to carbohydrate. With the development of photosynthesis and the pathways for the synthesis of necessary metabolites, organisms would become autotrophic.

The general picture of the origin of life and early evolution presented here is believed by many scientists to be basically correct. However, there is little detailed knowledge of any of the various steps in this process and no knowledge at all of some of the difficult steps.

Although this discussion is directed toward the events that have taken place on our planet, the same process could have taken place on other planets as well. Those planets with the proper temperature and atmosphere could undergo a similar process of chemical evolution. Mars is the nearest planet where life may be present, even though the temperature is barely high enough for life, as we know it, to persist. In a few years devices for the detection of life will be sent to Mars. The finding of life on Mars would confirm our ideas about the origin of life occurring under favorable conditions, and would be one of the greatest achievements of modern science.

It is likely that most stars have planetary systems. Life might also have arisen on many of these planets and may still be there. It follows that some of these planets may have very advanced civilizations that are attempting to communicate with other planets. Some attempts are being made to detect such signals. This is a very difficult technical problem, but the scientific results are of sufficient interest to warrant that some effort be made to detect these signals.

—Stanley Miller

BIBLIOGRAPHY

OPARIN, A. I. *The Origin of Life.* Dover Books, Inc., 1962.
SCHRODINGER, ERWIN. *What Is Life?* Cambridge University Press, 1963.

MICROBIOLOGY

Scope.—*Microbiology* is the study of microscopic living creatures. Generally, it is the study of viruses, *Rickettsiae*, bacteria, protozoa, yeasts, molds, and the small algae, thus including both plant and animal kingdoms. Some authorities do not use these kingdoms for the forms of life that show no tissue differentiation, but instead place them all in the kingdom *Protista*, a group established in 1866 by the German zoologist Ernst Heinrich Haeckel (1834–1919).

Cell Types.—Microorganisms, with the exception of viruses, are organized into two cell types, according to the structure of the nucleus. If there is a visible nucleus, the cell is *eucaryotic*. If the nucleus is not visible, the cell is *procaryotic*.

Eucaryotic cells have a definite outer cell membrane that varies from an unsupported, flexible membrane in animal-like cells to a fragile membrane inside a rigid cell wall in plant-like cells. The cell is filled with a more or less fluid material, *cytoplasm,* which contains a variety of granules (*plastids*) and membranes that function in the metabolism of the cell. The cytoplasm generally is in motion except during cell division.

■**PLASTIDS.**—There are two kinds of plastids. One, the *protoplast,* is a colorless granule that contains many of the cell's respiratory and synthetic functions assembled in a highly organized state. All eucaryotic cells have at least one protoplast and cannot live without it.

The other plastid, the *chloroplast,* occurs in plant cells in addition to the protoplast. The chloroplast contains chlorophyll and all mechanisms for synthesizing chemical compounds through the process of *photosynthesis*. The simplest eucaryotic algae contain one protoplast and one chloroplast. Chloroplasts are not essential for life —since some single-celled plants may lose their chloroplast and still be able to live on dissolved food materials. Once a chloroplast has been lost, there is no evidence of its regeneration from the cytoplasm.

■**NUCLEUS.**—The *nucleus* is suspended in the cytoplasm but is separated from it by a definite membrane. The nucleus contains the *chromosomes,* the hereditary material of the cell, which govern the structure and function of the rest of the cell. The cell usually multiplies by splitting in two. Prior to this, the chromosomes divide, half going into each new nucleus. Chromosomes are composed of *deoxyribonucleic acid (DNA),* which is not found in any other structure. Its sole function is to duplicate itself before cell division and to serve as a primary pattern or information center containing all the instructions that a cell or higher organism needs to grow and develop properly. If the DNA makes an error in duplicating itself, a mutation results. The mutant cell is either unable to function properly and therefore dies, or it lives on but is different from the parent cell; its *progeny,* or offspring, will

continue to be different in the same way. Since a mutation is always inheritable, evolution is thought to have occurred through a series of mutations. Some mutations add characteristics to the cell or higher forms of life that make the organism better able to compete for food and the other necessities of life. Most mutations, however, cause the loss or damage of a characteristic; such mutations usually are harmful to the species and have no value in its evolution.

■**EUCARYOTIC CELLS.**—Some eucaryotic cells either do not have a cell membrane, or have only an incomplete wall between nuclei. This is true of most of the molds. Such plants look and behave like a large cell with many nuclei. The eucaryotic microorganisms include most algae, protozoans, molds, and yeasts.

■**PROCARYOTIC CELLS.**—Procaryotic cells differ from eucaryotic cells primarily in lacking a definite nucleus surrounded by its own membrane. They do, however, contain nuclear material in the form of many small strands of DNA that behave as a single chromosome. The internal organization of procaryotic cells, such as those of bacteria and blue-green algae, is not well understood. However, the cytoplasm is free of plastids and does not move. The chlorophyll of the blue-green algae and the photosynthetic bacteria is not in special organs, but is organized in some unrecognized fashion. Procaryotic microorganisms include the blue-green algae, bacteria, and *Rickettsiae*.

Viruses.—*Viruses* are the smallest of the microorganisms and lack the structural complexity of a cell. Their unit is a particle that is able to cause a host plant, animal, or bacterium to make more virus. This infective unit, called a *virion,* ranges in size from about 0.025 micron (poliomyelitis virus) up to about 0.3 micron (smallpox virus). A *micron, μ,* is $\frac{1}{1,000}$ of a millimeter, or about $\frac{1}{25,000}$ of an

inch. Most viruses are too small to be seen with the light microscope, which has a maximum useful magnification of about 2,000 diameters. The electron microscope, which can produce magnifications of more than 100,000 diameters, can be used to photograph viruses. Some viruses are called *filterable viruses* because they can pass through a filter of unglazed porcelain that holds back bacteria.

A virus lacks usual cellular structure and instead consists of a nucleic acid associated with protein. The nucleic acid may be DNA, the material from which chromosomes are formed, or *ribonucleic acid (RNA)*, which serves as a secondary pattern for synthesis of cellular components.

A virus is not capable of independent life and reproduction, and must multiply within the cells of a host. Hence, viruses are *obligately parasitic*. Apparently, viral nucleic acid intrudes into a cell in such a way that the host cell's nucleic acid loses control of the cell's function. The cell then makes more virus particles instead of its own nuclear and cytoplasmic materials. The presence of a virus in a host usually causes changes recognizable as a disease, although animal viruses have been found that cause no recognizable symptoms in the host. These are called *orphan viruses*.

■**VIRAL PLANT DISEASES.**—Plant diseases of viral origin include the mosaics. The tobacco mosaic virus (TMV) was isolated by Wendell Stanley in a crystalline form and has remained infective after years of storage in a bottle. This virus has also been separated into its two components, protein and nucleic acid, and regenerated by their subsequent reunion. The protein, however, is not necessary for infection if it is possible for the nucleic acid to enter the cell without its aid. The protein may act as an enzyme, dissolving part of the cell wall to admit the nucleic acid fraction.

■**VIRAL ANIMAL DISEASES.**—Animal and human diseases caused by viruses

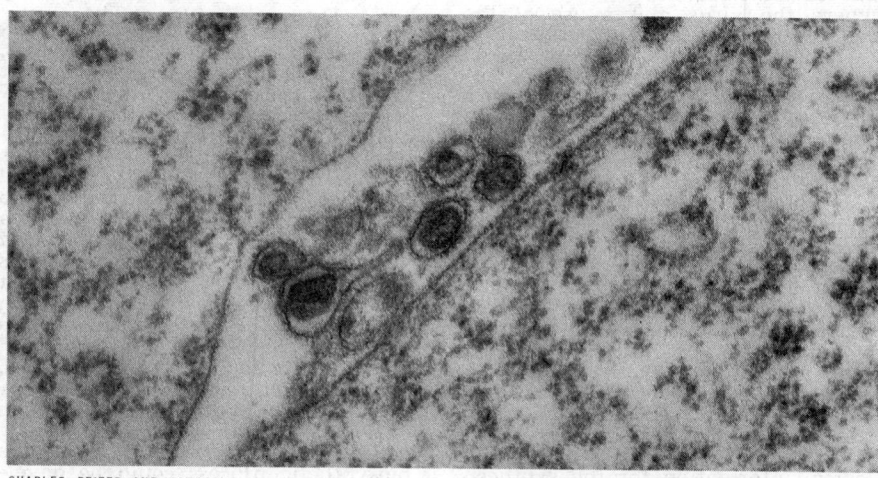

CHARLES PFIZER AND COMPANY

LEUKEMIA VIRUS in mouse tissue as seen through an electron microscope. Clearly visible are the outer shell of the virus, the dense nucleoid, and also the small, tail-like structure.

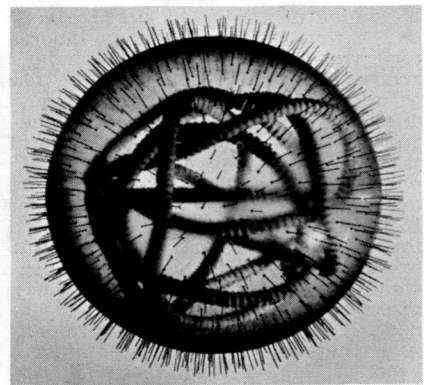

CHARLES PFIZER AND COMPANY

MEASLES VIRUS is classed as a cubic form. This model was designed from micrographs.

include yellow fever, distemper, hoof-and-mouth disease, influenza, psittacosis, measles, mumps, poliomyelitis, chickenpox, smallpox, and the common cold.

Viral diseases are transmitted to human beings and animals by various means. The virus that causes yellow fever is transmitted from person to person by the mosquito *Aedes aegypti*. The mosquito is infected when it bites a diseased person; if the mosquito later bites a healthy person, the virus may be transmitted. In the tropics, reservoirs of viral infection are maintained in monkeys, marmosets, and perhaps other species of animals. Psittacosis (parrot fever), primarily a disease of birds, is caused by a virus that infects parrots, parakeets, canaries, and other birds; human beings then contract it from infected birds. The disease, carried in bird droppings, is increasing in the United States as the sale of birds expands. The highly contagious hoof-and-mouth disease of livestock is of economic importance. The virus, transmitted by ingestion of contaminated particles, attacks the mouth and hoofs. Man may contract the disease in the same manner. Many viral diseases, such as measles, mumps, and influenza, are transmitted by simple contact with patients or by contact with infected materials. The virus of rabies is usually transmitted by the bite of an infected animal. Recently, an abundance of evidence has been found proving that some forms of animal cancers are caused by viruses. There is good reason to believe that some types of human cancer might also be caused by viruses.

Many human and animal viruses can be grown outside their normal hosts if they are inoculated into fertile chicken eggs before they hatch, or if they are inoculated into cultures of animal tissue cells maintained outside of the whole body. This use of chicken embryos and tissue cultures has made possible the laboratory cultivation of large quantities of viruses and has led to new methods of immunization against viral diseases.

A virus that appears to be of little if any importance to man, except as a tool, is the type that infects bacteria, a *bacteriophage*—literally, a "bacteria-eater." (The bacteriophages are treated more fully in the discussion of bacteria.)

Bacteria.—The *bacteria,* larger than viruses, are organized with a cellular structure contained within a rigid cell wall. They are usually divided into three large groups, depending on their shape. The spherical bacteria are *cocci* (singular, *coccus*), the cylindrical are *bacilli* (singular, *bacillus*), and the spiral ones are *spirilla* (singular, *spirillum*). Multiplication of bacterial cells occurs by simple splitting of the cell into two new cells, each of which can then grow and split again. Under ideal conditions this process can occur as often as every twenty minutes. Bacilli and spirilla usually split across the short diameter of the cell, and the newly formed cells seldom hang together for long. However, some species of bacilli form long chains of cells. The cocci have a more complicated system of multiplication that has led to their division into several groups. The *staphylococci* split in a random fashion, producing grapelike clusters. The *streptococci* always divide in the same plane and produce chains of cells. The *tetracocci,* or *gaffkya,* split alternately in two planes at right angles to each other, producing flat sheets of cells. The *sarcina* split successively in three planes at right angles to each other so that they tend to form cubical packets of eight cells.

The smallest bacteria are barely larger than some viruses, about 0.5 μ in diameter. Cocci are generally from 0.5 to 1.0 μ across. Bacilli vary in size, but most are from 0.5 to 1.0 μ across and 1 to 5 μ in length. Spirilla are about the size of bacilli or a little larger. A few giant bacteria will form cells over 50 μ long.

About 2,000 species of bacteria have been found. They are considered to be plantlike because of their rigid cell walls. Since there are so few basic shapes of bacteria, they are classified on the basis of size and shape, the materials they use as food, and the products formed from the food. The products are acids, alcohols, gases, pigments, and toxins. Oxygen relationship is also important. Those bacteria capable of growth only in the presence of air are called *aerobic;* those that cannot grow in the presence of air are called *anaerobic.* Bacteria able to grow in either situation are said to be *facultatively anaerobic.*

A few bacteria contain a special type of chlorophyll and hence are able to live photosynthetically in a manner similar to that of green plants. Bacterial photosynthesis differs from that of green plants mainly in that it is anaerobic and oxygen is not produced. Instead, oxidized organic compounds or sulfur compounds are the end products. Most photosynthetic bacteria contain a high concentration of *carotenoid pigments;* consequently, instead of appearing green, they are red or brown. There are a few green bacteria.

Most bacteria utilize nonliving organic materials for food and for growth, causing the materials' break-

down or decay. In fact, every naturally occurring organic material, including rubber, paraffin, and asphalt, can be used as a source of food by some microorganism. This breakdown is called *saprophytic action.* A few bacterial species are able to oxidize simple inorganic materials and secure their energy for growth from such processes. These processes include oxidations of ammonia, nitrites, sulfur, sulfides, hydrogen, carbon monoxide, iron, and manganese. Few, if any, bacteria are strictly parasitic. Many pathogenic (disease-causing) bacteria are unable to survive for long under natural conditions except in the host animal, but most of them have been cultivated in the laboratory on nonliving materials.

■**BACTERIAL MOVEMENT.**—Many bacteria cannot move by their own efforts. Some, however, have hairlike projections from the cell that enable them to swim rapidly in a liquid medium. These projections are called *flagella* (singular, *flagellum*). They may occur singly or in clusters at the ends of the cells, or may be scattered over the cell's surface. Bacterial species with a single terminal flagellum seem to swim as well as those having many flagella. How flagella are used to swim is not known. Most bacterial flagella are too small to be seen except when stained by a special method in which the stain accumulates around them so that they become visible under the microscope.

All bacteria have an outer slime layer that generally is thin and may be difficult to detect. Some bacteria, however, have a very thick gelatinous slime layer, a capsule, that can easily be seen. Some disease-causing bacteria, such as the *pneumococcus,* are able to resist defense mechanisms of the host because the latter react with the capsular material and do not

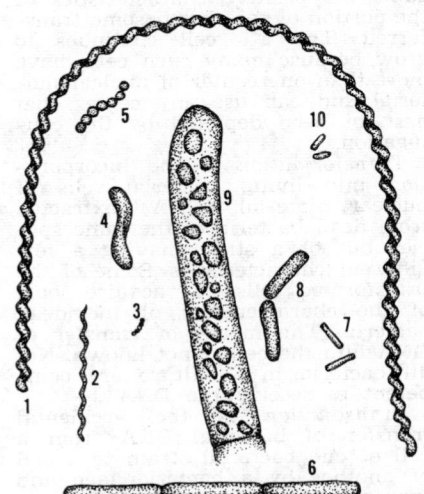

BACTERIA of various sizes and shapes: (1) *Spirochaeta plicatilis;* (2) *Treponema pallidum;* (3) *Peptostreptococcus parvulus;* (4) *Spirillum undula;* (5) *Streptococcus pyogenes;* (6) *Bacillus anthracis;* (7) *Mycobacterium tuberculosis;* (8) *Bacillus megatherium;* (9) *Beggiatoa alba;* and (10) *Bordetella pertussis.*

contact the bacterial cell itself.

A few species of the bacilli produce dormant forms that are more resistant to killing by heat, drying, and chemicals than are the original cells. These forms are called *spores* and are the most heat-tolerant form of life known. Spores of some species will survive boiling-water temperatures for several hours. The bacterial spore is thought to be a means of survival, not reproduction: a single cell usually forms but one spore, and when conditions are favorable for germination, that spore forms only one new growing cell.

The bacterial cell's nucleus is apparently not a clearly defined structure separated from the rest of the cell by its own membrane. The nucleus does, however, contain the cell's hereditary material (DNA), which controls the cell's processes in a manner that is probably similar to that in cells that have a well-defined nucleus. The bacteria that have been studied most completely appear to have only a single chromosome in the nuclear material. Since the chromosomes are not paired (*diploid*), the cell is *haploid;* and there are no dominant and recessive characteristics. Exchanges of nuclear material can occur in bacteria in at least three ways. These are recombination, transformation, and transduction. The latter two processes are apparently confined to bacteria.

■**NUCLEAR MATERIAL EXCHANGE.** — *Recombination* occurs when two bacterial cells conjugate, or mate, and part of a chromosome is transferred from one to the other. Donor (F+) strains always transfer to recipient (F−) strains. Usually conjugation is a rare process, but a few F+ strains combine readily with F− strains and are therefore called *high-frequency recombinants* (*HFR*). After conjugation, the F− cell becomes F+ and gains the positive characteristics of the portion of the chromosome transferred. The F+ cell continues to grow because many such cells have more than one center of nuclear material and can use any center that has not been depleted by the conjugation.

Transformation is the incorporation into living bacterial cells of nuclear material (DNA) extracted from dead bacteria of the same species but of a strain having a few different characteristics. Some of the transformed cells will acquire some of the characteristics of the dead bacteria. The means of transfer of DNA into the cell is not known. Not all bacteria in a culture are competent to receive the DNA.

Transduction is the accidental transfer of bacterial DNA from a cell of one bacterial strain to a cell of another by a bacteriophage and the incorporation of this DNA into the chromosome of the recipient bacterium. The resulting cell has the positive characteristics of both cells for the portion of the chromosome transferred. This transfer requires that the bacteriophage be propagated on a bacterial strain that is destroyed by the virus, and that the recipient strain of bacteria be one that har-

bors the virus but is not ordinarily destroyed by it. Bacteria of the latter type are called *lysogenic* and may carry the virus with little or no evidence of infection.

Most of the work on transfer of nuclear material among bacteria has been done on the genera *Escherichia, Salmonella,* and *Shigella.* There is evidence that these three processes occur in most genera of bacteria.

■**CLASSIFICATION.** — Bacteria have been classified in many ways. A completely *phylogenetic system,* one based upon obvious relationships and evolutionary patterns, is not possible with our present knowledge and perhaps may never be satisfactorily achieved. There are several large groups that have the status of orders and appear to be valid subdivisions of bacteria. The current system of classification, presented in the seventh edition of Bergey's *Manual of Determinative Bacteriology,* lists nine orders of bacteria. Four orders are listed below; the other five orders are of doubtful phylogenetic significance and may be listed as variations of true bacteria.

The *Eubacteriales* include the simple, or true, bacteria that have definite shapes and rigid cell walls. They multiply by transverse fission and do not show branching of cells. If they are motile, they move by means of flagella.

The *Myxobacteriales* are the slime bacteria that have no definite cell wall. They do not have flagella but are motile by a gliding motion, the explanation of which is unknown. The whole colony of cells may be motile and move across a surface in a small mound of secreted slime. The colony may organize into a complex fruiting body in which some cells form a base and others, a stalk. A few may become resting stages called *microcysts.* These dry and may be spread by the wind. New colonies of myxobacteria are started if they fall upon a suitable food source. Myxobacterial colonies are often found growing on animal dung deposits.

The *Actinomycetales* include the filamentous bacteria that often show true branching of the filaments. The intergradations between these and the eubacteria are so numerous that there is no clear line of demarcation.

The *Spirochaetales* form the order of the helical bacteria that are flexible, yet retain the coils of the helix. The spiral cell is wrapped around an axial filament that prevents the cell from straightening.

■**CONTROL OF BACTERIA.** — Bacteria can be useful, harmful, or of no known importance to man. They are present in large numbers in most soils and waters and are carried in the air by dust particles. They are abundant on the skin, in the mouth, and in the digestive system of all animals. All ordinary objects have bacteria or microorganisms on their outer surfaces. Since some bacteria cause disease and many contribute to food spoilage, it is important to be able to control their activities. It is necessary to sterilize equipment to be used during surgical treatment of patients and to sterilize foods that are to be preserved for long periods.

It is also necessary to sterilize containers for materials used in laboratory work when controlled changes are to be brought about by the use of a pure culture containing only one microbial species. The most common method of sterilization is use of steam under a pressure of about 15 pounds per square inch to give a temperature of 248° F. (121° C.) for 15 to 20 minutes. The apparatus used for this heat treatment is a large pressure cooker, an *autoclave.* Large containers of liquids or cans of dense, viscous material may have to be heated for an hour or more to ensure that all of the contents have been at 248° F. for the necessary length of time. Dry materials that should not be exposed to steam can generally be sterilized by heating them to 338° F. (170° C.) for two hours. If the material to be sterilized is severely altered by the heat treatment, chemical methods, although less convenient than heat, are available for sterilizing solid objects. Some liquids can be sterilized by passing them through a filter that holds back the bacteria. This will not, however, remove viruses; and if it is important that viruses be inactivated, this usually can be done by exposing thin layers of the liquid to high concentrations of ultraviolet light.

A reduction in the numbers of bacteria or complete sterility of water to be used for drinking, bottling, or industrial processes usually can be achieved by chemical treatment. Chlorine in a concentration of 0.1 to 1.0 parts per million bromine, or iodine is generally effective.

Where sterility is not as important as the destruction of disease-causing bacteria or the improvement of keeping quality by reducing the numbers of bacteria, pasteurization is the usual treatment. This relatively mild heat treatment was initiated by Louis Pasteur (1822–1895) to eliminate bacteria that spoil beer and wine. As it is commonly applied today to milk, pasteurization may use a temperature of 143° F. (61.3° C.) for 30 minutes or 161° F. (71.6° C.) for 15 to 20 seconds. Either process kills the bacteria that cause tuberculosis and brucellosis, as well as many of the common milk spoilage bacteria.

Early investigators did not understand that bacteria are everywhere and did not know that many of them can grow in the absence of air. Nor did they know that some species produce heat-resistant spores. Their crude methods of sterilization therefore generally failed, and subsequent growth of bacteria in the inadequately sterilized materials led them to believe that these living forms had originated spontaneously. The classical argument between J. T. Needham (1713–1781) and Lazzaro Spallanzani (1729–1799) in the eighteenth century pointed out the difficulties in establishing that spontaneous generation of life is not a common event under present conditions. The extensive experiments of Pasteur during the 1860's demonstrated that spontaneous generation of microorganisms does not occur— even bacteria must have ancestors.

■BACTERIAL DISEASES.

—The demonstration that bacteria can cause disease and that a particular bacterial species is always the cause of the same disease was made by the German physician Robert Koch (1843–1910) and his students during the period from 1870 to 1890. The rules for the establishment of this relationship are known as *Koch's postulates.* Four conditions must be achieved: (1) The suspected microorganism must be present in every case of the disease. (2) A pure culture of the microorganism must be obtained from a case of the disease. (3) The pure culture must cause the same disease when inoculated into a suitable experimental animal. (4) The original microorganism must be reisolated from the experimental case of the disease. These criteria often have been used to establish the cause-and-effect relationship between a particular bacterial species and a disease.

Some diseases in man caused by bacteria are scarlet fever, boils, diphtheria, bacillary dysentery, typhoid fever, whooping cough, pneumococcal pneumonia, asiatic cholera, tuberculosis, tetanus, gonorrhea, syphilis, and leprosy.

There are also many bacterial diseases of plants. Among these are fire blight of apple and pear trees, crown gall of trees and flowering plants, bean blight, tomato wilt, and soft rots of many vegetables.

Large quantities of foods are spoiled because of bacterial activities. Both stored fresh foods and canned foods that have been improperly sealed or processed are subject to spoilage. Several types of spoilage are of more than economic importance; poisonous toxins are sometimes produced and cause severe illness or death of persons who eat the affected food. *Staphylococci, streptococci, salmonellae,* and one of the anaerobic spore-forming bacilli, *Clostridium perfringens,* form toxins when they grow in food that has not been adequately refrigerated after preparation. These toxins may cause severe illness, but are seldom fatal. *Clostridium botulinum,* growing in canned or salted foods that have been inadequately processed, produces a toxin commonly fatal to man. Many cases of botulism have been caused by eating home-canned vegetables, but smoked fish have also been implicated. The toxin is destroyed by boiling food for ten minutes before it is eaten.

The manner in which a disease is transmitted depends in a measure on the living habits of the bacterium that causes it. Thus, the typhoid fever organism, *Salmonella typhosa,* which is carried in the feces, can contaminate meat, milk, shellfish, and water. It may infect subclinical carriers, who actually cause more outbreaks than persons with a full-blown case of typhoid. Infected food handlers are an important source of the disease. The gonococcus, *Neisseria gonorrhoeae,* attacks the mucous membranes of the genital tract and is usually transmitted during sexual intercourse. The whooping cough organism, *Bordetella pertussis,* is trans-

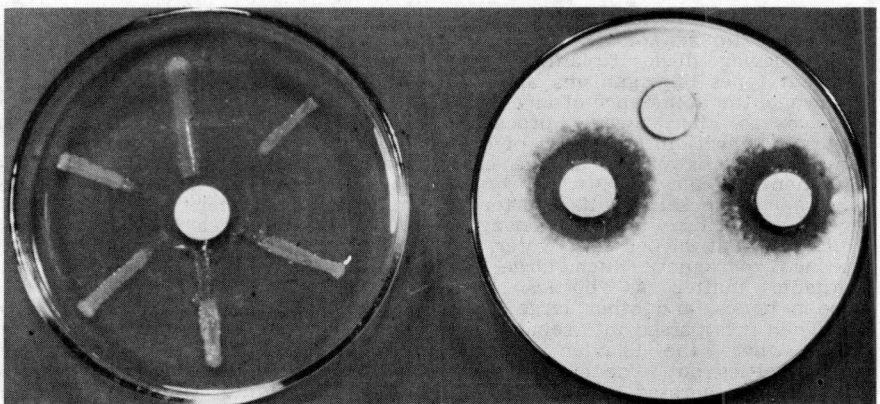

CHARLES PFIZER AND COMPANY

SCREENING PROCESS to test the antibiotic power of mold fluids. The dish on the left contains one mold fluid and six different germs; that on the right, four mold fluids and one germ organism. The dark rings signify fluids that are effective against the organisms.

mitted by inhalation of droplets from a coughing victim. Cholera is transmitted by contaminated water and food and by flies infected with the cholera organism, *Vibrio comma;* it may also be spread by person-to-person contact.

■INDUSTRIAL USES.

—Bacteria have important industrial uses. Indeed, many huge industries entirely depend upon bacterial action for their existence.

In the manufacture of cheese, cultures of bacteria are added to pasteurized milk. These bacteria slowly ferment the lactose to lactic acid and break down fats and proteins to produce substances that are responsible for the various flavors, textures, and aromas that characterize the different types of cheese. In fact, the "eyes" in Swiss cheese owe their existence to carbon dioxide made by bacteria.

To make commercial vinegar, the bacterium *Acetobacter* is used to oxidize alcohol to acetic acid, which in a concentration of about 4 per cent in water constitutes commercial vinegar. In the process, the alcohol trickles over a bed of shavings or other finely divided material that has been inoculated with the bacteria.

Bacterial fermentation is important in the manufacture of many other food products, such as sauerkraut, pickles, soy sauce, yogurt, and butter.

Bacteria are also used to make industrial chemicals. Species of the genus *Clostridium* ferment carbohydrates to produce butyl alcohol, isopropyl (rubbing) alcohol, acetone, and numerous other substances used in the manufacture of drugs, paints, synthetic rubber, explosives, and some plastics.

The brewing and related industries utilize bacteria. Species of the genus *Bacillus* produce enzymes from such organic wastes as soybean or peanut cake. These enzymes are used to convert raw starches into materials that can be fermented by yeasts. The textile and paper industries also make wide use of enzymes.

Mixtures of microorganisms are used in separating flax or hemp fiber from the woody plant tissue. Similarly, hides are subjected to bacterial action in leather-making. Bacteria

are even used to remove sulfur compounds from petroleum.

Following Sir Alexander Fleming's (1881–1955) discovery in 1929 of the antibacterial action of penicillin (derived from the mold *Penicillium notatum*), Selman Waksman, René Dubos, and others sought other types of antibiotics among bacterial species. They found that the soil bacterium *Streptomyces* is especially antagonistic to pathogenic organisms, and species of this organism have yielded streptomycin, chloramphenicol, erythromycin, neomycin, and many other antibiotics useful in the treatment of a host of infectious diseases. Bacitracin and subtilin derive from species of *Bacillus*. Xerosin comes from *Achromabacter*. Millions of lives have been saved during the past 20 years because of the discovery of antibiotics. Today, drug manufacturers sell more than $75,000,000 worth of antibiotics annually; as a class of medicals their sales are rivaled only by the vitamins.

■BACTERIA AND WATER.

—Microorganisms are used in one of the methods for the purification of municipal water supplies and also in the purification of sewage in sewage disposal plants. In purifying water supplies by the slow sand filter, the raw water, perhaps from a river, is filtered through sand and gravel beds. As filtration proceeds, a slimy, jelly-like film accumulates around each sand grain, particularly in the upper few inches of sand. This film is composed of billions of bacteria and protozoa; and as it develops, it slows the flow of water through the sand. The water is purified by the action of enzymes, by biological oxidation and reduction processes, and by the ingestion of bacteria by the protozoa in the film. The filter removes about 99 per cent of the impurities from raw water.

The more recent and more commonly used rapid sand filter method of purifying water depends upon a thin layer of a chemical gel on the sand and upon other chemical treatments for removal of organic compounds and bacteria from the water. Both processes are generally followed by the addition of chlorine to complete the sterilization of the water.

■BACTERIA AND SEWAGE.—Bacteria are vital to sewage disposal plants. Many different types of organisms abound in sewage; the abundance of any type changes as the sewage proceeds toward purification. One form of organism succeeds others as the environment changes.

Sewage disposal plants perform several functions. First, the sewage, which is about 95 per cent water, is screened to remove such large or inorganic matter as bottles and wooden boxes, and other large refuse. Then it is passed into separation tanks, where the heavier organic matter settles out. The supernatant liquid is then aerated by one of several processes to help the bacteria decompose the dissolved organic materials. This step is generally followed by another sedimentation, and the final water is chlorinated to remove harmful bacteria before it is discharged into a river, lake, or ocean.

The organic sediment from these treatments is pumped into closed tanks, or *sludge digesters,* and heated to about 100° F. Under these conditions the anaerobic bacteria produce a stable product that will not putrify later. The water from the sludge digesters is discharged with the other water; the sediment is dried and sold as fertilizer. The gases from the sludge digester are about 75 per cent methane, the same material as natural gas, which can be used to heat the digestion tanks and can be burned in gas engines to run the pumps in the sewage treatment plant.

Nearly all forms of organic materials are decomposed by bacteria during sewage treatment. Because of their slow rate of decomposition, however, greases and oils are usually skimmed off and burned.

■BACTERIA IN AGRICULTURE.— Agriculture is largely dependent upon microorganisms for decomposition of plant roots and other items in the soil and for conversion of nitrogen-, phosphorus-, and sulfur-containing materials into forms useful to plants. Some soil bacteria can take nitrogen from the atmosphere and build it into their bodies, thus eventually contributing to the fertility of the soil. This process, called *nitrogen fixation,* also occurs in root nodules of many plants in situations where the plants and bacteria of various types grow together in an association beneficial to both. The best example of such a *symbiotic* (living together) association is that found between the bacteria of the genus *Rhizobium* and the legumes, plants such as peas, beans, clover, alfalfa, and locust trees. When the proper strain of *Rhizobium* invades the plant rootlet, a nodule containing the bacteria develops on the root. The nodule is the site of nitrogen fixation, which enables legumes to grow well in soils deficient in nitrogen and therefore unable to support other plants. There are various other symbiotic associations.

■ANIMALS AND BACTERIA. — Although animals can live without bacteria in their environment, as has been shown by the raising of large colonies of "germ-free" animals, many animals benefit greatly from the presence of bacteria in their digestive systems. In the *rumen* (first stomach) of cattle, sheep, goats, deer, antelope, and other ruminant animals, bacteria and protozoa are responsible for the digestion of much of the food, especially the cellulose and other difficult-to-digest portions of the food. The microorganisms ferment these products and produce a number of acids from them. The acids, chiefly acetic, propionic, and butyric, are absorbed by the animal and metabolized as sources of energy. Microorganisms may help the animal by producing vitamins and proteins that can later be digested in the true stomach and utilized. A similar situation exists in the caeca of horses and some rodents.

Study of bacteria began as an applied science because of their relationship to disease, agriculture, and industrial processes. In recent years, investigators have attempted to study bacteria to learn more about the bacteria themselves. These studies have given much knowledge about the metabolism and genetics of higher plants and animals, because the basic chemical reactions of living creatures are all fundamentally similar. Because of rapid growth of bacteria, large crops of cells can be grown under carefully controlled conditions in a few hours. Similarly, genetic studies that need large populations or many generations have profited from observations of bacteria. The results of crossing various strains of bacteria can be observed in a few hours or days instead of the months or years that are required when higher plants or animals are used.

Rickettsiae.—*Rickettsiae* are intracellular parasites of the size and shape of small bacteria. They differ from bacteria in that they are dependent upon a host cell for part of their life processes. They have not been cultivated outside of a living host. Most *Rickettsiae* appear to be parasites of insects, ticks, or mites. They may or may not cause recognized illness in their normal host. Some, when transferred to other species, such as man, cause disease. Generally, rickettsial diseases are transmitted to man by the bite of their normal host—typhus fever by the body louse, tsutsugamushi fever by the mite, Rocky Mountain spotted fever by a tick. An exception to this is Q fever, caused by *Coxiella burnetii.* The fever is transmitted through milk from cattle to man, or by one's inhaling dust containing the dried manure of infected cattle. *Rickettsiae* usually can be cultivated in fertile chicken eggs; laboratory cultures are maintained in this manner.

Fungi.—The term *fungus* is poorly defined, but it includes those eucaryotic plantlike organisms that lack chlorophyll and the tissue differentiation of higher plants. Fungi vary in size from the single-celled yeasts, smaller than large bacteria, to mushrooms. Such related forms as puffballs may reach several feet in diameter.

The most commonly observed fungal growth is a cotton-like mass of filaments (*mycelium*) called *mold.* The individual filaments (*hyphae*) grow from the tip and may branch repeatedly. They have a chitin-like rigid wall and many nuclei. The nuclei may or may not be separated by cross walls (*septa*) in the hyphae; but even where septa are present, separation is generally incomplete, and the cytoplasm streams continuously through the mycelium.

Molds and other fungi with mycelia are abundant in the soil, where they are responsible for the decomposition of most dead plant material. Most of the mycelial structure is invisible to the naked eye. We become aware of it only when an unusually large amount of organic matter leads to the production of mycelia and mold fruiting bodies on its surface.

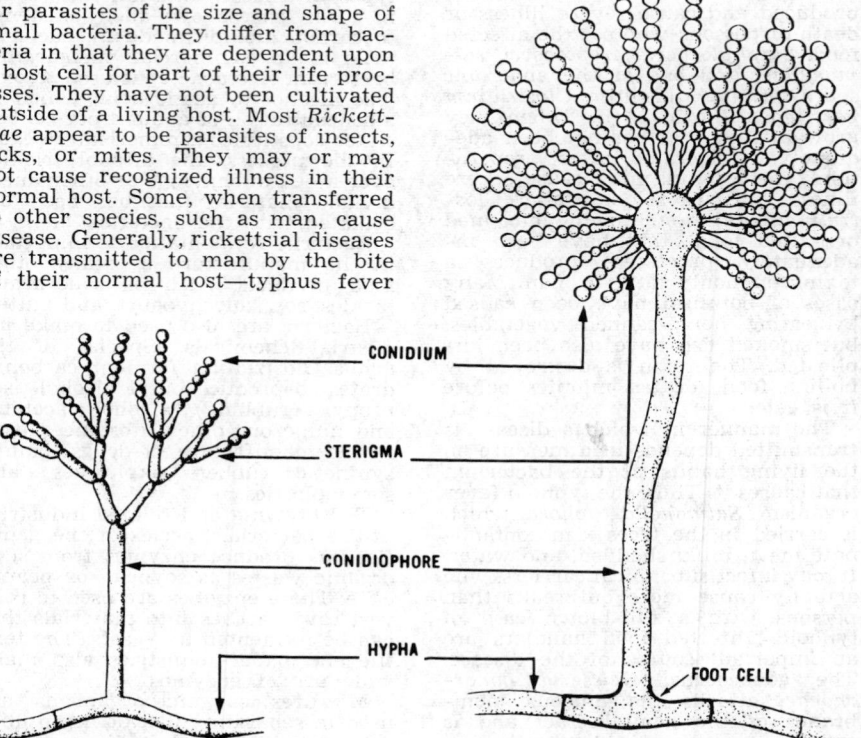

FUNGI occur in many types and forms. These two, *Penicillium* (*left*) and *Aspergillus* (*right*), are typical. Spores are produced at the tip of the branch called a *sterigma.*

■**REPRODUCTION OF FUNGI.**—Fungi reproduce by forming a variety of small bodies called *spores*. Many of these, such as those most often formed by molds of the genus *Penicillium*, are small spheres exuded from the tips of special mycelial cells. They are called asexual spores because no nuclear fusion is required for their formation. Spores of this mold can often be seen on moldy oranges or cheese. They are green or blue-green and give it its characteristic color.

Most fungi have a sexual process for forming spores after the fusion of nuclei from two different mycelia or within multinucleated mycelia. Some of these processes are complex and lead to special spore-bearing organs such as the mushrooms.

■**FUNGAL DISEASES.**—Many fungi cause diseases of plants; a few infect animals. Some fungi cause rust on grain and most other groups of plants.

than the feet, often the hands.

■**USES OF FUNGI.**—Fungi are useful in the production of drugs and chemicals. The first of the antibiotics, penicillin, was discovered as a product of *Penicillium notatum. P. chysogenum* is now used for commercial preparation of penicillin. Fungi are also used to produce commercial quantities of citric and gluconic acids and such enzymes as amylase, cellulase, and glucose oxidase.

Yeasts.—A large miscellaneous group of fungi that seldom form mycelia but that generally grow as oval or round cells is known as yeasts. Many have a spore stage that follows fusion of nuclei from two cells. Others show only asexual reproduction, generally by *budding*. A small knob grows from the cell. As it increases in size, the cell nucleus divides and one of the new nuclei migrates into the pro-

vitamins and protein. Food yeast may be recovered brewer's yeast, or it may be a special type, usually *Cryptococcus utilis,* grown on waste sugar solutions from a variety of industries.

■**YEAST INFECTIONS.**—A few yeasts, such as *Candida albicans,* cause infections of human mucous membranes. *Candida* infection is not thought to be communicable; most persons unknowingly harbor the organism. Sometimes, when antibiotics are administered, the normal microbial flora of the body are disturbed and a *Candida* flare-up occurs. It is thought that administration of some antibiotics may stimulate its growth. *Cryptococcus neoformans,* a yeast found in the soil, may cause a fatal meningitis.

Algae.—Closely related to fungi and bacteria are the *algae,* which are mainly aquatic and marine plants. The algae vary greatly in size and characteristics; they include the large marine kelps and tiny single-celled plants. All, except for the blue-green algae, are eucaryotic. They all carry out the same photosynthetic reactions as the higher green plants do with the aid of chlorophyll.

The algae are among the most abundant of living things. The mass of microscopic algae in the oceans exceeds that of all green plants on land, making the oceans the principal sites of photosynthesis. Algae constitute a principal part of the diet of the largest whales.

The green algae are the most closely related to higher plants. They have cellulosic cell walls and store starch as a reserve food supply. Some of the unicellular green algae, such as *Chlorella,* are nonmotile while others, *Chlamydomonas,* for example, have flagella and are motile.

Euglena and related algae are quite similar to the green algae. However, they have no rigid cell wall, and hence resemble the protozoans more closely than other algae.

Other algae belong to the groups called *dinoflagellates, brown algae, red algae,* and *diatoms.* The diatoms are of interest because their walls are composed of overlapping halves, as shown in the figure, reinforced with silica. Diatoms are particularly abundant in the oceans and give the brown color to the foam on beaches. Their chlorophyll is obscured by carotinoid pigments. Large deposits of diatom shells have been found where prehistoric seas existed. They form a soft, white, powdery stone called *diatomaceous earth,* which is a common base for scouring powders.

Blue-green algae lack the organization of the other algae. They are procaryotic, and their chlorophyll is scattered throughout the cell instead of being separated from the rest of the cytoplasm in a chloroplast. Many blue-green algae can use gaseous nitrogen from the air and are therefore among the most self-sufficient microorganisms on Earth. They are the first plants to recolonize areas devastated by volcanic action or other catastrophes that kill all forms of life. They also can live in association with certain fungi, producing a complex plant structure called a *lichen.*

FLEISCHMANN LABORATORIES, STANDARD BRANDS, INC.

REPRODUCTION OF YEASTS by budding. These photomicrographs, taken over a four-hour period, show the firm cell wall. It appears to be formed of a material similar to that found in the cell walls of molds. The yeast cell, however, is usually ovoid or ellipsoidal and produces no flagella. Motility of yeasts has not been observed in any experiment.

Many require different hosts for different stages of development. For example, black-stem wheat rust needs the common barberry for one phase of its sexual spore development. Another fungus, ergot, causes smuts of cereal crops and may cause death of animals and people who eat too much of the infected grain. However, ergot is also the source of a drug useful in controlling hemorrhage.

Human and animal diseases caused by fungi include athlete's foot, ringworm, and aspergillosis. Fungal diseases spread by contact with skin infected with the offending fungus. Athlete's foot is thought to be spread by the use of common showers and dressing rooms. In the course of this infection, the victim may become hypersensitive to the fungus or its products and develop allergic manifestations on parts of the body other

tuberance. The bud is then walled off from the cell and is capable of forming its own buds. As seen in the figure, many buds may be formed by one cell. If a mass of cells stays attached, it may give the superficial appearance of a mycelium. A few yeasts multiply by fission in a manner similar to that of bacteria.

■**USES OF YEASTS.**—Some of the yeasts, especially the species *Saccharomyces cerevisiae,* rapidly ferment sugars to carbon dioxide and alcohol. They have been used since antiquity to make beer and wine and to leaven bread. *S. cerevisiae,* variety *ellipsoideus,* is the yeast most often used in wine-making. Special distiller's yeast strains have been selected for making distilled alcoholic beverages and commercial ethyl alcohol. Yeasts also supplement human and animal diets because of their high content of B

Lichens grow in areas of extreme cold and dryness, such as the polar land masses and mountain heights.

Protozoa.—The *protozoa* are generally considered to be unicellular animals, but in some instances there is evidence that a protozoan has arisen from an alga that lost its ability to form chlorophyll. Most protozoans are sufficiently different from the algae so that no readily recognizable relationship can be established. Most protozoa lack a definite cell wall and vary greatly in size and shape. They are much larger than bacteria. *Paramecium*, a commonly studied form, is elliptical, with dimensions of 200 μ to 40 μ. Although they are regarded as the most primitive creatures in the animal kingdom, the protozoa are vastly more complex than the bacteria. The protozoa usually have well-defined portions that perform the functions of specialized organs in the more highly organized animals.

The four main groups of protozoa are *Sarcodina, Mastigophora, Sporozoa,* and *Ciliophora*. There are about 20,000 recognized species.

■SARCODINA.—*Sarcodina* include the *amoebae*, the *foraminifera*, and the *radiolaria*. The adult amoebae lack definite shape or form and are bounded by a poorly defined cytoplasmic membrane. They move by extending arms of cytoplasm called *pseudopodia* ("false feet"), followed by movement of the rest of the cytoplasm into the pseudopod. Pseudopodia may completely surround food particles, thus bringing them into the cell. Multiplication is generally by fission of a single cell. This may, however, be preceded by conjugation of two cells. Many amoebae form resting stages, known as *cysts*, that are resistant to drying. When the environment is favorable, the cyst grows, producing an adult cell.

Most of the amoebae are free-living forms, but many are also parasitic on man and other animals. Only one of these, *Endamoeba histolytica*, causes human disease. This organism is carried in the feces and causes amoebic dysentery, a fairly common intestinal disease spread by contaminated water and food.

The foraminifera have a more or less complex outer shell structure, usually formed of calcium carbonate.

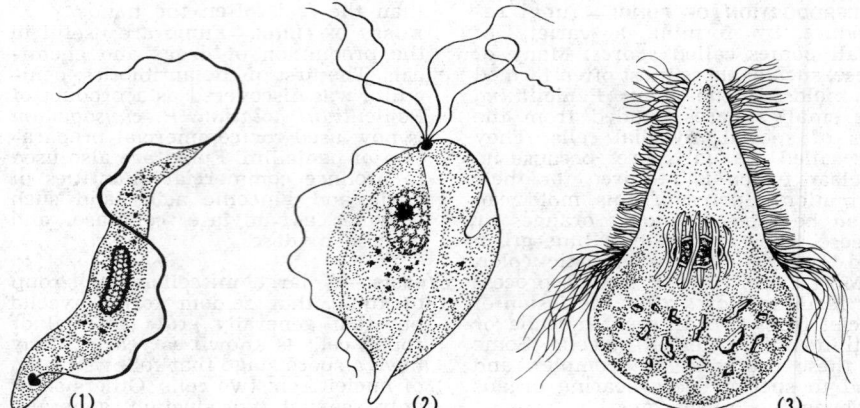

NONPHOTOSYNTHETIC PROTOZOA: (1) *Trypanosoma*; (2) *Trichomonas*; (3) *Trichonympha*.

Pseudopodia may extend through a mouth opening and also through holes in the shell to capture bacteria and other food materials. Geologists use the shells of foraminifera to determine geological age of rocks. Foraminifera occur only in salt water, and their skeletons make up a large part of the ooze of the ocean bottom. Throughout the world there are great chalk deposits, formed in the past geological ages, that consist largely of skeletons of foraminifera. The magnitude of these deposits is apparent when one considers that England alone produces over five million tons of chalk annually. The White Cliffs of Dover are shells of foraminifera.

The radiolaria have internal skeletons with radial spines that extend through and beyond the protoplasm. Their skeletons, which are siliceous, are almost indestructible. Their remains form the principal materials of millions of square miles of the bottoms of the Pacific and Indian oceans. They are thought to have been among the first animals on Earth; their skeletons form the oldest fossil-bearing rocks. Yet living forms closely resemble those of antiquity.

■MASTIGOPHORA.— The *Mastigophora* are protozoans that have from one to many long flagella in their principal phase. This group includes very simple organisms that appear to be flagellated amoebae and highly organized cells with definite shapes and internal structures; one finds protozoa that appear to be derived from algae. In fact, the protozoologist usually includes many species containing chlorophyll in the subclass *Phytomastigophora*, which contains the *Euglena* and related microorganisms. In this article all of the chlorophyll-containing protozoa have been classed as algae. Three important groups of flagellated protozoa are the trypanosomes, the trichomonads, and the trichonympha.

The *trypanosomes* and related protozoa have bladelike cells with a single terminal flagellum. An undulating membrane runs lengthwise along one side of the cell. Some of these protozoa cause diseases of insects and plants; others cause serious diseases in man and other animals. Among the latter are kala azar, caused by *Leishmania donovani* and thought to be transmitted by the bite of the sand flea. Another disease caused by a protozoan of this group is African sleeping sickness, caused by *Trypanosoma gambiense* and transmitted from man to man by an intermediate host, the tsetse fly. Most of the diseases of this group are spread by insects or other intermediate hosts.

Trichomonads are pear-shaped protozoans with four flagella at the smaller end. Many species of this group occur in animal intestines and can easily be observed in frogs and other amphibians. *Trichomonas vaginalis* causes an infection of the female genital tract; another form, *T. foetus*, causes abortion in cattle.

Trichonympha and related complex flagellates live in the digestive tracts of many insects, such as roaches and termites. In some instances they are beneficial to the insect, aiding in the digestion of such material as wood.

■SPOROZOA.—All *sporozoa* are parasitic protozoans that at some stage of their life cycle form spores. Each species is usually restricted to one or two hosts in which different stages of its life cycle may occur. All groups of animals have sporozoan parasites. The most common sporozoan disease of man is malaria. Part of the sporozoan's life cycle occurs in the Anopheles mosquito, which may become infected from feeding on blood of persons suffering from malaria. After a developmental stage in the mos-

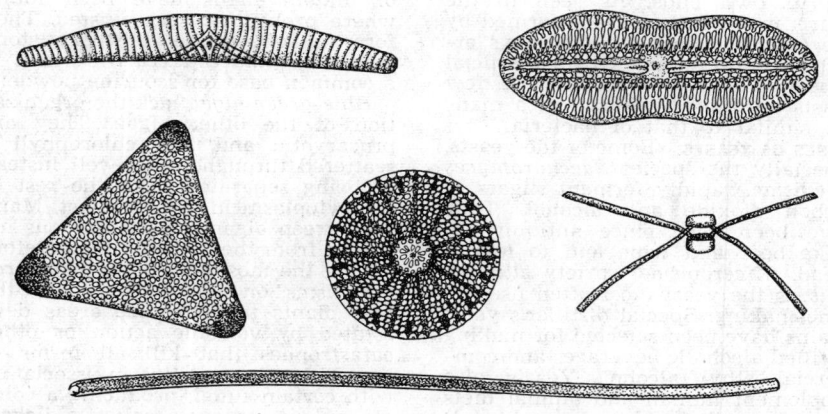

DIATOMS, a specific group of algae, occur in a wide variety of sizes, forms, and shapes.

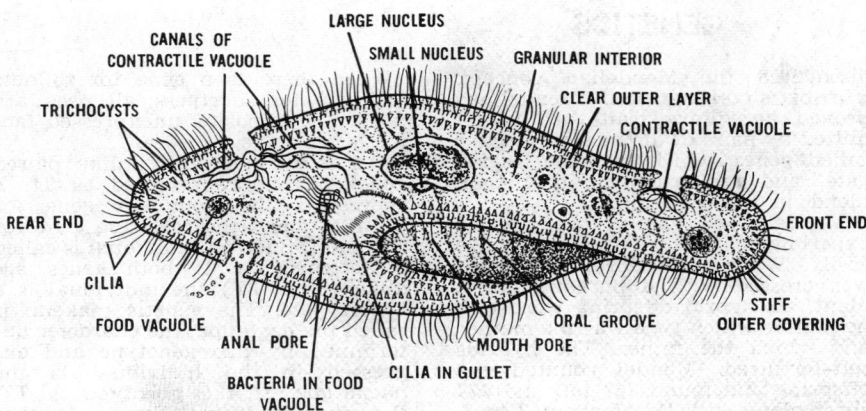

CANALS OF CONTRACTILE VACUOLE

LARGE NUCLEUS

SMALL NUCLEUS

GRANULAR INTERIOR

CLEAR OUTER LAYER

CONTRACTILE VACUOLE

TRICHOCYSTS

REAR END

CILIA

FOOD VACUOLE

ANAL PORE

BACTERIA IN FOOD VACUOLE

CILIA IN GULLET

MOUTH PORE

ORAL GROOVE

FRONT END

STIFF OUTER COVERING

THE PARAMECIUM is one of the most highly developed of all of the unicellular animals.

quito, malaria can be transmitted to man again.

■CILIOPHORA.—The *Ciliophora* (*Infusaria*) are protozoa with *cilia,* short protoplasmic threads, on their surface. These cilia may cover nearly the whole surface, acting as organs of locomotion, as in paramecia, or they may be restricted to certain areas, such as around an oral opening where they help collect food. Most ciliates are free-living aquatic animals, but some inhabit the digestive tracts of animals. Many of them, such as the paramecia, readily develop in stagnant water containing dead plant materials. They live largely on other microorganisms, such as bacteria.

Some of the most complex ciliates, belonging to the genus *Diplodinium,* are found in the rumen of cattle and other ruminant animals. They appear to aid in the digestion of food particles and thus are beneficial, although not essential, to the well-being of the animal.

Immunity to Disease.—*Immunology* is the science that is concerned with the study of immunity to disease. The field developed in the course of study of viruses, bacteria, and *Rickettsiae.* Prior to the eighteenth century, people recognized that most persons and animals that recovered from some diseases did not get a second attack of the same disease. They had what we now call acquired immunity. Observation of this fact led to the intentional propagation of a mild form of smallpox, *variola minor,* that killed very few persons. This prevented a larger number of deaths than would otherwise have been the case during epidemics of a more severe form of smallpox, *variola major.* The severe form often killed 50 to 75 per cent of its victims. However, the practice was too risky for wide acceptance.

The English physician Edward Jenner (1749–1823) observed that persons who had had a disease of cattle, cowpox, did not contract smallpox during epidemics. He dramatically demonstrated the value of this knowledge by artificially passing cowpox to a child and then later inoculating the child with material from a smallpox patient. The child did not contract smallpox. This dis-

covery in 1796 was soon put to practical use to control smallpox, although the reasons for its effectiveness were not known for about another century.

Further studies during the period of 1879 to 1900 showed that immunity to several animal and human diseases could be induced by injections of bacteria or viruses treated to make them noninfective. Diseases in which poisonous bacterial products, *toxins,* are involved can be prevented by repeated small injections of toxin. Further, the toxin-neutralizing effect can be passed from an immunized person to a nonimmunized person by a transfer of blood serum. All of these immunities have been found to be specific—they protect the person only against the disease-causing agent used to develop the immunity. Acquired immunity is now known to be caused by the formation of substances called *antibodies,* which are altered blood-serum proteins. The substance inducing antibody formation is called an *antigen.*

The reaction of serum antibodies with the corresponding antigen can be demonstrated in a test tube by one of several means. If the antigen is particulate, such as dead bacterial cells, the antibody will cause it to *agglutinate,* or form clumps, and settle out. If the antigen is soluble, such as egg white or some other protein foreign to the host animal, the antibody will cause a visible precipitate to form. If the antigen is a suspension of living bacterial cells, the antibody will increase the rate at which they can be engulfed by living white blood cells. If the antigen is a toxin, the antibody (*antitoxin*) will neutralize it so that it may safely be injected into an experimental animal that it would otherwise kill. These reactions can be used to identify either the antigen or the antibody if the other half of the system is known.

The exact means whereby antibodies protect an animal from a disease caused by its corresponding pathogenic antigen are not known. They may, however, involve some of the same reactions that can be demonstrated outside the body.

■IMMUNIZATION.—Studies of antibody formation have led to many procedures that can be used successfully

to protect man and domestic animals from disease. These include: (1) use of living but not virulent bacteria, such as the BCG (*bacille Calmette Guérin*) vaccine for tuberculosis; (2) use of dead bacteria to give immunity, as in vaccination against typhoid fever; (3) use of chemically modified extracts of bacteria, as in whooping cough vaccinations; (4) use of chemically modified toxins, *toxoids,* to form antitoxins against diphtheria and tetanus toxins; (5) use of dead *Rickettsiae,* as in vaccines for typhus fever and Rocky Mountain spotted fever; and (6) use of modified viruses to prevent such diseases as smallpox, measles, and poliomyelitis. Despite these many methods of immunization, present knowledge does not permit us to immunize against all diseases.

All of the above immunization procedures lead to what is called *active immunity;* the patient develops it himself. It is also possible to obtain *passive immunity* by transfer of antibodies, such as antitoxin, from one person to another or from an animal to a human being. Tetanus antitoxin is prepared by immunizing horses to tetanus toxin. The horse serum contains the antitoxin.

Active immunity is generally superior to passive immunity in preventing disease, since it lasts for a time from several months to the remainder of one's life; passive immunity disappears in a few weeks. Passive immunization is superior for treatment of a patient, since the maximum amount of antibody is present at the end of the injection. Active immunity generally requires several days or weeks to reach its maximum level.

The successful use of artificial immunity to prevent disease is dependent on an adequate vaccine, the length of immunity, the relative risk of immunization as compared with having the disease, and whether there are healthy carriers of the disease agent.

In addition to controlling disease, immunology includes studies of allergies and similar reactions and the response of a body to the transfer of material from a genetically different body of the same species.

—Richard H. McBee

BIBLIOGRAPHY

BROCK, THOMAS D. (ed.). *Milestones in Microbiology.* Prentice-Hall, Inc., 1961.

DUBOS, RENÉ JULES. *The Unseen World.* The Rockefeller Institute Press, 1962.

JACOBS, MORRIS B., and GERSTEIN, MAURICE J. *Handbook of Microbiology.* D. Van Nostrand, 1962.

STANIER, ROGER YATES, and others. *The Microbial World.* Prentice-Hall, Inc., 1963.

WALTER, WILLIAM G. *Dictionary of Microbiology.* D. Van Nostrand, 1962.

WALTER, WILLIAM G., and McBEE, RICHARD H. *General Microbiology.* D. Van Nostrand, 1962.

GENETICS

Continuity of Life.—*Genetics* is the study of the inheritance of biological characteristics in living things—characteristics that are passed from one generation to the next. What is inherited is a code message in the genetic material (*genes*) of egg and sperm. The code directs embryonic development and organization of cells into tissues and organs, and the function of each tissue and organ. The development is also influenced by external and internal environment. Thus, the organism is the product of interaction between genetic material and environment.

What is the nature of genetic material? How is it reproduced? What is the material's mechanism of action in the cell's function and the individual's development? How is the material transmitted? What is its role in the process of organic evolution? Each of these questions is complex, but progress has been made in answering them.

Mendelian Genetics.—The first problem to be solved is related to the mechanism of transmission of genetic material. This was the basis of Mendelian, or classical, genetics. Even in the nineteenth century, biologists knew an embryo develops from fusion of egg and sperm. Hence, the new organism is the product of materials from each parent. However, biologists were under the false impression that hereditary traits were transmitted in a bloodlike fluid from each parent and were mixed in the offspring. Hence we have the terms "half-blooded" and "full-blooded."

Gregor Johann Mendel (1822–1884), an Austrian monk, analyzed the basic laws of inheritance in 1866. The results were lost until 1900, when investigators in Holland, Germany, and Austria each independently rediscovered the Mendelian concept.

■MENDEL'S CONTRIBUTION.—Mendel had proved hereditary traits are transmitted by pairs of distinct units, later called *genes*, which reshuffle, segregate, and redistribute, rather than blend, in the offspring.

Mendel used garden peas in his experiments because they hybridize easily. When a purebred tall plant was crossed with a purebred short plant, all hybrid offspring were tall, no matter which type was the mother and which the father. The hybrids self-fertilized. Mendel counted the offspring and found 787 tall and 277 short plants, a ratio of about 3 to 1. When the short plants self-fertilized, they produced only short offspring, but when the tall plants self-fertilized, there were two types of offspring: one-third had only tall offspring, and two-thirds produced both tall and short in a ratio of 3 to 1. Mendel crossed six other characters: round and wrinkled peas, colored and uncolored flowers, and yellow and green peas. He had approximately the same results.

Mendel then formulated the *law of segregation.* Today this principle states that hereditary traits (such as tallness or shortness of peas) are transmitted by *zygotes* (fertilized eggs). One member of the pair of traits comes from the male parent; the other, from the female. In the mature plant, these paired genes segregate during the formation of *gametes* (sperms and eggs) so that just one of the pair is transmitted by a particular gamete. The gamete has only one gene of each pair, and is called *haploid.* When the male and female gametes unite to form the zygote, it is called *double* or *diploid.*

Mendel's studies showed the *principle of dominance.* The trait of tallness is dominant over shortness.

(When there is a gene for tallness and one for shortness, all peas are tall.) The opposite, unexpressed factor is *recessive.*

An individual with unlike paired genes can be represented as *Tt. T* represents the dominant gene for tallness, and *t* the recessive gene for shortness. Such an individual is called a *heterozygote.* If both genes are alike (*tt* or *TT*) the individual is a *homozygote.* The genetic makeup is called the *genotype;* the character determined by this genotype and expressed in the individual is the *phenotype.* If the genotype is *TT,* the phenotype is tallness. Another genotype that can give the phenotype tallness is *Tt.* The alternative forms of a gene are called *alleles.* This cross is illustrated in the diagram.

Mendel concluded that dominant and recessive genes do not affect each other; gametes are haploid and have only one of a pair of genes; each type of gamete is produced in equal numbers by a hybrid parent; and combination between gametes depends on chance—the frequency of each class of offspring depends on frequency of the gametes produced by each parent.

Mendel next determined how two or more pairs of genes would behave in crosses. He crossed plants with round, yellow seeds with those with wrinkled, green seeds. He knew a cross between round (*R*) and wrinkled (*r*) seeds produced round seeds in the F_1 generation and three round to one wrinkled seed in the F_2 plants; he knew crossing yellow (*Y*) with green (*y*) produced all yellow in the F_1 and three yellow to one green seed in the F_2 generation. This showed the dominance of roundness and yellowness over their respective contrasting alleles. When Mendel crossed round-yellow with

BROOKHAVEN NATIONAL LABORATORY

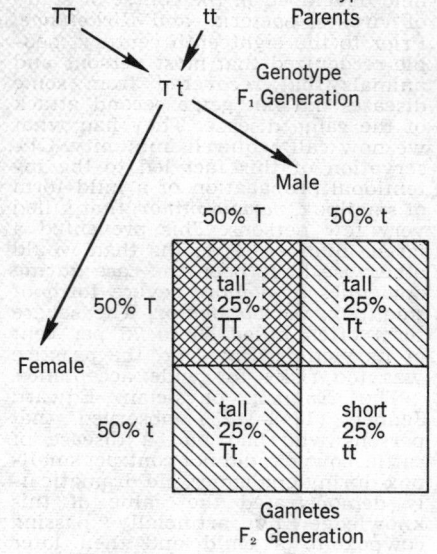

DROSOPHILA (FRUIT FLIES) aid geneticists in studying evolutionary characteristics. The Mendelian square (*right*) illustrates the principle of dominance. Since the trait of tallness is dominant, the combination *TT,tt* yields three tall individuals out of four offspring.

wrinkled-green, the F₁ produced all round-yellow seeds. In the F_2 generation, these seed types were obtained:

Two combinations, round-green and wrinkled-yellow, not present in either parental or the F₁ generation, have appeared. This result can be explained by Mendel's *law of independent assortment,* which states that members of one pair of genes segregate independently of other pairs. The various combinations are illustrated in the accompanying table.

Type	*Proportion*
Round-yellow	9/16
Round-green	3/16
Wrinkled-yellow	3/16
Wrinkled-green	1/16

Mendel also tested his F_2 plants to determine whether all of a single phenotype class, such as round-yellow, were alike in genotype. Accord-

Phenotype Parents — Genotype F₁ Generation — Gametes F₂ Generation

THIS MENDELIAN SQUARE shows the many genetic combinations possible in hybrid peas.

ing to his hypothesis, there should be four different genotypes in this group: RR, YY; RR, Yy; Rr, YY; and Rr, Yy. When F_2 plants self-fertilized, he found four classes of round-yellow seeded plants; the ratios fitted expectations. The breeding behavior of the F_2 round-green, wrinkled-yellow, and wrinkled-green were in accord with the hypothesis that each pair of genes segregates independently from other pairs of genes and is transmitted independently to the next generation.

Mendel's inheritance rules were later found to apply in other plants and in animals. More information explained the seeming exceptions.

In all characters studied by Mendel, the heterozygote was phenotypically identical with the homozygote dominant. In some cases, however, the heterozygote is intermediate. This is true in the color of the flower known as the "four o'clock." If a red parent is crossed with a white, all F₁ hybrids are intermediate in color, one-quarter of the F_2 offspring are red, one-quarter white, and one-half intermediate. In some cases, both alleles are equally "dominant," for example, those that determine the *MN* factors in blood. If one parent is *M* and the other *N,* all children will be *MN.* If both parents are *M,* or both *N,* all children will be *MM* or *NN,* respectively. If both parents are *MN,* one-quarter of the children are *M,* one-quarter *N,* and one-half *MN.* To understand other exceptions, where independent segregation does not seem to apply, one must consider the chromosomal basis of heredity.

Chromosomal Basis of Heredity.—All living things are composed of cells and begin life as a single cell. In organisms reproducing sexually, the cell is the fertilized zygote, which divides to form all the cells of the body of the organism (*somatic cells*).

Each cell has an inner body (*nucleus*) surrounded by a less dense semifluid material called *cytoplasm,* which is enclosed by a cell membrane. In the cytoplasm are various vital structures. In the nucleus, which is enclosed by its own membrane, are threadlike structures called *chromosomes,* and one or more bodies called *nucleoli,* which are dark when they are stained.

In 1902 a graduate student, W. S. Sutton, and a German cytologist, T. Boveri, decided independently that genes are in the chromosomes. Sutton's arguments were:

(1) Since sperm and egg give continuity from one generation to the next, the hereditary traits must be carried by the sperm and egg. (2) The sperm is almost all nucleus and yet contributes as much to heredity as does the egg, which has both cytoplasm and nucleus. Hence, the hereditary characters must be in the nucleus. (3) The visible nuclear parts that divide during cell division are chromosomes. The genes, then, must be on the chromosomes. (4) Chromo-somes occur in pairs, as do genes. (5) Chromosomes segregate during maturation of egg and sperm. Genes segregate during formation of the gametes (law of segregation). (6) Members of one pair of chromosomes segregate independently of other chromosome pairs. (Mendel showed that one pair of genes also segregates independently of other pairs.)

This gives a logical basis for the hypothesis that genes must be on chromosomes. In sixty years, evidence has accumulated proving the truth of this hypothesis and identifying the chemical nature of the hereditary chromosomal material. Chromosomes are equally distributed during cell division (*mitosis*) and each member of the chromosome pair segregates during maturation of egg and sperm (*meiosis*).

■**MITOSIS.**—Chromosomes are accurately reproduced and transmitted in a precise process that assures that each new cell formed receives one of each chromosome. The number of chromosomes characteristic of each species remains constant. Every somatic cell in the human being has 46 chromosomes; in the fruit fly, 8; in the garden pea, 14.

Although mitosis is a continuous process, it is described in terms of five phases:

Interphase. Chromosomes are usually not individually distinguishable; they are stretched out in long, diffuse threads. In this phase, each chromosome copies itself by a mechanism not yet understood.

Prophase. The chromosomes coil up and become short and thick. The nuclear membrane disappears and spindle fibers, denser than the cytoplasm, appear.

Metaphase. The chromosomes line up in a single plane across the center of the cell.

Anaphase. Each chromosome, at a fixed point on its body, has a minute structure called the *centromere,* attached to a spindle fiber. This fiber apparently contracts, and thereby guides each of the duplicated chromosomes away from the center of the cell in opposite directions.

Telophase. One complete set of chromosomes is in each half of the cell. The entire cell then divides between the two sets, and the chromosomes uncoil and lengthen. A new interphase is then begun in each daughter cell.

The number and make-up of chromosomes remain constant in each cell because successive chromosome duplication is followed by cell division.

■**MEIOSIS.**—Each cell's chromosomes occur in pairs, one from the mother and one from the father. Each member of the chromosomal pair has similar genes; they are called *homologous chromosomes,* or *homologues.* Human somatic cells have 23 pairs of chromosomes each.

The egg and sperm must each have half the somatic number of chromosomes, or be haploid, so that when they unite, the fertilized zygote will be *diploid,* as will be all cells derived from it by mitosis. The chromosome number of somatic cells remains constant from generation to generation

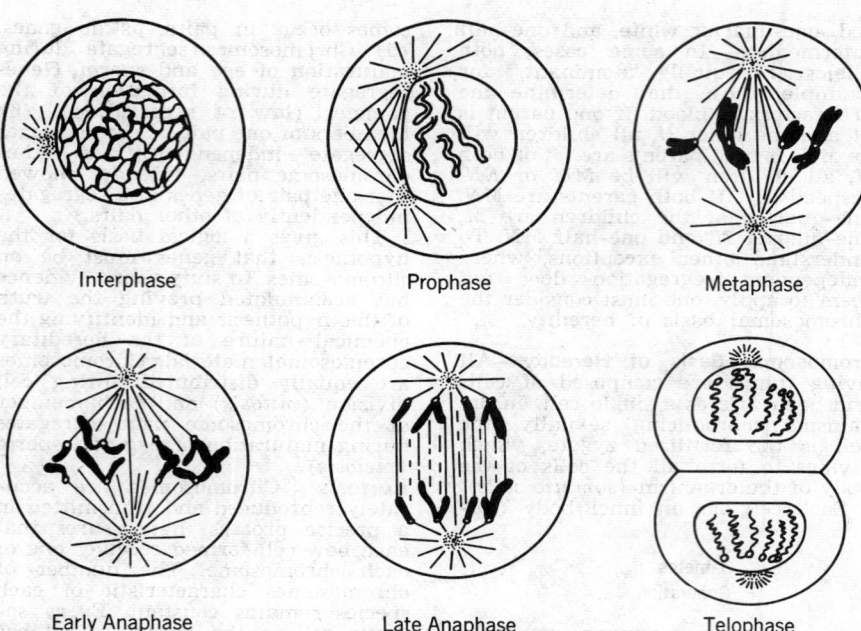

Interphase   Prophase   Metaphase

Early Anaphase   Late Anaphase   Telophase

MITOSIS, or cell division, is the process by which a cell splits into identical twins. The number and makeup of chromosomes remain constant in each cell during this process.

of the species and there is a mechanism to ensure that one member of each chromosome pair is in each gamete. The mechanism is known as *meiosis* and has two divisions:

First meiotic division. In this phase, each chromosome copies itself once, creating two *chromatids;* the chromatids are held together by the undivided centromere. The homologous chromosomes move toward each other and pair tightly, so that similar genes, or *alleles,* lie alongside each other. This makes a bundle of four chromatids and two centromeres. During this time the partner, or matching, strands twist around each other, break, and then reunite, thus exchanging homologous sections. As a result, chromosomes consist of parts from both paternal and maternal chromosomes. The centromere of each of the homologous chromosomes, attached to the spindle fiber and to the chromosome, is pulled to an opposite pole of the cell. The cell divides. Each new cell now has the haploid chromosome number, with either a maternally or paternally derived member of each chromosomal pair, depending on chance and on the random attachment of each centromere to the spindle fibers. This is the chromosomal basis for the independent assortment of each member of a pair of chromosomes with respect to the other.

Second meiotic division. In this phase, the centromeres divide so that each chromatid separates from its duplicate. Another division follows that is much like ordinary mitosis—two duplicate cells are formed.

Because of the two meiotic divisions, four cells are formed from the original cell; each has a haploid number of chromosomes, one of each homologous pair.

■**SEX-LINKAGE.**—Chromosomes occur in pairs, one maternal and one paternal.

All but one pair are identical in both sexes. In one sex (usually the male) there is one pair of unidentical chromosomes—X and Y. In the human male, there are 22 pairs of identical (nonsex) chromosomes called *autosomes,* and one X and one Y chromosome. The female has 22 pairs of autosomes and a pair of X chromosomes. The X and Y chromosomes are called *sex chromosomes.* If an egg is fertilized by a sperm bearing an X chromosome, it becomes female (XX). If it is fertilized by a Y-chromosome-bearing sperm, it becomes male (XY). Thus, sex determination occurs at the moment of fertilization. Since segregation of the sex chromosomes takes place during meiosis exactly as does segregation of the other chromosomes, and is completely random, the chance is even that any sperm will contain a Y chromosome. Since all eggs contain one X chromosome, the probability of the offspring's being either a boy or girl is exactly equal.

The Y chromosomes of organisms contain few or no genes. (None are known to occur on the human Y chromosome.) The X contains many genes.

Because of this, these genes are segregated differently in the two sexes, resulting in the phenomenon called *sex-linkage.*

Red-green color blindness is the most common sex-linked trait in human beings, occurring in about 8 per cent of men and in about .5 per cent of women. This is explained by the hypothesis that the recessive gene responsible is contained in the X chromosome and that there is no corresponding allele in the Y. A woman heterozygous for the trait married to a normal man would have daughters with normal vision, but probably half of her sons would be color-blind. The children of a homozygous (normal) woman married to a color-blind man would all be normal, but probably half the daughters would be heterozygous and would transmit the trait to half their sons.

■**X CHROMOSOME.**—It has long been a puzzle as to how males can function with only one X chromosome, and therefore only one set of sex-linked genes, whereas females have two X's and a double set of sex-linked genes.

Since 1949 geneticists have been able to distinguish between body cells from the male and female of many mammals, including human beings, by a simple staining technique. Cells from females contain a darkly staining body, the *Barr body* or *sex chromatin,* that is missing from male cells.

In 1961 the English geneticist, Mary Lyon, formulated a hypothesis based largely on experiments with mice, which resolved the riddle as to why a single X chromosome is enough for a male. She states that one X is also enough for a female, since only one of her two X's functions. The other is inactive and condensed, and so it stains deeply. This inactivation occurs early in the embryo's development. In some embryonic cells it may be the maternal X that is inactivated; in others, it may be the paternal X. All cells descended from the embryonic cells thus would only have the same single active X chromosome. The best evidence for this randomness of inactivation is the inheritance·of certain sex-linked coat-color genes in mammals. Females heterozygous for any of these always show a mottled or dappled phenotype, with patches of normal and mutant color, as in a tortoise shell cat.

The Barr bodies in female cells fit the theory of the single active X. The theory is that all inactive X's show up as Barr bodies. Males (XY)

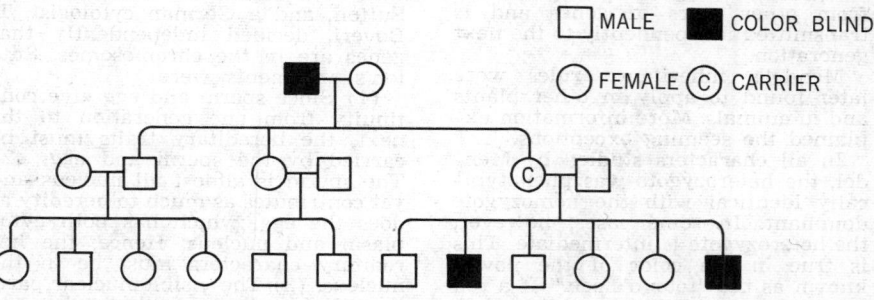

□ MALE   ■ COLOR BLIND
○ FEMALE   Ⓒ CARRIER

COLOR BLINDNESS is a common sex-linked trait in human beings. A color-blind male passes his recessive trait to a male grandchild through his daughter, who serves as a carrier.

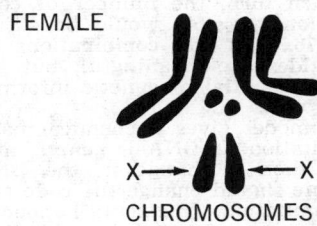

FEMALE

X ⟶   ⟵ X

CHROMOSOMES

MALE

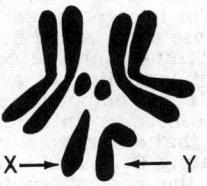

X ⟶   ⟵ Y

CHROMOSOMES

CHROMOSOMES in Drosophila. Two *X*'s combine to make a female; *X* and *Y*, a male.

and females with an abnormal chromosome complement of one *X* and no *Y* (*XO*) have none; normal females (*XX*) and males with an abnormal chromosome complement (*XXY*) have one. Other abnormalities in sex chromosome number have been found. There are females with three *X* chromosomes and two Barr bodies. Females with four *X*'s and three Barr bodies have also been reported.

The single active *X* chromosome hypothesis is not yet verified, but evidence indicates that it is true.

■**Y CHROMOSOME.**—Experiments with *Drosophila* (small two-winged flies) showed that two *X* chromosomes were necessary to produce a female, and one *X* to produce a male. The *Y* seemed to be neutral, as proved in certain flies with the *XO* chromosomal constitution (one *X* and no *Y*) that were sterile males. Female flies were found with two *X* chromosomes and a *Y* (*XXY*). Until recently, it was thought that sex was determined the same way in the human being. It is now known, however, that the *Y* chromosome is essential to determine maleness in human beings. Humans with rare chromosomal abnormalities have been studied, and those with the *XO* chromosome constitution (one *X* and no *Y*) are abnormal females. Some abnormal males have an *XXY* complement. Since the *Y* is essential in human beings for a male to develop, he will be abnormal if this is unbalanced by two *X*'s. One *X* will produce a female, but two are necessary for normality.

■**CHROMOSOME MAPPING.**—The principle of independent assortment is explained in that the maternal and paternal members of each homologous pair of chromosomes are distributed independently to the gametes at meiosis. The seven factors Mendel studied were carried by different chromosomes and were independently inherited. Each chromosome has many genes; in *Drosophila* there are hundreds of genes known, but only four pairs of chromosomes. Genes

located on the same chromosome tend to be inherited together and are said to be *linked*. During meiosis, when homologous chromosomes pair, they twist around each other with resultant breakage and reunion; hence, some parts of a chromosome segregated to the new cell can be either maternal or paternal. This process of chromosomal recombination is called crossover. There is indisputable evidence the crossover occurs at the stage of meiosis when there are four chromatids held together by the undivided centromeres.

Crossover occurs at random sites along the chromosome; the frequency is determined by the distance between the points—the closer the points, the less frequent the crossover; the farther apart, the more frequent.

This is the basis for mapping the locations (*loci*) of the genes; the crossover frequency is the unit of map distance between loci. To determine the order of the gene loci, crosses involving three different pairs of linked factors are used. Analysis of such crosses has proved that the genes within each chromosome are arranged linearly in a definite serial order at fixed loci.

Genetic maps of chromosomes are graphic representations of the relative distances of genes in each linkage group, as determined by the percentage of *recombination* (crossover) among the genes. The four pairs of chromosomes from *Drosophila melanogaster* have been extensively mapped. Corn has also been mapped; each of its ten linkage groups (corresponding to ten pairs of chromosomes) is represented by many genes. Other maps are available for pink bread mold (*Neurospora*), the colon bacillus (*Escherichia coli*), and the mouse. A few gene markers are mapped on the *X* chromosome of man, but the 22 autosomes (the non-sex chromosomes) are largely unmapped. New techniques in tissue culture may make possible mapping of all human chromosomes.

Correspondence between the genetic maps of chromosomes and morphologically detectable defects in the chromosomes has been good. The presence in the salivary glands of *Drosophila* of huge chromosomes has made possible detection of minor structural changes. Sometimes a portion of a chromosome is deleted; this defect is detected in salivary chromosomes. Flies missing a small region near one end of the *X* chromosome also lack the white eye gene; hence, the locus of the gene for white is in this region of the *X* chromosome. Likewise, the precise location of other genes has been ascertained; generally the relative distance as determined by linkage studies has been confirmed by cytological studies.

Nature of Genetic Material.—The chemical nature of genetic material and the chemical basis for its reproduction are important. Generally it is accepted that except for some viruses, genetic information is carried in *deoxyribonucleic acid* (DNA). Principally, the evidence is as follows:

DNA is unique to the chromosomes. The amount of DNA is remarkably constant from cell to cell within any organism and within a single species. Only the egg and sperm cells have a different amount; they contain half the normal amount of DNA (and half the somatic chromosome number). *Proteins* and *ribonucleic acids* (RNA), other substances found in chromosomes, vary considerably in amount in different tissues within a species. Inheritable changes, *mutations,* are in the genetic material. These seldom occur spontaneously, but the frequency may be greatly increased by exposure to X rays, ultraviolet light, and certain chemicals. DNA and the genes are normally stable. A wavelength of 260 μ ultraviolet light is effective in producing mutations because it is most absorbed by nucleic acids.

⁹ The best direct evidence that DNA is the genetic material comes from experiments in transformation of certain bacteria; these show that the so-called transforming principle is pure DNA. Classic work by O. T. Avery, C. M. MacLeod, and M. McCarty in 1944 was based on earlier observations that when an extract from dead cells of one strain of *Pneumococcus* was added to living cells of another strain, it transformed some characters of the living cells so they were identical to the extract strain. The new characters were inherited by progeny of the transformed strain as if the latter had extract genes. Avery's group analyzed the extract and proved that the active part of the transforming extract was pure DNA, so the genetic material must be DNA.

Evidence that DNA transmits genetic information was obtained by the 1952 studies of Hershey and Chase on viral infection of colon bacilli. *Bacterial viruses,* or *bacteriophages,* consist of a protein coat and a DNA core. When viral protein is labeled with a radioactive isotope of

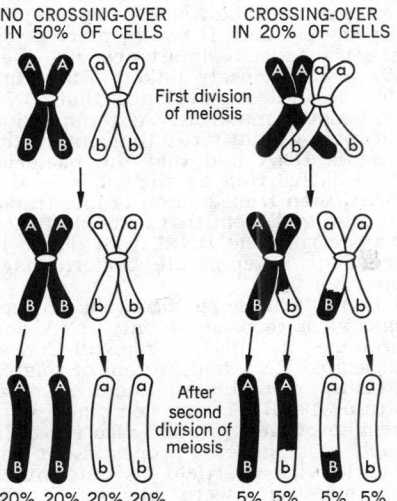

NO CROSSING-OVER IN 50% OF CELLS	CROSSING-OVER IN 20% OF CELLS

First division of meiosis

After second division of meiosis

20% 20% 20% 20%   5% 5% 5% 5%

CROSSOVER brings about new combinations of genes in the offspring. This allows the offspring to have their own traits.

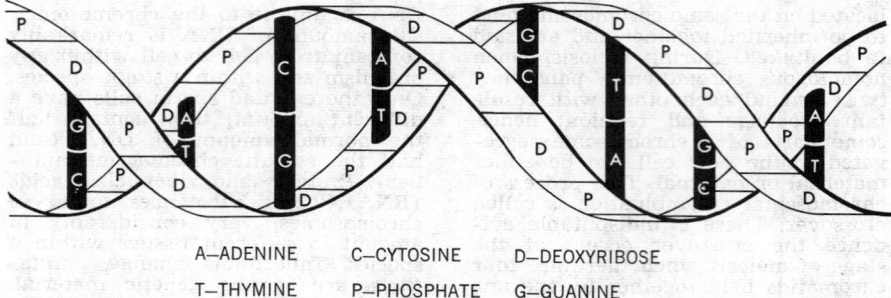

A—ADENINE   C—CYTOSINE   D—DEOXYRIBOSE
T—THYMINE   P—PHOSPHATE   G—GUANINE

WATSON-CRICK MODEL of the DNA molecule is formed from a few simple molecules repeatedly linked. These various combinations represent a complex genetic code of life.

sulfur (S-35) and the DNA with radioactive phosphorus (P-32) and each is allowed to infect the bacterial host, S-35 remains outside and P-32 inside the host. The P-32 is found in the new viruses released when the bacteria open. Since the viral part (*phage*) within the bacterium contains genetic information that directs its host to make more phage (both DNA and protein), it must be DNA that is the genetic material.

N. Zinder and J. Lederberg discovered bacterial transduction, providing more proof that DNA transmits genetic information. In *bacterial transduction*, a hereditary trait can be transferred from one bacterial cell to another via a virus that infects first one cell and then the other. In transduction, the viral DNA picks up a tiny bit of its host's DNA. When the host cell ruptures and the virus infects a new host, the virus carries the genes of the first host with it. These genes are expressed in the new host and its offspring. A streptomycin-resistant bacterium may be infected with a viral strain of low virulence, a temperate bacteriophage. The virus may multiply within it, and some viral particles may pick up the streptomycin-resistant gene. If the virus is allowed to infect a streptomycin-sensitive bacterial strain, some of these bacteria and progeny are then found to be streptomycin-resistant. If two or more genes are transduced simultaneously, they are always closely linked. Transduction is indirect evidence that DNA is genetic material. Assuming that the part of the virus that enters the host is DNA and that the bacterial material carried by the virus is also DNA, then transduction is like transformation, except that instead of man transferring the DNA from donor to recipient, a temperate bacteriophage does so.

Some viruses, such as tobacco mosaic virus, consist of only RNA and protein. In 1957, Fraenkel-Conrat separated RNA and protein of related strains, recombining them so that strain *A*'s RNA was combined with protein of strain *B*, and vice versa. In each case, genetic properties of the hybrid virus particle, as determined by infection, were always of the strain from which the RNA came.

The Watson-Crick Model.—A high-molecular-weight polymer, DNA is a large molecule formed from a few simple molecules linked repeatedly by chemical bonds. Repeating units are *nucleotides*, each of which consists of a phosphate group; a five-carbon sugar, *deoxyribose;* and one of four different nitrogenous bases. The four bases are two *purines* called *adenine* (A) and *guanine* (G), and two *pyrimidines, cytosine* (C) and *thymine* (T). In polymerized form, as in nucleic acids, nucleotides are connected by a chemical bond between the phosphate group of one nucleotide and the 3-hydroxyl of an adjacent deoxyribose. The DNA has a deoxyribose-phosphate backbone with bases projecting inward and perpendicular to the axis.

Chargaff and co-workers showed that the ratio of adenine to thymine, and of guanine to cytosine, is about 1/1 in any DNA preparation. However, the ratio of adenine (or thymine) to guanine (or cytosine) varies. They thought that since A = T and G = C, each was associated with the other in DNA.

This ratio, together with X-ray diffraction studies of DNA by M. H. F. Wilkins, led James Watson and F. H. C. Crick, in 1953, to propose a DNA structure. Their structure is essentially a twisted ladder or *double helix;* the sides are made of the sugar-phosphate backbone and the rungs are the *bases.* The *base sequence* in one strand determines that in the complementary strand; an A must always be matched with a T, and a C with G. Weak hydrogen bonds hold A to T and G to C, giving the ladder firmness and ability to separate when replication takes place during mitosis.

The *Watson-Crick model* makes it possible to understand how genetic information is duplicated and transmitted. If double helix strands separate, each is a *template,* or mold that specifies the replication of its complementary copy. This would result in two identical DNA molecules, each with an original and a newly synthesized strand.

The model explains how DNA could carry genetic information, or *code,* translated into protein-producing instructions. The code depends on the sequence of the four bases in relation to each other; in effect, a four-letter alphabet. Many configurations are possible, since there are ten base pairs in each complete turn of the double helix; and this is a small portion of the entire molecule.

For each turn, the number of configurations possible would be 4^{10}, or 1,048,576. Not all combinations of nucleotides are meaningful, but the storage potential of genetic information is vast.

The model gives a chemical basis for mutation. If DNA is genetic material, then a change in the DNA molecule should change the code and cause mutation. This could happen if an error is made during replication, or if A picks up C instead of T and the error is perpetuated. At one position, base pairs would be C-G instead of A-T, upsetting the code and preventing formation of a normal protein. If a compound similar to a normal base is introduced, a compound that differs so slightly that the replicating DNA could easily mistake it for the normal, mutations might occur. For example, 5-bromouracil can quantitatively replace thymine; in some cases this can produce mutation. Changing the code results in production of abnormal protein or of no protein.

The model fits requirements of linear arrangement of genes in linkage groups; the four bases are arranged linearly along the helix, forming a linear code.

The most direct work supporting the model is that done in 1958 by Meselson and Stahl. They grew many generations of bacteria in heavy nitrogen (N-15) and then transferred cells to ordinary N-14 medium for varying lengths of time. At specified times, they extracted the DNA from the cells and centrifuged it, using a technique that causes molecules to concentrate in bands at definite positions, depending on their density. DNA taken from bacteria grown for a long time in N-15 and allowed to divide once in N-14 formed a hybrid band halfway between that of DNA in bacteria grown in N-15 and in N-14. If the bacteria divided twice in N-14, two bands were visible, one a hybrid band and one the N-14 band. In succeeding divisions, the hybrid band became smaller and the N-14 band larger.

When the two strands of N-15 DNA separate, each is a template for information of a complementary N-14 strand. After one replication, two new DNA helices are formed—each a hybrid of N-14/N-15. At the next replication, each N-14 strand synthesizes another N-14 strand, forming a pure N-14/N-14 helix, and N-15 strands replicate, forming a hybrid N-14/N-15 helix. In succeeding generations, there is but one hybrid strand, but the number of pure N-14/N-14 molecules steadily increases. Facts and theory coincide, suggesting that the DNA helix unwinds into two single strands during replication.

Kornberg proved in a test tube the theoretical model of DNA synthesis. When he mixed a certain enzyme, triphosphates of each of the four nitrogen bases, and a primer, or starter, of a small amount of preformed DNA, more DNA would be synthesized. The DNA formed always had the same ratio of A, G, T, and C as the primer used had, showing that this had provided the template for new DNA.

Formation of Proteins.—DNA, now accepted as genetic material, is inactive in cellular metabolic processes, which are performed by proteins. Most proteins serve as enzymes and catalysts.

To translate instructions carried within DNA into protein structure, DNA within the chromosomes gives its message to an RNA form present in the nucleus; RNA acts as messenger and transmits the message to the site of protein synthesis within the cytoplasm. This site is another form of RNA found in many particles (*ribosomes*) in the cytoplasm. On the ribosome, an RNA template is formed according to the messenger RNA's code. Proteins are long chains of amino acids hooked together linearly by *peptide bonds*. The chains are *polypeptides*. Twenty amino acids occur in proteins; the smallest protein (*ribonuclease*) has a molecular weight of 13,500 and is a single chain of 124 amino acids. Many amino acids are repeated several times; not all need be present in any individual protein. Proteins have a definite shape, on which their function depends. Polypeptide chains form a helix that folds into a characteristic shape. The amino acid sequence is believed to determine the nature of this folding.

To synthesize proteins on the RNA template on the ribosome, the amino acids must be brought to their proper positions. This is done by a soluble RNA (S-RNA or transfer-RNA), of which there is a specific one for each of the twenty-odd amino acids. S-RNA picks up its own amino acid, which has been activated by its specific enzyme, and brings it to a specific site on the template that it "recognizes," presumably by some kind of complementarity.

Once each amino acid fits into place on the template, sequence is established, peptide bonds are formed, RNA is sloughed off, and protein zips off the template and takes on the shape necessary to carry out its function in the cell.

Genetic Code.—DNA carries genetic information and gives its message to one form of RNA; this message is translated into protein structure, with the help of other forms of RNA. Although less is known about RNA structure than about either DNA or protein, it is known to be similar to DNA in that it is also a polymer containing four kinds of nucleotides. These nucleotides are similar to those of DNA except that *uracil* (U) replaces thymine as a pyrimidine base, and that the five-carbon sugar is ribose instead of a deoxyribose. The other components are the same as those in DNA. DNA may transmit its information to messenger RNA through complementarity between the bases, which by their alignment in both DNA and RNA contain the key to the code. The problem is how a four-letter code consisting of nucleotides can give a dictionary that is thought to contain the twenty amino acid "words."

Nirenberg and Matthaei, and Severo Ochoa's group, made an RNA, "poly-U" (polyuridylic acid), all of

Summary of RNA Code Words

Amino Acid		RNA Code Words*		
Alanine	CCG	UCG†	ACG†	
Arginine	CGC	AGA	UGC†	CGA†
Asparagine	ACA	AUA	ACU†	
Aspartic acid	GUA	GCA†	GAA†	
Cysteine	UUG			
Glutamic acid	GAA	GAU†	GAC†	
Glutamine	AAC	AGA	AGU†	
Glycine	UGG	AGG	CGG	
Histidine	ACC	ACU†		
Isoleucine	UAU	UAA		
Leucine	UUG	UUC	UCC	UUA
Lysine	AAA	AAU		
Methionine	UGA			
Phenylalanine	UUU	CUU		
Proline	CCC	CCU	CCA	CCG†
Serine	UCU	UCC	UCG†	ACG
Threonine	CAC	CAA		
Tryptophan	GGU			
Tyrosine	AUU			
Valine	UGU	UGA†		

* Arbitrary nucleotide sequence.
† Probable.

whose bases are uracil (UUUU . . .). When poly-U was put in a test tube with ingredients needed for protein synthesis, a long chain of repeating units of only one kind of amino acid, phenylalanine, was formed. The RNA code for phenylalanine is thus an unknown number of uracil bases. The favored number is three.

Since then, RNA's have been synthesized containing all possible combinations of A, G, C, and U. These experiments and others by Crick, Brenner, and others lead to the following conclusions: (1) The code message is read in groups of three bases (triplets), although multiples of three are not completely ruled out. (2) The message is read in nonoverlapping triplets, starting from a fixed point, probably one end. (3) Most triplets are meaningful. They allow the gene to function; each triplet probably represents an amino acid. (4) Since four bases combine in groups of three, there is the possibility of $4 \times 4 \times 4$, or 64 triplets, more than enough to code the twenty amino acids found in protein.

In experiments with synthetic RNA, more than one triplet was found to code the same amino acid. A code such as the genetic code, in which more than one word can signify the same object, is called *degenerate*. This does not imply lack of specificity in protein structure; it simply means that more than one code word can direct the same amino acid to its specific site on the forming polypeptide chain. The accompanying table lists the RNA triplets that have been shown to code each of the twenty amino acids. This table must be viewed as tentative, since experiments to clarify it are in progress.

Present evidence suggests that the genetic code is universal—all species utilize approximately the same code.

Internal Structure of the Gene.—The gene, defined by classical genetics, is the unit of function, recombination, and mutation; the chromosome is pictured as a series of beads (genes) on a string. The genetic code resides in the nucleotide sequence of a long

DNA molecule; mutation and recombination can be detected within the borders of the genes of rapidly reproducing organisms. This changes the classical concept of the gene.

In recombination of genetic material, sexual reproduction brings about a great variety in the number of possible genotypes. Crossover results in further recombination of parts of chromosomes. Many microorganisms have alternatives to sexual reproduction that produce new combinations of genes in their progeny. Some bacteria mate, and there even is a form of gene recombination in bacteriophagic viruses.

Because great numbers of progeny can be obtained in bacterial and viral "crosses," it is possible to "dissect" the gene. The following ideas have emerged: (1) The gene locus may have more than one function. The function unit is called a *cistron*, and is perhaps a coded sequence of nucleotide pairs in a DNA molecule. This sequence carries information needed to specify the order of amino acids in a large polypeptide chain. (2) Mutation can occur in a cistron. The mutation unit may be as small as a single nucleotide pair. (3) Recombination may occur almost anywhere along the DNA molecule. The recombination unit is called a *recon*.

■**GENES AND CHROMOSOMES.**—Knowledge obtained from chemical, X-ray, and electron microscope studies of chromosomes is summarized as follows: (1) Chromosomes consist of a complex of DNA and protein, with a variable amount of RNA. (2) The nucleoprotein complex forms individual fibrous particles with a molecular weight of about 18,000,000 each, of which 8,000,000 is attributable to a single DNA molecule. (3) The chromosomes may consist of a *fibril bundle*; each fibril may have either two or four DNA double helices with associated protein or a large strand made up of 1,000 to 100,000 DNA molecules combined with proteins.

Biochemical Genetics.—Genes may control metabolic activity. In 1902 A. E. Garrod studied a human metabolic disease, alcaptonuria, a hereditary defect caused by a block in the normal series of metabolic reactions of the amino acid tyrosine. He called alcaptonuria and similar conditions "inborn errors of metabolism." This was the first example of recessive inheritance recognized in man, and since then other inborn metabolic diseases have been found. Each is controlled by one mutant gene locus.

Human beings are not usually subject to experimental manipulation and breeding. However, George W. Beadle and Edward L. Tatum found that by studying biochemical mutants in a mold, they could determine how genes act in producing such diseases and in normal metabolism. They formulated a hypothesis called the "one gene–one enzyme hypothesis." To paraphrase in terms of DNA: The DNA of each gene carries the information to specify the formation of a single protein—in most cases an enzyme that controls a specific chemical reaction in the organism. Today, based on very recent work, the hypothesis is modified to state that one gene specifies one polypeptide.

Beadle and Tatum chose an organism in which it was possible to prove unequivocally that single genes affect single enzymes—which govern single biochemical reactions. They looked for and found an organism simple enough to show the direct relationship between a gene and its product. The organism was *Neurospora*.

Neurospora is a fungus that usually reproduces asexually by means of spores called *conidia*. All nuclei are haploid; hence, every gene is expressed: no allele interacts or proves dominant. *Neurospora* also undergoes sexual reproduction, which requires fusion of two haploid nuclei to produce a diploid zygote. This occurs only through the union of two strains of opposite mating types. These strains are indistinguishable morphologically, but can be shown to differ. If strains of opposite mating types are grown together, characteristic black sexual spores (*ascospores*) are formed; strains of the same mating type, if grown together, do not form such spores.

Fungi like *Neurospora* grow on a simple synthetic medium, called a *minimal medium,* containing inorganic salts, sugar, and the vitamin biotin. The ordinary wild type of *Neurospora* thrives on this, synthesizing all the organic compounds of which protoplasm is made: amino acids, nucleic acids, fats, vitamins, etc.

Beadle and Tatum irradiated conidia to produce mutations and crossed them with a strain of the opposite mating type. The sexual spores produced were then isolated and each spore grown separately on a medium supplemented with one class of ingredients, either amino acids or vitamins. The germinated spores were tested on minimal medium. If they grew, they were the wild type, still able to synthesize all necessary growth factors. If unable to grow on minimal medium, but able to grow on minimal medium supplemented with, say, amino acids, they were deficient in the ability to synthesize one or more of these acids. Conidia of the new mutant were tested separately on minimal medium supplemented with each amino acid until the one that permitted growth was found. To test that this was truly a genetic defect, each mutant strain was crossed with a wild type and the offspring were tested; a ratio of one mutant to one wild type was found. A large number of mutants were isolated. When a single supplementary compound produced normal growth, it meant that a single gene was affected by the mutagenic treatment. Thus, Beadle and Tatum demonstrated that genes have a single primary function in the process of metabolism. It is, of course, assumed that the normal, or wild type, gene performs the function that is deficient in the mutant.

Essential compounds, the amino acids and vitamins, are synthesized by each cell through a series of reactions. If by mutation each of several strains loses the ability to synthesize a particular amino acid, such as arginine, would all the strains be mutants for the same gene? Would they all be affected at the same step in the synthesis of the amino acid? Could one deduce the order of the processes from a study of mutants and their nutritional requirements?

In the case of arginine, three classes of mutants, designated as X, Y, and Z, were found to grow in media as indicated in the following table. This study suggests that a linear series of reactions results in arginine synthesis: Prior substance X → ornithine → Y → citrulline → Z → arginine. Strain Z grows only on arginine and is blocked at the step lettered Z, conversion of citrulline to arginine; thus Z is unable to grow on any of the earlier compounds in the series, but will grow if arginine, which comes after the block, is supplied.

Mutant Strain	X	Y	Z
Arginine	+	+	+
Citrulline	+	+	−
Ornithine	+	−	−
No supplement	−	−	−

+ indicates growth.
− indicates no growth.

Strain Y can grow on either citrulline or arginine, each of which comes after the block; but it will not grow on ornithine or minimal medium with no supplement. Strain X will grow on all three; it is blocked at a step preceding ornithine production, and because of this blocked step is unable to grow on unsupplemented minimal medium. Each step is blocked because an enzyme needed to catalyze that specific step is missing or defective. Crosses involving mutants of each strain showed that each step involves mutation of one specific gene. Since there are three distinct enzymes, this is an example of the workability of the one gene–one enzyme hypothesis.

The same principle extends to all living organisms, including man. The hereditary disease *galactosemia* is caused by a single recessive gene that controls and prevents production of an enzyme essential for conversion of milk sugar, galactose, into glucose, the sugar that the body can use. A child homozygous for the galactosemia gene develops cataracts, mental retardation, and other defects because of abnormal accumulation of galactose in the body. By eliminating milk from the diet of children with galactosemia, the disease is controlled.

There is a test for the presence of the enzyme needed to convert galactose to glucose in red blood cells, and thus glactosemic infants can be identified before damage is extensive. A homozygote has virtually no enzyme, a normal person has a high level of enzyme, and a heterozygote usually has a level about halfway between. This intermediate level appears to be sufficient for normal function. If galactosemia runs in the family, parents and newborn infants can be tested.

There are many examples of inherited metabolic diseases that show that in man, as in microorganisms, genes control biochemical reactions.

■GENES AND PROTEIN STRUCTURE.—The best evidence for the precise effect of mutation on protein structure comes from a study of the abnormal hemoglobins produced in certain inherited anemias of man, particularly of sickle cell anemia. In *sickle cell anemia,* the red blood cells form a sickle-shaped structure when oxygen concentration is low. The disease is serious, usually fatal in childhood. There is also a mild form of abnormality called *sickle cell trait.*

Both sickle cell trait and sickle cell anemia tend to occur in certain families originating in Central Africa, the central Mediterranean area, the Persian Gulf, and India. Since it is an inherited disease, those with sickle cell anemia are homozygous for a partially dominant gene, S. They are designated SS. People with sickle cell trait are heterozygotes, AS, with A the normal gene. Only if both parents are heterozygotes would a child have the disease. The cross would be as follows:

$$AS \times AS$$

$\boxed{SS}$	AS	AA
anemia	*trait*	*normal*

Pauling and co-workers reported in 1949 that sickle cell anemia is a "molecular disease," since the large hemoglobin molecule of victims is different from that of normal people. More recent work by Ingram has defined the exact nature of the change. Hemoglobin, a globular protein with the molecular weight 66,200, consists of four polypeptide chains, two of one type (*alpha chains*) and two of another (*beta chains*). Each consists of about 140 amino acids. Ingram broke the hemoglobin molecule into small fragments and analyzed each fragment for its amino acid sequence. The two alpha chains of normal hemoglobin A fragments were identical with those of hemoglobin S. One fragment from the beta chain showed a difference. This difference resided in only one amino acid in the fragment concerned.

Hemoglobin A	Hemoglobin S
Val	Val
His	His
Leu	Leu
Thr	Thr
Pro	Pro
GLU	VAL
Glu	Glu
Lys	Lys

The only difference is the substitution of valine for glutamic acid. This single amino acid substitution also changes other hemoglobin properties, making the red blood cells abnormal.

Mutation, then, can result in an altered protein, as in the hemoglobin, or in no recognizable product at all, as in galactosemia and other diseases caused by metabolic blocks. It is possible that in cases where no enzyme activity is found, an altered, non-functioning protein is produced that is undetectable by means available today.

Cytogenetics.—Information can be obtained about the hereditability of traits from the analysis of pedigrees.

Twin studies have been useful in determining the relationship between heredity and environment. There are fraternal twins and identical twins. Fraternal twins result from separate fertilization of two different eggs produced by the mother at the same time. Each zygote develops separately and is no more like the other than any two siblings (brothers and/or sisters). They can be of the same or opposite sex, depending on the sperm that fertilized each egg. Identical twins come from one fertilized egg that divides and separates into two parts at some stage in development. Since both children come from one egg, they have identical genes and must, of course, be of the same sex. Any difference between them is due to environmental influences. Studies of identical twins raised apart have been useful in assessing the relative roles of hereditary and environmental influences. Certain traits—blood groups, fingerprints, eye color—are inherited and not noticeably influenced by environment. Body build, height, weight, and I.Q. are examples of traits that have a very large hereditary component, but are also much influenced by environmental factors.

This fits with the concept of the norm, or range of reaction. Genotypes of living things react with the environment in which they develop. There is a range of potentiality as to what the final phenotypes might be, depending on the interactions. A child potentially tall because of his genotype might be stunted in growth by poor food, disease, etc. But a child whose genotype limits his height to 5½ feet could never be six feet tall, regardless of all the food, vitamins, and good health that might be provided for him.

Another aspect of human genetics has developed because of new cytological techniques for study of human chromosomes. *Cytogenetics* is the study of the role played by cell components, particularly chromosomes, in heredity. Certain congenital abnormalities are associated with abnormal numbers of chromosomes. The normal number of chromosomes is 46. Mongolism, an abnormality accompanied by mental retardation, is associated with 47 chromosomes, the extra chromosome being one of the smallest autosomes.

■**GENES AND DEVELOPMENT.**—A challenging genetic problem is the gene's role in the development of the embryo. Each cell in an embryo has the same chromosomal complement because it is derived from the original zygote by mitosis. Yet some cells become spindle-shaped muscle cells whose major protein is myosin; some, red blood cells whose major protein is hemoglobin; some, glandular cells that secrete digestive enzymes. Each cell type has the same genes, but is different from other cell types. Genes control formation of proteins found in each cell; but some genes are active in muscle cells and inactive in liver cells, and vice versa. Differentiation involves a continual interaction between the nucleus and the cytoplasm, with substances in the cytoplasm acting on the genes in the nucleus to repress or stimulate certain activities. The nature of this interaction is of interest.

There are two approaches to the study of how gene action is regulated. One may trace the development of an inherited defect back to the earliest stage of the embryo. There is a mutation in chickens known as the *creeper fowl*, which when homozygous (*CpCp*) usually kills the chick in the egg after three days of incubation. The mutant lags behind the normal in growth at as early as 1½ days, and the limb rudiments fail to grow, although in normal chicks they grow rapidly at this time.

Transplantation and tissue culture studies have revealed that most tissue taken from day-old embryos will grow normally for many days. Had they developed within a creeper embryo, they would have died with it. Mutant chick cells can also live normally if the environment supplies something that could be missing in their usual environment.

Heart tissue from early creeper chicks is an exception. It will not grow normally in tissue culture, regardless of what is supplied. Thus, the gene *Cp* in some way produces a substance that affects the development of one embryonic organ, the heart. This leads to a defective circulatory system that cannot distribute food and oxygen to normal cells of the developing chick. Limb buds, which normally grow rapidly at 1½ days, are most in need of food and oxygen and are affected. The defect spreads and the chick dies.

A partial verification of this hypothesis comes from the following experiments. Limb buds from normal embryos grown in tissue culture with too few nutrients show many characteristics of creeper limb rudiments. Also, if certain chemicals that suppress normal metabolism are added to nutritive tissue culture media in which early limb rudiments are growing, development is suppressed in a manner that mimics the creeper phenotype.

Another approach is to start with the genes themselves in a less complex system, usually a microorganism, to determine how gene action is regulated. The method of regulation discovered may provide a model for gene regulation in differentiation. Jacob and Monod in Paris studied the bacillus *Escherichia coli* and its ability to metabolize the sugar lactose. They found two kinds of genes: —those that specify, via messenger RNA, the protein's structure and those that regulate the time and rate of activity of the structural genes. A regulator gene produces a repressor which enters the cytoplasm and inhibits the structural gene. When there are specific molecules present in the cell that combine with the repressor and thus inactivates it, the enzyme may be made. One such specific molecule would be the material on which the enzyme acts, called its *substrate*. This control prevents the cell's energy and amino acids from being wasted by producing unnecessary protein, and thus would have a selective advantage.

The particular system the French scientists studied in *E. coli* consists of four genes, three of which are closely linked to form a so-called *operon*, while the fourth is an unlinked regulator gene. The operon has two structural genes, one which controls the synthesis of an enzyme, called a *permease*, which permits the sugar to enter the cell. The second gene controls the synthesis of another enzyme, *beta-galactosidase*, which changes the lactose to simpler sugars. The third, an operator gene, does not control the enzyme structure; it coordinates the activity of the structural genes as follows: The unlinked regulator gene constantly produces a repressor substance (possibly an RNA) that keeps the operator inert. As soon as lactose is present in the cellular environment, the repressor combines with some of it and is no longer able to inhibit the operator gene. This gene starts a chain reaction along the operon, diagramed below; and the two structural genes produce their enzymes, permitting more lactose to enter the cell and to be metabolized to simpler sugars.

operator gene	beta-galactosidase gene	permease gene
O	O	O

This is an example of coordination of gene action and interaction between genes and substances within the cytoplasm, as well as control of the movement of substances through the cell membrane from the extracellular environment, all influencing one another. Such actions and interactions must take place in a regular sequence of time and space to produce each stage of the embryo until the fully developed organism is formed.

■**CYTOPLASMIC INHERITANCE.**—The primary mechanism of heredity is the self-duplicating gene of the chromosome. There are also cases of hereditary factors carried within the cytoplasm. Self-duplicating cytoplasmic factors are detected by a test in sexually reproducing organisms. Both egg and sperm contribute equal amounts of nuclear material to the zygote. The egg contributes the cytoplasm as well as the other haploid nucleus. If chromosomal genes are involved, no difference will be observed in offspring from reciprocal crosses. However, if a cytoplasmic factor is involved, it will be inherited through the cytoplasmic donor, the egg. As a result, there will be a difference between offspring from reciprocal crosses. The clearest examples are in plants and involve *plastids,* the small self-reproducing bodies that carry chlorophyll. This type of inheritance accounts for many of the green-and-white spotted leaves on ornamental plants.

Other small bodies in the cytoplasm, including the *centrosomes, mitochondria,* viruses, and virus-like bodies, are thought to be self-duplicating. In addition to green plants, maternal inheritance has been found in mice, *Drosophila, Paramecium,* some other one-celled animals, and molds, like *Neurospora* and yeast.

Genes and Evolution.—The theory of natural selection (developed by Charles Darwin) as the mechanism of organic evolution has been the integrating force common to all biology. It is of interest to observe how the mechanism has been applied to large populations. Consider, for example, the blood groups. The most common in the American white population is group O at 45 per cent; next is group A at 38.5 per cent; group B is 13 per cent; and AB is 3.5 per cent. Blood groups are inherited in a Mendelian fashion. One might question how mutations caused by radiation or chemicals would affect the frequency of the blood group genes, or whether the same frequency occurs in different geographic locations, or whether the frequency is changing with time. These questions belong to the realm of population genetics. Since organic evolution involves the changes in gene frequencies in populations in time and place, this branch of genetics strives to explain the mechanism of evolution.

The principle of population genetics was developed independently in 1908 by the Englishman Hardy and the German Weinberg, and hence is known as the Hardy-Weinberg law. It states that relative gene frequencies remain constant from generation to generation in an infinitely large interbreeding population in which mating is at random, and in which there is no selection, migration, or mutation.

How, then, could evolution, which involves change in the genetic composition of populations take place? Obviously, both mutation and selection do occur, as well as some migration and isolation of small populations. These are the factors that influence evolution.

Let us consider mutation first. Mutations occur spontaneously, for unknown reasons, at predictable but

AMERICAN MUSEUM OF NATURAL HISTORY

LEAFLIKE Kallima butterfly of India survives because of its natural camouflage.

low rates. Most mutations are harmful, because the genes already present in the populations have been the most successful survivors over millions of years that life has existed. Dominant lethal mutations are eliminated from the reservoir of genes in the population because the individuals in whom they occur die early in life. An occasional mutation is beneficial because it confers on the recipient a better chance to survive and pass the gene on to offspring. Such a gene is said to have a selective advantage.

Darwin observed that in most species of plants and animals the offspring produced are more numerous than their parents, yet most populations remain relatively stable in size. Also, many variations exist in nature, and most of these are inherited. As a result of the great numbers of offspring, competition exists; those best fitted by virtue of their variations will survive and pass on these variations to the next generation.

Beneficial genes remain in the gene pool, and dominant lethals are driven out. Unless they are disadvantageous to the heterozygote in the competition for food and mate, lethal recessive genes will be passed on, and not eliminated from the gene pool. If they are a disadvantage to the heterozygote, they will be eliminated very slowly over many generations. Many recessive harmful genes persist in populations because they are beneficial to the heterozygote. Sickle cell anemia is an example. The homozygote *SS* dies early, and the heterozygote *AS* has both normal and sickle cell hemoglobin. The trait is common in central Africa where a severe form of malaria exists. People with normal hemoglobin *AA* readily succumb to the disease, whereas heterozygotes *AS* are relatively resistant to this disease and have as much as a 25 per cent better chance of attaining adulthood than do the normal homozygotes.

Thus, a gene is maintained in the population even though individuals

homozygous for it die before reaching productive age. This is a case of *balanced polymorphism,* which maintains alternative genotypes in a population by a balance between forces selecting for and against the gene. It is closely related to *heterosis,* or hybrid vigor, exemplified in hybrid corn in which a combination of genes makes it better than any homozygous line.

Although evolution is usually too slow a process for a person to observe in a lifetime, there are some examples of evolutionary change that have been observed recently. One is the development of DDT-resistant strains of insects. No doubt there were always some insects that could have survived DDT, but this was not a selective advantage in a DDT-free world. Once the chemical came into wide use, they were the ones who survived and reproduced, while the DDT-sensitive insects died. Thus, a change in environment (use of DDT) brought about a change in the characteristics of the insect world.

An important question to the population geneticist is: What is the genetic basis of the origin of species? He defines a single species as one in which members can crossbreed and produce fertile hybrids. New species arise through isolation of one group from another. Within each region of different environment, the population over many generations will become unique because of the selection of traits adaptively advantageous in that particular area. After a long time, the individual groups will have diverged to the extent that they no longer can interbreed. They are then separate species, and will remain separate even if they should occupy the same environment. This has happened many times in the course of evolution.

Progress in Genetics.—The significant advances made in the study of genetics are reflected by the number of Nobel Prize awards received by geneticists in recent years. Thomas Hunt Morgan received the award in 1934; Hermann Joseph Muller in 1946; George Wells Beadle, Edward Lawrie Tatum, and Joshua Lederberg in 1958; Arthur Kornberg and Severo Ochoa in 1959; and most recently, Francis Harry Compton Crick, James Watson, and Maurice Hugh Frederick Wilkins in 1962.

—Selma Silagi

BIBLIOGRAPHY

CARSON, HAMPTON LAWRENCE. *Heredity and Human Life.* Columbia University Press, 1963.

DARWIN, CHARLES. *Evolution of Life.* The University of Chicago Press, 1960.

DOBZHANSKY, THEODOSIUS. *Genetics and the Origin of Species.* Columbia University Press, 1951.

ERLICH, PAUL R. *The Process of Evolution.* McGraw-Hill, Inc., 1963.

SAGER, RUTH and RYAN, FRANCIS JOSEPH. *Cell Heredity.* John Wiley & Sons, Inc., 1961.

BIOLOGICAL RELATIONSHIPS

Understanding Living Organisms.—In a world increasingly oriented toward technology it is sometimes difficult to remember our relationships to the earth and to other living things on it. Although it has become easy to make the false assumption that man is now independent of the old biological world, today we are almost as dependent upon our biological environment as our ancestors were thousands of years ago. We still require the same quantities of oxygen, water, and minerals from the soil that they did. We must still obtain the same quantity of energy from our food. The things that we eat must, as in the past, acquire this energy from sunlight and must still grow from the soil. We have not changed our tolerance to heat or cold, drought or humidity, radiation or pressure. Our advances have not come from any increased ability to adapt to a broader environment, but from learning how to maintain a suitable environment around us. Further technical advancement and survival in a world with an expanding population depend upon an understanding of ourselves as biological organisms and of our relationships with other organisms in the physical world.

In nature no living thing exists by itself. Each is part of an intricate structure composed of other living organisms and of the physical environment that encompasses them.

■ **ECOLOGY.**—The study of organisms in relation to each other and to their environment is known as *ecology.* One of the younger fields of biology, ecology has rapidly gained in importance; most of its developments have come since 1900 and more particularly since the 1940's. Ecology has been subdivided into two areas: *autecology,* concerned with the relation of the individual plant or animal to its environment; and *synecology,* concerned with the relation of populations of individuals to other groups and to their total environment.

Ecology has also been divided into the two fields of plant ecology and animal ecology, but one does not have to go very deeply into either field to realize that this separation is artificial. In studying the ecology of plants, an involvement with animals is inevitable. The study of animal ecology almost immediately entails the study of vegetation. There is fundamentally just one ecology, and it is concerned with the study of ecological systems, *ecosystems,* and the plants or animals of which these systems are composed.

Population, Community, Ecosystem.—Fundamental to the study of ecology are three different concepts: population, community, and ecosystem. A *population* is the total of all the individuals of a given species occupying a particular area. Each individual is necessarily part of a population; everything about it is affected by its place or status in the population; and even as an outcast it exists in rela-

tionship to the whole population.

But a population does not exist alone. Each occurs as part of a *biotic community,* a community of living creatures. Any species forms only a part of the community, for it is dependent upon other species for food or shelter, or in turn provides food or shelter for another species. Similarly, the biotic community is not an isolated entity, but bears relationships to other communities and to its physical environment. It cannot exist without the soil or rock, water, atmosphere, and sunlight. Thus each biotic community forms, in combination with its physical environment, an ecosystem.

■ **POPULATION.**—Although defined as the sum of individuals, a population is something more than the total of its parts and contains qualities not possessed by any individual member. Important properties of a population that are of interest to both ecologist and census-taker are the number of individuals and their relationship to the area occupied. Knowledge of these characteristics permits the calculation of *density,* which is the number of individuals per unit of area. Also important is the *structure* of the population. This refers to the sex and age composition of the whole: the number of males in relation to females and the age distribution of each sex. Finally, the student of population is interested in population *dynamics,* changes over a period of time and the forces that influence these changes. These are brought about by birth rates, or *natality;* death rates, or *mortality;* and *movements* of individuals into or out of the population.

In order to understand these movements, the factors influencing birth and death rates, and the determinants of population density, the student of animal population may investigate questions similar to those regarding the economic and social status of human populations. In a study of the Norway rat, investigators found that rat populations were essentially self-limiting. Even with abundant food and shelter their numbers were restricted by social factors, particularly an aversion to crowding. Other animals sometimes show no such aversion and, if their numbers are not checked by outside forces, eat themselves out of house and home.

Biotic Potential.—Populations that are not self-limiting are eventually checked in their growth by the pressures of environment. Each species is capable, if unchecked by mortality, of a high rate of increase, known as its *biotic potential.* Small animals with rapid breeding rates have a higher biotic potential than do large animals. But even the largest and slowest breeders could, if entirely unchecked, overrun the earth. Mankind, with a low biotic potential, currently shows signs of doing just that. But no population is long immune to mortality. Inevi-

tably factors in the environment will cause losses or inhibit the birth rate. Predators kill other animals; diseases and parasites decimate species; weather causes loss or checks gains from natality. If all other factors fail, the lack of food, water, or some other essential will limit population growth. The total of all agents in an environment that cause loss or arrest population growth is known as the *environmental resistance.*

A *stable population* is one in which the biotic potential and the environmental resistance are in balance. Interference with such a population can affect this stability and cause severe fluctuations. Some populations normally fluctuate in a regular and predictable manner. These are known as *cyclic populations.* The snowshoe hare and Canada lynx, for example, regularly reach a population peak at nine- to ten-year intervals. This is followed by a marked decline. Other populations are normally stable, but occasionally show a striking increase to "plague" proportions, followed by a major decrease. Such population changes are called *irruptions.* However, most populations are relatively stable. This indicates the presence of constant environmental resistance.

■ **COMMUNITY.**—Studies of any population soon lead to questions about the total community of which the population is a part. The community of the ecologist differs from the community of the sociologist in that the biotic community is always composed of more than one species: for example, populations of plants and of the animals that feed upon those plants. Communities vary in complexity. A simple community would be that of hardy lichens growing on an exposed rock surface along with the few associated organisms, mostly small to microscopic, that can find food and shelter among the lichens. The lichen itself is an example of the close ecological relationship between species. It is not a simple plant, but consists of two different kinds of plants living in close association and depending upon one another: a green alga that manufactures food from sunlight, water, and atmospheric gases; and a colorless fungus that shelters and anchors the algae and in turn receives food from the algal cells. Such a close association and mutual dependence between species is an example of a relationship known as *symbiosis* or *mutualism.*

At the other extreme of complexity from the simple lichen community is the tropical rain forest. Here the growing conditions are so nearly ideal for plants that hundreds of different species of trees sometimes occur within a small area. Associated with the trees are an even greater variety of other plants, including *epiphytes* (plants such as the orchids that grow high on tree trunks) and giant vines, or *lianas,* that also depend upon the trees for their support. Finding food and shelter in this mass of vegetation are a greater variety of birds, insects,

SIMPLIFIED ECOSYSTEM with its five basic components: an energy source (the sun), consumer organisms (animals designated *A, B, C,* and *D*), producer organisms (plants *E, F,* and *G*), reducer organisms (remains *H* and *I*), and abiotic, or nonliving, chemicals (*J, K,* and *L*). Reducer organisms return these abiotic chemicals to the soil or the sea.

and other forms of animal life than one can find in any comparable area.

Biotic communities do not spring suddenly into existence, but instead develop through a long process known as *biotic succession*. Succession, in its primary form, occurs in areas that have not previously supported life: bare rocks or newly formed lakes or ponds. The first invaders of such areas are always the more hardy plants and animals. They change the environment so that it can be occupied in turn by more demanding species. A predictable series of changes which lead to greater complexity usually occurs. The soil is further developed and becomes able to support a greater variety of life. Eventually a relatively stable community, in balance with the prevailing climate and adjusted to a mature soil, occupies the area until some disturbance destroys it. When this occurs, the process of succession begins again. This secondary succession may have fewer stages than a primary succession and usually resembles a primary succession's later stages. The relatively stable community resulting

from a succession is known as a *climax community*.

■ECOSYSTEM.—No biotic community exists apart from its physical environment. Each depends upon sunlight to provide energy, soil minerals, water, and atmospheric gases. Each is influenced by all the physical and chemical forces that characterize the area in which it is found. Since the interrelationship between the living portion of a community and the nonliving (*abiotic*) environment is so intricate that the two are virtually inseparable, it is necessary to consider them together as an ecological system. The ecosystem therefore becomes the fundamental unit of study for the ecologist. Ecosystems, like the communities that comprise them, can be simple or complex. However, even the most simple artificial system, set up in a laboratory test tube, often reveals complexities that require detailed study. Natural ecosystems may seem to defy any complete analysis or understanding.

Any ecosystem has five basic components: (1) *Energy,* usually derived from sunlight, but rarely and in small

quantities from other sources. This moves through the ecosystem along pathways known as food chains, which are described below. (2) *Abiotic chemicals,* including soil minerals, water, and atmospheric gases. (3) *Producer organisms,* usually green plants capable of capturing sunlight energy through the process of photosynthesis. They utilize the energy to construct the organic chemical compounds which form the plant body, or they store it in energy bonds and link the various atoms or molecules in these organic compounds. (4) *Consumer organisms,* such as some colorless, nongreen plants, and all animals in the community. Consumers do not obtain their energy directly, but acquire it secondhand from the sunlight energy originally stored in green plants. All animals are completely dependent upon the producers for energy and for the chemicals that they require for nutrition. Consumers are subdivided into two categories: *primary consumers,* or *herbivores,* that feed directly upon plants; and *secondary consumers,* or *carnivores,* that feed mainly on other animals and thus receive their energy or food chemicals after they have been processed through two other kinds of organisms. (5) *Reducer organisms,* mainly bacteria and fungi that decay and decompose the bodies of dead plants and animals. These organisms feed upon the plants' complex chemical compounds and in turn release simpler compounds. Through this process mineral materials that can be picked up and used once more by the roots of growing plants are eventually returned to the soil or water. Without such organisms an entire community would stagnate, choked by its own debris, and the fertility of the soil would be drained without being restored.

Concept of Niche.—Each of the many species within an ecosystem occupies a particular place in the environment. This place is known as the *ecologic niche* for the species and is not inhabited by any other group. In a broad sense the niche for a herbivore includes suitable green plants on which it can feed, and is influenced by the presence of secondary consumers that will in turn feed upon the herbivore. A herbivore such as the deer requires certain shrubs and herbs which are of a suitable height and contain essential nutritional elements in a palatable form. Drinking water should not be too far from the food supply, and both should be accessible. Shelter is also necessary so that the deer can escape from extreme heat or cold, avoid storms, and evade enemies. Salt licks to provide minerals lacking in food may also be essential. The presence and availability of these elements usually guarantee the deer's occupation of a place in the biotic community.

In turn, the deer's existence, along with other factors, will help create a niche for such other species as the mountain lion which feeds on the deer and the various parasites that depend upon the deer for food and shelter. Deer may also influence the vegetation and prevent the establishment of certain plants on which they feed too heavily, or alter the form or abundance of other plants.

Similar kinds of vegetation usually provide similar niches for animals. A tropical rain forest may harbor a leopard in Africa, a panther in Southeast Asia, and a jaguar in South America, each species occupying a similar niche. Grasslands everywhere provide niches for large, grazing herbivores. But the species of herbivore occupying the niche may vary from one continent to another.

Energy Flow.—The ancients worshipped the sun-god as the giver of life. Today's ecologists could have provided them with a much more complete justification for their religion than their high priest could have imagined. Until recently, all of the energy upon which life depended, and all of the power which made human civilization possible, came directly or indirectly from sunlight. With the discovery of atomic energy and the technology permitting its utilization, man has for the first time established a small degree of independence from solar energy. Complete independence, however, probably cannot be attained. The calories that sustain our work and maintain our bodies were originally sunlight calories. Heat given off by petroleum and coal runs our machinery. This heat was once trapped from solar energy by plants in the swamp forests and ocean waters. The water spinning the turbines in the hydroelectric dams was lifted from the oceans and transported to the streams by solar energy.

■PHOTOSYNTHESIS.—In ecosystems the source of energy is sunlight, and only green plants are equipped to utilize it. A few kinds of plants, the iron and sulfur bacteria, can exist without sunlight because they use energy stored in iron or sulfur compounds. But they do not contribute significant amounts of energy or chemicals to the earth's ecosystems. The mechanisms by which green plants use solar energy, known as *photosynthesis,* are extremely complex, and plant physiologists and biochemists have been unable as yet to work out all of the details. Suffice to say that the presence of a complex green compound, *chlorophyll,* permits the capturing of particles of sunlight energy and their storage in chemical bonds in the various parts of the plant. The simple sugar *glucose* is one of the first of these storage compounds. Through further use of sunlight energy, molecules of glucose are broken down and linked with other chemicals. This results in the formation of the various carbohydrates, proteins, vitamins, and other substances that constitute the body of a plant.

During photosynthesis two chemical compounds, carbon dioxide from the air and water from the soil, are combined into simple sugars. In the process, oxygen is released back into the atmosphere. The presence of this gas in the earth's atmosphere is believed to be a contribution from the past generations of plants. Without green plants or some other means of restoring atmospheric oxygen, the continued respiration by animals would eventually exhaust the supply of oxygen on which we all depend.

■LOSS OF ENERGY.—Green plants are the only organisms capable of storing large amounts of solar energy. Man has learned various ways of making direct use of this energy, but he has not yet devised effective ways of storing it in quantity. However, photosynthesis is not an efficient process. It has been calculated that only about 1 per cent of the total solar energy reaching the earth is actually fixed and stored by plants. The rest is lost, either because it is in wavelengths of light that plants cannot use; because it is reflected from the surface of plants or from bare soil, rock, or water; or because it is dissipated in the form of heat. Nevertheless, the total quantity of solar energy reaching the earth is so large that the 1 per cent remaining is more than adequate to maintain terrestrial life.

Inefficiency is also apparent in the step from plants to herbivorous animals. The energy stored within plant bodies cannot be transferred to animal tissues without loss. Some remains in the indigestible residue of plants; some is lost as heat generated in the process of digestion; and other fractions are lost during various metabolic processes in the animal's body. About 20 per cent of the energy is deposited in the body tissues of herbivores. A diminished amount of energy is thus available to the animals which feed on them. Further energy is lost in eating, digesting, and metabolizing the energy stored in a herbivore's body. Of the total herbivore supply of energy (which could be determined by burning tissues in a calorimeter), only a quarter or less will end up as energy stored in the body of a carnivore and available, therefore, to any creature that feeds upon carnivores.

It is obvious that this process cannot go on for long because one cannot have an unending chain of organisms feeding upon one another. Energy follows a one-way path through the ecosystem, with the initial supply rapidly dwindling as it passes from one organism to the next. In order for the system to function, energy must be supplied continually at the green end of the chain.

Energy relationships within an ecosystem illustrate the operation of the *second law of thermodynamics.* This law states that in any transfer of energy some energy is lost to the system and dispersed in a degraded form no longer capable of doing work. The various levels through which energy is transferred in a community are known as *trophic levels.* Producers, primary and secondary consumers, and reducers represent trophic levels. Food chains are the pathways over which energy is transferred from one organism to another.

Food Chains.—A simple predator food chain can be represented by the grass-steer-man linkage, where grass, steer, and man typify separate trophic levels and links. It is possible to have a longer food chain of this type. In a pond, for example, microscopic green algae are fed upon by small, floating animals (*zooplankton*). These in turn are fed upon by aquatic insects that provide food for small carnivorous fish. These small fish may in turn support a population of such large fish as bass or pike. Because of the energy relationships involved, it is rare to have more than five or six links in such a chain. In addition to predator food chains, other food chains go from large animals down through small. There are also food chains composed of reducer organisms which are involved in the breakdown of dead plant or animal tissues. Food chains are difficult to isolate in natural ecosystems because they are usually intertwined into complex

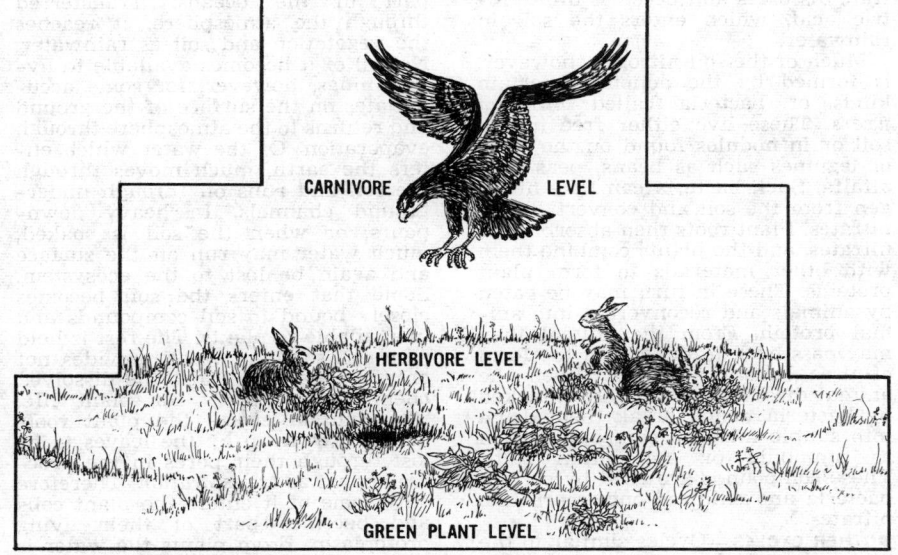

BIOTIC PYRAMID, which is based upon the diminishing quantities at each stage of the food chain, is illustrated by the large number of growths at the green-plant level, the three rabbits at the herbivore level, and the solitary eagle at the carnivore level.

food webs. Besides feeding a steer, a green plant furnishes food for a variety of small animals (including insects and microorganisms) which are then eaten by other species. Hence it is difficult to unravel the chains and webs in any complex community.

■**BIOTIC PYRAMIDS.**—The necessary loss of energy between links in each food chain has a direct effect upon the number of organisms that can be supported at any trophic level. Thus the number of green plants upon which deer will feed is always greater than the number of deer that will be supported by them. The number of deer is in turn always greater than the number of mountain lions that feed upon them. These relationships can be diagramed in the form of *biotic pyramids,* which may illustrate either the number of organisms, the total weight of organisms, or the calories of energy stored in each layer of organisms. In a pyramid of numbers there will be more green plants than herbivores supported by them, and more herbivores than carnivores. Therefore the pyramid will show a broad base of plants and a narrow apex of carnivores. The picture would be similar if the relative weights were charted. It would take about 12,000 pounds of range forage to support a 1,000-pound steer for a year, and the steer could be converted into beef and support a 170-pound man.

Man, an omnivorous creature, can support himself largely upon a predominantly plant or animal diet. If he acts as a herbivore, or *vegetarian,* more food energy is available to him because energy is not lost in the transfer through another herbivore. Less food, but of higher nutritional quality, is available when man functions as a carnivore. This is not just a matter of theoretical interest. In order to feed the mass of people in an overpopulated country such as China, the waste of energy involved in feeding cereal grains to domestic animals must be eliminated. People must consume food plants directly, and dietary quality must be sacrificed to provide the calories needed to sustain life.

Chemical Cycles.—Besides aiding the flow of energy, food chains provide pathways for the chemical materials required by the body tissues of plants and animals. Some of these chemical materials enter the soil when the rocks in which they originate are decomposed. Others are washed away to ponds and eventually come to rest in the oceans. From any of these substrates—soil, fresh water, or the sea— these minerals can be taken up by green plants and introduced into food chains. Unlike energy flow, however, the flow of chemical materials is not one-way, but circular. The same atom or molecule is used again and again. Moving from plant to animal, it is returned to the soil only to be taken up once more by some other plant. It is likely that the calcium and phosphorus in the bones of a living man were once part of the bones of a now extinct animal. These same elements doubtlessly passed through countless generations of prairie plants, ante-

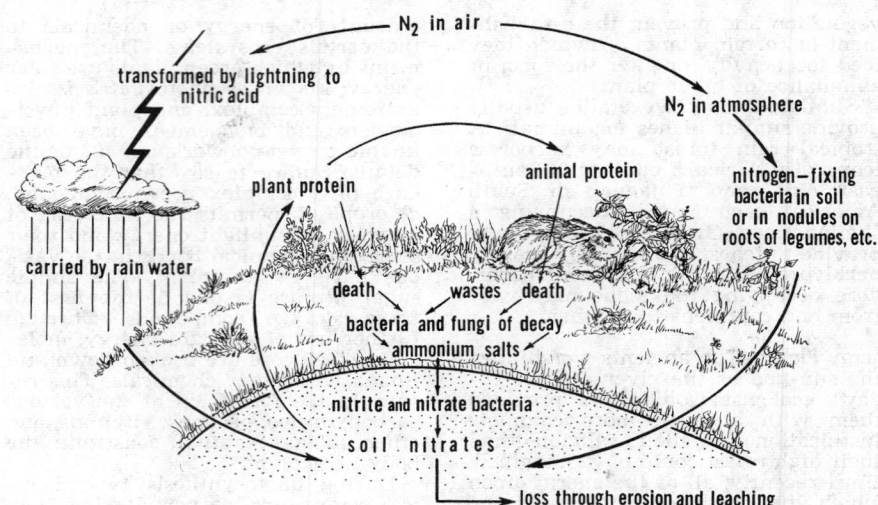

NITROGEN CYCLE shows how the nitrogen (N_2) in the air is transformed into the nitrates utilized by living organisms and then returned to the soil for further use. Nitrogen is essential to life because it is an integral part of the protein material present in living cells.

lopes, buffaloes, and wolves before being taken up by a wheat plant and later ground into flour.

■**NITROGEN CYCLE.**—One of the mineral pathways which have been thoroughly studied is the cycle through which nitrogen becomes available to living creatures. Nitrogen is essential for life because it forms an integral part of the proteins which must be present in each living cell. It is also one of the more common elements on earth and constitutes nearly 80 per cent of the atmosphere. Atmospheric nitrogen, however, is a relatively inert gas and does not combine readily with other elements. It cannot be used directly by most plants or animals, but must first be oxidized and converted to a nitrate. This conversion occurs when lightning ionizes atmospheric nitrogen and permits the gases to combine. The resultant nitrate dissolves and becomes dilute nitric acid, which enters the soil in rainwater.

Much of the soil nitrogen, however, is formed by the action of certain kinds of bacteria called *nitrogen fixers.* These live either free in the soil or in nodules found on the roots of legumes such as beans, peas, and alfalfa. Such bacteria can take nitrogen from the soil and convert it into nitrates. Plant roots then absorb these nitrates, and the plants combine them with other materials to form plant proteins. These in turn may be eaten by animals and reconverted into animal protein. From the animal they may pass back to the soil in the form of urea or other wastes. When the animal dies, its proteins are attacked by bacteria which break them down into simple nitrogen compounds such as ammonia or ammonium salts. These compounds are used by certain bacteria and oxidized once more into nitrates.

■**OTHER CYCLES.**—Cycles similar to the nitrogen cycle have been traced for various other elements. Since the chemicals required for life are numerous, and the supply in the soil is

not inexhaustible, there must be a continuous turnover of these materials if an area is to continue to grow living things and support living animals. In some complex biotic communities, such as dense, luxuriant forests, a high percentage of the chemicals derived from the soil may be within the bodies of the plants and animals. When soil nutrients are scarce, new growth depends upon the decay of dead plants and animals. Organisms such as earthworms process great amounts of plant litter through their bodies. Their actions accelerate decomposition and make available the materials necessary for new growth. Caterpillars that feed on leaves and add their excrement to the soil similarly hasten the rate of chemical turnover.

■**WATER CYCLE.**—Water, which is essential to life, originates for the most part in the oceans. Transferred through the atmosphere, it reaches the vegetation and soil as rainwater. Not all of it becomes available to living things, however, for some accumulates on the surface of the ground and returns to the atmosphere through evaporation. Of the water which enters the earth, much moves through the soil and runs off through underground channels. In heavy downpours, or when the soil is soaked, much water may run off the surface and again be lost to the ecosystem. Some that enters the soil becomes closely bound to soil compounds and unavailable to plants. The rest is held as a soil solution which provides not only the water but also the dissolved chemicals necessary for plant life. The solution enters the plant roots and is drawn up by the leaves to be lost through their pores in the process known as *transpiration.* Therefore only some of it enters the plant cells and becomes part of their living protoplasm. From plants the water is transferred to animals, which may also obtain a supply directly from runoff held for a time in streams or pools or from underground sources

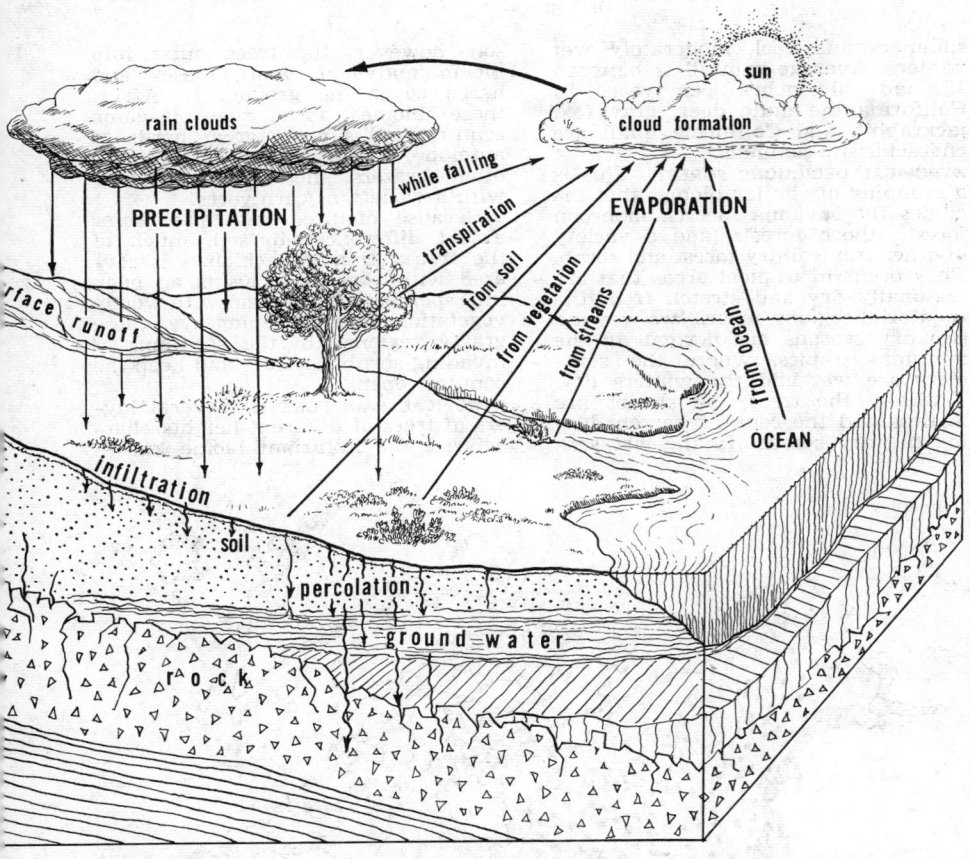

sun

rain clouds

cloud formation

while falling

PRECIPITATION

transpiration

EVAPORATION

from soil

from vegetation

from streams

from ocean

surface runoff

OCEAN

infiltration

soil

percolation

ground water

r o c k

HYDROLOGIC CYCLE is composed of (1) evaporation of water from the surface of the earth to form water-vapor clouds, (2) precipitation of the water in the form of rain and snow back to the surface, and (3) infiltration and percolation of the water into the ground.

that reach the surface as springs. Eventually, however, all of the water used by plants and animals returns to the soil or is lost directly into the atmosphere. In either event it re-enters the complex cycle.

Varieties of Ecosystems.—Because their distribution is determined largely by climate and topography, the kinds of ecosystems vary greatly from one part of the world to another. Classifications of ecosystems vary according to the emphasis that ecologists place upon their distinguishing features. Perhaps the most useful broad classification of terrestrial ecosystems is the *biome* system, which recognizes certain major natural communities distributed over the world in accordance with the occurrence of the major types of climate. Climate, vegetation, and animal life are so closely related that in the past, when meteorological records were scarce, geographers mapped the boundaries of climatic regions according to the occurrence of major changes in the vegetation.

■**DISTRIBUTION OF BIOMES.**—If you were to fly down the western coast of North America, starting at Point Barrow, Alaska, you would observe the sequence of biomes that extends between the Arctic and the tropics. First is an extensive region of treeless ground covered with low-growing vegetation. These arctic barren grounds are known as the *tundra*. In the vicinity of the Alaskan peninsula

are the first fringes of dark spruce forest, the *taiga*. Next, across the peninsula, beyond the open spruce, are the northward reaches of the *temperate rain forest*. This is a tall, dense forest of Sitka spruce, cedar, and hemlock that continues, with some changes in species, all the way south along the coast to the San Francisco Bay region.

North of San Francisco the forest is broken; and to the south it is replaced by a lower-growing woodland of evergreen oaks or, more frequently, by the dense brush known as *chaparral*. Chaparral and woodland dominate as far south as Baja California, where they are replaced by open desert vegetation. Still farther south, on the mainland of Mexico, the desert vegetation is supplanted by dry tropical scrub and woodland. In Central America this gives way to the dense, luxuriant rain forests of the humid tropics. A continuation of the journey south along the western coast of South America would reveal a similar pattern of vegetation. However, the biomes would appear in a reverse order. Rain forest would give way to woodland and scrub, these regions to desert. In central Chile chaparral would replace the desert, and still farther south would be a dense temperate rain forest not unlike that of the Pacific Northwest. These changes in vegetation represent the major biomes of the continental west coasts of the world and the principal cli-

matic regions of these coasts. Along the eastern coasts of continents some biomes will be different because of different climatic influences.

Ecologists classify the biomes of the regions of the world in a number of diverse ways. All of them, however, recognize the major divisions described below:

■**TUNDRA.**—The tundra characterizes regions of arctic climate with long, cold winters when the sun hardly appears above the horizon, short summer growing seasons of perpetual daylight, and relatively little precipitation. The soil is underlain in most places by permanently frozen ground, the *permafrost*, because summer temperatures are too low to thaw more than the surface layers of ground. Poor drainage causes boggy ground at lower elevations. The vegetation consists of dwarf shrubs and trees, matlike, broad-leaved herbs, grasses, sedges, and, in places, extensive stands of reindeer moss or lichen. This is the home of the caribou, reindeer, and musk ox; of the ptarmigan, white fox, arctic hare, and lemming. North of it lies the barren icefield of the Arctic Ocean. Above it on the mountains are bare rock, snowfields, and glaciers. Composed of those hardy species of plant and animal that have adapted to the extremes of climate, the tundra is the farthest extension of life to the north. It covers the northern fringe of Canada and Alaska and then extends in a band across northern Europe and Asia. Tundra is found also in the higher mountains, above timberline, extending south along mountain ranges into the temperate zone.

■**BOREAL AND MONTANE FORESTS.**—South of the tundra zone, or below it on the mountain ranges, is a forest dominated by needle-leaved evergreen conifers, mainly spruce and fir. This forest biome is the most extensive on the earth and covers much of Canada, Alaska, northern Europe, and Siberia. On its northern border the dark spruce trees are stunted and widely spaced where they merge with tundra. Farther south they grow in taller, denser stands and become mixed with fir, tamarack, or pine. In areas ravaged by fire the conifers are replaced by the broad-leaved birch and aspen. This biome occurs in regions of subarctic climate where winters are severe, but summer growing seasons are longer than in the tundra.

The summer heat is sufficient to prevent development of permafrost. Precipitation is higher than in the arctic region, averaging 15 to 30 inches a year. This biome is the home of the moose, snowshoe hare, northern grouse, goshawk, horned owl, red fox, and Canada lynx. Neither the tundra nor the boreal forest is found in the Southern Hemisphere, although some areas near the tip of South America are similar. This occurs because the southern continents do not have a large enough landmass close enough to the antarctic climatic regions to have the rigorous temperatures characteristic of the northern biomes. The climate of Antarctica is too extreme to support tundra.

■**TEMPERATE RAIN FOREST.**—This forest is dominated in the Northern Hemisphere by a dense, luxuriant stand of tall conifers, usually spruce, cedar, hemlock, Douglas fir, and redwood. In the Southern Hemisphere a forest of similar appearance is dominated by the southern beech (*Nothofagus*) and such southern conifers as *Araucaria* and *Podocarpus*. For sheer volume of wood supported by each acre of land, the forests of coastal North America are unsurpassed. Some of the world's largest trees are found among the redwoods and Douglas firs of California and the Northwest. The reason for this vegetative abundance is the climate, which presents no extremes of cold or drought. Mild temperatures and high rainfall characterize the winters; the summers are cool and seldom without moisture. The growing conditions are thus second only to those of the humid tropical rain forest. The temperate rain forest supports no great mass of animal life, but provides a home for a great variety of smaller species. Characteristic of the North American region are the Roosevelt elk, mountain beaver, and black-tailed deer.

Because of the Gulf Stream influence, the climate necessary for a temperate rain forest does not occur in Europe. Neither Africa nor Australia reaches far enough south to have the necessary weather conditions. Similar climate and vegetation occur, however, on the western coast of New Zealand's South Island.

■**TEMPERATE DECIDUOUS FOREST.**—In the eastern United States, western Europe, and northern China, the original vegetation was a forest of such broad-leaved trees as beech, maple, walnut, hickory, and oak. Man's influence has been felt more readily in these regions than in the others and has radically changed the environment. The climate of this biome is one of warm, wet summers and moderately cold, often snowy winters. A total rainfall of between 40 and 60 inches is adequate to support such a dense forest. Most of the trees adapt to the unfavorable winter growing conditions by shedding their leaves and becoming dormant. Unlike the conifers, which are mostly soft-wooded trees, the broad-leaved species are hardwoods and are considered among the most valued cabinet and furniture woods. In the United States this biome is the home of the white-tailed deer, wild turkey, gray squirrel, and cottontail rabbit.

■**MEDITERRANEAN FOREST AND SCRUB.**—This biome exists in much of California, central Chile, the Cape of Good Hope region in South Africa, and southern Australia. It occurs most widely around the Mediterranean Sea in Europe, Asia, and Africa. The vegetation consists of broad-leaved evergreens and is called *sclerophyll* because the leaves are hard and waxy. Live oak, madroña, and laurel are most widespread in the California woodland, but over much of this biome brush (known as chaparral in California and maquis in Europe) has replaced the forest or woodland. The climate of this biome is one of warm, rainless summers and cool, moderately wet winters. Average rainfall is between 15 and 30 inches per year. In California the mule deer, gray fox, jackrabbit, and California quail are characteristic animals.

■**TROPICAL DECIDUOUS FOREST.**—This is a grouping of similar biomes that includes the savanna forests, monsoon forests, thorn forests, and a variety of other tropical dry forest and scrub. They occur in tropical areas that are seasonally dry and stretch from the equatorial regions, where two wet and two dry seasons are normal, to the marginal tropics, where the summers are wet and the winters dry. Typically the trees and shrubs are leafless and the country barren during the dry season. In the wet season, however, the trees burst into bloom and leaf; and grasses and herbs cover the ground. In Africa these biomes form the big-game country and support great herds of antelope, zebra, buffalo, elephant, and other grazers and browsers, along with a variety of carnivores.

Because of fire, and to a lesser extent differences in soil, much of the area within these biomes is covered with *savanna*. This is an open interspersion of grassland with woody vegetation. Fires sweeping over these grassy regions kill the seedlings of invading shrubs or trees and keep the country open.

■**TROPICAL RAIN FOREST.**—Several layers of trees of different heights characterize the luxuriant biome known

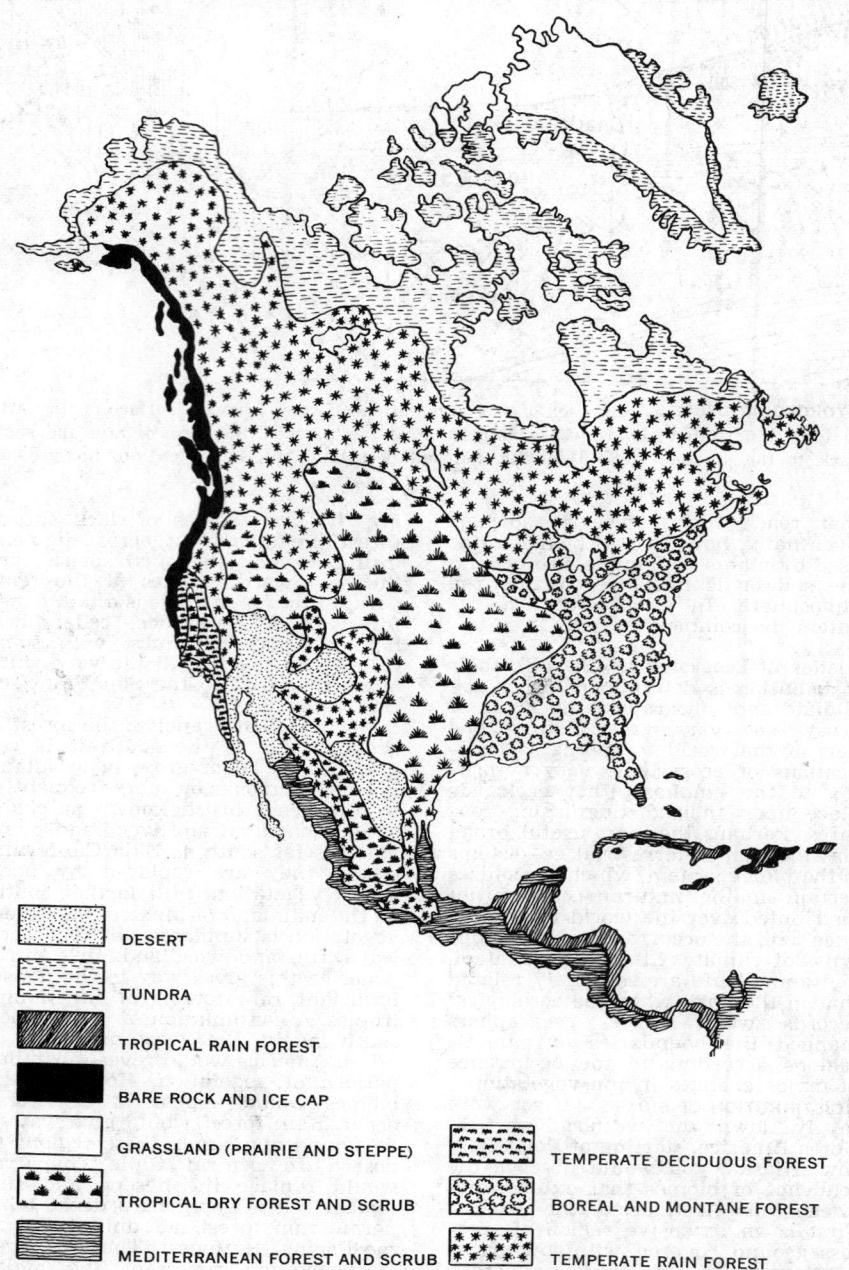

DESERT

TUNDRA

TROPICAL RAIN FOREST

BARE ROCK AND ICE CAP

GRASSLAND (PRAIRIE AND STEPPE)

TROPICAL DRY FOREST AND SCRUB

MEDITERRANEAN FOREST AND SCRUB

TEMPERATE DECIDUOUS FOREST

BOREAL AND MONTANE FOREST

TEMPERATE RAIN FOREST

BIOMES OF NORTH AMERICA

as the *tropical rain forest.* The trees are broad-leaved and evergreen, and in the mature forest the floor is relatively open. In some places one can walk on a dense mat of decomposing litter through aisles formed by the trunks of the rain forest trees. Where the mature forest has been cut or otherwise disturbed, however, a dense, almost impenetrable jungle springs up. This in turn is replaced, after many years, by another mature forest. Numerous species of trees occur within this region. However, it is unusual to find more than a few of each type in any one area. This has prevented the development of forest industries to any great extent, since the commercially valuable trees are widely scattered. Along with the great variety of plants, the rain forest supports more birds, insects, and small, tree-dwelling mammals than does any other biome.

This biome exists only in permanently warm and humid tropical areas. It is developed extensively in tropical areas with year-round rainfall; but in modified form, as gallery forest, it follows the banks of the larger permanent streams in the tropics. On tropical mountains, forests derived from the lowland rain forests occur, but these have fewer species and fewer layers of vegetation. The tropical rain forest is not as extensive as was once believed. It is found in the Amazon basin of South America and in other lowland areas of South and Central America. It occurs in the Congo basin and along the western coast of .Africa, and is developed also in Southeast Asia.

■**GRASSLANDS.**—*Grasslands* exist on all continents, either as extensive areas dominated exclusively by grasses and other herbaceous plants or as grassy areas interspersed among woodlands and scrub. North American grasslands once extended in an unbroken mass from Illinois to the Rocky Mountains and westward through the intermountain region to the Central Valley of California and the Palouse region of Washington. In Eurasia they stretched from Hungary to the Pacific. Formerly, huge herds of bison, antelope, and elk roamed the plains, and the North American grasslands supported the greatest mass of wild animal life on the continent.

Climatically, these areas are best developed in the zones between moist forests and arid deserts. Since this region is seasonally dry, it is subject to fires which suppress the invasion of woody vegetation. Grasslands can be divided into two general categories: the more humid prairies, dominated by tall grasses; and the dry steppes, where short grasses are the prevailing cover. Partly as a result of overgrazing, small shrubs such as the sagebrush (*Artemisia*) and saltbush (*Atriplex*) invaded widely and have changed the appearance of the dry steppes. Such areas of shrub invasion often look like deserts.

■**DESERTS.**—The warm, dry areas of the earth can be considered together as the desert biome or group of biomes. In these areas rainfall is seldom in excess of 5 inches per year and is so erratic that some places

often go without rain for a long time. The most barren deserts are lifeless, but when undisturbed by human influences the desert usually supports an open scrub vegetation. In the American deserts the creosote bush (*Larrea*) covers great areas in uniform, open stands. Elsewhere various cactuses or thorny leguminous shrubs are dominant. Deserts support an interesting and varied fauna including the desert fox, kangaroo rat, and desert jackrabbits in North America; and the oryx, gazelle, and jerboa in Asia and Africa. Many of these animals can live without drinking water and obtain all of their water from their food.

■**LIFE ZONES.**—Biomes occupy broad continental areas corresponding to the major climatic regions. In the higher mountains, however, it is possible to find in one small area the same series of biomes that would ordinarily be

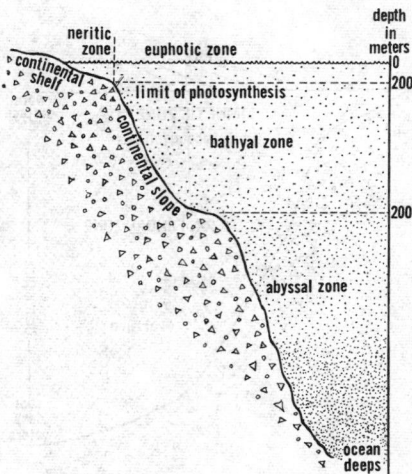

OCEAN is divided into the neritic zone, which lies above the continental shelf; the euphotic zone, in which all food is produced; and the bathyal and abyssal zones.

encountered in a journey over thousands of miles. The biomes in these mountain areas are distributed in altitudinally arranged belts known as *life zones.* In the western United States one can start at the base of a mountain range in the desert biome and pass successively through zones of grassland, Mediterranean scrub, and pine and fir forest until he finally reaches a tundralike zone above the timberline. Such life zone changes correspond to the decrease in temperature and increase in precipitation resulting from altitude changes.

Aquatic Ecosystems.—Most of the earth is covered with water, and most of the life on earth still finds its home in an aquatic environment. Life originated in the oceans and from them spread into fresh water, but relatively few of the many sea animals could adapt to the more rigorous conditions. Because the aquatic environment is much more uniform than that of dry land, it is difficult to divide it into separate biomes or easily recognizable

ecosystems. Nevertheless, there are marked differences among the life of arctic, temperate, and tropical seas, and between various freshwater environments.

■**MARINE ENVIRONMENT.**—Temperature and moisture are two major factors influencing the distribution of the major continental communities. In the oceans these are less important because of their tendency to be uniform and constant. On land, except beneath the canopies of dense forests, light is seldom a limiting factor. The distribution of life in the marine environment, however, is vitally determined by light. Much of the sunlight that strikes the face of the ocean is reflected back into the atmosphere. Only part of the total solar radiation penetrates the water; and of this, little reaches any great depth. To accomplish photosynthesis the green plants must live in the lighted surface layers of the water. Only here can they successfully produce the food and fix the energy that will support all other ocean life. Six hundred feet is the greatest depth at which this life-giving process can take place, and it usually occurs in more shallow water. Beyond that depth lie miles of water that are forever dark and unproductive. The lighted surface layer, termed the *euphotic zone,* produces all of the food and supports the greatest mass of marine life.

Since the organisms that live beneath the euphotic zone must depend for food upon materials that sink or are carried down from the surface, it was previously assumed that they were few in number. In recent decades, however, it has been found that this assumption is not necessarily true. Great layers of animal life have been located at depths well below the level of light penetration. Some of these layers consist of squid, which move to the surface to feed at night and submerge into the darkness during daylight. A great variety of other fish adjust to life in darkness in strange ways. In order to survive in their dark ocean homes they must feed either upon other organisms that move between the surface and the depths or upon materials that sink from above. Life can be found even in the great oceanic deeps, where animals must scavenge on the organic material that filters down through the upper layers of life. A diagram of life in the oceans, arranged according to mass, would be an inverted pyramid, with a broad base of living material near the surface and a narrow apex in the deeps.

The euphotic zone is not the only major life zone in the ocean. In the open ocean the zone below the euphotic, extending down to about 6,500 feet, is called the *bathyal region.* Still deeper lies the *abyssal region.* The principal way of life for plants and animals in the open ocean is termed *pelagic.* This is a free-swimming or free-floating existence, independent of contact with land. Of the pelagic types of life, those that have limited or no swimming ability are termed *plankton.* Their movements are dependent to a large degree upon the ocean currents, as opposed to those active swimmers that can move against or across currents.

Some animals in the open ocean region, however, live a *benthic* existence. This means that they are attached to, or moving over, the ocean floor. Around the edges of the main oceanic region is an extensive area called the *continental shelf*. This district represents the submerged portions of the continents. Life is usually more fruitful on a continental shelf than in the oceanic region beyond it. Here light can penetrate the water to support attached plants growing on the shelf's floor. These, in addition to the floating plants, constitute a great mass of productive plant material. Living a benthic existence on the continental shelf is also a much greater variety of attached or bottom-dwelling animal life than will be found on the main ocean floor. The water area on the continental shelf is classified as the *neritic zone*.

On its upper edge is the *intertidal zone*, that portion of the ocean with which most land dwellers are familiar. Here are found those plants and animals that can stand exposure to the air during periods of low tide. Although narrow by comparison with the great breadth of the oceans, the productive neritic zone occupies a considerable area. It follows the edges of all the continents, surrounds all of the islands, and occurs wherever there are submerged banks or reefs near the surface.

■ **CHEMICAL NUTRIENTS.**—Although light is the major factor limiting the distribution and amount of life in the ocean, chemical nutrients are also of great importance. Just as there are sterile soils on land that support little life, there are relatively sterile waters in the oceans. Those salts needed for plant nutrition are eroded from the land and carried in dissolved form down all of the streams and rivers to the oceans. Some come to rest in bays, in estuaries, or along the continental shelves. The salts that remain in the euphotic zone are available to green plants, but those that sink into the ocean depths are beyond the reach of food chains.

In a general sense there is no shortage of salt in the ocean. But not all of the salts necessary for nutrition are abundant. In particular, nitrates and phosphates are often in short supply. Those that are available are picked up by floating plants, *phytoplankton*, and pass from these to animals. When plants or animals die and their remains sink below the euphotic zone, the chemical nutrients in their bodies are removed from circulation. With a steady supply of nutrients flowing from the land and with an abundance of shallow, lighted water, it follows that the continental shelf areas are the most productive of life. Because mineral sources are unavailable, much of the oceanic euphotic zone is deficient in minerals and cannot support the mass of floating plankton on which larger marine organisms must feed.

The constant motion of the ocean waters encourages life in regions that would not ordinarily support it. Were it not for this motion, the required nutrients would have long ago sunk to the bottom and over the greater part of the seas the water would be lifeless. However, there are both deep and shallow currents in the ocean that keep the waters in constant movement and prevent stagnation. Deep currents can pick up those nutrients that have been lost to the surface waters. Where conditions are favorable, these deep currents can carry nutrient-rich water once more to the surface. Such favorable conditions exist along the western coasts of the major continents. Here the forces generated by the earth's rotation tend to push the warmer surface waters away from the land and to allow an *upwelling* of the cold waters from the depths. These fertile waters are then further distributed by surface currents. It is in

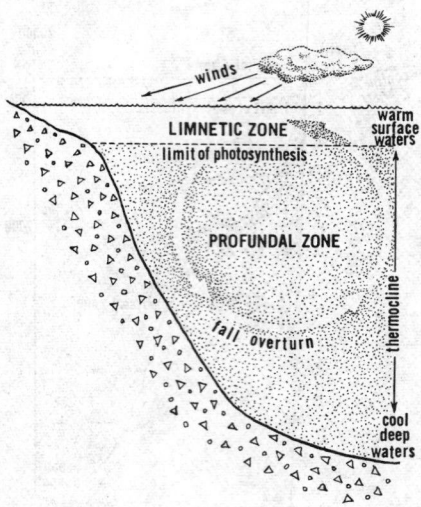

LAKES are divided into a limnetic and a profundal zone. The fall overturn replaces the nutrients that were depleted from the limnetic zone during photosynthesis.

these regions that some of the world's major fisheries are located.

■ **FRESHWATER ENVIRONMENTS.**—Since fresh water is less richly supplied with dissolved minerals than is the ocean, the availability of those minerals needed for plant and animal nutrition assumes a more controlling influence on the quantity and distribution of life. A common classification of freshwater environments separates the *oligotrophic* (low nutrient) waters from the *eutrophic* (high nutrient) waters. At one extreme is the glacial lake of the high mountains, fed by melting ice or snow, resting on a sterile substrate of granite; at the other, the farm pond in an area of rich soil, green with algae and teeming with animal life. Along with mineral content, the amount of dissolved oxygen in the water becomes limiting in fresh water more often than in the ocean. While photosynthesis occurs, shallow, eutrophic lakes are rich in oxygen; but in the winter light is screened out by a layer of

ice and snow, and the abundant animal populations may exhaust the oxygen supply. Temperature also is much more variable in fresh water than in the ocean. The trout that can survive in a cold, oxygen-rich stream cannot live in the warm waters of sluggish streams or shallow lakes. Passing through several kinds of microorganisms and small invertebrates before ending in some large predatory fish, food chains in fresh water are also frequently complicated.

■ **LAKES.**—Deep lakes present many of the same problems for life that are encountered in the oceans. Below the limit of light penetration, called the *limnetic zone* in lakes, is a deeper layer in which no photosynthesis takes place. This is called the *profundal zone*. Fish dwelling in this deep zone depend upon the production of the limnetic zone for their food supply. Periodic mixing of the upper and lower layers of water is essential if their united capability for sustaining life is to be maintained. During the winter, for example, lake waters cool. Since water reaches its maximum density at 4° Centigrade, the water that cools to this temperature will sink to the bottom. As winter progresses, however, the surface layer of water cools below 4° C., expands, and at 0° C. becomes ice. At this stage the bottom waters are cut off from the surface layer; and a sharp temperature gradient, the *thermocline*, exists between the surface and the depths. Since no new oxygen can be added from the surface, animal life dwelling in the profundal zone can exhaust the oxygen supply during the winter.

In the spring, surface waters warm once more and soon reach the same temperature as the bottom waters. At this stage the thermocline disappears. Wind action induces mixing of the waters from the surface and the depths and thereby restores oxygen to the deeper waters. However, as summer approaches, the surface waters continue to warm and a new thermocline develops. A layer of light, warm water occupies the surface of the lake and may not mix with the deeper, cool waters. This condition can continue until declining autumn temperatures encourage another period of mixing. Following the period of mixing in the spring, the *spring overturn*, the surface waters usually experience a blooming of the algae and a consequent increase in animal life. This can exhaust the available nitrates, phosphates, and other essential materials in the surface layer. If this happens, the summer is a period of low productivity because the nutrients in the surface area cannot be replaced until the *fall overturn*.

Although the supply of nutrients controls the abundance of life in fresh water, there are some continental aquatic environments where an excess of salts presents a problem. Great Salt Lake, for example, is so much more saline than the oceans that a swimmer has difficulty in submerging. Mono Lake in California has such a high salt concentration that only two species of organisms, a salt-tolerant fly larva and a brine shrimp, can survive. Because drainage is interior rather than toward the oceans, high levels of salinity or alkalinity are usually found in most lakes in the intermountain region of the American West.

Biology and Conservation.—Since the early days of civilization, when man first domesticated plants and animals, human societies have exploited natural communities. Sometimes man has taken only the few products which he has needed and has left the community to restore itself through natural succession. Often, however, the wild community has been deformed and reshaped into a tamed community intended to serve the human welfare. At times, and in some places, people have managed to strike a balance with the forces of nature and have created stable ecosystems that include civilized man as a component. Too frequently, however, through failure to understand the biological forces involved, the deformation and change wrought in natural communities have initiated chains of consequences that in time have worked against human society. Many old civilizations are buried in jungle or have left their ruins standing windswept in what are now barren wastes. These ruins often reflect the failure to balance human demands against the biological necessities of ecosystems.

Today conservation movements attempt to counterbalance the destructive effects that formerly accompanied the exploitation of nature. *Conservation* is concerned primarily with maintaining a suitable world in which man can live. It is less involved with the quantity of production than with the quality of living. It seeks to preserve at least the remnants of unmodified natural communities and to balance man's demands upon the land and the capabilities of the land to produce; to substitute careful management of resources for unbridled, destructive use. Where it is involved with those resources that form a part of ecological systems, conservation depends upon a knowledge of biological relationships.

It is a recognized tenet of biological conservation that all living things grow, reproduce, and therefore show an annual growth. In a stable community this yearly increase represents a quantity of living material that can be safely harvested by man without destroying the basic resource. If it is not used by man, it will sooner or later die of natural causes, for no living thing can exist forever. Consequently, if the annual production of wood in a forest, brought about by tree growth, is balanced against the amount that is cut and converted into lumber, and if reasonable care is taken in removing this crop, the forest can remain permanently productive. Conversely, if too little is cut, old age, disease, insects, or other natural forces will eventually destroy the surplus. Balancing growth against harvest leads to a *sustained yield* of forest products. Sustained-yield management characterizes all modern systems of conser-

vation-based forest management. The consequences of excessive harvesting and of careless handling of cut-over lands can be seen in the devastated hillsides of many parts of the world or in the scrubby growths of birch and aspen that have replaced the once magnificent pine forests of the Great Lakes states.

■**PRESERVATION OF WILD ANIMALS.**—A sustained-yield system of harvesting should characterize the commercial use of all living resources, including agricultural soils. Wild animal populations, for example, can be managed in this way. If the annual take by hunters is balanced against the annual replacement of adults by young, a game population can be permanently maintained. If an annual crop is not removed, the animals will die from natural causes; man's protection cannot make them eternal. In the United States game managers try to balance the annual increase of deer, quail, grouse, or rabbits against the annual demand from hunters. If game laws are tailored to allow a breeding stock to remain each year, the game populations will remain abundant. Game managers also attempt, through improving the vegetation or other aspects of the environment, to create a more suitable habitat for game and thus produce larger surpluses for the hunter.

In countries where hunting for sport is not extensive, as in Africa, it has been found that the annual crop of wild game can be taken for commercial purposes. The complex of wild grazers and browsers that forms a part of the biotic communities of Africa has been shown to produce more meat and other products of value, per acre, than can be produced when the same lands are used by domestic livestock. The Soviet Union has had similar experiences with some of its game animals. For example, the saiga antelope, an abundant game animal of the dry steppes

and desert margins, is now managed for meat production. A harvest is taken each year by hunters; and the meat, hides, and other by-products enter the domestic economy.

It has become obvious with many kinds of wild animals that excessive protection can do as much harm as excessive hunting. A population of deer or elk, when completely protected, overbrowses and destroys the food plants on which it depends. Before man modified the natural scene, wild predators helped to remove the annual surplus and to keep populations in balance. But in order to protect his domestic animals, man has destroyed most of the wild predators, with the result that the wild herbivores are left without adequate checks on their biotic potential.

■**DOMESTIC ANIMALS.**—It is in the handling of domestic animals that man has done the most damage to his environment. A sparse human population maintaining great herds of cattle, sheep, or goats can destroy a vast region in a surprisingly short time. Failure to realize that range forage, like timber or wildlife, produces an annual surplus, and that only this annual surplus can safely be cropped, lies behind this devastation. The arid steppe and savanna regions are most susceptible to damage by domestic livestock. Here the plant production during a wet season or good rainfall year must hold the soil during the long, dry periods that follow. Because plant growth is usually slow, the annual surplus that can safely be cropped without injury to the grasses or shrubs is small. Such areas can sustain only light grazing.

If the land is overgrazed, the plants are destroyed; and the bare ground is subject to rapid erosion by wind or rain. When the layer of more fertile topsoil is lost, vegetation is slow to reoccupy the ground, and damage continues. Over wide areas of the globe the desert has expanded

U.S. DEPARTMENT OF AGRICULTURE

MAN'S ACTIVITIES tend to overbalance ecosystems, thus destroying their symbiotic existence. The dust bowl of the American Midwest was the end product of such an overbalancing.

into formerly productive lands following the impact of too many hoofs or grazing mouths of domestic livestock. The Sahara, the Arabian Desert, the deserts of Pakistan and of our American Southwest have all spread into lands that formerly were more productive. *Range management* is a relatively new field of conservation. It attempts to instill a knowledge of how best to harvest the annual forage crop from grasslands without damage to the growing stock of range plants.

Faulty management of farming lands has also resulted from a failure to understand biological necessities. Soils that developed as part of natural ecosystems cannot for long be separated from those forces that contributed to their development and guaranteed their stability. In the virgin prairie soil, structure was maintained by a dense network of plant roots. Erosion was checked by the perennial cover of growing plants. Fertility was held in balance by the annual return of dead plant and animal materials to the ground that had originally produced them.

When these prairie soils were first plowed, they were remarkable in both fertility and stability. With continued cultivation and annual planting of the same kind of crop, and with no effort to protect them from wind or rain, they began to deteriorate. Surface soil was lost to erosion. Structure was destroyed because the roots of wheat or corn failed to provide the mechanical or chemical action that was necessary to maintain it. Fertility was lost through the steady drain of nutrients into crops that were subsequently transported to distant markets.

Recent soil-conservation activities have attempted to repair this damage. The original soil-forming and soil-holding functions of natural vegetation have been replaced by techniques compatible with agricultural production. Crop rotation, cover-cropping, contour cultivation, mulching, and fertilizing all are part of sound, conservation-based agricultural practices today.

■**FISHERIES.**—The early exploitation of the resources of fresh water and the oceans was based on a misunderstanding of the abundance of aquatic organisms. Too often fishermen have assumed that new sea fisheries can always be found to replace those that have been exhausted. In fact, commercially valuable fisheries are restricted to the few areas where nutrient supplies permit an abundant production of plants. Far from being inexhaustible, such localized fisheries can readily be overfished if sufficient pressure is placed upon them. Once it is reduced to a low population, a fishery may be a long time recovering, for the ocean environment cannot yet be controlled; and natural losses are high. Steady exploitation of depleted fish populations prevents any recovery. For the most part, excluding a few highly valued species of marine life, overfishing has been a localized problem. The ocean still has great resources of living materials suitable for human food. But

with the increasing demands of growing human populations, biologically sound management of these marine resources is essential if they are to remain productive.

■**PRESERVATION OF NATURAL AREAS.**—Since man is as dependent today upon the products of the lands and waters for his food as he was in ages past, it follows that much of the world must be used for the production of those things that people require. However, as more and more land comes into use, the value of the still wild, unmanaged parts of the world increases. Most nations have at least made gestures toward maintaining such natural areas in systems of national parks or wilderness reserves. However, no nation has gone far enough in this direction.

It is now clear that there is an acute need to preserve representative areas of all kinds of natural ecosystems, from humble tracts of bog or moor to vast areas of tropical rain forest. This is because it is important to have ecological check areas against which the progress or loss of the lands under management can be measured. In some parts of the world, devastation has been so complete that we do not know what the land could produce if it were left to recover. Some livestock owners have never seen an undamaged rangeland. They consistently settle for a lower productivity because they know no better. If natural grasslands of high productivity remained in each region, the range manager would better realize his goal.

Natural ecological systems contain the maximum variety and abundance of life that a climate and substrate will support. In development such ecosystems usually tend toward increased complexity. As each species moves in, it creates a niche for some new species that can feed or shelter upon it. Generally speaking, the more complex an ecosystem, the more stable it becomes and the less liable to extreme fluctuations in the abundance of any species. A herbivore that grows too numerous is fed upon by a variety of carnivores until its numbers are reduced. One that grows scarce is spared the pressure of predators that can turn to some other more abundant and readily available prey. Thus the entire system retains a natural balance.

Man, through his efforts at agriculture, pastoralism, logging, hunting, and fishing, tends to simplify complex ecosystems. The more they are simplified, the more likely they are to lose balance. A natural grassland is complex; a wheat field is simple. The wheat field provides an ideal environment for those things that prefer to live on, or feed upon, wheat—the wheat-destroying fungi and insect pests among them. Without natural enemies in this artificial system, these pests can increase to such proportions that they destroy the wheat crop. Similarly, an overgrazed range is simplified and supports fewer species of organisms than does a virgin rangeland. It is therefore out of balance. A species of rodent can increase to plague proportions and do

serious damage, whereas such an increase would be prevented by natural checks in an undisturbed grassland community.

■**CHEMICAL CONTROL OF INSECTS AND PESTS.**—Where agricultural or pastoral peoples have been, they have changed and simplified natural communities. Hence, they have often created an ideal environment for those pests, diseases, parasites, and predators that are the worst enemies of their crops and herds. In their efforts to control these pests that follow them, they have resorted to hunting, trapping, burning, and other techniques. Such attempts at regulation have usually been unsuccessful. With the development of the chemical industry, however, new weapons have been added to the battle against pests in the form of chemical insecticides, fungicides, and herbicides. For a while great progress was made by the use of these materials. Agricultural and pastoral losses were reduced, and production soared. Recently, however, it has become apparent that the use of poisonous chemicals on the land can, unless carefully controlled, wipe out the very species of plants and animals that man most wants to preserve. In the long run, the unrestrained and uninterrupted employment of some of these poisons could pollute the land and its waters to such an extent as to imperil man's very existence.

The pollution of the human environment, not just with pesticides but with all of the wastes and by-products of man's activities, creates the greatest problem for biological conservation today. As human populations increase, it will become even more severe. Perhaps it will finally force us to observe the biological rules of order that should govern our actions on this planet. It is the hope of the ecologist, who has an interest in natural things, that man will yet develop what Aldo Leopold has called an "ecological conscience." This involves a recognition that man is still a part of, not an enemy of, nature, and that other living things have as much right to a place on this earth in the future as they had in the past.

—Raymond F. Dasmann

BIBLIOGRAPHY

BATES, MARSTON. *Animal Worlds.* Random House, Inc., 1963.

BONNER, JOHN TYLER. *Cells and Societies.* Princeton University Press, 1955.

CARSON, RACHEL L. *Silent Spring.* Houghton Mifflin Co., 1962.

CLEMENTS, EDITH. *Adventures in Ecology: Half a Million Miles, from Mud to Macadam.* Pageant Press, 1960.

DASMANN, RAYMOND F. *Environmental Conservation.* John Wiley & Sons, Inc., 1959.

ODUM, EUGENE P. *Fundamentals of Ecology* (2nd ed.). W. B. Saunders Co., 1959.

WALLACE, BRUCE. *Ecology.* Prentice-Hall, Inc., 1961.

PHYSICS

Aspects.—Physics may be said to be the story of matter and radiation. This division of physics seems most appropriate at the present time. If it were possible to describe and predict the behavior of matter and radiation, the interaction between them, the energy exchanges among the forms of matter and between matter and radiation, the story would be complete.

There is little point in attempting to define the basic entities that are a part of the physical world. *Matter* appears everywhere in various forms. It has certain properties that characterize it. Everyone instinctively knows what matter is. There is nothing more basic than "stuff," or matter, or whatever one may call it.

In a similar sense, *radiation* is "radiation." It has certain characteristic properties. Man is constantly submerged in radiation, visible or invisible. There is no place from which all electromagnetic radiation is excluded. Even if no other objects are around him, man's own body emits heat radiation. Radiation is not matter, although it has some of the properties of matter. The futility of definition or description in terms of something else is illustrated by the so-called duality of radiation. Radiation has been described both as an electromagnetic wave (in the ether) and as a particle. Neither description alone is adequate, and the combination seems to involve contradictory parts. Thus radiation cannot be thought of as just a wave (in a medium) or as a particle, such as a grain of sand. It is "radiation," and it has its own characteristics.

The situation with respect to the basic concepts, such as time, length, and mass, used in physics is somewhat similar. How can one define *time?* In any attempt at definition, one finds the definition becomes circular—it is possible to describe methods of measuring time precisely, but one cannot define time in terms of something more basic.

Length is defined operationally. It is the number of times a standard length can be placed alongside an object being measured. *Mass* is determined by comparison with a standard mass. Attempts are often made to define mass as the quantity of matter in a body, but how does one determine the quantity of matter? He measures the mass of the object. *Electrical charge* is in the same category as time, length, and mass. The electrical charge in any situation is determined by comparison with a standard charge. *Electric currents* are measured by the magnetic effect of moving charges. There is no other physical entity or "stuff" in terms of which an electrical charge can be described or defined.

The physicist is in somewhat the same situation as a lexicographer who, in compiling a dictionary, defines all words in terms of those previously defined. He has little trouble with the words beginning with "X," "Y," or "Z" at the end of the book, but what can he do with the first half-dozen words? These must be taken as known, for they cannot be defined by words previously defined.

Today, the great majority of physicists adhere to the point of view developed by Percy Williams Bridgman (1882–1961), who wrote, "The concept is synonymous with the corresponding set of operations." The length of a table is the number of times a measuring rod can be placed along the edge of the table. One starts with one end of the rod coinciding with the end of the table and then, by marks on the table, moves the rod along until he arrives at the other end of the table. Time is measured by comparing an interval with the periods of some standard clock—the clock is the earth and the period its time of rotation.

The concepts of time and space upon which much of physics is based have been greatly modified since the early physicists, such as Sir Isaac Newton (1642–1727), first tried to define them. One might say they have been simplified. They are no longer considered abstract and beyond the realm of experiment. The physicist now is in the position Newton assigned to the common people who, as he said, "conceive those quantities (time, space, place, or motion) under no other notions but from the relation they bear to sensible objects."

Today the physicist realizes that his concept and measurement of time are associated with motion. Time is not something that "flows along without relation to sensible objects." Without motion—in a static universe in which nothing moves—the concept of time would not exist. There would be no change in any relationship that would permit a measurement of a time interval. When one attempts to measure an "absolute velocity," or a velocity with respect to an "ether," and then with this absolute velocity set an absolute time scale, his experiments yield no velocity that could be called absolute. All velocities are relative, and indeed a concept such as the simultaneity of two events at different places is found to be dependent on the observer and his motion relative to other observers.

This does not mean that the physicist no longer allows his imagination to operate or that he no longer makes postulates that have not been tested. Great advances are based on just such excursions of the mind—a notable example being Max Planck's (1858–1947) hypothesis regarding the quantum nature of radiation. But such projections must stand the severe test of experiment. Are they verified by experimental test? Do they predict phenomena that are later observed? If they do, then the physicist may say he has an "explanation," or a theory.

Scope of Physics.—Physics, once called "natural philosophy," is basic to several other sciences. *Astronomy* may be called the physics of the stars; *geology* (at least structural geology, as distinguished from historical geology), the physics of the earth. Indeed, the term "earth sciences" includes geology, *meteorology* (the physics of the air), and *oceanography* (the physics of the ocean). *Chemistry* might be called a branch of atomic physics. The composition of substances and the transformations they undergo are determined by the properties of the substance's atoms. There are well-recognized fields of science called *astrophysics, geophysics, physical chemistry,* and *biophysics.* The practice of medicine and medical research are becoming more and more dependent on physics. Isotopes, radioactivity, and electronic devices are familiar to the physician.

Engineering is now often called *applied physics.* The borderline between engineering and physics is often hard to distinguish. Engineering laboratories and courses in the engineering curricula in universities now resemble those in physics, especially those courses and laboratories that pertain to the properties and structure of matter in bulk.

The commonly recognized divisions of physics are mechanics, thermodynamics, electricity and magnetism, acoustics, optics, and a variety of topics often called "modern physics" to distinguish them from the classical divisions named above. The topics classed as *modern physics* include radioactivity and nuclear physics, atomic and molecular spectra, the quantum theory of matter and radiation, solid-state physics, relativity, and high-energy physics, which includes cosmic radiation coming to the earth from outer space.

The various categories are by no means separate and independent. Nature is not divided into nicely compartmentalized units. It is man's attempt to comprehend nature that leads to a division into subjects of areas of phenomena.

Mechanics, the oldest of the sub-

MAX PLANCK (1858–1947), German physicist, winner of the Nobel Prize in Physics.

jects dealt with in a quantitative manner, has three branches. The first is *kinematics*, the geometry of motion without regard to forces or energy. *Dynamics*, the second part of mechanics, includes the forces acting and the energy involved when bodies are in motion. The third branch, *statics*, deals with bodies in equilibrium. Mechanics is basic to much of engineering, certainly to structural engineering. Newton developed mechanics to the stage where he could (and did) determine what velocity and energy would be needed to put a satellite into orbit.

Thermodynamics involves heat and the behavior of matter with respect to thermal energy. Generalizations summarized by three laws of thermodynamics include the conservation of energy and the trend found in nature for the distribution and the availability of energy. Thermodynamics also encompasses the study of radiation.

The characteristics of electricity at rest and in motion are the starting topics for *electricity* and *magnetism*. These serve as the bases for the operation of electrical machinery of all kinds. They also lead to electromagnetic radiation and optics, which indicates the interdependence of the various divisions of physics. *Optics* also includes *geometrical optics*, in which the paths of light rays are traced through such devices as lenses.

It was an attempt to measure the difference in the velocity of electromagnetic radiation (light) in different directions as the earth moved about its orbit that led to the theory of relativity propounded by Albert Einstein (1879–1955), whose interpretation of the negative experimental result has had a profound effect on all of physical science and philosophical writings on science.

Acoustics, the phenomena related to sound, is one branch of a topic that might have been called elastic waves in solids, liquids, and gases.

Radioactivity was the first nuclear phenomenon studied by the physicist. In this he discovered that not all atomic nuclei are stable. Today nuclear physics engages the attention of thousands of scientists and large segments of industry. Atomic energy, more appropriately called "nuclear energy," is in the category of *nuclear physics*.

The characteristic radiation, visible and invisible, emitted by atoms and molecules under a variety of conditions is the major source of data on which our notions of atomic and molecular structure are based. The quantum theory of matter and radiation was initiated by Planck's hypothesis regarding the manner in which radiation is emitted from a solid. This was followed by the work of Neils Bohr (1885–1962) and Einstein. Today, quantum phenomena pervade all physics.

Engineers and physicists have recently given much attention to the electrical and mechanical properties of solids. Although solids have always been a part of man's environment, he has not, until recently, been able to relate the behavior and characteristics of solids to the properties of the atoms of which solids are composed.

For half a century the physicist has been aware of a penetrating radiation coming to Earth from outer space. Although called "radiation," the primary component that strikes the upper atmosphere is now known to be made up largely, if not completely, of atomic nuclei. Protons, the nuclei of hydrogen atoms, predominate. These come in with extremely high energies. Their origin and the source of their energy are not known. They are messengers that, with the radio signals detected by the recently constructed large radio telescopes, may yield previously unobtainable information about the stars and galaxies. The high energy of the primary components of cosmic rays has been approached but not equaled by the very large accelerators built in the United States, western Europe, and the Soviet Union.

Role of Physics.—Before an astronaut circles the earth, the energy required for launching, the direction of launching, and the direction of the final boost to his satellite must be accurately determined. Principles of physics supply the answers. The communication the astronaut has with Earth utilizes electronic apparatus and the knowledge of the behavior of electromagnetic radiation developed in the physics laboratories. Man's ability to communicate almost instantly with all parts of the world is the result of discoveries made by scientists in the past. Much of modern engineering is based on the products of the physics laboratory. The X rays, radium, heat therapy, radioactive isotopes, and electrocardigraphs used in hospitals had their origins, or were discovered, in the physics laboratories. Many of the comforts and conveniences in our homes—the temperature controls, the air conditioning, such kitchen devices as the refrigerator, the high-fidelity reproducer, and the television set—were not the objects of research but are by-products of such research.

The theory of relativity, with its prediction that mass and energy are in some respects equivalent, and that the relation between them is $E = mc^2$, where E is energy, m represents mass, and c is the velocity of light, may be called the achievement in physics that will characterize this century. The theoretical work has been confirmed by experimentation (fission and fusion of atomic nuclei) in which a small amount of mass "disappears" and in its place we have enormously large amounts of energy. The peaceful uses of nuclear energy will, no doubt, free man from fear that the fossil fuels will some day be exhausted.

PROPERTIES OF MATTER

Solids.—A body is said to be a *solid* when it retains its shape and offers resistance to forces tending to deform it. A solid has perceptible strength and does not flow. When described in this way, a solid is characterized by its *elastic properties*. There is no difficulty in differentiating a solid such as ice and a liquid such as water. But it is not always so easy to distinguish between a solid and a liquid. Suppose a piece of asphalt used in paving is broken from a large block. Its behavior while being broken seems to be that of a solid. But if the piece with rough edges and surface is placed in a container and kept at room temperature for a number of days, it will change its shape and appear to be flowing over the bottom of the container. It has not melted as ice melts, but it has not retained its shape. Is it a liquid or a solid? It behaves like very slowly moving molasses and has very high viscosity. Long pieces of glass tubing held in storage racks, with a support near each end of the tubing, will sag after some years. This behavior has led to the designation of glass as a supercooled liquid. Materials such as asphalt and glass, which do not exhibit all the properties of a true solid, are said to be *amorphous* because their molecules are randomly arranged. The molecules of true solids, on the other hand, have a definite pattern, called *crystal structure*. For this reason, solids are described as *crystalline* in structure.

■**CRYSTAL STRUCTURE.**—The molecules in a crystalline solid, such as ice or snow, are not arranged randomly. A definite geometrical spatial arrangement of the molecules is found in all crystals, although different arrangements are found in different crystals. A three-dimensional pattern of some type repeats itself regularly in all crystals. The definite pattern in snow is made evident in the large snow crystals that often can be seen during the first snowfall of the year. The beautiful "Jack Frost" figures formed on a cold window pane, and the crystals of salt formed when a saltwater solution is allowed to evaporate, show the crystalline nature of ice and salt. Metals in the solid state are usually composed of a myriad of tiny crystals, more or less randomly oriented and interlocking with one another. It is possible to grow large single metal crystals, each having dimensions of several centimeters. Such crystals have elastic properties differing markedly from the polycrystalline forms. A single crystal of copper, a centimeter in thickness and several centimeters long, can be bent easily. In copper, the atoms in the crystal are arranged in one of the ways (face-centered cubic) uniform spheres would be packed if the group was to occupy the smallest volume possible.

In common salt (sodium chloride) the atoms are not identical, as in copper; the sodium and chloride atoms are alternately placed in a cubic pattern, or *lattice*. The crystals may be very small or very large, but in every case the faces or surfaces of the crystals make definite angles with each other (90° in the case of sodium chloride).

Sometimes two or more crystalline forms of a substance are found. For example, although both the diamond and graphite are pure carbon, they have different crystal forms. In the diamond, each carbon atom is surrounded by four other carbon atoms at the corners of a regular tetrahedron. In graphite, the carbon atoms lie in planes, or flat sheets, and each atom is attached to three others in this plane to form a series of flat hexagons. The flat sheets of atoms are relatively easily separated or moved over one another. As a result of their respective structures, graphite acts as a lubricant, while diamond is the hardest naturally occurring substance known to man.

■AMORPHOUS SOLIDS.—Carbon is also found in the amorphous (noncrystalline) state as carbon black. Here, if crystals exist, they are microscopic, and the bulk substance does not behave as a crystal. There are numerous solids that are not crystalline in structure. Wood, for example, exhibits a growth pattern, but is not crystalline in the sense that metals are crystalline.

■PROPERTIES.—All solids, both crystalline and amorphous, resist change of shape and of volume. Many crystalline solids are *anisotropic;* that is, many of their properties are not the same in all directions. For example, the heat conductivity and optical properties (such as the speed of light as it passes through) vary with the direction in which these properties are measured. Amorphous solids and solids with a cubic crystal structure, on the other hand, are *isotropic;* that is, their properties are the same in all directions. Crystalline solids melt at definite, clearly defined temperatures. Amorphous solids do not melt at specific temperatures, but instead gradually soften and become more fluid with increasing temperatures.

Liquids.—A *liquid* is generally characterized as being in that state of matter in which the molecules are free to move among themselves without being able to separate from one another (as molecules of a gas do). A liquid will take the shape of any container into which it is placed. (Although a gas will also take the shape of any container into which it is placed, it differs from a liquid in that a gas will expand to fill all the available space in the container.) The volume of a liquid is relatively fixed; that is, it is changed only slightly by variations in temperature or pressure or both. The atoms in a liquid are about as closely spaced as those of a solid, but there is no long-range order as in a crystal.

■SURFACE TENSION.—This is the property of liquids that causes the surface to behave as if covered by a thin, elastic membrane under tension. This results from the fact that the molecules in the surface layer of the liquid are attracted downward by the molecules within the liquid with a greater force than they are attracted upward by molecules in the atmosphere. The surface of the liquid always tends to contract to the smallest possible area; thus, drops of liquid assume a shape as close to spherical as possible because the surface area is then minimum for a given volume.

■CAPILLARY ACTION.—This causes liquids to rise in tubes of very small diameter, and is a phenomenon related to surface tension. Because of

the difference in the magnitude of the forces between the molecules of the liquid themselves, and between these and the molecules of the solid composing the tube, the surface of the liquid is always curved. If the attraction of the liquid's molecules is greater than that of the solid's molecules, the surface curves downward. If the attraction of the liquid's molecules is less than that of the solid's molecules,

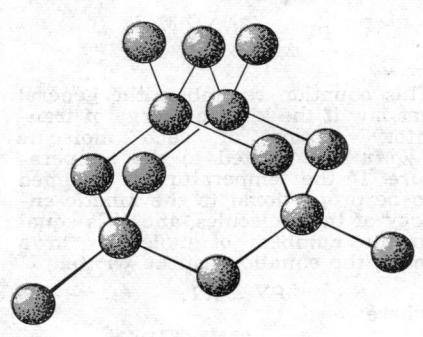

DIAMOND CRYSTAL

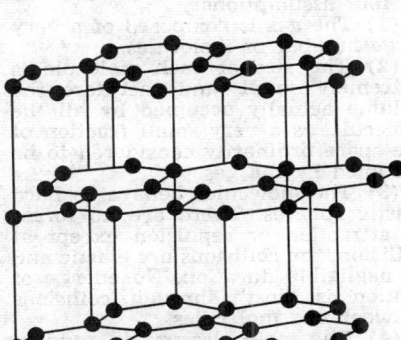

GRAPHITE STRUCTURE

CRYSTAL STRUCTURE of carbon can be either tetrahedral, as in the diamond (*left*), or in plane hexagons arranged in flat sheets bonded to one another, as in graphite (*right*).

the surface curves upward. In the latter case, if the radius of the curvature is sufficiently small, a pressure differential will cause the liquid to rise in the tube.

■VISCOSITY.—The measure of the resistance of a liquid to flow is called *viscosity.* Like surface tension, viscosity is caused by the attraction forces between layers of molecules. The greater the attractive forces, the more difficult it is for one layer to flow over another, and the greater the viscosity. The viscosity of a liquid usually decreases significantly with increasing temperatures.

Gases.—A *gas* is characterized as being that state of matter that has no bounding surface. A gas will take the shape of, and expand to fill, any container in which it is placed. Gases are also characterized by their sensitivity to changes of temperature and pressure. The behavior of most gases on a macroscopic (visible to the naked eye) scale is best described by some relatively simple laws. These are Boyle's law, proposed by Robert Boyle (1627–1691); Charles's law (sometimes called Gay-Lussac's law), proposed by Jacques Alexandre César Charles (1746–1823); Dalton's law of partial pressures, proposed by John Dalton (1766–1844); Joule's law, proposed by James Prescott Joule (1818–1889), and Gay-Lussac's law of combining volumes, proposed by Joseph Gay-Lussac (1778–1850).

Boyle's law.—If a given mass of gas is compressed into a smaller volume and its *pressure* (force on each unit area of the container) increased, or if it is expanded into a larger volume, the product of the pressure and the volume remains constant if the temperature is kept constant.

Charles's law.—If a fixed mass of gas is heated through a given tem-

perature range while the volume is kept constant, the fractional change in pressure will be the same for all gases. Also, if the pressure is kept constant while the temperature is changed over the same range, the fractional change in volume will be the same for all gases. In addition, the fractional change of pressure is equal to the fractional change of volume in the two cases described.

Dalton's law.—If two or more gases are placed in a container, the total pressure on the walls of the container is equal to the sum of the pressures each gas would exert if it were alone in the container.

Joule's law.—The energy associated with a given mass of gas is not a function of its volume or pressure if its temperature is kept constant; that is, the internal energy of a given gas depends only on its temperature.

Gay-Lussac's law.—The volumes of gases required for complete chemical combination to form new products bear a simple relation to each other and to the volume of the product if it is a gas.

The above "laws" are based on experiment. From these an Italian chemist, Amadeo Avogadro (1776–1856), proposed a hypothesis that was compatible with the experimental laws but was not subject to experimental verification by measurement of such macroscopic quantities as pressure or volume. The hypothesis, however, is now given the status of a "law" because it can be indirectly verified in a number of ways.

Avogadro's law.—All gases at a given pressure and temperature contain the same number of molecules per unit volume.

These laws are found valid for all gases if the temperature is not too low and the pressure is not too high. This suggests that under these conditions all gases have some common characteristics. A gas that is described accurately by these laws is called an *ideal gas.* One relation that combines several laws is: Pressure × Volume = Constant × Temperature, or $PV = RT$. The constant R is the same for all gases (at the appropriate temperature and pressure), providing one has a mass of gas numerically equal to its molecular weight. This mass is called a *gram molecular weight*, or *mole*. The relation $PV = RT$ is the *ideal gas law*.

Kinetic Theory of Gases.

—One of the earliest important achievements of theoretical physics was the *kinetic theory of gases*. By means of this theory, the laws describing the macroscopic behavior of a gas can be explained. The kinetic theory is based on four assumptions:

(1) The gas is composed of a very large number of molecules.

(2) The size of each molecule is extremely small, and therefore the volume actually occupied by all the molecules is a very small fraction of the space ordinarily considered to be occupied by the gas.

(3) The molecules behave as hard elastic spheres. There are no forces of attraction or repulsion except at collision; the collisions are elastic and of negligible duration. No energy of motion is "lost" through collisions between the molecules.

(4) The molecules are in random motion, and Newton's laws describe their motion.

On the basis of these assumptions, the macroscopic behavior of a gas can be explained. Assume the existence of a closed cubical box, with edges L centimeters long. Its volume is L^3 cubic centimeters. Within the box there are N identical molecules, where N is a very large number. Let M be the mass of each molecule and let u centimeters per second be its speed. For simplicity in calculation, assume that all the molecules have the same speed and that $\frac{1}{3}$ of them are moving vertically (along the z axis), another $\frac{1}{3}$ are moving horizontally (along the x axis), and the remaining $\frac{1}{3}$ are moving horizontally but perpendicular to the second group (that is, along the y axis).

On striking a wall (say the vertical wall), a molecule of mass M will bounce back with the same speed it had before striking the wall. Its momentum before collision is Mu and after collision is $-Mu$. The change in momentum $Mu - (-Mu)$ is $2Mu$. In the actual gas, this molecule may strike another before it crosses the box to the opposite side and, in so doing, communicate momentum to the other molecule. The net result, however, will be the same as if the molecule had traveled across the box without collision with another molecule and had struck the opposite side. It will then rebound and again strike the first side. The time for crossing the box twice is $2L/u$, and the number of collisions per second for one molecule with the side of the box will be $u/2L$. Each collision results in a change of momentum of the molecule of $2Mu$. Since $N/3$ of the molecules are moving across the box in this manner, the total change of momentum striking one side of the box will be $(N/3)\ (2Mu)\ (u/2L)$, or $NMu^2/3L$. This change in momentum per second of the molecules is, from Newton's laws, the force exerted on the side of the box. The pressure on the side of the box will be the force divided by the area (L^2) of the side.

Or the pressure, P, is given by

$$P = \frac{NMu^2}{3L^3}.$$

But L^3 is the volume of the box (V). Hence,

$$PV = \frac{NMu^2}{3}.$$

The kinetic energy of transitory motion of each molecule is $Mu^2/2$. Thus:

$$PV = \left(\frac{2N}{3}\right)\left(\frac{Mu^2}{2}\right)$$

This equation resembles the general gas law if the kinetic energy of transitory motion of each molecule ($\frac{1}{2}Mu^2$) is related to the temperature. If the temperature is assumed to be proportional to the kinetic energy of the molecules, and N is equal to the numbers of molecules in a mole, the equation can be written

$$PV = RT,$$

where:

$$RT = \left(\frac{2N}{3}\right)\left(\frac{Mu^2}{2}\right)$$

Sometimes the general gas constant R for N molecules is replaced by Nk where $R/N = k$. The constant k is called the gas constant for one molecule, or *Boltzmann's constant*.

The equation $PV = RT$ may be written:

$$PV = NkT = \left(\frac{2N}{3}\right)\left(\frac{Mu^2}{2}\right)$$

The kinetic energy per molecule is:

$$\frac{Mu^2}{2} = \frac{3kT}{2}$$

Thus, if the temperature T is related to the kinetic energy of the molecules, as in the last equation, the general gas law (for ideal gases) has been deduced from the assumptions regarding the nature of a gas. Boyle's law and Charles's law also are included, and Joule's law is predicted by the fact that the energy of the molecules is dependent only on the temperature (as shown by the last equation) and not on the volume occupied or on the pressure.

Since $PV = NkT$, one may write $P = NkT/V$. In this, k is a constant. Hence, if the pressure P and the temperature T are the same for two gases, then N/V, or the number of molecules per unit volume, must also be the same. This is Avogadro's law.

A gas's specific heat can also be predicted if it is assumed that the kinetic energy of motion is equally distributed among the *degrees of freedom* (the number of squared terms in the expression for its energy) of the molecules. For a *monatomic gas*, such as helium, the number of degrees of freedom is three; for a *diatomic gas*, such as oxygen, which may also tumble as a dumbbell, the number of degrees of freedom is five.

Triple Point.

—Depending upon the conditions of temperature and pressure, many substances can exist in any of the three states of matter—solid,

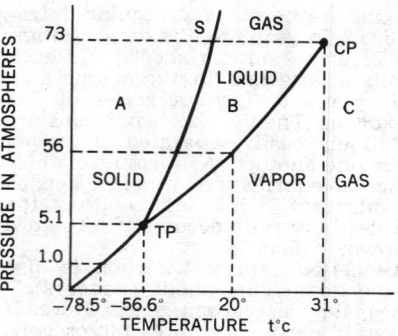

TEMPERATURE-PRESSURE (phase) diagram for carbon dioxide. (Scales not uniform.)

liquid, or gas. For any particular substance, the physical states in which it can exist are called *phases*. Thus, by varying the conditions, a substance in the solid phase can be converted into the liquid phase (melting); the liquid phase can be converted into the solid phase (freezing); the liquid phase can be converted into the vapor phase (evaporation); the vapor phase can be converted into the liquid phase (condensation); the solid phase can be converted into the vapor phase (sublimation); and the vapor phase can be converted into the solid phase (condensation).

The transition from one phase to another can be illustrated with carbon dioxide. Carbon dioxide (CO_2) is a gaseous constituent of the atmosphere. But it can be condensed, and at normal atmospheric pressure and a temperature of about $-80°$ C. it can be frozen into the solid commonly known as "dry ice." At a pressure of 5.1 atmospheres (75 pounds per square inch) and a temperature of $-56.6°$ C., the solid, liquid, and gaseous states may all exist simultaneously. This is known as the *triple point*. The illustration shows the temperature-pressure relations between the various phases of carbon dioxide.

At the temperature and pressure represented by the point A in the diagram and for any point above the lines O-TP-S, CO_2 is a solid. In the region between the lines TP-S and TP-CP (point B, for example) the substance is a liquid. At the temperature and pressure represented by points to the right of O-TP-CP (point C, for example) CO_2 is a gas for vapor. From this diagram it can be seen that CO_2 can exist as a liquid only when the pressure is above 5.1 atmospheres. This is the pressure at the triple point.

At a pressure of 1 atmosphere CO_2 (dry ice) will be in equilibrium with its vapor at a temperature of $-78.5°$ C.

Along the curve TP-CP (triple point-critical point) the vapor and liquid may exist in contact and in equilibrium. Thus at $20°$ C (room temperature) carbon dioxide stored in steel cylinders commercially will be in the liquid form with vapor above the liquid surface at a pressure of 56 atmospheres. The curve TP-CP is sometimes called the "boiling point" curve. It shows the temperatures at which the liquid will boil at various pressures. Points along

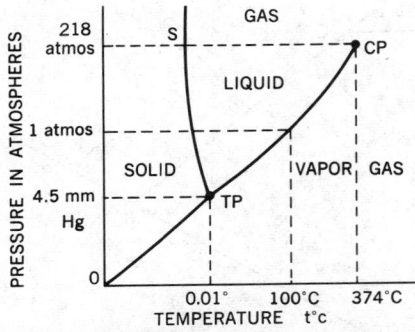

TEMPERATURE-PRESSURE (phase) diagram for water. (Scales not uniform.)

the line TP-S represent the freezing points of carbon dioxide when in contact with the liquid phase. As the pressure increases the freezing temperature rises.

Point CP is called the *critical point* at this point where the line from *TP* ends, the density of the liquid and the vapor are the same. No distinction can be made between them when the temperature is above 31° C. For all temperatures above 31° C. (say, for example, point *A*) the substance is a gas. No increase of pressure will cause it to become a liquid.

Diagrams such as this can be drawn for all substances. That for water is also shown. For water, the triple point temperature is just slightly above 0° C. The critical point is 374° C., and the corresponding pressure is about 218 atmospheres.

It should be noted that the line *TP-S* slopes backward; that is, the freezing point of water is lowered as the pressure is increased. It should also be noted that the line *TP-S* has no definite terminal point, as does *TP-CP*. As the pressure on water goes to very high values, water's behavior becomes more complex.

The terms "gas" and "vapor" refer to the substance in the region to the right of the line *TP-CP*. The term "vapor" is reserved for that state in which high pressure may condense a substance and "gas" is reserved for the condition of the substance when it is above its critical temperature and no increase of pressure is sufficient to condense the substance into the liquid state.

The portion of the curve below the triple point represents equilibrium between the solid and its vapor. All solids will evaporate: some, such as iron, extremely slowly at ordinary temperatures, but ice, even at temperatures well below 0° C., will readily evaporate.

The pressure-temperature diagrams are sometimes called *phase diagrams*.

—J. W. Buchta

MECHANICS

Measurement.—*Mechanics* is the division of physics that deals with force, motion, inertia, and energy. Of most interest are the laws that state what effect a *force*, which may be thought of as a push or a pull, will have upon the form and motion of an object. Mowing the lawn, for example, requires a force to push the mower. The engine of a car, truck, or locomotive exerts a pulling force to move the load. The laws of mechanics enable the prediction of the path of a space probe and the trajectory of an electron in a television tube. A study of mechanics is aided by an understanding of the division of mathematics called measurement.

In mechanics only three fundamental measurements are needed: length, mass or force, and time.

■**LENGTH.**—As it is commonly used in the United States, *length* specifies a distance in *inches, feet, yards,* or *miles.* Most other countries use the *metric system,* with the *meter* (m.) as the basic unit of length. From this base, 1/100 of a meter (0.01 m.) is called a *centimeter* (cm.); 1/1000 of a meter (0.001 m.) is a *millimeter* (mm.), and 1,000 meters is a *kilometer* (km.). The relationship between an inch and a centimeter is such that 1 inch equals 2.54 centimeters. The metric system is commonly used for measurements in mechanics.

■**MASS.**—The amount of material in an object as shown by its inertia is called *mass. Inertia* is the measure of resistance to change of motion. The fundamental unit of mass in the metric system is the *kilogram* (kg.), and the unit most used in mechanics is the *gram* (gm.)—1/1000 of the fundamental unit of mass. Other common values are the *milligram* (0.001 gm.), *centigram* (0.01 gm.), and *decigram* (0.1 gm.). In the United States the *pound* (lb.) is the basic unit of mass. The conversion to the metric system is as follows: 1 pound equals 453.6 grams, so that 1 kilogram equals 2.2046 pounds.

But a pound is also a weight. Sir Isaac Newton (1642–1727) found that besides possessing inertia (and thus having mass), all objects have the ability to attract all other objects. This is known as *universal gravitation.* Thus, everything on or near the surface of the earth is attracted to it. For example, a ball thrown into the air returns to earth. The force with which the earth pulls on a mass of 1 pound under standard conditions (at sea level) is called the weight of 1 pound, or 1 pound of force.

■**TIME.**—Regardless of country or the system of measuring length, or mass or force, *time* is measured in *hours, minutes,* and *seconds.*

As can be seen, there are several systems possible with the three fundamental measurements discussed. In the United States, the *foot, pound, second* (abbreviated as *f.p.s.*) *system* is generally used. This system is common to almost all engineering work except electrical engineering. There is a desire among some engineers and scientists in the United States to adopt the system generally used in scientific work throughout the world—the *c.g.s. system.* Here, the basic unit of length is the *centimeter;* of mass, the *gram;* and of time, the *second.* One problem in the c.g.s. system is the smallness of the values, although its decimal nature

makes it simple to convert values to other units.

A third system, which overcomes the small values of the c.g.s. system, is the *m.k.s. system*—based on the *meter, kilogram,* and *second.*

Regardless of which system is used, a few simple equivalents permit easy conversion to any of the other systems. The accompanying table gives some of the equivalents.

    1 foot = 0.3048 meter
    1 foot = 30.4801 centimeters
    1 inch = 2.5400 centimeters
    1 ounce = 28.350 grams
    1 pound = 453.6 grams

    1 kilometer = 3,281.8 feet
    1 meter = 39.37 inches
    1 centimeter = 0.3937 inch
    1 gram = 0.03527 ounce
    1 kilogram = 2.2046 pounds

Vectors.—In mechanics, there are two systems of addition that must be used. When adding two numbers (with identical units), an answer is easy. For example, it is easy to see that 8 feet and 2 feet equal 10 feet. But some answers also require a direction. If a direction is added—8 feet north and 2 feet east—the problem is no longer simple arithmetic.

A quantity that is specified by a number and its unit—8 feet, 50 miles per hour—is called a *scalar quantity.* A quantity that also has direction—8 feet north, 50 miles per hour east—is known as a *vector quantity.*

Vector quantities can be handled mathematically, but it is often easier to figure them graphically. For example, an object initially at a point *O* (Fig. 1) is moved 3 feet east and 4 feet north. The final position of the object is then distance *B* from the starting point *O,* or is displaced distance *OB. Displacement* of body is the direction and distance from the origin, and is a vector quantity.

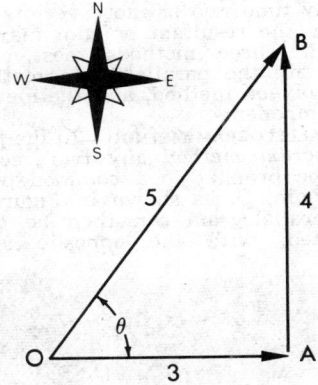

Figure 1.

This is indicated in Figure 1 by the arrow-tipped lines. The horizontal (east) line is 3 units long and shows the magnitude; the arrow head placement shows the direction and sense of the vector quantity. Similarly, the vertical (north) line locates the final point of the object. The resultant displacement from

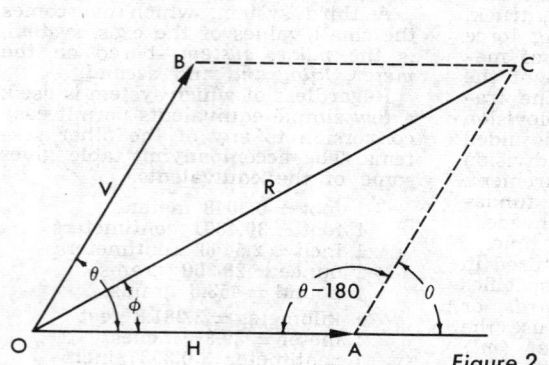

Figure 2.

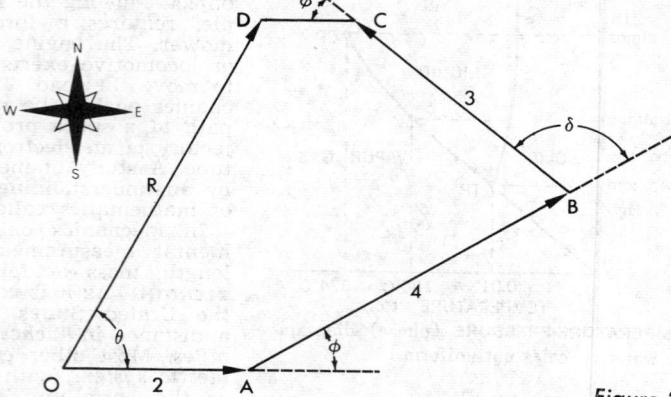

Figure 3.

point O is represented by vector OB, and the magnitude can be measured.

Mathematically, $3 + 4 = 5$ is not true. But vectors are added by a geometrical law that can be written as $\overrightarrow{OA} + \overrightarrow{AB} = \overrightarrow{OB}$, where the arrows show that the vector values are added in a special way.

In Figure 1, the vector OA is at right angles to vector AB. The resultant vector drawn from the origin to the head of the second vector closes the triangle OAB. Since it is a right triangle, and the Pythagorean theorem states that the sum of the squares of the two sides of a right triangle equals the square of the hypotenuse, then $(OA)^2 + (AB)^2 = (OB)^2$, which is $3^2 + 4^2 = (OB)^2$, or $9 + 16 = 25$. Hence, $OB = 5$ units.

Another way in which point B and the direction of vector OB can be described is by specifying the angle θ. The sine of the angle θ is the opposite side divided by the hypotenuse, or sine $\theta = AB/OB = 4/5 = 0.8 = 53°$ (approximately). Therefore, the resultant vector OB is 5 units long in a direction 53° northeast of point O.

Any time two or more vectors are given, the resultant or sum may be found. Three methods most often used are the parallelogram method, the polygon method, and the method of components.

■**PARALLELOGRAM METHOD.**—In the *parallelogram method* any two vectors can be brought to a common point or origin, O, as shown in Figure 2. A parallelogram can then be constructed, with the opposite sides parallel to the original vector and equal in length. Side $BC = OA = OB$ in Figure 2. The resultant, R, is the diagonal drawn from O to the intersection of the parallel sides at C. With a ruler the resultant is measured in the same units as those chosen for vectors V and H. Angle ϕ is measured with a protractor. This graphic solution is only as accurate as the drawing and care used in measuring the lengths of the vectors.

■**POLYGON METHOD.**— The parallelogram method is useful where only two vectors are involved. Where there are more than two vectors, the *polygon method* simplifies the number of lines that need be drawn. Here, the first vector is drawn from an origin, O, and each additional vector and its angle are drawn from the head of the succeeding one. Figure 3 illustrates the method.

For example, vector OA is drawn 2 miles east, and to its head is added vector AB, 4 miles northeast. Then BC is drawn 3 miles northwest, and finally CD, 1 mile west. The resultant OD is then drawn and its length measured in the units chosen for the other vectors. Angle θ is measured with a protractor. As can be seen, this is the parallelogram method but with each vector moved from the origin point parallel to itself until it coincides with the head of the previously drawn vector. Also, the vectors to be added follow each other head to tail. Only the resultant vector touches head to head with the last-drawn vector.

■**METHOD OF COMPONENTS.**—Probably the most useful process in mechanics is the *method of components*. It is used when a number of vectors at various angles to the origin must be combined into a single resultant. The method for achieving this is the reverse of that shown in Figure 1. In Figure 1 two vectors at right angles to each other were given and from these the resultant was found. Conversely, if the resultant (5 units) and its direction (θ) were given, the resultant could be resolved into its x and y components, namely 3 units and 4 units. This resolution into x and y is the method of components.

As an example, in Figure 4A there are four vectors acting at point O. Each vector can be resolved into x and y components (Fig. 4B) by drawing a line at right angles (*perpendicular*) from the vector head to the proper axis. If all the components along the x axis (A_x, B_x, C_x, D_x) are now added, the total is the *summation* of all x components and is written Σ_x. By performing the same operation for the y components, Σ_y is obtained.

Some values will be minus, such as D_x, C_x, A_x, and C_y, since their components point in a direction that, by convention, is negative. The resultant of the four forces is found by the Pythagorean theorem as in Figure 1, and is shown in Figure 4C.

Equilibrium.—Equilibrium is the state achieved when the resultant of all the forces upon a body, which are always represented by vectors, is zero. When equilibrium is attained, there is no change in the motion of the body. The body may be at rest,

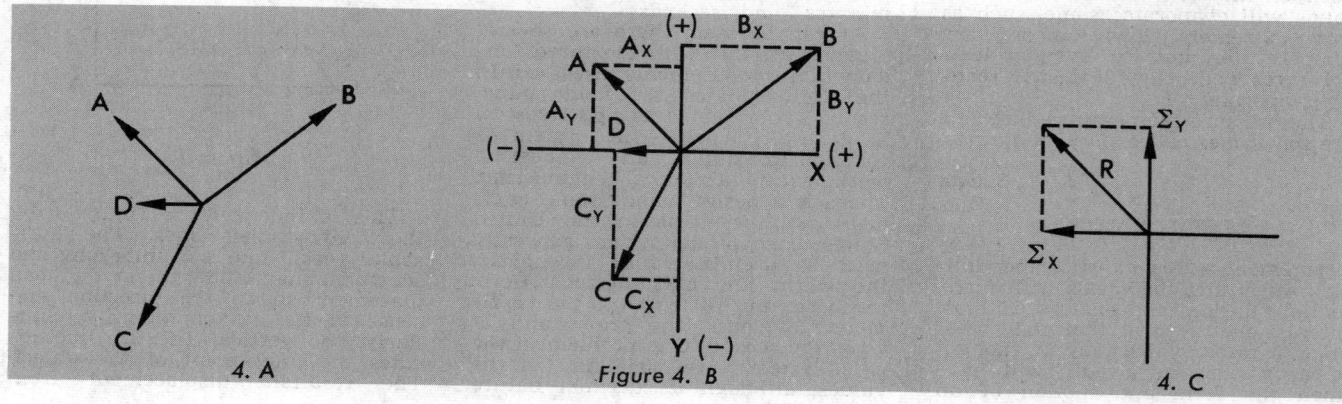

4. A   Figure 4. B   4. C

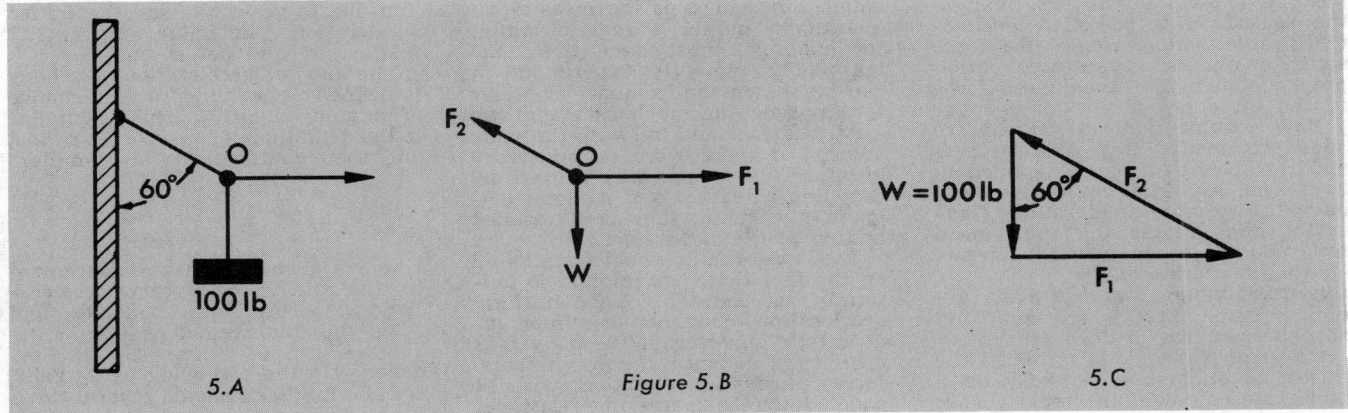

5.A   Figure 5.B   5.C

moving in a straight line at uniform speed, or rotating about a fixed axis at a uniform rate.

For example, assume a 100-pound object is suspended by a rope and held away from a wall by a second rope (Fig. 5A). If the first rope makes a 60° angle with the wall, what are the tensions in the rope? The system is in equilibrium if the vector sum of the forces acting upon it is zero. If a point O (Fig. 5B) is taken as the point in equilibrium, then the weight W and the forces F_1 and F_2 must equal zero.

The vector diagram (Fig. 5C) can be drawn to form a polygon that closes and the forces F_1 and F_2 can be measured to find the load, or the loads can be computed by trigonometric methods as follows:

$$\tan 60° = \frac{F_1}{100}$$
$$F_1 = 100 \ \tan 60°$$
$$= 173.2 \ \text{lb.}$$
$$\cos 60° = \frac{100}{F_2}$$
$$F_2 = \frac{100}{\cos 60°}$$
$$= 200 \ \text{lb.}$$

Therefore, to achieve equilibrium (to hold the system as drawn in Figure 5A), a pull of 173.2 pounds is needed on the horizontal rope, and tension in the hanging rope is 200 pounds.

This problem can be solved by the component method as well. If the horizontal component and vertical component of each force are found, the sums must equal zero if the system is in equilibrium. The x and y components of the 100-pound force are 0 and 100 pounds down, respectively. The components of F_1 are F_1 (right) and 0, respectively. The horizontal component of F_2 is $F_2 \cos 60°$ up. For equilibrium, these four forces must equal zero. Therefore

$$F_1 - F_2 \ \sin \ 60° = 0 \quad \text{(horizontal)}$$
$$F_2 \cos 60° - 100 \ \text{lb.} = 0 \quad \text{(vertical)}$$

Solving the second equation, F_2 equals 200 pounds as previously found. By substituting the F_2 value in the first equation, F_1 equals 173.2 pounds.

Velocity and Acceleration.—The discussion of equilibrium began with the supposition that the resultant, or summation, of the forces acting upon a body was zero. Equilibrium was defined as the state in which there was no change in the motion of a body. However, in mechanics one must also consider bodies upon which the resultant force is *not* zero, that is, upon which the forces do not result in a state of equilibrium. Since when the resultant force on a body is zero 'the motion of the body does not change, it logically follows that when the resultant force on a body is not zero the motion of the body must change.

The motion of a body is described by its velocity. *Velocity* is the rate of change of position, or rate of displacement; it is usually expressed in feet or centimeters per second. Velocity is a vector quantity. For its complete specification, both its magnitude and its direction must be stated. Thus, when a body is not in equilibrium and its motion is changing, its velocity must also be changing. The rate of change of velocity is *acceleration*. Acceleration is usually expressed in feet or centimeters per second per second, or feet or centimeters per second squared.

The study of mechanics is divided into three areas. One area, *statics*, deals with forces in equilibrium. A second area, *dynamics*, deals with the production and causes of motion. The third area, *kinematics*, treats motion without regard to the forces that produce it. The difference between statics, dynamics, and kinematics can be illustrated by the following discussion.

A box resting on the floor is in equilibrium. The weight of the box, W, is reacted by the ground, R (statics). If a rope is attached to the box and pulled (with a force, F), the box will move along the ground (kinematics). However, the force F must first overcome the weight of the box and the frictional force f between the box and the ground (dynamics). Once the friction is overcome, the box moves along as the force is continually exerted (statics). If F is increased, the box moves faster; if it is decreased, the box slows down and will stop when the force no longer overcomes friction (dynamics).

Motion, then, is velocity and acceleration. *Velocity* may be defined as the time rate of motion in a given direction, *acceleration* as the time rate of change of velocity. When, for example, a car speeds up, it is accelerating; when it slows down, it is decelerating. Acceleration may be expressed algebraically as the final velocity (v_f) minus the original velocity (v_o) divided by the time interval (t), or

$$a = \frac{v_f - v_o}{t}.$$

Newton's Laws of Motion.—The relationship of force to motion was described in three laws formulated by Sir Isaac Newton. Without these fundamental laws the science of mechanics might well be impossible.

■ **NEWTON'S FIRST LAW.**—A body at rest remains at rest, and a body in motion continues to move at constant speed along a straight line unless the body is acted upon, in either case, by an unbalanced force.

The first part of the law is simple enough. Forces act on a book placed on a table so that it remains at rest. Gravity pulls it down; the table pushes up. Hence, the forces are in equilibrium and the book remains stationary.

The second part of the law is more difficult, but consider the flights of the astronauts. An initial force accelerates the capsule to a constant speed in a vacuum where there is no opposing force. The capsule follows an orbit until the astronaut fires an unbalancing force (retro-rockets), impelling the capsule toward earth.

In both cases, whether the body is at rest or moving with constant speed along a line, its acceleration is zero. It follows that a body will not accelerate or decelerate unless an unbalanced force acts upon it.

■ **NEWTON'S SECOND LAW.**—An unbalanced force acting on a body causes the body to accelerate in the direction of the force, and the acceleration is directly proportional to the unbalanced force and inversely proportional to the mass of the body.

Expressed algebraically, the law states that a varies as F/M, where a is the acceleration, F is the force, and M is the mass. This proportion may be expressed as

$$a = \frac{F}{M} \quad \text{or} \quad F = Ma.$$

To illustrate the law, suppose two identical cars are driven along a road and more force, in the form of push, is applied to the first than to the second. This so-called push is really acceleration. Hence, the force acting on the car causes acceleration proportional to the unbalanced force in the direction of the force.

Now imagine that six persons are added to one of two identical cars and that equal forces are applied to both vehicles. The empty car will have the greater acceleration. Generally, the greater the unbalanced force and the less the mass, the greater the acceleration.

■NEWTON'S THIRD LAW.—For every action or force there is an equal and opposite reaction or force.

Of all of Newton's laws this is the easiest to understand. A book on a table presses down; the table pushes up. Action is the book pressing on the table; reaction is the table pushing against the book. Consider a missile being launched. The rocket engines fire hot gases downward. This is the action. The reaction is the upward motion of the missile away from the rocket-engine force.

Note that two bodies are involved in each case and that action and reaction, although equal and opposite, can never balance each other because, to balance each other, they must be exerted on the same body.

There are also forces at work on a body in circular or curvilinear motion. A body will move in a curve only when a lateral force is exerted upon it. The classic example is the stone whirled at the end of a string. The stone pulls outward on the string and, as the cord becomes taut, it pulls inward on the stone. In the same way an astronaut's capsule moves in an orbit around the earth because, as it is drawn inward by the pull of the earth's gravity, it maintains its position along a curved path due to its velocity.

Hence, the motion of a body traveling in a circular path with constant speed is of special interest. In such circular motion the moving object is pulled toward the center of the circle by a force called centripetal force. Since, by the first law of motion, an object in motion tends to travel along a straight-line path, the inertial tendency of the object opposes the inward pull. For many years, it was thought that the opposition to centripetal force caused by the body's inertial tendency was actually a reaction force, called centrifugal force, as stated in the third law. However, to repeat, action-reaction pairs are never exerted upon the same body.

■GRAVITATION.—Each particle of matter attracts every other particle with a force directly proportional to the product of their masses and inversely proportional to the square of the distance between them.

The most familiar example of universal gravitation is an object's falling when released. The amount of the earth's attraction is different for different bodies, varying with their mass; this attraction is known as the weight of the body. Weight is proportional to mass; if the same force (gravitational attraction) produces the same acceleration on two bodies, the weights of the two bodies are

equal. Since mass is the measure of quantity of matter, a quart of water, for example, must have twice the mass of a pint. By experiment, it can be shown that a quart of water weighs twice as much as a pint.

All bodies would fall with the same velocity if there were no resistance of air. This theory was proved by dropping a feather and a metal pellet in a vacuum; they both reached bottom at the same time.

The laws of falling bodies are based on the fact that their motion is uniformly accelerated. The uniform acceleration does not continue indefinitely, however. If the body falls a sufficient distance, the gravitational force causing acceleration will be equaled by the increasing resistance of the air. At this point, acceleration ceases and the body continues to fall at a uniform maximum velocity called terminal velocity.

A relationship exists between velocity, distance covered, acceleration, and time in uniformly accelerated motion. Based on the acceleration formula,

$$a = \frac{v_f - v_o}{t},$$

the formula for the final velocity is

$$v_f = v_o + at.$$

The distance traveled by a body having constant acceleration is found by averaging its velocities during the time interval t. Then distance traveled, s, may be found by the equation

$$s = v_{avg}t,$$
$$= \frac{v_o + v_f}{2} t.$$

Replacing v_f by $v_o + at$,

$$s = \frac{v_o + (v_o + at)}{2} t,$$
$$= v_o t + \tfrac{1}{2}at^2.$$

The third equation of uniformly accelerated motion is derived by eliminating time:

$$as = \left(\frac{v_f - v_o}{t}\right)\left(\frac{v_o + v_f}{2} t\right),$$
$$= \tfrac{1}{2}(v_f - v_o)(v_o + v_f),$$
$$v_f^2 = v_o^2 + 2as.$$

The substitution of gravitational acceleration, g, upon these uniformly

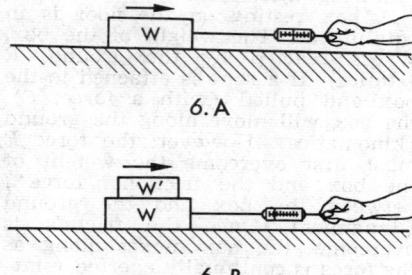

6. A

6. B

accelerated motion formulas yields

$$v_f = v_o + gt,$$
$$s = v_o t + \tfrac{1}{2}gt^2,$$
$$v_f^2 = v_o^2 + 2gs.$$

The only change is that accelera-

tion due to gravity is substituted for acceleration. The value of g is 32.2 feet per second per second.

The angular acceleration of a body is defined as its time rate of change of angular velocity. This is similar to the definition of linear acceleration, and the equations are also similar:

$$\omega_f = \omega_o + 2\alpha t$$
$$\theta = \omega_o t + \tfrac{1}{2}\alpha t^2$$
$$\omega_f^2 = \omega_o^2 + 2\alpha\theta$$

where θ is the angular displacement in time t; α is the angular acceleration; ω_o is the initial velocity; and ω_f is the final velocity.

Friction.—In the preceding paragraphs, friction has been named several times without being defined. When two bodies in contact are in motion relative to one another, a force—called frictional force, or the force of friction—opposes this motion; that is, the frictional force acts in a direction opposite to the direction of motion. There are several theories regarding the cause of friction. One theory contends that the cause of friction is the roughness of the two surfaces in contact. No matter how smooth the surfaces may appear, when they are observed under magnification, irregularities—looking like so many bumps—can be seen. It is thought that these "bumps" interlock to cause opposition to motion. A second theory contends that the same atomic forces that hold the molecules together in each surface also tend to hold the molecules of the two surfaces together. The magnitude of the frictional force depends upon the materials in contact, the condition of the surfaces, and the forces that are pressing the surfaces together.

To illustrate frictional force, imagine a box at rest to which a rope is attached and is pulled upon with a 1-pound force. If the box does not move, the resultant force is zero and the ground must be exerting a frictional force of 1 pound opposite to the force on the rope. If the pull is increased, the box will eventually move; and at the moment it does move and continues to move at constant speed, friction has been overcome. Any increase in the pull will then cause acceleration of the box.

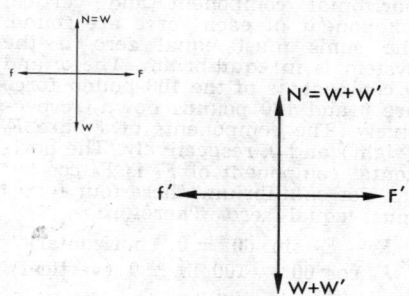

The Coefficient of Friction.—Figure 6A shows a box being moved to the right at a constant velocity by a force, F. The box pushes against the ground with a force equal to its weight, W, and the ground pushes back with an equal force called the normal, N.

Since the box is moving at a constant velocity, the system must be in equilibrium, and frictional force f must therefore equal F. If a second box is placed atop the first (Fig. 6B), to keep the system moving uniformly, the force to the right must be increased to a magnitude of F'. The boxes are pressing against the ground with a force equal to their combined weights, $W + W'$, and the ground is pushing back with the equal force N'. Since the system is still in equilibrium, the frictional force must have increased to f' to remain equal to F'. By experiment, it has been shown that the frictional force increases in the same proportions as the normal force:

$$\frac{f'}{f} = \frac{N'}{N}$$

or

$$\frac{f}{N} = \frac{f'}{N'} = \text{constant.}$$

The constant, which is designated as μ, is called the *coefficient of friction*, and has been determined for a large number of surface pairs. It can be used to determine the frictional forces in a system through the equation

$$f = \mu N.$$

As an example, assume a box weighs 100 pounds and the coefficient of friction is 0.1. How long would it take to move the box 100 feet if it were pulled with a constant force of 20 pounds? (Fig. 7.)

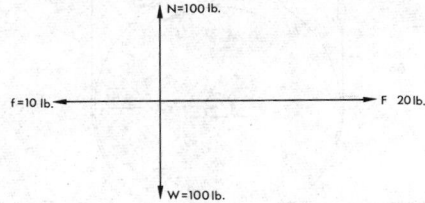

N=100 lb.

f=10 lb. ◄──────────────► F 20 lb.

W=100 lb.

Figure 7.

The frictional force on the box is:

$$f = \mu N$$
$$= (0.1)(100)$$
$$= 10 \text{ lb.}$$

The acceleration of the box, where $M = W/g$, is as follows:

$$a = \frac{F}{M}$$
$$= \frac{(F)(g)}{W}$$
$$= \frac{(20-10)(32.2)}{100}$$
$$= \frac{(10)(32.2)}{100}$$
$$= \frac{322}{100}$$
$$= 3.22 \text{ ft./sec.}^2$$

Substituting acceleration in the distance equation,

$$s = v_o t + \tfrac{1}{2}at^2.$$

Since the initial velocity, v_o, is zero,

$$s = \tfrac{1}{2}at^2;$$

and since $s = 100$ ft. and $a = 3.22$ ft./sec.^{2}, then

$$t = \sqrt{\frac{2s}{a}}$$
$$= \sqrt{\frac{200}{3.22}}$$
$$= \sqrt{62.1 \text{ sec.}^2}$$
$$= 7.88 \text{ sec.}$$

Work.—In physics, *work* is used to describe a situation where an applied force produces movement in the direction that the force is applied. A truck does not work in holding up a load of bricks, but it does work in moving the load up a hill. Work (W) can be expressed as the product of the applied force (F) times the distance (s) covered by movement in the direction of the force, or

$$W = Fs \cos \theta.$$

With a constant force applied in the direction of the displacement, $\cos \theta$ equals 1, and the work produced becomes the product of the force times the displacement, or

$$W = Fs.$$

The *foot-pound* is the unit of work in the f.p.s. system. One foot-pound is the work produced by a 1-pound force applied for a distance of 1 foot. In the c.g.s. system, the unit of work is the *erg*. One foot-pound is equal to 13,560,000 ergs. How much work is done while pulling a 650-pound log 20 feet with a chain that makes an angle of 30° with the ground? The coefficient of friction, μ, between the log and ground can be considered to be 0.40.

Thus,

$$F = \mu N$$
$$= (0.40)(650)$$
$$= 260 \text{ lb.}$$

and

$$W = Fs \cos \theta$$
$$= (260)(20)(\cos 30°)$$
$$= (5,200)(0.86)$$
$$= 4,472 \text{ ft.-lb.}$$

Energy.—The capacity for doing work, *energy,* can exist in many forms and can be converted from one form to another. *Potential energy* is the energy a body has by virtue of its position. *Kinetic energy* is the energy possessed by a body by virtue of its motion. Ignoring friction, the work done on a body equals the change in kinetic and potential energy. The energy change is expressed in the same units as work—foot-pounds in the f.p.s. system and ergs in the c.g.s system. It is converted or transformed by machines to a usable form. Although energy cannot be destroyed, it may be transformed into some unusable form and be dissipated. For example, electrical energy used to heat the coils in a toaster is irretrievably dissipated. Mechanical energy used to stop a moving car is converted into heat in the brakes and is dissipated. The energy used to operate any machine, therefore, can be said to follow a standard pattern: it is converted into a more usable or convenient form and finally dissipated as heat.

■**POTENTIAL ENERGY.**—The energy a body possesses by virtue of its location or configuration is referred to as *potential energy.* Water in a reservoir, or a weight lifted to an elevated position, has potential energy that can be converted by a machine into a more desirable or convenient form. *Gravitational potential energy* is the most common form of potential energy. Since the earth's gravity attracts every body, work is required to elevate a body to a higher level. The work expended on the body (weight of the body times the elevation) represents energy that is stored and can be recovered. This potential energy (P.E.) is the product of the weight (W) and the height (h) to which the body was raised, and can be stated as

$$\text{P.E.} = Wh.$$

If W is given in pounds and h is given in feet, the potential energy is expressed in foot-pounds. When a mass is elevated, its potential energy is increased; when a mass is lowered, its potential energy is decreased. In either case the potential energy is measured from an arbitrary zero point, such as sea level, the floor, or a table top. A stone on a table has no potential energy when the table top is selected as zero point. With the floor as zero point, the potential energy of the stone is equal to its weight times the height of the table.

■**KINETIC ENERGY.** — The energy a body possesses due to its motion is called *kinetic energy.* A bullet in flight, a spinning flywheel, and a speeding automobile all possess kinetic energy. The amount of work a moving body can do while being brought to rest or the work required to produce the velocity at which the body moves is a measure of its kinetic energy (K.E.).

A body at rest acted upon by an unbalanced force (F) through a distance (s) is accelerated (a) to a velocity (v). The work done to accelerate the body is equal to its kinetic energy, or

$$\text{K.E.} = Fs = mas.$$

From the earlier discussion of acceleration and velocity, it can be seen that the following substitutions can be made for a and s:

$$a = \frac{v_f - v_o}{t},$$
$$s = \frac{v_o + v_f}{2}t.$$

Thus,

$$\text{K.E.} = mas$$
$$= m\left(\frac{v_f - v_o}{t}\right)\left(\frac{v_o + v_f}{2}t\right).$$

Starting from rest, when v_o is zero,

$$\text{K.E.} = \frac{mv^2}{2}.$$

If the mass (m) is expressed in *slugs* and the velocity (v) in feet per second, the kinetic energy is expressed in foot-pounds. Using the above formula, the kinetic energy of a 3,200-pound elephant charging at 15 miles per hour (22 feet per second) can be calculated. In slugs the

3,200-pound animal's mass is:

$$m = \frac{W}{g}$$

$$= \frac{3,200 \text{ lb.}}{32 \text{ ft./sec.}^2}$$

$$= 100 \text{ slugs.}$$

Therefore,

$$\text{K.E.} = \frac{mv^2}{2}$$

$$= \frac{(100 \text{ slugs}) (22 \text{ ft./sec.}^2)}{2}$$

$$= 24,200 \text{ ft.-lb.}$$

Accelerating or decelerating a body requires the application of a force that produces a change in the kinetic energy. The change in kinetic energy (ΔK.E.) is equal to the total kinetic energy when the body is accelerated from rest or brought to a standstill.

To stop a moving object, its kinetic energy must be absorbed by work done in opposition to its motion. Since the kinetic energy is proportional to the square of an object's velocity, doubling the speed increases the kinetic energy four times. Therefore four times the amount of work is needed to bring the body to a stop.

Simple Machines. — Machines cannot create or destroy energy. Instead, they simply transform it or apply it in a more convenient or usable form. The energy received by the machine may be converted into useful work, but the work produced cannot exceed the energy received. Machines may be used to convert chemical energy (a gasoline engine), electric energy (an electric motor), or mechanical energy (a hydraulic jack) but only the conversion of mechanical energy will be considered in this discussion. In simple machines, energy is applied by a single force doing useful work against a single resisting force. Regardless of their complexity, all machines can be resolved into combinations of the wedge, or inclined plane, and the lever.

The *actual mechanical advantage* (A.M.A.) of any machine is the ratio of the force delivered (F_o) to the force applied (F_i), or

$$\text{A.M.A.} = \frac{\text{force out}}{\text{force in}}$$

$$= \frac{F_o}{F_i}.$$

To lift a 3,000-pound automobile with a 50-pound force requires an actual mechanical advantage of 3,000 lb./50 lb., or 60. Most machines are force multipliers and therefore have an A.M.A. of more than 1. Speed-increasing machines, such as a bicycle chain drive or a hand drill, have an A.M.A. of less than 1.

The *ideal mechanical advantage* (I.M.A.) is the ratio of the distance the applied force travels (s_i) to the distance the delivered force travels (S_o):

$$\text{I.M.A.} = \frac{\text{distance in}}{\text{distance out}}$$

$$= \frac{s_i}{s_o}.$$

Due to friction, the work produced is less than the work applied to any machine. Work in ($F_i s_i$) is greater than work out ($F_o s_o$):

$$F_o s_o < F_i s_i.$$

When each part of this expression is divided by $F_i s_i$, the result is:

$$\frac{F_o}{F_i} < \frac{s_i}{s_o}.$$

Therefore,

$$\text{A.M.A.} < \text{I.M.A.}$$

The actual mechanical advantage is therefore always less than the ratio of the input distance (s_i) to the output distance (s_o), or the ideal mechanical advantage. The ideal mechanical advantage is frequently referred to as the *velocity ratio*, since the forces are moved these distances in the same time period.

In a theoretical machine (without friction), the work in, $F_i s_i$, equals the work out, $F_o s_o$; thus A.M.A. equals I.M.A. In this case the ratio of forces in and out equals the ratio of distances the forces travel in and out, or

$$\frac{F_o}{F_i} = \frac{s_i}{s_o}.$$

Therefore,

$$\text{A.M.A.} = \text{I.M.A.}$$

The efficiency of a machine is a measure of the useful work produced, and it is usually expressed as a percentage. The useful work produced is always less than the energy input, and the loss, if no energy is stored in the machine, is caused by friction. Expressing this concept in terms of the principle of conservation of energy: the energy in equals the energy out plus the wasted energy.

Efficiency is expressed as the ratio of work output to work input, or

$$\text{efficiency} = \frac{\text{work out}}{\text{work in}}$$

$$= \frac{F_o s_o}{F_i s_i}.$$

The resulting fraction is multiplied by 100 and expressed as a percentage. The efficiency is always less than 1. The efficiency may also be calculated as one of the following ratios multiplied by 100:

$$\text{efficiency} = \frac{F_o/F_i}{s_o/s_i}$$

$$= \frac{\text{A.M.A.}}{\text{I.M.A.}}.$$

Power. — Power introduces a time element into the study of work. The time rate of doing work is *power*. By dividing the amount of work involved by the time required to complete the work, the average power can be determined. Both the work (W) and the time (t) must be measured to determine the average power (P).

$$P = \frac{W}{t} = \frac{Fs}{t}$$

It takes 20 seconds to carry a 3-pound ball to the roof of a building 30 feet tall. The same ball can be thrown to the roof in 2 seconds. The work done in either case is the same, but the power required to throw the ball is 10 times greater:

$$carrying \ P = \frac{Fs}{t}$$

$$= \frac{(3 \text{ lb.}) (30 \text{ ft.})}{20 \text{ sec.}}$$

$$= 4.5 \text{ ft.-lb./sec.}$$

$$throwing \ P = \frac{Fs}{t}$$

$$= \frac{(3 \text{ lb.}) (30 \text{ ft.})}{2 \text{ sec.}}$$

$$= 45 \text{ ft.-lb./sec.}$$

The units of power in the f.p.s. system are the same as those of work (foot-pounds), divided by time in seconds. Since 1 *horsepower* is defined as the energy needed to move a 550-pound weight 1 foot in 1 second (550 ft.-lb./sec.), the average horsepower can be expressed by dividing by this figure.

By absorbing the entire output of a machine with a friction brake, the power output can be measured. The energy absorbed is converted into heat and is dissipated. The band is tightened around the pulley (Fig. 8)

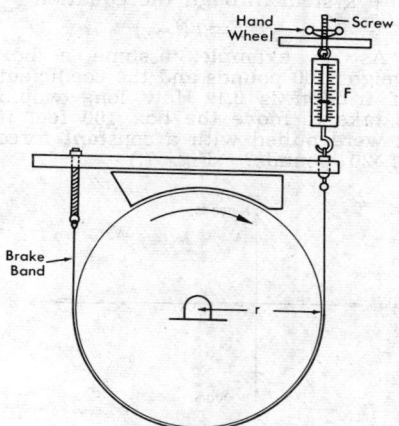

Figure 8.

by rotating the handwheel, and the scale measures the force of the friction produced. The work done by the machine in opposing the friction force F is equal to $F 2\pi r$ for each revolution. The work produced in unit time is $F 2\pi r n$, where n represents the number of complete revolutions made in unit time.

Torque. — A body at rest or in uniform motion can be said to be in equilibrium. A body will remain in equilibrium as long as all forces acting on the body pass through a common point and the sum of their vectors is zero. When the forces do not pass through a common point, the rotation as well as the linear motion will be changed. *Torque* is the force that produces or tends to produce rotation.

When opposing but equal forces act on a body (Fig. 9A), the resultant movement will be zero because the sum of the vector forces will be zero. If the same forces are applied to the body (Fig. 9B), the vector sum of the forces will again equal zero, but the body will rotate. When the vector sum of the forces is zero, the body will not move in a linear manner; but rotation is possible. Equilibrium is not assured, therefore, unless a second condition is satisfied. The second condition requires that the sum of the torques generated by the applied forces also be zero.

The *torque* (*L*) about a selected axis is a product of the force (*F*) and its moment arm (*s*). (The *moment arm* is the perpendicular distance from a selected axis to the line of the applied force.) Then

$$L = Fs.$$

When combined into the single quantity torque (or moment of force), the magnitude of the force and the length of the moment arm are of equal importance. For a given moment arm, increasing the force increases the torque; and for a given force, increasing the length of the moment arm increases the torque. Torque, being a product of force (pounds) and a measure of length (feet), is expressed in the f.p.s. system of units as *pound-feet* (*lb.-ft.*).

Since torque is a vector quantity, the selection of the axis is doubly important. First, the selection of the axis determines the algebraic sign of the vector, since altering the location of the axis can change rotation from clockwise (positive) to counterclockwise (negative). Second, the torque produced by a force of unknown magnitude can be reduced to zero by selecting an axis through which the unknown passes, thus simplifying problem solution.

Forces whose vectors intersect at a common point are called *concurrent forces*. The torque produced by each concurrent force, about an axis through their intersection, is zero. Selecting an axis at any other location will usually result in the sum of the torques being greater than zero. Should the sum of the torques around any axis outside the intersection equal zero, they will equal zero around any axis selected. Therefore torque does not enter into calculations involving concurrent forces in equilibrium. With nonconcurrent forces, no single axis exists about which the sum of the torques equals zero. It is essential, therefore, that the resultant torque be considered when analyzing a set of nonconcurrent forces in equilibrium.

The *center of gravity* is that point at which the entire weight of a body may be considered to be concentrated. The sum of all torque produced by the weights of all parts of the body around a horizontal axis through the center of gravity must equal zero. Locating the center of gravity of bodies is necessary in equilibrium problems to find the location of the single vector representing the body's weight.

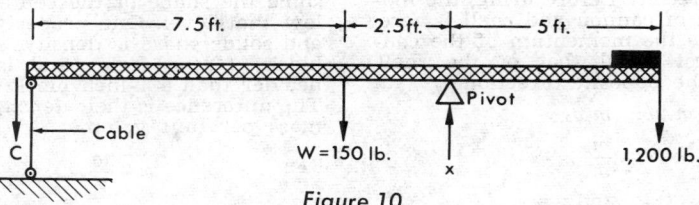

Figure 10.

A steel beam (Fig. 10) 15 feet long and weighing 150 pounds is supported 5 feet from its right end by a pivot. A 1,200-pound weight rests on the right end, and the left end is secured by a cable holding the bar in equilibrium. What is the load on the pivot (the downward force it must resist), and what force must the cable resist?

With a uniform bar such as this, the center of gravity (and its weight) can be considered to be concentrated at its center (*W*). A force (*x*) acts upward at the fulcrum, and the 1,200-pound weight acts downward at the right end. Since the system is in equilibrium, two conditions must be satisfied. First, the sum of all vector forces must equal zero:

$$-C - 150 \text{ lb.} + x - 1,200 \text{ lb.} = 0,$$

when *C* is the force on the cable.

With two unknowns this equation cannot be solved, so the second condition for equilibrium must also be considered. The sum of all torques (Σ_L) must equal zero in such a system. Taking the pivot (*x*) as the axis and starting at the right end, with counterclockwise torques taken as positive (+):

$$\Sigma_L = - (5 \text{ ft.}) (1,200 \text{ lb.})$$
$$+ (x) (0 \text{ ft.})$$
$$+ (150 \text{ lb.}) (2.5 \text{ ft.})$$
$$+ (C) (7.5 \text{ ft.}) + (2.5 \text{ ft.}) = 0$$
$$\Sigma_L = - 6,000 \text{ lb.-ft.}$$
$$+ 0 + 375 \text{ lb.-ft.}$$
$$+ (10 \text{ ft.}) C = 0$$
$$(10 \text{ ft.}) C = 5,625 \text{ lb.-ft.}$$
$$C = 562.5 \text{ lb.}$$

Having found one unknown—the force on the cable (*C*)—this can be substituted in the first equation and a complete solution arrived at:

$$-562.5 \text{ lb.} - 150 \text{ lb.} + x - 1,200 \text{ lb.} = 0$$
$$x = 1912.5 \text{ lb.}$$

Momentum.—During the study of basic mechanics, it must not be forgotten that the same laws apply to atomic particles that apply to larger objects. This is particularly true in the study of momentum, where application of basic laws enabled scientists to predict the movement and properties of atomic particles years before their existence was proved.

The *momentum* (*P*) of a body is defined as the product of its mass (*m*) times its velocity (*v*), or

$$P = mv.$$

Since they consist of mass and velocity, the units for momentum can be considered composite units. Following the f.p.s. system, mass (w/g) is given in slugs, velocity in feet per second, and momentum in slug-feet per second. Thus, the momentum of a 5,000-pound truck passing a point at 60 miles per hour (88 feet per second) is:

$$m = \frac{w}{g}$$
$$= \frac{5,000 \text{ lb.}}{32.2 \text{ ft./sec.}^2}$$
$$= 155.3 \text{ slugs}$$
$$P = mv$$
$$= (155.3 \text{ slugs}) (88 \text{ ft./sec.})$$
$$= 13,666.4 \text{ slug-ft./sec.}$$

A vector quantity, momentum takes its direction from the velocity. When two or more bodies are involved in a system, the momentum of each body must be added vectorially. If two balls of equal mass are rolled toward each other with equal velocity, the momentum of each is equal. Since the vectors are opposite in direction, the vector sum equals zero.

Newton's first law states that there is no change in the motion of a body unless a resistant force acts upon it. A body's mass is constant; therefore, its momentum will remain constant unless an external force is applied. Keeping this basic fact in mind will allow the behavior of everyday objects to be studied and analyzed. When a force is applied to a system of bodies, the system's momentum is altered; but some other set of bodies will gain (or lose) momentum equal to the loss (or gain) produced in the first system. This conservation of momentum can be expressed simply as: momentum lost = momentum gained. If the balls discussed previously collide, they will rebound (if they are elastic). Since the law of conservation of momentum applies to the system, the velocity of the rebounding bodies will be equal to, but not necessarily the same as, the original speed. The system's total momentum is still zero because the vector quantities cancel each other.

A system comprised of unequal masses, such as a projectile leaving

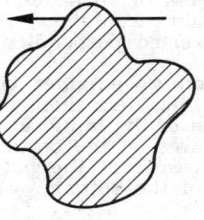

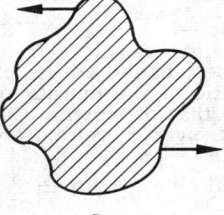

A   Figure 9.   B

a cannon, will also follow the same laws. For example, if a 12-pound shell leaves the muzzle at 2,400 feet per second, how fast will the 3-ton cannon recoil? Before firing, the momentum of cannon and shell is zero; therefore the momentum of the cannon must equal that of the shell, but in the opposite direction.

$$m_1 v_1 = m_2 v_2$$

$$v_1 = \frac{m_2}{m_1} \times v_2$$

$$m_1 = \frac{w_1}{g}$$

$$= \frac{6,000 \text{ lb.}}{32.2 \text{ ft./sec.}^2}$$

$$m_2 = \frac{w_2}{g}$$

$$= \frac{12 \text{ lb.}}{32.2 \text{ ft./sec.}^2}$$

$$v_1 = \frac{(12 \text{ lb.})/(32.2 \text{ ft./sec.}^2)}{(6,000 \text{ lb.})/(32.2 \text{ ft./sec.}^2)}$$
$$\times 2,400 \text{ ft./sec.}$$

$$= \frac{12}{6,000} \times 2,400 \text{ ft./sec.}$$

$$= 4.8 \text{ ft./sec.}$$

Impulse.—Impulse and momentum are related concepts. Indeed, impulse may be defined in terms of momentum: *impulse* is the product of the average value of a force and the time during which it acts, and this product is equal to the change in momentum produced in the force. Although this may sound complex, impulse can be shown to be derived from the second law of motion. Sir Isaac Newton originally stated his second law in terms of force, time, and momentum:

$$F = \frac{mv - mv_o}{t},$$

where F is the force, m is the mass, v is the terminal velocity, v_o is the starting velocity, mv and mv_o are the terminal and initial momentums, respectively, and t is the time. (This equation can be changed to its more familiar form by factoring out the mass:

$$F = \frac{m(v - v_o)}{t}.$$

Since

$$\frac{v - v_o}{t} = a,$$

$$F = ma.$$

By multiplying the above equation by t, it becomes

$$Ft = mv - mv_o.$$

This is called the *impulse equation:* Ft is the impulse, and $mv - mv_o$ is the change in momentum.

As an illustration of impulse, a hammer of mass m accelerating at a rate a to a velocity v strikes a nail with a force F. This force, which lasts for but a fraction of a second, drives the nail into the wood by impulse. The hammer has supplied an impulse equal to its loss of momentum. In the f.p.s. system, the unit of impulse is the *pound-second.* In the c.g.s. system, the unit of impulse is referred to as the *dynesecond.*

Liquids.—Liquids are unlike solid bodies because they have no definite size or shape. A liquid will fill any container to a certain level and assume the shape of the container below that level. One property liquids and solids share is density. A 1-inch block of lead feels (and is) much heavier than a 1-inch block of wood. The difference is their *density* (ρ), or mass per unit volume:

$$\rho = \frac{m}{V}.$$

In units of the f.p.s. system, density is expressed as *slugs per cubic foot.* (In the c.g.s. system, density is expressed in *grams per cubic centimeter.*) The weight per unit volume is called the *weight-density* (D):

$$D = \frac{W}{V}.$$

Since

$$W = mg,$$

$$D = \frac{mg}{V}$$

$$= \rho g.$$

Density (ρ) is used when problems involving mass are being considered,

NASA

LAUNCHING A MISSILE requires the combined knowledge of chemical, electrical, aeronautical, and mechanical engineers.

while weight-density (D) is used with respect to the effects of force.

The ratio of the density of a substance to that of water at 39.2° F. is called its *specific gravity,* and is expressed as:

$$\text{specific gravity} = \frac{\rho}{\rho_w},$$

where ρ_w is the density of water; and

specific gravity $= \dfrac{D}{D_w}$,

where D_w is the weight-density of water. Specific gravity has no units because the densities of both substances have the same units. Since specific gravity is frequently tabulated, it is convenient to find densities of specific substances by the formula

$$\rho = (\text{specific gravity})(\rho_w).$$

Densities obtained by this formula will be in the units of the system used for the density of water.

A liquid confined in a container exerts a force on the walls and bottom of the container. With a still liquid, the force is normal or perpendicular to the surface. This perpendicular force (F) per unit area (A) is called pressure (P), expressed as:

$$P = \frac{F}{A}.$$

A scalar quantity, pressure is exerted whenever force is applied over an area. Even a very light woman can exert high pressure if her weight is applied over a small area, such as a spike shoe heel. *Pounds per square inch* is the most commonly used unit in the f.p.s. system. (In the c.g.s. system, the unit of pressure is *dynes per square centimeter.*) The pressure concept is essential in work involving liquids and gases. A typical problem is: What is the pressure on a 10-inch by 10-inch plate at the bottom of a swimming pool 10 feet (120 inches) deep? The force perpendicular to the pool bottom is produced by the weight of the column of liquid resting on it. Water weighs 62.4 pounds per cubic foot, or 0.036 pound per cubic inch. Hence,

$$P = \frac{F}{A} =$$

$$\frac{(0.036 \text{ lb./in.}^3)(120 \text{ in.})(100 \text{ in.}^2)}{100 \text{ in.}^2}$$

$$P = 4.32 \text{ lb./in.}^2$$

When studying liquids at rest, several general statements that always apply should be kept in mind:

Every point within the body of a liquid is subjected to pressure.

Pressure is proportional to the vertical height of the liquid above the point in question.

Since the liquid is at rest, the force on a surface is the same regardless of the orientation of the surface, that is, how the surface is viewed.

Pressure is the same at any point selected on a horizontal plane through the liquid.

Regardless of shape or orientation of the fluid's container, pressure is always exerted perpendicular to the surface.

Force on a container bottom can be more than, less than, or equal to the weight of the liquid in a container. The force on the bottom is equal to the pressure at the bottom times the area of the bottom.

—Joseph J. Kelleher and Robert Abbott

ELECTRICITY AND MAGNETISM

History.—Electricity and magnetism are two very closely associated phenomena that play a vital part in nearly every aspect of modern living: in homes, in transportation, in communications, and in industry. Their impact on civilization has been tremendous and far-reaching. Because their many applications have made them commonplace, it perhaps is difficult to realize that electricity and magnetism have been harnessed for the benefit of mankind only within the last century and a half. This is true despite the fact that there are three natural manifestations of electricity and magnetism that are readily observable. These were known to the ancients, but were considered unrelated and of no apparent use to man.

One of these manifestations is electrical attraction. Records indicate that as early as 600 B.C. it was known that a piece of amber, which was used for ornamental purposes and called "electron," could be rubbed with wool or fur and made to attract small bits of straw. In 1600 Sir William Gilbert discovered that many other substances could be made to exhibit the same effect. He called the effect "electric," from "electron."

A second manifestation of electricity, lightning, has been observed since the dawn of history. However, its electrical nature was not recognized until 1751, when Benjamin Franklin performed his kite experiment.

A third natural manifestation, involving magnetism, was known to early Greek philosophers. A *lodestone* was known to attract iron and to orient itself in a north-south direction if freely suspended. The magnetizing of a steel needle from a lodestone, and use of the needle as a compass, were recorded by the Chinese at the beginning of the twelfth century. The connection between electricity and magnetism was discovered by Hans Christian Oersted in 1819. Other epoch-making discoveries followed rapidly, and the application of electricity and magnetism to the service of mankind soon began.

Static Electricity.—Static electricity is electricity at rest. It is responsible for the attraction between a bit of straw and a piece of amber that has been rubbed with wool or fur. Present theory holds that all matter is composed of tiny *molecules* that are themselves composed of even smaller structures called *atoms*. Atoms contain three principal types of particles—protons, neutrons, and electrons. Each *proton* carries a specific amount of *positive charge*, and each *electron* carries the same amount of *negative charge*. *Neutrons* carry no electric charge and therefore are electrically neutral. The protons and neutrons are located together at the center of the atom, to form the nucleus, while the electrons move about the nucleus in tiny orbits. Each proton or neutron has more than 1,800 times the mass of an electron. The number of protons and neutrons in the nucleus, and the number and arrangement of the orbiting electrons, determine the nature of the substance.

Normally each atom has the same number of electrons as protons; and since the total quantity of positive charge equals the total quantity of negative charge, the atom is electrically neutral. However, electrons can be removed to leave the atom with a net positive charge, or they can be added to give a net negative charge.

One method of altering the number of electrons in the atoms is by friction. Atoms have the ability to attract more electrons than the number normally moving about each nucleus; this attraction is of different strength for different materials. When two substances of different attractive power are rubbed together, some of the electrons in one will leave their orbits and move to new orbits in the other. The first substance will be left with a net positive charge, and the second will acquire a net negative charge (Fig. 1). Examples may be tabulated as follows:

Rubbed Material	Charge	Rubbing Material	Charge
Amber	—	Fur or wool	+
Rubber	—	Fur or wool	+
Glass	+	Silk	—

■**FORCES OF ATTRACTION AND REPULSION.**—The presence of a force acting between two charged bodies a little distance apart can be readily demonstrated by suspending one charged body by a thread and approaching it with another charged body held in the hand. Experimentation with the materials listed above will demonstrate the general law that like charges repel one another and unlike charges attract one another.

The uncharged bit of paper or straw is attracted to the charged body because a few of the electrons in the paper or straw are able to move about. Assume, for example, that a positively charged glass rod is brought near a bit of paper. Electrons, drawn toward the rod, will make the surface of the paper negatively charged and attract it to the rod. The more distant surface of the paper will be positively charged but, being farther away, it will be repelled with less force; therefore the paper is attracted. If the paper touches the rod, the movable electrons will go onto the rod, leaving the paper positively charged. The paper will then jump away. This involves another general law: the force between two charges is inversely proportional to the square of the distance between them, and directly proportional to the product of the values of the two charges.

■**ELECTRIC FIELDS.**—The force that acts between electric charges suggests that there is an electric field associated with every electric charge. For convenience, the *electric field* is considered to consist of electric lines of force, a *line of force* being a line along which a charge tends to move. The positive direction is that direction in which a positive charge would move. Lines of force may be thought of as extending radially outward in all directions from a positive charge, and radially inward from all directions toward a negative charge. The *intensity*, or strength, of the electric field is measured by the force that acts upon a unit electric charge at the point of measurement and is represented pictorially by the density with which the lines of force occur in the vicinity of the point. Electric lines of force never cross one another. They begin at a positive charge and terminate at a negative charge.

The effects of static electricity are of limited use. However, one use of increasing importance is in the electrostatic precipitator, which is used in some air-conditioning systems and in air-pollution control. In this device, dust and smoke particles are attracted and held to charged surfaces.

Current Electricity.—The most familiar uses of electricity involve electricity in motion, a flow of electric charges. A stream of moving electric charges constitutes an *electric current*.

■**CONDUCTORS AND INSULATORS.**—The electrons orbiting about atomic nuclei are not all unchangeably fixed in

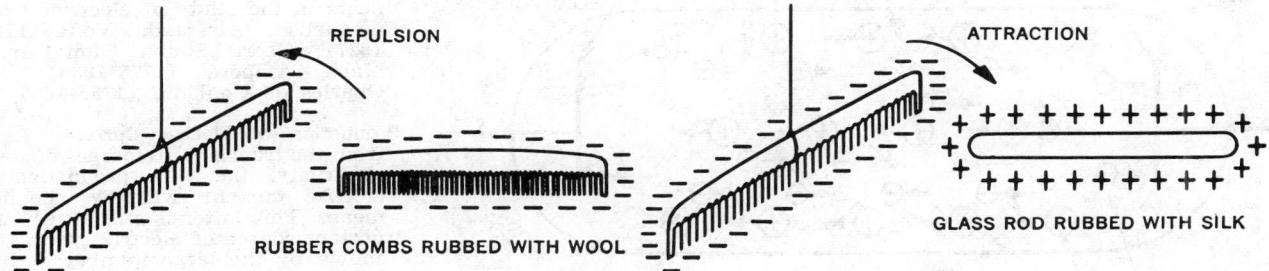

REPULSION   ATTRACTION

RUBBER COMBS RUBBED WITH WOOL   GLASS ROD RUBBED WITH SILK

Figure 1.

WIRE

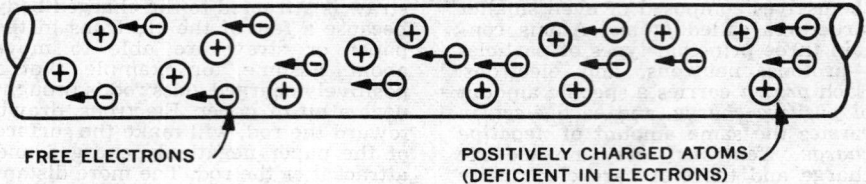

FREE ELECTRONS   POSITIVELY CHARGED ATOMS
                                  (DEFICIENT IN ELECTRONS)

Figure 2.

their orbits. In some materials there are electrons that move readily from atom to atom. Generally speaking, metals contain quantities of such free electrons, and are said to be good *conductors* (Fig. 2). In most nonmetallic substances, all the electrons are tightly bound in their orbits and can move from atom to atom only with great difficulty. These substances are called nonconductors, or *insulators*. Metals differ in the ease with which electrons can move about, and are said to differ in their electrical *conductivity*. The conductivities of several metals, relative to that of copper, are listed in the accompanying table. Of these metals, copper is the most widely used because it is relatively

Metal	Conductivity
Copper	100%
Silver	105%
Gold	71%
Aluminum	61%
Iron	18%
Low-carbon steel	8–13%
Some alloy steels	2%

inexpensive and an excellent conductor. Aluminum also is frequently used because it is relatively inexpensive and lightweight. High-power transmission lines frequently are constructed of a stranded steel cable around which aluminum strands are spiraled. This combination provides high strength, light weight, and good conductivity at a low total cost.

Resistivity, the converse (reciprocal) of conductivity, often is used to describe the property of a material as a conductor. Good conductors have low resistivity. Good insulators have very high resistivity. For example, plate glass has approximately 10^{19} times, and porcelain approximately 10^{20} times, the resistivity of copper. It

is this enormous difference in resistivity between good conductors and good insulators that makes possible the efficient control and distribution of electricity.

Under certain conditions a gas can become a conductor. The neon light is an example. Under the influence of an electric field, atoms of neon in the glass tube become positively charged ions and are drawn to the negatively charged conductor. At the same time, electrons that have left the neon atoms are drawn to the positive conductor (Fig. 3). A more spectacular example of an electric current through a gas (air) is a lightning flash.

Some liquids, principally water solutions of acids, bases, or salts, also are able to conduct electricity. A portion of the molecules of the solute (the acid, base, or salt) split, or *dissociate*, into two parts. One part has an excess of electrons, the other a deficiency, so that they are negatively and positively charged, respectively. Under the influence of an electric field between two conductors in the solution, these charged particles move, constituting a current. The solution is called an *electrolyte;* the conductors, *electrodes*. Pure water dissociates only to a very slight extent and therefore is a poor electrolyte (Fig. 4).

■**TYPES OF ELECTRIC CURRENTS.**—There are two basic types of electric currents: direct current and alternating current. *Direct current* is a stream of electrons past any one point in one, and only one, direction. *Alternating current*, on the other hand, alternates its direction, first flowing past a point in one direction and then in the opposite direction. The *frequency* of an alternating current is its number of cycles per second. A *complete cycle* is the interval during which a current starts from zero, pulses to a

maximum in one direction, drops back to zero, pulses to a maximum in the opposite direction, and returns to zero once again.

■**UNITS OF MEASURE.**—The unit of quantity of electricity is the *coulomb*. One coulomb is equivalent to the charge carried by 6.24×10^{18} electrons. Electricity flowing at the rate of 1 coulomb per second is a current of 1 *ampere*. Thus one ampere is equal to the passage through a given point of 6.24×10^{18} electrons per second.

The electric pressure, or *electromotive force (e.m.f.)*, which causes the flow of current, is measured in *volts*. The intensity of an electric field may be expressed as volts per centimeter or volts per inch.

The *resistance* of a conductor is measured in *ohms*. An e.m.f. of 1 volt applied to a resistance of 1 ohm will produce a current of 1 ampere. Ohm's law, named after its propounder Georg Simon Ohm (1787–1854), states that current is proportional to the voltage applied and inversely proportional to the resistance. Stated in the form of an equation, $I = E/R$, where

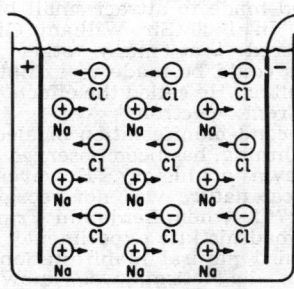

Figure 4.

ELECTROLYSIS consists of acid solution (electrolyte), electrodes, and container.

I is the current in amperes, E is the e.m.f. in volts, and R is the resistance in ohms. The converse of resistance, *conductance*, is measured in *mhos* —which is *ohm(s)* spelled in reverse. Resistance and conductance refer to the properties of a piece of material of a particular shape and size. The corresponding characteristics of the material itself, which do not depend on size or shape, are *resistivity* and *conductivity*. These are the resistance and conductance, respectively, of a cube of the material of unit size. The units mentioned above (the volt, ohm, ampere, and coulomb) are named in honor of the following pioneers in the study of electricity and magnetism: Alessandro Volta (1745–1827); Georg Simon Ohm; André Marie Ampère (1775–1836); and Charles de Coulomb (1736–1806).

Production of Electric Current.—Aside from the transient discharges of static electricity, the first production of electric current was by chemical means. This latter is still a very important source of electric current, as shown by the large number of battery-operated devices. The great bulk of electric power, however, is generated by electromagnetic induction in rotating machinery. The thermo-

SEALED GLASS TUBE   NEON GAS AT LOW PRESSURE

POSITIVE
ELECTRODE

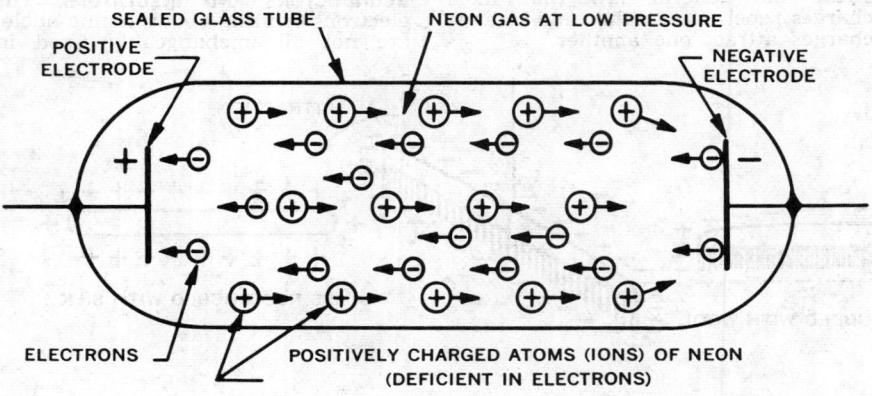

NEGATIVE
ELECTRODE

ELECTRONS   POSITIVELY CHARGED ATOMS (IONS) OF NEON
                   (DEFICIENT IN ELECTRONS)

Figure 3.

couple and the photocell are sources of current in small amounts.

■CHEMICAL CELLS.—If electrodes of two different materials, such as zinc and copper, are immersed in an electrolytic solution, one plate acquires a positive charge and the other a negative charge. If they are then connected externally by a wire, a current will flow through. This is a *voltaic cell*, discovered about 1800. Chemical action between the electrolyte and the electrodes causes atoms of one electode to go into solution, each atom leaving behind one or more electrons. This leaves the electrode with a negative charge. The electrolyte takes electrons from the other electrode, thus giving it a positive charge. The electrons flow through the external wire from the negative electrode to the positive electrode. A group of voltaic cells connected together form a battery.

The *dry cell* (Fig. 5) consists of a zinc container, which serves as the negative electrode; a carbon rod in the center, which serves as a current

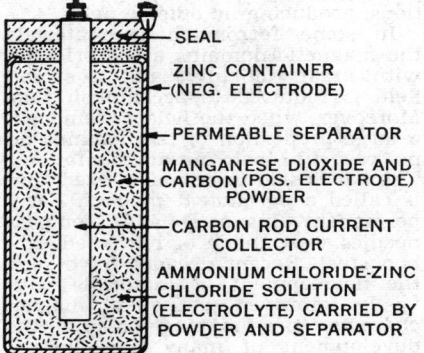

SEAL

ZINC CONTAINER (NEG. ELECTRODE)

PERMEABLE SEPARATOR

MANGANESE DIOXIDE AND CARBON (POS. ELECTRODE) POWDER

CARBON ROD CURRENT COLLECTOR

AMMONIUM CHLORIDE-ZINC CHLORIDE SOLUTION (ELECTROLYTE) CARRIED BY POWDER AND SEPARATOR

Figure 5.

collector for the positive electrode; and a paste made of ammonium chloride, zinc chloride, and water, which serves as electrolyte. Carbon and manganese dioxide powder are packed around the carbon rod to form the positive electrode. They also react with the hydrogen liberated there, and the zinc chloride reacts with the ammonia gas liberated at the zinc electrode to prevent build-up of gas pressure. These components are thoroughly sealed in, giving the cell its name. A present-day dry cell develops an e.m.f. of about 1.5 volts.

Dry cells and others of the same class are called *primary cells*. Primary cells must be discarded when one of the electrodes is consumed, or the consumed materials must be replaced. *Secondary cells*, such as those used in the *storage battery*, can be recharged by passing current through them in the direction opposite to that in which they produce current. The chemical action is reversed by this process, and the electrodes and electrolyte are restored to their original condition. A common example is the *lead-acid cell* used in automobile batteries and many other applications. The electrolyte is dilute sulfuric acid, and the electrodes are flat lead grids, the positive grid being filled with a porous paste of lead dioxide and the

negative grid with spongy lead. A fully charged cell of this type develops an e.m.f. of about 2.2 volts. Another widely used storage cell is the *Edison cell*, which was invented by Thomas Alva Edison (1847–1931); it has electrodes of nickel peroxide and spongy iron and a potassium hydroxide solution as electrolyte.

A more recent development is the *nickel-cadmium storage cell*, which is somewhat lighter than older types and has a longer life. It is capable of being completely sealed, since there is no evolution of gas during operation. Because of this feature it is used in satellites and space vehicles. It also is being used more and more in the development of battery-powered portable tools and appliances. Because there is no evolution of flammable gas or spillage of corrosive liquids, it is not a fire or corrosion hazard.

A development that may have great importance to industry is the *fuel cell*. This is a primary cell in which the chemical reactions are carried on between inexpensive and continually replaceable materials, such as hydrogen or hydrocarbons and oxygen or air. Successfully operating fuel cells have been built and demonstrated, but the development has not yet permitted widespread economic application. The over-all efficiency of converting the energy in the fuel cell to electricity promises to be much greater than that obtained in presently used turbines or diesel engines and generators.

■THERMOCOUPLES.—In 1822 Thomas J. Seebeck discovered that if two wires of dissimilar metals are joined at both ends and one junction is kept at a different temperature from the other, an electric current will flow. This is known as the *thermoelectric effect*, and the device is called a *thermocouple*. A number of thermocouples connected in series are a *thermopile*.

Thermocouples are widely used to measure temperature. One junction is maintained at a constant reference temperature, such as that of melting ice; the other, at the temperature to be measured. A sensitive electric instrument is used to indicate the voltage developed. Different combinations of metals are used to cover different temperature ranges. Thermopiles may be used as a source of electric power for some special applications, although they are inefficient. Combined with suitable reflectors, they may be used as sensitive detectors, indicating the presence of a hot object a considerable distance away.

■PHOTOCELLS.—The *photovoltaic cell*, or *photoelectric cell*, such as that used in photographic light meters, has been familiar for many years. More recently such cells have been combined into groups to form solar batteries that serve as power sources for the instrumentation of orbiting space satellites. By this means the operating life of the equipment in orbit is extended far beyond that which could be obtained with chemical batteries alone. Although they may become important for isolated applications requiring little power, solar batteries have not been a significant source of power in any quan-

tity for earthbound applications.

A photovoltaic cell consists of a very thin layer of semiconductor material deposited on the surface of another semiconductor material. (*Semiconductor materials* are so called because they lie in a range between good insulators and good conductors. Germanium and silicon are important examples.) When light falls upon the thin film, penetrating to the junction region between the two semiconductors, electrons move across the junction from one material to the other, forming a current.

Magnetic Fields.—The attraction and repulsion between magnets follows a set of principles similar to those described previously for electrostatic forces. Consider the familiar magnetic compass, the needle of which orients itself in a north-south direction. For convenience, the end

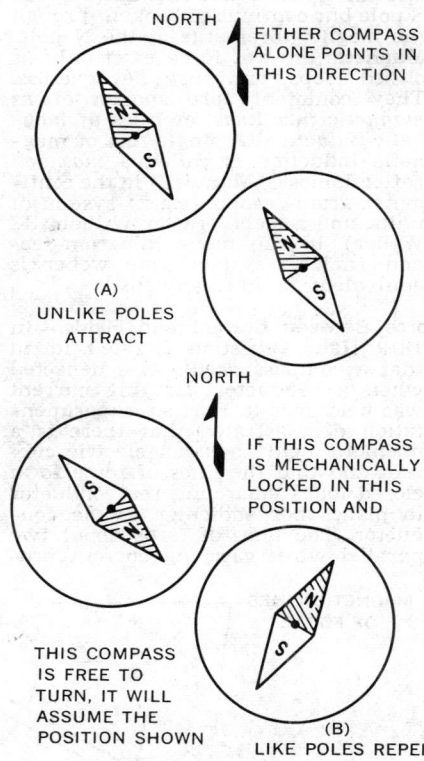

NORTH

EITHER COMPASS ALONE POINTS IN THIS DIRECTION

(A) UNLIKE POLES ATTRACT

NORTH

IF THIS COMPASS IS MECHANICALLY LOCKED IN THIS POSITION AND

THIS COMPASS IS FREE TO TURN, IT WILL ASSUME THE POSITION SHOWN

(B) LIKE POLES REPEL

Figure 6.

pointing north is marked N, or "north-seeking," and the other end S, or "south-seeking." When another compass is brought near the first and is moved about it, the two needles deviate from their north-south direction and tend to point toward each other. The attracting and repelling forces reside in the ends of the needles, and ends marked alike repel one another. The ends of the needles (and of all magnets) are called *poles*. Like poles repel one another and unlike poles attract one another, just as like electric charges repel and unlike electric charges attract (Fig. 6).

There is an important difference between a magnetized bar and a charged body, however. The charged body may carry the same polarity of charge over its entire surface, whereas the magnetized bar always has two poles of unlike polarity and of equal strength. A single magnetic pole does not exist by itself.

The forces that act between magnets at a distance suggest that the magnets are surrounded by a magnetic field. This field, like the electric field, is considered to consist of lines of force, a line of force being a line along which a magnet pole tends to move. The positive direction is that in which the N pole tends to move. Thus a compass needle in a magnetic field will orient itself parallel to the lines of force, with the N pole pointing in the positive direction. There is an important difference, however, between the concepts of the magnetic field and the electric field. Whereas the electric lines of force may emerge from a positive charge and terminate on a negative charge, the magnetic lines of force do not terminate at the S pole but continue unbroken through the magnet to emerge at the N pole. Magnetic lines of force exist only as closed loops, and they never cross. They commonly are spoken of as *magnetic flux lines*, or *lines of magnetic induction*. A single line of magnetic induction is called a *maxwell* (after James C. Maxwell) in the centimeter-gram-second (c.g.s.) system of units, and a *weber* (after Wilhelm E. Weber) in the meter-kilogram-second (m.k.s.) system. One weber is equivalent to 10^8 maxwells.

Force Between Current and Fields.—In 1819 Hans Christian Oersted found that a compass needle was deflected when a conductor carrying current was held over it. Further experimentation demonstrated that there is a magnetic field about an electric current and that the lines of force form closed loops encircling the conductor in planes perpendicular to the conductor. The lines of force about two parallel wires carrying current pro-

curving around outside to close upon themselves. Such a coil is called a *solenoid*, and it exhibits all the characteristics of a bar magnet (Fig. 9).

If a bar of soft iron is put inside the solenoid and current is then passed through the solenoid, the bar will exhibit all the characteristics of a strong magnet. When the current is turned off, the magnetic properties of the bar disappear. This device is called an *electromagnet*.

The discovery of the electromagnet and the development of the chemical cell as a source of electricity opened the way for the invention of the telegraph by Samuel F. B. Morse in 1837, and were essential to the invention of the telephone by Alexander Graham Bell in 1875. Electromagnets are used to open and close electric circuits, to operate valves, and to do a multitude of other mechanical tasks.

Ferromagnetism.—The magnetic characteristics exhibited when a core of soft iron is put into a solenoid are many times greater than those of the solenoid alone. The magnetic properties contributed by the iron are classed as *ferromagnetism*, and the iron is said to be *ferromagnetic*. Two other metals, nickel and cobalt, and a few nonferrous metal alloys also are ferromagnetic, but to a much lesser extent than iron. Some of the most widely used ferromagnetic materials are alloys of iron with nickel and cobalt. No other materials exhibit magnetic properties, except in extremely small amounts.

The increase in magnetic effects produced by putting iron in a solenoid indicates that it is much easier to establish magnetic flux in the iron bar than in the air that previously occupied the space. The iron is said to have a high *relative permeability*. For air and, practically speaking, for all materials other than ferromagnetic materials (and for space itself), the relative permeability is 1. As a

own axis as they orbit, producing a magnetic field along their axis. In all materials other than ferromagnetic materials, the electrons in each atom are so oriented that there is practically no magnetic field produced outside the atom. In ferromagnetic materials, however, there is a net unbalance in each atom so that the atom has a magnetic field about it. The ferromagnetic material thus is composed of a great many tiny magnets. Large groups of these tiny magnets are lined up in one direction, forming *domains*. Normally the domains are grouped together, forming closed loops; and no magnetic field appears outside the material. Under the influence of a fairly small magnetic field, however, these groups are altered until nearly all are oriented parallel to the magnetic field and add their own fields to it. The total field of all the tiny magnets in the material may be many thousand times greater than the field required to line them up. When the external field is removed, the tiny magnets revert approximately to their former orientations, producing no outside field.

In some ferromagnetic materials the magnetic domains are reoriented with great difficulty, and a strong field is required to accomplish this. Moreover, when the field is removed, a large proportion of the domains do not revert to their initial orientations. The bar is said to be magnetized, and is called a *permanent magnet*. Early permanent magnets and compass needles were made of hardened carbon steel. Recent decades have seen the development of materials with vastly improved permanent magnet characteristics, making possible the development of many new instruments and devices. Permanent magnets, when properly prepared and treated, exhibit great stability of their magnetic field and are used widely in electricity-measuring instruments. The watt-hour meters that measure

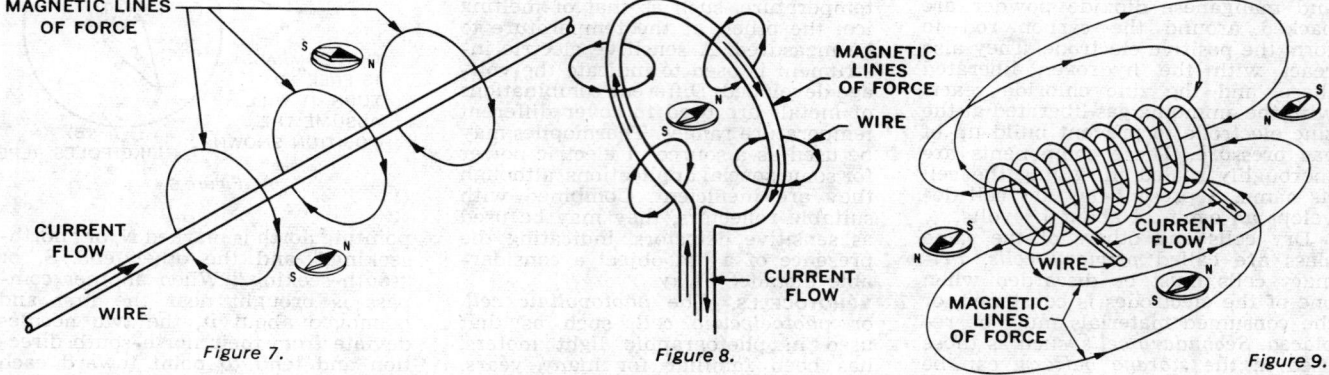

Figure 7.   Figure 8.   Figure 9.

duce a force between the two wires. They attract each other if the current flows in the same direction in both, and repel each other if the currents flow in opposite directions (Fig. 7).

If a wire is bent into a closed loop and current is passed through it, magnetic lines of force will form closed loops around the wire (Fig. 8). If a series of wire loops is joined to form a *helix*, or coil, lines of force will pass inside parallel to the axis,

comparison, for certain carefully prepared iron alloys it may be over 100,000. Some materials have relative permeabilities slightly greater than 1 and are called *paramagnetic materials*. Others have relative permeabilities slightly less than 1; they are called *diamagnetic materials*.

The source of ferromagnetic properties lies in the electrons orbiting about the atomic nuclei of the material. The electrons spin about their

household electrical consumption depend on the constancy of two permanent magnets for their accuracy.

Electromagnetic Induction.—In 1831 Michael Faraday discovered that when he plunged a magnet into a coil of wire, a current flowed in the wire, and that the current flowed only while the magnet moved. The principle thus illustrated is commonly stated in two forms. One says that the e.m.f. induced in a loop of wire is proportional to the rate at which the number of magnetic lines of force interlinking the loop increases or decreases. The other says that if a conductor is placed in a magnetic field perpendicular to the lines of force and moved in a direction mutually perpendicular to itself and the lines of force, an e.m.f. will be induced proportional to the rate of movement. The conductor is said to "cut" the lines of force. Actually, of course, they are not severed; they pass through the conductor as it moves.

If the magnetic flux interlinked by a loop of wire changes at the rate of 10^8 maxwells, or 1 weber, per second, the e.m.f. induced is equal to 1 volt. The generation of e.m.f. in this manner is spoken of as *electromagnetic induction*.

Generators.—Almost all the electricity used in homes and in industry is produced by machines, called *electric generators*, that make use of the principles of electromagnetic induction. In all such generators, conductors are moved through a magnetic field to produce an e.m.f. Consider a very simple arrangement in which a magnet is mounted on a shaft through its center so it can be turned end for end rapidly by turning the shaft. Imagine a coil of wire mounted close to the tumbling magnet so that each time a pole of the magnet passes the coil, its flux interlinks the turns of the coil for a brief time. Successive pulses of e.m.f. will be induced in the coil, and an alternating current will flow in a circuit connected to the coil. These are the various elements of an *alternating-current generator,* which produces current that changes direction many times a second. In practice there are several coils, and a laminated iron core is placed inside them to increase the flux from the magnet. In larger generators an electromagnet is used for the rotating magnet, and connection is made to it by means of carbon blocks or brushes that make sliding contact with insulated metal rings mounted on the shaft. The magnet may be arranged with two, four, six, or any even number of poles; the stationary coils must be provided to match. The stationary member is called the *stator;* the rotating one, the *rotating field* or *rotor*.

In order to generate direct current, a rotary switching device called a *commutator* is provided; it reverses the connection to the coils as the current in them reverses. In a *direct-current generator* the magnet is stationary, and the coils are mounted on the shaft with a laminated iron core. The coils are connected to copper bars insulated from one another and arranged to form a drum-type commutator revolving with the shaft. Two or more sets of stationary carbon brushes bear on the outside of the commutator and are located so that they always connect through the bars to coils in which an e.m.f. is being generated in the same direction. When a coil has turned halfway around and is generating e.m.f. in the opposite direction, its commutator bars are in contact with the brushes in the op-

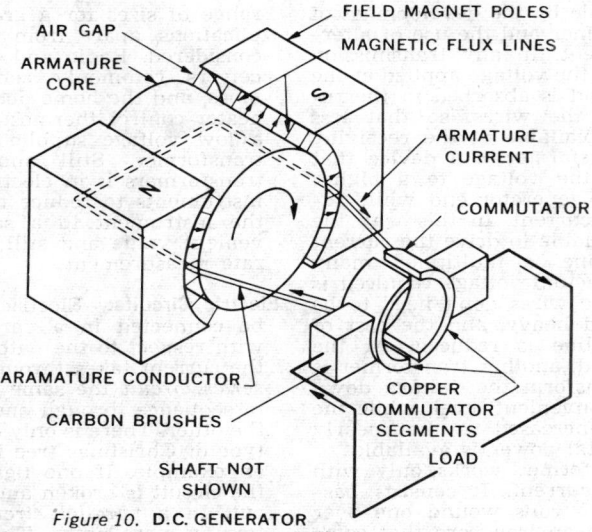

Figure 10. D.C. GENERATOR

posite direction. The combination of the rotating coil and its core is called the *armature*. The stationary magnet is called the *field*. Although it may be a permanent magnet, it is usually an electromagnet in larger generators, receiving its current from the armature through the brushes (Fig. 10).

Historically, direct-current generators came into use before alternating-current generators, although the latter may seem simpler. Direct-current generators provided a substitute for batteries, producing current in greater quantities, more economically, and in a form with which men were familiar. However, nearly all electric power now is generated as alternating current.

Motors.—Electric motors depend for their operation upon the force developed between electric currents and magnetic fields. Motors are very similar to generators in construction, and many may be used interchangeably as either. Consider the direct-current generator just discussed. If a current is passed through the armature, the brushes and commutator cause the current to pass through coils that are in the magnetic field, and a *turning moment* (torque) is produced. As the armature turns, the brushes and commutator always direct the current into coils that are passing through the magnetic field, and continuous torque is developed.

There are three basic types of alternating-current motors: the series, commutator-type motor; the induction motor; and the synchronous motor. A number of other types of alternating-current motors are used, but they are modifications or combinations of these three basic types.

The *series, commutator-type motor* is similar to the direct-current motor. The field electromagnet has a laminated iron core and is connected in series with the armature so that the same current passes through both. The magnetic field and the armature current alternate together so that the turning moment is always in the same direction. This type of motor is used extensively in appliances and portable tools. It has good starting torque

and operates over a wide speed range.

The *induction motor* is the most common type, particularly in motors of fractional horsepower and moderately larger sizes. The rotor consists simply of a soft iron cylinder carrying a short-circuited winding. There is no commutator. The alternating magnetic field produced by the stator current induces alternating current in the rotor coils; the alternating current reacts with the magnetic field to produce torque. These motors are very simple and sturdy.

The *synchronous motor* is similar to the alternating-current generator, with stationary coils and rotating field magnet. Suppose that the rotor is turning at just the right speed so that current in the stationary coils alternates in exact synchronism with the passing of the rotor poles. A turning moment is produced at each pole, always in the same direction. If a load sufficient to slow the rotor is applied, it will stop. Synchronous motors will not start of themselves, but must have auxiliary starting means provided. The familiar electric clock is driven by a synchronous motor. Some of the less expensive ones are not provided with a self-starting mechanism, but must be started by twirling a knob at the back. Synchronous motors are made in all sizes.

■**SINGLE-PHASE AND POLYPHASE MACHINES.**—Alternating-current generators and motors may be characterized as single-phase or polyphase, depending upon the arrangement of their stator coils. A *single-phase generator* has a single set of coils connected to the load circuit. A *polyphase generator* has two or three sets of coils spaced around the stator so that the voltage induced in the successive coils alternates in sequence rather than simultaneously. Synchronous and induction motors similarly may have single-phase or polyphase stator windings. The series, commutator-type motor is always single phase. Three-phase machines are more common than two-phase machines.

Transformers.—The large-scale, electric-power transmission systems were made possible by the development of the transformer and the use of alternating current. In any transmission line, part of the voltage applied at the generator end is absorbed in the resistance of the wires, so that less voltage is available at the receiving end. A *transformer* is a device that transforms the voltage to a higher level at the generator end while reducing the current. In this way the voltage available to drive the current over the line is multiplied many times, and actual voltage required is reduced. The wires don't need to be as large and heavy, and the cost of the entire line is reduced. At the receiving end, another transformer is used to transform the voltage down to a safe, convenient level, while the current is increased so that nearly the same total power is available.

The transformer works only with alternating current. It consists basically of two coils wound one over the other on an iron core that completely interlinks the coils, forming a closed path in the iron core for the magnetic flux. The voltage to be transformed is applied to one coil, called the *primary coil*. Alternating current flows in the primary coil, causing alternating magnetic flux in the core. This alternating flux, which interlinks the other, the *secondary coil*, induces an alternating voltage in that coil. The same flux induces a voltage in the primary coil that is very nearly equal and is opposite to the applied voltage. The voltage induced in the coils is proportional to the number of turns in the coils, so that if the secondary coil has, say, ten times as many turns as the primary coil, the voltage induced in the secondary coil will be very nearly ten times that applied to the primary coil. The current that flows from the secondary coil over the line produces in the transformer coil a magnetizing force that tries to change the flux there. This magnetizing force is proportional to the current and the number of secondary-coil turns. It is compensated for by an automatic increase in the current that flows in the primary coil, producing an almost equal and opposite magnetizing force. Thus, if the secondary coil has ten times as many turns as the primary coil, the current in the secondary coil will be only one-tenth its counterpart in the primary coil.

Transformer cores are made of thin sheets of a special alloy iron that has high permeability and resistivity. The sheets are insulated from one another by coats of insulating varnish. This reduces to a minimum the current that flows in the core itself as a result of the alternating flux.

Small transformers may consist simply of the coils and core with mounting brackets. Others may be in a case filled with pitch or other compound. Large transformers are mounted in tanks filled with a special grade of mineral oil or a liquid chemical compound. The oil or compound serves to insulate electrically the coils and their leads, and aids in transferring heat from the coils to the outside case.

Transformers are made in a wide range of sizes for a great many applications apart from the use just considered. Radio and television receivers commonly contain one or more, and the home doorbell and the heater-control thermostat operate on a low voltage supplied by a small transformer. Still another use of transformers is in electric-measuring instruments to reduce the voltage at the instrument to a safe and convenient value and still permit accurate measurement.

Electric Circuits.—Electric devices may be connected in a variety of ways with respect to the paths, or circuits, the current takes through them. In a *series circuit* the same current flows in sequence through one device after the other. There is only one path. One type of Christmas tree light string is an example. If one light burns out, the circuit is broken and all lights go out. In a *parallel circuit* there are two or more paths. The current divides, and part flows in each path simultaneously. In another type of Christmas tree lights, the bulbs are connected in parallel. The full supply voltage is applied to each bulb, and the current through each bulb comes directly from the source and returns to it. Thus, if one bulb burns out, only it goes out.

Many street-lighting and highway-lighting circuits are in series. However, most of the circuits normally encountered are parallel circuits. House wiring consists of several parallel circuits. When an appliance is plugged into an outlet, it is put in parallel with other appliances already in use. Circuits may become very complex, including branches of elements in series, forming various series-parallel combinations. The current flowing in parts of the circuit and the voltage across those parts depend upon the resistances of the circuit elements and the circuit complexity. The complexity is further increased in alternating-current circuits in that some of the elements may possess inductance or capacitance as well as resistance. *Inductance* appears when the current is interlinked by a magnetic field, as in an electromagnet. *Capacitance* appears when two parts of a circuit are close together and an alternating voltage establishes an electric field between them, continually building up electric charges of alternating polarity on them. The effect of the inductance is called *inductive reactance*, and that of the capacitance is called *capacitive reactance*. These combine *vectorially* (not directly) with the resistance to form *impedance*, which is the apparent resistance to current flow in an alternating-current circuit—or, to put it another way, impedance is to an alternating-current circuit what resistance is to a direct-current circuit. Both reactances depend upon the frequency of alternation, inductive reactance being directly proportional to frequency, and capacitive reactance inversely proportional to frequency.

Another type of circuit common to electromagnetic devices is the *magnetic circuit*. This describes the path of closed loops of magnetic flux. These circuits also may have series and parallel elements. Because the magnetic flux is not confined to specific paths, as electric current is confined to a conductor, there may be parallel paths, called *leakage paths*, beside or around the desired useful paths. Magnetic circuits may be difficult to calculate with accuracy because the actual extent of the leakage paths frequently is difficult to determine, and they may constitute a large part of the entire circuit.

Electronics.—In a broad sense the term *electronics* may seem relevant to all the applications of electricity, since they all involve the electron, its charge, and its movement. As commonly used, however, electronics applies to the use of electron currents in a vacuum or in a low-pressure gas. More recently it also has come to be used in connection with semiconductor devices.

■**DISCOVERY OF THE ELECTRON.**—The discovery of the electron in 1897 by Joseph John Thomson was a result of his study of the electric discharges in evacuated glass tubes. As the pressure is reduced in such a tube, the electric discharge first produces a blue glow. This changes to pink, dark areas appear, and the pink discharge disappears. Finally the glass itself glows with a faint greenish light. This is caused by invisible rays coming from the *cathode* (negatively charged electrode). They were first called *cathode rays*, and later were found to be tiny particles torn from the cathode by the strong electric field and drawn toward the *anode* (positively charged electrode). These particles now are known to be electrons.

■**ELECTRONIC EMISSION.**—A very strong field is required to tear electrons from the atoms in the surface of a metal at room temperature. As the metal is heated, a temperature is reached at which electrons are emitted spontaneously. This is called *thermionic emission*. It may require incandescence, as in the case of tungsten, or only a dull red glow, as with thorium oxide.

Electrons also are emitted at room temperature when light falls upon a metal. This is called the *photoelectric effect*. Most metals exhibit this effect only under ultraviolet light, but such metals as rubidium and cesium emit electrons in visible light.

■**THE FLEMING VALVE.**—The first important, successful application of thermionic emission was developed by Sir John Ambrose Fleming (1849–1945) in his Fleming valve. This consists of a wire filament surrounded by a metal cylinder in a highly evacuated glass bulb. The filament is heated to incandescence by an electric current, and electrons are emitted from it. If the cylinder is made positive with respect to the filament, the electrons are drawn to it, constituting a current. If the cylinder is made negative, the electrons are repelled and no current flows. The device that permits current to flow in only one direction is called a *rectifier*. It is also called a *diode* because it has two electrodes. In an important modification of this tube the glass bulb is filled with a gas, such as mercury

WESTERN ELECTRIC

TERMINAL for **transistorized video transmission,** prepared for HemisFair '68 by Southwestern Bell Telephone Company in San Antonio.

WESTERN ELECTRIC

GIANT 85-FOOT RADAR locates and tracks missiles being tested at the Pacific Missile Range in the vicinity of Point Mugu, California.

vapor or argon, at low pressure. Tubes of this type, both vacuum and gas-filled, are used in radio and television equipment, battery chargers, and other electronic devices. For example, large gas-filled rectifiers are used to provide direct-current power to electric railways.

■ **THE DE FOREST AUDION.**—A most important invention basic to present-day telephone and radio was made by Lee De Forest in 1907 when he placed a wire grid between the filament and plate of a Fleming valve and called the new tube an *audion.* Such a tube also is called a *triode,* indicating the use of three electrodes. A relatively small voltage applied to the grid has a strong controlling effect on the passage of electrons from filament to plate, much greater than if the voltage were applied directly to the plate. Through this effect the triode functions as an amplifier, by means of which very small amounts of power can be used to control large amounts of power. Additional grids may be added, making a *tetrode* or *pentode,* to modify the characteristics of the tube. Another important modification is the use of gas at low pressure in the tube. Such gas-filled tubes can control large amounts of power more efficiently than vacuum tubes.

Many modern tubes use indirectly heated cathodes. The filament is placed in two small holes along the axis of a ceramic rod, heating the rod. A metal cylinder coated with thorium, strontium, or cesium oxide fits snugly over the rod. These oxides are copious emitters of electrons when heated only to a dull red.

■ **TELEPHONY.**—The development of vacuum-tube amplifiers greatly extended the range of long-distance telephony. Amplifiers, called *repeaters,* are connected into the lines at intervals so that the strength of the signal is repeatedly restored to its original value. Amplifiers built to operate for twenty years without attention are built into transatlantic telephone cables at twenty-mile intervals. Through their use, telephone calls are transmitted for over 4,000 miles with full strength and clarity.

■ **RADIO COMMUNICATION.**—Vacuum tubes play a vital part in both the transmitting and receiving ends of radio communication. At the transmitter, a source of very-high-frequency alternating voltage is necessary to excite the antenna and generate the electromagnetic radiation that provides the means of communication. Early sources were the spark gap, the electric arc, and the high-frequency alternator. These were limited to relatively low frequency and could be used only for code transmission. The triode is capable of working as an oscillator, as well as an amplifier, thus providing a source of power that can cover a much wider range of frequency. The oscillator also is readily adaptable to the modulation of its output by tiny voltages generated by sound waves in a microphone, so that it can be used for transmission of voice as well as of code. Except for extremely high frequencies, where different types of electronic tubes are used, the triode or a modification is used universally in radio transmitters.

At the receiving antenna, the amount of energy is exceedingly small. By use of amplifiers this energy can be received and amplified to give adequate response in headphones or loudspeakers. An outstanding example of long-distance radio transmission and reception is the Mariner space probe, which transmitted signals to earth while passing the planet Venus. The transmitter was of relatively low power, but special high-sensitivity receivers were able to receive the signals reliably.

This transmission of signals from space vehicles in both manned and unmanned flights constitutes *telemetry,* a vitally important use of radio in which large quantities of data gathered by measuring devices on board the vehicle are automatically transmitted to observers on the ground and are recorded for analysis.

■ **TELEVISION.**—Television is a familiar example of the application of electronics. The basic principles are the same as those governing the transmission of sound by means of radio. A picture is focused on the photosensitive screen of a television camera. The screen is scanned by a sharply focused exploring beam of electrons moving rapidly across it in a succession of lines. Small electric currents are generated in response to the light and dark areas traversed by the end of the electron beam, and these currents are used to modulate the signal being transmitted. At the receiver a similar beam of electrons moves across a fluorescent screen, forming a tiny scanning spot. The brightness of the scanning spot varies in response to the received signal and reconstructs the picture as seen by the transmitter camera. Network programs may use both wire and radio transmission. Television transmission is tremendously more complex than sound transmission, for the frequencies generated by the scanning process are much higher and cover a broader range. Greater complexity yet is introduced in color television.

■ **RADAR.**—An extremely important application of radio came during World War II with the development of radar. A *radar transmitter* is a radio transmitter that emits a succession of short, sharp pulses. These signals are reflected by objects in their paths, and reflected signals return as echoes. A sensitive device receives these signals and measures the very short time they took to get back. This time is a measure of the distance to the object. The transmitting antenna concentrates its output into a beam that is constantly rotated so that the position at the instant the reflected signal is received gives the direction in which the object lies. Radar now is used as a means of navigation through fog by ships at sea, for the control of aircraft near airports, for military warning systems, and for the apprehension of speeding motorists by traffic police.

■ **RECORDING.**—Vacuum-tube amplification makes possible the high-fidelity recording and reproduction enjoyed today, and makes practical the slow-speed long-playing record. It also makes practical the tape recorder, both for sound recording and for the recording of television programs.

■ **INDUSTRIAL APPLICATIONS.**—Electronics plays a vital part in the rapidly increasing move to automation. Machine tools are automatically operated by electronic control devices. Steel mills are electronically operated to improve the product and reduce the cost. These controls may include computers that almost instantaneously process and analyze data received from measuring devices continually monitoring the operation, and automatically initiate corrections to be applied by controls.

Computers, which really are giant calculating machines, are used in design work to reduce the labor of calculation and to solve complex relationships that otherwise might require months of work. They are widely used in accounting procedures. As another example of their wide application, a flour milling company uses a computer to calculate formulas for cake mix and animal feed.

Semiconductor devices are competing strongly with vacuum tubes in radio and many other applications, particularly for portable use where small size and low battery drain are important. Examples are the transistor radio and the transistor hearing aid. Larger semiconductor devices are competing with gas-filled power rectifier tubes and other gas-filled tubes.

■ **X RAYS.**—X-ray machines are electronic devices. X rays are produced when a beam of electrons impinges on a metal target in a highly evacuated chamber. The penetrating power of the X rays is dependent upon the energy of the electron beam, expressed as the number of volts used to accelerate the electrons. Thus, a surgical X-ray machine may use 50,000–100,000 volts, while a therapeutic X-ray machine used for treating disease may require several hundred thousand volts. Machines using 10 million volts are used to X-ray large castings for detection of internal flaws or cracks. Even larger machines, requiring hundreds of millions of volts, are used for scientific investigation and research.

■ **ELECTRON MICROSCOPE.**—The electron microscope is a device in which a beam of electrons is used to examine and produce magnified images of objects that are many times smaller than the best light-beam microscope can see. This has been very useful in studying the structure of matter and the nature of viruses.

■ **PARTICLE ACCELERATORS.**—*Particle accelerators,* sometimes called "atom smashers," are huge electronic devices in which positively charged particles are accelerated to tremendous energy, measured in hundreds of millions—and billions—of volts. The radiations and new particles that are produced when these energetic particles bombard a target give new insights into the structure of matter.

■ **ELECTRONIC WELDING.**—Concentrated electron beams in evacuated chambers are used to heat and weld small parts. The heat applied can be precisely controlled, and materials that might be attacked or contaminated if heated in a gaseous environment can be welded.

■**ILLUMINATION.**—Several of the familiar types of electric lamps are electronic in nature. The neon lamp is a tube containing neon at low pressure through which an electric current passes. Mercury vapor lamps are widely used for highway lighting. Fluorescent lights are glass tubes filled with argon and mercury vapor at low pressure, and coated on the inside surface with a phosphorescent material. An electric current in the gas produces light containing wavelengths that cause the phosphorescent material to glow brightly. Fluorescent lights produce several times more light for the same expenditure of power than do incandescent lights, which must dissipate relatively large amounts of heat.

—Robert Ferguson Edgar

SEMICONDUCTORS

Classification.—Solid substances are classified, on the basis of their electrical behavior, as conductors, insulators, and semiconductors. Such substances as metals, which offer little resistance to the flow of electrons, are classed as *conductors*. Substances such as glass, which offer a great deal of resistance to the flow of electrons, are classed as *insulators*. Materials such as germanium and silicon, which offer more resistance to the flow of electrons than conductors, but less resistance than insulators, are classed as *semiconductors*. All metals show increased resistance as the temperature is increased. Semiconductors and insulators, on the other hand, drastically decrease their resistance as temperature increases.

Basic Principles.—In a good conductor, such as copper, electrons are free to move through the material when an electric field is applied. This flow of electrons is called *electric current*. Semiconductor materials, by contrast, hold their electrons more securely and normally do not have enough free electrons to carry electric current. However, if the temperature of a semiconductor is raised, electrons are freed and become available to conduct current; thus, the resistance in the semiconductor material is reduced.

If a small amount of an impurity, such as antimony, arsenic, or phosphorus, is added to a semiconductor material such as silicon, a small number of electrons are freed. These electrons flow through the material producing an electric current. Semiconductors of this type are called *n-type semiconductors*. The addition of small amounts of other impurities —aluminum, boron, or gallium—to a semiconductor material such as silicon takes electrons away from a few of the atoms of the semiconductor. This lack of an electron in an atom is called a *hole*. Just as an electron can flow through a material, so can a hole, and this flow of holes also produces an electric current. Semiconductors of this type are called *p-type semiconductors*.

Semiconductor Devices.—The first important application of semiconductors was to provide rectifiers for low-frequency alternating currents. A *rectifier* is a device that passes electric current in only one direction. *Selenium rectifiers* were used for this purpose even before 1900, but they did not find extensive use until much later. *Copper oxide rectifiers* were introduced in 1927. They were used in battery chargers and power supplies for radio sets. The large-scale development of the selenium rectifier, however, resulted in its replacing copper oxide types.

About 1904, the rectifying properties of semiconductors were used to provide a detector of the high-frequency currents set up in circuits by radio waves. The *crystal rectifier*, consisting of a fine metal wire, or cat-whisker, in contact with a crystalline piece of lead sulfide or silicon, was the best detector for radio waves in the early days of radio. Vacuum tubes replaced such devices, and during World War II metal point-contact silicon devices were used in radar.

■**P-N JUNCTION DIODE.**—More recently, crystal rectifiers have been developed that consist of a single piece of semiconductor containing both *p*-type and *n*-type materials. The junction between the *p*-type and *n*-type semiconducting regions, called a *p-n junction*, acts as a very good rectifier. *Silicon p-n junction diodes* are now widely used as rectifiers and logical elements in electronic equipment, particularly in computer systems.

■**TRANSISTORS.**—The most important development in the application of semiconductors came in 1948 with the discovery of the *germanium transistor* by John Bardeen and Walter H. Brattain at the Bell Telephone Laboratories. The *transistor* is an electronic device that can be used to control or amplify electric current. The earliest type consisted of two metal point contacts placed close together on the surface of a germanium crystal and a third soldered at its base. One of the point contacts is called the *emitter;* the other, the *collector;* the soldered contact is the *base*.

In 1949 William Shockley of the Bell Telephone Laboratories outlined many of the theories that led to a basic understanding of semiconductors, and subsequently, with his co-workers, developed the *junction transistor*. This device consists either of a thin section of *p*-type semiconductor between two parts of *n*-type semiconductor (known as an *n-p-n junction transistor*) or vice versa

(called the *p-n-p junction transistor*). Junction transistors and junction rectifiers caused a revolution in the electronics industry. Modern computers could not be built without these devices because of their superior reliability, speed, and useful life, as well as their small size and increased efficiency compared to electronic tubes. John Bardeen, Walter H. Brattain, and William Shockley received the 1956 Nobel prize for their work leading to the discovery of the transistor.

The transistor, since its invention in 1948, has had more impact on modern electronics than any other device. Modern electronic computers depend for their existence on transistors because tubes are too unreliable, slow-acting, and bulky to be used in a large-scale computer. Radios, hearing aids, military electronic systems, and space communications systems now use transistors as active circuit elements because of the many advantages the transistor has over the vacuum tube.

■**INJECTION LASERS.**—There are several other important semiconductor devices that use properties of special *p-n* junctions as the basis for their operation. The *injection laser,* the most recent of these devices, was developed simultaneously in 1962 by Marshall I. Nathan and co-workers at IBM and independently by Robert N. Hall and co-workers at General Electric. It consists of a *p-n* junction in a compound semiconductor, such as gallium arsenide, indium phosphide, or indium arsenide, that emits coherent light (light rays that stay in a tight beam rather than spread) when sufficient electrons are injected into the *p*-region (region of holes). The electrons recombine radiatively —fill the holes—and emit light in the process. (See MASERS AND LASERS.) This device requires a specific geometrical configuration to permit electrical current to be converted directly into a highly directional and pure beam of light through laser action. (*Laser* stands for Light Amplification by Stimulated Emission of Radiation.) The injection laser may ultimately be used in communications systems

■**TUNNEL DIODES.**—The tunnel diode was invented by Leo Esaki in 1957. A *tunnel diode* differs from an ordinary *p-n* junction diode in that both the *n*-region and *p*-region are 100 to 1,000 times more impure in the tunnel diode, creating a very thin, abrupt junction between the regions. Under certain conditions, because of the junction, electrons can go from the *n*-side directly to the *p*-side without having to "climb over" the junction barrier. This process is called *tunneling*. Because tunneling is inherently a very rapid process, tunnel diodes are being used in computer switching circuits where high speed is needed.

■**PHOTOCELLS.**—Semiconducting *photocells* are devices that detect light and convert its energy into electricity. There are three main types of semiconducting photocells: *photoconductive, photodiode,* and *photovoltaic.* Photoconductive and photodiode photocells are used as detectors of light, particularly of infrared light, while the photovoltaic type is used as a

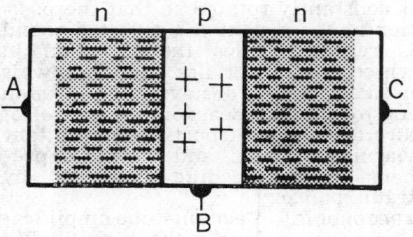

A JUNCTION TRANSISTOR can be used for amplification. Shown in simplified form: emitter (A), collector (C), and base (B).

power source. An example of the latter is the *silicon solar cell* that has been used to power electronic circuits in satellites by direct conversion of solar energy into electrical energy.

■**THERMOELECTRIC DEVICES.**—Semiconducting devices that can convert thermal (heat) energy into electrical energy and vice versa are called *thermoelectric devices*. In these devices, two dissimilar semiconducting materials, having junctions or joints between the two materials held at different temperatures, develop an electric current due to a heat flow through the systems. A reverse effect is achieved when current is passed through junctions of dissimilar materials; that is, one junction is cooled and the other junction is heated. The first of these effects may have application in the conversion of heat developed in a nuclear reactor into electrical energy; the second may have application in small refrigerators with no moving parts.

Methods of Device Fabrication.—Since the most important semiconductor devices—diodes and transistors—depend upon *p-n* junctions, some of the fabrication techniques for preparing junctions will be mentioned. Some semiconductors are frequently prepared by melting the pure material in a sealed system and pulling a crystal from the melt by slowly dipping and withdrawing a *seed crystal* affixed to a cooled rod. In this fashion it is possible to prepare pure material as a single crystal. If *dopants* (impurity atoms) are added to the melt before crystallization, the result is a *doped* (impure) crystal.

Some *p-n* junctions are *grown junctions* where first one type of impurity and then another is added during the growth process. A modern modification of a grown junction is accomplished by depositing semiconductor material from a vapor (gas) phase onto a semiconductor *substrate* (subsurface). This method is widely used for high-frequency silicon devices.

An *alloy junction diode* or *fused junction diode* is prepared by placing a small dot or pellet of an acceptor impurity, such as indium, on one surface of a wafer of *n*-type germanium. When this combination is heated to the proper temperature, part of the indium dissolves into a portion of the germanium and forms a *p-n* junction between the indium-germanium alloy and the original *n*-type germanium. A *diffused junction* is formed by exposing a piece of *n*-type germanium, silicon, or some other semiconductor to a gaseous *p*-type material. The atoms from the gas diffuse through the crystal lattice of the solid; and where the diffusion stops, a junction is formed. This method is by far the most widely used for preparing junctions.

Semiconductor Theory.—The electrical properties of all crystalline solids can be explained in terms of a unified concept called the *energy band theory*. According to atomic theory, electrons in an isolated atom are in stable orbits surrounding a nucleus that is made up of protons and neutrons. The electrons orbiting about the nucleus have exact energies. If a large number of atoms with discrete electronic energy levels are assembled into a three-dimensional array called a *crystal lattice*, the energy levels become perturbed and form bands of energy. These bands are made up of closely spaced electronic energy states that, according to the *Pauli exclusion principle*, can accommodate only two electrons per state. The bands are separated by forbidden gaps, or values of energy, that electrons cannot possess in a perfect lattice. The occupancy of these bands and the width of the forbidden gaps determine the electrical conductivity of solids.

Metals are solids in which the last occupied band (the one of highest energy) is only partially full. This is called the *conduction band*. When an electric field is applied to a piece of metal by a battery, the electrons near the top of the occupied energy states become excited and move into unoccupied energy states within the same band; thus they can move freely through the crystal. As the temperature is increased, the atoms of the lattice vibrate more due to thermal energy; and the electrons are scattered more, thereby decreasing the conductivity of the metal.

In insulators the last occupied band, called the *valence band*, is completely filled and the nearest unoccupied energy states are in the conduction band, which is at much higher energies. Transitions of electrons from the valence band across the energy gap to the conduction band cannot occur except under very high electric fields or at extremely high temperatures. The band gap for a good insulator is approximately 10 electron volts, compared to a thermal energy of the electrons at room temperature of 0.025 electron volt. Thus insulators have no electrons in the conduction band to conduct electricity and their conductivity is very low.

An *intrinsic* (pure) *semiconductor* at a temperature of absolute zero (−273° Centigrade) has a filled valence band and an empty conduction band. Therefore, at low temperatures an intrinsic semiconductor is an insulator. The band gap of semiconductors is much smaller than that in insulators. Typical band gaps range between 2.5 and 0.2 electron volts. Therefore, thermal energy available to electrons at room temperature and above is enough to excite a measurable number of electrons from the valence band to the conduction band. Then the negatively charged electrons in the conduction band and the holes in the valence band can be moved through the lattice by an electric field. The hole moves away from the electron, but also has an opposite charge and so adds to the total current. The number of holes is equal to the number of electrons in the conduction band of an intrinsic semiconductor because a hole is created every time an electron is excited to the conduction band. The reason the conductivity of intrinsic semiconductors increases markedly as temperature increases is that the number of electrons excited to the conduction band depends very strongly on temperature. The band gap of a semiconductor is an important property of the material. The table lists the room-temperature energy gaps of a few important semiconductors.

Semiconductor	Chemical Symbol	Energy Gap*
Germanium	Ge	0.66
Silicon	Si	1.09
Indium phophide	InP	1.29
Indium arsenide	InAs	0.36
Indium antimonide	InSb	0.175
Gallium phosphide	GaP	2.25
Gallium arsenide	GaAs	1.43
Gallium antimonide	GaSb	0.72
Cadmium sulfide	CdS	2.4
Cadmium telluride	CdTe	1.5
Lead sulfide	PbS	0.37
Lead telluride	PbTe	0.29

*Electron volts.

A polished wafer of semiconducting material illuminated with *monochromatic light* (light of only one frequency, or color) transmits or absorbs the light selectively. If the frequency of the light has an energy less than the band gap of a pure semiconductor, then the light is transmitted. However, if light is of sufficient optical energy to excite electrons across the gap, the material absorbs the light and is opaque. Consequently, it is possible to determine the energy gap of a semiconductor by observing the amount of optical energy transmitted.

In this discussion of the band theory of solids, the electrical behavior of metals, insulators, and intrinsic semiconductors has been covered. *Extrinsic* (impure) *semiconductors* are technologically much more important in the electronics industry than intrinsic material. The effects of impurity atoms in controlling the electrical behavior of semiconductors can also be explained by the band theory. When impurity atoms enter an intrinsic semiconductor lattice, in addition to the conduction band or valence band there are electron energy states in the forbidden gap that are close to either the conduction band or valence band.

Impurities that introduce electronic states that can give up electrons to the conduction band are called *donors*, while those that produce electronic levels that can accept electrons from the valence band are known as *acceptors*. Frequently the donor levels are near the conduction band in energy and can donate electrons to

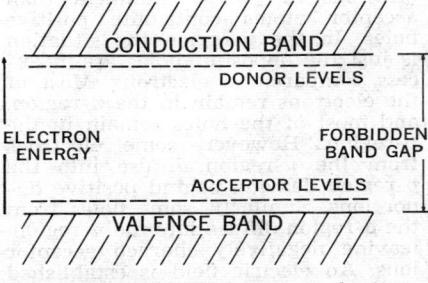

EXTRINSIC SEMICONDUCTORS rely upon impurities to control electrical behavior.

the conduction band when excited by a small fraction of the band-gap energy. Similarly, the acceptors are frequently near the valence band and can accept electrons excited from the valence band, leaving holes in the valence band. Because of the closeness of the impurity levels to the bands, small numbers of impurities donate or accept electrons, producing conduction electrons or holes that would not be available if the electrons had to be excited from the valence band to the conduction band. In an extrinsic semiconductor, when the number of donor impurities giving up electrons exceeds the number of acceptor impurities producing holes, the conduction is dominated by electrons and is *n*-type. The inverse situation occurs in *p*-type material, where holes dominate.

Since in most semiconductors the number of impurities is smaller than can be detected by chemical means, electrical measurements are used. In addition to conductivity or resistivity measurements, *Hall effect* measurements are also used. When a magnetic field is applied to a material that is carrying current, in a direction at right angles to the current, a voltage is produced across the sample at right angles to the current and the magnetic field. This effect, known as the Hall effect after Edwin H. Hall, who discovered it in 1879, is one of the most powerful tools for studying the electronic properties of semiconductors. By measuring the voltage produced, one can determine the sign and net number of carriers, hence the impurities in a semiconductor.

P-N Junctions.—It is possible to produce both an *n*-type region and a *p*-type region in a single crystal piece of semiconductor material. Such a

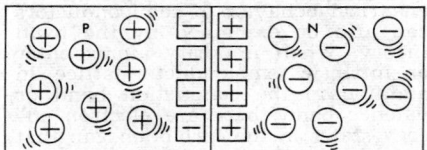

P-N JUNCTION in diagram form. The circles represent mobile electrons (−) and hole (+) carriers. The signs in the squares represent stationary ions at the junction.

combination is called a *p-n junction* and is the basis for many of the semiconductor devices. In the *n*-region, donor impurity atoms give up electrons in greater numbers than acceptor atoms contribute positive holes. In the *p*-region the situation is just the opposite: holes are in excess compared to electrons. Most of the electrons remain in the *n*-region, and most of the holes remain in the *p*-region. However, some electrons from the *n*-region diffuse into the *p*-region, leaving behind positive donor ions. Similarly, some holes from the *p*-region diffuse into the *n*-region, leaving negatively charged acceptor ions. An electric field is established at the junction due to the impurity ions, and this field inhibits additional

electrons from diffusing out of the *n*-type material or holes from diffusing out of the *p*-type material.

If a battery is connected with its negative terminal on the *n*-type material and its positive terminal on the *p*-type material, then electrons from the battery neutralize the positive ions on the *n*-side of the junction and electrons enter the positive terminal of the battery from the *p*-region, thereby decreasing the negative charge on the *p*-side. Consequently, the junction field is diminished and electrons can move from the *n*-type material through the junction to recombine with holes. The holes on the *p*-side carry the current from the positive battery terminal to the junction. A *p-n* junction connected to a voltage source in this fashion is said to be *forward biased*, and the device can carry appreciable current.

If, however, the *p-n* junction is *reverse biased* (with negative voltage applied to the *p*-side and positive voltage to the *n*-side), a field is present that causes the mobile holes and electrons to move away from the junction and each other, toward the *p*-contact and *n*-contact respectively. Electrons are added to the *p*-region and removed from the *n*-region by the battery, leaving a wider region near the junction charged with immobile impurity ions but depleted of mobile charge carriers. The junction field is enhanced by reverse biasing, but very little current flows because of the depletion of mobile charges. A small amount of current flows because of thermal excitation of holes and electrons in the junction region. These carriers contribute a small but finite reverse current. A *p-n* junction passes electrical current when forward biased, but opposes the flow when reverse biased.

Such a device is called a rectifier and can be used to convert alternating current into direct current. Solid-state rectifiers have wide commercial applications as radar or microwave detectors, computer switching diodes, television and radio diodes, and power rectifiers for battery chargers and electronic power supplies. Although vacuum-tube rectifiers were widely used for fifty years, the invention of the *p-n* junction rectifier and the vast needs of computer companies for reliable, small, efficient, and long-lived circuit elements have made semiconductor diodes dominant.

Junction Transistor.—The *junction transistor* is a solid-state device consisting of a thin region of *p*-type or *n*-type semiconductor between two regions of the opposite type semiconductor. Germanium and silicon are the most important semiconductor materials for transistors. While both *n-p-n* and *p-n-p* transistors are used commercially, only the *n-p-n* will be discussed here. Two *p-n* junctions exist that share a common narrow *p*-region. Three contacts called the *emitter, base,* and *collector* are made to the three regions. The *n-p* junction between the emitter and the base contact is the emitter junction and is forward biased. The junction between the collector and the

base is the collector junction and is reverse biased. Because the emitter junction is forward biased, electrons flow from the emitter contact through the *n*-region of the emitter to the emitter junction. There they are injected into the *p*-region. These injected electrons diffuse as minority carriers across the thin *p*-base region and are collected by the reverse biased collector junction.

The base region should be thin or narrow so that practically all the injected electrons are drawn across to the collector. They are swept into the collector by the large junction field of the reverse biased collector before they find their way to the base contact or recombine with holes. The emitter current also includes holes injected from the base into the emitter region. By introducing impurities more heavily in the *n*-region of the base, the electron injection can be made to dominate as required for an efficient transistor. The fraction

WESTERN ELECTRIC

TRANSISTORS on a printed circuit board.

of the emitter current that crosses the collector junction is known as the *alpha* (α) of the transistor. For junction transistors α can reach 0.99.

If the emitter current is varied by a signal voltage introduced at the input terminals, then there will be a corresponding variation of the collector current. Since the collector *impedance* (resistance) is high compared to the impedance of the forward biased emitter, a large-load resistor can be used in the output to get voltage amplification or power amplification. For example, if the impedances of the input and output circuits are 100 and 1,000,000 ohms respectively, then there is a power gain and a voltage gain of about 10,000 ohms.

For a more quantitative treatment of the junction transistor, let us assume that the input signal voltage increases in a negative amount of ΔV_i. The forward biased emitter has a low resistance, r_e, so that an increase in the emitter voltage will produce a corresponding increase in emitter current of

$$\Delta I_e = \frac{\Delta V_i}{r_e}.$$

The amount of this increased emitter current that reaches the collector depends on the current gain (α) of the transistor defined by

$$a = \frac{\Delta I_c}{\Delta I_e},$$

where ΔI_c is the change in the collector current. Thus

$$\Delta I_c = a\Delta I_e.$$

If the load resistor in the collector circuit is R_L, then the voltage gain of the transistor is

$$G_v = \frac{output\ voltage}{input\ voltage}$$

$$G_v = \frac{a\Delta I_e R_L}{\Delta I_e r_e} = a\,\frac{R_L}{r_e}.$$

If $a \cong 1$,

$$G_v = \frac{R_L}{r_e}.$$

The power gain is simply given by

$$G_P = \frac{power\ out}{power\ in} = \frac{\Delta I_c{}^2 R_L}{\Delta I_e{}^2 r_e}$$

$$= \frac{a^2 \Delta I_e{}^2 R_L}{\Delta I_e{}^2 r_e}$$

or

$$G_P = a^2\,\frac{R_L}{r_e},$$

but if $a \sim 1$,

$$G_P \cong \frac{R_L}{r_e}.$$

Because the junction transistor in different circuit configurations can produce voltage gain, power gain, or current gain, the transistor can be used as an amplifier in place of a vacuum tube. Transistors have many advantages over tubes. They are more reliable, more durable, more efficient, much smaller, and can work at lower signal levels with lower noise. They have no heater or cathode to fail and can be flexibly biased because of the existence of both the n-p-n and the p-n-p structures.

—William J. Turner

SOUND

Waves and Vibrations.—It is very difficult to realize that sound is a wave, yet it is. To visualize a wave, imagine you are holding one end of a rope whose other end is tied to a doorknob. If you make a sharp up-and-down motion with your hand, a bump starts moving down the length of the rope. The rope itself does not move forward—only the bump does. This is one of the very important characteristics of waves: the medium (in this case the rope) through which the wave travels does not move forward or back, it swings up and down across the direction of wave motion.

If a pebble is dropped in the center of a pond, the waves move away from the point of impact in ever-widening circles. The wave in the rope demonstrates a one-dimensional wave—it moves on a plane. Sound, on the other hand, like the waves in the pond, is a three-dimensional wave. The crests and troughs of sound are not bumps, but high-pressure areas (*compressions*) and low-pressure areas (*rarefactions*) of the spongy mass we know as air. Each pressure layer forms the surface of an ever-growing sphere. Each following rarefaction is a slightly smaller sphere just inside the pressure sphere and is itself followed by another sphere of high pressure.

A sound wave moves forward even though the air really only compacts a little and then thins out a little as the sound wave passes. The wave is started by the quick motion (*vibration*) of an object. When you rap the head of a drum, it moves away from the stick, creating a partial vacuum in the layer of air touching the surface of the drum. The surrounding air rushes in to fill this vacuum, leaving a partial vacuum in the second layer just above the drum head, and so on away from the surface. The drum head then returns from its depressed position and bounces to a level higher than normal. This compacts the air immediately above the drum, and the high-pressure area in this space also moves out into the air immediately behind the rarefaction. Thus a wave is created by the back-and-forth motion of the drum head. A radio speaker cone works in exactly the same way. It is pulled sharply back and forth in a quick series of vibrations (*oscillations*) that transmit themselves into the adjacent layers of air.

The sound waves move out on the surfaces of ever-growing spheres. Since the amount of energy carried by a single wave at the start remains with that wave throughout its existence, the amount of compression and rarefaction decreases as the area of the sphere increases. In theory, the wave never disappears entirely; in actuality, the rubbing of air molecules against each other slowly absorbs all of the initial energy and turns it into heat, so that eventually the sound wave is dissipated.

This dissipation of sound energy is even more pronounced in enclosed areas. In a room or auditorium the sound waves initiated on the stage strike the walls, the ceiling, and the floor. While some of the sound is reflected back into the room (causing *reverberation,* or echo), the rest is absorbed by such things as curtains, rugs, and clothes.

■**VOLUME AND PITCH.**—Sound has two important characteristics. The first is *volume* (loudness), which is the intensity of the pressure in the compression part of the wave and the reduction in pressure in the rarefaction. The greater the rise of pressure and the thinner the rarefaction, the louder the sound will seem. The second characteristic is *pitch,* which is the frequency of the waves. The more rapidly the sound waves follow each other, the higher the sound's pitch. A loudspeaker cone that moves back and forth very quickly produces a tone much higher in pitch than one that goes back and forth slowly.

■**VELOCITY.**—Regardless of the frequency of the wave, sound always travels through a particular medium at the same speed. The speed depends on the "springiness," temperature, and density of the medium. Since air is a relatively soft material, sound travels through it at the fairly slow speed of approximately 1,100 feet per second—about 750 miles per hour—at sea level at a temperature of 70° F. Water is stiffer and denser than air, so sound moves faster in the sea—4,800 feet per second. Sound moves fastest in a piece of hard steel—over 16,000 feet per second (more than 10,000 miles per hour).

■**WAVELENGTH.**—In air, sound waves always travel at about 1,100 feet per second, no matter how quickly a loudspeaker cone moves back and forth. Therefore, if a speaker completes one cycle in 1/30 of a second (forward in 1/60 of a second and back in 1/60 of a second), the wave that moves away from the speaker will have traveled about 37 feet by the time the cone is ready to start its second swing; that is, 1/30 (of a second) times 1,100 (feet per second). But if the speaker moves back and forth at the high pitch of 20,000 cycles per second, the wave would only be 1/20,000 times 1,100, or about 6½ inches long.

Engineers have discovered that if a sound wave is to be created efficiently—that is, if a reasonable amount of the energy needed to move the speaker cone back and forth is to be transformed into sound—the diameter of the speaker cone and the length of the sound wave must be approximately equal. This is why small speakers (*tweeters*) work very well for the very-high-frequency (very short) waves, while the deeper sounds require much larger speakers (*woofers*) coupled with large wooden enclosures to move an appreciable amount of sound energy into a room.

Resonance.—*Resonance* is the phenomenon by which sound waves are reinforced so that they sound louder. Resonance may take place in two specific ways, both of which work on the same principle. If the handle of a vibrating tuning fork touches a table, the sound emanating from the tuning fork becomes louder. The reason for this is that the tuning fork causes the particles of the table top to vibrate. Thus the table top also produces sound waves (by causing compressions and rarefactions of the air layers above it) of the same frequency as the sound waves coming from the tuning fork. The two sound waves join to produce a larger and louder sound wave. This type of resonance—one vibrating body causing another to vibrate—is called *sympathetic vibration.*

The other method of producing resonance can be illustrated by holding one end of a long cardboard tube in a bowl of water. If a vibrating tuning fork is held near the open end of the tube and the tube is moved slowly into the water, eventually (when the tube has reached the proper position) the sound will be amplified. This happens because the sound waves emanating from the tuning fork travel down the tube, bounce off the water, and travel back up the tube. When the length of the tube (measured from the open end to the water surface) is equal to the wavelength

DOPPLER EFFECT explains the apparent change in pitch of a train's whistle by the bunching and spreading of sound waves as the train moves toward and away from the listener. This principle is used by submarines to detect the speed and direction of other vessels.

of the sound waves produced by the tuning fork, the reflected waves will be *in phase* (the rarefactions and compressions will coincide) with the waves emanating from the tuning fork. This reinforces the sound waves and makes them sound louder. This resonance is an *echo phenomenon.*

Doppler Effect.—If an observer and a source of sound are moving relative to one another (one or both may be moving, but they cannot both be moving in the same direction at the same speed), the observed frequency or pitch of the sound waves differs from the frequency or pitch emitted. This is called the *Doppler effect,* after its discoverer, Christian Johann Doppler (1803–1853), an Austrian physicist. Picture a series of sound waves emanating from the whistle of a railroad locomotive. When the locomotive is standing still, the waves move out from the whistle in an ever-widening set of spheres. If the locomotive is moving, the sound waves going in front of the train travel at a speed of about 1,100 feet per second (the speed of sound waves in air) plus the speed of the locomotive, while the waves going behind the train are slowed by an amount equal to the speed of the locomotive.

A person standing alongside the track notices this difference. As the train comes toward him, its whistle seems to rise in pitch because the waves reach his ear at a frequency greater than the real one. But as soon as the train passes, the hearer is in the retarded sound area; the pitch suddenly drops and then slowly climbs to normal as the train moves into the distance. The Doppler effect is used to help submarines detect the speed and direction of surface vessels and even of other submarines through a device called *sonar.* (It is also used in astronomy, where the change in the frequency of light waves is measured to determine the velocities of distant stars.)

Hearing.—The human ear is sensitive to sound frequencies from about 30 cycles per second (the very low sounds that can be made by the enormous pipe organs in some old churches) up to 17,000 to 20,000 cycles per second, which are more like barely audible whistles or squeaks than real sound. Dogs are said to be

able to hear sounds in the range of 20,000 to 25,000 cycles per second—the reason why whistles producing sounds in that range can be heard by dogs but not by people. Bats use high-pitched squeaks, echoed from trees and walls, to fly between obstacles and even to locate and catch their prey on the darkest nights.

When a sound wave approaches the ear, it is directed down a horn-shaped duct that ends at a thin membrane called the *ear drum.* This membrane reacts to the alternating compression and rarefaction waves by moving back and forth, much as the speaker cone moves back and forth in making a sound wave. Just behind the ear drum, and attached to it at one point, is a tiny linkage composed of three small bones that provide a mechanical transfer of the motion of the ear drum across the middle ear. The *hammer* swings back and forth with the motion of the ear drum and transmits this motion to the *anvil;* the anvil in turn transmits it to the *stirrup,* the foot plate of which covers an oval window at the far side of the middle ear.

This bone linkage hangs in the middle ear from a set of ligaments that support and protect the hearing. When extremely loud sounds are received, causing the ear drum to bulge unduly in either direction, muscles holding the ligaments tense reflexively, limiting the motion of the linkage and thereby reducing the reaction at the sensitive inner ear.

Sound is actually sensed by the *cochlea,* a spiral organ shaped like a small snail shell, the larger end of which is attached to the middle ear. If the cochlea were unwound, it would make a hollow, tapered tube about 1½ inches long. Across the center of the tube, and running its full length, is a thin web carrying hundreds of nerve fibers that end in the roots of tiny hair cells standing crosswise in the web. The entire cochlea is filled with fluid.

When a pressure wave, received by the ear drum and transmitted through the linkage in the middle ear, arrives at the window to the cochlea, the window is driven into the fluid of the cochlea and pushes the dividing web down slightly. The extra pressure is relieved by a bulge in a second window to the cochlea from the middle ear. When the following rare-

faction pulls the ear drum and linkage away, the dividing web in the cochlea moves up slightly and the second communicating window bows inward to compensate.

Thus sound waves received at the ear drum are transmitted very efficiently to the sensitive web in the cochlea. In some way not precisely understood, the nerve endings in the web interpret these complex vibrations in terms of pitch and volume. When these are compared to the sounds received at the other ear, the brain can determine the direction from which the sound comes.

The most popular theory explaining how the ear hears is based on sympathetic vibration. Just as the strings of a piano start to vibrate when the same notes are sounded on another instrument so, it is thought, the tiniest hairs in the small end of the cochlea respond to the higher frequencies while the longer ones at the thick end respond to the lower frequencies. The chief objection to this theory is in the fantastic sensitivity of human hearing. The range of 30 to 20,000 cycles per second would require a much greater range in thickness of cochlea membrane and in length of hair cells than actually exists. Recent studies of the electrical signals sent out by ear nerve cells suggest that the frequency of impulses sent out by the nerve fibers themselves may be related to the frequency of sound waves.

Acoustics.—Since ancient times, instrument makers have created magnificent musical instruments with the sole purpose of producing beautiful sounds. Yet their skill was, and to a great extent still is, largely the result of trial and error. The knowledge of how best to shape the resonance chamber, the best woods for construction, the time required for seasoning, and the amount of varnish that will achieve the optimum sound quality is the result of hundreds of years of experimentation.

Over the last hundred years, however, the making, sensing, recording, and reproduction of sound have evolved into a science. Acoustic engineers know what sound is, how to detect it, and how to preserve it on records that can be played again and again. Sound waves are detected by microphones that work much as the ear does—a thin membrane is made to vibrate back and forth as the compressions and rarefactions impinge upon it. The vibrating membrane in the microphone may move a coil of wire in a magnetic field to create an electric voltage. Alternatively, it may move toward and away from a flat metal plate, changing the capacitance between the two and affecting an electric circuit accordingly. In another type it compacts a packet of finely ground carbon particles, thus changing the electric resistance of the packet and altering an electric circuit. Once the sound is transformed into an electric signal (that oscillates in voltage as sound waves do in pressure), it can then be *amplified.* (The voltage is increased while the relative strengths of loud and soft signals are maintained.) Amplification is necessary because the electric signal generated by the microphone is so weak that only the most sensitive electrical measuring instruments can detect any change at all.

■SOUND RECORDING.—There are many ways to preserve the pattern of rising and falling voltage. For example, the signal can be made to move a pen back and forth over a moving strip of paper to create a jagged trace; it can be used to swing a light beam back and forth across a moving photographic film, which is then developed to show the changing intensity and frequency by the sweep and density of lines. The signal can drive a pointed stylus back and forth as a soft plastic disk turns under the point, leaving a wavy groove; it can power an electromagnet to create magnetized and reverse-magnetized areas on either a strip of thin plastic tape coated with tiny iron oxide particles or an iron wire. All of these methods are practical. The photographic film is used in movies; the plastic disk is the master from which records are duplicated; the coated tape is used in tape recorders.

■SOUND REPRODUCTION.—Sound is recreated by simply reversing the recording process. In the tape recorder an electromagnet senses the changing magnetism of the coated tape passing across its face and reproduces the original electric signal. A stylus rides in the groove of the record disk; and as it moves back and forth, a tiny coil of wire builds up a similarly varying voltage. A light beam shines on the motion picture film and dims and brightens a tube that functions like an electric eye. Once again the weak electric signal must be amplified. It can then drive the electromagnet in the loudspeaker to move a speaker cone back and forth and reproduce a nearly exact duplicate of the sounds originally recorded.

■STEREOPHONIC SOUND.—One of the most recent advances in sound recording and reproduction is the achievement of a *stereophonic effect.* As stated before, the brain can recognize the direction from which sound comes by comparing the relative pitch and volume of the sound waves received by each ear. For example, if an orchestra has the brass section on the hearer's left and the percussion section on his right, the sound waves from the trumpets will reach his left ear before reaching the right ear; those from the tympani will reach the right ear before the left. By interpreting the time of arrival and the *intensity* (volume) of the sound reaching each ear, the brain can determine the position of the instruments. In stereophonic recording, two microphones are set some distance apart in front of the orchestra, one recording the sound waves emanating from the left side of the orchestra more strongly, and vice versa. The electric signals produced by each of the microphones are recorded on a separate *channel,* or track. When the sound is reproduced through two separated speakers, each channel is reproduced in only one speaker. Thus

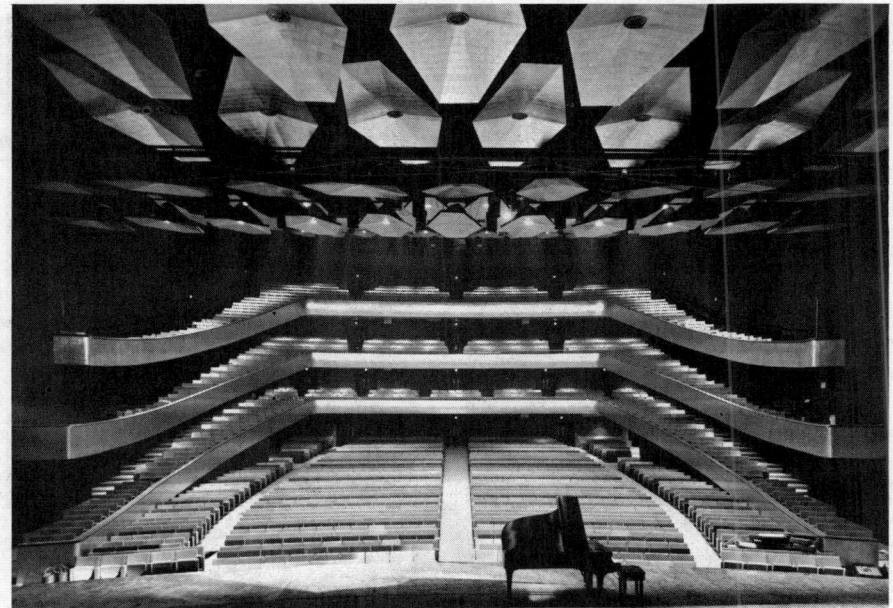

LINCOLN CENTER FOR THE PERFORMING ARTS

AN ACOUSTICALLY BALANCED AUDITORIUM of the Philharmonic Hall at Lincoln Center.

the sounds recorded by the left-hand microphone are reproduced by the left-hand speaker; those recorded by the right-hand microphone are reproduced by the right-hand speaker. In this way the listener can sense the direction of the sound, which creates a greater feeling of spaciousness and depth than is possible with *monaural* reproduction.

Room Acoustics.—Sound engineers face enormously difficult problems in designing concert halls. When the Philharmonic Hall at Lincoln Center for the Performing Arts in New York City was planned, studies were made of all the world's great concert halls to see if the best characteristics of each could be duplicated. The ideal hall would distribute music equally to all parts of the auditorium, so that there would be no seats where the music was either overly loud or inaudible. Furthermore, there would be no preferential treatment of some of the instruments at the expense of the others—the base drum would be heard as well as the piccolos. In addition, the *reverberation time*—the time it takes for all the echoes of a sharply struck note to die out—would have to be close to the ideal 1.7 to 2.0 seconds.

All of this can be accomplished by shaping the sides, roof, and floor of the hall so that the sound created on the stage is moved out into the auditorium. The back of the stage is usually shaped like a giant searchlight reflector, to reflect sound rather than light. In Philharmonic Hall carpeted floors, specially treated walls, and thousands of individually positioned reflectors mounted near the ceiling gave the designers an opportunity to change the acoustical characteristics almost at will. Dummy people—blocks of plastic foam with the same acoustic properties as people—were placed in the seats to simu-

late a filled hall; and engineers studied every area, checking sound levels and characteristics with special meters.

The work done on the Philharmonic Hall is typical of the work of acoustic engineers. They are called upon to design soundproof rooms, to construct rooms that will amplify sounds, to design offices that will minimize the clatter of typewriters, and to construct echo chambers. To meet these wide-ranging demands, a multitude of materials have been designed to meet the specific needs of room acoustics. Sound-absorbing panels for ceilings and walls, thick rugs and drapes, and reflecting panels have become commonplace, but their function in controlling undesirable noise and amplifying pleasant sounds has often gone unnoticed.

Musical Acoustics.—Every impact between two physical bodies, no matter how delicate, starts a pressure wave moving into the surroundings. Two leaves brush against each other, a tree falls in the forest, a moving wind flaps a shutter or whistles through a cracked windowpane—these are all naturally created sounds, but there are many ways to make sound artificially as well. The loudest artificial sound is probably that of the hydrogen bomb, which creates pressure waves so great that buildings are flattened and windows shattered miles from the center of the explosion. Thunder is the sound made when air rushes into the vacuum created by the passage of electric current in a lightning bolt. Sound travels much more slowly than light, so we see the lightning flash first. The sound follows, lagging by five seconds for every mile separating the observer and the lightning.

In an explosion or a thunderclap we are dealing with a single disturbance, possibly followed by echoes

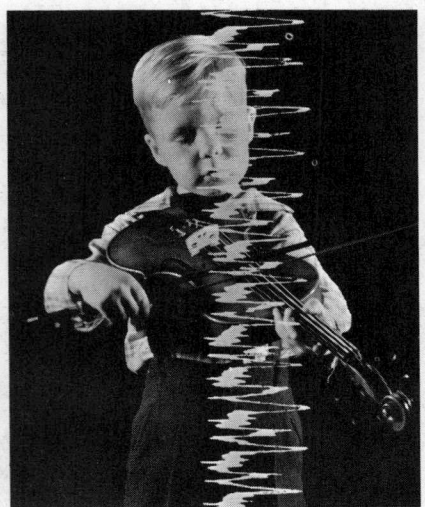

LOOK MAGAZINE

SOUNDS produced by reed (*left*), percussion (*center*), and stringed instruments (*right*) are characterized by the superimposed patterns.

from hills or large buildings nearby. The loudest continuous noise is that produced by sirens. A siren is made by drilling a series of holes in a metal cylinder and then aiming a jet of air at the holes. When the cylinder is turned at high speed, the air jet is broken into a series of *puffs,* or sound waves. The number of puffs per second (the number of holes that pass in front of the air jet in a second) determines the frequency or pitch of the siren.

Musical instruments create a very special type of sound. Music is made up of sounds of clearly defined pitch. Even drums and triangles (percussion instruments) are tuned so that, when struck, a distinct tone is created. The string instruments take advantage of the fact that a taut string will vibrate at a frequency dependent upon its tension, thickness, and length. The shorter, tighter, and thinner the string, the higher the frequency. This is how a violinist can change the notes. He strokes the string with a rosined bow (rosin increases the friction between the string and the bow), which starts the string vibrating and keeps it in motion as long as the bow is in contact with the string. The violinist can shorten the string and thus raise its pitch by clamping it with his finger against the fingerboard.

The wooden box of the violin, which is behind the strings, makes the sound louder and "colors" it as well. The pure note of the string alone in space would be barely audible if there were no wooden box to set larger volumes of air into motion. The differing shapes, sizes, and designs of violins, guitars, mandolins, and pianos create distinctly different sounds, even when strings of the same length and thickness are tightened to the same degree in two or more instruments. This occurs because these shapes do not merely amplify the single note vibrated by the string. They add other, higher notes (*harmonics*) of two, three, four, five, and more times the frequency of the basic

tone. The number of these harmonics give all musical instruments their distinctive character. They also cause some instruments to give a richness and mellowness to all the notes within their range, from the very lowest to the very highest.

The third major class of musical instruments is the horns. In these, sound is started by a flow of air moving past a flexible element (a reed in the oboe or clarinet, the musician's lip in the trumpet and tuba) so that the air passage is alternately opened and restricted. The pulsing flow travels down a metal or wooden tube and out a bell-shaped end. The length and diameter of the tube greatly determine the pitch of the note. When you blow across the open mouths of several bottles of different sizes, the larger bottles make the deeper tones; but a large bottle will give off a higher note than usual if it is almost filled with water. Some horns, such as the oboe or clarinet, have holes drilled along their length so that the musician can adjust the length of the tube by opening and closing different holes. Others, such as the trumpet and tuba, have valves that the musician can open or close to increase or decrease the length of the tube. In this way, combined with control of breath pressure, he changes notes.

The musical scale is no accident; it is a very carefully ordered set of frequencies. The intervals are based on the octave (c to C, for example), which is adjusted so that the higher note is precisely double the frequency, in cycles per second, of the lower note. In 1955 an international agreement set middle A at exactly 440 cycles per second; all other notes are based on this.

For many years the range between any two notes an octave apart has been divided into twelve parts. Originally these were not twelve equal divisions, but intervals determined by ratio. Thus G was always exactly 3/2 of the c below, and E was exactly 81/64 of the c below. This scale was invented by Pythagoras (died c. 497

B.C.) through his experiments with lengths of strings. Each additional note was set by stepping off the so-called *perfect fifths*—the ratio of 3/2 between G and c is a perfect fifth. The next ratio, between D and G, would be found by multiplying 3/2 by 3/2 and then dividing by 2 to reduce the D to the octave under consideration. Thus D is 9/8 above c, and so on.

Later this scale was modified for better harmony. D remained 9/8 of c, but E was made 5/4 (80/64 instead of 81/64) times c. However, all these modifications left the same problem. For example, the F sharp in the G scale is not quite the same frequency as the G flat in the D flat scale. Today all keyboard instruments are tuned to the *equal temperament scale.* In this, the twelve intervals are all equal, so that the frequency of each note is exactly $2^{1/12}$ (1.05946) times the preceding note. Middle A is 440; B flat is $440 \times 2^{1/12} = 466.2$; B is $440 \times 2^{2/12} = 493.9$; c is $440 \times 2^{3/12} = 523.3$; and so on up to A again, which is $440 \times 2^{12/12} = 880$ cycles per second.

The similarity and harmony of all A's, for example, occur because each is a simple multiple of all the others. There is a low A that is 55 cycles per second, another at 110, a third at 220, a fourth at 440, a fifth at 880, a sixth at 1,760, and the highest generally heard in written music at 3,520 cycles per second. Music does not generally take into account the ability of human ears to hear up to 20,000 cycles per second for two reasons. First, these high-pitched squeaks are not appealing to the ear unless they are accompanied by lower tones. Second, these higher frequencies do occur as harmonics (multiples), and they play a large part, as mentioned above, in giving a particular instrument its distinctive character.

■**CHORDS.**—Individual notes sound well when played together (*chords*) because there is a perfect match in the higher harmonics produced when the notes are sounded simultaneously. The similar harmonics of a chord do not appear until well up into the thousands-of-cycles-per-second range, yet this is enough to give them a melodious sound when played together. For example, take a simple major chord: c-e-g. The frequencies of the three basic notes are 261.6, 329.6, and 392.0 cycles per second. The third harmonic of c is 784.8; the second harmonic of g is 784.0—so close as to be undistinguishable. The fifth harmonic of c is 1,308.0; the fourth harmonic of e is 1,308.4—close enough to fool the human ear.

Ultrasonics.—Aviation engineers appropriated the word *supersonic* to define airplane speeds faster than the speed of sound (in air)—over 700 miles per hour. *Ultrasonic* refers to those frequencies of sound waves above the range of human hearing. These high-frequency waves are made with much the same equipment used to reproduce music in the home. However, for these very-high-frequency waves the area of the speaker face need not be so large (a 1,000,000-cycle-per-second ultrasonic signal has a wavelength of approximately the thickness of three pages of this book). Further, these very-high-frequency waves do not move from the sound producer in ever-widening spheres, but tend to stay in a narrow beam.

Certain crystalline materials, such as quartz and Rochelle salts, have the interesting property of changing shape when an electric voltage is applied across their opposite faces. This change in dimension is only a few thousandths of an inch, but that is all that is needed to start a sound wave in adjacent layers of air. These *piezoelectric crystals* are, therefore, the ideal sources of ultrasonic waves (*ultrasound*). The electronics specialist can make an electric signal oscillate through extremes of voltage a million or more times a second with little difficulty so it is quite easy to experiment with ultrasonic waves.

Ultrasound has some very peculiar effects. When it moves through water, it creates billions of tiny bubbles when the rarefaction part of the sound wave tries to thin out a layer of water. The water cannot thin out in this fashion without losing its basic liquid character and therefore turns into a vapor. But the vapor bubble lasts only a fraction of a second before a pressure wave snaps the bubble together with a bang. Scientists think that local pressures in the range of hundreds of thousands of pounds per square inch are generated in these tiny collapsing bubbles. Studies of *cavitation* (the creation and destruction of vapor bubbles) explained why high-speed ship propeller blades wear out faster than lower-speed propeller blades. The collapsing bubbles quickly destroy the surfaces of the metal blades with their extremely high local pressures. It is exactly like striking the blades with a sharply pointed hammer. The destructiveness of ultrasound is not limited to marine propellers. Fish are killed by the millions when their delicate nerve cells are exposed to a beam of high-frequency sound in the sea.

Ultrasonics also has a number of important uses. High-frequency waves are used to sterilize instruments in hospitals. Narrow pencil beams of ultrasonic energy can be aimed at specific parts of the human body to create warmth—as in the bone marrow—where no other heating device can reach. Ultrasound has been aimed through holes cut in the skull to reduce the pain and torment of the psychoneurotic patient. Ultrasound in air also has the effect of clumping small particles together, so that instead of floating in the air they grow heavy enough to fall. Hence, *ultrasonic precipitators* installed in industrial and incinerator chimneys help clear the air of dust and smoke. Ultrasound in water breaks up dirt and soil, and mixes the tiny particles well into the water. Ultrasonic waves are thus used to clean manufacturing grease and soil from metal parts. Eventually this principle may be used in home dishwashers and clothes washers.

—Richard M. Koff

HEAT

The term "heat" is one of the most misused words in the lexicon of science. An object cannot possess heat because heat is not a property of a material; a hot bar of steel cannot be said to possess more or less heat than a cupful of cold sea water. The unit of comparison between the two should be *energy*, for the concepts "heat" and "energy" are not identical. Energy may be stored in a system, whereas heat may not. The term *heat transfer* describes those processes in which energy is transferred from one object to another owing to a difference in their temperatures. This transfer process is basic to the concept of heat. Thus the definition of heat may be stated: *Heat is that energy which is transferred between two systems by virtue of a temperature differential.*

If a hot steel bar is plunged into cold water, the bar would cool and the water warm. The energies of the bar and water change as a result of heat transfer between them.

In order that we may understand more clearly the relationship between heat and energy, the latter concept must be more fully developed. A basic concept of mechanical energy is that a body in motion possesses *kinetic energy* proportional to the product of its mass and velocity squared. Another type of energy is *potential energy*, which results from movement against a restoring force; for instance, a ball rising against the earth's gravitational force increases in potential energy. Another example is the increase of potential energy of a spring as it is stretched.

All objects consist of molecules in motion, *molecular energy*, and consequently there exist discrete molecular energies. The sum of all the molecular energies of a body is its *energy*. In general, if molecular energies are large, then the *specific energy* (energy per unit of mass) is large; and this condition is reflected quantitatively in the statement that the temperature of the body is high. This concept of temperature is discussed more fully below, but for now, one can consider that the hotter (higher in temperature) a body is, the greater the energies of the molecules making up the body.

If two bodies of unequal temperature, such as a hot steel bar and cold water, are placed in contact with one another, the area of contact has highly energetic molecules (as the iron molecules) vibrating at a large amplitude contacting lower-energy water molecules. By collisions at this interface, the energy of the water molecules increases and the energy of the iron molecules decreases. In this process heat is transferred, and the energies of both systems change.

■**FIRST LAW OF THERMODYNAMICS.**—To express one of the most important and useful basic laws of physics: *The energy of a system can be changed by the transfer of heat.* The only other way in which energy within a system can be changed is by the system's doing work (such as the stretching of a spring or the expansion of a gas enclosed in a cylinder).

If Q is the heat transfer, W the work transfer, and ΔE the change in energy of a system due to these processes, then:

$$\Delta E = Q - W$$

where Q is positive when the heat transfer is such as to increase the energy of the body and W is positive when the body does work on its surroundings. This simple equation, in conjunction with the realization that the energy of any body is determined solely by the energies of its molecules and is independent of the way the molecules obtained these energies (either by work or heat transfer from other bodies), is called the *first law of thermodynamics.*

Historical Background

■**CALORIC THEORY.**—For many decades the manifestations of heat were attributed to an ethereal, invisible fluid called "caloric." This fluid was believed to have the power of penetrating, expanding, solidifying, and dissolving various materials, as well as the power of converting these materials from solid to liquid or from liquid to vapor. The caloric theory pictured heat as a fluid free to flow into a body when the body was heated and out of a body when it was cooled. The expansion of materials upon heating was attributed to the volume of the caloric fluid entering the material. This theory explained many of the known facts, and scientists were able to use it as a basis for the prediction of various phenomena in advance of their experimental discovery.

Although the caloric theory was accepted by many scientists, there remained certain incongruous observations that could not be explained by the postulation of this invisible, weightless, all-pervading fluid. For instance, the generation of heat by the friction arising from the motion of two mechanical objects contacting one another was attributed to a loss of caloric; the caloric was supposed to be ground or squeezed out of the objects. Many scientists of the late eighteenth century found this explanation inadequate.

In a classic experiment conducted in a Bavarian arsenal, Count Benjamin Rumford demonstrated the inadequacy of this explanation and in so doing prepared the way for the downfall of the caloric theory. Rumford's experiments were initiated by his observation that when cannons were bored, a large temperature rise accompanied the boring. In a series of experiments Rumford measured the energy gained by the cannon from the transfer of heat associated with the boring process. He also attempted to measure the weight of the caloric fluid picked up by the hot cannon. Finding none, he concluded that heat was some form of *motion*.

Rumford's experiments alone, however, were not sufficient to disprove the caloric theory. Not until Sir James Joule was able to determine accurately the mechanical equivalent of heat (by melting ice with friction) was heat recognized for what it is—energy in transit. Joule's experiments established beyond all doubt that heat and work are merely different manifestations of the same thing—energy.

Although the caloric theory was disproved more than a century ago, many erroneous concepts of heat that exist today in the mind of the layman are direct results of this theory. The terms associated with the concept of heat in our modern terminology reflect the hold the caloric theory had on scientists in the eighteenth and nineteenth centuries. We speak of heat "flowing" from one body to another, we talk erroneously about the "quantity of heat" in a body, and we measure the quantity in "calories" with a "calorimeter." Nevertheless, it must again be stressed that heat is neither a material object nor an ethereal one and that a body cannot possess heat. Like work, heat is a way to transfer energy from one system to another. Heat energy is transferred by virtue of a temperature difference existing between the systems.

Temperature.—It is common to associate the concept of temperature with the sensations of heat and cold. These physiological sensations can be very misleading. For example, if sheets of copper and paper are cooled by setting them on a dish of crushed ice until their temperatures equal that of the ice, the copper sheet will feel colder to the touch. This is caused by the high thermal conductivity of the copper. Physiological sensations are often deceptive and can lead at most to a qualitative temperature scale. To appreciate the meaning of the concept of temperature, however, we must first discuss quantitative temperature scales that are not associated with human sensations.

Although molecular energies may be used to define a temperature scale, it is extremely inconvenient to measure such energies. Within any given macroscopic system at any given time there exists a variety of molecular energies. It is the average of these molecular energies that we associate with the concept of temperature.

For gases at low pressures, the temperature is defined rather simply as being proportional to the square of the average molecular velocity. In high-pressure gases and in solids and liquids, the same general concept is accepted, although the reasoning is more complicated.

■**THERMOMETERS.**—To translate such molecular concepts into more practical measuring devices, one chooses to measure some other property that is related to molecular energies. It is known that the volume of most liquids and solids increases when they are heated. The same is always true of gases if the pressure is maintained constant. Thus the expansion of mercury, for instance, is used to indicate increases in temperature in the common mercury-in-glass thermometers. Other fluids are also used. It is obvious that there must be some standard for reference so that readings on all thermometers may be compared. These reference points are the freezing point of water (actually the triple point where solid, vapor, and liquid exist in equilibrium), the boiling point of water at one atmosphere of pressure, and the boiling and freezing points of several other materials.

These reference states are assigned numbers in any chosen temperature scale. The two scales with which we are most familiar are the *Centigrade scale* (C.) and the *Fahrenheit scale* (F.). They are thus related: $\frac{9}{5}$C. + 32 = F. The accompanying chart indicates the reference state temperatures. If the freezing point of water is chosen as 0° C. and the boiling point of water as 100° C., then each degree represents $\frac{1}{100}$ of the scale between 0 and 100. Since the volume change for each degree of temperature change is not constant over the entire scale, the actual distance between degree marks varies slightly on most liquid thermometers. In order that all thermometers may give the same temperature reading when placed in the same environment, they are calibrated against a low-pressure gas thermometer. The latter is used because the volume change of the gas is very nearly the same for each degree change in temperature.

Kelvin and *Rankine scales* are two other temperature scales that deserve mention. It has been previously stated that temperatures are indicative of molecular kinetic energies. As these energies decrease, one might expect some lower limit of temperature where all motion essentially stops. This lower limit is referred to as absolute zero, and the scales that use this point as a basis are the *Kelvin scale* (K.) and the *Rankine scale* (R.). These absolute temperature scales are related to the Centigrade and Fahrenheit scales: K. = C. + 273.16; R. = F. + 459.69. Thus, —273.16° C. represents the absolute lower limit of temperature on the Centigrade scale.

■**OTHER MEASURING DEVICES.**—In addition to the methods described above, numerous other techniques are used to measure temperature. A *thermocouple* consists of a circuit of two wires of different metals that generate a voltage and current flow when one junction is hotter than the other. The voltage is indicative of the temperature difference, and calibration charts have been prepared for many common thermocouple circuits. This method is generally used to measure temperature in industry.

A *resistance thermometer* measures the change in electrical resistance with change in temperature, and suit-

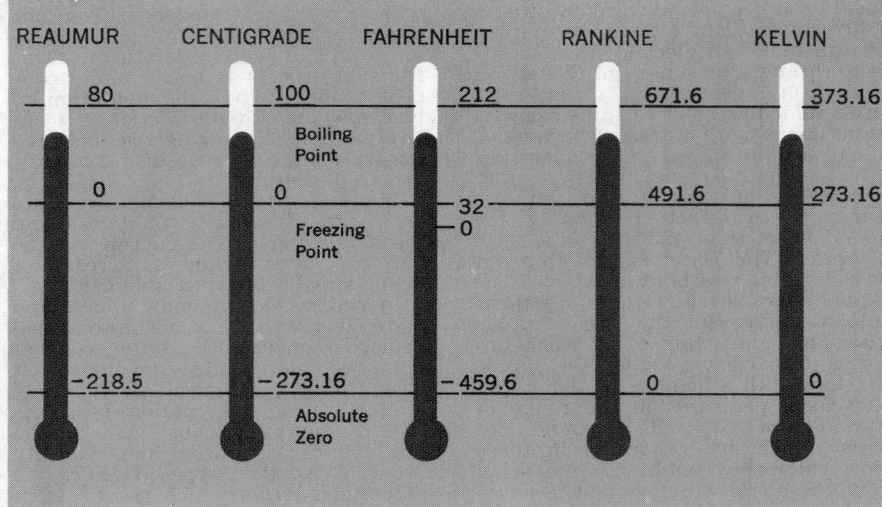

Reference State Temperatures

able calibration allows the resistance measurement to be converted to a temperature reading. This technique is useful for very accurate measurements in laboratory experiments.

At very high temperatures, an *optical pyrometer* is often used for temperature measurements. This instrument uses as a basis for comparison with a standard reference the "glow," or the visible light, that is emitted by a body at sufficiently high temperatures. There are literally hundreds of methods today to measure temperature, all of which measure the outward changes in some physical, optical, magnetic, or other property of a body as the molecular energy changes.

■ **UNITS OF ENERGY.**—The energy required to raise the temperature of one gram of water by one degree Centigrade is defined as *one calorie* of energy. If the units are one pound of water and one degree Fahrenheit, then the unit is *one British thermal unit* (Btu). One Btu is the equivalent of 252 calories. Calories are used by most scientists and by the general public in those countries employing the metric system. British thermal units are used by engineers in many English-speaking countries, including the United States. Other units of energy are used when desired (such as kilowatt-hour, joule, electron-volt, erg), but they are all proportional to the calorie or Btu.

■ **HEAT CAPACITY.**—The *heat capacity* of a substance is the change in energy necessary for a one-degree rise in its temperature. Values of heat capacities are needed whenever one desires to determine how much heat transfer is necessary to heat or cool a substance through a given temperature interval. Simply stated, the heat transfer requirement per unit of mass is the product of the heat capacity times the temperature change.

A calorie and a Btu were so defined that the heat capacity for water was approximately 1 in the units of calories/gram (C.) or Btu/lb. (F.). Heat capacities for other materials may be greatly different from that of water but are usually smaller. The term *specific heat* is the ratio of the heat capacity of a material to that of water. Since heat capacity is near unity, the two terms are often confused and used interchangeably. However, these terms are not synonymous, inasmuch as specific heats have no units and are simply numbers.

Heat capacities are related to the ability of a body to store energy from the transfer of heat. The more possible ways in which molecules can store this energy, the larger the heat capacity. For example, consider helium. The molecular energies of helium are related to how rapidly the molecules are moving—their velocity. If heat is transferred to helium, then the molecules move faster; this is the only way heat energy may be stored. The average molecular kinetic energy can be shown to be proportional to the absolute temperature (°K. or °R.); thus, if we double the average molecular energy, we double the absolute temperature.

As the heat capacity is the ratio of the energy increase to the temperature increase, it is a constant for helium, independent of temperature. The value is about 0.75 calories/gm for helium heated in a constant volume container. Instead of expressing heat capacities for a gram of matter, the unit of mole is used. A *mole* of any material is the mass that is equal to its molecular weight; since the molecular weight of helium is 4, one mole of helium has a mass of

4 grams. Each mole of any substance has the same number of molecules, so that when the heat capacity is given per mole, the number is simply related to that which would be given on a molecular basis. For helium, then, the heat capacity is about 3 calories/mole; therefore, if the temperature of 4 grams of helium in a closed container were raised one degree Centigrade, then the energy change of the helium would be 3 calories.

Consider next a more complicated molecule, such as ammonia gas, NH_3. There are four atoms in each molecule, the hydrogen atoms being chemically bonded to the nitrogen. Ammonia molecules can move, as could the helium, with various velocities. In this case, however, there are other ways in which energy may be stored. The molecule may rotate as a solid (as the earth does), or the bonds between the hydrogen and nitrogen may vibrate with increasing amplitude, as though the atoms were connected with springs. Each of these possibilities allows energy to be stored. Temperature, however, is still associated with the velocity of the molecule as a whole. Inasmuch as the rotational and vibrational energies increase with increasing temperature, any energy that is supplied to the system must be shared between these two forms of energy and the kinetic energy associated with translational molecular velocities. Consequently, for a given input of energy, less energy is available to increase the velocities of the ammonia molecules than was the case with helium. The result is a smaller temperature rise for ammonia than for helium. The heat capacity of ammonia per mole is thus considerably greater than that of helium. At room temperature the value is about 8.9 calories/mole. Although the true situation is somewhat more complicated, because some of the ways energy may be stored are not activated except at high temperatures, the essence of the above statements is correct.

Molecules in liquids and solids can store energy in various ways, and liquids and solids have much higher heat capacities than helium when expressed on the basis of a mole. No general rules may be given for liquids, but it can be shown that the heat capacities of all crystalline solid elements are approximately 6.2 ± 0.4 calories/mole. Thus iron, with a molecular weight of 56, has a heat capacity of $6.2 \times 1/56$ calories/gram.

■ **PHASE CHANGES.**—In most cases, materials expand when heated. For this expansion to occur, the molecules constituting the material must move farther apart. Just as work is required to stretch a spring, so in separating molecules there must be work done against the forces with which they attract one another. If one stretches a spring too far, the spring may lose its ability to return to its original position; in fact, the spring may break. Similarly, if the molecules in our analogy are moved far enough apart, a point will be reached at which the influence of

the attractive forces is almost completely overcome, and the molecules will no longer be constrained. In this condition the molecules can move about freely at random and completely fill the volume available.

The random kinetic energies corresponding to the high temperature are much greater than the potential energy of attraction between the molecules, and the material is a gas. Conversely, as a gas is cooled, the random kinetic energies of molecules decrease. Consequently, when a gas

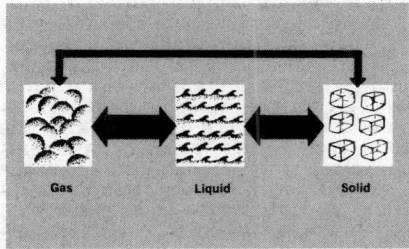

PHASE CHANGES as they occur among the three states of matter.

is cooling, a point is reached at which the attractive forces predominate and the gas collapses, with the molecules losing much of their potential energy of separation. This process, when the substance changes from a gas to a liquid, is called *liquefaction*.

In passing from a gas to a liquid, a substance releases energy. (When a stretched spring is released, it also releases energy.) The energy changes accompanying phase changes are known as *latent heat effects* and are quite large. For example, it was seen that the heat capacity of water is approximately 1 Btu/lb. The latent heat associated with the condensation of one pound of water is almost 1,000 Btu/lb. Clearly, a drastic change on the molecular level has occurred.

To extend this picture, if the liquid is further cooled, a temperature will be reached at which the attractive forces so dominate that another phase change occurs, this time one of *solidification*. The molecules are now almost completely prevented from movement because they have been locked in a semirigid structure. This change from a liquid to a solid is accompanied by another energy change, called the *latent heat of fusion*. Heats of fusion are usually much less than heats of vaporization; for instance, for water 133.5 Btu of energy must be removed to freeze one pound of water.

To complete the picture, if the original pressure had been sufficiently low, the cooling process would have resulted in a phase change directly from the gas to a solid. The energy change associated with this process is termed the *heat of sublimation*. The heat of sublimation is approximately equal to the sum of the heats of fusion and vaporization. Carbon dioxide, at one atmosphere of pressure, cannot exist as a liquid; and as the gas is cooled, solid carbon dioxide ("dry ice") is formed.

When certain liquids are rapidly cooled, solidification does not occur at a definite temperature, as occurs on slow cooling; that is, there is no assignable freezing-point temperature. Instead, the ability of the liquid to flow freely decreases steadily until a glassy substance is obtained. This glassy state is characterized by the absence of a regular crystalline structure and by *optical isotropy* (optical transparency) when not in a state of strain. On long standing, especially at high temperatures, glasses may undergo crystallization. This state in which certain substances can exist may be viewed as a condition lying between the liquid and solid states.

Vapor pressures of liquids represent a dynamic state of equilibrium with a continual interchange of molecules between the gaseous and the condensed phase. The higher the temperature, the higher the average kinetic energy of the liquid molecules and the more molecules that can break away from the strong attractive forces existing in the liquid. The vapor pressure thus increases with temperature, and vice versa. Thus, by increasing the pressure above a liquid, one increases the temperature at which a liquid will boil. The modern housewife takes advantage of this fact by using a pressure cooker that permits her to cook foods faster than ordinary pots and pans would permit.

■**CRITICAL TEMPERATURE.**—There is a limiting temperature, called the *critical temperature,* at which the kinetic energy of the liquid molecules exceeds the attractive forces, and no liquid phase can exist regardless of the pressure. At the critical point, the molecular energies of the liquid and gas are equal and the latent heat effects are zero.

It is obvious that in any operation in which a fluid is used to transfer energy, the amount of such fluid required is greatly decreased if a phase change can be utilized. This principle is used in most steam power plants and refrigeration cycles.

Heat Transfer Mechanisms.

Before a discussion of some practical uses of heat transfer can be opened, it is imperative to understand something about the underlying mechanism of heat transfer. Heat transfer will take place when two bodies of unequal temperature are brought together, the hot one becoming colder and the cold one hotter. This result is actually a statement of the *second law of thermodynamics.* However, even though no mention has been made of the rates of heat transfer that result, the size of all heat exchange equipment is based almost entirely on these rates. There are three general mechanisms through which heat transfer may take place.

■**CONDUCTION.**—The temperature of a solid is related to the amplitude of vibration of the molecules around some equilibrium position in the solid lattice. When two solid bodies of unequal temperature are placed in contact, some of the excess vibrational energy of the surface molecules of the hot body is communicated to the surface molecules of the cold body by collisions of the molecules at the points of contact. As a result of this exchange of energy, the surface molecules of the cold body acquire a higher average energy level (higher temperature) than those molecules in the underlying layers. Similarly, the surface molecules of the hot body are now at a lower temperature than those in the underlying solid. This energy exchange process is now repeated between the surface molecules and those just below the surface in both solids as well as between the original interacting surface molecules.

In this manner the heat transfer process is propagated through both solids until the transfer of vibrational energy occurs in both. After some time a condition is achieved in which the temperature of each body varies from point to point within the body and is a steadily increasing or decreasing function of the distance from the point of contact. Later, the energy transfer process is damped out and both bodies achieve a common temperature (approximately equal molecular energies), with no net heat transfer taking place. This type of energy transfer is termed *heat conduction;* no gross movement of any part of the materials occurs.

The rate of heat transfer by conduction has been found to be proportional to the area of contact and *temperature gradient,* the rate of change of temperature with distance. The constant of proportionality is called the *thermal conductivity.* The larger the thermal conductivity, the higher the heat conduction rate. Copper, for example, has a very high conductivity, whereas paper has a very low one. Thus, a piece of copper feels much colder to the touch than paper at the same temperature, since heat can be conducted through copper at a much higher rate than through paper. The rate of heat loss from one's body is greater in the case of copper, and thus copper will feel colder. It is obvious, then, why handles of cooking utensils are made of a material of low thermal conductivity, such as plastic or wood, while the pan bottoms are made of a metal with a high conductivity. Cold metal objects can actually freeze the moisture on a hand so rapidly that the hand will stick to them; nonmetallic objects, which have a low thermal conductivity, do not conduct body heat away at a sufficiently rapid rate to result in the freezing of the surface moisture.

Conduction processes may occur in liquids and gases by an identical mechanism; however, for these "fluids," it is difficult to prevent motion of parts of the material, a process that leads to the second form of heat transfer.

■**CONVECTION.**—Instead of contacting two solids as in the case of conduction, suppose a cold liquid is placed over a warm solid. The solid is cooled by the conduction process, which begins in the liquid phase. However, since liquids expand upon heating, the warmer liquid at the solid interface becomes buoyant and tries to rise over the colder, dense layers of liquid covering it. The liquid-solid surface is renewed with more cold liquid, and the process is repeated. This large-scale mixing of the heated fragments of liquid with the cooler bulk prevents any large temperature gradients from becoming established, and conduction processes (which depend upon such gradients) are small. Heat is transferred by actual movement of warm fluid being carried into and mixing with colder portions. The rate of heat transfer seems to be proportional to the temperature difference between the solid-liquid interface and the bulk liquid, and depends markedly on the degree of agitation near the surface. The convection process described above depends entirely upon the buoyant force of gravity to accomplish the mixing. Such a process is called *natural convection.*

If one were to accentuate the mixing by stirring, shaking, or flowing the liquid across the hot surface, then a similar result would be achieved; this process is called *forced convection.* Forced convection transfer is usually more rapid than natural convection, especially if the fluid has a high *viscosity* (is very syrupy). A thick pudding heated on a stove must be stirred to prevent burning, as natural convection and conduction rates are too low to cause sufficient heat to be transferred from the hot burner to the fluid.

To prevent convection, one inhibits the flow of fluid by packing material of low conductivity somewhat tightly on the interface. For example, for home insulation, wads of a low conductivity material such as fiber glass are tacked to the outer walls. The spacing of the fiber glass filaments prevents easy flow of convection air currents near the outer walls and thus decreases the heat loss due to convection.

■**RADIATION.**—Whereas convection and conduction heat transfer processes depend on molecules contacting molecules, radiation does not. Molecules by their very vibration can emit electromagnetic waves that, when absorbed by other materials, result in an energy transfer mechanism that is termed *radiation.* In a vacuum, radiation is the most efficient means of heat transfer. Materials must be at a rather high temperature before much emission of energy occurs; in fact, the intensity of the radiation (I) is proportional to the fourth power of the absolute temperature $(I \propto T^4)$. In general, then, radiation is important only at very high temperatures, or in those cases where heat is transferred between surfaces separated by a vacuum.

Electric heaters transfer heat primarily by radiation from the glowing coils, although some natural convection occurs simultaneously. All the sun's energy is transferred by radiation through the intervening vacuum of space. When radiation strikes a body, the radiation may be reflected, absorbed, or transmitted, depending upon the frequency of the radiation and the properties of the body's surface. Bright metallic surfaces, such as polished aluminum, are considered good reflectors. Black, rough surfaces are usually good absorbers. Glass may or may not be a good absorber or transmitter. The greenhouse effect results from the fact that the glass roof of a greenhouse transmits most of the radiation from the sun. However, this radiation is absorbed by the plants and re-emitted at a different frequency, which is not transmitted by the glass. Thus winter sunlight can be used rather efficiently to heat a greenhouse.

Applications of Heat Transfer.—Having developed the concept of heat as energy flowing from one system to another by virtue of a temperature difference, let us examine how man has managed to utilize this concept of energy transfer in his everyday life. Although such appliances as stoves, refrigerators, and furnaces come immediately to mind as examples of devices that utilize heat transfer processes, electric appliances are also the indirect result of man's ability to convert heat energy to work. Most of the electricity used in the United States is obtained from installations powered by heat engines. Since these devices play such a major role in our industrial society, it is important that we understand the principles by which they operate.

■**HEAT ENGINES.**—A *heat engine* is a machine that absorbs heat at a high temperature, uses some of the energy to perform work, and ejects a portion of this energy as heat at a lower temperature. Although the modern steam turbines used to generate electricity and the rocket engines used to place man in orbit are radically different in outward appearance from the early steam engines of Thomas Savery, Thomas Newcomen, and James Watt, all of these devices operate on the same basic principles. In order to understand these prin-

ciples, it is instructive to consider in some detail a very simple heat engine, as, for instance, a heat engine operating on a steam cycle.

The *steam power cycle* has continued in basically the same form from the days of Watt to the present. This cycle supplies the world with more power than any other man-made energy device.

The four basic components of a typical steam engine are shown in the figure below.

This basic arrangement is called a *Rankine cycle*. One of the simplest possible means by which thermal energy is converted into mechanical energy by means of this cycle is described below:

Starting at point (1), liquid at a temperature below its boiling point is injected at a high pressure into a boiler and heated by a combustion process or atomic reactor until it is vaporized. The high-temperature, high-pressure steam is piped out of the boiler into a prime mover (2), where it does work by being allowed to expand to a lower pressure against a piston or turbine wheel. The low-pressure exit steam is then condensed in a heat exchanger (3). The liquid water leaving the condenser is pumped (4) back to the boiler, and the cycle is repeated.

Since each pound of water has been returned to its original state, it undergoes no net energy change ($\Delta E = 0$), and the net result of the cycle may be stated as follows:

The system takes in heat (Q_1) at a high temperature in the boiler; some of this energy leaves the system as work (W) in the prime mover, and the remainder leaves the system as heat (Q_2) in the condenser. Thus this heat engine operates as shown in the below right figure, thus

$$0 = Q_1 - Q_2 - W.$$

Although this description has great-

ly oversimplified the actual situation as far as modern engines are concerned, it contains the elementary features used as a basis for the modern designs.

Steam cycles are often used for the production of electricity, but the *internal-combustion engine* is the type of heat engine that finds widespread application in the transportation industry. Automobiles, trucks, airplanes, and ships are powered by these engines.

In internal-combustion engines, the heat input is supplied by combustion of the working fluid itself—an air-gasoline mixture in the case of the automobile engine. The high-pressure, high-temperature mixture generated by the combustion processes does work by expanding against a piston or turbine. The residual high-temperature gases are then exhausted to the atmosphere. The internal-combustion engine thus operates on the same fundamental principle as the steam turbine. The corresponding portions of each cycle are as follows:

The *efficiency* (ζ) of a heat engine is the ratio of the mechanical work output (W) of the engine to the quantity of heat absorbed at the high temperature (Q_1). Thus:

$$\zeta = \frac{W}{Q_1}.$$

In general, heat engines are quite inefficient devices. A typical efficiency for a modern steam turbine power plant used in generating electricity is 35 per cent. Some of this inefficiency is due to irreversible losses of energy in the engine through friction of one type or another. The major reason for the low efficiencies of these devices, however, is the fact that the engine receives a quantity of heat at one temperature and ejects a smaller quantity at a lower temperature. By virtue of their nature, heat engines cannot be 100 per cent effi-

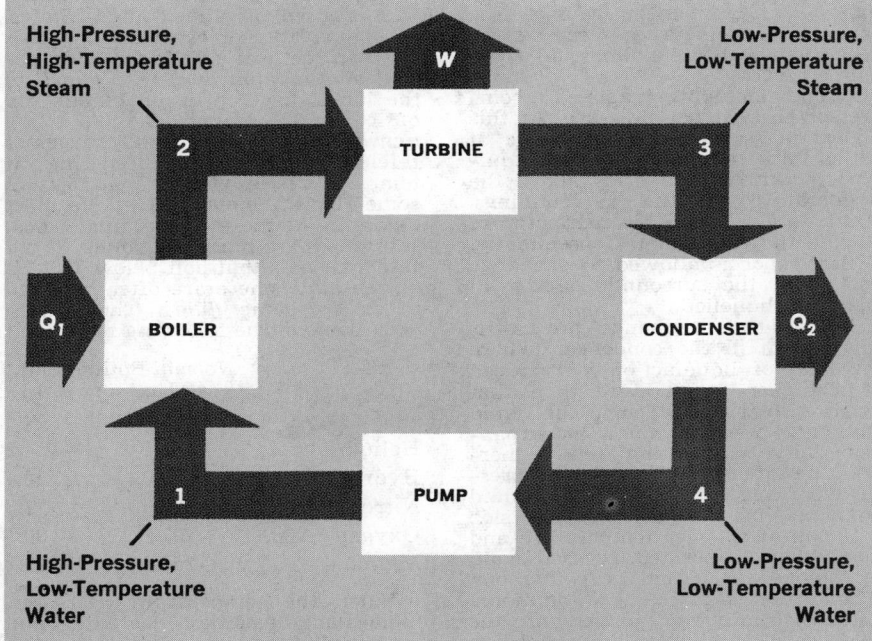

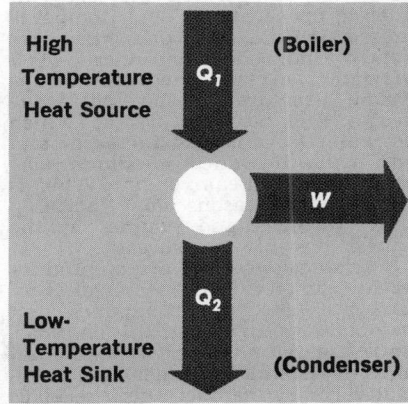

RANKINE CYCLE for the transfer of heat in a steam turbine is shown diagrammatically (*left*). The schematic diagram (*above*) shows that the heat input to the system, Q_1, which is added by combustion or atomic reactor at the boiler, is equal to the sum of the work performed by the turbine, W, and the heat removed from the system during the condensation of steam to water, Q_2.

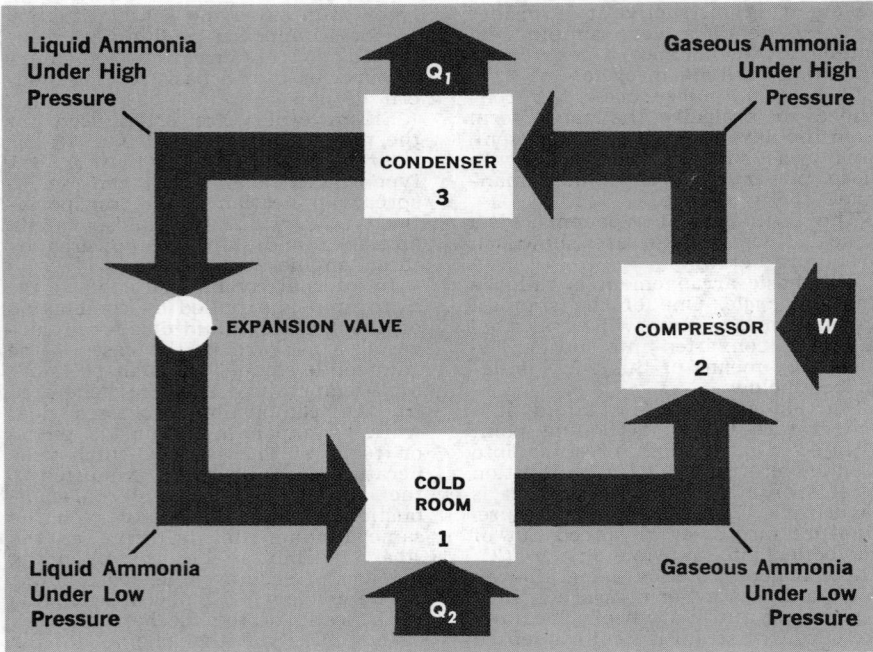

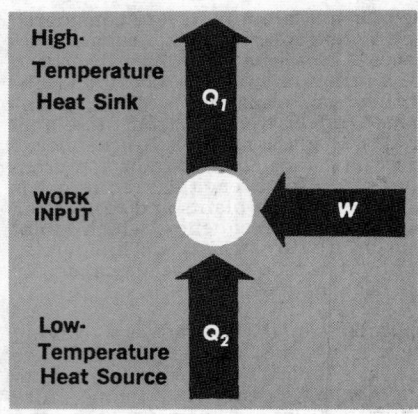

HEAT-TRANSFER CYCLE for an ammonia refrigeration unit (*left*). The schematic diagram (*above*) shows that the heat input, Q_2, which is abstracted by the liquid ammonia from the cold room during the vaporization process, plus the work input of the compressor, W, are equal to the heat liberated to the surroundings by the condensation of the gaseous ammonia, Q_1.

cient. There is a theoretical maximum efficiency at which these machines may operate. This theoretical maximum efficiency is uniquely determined by the temperatures at which the heat engine receives and ejects heat. For the steam cycle discussed earlier, this theoretical efficiency is given by:

$$\zeta \; theory = \frac{T_{boiler} - T_{condenser}}{T_{boiler}}$$

where the temperatures of the boiler and condenser are measured in degrees absolute (Kelvin or Rankine). From this relationship it is easily seen that the theoretical efficiency increases as the temperature at which the boiler is operated increases. In order to operate a boiler at temperatures above 212° F., boiler pressures greater than one atmosphere (14.7 psi) must be maintained. As the operating pressure of the boiler increases, the temperature at which the water is vaporized increases and with it the theoretical maximum efficiency of the steam engine. This is one of the reasons for operating steam turbines and engines at the highest possible pressures.

Refrigeration is the act of producing low temperatures. Most refrigerators are merely heat engines that are operated in reverse. In this sense, the refrigerator is a heat pump that takes in an amount of heat (Q_2) at a relatively low temperature, receives work from an external source, and ejects an amount of heat (Q_1) at a higher temperature. The relationship of this device to a heat engine is apparent from the figure above.

When a drop of ether, acetone, or other highly volatile substance is placed on one's skin, the skin in the immediate vicinity of the drop is cooled as the drop evaporates. The latent heat of vaporization is taken from the skin, causing a decrease in skin temperature in the vicinity of the drop. In the same manner, liquids with low boiling points can be used on a much larger scale to cool large rooms or closed boxes, such as the common household refrigerator. The most common working fluids used in modern refrigeration are ammonia, sulfur dioxide, and various *freons* (halogenated hydrocarbons). Heat from the area being refrigerated is transferred to the working fluid, and this energy is carried away by the vaporized liquid.

A simplified ammonia refrigeration cycle is shown above. The cycle shown is used to cool a room.

1. Cold liquid ammonia is vaporized by abstraction of heat from the room. With good heat transfer, the vaporized ammonia gas leaving the cold room is heated almost to room temperature.

2. The ammonia vapor is compressed to a higher pressure. At this higher pressure, the temperature at which liquid ammonia exists in equilibrium with its vapor is above the temperature of the surroundings, some easily attainable temperature outside the cold room. Consequently, if this vapor is allowed to exchange heat with the surroundings, it will again be liquefied.

3. This heat exchange process is carried out in the condenser, where the heat of liquefaction is removed at a higher temperature than that existing in the cold room. The liquid ammonia passes through an expansion valve separating the higher-pressure area from the lower-pressure portions of the system. Liquid ammonia in the low-pressure side will boil at a lower temperature and may, when evaporated, be used again to remove heat from the cold room.

In actual practice, the ammonia itself is usually not pumped into the cold room, but instead is pumped to a heat exchanger, where it is vaporized by contact with a cold brine solution that is continuously circulated between the cold room and the heat exchanger. The brine thus serves as a heat exchange medium for the liquid ammonia and the cold room.

The performance of refrigerating equipment is measured in terms of the ratio of the heat removed at the lower temperature to the work required to effect this removal. This ratio is termed the *coefficient of performance* (*COP*). Thus:

$$COP = \frac{Q_2}{W}.$$

In order to specify the capacity of a refrigeration unit, the standard ton is used in the United States. This quantity corresponds to a rate of heat removal of 288,000 Btu per day and is approximately equal to the latent heat of fusion of one ton of ice at 32° F.

■CRYOGENICS. — The term *cryogenics* refers to phenomena occurring at temperatures less than about 150° K., some 125° C. below the freezing point of water. At these temperatures most substances are liquids or solids. Those few materials that boil below 150° K. at one atmosphere are often referred to as *cryogenic fluids*. These comprise some of the following materials:

Fluid	Normal Boiling Point (at 1 atmosphere)	
	(°F.)	(°K.)
Helium	−452.1	4.2
Hydrogen	−423.0	20.4
Nitrogen	−320.5	77.3
Oxygen	−297.3	90.1
Methane	−258.6	111.7

When the temperature decreases, molecular velocities decrease, and liquefaction and/or solidification occur. At a temperature of absolute zero, molecular motion has essentially ceased. Now it is apparent, from observations of slow-motion movies, that one may study a particular process or event in more detail and thus gain more information from that event if one is able somehow to slow down the rate at which this event is occurring. Thus, by carrying out experiments at very low temperatures, scientists are able to gain information about the nature of the particular molecular species under investigation that would not otherwise be obtainable. Several unusual changes in the thermodynamic and electric properties of various materials also occur at these temperatures owing to the decrease in molecular motion. For example, the electrical resistance of some metals becomes zero below a certain temperature, a phenomenon known as *superconductivity*.

Because of the difficulties associated with the production and handling of cryogenic fluids, most of their early applications were in the area of basic research. However, as these difficulties have been surmounted by the development of modern techniques, cryogenic fluids have found increasing use in other areas.

The fields of practical application range from medicine to space research to transportation. Cryogenic fluids are used to obtain low temperatures in space-simulation chambers where components and instruments for space vehicles undergo testing. Liquid oxygen is often used as oxidizer in rocket propellant systems.

While man's conquest of space at present involves the most publicized application of cryogenics, some of the most promising applications for the future lie in the field of medicine. Medical researchers have in recent years successfully used cryogenic fluids in the treatment of stomach ulcers and Parkinson's disease. In the treatment of the latter, liquid nitrogen (77° K.) is used to destroy, by freezing, an area of the brain that is responsible for the shaking palsy characteristic of the disease. Cryogenic fluids have also been used in the preservation and storage of blood and various body organs.

In addition to the somewhat esoteric uses described above, cryogenic techniques are now being used in several basic industries. Liquid oxygen is often used in modern blast furnaces for the manufacture of steel. Liquid methane tankers have been developed to decrease long-distance transportation costs of this product. The quick freezing of foods is still another area in which cryogenic fluids are used today. As the techniques for handling these fluids are improved and as more people become aware of their commercial potential, these fluids will undoubtedly play an increasing role in our industrial society.

—Robert C. Reid and Charles Hill

LIGHT

Light in general may be simply defined as the form of radiant energy that produces visual sense impressions by stimulating the retina of the eye. Ultraviolet and infrared light are physically the same as visible light but cannot be seen by the human eye. *Ultraviolet light* is sometimes called black light; *infrared light* is often called heat radiation. The latter, however, is a misnomer.

Light is dualistic in nature; its properties must be explained by two separate and distinct theories—the wave theory and the quantum theory. These two theories are alike in only one respect; in both light has an *associated frequency*.

■**WAVE THEORY.**—The *wave theory* considers light as both electric and magnetic in character—and as transmitted through space as an *electromagnetic transverse wave*. This transverse wave motion may be compared to the motion of water molecules in a pond stirred by a stone thrown into it. The stone, striking the water, causes a series of ever-widening circles to ripple outward from the center of movement. Each circle consists of water molecules oscillating up and down, at right angles (transverse) to the direction of the wave's movement. These waves form a series of ridges (*crests*) and depressions (*troughs*). The distance between any two wave crests is the *wavelength;* and the *frequency* is the number of wavelengths passing a given point in a second. In a luminous body such as an incandescent bulb, the light waves travel out spherically (three-dimensionally) from the bulb, whereas the water waves travel out in circles (two-dimensionally) from the source of disturbance. However, an electromagnetic wave is transverse, like a water wave, and can be depicted as follows:

A represents the *amplitude* of the transverse wave (in the case of the electromagnetic wave, the maximum electric or magnetic intensity). The *period* (T) is the time it takes the wave to travel one wavelength (λ), or $\lambda = VT$. This can be written $V = \dfrac{\lambda}{T}$. Since the *frequency* (number of waves passing a point in one second) is equal to $\dfrac{1}{T}$, V (velocity) can be equated to frequency (f) times wavelength (λ).

Electromagnetic waves are classified by wavelength in the *electromagnetic spectrum*, which is divided into various regions. These regions, from long wavelengths to short, are radio waves, Hertzian waves or microwaves, infrared, visible light, ultraviolet rays, X rays, and gamma rays. In the visible-light region, the waves are classified by the colors that the human eye senses on receiving certain wavelengths—this region is called the *visible spectrum*. The wavelength is usually given in millimicrons (abbreviated $M\mu$). One millimicron is equal to 10^{-7} (.0000001) centimeters. Wavelengths, especially in the visible region, are also denoted in angstrom units. One *angstrom unit* (1 Å) is equal to 10^{-8} centimeters, or $1 M\mu = 10$ angstrom units. The visible region extends only from 760 $M\mu$ (7,600 Å)—the red region—to 380 $M\mu$ (3,800 Å)—the blue region. It is obvious, therefore, that the eye responds to a rather small portion of the over-all spectrum.

■**QUANTUM THEORY.**—The *quantum theory* explains effects that the electromagnetic theory cannot. It regards

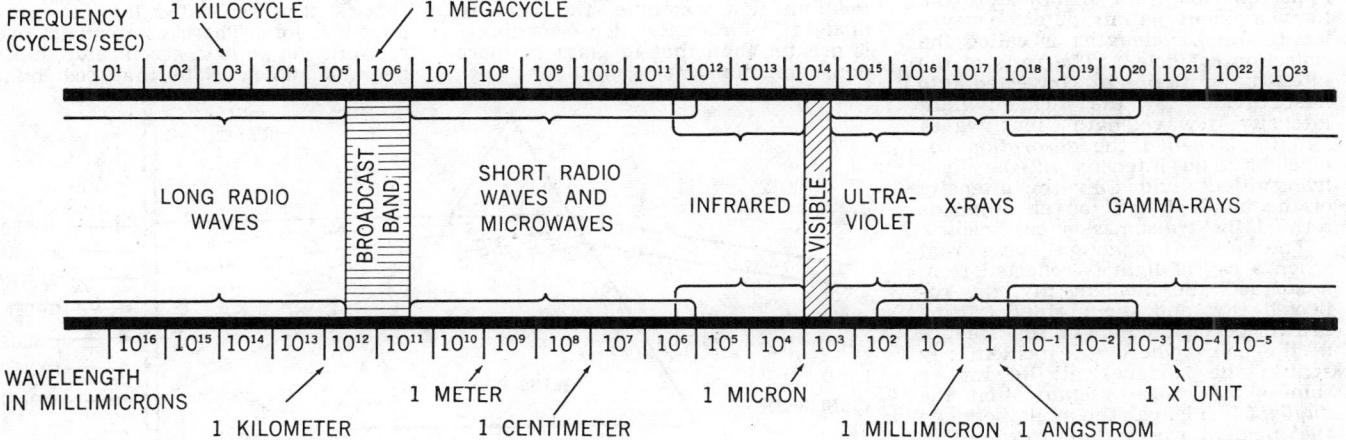

ELECTROMAGNETIC SPECTRUM categorizes the varied forms of electromagnetic radiation in terms of their frequencies and wavelengths.

electromagnetic energy as traveling in small packets. A single packet is called a *quantum* or *photon*. The energy in a quantum is given by the expression $e = hf$, where e is the energy in the photon, h is a constant (called *Planck's constant*), and f is the frequency. The existence of these discrete photons has been shown by the work of Niels Bohr (1885–1962), Albert Einstein (1879–1955), and Max Planck (1858–1947).

Velocity of Light.—Light travels at a *velocity* of approximately 186,283 miles per second in a vacuum and at practically the same speed in the atmosphere. The velocity, however, is less in all other transparent media. For example, in water the velocity is approximately 140,000 miles per second. The distance light travels in one second is roughly equivalent to seven times around the earth at the equator. The American physicist Albert A. Michelson (1852–1931) made the first precise measurement of the speed of light by using a mechanical device. Today, the speed of light in a vacuum is listed as 299,792,500 meters per second.

Reflection and Transmission.—When light strikes a material, it may be reflected, absorbed, or transmitted. An object appears blue because it reflects blue light and absorbs the other wavelengths. Objects appear red through a piece of red glass because the glass transmits red light and absorbs all other colors. A black object is black because it absorbs almost all the light that falls on it and reflects only a very small percentage. When light energy is absorbed by an object, it is imparted to the molecules of the object and consequently increases its temperature.

A substance therefore has a reflection coefficient, an absorption coefficient, and a transmission coefficient. These coefficients vary according to the wavelength of the incident light. For example, there are filters that transmit light in the visible spectrum and absorb light outside the visible spectrum. Such filters have a high transmission coefficient in the visible region, but a coefficient of practically zero elsewhere in the spectrum.

The ratio of the intensity of the light reflected from an object to the light incident on an object (wavelength for wavelength) is called the *reflection coefficient*. The ratio of the intensity of the light converted into heat divided by the incident light intensity (wavelength for wavelength) is called the *absorption coefficient*. The intensity of the light transmitted divided by the intensity of the incident light on an object is termed the *transmission coefficient*.

The *law of reflection* states that when a ray of light is reflected from a surface, the incident ray, the reflected ray, and the normal (a line drawn perpendicular to the surface at the point where the incident ray strikes the surface) all lie in the same plane. It also states that the *angle of incidence* (the angle between the incident ray and the normal) is equal to the *angle of reflection* (the

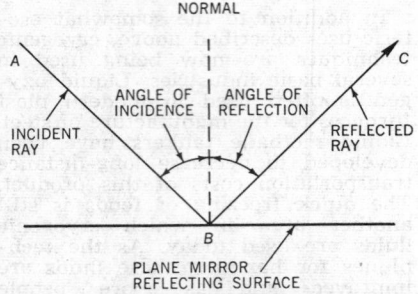

REFLECTION AND REFRACTION are changes in the path of an incident light ray. The angle of incidence equals the angle of reflection, but not the angle of refraction.

angle between the reflected ray and the normal). In geometrical optics, light rays are thought of as traveling in a straight line and as originating at the object.

When a ray of light from an object strikes a plane mirror, it is unchanged; it merely travels in a new direction. Therefore, when looking at a plane mirror, the eye sees an image that is identical to the object and that appears to be the same distance behind the mirror as the object is in front of it. A line joining the object and the image would be perpendicular to the mirror. In addition, the image is *virtual;* that is, the rays appear to be coming directly from the object, although they actually are not.

Of course, reflecting surfaces do not necessarily have to be plane mirrors. There are convex and concave spherical reflectors, convex and concave parabolic reflectors, convex and concave elliptical reflectors, and many others. Reflection takes place on these curved surfaces according to laws identical to those for plane surfaces, the normal now being the normal to the tangent plane of the surface at the point of reflection.

Refraction and Dispersion.—When light passes from a less dense medium into a denser medium, its path is altered. This change in the direction of a ray of light is called *refraction*. The velocity of light varies in different media; it is greater in a less dense medium than in a more dense medium. For example, the velocity of light in air (a less dense medium) is greater than that in glass (a more dense medium).

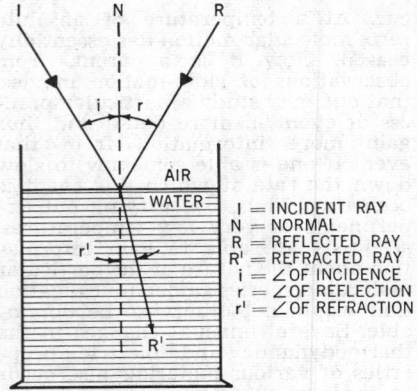

I = INCIDENT RAY
N = NORMAL
R = REFLECTED RAY
R' = REFRACTED RAY
i = ∠ OF INCIDENCE
r = ∠ OF REFLECTION
r' = ∠ OF REFRACTION

Every material that transmits light has an *index of refraction,* which is defined as the velocity of light in a vacuum for a particular wavelength, divided by the velocity of light at that wavelength in the material. This index of refraction is symbolized by n, so that mathematically,

$$n = \frac{\text{velocity of light in vacuum}}{\text{velocity of light in material}}$$

when the two velocities are for the same wavelength of light. The index of refraction depends, therefore, upon the kind of material and upon the wavelength.

The *law of refraction* is stated in two parts: When a ray of light passes from a less dense medium into a more dense medium, the ray is bent towards the normal (to the surface of the medium). Conversely, when the ray passes from a more dense medium into a less dense medium, it is bent away from the normal. Also, the incident ray, the normal, and the refracted ray all lie in the same plane. For any given wavelength, the index of refraction of the first medium multiplied by the sine of the angle of incidence is equal to the index of refraction of the second medium multiplied by the sine of the angle of refraction. This is known as *Snell's law.*

Since the index of refraction of a medium is different for different wavelengths of light, the component wavelengths that make up white light are bent by varying amounts when they pass through a prism. The light is then said to be *dispersed;* that is, it is separated into its component colors. These components are red, orange, yellow, green, blue, indigo, and violet. Note that red light

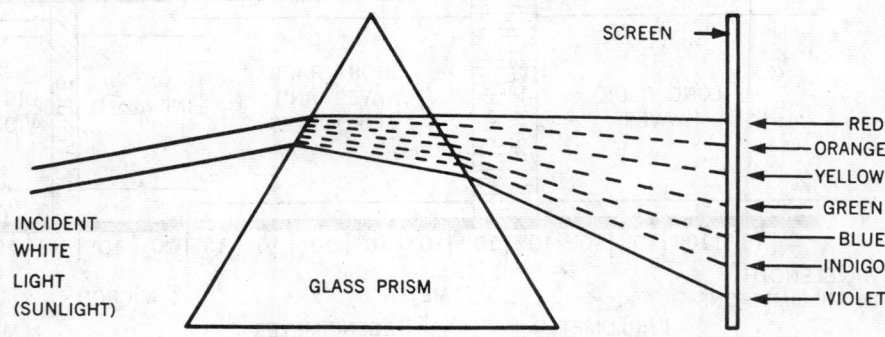

DISPERSION breaks multiwavelength white light into its component colors, or spectrum.

(with the longest wavelength) bends the least when passing through a prism, while violet light (with the shortest wavelength) bends the most.

Interference.—At any point where two or more light waves cross one another, they are said to *interfere*. This is not to be taken to mean that the waves impede one another, but refers to the combined effect at the point in question.

The accompanying illustration shows two transverse light waves emanating from the same source but having different path lengths. The top wave has traveled 1½ wavelengths while the bottom wave has traveled exactly one wavelength. If the amplitudes of the two waves are added, one will cancel the other and the resultant amplitude will be zero.

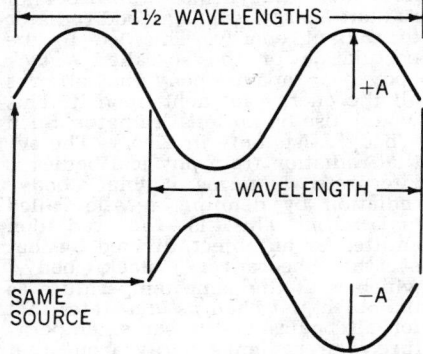

DESTRUCTIVE INTERFERENCE occurs when the crests and troughs of two light waves one-half wavelength apart cancel each other.

Physically speaking, the two waves have interfered; and complete *destructive interference* has taken place, because the two waves, added algebraically, are numerically equal but have opposite signs.

It is also possible to have *reinforcement* of the waves occur. This is not illustrated, but will occur when the path lengths differ by one wavelength or any multiple thereof.

The drawing shows the details of the experiment performed by an English physicist, Thomas Young, in 1804. The experiment was of great importance, for it verified the wave theory and the interference of light. Light from a monochromatic (single-wavelength) source illuminates slit s_1 and the light from this slit in turn illuminates slits s_2 and s_3. Since slits s_2 and s_3 are equidistant from s_1, it is as though s_2 and s_3 are identical sources but are displaced from one another by a distance d. The light from both s_2 and s_3 now falls on the screen. The light reaching P from both sources has traveled the same distance; therefore, at this point reinforcement will occur and a bright line will be observed. However, at a point such as E, the light from s_3 has traveled a distance greater than that from s_2 and interference will take place. If this path difference is one-half wavelength, *destructive interference* takes place; and a black line appears on the screen. The pat-

tern occurring on the screen thus consists of alternate light and dark lines called *interference fringes*.

The various colors observed when looking at a thin film of oil or a soap bubble are caused by interference effects at the surface of the medium. Since the light is reflected from the top and bottom surfaces of a film, interference takes place at the top surface and depends upon the wavelengths of the light, the index of refraction of the material, and the film thickness.

Diffraction.—If light travels in straight lines in a homogeneous material (a material whose composition is identical throughout), then one would expect that a beam of light passing through a slit would form an illuminated image of the slit. However, if the slit width is comparable to the wavelength of the light passing through the slit, a number of alternate light and dark areas will appear on the screen, similar to the light and dark areas produced by interference. The light is spread out in a *diffraction pattern*, consisting of a central bright band that may be much wider than the width of the slit, bordered by alternating dark and bright bands of decreasing intensity. In a sense, the light has bent around the corners of the slit. (This same diffraction effect takes place in the case of sound waves. Sound will travel around obstacles; but since sound waves are longer than light waves, the effect is greater.)

To increase the number of slits through which the beam of light must pass, a *diffraction grating* may be produced by ruling very narrow parallel slits on a piece of glass with a diamond point. When a beam of parallel rays of white light is incident on such a grating, the various wavelengths are spread out by the diffraction, producing a spectrum. This is similar to the color spectrum produced by a prism, except that in the case of diffraction the longest wavelength is bent the most. This is exactly opposite to the case of prism refraction, where red light is bent the least.

Gratings are produced with many thousands of lines per inch. The surface does not necessarily have to be transmitting; lines can also be ruled on reflecting surfaces, which become known as *reflection gratings*. Such ruled surfaces can be either plane or

concave. Many gratings of the latter type are used in spectographic systems. A grating system has less light loss and greater dispersion (colors are spread out more) than a prism.

Polarization.—Whereas interference and diffraction can occur with any sort of waves, polarization cannot. *Polarization* is a phenomenon that depends not only on the fact that light travels as a wave but also on the fact that light waves are transverse. Longitudinal waves, such as sound waves, cannot undergo polarization.

According to the wave theory, light is an electromagnetic transverse wave. Ordinary light consists of waves whose vibrations take place in all possible directions (*planes*) perpendicular to the direction of propagation. When light is polarized, all paths of vibration—except those in one direction—are eliminated. Therefore, in polarized light, the vibrations take place in only one plane perpendicular to the direction of propagation. Polarized light of this type, called *linearly polarized* or *plane-polarized* light, can be produced in a number of ways. For example, tourmaline, a transparent mineral containing aluminum, boron, silicon, and oxygen, possesses the property of transmitting vibrations in only one plane. Polaroid, a man-made material developed in 1934 and consisting of transparent sheets resembling cellophane, possesses the same property. Materials such as these are called *dichroic*.

Other crystalline materials, such as calcite and quartz, will split an ordinary light beam into two beams. These two beams will be plane-polarized light beams and the planes of polarization in the two beams will be at right angles to one another. Such crystalline materials are called *birefringent* or *double-refracting*.

Ordinary light can also be plane polarized by reflection. At a certain angle of incidence, vibrations in only one plane predominate in the reflected beam. The angle of incidence at which this occurs depends upon the index of refraction of the reflecting glass; the angle is called *Brewster's angle*. For ordinary glass this angle is approximately 57 degrees. Since light reflected from a road surface on a sunny day is partly polarized, polaroid glasses will decrease the glare.

If a source of light is observed

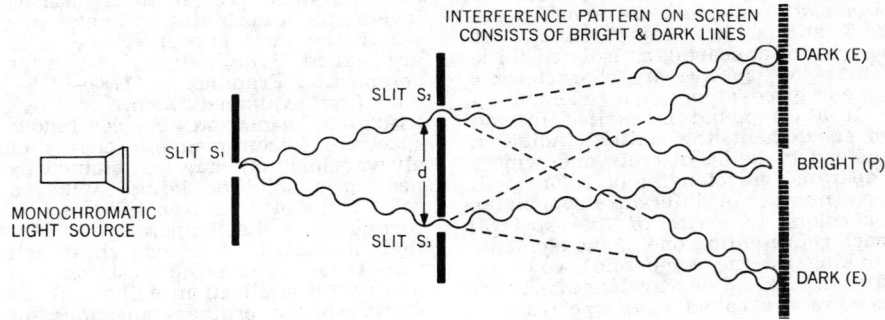

INTERFERENCE EXPERIMENT performed by the English physicist Thomas Young in 1804.

through a sheet of polaroid, the eye cannot detect polarization; and the source appears as it would to the naked eye. However, if the source of light is seen through two pieces of polaroid whose transmitting planes of vibration are perpendicular to one another, the light source is extinguished. For any other angle between the transmission planes of the two sheets of polaroid, some light from the source will reach the eye; and the amount of light will be maximum when the transmission planes are parallel to one another.

Much use is made of polarized light. In chemistry, for example, it is used to analyze sugar solutions because these solutions rotate the plane of polarization according to the concentration of sugar. Polarized light is also used in engineering. A transparent mechanical model may be constructed that, when placed between crossed polaroids and examined under stress, will show the points of greatest stress.

In addition to plane polarization, light can also be *circularly polarized* and *elliptically polarized*. In the former, the plane of the vibration rotates while the maximum amplitude of the wave remains the same as the wave progresses. In the latter, the plane of vibration rotates and the maximum amplitude of the wave varies as the wave progresses.

Luminescence and Incandescence.—
Light may be radiated by atoms and molecules if their electrons, excited by an increase in energy, suddenly lose that energy in the form of photons. When the energy is increased by heating, the resulting radiation is called *incandescence*. When the energy is increased by any means other than heating, the radiation of light is called *luminescence*.

When an electrical discharge travels through a gas at low pressure, or when a salt is volatized in a flame, light of a specific wavelength—called the *characteristic color*—is emitted. In the case of the electrical discharge passing through a vapor, familiar examples are the neon tube, the sodium vapor lamp, and the fluorescent lamp; the characteristic color of neon is reddish-orange; of sodium, yellow; and of the fluorescent lamp, bluish-white. If cadmium vapor were present in the tube, a red light would be emitted; and if other gaseous elements were present, colors characteristic of those elements would be emitted. The colors emitted when the atoms of an element are involved are few and widely separated in the spectrum, appearing as isolated lines. These *line spectra* are characteristic of energized atoms of an element.

If a compound is excited instead of an element, the emitted radiation, instead of being discrete and widely separated wavelengths or colors, will be a number of different wavelengths or colors (a series of line spectra, each representing one of the elements making up the compound) covering a span or band of wavelengths. These spectra are called *band spectra*.

If a solid or liquid is heated, all wavelengths of electromagnetic energy are produced. A spectrum of this type is called a *continuous spectrum*. (This phenomenon is described in THERMAL RADIATION.)

Luminescence occurs when the electrons in an atom are raised to a higher energy state by absorbing the energy in the photons of the light illuminating the material. The electrons, when raised to the higher energy states, are unstable and tend to return to their original state. When they do so, light of a frequency dependent upon the difference in energy states is emitted. Usually the light emitted is at a longer wavelength; that is, when materials luminesce, they usually absorb light of a shorter wavelength and emit light of a longer wavelength. For example, vegetation containing chlorophyll will emit orange light when illuminated by short-wavelength ultraviolet light.

Luminescence is categorized into *fluorescence* and *phosphorescence*. A fluorescent material emits light only while being illuminated and for a very short time afterward. A phosphorescent material emits light while being illuminated and may phosphoresce (continue to emit light) for hours and even weeks after the illumination is removed.

There are many ways to excite luminescence other than illuminating a material with light waves. A television screen is made to fluoresce by bombarding the front of the tube with electrons. This is called *cathode luminescence*. Luminescence can also be caused by the application of an electrical field to a material. This is called *electro-luminescence*. Luminescence may even be caused by chemical or physiological processes, as in the case of the firefly. It may even be spontaneous, as in the case of radium.

Elements emit their characteristic light waves when caused to luminesce. The science of *spectroscopy* is based on this fact. By determining the wavelengths emitted by a luminescing substance, it is possible to determine the elements of which the substance is composed.

Light will also be absorbed when it passes through a gaseous material; the wavelength absorbed will be the same wavelength that would be emitted if the gas luminesced. Before reaching the earth, sunlight must pass through the outer gaseous layers of the sun. When the spectrum of sunlight is studied, dark lines are observed in it, indicating that certain elements must exist in these gaseous layers to absorb the wavelengths where the lines appear. These lines are called *Fraunhofer lines,* after Joseph von Fraunhofer (1787–1826), who first explained them.

■**THERMAL RADIATION.**—A continuous spectrum (electromagnetic energy of all wavelengths) may be obtained by heating a solid or liquid. When a solid body such as iron is heated, it turns red; as the temperature is further increased, it turns white and then blue. Perhaps the most common and useful application of thermal radiation is the ordinary incandescent lamp. A tungsten filament is heated by an electrical current flowing through it; the filament then emits visible light. (The filament also emits light that is not in the visible region. If all the light were in the visible region, the luminous efficiency of the lamp would be greater.)

In the latter part of the eighteenth century, Pierre Prévost (1751–1839) investigated the radiation interchange from one body to another. He concluded that when radiant energy strikes a body, various portions of the energy are absorbed, transmitted, or reflected by that body. In 1792 he announced his *theory of interchanges,* which states that all bodies are continuously absorbing energy from surrounding bodies and in turn radiating energy to all surrounding bodies.

Gustav R. Kirchhoff (1824–1887) investigated absorption and radiation of energy by materials, and in 1859 he stated that a good absorber of radiant energy is also a good radiator of radiant energy. This led to the postulation of the so-called "black body"—an opaque body that absorbs all the energy incident upon it. This would also be an ideal radiator. Such a body exists only in theory. The actual radiation from physical bodies is interpreted in terms of "black body" radiation by defining a ratio called *emissivity*. This is the radiation emitted by an object, divided by that of the theoretical "black body," which is at the same temperature as the object. *Kirchhoff's law* states that for all bodies at the same temperature, the radiant energy from that body divided by the absorption of radiant energy of that body is a constant and equals the radiant energy of a "black body" at that temperature.

Units.—
The definition of light is based on our visual awareness of radiation in a very narrow band of the electromagnetic spectrum called the visible region. The eye is not equally sensitive to all visual light waves. The variation of sensitivity to each wavelength may be graphed as a *luminosity curve*. The luminosity curve for the average eye shows how the eye responds to equal amounts of energy at the various wavelengths within the visible region. Since the eye is more sensitive to wavelengths in the yellow region, yellows appear very bright as compared to the reds and blues. The most sensitive wavelength is at 555 millimicrons, and the curve is normalized by making the maximum ordinate at this point equal to one. Above and below, the maximum curve falls off sharply and drops to practically zero at 400 and 700 Mμ (the limits of the visible region).

Units based on the visual interpretation of radiant energy are called *photometric units* or *luminous units;* those based on the physical interpretation of radiation are called *radiometric units*. There would be no need for two sets of units if the eye responded equally to all the visible wavelengths; if this were the case, only the purely physical radiometric units would be needed.

The unit of luminous flux or power is called the *lumen;* that for radiant flux is the *watt*. The two are related by means of the luminosity curve.

At 555 Mμ, one watt equals 685 lumens; at any other visible wavelength one watt expressed in lumens will be less than 685 and will equal 685 times the luminosity curve ordinate at the particular wavelength. For example, at 600 Mμ the ordinate of the luminosity curve is 0.6; therefore, one watt of radiant energy of wavelength 600 Mμ is equal to 685 times 0.6, or 411 lumens.

The unit of luminous intensity is the *candle*. One candle equals one *lumen per steradian*. The *steradian* is the unit of solid angle and is so defined that the total number of steradians subtended at the center of a sphere is 4π. A point source of light having a uniform intensity of one candle in all directions therefore emits 4π lumens of luminous flux. This is true because the point source can be thought of as being at the center of an imaginary sphere and there are 4π steradians in the sphere. The analogous unit of radiant intensity is the *watt per steradian*.

The designation "candle" for luminous intensity came about because the first photometric standard for light intensity was a sperm-wax candle constructed in a specific way.

When light is incident on a surface, the surface is *illuminated;* and the unit of *illuminance* is the luminous flux per unit area. If the area is one square foot and the flux is one lumen, then there is one lumen per square foot; this is known as a *foot-candle*. The analogous radiant term is *irradiance*, and the unit is the watt per square foot.

A source of light does not necessarily have to be a point source; it can also be an extended source. For such sources, the larger area of the source is thought of as divided into smaller unit areas, each of which is pictured as emitting light. The total luminous flux emitted per unit area is termed the *luminous emittance* of the extended source, and the units become lumens per square foot, lumens per square meter, lumens per square centimeter, lumens per square inch, and so on. The corresponding radiant quantity is called *radiant emittance*, and the units are watts per square foot, watts per square meter, and so on.

The last unit of significance correspondingly associated with an extended light source is termed *brightness*, or *luminance*. This is the luminous intensity per unit area of the source (candles per square foot, candles per square meter, and such). Many surfaces appear equally bright no matter from which direction they are viewed; these obey *Lambert's law* and are called *perfectly diffuse emitters*. The sun is a good example, since the edge appears exactly as bright as the center. The analogous radiant quantity is *radiance,* radiant intensity per unit area of an extended surface.

The *inverse square law* states that the illuminance on a surface varies inversely as the square of the distance from a point source. For example, if the illuminance on a surface is one lumen per square foot when this surface is at a distance of one foot from a point source, the illuminance on the surface will be one-quarter lumen per square foot when the object is placed at a distance of two feet from the same source. The intensity of two point sources of light can be compared, or if one is known the other can be determined, by making use of this inverse square law. In essence, the sources are so placed that the illuminance on the screen is the same from either source. By measuring the distance of the screen from the sources, the relative intensities, or the unknown intensity, can be calculated. Instruments for making these measurements are called *photometers*.

Color.—The word *color* is commonly used in several different ways. It is used with reference to the sensation received in the brain when the retina of the eye is stimulated by light of a particular wavelength. It is used to describe a property of an object, for example, a "red" barn. Indeed, by definition, everything that is seen has a sensation of color associated with it. The only truly colorless things are those that are invisible, such as air.

■**ADDITIVE PROCESS.**—In passing through a prism, sunlight is dispersed and broken down into its constituent colors—the spectral colors red, orange, yellow, green, blue, indigo, and violet. Sunlight, which is essentially white light, is therefore an *additive color mixture* of all the spectral colors. If all these spectral colors are added in exactly the same amounts as they appear in the sunlight spectrum, sunlight or white light will be produced.

When colors are projected on a screen simultaneously by two or more projectors, different colors are obtained in regions where the colored images overlap. Similarly, if a disc made up of different-colored sectors is rotated rapidly in front of the eye, the eye will see a color different from that of either of the colored sectors. If half the disk is red and the other green, the disk will appear to be yellow. If a third of the disc is red, a third blue, and a third green, the disk will appear to be grayish white.

A color other than a pure spectral color can be reproduced by adding three spectral colors together in the correct luminous amounts. All colors cannot be produced by an additive mixture of the same three spectral colors, but it is always possible to find three spectral colors that, when added together in the right amounts, will produce the color desired. Since the greatest number of color variations can be produced by additively mixing red, yellow, and blue, these three are called the *primary colors*. In some cases it is possible to produce white light by adding two colored lights instead of three. Such colors are called *complementary colors*. Purple and green, for example, are complementary colors.

■**SUBTRACTIVE PROCESS.**—If white light is passed through an optical filter, the filter will transmit a percentage of the incident light at each particular wavelength in the visible region. If the filter is yellow, it will transmit a greater percentage of yellow light than light of other wavelengths. A blue filter will transmit a larger percentage of light in the blue region, and so on. If the incident light is passed through a blue filter and yellow filter in combination, the resultant light transmitted will be those wavelengths where the transmission curves of the two filters overlap. In the case of the blue and yellow filters, the greatest percentage of light transmitted is in the green region, and thus green light is observed through the two filters. Since each filter subtracts a certain amount of energy from the incident light, this method is called the *subtractive method* of color mixing.

■**COLORS OF PAINTS AND INKS.**—By mixing paints and inks of different colors, it is possible to obtain other colors through the subtractive process. If pigments (transparent and dyed) are suspended in a transparent, colorless base liquid such as linseed oil, a colored paint is produced. The color reflected from the paint is produced by the incident light passing through millions of suspended colored filters (pigments) in the base liquid. For example, if blue and yellow paint are mixed, the reflected light from the mixed paints will be green; and the paint produced will therefore be green. This is the same result produced by the blue and yellow filters in the subtractive method.

In the three-color printing process, three transparent, colored inks are used. The colored picture is produced by printing the three colors one on top of the other. The incident

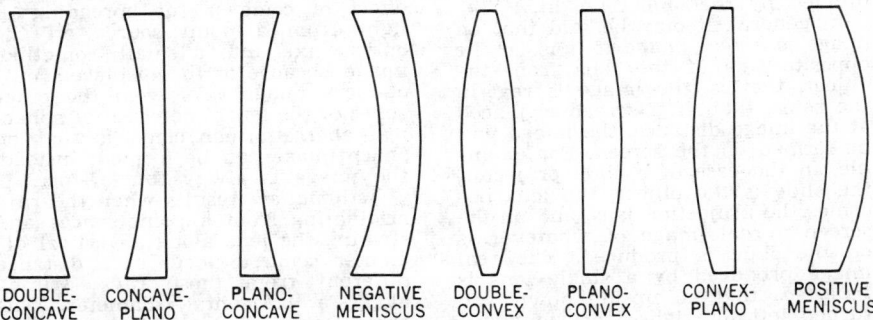

DOUBLE-CONCAVE CONCAVE-PLANO PLANO-CONCAVE NEGATIVE MENISCUS DOUBLE-CONVEX PLANO-CONVEX CONVEX-PLANO POSITIVE MENISCUS

POSITIVE AND NEGATIVE LENSES. All negative (concave) lenses are thinner in the middle than at the edges, while all positive (convex) lenses are thinner at the edges.

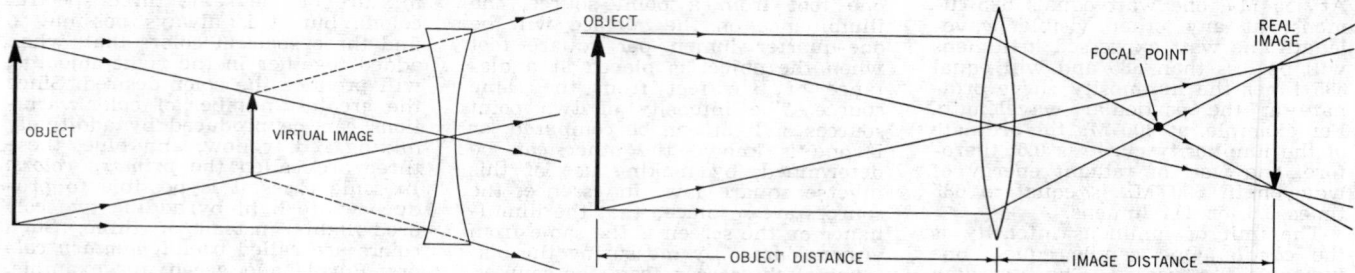

IMAGES formed by a negative lens (*left*) are always virtual, erect, and smaller than the object. Images formed by a positive lens (*right*) are always real, inverted, and smaller than the object when the object is more than twice the lens' focal length from the lens.

light on the picture thus passes through the three inks (filters, in effect), is reflected from the white paper on which the picture is printed, and then passes again through the same three inks to produce a colored picture by the subtractive method of color mixing.

Lenses.—A lens is made of a material that will transmit light. Its surfaces are shaped so that when light passes through it, the light will be refracted or redirected. Lenses are usually made to form images. In general, there are two types of lenses—*positive (convex)* and *negative (concave)*. A positive lens is thicker in the middle than at the edges. A negative lens is thinner in the middle than at the edges.

Positive (*converging*) lenses and negative (*diverging*) lenses are described by their optical axes, positions of their focal points, and their local lengths. (This is true if the lenses are considered to be thin lenses, meaning that the thicknesses of the lenses can be neglected in any computation involving them.)

The *optical axis* is an imaginary line that passes through the centers of the spherical lens surfaces. The *focal point* is that point through which all incident rays parallel to the optical axis and entering the lens will pass. (The focal point for the positive lens is real—the rays actually pass through this focal point. For the negative lens, the focal point is imaginary—the light rays appear to be passing through this focal point but actually do not.) The *focal length* is the distance of the focal point from the thin lens. The *linear magnification* of a lens is the image height divided by the object height.

In general, it may be said that an image is a *real image* if it is on the opposite side of the lens from the object; that is, the image is real in the sense that, if a screen is placed at the image distance, the image will be formed on the screen. For example, in the case of a slide projector, the slide is the object, the lens becomes the projection lens, and on the screen a real image of whatever is on the slide is produced. The real image produced by a single lens is *inverted,* that is, upside down and turned left for right (the right side of the object becomes, in effect, its left side in the image).

Virtual images only appear to be where they are seen. If a screen is placed at the point where the virtual image appears to be, no image is formed on the screen. However, to an eye looking through the lens, the image appears to be at that point.

With a positive lens, if the object is located between the first focus and the lens, the image is virtual, erect, and magnified. This is the principle of the simple magnifying glass. For an object located at a distance greater than two times the focal length of a positive lens, the image will be real, inverted, and reduced. Magnified, inverted, real images will be produced by a positive lens when the object is at a distance from the lens greater than one time, but less than two times, its focal length. At an object distance equal to two times the focal length of a positive lens, the image will be real, inverted, and the same size as the object.

Most lenses are made with spherical surfaces because these are the cheapest to produce. However, surfaces that are not spherical (*aspherical surfaces*) are becoming available. Such surfaces are used to overcome certain image defects of spherical surfaces. These image defects, called *aberrations,* include coma, spherical aberration, astigmatism, curvature of field, and distortion.

Coma and *spherical aberration* are the result of rays passing through the zones of the lens farther from the center being brought to a focus before those passing through the zones closer to the center. Coma results when the rays originate from a point not on the axis of the lens; spherical aberration, when they originate from a point on the axis. The effect of coma is the spreading of light from a point source off the optical axis into a small, cometlike image because of the displaced, out-of-focus image rays from the outer zones of the lens. The effect of spherical aberration or coma is that no sharp image can be formed; instead, the image is always out-of-focus.

Astigmatism results when the rays originating from a point source and striking the lens along a vertical diameter come to focus at a distance different from those rays striking along a horizontal diameter. The consequence of this is the formation of a line image (*primary image*) that progressively becomes an ellipse,

then a circle (called the *circle of least confusion*), and then an ellipse, and finally a line perpendicular to the first one (*secondary image*) as the beam moves outward from the lens. *Curvature of field* is a result of the rays crossing in the same manner as in astigmatism; however, in curvature of field the distance between the primary and secondary images is negligible. The images are curved instead of being in a plane. This is of special importance in photography, where the film is flat and the image must be made to fall upon it in a plane.

Distortion, unlike the other aberrations, does not refer to the inability of a lens to form a point image of a point source. Instead, distortion results from a variation of magnification with distance from the axis. In *pincushion distortion,* the magnification increases with increasing distance from the axis; and the outer parts of the object appear larger than they should. The result is that the sides of a square appear to be caving in toward the center. In *barrel distortion,* the magnification decreases with increasing distance from the axis; and the outer parts of the object appear smaller than they should. The result is that the sides of a square appear to bulge away from the center.

In general, aberrations are corrected by choosing particular radii of curvature for the lenses, by making the lens of two or more parts that have different refractive indices, by using aspherical surfaces, or by controlling the distances between the various lens elements. It is impossible to produce a perfect image, but by careful lens design it is possible to obtain images within the limits desired.

While all of the above-mentioned aberrations are *monochromatic* (occur for any one wavelength), there is also a form of aberration that takes place with only nonmonochromatic light; it is called *chromatic aberration* and occurs only when more than one wavelength is present. Chromatic aberration is explained by the fact that the index of refraction of any substance varies with the wavelength of the light. Therefore, when nonmonochromatic light passes through a lens, some wavelengths are bent more than others. The result is that each of the various colors or wavelengths has a different focal point. If a lens not corrected for chromatic aberration is used to form an image, the image will have a border of spectral colors. All single lenses, when used in nonmonochromatic light, exhibit chromatic aberration.

An *achromatic lens* is one designed to correct chromatic aberration. Such a lens actually consists of two lenses—a convex lens of crown glass and a concave lens of flint glass. These lenses are constructed so that the chromatic aberration produced by one is neutralized by the other.

Prisms.—Reflecting prisms are used in optical instruments for a number of reasons. They may be used to displace a beam of light through a certain distance, to deviate a beam of light through a known angle, to rotate an image, or to erect the image formed by a lens before the image enters another lens. Although there are many types of prisms, only those commonly used are described.

To fully understand prisms, one must know the meanings of reversion and inversion. It was mentioned in the section on lenses that a real image formed by a positive lens is inverted. An *inverted image* is one that is upside down with respect to the object and also is turned left for right. A *reverted image,* on the other hand, is an image that is reversed about only one dimension when compared to its object. When a person looks into a plane mirror or looking glass, for example, he sees himself right side up, but his left side becomes the right side and vice versa. Some prisms are capable of reverting the object, and others are capable of inverting it.

Another aspect of prisms (and other reflecting surfaces) ·that must be understood is the critical angle. If a ray of light passes from glass into air, and if that ray exceeds a particular angle (called the *critical angle*) at the glass-air interface, none of the light passes from the glass into the air. What happens is that all the rays are reflected back into the glass at the glass-air interface. At such a reflecting surface, it is not necessary to silver the glass because all the rays are reflected. One therefore sees many prisms with no silvered reflecting surfaces simply because the rays of light in the glass exceed the critical angle at the reflecting surface. However, in some prisms this is not the case; there are also prisms with silvered reflecting surfaces.

A *90° prism,* or *right-angle prism,* is used for deviating or bending the light beam through 90°. This prism reverts the image. The *Amici prism* accomplishes the same thing as the right-angle prism, except that the reflecting surface becomes a roof (two planes perpendicular to each other) and inverts the image. The *Porro prism* may cause some lateral displacement of the image, depending on how it is used. The rays of light entering from the object are reflected by the two reflecting surfaces, and the reflected rays come back out of the prism parallel to the entering rays. This is true even if the prism

is rotated about its horizontal axis. It should be noted that the image formed by a Porro prism is reverted. The *rhomboidal prism* merely causes a lateral displacement of the image, depending on the length of the prism. The *dove prism* causes an inline reversion of the image. "Inline" means that the rays leaving the prism are parallel to the rays that enter the prism. If one looks at an object through a dove prism and then rotates it, the image of the object will rotate through twice the angle that the prism is rotated through. This is also true if one looks at his reflection in a Porro prism and likewise rotates the Porro. The *Penta prism* bends or deviates the light beam through 90°. Penta prisms are sometimes made with a roof on one of the reflecting surfaces. If there is a roof, the image is reverted. If the Penta prism is rotated about its vertical axis, the entering and exiting rays will still make an angle of 90° with each other. This is a very important characteristic of the Penta prism. Penta prisms are used a great deal in large optical range finders to bend the ·rays of light entering the ends so that they pass along the axis of the instrument. They are also used to a great extent in optical alignment work. Penta prisms are sometimes called *optical squares.*

Often prisms are combined to make up a *prism system.* For example, two Porro prisms may be combined in such a way that the entering and exiting rays are parallel to one another although laterally displaced. The image formed by this system is inverted. A system such as this is commonly used in binoculars to reinvert the inverted image formed by the objective lens and eyepiece. This also permits higher magnification without increasing the length of the binocular housing.

—Edward F. Mackey and J. A. Mauro

MASERS AND LASERS

Masers.—Maser, an acronym for Microwave Amplification by Stimulated Emission of Radiation, is an amplifier or generator of electromagnetic waves. "Radiation" refers to electromagnetic radiation, a term that encompasses both visible light and invisible light. The latter includes frequencies higher than visible (ultraviolet and x-ray) as well as frequencies lower than visible (infrared, microwave, television, radio, and audio). Amplifiers from audio, radio, and up to microwave frequencies (about 10,000 million cycles per second) use condensers and inductances to make resonant circuits in which amplification or oscillation of electromagnetic radiation is possible. In order to design these resonant circuits to respond only over a particular band of frequencies, the circuits must be made smaller than a wavelength of the radiation, an increasingly difficult task at high frequencies. Shortly after World War II a number of scientists became convinced that the only practical solution to this prob-

lem was to use the natural molecular oscillations as the resonant circuits at the very highest frequencies.

Every system made of atoms—molecules and crystals, for example —has its characteristic energy levels. Although the system is almost always in the lowest state, it has the ability to absorb certain amounts of energy, and raise itself to a higher level. A molecule can be raised from a *lower state* to an *upper state* by absorbing radiation in the form of energy packets, or *quanta.* If E_u and E_1 are two molecular states, upper and lower respectively, the frequency of emitted or absorbed radiation is given by $E_u — E_1$, divided by the constant h, known as *Planck's constant.*

■**STIMULATED EMISSION OF RADIATION.**—One of the most important rules of quantum mechanics was first stated by Albert Einstein in 1917. He said that the ability of molecules to absorb radiation depends not only on the number of molecules in the system but also on whether the molecules are in their upper or lower energy states. If more molecules are in their upper states than in their lower states, more molecules are stimulated to emit rather than to absorb radiation. Hence, the intensity of the initial radiation is increased as it passes through the molecules. This is known as *stimulated emission of radiation* and is the principle on which all maser and laser amplifiers and oscillators work.

Of course, to produce useful devices, the molecular amplification must exceed various microwave or optical losses in the molecules through which the radiation is passed. The first molecular amplifier which solved these problems was designed and built in 1954 by Professor Charles H. Townes and a team of graduate students at Columbia University. The high-energy molecules were separated from the low-energy ones in a molecular beam of ammonia gas (NH_3) by passing the beam through appropriately designed electric fields. The frequency of the molecular transition was 23,870 megacycles (in the microwave region). The energy was removed from the molecules by passing them through a *microwave cavity* vibrating at the molecular frequency. This metal-walled "resonant cavity" for electromagnetic waves is like a resonant organ pipe for sound waves. In each case the dimensions of the structure determine the wavelength at which it will vibrate, or be *resonant.* For the simplest vibrations the cavity or pipe contains along its length an integral number of half wavelengths of light or sound, as the case may be. A stream of air excites the organ pipe acoustically; the stream of molecules excites the microwave cavity electromagnetically, building up a density of radiation which stimulates succeeding molecules in the molecular beam to emit more radiation, thus amplifying the radiation.

■**MASERS AS A STANDARD.**—In succeeding years many more molecular systems were made to oscillate or amplify in the microwave region, and means other than molecular beams

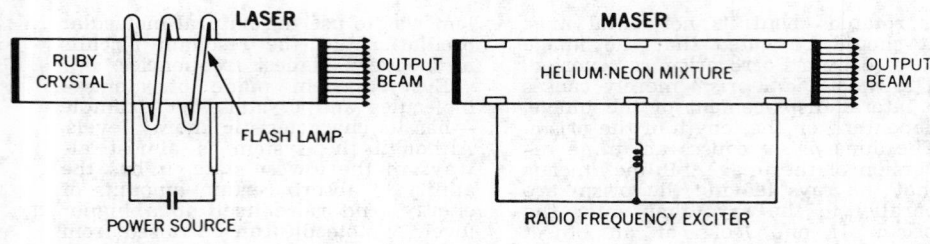

LASER

RUBY CRYSTAL — FLASH LAMP — OUTPUT BEAM — POWER SOURCE

MASER

HELIUM-NEON MIXTURE — OUTPUT BEAM — RADIO FREQUENCY EXCITER

PHOTON CASCADE

TOTALLY SILVERED REFLECTING SURFACE — PARTIALLY SILVERED REFLECTING SURFACE

LASERS AND MASERS (*above*) work on similar principles. They differ primarily in the nature of their excitation energy and their output beam. The laser amplifies visible light; the maser amplifies microwaves.

PHOTON CASCADE amplifies the excitation light in a laser (*left*). In *a*, the atoms (black dots) are in their ground state. The stimulating photons (arrows) have raised most of the atoms to their excited state (open dots) in *b*. The first photon spontaneously emitted parallel to the long axis of the crystal by an excited atom stimulates a second excited atom to emit its photon (*c*). (Photons emitted in other directions pass out of the crystal.) The stimulation continues as the photons are reflected between the ends of the crystal (*d*). When the amplification is great enough, some of the laser beam passes through the partially silvered end (*e*).

were found to selectively raise molecules to their upper states. Microwave masers possess two important electronic properties: as amplifiers they have very low noise figures, and as oscillators the molecular-beam masers in particular have very sharp, stable, and reproducible output frequencies because of collision-free oscillations. Hence the beam oscillators are used as frequency standards at the National Bureau of Standards, where frequency stabilities as great as one part in a million million have been achieved. Since all molecules of a given kind (such as ammonia) have the same oscillation frequency, which is independent of temperature, molecules serve as conveniently reproducible frequency standards.

■**MASERS AS LOW NOISE AMPLIFIERS.**— Despite their low noise features, microwave maser amplifiers have come into only limited use because they are relatively large and expensive. They are used, however, as sensitive low-noise receivers for radio astronomy experiments and in the Bell Telephone Laboratory's Telstar television relay link. In these applications a form of solid-state maser invented by N. Bloembergen of Harvard is used. Microwave energy of one frequency is absorbed by the material to "pump" the molecules or ions to the desired upper energy levels. These masers work best at temperatures of near −269°, the boiling point of liquid helium. A frequently used maser material is the trivalent chromium ion in Al_2O_3 (ruby). Some energy levels

of this ion are shifted by a magnetic field so that the transition frequencies lie in the microwave region.

Lasers.—Soon after the achievement of the microwave maser, scientists sought to extend this principle of operation to the visible region of the electromagnetic spectrum, where no true electronic amplifiers existed. The problems seemed formidable because optical wavelengths (around 5,000 angstrom units, or 0.02 thousandths of an inch) are much smaller than any resonant cavity in which the molecules are located. (As is evident from the discussion of the ammonia maser, it is often desirable to couple the molecular oscillations to some larger resonant structure.) At these optical frequencies, moreover, a new problem is encountered: when molecules are raised to high energy states, there is a great probability that they will radiate energy spontaneously, without requiring a stimulating input signal. Since this spontaneously radiated energy does not change when an input light signal is added, it does not contribute to an amplification of the light, but is wasted energy. The loss is proportional to the fourth power of the frequency, and hence is important at optical frequencies but negligible for most purposes at microwave frequencies.

Again the solution to the problem was proposed by Professor Townes, this time, in 1958, in collaboration with Dr. A. L. Schawlow of the Bell Telephone Laboratories. Their sug-

gestion: mirrors. They noted that if the molecular oscillators of a gas, for instance, are contained between two parallel mirrors, only the radiation bouncing back and forth between the mirrors passes through the molecules often enough to be amplified significantly. In the absence of mirrors, molecules can emit radiation spontaneously over a range of many millions of cycles near each resonant frequency. The mirrors are resonant to some of these frequencies, specifically those for which an integral number of half wavelengths of the radiation can be fitted into the space between the mirrors. (The product of light frequency times wavelength is the velocity of light, 3×10^{10} centimeters per second, or 186,000 miles per second.) Thus the combined mirror-plus-molecules system oscillates most strongly at one or more of these selected frequencies.

The first successful optical maser, or *laser*, an acronym for Light Amplification by Stimulated Emission of Radiation, was built in 1960 by T. H. Maiman of the Hughes Aircraft Company. Again the material was ruby, with mirror coatings of silver on the surfaces of accurately polished, parallel plane faces of the gem. For the ruby laser no magnetic field is required because different energy levels are used from maser levels. Operation is possible at room temperature, although lower temperature improves efficiency.

The laser oscillator emits a beam of light, with a very small angular spread, at right angles to the faces of the parallel mirrors. As the light energy bounces back and forth between the mirrored surfaces, energy is built up or amplified by stimulated emission. (One of the mirror's faces is partly transparent, allowing the amplified light energy to pass through.) As with the maser, this emitted radiation maintains an exact frequency, or is *monochromatic*.

In lasers using a gas (a mixture of helium and neon) as the molecular system, radiation monochromatic to 20 cycles out of 260 million million cycles (one part in 10^{13}) has been achieved, with an extremely small angular beam spread. These properties of narrow beam spread and sharp monochromaticity are the strong *coherence* features of a laser beam. Parts of the beam many wavelengths apart keep in step and thus maintain a flat wave front and a long wave path, or *train*. A very flat wave front possesses strong *space coherence*, and a long wave train has a long *coherence time*.

■**LASER APPLICATIONS.**—The proposed technical uses of lasers are many. The directional features suggest sending information over laser beams. Furthermore, since the frequency is very high, it should be possible to transmit many messages simultaneously. Theoretically, all the simultaneous telephone calls in the United States could be transmitted over a single laser beam. In practice, however, there are serious limitations in attaining this ideal—the laser must be *modulated*, that is, its light output must be changed to correspond to the message being sent.

Clouds in the atmosphere absorb and scatter the light, so signals on earth might have to be sent through pipes, although no such limitations are imposed on space communications. Indeed, lasers will probably be used first in space communications. Lasers are also planned for use in experimental tracking of some satellites. Laser radar echoes have been bounced off the moon and received on the earth. The high coherence features of laser beams, together with the fact that some lasers can be pulsed to emit their light in extremely short bursts, make them suitable for very precise measurements of distance and velocity of moving targets (determined from the *Doppler shift* in frequency of the return echo from the target).

Other laser applications result from the focusing properties of very coherent light beams: they can be focused to a spot about a wavelength in diameter and hence can be used to generate intense light, heat, and pressure in one spot. The pulsed output of a ruby laser has been used to punch holes through razor blades, diamonds, and other materials. Thus micromachining, welding, and photographic recording applications for lasers exist; and proposals have been made to use laser beams as antimissile weapons.

Some examples of all the phases of matter—gas, solid, and liquid—have now been made into lasers. Some feature direct conversion of energy from electrical to optical; and some, like the ruby, conversion from incoherent pump light to coherent laser light.

Although high power (ruby) and high coherence (gas) have been emphasized, for some purposes small size, high electrical efficiency, and ease of modulation are important. For these the *semiconductor injection laser*, developed in 1962 by Marshall I. Nathan and co-workers at International Business Machines and Robert N. Hall and co-workers at the General Electric Company, is a promising recent development.

—W. V. Smith

NUCLEAR PHYSICS

Scope.—*Nuclear physics* is a concerted study undertaken to determine what the nucleus of the atom consists of, how it behaves, and what holds it together. Attainment of a proper perspective requires an understanding both of the modern picture of the nucleus and of its properties.

Characteristics of the Nucleus.—An atom is about 10^{-8}, or 0.00000001 centimeter (cm.) in diameter. One can better imagine how small this is when it is realized that there are six sextillion (6 followed by 21 zeros) atoms in a drop of water. The nucleus of the atom, which is composed of neutrons and protons (except in the commonest form of hydrogen, in which it consists of a single proton), is much smaller—about 10^{-13} cm. in diameter. Outside the nucleus there are only electrons. The neutron and

the proton have almost identical masses, 1.67×10^{-24} gram. This is approximately 1,840 times the mass of an electron. Therefore, in the commonest form of hydrogen, which is composed of one electron and one proton, 1,840 times as much mass is found in the nucleus as is found in the region outside the nucleus. Since the region outside the nucleus is 100,000 times as big, it can be said that typically an atom is composed mostly of empty space, with only a very small region where all the mass is found. Although they have virtually the same mass, the neutron and proton differ in one important characteristic: the proton carries an electrical charge, and the neutron does not. The positive charge on a proton is the smallest electrical charge known in nature. In no experiments have charges of, say, half that on a proton been found. It is as if the charge on a proton were similar to the U.S. penny—no halfpennies are in circulation. Pairs of pennies can be found, but this would be similar to the case where two positive charges are found linked together in some way. The electron has an electrical charge of the same magnitude as that of the proton, but it is negative. Again, no experiment has detected a charge one-half or one-quarter the size of the electron's charge. There have been recent suggestions that "particles" called *quarks*, with one-third or two-thirds the electron's charge, do exist; but this has not yet been proved.

■ATOMIC STRUCTURE.—The structure of the hydrogen atom has been outlined above. The nucleus consists of one proton and therefore has a positive

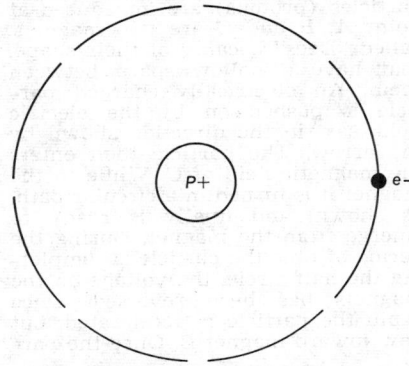

HYDROGEN ATOM consists of an electron, e^-, and a nucleus containing one proton, P^+.

charge. The electron has a negative charge, so the net charge on the hydrogen atom is zero, because the positive charge is equal to, but the opposite of, the negative charge. The force that holds the atom together, that binds the electron to the proton in some way, is the *coulomb force*, the attraction between positive and negative charges. The next smallest atom after hydrogen is that of helium, which has two protons and two neutrons in the nucleus; this results in its having a net positive charge of two units. Therefore, in order for helium to be electrically neutral, two

electrons must orbit the nucleus. The forces holding the electrons in the atom are once again the coulomb forces. At this point, however, a major problem of nuclear physics appears. There are two protons in the nucleus of helium. Since these two protons have identical positive charges, they would be expected to repulse each other, causing the nucleus to fly apart. What prevents this from occurring is a major concern of nuclear physics.

■BUILDING ELEMENTS.—The building of the atoms of elements by addition of protons and neutrons in the nucleus and of electrons outside the nucleus continues in orderly fashion until the heaviest naturally occurring element, uranium, is reached. The uranium nucleus contains 92 protons and 146 neutrons. Actually, there are several different forms of uranium, called *isotopes*, which differ in the number of neutrons in the nucleus. It should be noted that the isotopes of every element have been found. The number of electrons present in uranium is 92, again preserving the zero net charge of the atom. About a dozen elements having more than 92 protons in the nuclei have been created, but they are relatively unstable and do not exist in nature. These elements are called *transuranic elements*. Two of the more familiar are plutonium and neptunium.

Scattering Experiment.—A considerable amount has been said about what atoms look like, but nothing has been said about how the knowledge of the structure of the nucleus and the *nucleons* (the neutrons and protons) is obtained. The basic experiment of nuclear physics is the *scattering experiment*, in which projectiles (neutrons, protons, electrons, gamma rays, or various other nuclear particles) are accelerated to high energies and directed at a target consisting of atoms of the material to be studied. At positions around the target, *collectors* (or *detectors*) of various types are set up. This setup and experiment may be compared, in a simple way, to the game of pool or pocket billiards. The cue ball serves as the projectile, the racked balls or an individual ball as the target, the pockets as the collectors, and the pool cue as the accelerator. Some features of scattering immediately emerge. As anyone familiar with the game of pool knows, the effect of "scattering" the cue ball off several other balls is different from that of "scattering" it off a single ball. It is also clear that scattering off a cubic object, rather than a pool ball, would lead to a markedly different scattering pattern. The scattering experiment in nuclear physics differs from pool in that scientists do not know what the scatterers look like. They know what kind of "pool cue" they have (the various types of accelerators will be discussed later); they know what the "cue ball" looks like (the protons, neutrons, or other particles, which come out the end of the accelerator); they know what the pockets do because these collectors are built for a specific perform-

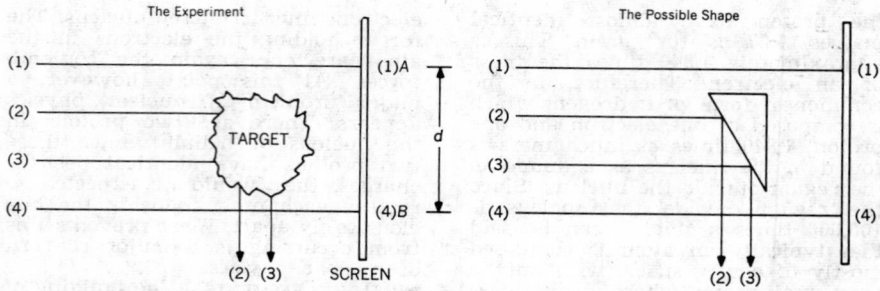

The Experiment   The Possible Shape

SIZE AND SHAPE OF AN UNKNOWN can be found by noting the way it deflects particles.

ance—but they do not know what the target looks like. However, from their knowledge of these three factors they can deduce the fourth. To see how this might be done in a simple case is shown in the accompanying illustration.

Thinking about a possible shape for the target leads to the following conclusions. The dimensions of the target have to be about the distance from point A to point B because the two balls passed straight through the target area without deflection. (This is an important concept in nuclear physics, and the dimension—the distance d—so obtained is called the *cross section of the target*. Obviously, nuclear physics deals with three dimensions and therefore the dimension, instead of being a length, is an area.) Balls (2) and (3) were scattered to their right. A possible means of accounting for the scattering of all four balls might be a target shaped like the one shown. The scattered paths are indicated. Thus, by observing the scattered particles, the shape and dimensions of targets can, at least in principle, be deduced.

One other phenomenon can be explained in terms of pool balls. All pool players know it is possible to put "English" on the ball. This causes the ball to rotate in one direction while moving in another. The effect of a ball being scattered with spin on it and without spin on it is different, and so indeed is the effect of scattering nuclear projectiles with this sort of spin off targets. Nuclear particles possess spin (and so do the targets), so it is possible that spin effects enter into the interpretation of scattering data. This useful result, although it somewhat complicates the interpretation of the scattering experiment data, does enable nuclear physicists to obtain more information than would otherwise be possible.

Accelerators.—One of the first accelerators used in a nuclear physics experiment was a naturally radioactive element that emitted *alpha particles*. (An *alpha particle* consists of two protons and two neutrons bound together, and thus is a helium atom stripped of electrons.) Ernest Rutherford (1871–1937) used radium as his "accelerator" to bombard thin foils of materials. The results indicated that some of the alpha particles were scattered backward, although most went through relatively undeviated. Backscattering could be explained only if the alpha particles were striking

something more massive than themselves. It was in these experiments that the picture of an atom as composed of a small but massive nucleus surrounded by a relatively vacant space was first deduced and then confirmed by Rutherford.

Other types of accelerators include the Cockroft-Walton accelerator, invented by J. Douglas Cockroft and Ernest Thomas Sinton Walton in 1932; the Van de Graaff accelerator, proposed by Robert Jemison Van de Graaff in 1931; the cyclotron, built by Ernest O. Lawrence in 1930; the synchrocyclotron; the synchroton; the bevatron; the betatron; the linear accelerator; and other special types of devices. In all these accelerators, the effect of electric and magnetic fields on charged particles is utilized to give the particles high velocities.

■**CYCLOTRONS.**—The effect of electric and magnetic fields can best be explained by reference to the *cyclotron*, where the effects of both types of fields are utilized to produce an energetic beam of particles. As shown in the accompanying diagram, charged particles (protons) are introduced at point A; B and C are two magnets, called "Dees" because of their shape, that have a hollow space between them. An electrically charged particle is pushed on by the electric field, say, in the direction shown by the arrow. The particle then enters the magnetic field of C. While in the magnet it is turned in a circular path, as shown, and finally is ready to emerge from the magnet. During the period of time the particle is completing the half circle, the voltage on the magnets has been reversed. Once again the particle is accelerated, but now toward magnet B. Once the par-

ticle enters magnet B it again is turned in a circular path. Upon emerging from the magnet B, the particle finds the direction of the electric field has again been reversed to cause acceleration toward C. This process continues until the particle emerges from the cyclotron.

■**SYNCHROCYCLOTRON.**—One characteristic of the cyclotron is that the rate at which the voltage on the magnets has to be reversed is independent of the radius of the accelerated particles' path and of their velocity, provided the mass of the accelerated particle remains the same. Relativity predicts that the mass of a particle will increase with its velocity, however, and this effect has been noted in the cyclotron. Such a mass change means that the rate at which the electric accelerating potential is changed must change as the accelerated particle increases in velocity. An accelerator that does this is the *synchrocyclotron*, a device put into operation after World War II. Its principles and those of the cyclotron are basically the same: the electric field accelerates the particles while the magnetic field steers them.

■**SYNCHROTRON.**—The basic operation of the *synchrotron* is also similar to the cyclotron and the synchrocyclotron. In the synchrotron the particles travel in nearly circular orbits whose radius does not change. The acceleration is performed between steering magnets, again by the use of electric fields. The largest synchrotron is located at the Brookhaven National Laboratory, Long Island, New York. It produces a beam of particles with an energy of 30 billion electron volts. (An *electron volt* is the energy equal to that acquired by an electron or protron in passing through an electric potential of 1 volt. Thus, it is as if the protons accelerated had passed through an electric potential of 30 billion volts.)

■**OTHER ACCELERATORS.**—A basically different type of accelerator is represented by the Van de Graaff, Cockroft-Walton, and linear accelerators. In these, magnetic fields are not used to bend the beam in a circular or almost circular path. Instead, the charged particles are accelerated in a straight line by the action of an electric field. In the case of the Van de Graaff and Cockroft-Walton accelerators, the electric field is static, while in the linear accelerator it is traveling. The linear accelerator now under construction at Stanford University is about two miles long.

■**NEUTRON PRODUCTION.**—After accelerated particles emerge from the accelerators, they are allowed to hit targets directly in order to study the targets themselves, or to hit targets in order to produce beams of particles of other than the original type. For example, neutrons, since they have no charge, cannot be accelerated or steered by electric and magnetic fields. Beams of neutrons must be produced by collisions of the primary beam with other targets.

■**ACCELERATOR RESEARCH.**—Attempts are being made to develop accelerators that can produce primary beams of higher and higher energies, per-

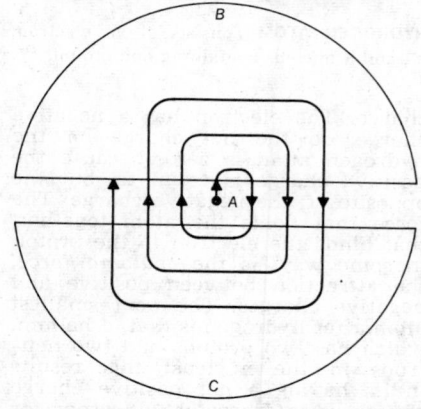

CYCLOTRON is used to accelerate particles.

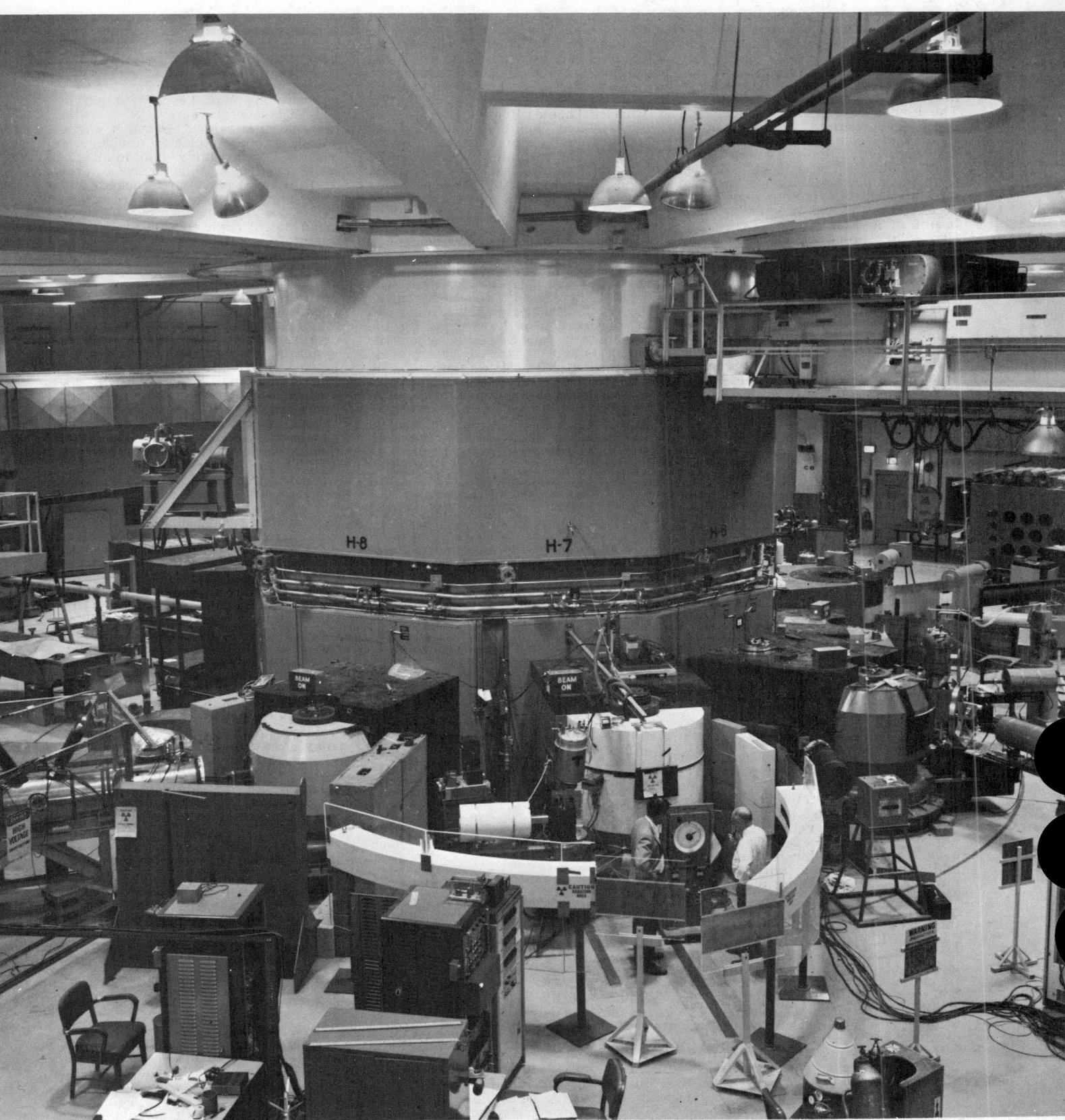

BROOKHAVEN NATIONAL LABORATORY

NUCLEAR BEAM RESEARCH REACTOR has a maximum power of 40 million watts. The reactor supplies intense beams of neutrons for use in nuclear research. The reactor is under the control of a digital computer with a memory of 32,000 words. The computer controls the reactor, handles all of the computations, accumulates and processes experimental data, and stores the results on a magnetic drum. The system shown has been in use since early 1966.

haps as much as 1,000 billion electron volts, in the next generation of accelerators. These accelerators will be used further to explore the nucleus, particularly in attempts to unravel the mystery of what holds the nucleus—and hence matter—together. The higher energies are needed because, in order to study the particles that scientists think hold the nucleus together, enough energy must be available to free these particles from the nucleus. Other workers are putting their efforts into developing accelerators that can produce primary beams of greater and greater intensity. The process of accelerating charged particles is a fairly wasteful one: the particles escape, collide, and so on, and do not emerge from the machines. The accuracy of the data obtained from scattering experiments depends to a great extent on the number of projectiles available. (In the example of the pool balls given above, eight balls would give more data and accuracy than would four.) For this reason, many scientists are concentrating on the intensity of the available beams rather than the absolute energy of emerging particles, although they also need relatively high energies. These machines would be used to find out more about the nucleus's structure and behavior than about what holds it together.

Collectors.—In the early days of nuclear physics, nuclear events were observed on photographic plates. In fact, radioactivity was discovered by Antoine Henri Becquerel in 1895 through the darkening of photographic film—charged particles expose film in passing through it. The use of photographic plates and their descendants, the *nuclear track plates*, continues to this day. The data obtained is accurate and useful. The methods, however, are slow; and the plates require developing and processing, steps that make obtaining and processing data more complex and difficult.

Electronic techniques have also been used. The *Geiger counter*, named after its inventor, Hans Geiger, uses the effect of energetic radiation in making an enclosed gas electrically conducting in order to measure the nuclear processes. Details of the events are not visible in the Geiger and similar counters; only the total number of events taking place is accessible to the user.

Scintillation counters make use of the fact that radiation produces flashes of light when it strikes certain crystals such as those of sodium iodide. Electronic circuitry, in conjunction with photomultiplier tubes, detects the flashes and counts them. Again, these devices, although extremely useful, measure only the quantity of a certain type of event rather than giving detailed information about the event. In some experiments in nuclear physics this type of information is extremely important, particularly in a case where accurate measurement of large numbers of events is desired. This is true, for example, in observations of the behavior and structure of the nucleus.

■CLOUD CHAMBER.—In some types of research involving the structure of the nucleus and the forces that hold it together, it is very important to observe individual nuclear events. To do this, a group of detectors has been developed. The first of these was the *Wilson cloud chamber*, designed by Charles Thomas Rees Wilson in 1911. A gas-filled chamber containing supersaturated vapor is exposed to radiation. The incoming particles cause the excess moisture to precipitate along the trail of the particle, creating a visible trail. Thus, the actual path of a particle can be seen. When the cloud chamber is used in conjunction with electric and magnetic fields and photographic films, the charge and momentum of the incident particles can be deduced. The basic difficulty with the cloud chamber is that relatively few events can be observed in a given time, for the chamber is sensitive only when the vapor is supersaturated. The process of supersaturation is a relatively long one, so the cloud chamber is "dead" a good part of the time.

■BUBBLE CHAMBER.—A device whose action is basically similar to the cloud chamber is the *bubble chamber*, which was designed in the 1950's. This

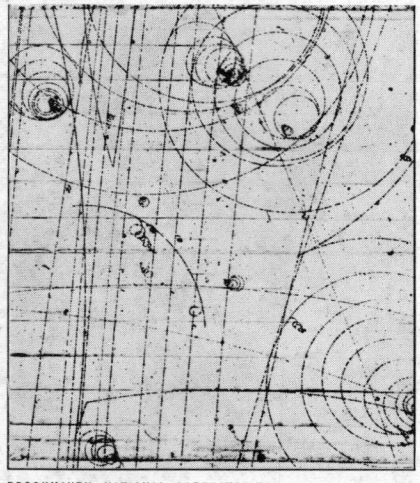

BROOKHAVEN NATIONAL LABORATORIES

VAPOR TRAILS of radioactive particles are seen in this bubble-chamber photograph.

chamber usually contains supersaturated liquid hydrogen; others possible include liquid xenon and helium. The action of the incoming radiation causes a row of bubbles along the trail of the incoming particle, provided the particle has an electrical charge. After supersaturation of the liquid is achieved, a light is flashed so that events of interest can be recorded on photographic film. However, the bubble chamber suffers from relative slowness and, since the picture does not necessarily coincide with a particular type of event, it is not very selective. Because the liquid hydrogen is dense compared to the gases used in the cloud chamber, many more events are photographed in a given volume of liquid than in an equal volume of gas in the cloud chamber. Furthermore,

since the nucleus of hydrogen is just a proton, scattering experiments are performed with the detector simultaneously being a very excellent target. Much information concerning scattering of various primary beams off protons has been obtained in the last several years.

■SPARK CHAMBER.—The *spark chamber* is another collector device used extensively to study individual nuclear events. In this device a series of thin metal plates are stacked, with each plate separated from its neighbor. The entire chamber contains neon gas. A high electric potential is maintained between each plate. When radiation enters the chamber, the neon gas along the trail is ionized—one or more electrons are separated from the neon atom. Therefore, the electrons and the neon atom, which now has a net positive charge, are free to be acted upon by the electric potential. Along the trail, neon gas makes visible the path of the incoming radiation through brief discharges. When the sparks occur, photographs are taken and later analyzed. Since the action of the spark chamber is electronically controlled, its action is relatively fast; supersaturation does not have to be achieved, although ions and electrons do have to be swept away. In various ways, through the use of auxiliary electronic circuits, the spark chamber can also be made somewhat selective about what events are recorded.

Nuclear Fission Reactions.—In *nuclear fission reactions* the nucleus of a heavy isotope of an element is ruptured into two segments of almost equal mass, with the resultant release of large quantities of energy and of neutrons. The two segments into which the nucleus splits are the nuclei of other, lighter atoms. The rupture occurs when the nucleus absorbs a free neutron. The neutrons released during the fission process may, in turn, cause other atoms of the heavy isotopes to undergo fission in a *chain reaction*. When the chain reaction is not inhibited in any way, an uncontrolled fission reaction takes place, releasing vast amounts of energy over a very short period; this is what happened in the atomic bombs exploded over Hiroshima and Nagasaki, Japan, in 1945. When the chain reaction is inhibited, a controlled reaction takes place and the same quantity of energy is liberated over a much longer period; this is what takes place in a nuclear reactor, such as in the Yankee power reactor at Rowe, Massachusetts, where electricity is produced, or in the one aboard the nuclear-powered merchant ship *Savannah*.

A typical fission reaction is the one undergone by uranium-235 to produce atoms of barium-141 and krypton-92, as shown in the following equation:

$$_{92}U^{235} + _0n^1 \rightarrow$$
$$_{56}Ba^{141} + _{36}Kr^{92} + 3_0n^1 + energy.$$

Nuclear Fusion Reactions.—The *fusion reaction* is virtually the exact opposite of the fission reaction. In a fusion reaction, the nuclei of two light

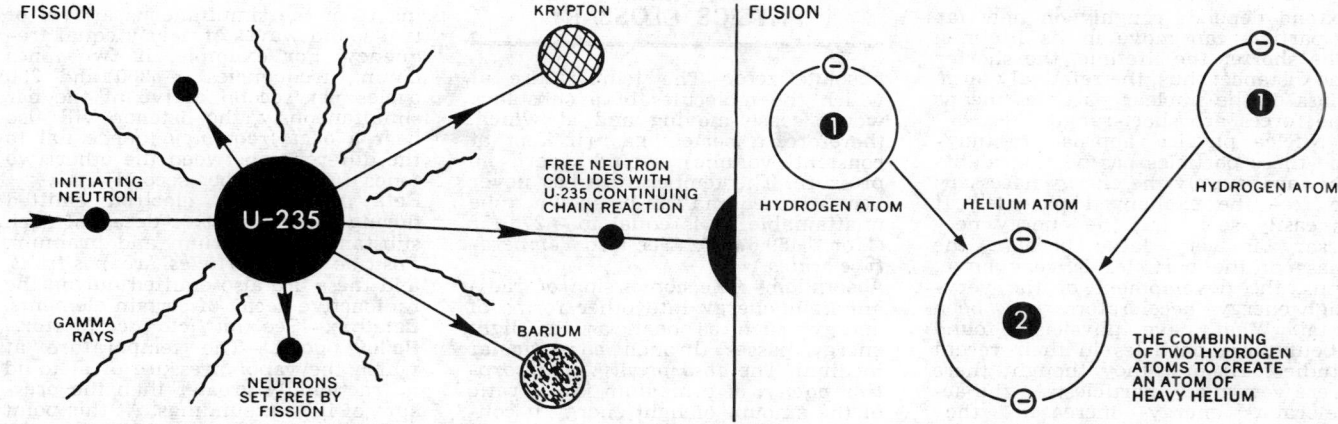

NUCLEAR REACTIONS can be of two types. In fission reactions (*left*), an atom of a heavy element—such as uranium-235—is split into atoms of lighter elements, while in fusion reactions (*right*), atoms of light elements combine to form an atom of a heavier element.

isotopes join to form a heavier isotope; here, too, the reaction results in the release of large quantities of energy. A typical uncontrolled fusion reaction is the one that takes place within the sun, where hydrogen nuclei combine to form a helium nucleus and release solar energy, a process called the *hydrogen-helium cycle*. The equation for this reaction is:

$$4_1\mathrm{H}^1 \rightarrow 2_2\mathrm{H}^4 + \mathrm{W}2_1\beta^0 + \text{energy},$$

where $_1\beta^0$ is a beta particle, or electron. Experiments are currently being conducted in an effort to produce a controlled fusion reaction. However, at the present time only limited success has been achieved.

Status of Knowledge.—With the accelerators and collectors that have become available in recent years, progress in understanding nuclear structure phenomena and forces has been rapid. A model of the nucleus has been developed that adequately explains many of the properties and the behavior of atoms. This is, of course, not to say that much more does not need to be done. More accurate measurements, improved theories, and greater variety, intensity, and energy of primary beams is still necessary.

The status of nuclear knowledge can be considered in three important areas that, while not the only areas of interest in nuclear physics, are typical of some of the most important: the structure and properties of the nuclei of atoms; the properties of *nucleons* (the protons and neutrons that make up the nucleus); and the forces that cause the nucleus to stay together (these are related to the "elementary" particles).

Properties of the Nuclei.—As a result of the research so far performed, it is now known that when a nucleus is bombarded by a primary beam from an accelerator, the resulting nuclear reaction can occur in two possible ways. In both of these the bombarding particle is essentially swallowed by the nucleus. The incoming particle and the nucleus stay in this joint state for about 10^{-22} second, after which time one of two things may happen.

The incoming particle may escape, or the incoming particle may literally combine with the bombarding nuclei. The processes have been described as one in which the intermediate state immediately proceeds to the final state by direct interaction without disturbing most of the nucleons in the system, and as one in which the intermediate state is transformed into a true compound that lasts for only about 10^{-13} second. The compound nucleus eventually decays by the emission of gamma rays or by evaporation of one or more nucleons to form a new product.

Structure of the Nucleons.—It was mentioned earlier that the proton and the neutron are the basic residents in the nucleus. For many years they, along with several others, were thought to be elementary particles, the simplest particles that could exist. The proton had a positive charge on it, and that was that; the neutron had no charge. However, some disconcerting facts eventually emerged. One of the most disconcerting was that the neutron was found to have a magnetic moment. A *magnetic moment* indicates the presence of charges in motion, and for a long time it was difficult to see how a particle with no charge could have a circulating charge. Robert Hofstadter, using a high-energy electron accelerator, was able to determine in scattering experiments that the neutron, although it has a net charge of zero, does have a *charge structure*. As a matter of fact, it possesses a fringe of positive charge and enough negative charges to make the net charge zero. While Hofstadter's findings cleared up one problem, they might have created others, in that the proton's charge was also found to have a structure. In other words, the charge is not concentrated all at one point. Thus, even though the charge on the proton is the smallest unit of charge so far found, it is "smeared" around to some extent. Hofstadter's findings also confirmed the basic similarity in the behavior of neutron and proton—except, of course, in terms of charge.

Nuclear Forces.—Finally, the investi-

gations of the fundamental forces holding the nucleus together are, at this moment, arranging themselves in order. The quandary of the "elementary" particles is being resolved. As has been mentioned, the search for elementary particles is an old one. These particles, which cannot be further subdivided, have been sought for many years. At first it was thought that they consisted of the electron, the proton, the neutron, the photon, and the neutrino. Then, in 1937, Hideki Yukawa predicted the existence of the *meson* as a carrier of the nuclear force. A *meson* is a particle having a mass approximately 250 times that of the electron. To show how a particle can be the carrier of a force, the following simple analogy may be made. Imagine two boys, each with a pillow. One of the boys throws the pillow to the other, who catches it. In catching it, he is pushed backward. The first boy is also pushed backward, and so the exchange of the pillow leads to a repulsive force. An attractive force occurs if each boy grabs the other's pillow and tugs on it. It is precisely in this way, using particles (mesons) rather than pillows, that Yukawa thought of nuclear forces. One other fact must be borne in mind, however. Creation of a particle to exchange requires energy. Einstein's familiar formula,

$$E = mc^2,$$

is well-known. E is the energy necessary to create a particle, m is the mass of the particle created, and c is a constant equal to the velocity of light. (The mass of an electron is equivalent to about 500,000 electron volts of energy.) The uncertainty principle of Werner Karl von Heisenberg (1901–   ) makes a prediction about how long particles of this type can survive unless enough energy is supplied literally to create them or to free them permanently. This principle states that the more massive the particle, the less time it can live if not freed. This has implications concerning over what distances nuclear forces can extend, for if the forces really arise due to an exchange, then the distance a force can extend depends roughly on how far a particle can move in its lifetime. The shorter the lifetime, the shorter the distance; thus, the relatively large mass of the nuclear particles means the forces are short-range.

Nuclear physics's approach to studying these particles has been straightforward; supply the energy necessary to free the exchanged particles. It is easily seen that the energy necessary is very large because the mass of the particles is very large; thus, the development of the very-high-energy accelerators has been vital. What have physicists found about these particles in their recent studies? At first they thought there were very many particles. As the accelerator energy increased, they found more and more particles. Finally, though, some order began to emerge out of the chaos. The situation is very similar to that which existed in atomic physics and spectra in the early days of research in that area. The spectrum of mercury, represented by lines in an illustration, can be taken as an example. Although a great many lines appear, the spectrum is only from mercury; each line represents transitions between excited energy states.

In the same way, current thinking is that the photons, the neutrino, the electron, the pi-mesons, the protons, the neutrons, and other particles are all related in simpler fashion, much as the line spectrum of mercury (or any atom) has its origin in the basic structure of a single atom. In addition, something should be said about the anti-particles. An *anti-particle* is merely another state of a known particle. For example, the anti-proton and the proton differ only in that their charges are opposite: the mass and other properties remain the same. For this reason, many physicists object to regarding the anti-particles as new particles. Their reasoning is that calling each anti-particle of a given particle a new particle is like doubling the number of animal species by calling the mirror image of each a new species.

A number of physicists maintain that there are only two elementary particles, the *baryon* and the *lepton*. The most familiar baryons are protons and neutrons; they are thought of as being merely different states of the same particles. Other particles, such as the *lambda-zero* and the *sigma-minus*, are excited states (states of higher energy) of the baryon. They can decay to a proton or neutron by emitting pi-mesons or K-mesons (kaons). The most familiar leptons are neutrinos, electrons, and mu-mesons. Again, decay is possible by emission of mesons.

Recently, Yuval Ne'eman and Murray Gell-Mann have independently devised an approach known as the "eight-fold way" to predict the differences in energies between certain excited states. To a large extent these relationships are correct, but physicists are still far from an understanding of the theory of why the relationships exist.

—Donald E. Cunningham

PHYSICS GLOSSARY

Absolute zero.—The temperature at which the molecules of a substance would cease moving and at which, therefore, a perfect gas (if kept at constant volume) would exert no pressure. The temperature has never been reached and can be shown to be unattainable. It is equal to —273.15° C. or —459.67° F. (See also *Temperature scales.*)

Absorption.—The conversion of radiant light energy into other forms of energy, such as heat, as the light energy passes through a particular medium. The *absorptivity,* or *absorptive power,* of a medium is the ratio of the amount of light energy it converts to the total amount of light energy passing through it.

Acceleration.—The change of velocity (speeding up or slowing down) with time. This change may be a change in speed, such as when a ball is dropped from a height, or a change in direction, such as when a runner moves around a curved track at a constant speed, or a combination of the two. *Angular acceleration* is the speeding up or slowing down of a rotating body. The *acceleration of gravity,* usually designated by the letter *g,* is the change in velocity caused by gravitational attraction; on Earth, it is equal to 32.2 feet per second per second, or 980.6 centimeters per second per second.

Acoustics.—The branch of physics that concerns itself with the production, conduction, measurement, perception, reproduction, and control of sound waves.

Adiabatic process.—Any change in matter that takes place without a loss or gain in the heat content of the system.

Alpha particle.—The nucleus of a helium atom. An alpha particle is composed of two protons and two neutrons and therefore has a positive charge. Alpha particles are one of the products of the radioactive decay of the elements radium and uranium.

Ammeter.—An indicating device used to measure the quantity of current in an electric or electronic circuit. Ammeters are always connected in series in the portion of the circuit in which they are used.

Ampere.—The unit of electrical current named after the French physicist André Marie Ampère (1775–1836). A *milliampere* is equal to 0.001 ampere, and a *microampere* is equal to 0.000001 ampere.

Amplitude.—The value measured from the mean, or interim, position to the highest, or extreme, position in any periodic or vibratory function, such as the swinging of a pendulum, the vibration of an alternating current, or the movement of a sound wave. It is sometimes called the *peak position.*

Avogadro's number.—(*Avogadro's constant.*) The total number of molecules present in 22.4 liters of any gas at standard temperature and pressure, named after the Italian physicist Amadeo Avogadro (1776–1856). Avogadro's number, usually designated as *N,* is equal to 6.0254×10^{23}.

Beat.—In acoustics, the tone result-

ing from the simultaneous arrival of two sound waves of nearly equal frequency. For example, if two tones having frequencies of 200 and 250 cycles per second arrive at the ear simultaneously, the listener will also hear a *beat frequency* tone equal to the difference between the other two tones (50 cycles per second).

Beta particle.—An electron emitted during the radioactive decay of such substances as thorium and uranium. *Positive beta particles* are *positrons,* and these are also emitted during the radioactive decay of certain elements.

Betatron.—See *Particle accelerator.*

Boiling point.—The temperature at which the vapor pressure of a liquid is fractionally greater than the pressure of its surroundings. At this point molecules of the liquid enter the gaseous state at a greater rate than they return to the liquid state, and the liquid boils off.

Calorie.—A unit quantity of heat energy. A *gram-calorie* is the quantity of heat that must be supplied to 1 gram of water to raise its temperature by 1° C. A *kilogram-calorie* is the quantity of heat that must be supplied to 1 kilogram of water to raise its temperature by 1° C.

Capacitance.—The ratio of the electrostatic charge on two bodies to the potential between them. A *capacitor,* or *condenser,* is a device consisting of two conducting plates separated by an insulating material, or *dielectric,* and thus having a high capacitance; it is used to store electric charges.

Carnot cycle.—The series of operations gone through by an ideal heat engine (called the *Carnot engine*), an engine that operates at maximum

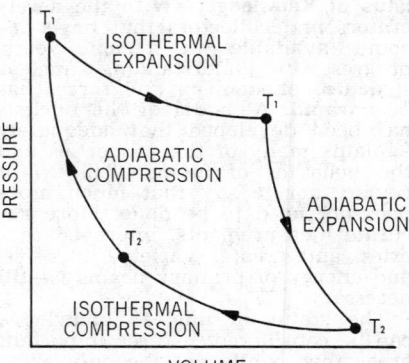

CARNOT CYCLE for an ideal heat engine. Since heat is evolved and taken up only during the two adiabatic parts of the cycle, the engine's efficiency is equal to 1 — (T_2/T_1); the greater the starting temperature, T_1, and the lower the interim temperature, T_2, the greater the efficiency.

efficiency. Proposed by Nicolas Léonard Sadi Carnot in 1824, the four phases of the cycle are *isothermal expansion, adiabatic expansion, isothermal compression,* and *adiabatic compression.* Work is done only during the two expansion phases of the cycle, which accounts for the high efficiency of the engine; energy is expended only when maximum energy (highest temperature) is attained in the expansion phases.

Cavitation.—The process of forming vapor bubbles in a liquid by the reduction of the pressure at a point within the liquid. A common example of this is the bubbles formed by the rotation of high-speed ships' propellers; cavitation results in the wearing of holes in the metal of the propeller, which are known as *cavitation damage*. When the vapor bubbles collapse in the liquid, the sound produced is called *cavitation noise*.

Celsius scale.—See *Temperature scales*.

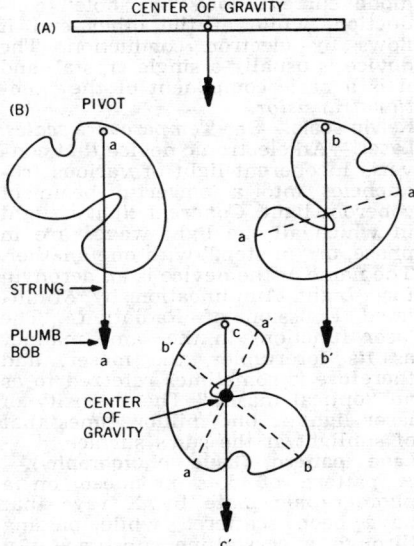

CENTER OF GRAVITY is the point of intersection of three plumb lines dropped from any body in three different orientations.

Center of gravity.—The point at which the weight of a body may be considered as being concentrated and at which the body may be supported by a single force to produce equilibrium. The center of gravity of a uniform beam is at its geometric center. The center of gravity of a nonuniform body may be determined by suspending a plumb line from it while it is in different positions. The center of gravity is the point of intersection of lines drawn through the plumb lines while the body is in any three different positions.

Centigrade scale.—See *Temperature scales*.

Circuit.—Any number of electrical conductors and components connected in such a way that current can flow. An *open circuit* is one through which current can normally flow but with a temporary break, such as an open switch, in it. A *closed circuit* is one through which current is flowing. A *series circuit* is one in which the total current, but only a fraction of the voltage, passes through every component of the circuit. A *parallel circuit* is one in which only a fraction of the current, but the total voltage, passes through every component. A *series-parallel circuit* is a parallel circuit in which some components are connected in series.

Cloud chamber.—A device in which rapidly moving charged particles, such as alpha and beta particles, leave a trail of condensed water-vapor particles. The trails may be photographed and studied to learn more about the particles that made them. The cloud chamber was invented by Charles Thomson Rees Wilson, a Scottish physicist, in 1911.

Color.—An inherent property of light apart from its form. Color is a sensation evoked in the eye in response to the wavelength of the light reaching it. In viewing a normal spectrum of light, going from long wavelength to short wavelength, the eye perceives the colors red, orange, yellow, green, blue, indigo, and violet; these are known as the spectral colors.

Condensation.—The change of a material from the gaseous to the liquid state, such as the condensation of water vapor to form rain.

Condenser.—See *Capacitance*.

Cosmic rays.—Radiation originating in interstellar space and reaching the earth's surface. The rays' exact origin is unknown. Cosmic rays consist primarily of protons, although electrons, mesons, and positrons have also been detected. Cosmic rays often rain upon the earth's surface in *bursts* or *showers*.

Cryogenics.—The branch of physics that deals with the properties of matter at temperatures approaching absolute zero.

Cybernetics.—The branch of physics that deals with the control and internal communication of information within automatic data-processing machines.

Cycle.—Any sequence of events at the end of which conditions have returned to the state that existed at the beginning. A cycle is generally recurrent; that is, the sequence generally repeats over and over. A familiar cycle is that of the four-stroke internal-combustion engine, in which the sequence of events is intake, compression, explosion, and exhaust. Other familiar cycles are found in electricity and in electronic communications: alternating electric current is usually designated in terms of both voltage and cycle rate, such as 120 volts, 60 cycles; and the frequency of radio waves is usually given in cycles per second (*c.p.s.*), thousands of cycles per second (kilocycles per second, *kc.p.s.*), or millions of cycles per second (megacycles per second, *mc.p.s.*).

Cyclotron.—See *Particle accelerators*.

Density.—The mass per unit volume of a material. Density is usually expressed in terms of pounds per cubic foot or grams per cubic centimeter.

Dewar vessel (Dewar flask).—A container used for the storage of liquid air. The vessel, named after its discoverer, Sir James Dewar, consists of a flask-within-a-flask (an arrangement called "double-walled"). The space between the inner and outer containers is a vacuum, and the walls enclosing the space are silvered. Thus, the construction is like that of the familiar vacuum bottle. The vacuum prevents the transfer of heat by conduction or by convection currents. The silvered surface minimizes the transfer of heat by radiation. Dewar vessels are used in cryogenics.

Diffraction.—In optics, the process by which "fuzziness" at the edge of a shadow is caused by the change in direction of light rays from a point source as they interact with the edge of an object. In acoustics, diffraction is the change in direction of a sound wave caused by its passing through layers of different densities or by the varying velocity of wind with altitude.

Diffusion.—The scattering of light in all directions during transmission or reflection. During transmission, it is caused by the light waves' striking minute particles. During reflection, diffusion is caused by irregularities in the reflecting surface.

Dispersion.—The separation of light into its component wavelengths. Dispersion may be accomplished through the use of a prism or a diffraction grating. The breaking of white light into the seven spectral colors (red, orange, yellow, green, blue, indigo, and violet) is a dispersion phenomenon.

Doping.—The introduction of a specified quantity of impurities, called *dopants*, into a solid material in order to produce certain properties. This process is very important in the production of semiconductors, such as transistors.

Echo.—A sound wave that has been reflected in such a manner as to arrive at the listener at a later time than a sound wave coming directly from the source. An *echo chamber* is a room used to produce intentionally a certain amount of reverberation, or echo, of the sounds on a phonograph record or tape recording.

Electroluminescence.—The direct conversion of electrical energy into light in a liquid or solid material. This process has been adapted by illumination engineers to provide a very efficient means of lighting large areas. It is also the basis of operation of the injection laser.

Electromagnetic spectrum.—See *Spectrum*.

Electromotive force (e.m.f.).—The pressure that causes the movement of electrons around an electric circuit. Electromotive force is produced by reversible processes of energy conversion, such as in a storage battery; and the device in which it is produced is called the *seat of electromotive force*. The unit of measurement of this force is the volt.

Electron.—An electrically charged particle that is one of the basic building blocks of the atom. The electron possesses the smallest amount of negative electric charge found thus far in nature. (However, three elementary particles, called *quarks*, with smaller charges have been postulated.) An electron has a mass only $\frac{1}{1,800}$ that of the proton, which is the basic particle of positive electric charge.

Electron-volt (e.v.).—A small unit of energy. It is defined as the kinetic energy possessed by an electron that has been subjected to an electromotive force of one volt. The energy of nuclear particles in particle accelerators is usually expressed in millions of electron volts (*M.e.v.*) or billions of electron volts (*B.e.v.*). An electron acted upon by one billion volts to give it a kinetic energy of 1 B.e.v. will travel at a speed close to that of light (186,300 miles per second).

Energy. — The ability to do work. There are many forms of energy, such as heat, light, chemical, radiant, mechanical, and nuclear energy. Any form of energy can be converted into any other form of energy, and matter and energy may be converted into one another. However, the total mass and energy of a system must always remain the same. There are two kinds of mechanical energy: a body possesses *kinetic energy* by virtue of its motion, and it possesses *potential energy* by virtue of its position in relation to any specified reference point.

Enthalpy. — The heat possessed by a body or system per unit mass. Enthalpy is an important concept in thermodynamics.

Entropy. — A thermodynamic property of a system that is a measure of the energy that the system has "used" and will, therefore, never be able to use again. Since all thermodynamic processes "use" energy in this way and the energy can never be recovered, the entropy of the universe is constantly increasing.

Fahrenheit scale. — See *Temperature scales.*

Fluorescence. — The absorption of energy of short wavelength and its prompt emission in the form of visible light. The energy absorbed may be from a chemical reaction, heating, ion bombardment, or exposure to light rays of short wavelength. If the energy is stored for a long period before the emission of the visible light, the process is called *phosphorescence.*

Force. — Any action that will impart an acceleration to any mass that is free to move.

Freezing point. — The temperature at which a liquid solidifies. Pure substances generally solidify at a constant temperature, while impure substances solidify over a small range of temperatures. The *melting point,* which is the temperature at which a solid turns into a liquid, is the same temperature as the freezing point.

Frequency. — The number of times an event will take place in a given unit of time. Thus, frequency may be measured in cycles per second, revolutions per minute, pulses per second, and so on. In acoustics, the *audiofrequency* is any sound-wave frequency that can normally be heard; audiofrequencies range from 15 to 20,000 cycles per second. An *infrasonic frequency* is one below the audiofrequency range; an *ultrasonic frequency* is one lying above the audiofrequency range.

Friction. — The inherent resistance to motion when an attempt is made to move one surface over another. The energy used to overcome friction is generally dissipated as heat.

Galvanometer. — An electric measuring instrument. It is generally used for the detection of electric currents. When properly connected to resistance elements and calibrated, galvanometers are called *ammeters* and *voltmeters.*

Gamma rays. — Very high energy X rays. Gamma rays are emitted by radioactive substances in decaying.

Half-life. — The period of time it takes for a radioactive material to lose one-half of its strength. Half-lives vary from trillions of years to fractions of seconds. For example, the half-life of samarium-152 is 1,000,000,000,000 years, while that of polonium-212 is 0.0000003 second.

Harmonic. — A frequency that is a multiple of another frequency to which it is related. A harmonic having a frequency four times that of the fundamental frequency, for example, is called the fourth harmonic. In acoustics, the harmonics of a sound that are heard simultaneously with the fundamental frequency are called *overtones.*

Heat. — A form of energy that is associated with the motions of the atoms and molecules within a substance. Thus, heat is a form of mechanical energy. The more rapid the motion of the atoms and molecules, the greater the heat content of the substance.

Hole. — An empty space in the crystal lattice of a semiconductor material, into which an electron may move. Current flows through a semiconductor by a process called *hole conduction,* in which an electron moves into a "hole," leaving a "hole" behind it; another electron moves to fill the new "hole," and so on.

Impedance. — In electronics, the apparent resistance to the flow of an alternating current that can be equated to the resistance to the flow of direct current through a circuit.

Image. — In optics, the likeness of an object caused by the viewing of the light rays proceeding from it. A *real image* can be shown on a screen, while a *virtual image* cannot.

Inductance. — An electrical property common to all circuits but primarily noticeable in A.C. (alternating current) circuits. Inductance can be seen in two separate effects. In one effect, a varying current tends to produce an electromotive force in its own circuit (called *self-inductance*) or in an adjoining circuit (called *mutual inductance*). In the other effect, inductance tends to even out the alternations in the current by causing a lag in building up to the maximum value and a lag once again in falling to the minimum value. The more rapid the alternations, the greater the inductance. An *inductor* is any electrical apparatus, usually an *inductance coil,* introduced into a circuit with the intention of producing inductance.

Inertia. — The inherent property of a body, as defined by Sir Isaac Newton's first law of motion, that tends to resist any change in the body's motion.

Infinity. — In optics, a distance sufficiently great so that light rays coming from a source located there will —for all practical purposes—be parallel to one another. Conversely, if an object is located at the focal point of a lens, the light rays proceeding from it will emerge from the lens parallel to one another, and the image is said to be formed at infinity.

Ion. — A charged particle that results when an atom or molecule gains or loses one or more electrons. A positive ion is an atom or molecule that has lost an electron; a negative ion is an atom or molecule that has gained an electron.

Isothermal process. — Any change in matter that takes place at a constant temperature; thus, it is a change in the pressure and/or volume of the substance.

Junction diode. — A semiconductor device that can carry current more easily in one direction than in the other; it is therefore widely used as a rectifier. At one end of a junction diode current flows by "hole" conduction, while at the other end it flows by electron conduction. The device is usually a single crystal, and it is a basic component of the *junction transistor.*

Kelvin scale. — See *Temperature scales.*

Laser. — An electronic device that converts incoherent light of various frequencies into a powerful beam of coherent light. *Coherent light* is light in which all the light waves are in phase, or "in step," with one another. The name of the device is an acronym for "*Light Amplification by Stimulated Emission of Radiation.*" The laser functions in the same manner as its forerunner, the maser, and therefore is sometimes referred to as an "optical maser." The intensity of laser light is one million times that of sunlight at the sun's surface.

Laue pattern (Laue photography). — A pattern of dots produced on a photographic plate by X rays that have been scattered while passing through a crystalline substance. An anaysis of the dot pattern allows the crystal structure of the substance to be determined. The technique is named for Max von Laue, who pioneered in the field in 1912.

Lens. — A transparent optical device with at least one curved surface that bends, or refracts, light rays. A *convex lens* is one in which the curved surface bulges outward; it converges the light rays that pass through it. A *concave lens* is one in which the curved surface bulges inward; it diverges light rays that pass through it.

Mach number. — Specifically, the ratio of the speed of a fluid to the speed of sound at that location. More generally, it is used to designate the ratio of the speed of an aircraft in flight to the speed of sound at the altitude at which the aircraft is flying. Thus, an aircraft flying at Mach 2 would have a speed twice that of sound, or about 1,400 miles per hour. If the Mach number is less than 1.0, the speed is called *subsonic;* if the Mach number is greater than 1.0 the speed is called *supersonic.*

Magnetohydrodynamics (M.H.D.). — The branch of physics that deals with the interaction of a magnetic field with an electrically conducting gas. The study of magnetohydrodynamics is closely related to many of the experiments with nuclear fusion.

Maser. — An electronic device that amplifies low-frequency electromagnetic waves (*microwaves*) by using these waves to stimulate the emission of similar waves from atoms and molecules. Its function is described by its name, which is an acronym for "*Microwave Amplification by Stimu-*

lated *Emission* of *Radiation.*" The inner workings of the maser are almost identical to those of its offshoot, the laser. In a simplified form, it is this:

The atoms of any material have a characteristic energy level, which is called the *ground state.* The atoms can absorb a quantum of energy, which raises them to a higher energy level. Under normal conditions, the atom will eventually emit the quantum it has absorbed and return to the ground state. However, in certain materials, the atom can be stimulated to give up the quantum of energy it has absorbed by exposing it to a second quantum. The unique property of maser and laser materials is that the quantum of energy emitted is in phase with and parallel to the quantum that stimulated its emission. It is this property that has made the maser and the laser the most significant breakthroughs in electronics since the transistor.

Mass.—An inherent property of matter that is a measure of the amount of matter present in a body. Masses are generally measured by comparing the force of gravitation acting upon them; this is called their *weight.* Thus, the weight of a body is proportional to its mass; in the English system, the mass of a body is $\frac{1}{32}$ of its weight.

Melting point.—See *Freezing point.*

Meson.—Any one of about a dozen subatomic particles whose mass lies between that of the electron and that of the proton, and that have electrical charges of 0, +1, or −1. Mesons are unstable, and their lifetime is only about 0.000001 second. Mesons are found in cosmic rays and are produced artificially in nuclear reactors. The two most prominent species are called *mu mesons* and *pi mesons.*

Momentum.—An inherent property of a body in motion that determines the amount of time it will take to bring the body to rest when a constant force is applied to the body. Momentum is the product of the body's mass multiplied by its velocity.

Neutron.—A neutral particle that is one of the basic building blocks of the atom. The mass of the neutron is equal to that of the proton.

Nuclear fission.—The splitting of the nucleus of an atom, caused by bombarding it with neutrons, into two parts; the splitting is accompanied by the release of more neutrons and large quantities of energy in the form of light and heat. Only the heavy isotopes, such as uranium-235 and plutonium-239, readily undergo fission, as in military uses.

Nuclear fusion.—The joining of the nuclei of two atoms to form the single nucleus of another heavier element, such as the fusion of two hydrogen nuclei in the sun to form a helium nucleus. When the nuclei of two light atoms, such as hydrogen or lithium, fuse, a large amount of energy is released, according to the formula proposed by Albert Einstein to equate mass and energy: $E = mc^2$, where E is the energy released, m is the mass, and c is a constant equal to the velocity of light.

Ohm.—The unit of electrical resistance named after the German physicist Georg Simon Ohm (1787–1854). The reciprocal of the ohm, the *mho,* is the unit of electrical conductance.

Optics.—The branch of mathematical physics that deals with light. *Physical optics* studies are based on the wave properties of light; studies in *geometric optics* are based on quantum properties.

Particle accelerator.—Any of several devices, sometimes referred to as "atom smashers," used to impart high velocities to such charged particles as alpha particles, electrons, and protons. The *betatron* is used to accelerate electrons. The *bevatron* is a proton accelerator. The *cosmotron* and the *cyclotron* are both used as proton accelerators. The *linear accelerator* is different from the others in that the particles within it always move in straight lines rather than in circles or spirals; it is used to accelerate electrons. The *synchrotron* is similar to the cyclotron, but it can accelerate protons to even higher energies. The *Van de Graaff accelerator* is the only electrostatic accelerator of the group; it is used to accelerate electrons.

Photon.—See *Quantum.*

Piezoelectricity.—An electric current developed in some crystalline materials when they are subjected to a strain in an appropriate direction. This property is utilized commercially in ceramic phonograph cartridges.

Pitch.—The subjective tone of a sound wave. The pitch of a sound wave is a function of its frequency.

Plasma.—The fourth state of matter. Plasmas are similar to gases in that the particles of which they are composed are at great distances from one another. The particles of a plasma have a very high internal energy. Plasmas are mixtures of neutral particles, ions (charged particles), and free electrons. Plasmas are found in the sun, in lightning bolts, and in a number of man-made devices, such as fluorescent lights.

Positron.—A positively charged subatomic particle that has a mass and a magnitude of charge equal to that of the electron.

Potential difference.—The difference in electrical potential at two points that causes an electrical current to flow between them. Potential difference is called *voltage.*

Potentiometer.—An electrical measuring device used to determine the potential difference between two points. It is more accurate than a voltmeter.

Printed circuit.—An electrically conducting wiring diagram deposited, etched, or otherwise superimposed on a nonconducting surface. Electrical components may be soldered to the conducting wiring diagram, as in most inexpensive radios.

Proton.—An electrically charged particle that is one of the basic building blocks of the atom. The proton has a positive electrical charge equal in magnitude to that of the electron. The proton has a mass of 1.66×10^{-24} grams, about 1,800 times larger than that of the electron and equal to that of the neutron.

Quantum.—The smallest indivisible quantity of energy. In an electromagnetic wave, such as light, a quantum is carried in a discrete packet called a *photon.*

Radioactive decay.—The breakdown of an unstable isotope through the emission of alpha and beta particles and gamma rays to form a stable isotope.

Réaumur scale.—See *Temperature scales.*

Rectification.—The conversion of an alternating electrical current into a direct electrical current. Any device that accomplishes this, such as a diode, is called a *rectifier.*

Refraction.—The change in direction of a light ray as it passes between substances of different densities. It results from the fact that the speed of light varies inversely with the density of the medium through which it is traveling.

Resistance.—The opposition offered to the flow of an electrical current by a substance through which it is passing. Those substances that have a low resistance, such as aluminum and copper, are called *conductors.* Those substances that have a high resistance, such as rubber and silk, are called *nonconductors,* or *insulators.* A *resistor* is a device placed in an electric circuit for the express purpose of providing a specified amount of resistance to the current flowing in it.

Semiconductor.—A material whose resistance to the flow of electrical current is greater than that of a conductor, such as aluminum or copper, but less than that of an insulator, such as rubber. Typical semiconductors are germanium and silicon.

Semimetal.—A material whose resistance to the flow of electrical current is greater than that of a conductor, such as aluminum or copper, but less than that of a semiconductor, such as germanium or silicon. Typical semimetals are antimony and bismuth.

Specific gravity. — The ratio of the weight of any substance to that of an equal volume of fresh water. A specific gravity of less than 1.0 indicates a density less than that of water; a specific gravity greater than 1.0, a density greater than that of water.

Spectrum.—The arrangement of any sequence of wave forms in order of increasing or decreasing wavelength or frequency. For example, in acoustics a study is made of the *audio-frequency spectrum,* which includes all sound waves of 15 cycles to 20,000 cycles per second. The term "spectrum," however, is generally taken as a reference to the visible portion of the *electromagnetic spectrum.* The electromagnetic spectrum consists of electromagnetic waves with wavelengths ranging from about 10^{-14} meter (cosmic rays) to about 10^7 meters (radio waves); the visible portion of the spectrum covers wavelengths from about 4×10^{-7} (violet light) to 7.5×10^{-7} (red light).

Speed.—See *Velocity.*

Temperature. — The average kinetic energy (energy of motion) of the atoms and molecules in a substance. Heat will always flow from a region of higher temperature to one of lower temperature.

Temperature scales.—Arbitrary calibrations of thermometers in order to establish convenient references for the determination of temperatures. There are three thermometric scales based on the boiling and freezing points of water: the Fahrenheit scale; the Celsius, or Centigrade, scale; and the Réaumur scale. The *Fahrenheit scale (F.)* was proposed by Gabriel D. Fahrenheit (1686–1736). He set the zero point as the temperature of a mixture of salt and ice water and the temperature of the human body as 96° (this latter measurement has since been proved erroneous, and the temperature of the human body on the Fahrenheit scale is 98.6°); on this basis, the *ice point* (the freezing point of water at a pressure of 1 atmosphere, or 980 millimeters) was 32° and the *steam point* (the boiling point of water at a pressure of 1 atmosphere, or 980 millimeters) was 212°. The *Celsius, or Centigrade, scale (C.)* was proposed by Anders Celsius (1701–1744). Celsius set the ice point of his scale at 0° and the steam point at 100°. The *Réaumur scale (R.)* was proposed by René A. F. Réaumur (1683–1757). Réaumur set the ice point of his scale at 0° and the steam point at 80°. The *Absolute (A.),* or *Kelvin (K.), scale* was proposed by Lord Kelvin (William Thomson, 1824–1907). The zero point is that temperature at which all molecular motion theoretically ceases. The ice point on the Absolute scale is 273° and the steam point is 373°. The scales are related to one another by the following formulas:

$$°F. = \frac{9}{5}°C. + 32$$

$$°F. = \frac{9}{4}°R. + 32$$

$$°C. = \frac{5}{9}(°F. - 32)$$

$$°C. = \frac{5}{4}°R.$$

$$°R. = \frac{4}{5}°C.$$

$$°R. = \frac{4}{9}(°F. - 32)$$

$$°K. = °A.$$

$$°K. = °C. + 273$$

$$°K. = \frac{5}{9}°F. + 255$$

$$°K. = \frac{5}{4}°R. + 273$$

Thermodynamics.—The branch of mathematical physics that deals with the relationship of heat energy to other forms of energy, primarily mechanical energy.

Transistor.—An electronic device, made of a doped semiconductor crystal, that is used to amplify an electrical current. Transistors are replacing vacuum tubes, such as the diode and the triode, in many applications.

Velocity.—The rate of displacement, or rate of change of position, per unit time. The difference between velocity and *speed* is that velocity includes direction, but speed does not. Thus, an airplane that has a velocity of 600 miles per hour east will have a speed of 600 miles per hour. The distinction between velocity and speed is not always made, especially in nontechnical usage, however. For example,

the velocity of light is generally given as 186,300 miles per second, but this is really its speed.

Volt.—The unit of electrical potential difference, named after the Italian physicist Alessandro Volta (1745–1827).

Voltmeter.—An indicating device used to measure the difference in potential between two points in an electric circuit. Voltmeters, which are not as accurate as potentiometers, are always connected in parallel between the two points.

Watt.—The unit of power named after the Scottish physicist James Watt (1736–1819). A *kilowatt* is equal to 1,000 watts; 1 *megawatt* is equal to 1,000 kilowatts, or 1,000,000 watts; and 1 *gigawatt* is equal to 1,000 megawatts, 1,000,000 kilowatts, or 1,000,000,000 watts. Electric power (measured in watts) is the product of the current (measured in amperes) and the potential difference (measured in volts).

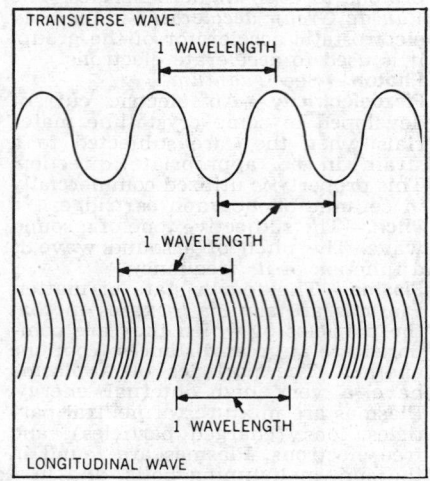

WAVELENGTH as it is measured in transverse and in longitudinal waves.

Wavelength.—The distance between similar, consecutive points along any wave form. Thus, in a *longitudinal wave,* such as a compressional sound wave, the wavelength is the distance between successive condensations and rarefactions; in a *transverse wave,* such as a sinusoidal light wave, the wavelength is the distance between successive crests and troughs. The different colors the eye senses when receiving light waves are due to the different wavelengths of the waves.

Weight.—See *Mass.*

Wheatstone bridge.—A device for determining the resistance in an electrical circuit invented by the English physicist Sir Charles Wheatstone in 1843.

Work.—In mechanics, the product of a force acting through a distance. Thus, work is done when a 5-pound weight is raised 10 feet above the ground, the amount of work being 50 (5 × 10) foot-pounds. In electricity, work is the electric power expended over a period of time. It is usually measured in watt-hours or kilowatt-hours, one kilowatt-hour equaling 1,000 watt-hours.

BIBLIOGRAPHY

GENERAL

ASIMOV, ISAAC. *Inside the Atom.* Abelard-Schuman, Ltd., 1961.

BLACKWOOD, OSWALD HANCE. *General Physics.* John Wiley & Sons, Inc., 1963.

COHEN, I. BERNARD. *The Birth of a New Physics.* Anchor Books, 1960.

DULL, CHARLES EDWARD. *Modern Physics.* Holt, Rinehart & Winston, Inc., 1964.

EINSTEIN, ALBERT and INFELD, LEOPOLD. *The Evolution of Physics.* Simon & Schuster, Inc., 1938.

GARDNER, MARTIN. *Relativity for the Millions.* The Macmillan Co., 1962.

REICHEN, CHARLES ALBERT. *History of Physics.* Hawthorn Books, Inc., 1963.

RIPIN, EDWIN M. *How to Solve Physics Problems.* John F. Rider Publisher, Inc., 1961.

WHITE, HARVEY E. *Modern College Physics* (4th ed.). D. Van Nostrand Co., Inc., 1962.

MECHANICS

BEER, FERDINAND PIERRE. *Mechanics for Engineers: Statics and Dynamics.* McGraw-Hill, Inc., 1962.

PHELAN, RICHARD. *Fundamentals of Mechanical Design* (2nd ed.). McGraw-Hill, Inc., 1962.

LIGHT

COLLIS, JOHN STEWART. *World of Light.* Horizon Press, Inc., 1960.

MONK, GEORGE SPENCER. *Light: Principles and Experiments.* Dover Publications, Inc., 1963.

OTIS, ARTHUR SINTON. *Light Velocity and Relativity.* Christian E. Burckel & Associates, 1963.

HEAT

BERGMANN, PETER GABRIEL. *Basic Theories of Physics: Heat and Quanta.* Prentice-Hall, Inc., 1951.

EFRON, ALEXANDER. *Heat.* John F. Rider, Publisher, Inc., 1957.

MOTT-SMITH, MORTON CHURCHILL. *Heat and Its Workings.* Dover Publications, Inc., 1962.

SOUND

RICHARDSON, EDWARD GICK. *Sound.* St. Martin's Press, Inc., 1953.

SEARS, FRANCIS WESTON. *Mechanics, Heat and Sound.* Addison-Wesley Publishing Co., Inc., 1950.

ELECTRICITY

ATKIN, RONALD HARRY. *Theoretical Electromagnetism.* John Wiley & Sons, 1962.

SUFFERN, MAURICE GRAYLE. *Basic Electric and Electronic Principles.* McGraw-Hill, Inc., 1962.

ATOMIC ENERGY

HARNWELL, GAYLORD P. and STEPHENS, WILLIAM E. *Atomic Physics.* McGraw-Hill, Inc., 1955.

HARRISON, GEORGE RUSSELL. *Atoms in Action.* William Morrow & Co., Inc., 1949.

JUKES, JOHN D. *Man-made Sun.* The Viking Press, Inc., 1961.

VOLUME TWENTY THREE

SOCIAL SCIENCE

Anthropology	1923
Sociology	1938
Psychology and Psychiatry	1947

THE AMERICAN MUSEUM OF NATURAL HISTORY

Social Science

ANTHROPOLOGY

Scope.—The term *anthropology* is derived from two Greek words: *anthropos,* meaning 'human being,' and *logos,* meaning 'ordered knowledge.' It is, in effect, *the science of man.*

Physical anthropology is the study of human beings as biological organisms varying in both time and space. It thus includes human evolution, various forms of adaptation to climate and culture, and racial variations in anatomy and physiology.

Prehistoric archaeology is the study of the caves, rock shelters, camp sites, village mounds, and other deposits in which human beings have lived and where they have left such remains as stone tools, broken animal bones, and pottery. A thin line separates this subject from the study of literate urban cultures, which fall under such separate headings as classical archaeology, Egyptology, and Assyriology, depending on the region, time span, and people concerned.

Cultural anthropology is the study of the habitual behavior patterns, or "cultures," of peoples before the impact of modern western civilization. A specific culture, as studied by anthropologists, consists of the sum total of the ways in which a certain people lives, transmitted from generation to generation. Most of these cultures are preliterate and considered primitive.

Relationship to Other Fields.—Anthropology stands midway between the natural and social sciences and includes aspects of many branches of learning. To many of the physical and social sciences it has contributed breadth of understanding and masses of comparative data, while it has also helped to prepare the leading nations of the world for the close interrelation of races and cultures created by the modern age.

At the same time, other disciplines have enriched anthropology. Anatomical studies have demonstrated some racial differences in certain physical characteristics, such as the positions of muscles, sizes of endocrine glands, and adaptation to heat and cold. Geneticists have found racial variations in blood groups, as well as in fingerprints and hand prints; they have also explained the principle of balanced polymorphism in which the "mixed" form of a gene may be more advantageous than either "pure" form. Population geneticists, working mostly with domestic animals, have thrown light on the structure of breeding units; zoogeographers have clarified the roles of marginal and nuclear populations in evolution; and animal taxonomists have helped to straighten out the tangled classification of human races, both living and extinct.

Systematic, scientific archaeological research has been made possible by studies in geology. Paleobotany has contributed knowledge of the flora of bygone times, and paleontology, that of the animals that men hunted; both have provided techniques of establishing the dates of fossil remains. Physicists have contributed the techniques of long-range dating by carbon-14, argon-potassium, the quantities of fluorine and nitrogen in ancient bone, and the amount of surface erosion in obsidian tools. Mine detectors and other electronic devices and skin divers are bringing new evidence to light.

In the field of cultural anthropology, modern transportation and communications, tape recorders, motion picture cameras, aerial photographs, and other mechanical devices have greatly helped the field worker. Year-round residence in a community enables the anthropologist to witness all seasonal aspects of a culture; the techniques of statistical analysis, using sorting machines and even computers, and the detailed mapping of villages have replaced earlier practices of making simple generalizations from hasty observation or the employment of single informants.

Psychology has contributed almost as much to anthropology as it has received in return. Some field workers have had themselves psychoanalyzed before going into the field in order to eradicate the biases that stem from their own cultures and personalities. The concept of the unconscious has taught field workers not to ask primitive people *why* they do this or that; the people themselves do not know, but in order to satisfy the inquirer, produce a variety of rationalizations and misleading answers.

Personality studies have been conducted on individuals in other cultures and on the whole cultures themselves, to determine, among other factors, what role infant training and child-rearing practices have on the cultural attitudes of the adults. Primate studies made on many species of monkeys and apes have also revealed the common behavioral background of man and his zoological kin, thus contributing to an understanding of human behavior; experiments in "handling" other animals have been made to supplement studies of infant training in human beings.

PHYSICAL ANTHROPOLOGY

The search for fossil man is one of the most exciting aspects of anthropology, and almost every year there are new finds that supplement or even change the human family tree. This tree, or *genealogy,* of man tells the story of his gradual evolution and his differentiation from the other descendants of a common primate ancestor. Man's evolution was not the direct, uninterrupted path it may seem in retrospect, but a series of staggering steps with many sideways leaps—and some disastrous dives down blind alleys. Many species that branched off, following one or more specializations and adaptations to specific environments, failed and slowly died out. Many of the fossil remains belong to these offshoots; the others, which stand in the line of the descent of man, constitute the story of the evolution of *Homo sapiens.*

Primates.—Man belongs to the order *Primates,* suborder *Catarrhinae,* superfamily *Hominoidea,* family *Hominidae,* subfamily *Homininae,* genus *Homo,* and species *sapiens.* Our nearest living relatives are the great apes, the *Pongidae,* which includes *Pongo,* the orangutan; *Pan,* the chimpanzee; and *Gorilla.* The gibbons are also closely related, monkeys, more distantly.

■**MAN'S EARLIEST ANCESTORS.**—The oldest known possible common ancestor of the great apes and man was *Proconsul,* who lived in East Africa during the Miocene period, between 26,000,000 and 14,000,000 years ago. Small and with a tiny brain, he lived among the trees but could also run along the ground on all fours and occasionally, on his hind legs. Another family of apes, the *Dryopithecines,* lived in Africa, Europe, and India; one of them may have been man's ancestor. Two of the likeliest candidates are *Ramapithecus* of India and *Kenyapithecus* of East Africa. Unlike the living apes, they both had short canine teeth similar to those of modern man.

After these apes there is a gap of more than 10,000,000 to 12,000,000 years to the *Pleistocene,* the last major period of geologic time. Until recently the Pleistocene was believed to have begun about 1,000,000 years ago. Recent work on argon-potassium dating of new finds in Africa and sea cores from the Atlantic and Indian oceans indicate that this date may have to be set back considerably—to 1,500,000 years ago. The Lower Pleistocene, or Villefranchian, may have begun twice as long ago, but this remains to be determined. In the event that these dates prove to be correct, the dates given later in this article should be correspondingly extended.

The Pleistocene was a period of extreme climatic changes, with four great ice ages interspersed with periods of warm temperatures in some areas, alternating moisture and drought in others. It is possible that the changing conditions of climate and environment may have induced the anatomical and social modifications that led to man.

The earliest fossil remains of the *Hominidae,* or hominids, belong to two subfamilies, the *Australopithecines,* or "near-men," and the *Homininae,* to which the first examples of the genus *Homo* belong. Although in general the Australopithecines preceded the *Homininae* by about 500,000 years, recent discoveries in Africa point to the possible contemporaneous existence of the two types.

■AUSTRALOPITHECINES.—Fossil remains of the Australopithecines have been found in Java (*Meganthropus*), South Africa (*Australopithecus*), and East Africa (*Zinjanthropus*). While the finds from Java and South Africa have been dated as being about 700,000 to 600,000 years old, the latter, discovered in 1960, may be as old as 1,250,000 years. The Australopithecines were less than five feet tall and walked upright, but had small brains about the size of those of living apes. They were probably capable of using, though not of making, crude pebble tools, with which they hunted small game. Their teeth, however, were more specialized than those of modern man, which would preclude their being our direct ancestors. The Australopithecines probably represent a variation in the general direction of man that failed to develop successfully and therefore became extinct.

■JAVA.—Among the earliest bones that can be considered those of true men are a series of skulls from Java, Pithecanthropus or *Homo erectus,* so called because the men walked upright. One of these, Pithecanthropus 4, has been dated at about 700,000 years. Over five feet tall, he had heavy, ape-like brow ridges and marked *prognathism* (forward projection) of the jaw. Pithecanthropus 4 was succeeded in Java by other Pithecanthropi, of whom three skulls have been dated as about 500,000 years old. Around 100,000 years ago (the date is very shaky) there appeared a type known as Solo Man; eleven Solo skulls have been discovered. An adolescent skull was found in Borneo and dated at about 40,000 years; two skulls were also found in Java, of the same or lesser age. These skulls show a gradual development of what was probably a single evolutionary line, the Australoid, culminating in the living Australian aborigines and in certain relict peoples of Southeast Asia and India.

■CHINA.—The oldest (about 400,000 years) human specimens from China are the fragmentary remains of about forty individuals quarried out of a former cave at Choukoutien, near Peking. Called variously *Pithecanthropus pekinensis, Sinanthropus* ("Chinese Man"), or, more simply,

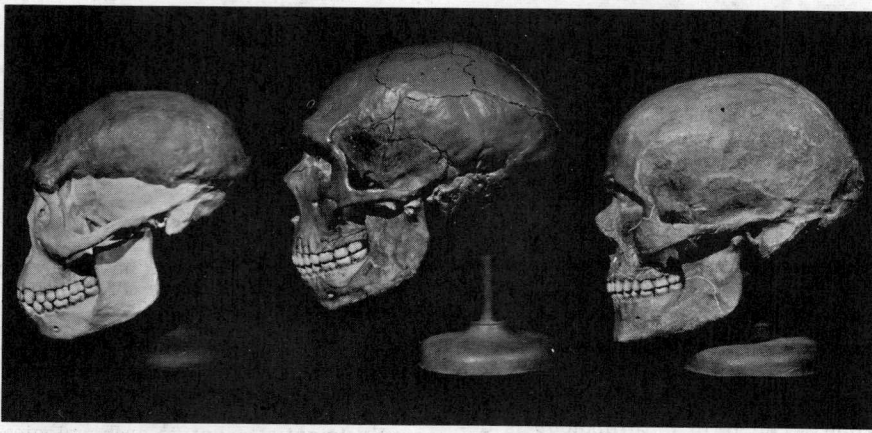

AMERICAN MUSEUM OF NATURAL HISTORY

SKULLS OF EARLY MAN show the evolutionary development of our species. The *Pithecanthropus* (*left*) dates back about 500,000 years. The *Neanderthal* (*center*) existed about 90,000 years ago, while the *Cro-Magnon* (*right*) may have lived only 30,000 years ago.

Peking Man, they are of about the same evolutionary stage as the Solo Man of Java. Heavily built and with a slightly larger cranial capacity, they show certain Mongoloid characteristics in the teeth and especially in the high cheekbones typical of modern Mongoloids. Remains in cave deposits where they were found indicate that they not only chipped rough stone tools but also used fire for warmth, protection against animals, and possibly for cooking.

These finds are followed by a late Pleistocene skull from Mapa (Kwangtung) in South China, dated at about 150,000 to 100,000 years ago; like Peking Man, it is still essentially a type of *Homo erectus.* A skull from Tze Yang in West China, of less than half that age, is much closer to the form of *Homo sapiens.* Finally, from the end of the Pleistocene, about 10,000 years ago, are three skeletons also found at Choukoutien; called the Upper Cave people, they are virtually modern Mongoloids.

■AFRICA. — The oldest man-ape yet found comes from Lake Chad on the edge of the Sahara. Small-brained but anatomically similar to man, it dates back to the dawn of the Pleistocene. Other Australopithecines have been found throughout Africa: *Australopithecus,* who gave the name to this type, at Sterkfontein; another at Kromdraai; and dozens more in caves of the Transvaal. The oldest of these, from the early Pleistocene, are small; but later examples are larger. Roughly shaped stones have been found with their remains, raising the possibility that these ape-men may have been primitive toolmakers. They became extinct toward the Middle Pleistocene, possibly as a result of the rise of true men.

The most recent discoveries at Olduvai Gorge in Tanganyika may shed some light on this problem. There, in 1963, on the site where *Zinjanthropus* was discovered, fossil remains of five individuals were found of the same time, earlier, and later than *Zinjanthropus.* They reveal a type about four feet tall, with an upright stance and a skull that is still small but

is larger than the Australopithecine skulls, and is shaped much like that of modern man. They have been named *Homo habilis* (meaning "able, handy, mentally skillful") by their finder, Dr. Lewis S. B. Leakey. He believes that they were the makers of the tools found in these layers and that *Zinjanthropus* represents an intruder (or a victim) on the *Homo habilis* living sites. Rough circles of stones have also been found in geologically contemporary strata, indicating that possibly they were able to make rough shelters.

Other finds in South Africa and East Africa follow the sequence from *Zinjanthropus* to *Homo erectus.* A skull cap found at Olduvai in the layer above *Zinjanthropus* is dated as about 400,000 years old. It is similar to the Pithecanthropines of Java and China, except that the brow ridges are curved instead of being straight, giving it a closer resemblance to a Caucasoid or Negroid type. Another *Homo erectus* skull, about 30,000 years old, was removed from a mine at Broken Hill, in Zambia (formerly Northern Rhodesia). It is the only truly primitive fossil skull yet found that is complete, and its facial structure is of a very primitive Negroid type. A series of four fragmentary skulls from Kanjera, Kenya, of uncertain date are also Negroid in type but more evolved than the Olduvai-Broken Hill examples. Aside from these specimens, we have nothing substantial with which to trace the origin of the African Negroes and their dwarf relatives, the Pygmies.

In North Africa the earliest *Homo erectus* remains are two lower jaws from Ternefine, Algeria, of about the same age as *Sinanthropus* and resembling him in form and tooth structure. A series of lower jaws from three sites in Morocco suggests that this local race survived until the early Late Pleistocene. Two skulls from Jebel Ighoud, Morocco, are heavy-browed, flat-faced and prognathous, similar to *Sinanthropus* and probably prototypes of the modern South African Bushmen. The upper jaw of a child, found in a cave of Tangier, carries this series into the Late Pleistocene, the time of modern Caucasoid men in Europe and the Near East.

■ EUROPE.—Very few examples of man have been discovered in Europe dating from the Early or Middle Pleistocene, but the record from the later eras is more detailed than on any other continent. The European (and associated Middle Eastern) sequence begins with the Heidelberg jaw, found in Germany, and dated at about 400,000 to 360,000 years ago. It roughly corresponds to the Pithecanthropines of Java and China. From about 250,000 years ago are two skulls, found at Steinheim, Germany, and Swanscombe, England; except for lingering apelike brow ridges, they are remarkably similar to skulls of modern man in both size and form. These two skulls establish the existence of *Homo sapiens* in Europe 250,000 years ago. Between this date and the final, or Würm, glaciation, Europeans changed little morphologically. The remains of 27 individuals have been discovered, all of whom are probably of the Caucasoid race.

■ NEANDERTHALS.—The Würm glacial period was the age of the Neanderthals, an enigmatic people concentrated in France and the Near East; the remains of 83 individuals had been unearthed by 1963. They were people of normal body build with deep chests and short, square-toed feet. They did *not* walk stooped over or with a shambling gait, as is commonly represented, but stood straight and held their heads erect. Like most fossil men, the Neanderthals had heavy brow ridges, long faces, and prominent noses; but they were not the brutish churls they are often made out to be, and their brain capacity was equal to that of many living Europeans. The teeth of the individual skulls studied are considerably worn down, possibly from using them to dress animal skins worn as protection against the cold.

Both the origin and the destiny of the Neanderthals is greatly disputed. Some scholars believe they were a race of *Homo erectus* who migrated to Europe and replaced the *Homo sapiens* living there, while others believe they evolved from their *sapiens* predecessors. They survived in both Europe and the Middle East throughout the first Würm glaciation, but with the temporary retreat of the ice they gradually disappeared, either replaced by the Caucasoid ancestors of living Europeans and Middle Easterners or genetically absorbed into the Caucasoid strain.

■ HOMO SAPIENS.—The strain *Homo sapiens* inhabited western Europe during the rest of the Pleistocene. Their practice of burying their dead has left many complete skeletons for physical anthropologists, and the rich and highly developed artistic tradition of their cave paintings provides both evidence to their culture and further clues to their appearance. A skeleton from Combe Capelle, a skull from Chancelade, the buried remains of a Cro-Magnon man found near Les Eyzies in France (all representing the Upper Paleolithic Magdalenian culture) are among the more than fifty skeletons recovered from this period. They range in height generally from five to six feet, and their skulls are almost identical to modern man's, with high foreheads and prominent chins; in general appearance they could nearly pass for contemporary Europeans. Their origin is still uncertain, although recent finds from Israel (a skull from Mt. Carmel and the Skhūl skeletons) show a mixture of Neanderthal and Caucasoid characteristics that indicate a Middle Eastern origin.

■ MIGRATIONS.—In Asia, by the end of the Pleistocene, and probably as early as 18,000 years ago, the Mongoloids had expanded from their home in China, crossed the Bering Strait, and entered the previously uninhabited New World, becoming the ancestors of the American Indian. Between 12,000 and 10,000 years ago, other Mongoloids spread southward into Southeast Asia and Indonesia, displacing the original Australoids. Some of these Australoids lived on as dwarfs in impenetrable forests, mountain refuges, and fringing islands; others moved out to sea across strings of small islands (exposed by the falling sea level during the glacial periods) from Indonesia to New Guinea and Australia.

At the time of this second Mongoloid expansion, Caucasoids coming from Europe or the Near East invaded North Africa, expelling many of the earlier inhabitants of the Jebel Ighoud race. The latter migrated southward as far as the Cape of Good Hope, where they became the ancestors of the modern Bushmen, now a partially dwarfed, partially infantile race. The Caucasoids who replaced them in North Africa were the ancestors of the living Berbers.

Living Races.—All living men belong to a single genus and species, *Homo sapiens*. Within this classification they fall into groups that differ in certain physical characteristics; these groups are called *races*. The differences between races are purely biological and are marked by the hereditary transmission of physical characteristics. Genetically, race can be defined as a group with gene frequencies differing from those of other groups of humans. The genes that determine hereditary racial differences are, however, very few when compared with the great number of genes common to all men. The overall differences between men of different races are much less than the similarities. The term "race" cannot be applied to national, cultural, religious, or linguistic groups, nor can different races be equated with mental characteristics of intelligence, character, or personality.

■ CLASSIFICATION.—Many attempts have been made to classify the living races of man on the basis of their physical characteristics, but no complete agreement has been reached. Other classifications based strictly on genetics have stressed such factors as blood groups. The various classifications have ranged from the commonly held, threefold, Caucasoid, Negroid, and Mongoloid to as many as ten or more divisions. Most recently, C. S. Coon has proposed a fivefold classification, based on the fossil history of man as outlined above. He recognizes five subspecies, or geographical races, as follows: Mongoloid, Australoid, Caucasoid, Capoid, and Congoid. The first three are clearly differentiated and generally accepted; there are less obvious differences between the last two races, which have the same hair form and similar blood groups. Mixture of Capoids and Congoids is probably the result of the translocation of the Capoids from North Africa to South Africa. The two races, however, have definitely separate histories.

■ MONGOLOIDS.—The principal characteristics of the Mongoloids are a flattish face, often with an internal eye fold, subnasal prognathism, and shovel-shaped incisors and canine teeth. They also have a minimum of beard and body hair; coarse, straight, black head hair; small wrists, ankles, hands and feet; and skin color varying from brunet white to dark brown. Many are of stocky build, with relatively short limbs.

■ AUSTRALOIDS.—The Australoids also have flattish faces, but their eyes are sunken like those of Caucasoids rather than flush like those of the Mongoloids. They also lack the characteristic Mongoloid eye folds. The jaws of Australoids are prognathous, their nasal tips broad and fleshy, and their teeth are large and unspecialized. They are bearded like Caucasoids; some have heavy body hair, and their hair form is straight, wavy, or curly. Australoid skin color varies from black to almost brunet white; dark skin is the result of one genetic factor, whereas in African Negroes at least two such factors are responsible for the characteristic pigmentation. As a rule, Australoids are of slender build, with limb proportions similar to those of Caucasoids. Unlike the Mongoloids, who show little *sexual dimorphism* (difference in body form between the sexes), the Australoid women are much smaller than the men. Both men and women also tend to become gray-haired early in life, and some of the men are bald; among Mongoloids baldness is almost unknown, except among the Japanese.

The "hairy" Ainu of northern Japan, Sakhalin Island, and the Kuriles, once thought to be Caucasoids, are probably the mixed remnants of an ancient Australoid people who moved north along the island chain before the Mongoloid expansion. Their resemblance to Europeans may be explained on two bases: convergence in hairiness and pigmentation owing to parallel climatic adaptation and the possibility that the oldest Caucasoid peoples were originally related to the Australoids.

■ CAUCASOIDS.—The Caucasoids are essentially the peoples of Europe, North Africa, the Arab countries of the Near East, Iran, Afghanistan, West Pakistan, much of India, and Ceylon. They also include settlers in the Americas, Australia, New Zealand, and South

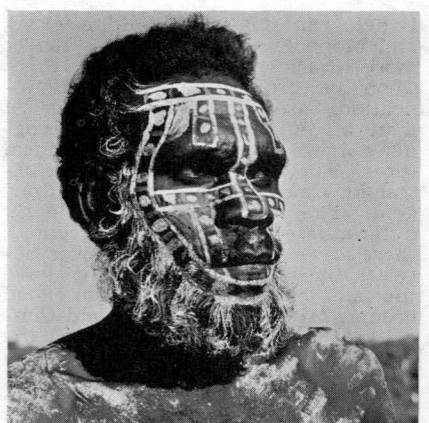

QANTAS

SATOUR

SATOUR

BROWN BROTHERS

THE RACES OF MAN cover the world with a wide variation on a single theme: *Homo sapiens*. The Australoids (*top left*) are the original inhabitants of the Australian subcontinent; the Congoid peoples of Africa are the Negroes and Pygmies; the Capoids are represented by a Bushman and a Zulu woman is another Congoid (*top center and right*). The Caucasoids shown here are five Iranian immigrants; the Mongoloids (*below, left to right*) include the pure Mongoloid Chinese and two offshoots, the Eskimo and the American Indian, who were the earliest immigrants to America.

NEW YORK PUBLIC LIBRARY

AMERICAN MUSEUM OF NATURAL HISTORY.

NEW YORK PUBLIC LIBRARY

Africa. Their physical characteristics are well-known. Their range in skin color is the greatest found in any subspecies, extending from the complete depigmentation of the Baltic peoples to the almost black skin color of the natives of southern India.

Essentially, the Causcasoids gravitate toward two morphological poles: the narrow-faced, thin-nosed extreme as seen in Europe among the Basques, and a broader, flatter-faced form with a low nasal bridge and widely separated eyes, as represented by Finns and Slavs. Although many anthropologists have seen in the latter form evidence of Mongoloid admixture, modern blood-group research has disproved this theory. The Lapps, who stand at the extreme in this respect, are not Mongoloid at all but purely European.

■CONGOIDS.—The classification of African peoples is confused by a scarcity of paleontological material and by the number of migrations along the highroads of the Sudan and the East African highlands. The Congoids include both the Negroes and the Pygmies, who apparently became dwarfs independently of the Asiatic and Philippine Negritos. We have absolutely no evidence of their beginnings. The historic center of the Negroes has extended from West Africa and the northern fringes of the Congo into the marsh country of the Sudan. From this point, some of them migrated in various directions, eventually reaching South Africa.

Their physical features are also well-known. They have less sexual dimorphism than either Australoids or Caucasoids, the same kind of hair as the Papuans and Melanesians (with whom they have no relation either historically or as shown by blood groups), long lower-leg and arm segments, and narrow pelves. The Pygmies, aside from being dwarfs, differ from the Negroes in having less everted lips, more body hair, and lighter skins, sometimes mahogany-colored or reddish.

■CAPOIDS.—The Capoids are represented today by the Bushmen of the Kalahari and a few relict tribes in Tanganyika; they are yellow-skinned, with flat faces, Mongoloid eye folds, and scanty body hair. Their local peculiarities include excessive steatopygia (fattening of the buttocks), a horizontal stance of the penis, and a great enlargement of the *labiae minorae*. Von Eickstedt, a modern classifier of races, places them with the Mongoloids, which may be justified if they are traced back far enough in time. Blood-group classifiers place them with Congoids, and Coon gives them separate status as a subspecies. In any case, they are the most enigmatic of the major living races of *Homo sapiens*.

■INTERMEDIATE PEOPLES. — Between these five subspecies live intermediate populations with mixtures of various features. They form what physical anthropologists call "clines": graded series of variations in bodily structure or function forming a kind of bridge or inclined slope between different races. Between the Mongoloids and Caucasoids in central Asia

AMERICAN MUSEUM OF NATURAL HISTORY

MAORI WOMAN of New Zealand. The tattooed chin is believed to be a sign of beauty.

are various intermediate Turkish-speaking peoples, such as the Turkmen and Uzbegs. On the southern slope of the Himalayas, a steep Mongoloid-Caucasoid cline is seen, particularly in Nepal. The Melanesians, Micronesians, and Polynesians probably are the product of a similar ancient cline in southern China and Indonesia, with the Polynesians being the most Mongoloid and the Melanesians the most Australoid.

Much of Africa is clinal country, with mixed Caucasoid-Congoid peoples in the Sudan and East Africa, and a special cline in Ethiopia. The Hottentots and Korana, cattle people who speak languages similar to those of the Bushmen, stand between the latter and Negroids.

■RACIAL MIXTURE.—Because the existence of interracial clines indicates a more or less constant flow of genetic material between centers of racial differentiation, the question naturally arises, Why do races continue to exist? Why did not mixture homogenize the human species long ago? The answer is, with man as with other animal species, that each race is adapted to its particular environment and to a certain extent, to its way of life. Natural selection compensates for the mixtures of genes.

■ADAPTATION.—Certain races are adapted for specific varieties of environmental stress. The Australian aborigines can sleep naked on the ground at 32° F. because the veins and arteries in their arms and legs exchange heat, reducing the caloric requirements of the body. The same kind of cold adaptation has been found among the Reindeer Lapps. The Indians of Tierra del Fuego and northern Canada, the Eskimo, and peoples of Siberia and Manchuria resist cold by having a high basal metabolism that burns a high-caloric diet. The Mongoloid Tibetans and Andean Indians can tolerate the thin air of their highland homes because their hearts are large and their blood thick. Such adaptations account for the persistence of races in their homelands despite intermingling with other

less adaptable racial types.

Regardless of race, certain other rules follow climatic zones. Within each race, stature and weight increase with isotherms of winter cold and decrease with heat. Pigment increases with the amount of sunlight, and tolerance to sunlight with pigmentation. Another kind of adaptation is the capacity to tolerate crowding, which is at its height in long-settled urban populations and at its minimum among those in isolated, thinly populated areas.

PREHISTORIC ARCHAEOLOGY

While physical anthropology deals with the changing body structure and biological adaptations of early men, prehistoric archaeology is concerned with man's developing *technology* and his first steps toward civilization. It is the record of what men made: the tools and weapons they fashioned first from stone, then ivory and bone, and later from metals.

During the Stone Age, the Bronze Age, and the Iron Age, men changed less in physical form than they had in previous eras. After the evolution of *Homo sapiens* in the Upper Paleolithic Age, man's adaptation became centered on the ways in which he added to his meager physical equipment by the use of clothing, tools, and weapons and by the application of his brain to work with other men in elementary forms of society, through speech and later through magic and art. This *cultural evolution,* which started with the manufacture of the first stone tool artifact, continued through the Pleistocene. Archaeologically, this prehistoric period is divided into the Old Stone Age (Paleolithic), Middle Stone Age (Mesolithic), and Late Stone Age (Neolithic). The Paleolithic is further subdivided into Lower (the earliest), Middle, and Upper. In Europe, the time span covered is more than 500,000 years, ending about 10,000 years ago. In some remote areas of the world it has continued.

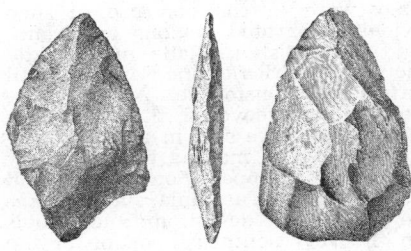

STONE IMPLEMENTS of prehistoric man.

Tool Making.—The earliest known tools are simple *pebble tools,* made by breaking a rounded pebble in such a way that a sharp edge will be formed. These have been found principally in Africa and Asia, and some exist in Australopithecine remains.

■CORE TOOLS.—The next step is the manufacture of *choppers,* which are shaped stones with a cutting edge produced by flaking on only one side, and *chopping tools,* made by flaking both sides. Both of these are called *core tools* because the central portion that remains after flakes are chipped off becomes the tool. They have been found in North Africa, East Africa, Israel, India, Southeast Asia, Java, China, Japan, and even in North America and South America. In modern times they were still made and used by Indians of the Great Basin of the American West and by some of the Australian aborigines.

While in the beginning choppers and chopping tools were as widely distributed as man himself, by the time of the first interglacial period, or roughly 500,000 years ago, the inhabited parts of the world diverged in the manufacture of tool types. In Europe, Africa, and western Asia as far as India, people began to make almond-shaped tools chipped on both sides, known as *hand axes,* and similar tools without points, known as cleavers. The manufacture of these so-called *bifacial* tools improved as time went on, reaching perfection by the first interglacial period, roughly 100,000 years ago. From India to China, choppers and chopping tools continued to be made for an even longer period.

■**FLAKE TOOLS.**—In both archaeological regions *flake tools* were also used, made by chipping flakes off the stone, then retouching the edges of these flakes to make many sharp-edged tools. From 150,000 to 75,000 years ago most of the world's tools were made of flakes, although in remote places such as South Africa, bifacial tools continued to be used until less than 25,000 years ago.

Some time between 75,000 and 30,000 years ago, men slowly perfected the technique of making *blades*—flat, parallel-sided strips of flint suitable for use as knives. Blades were made by carefully preparing a tubular piece of flint with a flat end so that a carefully aimed blow with a piece of horn or bone would break off long, thin slivers of stone. The first blades were probably made in the Near East, but by 30,000 B.C., they were in common use in such widely separated regions as France and Afghanistan. Blade making did not reach Africa or the Far East until after the Pleistocene. At the time they were discovered, the Australian aborigines were still in a technological Stone Age, making tools in many fashions: choppers on the island fringes and in Tasmania, simple flakes in parts of the desert, and blade tools in the very southeast portion of the continent. The American Indians made both chopping tool artifacts and elaborate flake tools (the finely pointed arrowhead); they also made blades with beautifully fluted points.

Paleolithic.—By far most of the work on the Paleolithic, or Old Stone Age, has been done in Europe, where detailed sequences have been established. The *Lower Paleolithic* is the period of bifacial tools, which served the rudimentary hunting needs of men whose primary diet was still roots, nuts, and fruits. The *Middle Paleolithic* is characterized by flake

tools of several industries and by the gradual elaboration of the flaking technique. This is the period of the culture of the various Neanderthals, more skillful hunters than their predecessors, who used fire and were beginning in some areas to bury their dead. From this latter practice we can infer the beginning of a rudimentary society and some dim concept of an after-life.

The *Upper* or *Late Paleolithic* began about 30,000 B.C., the time of a relatively warm interval in the last glaciation in Europe. It was essentially a time of blade making in both Europe and western Asia. The blade-makers, such as *Cro-Magnon* man, also made tools and weapons, including harpoons and needles, out of bone, ivory, and antler. They also clothed themselves with the skins of the beasts they killed, sewn together with

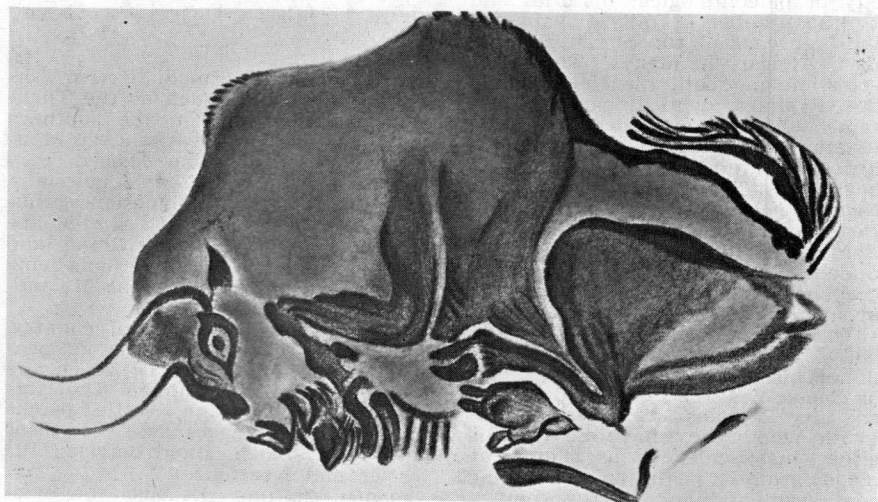

AMERICAN MUSEUM OF NATURAL HISTORY

CAVE DRAWING of a female bison was probably done about 50,000 years ago. This drawing, found near Altamira, Spain, gives some idea of the life that was led by the cave dwellers.

bone and ivory needles, which, together with crude buttons, have been found in some sites. Along with their developing technology they produced one of the most sophisticated representational art forms the world has known: the *Magdalenian cave paintings.* Figures of bison, mammoth, and reindeer were incised and painted with earth colors in the remote recesses of caves in southern France and in Spain; they undoubtedly served a magical purpose. The life-like representation of the animals they hunted, often shown pierced by arrows, became incantations to insure the success of the hunt. Likewise, the *Aurignacian Venuses,* similar to female figures found in existing primitive societies, were probably charms to increase human fertility. The practice of these arts, and of magic, together with the collective hunting required to kill the giant mammoths, show an increasing complexity of thought and activity that can for the first time be called *culture.*

Mesolithic.—The *Middle Stone Age* is the period of the European indus-

tries in the time span immediately following the Pleistocene. With the shrinking of the ice caps, forests invaded central and northern Europe, the sea level rose, and vast migrations of salmon and other fish filled the rivers and estuaries. The giant animals of the Pleistocene—mammoths, hairy rhinoceroses, cave bears, huge wild oxen—as well as the reindeer, were replaced by smaller game, particularly red deer. Bows and arrows and domestic dogs had been introduced, and fish weirs, nets, hooks, and spears were used. The stone industry was an offshoot of the Upper Paleolithic blade industry, with an emphasis on *microliths*—tiny blades that can be hafted in a row to produce a blade of any length. These tools later helped prepare the way for the practice of agriculture, since they could easily be adapted to use

as simple sickles. One important new tool was invented, the axe hafted onto a wooden or bone handle; it was both a product of, and the means of coping with, the new forest environment. These dense forests, which had replaced the open tundra of the Paleolithic, limited migration and communication between groups; thus the Mesolithic is not a single homogeneous culture but consists of a number of isolated separate cultures.

Neolithic.—The New Stone Age marks a change in way of life so decisive for man that it has been called the *Neolithic,* or *Agricultural Revolution.* For the first time men planted seeds and collected the harvest of their crops instead of gathering them where they could be found growing wild; they domesticated animals, spun and wove fibers into cloth, and made pottery. With polished stone axes they felled trees to clear the land, and built boats and houses. Villages grew up, industries and the arts flourished, and slowly the fabric of urban society evolved.

The initial date for the European

SATOUR ANDRE EMMERICH GALLERY

WEAPONS used by the South African Bushmen are very similar to the ancient bow and arrow pictured in this sixth-century B.C. drawing.

Neolithic is at least 4000 B.C.; in the Middle East it is much earlier. In Turkey it goes back to 7000 B.C., and the fortress of Jericho was once a Neolithic trading post. The Neolithic began in the Middle East, in the warm and well-watered areas of the great river valleys, and from there it spread to India and China, as well as to Europe and North Africa. In the New World, an apparently independent Neolithic culture arose in one or more centers of Central America and South America at about the same time. It spread northward as far as the St. Lawrence valley and south to Bolivia and Chile. Well into modern times the Neolithic was still the way of life of many of the earth's peoples, including the Polynesians, Micronesians, Melanesians, Papuans, and all of the agricultural Indians of North America and the forested regions of South America.

Ages of Bronze and Iron.—The discovery of the technique of extracting metal from ore and forging or casting metal tools marks the end of the Stone Age. Flint and bone were replaced by the more malleable and durable materials bronze and iron. The rise of metallurgy was soon followed by the invention of writing, with which man passed from prehistory into history.

While the Old World Bronze Age and Iron Age cultures were evolving, many peoples on the peripheries of the centers of origin of these techniques remained untouched by that development. They adopted metal work late in history, without passing through the regular sequences of cultural stages found in the Middle East and Europe. The Indians of Peru invented bronze metallurgy independently, and were in the Bronze Age when the Spanish *conquistadores* arrived. In Africa there was no proper Bronze Age outside of Egypt and a few sites along the Mediterranean coast. Iron followed stone tools in North Africa in Carthaginian and Roman times, having been introduced to the interior mostly by Jewish traders and craftsmen. In sub-Saharan Africa during the middle of the first millennium B.C., ironworking was set up on a large scale at Meroë by the Egyptians under Hittite influence.

From that center, and possibly also from Indonesian contacts on the Indian Ocean coast, techniques of smelting and forging iron spread over Negro Africa during the first millennium A.D.

CULTURAL ANTHROPOLOGY

Methods of Study.—*Cultural anthropology* can be studied in terms of individual cultures, such as those of the Hopi Indians of New Mexico or the Zulu of South Africa, or by subject matter such as marriage or religion. The first method is known as *ethnography*. Within the scope of ethnography is the study of groups of related cultures that occupy a geographical region and follow a common way of life. This is called the *culture area* method and includes such relatively small and homogeneous groups as the buffalo-hunting Indians of the American plains or the cattle people of East Africa; it also encompasses such a widespread and complex culture as that of the Islamic Middle East.

The study of cultures by subject matter is known as *ethiology*. It is broken down into studies of material culture, or *primitive technology,* and *social anthropology*, which emphasizes the human relationships binding men in a social fabric of behavior, custom, and institutions.

In studying the behavior patterns, beliefs, and customs of primitive cultures, anthropologists are hampered by the changes wrought on primitive peoples by the impact of modern civilization. Only rarely can the field worker find unspoiled cultures to examine and record; often he must reconstruct many of the details from elderly informants and early records. The *ethnographic present* is the term used to describe the period when a culture was still unspoiled, as yet unaffected by the various stages of acculturation.

Primitive Technology.—One of the working definitions of man is "the toolmaker," for from the beginning of his history man has used tools. There is no people on Earth who do not use some kind of tool, no matter how primitive. Toolmaking is in the material sense the beginning of civilization, for it is the root of technology, the means by which modern man so efficiently controls his environment.

The first tools used by men were stones thrown at small game, or sticks used in the same way a chimpanzee will use one to reach fruit beyond his grasp. The stones, were shaped and chipped to provide a cutting surface, as seen in the development of the Stone Age cultures, or tied in groups of two or three to form the *bolas,* a kind of thrown snare still used in South America. The stick pointed at one end became the digging stick, used to unearth edible roots and later, to plant and harvest cultivated crops. With a stone point at one end, it became the spear, the javelin, or the harpoon; later, the arrow was combined with the ingenious combination of the curved stick and tensed string that is the bow. A curved piece of wood alone, deftly shaped and accurately thrown, is a boomerang, which will return to the hand of the thrower if it fails to hit the target.

Where wood and stone were not available, man used whatever materials lay at hand: fish and animal teeth, coral, bamboo, clam shells, ivory, and whalebone. Without tools there would be no culture.

■**FIREMAKING.**—Another vital necessity to man is *fire,* which keeps him warm, protects him from predatory animals, and makes his food tender and easy to digest. It gives light and warmth at night to a group of people who can sit, talk, and dance together. Fire, which brings men together around a common center, is perhaps the beginning of social life.

Fire can be obtained from nature —from burning forests or smoldering volcanoes—or it can be made by man himself. The two commonest methods are by striking flint against iron pyrites to make a spark, or by friction of one piece of wood against another. Although almost all primitive peoples use a variation of one of these methods, there are a few who cannot make fire. When first discovered, the Andaman Islanders' only way of making fire was to kindle it from another piece of burning wood; certain Congo Pygmies cannot or will not make fire, but barter for it with neighboring tribes.

■**PROVIDING SHELTER.**—All peoples know how to make some kind of *shelter*. The most elementary protection is a *windbreak* of trees and brushwood, or a rectangle of skins or matting set at a slant with its back to the wind, the only shelter known to the Ona of Tierra del Fuego and the Great Andaman Andamanese. The simplest type of *hut* is made by bending over branches like croquet wickets, tying them together, and covering them with leaves or pieces of bark. In a cold climate, like that of the southern coast of Chile, skins are placed over such frames, and fires are built inside. In the northern regions of the Old World and New World, the commonest house type is a conical *tipi* made by leaning poles together and covering the surface with bark or skins. Desert nomads and the pastoral Tibetans dwell in tents of skin or goat hair, which are portable, durable, cool in summer, and warm in winter. But they are not as warm as the *yurt,* a demountable, portable house made by fitting sticks into a circular frame and covering the frame with sheets of felt. This is the traditional house of the Mongols and nomadic Turks.

Permanent houses everywhere are made of the best available materials, such as wood, straw, coconut fronds, stone, and earth, either poured and pounded between frames (pisé) or in the form of unburned (adobe) or burned bricks. Desert peoples have learned to build houses with thick walls and hidden windows; some tropical islanders make houses without walls. Northern fisherfolk and hunters in Siberia construct houses underground to conserve heat. The inland Chuckchi of Bering Straits, who breed reindeer, sleep in fur boxes suspended inside skin tents.

Some houses are single-family shelters, and others are communal dwellings in which each family has a cubicle or section. In primitive communities houses are built according to a single traditional plan. Usually a person in authority takes the first step, such as killing a cock and sprinkling its blood on the roof poles before building the roof, a practice in rural Morocco. Wherever permanent structures are to be erected, as many people as are available join in and help build each other's houses. This requires a certain amount of organization and is important in maintaining the mutual relationships of the persons concerned.

■**BODY COVERING.**—In most climates, people need some kind of portable protection, although they can become physiologically adapted to the extremes of their climate.

However, *body covering* serves another purpose besides protection: it is an important means of communication. By painting designs on their faces or wearing a special kind of clothing, people inform each other about their status, role, or condition. Even naked people use some kind of body paint, which may well be the oldest kind of body covering. Earth colors mixed with water, fat, or marrow offer a certain amount of incidental protection from wind and sun. In the Amazonian forests, where such mineral pigments are lacking and no such protection is needed, the Indians paint themselves with vegetable juices instead. Lacking mirrors, people who use body paint, paint each other, thus making this exercise an extension of grooming, one of the oldest forms of interpersonal activity among primates.

The habit of going naked is common among people who live in hot places, where extreme mobility is needed and nothing unnecessary to survival can be carried. It is also prevalent in chilly and wet climates, where clothing cannot be kept dry.

The simplest garments are the breech clout and the robe. A breech clout protects and conceals the genitals, and the robe keeps the body warm, although it impedes the use of the arms. These two are universal where clothes are worn at all and

METICULOUS GROOMING and concern for personal appearance occurs in all cultures.

where tailored garments have not been introduced.

Going barefoot is normal in most climates, at least in summer. In many regions, sandals are worn on hot and stony ground, and buskins, moccasins, and boots are worn in cold and wet climates. Many peoples go bareheaded. A simple and widespread kind of headgear is the fillet, a cord or band wrapped around the head, leaving the top bare. This may be combined with a dustcloth, as among desert Arabs. Visored caps, to protect the eyes from glare, are worn in Tibet, among the Aleuts of Alaska, and by Europeans. The Eskimo wear slitted wooden snow glasses as protection against snow blindness.

■**BODY MUTILATION.**—Many cultures habitually mutilate their bodies for symbolic purposes. Simple mutilations include tying bands around arms, legs, and waists so tightly that the trunk or limbs are deformed on either side, a practice found among the most primitive peoples. Those with black skins may decorate themselves with raised scars (Australians, Africans), and those with lighter skins with *tattooing* (Polynesians, Berbers, Ainu, modern Europeans, Japanese, and Malaysians).

Circumcision, a symbol of reaching manhood, is widespread in the Old World, but among Muslims and Jews it has been moved from puberty to infancy. Many kinds of head and facial *deformation* are practiced. Skulls are intentionally deformed with bands and boards in Africa and among many American Indian tribes. Among the Ubangi in Africa and one Indian tribe in Brazil, lips are pierced, stretched, and held out with discs like duck bills. Many peoples such as the Eskimo, wear labrets through holes in the lower lip, and some Indians of Brazil use cheek holes as receptacles for feathers. The piercing and stretching of nasal septa, nostrils, and earlobes is common. In Upper Burma, some tribesmen stretch the necks of women with brass rings. In sum, people put themselves to

SMITHSONIAN INSTITUTION

AMERICAN INDIANS OF THE PLAINS lived a nomadic life, as shown in this rare 1892 photograph of Kiowa Indians. The tepee was the typical shelter used by these tribes.

SAM MINSKOFF AND SONS

PAN AMERICAN AIRWAYS

MAN'S SHELTER can be a modern apartment building (*above left*), a regal castle (*above right*), or a nomad tent of cloth and hides (*below*).

UNITED NATIONS

THE STUDY OF MAN, his evolution and early history, his customs, his beliefs, and the sometimes puzzling patterns of his existence, is the province of the social sciences. Anthropology and sociology deal respectively with the physical and social aspects of culture—from the way a South African Xhosa woman paints her face with clay (*below*), to the living conditions in a Turkish slum (*right*). Psychology and psychiatry examine the inner life of man, the structure of the self, and the nature of human behavior. Together, these fields comprise a picture of man's past and present, seen through the eyes of modern science.

UNITED NATIONS

SATOUR

HELEN BUTTFIELD

LEON DELLER, MONKMEYER

SYMBOLS of the search for meaning, the churches which men build are the physical counterparts of philosophical and religious ideas. The Blue Mosque in Istanbul (*left*) embodies submission to the will of Allah; Le Corbusier's Chapel (*above*), a renewed Christianity.

every conceivable pain and discomfort, even mutilation, in order to transform their bodies into permanent symbols. Profiles of human hands with chopped-off fingers, found in Upper Paleolithic caves in France, show that this has been going on for a long time; and early Mesolithic skulls found in North Africa reveal the removal of incisor teeth in adolescence. Tooth-knocking is still practiced in Australia and Africa, and finger-chopping, until recently among the Plains Indians.

■CONTAINERS.—One of the conspicuous differences between man and other primates is that human beings habitually carry water and food, while the other primates (with few exceptions) drink and eat on the spot. Man alone uses containers. The Tasmanians carry water in seaweed bubbles; the Bushmen of South Africa use ostrich-egg shells. Human ingenuity is well demonstrated in the use of local materials: paper bark for baskets in Australia, birch bark in North America and northern Asia, bamboo nodes in Malaysia. The use of fibers, in the form of string bags, plaited baskets, and coiled baskets, is nearly universal, as is the craft of *pottery*. The invention of the potter's wheel, a time-saver in shaping pottery, in the Near East may have led to the invention of the wheel as a means of locomotion.

■FOOD PROCESSING.—Like most other primates, man eats a mixed diet of fruits, vegetables, and animal proteins. No other primate, however, eats as much meat as do human beings. The shift to a meat diet hundreds of thousands of years ago must have exposed our remote ancestors to many animal parasites and caused a rigorous selection of men with the greatest immunity. The invention of *cooking* reduced the hazards of infection. The simplest and probably the oldest method of cooking is simply to drop whole animals and roots on a fire and roast them. This is the usual system among such simple hunters and gatherers as the Australian aborigines, the Bushmen, and the Fuegian Indians. Refinements are grilling chunks of meat on spits, common among pastoral nomads, or grilling fish over fires of green sticks as do South American Indians. Some Australians encase a bird in clay and throw it on the fire; when they break off the clay, the feathers and skin come with it. Polynesians bake with hot stones in pits; Indians of the northern forests of North America boiled food in birch-bark kettles held off the flame. Malaysians boil food in green bamboo nodes; Eskimo, in soapstone kettles over blubber lamps; and Plains Indians, like the ancient Scythians, boil meat by dropping hot stones into a skin lining a hole in the ground.

Food is processed both for immediate consumption and for future use. Peoples who live in regions where there is little seasonal change store little food; where seasonal changes are marked, *food storage* is necessary for survival. Cereals can be stored without special attention. Many peoples dry meat, fish, and fruits, particularly in arid climates where they will not spoil. Smoking meat and fish, as is done with salmon in the Pacific Northwest, is more suitable in cool, wet climates. Where it is cold enough, as in the circumpolar region, whole carcasses can be frozen for the winter.

A common way to treat food materials, whether meat, fish, vegetables, or fruit, is to pulverize them in a mortar and pestle, on a hand grindstone (*metate*), or on a rotary *quern*, a primitive hand mill invented in Roman times.

Fermentation is another form of food preservation, for grapes will keep as well in the form of wine as in that of raisins; it is also a means of producing alcohol for ceremonial intoxication. This process, however, is virtually limited to agricultural and pastoral peoples, the only ones who have anything in bulk to ferment. *Distillation,* a relatively modern refinement of fermentation, is limited to the high cultures of the Old World and to those of Mexico.

■COLLECTING.—The simple collection of natural materials, such as picking berries or gathering nuts is common to animal life as a whole. Natural materials include roots, fruits, edible leaves, stalks, and tubers, insects in various forms, honey, eggs, and slow game (small, slow-moving mammals, snakes, lizards, and fledglings, which a woman or child can catch by hand or with a stick). Collecting as so described is as old as man—and older, for it was apparently done by the Australopithecines.

■HUNTING.—Hunting requires great endurance, keen observation, and a knowledge of animal behavior. Some hunters wear disguises that imitate the animal they are stalking; others lure animals to ambushes by imitating their mating calls. Agricultural people, for whom hunting is only part-time work, are very apt to employ *traps* in order to capture animals. These traps generally depend upon the ingenuity of the hunter in creating delicate trigger-release mechanisms. Some people catch birds by smearing sticky gums on favorite perches; another curiosity is the Eskimo's wolf trap—a piece of sharp-edged whalebone coiled and frozen in a piece of fat. The heat of the wolf's stomach melts the fat, and the whalebone uncoils.

Solo hunting is rare. Most successful hunters operate in small groups, in which coordination and direction are essential. A group of men can drive a herd of animals into an opening between two converging fences, leading to a butchering corral, and they can carry home and share the spoils of a successful hunt. There are elaborate rules governing both men's preparation for the hunt and the behavior of women while their hunter husbands are away. A common belief is that a wife's infidelity will spoil the men's luck.

■FISHING.—Primitive fishermen sometimes catch fish by hand, but more often by lines with or without hooks; a simple device is the fish gorge—a double-pointed spindle of bone or wood. In still waters, fishermen sometimes shoot fish with bows and arrows, and many use fish spears with barbed or pronged heads. More sophisticated fishermen, as in Melanesia and the Pacific Northwest, use elaborate traps and nets.

Such fishing gear is made by hand, and most fishing also requires only hand work, unless boats are used to reach the fishing grounds. In Fiji many people get together to operate nets, but the pattern of interaction needed for fishing is simple except when extensive voyages are made in large boats.

■HUSBANDRY.—*Husbandry* began when people first grew plants and bred animals in captivity. By so doing they sheltered the organisms, protecting them from predators and from the

HUNTING FOR FOOD is one of man's earliest technologies. Shown in this early print are American Indians draped in deer hide, trying to decoy deer that are close enough to kill.

rigors of the environment. They thereby preserved random mutations, which would otherwise have been quickly pruned off by natural selection. Some of these mutations, being useful to man, were selected deliberately, and the genetic structures of individual plant and animal species were changed. Grain that remains on the stalk after ripening, instead of scattering on the ground, is a mutation that provided primitive farmers with grain to reap and store.

The most useful and widely grown plants are *annuals*, which provide mainly starches; the *legumes*, including peas, beans, and lentils, grown principally for proteins; and the *oil seeds*, such as sesame, flax, and sunflower seeds. Seeds can be sown broadcast, harvested by reaping, threshed with flails or oxen, and easily stored—they can be handled by mass production methods. Only maize and wet rice require individual handling, but in compensation they have high yields. Also, the stalks and stems of seed plants can be used for fodder, bedding for animals, building materials, and fuel. A Neolithic family with a mixed crop of annuals, legumes, and oil seeds could be fed on a fraction of the land needed by seed collectors.

Primitive agriculture, however, is not limited to seed plants. Roots and tubers, such as yams, sweet potatoes, and manioc, grow best in the wet tropics, while white potatoes can be grown in moist, temperate climates. Temperate-land farmers get much of their sugar from fruits, such as apples, pears, figs, and peaches, while tropical gardeners get sugar from citrus fruits, persimmons, and papayas. Trees, particularly the coconut and the date palm, provide building and clothing materials; the coconut also yields drinking water. Without coconuts and other domestic plants, the Polynesians and Micronesians could not have settled their islands.

Compared to the number of plant species, very few species of animals have been domesticated, because the number of useful species is limited and because the requirements of catching, taming, feeding, and protecting animals is greater. The total is only 13 useful kinds of mammals, 11 of birds, 2 of insects, and 1 type of fish; and most of these were domesticated in the Old World. In the New World, only in the Andes did man tame economically valuable animals, the llama and the alpaca.

It is often stated that the dog was the first animal to be domesticated, but ancient dog bones are hard to tell from wolf bones. In the Neolithic, dogs became useful not only for hunting but also for guarding flocks. Some people ate them, and others sheared them for blanket material. Still others, including the Eskimo and Maritime Chuckchi, depend on dogs for winter transportation.

Domestic animals provide people with many substances—meat, skin, horn, bone, ivory, wool, hair, blood, guts, dung—but that is not their chief importance. They also provide a source of energy, as when oxen pull a plough across a field, camels draw

WALKING, the simplest form of land transportation, is predominant today in India.

water from deep wells, or donkeys turn grain mills.

■**TRANSPORTATION.**—The simplest form of land transport is *walking*. However, several ancient inventions facilitate walking under special conditions; the simplest are sandals and boots. Snowshoes and skis make traveling possible in deep snow; western Europeans and Chinese skate on ice, and Eskimos walk on it with ivory creepers. In Polynesia, southern France, and the Canary Islands, some people walk on stilts.

In different regions special ways of *carrying* things are characteristic. African Negroes prefer to carry loads on their heads; American Indians, on their backs. Many special carrying devices have been invented, such as the tumpline over the forehead (American Indies, Formosa) and the shoulder pole or shoulder yoke with loads hanging from each end (China, Japan, Europe, colonial United States).

The use of animals for transport involved *packing, riding,* and *traction*. Nearly every domestic animal is packed, and many ingenious packing devices have been invented. Those animals large and strong enough to hold a man have all been ridden, but the most widely used riding animals are the donkey, camel, and horse. Without the camel the great deserts could not have been efficiently crossed, and without the riding horse the great empires of the Old World could not have arisen. Long before the camel and horse were ridden, people used animals for traction. The simplest such device is the *travois,* an A-frame attached to an animal's back with the two poles dragging on the ground and the load fastened across the poles behind the

animal's rump. The Plains Indians first used the travois with dogs, later with horses.

In the Old World, the first known traction devices were land sleds, used long before the invention of the *wheel*. The use of wheeled vehicles was long limited to the Old World, and reached Oceania and Africa south of the Sahara only in modern times.

■**WATER TRANSPORT.** — Simple water craft are used by some of the world's most primitive peoples. The Tasmanians make rafts out of bundles of reeds that they tie together; the Andean Indians sail similar craft on Lake Titicaca. Some of the Australian aborigines make bark canoes with very crude tools; without such boats and simple rafts, the ancestors of these aborigines could not have reached Australia from Indonesia. Birch bark is the familiar canoe material of the Indians of northern North America, while the nomads of southern Iran make rafts of inflated skins and swim across swift streams on single skins.

People with Neolithic or metal tools hollow out large tree trunks, usually by alternately burning, quenching, and cutting the wood. Some very large hulls, carrying up to fifty people, have been made in this way. The next step is to raise the sides with plank gunwales (Polynesia), and the final one is to build the whole hull of planks on a single frame (China, India, Arabia, Europe).

The simplest way to propel a craft is to pole it in shallow water or to paddle it in deep water. When fifty men are paddling in stroke, a boat can move very fast. Rowing and sculling are European, West Asian, and Chinese techniques diffused to other peoples in recent times. Short of machine power, the only other ways of propelling boats are towing in canals and rivers, and sailing. Sails were first known in ancient Egypt and Mesopotamia.

Water transport is cheaper and more efficient than land transport. The ancient Egyptians sailed up and floated down the Nile; the Chinese long ago perfected a system of inland waterways; the Aztecs built their city on a large lake. Thus, the great civilizations of the Old World, and one of the greatest in the New World, arose in regions of efficient water transport. The ethnographic present, the time of autonomous native cultures, approached its end when European navigators crossed the great oceans and circumnavigated the world.

Techniques of transport on land and sea have influenced the growth of complex cultures in yet another way. A caravan crossing a desert needs careful organization and planning, a firm chain of command, and strict discipline, not only because of the rigors of travel but also because of hostile natives. The same is true of a ship at sea. Pastoral nomads, too, need organization and discipline in their annual migrations and are therefore more powerful than the sedentary peoples whom they sometimes conquer. Thus, the disciplines learned through techniques of transport may be transferred to those of government and warfare.

■**COMMUNICATION.** — Human beings communicate by means of mutually understood symbols. While gestures, body paint, clothing, religious objects, ritual procedures, and the like are all vehicles of communication, the prime medium of communication is language, and the study of language is *linguistics*.

■**LANGUAGE.**—Human *speech* is produced by the coordination of several organs that originally evolved in response to different needs. Neurological coordination of these organs for speech required the further evolution of the brain to a size and degree of complexity found among all normal human beings and probably all fossil men thus far discovered. Because the number of sounds capable of being produced and distinguished by the human ear far exceeds the number needed for a single language, no two languages have exactly the same sounds. And because languages are learned and people live in more or less isolated groups, different peoples have devoloped their own systems of speech.

Thus, the number of languages spoken in a given area is a function of the degree of isolation of the peoples concerned and the length of time they have lived together as cultural units. In aboriginal California and in Australia, where local tribes were small, self-sufficient, and relatively isolated, dozens of languages were spoken. The same is true of refuge areas, such as the Caucasus and the Himalayas. In contrast, English, Arabic, Spanish, and Chinese are spoken by millions, over vast regions.

Some linguists arrange languages in families and compare the basic vocabularies—words for family relationships and such universals as water and fire—to find out how long the

languages have been separated. A comparative study of whole vocabularies and of types of language also reveals borrowings and, hence, early cultural contacts. This is important in dealing with cultures without written history. The ways in which different languages classify concepts—by number, gender, size, shape, texture, chronological age, social classes—also reveal some of the psychological differences between cultures in their outlook on human relations and the outer environment.

■**EXTENSIONS OF LANGUAGE.**—Although many peoples habitually speak more than one language, they also come in contact with others with whom they cannot converse and therefore learn *sign languages,* as among the central Australians and the Plains Indians. Other extensions of language permit communication beyond the range of the spoken human voice. Examples are smoke signals, the West African drum languages, and the whistling language of the Canary Islands.

But the prime extension of language is *writing*, which not only permits sending messages but also provides an extension of the limits of memory, the accumulation of knowledge, and the accurate transmission of knowledge from generation to generation. Thus, the use of writing facilitates the growth and spatial expansion of cultures.

Mnemonic devices short of writing are used by many illiterate peoples. Australian aborigines send message sticks from camp to camp, inviting each other to meetings and ceremonies, with the meaning conveyed by simple carved designs and notches that indicate the number of intervening days. The Plains Indians painted pictures on skins to record events. In true writing, however, the symbols represent individual words or word components.

INDIA TOURIST OFFICE

SHEPHERD boy of 14 from Saurashtra, India.

Organization of Society.

—Since the acquisition and the preparation of food is the basic occupation of primitive societies, the division of labor is one of the most elementary forms of social organization.

■**DIVISION OF LABOR.**—The most fundamental *division of labor* is that based on *age*. In no society is a child expected to become fully self-reliant until after *puberty*. In any camp or village, children sort themselves out by age into natural grades and teach each other play activities, including games. As they reach puberty, they participate in the work of the society, performing different actions at successive periods; for instance, among the Galla of Ethiopia the men are first cattleherds, then warriors, and finally settle down as married men.

Because men specialize in hunting and the more exacting kinds of manufacturing, most social systems also have a clear division of labor based on *sex*. Among the simplest food gatherers, whose men neither hunt nor make anything very complicated, men and women do more or less the same things. Among hunting peoples, however, women collect wild vegetables and slow game, and fetch firewood and water. They are also usually responsible for tending the fire, while the men usually build shelters and handle meat. In agricultural societies the men fell and burn trees, and the women plant the crops; the men may go hunting or raiding while the crops are growing, and then come home to help the women with the harvest. Where the plow is used, however, planting becomes the province of the male.

In manufacturing, work relegated to women on a simple level becomes men's work when complex techniques require the skill of specialists. Thus, women make pottery by hand but men manufacture it on the potter's wheel. Women weave cloth on simple, usually vertical, looms and men, on complex horizontal looms.

In some countries, notably India, the contact between peoples of different racial and cultural origins and levels of cultural complexity has given rise to still another kind of divi-

HELEN BUTTFIELD

WATER TRANSPORTATION has been one of man's oldest means of trade and travel. These boats along Egypt's Nile River look today just as they did during the time of Christ.

AMERICAN MUSEUM OF NATURAL HISTORY

TRIBAL GAMES are an ancient device used to teach the methods of war. Often, neighboring tribes will compete against each other until the first man is killed. Both sides will then stop fighting, hold his funeral, and then continue the games until both sides have had enough.

sion of labor, the *ethnic*. Classes of people perform special tasks, which are inherited. This is the well-known *caste system,* also prevalent in many parts of Africa. It is characteristic in regions of interracial clines and in domestic and institutional slavery.

Many peoples keep household *slaves,* who are either war captives, as among Pacific Northwest Indians and Homeric Greeks; poor people who have sold themselves for debt, as described in the Old Testament; or children sold by poor parents, as in China. While *domestic slavery* is common to many relatively simple cultures, *institutional slavery* is confined to a few complex ones. The Romans kept large numbers of slaves at work on plantations, in grain mills, in mines, and in galleys; African slaves once worked on farms and plantations in Arabia, Brazil, and the United States.

■**INSTITUTIONS.**—An *institution* (in the sociological sense) is a group of persons who perform common activities regularly enough to develop a pattern of behavior and have their own rules and *esprit de corps.*

Anthropologists recognize several kinds of institutions based on the activities involved; and Coon has suggested that most, if not all, institutions can be traced to instincts held in common, not only with other primates but also with many other kinds of animals. The family is, in this sense, concerned with reproduction and child care; the political institution, with territoriality; the religious, with fear, deprivation, and ornament; the economic, with the food quest and possibly sharing and storing; and voluntary associations, with the pecking order, a basic status system.

■**KINSHIP AND THE FAMILY.**—In its simplest form the *family* consists of father, mother, and their children. But other relationships are recognized in all human societies, and each involves special *roles,* or patterns of behavior. Every language contains terms to indicate these relationships, vertically in age and laterally in *sibship.* (a *sib* is brothers and sis-

ters). The number of kin recognized by special names varies with societies. In the simplest cultures everyone is recognized by a *kinship* term; and if the actual relationship cannot be traced, as with a stranger, an appropriate one is given.

Every person need not be given a separate kinship term, because whole categories of kin are supposed to behave toward him in the same way—and vice versa—and they will be lumped under a single term. This operates through the principle of *the equivalence of brothers.* An individual's father's brother may also be called father, and his paternal grandfather's brother is also grandfather. Thus, he may expect the same kind of treatment from his paternal uncle that he received from his father, particularly if his father has died and, as is usual in some cultures, his paternal uncle has married his mother (*levirate*). Similarly, his mother's sister may be called mother, and his father may marry his deceased wife's sister (*sororate*) or be married to both of them at once.

Some cultures permit only monogamous marriages, but by far the greatest number permit *polygyny* (plural wives), which is usual among other primates and nearly all the hunters and food-gatherers. *Polyandry,* the marriage of one woman to two or more husbands, is usually confined to impoverished people.

Kinship terminology serves the function of specifying who should avoid whom, who may joke with whom, who must feed whom under certain circumstances, and particularly who may or may not marry whom. When these rules are studied carefully in terms of observed behavior, it is seen that they automatically perform two functions. Except in rare cases involving royalty, they forbid genetically deleterious *inbreeding,* as in brother-sister, father-daughter, and mother-son matings, and often specify the greatest possible outbreeding in small gene pools. But these *eugenic* aspects are no more deliberate than is the other function, that of so regulat-

ing the behavior of the community so that disturbances are kept at a minimum. Both have evolved through subconscious trial and error.

The family institution often reaches beyond the bounds of the local community to extend the range of the gene pool. In many cases it is the rule that a man is forbidden to marry within his own group, which may be designated as a *clan* or simply as a *marriage class.* This system is called *exogamy.* If, as sometimes happens in more elaborate cultures, social classes, and religious communities, he is obliged to marry within his group, this is called *endogamy.* Exogamy tends to foster amicable intergroup relations; endogamy, to strengthen the local unit and to accentuate its genetic peculiarities. Both systems can be useful.

■**POLITICAL INSTITUTIONS.**—The *political institution* differs from others in that it posseses the ultimate authority and is expected to use force in both internal and external crises. In its simplest form the *state* is no more than a band of a few related families living, hunting, and sharing food together. Its leadership is informal. The best hunter may divide the meat or feed the greatest number of people; the wisest and ablest man may settle disputes. Many such communities are really extended families, and the leader is simply the head of the family; further extensions of the family are clans and tribes.

In simple agricultural communities some form of *chieftainship* is usual in order to keep the peace in the village and to defend it against enemies. Such a chief may also act as judge. In some societies chieftainship is inherited, in others, normally acquired through competition.

In one Micronesian atoll early navigators found a small community ruled by a king. Although a monarch seemed unnecessary on so small an island, when a typhoon roared across the lagoon, shaking down the coconuts—the islanders' only source of drinking water—the king took charge of rationing, and order prevailed.

Pastoral nomads also require a firm political institution to regulate the times of migration, the routes followed, the position of each family and its flocks on the march, the assignment of pasture, and the use of water. So well-disciplined are nomads that they often defy established governments and even conquer cities and take over the reins of government. Many dynasties have been founded in this fashion, disappearing when a new group of nomads replaced them.

Whenever a sovereign state becomes so big that all its members do not know each other, formality creeps in; kings wear crowns or other insignia and follow a stereotyped pattern. Heralds run before them to clear the road, secretaries note conversations and prompt their master, jesters amuse them to break tension. The king may become so sacred that not even his shadow may be touched, as in Hawaii, or that he is not seen, as among Nilotic tribes.

■**GAMES AND WARFARE.** — Anthropologists sometimes find a village or tribe divided into two or more rival units that compete with each other in formal games, such as football, wrestling matches, or track events. These games are likely to be held at some relatively slack time of year, thus keeping idle men out of trouble.

Some games are rougher than others, and sometimes they are lethal. From games to formal warfare is a small but critical step, because primitive people usually fight according to gamelike rules. In New Caledonia, for example, rival armies used to meet at a prearranged place and time. The two forces would line up facing each other, hold an oratorical contest, and finally fight with clubs. After the first man was killed, they stopped and held his funeral, then continued to fight until they agreed both sides had had enough.

■**PRIMITIVE LAW.**—Every culture has its own rules for behavior in all aspects of human relations and in every kind of institution, but only those rules that are enforced by the political institution constitute *law*. The function of law is to prevent disturbances to the group. In modern nations, laws are made and repealed by governments; but in simple, mostly preliterate societies, laws are based on precedent and custom.

The usual explanation of a law, often related in the form of a myth, is that it was handed down by the tribal ancestors. During puberty ceremonies, when youthful minds are impressionable, the older men teach the boys rules of conduct toward women, children, older people, and each other. In more complex societies, where the body of law is great, men with particularly good memories memorize them, and recite them when needed.

In small, simply organized communities, everyone is under close observation by everyone else, and few breaches of custom pass unnoticed. In larger communities, however, the culprit may go undetected; and the chief or king may call in sorcerers and diviners to discover his identity. If the accused denies his guilt, trial by ordeal may follow. In West Africa, for example, he may be forced to drink a potion made from poisonous tree sap; if he is able to vomit it and thus to survive, he is considered innocent. Whether guilty or not, the victim is usually someone who disturbs the group. Among primitive peoples there are usually no facilities for imprisonment; punishment is death, exile, or enslavement. In the simplest societies, as in central Australia, the elders secretly meet and kill an offender under cover of darkness, disguising their tracks with emu-feather shoes.

■**PRIMITIVE ECONOMICS AND TRADE.**—In its most primitive form, *trade* is simply the practice of exchanging identical or similar goods between neighboring bands, in order to maintain friendly relations. Body paint and tool materials, owing to their uneven distribution, are particularly subject to trading. Obsidian was widely traded in both western Asia and Mexico; and Aztec traders, traveling through hostile territory in disguise, carried obsidian blades among many Central American tribes. Polished axe materials were traded even more extensively in the Pacific.

■**PRIMITIVE RELIGION.** — *Religion* is a broad category of phenomena involving symbols, beliefs, practices, ritual specialists, and organizations of various degrees of complexity. A principal function of religion is to restore equilibrium to individuals and groups after a disturbance. The only animal who knows death to be inevitable, man lives under constant if usually unconscious tension that increases at critical times of the individual's life: at puberty, marriage, childbearing, illness, and death. However, the disturbance affects the family and associates of the individual as much as, or even more than, it affects him. Among all peoples living in normal cultural situations, rituals are performed on at least some of these occasions, and they are called *rites of passage*. Changes in the work schedules of groups of people caused by the progression of the seasons occasion ceremonies of another kind, called *rites of intensification,* such as Thanksgiving and Hopi Snake Dance.

In most primitive societies there are religious specialists called *shamans, medicine men,* or *witchdoctors*. One of their functions to heal the sick; they sometimes succeed by use of herbs and other medicines, by massage, bloodletting, and the like, but their principal role is relieving the psychosomatic element, if any, of the patient's ailment.

A shaman may, for example, dance himself into a trance and talk in strange voices, which indicate that his spirit travels in the sky, and consult another spirit, who reveals the cause of the illness. The shaman's spirit now returns; the trance is over, and the shaman approaches the patient dramatically. He massages the affected part, sucks it, and spits out some strange object that, he states, was inside the patient's body, causing the disease. The audience, at least, feels better.

Nearly all peoples perform magic of some kind. Much more is done to protect from harm than to cause it; more is suspected than is performed.

As a culture becomes more complex, shamans begin to specialize; some are healers, while others try to influence the weather. The Maya priests, for example, kept a precise calendar, could predict the movement of the celestial bodies, including eclipses, and told the people the right time—before the rains were to begin—to plant crops.

■**PRIMITIVE ART.**—The creation and enjoyment of *art* is a universal human attribute that may be even older than our species. In its simplest forms it requires no artifacts, for even chimpanzees can make rhythmic sounds and can dance. Art's most primitive function is to communicate emotion, more basic than the communication of ideas and facts. Art is an element in all ritual—political, familial, and economic as well as religious. Each group of people is conditioned to respond agreeably to its own symbols and with distaste to the symbols of others; we revere our flag, but Muslims detest the sound of Christian church bells. Thus, art serves both to unite and to divide peoples at all cultural levels.

Art exists in space in the form of surface decoration and sculpture; in time as dance, music, and literature; and in space and time combined in the dance and drama. All of the most primitive peoples decorate their bodies and usually decorate their implements. Pottery is a natural art medium, as are textiles.

Since some individuals are more gifted in artistic expression than others, specialization in these media arises in relatively simple cultural levels, as for example, among the Australian aborigines of Arnhemland, where the Didjero-Doo Man, who blows a hollow-log trumpet, goes from band to band to perform and is fed by his audiences. In Polynesia there were whole companies of itinerant actors, and in North Africa troupes of religious students wander about as entertainers. Besides priests, ministers, and jesters, royal courts in many countries have their own staffs of musicians, just as Scottish chiefs used to walk preceded by pipers.

—Carleton S. Coon

BIBLIOGRAPHY

Anthropology Today: An Encyclopedic Inventory. Prepared under the chairmanship of A. L. Kroeber. The Univ. of Chicago Press, 1953.

CHILDE, V. G. *Man Makes Himself.* Penguin Books Inc., 1964.

COON, CARLTON S. *A General Reader in Anthropology.* Holt, Rinehart & Winston, Inc., 1950.

COON, CARLTON S. *The Story of Man.* Alfred A. Knopf, Inc., 1962.

KROEBER, A. L. *Anthropology.* Harcourt, Brace & World, Inc., 1948. and Dunlap, Inc., 1952.

OAKLEY, K. P. *Man the Tool-Maker.* British Museum of Natural History, 1952.

SOCIOLOGY

In 1838, the French philosopher Auguste Comte (1798–1857) coined the word "sociology," combining the Latin *socius* (associate) with the Greek *logos* (science). He envisioned a comprehensive science of social life, that is, all human life, since man is altogether a social creature. Comte believed that society necessarily progresses through a number of stages, each of which is an improvement on the preceding one. This view of social progress contributed to the one held by Karl Marx, the father of modern communism and socialism. Marx believed that society moves forward, back again, and forward once more—with a net forward movement that is necessarily determined by economic "laws of motion." Even later philosophers of history like Oswald Spengler and Arnold Toynbee, as well as socialists, communists, anarchists, and religious millenarians, still adhere to all-embracing schemes of the course of history. Sociologists, however, have abandoned such far-reaching speculations because they cannot be tested by observation. Unlike Comte and Marx, they concentrate on observable social activities.

Since sociologists formerly believed that the "progress" they were exploring was inherent in social development and thus *ipso facto* desirable, they saw no need to distinguish between their (scientific) description and their (moral) prescription. Sociology was dedicated to improvement —and sociologists thought there was no doubt as to where that improvement lay. Currently, sociologists generally confine themselves to description and prediction, to a study of what society is, was, might be, or will become. They try to refrain both from injecting their own moral views into their observations and from prescribing what should happen.

Sociologists are concerned with all aspects of group behavior. They focus on what the poet William Wordsworth called "The inscrutable workmanship that reconciles/discordant elements, makes them cling together/ In one society." For instance, when studying how people vote or marry, or who commits crimes, succeeds in college, or becomes an alcoholic, sociologists relate voting, marital choice, criminality, collegiate success, or alcoholism to group membership. To what extent is alcoholism or success in college related to residence in an urban or a rural community? to literacy? income? religion? sex? age? type of family? or to what extent is criminality or the rate of suicide, of fertility, or of radio listening related to change of group affiliation? How can the relationship be "explained"? What leads social groups to differ in fertility or in alcoholism rates?

Sociologists also inquire into the causes and effects of urbanization or of modifications in the techniques of production. Why are inventions made when and where they are made? (They seem to occur in clusters.) What leads to the application of inventions (innovation)? Surely the an-

cient Greeks were not less intelligent than we are, yet their technology was primitive compared to ours. Sociologists want to know what leads one group to behave in one way and another to behave in an entirely different way. They see each group as a strand in the social fabric and each personality is considered as a nexus of group influences.

Groups.—Every man is born into a group of men and throughout his life will belong to many groups. Such ex-

SAWDERS-CUSHING

THIS LAPP FAMILY from the northern part of Norway is one variation of the primary group that is common to all societies and cultures and is thus a universal institution.

ceptions as psychotics, hermits, and some geniuses do not disprove this rule. Voluntary isolation is part of the pathology of psychosis and of the uncommon but deliberate renunciations of the hermit. And, in the words of the Swiss historian Jacob Burckhardt (1818–1897), it is "the misfortune of genius to make him lonely in whom it dwells all too mightily." A genius, instead of sharing prevailing attitudes and ideas, creates new ones. His originality and depth are understood when what he pioneered is generally accepted and has lost its singularity. Only certain types of genius achieve recognition early enough to lead a group, usually when their innovations bring already accepted trends to full fruition.

■**PRIMARY AND SECONDARY GROUPS.**— Even the genius, hermit, or psychotic starts out as a member of a group by being born into a family. This primary group is itself part of a number of national, local, and religious communities into which the new family member will grow. Later he may also be drafted into a military group, be hospitalized with a group of patients or confined with a group of penitentiary inmates. He enters many groups without deliberation; he joins others by choice; still others

he joins through coercion by men or circumstances.

The term "group" may be used in a purely classificatory sense—regardless of how people feel and act. For instance, we can divide people into groups according to whether they have green or brown eyes. But classificatory orderings matter only when they can be related to the behavior of the group members toward each other and toward the social and natural environment, or to the behavior of others toward the group members. Every

group that behaves as a group or is felt to be one establishes—at least on some occasions—more, different, and perhaps closer relations among members than with outsiders.

Group members must have common attitudes. They create a structured relationship to each other by their distinctive attitudes to objects, persons, symbols, or actions. A physical or statistical aggregation of people can be called a (social) group only when the members are related by more than nearness or common traits. Nearness may, of course, lead to a group relationship without being one in itself. For example, the inhabitants of a village, a suburb, or a tenement, may be a group, but the tenants of an apartment house in a wealthy neighborhood probably are not. Often people become a group because of a common action they undertake; often they undertake the common action because of their group membership. The importance of the grouping depends on the importance of the behavior in relation to membership.

One may choose to become a member of a group formed mainly for the pleasures of group life, for instance, a college fraternity. As the name suggests, college fraternities are groups of elected "brothers" affiliated with the campus "family" and with the "parent" body of the national organization. Like many other groups, fraternities draw strength from the family, the original human association. They share some of its symbols and try to elicit sentiments associated with the family. However, fraternities must artificially provide the ties that grow quite naturally in actual families. Their initiation rites are imposed so that, through suffering a common experience, group solidarity and distinctiveness will be tightly strengthened.

■INITIATION RITES.—One may pay a high price for what one holds dear. Initiation rites are likely to be more demanding and harrowing where the need for solidarity is most strongly felt. Stringent initiations may also be required when those who undergo them have a great deal in common with nonmembers. The rite helps to weaken the bonds between the new group members and their nonmember friends (*adhesion*), as well as to strengthen ties between new and old group members (*cohesion*).

Pain is perhaps a more impressive experience than pleasure and is more easily inflicted. Although they end in feasts, initiations often feature pain. Pain may also be inflicted to purge the resentment of current members against the newcomers, who will compete with them and share in everything painfully created by them and by past generations.

The initiation ceremonies of primitive tribes may be interpreted analogously. In primitive puberty rites, however, additional motives are present; rites mark stages of biological maturity and usher age and sex groups into their social roles. In our own society, religious confirmations, school graduation ceremonies, and "coming-out" parties have a similar significance but a more limited scope.

■GROUP CHARACTERISTICS.—Groups may be both cause and effect of the common experiences undergone by members. For example, the cause of some group attitudes and characteristics may be the fact that members have received the same education. In turn, common education may be an effect of group membership. Families may be members of the same religious, or national, or economic groups; perhaps group members live in the same town or work together. Some groups are formed because of a common endeavor that may be also the effect of group formation. Other groups have no specific purpose. Group membership may be the result of people's dependence on each other for the satisfaction of their needs, or it may create the needs it satisfies, just as it may result from common characteristics or create them. Using the same after-shave lotion may not be sufficient reason to form a club—although advertisers seem convinced that it is—but how much more may be needed is unknown. Nearly any common experience may furnish the material for a common bond.

We become group-conscious almost as soon as we start differentiating ourselves from the rest of the universe, as soon as we become self-conscious. Our actions and feelings clearly distinguish our group from others, but the form of this distinction depends upon the culture into which we are born—the patterns of behavior transmitted to us. Culture also has a great deal to do with determining the common characteristics that lead to the formation of felt groups. Skin color, for example, may be important in one culture and political views, occupation, sex, or religion more important in another. Each group usually influences the behavior of members only in selected respects and on selected occasions. This is so because people hold membership in many groups. Only observation can tell which group membership will control individual behavior on a given occasion.

Groups may be ordered according to number and intimacy of members. The smallest and most intimate group is a pair—husband and wife, mother and child, or two friends. Then come families or classes in a boarding school—associations with personal, intimate, fairly enduring, and comprehensive contacts. These groups are called *primary groups* in order to distinguish them from such *secondary groups* as nations or labor unions. Relations in secondary groups are less personal, usually more purposefully concerned with fewer aspects of behavior, and frequently controlled by formal rules. The primary group often is formed spontaneously and is formally organized only when changed into a secondary one, which requires designation of officeholders, entrance requirements, and so forth. Within the secondary group there are numerous primary ones. Within the church there are congregations; within the fraternity there are chapters; and within each of these, there are still smaller and more intimate groupings. It is, of course, the primary group that is paramount in the formation of the individual personality.

■PERMANENT AND TEMPORARY GROUPS.—There are both permanent and temporary secondary groups. Such groups as nations or churches are permanent. They continue indefinitely because their characteristic patterns of behavior are transmitted to new members, and these patterns change slowly and continuously enough so that the group is able to retain its identity. Permanent groups are united by continuous habits—for instance, speaking a common language, residing in a given territory, being subject to the same laws, sharing common beliefs or traits. In contrast, mem-

UNITED NATIONS

THESE AFRICAN STUDENTS, members of a temporary learning group, also belong to a larger national group that is changing quite rapidly. The Greek Orthodox scribe (*right*) belongs to a permanent religious group that has changed very little over the centuries.

KRYN TACONIS, MAGNUM PHOTOS

GERT BERLINER

bers of temporary groups have only an *ad hoc* relationship that binds them together while they share an experience. The relationship—or the group as such—disappears with the experience that prompted it. Primary groups by definition dissolve with the death of the participants, if not before.

When the membership changes frequently, when the association is involuntary, or casual and sudden, and when it consists of people who have little in common, group solidarity (*cohesion*) is transient. Members may act as a group only during the temporary conditions that lead to group membership—being soldiers, or members of a crowd, or inmates of a penitentiary. Yet, while the activating condition exists, the solidarity of temporary groups can be as strong as that of permanent groups.

■**CROWDS.**—*Crowds (momentary groups)* differ according to the kind and binding power of their focus. Audiences sharing a spectacle (planned or accidental) or people sharing a bus ride form crowds. In a bus, the common ride is a means rather than an end, and it is not a strong bond. In the theater, the common enjoyment of the spectacle is the final purpose of the group. Members of crowds who come together to dance in a public hall or to go on a lynching are also each attuned to common sentiments. They often behave collectively as they would not individually, shedding personal characteristics and responsibilities, suspending individual judgment, and following their unbridled instincts. They are "beside themselves"; that part of their personality that they have in common with others overwhelms the ego and individuating traits and silences calmer counsel. They become anonymous not only to other members but also, one is tempted to say, even to themselves. Crowd members do not reason; they follow. Inflammatory speeches, martial music, or drinking may heighten and focus the anti-individual, anti-intellectual character of crowds; but they are not indispensable to crowd behavior. Any speaker knows that

what appears as a great joke to a crowd, owing to the near suspension of judgment, is not necessarily one.
■**PUBLICS.**—*Publics* should be distinguished from crowds and, in a sense, from groups. Unlike a crowd, the public is physically dispersed but is linked together by a common culture or, within the culture, by a common activity—reading a newspaper or looking at a television program. Being part of a public may contribute to a group membership, but by itself this is not enough to form a group except in the loosest sense. Yet the influence of the public on the conduct of individuals and groups is immense and, owing to the spread of mass media of communication, the influence of "public opinion" is rising.

It should be mentioned that the various relationships that we separate analytically—primary and secondary group, crowd and public, and many others—may coexist in the same aggregate of persons and blend into each other.

■**INSTITUTIONS.**—Groups cultivate behavior patterns that are more or less adapted to their distinctive functions. Permanent group behavior patterns, often accumulated over generations, are called *institutions*. Institutions are expected to generate appropriate sentiments that are often expressed through a cluster of symbolic and utilitarian paraphernalia. For example, such political institutions as the state elicit from the group members (citizens) sentiments of loyalty, patriotism, respect, and subordination. The state is symbolized by the flag, the national anthem, and numerous shrines and monuments. It is celebrated, and the sentiments reasserted, by rituals on such holidays as Washington's Birthday and Veterans Day. The state articulates and enforces its policies by laws, with the help of public officials, courts, schools, and armies.

Most institutions are similarly organized. The family, for example, inspires concern and mutual love. It is frequently symbolized by wedding rings or heirlooms, and is celebrated ritually on holidays, birthdays, and anniversaries, or on the occasion

of marriage, birth, or death. Family life takes place with the help of such equipment as furniture and living quarters, according to specifications laid down in laws and customs. Churches and schools are similarly operated. Such institutions as banks and labor unions are thought of mainly as means; therefore, the conscious sentiments of the groups involved, and the symbols, are likely to be more directly related to their material ends.

Poolrooms, colleges, prisons, hospitals, holidays, and athletic games are also institutions, each occupying a different place in the network of social relations. Some institutions bind people together continuously in a specific way; others, recurrently; some, exclusively; others only in a particular activity. However, each institution defines the related roles into which it fits its members. The family decides the limits of the roles played by parents, children, husbands, and wives. The state defines the roles of government and citizens; baseball, those of the player, the fan, and the coach. We may thus conceive of institutions as clusters of related roles outlining behavior patterns that are then interpreted by the participants.

Culture.—Groups are distinguished from each other by their institutions; societies, by the total systems formed by their institutions. The system is part of the culture of each society. Culture includes all transformation and control of the natural environment, as well as all the acquired traits shared by the members of a society; it does not include the inborn traits. It includes institutions, language, ideas, ideals, emotional and behavioral patterns, and such techniques as language, art, religion, science, and technology. Also involved are the abiding expectations we place on each other to associate, communicate, cooperate, and compete. None of our cultural heritage is innate, although we may think so because we are usually unaware of the informal processes through which we learn to master it. Culture, however, is not merely an aggregate of all these elements. They must be meshed together to permit the society to continue. No institution carries out its function by itself; it must be supported by other institutions. If the impact of some institutions is detrimental to others, we are faced with a "social problem" that can be resolved only by changing one or more of the institutions.

■**THE FAMILY.**—Although the culture of each society is different, all societies need certain institutions to perform the functions essential to any social life. Thus, all societies have the institution of the family. (Such groups as the Shakers and monastic orders can renounce offspring; but there are no societies that do.) Everywhere, the family is identified as the regulator of reproduction and of the biological propensity to sexual intercourse.

The family is seldom restricted to its basic reproductive function, but its additional functions differ from society to society. It may loom large or small as an economic or political unit. The family may decide who is to be whose bride or groom, or leave it to the individuals concerned. Sometimes only individuals of one sex—usually the male—are allowed to choose their own mates. Political and judicial power may be inherited through family membership, as it often was in the Middle Ages; or inheritance may be limited to wealth, as in the United States now.

The customs distributing power, respect, and income among family members also differ from society to society. Age may be decisive, or sex, or neither. Qualifications for membership (definitions of kinship) in families differ from one society to another, and so do eligibility requirements. Each culture prescribes different relations of family members to each other and to outsiders. Some societies have wide kinship systems; others, restricted ones. Some emphasize avuncular (relating to an uncle) relations; others, matrilineal; others, patrilineal; still others, adoptive family relations. Finally, some emphasize offspring; others stress ancestry; and still others, the conjugal mates.

The differences in accepted emotional relationships are also staggering. Among Eskimos and some other groups it is a matter of common courtesy to lend their wives to guests, but they will take great offense and kill each other for unauthorized wife-borrowing. (This is not as odd as it may appear: we, too, give gifts but punish anyone who takes anything without permission.) It has been suggested that this practice arose, at least in part, because the polar night is long and entertainment scarce. However, the Kiwei Papuans also have sexual hospitality, although their natural environment is very different from that of the Eskimos.

Some societies consider love the cause of marriage; others, the effect; and still others consider love irrelevant. It goes without saying that ideas and ideals of love differ enormously in different cultures, although some sort of attraction is always involved. Differences are so great that one might well say that love, as it has been defined since the Middle Ages, plays a significant role only in a few places and periods.

■**MARRIAGE.**—Types of marriage also vary. Some societies institutionalize *polygyny* (the practice of having more than one wife at a time); a few, *polyandry* (more than one husband at a time). Both of these types of marriage, of course, involve *polygamy*—plural wedlock. Byzantine Christendom had strict monogamy—even widowed persons could not remarry because there was some apprehension that a widower might be embarrassed by several wives at the Resurrection. Nonmarital relations, however, seem to have been rather free. Our own society has a somewhat looser monogamy. One can be married to only one person at a time, but the ease in changing partners brings us fairly near to serial polygamy: through divorce one is able to marry several persons successively without waiting for the death of any one. Marriage, moreover, is becoming mainly a union of two individuals that is meant to satisfy their psychological needs, while in the past it was largely a union of two families that was meant to continue them. For instance, in the fifth book of the Old Testament (Deuteronomy 25:5–9), it is stated that the duty of a brother is to marry his widowed sister-in-law. If he refuses: "Then shall his brother's wife come unto him . . . and spit in his face . . . and say, So shall it be done unto that man that will not build up his brother's house." The idea of the family as a device to continue the male's life (his name) through his descendants, and the many functions of the family beyond the union of two individuals, explain most of the characteristics it is now losing.

Also, the religious beliefs and social functions that once made marriage an indissoluble bond have lost their impact. Wedlock has become dependent upon the satisfaction of the needs felt by the married couple; thus, it is often temporary. Our high divorce rate (about 25 per cent of all marriages in the United States end in divorce) does not necessarily mean that husbands and wives get along less well now than before; however, it shows that when they do not get along, they can (and do) divorce more easily than they used to. Possibly the emotional demands made on marriage have increased as the material demands have decreased. Divorce is easy enough for many to prefer it to any serious attempts to overcome marital difficulties. There is some reason, finally, to suspect that many people expect from marriage a fulfillment that no human institution can yield.

■**SOCIETY.**—A society includes all people who share a common culture. However, parts of the culture may be diffused beyond the society, and

THE QUILTING BEE BY GRANDMA MOSES

COMMUNITY COOPERATION and homespun warmth are characteristic of rural society. In large urban areas, however, individuals can be lost in the city's mass shuffle (*left*).

not all its members share all its culture. Subcultures, variations that modify a great deal of behavior, distinguish the subgroups that compose large societies. The relationship is like that between a language and its dialects. Regional subgroups, occupational groups, classes, and social sets all may speak dialects, or lingos, indicative of their position in the general culture. Language is sometimes used spontaneously, sometimes willfully, to define subgroups. Children, as well as adults who feel the need to belong to a distinct group, may deliberately invent linguistic peculiarities intelligible only to insiders, thereby distinguishing themselves from outsiders ("squares" or "cornballs").

Large societies differ in stability or fluidity of relationships. The relationship of groups to each other, their composition, size, and their subcultures, may be stable, or quite changeable. Where members can move with ease from one group to the other, the continuity of identifiable subcultures is shortened.

Two related aspects can be found in every culture. First, each society selects different materials from the natural environment and employs them to create its own distinctive environment. This utilization of the natural world to provide particular types of shelter, food, clothing, ritual objects, and weapons always depends upon the second aspect of culture, which is acquired from the social past. Thus, land in America is used differently today from the way it was used by the Indians. Our European tradition and training led to a very different culture, although our innate impulses are not basically different from those of the Indians.

Each culture selects certain of

INTERNATIONAL NEWS

COLLECTIVE BEHAVIOR, when motivated by the common attitudes and beliefs shared by each of the individual members of a group, gives a true sense of unity and belonging.

man's inborn capacities to restrain or develop. Each subculture further stresses, elaborates, trains, or restricts some human abilities. Language illustrates how each culture selects and discards from the gamut of possibilities. The whole human race speaks with the same kind of mouth, yet there is an almost infinite variety of tongues. How different are the frequency, the meaning, and the patterns of sounds that English and Chinese cultures cause the same physical apparatus to produce! Yet language is only one form of communication, and communication only one of the many acquired techniques in which cultural differences appear.

Each culture narrows the wide range of action and feeling allowed by human nature and man's environment. The range of some cultures is limited by rigid boundaries; there is

general agreement on major preferences and a disdain for deviations. In other cultures, the range of choice is wide, and the boundaries are flexible. Cultures vary further by centering on different aspects of human potentialities. In each case, however, the range selected is believed to be the range granted or willed by nature. For instance, each culture somewhat narrows the choice of sexual relationships. One culture may foster and approve homosexual impulses while another condemns them; in both cultures, people feel that nature sanctions and dictates what is actually a cumulative, unconscious choice.

■**INDIVIDUALS AND CULTURE.**—For individuals, cultural limitation is produced in two ways. Culture guides the social influences that affect the formation of individual preferences and personalities. These influences, transmitted and modified by the family and other primary groups, affect the individual from birth. Later, culture continues to guide through social approval or disapproval of the developed preferences. Unapproved behavior incurs such penalties as conspicuousness, contempt, ostracism, or even legal punishment. Approved behavior is rewarded with success, popularity, power, or other advancement. Approved behavior includes a wide range; yet the patterns that develop individually may not be certain of approval beforehand—there is scope for innovation and risk. The range of variation and the heaviness of the risk depend on the particular culture and, within it, on the activity one engages in and the subgroup to which one belongs.

Society does not tell Americans to

dislike blubber or other Eskimo delicacies, but our tastes are so formed that Eskimo food appeals to us no more than Chinese music. Chinese ears and Eskimo taste buds do not differ from ours, but those cultures do. Again, no formal rule compels a stockbroker to wear trousers rather than leotards; no law prevents him from doing his hair in pigtails. But a male who wears what his society considers fit only for women or unacceptable for his role or for the occasion soon learns that he must move within the limits set by his culture. In every human activity cultural boundaries limit and direct individual choice, without eliminating it altogether. People do business, amuse themselves, create art, associate, perform rituals, and appraise conduct according to their preferences—within cultural bounds.

Culture also directs our perceptions; it sharpens our sensitivity in some ways and dulls it in others. Whether people strike us as black and white, or preeminently as men and women, or as rich and poor, depends on the socially influenced focus of our attention. Culture strongly affects how we evaluate what we see. Whether we find Gothic cathedrals ugly, as they were thought to be in the eighteenth century, or admirable, as they are thought of today; whether our respect for a person depends on age, color, sex, wealth, education, entertainment ability, physical strength, or individual character— all this is influenced by socially formed aesthetic, moral, and erotic ideals. We easily distinguish Chinese art from Italian art, and Renaissance painting from medieval painting because each is informed by different cultural ideals and executed in a style developed as part of a specific culture. Both the style and the ideal are cumulatively developed through individual contributions of different magnitudes.

Social ideals may even influence the actual human physique, not only by encouraging us to paint our lips, to extend them, or to deform our heads, but also by preferential selective breeding (not to be confused with planned selective breeding). Thus, some Chinese, some Burmese, and others for centuries have preferred and therefore married and procreated flat-chested women. Culturally formed ideals go a long way toward explaining the prevalence of different physical types among various ethnic groups.

The conduct of others, learned and reproduced by us since childhood, also helps determine the expression or repression of such feelings as respect or contempt, hate or love. It suggests the form in which they are expressed, as well as the occasion, the intensity, and the objects to which they may be attached. Notice, for instance, how emotional and sensual the heroes of Homer are, compared to modern heroes. The conduct and opinions of others influence the range and depth of our individual feelings, for our ideas about ourselves are influenced by the way others see us. Culture also includes the division of labor, the prevailing techniques of production, the distribution and evaluation of products, and the uses of political power. If the natural order makes work and human associations necessary, the social order—part of culture—determines how they are organized.

Culture follows us from the cradle to the grave. Our personality greatly depends on the way we are cradled, fondled, nourished, disciplined, and indulged as infants. In all of this, our parents follow the patterns of the culture to which they belong. Later, we learn more of our culture through education. Throughout life, custom continues to give us behavioral cues. Finally, custom helps us to be mourned and buried with proper ceremony, even telling the bereaved how to mark the grave.

However, culture should not be

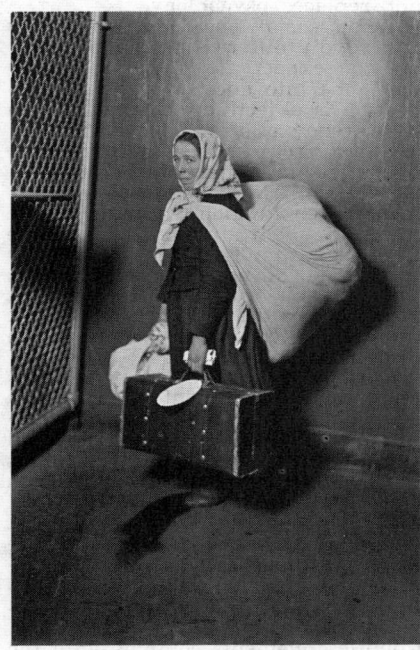

LEWIS W. HINE

ALIENATION from one's social or cultural group can mean temporary loss of identity.

regarded as a straitjacket. Its patterns are only one of the elements that affect individual fate. Although society limits the ability of individuals to choose, and stresses some decisions as more desirable than others, it does not altogether deprive us of choice. No two individuals have exactly the same pattern of group affiliations. Each defines himself by reference to the groups of which he is a member and by reference to the groups that are within his purview. Thus, each individual is differently located and uniquely defined within his culture.

History gathers customs, ideas, and institutions into a *network culture,* which molds individual attitudes before we are born and after we die. Like a sieve, culture strains our perceptions of internal and external stimuli. It suggests and channels re-

actions: "Notice this!" "Ignore that!" "Imitate this action!" "Shun that action!" Generally, these signals are so deeply internalized that we do not feel controlled by them. On the contrary, they enter our awareness as an inner ambition or as a "natural" expectation. Culture, after all, not only directs and controls the expression of our personalities, but also has a hand in shaping them.

We become aware of the directional signals of culture mainly when they are inconsistent or when they conflict with very strong congenital impulses that must be satisfied. Discord also arises when we are unprepared for a change of signals. Such a change may be due to developments within the culture or to contact between cultures. When we transfer from one group to another, as frequently happens in fluid cultures, friction and disorientation may also result. We become aware of our culture as the external source of orders and limitations when we find ourselves confronted with several alternative sets of customs, not one "natural" set.

Conflicts may be internalized if early conditioning is directed by people who have not sufficiently resolved their own conflicts, or by different persons with incompatible views and attitudes. One may then grow up torn by incompatible desires and inconsistent signals that seem to come from within. Even under the best conditions, conflicts between the demands of any culture and some of our innate impulses are unavoidable. Nor does a socially acceptable and individually bearable resolution depend only on conditioning. However they arise, conflicts always enhance awareness of cultural boundaries; they permit or compel us to see life as a problem. They also produce people who throw these cultural boundaries into relief and change them—artists, philosophers, and sometimes scholars.

Everyone experiences culture in his own way. Each of us develops his ways according to the models among his family, his friends, the books he reads, and the things he sees. However, culture does not provide patterns to meet all situations; at most, it provides cues for the more usual circumstances. Thus, in creating their future, men do more than reproduce the past. They learn from the experiences accumulated by past generations and weave old strands of behavior into new patterns. Of course, the new patterns need not be better than the old ones. The need to guard against such an implication arises in a society as keen on change as ours, where the very word "new" tends automatically to connote "better."

Stratification.—The survival of every society depends upon the performance of various tasks. Government, religion, law, defense, agriculture and industry, medicine, building, art, science, and other activities are present in all societies in more or less specialized form, together with such familiar tasks as bringing up children and preparing food. Every society must make reasonably sure that enough

persons—but not too many—perform each task and that they have the means and the incentive to render the services required. The incentive can be negative (punishment) or positive (reward). Societies have found many more or less efficient ways to make sure that essential services will be rendered; those that have altogether failed to do so have not survived.

In the main, the performance of tasks is assured by distributing prestige, power, and income so as to make the performance possible and profitable. Most services necessarily involve an unequal distribution of these incentives. Political and military tasks—government and war—necessitate an unequal distribution of power: subordination to officials and officers. Judges must have an unequal distribution of authority: the authority to control litigants and those suspected, or guilty, of law violations. Production leads to an unequal distribution of income: unequal control over goods and services. Different valuation of tasks leads to prestige: unequal deference, respect, and admiration enjoyed by people. Thus, prestige is by definition unequal. (In a sense, this is true of power, too; but unlike prestige, power need not be an end in itself.) Inequality of income is enjoyed because higher—as distinguished from high—income yields more prestige than does low income. Power, income, and prestige tend to coincide to some extent in all societies; but in no society are they identical or coextensive.

Although occasionally awarded directly to individuals, power, income, and prestige are usually attached to the services that people (selected on a hereditary basis or because of individual qualifications) are expected to perform. Activities that are important or demand rare talents and skills are usually invested with more power, prestige, or income than others. Thus, in each society, groups can be distinguished according to the power, prestige, and income they have because of the activities they engage in or the social stations they occupy. The classification of groups in these terms is called *stratification,* and the groups are called *strata* (layers).

Stratification seems as unavoidable as the division of labor, which to some extent is biologically given. The immature and the old cannot work as effectively as the mature. Women, because they bear and rear children, are more homebound than men. People have different abilities and disabilities. However, neither the dictates of nature nor those of economic rationality require either the specific elaboration that the division of labor receives or the specific power and prestige distribution among age and sex groups that characterizes each society. This is also true of stratification, which is closely allied to the division of labor. In all societies, stratification is required by the nature of the tasks performed and as an incentive to their performance. Further, where positions are not filled on a hereditary basis, stratification helps to attract the right per-

FREDERIC LEWIS

CLASS STRATIFICATION was fairly rigid in the Victorian era, when rank in the social hierarchy was largely determined by wealth; today's social structure is far more fluid.

sons in the right numbers to the tasks they can best perform. It does not follow that any given system of stratification is indispensable, but stratification itself is.

Societies have considerable leeway in cultivating or minimizing differences of position and the innumerable privileges and amenities attendant upon them. The rank assigned to each position also may vary from society to society, although similar tasks tend to lead to similar ranking in various societies. Finally, access to positions may depend either on a variety of personal qualifications, or on parental rank. Since there is leeway in all these matters, one may properly consider if and how any given system of stratification should be changed; from the possibility of abolishing any single rank order, it cannot be inferred that all rank orders can be abolished. This is a fallacy that many leftists who feel uneasy about inequality (including Marxists and anarchists) are loath to abandon. Rightists, on the other hand, are inclined to argue as though the impossibility of abolishing *all* rank orders proves the impossibility of abolishing *any* rank order. There is no evidence to show that sizable societies can exist without stratification, for none has. However, there also is no evidence to show that any particular system is indispensable—the most diverse kinds have existed. Naive defenders and opponents of the *status quo* also confuse the question, "Should a change be made?" with the question, "Can a change be made?" Change may be possible without being advantageous, or advantageous without being possible; inequality may be unjust without being unnecessary, or just without being necessary.

■INFLUENCE ON LIFE CHANCES.—Membership in a stratum comprehensively influences one's life chances. One's opportunity to survive the first year after birth, one's life span, nourishment, health, physical appearance, attire, abode, comfort, leisure, ability to communicate, chances of becoming a criminal and of receiving an education—in short, the duration, enjoyment, achievement, and style of life—are influenced by the privileges and characteristics of the stratum to which one belongs. A man's friends usually belong to his stratum. Also, strata are always somewhat endogamous. Even when exogamy is legally permitted, people usually marry within their own stratum.

Persons of equal or nearly equal rank in the social hierarchy form a stratum that is also the stratum of their families. The family is the basic constituent of the stratum. Regardless of whether a family's position has been achieved by its current head or is inherited, one belongs, at least until adulthood, to the stratum of one's family. In some systems, offspring remain permanently in the parental stratum. However, even when rank is not inherited, family membership influences what stratum one can belong to in later life—what opportunity for achievement one has—by providing such requirements as education.

Stratification involves not only an enduring rank order of social positions but also a tendency—greater than chance—for people to remain in the strata into which they are born. Logically, a stratified society in which rank is entirely independent of family and is not necessarily lifelong is possible. Plato's utopian *Republic* is a case in point.

The demarcation lines of strata

may be quite fluid, and subjective feelings of belonging need not be strictly correlated to objective lines. Nonetheless, objective inclusion—through, for instance, legal privileges or wealth—influences behavior and subjective outlook and generates subjective solidarity in the stratum. The members feel united in certain ways and separated from other strata—the less the individual members expect to move up vertically, the stronger the feeling. Also, a common fear of being pushed down may strengthen solidarity within a stratum. However, since position in the social hierarchy is only one of many influences leading to only one of many group memberships, its importance to the individual varies. All group memberships together (including membership in a stratum) do not exhaustively explain individual behavior: sociology adds to, but does not replace, psychology.

When social positions are highly and rigidly differentiated and people do not expect to move frequently from one into another—when stratification is objectively at a maximum —awareness of stratification and envy are far from intense. Antagonism among strata is inactive because society is split into noncompeting segments. People identify with people in their own stratum, not with people in other strata. They are not anxious to rise and do not form expectations that can be frustrated. Resentment grows when the ambition to change position is cultivated but is often disappointed.

Further, as stratification becomes more fluid, resentment rises. People compete strenuously and are necessarily envious of each other, since all run in the same race for positions that only a few can achieve. If an egalitarian ideology has taught them that men should be equal—at least when equally gifted—those in the lower positions are left to conclude either that their own gifts are inferior or that those who have superior positions do not deserve them. Countless elements combine with the stratification system to determine whether these difficulties are handled through political action or expressed in individual dissatisfaction.

■MAIN TYPES.—There are three main types of stratification: castes, estates, and classes. In caste and estate systems, the ranks are formally distinguished in law and custom; each stratum has different rights and obligations. In a class system, differences of strata are not legally recognized: except in the performance of occupational tasks, all citizens, regardless of class, are considered equal.

In a *caste system*, rank is ascribed by birth and retained throughout life. The newborn's caste depends on that of his parents. Vertical mobility is stunted—caste is not changed by personal achievement. People marry within the same caste, and numerous precautions are taken to minimize intercaste associations. Contact with the lowest caste is regarded as polluting, particularly with regard to bodily orifices: thus, common eating, defecating, and bathing are particularly feared. The system is rationalized in religious beliefs that hold that imperishable souls migrate from body to body (*metempsychosis*) and that the souls that have reached higher stages of purification are embodied in the higher castes, whereas those in the lower castes still have a long way to go. Mobility thus occurs—but the movement takes place in an invisible sphere. Analogous systems exist on a biological basis among many social insects, such as termites and bees. Among human societies, the caste system has existed for 3,000 years in Hindu India and for varying periods elsewhere, although it has never been as rigid as among the social insects.

Although the Indian caste system was, and still is, much more rigid than our own class system, we tend to overlook what flexibility there is. Each caste is divided into numerous subcastes, and the division changes over time and differs from region to region. Over 2,000 main castes were counted in India, and some of these were divided into 1,000 to 2,000 subcastes. So complex a system naturally had to change somewhat over a period of time, although even now most people expect to remain—and do remain—members of the caste into which they were born.

In an *estate system,* ordinarily part of the social system of feudalism, the individual inherits his rank. Even his attire may be regulated by the estate to which he belongs; the wife of an artisan may not be allowed to dress like the wife of a nobleman, even if she can afford to. However, the idea characteristic of a caste system—that a person of high rank is polluted by contact with a person of low rank—is alien to the estate system. Legally recognized rank depends upon land ownership and occupation, both largely inherited. But in an estate system, although stratification is rigid, there is some vertical mobility. The king may endow a subject with land and make him a member of the noble estate. Military and ecclesiastical careers are not closed to members of the lower estates, who may thus rise. However, mobility is generally low.

Compared with caste and estate systems, the position one achieves in a *class system* depends least on inherited rank or parental position—it depends most on one's ability. Legal, customary, and material barriers to mobility are minimized. Social strata are ranked essentially by income, however earned. (Classes may be defined and ranked by many criteria other than income, although income is usually included. For our present purpose, however, income alone will do.) Legally, all members of a class system are peers and subject to the same laws; and outside occupational spheres, there is little social recognition of rank. Political, military, judicial, and priestly positions are not inherited. This system, developed in Europe after the fall of the estate system, is the only one the United States has ever known, and it is replacing all others throughout the world.

Karl Marx distinguished classes according to ownership of means of production, such as land or capital. Some Marxists allege, therefore, that where private ownership of means of production is abolished, as in the Soviet Union, there is no class system. But this is a quibble over words. Differences in income, power, and prestige—in life chances—have not been abolished. The important class differences persist. Stratification in the Soviet Union proves that Marx was wrong in believing that differences in class originate exclusively with private ownership of means of production and are automatically abolished by socialization. The elimination of private ownership merely does away with one of many sources of income, one of many possible ways of achieving or inheriting rank.

Although income and rank are per-

HELEN BUTTFIELD

THE CASTE SYSTEM often keeps people in permanent subservience and poverty.

sonally achieved in a class system, the achievement is by no means independent of the class membership of one's parents; the ease of access to acquisitions—knowledge, skills, friendships—that facilitate achievement depends on parental position. Thus, life chances are never independent of the parental stratum.

In a caste system, people remain in the stratum into which they were born. They are trained accordingly and expect nothing else. In an estate system, only a few rather exceptional people move. However, in a class system everyone by right may enter the race for high rank; most people do, and many change their position.

Actual systems of stratification are never as pure as the theoretical constructs that help us to analyze them, just as the pure elements of chemistry are seldom found unmixed in nature. Although the American sys-

tem has always been predominantly a class system, slavery was obviously a caste element. There are still caste elements in our treatment of ethnic groups, particularly of Negroes. In Europe, there are many remnants of the estate system; hereditary nobility, including monarchy, is the most obvious. The systems become mixed through contacts with other systems or through changes within themselves. Further, each system originally contains some of the elements of the others. Even a caste system does not altogether exclude social mobility; in the course of time, some individual "passes" from one caste to another, and also ranking of castes changes. Since the caste system, like any system of social stratification, is based on socially recognized values on the one hand, and is linked to economic and political matters on the other, it is usually affected by religious, technological, and political changes.

Logically, the system by which positions are ranked is independent of the means used to select the people to occupy them. One can imagine a system in which ranks are inherited but not highly differentiated. And a society is logically possible in which ranks can be achieved individually and are highly differentiated; people of different ranks do not mix. However, experience indicates that when ranks are inherited, they are also highly differentiated. Each stratum keeps to itself; each has rigidly prescribed obligations and privileges. On the other hand, in a class society where rank is achieved individually, social strata ordinarily feel far less alienated from each other. As was pointed out, differences may be resented more, but they are smaller.

A general theory of stratification can do no more than indicate the functions that stratification can fulfill and the functions that cannot be fulfilled without stratification. To explain a particular system of stratification, historical elements must be added to the general theory. Each system will have elements that, although serving some function in it, need not be there or could be replaced by others without interfering with the survival of the society. At the same time, elements that could help the society to survive may be missing. This point may be generalized as follows: no analysis by the methods of any one social science exhausts all aspects of a social problem; the other social sciences are needed. No analysis by the methods of all social sciences exhausts a social problem; its historical setting and development must be considered. The problems of society are like those confronting the physician. Like each human organism, each society is a multidimensional historical system with intensive relationships among the parts. And there are nonrecurring elements in all societies.

■**STATUS.**—Unlike class, status is subjective; and each person has more than one status. *Status* refers to *personal prestige* (esteem) in each of many groups, large or small, family or co-workers, the community, friends, or the public at large; to the *imper-*

sonal prestige of each position, independent of who occupies it; to the behavioral expectations held by the occupants about themselves by virtue of the position they occupy; and to what is expected of them by others. The rank of "physician"—the status of the position—differs from that of "janitor." And the prestige of the position is independent of the personal prestige of John, the physician, or Jack, the janitor—although the occupant of each position is affected by, and expected to act in accordance with, the demands of the position. His prestige depends to some extent on how well he fulfills these demands.

Each position is located and ranked in a system of statuses. "System" here means the basis of ranking (occupation, color, kinship), the criteria used for the ranking on that basis (manual or nonmanual work), the actual allocation of ranks (the hierarchy), and the nonprestige expectations attached to each occupation. There are many status systems. Everybody, without respect for person, is ranked in them according to age, sex, kinship, occupation, and so forth, just as everybody is ranked in the class system according to income. But since there are many status systems, everybody occupies many statuses, although lodged in only one class. Age may bring deference regardless of personal merit. The father may be the head of the family regardless of who supports it. Status includes personal and official authority; but it goes beyond authority over others, formally established or derived from respect and esteem, to comprise all the expectations people place on each other by virtue of office, occupation, age, kinship, and the personal regard they have for each other.

■ **ROLE.**—The conduct expected in each status is called a *role*. The aged are expected to behave in one way, the young in another; parents play one role, children another. As the individual ages, his status and his role change. However, the role associated with each of the statuses he enters and leaves is expected to remain rather stable—although this is less so in our society than in others. The statuses directly related to biological matters, such as age or parenthood, were called *categories* by the anthropologist Ralph Linton (1893–1953). Other social statuses are mostly related to occupation—chief, priest, servant, policeman, merchant, physician. However, they are not unrelated to the categories: the priest is "father" and the chief has paternal authority. To hold together, a society must foster and then bend to social uses the sentiments that link a family together and are generated by it.

Status always occurs in a particular group and system; it is seldom the same in all groups, at all times, or in all systems. The prestige of positions, as distinguished from that of the persons occupying them, varies least from group to group when the positions are linked to occupations. Indeed, in industrialized countries the hierarchies of occupational prestige are quite similar.

In some hierarchies, the vertical order of status is formally established and indicated by standardized symbols. This is the case in the military hierarchy, in some ecclesiastic ones, and less explicitly in many hierarchies organized to perform definite functions. In the most formally organized hierarchies, rank officially defines both one's authority and the respect that others owe and are expected to pay in standardized ways. Hence, "status" sometimes refers to both authority and respect. But the power and the prestige of positions may diverge: the king (or the President of the German Republic) has less power, yet more prestige, than the prime minister. Analogously, the power and prestige of persons may diverge. We shall, therefore, use "status" to refer to prestige ranking (and to role expectations) and otherwise speak of "power"; "class" will be used to refer to income and, occasionally, wealth. Note, however, that "status" is colloquially used to refer to position on any scale and "class" is sometimes used to refer to quality or prestige (for instance, "high class"). Unavoidably, there is also some overlapping because the role expectations placed on a status may include the exercise of power. Still, the fact that power and prestige, although related, do not coincide with each other or with income makes separate terms convenient.

In informally organized groups the status hierarchy is implicit; and when they do not have functions that require a stable rank order, status is highly volatile and elusive. It can be described but shifts subtly. It depends both on how one behaves and on what criteria others apply to evaluate behavior. Hence, the same behavior brings different status in different groups and on occasions. And different behavior produces different statuses in the same group.

Class membership does not depend on anyone's opinion; the class hierarchy is ordered according to an objective, quantitative criterion—income. In contrast, except for the formal hierarchies mentioned, status hierarchies, being subjective, can be ascertained only by inquiring into people's opinions of each other as well as into their evaluations of social positions. Everyone's status depends on everyone else's opinion of others. Unlike stratum, status is a segmental matter. You have one standing in a particular group and, possibly, a different status in another group, or according to another system. Your status may be high on the ethnic prestige scale and low on the occupational scale if you are a white dog catcher in Alabama; the reverse may be true if you are a southern Negro physician. Status is an *ordinal ranking*—higher or lower. Unlike class, status is not a *cardinal ranking* —there is no way to measure the distance between adjacent ranks. Unless handled with great caution, the concept "total social status" (or "socioeconomic status") is an average of incommensurables that obscures as much as it enlightens. It is probably used, however, because people almost always feel that they themselves have one society-wide social status—usually the one they have in the group that ranks them highest. They cleave to that group because their status in it is actually higher than their "total social status" would be and because the ranking (and the group) is meaningful to them; it fits into their self-image and involves the activities with which they are concerned.

The many systems in which we occupy different statuses and the manifold expectations placed upon us by them were not designed according to a master plan. They grew separately and unevenly as society developed. In various periods they proliferated from one institution, sank roots in another, were grafted upon a third. Social institutions themselves do not necessarily develop in a harmonious order, nor do they mesh neatly. On the contrary, since they originate in different parts and groups of society, and develop at different rates of speed and sometimes in different directions, there is in all societies a need for overarching institutions that have the main task of unifying the others, adapting them to each other, and, where necessary, weeding them out. Religious, political, and economic institutions share this task, although they do not always perform it successfully.

—Ernest van den Haag

BIBLIOGRAPHY

Abrahamsen, David. *Psychology of Crime.* Columbia University Press, 1960.

Bierstedt, Robert. *The Social Order: An Introduction to Sociology.* McGraw-Hill, Inc., 1957.

Chase, Stuart. *The Proper Study of Mankind.* Harper & Bros., 1956.

Fairchild, Henry Pratt (ed.). *Dictionary of Sociology.* Littlefield, Adams & Co., 1955.

Gillin, John (ed.). *For a Science of Social Man.* The Macmillan Co., 1954.

Landis, Paul H. *Social Problems in Nation and World.* J. B. Lippincott Co., 1959.

Lerner, Max. *America As a Civilization.* Simon & Schuster, Inc., 1957.

Lynd, Robert S. and Helen M. *Middletown: A Study in Contemporary American Culture.* Harcourt, Brace & World, Inc., 1929.

Montagu, M. F. Ashley. *Man's Most Dangerous Myth: The Fallacy of Race.* Harper & Bros., 1952.

Mumford, Lewis. *The City in History: Its Origin, Its Transformations, and Its Prospects.* Harcourt, Brace & World, Inc., 1961.

Riesman, David and others. *The Lonely Crowd.* Yale University Press, 1962.

Ross, Ralph C. and van den Haag, Ernest. *Fabric of Society.* Harcourt, Brace & World, Inc., 1957.

Rumney, Jay, and Maier, Joseph. *Sociology: The Science of Society.* Abelard-Schuman Ltd., 1953.

Sirjamaki, John. *The American Family in the Twentieth Century.* Harvard University Press, 1953.

PSYCHOLOGY AND PSYCHIATRY

Introduction

Psychology is the science which studies the mental life of human beings and animals. More technically, psychology is the science that deals with the study of *behavior,* that is, with the facts and events arising from the interaction of a living creature and its environment by means of sense organs, nervous systems (including the brain), and such effector organs as glands and muscles.

Older writers defined psychology simply as the study of the mind or of the psychical processes, but the more modern definition given above includes all the mental phenomena embraced in the older definition, as well as all the processes seen in the adaptive and nonadaptive behavioral responses of the individual throughout his entire life span.

Psychiatry is the medical specialty dealing with the diagnosis, treatment, and care of those who are mentally ill or defective, as well as with the prevention of mental illness. Sometimes psychiatry is considered to include the study of the dynamic basis of personality adjustments of all human beings, both normal and abnormal.

■**PSYCHOTHERAPY.**—This is a method of treatment of mental and psychosomatic disorders by the use of various nonchemical and nonphysical psychological techniques. The term is usually reserved for types of treatment given by professional workers, such as psychiatrists, psychologists, or psychiatric social workers.

■**PSYCHOANALYSIS.**—This is the study and treatment of processes in the abnormal and the normal mental life of human beings as developed by Sigmund Freud (1856–1939) and his associates. This term is at times used somewhat loosely to include all dynamic psychiatric points of view. In this sense it includes *analytical psychology* as developed by Carl G. Jung (1875–1961), *individual psychology* as developed by Alfred Adler (1870–1937), and many other modern approaches to psychiatry.

■**PARAPSYCHOLOGY.**—This name covers the study of reported psychical phenomena that appear to fall beyond the known limits of the sciences of physics, chemistry, biology, or experimental psychology. Its subject matter is not easy to define, but it includes the consideration of alleged supranormal and extrasensory mental processes. It studies telepathy and the activities of self-styled "mediums." *Psychic research* is the investigation of the phenomena that make up the field of parapsychology.

PSYCHOLOGY

History.—The word "mind" was once used to designate all conscious human processes, including mental faculties, powers, aptitudes, and dispositions, whether acquired or innate. Philosophers considered mind and body two ultimately distinct aspects of life. They gave much time to speculation about the body-mind problem and how consciousness is related to the physical matter of the brain and body.

Today "mind" is regarded by scientific psychologists as a collective noun used to describe all the aspects of what is commonly called *mental life.* These mental phenomena include memory, perception, and thought as well as all the behavior, unlearned or learned, related to the individual's adaptation to his environment.

Mental life, the subject matter of psychology, has long interested and

LOOK MAGAZINE

THE MIND, when withdrawn from the external world, has the power to create its own realm—which may become a prison.

puzzled human beings. Some primitive men thought of breath as having a special significance in connection with mental processes, a concept described by anthropologists as belief in a thin, unsubstantial vapor, film, or shadow which was regarded as basic to the actions and thought of the individual. Breath, in this special sense, was sometimes considered the animating principle of the body. In dreams it might journey from the body and return, but at death it left the body forever. This concept is known as *primitive animism.* Today, this animistic or vitalistic view is not generally accepted, principally because scientists have never been able to determine how a nonmeasurable or not directly observable mental force of any kind can act upon any part of the living body, such as the cells of the brain, and thereby initiate observable changes in, or modify, behavior. This is further dealt with under parapsychology.

The term "consciousness" is not used today in the writings of many scientific psychologists because the word has proved difficult to define. Those who still wish to use this term tend to think of it as a name for the sum of those private processes, such as sensations, feelings, thoughts, and impulses to action, that an individual himself knows and is able to report upon, but that are never directly observable to others.

Experimental Psychology.—Scientific experimental psychology began in the laboratory studies of a number of physicians and physiologists who explored the structure and function of the human nervous system. Sir Charles Bell (1774–1842) was the first to demonstrate the existence of two anatomically distinct types of nerves: those which transmit sensory impulses from the outside world to the brain and those which send motor impulses out from the brain to the muscles. His studies of retinal sensitivity led to the realization that the sense organs, or receptors, of the body are each specialized to be stimulated by one sort of energy rather than by others. This means that human beings are aware of, and respond to, the activities set up in their own nerves (the optic nerve, the auditory nerve, and so on) and not to the physical or chemical characteristics of the stimuli. For example, an individual who has congenital red-green blindness cannot discriminate these colors, even though the stimuli for red and for green are acting on his eyes.

■**WUNDT.**—Although many physiologists, physicists, doctors of medicine, and philosophers made early contributions to the science of psychology, the founder of experimental or scientific psychology is considered to be Wilhelm Wundt (1832–1920), who founded the first formal psychological laboratory in 1878 at the University of Leipzig in Germany.

■**JAMES.**—The great American psychologist William James (1842–1910) also started his scientific work as a physiologist, and as early as 1875, he organized at Harvard an informal laboratory to demonstrate phenomena in the field of psychology to his students. This was not, however, a formal scientific research laboratory of the sort that Wundt founded, one dedicated to the discovery of new facts. Following these early experimental and demonstrational laboratories, many similar centers were established in other universities. Today, scientific psychology is largely made up of the facts and theories developed in such laboratories.

Schools of Psychology.—The organized teachings of philosophers on the nature of the physical and mental worlds and of man's place in nature have long been called "systems" or "schools" of philosophy. Toward the end of the nineteenth century there was a tendency also to use the term "school" to describe different systems of organizing the observed facts and the general theories of psychology. Today, many scientific students of psychology tend to be much less concerned with schools than was formerly the case. Nevertheless, it is worthwhile to mention briefly some of these systems because they are so frequently referred to.

■STRUCTURAL SCHOOL. — Psychologists who emphasize the study of conscious experience are called *introspective psychologists*. Those who attempt to analyze the content of immediately given conscious experience (or experience in the phenomenal field) into mental elements are said to belong to the *structural school*. Structure in this sense does not refer to the make-up of the cells of the brain or of the rest of the body, but rather to the assumed structure of conscious experience. The units resulting from the analysis are called by such names as sensations, images, and feelings. The leading American exponent of the structural school was Edward B. Titchener (1867–1927), an English psychologist who studied with Wundt.

NEW YORK PUBLIC LIBRARY

WILLIAM JAMES, an American psychologist.

■ACT SCHOOL.—Certain psychologists soon came to feel that man's conscious life is not made up exclusively of mental building blocks, as described by the structuralists. They became concerned with the active processes of motivation and "set," or a readiness to perceive or to respond in a certain way, that steer and direct human experience and thought. These psychologists, represented by O. Külpe in Germany and R. M. Ogden in America, were classed as members of the *act school* of psychology.

■FUNCTIONAL SCHOOL.— Some American psychologists rebelled against the idea that psychology was exclusively concerned with an analysis of conscious experiences. They were very much influenced in this view by the study of Darwinian evolutionary biology. They investigated the role of intelligence, emotion, learning, and so-called instinct in the adaptive and maladaptive behavior of animals and man. This point of view came to be called the *American functional school*. William James, whose great and stylistically elegant two-volume *Principles of Psychology* was published in 1890, did much to make this approach dominant in the United States, although as a "school" it may be better to associate it with the

names of John Dewey (1859–1952) and J. R. Angell (1869–1949).

■BEHAVIORIST SCHOOL.—Gradually laboratory studies of human reactions and the intensive scientific investigation of animal behavior led to the study of bodily responses for their own sake. Ultimately some students came to think of this objective study of behavior as the main, or indeed the only proper, subject matter of psychology. Holders of an extreme form of this belief, the *behaviorists*, came to hold that conscious phenomena cannot really be studied scientifically and are thus irrelevant in a scientific study of psychology. Some behaviorists are greatly interested in the neural and other bodily structures that make responses possible, while others are mainly concerned with a quantitative correlation between measured stimuli and measured responses, without reference either to intervening conscious processes or the nervous system.

■GESTALT SCHOOL.—The German word for form, shape, or pattern is *Gestalt,* and this has been used to name a school of psychology. Gestalt psychology emphasizes the fact that behavior and experience must be studied as organized wholes and cannot be analyzed into independent units. All responses, they insist, are not a sum of independent reflexes and all perceptions are not a mere adding together of independent sensations. The Gestalt psychologists see relationships, patterns, and grouping as primary elements of perception. Wolfgang Köhler is one of the greatest exponents of this view. Another position that has developed, at least in part, out of Gestalt psychology is called *psychological field theory*. This is a way of looking at some parts of psychology on the basis of a description of a so-called *life space*, which includes the individual and the conceptualized forces of the environment in which he exists. This school, which owes much to K. Lewin, uses terms such as goals, barriers, and boundaries and is interested in the mathematical concepts of topology as applied to psychology.

General Scientific Psychology.—The name *general psychology* is often given to the consideration of all the psychological processes of normal adult humans without special reference to any limited school. Once, it is true, the study of general psychology was almost wholly concerned with an analysis of human conscious experience; but now this conscious

experience is discussed under such headings as sensation, perception, feeling, emotion, and thought. *Perception,* for example, is recognized as primarily controlled by the present excitation of an individual's sense organs. Yet a full study of every perception shows that all such processes are also influenced by the inborn makeup of the organism and by previous behavior and learning. In any perceptual experience, such as seeing, hearing or touching, it is difficult to distinguish between the raw sensory data and the recognition of these data as an object or a person. Part of the experience is immediately and clearly given; but a large part is derived from previous experience and learning. A consideration of geometrical visual illusions may make this clear. Because of the way their eyes and brains work, all normal people "see what is not there" if measurement is taken as a test of reality in such illusions. Also, the influence of other people, past and present, is recognized as playing a special part in much perception. It has even been shown that children of poor families tend to judge coins as larger than do rich children similarly tested.

■SENSATION.—In the older "structural" experimental psychology the basic unit of perceptual experience was considered to be the sensation. A *sensation* was defined as applying to an elementary and generally not further analyzable item or fixed unit of experience that could be shown to be related to present receptor activity. Specific colors, sounds, odors, tastes, temperature experiences, pains, and pressures are examples of types of sensations. Each sensory experience, such as that of a particular color, can be further described in terms of its conscious dimensions or attributes. Every seen color has a particular hue (red or green, for instance), a particular brightness (relation of the color to a point on the black-white continuum), and a particular saturation (purity of color, freedom from admixture with white). Other visual attributes have been isolated, and auditory and other types of sensory experience described.

■AFFECTION.—The word *affection* is used by some psychologists to distinguish emotions and their attendant feelings from the cognitive, perceptual or sensory experiences just considered. Feeling tones are typically pleasant or unpleasant. Emotional experiences are thought of as involving conscious experiences and ways of acting commonly called fear, an-

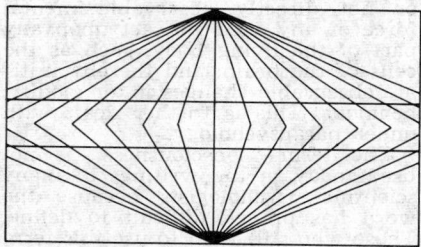

VISUAL ILLUSIONS show how our sensory organs may perceive things differently from the way they actually are. The horizontal lines are parallel though they do not appear so.

ger, joy, disgust, pity, and so forth. It is known that special parts of the brain, such as the hypothalamus, are active in emotions and that the complex autonomic nervous system is involved in bringing about the bodily activities characteristic of emotional experiences.

■CONATION.—In the older psychology, *conation* was used to describe those aspects of mental life which are related to action and striving. In some writings on psychology the terms cognition, affection, and conation are spoken of as basic mental processes.

General psychology traditionally considers all the topics just mentioned and also gives special emphasis to a study of behavior changes resulting from growth, that is, maturation, or from learning. When one attempts to analyze learning, it becomes clear that only an active or motivated organism learns. Today, as a result of this understanding, much of general psychology is devoted to a consideration of the factors that explain the basis of human responses and patterns of action and the way in which organisms are modified by the processes of habit formation.

■MOTIVATION.—The term *motivation* is frequently used to describe a continuing physiological condition or drive of an organism which impels it to activity, persisting until the organism reacts in such a way as temporarily or permanently to satiate or eliminate the drive. Physiological drives of this sort provide the most basic motivation. In an organism that has had an opportunity to acquire habits, drive-satiation behavior may be seen as having an end in view, or as *goal-seeking*. Sometimes an internal drive must reach a certain level before other stimuli, often in the external world, are able to start or direct behavior. For example, an organism must often be in a certain definite state of hunger before the presence of food in its environment will cause it to eat.

Among the basic drives are those connected with the need for food, water, sexual partners, oxygen, the elimination of waste materials, and the securing of an external temperature that is neither too warm nor too cold. In the adult human, however, motivation is by no means limited to such physiological drives. All those aspects of human mental life that are related to acquired desires, preferences, and purposes act as motives. Many of these motives take their form from the normal social experience of the group to which the individual belongs.

Learning.—Motives are basic in producing the behavior which can be modified by the processes called *learning*, a word used in psychology as a name for any change in an individual's experience or behavior that can be shown to be brought about by previous responses or activities that the individual organism has carried out, and that would not have developed by maturation alone. The physiological process of learning in the higher animals is generally considered to consist of some alteration

in the brain structure. This change takes place in the cortex, or outer part of the cerebral hemispheres. When a motivated organism reacts, the brain is involved, and under certain conditions such brain activity produces more or less permanent changes in the brain's living cells. What these changes are is not at present well understood, but their effect is to modify the subsequent reaction of the organism. When the stimuli are repeated later the organism that has "learned" reacts as it would not have reacted if the brain changes had not taken place.

During the twentieth century much experimental study of learning has involved investigation of what are called *conditioned reflexes,* or, to use

HARVARD UNIVERSITY

CONDITIONED RESPONSES have enabled these pigeons to play a game. If the ball falls into the slot, the defending pigeon receives a mild shock; the other pigeon receives food.

the more common term, *conditioned responses*. This approach to the study of learning developed out of the investigations of a Russian physiologist, Ivan P. Pavlov (1849–1936), in the physiology of digestion. He discovered that a dog that salivated when given food could later be made to salivate when another stimulus, such as a bell, was sounded. This took place, however, only when the bell had been sounded at the same time or just before the food was given to the dog. When the bell-food sequence was repeated a number of times, the bell alone could elicit the salivary response, even when food was not present. Food, in this example, which causes salivation without previous laboratory experience, is called the *unconditioned stimulus*. The bell that elicits the response which is acquired after the two stimuli have been presented to the organism together is called a *conditioned stimulus*. The response elicited by this stimulus is termed the *conditioned response*.

A second type of conditioning, called *instrumental* or *operant conditioning*, describes a modification of behavior that is different in certain respects from the classical conditioning described above. If a situation is established in which a hungry animal may respond in any way that is natural to it, and if one of these responses leads to the reward of securing food, it often turns out that the specific response which leads to the securing of food is repeated and thus learned. The behavior that has been instrumental in obtaining the

reward is thus especially important to the organism. The second type of conditioning is also applied to an action that, when carried out, allows the organism to escape from painful or noxious stimuli. Operant conditioning of all types has been studied in great detail by B. F. Skinner and his students and has been made the basis of a general theory that is seen to have much relevance to an understanding of normal and even abnormal human and animal behavior.

When some previously conditioned responses can no longer be elicited, they are said to be *extinguished*. The establishment and the extinction of responses can be determined by the way *reinforcers*, or rewards, are given. This pattern of reward-giving, both in time and frequency, is a *schedule of reinforcement*. For example, in the case of certain animal experiments, the presentation or withholding of a pellet of food after an animal has pressed a lever which sometimes releases the food will determine the rate of learning and, to a degree, the rate of extinction. One rate will follow if each lever press produces food; another, if every other press produces food; and still another if the reinforcement is irregular.

The idea of conditioning is a modern, objective behavioristic extension of what the older writers called the *association of ideas*. This phrase was used to describe a functional relationship that made possible the recall of words or ideas. In a typical case of association, a sight, sound, odor, or word may recall a specific memory. Laws of association were developed to explain differences in recall. For example, it was noted that items were associated if they were similar or contrasting, or if they were presented at the same time or in immediate succession. In general, associationistic psychologists concluded, as do students of conditioned responses, that if two presentations occur simultaneously or in close succession, recall is most apt to take place. If such presentations are related to intense stimulation, recall is also especially apt to occur.

■MEMORY.—The word *memory* is employed not only in cases of association, but also to describe some types of conditioning. Classically, memory has been recognized as involving four logically separate stages: *impression* or *presentation,* sometimes called *memorization; retention,* probably involving the maintenance of an established brain trace; *recall* or *retrieval,* hypothetically the reactivation of the brain trace; and *recognition,* that is, placing and dating, or a knowledge that "this has been experienced before."

Much experimental study of learning and memory has been conducted by requiring subjects to memorize lists of words or of "nonsense" syllables such as zug and yarp. The factors that influence the subjects' ability to recall these associations can thus be measured or "quantified" and curves of recall can be drawn to show the effect of time and other factors on forgetting. For example, it is found that the normal effects of learning may be impaired if the first presentation is followed closely by another activity, especially if it is very similar to the first. This has been called *retroactive inhibition,* and is important in much active forgetting. Forgetting is known to be a complex process which depends on many factors besides the mere passage of time. In the older psychology, memories were thought to be composed of images, that is, impressions which remain after an external stimulus has been removed. Images were seen as fundamental also in thought, including reasoning and constructive imagination, and in dreams. When images are confused with perceptions the individual is said to have hallucinations. The famous pink elephants of persistent alcoholic intoxication are examples of this process.

The term *trial-and-error learning* describes a situation in which a human being or an animal that has not established a way of satisfying a drive responds with a series of varied actions until one response proves rewarding. This is *accidental success.* As the situation is repeated, the adaptive act appears more and more quickly until, when it is learned, it is the only response that appears. Certain Gestalt psychologists have emphasized the fact that some learning is not based on many repetitions of blind trial and error, but may involve only one immediate response that is correct the first time. This is said to result from insight into what must be done in order to meet the situation adaptively. *Insight* is thus learning guided by all relevant existing relations. Sometimes it seems as though the solution to the problem were already prepared, and the adding of one item leads to "closure." The study of thought and the psychological investigation of language, both spoken aloud and said to oneself (sometimes called *subvocal*), are closely related to the study of learning. The psychology of language is a specialized and important topic. Reasoning and thought are also fields now much studied by psychologists. Reasoning has been seen sometimes to be like trial-and-error learning and sometimes like insight learning. In reasoning, symbolic representations such as images, rather than overt acts, are manipulated.

SYMMETRICAL INKBLOT is similar to the type used in the Rorschach personality test.

Intelligence.—The term "intelligence" has been used in many different senses in technical psychology. As applied to man, *intelligence* is often used to describe differences in ability to solve problems or to deal with new life situations. The rate at which the individual develops the capacity to learn the solutions to new problems and his ability to deal effectively with linguistic, numerical, or other abstractions when solving problems are both spoken of as depending on intelligence or as constituting intelligence.

■**INTELLIGENCE TESTS.**—Sets of problems have been devised that can be given to persons of different ages to determine the individual's capacity to solve them. When such tests are given to large numbers of individuals and the results are carefully tabulated, it is possible to establish norms against which an individual can be tested or judged, or, in a sense, measured. Errors resulting from different linguistic and social backgrounds and prior opportunities for learning must be guarded against in evaluating such test scores. It is known that an individual's scores on intelligence tests or specialized verbal or mathematical aptitude tests are a result of both his inborn capacity and his experiences, including his formal education. The most famous of all intelligence tests is the Binet or Binet-Simon scale, so named because of the psychologists who developed it and first used it to test French school children in 1905. In all its forms this test battery consists of a series of problems that are so arranged that they can be solved by average children of different chronological ages. By the use of this scale a mental age may be computed for the child being tested as compared with those on whom the test was standardized. The *I.Q.,* or *intelligence quotient,* is calculated by dividing the mental age secured on the test by the chronological age of the sub-

ject and multiplying by 100. If the chronological age and the mental age are the same, the I.Q. is 100. If the child's mental age is 12 and his chronological age is 10, he has an I.Q. of 120. If his mental age is 8 and his chronological age is 10, he has an I.Q. of 80.

Personality.—"Personality" is a term used in modern psychology in many different ways. Human personalities are, it is agreed, always a result of inborn characteristics and of the learning that has molded the individual during his formative years. The word "personality" derives its meaning from the Latin *persona,* meaning 'theatrical mask.' Thus, the term is often used to describe what may be spoken of as the "mask" that an individual wears for others and, indeed, for himself. Each personality, when studied, is seen to be an organization and, to a degree, a unification, of motives, dynamic tendencies, perceptual sensitivities, intellectual capacities, and aesthetic and other characteristics. Many people who have investigated the topic of personality have found that it is illuminating to study and increase the specific types of differences in characteristics that exist among individuals. Students of abnormal psychology are anxious to define the limits of what may be called socially normal personalities.

■**PERSONALITY TESTS.**—Psychiatrists and clinical psychologists are interested in what are called *projective tests,* in which personality characteristics are revealed in relatively free, constructive, and imaginative situations. The Rorschach inkblot test is a well-known projective test. In this test, subjects are shown ten inkblots, one at a time; their replies to such questions as "What could that be?" are recorded. These replies are then scored in a standard and elaborate way, and the results provide clues to some of the basic personality mechanisms of the individual.

Physiological Psychology.—The name *physiological psychology* is given to the study of the correlation between anatomical and physiological processes of the body and the behavior and reported experience of individuals. Some authors prefer the term *psychophysiology* for this study. Physiological psychologists have learned much about mental life and have described in detail how the sense organs work. Much of this study, as carried on by psychologists today, involves the use of very complex electronic devices, both to control and measure stimulation and to record the electrical reactions of active nerve and other cells. In their studies of emotion they have described the activities of the smooth muscles (typical of the viscera) and the glands in relation to responses seen in different psychological states. The effect of inherited physique has also been examined by some physiological psychologists. Above all, such students have been interested in the brain in relation to conscious experience and behavior, including language and defects of speech such as aphasia, or specific difficulties in reading, such as alexia. Certain large areas of the cortex of the brain are equipotential (one part is as important as another part) in facilitating certain types of learning and behavior. However, some processes, such as those dependent on the brain mechanisms fundamental to vision, are precisely localized. The electrical waves accompanying brain activity can be detected by placing electrodes on the scalp of subjects and recording the patterns on an *electroencephalograph*. These tracings of brain waves, or *electroencephalograms*, have been found to have many clinical uses, such as in the identification of types of epilepsy.

The study of physiological psychology is closely related to *psychophysics*, which is the study of the relation between the measurable characteristics of the physical energies of stimuli and the quantitative attributes of sensory or other experiences or of behavior. *Weber's law* or, in its development, the *Weber-Fechner law* holds that in a general way and in certain ranges of the strength of stimulation, the intensity of a sensory experience or the magnitude of a response has a definite mathematical relation to the intensity of the stimulus.

Comparative and Animal Psychology.—

The term *comparative psychology* is given to the branch of psychology which studies and compares the behavior and mental life of different animal species, including man. This is actually *phylogenetic psychology*. *Comparative psychology* is also used, but less frequently, in the comparison of typical patterns of mental life of different human races or of different development stages in the growth of the individual. The latter, however, is better called *child psychology, developmental psychology,* or *ontogenetic psychology*. The term *genetic psychology* is used by some writers as a synonym for both phylogenetic and ontogenetic psychology.

As we have seen, behavior is the main field of study of many present-day scientific psychologists. Behavior also is a subject studied by some modern zoologists who are interested in *taxonomy*—the classification of animal species—and in the natural history of living organisms. Students of behavior who are primarily trained in zoology tend to be especially interested in what has sometimes been called the *ecology of behavior;* they consider the all-inclusive environment that makes an animal's life what it is as a basis for understanding the natural responses of organisms. The term *ethology* is generally used for zoologically oriented study of the complete behavior of animals, especially in their natural habitats. Modern ethologists tend to avoid terms referring to consciousness in their scientific reports, but they do speak of instincts and of the characteristic responses of different types of organisms. Responses of this type are referred to frequently as categories of *species-specific* behavior.

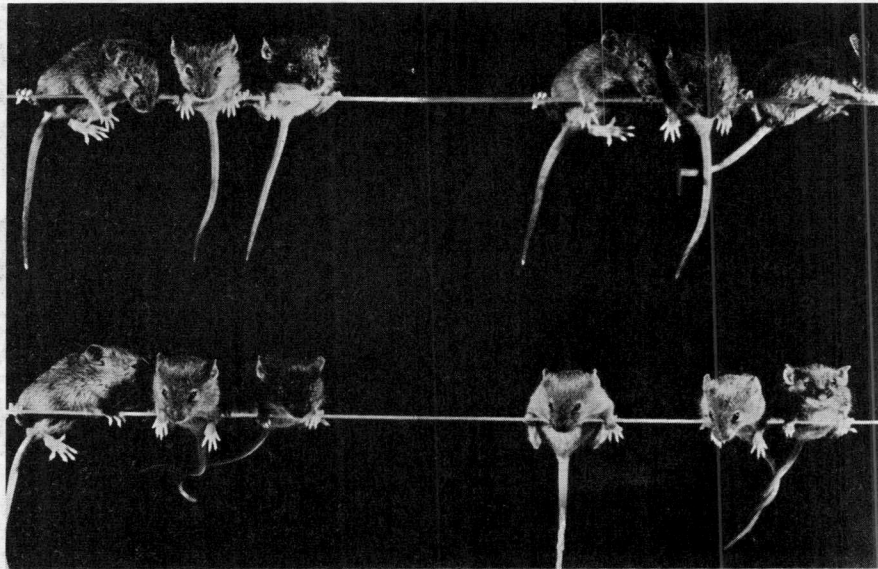

WORLD HEALTH ORGANIZATION

SOCIAL BEHAVIOR OF ANIMALS can be studied under a variety of controlled laboratory conditions. These two groups of mice are living in various radioactive environments.

Ethologists refer to the quick learning or lasting change of behavior under specific conditions as *imprinting*.

■ **INSTINCT.**—The word "instinct" has had a checkered career in scientific psychological work since the 1860's. At first, after Darwin's concepts of evolution had become important in psychology, it was assumed that all animals, including man and the other mammals, displayed many specific and identifiable tendencies or dispositions to action which were inherited. Some of these were called *instincts*. The older psychologists often gave long lists of instincts, such as pugnacity and maternal behavior. But the difficulty of proving that such classes of response, particularly in human beings, are inborn, rather than learned, led to a strong opposition to the use of the term "instinct" in psychology. Today, it is once again recognized that a concept such as "instinct" may be useful in describing many forms of behavior in insects and vertebrates, and in man. In Freudian psychiatry "instinct" is used to characterize the basic tendencies of the individual, the *life* (or *love* or *sex*) *instinct* and the *death instinct*.

Other Fields of Psychology

Differential psychology is the name given to the branch of psychology in which tests to measure or define intelligence and personality are used, as well as tests that measure differences in sensory thresholds, motor skills, musical ability, and many other capacities. In general, such tests give the person being tested a rating so that he can be compared to others being tested. Personality tests, vocational aptitude tests, and various measures used by psychologists interested in selecting individuals to play a part in complex man-machine systems are all part of this branch.

Human engineering is the field concerned with man-machine organizations. The work of human engineers is of especial importance to industries in which automation is extensively used, such as aviation, space programs, and weapons systems and other military devices.

Child psychology is the branch of psychology which considers the psychological processes of the developing human being from the first responses of prenatal life until he has reached adult life. Psychologists also study the behavior characteristics of senescence which result, in part, from the brain and body changes due to tissue deterioration in old age.

Social psychology is the branch of psychology which considers the reactions of the individual that depend on his inborn character and the learning that has taken place during his growth in a world made up of other people. Social psychology emphasizes the importance of the interstimulation and response between the individual and the small, as well as the large, groups of people of which he is a part. It studies the reactions found in regimented authoritarian situations as contrasted with those that take place in congenial and permissive environments. Special social situations, such as the essentially pathological reactions brought out in individuals when they become part of a mob, have been studied.

Abnormal psychology is the branch of psychology given to a scientific consideration of the mental life and the reactions of atypical or abnormal individuals. To some degree, practically every person may be considered as not fully normal in all respects, but the term "abnormal" is most often used to describe persons with personality characteristics which lead them into obvious social maladjustments and, in extreme cases, require their confinement in mental hospitals.

Educational psychology occupies itself with the study of the human individual in learning situations, especially in formal school life. It is concerned with the nature of the academic learning of such skills as those required in reading and arithmetic and with the use of various differential tests, which assist in assessing the educational capacity of each pupil. In education, scholastic aptitude is tested for by examinations very similar to those for measuring intelligence. Modern educational psychologists are interested in the social climate of the classroom and in the proper and constructive use of rewards, punishments, and discipline in connection with education. They are also concerned with the overall mental hygiene of pupils. Educational psychologists have given much attention to visual aids to education, such as television, and to programmed learning made possible in teaching machines.

Clinical psychology is directly concerned with the study and treatment of individuals who have psychological problems of various kinds. The term is often used today to describe those psychological processes which are important in diagnosing and correcting the behavior maladjustments which interfere with the individual's educational or social life. An important modern technique of clinical psychology is *nondirective counseling,* as developed by C. R. Rogers and his students. By the use of this technique individuals are helped to "talk out" and solve their own, often deepseated problems, enabling them to develop better-adjusted personalities and thus to live more effective lives.

Vocational psychology includes all those techniques by means of which the psychologist assists in selection, classification, training, and effective use of the aptitudes and skills of individuals in their vocations. Certain specific vocational tests, such as those for clerical aptitude, musical aptitude, and for the performance of various military tasks, such as those of aircraft pilots, have been used with marked success.

Parapsychology, also called *psychical research,* is the study of seemingly supranormal phenomena. It is not, as yet, an accepted part of a recognized field of science. It includes such phenomena as the *transmittance* of impressions from one person to another by channels outside the known means of sense perception; *psychometry,* the supposed capacity to receive supranormal knowledge of an object's history or that of the present owner while holding it; *precognition,* the ability to forecast specific occurrences without scientific explanations of such predictions; and *mediumship,* the reported ability of persons to mediate communications between the living and the deceased; and phenomena such as movement of objects without visible contacts.

PSYCHIATRY

Introduction.—*Psychiatry* is the branch of medicine dealing with the prevention, treatment, and cure of mental diseases and emotional disorders. Both psychiatry and the specific

NEW YORK PUBLIC LIBRARY

NINETEENTH-CENTURY MENTAL HOSPITALS were often no better than penal institutions. In this hospital in Paris the patients were free to roam the grounds under supervision.

method of treatment developed by Freud, psychoanalysis, are deeply involved in the study of the nature and development of the mental and emotional life. Although studies in these fields are drawn from the examination of disturbed and mentally ill individuals, the findings have contributed greatly to man's understanding of himself and of his often mystifying behavior.

Psychiatry emerged as a branch of *neurology,* the study of the anatomy and physiology of the nervous system, including the brain. Most of the early pioneers were themselves neurologists. Medically, the *neurologist* is a physician who treats organic diseases of the nervous system. *Neurosurgeons* specialize in operations on the nervous system and brain, and often treat such illnesses as the convulsive disorders of the epilepsies which have various psychological symptoms. Since some mental illness is related to pathology of the brain, neurologists are sometimes thought of as physicians who specialize in the treatment of those aspects of mental illness that are directly related to brain disease.

■**CLASSIFICATION.**—*Mental illness* can roughly be classified according to two general categories: the organic and the functional. Basically, the *organic* illnesses are those which derive from a physical disorder, deficiency, or malfunctioning of the nervous system, especially the brain. This may be caused by a failure to develop normally (*amentia*), or by some later damage to or deterioration of the brain through disease, accident, or the process of aging (*senescence*). This category involves mental deficiencies and many of the severe psychoses. The *functional* diseases are those in which there is no apparent physical change in the brain; these include some psychoses and most neuroses

and so-called character disorders.

■**MENTAL DEFICIENCY.**—The term *mental deficiency* is used to describe all levels of subnormal intellectual development, the range of which is measured in terms of intelligence quotient (*I.Q.*). The term *idiot* is applied to an individual with an I.Q. generally below 25. Typically, idiots are not able to learn effective speech and cannot guard themselves from the common physical or social dangers. An *imbecile* is an individual with an I.Q. of roughly between 25 and 49. Imbeciles can be taught simple habits, and may learn to protect themselves against the dangers of the environment; however, they cannot become self-supporting members of society. The *moron* is an individual whose I.Q. is approximately between 50 and 69. Under favorable and protected conditions, morons can be taught to earn a living; but in general they cannot compete on equal terms with normal individuals or demonstrate necessary prudence in managing their lives. *Borderline deficiency* describes the mental state of individuals with I.Q.'s of approximately 70 to 80. Such individuals, in general, may be considered as legally competent, but they are slightly subnormal in their ability to deal with intellectual problems and to adjust themselves in social situations. An individual whose test performance is *normal* has an I.Q. of between 90 and 110. Individuals with I.Q.'s between 80 and 90 are sometimes spoken of as having *low normal* intelligence. Individuals with I.Q.'s above 120 are generally classified as *superior,* and in much earlier writing those with an I.Q. of 140 or more were spoken of as having the ability of a *genius.* All these definitions are subject to the qualification that the determination of the I.Q. is far from fixed or absolute.

Mental deficiency is generally considered a result of an inborn failure of the brain to develop normally. It is believed to depend on atypical chromosomes or upon disease or other environmental factors affecting the individual in prenatal or early postnatal life. Some types of mental retardation are related to brain injuries sustained during the birth process, but such injuries characteristically show themselves in motor disabilities rather than in intellectual defects. The term *mongolism* is given to one type of inborn failure to develop in a normal way. Good evidence is available that this condition is a result of an extra chromosome. The condition of a child who characteristically has a dwarfed physique and limited intelligence seldom rising above the imbecile level is called *cretinism*. If this condition is diagnosed early and the hormone from the thyroid gland, thyroxin, is regularly administered, the child may be normal, mentally and physically.

Psychoses.—The most serious types of mental illness are *psychoses*, which severely hamper the individual's ability to function socially, to express himself, or to deal with reality. The *psychotic* often creates his own special environment in which his perceptions are grossly distorted, as in delusions and hallucinations. Such a condition is known legally as *insanity* and requires very specialized treatment, often in a mental hospital.

■**SCHIZOPHRENIA.** — One of the most severe and widespread of all psychoses is *schizophrenia;* it is also one of the most baffling to psychiatrists, for although it has been prevalent since early times, its causes and cure are still largely unknown. It was formerly called *dementia praecox,* the "precocious disease," because it

LOOK MAGAZINE

SCHIZOPHRENIA patient in a mental hospital has withdrawn completely from society.

often occurs in middle or late adolescence; the term now used is *schizophrenia,* meaning a "splitting of the mind" or personality. In the early stages it is characterized by a *dissociation of affect,* a general decline in intelligence, emotional blunting, and withdrawal from normal social relations. His feelings become separated from and often at variance with his thoughts; he may laugh when his normal feeling would be one of sadness, or cry at an instance of great humor. His powers of association deteriorate and his speech frequently takes on a characteristic disorderly, incoherent, and utterly irrelevant quality. This endless chain of discourse may not, as it so often does in less severe mental states, represent a hidden or private meaning; it is so totally disconnected and meaningless that it has been likened to a tangled, interminable string which, no matter how long it is pulled, has no end. In its extreme form schizophrenia is marked by severe mental deterioration and increasing withdrawal from reality ending in complete separation from the outside world. It is the most serious of all psychotic disorders and accounts for the great majority of patients in mental hospitals. Medical treatments include the early use of tranquilizers, with effectiveness increased by electroshock therapy.

Manic-depressive psychosis is another grave form of mental illness, in which the victim suffers alternate periods of great excitement and severe depression with or without intervals of normality. In the *manic phase,* the individual is in an excited state in which restlessness, feelings of elation, flights of ideas, and sometimes a destructive violence appear. In the *depressive phase,* the person shows deep feelings of sadness, anxiety, and hopelessness, often with the conviction that the body and even the person are disappearing; sometimes these symptoms are accompanied by attempted or successful suicide or by a deep stupor.

Paranoia is the term used to describe a severe mental illness which, in its pure form, is relatively rare and is characterized by delusions such as an unsubstantiated belief in the person's own grandeur ("I am Napoleon, you know") or in fancied persecution ("Wall Street is trying to get me"), but with little or no accompanying dementia. Sometimes individuals with strong paranoiac tendencies have personalities which in other ways are relatively unaffected. On the other hand, paranoia is often associated with schizophrenia, in which case the most prominent symptom is a well-developed delusional system with hallucinations and feelings of persecution. People who are relatively normal, but who tend to be unduly pompous, sensitive to criticism, and suspicious of those around them, are sometimes half-jokingly spoken of as paranoid.

Involutional melancholia or *involutional psychotic reaction* is a form of mental illness which occurs most frequently at the time of the climacteric. The symptoms of this illness are often complex, involving deep worry, feelings of guilt, delusional ideas, and a prolonged and intense general depression. Special psychotic conditions of short or very long duration sometimes follow childbirth or severe infectious diseases.

Senile psychosis refers to a chronic condition of the aged which is almost certainly related to an impairment of the structure and function of the brain. It often is characterized by marked loss of memory, stubbornness, irritability, and irresponsibility. The term *paresis* is given

THAMES & HUDSON, LONDON

DRAWINGS BY MENTAL PATIENTS both enable psychiatrists to learn more about the patient and allow the patient the opportunity to express all of his inner feelings in visual terms.

to a psychosis in which a progressive loss of intellectual capacity is accompanied by various types of motor paralysis and specific psychotic manifestations. General paresis or general paralysis of the insane (*dementia paralytica*) is typically a result of deterioration of the brain brought about by syphilitic infection.

Neuroses.—The *psychoneuroses,* or *neuroses,* are functional behavior disorders of a generally less severe order. While deeply troublesome to the individual and often to his close associates, they do not exhibit the flagrant disturbances of external behavior characteristic of the psychoses, and are usually not severe enough to require commitment to a mental hospital. The neurotic usually maintains contact with his environment; both his thinking and feeling are distorted, but he is not delusional.

Character Disorders.—A third category used by some psychiatrists is that of *character disorders* or *personality disorders,* closely associated with neuroses, in which the basic character structure of the individual is distorted or deformed. This condition is characterized by patterns of inadequate or antisocial behavior, emotional instability, excessive reaction to stress, extreme dependence or aggressiveness, and, above all, anxiety. In this category are many individuals called *sociopaths,* who act out their hostility on society; many criminals, delinquents, and sexual deviates are often included in this category.

The distinctions between these categories are not rigidly defined and are interpreted differently by various schools of psychiatry and psychoanalysis. The distinction between the psychoses and neuroses is not as clearly defined as it once was, especially in the view of some psychoanalytically oriented psychiatrists.

The term *psychosomatic disorders* is given to the physical illnesses which are considered to have full or partial base in the abnormal mental life of the individual. Many experts in psychosomatic medicine rely largely on the techniques of psychoanalysis in their clinical procedures. There is evidence that certain allergies at times have a psychosomatic origin, and some types of stomach ulcer have been treated successfully by psychosomatic techniques. The term *conversion hysteria* is sometimes used to name a condition, such as paralysis, which results from emotional conflict and which may be treated by psychosomatic procedures.

The terminology of mental illness is not as fixed as those of many other classes of disease, due to the very complex nature of the symptoms of mental illness. The present terminology owes much to the work of Emil Kraepelin, a student of Wundt, whose categorization of mental symptoms, as early as 1883, helped bring a scientific viewpoint to psychiatry.

The Growth of Psychiatry.—Modern psychiatry and psychoanalysis have had a complex and fascinating history. In primitive society, in classical times,

and almost down to the modern era, mental illness was believed to result from the activities of a malevolent spirit inhabiting the human body. This concept was an extension of the primitive animism prevalent in almost all early societies. The causes and cure of this "possession" were the province of magic, and the first professional psychiatrists were the witch doctors and charmers. Later, the clergy performed rites of exorcism which, if successful, drove out the evil spirits. The term *lunacy* is now only a legal term denoting a deviation from normal mental life that makes it necessary to appoint a guardian for the afflicted individual. The term comes from the Latin word

CLARK UNIVERSITY

PSYCHIATRY PIONEERS. (*Left to right, standing*) A. A. Brill, Ernest Jones, Sandor Ferenczi; (*seated*) Sigmund Freud, G. Stanley Hall, and Carl G. Jung. Photo was taken in 1909.

luna, 'the moon,' whose changing phases were believed to cause the waxing and waning of symptoms in some types of mental disease. Many of the witches who were burned in medieval times, or executed in colonial America, were undoubtedly mentally ill individuals. *Bedlam,* the earliest insane asylum in England, was really a prison for the insane. Londoners, even in the eighteenth century, considered it an amusement to visit Bedlam and to poke fun at and excite the unfortunate inmates. Humanitarianism, reinforced by religious feelings, led to a gradual transformation of the old inhuman custodial madhouses of Europe and America into much more humane asylums for the insane in the latter part of the eighteenth century and first half of the nineteenth century. The great French physician Philippe Pinel gave impetus to this movement when, in 1795, he removed the shackles from the inmates of Paris' notorious Bicêtre, the hospital for the insane, and initiated their treatment as patients instead of as prisoners. In America progress in reforms owes much to Dorothea Lynde Dix.

The modern scientific study of mental illness at first placed great emphasis on the investigation of the forms of brain pathology seen at the autopsies of the mentally ill. Much new and important information was

secured by such studies, for instance, the base of some forms of mental illness, such as those caused by syphilis and by the brain deterioration resulting from old age.

■ **NEUROSIS.**—The diagnosis and treatment of *neurotic disorders,* as distinguished from the psychoses, have been especially important in the history of psychiatry and psychology. Such illnesses also have not been shown to be related to easily demonstrable changes in the brain. They are sometimes described as functional, although it is recognized by scientists that all human functions have an organic base.

The condition known as *hysteria* early attracted medical attention. In extreme cases such neurotics may suddenly become blind or deaf, lose feeling in their limbs, become wholly or partially paralyzed, or even forget who they are. As early as 1766, Friedrich Mesmer began the use of *hypnosis* in the treatment of hysteria, and the term *mesmerism* has often been used as a synonym for hypnosis. It is a trancelike state induced by the hypnotist through suggestions. The subject becomes sleepy, relaxes his muscles, and performs various acts as directed by the hypnotist. Josef Breuer in 1880–1882 relieved a patient's hysterical symptoms by causing her to relive, under hypnosis, certain scenes associated with the onset of her illness. At the same time in Paris the French neurologist J. M. Charcot was using hypnosis in the study and cure of hysterical patients. One of Charcot's students, Theodore Janet, developed the teachings of his master into a new psychological view of the importance of the integration of the personality and insisted on psychological treatment for hysteria. He pointed out that neurotics tend to have divided personalities, whereas those of normal individuals are more fully integrated. Another student of Charcot was Morton Prince, a distinguished American neurologist and psychiatrist who did much to advance the understanding of dissociated and

NATIONAL ASSOCIATION FOR MENTAL HEALTH

NATIONAL ASSOCIATION FOR MENTAL HEALTH

RESEARCH. Scientists study the relationship of body chemicals (*above left*) and brain waves (*above right*) to behavior disorders. Machines can stimulate and record electrical activity in the nervous system. (*below*).

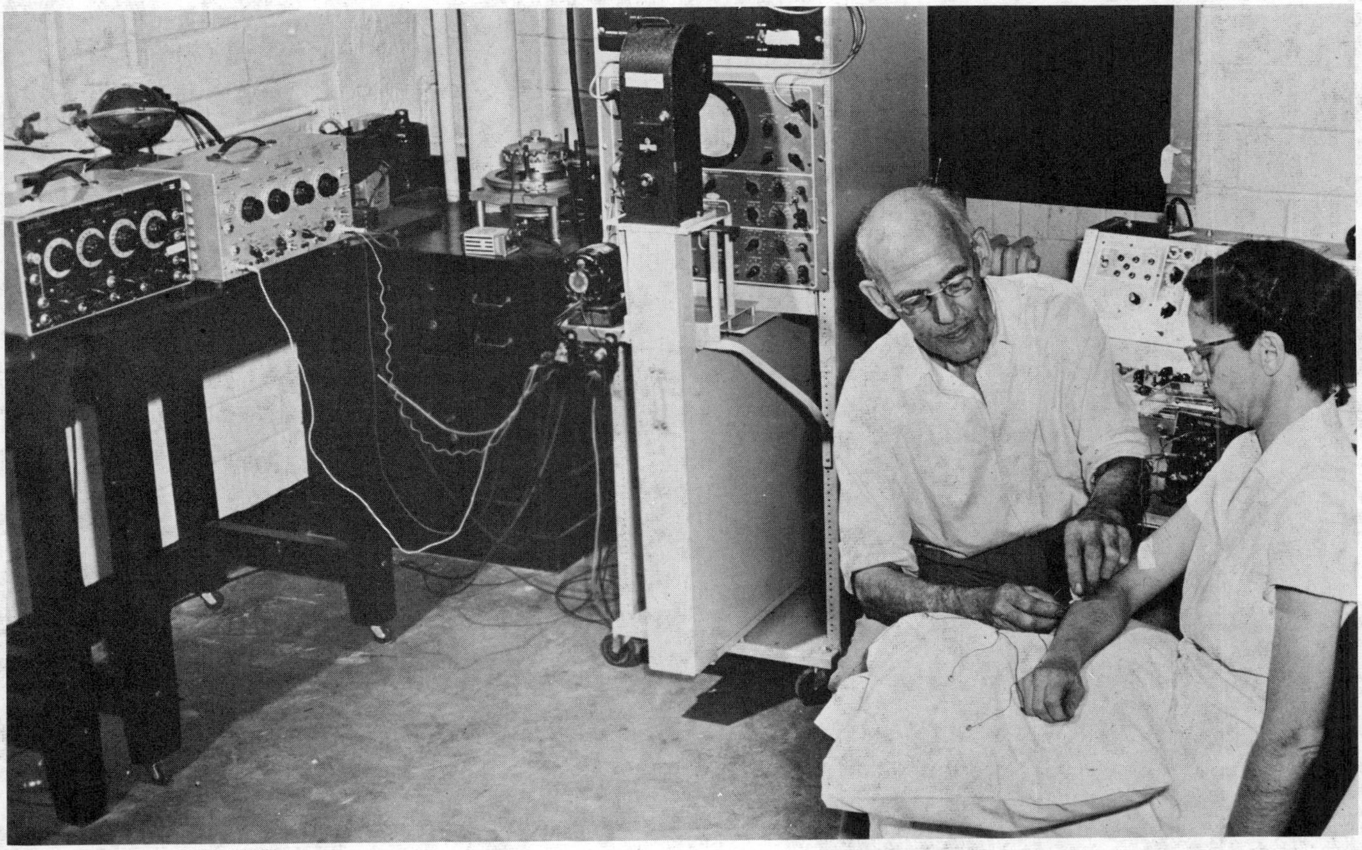

NATIONAL ASSOCIATION FOR MENTAL HEALTH

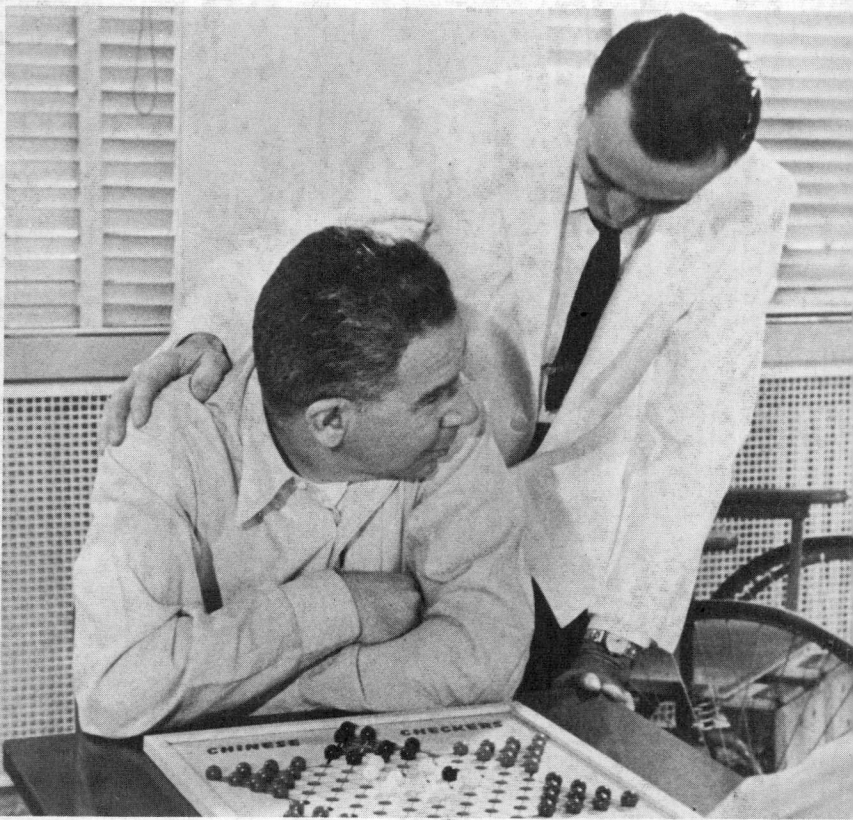

NATIONAL ASSOCIATION FOR MENTAL HEALTH

TREATMENT. Group discussions (*above*) help to increase understanding. Crafts (*below left*) and games (*below right*) afford relaxation.

NATIONAL ASSOCIATION FOR MENTAL HEALTH

NATIONAL ASSOCIATION FOR MENTAL HEALTH

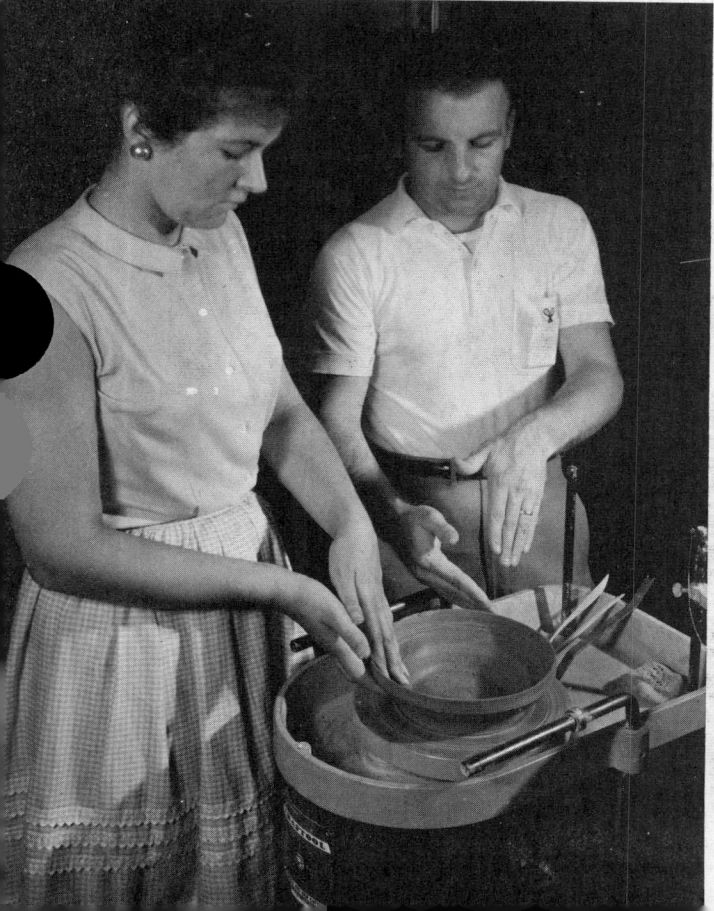

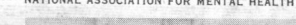

multiple personalities. *Dissociative reactions* such as fugue and amnesia are attempts to escape from tension by unconsciously blocking off part of one's conscious recognition. The term *multiple personality* describes a condition in which two or more personalities inhabit an individual, alternating with one another, appearing and disappearing, with no awareness on the individual's part.

■**FREUD.**—By far the most important student to work with Charcot was Sigmund Freud (1856–1939), considered by many to be one of the greatest figures of our time. Born in Czechoslovakia, he lived almost all his life in Vienna, where he made his studies and his far-reaching discoveries concerning the mental life. As a young student, he began the microscopic study of nerve cells in connection with the physiology and pathology of the brain. In his study of mental disease, he became especially puzzled by the neuroses, and in 1885 went to Paris to study with Charcot. For a time Freud adopted Charcot's technique of hypnosis, and on returning to Vienna he became associated with Breuer in the treatment of neurotic patients by this method. They observed that certain patients were relieved of their symptoms by the recalling of an otherwise forgotten event, as had first been noted, but not pursued, by Breuer. This *mental catharsis,* or "talking-out treatment," as one patient named it, was dropped by Breuer; but Freud continued in the work that led to the development of psychoanalysis.

■**PSYCHOANALYSIS.** — Noting that patients talked freely even when not under hypnosis, Freud soon abandoned that technique, which he found too controlling, and urged his patients to say whatever came into their minds without concern for relevance or propriety. By this method of *free association* and by the study of the dreams which they reported, he assisted his patients in recovering previously forgotten memories. At certain times, however, patients had great difficulty in speaking freely, and Freud concluded that this occurred in instances where an experience had been so painful and disturbing that it was *repressed* from awareness and memory by the conscious self. Such experiences are called *traumatic* because they appear to cause a mental wound or shock. Freud also noted that many of these repressed experiences were sexual in nature and occurred very early in childhood; and he therefore concluded that in most cases these sexual experiences were the primary cause of the neurosis. This discovery, on which the theory of the *sexual origin* of neuroses is based, is one of the most fundamental and controversial of all Freud's discoveries. It led to the theory of *infantile sexuality*—that the first sexual feelings appear not at puberty, but in early childhood. Freud believed that the child's sexual development passes through three stages: the *oral,* associated with sucking and mouth activity; the *anal,* in which pleasure is derived from the excretory functions; and finally the locali-

zation of sexuality in the *genital* region, leading to full adult sexuality and finally to reproduction. If the individual's development is arrested, or *fixated,* at one of the earlier stages, it may cause a serious *regression* of the adult to that stage, thus determining the form of his neurosis.

In general, Freudian psychoanalysis may be described as a form of *depth psychiatry* or *depth psychology* in which an attempt is made to bring "into consciousness" the impulses and mental processes that have been active in ordinarily hidden parts of the individual's mental life. These deep mechanisms are spoken of as existing in the patient's *unconscious,* whose existence was one of Freud's most important postulations. In treating patients, psychoanalysts believe that it is necessary to break through *resistances* in order to bring some of these hidden, previously unconscious, but important and powerful mental processes into awareness. The physician who conducts the psychoanalysis therefore helps the patient to break down various forms of resistance and later assists him in reorganizing his life by facing reality in a constructive way. The patient comes to avoid the emotional conflicts that had previously led to obstructive and damaging behavior.

What is known as *motivation* in psychological terms is a fundamental concept in psychoanalysis. Freud believed that the basis of all human motivation was to be found in the *libido,* the manifestation of the sexual instinct, or Eros, a term which he closely identified with the *life instinct.* Mental and emotional life results from the interplay of libidinal energy with other factors in the individual and in his environment.

One of the most important of these factors is the *pleasure-pain principle,* which describes the individual's striving toward pleasure and withdrawal from or avoidance of pain. During growth and development, the original pleasure principle is modified by its contact with the *reality principle,* the sum total of outside forces leading to new developments in the individual's mental life.

Toward the end of his life, Freud posited a second great principle which he believed acted in opposition to Eros, the "life-instinct"; he called it *thanatos,* the "death instinct" or wish for death. Thus the process of life represents a struggle of counterbalancing forces, the constructive, or life-creating, force, versus the destructive, or life-destroying, force.

In psychoanalysis the mental life of the individual is often considered to consist of three interacting parts: the id, the ego, and the superego. The *id* is the division of the psyche from which arise blind, impersonal, instinctual impulses related to the gratification of primitive needs. These impulses dominate the earliest life of the individual, but during later life are forced into various forms of submission and conformity. The *ego* is the aspect of the personality which is in contact with the external world through perception and *reality-regulated striving,* the struggle be-

tween the pleasure principle and the reality principle. As the individual develops, the ego is further differentiated and a superego develops. The ego comes to mediate between the superego and the id by building up what have been called *ego defenses.* The *superego* represents the inhibitions of instinct in man, the system within the individual's total mental life developed by incorporating parental standards as perceived by the ego. Thus, moral standards as perceived by the ego become part of the personality. Sometimes the superego is considered as having two parts, the *ego ideal* and the *conscience.*

It can be seen in a dynamic theory of depth psychiatry of the sort de-

MUSEUM OF MODERN ART

FREE ASSOCIATION in Chagall's *I and the Village* resembles psychoanalysis.

veloped by Freud that conflict and repression are inevitable as an individual develops. Various complexes are thus characteristic of the growth of the normal, as well as of the neurotic, individual. In the neurotic, however, this conflict leads to an arousal of *anxiety* against which the individual erects *defense mechanisms* which severely impede his personal and social life. Basically, the differences between normal and abnormal are in degree or quantity, and not in kind. Psychoanalysis is a clinical method used by properly trained physicians or other qualified professional persons in treating many neurotic conditions and personality disorders. In America virtually all qualified psychoanalysts are physicians. Today psychoanalysis is held by many psychiatrists to have an important place also in dealing with aspects of the graver psychoses.

■**JUNG.**—Carl G. Jung, a psychiatrist in Zurich, developed a school described as *analytic psychology.* In his early years, Jung was personally associated with Freud in the development of psychoanalysis but later broke with Freud over the question of the sexual basis of neurosis. Jung gives less emphasis to sex in his treatment of the basic dynamics of personality than does Freud and instead sees a general life urge as fundamental in motivation. The concepts of *introversion* and *extroversion* were developed by Jung to describe the characteristics of individuals whose attention and interest are centered internally upon themselves or externally upon the social and physical world. For Jung, depth psychology and the concept of the unconscious are just as important as they are for Freud, but Jung deals not only with an individual's unconscious but also with the concept of a *collective* or *racial unconscious*, which he considered to be inherited by all human beings. Primitive notions related to birth, death, and other magical phenomena are described by Jung as natural ways of thinking and as inherited in the unconscious. The system developed by Jung, like that of Freud, is very complicated and important for the modern student. Jung emphasizes the deep significance of religion in human life, and his system is of great importance to the *psychology of religion*. Those who have studied Jung's work in detail and who know of his clinical procedures are convinced that he brought great wisdom to the assessment and cure of individual personality disorders—disorders arising from the complex demands of today's world.

■**ADLER.**—Alfred Adler, a Viennese physician who was an early associate of Freud, developed another system which is characterized as *individual psychology*. Adler believed that the fundamental fact in a neurosis is a feeling of inferiority and that the most important striving is for power. He did not deny the importance of sex, but like Jung placed less emphasis on it than did Freud. Adler taught that individuals who have fancied inferiorities try to compensate or sometimes to overcompensate for these intensely felt self-deficiencies and thus develop an urge for power and domination over others. The commonly used term *inferiority complex* was coined by Adler to describe the style of life of weak individuals which allows them to avoid at least certain of the realistic demands of their environments. Adler held up as the human ideal a balanced emotional life in which each person thinks of those with whom he is associated not as superiors to whom he should be subservient nor as inferiors who should be dominated by him, but rather as equals. Adler's teaching, much less complexly formulated than that of Freud, has had a strong effect in reinterpreting some of the fundamental meaning of democracy for today's generations.

■**RANK.**—Another psychoanalyst whose work has had wide influence, Otto Rank stressed what is called the *birth trauma*, which is defined as the effect upon the individual's psyche of the strain of being born. Emphasis is given not so much to the actual pain of delivery as to the fact that the newborn child must begin his difficult adaptation to a hostile environment. The child is, as it were, removed by birth from the security of the mother's body and from the first object of its libido, the mother. Adult anxiety neuroses and other

neurotic symptoms, it is held, may at times be traced back to this initial trauma. Rank emphasized the importance of observation of the full environment, the complete present state of life of his patients. This point of view has been found helpful by many clinicians and social workers who must help individuals to adjust in difficult family and social situations.

■**SULLIVAN.**—The American psychiatrist Harry Stack Sullivan emphasized the interaction between the growing child and his parents, and between the adult and other individuals, or society. He believed that these *interpersonal relations* were of greater importance in the origin and treatment of mental illness than were developments and relationships within the individual psyche.

The preceding paragraphs have given in barest outline some suggestions of modern dynamic psychoanalytic approaches to an understanding of mental life. These psychoanalytic theories and others related to them have had an important influence upon modern thought. Sociology, legal history, and the criticism of literature and art have all been affected by different schools of psychoanalysis. Today, as the pioneer workers in these specialized schools, who were trained by Freud, Jung, or Adler, or the other pioneers in depth psychology, are being replaced by men and women fully trained in modern medicine and experimental and clinical psychology, there is an inevitable reorientation of the basic concepts of these dynamic approaches to an understanding of mental life and mental illness. For example, a new biological orientation in dynamic psychology seems to be developing. New psychopharmacologic knowledge, based on an understanding of the effects of tranquilizing drugs, must be considered in connection with basic psychological and analytical approaches to the personality. Drugs that produce hallucinations and motivational changes must be assessed in the same context. In general, drugs are seen as aids in enabling a patient to profit by psychotherapy and not as a substitute for professional care.

Mental Hygiene.—All these facts and theories are considered in the new approach to mental hygiene, that is, the study of techniques that may be used in the prevention of mental illness. Indeed, growing knowledge of the anatomy of the brain, the physiology of the nervous system, experimental psychology, general psychiatry, psychoanalysis, and psychopharmacology are all making contributions to the techniques that may be used in preventing, insofar as possible, incapacitating mental illness and in its cure. The dream of a world without mental hospitals may not be a realizable one, but there can be no doubt that modern scientific approaches to the understanding of mental life and of mental illness will not only reduce the number of patients who must be sent to such institutions, but will also cut down the duration of confinement. Part of the present-day improvement in the care

of mental illness is related to new drugs, a wide variety of techniques of psychotherapy, and the use of imagination to improve the lives of patients while they are in mental hospitals. Above all, many types of mental patients must be made to feel that they are important to those treating them, no matter by what "system." Useful treatment techniques are occupational therapy and the creative use of drama, dance, music, and painting. All these approaches help to bring about the readjustment of the patient to the real world and many emphasize the importance of an understanding of learning in the reeducation of patients.

A generation ago Adolf Meyer, of Johns Hopkins, who originated the term "mental hygiene," taught that understanding of mental illness depended upon greater scientific knowledge in psychology and in all aspects of medicine. This approach, called *psychobiology*, gives full attention to the findings of all schools of psychology, psychoanalysis, pharmacology, and physiology. It promises great strides in mental medicine. Today advances are being made that will enable man to achieve a better understanding of one of the most important and complex of all subjects —the human mind.

—Leonard Carmichael

BIBLIOGRAPHY

Carmichael, Leonard. *Basic Psychology: A Study of the Modern Healthy Mind*. Random House of Canada, Ltd., 1957.

English, Horace B. and Ava C. *A Comprehensive Dictionary of Psychology and Psychoanalytical Terms*. Longmans, Green & Co., Ltd., 1958.

Freud, Sigmund. *Collected Papers*. Phillip Rieff, ed. 10 vols. Collier Books, 1963.

Hendrick, Ives. *Facts and Theories of Psychoanalysis* (3rd ed.). Alfred A. Knopf, Inc., 1958.

Jones, Ernest. *The Life and Work of Sigmund Freud*. Edited and abridged by Lionel Trilling and Steven Marcus. Basic Books, Inc., 1961.

Jung, Carl Gustav and Kerenyi, Károly. *Essays on a Science of Mythology*. Translated by R. F. C. Hull. Harper & Row, Publishers, 1963.

Krech, David and Crutchfield, Richard S. *Elements of Psychology*. Alfred A. Knopf, Inc., 1958.

Reik, Theodore. *Of Love and Lust*. Grove Press, 1959.

Roberts, William H. *Psychology You Can Use*. Harcourt, Brace World, Inc., 1943.

Strecker, Edward A. and Appel, Kenneth E. *Discovering Ourselves: A View of the Human Mind and How It Works* (3rd ed.). The Macmillan Co., 1958.

Whyte, Lancelot Law. *The Unconscious Before Freud*. Basic Books, Inc., 1963.

Geography	1961
Census	1970
States	1974
Territories	2000
Cities	2005
Natural features	2016
History	2021

VOLUME TWENTY FOUR

UNITED STATES

ROBERT REIB

United States

GEOGRAPHY

The United States of America occupies the entire width of the North American continent between approximately the 30th and 49th parallels of latitude, and also the northwestern corner of the continent, Alaska. The island state of Hawaii lies in the Pacific Ocean, about 2,000 miles southeast of San Francisco, between 19° and 29° north latitude.

The territory of the old 48 states, that is, excluding Alaska and Hawaii, was formerly called the "continental United States," and now is known as the "conterminous United States." It forms a rough rectangle extending some 2,700 miles from east to west and 1,300 miles from north to south. It is bounded on the north by Canada and on the southwest by Mexico.

The United States is the world's fourth largest nation in area and the fourth largest in population. Its area of 3,615,211 square miles is exceeded only by that of the Soviet Union, Canada, and China. And its mid-1967 population of 199,118,000 was exceeded only by that of China, India, and the Soviet Union.

Another 13,000 square miles and 3 million people could be added to the U.S. figures if Puerto Rico, the Virgin Islands, Guam, Samoa, and other U.S. territories were included. But these areas are discussed in the section Territories.

The simple area and population figures do not accurately reflect the power of the United States, however. The United States is a world leader in terms of wealth, military power, and technical achievement. This leading position is largely the result of the development at just the right time of exceptionally rich resources by unusually able and energetic settlers from overseas.

PHYSICAL GEOGRAPHY

North America is basically a large continental platform, or bloc, of very ancient rock, at least 2 billion years old. Most of this ancient bloc is covered by material deposited in more recent times.

The "continental basement" is visible in the United States in the Black Hills, the Rockies, and at the bottom of the Grand Canyon. But the most extensive area of the ancient rock is in the Canadian Shield area of North America, which projects into northern Minnesota, Michigan, Wisconsin, and New York.

The physical geography of the United States cannot be understood without taking into account the huge ice sheets that covered large areas during the Pleistocene Glacial Period between 1 million and 10,000 years ago. The land east of the Missouri River and north of the Ohio River was covered four times during this glacial period.

The moving ice sheets scooped out the basins of the Great Lakes, formed thousands of other lakes, scraped soil from some areas and deposited it in other places, and radically changed the patterns of rivers.

Beyond the edge of the huge ice sheets that covered the northeast, there were smaller, but still impressive, glaciers in the higher portions of the Rockies, the Sierra Nevadas, Cascades, and other western mountains.

LAND REGIONS

The bulk of the United States may be divided into three major zones in which rock formations of more recent origin prevail—the Appalachian Zone; the Central Lowlands and Plains; and the Western Cordilleran Region. Each of these three major zones contains several subregions.

APPALACHIAN ZONE. The smallest of the three major regions is the Appalachian Zone. It includes the Appalachian Mountains, the Appalachian Piedmont, and the Atlantic Coastal Plain.

The Appalachian Mountains is a system of low hills and mountains and of plateaus extending northeast from central Alabama into New England and across the border into eastern Canada. The Blue Ridge, Great Smokies, and other parallel ridges form the highest part of the Appalachians.

Although they seldom exceed elevations of 5,000 feet above sea level and generally crest at about 2,000 or 3,000 feet, the Appalachians remain formidable barriers to east-west travel. Low-level passes are found only in the Hudson-Lake Champlain and Mohawk valleys in New York.

South and east of the mountains lies the Appalachian Piedmont, a low plateau with an elevation of some 500 to 1,000 feet above sea level. Its hard-rock surface is the worn-down base of former mountains. Seaward of the plateau is the Fall Line, which marks the meeting of hard Piedmont rock and the softer rock of the coastal plain with a series of waterfalls.

The low, relatively featureless, Atlantic Coastal Plain is composed of rather soft materials washed down from the Appalachians. The plain is quite broad through Georgia, South and North Carolina, and Virginia. It narrows considerably to the northeast and finally peters out along New England's southern coast.

The coastal plain, and thus the North American continent, continues beyond the shoreline of the Atlantic Ocean as the Continental Shelf. The Florida peninsula, a nearly flat, poorly drained part of the Continental Shelf covered by young, limey materials, rises only a few feet above sea level.

U.S. NATIONAL PARK SERVICE

THE APPALACHIAN SYSTEM near the east coast, includes these mountains of the Blue Ridge.

South of Hampton Roads, Virginia, the Atlantic coast is fringed by long, narrow sand bars and has few usable harbors. To the north, however, particularly in New England where the Appalachian hills meet the sea, there are many excellent natural harbors.

Northwest of the Appalachian Mountains is a rough plateau, called the Allegheny in the north and the Cumberland in the south. The plateau gradually loses both elevation and roughness as one travels northwestward.

CENTRAL LOWLANDS AND PLAINS.
The great Central Lowlands and Plains of the United States extend far northward into Canada and account for more than half the width of the United States. This broad, generally saucer-shaped zone is structurally one vast geosyncline, or basin. It is asymmetrical in profile, for the lowest part, the north-south line followed by the Mississippi River, lies well to the east of its center.

Much of the huge region is quite low, less than 500 feet above sea level, and nearly level, especially the valley of the Mississippi below Cairo, Illinois, and the broad Gulf Coastal Plain stretching from Mexico across Texas into Alabama. The Gulf Coastal Plain is quite similar in nature to the Atlantic Coastal Plain.

Elsewhere in the region, as in the area drained by the Ohio and upper Mississippi rivers, the land is gently to moderately rolling. Occasionally low uplands and some broken country are encountered, as in the Ozark-Ouachita highlands and in isolated hill regions in the middle west. Only rarely do landforms in the region create serious transportation problems, however.

Most of the Central Lowlands and Plains is drained by the Mississippi and its tributaries, including the Missouri, Ohio, Tennessee, Red, Arkansas, and Platte rivers. A number of short streams flow into the Great Lakes, however, and parts of Minnesota and North and South Dakota are drained into the Red River of the North, and thus eventually into Hudson Bay, in Canada. Most of the streams of the Gulf Coastal Plain flow directly into the Gulf of Mexico.

West of about the 95th meridian and between the border with Canada and Mexico, the land rises slowly but steadily from elevations of only several hundred feet to 5,000 feet or more above sea level. This gently tilted surface is crossed by eastward flowing tributaries of the Mississippi and is known as the Great Plains, or the High Plains.

Aside from the Llano Estacado of western Texas and eastern New Mexico, the Great Plains region is as nearly level as its name implies, and a rolling, often broken surface is the rule. In northwestern Nebraska there are extensive areas of low sand dunes. Northeast of the Missouri River there are occasional deposits of material left by a retreating glacier some 10,000 years ago.

The great expanse of the Central Lowlands and Plains zone, combined with the extensive Atlantic Coastal Plain and the isolated but important plains areas of the western United States, gives the nation a vast quantity of relatively low, level terrain—a fortunate geological situation that has been a major asset in the economic development of the United States.

WESTERN CORDILLERAN REGION.
The western third of the United States, and virtually all of Alaska, are occupied by a complex series of mountains, plateaus, and basins collectively known as the Western Cordilleran Region. The region contains three major subregions—the Rocky Mountains, in the east; two parallel chains of mountains flanking the Pacific coast; and the zone of basins and plateaus lying between the two mountain systems.

The Rockies consist of an irregular series of high ranges and valleys that generally trend north-south. Peaks of 10,000 feet or more, many of them snow-capped, are common, especially in the impressive ranges of Colorado, western Montana, and northern Idaho. Although drained by many eastward-flowing streams, the Rockies present serious difficulties to travelers, and they are easily crossed only in southern New Mexico or through South Pass, in central Wyoming.

Along the western side of North America, a continuous line of hills and mountains called the Coast Ranges extends from Canada to Lower (Baja) California, in Mexico. The Coast Ranges run very close to the Pacific, and there is only a very poorly developed coastal plain. The Pacific Continental Shelf, unlike its Atlantic counterpart, is quite narrow.

The Coast Ranges are breached only by the Sacramento-San Joaquin river system in central California and the Columbia River and Puget Sound in Washington. Southern Alaska has many fine harbors. But except for Puget Sound, San Francisco Bay, and San Diego Bay, the Pacific Coast of the conterminous United States has almost no good harbors.

The Coast Ranges together with the even higher ranges of north-south mountains further inland, called the Sierra Nevada in California and the Cascade Range in Oregon and Wash-ington, present serious problems for highway and railroad builders.

The Western mountain system is still quite active geologically, and earthquakes are much more frequent and damaging there than in other parts of the country. Volcanic eruptions occur only at long intervals in the Pacific Northwest, but they are fairly frequent in the Alaskan coastal ranges.

Some long, narrow valley basins lie between the two parallel mountain ranges. The largest and most important is the Central Valley of California, which contains the Sacramento-San Joaquin river system. To the north, the Willamette and Puget Sound valleys are of great local economic significance.

The region between the mountains, the "intermontane" region, is known as the Basin and Range Province. It contains a series of high and low plateaus and basins occasionally interrupted by minor mountain ranges. There are landforms there quite different from those found in other parts of the United States that must be explained by past earthquake or volcanic activity and the present dryness of the climate.

Most of the region has dry-channel streams that contain water only just after the infrequent showers. Few of the streams reach the sea, and many drain into salt lakes that may evaporate during periods of drought. Only when major streams are fed by moisture from mountain rainsheds, as happens with the Snake, Rio Grande, and Colorado, do large, permanent rivers wind their way to the ocean.

CLIMATE

The United States is fortunate in both its middle-latitude location and in the moderating effects of the three major bodies of water along its shores —the Atlantic and Pacific Oceans, and the Gulf of Mexico.

As in other middle-latitude land areas, there are major temperature differences between winter and summer. These differences become sharper the further inland one travels, for the central portion of the United States is shielded by mountains and distance

U.S. BUREAU OF RECLAMATION
ROCKY MOUNTAIN PEAKS in Wyoming's Teton Range are snow covered throughout the year.

from the modifying effects of the oceans, the phenomenon of *continentality.*

An average January temperature below 10°F prevails in North Dakota, and there are frequent subzero winter cold snaps over much of the U.S. interior. Average midsummer temperatures of 80°F to 90°F are common over much of the country, with even higher temperatures in the southwest.

Frosts occur everywhere in the conterminous United States, except in southernmost Florida. Growing seasons range from 90 to more than 300 days a year, and the warm to hot summer temperatures make it possible to cultivate a wide variety of crops. Alaska, however, is handicapped by extremely long, cold winters, very short summers, and unreliable growing seasons—except where its shores are bathed by the warm waters of the Pacific Ocean. Hawaii, in contrast, enjoys year-round warmth with only slight seasonal variations in temperature.

CLIMATIC ZONES. The many distinct climatic regions of the United States can be grouped into three great climatic zones—the east, the Pacific, and the west-central.

Eastern Zone. Half of the country east of the 100th meridian is humid. With annual precipitation ranging between 25 and 80 inches, it normally has adequate amounts of moisture and thus, where temperatures permit, a wide variety of agricultural activities. This moisture is derived primarily from the Gulf of Mexico and only secondarily from the Atlantic Ocean.

Within the eastern zone, precipitation tends to increase eastward and southward, whereas thermal belts run east-west, so that temperatures and growing seasons decrease toward the north. Temperatures and precipitation generally reach their peak during the warm-weather months.

Pacific Zone. A second, much smaller humid region extends north from central California to the Canadian border and generally reaches less than 200 miles inland from the Pacific.

This region differs markedly from the eastern zone. Its seasonal temperature shifts are rather moderate, and precipitation peaks during the winter months. This is caused by the nearness of the relatively equable Pacific Ocean and the westerly drift of air which dominates the middle latitudes, thus ensuring mild, almost frostless winters and cool summers.

There is a pronounced summer drought along the entire Pacific Coast, and in southern California it is so protracted that true desert conditions are approached. The generally mild, pleasant climate prevailing in central and southern California is of the Mediterranean type found on the west coasts of other continents in the same latitudes.

West-Central Zone. The third climatic zone lies between the eastern edge of the Great Plains and the Sierra Nevada-Cascade ranges. Semiarid to arid conditions prevail, and temperature regimes vary considerably, depending on both latitude and altitude.

Water supply is inadequate and is an acute problem everywhere except at higher elevations or in tracts close to the region's few major streams.

WEATHER PROBLEMS. Although nature has generally been kind to the United States in arranging its climates, weather problems do occur. There have been floods in almost every part of the country, even in some of the driest sections. Year-to-year fluctuations in the amount of rainfall can be particularly serious in regions lying along the margins between humid and arid climates, such as the Great Plains region.

Occasionally, a cycle of dry years, such as those of the early 1930s or mid-1950s, will cause major distress to farms, ranches, and urban water supplies in normally moist areas.

The United States also seems to be unusually susceptible to the most violent windstorm known anywhere—the tornado. These small, rapidly moving, highly destructive storms have occurred in every part of the conterminous United States. They are especially likely to strike in the central states during the warmer months.

Each summer and fall the Gulf and South Atlantic coasts are hit by an average of two or three destructive hurricanes. These storms of tropical origin seldom penetrate far inland, however.

VEGETATION

The natural plant cover of the United States has been altered almost beyond recognition in most areas, but where it has survived it is still of great importance. The original pattern, the result of climate, soils, landforms, plant migrations, and aboriginal land use, is best preserved in the driest and roughest parts of the western half of the nation. There a variety of sparse desert shrubs and short grasses appear over extensive reaches of dry to semiarid land.

Fairly tall, dense stands of coniferous trees are found in the higher, damper uplands and on the slopes of the Coast Ranges, Sierras and Cascades, except where they have been cut down or burned off. Many large stretches of grassland, such as in California's central valley or on the Columbia Plateau, in eastern Washington and Oregon and southern Idaho, are now under cultivation.

Great changes have also occurred in the former vast grasslands of the Great Plains, for they are now largely farmland and pasture. The tall grass prairie that covered much of the western Middle West and extended eastward into central Illinois and Indiana has been largely replaced by corn, soybeans, hay, and other crops.

East of the Mississippi, the land was once almost wholly forested, except for Indian clearings and some salt marshes. In northern Michigan and Wisconsin, northern New England, and much of New York and Pennsylvania, there stood a mixed deciduous and evergreen forest that in places yielded to pure evergreen—pine, spruce, or fir. Although heavily exploited and impoverished, this kind of forest persists where farming has proved unfeasible.

Such is not the case with the magnificent deciduous hardwood forest that once filled the territory south of the Great Lakes and well into Georgia, Alabama, Mississippi, and east-central Texas. Farming and logging activities now limit the remnants of this forest to the more inaccessible mountain areas.

Most of the Deep South, the states bordering on the Gulf of Mexico, was covered by piney woods where drainage was good and by swamp hardwood forests where it was not. Over that large portion of the Deep South that is not now cultivated, much the same formations remain, although usually in second or third growth.

All in all, the trees and grasses that initially covered much of the land were a prime economic asset, even though the pioneer farmer had to expend much energy ridding himself of unwanted forest or sod.

SOILS

The character and quality of the soil resources of the United States are highly varied, for the effects of parent material, plant life, climate, and terrain operating through time are quite complex.

On the one hand, there are the thin, stony soils of upland New England, the sterile sandy soils of southern Alabama, and the virtually lifeless soils of the salt flats of northern Utah. On the other hand, there are the rich, black prairie soils of central Illinois and Iowa, the highly fertile alluvial soils of the Mississippi Delta, and the productive soils of Lancaster County, Pennsylvania.

On balance, the United States has been unusually fortunate in the extent of its good to excellent soils. It has been less fortunate in the way many of them have been carelessly cultivated. Natural fertility has been appreciably reduced in many areas, and many millions of tons of earth have been washed downhill or out to sea.

MAINE DEPARTMENT OF ECONOMIC DEVELOPMENT
NORTHEASTERN FOREST of tall evergreens mixed with other smaller deciduous trees.

VIRGINIA STATE TRAVEL SERVICE

COLONIAL WILLIAMSBURG is a restoration of an early British settlement in Virginia.

HISTORICAL GEOGRAPHY

At the time of its discovery by Europeans in the 1500s, the present territory of the conterminous United States was thinly peopled by several dozen distinct Amerindian groups with a total population estimated at between 500,000 and 2 million. Although all were members of the same racial stock, the Indian tribes differed greatly in language, customs, and way of life.

The Indians living east of the Rockies and in parts of New Mexico and Arizona practised farming, which they generally combined with hunting and fishing to provide a basic livelihood. In the rest of the nation, the aboriginal peoples existed at a less advanced level in a hunting and gathering economy. In certain food-rich areas along the Pacific coast, fairly dense populations had developed, however.

Even the more advanced farming groups of the southeast and southwest failed to develop cities or political organizations much above the tribal level. And in terms of economic or military technology, the Indians were no match for the invading Europeans, even though they may locally have slowed the advance of the frontier. Warfare, disease, and loss of land and morale decimated Indian numbers. By 1900, the 250,000 or so Amerindians who remained had been herded into reservations.

DISCOVERY AND EXPLORATION

The United States was "discovered" many times by voyagers from other lands before the written accounts and maps of European explorers of the 1500s appeared. It is quite certain the Norsemen, or Vikings, visited and briefly settled parts of the northeastern United States in the 1000s. It is less certain, but still possible, that other medieval European, as well as Chinese and Japanese, seafarers reached the shores of the United States. But little came of such casual visits.

It was shortly after Christopher Columbus and other Spanish navigators reached the Caribbean islands and mainland that ships from Spain, France, Britain, and other European countries began to cruise and chart the Atlantic and Gulf coasts of North America, and, a few decades later, the Pacific coast.

But despite a few spectacular expeditions, such as those of Hernando de Soto and Francisco Vásquez Coronado, the North American interior was left almost unexplored until the early 1600s, when serious settlement began.

The discovery and exploration of Alaska and Hawaii came much later. Vitus Bering, sailing under Russian auspices, reached Alaska in 1741, and the British navigator, Capt. James Cook, came upon Hawaii and its relatively advanced Polynesian people in 1779.

SETTLEMENT

From 1607 onward, four northwestern European powers—Britain, France, the Netherlands, and Sweden—began to claim, settle, and exploit various parts of eastern North America. By 1664 the British managed to oust the Dutch from the Hudson and Delaware valleys. The Dutch had earlier wrested the Delaware territory from the Swedes.

By 1733, a string of 13 British colonies filled nearly the entire Atlantic seaboard from Maine to Georgia, and settlement had begun to creep inland, in some cases as far as the Appalachians. After a series of wars, French holdings in the St. Lawrence and Great Lakes regions and along the Mississippi River were taken by Britain and Spain.

On the eve of the American Revolution, there were approximately 2 million persons living in the future United States. The great majority were of English extraction, but after about 1700 there began to arrive large numbers of Scotch-Irish immigrants, mostly Presbyterian Scots who came by way of northern Ireland.

In Pennsylvania and Maryland, Germans from the Rhineland and Switzerland settled. Smaller numbers of Welsh and Irish were also present, and there were a few Dutch and French. Roughly one-fifth of the colonial population was made up of Negro slaves.

TERRITORIAL EXPANSION

After the achievement of independence in 1783 and the ceding by Britain of all its land east of the Mississippi and south of Canada, the new nation rapidly expanded its territory. Territorial expansion matched the growth of population and of national economic strength.

The immense Louisiana Territory was purchased from France in 1803, an act that doubled the size of the country. Florida was acquired from Spain in 1819, and the short-lived Republic of Texas was annexed in 1845. Then, following a brief war with Mexico in 1848, the country acquired a huge block of territory comprising present-day California, Nevada, and Utah; most of Arizona; and much of New Mexico, Colorado, and Wyoming.

In 1846, after a long and bitter dispute, Britain recognized the U.S. claim to all of the Pacific northwest below the 49th parallel. Earlier disagreements over Maine's and Minnesota's borders with Canada had already been settled. The present-day boundaries of the conterminous United States were finally rounded out in 1853 by the acquisition from Mexico of southern Arizona and New Mexico in the Gadsden Purchase.

Although the Russians had once been active in western North America as far south as California, they were delighted to sell their unprofitable territory of Alaska to the United States in 1867. In 1898 the Hawaiian islands were annexed at the request of the Hawaiians, and in the same year Puerto Rico, the Philippines, and Guam were acquired from Spain as the spoils of war.

The unsettled western portions of the newly independent United States were claimed by several of the original colonies. But gradually over the period 1784–1802, the claims were relinquished to the federal government, and the lands unoccupied were placed in the public domain.

The western areas, with the exception of Vermont, Kentucky, and Tennessee, which had already been partially settled, along with other lands later acquired by purchase or treaty, were surveyed quickly and efficiently. Blocks and parcels of land were sold or given to pioneer settlers under generous terms.

At first the western areas were divided into federally administered territories. But as their populations and economies developed, statehood was granted by Congress. The process of state-building was completed in 1912 in the conterminous United States with the admission of Arizona and New Mexico. Alaska and Hawaii achieved statehood in 1959.

The settlement of the central and western parts of the country was accomplished almost wholly by migrants from the older Eastern seaboard settlements and by Europeans entering through the same region. The advance of the frontier, although slow in colonial times, accelerated sharply after independence and reached a climax in the period 1850–1890. By 1890 the frontier had ceased to exist as a distinct zone, but a few tracts of good land remained to be claimed in Oklahoma and eastern Montana in the early 1900s.

POPULATION GROWTH

The spectacular growth of population from some 3.9 million in 1790, when the first of the regular 10-year censuses was taken, to nearly 10 million in 1820, 23 million in 1850, 50 million in 1880, and past the 100 million mark by about 1916, was brought about by two major factors—natural increase and immigration.

First, there was a vigorous natural increase, that is, a greater number of births than deaths. And it is suspected that roughly half the present-day population is descended from the less than 4 million persons present in 1790. Secondly, the United States received the greatest flood of immigrants any country has ever known, a total of 40 to 50 million persons. This great movement began in earnest only after 1820. The influx of Africans had virtually come to a halt in 1808 with the outlawing of the slave trade.

IMMIGRATION. At first, immigration was largely from Britain, but beginning in the 1830s and 1840s, the trickle of Irish and German newcomers became a flood. After the mid-1800s they were joined by large numbers of Scandinavians. The composition of immigration changed again after about 1880, when many people from eastern and southern Europe arrived. There was also a smaller, but still notable, immigration of Chinese, Japanese, and other Asians directed mainly toward the western states.

Nearly without exception, the immigrants avoided the south and moved into urban and rural areas of the northeast, middle west, and western parts of the country.

Congress limited immigration in 1924, both in numbers and in origin. But immigration still continues, although on a more moderate scale. In recent years, large numbers of people have come from the Caribbean and from Mexico, and the southern drift of French-Canadians into New England and New York continues.

With the growth in national population, U.S. cities experienced truly remarkable growth. In 1790 scarcely one of every 20 people lived in a city. On the eve of the Civil War, in 1860, about one of every five people lived in a city. Now, more than seven of every 10 people live in cities. The expansion came not only in total urban population, but also in the number and size of cities, and in many regions the density, or closeness, of cities has increased notably.

HUMAN GEOGRAPHY

The outstanding factor in the human geography of the United States is the unrivaled level of technological achievement and material prosperity achieved. Thus much of the study of U.S. human geography consists of the analysis of economic regions and the pattern of distribution of economic activities.

But there are two other major factors, only partly linked to economic activities, that are important in understanding the geography of the United States. They are cultural regions and population regions.

CULTURAL REGIONS

Although the settlers of the Atlantic Seaboard were largely English in origin, and thus generally similar in background, three distinct culture areas appeared early in the colonial period—New England, the Middle Atlantic (or Midland), and the South.

The differences among the three areas, which may have sprung from dissimilarities in religious, political, and social systems or in physical and economic conditions, have persisted. They have also helped mold the cultural character of the central and western portions of the nation. Today there are still noticeable distinctions among these three colonial culture areas in terms of speech, religion, diet, and the physical details of settlement.

NEW ENGLAND. New England migrants and ideas have been influential in New York State, much of the northern Midwest, and even further west.

MIDDLE ATLANTIC. The Middle Atlantic region is essentially Pennsylvania and New Jersey, but it also includes parts of New York, Maryland, and Delaware. It is the principal progenitor of the Middle Western region, although the Midwest is also much affected by New England and the South.

SOUTHERN. From its origin in Virginia, North and South Carolina, and Georgia, the Southern culture area spread south into northern Florida. Southern Florida is culturally hybrid, having been settled by persons from both the South and the Northeast. It also spread westward within a zone roughly bounded on the north by the Ohio River and the Ozarks and reaching into Oklahoma and Texas.

There are several subregions within the large Southern culture area, including the Kentucky Bluegrass, the Southern Appalachians, and the Cajun section of Louisiana.

WESTERN. In the far west (California, Oregon, and Washington), the cultural patterns are more strongly "American" and less European than elsewhere. They are derived from a fusion of influences from the central and eastern United States.

In most of the Great Plains, Rocky Mountain, and Intermontane areas, settlement is so thin that recognizable cultural patterns have scarcely appeared, with two major exceptions—the Mormon and the Spanish-American cultural areas.

Utah and portions of neighboring states comprise the distinctive Mormon cultural area, reflecting the special religious, economic, and settlement patterns of the vigorous, well-organized Mormon population centered there since the late 1840s. In parts of New Mexico, Arizona, Colorado, and Texas, Spanish-American influences, some dating back to the 1600s, are so strong that a distinct regional culture must be recognized.

POPULATION DISTRIBUTION

The citizens of the United States are quite unevenly distributed within their country. By the 1960 census, the 70 percent of the population classed as urban, including those living in urban fringe areas and unincorporated places with 2,500 or more inhabitants, lived on only 1.13 percent of the land in the conterminous United States.

Within the remaining 98.87 percent of the land lived 30 percent of the population. There were about 6.5 mil-

lion people in small villages (1,000 to 2,500 persons). Some 20 million persons, largely dependent on agriculture, were dispersed over the countryside. There were seldom more than 20 to the square mile, even in the more productive, fully occupied tracts of farmland.

The remaining population lived in hamlets or villages of less than 1,000. They were engaged in nonagricultural rural occupations, or were city workers who lived in the countryside.

Thin as it is, particularly compared to agrarian settlement in much of Europe and Asia, the U.S. farm population still continues the rapid decline in absolute numbers begun a quarter century ago. The average farm size keeps increasing, and many farmers enter other occupations.

Settlement, both rural and urban, is virtually continuous east of the 100th meridian, except in very rough areas and those with poor drainage or especially poor soil. West of the 100th meridian settlement is much more patchy.

The Central Valley and the various coastal valleys of California are well settled, as are the Willamette and Puget Sound areas and the Columbia Basin in the Pacific Northwest. Elsewhere in the western half of the country, rural and urban settlement is limited to areas where rainfall is adequate, irrigation is possible, or where rich mineral resources have attracted interest.

In most of Alaska's territory, there is no permanent settlement. The 86,000 city dwellers and 140,000 rural inhabitants are restricted to a few small areas with favorable physical or transport facilities.

URBAN AREAS. The United States is now a highly urbanized nation, with about one third of the population living in cities of 100,000 or more, and more than 17 million persons in metropolitan areas of 1 million or more. It is in these places that most of the rather brisk population growth now occurs. The bulk of the large and medium-sized cities tends to be clustered within the northeastern quarter of the nation.

The recent "metropolitan explosion"—the rapid outward spread of cities, suburbs, and other fringe development—has caused the appearance of several major "conurbations," that is, urban zones within which several growing cities now touch and have merged physically, if not yet politically.

By far the greatest conurbation, or megalopolis, indeed easily the world's largest metropolitan development, with some 30 million residents, is a strip of continuous urban settlement along and near the Atlantic shore from Portland, Maine, southwest to Washington, D.C. New York City, Boston, Philadelphia, Baltimore, Washington, Wilmington, and Providence are only the largest of the urban centers in a zone that includes some scores of other sizeable population centers.

Elsewhere in the eastern half of the United States there are at least five other notable conurbations. The one centered on Pittsburgh is now merging with the one along the south shore of Lake Erie centered on Cleveland. In the midwest, three clusters of cities are grouped around Detroit, Cincinnati, and Chicago.

In the south, there is a nearly continuous string of urban centers along the east coast of Florida from Jacksonville to Miami. Closely spaced medium-sized and small cities cluster in the upper Piedmont from southern Virginia to South Carolina.

The largest conurbations of the west are located in California. A vast, sprawling "Southern California City" centers on Los Angeles, extending from Santa Barbara south to San Diego. There is another cluster of cities around San Francisco Bay.

Outside these and a few lesser conurbations, U.S. cities show a decided tendency toward even spacing in zones of continuous rural occupancy.

Location of Cities. The location of U.S. cities is closely related to their past or present functions. Strategic location with regard to rivers or canals and lake or ocean harbors in earlier times, and railroads in more recent times, has been crucial for the growth of most cities. This is because virtually all cities perform significant wholesale, retail, and transportation functions.

Many other cities that are mainly dependent on manufacturing are situated in places with good access to raw materials, labor, and markets, as well as transport.

The advanced evolution of U.S. society is shown by the increasing number of places now specializing in skilled services, such as government, education, research and development, publishing, finance and insurance, communications, advertising, and business administration. These include some of the largest cities, as well as a considerable number of college centers and state capitals.

Another sign of affluence is the growing number of cities catering to pleasure-seekers. The recreation industry accounts for most of the cities in Florida and Nevada and many in Colorado, New Mexico, Arizona, California, and elsewhere.

MOBILITY. The U.S. population has always been highly mobile. The frequency of migration has increased since the closing of the frontier. Many millions of persons from farms and villages have been moving to the cities; and there has been a vigorous exchange of migrants among the cities as well. The rural exodus has been so pronounced that during the 1950s the majority of American counties, most of them rural, lost population.

In regional terms, there has been a heavy movement from the rural southeast to the urban northeast and west, a migration in which Negroes have been particularly important. But some southern areas, notably Florida and the industrial sections of Texas and Louisiana, have drawn large numbers of migrants.

The historic westward drift of the population continues. In the period from 1950 to 1960 the nation's center of population shifted westward by 50 miles to a point near Centralia, Illinois. The western states of Cal-

U.S. DEPARTMENT OF TRANSPORTATION

MOBILITY IS INCREASED by automobile travel on superhighways that lace the United States.

ifornia, Washington, Oregon, Hawaii, Colorado, Arizona, and New Mexico have been the chief beneficiaries of the westward drift.

ETHNIC GROUPS. The ethnic and racial makeup of the United States varies considerably from region to region. The foreign-born and their children and grandchildren are found mostly in the northeast, predominantly in the cities, and also in significant numbers in many parts of the west. In the south foreign stock is conspicuously rare with the exception of parts of Florida and Texas.

The Negro population, now accounting for more than 10 percent of the national total, was limited largely to the cotton, tobacco, and rice plantation areas of the south before the Civil War. But the massive northward and westward movement into the cities that got well under way in the 1910's has reached the point where the Negro population as a whole is more urbanized than the white population.

RELIGION. The United States easily leads the world in religious diversity. There are more than 250 distinct religious denominations and many of them are of U.S. origin. The Protestant majority is splintered into scores of groups, each with a distinct spatial pattern. It is most strongly dominant in the southeast and in the Morman region.

The approximately 25 percent of the population that is Roman Catholic is unevenly bunched within tracts settled heavily by immigrants from Catholic nations in Europe and Latin America. A Jewish population of more than 5.6 million is strongly concentrated in the larger cities, mostly in the northeast, Florida, and California.

INCREASE. Other demographic characteristics of the U.S. people, such as the median age of the population, sex ratio, and occupation, vary between city and countryside and among various regions. One set of characteristics, however, is of particular importance—the pattern of births, deaths, and natural increase.

In 1966 the crude birth rate (number of births per 1,000 persons) was reported as 18.5, but there were major regional differences. Rural birth rates

are still higher than urban, although much less so now than previously. The southern, west-north-central, and southwestern states have much higher birth rates than the northeast or the Pacific coast states.

A crude death rate of 9.5 was reported in 1966 and with much less regional variance than reported for the birth rate. Although this rate is low by world standards, it compares unfavorably with other well-to-do nations having social and health services that are more advanced than those in the United States.

Thus an infant mortality rate (number of babies dying during first year of life per 1,000 born) of about 23.4 currently prevails. But a rate of less than 15 is reported in Sweden, the Netherlands, and New Zealand.

Although there is still room for improving the mortality situation, United States birth rates are also rather higher than in most other advanced nations, so that the present annual rate of natural increase is high enough, if present trends continue, to double the population within 50 years. A figure of more than 300 million will probably be reached before the end of the century.

ECONOMIC GEOGRAPHY

However measured, the prosperity of the United States is tremendous. In 1966 the gross national product was approximately $740 billion, or about $3,760 per person. These sums are more than double those of most other developed nations. This wealth is the product of many factors, physical—land forms, climate, soils; human—a large, active, industrious population; and material—rich resources of minerals, forests, and other materials.

MINERALS

The mineral wealth of the United States is phenomenal in both its diversity and its abundance. In part this is a matter of simple territorial size, but there is again a strong element of sheer geological luck. The most important U.S. mineral resources are undoubtedly the mineral fuels.

U.S. BUREAU OF MINES

MINERAL RESOURCES include metals like copper, tapped by this New Mexico open-pit mine.

But the variety and quantity of other minerals, metallic and non-metallic, are almost ideal.

FUELS. Tremendous amounts of high-quality bituminous coal are found in the Appalachian Plateau from northern Pennsylvania to northern Alabama. Despite decades of intensive exploitation, reserves are still adequate for a good many centuries. A second important coal region is found in central and southern Illinois and in the margins of adjacent states.

Two other extensive coal fields, one running southward in a broad band from central Iowa to central Oklahoma and another in western North and South Dakota and eastern Montana, are poorer in quality but may be of value in the future. There are also a number of smaller, but locally important, deposits scattered through the Rocky Mountain regions and the plateaus to the west of the Rockies. And eastern Pennsylvania boasts what is probably the largest, finest anthracite deposit in the world.

The United States is so well endowed with petroleum and natural gas that it has at times been the world's leading producer of both. By far the largest part of the known and exploited oil and gas reserves are in the south-central states, especially Texas, Louisiana, Oklahoma, and Kansas. What was once a major field in Southern California has declined in importance.

Secondary, but still noteworthy, petroleum fields exist in the Appalachian Plateau, several places in the middle west, western North Dakota, northern Alaska, and various basins in the Rocky Mountains. Even after all the intensive exploration that has already taken place, it is not unlikely that some additional major fields remain to be found.

METALS. Among the metals, the United States must rely primarily on foreign sources only for bauxite (aluminum), nickel, tin, and a few ferroalloys. Of particular importance is the U.S. supply of iron ore. Large, rich deposits in the Lake Superior region once ensured U.S. primacy in iron ore output. But continued heavy use depleted those reserves, and iron

and steel producers have been forced to develop other domestic fields and to import large quantities of foreign ore.

The Adirondacks have deposits of iron ore that have long been exploited on a modest scale, and production has steadily grown in Alabama fields near Birmingham. Recent explorations in the eastern Ozarks have been promising, and there are several large reserves in the western states whose use is limited only by high transportation costs.

OTHER MINERALS. Domestic supplies of a few nonmetallic minerals, such as industrial diamonds and asbestos, are deficient. But most important nonmetals, such as sulfur, salt, limestone, phosphates, and potash are in more than adequate supply.

ECONOMIC REGIONS

The United States can be divided into three major economic zones—the Primary Zone, or Core Region; the Secondary Zone; and the Tertiary Zone.

PRIMARY ZONE. The smallest, and by all means the most important, is the Primary Zone, or Core Region. This is a roughly rectangular area whose corners are located at Portland, Me., Minneapolis, Minn., St. Louis, Mo., and Washington, D.C. It also includes the southern, economically dominant fringe of Canada's Ontario and Quebec provinces.

Within the Primary Zone, a scant one-eighth of the conterminous United States in area, are found about half the nation's population, nearly three-quarters of the total manufacturing activity, and even higher fractions of the more advanced forms of business.

The Primary Zone is a prosperous, densely settled, highly urbanized, strongly industrialized area that dominates the continent economically and in other ways. It owes this dominance to a strong early start; superb internal and external transport facilities, including good access to the Atlantic and thus to Western Europe; good to excellent terrain and climatic conditions; and, quite significantly, the enterprise and vigor of its population.

The Primary Zone is provided with ample supplies of agricultural materials, either from local sources or from other areas by means of cheap transport. It also has water, energy, minerals, and forest products.

The outer boundaries of this Core Area have been rather stable for some time; but in recent years a secondary Core Area, largely peopled by migrants from the first one, has sprung up and grown rapidly in central and southern California. It plays much the same role for the western half of the country (including Alaska and Hawaii) that the older Core Area plays for the entire nation.

SECONDARY ZONE. There is next a Secondary Zone, roughly the remainder of the area east of the 100th Meridian. In this zone land-use and settlement are nearly continuous, but population densities are much lower on the average. Cities and industrial centers, while important, are generally widely scattered. Agriculture and forestry are relatively more important there than in the primary zone.

TERTIARY ZONE. Most of the western United States and Alaska is included in the Tertiary Zone, which may be considered a peripheral, or "colonial," area in an economic sense. Because of climate, terrain, or general inaccessibility, much of its surface is not regularly used at all. There are relatively few cities, farms, or other populated areas.

Economically, the Tertiary Zone acts as a source of raw materials, particularly minerals, and some farm, ranch, forest, and marine products. Manufacturing and other advanced activities are of slight importance.

TRANSPORTATION AND COMMUNICATIONS

The transportation network that is so basic to the economy of any country is unusually well-developed in the United States. The system is essentially land-based, for the generous endowment of natural resources has enabled the United States to depend upon foreign, or ocean, commerce less than other advanced nations.

Furthermore, a large part of the national territory happens to be distant from usable ocean harbors or navigable streams and lakes.

WATER TRANSPORT. Locally, however, water transport is extremely important, as in the port cities extending from New England to Hampton Roads or those around Puget Sound and San Francisco Bay, along the shores of the Great Lakes, and along the major streams of the Mississippi system.

A huge volume of domestic, U.S.-Canadian, and now overseas freight is carried on the Great Lakes-St. Lawrence Seaway system. This movement has been facilitated by the building of the Wellandship Canal, the Soo Canal, and other improvements in the connecting channels.

Water connections with other areas are maintained through the New York State Barge Canal, the rebuilt Erie Canal, and the Illinois Waterway which links Lake Michigan to the Mississippi via the Illinois River and the Chicago Sanitary and Ship Canal.

In recent years, major engineering efforts have made the entire length of the Ohio River an important waterway. Barge traffic is heavy along the Mississippi from the Twin Cities to the mouth and along such important tributaries as the Tennessee, Kanawha, Monongahela, and Red rivers as well.

The unique intracoastal Waterway is a combination of natural lagoons and improved channels immediately behind barrier beaches and islands. It stretches all the way from Long Island Sound to the Mexican border, except for a stretch in western Florida. Locally, it is used heavily by barge lines as well as by pleasure craft.

RAIL TRANSPORT. With a total of 211,384 miles of track in operation at the end of 1965, and despite the abandonment of about 40,000 miles in recent decades, the United States remains the world's first-ranking railroad power. The great bulk of trackage and other rail facilities is located in the eastern half of the country, where it forms a generally dense network.

The U.S. railroad system is composed of a large number of privately owned regional systems that are quite competitive locally but cooperate nationally for the efficient transfer of freight and equipment. Railroads were instrumental in the settlement of vast areas, the location of many towns and factories, and were for a long time a major factor in the economic geography of the country.

Recently the railroads have lost much ground to other means of transportation, particularly trucks, barges, and pipelines. In 1965, only 43.4 percent of ton-miles of intercity freight were transported by rail, as compared to 63.2 percent in 1940.

Trucks carried 22.3 percent, pipelines 18.7 percent, and inland waterways 15.4 percent. The pipelines handle petroleum, natural gas, refinery products, and liquid chemicals cheaply over long distances. Most of the former railroad passenger business has passed over to private autos, buses, and airlines.

ROAD TRANSPORT. With some 3.7 million miles of road, both rural and municipal, about 74 percent of them paved, the United States is exceptionally well equipped for the automotive age. The completion in the 1970s of a 43,000-mile interstate highway system linking all major cities with four-lane, limited-access roads will further facilitate the rapid movement of people and goods.

AIR TRANSPORT. The bulk of intercity passenger movement by commercial transportation now takes place by means of air service that reaches all cities with more than a few thousand inhabitants. For physical reasons, air traffic is especially important in Alaska and Hawaii, and it is increasing in importance in the more remote portions of other states, as well.

COMMUNICATIONS. Both telephone and wireless communications are exceptionally well developed. Few U.S. communities are beyond the range of one or more radio or television transmitters.

AGRICULTURE

In the United States agriculture is less important than manufacturing in terms of number of operators or value of products. A farm population of some 11.6 million received $42.9 billion for crops, livestock, and livestock products in 1966. Almost half of the area of the 50 states is in farms.

Subsistence farming has virtually disappeared. Agriculture has become a highly commercial venture, involving heavy capital investment in real estate, buildings, and machinery on ever larger parcels of land for the production of those items that will bring the greatest cash return.

There are two general features that characterize most U.S. farms. First, most operators grow a variety of products to guard against the hazards of weather and the market rather than relying upon a single commodity.

Second, the prevailing pattern stresses the growing of animal products—particularly beef, pork, poultry, eggs, and dairy products—and of livestock feeds rather than the growing of plant foods for direct human use. Thus corn, oats, soybeans, hay, and various other fodder crops play a large role in agriculture in the United States.

AGRICULTURAL REGIONS. The physical geography of the country—specifically growing season, rainfall regime, soil types, terrain, and drainage—and location with respect to markets have divided the country into distinct farming regions.

Corn Belt. Perhaps the wealthiest, and certainly the most famous region, is the corn belt. This belt stretches across the southern half of the middle west from central Ohio to eastern Nebraska and Kansas. The growing of corn, soybeans, oats, and hay for conversion into animal products predominates. But wheat and various fruits and vegetables are also of some importance.

Dairy Belt. A large dairy belt runs from New England, New York, Pennsylvania, through the northern middle west as far west as Minnesota. This area is largely devoted to whole milk production in districts accessible to the larger urban centers, and to butter and cheese elsewhere. Important milksheds also occur in other parts of the nation in proximity to major cities.

Cotton Belt. The cotton belt that once crossed the deep south from southern Virginia to east Texas has shrunk in size and importance in recent years. It still remains recognizable, however, despite the introduction of livestock on a large scale and other land-use changes. Cotton production has recently made a major shift westward into southern California, Arizona, and west Texas.

Wheat Belt. Comparable in size with the corn, dairy, and cotton belts are the wheat belts that occupy major portions of the Great Plains and the Columbia Basin in Washington and Idaho. They produce wheat as well as other small grains and hay.

Other Regions. The remaining farming regions are relatively small specialty areas. Among the more notable are the bright tobacco belt of Virginia, North Carolina, and Kentucky; the fruit belt of western Michigan; the irrigated sugar beet district of the Rocky Mountains and western Great Plains.

Other districts include the sugarcane and pineapple areas in Hawaii; the citrus fruit areas of Florida, south Texas, Arizona, and California; and the small districts in the same states given over to many kinds of fruits, nuts, berries, and vegetables for shipment fresh, canned, or frozen.

U.S.D.A.—SOIL CONSERVATION SERVICE

DAIRY BELT FARMER in Wisconsin raises Ayrshire cattle to produce milk and milk products.

Regions too dry or rough for cultivation—mostly in the western Great Plains, the Rocky Mountains, and the Intermontane Region—are used, where they are used at all, for the breeding and grazing of cattle and sheep on large ranches. These livestock are usually shipped to feedlots in farming districts before a final trip to the slaughterhouse.

FORESTRY

The growing of trees for lumber and paper mills continues to be the major form of land use in those relatively humid parts of the United States where farming is difficult for reasons of soil or terrain.

In northern New England and in the "Cutover Area"—northern Michigan, Wisconsin, and Minnesota—lumbering was dominant during the last century. But the ruthless cutting of the past has drastically reduced the value of the forests and the extent of present-day activity.

Most of the country's wood products now come from the pine forests of the southeast and the coniferous forests of the Pacific northwest. In both areas the climate favors the rapid growth of dense stands of valuable species.

FISHING

Despite the wealth of marine resources along much of the long shoreline of the United States, the fishing industry has lagged far behind other parts of the economy. Highly effective foreign competition has been a major factor, but the relative unimportance of fish in the U.S. diet and the difficulty of shipping highly perishable material far inland also discourage full exploitation of this rich potential.

Fishing is a major source of income only in parts of New England, Florida, the Pacific northwest, and Alaska.

INDUSTRY

The United States is the world's leading industrial nation by a wide margin. Its more than 312,000 manufacturing establishments employ 18 million persons, account for over $225 billion of value added by manufacture, and fabricate every conceivable variety of mass-produced commodity.

Most manufacturing activity takes place in the northeastern Core Area. But there has been a significant recent dispersion of factories to the southern Piedmont, California, Texas, Louisiana, and elsewhere.

Many kinds of factories, particularly those in the heavy industrial class —those producing metals, chemicals, glass, paper, oil refining, and the bulkier types of machinery—are located so as to minimize the costs of production and delivery.

Thus, major steel mills are found in the Pittsburgh-East Ohio and Chicago-Gary districts, at Baltimore, and along the south shore of Lake Erie. These locations have access to large quantities of ore, coal, limestone, and scrap metal, a good water supply, and both labor supply and market.

The location of some industries, however, must be explained largely by historical factors. This is the case with the textile mills of New England,

the rubber industry of the Akron, Ohio area, and the strong automotive concentration in southeastern Michigan.

The pattern of industrial activity in any given area is so complex that it is difficult to single out definite regions, but several areas tend to specialize in certain products, depending upon resources, markets, and local enterprise. Thus, in addition to textiles, New England is noted for electronic products and various advanced kinds of engineering.

In the southern Piedmont factories produce clothing, furniture, and tobacco products as well as great quantities of textiles. On the coastal plains of Texas and Louisiana, metal refineries and petrochemical plants predominate, and the Kanawha Valley is outstanding for chemicals.

Consumer-oriented products are especially important in California and Florida plants. Toward the western fringe of the manufacturing belt there is a specialization in farm machinery and in the processing of farm products. Wood products are conspicuously important in Puget Sound centers.

RECREATION

An increasing share of the U.S. labor force, income, and territory is being devoted to leisure activities. Within commuting range of the larger cities, most tracts suitable for hunting, fishing, boating, skiing, and other outdoor sports are already in use.

Throughout the country most of the suitable seashore and lakefront properties and especially scenic or attractive areas have been developed, either privately or by some government agency. In northern New England, the "Cutover Area," much of Florida, Arizona, and New Mexico, and many mountainous areas in the west, income from tourists and vacationers is the mainstay of the economy.

INTERNATIONAL TRADE

Although the United States is far less reliant on foreign commerce than many other advanced nations, the volume of such trade is far from trifling. In 1966 this volume meant $30.9 billion in exports and $25.7 billion in imports.

COMPOSITION. During its earlier history, the United States was an exporter of raw materials and depended on Europe for most of the industrial products it consumed. Since about 1890, however, the foreign trade pattern has been that of a highly advanced economy.

This means the export of highly processed industrial products, machinery, and transportation equipment, and the import of such raw materials as are not available domestically or only available at a relatively high price. Thus there is a heavy outflow of industrial and electrical machinery, vehicles, chemicals, food and beverages, and metal products of all sorts, and the receipt from foreign sources of rubber, wool, wood and pulp, petroleum, metallic ores and metals, sugar, furs, tropical fruits, coffee, tea, and sugar.

At the same time, however, the

United States still exports major quantities of coal, some metals, grain and flour, cotton, and tobacco, and receives many high-value industrial products and machines from the more advanced countries of Western Europe, Canada, and Japan.

DIRECTION. Europe accounts for the lion's share of American foreign trade with a total of $17.5 billion in 1966. Britain, West Germany, Italy, and France are the leading European trading partners of the United States.

Canada is by far the most important single customer and supplier with $12.7 billion of trade in 1966. Latin America had a total value of trade in 1966 of $9.4 billion. Mexico, with $1.9 billion, and Brazil, with $1.2 billion, are the most active Latin American participants in U.S. trade.

In Asia, Japan has strong trading ties with the United States. A total of $5.3 billion worth of goods was exchanged in 1966. India, with $1.3 billion, and the Philippines with $0.7 billion, are also important. The other Asian countries trail far behind.

Trade with Africa has been relatively light, amounting to $2.3 billion in 1966. Of this, South Africa's share was $700 million.

GEOGRAPHIC PROBLEMS

Despite a great and growing prosperity, students of the U.S. scene are concerned about a number of problems of a geographic character. Much of the present wealth enjoyed by the people of the United States has been gained by reckless exploitation of natural resources—soils, forests, water, and minerals— that cannot be fully replaced.

Much has been done recently to check unnecessary soil erosion, but much more remains to be done. It is doubtful, in any event, in the face of its own rapidly growing population whether the United States can continue indefinitely to export food products.

Inadequate protection and management of forest resources has brought about an increasing reliance on foreign sources for paper and wood products. The domestic supply of many minerals is no longer adequate, and large amounts of petroleum, iron ore, and copper, lead, and zinc are now being imported.

The problem of the contamination of lakes, streams, and underground water supplies by industrial and municipal wastes is increasingly acute as is the matter of assuring adequate quantities of water for growing urban, industrial, and agricultural use. The problem of atmospheric pollution has arisen in many metropolitan areas, and the solutions are by no means simple.

But the largest problem of all is perhaps how to arrange the optimum use of a finite amount of space, both in and near scores of sprawling metropolises and in the open countryside for a large, ever wealthier, and ever more mobile population. And this in turn is part of the even larger challenge of how to make U.S. life qualitatively as well as quantitatively superior.

—Wilbur Zelinsky

Total Population of the United States is 179,323,175

ALABAMA
3,266,740

Albertville	8,250
Alexander City	13,140
Andalusia	10,263
Anniston	33,657
Athens	9,330
Atmore	8,173
Attalla	8,257
Auburn	16,261
Bessemer	33,054
Birmingham	340,887
Brewton	6,309
Chickasaw	10,002
Cullman	10,883
Decatur	29,217
Demopolis	7,377
Dothan	31,440
Enterprise	11,410
Eufaula	8,357
Fairfield	15,816
Florence	31,649
Fort Payne	7,029
Gadsden	58,088
Greenville	6,894
Guntersville	6,592
Homewood	20,289
Huntsville	72,365
Jasper	10,799
Lanett	7,674
Leeds	6,162
Mobile	202,779
Montgomery	134,393
Mountain Brook	12,680
Opelika	15,678
Ozark	9,534
Phenix City	27,630
Prattville	6,616
Prichard	47,371
Russellville	6,628
Selma	28,385
Sheffield	13,491
Sylacauga	12,857
Talladega	17,742
Tarrant City	7,810
Troy	10,234
Tuscaloosa	63,370
Tuscumbia	8,994

ALASKA
226,167

Anchorage	44,237
Fairbanks	13,311
Juneau	6,797
Ketchikan	6,483
Kodiak	2,628
Sitka	3,237
Spenard	9,074

ARIZONA
1,302,161

Ajo	7,049
Avondale	6,151
Bisbee	9,914
Casa Grande	8,311
Chandler	9,531
Douglas	11,925
Flagstaff	18,214
Glendale	15,696
Globe	6,217
Mesa	33,772
Nogales	7,286
Phoenix	439,170
Prescott	12,861
Scottsdale	10,026
South Tucson	7,004
Tempe	24,897
Tucson	212,892
Winslow	8,862
Yuma	23,974

ARKANSAS
1,786,272

Arkadelphia	8,069
Batesville	6,207
Benton	10,399
Blytheville	20,797
Camden	15,823
Conway	9,791
El Dorado City	25,292
Fayetteville	20,274
Forrest City	10,544
Fort Smith	52,991
Harrison	6,580
Helena	11,500
Hope	8,399
Hot Springs	28,337
Jacksonville	14,488
Jonesboro	21,418
Little Rock	107,813
Magnolia	10,651
Malvern	9,566
Newport	7,007
North Little Rock	58,032
Osceola	6,189
Paragould	9,947
Pine Bluff	44,037
Russellville	8,921
Searcy	7,272
Springdale	10,076
Stuttgart	9,661
Texarkana	19,788
Van Buren	6,787
Warren	6,752
West Helena	8,385
West Memphis	19,374

CALIFORNIA
15,717,204

Alameda	61,316
Alhambra	54,807
Altadena	40,568
Anaheim	104,184
Arcadia	41,005

CALIFORNIA—Continued

Arden-Arcade	73,352
Azusa	20,497
Bakersfield	56,848
Baldwin Park	33,951
Bellflower	44,846
Bell Gardens	26,467
Berkeley	111,268
Beverly Hills	30,817
Buena Park	46,401
Burbank	90,155
Burlingame	24,036
Carson	38,059
Castro Valley	37,120
Chula Vista	42,034
Compton	71,812
Concord	36,208
Costa Mesa	37,550
Culver City	32,163
Daly City	44,791
Downey	82,505
East Los Angeles	104,270
El Cajon	37,618
El Cerrito	25,437
Eureka	28,137
Florence-Graham	38,164
Fremont	43,790
Fresno	133,929
Fullerton	56,180
Gardena	35,943
Garden Grove	84,238
Glendale	119,442
Hawthorne	33,035
Hayward	72,700
Huntington Park	29,920
Inglewood	63,390
La Habra	25,136
Lakewood	67,126
La Mesa	30,441
Lancaster	26,012
La Puente	24,723
Lawndale	21,740
Lennox	31,224
Lodi	22,229
Long Beach	344,168
Los Angeles City	2,479,015
Lynwood	31,614
Manhattan Beach	33,934
Menlo Park	26,957
Merced	20,068
Mirada Hills	22,444
Modesto	36,585
Monrovia	27,079
Montebello	32,097
Monterey	22,618
Monterey Park	37,821
Mountain View	30,889
Napa	22,170
National City	32,771
Newport Beach	26,564
Norwalk	88,739
Oakland	367,548
Oceanside	24,971
Ontario	46,617
Orange	26,444
Oxnard	40,265
Palo Alto	52,287
Pasadena	116,407
Pico Rivera	49,150
Pleasant Hill	23,844
Pomona	67,157
Redondo Beach	46,986
Redwood City	46,290
Richmond	71,854
Riverside	84,332
Sacramento	191,667
Salinas	28,957
San Bernardino	91,922
San Bruno	29,063
San Buenaventura	29,114
San Diego	573,224
San Francisco	742,855
San Jose	204,196
San Leandro	65,962
San Mateo	69,870
Santa Ana	100,350
Santa Barbara	58,768
Santa Clara	58,880
Santa Cruz	25,596
Santa Monica	83,249
Santa Rosa	31,027
South Gate	53,831
South San Francisco	39,418
Stockton	86,321
Sunnyvale	52,898
Temple City	31,838
Torrance	100,991
Vallejo	60,877
W. Covina	50,645
West Hollywood	28,870
Whittier	33,663

COLORADO
1,753,947

Alamosa	6,205
Arvada	19,242
Aurora	48,548
Boulder	37,718
Brighton	7,055
Canon City	8,973
Colorado Spgs.	70,194
Commerce Town	8,970
Cortez	6,764
Denver	493,887
Derby	10,124
Durango	10,530
Englewood	33,398
Fort Collins	25,027
Fort Morgan	7,379
Golden	7,118
Grand Junction	18,694
Greeley	26,314
Ivywild	11,065
La Junta	8,026
Lakewood	19,338
Lamar	7,369

COLORADO—Continued

Littleton	13,670
Longmont	11,489
Loveland	9,734
Pueblo	91,181
Security	9,017
Sterling	10,751
Thornton	11,353
Trinidad	10,691
Westminster	13,850
Wheat Ridge	21,619

CONNECTICUT
2,535,234

Ansonia	19,819
Branford	16,610
Bridgeport	156,748
Bristol	45,499
Cheshire	13,383
Danbury	39,382
Darien	18,437
East Hartford	43,977
East Haven	21,388
Enfield	31,464
Fairfield	46,183
Glastonbury	14,497
Greenwich	53,793
Groton	29,937
Hamden	41,056
Hartford	162,178
Killingly	11,298
Manchester	42,102
Mansfield	14,638
Meriden	51,850
Middletown	33,250
Milford	41,662
Naugatuck	19,511
New Britain	82,201
New Canaan	13,466
New Haven	152,048
New London	34,182
Newington	17,664
Newton	11,373
North Haven	15,935
Norwalk	67,775
Norwich	38,506
Plainville	13,149
Shelton	18,190
Southington	22,797
Stamford	92,713
Stonington	13,969
Stratford	45,012
Torrington	30,045
Trumbull	20,379
Vernon	16,961
Wallingford	29,920
Waterbury	107,130
Watertown	14,837
West Hartford	62,382
West Haven	43,002
Westport	20,955
Wethersfield	20,561
Windham	16,973
Windsor	19,467

DELAWARE
446,292

Dover	7,250
Elsmere	7,319
Lewes	3,025
Milford	5,795
Newark	11,404
New Castle	4,469
Seaford	4,430
Wilmington	95,827

DISTRICT OF COLUMBIA
763,956

Washington	763,956

FLORIDA
4,951,560

Avon Park	6,073
Bartow	12,849
Belle Glade	11,273
Boca Raton	6,961
Boynton Beach	10,467
Bradenton	19,380
Brownsville	38,417
Carol City	21,749
Chattahoochee	9,699
Clearwater	34,653
Cocoa	12,294
Coral Gables	34,793
Crestview	7,467
Dania	7,065
Daytona Beach	37,395
Deerfield Beach	9,573
De Land	10,775
Delray Beach	12,230
Dunedin	8,444
Eau Gallie	12,300
Fernandina Beach	7,276
Fort Lauderdale	83,648
Fort Meyers	22,523
Fort Pierce	25,256
Fort Walton Beach	12,147
Gainesville	29,701
Gulfport	9,730
Haines City	9,135
Hallandale	10,483
Hialeah	66,972
Hollywood	35,237
Homestead	9,152
Jacksonville	201,030
Jacksonville Beach	12,049
Key West	33,956
Lake	9,465
Lakeland	41,350
Lake Wales	8,346
Lake Worth	20,758
Leesburg	11,172
Melbourne	11,982
Miami	291,688

FLORIDA—Continued

Miami Beach	63,145
Miami Springs	11,229
North Miami	28,708
North Miami Beach	21,405
Ocala	13,598
Opa-Locka	9,810
Orlando	88,135
Ormond Beach	8,658
Palatka	11,028
Palm Beach	6,055
Panama City	33,275
Pensacola	56,752
Perrine	6,424
Perry	8,030
Pinellas Park	10,848
Plant City	15,711
Pompano Beach	15,992
Quincy	8,874
Riviera Beach	13,046
St. Augustine	14,734
St. Petersburg	181,298
St. Petersburg Beach	6,268
Sanford	19,175
Sarasota	34,083
South Miami	9,846
Tallahassee	48,174
Tampa	274,970
Tarpon Springs	6,768
Titusville	6,410
Vero Beach	8,849
Warrington	16,752
West Palm Beach	56,208
Westwood Lakes	22,517
Wilton Manor	8,257
Winter Haven	16,277
Winter Park	17,162

GEORGIA
3,943,116

Albany	55,890
Americus	13,472
Athens	31,355
Atlanta	487,455
Augusta	70,626
Bainbridge	12,714
Brunswick	21,703
Carrollton	10,973
Cartersville	8,668
Cedartown	9,340
College Park	23,469
Columbus	116,779
Cordele	10,609
Covington	8,167
Dalton	17,868
Decatur	22,026
Douglas	8,736
Dublin	13,814
East Point	35,633
Fair Oaks	7,969
Fitzgerald	8,781
Forest Park	14,201
Fort Valley	8,310
Gainesville	16,523
Griffin	21,735
Hapeville	10,082
Jesup	7,304
La Grange	23,632
Mableton	7,127
Macon	69,764
Marietta	25,565
Midway Hardwick	16,909
Milledgeville	11,117
Moultrie	15,764
Newnan	12,169
North Atlanta	12,661
Perry	6,032
Rome	32,226
Savannah	149,245
Smyrna	12,038
Statesboro	8,356
Thomaston	9,336
Thomasville	18,246
Tifton	9,903
Toccoa	7,303
Valdosta	30,652
Vidalia	7,569
Warner Robins	18,633
Waycross	20,944

HAWAII
632,772

Aiea	11,826
Ewa	3,257
Hilo	25,966
Honolulu	294,179
Kahului	4,223
Kailua-Lanikai	25,622
Kaneohe	14,414
Kapaa	3,439
Lahaina	3,423
Lihue	3,908
Lualualei-Maili	5,045
Puunene	3,054
Wahiawa	15,512
Waianae-Makaha	6,844
Wailuku	6,969
Waimanalo	3,011

IDAHO
667,191

Alameda	10,660
Blackfoot	7,378
Boise	34,481
Burley	7,508
Caldwell	12,230
Coeur d'Alene	14,291
Franklin	7,222
Idaho Falls	33,161
Kellogg	5,061
Lewiston	12,691
Lewiston Orchards	9,680

IDAHO—Continued

Moscow	11,183
Mountain Home	9,344
Mountain View	4,898
Nampa	18,013
Pocatello	28,534
Preston	3,640
Rexburg	4,767
Sandpoint	4,355
Twin Falls	20,126
Whitney	13,603

ILLINOIS
10,081,158

Alton	43,047
Arlington Hts.	27,878
Aurora	63,715
Belleville	37,264
Bellwood	20,729
Belvidere	11,223
Bensenville	9,141
Berwyn	54,224
Bloomington	36,271
Blue Island	19,618
Brookfield	20,429
Cahokia	15,829
Calumet City	25,000
Canton	13,588
Carbondale	14,670
Carpentersville	17,424
Centralia	13,904
Champaign	49,583
Centreville	12,769
Charleston	10,505
Chicago	3,550,404
Chicago Heights	34,331
Cicero	69,130
Collinsville	14,217
Danville	41,856
Decatur	78,004
Deerfield	11,786
De Kalb	18,486
Des Plaines	34,086
Dixon	19,565
Dolton	18,746
Downers Grove	21,154
East Moline	16,732
East Peoria	12,310
East St. Louis	81,712
Elgin	49,447
Elmhurst	36,991
Elmwood Park	23,866
Evanston	79,283
Evergreen Park	24,178
Forest Park	14,452
Franklin Park	18,322
Freeport	26,628
Galesburg	37,243
Glencoe	10,472
Glen Ellyn	15,972
Glenview	18,132
Granite City	40,073
Harvey	29,071
Highland Park	25,532
Hinsdale	12,859
Homewood	13,371
Jacksonville	21,690
Joliet	66,780
Kankakee	27,666
Kewanee	16,324
La Grange	15,285
La Grange Park	13,793
Lake Forest	10,687
Lansing	18,098
La Salle	11,897
Lincoln	16,890
Lincolnwood	11,744
Lombard	22,561
Macomb	12,135
Marion	11,274
Markham	11,704
Mattoon	19,088
Maywood	27,330
Melrose Park	22,291
Moline	42,705
Monmouth	10,372
Morton Grove	20,533
Mount Prospect	18,906
Mount Vernon	15,566
Mundelein	10,526
Naperville	12,933
Niles	20,393
Normal	13,357
Norridge	14,087
Northbrook	11,635
North Chicago	20,517
North Lake	12,318
Oak Lawn	27,471
Oak Park	61,093
Ottawa	19,408
Palatine	11,504
Park Forest	29,993
Park Ridge	32,659
Pekin	28,146
Peoria	103,162
Peru	10,460
Quincy	43,793
Rantoul	22,116
Riverdale	12,008
River Forest	12,695
Rock Falls	10,261
Rockford	126,706
Rock Island	51,863
Rolling Meadows	10,879
St. Charles	9,269
Skokie	59,364
South Holland	10,412
Springfield	83,271
Sterling	15,688
Streator	16,868
Summit	10,374
Urbana	27,294
Villa Park	20,391
Waukegan	55,719
Westchester	18,092

ILLINOIS—Continued

Western Spgs.	10,838
West Frankfort	9,027
Wheaton	24,312
Wilmette	28,268
Winnetka	13,368
Wood River	11,694
Woodstock	8,897
Zion	11,941

INDIANA

4,662,498

Anderson	49,061
Auburn	6,350
Bedford	13,024
Beech Grove	10,973
Bloomington	31,357
Brazil	8,853
Columbus	20,778
Connersville	17,698
Crawfordsville	14,231
East Chicago	57,669
East Gary	9,309
Elkhart	40,274
Elwood	11,793
Evansville	141,543
Fort Wayne	161,776
Frankfort	15,302
Franklin	9,453
Gary	178,320
Goshen	13,718
Greencastle	8,506
Greenfield	9,049
Greenwood	7,169
Griffith	9,483
Hammond	111,698
Highland	16,284
Hobart	18,680
Huntington	16,185
Indianapolis	476,258
Jeffersonville	19,522
Kokomo	47,197
Lafayette	42,330
La Porte	21,157
Lawrence	10,103
Lebanon	9,523
Logansport	21,106
Madison	10,097
Marion	37,854
Michigan City	36,653
Mishawaka	33,361
Muncie	68,603
Munster	10,313
New Albany	37,812
New Castle	20,349
Noblesville	7,664
Peru	14,453
Plymouth	7,558
Portage	11,822
Portland	6,999
Princeton	7,906
Richmond	44,149
Rushville	7,264
Seymour	11,629
Shelbyville	14,317
South Bend	132,445
Speedway	9,624
Terre Haute	72,500
Valparaiso	15,227
Vincennes	18,046
Wabash	12,621
Warsaw	7,234
Washington	10,846
West Lafayette	12,680
Whiting	8,137

IOWA

2,757,537

Algona	5,702
Ames	27,003
Atlantic	6,890
Bettendorf	11,534
Boone	12,468
Burlington	32,430
Cedar Falls	21,195
Cedar Rapids	92,035
Centerville	6,629
Charles City	9,964
Cherokee	7,724
Clinton	33,589
Council Bluffs	54,361
Creston	7,667
Davenport	88,981
Des Moines	208,982
Dubuque	56,606
Estherville	7,927
Fairfield	8,054
Fort Dodge	28,399
Fort Madison	15,247
Grinnell	7,367
Independence	7,069
Indianola	7,062
Iowa City	33,443
Keokuk	16,316
Knoxville	7,817
Marion	10,882
Marshalltown	22,521
Mason City	30,642
Mount Pleasant	7,339
Muscatine	20,997
Newton	15,381
Oelwein	8,282
Oskaloosa	11,053
Ottumwa	33,871
Pella	5,198
Perry	6,442
Red Oak	6,421
Shenandoah	6,567
Sioux City	89,159
Spencer	8,864
Storm Lake	7,728
Urbandale	5,821
Washington	6,037
Waterloo	71,755
Waverly	6,357
Webster City	8,520
West Des Moines	11,949
Windsor Heights	5,906

KANSAS

2,178,611

Abilene	6,746
Arkansas City	14,262
Atchison	12,529
Augusta	6,434
Chanute	10,849
Coffeyville	17,382
Concordia	7,022
Derby	6,458
Dodge City	13,520
El Dorado	12,523
Emporia	18,190
Fairway	5,398
Fort Scott	9,410
Garden City	11,811
Great Bend	16,670
Hays	11,947
Haysville	5,836
Hutchinson	37,574
Independence	11,222
Iola	6,885
Junction City	18,700
Kansas City	121,901
Larned	5,001
Lawrence	32,858
Leavenworth	22,052
Leawood	7,466
Liberal	13,813
McPherson	9,996
Manhattan	22,993
Merriam	5,084
Newton	14,877
Olathe	10,987
Ottawa	10,673
Overland Park	21,110
Parsons	13,929
Pittsburg	18,678
Prairie Village	25,356
Pratt	8,156
Roeland Park	8,949
Russell	6,113
Salina	43,202
Shawnee	9,072
Topeka	119,484
Wellington	8,809
Wichita	254,698
Winfield	11,117

KENTUCKY

3,038,156

Ashland	31,283
Bellevue	9,336
Bowling Green	28,338
Campbellsville	6,966
Corbin	7,119
Covington	60,376
Cynthiana	5,641
Danville	9,010
Dayton	9,050
Elizabethtown	9,641
Erlanger	7,072
Florence	5,837
Fort Thomas	14,896
Frankfort	18,365
Franklin	5,319
Georgetown	6,986
Glasgow	10,069
Harrodsburg	6,061
Hazard	5,958
Henderson	16,892
Hopkinsville	19,465
Lexington	62,810
Louisville	390,639
Ludlow	6,233
Madisonville	13,110
Mayfield	10,762
Maysville	8,484
Middlesborough	12,607
Mount Sterling	5,370
Murray	9,303
Newport	30,070
Owensboro	42,471
Paducah	34,479
Paris	7,791
Pleasure Ridge Park	10,612
Princeton	5,618
Richmond	12,168
Russellville	5,861
St. Matthews	8,738
Shively	15,155
Somerset	7,112
Valley Station	10,553
Versailles	4,060
Winchester	10,187

LOUISIANA

3,257,022

Abbeville	10,414
Alexandria	40,279
Bastrop	15,193
Baton Rouge	152,419
Bogalusa	21,423
Bossier City	32,776
Bunkie	5,188
Covington	6,754
Crowley	15,617
Denham Spgs.	5,991
De Ridder	7,188
Donaldsonville	6,082
Eunice	11,326
Franklin	8,673
Goosport	16,778
Gretna	21,967
Hammond	10,563
Harahan	9,275
Houma	22,561
Jefferson Hts.	19,353
Jennings	11,887
Kenner	17,037
Lafayette	40,400
Lafayette Southwest	6,682
Lake Charles	63,392
Mansfield	5,839
Minden	12,785
Monroe	52,219
Morgan City	13,540

LOUISIANA—Continued

Natchitoches	13,924
New Iberia	29,062
New Orleans	627,525
North Shreveport	7,701
Oakdale	6,618
Opelousas	17,417
Pineville	8,636
Plaquemine	7,689
Port Allen	5,026
Rayne	8,634
Ruston	13,991
St. Martinville	6,468
Shreveport	164,372
Slidell	6,356
Springhill	6,437
Sulphur	11,429
Tallulah	9,413
Thibodaux	13,403
Ville Platte	7,512
West Monroe	15,215
Westwego	9,815
Winnfield	7,022

MAINE

969,265

Auburn City	24,449
Augusta City	21,680
Bangor City	38,912
Bath City	10,717
Biddeford City	19,255
Brewer City	9,009
Brunswick	15,797
Caribou	12,464
Gardiner City	6,897
Houlton	8,289
Kittery	10,689
Lewiston City	40,804
Limestone	13,102
Millinocket	7,453
Old Town City	8,626
Orono	8,341
Portland City	72,566
Presque Isle City	12,886
Rockland City	8,769
Rumford	10,005
Saco City	10,515
Sanford	14,962
Scarborough	6,418
Skowhegan	7,661
South Portland City	22,788
Waterville City	18,695
Westbrook City	13,820

MARYLAND

3,100,689

Aberdeen	9,679
Arbutus-Halethorpe-Relay	22,402
Annapolis	23,385
Baltimore	939,024
Bethesda	56,527
Cambridge	12,239
Catonsville	37,372
Cheverly	5,223
College Park	18,482
Cumberland	33,415
District Hgts.	7,524
Dundark	82,428
Easton	6,337
Essex	35,205
Frederick	21,744
Frostburg	6,722
Greenbelt	7,479
Hagerstown	36,660
Havre de Grace	8,510
Hillcrest Hgts.	15,295
Hyattsville	15,168
Langley Pk.	11,510
Lansdowne-Baltimore-Highlands	13,134
Laurel	8,503
Lexington Pk.	7,039
Lock Haven	23,278
Middle River	10,825
Mt. Rainier	9,855
Overlea	10,795
Parkville-Carney	27,236
Pikeville	18,737
Rockville	26,090
Salisbury	16,302
Silver Spring	66,348
Sparrows Point-Ft. Howard-Edgemere	11,775
Stoneleigh-Rodgers Fge.	15,645
Suitland-Silver Hills	10,300
Takoma Park	16,799
Towson	19,090
Westminister	6,123
Wheaton	54,635
Woodlawn-Rockdale-Millford Mills	19,254

MASSACHUSETTS

5,148,578

Abington	10,607
Agawam	15,718
Andover	15,878
Arlington	49,953
Attleboro City	27,118
Auburn	14,047
Ayer	14,927
Barnstable	13,465
Bedford	10,969
Belmont	28,715
Beverly City	36,108
Billerica	17,867
Boston City	697,197
Braintree	31,069
Bridgewater	10,276
Brockton City	72,813
Brookline	54,044
Burlington	12,852
Cambridge City	107,716
Chelmsford	15,130

MASSACHUSETTS—Continued

Chelsea City	33,749
Chicopee City	61,553
Clinton	12,848
Concord	12,517
Danvers	21,926
Dartmouth	14,607
Dedham	23,869
Dracut	13,674
Everett City	43,544
Fairhaven	14,339
Fall River City	99,942
Falmouth	13,037
Fitchburg City	43,021
Foxborough	10,136
Framingham	44,526
Gardner	19,038
Gloucester City	25,789
Greenfield	17,690
Haverhill City	46,346
Hingham	15,378
Holyoke City	52,689
Lawrence City	70,933
Leominster	27,929
Lexington	27,691
Lowell City	92,107
Ludlow	13,805
Lynn City	94,478
Malden City	57,676
Marblehead	18,521
Medford City	64,971
Melrose City	29,619
Methuen	28,114
Milton	26,375
Natick	28,831
Needham	25,793
New Bedford City	102,477
Newburyport City	14,004
Newton City	92,384
North Adams City	19,905
Northampton City	30,058
No. Attleborough	14,777
Norwood	24,898
Peabody City	32,202
Pittsfield City	57,879
Plymouth	14,445
Quincy City	87,409
Randolph	18,900
Reading	19,259
Revere City	40,080
Salem City	39,211
Saugus	20,666
Shrewsbury	16,622
Somerville City	94,697
Southbridge	16,523
Springfield City	174,463
Stoneham	17,821
Stoughton	16,328
Taunton City	41,132
Tewksbury	15,902
Walpole	14,068
Waltham City	55,413
Watertown	39,092
Wellesley	26,071
Westfield City	26,302
West Springfield	24,924
Weymouth	48,177
Winchester	19,376
Winthrop	20,303
Woburn City	31,214
Worcester City	186,587

MICHIGAN

7,823,194

Adrian	20,347
Allen Park	37,052
Alpena	14,682
Ann Arbor	67,340
Battle Creek	44,169
Bay City	53,604
Benton Harbor	19,136
Berkley	23,275
Birmingham	25,525
Cadillac	10,112
Center Line	10,164
Clawson	14,795
Dearborn	112,007
Detroit	1,670,144
East Detroit	45,756
East Lansing	30,198
Eastlawn	17,652
Ecorse	17,328
Escanaba	15,391
Ferndale	31,347
Flint	196,940
Garden City	38,017
Grand Rapids	177,313
Grosse Pointe Farms	12,172
Grosse Pointe Park	15,457
Grosse Pointe Woods	18,580
Hamtramck	34,137
Harper Woods	19,995
Hazel Park	25,631
Highland Pk.	38,063
Holland	24,777
Inkster	39,097
Ironwood	10,265
Jackson	50,720
Kalamazoo	82,089
Lakeview	10,384
Lansing	107,807
Lincoln Park	53,933
Livonia	66,702
Madison Hts.	33,343
Marquette	19,824
Melvindale	13,089
Menominee	11,289
Midland	27,779
Monroe	22,968
Mount Clemens	21,016
Mount Pleasant	14,875
Muskegon	46,485
Muskegon Hts.	19,552
Niles	13,842
Oak Park	36,632
Owosso	17,006
Pontiac	82,233
Port Huron	36,084

MICHIGAN—Continued

River Rouge	18,147
Roseville	50,195
Royal Oak	80,612
Saginaw	98,265
St. Clair Shores	76,657
St. Joseph	11,755
Sault Ste. Marie	18,722
Southfield	31,501
Southgate	29,404
Traverse City	18,432
Trenton	18,439
Troy	19,058
Warren	89,246
Wayne	16,034
Wyandotte	43,519
Wyoming	45,829
Ypsilanti	20,957

MINNESOTA

3,413,864

Albert Lea	17,108
Anoka	10,562
Austin	27,908
Bemidji	9,958
Blaine	7,570
Bloomington	50,498
Brainerd	12,898
Brooklyn Center	24,356
Brooklyn Park	10,197
Chisholm	7,144
Cloquet	9,013
Columbia Hts.	17,533
Coon Rapids	14,931
Crookston	8,546
Crystal	24,283
Duluth	106,884
Edina	28,501
Fairmont	9,745
Faribault	16,926
Fergus Falls	13,733
Fridley	15,173
Golden Valley	14,559
Hastings	8,965
Hibbing	17,731
Hopkins	11,370
Little Falls	7,551
Mankato	23,797
Maplewood	18,519
Minneapolis	482,872
Minnetonka	25,037
Moorhead	22,934
New Ulm	11,114
Northfield	8,707
North St. Paul	8,520
Owatonna	13,409
Plymouth	9,576
Red Wing	10,528
Richfield	42,523
Robbinsdale	16,381
Rochester	40,663
Roseville	23,997
St. Cloud	33,815
St. Louis Park	43,310
St. Paul	313,411
St. Peter	8,484
Shoreview	7,157
So. St. Paul	22,032
Stillwater	8,310
Thief River Falls	7,151
Virginia	14,034
West St. Paul	13,101
White Bear Lake	12,849
Willmar	10,417
Winona	24,895
Worthington	9,015

MISSISSIPPI

2,178,141

Biloxi	44,053
Brookhaven	9,885
Canton	9,707
Clarksdale	21,105
Cleveland	10,172
Columbia	7,117
Columbus	24,771
Corinth	11,453
Greenville	41,502
Greenwood	20,436
Grenada	7,914
Gulfport	30,204
Hattiesburg	34,989
Jackson	144,422
Laurel	27,889
McComb	12,020
Meridian	49,374
Natchez	23,791
Pascagoula	17,139
Picayune	7,834
Starkville	9,041
Tupelo	17,221
Vicksburg	29,130
West Point	8,550
Yazoo City	11,236

MISSOURI

4,319,813

Bellefontaine Neighbors	13,650
Berkeley	18,676
Brentwood	12,250
Cape Girardeau	24,947
Carthage	11,264
Caruthersville	8,643
Chillicothe	9,236
Clayton	15,245
Columbia	36,650
Crestwood	11,106
Ferguson	22,149
Florissant	38,166
Fulton	11,131
Gladstone	14,502
Hannibal	20,028
Independence	62,328
Jefferson City	28,228

MISSOURI—Continued

Jennings	19,965
Joplin	38,958
Kansas City	475,539
Kennett	9,098
Kirksville	13,123
Kirkwood	29,421
Ladue	9,466
Lebanon	8,220
Lees Summit	8,267
Liberty	8,909
Maplewood	12,552
Marshall	9,572
Mexico	12,889
Moberly	13,170
Nevada	8,416
Olivette	8,257
Overland	22,763
Poplar Bluff	15,926
Raytown	17,083
Richmond Hts.	15,622
Rolla	11,132
St. Ann	12,155
St. Charles	21,189
St. Joseph	79,673
St. Louis	750,026
Sedalia	23,874
Sikeston	13,765
Springfield	95,865
University City	51,249
Warrensburg	9,689
Webster Groves	28,990

MONTANA
674,767

Anaconda	12,054
Billings	52,851
Bozeman	13,361
Butte	27,877
Glasgow	6,398
Glendive	7,058
Great Falls	55,357
Havre	10,740
Helena	20,227
Kalispell	10,151
Lewistown	7,408
Livingston	8,229
Miles City	9,665
Missoula	27,090

NEBRASKA
1,411,330

Alliance	7,845
Beatrice	12,132
Bellevue	8,831
Columbus	12,476
Fremont	19,698
Grand Island	25,742
Hastings	21,412
Kearney	14,210
Lincoln	128,521
McCook	8,301
Nebraska City	7,252
Norfolk	13,111
North Platte	17,184
Omaha	301,598
Plattsmouth	6,244
Scottsbluff	13,377
Sidney	8,004
South Sioux City	7,200
York	6,173

NEVADA
285,278

Boulder City	4,059
Carson City	5,163
Elko	6,298
Ely	4,018
Henderson	12,525
Las Vegas	64,405
North Las Vegas	18,422
Reno	51,470
Sparks	16,618
Winnemucca	3,453

NEW HAMPSHIRE
606,921

Berlin City	17,821
Claremont City	13,563
Concord City	28,991
Derry	6,987
Dover City	19,131
Durham	5,504
Exeter	7,243
Franklin City	6,742
Goffstown	7,230
Hampton	5,379
Hanover	7,329
Hudson	5,876
Keene City	17,562
Laconia City	15,288
Lebanon City	9,299
Littleton	5,003
Manchester City	88,282
Nashua City	39,096
Newport	5,458
Portsmouth City	25,833
Rochester City	15,927
Salem	9,210
Somersworth City	8,529

NEW JERSEY
6,066,782

Asbury Park	17,366
Atlantic City	59,544
Bayonne	74,215
Belleville	35,005
Bergenfield	27,203
Bloomfield	51,867
Bridgeton	20,366
Camden	117,159
Carteret	20,502
Clark	12,195
Cliffside Park	17,642
Clifton	82,084

NEW JERSEY—Continued

Collingswood	17,370
Cranford	26,424
Delaware	31,522
Dover	13,034
Dumont	18,882
East Orange	77,259
East Paterson	19,344
Edison	44,799
Elizabeth	107,698
Englewood	26,057
Ewing	26,628
Fair Lawn	36,421
Fort Lee	21,815
Garfield	29,253
Gloucester City	15,511
Hackensack	30,521
Haddon	17,099
Hamilton	65,035
Hasbrouck Heights	13,046
Hawthorne	17,735
Hillside	22,304
Hoboken	48,441
Irvington	59,739
Jersey City	276,101
Kearny	37,472
Linden	39,931
Livingston	23,124
Lodi	23,502
Long Branch	26,228
Lyndhurst	21,867
Maplewood	23,977
Maywood	11,460
Metuchen	14,041
Middletown	39,675
Millburn	18,799
Millville	19,096
Montclair	43,129
Morristown	17,712
Mt. Holly	13,271
Neptune	21,487
Newark	405,220
New Brunswick	40,139
New Hanover	28,528
New Milford	18,810
No. Arlington	17,477
No. Bergen	42,387
No. Plainfield	16,993
Nutley	29,513
Orange	35,789
Palisades Park	11,943
Paramus	22,238
Parsippany-Troy Hills	25,557
Passaic	53,963
Paterson	143,663
Paulsboro	8,121
Pennsauken	33,771
Perth Amboy	38,007
Phillipsburg	18,502
Plainfield	45,330
Pleasantville	15,172
Princeton	11,890
Rahway	27,699
Red Bank	12,482
Ridgefield	10,788
Ridgefield Park	12,701
Ridgewood	25,391
River Edge	13,264
Roselle	21,032
Roselle Park	12,546
Rutherford	20,473
Saddle Brook	13,834
Sayreville	22,553
Scotch Plains	18,491
South Orange	16,175
So. Plainfield	17,879
South River	13,397
Springfield	14,467
Summit	23,677
Teaneck	42,085
Tenafly	14,264
Trenton	114,167
Union	51,499
Union City	52,180
Verona	13,752
Vineland	37,685
Wayne	29,353
Weehawken	13,504
Westfield	31,447
West New York	35,547
West Orange	39,895
Woodbridge	78,846
Woodbury	12,455
Wyckoff	11,205

NEW MEXICO
951,023

Alamogordo	21,723
Albuquerque	201,189
Artesia	12,000
Aztec	4,137
Belen	5,031
Bernalillo	2,574
Carlsbad	25,541
Clayton	3,314
Clovis	23,713
Deming	6,764
Eunice	3,531
Farmington	23,786
Gallup	14,089
Grants	10,274
Hobbs	26,275
Jal	3,051
Las Cruces	29,367
Las Vegas (city)	7,790
Las Vegas (town)	6,028
Lordsburg	3,436
Los Alamos	12,584
Lovington	9,660
Milan	2,658
Portales	9,695
Raton	8,146
Roswell	39,593
Sante Fe	34,676
Silver City	6,972
Socorro	5,271
State College-Mesilla Park	4,387
Truth or Consequences	4,269

NEW MEXICO—Continued

NEW YORK
16,782,304

Tucumcari	8,143
Tularosa	3,200
Zuni Pueblo	3,585
Albany	129,726
Amityville	8,318
Amsterdam	28,772
Arlington	8,317
Auburn	35,249
Babylon	11,062
Baldwin	30,204
Batavia	18,210
Beacon	13,922
Bellmore	12,784
Bethpage-Old Bethpage	20,515
Binghamton	75,941
Brentwood	15,387
Buffalo	532,759
Canandaigua	9,370
Cheektowaga-Northwest	52,362
Cheektowaga-Southwest	12,766
Cohoes	20,129
Commack	9,613
Copiague	14,081
Corning	17,085
Cortland	19,181
Deer Park	16,726
Depew	13,580
Dobbs Ferry	9,260
Dunkirk	18,205
East Massapequa	14,779
East Meadow	46,036
East Rockaway	10,721
Eggertsville	44,807
Elmira	46,517
Elmont	30,138
Endicott	18,775
Floral Park	17,499
Freeport	34,419
Fulton	14,261
Garden City	23,948
Garden City Pk-Herricks	15,364
Geneva	17,286
Glen Cove	23,817
Glens Falls	18,580
Gloversville	21,741
Great Neck	10,171
Hamburg-Lake Shore	11,527
Hempstead	34,641
Hicksville	50,405
Hornell	13,907
Hudson	11,075
Huntington	11,255
Huntington Station	23,438
Ilion	10,199
Inwood	10,362
Ithaca	28,799
Jamestown	41,818
Jericho	10,795
Johnson City	19,118
Johnstown	10,390
Kenmore	21,261
Kingston	29,260
Lackawanna	29,564
Lancaster	12,254
Levittown	65,276
Lindenhurst	20,905
Lockport	26,443
Locust Grove	11,558
Long Beach	26,473
Lynbrook	19,881
Malverne	9,968
Mamaroneck	17,673
Massapequa	32,900
Massapequa Park	19,904
Massena	15,478
Merrick	18,789
Middletown	23,475
Mineola	20,519
Mt. Vernon	76,010
Newark	12,868
Newburgh	30,979
New Hyde Pk	10,808
New Rochelle	76,812
New York	7,781,984
Niagara Falls	102,394
North Bellmore	19,639
North Merrick	12,976
North New Hyde Park	17,929
North Tonawanda	34,757
North Valley Stream	17,239
Oceanside	30,448
Ogdensburg	16,122
Olean	21,868
Oneida	11,677
Oneonta	13,412
Ossining	18,662
Oswego	22,155
Peekskill	18,737
Plainedge	21,973
Plainview	27,710
Plattsburgh	20,172
Port Chester	24,960
Port Jervis	9,268
Port Washington	15,657
Potsdam	7,765
Poughkeepsie	38,330
Rensselaer	10,506
Rochester	318,611
Rockville Centre	26,355
Rome	51,646
Roosevelt	12,883
Rotterdam	16,871
Rye	14,225
San Remo	11,996
Saratoga Springs	16,630
Scarsdale	17,968
Schenectady	81,682
Seaford	14,718
Solvay	8,732
South Farmingdale	16,318
South Westbury	11,977

NEW YORK—Continued

Syracuse	216,038
Tarrytown	11,109
Tonawanda	21,561
Tonawanda (uninc.)	83,771
Troy	67,492
Uniondale	20,041
Utica	100,410
Valley Stream	38,629
Wantagh	34,172
Watertown	33,306
Watervliet	13,917
Westbury	14,757
West Hempstead-Lakeview	24,783
West Seneca	23,138
White Plains	50,485
Woodmere	14,011
Yonkers	190,634

NORTH CAROLINA
4,556,155

Albemarle	12,261
Asheboro	9,449
Asheville	60,192
Burlington	33,199
Chapel Hill	12,573
Charlotte	201,564
Clinton	7,461
Concord	17,799
Dunn	7,566
Durham	78,302
Elizabeth City	14,062
Fayetteville	47,106
Gastonia	37,276
Goldsboro	28,873
Greensboro	119,574
Greenville	22,860
Henderson	12,740
Hickory	19,328
High Point	62,063
Jacksonville	13,491
Kannapolis	34,647
Kings Mountain	8,008
Kinston	24,819
Laurinburg	8,242
Lenoir	10,257
Lexington	16,093
Lumberton	15,305
Monroe	10,882
Morganton	9,186
Mount Airy	7,055
New Bern	15,717
North Belmont	8,328
Raleigh	93,931
Reidsville	14,267
Roanoke Rapids	13,320
Rocky Mount	32,147
Salisbury	21,297
Sanford	12,253
Shelby	17,698
Statesville	19,844
Tarboro	8,411
Thomasville	15,190
Washington	9,939
Wilmington	44,013
Wilson	28,753
Winston-Salem	111,135

NORTH DAKOTA
632,446

Bismarck	27,670
Devils Lake	6,299
Dickinson	9,971
Fargo	46,662
Grafton	5,885
Grand Forks	34,451
Jamestown	15,163
Mandan	10,525
Minot	30,604
Valley	7,809
Wahpeton	5,876
Williston	11,866

OHIO
9,706,397

Akron	290,351
Alliance	28,362
Ashland	17,419
Ashtabula	24,559
Athens	16,470
Barberton	33,805
Bay	14,489
Bedford	15,223
Bellaire	11,502
Bellefontaine	11,424
Berea	16,592
Bexley	14,319
Bowling Green	13,574
Brooklyn	10,733
Brook Park	12,856
Bucyrus	12,276
Cambridge	14,562
Campbell	13,406
Canton	113,631
Cheviot	10,701
Chillicothe	24,957
Cincinnati	502,550
Circleville	11,059
Cleveland	876,050
Cleveland Heights	61,813
Columbus	471,316
Conneaut	10,557
Coshocton	13,106
Cuyahoga Falls	47,922
Dayton	262,332
Defiance	14,553
Delaware	13,282
Dover	11,300
East Cleveland	37,991
Eastlake	12,467
East Liverpool	22,306
Elyria	43,782
Euclid	62,998
Fairborn	19,453
Fairview Park	14,624

OHIO—Continued

Findlay	30,344
Fostoria	15,732
Fremont	17,573
Galion	12,650
Garfield Hgts.	38,455
Girard	12,997
Hamilton	72,354
Ironton	15,745
Kent	17,836
Kettering	54,462
Lakewood	66,154
Lancaster	29,916
Lima	51,037
Lorain	66,932
Lyndhurst	16,805
Mansfield	47,325
Maple Heights	31,667
Marietta	16,847
Marion	37,079
Martins Ferry	11,919
Massillon	31,236
Mayfield Hgts.	13,478
Middletown	42,115
Mt. Vernon	13,284
Newark	41,790
New Philadelphia	14,241
Niles	19,545
No. Olmstead	16,290
Norwalk	12,900
Norwood	34,580
Oakwood City	10,493
Oregon	13,319
Painesville	16,116
Parma	82,845
Parma Hgts.	18,100
Piqua	19,219
Portsmouth	33,637
Ravenna	10,918
Reading	12,832
Rocky River	18,097
Salem	13,854
Sandusky	31,989
Shaker Hgts.	36,460
Sidney	14,663
South Euclid	27,569
Springfield	82,723
Steubenville	32,495
Stow	12,194
Struthers	15,631
Tiffin	21,478
Toledo	318,003
Troy	13,685
Upper Arlington	28,486
Urbana	10,461
Wadsworth	10,635
Warren	59,648
Warrensville Heights	10,609
Washington	12,388
Westlake	12,906
Whitehall	20,818
Wickliffe	15,760
Willoughby	15,058
Willowick	18,749
Wooster	17,046
Xenia	20,445
Youngstown	166,689
Zanesville	39,077

OKLAHOMA
2,328,284

Ada	14,347
Altus	21,225
Ardmore	20,184
Bartlesville	27,893
Bethany	12,342
Blackwell	9,588
Chickasha	14,866
Clinton	9,617
Cushing	8,619
Del City	12,934
Duncan	20,009
Durant	10,467
Edmond	8,577
Elk City	8,196
El Reno	11,015
Enid	38,859
Guthrie	9,502
Lawton	61,697
McAlester	17,419
Miami	12,869
Midwest City	36,058
Muskogee	38,059
Norman	33,412
Oklahoma City	324,253
Okmulgee	15,951
Ponca City	24,411
Sand Springs	7,754
Sapulpa	14,282
Seminole	11,464
Shawnee	24,326
Stillwater	23,965
The Village	12,118
Tulsa	261,685
Warr Acres	7,135
Woodward	7,747

OREGON
1,768,687

Albany	12,926
Altamont	10,811
Ashland	9,119
Astoria	11,239
Baker	9,986
Bend	11,936
Corvallis	20,669
Dalles City	10,493
Eugene	50,977
Grants Pass	10,118
Klamath Falls	16,949
La Grande	9,014
Medford	24,425
Milwaukie	9,099
Pendleton	14,434
Portland	372,676
Roseburg	11,467
Salem	49,142
Salem Hgts.	10,770
Springfield	19,616

PENNSYLVANIA
11,319,366

Abington	55,831
Aliquippa	26,369
Allentown	108,347
Altoona	69,407
Ambridge	13,865
Aston	10,595
Baldwin	24,489
Beaver Falls	16,240
Bellevue	11,412
Berwick	13,353
Bethel	23,650
Bethlehem	75,408
Bloomsburg	10,655
Braddock	12,337
Bradford	15,061
Brentwood	13,706
Bristol	12,364
Bristol (uninc.)	59,298
Butler	20,975
Canonsburg	11,877
Carbondale	13,595
Carlisle	16,623
Carnegie	11,887
Castle Shannon	11,836
Chambersburg	17,670
Cheltenham	35,990
Chester	63,658
Clairton	18,389
Coatesville	12,971
Collingdale	10,268
Columbia	12,075
Connellsville	12,814
Conshohocken	10,259
Darby (borough)	14,059
Darby (township)	12,598
Donora	11,131
Dormont	13,098
Du Bois	10,667
Dunmore	18,917
Duquesne	15,019
Easton	31,955
Ellwood City	12,413
Emmaus	10,262
Erie	138,440
Falls	29,082
Farrell	13,793
Greensburg	17,383
Hanover	15,538
Harrisburg	79,697
Harrison	15,710
Haverford	54,019
Hazleton	32,056
Hempfield	29,704
Indiana	13,005
Jeannette	16,565
Johnstown	53,949
Kingston	20,261
Lancaster	61,055
Lancaster (uninc.)	10,020
Lansdale	12,612
Lansdowne	12,601
Latrobe	11,932
Lebanon	30,045
Lewistown	12,640
Lock Haven	11,748
Lower Burrell	11,952
Lower Merion	59,420
Lower Southampton	12,619
McKeesport	45,489
McKees Rocks	13,185
Marple	19,722
Meadville	16,671
Middletown	11,182
Middletown (uninc.)	26,894
Millcreek	28,441
Monessen	18,424
Monroeville	22,446
Mount Carmel	10,760
Mount Lebanon	35,361
Munhall	17,312
Nanticoke	15,601
Nether Providence	10,380
New Castle	44,790
New Kensington	23,485
Norristown	38,925
Northampton	8,866
North Braddock	13,204
North Versailles	13,583
Oil City	17,692
Penn Hills	51,512
Philadelphia	2,002,512
Phoenixville	13,797
Pittsburgh	604,332
Pittston	12,407
Plum	10,241
Plymouth	10,401
Pottstown	26,144
Pottsville	21,659
Radnor	21,697
Reading	98,177
Ridley	35,738
Ross	25,952
Scott	19,094
Scranton	111,443
Shaler	24,939
Shamokin	13,674
Sharon	25,267
Shenandoah	11,073
Springfield (Del. County)	26,733

PENNSYLVANIA—Continued

Springfield (Erie County)	20,652
Spring Garden	11,387
State College	22,409
Steelton	11,266
Stowe	11,730
Sunbury	13,687
Swissvale	15,089
Tamaqua	10,173
Turtle Creek	10,607
Uniontown	17,942
Upper Darby	93,158
Upper Moreland	21,032
Warminster	15,994
Warren	14,505
Washington	23,545
Waynesboro	10,427
West Chester	15,705
West Mifflin	27,289
Whitehall	16,075
Wilkes-Barre	63,551
Wilkinsburg	30,066
Williamsport	41,967
York	54,504

RHODE ISLAND
859,488

Barrington	13,826
Bristol	14,570
Central Falls City	19,858
Coventry	15,432
Cranston City	66,766
Cumberland	18,792
East Providence City	41,955
Johnston	17,160
Lincoln	13,551
Middletown	12,675
Newport City	47,049
North Kingstown	18,977
North Providence	18,220
Pawtucket City	81,001
Providence City	207,498
So. Kingstown	11,942
Warwick City	68,504
Westerly	14,267
West Warwick	21,414
Woonsocket City	47,080

SOUTH CAROLINA
2,382,594

Aiken	11,243
Anderson	41,316
Cayce	8,517
Charleston	65,925
Clinton	7,937
Columbia	97,433
Conway	8,563
Easley	8,283
Florence	24,722
Gaffney	10,435
Georgetown	12,261
Greenville	66,188
Greenwood	16,644
Greer	8,967
Lancaster	7,999
Laurens	9,598
Marion	7,174
Myrtle Beach	7,834
Newberry	8,208
No. Augusta	10,348
Orangeburg	13,852
Rock Hill	29,404
Shannontown	7,064
Spartanburg	44,352
Sumter	23,062
Union	10,191

SOUTH DAKOTA
680,514

Aberdeen	23,073
Brookings	10,558
Huron	14,180
Lead	6,211
Madison	5,420
Mitchell	12,555
Pierre	10,088
Rapid City	42,399
Sioux Falls	65,466
Vermillion	6,102
Watertown	14,077
Yankton	9,279

TENNESSEE
3,567,089

Athens	12,103
Bristol	17,582
Chattanooga	130,009
Clarksville	22,021
Cleveland	16,196
Columbia	17,624
Cookeville	7,805
Donelson	17,195
Dyersburg	12,499
East Ridge	19,570
Elizabethton	10,896
Fountain City	10,365
Gallatin	7,901
Greeneville	11,759
Humboldt	8,482
Inglewood	26,527

TENNESSEE—Continued

Jackson	33,849
Johnson City	29,892
Kingsport	26,314
Knoxville	111,827
Lawrenceburg	8,042
Lebanon	10,512
McMinnville	9,013
Madison	13,583
Maryville	10,348
Memphis	497,524
Morristown	21,267
Murfreesboro	18,991
Nashville	170,874
Oak Ridge	27,169
Paris	9,325
Red Bank-White Oak	10,777
Shelbyville	10,466
Springfield	9,221
Tullahoma	12,242
Union City	8,837
Whitehaven	13,894
Woodbine-Radnor-Glencliff	14,485
Woodmont-Green Hills Glendale	23,161

TEXAS
9,579,677

Abilene	90,368
Alice	20,861
Amarillo	137,969
Arlington	44,775
Austin	186,545
Baytown	28,159
Beaumont	119,175
Bellaire	19,872
Big Spring	31,230
Borger	20,911
Brownsville	48,040
Brownwood	16,974
Bryan	27,542
Cleburne	15,381
Corpus Christi	167,690
Corsicana	20,344
Dallas	679,684
Del Rio	18,612
Denison	22,748
Denton	26,844
Edinburg	18,706
El Paso	276,687
Fort Worth	356,268
Gainesville	13,083
Galveston	67,175
Garland	38,501
Grand Prairie	30,386
Greenville	19,087
Groves	17,304
Halton City	23,133
Harlingen	41,207
Highland Park	10,411
Houston	938,219
Hurst	10,165
Irving	45,985
Killeen	23,377
Kingsville	25,297
Lamarque	13,969
Lamesa	12,438
Laredo	60,678
Longview	40,050
Lubbock	128,691
Lufkin	17,641
McAllen	32,728
McKinney	13,763
Marshall	23,846
Mercedes	10,943
Mesquite	27,526
Midland	62,625
Mineral Wells	11,053
Mission	14,081
Nacogdoches	12,674
Nederland	12,036
New Braunfels	15,631
Odessa	80,338
Orange	25,605
Palestine	13,974
Pampa	24,664
Paris	20,977
Pasadena	58,737
Pecos	12,728
Pharr	14,106
Plainview	18,735
Port Arthur	66,676
Richardson	16,810
San Angelo	58,815
San Antonio	587,718
San Benito	16,422
San Marcos	12,713
Seguin	14,299
Sherman	24,988
Snyder	13,850
Temple	30,419
Terrell	13,803
Texarkana	30,218
Texas City	32,065
Tyler	51,230
University Park	23,202
Uvalde	10,293
Victoria	33,047
Waco	97,808
Westaco	15,649
West University Place	14,628
Wichita Falls	101,724

UTAH
890,627

Bountiful	17,039
Brigham City	11,728
Cedar City	7,543
Clearfield	8,833
Kearns	17,172
Layton	9,027
Logan	18,731
Murray	16,806
Ogden	70,197
Orem	18,394
Provo	36,047
Roy	9,239
Salt Lake City	189,454
South Ogden	7,405
South Salt Lake	9,520
Springville	7,913
Tooele	9,133

VERMONT
389,881

Barre City	10,387
Bennington	13,002
Brattleboro	11,734
Burlington City	35,531
Essex	7,090
Hartford	6,355
Middlebury	5,305
Montpelier City	8,782
Newport City	5,019
Rockingham	5,704
Rutland City	18,325
St. Albans City	8,806
St. Johnsbury	8,869
South Burlington	6,903
Springfield	9,934
Winooski City	7,420

VIRGINIA
3,966,949

Alexandria	91,023
Arlington Co. (uninc.)	163,401
Blacksburg	7,070
Bristol	17,144
Charlottesville	29,427
Colonial Hgts.	9,587
Covington	11,062
Danville	46,577
Fairfax	13,585
Falls Church	10,192
Franklin	7,264
Fredericksburg	13,639
Front Royal	7,949
Hampton	89,258
Harrisonburg	11,916
Hopewell	17,895
Lexington	7,537
Lynchburg	54,790
Marion	8,385
Martinsville	18,798
Newport News	113,662
Norfolk	305,872
Petersburg	36,750
Portsmouth	114,773
Pulaski	10,469
Radford	9,371
Richmond	219,958
Roanoke	97,110
Salem	16,058
South Norfolk	22,035
Springfield	10,783
Staunton	22,232
Suffolk	12,609
Vienna	11,440
Virginia Beach	8,091
Waynesboro	15,694
Winchester	15,110

WASHINGTON
2,853,214

Aberdeen	18,741
Anacortes	8,414
Auburn	11,933
Bellevue	12,809
Bellingham	34,688
Bremerton	28,922
Centralia	8,586
Clarkston	6,209
College Place	4,031
Edmonds	8,016
Ellensburg	8,625
Ephrata	6,548
Everett	40,304
Hoquiam	10,762
Kelso	8,379
Kennewick	14,244
Kent	9,017
Kirkland	6,025
Lacey	6,630
Longview	23,349
Lynnwood	7,207
Moses Lake	11,299
Mountlake Terrace	9,122
Mount Vernon	7,921
Olympia	18,273
Opportunity	12,465
Pasco	14,522
Port Angeles	12,653
Pullman	12,957
Puyallup	12,063
Renton	18,453

WASHINGTON—Continued

Richland	23,548
Seattle	557,087
Spokane	181,608
Sunnyside	6,208
Tacoma	147,979
Vancouver	32,464
Walla Walla	24,536
Wenatchee	16,726
Yakima	43,284

WEST VIRGINIA
1,860,421

Beckley	18,642
Bluefield	19,256
Buckhannon	6,386
Charleston	85,796
Clarksburg	28,112
Dunbar	11,006
Elkins	8,307
Fairmont	27,477
Huntington	83,627
Keyser	6,192
Martinsburg	15,179
Morgantown	22,487
Moundsville	15,163
Nitro	6,894
Parkersburg	44,797
Princeton	8,393
Saint Albans	15,103
South Charleston	19,180
Vienna	9,381
Weirton	28,201
Weston	8,754
Wheeling	53,400
Williamson	6,746

WISCONSIN
3,951,777

Appleton	48,411
Ashland	10,132
Beaver Dam	13,118
Beloit	32,846
Brookfield	19,812
Brown Deer	11,280
Chippewa Falls	11,708
Cudahy	17,975
De Pere	10,045
Eau Claire	37,987
Fond du Lac	32,719
Franklin	10,000
Green Bay	62,888
Greenfield	17,636
Janesville	35,164
Kaukauna	10,096
Kenosha	67,899
La Crosse	47,575
Madison	126,706
Manitowoc	32,275
Marinette	13,329
Marshfield	14,153
Menasha	14,647
Menomonee Falls	18,276
Menomonee	8,624
Milwaukee	741,324
Neenah	18,057
New Berlin	15,788
Oshkosh	45,110
Racine	89,144
Rhinelander	8,790
Rice Lake	7,303
St. Francis	10,065
Sheboygan	45,747
Shorewood	15,990
South Milwaukee	20,307
Stevens Point	17,837
Sturgeon Bay	7,353
Superior	33,563
Two Rivers	12,393
Watertown	13,943
Waukesha	30,004
Waupun	7,935
Wausau	31,943
Wauwatosa	56,923
West Allis	68,157
West Bend	9,969
Whitefish Bay	18,390
Whitewater	6,380
Wisconsin Rapids	15,042

WYOMING
330,066

Casper	38,930
Cheyenne	43,505
Cody	4,838
Evanston	4,901
Gillette	3,580
Green River	3,497
Lander	4,182
Laramie	17,520
Newcastle	4,345
Powell	4,740
Rawlins	8,968
Riverton	6,845
Rock Springs	10,371
Sheridan	11,651
Thermopolis	3,955
Torrington	4,188
Worland	5,806

Trend of U. S. Population

Following is a projection of the population of the fifty states in 1975 and 1980. It is based on the assumption that the fertility rate of 179 births a year for each 1,000 women capable of bearing children will continue, as it has for the last five years.

Population, Total and Under 20

	1960	1975	1980
All ages	180,677,000	235,275,000	259,584,000
Under 5 years	20,318,000	28,735,000	32,505,000
5 to 9 years	18,789,000	25,172,000	28,762,000
10 to 14 years	16,985,000	22,271,000	25,223,000
15 to 19 years	13,424,000	20,443,000	22,312,000

Male Population, Total and Under 20

	1960	1975	1980
All ages	89,323,000	116,001,000	128,140,000
Under 5 years	10,330,000	14,690,000	16,621,000
5 to 9 years	9,554,000	12,859,000	14,697,000
10 to 14 years	8,632,000	11,368,000	12,879,000
15 to 19 years	6,793,000	10,362,000	11,370,000

Female Population, Total and Under 20

	1960	1975	1980
All ages	91,354,000	119,274,000	131,444,000
Under 5 years	9,988,000	14,045,000	15,884,000
5 to 9 years	9,235,000	12,313,000	14,065,000
10 to 14 years	8,353,000	10,903,000	12,344,000
15 to 19 years	6,631,000	10,081,000	10,942,000

STATES AND THE DISTRICT OF COLUMBIA

ALABAMA

Area: 51,609 square miles (including 758 square miles of water)
Population: (1960 census) 3,266,740; (1967 est.) 3,540,000
Capital: Montgomery
State bird: Yellowhammer
State tree: Southern pine
State flower: Camellia
State motto: Audemus iura nostra defendere (We dare defend our rights)

Alabama, one of the East South Central states, lies between Georgia on the east and Mississippi on the west. To the north is Tennessee, and to the south are the long western arms of upper Florida and the Gulf of Mexico. Alabama is in the heart of the old cotton belt, now an area of mixed farming and manufacturing. Alabama entered the Union as the 22nd state on Dec. 14, 1819.

THE LAND. Alabama can be divided into five major geographic regions. At its northern border is the Interior Low Plateau, a part of the Tennessee River valley. It is an area of prosperous farms, busy river traffic, and hydroelectric power production. To its south lies the Cumberland Plateau, sloping from about 1,800 feet to some 500 feet. It is a mixed farming region.

South and east of the Cumberland Plateau is the Appalachian Ridge and Valley Region. It is rich in coal, iron ore, and limestone, and its cities are iron and steel producing centers. Further south is the Piedmont, a region of low hills and valleys. Forests cover much of the land. The highest point in the state, Cheaha Mountain, 2,407 feet, is located in the northwestern corner of the Piedmont.

The southern two-thirds of Alabama is occupied by the East Gulf Coastal Plain. It reaches from the western part of the Interior Low Plateau to the state's southern border. In the northern part of the coastal Plain are rolling hills covered by pine forests. The Black Belt, a subregion rich in black clay soils, is found in the central part of the East Gulf Coastal Plain. In the southwest is the Mobile River Delta, an area of low, swampy land.

The rivers of Alabama reach almost every part of the state and are used for both transportation and power. The Tennessee River flows from northern Alabama into Tennessee. Along the eastern border is the Chattahoochee. The Tombigbee flows from Mississippi into Alabama and empties into the Mobile River. The Mobile River, in turn, flows into Mobile Bay, where Mobile, the state's only seaport, is located.

Alabama has short, mild winters and long, hot summers. January temperatures average about 52°F in the south and 46°F in the north. July temperatures average about 80°F throughout the state.

THE PEOPLE. Nearly all of Alabama's people were born in the United States. About 30 percent are Negro. More than 55 percent of the people live in urban communities.

About half of Alabama's population lives in the state's six Standard Metropolitan Statistical Areas: Birmingham, Gadsden, Huntsville, Mobile, Montgomery, and Tuscaloosa. Birmingham, one of the nation's leading steel centers, is the state's largest city. Huntsville is an important missile and space-flight center.

ECONOMY. Although Alabama has an abundance of natural resources, the state's 1966 per capita personal income level of $2,039 ranked it 47th among the states. Much of the once-fertile soil has been eroded, although conservation methods are now curbing the loss.

Pine forests cover some two-thirds of Alabama's land. In addition to considerable coal, iron ore, and limestone deposits, there are oil fields in southwestern Alabama.

Agriculture contributes about one-fifth of the value of goods produced. Over half of this is supplied by livestock, dairy products, and poultry. Cotton, once Alabama's leading crop, now accounts for only one-fifth of farm income. Other crops include peanuts, corn, potatoes, and fruit.

Commercial fishing in the Gulf of Mexico yields large catches of shrimps, red snappers, crabs, mullet, and oysters. From the forests come more than 1 billion board feet of lumber annually, as well as pulpwood, rosin, and turpentine.

The chief industry is the manufacture of metals and metal products, which provides about one-quarter of the value of manufactures. Most important is the production of iron and steel. Aluminum is also significant. The state's textile industry is supplied by Alabama-grown cotton.

GOVERNMENT. Alabama's governor is elected to a four-year term and may not succeed himself. The state legislature includes a senate, with 35 members, and a house of representatives, with 106 members. All legislators serve four-year terms.

ALASKA

Area: 586,412 square miles (including 19,980 square miles of water)
Population: (1960 census) 226,167; (1967 est.) 272,000
Capital: Juneau
State bird: Willow ptarmigan
State tree: Sitka spruce
State flower: Forget-me-not

Alaska, one of the Pacific states, occupies the extreme northwestern corner of the North American continent. It is bounded on the south and southwest by the Pacific Ocean, on the west by the Bering Sea, and on the north by the Arctic Ocean. To the east is Canada. Although Alaska is the largest state in the area, it has the smallest population. It entered the Union on Jan. 3, 1959, as the 49th state.

THE LAND. Alaska may be divided into four roughly equal geographic regions. At the north is the Arctic Coastal Plain, which rises from sea level along the Arctic Ocean beaches to about 600 feet at its southern edge. Its permanently frozen subsoil prevents trees from growing. In summer, however, grass and flowers cover the region.

South of the Arctic Coastal Plain lies the Rocky Mountain System. There peaks rise as high as 9,000 feet. Further south lies the Central Uplands and Lowlands. It has low, rolling hills and wide river valleys.

Southern Alaska is occupied by the Pacific Mountain Region. The region consists of a group of ranges that run from the Aleutian Islands east along Alaska's southeastern coast and then south along the Pacific coast to southern California. Mount McKinley, 20,-320 feet, the highest peak in North America, is in the Pacific Mountain Region.

Thousands of lakes dot Alaska's land, and thousands of glaciers fill its valleys and canyons. The 1,875-mile-

PAN AMERICAN AIRWAYS

JUNEAU, THE CAPITAL OF ALASKA, lies on the slopes of Mount Juneau and Mount Roberts.

ARKANSAS PUBLICITY AND PARKS DIVISION
ARKANSAS BAUXITE supplies the U.S. aluminum industry.

SANTA FE RAILWAY
ARIZONA'S PAINTED DESERT, a region in the Colorado Plateau.

long Yukon River crosses Alaska from east to southwest. One of the longest rivers in North America, the Yukon is ice-free from June to October.

THE PEOPLE. Alaska is sparsely populated, with an average of fewer than four people per square mile. More than 60 percent of the population lives in rural communities. About one-third of Alaskans are born in Alaska.

Eskimos live in the north; Indians live in the south; and Aleuts live on the Alaska Peninsula and in the Aleutian Islands. Most other Alaskans live in Anchorage, Fairbanks, and other coastal cities. Many are members of the U.S. armed forces assigned to bases in Alaska.

ECONOMY. The per capita personal income in Alaska is high, and in 1966 Alaska ranked 9th among the states, with $3,272. The U.S. government is important to the economy. Military bases employ thousands of civilian workers in addition to military personnel. Federal scientific, strategic, and commercial projects are also of economic significance.

Alaska's natural resources include rich stores of oil and natural gas. The state has long been a source of gold-bearing ores, and it is also noted for large deposits of iron and tin ores.

Salmon and halibut abound in the coastal waters, as do clams, cod, crabs, herring, and shrimps. Wildlife includes brown, grizzly, and polar bears; caribou, reindeer, deer, elk, and moose; mountain goats and sheep; and seals.

Alaska's manufacturers work largely with the state's own resources. The most important manufacturing industry is fish processing. The forests yield about 350 million board feet of timber a year, most of which is made into pulp. Sand and gravel mined in Alaska are used in highway construction and in the manufacture of cement and concrete blocks.

Alaska has only a few hundred farms. The growing season is short, and much of the land is unsuited to agriculture. In the summer, however, farmers take advantage of 20 hours of daylight each day to grow extraordinarily large vegetables.

GOVERNMENT. Alaska's governor is elected to a four-year term. The state legislature consists of a senate, whose 20 members serve four-year terms, and a house of representatives, whose 40 members serve two-year terms.

ARIZONA

Area: 113,909 square miles (including 346 square miles of water)
Population: (1960 census) 1,302,161; (1967 est.) 1,634,000
Capital: Phoenix
State bird: Cactus wren
State tree: Paloverde
State flower: Saguaro
State motto: Ditat Deus (God enriches)

Arizona, one of the Mountain states, is bordered by Utah on the north, New Mexico on the east, Mexico on the south, and California and Nevada on the west. Arizona entered the Union as the 48th state on Feb. 14, 1912. It became one of the fastest growing states, more than doubling its population in the 20 years following World War II.

THE LAND. Arizona has two major geographic regions: the Colorado Plateau and the Basin and Range Region.

The Colorado Plateau covers most of the northern two-fifths of the state. It is made up of level plateaus broken in a few places by mountains and canyons. Humphreys Peak, 12,633 feet, is the highest point in the state. The Grand Canyon of the Colorado River is one of the world's most spectacular natural features. The scenic Painted Desert and the Petrified Forest are also in the Colorado Plateau region.

The Basin and Range Region covers southern Arizona and extends into the northwest. Mountain ranges cross the region from northwest to southeast. In the far west and south are low mountains separated by wide deserts.

Arizona is drained by the Colorado River, which flows through the state for 688 miles. There are many manmade lakes, formed by streams dammed for conservation and irrigation. Lake Mead, behind Hoover Dam, is partly in Nevada. Lake Powell, formed by the Glen Canyon Dam, is partly in Utah.

The climate of Arizona varies. In the desert region temperatures range from a January average of about 50°F to a July average of about 90°F. In the plateau region temperatures average about 25°F in January and about 65°F in July. Average annual precipitation is about 30 inches, most of it falling in the plateau region. The air is very dry throughout the state.

THE PEOPLE. Most of Arizona's people live in urban areas, and some 70 percent live in two Standard Metropolitan Statistical Areas—Phoenix and Tucson. Nearly all Arizonans were born in the United States. About 7 percent are Indian, and 3 percent are Negro. Many residents are of Mexican descent.

ECONOMY. The federal government plays a vital role in the economy. It owns nearly half of Arizona's land and controls another quarter. Dams constructed or financed by the federal government provide irrigation for farms and hydroelectric power for cities and industries.

Arizona's farms produce large crops of cotton, vegetables, feed grain, and citrus fruits. Cattle and sheep account for about 25 percent of agricultural income.

Metal smelting is one of the leading industries, and Arizona produces more than half of the country's copper. Important manufactures include electronic and electrical machinery, aircraft, and military weapons. Tourism is a major source of income. Per capita personal income in 1966 was $2,528, placing Arizona 32nd among the states.

GOVERNMENT. Arizona's governor is elected to a two-year term and may be reelected an indefinite number of times. The state legislature consists of a 28-member senate and an 80-member house of representatives. Legislators serve two-year terms.

ARKANSAS

Area: 53,104 square miles (including 929 square miles of water)
Population: (1960 census) 1,786,272; (1967 est.) 1,968,000
Capital: Little Rock
State bird: Mockingbird
State tree: Pine
State flower: Apple blossom
State motto: Regnat populus (The people rule)

Arkansas, one of the West South Central states, lies on the west side of the Mississippi Valley. To the north is Missouri. To the east, across the Mississippi River, are Tennessee and Missouri. To the south is Louisiana, and to the west are Oklahoma and the northeastern corner of Texas. Arkansas entered the Union on June 15, 1836, as the 25th state.

THE LAND. Arkansas can be divided into five major geographic areas. In the northwest and north-central part of the state is the Ozark Plateau, a region that reaches across Illinois, Missouri, and Oklahoma. The plateau is marked by forests, hills, and valleys. The wooded hills on its southern edge are called the Boston Mountains.

South of the Ozark Plateau is the Arkansas Valley. Although generally lower than the regions to its north and south, the valley has several mountains. Among them is Magazine Mountain, 2,753 feet, the highest point in the state.

Further south are the Ouachita Mountains, which enter Arkansas from the west. Dams along the Ouachita River form a chain of lakes. The region is known for its hot springs.

The southwestern corner of Arkansas is occupied by the West Gulf Coastal Plain, which extends into Louisiana and Texas. It is a region containing forests, petroleum, and bauxite ore, from which aluminum is made. In the eastern third of the state is the Mississippi Alluvial Plain, which runs along the Mississippi River for the length of the state. It is a level region made fertile by soil deposited by the river.

Arkansas has cool winters and warm summers. July temperatures average about 80°F, and January readings are between 30°F and 40°F. Precipitation averages some 42 inches a year.

THE PEOPLE. Virtually all Arkansans were born in the United States. About 20 percent of the population is Negro. More than half of the state's residents live in urban areas, and about one-fourth live in one of four Standard Metropolitan Statistical Areas—Fort Smith, Little Rock–North Little Rock, Pine Bluff, and Texarkana.

The population of Arkansas fell by seven percent between 1950 and 1960, but it showed a slight increase in the first half of the 1960s.

ECONOMY. The Arkansas economy is divided almost equally between agriculture and industry. Although rich in natural resources, Arkansas in 1966 ranked 49th among the states in per capita personal income, with an average of $2,015.

Natural resources include excellent farm lands along the river valleys; forests, which cover some three-fifths of the land; and extensive petroleum, bauxite, and coal deposits. Arkansas supplies the bulk of the bauxite used in U.S. aluminum production.

Virtually all of the cleared land is covered by farms. Ten percent of the nation's cotton is grown in Arkansas. Other important farm products are soybeans, rice, poultry, and livestock.

Food processing is the leading manufacturing industry, with raw materials supplied by the state's farmers. Lumber and paper are produced from local resources.

GOVERNMENT. The governor of Arkansas is elected to a two-year term. He may succeed himself any number of times. The state legislature, the General Assembly, is divided into a 35-member senate and a 100-member house of representatives. Senators serve four-year terms, and representatives serve two-year terms.

CALIFORNIA

Area: 158,693 square miles (including 2,156 square miles of water)
Population: (1960 census) 15,717,204; (1967 est.) 19,153,000
Capital: Sacramento
State bird: California valley quail
State tree: California redwood
State flower: Golden poppy
State motto: Eureka (I have found it)

California, one of the Pacific states, is bounded on the west by the Pacific Ocean, on the north by Oregon, on the east by Nevada and Arizona, and on the south by Mexico. California was admitted to the Union on Sept. 9, 1850, as the 31st state.

THE LAND. California is about twice as long as it is wide, and has a Pacific coastline of 840 miles. The state can be divided into eight major geographic regions. In the northwestern corner are the Klamath Mountains, which form a region of forested ranges with high peaks, deep canyons, and some broad valleys.

In north-central California are the Cascade Mountains, which were formed by volcanoes. Lassen Peak, in the southern part of the Cascades, is an active volcano. Much of the eastern part of the state is in the Basin and Range Region. In the northern part of this region is a lava plateau. Much of the southern part is taken up by the Mojave and Colorado deserts. Death Valley, 282 feet below sea level, the lowest point in North America, is in the Basin and Range Region.

South of the Klamath Mountains are the Coast Ranges, which extend southward along the coast to the Los Angeles area. The ranges include both the vast redwood forests and the San Andreas Fault, where occasional earthquakes are generated. East of the Coast Ranges is the Central Valley, the richest farm area west of the Rocky Mountains. The Sacramento River is in the north end of the valley, and the San Joaquin River is in the south.

East of the Central Valley looms the Sierra Nevada. Its peaks include Mount Whitney, 14,494 feet, the highest point in the United States south of Alaska.

In the southwestern corner of California are the Los Angeles Ranges and the San Diego Ranges. These groups of low mountains reach south into Lower (Baja) California, a part of Mexico.

California's climate varies greatly. The southern coast is mild; the southeastern deserts are hot. Temperatures in San Francisco only vary from a January average of 50°F to a July average of 59°F. Winters in the Sierra Nevada are extremely cold, with temperatures below 0°F and average yearly snowfall of about 450 inches.

THE PEOPLE. In 1963 California passed New York to become the most populous state. More than 85 percent of the people live in urban communities. Well over half of Californians live in either the Los Angeles–Long Beach or the San Francisco–Oakland Standard Metropolitan Statistical Areas.

LOCKHEED AIRCRAFT CORPORATION
CALIFORNIA'S AIRCRAFT INDUSTRY.

U.S. AIR FORCE
THE U.S. AIR FORCE ACADEMY IN COLORADO, with the Rocky Mountains in the background.

About 90 percent of California's residents were born in the United States. The largest foreign-born group is of Mexican origin. There are also large numbers of people of Chinese and Japanese descent.

ECONOMY. California is a prosperous state. In 1966 the per capita personal income level of $3,499 ranked it fifth in the nation. California ranks first among the states in total value of products. Its rich natural resources include fertile soils, thick forests, and abundant deposits of petroleum, natural gas, and tungsten.

More than three-fourths of the value of goods produced annually comes from manufacturing. About one-sixth comes from agriculture, and most of the remainder is provided by extractive industries—fishing and mining.

California's farm income is the highest in the United States. Most of the farmland is irrigated, and more than 200 crops are grown. Over one-third of farm income is derived from livestock, principally dairy cattle, poultry, and sheep.

California ranks second among the states in manufacturing. Its leading manufacture is transportation equipment, mainly aircraft. Southern California's warm, dry climate is ideal for testing new planes.

Processing the food products of California's farms, ranches, orchards, and vineyards is the second most important industry. The manufacture of electrical machinery, including electronic components, is third. The motion picture and television industries are also notable.

GOVERNMENT. The governor of California is elected to a four-year term and may succeed himself any number of times. The state legislature consists of a senate, whose 40 members serve four-year terms, and an assembly, whose 80 members serve two-year terms.

COLORADO

Area: 104,247 square miles (including 453 square miles of water)
Population: (1960 census) 1,753,947; (1967 est.) 1,975,000
Capital: Denver
State bird: Lark bunting
State tree: Blue spruce
State flower: Rocky Mountain columbine
State motto: Nil sine Numine (Nothing without Providence)

Colorado, one of the Mountain states, is bordered on the north by Wyoming, on the northeast by Nebraska, on the east by Kansas, on the southeast by Oklahoma, on the south by New Mexico, and on the west by Utah. Colorado entered the Union on Aug. 1, 1876, as the 38th state.

THE LAND. Colorado has four major geographic regions. Along the western boundary is the Colorado Plateau, an area of hills, plateaus, and valleys. To the north is the Intermontane (between the mountains) Basin, a region of forested hills and brush covered plateaus.

Beginning in the northwestern corner and continuing into the central part of the state is the Rocky Moun-

AMERICAN AIRLINES

HARTFORD, CONNECTICUT'S Constitution Mall is part of an urban development project.

tain region. It is interrupted by the Continental Divide, which runs roughly north and south through the mountains. East of the Divide, water flows toward the Gulf of Mexico and the Atlantic Ocean; west of the Divide, water flows toward the Pacific. In the Sawatch Range of the Rockies is Mount Elbert, 14,431 feet, the highest peak in the state.

Covering eastern Colorado is the Great Plains region. Once called the "great American desert," the area is subject to drought. The Arkansas, South Platte, and Republican rivers flow through it on their way to the Missouri-Mississippi system.

The climate is usually dry and sunny, with the mountains cooler than the plateaus and plains. The record low temperature is −60°F; the record high is 118°F. Precipitation averages 15 inches a year.

THE PEOPLE. Almost all Coloradans were born in the United States. About three-fourths of them live in urban communities. Two out of every three people live in one of three Standard Metropolitan Statistical Areas: Colorado Springs, Denver, and Pueblo. Per capita personal income was $2,872 in 1966, ranking Colorado 21st among the states.

ECONOMY. Colorado has a wealth of natural resources. Its minerals include valuable metals and fuels, including petroleum, molybdenum, and coal. Forests cover some 20 million acres, but only about 40 percent is of commercial use.

The U.S. government owns more than one-third of Colorado's land, including 6 million acres of commercial forests, vast grazing and mining areas, and national parks. It also operates the Air Force Academy near Colorado Springs.

The value of goods produced is about equally divided between manufacturing and agriculture, with about 14 percent coming from mining. Cattle and sheep account for some two-thirds of farm income. Petroleum is the main source of mining income.

The leading manufacture is processed foods, especially beef and beet sugar. Military weapons, notably missiles, are next in importance.

GOVERNMENT. The governor of Colorado serves a four-year term and may succeed himself any number of times. The state legislature, the General Assembly, consists of a senate, with 35 members elected to four-year terms, and a house of representatives, with 65 members elected to two-year terms.

CONNECTICUT

Area: 5,009 square miles (including 139 square miles of water)
Population: (1960 census) 2,535,234; (1967 est.) 2,925,000
Capital: Hartford
State bird: Robin
State tree: White oak
State flower: Mountain laurel
State motto: Qui transtulit sustinet (He who transplanted will sustain)

Connecticut, the southernmost of the New England states, is bordered on the north by Massachusetts, on the east by Rhode Island, on the south by Long Island Sound, and on the west by New York. One of the original 13 colonies, Connecticut entered the Union on Jan. 9, 1788, as the fifth state.

THE LAND. Connecticut can be divided into five major geographic regions. In the northwestern corner is the Taconic Section, which contains Mount Frissell, 2,380 feet, the highest point in the state. The western third of Connecticut is covered by the Western New England Upland, which extends into Massachusetts and Vermont.

Running north and south in a wide central strip is the Connecticut Valley Lowland. The region's rivers cut through lava ridges. Most of eastern Connecticut is occupied by the Eastern New England Upland, which stretches north to Maine. This region is marked by forested hills and river valleys.

Along the southern shore is a belt formed by the Coastal Lowlands. The coast has numerous beaches, and many of its harbors are the mouths of Connecticut rivers, such as the Housatonic, the Connecticut, and the Thames rivers.

The climate is moderate, with January temperatures averaging 27°F and July readings averaging 72°F. Precipitation is about 46 inches a year. Rainfall is distributed evenly throughout the state, but annual snowfall ranges from 25 inches in the southeast to as much as 80 inches in the northwestern hills.

THE PEOPLE. More than 80 percent of the population is concentrated in nine Standard Metropolitan Statistical Areas: Bridgeport, Hartford, Meriden, New Britain, New Haven, New London–Groton–Norwich, Norwalk, Stamford, and Waterbury. Almost all of Connecticut's inhabitants were born in the United States. The largest group of foreign-born residents is of Italian origin.

ECONOMY. Connecticut ranked first in the United States in per capita personal income in 1966, with an average of $3,678. Connecticut is primarily an industrial state. Over 95 percent of the value of goods produced comes from manufacturing, and over 40 percent of the state's workers are employed in manufacturing.

The leading manufacture is transportation equipment. Connecticut is the nation's largest producer of helicopters, jet airplane engines, and submarines. It is also a major supplier of propellers and small boats.

Nonelectrical machinery, such as machine tools, ball and roller bearings, and typewriters, ranks second. Third is electrical machinery, followed by fabricated metal products, such as silverware.

Connecticut's natural resources are meagre. The forests do not yield commercial timber, although they cover 60 percent of the land. There are few mineral resources, and most of the soil is dry. Tobacco and vegetable crops are substantial, however. Commercial fishermen make large catches of clams, flounder, lobsters, and oysters in Long Island Sound.

GOVERNMENT. Connecticut's governor is elected to a four-year term. He may succeed himself any number of times. The state legislature, the General Assembly, consists of a senate and a house of representatives. Legislators are elected to two-year terms. The senate has between 30 and 50 members, and the house has between 125 and 225 members.

DELAWARE

Area: 2,057 square miles (including 75 square miles of water)
Population: (1960 census) 446,292; (1967 est.) 524,000
Capital: Dover
State bird: Blue hen chicken
State tree: American holly
State flower: Peach blossom
State motto: Liberty and independence

Delaware, one of the South Atlantic states, is located on the eastern part of the Delmarva Peninsula, which lies between Chesapeake Bay and Delaware Bay. Pennsylvania is to the north and northwest, the Delaware River and Bay and the Atlantic Ocean are to the east, and Maryland is to the south and southwest. Delaware entered the Union on Dec. 1, 1787. It is considered the first state because it was the first to ratify the U.S. Constitution.

THE LAND. Delaware has two major land regions—the Piedmont and the Atlantic Coastal Plain. The Piedmont, which reaches from New Jersey south to Alabama, crosses the northern tip of the state. It is covered by hills and valleys and includes the highest point in the state, Ebright Road, with an elevation of 442 feet.

The Atlantic Coastal Plain runs along the Atlantic coast from New Jersey to Florida and covers most of Delaware. Altitudes on the plain rarely exceed 60 feet. Its sandy soil makes good farmland.

Delaware has mild winters and hot, humid summers. Winter temperatures average about 35°F, and summer readings are about 75°F. The Atlantic beaches are about 10° cooler than the inland areas. Precipitation averages about 45 inches yearly.

THE PEOPLE. Over 95 percent of Delaware's residents were born in the United States. The rest came mainly from Britain, France, Germany, and Italy. Almost 15 percent are Negro.

More than two-thirds of Delaware's residents live in urban areas, primarily in the Wilmington Standard Metropolitan Statistical Area.

ECONOMY. Delaware is a prosperous industrial state. The average per capita personal income in 1966 was $3,563, second only to Connecticut. Manufacturing yields some 80 percent of the value of goods produced. Agriculture accounts for most of the rest, and a small share is derived from fishing and mining.

The chief manufactures are chemicals and related products. Wilmington has been described as the chemical capital of the world. It is the home of E. I. du Pont de Nemours & Company, the world's largest chemical producer. Other leading chemical firms are also located in Delaware.

Food and food products are the second most important manufactures. Chickens, fruits, and cucumbers are the principal processed foods. Other significant industries include the manufacture of leather products and ships.

Delaware has good soils, and the Delaware River provides a plentiful water supply. Forests cover about one-third of the state, and much of the rest is farmland. The leading agricultural products are poultry and beef cattle. Major cash crops include soybeans, corn, and potatoes.

GOVERNMENT. The governor of Delaware serves a four-year term and may succeed himself only once. The state legislature, the General Assembly, consists of an 18-member senate and a 35-member house of representatives. Senators are elected to four-year terms, and representatives to two-year terms.

DISTRICT OF COLUMBIA

Area: 67 square miles
Population: 1960 census, 763,956; Metropolitan Stat. Area, 1965 est., 2,408,000

The District of Columbia, officially Washington, District of Columbia, is the capital of the United States. Washington lies on the Potomac River between the states of Maryland and Virginia.

Washington occupies a low, mostly flat region that was ceded to the federal government by Maryland in 1790. The climate is cool in winter and hot and humid in summer. Temperatures average 37°F in January and 78°F in July. Yearly precipitation averages over 40 inches.

THE PEOPLE. The District of Columbia is densely populated and highly cosmopolitan. Over 50 percent of the population is Negro, and there are people from almost every country in the world living in Washington. The

THE WHITE HOUSE

THE DISTRICT OF COLUMBIA, with the White House in the foreground, as seen from the air.

Washington, D.C., Standard Metropolitan Statistical Area includes parts of Maryland and Virginia.

ECONOMY. The federal government, with its legislative, executive, and judicial headquarters in Washington, is the District's most important business. In 1966 the District of Columbia had a higher annual per capita personal income than any of the states, with an average of $3,969.

Washington has embassies of most countries of the world, and the city is the headquarters for many U.S. organizations. Tourism is a significant source of income. Industries not directly related to government include building, printing and publishing, food processing, and retailing.

GOVERNMENT. Under the provisions of a 1967 bill, the District of Columbia is governed by a District Commissioner, or mayor, and a 9-member City Council. The mayor and councilmen are nominated by the president and must be approved by the Senate. The mayor is appointed to a 4-year term, and the councilmen are appointed to staggered 3-year terms.

FLORIDA

Area: 58,560 square miles (including 4,424 square miles of water)
Population: (1960 census) 4,951,560; (1967 est.) 5,995,000
Capital: Tallahassee
State bird: Mockingbird
State tree: Sabal palm
State flower: Orange blossom
State motto: In God we trust

Florida, a South Atlantic state, is a peninsula bounded on the east by the Atlantic Ocean; on the south by the Straits of Florida and the Gulf of Mexico; on the west by the Gulf of Mexico; and on the north by Alabama and Georgia. Florida entered the Union on March 3, 1845, as the 27th state.

THE LAND. Florida has three major geographic regions. The Florida Uplands begin in the northwestern corner of the state, turn eastward, and then turn south. The northern part of this region is forested, and there are valleys and low hills of red clay. The highest point in the state, 345 feet, is in this northern area. The southern part of the Uplands is studded with lakes.

The East Gulf Coastal Plain is part of a region that reaches westward to Mississippi and northward to Illinois. In Florida the region is divided into two parts, separated by the Florida Uplands. One part borders the northern edge of the Gulf of Mexico on Florida's western shore, the other borders the gulf on the southwestern shore.

The Atlantic Coastal Plain covers the whole eastern section of Florida. Part of a larger region that begins in New Jersey, it includes the Florida Keys, small islands that extend to the south and west from the tip of the peninsula.

Florida has warm summers, with July temperatures averaging in the low 80's F, and mild winters. Miami's January temperatures average 67°F, and Jacksonville's January readings

FLORIDA CITRUS COMMISSION

FLORIDA. Packing oranges for shipment.

average 56°F. Precipitation averages 53 inches a year.

THE PEOPLE. Between 1950 and 1960 Florida had the largest population increase of any state, and growth continued through the 1960s. Many people came to live in retirement communities; others came to work in the state's expanding industries.

About three-quarters of the people live in urban areas. Most urban residents live in one of the state's eight Standard Metropolitan Statistical Areas: Fort Lauderdale–Hollywood, Jacksonville, Miami, Orlando, Pensacola, Tallahassee, Tampa–St. Petersburg, and West Palm Beach. About one in five Floridians is Negro.

ECONOMY. Sun, fine beaches, forests, sandy soils, and giant limestone deposits are among Florida's wealth of natural resources. These combine to bring a good income from tourism, manufacturing, farming, and mining. The annual per capita income in 1966 averaged $2,576, ranking Florida 31st among the states.

Tourism is the major source of income. The Atlantic and Gulf coasts and central Florida all cater to visitors, both winter and summer. A prime attraction is the government space and missile center at Cape Kennedy.

About 65 percent of the value of goods produced in Florida comes from manufacturing. The leading product is processed foods derived from citrus fruits. Next in value are chemicals and related products and paper and paper products.

Agriculture accounts for about 25 percent of the value of goods produced. The largest cash crop is oranges, followed by grapefruits and tomatoes. Mineral products, especially phosphate rock, and commercial fishing are also significant.

GOVERNMENT. The governor of Florida is elected to a four-year term. He must skip a term before he may run again. The state senate has 48 members elected to four-year terms. The state house of representatives has 119 members elected to two-year terms.

GEORGIA

Area: 58,876 square miles (including 679 square miles of water)
Population: (1960 census) 3,943,116; (1967 est.) 4,509,000
Capital: Atlanta
State bird: Brown thrasher
State tree: Live oak
State flower: Cherokee rose
State motto: Wisdom, justice, and moderation

Georgia, one of the South Atlantic states, is bordered on the north by Tennessee and North Carolina, on the east by South Carolina and the Atlantic Ocean, on the south by Florida, and on the west by Alabama. The largest state east of the Mississippi River, Georgia is also one of the 13 original states. It entered the Union on Jan. 2, 1788, the fourth state to ratify the U.S. Constitution.

THE LAND. Georgia can be divided into six major land regions. The three northerly regions are part of the Appalachian Mountains. The Appalachian Plateau, in the northwestern corner, is an area of forested ridges and valleys. The Appalachian Ridge and Valley Region, a good farming area, lies south of the plateau. The Blue Ridge, with high peaks and wooded slopes, is in the northeast. In the Blue Ridge region is Brasstown Bald, 4,784 feet, the highest point in the state.

The Piedmont covers the central third of the state. It is a hilly region that slopes from 1,500 feet in the north to less than 400 feet in the south. The southern half of Georgia is divided into the East Gulf Coastal Plain and the Atlantic Coastal Plain. Both are good farming regions.

The state is drained by the Savannah River, which forms the boundary with South Carolina; the Chattahoochee, along the Alabama border, and the St. Mary's along the Florida border.

Georgia's winters are mild and its summers hot. January temperatures average about 50°F, and July readings are about 80°F. Precipitation averages almost 50 inches a year.

THE PEOPLE. Slightly more than half the population lives in urban communities. Georgia has six Standard Metropolitan Statistical Areas: Albany, Atlanta, Augusta, Columbus, Macon, and Savannah. Nearly one-fourth of the state's residents live in or around Atlanta. About three out of ten Georgians are Negro.

ECONOMY. Georgia ranks low among the states in annual per capita income. In 1966 it was 40th, with an average of $2,311. The state's natural resources include some fertile soils, good water supplies, several commercial minerals, and thick forests covering about 70 percent of the land. The forests make Georgia a leading producer of timber, pulp and paper, and wood products.

Manufacturing accounts for nearly three-fourths of the value of goods produced. Most of the remainder comes from farm products. The most important manufacture is textiles.

The chief farm product is cotton, but other important crops are peanuts, corn, tobacco, and peaches. Beef cattle are an increasingly significant source of farm income.

Other valuable resources are clays such as kaolin and fuller's earth. Shrimps, caught along the Atlantic coast, are another source of income.

GOVERNMENT. Georgia's governor is elected to a four-year term, but he must skip one term before he runs again. The General Assembly consists of a 54-member senate and a 205-member house of representatives. All legislators serve two-year terms.

HAWAII

Area: 6,450 square miles (including 25 square miles of water)
Population: (1960 census) 632,722; (1967 est.) 739,000
Capital: Honolulu
State bird: Nene (Hawaiian goose)
State tree: Kukui (Candlenut)
State flower: Hibiscus
State motto: Ua mau ke ea o ka aina i ka pono (The life of the land is perpetuated in righteousness)

Hawaii, one of the Pacific states, lies in the north-central Pacific Ocean, some 2,000 miles southwest of San Francisco. It is made up of 122 islands, of which seven are inhabited. Hawaii entered the Union on Aug. 21, 1959, as the 50th state.

THE LAND. The islands of Hawaii were formed by volcanic action. There are eight main islands, all of which are in the southeast. The island of Hawaii, which was formed by the eruption of five volcanoes, is the largest. One of these volcanoes, Mauna Kea, has an altitude of 13,796 feet, the highest point in the state. There are two active volcanoes, Mauna Loa and Kilauea.

Oahu, formed by two mountain ranges with a broad valley between them, is the most populous island. On the south end of Oahu is Pearl Harbor, one of the biggest harbors in the Pacific. Honolulu, the state's capital, also is on Oahu.

Molokai Island is divided into three geographical areas. In the east are high mountains and steep valleys. In the

center is a fertile plain. In the west is a dry plateau. Niihau Island is covered by one large cattle ranch, owned by a single family. Low plains at the ends of Niihau rise to a high plateau in the center of the island.

The other major islands are Maui, which was formed by two volcanic mountains; Kahoolawe, which is the smallest and only uninhabited major island; Lanai, which is one huge pineapple plantation; and Kauai, which is roughly circular in shape.

Hawaii's temperature shows very little variation throughout the year. Day and night temperatures remain in the 70's F. Hundreds of inches of rain each year fall on many mountain peaks, but only about 15 inches falls on the plains.

THE PEOPLE. The original Hawaiians were Polynesians, a people of the Pacific islands. They mixed with many other ethnic stocks, including Japanese, Chinese, Filipinos, Koreans, and Europeans.

About three-quarters of Hawaii's people live in urban areas. The only Standard Metropolitan Statistical Area is Honolulu, which covers the entire island of Oahu.

ECONOMY. Hawaii has a high per capita personal income. In 1966 it ranked 13th among the states, with an average of $3,143.

Agriculture accounts for nearly three-fifths of the value of the state's products. Most farms, ranches, and plantations are large corporate enterprises that process and market their output. Sugar, pineapples, and beef cattle are the chief products of Hawaiian agriculture.

The main manufacturing industry is food processing. Tourism is a significant source of income, as is the cultivation of orchids. The U.S. government maintains military bases in Hawaii and is the largest employer in the state.

GOVERNMENT. Hawaii's governor is elected to a four-year term. The state legislature consists of a senate, whose 25 members serve four-year terms, and a house of representatives, whose 51 members serve two-year terms.

IDAHO

Area: 83,557 square miles (including 880 square miles of water)
Population: (1960 census) 667,191; (1967 est.) 699,000
Capital: Boise
State bird: Mountain bluebird
State tree: White pine
State flower: Syringa
State motto: Esto perpetua (May she endure forever)

Idaho, one of the Mountain states, is bordered on the east by Montana and Wyoming, on the south by Utah and Nevada, and on the west by Oregon and Washington. To the north is British Columbia, Canada. Idaho entered the Union on July 3, 1890, as the 43rd state.

THE LAND. Idaho is shaped roughly like a frying pan, squared off on three sides, with a "panhandle" pointing north. It can be divided into three main geographic regions. The Rocky Mountains form the largest region, starting in the panhandle and continuing into central Idaho. It is a rugged area, pitted with canyons and gorges, and contains the highest point in the state, Borah Peak, 12,662 feet.

The Columbia Plateau edges along the western border and then turns east to include much of southern Idaho. The plateau has good crop and grazing lands. The Basin and Range Region covers part of the southeastern corner of the state. It is mainly valleys and plateaus.

Idaho is drained by the Snake River, flowing from the southeastern section west and then north along the Oregon boundary. Hells Canyon, the deepest gorge in the United States, is on the Snake River.

January temperatures in Idaho average about 24°F and July readings are about 68°F. Average annual precipitation is about 16 inches, much of it in the form of snow.

THE PEOPLE. About half of Idaho's residents live in urban communities. The only Standard Metropolitan Statistical Area is Boise, the capital. There are more than 5,000 Indians in Idaho, most of whom live on reservations. The largest reservation is Fort Hall.

ECONOMY. In 1966 Idaho ranked 36th among the states in per capita personal income, with an average of $2,441. The state's natural resources include rich soils, huge mineral deposits, thick forests, and a vast supply of water.

Well over half the value of goods produced comes from agriculture. Beef cattle are the major source of income, and dairy products rank high. Idaho is an important potato-growing state. Other leading crops are wheat, sugar beets, and hay.

About one-third the value of goods comes from manufacturing. Processed foods are the leading products. Mining is also important. Idaho is the leading producer of silver in the United States, and it ranks high in lead and zinc production.

Tourism is of increasing significance. Sun Valley, one of the world's leading ski resorts, is located in south-central Idaho.

HAWAII VISITORS BUREAU
MAUI ISLAND, HAWAII, is the site of Lahaini, a busy boat harbor throughout the year.

BUREAU OF RECLAMATION, DEPARTMENT OF THE INTERIOR

IDAHO FARMS irrigated by water drawn from the Snake River in the Minidoka Project.

GOVERNMENT. Idaho's governor serves a four-year term and may be reelected an indefinite number of times. The state legislature consists of a 35-member senate and a 70-member house of representatives. Legislators serve two-year terms.

ILLINOIS

Area: 56,400 square miles (including 523 square miles of water)
Population: (1960 census) 10,081,158; (1967 est.) 10,893,000
Capital: Springfield
State bird: Cardinal
State tree: Native oak
State flower: Native violet
State motto: State sovereignty—national union

Illinois is an East North Central state. It is bounded on the north by Wisconsin, on the east by Lake Michigan and Indiana, on the southeast by Kentucky, on the southwest by Missouri, and on the west by Iowa. Illinois entered the Union on Dec. 3, 1818, as the 21st state.

THE LAND. Illinois has four major geographic regions. One of these, the Central Lowlands, covers nine-tenths of the state and can be divided into three sub-regions. In the northwestern corner of the Central Lowlands is the Driftless Area, which contains the state's highest point, Charles Mound, 1,235 feet. In the northeast are the Great Lakes Plains. In the central region are the fertile Till Plains.

The Ozark Plateau enters the southwestern corner of Illinois from Missouri. The Interior Low Plateau, or Shawnee Hills, enters southeastern Illinois from Kentucky. The Gulf Coastal Plain, at the southern tip of Illinois, is the northern end of a plain that begins at the Gulf of Mexico.

The most important rivers are the Mississippi, which forms the western boundary; the Ohio, which forms the southeastern boundary; and the Wabash, which forms part of the eastern boundary.

Illinois has cold winters and hot summers. Lake Michigan exerts a modifying influence on the climate. In the north, January readings are about 25°F, and July temperatures are about 75°F. In the south, readings are about 36°F in January and 79°F in July. Annual precipitation varies between 34 inches in the north and 40 inches in the south.

THE PEOPLE. More than 80 percent of the population lives in urban communities, mainly in the Chicago metropolitan area. There are seven other Standard Metropolitan Statistical Areas. Bloomington–Normal, Champaign–Urbana, Decatur, Peoria, Rock Island–Moline–Davenport (Iowa), Rockford, and Springfield.

About seven percent of Illinois residents were born in foreign countries, mainly Germany and Poland. Most of the foreign-born live in the Chicago area.

ECONOMY. Illinois is a major industrial state, with more than 80 percent of the value of goods produced coming from manufacturing. In 1966 it ranked third among the states in per capita personal income, with an average of $3,511. Natural resources include rich soils left by Ice Age glaciers and valuable deposits of coal and petroleum.

The leading manufacture is nonelectrical machinery. Electrical equipment, including appliances, telephones, and lighting fixtures, is also important. Iron and steel are produced from ores carried by Great Lakes vessels.

Agriculture contributes about one-seventh of the value of goods produced. Illinois is one of the nation's leading corn-producing states. Other crops are soybeans, hay, and wheat. Hogs, fattened on home-grown corn, are also important.

GOVERNMENT. The governor of Illinois is elected to a four-year term and may succeed himself any number of times. The state legislature, the General Assembly, consists of a 58-member senate and a 177-member house of representatives. Senators serve four-year terms; representatives serve two-year terms.

INDIANA

Area: 36,291 square miles (including 102 square miles of water)
Population: (1960 census) 4,662,498; (1967 est.) 5,000,000
Capital: Indianapolis
State bird: Cardinal
State tree: Tulip tree
State flower: Peony
State motto: The crossroads of America

Indiana is one of the East North Central states. It is bordered on the north by Lake Michigan and the state of Michigan, on the east by Ohio, on the south by Kentucky, and on the west by Illinois. Indiana was admitted to the Union on Dec. 11, 1816, as the 19th state.

THE LAND. Indiana can be divided into three major geographic regions. The Lake, or Great Lakes, Plains are in the north. The plains are dotted with small lakes and moraines, which are low hills formed by glaciers. Huge sand dunes line the Lake Michigan shore.

The Till, or Central, Plains form a fertile farming and grazing region in central Indiana. The highest point in the state, 1,257 feet, is in the Till Plains. The Southern Hills and Lowlands, also called the Interior Low Plateaus, lie in the south-central part of Indiana. The region contains ridges and valleys with rocky hills and mineral springs.

The climate is humid with hot summers and rather cold winters. January temperatures vary from 27°F in the north to 34°F in the south. July readings are in the 70°s F throughout the state. Precipitation averages about 39 inches yearly.

THE PEOPLE. Nearly two-thirds of the people live in urban communities. Indiana has eight Standard Metropolitan Statistical Areas: Anderson, Evansville, Fort Wayne, Gary-Hammond-East Chicago, Indianapolis, Muncie, South Bend, and Terre Haute.

About 2 percent of the residents were born in foreign countries. Germans form the largest foreign-born group. About 9 percent of the people are Negro.

ECONOMY. Indiana is primarily an industrial state, with nearly 85 percent of the value of goods produced coming from manufacturing. In 1966 it ranked 14th among the states in per capita personal income, with an average of $3,061.

The most important manufacture is steel. Lake freighters transport iron ore from Canada, Minnesota, and upper Michigan to plants along Indiana's Lake Michigan shore.

The chief manufactures are automotive and aircraft parts and equipment. Electrical equipment and processed foods are also significant products.

Good soil and abundant water make Indiana well suited to agriculture. The chief crops are corn, soybeans, wheat, and hay, and hogs are raised. Mineral resources include coal, cement, stone, and petroleum.

GOVERNMENT. The governor of Indiana is elected to a four-year term and must skip a term before he may

USDA-SOIL CONSERVATION SERVICE

IOWA CROPS of corn and hay are planted in contour strips in order to prevent erosion.

USDA

KANSAS FARMERS harvesting their wheat.

run again. The state legislature, the General Assembly, consists of a 50-member senate and a 100-member house of representatives. Senators serve four-year terms, and representatives serve two-year terms.

IOWA

Area: 56,290 square miles (including 247 square miles of water)

Population: (1960 census) 2,757,537; (1967 est.) 2,753,000

Capital: Des Moines

State bird: Eastern goldfinch

State tree: Oak

State flower: Wild rose

State motto: Our liberties we prize and our rights we will maintain

Iowa, one of the West North Central states, is bordered on the north by Minnesota, on the east by Wisconsin and Illinois, on the south by Missouri, and on the west by Nebraska and South Dakota. Iowa entered the Union on Dec. 28, 1846, as the 29th state.

THE LAND. Iowa forms a single major geographic region, the Central Lowland. The region can be subdivided into three subregions: the Dissected Till Plains, the Young Drift Plains, and the Driftless Area.

The Dissected Till Plains begin in the northwest and extend south to include all of southern Iowa. The plains were formed by glacial deposits of rock and soil cut through by streams, forming low hills. The highest point in the state, 1,658 feet, is in the northwest corner of the sub-region.

The Young Drift Plains, which cover much of northern and central Iowa, were also formed by glaciers. The Driftless Area in northeastern Iowa is marked by hills and cliffs.

Iowa is drained by the Mississippi River, which forms its eastern border, and the Missouri River, which forms its western border.

Iowa has hot summers and cold winters. Winds from the northwest or the south cause rapid changes in temperatures. In January readings average 18°F in the north and 24°F in the south; in July readings are in the middle to upper 70's F throughout the state. Annual precipitation varies from 26 inches in the northwest to 36 inches in the southeast.

THE PEOPLE. More than half of Iowa's people live in urban communities. There are six Standard Metropolitan Statistical Areas: Cedar Rapids, Davenport–Rock Island (Ill.)–Moline (Ill.), Des Moines, Dubuque, Sioux City, and Waterloo.

About two out of every 100 Iowans were born in a foreign country. One-third of the foreign-born are from Germany.

ECONOMY. Iowa has excellent farm land and a good supply of water, and it is one of the country's most productive agricultural states. Farm products account for over half the total value of goods produced. In 1966 Iowa ranked 20th among the states in per capita personal income, with an average of $2,931.

Corn is Iowa's chief crop. It is used mostly to feed hogs and cattle, both of which are important to the state's economy. Other important crops include soybeans, hay, and oats.

Meat packing is the leading manufacturing industry, and the manufacture of corn products is significant. Farm implements, laundry machines, and refrigeration equipment are produced. Large printing plants turn out magazines and catalogues.

GOVERNMENT. Iowa's governor is elected to a two-year term. He may succeed himself an unlimited number of times. The state legislature, the General Assembly, is made up of a 61-member senate and a 124-member house of representatives. Senators serve four-year terms, and representatives serve two-year terms.

KANSAS

Area: 82,264 square miles (including 208 square miles of water)

Population: (1960 census) 2,178,611; (1967 est.) 2,275,000

Capital: Topeka

State bird: Western meadowlark

State tree: Cottonwood

State flower: Wild sunflower

State motto: Ad astra per aspera (To the stars through difficulties)

Kansas, one of the West North Central states, lies midway between the Atlantic and Pacific oceans. It is bordered on the north by Nebraska, on the east by Missouri, on the south by Oklahoma, and on the west by Colo-

rado. Kansas joined the Union on Jan. 29, 1861, as the 34th state.

THE LAND. Kansas has three major geographic regions. In the northeastern corner of the state are the Dissected Till Plains, which were covered by glaciers during the Ice Age. In the southeastern part of the state are the Southeastern, or Osage, Plains, which extend southward to the Oklahoma border.

The western two-thirds of the state is covered by the Great Plains. This region is very dry and often suffers from dust storms and soil erosion. The highest point in Kansas, Mt. Sunflower, 4,039 feet, is in the northwestern part of the Great Plains.

Kansas is drained by the Kansas River, which flows east through the northern part of the state, and the Arkansas River, which flows southeast through the southern part of the state.

Cold winter winds move down on Kansas from the north, and hot summer winds blow up from the south. Temperatures average 32°F in January and 97°F in July. Annual precipitation varies from 40 inches in the southeast to about 17 inches in the west.

THE PEOPLE. More than three out of every five Kansans live in urban communities. Kansas has three Standard Metropolitan Statistical Areas: Kansas City, Wichita, and Topeka.

Only about 2 percent of the people were born outside the United States. The state has over 90,000 Negro and 5,000 Indian residents.

ECONOMY. Kansas is both an agricultural and industrial state. In 1966 it ranked 25th among the states in per capita personal income, with an average of $2,814.

Agriculture accounts for more than 40 percent of the value of goods produced. Kansas is the nation's leading producer of wheat and also provides large crops of sorghum grain, hay, and corn. Livestock, especially hogs, are raised.

Manufacturing accounts for about 40 percent of the value of goods produced. The leading product is transportation equipment, including aircraft, railroad cars, and truck trailers. Food processing is also important, and Kansas is a major flour milling and meat packing center. Other products include animal feed, processed meats, and canned vegetables and fruits.

Minerals of economic significance include petroleum and natural gas, and cement and stone.

GOVERNMENT. The governor of Kansas is elected to a four-year term and may succeed himself any number of times. The state legislature consists of a senate, whose 40 members serve four-year terms, and a house of representatives, whose 125 members serve two-year terms.

KENTUCKY

Area: 40,395 square miles (including 544 square miles of water)
Population: (1960 census) 3,038,156; (1967 est.) 3,189,000
Capital: Frankfort
State bird: Cardinal
State tree: Tulip poplar
State flower: Goldenrod
State motto: United we stand, divided we fall

Kentucky is one of the East South Central states. It is bordered on the north by Illinois, Indiana, and Ohio; on the east by West Virginia and Virginia; on the south by Tennessee; and on the west by Missouri. Kentucky entered the Union on June 1, 1792, as the 15th state.

THE LAND. Kentucky may be divided into five major geographic regions. In the western corner is the East Gulf Coastal Plain, covered by swamps, lakes, and low hills. The central and southwestern parts of the state are covered by the Pennyroyal Region, named for a mint herb found there. The Pennyroyal is flat except for its northern corner, which has limestone ridges and bluffs.

In the northwestern part of Kentucky is the Western Coal Field, a region of good farm lands and bituminous coal deposits. The north-central part of Kentucky is called the Bluegrass Region and is noted for its rich pastures.

Eastern Kentucky is covered by the Appalachian, or Cumberland, Plateau, part of a region that reaches from New York to Alabama. The

plateau is marked by mountain ridges and valley streams. The highest point in Kentucky, Black Mountain, 4,145 feet, is in this region.

The Mississippi River forms the western boundary of Kentucky. The Ohio River, part of the dividing line between the northern and southern states, forms the northern boundary.

In Kentucky, summers are warm and winters are cool. January temperatures average in the high 30's F and July readings are in the high 70's F. Annual precipitation is about 46 inches.

THE PEOPLE. About 45 percent of the people live in urban communities. Kentucky has three Standard Metropolitan Statistical Areas: Ashland-Huntington (W. Va.), Lexington, and Louisville.

ECONOMY. Kentucky's ample natural resources include good crop and pasture lands, rich coal deposits, and heavy forests. Nonetheless, the state ranked 44th in per capita personal income in 1966, with an average of $2,205.

Manufacturing provides about 65 percent of the value of goods produced. Food products are an important source of income, and Kentucky leads the nation in whiskey distilling. It is also a leading manufacturer of cigars and cigarettes, petrochemicals, and electrical machinery.

Agriculture accounts for about one-quarter of the value of goods produced. Tobacco is the leading crop, followed by grass seed, corn, and hay. Many farmers raise livestock, and Kentucky is famous for breeding race horses.

Minerals also contribute heavily to the economy. Most important are bituminous coal, petroleum, and natural gas. Fluorite, clay, and limestone are also significant.

GOVERNMENT. Kentucky's governor is elected to a four-year term and must skip a term before running again. The state legislature, the General Assembly, consists of a senate, whose 38 members serve four-year terms, and a house of representatives, whose 100 members serve two-year terms.

LOUISIANA

Area: 48,523 square miles (including 3,368 square miles of water)
Population: (1960 census) 3,257,022; (1967 est.) 3,662,000
Capital: Baton Rouge
State bird: Brown pelican
State tree: Bald cypress
State motto: Union, justice, and confidence

Louisiana, one of the West South Central states, is bordered on the north by Arkansas, on the east by Mississippi, on the south by the Gulf of Mexico, and on the west by Texas. Louisiana entered the Union on April 30, 1812, as the 18th state.

THE LAND. Louisiana is crossed by several major water routes. The Mississippi River, which forms part of the eastern boundary, and the Sabine River, which forms part of the western boundary, both flow into the Gulf of Mexico. The Intracoastal Waterway crosses Louisiana from east to west.

The state is divided into three major geographic regions: the West Gulf Coastal Plain, the Mississippi Alluvial Plain, and the East Gulf Coastal Plain.

The West Gulf Coastal Plain covers the western half of the state. It is a region of coastal beaches, marshes, and prairies. The highest point in the state, Driskill Mountain, 535 feet, is in this region. The East Gulf Central Plain, in the east central corner of Louisiana, is a region of marshes and low hills.

The Mississippi Alluvial Plain lies along the lower Mississippi River. It includes the state's most fertile area, the Mississippi Delta, formed by silt at the river's mouth.

Louisiana has a hot, wet, sub-tropical climate. January temperatures average 49°F in the north and 55°F in the south. July averages are about 82°F throughout the state. Annual precipitation is high, about 56 inches, making Louisiana one of the wettest states.

THE PEOPLE. More than 60 percent of Louisiana's residents live in urban communities, mostly in the New Orleans area. The state has six Standard Metropolitan Statistical Areas: Baton Rouge, Lafayette, Lake Charles, Monroe, New Orleans, and Shreveport.

Among the distinctive groups in Louisiana are the Creoles and the Cajuns. The Creoles are descendants of early French and Spanish settlers; the Cajuns are descended from Frenchmen who first settled in Canada and came south to Louisiana in the 1700s. About one-third of the population is Negro.

ECONOMY. Louisiana depends heavily on its rich mineral resources. But despite vast reserves of petroleum and natural gas, the annual per capita income is low. In 1966 Louisiana ranked 42nd among the states, with an average of $2,257.

Mineral products account for slightly more than half the total value of goods produced. Nearly all of the income is from petroleum and natural gas, which are found throughout the state. Sulfur and salt are also of importance.

KENTUCKY DEPARTMENT OF PUBLIC INFORMATION

KENTUCKY HORSES, famous as racers, are raised on the farms of the Bluegrass Region.

MAINE DEPARTMENT OF ECONOMIC DEVELOPMENT

MAINE LIGHTHOUSE, at Penobscot Bay.

BALTIMORE ASSOCIATION OF COMMERCE

MARYLAND'S CHESAPEAKE BAY BRIDGE links the state's eastern and western shores.

Manufacturing accounts for over one-third the value of goods produced. Refined petroleum and petrochemicals are important, as are processed rice, cotton fibers, and cottonseed oil.

Louisiana has extremely fertile soils, but agriculture contributes only about 10 percent of the value of goods produced. Leading cash crops are rice, cotton, sugarcane, and soybeans. Commercial fishing is another source of income.

GOVERNMENT. Louisiana's governor is elected to a four-year term. The state legislature consists of a 39-member senate and a 105-member house of representatives. Both senators and representatives are elected to four-year terms.

MAINE

Area: 33,215 square miles (including 2,282 square miles of water)
Population: (1960 census) 969,265; (1967 est.) 973,000
Capital: Augusta
State bird: Chickadee
State tree: White pine
State flower: White pine cone and tassel
State motto: Dirigo (I direct, or I guide)

Maine is the largest of the New England states. It is bounded on the northwest, north, and east by Canada; on the south by the Atlantic Ocean; and on the west by New Hampshire. At one time Maine was part of Massachusetts. In 1819 it voted to become a separate state, and on March 15, 1820, Maine entered the Union as the 23rd state.

THE LAND. Maine has three major geographic regions. The White Mountains Region, which stretches over northwestern Maine, is a mountainous area dotted with lakes. The White Mountains Region extends into neighboring New Hampshire and nearby Vermont.

The Eastern New England Upland covers much of the central and northern parts of the state. The Upland is part of a system that reaches from Connecticut to the Canadian border.

The highest point in Maine, Mount Katahdin, 5,268 feet, is in the Upland region.

The Coastal Lowlands, part of a region that runs along the whole New England coast, cover eastern Maine. The coast has innumerable bays, coves, and inlets, and there are many off-shore islands.

Maine has cold winters and cool summers. January temperatures average 24°F, and July readings average 67°F. Annual precipitation is about 43 inches.

THE PEOPLE. Only slightly more than half the people of Maine live in urban communities. About one-fifth of the population lives in one of two Standard Metropolitan Statistical Areas: Lewiston-Auburn and Portland.

The vast majority of Maine's residents were born in the United States. Many are the descendants of French-Canadians.

ECONOMY. Maine is an industrial state, and it depends heavily on the forests that cover nearly 90 percent of the land for raw materials. Maine's 1966 per capita personal income of $2,438 ranked it 37th among the states.

Manufacturing accounts for about three-fourths of the value of goods produced. Wood processing is the most important industry. Products include pulp and paper, lumber, toothpicks, matches, furniture, and newsprint. Other important manufactures are shoes, canned and frozen foods, and textiles.

Agriculture accounts for about 20 percent of the value of goods produced. Most important are livestock, especially broiler chickens. Potatoes are the chief cash crop. Fishing is also important, and Maine is noted for its lobsters.

GOVERNMENT. The governor of Maine is elected to a four-year term. He may succeed himself once and then must skip a term before running again. The state legislature is composed of a 34-member senate and a 151-member house of representatives. Legislators are elected to two-year terms.

MARYLAND

Area: 10,577 square miles (including 686 square miles of water)
Population: (1960 census) 3,100,689; (1967 est.) 3,682,000
Capital: Annapolis
State bird: Baltimore oriole
State tree: White oak
State flower: Black-eyed Susan
State motto: Fatti maschii, parole femine (Manly deeds, womanly words)

Maryland is one of the South Atlantic states. It is bounded by Pennsylvania on the north, Delaware and the Atlantic Ocean on the east, Virginia and West Virginia on the south and west, and the District of Columbia on the southwest. Maryland was one of the original 13 colonies. It entered the Union on April 28, 1788, as the seventh state.

THE LAND. Maryland can be divided into five major geographic regions. The Atlantic Coastal Plain, part of a region that reaches from New Jersey to Florida, extends from the northeastern corner of the state to the south-central boundary.

The Piedmont region runs west of the Atlantic Coastal Plain. It is part of a region that stretches from New Jersey to Alabama. The Blue Ridge Region is a narrow rugged strip west of the Piedmont.

The Appalachian Ridge and Valley Region lies west of the Blue Ridge. The Appalachian Plateau is Maryland's most westerly region. Much of the Plateau is covered by the Allegheny Mountains. The highest point in the state, Backbone Mountain, 3,360 feet, is in this region.

Chesapeake Bay cuts through eastern Maryland from the south and extends almost to the northern border. The Susquehanna River, which flows from Pennsylvania, and the Potomac, which forms part of the southern border of Maryland, both flow into Chesapeake Bay.

Maryland has hot, humid summers and mild winters. Average January temperatures range from 39°F along the coast to 29°F in the northwest.

July temperatures vary from the mid-70's F near Chesapeake Bay to 68°F in the northwest. Annual average precipitation is about 44 inches.

THE PEOPLE. Almost 75 percent of Maryland's people live in urban communities. Baltimore is the only Standard Metropolitan Statistical Area in the state, but parts of Maryland are included in the Washington, D.C., metropolitan area. About 3 percent of the residents are foreign-born. Most came from Poland and Italy.

ECONOMY. Maryland is a prosperous state. The average per capita income in 1966 was $3,220, ranking Maryland 11th among the states.

Manufacturing provides over 85 percent of the value of goods produced. Maryland is a major producer of steel and an important manufacturer of transportation equipment. Other products include processed foods, chemicals, and electrical machinery.

Agriculture contributes over 10 percent of the value of goods produced. Broiler chickens and dairy products are important. Major cash crops include corn, tobacco, hay, and soybeans.

GOVERNMENT. The governor of Maryland is elected to a four-year term. He may succeeed himself once but must be out of office for at least one year before he may serve again. The state legislature, the General Assembly, consists of a 42-member senate and a 142-member house of delegates. Legislators are elected to four-year terms.

MASSACHUSETTS

Area: 8,257 square miles (including 424 square miles of water)
Population: (1960 census) 5,148,578; (1967 est.) 5,421,000
Capital: Boston
State bird: Chickadee
State tree: American elm
State flower: Mayflower
State motto: Ense petit placidam sub libertate quietem (By the sword we seek peace, but peace only under liberty)

Massachusetts is one of the New England states. It is bounded on the north by Vermont and New Hampshire; on the east by the Atlantic Ocean; on the south by the Atlantic Ocean, Rhode Island, and Connecticut; and on the west by New York. Massachusetts was one of the 13 original colonies. It entered the Union on Feb. 6, 1788, as the sixth state.

THE LAND. Massachusetts can be divided into six major geographic regions. Along the western border is the Taconic Mountain Region, which extends into Vermont. This region is only six miles across at its widest point. East of the Taconic region is the narrow Berkshire Valley, which reaches south into Connecticut.

Further east is the Western New England Upland, or Berkshire Hills, part of a region that runs from Vermont to Connecticut. The highest point in the state, Mount Greylock, 3,491 feet, is in this region. East of the Berkshire Hills is the Connecticut Valley Lowland, which is drained by the Connecticut River.

Lying east of the Connecticut Valley Lowland is the Eastern New England Upland, part of a region that extends from Maine to New Jersey. Still farther east are the Coastal Lowlands, which run along the Atlantic coast and include several off-shore islands. The shoreline contains many good harbors.

The climate of western Massachusetts is cooler than that of the east. Temperatures in the west average 21°F in January and 68°F in July. Annual precipitation varies from 44 inches in the west to 40 inches along the coast.

THE PEOPLE. Nearly 85 percent of the people of Massachusetts live in urban communities. Almost all urban dwellers live in one of the 10 Standard Metropolitan Statistical Areas: Boston, Brockton, Fall River, Fitchburg-Leominster, Lawrence-Haverhill, Lowell, New Bedford, Pittsfield, Springfield-Chicopee-Holyoke, and Worcester.

About 10 percent of the people in Massachusetts were born in foreign countries, mainly Canada, Ireland, Italy, and Britain. Slightly more than 2 percent of the state's residents are Negro.

ECONOMY. Massachusetts is a highly industrialized state, and more than 95 percent of the value of goods produced comes from manufacturing. In 1966 Massachusetts ranked 10th among the states in per capita personal income, with an average of $3,271.

The leading manufacture is machinery, both electrical and nonelectrical. Electronics research laboratories, concentrated in the Boston area, are an important source of income. Other significant manufactures are textiles, apparel, and shoes and other leather goods.

Farm revenue is produced by dairy products, poultry and eggs, hay, tobacco, and cranberries. Commercial fishermen bring in catches of scallops, cod, ocean perch, and whiting. Other sources of income are tourism and the mining of building stone, gravel, and sand.

GREATER BOSTON CHAMBER OF COMMERCE

MASSACHUSETTS STATE HOUSE, built in 1795, is one of Boston's noted landmarks.

GOVERNMENT. The governor of Massachusetts serves a four-year term and may succeed himself. The state legislature, the General Court, consists of a 40-member senate and a 240-member house of representatives. Legislators are elected to two-year terms.

MICHIGAN

Area: 58,216 square miles (including 1,398 square miles of water)
Population: (1960 census) 7,823,194; (1967 est.) 8,584,000
Capital: Lansing
State bird: Robin
State tree: White pine
State flower: Apple blossom
State motto: Si quaeris peninsulam amoenam circumspice (If you seek a pleasant peninsula. look about you)

Michigan, one of the East North Central states, is divided into two parts: the Upper Peninsula, in the northwest, and the Lower Peninsula, in the southeast. The Straits of Mackinac divide the two parts.

The Upper Peninsula is bounded on the north by Lake Superior, on the east by Canada, on the south by Lake Michigan and Lake Huron, and on the south and southwest by Wisconsin. The Lower Peninsula is bounded on the northeast and east by Lake Huron, on the southeast by Canada, on the south by Indiana and Ohio, and on the west and northwest by Lake Michigan.

Michigan entered the Union on Jan. 26, 1837, as the 26th state.

THE LAND. Michigan can be divided into two major geographic regions—the Superior Upland and the Lake, or Great Lake, Plains. The Superior Upland covers the western half of the Upper Peninsula. Most of the region is a rough plateau, with mountains in the northwest corner. The highest point in the state, Mt. Curwood, 1,980 feet, is in this region.

The Lake, or Great Lakes, Plains cover the remainder of Michigan. These are part of a larger region known as the Interior Lowland. In the Lake Plains are thousands of small lakes and several rivers that drain into the Great Lakes.

Winters are cold throughout Michigan. Summers are warm in the south and cool in the north. Average January temperatures vary from 15°F in the Upper Peninsula to 26°F in the Lower Peninsula. July temperatures range from 65°F in the north to 73°F in the south. Annual precipitation ranges from 25 to 35 inches.

THE PEOPLE. Michigan's population is heavily concentrated in the Lower Peninsula. Almost 75 percent of the people live in urban communities. Michigan has 10 Standard Metropolitan Statistical Areas: Ann Arbor, Bay City, Detroit, Flint, Grand Rapids, Jackson, Kalamazoo, Lansing, Muskegon-Muskegon Heights, and Saginaw.

Some 6 percent of Michigan's residents are foreign-born. They came mostly from Canada, Poland, and Germany. About 10 percent of the population is Negro.

ECONOMY. An industrial state, Michigan ranked 12th among the states in per capita personal income in 1966 with an average of $3,219.

U.S. DEPARTMENT OF AGRICULTURE

GRAIN FROM MINNESOTA and other midwestern states is stored in elevators at Duluth, where it is loaded into ships for transport.

USDA—SOIL CONSERVATION SERVICE

MISSISSIPPI COTTON, planted on extensive, contoured fields. Cotton represents the state's most important commercial farm crop.

More than 90 percent of the value of goods produced comes from manufacturing. Transportation equipment is the chief product. Detroit, sometimes called the "Automobile Capital of the World," turns out cars, trucks, and buses. Michigan also manufactures industrial goods used to supply the automotive industry.

Agriculture accounts for about 6 percent of the value of goods. Milk and dairy products, livestock, corn, hay, and dry beans are leading sources of farm income.

Michigan is a major source of iron ore. It is also a fishing state, noted for carp, chub, whitefish, perch, pike, and smelts.

GOVERNMENT. The governor of Michigan is elected to a four-year term and may succeed himself any number of times. The state legislature consists of a 38-member senate and a 110-member house of representatives. Senators are elected to four-year terms; representatives to two-year terms.

MINNESOTA

Area: 84,068 square miles (including 4,779 square miles of water)
Population: (1960 census) 3,413,864; (1967 est.) 3,582,000
Capital: St. Paul
State bird: Common loon
State tree: Norway pine
State flower: Pink and white lady's slipper
State motto: L'etoile du nord (The star of the north)

Minnesota, one of the West North Central states, is bounded on the north by Canada, on the east by Lake Superior and Wisconsin, on the south by Iowa, and on the west by North Dakota and South Dakota. Minnesota entered the Union on May 11, 1858, as the 32nd state.

THE LAND. Minnesota has four main geographic regions. The Young Drift Plains begin in the northwest and extend south to cover most of the southern half of the state. Glaciers passing over the land left rich deposits of fertile soil.

The Superior Upland covers the northeastern and north-central part of Minnesota. The Superior Upland is part of a rocky region that covers much of eastern Canada. The highest point in the state, Eagle Mountain, 2,301 feet, is located in the Superior Upland.

The Dissected Till Plains, a region crossed by many streams, are in the southwestern corner of the state. The Driftless Area, a flat region cut by swift streams, is in the southeast.

Minnesota has thousands of lakes and many rivers. The Mississippi River starts in north-central Minnesota and, with the St. Croix, forms the boundary with Wisconsin. The Red River forms the boundary with North Dakota.

Minnesota has severe winters and moderately warm summers. January temperatures average 2°F in the north and 15°F in the south. July averages range from 68°F in the north to 72°F in the south. Precipitation in the state averages about 25 inches annually.

THE PEOPLE. Nearly 70 percent of the population live in urban communities. Minnesota has three Standard Metropolitan Statistical Areas: Duluth-Superior (Wis.), Minneapolis-St. Paul, and Moorhead-Fargo (N. Dak.).

Foreign-born residents account for about 4 percent of the population. Germans, Swedes, and Poles make up the largest groups.

ECONOMY. Minnesota has a diversified economy based on manufacturing, agriculture, and mining. In 1966 the average annual per capita personal income was $2,871, ranking Minnesota 22nd among the states.

Manufacturing accounts for almost 60 percent of the value of goods produced. Food processing is the chief industry, followed by the production of non-electrical machinery. Minnesota's forests supply the raw material for the state's important paper industry.

Agriculture provides more than one-third of the value of goods produced. Dairy products, eggs, hogs, and turkeys contribute heavily to farm income. Crops include corn, soybeans, hay, and oats.

Iron ore is the state's most valuable mineral product. Although Minnesota produces about two-thirds of the iron ore mined in the United States, much of the ore is of low grade.

GOVERNMENT. The governor of Minnesota is elected to a four-year term and may succeed himself. The state legislature consists of a 67-member senate and a 135-member house of representatives. Senators are elected to four-year terms; representatives to two-year terms.

MISSISSIPPI

Area: 47,716 square miles (including 358 square miles of water)
Population: (1960 census) 2,178,141; (1967 est.) 2,348,000
Capital: Jackson
State bird: Mockingbird
State tree: Magnolia
State flower: Magnolia
State motto: Virtute et armis (By valor and arms)

Mississippi, an East South Central state, is bounded on the north by Tennessee, on the east by Alabama, on the south by the Gulf of Mexico and Louisiana, and on the west by Louisiana and Arkansas. The Mississippi River forms the boundary with Arkansas and part of the boundary with Louisiana. Mississippi entered the Union on Dec. 10, 1817, as the 20th state.

THE LAND. Mississippi can be divided into two major land regions—the Mississippi Alluvial Plain and the Gulf, or East Gulf, Coastal Plain. The Mississippi Alluvial Plain runs along the western edge of the state. Also known as the Delta, it is a region made rich by the periodic deposits of fertile soil left by the flooding Mississippi River.

The Gulf, or East Gulf, Coastal Plain covers the rest of the state. The western part of this region is made up of low hills. The northeastern area contains the Tennessee River Hills, where the highest point in the state, Woodall Mountain, 806 feet, is located. In the southeast are the Pine Hills, and in the northeast is the Black Belt, an area of mixed grazing and cropland.

Mississippi has long, hot summers and short, moderate winters. Temperatures average about 48°F in January and about 82°F in July. Annual precipitation varies from 50 to 65 inches.

THE PEOPLE. About 60 percent of the population lives in rural communities or on farms. Jacksonville is the only Standard Metropolitan Statistical Area. About 40 percent of Mississippi's residents are Negro.

ECONOMY. Mississippi is a poor state. In 1966 it ranked last among the states in per capita personal income, with an average of $1,751.

Less than half the value of goods produced comes from manufacturing. Food processing is the chief manufacturing industry. Dairy products and canned and frozen crabmeat, oysters, and shrimps are produced. Paper, lumber and wood products, industrial chemicals, and clothing are also significant.

More than 40 percent of the value of goods comes from agricultural products. Cotton, grown on the Delta, is the most important crop. Mississippi also produces soybeans, cottonseed, corn, and sweet potatoes. Cattle and poultry are raised.

The most important mineral assets are petroleum and natural gas. Mississippi has thousands of oil wells and gas fields. Commercial fishing yields shrimps, crabs, and oysters from the Gulf of Mexico, and carp and catfish from the Mississippi River.

GOVERNMENT. Mississippi's governor is elected to a four-year term and may not succeed himself. The legislature consists of a 52-member senate and a 122-member house of representatives. Legislators are elected to four-year terms.

MISSOURI

Area: 69,686 square miles (including 640 square miles of water)
Population: (1960 census) 4,319,813; (1967 est.) 4,603,000
Capital: Jefferson City
State bird: Bluebird
State tree: Flowering dogwood
State flower Hawthorn
State motto: Salus populi suprema lex esto (Let the welfare of the people be the supreme law)

Missouri, one of the West North Central states, is bounded on the north by Iowa; on the east by Illinois, Kentucky, and Tennessee; on the south by Arkansas; and on the west by Oklahoma, Kansas, and Nebraska. Missouri entered the Union on Aug. 10, 1821, as the 24th state.

THE LAND. Missouri can be divided into four major geographic regions. The northern third of the state is occupied by the Dissected Till Plains, which were cut by glaciers and left with a cover of fertile soil. Entering the state from the west are the Osage Plains, a region of prairies and low hills.

Most of southern Missouri is covered by the Ozark Plateau. It is a region of hills, mountains, river valleys, and tablelands. In the southeastern Ozarks are the St. François Mountains, which contain the highest point in the state, Taum Sauk, 1,772 feet. In the southeastern corner of Missouri is the Mississippi Alluvial Plain, a fertile region whose distinctive shape has given it the name of Boot Heel.

The two largest rivers in North America, the Mississippi and the Missouri, flow through Missouri. The Mississippi forms the state's eastern boundary. The Missouri enters the state from the west and joins the Mississippi in the east, just north of St. Louis.

Missouri has warm summers and moderate winters. July temperatures average about 80°F, and January averages vary from 38°F in the Boot Heel to 29°F in the north. Annual precipitation averages from 30 inches in the north to 50 inches in the south.

THE PEOPLE. About two-thirds of the population live in urban communities. Missouri has four Standard Metropolitan Statistical Areas: Kansas City, St. Joseph, St. Louis, and Springfield.

Virtually all Missourians were born in the United States. About 9 percent of the population is Negro.

ECONOMY. Missouri's economy depends on manufacturing for some 74 percent of the value of goods produced. Agriculture contributes about 24 percent, and mining most of the remainder. The average annual per capita income in 1966 was $2,845, ranking Missouri 23rd among the states.

Transportation equipment and processed foods are Missouri's leading manufactures. The state makes aircraft, spacecraft, missiles, and rockets as well as railroad cars, trucks, buses, and automobiles. Meats, dairy products, beer, and flour are among the foodstuffs produced.

The chief farm product is livestock, fattened on Missouri-grown corn. Corn, soybeans, hay, and wheat are the leading crops.

Missouri is a leading producer of lead and is also a source of stone, cement, and iron ore.

GOVERNMENT. The governor of Missouri is elected to a four-year term and may not succeed himself. The state legislature, the General Assembly, consists of a senate, with 34 members elected to four-year terms, and a house of representatives, with 163 members elected to two-year terms.

MONTANA

Area: 147,138 square miles (including 1,535 square miles of water)
Population: (1960 census) 674,767; (1967 est.) 701,000
Capital: Helena
State bird: Western meadowlark
State tree: Ponderosa pine
State flower: Bitterroot
State motto: Oro y plata (Gold and silver)

Montana, a Mountain state, is bounded on the north by Canada, on the east by North Dakota and South Dakota, on the south by Wyoming, and on the southwest and west by Idaho. Montana entered the Union on Nov. 8, 1889, as the 41st state.

THE LAND. Montana can be divided into two main geographic regions. The Great Plains, or Missouri Plateau, Region covers the eastern three-fifths of the state. The region contains rolling hills and wide valleys, broken by mountains in the west. The Continental Divide cuts through the mountain-

U.S. BUREAU OF RECLAMATION
WESTERN MONTANA BLUFFS ring the barren Big Hole River valley in the Rocky Mountains.

ous western part of the region. Water west of the divide flows to the Pacific Ocean; water east of the divide flows toward the Gulf of Mexico or the Atlantic Ocean.

The Rocky Mountains Region covers the rest of the state. Among the more than 50 mountain ranges found there is the Absaroka Range which includes the highest point in the state, Granite Peak, 12,799 feet. The Rocky Mountains Region is subject to earthquakes, and the higher ranges still have some glaciers.

Montana's climate west of the Continental Divide is less severe than it is in the east. Temperatures in the west average 64°F in July and 20°F in January; in the east temperatures average 71°F in July and 14°F in January. Precipitation is about 14 inches a year except in the western mountains, which receive up to 45 inches.

THE PEOPLE. About half of Montana's people live in urban areas. There are two Standard Metropolitan Statistical Areas: Billings and Great Falls.

Most of the small number of residents born in foreign countries came from Canada. There are about 21,000 Indians, most of whom live on one of seven reservations in the state.

ECONOMY. Montana's economy is heavily dependent on agriculture, but manufacturing and mining are important. In 1966 Montana ranked 28th among the states in per capita personal income, with an average of $2,615.

More than half the value of goods produced comes from agriculture. The leading farm product is livestock. Beef cattle and calves are the most important, but there are also large herds of sheep. Montana is an important wheat state and also produces hay, barley, sugar beets, and dairy products.

Manufacturing accounts for about one-fourth the value of goods produced. Metal smelting and refining and petroleum refining are important industries. Other significant manufactures are lumber products and processed foods.

Minerals yield over one-fifth the value of goods produced. Although petroleum and natural gas are the most valuable, considerable quantities of copper, gold, silver, zinc, lead, and manganese ore are mined.

GOVERNMENT. Montana's governor is elected to a four-years term and may succeed himself. The state legislature, the Legislative Assembly, consists of a senate and a house of representatives. The 55 senators are elected to four-year terms; the 104 representatives are elected to two-year terms.

NEBRASKA

Area: 77,227 square miles (including 705 square miles of water)
Population: (1969 census) 1,411,330; (1967 est.) 1,435,000
Capital: Lincoln
State bird: Western meadowlark
State tree: American elm
State flower: Goldenrod
State motto: Equality before the law

Nebraska, one of the West North Central states, is bounded on the north by South Dakota, on the south by Kansas and Colorado, and on the west by Wyoming. The Missouri River forms the eastern border. Nebraska entered the Union on Mar. 1, 1867, as the 37th state.

THE LAND. Nebraska can be divided into two main geographic regions—the Dissected Till Plains and the Great Plains. The eastern 20 percent of the state is covered by the Dissected Till Plains, which extend along the Missouri River. Ages ago glaciers left a fertile soil cover called till, which since that time has been cut, or dissected, by streams.

The rest of Nebraska is part of the Great Plains, a region that reaches into neighboring Wyoming and Colorado. Much of the Great Plains is covered by windblown dust called loess. In the central part of the region are the Sand Hills. In the west are the very dry High Plains. The highest point in the state, 5,424 feet, is in the southwest corner.

Nebraska has hot summers and cold winters. It is subject to blizzards, tornadoes, hailstorms, and thunderstorms. Temperatures average about 77°F in July and about 25°F in January. Average annual precipitation ranges from 16 inches in the west to 34 inches in the southeast.

THE PEOPLE. About 55 percent of the people live in urban communities. There are two Standard Metropolitan Statistical Areas: Omaha and Lincoln.

About 3 percent of the population was born in foreign countries. Germans form the largest foreign-born group. About 2 percent of Nebraska's people are Negro, and there are more than 5,000 Indians, most of whom live on reservations.

ECONOMY. Nebraska is one of the few states in which the economy depends more heavily on agriculture than on manufacturing. The 1966 average per capita personal income was $2,819, ranking Nebraska 24th among the states.

Agriculture provides almost two-thirds of the value of goods produced. Nebraska is an important producer of cattle and calves, hogs, corn, hay, wheat, sorghum, and sugar beets. Cattle and calves provide the greatest income. They are raised on ranches in the west and fattened in feed lots in the east.

Manufacturing accounts for about one-third of the value of goods produced. Most important are processed foods, including meats, dairy products, flour, and beet sugar.

Mining provides about 4 percent of the value of goods produced. Of this, more than half comes from petroleum and natural gas.

GOVERNMENT. The governor of Nebraska is elected to a four-year term and may succeed himself. Nebraska is the only state with a one-house legislature. The 49 legislators are called senators. They are elected to four-year terms on a ballot that does not list party affiliations.

NEVADA

Area: 110,540 square miles (including 651 square miles of water)
Population: (1960 census) 285,278; (1967 est.) 444,000
Capital: Carson City
State bird: Mountain bluebird
State tree: Single-leaf piñon
State flower: Sagebrush
State motto: All for our country

Nevada, a Mountain state, is bounded on the north by Oregon and Idaho, on the east by Utah and Arizona, and on the southwest and west by California. It entered the Union on Oct. 31, 1864, as the 36th state.

THE LAND. Nevada can be divided into three major geographic regions. The largest of these is the Great Basin, which covers almost the entire state. A vast desert cut by mountain ranges, the Great Basin is part of the Basin and Range Region that runs between the Rocky Mountains on the east and the Sierra Nevada on the west. The highest point in Nevada, Boundary Peak, 13,140 feet, is in this region, on the California border.

The Sierra Nevada covers a small part of the southwestern corner of the state. It is a rugged mountain region towering above scenic Lake Tahoe. The Columbia Plateau covers a small part of the state's northeastern corner.

It is a part of a tableland that reaches into Oregon and Idaho.

In the north and in the mountains, winters are long and cold, and summers are long and hot. In the south, winters are mild, and summers are long and hot. Temperatures in the north average about 24°F in January and 70°F in July; in the south they average 43°F in January and 86°F in July. Nevada is extremely dry, with precipitation averaging only seven to nine inches a year.

THE PEOPLE. Nevada is sparsely populated, with an average of fewer than three people per square mile. About 70 percent of the population lives in urban communities. The state's two Standard Metropolitan Statistical Areas are Las Vegas and Reno.

About 5 percent of the population was born in foreign countries. Negroes make up about 5 percent of the people, and there are some 7,000 Indians, who live mostly on reservations.

ECONOMY. Nevada's economy is based largely on tourism, which yields nearly three times as much income as the total value of goods produced. The average annual per capita personal income in 1966 was $3,330, ranking Nevada seventh among the states.

Each year millions of tourists visit Nevada, attracted by the dry climate and beautiful scenery, as well as legal gambling and lenient divorce laws. Las Vegas is noted for its casinos and nightclubs, and Reno is known as a divorce center.

The U.S. government owns over 85 percent of the land in Nevada. Most of it is occupied by national forests, rangelands, and game preserves.

Agriculture accounts for about one-fifth of the value of goods produced. Cattle and calves are the most important source of farm income. Ranchers pay a small fee to let their livestock graze on public lands. Water from reservoirs and wells is used to grow crops of hay, wheat, and alfalfa seed.

More than one-third of the value of goods produced comes from mining. Copper is the leading mineral, followed by sand and gravel and iron ore.

STATE OF NEW HAMPSHIRE

NEW HAMPSHIRE COVERED BRIDGE, at West Hopkinton is over 100 years old.

STATE OF NEW JERSEY

NEW JERSEY MONUMENT, in Sussex County, marks the state's highest point, 1,803 feet.

Manufacturing provides more than 40 percent of the value of goods produced. Most important is the processing of metals.

GOVERNMENT. The governor of Nevada is elected to a four-year term and may succeed himself. The state legislature consists of a 20-member senate and a 40-member assembly. Senators are elected to four-year terms; assemblymen are elected to two-year terms.

NEW HAMPSHIRE

Area: 9,304 square miles (including 271 square miles of water)
Population: (1960 census) 606,921; (1967 est.) 686,000
Capital: Concord
State bird: Purple finch
State tree: White birch
State flower: Purple lilac
State motto: Live free or die

New Hampshire, one of the New England states, is bordered on the north by Canada, on the east by Maine, on the southeast by the Atlantic Ocean, on the south by Massachusetts, and on the west by Vermont. One of the original 13 colonies, New Hampshire became the ninth state when it ratified the U.S. Constitution on June 21, 1788.

THE LAND. New Hampshire may be divided into three major geographic regions. The White Mountains, a part of the Appalachian Highlands, cover the northern third of the state. The highest point in New Hampshire, Mt. Washington, 6,288 feet, is in the White Mountains region.

The Eastern New England Upland covers most of the remainder of the state. It is part of a region that runs from Maine to Connecticut, and it contains low ranges, river valleys, and many lakes. The Coastal, or Seaboard, Lowlands are in the southeastern corner of the state.

New Hampshire's climate is marked by cool summers and cold, snowy winters. January temperatures vary from 16°F in the north to 22°F in the south. July readings range from 66°F in the north to 70°F in the south. Annual precipitation averages 40 to 42 inches.

THE PEOPLE. Almost 60 percent of New Hampshire's residents live in urban communities. Manchester is the state's only Standard Metropolitan Statistical Area. Foreign-born residents, mostly of Canadian origin, make up about 7 percent of the population.

ECONOMY. New Hampshire is an industrial state, and manufacturing provides about 90 percent of the value of goods produced. In 1966 it ranked 26th among the states in per capita personal income, with an average of $2,761.

The leading manufactures are leather and leather products, principally shoes. Also of importance are textiles, machinery, paper, and lumber.

Agriculture accounts for only 10 percent of the value of goods produced. About one-third of farm income comes from dairy products, and another third comes from poultry. Much of the nation's maple syrup is produced in New Hampshire.

Tourism provides a sizable income each year. The White Mountains attract skiers, and the lakes and seacoast attract water sports enthusiasts.

GOVERNMENT. The governor of New Hampshire is elected to a two-year term and may succeed himself. The state legislature, the General Court, consists of a senate with 24 members and a house of representatives with not fewer than 375 nor more than 400 members. Legislators are elected to two-year terms.

NEW JERSEY

Area: 7,836 square miles (including 304 square miles of water)
Population: (1960 census) 6,066,782; (1967 est.) 7,003,000
Capital: Trenton
State bird: Eastern goldfinch
State tree: Red oak
State flower: Purple violet
State motto: Liberty and prosperity

New Jersey is one of the Middle Atlantic states. It is bounded on the north by New York, on the east by New York and the Atlantic Ocean, on the south by Delaware Bay, and on the west by Delaware and Pennsylvania. The Hudson River forms the northeastern boundary, and the Delaware River forms the western boundary.

New Jersey was one of the 13 original colonies. It ratified the U.S. Constitution on Dec. 18, 1787, to become the third state.

THE LAND. New Jersey can be divided into four major geographic regions. In the northwestern corner is the mountainous Appalachian Ridge and Valley Region, part of a larger region that extends from New York to Alabama. In the western corner of the region is the Delaware Water Gap, formed where the Delaware River cuts through the mountains. In the northern corner is High Point, 1,803 feet, the highest point in the state.

Southeast of the Appalachian Ridge and Valley is the New England Upland, a region marked by rocky ridges and numerous lakes. South of the New England Upland lies the Piedmont Plateau. The plateau forms a 20 to 30 mile-wide belt running from northeastern to southwestern New Jersey.

The southern part of New Jersey is part of the Atlantic Coastal Plain, a lowland region that stretches from New York to Florida. In the west and southwest there are fertile soils, and in the east there are forests and salt marshes.

New Jersey has a mild climate. Average July temperatures range from 76°F in the south to 70°F in the north. January readings range from 34°F in the south to 26°F in the north. Precipitation averages about 46 inches a year.

THE PEOPLE. New Jersey lies in the middle of a vast urban complex that stretches from Washington, D.C., in the south to Boston in the north. Some 90 percent of New Jersey's residents live in urban communities.

There are five Standard Metropolitan Statistical Areas wholly within New Jersey: Atlantic City, Jersey City, Newark, Passaic-Paterson-Clifton, and Trenton. In addition, the Pennsylvania metropolitan area of Allentown-East on-Bethlehem and the Delaware metropolitan area of Wilmington include parts of New Jersey.

Northeastern New Jersey, once part of the New York City Standard Metropolitan Statistical Area, still has strong ties with New York. Many residents commute to jobs in New York City.

About 10 percent of New Jersey's residents were born in foreign countries. One-fourth of the foreign-born are of Italian origin. Almost 10 percent of the population is Negro.

ECONOMY. New Jersey is a prosperous state. In 1966 it ranked sixth among the states in per capita personal income, with an average of $3,414.

Manufacturing accounts for over 95 percent of the total value of goods produced. The chief manufacturing industries produce chemicals and chemical products, electrical machinery, and processed foods.

Agricultural products include eggs and poultry, vegetables, and dairy products. Fishermen make substantial catches of clams and oysters in New Jersey's coastal waters.

GOVERNMENT. The governor of New Jersey is elected to a four-year term. He may succeed himself once but must then skip a term before running a third time. The state legislature consists of a senate, with 40 members elected to four-year terms, and a general assembly, with 80 members elected to two-year terms.

NEW MEXICO

Area: 121,666 square miles (including 221 square miles of water)
Population: (1960 census) 951,023; (1967 est.) 1,003,000
Capital: Santa Fe
State bird: Roadrunner, or chaparral
State tree: Piñon, or nut pine
State flower: Yucca
State motto: Crescit eundo (It grows as it goes)

New Mexico, one of the Mountain states, is bounded on the north by Colorado, on the east by Oklahoma, on the south by Texas and Mexico, and on the west by Arizona. New Mexico entered the Union on Jan. 6, 1912, as the 47th state.

THE LAND. New Mexico can be divided into four major geographic regions. The Colorado Plateau covers the northwestern portion of the state. A region of cliffs and valleys, the plateau is broken by the Continental Divide. West of the divide water flows to the Pacific Ocean: east of the divide water flows toward the Gulf of Mexico and the Atlantic.

The Rocky Mountains extend south from Colorado into north-central New Mexico. The Rio Grande flows south through the mountains. East of the river is the highest point in the state, Wheeler Peak, 13,161 feet.

The Basin and Range Region occupies the southwestern third of the state. The Rio Grande continues south through this region of desert basins and rugged mountains.

The Great Plains, which cover eastern New Mexico, are part of a region that stretches between Canada and Mexico. The plains contain deep canyons, cut by the movement of swift streams.

New Mexico's climate is marked by warm dry days and cool nights. January temperatures average 55°F in the south and 35°F in the north. July temperatures average about 74°F throughout the state. Precipitation averages about 14 inches a year.

THE PEOPLE. About two-thirds of the people live in urban communities. New Mexico has one Standard Metropolitan Statistical Area, Albuquerque, which contains one-fourth of the population.

Some 98 percent of the people in New Mexico were born in the United States. Indians make up about 5 percent of the population. People of Mexican origin form a large part of the population. Spanish is widely spoken, and Mexican customs, foods, and holidays are popular.

ECONOMY. Although New Mexico has many valuable mineral resources, it is not one of the more prosperous states. In 1966 the average per capita personal income was $2,310, ranking New Mexico 41st among the states.

Mineral production accounts for three-fifths of the value of goods produced. Petroleum provides about half of this, with natural gas second in value. New Mexico is the largest producer of uranium and potash in the United States. Copper, gypsum, and helium gas are also important.

Agriculture contributes about one-fourth the value of goods produced. Cattle and sheep are the chief products. Crops include cotton, hay, and sorghum grains. About one-third of the croplands are irrigated.

Manufacturing provides only one-eighth the value of goods produced. Processed foods, lumber, and petroleum products are all important. Nuclear energy facilities, both governmental and private, are also of major significance. New Mexico has been an atomic center since 1945, when the first atom bomb was built and tested in the state.

GOVERNMENT. The governor of New Mexico is elected to a two-year term. He may succeed himself once but must then skip two years before holding any state office. The state legislature consists of a senate, with 42 members elected to four-year terms, and a house of representatives, with 70 members elected to two-year terms.

NEW YORK STATE DEPARTMENT OF COMMERCE

NEW YORK'S WHITEFACE MOUNTAIN is located in a popular tourist and resort area.

NEW YORK

Area: 49,576 square miles (including 1,707 square miles of water)
Population: (1960 census) 16,782,304; (1967 est.) 18,336,000
Capital: Albany
State bird: Bluebird (unofficial)
State tree: Sugar maple
State flower: Rose
State motto: Excelsior (Ever upward)

New York, one of the Middle Atlantic states, is bounded on the north by Lake Ontario and Canada; on the east by Vermont, Massachusetts, and Connecticut; on the south by the Atlantic Ocean, New Jersey, and Pennsylvania; and on the west by Lake Erie and Canada. In the state's southeastern corner lies Long Island, which extends east into the Atlantic Ocean.

New York was one of the 13 original colonies. It ratified the U.S. Constitution on July 26, 1788, to become the 11th state.

THE LAND. New York has seven major geographic regions and is drained by an excellent river system. The main rivers are the Hudson, which flows south through the eastern part of the state; the Mohawk, a branch of the Hudson, which flows southeast; and the St. Lawrence, which forms part of the border with Ontario.

The Atlantic Coastal Plain, part of a region that runs from Massachusetts to Florida, covers Staten Island and Long Island in the southeastern part of the state. The New England Upland covers a strip along the southern half of New York's eastern border, including Manhattan and the lower Hudson River Valley.

The Hudson-Mohawk Lowland occupies the rest of the Hudson River Valley and most of the Mohawk River Valley. The Adirondack Upland covers a roughly circular area north of the Mohawk River Valley. A region of hills and mountains, the Adirondack Upland contains Mt. Marcy, 5,344 feet, the highest point in the state.

The St. Lawrence Lowland covers a strip north of the Adirondack Upland. The Erie-Ontario Upland, west of the Adirondack Upland, borders Lake Erie and Lake Ontario. The Appalachian Plateau covers most of the southern and western parts of the state. The Catskill Mountains and the Finger Lakes are part of the Appalachian Plateau.

The climate varies widely throughout the state. Temperatures are cooler in the mountain areas than they are along the shore. In New York City temperatures average 32°F in January and 77° in July. In Buffalo temperatures average 25°F in January and 70°F in July. Precipitation varies from a yearly average of 32 to 54 inches in different areas.

THE PEOPLE. About 85 percent of New York's residents live in urban communities. There are seven Standard Metropolitan Statistical Areas: Albany-Schenectady-Troy, Binghamton, Buffalo, New York, Rochester, Syracuse, and Utica-Rome.

Because New York City is the major port of entry for immigrants to the United States, the state has a large foreign-born population. In the early 1960s, almost 15 percent of the residents were born abroad, the largest group being those of Italian descent. There are some 1.5 million Negroes in New York and some 16,000 Indians.

ECONOMY. New York is a highly industrial state. It provides about 10 percent of the nation's total value of goods produced. In 1966 New York ranked fourth among the states in annual per capita personal income, with an average of $3,480.

Manufacturing accounts for almost 95 percent of the total value of goods produced in New York. There is a wide variety of industries. Among the most important are clothing and printing and publishing. Other important industries produce processed foods, machinery, and chemicals.

Agriculture provides almost all the remaining value of goods produced, although mining and fishing add a small share. Dairy products and poultry and eggs are valuable, as are such crops as hay, potatoes, and apples.

GOVERNMENT. New York's governor is elected to a four-year term and may succeed himself. The state legislature consists of a 57-member senate and a 150-member assembly. All legislators are elected to two-year terms.

NORTH CAROLINA

Area: 52,586 square miles (including 3,706 square miles of water)
Population: (1960 census) 4,556,155; (1967 est.) 5,029,000
Capital: Raleigh
State bird: Cardinal
State tree: Pine
State flower: Flowering dogwood
State motto: Esse quam videri (To be rather than to seem)

North Carolina, a South Atlantic state, is bordered on the north by Virginia, on the east and southeast by the Atlantic Ocean, on the south by South Carolina and Georgia, and on the west and northwest by Tennessee. One of the original 13 colonies, North Carolina ratified the Constitution on Nov. 21, 1789, to become the 12th state.

THE LAND. North Carolina can be divided into three major land regions: the Atlantic Coastal Plain, the Piedmont Plateau, and the Blue Ridge, or Mountain, Region.

The Atlantic Coastal Plain, part of a region that reaches from New Jersey to Florida, occupies the eastern two-fifths of North Carolina. It includes offshore capes and islands, known as the Outer Banks. The plain contains swamps, prairies, and fertile cropland.

The Piedmont Plateau runs from north to south through the center of the state. In the west it is hilly; in the east, gently rolling. About half the Piedmont is forested.

The Blue Ridge Region covers western North Carolina. Its mountain ranges, part of the Appalachian system, contain Mt. Mitchell, 6,684 feet, the highest point east of the Mississippi River.

North Carolina's climate varies from subtropical in the southeast to temperate in the northwest. Temperatures in July average 80°F in the southeast and 60°F in the northwest; readings in January average 48°F in the southeast and 28°F in the northwest. Precipitation averages about 49 inches a year.

THE PEOPLE. Only about 40 percent of the people in North Carolina live in urban communities. The state has eight Standard Metropolitan Statistical Areas: Asheville, Charlotte, Durham, Fayetteville, Greensboro-High Point, Raleigh, Wilmington, and Winston-Salem.

Almost all residents of North Carolina were born in the United States. About one-fourth of the population is Negro.

THE ECONOMY. Despite its rich soils and fine forests, North Carolina is one of the less prosperous states. In 1966 it ranked 43rd among the states in annual per capita personal income, with an average of $2,235.

Manufacturing provides about three-quarters of the value of goods produced. North Carolina leads all other states in the manufacture of textiles and related products and tobacco products. The state is also a leading producer of furniture.

DURLINGTON INDUSTRIES

NORTH CAROLINA'S TEXTILE MILLS have a spinning frame and other automation.

ROBERT PACKO-TOLEDO

TOLEDO, OHIO. The city's grain elevators have a storage capacity of 7.5 million bushels.

Agriculture provides almost all the remaining value of goods produced. The chief farm product is tobacco, followed by corn, cotton, and peanuts.

GOVERNMENT. The governor of North Carolina is elected to a four-year term and may not succeed himself. The state legislature, the General Assembly, consists of a 50-member senate and a 150-member house of representatives. Legislators are elected to two-year terms.

NORTH DAKOTA

Area: 70,665 square miles (including 1,385 square miles of water)
Population: (1960 census) 632,446; (1967 est.) 639,000
Capital: Bismarck
State bird: Western meadowlark
State tree: American elm
State flower: Wild prairie rose
State motto: Liberty and union, now and forever, one and inseparable

North Dakota, a West North Central state, is bounded on the north by Canada, on the east by Minnesota, on the south by South Dakota, and on the west by Montana. North Dakota entered the Union on Nov. 2, 1889, as the 39th state.

THE LAND. North Dakota can be divided into three major geographic regions: the Red River Valley, the Young Drift Plains, and the Great Plains or Missouri Plateau. Among the rivers that drain the state are the Red, which forms the eastern boundary; the James, which flows south from central North Dakota; and the Missouri, which flows southeast through the western part of the state.

The Red River Valley is the easternmost region. It narrows in width from 40 miles in the north to 10 miles in the south. The valley's fertile black soil yields huge quantities of wheat. The Young Drift Plains cover much of the east and center. River valleys cut through the region's rolling hills.

The Great Plains lie in the western half of the state, broken by the Missouri River. In the southwest are the Badlands, a rough area famous for its strange rock formations. The state's highest point, White Butte, 3,506 feet, is in the Badlands.

Summers in North Dakota are short and hot, and winters are long and severe. July temperatures average about 70°F, January averages about 10°F. Average yearly precipitation is about 17 inches.

THE PEOPLE. Only a little more than one-third of North Dakota's people live in urban communities. There is one Standard Metropolitan Statistical Area, Fargo-Moorhead (Minn.).

Some 95 percent of the population was born in the United States. Indians number about 12,000.

ECONOMY. North Dakota derives a greater percentage of its income from agriculture than does any other state. In 1966 it ranked 38th among the states in annual per capita income, with an average of $2,400.

More than 80 percent of the value of goods produced in North Dakota comes from farming. Spring wheat is the major crop. Other important crops include barley, hay, oats, rye, flax, and potatoes.

Slightly over 10 percent of the value of goods produced comes from mining. The chief mineral is petroleum, and lignite, a form of soft coal, is also significant. Only a small percentage of the value of goods produced comes from manufacturing. Processed foods and petroleum products are the chief manufactures.

GOVERNMENT. The governor of North Dakota is elected to a four-year term and may succeed himself. The state legislature, the Legislative Assembly, consists of a 49-member senate and a 98-member house of representatives. Senators are elected to four-year terms, and representatives are elected to two-year terms.

OHIO

Area: 41,222 square miles (including 204 square miles of water)
Population: (1960 census) 9,706,397; (1967 est.) 10,458,000
Capital: Columbus
State bird: Cardinal
State tree: Buckeye
State flower: Scarlet carnation
State motto: With God, all things are possible

Ohio, an East North Central state, is bounded on the north by Michigan and Lake Erie, on the east by Pennsylvania, on the southeast by West Virginia, on the south by Kentucky, and on the west by Indiana. The Ohio River separates it from West Virginia and Kentucky. Ohio entered the Union on Mar. 1, 1803, as the 17th state.

THE LAND. Ohio can be divided into four major geographic regions. In the north are the Great Lakes Plains, a lowland strip that follows the shore of Lake Erie and then broadens into a valley at its western end.

In the west, south of the Great Lakes Plains, are the fertile Till, or Interior, Plains. The highest point in the state, Campbell Hill, 1,550 feet, is in this region.

In south-central Ohio is the Bluegrass Region, a small triangular area that extends northward from Kentucky. Eastern Ohio is part of the Appalachian, or Allegheny, Plateau, a region of rich mineral deposits, thick forests, and beautiful scenery.

Ohio has a continental climate, with hot, humid summers and cold winters. Temperatures average 31°F in January and 74°F in July. Precipitation averages 37 or 38 inches a year.

THE PEOPLE. More than three-fourths of the population lives in urban communities. Ohio has 13 Standard Metropolitan Statistical Areas: Akron, Canton, Cincinnati, Cleveland, Columbus, Dayton, Hamilton-Middletown, Lima, Lorain-Elyria, Springfield, Steubenville-Weirton (W. Va.), Toledo, and Youngstown-Warren.

About 4 percent of the state's residents were born in foreign countries. Nearly 10 percent of the population is Negro.

ECONOMY. Ohio's economy depends heavily on manufacturing. In 1966 Ohio ranked 15th among the states in annual per capita personal income, with an average of $3,027.

About 90 percent of the value of goods produced in Ohio comes from manufacturing. Transportation equipment is the leading manufacture, and Ohio is noted for the production of truck and bus bodies, truck trailers, and motorcycles. Other important industries produce iron and steel, machinery, and rubber tires.

Agriculture accounts for about 8 percent of the value of goods produced. Hogs, beef cattle, sheep, and poultry are raised, and corn, soybeans, hay, and wheat are grown in large quantities.

Mining provides most of the remainder of the value of goods produced. Bituminous coal is the chief mineral. Oil and natural gas rank high, and Ohio also produces clays, sandstone, limestone, and lime.

GOVERNMENT. The governor of Ohio is elected to a four-year term and may succeed himself. The state legislature, the General Assembly, is made up of a 33-member senate and a 99-member house of representatives. Senators are elected to four-year terms, and representatives are elected to two-year terms.

OKLAHOMA

Area: 69,919 square miles (including 935 square miles of water)
Population: (1960 census) 2,328,284; (1967 est. 2,495,000
Capital: Oklahoma City
State bird: Scissor-tailed flycatcher
State tree: Redbud
State flower: Mistletoe
State motto: Labor omnia vincit (Labor conquers all things)

Oklahoma, a West South Central state, is bounded on the north by Kansas and Colorado, on the east by

Missouri and Arkansas, on the south by Texas, and on the west by Texas and New Mexico. Oklahoma entered the Union on Nov. 16, 1907, as the 46th state.

THE LAND. Oklahoma is shaped like a pan with its handle extending west. The state, whose southern border is formed by the Red River, can be divided into five major geographic regions.

The Great Plains, which cover the Panhandle, are part of a larger region that stretches across the continent east of the Rocky Mountains. The highest point in the state, Black Mesa, with an elevation of 4,973 feet, is in the Great Plains.

The Central Plains cover much of the rest of Oklahoma. A rolling grassland, the region includes the Arbuckle Mountains in its south-central area and the Wichita Mountains in the southwest.

The Ozark Plateau, a region of steep hills and river valleys, lies in the northeastern corner of Oklahoma. The Ouachita Mountains Region, which lies south of the Ozark Plateau, is a series of forested ridges.

The Gulf Coastal Plain runs along the Red River Valley in the southeast. It is part of the lowlands region that extends south to the Gulf of Mexico.

Most of Oklahoma has a warm, dry climate. January temperatures average about 39°F, and July readings are about 83°F. Precipitation varies from more than 50 inches yearly in the humid Gulf Coastal Plain, to less than 20 inches in the Panhandle.

THE PEOPLE. Nearly two-thirds of the population lives in urban communities. Oklahoma has three Standard Metropolitan Statistical Areas: Oklahoma City, Tulsa, and Lawton.

The great majority of the state's residents were born in the United States. The population includes some 50,000 Indians and about 150,000 Negroes.

ECONOMY. Oklahoma's economy is based on manufacturing, mining, and agriculture in roughly equal proportion. In 1966 Oklahoma ranked 35th among the states in per capita personal income, with an annual average of $2,456.

Agriculture provides about 30 percent of the value of goods produced. Oklahoma is a leading beef cattle producer and ranks high in the production of winter wheat, cotton, peanuts, and barley.

Mining activities yield about one-third of the value of goods produced. The most valuable mineral is petroleum, followed by natural gas and coal. Also important are gypsum, sand and gravel, and stone.

Manufacturing accounts for almost 40 percent of the value of goods produced. Processed foods are the leading manufacture. Petroleum refineries and natural gas processing plants are of major importance. The production of nonelectrical machinery, fabricated metal products, and aircraft is also significant.

GOVERNMENT. The governor of Oklahoma is elected to a four-year term and may not succeed himself. The state legislature consists of a 48-

member senate and a 99-member house of representatives. Senators are elected to four-year terms, and representatives are elected to two-year terms.

OREGON

Area: 96,981 square miles (including 772 square miles of water)
Population: (1960 census) 1,768,687; (1967 est.) 1,999,000
Capital: Salem
State bird: Western meadowlark
State tree: Douglas fir
State flower: Oregon grape
State motto: The union

Oregon, a Pacific state, is bordered on the north by Washington, on the east by Idaho, on the south by Nevada and California, and on the west by the Pacific Ocean. Oregon entered the Union on Feb. 14, 1859, as the 33rd state.

THE LAND. Oregon can be divided into six major geographic regions. The Coast Ranges lie along the northern two-thirds of the Pacific shore. They are low, rolling mountains covered with evergreen forests. The Klamath Mountains occupy the southern third of the coastal area.

The Willamette Lowland lies east of the northern part of the Coast Ranges. The lowland forms a narrow strip of fertile farmland along the Willamette River.

The Cascade Mountains, a region of rugged peaks and volcanoes, run from north to south in central Oregon. The highest point in the state, Mt. Hood, 11,235 feet, is in the Cascades.

The Basin and Range Region covers the southern part of eastern Oregon. It is a dry, almost desertlike area. The Columbia Plateau occupies the rest of eastern Oregon. The plateau contains mountains and deep canyons cut by the action of rivers.

Oregon's most important rivers are the Columbia, which forms most of the boundary with Washington, and the Snake, which forms much of the boundary with Idaho.

Oregon has two distinct climate zones. West of the Cascade Mountains temperatures range from the 40°s F in winter to the 60°s F in summer. Precipitation varies from 60 to 120 inches a year. East of the Cascades, winters are cold and summers are hot. Precipitation ranges from only 6 to 12 inches yearly.

THE PEOPLE. Slightly less than two-thirds of the people in Oregon live in urban communities. There are three Standard Metropolitan Statistical Areas: Portland, Eugene, and Salem.

Foreign-born residents, mostly of Canadian and Scandinavian origin, make up about 4 percent of the population. There are some 10,000 Indians and about 10,000 Negroes.

ECONOMY. Oregon's most important natural resource is its forests, which are important to the country's economy. In 1966 Oregon ranked 18th among the states in annual per capita personal income, with an average of $2,938.

Nearly three-fourths of the value of goods produced comes from manu-

BIRD-IN-HAND, PENNSYLVANIA, in Amish country, has horse-drawn transportation.

RHODE ISLAND'S famed Brown University.

facturing. Wood processing is the leading industry, with Oregon supplying nearly one-fourth of the nation's timber. Plywood, hardboard, fiberboard, shingles, and vast quantities of pulp and paper are produced. Food processing is the second most important manufacturing industry.

Almost one-quarter of the value of goods produced comes from agriculture. Cattle and calves, dairy products, and wheat, hay, fruit, and truck crops are all important.

Less than 5 percent of the value of goods produced come from mining and fishing. Stone, sand, gravel, and nickel are the chief minerals, and salmon, tuna, crabs, and sole are the most important fish.

GOVERNMENT. The governor of Oregon is elected to a four-year term. He may not serve for more than 8 years in any 12-year span. The state legislature, the Legislative Assembly, consists of a 30-member senate and a 60-member house of representatives. Senators are elected to four-year terms, and representatives are elected to two-year terms.

PENNSYLVANIA

Area: 45,333 square miles (including 308 square miles of water)
Population: (1960 census) 11,319,366; (1967 est.) 11,629,000
Capital: Harrisburg
State bird: Ruffed grouse
State tree: Hemlock
State flower: Mountain laurel
State motto: Virtue, liberty, and independence

Pennsylvania, a Middle Atlantic state, is bounded on the north by New York and Lake Erie; on the east by New York and New Jersey; on the south by Delaware, Maryland, and West Virginia; and on the west by West Virginia and Ohio. One of the 13 original colonies, Pennsylvania ratified the Constitution on Dec. 12, 1787, to become the second state.

THE LAND. Pennsylvania can be divided into seven major geographic regions. The Erie Lowland is a narrow region lying along the Lake Erie shore. The Appalachian, or Alle-

gheny, Plateau covers most of the western and northern parts of the state and reaches into the northeast. The plateau, which is cut by deep river valleys, contains Mt. David, 3,213 feet, the state's highest point.

The Appalachian Ridge and Valley Region lies east of the Appalachian Plateau. It contains the Great Valley, made up of three fertile valleys. In the eastern part of the region are coal and slate fields. The mountainous Blue Ridge enters Pennsylvania from Maryland and forms a small region along the central part of the southern border.

The New England Upland covers a small portion of east-central Pennsylvania. Rolling plains and low hills alternate with fertile valleys. The Atlantic Coastal Plain, a level and fertile area, occupies the southeastern corner of the state.

Pennsylvania's winters are cold, and its summers are hot. Temperatures in January range from 26°F in the north to 34°F in the south. Temperatures in July vary from 70°F in the north to 77°F in the south. Precipitation averages about 42 inches a year.

THE PEOPLE. About three-fourths of the people of Pennsylvania live in urban communities. There are 12 Standard Metropolitan Statistical Areas: Altoona, Bethlehem-Easton-Allentown, Erie, Harrisburg, Johnstown, Lancaster, Philadelphia, Pittsburgh, Reading, Scranton, Wilkes Barre–Hazleton, and York.

About 5 percent of the population was born in foreign countries. Pennsylvania also has colonies of people of German descent, known as Pennsylvania Dutch. The population includes more than 800,000 Negroes.

ECONOMY. Pennsylvania is a highly industrialized state. In 1966 it ranked 17th among the states in annual per capita personal income, with an average of $2,951.

About 90 percent of the value of goods produced comes from manufacturing. Pennsylvania leads the nation in the production of pig iron and steel and produces large quantities of coke, used in smelting iron ore. Other important industries produce processed foods and machinery.

The remaining 10 percent of the

value of goods produced is equally divided between agriculture and the extractive industries—fishing and mining. Pennsylvania produces dairy goods, eggs, hay, and corn. One of the most important coal-producing states, it is the source of almost all the hard coal in the United States.

GOVERNMENT. The governor of Pennsylvania is elected to a four-year term and may succeed himself once. The General Assembly consists of a 50-member senate and a 203-member house of representatives. Senators are elected to four-year terms and representatives are elected to two-year terms.

RHODE ISLAND

Area: 1,214 square miles (including 165 square miles of water)
Population: (1960 census) 859,488; (1967 est.) 900,000
Capital: Providence
State bird: Rhode Island red
State tree: Red maple
State flower: Violet
State motto: Hope

Rhode Island, officially the State of Rhode Island and Providence Plantations, is one of the New England states. It is bounded on the north and east by Massachusetts, on the south by the Atlantic Ocean, and on the west by Connecticut. One of the 13 original colonies, Rhode Island ratified the Constitution on May 29, 1790, to become the 13th state.

THE LAND. Rhode Island, the smallest state in area, is cut almost in two by Narragansett Bay. The state has two major geographic regions—the Coastal Lowlands and the Eastern New England Upland.

The Coastal Lowlands, which cover eastern and southern Rhode Island, are part of a larger region that extends across the whole New England coast. The region is marked by sandy beaches and lagoons along the shore, and rising ground inland.

The Eastern New England Upland stretches across the rest of the state. Rough and hilly, the region has many lakes and ponds and contains the highest point in the state, Jerimoth Hill, 812 feet.

Rhode Island has a mild, moist climate. Temperatures are warmer near the coast than inland. January readings average about 30°F, and July temperatures average about 70°F. Precipitation averages some 42 inches a year.

THE PEOPLE. Nearly nine out of every ten people live in urban communities. Rhode Island has one Standard Metropolitan Statistical Area, Providence-Pawtucket-Warwick.

ECONOMY. Although Rhode Island has few natural resources, it is a relatively prosperous state. In 1966 the annual average per capita personal income was $2,980, ranking Rhode Island 16th among the states.

Manufacturing contributes about 97 percent of the value of goods produced. Textiles are the most important product, and Rhode Island mills turn out cotton, woolen, worsted, synthetic, and lace fabrics. Other valuable manufactures include jewelry and silverware, rubber and plastics products, and precision instruments.

Only about 2 percent of the value of goods produced comes from agriculture. Milk and eggs are the most important farm products, followed by potatoes and broiler chickens.

GOVERNMENT. The governor of Rhode Island is elected to a two-year term and may succeed himself. The state legislature, the General Assembly, consists of a 50-member senate and a 100-member house of representatives. Legislators are elected to two-year terms.

SOUTH CAROLINA

Area: 31,055 square miles (including 775 square miles of water)

Population: (1960 census) 2,382,594; (1967 est.) 2,599,000

Capital: Columbia

State bird: Carolina wren

State tree: Palmetto

State flower: Carolina jessamine

State mottoes: Animis opibusque parati (Prepared in mind and resources); Dum spiro spero (While I breathe I hope)

South Carolina, a South Atlantic state, is bounded on the north by North Carolina; on the east and southeast by the Atlantic Ocean; and on the south, southwest, and west by Georgia. One of the 13 original colonies, South Carolina ratified the Constitution on May 23, 1788, to become the eighth state.

THE LAND. South Carolina can be divided into three geographic regions: the Atlantic Coastal Plain, the Piedmont, and the Blue Ridge. The Atlantic Coastal Plain is known as the low country, and the other two regions are known as the up country. The two "countries" are divided by the fall line, a line of low hills crossed by rivers that form rapids and falls.

The Atlantic Coastal Plain stretches across the eastern two-thirds of the state. The plain is a lowland, containing bays and islands along the coast and swamps inland.

The Piedmont extends over much of northwestern South Carolina. It is a region of granite and other rocks worn down into rolling hills that form a plateau. Many swift rivers run

across the Piedmont from northwest to southeast.

The Blue Ridge occupies the northwestern corner of the state. Part of a larger region that reaches from Pennsylvania to Georgia, it contains the highest point in South Carolina, Sassafras Mountain, 3,560 feet.

The climate of South Carolina is mild. July temperatures average 81°F in the south and 72°F in the northwest. January readings range from 51°F in the south to 41°F in the northwest. Precipitation averages 45 inches a year.

THE PEOPLE. Only slightly more than 40 percent of the state's residents live in urban communities. There are three Standard Metropolitan Statistical Areas: Charleston, Columbia, and Greenville. About one-third of the population is Negro.

ECONOMY. South Carolina is one of the less prosperous states. In 1966 it ranked 48th in per capita personal income, with an average of $2,027.

Manufacturing accounts for four-fifths of the value of goods produced. Textiles are the most important manufacture, and South Carolina produces cottons, silks, wools, and synthetic fabrics. Other important products are chemicals and allied goods, clothing, and pulp and paper.

Agriculture accounts for slightly less than one-fifth of the value of goods produced. Tobacco is the chief crop, followed by cotton, soybeans, and corn.

Commercial fishing and mining provide some income. South Carolina is a leading shrimp state, and it is a producer of cement and granite.

GOVERNMENT. The governor of South Carolina is elected to a four-year term and may not succeed himself. The General Assembly consists of a 50-member senate and a 124-member house of representatives. Senators are elected to four-year terms, and representatives to two-year terms.

SOUTH DAKOTA

Area: 77,047 square miles (including 1,091 square miles of water)

Population: (1960 census) 680,514; (1967 est.) 674,000

Capital: Pierre

State bird: Ring-necked pheasant

State tree: Black Hills spruce

State flower: American pasqueflower

State motto: Under God the people rule

South Dakota, a West North Central state, is bounded on the north by North Dakota, on the east by Minnesota and Iowa, on the south by Nebraska, and on the west by Wyoming and Montana. The Missouri River flows south through the center of the state. South Dakota entered the Union on Nov. 2, 1889, as the 40th state.

THE LAND. South Dakota can be divided into four major geographic regions. The Black Hills, which run along the Wyoming border, are thickly forested and pitted with deep canyons. They include the highest point in the state, Harney Peak, 7,242 feet.

The Great Plains extend across most of the western two-thirds of South Dakota. In the east are rolling hills, and in the west are ridges, val-

leys, and flat-topped solitary hills known as buttes.

The Dissected Till Plains, in the southeastern corner of the state, are rolling prairies cut by streams. The Young Drift Plains, in much of eastern South Dakota, are distinguished by low hills and glacial lakes.

South Dakota's summers are short and hot and winters are long and cold. Average July temperatures vary from 68°F to 78°F, and January readings range from 10°F to 22°F. Precipitation averages about 13 inches in the northwest and about 25 inches in the southeast.

THE PEOPLE. Only about 40 percent of South Dakota's people live in urban communities. There is one Standard Metropolitan Statistical Area, Sioux Falls.

About 3 percent of the state's residents were born in foreign countries. They are mostly of Scandinavian, German, and Russian origin.

ECONOMY. The economy of South Dakota rests largely on agriculture. In 1966 the average annual per capita personal income was $2,355, ranking South Dakota 39th among the states.

More than four-fifths of the value of goods produced comes from agriculture. Livestock and livestock products provide the bulk of farm income. Cattle graze on the state's enormous pastures and are then sent to feeding lots to be grain-fattened before being slaughtered. South Dakota is a leading producer of corn, hay, wheat, and oats, much of which is used as livestock feeds.

Some 15 percent of the value of goods produced is derived from manufacturing. Meat packing is the most important industry. Mining is also important, and South Dakota is the nation's leading gold-mining state, producing about two-fifths of the gold mined in the United States. Petroleum is of increasing significance.

GOVERNMENT. South Dakota's governor is elected to a two-year term and may succeed himself once. The state legislature consists of a 35-member senate and a 75-member house of representatives. Legislators are elected to two-year terms.

TENNESSEE

Area: 42,244 square miles (including 879 square miles of water)

Population: (1960 census) 3,567,089; (1967 est.) 3,892,000

Capital: Nashville

State bird: Mockingbird

State tree: Tulip poplar

State flower: Iris

State motto: Agriculture and commerce

Tennessee is an East South Central state. It is bounded on the north by Kentucky and Virginia; on the east by North Carolina; on the south by Georgia, Alabama, and Mississippi; and on the west by Arkansas and Missouri. The Mississippi River forms the western boundary. Tennessee entered the Union on June 1, 1796, as the 16th state.

THE LAND. Tennessee has seven major geographic regions. The Blue Ridge lies along the state's eastern border. A mountainous region, it contains the

ATOMIC ENERGY COMMISSION

OAK RIDGE, TENNESSEE, is the site of a government plant for production of uranium-235.

highest point in Tennessee, Clingmans Dome, 6,642 feet.

The Appalachian Ridge and Valley Region lies west of the Blue Ridge. Valleys alternate with forested ridges. To the west the Appalachian, or Cumberland, Plateau runs parallel to the Ridge and Valley Region. The plateau is made up of flat-topped mountains cut by valleys.

The Nashville Basin forms a rough circle in central Tennessee. It is a rich pasture and cropland. The Highland Rim is a plain that circles the Nashville Basin. The land slopes from the rim to the basin.

The Gulf Coastal Plain, west of the rim, is part of a larger region that runs from Illinois to the Gulf of Mexico. The Mississippi Alluvial Plain, in the far western corner, is bottomland that runs along the bank of the Mississippi River.

Tennessee has a moderate, rather humid climate. Western parts of the state are generally warmer than the more mountainous east. Temperatures in the west average 40°F in January and 79°F in July. Readings in the east average 37°F in January and 71°F in July. Precipitation averages about 50 inches a year.

THE PEOPLE. Slightly more than half the people of Tennessee live in urban communities. There are four Standard Metropolitan Statistical Areas: Memphis, Knoxville, Nashville, and Chattanooga. About 16 percent of the population is Negro.

ECONOMY. Tennessee is an industrial state whose development is due in large part to the Tennessee Valley Authority (TVA). The TVA, an electric power system sponsored by the federal government, provides inexpensive electricity to many industries. In 1966 Tennessee ranked 45th among the states in per capita personal income, with an everage of $2,199.

Manufacturing yields about 80 percent of the value of goods produced. Chemicals and allied products are the chief manufactures, followed by metals and metal products, textiles, and processed foods. There is also a major U.S. Atomic Energy Commission installation at Oak Ridge.

Agriculture provides less than 20 percent of the value of goods produced. Cotton is the chief crop, and tobacco, corn, and hay are also important. Cattle, calves, and hogs are raised.

Mining contributes a small share of the total value of goods produced. Stone is the leading item, and zinc and coal are significant.

GOVERNMENT. The governor of Tennessee is elected to a four-year term and may not succeed himself. The General Assembly consists of a 33-member senate and a 99-member house of representatives. Legislators are elected to two-year terms.

TEXAS

Area: 267,339 square miles (including 4,369 square miles of water)
Population: (1960 census) 9,579,677; (1967 est.) 10,869,000
Capital: Austin
State bird: Mockingbird
State tree: Pecan
State flower: Bluebonnet
State motto: Friendship

Texas is one of the West South Central states. It is bounded on the north by Oklahoma and Arkansas, on the east by Arkansas and Louisiana, on the southeast by the Gulf of Mexico, on the south and southwest by Mexico, and on the west by New Mexico. Once a part of Mexico, Texas became an independent republic in 1836. It joined the Union on Dec. 29, 1845, as the 28th state.

THE LAND. Texas, which may be divided into four geographic regions, has an extensive river system. Among the major rivers are the Rio Grande, which forms the boundary with Mexico; the Red River, which forms part of the boundary with Oklahoma; the Sabine, which forms part of the boundary with Louisiana; and the Brazos, which flows southeast through central Texas to the Gulf of Mexico.

The Basin and Range, or Trans-Pecos, Region covers the extreme western part of Texas. It contains high plains crossed by spurs of the Rocky Mountains. Mountain gorges are found along the upper Rio Grande. The Great Plains cover much of northwestern Texas. They contain the highest point in the state, Guadalupe Peak, 8,571 feet. The plains are rich in wheat and oil.

The North-Central Plains, which lie in north-central Texas, are broken by low hills. The region contains rich cropland and large petroleum deposits. The West Gulf Coastal Plain covers eastern and southern Texas. It is part of a fertile lowland crescent that fans out around the Gulf of Mexico.

The climate of Texas varies from temperate in the northwest to subtropical along the Mexican border. It is warm and damp along the Gulf of Mexico, mild in central Texas, damp and cool in the northeast, and dry in the west. Average January temperatures range from 35°F to 60°F, and July readings range from 79°F to 85°F. Precipitation averages 28 inches a year.

THE PEOPLE. About 75 percent of the people live in urban communities. Texas has 21 Standard Metropolitan Statistical Areas: Abilene, Amarillo, Austin, Beaumont-Port Arthur, Brownsville-Harlingen-San Benito, Corpus Christi, Dallas, El Paso, Fort Worth, Galveston-Texas City, Houston, Laredo, Lubbock, Midland, Odessa, San Angelo, San Antonio, Texarkana-Texarkana (Ark.), Tyler, Waco, and Wichita Falls.

About 3 percent of the people of Texas are foreign-born. Most are of Mexican origin, and many U.S.-born Texans are of Mexican descent. About 10 percent of the state's population is Negro.

ECONOMY. Although Texas is the leading state in mineral production, in 1966 it ranked 33rd in annual per capita personal income, with an average of $2,511.

About 30 percent of the value of goods produced in Texas comes from minerals. Petroleum and natural gas are most valuable, but sulfur, salt, and helium are also important.

Some 20 percent of the value of goods produced comes from agriculture and commercial fishing. Texas is a leading producer of cotton, sorghum, rice, and wheat. Large herds of cattle are raised, and shrimp and other fish are caught along the Gulf coast.

About half the total value of goods produced comes from manufacturing. Leading industries produce chemicals and allied products, food products, and refined petroleum.

GOVERNMENT. The governor of Texas is elected to a two-year term and may succeed himself. The state legislature consists of a 31-member senate and a 150-member house of representatives. Senators are elected to four-year terms, and representatives are elected to two-year terms.

UNITED STATES DEPARTMENT OF THE INTERIOR

UTAH'S CANYONLANDS NATIONAL PARK contains the huge Druid Arch, in Needle Country.

VERMONT DEVELOPMENT DEPARTMENT

VERMONT SKIERS at Madonna Mountain.

UTAH

Area: 84,916 square miles (including 2,535 square miles of water)
Population: (1960 census) 890,627; (1967 est.) 1,024,000
State bird: Sea gull
State tree: Blue spruce
State flower: Sego lily
State motto: Industry

Utah, a Mountain state, is bounded on the north by Idaho and Wyoming, on the east by Colorado, on the south by Arizona, and on the west by Nevada. Utah entered the Union on Jan. 4, 1896, as the 45th state.

THE LAND. Utah has three major geographic regions: the Colorado Plateau, the Basin and Range Region, and the Rocky Mountains Region.

The Colorado Plateau covers most of the eastern three-fifths of the state. It is part of a larger region that extends into Arizona, Colorado, and New Mexico. The Colorado Plateau contains wide uplands sliced by canyons and valleys.

The Basin and Range Region, one of the most arid regions in the nation, covers the western third of Utah. Great Salt Lake is in the northeast and the Great Salt Lake Desert is in the west and southwest.

The Rocky Mountains Region lies in the northwestern corner of Utah. It is made up of two ranges, the Uinta and the Wasatch, and contains the highest point in the state, Kings Peak, 13,528 feet.

Utah has a varied climate. In the northeast, July temperatures average 60°F, and January temperatures average 20°F. In the southwest, July readings average 84°F, and January readings average 39°F. Precipitation varies from less than five inches in the Great Salt Lake Desert to over 40 inches in the northeast.

THE PEOPLE. About three-quarters of the people of Utah live in urban communities. The state has three Standard Metropolitan Statistical Areas: Ogden, Provo-Orem, and Salt Lake City. Foreign-born residents, mostly of Canadian and British origin, make up some 5 percent of the population.

ECONOMY. Manufacturing, mining, and agriculture all contribute significantly to Utah's economy. In 1966 Utah ranked 34th among the states in annual per capita personal income, with an average of $2,500.

Over half the value of goods produced comes from manufacturing. The most important industries produce metals and metal products, missiles and missile parts, and processed foods.

About one-third of the value of goods produced comes from mining. Utah produces sizeable quantities of copper, petroleum, coal, and uranium. Gold, iron ore, lead, and zinc are also found in the state.

Some 15 percent of the value of goods produced is derived from agriculture. Cattle and calves are the chief farm product. Crops include hay, wheat, barley, and sugar beets. Turkeys, sheep, and lambs are other important sources of income.

GOVERNMENT. The governor of Utah is elected to a four-year term and may succeed himself. The state legislature consists of a 28-member senate and a 69-member house of representatives. Senators are elected to four-year terms, and representatives are elected to two-year terms.

VERMONT

Area: 9,609 square miles (including 335 square miles of water)
Population: (1960 census) 389,881; (1967 est.) 417,000
Capital: Montpelier
State bird: Hermit thrush
State tree: Sugar maple
State flower: Red clover
State motto: Freedom and unity

Vermont, a New England state, is bounded on the north by Canada, on the east by New Hampshire, on the south by Massachusetts, and on the west by New York. The Connecticut River runs along the eastern border, and Lake Champlain forms the northern part of the western border. Vermont entered the Union on Mar. 4, 1791, as the 14th state.

THE LAND. Vermont can be divided into six major geographic regions. The Champlain Valley, a region of rolling hills and lowlands, runs along the northwestern border near Lake Champlain. The Taconic Mountains Region, marked by tall peaks, swift rivers, and lakes, lies along the southwestern border.

The Vermont Valley, lying just east of the Taconic Mountains, contains the valleys of several small rivers. The Green Mountains run from north to south through the center of the state. They contain the highest point in Vermont, Mt. Mansfield, 4,393 feet.

The Western New England Upland extends across most of eastern Vermont. The lowlands of the Connecticut River are in the eastern part of the region, and low hills cover the western part. The White Mountains Region lies in the northeastern corner of Vermont. It contains rocky hills and swift streams.

Summers in Vermont are short and cool, and winters are long and cold. Temperatures average 60°F in July and 19°F in January. Precipitation averages some 40 inches a year.

THE PEOPLE. Some 60 percent of the people of Vermont live in rural communities or on farms. Unlike most states, Vermont has no Standard Metropolitan Statistical Areas. Foreign-born people, mostly of Canadian origin, make up about 6 percent of the population.

ECONOMY. Manufacturing and tourism are the two most important factors in Vermont's economy. In 1966 Vermont ranked 29th among the states in per capita personal income, with an average of $2,590.

Tourism is one of Vermont's leading industries. In the summer visitors come to the lakes and mountains, in autumn they come for the beautiful foliage, and in winter they gather in the numerous mountain ski resorts.

Manufacturing provides about 65 percent of the value of goods produced. The leading manufactures are machinery, processed foods, and paper and paper products. Also of importance are stone, clay, and glass products.

Agriculture provides about 30 percent of the value of goods produced. Milk, much of which is made into cheese, is the leading farm product. Calves, poultry, and eggs are also important.

Potatoes are the state's biggest vegetable crop, and apples are the leading fruit. Vermont is also noted for the production of maple syrup.

Some 5 percent of the value of goods produced comes from mining. Vermont produces stone, asbestos, talc, limestone, and granite.

GOVERNMENT. The governor of Vermont is elected to a two-year term and may succeed himself. The state legislature is made up of a 30-member senate and a 150-member house of representatives. Members of the state legislature are elected to two-year terms.

VIRGINIA

Area: 40,817 square miles (including 976 square miles of water)
Population: (1960 census) 3,966,949; (1967 est.) 4,536,000
Capital: Richmond
State bird: Cardinal
State flower: Flowering dogwood
State motto: Sic semper tyrannis (Thus always with tyrants)

Virginia is one of the South Atlantic states. It is bounded on the north by Maryland and West Virginia; on the east by Maryland, Chesapeake Bay, and the Atlantic Ocean; on the south by North Carolina and Tennessee; and on the west by Kentucky and West Virginia. One of the original 13 colonies, Virginia ratified the Constitution on June 25, 1788, to become the 10th state.

VIRGINIA DEPARTMENT OF CONSERVATION
VIRGINIA'S JAMESTOWN FESTIVAL PARK shows exact copies of 1607 English settler ships.

THE LAND. Virginia can be divided into five major geographic regions. In the southwestern corner is the Appalachian Plateau, a forested region crossed by westward flowing streams.

Running from northeast to southwest is the Appalachian Ridge and Valley Region, a string of river valleys divided by knobs and ridges.

East of the Ridge and Valley Region, and parallel to it, is the Blue Ridge. Part of the Appalachian Mountain system, the Blue Ridge contains the highest point in Virginia, Mt. Rogers, 5,729 feet.

East of the Blue Ridge is the Piedmont. It is a rolling plain cut by rivers that become rapids and falls at its eastern edge. Still farther east is the Atlantic Coastal Plain, also called the Tidewater. It is a low, swampy region that runs along the coast.

Virginia has a mild climate. January temperatures average 41°F in the east and 32°F in the west. July temperatures vary from 78°F in the east to 68°F in the west. Yearly precipitation ranges from 36 inches in the north to 44 inches in the south.

THE PEOPLE. Over half of Virginia's residents live in urban communities. There are five Standard Metropolitan Statistical Areas: Lynchburg, Newport News-Hampton, Norfolk-Portsmouth, Richmond, and Roanoke. More than one-fifth of the people are Negro.

ECONOMY. Virginia's economy is based largely on manufacturing, and the state is moderately prosperous. In 1966 the average annual per capita personal income was $2,581, ranking Virginia 30th among the states.

Manufacturing industries yield about three-fourths of the value of goods produced. The leading manufactures are chemical products, including man-made fibers such as nylon and rayon. Other important industries produce processed foods and tobacco products.

Agriculture provides over 15 percent of the value of goods produced. More than half of this comes from livestock, dairying, and poultry. Tobacco is the chief cash crop, and hay, corn, peanuts, apples, and soybeans are also important.

The extractive industries—mining and commercial fishing—supply less than 5 percent of the value of goods produced. Virginia's minerals include soft coal, stone, sand, and gravel. Fishermen make large catches of crabs, oysters, shrimps, clams, and flounder.

GOVERNMENT. The governor of Virginia is elected to a four-year term and may not succeed himself. The state legislature, the General Assembly, is made up of a 40-member senate and a 100-member house of delegates. Senators are elected to four-year terms, and delegates are elected to two-year terms.

WASHINGTON

Area: 68,192 square miles (including 1,529 square miles of water)
Population: (1960 census) 2,853,214; (1967 est.) 3,087,000
Capital: Olympia
State bird: Willow goldfinch
State tree: Western hemlock
State flower: Coast rhododendron
State motto: Alki (By and by)

Washington, one of the Pacific states, is bounded on the north by Canada, on the east by Idaho, on the south by

WASHINGTON'S GRAND COULEE, on the Columbia River, is one of the world's largest dams.

Oregon, and on the west by the Pacific Ocean and Puget Sound. Washington entered the Union on Nov. 11, 1889, as the 42nd state.

THE LAND. Washington can be divided into six major geographic regions. The Olympic Mountains, which lie in the northwestern corner of the state, form a wild region that has been only partly explored. The Coast Range covers the state's southwestern corner. Much of the range is taken up by the forested Willapa Hills.

The Puget Sound Lowland, which forms a strip east of the Olympic Mountains and Coast Ranges, has a western extension between those two mountain regions. Waters from Puget Sound run far into the lowland. The Cascade Mountains lie east of the Puget Sound Lowland. The Cascades, part of a mountain chain that runs from Canada to California, contain the highest point in the state, Mt. Rainier, 14,410 feet.

The Rocky Mountains Region is in the northwestern corner of Washington. The Rockies are part of a mountain chain that extends from Canada to Mexico. The Columbia Plateau extends over the central and southeastern parts of the state and is part of the world's largest lava plateau.

Western Washington has a mild climate. January temperatures average 41°F, and July temperatures average 66°F. Eastern Washington has colder winters and warmer summers. Temperatures there average 25°F in January and 72°F in July. Yearly precipitation varies from 135 inches in the northwest to 6 inches in the central plateau.

THE PEOPLE. More than two-thirds of the people live in urban communities. Washington has three Standard Metropolitan Statistical Areas: Seattle-Everett, Spokane, and Tacoma.

Some 10 percent of the people are foreign-born. The largest groups are of Canadian and Scandinavian origin. Some 30,000 Negroes and 20,000 Indians live in Washington.

ECONOMY. Washington is a prosperous state. In 1966 it ranked eighth among the states in per capita personal income, with an average of $3,200.

About four-fifths of the value of goods produced comes from manufacturing. The leading manufacture is transportation equipment, including jet aircraft, space vehicles, and ships. Wood and wood products and processed foods are also important.

Less than one-fifth of the value of goods produced comes from agriculture. Wheat is the biggest cash crop, and milk is a leading product. Washington also produces large quantities of apples and potatoes.

Less than 5 percent of the value of goods produced is derived from fishing and mining. Salmon and halibut are among the fish caught in Washington's waters. Sand, gravel, and stone are significant.

GOVERNMENT. The governor of Washington is elected to a four-year term and may succeed himself. The state legislature consists of a 49-member senate and a 99-member house of representatives. Senators are elected to four-year terms, and representatives are elected to two-year terms.

WEST VIRGINIA

Area: 24,181 square miles (including 97 square miles of water)
Population: (1960 census) 1,860,421; (1967 est.) 1,798,000
Capital: Charleston
State bird: Cardinal
State tree: Sugar maple
State flower: Rhododendron
State motto: Montani semper liberi (Mountaineers are always free)

West Virginia, a South Atlantic state, is bounded on the north by Ohio, Pennsylvania, and Maryland; on the east and south by Virginia; and on the west by Kentucky and Ohio. West Virginia entered the Union on June 26, 1863, as the 35th state.

THE LAND. West Virginia can be divided into three major geographic regions: the Blue Ridge, the Appalachian Ridge and Valley, and the Appalachian Plateau.

The Blue Ridge, a mountainous region, occupies a small portion of eastern West Virginia. The Appalachian Ridge and Valley Region runs along the state's eastern border. Forested ridges alternate with river valleys. The highest point in the state, Spruce Knob, 4,862 feet, is in the Ridge and Valley region.

The Appalachian Plateau covers the rest of the state. The plateau's rough surface is cut by narrow river valleys, forming uplands and hills rich in minerals.

Summers in West Virginia are warm, and winters are moderate. January temperatures average 33°F, and July readings average about 75°F. Yearly precipitation varies from 32 to 56 inches across the state.

THE PEOPLE. Over 60 percent of the population lives in rural communities or on farms. West Virginia has four Standard Metropolitan Statistical Areas: Charleston, Huntington-Ashland (Ky.), Weirton-Steubenville (Ohio), and Wheeling.

About 5 percent of the population of West Virginia is Negro.

ECONOMY. Although West Virginia has rich mineral resources, it is not a prosperous state. In 1966 it had an average per capita personal income of $2,195, ranking it 46th among the states.

Mining accounts for nearly 30 percent of the value of goods produced. Bituminous coal is the most important mineral, and natural gas is significant. Natural gas fields also produce natural gasoline, which is liquified natural gas. Great quantities of limestone, sandstone, and sand, gravel, clay, and salt are also mined.

Manufacturing provides about 65 percent of the value of goods produced. Chemical products, many of which are derived from West Virginia's minerals, are the chief manufacture. Iron and steel are produced from ore shipped to West Virginia from Minnesota and Michigan. Other items are stone, clay, and glass products.

Agriculture supplies only about 5 percent of the value of goods produced. Beef and dairy cattle, sheep, hogs, and poultry are raised, and apples, corn, tobacco, and peaches are grown.

GOVERNMENT. The governor of West Virginia is elected to a four-year term and may not succeed himself. The state legislature consists of a 34-member senate and a 100-member house of delegates. Senators are elected to four-year terms, and delegates are elected to two-year terms.

WISCONSIN

Area: 56,154 square miles (including 1,690 square miles of water)
Population: (1960 census) 3,951,777; (1967 est.) 4,189,000
Capital: Madison
State bird: Robin
State tree: Sugar maple
State flower: Violet
State motto: Forward

Wisconsin is an East North Central state, bounded on the north by Michigan and Lake Superior, on the east by Lake Michigan, on the south by

WEST VIRGINIA INDUSTRIAL AND PUBLICITY COMMISSION
HARPER'S FERRY, WEST VIRGINIA, lies where the Shenandoah River joins the Potomac River.

U.S. SOIL CONSERVATION SERVICE

WISCONSIN, well known for its dairy-farming, also raises crops using contour strip-cropping.

U.S. DEPARTMENT OF THE INTERIOR

WYOMING'S huge Grand Teton Mountain.

Illinois, and on the west by Iowa and Minnesota. The St. Croix and Mississippi rivers form most of the western boundary. Wisconsin entered the Union on May 29, 1848, as the 30th state.

THE LAND. Wisconsin can be divided into five major geographic regions. The Lake Superior Lowland is a narrow region along the lake shore. The Superior Upland, which stretches across much of northern Wisconsin, is a region of lakes and forests. It includes the highest point in the state, Timms Hill, 1,952 feet.

The Central Plain forms an arc south of the Superior Upland. The Western Upland runs from northwest to southwest, along the Mississippi River. The Great Lakes Plain, a rich agricultural region, covers eastern Wisconsin.

Wisconsin has warm summers and long, cold winters. July temperatures average in the low 70°s F; January temperatures are in the high teens. Yearly precipitation is about 30 inches.

THE PEOPLE. Nearly two-thirds of Wisconsin's residents live in urban communities. There are six Standard Metropolitan Statistical Areas: Green Bay, Kenosha, Madison, Milwaukee, Racine, and Superior-Duluth (Minn.).

About 4 percent of the people were born in foreign countries. The largest foreign-born groups are of German, Norwegian, Polish, and Russian origin.

ECONOMY. In 1966 Wisconsin ranked 19th among the states in per capita personal income, with an average of $2,935.

About four-fifths of the value of goods produced comes from manufacturing. Nonelectrical machinery is the most important product. Also important are processed foods, including cheese and canned vegetables. Wisconsin is a major producer of transportation equipment and paper products.

Less than one-fifth of the value of goods produced comes from agriculture. Milk and hay are the most important farm products. The state is

also an important source of corn, oats, eggs, and truck crops.

Tourism is a significant source of income. Wisconsin's lakes, streams, and forests attract summer visitors, and its skiing facilities bring winter sports enthusiasts.

GOVERNMENT. The governor of Wisconsin is elected to a two-year term and may succeed himself. The state legislature consists of a 33-member senate and a 100-member assembly. Senators are elected to four-year terms, and assemblymen are elected to two-year terms.

WYOMING

Area: 97,914 square miles (including 633 square miles of water)

Population: (1960 census) 330,066; (1967 est.) 315,000

Capital: Cheyenne

State bird: Meadowlark

State tree: Cottonwood

State flower: Indian paintbrush

State motto: Equal rights

Wyoming, a Mountain state, is bounded on the north by Montana, on the east by South Dakota and Nebraska, on the south by Colorado and Utah, and on the west by Utah and Idaho. Wyoming entered the Union on July 10, 1890, as the 44th state.

THE LAND. Wyoming has three major geographic regions—the Rocky Mountains, the Intermontane Basins, and the Great Plains.

The Rocky Mountains Region is broken into two parts. One section enters the state from the west and extends into the south-central region. The other section enters the state in the southeast and extends north. The region's many mountain ranges include the highest point in Wyoming, Gannett Peak, 13,785 feet.

The Intermontane Basins are flat stretches between the mountain ranges. The basins are good grazing land. The Great Plains, part of a larger region that runs from Canada to Mexico, extend along the eastern border.

Wyoming summers are warm and dry, and winters are cold. Temperatures are lower in the mountains than in the basins. Average July temperatures range from 59°F to 71°F, and average January temperatures vary from 12°F to 22°F. Yearly precipitation varies from an average 5 inches in the mountains to 50 inches in the basins.

THE PEOPLE. Nearly 6 out of every 10 people in Wyoming live in urban communities. Wyoming, unlike most other states, has no Standard Metropolitan Statistical Areas.

Foreign-born people, mostly of British, German, and Russian origin, make up about 3 percent of the population. There are about 4,000 Indians, most of whom live on the Wind River Reservation.

ECONOMY. Wyoming's economy rests on the state's mineral resources, which provide about two-thirds of the value of goods produced. In 1966 Wyoming ranked 27th among the states in annual per capita personal income, with an average of $2,686.

The leading mineral in Wyoming is petroleum, which provides about three-fourths of mining income. Natural gas, uranium ore, and iron ore are also important.

Agriculture accounts for about one-fourth of the value of goods produced. Cattle, sheep, hogs, and poultry are a major source of farm income. Crops, grown on irrigated land, include sugar beets, wheat, dry beans, and potatoes.

Manufacturing provides less than 10 percent of the value of goods produced. The most important industries refine and process the petroleum, natural gas, and uranium ore found in the state. Food processing is also a major industry.

GOVERNMENT. The governor of Wyoming is elected to a four-year term and may succeed himself. The state legislature consists of a 30-member senate and a 61-member house of representatives. Senators are elected to four-year terms and representatives are elected to two-year terms.

The outlying territories of the United States are of several different types. Puerto Rico, for example, is a self-governing commonwealth. Guam is an unincorporated territory administered by the Department of the Interior. The Ryukyus are islands administered by the United States, although sovereignty rests with Japan.

There are 25 islands in the south-central Pacific Ocean over which the United States claims to sovereignty are disputed. Islands in the Line, Ellice, and Phoenix groups are claimed by both the United States and Britain. Islands in the Tokelau (Union) and Northern Cook groups are claimed by both the United States and New Zealand.

There are also some islands in the Pacific which, like the Ryukyus, are owned by Japan and administered by the United States. These are the Daito, which are administratively part of the Ryukyus, the Bonins, the Volcanos, Marcus Island, Rosario Island, and Parece Vela.

AMERICAN SAMOA

Area: 76 square miles
Population: (1960 census) 20,051
Capital: Pago Pago

American Samoa, a group of islands in the South Pacific Ocean, lies some 1,500 miles northeast of Australia and 4,000 miles southwest of San Francisco. The islands are part of the Samoan archipelago, which is divided between Western Samoa, an independent nation, and American Samoa, a U.S. territory.

THE LAND. American Samoa consists of five islands in the Samoan archipelago and Swain's Island, some 200 miles to the north. Four of the islands are of volcanic origin and contain rugged peaks. Swain's Island and the uninhabited Rose Atoll are coral atolls.

The islands have a hot, wet climate. Average temperatures range from about 75°F in August to 90°F in February. Well over 100 inches of rain fall each year, mostly from December through March. Gales are frequent, and hurricanes occur at times.

THE PEOPLE. The people of Samoa are mainly of Polynesian descent. Samoan is the national language, but official documents are printed in English.

THE ECONOMY. The economy of American Samoa rests heavily on agriculture, but manufacturing and tourism are of increasing significance. Copra, fruits and vegetables, coffee, and cocoa are the chief crops, and livestock are raised. Tuna canneries are the most important industrial establishments.

Pago Pago has an excellent natural harbor and is a transportation and commercial shipping center. Copra is the most valuable export.

GOVERNMENT. American Samoa is an unincorporated territory of the United States under the jurisdiction of the Department of the Interior. The governor is appointed by the U.S. secretary of the interior with the approval of the president.

The legislature, the Fono, consists of a popularly elected lower house and a tribally selected upper house. The Fono is an advisory body with limited powers.

American Samoans are nationals of the United States, but they must fulfill requirements of the Immigration and Nationality Act to become U.S. citizens.

HISTORY. The Samoan Islands were visited by Europeans in 1772 and 1768. During the 1800s the United States, Britain, Germany, and Hawaii all tried to gain control of the islands. In 1880 the United States, Britain, and Germany recognized a local king and set up a three-power executive council.

Local factions soon developed, however, and in 1898 civil war broke out. A treaty in 1899 divided the Samoan Islands, giving the western islands to Germany and the eastern islands to the United States.

For the first half of the 1900s American Samoa was administered by the Department of the Navy. In 1951 the islands were placed under the Department of the Interior. In recent years there has been a breakdown in Samoan tribal life, and American Samoa has become Westernized.

BONIN ISLANDS

Area: 41 square miles
Population: (1960 census) 215

The Bonin Islands are a group of volcanic islands in the western Pacific Ocean. The islands are administered by the U.S. Navy, although Japan has residual sovereignty over them.

In the early 1800s both the British and the Japanese claimed the Bonins, but in 1876 they were annexed by Japan. The islands were occupied by U.S. forces at the end of World War II, and are administered by the United States under the terms of the peace treaty with Japan, signed in 1952.

CANTON AND ENDERBURY

Area: 27 square miles
Population: (1960 census) 320

Canton and Enderbury are two islands in the Pacific Ocean administered as a condominium by the United States and Britain. The islands are part of the Phoenix Island group. Enderbury is uninhabited.

The islands were discovered and claimed by various nations in the early 1800s. In the 1900s claims to the islands were put forth by New Zealand, Britain, and the United States. In 1939 an agreement was reached by Britain and the United States to govern the islands jointly for 50 years. U.S. affairs on the islands are under the jurisdiction of the Department of the Interior.

The islands were considered a valuable source of guano, a fertilizer, in the 1800s. Today, however, Canton is important for its airfield.

CORN ISLANDS

Area: 4 square miles
Population: (1960 census) 1,872

The Corn Islands, two islands off the coast of Nicaragua, were leased to the United States in 1914 by Nicaragua. Although the United States has authority over the islands' administration, local government has remained under the direction of Nicaragua.

The islands were leased from Nicaragua for a period of 99 years to protect U.S. interests in a proposed canal across Nicaragua.

GOVERNMENT OF AMERICAN SAMOA

AMERICAN SAMOA'S TUTUILA ISLAND, showing Rainmaker Mountain and Pago Pago Bay.

GUAM

Area: 209 square miles
Population: (1960 census) 67,044
Capital: Agana

Guam lies in the northwestern Pacific Ocean and is the largest and southernmost island of the Marianas Archipelago. Guam is about 1,500 miles east of the Philippines and more than 5,000 miles southwest of San Francisco.

THE LAND. Guam is over 30 miles long and between 4 and 10 miles wide and is surrounded by a coral reef. The island is of volcanic origin. Its center is flat, and hills rise in the north. There are mountains in the south that include the highest point on the island, Mt. Lamlam, 1,329 feet. Much of the island is covered by dense forests.

The island has a tropical climate, hot and humid, with temperatures moderated by northeasterly winds. Average temperatures range from the 70's F to the 90's F. Rain, which falls mostly between July and September, averages over 80 inches a year. Typhoons are common, and earthquakes occur from time to time.

THE PEOPLE. The people of Guam are predominantly Chammoro, who are descended from Micronesian stock heavily mixed with Filipino and Spanish. Americans, Italians, Britains, Chinese, Japanese, and Mexicans have also intermarried with the Chammoro.

English is the official language, but Chammoro is widely spoken. The main religion is Roman Catholicism.

THE ECONOMY. Guam's economy is heavily dependent upon U.S. military establishments on the island. Employment at the naval and air bases has drawn many people from the traditional economic mainstay, agriculture.

Thick jungle and the size of the military bases have limited the amount of land available for farming. Guam does produce fruits and vegetables for export, but most produce is grown for home consumption. Corn, rice, sweet potatoes, taro, and cassava are the chief crops. Livestock are raised, and eggs are an important source of farm income.

Manufacturing is limited largely to food processing. There is little commercial fishing, and there are no important mineral industries. Guam is heavily dependent on imported goods, most of which come from the U.S. mainland.

GOVERNMENT. Guam is an unincorporated territory of the United States administered by the Department of the Interior. There is a governor, appointed by the U.S. president, and a 21-member legislature, which is popularly elected. The governor is appointed to a 4-year term, and legislators are elected to 2-year terms.

Although the people of Guam are citizens of the United States, they have no representative in Congress.

HISTORY. Ferdinand Magellan discovered Guam in 1521, and Spain claimed the island in 1565. Spanish settlement, which took place in the mid-1600s, met with resistance from the local people. In 1898 Guam was ceded to the United States under the terms of the Treaty of Paris, which ended the Spanish-American War.

Guam was a strategic naval outpost and was governed under the jurisdiction of the U.S. Department of the Navy. During World War II the island was occupied by Japanese forces (1941–1944). In July 1944 the United States regained control of Guam after a lengthy battle.

The people of Guam were granted U.S. citizenship and internal self-government under the terms of the Organic Act of Guam, passed by Congress in 1950. In recent years attempts have been made to promote tourism and industry and to develop further the island's agricultural resources.

HOWLAND, BAKER, JARVIS

Area: 3 square miles
Population: no permanent population

Howland, Baker, and Jarvis are three widely separated islands in the Pacific Ocean lying near the equator. The islands form an unincorporated territory of the United States. They were claimed by the United States in 1857 and proclaimed a U.S. territory in 1935–1936.

JOHNSTON AND SAND

Area: less than 1 square mile
Population: (1960 census) 156

Johnston and Sand are two coral islands in an atoll in the North Pacific Ocean about 750 miles southwest of Honolulu, Hawaii. The islands are administered by the U.S. Navy.

The islands were discovered in 1807 by a British sea captain. The United States claimed possession of them in 1858. Johnston Island has served as a bird sanctuary and a U.S. naval base.

KINGMAN REEF

Area: less than 0.5 square miles
Population: no permanent population

Kingman Reef is a reef lying in the Pacific Ocean about 900 miles southwest of Honolulu, Hawaii. It was discovered by the United States in 1874 and annexed as an unincorporated territory in 1922.

MIDWAY ISLANDS

Area: 2 square miles
Population: (1960 census) 2,356

Midway Islands, a group of islands in the northern Pacific Ocean some 1,300 miles northwest of Honolulu, Hawaii, are under the jurisdiction of the U.S. Navy. The group consists of an atoll with two small coral islands—Sand Island and Eastern Island.

Midway was uninhabited in 1859, when it was discovered and claimed for the United States. In the 1930s the island became a stopping place for planes flying between Hawaii and the Philippines. U.S. air and naval bases were established on Midway in the late 1930s.

The islands were a target for Japanese attack during World War II. The Battle of Midway, fought in 1942, was a decisive defeat for the Japanese. U.S. military installations have been maintained there since World War II.

NAVASSA

Area: 2 square miles
Population: no permanent population

Navassa, an unincorporated territory of the United States, lies in the Caribbean Sea between Jamaica and Haiti. The United States claimed the island in 1865 to exploit its guano, used as fertilizer.

Navassa officially came under U.S. jurisdiction in 1916, and the following year a lighthouse was established on the island.

PALMYRA ISLAND

Area: 4 square miles
Population: no permanent population

Palmyra Island, lying in the Pacific Ocean some 960 miles southwest of Honolulu, Hawaii, is actually an atoll made up of 50 small islands. The area has been claimed at various times by Britain, Hawaii, and the United States.

Palmyra was annexed to the United States as an unincorporated territory in 1912. The area was administered from Honolulu until 1959, when Hawaii became a state. Palmyra, which is privately owned, was not included in the new state.

PANAMA CANAL ZONE

Area: 553 square miles
Population: (1960 census) 42,122

The Panama Canal Zone is a strip of land, about 10 miles wide, which borders the Panama Canal. The Canal Zone is leased by Panama to the United States. Most of its inhabitants were born in the United States.

PAN AMERICAN AIRWAYS
THE PANAMA CANAL provides a waterway connecting the Atlantic and the Pacific.

The Canal Zone is under the jurisdiction of the U.S. Army and is administered by a governor appointed by the U.S. president. Since 1950 the Panama Canal has been run by the government-owned Panama Canal Company. The governor is president and director of the company.

The Canal Zone was leased to the United States in perpetuity by the Republic of Panama in 1903. The lease was granted primarily in return for a guarantee of protection for the newly established republic. In 1967 the governments of the United States and Panama negotiated a new treaty recognizing Panama's sovereignty over the Canal Zone and establishing a joint board to govern the canal.

PUERTO RICO

Area: 3,435 square miles
Population: (1960 census) 2,349,544; (1967 est.) 2,697,000
Capital: San Juan

Puerto Rico, an island nation in the Caribbean Sea some 1,000 miles southeast of Miami, Florida, is a self-governing commonwealth of the United States. Its official name is the Commonwealth of Puerto Rico. In Spanish it is called the *Estado Libre Asociado de Puerto Rico,* which may be translated as the "free associated state of Puerto Rico." Puerto Rico is sometimes referred to by its Indian name, Boriquén.

THE LAND. Puerto Rico is the smallest and easternmost major island of the Greater Antilles. The commonwealth of Puerto Rico includes several small nearby islands, including Vieques and Culebra.

Puerto Rico may be divided into four major geographic regions. The Coastal Lowlands run along the island's northern and southern shores. The Coastal Valleys extend along most of the eastern and western shores.

The Foothills form two chains of hills—one south of the northern Coastal Lowlands and one north of the southern Coastal Lowlands. The Central Mountains cover the center of the island and contain the highest point in Puerto Rico, Cerro de Punta, 4,389 feet.

Several rivers run down from the mountains in northern Puerto Rico. The most important of these are the Río Grande de Loíza, Río de Bayamón, Río Grande de Arecibo, and Río La Plata. The southern part of the island is drained by small streams that are often dry during part of the year.

Puerto Rico has a warm, pleasant climate, which varies only slightly from season to season. Temperatures in San Juan average 81°F in January and 87°F in July. Yearly precipitation varies from less than 20 inches along the southern coast to over 200 inches in the mountains. In many areas small amounts of rain fall each day. The hurricane season lasts from June to November.

THE PEOPLE. Puerto Rico was originally inhabited by Arawak Indians. In the 1500s the island was colonized by Spaniards who brought Negro

COMMONWEALTH OF PUERTO RICO
PUERTO RICO'S HARBOR has been guarded for centuries by El Morro in Old San Juan.

slaves with them. Most Puerto Ricans are of mixed descent.

Spanish is spoken by most of the people, although both English and Spanish are official languages. Roman Catholicism is the predominant religion.

Puerto Rico is densely populated, with an average of over 685 people per square mile. Almost half of the people live in urban areas. There are three Standard Metropolitan Statistical Areas: Mayagüez, Ponce, and San Juan.

In the 1940s large-scale migration to the U.S. mainland began. During the 1950s an average of 19,000 Puerto Ricans emigrated each year.

THE ECONOMY. Puerto Rico, once almost totally dependent on subsistence farming, has a balanced economy based on tourism, manufacturing, and agriculture. In 1967 the annual average per capita income was $1,047. Although this figure was lower than that of any U.S. state, it was high in relation to most other Caribbean countries.

Tourism developed in Puerto Rico in the 1940s and is now a major industry. Fine beaches and a warm, sunny climate attract hundreds of thousands of visitors each year.

A highly successful government program, Operation Bootstrap, has attracted many manufacturers to the island. The program includes tax incentives, liberal credit arrangements, and labor recruitment and training for new industries.

By the mid-1960s manufacturing accounted for over half the value of goods produced. The most important manufactures include processed foods, apparel, and metal products and machinery. Other major industries produce chemical products; stone, clay, and glass products; and textiles.

Agriculture accounts for some 40 percent of the value of goods produced. Sugarcane is the leading crop, followed by coffee, tobacco, plantains, bananas, and pineapples.

The extractive industries—fishing and mining—account for less than 5 percent of the value of goods produced. Sand, gravel, and stone are mined, and salt is evaporated from sea water. Fisherman catch a variety of fish, including barracuda, herring, marlin, and oysters.

Puerto Rico's trade is carried on almost exclusively with the United States, and there are no customs duties on goods imported from the mainland. In the mid-1960s Puerto Rico's yearly imports were valued at $1.5 billion, and its exports at almost $1 billion.

GOVERNMENT. Puerto Rico is autonomous in domestic affairs, but functions as part of the United States in international affairs. The constitution of Puerto Rico provides for a governor, popularly elected to a four-year term, and a legislature composed of a 27-member senate and a 51-member house of representatives. Legislators are also elected to four-year terms.

Puerto Rico sends an elected, non-voting Resident Commissioner to the U.S. Congress. Puerto Ricans are citizens of the United States and may enter the mainland without restriction. They may not, however, vote in U.S. presidential elections while living in Puerto Rico.

HISTORY. Columbus discovered Puerto Rico in 1493 during his second voyage to the New World. Colonization began in 1508, when Ponce de Leon established a Spanish settlement across the bay from present-day San Juan. The Arawak Indians, who occupied the island before the arrival of Columbus, were enslaved by the Spanish. As the Arawak began to die out, Africans were imported as slaves.

Spanish Rule. The Spanish established a strict military government. Puerto Rico could trade only with Spain, and the island was supported by Spanish taxes on Mexico. Puerto Rico was frequently raided by Carib Indians from neighboring islands and by the Dutch, English, and French.

The Spanish relaxed trade restrictions in the early 1800s, but discontent in Puerto Rico had become widespread. The influence of revolutions in the United States and France contributed to the development of a movement for independence from Spain, and in 1868 an abortive rising took place. A band of insurgents proclaimed Puerto Rico an independent republic in the *Grito de Lares* (The Cry of Lares). Although the revolution was quickly crushed, it began an era of unrest.

Soon after the 1868 revolution the Liberal Party, led by Luis Muñoz Rivera, grew up and began to press for reforms. Spain made some concessions. In 1869 Puerto Rico was given the status of a Spanish province, and in 1873 slavery was abolished. In 1876 the island gained representation in the Spanish legislature, and in 1897 Spain granted the island a large degree of autonomy.

U. S. Control. The outbreak of the Spanish-American War in 1898 put an end to Puerto Rican autonomy. In the Treaty of Paris, which ended the brief war, Puerto Rico was ceded to the United States. For the next two years Puerto Rico lived under U.S. military occupation.

The Foraker Act, passed by the U.S. Congress in 1900, ended the occupation. It established a civil administration and provided for free trade with the United States. The island's status remained unclear, however. A governor was appointed by the U.S. president, and a legislature, partly elected and partly appointed, was established. In 1917 the Jones Act made Puerto Ricans U.S. citizens and allowed for a fully elected legislature.

In the early 1900s the Liberal Party split into two groups—followers of Luis Muñoz Rivera advocated independence, and followers of José Celso Barbosa called for statehood. During the world economic depression of the 1930s, the Nationalist Party, led by Pedro Albizu Campos, gained power. The Nationalists demanded immediate independence. In 1936 Nationalists assassinated the chief of police,

and in 1937 a Nationalist Party parade erupted into a riot in which over 100 people were injured.

In 1938 Luis Muñoz Marín, the son of Luis Muñoz Rivera, helped form the Popular Democratic Party, which won control of the island's legislature in 1940. The Popular Party enacted broad social and economic reform measures.

In 1946 Muñoz Marín committed himself to retaining ties with the United States for economic reasons. In 1947 the federal Elective Governor Act permitted Puerto Ricans to choose their own governor, and in 1948 Luis Muñoz Marín was elected to the position.

The Commonwealth. In 1952 a constitution for Puerto Rico was written and approved by both Puerto Rican voters and the U.S. Congress. On July 25, 1952, the Commonwealth of Puerto Rico was proclaimed.

The Popular Democrats remained the leading political party, and Muñoz Marín remained the dominant political figure. When he retired in 1964, after four terms as governor, he was succeeded by Roberto Sánchez Vilella, also a Popular Democrat.

Under the leadership of the Popular Democrats, Puerto Rico experienced a period of unprecedented growth. The success of Operation Bootstrap continued to attract new industries, and the 1960s saw a sharp reduction in emigration and an increase in the number of Puerto Rican emigrants returning to the island.

In 1967 a plebescite was held in which voters were given the choice of remaining a commonwealth, becoming a U.S. state, or becoming independent. Over 60 percent of the voters supported continuing Puerto Rico's status as a commonwealth.

QUITA SUEÑO, RONCADOR, SERRANA

Area: less than 0.5 square miles
Population: No permanent population

Quita Sueño Bank, Roncador Cay, and Serrana Bank are a group of banks and cays in the Caribbean Sea about 120 miles east of Nicaragua. Both the United States and Columbia claim sovereignty over the area.

Quita Sueño Bank, the most westerly of the group, contains a 23-mile long reef. Roncador Cay, the most southerly of the group, contains a small piece of land rising 13 feet above sea level. Serrana Bank, the northeastern part of the group, is formed by four cays.

U.S. interest in the group began in the 1800s, and a claim to the islands was made under the Guano Act of 1856.

RYUKYU ISLANDS

Area: 848 square miles
Population: (1960 census) 934,176
Administrative center: Naha

The Ryukyu Islands are a chain of islands in the western Pacific Ocean composed of three main groups —Sakishima, Okinawa, and Amami. The Sakishima and Okinawa groups

are under U.S. military government, although residual sovereignty rests with Japan, which administers the Amami group.

A major source of income and employment is the U.S. government. Before World War II farming was the most important economic activity, and it is still significant. The chief crops include sugarcane, vegetables, rice, sweet potatoes, pineapples, and tobacco. Commercial fishing and food processing are also important in the islands.

The Ryukyus are under the jurisdiction of the U.S. Army. There is an appointed military high commissioner and a popularly elected chief executive. A popularly elected 32-member legislature has some local autonomy.

The islands were annexed by Japan in 1879. During World War II they were the scene of heavy fighting. After the war all the Ryukyus were placed under U.S. jurisdiction, but in 1953 the Amami group was returned to Japan. In 1967 plans for returning the remaining islands to Japan were discussed by U.S. Pres. Lyndon B. Johnson and Japanese Premier Eisaku Sato during a visit to Washington by the premier.

SWAN ISLANDS

Area: 1 square mile
Population: (1960 census) 28

The Swan Islands, an unincorporated territory of the United States, lie in the western Caribbean Sea. Two islands—Little Swan and Great Swan—make up the territory.

In the 1860s the islands were worked as a source of guano, used as fertilizer. Later they were used for coconut plantations, and in the 1960s U.S. navigation and communications installations were constructed.

TRUST TERRITORY OF THE PACIFIC

Area: 8,484 square miles (including 7,797 square miles of water)
Population: (1966 est.) 94,000
Administrative center: Saipan

The Trust Territory of the Pacific Islands, a group of 2,141 islands in the western Pacific Ocean, is a UN trusteeship administered by the United States.

THE LAND. The trust territory includes three main groups of islands —the Carolines, Marianas, and Marshalls. The territory has a tropical climate, hot and humid throughout the year. Average rainfall varies from about 80 inches in the northern Marianas to over 180 inches in the eastern Carolines. The typhoon season lasts from July through November.

THE PEOPLE. Most of the people of the territory are Micronesians. There are several different groups on the islands, and there are 9 Micronesian languages, each with several dialects, in use. English is the official language and Japanese is widely spoken.

THE ECONOMY. The main economic activity is subsistence farming. Crops include yams, arrowroot, tapioca, taro,

U.S. VIRGIN ISLANDS GOVERNMENT

ST. THOMAS, one of the U.S. Virgin Islands, has a beautiful harbor and busy yacht basins.

cacao, and black pepper. Livestock are raised, and there is some commercial fishing for tuna.

In recent years attempts have been made to increase agricultural output and to develop industry. The most important exports are copra, a source of coconut oil, and trochus shell, used in making pearl buttons.

GOVERNMENT. The Trust Territory of the Pacific Islands is under the jurisdiction of the U.S. Department of the Interior. A high commissioner, appointed by the U.S. president, and six district commissioners, appointed by the high commissioner, administer the islands.

A popularly elected legislature with limited powers was established in 1964. It consists of a 12-member house of delegates and a 21-member general assembly.

HISTORY. Most of the islands of the trust territory were unknown to Europeans until the 1800s, although the Portuguese explorer Ferdinand Magellan had discovered the Marianas in 1565. Each of the main island groups has been under Spanish, German, and Japanese control. The Japanese held the islands at the start of World War II, but during the course of the war they lost many of them to the United States.

In 1947 the islands became a UN trust and were placed under U.S. administration. Two atolls in the territory have been used as U.S. test sites for nuclear weapons. The first test was held on Bikini in 1946. Later tests were held on Eniwetok, which was designated an atomic proving ground in 1947.

VIRGIN ISLANDS

Area: 133 square miles
Population: (1960 census) 32,099
Capital: Charlotte Amalie

The Virgin Islands, which lie in the Caribbean Sea some 40 miles east of Puerto Rico, are the northernmost extension of the Lesser Antilles.

The western Virgin Islands are a possession of the United States, and the eastern Virgin Islands belong to Britain. There are three main islands in the U.S. group—St. Croix, St. John, and St. Thomas—and several small uninhabited islands.

THE LAND. The U.S. Virgin Islands are of volcanic origin, and all except St. Croix contain rugged mountains.

St. Croix, the southernmost major island, has an area of 80 square miles. St. John, the easternmost, has an area of 20 square miles. St. Thomas, the westernmost, has an area of some 30 square miles and includes the highest point in the U.S. Virgin Islands, Crown Mountain, 1,556 feet.

The climate of the Virgin Islands is tropical. Average temperatures in St. Thomas range from the 70°s F to the low 80°s F, and yearly rainfall is usually between 40 and 45 inches. The Trade Winds cool all the islands.

THE PEOPLE. When Europeans arrived in the Virgin Islands in the late 1400s, they found them inhabited by Carib Indians. Spanish settlers brought Negro slaves to the islands in the 1600s, and over 65 percent of the present population is of African descent. Some 20 percent of the population is white, and the remainder is of mixed origin.

St. Thomas is the most populous island, with over 16,000 people in 1960. It contains Charlotte Amalie, the capital of the U.S. Virgin Islands, which had a 1960 population of about 13,000. In the same year St. Croix had some 15,000 people, and St. John had under 1,000 people.

THE ECONOMY. Tourism is the most important industry. Some 750,000 people visited the islands in 1967, and many cruise ships stop at St. Thomas. Manufacturing and agriculture are limited, and most foodstuffs and manufactured goods must be imported.

The islands' most important manufactures are bay-leaf oil, clothing and textiles, and watch parts. Sugarcane is the leading crop, and cattle are raised.

In 1966 the value of imports to the Virgin Islands was over $138 million, and the value of exports was $56 million. Almost all exports are sent to the U.S. mainland, which supplies some two-thirds of imports.

GOVERNMENT. The U.S. Virgin Islands are an unincorporated territory under the jurisdiction of the Department of the Interior. The islands have a governor, appointed by the U.S. president, and a popularly elected legislature, whose 11 members are elected to two-year terms.

HISTORY. Columbus discovered the Virgin Islands in 1493 during his second voyage to the New World. For over 100 years the islands were used as a meeting place for pirates.

The first island to be colonized by Europeans was probably St. Croix. It was settled by both the Dutch and the British in the early 1600s. In the mid-1600s the Spanish drove out the English and Dutch. Some 20 years later the French drove out the Spanish, and in 1733 the French sold St. Croix to the Danes.

St. Thomas was first in the possession of the Dutch, who lost it to the British in 1667. The British then abandoned the island to the Danes, who had a trading post there.

St. John became part of Denmark in 1716. In 1733 there was a slave revolt on the island. The Virgin Islands at that time formed one of the largest slave markets in the world. In 1792 the Danes prohibited the slave trade, but emancipation did not come until 1848, when a slave revolt took place on St. Croix.

Denmark held possession of the three islands until 1917, except for two brief periods in the 1800s when the British took control. In 1917 Denmark sold the islands to the United States, and 10 years later the people became U.S. citizens.

The islands were considered important in the defense of the Panama Canal at the time of purchase, and they were of strategic value during World War II. Since the war the U.S. Virgin Islands have been most significant as a tourist resort.

WAKE ISLAND

Area: 3 square miles
Population: (1960 census) 1,097

Wake Island, a U.S. possession in the northern Pacific Ocean is under the jurisdiction of the Department of the Interior. Wake, which lies some 2,300 miles west of Honolulu, Hawaii, is actually a coral atoll with three small islands—Wake, Peale, and Wilkes.

The uninhabited islands were discovered by the British in 1796. In 1898 they were visited by a U.S. naval expedition, and in 1900 they were formally claimed by the United States.

Wake served as a commercial air stop-over in the 1930s and as a U.S. air and naval base at the beginning of World War II. In 1941 the Japanese captured the islands, which they held until 1945. Since the war, Wake has served as an air base and a stop-over point for commercial trans-Pacific flights.

CITIES AND URBAN AREAS

AKRON, a city in northeastern Ohio, the seat of Summit County. Akron is on the Little Cuyahoga River. Its major industry is the manufacture of rubber products, especially automobile tires. Other products include breakfast foods, automobile and aircraft parts, clay and metal products, industrial machinery, and chemicals. Pop., 1960 census, 290,351; Metropolitan Stat. Area, 1965 est., 650,000.

ALBANY–SCHENECTADY–TROY, an industrial complex in New York State. Albany, on the west side of the Hudson, is the state capital. Schenectady, the seat of Schenectady County, is located on the Mohawk River and the New York State Barge Canal. Troy, the seat of Rensselaer County, is on the east side of the Hudson River.

The area produces chemicals, textiles, paper, wood products, apparel, valves, and electrical machinery. There are also grain elevators and oil refineries. Pop., 1960 census, Albany, 129,726; Schenectady, 81,682; Troy, 67,492; Metropolitan Stat. Area, 1965 est., 697,000.

ALBUQUERQUE, a city in west-central New Mexico, the seat of Bernalillo County. Albuquerque is located on the Rio Grande. It is the largest city in the state, and its population more than doubled between 1950 and 1960.

Albuquerque has lumber mills, food processing plants, and railroad shops, and produces tiles and bricks. The surrounding area, for which it is the industrial and transportation center, produces farm products and timber. Pop., 1960 census, 201,189; Metropolitan Stat. Area, 1965 est., 288,000.

ALLENTOWN–BETHLEHEM–EASTON, an urban industrial complex in eastern Pennsylvania overflowing into New Jersey, across the Delaware River. Both Allentown, the seat of Lehigh County, and Bethlehem, in Lehigh and Northampton counties, are on the Lehigh River. Easton, the seat of Northampton County, is on the Delaware River.

Industrial products of the area include steel, cement, textiles, machinery, electrical appliances, truck and bus bodies, iron, and chemicals. Pop., 1960 census, Allentown, 108,347; Bethlehem, 75,408; Easton, 31,955; Metropolitan Stat. Area, 1965 est., 515,000.

ANNAPOLIS, a city in central Maryland, the capital of the state and the seat of Anne Arundel County. Annapolis is located near the western shore of Chesapeake Bay. The United States Naval Academy is in Annapolis. The city's major industries include shipbuilding, fishing, and seafood packing. Tourism is important to the city. Pop., 1960 census, 23,385.

ATLANTA, a city in northwestern Georgia, the state capital and the seat of Fulton County. It is the largest city in the state. Atlanta is a commercial and transportation center and a port of entry. During the Civil War, Atlanta was a major Confederate center.

Many U.S. federal government departments have offices in Atlanta. Industrial products include furniture, textiles, and food products. Pop., 1960 census, 487,455; Metropolitan Stat. Area, 1965 est., 1,216,000.

AUGUSTA, a city in southwestern Maine, the capital of the state and the seat of Kennebec County. Augusta is a manufacturing city located at the head of navigation of the Kennebec River. The city's major industries include poultry processing, printing, and the manufacture of cotton goods, textiles, paper, and shoes. Pop., 1960 census, 23,385.

AUSTIN, a city in east-central Texas, the capital of the state and the seat of Travis County. Austin is located on the Colorado River. The city produces scientific instruments, boats, and books. It is the distribution and trade center for the surrounding agricultural area. Pop., 1960 census, 186,545; Metropolitan Stat. Area, 1960 census, 212,136.

BALTIMORE, a city in central Maryland, the largest city in the state and one of the largest cities in the United States. Baltimore is located on the Patapsco River where it flows into Chesapeake Bay. It is a major seaport and a port of entry.

Important industries are shipbuilding, food processing, and oil refining. Apparel, aircraft, chemicals, and steel are manufactured. Pop., 1960 census, 939,024; Metropolitan Stat. Area, 1965 est., 1,854,000.

BATON ROUGE, a city in southeastern Louisiana, the state capital and the seat of East Baton Rouge Parish

AMERICAN AIRLINES

BOSTON SKYSCRAPER near the Charles River

(county). It is located on the east bank of the Mississippi River and is a port of entry. Industrial products include chemicals and wood and food products. Oil refining is important. The surrounding area produces cotton, sugar, vegetables, fruit, dairy products, oil, and natural gas. Pop., 1960 census, 152,419; Metropolitan Stat. Area. 1960 est., 230,058.

BETHLEHEM. See Allentown-Bethlehem-Easton.

BILLINGS, a city in southern Montana on the Yellowstone River, the seat of Yellowstone County. Billings is located in an area in which oil and wool are produced, and poultry and livestock are raised. The major industries of the city are meat packing, sugar and oil refining, and flour milling. Pop., 1960 census, 52,851; Metropolitan Stat. Area, 1960 est., 79,016.

BIRMINGHAM, a city in north-central Alabama, the seat of Jefferson County. It is the largest city in the state. Birmingham is a railroad center. Nearby are great deposits of coal and iron, and the city's major industries produce iron and steel. Other products include textiles, machinery, tanks, cigars, soap, cement, chemicals, and electrical equipment. Pop., 1960 census, 340,887; Metropolitan Stat. Area, 1965 est., 644,000.

BISMARCK, a city in south-central North Dakota, the capital of the state and the seat of Burleigh County. Bismarck is located on the Missouri River. Rail, air, and highway transportation lines converge at Bismarck.

The city serves as a trading and processing center for agricultural products from the surrounding area. The manufacture of farm machinery is the major industry. Pop., 1960 census, 27,670.

BOISE, a city in southwestern Idaho, the capital of the state and the seat of Ada County. Boise, located on the Boise River, is the headquarters for the Columbia River Basin Project. The Arrowrock, Lucky Peak, and Anderson Ranch dams provide water for irrigation in the area. Boise's major industries include food processing and light manufacturing. Pop., 1960 census, 34,481; Metropolitan Stat. Area, 1960 census, 93,460.

BOSTON, a city in eastern Massachusetts, the state capital and the seat of Suffolk County. Boston, a major seaport and port of entry, is located on Boston Bay at the mouths of the Charles and Mystic rivers. It is the largest city in the state. Boston played a major role in the American Revolution and was long the cultural center of the nation.

Industrial products include shoes, machinery, electronics equipment, textiles, and foods. Publishing and shipbuilding are also important. Boston is a large market for wool and fish. Pop., 1960 census, 697,197; Metropolitan Stat. Area, 1960 census, 2,595,481.

BUFFALO, a city in western New York State, the second largest city in the state. Buffalo is located at the eastern end of Lake Erie on the Niagara River. The western end of the New York State Barge Canal is at Buffalo.

Buffalo is an important Great Lakes port, a port of entry, and a major railroad center. Power from Niagara Falls is used for varied industries. Buffalo produces steel, pig iron, flour, and rubber. Pop., 1960 census, 532,-759: Metropolitan Stat. Area, 1965 est., 1,320,000.

BUTTE, a city in southwestern Montana. Butte is located on a plateau in the Rocky Mountains. It is one of the largest cities in the state. Butte was founded in 1864 during a gold rush. Its subsequent growth was the result of mining operations. Major mineral deposits include copper, silver, zinc, and manganese. Pop., 1960 census, 27,877.

CARSON CITY, a city in west-central Nevada, the capital of the state and the seat of Ormsby County. Carson City is located about 10 miles east of Lake Tahoe in a popular resort area. There are gold, silver, and copper mines in the surrounding area. Livestock are raised and lumber is produced in the region. Pop., 1960 census, 5,163.

CHARLESTON, a city in west-central West Virginia, the capital of the state and the seat of Kanawha County. Charleston is the largest city in the state. It produces metal and glass products, chemicals, and furniture. Charleston is the railroad center for an area producing salt, hardwood, coal, oil, and natural gas. Pop., 1960 census, 85,796; Metropolitan Stat. Area, 1965 est., 345,000.

CHATTANOOGA, a city in southeastern Tennessee, the seat of Hamilton County. Chattanooga spreads over into Georgia. The city, which is located on the Tennessee River, is a port of entry.

Chattanooga produces chemicals, textiles, hosiery, metal products, and farm implements. It serves as the industrial and market center for an area that produces coal, timber, strawberries, and cotton. Pop., 1960 census, 130,009; Metropolitan Stat. Area, 1965 est., 292,000.

CHEYENNE, a city in southeastern Wyoming, the capital of the state and the seat of Laramie County. It is the largest city in the state. Cheyenne is the railroad and commercial center for a sheep and cattle-raising area. The major industries include meat packing, oil refining, and the manufacture of aircraft. Pop., 1960 census, 43,505.

CHICAGO, a city in northeastern Illinois, the seat of Cook County. Chicago is located on the southwestern shore of Lake Michigan. It is the largest city in Illinois and the second largest city in the United States. Chicago is a major Great Lakes port, a port of entry, and a great transportation center.

CHICAGO ASSOCIATION OF COMMERCE AND INDUSTRY

CHICAGO SKYLINE, a complex of apartments and offices, towers over Lake Michigan's shores.

Industrial products include electrical equipment, machinery, furniture, chemicals, apparel, and railroad cars. Chicago is a major center for meat packing, flour milling, and steel production. Pop., 1960 census, 3,550,404; Metropolitan Stat. Area, 1965 est., 6,689,000.

CINCINNATI, a city in southwestern Ohio, the seat of Hamilton County. Cincinnati is located on the Ohio River. It is the second largest city in the state.

Cincinnati produces transportation equipment, machine tools, electrical machinery, cosmetics, and radar equipment. There are also meat packing, brewing, and slaughtering industries. Coal, lumber, salt, and iron are distributed from the surrounding area.

Pop., 1960 census, 502,550; Metropolitan Stat. Area, 1965 est., 1,347,000.

CLEVELAND, a city in northern Ohio, the seat of Cuyahoga County. Cleveland is located on Lake Erie at the mouth of the Cuyahoga River. It is the largest city in the state.

The city produces iron, steel, automobiles and parts, freight-handling equipment, gas and electric fixtures, batteries, and paint. Other industries include slaughtering, meat packing, and publishing. Cleveland is a distribution center for an area that produces iron, coal, lumber, and grain. Pop., 1960 census, 876,050; Metropolitan Stat. Area, 1965 est., 2,000,000.

COLUMBIA, a city in central South Carolina, the capital of the state and the seat of Richland County. Columbia is located at the head of navigation of the Congaree River. It is the largest city in the state, and is an educational and retailing and manufacturing center.

Columbia produces textiles, apparel, foodstuffs, fabricated steel, and chemicals. Corn and cotton are grown in the surrounding area. Pop., 1960 census, 97,433; Metropolitan Stat. Area, 1965 est., 289,000.

COLUMBUS, a city in central Ohio, the capital of the state and the seat of Franklin County. Columbus is located on the Scioto River. It is a port of entry and a railroad and highway center.

Columbus produces automobile parts, mining machinery, aircraft, foundry products, shoes, and paper. The surrounding area produces agricultural products, coal, natural gas, iron, limestone, and clay. Pop., 1960 census, 471,316; Metropolitan Stat. Area, 1965 est., 847,000.

CONCORD, a city in south-central New Hampshire, the capital of the state and the seat of Merrimack County. Concord is located on the Merrimack River. The city is a manufacturing center with electronics and printing plants and factories that produce leather products. Building granite is quarried nearby. Pop., 1960 census, 28,991.

DALLAS, a city in northern Texas, the seat of Dallas County. Dallas is located on the Trinity River. With Fort Worth, some 30 miles to the west, it forms a major Texas industrial area.

Dallas produces textiles, leather, machinery, electronic equipment, and aircraft. Other important industries are oil refining, meat packing, publishing, and the assembly of automobiles. There are also many insurance offices in the city. Pop., 1960 census, 679,684; Metropolitan Stat. Area, 1965 est., 1,289,000.

DENVER, a city in north-central Colorado, the capital of the state. Denver is located on the South Platte River and Cherry Creek. It is Colorado's largest city and the trade center for an agricultural area.

Denver has aircraft and missile plants, a U.S. mint, railroad shops, flour and feed mills, canneries, and plants producing leather and rubber goods, mining machinery, and electronic equipment. Pop., 1960 census, 493,887; Metropolitan Stat. Area, 1965 est., 1,073,000.

DES MOINES, a city in south-central Iowa, the capital of the state, and the seat of Polk County. Des Moines is located at the junction of the Des Moines and Raccoon rivers. It is the largest city in Iowa.

Industrial products include apparel, food products, tires, and aircraft parts. Printing and publishing are also important. The area around the city produces coal and corn. Pop., 1960 census, 208,982; Metropolitan Stat. Area, 1965 est., 271,000.

DETROIT, a city in southeastern Michigan, the seat of Wayne County. Detroit is located on the Detroit River, near Lake Erie. It is the largest city in Michigan and one of the largest cities in the United States. Detroit is a Great Lakes port, a port of entry, and a railroad and shipping center.

Detroit is the center for the major automobile-producing area in the country. Other industries include food

El Paso is a commercial center for an agricultural area producing cotton, fruit, and vegetables. It has copper and oil refineries and ore smelters. Cement and apparel are produced. Pop., 1960 census, 276,687; Metropolitan Stat. Area, 1965 est., 344,000.

FARGO–MOORHEAD, a metropolitan complex formed by Fargo, in eastern North Dakota, and Moorhead, in western Minnesota. The two cities are on opposite sides of the Red River. Fargo is the largest city in North Dakota and a river port.

The two cities serve an agricultural area that produces spring wheat, potatoes, livestock, poultry, and dairy products. Industries include food processing, shipping, and the manufacture of farm machinery, steel, and glass and wood products. Pop., 1960 census, Fargo, 46,622, Moorhead, 22,-934; Metropolitan Stat. Area, 1960 census, 106,027.

land in the mouth of Galveston Bay, an inlet of the Gulf of Mexico. It is connected with Texas City, on the mainland, by causeways.

Galveston is a port of entry. It manufactures wire, nails, cement, and apparel. Shipbuilding and oil refining are important industries. Texas City has oil and sugar refineries, tin smelters, and chemical plants. Oil, sulfur, and cotton are shipped through the ports.

Pop., 1960 census, Galveston, 67,175, Texas City, 32,065, Metropolitan Stat. Area, 1960 census, 140,364.

GARY–HAMMOND–EAST CHICAGO, an urban industrial complex in northwestern Indiana on Lake Michigan. The Grand Calumet River flows through Hammond. East Chicago is the largest port in the state.

Steel production is the major industry of the region. The area also produces railroad equipment, hospital

DENVER CHAMBER OF COMMERCE

DENVER lies high in the foothills of the Rocky Mountains

AMERICAN AIRLINES

DETROIT'S DOWNTOWN SKYLINE reflects its commercial importance.

processing and the manufacture of steel, chemicals, and machinery. Pop., 1960 census, 1,670,144; Metropolitan Stat. Area, 1965 est., 1,073,000.

DOVER, a city in central Delaware, the capital of the state and the seat of Kent County. Dover is located on the St. Jones River. The city is a retailing and trading center for the surrounding agricultural area. The main industries include meat canning and the manufacture of rubber goods. Pop., 1960 census, 7,250.

EAST CHICAGO. See GARY–HAMMOND–EAST CHICAGO.

EASTON. See ALLENTOWN–BETHLEHEM–EASTON.

EL PASO, a city in west-central Texas, the seat of El Paso County. El Paso is located on the Rio Grande opposite Ciudad Juárez, Mexico. It is a port of entry.

FORT WORTH, a city in north-central Texas, the seat of Tarrant County. With Dallas, some 30 miles to the east, it forms a major industrial area in Texas. Fort Worth's principal industries are meat packing, grain milling, shipping, and oil and gas refining. Aircraft, oil field equipment, metal products, and apparel are manufactured. Pop., 1960 census, 356,268; Metropolitan Stat. Area, 1965 est., 627,000.

FRANKFORT, a city in north-central Kentucky, the capital of the state and the seat of Franklin County. Frankfort is located near the Kentucky River in the Bluegrass region. Many horses are raised in the surrounding area. The city produces bourbon whisky, shoes, and twine. Pop., 1960 census, 18,365.

GALVESTON–TEXAS CITY, an industrial and port area in southeastern Texas. Galveston is located on Galveston Is-

supplies, tinplate, soap, and shortening. There are printing, oil refining, and sacking plants.

Pop., 1960 census, Gary 178,320, Hammond, 111,698, East Chicago, 57,-669; Metropolitan Stat. Area, 1965 est., 596,000.

GREAT FALLS, a city in north-central Montana, the seat of Cascade County. It is the largest city in the state. Great Falls is located on the Missouri River and has well-developed hydroelectric power facilities. Industries include copper and oil refining, zinc reduction, and flour milling and packing, and the city is an important river port.

The area the city serves produces coal, petroleum, lead, silver, zinc, and copper. There are irrigated farms and livestock ranches in the region. Pop., 1960 census, 55,357; Metropolitan Stat. Area, 1960 census, 73,418.

HAMMOND. See GARY–HAMMOND–EAST CHICAGO.

HAWAII VISITORS BUREAU
HONOLULU'S WAIKIKI BEACH.

NASA
HOUSTON'S MANNED SPACECRAFT CENTER, important in space research and development.

HARRISBURG, a city in southeastern Pennsylvania, the capital of the state and the seat of Dauphin County. Harrisburg is located on the Susquehanna River. The city is a railroad center.

Harrisburg's major industry is the manufacture of steel. Other industries produce jet engine parts, metal products, apparel, electrical equipment, food products, and lumber products. The surrounding area produces coal and iron. Pop., 1960 census, 79,797; Metropolitan Stat. Area, 1965 est., 391,000.

HARTFORD, a city in northern Connecticut, the capital of the state and the seat of Hartford County. Hartford is located at the head of navigation of the Connecticut River. It is the state's largest city and a port of entry.

The city has many insurance companies. Industrial products include typewriters, guns, turbines, engines, brushes, and tools. Printing and bookbinding are also important. Pop., 1960 census, 162,178; Metropolitan Stat. Area, 1960 census, 549,249.

HELENA, a city in west-central Montana, the capital of the state and the seat of Lewis and Clark County. Helena is located near the Missouri River. The city is a retailing and trading center for the Prickly Pear Valley, an agricultural region in which cattle and sheep are raised and vegetables are grown. Some gold and silver is mined nearby. Pop., 1960 census, 20,227.

HONOLULU, a city in the southeastern part of Oahu Island, Hawaii. It is the capital of the state and the seat of Honolulu County. Honolulu is the population center of the Hawaiian Islands.

The city has an excellent harbor and is a major Pacific port. Large numbers of tourists visit Honolulu each year. The major manufacturing industries are sugar refining and pine-

apple canning. Pop., 1960 census, 294,179; Metropolitan Stat. Area, 1965 est., 571,000.

HOUSTON, a city in southeastern Texas, the seat of Harris County. It is the largest city in Texas. Houston is connected to the Gulf of Mexico by the Houston Ship Channel. Petroleum products, lumber, cotton, rice, and sulfur are shipped from Houston, which has a deepwater harbor.

The major industries include meat packing, publishing, petroleum and sugar refining, and rice processing. Other industries produce chemicals, cottonseed oil products, oil well machinery, cement, and paper. Houston is an important space-research center. Pop., 1960 census, 938,219; Metropolitan Stat. Area, 1965 est., 1,696,000.

INDIANAPOLIS, a city in central Indiana, the capital of the state and the seat of Marion County. Indianapolis, on the White River, is the state's largest city. It is a railroad center with flour-milling and meat-packing industries.

Indianapolis also produces hosiery, road construction machinery, automobile and aircraft parts, textiles, chemicals, pharmaceuticals, and electronic and electrical equipment. Pop., 1960 census, 476,258; Metropolitan Stat. Area, 1965 est., 984,000.

JACKSON, a city in south-central Mississippi, the capital of the state and the seat of Hinds County. Jackson is located on the Pearl River. It is the largest city in the state and is a railroad center. Jackson produces lumber, textiles, and cottonseed. Cotton and natural gas from the area are shipped from Jackson. Pop., 1960 census, 144,422; Metropolitan Stat. Area, 1960 census, 221,367.

JACKSONVILLE, a city in northeastern Florida, the seat of Duval County. Jacksonville is located on the St. Johns River, near the Atlantic Ocean.

It is a port of entry and an important transportation center. The city produces paper, cigars, and chemicals. Shipbuilding and food processing are also important. Pop., 1960 census, 201,030; Metropolitan Stat. Area, 1965 est., 497,000.

JUNEAU, a city in southeastern Alaska, the capital of the state and the seat of the Southeastern District. The Greater Juneau Borough includes Juneau and the city of Douglas on nearby Douglas Island. Juneau is located on the slopes of Mt. Juneau and Mt. Roberts.

Juneau is a port on the Gastineau Channel of the Inland Waterway, and pulp and lumber are shipped from the city. It is the trade center for the panhandle of Alaska. Pop., 1960 census, 6,797.

JEFFERSON CITY, a city in central Missouri, the capital of the state and the seat of Cole County. Jefferson City is located on the Missouri River. The city's major industries include printing and the production of wood products, shoes, and electrical appliances. Poultry are raised and fruit and grain are grown in the surrounding agricultural region. Pop., 1960 census, 28,228.

KANSAS CITY, an urban industrial complex formed by Kansas City, in eastern Kansas, and Kansas City, in western Missouri. The two cities are located at the junction of the Kansas and Missouri rivers. They are both ports of entry and railroad centers.

The major industries are meat packing, flour milling, oil refining, and the assembly of automobiles. Steel, soap, and agricultural machinery are also produced. There are stockyards and grain storage facilities in the two cities.

Pop., 1960 census, Kansas City, Kan., 121,901, Kansas City, Mo., 457,539; Metropolitan Stat. Area, 1965 est., 1,183,000.

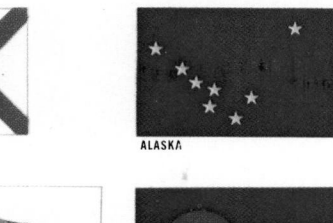

ALABAMA

ALASKA

ARIZONA

ARKANSAS

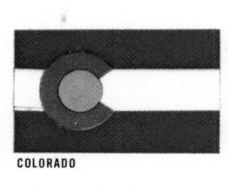

CALIFORNIA

COLORADO

CONNECTICUT

DELAWARE

DISTRICT OF COLUMBIA

FLORIDA

GEORGIA

HAWAII

IDAHO

ILLINOIS

INDIANA

IOWA

KANSAS

KENTUCKY

LOUISIANA

MAINE

MARYLAND

MASSACHUSETTS

MICHIGAN

MINNESOTA

MISSISSIPPI

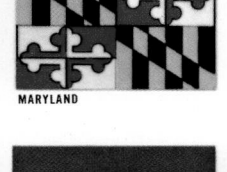

MISSOURI

MONTANA

NEBRASKA

NEVADA

NEW HAMPSHIRE

NEW JERSEY

NEW MEXICO

NEW YORK

NORTH CAROLINA

NORTH DAKOTA

OHIO

OKLAHOMA

OREGON

PENNSYLVANIA

RHODE ISLAND

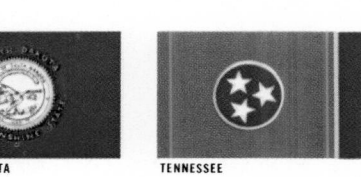

SOUTH CAROLINA

SOUTH DAKOTA

TENNESSEE

TEXAS

UTAH

VERMONT

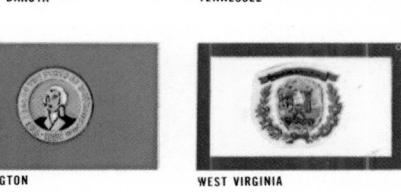

VIRGINIA

WASHINGTON

WEST VIRGINIA

WISCONSIN

WYOMING

AMERICAN SAMOA

GUAM

PUERTO RICO

VIRGIN ISLANDS

AMERICA'S NATIONAL PARKS. A vast array of unusual geographic features characterize these sites, the first of which was established by Congress in 1872. Excellent views of the Grand Canyon, in Arizona, can be had from almost any spot, including the North Rim. The dull red walls of the Canyon, an immense and deep gorge cut by the Colorado River, give off a glow when lit by the sun.

KNOXVILLE, a city in eastern Tennessee, the seat of Knox County. Knoxville is located on the Tennessee River. It is the administrative center of the Tennessee Valley Authority (TVA).

Knoxville produces furniture, textiles, flour, feed, apparel, iron, and plastics. The surrounding area produces grain, iron, marble, coal, zinc, timber, and tobacco. Pop., 1960 census, 111,872; Metropolitan Stat. Area, 1965 est., 390,000.

LAS VEGAS, a city in southern Nevada, the seat of Clark County. It is the largest city in the state. Las Vegas is a tourist center famous for its gambling casinos and nightclubs. It is also the commercial center for a mining and livestock raising area. Pop., 1960 census, 64,405; Metropolitan Stat. Area, 1960 census, 127,016.

LINCOLN, a city in southeastern Nebraska, the capital of the state and the seat of Lancaster County. Lincoln's industries include meat packing, canning, and printing. The city produces bricks, tiles, motor scooters, conveyor belts, engines, rubber tires, telephone equipment, freight cars, and creamery products.

Lincoln is a distribution center for poultry, grain, and livestock raised in the surrounding area. Pop., 1960 census, 128,521; Metropolitan Stat. Area, 1960 census, 155,272.

LITTLE ROCK–NORTH LITTLE ROCK, an urban industrial complex in central Arkansas on the Arkansas River. Little Rock is the capital of the state and the seat of Pulaski County. The cities produce cottonseed oil, furniture, chemicals, concrete, sheet metal, and electrical appliances. There are also railroad repair shops.

The surrounding area produces cotton, dairy products, bauxite, coal, oil, natural gas, clay, and marble. Pop., 1960 census, Little Rock, 107,813, North Little Rock, 58,032; Metropolitan Stat. Area, 1965 est., 279,000.

LONG BEACH. See Los Angeles–Long Beach.

LOS ANGELES–LONG BEACH, an urban area in southern California, near the Pacific Ocean. Los Angeles is one of the largest cities in area in the United States. Los Angeles-Long Beach is a transportation center.

The major industries include oil refining and food processing. The cities manufacture aircraft, machinery, chemicals, apparel, electronic equipment, and steel. Hollywood, a district of Los Angeles, is a motion picture and television center. Pop., 1960 census, Los Angeles, 2,479,015, Long Beach 344,168; Metropolitan Stat. Area, 1965 est., 6,765,000.

LOUISVILLE, a city in northwestern Kentucky, the seat of Jefferson County. Louisville is located at the falls of the Ohio River. It is the largest city in the state, a port of entry, and a railroad center.

The major industries include tobacco processing, oil refining, distilling, meat packing, and flour milling. The Kentucky Derby, an annual horse race of international renown, is held at Churchill Downs in Louisville. Pop., 1960 census, 390,639; Metropolitan Stat. Area, 1965 est., 771,000.

LANSING, a city in the south-central lower peninsula of Michigan, the capital of the state. Lansing is located at the confluence of the Grand and Red Cedar rivers. The city produces motor vehicles, metal products,

MIAMI BEACH NEWS BUREAU

MIAMI BEACH, a luxurious Atlantic resort.

pumps, and engines. Pop., 1960 census, 107,807; Metropolitan Stat. Area, 1965 est., 366,000.

MADISON, a city in south-central Wisconsin, the capital of the state and the seat of Dane County. Madison is located between lakes Monona and Mendota. It produces machine tools, batteries, meat products, surgical equipment, farm machinery, tin containers, and air conditioning equipment. An agricultural area surrounds the city. Pop., 1960 census, 126,706; Metropolitan Stat. Area, 1960 census, 222,095.

MEMPHIS, a city in southwestern Tennessee, the seat of Shelby County. Memphis is located on the Mississippi River. It is the largest city in the state, a port of entry, and a railroad center.

Memphis produces cottonseed oil, farm machinery, textiles, drugs, feed, and wood and rubber products. There are hardwood forests in the surrounding area. Livestock and cotton are raised in the region. Pop., 1960 census, 497,524; Metropolitan Stat. Area, 1965 est., 740,000.

MIAMI, a city in southeastern Florida, the seat of Dade County. It is the largest city in Florida. Miami is located at the mouth of the Miami River and is a port of entry.

Tourism is the major industry. Miami is the center of an extensive resort area including Miami Beach, Hialeah, and Coral Gables. The city manufactures electronic equipment, apparel, and aluminum products. Pop., 1960 census, 291,688; Metropolitan Stat. Area, 1965 est., 1,061,000.

MILWAUKEE, a city in southeastern Wisconsin, the seat of Milwaukee County. Milwaukee is located on Lake Michigan. It is the largest city in the state

LOS ANGELES CHAMBER OF COMMERCE

ALL ROADS LEAD TO LOS ANGELES, a city noted for its extensive system of expressways.

and a port of entry. Milwaukee produces construction machinery, electrical equipment, diesel and gasoline engines, beer, hosiery, shoes, and tractors. Pop., 1960 census, 741,324; Metropolitan Stat. Area, 1965 est., 1,275,000.

MINNEAPOLIS–ST. PAUL, an urban area in eastern Minnesota. Minneapolis is the seat of Hennepin County and the largest city in the state. St. Paul is the seat of Ramsey County and the state capital. Minneapolis and St. Paul, the Twin Cities, face each other across the Mississippi River, at the head of navigation. Both cities are ports of entry.

The area produces machinery, electronic and aerospace equipment, chemicals, abrasives, and metal, wood, and rubber products. Dairy and grain products, beer, and soybean oil are also produced. Pop., 1960 census, Minneapolis, 482,872, St. Paul, 313,411; Metropolitan Stat. Area, 1965 est., 1,612,000.

MOBILE, a city in southwestern Alabama, the seat of Mobile County. Mobile is located at the mouth of the Mobile River, at its entrance to Mobile Bay, and is Alabama's only sea port. Mobile is a port of entry.

The city ships agricultural products, cotton, naval stores, and lumber. Its major industries include the processing of food, aluminum, and asbestos, and the production of paper and chemicals. Pop., 1960 census, 202,779; Metropolitan Stat. Area, 1965 est., 391,000.

MONTGOMERY, a city in central Alabama, the capital of the state and the seat of Montgomery County. Montgomery is located on the south bank of the Alabama River. The city was a temporary capital of the Confederate States of America during the Civil War and has been called the "Cradle of the Confederacy."

Montgomery is a transportation center. The city's stockyards and meat-packing plants serve the surrounding area. There are also lumber mills, fertilizer plants, and textile mills. Montgomery produces syrups, furniture, glass, chemicals, and rail equipment. Pop., 1960 census, 134,393; Metropolitan Stat. Area, 1965 est., 207,000.

MONTPELIER, a city in central Vermont, the capital of the state and the seat of Washington County. Montpelier is located on the Winooski River. The city produces textiles, building granite, wood products, and machinery. Pop., 1960 census, 8,782.

MOORHEAD. See FARGO–MOORHEAD.

NASHVILLE, a city in central Tennessee, the capital of the state and the seat of Davidson County. Nashville is located on the Cumberland River. It is a port of entry and a shipping center.

The city manufactures shoes, cellophane, rayon, bricks, cement, flour, lumber, and food and tobacco products. Nashville also has railroad shops and publishing houses, and it

CHAMBER OF COMMERCE OF THE NEW ORLEANS AREA

NEW ORLEANS, looking through traditional lacey ironwork toward St. Louis Cathedral.

is a major center of the entertainment industry. Productive farmlands surround the city. Pop., 1960 census, 170,874; Metropolitan Stat. Area, 1965 est., 512,000.

NEW ORLEANS, a city in southeastern Louisiana, the seat of Orleans Parish (county). New Orleans, located at a bend of the Mississippi River, is a port of entry. Bauxite, bananas, coffee, and sugar are shipped into New Orleans, and petroleum, chemicals, cotton, lumber, grain, iron, and steel are shipped from the city.

New Orleans produces food products, textiles, aluminum, furniture, and construction materials. Many tourists come to the city's yearly carnival, the Mardi Gras. Pop., 1960 census, 627,525; Metropolitan Stat. Area, 1965 est., 1,027,000.

NEW YORK, a city in southeastern New York State. New York is located at the mouth of the Hudson River. It is the largest city in the United States and one of the largest cities in the world. The United Nations has its headquarters in the city.

New York is made up of five boroughs—Manhattan, Brooklyn, the Bronx, Queens, and Richmond (Staten Island)—each of which is coextensive with a county. The New York metropolitan area extends into Connecticut, New Jersey, and New York State.

New York is the largest U.S. port and a major world port. It is also a major airline, railroad, and highway center. The city is the trade and financial hub of the United States. Its diverse products include apparel, metal products, chemicals, and food products. New York is a center for publishing and television and radio producing. Its many museums, colleges, and theaters make it a cultural center of the United States. Pop., 1960 census, 7,881,984; Metropolitan Stat. Area, 1965 est., 11,366,000.

NORTH LITTLE ROCK. See LITTLE ROCK–NORTH LITTLE ROCK.

OAKLAND. See SAN FRANCISCO–OAKLAND.

OGDEN, a city in northern Utah, the seat of Weber County. Ogden is located at the junction of the Weber

and Ogden rivers. It is a major railroad center of the West. Its industries include meat packing, canning, and the production of jet engines and textiles. There are farms and livestock ranges in the surrounding area. Pop., 1960 census, 70,197; Metropolitan Stat. Area, 1960 census, 110,744.

OKLAHOMA CITY, a city in central Oklahoma, the capital of the state and the seat of Oklahoma County. Oklahoma City is located on the North Canadian River. It is the largest city in the state. Its industries produce transportation equipment, oilfield equipment, and storage batteries.

The city processes grain and dairy goods produced in the surrounding area. It is also a livestock market. Oil wells are located in the metropolitan area. Pop., 1960 census, 324,253; Metropolitan Stat. Area, 1965 est., 585,000.

OLYMPIA, a city in west-central Washington, the capital of the state and the seat of Thurston County. Olympia is located on Budd Inlet at the southern end of Puget Sound. Agricultural products, oysters, and lumber are shipped from Olympia. The city's major industries include shipbuilding, canning, brewing, and lumber and plywood manufacturing. Pop., 1960 census, 18,273.

OMAHA, a city in eastern Nebraska, the seat of Douglas County. Omaha is located on the Missouri River and is a port of entry. It is the largest city in the state. Omaha is a market for livestock and farm products. It produces apparel, chemicals, and metal and food products. Pop., 1960 census, 301,598; Metropolitan Stat. Area, 1965 est., 516,000.

PAWTUCKET. See PROVIDENCE–PAWTUCKET.

PHILADELPHIA, a city in southeastern Pennsylvania. Philadelphia is located on the Delaware River. It is the largest city in Pennsylvania and one of the largest cities in the United States. Philadelphia was founded as a Quaker colony by William Penn in 1682. The Declaration of Independence was signed there in 1776.

Philadelphia is a major U.S. port and an important commercial center. The city produces chemicals, machinery, textiles, apparel, and carpets. Publishing is also important. The city's metropolitan area extends into New Jersey. Pop., 1960 census, 2,002,512; Metropolitan Stat. Area, 1965 est. 4,664,000.

PHOENIX, a city in south-central Arizona, the capital of the state and the seat of Maricopa County. It is the largest city in the state. Phoenix is located in the Salt River Valley, where irrigated farms produce cotton, melons, citrus fruits, olives, lettuce, and grapes.

Phoenix produces aircraft, steel products, chemicals, furniture, aluminum, and flour. There are also plants for research in electronics. Phoenix is a famous health and winter resort. Pop., 1960 census, 439,170; Metropolitan Stat. Area, 1965 est., 818,000.

PIERRE, a city in central South Dakota, the capital of the state and the seat of Hughes County. Pierre is located on the east bank of the Missouri River. Pierre markets and ships grain and livestock raised in the surrounding region. Pop., 1960 census, 10,088.

PITTSBURGH, a city in southwestern Pennsylvania, the seat of Allegheny County. Pittsburgh is located at the junction of the Allegheny and Monongahela rivers where they meet to form the Ohio River. It is a port of entry. Steel production is the major industry.

Other important industries include the production of iron, glass, coke, clay products, air brakes, aluminum, chemicals, explosives, and machinery for steel mills. Oil refining, printing, and publishing are also significant. Pop., 1960 census, 604,332; Metropolitan Stat. Area, 1965 est., 2,372,000.

PONCE, a city in south-central Puerto Rico, the island's second largest city. Ponce lies four miles north of Playa, its port.

Ponce is a shipping center for sugar, coffee, tobacco, and rum. Its manufactures include textiles, cement, and chemicals and pharmaceuticals. There are oil refineries in the area. Pop., 1960 census, 114,286; Metropolitan Stat. Area, 145,586.

PORTLAND, a city in southwestern Maine, the seat of Cumberland County. Portland is located on Casco Bay. It is a port of entry and the commercial and transportation center of the state. Portland produces textiles, shoes, and metal products.

The surrounding area produces farm products, lumber, and paper. Fish caught in nearby waters are processed in Portland. Pop., 1960 census, 72,566; Metropolitan Stat. Area, 1960 census, 139,122.

PORTLAND, a city in northwestern Oregon, the seat of Multnomah County. Portland is located on the Willamette River near its junction with the Columbia River. It is the largest city in the state and a port of entry.

The city produces paper, wood products, textiles, machinery, metals, flour, cereals, canned foods, and cheese. Portland ships wool, wheat, and lumber produced in the surrounding area. Pop., 1960 census, 372,676; Metropolitan Stat. Area, 1965 est., 897,000.

PROVIDENCE–PAWTUCKET, an urban industrial complex in eastern Rhode Island that also includes East and North Providence and parts of Massachusetts.

Providence is the capital and largest city of the state and is a port of entry. It produces jewelry, silverware, metal products, machinery, rubber goods, and textiles. Pawtucket produces thread, textiles and textile machinery, and metal products.

Pop., 1960 census, Providence, 207,498, Pawtucket, 81,001; Metropolitan Stat. Area, 1960 census, 821,101.

RALEIGH, a city in central North Carolina, the capital of the state and the seat of Wake County. Raleigh is the commercial center for eastern North Carolina and is located in a fertile agricultural region. The city produces textiles, cottonseed oil, refrigerators, and farm implements. Pop., 1960 census, 93,931; Metropolitan Stat. Area, 1960 census, 169,082.

RENO, a city in western Nevada, the seat of Washoe County. It is located on the Truckee River. Reno is widely known for its liberal residency requirements for divorce. Its vacation facilities and pleasant climate have made Reno a prosperous resort city.

Reno's industries include lumber milling, meat packing, and flour milling. Bricks, soap, and stoves are also produced. Pop., 1960 census, 51,470; Metropolitan Stat. Area, 1960 census, 84,743.

RICHMOND, a city in east-central Virginia, the capital of the state and the seat of Henrico County. Richmond is located on the James River. It is a port of entry. During the Civil War, Richmond was the capital of the Confederacy.

Richmond is a leading tobacco market. The city manufactures tobacco products, textiles, apparel, steel products, paper, machinery, fertilizer, and flour. Printing is also important. Pop., 1960 census, 219,958; Metropolitan Stat. Area, 1965 est., 484,000.

ROCHESTER, a city in northwestern New York State, the seat of Monroe County. Rochester is located near Lake Ontario and the New York State Barge Canal. The Genesee River flows through the city. Rochester is a port of entry.

The city produces cameras and photographic supplies, optical equipment, office supplies and equipment, telephone equipment, and radios. There are truck farms and fruit orchards in the surrounding area. Pop., 1960 census, 318,611; Metropolitan Stat. Area, 1965 est., 804,000.

SACRAMENTO, a city in north-central California, the capital of the state and the seat of Sacramento County. Sacramento is located in the Sacramento Valley, at the confluence of the Sacramento and American rivers. It was settled during a gold rush in 1849.

Sacramento's main industries include meat packing and canning. The city is also noted for missile research and production. It is a distribution and trade center for the fertile Sacramento Valley. Pop., 1960 census, 191,667; Metropolitan Stat. Area, 1965 est., 737,000.

ST. LOUIS, a city in east-central Missouri, the largest city in the state. St. Louis is located on the west bank of the Mississippi River. During the 1800s the city was a major river port and railroad center. It is still a transportation center, as well as a fur, grain, livestock, and produce market.

St. Louis produces stoves, brick, beer, chemicals, machinery, aircraft,

THE PORT OF NEW YORK AUTHORITY

NEW YORK CITY SKYLINE showing lower Manhattan with the Hudson and East River docks.

SAN FRANCISCO CONVENTION AND VISITORS BUREAU
SAN FRANCISCO, famous for its cable cars.

PUERTO RICO INFORMATION SERVICE
SAN JUAN'S FORT SAN GERONIMO looking toward the modern Condado Beach area.

and shoes and leather goods. Pop., 1960 census, 750,026; Metropolitan Stat. Area, 1965 est., 2,249,000.

ST. PAUL. See MINNEAPOLIS-ST. PAUL.

ST. PETERSBURG. See TAMPA-ST. PETERSBURG.

SALEM, a city in northwestern Oregon, the capital of the state and the seat of Marion County. Salem is located at the head of navigation of the Willamette River and is the commercial center for the fertile Willamette Valley. The city produces storage batteries, machinery, paper, and paint. Pop., 1960 census, 49,142; Metropolitan Stat. Area, 1965 est., 172,000.

SALT LAKE CITY, a city in north-central Utah, the capital of the state and seat of Salt Lake County. Salt Lake City is located on the Jordan River, 13 miles from the Great Salt Lake. The city was founded by the Mormons in 1847.

The city's major industries include food processing, oil refining, printing and publishing, smelting, and the production of textiles, radios, and metal and clay products. There are mines and irrigated farms in the area. Pop., 1960 census, 189,454; Metropolitan Stat. Area, 1965 est., 523,000.

SAN ANTONIO, a city in south-central Texas, the seat of Bexar County. San Antonio is located on the San Antonio River and is a port of entry. The Alamo, an historic fort, was the scene of a battle between Texans and Mexican soldiers in 1836.

The city is the trade and distribution center for a livestock-raising and crop-growing area. Cotton, vegetables, and fruit are grown. The major industries include oil refining, food processing, and the production of apparel, refrigeration equipment, soap, and iron and steel products. Pop., 1960 census, 587,718; Metropolitan Stat. Area, 1965 est., 808,000.

SAN DIEGO, a city in southern California, the seat of San Diego County. The city is located on San Diego Bay. It is a port of entry and a military center. San Diego was the site of California's first permanent white settlement.

San Diego has a good, natural harbor and is a major fishing port and shipbuilding center. Other important industries include sugar refining and brewing. San Diego also produces electronic equipment, aircraft, and missiles. Pop., 1960 census, 573,224; Metropolitan Stat. Area, 1965 est., 1,136,000.

SAN FRANCISCO–OAKLAND, an urban area in western California that includes Berkeley, Alameda, and many other towns. San Francisco is located on the Pacific Ocean. Oakland is to the east of San Francisco, across the San Francisco Bay. The two cities are connected by the San Francisco-Oakland Bay Bridge. San Francisco's Chinatown is the largest Chinese settlement in the United States.

The area is a major West Coast port, and a financial, insurance, and cultural center. Major industries include shipbuilding, meat packing, sugar refining, printing, publishing, and canning. The area produces paint, iron and aluminum products, diesel engines, and chemicals. Pop., 1960 census, San Francisco, 742,855, Oakland, 367,548; Metropolitan Stat. Area, 1965 est., 2,918,000.

SAN JUAN, a city in northeastern Puerto Rico, the island's capital and largest city. San Juan consists of Old San Juan, which lies on an offshore island, and Santurce and Río Piedras on the mainland.

San Juan's excellent harbor is used by commercial vessels, cruise ships, and fishing boats. The city is the commercial center of Puerto Rico. Its many products include chemicals and pharmaceuticals, textiles and apparel, and electronic equipment. Pop., 1960 census, 432,777; Metropolitan Stat. Area, 588,805.

SANTA FE, a city in north-central New Mexico, the capital of the state and the seat of Santa Fe County. The city is almost completely surrounded by mountains. Santa Fe was founded by the Spanish in the 1600s. Tourism is important to the city, and Indian jewelry, blankets, and rugs are produced. Pop., 1960 census, 33,394.

SAULT STE. MARIE, a city in the northeastern end of the upper peninsula of Michigan, the seat of Chippewa County. Sault Ste. Marie is located on the St. Marys River, which connects lakes Superior and Huron. It is a port of entry. The Soo Locks, near Sault Ste. Marie on the St. Marys River, is a heavily used shipping route.

The city produces carbide, wood products, machinery, and clothing. The surrounding area produces dairy products and grows hay and grain. It is also a resort area. Pop., 1960 census, 18,722.

SAVANNAH, a city in southeastern Georgia, the seat of Chatham County. Savannah is located near the Atlantic Ocean, on the Savannah River. It is a port of entry.

Savannah produces paint, chemicals, wood and paper products, and fertilizer. The city is a distributing center for an area that produces naval stores, petroleum, tobacco, cotton, sugar, and lumber. Pop., 1960 census, 149,245; Metropolitan Stat. Area, 1960 census, 188,299.

SCHENECTADY. See ALBANY-SCHENECTADY-TROY.

SEATTLE, a city in west-central Washington, the seat of King County. Seattle is located between Elliot Bay of Puget Sound and Lake Washington. It is the largest city in the state and is an important port.

Major industries include fishing, food processing, shipbuilding, lumbering, and the production of paper, flour, aircraft, machinery, metal products, and chemicals. Pop., 1960 census, 557,087; Metropolitan Stat. Area, 1965 est., 1,179,000.

SPOKANE, a city in eastern Washington, the seat of Spokane County. Spokane is located at the falls of the Spokane River. It is a port of entry.

The city's industries include aluminum smelting, metal refining and casting, lumber milling, and meat packing. There are also railroad shops and grain elevators in Spokane.

The surrounding area, called the "Inland Empire," produces agricultural and dairy products, minerals, and lumber. Pop., 1960 census, 181,608; Metropolitan Stat. Area, 1965 est., 267,000.

SPRINGFIELD, a city in central Illinois, the capital of the state and the seat of Sangamon County. Springfield is located on the Sangamon River. The city produces castings, mattresses, paint, feed, flour, cereal products, electronic equipment, boilers, automotive equipment, and electric meters. Many tourists visit the memorials built to Abraham Lincoln, who lived in Springfield. Pop., 1960 census, 83,271; Metropolitan Stat. Area, 1960 census, 146,539.

SYRACUSE, a city in central New York State, the seat of Onondaga County. Syracuse is located on Onondaga Lake and the New York State Barge Canal and is a port of entry.

Syracuse produces steel, motor vehicle parts, soda ash, electrical machines and appliances, air conditioning equipment, typewriters, agricultural machinery, china, and cans. Printing and publishing are also important industries. Syracuse is the commercial center for an agricultural area. Pop., 1960 census, 216,038; Metropolitan Stat. Area, 1965 est., 606,000.

TACOMA, a city in west-central Washington, the seat of Pierce County. Tacoma is located on Puget Sound at the mouth of the Puyallup River. It is a seaport and railroad center.

Major industries include lumber milling, smelting, fishing, fish processing, and flour milling. Tacoma produces logging machinery, furniture, plywood, and paper products. It is the electrochemical center of the West Coast. Pop., 1960 census, 147,979; Metropolitan Stat. Area, 1965 est., 343,000.

TALLAHASSEE, a city in northwestern Florida, the capital of the state and the seat of Leon County. The city is an educational center. It produces lumber, naval stores, feed, and mobile homes. Cotton, pecans, and cattle are raised in the surrounding area. Pop., 1960 census, 58,022; Metropolitan Stat. Area, 1960 census, 74,225.

TAMPA–ST. PETERSBURG. a metropolitan area in western Florida. Tampa is the seat of Hillsborough County. The two cities are located on opposite shores of Tampa Bay and are connected by two bridges. The area is a popular winter resort.

The major industries include cigar making, and citrus fruit, shrimp, and vegetable processing. The cities produce metal and cement products, beer, and electrical and electronic equipment. Pop., 1960 census, Tampa, 274,970; St. Petersburg, 181,298; Metropolitan Stat. Area, 1965 est., 873,000.

TEXAS CITY. See Galveston-Texas City.

TOPEKA, a city in northeastern Kansas, the capital of the state and the seat of Shawnee County. Topeka is located on the Kansas River. It is the commercial center for a cattle-raising and wheat-growing area.

Major industries include meat packing and flour milling. There are tire companies, railroad shops, insurance companies, and printing and publishing concerns in the city. Topeka is also a center for psychiatric research and therapy. Pop., 1960 census, 119,484; Metropolitan Stat. Area, 1960 census, 141,286.

TRENTON, a city in west-central New Jersey, the capital of the state and the seat of Mercer County. Trenton is located on the Delaware River. Important battles were fought in Trenton during the American Revolution.

The city produces cable, wire rope, cigars, rubber goods, porcelain, pottery, linoleum, woolen goods, parachutes, airplane equipment, and machinery. Pop., 1960 census, 114,167; Metropolitan Stat. Area, 1965 est., 296,000.

TROY. See Albany-Schenectady-Troy.

TUCSON, a city in southeastern Arizona, the seat of Pima County. Tucson is located on the Santa Cruz River. Because of its clear, dry climate, Tucson is popular as a health resort and for winter sports and tourism. It is a railroad center for an area of mines, irrigated farms, and livestock ranches.

The city produces missile parts and processes food. It is also a center for electronics research and production and for railroad repair. Pop., 1960 census, 212,892; Metropolitan Stat. Area, 1965 est., 307,000.

TULSA, a city in northeastern Oklahoma, the seat of Tulsa County. Tulsa is located on the Arkansas River. The major activities of the city are concerned with oil exploration, drilling, marketing, and research.

Tulsa manufactures oil-field equipment and refines petroleum. Aircraft are among the many products manufactured. The surrounding area produces a variety of agricultural products. Pop., 1960 census, 261,685; Metropolitan Stat. Area, 1965 est., 433,000.

WHEELING, a city in northern West Virginia, the seat of Ohio County. The Wheeling metropolitan area includes Belmont County in Ohio. Wheeling is located on the Ohio River and is a port of entry.

Wheeling manufactures steel and iron products, food products, tin plate, glassware, porcelain, textiles, and paper products. The area produces coal and natural gas. Pop., 1960 census, 53,400; Metropolitan Stat. Area, 1960 census, 190,342.

WICHITA, a city in south-central Kansas, the seat of Sedgwick County. Wichita is located at the confluence of the Arkansas and Little Arkansas rivers. It has grain elevators, stockyards, packing houses, flour mills, and oil refineries serving the surrounding agricultural and oil region.

Wichita produces aircraft, farm machinery, air conditioning equipment, machine tools, transportation equipment, pharmaceuticals, chemicals, apparel, and stoves. Pop., 1960 census, 254,698; Metropolitan Stat. Area, 1965 est., 389,000.

WILMINGTON, a city in northern Delaware, the seat of New Castle County. The metropolitan area includes Salem County, New Jersey, and Cecil County, Maryland. Wilmington is located at the confluence of Brandywine Creek and the Christina and Delaware rivers. It is a port of entry and the largest city in the state.

The city is the home of the E. I. du Pont de Nemours Company and other major chemical research companies. Wilmington produces aircraft, farm machinery, air conditioning and transportation equipment, machine tools, pharmaceuticals, chemicals, apparel, and stoves. Pop., 1960 census, 95,827; Metropolitan Stat. Area, 1965 est., 468,000.

AMERICAN AIRLINES

TUCSON'S MISSION SAN XAVIER DEL BAC, founded in 1700 by Father Eusebio Kino.

NATURAL FEATURES

ADIRONDACK MOUNTAINS, a group of mountains in northeastern New York State lying west of Lake Champlain and Lake George and north of the Mohawk River. The highest point in the Adirondacks is Mt. Marcy, 5,344 feet.

There are many lakes in the Adirondacks, including Lake George, Lake Placid, Saranac Lake, and Racquette Lake. The headwaters of the Black, Ausable, and Hudson rivers are in the Adirondacks. The Adirondack Forest Preserve, a state park, covers more than 2 million acres of the mountain region.

ALEUTIAN ISLANDS, a chain of islands extending about 1,700 miles west of the Alaska Peninsula, separating the Pacific Ocean from the Bering Sea. The Aleutians are divided into four main groups—the Fox, Adreanoff, Rat, and Near islands. They are mountainous and contain many volcanoes. The Aleutians were purchased from Russia in 1917 and are now a district of Alaska.

APPALACHIAN MOUNTAINS, a mountain system stretching along the east coast of North America from Canada's Quebec Province to northern Alabama. The highest peak is Mt. Mitchell, in North Carolina, 6,684 feet.

The Appalachian system includes the Green Mountains of Vermont, the White Mountains of New Hampshire, the Catskill Mountains of New York, the Blue Ridge of Virginia and North Carolina, and the Cumberland Mountains of Tennessee.

ARKANSAS RIVER, one of the longest rivers in the United States. It rises in the Rocky Mountains of central Colorado and flows in a generally southeasterly direction for 1,450 miles, emptying into the Mississippi River in southeastern Arkansas.

The Arkansas, which is navigable for about 650 miles, passes through Colorado, Kansas, Oklahoma, and Arkansas. Its two major tributaries are the Canadian River and the Cimarron River.

BADLANDS, a dry plateau in southwestern South Dakota and northwestern Nebraska. The surface of the Badlands is highly eroded and contains deep gullies and fantastic land formations. There are extensive fossil deposits in the area.

BLACK HILLS, a group of mountains in southwestern South Dakota and northeastern Wyoming. The highest point in the Black Hills is Harney Peak in South Dakota, 7,242 feet. The mountains are drained by the Belle Fourche River and a branch of the Cheyenne River. Mineral resources include gold, silver, mica, uranium, and feldspar.

Much of the Black Hills is included in national parks, including the Black Hills National Park, Wind Cave National Park, Mt. Rushmore National Park, and Devil's Tower National Monument.

BLUEGRASS, a region in central Kentucky that reaches into parts of Ohio, Indiana, and Tennessee. It is named after a species of flowering pasture grass. The area is underlain by limestone with sinkholes and caverns. The Bluegrass is famous as a horse-breeding region.

BRAZOS RIVER, one of the major rivers of the southwest, 1,210 miles long. It originates in north-central Texas and flows southwest through the state to the Gulf of Mexico.

CAPE COD, a sandy peninsula extending east and then north from southeastern Massachusetts. It is touched by Cape Cod Bay on the north, the Atlantic Ocean on the east, Nantucket Sound on the south, and Buzzards Bay on the southwest. The Cape Cod Canal cuts through the base of the peninsula, separating it from the rest of Massachusetts. Offshore islands include Nantucket, Martha's Vineyard, and the Elizabeth Islands.

Cape Cod was formed by glacial deposits. Its many beaches and sand dunes make it a popular resort area. Cranberries grow on the peninsula, and fish are plentiful in the offshore waters.

CAPE HATTERAS, a sandbar off the Atlantic coast of North Carolina. It lies at the end of a series of small islands that form a barrier beach extending parallel to the coast. The region is dangerous for navigators.

CAPE KENNEDY, formerly Cape Canaveral, a cape on the east coast of the Canaveral Peninsula, which lies on the east coast of Florida. The cape is the site of an air force base and a major missile testing and launching center.

CASCADE RANGE, a mountain range in the western United States and Canada. It lies between 100 and 150 miles inland from the Pacific Ocean and is some 700 miles long. The range covers parts of California, Oregon, and Washington and extends into British Columbia.

The peaks of the Cascades, some of which are snow-capped, are among the highest in the United States outside of Alaska. The highest point is Mt. Rainier, Washington, 14,410 feet.

CHAMPLAIN, a lake on the New York-Vermont border extending into Quebec, Canada. The lake has a surface area of 490 square miles, of which 473 square miles are under U.S. jurisdiction.

COAST RANGES, a group of mountain ranges along the west coast of North America. They extend from northern Mexico through the western states and Canada to Alaska.

Among the mountain groups in the Coast Ranges are the St. Elias Mountains, the Coast Mountains, the Olym-

U.S. DEPARTMENT OF THE INTERIOR—NATIONAL PARK SERVICE
THE APPALACHIAN MOUNTAINS are divided into many sections. Seen here is part of the Blue Ridge, one of the southeastern ranges.

NATURAL FEATURES

pic Mountains, the San Bernardino Mountains, the San Jacinto Mountains, the San Rafael Ranges, and the Santa Monica Range.

COLORADO RIVER, a major U.S. river, 1,450 miles long. It rises in northern Colorado and flows southwest and south through Colorado, Utah, Arizona, and Mexico into the Gulf of California. The Colorado forms the boundary between Arizona and California and part of the Arizona-Nevada border.

COLUMBIA RIVER, a major waterway originating in southeastern British Columbia, Canada, and flowing generally south and then west for 1,214 miles. It empties into the Pacific Ocean, north of Portland, Oregon, where it forms a deepwater port.

The Columbia forms the boundary between Washington and Oregon. Its major tributary is the Snake River. Dams along the Columbia, including the Grand Coulee and Bonneville, provide hydroelectric power and water for irrigation.

CONTINENTAL DIVIDE, the line in North America dividing waters that flow west toward the Pacific Ocean from those that flow east toward the Gulf of Mexico and the Atlantic Ocean. In the United States, the Continental Divide runs mainly along the Rocky Mountain ranges.

CRATER LAKE, in the Cascade Range of southwestern Oregon, formed in the crater of an extinct volcano, Mt. Mazama. The lake is about 6 miles long, 5 miles wide, and 1,900 feet deep, and is ringed by cliffs. Crater Lake lies more than 6,100 feet above sea level.

Wizard Island, a small cinder cone, rises from the floor of the crater to a height of 750 feet above the lake. There are no surface inlets or outlets to Crater Lake, and the water level is maintained by rain and snow. The region is maintained by the U.S. government as Crater Lake National Park.

U.S. DEPARTMENT OF THE INTERIOR—NATIONAL PARK SERVICE

THE CASCADE RANGE, with its snow-capped peaks, stretches from California to Washington.

DELAWARE RIVER, a major waterway of the east. It originates in the Catskill Mountains of southeastern New York at the junction of the East Branch and the West Branch. The river flows generally south for about 300 miles, emptying into Delaware Bay.

The Delaware forms part of the borders between New York and Pennsylvania, Pennsylvania and New Jersey, and New Jersey and Delaware. Cities along its course include Easton and Philadelphia, Pennsylvania; Trenton and Camden, New Jersey; and Wilmington, Delaware. Its scenic gorge, the Delaware Water Gap, cuts across Kittatinny Ridge on the Pennsylvania-New Jersey border.

The Delaware River Basin Compact between New York, New Jersey, Pennsylvania, and Delaware provides for supervision and development of the river's power and recreation potential, and for flood control.

ERIE, the fourth largest and southernmost of the Great Lakes. It is bounded by New York, Pennsylvania, and Ohio on the east and southeast; Michigan on the southwest; and Ontario Province, Canada, on the northwest and north.

Lake Erie has a surface area of 9,940 square miles, of which 4,990 square miles are under U.S. jurisdiction. It is about 240 miles long and 60 miles wide, and has a maximum depth of 210 feet.

EVERGLADES, an area in southern Florida, characterized by water and sawgrass underlain by thick black muck. The Everglades stretch from south of Lake Okeechobee to the end of the Florida peninsula. Everglades National Park, established in 1947, covers the southwestern part of the area.

FINGER LAKES, a group of lakes in west-central New York formed by glacial action. The lakes were once

rivers, but as glaciers deepened valleys and dammed rivers, they became lakes.

The Finger Lakes vary from 10 to 40 miles long and from 1 to 3.5 miles wide. There are many falls and glens, including Watkins Glen, which reaches a depth of 700 feet. Among the Finger Lakes are lakes Canadice, Canandaigua, Cayuga, Conesus, Hemlock, Honeoye, Keuka, Otisco, Owasco, Seneca, and Skaneateles.

GOLDEN GATE, a strait on the west coast of California separating San Francisco Bay from the Pacific Ocean. It is about 5 miles long and from 1 to 2 miles wide. San Francisco is on the southern shore, and Sausalito is on the northern shore. The strait is crossed by the Golden Gate Bridge.

GRAND CANYON, a gorge in northwestern Arizona formed by the Colorado River. It is 217 miles long, from 4 to 18 miles wide, and about 1 mile deep.

Grand Canyon, with its immense dimensions and unusual rock formations, is a spectacular natural feature. Over 100 miles of the canyon are included in Grand Canyon National Park.

GREAT LAKES, a group of five lakes in central North America. Of the five, only Lake Michigan is wholly within the United States. The others—lakes Huron, Ontario, Erie, and Superior—form part of the U.S.-Canada border.

The Great Lakes are drained by the St. Lawrence River, which runs from the eastern end of Lake Ontario to the Gulf of St. Lawrence. The lakes are an important water route connecting the northeast and the midwest.

GREAT PLAINS, a generally level and treeless grassland in the west-central United States and Canada. The plains slope eastward from the Rocky Mountains to the prairies of the Mississippi Valley.

U.S. DEPARTMENT OF THE INTERIOR—NATIONAL PARK SERVICE

THE BADLANDS, a region famous for its fantastic land and weird rock formations.

The Great Plains cover the eastern parts of New Mexico, Colorado, Wyoming, and Montana and the western parts of Oklahoma, Kansas, Nebraska, North Dakota, and South Dakota. Most of the land is semiarid rangeland and is not well suited to agriculture.

GREAT SALT LAKE, the largest body of salt water in the United States. It lies in northwestern Utah and is a remnant of Lake Bonneville, which was formed during the Ice Age, about 1 million years ago.

The U.S. Geological Survey gives the area of Great Salt Lake as about 1,000 square miles, but the area varies considerably from year to year. In the 1870s it had a surface area of 2,400 square miles, and in the early 1960s its area was 950 square miles. The lake has no outlet, and evaporation is an important factor in determining its size.

HUDSON RIVER, a major waterway in New York State. It originates in the Adirondack Mountains of northeastern New York and flows south into Upper New York Bay at New York City. It forms part of the New York-New Jersey boundary at its southern end.

The Hudson is about 300 miles long. Its main tributary is the Mohawk River. The Hudson is connected with Lake Erie, Lake Ontario, the St. Lawrence River, and Lake Champlain by parts of the New York State Barge Canal.

HURON, the second largest of the Great Lakes. It is bounded on the north, east, and southeast by Ontario, Canada; and on the southwest and west by Michigan.

The surface area of Lake Huron is about 23,010 square miles, of which 9,110 square miles are under U.S. jurisdiction. Lake Huron, which is about 250 miles long and 100 miles wide, has a maximum depth of 750 feet.

ILIAMNA LAKE, in southwestern Alaska, the largest lake in the state and one of the largest lakes in the United States. It is about 75 miles long and 25 miles wide and has a surface area of some 1,000 square miles.

IMPERIAL VALLEY, in southern California and Lower California, Mexico. Most of the valley is below sea level. It was once desert, but since 1902 extensive irrigation has made the valley a rich agricultural area. Water is brought from the Colorado River by the All-American Canal.

LAKES. The largest lake entirely within the United States is Lake Michigan, one of the Great Lakes, with an area of 22,400 square miles. Other major U.S. lakes are Great Salt Lake in Utah and Iliamna in Alaska, both about 1,000 square miles in area; Okeechobee in Florida, 700 square miles; and Pontchartrain in Louisiana, 625 square miles.

The largest lakes in North America are shared by the United States and Canada. These are the remaining Great Lakes—Superior (31,820 square miles), Huron (23,010 square miles), Erie (9,940 square miles), and Ontario (7,540 square miles). Other major lakes shared by the two countries are Lake of the Woods in Minnesota and the provinces of Ontario and Manitoba (1,485 square miles); Lake Champlain in New York and Quebec Province (490 square miles); and Lake St. Clair in Michigan and Ontario (460 square miles).

LONG ISLAND, an island extending east-northeast from southeastern New York. Long Island Sound is to the north, and the Atlantic Ocean is to the south. The East River separates Long Island from the Bronx and Manhattan, and the Narrows separates it from Staten Island.

Long Island is over 118 miles long and is 23 miles wide at its widest point. There are many fine beaches along its shores.

MAUNA KEA, an extinct volcano in the north-central part of Hawaii Island, Hawaii. It is the highest island mountain in the world, rising 13,796 feet above sea level. Snow covers the upper parts during most of the year, and coffee is grown on the lower parts.

MAUNA LOA, an active volcano in the south-central part of Hawaii Island, Hawaii. It rises 13,680 feet above sea level. Kilauea, a crater on the eastern slope, has a circumference of 8 miles. Within Kilauea is Halemaumau, a lake of molten lava. Another large crater is Mokauweoweo.

MESABI RANGE, a range of hills in northeastern Minnnesota. The hills average between 200 and 500 feet in height, although at one point they reach almost 2,000 feet. The range contains rich deposits of iron ore.

MICHIGAN, the third largest of the Great Lakes, is bounded by Michigan on the northwest and east, Indiana on the southeast, and Illinois and Wisconsin on the west. It is the only one of the Great Lakes entirely within the United States.

Lake Michigan has a surface area of about 22,400 square miles. It is about 320 miles long and 120 miles wide and has a maximum depth of over 920 feet.

MISSISSIPPI RIVER, the major river of the United States. Its drainage basin includes all or parts of 31 states and 2 Canadian provinces. The Mississippi, which is 2,348 miles long, originates in northern Minnesota and flows south into the Gulf of Mexico, forming the Mississippi River delta.

The Mississippi is divided into two parts by the Missouri River, its main tributary. The Upper Mississippi lies above the mouth of the Missouri, and the Lower Mississippi lies below it. Other major tributaries of the Mississippi are the Arkansas, Illinois, Minnesota, Ohio, Red, St. Croix, White, and Wisconsin rivers.

The Mississippi River exerted its greatest economic influence in the 1800s, when steamboats were a major carrier of commercial traffic. Among the larger cities along the river are Minneapolis and St. Paul, Minnesota; St. Louis, Missouri; Memphis, Tennessee; Vicksburg, Mississippi; and Baton Rouge and New Orleans, Louisiana.

MISSOURI RIVER, one of the major rivers of the United States. It flows south and east through the northwest-central and central states and is a major tributary of the Mississippi River.

The Missouri originates in southern Montana at the confluence of the Jefferson, Madison, and Gallatin rivers. Its 2,315 mile course passes through North Dakota and South Dakota and forms all or part of the boundaries between South Dakota and Nebraska, Nebraska and Iowa, Nebraska and Missouri, and Kansas and Missouri. The Missouri then flows across the state of Missouri entering the Mississippi River near St. Louis.

Tributaries of the Missouri include the Big Sioux, Cheyenne, Osage, Platte, White, and Yellowstone rivers. Among the cities along the Missouri are Great Falls, Montana; Bismarck, North Dakota; Pierre, South Dakota;

NEW YORK STATE DEPARTMENT OF COMMERCE

THE HUDSON RIVER, as seen from Bear Mountain State Park, in New York State.

BUFFALO CHAMBER OF COMMERCE

NIAGARA FALLS consists of American Falls on left and Canadian (Horseshoe) Falls.

Omaha, Nebraska; Kansas City, Kansas; and Kansas City and Jefferson City, Missouri.

The Missouri River Basin Project deals with flood control and navigation problems and the development of power resources and irrigation facilities.

MOJAVE DESERT, an arid basin in southern California. It lies between the Sierra Nevada on the north, the Tehachapi Mountains on the northwest, the San Gabriel and San Bernardino mountains on the southwest, and the Colorado Desert on the southeast.

The Mojave is almost uninhabited, although it contains borax and gold deposits. Over 650 thousand acres in the southern part of the Mojave are included in Joshua Tree National Monument.

MOUNTAINS. In the United States, the mountains are generally higher in the west than in the east. Among the most important U.S. ranges are the Appalachians and Ozarks in the east and the Rockies, Cascades, Sierra Nevada, and Coast Ranges in the west.

The highest peaks in the United States are in Alaska, California, Colorado, and Washington. The 16 highest peaks are in Alaska. The highest of these are Mt. McKinley, 20,320 feet; North Peak, 19,470 feet; and Mt. St. Elias, 18,008 feet.

The highest point in the United States outside of Alaska is Mt. Whitney, in California, 14,494 feet. Next in height are three Colorado peaks—Mt. Elbert, 14,431 feet; Mt. Harvard, 14,-420 feet; and Mt. Massive, 14,418 feet. These are followed by Mt. Rainier, in Washington, 14,410 feet.

The highest point east of the Mississippi is Mt. Mitchell, in North Carolina, 6,684 feet.

MT. HOOD, an extinct volcanic peak in the Cascade Range. It lies in northwestern Oregon, and is the highest point in the state, 11,235 feet. Mt. Hood has eight glaciers, an icecap, and a crater at its summit.

MT. McKINLEY, the highest point in Alaska, the United States, and North America, 20,320 feet high. The mountain, which is snow-capped throughout the year, rises from a plateau that is between 2,500 and 3,000 feet above sea level. Mt. McKinley is part of the Alaska Range.

MT. RAINIER, in west central Washington, the highest peak in the Cascade Range and in the state. It rises 14,410 feet above sea level. Mt. Ranier is an extinct volcanic peak with 26 glaciers and a snow cap. The surrounding area is part of Mount Rainier National Park.

MT. SHASTA, in northern California, a peak of the Cascade Range. It rises 14,162 feet above sea level. Mt. Shasta is an extinct volcano noted for its hot sulfurous springs and steam vents. There are five glaciers on its slopes.

MT. WASHINGTON, in northern New Hampshire, the highest point in the northeastern United States, 6,288 feet above sea level. It is a peak in the Presidential Range of the White Mountains.

MT. WHITNEY, the highest peak in the United States outside of Alaska, 14,494 feet above sea level. It lies in the Sierra Nevada of southern California, and is included in Sequoia National Park.

NIAGARA FALLS, the great falls of the Niagara River, on the boundary between western New York and southern Ontario, Canada. The falls are divided into two sections—the American Falls and the Horseshoe, or Canadian, Falls—separated by Goat Island in the Niagara River.

The Canadian Falls are wider, but the American Falls are higher. Famous features include the Cave of the Winds and the Whirlpool Rapids. Both the United States and Canada use the falls to generate hydroelectric power.

OHIO RIVER, a major waterway in the east-north-central United States. It is formed at Pittsburgh, Pennsylvania, by the confluence of the Allegheny and Monongahela rivers. It flows southwest and west and forms the boundaries between Ohio and West Virginia, Ohio and Kentucky, Indiana and Kentucky, and Illinois and Kentucky.

The Ohio flows for 981 miles and then empties into the Mississippi River at Cairo, Illinois. Its main tributaries are the Cumberland, Kanawha, Kentucky, Licking, Muskingum, Tennessee, and Wabash rivers. Major cities along the Ohio are Pittsburgh, Pennsylvania; Cincinnati, Ohio; Evansville, Indiana; Cairo, Illinois; Wheeling, West Virginia; and Louisville, Kentucky.

OKEECHOBEE, a lake in southern Florida and the largest lake in the southern United States. It is between 35 and 40 miles long and 25 and 30 miles wide. It has a surface area of some 700 square miles.

Lake Okeechobee is drained by the Kissimmee River from the north. Its waters empty into the Everglades.

OLYMPIC MOUNTAINS, a section of the Coast Ranges in northwestern Washington on the Olympic Peninsula west of Puget Sound. The mountains are rugged and have many lakes, streams, and glaciers, and dense forests. The area is part of Olympic National Park.

ONTARIO, the smallest and easternmost of the Great Lakes. It is bounded by New York on the east and south, and Ontario, Canada, on the west and north.

The lake has a surface area of over 7,540 square miles of which 3,560 square miles are under U.S. jurisdiction. Lake Ontario is about 190 miles long and 50 miles wide and has a maximum depth of over 775 feet.

PONTCHARTRAIN, a lake in southeastern Louisiana. It is a salt lake about 40 miles long and 25 miles wide, with a surface area of some 625 square miles. The lake is connected by canal with the Mississippi River. New Orleans lies along the south shore of Lake Pontchartrain.

POTOMAC RIVER, a river flowing southeast into Chesapeake Bay, formed by the confluence of the North Branch and the South Branch at Cumberland, Maryland. Its major tributary is the Shenandoah River. The Potomac forms parts of the boundaries between Maryland and West Virginia, Maryland and Virginia, and Virginia and the District of Columbia.

The Potomac is about 285 miles long and is navigable to Washington, D.C., by means of a dredged channel. North of Washington it forms a series of rapids and falls known as the Great Falls.

PRIBILOF ISLANDS, four islands in the southeastern part of the Bering Sea, north of the Aleutian Islands. The four islands—St. George, St. Paul, Walrus, and Otter—are part of the state of Alaska.

The islands are inhabited by white and blue foxes and many varieties of birds. St. George and St. Paul are breeding places for fur seals. Since 1911 commercial killing of seals has been under U.S. government control.

PUGET SOUND, an extension of the Pacific Ocean reaching into north-western Washington through the Juan de Fuca Strait. The sound, which has many navigable branches, extends south for about 100 miles. Port cities on Puget Sound include Tacoma, Seattle, and Everett.

RED RIVER, a major waterway of the southwest, 1,222 miles long. It originates in New Mexico and flows east across the Texas Panhandle and along the Texas-Oklahoma border into Louisiana. In Louisiana, the river turns southeast and flows into the Mississippi.

RIO GRANDE, a major U.S. river flowing for 1,885 miles from the San Juan Mountains of southwestern Colorado to the Gulf of Mexico. The river flows south through New Mexico and then turns southeast to form the boundary between Texas and Mexico.

The Rio Grande is used extensively for irrigation. Among the dams along its course are Elephant Butte Dam and Caballo Dam in New Mexico and Falcon Dam in Texas.

RIVERS. U.S. rivers can be divided into three main groups: those on the Atlantic coast, those between the Appalachian Mountains and the Continental Divide, and those on the Pacific coast.

Many of the rivers between the Appalachian Mountains and the Continental Divide are part of the Mississippi River system, the greatest drainage system in the United States. The two longest U.S. rivers—the Mississippi, 2,348 miles, and the Missouri, 2,315 miles—are the main branches of the Mississippi system.

The third longest river in the United States is the Rio Grande, 1,885 miles long, which flows across the south-western part of the country and empties into the Gulf of Mexico. Next in size is the Yukon River, which flows 1,875 miles in Canada and Alaska.

The next longest U.S. rivers are the Arkansas, 1,450 miles; Colorado, 1,450 miles; Red, 1,222 miles; Columbia, 1,214 miles; Brazos, 1,210 miles; and Snake, 1,000 miles.

ROCKY MOUNTAINS, a complex mountain system in the western United States and Canada. The mountains extend from New Mexico through Arizona, Colorado, Utah, Nevada, Montana, Idaho, Alberta, British Columbia, the Yukon Territory and into Alaska. The Great Plains lie east of the Rockies, and the Coast Ranges lie west of them. The highest point in the Rockies is Mt. Elbert, in Colorado, 14,431 feet.

The Rocky Mountains mark the Continental Divide. Waters west of the divide flow toward the Pacific Ocean, while waters east of it flow toward the Gulf of Mexico and the Atlantic Ocean.

Ranges in the Rocky Mountain system include the Laramie Mountains, the Teton Range, the Medicine Bow Mountains, and the Bighorn Mountains in the United States; and the Selkirk, Stikine, and Cariboo mountains in Canada.

U.S. national parks in the Rockies include Glacier, Yellowstone, Grand Teton, and Mesa Verde. Canadian parks include Banff, Jasper, Yoho, Waterton, and Kootenay.

ST. LAWRENCE RIVER, a major waterway flowing northeast from Lake Ontario into the Gulf of St. Lawrence, a distance of about 750 miles. It forms part of the boundary between New York and Ontario, Canada. The Thousand Islands and three large lakes—St. Francis, St. Louis, and St. Peter—lie along its course.

The chief tributaries of the St. Lawrence are the Richelieu, St. Francis, Ottawa, St. Maurice, and Saguenay rivers. Cities on the river include Montreal and Quebec, Canada, and Ogdensburg, New York.

The St. Lawrence Seaway and Power Project, a joint U.S.-Canadian enterprise, controls power and navigation development.

SALTON SEA, formerly Salton Sink, a salty body of water in southeastern California about 80 miles northeast of San Diego. It was formerly a salt flat, and lies 280 feet below sea level. The sink was periodically flooded by the Colorado River, and in 1905 an irrigation levee broke, flooding it for two years. Both the water level and area of the Salton Sea are variable.

SNAKE RIVER, a 1,000-mile-long river tracing a roughly semicircular course through the northwestern United States.

The Snake originates in Yellowstone National Park in Wyoming. It flows southwest through Idaho and then north and northwest to form parts of the Idaho-Oregon and Idaho-Washington borders. The river then turns west and slightly south to join the Columbia River in Washington.

Among the features along the Snake River are Hells Canyon, Twin Falls, and Shoshone Falls. The river is dammed at American Falls in southeastern Idaho, and the waters are used for irrigation.

SUPERIOR, the largest and most northerly and westerly of the Great Lakes, and the world's largest fresh water lake. It is bounded by Ontario, Canada, on the north; Michigan and Wisconsin on the south; and Minnesota on the west.

Lake Superior has a surface area of 31,820 square miles, of which 20,710 square miles are under U.S. jurisdiction. The lake is about 380 miles long and 160 miles wide and has a maximum depth of about 1,300 feet.

TENNESSEE RIVER, an important waterway in the southeast. It flows a distance of 652 miles from the confluence of the Holston and French Broad rivers in eastern Tennessee into the Ohio River in western Kentucky. The Tennessee runs from eastern Tennessee southwest into Alabama, then northwest into western Tennessee and west into Kentucky.

The Tennessee Valley Authority (TVA) was created by the U.S. government in 1933 to direct development of flood control, navigation, and power facilities in the river basin. Muscle Shoals, an area of rapids in Alabama, has been used to generate hydroelectric power since World War I.

YUKON RIVER, one of the longest rivers in the United States, 1,875 miles. It originates in the southern part of the Yukon Territory, Canada. The Yukon flows northwest into Alaska and then turns southwest, flowing into the Bering Sea. Much of the river is navigable during the summer months, but is blocked by ice in winter.

WASHINGTON STATE DEPT. OF COMMERCE AND ECONOMIC DEVELOPMENT

PUGET SOUND, in northwestern Washington, is a favorite area with boating enthusiasts.

HISTORY OF THE UNITED STATES

A wise man once wrote, "He little knows of England who only England knows." Everyone agrees that it is necessary to know European history in order to understand properly the history of France, Germany, or England. However, there are very few who realize that the history of the United States or Canada or Argentina takes on new and deeper meaning if it is viewed as part of the history of the Americas. This failure to think in terms of America as a whole is curious, because so many of the experiences, so many of the problems encountered, and so many of the controlling forces were essentially the same in all parts of the Western Hemisphere.

The Red Man's America. — Even before the first Europeans reached the New World the Indians gave the Americas a certain degree of unity. Exactly where the Indians originated is not definitely known, but the most generally accepted theory is that they came from Asia by way of Alaska. This must have occurred many centuries prior to the discovery of America, because they had spread over the two continents and had erected different civilizations. Most of the Indians were still very primitive at the time of the first voyage by a European to the New World. Like other peoples in the hunting stage, many tribes wandered from place to place, following the wild animals that furnished their food and clothing. Other Indians had reached higher cultural levels. Some were partially agricultural, some entirely so, and some had rich civilizations with large cities and complex societies.

■ MAYAN CIVILIZATION. — The Indians in the temperate and colder sections of both North America and South America were more primitive than those in the tropical sections. Probably the most advanced of all were the Maya, who lived in what is now Yucatán, which comprises the southeastern part of Mexico and the northern section of Guatemala. From their cities and other remains that are now being excavated, it appears that the Maya reached that region about 1000 B.C. Their complex civilization was marked by elaborate farming methods, good roads, large cities with beautiful buildings, skillful weaving of textiles, expert work with metals, and artistic achievements of a high order. The Maya developed the most advanced system of recording thought in aboriginal America, and were particularly advanced in mathematics: they invented a calendar that some scholars say was more accurate than the one then used in Europe. The Mayan civilization had passed its peak before the Europeans arrived, and the Maya had been conquered by the Toltecs, who built up a flourishing empire, until it, in turn, was conquered. The victorious Aztecs, with their capital at Mexico City, were the first rich, densely populated Indian civilization to dazzle the eyes of the Spanish newcomers. The only rivals of the Aztecs were the Incas, who had an equally elaborate and rich civilization in what is now Peru.

BETTMAN ARCHIVE

A stone calendar invented by the Maya, who were very advanced in mathematics.

The Europeans. — It was the white man, not the Indian, who gave real unity to the history of the Americas. The desires, forces, and preparations that resulted in the voyage of Columbus in 1492 were not confined to Spain, but were common to many of the peoples of Europe. The consequences of his voyage were equally international. The Europeans thought in terms of the New World as a unit, at first regarding it as an obstacle barring them from a direct and cheap water route to the wealth of India and Asia. Spanish, Portuguese, French, Dutch, and British navigators tried again and again to find a passage through or around the barrier. Soon, however, the new lands were prized for themselves — particularly after Cortez had proved in Mexico that great wealth could be won by an audacious plunderer. In spite of their efforts, no European country except Spain and Portugal succeeded in establishing permanent settlements in the New World for more than a century after the discovery by Columbus. The great power of Spain kept the others out. Once Spanish sea power was broken by the defeat of the *Armada* in 1588, other nations rushed into the New World. England, France, and Holland quickly began their American empires. Although much smaller than the Spanish possessions, which extended from California and the southwestern part of the United States through Mexico, Central America, and all of South America except Brazil (Portuguese), these other empires were not confined to one portion of America. The thirty or more colonies that the English ultimately established included portions of frigid Canada, of the temperate United States, and of tropical areas in the Caribbean. So, too, did the French and Dutch settlements.

■ A WORLD MIGRATION. — The migration of Europeans to the Americas, started by Columbus, became one of the largest and most important movements of people in the history of the world. At first only a thin stream of people flowed across the Atlantic, for the hardships were great, and many died on the way. The stream gradually increased, and

after the development of the steamship and railroad, with all of the accompanying economic changes, wave after wave of humanity reached the shores of America from Europe. Although it is often thought that the United States is the only country whose history has been vitally and continuously affected by a steady influx of immigrants from Europe, every large country in the New World has had some of the same experiences and problems. Although only estimates can be made for the early period, there are fairly accurate figures showing that from 1846 to 1935 over 50,000,000 persons moved from Europe to the Americas, and that from 1821 to 1935 about 36,000,000 came to the United States. In the 70 years after 1857, when Argentina began collecting immigration statistics, nearly 6,000,000 persons entered that country, and 47 per cent of them were Italian. According to the census of 1914, about 30 per cent of the Argentine population were foreign-born; this is a proportion twice as large as that in the United States in 1910, when the immigrant population reached its maximum. The movement of European peoples to the New World was intercontinental and can be better understood if it is so viewed.

■ SIMILAR COLONIAL EXPERIENCES. — Not only was the arrival of Europeans common to all of the Americas, but the experiences of the newcomers in each part of the Western Hemisphere were strikingly similar. For about 300 years after Columbus the New World consisted entirely of European colonies. The Europeans who came to America as well as those who stayed in Europe busied themselves with plans for getting wealth out of this fabulous New World. Their first thought was for gold and silver, but only the Spanish were lucky enough to find such precious metals. Attention was then given to other products, and because labor was the lagging factor in production, every European country established some kind of system of forced labor, Negro slavery being the most common.

The ruling European countries all shared the same fundamental ideas regarding the relationship between colonies and mother country. Each believed in *mercantilism*, the national policy of promoting economic self-sufficiency so that the country would not have to buy from other countries. Each mother country wanted its colonies to produce the kind of articles that would otherwise have to be imported. Accordingly, the English and all the other colonizing nations passed laws to compel — or at least to encourage — her colonies to produce, among other things, wine and silk. Naturally the mother country was most important in their eyes, and in adopting policies for their empires they tried to arrange things so that the mother country would receive the greatest benefit.

These commercial regulations differed in details, but English, Spanish, French, and Dutch empires had essentially the same policies, and everywhere in America the effect was the same. The colonists, believing their interests were being sacrificed for the benefit of the home countries, protested and finally sought through independence the economic freedom and opportunity for growth that they felt were being denied them. Other factors played a part in the various colonial revolutions occurring in America between 1776 and 1826, but opposition to imperial commercial policies was fundamental to all.

Revolt and Democracy. — The American revolutions that resulted in the independence of most of America from Europe had other important elements in common. All were based on the same political philosophy. The English colonists who announced the independence of the United States in 1776 gave those ideas their classic form in the Declaration of Independence. The ideas did not originate in the New World. Indeed, they had already been used by John Locke (1632-1704) and others to justify another revolution, that of 1688 in England. The colonists had taken them to America along with their other intellectual baggage. The Spanish colonists also justified their acts by the same principles, which they received not so much from the United States as from Europe and the French Revolution. In both English and Spanish colonies, the settlers, influenced by and attached to the new environment, had grown apart from the peoples in the European mother countries. They began to think themselves different and to resent being treated as inferiors and provincials.

■ **FORMS OF GOVERNMENT.** — The character of the successful revolutions committed, in principle at least, all of the newly-independent countries to democracy. Spanish America is still democratic in theory, but in practice there has been a marked contrast with English America. Throughout the history of these various Spanish-American countries there has been a series of dictators; although the outward forms of democracy have been and still are preserved, actual democracy has been partial and intermittent. In Canada the situation is just the reverse. The form of Canadian government is different, but the spirit and the essentials are the same as in the United States. Although Canada, a dominion of the British Empire, has a queen, its government and political practices are closer to those of the United States than are those of Spanish America. Democracy was established in Canada within the Empire, and Canadian independence, real independence with full control over its own destiny, was achieved, not by revolution and war, but by gradual and peaceful means.

■ **ATTITUDES TOWARDS EUROPE.** — Immediately after they won their independence, the Latin and South American republics, as well as the United States, feared that the European powers might attempt to regain their lost empires in America. These fears led to the Monroe Doctrine, which declared that any European intervention in the Western Hemisphere would be considered an unfriendly act. At first, because the doctrine offered them protection, the Latin American republics looked favorably upon it; but as conditions changed and the threat of European intervention disappeared, resentment toward

the unilateral policy arose. Over the years, however, the animosity subsided. Numerous attempts were made to bind all American nations into a cooperative league, the main object of which was to promote the safety and prosperity of all. During the 1930's, as a result of President Franklin D. Roosevelt's "Good Neighbor Policy," mutual trust and friendship among all members of the Western Hemisphere were attained.

American Frontiers. — The key to the history of the United States during the nineteenth century is the westward expansion of its population across the almost empty and fabulously rich continent to the Pacific. Nearly every major problem faced by the people of the United States from 1815 to 1914 either arose from that westward expansion or was connected with it. The strong and often decisive influence exerted by the frontier has long been recognized, but what is forgotten is that other American peoples were also on the march. In the larger countries — Canada, Brazil, and Argentina — migration moved westward; elsewhere the movement was southward or eastward from the Pacific; in Mexico it was northward. In all places the settlers pressed on to the unoccupied lands. Everywhere they were extending their institutions and adjusting themselves to the frontier.

■ **PARALLEL EVENTS.** — Many types of historical events were repeated in each country. The results were much the same in the United States and Canada, but quite different in most of Latin America. The type of explorations made by Lewis and Clark and Pike for the United States were paralleled by Alexander Mackenzie and Duncan McGillivray in Canada and by earlier Spanish and Spanish-American explorers throughout the rest of the two continents. The dramatic story of the building of the Union Pacific Railroad was matched by the construction of the Canadian Pacific. There was the same heroic vision, the same rugged endurance by the men who did the job, the same Indian troubles, the same engineering difficulties, the same financial problems — and the same success. The history of the Union Pacific could almost be taken for that of the Mexican National Railways or that of the Transandine Railroad. The United States had a period of flush mining when mushroom towns sprang up overnight, when law and order were conspicuously lacking, and when things occurred that can now be found only in the stories of Bret Harte. But so, too, did Canada; so, also, Mexico; and long before this, Peru. The rancher and the cowboy have become symbols of nineteenth-century life in the United States, yet the ranches of Canada, of Mexico, and of Argentina could scarcely be distinguished from their counterparts in the United States.

■ **ENGLISH AND LATIN CULTURES.** — As numerous as are the features that appear in the histories of all the countries in the Americas, there is one area in which there are two distinct groups. Notwithstanding the large number of immigrants to North America from southern and eastern Europe, it is clear that the culture, the literature, the

family life, and most of the social customs in the United States and Canada are definitely English or Anglo-Saxon. It is equally clear that the literature, the family life, and most of the social customs of the rest of the Western Hemisphere are Latin in origin. People living in the United States are hardly aware of the books written in Latin America. Latin Americans, on the other hand, find their literary models in Spain, France, Portugal, and Italy. Their art reveals these same influences. Their young men, as a rule, have gone to France or Spain to study, not to the United States or England or Germany. Their young women, again as a rule, have not received an academic education — another difference in social custom from the United States and Canada.

Whatever the individual peculiarities, however, each is not isolated, but is part of the greater epic: the expansion of the European peoples in the New World.

America. — The name "America," employed to designate the entire known western world, was first employed by the Flemish geographer Gerhardus Mercator in 1541. Originally, the name "America" was used only for central Brazil, in honor of Americus Vespucius, or Amerigo Vespucci, an Italian navigator who wrote an account of a voyage he made in 1497-98 along the coast of South America (Brazil, apparently). Columbus's earlier discovery of the mainland was a secret when Vespucci made his claim.

Early European Background. — During the latter half of the fifteenth century, Europe was passing from the Middle Ages into the modern period. The transition is called the *Renaissance*, which means "rebirth." Some scholars say the Renaissance began with the fall of Constantinople in 1453 and the spread of classical culture through western Europe; others say it began with the invention of typography in 1440. Certainly both of these played a large part in awakening western Europe to art and learning — to astronomy, geography, and invention — and in stimulating the curiosity of the nations concerning the wide world as a human habitation. In western Europe, Spain particularly was fired with the dream to find a new route to that rich land visited by Marco Polo in 1269-1295 and described in the book he wrote while he was a prisoner in Genoa in the year 1298.

The marriage of Ferdinand and Isabella in 1469 led to the union of Castile and Aragon in 1479 — Spain thus was becoming one nation. When the conquest of Granada in January, 1492, pushed the Moors from their last stronghold on the continent back into North Africa, a strong, united Spain was ready to reach still farther afield for gold, riches and dominions. As a result, Isabella, after eight years of indifference, finally lent a willing ear to the disheartened Christopher Columbus of Genoa, who had failed also at the court of Portugal to find patronage for a voyage into the West that he (and other geographers) believed would lead to the Indies.

Isabella foresaw in this venture glory and wealth for Spain, as well as the chance to establish her church in a heathen land. But no one, not even Columbus himself, dreamed what an empire Spain was soon to hold as the three small vessels provided by Isabella, the *Nina*, *Pinta*, and *Santa Maria*, started out of Palos, Spain, on August 3, 1492, making into the trackless sea toward an unknown west.

The Discovery. — The voyage of Columbus was one of hardship and discouragement. Terror and mutiny gripped the sailors as the ten long weeks went by and no land appeared. On October 12, 1492, Columbus sighted land, but he did not know that he had discovered a new continent. Even the learned geographers, who also believed that Marco Polo's Indies could be reached by sailing west, had no idea that between that rich land and Spain lay yet another larger, richer, unknown, unnamed world. And it was many years before Europe could believe that the new domains were new indeed.

Columbus believed that he had found the Indies, the very islands Polo described as being located off the east coast of Asia. Actually, however, he had landed on a small island now identified as Watling Island in the Bahamas. He named it San Salvador, raised the flag of Spain, and formally claimed it in the names of their majesties, Ferdinand and Isabella. He then returned home, eager to make known his success. He was received with honor and ceremony and rewarded with the title "Admiral of the Ocean."

The Explorers. — If southern Europe had ever heard of the legendary voyages to a new country made by the Viking, Leif Ericson, about A.D. 1000, it had forgotten them long before 1492. Columbus made four voyages between 1492 and 1504, but at no time did he set foot on the continent of North America. It was another Genoese, John Cabot (1450-1498), under the patronage of Henry VII of England, who landed on the mainland.

In 1497, Henry VII, though burdened with debt, outfitted an expedition under the command of John Cabot to search for the western passage to India. Exactly where Cabot landed is not known, but most historians agree that it was on Cape Breton Island, Nova Scotia. Cabot took possession in the name of the king of England, and the following year continued his explorations southward, possibly as far as South Carolina.

■ PORTUGUESE AND SPANISH. — In 1501 and 1502, two Portuguese brothers, Caspar and Miguel Cortereal, made voyages that touched the shores of Newfoundland and Labrador. But Spain was foremost in expressing the Old World's zeal for New World exploration. Alonzo de Ojeda (c. 1465-1515) established in 1509 the first Spanish settlement in Darien in eastern Panama. Juan Ponce de Leon (c. 1460-1521), who had been with Columbus on his second voyage in 1493 and had become governor of Puerto Rico in 1509, learned from the Indians of a wonderful island named Bimini, where flowed the "fountain of youth." He set sail in 1512 to discover and claim this island; on Easter Sunday (*Pascua Florida* in Spanish) he found a new land and he named it "Florida."

The Spaniard Vasco Núñez de Balboa (1475-1517) crossed the Isthmus of Darien in 1513 and was the first white man to behold the Pacific Ocean. In 1518 Hernandez de Córdova discovered Yucatan, while Juan de Grijalva (c. 1489-1527) pushed on northward to Vera Cruz. Hernando Cortez (1485-1547) conquered Mexico in 1519-21 and gave the coveted gold of that new territory to Spain.

In 1520, Ferdinand Magellan (1480-1521), the famous Portuguese navigator, sailed the Pacific Ocean through the straights that now bear his name and removed the last doubt that a new continent lay between Europe and the east coast of Asia, at the same time giving the first physical demonstration that the world is round.

Other Spaniards, among them, Coronado and De Soto, pushed through the wilderness into the interior of North America. During 1540-42, Francisco Vásquez de Coronado (1510-1554), seeking the seven cities of Civola, planted the flag of Spain in what is presently Arizona and New Mexico. Hernando De Soto (c. 1500-1542) pushed westward and northward from Florida and came upon the Mississippi River in 1542.

■ FRENCH. — In the meantime, France was realizing that a new world was there for the taking, and in 1524, the Italian navigator Giovanni da Verrazano (c. 1485-c.1528) explored, with a French commission, the new coasts and entered New York bay. Between 1534 and 1542, Jacques Cartier (1491-1557) explored the new lands. He found the Strait of Belle Isle; he discovered and named the St. Lawrence River and followed it inland to a little Indian village, which he named "Mont Real" (Mount Royal), now Montreal. He took possession of all of that northern territory in the name of France. He was on his way home when he passed the shipload of French colonists under the Sieur de Roberval coming to attempt the first, ill-fated settlement. Later, Samuel de Champlain, Louis Joliet, Robert Cavelier La Salle, and others were to move westward and establish New France in Canada.

■ ENGLISH. — England was no laggard in its interest in the New World. Its ships roved the seas and traded in the West Indies, defying Spain's right to forbid this. With Queen Elizabeth's accession to the throne, definite expeditions were resumed. Sir Martin Frobisher (c. 1535-1594) made three voyages between 1576 and 1578, looking for that northwest passage to India that all of Europe still believed must exist. He found Frobisher Bay in South Baffin Island and entered Hudson Strait. In 1577, with the secret consent of Elizabeth, Sir Francis Drake (c. 1540-1596) set out to raid the rich Spanish towns along the Pacific coast. He went through the Straight of Magellan, plundered the South American Pacific settlements, and sailed north along the coast of South America, taking possession of the California coast in the name of Queen Elizabeth.

In 1609, Henry Hudson, an Englishman employed by the Dutch East India Company, was another to take up the search for the Northwest Passage. He entered Chesapeake Bay, Delaware Bay, and finally the great river that now bears his name, claiming the land as far as Albany for the Dutch. His voyage in 1610 in an English ship resulted in the exploration of Hudson Bay; he perished on its shores (1611) after being marooned by mutineers.

Colonization. — Out of the great sweep of adventure and exploration in the new continent, ideas of empire gradually took shape. Here was wealth to be had undisputed; here were inexhaustible resources for trade and commerce; here was vast, uncharted territory to be peopled and possessed. The three great rival powers of Europe — Spain, England, and France — extended their rivalry to the new world. Spain took Florida; St. Augustine, the oldest city in America, was founded in 1565. Spain occupied Texas, the whole Southwest of the present United States, and upper California. The Spanish missions became rooted, and Spanish dominion prevailed until Mexico took over in 1822. France took the Northeast, or what is now Canada; Port Royal, Nova Scotia, was founded in 1605, Quebec in 1608. From there France blazed trails along the Great Lakes to Hudson Bay, to Illinois, to the Mississippi, and to the Gulf of Mexico. Louisiana, claimed for France by La Salle in 1682, was settled in 1699. England took the Atlantic coast and was content to prosper east of the Alleghenies. The story of the struggle of these three powers, ending in the supremacy of the English colonies and their final separation from the parent country, is the story of all of the wars, large and small, fought on American soil up to and including the American Revolution.

■ "THE LOST COLONY." — England was the last of the three great nations to send permanent settlers to America. In 1584, Sir Walter Raleigh sent out the expedition that claimed and named Virginia for the Virgin Queen, Elizabeth I. In 1585 he outfitted a band of 108 colonists to go to Virginia under Ralph Lane (c. 1530-1603). They landed in August of that year on Roanoke Island on the coast of what is now North Carolina. The ships returned at once to England for supplies, but the small group that remained on the island was threatened with starvation. In 1586 the colonists returned to England with Sir Francis Drake.

Bitterly disappointed but undaunted, Raleigh sent out another group; 121 people led by John White landed once more on Roanoke Island in July, 1587. Here the first child was born in America of English parents; Virginia Dare, granddaughter of Governor John White, was born on August 18, 1587. Nine days later John White sailed to England, expecting to return at once with the supplies and equipment essential to existence in a wild land. The Spanish war prevented the return of any ships until 1591, and by then all trace of the colony had vanished. A search of the island revealed only the word "Croatan" carved on a tree. It was the name of a tribe of Indians of that region. The fate of these colonists has remained undetermined.

THE THIRTEEN COLONIES

Virginia.—Failure had never meant "give up" in English; and the work of planting English colonies in America continued. In 1606, King James I divided the tract called "Virginia" into North Virginia and South Virginia. South Virginia included the land from Cape Fear (now in North Carolina) to the Potomac River. North Virginia included everything between the Hudson River and Newfoundland.

A charter to settle South Virginia was given to the London Company, which sent out the expedition destined to be the first permanent English colony in America. They landed at Jamestown on May 13, 1607. Two years of suffering and want went by; old records refer to this period as "the starving time." Had it not been for Captain John Smith, whose good sense and high courage pulled them through, the fate of that small group at Jamestown might have been like that of the Lost Colony.

This initial colony in Jamestown created what was perhaps the first industry in the New World. A group composed of eight Poles and Germans built a glass-house to manufacture various types of glassware. Some of their glass was shipped to England among the New World's first exported commodities. These men were artisans who kept their glass making process secret even from the curious Indians who would wander in and around the new settlement. Unfortunately, the Indians became irritated, and in 1622 massacred the inhabitants of the glasshouse, leaving Virginia to wait over a hundred years for its next glass works.

In 1609, the London Company received a new charter that enlarged the South Virginia territory. Sir Thomas Gates was commissioned the first governor, and 150 new colonists were sent out. But when they arrived, May 23, 1610, they were greeted with tales of hunger and sights of privation and hardship that quickly disheartened them. The whole colony set sail for home less than a month after the newcomers landed. The little fleet had barely reached the mouth of the James River when they sighted English ships. It was Lord De La Warr (1577-1618) arriving with more colonists and enough supplies to give them hope. They turned back and once more took up the hard task of making a home in the wilderness. This time they settled at Hampton; thus Virginia was settled.

The next year 650 more colonists joined them. Settlements spread out, up and down the James River, up and down the Appomattox, and farther and farther inland, until Virginia prospered, becoming a tobacco-growing colony.

Massachusetts.—The second permanent English colony in America was Plymouth Colony, founded in 1620. The *Mayflower* sailed out of Plymouth, England, in September of that year, with 41 families on board. These were the Pilgrims: the 102 men, women, and children who left the Old World, seeking the freedom to think and worship as they pleased. They landed on the Massachusetts coast on December 21 and founded the settlement that they named "New Plymouth."

The story of this colony is one of hardship. The first long, terrible winter dragged by and many died from disease or exposure, until only 50 were left alive. The survivors buried their dead, stoically flattened the tops of the graves, and in the spring sowed grain across Burial Hill to keep the Indians from knowing how many had died.

In 1621, more settlers came to cast their lot with those courageous few. After the small harvest was gathered, the pilgrims celebrated the first Thanksgiving Day. The religious devotion of the Plymouth settlers prevented them from abandoning the colony.

John Carver, the first governor of Plymouth Colony, died the first year. William Bradford (1590-1657) was chosen in his place and the colony was strengthened by his integrity and firm idealism. According to the provisions of the Mayflower Compact, Plymouth was governed "for the general good of the colony." This brief but extremely important compact provided for a democratic system of government; it was signed on board ship a month before the Pilgrims landed, when it was realized that they had no title to the land they had mistakenly reached.

■ **MASSACHUSETTS BAY COLONY.**—The larger and more important Massachusetts Bay Colony was founded at Salem in 1628 under John Endecott. Boston was founded by Governor John Winthrop in 1630 and became the capital in 1632. In 1691, the government at Plymouth joined the government at Boston and the Massachusetts colony throve on the union. New England towns are governed today by the town meeting system that grew up from these first meetings.

New York.—Dutch fur-trading posts had already been organized on the Hudson River before the Massachusetts people took root. After Henry Hudson's enthusiastic prediction of the rich traffic in furs that might be established with the Indians, the Netherlands lost no time in sending out a vessel (1610) loaded with merchandise to be exchanged for the prized skins. In 1614, Fort Nassau was built on Castle Island near Albany, and another trading post was subsequently built on lower Manhattan Island.

The first permanent colonists, about thirty families, came to New Netherland in 1624 and founded Fort Orange, which is now Albany, with Cornelis Mey as governor. The first director-general of the colony was Peter Minuit (1580-1638), who arrived in 1626 with more colonists. It was Minuit who bought Manhattan Island from the Indians for a fantastic $24 worth of bright red cloth and trinkets and built Fort Amsterdam at the lower end of it.

There are many colorful stories about the last Dutch Governor of New Netherland—the wooden-legged and hot-tempered Peter Stuyvesant (1592-1672). Although he was a moody and hated despot, he strengthened, enriched, and expanded the colony until, in 1664, it contained 10,000 people.

Brooklyn, New Haarlem, Bronx, and Staten Island were other thriving Dutch settlements.

There had been a long dispute with the English over the possession of New Netherland. King Charles II bestowed it by grant upon his brother James, the Duke of York. English ships appeared in August, 1664, in the harbor of New Amsterdam, demanding the colony. In a rage, Peter Stuyvesant tore up the English letter. However, the citizens were tired of his iron rule and refused to fight. The colony was transferred to the English on September 9, 1664, and was renamed "New York." Richard Nicolls was the first English governor. From these three English colonies in Virginia, Massachusetts, and New York grew the United States. Gradually the settlements spread out and formed their governments. One hundred and twenty-five years after the founding of Jamestown there were thirteen colonies, destined to become one nation.

New Hampshire.—Permanent settlements were made at Rye and Dover, New Hampshire, as early as 1623, but that colony was not named until 1629, when the vast "province of Maine" was divided between the two original grantees. John Mason received the land between the Merrimac and Piscataqua rivers and named it "New Hampshire." Although it was a proprietary colony, New Hampshire became a royal colony in 1679. Under the charter provisions of the former, the proprietor was authorized to dispose of the land as he wished and to make all the laws of the colony, subject only to the advice and assent of the people. In contrast to this, however, royal colonies were ruled by a governor and council, named by the king, which could veto acts of an assembly elected by the people.

Delaware.—The first settlement in Delaware was made by the Dutch in 1631. In 1638, Fort Christina (near Wilmington) was founded for the Swedish Royal Trading Company by the same Peter Minuit who purchased Manhattan Island for the Dutch. He bought all of the land between the mouth of the Delaware and the Schuylkill River from the Minqua Indians and named it "New Sweden." In 1643, Johan Printz became the first Swedish governor and proceeded to remove the Dutch traders from their posts up and down the river.

The Dutch, of course, protested the seizure of what they considered their own by first claim and possession. When fiery Peter Stuyvesant became governor of New Netherland, he speedily took New Sweden back into Dutch possession (1655), only to lose it to the British in 1664 with the rest of New Netherland. It was granted to William Penn in 1682 and remained under a Pennsylvania governor until 1776, when the lower counties became Delaware State.

Maryland.—Maryland was intended as a refuge for persecuted Catholics of England. Leonard Calvert, brother of the second Lord Baltimore, governed the first colonists in 1634. They made a settlement between the Potomac and the Chesapeake rivers, which they called "St. Mary's." Having experienced persecution himself, Lord Baltimore encouraged non-Catholics in the colony and in 1649 proposed the Toleration Act, the first attempt at religious toleration in America.

The granting of Delaware to William Penn in 1682 resulted in almost a century of squabbling over the northern boundary of Maryland. In 1763, two English mathematicians, Charles Mason and Jeremiah Dixon, were hired to settle the dispute. It took them four years to survey the territory and run the famous Mason-Dixon line, which separates not only Maryland from Pennsylvania, but the North from the South.

New Jersey.—The history of New Jersey overlaps the histories of New York and Pennsylvania. The first settlers were a few Dutch families from New Amsterdam who, in 1623, established themselves on the Delaware and Hudson rivers where Gloucester and Hoboken now stand. Dutch control prevailed over these and certain Swedish settlements (taken in 1655) until 1664, when the British took New Netherland and these river towns.

The settlement was named "New Jersey" after the Channel Island of Jersey to honor Sir George Carteret, former governor of the English islands and one of the original grantees of the land between the Delaware River and the Atlantic shore running north from Cape May. New Jersey was part of the English consolidation of New York and New England under one governor, Sir Edmund Andros, who served from 1685 to 1689. It was a royal colony from 1702 to 1776.

Connecticut.—A growing discontent with the high-handed and intolerant government in the Massachusetts Bay Colony resulted in the movement of about 100 people from the Massachusetts towns into Connecticut. Withersfield was settled in 1634, Windsor and Hartford in 1635. Strangely enough, the new government that the people formed in 1639—the famous Fundamental Orders of Connecticut—differed from the Massachusetts government in only one important respect: a man's right to citizenship was not based on religious creed. It is interesting that this document mentioned neither the English king nor country.

In 1638, New Haven was settled by a group from Boston, Massachusetts. The government of New Haven was even more theocratic than the one the settlers had left; the New Haven Plantation Covenant provided for a government according to "the laws of God as given by Moses." No one could be a citizen who was not a church member. Other severe and strange laws are recorded, although most of the "blue laws" that are attributed to the New Haven colony were made up by a Connecticut historian, Samuel A. Peters, and had never been heard of in old New Haven.

The colonies of Connecticut, New Haven, Massachusetts, and Plymouth joined the New England confederation in 1643. This union was established for purposes of mutual defense; it left the autonomy of each member colony intact. Connecticut and New Haven became one colony in 1664 under the royal charter of 1662, which was preserved until Connecticut became a state in 1788.

Rhode Island.—The first settlement in Rhode Island was made by Roger Williams (c. 1603-1683) in 1636. It was called "Providence Plantations." Williams was a refugee from the Massachusetts Bay Colony, where, because he so passionately and publicly had opposed the right of civil government to dictate to the human conscience, the Puritans had banished him. They had tried to deport him to prevent his founding a new colony on such "dangerous" principles, but Williams escaped into the forests and founded Providence "especially for such as are troubled elsewhere about the worship of God." Other liberals followed in 1638, settling Portsmouth on the island of Aquidneck (Rhode Island). Newport was settled in 1639 and Warwick in 1643. Roger Williams worked for the union of the scattered towns, and in 1644 brought back from England the charter that made Providence Plantations and Rhode Island one colony. In 1663, Rhode Island received a charter from Charles II.

North Carolina.—A huge piece of territory south of Virginia was granted in 1629 to Sir Robert Heath by Charles I. It was named "Carolina" for the king. The first permanent colony was established at Albermarle in 1660, but little was done about colonizing until 1663, when Charles II gave Carolina to the Duke of Albermarle and seven other nobles, thereafter designated as the lord's proprietors. There followed an incessant struggle between the people and proprietors. Out of sixteen governors appointed by the proprietors, six were jailed, forced to abdicate, or openly driven out of office by the people for their unjust and severe taxation or for their incompetency.

By 1729 the proprietors, glad to be rid of a troublesome bargain, sold their grants back to the Crown; the land was officially divided into North and South Carolina, and North Carolina became a royal colony. With this change, the land began to fill up with settlers from Virginia and Pennsylvania. By 1776 there were 300,000 inhabitants. A tradition of dissent, a passion for democracy, and an independent spirit that would tolerate neither imposition nor interference persisted throughout the history of the colony. In 1768 and 1770, these characteristics were manifest in the Regulator uprisings. A dissatisfied group of frontiersmen in the colony's western counties protested the high taxes, unfair judges, and general political corruption. In 1775, Governor Martin was forced to flee, and on May 10 a committee representing the militia of Mecklenburg county is said to have adopted the Mecklenburg Declaration, which asserted the independence of America from England. This occurred almost fourteen months before the Declaration of July 4, 1776.

South Carolina.—South Carolina was named "Carolina" a century before the 1663 grant of Charles II included it in the Carolina given to Sir Robert Heath. In 1562, Jean Ribaut brought to Port Royal 150 Huguenots, who named the region Carolina for Charles IX of France. This settlement was short-lived due to lack of supplies and support.

The first English colonists settled at Albemarle Point in 1670; they moved up to the head of the harbor and founded Charleston in 1680. As in North Carolina, the people bitterly resented the deliberate attempt of the proprietors to curb popular government. They insisted on the letter of the charter—that the colony be governed "by and with the advice and assent of the Freedmen." Half a century of discord followed, with the people demanding and petitioning and the proprietors ignoring and denying. Finally in 1719 the proprietors vetoed so many of the laws that the people had fought to establish, among them freedom of franchise, that the colonists overthrew the proprietary government and put up their own man, James Moore, as governor "for the king." England immediately recognized the appeal and South Carolina became a royal colony, although the landed proprietors were not officially bought up until 1729. From 1729 on, the colony prospered; trade, culture, and social ease increased. Schooled in the struggle for personal and civil liberty, the Carolinians' sympathies were quickly enlisted on the side of their New England neighbors when the issue of "no taxation without representation" arose.

Pennsylvania.—In 1680, William Penn, an English Quaker of wealth and family who had been imprisoned many times for defending his principles, asked the king for "a tract of land in America, north of Maryland, west of the Delaware and northward as far as plantable," which he intended as a refuge for persecuted English Quakers. Charles II, who owed the Penn family $16,000, saw this as an easy way to pay an old debt, and gave the grant. Penn sailed for the New World in 1682 with 100 colonists. He wrote the constitution for the new colony, laid out the city of Philadelphia, and in 1683 negotiated the "Great Treaty" with the Indians, "not sworn to and never broken," which insured peace for the colony and safety from the Indians during Penn's lifetime. His government established complete religious freedom and "just and friendly conduct toward the natives," and it also gave the people full power to make and repeal their own laws.

The Quaker commonwealth holds a place in history because it made an actuality of the ideal of religious toleration, and because it harbored more races and creeds than any other English colony. English, Germans, Dutch, Swedes, Welsh, Irish, Scotch, and Swiss lived side by side and worshipped freely. Here lived a people unarmed and unmolested in a wilderness surrounded by savage tribes; here no oaths were asked or given in the people's courts, and there was no capital punishment except for the crimes of treason and murder. To English statesmen, any *one* of these practices was enough to spell folly or failure, but the Pennsylvania colony flourished. By 1685 there were 8,000 inhabitants; by 1702 there were 12,000 white people alone; in 1709, 12,000 more arrived and took up farming in the rich country north of Philadelphia. By 1776 Pennsylvania had a population of 300,000.

When England heard of threats of war with the French, the defenses of the American colonies were investigated, and the king was told that the "insane colony" had no defenses whatever and that its assembly refused to contribute either men or money to any military project. Because of this, Penn lost his charter in 1692, and Governor Benjamin Fletcher of New York became governor of Pennsylvania. The colony was returned to Penn in 1694, however, on his promise to "police" the frontiers. Quaker conscience could sanction police defenses but not full preparation for war. Hence, when the French and Indian War actually broke out the king proposed that Pennsylvania become a Crown colony.

Penn left for England to negotiate, and never returned. Before he left (1701) he had made Philadelphia a city and revised the constitution, which then served the colony unaltered until 1776. He died in 1718 and his sons became proprietors of Pennsylvania.

Pennsylvania sent delegates to the First Continental Congress, held in Philadelphia in 1774, subscribed money to aid Massachusetts, and adopted the Declaration of Independence. In September, 1776, a new state constitution was adopted and the Penn proprietorship came to an end.

Georgia. — Georgia, the last of the thirteen mainland colonies, was founded to serve as a buffer state between the Carolinas and Spanish Florida, as well as to receive and repulse the harrying French and Indian attacks from the West. It was also to serve as a haven for persecuted European Protestants and as a refuge for the debtors who clogged England's jails. Finally, it was to have an economic function; England, in need of silk, planned to have Georgia's settlers raise silkworms for the mother country.

In 1732 James Oglethorpe, a prominant humanitarian, obtained a charter from George II for a tract of land (originally part of South Carolina) between the Savannah and Altamaha rivers, which was named "Georgia" in honor of the king. The first settlement at Yamacraw Bluff, in 1733, led to the founding of Savannah. The colony grew slowly because English debtors did not migrate in the numbers expected, and constant conflicts with hostile neighbors deterred more timid settlers. Moreover, since land holders were restricted to 500 acres as a defense measure, and Negro slaves were forbidden, the growth of a plantation economy was impeded. Dismal economic failure resulted. These restrictions were soon modified, however, and after it became a royal colony in 1751, Georgia prospered. Her loyalties, more than those of any other colony, were divided between allegiance to the king and self-determination at the beginning of the separation issues; Georgia signed the Declaration of Independence, however, and fought against the British to maintain her own rule within her borders.

The Preparation for Independence. — In a new country where mere survival depended on each man's endurance, his ingenuity, and his independence, men would not be likely to accept dictation. Homes they had hewn and made together with their laws, good or bad,

were their own; their labors and their dead bestowed on them the right to live their own lives.

Although many of the participants were unaware of it at the time, the drama of independence had already begun. The desire for individual and civil freedom that had actuated the early American settlements was not only growing stronger, but also undergoing subtle change. At first, it had been believed that freedom could be achieved within the British Empire. Due to the American environment and British neglect, however, the notion of allegiance to the mother country was weakening and being replaced by the new idea of independence. The growth of this feeling, which gained enormous strength after 1763, can be traced through a long series of assemblies, documents, and rebellions:

(1) The Virginia House of Burgesses (1619), which grew from the harsh rule of deputy-governors, was the first representative legislative body in America.

(2) The Mayflower Compact (1620), which took for granted that the people were to "combine together into a civil body politic—to enact, constitute and frame just and equal laws—for the general good of the colony."

(3) The town meetings of New England, whereby the town governed itself and each town was represented in the general court.

(4) The bitter struggle in Maryland between the people's assembly and the proprietors for the right to make laws.

(5) The Fundamental Orders of Connecticut (1639), "the first written constitution of a self-governing people," which gave all authority to the people and forgot to mention the king.

(6) The New England Confederation (1643-84), the first step toward uniting for mutual strength taken by separate, autonomous colonies.

(7) Bacon's rebellion (Virginia, 1676), the first violent uprising against unjust, indifferent, and aristocratic government.

(8) The continuous disposal by North and South Carolina settlers of obnoxious proprietary governors for the sake of popular representation; and the constant contest between settlers and Crown or settlers and proprietors that was evident even in the comparatively peaceful colonies of Pennsylvania and Maryland.

(9) The Albany Congress (1754), representing seven colonies, which favored Benjamin Franklin's plan for union of the colonies.

(10) The Virginia Parsons' Case (1759), the protest of underpaid country clergy, which brought forth Patrick Henry's daring assertion that a king's class-favoring laws brand a king a tyrant who "forfeits all right to obedience."

(11) The Sons of Liberty (1764), intercolonial secret societies that fanned the flame of rebellion against taxation tyranny.

(12) The Regulator Movement (1765-76), an organization of thousands of farmers in North Carolina who took up arms against taxation and extortion.

(13) The Stamp Act Congress (1765), representing nine colonies, the first intercolonial meeting that registered indignation against English policy and adopted its own Declaration of Rights.

(14) The First Continental Congress, 1774 (representing every colony but Georgia), which agreed to boycott English imports.

(15) The Second Continental Congress (1775), which renounced loyalty to England, advocated defiance, and adopted in 1776 the unanimous Declaration of Independence of the thirteen United States.

European Wars. — For approximately 75 years during the seventeenth and eighteenth centuries, England and France were involved in a series of four European wars. Each one precipitated in America a flare-up of the ill-hidden spark of colonial jealousy between these two rival powers. The intercolonial, or French and Indian, wars settled once and for all the supremacy of England over France in America, but more important, they revealed to the colonists their own strength and importance. These wars were another step in the growth of colonial self-consciousness. Thus the war *for* England helped to pave the way for the war *against* England.

■ KING WILLIAM'S WAR. — The North American echo of the war against Louis XIV, known as the War of the League of Augsburg (1688-97), which William of Orange (William III) involved England in almost immediately after he ascended the English throne, was the first in which the colonists became involved. Actual conflict in America began in 1690 with the French and Indian attack on Schenectady, New York; this was followed by a series of massacres throughout New England. Sir William Phipps with 855 men took Port Royal, Acadia, from the French in 1690. The peace treaty of Ryswick in Europe (1697) brought a five-year respite to the conflict, but there was no real peace.

■ QUEEN ANNE'S WAR. — The American aspect of the War of the Spanish Succession in Europe (1701-14) was Queen Anne's War in America (1702-13). Once again the French and Indians attacked New England. The terrible massacre and burning of Deerfield, Massachusetts, in 1704 is one of the horrors of this period. There were also battles in the south with the Spanish. Peace came with the Treaty of Utrecht (1713), which gave all of the Hudson Bay region to the British and reconfirmed British possession of Acadia (Nova Scotia). Port Royal was renamed Annapolis in honor of Queen Anne.

■ KING GEORGE'S WAR. — The next French and English clash in America came with King George's War (1745-48), the North American counterpart of the War of the Austrian Succession (1740-48). About 4,300 New England men fought in this war of futile bloodshed. Louisburg, on Cape Breton Island, Nova Scotia, was taken from the French, but was eventually returned to them by the treaty of Aix-la-Chapelle.

Still there was no peace. The French had taken the Ohio Valley and forced a young officer named George Washington to depart from his stronghold at Great Meadows in western Pennsylvania, where he had endeavored to stem the French advance. His surrender (1754) was the beginning of the fourth and last French and Indian War.

The European counterpart of this war was the Seven Years' War (1756-63), with France, Spain and Austria in alliance against England and Prussia. The English colonists took Louisburg (1758) and all of the St. Lawrence region. They also took Fort Duquesne, now Pittsburgh. Ticonderoga fell in 1759, the year of the memorable battle on the Plains of Abraham between Wolfe and Montcalm, in which both great generals fell and the English won Quebec. The Peace Treaty of Paris in 1763 established English colonial supremacy in America. Canada came into the possession of England; Spain gave up Florida; and though French Louisiana was given to Spain, the English now held all of North America east of the Mississippi.

■ **THE PEACE OF PARIS.** — The Treaty of 1763 marked an important turning point in American history. In many respects it brought an end to the "colonial period" and opened the door to independence. The French and Indian War, fought because the Crown had finally become fully conscious of the existence and value of the colonies and was determined not to share their trade and lands with any other power, brought about two fundamental changes in Anglo-American relations. Since the war was expensive, and Great Britain had incurred a large debt during the conflict, the Crown was determined to have the colonies share the cost of the struggle, which, it was argued, was fought for the benefit of the colonists. In order to raise the needed money, England tried for the first time to exercise complete control over the colonies — a right that it had long had in theory, but had never practiced. The colonies, resentful of this new tightened control and no longer dependent upon the mother country for military aid against the French and Indians, began to change their attitude toward independence; the previous idle speculation about independence turned to serious debate after 1763.

Navigation Acts.
— With the Restoration of Charles II to the throne in 1660, England launched a definite colonial program. In 1651 Parliament had passed the first Navigation Act, requiring that colonial trade be carried in English or colonial vessels, and colonial products (sugar, tobacco, cotton, ginger, indigo) be shipped only to England. A new Navigation Act, almost identical to the old, was passed in 1660, and it was strengthened each year by additional legislation. The act of 1663 required all colonial products intended for foreign sale to be shipped first to England, where a duty could be collected before reshipment. The same requirement was placed on foreign goods going into the colonies. Smuggling flourished and the acts were largely ignored, but in 1673 and 1696 measures were passed by Parliament in an effort to check the smuggling and prevent frauds and abuses.

The Dominion of New England.
— In 1686 the New England colonies were united under one charter with Sir Edmund Andros as royal governor. All of the colonies north of the Delaware River were joined under his rule into one Dominion of New England. This move was primarily for defense against the French, but to the people it seemed a violation of all they had labored to create. They resented giving up their individual colonial charters; they resented being taxed by a royal council instead of by their own assemblies; and they found intolerable the disassembling of representative bodies. Bred as they were to wrest what they needed from a hard environment, they could not sit patiently for long. In 1689 they sent Andros and his officers back to England aboard an English ship, and the Dominion of New England was dissolved.

The single royal charters were gradually restored to the colonies, but revenue acts and irksome trade restrictions continued as England's consciousness of empire grew.

The Stamp Act.
— The Molasses Act (1733) put so high a duty on molasses and sugar imported from the West Indies that the colonists could not manufacture rum. Smuggling was successful until the Sugar Act (1764) indicated that England meant to collect the duty with the aid of Admiralty Courts — medieval naval tribunes that left court decisions to military judges rather than to civilian juries. The indignation on both sides might have finally subsided into a grumbling acceptance had there not been the added burden of the Stamp Act (1765). This was an English attempt to collect $100,000 a year from the colonies for their defense and administration by requiring a revenue stamp on all legal documents.

Resistance flared in every colony. The assemblies passed measures of protest. The New England town meetings were unanimously against the Act. The Sons of Liberty spread the gospel of defiance and staged mob scenes in Boston. The officers appointed to distribute the stamps were violently handled. English goods were boycotted. The newspapers spoke the mind of the people with extravagance. The Stamp Act Congress, representing nine colonies, met in New York to consider methods of opposition and came to one decision: the Stamp Act violated the just principle of "no taxation without representation." The colonists would be taxed by their own assemblies, not by Parliament. Protesting, the people carried on business as usual without stamps. The Act was repealed in 1766, but it was too late to arrest the leaven of alienation already at work.

Boston's Defiance.
— The Townshend Acts were passed in 1767. These were revenue acts giving England the right to collect a duty on all glass, lead, paper, pepper, and tea brought into the colonies, and they were met by rioting in the streets of Boston. English soldiers were sent to keep the peace and enforce the tax, and four people were shot in one of the outbreaks that their presence provoked. This incident is called the Boston Massacre.

England withdrew her troops and repealed all duties except the one on tea. This was left as an assertion of right. However, the people had been goaded beyond the point of compromise. A group of citizens made up as Indians stealthily boarded three vessels in Boston harbor one night in 1773 and dumped chest after chest of good tea into the water. The Boston Tea Party made it impossible for the British to collect any tax on the tea aboard the ships, but England retaliated with the Boston Port Bill (1774), which closed the harbor.

First Continental Congress.
— What was intended to punish and isolate Massachusetts served only to rally the other colonies to her support and defense. At the first news of Boston's fate, the intercolonial congress (already proposed) was summoned.

This First Continental Congress met in Philadelphia in 1774. From every colony but Georgia came delegates ready to decide their future. Although the delegates were narrowly divided between radicals, who favored resistance to the mother country, and moderates, who advocated conciliation, ultimately they reflected a mood of unity and independence. They rejected Joseph Galloway's proposal for a colonial congress that would accept or reject legislation enacted by the British Parliament. Instead, they adopted the Suffolk Resolves and the Declaration of Rights and Grievances, which pledged members to disobey the "unconstitutional" coercive acts and denied Parliament's right to tax the colonies. Equally significant was the formation of a Continental Association, whereby the colonies agreed not to import English goods or export their own to England. The congress adjourned to meet again in 1775.

Declaration of Independence.
— When the Second Continental Congress met in May, 1775, all thirteen colonies were represented; they were destined to preside for six years over a war for independence. The Revolution was at hand; blood had already been shed at Lexington and Concord in April. George Washington was made commander-in-chief of the colonial armies in June. The Battle of Bunker Hill, June 17, though a British victory, was no American defeat. Outnumbered yet unbeaten, the colonists learned that courage was greater than technique, and their confidence grew. The royal governments throughout the colonies were at an end and the only government was that of the local committees of correspondence.

Even up to this time the sympathies of the colonists were divided. The radicals preached independence, the loyalists stood staunchly for the mother country, while another intensely pro-colonial group still hoped for some solution other than complete independence. Congress, however, went about the work that was to bring the break with England. Defenses were built and recruits were drilled on the village greens. Nine thousand men were sent to New York, where it was plain that the British intended to concentrate. Privateers were financed to harass British merchant vessels. All trade restrictions were ignored and traffic was resumed with foreign countries. Loyalists were watched and disarmed. Overtures for help were made to France.

By May of 1776, the colonies found that they had been abandoned by the king. No answer came to their petitions, no redress for their wrongs. The time had come to adopt some form of representative government for their individual and mutual good. In June it was resolved "that these united colonies are and of right ought to be free and independent states." Ten colonies voted for full independence from England and the Crown. New York, South Carolina, and Georgia still wavered. Then Charleston, South Carolina, was attacked by the British fleet; General William Howe was approaching Staten Island. Indecision suddenly came to an end, and the Declaration of Independence was adopted, July 4, 1776. The historic document was composed of two parts: (1) a preamble justifying rebellion on the basis of natural rights, and (2) a list of grievances demonstrating that the natural rights of Americans had been violated by the tyrannical King George III. It is worth noting that the second section was directed at the king, rather than Parliament, because the colonists contended that Parliament had no authority over them.

The American Revolution. 1775-1781. — England was unaware of the initiative and calibre of the colonists. Had it known the Minute Men were to rise up 16,000 strong for the siege of Boston, General Gage might have had the 20,000 men he originally demanded, but was refused, for the chastisement of the colonists.

■ **1775.** — The phrase "Lexington and Concord" flew through the colonies and started the war. The Battle of Bunker Hill on June 17 proved the mettle of the American troops. The siege of Boston (July, 1775-March 17, 1776) ended with General Howe's retreat to Halifax, Nova Scotia, in March, 1776. (He had replaced Gage as commander-in-chief of the British forces.) In the meantime, the British had failed to take Charleston, South Carolina; the Vermont patriot, Ethan Allen, had taken Ticonderoga; although Benedict Arnold was defeated at Quebec, he nevertheless served to stop the British from moving south out of Canada.

■ **1776.** — The year commenced with an attack on North Carolina. In January, Sir Henry Clinton sailed from Boston with a considerable fleet, aided by 1,600 Tories who marched toward the coast. The Tories were beaten at Moore's Creek by a force of volunteers. The state was then aroused, and so many armed men had assembled that when Clinton arrived he decided not to attack. Instead, he proceeded against South Carolina; his fleet reached Charleston late in June. Clinton decided to reduce Fort Moultrie by attacking it on sea and land, but the land attack was repulsed. The accurate return fire of the fort so badly damaged the British ships that they were compelled to withdraw. The expedition then sailed to aid Howe, who reappeared off the Long Island coast with 34,000 men. He landed on Staten Island on July 5, 1776. General Washington was waiting for him with a line of defenses stretched from Brooklyn across lower Manhattan; but Howe's advance was too

strong, and Washington was pushed from Brooklyn Heights to Manhattan to White Plains. Howe took Forts Washington and Lee and 3,000 prisoners and sent three regiments after Washington as he retreated across New Jersey into Pennsylvania.

It was during this retreat that Washington suddenly stopped and, on Christmas night, 1776, moved 6,000 men across the ice-packed Delaware in boats. The place where the troops crossed, eight miles above Trenton, is still called Washington's Crossing. He surprised the Hessian mercenaries under Colonel Rall at Trenton and took 1,000 prisoners. He followed this coup by defeating Cornwallis at Princeton, and then proceeded to Morristown to camp for the winter. Washington thus controlled northern New Jersey, and the British were held back to eastern New Jersey and New York. Colonial spirits soared with these sudden successes after Washington's long, discouraging retreat. By March, 1777, new enlistments had raised Washington's strength from 1,500 to 4,000 men.

■ **1777.** — In 1777 the British made their fatal mistake. They had planned to split the colonies by seizing the whole waterway from the St. Lawrence to Lake Champlain and the length of the Hudson to New York. Howe moved toward Philadelphia by sea. He landed at the head of the Chesapeake, advanced over land into Pennsylvania, defeated Washington in the battles of Brandywine and Germantown, and moved into the American capital. This partial success netted the British little gain, however, for the forces left in New York under Clinton were inadequate for the northward push up the Hudson to meet General Burgoyne. Burgoyne's army was forced to surrender before the English troops from New York got halfway to Albany.

■ **THE TURNING POINT IN THE REVOLUTION.** — Burgoyne, coming down from Canada with 7,600 men, expected to meet Colonel Barry St. Leger advancing to the southeast from Ontario, and to join forces with him at Albany. They never met. St. Leger, stopped at Oriskany, New York, by Herkimer, turned back to Canada. Burgoyne took Ticonderoga, was beaten at Bennington, yet continued the hard push through the thick, unbroken forests. He was delayed and obstructed at every step by General Schuyler, but he finally reached Stillwater, above Albany. Cut off from reinforcements from Canada, his supplies captured, waiting in vain for Clinton to come up the Hudson from the south, his 5,000 men surrounded by 16,000, Burgoyne finally surrendered to General Horatio Gates after the hard battle at Saratoga on October 17, 1777. The Battle of Saratoga was the turning point in the Revolution because it frustrated the one campaign that would have given the British sweeping control from the St. Lawrence to New York and so put an end to the war.

■ **1778-1779.** — The winter of 1777-1778 was the terrible winter of starvation, disease and suffering, courage and endurance, that Washington spent with the remnants of his army at Valley Forge. The British held the Delaware. The capital had been moved from Philadelphia to Lancaster, and from

there to York, Pennsylvania. The men at Valley Forge starved and drilled and died under Washington and the German military genius Baron von Steuben.

In the spring, Clinton, who replaced Howe as British commander-in-chief, decided to leave Philadelphia and march across New Jersey to New York. His haste was due to the signing of the American-French alliance. He wanted to get back within the protecting range of the British navy before the French fleet arrived in American waters. Washington fought a long battle with him at Monmouth, New Jersey, but did not prevent his reaching New York.

With Clinton well settled in New York, Washington flung his defenses to the north and west and made his own headquarters at West Point. Here he could keep an eye on the British and forestall any move they might make north into New England or west toward Philadelphia. There was almost no fighting. Clinton was in New York, Washington at West Point: this remained the situation for three years.

From 1778 on, the British difficulties increased. They had had the advantage of approach by sea until France entered the war, but the Americans knew the interior and could play a waiting game. The colonists could give battle or disappear. In 1778, while England could not find a single ally, Benjamin Franklin signed the American pact with France. By 1780 Great Britain was at war with Spain, Holland, and France.

The British took Savannah late in 1778 and extended their influence through most of Georgia. They held Savannah against the combined attack of the French by sea and the Americans by land.

■ **1780.** — In 1780 the British captured Charleston and began subjugating the Carolinas. There was little real resistance. Gates was defeated by Cornwallis at Camden, South Carolina, and only small, raw patriot bands were left to prevent the South from being overrun. The British might have kept Georgia, North Carolina, and South Carolina forever separate from the union if they had not started *forcing* military service in the conquered area. This coercion stirred up a storm of partisan protest. Thus one British hold was broken in the South and Cornwallis's intended northward march was finally postponed. The sharp battle of King's Mountain in October, 1780, between the British and the Carolina backwoods riflemen left Cornwallis no troops to spare. By 1781, the British were confined to the coast, to Charleston, and to Savannah.

■ **1781.** — General Nathanael Greene, who replaced Gates, proceeded to entice Cornwallis away from the coast. He gradually drew the British across North Carolina. General Daniel Morgan defeated the British at Cowpens, North Carolina, in January, 1781. At Guilford Court House in March of that year, Greene, although defeated, inflicted such heavy losses on the English that Cornwallis retreated to Virginia. He fortified himself at Yorktown, where he thought aid from Clinton in New York could easily reach him by sea.

Washington, in the meantime, was faking activity for Clinton's attention. Clinton fully expected some new campaign and dared not weaken his

In the following listing of battles and events in the American Revolution, (A) indicates an American force and (B) a British force. The winning generals appear in boldface italics. The symbol (k) denotes killed in action.

1766–1774

March 8, 1766–Repeal of the Stamp Act.
March 5, 1770–Boston Massacre.
June 9, 1772–Burning of the Gaspé.
Dec. 16, 1773–Boston Tea Party.
Sept. 5 to Oct. 6, 1774–First Continental Congress.

1775

April 18–Paul Revere's Ride.
April 19–Fight at Lexington and Concord–*Capt. John Parker* (A); Major John Pitcairn (B).
May 10, 1775 to March 3, 1789–Second Continental Congress.
May 10–Capture of Ticonderoga–*Ethan Allen* (A); Capt. Delaplace (B).
May 12–Capture of Crown Point–*Seth Warner* (A).
June 17–Battle of Bunker Hill–*William Prescott* (A); Gov. Thomas Gage (B).
July 3–Washington assumes command of the Continental Army at Boston.
July 1775 to March 1776–Siege of Boston–*Washington* (A); Sir William Howe (B).
Sept. to Dec., 1775–American Invasion of Canada–Richard Montgomery (A); Sir Guy Carleton (B).
Nov. 12–Capture of Montreal–*Gen. Richard Montgomery* (A); Sir Guy Carleton (B).

1776

March 17–British evacuate Boston.
July 4–Declaration of Independence adopted by Continental Congress in Philadelphia.
Aug. 27–Battle of Long Island, N.Y.–Washington (A); *Sir William Howe* (B).
Sept. 15–Occupation of New York City by British.
Sept. 16–Battle of Harlem Heights–Washington (A); *Sir William Howe* (B).
Sept. 22–Execution of Nathan Hale (A) as a spy.
Oct. 11-13–Naval battle on Lake Champlain–Benedict Arnold (A); *Sir Guy Carleton* (B).
Nov. 16–Loss of Fort Washington, N.Y.–Col. Robert Magaw (A); *Sir William Howe* (B).
Nov.-Dec.–Washington's retreat through New Jersey.
Dec. 25–Washington crosses the Delaware River.
Dec. 26–Battle of Trenton, N.J.–*Washington* (A); Johann G. Rall (B).

1777

Jan. 3–Battle of Princeton, N.J.–*Washington* (A); Lt. Col. Mawhood (B).
April 25-26–British raid and burn Danbury–*Benedict Arnold and David Wooster* (A); Col. William Tryon (B).
July 6–Americans evacuate Ticonderoga–Arthur St. Clair (A).
Aug. 4-22–Siege of Ft. Stanwix (Schuyler–now Rome), N.Y.–*Peter Gansevoort* (A); Barry St. Leger (B).
Sept. 11–Battle of Brandywine, Pa.–Washington (A); *Sir William Howe* (B).
Sept. 18–Continental Congress flees Philadelphia to York, Pa.
Sept. 21–The Paoli "Massacre,"–Pa.–Anthony Wayne (A); *Gen. Grey* (B).
Sept. 25–British occupy Philadelphia, Pa.
Oct. 4–Battle of Germantown, Pa.–Washington (A); *Sir William Howe* (B).
Oct. 6–British capture Forts Montgomery and Clinton, N.Y., on the Hudson–James Clinton (A); *Henry Clinton* (B).
Oct. 17–Surrender of the British Army at Saratoga, N.Y., by Sir John Burgoyne.
Nov. 15–Articles of Confederation submitted to the States for ratification.
Dec. 19, 1777 to June 17, 1778–Washington's army encamped at Valley Forge, Pa.

1778

January–Exposure of the Conway Cabal seeking removal of Washington from command of American Army.
Feb. 6–Franco-American treaty of alliance signed in Paris.
June 18–British evacuate Philadelphia.
June 28–Battle of Monmouth, N.J.–*Washington* (A); Sir Henry Clinton (B).
July 4–Wyoming (Pa.) Massacre–Col. Zebulon Butler (A); *Col. John Butler* (B).

July 4–Aug. 12–Court Martial of Gen. Charles Lee for conduct at battle of Monmouth.
July 11–Arrival of French fleet under Comte d'Estaing off Sandy Hook, N.Y.
Aug. 8-11–Siege of Newport, R.I.–Washington (A); *Sir Henry Clinton* (B).
Nov. 11–Cherry Valley (Pa.) Massacre–by Indians led by Chief Joseph Brant (B).
Dec. 29–Capture of Savannah, Ga., by British–Gen. Robert Howe (A); *Lt. Col. Archibald Campbell* (B).

1779

Jan. 29–British conquest of Georgia completed–Gen. Robert Howe (A); *Lt. Col. Archibald Campbell* (B).
Feb. 24–Capture of Vincennes, Ind.–*George Rogers Clark* (A); Henry Hamilton (B).
March 3–Battle of Briar Creek, Ga.–Col. John Ashe (A); *Lt. Col. Prevost* (B).
July 5–Plundering and burning of New Haven, Conn., by British led by Gov. William Tryon.
July 16–Storming of Stony Point, N.Y.–*Anthony Wayne* (A); Lt. Col. Henry Johnson (B).
July 25–Penobscot (Me.) Expedition–Solomon Lowell (A).
Sept. 23–Naval action, "Bon Homme Richard" and "Serapis"–*John Paul Jones* (A); Richard Pearson (B).
Sept. 29 to Oct. 9–American Siege of Savannah, Ga.–Benjamin Lincoln (A); *Sir James Wright* (B).
Oct. 9–American assault at Savannah and death of Pulaski–Lincoln (A); *James Wright* (B).

1780

April 10-May 12–British Siege of Charleston, S.C.–Benjamin Lincoln (A); *Sir Henry Clinton* (B).
May 12–American surrender of Charleston, S.C.–Lincoln (A); *Henry Clinton* (B).
July 10–Arrival of French troops under Rochambeau at Newport, R.I.
July 25–Gen. Horatio Gates assumes command of American army in the South.
Aug. 6–Battle of Hanging Rock, S.C.–*Thomas Sumter* (A); Banastre Tarleton (B).
Aug. 16–Battle of Camden, S.C.–Horatio Gates (A); *Lord Cornwallis* (B).
Sept. 21–Benedict Arnold's (A) treason.
Oct. 2–Execution of John André (B) at Tappan, N.Y., as a spy.
Dec. 4–Gen. Nathanael Greene assumes command of the American army in the South.

1781

Jan. 1–Mutiny of Pennsylvania Line in Washington's army at Morristown, N.J.
Jan. 17–Battle of Cowpens, S.C.–*Col. Daniel Morgan* (A); Tarleton (B).
Jan. 20–Mutiny of the New Jersey Line in Washington's army at Morriston, N.J.
March 1–Articles of Confederation become effective.
March 15–Battle of Guilford Courthouse, N.C.–Greene (A); *Lord Cornwallis* (B).
May 22 to June 5–Siege of Augusta, Ga.–*Andrew Pickens* (A); Lt. Col. Thomas Browne (B).
Sept. 8–Battle of Eutaw Springs, S.C.–*Greene* (A); Lt. Col. Alexander Stewart (B).
Sept. 28 to Oct. 19–Siege of Yorktown, Va.–*Washington* (A); Lord Cornwallis (B).
Oct. 19–Surrender of Yorktown, Va.–*Washington* (A); Cornwallis (B).

1782

July 11–British evacuate Savannah, Ga.
Nov. 30–Preliminary Treaty of Peace between United States and Great Britain signed in Paris.
Dec. 14–British evacuate Charleston, S.C.

1783

March–The Newburgh Addresses to Congress.
Sept. 3–Definitive Treaty of Peace between the United States and Great Britain signed at Paris.
Nov. 25–British evacuate New York City.
Dec. 2–Washington delivers his Farewell Address to his officers in Fraunce's Tavern, New York City.
Dec. 23–Washington resigns as Commander-in-Chief of the American army.

strength to reinforce Cornwallis; but Washington and the French under Marshall Rochambeau were planning to advance into Virginia. They so informed De Grasse, the French admiral then in the West Indies. He replied, "Look for me in the Chesapeake." Washington, Rochambeau, and Lafayette then went into Virginia and stood in full force before Yorktown. De Grasse, true to his promise, appeared in the Chesapeake and cut off Yorktown from the British fleet. The move was a checkmate for Cornwallis. He surrendered on October 19, 1781. The American War of Independence was over. The United States of America had become a new nation.

The war would have ended sooner except for the fact that there was a powerful and influential group in every colony that had not joined the move for independence. These groups were comprised of the Loyalists, or Tories, who hated the idea of rebellion and remained firm in their allegiance to established government, even though they had to sacrifice their homes and their property.

Articles of Confederation.—The passion for personal liberty was reflected in the fear of a strong and thus potentially coercive government. Congress, however, immediately foresaw the need for some centralized control in the new nation and realized the necessity for an understanding between Congress and the states about their relations.

A committee was appointed in June, 1776, to draft plans of confederation for the consideration of the separate colonies. John Dickinson of Delaware, the "penman of the Revolution," wrote the first draft and submitted it to Congress in July. A "firm league of friendship" between the states was proposed. The Articles went to the state legislatures in 1777 and the document was adopted by Congress in 1778; by 1779 every state had signed it but Maryland. It held out to the bitter end, insisting that the states (Massachusetts, Connecticut, Rhode Island, New York, Virginia, the Carolinas, and Georgia) must give up their claim to western territory. When these "large" states agreed to cede those claims to Congress and Congress decided that new states should be created from this western territory, Maryland ratified (March 1, 1781) and the Articles went into effect.

The Articles provided for the continuation of the Congress, with state delegates appointed and paid by each state. The document gave Congress the right to declare and carry on war, build a navy, manage all foreign and all Indian affairs, settle interstate disputes, coin money, and create post offices.

Although the Articles of Confederation was a big step toward a unified government, and although this document provided the basis for the more workable union that was soon to emerge, it was not equal to the need. It merely established what was tantamount to a league of sovereign nations linked together to solve common problems. More centralization of power was needed. Congress was still child, not father, to the nation. Congress could neither levy nor collect taxes; all it was empowered to do was name the amount needed and wait for the states to supply it. It could not make good its own decrees, had no way of enforcing treaty obligations, and consequently could not command respect abroad. No change or improvement could be made in the Articles without the unanimous vote of all of the states, thus 12 states could be held to the rule of one.

Delegates from Maryland and Virginia met in 1785 at Alexandria and at Washington's home in Mount Vernon to regulate trade on Chesapeake Bay. These delegates invited the other states to join in a subsequent meeting on trade and commerce at Annapolis, but only five states (New York, New Jersey, Pennsylvania, Delaware, and Virginia) attended the Annapolis Convention in September, 1786. Nothing could be done immediately, but the group that met at Annapolis called a convention of delegates from all of the states to meet in Philadelphia in May, 1787, "To take into consideration the situation of the United States." In February, 1787, Congress repeated this call, explaining that the purpose was to revise the Articles of Confederation.

Ordinance of 1787.—Before the federal convention met, the Congress of the Federation adopted its most important and far-reaching measure—the Ordinance of 1787, which shaped the government of the vast Northwest Territory and provided for its division into self-governing states.

Virginia, New York, Massachusetts, Connecticut, North and South Carolina, and Georgia all claimed huge tracts of land stretching west and north to the Mississippi and the Great Lakes. These claims had delayed ratification of the Articles of Confederation for five years (1776-1781). One by one, however, the states ceded their western lands to Congress; New York did so in 1781, Virginia in 1784, and the others soon after.

The Ordinance declared that the region become self-governing as fast as the population warranted. It divided the land into territories under one territorial governor. Slavery was forbidden, but this provision did not affect slaves already in the region. Congress was to govern the territory until its free male inhabitants of full age numbered 5,000. Each territory was then to elect its own legislature and be represented in Congress; it could apply for statehood when the population reached 60,000.

Five states grew out of the old Northwest: Ohio (1802), Indiana (1816), Illinois (1818), Michigan (1837), and Wisconsin (1848). The major import of the ordinance, however, lies in its provisions for the creation of new states on a par with the old, in its framing of a method by which the whole West came into the Union, and in its exclusion of Negro slavery from this territory.

Constitutional Convention.—The Convention that met in Philadelphia in May 1787, represented every state except Rhode Island. The leaders of the nation were there: George Washington, who was chosen president of the Convention, James Madison, Alexander Hamilton, Benjamin Franklin, and Gouverneur Morris. Fifty-five of America's ablest statesmen were sent to inquire into the state of the Union and to frame a new national government. It was at once found that to revise the old Articles of Confederation was impossible; it failed on too many points. The statesmen set to work on a new constitution.

There were problems at once. Large state and small state ambitions clashed. Representation in proportion to population was favored by Virginia and other large states, for this would assure their own control of Congress and the nation. The little states wanted a congress with an equal representation of states. It seemed as if the Convention would divide and fail, but Connecticut's proposal saved the day. The proposal provided for two houses in Congress: one, the House of Representatives, representing the people according to the population of each state; the other, the Senate, giving each state equal voting power. The large states finally agreed to this plan, and the first stumbling block was surmounted.

An electoral college, composed of representatives from each state, was provided to cast the votes for president. The population of slave states was counted as including three-fifths of the slaves. When other compromises were reached the 13 states finally agreed upon an outline for a federal government equipped with a system of federal courts empowered to deal at home with individuals and with the states and strong enough to conduct itself in a world of other nations.

The Convention adopted the Constitution and adjourned in September, 1787, having resolved that ratification by nine states would make it effective. The new form of government was reported first to the old Congress of the Confederation, which submitted it to the 13 states for their approval.

Ratification.—The Constitution met a great deal of opposition in the various states. Numerous groups opposed it, as did some prominent patriots who had been eager for and active in seeking independence. Many small farmers and debtors opposed the new instrument of government because they disliked restrictions on the states' power to issue paper money. Some westerners were against the measure because they feared the new government would barter away their right to navigate on the Mississippi River. Finally, some revolutionary liberals, including such leaders as Patrick Henry and Samuel Adams, fought against ratification because they believed that strong central government tends toward tyranny. The *Federalist* papers, a series of essays written by Alexander Hamilton, James Madison, and John Jay, defended the Constitution and helped secure its ratification. Eight states had ratified it by May, 1788. On June 21, 1788—about nine months after the Convention had adopted it—the vote of the ninth ratifying state (New Hampshire) made the Constitution "the supreme law of the land"; and "we, the people" became sovereign in the United States.

The first Wednesday in January, 1789, was set apart for the selection of electors by the states, the first Wednesday in February for the meeting of the electoral college to choose the president and vice-president, and the first Wednesday in March as inauguration day.

GEORGE WASHINGTON
(1789–1797)

When George Washington was twenty-one, the royal governor sent him to Pennsylvania to negotiate with the French. Though the French refused to talk with the young Virginian, he gained political recognition upon returning home. In 1775, he was sent to the Second Continental Congress, where, to his surprise, he was chosen to lead an American force against the British near Boston. Eight years later, as head of the armies, he triumphantly returned to New York and there bade his generals and officers farewell in Fraunces Tavern (*below*). During his presidency, a youthful Yale graduate, Eli Whitney, invented the cotton gin, and within a decade, cotton (*left*) became the economic foundation of the southern states.

PICTURES: LIBRARY OF CONGRESS

ADMINISTRATIONS OF THE PRESIDENTS

George Washington—1789-1797

Whatever the differences of the states during the framing of the Constitution, they were of one mind when it came to a president. The votes of the electoral college were cast unanimously for George Washington for first president of the United States.

Organization.—Congress created three executive departments: state or foreign affairs, treasury, and war; it also provided for an attorney general and a postmaster general. Washington's first cabinet consisted of Secretary of State Thomas Jefferson, Secretary of the Treasury Alexander Hamilton, Secretary of War General Henry Knox, and Attorney General Edmund Randolph. The head of the postal service was not then considered an executive officer; not until 1829 did the postmaster general become a member of the cabinet.

The new Congress, a potent body, soon set about governing the nation. It created a national bank and a United States mint, laid high import duties to protect American industries and raise government funds, and took over state debts. Using economic pressure, Congress compelled the two still resistant states to ratify the Constitution: North Carolina ratified it in 1789, Rhode Island in 1790. To carry out the wishes made by five of the states during the ratification controversy, it adopted and submitted to the states a Bill of Rights the first ten amendments to the Constitution. These amendments, adopted by December 15, 1791, protected the people's liberties and the states' rights from federal encroachment. The ten amendments pledged to the people freedom of worship, speech, and press; freedom of appeal to the government for redress of wrong; freedom from search without warrant; the right of assembly, to trial by jury; and protection against excessive fines and "cruel punishment."

Federalist and Republican.—Very soon two bitterly opposed political factions began to develop. One, headed by Alexander Hamilton, represented the wealthy, landed class and favored a strong central government. Known as the Federalists, this group advocated national power over individual or strong state rights. The other group, headed by Thomas Jefferson, represented the common people and believed in strong state powers as the surest medium for gaining individual rights. Jefferson detested the flavor of monarchy and was strongly for the "rights of man," the ideals of the French Revolution that he had encountered in France, and the principles of the English Whigs that he admired. The group that rallied to his views called themselves Republicans.

The Second Term.—George Washington was unanimously reelected for his second term, but the peaceful business of organization was over. Troublous foreign problems brought differing political views to violent expression, and Washington received a full dose of criticism as a rank aristocrat and even usurper.

Neutrality.—During the war between England and France in 1793, Jeffer-son's sympathies were with France; he withdrew from the cabinet in protest against Washington's proclamation of neutrality. He had a large following who felt neutrality was sheer ingratitude to a former ally. "Citizen" Edmond Charles Genêt, French minister to the United States, defied Washington's strict neutrality stand and proceeded to outfit privateers to harass British ships and to enlist troops. Washington and his cabinet, realizing that any meddling in European wars would be suicidal to the new nation, insisted on neutrality; when Genêt demanded an appeal to Congress, Washington insisted on his recall to France. When commercial conflicts intensified antagonism between England and the United States, Washington sent John Jay to England to negotiate a treaty with the British. The result was Jay's Treaty, which was extremely unpopular because it accepted England's contention that food was contraband and it made no mention of either the British seizure of American ships or the impressment of American seamen. Pro-British Federalists had difficulty, but finally succeeded in, convincing the Senate to ratify the measure and the House to provide the appropriations.

Whisky Rebellion.—Internal problems also confronted Washington's second administration. When Congress levied a tax on the manufacture of whisky, the western Pennsylvania farmers refused to pay it. They could not market their grain, but they could, and did make whisky on their farms at a profit. The tax seemed to them a personal as well as an economic insult and they resisted it for three years, to the point of bloodshed in 1794. This incident was

JOHN ADAMS
(1797–1801)

PICTURES: LIBRARY OF CONGRESS

The north wing (*right*) of the new Potomac capitol was completed in 1800, and Adams gave his first address on November 22 in this Senate wing. In 1800 and 1801, Congress appropriated funds to fight the French; powerful frigates were made ready (*upper right*) to defend America's trading interests abroad.

called the Whisky Rebellion. Washington called out 15,000 militia to enforce the tax and put down the uprising. The defiant farmers took the required oath of allegiance and the strength of the federal law was proved.

Other Events. — Trouble also arose in the West with the Indians. General Harmar in 1790 and General St. Clair in 1791 both failed against them, but General Anthony Wayne defeated the Indians at Fallen Timbers in 1794. This resulted in the Greenville Treaty and the cession of 25,000 square miles to the United States.

A treaty with Spain in 1795 gave the United States free navigation of the lower Mississippi. Eli Whitney's invention of the cotton gin in 1793 initiated the industrial revolution in America. Three new states joined the Union under Washington: Vermont (1791), Kentucky (1792), and Tennessee (1796).

Washington refused to accept a third term and in September, 1796, delivered a moving *Farewell Address* with the famous warning against "entangling alliances."

John Adams — 1797-1801

John Adams of Massachusetts was one of the most fervent patriots of the colonial and revolutionary periods and one of the most able statesmen that America had produced. When Washington laid down the cares of office after two terms, Adams, who had served as vice-president for eight years, was his logical successor. He received 71 electoral votes and Thomas Jefferson received 68. Under the constitutional provision (not changed until 1804) giving the vice-presidency to the candidate receiving the second highest number of electoral votes, Jefferson became vice-president although he and Adams belonged to opposing political parties.

Resenting the Jay Treaty with England that was so favorable to its greatest rival, France broke off diplomatic relations with the United States. Charles C. Pinckney, the American minister, was refused a hearing. When French privateers attacked and took American ships, Adams sent a special commission composed of Pinckney, Elbridge Gerry, and John Marshall to France to reestablish peace.

XYZ Affair. — Talleyrand, French minister of foreign affairs, would not meet with the commission, but instead sent three men demanding huge sums of money for a peaceful settlement. The Americans scorned the offer; Pinckney is said to have made the spirited answer, "millions for defense, but not one cent for tribute." This incident was reported in detail throughout America, but the identity of the three Frenchmen was concealed under the signatures X, Y, and Z. The cry for war was immediately heard in the nation; there were battles at sea, and Washington was called from Mount Vernon to take command of the army.

Adams, however, was determined to avert war. Despite Hamilton's and the cabinet's intense hatred of France, President Adams succeeded in preventing hostilities. In 1800, a year after Napoleon supplanted the Directory and became first consul of the country, a treaty of peace was signed with France.

Alien and Sedition Acts. — The violence of popular feeling and writings at the height of the French crisis led Congress to pass the Alien and Sedition Acts in 1798. The first gave the president power to deport any foreigner who seemed a menace to the nation; the second imposed fines and imprisonment upon anyone who opposed government measures or published "false and malicious" attacks upon Congress, the president, or the government. These Acts, which grew out of the Federalist fear that the Constitution would be overthrown, resulted in the arrest of ten Republican newspaper editors. There was a wave of popular fury because the freedom of press and speech pledged by the Constitution had been suddenly swept away. The Kentucky and Virginia Resolutions adopted in 1798 denied the federal government any powers not explicitly given by the Constitution, and declared that the states had the right to nullify what they believed to be unconstitutional acts of Congress.

In November, 1800, Congress moved from Philadelphia, where it had met since 1790, and met for the first time in the new, rough city of Washington, in a Capitol building erected in the woods. John Marshall, Adams's secretary of state, was appointed chief justice of the Supreme Court a few weeks before the close of Adams's administration.

Thomas Jefferson — 1801-1809

John Adams, the Federalist, was not reelected; Thomas Jefferson, the Republican, succeeded him. Of the electoral votes, Adams received 65, Jefferson and Aaron Burr 73 each. There was no majority and the election was therefore thrown into the House of Representatives, where six days of bal-

BROWN BROTHERS

THOMAS JEFFERSON
(1801–1809)

The most important of Jefferson's contributions was his purchase, in 1803, of the Louisiana Territory from France. The next year he dispatched Lewis and Clark to investigate the huge land (*below*), and records show that the explorers had considerable help along the way. In 1807, Robert Fulton assembled the first successful steamboat, the *Clermont* (*left*), which plied the Hudson between New York and Albany.

LIBRARY OF CONGRESS

JOHN MORRELL AND COMPANY

loting gave Jefferson the vote of ten states and Aaron Burr the vote of four. Two states did not record their votes. Jefferson became president, Burr vice-president. This was the deadlock that gave rise to the twelfth amendment to the Constitution in 1804, providing for the election of president and vice-president on separate ballots in the electoral college.

Although Jefferson's election is often referred to as the "Revolution of 1800," in reality there was no striking reverse in national politics. Despite his espousal of democracy and his belief in the improvability of man, Jefferson did not turn the government over to the people. He felt that rule must be entrusted to an educated, agrarian-minded elite, and the main effect of his election was that it shifted control from a moneyed aristocracy of the Northeast to an agrarian aristocracy of the South. European conflicts kept the United States constantly embroiled in foreign affairs and prevented Jefferson from translating most of his democratic theories into practice. In the long run, Jefferson's faith in the perfectability of man and his insistence on strong local governments to check what he believed to be monarchical trends in the national government both helped to pave the way for and sometimes hindered the democratic gains that came later.

Louisiana Purchase.—Although Jefferson believed that the federal government had no power not expressly given it by the Constitution, thus becoming known as a "strict constructionist," he had the sense and greatness of mind to enlarge his views when Napoleon offered the Louisiana Territory to the United States for $15,000,000. Jefferson quickly pushed through a treaty securing New Orleans, West Florida, and all the French lands west of the Mississippi. He then asked for a constitutional amendment to ratify what he had done. This was unnecessary, for he was already clothed with the full power to make treaties ("by and with the advice and consent of the Senate").

New England objected to this purchase because it so greatly expanded the power of the South; but since it guaranteed the Mississippi River to the United States forever, the rest of the country approved, and Louisiana was purchased in 1803. The value of this vast region was little realized at the time, although it more than doubled the area of the United States. To ascertain something of the character of the lands purchased, Jefferson commissioned Meriwether Lewis (1774-1809) and William Clark (1770-1838) to explore the territory.

The Right of Search.—The United States had been suffering directly from the Napoleonic wars between England and France. England declared a blockade on European ports; Napoleon blockaded the British coasts. England did not recognize the right of any Englishman to change his citizenship, and captains of English war vessels claimed the right to search American ships for escaped English sailors and to impress them into her own service.

In 1807 the English frigate *Leopard* demanded the right to search the American frigate *Chesapeake*. The request was refused; the *Leopard* fired on the *Chesapeake* and forced the American ship to submit.

Embargo Act.—The Chesapeake affair was the last straw. Congress passed the ill-fated Embargo Act in December, 1807, to show England and France that they could not interfere with neutral vessels. The act was a sweeping ban on all foreign trade: foreign ships were not to bring goods to American ports, and American ships were not to trade in foreign ports. The act, however, failed in its purpose and only crippled America's own shipping. So great was the opposition to it in New England and New York, the American shipping centers, that it was repealed in 1809 and replaced by the Nonintercourse Act, which forbade trade with England and France only.

Burr's Dream of Empire.—When Aaron Burr was defeated for the presidency, he charged that Alexander Hamilton had thrown his influence to Jefferson, which was in fact the case. In 1804, while he was still vice-president, Burr lost the election for governorship of New York and he again blamed Hamilton for his defeat. Embittered by the long-standing feud, Burr challenged Hamilton to a duel on the New Jersey side of the Hudson River, opposite New York, and killed him (July 11, 1804).

Burr fled to Georgia, but returned to his post at Washington. After his term was over he was politically ostracized in the North and went South. His opponents charged that he was planning to raise a force to conquer the great Southwest and to establish there a new republic, with himself as its president. He did muster a party of men, but was arrested and tried for treason. Chief Justice Marshall directed his acquittal to the great disappointment of Jefferson and his friends.

LIBRARY OF CONGRESS

JAMES MADISON
(1809–1817)

NEW YORK PUBLIC LIBRARY

LIBRARY OF CONGRESS

Madison's administration was greatly enlivened by the brilliant parties given by his wife Dolley, a charming daughter of a widowed Philadelphia boardinghouse keeper; she fully enjoyed her new station in society. Popular feeling against Britain's policy of impressment (*lower right*)—taking American seamen of English birth off United States' ships—was not enough for Madison to declare war. But soon more pressing forces led to the War of 1812, which ended in Andrew Jackson's great victory over 10,000 British troops at New Orleans in 1815 (*upper right*).

Other Events.—Other outstanding events of Jefferson's administation included: the act preventing the importation of slaves after 1807; the construction of the National Road from Cumberland, Maryland, to Ohio; and the admission to the Union in 1803 of Ohio. In 1807, Robert Fulton's steamboat made its first successful trips.

Having served two terms, Jefferson followed the example of Washington and refused to accept a third. The election of 1808 resulted in the choice of James Madison of Virginia as president and George Clinton of New York as vice-president.

James Madison—1809-1817

James Madison, the fourth president, stepped into a hornet's nest of trouble. American grievances against England increased and English impressment of American seamen continued. The westerners accused the British of stirring up Indian warfare against them. The French and English blockades were still in effect and the Nonintercourse Act of 1809 was repealed and replaced by Macon's Bill No. 2 (1810); this gave the president power to renew nonintercourse against one belligerent the minute the other lifted its restrictions against American shipping. Napoleon was quick to take advantage of this and led Madison to believe France had withdrawn her decrees against neutral vessels. Hence nonintercourse was maintained more strictly against England and against England only.

Relations with England grew more and more tense. The Republican party wanted war with England, insensible of the fact that America was not prepared for war against so strong a nation. The

president advocated keeping the peace, but the war party grew and war psychology prevailed under the eloquence of a popular group of young congressmen known as "war hawks." Led by Henry Clay of Kentucky and John C. Calhoun of South Carolina, the group clamored for war. Mostly westerners, the war hawks were both nationalists, wishing to avenge the nation's honor, and expansionists, desirous of using the war as a means of acquiring British Canada and Spanish Florida. On June 1, 1812, Madison was persuaded to ask Congress to declare war on the grounds of impressment, of blockade, and of B ·it-ish incitement of Indian wars. War was declared June 18, 1812.

War of 1812.—The War of 1812 was a sorry story from the start. Like the boastful little tailor who claimed to kill twenty at a blow, the Americans expected to take Canada quickly and easily. Instead, the first move was inglorious defeat. General William Hull advanced into Canada with 2,000 men in August, 1812. Forced back by General Isaac Brock and a handful of British and Indians, he surrendered Detroit and with it all of the Michigan Territory. In October, Stephen Van Rensselaer met with another spectacular failure when he invaded Canada at Queenstown on the Niagara River.

■ **1813.**—January, 1813, witnessed General James Winchester's defeat at Raisin River by the British General Henry Proctor and the terrible massacre of abandoned wounded by the Indians. The Americans took York (now Toronto) in May, but failed at Montreal. The Americans were encouraged, however, by William Henry Harrison's victory over Proctor at the Thames

River, which won the Detroit frontier and broke the British hold in Michigan Territory. In September, Lieutenant Oliver Hazard Perry had defeated the British fleet on Lake Erie and cleared the British out of that region.

■ **AT SEA.**—America's nautical prowess during the war surprised both the enemy and itself. Its privateers captured some 300 British vessels, and its navy out-maneuvered the British fleet in seamanship and battle-tactics. In 1812, the frigate *Constitution* took the British *Guerriere* and added the legend of "Old Ironsides" to American lore.

■ **1814.**—In 1814, Jacob Brown and Winfield Scott were in command of the inland armies and America's fortunes began to improve. Brown defeated the British at Chippewa, Ontario, on July 5. Brown and Scott together met the enemy at Lundy's Lane, Ontario, in a hard battle that was neither victory nor defeat. In August, the British fleet sailed up the Chesapeake and landed 4,000 soldiers under General Ross to march against the capital. They easily took Washington and burned the federal buildings. They could not, however, take Baltimore by either land or sea, and this American victory (September 12), during which the national anthem "The Star Spangled Banner" was written, made England think that the war would be indeterminate. On September 11, an American naval force under Thomas Macdonough saved Plattsburg from a British land and naval attack and further impressed upon the British that nothing was to be gained by continued warfare.

■ **AMERICAN DISCONTENT.**—America seemed ready to end the war. The situation was very bad: the government had no money; the English had more men

JAMES MONROE
(1817–1825)

The Missouri Compromise of 1820 allowed slavery in Missouri but prohibited slavery in the remainder of the Louisiana Purchase land north of 36°30′. In 1823 Monroe proclaimed his doctrine (*below*) that the American continents "are henceforth not to be considered . . . for future colonization by any European powers."

LIBRARY OF CONGRESS

(released by the end of the Napoleonic war); and New England was threatening to withdraw from the Union to save her own shipping. Connecticut had already withdrawn her troops, while Vermont kept hers within her borders; also, the federal loan received no support in New England. The Hartford Convention (all New England delegates) met on December 15, 1814, to repudiate "Mr. Madison's War" and to consider a separate peace with England.

■ **THE TREATY OF GHENT.** — Thus the final peace treaty, the Treaty of Ghent, was signed on December 24, 1814. The news of the peace, however, did not reach either side until after the British had landed 10,000 troops at New Orleans. Andrew Jackson, who had been delegated to defend the city, met and drove back the invaders at the Battle of New Orleans; 2,000 British casualties were suffered, while American casualties were fewer than 100. This battle, fought after the war had technically ended, made Jackson a national hero and later played an important role in his election to the presidency.

The Treaty of Ghent provided for the mutual restoration of all conquests, but made no mention of maritime rights or the other issues for which the United States supposedly had gone to war. Actually, then, the War of 1812 ended in defeat for the United States; yet the nation benefitted greatly from the affair. The failure of the United States to win the adoption of its interpretation of maritime law proved unimportant, for Europe remained relatively peaceful for the rest of the century. Most important, the war was over. The Union was intact. The decisive defeats of the Indians of the North and Southwest and the amicable settlement of dif-

ferences with Great Britain assured peace and tranquility on the frontier for a generation. The settlement allowed the United States to enter upon a long period of uninterrupted westward expansion and development; America took its place as a full-fledged nation, and for the remainder of the nineteenth century the American people effected the final conquest of their continent.

Postwar Events. — The new sense of unity and national selfhood bore fruit in the chartering of a second national bank (1816); the building of new national fortifications, roads, and canals; and the laying of a stiff new tariff to protect American manufacturing.

Louisiana was admitted as a state in 1812, Indiana in 1816.

The Federalists had faded into oblivion and there were no sharp party differences. Of one mind, the country elected James Monroe fifth president of the United States with almost the unanimity that had marked the choice of Washington.

James Monroe — 1817-1825

The manifest unity of the people in their desire to uphold and build a nation caused Monroe's administration to be called the "era of good feeling." An unbroken line of settlers marched west to settle and organize the rich lands of the Louisiana Purchase. Five states came into the Union, four of them the result of this westward movement: Mississippi (1817), Illinois (1818), Alabama (1819), Maine (1820), and Missouri (1821). Steamboats were the only highly developed means of communication and transport, but roads were built and the Erie Canal (1825), extending from Lake Erie to New York, helped to knit

together inland producers and seaboard markets. Andrew Jackson stopped the Seminole Indians' plundering raids of Georgia. He marched into Florida, took the Indian towns, and also let his vengeance fall on Spanish and British troublemakers. Florida was bought from Spain for $5,000,000 in 1819.

Missouri Compromise. — In 1818, when Missouri applied for admission to the Union as a state, slavery became a national problem for the first time. Missouri had been settled by people from the South who expected it to become a slave state. The House of Representatives added the Tallmadge amendment to the Missouri bill; this prohibited the importation of more slaves and provided for the freeing of those born in the state. The Senate, however, rejected this amendment. The country was suddenly divided between advocates of slavery and those opposed to the extension of slavery to areas where it did not already exist; this controversy engendered much bitterness.

Up until this time, slave states and free states had been evenly represented in the Senate. When Maine was admitted in 1820 as a free state, Missouri could come in as a slave state without endangering the balance of the Senate vote. Missouri was admitted to the Union (1821) under the Missouri Compromise, which allowed it to come into the Union as a slave state but prohibited slavery in the remaining lands of the Louisiana Purchase north of the line 36°30′ (boundary of Missouri).

The Monroe Doctrine. — The Holy Alliance, a union of European nations ostensibly formed to preserve the peace of the Continent after the downfall of

NEW YORK PUBLIC LIBRARY

BETTMANN ARCHIVE

LIBRARY OF CONGRESS

JOHN QUINCY ADAMS
(1825–1829)

The sixth president of the United States began his distinguished career at the age of 14 as a Russian interpreter. Although he was the first president not elected by popular majority, he remained an independent man, swayed by none. During Adams' administration, America's first horse-drawn railway (*left*) was built in 1826 at Quincy, Massachusetts, and the 352-mile-long Erie Canal (*above*) was opened.

Napoleon, but actually aiming to preserve the old monarchical orders against the rising tide of republicanism, became concerned over the Spanish and Portuguese colonies in South America. One by one these small states were declaring their independence, and Europe was ready to use force to hold them in subjection. England proposed to the United States that the two countries join together to prevent Spain, Portugal, or France from annexing territory on this side of the Atlantic. In 1823, at the advice of Secretary of State John Quincy Adams, who did not trust British intentions, President Monroe enunciated the doctrine in his annual message to Congress. The Monroe Doctrine, issued unilaterally and aimed at England as well as at other European nations, warned against any foreign attempt at territorial expansion or interference in the new world. Colonization or intervention in either of the Americas on the part of European nations would be looked upon as an "unfriendly disposition toward the United States." Another important, but often-forgotten, part of the doctrine was the statement that the United States would likewise not intervene in European affairs. Although never embodied in the actual law of the land, the Monroe Doctrine became part of the national mind and practice. It assumed its greatest importance in the recent years of the twentieth century.

Election of 1824. — No party issues marked the election of 1824. Four Republicans ran for president: John Quincy Adams, Henry Clay, William H. Crawford, and Andrew Jackson. The differences were strictly personal ones, and the country lined up behind the

candidates without party consciousness. Adams was supported by the commercial interests of the East, Clay by the commercial interests of the West, and the leanings of both were toward nationalism. Crawford represented the South and its interests. Jackson, the champion of the common man, was to be elected president in a subsequent election. But in 1824, none of the four candidates received a majority vote and the election was thrown into the House of Representatives. John Quincy Adams was chosen president and Calhoun was almost unanimously elected vice-president.

John Quincy Adams — 1825-1829

John Quincy Adams, like his father John Adams, was destined to a single term in office. Soon after his inauguration, party differences became marked. Andrew Jackson's following charged that Adams had been elected in the House of Representatives through a corrupt bargain between Adams and Clay. A split occurred, and the party that had been called Republican or Republican-Democrat now became the Democratic party, with Jackson as its leader. The National Republican party was formed in opposition headed by Clay. It became the Whig party in 1832. The Jackson faction thwarted the administration at every turn.

The Tariff of Abominations. — New England was rapidly becoming a manufacturing center, and through Adams' efforts a high tariff was passed in 1828 to protect American industry against the cheaper products of Europe. Opposition immediately developed in the South, where there was little manufacturing and no demand for

protective tariffs. South Carolina opposed the measure as a "sectional benefit" and asserted her right to nullify the tariff law within her own domain. The rest of the South took similar action and nullification was to become once more a vital issue.

Election of 1828. — The politicians who organized this campaign to discredit Adams did a thorough job. The election of 1828 resulted in victory for Jackson; he received 178 electoral votes to Adams' 73. Jackson, the "symbol of his age," appealed to many different types of Americans. Into his ranks were marshalled (1) westerners who detected and disliked the "aristocratic" tendencies in Adams, (2) southerners who remembered him as the savior of the South in the War of 1812 and who, eager to defend "states' rights," believed that Jackson, a southerner, would help them, and (3) eastern wage earners who demanded recognition of their claims to political power and saw in Jackson the self-made man who would help them.

Andrew Jackson — 1829-1837

With Andrew Jackson and the election of 1828 a new era in American history began; the conservative trend in politics and thought that had been so marked was reversed. Jackson was a fervent believer in individualism and democracy, and under his leadrship the nation witnessed a sweeping change toward a *people's* government: suffrage was broadened, aristocratic institutions discarded, popular controls extended, and cultural life adjusted to the needs of the masses. The Jacksonian era had a dual nature. It was both a return to the true principles of

ANDREW JACKSON
(1829–1837)

Jackson grew up as wild as the frontier itself— notorious for brawls and gambling—yet was admitted to the bar when he was only 20. He became Nashville's most successful lawyer; and when Tennessee joined the Union, he was elected its first representative. The troublesome Creek nation succumbed to his civilian army, and a few months later he won a victory against unfavorable odds at New Orleans. Popular sentiment was for him, and it was inevitable that he became president. During his term, McCormick invented the reaper (*below*), which revolutionized farming. Samuel Morse (*left*), who invented the telegraph, was also the first instructor of Mathew Brady, who took this early daguerreotype of the inventor.

LIBRARY OF CONGRESS

MATHEW BRADY: LIBRARY OF CONGRESS

NEW YORK PUBLIC LIBRARY

the American Revolution and the Declaration of Independence, and at the same time a step forward that freed the American people from previous restraints, allowing them to pursue their interests and develop the nation's resources without government interference.

The Spoils System.—Jefferson had complained of government officials that "few die and none resign" and forthwith replaced John Adams' last-minute appointees with men to his own liking. President John Quincy Adams had made no removals for partisan purposes, not even of his avowed enemies.

Partly because of a strengthened partisan sympathy resulting from his bitter conflict with Adams, but primarily because he felt that rotation in office was a much-needed democratic reform, Jackson extended the already longstanding practice epitomized by the phrase, "to the victor belongs the spoils." He removed 121 government officeholders the first year. Ignoring the severe censure of his enemies, Jackson eventually removed approximately 1,000 out of over 10,000 federal employees. When the Whigs came into office they continued and enlarged the spoils system, which was not checked until the Civil Service Act of 1883.

The Kitchen Cabinet.—Jackson's abilities were those of war, not peace. He had studied law, had taken a prominent part in frontier disputes and development, had been a country storekeeper, lawyer, district attorney, judge, congressman, and senator before he was thirty-two years old. Jefferson said of him that he never could speak in the Senate "on account of the rashness of his feelings . . . he would choke with rage." As president, Jackson rarely held a cabinet meeting, but was advised by his personal friends, who became known as "The Kitchen Cabinet."

United States Bank.—The United States Bank had been chartered in 1816 for 20 years, chiefly as a depository for government funds. In 1832, Congress voted to renew the charter. Jackson, who disliked the bank's able but conservative president, Nicholas Biddle, opposed rechartering the Bank. He felt it was a tool of the rich to oppress the poor and to prevent state banks and small businessmen from expanding their commercial activities. Among other things, the national bank ruthlessly foreclosed mortgages when debtors fell behind in the payments, and kept state banks from issuing currency needed by debtor farmers and small businessmen. Consequently, Jackson vetoed the new bank bill, challenging it on constitutional grounds. The bank became the great issue in the next election; and when Jackson was returned to office with 219 electoral votes to Clay's 49, he felt that he had indeed executed the will of the people. In 1835, he ordered all government money removed from the United States Bank and distributed in state banks throughout the country. The national bank thus was crippled and failed.

Nullification.—Adams' high tariff of 1828 had antagonized the South, and another act in 1832 reinforcing it added to the southern grievance. South Carolina passed a law in November, 1832, declaring the tariff null within that state and prepared to defend her stand by force of arms if necessary. Jackson was personally opposed to the tariff, but would not tolerate any disruption of the Union. He sent South Carolina a sharp warning emphasizing that the law would be enforced, and sent two warships into Charleston Harbor in support of his threat. Conflict seemed imminent until Henry Clay pushed a compromise tariff through Congress that provided for a ten-year decrease in the duties until none would exceed 20 per cent. This satisfied South Carolina and talk of nullification ceased.

The nullification issue gave rise to a series of great debates in the Senate on state rights, the Constitution, and the preservation of the Union; during these debates Daniel Webster made his stirring *Reply to Hayne,* repudiating "Liberty first and Union afterwards" and exalting "that other sentiment, dear to every true American heart— Liberty *and* Union, now and forever, one and inseparable."

Other Events.—The Cherokee Indians in Georgia protested that the state had unjustly taken their lands, but the federal government upheld the state on this issue, and the Cherokees were obliged to move west of the Mississippi River. In Illinois, Chief Black Hawk was in insurrection against the whites for encroaching on tribal lands (1832). In 1835, the Seminoles in Florida warred against the government and were not defeated for several years. William Lloyd Garrison gave impetus to the antislavery movement by beginning publication of *The Liberator* in 1831. In 1834, Cyrus McCormick invented the reaping machine, which was to revolutionize the agricultural world. Samuel F. B. Morse announced the principle of the telegraph and demonstrated its practicability in 1835. The steam

UNITED STATES RUBBER COMPANY

LIBRARY OF CONGRESS

MARTIN VAN BUREN
(1837–1841)

This innkeeper's son had a limited education, but managed to win success in both law and politics. In 1828 he was governor of New York and shortly afterward became secretary of state under Jackson. During this time the industrial revolution was in fullest swing, and discoveries such as Charles Goodyear's process for vulcanizing rubber (*above left*), further accelerated the rapidly expanding economy. Overextension of credit was partly responsible for the Panic of 1837 (*right*); this and the depression that followed was a problem of major proportions that Van Buren encountered upon taking office.

LIBRARY OF CONGRESS

locomotive had become a success in England; two locomoties were imported into Pennsylvania in 1829, and when America began to build her own engines in 1830, railroad mileage jumped from three to 23 miles. By 1835 there were 1,098 miles of track in the East, and by 1840 there were 2,800. In 1833 the steamship *Royal William* crossed the Atlantic in 17 days.

Arkansas joined the Union in 1836, Michigan in 1837.

The dynamic and beloved Jackson had established the Democratic party so firmly in power that in 1836 Martin Van Buren, Jackson's trusted lieutenant, the party's presidential candidate, was chosen by an electoral vote of 170 to 73 for William Henry Harrison.

Martin Van Buren—1837-1841

Panic of 1837.—When Jackson ordered the cessation of deposits of the national funds in the United States Bank, certain other banks were chosen to handle government funds; these were called "pet banks," and they began circulating large amounts of bank notes, which fostered speculation to the extent that soon there was no money with proper backing and a serious inflation resulted. The banks issued bills payable in gold and silver without the specie with which to meet the obligations. Wildcat banks were formed with little or no capital; this was the legacy left to the Van Buren administration by Jackson. Since the greater part of the speculation was in public lands, Jackson's order that agents should receive nothing but gold for land had precipitated a panic that extended to all branches of trade. Banks failed everywhere, and the treasury was compelled to issue notes up to $10,000,000.

Repudiation (1837).—During the period of speculation, states had undertaken the construction of railroads, canals, and other public works, issuing bonds on which they could no longer pay even the interest. In some cases the money had been squandered, in others, plundered. Some states refused to pay their debts, taking refuge behind the clause of the Constitution that forbids a state to be sued by an individual. Some states eventually paid their debts, as did Pennsylvania, but others never did. Since much of this money had been borrowed in Europe, American honor received a strong blow and American credit fell so low that for years afterward the United States government was unable to secure a loan in Europe.

Subtreasury Established (1840).—Van Buren, who had run for office hoping to walk in the footsteps of his illustrious predecessor, hurried to find a way to remedy Jackson's mistakes. He proposed the Subtreasury System, which severed all connection between the government and the banks of issue and allowed the government to do its own banking. Vaults were built and government moneys deposited, to be paid out by government agents under heavy bonds; this scheme had the disadvantage, however, of holding such money out of circulation, except through payment of salaries and interest and the purchase of its own bonds.

The Abolition Movement (1834-1840).—Abolitionism, a product of the reforming zeal of the Jacksonian era, differed from the earlier antislavery movement in its emphasis on racial equality. Whereas earlier antislavery reformers encouraged sending the freed slaves to Africa, in the 1830's a small but active band of abolitionists talked of freeing the slaves, by force if necessary, and then educating them to take their equal place in American society. This program met with opposition in the North as well as in the South, the majority in both sections determined to maintain "white supremacy." Riots and bloodshed frequently resulted. The controversy grew in depth and power in both North and South and was hastening the day of reckoning, which even then seemed to be inevitable. John Quincy Adams had said long before that the Union would ultimately split on the slavery issue.

Other Events.—Before the end of Van Buren's term, regular steamship routes were established between the United States and Europe—this occurred less than 20 years after the first steamboat had made the Atlantic crossing (1819).

Election of 1840.—Misfortune had marked the greater part of Van Buren's four years as president, and though the Democrats nominated him for a second term, he was easily defeated. The Whigs took advantage of the financial distress of the common people to wreck their already weakening faith in Van Buren's party. General William Henry Harrison, the Whig candidate, was elected on the wave of hysteria known as the "log cabin and hard cider" Campaign. He received 234 electoral votes to 60 for Van Buren. John Tyler, another Whig candidate, was elected vice-president.

One of the most memorable aspects of the election of 1840 was Harrison and Tyler's campaign slogan, "Tippecanoe and Tyler too."

JOHN TYLER
(1841–1845)

John Tyler (*right*) was a willing man, but he had less than mediocre ability to handle the presidency. Irreconcilable differences arose between him and the Whigs, and eventually his entire cabinet walkd out. To his credit, he settled a boundary dispute between Canada and the United States. In 1842, John C. Frémont (*below*) began an official survey of the Indian route that was known as the Oregon Trail.

LIBRARY OF CONGRESS

LIBRARY OF CONGRESS

WILLIAM H. HARRISON
(1841)

Harrison (*above*) was nominated by the Whigs because of his success at Tippecanoe, Indiana, where he defeated the great Shawnee chief, Tecumseh, and also because of his politically neutral viewpoints. He died barely a month after inauguration.

BETTMANN ARCHIVE

William Henry Harrison—1841

Harrison died one month after his inauguration, having had time to accomplish little except appoint Daniel Webster secretary of state and call a special session of Congress to plan a way out of the financial distress of the nation.

John Tyler—1841-1845

John Tyler, vice-president, automatically became chief executive. He was a Virginian bred in a democracy that had idolized Jefferson, and was at heart a states' rights man, not a nationalist. Harrison's victory at the polls had naturally filled Congress with a Whig majority, but when the two groups began to legislate for party policies, they found Tyler not only unsympathetic but immovably against them. He at once (in August, 1841) vetoed the bill providing for a new United States Bank with various state branches, charging it unconstitutional and an infringement upon states' rights. The bill was reworded to meet the president's objections, but he vetoed it again in September. Frustrated and indignant, the whole Whig cabinet resigned, except for Daniel Webster, who remained to negotiate the pending treaty with Great Britain. When this had been signed he too stepped out of office, and Tyler stood alone—disowned by the Whigs, unclaimed by the Democrats.

Webster-Ashburton Treaty.—The treaty with Great Britain, known as the Webster-Ashburton Treaty, was signed in 1842. It fixed the Maine-Canada boundary line and provided for joint suppression of the African slave trade and for the exchange of refugee criminals.

Annexation of Texas.—In 1844 the Republic of Texas applied for admission to the Union. As Texas was largely settled by slave-holding southerners, the annexation issue brought the slavery question into major focus. The South was solid for annexation; the North feared it; Tyler approved it. The annexation treaty was defeated in the Senate (1844), however, and it became the main issue of the next election. The Democrats nominated James K. Polk of Tennessee for president on an annexation platform.

Before the new president came in, however, Congress passed another resolution to annex Texas as a state. Tyler approved it just before he went out of office. The provisions of the Missouri Compromise left Texas open to slavery because it was south of the 36°30′ line. Texas became a state in 1845.

Long-Distance Telegraph.—In 1844 Congress gave Samuel F. B. Morse an appropriation to set up an electric telegraph line between Baltimore and Washington—the first successful long-distance line in the world.

James Knox Polk—1845-1849

James Knox Polk, the eleventh president, came into office with 170 electoral votes to 105 for Henry Clay. Clay might have been elected had not the Liberty party in New York swung its full strength from Clay to James G. Birney, the antislavery candidate. George M. Dallas was elected vice-president.

Mexican War (1846-1848).—Soon after the annexation of Texas came the Mexican War. The immediate cause of the war was Texas' claim that the Rio Grande was its southwestern boundary; Mexico claimed the region as far north and east as the Nueces River. In May, 1845, General Zachary Taylor was sent with troops to the border, and in July he advanced to the Rio Grande. The Mexicans under General Arista attacked him (April, 1846) but Taylor drove them back across the river, and though outnumbered 3 to 1, scored two decisive victories: Palo Alto, May 8, and Resaca de la Palma, May 9. Congress declared war on Mexico, May 13, 1846; Mexico's formal declaration followed, May 23. Actually, United States relations with Mexico had reached the breaking point long before this time. President Polk had come into office determined to defend American annexation of Texas, an act that Mexico refused to recognize. More important, Polk and the American people, believing in "manifest destiny," the natural expansion of U.S. geographic boundaries, desired to add to United States territory the province of California, which Mexico refused to sell. The outbreak of hostilities, therefore, was no surprise. Although the western and southern states responded enthusiastically to the conflict, many northerners were either apathetic or hostile. New England abolitionists, in particular, were severely critical of the administration's policy, which they viewed as a southern conspiracy to secure more territory for the extension of slavery.

■ WAR STRATEGY.—Militarily, four moves were planned. General Taylor was to hold the Rio Grande; General Scott was to advance on Mexico City from Vera Cruz; Colonel Stephen Kearny was to take and hold New Mexico, then push

MATHEW BRADY; LIBRARY OF CONGRESS

Polk, the first "dark horse" candidate, proved to have great initiative. He considered Texas annexation right and necessary, and in 1845 dispatched troops to the border to avert a possible Mexican attack; he then conceived the idea of obtaining all the Mexican land west of Texas. Fighting broke out "spontaneously," and war was declared on Mexico. In 1848 Commodore Perry successfully landed troops in Tobasco, Mexico (*below*); the United States eventually gained all the Southwest as well as Texas from Mexico. The first sewing machine (*below right*) was developed by Elias Howe in Polk's term.

JAMES K. POLK
(1845–1849)

LIBRARY OF CONGRESS

LIBRARY OF CONGRESS

on to California to join the army there under Captain John C. Frémont, whose safety would be assured by a fleet in the Pacific commanded by Commodore Stockton. All four campaigns were marked with success.

Taylor followed up his first two victories by taking Matamoras and in September, 1846, attacking and capturing Monterey. He then sent some 10,000 men south to reinforce Scott's march from the coast to Mexico City. General Santa Anna with an army of 20,000 attacked Taylor's weakened forces, (about 4,000 men) at Buena Vista—but the 4,000 did not yield, and a desperate two-day battle (February, 1847) sent the Mexicans fleeing. This battle made Taylor the hero of the war and as a result put him in the White House in 1849.

In March, 1847, Scott landed at Vera Cruz, took the city, and began his march on the Mexican capital. He drove Santa Anna from the pass at Cerro Gordo and continued his advance, taking city after city. On September 14, Santa Anna retreated from Mexico City, Scott's army entered and kept possession until the peace treaty was signed in February, 1848.

New Mexico was occupied by Colonel Kearny (1846) who later proceeded into Upper California, where Commodore Stockton's Pacific fleet had taken Los Angeles and San Diego and had secured the occupation of the area by Frémont's land forces.

■ **TREATY OF GUADALUPE HIDALGO.**—February 2, 1848, the peace treaty was signed at Guadalupe Hidalgo. Mexico conceded the border question: the Rio Grande henceforth would be Texas' southwestern boundary. It also ceded to the United States, for $15,000,000, territory now known as California, Utah, Arizona, and New Mexico.

Gold Rush.—Shortly after the treaty was signed, word came from California that gold had been discovered in the Sacramento Valley; this was the signal for a phenomenal migration to the Pacific coast. More important, however, the addition of new western land resulted in a renewal of the slavery question and launched the nation on a debate in which the opposing sections drifted even more widely apart.

Oregon Question.—A convention with Britain in 1818 fixed the northeast boundary between America and Canada, but did not settle the northwest boundary dispute. Oregon was filling up. In 1842 the first Oregon-bound wagon train made its way over the Oregon trail. In 1843 began the "great emigration" of 900 people and 120 wagons. By 1845, 3,000 emigrants had settled in Oregon; British-American interest in the territory increased and British-American jealousy for its possession grew increasingly intense. The American people wanted 54°40' for the northern boundary, and "Fifty-four forty or fight" became the cry. Polk, who had been elected partly on a platform "to reoccupy Oregon," wanted to fulfill that pledge without involving America in two wars at once. Great Britain had refused to accept the 49° line as a boundary compromise. The settlers had made their own stand against the presence of the British by setting up their own government (1843), but Polk would not let them arm. He persisted in negotiating for the 49° compromise treaty until England finally agreed (1846).

Walker Tariff.—In 1846, Polk's secretary of the treasury, Robert G. Walker, framed the lowest tariff measure the country had ever known. The bill was to raise revenue for government expenses, omitting all protective features. Previously, every important tariff bill had been framed to protect American industries, but Congress and President Polk passed Walker's bill, which immediately increased British-American trade. "Tariff for revenue only" was the Democratic party's policy for the next 80 years.

Other Events.—During Polk's administration, Iowa was admitted as a state in 1846 and Wisconsin in 1848. In 1847 postage stamps were authorized for the first time by the government. Elias Howe invented the sewing machine in 1846. The Wilmot Proviso (abolishing slavery in the territory newly acquired from Mexico) was debated (1846-47) and kept in ferment. In 1846 Congress re-created the independent treasury department, which had been established by Van Buren after the Panic of 1837 when government funds were removed from state banks, but was discarded by the Whigs in 1841. The Free-Soil Party was formed (1848) to keep the territories closed to slavery.

Election of 1848.—The Mexican War hero General Zachary Taylor was nominated for president on the Whig ticket; Millard Fillmore was nominated for vice-president. They won the election over Lewis Cass, the Democratic nominee. The new Free-Soil Party was headed by Martin Van Buren. However this political group did not receive any electoral votes.

ZACHARY TAYLOR
(1849–1850)

Zachary Taylor was the first active army man to become president. Although a southerner and a slaveholder, he took no stand on this issue. He assured the South they need not fear attacks against slavery, yet he opposed their threatened secession and thus incurred opposition of his southern Whig supporters. He died unexpectedly after holding office for sixteen months.

UNCLE TOM'S CABIN;

OR,

LIFE AMONG THE LOWLY.

BY

HARRIET BEECHER STOWE.

VOL. I.

BOSTON:
JOHN P. JEWETT & COMPANY.
CLEVELAND, OHIO:
JEWETT, PROCTOR & WORTHINGTON.
1852.

FIRST EDITION, IN THE EXCESSIVELY RARE
RED CLOTH PRESENTATION BINDING

[NUMBER 210]

MILLARD FILLMORE
(1850–1853)

Millard Fillmore took office upon Taylor's death. He appointed a new cabinet, signed the Compromise of 1850 and enforced the Fugitive Slave Law. Defiance of the law widened the right between North and South and marked the end of Fillmore's political career. Mrs. Stowe's controversial and successful book (*left*), gained a great deal of northern support for abolitionists.

Zachary Taylor—1849-1850

Taylor came to the presidency without political experience at a time when sentiment regarding slavery was rapidly causing a breach between the North and the South. He was scarcely more than an observer of the course of events, and his career as chief executive was cut short by his death 16 months after his inauguration.

Compromise of 1850.—California was applying for admission to the Union with a state constitution prohibiting slavery. The slave and free states in the Union were still equal in number—15 each. If California were admitted as a free state, this balance would be broken; the 16 free states would have 32 senators to 30 from the 15 slave states. Henry Clay, known as "the great pacificator," drafted a compromise bill loaded down with so many distinct measures that it was called by its enemies the "Omnibus Bill." History records it, however, as the "Compromise of 1850."

Clay's bill, intended to satisfy both North and South, provided that California be admitted as a free state, New Mexico and Utah be organized as territories empowered to decide for themselves the slavery question, and that Texas receive $10,000,000 as indemnity for the territory it claimed from New Mexico. A second bill in the compromise group excluded the slave trade from the District of Columbia and provided for the enforcement of fugitive-slave laws by federal officers, whose duty it became to return to their masters runaway slaves who escaped to free states.

Before Congress could act upon these measures, President Taylor died (July 9, 1850) and Vice-President Millard Fillmore became president.

Millard Fillmore—1850-1853

Fillmore had presided over the Senate as vice-president on the heated question of slavery in a manner highly satisfactory to both sides; he had been impartial, as his position required him to be. As president, however, he became the leader of the Whigs, who were opposed to the extension of slavery.

During the summer of 1850 the Compromise bills were heatedly discussed, and they were passed early in September. California was admitted to the Union on September 9. When Fillmore signed the Fugitive Slave Law, which had been demanded by the South, he weakened his leadership of the Whigs and never fully regained it. He believed, however, that he was taking the only possible course to preserve the Union.

Other Events.—One of the circumstances leading to the crystallization of northern sentiment against slavery was the publication in 1852 of Harriet Beecher Stowe's novel *Uncle Tom's cabin*, which was unsympathetic toward slavery.

Election of 1852.—Fillmore wanted the Whig nomination for the presidency, as did General Scott and Daniel Webster. Scott was nominated but defeated in the November election by Franklin Pierce, a Democrat, who received 254 electoral votes to 42 for Scott.

Franklin Pierce—1853-1857

The lull that followed the assertion that the Compromise of 1850 was "final" was only the stillness that precedes a storm. Pierce's whole administration was filled with bitter feeling, violent debate, and actual bloodshed over the slavery issue. The lands west of Missouri were ready to be organized into territories, and according to the Missouri Compromise (prohibiting slavery north of 36°30′), would automatically become free states when they entered the Union. The initiation of surveys (1853) for the first transcontinental railroad alarmed the slave-holding South, which feared any increase in free-state representation in Congress and felt that easier intercourse with antislave sections would be a contamination and a danger. In the North, the enforcement of the fugitive slave laws had made apparent the inhumanity of the commercial slave system. The question of slavery became one of increasingly intense feeling.

Kansas-Nebraska Bill.—In 1854, Senator Stephen A. Douglas attempted to solve the western slavery question by introducing the Kansas-Nebraska Act. Douglas was motivated by many considerations. He hoped that the bill, which proposed repealing the Missouri Compromise and creating the territories of Nebraska and Kansas, would promote his presidential ambitions by securing the support of southern Democrats who disliked the compromise. He was also anxious to have the Nebraska region organized and settled so as to stimulate the growth of the Northwest. This would help promote the building of a transcontinental railroad that would have its eastern terminal in Chicago, and thus benefit his native state of Illinois. Douglas had no moral convictions against slavery; he preferred to leave the question in the new

LIBRARY OF CONGRESS

BETTMANN ARCHIVE

LIBRARY OF CONGRESS

FRANKLIN PIERCE
(1853–1857)

General Pierce had a good military record, an attractive personality, and no troublesome political ties; he was elected because he was acceptable to both North and South. His indecisive leadership, however, made an uneventful administration. Since his wife hated Washington and rarely attended social events, White House life was never duller. In Pierce's term, Commodore Matthew Perry twice visited Japan (*left*) to gain trading rights; he was successful in 1854. That year, the Republican party was formed as a reform party and held its first national convention in Pittsburgh, Pennsylvania, in 1856 (*above*).

territories to the settlers themselves. As a result, "popular," or "squatter's sovereignty," as this plan came to be known, was written into the Kansas-Nebraska Bill, which was passed in May, 1854. Instead of solving the slavery conflict, however, the act merely stimulated all of the old and sore questions that had been temporarily solved by the Missouri Compromise.

At once pro-slave and anti-slave interests propelled armed settlers to the new territories, particularly Kansas, which became the stage for a violent drama. Westbound free-soil settlers found their way obstructed by armed pro-slave Missouri men, the same men who dashed over the border and carried the first Kansas territorial elections. Each side set up a government and sent delegates to Congress. Murders, pillagings, and burnings prevailed. Kansas was in a state of civil war, which continued into 1858.

Gadsden Purchase.—To settle a boundary dispute with Mexico, the United States purchased the territory in question for $10,000,000. This purchase, effected by James Gadsden, United States minister to Mexico, covered the 45,535 square miles that now form the southern parts of New Mexico and Arizona.

Proposed Annexation of Cuba.—The South greatly desired the annexation of Cuba to the United States in the interests of slavery extension. The Pierce administration, although not opposed to the movement, proceeded slowly. The American ministers to Spain, France, and England were instructed to confer on the subject in Europe. They issued the Ostend Manifesto, a proclamation

claiming that the United States would be justified if it took Cuba from Spain by force.

Other Events.—A Tennessee adventurer, William Walker, took possession of the Central American state of Nicaragua, over which Great Britain desired to establish a protectorate, in 1855. The United States recognized Walker's government, which restored slavery in Nicaragua, but the government was overthrown in 1857. Commodore Perry's treaty with Japan (1854) opened two Japanese ports to American ships and established a United States consul in Japan.

Election of 1856.—The passage of the Kansas-Nebraska Bill was directly responsible for the rise of a new party—the Republican party, formed in the North in 1856 to oppose the further spread of slavery. John C. Frémont was named as its candidate for president; the Democrats nominated James Buchanan of Pennsylvania, who received 174 electoral votes to Frémont's 114; 8 votes were cast for Fillmore, who ran as candidate of the American party and of the few Whigs who had not become Republicans.

James Buchanan—1857-1861

Buchanan's administration began with the Supreme Court decision in the Dred Scott case and ended with the secession of the South from the Union. In the case of Dred Scott, the Supreme Court declared (March 6, 1857) that no slave and no individual of slave ancestry could be a citizen of the United States or appeal to a federal court, that slaves were "property" to be transported from state to state like any property,

and that Congress could not prohibit slavery in the territories and was bound by the Constitution to protect it. More important was an additional ruling in which the Court announced that Congress had no right to prohibit slavery in the territories. This decision, which delighted the South, was extremely significant, for it implied that slavery was protected throughout the nation by constitutional guarantees. In its attempt to settle the slavery controversy by judicial decision, however, the Supreme Court merely succeeded in losing a good deal of its own prestige and increasing the hostile feelings between the two sections. Northerners were outraged at the ruling, and the newly-formed Republican party continued to insist upon congressional legislation against the extension of slavery into the territories. Republicans knew, however, that they could reverse the ruling only by winning control of the government and then staffing the Court with their own appointees.

The break between North and South was hastened by the four-year-long agitation over the two territorial constitutions of Kansas, one pro-slavery, and the other anti-slavery. Congress was split wide open on the question: the gentlemen from the South were as determined to prevent the admission of Kansas as a free state as the northern representatives were unwilling to see a pro-slave constitution railroaded through. The result was the break up of the Democratic party into northern and southern Democrats. Minnesota came into the Union as a free state in 1858, Oregon as a free state in 1859. By this time there were 19 free and 12 slave states represented in the national Con-

NEW YORK PUBLIC LIBRARY

CULVER

CULVER

JAMES BUCHANAN
(1857–1861)

A northerner with southern sympathies, Buchanan so enraged Senator Douglas of Illinois over the slave issue that Douglas broke with the pro-South administration and had to fight desperately to keep his Senate seat; Douglas was delighted when Lincoln challenged him to a series of debates (*above*) in 1858. The next year, John Brown, in a wild attempt to incite a slave rebellion, led an attack on the arsenal at Harpers Ferry (*left*); he was arrested by Colonel Robert E. Lee, tried for treason, and was hanged on the gallows in December, 1859.

gress. Kansas further upset the balance by signifying her will to become a free state (1859) with the adoption of the Wyandotte Constitution prohibiting slavery, but she was not admitted until January of 1861.

John Brown.—In the midst of this ferment came John Brown's attack on the U.S. arsenal at Harper's Ferry, Virginia (1859). This was the first step in his fanatic design to arm the slaves to attack their masters. With a band of only 21, he attacked and took the armory at Harper's Ferry, but he was captured by Colonel Robert E. Lee with a small force of Marines, was tried for treason, and hanged, December, 1859. The episode electrified the nation. The possibility of slave uprisings horrified and terrified the South. In the North, the hanging of John Brown put his name first on the list of abolitionist martyrs. The South now felt that its existence as a slave-holding territory depended on separation from an antislavery union.

Election of 1860.—Not only the South, but the entire nation anxiously awaited the next election. When the Democratic convention met to nominate its presidential candidate, Stephen A. Douglas and his followers, advocating "popular sovereignty," were in the majority. This so disrupted the southern Democrats, who thought that the slavery issue had been solved by the Dred Scott case, that the convention adjourned without having nominated a candidate. When it reassembled two months later, delegates from the deep South were absent. Those who attended the convention nominated Douglas for president on a platform that supported "popular sovereignty." In the meantime,

southern Democrats chose their own standard bearer, John C. Breckinridge of Kentucky, on a platform endorsing the Dred Scott decision. The jubilant Republicans, sensing victory over a divided opposition, nominated a relatively unknown and moderate candidate: Abraham Lincoln of Illinois. In an attempt to attract a wide following, particularly among agricultural and business interests, their platform promised: (1) not to abolish, but to restrict slavery to the states where it already existed; (2) to adopt a protective tariff and provide government support for transcontinental railroad building; and (3) to pass a homestead law. A fourth candidate, John Bell of Tennessee, was nominated to represent the Constitutional Union party on a platform demanding the preservation of the Union by compromise.

Lincoln secured 180 electoral votes, Breckinridge 72, Bell 39, and Douglas only 12. Lincoln won only 40 of the popular votes and thus was a "minority" president. Nevertheless, it was significant that the electorate, North and South, obviously favored decisive action, for Lincoln and Breckinridge together polled an overwhelming majority of the votes.

Secession.—With the election of Lincoln the southern states seceded from the Union and formed the Confederate States of America. The movement for secession, which was opposed by many southerners, had been afoot for over a decade. Southern "fire-eaters," disturbed by the belief that (1) the South was losing its commanding position in federal affairs, and (2) that southerners would be unable to protect themselves against the economic power of the in-

dustrial North, preached secession. Despite Republican promises that they would not interfere with slavery in the South, many southerners were afraid that party machinery might fall into the hands of the abolitionists. The Republican intention to exclude slavery from the territories would, if carried out, result in a permanent majority of free states in Congress. Furthermore, Republicans championed a protective tariff, a homestead act, and a transcontinental railroad—all measures that the South had consistently opposed. For these and other reasons, southern extremists became popular. To reassure more timid southerners, they maintained that secession would not lead to civil war because the North, threatened with the loss of cotton and the southern market, would not dare to forcibly oppose secession.

South Carolina led the movement for secession by calling a popularly elected convention (December, 1860) that adopted an Ordinance of Secession and issued a Declaration of Causes. By February, 1861, all other states of the lower South—Mississippi, Florida, Alabama, Georgia, Louisiana, and Texas—had acted; Virginia, Arkansas, North Carolina, and Tennessee followed. In each case, however, secession triumphed only after the defeat of strong unionist sentiment.

The Confederacy.—Delegates of the first seven seceding states met at Montgomery, Alabama, on February 8, 1861, to frame a constitutional government. On February 18, Jefferson Davis was inaugurated president of the Confederate States of America with Alexander H. Stephens as vice-president. The Confederate constitution differed from the

MATHEW BRADY

PICTURES: LIBRARY OF CONGRESS

ABRAHAM LINCOLN
(1861–1865)

Lincoln's debates with Stephen Douglas on slavery gained him national attention, and in 1860 the lawyer from Illinois was nominated for president. His object at the outset of the Civil War was to restore the Union, but by 1862 northern agitation grew against continuing the importation of slaves (*above*), and he issued the historic Emancipation Proclamation (*left*). On April 14, 1865, shortly after starting his second term, he was assassinated by John Wilkes Booth (*upper left*) while at Ford's Theater.

Constitution of the United States in that it stressed state sovereignty, prohibited high protective tariffs, and recognized "the institution of Negro slavery as it now exists in the Confederate States."

War Postponed.—Buchanan could do little but look on. He spoke his mind, declaring that no state had the right to secede, but he had no way of compelling the rebellious states to return to the Union. When South Carolina's delegates came to him demanding the transfer of United States property within the state *to* the state, he refused to confer with them as officials of a recognized government, but said he would "receive them as private gentlemen of the highest character." He was intent on avoiding war and warned the men in command of the threatened Fort Pickens at Pensacola and of the three forts in Charleston Harbor to do nothing that could be interpreted as an act of war. Major Robert Anderson was thus forced to remain inactive while South Carolina's guns drove away a vessel of supplies for Fort Sumter in Charleston Harbor. Not until Anderson moved from Fort Moultrie to Fort Sumter (which was less certain to be crushed by the South Carolina batteries) did Buchanan send tardy reinforcements. Buchanan postponed the war in his own administration, but he knew that Lincoln "had no alternative but to accept the war."

Abraham Lincoln—1861-1865

Believing that John Brown's raid was a Republican party plot, the South chose to see doom in Lincoln's election. Actually, neither slavery nor the South were endangered by Lincoln's election,

for the president was no abolitionist and both Congress and the Supreme Court remained in the hands of Democratic majorities. Moreover, southerners failed to see that secession would not protect slavery. On the contrary, by leaving the Union, the South left the territories and the federal government entirely in the hands of northerners, thus opening the way for antislavery activities through economic policy, military conquest, and eventual emancipation. Sober argument, however, bore little weight. Northerners and southerners alike were now ruled by emotion rather than reason. Secession was already in effect when Lincoln entered office.

Two years before assuming the presidency, Lincoln had said, "A house divided against itself cannot stand. I believe this government cannot endure permanently half slave and half free. I do not expect the Union to be dissolved I do not expect the House to fall—but I do expect it will cease to be divided." On countless other occasions, however, this shrewd politician also made it clear that his sole objective was the preservation of the Union "with or without slavery," as he said in his inaugural address. "If there be those," he said after he became president, "who would not save the Union, unless they could at the same time *destroy* slavery, I do not agree with them. My paramount objective . . . is to save the Union" and if "I could save the Union without freeing *any* slave I would do it. . . ."

Lincoln did not believe in racial equality. In 1858 he had said, "I am not, nor ever have been in favor of bringing about in any way the social and political equality of the white and black races." As long as both races remained in the United States, he de-

clared, "there must be a position of superior and inferior, and I . . . am in favor of having the superior position assigned to the white race." Nevertheless, he also believed that slavery was unjust, cruel, and inhuman. He favored a conservative plan that called for the gradual and voluntary emancipation of the slaves, compensation to slaveholders for the loss of their "property," and some federal assistance to the states in implementing the plan. Because he believed in the inferiority of the Negro race and the inability of the two races to live together peacefully, Lincoln's plan also called for overseas colonization of the freedmen.

Fort Sumter, April, 1861.—During the first three months of secession the seceding states had taken over many forts belonging to the national government almost without protest from those in charge. Waiting and hoping for compromise measures that would undo secession, fort commanders had abstained from warlike action. When Lincoln came into office, Fort Sumter alone of the three forts in Charleston Harbor still flew the United States flag. Under the command of Major Robert Anderson, the fort was, however, in a state of seige and in dire need of supplies and provisions. Confronted directly with the question of Fort Sumter, and more generally with the entire question of secession, Lincoln had to decide whether or not to employ coercion, and, if so, how to do it without alienating the border states that had remained within the Union. His decision to employ force was determined by his desire to preserve the Union and by his realization that the principle of secession was both illegal and dangerous; it would lead to further disunion if disgruntled minorities could leave the Union at will. For this reason, and possibly in the hope of goading the Confederacy into firing the first shot, Lincoln decided to send supplies to the besieged garrison at Fort Sumter. When news of the expedition reached the Confederates at Charleston, they opened fire on Fort Sumter (April 12, 1861), forcing its surrender before the supply ships arrived. Thus began the Civil War.

The Civil War. Causes. — Although more than a full century has elapsed since the Civil War occurred, the explanation of its causes are still uncertain and highly controversial. Certainly, the causes were many and more complex. Whether looked upon as a moral or as a social problem, the root of the conflict was the question of slavery. Intimately related to this were the economic differences between the two sections: the North was rapidly industrializing while the South tenaciously clung to its agrarian way of life. Each side, believing that it was following the right path, fought for control of the government in order to preserve its system. With fanatics on both sides, the divided nation was plagued by bitter sectional disputes and a refusal by either side to face problems squarely and work out a peaceful compromise. Under these circumstances, war was inevitable. It came when the South believed that Lincoln's election endangered its chosen way of life and it was therefore justified in withdrawing from the Union.

■ PREPARATIONS. — The day after the surrender of Fort Sumter, Lincoln made a formal proclamation of war and called for 75,000 volunteers. Regiments sprang up overnight. In the first call 90,000 men were enlisted, and still more volunteered. By December, 1861, 600,000 men were in the Union army.

In the South the call for volunteers met with an equally ardent response, and many brilliant officers resigned from the U.S. army to go home and serve their states. Among these were Albert S. Johnston and the unparalleled Robert E. Lee, who refused the command of the Union army to serve the South. Four more states went over to the Confederacy. Virginia passed her ordinance of secession on April 17, two days after the Union call to arms, but the western section of Virginia remained loyal to the Union and was admitted as the state of West Virginia (June 20, 1863). Arkansas seceded May 6, North Carolina on May 20, and Tennessee, June 18. The capital of the Confederacy was moved from Montgomery, Alabama, to Richmond, Virginia. President Davis issued a proclamation (April 17) licensing southern privateers to seize U.S. vessels. Lincoln proclaimed the blockade of southern ports, April 19.

On July 4, 1861, Lincoln called a special session of Congress to plan for war. All other business was dropped. Congress issued a call for 500,000 additional volunteers; it also voted a $500,000,000 loan, levied new and higher tariff duties to pay for the war, provided for the punishment of any who worked against the government,

and proclaimed the property of states in rebellion subject to confiscation. In May, Lincoln stationed Federal troops on the south bank of the Potomac to protect the capital. This force, called the Army of the Potomac, was under General Irvin McDowell. Davis protected his capital in a similar manner: two Confederate armies stood between Washington and Richmond under Generals Beauregard and Joseph E. Johnston.

■ MANASSAS (BULL RUN). — Once committed to the war, the people were eager for it. "On to Richmond" could be heard everywhere. The people and the Congress still believed one decisive battle would end the Confederacy; the army and the administration were under a cloud of disfavor for the delay. Lincoln knew the troops were still too green to fight, but he believed the Confederate troops were equally unprepared. On July 21, 1861, he allowed McDowell to advance against Beauregard's forces at Manassas Junction, about 30 miles south of Washington, while spectators drove out to watch "their boys" win.

The battle was fought along the little creek called Bull Run. North and South seemed evenly matched. The men on both sides were equally raw, equally brave; but the Union generals were conspicuously out-generaled. The plan had been for Patterson and 18,000 men to prevent General J. E. Johnston's Shenandoah army from joining Beauregard. The Union troops were about to gain an easy victory when five new regiments appeared before them, standing "like a stone wall" and giving their commander, General Thomas J. Jackson, the nickname "Stonewall." Still another brigade from Johnston's forces arrived to confound the federal troops, whose retreat turned into panic and a run for Washington.

Gloom succeeded assurance in the public mind; this war was not to be decided by the turn of a battle. The next day (July 22) Lincoln sent west for McClellan to organize the army. This young Major-General had successfully helped West Virginia establish her Unionist stand, during June and July, and seemed the one man into whose hands the Union cause might be delivered.

■ THE TRENT AFFAIR. — On November 8, 1861, an incident took place that very nearly cost the Union the neutrality of England. Two Confederate agents, Mason and Slidell, were on board the English mail steamer, *Trent*, bound for England to solicit aid for their cause. The ship was stopped and boarded by officers from the U.S. frigate *San Jacinto*. Mason and Slidell were taken off and sent as prisoners to Boston. Before the United States had time to disavow the act as unauthorized, Great Britain demanded the release of the two men and the apology of the United States government. To have England aligned with the Confederacy was the last thing the Union wanted, and cotton manufacturing interests of England had already predisposed her to side with the South. Freedom of neutral vessels and nonmilitary persons from search or capture was "an old, honored and cherished American cause," as Secretary of State Seward admitted. The prisoners were released and allowed to go to England,

where they secured, not the official aid they sought, but a great deal of sympathy.

■ 1862. THE WESTERN CAMPAIGN. — All winter McClellan drilled his men in the East. In the West, General Halleck was in command, and the successes of a hitherto unknown subordinate officer named Grant were gaining attention.

Albert S. Johnston was in command of the Confederate army in the West. He had fortified the Tennessee and Cumberland rivers and had extended the Confederate line up into Kentucky. Grant was in command at Cairo on the Mississippi; he had taken the mouth of the Tennessee River and the mouth of the Cumberland where they flowed into the Mississippi. He planned to strike quickly at Fort Henry on the Tennessee, then take Fort Donelson on the Cumberland. This would leave Nashville undefended and give Tennessee over to Union operations.

Halleck, however, did not give the command until February 1. Grant started the next day through the mud and rain. His advance by land was backed up by gunboats in the Tennessee under Commodore Andrew H. Foote, and on February 6 Fort Henry surrendered. Grant then pushed overland to Fort Donelson on the Cumberland. Foote's gunboats hurried down the Tennessee and up the Cumberland again to help him. On February 15 he surrounded Fort Donelson and discovered that the garrison was leaving. He attacked at once. The fort surrendered on February 16, and Grant took 15,000 prisoners. On February 25 the Union troops were in Nashville; west Tennessee was won.

Washington rejoiced and made Grant a major-general. Halleck, however, jealously forbade Grant's further advance southward, which was designed to cut the Memphis-Charleston railroad. Delay gave Johnston time to strengthen and make sure of his defenses on that line all the way from Memphis to Chattanooga.

The next step was to break the Confederate blockade on the Mississippi, and in March this job was given to General John Pope and his 20,000 men. Supported by Commodore Foote from the river, he took New Madrid, and after long siege, captured Island No. 10 (April 7). Missouri was thus isolated from further Confederate activity.

■ SHILOH. — Halleck then undertook to complete the task so spectacularly begun by Grant in February. Whichever side held Corinth (a Mississippi town between Memphis and Chattanooga), could control the Mississippi down to Vicksburg. Halleck had already given Johnston plenty of time to move west and take his stand with Beauregard at Corinth. Against the odds stacked up by his own superior officer, Grant undertook the movement. He marched up the Tennessee and stood at Pittsburg Landing. General Don Carlos Buell was on his way to join him from Nashville, but an unexpected attack by Johnston on April 6 nearly ended in defeat for Grant's recruits. After one of the most terrible battles of the war, Grant retreated during the night, leaving Johnston dead on the field of battle. Buell arrived before daybreak with 20,000 men to meet a new assault led by Beauregard, and the Confederates

U. S. VOLUNTEERS.

E Pluribus Unum!

"The Union now and forever, one and inseparable!"

SEIDMAN PHOTO SERVICE

CIVIL WAR (1861–1865), the battle between the American Union (northern states) and the Confederate States of America, which consisted of eleven southern secessionist states. Following the call for volunteers, regiments on both sides soon overflowed with enthusiastic enlistees—with men eager for excitement, anxious for action. The posters promised that regiments, once full, would "march immediately to the seat of war and do duty as active riflemen." As in all wars entailing strategic planning, however, the active, able-bodied men spent much time sitting in the trenches and simply waiting for orders to push forward.

NATIONAL ARCHIVES

PRESIDENT ABRAHAM LINCOLN and his generals, following the battle of Antietam, September 17, 1862. As commander-in-chief of the Union forces, Lincoln's major problem was in finding a capable chief of staff and in establishing a successful system of command. This, however, was not achieved until the last year of the war, when Ulysses S. Grant was appointed general-in-chief. Prior to this, from 1861 to 1864, Generals Scott, George McClellan, and Halleck succeeded each other in this post. The Army of the Potomac, pictured here, also saw a series of leaders. McClellan (facing Lincoln) was relieved of his command twice; the first time he was replaced by General John Pope. The second time he was succeeded by Generals Burnside, "Fighting Joe" Hooker, and Meade, in that order.

RIVER CAMPAIGNS were staged by iron-clads, armored vessels that had a paddle wheel built into the stern and were expected to fight head-on. The main functions of the Union Navy, which both outnumbered and outmaneuvered that of the Confederates, were to stage blockades against the South and to supply the northern troops. Ships such as this one also lent aid to land operations along the inland rivers, particularly the Mississippi and its tributaries. One fleet followed General Grant on all of his western campaigns and, by landing troops south of the city, was partially responsible for his success at Vicksburg.

LIBRARY OF CONGRESS

NATIONAL ARCHIVES

THE RAVAGES OF WAR left scars throughout the South; since most of the war was fought on southern ground, it was here that the toll in lives and property was most clearly evidenced. The countryside was decimated and cities were destroyed. Charleston, South Carolina, pictured here, was left in ruins by General Sherman and his troops. The number of dead in the Civil War ran into the hundreds of thousands, and graveyards, such as this one at the notorious Andersonville prison in Georgia, numbered the dead with rows and rows of tombstones. Here, 1,040 of the 13,737 graves are marked "unknown." The total number of casualties in the Union forces alone was estimated at 646,392; this appalling figure represents twice that of the total United States losses during World War I.

were forced back toward Corinth (April 7). Halleck then took command of the armies of Grant and Buell, reinforced them with Pope's troops, and slowly advanced toward Corinth, which was evacuated on May 30. Memphis fell in June. The North now held the Mississippi from Cairo to Vicksburg. New Orleans had fallen to Farragut's fleet on April 24, and General Benjamin Butler had taken possession of the city, May 1.

■ 1862. SEVEN DAYS' BATTLES. JUNE 26-JULY 2. — No remarkable victories featured the eastern campaign, however, and McClellan was partly to blame. Instead of marching from Washington directly toward Richmond and probably fighting an important battle near Fredericksburg, he decided to approach the Confederate capital by water. Early in April his army of 100,000 men was crowded on the little peninsula between the York and James rivers, ready for a march on Richmond. McDowell's corps of 50,000 men were left to guard Washington and quiet the fears of the politicians. General Nathaniel P. Banks had about 10,000 men in the Shenandoah Valley guarding against a raid from that quarter.

McClellan advanced with caution, besieging Yorktown for a month and giving the Confederates ample time to evacuate; they did so on the night of May 3, retreating to Williamsburg. The battle sent the outnumbered Confederates retreating across the Chickahominy. McClellan followed, establishing his camps on both sides of the river. Joseph E. Johnston, in command of the Confederate troops, decided to attack two corps south of the Chickahominy, hoping to defeat them before assistance could arrive. A fierce two-day battle resulted (Seven Pines, May 31-June 1). The Confederates were defeated, and Johnston, badly wounded, was replaced by Robert E. Lee.

Meanwhile, amazing Confederate victories marked the Shenandoah Valley. By a series of swift and bewildering marches, Stonewall Jackson had defeated the Union forces under Banks at Front Royal; he beat them again at Winchester, and drove them in disorder back to the Potomac and out of the Valley. Lincoln ordered McDowell to detach 20,000 men to the Valley to catch Jackson, but Jackson eluded these troops, as well as others led by Frémont and Shields.

Lee then planned to crush the single corps stationed north of the Chickahominy, the other two corps having already withdrawn to south of the stream. The plan failed; Jackson's troops did not arrive when promised. General Ambrose P. Hill launched a fierce attack on the corps of General Fitz-John Porter. Although undefeated, Porter retreated that night and was attacked the next morning by nearly all of Lee's army, Jackson having at last arrived. Outnumbered, the Union soldiers crossed the Chickahominy on the night of June 27 and burned their bridges behind them. The next day Lee's troops were busy repairing the bridges while the Union army was marching south through White Oak Swamp. Emerging from this morass on the twenty-ninth, they were attacked at Frayser's Farm. They held off the Confederates until dark and then safely retreated to Malvern Hill. Here, on July 1, Lee made a serious blunder: his attack on an impregnable position resulted in a bloody defeat, and more than 5,000 dead and wounded men were left on the slopes of the hill. McClellan resumed his retreat that night and did not halt until his army was under the protection of the Federal gunboats on the James River.

■ 1862. SECOND BULL RUN. — While McClellan remained on the James, demanding vast reinforcements before he again advanced against Lee, Lincoln made Halleck commander-in-chief of all the Union armies. General Pope took command of a new eastern army composed of the troops guarding Washington and those in the Shenandoah Valley. Despite the reinforcements sent him from McClellan, Pope was badly defeated near Manassas Junction on August 20-30. His troops retreated to Washington and began to disintegrate. Lincoln was compelled to restore McClellan to the command not only of the Army of the Potomac, but also of the Pope army, known as the Army of Virginia.

■ 1862. ANTIETAM. — Believing that Union forces were too seriously shaken to offer resistance, Lee began to invade Maryland after resting only one day. Jackson's corps crossed the Potomac on September 5. Confident that he would not be attacked by McClellan, Lee divided his army, sending about half of his troops to capture the garrisons at Harper's Ferry and Martinsburg. McClellan learned of this through a captured dispatch and attacked Lee at Sharpsburg on September 17. The bloodiest one-day battle of the war followed, and the result was a deadlock. Lee, however, was compelled to retreat across the Potomac. Disappointed in McClellan's failure to pursue Lee, Lincoln replaced him with General Ambrose E. Burnside.

■ 1862. FREDERICKSBURG. — Burnside decided to march the Army of the Potomac directly toward Richmond and to attack Lee whenever he was found. The attack, on December 13, was made at Fredericksburg against a well fortified position. A bloody defeat followed, with the Union loss exceeding 12,000 dead or wounded. A more able general than Burnside was needed.

Emancipation Proclamation. — That the Union must "cease to be divided" had remained Lincoln's aim from the beginning. "The Union must be preserved, with or without slavery," he had said. Now Lincoln sensed, however, that the long, discouraging war could be won only with the impetus provided by a new emotional lift. He decided that *now* was the time to take a moral stand and raise the banner for the slave.

On September 22, Lincoln issued a preliminary proclamation (ready since July) that all slaves within the states still in rebellion by January 1, 1863, would be freemen from that day. Not one state returned to the Union, and the final proclamation was accordingly issued on January 1, 1863.

Few people realize that this proclamation freed no slaves. (It was not until the thirteenth amendment was passed, at the end of the Civil War, that slavery was in theory abolished.) It did not apply to the loyal slave states, only to those in rebellion. It did not apply to slave territory recaptured in the war, and it was totally ignored within the Confederacy. What it did do, however, was to change the war from one of political patriotism to one of a crusade for the oppressed. Lincoln's proclamation also enlisted the wavering sympathy of Europe. A war waged by the North to end slavery had England's full approval, while in a political squabble her leanings were to the South.

■ 1863. CHANCELLORSVILLE. — Following its December disaster at Fredericksburg, the Army of the Potomac remained in its winter camps along the Rappahannock River. Joseph Hooker, who replaced Burnside, planned an ambitious campaign against Lee, intending nothing less than the capture of Lee's entire army. The outcome was utter defeat for Hooker: 11,000 of his 130,000 men were killed or wounded and 6,000 were taken prisoner. More than 10,000 of Lee's 60,000 men were killed or wounded and about 2,000 were captured, but Lee's greatest loss was Stonewall Jackson. Mistaken for a Union officer, he was shot by his own troops.

■ 1863. GETTYSBURG. — Despite a brilliant victory, the South was in a desperate situation after the Battle of Chancellorsville. The strangling effect of the sea blockade made it difficult to ship cotton abroad or to obtain munitions and other supplies from Europe. A victory was necessary to win an alliance with France.

Lee decided to invade Pennsylvania. The army was to march down the Shenandoah Valley and up the valley of the Cumberland to Harrisburg. After the capture of that city, if the North did not sue for peace, Philadelphia and New York were to be captured.

Unknown to Hooker, Lee began to detach his troops, with Longstreet's corps leaving for the Shenandoah on June 3. Within three weeks the entire Confederate army was across the Potomac, and two days later the extreme advance was approaching Harrisburg. When he learned that Lee was on his way north, Hooker wanted to march directly for Richmond, but Lincoln would not permit it. Instead, he was ordered to go after Lee's army, but not to leave Washington unprotected. On June 28, shortly after the Army of the Potomac had entered Maryland, Hooker was relieved from command and replaced by General George C. Meade.

Realizing that Meade would soon be on his line of communications, Lee began to gather his army. Neither Lee nor Meade planned a battle at Gettysburg; it was only by chance that it occurred there. The bloody struggle continued for three days (July 1-3). The Confederates, victorious the first two days, confidently charged the Union center on the third day. Here the Confederates met defeat, and George E. Pickett's division, which led the charge, was almost annihilated. It is estimated that the total number of losses was between 40,000 and 50,000.

■ 1863. VICKSBURG. — Surrounded by many swamps and rivers, the Confederate fortress at Vicksburg was very difficult to attack. Ever since October, 1862, Grant had been in command of the Union armies in this central area. His most important task was the opening of

1861 — THE AMERICAN CIVIL WAR — 1865

In the following listing of battles and events in the Civil War, (U) represents the Union (northern) army, while (C) represents the Confederate (southern) army. Boldface italics denote winning generals; (k) signifies killed.

1860

Nov. 6—Election of Lincoln.
Dec. 20—Secession of South Carolina.

1861

Feb. 9—Jefferson Davis elected President of "The Confederate States of America."
Feb. 18—Davis inaugurated at Montgomery, Ala.
Mar. 4—Lincoln inaugurated at Washington, D.C.
Apr. 12-13—Bombardment and Surrender of Ft. Sumter, Charleston Harbor, S.C.
Apr. 19—Blockade of Southern ports declared by Pres. Lincoln.
May 6—Confederate Congress passes act recognizing state of war between the U.S. and the C.S. of A.
May 26—Richmond, Va., becomes capital of the C.S. of A.
July 21—Battle of First Bull Run (Manassas, Va.): McDowell (U); *J. E. Johnston and Beauregard* (C).
Aug. 10—Battle of Wilson's Creek, Mo.: Lyon (U); *Ben McCulloch* (C).
Oct. 21—Battle of Ball's Bluff, Va.: C. P. Stone (U); *N. G. Evans* (C).
Nov. 7—Battle of Belmont, Mo.: U. S. Grant (U); *L. Polk* (C).
Nov. 8—Removal of Mason and Slidell from the British steamer *Trent*.
Nov. 20—Creation of Committee on the Conduct of the War by Union Congress.

1862

Jan. 19—Battle of Mill Springs (or Logan's Cross Roads), Ky.: *G. H. Thomas* (U).; G. B. Crittenden (C).
Feb. 6—Fall of Fort Henry, Tenn.: *U. S. Grant* (U); L. Tilghman (C).
Feb. 14-16—Siege and Surrender of Ft. Donelson, Tenn.: *Grant* (U); Buckner (C).
Feb. 21—Battle of Valverde, New Mexico: E. R. S. Canby (U); *H. H. Sibley* (C).
Mar. 9—Battle of Monitor and Merrimac in Hampton Roads, Va.: *J. L. Worden* (U); Catesby ap Roger Jones (C).
Apr. 5-May 4—Siege of Yorktown, Va.: *G. B. McClellan* (U); J. B. Magruder (C).
Apr. 6-7—Battle of Shiloh (or Pittsburgh Landing), Tenn.: *Grant* (U); A. S. Johnston (k) and Beauregard (C).
Apr. 16—First Confederate Conscription Act.
Apr. 29—Surrender of New Orleans, La.: *B. F. Butler* (U); Mansfield Lovell (C).
May 8-25—Jackson's Valley (Va.) Campaign: N. P. Banks (U); *T. J. Jackson* (C).
May 31-June 1—Battle of Seven Pines (or Fair Oaks), Va.: *McClellan* (U); J. E. Johnston (w) and G. W. Smith (C).
June 1—R. E. Lee (C) appointed to command Army of Northern Virginia.
June 25-July 1—Seven Days battles, Va.: McClellan (U); *Lee* (C).
Aug. 29-30—Battle of 2d Bull Run (or Groveton), Va.: John Pope (U); *Lee* (C).
July 17—Second Confiscation Act (U) passed.
Sept. 16-17—Battle of Antietam (or Sharpsburg), Md.: McClellan (U); Lee (C). *Draw*.
Sept. 19—Battle of Iuka, Miss.: *W. S. Rosecrans* (U); Sterling Price (C).
Sept. 24—Presidential (U) suspension of writ of *habeas corpus*.
Oct. 3-4—Battle of Iuka, Miss.: *Rosecrans* (U); Van Dorn (C).
Oct. 8—Battle of Perryville, Ky.: D. C. Buell (U); *Braxton Bragg* (C).
Nov. 16-July 4, '63—Vicksburg (Miss.) campaign: *Grant* (U); J. C. Pemberton (C).
Dec. 13—Battle of Fredericksburg, Va.; A. E. Burnside (U); *Lee* (C).
Dec. 20—Holly Springs, Miss., depot captured and burned: R. C. Murphy (U); *Van Dorn* (C).
Dec. 31-Jan. 1, '63—Battle of Stone River (or Murfreesboro), Tenn.: Rosecrans (U); Bragg (C). *Draw*.

1863

Jan. 1—Emancipation Proclamation (U).
Jan. 1—Galveston, Texas recaptured: I. S. Burrell (U); *Magruder* (C).
Feb. 25—National Bank Act effective (U).
Mar. 3—Federal (U) Draft Act.
Apr. 11-May 4—Siege of Suffolk, Va.: *John J. Peck* (U); James Longstreet (C).
May 20-July 4—Siege and surrender of Vicksburg, Miss.: *Grant* (U); Pemberton (C).
May 27-July 8—Siege and Surrender of Port Hudson, La.: *Banks* (U); Franklin Gardner (C).
Apr. 27-May 5—Campaign and battle of Chancellorsville, Va.; Joseph Hooker (U); *Lee* (C).
June 9—Cavalry battle of Brandy Station, Va.: Alfred Pleasanton (U); *Jeb Stuart* (C).

June 20—West Virginia admitted to the Union.
June 23-30—Tullahoma (Tenn.) campaign: *Rosecrans* (U); Bragg (C).
July 1-3—Battle of Gettysburg, Pa.: *G. G. Meade* (U); Lee (C).
July 4—Surrender of Vicksburg, Miss.: *Grant* (U); Pemberton (C).
July 8—Surrender of Port Hudson, La.: *Banks* (U); Gardner (C).
July 13-16—New York City draft riots.
Sept. 19-20—Battle of Chickamauga, Ga.: Rosecrans (U); *Bragg* (C).
Sept. 21-Nov. 24—Siege of Chattanooga, Tenn.: *Rosecrans and Thomas* (U); Bragg (C).
Oct. 25-Nov. 27—Chattanooga, Tenn. campaign: *Grant* (U); Bragg (C).
Nov. 17-Dec. 5—Siege of Knoxville, Tenn.: *Burnside* (U); Longstreet (C).

1864

Feb. 3-Mar. 5—Meridian (Miss.) Campaign: Sherman (U); Polk (C). No decision.
Feb. 20—Battle of Olustee (or Ocean Pond), Fla.: Truman Seymour (U); *Jos. Finegan* (C).
Mar. 12—Grant appointed General-in-Chief of Union armies.
Mar. 10-May 22—Red River (La.) campaign: Banks (U); *Richard Taylor* (C).
Apr. 12—Capture of Fort Pillow, Tenn.: L. F. Booth (k); *N. B. Forrest* (C).
May 5-7—Battles in the Wilderness, Va.: *Grant* (U); Lee (C).
May 8-21—Operations about Spotsylvania Court House, Va.: *Grant* (U); Lee (C).
May 11—Cavalry battle at Yellow Tavern, Va.: *P. H. Sheridan* (U); Jeb Stuart (k) (C).
May 5-Sept. 1—Atlanta Campaign, Ga.: *W. T. Sherman* (U); J. E. Johnston and J. B. Hood (C).
May 15—Battle of New Market, Va.: Franz Sigel (U); *C. Breckinridge* (C).
May 27—Battle of New Hope Church, Ga.: Joseph Hooker (U); *P. R. Cleburne* (C).
June 3—Battle of Cold Harbor, Va.: Grant (U); *Lee* (C).
June 10—Battle of Brice's Cross Roads, Miss.: S. D. Sturgis (U); *N. B. Forrest* (C).
June 17-April 1, 1865—Siege of Petersburg, Va.: *Grant* (U); Lee (C).
June 19—Naval battle, "Alabama" and "Kearsarge," off French coast: *John A. Winslow* (U); Raphael Semmes (C).
June 27-Aug. 7—Early's (C) raid on Washington, D.C.
July 9—Battle of Monocacy, Md.: Lew Wallace (U); *J. E. Early* (C).
Aug. 5—Naval battle in Mobile Bay, Ala.: *D. G. Farragut* (U); Percival Drayton (C).
Aug. 7-Oct. 25—The Shenandoah Valley (Va.) campaign: *P. H. Sheridan* (U); Early (C).
Sept. 1—Evacuation of Atlanta, Ga.—*Sherman* (U); Hood (C).
Sept. 27—Battle of Pilot Knob, Mo.: *Thomas Ewing, Jr.* (U); Price (C).
Oct. 19—Battle of Cedar Creek, Va.: *Sheridan* (U); Early (C).
Oct. 23—Battle of Westport, Mo.: *S. R. Curtis* (U); Price (C).
Nov. 16-Dec. 20—Raid through Georgia from Atlanta to Coast: *Sherman* (U); G. W. Smith and W. J. Hardee (C).
Nov. 8—Lincoln reelected President.
Nov. 20-Dec. 17—Hood's Tennessee campaign: *Thomas* (U); Hood (C).
Dec. 15-16—Battle of Nashville, Tenn.: *Thomas* (U); Hood (C).
Dec. 20—Capture of Savannah, Ga.: *Sherman* (U); Hardee (C).

1865

Jan. 13-15—Battle of Ft. Fisher, N.C.: *A. H. Terry* (U); W. H. C. Whiting (k) (C).
Feb. 5—Hampton Roads (Va.) Peace Conference.
Feb. 6—Lee appointed General-in-Chief of all Confederate forces.
Feb. 17—Charleston, S.C., evacuated by Confederate troops.
Feb. 17—Columbia, S.C., burned by Sherman's troops (U).
Mar. 4—Lincoln inaugurated for second term.
April 1—Battle of Five Forks, Va.: *Sheridan* (U); G. E. Pickett (C).
April 2—Capture of Selma (Ala.): *J. H. Wilson* (U); N. B. Forrest (C).
April 2—Confederate evacuation of Richmond, Va.
April 9—Confederate surrender at Appomattox Court House, Va.: *Grant* (U); Lee (C).
April 12—Capture of Mobile, Ala.: *Canby* (U); D. H. Maury (C).
April 15—Death of President Lincoln—Andrew Johnson inaugurated as President.
April 26—Confederate surrender at Durham, N.C.: *Sherman* (U); J. E. Johnston (C).
May 4—Surrender of Confederate forces in Louisiana: *Canby* (U); Taylor (C).
May 10—Jefferson Davis captured at Irwinsville, Ga.
May 26—Surrender of Trans-Mississippi Dept.: *Canby* (U); E. Kirby Smith (C).
June 2—Surrender of Galveston, Texas: *Henry K. Thatcher* (U); Kirby Smith (C).
Nov. 6—Final Confederate surrender—"Shenandoah," Capt. James Waddell, to British authorities at Liverpool, England.

the Mississippi River—impossible without the surrender of Vicksburg. Grant's plan to transport a large army along the railroad from Holly Springs, Mississippi, to Vicksburg failed. The redoubtable Confederate cavalry leader Nathan B. Forrest wrecked beyond repair the railroad Grant depended on for his supplies.

After several other failures, Grant decided to attack Vicksburg from the south. Late at night on April 16, Admiral David D. Porter ran 11 vessels past the batteries at Pittsburg, losing only one. Six nights later several more boats passed safely down the stream. Grant then landed about 20,000 men on the west bank of the Mississippi above Vicksburg. These troops marched south, and then at a landing below Vicksburg, Porter's fleet ferried them to the east bank of the Mississippi.

Grant left his line of supplies and improvised an ammunition and supply train, using every sort of vehicle and draft animal to be found on the surrounding plantations and farms. Marching north toward Vicksburg, with his left flank protected by the Big Black River, he suddenly turned his columns to the right—away from Vicksburg. Driving before him the few Confederate troops General Johnston had collected, on May 14 Grant captured and destroyed Jackson, an important railroad and munition center.

The next day Grant turned his columns to the west and on May 16, at Champion Hill, defeated a considerable part of the Vicksburg garrison. Two days later Grant had completely surrounded Vicksburg, and 47 days later the fortress surrendered.

The Turn of the War.—The two victories of Vicksburg and Gettysburg, a day apart, marked the turn of the war. Union forces now controlled the Mississippi. Lee had at last suffered a defeat. West Virginia was readmitted to the Union, June 20, 1863. By December, the recaptured sections of Louisiana, Tennessee, and Arkansas were ready for reconstruction, and Lincoln was already dedicating himself to that "great task remaining." His proclamation of December, 1863, offered the oath of allegiance to every one in the retaken sections except Confederate military and government officers and those who had mistreated prisoners of war. When the number of loyal citizens reached ten per cent, state governments were to be established, recognized, and readmitted to the Union.

■ **1864. THE BATTLE OF THE WILDERNESS.**—Two armies were left to the Confederacy: Lee's in Virginia and Johnston's in Georgia. Ulysses S. Grant was made commander-in-chief of Union armies in March, 1864. He put Sherman in command in the West and took over the Army of the Potomac himself, retaining Meade in the field. Grant knew his soldiering, and neither the politicians nor public pressure could dissuade him from his own plans.

Grant headed straight for Richmond. He and Meade crossed the Rappahannock, May 4, and were attacked by Lee in the difficult, unbroken forest land that gave the region its name "the Wilderness." For 16 days Lee held fast. This Battle of the Wilderness, May 5-6,

resulted in no gain. Union forces achieved nothing in the battle at Spotsylvania Court House, and the long struggle at Cold Harbor brought them nothing but the loss of 12,000 men, with Lee still standing strong.

Grant crossed the James River, planning to approach Richmond by way of Petersburg, 20 miles south. By June 15 he had surrounded Richmond and begun the long siege that would open the way to the Confederate capital.

■ **1864. WESTERN CAMPAIGN.**—In the meantime, General Sherman was pressing Johnston backwards into Georgia. On May 5, he left Chattanooga, beginning the move that was to unite his army with Grant's, tie up the Confederacy in a loop knot, and end the war. An engagement at Kenesaw Mountain was won by Johnston, but by July he was forced back to Atlanta. Johnston's long maneuver of impeding, but not fighting, the invader and inevitably retreating did not seem adequate to President Davis, who sent General John B. Hood to replace him. Hood wearied and depleted his small army by constant and fruitless fighting in July. Sherman defeated him in three battles, cut the railroad lines that kept Hood in Atlanta in communication with the Confederacy, and moved into that city on September 2. Hood tried to lure him north again into Tennessee, but Sherman would not be tricked and stayed in Atlanta. General George Thomas defeated Hood at Nashville (December 15-16) so effectively that Hood's army was never unified again.

■ **ELECTION OF 1864.**—Lincoln's reelection was dependent upon the success of Grant. While the army fought and died in the Wilderness, tongues wagged and bitterness prevailed. Hardly a good word was said for Lincoln, who was at once "too tyrannical" and "too lenient" for his critics. Secret societies sprang up, conspired against the government, and encouraged army deserters.

Both the Republicans and Democrats popularized other candidates. The Democrats nominated McClellan; the radical Republicans tried to run Frémont. The conservative Republicans wanted to nominate Salmon P. Chase, Lincoln's own secretary of the treasury. But the Republican convention that met in Baltimore, June 17, renamed its party the Union Party, nominated Abraham Lincoln, Republican, and Andrew Johnson, Democrat, on the same ticket, and pledged itself to Union interests.

By September Lincoln's chances had increased. Farragut had taken Mobile harbor in August. Sherman entered Atlanta, September 2, and Lincoln issued a proclamation of Thanksgiving on September 3, which lifted dissatisfaction. He was elected with 2,200,000 votes to McClellan's 1,802,000.

■ **SHERMAN'S MARCH TO THE SEA.**—Once inside Atlanta, from which the inhabitants had fled, Sherman destroyed the famous mills and factories, burned tons of cotton in the storehouses, and marched out, leaving the great Confederate industrial city a wasteland. He was eager to strike out for Savannah. "I can make this March," he told Grant; but even Grant, who ignored most hazards, was loath to let him cut loose from his base and advance 300 miles

into enemy territory without a food supply. Grant did consent, however, and Sherman handpicked his men. No sick, no laggards, no doubtful spirits, no baggage could impede this march.

On November 15, the 60,000 men began marching, foraging, singing through Georgia. They cut a swath 60 miles wide, destroyed 160 miles of railroad, and isolated Georgia's grain from Lee's army. They ate what they found, burned what remained, and arrived at Savannah on December 10. They entered the city on December 20.

1865. End of the War.—Sherman turned north in February, 1865, and headed for Columbia, South Carolina, which he took on February 17. South Carolina suffered horrors of destruction from the hands of this army, which had plundered its way through Georgia. Stories of homes in flame, families scattered and lost, as well as the news of military defeats, broke the remaining morale of the Confederate armies. Men deserted by the hundreds to find and help their families at home. Charleston had already fallen to the U.S. fleet in February. Sherman entered Fayetteville, North Carolina, March 11, and continued northeast toward Goldsboro. Johnston attacked him (March 19) but was forced to retire to Raleigh. Here Sherman moved in on him (April 10) and took the city on April 13. This was the end, but Johnston did not formally surrender until April 26 at Greensboro, North Carolina.

All this time Grant was besieging Petersburg. He had put Sheridan in command of the cavalry in the East in April, 1864, and Sheridan had distinguished himself in the Shenandoah Valley by a series of victories and an utter destruction of the region, which gave the Union permanent control of the valley.

Sheridan turned south again in the Spring to help Grant close in on Richmond, and both armies began to move on March 22, 1865. On April 1 Sheridan, in his victory over Lee's forces at Five Forks, took 6,000 prisoners and the South Side Railroad, cutting the last supply line of the Confederacy. On April 2 Petersburg was abandoned to Grant's advance. Richmond surrendered on April 3. Lee withdrew toward Lynchburg, the one avenue of refuge where the dwindling Confederate army might still hold the mountain passes. Lee was in definite retreat; his supplies had miscarried, and between April 1 and 7 he had lost 14,000 men. Sheridan intercepted him (April 8) at Appomattox Court House, and here Lee surrendered to Grant on the ninth.

■ **TWO GREAT MEN.**—No rancor marked the meeting of these two generals, who held each other in deep mutual respect and esteem. Grant talked on, unable to mention surrender to a foe "who had fought so long and valiantly." Lee had to broach the subject, and Grant's terms were generous. Surrender, unconditional, came first, but officers and men were to go home unmolested, no personal property was to be given up, and no swords were to be laid down. Each man could take his own horse or mule home for the spring plowing, and the starved southern army was to be fed at once, before disbanding. The war was over.

Why the North Won the War. — Many reasons account for the North's victory. Perhaps the most important was the North's overwhelming preponderance of war-making potential — people, wealth, and economic power. The victory, however, resulted from southern internal weaknesses as well. The Confederacy never really developed the nationalistic sentiment so necessary to wage effective warfare, and this contributed to the breakdown of the southern transportation and financial systems. Southern states had seceded from the Union in order to defend and enjoy states' rights, and thus preserve a way of life based upon Negro slavery. The very principle of states' rights, however, by its nature decentralizing and disintegrating, meant that the South could have no strong central government: an insurmountable handicap in waging war. Finally, while southern military leadership compared favorably with the Union's, it is conceded that its political leadership did not. Jefferson Davis lacked the statesmanlike qualities of Abraham Lincoln.

Lincoln's Death. — North and South were one again. The thirteenth amendment was passed in February, 1865; all slaves were free, and no human being could ever again be enslaved under the law of the United States. Washington was still rejoicing when Lincoln stepped into a box at Ford's Theater about ten o'clock the night of April 14 to watch the performance of *Our American Cousin.* A shot rang out. "*Sic semper tyrannis!*"[1] someone cried, "The South is avenged!" A man leaped to the stage, ran off behind the scenes and disappeared. John Wilkes Booth, once an actor, was the crazed, fanatic assassin of the one man who might have put through the difficult postwar policy of "malice toward none; charity for all." The war was over, but Lincoln was dead.

Results of the War. — The Civil War is a landmark in American history because of both the questions it settled and the new problems it created. Two consequences were most important. First, the Union victory, emphasizing the supremacy of the federal government over the states, ended the doctrines of nullification and secession and laid down the principle of an "indestructable union of indestructable states." Since that time the federal government has increasingly asserted its supremacy over the states. Second, the war transferred national political dominance from southern planters to northern industrialists, and so enhanced the prestige of the Republican party that it controlled the federal government until well into the twentieth century. As a result, businessmen so securely entrenched their national influence that they carried the nation into a new period of history, which was characterized principally by a trend toward industrialization and westward expansion.

[1] "*Thus ever to tyrants*" — the state motto of Virginia.

Andrew Johnson — 1865-1869

Had Lincoln lived, it is likely that he would have had difficulty implementing his plans for reconstructing the nation. Determined to reunite the nation as quickly as possible, and believing that this was an executive function, Lincoln had met congressional opposition to his "ten per cent plan" long before his death. This plan was for the organization of new state governments once ten per cent of the qualified voters had taken an oath of future loyalty to the United States. The radicals countered by passing the Wade-Davis Bill (July 8, 1864), which required a majority of voters to take an oath of past loyalty. When Lincoln pocket-vetoed this bill, he was castigated by the Wade-Davis Manifesto (August 5, 1864) for usurping congressional authority, indicating that a growing conflict was in process. In any event, whereas there was a possibility that Lincoln's political skill may have enabled him to avert such a struggle, Johnson's political ineptness made one inevitable. While to forget everything and *build* was to have been Lincoln's policy, Johnson held that "treason must be made odious, and traitors must be punished and impoverished." The radicals who had deplored Lincoln's leniency cheered this attitude, only to be dashed when Johnson reversed his position and (1) espoused the plans Lincoln had already put into operation in Virginia, Arkansas, Louisiana, and Tennessee, and (2) fought the drastic Reconstruction measures that Congress put through over his head.

The Presidential Plan. — Johnson's plan, like Lincoln's, was to restore civil government throughout the broken South as rapidly as possible. In May, 1865, he proclaimed a general amnesty, a full pardon to all who would take the oath of allegiance to the United States. There were, however, certain exceptions. Beginning with North Carolina, he started provisional governments in the seven southern states not already recognized by Lincoln. The provisional governments were to organize state conventions representing that percentage of the people eligible to vote, they were to embody in their constitutions the abolition of slavery, to ratify the thirteenth amendment, and to repudiate all debts incurred in the furtherance of rebellion. Johnson's plan differed from Lincoln's only in the enlargement of the list of exceptions. Lincoln's amnesty was withheld from civil and military Confederate officers. To these leaders Johnson added "all persons whose taxable property is over twenty thousand dollars," for Johnson was a poor white and small farmer, bred to jealousy and distrust of the plantation aristocracy. By fall, 1865, all the southern states except Texas were organized and ready to send representatives to Congress. The only difficulty, however, was the fact that these reorganized southern state governments were largely controlled by former Confederates.

Congress Steps In. — Most southern states also passed odious "black codes," which denied the freedmen many rights of citizenship, including suffrage. These codes also forbade them from carrying arms, required that they serve an apprenticeship while under age, governed their employment by strict labor contracts, and instituted curfews; thus the Negro was once again relegated to social, economic, and political inferiority. Moreover, by ratifying the thirteenth amendment, which abolished slavery, and thus increased their "free population," the southern states were entitled to more congressional representation. Republicans, primarily the representatives of business and industrial interests, were unwilling to be outnumbered and subsequently overruled in Congress by western and southern agrarian-minded Democrats. They therefore decided that the South could reenter the Union only after it enfranchised the Negro, who no doubt would vote Republican. As a result, when Congress reconvened in 1866 it refused to seat the representatives from the reorganized southern states, many of whom had been Confederate officers. Because of the black codes and the fear of excessive representation, Congress refused to admit the new southern representatives.

Reconstruction Legislation. — Congress immediately appointed a joint Committee on Reconstruction to inquire into the loyalty of the South and its fitness to be represented. It passed a bill prolonging and enlarging the powers of the Freedman's Bureau — a government organ that had been created in March, 1865, to uplift and educate the freedmen, to assign them to abandoned lands, and to protect them in their labor contracts and their local troubles. Its existence had originally been limited to one year, and Johnson vetoed the measure to extend its time of powers.

Congress answered the veto with the Civil Rights Bill, passing it over Johnson's next veto (April, 1865). This act raised the Negroes to full and equal citizenship with the whites, and entitled them to federal protection against discriminating laws, thus nullifying the black codes. The fourteenth amendment, designed to make permanent the proposition of the Civil Rights Bill, was sent to the states for ratification in June. In July, the passage of a new Freedman's Bureau Bill, also over Johnson's veto, continued that institution for two more years and extended federal protection to Negroes. While the Bureau engaged in some corruption, it nevertheless did a great deal to implement the lofty program for which it was established — to guide the Negro in the difficult process of social readjustment to freedom.

Fourteenth Amendment. — The fourteenth amendment, passed by Congress in June, 1866, gave full citizenship to the freedmen, reduced the representation in Congress of any state denying the franchise to any male citizen twenty-one years old, and disqualified for office (until Congress should pardon them) the leaders of the South in the war. Ratification of the fourteenth amendment became the price of readmission to representation in Congress, but it was too high a price for the proud old order; the South chose to remain un-

M. BRADY

LIBRARY OF CONGRESS   BETTMANN ARCHIVE

ANDREW JOHNSON
(1865–1869)

His flair for oratory got him into politics, where he battled his way to the Senate. He had courage enough to fight the South, but the North saw him as a "turncoat." Although honest and resolute, Johnson lacked political skill and self-control. In 1868, conflicts with Congress resulted in his impeachment; the Senate, however, acquitted him (*above*). His presidency was beset by difficult Reconstruction problems. Hordes of carpetbaggers (*right*) swarmed from the North into the South, taking economic and political advantage of the confusion and disruption left in the aftermath of the war.

represented. Every southern state defeated the amendment except Tennessee, which was restored to statehood; its senators and representatives re-entered Congress on July 24, 1866.

Johnson's Failure.—Meanwhile, the investigative Joint Committee on Reconstruction reported outrages of various types, instability of state conventions, and defiance of the thirteenth amendment.

Johnson had alienated Congress by opposing and vetoing every extreme Reconstruction measure Congress put through. In the 1866 congressional campaign he hoped to win enough Democrats and conservative Republicans so that the new Congress would support his policies, but he lost his own cause by intemperate and abusive attacks on Congress and his personal enemies. Johnson estranged both the politicians and the public, and brought discredit and distrust upon himself. The new Congress became more anti-Johnson and anti-southern than the old.

Reconstruction Act, 1867.—As a result of the 1866 elections, Congress finally seized control of Reconstruction. Over presidential vetoes, Republican legislators passed a series of bills to protect the freedmen and extend to them all the rights and privileges of citizenship. Perhaps the most significant measure, and one that dealt the death blow to presidential reconstruction, came when Congress overrode Johnson's veto and passed the Reconstruction Act.

The Reconstruction Act (March 2, 1867) put the South under military rule (with the exception of Tennessee). The ten ex-Confederate states were divided into five military districts, and the mili-

tary commander of each district was put in direct control of Reconstruction. He was to register the voters, excluding prominent southern leaders and including all other male citizens "of whatever race, color, or previous condition of servitude." To these voters was entrusted the election of a state convention to frame a state constitution. If this constitution satisfied Congress and if its legislature ratified the fourteenth amendment, then that state was to be readmitted to the Union.

Other congressional acts, such as the Command of the Army Act, which gave Congress control of the army, and the Tenure of Office Act, which denied the president the right to dismiss civilian government officials without the consent of the Senate, stripped Johnson of power. Over the appointment of military commanders to the southern military districts Johnson came into direct conflict with Secretary of War Edwin M. Stanton, removed him from his post, and appointed General Grant in his place. As the president's act was a violation of the Tenure of Office Act, the Senate would not approve the appointment of Grant, and Stanton was returned to his post. Within five months Stanton was again discharged.

Impeachment and Trial of Johnson.—Congress again declared Stanton's removal illegal, and the House of Representatives passed articles of impeachment against Johnson (February 2, 1868) in which all of the president's "misdemeanors and crimes" were recited. In the spring of 1868, the Senate sat as a jury to try the impeachment, with Chief Justice Salmon P. Chase presiding. Thirty-five senators voted Johnson guilty, 19 voted for his acquittal.

Had the vote been 36 to 18, the president would have been removed. Johnson's milder policy had been defeated and Congress continued its own severe course of Reconstruction.

Reconstruction, 1867-1876.—The period of Reconstruction, frequently called by southerners the "reign of terror," was, in fact, a remarkably calm and prosperous period in southern history. The new electorate of freedmen proved extremely modest in their demands, unaggressive in their conduct, and deferential in their attitude. Although Negroes held a variety of political offices, in no state did they hold place and power in any way approaching their actual numbers and relative voting strength. The success that a people of such meager resources and limited experience enjoyed in producing so many honest and capable leaders and public servants is impressive.

In addition, despite some shortcomings, the "radical" governments were more democratic than any the South had ever known. The social history of the South shows that during Reconstruction many sane and constructive acts dealing with educational, constitutional, economic, and political reforms were passed. These advances, which, significantly, were not later repealed, helped bring many backward southern states in line with the progressive spirit of the late nineteenth century. The ideal of social services for the public welfare and the extension of democracy was brought to the South during this period, and not at a particularly high financial or moral burden. In short, most of the frequently condemned aspects of "radical Reconstruction" were merely the mani-

M. BRADY

ULYSSES S. GRANT
(1869–1877)

Grant was a thoroughly relentless general who rose quickly in the Civil War but disliked his soldiering and was at heart a pacifist. During Reconstruction, the conservative whites looked with disgust upon their nearly half-Negro legislatures and many turned to the Ku Klux Klan, the terrorist organization that is pictured planning a murder (*left*). On October 8, 1871, fire gripped Chicago (*above*) for two days, consuming the entire business section of the city at a tremendous cost in both lives and property.

PICTURES: LIBRARY OF CONGRESS

festations of a much-needed democratic revolution in a region habituated to aristocratic control.

Other Events. — Alaska was purchased from Russia (1867) for $7,200,000. Secretary of State William H. Seward was severely censured in many quarters for the extravagant price paid for "500,000 square miles of ice and polar bears," but "Seward's Folly" proved a profitable government investment.

Nebraska was admitted to the Union in March 1, 1867.

Election of 1868. — The Republicans unanimously nominated Ulysses S. Grant; the Democrats nominated Horatio Seymour. Grant received 214 electoral votes, Seymour, 80. For the first time a large number of former Negro slaves voted in a presidential election.

Ulysses S. Grant — 1869-1877

Grant came into office beloved and acclaimed, the hero of the war, a military genius, but a political novice. His administration epitomized the new relationship between business and politics that emerged after 1865. From the close of the Civil War until the end of the nineteenth century, the nation's political history declined. During these years the leading political parties ignored the vital issues facing the American people. The true national leaders, the captains of industry, were primarily concerned with perpetuating a *laissez-faire* political system that left them free to exploit the nation's abundant natural resources and to amass huge personal fortunes.

The deterioration of American politics was clearly shown in Grant's administration. Politically inexperienced and worshipful of wealthy industrialists, Grant, although personally honest, unwittingly became a tool of unscrupulous businessmen and crooked politicians. Yet the nation continued to prosper, and although his record as president caused some dissatisfaction, even within his own party, Grant was reelected in 1872.

Fifteenth Amendment. — In March, 1870, the fifteenth amendment, which guaranteed the Negro the right to vote, became law. The four states still out of the Union (Virginia, Mississippi, Texas, and Georgia) were compelled to ratify this amendment to be readmitted.

Ku Klux Klan. — Reconstruction continued apace during Grant's two administrations. The South, determined to rise in arms and overthrow congressional control, was prevented from doing so only by the United States army, which still held encampments in the region. Southerners organized the Ku Klux Klan to intimidate Negroes and their supporters, in the hope of preventing them from voting and using their other rights and privileges. Klansmen, white-hooded and white-robed, frequently met at night to burn crosses, and to frighten, beat, and sometimes lynch more aggressive Negroes. Other secret organizations swept through the South. Local bands of vigilantes unified by the single aim of terrorizing the freedmen and their sympathizers sprang up everywhere.

The Ku Klux Acts (1871 and 1872) were passed for the suppression of this group. Grant suspended the writ of *habeas corpus* in some sections of the South, and federal troops arrested hundreds of the Klansmen, but the movement could not be stopped.

End of Reconstruction. — The radical Republicans were already beginning to lose their hold on the South when the Amnesty Act of 1872, which reduced the number of southerners banned from holding public office to approximately 500, hastened the turnover. The gradual return of an all-white government in the South and the virtual reenslavement of the freedmen came about through bribery and reward in elections, force, bloodshed, and intimidation. In short, Reconstruction did not fail because of the shortcomings and corruption of the state and local governments in which the Negro participated, as some believe. Rather, it failed because of the lessening of federal concern for the Negro and, more important, because many southerners would not tolerate complete racial equality, which sometimes meant Negro rule. As a result, the "natural order" was gradually restored in Virginia, North Carolina, and Georgia. By 1876 only Florida, Louisiana, and South Carolina were still under federal control; but the contested federal election of that year gave the South the opportunity to bring a complete end to reconstruction.

Foreign Policy. — The outstanding international event of Grant's administration was the conclusion of the Treaty of Washington, signed in May, 1871, which settled the Alabama Claims: the losses suffered by the United States at the hands of the Confederate cruiser *Alabama*, which was built in England during the Civil War. The United States government demanded that England

LIBRARY OF CONGRESS

U.S. DEPT. OF INTERIOR

NEW YORK PUBLIC LIBRARY

RUTHERFORD B. HAYES
(1877–1881)

Hayes had a smooth, untarnished career, and his confirmed reputation for honesty and efficiency made him the best Republican of his day. His wife, known as "Lemona de Lucy," would never serve alcohol in the White House. When railroad strikes caused nation-wide rioting, soldiers were sent to quell the fighting, but often they were turned upon by angry mobs (*left*). Thomas Edison was the genius of the day, and this photograph (*above*), taken May 13, 1880, documented the first running, at Menlo Park, N.J., of his latest invention, the electric railroad.

pay for the damage caused by the cruiser. The question was submitted to a tribunal of five nations, which decreed that England pay the United States $15,500,000.

Civil Service Reform.—The custom whereby the president, upon taking office, place new men in all government positions, had resulted in a vast amount of corruption by the time of Grant's accession in 1869. In 1871, the pressure of public opinion caused Congress to pass the first law of civil service reform, authorizing the president to organize a system for regulating appointments to minor civil service positions. The president appointed a commission that arranged competitive examinations for applicants to the civil service. This method of appointment was in practice for three years, when the influence of politicians in Congress succeeded in withdrawing financial support from the commission.

Reelection.—As Grant's first term drew to a close, many Republicans believed he could not be reelected because he was unpopular in the South for his harsh Reconstruction methods and because the dominant element of his party was corrupt. The regular Union-Republican convention gave him the nomination, but a convention of liberal Republicans nominated Horace Greeley, whom the Democrats also named. Greeley died after the election and before the meeting of the electoral college; the Democrats then gave his successor, Hendricks, 42 electoral votes; however, Grant was elected with 286 votes.

Panic of 1873.—The postwar period of overexpansion in industry, overinvest-

ment in railroads and new lands, unstable currency, and overexpansion of credit ended in a sweep of failures in banking, railroads, and private businesses. A serious panic resulted. Congress tried to stay the tide of national insolvency with the Inflation Bill (1874), ordering the printing of $400,000,000 in unsecured paper money; but Grant vetoed the bill. To bring financial order out of the existing chaos, the Resumption Act was passed (1875), providing for resumption of specie payments in 1879.

The Scandals of 1873-1875.—Grant's administration was marred by the first and worst political and financial graft brought to public knowledge. Time and again Grant was implicated, though innocent, because his own forthrightness made it impossible for him to suspect dishonor in others and his loyalty made it impossible for him to believe evil of his friends. His second term was darkened by charges that congressmen had been bribed with stock of the Crédit Mobilier, a railroad construction company. Investigation left two prominent Republican congressmen and Vice-President Schuyler Colfax under suspicion.

Soon after the Crédit Mobilier scandal, the "Salary Grab" Act (1873) increased the salaries of the president, the cabinet, federal judges, senators, and representatives. It provided increases in pay for the terms congressmen were then serving; thus they had raised their own pay. So great was the outcry against this "back-pay grab" that there was an undignified scramble in Congress to return the back-pay increases and to reduce the raised congressional salaries.

■ **THE WHISKY RING.**—In 1875, the existence of the Whisky Ring was first

disclosed. This was an agreement between distillers of whisky and internal revenue officers to rob the government of the tax on whisky. Suspicion centered about Grant's private secretary, Orville E. Babcock, as one of the ringleaders, but his guilt was not proved and he was acquitted.

By the end of the second term so many frauds had been brought to light and so many of the suspects were intimates of Grant that extreme reaction and opposition ensued. Grant's secretary of war, William W. Belknap, was impeached on the charge of selling army supply contracts and appointments to frontier trading posts. Belknap resigned to escape trial, a move that did not improve Grant's public image.

■ **TWEED RING.**—Fraud and corruption were not confined to the federal government. New York City, run by the scandalous Tweed Ring, was a hotbed of political corruption. Under the leadership of Boss Tweed, this society of political crooks had been ruling the elections of New York State and influencing those of the nation since before 1860. With headquarters at Tammany Hall, the Ring's strength lay in its control over the foreign vote and in the band of thugs it employed to cast many times its given number of votes. The corrupt politicians influenced the lawmaking of the state by bribing legislators and amassed great fortunes by appropriating public funds.

Other Events.—Grant favored the annexation of Santo Domingo when that small state asked to be admitted to the Union, but the Senate defeated the proposal.

Alexander Graham Bell completed the invention of the telephone and secured patents on his invention in 1876.

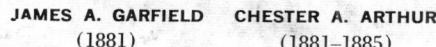

FOR PRESIDENT — FOR VICE-PRESIDENT

UNION & LIBERTY NOW & FOR EVER — GEN. JAS. A. GARFIELD OF OHIO — E PLURIBUS UNUM — GEN. CHESTER A. ARTHUR OF NEW YORK — LOYALTY-JUSTICE PUBLIC FAITH

LIBRARY OF CONGRESS

JAMES A. GARFIELD   CHESTER A. ARTHUR
(1881)   (1881–1885)

Garfield was the highly-esteemed leading Republican in the House. His administration was barely underway when a disappointed office seeker shot him. He left the White House to convalesce (*lower right*), but died two months later. When Arthur became president he worked for civil service reform. In 1883 Chester Arthur and Grover Cleveland took the first walk over the newly-constructed Brooklyn Bridge (*lower left*).

BETTMANN ARCHIVE

LIBRARY OF CONGRESS

The telephone attracted much attention at the Centennial Exposition held in Philadelphia that year in commemoration of the one-hundredth anniversary of the signing of the Declaration of Independence.

Colorado was admitted to the Union in 1876.

Election of 1876.—Intense feeling and violent action marked this election. Grant's friends tried to secure his nomination for a third term, but without success. Rutherford B. Hayes of Ohio was nominated by the Republicans, Samuel J. Tilden of New York by the Democrats.

On the basis of the election returns, a majority of the electoral college was Democratic, but charges of fraud were raised in three states. An electoral commission (containing eight Republicans and seven Democrats) was named by Congress to decide the contest. Hayes, due to a political deal made with southern "redeemers," was declared the victor, with 185 electoral votes to 184 for Tilden. The deal involved a promise by Hayes to (1) remove the remaining federal troops in the South, (2) give a lucrative cabinet position to a southerner, and (3) be "exceptionally liberal" in bestowing federal funds on the South for internal improvements and for railroad construction; these promises were made in return for support by southern members of the electoral commission.

Rutherford B. Hayes—1877-1881

Hayes carried out the promises he and the Republican party had made to the South's new leaders, men who saw the future of their region intimately linked with the triumphant northern business interests. Hayes appointed David M. Key, an ex-Confederate officer, as postmaster general, Congress prepared itself to extend federal subsidies to promoters of southern railroads, and Hayes removed the remaining federal troops from the South. Thus Reconstruction came to an end and "redemption" started—the former Confederate states were restored to white rule. The 1877 election promises laid the political and psychological foundation for reunion and marked the abandonment of principles for a return to expediency in determining the future of the four million southern freedmen.

Hayes was ardently interested in civil service reform but he accomplished little in this field. Instead, he alienated party leaders on both sides by his independence in removing certain ineffectual officers and by his refusal to take care of others who felt they had done him campaign service.

Labor Troubles.—Hayes inherited the aftermath of the Panic of 1873. Business was in a condition of stagnation, and thousands of laborers were unemployed or at work only part of the time. The unrest induced railroad strikes and riots all over the United States. Federal troops were required to maintain order.

The Bland-Allison Act.—To placate both clamoring, debt-ridden farmers interested in inflating the currency supply, and western silver miners desirous of selling their silver to the government since its value on the open market had fallen below the government price, in 1878 Congress passed the Bland-Allison Act. This measure authorized the government to purchase $2,000,000

worth of silver bullion a month to be coined into silver dollars. It was passed over Hayes's veto, but the revival of trade, plus the sound sense of Secretary of the Treasury John Sherman, brought hard money from abroad. By January 1, 1879, when specie payments were resumed, the United States had an excess reserve, and greenbacks were equal in value to gold.

Election of 1880.—Hayes refused to be a candidate for reelection, for he was aware that strong elements of his party did not want another reform administration. The Republicans nominated James A. Garfield of Ohio for president and Chester A. Arthur of New York for vice-president. The Democrats named General Winfield S. Hancock, of Civil War fame. The Republican ticket received 214 electoral votes; the Democratic, 155.

James A. Garfield—1881

The "Stalwarts," the pro-Grant wing of the Republican party, had supported Garfield for president only because they expected a major share of patronage. Garfield's choice for collector of the port of New York so angered Senators Conkling and Platt of New York, both prominent Stalwarts, that they resigned (May, 1881). They did not receive the justifying reelection favors they demanded, and bitter feuds raged in the party for many months.

Assassination of Garfield.—To what extent the viciousness accompanying the spoils system could go was shown on July 2, 1881, when the president was shot by Charles J. Guiteau, a disappointed office seeker. Garfield died on September 19.

GROVER CLEVELAND
(1885–1889, first term)

As mayor of Buffalo, Cleveland, a Democrat, so ably carried out reforms that he was elected governor of New York in 1882. He ignored Tammany, the New York City Democratic machine, and was supported by the better elements of both parties. In 1886, at a meeting of anarchist labor leaders in Chicago (*below*), a bomb exploded amidst policemen, killing seven; this helped to delay the eight-hour day a generation. Reform movements were gaining momentum, and it was common to see women, called suffragettes, demonstrating for voting rights (*right*).

PICTURES: LIBRARY OF CONGRESS

Chester A. Arthur – 1881-1885

Chester A. Arthur, vice-president, stepped into office and fought against the spoils system. A National Civil Service Reform League was organized (1881). In 1883 a law providing for government employees to be placed in classified lists, requiring appointments to be made by competitive examination, and forbidding recommendations to be made by congressmen was passed.

Other Legislation. – As early as 1870, many American laborers, resentful of foreign competition for jobs, began agitating for revision of the national policy of free and unrestricted immigration. Due specifically to the demands of unemployed native workers in California, the Chinese Exclusion Act was passed in 1882. The measure prohibited Chinese from entering the United States for ten years, and denied the right of naturalization to Chinese immigrants already in this country, most of whom were living in California. The Edmunds Anti-Polygamy Act (directed particularly against the Mormons in Utah), prohibiting the practice of polygamy in the United States, was also passed in 1882.

Other Events. – A great engineering triumph was the completion of the Brooklyn Bridge in 1883. In 1884, Alaska was organized as a district.

Election of 1884. – Arthur sought the presidential nomination, but was defeated in the Republican convention by James G. Blaine of Maine, secretary of state under Garfield and an active candidate in two preceding Republican conventions. The Democrats nominated

Grover Cleveland, whose career as governor of New York strongly recommended him; Cleveland was committed to the "new issues born of time and progress." Cleveland won with 219 electoral votes to 182 for Blaine.

Grover Cleveland – 1885-1889

Cleveland came into office as a champion of civil service reform, but on this issue he satisfied nobody completely. He did not dismiss *every* Republican officeholder in the civil service system, as his Democratic supporters wished, nor did he make all his appointments strictly nonpartisan. His policy had the good effect, however, of compelling the Republicans to decry the spoils system and of curbing the political activity of many holding civil service positions. The Tenure of Office Act was repealed during his administration.

Legislation. – The death of Vice-President Hendricks prompted the passage of the Presidential Succession Act (1886), which declared the line of succession to the presidency: first, the vice-president, and then, in order, the secretaries of state, treasury, and war, the attorney general, and the secretaries of the navy and the interior. In 1947, at President Truman's insistence, Congress passed a new Presidential Succession Act that placed the speaker of the House of Representatives and the president pro tempore of the Senate ahead of the secretary of state in the line of presidential succession after the vice-president.

The Interstate Commerce Act of February, 1877, was an attempt to correct the abuses by which the railroad com-

panies were growing rich. This act forbade the railroads to give rebates to favored shippers, to pool their freight revenues, or to charge relatively more for a short haul than for a long haul, and it declared that all rates and tariffs must be kept public. A permanent but relatively powerless Interstate Commerce Commission was appointed to investigate railroad management and fine offenders, and to work out a system of railroad accounting. With very little power of its own, the commission had to rely upon the courts to enforce its action, but it was not sufficiently supported. The Supreme Court, for example, handed down decisions favorable to the railroad interests in fifteen of the sixteen cases it reviewed between 1887 and 1905. For this reason, as well as the fact that most administrations at the time favored big business and frequently staffed the commission with conservative members, the measure failed. Nevertheless, it had significance in that it was the first important national departure during this period from the principle of *laissez-faire*.

Labor Troubles. – Due to the industrial revolution and the development of the corporate system in post Civil War America, individual workers, dependent for their livelihood upon meager daily wages, could not expect to bargain on equal terms with wealthy and powerful employers. Only by organizing and presenting their demands as a group could the workers hope to secure higher wages, a shorter working day, improved working conditions, and protection from being fired without just cause. Whereas in the early nineteenth century there were some small, local unions, during the second half of the

LIBRARY OF CONGRESS

BENJAMIN HARRISON
(1889–1893)

The grandson of the ninth president studied law, rose to brigadier general in the Civil War, and gained the presidency through the electoral college. His regime was honest and free from scandal, though responsive to wealthy "special interest" groups. In 1889, the worst peacetime disaster occurred when the Conemaugh Dam broke, flooding Johnstown, Pennsylvania (below). The first great strike, in 1892 at Homestead, Pa., saw ten killed; then some 300 armed Pinkerton men surrendered to strikers (left).

BETTMANN ARCHIVE

LIBRARY OF CONGRESS

century strong national labor unions grew. Employers, unwilling to accede to the demands of organized labor, did all they could to crush these rapidly rising organizations. With the courts and the federal government on their side, business leaders managed to break most strikes that occurred during these troubled years—frequently, however, only after the outbreak of violence and the destruction of both property and lives. The Knights of Labor, an idealistic national industrial union open to all laborers, had a membership that totaled close to a million in 1886; by the end of the century, however, it had declined. Strongest among the remaining labor organizations was the practical but conservative American Federation of Labor, a trade union of skilled workers under the leadership of Samuel Gompers. Formed in 1886, the AF of L was devoted solely to improving the working conditions of its members.

Pension Vetoes.—By 1885 there were 345,125 war veterans receiving pensions from the United States. Among those legally entitled to government aid were many who had been dishonorably discharged from the army, and even some deserters. Cleveland vetoed 233 private pension bills and won the name of the "veto president" and a reputation for being anti-veteran.

Tariff Issue.—Cleveland devoted his annual message in 1887 to the tariff question. There was a surplus of $140,000,000 in the treasury and, according to Cleveland, high protective tariffs were no longer necessary or expedient. Although he advised tariff revisions in order to reduce the revenue, he did not propose "free trade," as is often thought. The Mills Bill passed the House (1888) and provided for a reduction in protective duties; but the Republican Senate made a counter-proposition to keep down the revenue by eliminating taxes on tobacco and limiting the importation of all articles produced in the United States. The tariff question was finally resolved in the McKinley Tariff Act.

Election of 1888.—The election campaign centered on the tariff question. Cleveland was renominated by the Democrats; Benjamin Harrison was nominated by the Republicans. Capitalizing on manufacturers' fears of tariff reduction, Harrison supporters raised a vast campaign fund from industrialists. This, plus veterans' resentment of Cleveland's pension vetoes and the loss of liberal support because of the generally conservative nature of his administration, cost Cleveland the election. Harrison received 233 electoral votes to 168 for Cleveland.

After the passage of the McKinley Tariff Act in 1890, there was a movement to renominate Cleveland. In 1892 he again became president.

Benjamin Harrison—1889-1893

Benjamin Harrison was elected in a campaign tariff fight and political turnover, which convinced him and his Republican supporters that the people wanted a protective tariff. Harrison's administration passed the McKinley Tariff Act, which put higher duties on imports for the protection of American industries than any yet known in the history of the country. The tariff put staggering duties on almost everything that could be produced in the United States, including agricultural products. This raised the prices of so many necessities of everyday life that "the high cost of living" became for the first time a bugaboo of American life; this also contributed to the defeat of the Republicans in the next election.

Legislation.—To keep another of its campaign promises to the people—that it would restrain the growing power of the great trusts that were stifling small business—the Republican Congress passed the Sherman Antitrust Act, July, 1890. This act outlawed and penalized the big monopolies insofar as they interfered with interstate or international commerce. It was aimed at the sugar trust, the Standard Oil trust, and Armour's meatpacking company, and the huge, nonpartisan vote with which it passed revealed how widespread was the oppression felt from monopoly prices. Unfortunately, the Sherman Antitrust Law was not rigidly enforced, and the trusts soon devised loopholes for reducing competition.

Another important law of 1890 was the Sherman Silver Purchase Act, which bound the treasury to purchase 4,500,000 ounces of silver each month and to issue in payment treasury certificates redeemable in gold or silver. This double standard of currency, called "bimetallism," became an important political issue.

Foreign Affairs.—Since industrialization led to a demand for foreign markets and raw materials, it was partly responsible for a transformation in American foreign policy. Every year after the Civil War the United States played a larger role in world affairs, until by the turn of the century it had become a

LIBRARY OF CONGRESS

NIAGARA MOHAWK POWER CORPORATION

GROVER CLEVELAND
(1893–1897, second term)

In his second term, Cleveland was elected by an astounding majority. But public approval was short-lived, as the world-wide depression seemed to have crossed the ocean. Chicago hosted the world with the Fair of 1893 (*above left*), but in 1894, Jacob S. Coxey led an "army" of unemployed to Washington (*above right*) seeking work and federal aid. Niagara's power was harnessed in 1896 (*right*).

leading world power and an imperialistic nation with possessions scattered all over the globe. On the whole, Americans were more interested in Latin America and Asia than in Europe or Africa, for these underdeveloped areas represented the best potential markets for American manufactured articles and investment capital. In 1889, Germany, England, and the United States established a joint control over the Samoan Islands, to continue for ten years. The monarchy in Hawaii was overthrown and a republic set up, largely through the efforts of American businessmen who wanted Hawaii annexed to the United States. Harrison prepared an annexation treaty, which was later rejected by Cleveland on the grounds that the U.S. had taken too serious a part in the revolution.

Other Events. — The first Pan-American Conference met in Washington, D.C., in 1889 to encourage good will and reciprocity between the United States and the South American governments.

In November, 1889, North and South Dakota, Montana, and Washington were admitted to the Union; in July, 1890, Idaho and Wyoming also became states.

Billion Dollar Congress. — The Republican Congress lost no time spending the surplus in the treasury. It reduced the excess from $10,000,000 in 1892 to $2,000,000 in 1893, and was therefore dubbed by the Democrats the "billion dollar Congress." By the Dependent Pension Act it granted enough additional pensions to double the number of Civil War veterans and dependents on the list. It appropriated large sums for river and harbor improvement, and

authorized the building of a new navy as speedily as possible; the United States jumped from twelfth to fifth place among world navies.

More Unrest. — Increasing discontent pervaded the labor element throughout the country. A terrible strike in the steel works at Homestead, Pennsylvania (June, 1892), was handled with ruthless bloodshed, thus adding to the public sentiment against the administration. The western farmers, too, were short of money and saddled with mortgages. They wanted lower freight rates and more silver put into circulation. Their strong influence was channeled into the People's Party (or Populists, which, in part, had sprung from the farmers' alliances).

Election of 1892. — During the next presidential campaign, the Democrats vehemently attacked the McKinley Tariff; it was "fraud and robbery" and the root of all evil. The Populists agitated for a return of the government to the hands of the "plain people." Grover Cleveland was routed out of private life and nominated on the Democratic ticket, with Adlai E. Stevenson (1835-1914) for vice-president. Harrison again became the Republican nominee. The Populists named James B. Weaver of Iowa, who polled more than 1,000,000 votes. Cleveland was elected with 277 electoral votes to 145 for Harrison and 22 for Weaver.

Grover Cleveland — 1893-1897

Cleveland walked into the midst of the financial havoc wrought in Harrison's administration, and received all the blame for it. He had promised to revise the McKinley Tariff, but by the

time he secured the passage of the Wilson Bill (1893), which increased the number of free entries and reduced several high duties, it was no longer wise to reduce the tariffs. The treasury had a deficit, not a surplus, and drastic measures had to be taken to pull the country out of panic and depression.

Panic of 1893. — Panic was at hand. The gold reserve in the treasury was only $80,000,000, far too low for the United States to continue redeeming currency in gold. Cleveland called a special session of Congress in August, 1893, to repeal the Silver Purchase Act that was depleting the reserve. He was bitterly opposed by the silver contingent of his own party. The act was repealed, but no other legislation was passed to protect the reserve.

People began to hoard gold. Businesses failed and banks closed everywhere. National bank deposits fell $378,000,000. The silver dollar dropped from 67 to 60 cents in value; the western silver mines closed. By winter (1893-94) thousands were jobless, hundreds hungry. "Coxey's army," a spectacular horde of the unemployed, marched to Washington to plead redress. They arrived in front of the White House on May 1, 1894, but instead of aiding them, Clevelend had them arrested for walking on the grass.

Pullman Company workers in Chicago went on strike in protest against wage cuts. The strike spread to 27 states and involved 23 railroads. Railroad property was burned, trains were stopped, and mail was obstructed. Governor John Altgeld of Illinois, who sympathized with the strikers, would do nothing; but President Cleveland sent federal troops to quell the agitation and

LIBRARY OF CONGRESS

CULVER

WILLIAM McKINLEY
(1897–1901)

William Jennings Bryan, the Progressive Democrat candidate, alarmed the business community (represented by the spindletop oil rigs throughout Texas, *above*) with his opposition to tariffs and the repeal of the Sherman Silver Purchase Act—and the election went to McKinley. The main event in McKinley's prosperous administration, the Spanish-American War, was touched off by the sinking of the battleship *Maine* (*right*). The president is shown (*above left*) at work with his secrètary Cortelyou in 1897. In 1901, McKinley was shot by anarchist Leon Czolgosz.

LIBRARY OF CONGRESS

keep the mail moving. The Supreme Court issued an injunction forbidding interference with the movements of trains. Bloodshed marked clashes between the troops and the strikers. Quiet was restored by the end of July, 1894, but Cleveland's interference cost him the support of organized labor and its sympathizers.

Wilson-Gorman Tariff Act.—Attempting to fulfill their promise to reduce the high tariffs of the McKinley Tariff Act, the Democrats framed the Wilson-Gorman Tariff Bill, which allowed wool, coal, lumber, iron ore, and raw sugar to come into the country free. It reduced the duties on silks and cottons and provided for a two per cent income tax on all incomes over $4,000. The bill passed the House (February, 1894) but met serious trouble in the Republican Senate. There it was changed and amended beyond recognition: duties were put on sugar, coal, and iron ore. All the Changes were suspiciously favorable to "big interests." When finally passed, it differed little from the McKinley Tariff Act. Cleveland would not sign it, but he let it become law. By that time the deficit in the treasury prohibited any lower tariff.

Foreign Affairs.—Great Britain declared that the United States had no right to invoke the Monroe Doctrine in a boundary dispute between Venezuela and British Guiana. Cleveland demanded that the quarrel be settled by arbitration and for a time there was danger of war, but the British government finally agreed to arbitrate.

Election of 1896.—By repealing the Silver Purchase Act, Grover Cleveland had

alienated the pro-silver element of his own party and the western and southern Populists who still thought free silver the cure-all for bad times. Labor was hostile toward him because of his interference in the Pullman strike. Republicans and Democrats alike turned against him for the four bond issues with which he strove to keep the U.S. gold reserve up to its $100,000,000 mark.

The election campaign of 1896 centered entirely on the silver issue. The Democratic convention, captivated by a former congressman from Nebraska, William Jennings Bryan, and his impassioned free-silver declamations, nominated him for the presidency. The Republicans, nominating William McKinley of Ohio, directly opposed the free-silver platform and supported the gold standard. "Back to prosperity" and "Vote for McKinley and go back to work" were the slogans. McKinley was elected with 271 electoral votes to Bryan's 176.

William McKinley — 1897-1901

Dingley Tariff. 1897.—After the Senate's revision of the Wilson-Gorman Bill during Cleveland's administration, no additional tariff was really needed to bring in revenue. The business interests that had put the Republicans in power, however, were demanding that the government go through the motions of victory, and so the Dingley Tariff Bill was framed and became law (July, 1897). It differed little from the old McKinley Tariff of 1890, and the duties were so high that foreign trade was almost prohibited. The clauses giving the president power to make limited reciprocity treaties were intended to temper the burden of the high rates.

Seven such reciprocity treaties were prepared, but the Senate refused to ratify them.

Cuban Insurrection.—An outburst of American interest and sympathy met the Cuban uprising against Spain; there was indignation over Spain's inhuman herding of Cuban noncombatants into garrisoned towns, where they died by the thousands.

Spain had long been enriching itself at the expense of Cuban agriculture, and its rigid rule in the island resulted in an inevitable people's uprising for self-government. After the Ten Years' War (1868-78), Cuba had won certain grants and concessions from Spain that were less strictly enforced as time went by. Another insurrection occurred in 1895. The natives could not cope with professional Spanish troops, and guerilla warfare raged (1896-97). Spain put General Weyler in charge of the island in 1896; his pitiless system of concentrating the people inside the towns to starve earned him the title of "Butcher."

American sympathy with the native uprising was not at all lessened by the fact that $50,000,000 of American capital was tied up in Cuba. In addition, many important and influential Americans, most notably Assistant Secretary of the Navy Theodore Roosevelt and Senator Henry Cabot Lodge, wished to oust Spain from the Western Hemisphere and, for economic and strategic reasons, to acquire her possessions both in the Caribbean and the Pacific. There was much talk of intervention, but strict neutrality was maintained. Crises soon arose, however. A letter from the Spanish minister to a Cuban friend, mentioning

McKinley in insulting terms, was published in February, 1898. The U.S. battleship *Maine* was blown up in Havana harbor (February 15) and 266 American sailors were killed.

Although it was never proven that Spain was responsible for the *Maine* disaster, and in fact there was good reason to believe she was innocent, newspapers played up the incident until the American public was eager for war. European powers intervened to prevent it. On April 10 the United States was informed that Spain had suspended hostilities in Cuba, but on April 11 McKinley asked Congress for the right "to intervene" and received enthusiastic consent. On April 19 Congress passed resolutions (1) declaring Cuba free and independent, (2) asserting the right of the United States to demand that Spain Relinquish the Island, (3) disclaiming any intentions beyond the restoration of peace, and (4) declaring its "determination, when that is accomplished, to leave the government and control of the island to its people." On April 24 Spain declared war; on April 25 the United States resolved that a state of war had existed since April 21.

Spanish-American War. 1898. — Activities began at once. Captain William Thomas Sampson, in charge of the North Atlantic squadron, was ordered to blockade Cuba and head off the Spanish fleet known to be en route from the Cape Verde Islands since April 29, destination unknown. Commodore George Dewey, in command of the Pacific squadron, had been ordered to the Philippine Islands to destroy the Spanish fleet stationed there. Dewey was in Manila Bay by midnight, April 30. He began his bombardment about 5 A.M. and had won the engagement by 12:30 with no losses. The Spanish fleet had been destroyed.

The elusive fleet for which Sampson had been searching finally sailed into Santiago harbor in Cuba under the command of Admiral Cervera. Commodore Winfield S. Schley had the harbor blockaded by May 28 and then stood by to wait for Sampson.

General William R. Shafter and 17,000 troops (including the famous Rough Riders led by Theodore Roosevelt) landed at Daiquiri near Santiago in June. El Caney was taken by General Henry Lawton on July 1. The same day the Rough Riders stormed and captured San Juan Hill. Fearing the destruction of Cervera's fleet, which was caught between land and sea, General Blanco in Santiago ordered it to make a run for the open sea. On July 3 Cervera sailed out of the harbor to dare the blockade, and the battle that followed left not one Spanish vessel afloat. Sampson then bombarded Santiago unhindered, and the city surrendered on July 17.

An armistice was signed, August 12; on December 10, 1898, a peace treaty was signed in Paris. Spain gave up all claims to Cuba, Puerto Rico, and Guam, and sold the Philippine Islands to the United States for $20,000,000.

The Open Door. — After the Spanish-American War, the U.S. became involved in an international trade problem requiring the utmost diplomacy. The European nations were engaged in the partition of China— dividing it into portions convenient and favorable to their respective interests. American-Chinese trade was thus threatened, as was America's position in the newly acquired Philippines.

On September 6, 1899, Secretary of State John Hay sent a message to the nations involved, urging that the ports of China be kept open to the trade of the world. He asked each nation for a statement guaranteeing that it would not interfere with any treaty, port, or vested interests in its so-called "sphere of influence"; that it would likewise not interfere with Chinese customs, which would be collected by Chinese officials; and that it would not discriminate against other powers in matters of port dues or railroad rates. European powers were thus compelled to disavow their acquisitive intentions in China.

The New Possessions. Hawaii. — Hawaii's request for annexation to the United States had been turned down in Cleveland's administration, but the Spanish-American War had revived America's old spirit of expansion. The Hawaiian Islands were annexed by a joint resolution of Congress, signed by the President, July 7, 1898. Formal transfer of sovereignty took place on August 12, and in June, 1900, the islands were organized as a territory with Sanford B. Dole as governor.

■ CUBA. — Cuba received a provisional government under General Leonard Wood, whose military rule greatly improved education and sanitation on the island. Yellow fever was wiped out, due to the sacrifices of Major Walter Reed, a U.S. army surgeon. The provisional government developed, with self-government as its goal. In February, 1901, Cuba framed a constitution patterned after the U.S. Constitution. The Platt Amendment was incorporated into this constitution as a condition of American withdrawal from the island; the amendment guaranteed that Cuba would permit no foreign interference or control by treaty of any kind, and reserved for the United States the right to intervene, at its own will, in behalf of Cuba's peace or independence.

■ PUERTO RICO. — Puerto Rico remained under U.S. military control until the Foraker Act, April, 1900, established a civil government with an American governor and executive council appointed by the president, and a house of representatives elected by the natives. This was far from satisfactory to the Puerto Ricans, because control of their government actually rested with the American executive council, and because U.S. citizenship was denied them. Finally, an act passed in 1917 gave them their own legislature and U.S. citizenship.

■ THE PHILIPPINES. — American desire for overseas expansion came to a head over the question of the Philippines. Living on approximately 80 islands more than 6,000 miles from America's west coast were some 7,500,000 half-christianized natives from over 80 tribes. A common desire to be free from United States rule united them. Under the leadership of Emilio Aguinaldo, the Filipinos tried, in February, 1899, to oust the temporary American regime established in Manila. The United States countered mercilessly with a force of 50,000 troops that engaged in a three-year guerilla war, killing hundreds of thousands of natives before putting down the revolt and restoring order. Despite opposition to annexing the islands by "anti-imperialists," who denounced the attempt to subjugate and rule distant peoples against their will, expansionists succeeded, and the administration secured possession of the Philippines, as well as of Puerto Rico and Guam. Imperialists argued that the United States would now increase its national prestige, promote new business enterprise, tap the expanding trade with the Orient, frustrate the designs of other expanding powers, particularly Germany, in the Pacific, and finally, "uplift and civilize" the backward people of these islands.

In July, 1901, William Howard Taft, who had previously headed a commission to organize a civil government for the Philippines, became the islands' first civil governor. Although they were promised independence in 1916, the Filipinos did not achieve that coveted goal until 1946.

Other Events. — Congress passed the Gold Standard Act (March, 1900), which put the country's currency back on the gold standard. It reserved $150,000,000 in gold and provided for the sale of bonds whenever necessary to maintain the reserve.

Samoa, which had been occupied jointly by Great Britain, Germany, and the United States, was divided in 1899, and the United States acquired the island of Tutuila with its harbor at Pago Pago, and four smaller islands.

Election of 1900. — As the end of McKinley's first term approached, the Democrats put their demand for free silver second only to their criticism of the administration's imperialism and the expansion of the nation beyond its continental borders. McKinley was renominated by the Republican party with Theodore Roosevelt on the ticket for vice-president; Bryan was again the choice of the Democrats. McKinley won a more pronounced victory than in 1896, receiving 292 electoral votes to 155 for Bryan.

Assassination of the President. — Half a year after his second inauguration, President McKinley was shot by anarchist Leon Czolgosz at the Pan-American Exposition at Buffalo, New York. He died eight days later, on September 14, and Theodore Roosevelt became the new head of the administration.

The Progressive Era. — The consequences of the triumph of conservative forces and big business in the 1890's forced Americans to re-examine their beliefs and ask important questions. Most pressing was whether or not the results of industrialization should be farm distress, labor violence and poverty, poor social conditions, and political corruption. The answer was an emphatic "no." The way to remedy these conditions, many Americans argued, was to restore government to the hands of the

WIDE WORLD

THEODORE ROOSEVELT
(1901–1909)

'T.R.' was one of the most colorful men ever to hold the presidency. He organized cowboys and Indians into the Rough Riders and fought with them in Cuba. His books are on such varied subjects as hunting and Oliver Cromwell. When he entered office, many cartoons (*below*) attacked the growing power of the trust magnates; monopolies were rudely awakened by his trust-busting. He received the 1906 Nobel Peace Prize for negotiating peace between Russia and Japan (*left*).

LIBRARY OF CONGRESS

POPULAR PLAYS FOR THE PEOPLE—TEN NIGHTS IN A BAR-ROOM

NEW YORK PUBLIC LIBRARY

people and then to use that popularly controlled government to regulate industry, finance, transportation, and agriculture in the interests of the many, rather than the few. The accession of Theodore Roosevelt to the presidency initiated the implementation of this program on the national level; it had already begun on the municipal and state levels. This phase of American history, particularly the early years of the twentieth century, is known as the Progressive Period.

Theodore Roosevelt—1901-1909

When Theodore Roosevelt so unexpectedly became president he announced his readiness to take up and continue the policies of McKinley; but the difference between the two men was great. Young Roosevelt seemed "unsafe" to the conservative leaders of big business; however, the vigor and picturesqueness of his personality at once captured the mass of the people.

Coal Strike.—Opportunity came quickly to test Roosevelt's leadership. The Pennsylvania anthracite coal mines had fallen into the hands of a combination of coal-carrying railroads that was concealing profits, cutting wages, and raising the price of coal. The railroads would not arbitrate the wage cut, and the inevitable strike followed (May, 1902) putting 150,000 miners out of work. With the advance of cold weather in autumn, discomfort spread. Schools, hospitals, orphan asylums, rich and poor suffered alike; no one could buy a ton, or even a bag, of coal. When the mine owners tried to make the strike unpopular by withholding coal already mined, the people appealed to the president, who called owners and workers

to Washington to settle the dispute in the name of humanity. The owners again refused to arbitrate, but when Roosevelt threatened to take over the mines in the form of "government receivership" to keep them working, they were forced to come to terms. A presidential arbitration board granted the miners a shorter work day and a ten per cent pay increase, but not, as the miners wished, recognition of their union as a bargaining agency. Although not a complete victory for the workers, it was the first time the federal government had come to the aid of the striking workers.

Panama Canal.—Through the Second Hay-Pauncefote Treaty with Great Britain (1901), the United States secured the exclusive right to build and operate a canal across the Isthmus of Panama. In January, 1903, the Hay-Herrán Treaty between Colombia and the United States provided that the United States would buy a strip of land six miles wide across the isthmus. The U.S. Senate readily ratified this treaty, but Colombia rejected it. The inhabitants of Panama rebelled against Colombia and established an independent republic of their own—apparently with the tacit assistance of President Roosevelt.

The U.S. naval forces, arriving close on the heels of Colombian troops, prevented them from opening fire in Panama to quell the rebellion. The new government was recognized within three days by the United States, and its independence was immediately guaranteed. In February, 1904, the Hay-Bunau-Varilla Treaty between the United States and the new Panamanian government was ratified; Pa-

nama by the treaty leased permanently a zone ten miles wide across the isthmus for $10,000,000 and a perpetual annuity of $250,000. The coasts and certain islands were also ceded to the United States for the building of defenses.

Digging began at once but no great progress was made until 1907, when Roosevelt transferred the job to the army engineers under George W. Goethals. The project took ten years (1904-1914).

Roosevelt Corollary to the Monroe Doctrine.—Germany, Italy, and France had announced their intention to collect by force from Venezuela and Santo Domingo certain debts long owing to their citizens. Roosevelt secured arbitration at the Hague Tribunal (1904), and the claims were declared valid. Venezuela agreed to pay the debts in part and to set aside a percentage of her customs receipts for the remainder. In his 1904 annual message to Congress, Roosevelt announced that since the United States had taken it upon herself to be the guardian of the Western Hemisphere, according to the provisions of the Monroe Doctrine, she must also have the right to police all international difficulties in the area. This meant that if any Caribbean or Central American nation was unable to meet its financial obligations, or protect the lives and property of European nationals, the United States would intervene to forestall intervention by other powers. Known as the Roosevelt Corollary to the Monroe Doctrine, this principle was applied for the first time in 1905 when the Dominican Republic was unable to pay its European debts.

Reforms.—In 1903 the president caused the government to bring suit against the Northern Securities Company, a holding company for three great railroads controlled by two or three financial interests. By a 5 to 4 decision, the Supreme Court declared the combination illegal and it was dissolved.

The Elkins Act (1903) empowered the Interstate Commerce Commission to prosecute violators of rebate laws.

The Square Deal Campaign. 1904.—Roosevelt had proven himself a capable, effective politician who for the first time asserted some federal regulation of the big trusts. Although there was a movement within the Republican party to nominate Mark Hanna, the capitalist who had engineered McKinley's entire career, Roosevelt was nominated for the presidency on the Republican ticket. The Democrats forgot their free-silver issue and also came out for trust reform, nominating Judge Alton B. Parker of New York. Roosevelt was elected by the largest popular plurality yet counted, 2,500,000, with 336 electoral votes to Parker's 140.

Trust-Busting.—During Roosevelt's second term his reform activities increasingly threatened the law-breaking combinations known as trusts. During his administrations (1901-09) 44 prosecutions against trusts were decided in favor of the government. In June, 1906, the Hepburn Rate Bill was passed, increasing the Interstate Commerce Commission's power to investigate and fix railroad rates; many railroads and shippers were convicted of rebating.

Among the most famous trust exposures of this period was the suit against the Standard Oil Company, which, convicted of receiving and granting rebates, was ordered to dissolve (1907). The suit against the American Tobacco Company (1906) ended in an order for its dissolution in 1911. The New York Central and Hudson River Railroad was also convicted of granting illegal rebates.

Cuban Insurrection.—In August, 1906, a Cuban uprising ousted the government then in control. The United States felt obliged to intervene under the terms of the Platt Amendment. Roosevelt sent Secretary of War William H. Taft to investigate, and he found the situation sufficiently chaotic to warrant U.S. military occupation until a new government could be organized. The U.S. troops were recalled in 1909, when the newly installed government, favorable to the United States, was strong enough to stand alone.

Other Events.—A department of commerce and labor was created in 1903, adding a new member to the president's cabinet. In 1906 the Pure Food and Drug Act made it illegal to misbrand or adulterate food and drugs. A Bureau of Immigration was instituted (1906) and naturalization laws were revised and strengthened.

In the hope of maintaining a "balance of power" in the Far East to protect American interests and to prevent a possible war, Roosevelt desired to end the Russo-Japanese War before either of the combatants was completely crushed. In 1905 he induced both nations to send peace negotiators to Portsmouth, New Hamphire, where he successfully arranged a treaty that ended the conflict. For his masterly mediation, Roosevelt received the Nobel Peace Prize (1909).

San Francisco suffered great loss by earthquake and fire in 1906; 200,000 were left homeless and property damage was close to half a billion dollars. The first Pacific cable was laid, touching at Guam, Hawaii, and the Philippine Islands, and extending to the Asiatic Mainland by way of Japan to Shanghai.

The panic of 1907, which started with the Knickerbocker Trust Company failure in October, was over before the end of December. The amount of money in circulation was increased as a result of government activity and intervention on the part of high financial circles. The Root-Takahira note (1908), in which the United States and Japan agreed to respect each other's territorial possessions in the Pacific, China's independence, and the Open Door, temporarily calmed the fears of American-Japanese hostility that had arisen over American maltreatment of Japanese immigrants in California.

Conservation.—Before he went out of office, Roosevelt called the Conservation Congress (May, 1908) to take up the question of saving America's dwindling natural resources. The Reclamation Act (1902) had already provided for the irrigation of western arid areas. The renewal of forests, the protection of wild life, and the development of water power were provided for as a result of the congress.

Election of 1908.—Despite some conservative opposition to his reform measures, the popular Roosevelt, having decided not to seek reelection, was able to secure the Republican presidential nomination for his close friend, Secretary of War William H. Taft. The Democrats nominated William Jennings Bryan for the third time. It was an uneventful campaign except for the Republican promise of a downward tariff revision. Taft received 321 electoral votes; Bryan, 162.

William Howard Taft—1909-1913

Taft began his duties under very favorable conditions. He was Roosevelt's friend and Roosevelt's choice, he had a background of wide governmental experience, and he possessed the good will of the people to an extraordinary degree. He pursued the antitrust activities begun by Roosevelt and furthered much civil service reform; but his popularity waned with the enactment of the Payne-Aldrich Tariff and with his dismissal of Roosevelt's friend, Gifford Pinchot, from the forestry service after the Ballinger-Pinchot conservation controversy.

Tariff Act of 1909.—Although the people had been led to expect a downward revision of the tariff, the Payne-Aldrich Tariff Act passed in August, 1909, reduced only 650 of some 2,000 duty rates, while it raised 220 and left the rest as they were. The people felt that their wishes had been ignored, and the new president was at once categorized in the public mind with the old conservative factions.

Ballinger versus Pinchot.—The Ballinger-Pinchot controversy the same month added to this impression. Chief Forester Pinchot accused Secretary of Interior Ballinger of reentering for private ownership large tracts of coal land in Alaska. Ballinger was known to have no sympathy with Roosevelt's conservation program, yet Taft backed Ballinger and dismissed Pinchot. Taft was actually strongly pro-conservation, but by this seeming repudiation of Roosevelt's ideals he alienated the nation's progressive sentiment.

Roosevelt returned from Central Africa on June 10, and his unconcealed displeasure with the current situation served to strengthen the reaction against Taft. The 1910 congressional election seated many Democrats, as well as "insurgent" anti-Taft progressive Republicans, in both the House and Senate.

Constructive Legislation.—Many important progressive measures were enacted during Taft's four years. Postal savings banks were established (1910). The Mann-Elkins Act (1910) further enlarged the powers of the Interstate Commerce Commission. The Mann-White Slave Act was adopted in the same year, and in 1912 the parcel post was established. Civil government was recognized in Alaska (1912). The Drug Label Act was adopted in an attempt to prevent the adulteration of drugs. Another act in 1912 provided that U.S. coast-trade vessels go toll-free through the Panama Canal. The department of labor was created, and a secretary of labor was added to the president's cabinet in 1913.

Mexican Revolution.—A revolution in Mexico led by the democratic Francesco Madero drove out the Diaz government in 1911. Madero was unable to uphold his reform promises, however, and in two years was overthrown and murdered by Victoriano Huerta, who proclaimed himself president. Taft had sent U.S. troops to patrol the border, but permitted no intervention beyond an embargo on arms and ammunitions that were being shipped across the border (1912). He refused to recognize the Huerta government and left the Mexican problem to his successor.

Constitutional Amendments.—Two constitutional changes were made effective during the latter part of Taft's term. The sixteenth amendment (in effect February, 1913) empowered Congress to levy an income tax. The seventeenth (in effect May, 1913, after Taft went out of office) changed the method of choosing United States senators from election by state legislatures to direct election by the people.

Election of 1912.—Taft's judicial temperament, which directed him into conservative channels, and his unaggressive support of progressive principles alienated Roosevelt and other progressive leaders. In 1912, when the Repub-

UNITED PRESS INTERNATIONAL

LOOK MAGAZINE

LIBRARY OF CONGRESS

WILLIAM H. TAFT
(1909–1913)

When Roosevelt refused a third term, he threw all his support behind Taft, whose ability lay in the courts rather than in executive office. Taft defeated Bryan by an electoral vote of 321 to 162. During his administration, he introduced a new cabinet post, that of secretary of labor. Further, he signed the sixteenth and seventeenth amendments, instituting graduated income tax and direct senatorial election, respectively. Admiral Peary (*left*), after many attempts, finally reached the North Pole in 1909. In 1912, the liner *Titanic* struck an iceberg and sank (*above*).

licans nominated Taft at the national convention, the Roosevelt forces withdrew and formed the Progressive party (also known as the Bull Moose party), nominating their leader on this new ticket. Roosevelt called his program, which emphasized govenment regulation of big business, the "New Nationalism." The Democrats nominated Woodrow Wilson, whose "New Freedom" program stressed the elimination of trusts and the restoration of free competition. The Socialist party entered the race with Eugene V. Debs as its standard-bearer. A stirring campaign found Taft, the only conservative candidate, standing firm, while Roosevelt, Wilson, and Debs, all calling for increased social and industrial justice, competed for the liberal vote. With the Republican vote split, Wilson had little difficult capturing the election, winning 435 electoral votes to 88 for Roosevelt and 8 for Taft. Most significant was the fact that the progressive measures supported by Wilson, Roosevelt, and Debs (who polled nearly a million votes) commanded the support of three-fourths of all the voters, indicating the triumph of progressivism among the people.

Woodrow Wilson—1913-1921

Progressivism reached its climax under Woodrow Wilson's leadership. A devout Presbyterian and a descendent of a long line of ministers, President Wilson had a strong moral sense, which he applied to his task as chief executive. A trained political scientist and author of a book on *Congressional Government* (1885), Wilson realized that strong executive leadership was necessary for progress. He had been a professor of jurisprudence and political economy at

his alma mater, Princton University, before becoming president of that institution. After unsuccessfully championing the cause of democracy in several university squabbles, he resigned and was elected governor of New Jersey. There he surprised the politicians who had supported his candidacy in the belief that he would be a docile party tool; he openly defied their political machine.

It was largely the success of Wilson's reform program in New Jersey that won him the support of the people. He came into office with avowed intentions to break the monopolies and to restore individual competition; to battle, in fact, "everything which bears even the semblance of privilege or of any kind of artificial advantage."

Helped by a fairly friendly and liberal Congress, President Wilson was able to secure passage of a volume of reform legislation unequalled by any previous administration.

Legislation. Tariff. —The Democrats had promised to lower the high protective tariffs established by the Payne-Aldrich Act, and in April, 1913, Wilson called a special session of Congress for tariff revision. The Underwood-Simmons Tariff Act, passed in October, 1913, put raw wool, lumber, iron ore, and steel rails on the free list, lowered the duties on sugar and some 900 other articles by about 27 per cent, established free trade with the Philippines, and provided for a graduated income tax.

■ CURRENCY REFORM. —The Federal Reserve Bank Act (December, 1913) was framed to make the American currency system more flexible. It organized all the national banks of the country into 12 regional reserve banks under a

Federal Reserve Board, composed of the secretary of the treasury, the comptroller of currency, and five other members appointed by the president. This board was given the power to command the transfer of funds from one bank to another and to permit the issue by any member bank of Federal Reserve notes, a new system of paper money designed to eventually replace all old national bank notes. This important law did away with the old subtreasury system that withheld vast sums from circulation, and provided that enough money to meet the needs of any special section would always be in circulation. It put all of the nation's money on call in time of regional panic, and prevented the monopoly of currency by big bankers or groups of bankers by keeping the banks under government control. It was reinforced by the Rural Credits Act (1916) that arranged for certain groups of banks to lend money to farmers.

■ TRUST CONTROL. —The Federal Trade Commission Act (September, 1913) established a five-member commission to check all big corporations (except banks and railroads) engaged in interstate or foreign trade. It was required to publish violations and abuses and to enforce the laws against unfair competition.

The Clayton Antitrust Act (1914) was framed to help the government further restrict the trusts. It listed in detail all the practices condemned by the courts, particularly forbidding rebates, secret agreements, price privileges, and interlocking directorates between banks, railroads, coal companies. It asserted that the labor of a human being is not a commodity, and it exempted from antitrust laws all non-profit-making labor and farm groups.

U.S. SIGNAL CORPS, NATIONAL ARCHIVES

NATIONAL ARCHIVES

KEYSTONE

PORTLAND OREGON, OREGONIAN

WOODROW WILSON
(1913–1921)

Woodrow Wilson, the "ex-college professor," was elected president in 1912. The terrible years of World War I occurred during his term and he is best remembered for his efforts to establish the League of Nations. In 1919, Wilson headed the victory march in Washington (*above right*) and in June, following lengthy negotiations, signed the Treaty of Versailles (*above left*). He was awarded the Nobel Prize for peace in 1919. Prohibition saw federal revenue agents pouring confiscated liquor into the sewers of New York (*far left*).

■ **OTHER LAWS.**—The Adamson Act of 1916 fixed eight hours as the normal working day for employees on interstate railways actually engaged in train operation; this constituted a victory for the railroad unions. Immediately after the passage of the Adamson Act, Congress created the employees Compensation Commission to administer benefits to civil employees of the federal government. The Literacy Test Act was passed in 1917 over Wilson's veto. This law excluded from the United States all immigrants who could not read; it was another measure urged by organized labor to keep out competing immigrant labor. A Federal Board of Vocational Education was created (1917) by an act that appropriated federal money to the states for teaching home economics, trades, and industrial subjects.

Mexico.—Taft had left the touchy Mexican situation for Wilson to deal with. The president's determination to maintain democratic rule and cultivate the friendship and confidence of our Central and South American neighbors was the basis of his well-intentioned but unsuccessful policy in dealing with Mexico. In his relations with that country, Wilson tried to introduce a strong moral tone; although 25 nations accepted Huerta as the *de facto* president of Mexico, Wilson refused to recognize the new regime, charging that it did not represent the will of the Mexican people, that it was responsible for the murder of Madero, and that it rested on force. This represented a departure from traditional American policy, which had been to recognize any government firmly in power, regardless of how it was installed. Wilson went so

far as to engage in various efforts to bring down the Huerta regime. Huerta retaliated with acts of reprisal on American citizens and their property, which culminated in the arrest of several American marines at Tampico in April, 1914. When the United States promptly seized Vera Cruz to prevent a shipment of arms from reaching Huerta, war seemed imminent.

To avert the outbreak of war, the "ABC" powers (Argentina, Brazil, and Chile) offered to mediate the controversy, and proposed the retirement of Huerta and the installation of a reform government. After several weeks, however, the deliberations broke down, Huerta lost public support and was forced to flee Mexico, and the leader of the Popular party, Venustiano Carranza, seized power. When Carranza promised to establish an orderly government, Wilson abondoned his "watchful waiting" and accorded the new regime *de facto* recognition. Mexico remained chaotic for several years, however, largely because of the government's failure to inaugurate much-needed and promised land reforms. Pancho Villa, a former bandit who led constant attacks aganst the Carranza government, was the principal agitator. When the United States refused to come to Villa's aid, he retaliated by raiding Columbus, New Mexico (March, 1916), and killing seventeen Americans. The United States sent a punitive military expedition under General John J. Pershing into Mexico to capture Villa, but Pershing failed and was withdrawn in January, 1917. Latin Americans strongly disliked American intervention in their sovereign domestic affairs, and not until the "Good Neighbor Policy" of Franklin D.

Roosevelt was instituted were cordial relations with Latin America restored.

World War I.—World War I had begun in 1914, with Austria-Hungary's declaration of war on Serbia, on July 28. By the end of 1916, Serbia, Russia, France, Belgium, England, Japan, Montenegro, Italy, Portuagal, Rumania, and Greece were allied against the Central Powers Germany, Austria-Hungary, Turkey, and Bulgaria. Wilson stood for the strict neutrality both by proclamation (August 4, 1914) and by popular appeal (August 18), when he exhorted the people to abstain from heated discussions and to be neutral "not only in act but in word and thought."

American neutrality was impossible to maintain, however, for its basic sympathies and the early events of the war inclined the American people to favor the Allies rather than the Central Powers. Most Americans had a cultural affinity with England, based on common background, language, and traditions. In addition, many Americans felt an obligation to aid France in her hour of need, for she had supported them during the American Revolution. In addition, German militarism offended the American people's sense of democracy, while the ruthless invasion of Belgium aroused resentment. Effective British propaganda emphasized what were later found to be only imaginary German atrocities; but as the war progressed this propaganda intensified the conviction that England and France were fighting for human decency while Germany sought to extend autocracy and militarism. The Allies' cause was further strengthened because (aside form the wireless) Great Britain controlled the only means of communication between Europe and the United States. Economic conditions also influenced American opinion. Since Great Britain controlled the seas and her navy blockaded the Central Powers, nearly all American overseas trade was confined to the Allied nations. Trade, particularly in munitions, increased rapidly as American factories and farms assumed the task of sustaining the Allied armies and their civilian populations. These purchases, which brought the nation out of a depression, were financed largely by American loans; thus, many American citizens and the United States government had a vital economic stake in an allied victory.

Neutrality. — Efforts by the warring groups to control the sea eventually forced the United States into the conflict. England's attempt to starve the Central Powers into submission led her to violations of all rules of international law, to raise havoc with American shipping, and to seize much American property. In each case President Wilson protested the illegal British acts, but pro-Allied sentiment and Wilson's determination to keep America out of the war prevented his taking action.

Faced with economic strangulation unless the Allied blockade was broken, Germany was forced to resort to unrestricted submarine warfare, which also constituted violation of international law. German acts eventually brought the United States into the war, for not merely American property, but American lives were destroyed. In February, 1915, Germany announced that all enemy ships in the waters surrounding the British Isles would be sunk on sight, and that neutral ships should avoid the area to prevent "unfortunate mistakes." Although Wilson warned the Germans that they would be held to "strict accountability" for the loss of American lives or property, Germany refused to abandon her submarine policy. Several ships were sunk and a number of Americans killed. The climax came on May 7, 1915, when the English liner the *Lusitania*, was sunk without warning off the Irish coast; 1,200 lives were lost, including 128 Americans.

Wilson sent a series of notes to Germany demanding reparations for damages and abandonment of her lawless practices. In protest to Wilson's second note, a war-like threat, Secretary of State William Jennings Bryan resigned, maintaining that Americans should not travel on belligerent ships. Wilson replaced him with Robert Lansing, who was outspoken in his sympathies with the Allied cause. Meanwhile, more ships were torpedoed with further American losses. Wilson's protests were so violent that on September 1, 1915, Germany promised not to sink passenger ships without provision for the safety of the passengers. This had been the main point of contention between the two countries.

When, on March 24, 1916, the British steamer *Sussex* was torpedoed and American citizens were killed, Wilson sent his ultimatum: Germany must repudiate and abandon unrestricted submarine warfare or all relations would be severed. Germany promised

on May 5 that merchantmen "shall not be sunk without warning and without saving human lives." This quieted the submarine controversy for nine months.

Election of 1916. — The Democratic party nominated Wilson on a platform boasting of his domestic reforms, tariff policy, and efforts to keep the peace. The Republicans chose as their candidate Charles Evans Hughs, a supreme court justice and former governor of New York. Wilson's domestic program, which won him the support of most progressives, as well as the Democratic slogan, "he kept us out of war," proved decisive. Wilson was re-elected by a close vote when California's thirteen electoral votes, long in doubt, gave him 277 to Hughes' 254.

Efforts Toward Mediation. — Wilson's hope was that Europe would listen to his proposals of peace. On December 18 he sent identical notes to the warring nations, proposing mediation. Germany was again evasive, and the Allies would consider peace on no terms except "complete restitution, full reparation, and effectual guarantees." Wilson's convictions that the only just peace would have to be a "peace without victory" found utterance in his speech of January 22, 1917, in which he expressed the world's need for a League of Nations.

Nine days later plans for mediation were made impossible by Germany's change of policy. Although it realized that the United States would be forced to enter the war, on January 31, 1917, the German high command announced the immediate resumption of unlimited submarine warfare. In February, 1917, the United States obtained a copy of the Zimmerman Note, a communication from Germany to Mexico promising it Texas, Arizona, and New Mexico in return for entering the war against the Allies and the United States. When published on March 1, 1917, the note aroused a great deal of popular resentment against Germany.

America Joins the Allies. — Three American vessels were deliberately and defiantly sunk by German submarines in mid-March. On April 2, 1917, Wilson asked Congress to declare that war already existed, and Congress promptly "resolved . . . that the state of war between the United States and the Imperial German Government which has thus been thrust upon the United States is hereby formally declared." Wilson asserted that this "war to end all wars" was being fought for "the ultimate peace of the world." National sympathy fully supported Wilson's position and entrance into the war.

The United States was totally unprepared for war, but organization was rapid. Instant and overwhelming was the public response to Wilson's "call to service." Of prime importance were production and distribution of food and clothing, coal for ships and factories, steel for arms and ammunition, ships to carry men and supplies, rails and locomotives, horses, mules, and cattle: all were essential for the army, the navy, and the impoverished Allies. Competition was largely suspended, as was most personal luxury; and Wilson

reflected the feeling of national unity with the phrase "politics is adjourned." Manufacturers vied with each other to give over their plants to government service. Class vied with class and laborer with artisan to measure up to the need. Some profiteering resulted from the sudden demand for big production, but this was said to be almost minimal.

■ MOBILIZATION. — Within three months over a million men had volunteered, but Wilson felt that a more effective army could be raised and trained by more scientific means. The Selective Service Act was passed, May 18, to enlist a million men 21-30 years old. By June 5, 1917, 9,586,000 were registered; by June, 1918, a million more, and by September, 1918, 13 million (18-45 years of age). General John J. Pershing was made commander-in-chief of the American Expeditionary Forces. He was in France by June 13, 1917, and sent word that 3,000,000 men were needed. The first small U.S. contingent set foot in France on June 26. By the end of 1917 troops were going over at the rate of 30,000 a month; by the end of the war (November, 1918) the U.S. army numbered 3,665,000 men, and 2,086,000 of these were in Europe.

The Council of National Defense was created to organize and centralize the war activity of the nation. Headed by the secretaries of war, navy, interior, agriculture, commerce, and labor, it operated through state councils of defense and specialized committees on transportation, communication, and public information, as well as a women's committee that coordinated the war work of American women.

The American National Red Cross knitted, rolled surgical dressings, made hospital garments, and ministered to fighting men, the wounded, and starving refugees.

The Espionage Act (June, 1917) prohibited interference with the draft or the sale of government bonds, provided punishment for disloyalty in speech or printed word, and suppressed several ultraliberal publications. The measure raised important constitutional questions, however, for its enforcement frequently led to the violation of basic civil liberties. It created the Exports Administrative Board, gave the president power to limit exportation to neutrals of goods that might be ultimately destined for the enemy, and published a list of business houses with which U.S. firms were warned not to trade. By February, 1918, all foreign trade was controlled by the government.

■ LIBERTY LOANS. — The United States needed huge sums to prepare for and wage war; the Allies needed huge sums in order to continue their efforts. By June, 1917, the American people had loaned $3,000,000,000 to the government by buying liberty bonds. In four war issues and a fifth called the "victory loan," almost 21½ billion dollars were subscribed to pay for the war; in June, 1919, the interest-bearing debt of the United States was almost 25¼ billion.

■ THE WAR BOARDS. — Six War Boards were established to meet the emergencies of war. The Lever Act (August, 1917) created the Food Administration, headed by Herbert C. Hoover, and the Fuel Administration, headed by Harry A. Garfield. "Food will win the war" was the cry from coast to coast; the people gladly skimped on sugar, observed wheatless and meatless days to aid in a just distribution, planted and harvested, and frowned upon hoarders. The Fuel Administration was not as popular. Manufacturers objected to compulsory fuelless Mondays—January to March, 1918;—but cooperation won out and in only four weeks 30,000,000 tons of coal were made available to keep war goods moving by rail and transport. The appeals to save gasoline by giving up Sunday pleasure driving met with instant and enthusiastic response. In two months a million barrels of gasoline had been saved and ten shiploads had gone overseas.

In December, 1917, the Railroads War Board was taken over by the government with William G. McAdoo as director. Drastic economies were enforced and all operations were subordinated to the mobilization of troops and war supplies. The War Trade Board under Vance McCormick took charge of foreign and domestic trade with war success its sole aim. The Shipping Board, under Edward N. Hurley, was one notable failure in the otherwise successful effort at mobilizing the American economy. While it did succeed in confiscating enemy ships in American ports and in adding some 3,000,000 pounds of tonnage to the United States merchant marine by commandeering neutral ships being constructed in this country, the first ship it actually constructed was not completed until after the war had ended. The War Industries Board was put in the able hands of Bernard M. Baruch, who organized and unified all American industry to wartime pace. He fixed prices, kept competition secondary to the speeding up of production, and was successful in maintaining supplies of high quality and keeping them adequate to the demand.

■ THE AEF.—Money and unlimited material aid, rather than real help on the battlefield, was what the Allies expected of the United States. U.S. fighting ability was at first underestimated by Germany and the Allies alike, for the inexperienced American army had been recruited suddenly from farm and city street, and had been only briefly trained.

Men were needed, however. Russia had withdrawn from the war in 1917, and Germany was preparing a tremendous drive for the spring of 1918. At least 3,000,000 men were needed at the front, but 3,000 miles of Atlantic infested with submarines lay between the United States and the enemy. The American Expeditionary Forces (AEF) got through, however, and were on the line 500,000 strong by the end of the first year; 10,000 troops were landing daily in 1918. In the last engagement of the war (September 20-November 11, 1918) 1,200,000 U.S. troops took part.

Through the winter of 1917-18, American divisions were brigaded with divisions of the French and British armies. Pershing's great struggle was for recognition of the AEF as an independent combat army, but in the fateful days of the German offensive

(1918) he subordinated this aim to the crisis and sought only to aid in halting the grilling advance. He pledged to General Foch (March 28), "Infantry, artillery, aviation—all that we have are yours to dispose of as you will," and the offer was accepted.

■ SPRING, 1918.—Germany had launched her final desperate offensive to break the Allied line before the American forces could be massed against her. German strength was concentrated entirely on the western front from Ypres to Chateau-Thierry. The channel ports were in danger; Paris was threatened. The best of the American divisions were hurried into Picardy, for the allies were all but exhausted.

By April 1 the Germans had almost reached Amiens and were within two miles of the French-British transportation railroad, but the Allied line held; within three weeks the American First Division (28,000 men) was on the front near Montdidier. On May 28 they attacked the German positions, took Cantigny, and held it in the face of a vicious three-day bombardment.

■ BELLEAU WOOD.—In June, two regiments of the U.S. marines of the Second Division pushed the Germans out of the Belleau woods. This impenetrable forest, filled with thick brush and jagged rocks, was one of the most vital strongholds in Germany's intended drive toward Paris. For three days the marines fought with utmost bravery and sweeping losses—and gained a mile; it was one of the most bitter battles of the war. After another attack (June 9) and two additional weeks of bitter fighting, the woods were finally taken. Vaux and Boureshes were taken, and the German advance was stopped.

■ THE TURNING POINT.—The Third Division was on the bank of the Marne River east of Château-Thierry. Here, on July 15, the thirty-eighth regiment held and drove back two German divisions so decisively that the engagement has been called the turning point of the war. The morale of the German private had been broken; the German army was in retreat and could not again undertake the offensive.

■ FIRST AMERICAN ARMY.—Foch finally consented to the integration of the First American Army as an independent unit. By August 10 about 600,000 men had been organized under Pershing's full command. On September 13 the army took the Saint-Mihiel salient, easily reducing in a day a position for four years considered impregnable. The American forces took 16,000 prisoners and 443 guns, reoccupied 175 square miles and 70 towns, and restored the main Paris-Verdun-Toul-Nancy railroad.

Two weeks later the U.S. unit was on the Meuse-Argonne front, with Sedan, the crucial railhead of the German communications, as its objective. Germany considered the Argonne Forest her strongest defense: it was a death-trap of machine gun pits and cannon-swept roads. The American advance moved northward between the eastern edge of the Forest and the Meuse River. By September 28 many villages had been retaken by bitter man-to-man fighting, rifle and bayonet against machine gun fire. The Forest was won by October 10, and the last advance to shatter the Kriemhilde line began on

November 1. On the sixth, two American divisions were opposite Sedan. The German army was unnerved and in retreat, and only the Armistice (November 11) saved it from annihilation.

■ ARMISTICE.—The allies of Germany had already sued for peace prior to the fall of Sedan. Bulgaria had surrendered on September 29; Turkey, October 30. Austria-Hungary asked for an armistice on October 30 and signed on November 4. As early as October 3 Hindenburg had claimed that "the gravity of the military situation admits of no delay," and had appealed to Wilson for an armistice based on the Fourteen Points. "Retire at once from France and Belgium. Guarantee representation of the German people" were among the conditions cited by Wilson. He would accept no peace that might later be repudiated by a ruling few.

Far more than the "gravity of the military situation" forced Germany's surrender. Shock and surprise at the news of impending military defeat worked a tremendous reaction among the German people, who suddenly realized they had been duped by their leaders. Wilson's peace propaganda had seriously undermined the popular militarism. By November 4 there was revolution in Germany, quickened daily by the kaiser's reluctance to abdicate. By November 9 Germany had formed a republic.

On November 8 Foch handed the written terms of the armistice to the German representatives. The armistice was signed at 5 A.M. on November 11, 1918, and by 11 A.M. the war was over.

The terms were severe. Germany was to get out of Belgium at once, surrender 10 battleships, 14 cruisers, 50 destroyers, and all her submarines (129). She had to give up thousands of machine guns, airplanes, railroad cars, and munitions, and tolerate U.S. and Allied armies of occupation on the west bank of the Rhine. The Fourteen Points of Wilson's world-peace theories were to be incorporated into the peace treaty, but the Allies reserved the right to interpret for themselves the "freedom of the seas" and "restoration" clauses.

The Fourteen Points.—The Fourteen Points that Wilson considered the necessary basis of a "just and lasting peace" were set forth in his idealistic speech to Congress, January 8, 1918. How deeply the words took root in the warring world was not revealed until the failing Central Powers looked to him to hold the coming peace to justice.

The Fourteen Points guaranteed: (1) "open covenants openly arrived at"; (2) "absolute freedom of navigation on the high seas" in peace and war; (3) "equality of trade conditions among all nations"; (4) "reduction of national armaments"; (5) settlement of colonial claims in justice to native and claimant alike; (6) evacuation of all Russian territory; (7) evacuation and restoration of Belgium; (8) return of Alsace-Lorraine to France; (9) readjustment of the Italian frontier in justice to adjacent nationalities; (10) autonomous development of all of the nationalities of Austria-Hungary; (11) the realignment of the Balkan boundaries according to nationalities;

INTERNATIONAL NEWS PHOTO

AMERICA'S ENTRY into World War I finally broke the long stalemate between Allied and German forces. American soldiers cheerfully embarked for France in 1917, answering Uncle Sam's pointed plea. Once "over there," however, months of hardship sapped much of the initial enthusiasm. World War I was the war of the trenches, a war of crawling through miles of mud and barbed wire, a war of sleeping in improvised bunks dug out of the mud. At home, after the war, a victory parade down Fifth Avenue commemorated dead comrades with a horse-drawn, wreath-decorated caisson.

I WANT YOU FOR U.S. ARMY
NEAREST RECRUITING STATION

INTERNATIONAL NEWS PHOTO

CULVER PICTURES, INC.

OUR "ACE OF ACES," Eddie Rickenbacker, credited with downing 26 enemy craft. Air attack replaced the glamour of the cavalry.

(12) the autonomy of all Turkey's subject peoples; (13) establishment of an independent Poland; and (14) "an association of nations formed under specific covenants" to afford "mutual guarantees of political independence and territorial integrity to great and small states alike."

Peace Conference.—Wilson sailed for Paris (December 4, 1918) to attend the Peace Conference in person. To those who criticized this unprecedented step he replied only that he knew of no business that should take precedence over the peace of the world. He had the League of Nations at heart, for he was its spokesman, its prophet, and its engineer, all in one.

Wilson, however, hindered his cause by engaging in some questionable practices before sailing. In 1918, just before the armistice, he mistakenly appealed to the American people to elect a Democratic Congress. His partisan appeal resulted only in sweeping Republican victories, giving the Republicans control of both houses of Congress. When Wilson left for Europe, therefore, it appeared as though he was no longer able to speak for the American public. Furthermore, hoping and expecting to write the peace treaty himself, Wilson deliberately chose a weak delegation to accompany him to the Paris conference; the American delegation contained only one unimportant Republican and no member of either the House of Representatives or the Senate. Wilson would meet certain difficulty in trying to secure ratification of the treaty by the Republican-dominated Senate.

Europe received Wilson with wild enthusiasm. Half the world looked to him to frame a just peace, the other half to save them from an unjust one; but it was easier to plan for than to make a peace. Of the 39 governments that sent delegates, only the United States seemed to have no special selfish purpose. Each nation held to its own nationalistic interests, and the victors were eager to crush the defeated foe.

The Fourteen Points survived the Conference but with drastic alterations. To preserve a League of Nations, Wilson compromised on certain details after long and bitter debate. He finally had to accept Japan's remaining in Shantung, a German concession in China that Japan took during the war, and the separation of the Saar River from Germany. He was forced to let the Allies exact crippling reparations from Germany, for they were moved by no appeal to temper the sum to her ability to pay.

Wilson had lost face in all quarters: with the Allies for his stand against some of their most important aims; with his own country, where his political enemies were fanning the agitation for a "strong peace" to destroy Germany; and with liberals everywhere for his failure to put through the promised "peace of conciliation." For such a peace "the ingredients were lacking at Paris," said Colonel House, Wilson's friend and counsellor. Unsatisfactory as the treaty was, it was far better and less harsh than it would have been had Wilson not gone to Paris. In fact, it probably was the best possible peace treaty under the circumstances.

Treaty of Versailles.—In Paris, Wilson won what he considered to be the most important battle—the fight over the League of Nations. As he had insisted from the outset, the Covenant of the League was written into the Treaty of Versailles, signed in June, 1919. As Wilson envisioned it, the League would provide the cure for all other Treaty ills. He came home to present the Treaty and the Covenant to the American people for their ratification.

Wilson found a hostile Republican Senate and a rather apathetic American public waiting to hear and judge the treaty with its League Covenant. For various reasons—personal, partisan, and other—the Senate would not have the treaty without changes; Wilson, stubborn, exhausted, and ill, certain he was right and unwilling to compromise, would accept no reservations in the document.

Article X of the Covenant was the stumbling block: it stated that League members were "to respect and preserve as against external aggression the territorial integrity and political independence of all members of the League." This was particularly opposed by isolationists as an "entangling alliance."

Disappointed and disillusioned, but undeterred, Wilson set out on a speaking tour of the United States (September, 1919). He sought to secure the people's support of his peace in order to force the Senate's ratification. At Wichita, Kansas, September 26, he suffered a complete nervous collapse, from which he never fully recovered. The nation lost its inspiration and its leader, the League its advocate. The United States never joined the League or the World Court for which the League provided.

Other Events.—During Wilson's second term two amendments to the Constitution were adopted by Congress and shortly thereafter ratified by the states. The eighteenth amendment, ratified in 1919, prohibited the manufacture, sale, and transportation of intoxicating liquors. The nineteenth amendment, granting women the right to vote, was adopted by Congress in 1919 and ratified by the states in 1920.

Election of 1920.—The Republicans nominated Senator Warren G. Harding, a "regular" who could be controlled by party bosses in the Senate. The platform attacked Wilson, hedged on the League of Nations question, and avoided most of the important issues. Calvin Coolidge, reactionary governor of Massachusetts, was chosen as Harding's running mate. The Democrats named Governor James M. Cox of Ohio, a mild liberal, and Franklin D. Roosevelt as their presidential and vice-presidential candidates. Their platform praised Wilson and unequivocally endorsed the League. To Wilson's disappointment, because Harding either avoided, evaded, or took conflicting stands on the issue, the election was not a "solemn referendum" on the League. Rather, reacting against wartime controls, Wilsonian idealism, and the harsh peace treaty, the voters gave Harding an overwhelming majority. It was less a pro-Harding than an anti-Wilson vote; Cox faced insurmountable odds due to his association with Wilson.

Warren G. Harding—1921-1923

Harding had not sought the presidency; he received it because fortuitous circumstances made his candidacy a good one for Republicans. For many years, Harding had been a small-time Ohio politician who had fulfilled his political ambitions when elected Senator. A weak and incompetent legislator who added nothing of importance to Senate debate during the six years he served in Washington, he nevertheless was personable, handsome, popular, and a good speaker. Since he had no moral scruples or strong beliefs, and recognized his deficiencies, Harding was quite willing to take orders from others. He was, in short, the very opposite of Wilson. In 1920 the American people wanted a change—in Harding's words, "a return to normalcy." A tool of the business interests, Harding promised the American people what they wanted: business stabilization, and end to government controls, and increased prosperity.

The Cabinet.—Harding's cabinet was the talk of the nation and continued so into the years of Coolidge's administration. Some of the men he chose had unquestionable ability, in particular Secretary of State Charles E. Hughes, and Secretary of Commerce Herbert C. Hoover. Most of the others, however, were undistinguished men, personal friends too greatly trusted or political associates to whom office was due. Harding's secretary of the interior, Albert B. Fall, was forced to resign in 1923 and later served a penitentiary sentence for leasing the Teapot Dome oil lands (a navy oil reservation) to private interests. (He secretly transferred the reserves to a prominent oil man, Harry F. Sinclair, in return for a $100,000 "loan"). Harding's friend, Attorney General Harry M. Daugherty, was discovered in shady and unexplainable practices and forced to resign (1924). Harding's secretary of the navy, Edwin Denby also resigned from office.

Foreign Relations.—Harding's first task was to officially end the state of war still existing between Germany and the United States. Three separate treaties were signed by Germany, Austria, and Hungary and ratified by the Senate (October 18, 1921). Parts of the Treaty of Versailles were incorporated into these, but they were carefully worded to keep the United States uninvolved in the League of Nations.

Washington Naval Conference.—The most significant event of Harding's administration was the conference for the limitation of naval armaments (November 12, 1921-February 6, 1922). He called together those nations interested in Pacific Ocean problems: the United States, Great Britain, France, Italy, Japan, China, Holland, Belgium, and Portugal. The first agreement was for a naval holiday: no capital ships (ships of 10,000 tons or more with eight-inch calibre guns) were to be built

LIBRARY OF CONGRESS

WARREN G. HARDING
(1921–1923)

Harding's spirit of "return to normalcy" was seen in the International Armament Limitation Conference (right). To trim the U.S. Navy, the U.S.S. *Iowa* was used for target practice (above). The Teapot Dome scandal involved A. B. Fall (upper right) who "gave" oil rights to private interests for a $100,000 "loan."

UNITED PRESS INTERNATIONAL

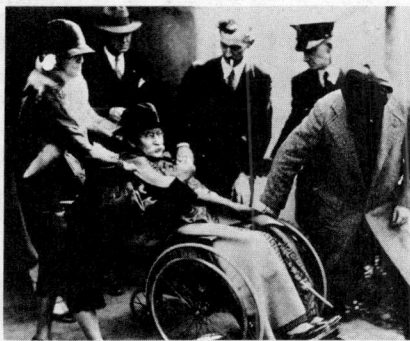

UNITED PRESS INTERNATIONAL

LIBRARY OF CONGRESS

before 1936 by the United States, Great Britain, Japan, France, or Italy. This Five-Power Naval Pact allowed Great Britain and the United States each 525,000 tons, Japan 315,000 tons, and France and Italy each 175,000 tons of capital ships. It also called for the scrapping of 66 capital ships in each of the navies of the United States, Japan, and Great Britain.

Five other treaties were negotiated at this conference. The Four-Power Pacific Treaty, signed December 13, 1921, was an agreement between the United States, Great Britain, France, and Japan to respect and protect each other's insular rights in the Pacific. The Five-Power Treaty bound the signers to observe the international code in submarine warfare and to forswear the use of poisonous gas. By the Sino-Japanese Treaty, Japan agreed to evacuate its troops from Shantung within six months and to return to China all former German interests in Tsingtao. China agreed to pay for the improvements made there by Germany and Japan. A Chinese Customs Treaty was also passed. The Pacific Cable Treaty upheld Japan's mandate over Yap but gave the United States equal rights in the laying of trans-Pacific cables.

These treaties had many shortcomings. The limitations applied only to capital ships, and by surrendering the right to fortify its Pacific possessions, the United States had conceded Japanese supremacy in that area. Despite this, the treaties were hailed as a brilliant achievement of American diplomacy and a sincere effort to bring about world peace. It is important to note that these treaties, and other events in the decade, indicate that, contrary to the usual assumption, the United States did not retreat into an isolationist shell during the 1920's. Rather, America was quite active diplomatically. Unfortunately, however, the nation chose to pursue a unilateral, and often ambivalent, foreign policy.

World Court.—Ever since the Hague Tribunal was established (1899) certain presidents of the United States, (notably Roosevelt, Taft, and Wilson) had been in favor of compulsory arbitration. In 1920 Elihu Root proposed a court of arbitration very similar to the actual Permanent Court of International Justice (popularly called the World Court), established by the League of Nations in December of that year. Popular opinion in America held out for a *qualified* membership, however, even though Harding urged that the United States join the World Court in a strong message to the Senate (February, 1923). The question remained undecided at the time of his death in August.

Other Events.—Harding favored economy in government and pushed through the first Federal Budget Bill (June, 1921). In February, 1923, an important agreement was made with England to eliminate England's war debt to the United States within 62 years.

Harding's Death.—Harding had surrounded himself with old cronies and mediocre politicians, many of whom were members of his earlier "Ohio gang." The result was a series of scandals that rivaled those of Grant's administration. Millions of dollars of the public's money were squandered and several Harding-appointed government officials were sentenced to prison terms. Although personally innocent, Harding was greatly demoralized and disillusioned by these and other incidents. He died in San Francisco on August 2, 1923, while away on a trip to the west coast in order to "escape" from the White House.

Calvin Coolidge—1923-1929

Calvin Coolidge, the New England Yankee, was visiting his father's home in Plymouth, Vermont, when the news came of President Harding's death. He took the oath of office from his father, the local justice of the peace, at two o'clock in the morning on August 3, 1923, and left at once for Washington.

Coolidge's Position.—A dull man known for saying very little, "Silent Cal" had a reputation for honesty. He quickly won the confidence of most Americans through a well-publicized statement that summed up the conservative, pro-business philosophy that was to govern his administration, "The business of America is business." He earnestly wished to continue Harding's government economy program. He believed in the tariff, not in vacillating revisions. He believed in reducing taxes. He was against the soldiers' bonus, for which there was much agitation, and against government relief for farmers. He opposed the League of Nations but supported the World Court.

Coolidge made no active move for the administration housecleaning for which the people were clamoring, as corrupt transactions by members of Harding's cabinet were rapidly revealed. He encouraged the investigations but would make no hasty dismissals until malfeasance was proved.

WIDE WORLD

LIBRARY OF CONGRESS

LIBRARY OF CONGRESS

CALVIN COOLIDGE
(1923–1929)

Coolidge's rigid government economy reduced taxes. He and Secretary of State Kellogg signed the 15-nation Kellogg-Briand Peace Pact on January 17, 1929 (*left*). Lindbergh's New York-Paris flight in May, 1927 (*far left*), made him a national hero.

Legislation. Mellon Plan.—Since World War I, taxation on the war-profit incomes of individuals and corporations had provided the bulk of the national revenue. When the war was over, Harding, not Wilson, was in the White House. Freed from the fear of federal regulation, businessmen were gradually relieved of the high taxes of the war period. Secretary of the Treasury Andrew Mellon, former head of the Aluminum Company of America and one of the richest men in the world, set out to revise the tax structure for the benefit of the upper-income brackets. He immediately sponsored a tax bill that repealed the excess profits tax and sharply reduced the surtaxes on personal income. After overcoming opposition from the progressive Republican farm-bloc and Senate Democrats, the measures were passed with some unimportant amendments. By 1929 four subsequent revenue acts were passed that further cut the surtax on high incomes, ended the gift tax, cut the estate tax in half, and reduced corporation taxes. Mellon's tax program had almost entirely reversed the progressive tax policies of the Wilson years and saved the secretary of the treasury approximately one million dollars annually.

■ THE IMMIGRATION ACT.—The Immigration Bill of 1924 established a quota system that gave entry annually to only two per cent of the number of natives of any one country living in the United States in 1890. The bill not only drastically reduced the number of foreigners allowed into this country each year, but as intended, discriminated against certain kinds of immigrants: it barred Orientals entirely and nearly eliminated immigrants from southern and southeastern Europe—mainly Catholics

and Jews. Immigration from Canada and Mexico was not restricted. The yearly influx of immigrants was reduced to 150,000.

■ THE SOLDIERS' BONUS.—Like Harding, Coolidge was opposed to veterans' compensation. The government had already hailed the returned disabled soldier with free hospitalization, rehabilitation programs, and prolongation of the privileges of War Risk Insurance for the fit. Seventeen states had come forward with cash bonuses, but many ex-servicemen continued jobless and Congress was flooded with bill after bill proposing adjusted compensation. "I am opposed to the bonus," was Coolidge's reply to public insistence, but the World War Adjusted Compensation Act was passed over this veto (May 17-19, 1924).

Election of 1924.—The Republican convention nominated Coolidge almost without opposition, and Charles Gates Dawes of Illinois (author of the Dawes Plan) was named for vice-president. The Democrats were divided into an immigrant-labor-city-anti-prohibition faction, led by Governor Alfred E. Smith of New York, and a rural-southern—western-prohibition faction under William G. McAdoo of California. When these two candidates remained deadlocked at the convention for over one hundred ballots, they withdrew from the race and the nomination was finally given to a darkhorse, John W. Davis of New York. Liberals, unhappy over the choice of both major candidates and their party platforms, joined with Socialists to form the Progressive party, which nominated Senator Robert LaFollette of Wisconsin. Content with the prosperity, the voters

gave Coolidge an overwhelming victory. He received 328 electoral votes to Davis' 136 and LaFollette's 13. The Republicans also won control of both houses of Congress.

Dawes Plan.—Germany had ceased to pay the reparations exacted of her under the Treaty of Versailles for "all the loss and damage" sustained by the Allies. France had accordingly moved into the Ruhr mining regions (1921) in an attempt to compensate herself for Germany's default. Dispute followed dispute, and in 1923 the United States proposed a commission to work out a settlement. Charles G. Dawes headed this investigation into Germany's budget and reported to the Reparations Commission regarding Germany's exact ability to pay. The Dawes Plan revised the entire reparations schedule: it extended the time, pared down the amounts due, and arranged for the collection and distribution of the payments.

World Court.—In January, 1926, Coolidge again took up the matter of joining the World Court. Public sentiment had strengthened in favor of the world peace movement, and when the Senate voted again (January 27, 1926) there were only 17 adverse votes. Five reservations were made, however. The most important, the fifth, stipulated that the Court shall not "without the consent of the United States entertain any request for an advisory opinion touching any dispute or question in which the United States has or claims an interest." When the Court conferred in Geneva (September, 1926) it decided that the fifth reservation could not be granted. Coolidge would not urge the

DESERT SEA NEWS BUREAU

INTERNATIONAL NEWS

WIDE WORLD

HERBERT HOOVER
(1929–1933)

Hoover had barely taken office when, on October 29, 1929, the Wall Street crash stunned the country (*left*). An engineering marvel, Hoover Dam (*far left*) generates power for over eight million people.

Senate to retreat from its demands. The United States remained outside, with "no prospect of adhering to the World Court."

Agriculture.—Despite relatively widespread prosperity, there were many "sick" industries and depressed sectors of the economy, such as the coal mining and textile industries. Most seriously depressed, however, was agriculture. Farmers never recovered from a recession in 1920 and farm prices decreased almost 75 per cent between 1920 and 1932; farm income declined from approximately fifteen to five billion dollars. The slump was caused by the contraction of European markets and increased world production. At the same time, higher prices for manufactured goods further reduced the farmer's profits, and he still faced large debts incurred during the prosperous war years. Acting in Congress through a bipartisan "farm bloc," the farmers sought relief through various devices; on the whole, however, due to Coolidge and Harding's lack of concern for the farmer, no relief came.

Election of 1928.—Coolidge was still popular in 1928 but he did not "choose to run" for president. He gave his support to the Republican nominee, Herbert C. Hoover, who had won public admiration as wartime food administrator, and public confidence as secretary of commerce. Alfred E. Smith won the Democratic nomination. Although the party platforms were fairly similar, the contest was a colorful and exciting one. Smith was handicapped, particularly in rural areas, by his Catholic religion, his opposition to prohibition, and his Tammany background. None of these fac-

tors cost him the election, however. The country was prospering and the people wanted to remain under the spell that seemed to have been induced by Republican rule. Smith won only 87 electoral votes to 444 for Hoover. Even several states in the "solid south" voted Republican.

Herbert C. Hoover—1929-1933

That the wheels of prosperity could stop revolving evidently did not occur to the new president any more than it did to the people. "I have no fears for the future of our country," Hoover asserted in his inaugural speech in 1929.

Agricultural Marketing Bill.—Although the prolonged distress of the farmers was not interpreted as a sign of danger, to keep a campaign promise Hoover called a special session of Congress (April 16, 1929) to take up farm relief and revise the tariff. The Agricultural Marketing Bill, passed June 15, established a Federal Farm Board and set aside $500,000,000 for loans to farmers' cooperative groups. Agricultural prices remained extremely low in foreign markets, however. The government stepped in and spent billions of dollars on bushels of wheat and bales of cotton in order to forestall surpluses. Nevertheless, farmers still could barely meet production costs.

Smoot-Hawley Tariff.—The remedy to the farm problem might have been to lower the tariff barriers and thus facilitate world buying and selling. Instead, Congress passed the highest protective tariff in its history, the Smoot-Hawley Tariff Act, which raised the rates on approximately a thousand commodities. Hoover had advised increasing the

rates on farm products only, but duties on manufactured goods were also raised. When the bill went through again in a revised form, all rates were raised again and 25 nations retaliated with high tariffs on U.S. goods. Consequently, within two years the U.S. lost $5,326,000,000 in world trade.

Wickersham Commission.—Hoover came into office believing that crime prevention was the "dominant national problem." He was aghast at the prevalence of bootleggers and machine gun bandits, at the murders, kidnappings and holdups. He appointed a commission (May, 1929), headed by George W. Wickersham, to investigate lawlessness and law enforcement. The first report, submitted January, 1931, found the methods of prohibition enforcement at the root of the problem. The recommendations of the commissioners themselves, however, were so confused—at once opposing and recommending the repeal of the eighteenth amendment—that the Wickersham Commission's report was not taken seriously.

The Stock Market Crash: 1929.—Blind confidence that prosperity begets prosperity lured the nation deeper and deeper into speculation. "Buy stocks today and be a millionaire tomorrow" was the prevailing psychology. Then, in October, 1929, the crash came. The stock market went to pieces; 16,410,030 shares were suddenly for sale. Huge fortunes and modest lifetime savings were lost overnight; men and women were left penniless.

The government began a crusade of optimism, telling the people that "everything is fundamentally sound," and, six months later, that the nation had "passed the worst." Closed banks and factories reflected the truth, however. The unemployed numbered 7,000,000 within a year, and 15,000,000 by 1933. People were without money, without homes, without work, without spirit. Local and state charities could not deal with the widespread destitution.

■ ANTI-DEPRESSION MEASURES. — Hoover was opposed to measures for federal relief on various political and moral grounds, but he launched a huge program of public works in 1930 in order to stem unemployment. He proposed the bankers' pool of $500,000,000 (1931) in an attempt to save the little banks, and in 1932 secured passage of the bill for the Reconstruction Finance Corporation, which lent $2,000,000,000 to banks, railroads, and other industries. Charles G. Dawes headed this Corporation, which was intended to lift industry and the nation out of the depression.

Nothing short of world recovery, however, could stem the economic disaster that had struck the entire world as well as the United States. Federal relief was needed to give the millions of homeless and jobless enough to eat, to wear, to do.

The treasury deficit, $900,000,000 in 1931, grew to $2,000,000,000 by June of 1932. Taxes had to be increased. Luxuries, such as automobiles and theater tickets were taxed, as were bank checks and telephone and telegraph messages. Income taxes were raised with a surtax on million-dollar incomes, but revenue remained inadequate.

■ DEBT MORATORIUM. — The world situation was intensified by the problem of foreign debts. Europe owed the United States $238,000,000 and found it impossible to pay. In June, 1931, Hoover proposed a one-year moratorium on *all* international debts, partly to save Germany from utter collapse and partly to give America's own debtors a chance to recuperate and eventually pay. When the year was over, however, the payments became increasingly smaller or were postponed indefinitely. Finland alone paid in full.

Foreign Affairs. Young Plan. — In 1929 Owen D. Young became chairman of the International Reparations Committee. He revised the system of payments, making them collectable through a Bank of International Settlements at Basel, Switzerland. Germany's reparations were again drastically cut.

London Naval Conference. — America joined Great Britain, France, Italy, and Japan in a naval conference in London (January 21-April 22, 1930). This conference halted until 1936 the renewed activity in war construction, particularly of cruisers and submarines. The United States, Great Britain, and Japan signed the treaty while France and Italy, apprehensive of their Mediterranean interests, did not. The treaty called for naval parity between Great Britain and the United States, but allowed either one to increase her strength in an emergency.

League of Nations; The World Court. — Hoover's position on the League of Nations stated that the United States would be "glad to cooperate with . . . endeavors to further scientific, economic, and social welfare and to secure the limitation of armaments." By 1931 the United States was participating in some League activities, although technically it was not a member.

In 1928 Elihu Root had framed a formula that would satisfy the contested fifth reservation of the United States and at the same time be acceptable to the League and the Court. The Root Protocol granted the United States the privilege of consultation with the Court Council to learn whether American interests were involved, before any question came before the Court. This seemed a basis for agreement, but the Senate would not adopt it.

Other Events. — In February, 1933, the twentieth amendment to the Constitution was ratified. It abolished the "lame duck Congress" (the session starting in December, after a November election in which members not reelected still had seats; new members were not seated until 13 months after election), and changed inauguration day from March 4 to January 20.

Election of 1932. — Hoover was nominated again by the Republican party, and the Democrats nominated Governor Franklin D. Roosevelt of New York. Roosevelt toured the country, promising the people relief and recovery through a "New Deal," and the people responded by giving him a landslide victory. Roosevelt's election, however, was not so much a vote of confidence in the Democratic party and its leaders as it was a measure of the resentment, inspired in large part by the economic depression, against the Hoover administration. Roosevelt received 472 electoral votes to Hoover's 59, and 22,821,857 popular votes to Hoover's 15,761,841.

Franklin D. Roosevelt — 1933-1945

Franklin D. Roosevelt, an aristocrat and the fifth cousin of Theodore Roosevelt, was raised on a country estate at Hyde Park, New York and educated at Harvard and Columbia University Law School. In 1910 he entered politics and was elected to the New York State Assembly, where he was a progressive reformer and an early supporter of Woodrow Wilson. When Wilson was elected to the presidency, he appointed the knowledgeable and personally appealing Roosevelt assistant secretary of the navy. After holding that position for eight years, gaining a great deal of administrative experience and making many important political contacts, Roosevelt was nominated for the vice-presidency by the Democratic party (1920). Shortly after his defeat he contracted a severe case of infantile paralysis, but by 1924 he had made a remarkable recovery and appeared, on crutches, at the Democratic convention to make the nominating speech for Alfred E. Smith. In 1928, at Smith's urging, Roosevelt ran for governor of New York, carrying the state by a small majority. In 1930, after a term as an effective, liberal governor, he was reelected by a record-breaking vote. By 1932 he had demonstrated superb skill as a politician, administrator, and governor; by using government as a positive tool for the welfare of people in need, he had made New York into a model progressive state.

The New Deal. — Roosevelt's "New Deal," a domestic program from 1933-1939, continued and expanded the progressive trend evident in America since the 1880's. The American government had assumed an increasingly positive role in safeguarding human welfare, and on both the state and national levels an impressive body of legislation had been passed that sought to regulate business and to prevent or alleviate economic hardship. This progressive tradition was furthered during the war years, when the federal government successfully engaged in full-scale economic planning; many of these ideas survived the "era of normalcy." Due to the depth of the depression Roosevelt had to act quickly, and although he relied heavily upon older ideas in his attempt to bring the economy and government abreast once again, the impression was falsely created that the New Deal was revolutionary rather than evolutionary. Recently it has been maintained, with some truth, that the New Deal was actually quite conservative. Franklin Roosevelt himself continually asserted that he was determined merely to preserve the existing American free enterprise, capitalistic system. On the other hand, he certainly went much further than his predecessors in helping the "forgotten man" and in stressing the government's responsibility to promote the well-being of the majority of the nation's citizens. With the aid of a group of unofficial advisors, popularly referred to as the "brain trust," Roosevelt indicated that the nation would move away from the old principle of economic individualism toward a planned economy in an effort to balance conflicting interests and classes in the economic system.

The First Hundred Days. — The New Deal had three main objectives: relief for workers, farmers, and the unemployed; recovery for the nation's economy; and reform that would prevent future economic maladjustments.

The famous first "one hundred days" stressed recovery: Congress, called into special session on March 9, 1933, enacted a series of essential measures to meet the immediate needs of a discouraged and destitute people. The most important recovery measures dealt with banking, industry, and agriculture.

Runs on banks had forced most of them to suspend operations. Fearful that the banking system was on the verge of collapse, President Roosevelt declared a bank holiday (March 5-9, 1933) that closed all national banks and affiliated institutions. Congress quickly passed the Emergency Banking Law, giving the president the power to reorganize insolvent national banks; most bank resumed successful operation under this measure.

One of the most sweeping and important New Deal measures was the National Industrial Recovery Act

U.S. ARMY

FRANKLIN DELANO ROOSEVELT
(1933–1945)

During his three and a half terms in office, Franklin D. Roosevelt encountered major problems, both at home and abroad. He was faced with the greatest depression to beset the land (*right*). In 1939 war broke out in Europe. On December 7, 1941, Japan attacked Pearl Harbor without warning; within a few days the United States was at war with Japan and Germany. In February of 1945, Churchill, Roosevelt, and Stalin met at Yalta in the Crimea (*above*) to discuss plans for the defeat of Germany and its fate after the war. The "Big Three" also announced plans for the San Francisco Conference, where the U.N. was charted.

JOHN VACHON

WALKER EVANS

(1933). Under the provisions of this act, a National Recovery Administration (NRA) was created to help representatives of government, business, and the public prepare codes in each industry; these codes, if enforced, would eliminate unfair competition practices, abolish child labor and sweat shops, establish minimum wages and maximum hours, create additional jobs for the unemployed, and assure labor the right to bargain collectively. Hundreds of codes were drafted by the NRA under the chairmanship of General Hugh Johnson, but few proved effective. Small businessmen soon complained that the codes discriminated against them, while liberals charged that the NRA was creating giant monopolies and conservatives complained about the rights given labor (in Section 7a). In 1935 the Supreme Court ruled the National Industrial Recovery Act unconstitutional.

■ THE AAA. — Another important piece of legislation was the Agricultural Adjustment Act, passed in May, 1933. This act created an Agricultural Adjustment Administration (AAA) authorized to (1) control production of certain enumerated commodities by paying cash subsidies to farmers who voluntarily restricted acreage or reduced the numbers of their livestock; (2) impose taxes on the processors of certain agricultural commodities in order to secure the funds to pay the farm subsidies; and (3) pay farmers to sow grass on untilled land that would provide cover for top soil and prevent dust storms. While the act did increase farm prices and raise the income of large farmers, it incurred a hardship on small farmers, particularly tenant farmers, many of whom were forced off

the land as a result of the cut-back in farm acreage. Opposition to the AAA was also voiced by consumers who resented increased prices, processors who objected to the tax on their services, and liberals who felt that an "economy of scarcity" was ill-suited to a land where millions were underfed. Like the NIRA, the Agricultural Adjustment Act was ruled unconstitutional (1936).

■ OTHER RELIEF ORGANIZATIONS. — Although the relief program concentrated primarily upon work relief, there was also some direct relief. The Federal Emergency Relief Administration (FERA) was created to assist the states in caring for the unemployed. It was authorized to match funds with state and local governments for distributing aid to the jobless. The Civilian Conservation Corps (CCC), a bold relief measure, was created to employ destitute young men. Scattered in 2,600 "work camps" throughout the country, the workers provided an invaluable service in the national parks, forests, and reclamation projects in wilderness areas throughout the nation. The Civil Works Administration (CWA), which gave temporary work relief to four million jobless men through the 1933-34 winter, was replaced by such long-range relief agencies as the Public Works Administration (PWA) and the Works Progress Administration (WPA). Under Secretary of the Interior Harold Ickes, the PWA was assigned numerous heavy construction projects that eventually relieved much unemployment. The WPA, under Harry Hopkins, returned the problem of unemployables to the states, but put employables to work on socially valuable projects, rather than trivial tasks. By March, 1936, four million persons employed by

the WPA were building schools, parks, roads, irrigation dams, and other important civic-improvement projects.

At the same time, Congress was dealing with long-range economic reforms and serious problems only indirectly related to the great depression. One project resulted in the passage of the Tennessee Valley Authority Act, which represented a long-sought triumph for those who desired to place the power resources of the Tennessee River at the disposal of the people rather than private interests. The act created an independent public corporation, the Tennessee Valley Authority (TVA), to develop the economic and social well-being of an area embracing parts of seven depressed states. Through construction of dams, power plants, and transmission lines, many farms and villages in the Tennessee Valley were supplied (in most instances for the first time) with electric power at low rates. One of the most successful of all New Deal measures, the TVA launched an important experiment in government ownership, led to the rehabilitation of the area, and served as a public "yardstick" that forced private power companies in the area to lower their rates. It also served as a blueprint for projects throughout the nation.

■ FINANCIAL MEASURES. — To protect the investing public against fraudulent practices, Congress passed the Truth in Securities Act (1933) and the Securities Exchange Act (1934), which created the Securities and Exchange Commission (SEC). These measures gave the federal government broad powers in regulating the activities of the stock exchange.

Another important area of reform was in banking. The Glass-Steagall

Banking Act (1933) was designed to prevent future collapses of the private banking system. It forbade banks to engage in the investment business, restricted the speculative uses of bank credits, and expanded the federal reserve system to banks previously excluded. Its most popular provision established the Federal Deposit Insurance Corporation (FDIC) to insure all deposits up to $5,000. National control of the banking system was further strengthened by the banking act of 1935.

The Second New Deal.—Many businessmen and political leaders began to resist what they considered to be the "radical" policies of the New Dealers, charging that the administration was destroying private enterprise and undermining the capitalistic system through interference in every phase of business activity. Nevertheless, the administration received the endorsement of the American people in the 1934 congressional elections, and the Democratic party increased its strength in both houses of Congress. After the returns were known, Roosevelt indicated that he was ready to sponsor a comprehensive program to assist the underprivileged throughout the nation. Of the many new pieces of legislation that resulted (National Youth Administration, Resettlement Administration, Farm Security Administration), two measures stand out. Most important was the Social Security Act (1935). A great deal of pressure had been put on the administration to provide some measure of security for the nation's citizens, particularly its older ones. To meet these demands, the SSA was enacted. It provided for (1) old age insurance, financed jointly by workers and employers; (2) unemployment compensation, administered by the states but financed by a federal tax on payrolls; and (3) federal aid to the states for destitute persons, child health, maternity care, crippled children, the aged, and the blind. Although attacked by conservatives as "radical" and by liberals as too conservative, the measure was welcomed by a majority of the people and upheld by the Supreme Court.

■ LABOR LEGISLATION.—After the NIRA was declared unconsitutional, Senator Wagner of New York sponsored a bill to protect labor's right to organize and to bargain collectively. The National Labor Relations Act (1935) created a National Labor Relations Board (NLRB), which was empowered to determine suitable units for collective bargaining, to conduct elections for the choice of laborers' representatives, and to prevent interference with such elections. The NLRB was also empowered to investigate complaints of unfair labor practices and to issue restraining orders, which it could petition federal courts to enforce. Through this and other "labor" legislation, the New Deal both changed and made lasting contributions to the growing movement of organized labor.

Opposition to the New Deal.—Although the New Deal was popular with a majority of the people, opposition to it continued to grow. The administration was attacked by both Republicans and conservative Democrats, who formed the Liberty League, among other organizations, to combat Roosevelt. Radical opposition was manifest in such rabble-rousers as Senator Huey P. Long of Louisiana, whose "Share Our Wealth" program promised to divide the nation's wealth among the poor; Dr. Francis E. Townsend, who promised pensions of $200 monthly to all citizens over sixty years of age; and the anti-Semitic Reverend Charles E. Coughlin, Detroit's radio priest who demanded an expulsion of all Jews from public office and a nationally controlled currency system. Several million Americans followed these and other false prophets, all of whom were pledged to the defeat of Roosevelt in 1936.

Election of 1936.—The Republicans nominated Alfred M. Landon of Kansas on a platform that seemed to call for a continuance of all New Deal measures, yet somehow without extra cost and with no danger to the Constitution. Roosevelt was renominated by the Democrats on a platform pledging to carry on the New Deal. Despite almost solid opposition from the press, Roosevelt carried every state in the Union except Maine and Vermont, winning 523 electoral votes to Landon's 8.

Court Reorganization.—In 1935, seven of the nine judges serving on the Supreme Court had been appointed to their position by Republican presidents, and six of them were over seventy years old. During the next two years, the Court, by narrow majorities, held seven basic New Deal pieces of legislation unconstitutional; four of the judges often allowed prejudice and blind tradition rather than reason dictate their decisions. Accordingly, in February, 1937, President Roosevelt asked Congress to reorganize the Court by enlarging it from nine to fifteen members, depending upon the number of judges that declined to retire at age seventy. Already beginning to react against executive control, Congress denounced this measure as "court packing" and refused, amidst great controversy, to heed Roosevelt's wishes. While the debate raged, however, the Court suddenly reversed itself and handed down favorable decisions on several important New Deal measures. During the next few years, Roosevelt achieved his end as the death or retirement of older justices allowed him to place younger and more liberal men on the bench. Nevertheless, the incident aroused further public and official opposition to his administration.

Climax of the New Deal.—A sharp business recession, caused by Roosevelt's conservative policy of curtailing government relief spending in an effort to balance the budget, brought a return of hard times between August, 1937 and June, 1938. Although revived federal spending restored conditions rather quickly, the new recession further alienated some of the electorate. Another important incident with the same effect was Roosevelt's attempt to "purge" conservative anti-New Deal Democrats from Congress by appealing to constituents for their defeat. The plan did not work; not only were many of these Democrats reelected, but for the first time since 1933 Democratic majorities were reduced in both congressional houses. Although the Democrats still controlled the federal legislature, the Republicans now had enough strength to operate as an effective minority; in alliance with conservative Democrats they could control Congress.

In actuality, the New Deal came to an end after the 1938 congressional elections. Roosevelt continued in office until his death in 1945, but during these last years effective opposition plus Roosevelt's preoccupation with foreign affairs brought domestic reform virtually to an end.

Results of the New Deal.—Franklin D. Roosevelt's years as president constituted one of the most controversial periods in American history. Just as Roosevelt was both greatly loved and bitterly hated, the New Deal had both good and bad points. It vastly increased the federal debt, fostered bureaucracy, aroused class consciousness, and left many serious problems unsolved. On the other hand, its benefits far outweighed its shortcomings. Because of the New Deal, the nation came through its most serious economic crisis without upsetting its capitalistc system. The New Deal brought labor and agriculture, long ignored, into better balance with industry, and for the first time gave various minority groups, particulary the Negro, an important place in the American system. It also fostered a more equitable distribution of wealth and conserved the nation's resources, both physical and human. Finally, and most important, the New Deal permanently established the principle of *positive* government—the obligation of the federal government to provide for the general welfare of all its citizens in time of need.

The Road to World War II.—International developments between World War I and World War II were shaped largely by the breakdown of collective security, for which the United States was in large part responsible. Rejecting their world responsibilities through an unwillingness to accept any foreign commitments, the American people intended to remain aloof from world events, except in matters of economic or military self-interest. By refusing to join the League of Nations or the World Court and by passing high tariffs, Americans contributed to the rise of nationalism and thus helped to undermine faith in collective efforts to preserve the peace. This, in turn, helped dictators who sought to expand their influence and territory at the expense of others, and eventually led to another major war.

American Neutrality.—During the 1920's and 1930's dictatorial powers threatened the democracies and world peace. The Soviet Union, under Joseph Stalin, Italy, under Benito Mussolini, and Germany, under Adolph Hitler were all intensely nationalistic (despite Stalin's professions of "world" communism) and determined to expand at the expense of weaker neighbors. When the

WORLD WAR II began September 1, 1939, when Germany invaded Poland. The United States entered the conflict in Europe on December 8, 1941, by declaring war on Japan. Germany and Italy then declared war on America. The preceding day, December 7, th United States naval base at Pearl Harbor had been attacked without warning by a Japanese task force (*upper right*). In Europe, Allied Flying Fortresses (*center right*) bombarded Germany almost daily. The heavy concentration of air power plus the Allied invasion of Normandy, June 6, 1944, led to the eventual dismemberment of Germany's war machine. Allied soldiers (*center left*) fought from farmhouse to farmhouse, from town to town, and by May 7, 1945, the war in Europe was over. In the Pacific, the war was fought on many small coral islands. One such island, Iwo Jima (*bottom*), was invaded on February 19, 1945. The island fell less than a month later, at a cost of 19,935 American casualties. After Iwo Jima, Okinawa fell, and the American forces began to concentrate on the islands of Japan itself. An atomic bomb was dropped on Hiroshima, another on Nagasaki—Japan signed the surrender on September 2, 1945 aboard the U.S.S. *Missouri*.

LOOK MAGAZINE

U.S. ARMY

LOOK MAGAZINE

QUICK

depression played into the hands of its military leaders, Japan also showed aggressive tendencies in the 1930's. Advocating territorial expansion as the only cure for its problems, Japanese generals won control of the nation and committed it to a program of expansion.

While these nations engaged in aggression during the 1930's, Americans became convinced that they should separate themselves from the rest of the world. Isolationist sentiment was fostered by the depression, which forced most Americans to concentrate on domestic affairs; by the existence of some fascist and communist sentiment in the country; by the failure of our World War I Allies to repay their debts to us; and by the disclosure of a Senate investigating committee, under the chairmanship of Gerald P. Nye (1934-1936), that during World War I American bankers and munitions manufacturers made huge fortunes. This led many Americans to believe that the nation had been forced into the war by these economic interests, and they were determined to prevent this from happening again.

Accordingly, Congress passed a series of laws known as the "Neutrality Acts," which were designed to prevent American involvement in future "European" wars. Based on the assumption that economic motives had been responsible for America's entrance into World War I, these acts stipulated that, should another war occur, America would no longer insist upon maintaining its neutral rights; thus, they represented a reversal of traditional American policy. President Roosevelt had no sympathy for the measures. He continually maintained, in vain, that the United States could remain at peace only by preventing another European war through collective security: cooperation with democracies to check dictators and aggressive nations before they became strong enough to bid for world power.

Approach to War. — Hitler, using well-trained, well-armed troops and skillfull diplomacy, added both Austria and Czechoslovakia's Sudetenland to German territory in 1938 and 1939. Italy overran Albania. After the signing of a non-aggression pact with Russia, Hitler's troops invaded Poland, and World War II began. Russia annexed the Baltic countries and then launched an aggressive war against Finland. In the spring of 1940 Hitler carried out his "blitzkrieg"; Denmark and Norway fell in April, 1940, the Netherlands and Belgium fell in May, and France capitulated in June. Only England held out against Germany, although Russia soon joined the Allies after Hitler unexpectedly attacked her.

These events finally convinced Americans that the time for preparedness was at hand, for the Western Hemisphere was endangered and would become more so if England fell before the German assault. Military and industrial mobilization began. After Franklin Roosevelt was reelected in 1940 the United States became, in the president's words, the "arsenal of democracy." The president had already traded fifty American destroyers to Britain in exchange for naval bases in the Caribbean. According to the provisions of the Lend Lease Act, passed in March, 1941, the United States transferred a great deal of military equipment and an unlimited amount of other aid to Great Britain and other nations resisting German forces. By autumn of 1941 Congress had repealed the Neutrality Acts and the nation was engaged in an undeclared naval war with Germany, as armed American ships freighted supplies across the Atlantic to England. America's entrance into the war, however, was caused, not by events in the Atlantic, but by events on the other side of the globe.

The Attack by Japan. — Japanese-American relationships were strained throughout the 1930's, particularly between 1939 and 1941. After signing a ten-year alliance with Germany and Italy in September, 1940, the Japanese became more aggressive. Attempting to take advantage of the Allied Powers' preoccupation with the European war, Japan invaded and occupied French Indo-China and thus endangered American, Dutch, and British possessions in southern Asia. In retaliation for this and for other aggressive acts, the United States froze Japanese assets in this country and embargoed shipments to Japan of fuel oil and scrap iron. Prolonged but unsuccessful negotiations followed between the two countries, while Premier Tojo at the same time secretly prepared for an attack on American-owned Pearl Harbor. The attack occurred on the afternoon of December 7, 1941. Completely surprised and unprepared, the United States suffered heavy losses, particularly to its naval fleet. On December 8 Congress declared the existence of a state of war between the United States and Japan. Germany, and Italy, adhering to the provisions of their Tripartate Pact, declared war on America several days later. The United States had entered World War II.

World War II. — The attack on Pearl Harbor quickly quieted arguments over American foreign policy and united the nation in a solemn determination to successfully meet a great crisis. By the spring of 1943 the American people had converted their peacetime industrial establishment into the mightiest wartime arsenal the world had ever seen. Labor worked ceaselessly; food production reached new all-time highs. A two-ocean navy was hastily constructed, and ten million men served in the armed forces. (For an account of World War II see p. 809.)

Allied Cooperation. — Among the most notable achievements of the war were Allied cooperation and the evolution and establishment of the United Nations. The leaders of the three major Allied Powers, Roosevelt, Winston Churchill, and Joseph Stalin, and their representatives, met regularly to work out military strategy and plans for peace. At the Moscow Conference (October, 1943), the Cairo Conference (November, 1943), and the Teheran Conference (November, 1943), such important matters as the details of the invasion of Normandy and the establishment of a second military front, the creation of international organization, and the acceptance of the principle of continued Russian cooperation with the Western Powers after the war, were worked out.

Several conferences were held specifically to discuss postwar problems. The most important and controversial was the conference conducted at Yalta in January, 1945. Roosevelt, determined to establish a United Nations Organization with Russian participation, made some concessions to Stalin: three Russian votes in the United Nations Assembly, territorial concessions in eastern Poland (which was already under the domination of the Russian army), and Russian dominance over Manchuria. On the other hand, Roosevelt and the West won equal, if not greater concessions from Russia: the promise of democratic governments in Poland and Yugoslavia; support for the United Nations; the division of postwar Germany into four temporary occupation zones, one of which was to go to France; and Russian entrance into the war against Japan after Germany's defeat. This last point was extremely important, since United States military experts estimated that without Russian aid, it would take approximately 18 months and the loss of over a million American lives to conquer Japan after Germany's defeat. Considering the military realities of the situation, Yalta represented a diplomatic triumph for Western statesmanship, and was hailed as such by a majority of the American people at the time. Had Russia adhered to the promises made at Yalta, the basis would have been laid for world peace and international cooperation.

End of the War. — The war was rapidly coming to an end while the "Big Three" met at Yalta. In January, 1945, the Russian Army moved into Germany from the East; by March 1, they were 30 miles from Berlin. Anglo-American armies from the West crossed the Rhine on March 7, 1945. Hitler and his top officials committed suicide or fled, and Germany surrendered unconditionally on May 8, 1945. The official document was signed in Allied headquarters, Reims.

Japan's surrender came in August, 1945, after atomic bombs were dropped for the first time on Hiroshima and Nagasaki, two military-industrial targets, and immense destruction was caused. The dropping of the bombs ended the war but ushered in the atomic age, making clear to the people of the world that another full-scale war might destroy civilization. The decision to use atomic weapons for military purposes rested solely with President Truman. He was under great pressure from both military leaders and scientists, who disagreed among themselves on what policy to follow.

Death of President Roosevelt. — President Roosevelt did not live to see the end of the war or the actual creation of the United Nations, two events to which he had contributed so much. On April 12, 1945, as delegates met in San Francisco to draft the charter of the world organization, Franklin Roosevelt died suddenly at his vacation home in Warm Springs, Georgia.

LIBRARY OF CONGRESS

HARRY S. TRUMAN
(1945–1953)

WIDE WORLD

DEFENSE DEPT. U.S. MARINE CORPS.

On June 26, 1945, Truman watched his secretary of state sign the document establishing the United Nations (*upper right*). Five years later, U.S. marines (*right*) went to the defense of South Korea.

Harry S. Truman—1945-1953

When Harry S. Truman was sworn in as the thirty-third president by Chief Justice Harlan Stone, his immediate objective was the successful completion of the war against Germany and Japan. The United States was emerging from World War II as the leading power among the Western nations, however, and as president of such a world power, Truman also inherited the long range objective and far greater responsibility of shaping the postwar world. Fortunately, he was aided in that task by the United Nations, which was formally created in June, 1945, when the Charter was signed by fifty nations.

Postwar America.—The United States reconverted to peace with surprising ease. The tremendous army and navy were rapidly and efficiently demobilized. Returning military men were aided by the farsighted G.I. Bill of Rights, which provided veterans with unemployment insurance, government-guaranteed loans for business or home building purposes, and free education in colleges, universities, and vocational schools. War contracts had been canceled, but the demand for scarce goods kept factories busy. Control of rationed materials was discontinued soon after the war ended, and price ceilings on various foods, such as dairy products and meats, were removed as soon as it was practical to do so.

Meanwhile, the United States was taking a leading part in the postwar administration of Japan and Germany. Truman was praised for placing exceptional men in charge of these occupied countries and allowing them full responsibility for carrying out their policies. In 1947 the state department announced that reciprocal trade agreements had been negotiated with many other countries. After World War I Wilson had made the grave error of presuming to decide our foreign policy according to his own ideas. Truman, careful to avoid Wilson's blunders, consulted with leading Republicans on all international questions.

Both James F. Byrnes and George C. Marshall, who served consecutively as secretary of state during Truman's first administration, were capable men. Marshall in particular was respected by both Republicans and Democrats, and this proved to be of paramount importance after January, 1947, when Republicans controlled both houses of Congress.

■ **THE TAFT-HARTLEY ACT.**—It was inevitable, once the war had ended, that strikes would occur throughout the nation. Farm prices were rising rapidly, due principally to the exportation of food to destitute nations. Prices of consumer goods also rose after the Office of Price Administration (OPA) was dissolved. Labor struck for higher wages and an upward revision was granted in almost all cases. It was at this time that the Taft-Hartley Act was approved by Congress. Although denounced by labor as a "slave bill" and rejected by Truman, the measure was passed over the president's veto. The Taft-Hartley Act deprived labor of much of the power it had gained during the New Deal. It banned the closed shop, permitted employers to sue unions for broken contracts or for damage inflicted during strikes, forced unions to abide by a "sixty-day cooling off period" before striking in vital industries, required unions to make public their financial statements, and forbade them to contribute to political campaigns.

■ **THE TRUMAN DOCTRINE.**—By 1947 it was evident that Russian influence in Europe was expanding. Communist minorities in France, Italy, Turkey, and elsewhere gained strength due to postwar economic chaos. It was feared that Russian influence, perhaps even dominance, would soon engulf the Continent. As a result, the president announced the famous "Truman Doctrine" in March; he asked Congress for American aid to Greece and Turkey to resist the spread of communism in those areas. Truman declared that it "must be the policy of the United States to support free people who are resisting attempted subjugation by armed minorities or by outside pressure." This should be done, he continued, through economic and financial aid to maintain order and stability in the affected nations. The Truman Doctrine received bipartisan political support.

Truman's policy was carried even further by Secretary of State George C. Marshall; on June 5, 1947, during a Harvard University commencement address, he stated that the American government was willing to aid any country that agreed to aid in its own recovery. This principle was the basis for the successful European Recovery Plan (ERP) for the reconstruction and rehabilitation of Europe.

The Second Term.—As the presidential election of 1948 approached, Truman was conceded but little chance against Thomas E. Dewey. First, the end of World War II was expected to bring an end to the previous "war emergency" voting that had kept Roosevelt in office. Secondly, southern Democrats had split the Democratic ranks by forming the States' Rights party. Truman campaigned vigorously, however, and was swept in. He appointed Dean Acheson as secretary of state to succeed General Marshall, who wished to retire.

Repeal of the Taft-Hartley Act had been a major contention of the campaign, but a coalition of Republicans and southern Democrats defeated the repeal. Truman and the "Fair Deal" Democrats proposed civil rights for Negroes, but southern congressmen filibustered the bill to death.

The discord between East and West grew increasingly intense and continued to shape American foreign policy; diplomatic moves were directed toward uniting the free nations of the world and providing protection for them against communist aggression. The "cold war," however, suddenly grew hot.

Korean War. — In 1949 both Russia and the U.S. had withdrawn their occupation troops from Korea. On June 25, 1950, the Communist North Korean army crossed the 38th parallel and attacked South Korea. The United States immediately joined with the United Nations in sending troops, ships, and planes to fight on the side of the South Koreans. After a year of bitter warfare, fighting slowed down while long truce conferences were held.

NATO. — The Korean War proved that the U.S. was willing to assume leadership in resisting Communist aggression. Truman took another step in this direction when he sent General Eisenhower to Europe to implement the North Atlantic Treaty Organization (NATO), created to integrate western Europe's military forces. NATO grew out of the North Atlantic Treaty of April, 1949, in which twelve western nations agreed that an attack against one would be considered an attack on all. They also bound themselves to use force, if necessary, to maintain the security of the North Atlantic area; to this end Congress passed the largest military appropriations bill ever voted in peacetime. President Truman had made the nation and the world aware of "the communist threat."

Other Events. — In domestic affairs, wage and price controls were put into effect, and the draft was extended. An excess-profits tax was passed and the twenty-second amendment limited future presidents to two terms of office.

The costs of fighting a cold war throughout the world and an actual war in Korea forced living costs and taxes higher. These factors, plus the corruption found in some departments of the government, became the issues of the 1952 presidential campaign.

Dwight David Eisenhower — 1953-1961

Responding to the demands of the liberal wing of the Republican Party, in 1952 General Dwight D. Eisenhower resigned as supreme commander of the allied forces in Europe to become a candidate for the presidential nomination. He finally decided to seek the presidency largely for one reason — to make certain that no conservative-isolationist, particularly Senator Robert A.

Taft of Ohio, captured the position. Eisenhower strongly believed that the United States had an important and inescapable role to play in world affairs; retreat, in his opinion, would be a tragic mistake. He succeeded in securing control of the Republican national convention and obtaining the nomination.

At the Democratic convention, the eloquent governor of Illinois, Adlai E. Stevenson, was "drafted" for the nomination. Stevenson, however, could not overcome Eisenhower's personal popularity, or escape the Republican charge that the Democrats had condoned corruption in the administration and that it was "time for a change." Most effective, however, was Eisenhower's campaign promise to go to Korea to end the war. The Republicans gained a substantial victory, their first in 20 years. Eisenhower captured 442 electoral votes to Stevenson's 89.

With the election of Eisenhower to the presidency, one great period of U.S. political power ended and another began. The Korean War was at a standstill, with no prospect of being brought to a close after two and a half years of fighting and 128,530 U.S. casualties. The situation in the Far East brought constant threat of the spread of communism and loss of U.S. prestige. In the Arabian Middle East, where Arab opposed Jew, communism was gaining ground because of the anti-Semitic drive by the Kremlin. The North Atlantic Treaty Alliance, established during the Truman administration and guided by General Eisenhower, had not fulfilled its purpose — rearmament schedules were lagging.

Taxes and living costs were at a high peak because of the defense program. The problem was to arrest inflation without endangering the safety of the country. One of the first acts of the Eisenhower administration was to end all economic controls except those on rent and strategic material. All wage and salary controls were abolished, and a gradual removal of controls on consumer goods was inaugurated. Certain regulations remained, such as debt and credit controls by the treasury and the Federal Reserve Board.

President Truman had requested in 1950 that a Federal Security Agency be made a major department of the government. In 1953, President Eisenhower appointed Mrs. Oveta Culp Hobby (wartime commander of the Women's Army Corps) as administrator of the Federal Security Agency; at Eisenhower's request Congress made this agency a cabinet post, to be called the department of health, education, and welfare.

The Korean War was brought to an end by an armistice signed at Panmunjom, Korea, in 1953. The threat of U.S. participation in the Indo-Chinese War was removed by an armistice signed at Geneva in 1954. At the same time, the Communist Control Act of 1954 was passed, outlawing the Communist party in the United States.

Civil Rights. — In May of 1954, the Supreme Court, presided over by Chief Justice Earl Warren, handed down a momentous, unanimous decision outlawing segregation in the public

schools. This ruling, set forth in *Brown v. Topeka,* reversed the *Plessy v. Ferguson* decision of 1896, which said that "separate but equal" facilities were constitutional. Maintaining that "separate educational facilities are inherently unequal," the court ruled that school desegregation should proceed carefully, but at once. Despite southern resistance, particularly from hostile state governors, the process of integration began. The pace was slow at first but soon increased, especially after 1957 when Eisenhower used federal troops to enforce the law at Little Rock, Arkansas.

■ **OTHER LEGISLATION.** — A bill was passed permitting the United States to join Canada in construction of the Saint Lawrence Seaway, which would open the Great Lakes to ocean commerce. Additional legislation increased the minimum wage and extended by nearly ten million the number of people receiving social security benefits, thus continuing the New and Fair Deal principle that the federal government is responsible for the welfare and security of its citizens. After a long congressional debate, with divisions drawn on sectional rather than party lines, the movement to extend civil rights made limited advances. The federal government was empowered to seek court orders, if necessary, to guarantee all individuals the right to vote. President Eisenhower also appointed a bipartisan Civil Rights Commission to examine abuses of civil rights and to make recommendations for new legislation. Reflecting the president's inherent conservatism and his "business" philosophy, an act was passed in 1955 that for the first time licensed private corporations to use atomic material. An income tax revision, favoring the upper-income brackets, was also effected.

Internal Security. — One of the most prominent aspects of the Eisenhower years was an increased concern with the question of internal security. The apparent communist threat aroused the American people to take action against individuals and groups considered subversive. Feeling against such people was heightened when a former state department official, Alger Hiss, was convicted of passing secret documents to communist agents. Former communists, persons who had been associated with communists, and others suspected of radical tendencies became the objects of public and private investigations throughout the country. Many people were unfairly dismissed from their jobs, loyalty oaths and investigations were required by public and private employers, and although very few people were ever proven to be communists, many were dismissed as "security risks." The most spectacular "Red hunt" was conducted by the reckless and demagogic chairman of the Senate Committee on Un-American Activities, Joseph R. McCarthy of Wisconsin. McCarthy's charges, which were eventually hurled against the Eisenhower administration, finally resulted in his censure by a bipartisan Senate resolution.

Election of 1956. — President Eisenhower's poor health was a matter of deep

WIDE WORLD

WIDE WORLD

DWIGHT D. EISENHOWER
(1953–1961)

The World War II hero was a natural to win the 1952 presidential election. War was still raging in Korea, and the American people believed Eisenhower could bring it to an end. Six months after his inauguration the armistice was signed. "Ike" then turned to domestic problems. In 1954 the Supreme Court ruled school segregation illegal (*left*). On February 1, 1958, America's first satellite, *Explorer I*, was launched into orbit (*far left*) from Cape Canaveral.

concern to Americans and the rest of the world. Nevertheless, he was determined to seek a second term. Running again with Richard M. Nixon, who had gained fame as a congressman by his crusade against supposed communist infiltration in the civil service, Eisenhower once again won a landslide victory over Adlai Stevenson: he polled 457 electoral votes to his opponent's 73. The overwhelming endorsement of the president was largely a measure of his personal popularity, however, and was not an endorsement of the Republican party; for the first time in American history a reelected president lost both the House and the Senate to the opposing party.

Eisenhower's Second Term.—After his reelection, Eisenhower continued his legislative program. The Pentagon was reorganized, a reciprocal trade program was extended, and amendments to the Social Security Act once again increased its scope and its coverage Through large federal expenditures for public works in 1958, the nation began to recover from its most serious economic recession since World War II.

Space Exploration.—Of greatest importance was the continuing Soviet challenge, particularly in the new field of outer space. Announcement by Russia in October, 1957, that its scientists had successfully launched a satellite that was revolving about the earth strengthened the administration's determination to overcome America's apparent lag in this field. Several space programs were launched. By January, 1958, the United States successfully sent several earth satellites into orbit; in May, 1961, after the Soviet Union

had already done so, the United States sent its first human astronaut, navy commander Alan B. Shepard, into outer space and returned him safely to earth. While disarmament negotiations were being carried on in Geneva in an effort to achieve enduring peace, both the United States and Russia competed furiously in the construction of new and more potent nuclear weapons. Rockets carrying nuclear warheads and atomic submarines equipped with Polaris missiles became formidable weapons in the arms arsenals.

■ THE SUMMIT CONFERENCE.—After much preparation a Summit Conference was proposed for 1960, and it was hoped that this high-level meeting would result in the easing of world tensions and threats of nuclear destruction. In September, 1959, at Eisenhower's invitation, Premier Khrushchev of Russia visited the United States and was warmly greeted. Khrushchev's cordial personal negotiations with the president led to hopes that the basis had been laid for another and more fruitful meeting to discuss disarmament. A few weeks before the second conference was to convene, however, a United States U-2 reconnaisance plane was brought down within the Soviet Union. When U-2 pilot Francis G. Powers admitted to Soviet officials that he had been mapping military targets, and the administration, after retracting earlier denunciations of the story, refused to apologize for the incident, Khrushchev then refused to negotiate with President Eisenhower.

Castro in Cuba.—Before Eisenhower left office, communism came to United States shores for the first time. Cuban Premier Fidel Castro, who had led a

successful revolution against dictator Fulgencio Batista, began to turn to communist nations for economic and military support after he encountered opposition from the American public and United States government; this began early in 1959 after wholesale executions of Castro's former enemies. Cuban-American relations were further aggravated in May, 1959, after Castro promulgated an Agrarian Reform Law, which empowered the Cuban government to expropriate, without compensation, American-owned property on the island. Whether or not Castro was a communist when he seized power in mid-1958 is debatable; that he had strong communist connections and convictions by 1961 is certain. While at first Eisenhower was patient with the new Cuban regime, he broke off diplomatic relations with Cuba just before leaving office in December, 1960.

Election of 1960.—The Democrats nominated Senator John F. Kennedy of Massachusetts for president, and Senator Lyndon B. Johnson of Texas for vice-president. The Republican nominees were Vice-President Richard M. Nixon and Henry Cabot Lodge, United States ambassador to the United Nations. The election was decided by the closest popular vote since 1884; the Democratic ticket received a plurality of only 112,000 votes out of a total of more than 69 million ballots. Born in 1917, Kennedy became the youngest man and the first Catholic ever elected president of the United States.

During the campaign, Kennedy had promised the voters that he would name a "ministry of talent" as cabinet advisers. Fulfilling that promise, he gathered around him advisers distin-

LOOK MAGAZINE

JOHN F. KENNEDY
(1961–1963)

THREE PROMINENT GEOGRAPHICAL LOCATIONS during John F. Kennedy's first year in office were Cuba, Berlin, and Vienna. The fierce-looking soldiers (*upper left*), are supporters of Castro's regime in Cuba. Equally ominous is the scene at the Brandenburg Gate at the East-West Berlin border (*lower left*). On August 14th, the East German government strengthened its defenses. In his conference with Nikita Khrushchev in Vienna (*right*), President Kennedy unsuccessfully attempted to improve the cold war situation.

WIDE WORLD

WIDE WORLD

guished by their youthfulness, academic background, informality, and penchant for action. Adlai Stevenson, still enormously popular although twice-defeated for the presidency, accepted the position as ambassador to the United Nations. The new, young president and his advisers worked closely with the outgoing Eisenhower administration to insure a smooth transfer of government, and the continuity with which that task was carried out immediately won for Kennedy the public's confidence. His historic inaugural address was an inspiring appeal to his fellow countrymen to join him in pushing toward a "New Frontier," both at home and abroad.

John F. Kennedy—1961-1963

President Kennedy, an experienced congressman and senator, showed great insight into the nature and potentialities of his office. He pressed hard for new programs in housing, education, agriculture, minimum wage, urban renewal, and medical care for the aged. After succeeding in increasing the size of the conservative House Rules Committee, he marshaled narrow majorities for housing, urban renewal, depressed areas, and an increase in minimum wages.

Kennedy also sought to broaden and strengthen America's defenses by increasing the nation's missile supply, raising the level of conventional arms, and strengthening NATO. He pressed for new and better relations with Latin America through a ten billion dollar Alliance for Progress, and he advocated a fresh approach to arms control and a nuclear test ban. To strengthen the image of the United States abroad, and at

the same time help underdeveloped nations, he suggested and implemented the unique and enormously successful Peace Corps. The Corps was composed mainly of youthful volunteers who served overseas at subsistence wages as teachers, farm helpers, public health workers, and a host of other occupations. This organization, under R. Sargent Shriver, helped foreign countries meet their urgent needs for skilled manpower.

Cuban Invasion.—The high hopes that greeted the first months of the Kennedy administration were dampened by some notable failures, the most important of which was the Cuban invasion fiasco. On April 17, 1961, approximately 1,500 anti-Castro forces, trained under the supervision of the United States Central Intelligence Agency (CIA), unsuccessfully attempted to invade Cuba. Most of the invaders were captured on the landing beach at the Bay of Pigs when the Cuban people failed to rise in support of the rebels. Anti-United States demonstrations flared throughout Latin America, and the president, who took full responsibility for the decision to back the invasion (plans for which had actually begun under Eisenhower), became the target of bitter comments and questions about the wisdom of the plan; the administration's popularity quickly but temporarily waned.

At almost the same time, civil war broke out in Laos, the Congo was in a state of open warfare, and the administration was faced with repeated threats by Khrushchev that Russia would sign a separate peace treaty with East Germany. To halt the flow of Germans escaping from communist rule,

on August 13, 1961, military police suddenly constructed a wall between East and West Berlin, thus dividing the city, closing the border, and cutting off escape routes to the West.

Kennedy also suffered domestic setbacks. Congress defeated his farm bill, blocked his proposals for federal aid to education, gutted his tax reform measure, and rejected a bill to extend compulsory social security to include hospital care for the nation's senior citizens (Medicare). In addition, the most serious stock market decline since 1929 raised serious doubts about the effect of Kennedy's economic policies on business. His single important legislative victory came in 1962 with the passage of a foreign trade bill, the Trade Expansion Act, which granted the president new power to negotiate tariff reductions with other nations.

Outer Space.—Kennedy took a great interest in the field of space exploration. In an attempt to meet Soviet competition, he signed a bill doubling United States space appropriations for 1962. The nations's hope of putting a man into orbit was realized on February 20, 1962, when Lieutenant Colonel John H. Glenn circled the globe three times in a Mercury space capsule. Although this feat fell far short of an earlier Soviet achievement, Glenn became a national hero and was awarded the Distinguished Service Medal by President Kennedy. Glenn's effort triggered several more notable American space successes, which, in contrast to Soviet secrecy, were viewed live by the entire world via television.

The Cuban Crisis.—Kennedy faced growing criticism over his inaction with regard to Cuba, where Castro, with Russian aid, was strengthening his communist state and threatening the peace of the hemisphere. A serious crisis occurred in October, 1962, when the president learned from the CIA that the Soviet Union was arming Cuba with Russian-manned offensive missiles that could carry nuclear warheads to the United States. Kennedy's reply was quick, decisive, and bold: a naval quarantine was ordered against all ships carrying offensive weapons to Cuba. In an address to the nation during the crisis period, the president said that the United States intended to prevent the use of the missiles, and he warned that "any nuclear missile launched from Cuba at any nation in the Western Hemisphere" would be regarded by the United States as an attack by the Soviet Union and would bring a full-scale nuclear reprisal against Russia.

World tension mounted as Soviet ships headed toward Cuba. After several days, the ships were finally ordered home; as Kennedy firmly insisted upon the withdrawal of the missiles, Khrushchev capitulated, announcing that he would stop building missile launching bases in Cuba, dismantle the offensive weapons there, and return them to Russia under United Nations verification. Although United Nations inspection was never carried out, American reconnaisance flights indicated that the Soviet premier had honored his commitments. Thus, in his first important confrontation with Soviet power, Kennedy won a significant victory for America and the rest of the free world. From the moment the bases were dismantled and the missiles withdrawn from Cuba, a period of comparative relaxation in cold war tensions began.

1962 Elections.—The "Cuban crisis" affected the 1962 midterm elections. By acting vigorously and decisively, the president gained great popularity and respect, quieted the criticism of his Cuban policy, and thus removed the Republican's strongest campaign issue. The outcome of the election was a triumph for Kennedy; the Democrats achieved the most successful showing for a party in power since 1934. Although still plagued by a conservative southern Democratic-Republican coalition strong enough to block most legislation, Kennedy anticipated success in attacking domestic issues.

Nuclear Test Ban.—Kennedy at once took advantage of the temporary calm in the cold war to ease the threat of nuclear destruction. In the spring of 1963 a "hot line" communications link was established between Moscow and Washington for the exchange of messages in the event of a threat of war. When it appeared that both sides were willing to explore new approaches to long-deadlocked questions, Kennedy achieved what no doubt will be considered one of the most important successes of his administration. Still recoiling from the rebuff suffered in Cuba and threatened by internal difficulties and disagreements with other members of the Communist bloc (particularly with Red China) the Soviet Union seemed receptive to new accommodations with the United States. After great effort, in August, 1963, the United States, the Soviet Union, and the United Kingdom signed a treaty that banned nuclear testing in space, in the atmosphere, and underwater. The treaty did not bar underground testing because of continued Soviet opposition to on-site inspection. Nevertheless,

representing the culmination of five years of negotiations, the treaty was an important breakthrough in East-West relations. It was later signed by additional countries.

Kennedy's Death.—On the afternoon of November 22, 1963, the nation and the entire world were shocked and grief-stricken by tragic and sudden news. While in Texas on a political fund-raising tour, President Kennedy was fatally shot by an assassin's bullet. Kennedy was officially pronounced dead half an hour after he received a brain wound from a rifle bullet that was fired at him as he rode in a motorcade through downtown Dallas.

Shortly after the assassination, Lee Harvey Oswald, a twenty-four year old one-time defector to the Soviet Union was arrested by Dallas police, accused of the killing, and charged with the murder. Two days later, the accused assassin was fatally shot by a Dallas nightclub owner, Jack Ruby. The shooting, witnessed by millions of television viewers, occurred as the police attempted to move Oswald from the city jail to the county jail. After a short but much publicized and highly controversial trial, on March 21, 1964, Ruby was found guilty of killing Oswald and sentenced to death.

Lyndon Baines Johnson—1963

On November 22, 1963, Lyndon Baines Johnson became the thirty-sixth president of the United States, only 98 minutes after his predecessor, John F. Kennedy, had been assassinated. Shadowed by the popularity, vigor, and youth of the urbane Kennedy, little was known about the tall Texan who was so suddenly catapulted into the most important position in the United States.

LOOK MAGAZINE

PIX INCORPORATED

LOOK MAGAZINE

". . . the torch has been passed to a new generation of Americans" is his legacy. The young father (with John, Jr., *above*) venerated the youth of America; the Peace Corps (*above right*) is a monument of his faith. The Kennedy tradition is still carried on by his family (*right*).

WIDE WORLD

LOOK MAGAZINE

LOOK MAGAZINE

LYNDON B. JOHNSON
(1963–   )

VIETNAM, POVERTY, AND CIVIL RIGHTS were three of the more important problems that Lyndon Johnson had to deal with during his administration. The Vietnamese situation remains unsettled, as its internal political climate continually fluctuates. Domestically, President Johnson has persuaded Congress to enact legislation to reduce poverty and racial discrimination.

Before he ran for vice-president in the 1960 national election, Johnson had had a long career in Congress. He was elected to the House of Representatives in 1937, and in 1948 to the Senate. In 1953 he became Senate majority leader, a position that gave him both prestige and power in Congress. It was this long and intimate association with Congress that helped the new president to "carry forward the plans and programs of John Fitzgerald Kennedy" and to initiate his own massive program of legislation.

Prior to the 1964 election, Johnson and the eighty-eighth Congress passed three "New Frontier" bills: (1) a major tax cut, decreasing individual income tax rates (passed February, 1964); (2) a federal pay raise; and (3) the Civil Right Act of 1964, a major bill covering discrimination in public accommodations, school integration, fair employment practices, and voter registration.

In November of 1964, Johnson defeated the Republican candidate, Barry Goldwater, in the presidential election, receiving 486 electoral votes to Goldwater's 52. The overwhelming landslide for the president and his running mate Hubert Humphrey brought with it the biggest Democratic majority in Congress since 1936 (295 to 140 in the House; 68 to 32 in the Senate).

Domestic Issues.—In his State of the Union message of January, 1965, Johnson outlined a massive domestic program aimed at the establishment of a "Great Society." By the end of the summer, the eighty-ninth Congress, in an extraordinary display of presidential-congressional concordance, had passed most of the legislation proposed. (1) *Education:* the Elementary and Secondary Educa-

tion Act of 1965, providing over $1 billion in grants to public school districts serving low-income families; $100 million in grants for texts and library books for both public and parochial school children, and $100 million for the creation of education centers shared by public and parochial school children. A second $4.7 billion higher education aid bill, providing scholarships for needy college students and the establishment of a national teachers corps. (2) *Medicare:* a highly controversial bill, first proposed in 1945 by President Truman, and one that the Kenneday administration had been unable to pass in 1961, providing federal health insurance under Social Security for persons over sixty-five years old. (3) *Anti-poverty:* the Johnson program to alleviate poverty-stricken areas, expanded with the Appalachian bill, providing $1.1 billion in aid to impoverished areas in 11 eastern states. A housing bill, by which the federal government pays part of the rent for families with low incomes. (4) *Tax cut:* a $47 billion excise tax cut. (5) the creation of a new cabinet level department—that of housing and urban development. (6) *Voting rights:* the Voting Rights Act, providing for federal voting examiners to prevent the use of the poll tax as a means of denying Negroes their vote. The passage of this bill was in part the result of persistent and dramatic action by Negroes across the nation during the past several years. The most recent event had been a five-day, fifty-four-mile march from Selma to Montgomery, Alabama, in which Dr. Martin Luther King led 25,000 Negroes and whites in silent but forceful protest against Governor George Wallace's long denial of Negro civil rights.

Foreign Policy. — Although most of Johnson's domestic policy met with remarkable success, his foreign policy did not have such vast approval. In May of 1965 President Johnson declared that the "old distinction between the civil war and international war has already lost much of its meaning." In accordance with this, he sent 21,000 men into the Dominican Republic to quell politically-inspired rioting and to prevent a possible communist-infiltrated takeover.

In the same State of the Union message that so carefully outlined the details for the establishment of a "Great Society," President Johnson said very little of a specific nature about the American role in foreign affairs. He proclaimed that America would work toward "peaceful understanding" with the U.S.S.R., and he reaffirmed America's commitment to Southeast Asia.

Despite protests from Red China, the U.S.S.R., and France, the United States continued in 1965 and 1966 to escalate its involvement in the Vietnamese war. In February, 1965, the U.S. began systematic air raids on military installations and transportation lines in North Vietnam. During the spring and summer of 1965 the number of Americans mobilized was increased, and by the end of that year close to 100,000 men had been deployed. In July of 1966 the oil depots at Haiphong, North Vietnam's largest port, were bombed and by October the number of Americans fighting in Vietnam was approximately 320,000 (as compared with 105,000 in 1961). It was this involvement in Southeast Asia that caused a resurgence of tension between the Communist bloc and the United States. **—Walter Trattner**

Countries of the world 2085
Colonies and
 dependencies 2306
Natural features 2325
Cities 2344
Bibliography 2377

VOLUME TWENTY FIVE

WORLD

COUNTRIES OF THE WORLD

AFGHANISTAN

Official name: Kingdom of Afghanistan
Area: 249,934 square miles
Population: (1966 est.) 15,960,000
Capital: Kabul (Pop., 1965, 449,000)
Language: Pashto, Dari
Religion: Islam
Currency unit: Afghani
National holiday: Independence day, May 27

Afghanistan, a landlocked, mountainous country in south Asia, is bordered on the north by the Soviet Union, on the east by China, on the south by Pakistan, and on the west by Iran.

THE LAND. Afghanistan is a high country, with an average elevation of about 6,000 feet above sea level. A great central mountain core dominates the landscape. In the east, the Hindu Kush ranges rise to more than 20,000 feet. The Koh-i-Baba and Paropamisus ranges, with elevations of 10,000 to 15,000 feet, fan out toward the west.

Near the western border the land drops to Seistan, a barren plateau at an elevation of 1,500 feet. East of Seistan are two deserts, the Dasht-i-Margo and the Registan.

Four major rivers flow from the central mountains through the country's major inhabited regions. The Amu Darya (Oxus) drains the hilly northeast and forms part of the border with the Soviet Union. The Hari flows west from the Paropamisus. The richest regions are the valleys of the Helmand and its tributaries, in the southwest, and the valley of the Kabul, which flows east to the Indus.

Afghanistan's climate is characterized by extremes. In the lower regions average temperatures range from over 115°F in summer to –10°F in winter. Mountain temperatures may vary by as much as 50°F in one day, although south of the mountains temperatures are more moderate. Winds are high throughout the country. Average precipitation ranges from 2 inches a year in the west to 12 inches in the east.

THE PEOPLE. Afghanistan's central position in Asia has given it a varied population. Over half the people are Pashtun, or Pathan, a tribal group related to the Persians and Indians. Their language, Pashto, is one of Afghanistan's official languages. Other major groups are the Hazara, who speak a mixed Persian-Turkish dialect, the Turkic-speaking Uzbek and Turkoman, and the Tajik, whose language is a dialect of Persian.

Almost all Afghanis live in rural villages, although by the mid-1960s urbanization was increasing. The major cities are Kabul in the east, Herat in the west, and Kandahar in the south.

ECONOMY. Afghanistan's economic life is based on farming and herding, although no more than 15 percent of the land can be cultivated and less than half of that is farmed. Mineral resources include coal, oil, gas, iron, salt, copper, gold, and lapis lazuli. Exploitation of these resources began only in the 1950s and 1960s.

Karakul sheep are Afghanistan's most valuable agricultural commodity, providing meat, milk, and fat for domestic consumption and skins for export. Goats, cattle, horses, donkeys, and camels are also raised. The leading crops are wheat, barley, and other grains; cotton; sugar beets; and a great variety of fruits and vegetables.

Leather processing, textile weaving, and flour milling are the only well-established manufacturing industries. The development of heavy industry began in the 1950s and 1960s with assistance from the United Nations, the United States, and the Soviet Union.

Projects have been initiated to develop hydroelectric resources, to expand transportation and communications facilities, and to improve education and health services.

Afghanistan's exports, valued at about $70.7 million in 1964–1965, include fresh and dried fruits, skins and hides, wool, cotton, and rugs. Fuel, fabrics, machinery, and metal and rubber products were among the $141.4 million worth of goods imported in 1964–1965. In the 1950s and 1960s the Afghan economy was supported by financial and trade assistance from the United States, the Soviet Union, and other countries.

GOVERNMENT. Afghanistan is a constitutional monarchy. The head of state is the padshah, or king. Under Afghanistan's 1964 constitution a prime minister appointed by the king chooses a cabinet, which requires the support of the lower house of parliament.

Members of the lower house are popularly elected to four-year terms. The upper house is partly appointed, partly elected, and partly chosen by provincial legislatures.

Afghanistan is a member of the United Nations.

HISTORY. Afghanistan lies at the crossroads of ancient Asian migration routes, and its early history is a story of invasions and conquests. The country has been inhabited since prehistoric times, but the first known settlers were Aryans, who passed through Afghanistan on their way to India in about 1500 BC.

By the 500s BC, Aryana, as the area was then called, was part of the Persian Empire. In 328 BC it was conquered by the Greek armies of Alexander the Great. After Alexander's death, it was divided between the Seleucid Empire of Persia, and Bactria, a kingdom in the east.

In the 100s BC these kingdoms fell before invasions from the north by nomadic tribes from central Asia, including the Yueh-chi. The Kushan dynasty of the Yueh-chi established a Buddhist empire centering on Afghanistan in the 100s AD. The Kushan empire was overthrown in the 400s by the White Huns.

Islam. At the end of the 600s and in the early 700s Arab armies invaded the country and converted the people to Islam. During the next several centuries many small kingdoms arose in Afghanistan, most of them ruled by Muslims. These kingdoms were dominated in the 900s by Turkic tribes, who made Afghanistan a center of culture and learning.

In the 1200s the Turkic kingdoms were destroyed by the Mongol armies of Genghis Khan. The Turkic-Mongol conqueror, Tamerlane, made Afghanistan part of his Asian empire in the 1300s. Two hundred years later Tamerlane's descendant, Babur, ruled the vast Indian Mughal (Mogul) Empire.

The Mughals lost most of Afghanistan to the Safavid rulers of Persia in the 1600s. But in the early 1700s Afghanistan asserted its independence and drove the Persians out. In 1747 the Afghan tribes jointly chose Ahmad Durrani of the Sadozay tribe as the first ruler of their newly united country. Many tribes were dissatisfied, however, and in the early 1800s rebellions toppled the dynasty.

Foreign Interference. Several civil wars were fought for control of the throne, leaving the country vulnerable to foreign invasion. For by the 1800s control of Afghanistan, long sought by Persia, also had become a goal of Russia and Britain, whose Indian territory bordered Afghanistan. In 1834 Dost Muhammad, a

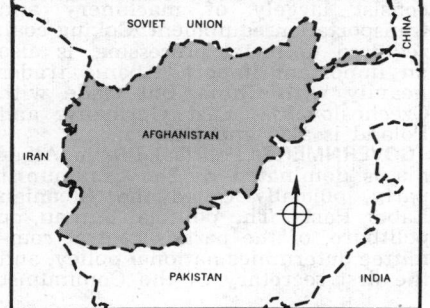

Barakzay tribal leader strongly opposed to foreign control, took the throne. To protect its position in India and the Near East, Britain sought to place a more friendly ruler in power. This led to an Anglo-Afghan war between 1839 and 1842.

The British captured Dost Muhammad, but could not put down a rebellion in the country and they withdrew. For the next 36 years Afghanistan's history was marked by civil war, Russian advances, Persian invasions, and, in 1878, by renewed war with Britain. In 1879, having won the war, Britain in effect made Afghanistan a buffer state between British and Russian imperialist ambitions.

In 1880 a new amir, Abd-ar-Rahman, came to the throne and cooperated with the British whenever it benefited Afghanistan. During his reign rebellious tribesmen were pacified and the present boundaries were set between Afghanistan, Russia, and British India. By the beginning of World War I, Britain was dominant in Afghanistan and the Russians and Persians had agreed to end their involvement there.

Afghanistan remained neutral during the war, but a spirit of nationalism developed and in 1919 nationalists led a war against Britain. Neither side was able to win the war, but the British allowed the country to conduct its own foreign affairs.

Modernization. After the war a new king, Amanullah, began to modernize the country. His reforms proved extreme, costly, and unpopular, and in 1929 he was deposed during a widespread tribal rebellion. Muhammad Nadir, a Pashtun leader, defeated rival contenders for power.

Under Nadir Shah and his successors Afghanistan was modernized very gradually. Many democratic forms and processes were introduced, the economy was developed, and the traditional society began to change as Western ideas penetrated the country.
—Thomas Ennis; M. G. Inaba; Louis Dupree

ALBANIA

Official name: People's Republic of Albania
Area: 11,020 square miles
Population: (1966 est.) 1,914,000
Capital: Tiranë (Pop., 1964 est., 156,950)
Language: Albanian
Religion: Islam, Orthodox Christianity, Roman Catholicism
Currency unit: Lek
National holiday: Liberation day, November 29

Albania, a small nation in southeastern Europe, lies along the western coast of the Balkan peninsula. It is bounded on the north and northeast by Yugoslavia, on the southeast and south by Greece, and on the west by the Adriatic Sea. Albania is separated from southern Italy by the narrow Strait of Otranto, at the entrance to the Adriatic. Albanians call their country *Shqiperia,* or "Eagle's land."

THE LAND. Albania is a mountainous land, and mountains cover more than two-thirds of the country. Level land is found only along rivers and near the coast. Albania's rivers are few and short, and they flow westward, to the Adriatic. Three large lakes lie astride Albania's borders—Scutari, in the northwest, and Ohrid and Prespa, in the east.

The climate along the coast is Mediterranean, with warm, dry summers and mild, damp winters. The vegetation there is of the *maquis* type—dry evergreen bushes and small trees. Further east the rainfall is considerably higher, and part of the original forest of oak, beech, and evergreens still stands.

THE PEOPLE. Almost all of the people are Albanians, but there is a small Greek minority in the south, along the Albanian-Greek border. About 1 million Albanians live across the border in Yugoslavia's Kosovo-Metohija region, and about 200,000 live in Greece. The population of Albania is increasing at a very rapid rate, estimated at more than 3 percent a year between 1958 and 1965.

The Albanians are divided into two main groups, each with its own dialect. The Ghegs live in the northern half of the country, and the Tosks live in the southern half. Most Albanians are Muslims. About 20 percent of the people are Orthodox Christians, and 10 percent are Roman Catholics.

ECONOMY. Albania's economy is controlled by the government, which directs economic life through a series of five-year plans. The government has sought to transform the country from an agricultural to an agricultural-industrial nation. Economic development has required support from abroad. Up to the early 1960s, Albania depended on the Soviet Union for economic and technical aid. Since then, it has depended on China.

Agriculture is the major employer of Albania's people, although there is little land that can be cultivated and soils are poor. Wheat and corn are the principal grain crops, and cotton, tobacco, and sunflowers are the main industrial crops. Large quantities of fruit are produced. Livestock includes cattle, goats, and sheep. Sheep are the most important.

Albania has considerable mineral resources, but the rough landscape makes it difficult to exploit them. The major minerals include oil, lignite, chromium, and copper. The country's fast-flowing rivers are used to provide hydroelectric power for industry. The basic industries process the nation's agricultural and mineral products.

In 1964 Albania's exports earned $60 million and its imports cost $98 million. The major exports are minerals and metals and agricultural products—fruit, wine, and tobacco. Imports consist largely of machinery and transportation equipment. Coking coal, required in metal processing, is also an important import. Abania trades heavily with China, but trade with Czechoslovakia, East Germany, and Poland is also important.

GOVERNMENT. Political life in Albania is dominated by the Communist party, officially called the Albanian Labor Party. The political bureau, or politburo, of the party's central committee determines national policy, and the first secretary of the Communist party is the key figure in the government.

The Albanian constitution provides for a popularly elected legislature of one house, the People's Assembly. Assembly candidates are nominated by the Albanian Democratic Front, which is controlled by the Communist party. The assembly chooses a small committee, or presidium, to act for it between its relatively short sessions.

The chairman of the presidium is the head of state. A council of ministers functions as a cabinet. It is headed by a chairman, who is equivalent to a prime minister.

HISTORY. Illyrian tribes from central Europe migrated into the area of present-day Albania in about 2000 BC. The region was called Epirus by the Ancient Greeks, who established colonies along the coast. In the 200s BC Pyrrhus of Epirus built a powerful state and in 280 invaded Italy. He was defeated, and internal unrest led to the disintegration of the state.

Roman Era. Rome conquered the Illyrian states by 167 BC, and the region became fairly prosperous from its geographic position astride Rome's trade routes to the East. Many Albanians became prominent in Roman life, and the towns generally became Roman in culture. In 395 the Roman

Empire was divided into eastern and western halves, and Albania became part of the Eastern, or Byzantine, Empire.

During the 400s AD a number of barbarian tribes invaded the region, and during the 600s and 700s Slavic peoples began to settle in the lowland areas. During the 800s and 900s the region was included in a Bulgarian state, but Byzantine rule was reestablished in 1018.

In 1054, a schism in the Christian church led to a new era of conflict. Normans and Crusaders, representatives of the Western, or Roman Catholic, church, invaded the country and fought against adherents of the Eastern, or Orthodox, church.

The decline of Byzantium in the 1100s was accompanied by the establishment of Albanian principalities, and in 1230 by the reimposition of Bulgarian rule. During the later 1200s, the Anjou rulers of Sicily established themselves in parts of Albania, and in the mid-1300s the region was included in a Serbian empire.

Ottoman Rule. The Ottoman Turks began the conquest of Albania in the 1300s, and by 1389 most of the country was under Ottoman control. Albania remained under Turkish control until 1912. There were many risings against Ottoman rule during the 1400s, and in 1443 a major rising was led by Gjergj Kastrioti (George Castriota), popularly known by his Turkish name, Skander, and title, beg ("Skanderbeg").

In 1444 a general assembly of Albanian notables created an Albanian league with Skanderbeg as president. The Albanian state collapsed after the death of Skanderbeg in 1468.

During the period of Ottoman rule, local officials, often Albanians, gained control of large areas, and they made these lands hereditary possessions. The population came to be divided into three main groups—Muslims, educated in Turkish; Orthodox Christians, educated in Greek; and Roman Catholics, educated in Italian.

In the 1800s the Ottoman Empire was near collapse, and Albania became a focal point for the ambitions of several states. Serbia and Montenegro, both part of present-day Yugoslavia, and Greece, staked out claims to Albanian lands.

In 1912 the first Balkan War was fought against Turkey by Bulgaria, Greece, Serbia, and Montenegro. The Greeks, Serbs, and Montenegrins planned to divide Albania among themselves. But the Albanians proclaimed their independence in the city of Vlorë in November 1912 and petitioned the great powers of Europe for recognition.

The powers agreed to the establishment of an autonomous Albanian state under the suzerainty of the Ottoman sultan, and set out the boundaries of the new state. The boundaries included only about one half the area and one half the people traditionally considered Albanian by the Albanians.

Independence. In 1913 the powers recognized Albania as an independent nation, but under a 10-year period of control by the powers. The new nation was to be a monarchy, and the powers chose a German prince, William of Wied, to head the new state. World War I broke out in 1914, and William left the country.

After the war, Italy, Serbia, Greece, and Montenegro all put forth claims to Albanian territories. But in 1920 Albania won recognition of its full independence and membership in the League of Nations.

The new Albanian government was weak. The country was poor, most of the people were illiterate, and neighboring nations interfered in the country's troubled politics. During the 1920s a regional chieftain, Ahmed bey Zogolli, or Achmed Zogu, emerged as the most powerful force in the government. He was briefly driven from the country in 1924 by a liberal rising, but regained power and in 1925 became president of Albania. In 1928 he transformed the government into a monarchy with himself as King Zog I. During the 1930s, Italian influence became dominant in the economically hard pressed country, and in 1939

Italy moved to take full control of Albania. Italian troops were landed on Apr. 7, 1939, and on April 12 the union of Albania with Italy was proclaimed.

During World War II, Albania formed a part of the Italian empire. Traditionally Albanian areas in Yugoslavia (Kosovo) and in Greece (Cameria) were added to the puppet Albanian state. But Italian efforts to win Albanan support met with little popular success.

Communist Rule. In 1942 a national resistance movement, the National Liberation Front, was organized under Communist control. Although the Communist Party had been founded only in 1941, its leader, Enver Hoxha, was able to maintain leadership of the front and eliminate opposition from nationalist organizations. By the end of 1944, when German troops had been driven from the Balkans, the Hoxha group was in firm control of the country.

The Communist regime established in Albania had close ties with Yugoslavia, which had also come under Communist control. The Yugoslav Communist-led resistance movement had given significant aid to the Albanians during the war, but in 1948, when Yugoslavia and the Soviet Union split, the Albanians supported the Soviet Union.

Ties with the Soviet Union remained close until after the death in 1953 of the Soviet dictator, Joseph Stalin. The new leaders of the Soviet Union gradually moved to heal the breach with Yugoslavia, which again had become an enemy for the Albanians.

The development of a split in the Communist world between the Soviet Union and China in the early 1960s further troubled Soviet-Albanian relations. Despite its heavy dependence on Soviet economic aid, Albania supported China in the dispute.

—Robert F. Byrnes; George Kish

ALGERIA

Official name: Democratic and Popular Republic of Algeria

Area: 919,352 square miles

Population: (1966 est.) 12,150,000

Capital: Algiers (Pop., 1966, urban area, 943,-142)

Language: Arabic, French

Religion: Islam

Currency unit: Dinar

National holiday: November 1

Algeria, a republic in northern Africa, is bounded on the north by the Mediterranean Sea, on the east by Tunisia and Libya, on the south by Niger and Mali, and on the west by Mauritania, Spanish Sahara, and Morocco. Algeria became independent in 1962 after more than a century of French rule.

THE LAND. Most of Algeria is part of the vast desert waste of the Sahara. A narrow northern zone, where the bulk of the people live, is dominated by two parallel east-west mountain chains—the Tell Atlas and the Saharan Atlas. Both are part of the massive Atlas Mountains, which stretch across northern Africa. The

LOOK MAGAZINE

MARKET IN ALGIERS, capital of Algeria.

Tell Atlas is a series of coastal mountains and valleys parallel to the Mediterranean Sea. The Saharan Atlas lies about 200 miles inland. Between the two ranges is a plateau area.

Most of the desert surface of southern Algeria is composed of rock and gravel, but there are some large sand areas. In the southeast are the Ahaggar Mountains, a volcanic rock mass that reaches above 9,600 feet. The Sahara region is sparsely populated.

In Algeria's coastal region, the winters are mild and rainy and the summers are hot and dry. The plateau region receives little rain. The Sahara is hot and dry and receives less than four inches of rain a year.

THE PEOPLE. Most of Algeria's rapidly growing population is Muslim of Arab-Berber stock. More than 1 mil-

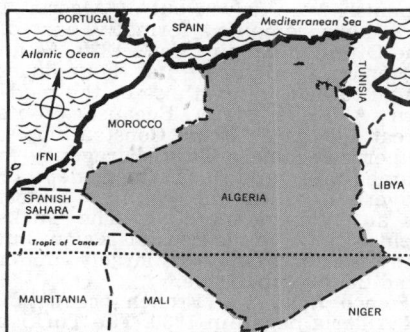

lion people of European origin left Algeria after independence was won in 1962. The Europeans had operated the most profitable and efficient farms and had filled most of the administrative, technical, and management positions. Their loss deprived the new nation of badly needed skilled personnel.

ECONOMY. Algeria has traditionally been an agricultural country, although there is relatively little good farm land. The bulk of its produce, which consists of wheat and barley and a variety of vegetables and fruits, comes from the region between the Tell Atlas and the Mediterranean.

In 1964 Algeria's imports cost $703 million and its exports earned $727 million. The most valuable Algerian export for many years was wine. The major exports today are petroleum and natural gas from rich fields discovered in the Sahara in the 1950s.

GOVERNMENT. Algeria's constitution provides for a national assembly and a president. A military coup overthrew the president in 1965, however, and governmental powers were assumed by a Revolutionary Council composed of army officers.

Algeria is a member of the United Nations and the Arab League.

HISTORY. The territory of present-day Algeria was invaded many times and dominated by many peoples before the country won its independence in 1962. Until the modern era, Algeria was often included in larger units that included parts of present-day Morocco and Tunisia.

The earliest known settlers were Berber-speaking peoples. The Phoenicians, who arrived in about 1200 BC, established control over part of North Africa. Their rule ended in 146 BC with the fall of Carthage to Rome.

Roman domination ended with invasions by Vandals in the 400s AD. In the 500s the region came under Byzantine rule. In the 600s the Arabs began to sweep through North Africa, and Algeria became part of the Arab-dominated Muslim world that stretched from Spain to Arabia.

Ottoman Era. In the early 1500s the Spanish, crusading against the Muslims who had withdrawn from Spain to North Africa, captured several Algerian cities. The inhabitants of Algeria appealed for help to a Muslim commander, Khayr-ad-Din, who drove the Spanish from Algiers in 1519. He offered allegiance to the Ottoman Empire in return for men and supplies. With Turkish aid, the Spanish were driven out of Algeria.

Algeria remained formally part of the Ottoman Empire until 1830. As an Ottoman province, its boundaries came to be roughly those of the modern Algerian state. Because of its great distance from Constantinople, Algeria became a Turkish regency in name only, and a Turkish *dey*, or governor, ruled the country almost as an independent state. The Turks held control of the coastal region, but the interior remained largely under traditional tribal rule.

French Rule. The French occupation of Algeria began in 1830. The Turkish dey quickly capitulated, but native Algeria, led by Abd al-Qadir (Abd-al-Kader), resisted. Not until 1847, when Abd al-Qadir was captured, did France secure control over most of Algeria.

Large numbers of French and other Europeans settled in Algeria soon after the defeat of Abd al-Qadir, and by 1900 Europeans made up 14 percent of Algeria's total population. The new settlers built up the Algerian economy, developing commercial agriculture for the French market. But the development basically served the needs of only the French Algerians,

who gradually gained control of most of the best land.

By the early 1900s, the lack of economic opportunities and political inequalities created growing unrest within the Muslim majority. France attempted piecemeal reforms, but none succeeded in meeting the needs of the people.

Algerian desire for self-determination grew following World War II. In 1954 an armed rebellion against the French was begun by the National Liberation Front (FLN). The FLN slowly won the allegiance of most of the non-European Algerian population during a bitter struggle against the French in the years that followed.

Finally, in 1960, after a military effort that brought 500,000 French troops to Algeria and resulted in a series of French domestic political crises, French President de Gaulle agreed to negotiate with the FLN.

The two countries reached agreement only after months of bargaining. During that period part of the French army based in Algeria attempted a military coup against De Gaulle and a last-ditch terrorist campaign against a French withdrawal was waged by the European Secret Army Organization (OAS). On July 3, 1962, after 132 years of French rule, Algeria became independent.

Independence. The fruits of victory were almost lost in a near civil war that erupted immediately after independence was granted. Ahmed Ben Bella, a leader of the FLN who had been imprisoned in France since 1956, made a successful bid for power with the support of the FLN army.

By the end of 1962 Ben Bella had been elected premier by a newly formed national assembly, and he appeared to be securely in power. In June 1965, however, Ben Bella was deposed in a bloodless coup led by the army, and Houari Boumedienne, a military leader of the independence struggle, emerged at the head of a provisional military regime.

The emigration of most of Algeria's European population, which began when the country achieved independence, left Algeria stripped of its trained personnel and deepened the economic crisis that followed the years of civil war. Increasing production of Saharan oil and gas, however, somewhat brightened Algeria's economic future.

—L. Carl Brown; Hibberd V. B. Kline, Jr.

ANDORRA

Official name: Andorra
Area: 175 square miles
Population: (1966 est.) 11,000
Capital: Andorra la Vella
Language: Catalan
Religion: Roman Catholicism
Currency units: French franc, Spanish peseta

Andorra, one of Europe's smallest states, is a principality lying high in the eastern Pyrenees between Spain and France.

THE LAND AND PEOPLE. Andorra has a rugged landscape dominated by mountains rising from 6,500 to over 9,000 feet and cut by steep gorges. The climate is dry and rather mild.

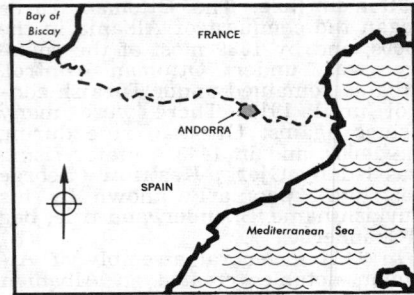

Andorrans are descendants of a people known to the ancient Romans. They speak Catalan, the language of Catalonia, a region in northeastern Spain. The population also includes Spanish and French minorities. Andorra la Vella, the capital, is the only large town.

ECONOMY. Although tiny, Andorra is quite prosperous. Its major natural resources are waterpower, from several lakes and the Valera River; small deposits of iron and lead; and timber. Only a small part of the land can be farmed. Rye, wheat, vegetables, and a valuable tobacco crop are grown, but Andorra depends on Spain and France for most of its food.

Tourism and trade contribute heavily to the economy. Andorra exports tobacco, cigarettes, and timber. Andorra's principal trading partners are Spain and France.

GOVERNMENT. Sovereignty over Andorra is exercised jointly by the Roman Catholic bishop of Urgel, in Spain, and by the head of the French state. Each is represented locally by a delegate called a *viguier*. Actual government is administered by a general council elected every four years by heads of households. The council chooses a nonmember as *syndic,* or chief executive.

HISTORY. Andorra's history as a state traditionally extends back to Charlemagne, who is said to have driven the Muslims from the region. The country gained semi-independent status in 1278, when the bishop of Urgel and the French counts of Foix assumed joint sovereignty over the "Valleys of Andorra," with the right to collect tribute.

The arrangement endured, but the counts were replaced by the princes and kings of Navarre, the kings of France, and then the presidents of France. Nominal tribute is still paid to the co-sovereigns.

Because of its small size and geographic isolation, Andorra escaped involvement in modern European wars, including the Spanish Civil War of 1936–1939. In the 1950s and 1960s, however, the increasing importance of the tourist trade led the principality to fuller involvement in European affairs.

In the early 1960s Andorra began to meet formally with other small European states, including Liechtenstein, Monaco, and San Marino, to discuss matters of mutual concern.

In 1967 French Pres. Charles de Gaulle paid a state visit to Andorra, the first visit by a French head of state since the 1200s.

—Charles Nowell

ARGENTINA

Official name: Argentine Republic
Area: 1,072,067 square miles
Population: (1967 est.) 23,031,000
Capital: Buenos Aires (Pop., 1960, urban area, 7,000,000)
Language: Spanish
Religion: Roman Catholicism
Currency unit: Peso
National holiday: Independence day, May 25

Argentina, a republic in the southern part of South America, is the second largest Latin American country in area and the third largest in population. It is bounded on the north by Brazil, Paraguay, and Bolivia; on the east by Brazil, Uruguay, and the Atlantic Ocean; on the west by Chile; and on the south by Chile and the Atlantic Ocean.

THE LAND. Argentina has four major land regions: the pampas, the North, the Andes, and Patagonia.

The pampas, great level plains, are divided into the Humid Pampa, in the east of Argentina's central region, and the Dry Pampa, in the west. The rich, black soil of the Humid Pampa makes it one of the most fertile agricultural areas in the world.

The pampas form the economic, political, and social heartland of the nation. The half circle around Buenos Aires, with a radius of 250 miles, includes only 24 percent of the country's total area but contains some 75 percent of the total population.

The North contains the semiarid, forested plains of the Chaco, the rolling hills and the floodplains of Mesopotamia, which lie between the Paraná and Uruguay rivers, and the Paraná Plateau.

The Andes region includes the "Monte," or foothill zone, with elevations below 2,500 feet, and the Andes cordillera (range) itself. In the northwest the cordillera reaches a height of 22,834 feet at Mt. Aconcagua, the highest point in the western hemisphere. The Argentine Andes are steep and have permanent snow caps. In the northwest the Andes are very dry, but in the extreme southwest they are covered by glaciers.

Patagonia is a dry, windswept plateau south of the Río Colorado. Rainfall ranges between 20 inches a year near the Andes and less than 8 inches along the Atlantic Coast. Patagonia's dryness is an obstacle to both farming and grazing, and it is sparsely populated.

THE PEOPLE. About nine out of every ten of Argentina's people are of European descent, and approximately one out of five Argentinians was born in Europe. In the 1800s a large number of Europeans, primarily Italians and Spaniards, emigrated to Argentina and their influence has made the country in many ways more European than Latin American. The dwindling indigenous population consists of small groups of Guaraní Indians in the north and Patagonian Indians in the south.

One third of the people of Argentina live in the metropolitan area of Buenos Aires, the capital. Population density decreases as one moves away from Buenos Aires, and other cities are small in comparison.

The larger provincial cities include Mar del Plata, about 250 miles from the capital, a beach resort; Rosario, the country's wheat exporting center, about 200 miles from Buenos Aires on the Río Paraná; Cordoba, an educational and commercial center in the heart of the country that has recently become important in manufacturing; and Tucumán, the major metropolis of northwestern Argentina and capital of the sugar-growing area.

ECONOMY. Agriculture is the chief source of income in Argentina. Most farming activity occurs in the Humid Pampa, where corn, wheat, oats, barley, and potatoes are grown. Argentina is a world leader in wheat, corn, and cotton production. Livestock raising, formerly the dominant economic activity, is now on a level with farming. Beef cattle are raised in the pampas, and sheep in Patagonia.

Mining had been limited mainly to copper, lead, and zinc, in the northwestern Andes, and coal in the Río Turbio area. Petroleum is now Argentina's major mineral resource.

Industry. After World War II Argentina made an effort to increase industrialization to broaden the base of its economy. Industrial development has been slow, however, and by the 1960s less than two fifths of the labor force was employed in industry, most of which is centered in Buenos Aires. The growth of heavy industry has been limited by inadequate mineral resources, especially coal.

Argentine industry is largely confined to the processing of food and agricultural products. Meat packing, flour milling, sugar refining, and wine making play an important role. Argentina also produces large quantities of cement, vegetable oil, soap, rubber goods, glass, pharmaceuticals, and chemicals.

Trade. In 1966 Argentina's imports were valued at $1,124 million and exports earned $1,593 million. By and

PAN AMERICAN AIRWAYS
PLAZA DEL MAYO, in Buenos Aires, capital of Argentina, faced by the presidential palace.

large Argentina trades its agricultural products for manufactured goods. Major imports include vehicles, machinery, petroleum, wood, chemicals, and manufactured iron and steel goods. Major exports are grain, meat and meat products, wool, and vegetable and linseed oil.

Argentina imports mainly from the United States, Brazil, West Germany, Italy, France, and Japan. Exports go primarily to Italy, the Netherlands, Britain, Brazil, West Germany, the United States, and Communist China.

GOVERNMENT. Argentina has been a republic since 1853, when its first constitution was drawn up. But democratic processes have frequently been disrupted by the military. Traditionally, the government has been headed by a popularly elected president, the head of state and chief executive. The legislative branch of government has included a senate chosen by provincial legislatures and a directly elected house of deputies.

Argentina is a member of the United Nations and the Organization of American States (OAS).

HISTORY. In the 1400s the Inca empire extended into the northern corner of what is now Argentina. Its drive south, however, was halted by Argentina's more primitive Indians, who were largely nomadic.

The first European to explore Argentina was the Spaniard Juan Díaz de Solís, who discovered the Río de la Plata in 1516. Exploration of the coast continued, and in 1536 an expedition headed by Pedro de Mendoza built a village on the site of present-day Buenos Aires. A majority of the early settlers, however, were Spanish colonists who crossed the Andes from Chile and Peru in the late 1500s.

The hostility of the Indians and the relative lack of precious metals at first made Argentina a neglected and sparsely settled part of the Spanish empire. It was not until the late 1700s that the colony acquired major economic importance as an exporter of cattle products, principally hides. In 1776 its capital, Buenos Aires, became the seat of the Spanish colonial viceroyalty of La Plata, which also included modern-day Bolivia, Paraguay, and Uruguay.

Independence. Argentinians acquired a new sense of their own power and importance in 1806 during the Napoleonic wars, when they expelled a British force that had seized Buenos Aires. Four years later, on May 25, 1810, they established an autonomous junta to rule during the captivity in France of Spain's King Ferdinand VII. Although independence was not formally declared until 1816, in practice the Argentinians had been self-governing since 1810.

Internal stability proved harder to achieve than independence. Not only were Argentine patriots unable to retain control over the outlying sections of the viceroyalty of La Plata, but within Argentina itself strong rivalry had developed between Buenos Aires and the inland provinces.

The capital favored a centralized government and was receptive to liberal reforms; the interior desired a federal system that would provide almost complete local autonomy and was politically conservative. For many years no really effective national administration could be established.

In the early 1820s, the liberal and centralist faction, the Unitarios, consolidated its control of the city and surrounding province of Buenos Aires under the leadership of Bernardino Rivadavia. The Unitarios encouraged immigration and investment, reformed the tax system, and restricted the influence of the Roman Catholic Church.

But they were unsuccessful when they tried to establish a centralized government over the entire country. The move provoked bitter Federalist resistance, which coincided with a war fought against Brazil over control of Uruguay (1825–1828).

Rosas Era. In 1829 the Unitarios lost even Buenos Aires, which came under the control of the wealthy rancher and Federalist leader, Juan Manuel de Rosas. Rosas ruled the Buenos Aires province as dictator from 1829 to 1832 and from 1835 to 1852. He brutally suppressed political opponents, repealed many of the reforms of the Unitarios, and governed in the interest of his own class of great ranchers.

Although his primary position was always that of provincial governor, Rosas joined with Federalist leaders of the interior to form a loose Argentine confederation. The confederation had no president or constitution, but Rosas was its unquestioned leader; it authorized him to direct defense and foreign relations for all the provinces.

Rosas fought a brief war with Bolivia in 1837–1838 and continually intervened in Uruguay's affairs. He also engaged in disputes with France and Britain, which resulted in a blockade of the Argentine coast from 1845–1848.

The European powers failed to humble Rosas, but eventually some of his own collaborators in the interior provinces turned against him. One of these, Gen. Justo José de Urquiza, formed a coalition with the Unitarios and in 1852, with aid from Brazil, drove Rosas from power.

Federalism. Urquiza sought to reorganize the government of Argentina, and in 1853 a new constitution providing for a federal system was adopted. The province of Buenos Aires at first remained outside the union, but it agreed to join in 1859. In 1862 its governor, Bartolomé Mitre, became the first president of a fully united Argentina, serving from 1862 to 1868. During his administration, Argentina joined Brazil and Uruguay in the War of the Triple Alliance against Paraguay (1865–1870), when Paraguayan troops ignored Mitre's refusal to allow them to cross Argentine territory.

Domingo F. Sarmiento, president from 1868 to 1874, was an ardent admirer of the United States and especially of U.S. educational methods. Sarmiento established a public school system that became the best in Latin America. Moreover, the nation experienced a period of rapid economic expansion during the latter 1800s and early 1900s. Argentina built up an elaborate railway network, attracted a flood of European immigrants, and became a major world supplier of meat and wheat.

Argentina's wealth was largely derived from the land, but there developed a large urban middle and working class, which gained its livelihood from commerce and transportation, public services, processing, and light manufacturing. Such groups had little voice in the Argentine government, which was dominated by the great landowners and allied business interests.

This ruling class was in many respects able and progressive, but it frequently stayed in power by irregular election practices and the use of arbitrary federal intervention in provincial affairs. The result was a gradual increase in political unrest, which found its most important expression in the Radical party, organized in the 1890s. The Radicals had special appeal for the middle class.

Enactment of an electoral reform law in 1912 finally opened the way for the Radicals to elect a president, Hipólito Irigoyen, in 1916. Once in power, the Radicals did not introduce any fundamental changes in social and economic policy, and Irigoyen, the first Argentine president ever chosen in a truly democratic election, was best known outside Argentina for his course of strict neutrality in World War I.

Irigoyen resigned in 1922, but was reelected in 1928. He was overthrown by a military coup in 1930, however, amid the crisis of the world economic depression.

This first revolutionary change of government in almost 70 years was followed in 1932 by the resumption of an outwardly constitutional government under a wealthy oligarchy similar to the one that had ruled prior to 1916. Another revolt occurred in June 1943, however, and led to the establishment of a military regime under Gen. Pedro Ramírez and later under Gen. Edelmiro Farrell, in which Juan D. Perón ultimately emerged as the leading figure.

Perón Dictatorship. The new regime was politically repressive, but through Perón's inspiration it gained working class support by expanding social security and other benefits. During World War II it continued the neutrality policy that it had inherited from the preceding administration, but with pro-Axis overtones. In March 1945, however, when the conflict was almost over, Argentina declared war on Germany and Japan.

Perón was briefly stripped of power in October 1945, but he scored an impressive victory early in 1946 in a free election and officially became president. Although opposition was never wholly suppressed, Perón's government was a dictatorship.

As president, Perón expanded his labor policy into a doctrine called *justicialismo*, which claimed to be a middle course of true social justice between the extremes of communism and capitalism. Workers received a steady stream of wage increases and benefits.

Perón also gave special encouragement to industry. His extravagant spending and economic favoritism, however, severely damaged grazing and agriculture and produced grave inflation. In addition, he quarreled with the Roman Catholic Church and alienated the army. Dissatisfaction with his policies steadily increased, and he was finally overthrown by a military coup on Sept. 19, 1955.

Contemporary Argentina. A series of provisional military governments ruled from 1955 until 1958, when the Radicals returned to power with the election of Dr. Arturo Frondizi to the presidency. His government was troubled by military interference, unrest in the ranks of labor, where *peronista* influence remained strong, and inflation and other economic problems inherited from the Perón regime.

Frondizi allowed the peronistas to enter candidates of their own in off-year elections in March 1962. When they won pluralities in a large number of provinces, antiperonista members of the military installed Senate leader José María Guido in the presidency.

In 1963 presidential elections were won by Dr. Arturo Illía, a Radical. The peronistas continued to be a disruptive force, however, and in 1964 Perón himself unsuccessfully tried to return to Argentina.

Peronista strength registered an increase in the 1965 congressional elections, and on June 28, 1966, the Illía government was overthrown by the military, which established a new regime headed by Gen. Juan Onganía.
—David Bushnell; Kempton E. Webb

AUSTRALIA

Official name: Commonwealth of Australia
Area: 2,967,909 square miles
Population: (1967 est.) 11,751,000
Capital: Canberra (Pop., 1966, urban area, 95,913)
Language: English
Religion: Anglicanism, Roman Catholicism, Protestantism
Currency unit: Dollar
National holiday: Australia day, January 26

Australia, an island-continent in the southern hemisphere, is bounded on the north by the Timor Sea and the Arafura Sea, on the east by the Coral Sea, the Pacific Ocean, and the Tasman Sea, and on the south and west by the Indian Ocean. Bass Strait separates the island of Tasmania from the Australian mainland.

The Commonwealth of Australia is composed of six states and two mainland territories. The states are New South Wales, Queensland, South Australia, Tasmania, Victoria, and Western Australia. The two internal territories are the Northern Territory and the Australian Capital Territory.

THE LAND. Australia contains some of the oldest and most stable portions of the earth's surface. It may once have formed part of an ancient continent known as Gondwanaland, consisting of Africa, parts of the Indian subcontinent, and Brazil, as well as Australia.

Regions. Australia has three main land regions—the Western Plateau, the Central Lowlands, and the Eastern Highlands.

The Western Plateau occupies approximately the western half of the continent. It has an average elevation of about 1,200 feet above sea level. It

SNOWY MOUNTAINS AUTHORITY

EUCUMBENE DAM. One of the highest dams in the world, Australia's Eucumbene stands more than 381 feet high and is nearly half a mile thick at its base. Lake Eucumbene, the reservoir formed by the dam, contains eight times as much water as does Sydney Harbor.

is flat and monotonous for the most part, but there are some isolated mountain ranges, such as the Macdonnell and Musgrave ranges, which rise to almost 5,000 feet above sea level.

The Central Lowlands, lying east of the Western Plateau, have an average elevation of about 500 feet, although Lake Eyre, in the southern part of the region, lies about 40 feet below sea level. Marine sediments, laid down about 50 million years ago, cover much of the region.

Sedimentary rocks in the northern part of the Central Lowlands form the Great Artesian Basin, an important source of underground water in an area that receives very little rain. The Murray-Darling-Murrumbidgee Basin, Australia's most extensive river system, occupies the southeastern portion of the lowlands. The Great Australian Bight cuts into the southern coast, and the Gulf of Capentaria cuts inland on the north.

The Eastern Highlands, sometimes known as the Great Dividing Range, are a collection of many mountain ranges and plateaus that run parallel to Australia's east coast. Among the ranges are the Australian Alps, Hunter Mountains, Blue Mountains, Liverpool Range, and Darling Downs. Mount Kosciusko, which rises more than 7,300 feet in the Australian Alps, is Australia's highest peak.

The island of Tasmania, about 130 miles from the Australian mainland, contains an extension of the Eastern Highlands. The highlands on Tasmania form a central plateau containing many natural lakes.

The Great Barrier Reef, a collection of islands, cays, and reefs, stretches for some 1,250 miles along the northern half of the east coast. Some parts of the reef are formed from the same rocks as the adjacent

mainland; others are made up of the skeletons of millions of tiny coral polyps which have solidified into reefs and islands.

Climate. Australia's winter season extends from June through August, and summer from December to February. Winters are mild almost everywhere; summers are warm to hot. Precipitation is of greater concern in Australia than temperature, since much of the continent is deficient in rainfall.

The interior parts of the Central Lowlands and Western Plateau are extremely arid, and Lake Eyre is usually completely dry. The northern coastal region receives heavy seasonal rainfall. Australia's southwestern corner receives winter rain. The only area to receive year-round rain is the southeastern corner. Rainfall over most of the interior averages less than 10 inches a year.

Plant Life. Because of Australia's dryness, forest areas are composed of trees that are drought resistant. Forests occur only in the southeast and southwest and in isolated patches along the east coast. Almost half the continent is covered with semi-desert scrub or sand dunes. Another large portion has mixed grass and tree cover.

Australia's dryness, coupled with the continent's long isolation from the rest of the world, have led to the development of many unique species of plants and animals. Typically Australian are the eucalyptus and acacia types of plants, which together account for more than 1,000 different species. These plants, which may vary from low shrubs to tall trees, form the dominant non-grass vegetation.

Animal Life. The continent is also famous for its distinctive animal life, especially the platypus, kangaroo, wallaby, and koala. Rabbits, although not native to Australia, are so numerous that they have been labeled pests.

The kookaburra, emu, Australian lyrebird, and black swan are among the more famous of some 650 species of birds found in Australia.

THE PEOPLE. When the first European settlers arrived in Australia in the 1700s, they found an estimated 300,-000 aborigines living there. The aborigines are related to small groups of people living in other areas of southern Asia.

Many of the aborigines died as a result of diseases introduced by the Europeans, and in 1961 there were only about 40,000 full-blooded aborigines living in Australia. There were, however, a larger number of people of mixed aboriginal and European origin. Most of the full-blooded aborigines live in the Northern Territory and in Western Australia.

About 95 percent of the Australian population is of British origin. After World War II Australia sought to double its immigration rate. Immigration restrictions were eased and over 665,000 people came to Australia between July 1947 and June 1966.

The population of Australia is unevenly distributed. More than 80 percent of the people live in urban areas that are, for the most part, on or near the coast. The interior of the continent has almost no permanent population.

Over half the people live in the capital cities of Australia's six states, and the capital cities are of vast importance in each of the states. Sydney, the capital of New South Wales, is the largest of Australia's cities and an important economic center. Melbourne, the capital and largest city of Victoria, is also a major economic center. Canberra, the national capital, is located in the Australian Capital Territory, approximately 180 miles south of Sydney.

ECONOMY. Although long famous for its agricultural products, wool, wheat, and cattle, Australia is also an important manufacturing nation. The smelting of iron and the production of machines, tools, and vehicles today constitute the largest group of Australian manufacturing industries. By 1948 the value of Australia's manufacturing production had surpassed the value of its agricultural output, and by 1963 manufacturing contributed 28 percent of the country's gross domestic product.

Manufacturing is concentrated in the southeastern corner of the continent. Sydney is a major industrial center, with clothing, metal, machinery, and food processing plants. Melbourne also has many industries, and its neighboring cities of Geelong and Broadmeadows are major centers of the automobile industry.

Agriculture. Agriculture accounted for 14 percent of the gross domestic product in 1963, as compared with 29 percent in 1950. Although the range of products is very great, wheat, wool, and meat continue to dominate the agricultural part of the economy.

Wheat is produced mainly in a crescent-shaped area beginning in New South Wales, running southwestward through Victoria and South Australia, jumping the Great Australian Bight, and continuing through the southern portion of Western Australia to the Indian Ocean.

Cattle are raised in all of the Australian states, although Queensland accounts for more than one third the national total. Sheep are also found in all of the states, although New South Wales and Victoria account for well over half of the country's total. In many cases wheat and sheep or cattle are raised in the same area. Other agricultural products include sugar cane, grapes and wine, fruits and vegetables, and dairy products.

Mining. Mining is important to Australia's economy. In recent years the mining industry has been dominated by coal, lead, zinc, copper, gold, and iron ore. The principal coal producing state is New South Wales, especially the Hunter Valley. Lead and zinc come primarily from New South Wales and Queensland.

Copper is mined in several places, including Queensland, the Northern Territory, and Tasmania. Most of the gold comes from Western Australia. Whyalla, in South Australia, and Yampi Sound, in Western Australia, are the principal producers of iron ore.

Transportation. Australia is well served by modern road, rail, and air networks. The greatest density of roads is in the southeast.

Australian railroad tracks were built to three different widths and this has created problems in shipping goods from one part of the continent to another. But a program of rebuilding many of the lines to a standard gauge was well underway by the mid-1960s.

Trade. In 1966 Australia's imports were valued at almost U.S.$3,200 million and exports earned slightly more than U.S.$3,000 million. Wool is the most valuable single export item, accounting for about 30 percent of the total income from merchandise exports. Other important exports are wheat, flour, and meat. Australia's major imports include chemicals and fertilizers, petroleum products, paper products, and fabrics, as well as machinery.

Australia's main trading partners include Britain, New Zealand, the United States, and Japan.

GOVERNMENT. Australia's federal system of government is patterned on the governments of Britain and the United States. The nominal head of the Australian government is the British Queen, who is represented by a governor-general. Actual executive power is wielded by a cabinet, headed by a prime minister, responsible to the national legislature.

Legislative power is vested in Parliament. Parliament has two houses—the 60-member Senate, with 10 senators elected from each of the 6 states to 6-year terms, and the House of Representatives, popularly elected to a 3-year term.

The British sovereign also appoints individual state governors. Each state has its own parliament to deal with local matters. The organization of the state parliaments varies from state to state, according to the various state constitutions.

Australia is a member of the Commonwealth of Nations, and close ties are maintained with Britain and other Commonwealth countries. Australia is also a member of ANZUS, a defense pact linking Australia, New Zealand, and the United States, and of the South East Asia Treaty Organization (SEATO). Australia was a charter member of the United Nations, and it plays an active role in UN affairs.

HISTORY. The original settlers of Australia were aborigines, who came to the continent about 12,000 years ago from Southeast Asia. These people lived at an extremely primitive level, with very little in the way of material culture, but with a highly developed ability to survive in a hostile natural environment.

In the 1600s Portuguese, Spanish, and Dutch navigators explored the southern hemisphere. In 1606 a Spanish commander, Luis Vaez de Torres, sailed through the strait which now bears his name off the northeastern tip of the mainland. In the same year Willem Jansz explored the region around the Gulf of Carpentaria.

Abel Tasman discovered the island of Tasmania in 1642. In 1770 Captain James Cook made extensive explorations of the continent's east coast, and landed at Botany Bay in southeastern Australia. He later sailed north, landed on an island off the northeastern tip of Australia, and claimed the eastern part of the continent for England.

Settlement. Britain made the first settlement in Australia in 1788, when 11 ships under the command of Capt. Arthur Phillip landed at Botany Bay. The 1,030 people carried by the ships included 726 convicts. A settlement was made at Port Jackson, which eventually became the great city of Sydney. Britain established a second colony in 1803-1804 in Tasmania.

The early history of the settlements was dominated by the convict system, and by the struggle of the free settlers to establish their rights as Englishmen. The colony's first economic objective was agricultural self-sufficiency, and when a convict's time expired, he was encouraged to set up a small farm.

Farming did not provide an exportable surplus, however, and free officers in the colony set up a profitable business in rum. The colony's governors unsuccessfully tried to put an end to the rum trade, and in 1808 the officers forcibly ousted Gov. William Bligh, who had tried to end the rum trade.

Lachlan Macquarie, governor from 1809 to 1821, energetically reorganized the community and ended the officers' power. He emphasized agricultural development and convict rehabilitation. He developed aesthetically appealing public buildings, useful roads, and a bank. The colony's population increased considerably, but London recalled Macquarie and rebuked him because of claims that he had overstepped his official authority.

By 1796 Merino sheep had been introduced into the colony, and wool soon became an important industry and changed Australia's economic base. The dynamic wool industry spread rapidly after the 1820s and provided an export commodity that has since been basic to the Australian economy. With the industry's spread over the continent's usable land, businessmen and free workingmen came to settle.

Because sheep farming requires broad fields and a small work force, each colony tended to develop a single urban center, usually near a port. In 1829 settlers founded Perth, in Western Australia; in 1835, Melbourne, in the Port Phillip district of what was then New South Wales; and in 1836, Adelaide, in South Australia. Except for Western Australia, the new colonies were for free men only.

The early 1800s were also marked by further efforts of the former convicts to establish their civil rights and of the colonies to achieve self-government. Many of the free colonists and the authorities were unwilling to grant political rights to the large number of ex-convicts and feared the end of the convict system, which provided cheap labor.

Nevertheless, many Australians and Englishmen strongly attacked the convict system on the grounds that it morally damaged Australian society, it had ceased to be a punishment for English criminals, it did not rehabilitate the prisoners, and it unfairly competed with free labor. Britain ceased sending convicts to New South Wales in 1840, to Tasmania in 1853, and to Western Australia in 1868.

Self-rule. Progress toward self-rule developed as the number of free colonists grew. In 1850 the British Parliament passed the Australian Colonies Government Act, which allowed the Australian colonies to organize legislatures. The act formed the Port Phillip district of New South Wales into the separate colony of Victoria, and provided for the separation of Queensland from New South Wales in 1859. Western Australia waited until 1890 for responsible government, however.

In 1851 gold was discovered in eastern Australia, and the ensuing gold rush brought a rapid rise in the population, which grew from some 400,000 in 1850 to 1,146,000 in 1860. Australians faced both an economic struggle to develop an economy diverse enough to allow for the successful assimilation of an increasing population and a political struggle for stability.

Economic development involved the investment of both government and private capital. Industrialists invested earnings from the wool industry in wheat, sugarcane, irrigation, dairy farming, gold mining, and base metal mining.

Cities expanded and the government built railways in each colony. Victoria and New South Wales developed at faster rates than the other parts of Australia. Base metal mining stimulated the Tasmanian economy, but Western Australia stagnated until the development of gold mining there in the 1890s and the later development of wheat and wool.

In the 1890s, in the midst of a world-wide financial depression, a serious shipping, shearing, and mining strike erupted in Australia. The ef-

AUSTRALIAN NEWS AND INFORMATION BUREAU

SYDNEY HARBOR, showing the modern terminal wharves and the elevated Cahill Expressway. Berthed at the overseas passenger terminal, seen at the left, is the S.S. Canberra.

fects of the strike were intensified by a tremendous drought, which reduced the numbers of sheep and cattle. At that time trade unions grew in importance, and the first politically oriented labor parties emerged.

Recovery from the depression of the 1890s was reasonably quick, largely the result of rising export prices. The government extended the railway system, and wheat farming and sheep raising expanded. In the 1890s the government established free, compulsory state schools. The number of universities grew, and authentically Australian schools of painting and writing appeared.

Commonwealth. In 1897–1898, a convention met to draft a federal constitution. In 1900 Britain accepted a federal, political framework for Australia, and the Commonwealth of Australia came into being on Jan. 1, 1901.

A significant development between 1901 and the outbreak of World War I was the political impact of the Labor party, organized in 1891. Trade unions saw the need for political support for social welfare legislation, but the Labor party, representing the trade unions, entered federal politics reluctantly. It felt the best prospects for success lay in influencing the state governments.

In 1902 the Labor party allied itself with Alfred Deakin, who became prime minister, although Labor's views were more socialistic than Deakin's. Labor supported a White Australia position; that is, they wanted to keep out Orientals, whom they feared as cheap labor. Deakin also convinced Labor of the need for a high protective tariff.

By 1910 the Labor party held a majority of seats in the House of Representatives, but implementation of the full Labor program was frustrated by the electorate's refusal to approve necessary constitutional changes.

At the outbreak of World War I, Australia was weak in manufacturing. After foodstuffs and raw materials, its

major export for war was manpower. Of a total population of about 4 million, Australia mobilized some 400,000 men and sent 332,000 volunteers overseas. The men served in the Middle East and in France. The federal government increased its authority over the states during the era of war preparation.

In 1915 William Morris Hughes, leader of the Labor party, became prime minister. Hughes advocated conscription for overseas service, but a popular referendum twice defeated his attempts. A rift developed within the party following the defeat, and Hughes and his colleagues broke from the Labor party. Hughes organized a National War Government, and his followers formed the Nationalist party, politically opposed to the Labor party.

Interwar Era. Hughes represented Australia at the peace conference at the end of World War I. He sought punitive measures against Germany and heavy reparations for Australia. Hughes also fought successfully a League of Nations proposal to establish racial equality and thereby compromise the White Australia policy.

After the war the Commonwealth came under the rule of a coalition of the Nationalists and a new group, the Country party. The Country party was formed in 1918 by farmers who felt that rural areas were not adequately represented.

War production over, the government emphasized land industries, but although men and money were forthcoming, the markets failed. There was a postwar recession, exports declined, and tremendous imports left companies without means to finance purchases. The rural industries, except for wool, had to be supported by high, government-fixed domestic prices.

The world-wide depression of the 1930s hit Australia hard because of the sharp drop in prices for its exports—foodstuffs and raw materials. Labor regained federal power in 1929 but lost in 1931, unable to master the depression situation. Former Nationalist and Labor party members formed the United Australia party to meet the results of the depression with sound finance.

In the 1920s there had been a concentration on material development and a lack of experimentation. In the 1930s, however, activity in painting, literature, and education all showed a renewed vitality.

World War II. At the opening of World War II, Australia's industrial war potential was considerable. The prime minister, Robert Gordon Menzies, prepared Australia for war. He assisted Britain with supplies and food, increased war production, and raised an army. The country became a heavier exporter of foodstuffs and raw materials than it had been during World War I. Its manpower was also greater.

Australians early realized the great importance of war developments in the Pacific. From 1939 to the bombing of Pearl Harbor by the Japanese in 1941, Australians anxiously watched developments in the Pacific. At the same time they sought to organize their industrial war potential and deployed their armed forces in North Africa.

Because of Britain's inability to provide for Australia's security in the Pacific, ties with the United States were fostered. In 1940 a representative was sent to Washington, and a U.S. representative went to Canberra. When Singapore fell to the Japanese in 1942, a course was set for Australian-U.S. collaboration.

The Australians elected the Labor party to office in 1941. Labor confirmed the steady growth of federal power, worked to diversify the economy, and stressed industrialization and social welfare.

Contemporary Australia. In 1949 the Labor party lost to Robert Gordon Menzies. Menzies led a coalition of the Country party and the Liberal party, which had supplanted the United Australia party in 1944. The Menzies government kept the emphasis on manufacturing growth but also looked to develop land industries to provide basic exports. The government strengthened ties with the United States through U.S. capital investment in Australia.

Federal responsibility was extended to include internal transportation, water resource development, and higher education. The government maintained control over state finances and relaxed immigration restrictions. The national product rose sharply, and Australians acquired a new affluence.

Menzies retired in 1966, and the Liberal party leader, Harold Holt, became prime minister. Holt continued the policy of cooperation with the United States and strongly supported the U.S. position in the Vietnam conflict.

Prime Minister Holt lost his life in a swimming accident in December 1967, and in January 1968 John Gorton was chosen to succeed him as leader of the Liberal party and as prime minister. Gorton pledged to continue Holt's program.

—David A. Smith

AUSTRIA

Official name: Federal Republic of Austria
Area: 32,371 square miles
Population: (1966 est.) 7,290,000
Capital: Vienna (Pop., 1965 est., 1,640,100)
Language: German
Religion: Roman Catholicism
Currency unit: Shilling
National holiday: October 26

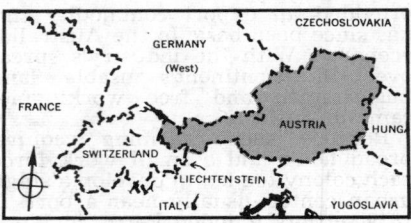

Austria, a landlocked nation in central Europe, is bounded on the north by Germany and Czechoslovakia, on the east by Hungary, on the south by Yugoslavia and Italy, and on the west by Switzerland and Liechtenstein. Although Austria today is a small republic, it was once the center of the mighty Holy Roman and Austro-Hungarian empires, and Vienna was a cultural and intellectual capital of the world.

THE LAND. Austria is a mountainous land. The Austrian Alps run west to east from the Swiss border and occupy nearly all of central and southern Austria. Aside from a few prosperous valleys, the Alps are rugged and barren, with many ice-covered peaks rising above 10,000 feet.

North of the Alps lies the crescent-shaped Alpine Foreland, a hilly area that grades into a forested plateau region between the Danube River and the Czech border. In the northeastern corner of the plateau is the fertile and heavily populated Vienna basin. The navigable Danube crosses northern Austria on its way to the Black Sea, and its many tributaries thread the country.

The Austrian climate varies greatly from region to region. For the country as a whole, the average temperature in January is 22°F, and in July 64°F. The Alps, however, are much colder in winter and cooler in summer than the rest of Austria. Rainfall averages between 30 and 40 inches a year.

THE PEOPLE. The people of Austria are almost entirely German-speaking, but there are some who speak other languages, including Croatian, Czech, and Slovene. Over 90 percent of the people are Roman Catholic, and about 6 percent are Protestant. There is a small Jewish minority.

The most densely populated areas are on the northern and southern edges of the Alps, especially along the Danube River in the north. Vienna, in the northeast, is Austria's largest city, with over 20 percent of the country's total population. The mountainous central part of the country is sparsely settled.

THE ECONOMY. Austria is a prosperous nation. Industry is the most important part of the Austrian economy, contributing more than 40 percent of the national product in the mid-1960s.

PAN AMERICAN AIRWAYS

AUSTRIA'S ALPINE SCENERY attracts thousands of tourists to the country each year.

AUSTRIAN TOURIST BUREAU

SCHOENBRUNN CASTLE, originally built for Emperor Leopold I (1658–1705) by the baroque architect Johann Bernhard Fischer von Erlach, was reconstructed in its present form by Empress Maria Theresa (1740–1780) after plans by the architect Nicolas Pacassi.

An important factor in industrial growth has been the availability of water power. Austria's hydroelectric power potential has been greatly developed, and large quantities of electricity are exported to neighboring nations. Austria's moderate mineral resources include iron, oil, magnesite, lead, and copper.

Since World War II, industry has shifted from the production of luxury articles to the manufacture of iron and steel, metal goods, aluminum, chemicals, and forest products.

Agriculture and forestry are important in the economy. Dairying is the leading farm activity, and wheat, corn, barley, oats, sugar beets, and potatoes are the principal crops.

Trade, mainly with West Germany and other western European nations, is vital to Austrian prosperity. In 1966 the country imported $2,328 million worth of goods and exported goods valued at $1,684 million. Imports consist mainly of machinery, foodstuffs, vehicles, electrical equipment, and textile raw materials. Exports include iron and steel, machinery, wood and wood products, and textiles. Tourism is an important source of income.

GOVERNMENT. Austria is a federal republic made up of nine provinces. A president, elected to a six-year term, is head of state. He appoints the chancellor, or prime minister, who heads the cabinet. The chancellor and cabinet are responsible to the lower house of the legislature. Members of the lower house are popularly elected; those of the upper house are chosen by provincial legislatures.

By the 1955 treaty restoring its sovereignty, Austria may possess only defensive weapons and must maintain neutrality in world affairs. It is a member of the United Nations and the Council of Europe.

HISTORY. The Danube Basin was an important roadway for peoples migrating from the east many centuries ago. The Romans established military posts in the area, but by the 400s AD migrating Germanic tribes had forced the Romans out of the region. By about 800 the area had become part of the empire of Charlemagne, who made it the eastern kingdom, the "Ostmark" or "Osterreich," of his realm.

In 1282 Austria, then part of the Holy Roman Empire, became a possession of the Hapsburg family. The Hapsburgs, Holy Roman emperors for 400 years, ruled Austria for over 600 years. Through the strength of their dynasty the country achieved a position of leadership in Europe during the 1500s, 1600s, and 1700s. During that time Austria was the center of a Hapsburg empire that controlled territory throughout Europe.

The Empire. In 1804, two years before the Holy Roman Empire was dissolved, the Hapsburg Francis II declared himself emperor of Austria and Austria itself became an empire. In the following 50 years, the Austrian Empire, led by its foreign minister, Prince von Metternich, played a major role in the complex series of military and political alliances that characterized European affairs during the Napoleonic and post-Napoleonic eras.

The Austrian Empire included Galicia, Bohemia, Hungary, northern Italy, and part of the Balkan peninsula, and the many different and often restless nationalities that lived in those regions. Austria's government was highly centralized and conservative.

In the 1840s and 1850s liberal and nationalist revolutions broke out in the Austrian Empire. These rebellions weakened the government's power and led to reforms that only partly satisfied the empire's subject peoples —particularly the Croatians, Czechs, and Hungarians. Austria's loss of absolute control over its people weakened its international position.

In 1867 the many separate German states were united under Prussia, Austria's rival in German politics. The German union excluded Austria. The unification of Germany forced Austria, in order to retain some internal stability and international power, to make the restive Hungarian region of the empire an equal partner with the German part. The two states were joined in the Dual Monarchy of Austria-Hungary in 1867.

Creation of the Dual Monarchy, controlled by the Germans of Austria and the Magyar people of Hungary, left the Slavic subject peoples in Bohemia and the Balkans dissatisfied. The discontent of the Slavs was an important cause of World War I, which began when a Slav from Serbia assassinated Archduke Francis Ferdinand, the heir to the Austro-Hungarian throne. Austria-Hungary declared war on Serbia, and was joined by Germany.

The German allies were defeated, and at the end of the war in 1918 the Hapsburg empire lay in ruins. In 1918 the emperor abdicated and was replaced by a provisional government. The provisional assembly declared its desire to unite with Germany, but the Allied powers prohibited Austrian-German unification by the Treaty of St. Germain (1919).

The Allies divided much of Austria's old territory among Italy, Hungary, a restored Poland, and the new states of Czechoslovakia and Yugoslavia. The treaty also proclaimed Austria a republic.

The First Republic. In 1920 a permanent government was formed, and its members drafted a constitution. Austria, now a small, overwhelmingly German-speaking nation, was made a federal state with a president as chief of state and a cabinet led by a chancellor. A two-house legislature was elected democratically.

Two political parties dominated the republic—the Christian Socialists and the Social Democrats. The Christian Socialist party drew its principal support from the wealthy landowners and manufacturers, the clergy, and the farmers. It favored some form of authoritarian government. The Social Democrats represented mainly the urban workers and followed a socialist program. A small, nationalistic faction favoring union with Germany grew rapidly in size and power during the 1920s.

The first republic faced serious difficulties from its earliest years. In 1920 the government had to use force to prevent parts of the country from seceding and joining Germany. Pressure for unification with Germany, or *Anschluss,* was to plague the republic continually. The Austrian economy was weak. It avoided total collapse only by receiving financial grants from the League of Nations between 1922 and 1925.

Party politics created the most severe problems, however. In 1926 a serious conflict opened between the Christian Socialist national government and the Social Democrats. The Social Democrats governed the province that included the capital city, Vienna, where one quarter of the country's population then lived.

In Vienna the Social Democrats had financed experimental social welfare programs for the workers by heavily taxing the rich. The conservative

Christian Socialists objected strongly to these programs. The conflict, centered in Vienna, led to frequent riots. Each party had its own private army, and the riots were usually bloody.

A new Christian Socialist national government elected in 1929 set the restoration of order as its primary goal. It outlawed the bearing of arms and banned the political parties. In 1930 it signed a treaty of friendship and protection with Benito Mussolini's fascist government of Italy.

To strengthen Austria's economy the government in 1931 tried to enter a customs union with Germany. Both countries gave up the attempt when the World War I Allies protested. Without the agreement, the Austrian state bank collapsed. The League of Nations granted funds again in 1932 on the condition that Austria would form no economic union of any kind for 20 years.

The financial crisis had seriously weakened the national government, which proved unable to handle the continuing political conflicts. The National Socialist (Nazi) party's growing power in Germany inspired the Austrian nationalists. They held demonstrations in Austria and in 1932 nearly succeeded in taking over the government of one province. The nationalists' strongest opposition came from the Social Democrats, and the conflict between the two parties grew violent.

Dictatorship. A Christian Socialist cabinet formed in 1932 by Chancellor Engelbert Dollfuss determined to restore order. In 1933 Dollfuss dissolved parliament and restricted the rights of free speech, press, and assembly. He tried to ban the Austrian Nazis in 1933, but when Germany strongly objected, he turned his attack on the Social Democrats.

After 1934 an undeclared civil war raged between the nationalists and the socialists, and Dollfuss lost the support of the working class when he destroyed a new Social Democratic housing project in Vienna. In a last effort to restore order, Dollfuss rewrote the constitution and made himself a dictator. The chancellor's aim was to make Austria strong enough to prevent a German conquest.

Austria's international situation became desperate, as Germany's growing power threatened Austria's very existence. In 1934 Dollfuss entered an alliance with Hungary and Italy, despite the provisions of the treaty of St. Germain. He hoped to gain Italy's support against Germany, where Adolf Hitler's Nazi party had come to power in 1933. On July 25, 1935, however, Austrian Nazis assassinated Dollfuss in an attempt to take over the government. Germany was unable to aid the Austrian Nazis because of a military threat from Italy, and Austria won one more chance for independence.

Dollfuss' associate, Kurst Schuschnigg, who succeeded him as chancellor in 1934, continued the dictatorship. He relied even more heavily on Italy for military and economic aid. Schuschnigg, too, hoped that with order at home and Italy's aid abroad, Austria could escape conquest by Germany. Domestic disorder continued, however, and Italy's effectiveness as a protector

decreased rapidly as Mussolini and Hitler drew closer.

In 1938 Hitler forced Schuschnigg to recognize the Austrian Nazi party and to admit a Nazi, Arthur Seyss-Inquart, to the cabinet. Increased Nazi activity followed and brought more violence to Austria. The Christian Socialist government could not control the Nazi outbreaks alone, and Schuschnigg attempted to unite with his party's old rivals, the Social Democrats. The Social Democrats, however, refused to join him.

Anschluss. In a last effort to save Austria, Schuschnigg tried to show the world that Austrians did not want to join Germany. He planned an election in which the citizens would vote for either independence or union. By the chancellor's arrangement, a "yes" vote for independence would have been easy to cast; a "no" vote almost impossible.

Hitler responded to this plan with an ultimatum. Austria must either accept Nazi rule peacefully, or face military conquest. Hitler then began massing troops on the Austrian border. Schuschnigg resigned, and Seyss-Inquart, the Nazi minister of the interior, replaced him as chancellor. In March 1938, Seyss-Inquart announced Austria's union with Germany and invited the German army into the country. The *Anschluss* had been accomplished.

The Allies, who had the treaty right to oppose the German occupation of Austria, did not protest. They hoped to avoid a second war by letting Hitler take Austria. In 1939, when World War II did begin, Austria, as part of Germany, shared Germany's fate. The early years of victory ended in 1945 with the defeat of the Axis, the German allies.

Contemporary Austria. After the war, the Allies treated Austria as a liberated country rather than as a conquered enemy. But Austria was divided into four zones, each occupied by one of the major Allied powers—the Soviet Union, Britain, France, and the United States.

The democratic constitution of 1920 was restored, and the Socialist and the People's parties, the more moderate successors of the prewar Social Democratic and Christian Socialist parties, formed a coalition government. The coalition avoided the destructive political conflicts of the first republic, and, with Allied aid, Austria rebuilt and expanded its economy.

Austria was not fully independent, however, until a final peace treaty with the Allies was signed. Peace negotiations were hampered by the Soviet Union, which wanted large war damage payments from Austria and which was unwilling to withdraw its occupation troops. Finally, in 1955, Austria once more became independent with the signing of the Austrian State Treaty.

Austria grew steadily stronger economically and politically. In 1966 Chancellor Josef Klaus' People's Party won an election by enough votes to allow a one-party government to replace a coalition cabinet for the first time since the war.

—George M. Kren

BAHRAIN

Official name: Bahrain
Area: 231 square miles
Population: (1966 est.) 193,000
Capital: Al Manamah (Pop., 1959, urban area, 61,700)
Language: Arabic
Religion: Islam
Currency unit: Dinar

Bahrain is a tiny, oil-rich island nation in the Gulf of Bahrain, an inlet of the Persian Gulf between the Qatar peninsula and the Saudi Arabian coast. The country's major islands are Bahrain, the largest, Sitra, Al Muharraq, Umm an Nasan, Jidda, and Hawar.

THE LAND AND PEOPLE. All of the islands are deserts with an extremely hot and humid climate. Almost no rain falls on them, and their only water comes from a few underground springs. Cities developed around these springs, and in the mid-1960s about two-thirds of Bahrain's people lived in two major cities, Al Manama, on Bahrain Island, and Muharraq.

Native Bahrainis are Muslim Arabs, and they constitute about 80 percent of the population. There are also Arabs from other countries, Iranians, Indians, and European oil workers.

ECONOMY. Oil is the small country's principal natural resource and chief export. In 1966 more than 3.1 million metric tons of oil were pumped from beneath Bahrain's deserts and coastal waters. A refinery on Bahrain Island processes oil from Bahrain and from Saudi Arabia. Royalty fees paid by oil companies have financed educational and medical programs, communications and power development projects, and agricultural modernization programs.

Dates, grain, vegetables, and citrus fruits are raised in the islands' oases. Trade passing through Al Manama, one of the best ports in the Persian Gulf, is an important source of income. Pearling, once the mainstay of the economy, is still of some significance.

GOVERNMENT. Bahrain is ruled by a sheikh, who is a hereditary monarch with absolute power. He heads a government council formed of members of his family and appointed cabinet members.

A British political agent advises the government, and Britain is responsible for the country's foreign affairs and defense.

HISTORY. Bahrain's islands may have been inhabited as early as 3000 BC, and they were known to the ancient Greeks. Their strategic location for trade and rich beds of pearl oysters attracted several conquerors. In 1507 Portugal occupied the islands and held them until 1602, when the Persians conquered them.

In 1782 Arab tribes seized power and founded the Khalifa dynasty. In 1820 Bahrain entered into treaty relations with Britain, and in 1861 the two countries concluded a treaty of protection for Bahrain.

The discovery of oil in 1932 brought Bahrain sudden international importance and radically changed the islanders' traditional way of life. Iran laid claim to the islands and protested the British presence there.

In the mid-1950s and mid-1960s Bahraini pan-Arab nationalists incited anti-British riots and called for union with other Arab states. But the Khalifa dynasty maintained its control, and Bahrain remained under British protection. But British plans to withdraw from the Persian Gulf by 1970 led Bahrain to draw closer to Saudi Arabia. In 1968 they agreed to build a causeway linking Bahrain Island to the Arabian mainland.
—Charles Issawi; Alexander Melamid

BARBADOS

Official name: Barbados
Area: 166 square miles
Population: (1966 est.) 245,000
Capital: Bridgetown (Pop., 1960, 11,452)
Language: English
Religion: Anglicanism, Protestantism
Currency unit: East Caribbean dollar
National holiday: November 30

Barbados, a small island nation at the extreme eastern end of the West Indies, lies about 300 miles north of Guyana, on the South American mainland. Barbados achieved its independence in 1966 after some 300 years of British control.

THE LAND. Barbados is a triangular-shaped island about 20 miles long and 14 miles across at its widest point. Most of the island is a low-lying plateau, but there is a small highland area in the northeast. There are good beaches along the western and southwestern coasts.

Barbados has an adequate supply of fresh water, but there is little natural vegetation. The climate is comfortable. Temperatures range between 70°F and 87°F, and the trade winds blow across the island all year.

THE PEOPLE. Most of the island's people are of African origin. Persons of mixed African and European background make up about 17 percent of the total, and those of European origin represent about 3 percent.

The island is densely populated, and population growth creates serious economic and social problems.

ECONOMY. Sugar is the basis of the economic life of Barbados. Sugarcane is grown on about 80 percent of the cultivatable land, and sugar and sugar products—rum and molasses—account for approximately 80 percent of export earnings. Yams, peas, beans, and corn are grown for local food needs.

PAN AMERICAN AIRWAYS
THE HARBOR AT BRIDGETOWN, capital of Barbados, is a sight familiar to many tourists.

The government has worked to diversify the economy. Light industry has been growing, and other activities, such as fishing, have been promoted. Tourism is an important source of income.

GOVERNMENT. The head of state is the British monarch, represented on the island by a governor-general, the nominal chief executive. Actual executive powers are exercised by a prime minister and cabinet. The prime minister is normally the leader of the majority party in the legislature.

The legislature, or parliament, has two houses, the Senate and the House of Representatives. The 21 members of the Senate are appointed by the governor-general. Twelve are named on the advice of the prime minister, 2 on the advice of the leader of the opposition party, and 7 to represent religious, economic, and other interest groups. The 24 members of the House of Representatives are popularly elected.

Barbados is a member of the United Nations, the Commonwealth of Nations, and the Organization of American States (OAS).

HISTORY. Arawak Indians lived on Barbados until about 100 years before the arrival of the first British voyagers in 1625. An English merchant group had won control of the island by 1629, but during the English civil wars of the 1600s the English government took direct control. In doing so, the British granted the islanders the Charter of Barbados, which provided for government by a governor, council, and elected assembly, and taxes levied only with the consent of the inhabitants.

British Rule. Barbados was a prosperous island. Coffee, tobacco, cotton, and other crops were grown for export, and cassava and corn were raised for local needs. In the late 1600s sugar became the major crop, and large numbers of African slaves were brought to Barbados to work on sugar plantations.

The abolition of slavery in 1834 had little effect on the island's economic,

social, or political life. Prosperity continued until late in the 1800s, when home-grown sugar beets began to meet Europe's sugar needs, and the world price of sugar dropped.

The economy revived in the early 1900s as a result of British financial aid, improvements in sugar production, and the beginnings of the export of labor. Many Barbadians went to Central America to work on the construction of the Panama Canal. They were able to send money home, and many saved enough to buy small farms on their return.

The emigration of Barbadians to Panama ended in 1913, but World War I led to a great demand for sugar. Prosperity continued until the onset of the world economic depression of the 1930s.

Federation. Political progress was rapid after World War II, and universal suffrage was introduced in 1951. Political parties were formed during the postwar years, and elections held in 1951 were won by the Barbados Labor Party (BLP), led by Grantley Adams.

In 1958 Barbados became a member of the short-lived Federation of the West Indies, which united ten of Britain's West Indian and Caribbean territories, and Adams became the federation's prime minister. Adams' BLP lost elections held in Barbados in 1961. The victor was the Democratic Labor Party, led by Errol Barrow, which had been formed in 1955 by dissident BLP members.

Independence. The Federation of the West Indies began to break up in 1962, when Jamaica and Trinidad withdrew to become independent nations. In 1965 Barbados decided to seek its own road to independence, and on Nov. 30, 1966, Britain granted the island its freedom.

Prime Minister Barrow quickly brought the new country into the United Nations and the Commonwealth of Nations. In 1967 Barbados became a member of the Organization of American States (OAS).
—Robert J. Feldman

BELGIUM

Official name: Kingdom of Belgium
Area: 11,781 square miles
Population: (1966 est.) 9,528,000
Capital: Brussels (Pop., 1965 est., urban area, 1,065,900)
Language: Flemish, French
Religion: Roman Catholicism
Currency unit: Franc
National holiday: Independence day, July 21

Belgium, a small nation in western Europe, is bounded on the north by the Netherlands, on the east by West Germany and Luxembourg, on the south by France, and on the west by the North Sea.

In 1922 Belgium and Luxembourg formed an economic union that abolished the customs frontier between them. The union was dissolved in 1940, but was reestablished in 1945. In 1948 a customs union went into effect linking Belgium and Luxembourg with the Netherlands, which is known as the Benelux Customs Union. Full economic union of the three countries has existed since 1960.

THE LAND. Most of Belgium consists of low-lying plains. In the southeast, however, the country is quite hilly, and this highland pasture zone—the Ardennes—is rather sparsely settled. The main rivers in Belgium are the Schelde, the Sambre, and the Meuse.

Belgium has little variation in climate. Its mild winters and cool summers are characterized by light rainfall, high humidity, and partial cloudiness. In the southwest, however, the higher elevations cause somewhat cooler summers and distinctly colder winters, and the precipitation is much heavier.

THE PEOPLE. Belgium can be nearly evenly divided linguistically, and, to a certain extent, culturally, by an east-west line. In the north are Flemings, who make up about 55 percent of the population. They speak Flemish, a language closely related to Dutch. In the south, French-speaking Walloons are dominant. Brussels is bilingual. Flemish and French are the official languages, and both are used for highway signs, public announcements, and official documents. Belgium is overwhelmingly Roman Catholic.

The population is relatively stable, having increased on the average by only 0.6 percent a year between 1958 and 1966. Population is densest in the central district and sparsest in the southeastern quarter of the country. Belgium is highly urbanized. Its major cities include Brussels, Antwerp, Liège, Charleroi, Ghent, and Louvain.

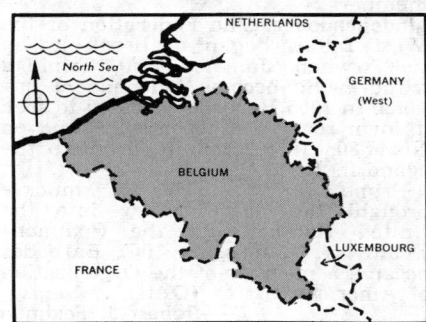

ECONOMY. Belgium is primarily an industrial nation, and, although it is small, it ranks high among European nations in the manufacture of such products as refined copper, pig iron, steel, and textiles. Belgium's only important mineral is coal, and this vital industrial requirement has been the basis of much of the country's industry.

Industry. The western cities, of which Ghent is the largest, specialize in textiles and food processing. Antwerp's industries, with access to the endless variety of raw materials unloaded at its great port, range from diamond cutting to smelting and shipbuilding.

Brussels concentrates on a wide variety of light industries. The coal-rich Sambre-Meuse area contains the country's heavy industry. Metallurgy and metal fabrication are important and cement, glass, chemicals, rubber goods, and paper are all produced there in large quantities.

Agriculture. Although agriculture plays a secondary role in Belgium's economic life, employing only a small share of the labor force, the country's farms meet about 80 percent of domestic food requirements and provide an important share of raw materials for industry.

Trade. International trade is of great importance to the country, and Belgium has a sizable merchant fleet. Antwerp, on the River Schelde, is one of Europe's busiest ports. Belgium and Luxembourg trade as a unit, and in 1966 their exports earned $6,811 million, and their imports were valued at $7,054 million.

Major exports include iron and steel products, machinery, chemicals and pharmaceuticals, and textiles. Major imports include textiles, chemicals, machinery, and petroleum. Exports go chiefly to the Netherlands, West Germany, France, the United States, Britain, Italy, and Switzerland. The principal suppliers of imports are West Germany, France, the Netherlands, the United States, and Britain.

GOVERNMENT. Belgium is a constitutional monarchy. The king is head of state. Executive power is exercised by the king and his ministers. No act of the king is effective, however, unless countersigned by a minister. Ministers are appointed by the king from among the members of the majority party in parliament, and they are responsible to parliament. Since World War I the government has been headed by a prime minister, who coordinates national policy.

Legislative power is exercised by the parliament, which consists of two houses, the Senate and the Chamber of Representatives, and by the king, who sanctions and promulgates the laws. Members of the Chamber of Representatives are popularly elected on the basis of proportional representation. The Senate includes 46 members chosen by local government councils, 109 directly elected members, and 23 chosen by their fellow senators.

Belgium, in addition to inclusion in Benelux, belongs to the European Communities, the United Nations, and the North Atlantic Treaty Organization (NATO).

HISTORY. The Belgae, or Belgians, were one of the Gallic tribes conquered by Julius Caesar in the first century BC, and the area that is now Belgium became part of the Roman Empire. Roman occupation was followed by invasions of Franks between the 200s and 400s AD. After 476 Belgium was ruled by the Merovingians, and later it became part of Charlemagne's empire (800–843).

During the Middle Ages Belgium existed as a group of duchies, which in 1384 came under the control of the dukes of Burgundy. Belgium passed to the Hapsburgs through marriage in 1477 and subsequently became part of the Holy Roman Empire. On the resignation of the Holy Roman Emperor Charles V in 1556, Belgium, along with the Netherlands, passed to Philip II of Spain.

The northern provinces of the Netherlands, or Holland, formed the Union of Utrecht and declared their independence in 1581. But the provinces that constitute modern Belgium continued to be ruled by Spain and then by Austria (1713) until conquered by France in 1792.

Belgium became part of Napoleon's empire in 1801. The Congress of Vienna (1814–1815), which redrew the map of Europe after Napoleon's defeat, united Belgium with Holland in the Kingdom of the Netherlands.

The union failed to take into consideration the difference in character between the two regions, however. Holland was Protestant, Germanic, agricultural, and commercial, whereas Belgium was Roman Catholic, French-oriented, and industrial. Holland favored a policy of free trade, and Belgium sought high tariffs to protect its industry.

Independence. In 1830 the Belgians revolted. King William I sent Dutch troops into Brussels to suppress the revolution, but they were unsuccessful. A provisional government was established, and Prince Leopold of Saxe-Coburg-Gotha was elected king. Within a year, after several conferences, the Great Powers recognized

BELGIAN GOVERNMENT INFORMATION CENTER

BRUGES, capital of Belgium's West Flanders province, derives its name from the Flemish word, *brug*, which means bridge.

the independence of Belgium and in 1839 guaranteed its neutrality.

Under Leopold I, who ruled from 1831 to 1865, Belgium's economy expanded rapidly, and under Leopold II (1865–1909) Belgium acquired a vast empire in Africa. By the end of the 1800s Belgium had transformed itself from an oligarchy governed by a small middle class to a democracy based on universal suffrage with very advanced social welfare programs.

Belgian neutrality was violated by Germany during both World War I and World War II. German troops first entered Belgium on Aug. 4, 1914, after Germany repudiated the treaty guaranteeing Belgian neutrality. The resulting destruction and death toll were enormous, and the country was plundered to the extent that the people were reduced to starvation.

Belgian war damage amounted to more than $7 billion, and the tremendous cost of reconstruction after the war caused a rapid rise in the national debt, inflation, and other financial problems that were to plague the country for almost 20 years. Economic problems increased demands for social legislation, and popular dissatisfaction was expressed politically. As a result, the interwar period was characterized by a series of short-lived governments.

During World War II the Germans attacked Belgium on May 10, 1940, and on May 28, King Leopold III surrendered to avoid further bloodshed. It was felt, however, that his early surrender had weakened Allied strategy. The patriotic feelings of many Belgians were outraged, and Leopold was deposed. The second German occupation was far worse than the first. Material damage was more extensive and many more lives were lost.

After World War II the Belgians voted on Mar. 12, 1950, to recall King Leopold to the throne. Socialist opposition proved so bitter, however, that Leopold abdicated on June 16, 1951, in favor of his son, who became King Baudouin.

Contemporary Belgium. Early during the postwar period, Belgium recognized the need for economic cooperation among the nations of Europe. It was a founding member of the European Monetary Agreement (1950), the European Coal and Steel Community (1951), and the European Economic Community (1958). In 1957 Belgium, along with five other nations, signed the treaty establishing the Common Market.

One of the main concerns of the government during the 1950s was the increasing political unrest in the mineral-rich Belgian Congo. Independence was granted to the Congo on June 30, 1960, and the loss of this important market and source of raw materials dealt a severe blow to the Belgian economy. The government initiated an austerity program to offset the loss, but the program was met by a series of strikes and antigovernment demonstrations.

The austerity program also contributed to a revival of the long-standing hostility between French and Flemish-speaking Belgians. Each claimed the government exhibited economic favoritism toward the other.

Demonstrations aimed at bringing about an official linguistic, if not political, division, between Wallonia and Flanders occurred in 1961 and 1962. In November 1962 the legislature passed a bill making Flemish the official language in the north and French the language in the south. But Flemish-Walloon animosity continued, and in 1968 led to the resignation of the prime minister and cabinet.

In 1967 Belgium met with the Netherlands and Luxembourg to discuss extending the integration of their countries beyond the field of economics, hoping thus to encourage closer cooperation among the other members of the European Community.

—George M. Kren

BHUTAN

Official name: Kingdom of Bhutan
Area: 18,000 square miles
Population: (1966 est.) 750,000
Capital: Thimbu
Language: Dzongkha
Religion: Buddhism
Currency unit: Indian rupee

Bhutan is a small kingdom on the northeastern border of the Indian subcontinent. It is bounded on the north by China, on the east and south by India, and on the west by Sikkim. India manages Bhutan's foreign affairs and is responsible for its defense.

THE LAND. Bhutan is no more than 190 miles long and 90 miles wide, but it has three distinct geographical zones. Within 20 miles of its northern border is a wild and snowy region, where peaks of the eastern Himalayas tower to almost 25,000 feet. A central zone, about 40 miles wide, ranges in elevation from 3,500 feet to 10,000 feet and is forested with evergreens. The southern region, which grades into the valley of the Brahmaputra River, is low and mostly covered with dense semitropical forest.

Several Himalayan rivers flow south through Bhutan. The most important are the Amo Chu, the Ma Chu, and the Manas.

Bhutan's climate varies with elevation. In the north, where alpine tundra conditions prevail, the cold is extreme, and glaciers fill the higher valleys. The central zone is temperate, and rainfall averages 40 to 60 inches a year. The southern region has a semitropical climate—heat and humidity are extreme, and up to 300 inches of rain may fall in a year.

THE PEOPLE. Bhutan's population is concentrated in the river valleys of the temperate central region. Approximately 70 percent of the people are Bhotia, a Tibetan-speaking people. A Nepali minority makes up about 20 percent of the population, and there is a small group of Mongols. Bhutanese are Mahayana Buddhists.

ECONOMY. Agriculture is the basis of Bhutan's economy. Bhutan's forests are valuable, and there are deposits of gypsum and limestone, but these remained unexploited in the mid-1960s. Farms are concentrated in the rich river valleys, and although small, they produce a surplus of food. The major crops are rice, corn, barley, and millet. Fruits and vegetables are also raised.

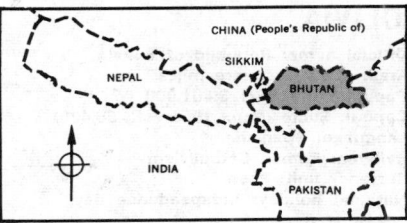

Yaks, goats, and ponies are herded. Traditional handicrafts include weaving, woodworking, and metalworking.

In the 1950s and 1960s development projects were undertaken jointly with India to begin exploiting the country's natural resources, especially its vast hydroelectric potential.

Bhutan exports grains, wax, lac (the base for lacquer), and musk (a perfume base). Almost all of its trade is with India. By treaty, India makes an annual contribution to Bhutan of 500,-000 rupees—about $66,000 at the 1968 rate of exchange.

GOVERNMENT. Bhutan is a monarchy ruled by a hereditary maharaja, or king. He is limited by no constitution, but there is an advisory council of elected village headmen and appointed officials.

HISTORY. Little is known of Bhutan's early history. In the 1500s Tibetans conquered the Mongol tribes that inhabited the land and settled there. Tibetans governed Bhutan and placed it under the spiritual authority of the Dalai Lama of Tibet. In the 1700s China conquered Tibet and assumed control over Bhutan jointly with the Dalai Lama, but the country actually was governed by local tribal chieftains.

In 1774, after several raids by Bhutanese hill tribesmen on British India, the British East India Company forced Bhutan to grant it trading privileges through the important Himalayan passes that Bhutan controlled. But the raids continued, and in 1865 British troops subdued the hill tribesmen and annexed Bhutan's eastern region, which included the major passes.

In 1885, after years of feuding among the tribal chieftains, one leader, Ugyen Wangchuk, gained dominance over all the tribes. He cooperated with the British and by 1907 had established himself as the maharaja of Bhutan. During the early 1900s China tried unsuccessfully to reassert control over the country, but in 1910 an Anglo-Bhutanese treaty recognized Bhutan's sovereignty. Its foreign affairs were to be managed by Britain, which also agreed to pay compensation for the territory annexed in 1865. Bhutan remained largely isolated from the rest of the world for half a century.

The Chinese Communist conquest of Tibet in 1950 greatly increased Bhutan's strategic importance to China and India. India, which in 1949 had agreed to assume Britain's responsibilities in Bhutan, lent technical and financial assistance for the development of Bhutan's economy. During the 1950s and 1960s Bhutan's society and government began to be modernized, and the country began to participate more fully in the affairs of the modern world.

—Charles H. Heimsath; George Inaba

BOLIVIA

Official name: Republic of Bolivia
Area: 424,162 square miles
Population: (1967) 3,801,000
Capital: Sucre (Pop., 1965 est., 58,400)
Language: Spanish
Religion: Roman Catholicism
Currency unit: Peso
National holiday: Independence day,
   August 6

Bolivia, a landlocked country in west-central South America, is bounded on the north and east by Brazil, on the west by Peru and Chile, and on the south by Argentina and Paraguay. Lake Titicaca, on the Peru-Bolivia border, is the largest lake in South America.

THE LAND. The basic natural division of the country is between Lowland Bolivia and Mountain Bolivia. The lowlands, or Oriente, in the east, occupy about 70 percent of the country. Mountain Bolivia includes four regions—the Altiplano, the Western Cordillera, the Northeastern Cordillera and Yunga Zone, and the Eastern Bolivia Highland.

Lowland Bolivia. The lowlands are sparsely inhabited, although pioneer activity begun in the 1950s attracted a number of people from the overpopulated upland areas. The humid, tropical condition of the north, situated within the southern part of the Amazon Basin, contrasts with the southeastern Chaco, which has frosts as well as temperatures of over 100°F. Rainfall can vary as much as 25 inches a year from an average of 38 inches.

Mountain Bolivia. The core of Mountain Bolivia is the vast central plateau of the Bolivian Andes, the Altiplano (literally, "high flat area"). The Altiplano, averaging 12,000 to 13,000 feet above sea level, is composed of a series of high and gently rolling basins surmounted here and there by snow-capped mountains. The region is cool and dry in the south but more humid in the north.

The Western Cordillera, separating Bolivia from Chile, is a long series of dry slopes among which are several extinct volcanoes. The Northeastern Cordillera, or Cordillera Reál, forms the edge of the Altiplano. Its streams have carved steep valleys in the course of their rapid descent to the broad Beni River system, which empties into the enormous Amazon River. Also known as the Yungas (semitropical mountain valleys), the area has a large population and supplies food to the highland communities.

The remaining area of Mountain Bolivia is the Eastern Bolivia Highland, or the Puna, a sloping region connecting the Northeastern Cordillera with the plains. The important regional centers of Cochabamba, Sucre, and Tarija provide markets for the corn, wine, and fruit grown in the area.

THE PEOPLE. Over half of the people of Bolivia are Indians. A small percentage of the population is of European descent. The remainder of the people are mestizo, of mixed Indian and European origin.

The Indians in the Lake Titicaca area speak Quechua, the Inca language, but the majority of the Andean

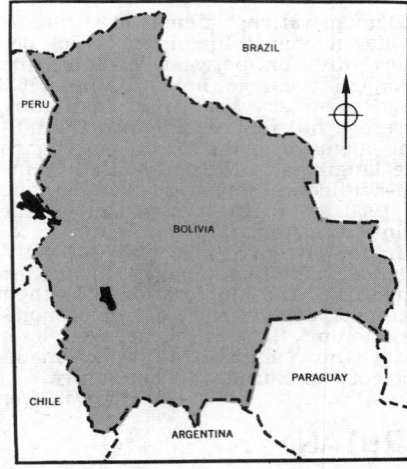

Indians speak Aymara. Most of the mestizo and white population is found in the eastern valley towns of the Yungas and in the south.

La Paz, lying more than 12,000 feet above sea level, is the social, political, and economic center of the country and occupies the position formerly held by Sucre, which is still the administrative capital of Bolivia. The population of La Paz in 1965 was estimated at more than 360,000.

Bolivia's second largest city is Cochabamba, the focus of the road and rail routes that link Mountain Bolivia with the lowlands. It is also the center of a populous farming area.

Other important cities include Santa Cruz, the capital of the department of Santa Cruz; Oruro, which refines half the tin produced in the country; Potosí, in the center of the tin mining region; and Tarija, one of the oldest cities in Bolivia.

ECONOMY. Bolivia's economy is based on mining. The country depends on the export of its mineral resources, particularly tin, to earn the foreign exchange necessary to import essential goods. Bolivia is the second largest tin-producing country in the world, and in 1966 production was 25,920 metric tons. There are also large deposits of lead, copper, silver, and oil.

Approximately three out of every four workers are engaged in agriculture, but farm production meets only about 75 percent of Bolivia's food needs. The Altiplano, where most of the people live, is ill-suited for agriculture. Nevertheless, some barley wheat, corn, beans, and potatoes are grown there. Coffee is a major crop and is produced in the Yungas, where sugarcane is also grown.

Industry is limited and mainly produces simple consumer goods for domestic needs. La Paz is the country's manufacturing center. The lack of an adequate transportation system has been a major obstacle to economic growth. The cost of building roads and railroads over the steep, mountainous terrain is extremely high.

Bolivia usually imports more than it exports, and the resulting deficit has been met by foreign economic aid, principally from the United States. In 1965 Bolivian exports were valued at $110 million, and imports cost $126 million.

Minerals are Bolivia's major export, and foodstuffs and manufactured goods make up the bulk of imports. Bolivia exports primarily to the United States and Britain. Most imports come from the United States, although Japan is increasingly important as a supplier of imports.

GOVERNMENT. The chief executive and head of state is the president, who is popularly elected to a four-year term of office. The Congress consists of the Senate and the Chamber of Deputies. Senators are elected to six-year terms and deputies to four-year terms.

Bolivia is a member of the United Nations and the Organization of American States (OAS).

HISTORY. The Andean portion of what is now Bolivia was long a center of advanced Indian civilization. It formed part of the Inca empire from the 1300s to the 1500s. The Inca empire was overthrown by the Spanish in 1533, and in 1538 an expedition led by Gonzalo and Hernando Pizarro conquered Bolivia.

In 1559 Bolivia became part of the Spanish colonial viceroyalty of Peru and was known as Upper Peru. It later became important to Spain as a supplier of precious metals, especially silver. Spanish rule was harsh, and from 1661 to 1780 there were many Indian uprisings.

Independence. In 1809, after Napoleon had conquered Spain, the people of the city of La Paz deposed the Spanish authorities and established a junta under the leadership of Pedro Domingo Murillo. Murillo was soon overthrown by the Spanish, and attempts by Argentine patriots to liberate Bolivia from the south met with failure. Nevertheless, scattered guerrilla activity against Spain continued.

In December 1824, Simón Bolívar's forces, under the command of Antonio José de Sucre, won a decisive victory at Ayacucho, Peru, that set the stage for the final defeat of the Spanish in Bolivia the following year. Bolivians were then faced with the alternatives of joining Argentina, of joining Peru, or becoming a separate nation. An assembly in 1825 chose independence for the country and adopted the name Bolivia.

The Early Republic. Antonio José de Sucre was elected Bolivia's first president in 1826. His administration was enlightened but brief. Unrest among his own troops combined with an invasion by Peru forced him from power in 1828. Sucre was succeeded by Andrés Santa Cruz, who remained in office until 1839. For roughly the next 50 years government consisted largely of a rapid succession of dictatorships.

One recurring feature of the mid-1800s was the interference in each other's affairs by Bolivian and Peruvian military dictators. From 1835 to 1839 Santa Cruz united both countries in a confederation, but a war with Chile brought about its collapse.

Bolivia again fought Chile in the War of the Pacific (1879–1884), which resulted from Chilean designs on the nitrate deposits controlled by Bolivia and Peru in the Atacama desert along the Pacific coast. Bolivia was defeated and lost its portion of the Atacama desert, which included Bolivia's only outlet to the sea.

Modernization. Bolivia began to modernize rapidly in the early 1900s under presidents Ismael Montes (1904–1909; 1913–1917) and Eleodoro Villazón (1909–1913). Railroads were constructed, industries developed, and tin mining greatly expanded. During World War I Bolivia remained neutral until 1917, when it broke off diplomatic relations with Germany.

In the late 1920s an old boundary dispute with Paraguay over the Chaco region was renewed. War broke out in 1932, and in 1935 Bolivia was defeated. The final settlement, negotiated in 1938, gave three-fourths of the disputed territory to Paraguay. The land lost was not valuable, but the humiliation of defeat caused widespread bitterness against the nation's traditional ruling class, and participation in the struggle awakened many Bolivians to the modern world.

Dissatisfaction with the traditional social, economic, and political domination by Bolivians of European descent coupled with economic difficulties brought on by the world economic depression of the 1930s resulted in a rapid turnover of governments.

New political parties arose with programs aimed at modernizing the country and improving the condition of the masses of the people. One of these, the National Revolutionary Movement (MNR), came to power in 1943 with a program calling for sweeping economic and social reforms.

Contemporary Bolivia. The MNR was overthrown in 1946 before it could accomplish a great deal, but it staged a successful uprising in 1952 after its leader, Victor Paz Estenssoro, had been cheated of his victory in a presidential election. The MNR managed to consolidate its position and carried out a series of reforms that included nationalization of the tin mines and distribution of large private estates among the Indian peasantry.

The MNR incurred huge deficits in operating the tin industry, and the drastic land reforms resulted in a sharp drop in production. Severe food shortages in the cities followed. Only massive U.S. aid kept the government functioning and saved many Bolivians from starvation. Nevertheless, progress was made in expanding education and in developing the fertile but sparsely populated eastern lowlands.

Paz Estenssoro himself remained in power from 1952 until 1956, when he resigned in favor of a party colleague, but he returned as president in 1960. After a period of strikes and rioting, especially in the tin mining region, he was overthrown in 1964 by the military, and a junta took power.

The new regime was committed to carrying out much the same objectives as the Paz Estenssoro administration. In 1965, the junta promised free elections, and in the following year Gen. René Barrientos Ortuño, who had been one of the junta leaders, was elected president.

—David Bushnell; Kempton E. Webb.

BOTSWANA

Official name: Republic of Botswana
Area: 219,915 square miles
Population: (1967 est.) 593,000
Capital: Gaberones (Pop., 1965 est., 4,200)
Language: English, Tswana
Religion: Traditional religions, Christianity
Currency unit: South African rand
National holiday: Independence day, September 30

Botswana, a republic in southern Africa, is bordered on the northeast by Rhodesia, on the east and south by South Africa, and on the west and north by South West Africa. A large, sparsely populated country, Botswana was the British protectorate of Bechuanaland before receiving its independence in 1966.

THE LAND. The Kalahari Desert occupies most of central and western Botswana. This dry region, covered with sand, grass, and thorn bush, has no rivers. The land in eastern Botswana is well-watered and fertile. The Okavango River flows into northern Botswana and forms an area of swamps and marshes. The Molopo and Limpopo rivers run along the southern border.

Northern Botswana has a tropical climate. Further south, the climate is generally hot and dry. The north receives an average of 27 inches of rain a year, but the south receives less than 9 inches.

THE PEOPLE. Most of Botswana's people are Bantu-speaking Africans. There are eight principal tribes in Botswana, each with its own traditional tribal area. The Bamangwato is the largest tribal group. Eighty percent of the people live in villages in the eastern part of the country.

ECONOMY. Cattle are the basis of Botswana's traditional economic life. Most of the people are herdsmen, and livestock contributed some 85 percent of the value of exports in the mid-1960s. Some minerals, including gold and manganese, are also exported. The basic food crops of Botswana include corn, sorghum, and peanuts.

Botswana's economy is closely linked with South Africa's. South Africa levies and collects Botswana's customs duties, and in return Botswa-

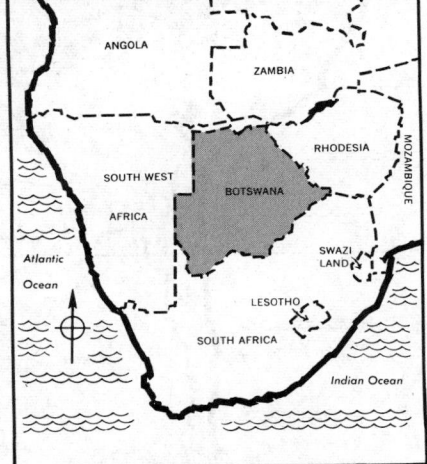

na receives a fixed share of South Africa's customs revenue. Botswana also uses South African currency, the rand.

GOVERNMENT. The head of state and chief executive of Botswana is the president, who is elected along with the legislature, the National Assembly. Assembly candidates must indicate their choice for president, and the presidential candidate with the greatest number of supporters elected to the assembly becomes president. A House of Chiefs, composed of members of the eight dominant tribes, serves as an advisory body to the National Assembly.

HISTORY. Botswana's dry, thornbush grassland attracted few immigrants until the early 1800s, when Tswana-speaking people entered the area. The Tswana were driven from the Transvaal, in present-day South Africa, by invading Zulus. In the years following, there were tribal wars and conflicts with Boer pioneers from the Transvaal.

British Rule. In 1885 the British placed present-day Botswana under their protection. They viewed the area as economically useless, but strategically important because it served as an access route to the north, which was then unoccupied by whites. The land served also as a wedge between the Germans, then in South West Africa, and their Boer allies, in the Transvaal.

In 1895 the British government incorporated the land south of the Molopo River into the Cape Colony, later a part of South Africa. The British instituted indirect rule in the protectorate, allowing the Botswana chiefs to retain their authority under the protection of the British Crown. The protectorate became economically dependent upon South Africa, into which the British assumed Bechuanaland would eventually be incorporated.

The protectorate progressed slowly until after World War II, when political change became rapid, spurred by the development of nationalism in other parts of Africa. A serious issue arose in 1948, when Seretse Khama, chief of the Bamangwato tribe, married a white Englishwoman. Although a tribal council had approved the marriage, the British refused to allow him to return to the country until 1956, after he surrendered his claim to the chieftaincy.

Independence. A constitution promulgated in 1960 allowed elections for a legislative assembly, and Seretse Khama became the country's leading political figure. He founded the Bechuanaland Democratic Party and became an advocate of moderation.

Early in 1965 the capital was moved from Mafeking, in South Africa, to Gaberones, and in March general elections were held. Seretse Khama's party won an overwhelming majority of seats in the new legislature, and Seretse Khama became the first prime minister. Britain granted the country its independence on Sept. 30, 1966, and Seretse Khama became Botswana's first president.

—Hibberd V. B. Kline, Jr; Gary A. Weissman

BRAZIL

Official name: Republic of Brazil
Area: 3,286,470 square miles
Population: (1967) 85,655,000
Capital: Brasília (Pop., 1965 est., 200,000)
Language: Portuguese
Religion: Roman Catholicism
Currency unit: Cruzeiro
National holiday: Independence day, September 7

Brazil, South America's only Portuguese speaking nation, covers almost half the South American continent and contains nearly half its people. Brazil borders every country in South America with the exception of Chile and Ecuador. It is bounded on the north by Colombia, Venezuela, Guyana, Surinam, and French Guiana; on the northeast and east by the Atlantic Ocean; on the south by Uruguay; and on the west by Argentina, Paraguay, Bolivia, and Peru.

THE LAND. Brazil has a widely varied landscape, but there are two major types of terrain: the broad lowlands of the northern third of the country, which include the Amazon Basin, and the Brazilian Highlands, which consist of low plateaus and mountains.

Brazil's land surface is unusual in that the highest areas lie just behind the Atlantic coast, and most of the rivers flow toward the interior, where they eventually empty into the Amazon River or the Paraná-Paraguay river systems.

Major Regions. Brazil has five major land regions: the North, the Northeast, the East (the coast), the South, and the Central West.

The North, which includes more than half the nation's land area, has less than 10 percent of its total population. The area's few inhabitants live mainly within the floodplains of the Amazon River and its numerous tributaries. Since the 1950s, the exploitation of jute, cacao, tropical hardwoods, medicinal plants, oil-bearing nuts, and black pepper has improved the economic situation of the North. A number of Japanese immigrants have settled in the North, particularly in the Amazon Delta.

The Northeast is a region of great physical diversity. A wet, tropical, coastal plain is separated from desert, or *sertão*, by a dry forest area, the *agreste*, which forms a narrow zone between the two. Droughts have always afflicted the desert, and it is only within the last two or three decades that the building of reservoirs and the development of drought-resistant forage plants for cattle have lessened the effects of the dry periods.

The Northeast is the poorest area of Brazil. Few farmers own land and the general level of productivity is extremely low. Modern agricultural techniques are still alien to the traditional thinking of most farmers of the Northeast. In the 1960s the Brazilian government began a large-scale development program in the area.

The Eastern region contains the states of Minas Gerais and Bahia. Minas Gerais is agricultural in the south and west and pastoral in the north. The areas near the city of Rio de Janeiro are devoted to dairy products. The region's western area is one of Brazil's principal food-producing zones, supplying both Rio de Janeiro and São Paulo, the country's largest cities. Belo Horizonte, the capital of Minas Gerais, is a leading manufacturing center, and has numerous metallurgical industries.

The South contains over one third of the nation's population although it constitutes only 10 percent of Brazil's total area. It is Brazil's richest and most productive region and received the major portion of European immigrants. The South is composed of a series of plateaus which rise abruptly from the sea and dip slightly in the west to the lower basin of the Paraná River. It is the center of coffee production and is also important for its forests, which provide softwoods.

The Central West, the fifth region, includes almost 22 percent of the total area, but is occupied by only 3 percent of the country's population. It is an area of extensive grasslands with scattered trees, known as *campo cerrado*, or savanna. These *cerrados* occupy high plateaus at elevations of between 2,000 and 3,000 feet and are dry for most of the year.

In the south, it snows during the winter months in the highest areas, but usually the snow does not stay on the ground for more than a day. The vast western central interior of Brazil experiences sporadic showers three to four months a year, from November through March or April, followed by a dry season during which the scrub vegetation turns brown.

THE PEOPLE. Brazil's population is composed of three main stocks: Indians, descendants of the original inhabitants; whites, descended from Portuguese and other European colonists; and Negroes, brought as slaves from Africa by the Portuguese in the 1500s.

The bulk of the population is concentrated along the coast in a strip extending approximately 250 miles inland. The few remaining pureblooded Indians live within the remote interior, particularly in the Amazon Basin. Negroes live primarily in the Northeast, especially near the coast, where once there were many sugar plantations.

The major cities of Brazil are on or near the coast. The largest city is São Paulo, which had almost 5 million inhabitants in 1965. Rio de Janeiro, the capital of Brazil until 1960, is the country's second largest city, with almost 4 million people in 1965. Rio remains the artistic and cultural center of the country, although it has been superseded in economic importance by São Paulo.

The capital, Brasília, in the Central West, is a model of modern architecture and city planning. It is designed to link the heavily populated coast with the still underdeveloped interior.

ECONOMY. Historically, Brazil's economy has depended heavily on the export of one commodity at a time. Sugar was the mainstay in the 1500s and 1600s, minerals, gold, and diamonds in the 1700s. In the mid-1800s coffee became Brazil's most important product. Although the coffee boom declined, the country has continued to rely heavily on the export of coffee for foreign exchange.

Brazil is rich in natural resources, including a vast, largely untouched

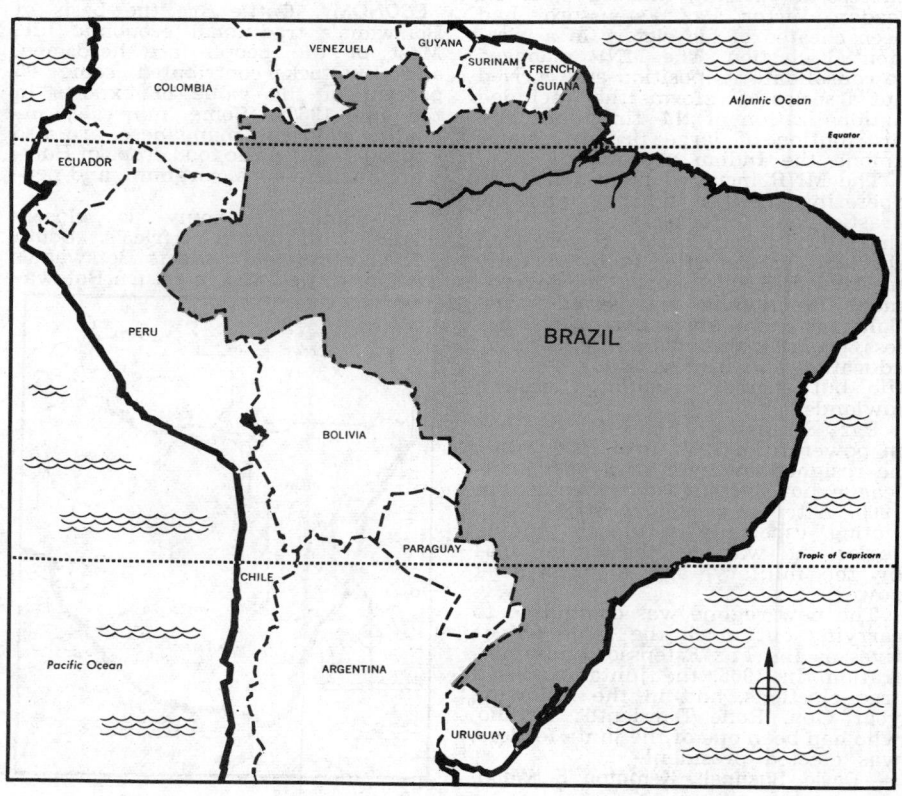

LUFTHANSA
HARBOR OF RIO DE JANEIRO. The rock rising 1,270 feet above the sea is Sugarloaf.

supply of minerals. Their distribution in relation to the distribution of population and markets, however, is poor. Brazil's potential for hydroelectric power is enormous, but many sites, such as the Iguaçu falls, are too far from inhabited areas to prove useful.

Mining has changed from the production of gold and diamonds to exploitation of iron ore and manganese. Coal is mined in southern Brazil, principally in Santa Catarina, but it is of poor quality. The iron ore and coal are consumed in the various iron and steel mills located at Volta Redonda, on the route between Rio de Janeiro and São Paulo, and in Minas Gerais.

Agriculture. Agriculture employs about 3 out of every 5 workers, and 90 percent of Brazil's exports are derived from agriculture. But the productivity of the farm worker is less than half that of the industrial worker, and only 2 percent of the land was cultivated in the mid-1960s.

In addition to coffee, Brazil produces much of the world's cacao and considerable amounts of sugar, vegetable oils, and tobacco. Brazil is also a world leader in cotton production.

Industry. Since World War II there has been an accelerated growth of both light and heavy industry, centered primarily in the state of São Paulo. The major Brazilian industries produce textiles, iron, steel, motor vehicles, and foodstuffs.

Transportation. The transportation situation in Brazil has changed markedly since World War II. The physical integration of the country is being accomplished by building roads to the cities of the interior. Airlines have also come to serve the entire country. As a result, physical isolation, one of the primary barriers to development, is rapidly being overcome.

Trade. In 1966 Brazil's exports earned $1,742 million and its imports cost $1,496 million. Coffee normally makes up about half the value of Brazil's exports. Other major exports include cacao, sugar, pinewood, iron and manganese ores, and cotton. Brazil imports large quantities of manufactured goods, machinery, fuels, vehicles, industrial raw materials, and foodstuffs.

Brazil exports chiefly to the United States, Argentina, West Germany, and the Netherlands. Imports come largely from the United States, West Germany, Venezuela, and Argentina.

GOVERNMENT. Brazil was proclaimed a republic in 1889, but democratic processes have often been disrupted. The military overthrew the constitutional government in 1964 and in 1967 put into effect a new constitution.

The 1967 constitution strengthened the central government considerably, changing Brazil from a federal union of states into a centralized republic. It vested executive powers in the president, no longer elected by popular vote but chosen indirectly, by the congress. Strong powers were given to the president, including the right to appoint state governors and declare legislation initiated by him law if not passed by congress within 30 days.

The congress, consisting of the Senate and the Chamber of Deputies, continued to be elected by popular vote, but the franchise was restricted to those able to read and write.

Brazil is a member of the United Nations and the Organization of American States (OAS).

HISTORY. In 1494 Spain and Portugal, rivals in the establishment of colonies, signed the Treaty of Tordesillas, which granted Portugal all the territory east of a north-south line that extended from the mouth of the Amazon River to the São Paulo coast,

neither of which had then been discovered. Thus, in 1500, when the Portuguese explorer Pedro Alvares Cabral claimed Brazil for the Portuguese crown, the claim was incontestable.

Brazil was at first overshadowed by Portugal's Asian and African possessions. It had no great Indian civilization or readily apparent mineral wealth, and early Portuguese contacts consisted mainly of sporadic expeditions to obtain dyewood and to trade with the Indians. Other Europeans, however, especially the French, began frequenting the Brazilian coast for the same reasons, and the rivalry spurred Portugal into taking more effective possession of the vast land.

Colonial Administration. In 1534, Portugal carved Brazil into a series of "captaincies," under proprietary governors called "captains donatary," who were authorized to colonize and rule in the name of the king. In 1549 Portugal also sent out a royal governor-general to the city of Salvador, on Brazil's northeast coast, to exercise general jurisdiction over the entire colony.

Gradually, from the mid-1500s through the 1600s, sugar plantations worked by African slaves took root in the northeastern coastal belt. The export of sugar yielded huge profits and became the backbone of Brazil's economy. It was basically sugar that enticed the Dutch to carve out a short-lived colony in northeastern Brazil in the second quarter of the 1600s. Farther south, there arose a more varied agricultural and grazing economy which relied on Indians and mestizos rather than on Negro slaves for labor.

At the same time, some settlers, especially those of São Paulo, ranged far and wide through the interior seizing Indians to work as slaves and searching for gold. In the process they pushed the boundaries of the colony far to the west of the zone allotted to Portugal by the Treaty of Tordesillas. In the late 1600s they found gold and diamonds in the region of Minas Gerais.

In the 1700s population growth and the increased importance of the south with its gold and diamond deposits brought a number of administrative changes. The last vestiges of the powers of the captains donatary, already largely superseded by royal officials, were eliminated, and in 1763 the capital was transferred from Salvador to Rio de Janeiro. It was also at that time that the first agitation for independence, which drew inspiration from the revolutions in France and the United States, began to occur.

In 1789 in Minas Gerais a militia subaltern nicknamed Tiradentes, meaning "toothpuller," headed a conspiracy against the government. The Tiradentes conspiracy was easily suppressed, but it set a precedent for later attempts.

Brazil's status was altered without a struggle early in 1808, when Prince Regent Dom João and the Portuguese court arrived on Brazilian soil in flight from the armies of Napoleon. Rio de Janeiro became the temporary capital of the Portuguese empire, and Brazil obtained many of the advantages of independence. Moreover, Dom João lingered in Brazil even after Portugal was evacuated by Napoleon's forces. When he did return to Portugal in 1821, he left his eldest son, Pedro, in Brazil as regent, and advised him to become an independent monarch if a final separation of the two countries should prove unavoidable.

The Empire. The eventuality feared by Dom João became a reality in 1822, when the Portuguese government attempted to return Brazil to a subordinate position within the empire. A resistance movement developed, and on Sept. 7, 1822, Pedro declared Brazil independent. On Dec. 1, 1822, he was crowned Emperor Pedro I of Brazil.

Although Brazil was organized as a limited, constitutional monarchy, Pedro I was unable to work smoothly with the parliament. His government's popularity also suffered because of an unsuccessful war with Argentina over control of Uruguay and dislike of Pedro's numerous Portuguese advisers. In 1831 the emperor was forced to abdicate in favor of his infant son, Pedro II. From then until 1840 Brazil was governed by a series of regencies chosen by parliament.

The regency period was marked by outbreaks of republicanism, regional separatism, and general political turmoil, but the monarchy survived. Demands for regional autonomy were partially met by the Additional Act of 1834, which amended the constitution to grant limited self-government to the provinces.

Pedro II. In 1840 Pedro II was declared of age, and he began performing his duties personally. During his reign of almost 50 years, Brazil attained a high degree of political freedom and stability. Brazil's two political parties, the Conservatives and the Liberals, peacefully alternated in power under prime ministers chosen from first one and then the other.

Pedro II wielded substantial personal power, but civil liberties were guaranteed even to the small republican minority. However, the monarchy was slow to deal with the problem of Negro slavery. The slave trade had been outlawed by a treaty signed with Great Britain in 1827, but it continued in practice until the mid-1800s.

Slavery itself was completely ended only in 1888. The fact that slavery was abolished without compensation alienated the slave-owning aristocracy. By that time, moreover, the monarchy had also begun to weaken in other ways.

In the 1870s a serious clash with the Roman Catholic Church had occurred as a result of government interference with an anti-Masonic campaign launched by a group of bishops. Brazil's participation in the war of the Triple Alliance against Paraguay (1865–1870), although it ended in victory, added little to the empire's prestige.

Nevertheless, after the war the army aspired to a greater role in Brazilian life, and thus came into conflict with the civilian-minded emperor and his ministers. Finally, republicanism increased steadily after 1870. The aging Pedro II still retained great personal popularity, but there was no serious resistance on his behalf when a military coup led by Marshal Manoel Deodoro da Fonseca overthrew the monarchy in 1889.

The Republic. In 1891 the new Brazilian republic adopted a federal constitution modeled after that of the United States. The first two presidents, however, were military officers, and both showed arbitrary tendencies that provoked wide unrest. The first president to serve a full term was a civilian from São Paulo, Prudente José de Moraes Barros (1894–1898). His administration was harassed by military upheavals and by a revolt in the back country of northeastern Brazil led by a religious fanatic, Antônio Conselheiro. But when Barros left office, the republic appeared to be firmly established.

Subsequent administrations until 1930 were mostly controlled by a narrow oligarchy representing the large and wealthy states of São Paulo and Minas Gerais. Nonetheless, constitutional forms were generally maintained.

During the mid-1800s coffee had replaced sugar as Brazil's chief crop and major export. Coffee production steadily increased until in the early 1900s serious overproduction appeared. The government then began to restrict coffee planting and later to buy up surplus stocks, hoping to support coffee prices. Meanwhile a great rubber boom had swept the Amazon basin, only to collapse on the eve of World War I in the face of Asian competition.

The economy recovered with the wartime and early postwar demand for Brazilian products, but slumped with the later return to normal conditions. The 1920s were characterized by serious social and economic unrest.

The world economic depression of the 1930s caught Brazil in a highly vulnerable position because of its heavy dependence on coffee as an export. The government was unable to halt a disastrous drop in coffee prices. Moreover, the economic crisis coincided with an attempt in 1930 by the outgoing president, Washington Luís Pereira de Souza, to assure the election of Julio Prestes as his successor. Prestes won, but a revolution by the military installed the more popular opposition candidate, Getulio Vargas, in the presidency.

The Vargas Era. Although he had condemned undemocratic practices of the previous regime, Vargas himself ruled by decree, which provoked demands for a return to constitutional procedures and an uprising in São Paulo in 1932. The revolt failed, however, and Vargas remained in power as dictator.

From the beginning Vargas recognized the need for social and economic reforms. On assuming office, he initiated labor legislation, supported labor unions, and expanded educational facilities and social services in the larger towns and cities. He also encouraged industrialization in an attempt to diversify the economy, and with foreign financial assistance began the creation of a Brazilian steel industry.

In World War II Vargas sided with the Allies and sent Brazilian troops to fight in Italy. Toward the end of the war Vargas found himself subject to increasing public pressure to observe in Brazil the democratic principles for which he was ostensibly fighting abroad. He therefore began to modify his dictatorship and promised free presidential elections in 1945.

Fearing that Vargas would go back on his word, the military ousted him from office in October 1945. The 1945 elections were won by Enrico Gaspar Dutra, who took office on Jan. 1, 1946. In September a new constitution completed the restoration of political freedom and representative government.

In 1951 Vargas returned to the presidency by popular election. His new administration, however, was characterized by blatant corruption and demagoguery. Vargas did create a government petroleum monopoly, Petrobras, which was designed to save Brazil from exploitation by foreign oil interests. Nonetheless, he was generally unable to solve Brazil's postwar economic problems.

An attempt by men close to the president to assassinate an opposition publisher brought forth a new move by the military to oust Vargas. Rather than resign as demanded he committed suicide in August 1954.

Contemporary Brazil. After a period of political confusion, Juscelino Kubitschek took office as president for the next full term (1956–1961). Kubitschek's main accomplishments were the creation of a new capital city, Brasília, located near the geographic center of the country, and the building of highways and hydroelectric works.

To finance these and other expenditures, Kubitschek issued vast amounts of paper money. By doing so he added to an inflationary spiral that had begun before his presidency. Economic growth nonetheless continued.

Jânio da Silva Quadros was elected president in 1960. His government resumed diplomatic relations with the Soviet Union and decorated the Argentine-born Cuban guerrilla expert Ernesto "Ché" Guevara. In general, Quadros proved to be a highly erratic leader, and he resigned in less than a year. The military unsuccessfully tried to prevent Vice President João Goulart from succeeding him because of Goulart's strong leftist leanings.

Under President Goulart (1961–1964), inflation increased. Much was said about fundamental social reforms, including agrarian reform, but little was accomplished. In March 1964, a new military coup ousted Goulart.

A provisional military government had some success in slowing the pace of inflation. It conducted a wide-spread purge of prominent politicians, and gained control of the congress by barring opponents. Gen. Humberto Castello Branco was elected president by the purged congress on Apr. 11, 1964.

On Oct. 3, 1966, Marshal Artur da Costa e Silva was elected by congress as Castello Branco's successor. In December 1966 Castello Branco had pushed through congress a new constitution providing for the consolidation of federal power and the election by congress of the president, who was granted semi-dictatorial powers. The new constitution went into effect on Mar. 15, 1967, when President Costa e Silva took office.

—David Bushnell; Kempton E. Webb

BULGARIA

Official name: People's Republic of Bulgaria
Area: 42,823 square miles
Population: (1966 est.) 8,257,000
Capital: Sofia (Pop., 1965, urban area: 793,-300)
Language: Bulgarian
Religion: Orthodox Christianity
Currency: Lev
National holiday: National liberation day (Anniversary of the socialist revolution in Bulgaria), September 9

The People's Republic of Bulgaria, a nation in southeastern Europe, occupies the northeastern corner of the Balkan peninsula. It is bounded on the north by Romania, on the east by the Black Sea, on the south by Turkey and Greece, and on the west by Yugoslavia.

THE LAND. Mountains and plains alternate in Bulgaria to form four major geographical regions. In the north is the Danube Basin, a low, fertile plateau crossed on the north, at the Bulgarian-Romanian boundary, by the Danube River.

At the eastern end of the Danube Basin is the Dobruja, a large limestone plateau region. To the south of the basin, arching southeastward from Bulgaria's northwestern corner to the Black Sea, are the Balkan Mountains (the Stara Planina), ranging from 3,000 feet to over 7,000 feet in elevation. The entire southwestern corner of the country is also mountainous, with the Rila, Pirin, and Rhodope ranges rising to over 9,000 feet.

Between the two mountainous regions, in central Bulgaria, is the basin of the Maritsa River. At its eastern end, the basin widens and opens into the Black Sea. At its western end is the heartland of Bulgaria, the Sofia Basin. The basin is one of the great crossroads of the Balkan peninsula, connected by river valleys to the Danube on the north, the Morava River in Yugoslavia on the west, and with the Aegean Sea on the south.

The Bulgarian climate varies from region to region. The Danube plateau has cold, snowy winters and hot summers. The Maritsa basin, further south, is protected by the mountains to the north and has milder winters. The mountains throughout the country tend to have harsher weather, with yearly variations in temperature and rainfall.

THE PEOPLE. Nearly 90 percent of the people are Bulgarians. They speak Bulgarian, a south Slavic language, and use an alphabet similar to the Russian. The larger minority groups include Turks, Macedonians, Romanians, Armenians, and Gypsies. Most of the people belong to the Bulgarian Orthodox Church, an independent Eastern Christian body. Islam is the largest minority religion.

Population is densest in the Sofia Basin, especially around Sofia, the capital, which is a rapidly growing industrial center as well as the administrative and intellectual heart of the country. Other large urban centers are Plovdiv in the Maritsa valley; Varna and Burgas, the leading Black Sea ports; and Ruse, the largest Danubian port.

ECONOMY. Bulgaria's economy, traditionally based on agriculture, became increasingly industrialized in the 1950s and 1960s under the direction of the Communist party, which came to power during World War II.

The country has a good supply of natural resources. They include low-grade coal, useful for generating electric power, as well as uranium, petroleum, iron ore, lead, zinc, copper, and manganese.

Rich soil, especially in the Danube and Maritsa basins, is also a vital resource, and in 1965 agriculture contributed one-third of the national product. Bulgarian agriculture is almost entirely collectivized.

Wheat and corn are the leading cereal crops, occupying about 75 percent of the total cultivated area. Rye, barley, and oats are also important. Tobacco is the leading industrial crop, and Bulgaria is one of the world's largest producers of the Oriental type of tobacco. Sunflowers, sugar beets, cotton, and soybeans are also grown in substantial quantities. Because of its climatic advantages, including an early spring, the Maritsa basin is known for such specialty crops as early vegetables and fruits and especially for rose oil, pressed from rose petals and used as a base for perfumes.

Livestock is grazed on mountain pastures. Fishing and forestry are of importance.

Industry expanded greatly during the 1950s and early 1960s, and in 1965 contributed 45 percent of the national product. The leading industries include metal working, oil refining, iron and steel production, machinery manufacture, chemical production, and the production of electricity. The traditionally important light industries, including textiles and weaving, leather tooling, woodworking, and tobacco processing, thrive on a smaller scale.

Bulgaria's international trade increased greatly in the 1950s and 1960s, and in 1966 imports cost $1,474 million and exports earned $1,305 million. Farm products, especially tobacco, are the leading exports, and clothing, fruits, and ship parts are also important. Leading imports are machinery, fuel, minerals, metals, and other raw materials.

Over 75 percent of Bulgaria's trade is with other communist countries, but by the mid-1960s trade had increased with western Europe, especially with Italy, West Germany, and Britain.

Tourism also increased rapidly during the early 1960s. The most popular tourist attractions are the Black Sea beach resorts.

GOVERNMENT. The Communist party dominates Bulgarian political life. At the head of the party is a central committee, whose political bureau, or politburo, determines national policy. The first secretary of the party is normally the key figure in government.

The constitution formally vests governmental powers in the popularly elected National Assembly. But assembly candidates are nominated by the Fatherland Front, a mass organization controlled by the Communist party. The National Assembly elects an executive committee, or presidium, to function for it between its short sessions. The chairman of the presidium is the official head of the state. The assembly also elects a council of ministers, or cabinet, and its chairman, the prime minister.

Bulgaria is a member of the United Nations and the Warsaw Pact, a military alliance of communist-dominated European nations.

HISTORY. Bulgaria's location has made the country subject to competing Slavic, Byzantine, Ottoman Turkish, and West European influences, and Bulgaria's history has been marked by frequent conquest and domination by foreign powers. Present-day Bulgaria was part of the Roman Empire by the middle of the first century AD. By the 500s a variety of Slavic tribes had settled in the region.

In the 600s the Bulgars, a warlike people from the northern shores of the Black Sea, conquered the Slavs and settled in the territory. By the 700s the Bulgars had organized a state, the first Bulgarian Empire, and for the next 100 years they resisted conquest by the Byzantine Empire. In 817 a Bulgarian-Byzantine treaty established peace between the two nations.

During the mid-800s, under Emperor Boris, the Bulgarian Empire reached its height. Boris consolidated his power by putting down rebellious nobles, and his armies conquered new territory. During that time the Bulgars were converted to Christianity. In the late 900s Bulgarian territory began to fall to Byzantine armies, and by 1018 the entire nation had been conquered. During the 1100s, when the Byzantine Empire had begun to disintegrate, a second Bulgarian empire was established. By the 1200s it had become a great power.

Ottoman Rule. The brief period of brilliance and expansion of the second empire was followed by 500 years of rule by the Ottoman Turks. Under the Ottomans, Bulgaria was isolated from both the Western and the Slavic worlds. Ottoman control of the country was complete, and only those Bulgarians who became Muslims could achieve positions of authority. But the life of the peasants—the bulk of the population—was probably no more difficult than under Bulgarian rulers.

During the second half of the 1800s, Bulgarian nationalism became an active force. The Ottoman Empire had

become weak, and Bulgarians were able to assume greater control over their own affairs. They established a national school system, an active press, and an independent Bulgarian church. In 1876 a revolt against the Turks was crushed with vicious ferocity. This provided Russia, an enemy of the Ottomans, with an excuse to go to war with Turkey in 1877.

Independence. Russia was victorious, and in 1878 the Treaty of Berlin granted independence to the principality of Bulgaria, the northern section of present-day Bulgaria. The southern two-thirds, known as Eastern Rumelia, received independence separately. The area remained the center of international political and territorial disputes, however, until 1885, when the two regions were united as Bulgaria.

The new nation was governed by nationalist leaders until 1908, when Prince Ferdinand proclaimed it a kingdom. In the years between 1886 and 1912, Bulgaria made substantial economic and political progress under a democratic constitution. Domestic progress was continually jeopardized by territorial quarrels, however. Bulgaria claimed Macedonia from Serbia and Greece, Thrace from Greece and Turkey, and southern Dobruja from Romania.

These territorial disputes led in 1912 to the first Balkan War, which Bulgaria and its Balkan allies won against Turkey. In the second Balkan War, in 1913, Bulgaria lost territories to its former allies, Greece and Serbia, and to Romania and Turkey. When Germany and Austria promised the return of these territories, Bulgaria sided with them in World War I. Germany and its allies lost the war, and the 1919 treaty of Neuilly forced Bulgaria to cede still more territory—to Yugoslavia, Greece, and Romania.

The losses embittered Bulgaria's domestic politics and foreign relations during the decades between the two world wars. Relations with Greece and Yugoslavia were especially uneasy, and border disputes were frequent. Resentment within Bulgaria led to the loss of many social and economic gains. Premier Aleksandr Stamboliski, the effective political leader of the time, instituted many reforms, but his methods were unpopular and aroused further resentment.

In 1923 a militant nationalist organization, IMRO (Internal Macedonian Revolutionary Organization) helped overthrow the Stamboliski government. IMRO played a large part in precipitating a series of government crises during the next ten years. After a decade of disorder, the military seized control in 1934.

A second coup staged by the king took place in 1935. The king suspended the constitution and made himself a dictator. Bulgaria's continuing territorial ambitions and close trade ties with Germany brought it into World War II on the German side in 1941.

Communist Rule. Toward the end of the war, in September 1944, the Soviet Union declared war on Bulgaria, and within a week Soviet forces had occupied the country. In 1945 elections were held under communist rule, and

a government dominated by the communist-controlled Fatherland Front came to power. In 1946 Georghi Dimitrov, long prominent in the international communist movement, became prime minister.

Bulgarians voted in 1946 to abolish the monarchy, and a socialist republic was proclaimed. A constitution establishing a people's republic was adopted in 1947, and by the end of 1947 communist rule was abosolute. The nationalistic Bulgarian communists who had organized the republic gradually were replaced by those controlled from the Soviet Union.

During the late 1940s and early 1950s industries were nationalized and farms were collectivized. The government concentrated on ending Bulgaria's traditional dependence on agriculture and transforming the country into an industrial state. During the 1950s Bulgaria grew increasingly dependent politically and economically on the Soviet Union.

In the early 1960s, when other Soviet bloc countries began to move away from Soviet domination, Bulgaria's ties with the Soviet Union remained close. In 1960, however, diplomatic relations with the United States, which had been severed in 1950, were resumed, and during the 1960s trade and diplomatic contacts were expanded with Western Europe.

Progress was made toward industrialization, but the general standard of living remained low. Moreover, in the drive to industrialize, agriculture had been neglected. A farm crisis in the early 1960s led in 1963 to rationing and in 1964 to the encouragement of private farming.

In 1962 Todor Zhivkov, first secretary of Bulgaria's Communist party since 1957, was named premier as well. In 1965 an alleged plot by a pro-Chinese Communist group to overthrow the government was thwarted. The attempted coup was followed by a purge of the party and a reorganization of the government.

—Robert F. Byrnes; George Kish

BURMA

Official name: Union of Burma
Area: 261,787 square miles
Population: (1966 est.) 25,246,000
Capital: Rangoon (Pop., 1966 est., 821,800)
Language: Burmese, English
Religion: Buddhism
Currency unit: Kyat
National holiday: Independence day, January 4

Burma, an independent nation in Southeast Asia, is bounded on the northeast by China, on the east by Laos and Thailand, on the south by the Andaman Sea, and on the west by the Bay of Bengal, Pakistan, and India. Burma received independence from Britain in 1948 as a union of Burma proper and the Shan, Chin, Kachin, Kayah, and Karen states.

THE LAND. Burma is a diamond-shaped country with a long, narrow extension stretching southward into the Malay Peninsula. The Tenasserim coast, in the south, and the Arakan coast, to the north, are rocky and steep. The central coast is shallow

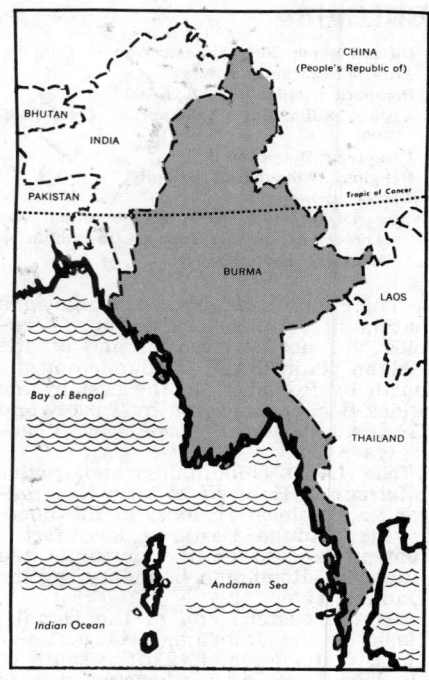

and filled with sandbars. Many small islands dot the long coastline.

Along the coast the densely forested Arakan mountain range rises more than 10,000 feet and extends into a region of hills in the country's northwest corner. Central Burma is a low basin through which flows the Irrawaddy River and, east of a low range of hills, the Sittang River. In the east is the hilly Shan Plateau, about 3,000 feet in elevation, threaded by the Salween River and its tributaries.

The Irrawaddy River dominates Burma's terrain. It rises in the far north and flows southward for approximately 1,400 miles before entering the Gulf of Martaban at the head of the Andaman Sea. It is navigable for about 875 miles inland, and it leaves a deposit of rich soil in its valley and delta. The delta is 150 miles wide and extends about 180 miles inland from the sea.

Burma has a tropical climate. Average winter temperatures range from 70°F along the coast, where humidity is very high, to 60°F in the interior. Summer temperatures rise above 100°F. In southwestern and northeastern Burma, monsoons are common and rainfall is generally heavy—about 80 inches a year in the northeast and up to 200 inches in the southwest. Tropical forests cover these wet regions. Central Burma is a treeless, grassy plain that receives only about 25 inches of rainfall a year.

THE PEOPLE. The people of Burma are divided into a number of traditional tribal and language groups. The dominant people are the Burmans, who speak Burmese, a Sino-Tibetan language, and use an alphabet similar to that of Sanskrit. The larger minority groups are Chin, Shan, and Kachin peoples of the hill regions and the Karen of lower Burma. Population is densest in the river valleys. Rangoon and Mandalay are the largest of the country's few cities.

ECONOMY. Burma is a country with rich natural resources. Over half of the country is forested, and there are valuable stands of teak and ironwood. Burma's mineral riches include petroleum, lignite, lead, tin, tungsten, copper, iron, nickel, zinc, silver, gold, jade, amber, and rubies. All are mined to some extent but none has been fully exploited.

Burma's most valuable resource is its soil, which is extremely fertile in the river valleys. The economy is dominated by agriculture, which contributed one-third of the national income in the early 1960s. The chief crop is rice, which is grown on approximately two-thirds of the cultivated land, mostly in the rich, moist delta region. Rice is also grown on irrigated land in the drier central region, where peanuts, millet, beans, cotton, and tobacco are also raised. Fishing is important along the coast.

Most of Burma's few industries are concerned with the processing of agricultural goods or the extraction of such natural resources as timber and oil. Although industrialization increased during the late 1950s and early 1960s, manufacturing is limited to the production of such light consumer items as textiles and cigarettes.

International trade is second only to agriculture in economic importance, and contributed 20 percent to the national product in the early 1960s. In 1966 exports earned $193 million, and imports cost $160 million.

Rice and teak are the chief exports. Oil, rubber, and cotton are also important. Finished goods and machinery must be imported. India, Japan, Indonesia, Pakistan, Britain, and Ceylon receive most Burmese exports. Britain, Japan, China, India, West Germany, and the United States are the main sources for imports.

GOVERNMENT. Burma's 1948 constitution provided for a parliamentary democracy with a president as head of state and with executive powers exercised by a prime minister and a cabinet responsible to a popularly elected legislature. In 1962 the military overthrew the constitutional government and established a Revolutionary Council to govern Burma.

Burma is a member of the United Nations.

HISTORY. The easy migration and invasion routes along the Sittang and Irrawaddy river valleys have helped make Burma's history turbulent. The earliest known settlers were the Pyu, probably a Tibetan people, who had moved into the region by the late 600s. In the late 700s, a more powerful people, the Mon, settled in the delta region of lower Burma and in the 800s conquered the Pyu.

The Burmans. The Burman people immigrated from northeastern Tibet during the 900s. They came in such large numbers that they were able to occupy all of central and southern Burma and parts of Siam, and they soon dominated the entire region. At first the Burmans were divided into many small clans, but in the mid-1000s one clan chieftain, Anawrahta, united all the Burmans into one empire.

The Burmans conquered the Mon and adopted much of their culture, which was focused on warfare and religion. The king was deified, and many great temples were built in their fortress-like capital, Pagan, in central Burma.

In 1287 Pagan fell to the Mongols, and the empire collapsed. The Mongols took over central Burma, the Mon reestablished their southern kingdom, and a newly powerful people, the Shan, established a group of states in the northeastern hills. The Shan led the Burmans in resistance to the Mongols and drove them out of the region in the early 1300s.

Once more the region was divided among numerous rulers, and for the next several centuries the Shan, the Burmans, and the Mon competed for control of Burma while holding off attacks from Chinese, Laotian, and Siamese invaders. During the 1500s a Burman dynasty briefly united the kingdoms.

In the late 1500s and the 1600s, the Portuguese, Dutch, and English all attempted to establish trading posts in Burma. But the almost continuous warfare in the country contributed to the failure of the trading colonies and discouraged the Europeans.

In the 1750s a powerful Burman dynasty arose under Alaungpaya, who reunited the kingdoms and conquered portions of India and Siam. The destruction wrought by centuries of violence and the stagnation created by an archaic system of government had weakened the country, however, and it was unable to meet a strong challenge from British merchant interests.

British Rule. Between 1824 and 1826 the British drove the Burmese out of northeastern India and occupied the Arakan and Tenasserim coasts. The Burmese refused to grant trading privileges to the British, and by 1886 the British had conquered all Burma and made it a part of British India.

Burma's economy and government were modernized under British rule. Burma became the world's greatest exporter of teakwood, and the Irrawaddy delta became one of the world's largest producers of rice. Missionaries, especially from the United States, began working in Burma's upland areas, and many of the hill peoples were converted to Christianity and brought into contact with the modern world.

Many Burmese resented the British and the Indians, who had come to play a prominent role in economic affairs. After World War I a wave of nationalism led to strikes, riots, and, in 1931, to a brief but large-scale rebellion. The British introduced democratic forms of government in the 1920s and 1930s, and in 1937 granted a constitution separating Burma from India and permitting a good deal of self-government.

By the beginning of World War II, Burma had a prosperous economy and a fairly stable political system, but Japanese occupation in 1942 and British reconquest in 1944 caused great economic destruction.

Independence. After the war a group of nationalists who had organized an anti-Japanese army and a political network during the occupation led a drive for independence. As the Anti-Fascist Peoples Freedom League (AFPFL), they emerged as the dominant political party after the British granted Burma its independence in 1948.

Violent political disputes and tribal rebellions kept the nation in disorder from 1948 until 1952, when the Burmese government, under Prime Minister U Nu, succeeded in restoring its authority. Some social and economic gains were made during the 1950s, but corruption and lack of skills slowed progress. Moreover, the national government was too weak to

LOOK MAGAZINE

BURMESE BUDDHIST MONKS IN PRAYER. Most of Burma's people are Buddhists, and Buddhism exerts a strong influence on Burmese cultural and political life.

cope with the demands of the minorities for greater autonomy or with communist-led insurrections.

In 1958, faced with dissension within the ruling AFPFL, conflict among Burma's other parties, and the imminence of rebellion and civil war, U Nu asked Gen. Ne Win to take power. Army rule brought a measure of peace to the country, and elections in 1960 restored civilian government under U Nu.

In 1962, with a rebellion among the Shan and a threat of total civil war, Ne Win led an army coup and again took control of the government. The army governed through the Revolutionary Council. In 1963 and 1964 most large businesses were nationalized and the repatriation of many Indians and Pakistanis was ordered.

The Revolutionary Council adopted a neutralist policy in international affairs, attempting to steer clear of alignment with either East or West. In 1967, despite Burma's neutralist position, Communist China broke relations with the Burmese government.
—M. G. Inaba

BURUNDI

Official name: Republic of Burundi
Area: 10,747 square miles
Population: (1966 est.) 3,274,000
Capital: Bujumbura (Pop., 1965 est., 71,000)
Language: Kirundi, French
Religion: Roman Catholicism
Currency unit: Franc
National holiday: Independence day, July 1

Burundi, a small, densely populated highland country in central Africa, is bordered on the north by Rwanda, on the east and south by Tanzania, and on the west by the Democratic Republic of the Congo. Burundi was united with present-day Rwanda as the Belgian-administered UN trust territory of Ruanda-Urundi until 1962, when it became independent.

THE LAND. Plateaus, lying at elevations of between 2,500 and 3,500 feet, cover most of Burundi. The Great Rift Valley, which stretches along Burundi's western boundary, is bordered by peaks that rise above 7,000 feet. The country's land surface is badly eroded, and soil erosion is a basic problem almost everywhere in Burundi. The climate is temperate throughout the year.

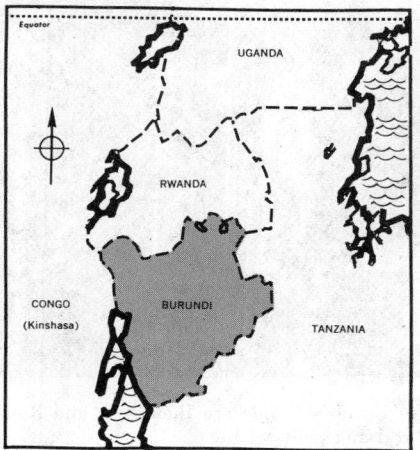

THE PEOPLE. Two tribal groups are dominant in Burundi, the Hutu and the Tusi, or Watusi. The Hutu, comprising about 85 percent of the population, are mostly farmers. The Tusi, who make up about 15 percent of the total, are traditionally herdsmen and warriors. The Tusi long dominated the Hutu and provided the country's rulers.

ECONOMY. Burundi is chiefly an agricultural country, and coffee is the main export. Cotton and rice are also grown.

GOVERNMENT. In 1966 Burundi's constitutional monarchy was overthrown, and a republic proclaimed. Governmental powers were assumed by a 12-member National Revolutionary Committee.

HISTORY. The Tusi, who probably came south from the area of Ethiopia, overran Burundi and Rwanda in the 1500s. A Tusi aristocracy headed by a *mwami*, or king, established its rule, and the Hutu became a subject people.

In 1890 Germany seized the area of present-day Burundi and Rwanda, which became known as Ruanda-Urundi. Belgium occupied the region in 1916 during World War I, and after the war Ruanda-Urundi became a Belgian mandate under the League of Nations. Ruanda-Urundi became a UN trust territory in 1946.

Burundi became independent on July 1, 1962. Moderate Tusi and Hutu formed the National Union and Progress Party (UPRONA), which became the majority party in Burundi. Mwami Mwambutsa IV, who had come to the throne in 1915, became chief of state.

Rivalry among factions within the government caused political instability in the period following independence. Premier Pierre Ngendandumwe was assassinated by extremists in January 1965. His successor, Joseph Bamina, was ousted by the king in July 1965, and in September the king appointed Léopold Biha premier.

In July 1966, the king's son, Prince Charles, seized power from his father and ousted Premier Biha. Charles appointed Michel Micombero premier. In September 1966, the prince was proclaimed Mwame Ntare V. Two months later the army, led by Micombero, overthrew the king and declared Burundi a republic.
—Hibberd V. B. Kline, Jr.;
Vera L. Zolberg

CAMBODIA

Official name: Kingdom of Cambodia
Area: 69,898 square miles
Population: (1966 est.) 6,320,000
Capital: Phnom Penh (Pop., 1962, urban area: 403,500)
Language: Cambodian (Khmer), French
Religion: Buddhism
Currency unit: Riel
National holiday: Independence day, November 9

Cambodia, a kingdom in southeast Asia, is bounded on the north by Thailand and Laos, on the east and south by Vietnam, and on the west by the Gulf of Siam and Thailand.

THE LAND. Cambodia occupies the mountain-rimmed basin of the lower Mekong River. At the center of the

basin, only a few feet above sea level, is Tonle Sap, a lake that serves as an overflow basin for the floods of the Mekong. It has an area of about 1,000 square miles and a depth of 5 feet during the dry season, but increases to four times that area and ten times that depth during the rainy season.

Cambodia's highest point, in the Chaine des Cardamomes along the southwest border of the basin, is only slightly under 6,000 feet. Separated from the Cardamomes by a narrow lowland corridor in the northwest is the Dang Raek plateau, over 2,000 feet high, which rims the basin on the north. East of the basin, the Moi plateau rises to between 1,500 and 4,000 feet.

Cambodia has a tropical climate, with rainy summers and dry winters. Year-round temperatures range from 70°F to 100°F, and the humidity is high. An average of 60 inches of rain a year falls in the basin, and the mountains receive about 80 inches a year.

THE PEOPLE. Cambodia's population is quite homogeneous. Most of the people are Khmers, or native Cambodians. They are Theravada Buddhists and speak Khmer, or Cambodian. There are minorities of Vietnamese, Chinese, and Chams—Muslims of Indonesian origin—as well as some small tribal groups in the hills.

Population is concentrated around the shores of Tonle Sap. About one-tenth of Cambodia's people live in or near the capital, Phnom Penh.

ECONOMY. The Cambodian economy is underdeveloped, but the country can support itself. Natural resources include valuable hardwood forests, iron ore deposits, and rich soil, especially in the central basin. Agriculture is the mainstay of the economy, and the chief crop is rice. Livestock is raised, and cotton, tobacco, pepper, beans, kapok, and rubber are grown. Fishing is second in importance only to farming, and Tonle Sap and the Gulf of Siam yield abundant catches.

Cambodia has few major industries other than traditional handicrafts and rice processing. In the early 1960s, with foreign technical and financial aid, a hydroelectric development project was initiated and some industrialization was undertaken. By the mid-1960s, cigarette plants, a rubber tire factory, paper mills, sawmills, and textile mills were in operation.

The country depends on foreign trade for many commodities. In 1966 Cambodian exports earned $67 million, and imports cost $111 million. Rice and rubber are the only important exports, and transportation equipment, machinery, and textiles are imported.

Most Cambodian trade is with neighboring Asian countries and with France. Almost all of Cambodia's trade passes through the modern port of Sihanoukville, on the Gulf of Siam, which was built with French aid in the early 1960s.

GOVERNMENT. Cambodia is a constitutional monarchy. Its constitution provides for a monarchy limited by a cabinet that is responsible to the parliament. It requires that the more powerful lower house of parliament be popularly elected and that the upper house be elected by limited suffrage to represent certain groups. Another representative body, the National Congress, holds semiannual meetings in which all Cambodians may participate directly.

During the early 1960s the former king, Prince Norodom Sihanouk, assumed more direct control as chief of state but did not rule absolutely.

HISTORY. Cambodia's history extends back at least as far as the 100s AD, when the Kingdom of Funan, in southern Cambodia, was established. It gained power over territory in present-day Thailand, Malaya, Vietnam, and Laos. During the 500s, the kingdom of the Chenla, to the north, overthrew the Funan empire.

By about 800, the Khmers, inhabitants of southern Cambodia who may have been descended from Indians, united with the Cham, an Indonesian people of the northern Malay peninsula. They conquered the Chenla and established an empire centered at Angkor, on the plain northeast of Tonle Sap. Their culture was predominantly Indian and their religion similar to Hinduism.

For the next 400 years Khmer god-kings ruled an empire that included large areas of southeast Asia. Their rice-growing civilization was quite advanced, and evidence remains of great temples, roads, irrigation projects, and public buildings. Khmer power declined during the 1300s. In 1431 the Siamese conquered and sacked Angkor, and the Khmer kings retreated to the region near Phnom Penh.

During succeeding decades, the Khmers fought several disastrous wars with their former subject peoples, the Cham, the Thais, and the Vietnamese, and lost much of their territory. By the mid-1800s, when French colonists began to settle in Indochina, Cambodia was a minor principality plagued by dynastic disputes and in danger of being divided between the Siamese and the Vietnamese.

French Control. In 1863 France made Cambodia a protectorate. Except for preventing its partition, the French generally ignored Cambodia. They fostered little social or economic change and allowed the Cambodian monarchy to continue to function. During the 1930s Cambodian nationalism began to grow, and it turned into

anti-French feeling during World War II, when Vichy France allowed Japan to use bases in Cambodia and permitted Thailand to occupy Cambodian territory.

In 1945 Japan took direct control of the Cambodian government, but Prince Norodom Sihanouk proclaimed his country's independence. In 1953 the French, having allowed Cambodia complete internal self-government, turned control of the military over to the Cambodians. In 1954 Vietnamese communist forces invaded Cambodia, joining anti-French guerrillas who had been active there since 1945. A Geneva conference held late in the year ended the fighting, and the troops were withdrawn along with all remaining French troops.

Independence. In 1955 King Sihanouk abdicated in favor of his parents and assumed the title of prince. He consolidated the nation's political strength and founded a political party, the Peoples' Socialist Community, which dominates Cambodia's political life. In 1960, when Sihanouk's father died, the prince was elected chief of state. He was chosen to lead a council to act as regent for his mother.

The country concentrated on social and economic development and remained at peace despite violent conflicts raging in neighboring Southeast Asian nations. In the early 1960s, however, when the Vietnam war intensified, Cambodia feared for its safety and sought international guarantees of its independence and neutrality.

Although Cambodia did not become directly involved in the Vietnam war, eastern Cambodia was used as a military staging area. In 1965 Cambodia severed relations with the United States after the bombing of a Cambodian village. In 1967, as the border situation worsened, Prince Sihanouk assumed special powers and took firmer control of the government.

—M. G. Inaba

PAN AMERICAN AIRWAYS

THE RUINS OF ANGKOR remain as a symbol of the rich heritage of Cambodia's people.

CAMEROON

Official name: Federal Republic of Cameroon
Area: 183,568 square miles
Population: (1966 est.) 5,229,000
Capital: Yaoundé (Pop., 1965 est., 101,000)
Language: French, English, African languages
Religion: Christianity, Islam, traditional religions
Currency unit: Franc CFA (African Financial Community)
National holiday: Independence day, January 1

Cameroon, a federal republic in western Africa, is bordered on the northeast by Chad, on the east by the Central African Republic, on the southeast by the Congo (Brazzaville), on the south by Gabon and Equatorial Guinea (Río Muni), and on the west by the Atlantic Ocean and Nigeria. Cameroon is a federation of two former UN trust territories—one French-administered, now East Cameroon, and the other under British control, West Cameroon.

THE LAND. Cameroon has a varied landscape. In the north are broad grasslands. In the center of the country is the Adamawa Plateau, with elevations of between 2,600 and 5,000 feet above sea level. In the south is a densely forested plateau averaging 2,000 feet in elevation. The volcanic Mt. Cameroon, which rises over 13,300 feet, is near the coast. The coastal region is forested and marshy.

The climate throughout the country is hot and humid. Some regions in the south receive as much as 180 inches of rain each year.

THE PEOPLE. Many different tribes live in Cameroon. Bamileke, Kirdi, and Fulani peoples live in central and northern Cameroon. Bantu-speaking people inhabit parts of southern Cameroon. Some pygmies live in the forests of the south. Cameroon's largest cities include Yaoundé, the capital, and Douala, the major port.

ECONOMY. Cameroon has a variety of resources and products. Cacao, coffee, cotton, and bananas are grown. Forestry provides an important source of revenue. Mineral resources are limited, but in the 1960s exploitation of bauxite deposits was begun.

A large aluminum factory has been built at Edéa, in the west, where there is a major hydroelectric power station. But industrial development elsewhere has been hampered by a lack of power, although small, local hydroelectric plants have been built in various parts of the country. A 20-year economic development program was begun in 1961 to improve the standard of living and ensure a stable economy.

In 1965 imports cost $152 million and exports earned $139 million. The chief exports are cacao and coffee. Cameroon imports manufactured goods, machinery, transportation equipment, chemicals, and petroleum products.

Cameroon maintains close economic relations with France, and it has a customs union with some of its neighbors.

GOVERNMENT. The federal government of Cameroon is headed by a president and a vice-president, both popularly elected to five-year terms. Legislative powers rest with the Federal National Assembly. The assembly includes one representative for every 80,000 people. The assembly elected in 1964 had 50 members, 40 from East Cameroon and 10 from West Cameroon. Assembly members are directly elected to five-year terms.

Cameroon is a member of the United Nations and the Organization of African Unity (OAU).

HISTORY. Cameroon was the original home of the agricultural Bantu-speaking people, who swept westward across central Africa in prehistoric times. Between the 1600s and 1800s, the Portuguese and British established trading posts in the area. In 1884 Germany established the Kamerun protectorate, which covered approximately the same area as the present-day republic.

After World War I the German protectorate was divided into separate French and British mandates under the League of Nations. The two mandates later became UN trust territories. France acquired the larger share of the former German territory. Britain acquired two disconnected land areas, one in the north, inhabited by Muslim Fulani with a feudal system closely allied to that of northern Nigeria, and a part of the southwest, a humid, tropical rain forest area with Bantu-speaking inhabitants.

France administered its territory as part of the Federation of French Equatorial Africa. East Cameroon received internal autonomy from France in 1958, and full independence in 1960 under the administration of Ahmadou Ahidjo. Britain administered its territory with Nigeria, using local chiefs in the administration and permitting some representation in Nigerian assemblies.

In 1961, in a UN-sponsored plebiscite, the northern region expressed the desire to remain with Nigeria, but the southern region voted to join the Republic of Cameroon. A federal republic was formed on Oct. 1, 1961, with Ahidjo as president and John Ngu Foncha, prime minister of the former British region, as vice-president.

—Hibberd V. B. Kline, Jr.;
Vera L. Zolberg

CANADA

Official name: Dominion of Canada
Area: 3,851,809 square miles
Population: (1967 est.) 20,441,000
Capital: Ottawa (Pop., 1965 est., urban area: 482,000)
Language: English, French
Religion: Roman Catholicism, Protestantism, Judaism
Currency unit: Dollar
National holiday: Dominion day, July 1

Canada occupies all of the northern half of North America with the exception of Alaska in the northwest and the Danish island of Greenland to the northeast. Canada is the world's second largest nation in area, but it ranks far lower in population. The enormous area of the country and its relatively small population have at times brought into question Canada's very existence as a separate nation in North America.

Few countries have been so deeply affected by their geography as has Canada. The vast, rock-strewn Canadian Shield, which covers the northeastern half of the country, and the harsh climate in the north created a pattern in which three-quarters of the population live within 200 miles of the U.S. border. But the habitable regions—the Maritime area, the St. Lawrence Valley, the prairies, and the Pacific slope—are separated from each other by formidable land barriers, and each of the regions is more closely linked geographically with U.S. areas to the south than with other parts of Canada.

The major forces helping to preserve a separate Canadian nation have been historical and cultural. These include the military and diplomatic protection provided Canada by membership in the British Empire and later in the Commonwealth of Nations, the determination of most English-speaking Canadians to retain their British heritage, and the French-speaking Canadians' fear of assimilation by the numerically overpowering culture of the United States.

Within Canada, however, the problem of establishing and maintaining a national identity has been complicated not only by the influence of the United States, but also by the division between English and French Canadians. The existence of these two

distinct and often competing cultural groups has been a source of dissension throughout Canada's modern history.

THE LAND. A northerly location and continental dimensions are basic elements in Canadian geography. From the northern tip of Ellesmere Island, in the Arctic Ocean, to southernmost Ontario, thrust deep into the Great Lakes region, Canada extends for a distance of some 2,800 miles, most of it within Arctic and subarctic regions. At its widest, Canada extends 3,200 miles from east to west and stretches across seven time zones.

This huge area is divided into ten provinces and two territories. Newfoundland, New Brunswick, Prince Edward Island, and Nova Scotia—the Maritime Provinces—lie along the Atlantic coast. The provinces of Quebec and Ontario occupy the southeast. Manitoba, Saskatchewan, and Alberta—the Prairie Provinces—lie in the center of the country. British Columbia is on the Pacific coast. The Northwest and the Yukon territories lie in the north and northwest.

The country is fringed with islands along its three ocean shorelines. To the east, in the Atlantic, lie Newfoundland, Cape Breton Island, Prince Edward Island, and Anticosti. To the north, in the Arctic Ocean, there stretches a vast archipelago containing some 20 large islands, of which Baffin and Ellesmere are the largest and most rugged. The mountainous, deeply indented Pacific coast is rimmed by rocky islands, including Vancouver Island and the Queen Charlotte and Alexander archipelagos.

Landscape. The country's dominant physical feature is the Canadian Shield, a great mass of ancient rock that covers roughly the northeastern half of the country. At its southern end it reaches the north shore of Lake Superior and extends into the United States in northern Minnesota and the Adirondack section of New York. The shield is a low plateau that rises to a fringe of hills and mountains in the east along the Labrador coast and in the south to the Laurentian Highlands overlooking the Gulf of St. Lawrence.

The center of the shield is a depressed basin, most of which is occupied by the broad, shallow Hudson Bay. The shield reflects the most obvious effects of glaciers that covered virtually all of Canada during the Pleistocene Period, from about 1 million to 10,000 years ago. Except for thin patches of poor soil and two major pockets of sedimentary material, in the Ontario-Quebec Clay Belt and around Quebec's Lake St. John, the shield's surface is largely ice-scoured, boulder-strewn rock marked by a maze of swamps, lakes, and streams. Although its agricultural resources are extremely meager, the Canadian Shield is one of the world's greatest sources of minerals and waterpower.

To the south and east of the shield is a zone of plains reaching from the Gulf of St. Lawrence to the Arctic Ocean. The southern Ontario and Quebec segment of the plains, which includes the Great Lakes and the St. Lawrence Valley, is small in area,

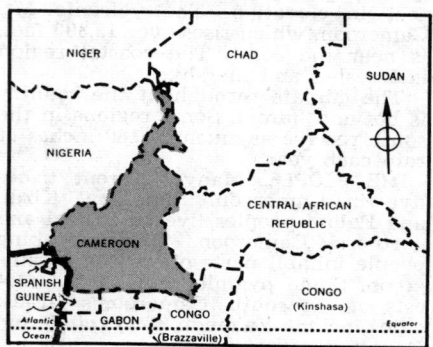

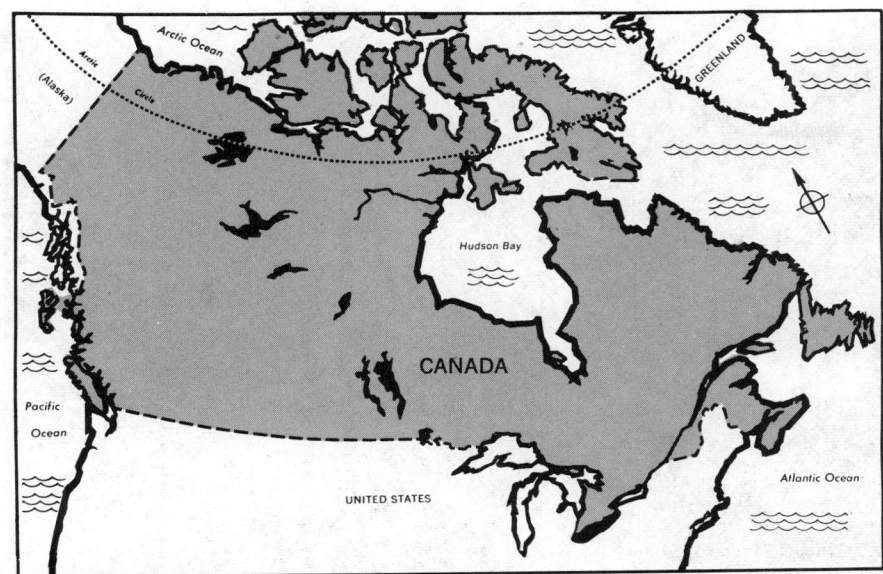

NATIONAL FILM BOARD
CANADA'S MAPLE LEAF FLAG

but enjoys some of Canada's best climate and forms the economic heartland of the nation. As the Prairie Region, the plains zone extends westward into southern Manitoba, Saskatchewan, and Alberta. This belt of plains contains some of the best Canadian soils as well as the country's principal reserves of petroleum, natural gas, and coal. The plains extend further north as the Mackenzie Valley of the Northwest Territory, a less developed area containing oil and coal.

Westward to the Pacific and the Alaska border lies the extremely mountainous Cordilleran Region. This region contains three major divisions —the Canadian Rockies on the east, the Coastal Ranges on the west, and, between them, a high, deeply dissected plateau drained by the Columbia, Fraser, and other westward-flowing rivers. There are some important deposits of metallic ores in British Columbia.

In southeastern Canada, an upland belt lies between the narrow St. Lawrence lowland and the Atlantic Ocean. This Appalachian system, extending northeast from New England, is a zone of hills and low plateaus and is deeply indented by the sea. The mineral wealth of the east is moderate in comparison with that of the west.

Climate. Low temperatures and a short or sometimes nonexistent growing season have been major hindrances to Canada's economic development. The frost-free season exceeds 120 days only in southern Ontario and Quebec and in southern and coastal British Columbia. But even in the Great Lakes-St. Lawrence inland water system, ice impedes navigation for four or five months each winter.

In the Prairie Region, along the U.S. border, a moderately long, warm to hot summer combines with rather low precipitation, 15 to 20 inches a year, to bring about a natural grass cover. This region and the British Columbian "rain-shadow" to the east of the humid Coastal Ranges are the only areas in Canada in which

drought is common. Further eastward in southeastern Canada, greater precipitation—30 to 50 inches a year—generates a rich, mixed forest cover.

Further north, as the temperature drops, both prairie and mixed forest give way to a vast, continent-wide belt of spruce, fir, and pine. This, in turn, thins out gradually until finally a treeless, truly Arctic tundra is reached. Winters are so long and bitterly cold (*average* January temperatures may be as low as –30°F) that only the topmost layers of the earth thaw during the few weeks of summer, and there is a permanently frozen subsurface, or "permafrost."

Icebergs are a major hazard off the Labrador coast, Hudson Bay is ice-jammed for as many as nine months of the year, and only rarely can ships force their way through the nearly permanent icefields bordering Canada's Arctic coast.

THE PEOPLE. Canada's people are of varied origins, for Canada has been one of the major destinations for the great European migrations of recent times. About 30 percent of the total population is of French origin. Although concentrated strongly in Quebec, French Canadians live in all the provinces and are particularly numerous in Ontario and New Brunswick. About 44 percent of Canada's people are of British origin—Irish, Scot, and Welsh, as well as English. They are widely distributed outside the French-speaking region.

Other important groups—Germans, Italians, Ukrainians, Dutch, Scandinavians, Poles, and Russians—are represented in Ontario, the Prairie Provinces, British Columbia, and the city of Montreal. They have been partly or wholly assimilated into the English-speaking community. Approximately 120,000 Canadians are of Asian descent—mostly Chinese and Japanese. Once almost entirely confined to British Columbia, they have begun to migrate eastward.

Some 220,000 Indians and Eskimos were counted in the 1961 census. About three-quarters of them live on government-administered reservations.

Religious life is also highly varied. About 45 percent of the population is Roman Catholic. Most live in Quebec, but all the other provinces have large Roman Catholic minorities. The major Protestant denominations—United Church, Anglican, Presbyterian, Lutheran, Baptist, Mennonite, and Pentecostal—are well represented outside Quebec, as are Greek Orthodox and Ukrainian Catholics. Canadian Jews are concentrated in the larger cities.

Distribution. The distribution of population is extremely uneven. Some 90 percent of all Canadians live within 10 percent of the country's area, a long, narrow, fragmented strip of territory along the southern boundary. In addition to being quite narrow, the populous region is split into four physically and socially isolated areas of settlement.

In the west, there is a relatively dense urban and rural settlement in southern British Columbia, especially within the Fraser and Columbia valleys. This is separated by the rugged Rocky Mountains from the thinly, but continuously, settled Prairie zone bounded on the east by the Canadian Shield and on the north by a forested zone of poor soils.

Canada's main concentration of population and wealth lies several hundred miles to the east in the lowlands wedged between the Canadian Shield, the Great Lakes, and the Appalachian uplands. This Canadian "heartland" is sharply divided culturally between a French-speaking, Roman Catholic Quebec and an English-speaking, ethnically and religiously diverse Ontario. Lastly, the Maritime area of settlement is isolated from the St. Lawrence-Great Lakes region by the Gaspé uplands and U.S. territory.

North of the main population belt, settlement is limited to a few areas such as Alberta's Peace River Valley, the Clay Belt, the Lake St. John basin, and various mining districts. Much of the Arctic is uninhabited. The total population of the Yukon and Northwest territories was only some 27,000 in the mid-1960s.

Growth. Canada's population has been growing rapidly, more so than that of almost any other economically developed nation. Between 1958 and 1965 the rate of increase was 2 percent a year. The government encourages the immigration of people with skills needed for the development of Canada's resources. Most of the increase has occurred in the relatively prosperous portions of Ontario and Quebec and in the two western provinces of British Columbia and Alberta.

Impressive growth has been limited almost wholly to cities and suburbs. By the early 1960s some 70 percent of the population was officially classified as urban and almost 45 percent lived in the 17 largest metropolitan areas. Among the relatively small number of large cities, two giants dwarf all others — Montreal, with more than 2.3 million people in its metropolitan area in 1965, and Toronto, with over 2 million.

ECONOMY. Canada is one of the most prosperous of the world's nations. In good part, this results from the combination of a small but highly skilled and well-educated population, rich natural resources, and the availability of investment capital from Europe and the United States.

Resources. Canada has abundant mineral and power resources. With thousands of miles of developed rivers and streams, the country is one of the world's leading producers of hydroelectric power. Waterpower produces approximately 80 percent of Canada's output of electricity, which in 1966 totaled nearly 160 billion kilowatt hours.

Large reserves of petroleum, gas, and coal lie in the Prairie Provinces. The Maritime Provinces also have important coal deposits.

Iron ore, copper, lead, zinc, nickel, cobalt, uranium, radium, and other metallic ores are mined in the shield. The western mountains are rich in zinc, lead, copper, gold, nickel, and silver.

In addition to these resources, forests cover almost 2 million square miles of Canada, and Canadian rivers and coastal waters are well stocked with fish.

Agriculture. Poor soils and harsh climate limit Canada's agricultural area, and in 1966 only some 7 percent of the land was under cultivation. Two regions are quite fertile—the prairies and the St. Lawrence lowlands.

Agriculture is the mainstay of the Prairie Provinces, where wheat and other small grains are grown in enormous quantities. Flaxseed, hay, sugar beets, cattle, and sheep are also

NATIONAL FILM BOARD

SORTING LOGS in British Columbia to feed the country's key pulp and paper industries.

major sources of farm income. Southern Quebec and Ontario produce grains and vegetables as well as meat and dairy products.

The Great Lakes region of Ontario raises the greatest variety of crops. Corn, tobacco, fruits, and vegetables are added to the usual grain, hay, and root crops. In southern British Columbia vegetable-growing, dairying, berry-farming, bulb-raising, and cattle herding are all important. In the Maritimes general farming is profitable only in a few localities, but fruit farms prosper.

Manufacturing. Manufacturing makes the largest contribution to Canada's economy, accounting for more than one quarter of the gross national product in 1966. Pulp and paper milling, ore processing, and oil refining are the leading industries. The processing of meat, grains, milk, and other farm products is also important.

Plants manufacturing machinery, vehicles, electrical equipment, chemicals, and textiles are concentrated in the urban centers of southern Ontario and Quebec. Many are affiliates of U.S. corporations.

Extractive Industries. The fur trade is still carried on in large sections of northern Canada. Forest industries continue to expand in areas with easy access to markets, and Canada is a major producer of pulp and paper.

Mining is increasing with further exploration, improved transportation, and rising world demand. Iron ore production rose sharply in the early 1960s with the development of mines in Labrador and north of Lake Superior.

Fishing remains important to the economies of Newfoundland and Labrador, but it is less significant than in earlier years. Newfoundland, for example, has started major forest and mineral industries. Deep sea fishing, especially for salmon, is important in coastal British Columbia.

Tourism. Tourism is an increasingly important source of income. Throughout the nation, during the early 1960s tourist and recreation facilities were being developed rapidly for Canadians and for European and U.S. visitors.

Transportation. The Canadian economy depends upon a transport system capable of coping with enormous distances and bad weather. Canada's highway network is adequate only within the well-populated regions. The Trans-Canada Highway runs from the Atlantic to the Pacific, and the Alaska Highway links Canada's northern and southern boundaries.

Much of Canada's freight travels by rail, on the government-owned Canadian National and the private Canadian Pacific, or by boat. Canada has many good natural harbors, especially along the Great Lakes-St. Lawrence system, but many ports are closed by freezing weather during most of the winter.

Trade. Canadian economic well-being depends heavily upon international trade. In 1966 the country's exports were valued at just over $9,500 million and its imports cost slightly more than $9,000 million.

Major Canadian exports include paper, newsprint, wheat, lumber, wood pulp, nickel and nickel products, aluminum, copper, uranium, petroleum, iron ore, asbestos, synthetic rubber, plastics, machinery, and whisky. Imported goods include petroleum and coal for eastern Canada, raw sugar, bauxite, coffee, cotton, rubber, fruits, and a broad range of industrial products.

Most of Canada's trade is with the United States. Britain, once Canada's principal market, ranked second in the 1960s.

GOVERNMENT. Canada, a federation of ten provinces, is a parliamentary democracy. Although it is an independent nation, Canada is a member of the Commonwealth of Nations and recognizes the British monarch, or the Crown, as head of state. A governor-general represents the Crown in Canada and is the nominal chief executive.

A prime minister, normally the leader of the majority party in the parliament, is the functioning chief executive of the national government. He heads a cabinet responsible to the House of Commons, the lower house of parliament. Members of the House of Commons are popularly elected to a normal term of five years. Members of the upper house, the Senate, are nominated by the prime minister and appointed for life by the governor-general.

A lieutenant-governor appointed by the governor-general in council with the prime minister formally leads the government in each province. Actual provincial executive power is in the hands of a prime minister, or premier, and cabinet responsible to the provincial legislature.

The legislatures are unicameral in every province but Quebec, where the assembly has two houses, and all are popularly elected. Federally appointed commissioners and small elected councils govern the Yukon Territory and the Northwest Territories. The Dominion government has direct authority over many territorial matters, however.

Canada is a member of the United Nations. It has close ties with Britain and with other members of the Commonwealth. Canada is also a member of the North Atlantic Treaty Organization (NATO).

HISTORY. The history of Canada has been called a story of challenge. First, New France, as the French possessions in North America were called, strug-

gled for survival against the wealthier British colonies to the south, in the present-day United States. Then, after the British conquest of New France in 1763 and the American Revolution, British Canada began its own long struggle against the powerful military, economic, and cultural forces exerted by the United States. While struggling to maintain itself as a nation, Canada has also struggled to establish a national identity, to be Canadian.

Early Exploration. The first Europeans to reach America were the Vikings, who came in the 1000s by way of Iceland and Greenland. The extent of Viking penetration of the continent and the fate of Viking settlements have remained uncertain. Norse sagas and maritime traditions preserve much knowledge of those early discoveries and a map of "Vinland," published in the 1960s, indicates that they explored Newfoundland, at the least.

It was not until the late 1400s that English, French, Spanish, and Portuguese ships began to cross the Atlantic. The first voyages were undertaken by John Cabot in 1497 and 1498. With permission of England's King Henry VII, Cabot sailed on behalf of a group of English merchants who wished him to find a Northwest Passage to the Orient. No shortcut to the riches of Asia was found, but Cabot's party did discover the great North Atlantic fishing banks near the Gulf of St. Lawrence.

The fame of the fisheries spread among Europe's seafaring nations, but by the end of the 1500s the fishermen of England and France were taking the greatest advantage of the fishing banks. The main catch was cod, and as the fish had to be dried, fishermen built storehouses and dwellings on the shore.

The fishermen began to trade with Indians eager to exchange their fur clothing for European trinkets. This sideline soon proved enormously profitable. It led to the founding of posts devoted to the fur trade, and the demand for furs gradually lured trappers deeper into the continent. Fish and furs became the two great staples of the Canadian economy.

In 1534 and 1535 Jacques Cartier undertook exploratory voyages on behalf of France's King Francis I. On his second voyage, Cartier discovered the mighty St. Lawrence River. He sailed up the St. Lawrence as far as the Iroquois villages then located on the sites of the present-day cities of Quebec and Montreal.

As a result of Cartier's voyages, France attempted to colonize the area near Quebec in 1541–1543. The failure to discover hoped-for treasures of gold and jewels discouraged the French, and their first attempt to found a colony in Canada failed. Cartier's efforts were not in vain, however, for his voyages established a clear title for later French claims to the whole area of the St. Lawrence gulf and valley.

New France. During most of the remainder of the 1500s internal religious and political struggles distracted France from further efforts to colonize Canada. Fishing and fur trading continued, however, and the popularity of beaver hats in France spurred the fur trade.

When Henry IV became king of France in 1589, stability began to return and important commercial interests looked to Canada for fur to meet the continuing European demand for fur clothing. Henry IV was personally interested in resuming the exploration and settlement of Canada, and he used the interest of French merchants in the fur trade to accomplish his ends. In 1599 the merchants of Honfleur received the first of a series of royal monopolies of the fur trade.

The French controlled New France through these monopolies until King Louis XIV took direct control in 1663. A monopoly of the fur trade in a particular region was granted to a company in return for its undertaking settlement and missionary work. This policy succeeded in planting French colonies in North America, but the hostility of the Iroquois, the lack of interest in settlement among the monopolists, and the harshness of the climate led to their failure and to the revocation of the monopolies.

Much of the credit for the colonization that was achieved belongs to Samuel de Champlain (c.1567–1635). Soldier, geographer, and fervent Roman Catholic, Champlain was the true founder of New France. He surveyed the explored territories for possible settlement sites, and after the original coastal colonies had failed he persuaded the monopolists to concentrate on developing the St. Lawrence Valley. The energy and initiative with which he guided the destinies of New France from 1608, when he founded a trading post at Quebec, until his death in 1635 were responsible for the colony's survival in the face of the same obstacles to which earlier settlements had surrendered.

NATIONAL FILM BOARD

SHIPPING FREIGHT at St. John, New Brunswick, in southeastern Canada's Maritime region.

Other forces also worked to insure success. The religious zeal of the Catholic Counter-Reformation in France soon spread to Canada. The enthusiasm of the Jesuit and other religious orders to convert the Indians led to the establishment of missions and kept the colony active.

In 1627 Cardinal Richelieu, the chief minister of Louis XIV, organized a new monopoly, the Company of New France, also known as the Company of One Hundred Associates. It assumed direction of the colony and permitted only Catholics to come to New France.

The church founded and conducted the colony's social and educational institutions and in 1642 established a mission and hospital for the Indians on the site of what is now Montreal. But the zeal of the missionaries alone could not maintain the colony, even though many new settlements were being founded.

By 1663 New France faced grave problems. The fur trade did not encourage settlement. It depended on single men rather than on families, and in fact the fur companies had established only about two thousand people in the colony. In addition, the Iroquois were a constant threat. Thus the colony remained little more than a fur-trading station dependent on France for almost all its supplies.

Royal Rule. At that critical moment, Louis XIV, having firmly established his power in France, initiated an entirely new policy designed to turn the colony into a source of strength for the crown. The Company of New France was persuaded to surrender its monopoly in 1663, and Louis XIV assumed personal control through his finance minister, Jean Baptiste Colbert.

Government was placed in the hands of three officials, each directly responsible to the king. A governor was to direct military affairs, especially defense against the Indians; a bishop was to direct the church; and an *intendant*, a new official in Canada, was to regulate economic and judicial matters. All three officials sat on a supreme council that included five other appointed members. The council handled administration and acted as a court of appeals. This government endured until the loss of the colony in 1763.

In 1665 the king ended the immediate threat from the Indians by sending more than a thousand well-trained soldiers to Canada. A revival of the fur trade soon followed the victories over the Indians. The first intendant was Jean Talon, who served from 1665 to 1672. His bold plans transformed the colony. Encouragement of immigration and rewards for early marriage helped raise the population from about 3,000 in 1666 to almost 7,000 by 1673.

Social organization in New France was a modification of that in the mother country. Colonial strength resulted from social changes made possible or necessary by the conditions of pioneer life. France's feudalistic seignorial system of landholding was reorganized.

Some of the rigid restrictions on the peasants were relaxed to allow them more freedom from their seigneur, or landlord. As semi-independent small farmers, the peasants became a source of social stability. Agriculture began to prosper, and the long, narrow farms fronting on the St. Lawrence gave New France the appearance of a continuous village with a single street, the river. Law was based on the French code, but it included statutes passed by the council and decrees made by the intendant.

Talon tried to make the colony less dependent on the fur trade, and he promoted lumbering, fishing, shipbuilding, hemp-growing, brewing, tanning, and the mining of potash. He was only partially successful in this, however, and trade with France and the French West Indies never reached substantial proportions. By the end of the 1670s, royal interest in the colony had waned once more and New France was again forced to rely on its own resources.

The fur trade and rivalry with the expanding British colonies to the south pushed the French ever deeper into the interior of North America. Louis Joliet and the Jesuit missionary Father Jacques Marquette explored the Mississippi area in 1673. The Sieur de la Salle explored the Ohio River in 1669 and the Mississippi River in 1682, claiming the entire Mississippi Valley, "Louisiana," for France.

By 1700 French possessions stretched north to Hudson Bay, west beyond Lake Superior, and south to the Gulf of Mexico. But this great territorial expansion contributed to the fall of New France, for the area was large and had few French settlers.

French-British Rivalry. Conflict between Britain and France for dominance in Europe had started in 1689 and continued with only occasional periods of peace until 1763. The French-British conflict also involved the American colonies. The vast territories of France were held in spite of the colony's small population and economic weakness.

New France in the 1750s had only about 60,000 inhabitants, whereas the population of the wealthier British colonies approached 2 million. But New France relied on the ability of a united colony organized along military and authoritarian lines to mobilize swiftly its entire strength.

French ability to win Indian support, the warlike qualities of the French nobility and militia, and French pride, daring, and vigor long enabled New France to withstand British power in North America.

French expansion received its first check in 1713, when the Treaty of Utrecht gave Britain Newfoundland, Acadia (Nova Scotia), and Hudson Bay. Although New France made an impressive recovery from this setback, British numerical and naval superiority in the New World made final defeat inevitable.

The tide turned in favor of the British in 1758, and in 1759 British Gen. James Wolfe defeated Commander Louis Montcalm on the Plains of Abraham. This led to the fall of Quebec, the strategic center for French power in America. The Treaty of Paris, signed in 1763, brought the struggle of empires to a close. France surrendered its mainland possessions in North America and formally transferred Canada to Britain.

British Canada then included the Atlantic Coast maritime region, part of which England had possessed before the treaty; "Canada," part of the present-day Quebec and Ontario provinces, won under the treaty; and the Northwest Territories, north and west of Hudson Bay. Britain also had access, if not absolute title, to the largely unsettled wilderness between the Great Lakes and the Pacific.

British Canada. Britain was faced with the problem of governing a French-speaking community in the British Empire. In the Proclamation of 1763, Britain announced the goal of assimilating the French into British culture. To increase the English-speaking population, Britain sought immigrants from the 13 American colonies. The government promised

BRITISH TAKING THE CITY OF QUEBEC in 1759, from an old print by an unknown artist.

English law and institutions to all colonists and rule by Protestants, not by Catholics.

The expected heavy immigration did not occur, however, and British officials began to doubt the wisdom of turning Canada into a typically British colony at a time when the other British colonies in North America were becoming increasingly rebellious. Sir Guy Carleton, who governed Canada for much of the critical period between 1766 and 1796, avoided enforcing the assimilation policy. He had come to see Canada as a strategic outpost for England and as a potential source of manpower for subduing the American colonies if they should rebel.

The assimilation policy was officially abandoned by the Quebec Act of 1774 in a move to win the loyalty of the French Canadians. The act guaranteed the continuance of French civil law along with English criminal law, the maintenance of the French seigniorial system of landholding, the admission of Catholics to public office, and the right of the Church to collect tithes.

The act also extended the boundary of Quebec south to the Ohio River. American colonists felt that this provision was meant as punishment, although it was not so intended.

At the outbreak of the American Revolution, the American colonies hoped to win both Quebec and Nova Scotia to their cause, and the British looked to Quebec for military support. Both sides were disappointed.

French Canadians were weary of war and, with few exceptions, remained neutral. Nova Scotia, although inhabited by many recent immigrants from New England, was still economically dependent on trade with England and was intimidated by the great British naval and military base at Halifax. The American Revolution found little active support there, either.

The only major battles of the revolution fought on Canadian soil occurred in 1775, when American forces attacked Montreal and Quebec. The American colonists moved an army under Richard Montgomery toward Quebec to meet a second American force led by Benedict Arnold. Although Montreal fell to Montgomery's army, Quebec withstood the American siege. In the spring, when ships of the British navy sailed up the St. Lawrence, the Americans retreated.

The boundary agreed upon at the close of the American Revolution in the Treaty of Paris (1783) affected Canada as much as the United States. Most Canadians believed it a surrender of their interests. It abandoned much of the Ohio territory, on which the fur trade depended, and it left undetermined Canada's southern boundary west of the Mississippi. But the war had brought new settlers to Canada—some 40,000 Loyalists from the United States.

In Nova Scotia, nearly 30,000 Loyalists swelled the original population, transforming the region into a fiercely loyal British colony. To assist the immigrants, the British government assigned a liberal portion of land to each

family. On Aug. 16, 1784, New Brunswick, where the largest number of Loyalists had settled, was formed from the western part of Nova Scotia. It became the most loyally British and the most conservative province in Canada. West of the Maritimes, the Loyalists settled in three main areas: along the upper St. Lawrence; on the north shore of Lake Ontario; and on the Niagara peninsula.

The Loyalists throughout Canada soon claimed the right to have an elected assembly, and in 1791 the British Parliament passed the Constitutional Act establishing representative government in the Canadian colonies. The act also divided the colony of Canada into two separate sections—Upper Canada and Lower Canada.

Upper Canada, now the province of Ontario, was where most of the Loyalists had settled. Lower Canada, now the province of Quebec, lay nearer the mouth of the St. Lawrence and had remained predominantly French. Each had an appointed governor, a legislative council chosen by the governor, and an elected assembly. In Upper Canada, English common law formed the basis for government. Lower Canada retained much of the old French civil code.

The resolve of the Loyalists to remain British was tested in 1812 by the renewal of war with the United States. Although the war achieved little for either England or the United States, it had some important results for Canada. Canadian nationalism, as distinct from loyalty to England or to France, began to be felt as French and English Canadians fought side by side and, with the help of British regulars, fought off a U.S. invasion.

The war also reinforced Canadian conservatism, and for decades afterward forces of social and political reform could be greatly weakened by an accusation that they were American-inspired.

Until 1867 Upper and Lower Canada and the Maritime Provinces developed as separate units, but all were experiencing rapid social change, commercial expansion, and population growth. After the Napoleonic Wars, hard times in Britain drove immigrants to British America and the population level rose from under 500,000 in 1815 to 2.5 million in 1850. This rapidly transformed the colony from a comparative wilderness into a region of settled communities.

Fur, the chief industry of the wilderness, was no longer the basis of Canadian economic life. New activities were making important contributions to Canada's growth — lumbering and grain-growing in Upper and Lower Canada, and lumbering, shipbuilding, and fishing in the Maritimes.

Improved transportation became a necessity, and a program of canal-building, centered on the St. Lawrence River and its tributaries, was undertaken to tap the trade of the U.S. west. Although in the 1830s Canada completed the Welland Canal, which joined Lake Erie to Lake Ontario, the U.S. Erie Canal system easily maintained its superiority over the St. Lawrence route.

A world-wide depression in 1837

dealt a heavy blow to Canadian prosperity. Canada's economy was weakened further when Britain removed its protective trade system in the 1840s. Economic despair was reflected in the Annexation Manifesto requesting union with the United States, which was signed by numerous merchants in 1849 but never acted upon.

In the 1850s, railway-building helped bring renewed prosperity to British North America. The Reciprocity Treaty, signed in 1854, established freer trade between Canada and the United States and opened new markets for Canadian produce.

Canadian-American relations had already been improved by settlement of old boundary disputes in the 1840s. The Webster-Ashburton Treaty of 1842 set the line between New Brunswick and Maine at its present position, and the Oregon Treaty of 1846 set the U.S.-Canadian boundary west of the Mississippi along the 49th parallel.

During the 1800s Canada matured politically as widely separated struggling pioneer settlements grew into robust provincial societies. For several years after the War of 1812 the governments of Upper and Lower Canada were dominated by small, powerful groups called "family compacts" or "cliques." They controlled the legislative councils, the colonial cabinets.

The compacts often won popular support and adopted reasonably progressive policies, but too often they used their power to promote their own interests. Reform groups demanded that power be concentrated in the popularly elected assemblies. The political situation in Lower Canada was further complicated by an ethnic struggle. The ruling clique was almost entirely British, and the opposition, which controlled the assembly, was primarily French.

Robert Baldwin, a member of the legislature of Upper Canada, led the drive to obtain responsible government, with the executive responsible to the majority in the elected assembly. The local compacts opposed this threat to their power. They were supported by the British Colonial Office, which feared that responsible government would reduce the governor to a mere agent of the local assembly and would have almost the same effect as granting independence.

To these political grievances were added the severe financial crisis in 1837 and general economic hardship caused by widespread crop failures. Discontent led in 1857 to rebellions in Upper and Lower Canada.

The rising in Upper Canada involved only the more radical reformers, led by the Upper Canadian legislator William Lyon Mackenzie, and was primarily a protest against rule by the compacts. The rising was quickly suppressed, and the majority of the population remained loyal to the government.

In Lower Canada the revolt was more widespread, particularly among the French Canadians, who resented what they felt was unjust treatment by British officials. There, the untrained rebel forces were soon routed by British regular troops. The rebellions caused friction along the U.S. border and resulted in several ill-organized raids on Canada by misinformed American patriots. The uprisings dealt the British government a severe blow and in 1838 led to the dispatch of the Earl of Durham, John George Lambton, to report on unrest in the colonies.

Responsible Government. Lord Durham's *Report on the Affairs of British North America* (1839) was a denunciation of rule by compacts. The report recommended the institution of responsible government, a clear division between imperial and local functions, and the union of Upper and Lower Canada. But these were only partially put into effect by the British Parliament's Union Act of 1840.

The Canadas joined in 1841 to become the Province of Canada. Durham had intended the union of Upper and Lower Canada to solve the French-British cultural conflict by assimilating French Canadians into British culture. The proposal for a united legislative assembly was carried out, but the attempted assimilation did not succeed. The Union Act gave each equal representation in the legislature, despite their unequal populations, and the idea of two distinct sections was kept alive.

Responsible government began in 1848. It came first to Nova Scotia, which had not been disturbed by the rebellion. A few months later the Province of Canada followed. Robert Baldwin, the attorney general of Upper Canada, joined Louis H. Lafontaine, a prominent French Canadian, to form a government. But Canadian politics continued to be plagued by sectional strife based on historical and cultural differences. With each section stubbornly opposed to the other, Canada could make little progress.

The French-Canadian element, because of its solidarity, had great political strength. It campaigned for objectives of its own, such as separate Roman Catholic schools, and against the programs of the more liberal element.

By the early 1850s Upper Canada, then called Canada West, had a larger population than Canada East, the predominantly French-Canadian portion of the union, but each had equal representation in the assembly. George Brown, publisher of the Toronto *Globe* and a Liberal member of the Canadian parliament from Canada West, led the campaign to end what was called "French domination" by achieving representation on the basis of population.

French Canadians responded by staunchly supporting Brown's opponents in the Conservative Party. As a result, there were three changes of government between 1861 and 1864. The sections were so evenly balanced that the deadlock would only have continued after another election.

Confederation. To break the stalemate, the Liberal and Conservative parties formed a coalition to promote the union of all the British North American colonies. At that same time the Maritime Provinces had planned a conference to discuss a limited union

among themselves, and delegates from Canada East and Canada West attended the meeting, held in September 1864.

At another meeting held at Quebec City the following month, the Canadas won over the Maritimes to their plan of union. Both Canada and the Maritimes faced common problems, which Confederation was expected to solve. In Canada, the agricultural frontier had reached its limits and a stronger political authority was needed to promote settlement of the western plains, an area already threatened by U.S. expansionism.

Moreover, the nation had a great need for railroads and other major transportation facilities. Projects of such vast proportions could be handled and financed more easily by a centralized government than by the individual provinces. In the Maritime Provinces prosperity based on the timber trade, wooden-ship building, and fishing was threatened by the new economy based on coal and steel.

When the United States showed its determination to cancel the Reciprocity Treaty of 1854, all Canadians became aware of the need for a united country to resist U.S. economic pressure and to seek new markets. Other external pressures also made a united front desirable. During the U.S. Civil War most Canadians favored the South. Fear of attack by Union armies led many to support Confederation as a defense against U.S. invasion.

British support made Confederation almost inevitable. The British government realized that a united British North America could take more vigorous defensive measures against U.S. pressure and, in addition, could relieve the mother country of much of the colonies' financial burden. Britain therefore used all its influence and power to bring about confederation and it pressured the reluctant Nova Scotia and New Brunswick into joining the union. Nevertheless, Newfoundland and Prince Edward Island refused to join.

The Dominion. The British North America Act of 1867 united Canada East and Canada West with New Brunswick and Nova Scotia to form the Dominion of Canada. Canada East became Quebec province, Canada West became Ontario, and Nova Scotia and New Brunswick retained their former boundaries and provincial organization. Ottawa, in Ontario but near the Quebec border, was chosen as the dominion capital.

In response to the French Canadians' desire to protect their language and religious rights, the new dominion was a federal and not a unitary state. In contrast with the U.S. example, however, the central government, not the provinces, received all powers that the constitution did not specifically grant to one or the other.

The aim of the planners was to create a strong central administration that would control most of the important functions of governing the dominion. The new dominion combined the British parliamentary form of government with the U.S. principle of federalism in a government that still remained subordinate to Britain.

John A. Macdonald, the dominion's first prime minister, and his Conservative Party dominated the political history of Canada from Confederation until 1891. Macdonald's task was to build a nation. His first great achievement was to prevent Nova Scotia's attempted withdrawal from Confederation in 1869 by granting needed economic assistance to the province.

In foreign affairs, Macdonald ably represented Canadian interests in negotiations between Britain and the United States that resulted in the Treaty of Washington of 1871. The treaty resolved a U.S.-Canadian dispute over fishing rights in the waters off Nova Scotia. It also set the boundary between Washington state and British Columbia firmly at the 49th parallel in accordance with the Oregon Treaty of 1846.

During Macdonald's ministry, three new provinces entered Confederation. In 1869 the Hudson's Bay Company sold its rights in the West to the Canadian government, but before the transfer was completed the largely French-Indian, or *métis* population of the territory of Red River, led by Louis Riel, rose in protest.

The *métis* feared for the survival of their cultural and property rights if they were forced into Confederation. Macdonald negotiated with Riel and sent troops to nearby Fort Garry to enforce order. Red River entered Confederation on July 15, 1870, as the province of Manitoba.

On July 1, 1871, British Columbia, on the Pacific coast, attracted by generous offers of economic aid and the promise of a transcontinental railway, entered Confederation and completed the rapid expansion of the new Dominion from coast to coast. This milestone was followed on July 1, 1873, by the addition of the Atlantic coast colony of Prince Edward Island, where a financial crisis had overcome earlier opposition to Confederation.

Macdonald's Conservative government, implicated in a railway scandal, lost to the Liberals in 1873. The Liberals' period in office, under Alexander Mackenzie, coincided with an international economic depression. The Liberal government appeared helpless in the face of the crisis, and in 1878 Macdonald was returned to power.

Macdonald's platform in the 1878 election race promised a "national policy" to rebuild the economy. It proposed high protective tariffs, increased railway building, and a stepped-up immigration program. A protective tariff instituted after the election became a central feature of Canadian economic policy, and the Canadian Pacific Railway, with the help of generous government grants, was completed to the Pacific in 1885.

Unfortunately, the expected immigration, without which the railway and the tariff could be of little value, failed to materialize. In addition, the return of world economic depression in the 1880s led to the stagnation of the Canadian economy, which was vulnerable because of its heavy dependence on exports.

Disunity. At that critical time, Canada once again faced old problems. The last two decades of the 1800s were

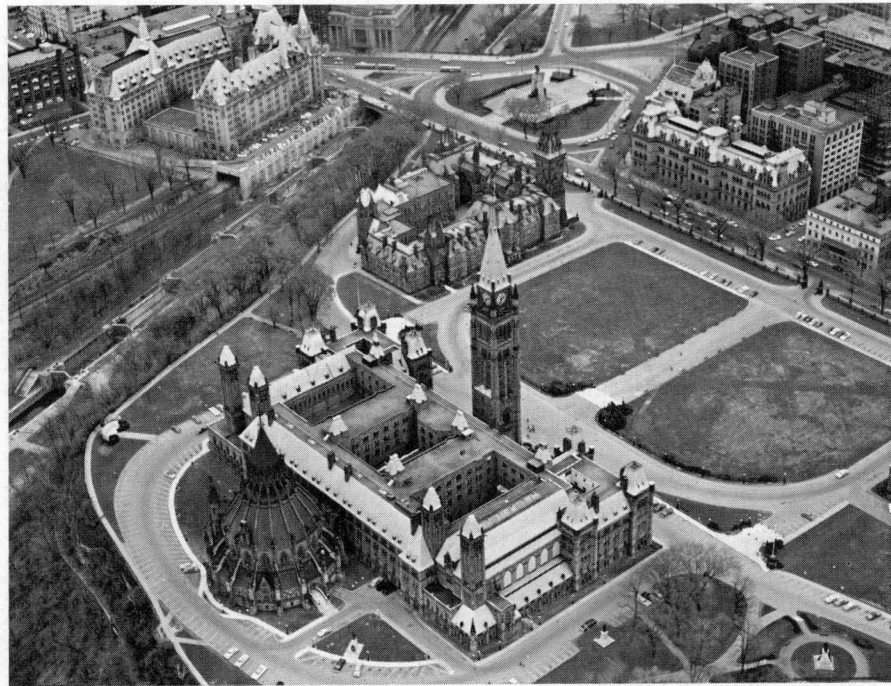

CANADIAN GOVERNMENT TRAVEL BUREAU

THE PARLIAMENT BUILDINGS of the Dominion of Canada, in Ottawa, the nation's capital. The buildings house Canada's federal legislature, the Parliament, which has two houses—the Senate and the House of Representatives.

marked by the renewal of bitter cultural conflicts between French-speaking Roman Catholics and English-speaking Protestants. This conflict and a strong movement for provincial rights challenged the centralizing policies of Macdonald's nationalism.

In 1885 the *métis* and Indians again joined behind Louis Riel in a second and more serious rebellion, this time in the Northwest Territories. Riel was executed in 1885, and French Canadians blamed his death on political pressure from Ontario Protestants, who sought revenge for Riel's execution of a Protestant during the 1869 revolt.

A new wave of anti-British feeling swept Quebec, and in 1886 the province elected a fiery French-Canadian nationalist, Honoré Mercier, as premier. French Canadians began to turn away from a national government controlled by British votes and toward their own provincial government for protection of their rights.

The English-speaking provinces also experienced strong localist sentiment. Opposition in Manitoba and the Maritimes to Macdonald's centralizing nationalism probably originated in economic depression. Wealthy Ontario, led by the Liberal Premier Oliver Mowat, also challenged the centralist policies of the Conservatives in power at Ottawa.

At the Interprovincial Conference of 1887 the premiers of five of the seven provinces passed resolutions attacking federal interference in provincial matters. Under attack, Macdonald's government partially abandoned such federal policies as the disallowing of laws passed by provincial legislatures.

Provincial power also was enhanced by a series of decisions handed down by the judicial committee of the Privy Council in England, the empire's highest court. By 1896 the central government retained little of the great power provided it by the constitution of 1867.

Macdonald won his last election in 1891, defending his "national policy" against the Liberal's advocacy of provincial rights and of unlimited reciprocity with the United States. His death later in 1891 removed the leading figure in Canadian politics.

Macdonald's Conservative successors were unable to cope with renewed economic depression in the 1890s or with the continuing quarrel between French- and English-speaking Canadians. In 1896 the nation turned to the Liberal Party and its distinguished leader, the French Canadian Wilfrid Laurier.

Laurier Administration. Laurier was dedicated to achieving harmony among the different elements of Canada's population. To reduce cultural conflicts, he advocated stronger provincial rights, and he reconciled many of the conflicts between French- and English-speaking Canadians.

World prosperity enabled the Liberals to succeed on the basis of economic policies introduced by Macdonald's Conservatives. Two new transcontinental railways were constructed with government aid, opening new forest lands and exposing untapped mineral wealth.

Settlers from the United States and Europe moved to the Canadian west in response to an imaginative immigration program. The planting of new types of early-maturing grain and the

development of mechanized farming made possible a great wheat boom in the early 1900s. On Sept. 1, 1905, Saskatchewan and Alberta provinces, formed from part of the Northwest Territories, entered Confederation. Canada was filled with an unprecedented sense of self-confidence.

An equally important feature of Laurier's administration was his attitude toward a growing sentiment in Britain for a stronger, more unified empire. Laurier recognized Canada's great need for British support to balance U.S. influence, but he was fully aware of the danger to Canada's national unity and independence in the new British imperial policy. At a series of Imperial Conferences Laurier gradually won a measure of world recognition of Canadian independence without seriously affronting the imperialist element within Canada.

Laurier dealt less successfully with the controversial question of imperial defense. Pressure had been put on him from both Canada and Britain to contribute to the imperial navy, but French Canadians opposed the move. When Laurier attempted to compromise by building a separate Canadian navy, Ontario Conservatives attacked him for doing too little and French Canadians condemned his policy as a surrender to imperialist interests.

Laurier also lost popularity over the Reciprocity Agreement of 1911 that he had negotiated with the United States. Had it been passed, the agreement would have greatly lowered tariffs on goods traded with the United States, but the nation's Liberal manufacturers opposed the agreement. Opposed by French Canadians, Nationalists, some Liberals, and the Conservatives, Laurier lost the election of 1911, and Robert Borden, a Conservative, became prime minister.

World War I. Prime Minister Borden was soon faced by the outbreak of World War I. Canada responded to the war quickly. Over 600,000 men were mobilized, and more than 400,000 went overseas. About 40,000 of them did not return. Canadian farms supplied food for British armies, and Canadian industries provided equipment. French Canadians, however, were not as enthusiastic in their support of the war as were English-speaking Canadians.

A coalition government of Liberals and Conservatives that included no French Canadians called for compulsory military service. The French-speaking population objected, often violently, to being forced to submit to a conscription act of an all-British government. Quebec blamed the Conservative Party for the draft act, and for decades afterward the party was weak in that province.

Interwar Era. After its war effort, Canada was in a position to assert its independence within the British Empire. At the Imperial War Conference of 1917 Prime Minister Borden insisted upon full autonomy for Canada and the right to an equal voice in foreign affairs and imperial defense.

The conference passed a resolution drafted by Borden and Gen. Jan Christiaan Smuts of South Africa, which for the first time officially used the term "Commonwealth." The resolution laid the basis for what was soon called the "dominion status" of certain former colonies of the British Empire.

At the end of the war, Canada signed the Treaty of Versailles, and on Borden's insistence Canada's parliament ratified the treaty separately from Britain. Largely through Borden's efforts, Canada and the other British dominions received the right to sit as independent members of the League of Nations.

Borden's health forced him to retire in 1920, and his successor, Arthur Meighen, was defeated in 1921 by the Liberals led by Mackenzie King. King, Laurier's successor as leader of the Liberals continued and extended Borden's policies of autonomy. In 1931 Canadian independence received legal and constitutional acceptance by the British Parliament in the Statute of Westminster.

Prime Minister King demonstrated a political skill that demoralized opposition parties and an administrative ability that attracted strong leaders to the federal government. King was a sincere social reformer who moved Canada slowly and cautiously towards a system of social welfare.

King introduced old-age pensions, family allowances, and unemployment insurance. In many areas, however, the central government was unable to take action. Responsibility for education, labor relations, highway building, and other government services rested upon the individual provinces.

The constitution had given the federal government the wider powers of taxation, and the provinces—especially those in the poorer Maritime and Prairie regions—found it difficult to maintain the services for which they were constitutionally responsible.

Economic Crisis. The world economic depression of the 1930s worsened the economic problems caused by this imbalance of power and responsibility. The wheat-exporting Prairie Provinces were financially crippled, and the high tariff remedy of the Conservatives, in power under Prime Minister Richard Bennett from 1930 to 1935, was of little help.

Facing an election in 1935, Bennett suddenly introduced his "new deal," consisting of national marketing, wages and hours legislation, and an employment and social insurance law. But the Conservatives were overwhelmingly defeated in 1935, and in 1936 the courts declared the programs unconstitutional.

Mackenzie King's Liberals were returned to power in 1935 and they sought a solution to the depression and to the imbalance between federal taxing power and provincial responsibilities.

In 1937 the federal government appointed the Royal Commission on Dominion-Provincial Relations, which in 1940 recommended that the central government be given the authority to deal with the country's more pressing social needs and that it pay the poorer provinces a series of "adjustment grants" to enable them to maintain the less urgent remaining services. The richer provinces—Ontario, British Columbia, and Alberta—rejected these proposals. World War II provided a temporary solution, however, by allowing the federal government greater power.

Contemporary Canada. Canada entered World War II on Sept. 10, 1939, and Canada's war effort was intense. The country raised $12 billion and completely mobilized its industrial and human resources. Canada emerged from the war with increased prestige and with a new willingness to play its role in the international organizations of the postwar world. After the war the dominion government negotiated temporary agreements with the provinces that included adjustment grants similar to those of the rejected program.

Louis St. Laurent, a French Canadian, succeeded Mackenzie King as prime minister in 1948. The Liberal Party continued its political dominance over the Conservatives as well as over two new protest parties born in the 1930s—the socialist Cooperative Commonwealth Federation and the Social Credit Party. In 1949 Canada gained its tenth province when Newfoundland entered Confederation.

Renewed immigration, rapid industrialization, increased urbanization, and a booming economy created a high standard of living and a stable political situation. Canadians, aided by heavy foreign investment, opened new mining frontiers, developed new oil fields, initiated vast hydroelectric projects, and with the United States began construction of the St. Lawrence Seaway in 1954.

Canada, a founding member of the North Atlantic Treaty Organization (NATO), also played an active role in the United Nations as a "middle power," balancing between the two mighty power blocs of East and West. Under Lester Pearson's guidance as minister of external affairs, Canada took a full share of international responsibilities, including heavy participation in military action with UN forces in Korea.

During the 1950s and 1960s Canada moved ever closer to the United States economically, culturally, and militarily. Many Canadians feared the loss of their national identity as their economy grew more dependent on the United States for markets, imports, and capital. Unrest caused by the increasing speed of movement into the U.S. orbit contributed to a political upheaval in 1957 that swept the Conservatives into power after 22 years of Liberal government.

Economics also played a part in the defeat of the Liberals. Although the country as a whole was enjoying prosperity, not all regions shared in the economic boom. The poorer Atlantic coast and the grain-growing areas in the west had both turned to Conservative provincial governments before the national election. Moreover, Liberal foreign policy was greatly criticized, particularly when the Canadian government sided with the United States in the UN against British action in the 1956 Suez Canal crisis.

John Diefenbaker, a Conservative, became prime minister in 1957, and he offered the country a plan for national development apart from the Canadian-U.S. partnership promoted by the Liberals. Skillfully using Canadian fear of excessive U.S. influence, Diefenbaker represented a resurgence of Canadian national feeling. He presented an attractive alternative to a government many felt had been too long in office.

In power from 1957 to 1963, the Conservatives made substantial achievements. These included enormous wheat sales to communist countries, extended social welfare measures, new tax agreements with the provinces, and the passage of a bill of rights for Canadians. Conservative popularity waned, however, as an economic recession developed. Exports declined, and unemployment rose.

The Conservatives proved themselves particularly inept in foreign affairs. They antagonized Britain by opposing its plans to enter the European Common Market, and irritated the United States by lengthy indecision on an offer to provide nuclear weapons for Canadian forces. In addition, Conservative failure to understand or cope with a new surge of French-Canadian nationalism weakened the government in Quebec.

In 1963, after a bitter campaign, Lester Pearson's Liberal Party returned to power, but without a clear majority in the House of Commons. The Liberals again failed to win a solid majority after another election in 1965, and they were prevented from taking effective action on many important issues.

In 1964 and 1965, despite partisan political quarrelling and several governmental scandals, Canada made progress in reforming parliamentary organization, in further extending social welfare programs, and in insuring the conservation of the nation's vital natural resources. In 1964 parliament decided on a new national flag, a single maple leaf on a field of white and red, to replace the former modified British flag. The change, achieved only after much debate, symbolized Canada's independent nationhood.

In Canadian-U.S. affairs, meetings between Prime Minister Pearson and Pres. Lyndon B. Johnson led to the formation of a joint commission to study the relationships of the two nations and the negotiation of new trade agreements.

Centennial. As Canada celebrated the centennial year of confederation in 1967 with "Expo '67," a world's fair at Montreal, it maintained its position as a middle power in the world and was experiencing tremendous prosperity at home. But many of the same problems that had plagued the nation since its earliest years remained unsolved.

Conflict between French-speaking and English-speaking citizens still smoldered, and a small group of separatists even argued for an independent French-speaking state. The conflict was aggravated in 1967 by France's Pres. Charles de Gaulle's open support for a "free Quebec." Nonetheless, in 1968 a French Canadian, Pierre Elliot Trudeau, was chosen to succeed retiring Prime Minister Pearson.

The relationship between the federal government and the provinces also remained a matter of dispute. Various new proposals were put forth for increasing government services to the poorer provinces without restricting their provincial rights. At the same time, the wealthier western provinces objected to some of the more progressive federal activities in the provinces and turned to conservative leaders.

Canadians still feared domination by the U.S. dollar, and businessmen and politicians debated the effects of foreign investment and U.S. economic influence. But they conceded the contribution of U.S. investment to Canadian prosperity.

Despite its unresolved problems, Canada continued the struggle to maintain its independent existence and to forge a unique, Canadian national identity.

—Peter Oliver; Wilbur Zelinsky

CENTRAL AFRICAN REPUBLIC

Official name: Central African Republic
Area: 239,534 square miles
Population: (1967 est.) 1,459,000
Capital: Bangui (Pop., 1964, urban area, 126,602)
Language: French, Sangho and other African languages
Religion: traditional religions
Currency unit: Franc CFA (African Financial Community)
National holiday: Independence day, December 1

The Central African Republic, a landlocked country in central Africa, is bounded on the north by Chad, on the east by Sudan, on the south by the Congo (Kinshasa) and the Congo (Brazzaville), and on the west by Cameroon. Before receiving its independence from France in 1960, the territory was known as Ubangi-Shari because of its location near the Ubangi and Shari (Chari) rivers.

THE LAND. The Central African Republic lies on a plateau with an average elevation of 2,000 feet above sea level. In the east are mountains with heights ranging up to almost 4,600 feet. There are forests in the south, but savanna woodlands and grasslands cover most of the country. Tributaries of the Shari River, in the north, and of the Ubangi River, to the south, flow through the country.

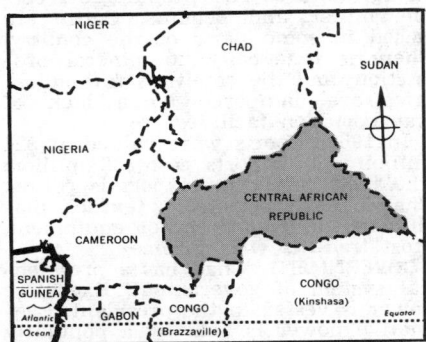

Because of the altitude, the climate is quite mild. Temperatures average between 70°F and 80°F.

THE PEOPLE. The Central African Republic is a sparsely populated country inhabited by peoples of the Mandjia-Baya, Banda, M'Baka, and Zande tribes. The people are mostly farmers. A few thousand Europeans live in Bangui and in other smaller towns.

ECONOMY. The Central African Republic traditionally has been an agricultural country. The main crops are cassava, cotton, and coffee. In the early 1960s diamond mining became important, and by 1965 diamonds accounted for half of the country's exports.

In 1966 imports were valued at $35 million and exports earned $31 million. The Central African Republic is a member of a customs union that includes Cameroon, Chad, the Congo (Brazzaville), and Gabon.

GOVERNMENT. Until 1966 the Central African Republic had a presidential form of government. The president was elected by universal suffrage to a seven-year term of office. Legislative power was vested in a popularly elected, 50-member National Assembly. In 1966 army officers seized control, overthrew the president, and abolished the National Assembly.

The Central African Republic is a member of the United Nations and of the Organization of African Unity (OAU).

HISTORY. Little is known of the early history of the present-day Central African Republic. The French entered the region in the mid-1800s and gave it the name Ubangi-Shari. They met with little opposition from the tribesmen who live there.

In 1899 France permitted private companies to develop the region. Company abuses led to loss of life from forced labor and disease, and loss of capital because of inefficient management. In 1910 France united Ubangi-Shari with present-day Chad, the Congo (Brazzaville), and Gabon in the Federation of French Equatorial Africa.

In 1946 France reorganized the administration and introduced territorial assemblies. Barthelemy Boganda, a political leader in Ubangi-Shari, created the Movement for the Social Evolution of Black Africa (MESAN). Boganda was elected to the territorial assembly in 1952, and by 1956 MESAN had won all the seats in the territorial assembly.

Ubangi-Shari voted to join the French Community in 1958 as an individual member, thus ending the federation of Equatorial Africa. Boganda became the nation's first premier. Ubangi-Shari changed its name to the Central African Republic. Boganda was killed in an airplane crash in 1959, and the assembly elected Boganda's cousin and political associate, David Dacko, president of the republic. Complete independence came on Aug. 13, 1960. Dacko dissolved all opposition parties in 1962, leaving MESAN the sole legal political party.

In 1966, the army chief of staff, Col. Jean Bedel Bokassa, deposed Dacko and assumed the position of chief of state.
—Hibberd V. B. Kline, Jr.; Vera L. Zolberg

CEYLON

Official name: Dominion of Ceylon
Area: 25,332 square miles
Population: (1966 est.) 11,491,000
Capital: Colombo (Pop., 1963, 510,947)
Language: Sinhalese, Tamil, English
Religion: Buddhism, Hinduism
Currency unit: Rupee
National holiday: Independence day, February 4

Ceylon is an island nation lying off the southeastern tip of India. It is separated from India by the Gulf of Mannar and Palk Strait. The Bay of Bengal lies off Ceylon's east coast, and the Indian Ocean lies to the south.

THE LAND. Ceylon's coastline is low and sandy except for the area around the Jaffna Peninsula, in the north, and at Trincomalee, in the east. Both have excellent natural harbors. In the interior of southern Ceylon, mountainous highlands rise from the coastal plain to a peak of over 8,000 feet. The north is largely a flat plain with an elevation only slightly above sea level.

Ceylon has a tropical climate, with average year-round temperatures ranging between 80°F and 100°F. It is cooler in the mountains. Humidity is high throughout the country, but especially in the southwest, where as much as 200 inches of rain a year may fall. About 50 inches falls yearly on the rest of the country.

THE PEOPLE. More than two-thirds of the people of Ceylon are Sinhalese, and speak Sinhalese, an Indic language. Most are Buddhist. Almost one-quarter of the people are Tamils, a people of southern Indian origin who speak Tamil, a Dravidian language. Most Tamils are Hindus. The Tamils are divided between "Ceylon Tamils," those who have been Ceylonese for many generations, and "Indian Tamils," the descendants of Indian laborers brought to the island in the 1800s.

Smaller minorities include Muslim Arabs, "Burghers"—descendants of Dutch colonists, Eurasians, Muslim Malays, and Veddas, descendants of the island's first settlers. Relations among the various groups have not always been good, and there have been bitter conflicts between the Sinhalese and the Tamils.

The population is concentrated in the southwestern corner of the island and in places along the coasts. The population is growing at a rapid rate, 2.6 percent a year between 1958 and 1965.

ECONOMY. Ceylon's economy is based almost completely on agriculture, and the soil is Ceylon's most important natural resource. There are deposits of graphite and precious gems. The leading crops, tea, rubber, coconuts, and spices, are grown on large plantations. Tea is grown in the highlands, rubber in the wet lowlands, and coconuts in drier coastal regions. Small farms produce rice and vegetables. Fish are abundant off the coasts.

Ceylon's few industries are mainly concerned with processing tea, rubber, and coconuts. Manufacturing increased during the 1960s, and there are factories producing textiles, cement, soap, and other consumer items. In 1967 construction began on an oil refinery.

UNITED NATIONS

PICKING TEA IN CEYLON. Tea is one of Ceylon's major crops and an important export.

Ceylon relies heavily on foreign trade for many commodities. In 1966 its exports earned $357 million and its imports cost $426 million. Tea, rubber, and coconut products make up more than 90 percent of exports. The major imports include foodstuffs, petroleum products, fertilizers, textiles, and machinery. Ceylon trades mainly with India, Britain, the United States, and China. Technical and financial aid from the United States, Britain, and west and east European countries is important to Ceylon.

GOVERNMENT. Ceylon has a parliamentary system of government. The British monarch is head of state, and is represented in Ceylon by a governor-general. Actual executive power is wielded by a prime minister and cabinet responsible to parliament. Ceylon's parliament has two houses. Members of the lower house are popularly elected. The upper house is partly appointed by the governor-general and partly elected by the lower house.

Ceylon is a member of the United Nations and of the Commonwealth of Nations.

HISTORY. Ceylon's first known inhabitants were a primitive people, the Veddas. In the 500s BC they were conquered by the Sinhalese, an Aryan people from northern India. The Sinhalese established a kingdom in the north central portion of the island, constructing irrigation works to enable them to grow rice in the dry region. By the 200s BC Sinhalese civilization was quite advanced, and its culture, centered on Buddhism, had produced many magnificent temples, especially in the capital at Anuradhapura.

The kingdom was subjected to repeated attacks and invasions by peoples from southern India, and it was conquered in the 900s AD by the Chola empire. The Chola were driven out in the 1000s, but some Chola cultural influences remained. During the 1000s Arab traders began to stop at Ceylon, and some settled on the island.

Between the 1200s and the 1400s the island was attacked repeatedly by Malay and Chinese adventurers, as well as by Indians. In the 1300s the Hindu Tamil people of southern India invaded Ceylon and settled in the northern part of the island, forcing the Sinhalese to the south.

European Influence. In the 1500s Portuguese traders arrived in Ceylon, drawn by the high quality of the cinnamon that the islanders grew. They destroyed the Tamil kingdom and established control over the coastal regions of Sinhalese territory. The Sinhalese retreated to the highland interior, around Kandy. In 1638 traders of the Dutch East India Company arrived.

By 1658, aided by the king of Kandy, the Dutch had driven out the Portuguese and taken over the spice trade. The Dutch exerted little control over the island's government. During the 1600s and 1700s the Sinhalese Kingdom of Kandy underwent a cultural revival and grew in power, controlling some smaller islands in the Indian Ocean.

In 1796 the British replaced the Dutch in the coastal areas, and in 1802 made them a crown colony. By 1815, with the aid of some of the Kandyans, the British took control of the entire island, including Kandy. The British expanded the area of cultivated land, planted tea and rubber, and improved irrigation facilities in the drier north. They established schools and introduced Western forms of government.

In 1931 Ceylon was granted limited self-government. Parliamentary elections were held in 1947, and on Feb. 4, 1948, Ceylon was granted sovereignty as an independent member of the Commonwealth of Nations.

Independence. Independent Ceylon concentrated on developing its economy and improving the lot of its people through social welfare programs. From the mid-1950s to the mid-1960s Ceylonese politics were dominated by the socialist Sri Lanka Freedom Party (SLFP). S. W. R. D. Bandaranaike, leader of the SLFP, was prime minister from 1956 until his assassination in 1959. Under his widow, who became prime minister in 1960, the country followed strongly socialist policies, and many businesses were nationalized. The government's methods were unpopular, and it fell in 1964.

Under the more moderate United National Party (UNP) elected in 1965, the socialist program continued, but encouragement was given to private business in an effort to speed economic growth. The UNP government con-

centrated on uniting the many factions of Ceylon's society.

Rioting broke out in 1966 when the government introduced legislation permitting the official use of the Tamil language in Tamil areas, but the legislation was passed. A graver problem, the citizenship of Indian Tamils, was resolved in 1967, when an agreement was ratified by which India agreed to repatriate some Indian Tamils and Ceylon agreed to grant citizenship to the rest.

—Thomas E. Ennis; M. G. Inaba

CHAD

Official name: Republic of Chad
Area: 495,752 square miles
Population: (1966 est.) 3,361,000
Capital: Fort-Lamy (Pop., 1964 est., urban area, 99,000)
Language: French, Arabic, Sara
Religion: Christianity, Islam, traditional religions
Currency unit: Franc CFA (African Financial Community)
National holiday: Independence day, January 11

Chad, a large, landlocked republic in central Africa, is bounded on the north by Libya, on the east by Sudan, on the south by the Central African Republic and Cameroon, and on the west by Nigeria and Niger. The country derives its name from Lake Chad, which is located on its western border.

THE LAND. Most of Chad is a vast plain. The northern region of the country forms part of the Sahara. Grasslands cover central and southern Chad. The country's lowest point is the dry Bodele Depression, in north-central Chad. In the extreme north is the Tibasti Massif, with elevations of about 11,000 feet. The country's most important rivers are the Shari and the Logone.

Northern Chad is hot and dry and receives less than 10 inches of rain a year. The climate in the south is more tropical, and rainfall averages about 40 inches a year.

THE PEOPLE. Chad is a sparsely populated country. The composition of Chad's population differs in each part of the country. Arabs and Hamitic people live in the north. People of the Sara tribe, the largest tribal group in Chad, live in the south.

Most of the people are either farmers or herdsmen. Chad's major cities are concentrated in the southern part of the country. They include Fort-Lamy, the capital, and Moundou.

ECONOMY. Chad's economy depends on agriculture. The people grow cotton, millet, and peanuts. Cattle are raised in some parts of the country. There is practically no mineral production, and the country's few industries are hampered by a lack of transportation facilities.

In 1966 exports were valued at $24 million and imports cost $32 million. The most important export is cotton. Chad imports petroleum, textiles, machinery, and transportation equipment. Most trade is with France.

GOVERNMENT. Chad has a presidential system of government. Executive power is vested in the president. Legislative power is held by a popularly elected National Assembly. The National Assembly votes on the presidential candidate proposed by the country's sole legal political party, the Chad Progressive Party. The people then vote for or against the candidate. The president holds office for an indefinite term.

Chad is a member of the United Nations and of the Organization of African Unity (OAU).

HISTORY. The area that is now Chad was for many centuries an important crossroads. From about 200 BC to AD 1000, its inhabitants maintained close contacts with the peoples of the Nile Valley, with whom they shared a fairly similar culture.

Christianity flourished in central Chad in about 300 AD. Later, nomadic peoples from Darfur, in Sudan, overran Chad, dispersed the indigenous inhabitants, and created an empire known as Kanem in the region near Lake Chad. In the 1000s Islam penetrated the area. From about that time the peoples of Chad strengthened their commercial ties with the Mediterranean coast.

In the period from about 1000 to 1600 there were a number of violent internal and foreign wars. As a result of those conflicts, the Kanem empire moved its center to Bornu, on the southwestern side of Lake Chad in what is now northern Nigeria.

Both the sultanate of Bagirmi and the Wadai empire became powerful in Chad, and maintained their control until the late 1800s. At that time Rabeh, a warlord and slave trader from Sudan, gained control of Chad.

The French, who had established themselves in Chad in the 1890s, defeated Rabeh in 1900 and proceeded to conquer all of Chad. The present boundaries of Chad were established in 1913, and in 1920 Chad became a member of the Federation of French Equatorial Africa.

During World War II Chad supported Free France and contained important Allied bases. Postwar politics were at first largely controlled by the French. After 1958, however, African leaders rapidly gained prominence. France gave Chad its independence in August 1960, and François Tombalbaye became the country's first president.

—Hibberd V. B. Kline, Jr.; Robert I. Rotberg

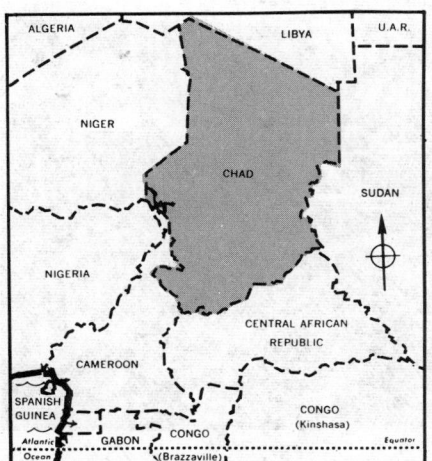

CHILE

Official name: Republic of Chile
Area: 292,256 square miles
Population: (1966 est.) 8,750,000
Capital: Santiago (Pop., 1965 est., urban area, 2,248,400)
Language: Spanish
Religion: Roman Catholicism
Currency unit: Escudo
National holiday: Independence day, September 18

Chile is a long, narrow country on the western coast of South America. It stretches 2,650 miles from north to south, but averages only 100 miles in width. The country has imposing natural boundaries. On the north the Atacama Desert separates Chile from Peru; on the northeast and east the Andes separate the country from Bolivia and Argentina; on the south the Drake Passage separates Chile from Antarctica; and on the west is the Pacific Ocean.

THE LAND. The highest mountain in the western hemisphere, Mt. Aconcagua (22,834 feet), lies on the Chile-Argentina border. The Chilean Andes form a single mountain range in the east, and there is a low coastal mountain range in the west. A central valley nearly 500 miles long nestles between the two parallel ranges.

Northern Chile, the desert region, is very dry, and there are weather stations there that have no record of rain ever having fallen. The region has rich mineral resources. The central valley has a mild climate, with a winter rainy season and summer drought. It is the heartland of the country. Almost 90 percent of the people live there, and it produces most of the country's domestic food supply.

Southern Chile is wet and heavily forested. The land is said to resemble Switzerland because of its high, snow-capped mountains and glacial lakes. Temperatures average in the low 50's F. In the extreme south, at the end of the continent, are Patagonia and Tierra del Fuego. The area has steep slopes, heavy rainfall, low temperatures, and high winds. It is very sparsely populated.

THE PEOPLE. Approximately 25 percent of Chile's population is of European descent. Most of the rest is mestizo, of mixed Spanish and Indian heritage.

About 100,000 Araucanian Indians live in the forests of south-central Chile. Changos live along the northeastern frontier and are employed in the mines. Groups of nomadic Fuegians inhabit Tierra del Fuego.

A dominant trend in Chile is the movement of people from the rural areas to the urban centers. The capital, Santiago, has sizable suburbs, as does Valparaiso, the principal port, which had a 1964 population of over 270,000. The country's third major city is Concepción, located in the center of Chile on the Bío-Bío River. Smaller cities such as Talcahuano, Puerto Montt, and Punta Arenas, the most southerly city, are important ports.

ECONOMY. Chile is largely dependent on the exploitation of its mineral resources, which are found primarily within the Atacama Desert. In 1965,

for example, copper, iron ore, and nitrates made up four-fifths of the total value of Chilean exports.

Chile has long been a world leader in copper and nitrate production, but in the early 1960s iron ore replaced nitrates as the country's second most important export. In 1965 Chile ranked third in world copper production and tenth in the production of iron ore. Iodine, a by-product of nitrate, has also become an important export, and by the mid-1960s Chile was producing 75 percent of the world's supply.

Agreements with foreign mining companies provide for a portion of the profits to remain in Chile, and the income has aided the development of the entire economy.

Only a fraction of Chile's total land area is suitable for cultivation, and only a small part of that is used. Chile's Central Valley is the main agricultural region. The principal crops are wheat, barley, and oats. Livestock raising is also important, but neither cattle nor crop production is adequate for Chile's needs, and foodstuffs must be imported.

Chile is one of the most industrialized countries in South America. The Huachipato steel plant, inaugurated in 1951, meets almost all Chile's requirements. Chile also manufactures a variety of consumer goods for domestic consumption including textiles, medicines, shoes, paper, and cement. Major industrial centers are in the provinces of Santiago, Valparaiso, and Concepción.

In 1966 Chile's exports were valued at $878 million and imports cost $755 million. Major exports are copper, iron ore, nitrates and iodine, fish meal, beans, lentils, wool, and paper. Principal imports include industrial raw materials, industrial and agricultural machinery and equipment, vehicles, petroleum, and consumer goods.

Most exports go to the United States, Britain, West Germany, the Netherlands, and Japan. Imports come largely from the United States, Argentina, West Germany, and Britain.

GOVERNMENT. Chile is a republic with a strong tradition of constitutional government. The head of state and chief executive is the president, who is popularly elected to a term of six years and is not eligible for reelection.

Legislative power is vested in the National Congress, which consists of a Senate and Chamber of Deputies. The Senate has 45 members, but the number of members of the Chamber of Deputies, which is based on the size of the population, varies. Senators and Deputies are directly elected, senators to a term of eight years and deputies to a term of four years.

Chile is a member of the United Nations and the Organization of American States (OAS).

HISTORY. During the 1400s, the northern part of Chile had come under the influence of the Inca empire. The extent of Inca control is not known, but it did not extend to the warlike Araucanian Indians who lived in the southern forest region. The Spaniards, under Pedro de Valdivia, conquered Chile in 1541 but were unable to defeat the Araucanians, who were not completely subdued until the late 1800s.

In the more open central portion of Chile Spain created a stable agricultural colony, and Chile was part of the Viceroyalty of Peru until the 1800s.

The first move toward independence was made in September 1810, when Chileans established an autonomous junta to rule during the absence of the Spanish king, Ferdinand VII, who was held prisoner by Napoleon. The patriot regime was suppressed in 1814 by loyalist forces from Peru.

The Spanish were finally defeated in 1817–1818 by the army of José de San Martín, which crossed the Andes from Argentina. San Martín's Chilean comrade-in-arms, Bernardo O'Higgins, was made provisional ruler of Chile with the title of Supreme Director.

Independence. O'Higgins gave Chile a generally sound and progressive administration. Nonetheless, he antagonized Chile's powerful class of wealthy landowners by his efforts at mild social reform and his concentration of authority in his own hands. In 1823 he was forced to resign. Chile was then plunged into a brief period of turmoil during which rival political factions battled for control.

In 1830 the Conservatives came to power under the leadership of Diego Portales. Although he never assumed the presidency, Portales nonetheless created a strong centralized government while holding various cabinet posts. Portales was assassinated in 1837 while organizing a military campaign against a confederation of Peru and Bolivia, which he believed posed a threat to Chile. Chile won the war and broke the confederation in 1839.

An Era of Growth. From the 1840s through the 1880s, Chile made notable social and material progress, although those who benefited most were the upper and middle classes. Educational facilities were expanded, religious toleration and the abolition of entailed estates were peacefully achieved. Economic development was aided by the extension of railway and coastal steam navigation, and by the final subjugation of the Araucanians.

From 1879 to 1883 Chile fought Bolivia and Peru in the War of the Pacific, which began as a dispute over Bolivia's treatment of Chilean nitrate interests in the Atacama region. Chile won the war and annexed the nitrate-producing provinces of Peru and Bolivia. A Chilean nitrate boom followed and lasted until the development of synthetic nitrates during World War I.

Commerce, manufacturing, and coal and copper mining grew during the same period. This progress was accompanied by the rapid growth of an urban and mining proletariat, whose poor working conditions led to serious unrest in the early 1900s.

Call for Reforms. Chile had moved toward a system of constitutional rule in which the legislative branch established its supremacy over the executive. Confirmation of this trend was assured by a civil war in 1891, in which an attempt by Pres. José Manuel Balmaceda to reassert presidential authority was defeated. Congress was controlled by parties representing the landed aristocracy and the allied urban upper class, and little was done to improve the conditions of Chilean labor.

Chile remained neutral during World War I. The economy was stimulated by the wartime need for nitrates, but was badly hurt when prices dropped after peace was declared. Social and political dissatisfaction on the part of the middle and working classes increased and resulted in the election in 1920 of Arturo Alessandri, who had run on an ambitious reform platform. Once in office, however, Alessandri had little success in carrying out his program and was forced to resign.

From 1924 to 1932 constitutional government was severely shaken. There were numerous changes of administration and even a mild dictatorship from 1927–1931 under reform-minded Gen. Cárlos Ibañez. Nevertheless, Chile emerged from this period of turmoil with a start in labor legislation and a new constitution designed to end congressional domination of the executive.

Alessandri, allied with both Conservatives and Liberals, returned to the presidency in 1932 and successfully restored the pattern of constitutional government. He was succeeded in 1938 by Pedro Aguirre Cedra, whose Popular Front administration drew support from both socialists and communists, although Aguirre Cedra himself was from the generally moderate Radical party.

The Popular Front sponsored additional benefits for labor, including government medical programs and low-cost housing. It collapsed during World War II, and for the following 20 years Chile was ruled by a succession of middle-of-the-road and right-of-center administrations.

Contemporary Chile. Despite a high degree of political freedom and stability, and a seemingly impressive body of social legislation, Chile still had not really solved its social problems. Almost nothing had been done for the landless rural masses, and the standard of living of urban workers did not keep pace with overall national economic gains.

Persistent inflation became a major problem, and in the late 1950s a vigorous socialist-communist alliance showed signs of growing political strength. This was counterbalanced by the rapid rise of the Christian Democratic Party, which called for fundamental changes in social structure—including land redistribution—while rejecting both communism and traditional capitalism.

The Christian Democrats finally gained power in 1964, when their leader, Eduardo Frei Montalva, was elected president. Frei set about effecting basic changes in Chile's economic and social life under the slogan "revolution within liberty and law." His program called for part ownership by the government of the copper mines and included a broad agrarian reform program.

—David Bushnell; Kempton E. Webb

UNITED NATIONS

CHILEAN STEEL PLANT at Talcahuano, near the important industrial city of Concepción.

LOOK MAGAZINE

CHINESE SAMPANS dock in the harbor at Shanghai, near modern office buildings.

LOOK MAGAZINE

AGRICULTURE IN COMMUNIST CHINA still depends heavily on human labor. Despite the country's rapid industrialization, agriculture remains the prime factor in the economy.

CHINA

COMMUNIST CHINA

Official name: People's Republic of China
Area: 3,692,000 square miles
Population: (1966 est.) 710,000,000
Capital: Peking (Pop., 1957 est., 4,010,000)
Language: Chinese
Currency unit: Yuan

NATIONALIST CHINA

Official name: Republic of China
Area: 13,886 square miles
Population: (1967 est.) 13,142,000
Capital: Taipei (Pop., 1964 est., 1,085,100)
Language: Chinese
Currency unit: New Taiwan dollar
National holiday: National Day, October 10

China, an ancient land of East Asia, is one of the world's largest nations and contains nearly one quarter of the world's people. Since 1949 two governments have claimed to represent China's people—one, the People's Republic of China, a communist state controlling the mainland of China; and the other, the Republic of China, occupying Taiwan, or Formosa, an island off the mainland's east coast.

The Republic of China, or Nationalist China, is recognized as the legal government of China by the United States and represents China in the United Nations. The People's Republic of China, called Communist China or Mainland China, is recognized by the Soviet Union and the world's communist-ruled nations as well as by many other countries, including Britain and France.

Mainland China is bounded on the north by the Mongolian People's Republic and the Soviet Union; on the east by North Korea, the Yellow Sea, the East China Sea, and the Formosa Strait; on the south by British Hong Kong and Portuguese Macao, the South China Sea, North Vietnam, Laos, Burma, India, Bhutan, Sikkim, and Nepal; and on the west by India, Pakistan, Afghanistan, and the Soviet Union. Many of the boundaries are disputed. The large island of Hainan off China's southern coast is controlled by the mainland.

The Republic of China, on Taiwan, is bordered on the north by the East China Sea, on the east by the Philippine Sea, on the south by the South China Sea, and on the west by the Formosa Strait. The P'enghu archipelago (the Pescadores Islands) in the Formosa Strait are controlled by the republic.

THE LAND. China is an immense country, and only the Soviet Union and Canada are larger in area. Mainland China's length from east to west is approximately the same as that of the United States, and its range from north to south is equivalent to that from Puerto Rico to Labrador.

China's 4,000-mile-long coastline is deeply indented and dotted with small islands. The North China coast is flat and shallow, the South China coast is steep and rocky. The North China coast has few harbors, but there are many good harbors along the south coast.

The huge area of Mainland China is divided into 21 provinces, five autonomous nationality regions, and two municipalities—Peking, the capital, and Shanghai. The autonomous regions are more than administrative units. Each of the five—Kwangsi-Chuang, Tibet, Sinkiang-Uighur, Ningsia-Hui, and Inner Mongolia—contains a majority of non-Chinese people, and each has a history and culture different from China's.

Nor are the provinces merely administrative subdivisions. There is a cultural connotation to the units, which have recognizable dialects, if not individual languages, and customs, social patterns, and traditions, within the larger framework of Chinese culture. Identification with provincial birthplace and the banding together of provincial compatriots have long characterized Chinese society.

Regions. Geographically, it is conventional to divide Mainland China into five regions—China Proper, Manchuria, Tibet, Sinkiang, and Mongolia. China Proper, the region south of the Great Wall and east of Tibet, occupies a third of the land. It is the geographical and historical core of the country, containing the bulk of the population and the roots of Chinese civilization.

The other four regions comprise what is often called Outer China. Manchuria, northeast of China Proper, is more sparsely populated and contains rich mineral deposits. Tibet, in the southwest, lies high in the Himalayas and has a very small population. Sinkiang, in the northwest, is arid and inhabited mainly by Uighur peoples. The Mongolian region, Inner Mongolia, north of China Proper, is arid and peopled primarily by Mongols.

Uplands. Highlands dominate China's terrain. High mountains thrusting eastward from the southwest include the Himalayas and their foothills, the Thanglha Ri, the Kunlun, the Astin Tagh, and the Nan Shan, with many peaks over 20,000 feet.

These mountain systems and the high, barren plateau of Tibet in their center form the world's most formidable land barrier, separating the Hindu civilization of South Asia from the Chinese civilization of East Asia. The eastern edge of these mountains also contains the sources of China's two great rivers, the Yangtze and the Hwang Ho, the Yellow River.

Between this mountainous mass and a northern spur, the towering Tien Shan in Sinkiang, is the Takla Makan, a desert lying about 8,000 feet above sea level. The center of the Dzungarian Basin in northern Sinkiang is also desert, separating the Tien Shan from the Altai mountains, which mark the Sinkiang-Soviet-Mongolian border.

Arid, flat or rolling highlands continue across the northern rim of China. They include the Alashan desert, bordered on the south and east by the

Ala mountains; the Ordos desert, east of the Alashan desert; and the eastern fringe of the Gobi desert, bounded on the east by the Greater Khingan range, which marks the western edge of Manchuria.

South and east of these barriers of towering mountains and barren deserts, China Proper and Manchuria are crisscrossed by less formidable highlands that follow two major sets of intersecting structural areas, one trending northeast to southwest and the other intersecting it from east to west.

The northeast-southwest axis is marked in the east by the Fukien Massif of hills along the southeast coast, the rounded mountains of the Shantung and Liaotung peninsulas, and the Manchurian highlands bordering Korea in the northeast. The central portion of this axis is formed by the Greater Khingan range in Manchuria and the Wut'ai and Luya ranges in Shansi province further south.

This line is a major physical and cultural division of eastern Asia. To the west of it elevations are from 3,000 to 6,000 feet higher than to its east. The west is arid, the east is humid; the western economy is based upon pastoral activities, the eastern on sedentary agriculture. Following the axis west of this core section are the Ala Shan.

The series of east-west trending chains is represented at the far north by the Lesser Khingan mountains, at the southern edge of Mongolia by the Yin Shan, and in the far south by the Nan Ling mountains, a series of hills and low mountains between the Yangtze and the Hsi rivers. By far the most important mountains of the east-west axis are those of the Ch'in Ling, which bisect China Proper.

The Ch'in Ling has a physical and cultural significance similar to that of the north-south Khingan divide. South China, below these mountains, is generally warm and humid whereas north China tends to be cold and dry.

Lowlands. China's few major lowlands and plateaus lie in China Proper and Manchuria, among the intersecting lines of highlands. In the northeast the Manchurian Plain, about 130,000 square miles in area, is bounded by the Khingan mountains, the East Manchurian Highlands, and the Gulf of Liaotung. It is drained by the Sungari River in the north and the Liao River in the south. Its grasslands contain some of China's most fertile soils.

The flat and fertile North China Plain, also about 130,000 square miles in area, is essentially a giant compound delta of the Hwang, the Huai, and the Yangtze rivers. The loess plateau is a dissected region in North China. About 120,000 of its 200,000 square miles is covered with loess, a deep layer of loose dust and silt. It is watered by the Hwang Ho, to which its dust imparts a yellow color.

The 100,000-square-mile Yangtze Basin contains lakes Tungt'ing and P'oyang, which serve as natural reservoirs for the Yangtze River. The basin is rich with alluvial soils. The mountain-ringed Szechwan basin on the upper Yangtze River includes about 75,000 square miles of rolling terrain.

The most important region in south China, the Canton lowlands, is the compound delta of the Hsi, Pei, and Pearl rivers, bordering on the South China Sea. Although only some 3,000 square miles in area, it is a key agricultural, industrial, and commercial center.

Rivers. Almost all of China's rivers, which are concentrated in the eastern portion of the country, flow east or south toward the sea. The most important in the south is the Hsi, formed by the Yu, the Li, and other streams flowing from the eastern Tibetan foothills.

The Yangtze rises in the east Kunlun mountains and twists some 3,200 miles through south-central China, passing through deeply etched gorges in Szechwan and emptying into the East China Sea at Shanghai.

The Hwang Ho rises near the Yangtze and flows north along a winding course, making a great bend northward around the Ordos desert and on eastward between Shansi and Honan provinces. It empties into the Gulf of Chihli, an inlet of the Yellow Sea.

Both the Huang and the Yangtze are subject to frequent and vicious floods and sudden changes of course, but both supply the water and the soil to raise food for the huge concentration of people in their valleys.

Climate. Most of Mainland China lies within the temperate zone, but the climate varies greatly from region to region. Manchuria has a subhumid continental type of climate. Winters there are long and severe. A mild growing season lasts for about 5 months, and rainfall is generally less than 20 inches a year.

Northwestern China, the region bordering Mongolia, has a semi-arid to arid climate. Precipitation is under 20 inches a year and frequently less than 10 inches. Winters are long and severe, and the growing season is less than 200 days.

North China, the southern portions of Manchuria, the loess highlands, and the northern half of the North China Plain form a transitional region between the arid continental north and the humid subtropical south. The growing season ranges from 150 to 225 days, and the annual precipitation averages 15 to 30 inches.

Within the Yangtze lake region and the delta of the Yangtze Basin, the summers are hot and humid and the winters are generally mild. The frost-free period is 225 to 280 days. Precipitation averages 45 to 80 inches a year with the peak rainy period in June and July.

South China, except in its higher elevations, is a warm and humid region. The frost-free period is 300 to 365 days. There is no dry period, and average annual precipitation varies from 50 to 80 inches. Along the coast typhoons bring high winds and heavy downpours from July to October. In the far south, including Hainan Island, the climate tends toward the tropical.

Climatic conditions in southwest China are intermediate between those of subtropical China and Tibet. Temperatures are generally mild. Precipitation ranges from 40 to 60 inches a year, with the peak period coming during the summer season.

Much of Tibet above 16,000 foot elevations has a tundra-type climate with less than 4 inches of precipitation yearly. Temperatures average about 10°F in January and 45°F in July.

Large parts of Sinkiang and Mongolia are occupied by midlatitude continental deserts. Precipitation is extremely limited, and many areas in the two regions receive less than 5 inches of rain a year.

Taiwan. Nationalist China's island of Taiwan is also mountainous. Its major range, the Chungyang, runs from north to south in the eastern third of the island. It contains many peaks over 10,000 feet high, and its highest peak, Yü Shan, is more than 13,000 feet high. To the east, across a narrow rift valley, a coastal range rises to a maximum of 7,000 feet and then drops sharply into the sea. Many rivers flow east and west from the Chungyang.

To the west of the mountains the land slopes to a fertile coastal plain that is the heartland of the island. It is only some 25 miles at its widest, but its width is being extended by continuous sedimentation along the shallow west coast. The west coast contains the island's best harbors.

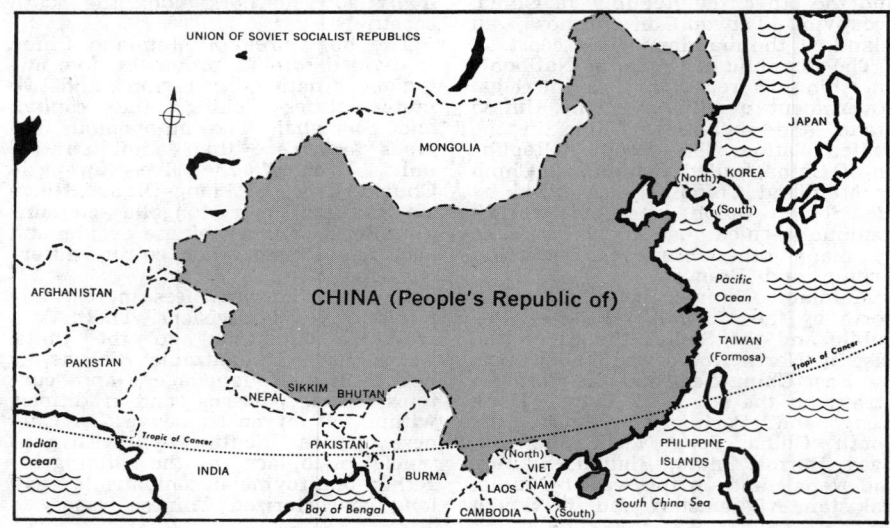

Taiwan's climate is semitropical. Annual precipitation varies from 50 inches in the mountains to 200 inches on the coasts. During winter, from October to April, north to northeast winds bring much rain to the northern areas. In summer, the winds are chiefly from the south and southwest, and it is during this period that most of the south receives its maximum rain. From May to November, the island may be struck by typhoons.

Temperatures in the lowlands rarely drop below 60°F. The higher elevations are colder, and the higher peaks have prolonged snow cover.

THE PEOPLE. With a 1966 population estimated by the United Nations at 710 million and by the U.S. census bureau at between 760 and 894 million, Communist China contains approximately one-quarter of the world's people. Its rate of population growth was estimated by the UN at 1.5 percent a year in the 1950s and 1960s, representing a tremendous numerical increase each year.

About 90 percent of the people live in the eastern third of China, where population density averages more than 500 people per square mile. Over the years, many thousands of Chinese have emigrated, largely from South China, and formed large communities in Southeast Asia and elsewhere throughout the world.

Although many ethnic groups make up China's population, more than 90 percent of the people are of the Han group, the people commonly considered "Chinese." The Han have great cultural unity and share the same written language, but they speak innumerable regional dialects of Chinese.

The Cantonese dialect, for example, is widely spoken in the south, and the Peking dialect, or Mandarin, is the national language (*Kuo-Yü*) and is taught in the schools throughout China. Most people adhere to a Chinese religious pattern that is a combination of Buddhism, Taoism, Confucianism, and animism.

About 6 percent of China's people are non-Han Chinese. They belong to more than 50 different ethnic groups that live in the areas surrounding China Proper. The Chuang, a Thai-speaking people in southeastern China, are the largest minority. The Yi, also in the south, is another large group. Along the western and northwestern frontiers Tibetans, Uighurs, and Mongols are in the majority, and the Manchu peoples, related to the Mongols, are concentrated in the northeast.

Taiwan. Taiwan was settled by Chinese from Fukien and Kwantung provinces during the period from the 1600s to the 1900s. There was a large influx of people from all parts of the mainland in the late 1940s and early 1950s. There are also small numbers of aborigines who come from Polynesian stock.

Taiwan is densely populated, with over 900 people per square mile in 1966. A very high rate of population growth slowed to a still rapid 3.4 percent a year increase between 1958 and 1965.

ECONOMY. China has traditionally been an agricultural land, and this remains true for Mainland China despite considerable industrialization since the advent of the communist regime in 1949.

Natural Resources. Exploration and development of the mainland's mineral resources was not undertaken on a large scale until the 1950s and 1960s. The country has oil, iron ore, and coal in Manchuria, Sinkiang, and in the central Yangtze basin.

There are also large supplies of tungsten, antimony, manganese, tin, bauxite, copper, mercury, molybdenum, lead, and zinc. Magnesite, sulfur, bismuth, mica, and graphite deposits are also worked, mostly in Manchuria. The extent of mineral resources in remote regions is unknown.

Agriculture. Farming occupies about 80 percent of the population, and in 1965 agriculture contributed one-half of the national product. The poor climate, rough terrain, and inadequate soils or water prohibit farming in much of China. With an estimated 270 million acres, or about 11 percent of China's total area, under cultivation, there is less than half an acre of farm land per person.

The major growing regions are in Manchuria, the North China Plain, the Lower Yangtze basin and delta, the Szechwan basin, the Wei and Fen river valleys, the Han river valley, the Canton delta, and the lower Hsi valley. Most of these are both dependent upon floods for soil and water and endangered by heavy flooding.

During the 1950s the communist government initiated a program of total collectivization of agriculture. Most farm households were organized into communes, and private property was virtually eliminated. The project was a failure, however, and in the early 1960s most of China's peasant farmers had returned to more traditional patterns of living. China's farmers remained organized into local cooperatives, however.

The chief crops are wheat, raised chiefly in North China and Manchuria, and rice, grown mainly in the Yangtze basin and South China. Other important crops include barley, millet, kaoliang, soybeans, cotton, tobacco, and tea. There is little livestock raising, but there is some fishing off the coasts and in the rivers.

Industry. The communist regime of Mainland China has emphasized the development of heavy industry and transportation, and by 1965 industry contributed an estimated 26 percent of the national product of Communist China. China's traditional industries, such as textiles, continued to play an important role in the economy.

Industrial development advanced rapidly in the 1950s with financial and technical aid from the Soviet Union. But attempts to move ahead too rapidly created serious problems in the late 1950s. The economy had recovered by the early 1960s, but political and social upheavals associated with the Red Guard movement in the mid-1960s again slowed development.

By the mid-1960s, however, Chinese manufactured goods could be found in the markets of Southeast Asia, and many nations looked at Communist China as a potential competitor.

Trade. Agriculture provides about two-thirds of Mainland China's exports, although precise trade figures are not available. Textiles, minerals, light manufactures, and parts for machinery are also exported. Foodstuffs, machinery, and industrial raw materials are major imports.

Communist China's trade was once solely with communist countries, especially the Soviet Union. By the mid-1960s, however, about two-thirds of the Mainland's trade was with noncommunist nations, notably Japan, the Southeast Asian countries, France, Britain, and Canada.

Taiwan. The Republic of China had more success in moving from an agricultural to an agricultural-industrial economy in the 1950s. By the mid-1960s it was a very prosperous country with one of the highest per capita incomes in Asia.

The island's mineral resources are limited. Coal is mined in the north, and there is some petroleum, natural gas, sulfur, and salt.

The island's chief natural resource is the water power of streams that rush from the Chungyang mountains. Between 1958 and 1965 the production of electricity rose sharply, from 2.7 billion kilowatt hours (kwh) in 1957 to 6.6 billion kwh in 1965.

Agriculture continued to play an important role in the economy, however, contributing over 26 percent of the domestic product in 1965 and employing a little more than half the labor force. As only one-quarter of the island's land can be cultivated, farming is intensive and two or three crops a year are raised on the same land.

Rice is the major crop, and the staple of the diet. Sugarcane, raised primarily for export, is second in importance. Sweet potatoes, soybeans, tea, peanuts, and fruits are also significant items.

Industry contributed 24 percent of the island's domestic product in 1965. Most of the industry, developed with large-scale foreign aid, especially U.S. aid, consists of light manufacturing. Food processing is the most important industry, but textiles, machinery parts, glass, and rubber goods are also leading products.

Taiwan has a rather poor balance of trade. In 1966 imports cost $623 million and exports earned only $536 million, but the gap was closing. Sugar, fruit, textiles, and light manufactures are exported. Foodstuffs, machinery, fuels, and textile fibers are imported. The United States and Japan are Taiwan's leading trading partners.

GOVERNMENT. The government proclaimed for Communist China in 1949 and embodied in a constitution in 1954 is a People's Republic, which is democratic in form but in fact dominated by the Communist party.

Supreme legislative and executive power is vested in the National People's Congress, which is elected every four years. The congress chooses a standing committee to act for it between its short yearly sessions. The congress also elects a state council, or cabinet, led by a prime minister, to administer the government, and a Chairman of the Government, who acts as head of state.

The actual seat of power is the Chinese Communist party's Political Bureau, or Politburo, of the party's Central Committee. It determines national policy, and its chairman is usually the key figure in the government. Only party-supported candidates are elected to public office, although party membership is not required for election. Most important government posts are held by party leaders.

A "cultural revolution" launched in 1966 to reorganize and "purify" Chinese society turned into a mass upheaval that disrupted the Chinese social order, economy, and established patterns of government.

Taiwan. Taiwan has a republican form of government. The island has two elected legislatures—one theoretically for all China, and one "provincial" assembly for Taiwan affairs.

The executive branch of government is quite strong. It consists of a president and vice president elected by the National Assembly and a premier, or prime minister, appointed by the president and responsible to the assembly. The Kuomintang, or Nationalist party, is the island's dominant political organization.

HISTORY. China has a long continuous history. Remains of prehistoric "Peking man," found in North China, date back as far as 1 million years and indicate that this early man was probably an ancestor of the modern Chinese. The valley of the Yellow River on the North China Plain was the site of one of the earliest human societies, which developed its own, unique culture.

First Dynasties. Heroic legends tell of a Hsia dynasty founded by an emperor Yü in 2205 BC. There is no concrete evidence of its existence, however, and the first documented Chinese dynasty is the Shang, or Yin. Exact dates of ancient Chinese events are often disputed, but the Shang dynasty was founded in 1766 or 1523 BC on the North China Plain.

Remains of the Shang dynasty show that the basis for the present-day Chinese language already had been formed, and the early characters are similar to those in use in modern China. The Shang controlled many smaller principalities on the North China Plain. One of these, the western kingdom of the Chou, under its king, Wu, overthrew the Shang in 1122 or 1027 BC.

The Chou. The Western Chou (1122–771 BC) is the first dynasty for which a quantity of detailed records exist. Early Chou kings expanded their rule from the North China plain northward to the Liaotung peninsula, southward to the Yangtze valley, and westward to the Himalayan foothills.

Although control of this area was actually divided among many petty states, often in conflict with each other, the Chou dominated them all and was the most influential state for about 300 years.

During the early Chou period society came to be organized along a feudalistic pattern, with wealth based on land ownership and the economy based on agriculture. Warrior-nobles formed the upper class, and village peasant society was communal.

In the 700s BC an eastern branch of the Chou took the throne. The Eastern Chou (770–256 BC) held little power over the nobles and China was actually a federation of states. But during 500 years of Eastern Chou rule, China experienced its classical age of culture and considerable prosperity.

Agricultural and military technology improved, canals were built, a money economy developed, population grew, contact was made with western Asian countries, and trade prospered. Art, music, and literature all flourished, but the Eastern Chou is known primarily for its philosophers. Indeed, so many philosophies, ethical codes, and religions developed during the later Chou that it is known as the era of the "One Hundred Schools."

The Philosophers. Three of the most important philosophers who founded schools of thought between 600 and 300 BC were Lao Tzu, Confucius

ordered, well-educated, and mutually cooperative society that he envisioned stood as the ideal Chinese state for many centuries.

Hsüntzu laid the basis for the "legalist" school of thought, which provided the philosophical foundation for an authoritarian state led by an absolute ruler and ordered by strict laws. The states which followed the legalist pattern were feudalistic and militaristic.

The Ch'in. One state that benefited directly from the legalist doctrine was the Ch'in. It was the westernmost of the many warring states under Chou influence, and it rose to power in the 300s BC. The Ch'in grew prosperous with an excellent system of irrigation, which made agriculture more productive, and a strong central government, which contributed to social stability and military strength.

The Ch'in made alliances with warlike nomadic "barbarian" (non-Chi-

CHINA NEWS SERVICE

GREAT WALL OF CHINA extends 1,500 miles across the country's northeastern border region.

(K'ung-fu-tzu), and Hsüntzu. Lao Tzu, probably in reality several writers, in the *Way of Power (Tao Te Ching)* taught that there was a natural order to the universe of which man was a part. Man could fulfill himself by achieving balance and harmony within himself and with his environment.

Confucius and his student and interpreter Mencius (Mengtzu) laid the foundation for much of China's subsequent social order, moral code, and political development. Confucius taught that leaders could rule through good example, education, moderation, and justice.

The Confucian idea that man could find fulfillment through self-discipline and brotherly love extended to all of society. And the paternalistic, well-

nese) states beyond the fringes of Chou civilization and extended its territory north of the Chou. The Ch'in conquered all of the Chou subject states, and in 256 BC Ch'in armies crushed the Chou.

The Ch'in dynasty gave China its name and marked the first Chinese empire. The Ch'in ruler adopted the title Shih Huang-ti, or "First Emperor," in 221 BC. Ch'in administrators unified the formerly warring states and centralized the government.

The Ch'in emperors extended Chinese rule south to modern Canton and west across the plateau of Yünnan. By linking short walls built earlier, the First Emperor built the Great Wall to keep out invaders from the north, the only exposed frontier.

The centralized government of the Ch'in depended heavily on the central ruler, and when the First Emperor died in 210 BC and the succession was disputed, China was once more plunged into political chaos. In 206 BC Liu Pang, a leader from the Ch'in territory of the Wei valley, became the first emperor of the Han dynasty (206 BC–AD 220).

The Han. The Han emperors worked from the firm political, social, and territorial base laid by the Ch'in. They built an empire that was, with Rome, one of the world's greatest states.

Early Han rulers consolidated the power of the central government over national affairs and successfully beat off attempted invasions by the "barbarians." Han administrators maintained political order by giving all governmental responsibility in distant regions of the empire to the vassals of the emperor.

By the beginning of the reign of Wu Ti, in 141 BC, China's social organization and political system were strong enough for the country to expand its territory and further develop its cultural life. Wu Ti conquered territory almost equal to that of modern China—excluding only mountainous Tibet, Manchuria, and the coastal area around Shanghai, but including northern Korea and part of Indochina.

Thus China had a route north of the Kunlun Mountains into western Asia and then to the Mediterranean. The Chinese traded with the Romans and received artistic and cultural influences from the west.

China grew prosperous under the later Han emperors, who introduced state monopolies and the licensing of certain commodities and state control of parts of the economy. Trade expanded, and roads, canals, and irrigation works were built. Education widened, and Confucianism, with its ideals of discipline, balance, and moderation found expression in all aspects of Chinese society and culture.

In about 8 AD a government official, Wang Mang, usurped the throne. He attempted wide-scale land reform to improve the lot of the peasants and to increase tax revenue. He nationalized landed estates and instituted fiscal reforms that were unpopular with the great landowners. In 23 rebel lords sacked the palace and killed Wang Mang.

The Han dynasty was restored, and although it made some subsequent territorial gains it had lost power to local lords. The lords had been the government's main source of money and manpower, and the dynasty had to compensate for their loss by taxing the peasants more heavily.

Peasant rebellions and fighting between rival lords were frequent in the 100s AD. Professional armies moved into local areas to keep the peace and soon came under the control of the local lords.

Three leaders of these armies grew to such power that they divided the empire into three semi-independent kingdoms—the Wei, the Wu, and the Shu Han. Imperial power disintegrated, and the last Han emperor died in 220.

The Six Dynasties. For the next 370 years China was merely a collection of petty states, most of them at war with one another, and none able to dominate the others. The period was known as the era of the "six dynasties," as six houses in succession managed to gain the throne, but none actually ruled China.

The Chinese had to face both invasion from the north by nomadic non-Chinese peoples and the challenge of strong non-Chinese cultural influences from the south and west. In the 300s and 400s nomads conquered China's northern frontier region, although the natural mountain and desert barriers prevented them from penetrating further. Many northern Chinese migrated southward, and during the 300s and 400s they spread their culture into Southeast Asia.

While military invasion from the north disrupted China, the spread of Buddhism, the Indian religion from the south, altered China's traditional social base. Confucianism had fallen from favor because of the failure of the Han dynasty, which had been built upon it. Taoism also grew in strength and soon rivaled Confucianism in importance.

The Sui. By about 550 one dynasty, the Sui, had emerged dominant among the Chinese kingdoms in the south. In the late 500s and early 600s Sui rulers, allied with Turkic-speaking people, led the reconquest of the northern territories held by the barbarians, who by then had absorbed Chinese culture. During the brief Sui dynasty (589–618) the central government was restored to its former power, the Great Wall was rebuilt, and the economy was put on its feet again.

In trying to expand Chinese territory the Sui met disastrous defeats at the hands of the Koguryo people of Korea in the north and Turkic tribes in the west. Following these defeats, a rebellion toppled the Sui.

A brief period of turmoil followed the end of the Sui. Li Yüan, a Sui bureaucrat of Chinese and "barbarian" descent, with the support of Turkic tribes from central Asia became emperor of China in 618, founding the T'ang dynasty (618–907).

The T'ang. The 300-year T'ang era was one of China's most brilliant. In the 600s T'ang rulers consolidated their control of the government and made China's borders secure against further invasion by forming an alliance with the powerful, warlike Uighurs. T'ang government was efficient, economical, and more just to all classes.

Agriculture and trade prospered. Chinese thinkers assimilated Buddhism, Taoism, and Confucianism and developed a unified philosophical base for society. Under the T'ang, poetry, painting, sculpture, scholarship, and science flourished and attracted artists and scholars from other lands.

T'ang peace and prosperity were interrupted in the mid-700s by a revolt led by An Lu-shan, a "barbarian" who commanded some Chinese armies. The rising resulted in a bloody civil war and caused the emperor to flee his capital, Ch'ang-an. Thus weakened, the empire was open to attack by its neighbors, and the late 700s were marked by invasions by such peoples as the Uighurs and Tibetans.

In the 800s the empire disintegrated into political anarchy once more, and in the 900s effective power was divided among many rival warriors. The Khitan Mongols, a newly powerful northern tribe, seized present-day Mongolia, Manchuria, and Korea from China.

The Sung. The Sung dynasty (960–1279), which finally won the competition for power in 960, led China into the modern age. Sung leaders reformed the military and reorganized the government by creating a large, well-salaried, honest, and efficient civil service. They won the support of the masses by reducing taxes, by abolishing the traditional forced labor, by providing loans to farmers, and by initiating public works projects.

The arts and sciences continued to advance, spurred by the widespread use of printing. The Sung empire was not a strong military state, however. By 1234 the north had fallen before the Mongols, who had begun in the 1100s to conquer an empire that eventually included all of Asia north of India.

The Yüan. In 1260 Kublai Khan, a leader of the Mongols, established the Yüan dynasty (1271–1368) in northern China. By 1279 the dynasty controlled the entire country, and China was a subdivision of the Mongol empire. Although Chinese cultural development was slowed or suspended during the 100 years of Mongol rule, Kublai Khan expanded and developed the Chinese economy.

He improved agricultural techniques, built roads, established a postal system and instituted a system of public relief and care for the aged and indigent. He greatly extended Chinese trade with other Asian states and with Europe. One European adventurer, Marco Polo, from Venice, visited Kublai Khan's court, and his reports excited European interest in the empire.

Despite rule by non-Chinese, central China retained its traditional culture and social organization and remained remarkably unified. In the 1300s Chinese antagonism to foreigners sparked rebellions against the Mongols. These rebellions and rivalries among the Mongols themselves led to the disintegration of the Yüan dynasty in the late 1300s.

The Chinese leaders of the rebellion against the Mongols competed among themselves for the throne. Chu Yüan-chang, a Buddhist from northwestern China, emerged dominant and in 1368 established himself as the first emperor of the Ming dynasty (1368–1644).

The Ming. By 1382 Ming rulers had driven the Mongols out of China Proper, and by the 1400s they had regained control of all but the western third and the northern fringe of present-day China. In 1421 Yung-lo moved the capital from Nanking, where it had been since the founding of the dynasty, to Peking, where a walled "forbidden city" became the center of imperial rule.

The Ming emperors proclaimed China supreme in all the world, and indeed China wielded great power throughout Asia. From its Asian neighbors China demanded tribute, either token or actual, that indicated that China was superior to the tributary states. China also gained the right to approve the rulers of the tributary states. In return for this recognition of China's pre-eminence, China gave financial aid and military protection to the tributary states.

Under rules of conduct established by China, the empire opened diplomatic relations with neighboring states. Ming expansion of foreign contacts improved Chinese prosperity and influenced the country's cultural growth.

For the first time large numbers of Christian missionaries and Western merchants visited China. Chinese literature and art flourished, but in the 1600s the Ming declined. Corruption paralyzed the government and left it incapable of managing the affairs of the empire.

Opposition to the dynasty arose from many groups, which formed into rival parties. In the 1630s a bandit, Li Tzu-ch'eng, gained control of northern China, and his rebellion soon spread. He gained the support of many groups in society, won control of most of China, and soon conquered Peking.

Added to this rebellion was an external threat from the Manchus, a non-Chinese people who lived in the region northeast of China proper. Manchu society was based on farming and herding, but the Manchus had been strongly influenced by China, and their culture was quite similar to that of China. In the 1500s they began expanding their territory, building alliances with their non-Chinese neighbors, streamlining their government, and strengthening their military organization.

By the 1640s the Manchus had begun to invade China and were poised to attack Peking just as a Chinese army was preparing to drive out the rebel forces of Li Tzu-ch'eng. The Manchus joined the government troops in defeating the rebels and then used their position of power to establish the Ch'ing dynasty (1644–1912).

The Ch'ing. Much of the first 100 years of the Ch'ing dynasty was spent in putting down resistance by supporters of the Ming and in subduing the non-Chinese neighbors of China and annexing their territory.

By about 1800 the Ch'ing had expanded to the boundaries of present-day China, and beyond, to Taiwan in the east, across Mongolia and coastal Siberia in the north, and to Tibet in the west. These non-Chinese areas were administered by governors under the control of Peking.

The Manchus ruled China with Chinese assistance. They did not attempt to replace Chinese customs, rather, they continued the political and economic policies of their Ming predecessors, maintaining strict state control over all areas of Chinese life. Chinese culture and scholarship continued to flourish in the traditional pattern through the 1700s.

Chinese society remained too stable, in fact, and tradition permitted little progress or modernization. The end of the 1700s brought unprecedented problems to China. The Western world was beginning to take an active interest in the Far East, and European states were beginning to establish trading colonies in the nations around China.

The Portuguese in the 1500s were the first to trade with China, and they were followed by the Dutch and the British. The British East India Company established a trading station at Canton in the late 1600s and throughout the 1700s carried on a brisk trade in tea through Canton.

At the same time as this new factor was posing a threat to traditional Chinese society, Chinese leadership entered a decline. The Ch'ing rulers became mired in fruitless military activity, and their court became riddled with corruption. Chinese prosperity began to wane as the population level began to soar and the traditional economy could not support it.

Western Impact. At the turn of the century rebellions broke out throughout China, caused by hardship and poverty and directed at the lax government administration. As the old ways were proving to be inadequate, new ideas flooded China. Western merchants and settlers brought with them Western technology and science. Western missionaries brought Western ideals of culture along with Christianity.

Unable to meet these challenges, the Ch'ing rulers tried to frighten them away. They banned Christian missionaries and literature, and they refused contact with western diplomats and merchants. Western pressure only grew stronger.

By the early 1800s the British East India company virtually controlled Canton, China's major port, on the Pearl River. In addition to the tea trade, the British carried on a brisk, illegal trade in opium. The narcotic was grown in British India.

Peking banned the opium trade in the early 1800s, partly because the habit was becoming so widespread that it seriously endangered the health of China, and partly because it was too costly and placed too great a strain on China's silver supply.

A deeper reason for Peking's attempts to control the opium trade with Britain was its anger that foreigners should not only not violate their status as guests in the country by breaking its laws, but should refuse to pay tribute to the emperor as other foreign nations did. This was only the first of many Western blows to China's pride.

The Ch'ing rulers attempted to enforce their prohibition of the opium trade in 1839 by seizing and burning a shipment of opium. British warships moved into Canton harbor, and the British occupied the river forts to force the Chinese to continue the trade, and, necessarily, admit British military superiority. Negotiations began between British and Ch'ing representatives, but no agreement was reached.

The Ch'ing cut off all legal trade with Britain, blockaded river mouths and harbors, and finally attacked British-held posts. China's rulers gained little support from the people of Canton, who, despite a growing anti-foreign sentiment, liked their ineffectual, corrupt Manchu rulers even less.

The British defeated the poorly armed and trained Ch'ing forces, and the government finally agreed to British demands. In the Treaty of Nanking of 1842 China ceded Hong Kong, an island at the mouth of the Pearl River, to the British and opened five other ports to foreign trade. The Ch'ing relinquished their claim to superiority and much of their right to control foreign traders. Finally, they granted a low import tariff and paid an indemnity to the British.

In 1844 another treaty granted extra-territorial rights to foreign nations in the treaty ports—foreigners were not subject to Chinese law. Under pressure from missionaries, Christianity was granted official toleration in 1845. Although merchants and missionaries were not permitted outside the treaty ports, Chinese who traded with the merchants and were converted by the missionaries spread Western influence.

China was humiliated. It was no longer supreme even within its own boundaries. China was revealed to be technologically backward and unable to meet the Western challenge, and the empire was thus opened to further intrusion and insult from abroad. Moreover, the Ch'ing dynasty was revealed to the Chinese people to be too weak even to handle its domestic problems or to put down rebellion.

Rebellions. In 1850 an insurrection broke out in Kiangsi, where floods and crop failures had aggravated problems caused by government mismanagement. Led by a religious mystic with the aid of a military officer, a large force of rebels marched toward Peking, conquering the territory along their route. This, the Taiping Rebellion, nearly succeeded in overthrowing the Ch'ing.

The rebels founded the Taiping kingdom in southeastern China, but they were unable to administer it. After approximately 14 years of destructive civil war, the rebellion was finally put down.

Southeastern China was not the only restless part of the country. Rebellions broke out throughout China in the 1850s. In 1853 the Nien began 15 years of terror and plunder in the north-central provinces of Anhwei, Kiangsu, Shantung, and Shansi. The army and the capital were too busy with the Taiping and foreign intrusions to suppress them.

In 1855 Muslims in southwestern Yünnan rebelled and set up a separate Muslim state, and non-Chinese Miao tribesmen in neighboring Kweichow province opened a 26-year rebellion. The destruction of years of violence set China's economy back still more.

Treaty System. Problems raised by the presence of foreigners worsened. Canton, where most of the Westerners were concentrated, was especially rebellious because of its resentment at the British conquest in the Opium War. Friction between the Cantonese and the foreigners grew so intense that in 1857 and 1858 French and British troops, using the need to protect their interests as an excuse, seized and occupied the city.

In settlement of this conflict, the treaties of Tientsin opened more ports to foreigners, legalized the importation of opium, permitted the establishment of European diplomatic missions at Peking, allowed missionaries and traders to enter the interior of the country, and exacted further indemnities from the Chinese.

The Ch'ing rulers, giving the matter second thought, refused to admit foreign ambassadors to Peking. In reprisal, British and French armies stormed Peking in 1860 and burned the summer palace.

Having thus proved the weakness of the imperial government, the British and French saw an advantage in maintaining a weak dynasty, which they could control, and they assisted the Ch'ing rulers in putting down the bloody rebellions throughout the country. The Ch'ing remained on the throne, but they and China were dependent on the Westerners who flooded the once isolated empire after 1860.

By 1890 China had established formal diplomatic relations with Britain, France, Russia, the United States, and other nations. With foreign aid, cable and rail lines were laid connecting China with the "outside world," and the building of a navy was begun. Friction between China and the foreigners did not lessen, however, and ranged from the persecution of missionaries to protests over Japanese involvement in Taiwan and Korea, a tributary of China.

The imperial government still made no major attempts to reform its administration or modernize its economy and society, and China continued to be humiliated as it became more and more subservient to the foreign powers.

Renewed Conflict. In 1874 the Ch'ing proved unable to prevent Japan from invading Taiwan, and they avoided losing the island only through Western diplomatic maneuvers. In the 1880s France, ostensibly in retaliation for the killing of French citizens, occupied Indochina, part of the traditional Chinese tribute system, and forced China to recognize France's position there. In 1887 Portugal was granted Macao, a port near Hong Kong.

Relations with Japan, which had made a rapid transition from its traditional ways to the technological and political sophistication of the 1800s, grew tense. Korea, long a tributary of China, slipped into Japanese control in the 1860s and 1870s, when China refused to take responsibility for Korean actions and later did not protest Japan's recognition of Korea as an independent state.

In 1885 both China and Japan agreed to withdraw their troops from Korea, but continuing intrigue and growing Korean nationalism led in 1894 to war between Korea and China and to a Sino-Japanese war.

By early 1895 Japanese troops had all but destroyed China's army and navy. Further humiliation was added in 1895 by the Treaty of Shimonoseki, by which China was forced to recognize Korean independence, cede Taiwan, the Liaotung Peninsula, and the Pescadores to Japan, pay a huge indemnity, and open more ports to foreigners.

This defeat was a final blow to the pride and patience of many Chinese. Chinese intellectuals realized that a revolution was needed to force China out of its traditional ways and into modern ways if the country was to survive the competition from the technologically advanced nations of the world.

Although a young emperor sat on the throne, actual power rested with his aunt, the dowager empress, Tz'u-hsi, who had ruled for him when he was an infant and who had ruled as regent for much of the reign of the previous emperor, her son. The dowager empress was extremely conservative and held to an archaic ideal of China's grandeur.

Reform Efforts. In 1894 Dr. Sun Yat-sen (Sun Wen) organized one of the earliest secret revolutionary societies whose goal was the overthrow of the Ch'ing. After the Treaty of Shimonoseki in 1895, reformers who had been demanding modernization voiced their demands even more loudly.

Students organized "study societies" such as the "society for the study of self-strengthening," to develop theories of reform. Philosophers reinterpreted Confucianism to permit modernization and reform within Chinese traditional ideology. It seemed that even quite radical reform programs would be adopted.

K'ang Yu-wei, a reformer with a positive program for modernizing China, convinced the emperor that reforms were necessary. In 1898 the emperor gave the reformers the power to enact reform measures. In the so-called "One Hundred Days of Reform," edicts were issued to make the schools effective for all classes, remove extra-territorial rights, develop China's natural resources, improve agricultural technology, better national health, expand trade, begin industrialization, and modernize the police and the military.

Conservative opposition to these projected programs was immediate. The dowager empress supported the conservatives, and in September 1898 she had the emperor imprisoned, revoked the reform edicts, and placed conservatives in power.

Foreign Encroachments. While China's domestic policies were in upheaval, Chinese entanglements with foreign powers grew more complex. In 1896 China and Russia concluded a secret treaty by which Russia guaranteed to defend China from attack in return for the right to build and manage a railway across Manchuria to the Russian city of Vladivostok.

The concession to Russia was followed by a commercial treaty with Japan and in 1897 by commercial concessions to Britain. Germany, hoping for equal benefits, used the murder of Germans in China as a pretext for seizing Kiaochow Bay in 1897. It forced China to grant Germany a 99-year lease on the bay and the right to operate mines and build railroads in Shantung.

The other European powers were quick to demand similar favors. Britain gained exclusive rights to much of China's inland river trade, and Russia forced the granting of a 25-year lease on the southern tip of the Liaotung Peninsula. France gained the 99-year lease on Kwangchow Bay, Japan gained a guarantee of prominent influence in Fukien province, and Britain was granted Kowloon, on the mainland across from Hong Kong.

The reactionaries who had come to power with the defeat of China's attempts at domestic reforms hoped to restore China to its position of isolation. Thus, in 1899 when Italy sought concession of a port, the demand was rejected violently. An anti-foreign militia was organized in Eastern China called the "Righteous and Harmonious Fists," or "Boxers."

The Boxer Rebellion. The Boxers sought to drive foreigners and foreign influence out of China by violence. The Boxers received the support of the empress dowager, and by 1900 they were at the core of Peking mobs that attacked foreigners and foreign diplomatic missions. The uprising also sparked anti-foreign incidents elsewhere in China.

In response to the Boxer rising, Germany, Russia, and a joint force of Western European allies attacked China, occupied areas in many provinces, and seized Peking. The empress dowager and the government fled. In 1901 the Boxer Protocol ended the fighting. It exacted further indemnities, apologies, and trade, territorial, and diplomatic concessions from China.

That China was actually divided into foreign "spheres of influence"— regions in which one nation held dominant influence—was pointed out by the United States, which had no sphere of influence in China. The United States urged that an "Open Door" be left for other nations to trade with China.

New Reforms. The utter failure of the conservatives' methods forced the dowager empress to allow some reforms. In 1902 imperial edicts were issued to expand education, modernize the army, and reform the economy.

These reforms were too little, too late, and too slow in materializing for the more radical Chinese reformers. Moreover, opponents of the regime felt that no reform program could be effective without bringing under Chinese control the foreigners who held vital portions of the nation's economy.

In 1905 Sun Yat-sen, who had been seeking support from Chinese throughout the world for his campaign against the Ch'ing dynasty, united in Japan many Chinese reform societies into one revolutionary organization, the T'ung-meng hui, or United League.

Government-sponsored reform continued at a slow pace. Preparations begun in 1906 for the institution of constitutional government were hindered in 1908, when both the dowager empress and the emperor died. The regent for the infant heir to the throne was a conservative, who dismissed the liberal reformers in the government and appointed conservative Manchus as the chief ministers. The meeting of a parliament was put off until 1913.

Republican Revolution. This stalling increased the restlessness of the revolutionaries, who by 1910 had established a network throughout China. The spark that ignited the revolution was the discovery of the revolutionary headquarters by government police in October 1911. Within a month, most of the country had risen against the Manchus.

A truce was signed in December between the rebels and the government, and a revolutionary provisional assembly met in Nanking. It elected Dr. Sun Yat-sen president of China. In February 1912 the Manchus acknowledged defeat. The abdication of the boy emperor was announced, and the assembly proclaimed the Republic of China.

Yüan Shih-K'ai was elected provisional president of the republic in February 1912. A provisional constitution was adopted which would have made the national assembly the supreme organ of government, and a dispute immediately began between President Yüan, who wanted to head a strong executive, and the assembly. Opposition parties grouped around this issue.

Liang Ch'i-ch'ao formed the Progressive party, which supported Yüan's government. Sun Yat-sen led the Kuomintang (KMT), or Nationalist party, which favored parliamentary supremacy. Thus, in disarray within a month of its formation, the republic began to disintegrate.

The first elected parliament was convened in April 1913. A loan received by Yüan from Britain, France, Russia, and Japan, which would serve to finance his drive for increased power, caused his opponents to lead a second revolution. It was quickly suppressed, and Kuomintang leaders were forced to flee to Japan.

Yüan, who was formally elected president of the republic in October 1913, consolidated his power by expelling Kuomintang members from the parliament and then by dissolving parliament itself in January 1914. In place of the constitution, which was to have been ratified by the parliament, Yüan governed under a "constitutional compact," which he announced in 1914 and which gave him a 10-year term as a powerful president.

The establishment of the republic did not lessen the financial and political power wielded by foreign nations, however, and Chinese political instability left China even more unprepared to cope with foreign interference. When World War I broke out in 1914, China became the diplomatic and occasionally the military battleground for Russia, Japan, and Germany.

Nor was the war the only source of violence in China. A successful rebellion broke out in 1915 in Yünnan, led by Yüan's opponents in response to Yüan's assumption of the title of emperor. Yüan died in 1916, shortly after he had renounced the imperial title. He was succeeded by Li Yüanhung.

Li restored the constitution, but in 1917 military leaders rebelled and restored the Ch'ing dynasty for two weeks. In July 1917 Sun Yat-sen established a military government in the south, with its capital at Canton.

With China itself divided, the end of World War I also found Manchuria in the hands of Japan and Mongolia under Russian domination. The Versailles Treaty, which ended the war, allowed Japan to retain Shantung, and China refused to sign the document.

At the Washington Conference in 1922, the Allied powers agreed to reconsider their demands for extraterritorial rights, to respect China's territorial integrity, and to assist China in the formation of a stable government. A Sino-Japanese treaty was arranged, by which Japan was to withdraw from Shantung.

This official end to foreign intervention came too late, however. No one government led China, and in 1920 the country was plunged into open civil war among warlords—military leaders who held sway over districts, even provinces—while in the larger cities, anti-foreign mobs rioted.

Kuomintang. In 1924 a Kuomintang congress met to plan the party's future. It accepted communists as members and employed Soviet advisors to train members in military and political tactics. Sun Yat-sen died in 1925, and leadership of the Kuomintang passed to Chiang Kai-shek. Dr. Sun's wife, Soong Ch'ing-ling, supported a radical left-wing of the nationalist movement, however.

With Soviet aid, Chiang suppressed the warlords and gained control of northern China. Soon, however, a split opened between the conservative nationalists, led by Chiang, and the radicals and communists. The radicals and communists established a government at Wuhan, and the nationalists set up a government at Nanking.

After a brief reconciliation, the two factions split widely apart. In 1927 Mao Tse-tung, a Communist party leader, organized a peasant uprising in Hunan province. When the uprising was suppressed, the communists retreated into the interior and organized an anti-Kuomintang revolutionary army. In June 1928 Chiang and a purged Kuomintang captured Peking and proclaimed a single government for the whole of China with its capital at Nanking.

Since the revered Dr. Sun had recommended that a strict, authoritarian regime strengthen the country before democracy was introduced, a strong central executive was established under Chiang and the now moderate-conservative Kuomintang. From 1928 to 1930 the Nanking government consolidated its international position by negotiating treaties recognizing Chinese sovereignty.

The Kuomintang did not rule all of China, however. Warlords had risen to power again in the north, and communists controlled the southwest.

In 1931 Japan invaded and occupied Manchuria. Chiang's government was able to put up little effective resistance, and in 1932 Japan proclaimed Manchuria independent as Manchukuo (Manchu-nation), with a puppet government headed by the former Ch'ing emperor of China.

Japan used Manchukuo as a base for further military operations in China and by 1933 had gained control of Jehol province and claimed the provinces of the North China Plain for Japan.

Late in 1934 Mao Tse-tung and his communist followers began a "Long March" from the south, where the pressure of government forces had made their position untenable. They walked 5,000 miles into Shensi province in the northwest. The march, accomplished over difficult terrain and under almost constant attack by government troops, took nearly a year.

Communist losses were heavy, but the survivors formed a tightly knit, dedicated unit. In late 1935 the communists established a government headed by Mao at Yenan, in Shensi.

Chiang, without control of the entire nation, felt unprepared to go to war against Japan, although it was apparent that Japan was preparing for total war with China. In 1936 Chiang was kidnapped by nationalists who attempted to force him to postpone internal struggles to meet the threat posed by Japan. After his release, Chiang concluded a truce with the communists, and the nationalists and communists formed a united front against Japan.

War with Japan. In 1937 Japan opened a major offensive against China. Japanese troops met surprisingly strong resistance from both communist and nationalist forces, but by 1939 they had conquered and occupied the eastern third of China, the country's heartland. From this large mainland base, Japan entered World War II.

During the war the British, Soviet, and U.S. governments aided the Chinese by sending supplies through western China. In 1943 Britain and the United States abrogated all treaties giving them special rights in China and promised President Chiang that they would force Japanese restitution of Chinese territories after the war.

During the Japanese occupation, however, the communist forces gained widespread popular support and won control of most of the northeast. The nationalist regime, having been pushed inland, made the city of Chungking its capital. It was weakened by internal division and corruption, and was separated from the vital coastal areas from which it had drawn its support. Late in the war Soviet troops occupied Manchuria and stripped the industrially developed area of its machinery.

When the war ended in 1945, civil war again broke out between the nationalists and the communists. A U.S. mission led by Gen. George C. Marshall tried without success to mediate the conflict.

The communists won most of the battles and in 1949 captured the nationalists' restored capital, Nanking, and proclaimed the People's Republic of China from Peking. Chiang Kaishek and his government fled to the island of Taiwan, where they established themselves at Taipei.

Communist Regime. The outbreak of the Korean war (1950–1953) aided the communist government. It rallied popular support against the U.S. and UN forces and gained prestige by successfully repelling an invasion across the Yalu River and pushing back the U.S.-UN forces led by Gen. Douglas MacArthur.

By 1952 the Communist party had consolidated its control of the mainland, and in 1953 it announced the first five-year economic plan to industrialize China. However, plans for enacting the program were not drawn up until 1955.

With aid from the Soviet Union, Communist China's strong central government and well-disciplined party, backed by a strong army, made great strides in repairing the damage done by years of warfare. The communist government collectivized agriculture and worked for the rapid industrialization of China.

In 1956 the government called for a "Great Leap Forward," which aimed at replacing family and village life with communal life and which hoped to have each citizen participate in all phases of the economic development program.

But the first plan and the subordination of agriculture to industrial growth proved to be disastrous mistakes. Combined with floods and poor initial organization, they caused a great decline in crop production. Moreover, industrialization did not proceed at the pace the communist planners had hoped, and it was not until the early 1960s that China's economy seemed based on a firm foundation.

In foreign affairs Communist China concentrated on extending its influence throughout eastern and Southeast Asia. Communist Chinese troops had aided North Korean forces in the Korean war and supported communist guerrilla bands in Laos, Vietnam, Cambodia, and elsewhere. Also, despite its own need for food and funds, the communist government sent foreign financial and technical aid to other nations.

China's progress toward stability, prosperity, and prestige was interrupted in the mid-1960s by events stemming from an ideological conflict that had been growing between the Soviet Union and China since the mid-1950s. The dispute became an open break in the early 1960s.

The Chinese government declared itself ideologically purer than the Soviet Union, and made the Soviet Union and its leaders the target of abuse. By the mid-1960s the two nations had ended most contacts and were in open competition for the leadership of the world communist movement.

Chairman Mao carried his ideological campaign further in 1966 by proclaiming a "proletarian cultural revolution" to purge China of "revisionist," or regressive, tendencies. The movement, spearheaded by Red Guards, as the pro-Mao activists were called, grew into an orgy of anti-Western, anti-Soviet violence.

Schools were closed, agricultural

and industrial production interrupted, and the government's administrative machinery disrupted. Nonetheless, China successfully continued its research and development programs in atomic weapons, and exploded its first thermonuclear device.

Taiwan. In 1945, when the nationalists took over the government of Taiwan, they were faced immediately with difficulties in governing the island. Descendants of the mainland Chinese who had settled Taiwan in the 1600s regarded themselves as native Taiwanese, different from the mainland peoples. And some had hoped for complete independence for Taiwan after the Japanese withdrew.

Japan had made the island a colony after winning it from China in 1895, and although Japanese rule improved the economy considerably, it was oppressive and unpopular. The island had become a strategic base for Japan's military operations, and during World War II Japanese bases on the island were heavily bombed by Allied forces.

The sufferings of the Taiwanese under alien rule, their unmet demands for independence, and the ineptitude and harshness of the Nationalist government after 1945 combined to create severe friction between the Taiwanese and the mainlanders. The situation worsened, and in 1947 the Taiwanese rebelled. The revolt was crushed ruthlessly.

When the nationalists lost to communist forces on the mainland in 1949, they moved their government, their army, and some 3 million of their citizens to Taiwan. There, President Chiang proclaimed a government of all China and declared his intention to return to the mainland.

In 1950 Communist China declared Taiwan to be a part of its territory and announced its intention to reclaim it. The U.S. Navy protected the island and prevented any mainland invasion attempt. Both sides have a claim to the island, for in the peace treaty that Japan signed in 1951, it

relinquished all its claims to Taiwan without ceding it to any particular state.

Taiwan's history in the 1950s and 1960s was shaped by the claim of both Chinas to be the sole representative of the Chinese people. Because of the rivalry, low level military activities continued between the two Chinas in the 1950s and 1960s, flaring up into several major crises—the battle for the tiny offshore islands of Quemoy and Matsu in the late 1950s, and the large-scale buildup of communist and nationalist troops on facing coasts in the early 1960s.

The division radically affected the nation's foreign affairs as well. Taiwan committed itself to maintaining its position in the noncommunist world as the sole legal government of China, and it refused to deal officially with any nation that recognized Communist China.

The United States not only protected the island with U.S. naval forces, but gave the nationalists their main diplomatic support, trained the nationalist army, and provided the aid that made possible Taiwan's economic growth. Taiwan was frequently used as a symbol of the larger conflict between the United States and the communist world, and Taiwan benefited greatly from U.S. interest in limiting the spread of communism in Asia.

Taiwan's growing prosperity helped to ease the friction between the native Taiwanese and the mainland-dominated government. But the movement for Taiwanese independence continued.

The Kuomintang claim to all China affected Taiwan's domestic politics in other ways. Full-scale national elections were postponed until the return to the mainland, and the republic's affairs remained in the hands of the National Assembly, which elects the president. Twice it amended the constitution to permit President Chiang to be reelected.

No party other than the Kuomintang was active in Taiwan until 1960, when opposition leaders attempted to form the China Democratic party. Direct and indirect suppression by the Nationalist government, consisting only of Kuomintang members, caused the collapse of the new party. Its role was taken by politicians calling themselves "independents" who managed to win several contests for local and provincial offices in the 1960s.

In the early 1960s the Kuomintang moved to strengthen its control over Taiwan politics in response to this widening of opposition activities. In 1966 the National Assembly greatly increased the powers of the presidency, at the same time promising that elections would be held for the assembly on Taiwan.

The advanced age of President Chiang, the center of the nationalist movement for over 50 years, led in the early 1960s to speculation over Taiwan's future. The appointment of President Chiang's son, Chiang Kuo, as minister of defense in 1965, however, seem to indicate a continuance of Chiang's policies.

—Thomas E. Ennis; M. G. Inaba

U.S. ARMY

NATIONALIST CHINESE airmen overhaul an aircraft engine at air cadet training school.

UNITED NATIONS

COLOMBIAN INDIAN FARMERS. Agriculture employs about half of Colombia's people.

COLOMBIA

Official name: Republic of Colombia
Area: 439,512 square miles
Population: (1966 est.) 18,650,000
Capital: Bogotá (Pop., 1964, 1,697,311)
Language: Spanish
Religion: Roman Catholicism
Currency unit: Peso
National holiday: Independence day, July 20

Colombia is unique among the South American nations in facing both the Caribbean Sea and the Pacific Ocean. Colombia is bordered on the north by the Caribbean, on the east by Venezuela and Brazil, on the south by Peru and Ecuador, and on the west by the Pacific Ocean and Panama.

THE LAND. The country is crossed by three distinct ranges of the Andes, which create serious barriers. Most of the country's people and economically important areas lie in scattered valleys, separated not only by the Andes but also by climate and different ways of life.

Physical Regions. Colombia has two main land regions—the Andes, in the west, and the lowlands, in the east. The Andean region is a continuation of the broad Andes mountain system which runs almost the entire length of the western side of the South American continent. The Colombian Andes fan out in an east-west direction in the southwest to form three separate ranges: the Cordillera Occidental, the Cordillera Central, and the Cordillera Oriental.

The Cordillera Central has peaks that rise more than 18,000 feet above sea level. The cordilleras Occidental and Oriental are somewhat lower. The Cordillera Oriental widens in the north and forms a narrow plateau in the vicinity of Bogotá. The Magdalena River separates the Cordillera Oriental from the Cordillera Central, and the Cauca River separates the Cordillera Central from the Cordillera Occidental. Both rivers flow northward and empty into the Caribbean Sea.

The eastern lowlands drain into the Amazon and Orinoco river systems. The southern section of the region is tropical rain forest and is sparsely populated. The northern section consists of savannas, or *llanos*. Although flooded for a large portion of the year, it is suitable for livestock raising.

Climatic Zones. Climate in Colombia varies with altitude. The lower areas, from sea level to about 3,000 feet, comprise the *tierra caliente*, or hot country. It has average temperatures of from 75°F to 85°F, and tropical crops such as rice and bananas are grown there.

The *tierra templada*, or temperate country, lies between 3,000 and 6,500 feet above sea level. It has year-round temperatures of 65°F to 70°F, and coffee flourishes on the Andean slopes of the region.

The third level is the *tierra fría*, or cold country, between 6,500 and 10,000 feet above sea level. Wheat, maize, and fruit are grown there. Above 10,000 feet but below the 15,000-foot snow line the land is unsuitable for cultivation and is devoted to pasturing livestock.

THE PEOPLE. About 70 percent of the Colombian population is mestizo, of mixed Spanish and Indian descent, and mulatto, mixed Negro and white. Whites constitute about 20 percent of the total and are concentrated in the major cities. Negroes make up less than 7 percent of the population and live mainly along the Caribbean and Pacific coasts. Indians represent about 3 percent of the population.

Most Colombians live in the Andean valleys. Bogotá, the capital, lies more than 8,500 feet above sea level. Cali, in the fertile Cauca Valley, is a market point for agricultural products and an industrial center. It had a population of almost 638,000. The city of Medellín, located in the Cordillera Central, is the center of the coffee and textile industries. It had a 1964 population of almost 773,000.

Barranquilla, on the Caribbean coast, is the country's largest port. It had a population of approximately 500,000 in 1964. Cartagena, one of the oldest South American cities, is Colombia's foremost tourist center. It is also the shipping point for petroleum and petroleum products from a large local refinery. In 1964 it had more than 242,000 inhabitants.

ECONOMY. Agriculture is the most important part of Colombia's economy. Although only 2 percent of the nation's total land area is cultivated, about half the population is employed in agriculture. Coffee is the chief crop, and Colombia relies heavily on its export to earn foreign exchange. Other major commercial crops are bananas, sugarcane, tobacco, cotton, and cacao. Cattle are also important and are raised on the *llanos* of the country's eastern lowlands.

Colombia is rich in mineral resources, and mining plays an important role. Petroleum is the country's second most valuable export, and in 1966 Colombia ranked third among South American oil producers. Colombia leads South America in gold production and is the world's most important source of emeralds.

Although by the mid-1960s industry was not highly developed, it has been growing. Manufacturing is largely devoted to textiles and food processing, but beverages, shoes, steel, and a variety of chemicals are also produced. The growth of both industry and mining, however, is hampered by a lack of capital for investment, poor transportation facilities, a small domestic market, and political instability.

In 1966 Colombian exports were valued at $508 million and imports cost $673 million. Coffee accounts for about 65 percent of the value of all exports. Other exports include petroleum, bananas, tobacco, cotton, and sugar. Chemicals, machinery, steel products, paper, and vehicles are the country's main imports. Colombia's major trading partner is the United States. Other important trading partners are West Germany, Britain, Spain, and Sweden.

GOVERNMENT. Colombia is a constitutional republic. The chief executive and head of state is the president, who is popularly elected to a term of four years. He may not serve consecutive terms.

The Congress is composed of the Senate and the House of Representatives. Senators serve for four years, and representatives for two.

Colombia is a member of the United Nations and the Organization of American States (OAS).

HISTORY. Before the Spanish Conquest in the 1500s, the high Andean region of Colombia stretching northeastward from Bogotá was the home of the Muiscas, a Chibcha-speaking American Indian people who had evolved a stable agricultural society and were highly skilled at goldwork. They were easily subdued by the Spaniards, who began exploring the Caribbean coast as early as 1500.

Spanish Era. The first permanent Spanish communities were established at Santa Marta in 1525 and Cartagena in 1533. Santa Marta later served as the base for an expedition under Gonzalo Jiménez de Quesada that moved inland to conquer the Muiscas and resulted in the founding of Bogotá in 1538.

To the west, the Spaniards discovered what was to become the chief gold-producing area of their empire, and Cartagena, on the Caribbean coast, became the principal naval base of the Spanish Main. Nonetheless, most of Colombia remained virtually uninhabited throughout the Spanish colonial period. Its few people were engaged chiefly in raising cattle and growing crops for local consumption.

Colombia's struggle for independence began in 1810, when local leaders deposed the Spanish authorities and established a number of juntas, ostensibly to rule in the absence of Spain's King Ferdinand VII, who was held captive by Napoleon. Spanish armies reoccupied the principal regions of the country in 1815–1816, but in 1819 Simón Bolívar returned from Venezuela and decisively routed the Spanish forces at the battle of Boyacá.

Independence. In the same year, 1819, the former Viceroyalty of New Granada—which included modern Colombia, Panama, Venezuela, and Ecuador—was organized by the leaders of the independence movement into the republic of Gran Colombia. Bolívar was elected president, but he left to continue the war against Spain and turned over the government to his vice president, Francisco de Paula Santander.

Santander proved an able administrator, but was harassed by separatist movements in Venezuela and Ecuador. Not even the return of Bolívar could prevent the final dissolution of the republic of Gran Colombia in 1830.

In 1831 the territory of modern Colombia and Panama was established as the Republic of New Granada. Santander became its first elected chief executive in 1832. Soon, however, a long and often violent struggle began between Liberals and Conservatives over church policy and constitutional organization.

Era of Conflict. During the 1850s and 1860s, the Liberals established freedom of worship and separation of church and state, but they also seized church lands, abolished monastic orders, and placed restrictions upon the Roman Catholic clergy. Politically, they carried the concept of states' rights to such extremes that the national government itself was often rendered ineffective.

The Liberals' extreme approach to local autonomy and their church policy brought a strong reaction against them in the 1880s. Although originally a Liberal, President Rafael Núñez joined forces with the Conservatives to adopt a rigorously centralist constitution in 1886 and removed the major restrictions placed upon the church.

The policies of Núñez did not end internal strife. Liberals fought to undo his work by launching civil wars, the longest and bloodiest of which raged from 1899 to 1902. This war, plus the secession of Panama in 1903, shocked the leaders of both parties into laying aside at least some of their former bitterness.

Civil wars abruptly ceased, and for nearly 50 years Colombia enjoyed relative stability and constitutional government. Meanwhile, economic growth continued. The production of coffee increased and new commodities, such as bananas and petroleum, and the beginnings of manufacturing, especially of textiles, served to broaden the base of the economy.

Reforms. Until the Liberal administration of Alfonso López (1934–1938), however, neither party had given much attention to the great majority of Colombians, who remained illiterate, impoverished, and beyond the reach of modern health facilities and social services. To deal with this problem López launched a program that included labor reform and social welfare legislation.

Although his program was generally moderate, it aroused strong opposition from wealthy Colombians. At the same time, it aroused among the working class hopes that could be only partially satisfied. Colombia thus faced a new period of strife in which inherited political rivalries were aggravated by new social and economic conflicts.

Tensions reached a climax on Apr. 9, 1948, when the leftist Liberal leader Jorge E. Gaitán was assassinated in Bogotá and his followers staged an orgy of rioting in protest. A year later, inter-party relations broke down entirely, and violence spread to large areas of Colombia. Beginning as a struggle between Liberals and Conservatives, it often degenerated into banditry.

Contemporary Colombia. A dictatorship by Gen. Gustavo Rojas Pinilla, from 1953 to 1957, brought a slight decline in civil strife but failed to stop the violence, which in the decade following Gaitán's death claimed roughly a quarter million lives. The violence of the 1950s and the growing unpopularity of the Rojas regime led Liberal and Conservative leaders to cooperate once again.

After joining to overthrow the dictator in May 1957, the two parties created a National Front coalition government. The terms of the coalition agreement provided for the alternation of Liberals and Conservatives in the presidency and the division of other offices on a 50-50 basis for a 16-year period. Under the National Front, violence decreased but did not completely disappear.

A new approach was made to the nation's fundamental social and economic problems, including efforts at agrarian reform. But Colombia's difficulties were compounded by an extremely high rate of population increase, large-scale migration to the cities, and a sharp drop in the world price of coffee, which limited the financial resources available for carrying out reform programs.

Popular dissatisfaction was reflected in the loss of support for both traditional parties in elections held in 1966. Many Colombians abstained from voting and others backed the forces of ex-dictator Rojas Pinilla, which made strong gains. Nonetheless, the Liberal party candidate, Carlos Lleras Restrepo, was elected president by a safe majority.

—David Bushnell; Kempton E. Webb

CONGO (Brazzaville)

Official name: Republic of Congo
Area: 132,047 square miles
Population: (1966 est.) 850,000
Capital: Brazzaville (Pop., 1962, urban area, 136,200)
Language: French, African languages
Religion: Christianity, traditional religions
Currency unit: Franc CFA (African Financial Community)
National holiday: National day, August 15

The Congo (Brazzaville), a republic in central Africa, is bordered on the north by the Central African Republic, on the east and southeast by the Congo (Kinshasa), on the southwest by the Cabinda region of Angola and the Atlantic Ocean, on the west by Gabon, and on the northwest by Cameroon. The Congo, formerly a territory in French Equatorial Africa, received its independence from France in 1960.

THE LAND. The Congo has a varied geography. Along the coast is a relatively cool and practically treeless plain. Farther inland is the wet and forested Mayombé Escarpment, which is cut by the Kouilou River. The Niari Basin, a region of woodlands and grassy plains, lies east of the escarpment.

To the north of the escarpment are the grassy Batéké plateaus. There are swamps along the Sangha River in the northern part of the country. The Congo and Ubangi rivers border the Congo on the east.

The Congo has a hot, tropical climate. The coastal area, cooled by ocean currents, has generally lower temperatures than the rest of the country.

THE PEOPLE. There are many different ethnic groups in the Congo. The Bacongo people make up almost half the population. Other important groups are the Vili, the Batéké, the M'Bochi, and the Sangha.

Most of the people live in rural areas. The country's major cities include Brazzaville, the capital and major river port, and Pointe Noire, a port city on the Atlantic Ocean.

ECONOMY. The economy of the Congo is based largely on agriculture, and about 60 percent of the people are farmers. Bananas, manioc, peanuts, rice, tropical fruits, and corn are grown for local consumption. Forestry is very important to the Congo's economy. The Congo is poor in mineral resources, apart from large potash deposits near Pointe Noire, and there is little industry.

The Congo has a well-developed transportation system. The Congo-Ocean railroad links Brazzaville and Pointe Noire, and the Congo and Ubangi rivers provide excellent water routes for the Congo and neighboring countries.

In 1966 imports cost $70 million and exports were valued at $43 million. The Congo imports machinery and consumer goods. The major exports include diamonds mined in neighboring countries and timber.

GOVERNMENT. The Congo has a modified presidential system of government. The chief of state is the president, chosen by an electoral college composed of members of the national legislature and local government councils. The chief executive is the prime minister, responsible to the legislature, the National Assembly. Assembly members are popularly elected to five-year terms.

The Congo (Brazzaville) is a member of the United Nations and of the Organization of African Unity (OAU).

HISTORY. The Balali people, an offshoot of the Bacongo kingdom centered in nearby Angola, overran the M'Bochi and Vili people living in the present-day Congo many centuries ago. Portuguese explorers had begun trading with these people in the 1400s. The original trade in gold and ivory was replaced by the slave trade. British, Dutch, and French companies joined the trade until slaving was abolished in the 1800s.

French Rule. The French explorer Pierre Savorgnan de Brazza reached the area in 1873, and signed an agreement with the Batéké king. The French obtained European recognition of their influence over the region of the present-day Congo at the Berlin Conference on African Affairs in 1884.

The French called the area Middle Congo. In 1910 France joined Middle Congo with present-day Gabon, Chad, and the Central African Republic to form the Federation of French Equatorial Africa.

France gave private companies control of developing the country, but company rule was harsh. Africans were deprived of legal rights, and in the 1920s African political dissatisfaction was expressed in the rise of various local religious sects. The most important sect was the Matswa movement among the Bacongo.

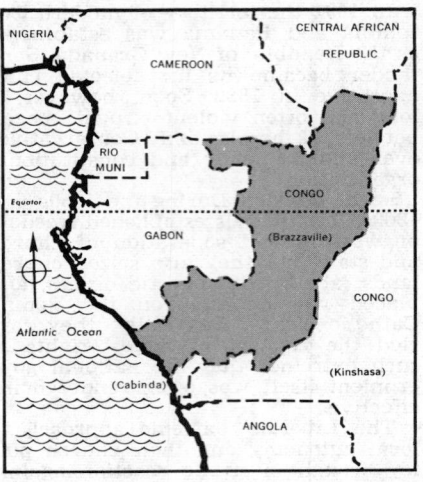

Middle Congo supported Free France during World War II. In 1944, in gratitude for their support, France held a conference to discuss colonial reforms in Brazzaville. Shortly after, Middle Congo became an overseas territory within the French Union, and many political parties developed, largely along tribal lines.

Independence. In the mid-1950s Fulbert Youlou became the dominant political figure in the country. Youlou, a Bacongo and a Roman Catholic priest, had gained the support of the Matswa movement. In 1958 Middle Congo agreed to join the French Community and changed its name to Republic of Congo. In 1959 Youlou became the first president, and the Republic of Congo became independent on Aug. 15, 1960.

Youlou attempted to establish a one-party state, but in 1963 his opponents staged a successful coup, and Alphonse Massamba-Debat became president under a new constitution.

—Hibberd V. B. Kline, Jr.;
Vera L. Zolberg

CONGO (Kinshasa)

Official name: Democratic Republic of the Congo
Area: 905,562 square miles
Population: (1966 est.) 15,986,000
Capital: Kinshasa (Pop., 1966 est., 507,868)
Language: French, African languages
Religion: Christianity, Islam, traditional religions
Currency unit: Zaire
National holiday: Independence day, June 30

The Democratic Republic of the Congo, a nation in central Africa, is bordered on the north by the Central African Republic and Sudan, on the east by Uganda, Rwanda, Burundi, and Tanzania, on the south by Zambia and Angola, and on the west by the Congo (Brazzaville) and the Cabinda region of Angola. The country was a colony of Belgium until 1960, when it received its independence.

THE LAND. Tropical grasslands and forests are typical of most of the Congo's landscape. The interior of the country is a vast plain with swamps in some places. There are highlands along the eastern border, including

Mount Ruwenzori, which has an elevation of about 16,800 feet. There are also highlands in the south.

There are many lakes along the Congo's eastern border, including lakes Albert, Edward, Kivu, Tanganyika, and Mweru.

The Congo River flows through part of the northeastern Congo and along the western border. The wide, navigable lower part of the river drops nearly 1,000 feet between Kinshasa and the sea. The Ubangi and Kasai rivers are the main tributaries of the middle Congo River. The climate throughout the country is tropical.

THE PEOPLE. Most of the Congo's indigenous population is Bantu-speaking. Many different groups of people, including the Bacongo, Lulua, and the pygmies, live in the Congo. About one-third of the people are Christian, a small number are Muslim, and most of the remainder follow traditional tribal religions.

In 1966 the Congo renamed its cities that had Belgian names. Leopoldville, the capital, became Kinshasa, and the important city of Elisabethville was renamed Lubumbashi. Stanleyville became Kisangani.

ECONOMY. Since independence in 1960, the economy of the Congo has been seriously disrupted by political instability and civil wars. The Belgians had developed the country's rich mineral resources and had built railroads to complement river navigation. Most of the technically trained Belgians left during the political disorder following independence.

The Congo's mineral riches include copper, cobalt, zinc, gold, and diamonds. In 1965, 288,600 metric tons of copper ore, about 8,400 metric tons of cobalt ore, 117,400 metric tons of zinc ore, and 72,850 ounces of gold were mined. Diamond production in 1965 reached 26.6 million carats, more than half the world's total.

There is little industry in the Congo apart from the processing of minerals and agricultural products. Most of the Congo's people are engaged in subsistence farming. The main crops are corn, millet and sorghum, peanuts, coffee, and fruits.

In 1965 imports cost $320 million and exports were valued at $330 mil-

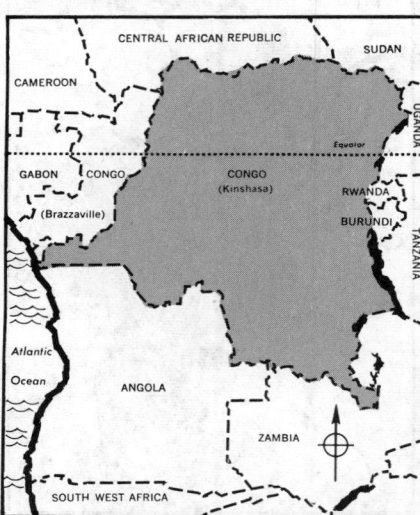

lion. The Congo's main exports include copper, cobalt, diamonds, tin, palm oil, and coffee. The main imports are foodstuffs, petroleum products, transportation equipment, and textiles.

GOVERNMENT. A constitution promulgated in 1967 established a presidential system of government. Executive power is vested in a president elected to a seven-year term. Legislative power is held by a National Assembly elected to a five-year term. The constitution called for the establishment of a two-party system.

The Congo is a member of the United Nations and of the Organization of African Unity (OAU).

HISTORY. Many different tribal peoples have lived in the vast region of the present-day Congo. Among the earliest inhabitants were the pygmies and the Bacongo peoples. Portuguese sailors reached the region in 1482, but the area remained largely unknown until the late 1800s. Between 1874 and 1877 the British explorer Henry Stanley explored the area. In 1884 Belgium's King Leopold II obtained European recognition of a Congo Free State at the Berlin Conference on African Affairs.

Colonial Rule. Between 1885 and 1908 Leopold's agents used unscrupulous methods to secure labor to exploit the Congo's rubber and ivory resources. Mistreatment of the people created an international scandal, and in 1908 Leopold turned over control of the area to the Belgian parliament.

From then until 1960, large companies controlled the economy, Roman Catholic missionaries with government subsidies controlled education, and Belgian administrators ran the government.

Under Belgian rule there was economic advancement, and a high literacy rate was achieved. But there was little secondary education and no higher education until the founding of Lovanium University in 1954.

The administration encouraged vocational training and the breaking of tribal ties, but did not allow the inhabitants to gain political experience. Early African political expression took the form of national religious sects. After World War II, however, Belgium slowly liberalized its colonial rule.

In 1954 the Bacongo people, led by Joseph Kasavubu, demanded political rights and autonomy from the rest of the country. From then on the tempo of political change greatly accelerated. In 1955 Belgium discussed a plan for citizenship, but in response to growing African pressure, Belgium announced in January 1960 that independence would be granted June 30.

Independence. The country held elections in the midst of turmoil. Parties were hastily organized by almost every ethnic group, and the elections failed to produce a clear majority for any single party or group. Patrice Lumumba, leader of the National Congolese Movement, which won the most seats in the assembly, became prime minister, or chief executive, of the new republic. His closest election rival, Joseph Kasavubu, became president, or head of state.

Lumumba's government faced both a mutiny in the army and the flight of most of the country's European technicians and administrators. The Congo's richest province, Katanga, under the leadership of Moise Tshombe, seceded from the new republic in July 1960.

Lumumba then appealed to the United Nations for aid in restoring order. A military coup, led by Col. Joseph Mobutu, overthrew Lumumba in September 1960, and he was assassinated in February 1961.

In July 1961 Kasavubu designated Cyrille Adoula as prime minister, but the new government could not stabilize the situation. In 1963 UN forces finally ended Katanga's secession. In June 1964 Adoula resigned, and in July Tshombe became prime minister despite the objections of many African states, which saw him as a tool of European mining interests.

In August 1964 a newly adopted constitution vested increased powers in the president, and Tshombe showed signs of wanting the office. In October 1965 Kasavubu claimed that Tshombe had violated constitutional procedures and ousted him from office. Evariste Kimba was appointed prime minister in Tshombe's place.

In November 1965 army chief of staff Joseph Mobutu ousted both Kimba and Kasavubu and named himself president. In 1966 Mobutu took over all legislative powers from parliament, and in 1967 he proclaimed a new constitution providing for a strong presidential system of government. Mobutu also instituted needed economic reforms.

—Hibberd V. B. Kline, Jr.;
Vera L. Zolberg

COSTA RICA

Official name: Republic of Costa Rica
Area: 19,575 square miles
Population: (1966 est.) 1,486,000
Capital: San José (Pop., 1965 est., urban area, 339,100)
Language: Spanish
Religion: Roman Catholicism
Currency unit: Colón
National holiday: Independence day, September 15

The Republic of Costa Rica, a small country in Central America, is bounded on the north by Nicaragua, on the east by the Caribbean Sea and Panama, and on the south and west by the Pacific Ocean.

THE LAND. Costa Rica has three major regions: a Caribbean coastal plain, a mountainous central area, and a Pacific coastal plain.

The Caribbean coast is rainy and covered with tropical evergreen forests and swamps. The central region, which has a temperate climate, consists of high flat basins formed by three mountain ranges—the Cordillera de Guanacaste, the Cordillera Central, and the Cordillera de Talamanca. The *Meseta Central,* or central plateau, the largest basin of the region, lies between the Cordillera de Guanacaste and the Cordillera de Talamanca.

The Pacific coastal plain, a region of tropical forests and savanna, has alternating wet and dry seasons.

THE PEOPLE. With the exception of a relatively small Negro population concentrated in the Caribbean coastal area, Costa Ricans are almost all of European, largely Spanish, descent. Most people live in the Meseta Central, the site of San José, the industrial and cultural center as well as the capital of the country.

Costa Rica has a very high population growth rate, estimated at more than 4 percent a year between 1958 and 1965.

ECONOMY. Costa Rica's rapid rate of population increase creates serious economic problems. Although the total national income increased considerably between 1960 and 1965, population growth absorbed most of the gain, and living standards rose but little.

In 1963 Costa Rica entered the Central American Common Market, and agricultural production, the main source of national income, and manufacturing expanded rapidly. By the mid-1960s Costa Rica had become the most industrialized nation of Central America. The most important industrial products are foodstuffs, cotton, textiles, synthetic fibers, and pharmaceuticals.

In 1966 Costa Rica's exports earned $138 million and its imports cost $179 million. Coffee, bananas, cacao, abaca, cotton, and cattle are the major agricultural exports. Other exports are fish, lumber, gold, and manganese.

Costa Rica's economic progress is heavily dependent on foreign aid and investment. Through the Alliance for Progress the United States has helped finance Costa Rica's efforts to industrialize further.

GOVERNMENT. Costa Rica has a presidential form of government. The head of state and chief executive is the president, who is popularly elected to a four-year term of office. Legislative powers rest with the unicameral Legislative Assembly, which is also popularly elected to a four-year term.

Costa Rica is a member of the United Nations, the Organization of American States (OAS), and the Organization of Central American States.

HISTORY. Columbus discovered Costa Rica in 1502 on his last voyage to America. Expecting to find gold, he named it *Costa Rica,* or rich coast. Disappointed treasure hunters who followed him stayed only long enough to pillage the land. The first permanent European settlement was established in 1564 at Cartago, on the Meseta Central, by Juan Vásquez de Coronado.

Costa Rica was part of the Spanish colonial province ruled by the captain general of Guatemala. When Agustín de Iturbide proclaimed Mexico's independence from Spain in 1821, the Spanish Captain General Gabino Gaínza declared Central America independent. In 1822 Gaínza was overthrown and the region was annexed to Mexico.

Iturbide fell in 1823, and Costa Rica joined Guatemala, El Salvador, Honduras, and Nicaragua to form the United Provinces of Central America. Dissatisfaction with Guatemala's domination of the union soon developed, and in 1839 Costa Rica withdrew from the federation and became a separate nation.

Independence. Braulio Carrillo, a dynamic president, who served from 1834 to 1837 and again from 1838 to 1842, promoted the cultivation of coffee, which became a major export, and subdivided many large estates, thus increasing the number of small landholders.

In 1842 Carrillo's dictatorial methods led to a successful revolt under the leadership of Francisco Morazán. Morazán was himself shortly overthrown, and a period of anarchy followed. Order was finally restored in 1849.

In 1870 Tomás Guardia overthrew the government and dominated national affairs until his death in 1882. He modernized the economy and increased unity, partly through a vast program of railroad construction.

Under Pres. Bernardo Soto (1885–1890), free compulsory education was established and in 1889 the first free elections were held. Costa Rican support of democratic principles was expressed in public hostility to a coup in 1917 led by Federico Tinoco Granados, and his regime lasted for less than two years.

Conflict with Panama over Coto, a border region on the Pacific coast, dominated foreign affairs during the 1920s and 1930s. Costa Rica invaded the Panamanian-occupied territory in 1921, and the United States pressured Panama to accept Costa Rican control of Coto. The issue was finally settled in 1941, when both countries agreed to redefine their common boundary.

Contemporary Costa Rica. In 1948 a communist-supported attempt to elect fraudulently former president Calderón Guardia over the moderate Otilio Ulate was frustrated by rebels under the leadership of José Figueres. The Figueres victory was followed by 18 months of rule by a junta. During that period many progressive social reforms were enacted into law. Otilio Ulate was inaugurated in 1950 after Figueres restored civilian rule.

At the end of Ulate's term in 1953, Figueres was elected president. Figueres, a liberal, was a severe critic of Latin American dictators, in particular of Pres. Anastasio Somoza of Nicaragua. Early in 1955 a Nicaraguan-instigated rebellion broke out, but the rebels were crushed.

Francisco Orlich, a supporter and friend of Figueres, was defeated in the 1958 election by Mario Echandi Jiménez, a conservative. In 1962, however, Orlich won the presidency and, a year later, brought Costa Rica into the Central American Common Market. The resulting economic progress led to greater political stability and unity.

Economic growth continued under Pres. José Joaquín Trejos Fernández, elected in 1966 as the candidate of a coalition that included Ulate, Echandi, and Calderón Guardia.

—George W. Carey; Jerome Fischman

CUBA

Official name: Republic of Cuba
Area: 44,218 square miles
Population: (1967 est.) 8,033,000
Capital: Havana (Pop., 1965 est., urban area, 1,543,900)
Language: Spanish
Religion: Roman Catholicism
Currency unit: Peso
National holiday: Independence day, May 20

Cuba, the largest island in the Greater Antilles, occupies a strategic position dominating the sea lanes that link the Atlantic Ocean, the Caribbean Sea, and the Gulf of Mexico. The island lies about 100 miles southeast of the United States, from which it is separated by the Straits of Florida. There is a major U.S. naval base in southeastern Cuba, at Guantanamo Bay.

A revolutionary government was established in Cuba in 1959 under the leadership of Dr. Fidel Castro Ruz. Under Castro's leadership, Cuba became closely tied to the communist bloc of nations.

THE LAND. Cuba is made up largely of level or rolling land. There are only three mountain areas—all small. The Sierra Maestra and associated highlands lie in the extreme south-

east and reach a maximum elevation of about 6,500 feet. The heavily eroded, limestone Sierra de los Organos, with a maximum elevation of some 2,500 feet, is in the dry and barren northwest. The Trinidad Mountains, rising less than 4,000 feet, are on the south coast, east of Cienfuegos.

The island has two rainy seasons, one in summer and one in winter. Hurricanes frequently occur in the fall and winter.

THE PEOPLE. The people of Cuba are largely of Spanish, African, and mixed origins. More than half the population lives in urban areas. The major cities include Havana, the capital; Camaguey, a center of the sugar industry; and Santiago, a major port.

The rate of population increase is high, but there has been a heavy emigration since the early 1960s, when the Castro government launched a socialist program. Many of the émigrés settled in the United States. They included large numbers of professional people, managerial personnel, and technicians.

ECONOMY. Cuba is a rich country, and it is among the most economically developed nations of Latin America. The island has rich soils and considerable mineral wealth. There are abundant deposits of iron ore, chromite, manganese, nickel, cobalt, and copper ore. There is also some petroleum, although not enough to meet the country's needs. There is a good transportation system, with an excellent road and rail network and a number of well equipped ports.

Cuba has long been one of the world's leading producers of sugar, and is also known for its tobacco, which is grown in the region east of the Sierra de los Organos. Coffee is produced in southeastern Cuba. Other important crops include henequen, sweet potatoes, citrus fruits, vegetables, and pineapple.

LOOK MAGAZINE

MODERN BUILDINGS RISE ABOVE THE SLUMS in Havana, Cuba's capital and largest city.

WIDE WORLD

FIDEL CASTRO in the Sierra Maestra in 1957.

Manufacturing is significant and growing. Sugar processing is the most important activity, but Cuba is on a par with several European countries in the production of several types of goods—synthetic fibers, for example. Steel and power consumption are also high. But industry has been hampered by a shortage of technicians and parts since the Castro revolution.

In 1965 Cuba's exports earned $686 million and its imports cost $865 million. Sugar represents about 85 percent of export earnings. Tobacco; ores, especially nickel; and chemicals are also significant exports. Imports consist largely of machinery and transportation equipment, foodstuffs, and manufactured goods.

Before the establishment of the Castro regime, the United States was Cuba's major trading partner. By 1965 the Soviet Union had replaced it. China and other communist-controlled countries are also important trading partners.

GOVERNMENT. Cuba has traditionally been a republic with democratic institutions. But the country has experienced long periods of dictatorship. The constitution of 1940, which was suspended in 1959, provided for an elected president and a legislature of two houses. The upper house, the Senate, included 54 members elected to four-year terms, and the lower house had 140 members, half of whom were elected every two years.

Dr. Castro instituted a dictatorship under his personal control. The head of state was still nominally the president, but power rested in Castro's hands as prime minister and first secretary of the Communist Party of Cuba, or PCC, from its initials in Spanish.

The United Party of the Cuban Socialist Revolution (PURSC), formed in 1962 by the merger of Cuba's old Communist party with Castro's Integrated Revolutionary Organizations (ORI), was renamed the Communist Party of Cuba in 1965. Castro's followers remained the dominant group. In 1967 Castro promised that Cuba would have a new, "socialist," constitution by 1970.

Cuba is a member of the United Nations.

HISTORY. Christopher Columbus claimed the island of Cuba for Spain in 1492, on his first voyage to the new world. At that time the island was inhabited by Arawak Indians. The Arawak had been weakened by raids by the warlike Carib Indians and they were soon enslaved by the Spanish.

Spanish Rule. Under the leadership of Gov. Diego Velázquez, Cuba became an important base for Spanish exploration and conquest of the American mainland. Cities were built and slaves were brought from Africa to replace the fast-disappearing Arawak as a source of labor. The island grew rich from sugar and was the object of pirate raids during the 1500s and 1600s. During a war with Spain in the 1700s the British briefly gained control of Havana.

Cuba remained aloof from the general struggle for independence from Spanish rule that occupied the mainland during the early 1800s. Although in 1812 a slave revolt was led by José Aponte, Spanish rule remained secure, based on capable administrators, loyal troops, and an aristocracy that feared the loss of its wealth should relations with Spain be changed. Resentment against Spain developed by the mid-1800s, however, as Spanish rule became increasingly corrupt.

The first serious attempt to organize an independence movement was made by Narciso López, a veteran of the mainland independence struggles. López was captured and executed, but his death served to strengthen Cuban nationalism. In 1868 a group of Cuban patriots, including Carlos Manuel de Céspedes, drew up the *Grito de Yara*, or "Cry of Yara," a call for independence. The new movement fought a bitter ten-year struggle, the Ten Years' War (1868–1878), which ended in a truce.

Resentment against Spanish rule intensified in the early 1890s, when the island was struck by an economic depression and North American tariff restrictions were raised against Cuban tobacco and sugar exports. In 1895 a new rebellion broke out, sparked by the poet and journalist José Martí, Cuba's national hero.

The rebel forces were led by men such as Máximo Gómex, Antonio Maceo, and Calixto García. The Spanish colonial troops were commanded by Gen. Valeriano Weyler. Within a short time, Weyler had the rebellion under control, and he launched a bitter campaign of repression, during which many thousands of Cubans died of mistreatment.

U.S. Rule. The Spanish repression kindled cries in the United States for support of the Cubans, and in 1898 war broke out between the United States and Spain after the U.S. battleship Maine blew up in Havana harbor. The Spanish-American War lasted but 100 days. Spain gave up Cuba, but instead of granting Cuba independence, the United States sent forces to occupy the island, remaining until 1902.

During the U.S. occupation, Cuba benefited from improved sanitary conditions and public education was extended. Yellow fever was wiped out after a Cuban doctor, Carlos Finlay, discovered that it was carried by a mosquito. But Cuban resentment grew as the United States continued to refuse to withdraw its troops.

The United States set as a condition for withdrawal the inclusion in the Cuban constitution of the Platt Amendment. The amendment provided the United States with naval bases in Cuba, including a base at Guantanamo Bay, and allowed the United States to intervene if it felt Cuban sovereignty threatened.

Independence. The Cuban constitution was promulgated in 1901, and in 1902 a conservative, Tomás Estrada Palma, became Cuba's first president. Liberal opposition and popular unrest led to the resignation of Estrada in 1906, and U.S. forces were again landed in Cuba.

In 1909 José Gómez, a liberal, was elected president. Instability continued, and in 1917 U.S. troops again returned. In 1925 Gen. Gerardo Machado won the presidency, and changed the constitution to maintain himself in power. Machado instituted an era of tyranny that lasted until 1933, when he was toppled by an army revolt led by Sgt. Fulgencio Batista.

Batista remained in control of Cuba until 1944, when he unexpectedly allowed fair elections. Dr. Ramón Grau San Martín, once an associate of Batista but by then a bitter political foe, was elected president. Grau was succeeded in 1948 by Carlos Prío Socarrás. In 1952 Batista again seized power and gradually instituted a repressive regime that became increasingly unpopular.

Castro Revolution. In 1953 a young law-school student, Fidel Castro, and his brother, Raúl, led a revolt against Batista. On July 26, the rebels unsuccessfully tried to seize the Moncado army base in Santiago. Captured, but later pardoned in a general amnesty, the Castros went into exile.

In 1956 Castro returned with a small band of followers that included an Argentinian, Ernesto (Ché) Guevara. They succeeded in reaching the rugged Sierra Maestra, and gradually their strength grew as students and peasants from Oriente Province joined them. Large-scale fighting broke out in 1958, and on Jan. 1, 1959, Batista fled the country.

Castro took power on a wave of popular support, but his popularity quickly waned at home and abroad. Former associates broke with him over communist influence in the new government, and in 1960 a socialist program was launched with the nationalization of much of the economy. Hundreds of thousands of Cubans fled, most of them finding refuge in the United States.

U.S. property was among that seized, and the United States retaliated by reducing sugar imports from the island. In 1961 Cuba signed a trade agreement with the Soviet Union, and Castro announced his acceptance of Marxist-Leninist doctrine.

U.S. diplomatic relations with Cuba were severed in 1961, and in that year the United States sponsored an invasion of Cuba by a force of Cuban exiles. The force landed at the Bay of Pigs, and was soon destroyed. In 1962 Castro exchanged the survivors of the invasion for needed foodstuffs and medical supplies from the United States.

A new crisis in Cuban-U.S. relations occurred in 1962, when U.S. Pres. John F. Kennedy charged that Soviet missiles were being installed in Cuba. A blockade of Cuba was announced by the United States, and the Soviet Union agreed to dismantle the missile bases.

Castro attempted to spread his form of revolution throughout Latin America, and Cuban-supported insurrections broke out in many countries. In 1962 the Organization of American States (OAS) suspended Cuba's participation in the work of the organization. Prominent among the Cuban revolutionaries active in promoting Castro-type revolutions in other countries was Ché Guevara, who lost his life fighting with a rebel band in Bolivia in 1967.

—George W. Carey; Jerome Fischman

CYPRUS

Official name: Republic of Cyprus
Area: 3,572 square miles
Population: (1967 est.) 614,000
Capital: Nicosia (Pop., 1964, urban area, 103,000)
Language: Greek, Turkish
Religion: Orthodox Christianity, Islam
Currency unit: Pound
National holiday: Independence day, October 1

Cyprus, an independent island republic in the eastern part of the Mediterranean Sea, lies about 40 miles south of Turkey.

THE LAND. The island of Cyprus is mountainous. Two ranges rim the coasts—the Kyrenia Mountains in the north and the Olympus Mountains in the south. A wide, fertile plain occupies the center of the island. Summers are hot and dry, and winters are cool with occasional rain.

THE PEOPLE. About four-fifths of the Cypriots are Greek Christians, and about one-fifth are Turkish Muslims. The island's population is concentrated in the central plains, especially around Nicosia, and along the southern coast, in the port cities of Limassol and Famagusta.

ECONOMY. Copper, asbestos, and iron mined in the Olympus Mountains are among Cyprus' principal exports. Vegetables, oranges, and wines produced for the European market are also important. Wheat, olives, and carobs (a cattle fodder) are grown. The island has not developed any heavy industry, but there are many light-manufacturing plants.

Tourism is encouraged by the government and has been an important source of income. In 1966 Cyprus' exports earned $78 million and its imports cost $154 million.

GOVERNMENT. Cyprus' constitution, adopted at the time of independence, established a republic with government posts divided proportionally between the Greek and Turkish communities. The president was to be a Greek-speaking Christian, the vice president, a Turkish-speaking Muslim. The parliament was also divided —70 percent Greek and 30 percent Turkish.

Cyprus is a member of the United Nations and of the Commonwealth of Nations.

HISTORY. People have lived on Cyprus since before 4000 BC. The ancient Greeks traded with Cyprus and established colonies on the island. From about 800 BC to modern times, Cyprus was ruled by whatever nation dominated the adjacent seas. Phoenicians, Assyrians, Persians, Romans, Byzantines, Arabs, Crusaders, and Venetians all occupied the island.

In 1571 the Ottoman Turks conquered Cyprus and held it until 1878, when Britain took control. During the period of Ottoman rule a Turkish-speaking Muslim minority developed alongside the original Greek-speaking Christian majority. In 1914, at the beginning of World War I, Britain formally annexed Cyprus from the Ottoman Empire, an ally of Germany. In 1925 the island became a British crown colony.

During the years of Venetian and Ottoman government the island had undergone an economic and cultural decline, but as a British colony it experienced a revival. With this revival came an awakening of national consciousness and a rising demand on the part of Greek Cypriots for union with Greece, *Enosis,* a demand Turkish Cypriots opposed. In 1955 Greek Cypriots began a guerrilla war against the British.

Independence. In 1959, after years of bloody fighting, an agreement signed by Britain, Greece, and Turkey granted Cyprus independence with strict safeguards for the rights of the Turkish minority and for British military interests.

Archbishop Makarios, head of the Cypriot Orthodox Church and leader of the Greek community, became president, with a Turkish Cypriot leader as vice president. Increasing friction between the Greek and Turkish communities soon paralyzed the new government, however.

At the end of 1963, a dispute arose over a proposed constitutional change that would have reduced the power of the Turkish minority. Turkish officials withdrew from the government, and civil war broke out between the two communities. Turkey and Greece became involved in the conflict and came close to war over Cyprus.

In 1964 a UN force arrived on the island and secured a ceasefire, but the United Nations failed to achieve a permanent solution to the island's communal problem. Fighting again erupted in late 1967, and Greece and Turkey were again drawn into the conflict. Despite the crisis, the Greek Cypriot administration held elections in 1968, and Archbishop Makarios was reelected president.

—Charles Issawi; Alexander Melamid

CZECHOSLOVAKIA

Official name: Czechoslovak Socialist Republic
Area: 49,370 square miles
Population: (1966 est.) 14,240,000
Capital: Prague (Pop., 1965 est., 1,023,000)
Language: Czech, Slovak
Religion: Protestantism, Roman Catholicism
Currency unit: Koruna
National holiday: Liberation day, May 9

The Czechoslovak Socialist Republic is a landlocked nation in east-central Europe. It is bounded on the north by Poland, on the east by the Soviet Union, on the south by Hungary and Austria, and on the west by West Germany and East Germany.

The country consists of three historic regions—Bohemia, or Czecy, in the west, Moravia in the center, and Slovakia in the east. These regions were united in 1918 to form Czechoslovakia.

THE LAND. Uplands dominate Czechoslovakia's terrain. In Bohemia, the western third of the country, the rolling plateau of the Bohemian Quadrangle is rimmed with mountains. The Bohemian Forest in the southwest, the Erz (Ore) Mountains in the northwest, and the Sudeten range in the north all rise above 4,000 feet, and the hills of the Czech-Moravian Uplands (Ceskomoravská Vysočina) form the eastern limit of the plateau. The Elbe River and its tributaries drain the entire region. Flowing northwest, the Elbe provides a route to the North Sea.

Moravia, in central Czechoslovakia, is a wide passageway of river valleys and low hills drained by the Morava and Oder rivers. The Morava flows south toward the Danube River, which provides access to the Black Sea. The Oder flows north toward the Baltic.

Higher mountains rise in Slovakia, the eastern third of the country. The Carpathian range reaches a peak of more than 8,000 feet. From this mountainous core a series of lower ranges, hills, and plateaus descends toward lowlands in the southeast.

Czechoslovakia's climate is moderate, with temperatures averaging about 70°F in summer and 20°F in winter. Between 20 and 40 inches of rain fall each year, most of it in the winter.

THE PEOPLE. Slightly less than two-thirds of the people are Czech, and just under one-third are Slovak. There are small groups of Hungarians, Ukrainians, Germans, and Poles. Czech and Slovak, the official languages, are West Slavic tongues.

Slovaks are concentrated in the east, Czechs in the center and west. Friction between the two groups has created serious problems.

Population is densest in central Bohemia, especially around Prague, the capital, largest city, and cultural and economic center of the country.

ECONOMY. Czechoslovakia is one of the most prosperous countries in eastern Europe. Its prosperity stems largely from industry, which is based on the country's location along many excellent transportation routes, its industrious and skilled population, and its rich natural resources.

Mineral resources include large deposits of brown coal, more limited amounts of hard coal, and uranium. There are also smaller deposits of antimony, mercury, graphite, glass sands, silver, iron ore, lead, and zinc.

Agriculture. Although there is rich soil, agriculture is limited to the lowland areas and contributed only 13 percent to the national product in 1965. Most of the land is cultivated by collective farms. The limited amount of good farmland is partially compensated for by the use of advanced agricultural techniques.

Wheat, rye, barley, oats, sugar beets, and potatoes are the leading crops. Meadows and fields devoted to fodder crops support large herds of livestock.

Industry. Czechoslovakia is one of eastern Europe's most industrialized nations, and in 1965 industry contributed 65 percent of the national product. All large-scale industries and businesses are operated by the government.

Chemicals, iron and steel, heavy machinery, and electricity are the country's major products. Traditional light industries, including leather working, glass making, textile weaving, brewing, and food processing, still thrive but have declined in importance as heavy industry expanded during the 1950s.

Industrial activity is concentrated around Prague and Plzen, in central Bohemia, Brno, in central Moravia, and Bratislava, in southwestern Slovakia on the Danube.

Trade. In 1966 imports cost $2,729 million, and exports earned $2,745 million. Iron, steel, machinery, and chemicals are the leading exports, and fuel oil, raw materials, and foodstuffs are imported. The Soviet Union is the country's leading trading partner, followed by other eastern European states. In the early 1960s, trade was expanded with some western European, Asian, and African countries.

GOVERNMENT. The Communist party dominates political life. At the head of the party is a central committee, whose presidium, or executive committee, determines national policy. The first secretary of the central committee is the key political figure in the country.

A constitution places executive power in a president, who is chosen for a five-year term by the popularly elected 300-member National Assembly. The president appoints a cabinet of ministers. Candidates for the assembly are chosen by the National Front, a mass organization controlled by the Communist party.

Czechoslovakia is a member of the United Nations; the Warsaw Pact, a military grouping of European communist-controlled states; and the

PETER SPRAGUE

PRAGUE'S CHARLES BRIDGE, a city landmark, was built by King Charles IV in 1357.

Council for Mutual Economic Assistance (COMECON), which attempts to coordinate economic programs within the Soviet bloc.

HISTORY. Czechoslovakia came into existence as a single independent state in 1918. Prior to that, the history of the Czechs of Bohemia and Moravia and that of the Slovaks differed, but each was characterized by domination by other nations.

The basins of the Elbe, Oder, and Morava rivers, protected by the surrounding mountains, had been settled by Slavic peoples by the 500s. By the 600s some tribal and geographical distinctions had been made between Czechs, Moravians, and Slovaks.

Moravia developed most quickly, and by the end of the 800s Moravian princes ruled an empire that included Slovakia and parts of present-day Austria and Hungary. Moravian subjects became Christians during the 800s. In the early 900s, the Moravian empire was conquered by the Magyar people of Hungary.

Hungary ruled Slovakia and the eastern part of old Moravia for 1,000 years, until the defeat of Austria-Hungary in World War I. The Czech tribes of Bohemia were gradually united during the 800s and 900s. By the end of the 900s one leader ruled Bohemia and western Moravia.

In the 1000s the kingdom of Bohemia became part of the Holy Roman Empire, but its military power and political strength was great enough to permit the state a great deal of independence. Its wealth, prestige, and cultural and political leadership reached a peak in the 1300s, when Prince Charles of Bohemia became Holy Roman emperor.

Hapsburg Rule. During the 1400s, especially after the execution in 1415 of a Bohemian religious reformer, John Hus, conflict within Bohemia and between Bohemia and the empire led to a gradual decline in the kingdom's prestige. In 1526 a Hapsburg of Austria was elected king of Bohemia, and in 1547 the Bohemian crown became the hereditary possession of the Hapsburgs, who ruled Bohemia together

with Austria and Hungary. Hapsburgs also ruled the Holy Roman Empire.

The Bohemian nobles resented the Hapsburg king. Not only because he was not Czech, but also because he was a Roman Catholic and during the late 1500s many Bohemians had become Protestants. In 1618 the Bohemian nobles rebelled. The rebellion raged for two years, until 1620, when the Bohemians were defeated at the battle of White Mountain, near Prague.

Through the 1600s and 1700s Bohemia was included in the Hapsburg Holy Roman Empire, which was succeeded by the Hapsburg-ruled Austrian Empire. Catholic German rule impoverished Bohemia and crushed Czech spirits and Czech prospects. In the early 1800s the pan-Slav movement developed in Bohemia and Slovakia, and in 1848 it contributed to a Slavic revolt against the German-speaking Austrians.

The rebellion was put down by 1849, but the movement gained strength as Austria lost power to Prussia and gradually relaxed its rule. In 1867 Austria's reception of the Magyars of Hungary into an equal partnership in a dual Austrian-Hungarian monarchy served to spur the Slavic independence movement. By the last decades of the 1800s, Austria-Hungary's encouragement of industrialization in Bohemia had made the Czechs among the most prosperous people of Europe.

Austria-Hungary went to war with Serbia in 1914, and World War I began. The Czechs were economically, emotionally, and politically ready to take advantage of the turmoil the war caused in Austria-Hungary. Czech and Slovak soldiers surrendered independently to the Allied armies and fought against Austria-Hungary, thus wining support for their independence movement in the Allied countries.

During the war Tomáš Masaryk, the leader of the Czech national movement, and Slovak leaders agreed to unite in a new country and formed a provisional government. After the war the Allies recognized the provisional government as the representative of the Czech and Slovak peoples, and in

1918 Czechoslovak independence was proclaimed.

Independence. The new state was formally recognized in 1919 in the Treaty of St. Germain. A democratic constitution was adopted, and Masaryk became the first president. He was succeeded in 1935 by his associate, Eduard Beneš.

Czechoslovakia was the most promising new parliamentary democracy in Europe, and in many ways Czechoslovakia more than fulfilled its promise. It became the most democratic and prosperous country in eastern Europe.

Although equal status had been granted to Czechs and Slovaks, the new state was based largely on Czech political and economic leadership centered in Prague. The Slovaks, after 1,000 years of rule by Hungary, were not as advanced as the Czechs politically or economically.

Friction between Czechs and Slovaks mounted over political, economic, religious, educational, and social issues. To these difficulties was added the dissatisfaction. Suffering the effects of nority included in the new state. The Germans, concentrated in the strategic Sudeten region of northwestern Czechoslovakia, resented rule by Czechs and Slovaks, whom they had dominated for centuries. They charged discrimination and claimed that they had no effective voice in government.

The problems of Czechs and Slovaks and of Slavs and Germans might have been solved if Adolf Hitler and the Nazi party of Germany had not taken advantage of the German minority's dissatisfaction. Suffering the effects of the world economic depression of the 1930s and excited by Hitler's brand of German nationalism, Sudeten Germans served as German agents within Czechoslovakia. Their complaints and Hitler's diplomatic and military pressures created an international crisis that led in 1938 to the Munich agreement.

Britain and France agreed at Munich to the division of Czechoslovakia and the transfer of one-third of its population and its vital defenses to Germany. Poland and Hungary also took areas they had long claimed. In return, Hitler promised to leave untouched the remainder of Czechoslovakia. In 1939, despite Munich, German troops occupied the rest of Czechoslovakia.

During the war, a major Czechoslovakian resistance movement was organized in which Czechoslovakian communists played a prominent role. In 1944–1945 Soviet troops liberated Slovakia, Moravia, and most of Bohemia from the Germans. U.S. forces liberated western Bohemia in 1945, but the Soviets insisted that Soviet troops be allowed to free the capital, Prague. This gained for the Soviet Union the bulk of the prestige associated with the country's liberation.

Communist Rule. The presence of Soviet troops and the desire of President Beneš and other Czechoslovak leaders to cooperate with the Soviet Union allowed the communists to make their leader, Klement Gottwald, prime minister. The communists also gained control of the key departments of defense, which controlled the army, and of interior, which controlled the police.

In elections held in 1946, however, the Communist party received only 38 percent of the votes. In 1948, because of Soviet refusal to allow Czechoslovakia to receive U.S. economic aid under the Marshall Plan, it seemed likely that the communists would receive even fewer votes. In 1948, before elections could be held, the communists staged a successful coup d'etat. They took control of the government and made Czechoslovakia part of the Soviet bloc.

During the 1950s the communist-controlled government nationalized all large-scale business and industry and collectivized agriculture. The government concentrated on developing Slovakia and on building up heavy industry in Bohemia. Czechoslovakia became one of the most productive states in the Soviet bloc, and its industry contributed heavily to Soviet economic aid projects in Africa and the Middle East.

But inefficient state management led to a sharp decline in Czechoslovakian output in the late 1950s and early 1960s. In 1965 the party reorganized its economic control programs and established a new management plan emphasizing profits and wage incentives. In 1967 economic reforms were carried still further, and in 1968 leading party and government posts were filled by more liberal communists.

—George Kish; Robert F. Byrnes

DAHOMEY

Official name: Republic of Dahomey
Area: 43,483 square miles
Population: (1966 est.) 2,410,000
Capital: Porto-Novo (Pop., 1964 est., 69,500)
Language: French, African languages
Religion: Christianity, Islam, traditional religions
Currency unit: Franc CFA (African Financial Community)
National holiday: Independence day, August 1

Dahomey, a republic in west Africa, is bounded on the east by Nigeria, on the south by the Atlantic Ocean, on the west by Togo, and on the north by Upper Volta and Niger. Dahomey, a former French territory, received its independence in 1960.

THE LAND. Most of Dahomey lies at an elevation of less than 1,000 feet above sea level. Dahomey has a narrow, sandy coastline. Behind the coast are marshes and lagoons. The mainland begins in a low-lying clay plain, which is intensively cultivated. There are grasslands in the north.

A low dividing ridge crosses the country at its greatest width. Rivers south of the ridge drain into the sea. To the north they are tributaries of the Volta and Niger rivers.

The climate in the coastal region is hot and wet. In the north it is dry from November to June, and rainy from June to November.

THE PEOPLE. The population of Dahomey includes many ethnic groups. The Fons live in the southern part of the country. The Nagots live in western Dahomey and in the districts of Porto-Novo and Abomey. The Baribas live in the north. Other ethnic groups

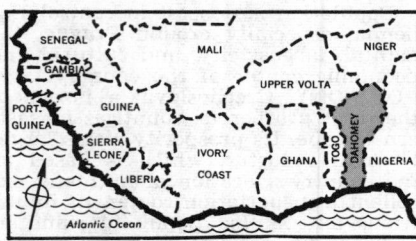

are the Peuhls, the Sanbas, the Azios, and the Adjas. There is a small European population.

Dahomey is densely populated, and numbers of men emigrate to neighboring countries in search of work.

Most people live in rural areas. The port of Cotonou is Dahomey's largest city and economic center. Porto-Novo, the capital, is the second largest city.

ECONOMY. Dahomey's economy depends on agriculture. Most of the people are farmers who grow corn, coffee, peanuts, and millet. Fishing provides an additional source of income for the people of the coastal region. Livestock are also raised. Although there are deposits of iron, gold, and chromite, mineral resources are not exploited to any great extent. There is little industry, but handicrafts are important.

In 1965 exports earned $14 million and imports cost $34 million. Exports consist largely of oil palm products. Imports include foodstuffs, motor vehicles, machinery, petroleum products, and cotton fabrics. Most trade is conducted with France.

GOVERNMENT. Until 1965 Dahomey elected a president and vice-president, each to a five-year term. The president served as chief of state. The vice-president held actual executive power. Legislative power was vested in a single-chambered National Assembly, which consisted of 42 members. In 1965 the army took power.

Dahomey is a member of the United Nations and of the Organization of African Unity (OAU).

UNITED NATIONS
DAHOMEAN WEAVER working on a tapestry.

HISTORY. Many rich and highly organized kingdoms existed in the area of present-day Dahomey. The most famous was the Fon kingdom of Abomey, whose ruler had conquered other coastal states by the early 1700s.

Portuguese traders came to what is now Porto-Novo in the 1600s. With the rise of the slave trade the English, Dutch, Spanish, and French also came to the area. European slave companies dealt largely with the foreign minister of the kingdom of Abomey.

French Rule. In 1851 the French established themselves at Cotonou, and in 1890 hostilities broke out between France and Abomey. In 1890 France established a protectorate over the area and exiled the king, although France continued to use tribal chiefs in administering the region. The boundaries of Dahomey were defined by 1898, and in 1904 Dahomey became part of the Federation of French West Africa.

Local conflicts dominated Dahomey's politics after World War II. In 1947 France introduced a territorial assembly, and Sourou-Migan Apithy, a southern leader, and Hubert Maga, a northerner, were elected to the French National Assembly. But regional movements did not solidify into a single national organization.

France granted Dahomey internal autonomy in 1957, and Apithy was elected prime minister. In 1958 Dahomey voted to become a member of the French Community.

Independence. France granted Dahomey its independence in August 1960. Several parties merged, and Maga was elected president. Party unity did not last, however, and a military coup overthrew Maga in October 1963.

The army set up a provisional government which, although headed by Col. Christophe Soglo, also included Maga, Apithy, and Justin Ahomadegbé. In January 1964 the people elected Apithy, the sole candidate, president and Ahomadegbé premier. In November 1965 Soglo ousted Apithy and Ahomadegbé, and assumed executive power the following month.
—Hibberd V. B. Kline, Jr.;
Vera L. Zolberg

DENMARK

Official name: Kingdom of Denmark
Area: 16,629 square miles
Population: (1966 est.) 4,797,000
Capital: Copenhagen (Pop. 1965, urban area: 1,377,605)
Language: Danish
Religion: Protestant
Currency unit: Krone
National holiday: Birthday of the king, March 11

Denmark, a small kingdom in northern Europe, lies between the North Sea, to the west, and the Baltic Sea, to the east. Its only land boundary is with West Germany, to the south. Denmark consists of the Jutland peninsula, four main islands—Fyn, Sjaelland, Lolland, and Bornholm, and 478 smaller islands, 99 of which are inhabited. The self-governing Faeroe Islands and Greenland are dependencies of Denmark.

Denmark occupies a strategic position in northern Europe controlling the Kattegat and the Skagerrak, the waterways that connect the Baltic Sea with the North Sea. The narrow Sound, the only easily navigable waterway between the Kattegat and the Baltic, passes between Sjaelland and Sweden and is the major route for shipping between the Baltic and North seas.

THE LAND. Denmark has a long, deeply indented coastline with many fine harbors. Almost all of Denmark is low plains. The highest point, on hilly East Jutland, is less than 600 feet above sea level. There are many small lakes and streams throughout Denmark.

Denmark's climate is generally mild and moist. Average temperatures range from about 32°F in January to 62°F in July, and rainfall averages about 24 inches a year in the east, and about 30 inches in the west. In the western part of the country, winters are slightly warmer, summers cooler, fog more frequent, and the humidity higher.

THE PEOPLE. The Danish population is quite homogeneous. Danish is the universal language, and 97 percent of the Danes belong to the Danish Lutheran Church.

Overall population density is high, but the rate of population growth is low. The most heavily populated regions are northern Fyn, East Jutland, and eastern Sjaelland, especially the Copenhagen area, where almost 20 percent of the population lives. Western Jutland, which is rather barren, is sparsely settled.

ECONOMY. Denmark's prosperity is based on its very efficient farming, light industry, and commerce. There are few mineral resources other than building stone, sands, and clays.

Over half of Denmark's land is cultivated. Agriculture employs about 25 percent of the population, and in 1965 it contributed 11 percent to the national product. Farms are small and privately owned, but farmers are organized into cooperative societies for purchasing, for processing and marketing their produce, and for improving production.

Dairying and the production of meat, especially pork, are the most important farm activities. Cereals, particularly barley, account for about 50 percent of the cultivated land. Fishing is also an important activity.

Manufacturing contributed 30 percent to the Danish national product in 1965, and between 1960 and 1965 industrial output increased at a rapid rate. The leading industrial products are processed foods, furniture, textiles, pharmaceuticals, chemicals, china and glassware, light machinery, and machine parts. Tourism is an important source of income. Shipping is a major activity, and in 1966 Denmark's fleet totalled almost 3 million gross registered tons.

Denmark generally has a slightly unfavorable balance of trade. In 1966, for example, exports earned $2,454 million and imports cost $3,003 million. The deficit is usually covered by such "invisible" items as shipping and tourism.

Denmark's leading imports are heavy machinery, petroleum products, motor vehicles, iron and steel products, textiles, and foodstuffs. The major exports are meat and meat products, fish and fish products, dairy products and other processed foods, and machinery. Most Danish trade is with Great Britain, the western European countries of the European Economic Community, and the United States.

GOVERNMENT. Denmark is a constitutional monarchy with a hereditary king as head of state. A prime minister and a State Council wield executive power and are responsible to the parliament, the Folketing. The parliament has one house and is popularly elected. Greenland and the Faeroe Islands are represented in the Folketing.

Denmark is a member of the United Nations, the North Atlantic Treaty Organization (NATO), and the Nordic Council, an association of the Scandinavian states.

DANISH NATIONAL TOURIST OFFICE

COPENHAGEN'S NYHAVEN, where centuries old buildings face the four-block-long canal.

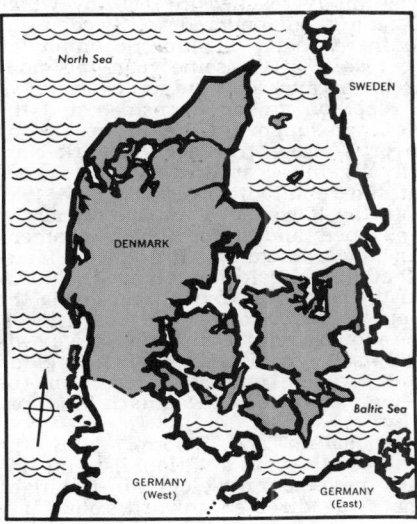

HISTORY. Archeological evidence indicates that the region of present-day Denmark has long been inhabited by man. Primitive civilization may have existed there as early as 10,000 years ago, and beginning about 2500 BC a society based on agriculture developed in the area. Early Danish peoples may have included the Cimbri and Teutons, warlike tribes described by Roman histories as inhabiting the region in the first century BC.

By the 800s AD, Danish Vikings had developed a society with a complex social organization. The Viking period, between about 800 and 1050, was turbulent. Scandinavian adventurers —raiders, merchants, and eventually settlers—visited the Caspian Sea, Iceland, Greenland, and possibly even North America. During the 900s Christianity was introduced into the region, and by about 1035 it had become the dominant religion.

The inhabitants of Denmark remained divided into separate communities until about 950, when one chieftain, Harold Bluetooth, began uniting the tribal kingdoms. The consolidation continued gradually until the 1000s, when King Canute (1014-1035) ruled a single Danish kingdom. Canute also expanded his power over England and Norway, but this Anglo-Scandinavian empire did not survive his death.

By the mid-1200s a highly organized, semi-feudal society had developed, with a strong central monarchy limited by a council of royal advisors firmly based on a middle class of farmers and artisans. During the 1200s and 1300s Denmark extended its control over territory in the Baltic area, Norway, and Sweden.

Union. By 1388 both Norway (with its possessions—the Faeroe Islands, Greenland, and Iceland) and Sweden were united under the Danish crown. This union survived, at least in form, for over a century. At the beginning of the Protestant Reformation in the early 1500s, Scandinavia was torn by religious disputes and social conflicts. As a result, Sweden in 1523 asserted its independence, but Norway remained under Danish rule.

Wars with Sweden were frequent well into the 1600s. A peace settlement was finally reached in 1660, by which Denmark surrendered to Sweden the southern part of the Scandinavian peninsula. In the same year, the monarchy became absolute as the result of a rebellion among townsmen and the clergy in support of the throne. Led by several strong rulers, Denmark-Norway regained lost territory from Sweden and rebuilt its strength.

In the 1700s, however, the monarchy weakened and a form of parliamentary government was introduced. Many other liberal reforms followed, and industry and trade expanded. During the Napoleonic period of the early 1800s, the monarchy of Denmark-Norway allied itself with France against England and Sweden, and as a result of the defeat of Napoleon, Denmark lost Norway to Sweden.

Nationalism and Reform. After the Napoleonic wars a nationalist and liberal movement developed in Denmark that was directed toward rebuilding and reforming the country. Representative local government was introduced in the 1830s, and in 1849 a constitution was adopted that limited the monarchy, created a national assembly, and guaranteed civil liberties.

The Danish nationalist movement was partly responsible for attempts to bring under Danish rule the duchies of Schleswig and Holstein, at the southern end of the Jutland peninsula. Although the duchies had once been ruled by Danes, all but the predominantly Danish northern section of Schleswig was German in language and loyalty, and the German states disputed Danish claims to the territory. The conflict led to two Danish-German wars, one in 1848-1850 and the second in 1864. A peace settlement in 1864 forced Denmark to relinquish all claims to the duchies.

The latter half of the 1800s was an era of continuing reform in Denmark. The cooperative movement was organized, and broad social welfare measures were introduced. The constitution underwent several revisions, and by 1914 Denmark had a fully democratic parliamentary government.

Modern Denmark. Denmark remained neutral during World War I. In 1918 Iceland was granted independence, but it remained united with Denmark under the Danish crown. In 1920, in a plebiscite required by the Treaty of Versailles, the Danes of Schleswig voted to rejoin Denmark.

During the 1920s Denmark entered agreements with other Scandinavian states for mutual aid and defense, and in 1926 Denmark began complete disarmament. During the 1930s Denmark had marked success in repairing the damage done by the world economic depression. Advanced social legislation was passed that remained in effect long after the depression had ended.

Denmark again proclaimed its neutrality at the beginning of World War II, but in April 1940 German forces invaded and occupied the country. King Christian X refused to go into exile or to yield to the Germans, and the Danes governed themselves until 1943, when the Germans assumed direct control. In 1944 Iceland severed its ties with Denmark and proclaimed itself an independent republic.

The Danish resistance movement was strong throughout the war. It successfully sabotaged German facilities and helped almost all of Denmark's Jews to escape German persecution. In 1945 the country was liberated.

Denmark's economy had been badly damaged during the German occupation, but by the early 1950s, prosperity had returned. In 1953 a new constitution was adopted. It removed Greenland from colonial status, and it substituted a unicameral for a bicameral legislature.

Danish politics in the 1950s and 1960s were complex, and the existence of a large number of political parties made majority governments rare. In 1968 Denmark's voters swung to the right, and 15 years of government by Social Democratic-led coalitions came to an end. A new right-of-center government headed by Hilmar Baunsgaard took over from Social Democrat Jens Otto Krag.

DOMINICAN REPUBLIC

Official name: Dominican Republic
Area: 18,816 square miles
Population: (1967 est.) 3,889,000
Capital: Santo Domingo (Pop., 1966 est., 560,600)
Language: Spanish
Religion: Roman Catholicism
Currency unit: Peso
National holiday: Independence day, February 27

The Dominican Republic occupies the eastern two-thirds of the Caribbean island of Hispaniola. The western third of the island is occupied by Haiti. Hispaniola is situated between Cuba on the west, Jamaica on the southwest, and Puerto Rico on the east.

Santo Domingo, the country's capital, was founded in 1496 by Bartholomew Columbus and is the oldest permanent European settlement in the Western Hemisphere.

THE LAND. The Dominican Republic has four mountain ranges, which lie roughly parallel to each other. The narrow Cordillera Septentrional is the northernmost range. The Cordillera Central, with peaks over 10,000 feet, is the backbone of the country. To the south are the Sierra de Neiba and the Sierra de Bahoruco.

The Cibao plain, the largest lowland in the republic, separates the Cordillera Septentrional from the Cordillera Central. In the eastern part of the plain is the humid and rich Vega Real, which is drained by the Río Yuna in the east and by the Río Yaque del Norte in the northwest.

Southwest of the Cordillera Central is the San Juan Valley, and south of the Sierra de Neiba lies the Cul de Sac, a semi-arid lowland area watered by Lake Enriquillo. A broad Caribbean coastal plain is the site of Santo Domingo.

The climate of the Dominican Republic is generally subtropical. Extremes in temperature do not often occur, and rain is abundant in most areas. The higher inland regions, however, are cooler, and rainfall is greatest on the slopes facing northeast, toward the trade winds.

THE PEOPLE. Most Dominicans are mulatto, of mixed white and Negro origin, but there are white and Negro minorities. The Vega Real and the Caribbean coastal plain are the most heavily populated regions.

ECONOMY. Fertile soil and a favorable climate have made agriculture and stock raising the principal economic activities. Sugar, cacao, coffee, tobacco, and bananas are grown for export. Meat and dairy products are also exported.

There is a great variety of mineral resources, and gold, silver, copper, iron, and bauxite are mined for export. Textiles and lumber are manufactured mainly for domestic use.

In 1966 exports earned $137 million and imports cost $159 million. Sugar and sugar products, such as molasses and rum, make up about 50 percent of all exports. The major imports are machinery, textiles, iron and steel products, and petroleum products.

Civil conflict in 1965 resulted in serious reductions in the volume of the

Dominican Republic's trade. As a result, the country faced serious economic problems and was forced to rely heavily on foreign economic aid.

GOVERNMENT. The head of the government is the president, who is popularly elected to a four-year term of office. He is assisted by a cabinet, whose members are appointed by him. Legislative power rests with the Legislative Assembly, whose members are also elected to four-year terms.

The Dominican Republic is a member of the United Nations and the Organization of American States (OAS).

HISTORY. Christopher Columbus discovered the island of Hispaniola in 1492 and claimed it for Spain. In 1697 Spain ceded the western third of Hispaniola to France, and in 1795 it also surrendered the eastern two-thirds of the island, Santo Domingo. Spain regained Santo Domingo in 1809 with British and Dominican help.

Independence. In 1821 the middle class rebelled against Spain and proclaimed the country's independence. But in 1822 Haitian forces occupied Santo Domingo, and for 22 years Dominicans suffered under oppressive Haitian rule. In 1844 the Dominicans expelled the Haitians and established the Dominican Republic with Pedro Santana as president.

During the following years, a fierce power struggle between Santana and Buenaventura Báez and the continued fear of Haitian aggression threatened the existence of the republic. To protect the state and maintain himself in office, President Santana in 1861 proclaimed the reannexation of the Dominican Republic to Spain with himself as governor-general. Spanish forces occupied the country, but sporadic uprisings, called the War of Restoration, forced the withdrawal of the Spanish troops in 1865.

Under Báez's intermittent rule, from 1865 until 1878, the country continued to be poor and backward and accumulated large foreign debts. In 1869 Báez negotiated a treaty of annexation with the United States. Although the measure was supported by Pres. Ulysses S. Grant, it was rejected by the Senate.

In 1882 Ulises Heureaux gained the presidency and ruled the country until he was assassinated in 1899. Although he greatly increased the foreign debt, he maintained internal peace, launched public works programs, and developed industry.

U.S. Role. With the death of Heureaux, violence and disorder again erupted. In 1905 Pres. Theodore Roosevelt, fearing aggression by foreign nations demanding repayment of loans, agreed to place Dominican customs duties under the control of U.S. collectors, who would use the customs revenues to pay the foreign debts. In addition, U.S. loans reassured both foreign creditors and Dominicans.

Political instability continued, however, and in 1911 President Ramón Cáceres was assassinated and a military government installed. Peace was temporarily restored in 1912 by a U.S. mission, and in 1914 by U.S. supervision of elections.

Further difficulties in 1916 led Pres. Woodrow Wilson to send troops and to establish a U.S. military govern-

ment in the Dominican Republic. Although material improvements were made during the occupation, Dominicans resented foreign rule. The occupation forces were withdrawn in 1924, but U.S. control of Dominican customs continued until the 1940s.

Trujillo Regime. Horacio Vásquez was elected president of the republic in 1924. When he attempted to remain in power indefinitely, his government was overthrown in 1930 by Rafael Leonidas Trujillo Molina. Trujillo ruled the country, directly or indirectly, until he was assassinated in 1961.

Trujillo achieved political stability and economic progress at the expense of civil liberties. Dominicans had the highest per capita income of any of the small Caribbean republics, the budget was balanced, and debts were paid. The expansion of industry and public works projects broadened the economy and raised the standard of living.

Nonetheless, no opposition was tolerated and Trujillo, supported by the army, ruled by means of a system of terror. In 1960 the Trujillo regime was censured by the Organization of American States (OAS) for trying to assassinate Pres. Romulo Bétancourt of Venezuela.

Trujillo was assassinated in 1961, and the army and the bureaucracy, both controlled by the Trujillo family and their supporters, seized power. But they were forced out when the United States threatened to intervene.

Search for Stability. A provisional council of state governed until 1962, when elections were held. Juan Bosch, a popular intellectual and a member of the Dominican Revolutionary Party, became president.

Seven months later the military deposed Bosch and established an army-backed civilian triumvirate, headed by Donald Reid Cabral, which initiated considerable economic reforms. On Apr. 24, 1965, however, civil war broke out between government forces led by Gen. Elías Wessin y Wessin and Bosch supporters under Col. Francisco Caamaño Deñó.

Pres. Lyndon B. Johnson, fearing communist infiltration of the pro-Bosch faction, sent troops to the republic. After bitter fighting, a military occupation of U.S. and OAS forces was established. Despite the condemnation by some Latin American countries for this violation of the non-intervention provisions of the OAS charter, an OAS-sponsored provisional government headed by Dr. Héctor García-Godoy was formed.

Elections were held in June 1966, and Joaquim Balaguer, a former puppet president under Trujillo, defeated ex-President Bosch. The U.S. and OAS forces were withdrawn by September 1966, and the country set about restoring its war-shattered economy and developing democratic processes.

—George W. Carey; Jerome Fischman

PANAGRA

ECUADOR'S SAN FRANCISCO CATHEDRAL

ECUADOR

Official name: Republic of Ecuador
Area: 109,483 square miles
Population: (1966 est.) 5,326,000
Capital: Quito (Pop., 1965 est., 401,811)
Language: Spanish, Quechua
Religion: Roman Catholicism
Currency unit: Sucre
National holiday: Independence day, August 10

Ecuador, a republic in northwestern South America, is bordered on the north by Colombia, on the east and south by Peru, and on the west by the Pacific Ocean. Ecuador's territory also includes the Galapagos Islands, situated about 600 miles from the mainland.

THE LAND. Ecuador has three major geographical zones: the coastal lowlands in the west, the Andes, and the eastern lowlands.

The Andes in Ecuador form two parallel chains: the Cordillera Occidental and the Cordillera Oriental. The mountains of these ranges, which have elevations of between 10,000 and 20,000 feet above sea level, are frequently volcanic. The ranges are highest in the north, where there are three towering, dormant volcanoes—Chimborazo, Cotapaxi, and Sangay.

Between the ranges is nestled a long trough, with an elevation of between 6,000 and 9,000 feet. This trough is composed of a series of interconnected mountain basins cut by rivers flowing west to the Pacific or east to the Amazon. Over three-fourths of the population lives within this central valley region. Livestock, poultry, grains, and vegetables are produced there, mainly for local consumption. Cotton and sugarcane are also cultivated in the lower basins.

The Cordillera Occidental descends abruptly to a warm coastal plain that is 40 to 50 miles wide. The northern

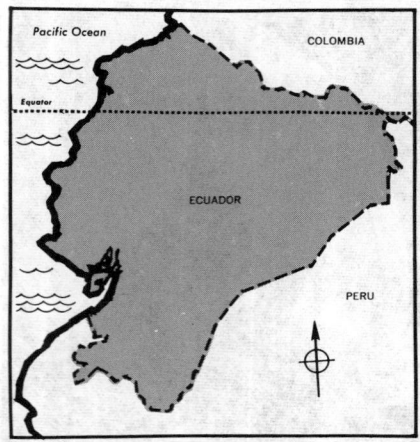

part of the plain is well watered and forested, but the southern region is semi-arid and grades into the desert of the Peruvian coast.

The coastal plain is crossed by rivers, the most important of which is the Guayas, which flows south and empties into the Gulf of Guayaquil. It is in this region that Ecuador's banana, coffee, and cacao plantations are found.

The eastern lowlands form a humid, tropical area that is almost uninhabited, except for the primitive Jivaro Indians.

THE PEOPLE. Most of the people of Ecuador are Indian or mestizo, of mixed Indian and European origins. About 10 percent of the population is of European origin, and some 10 percent is Negro. The Indians live mainly in the Andes, and the mestizos are concentrated in the Andes and in the coastal areas. The Europeans, largely of Spanish descent, live primarily in the large cities, particularly Quito and Guayaquil, and the Negroes live mainly along the coast.

The capital, Quito, lies at an elevation of about 9,500 feet above sea level. The chief commercial center and largest city is Guayaquil, located on the warm coastal plain. It had a 1965 population of over 650,000. Guayaquil sends out about 75 percent of Ecuador's exports and receives about 90 percent of all imports. It is linked with Quito by a narrow-gauge railroad, the country's major rail line.

ECONOMY. Agriculture is the mainstay of Ecuador's economy and employs most of the country's labor force. Bananas, coffee, and cacao have been the chief crops since World War II. Although some petroleum is produced, there is no large-scale mining industry. Manufacturing, with the exception of textiles, is limited.

Ecuador's exports and imports for 1964 were each valued at $148 million. Ecuador's major export is bananas. Other important exports are coffee, cacao, fish products, rice, sugar, and balsa wood. Ecuador also exports "Panama hats," so named because they were shipped through the Panama Canal. Ecuador's imports consist primarily of manufactured goods—machinery, motor vehicles, chemicals, textiles, and paper.

Ecuador's major trading partner is the United States, which supplies

about half its imports and buys about half its exports. Ecuador also trades extensively with West Germany and Belgium.

GOVERNMENT. Ecuador is officially a republic, but it has a long tradition of political upheaval and coups d'etat have been frequent. Traditionally, the head of state and chief executive is a popularly elected president. Legislative powers have rested with a congress consisting of a senate and chamber of deputies.

Ecuador is a member of the United Nations and the Organization of American States (OAS).

HISTORY. Present-day Ecuador was originally the Indian kingdom of Quito. The Incas, however, conquered Quito and incorporated it into their empire. After the Spanish conquest of Peru by Francisco Pizarro in 1533, an army led by one of his captains, Sebastián de Belalcázar, conquered Ecuador and in 1534 established the city of San Francisco de Quito on the site of the ancient Indian capital. At first Ecuador was part of the Spanish colonial Viceroyalty of Peru, but after 1740 it belonged to the Viceroyalty of New Granada.

During the Spanish American struggle for independence in the early 1800s, Quito was one of the first cities to establish an autonomous government, or junta (August 1809). This junta was quickly suppressed by forces loyal to Spain.

A second patriot government created in 1810 was also suppressed. In 1820, however, the port of Guayaquil threw off Spanish rule. Two years later, the rest of Ecuador was liberated with the help of one of Simón Bolívar's lieutenants, Antonio José de Sucre, who decisively defeated the Spaniards at the battle of Pichincha.

Independence. After gaining its freedom, Ecuador joined with Venezuela and Colombia to form the republic of Gran Colombia. But separatist feeling was strong, and in 1830, with the dissolution of Gran Colombia, Ecuador became an independent republic.

Ecuador's first president was Gen. Juan José Flores, another of Bolívar's lieutenants and a Venezuelan by birth. Flores remained a dominant figure until 1845, serving twice as president (1830–1835, 1839–1845) and keeping control of the army even during the four years he was out of office. His last administration was followed by 15 years of political instability. Some attention, however, was given to liberal reforms—slavery, for example, was completely abolished in 1854.

A new era began in 1860 with the election of Gabriel García Moreno as president. From then until 1875 he exercised firm control over Ecuador. García Moreno launched an ambitious public works program and expanded the school system, but his rule is remembered chiefly for its close alliance with the Roman Catholic Church, to which García Moreno gave wide control over both education and cultural life.

García Moreno was assassinated in 1875, and during the following two decades political anarchy reigned. In 1895 Ecuadoran Liberals, led by Gen. Eloy Alfaro, gained control of the

government. Over the next few years they attempted to weaken the influence of the church and enacted a series of laws that included the legalization of divorce and the granting of religious freedom. In addition, the completion in 1908 of a railroad from Guayaquil to Quito was a major step toward the modernization of the country.

Various factions of the Liberal party generally remained in control until the mid-1940s, despite numerous coups and periods of political chaos. During the period 1925–1948, for example, Ecuador had more than 20 presidents or chiefs of state, and none completed a normal term of office.

Contemporary Ecuador. An undeclared border war with Peru broke out in 1941. The conflict was settled by the Rio de Janeiro Protocol of 1942. Under its terms Ecuador was forced to give up most of its claims to territory in the Amazon basin, Ecuador's Eastern Region. In 1961 Ecuador unilaterally denounced the agreement, however, and renewed its claims.

In 1956 Camilo Ponce Enríquez was elected president. He was the first Conservative to hold the office in 60 years. He was succeeded in 1960 by José María Velasco Ibarra, a political independent with demagogic tendencies, who had broad popular support and had been president three times previously. In 1961 a series of violent anti-government demonstrations broke out, and Velasco Ibarra resigned in favor of Vice President Carlos Julio Arosemena Monroy.

Arosemena was overthrown by a military junta in 1963. In March 1966 the junta was replaced by an interim civilian president, Clemente Yerovi Indaburu. The Yerovi administration held elections for a constituent assembly, which convened in November and chose a civilian, Otto Arosemena Gómez, as provisional president of Ecuador.

—David Bushnell; Kempton E. Webb

EL SALVADOR

Official name: Republic of El Salvador
Area: 8,260 square miles
Population: (1966 est.) 3,037,000
Capital: San Salvador (Pop., 1963 est., 281,-122)
Language: Spanish
Religion: Roman Catholicism
Currency unit: Colón
National holiday: Independence day, September 15

The Republic of El Salvador is the smallest and most densely populated of the Central American states. It is bounded on the north and east by Honduras, on the southeast by the Gulf of Fonseca, on the south by the Pacific Ocean, and on the northwest and west by Guatemala.

THE LAND. The backbone of El Salvador is formed by two volcanic mountain ranges, which run parallel to the Pacific coast. Between the two ranges is a large, high plateau with rich volcanic soils. The plateau is the most densely populated region of the country. There is a narrow plain along the Pacific coast. The Río Lempa, cuts El Salvador in two and pro-

UNITED NATIONS

THE SQUARE IN IZALCO, in western El Salvador, lies in the shadow of Izalco Volcano.

vides hydroelectric power and water for irrigation.

The climate of El Salvador is tropical, but the heat is modified by elevation. Rainfall is heavy from May to October and slight from November to April. There are frequent earthquakes and volcanic eruptions.

THE PEOPLE. Most of the people are mestizo, of mixed European and Indian origin, but there are white and Indian minorities. The population is growing at a very rapid rate, estimated at 3.4 percent a year between 1958 and 1965.

ECONOMY. Agriculture is El Salvador's main source of income and the source of most of the country's exports. Coffee, cotton, sesame, and balsam are grown for export, and corn, sorghum, beans, rice, sugarcane, and fruits are raised largely for domestic consumption. Cattle raising is also important.

Mineral resources include gold, lead, zinc, mercury, sulfur, gypsum, alum, limestone, iron, and coal. The major manufactured products are cement, refined sugar, cotton textiles, coffee concentrates, and henequen bags for the coffee industry.

In 1966 El Salvador's imports cost $220 million and its exports earned $192 million. Coffee and cotton are the major exports. Other exports include gold, silver, and balsam. The chief imports are machinery, chemicals, textiles, wheat, and petroleum products. El Salvador is a member of the Central American Common Market.

GOVERNMENT. The constitution of El Salvador provides for a system of checks and balances similar to that of the government of the United States. Executive power is vested in a president, who is popularly elected to a five-year term. Legislative power rests with the Legislative Assembly, which has a single house, or chamber. Assembly members are popularly elected to two-year terms.

El Salvador is a member of the United Nations, the Organization of American States (OAS), and the Organization of Central American States.

HISTORY. In 1524 Pedro Alvarado led an expedition southeast from Guatemala into El Salvador to continue the Spanish conquest of the area. In 1525 Alvarado founded San Salvador de Cuscatlán.

As a Spanish colony, El Salvador was part of a province under the control of the captain-general of Guatemala. The province, including El Salvador, declared its independence from Spain on Sept. 15, 1821.

Soon after, Augustín de Iturbide, who had been crowned emperor of Mexico, sent troops to El Salvador and incorporated the country into his empire. In 1822, however, the government in El Salvador petitioned to be included in the United States as a sovereign state, but the U.S. Congress rejected the appeal.

In 1823 Iturbide's empire fell and El Salvador joined the other Central American states to form the United Provinces of Central America. In 1828 El Salvador, prompted by the threat of Guatemalan dominance within the federation, withdrew and in January 1841 independence was proclaimed.

Independence. The history of the republic has been turbulent. During the 1800s, there were frequent presidential successions and revolutions reflecting factional strife between liberals and conservatives. Internal unrest was complicated by foreign aggression and the country's participation in numerous wars. The period from 1900 to 1930 was relatively peaceful, however. The coffee industry grew and the country prospered.

In 1931 Gen. Maximiliano Hernández Martínez seized power, ruling until 1944. Although he instituted one of the most brutal regimes in the country's history, the period was one of the most prosperous for El Salvador.

Contemporary El Salvador. The overthrow of Martínez in 1944 was followed by a new period of political instability. In 1945 Gen. Salvador Castañeda Castro became president. Castro was removed from office at the expiration of his term in 1948, however, when he tried to alter the constitution to retain power indefinitely.

Castro was replaced by a junta, and in 1950 Maj. Oscar Osorio, a member of the junta, was elected president. His administration grew increasingly autocratic, and in 1956 a follower of his, Lt. Col. José Mariá Lemus, was chosen president.

Lemus ruled until 1960, when he was deposed by a military-civilian junta, which promised democratic reforms including free elections in 1962. In January 1961, however, a military directorate seized control of the government. In elections, held in 1961, Lt. Col. Julio Adalberto Rivera, a member of the directorate, was the only candidate.

Although Rivera's government depended on the military, there were some political reforms. Local elections held in 1964 and 1966 were free from military interference, and in 1967 Col. Fidel Sanchez Hernández was chosen president.

—George W. Carey; Jerome Fischman

ETHIOPIA

Official name: Empire of Ethiopia
Area: 471,776 square miles
Population: (1966 est.) 23,000,000
Capital: Addis Ababa (Pop., 1965 est., 560,-000)
Language: Amharic, English
Religion: Coptic Christianity, Islam
Currency unit: Dollar
National holiday: Birthday of the emperor, July 23

Ethiopia, an ancient kingdom in east Africa, is bordered on the north by the Red Sea, on the east by the French Territory of the Afars and the Issas (French Somaliland) and the Somali Republic, on the south by Kenya, and on the west by Sudan. The former Italian colony of Eritrea was incorporated into Ethiopia in 1962.

THE LAND. Most of Ethiopia is occupied by the Ethiopian Highlands, a region formed of tremendous thicknesses of volcanic lava split by deep gorges and canyons. The Great Rift Valley divides the highlands along a line running southwest from the east-central part of the country.

A large mountain mass northwest of the Great Rift Valley rises more than

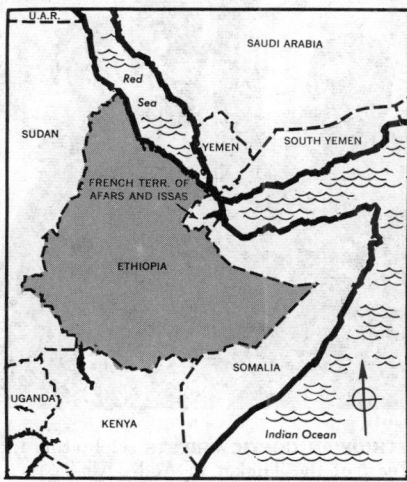

15,000 feet. There is a plateau in the southeast with elevations above 10,000 feet. In the northern part of the country, near the Red Sea, is a low-lying desert region, the Danakil Depression.

There are many rivers and lakes in Ethiopia. At the western end of the Rift Valley is the Omo River, which drains into Lake Rudolf, along the border with Kenya. Lake Tana, near the center of the Ethiopian Highlands, is the source of the Blue Nile. The Takkaze River, another Nile tributary, originates near the eastern slope of the highlands. The Awash River in the eastern end of the Rift Valley flows northeast through a dry plain to its final destination in Lake Abbe.

Ethiopians distinguish three major natural regions—the Kolla, the Woina Dega, and the Dega. The Kolla is a zone of desert plants, dry shrubs, and savanna grasslands with elevations up to 6,000 feet. The Woina Dega reaches elevations between 6,000 and 8,000 feet and is well cultivated. The Dega is a region of mountain grasslands lying above 8,000 feet.

THE PEOPLE. There are many ethnic groups in Ethiopia. Among the most important are the Amhara, Tigrean, and Galla peoples. The Amhara people live in the central highlands, and the Tigrean people live in the northern part of the country.

Both the Amhara and Tigrean peoples are Coptic Christians, and they form the ruling groups in Ethiopia. Some Galla people are Muslim, some are Christian, and some are pagan. They live in the south and also in parts of central Ethiopia.

Most of the people are farmers. Ethiopia's major cities include Addis Ababa, the capital, and Asmara, in the northern part of the country.

ECONOMY. Ethiopia's economy depends on agriculture, and the most important crop is coffee. Most farmers, however, are engaged only in producing basic food crops, and about one-half the farmland is planted in grains.

Although Ethiopia has deposits of gold, platinum, and other minerals, mining is poorly developed, partly due to the high costs of overland transportation. Industrial production greatly increased in the 1960s, and the country has textile and food processing plants. Ethiopia's many rivers provide a potential source for hydroelectric power, vital to further industrialization.

In 1966 imports cost $152 million and exports earned $112 million. Coffee is Ethiopia's major export. Ethiopia's major imports include petroleum products, textiles, transportation equipment, and machinery. Ethopia's main trading partners are the United States, Italy, and Japan.

GOVERNMENT. Ethiopia is a constitutional monarchy. Supreme political power is vested in the emperor. A constitution promulgated in 1955 provides for a bicameral parliament consisting of a Senate and a Chamber of Deputies. Senators are appointed by the emperor. Deputies are elected by universal suffrage to four-year terms. An appointed Council of Ministers, or cabinet, is responsible to the emperor.

Ethiopia is a member of the United Nations and of the Organization of African Unity (OAU).

HISTORY. Ethiopia is one of the world's oldest kingdoms, and the historical and archaeological records of Ethiopian culture go back to about 500 BC. The present-day rulers claim descent from the Queen of Sheba, whose descendents ruled over the ancient Semitic-speaking Sabaean people, whose origins are in southern Arabia.

Ethiopia was under Semitic influence until 324 AD, when the emperor Azana was converted to Christianity. Muslims invaded Ethiopia in the 600s. The Muslims converted the Galla people and pushed the Amhara people to the highlands, where they remained cut off from the rest of the world until the early 1500s.

In the 1400s Portugal sent an expedition to Ethiopia. In 1527 Muslims overran Ethiopia, but with the aid of Portugal, Ethiopia expelled the Muslim sultan in 1541. Portuguese Jesuits came to Ethiopia and tried to bring the Ethiopian Christians into the Roman Catholic Church. In 1632 the emperor, Fasilidas, expelled the Jesuits.

Political unrest, poor relations with Britain, and religious wars marked the period until 1887. At that time Italy attempted to gain territory in Ethiopia. Italy proclaimed Ethiopia a protectorate in 1889, and in 1895 the Italian army invaded Ethiopia. Italy was defeated at the Battle of Adua in 1896, but retained the coastal region of Eritrea.

Modern Ethiopia. In 1916 Ras Taffari became the regent for the Empress Zauditu. He succeeded to the throne at her death in 1930, and took the name Haile Selassie I.

In 1935 Italy, then under the rule of Benito Mussolini, renewed its claims on Ethiopia and invaded the country. The emperor unsuccessfully appealed to the League of Nations for help, and the Italians were victorious. In 1936 Italy united Ethiopia, Eritrea, and Italian Somaliland to form Italian East Africa.

In 1941 English and Ethiopian troops defeated the Italian occupation forces, and Haile Selassie returned to the throne. In 1950 the United Nations approved the federation of Eritrea with Ethiopia, and in 1962 Eritrea was integrated fully into Ethiopia.

In 1960 the Imperial Guard revolted against Haile Selassie in protest against a lack of social and political reforms. The army, loyal to the emperor, suppressed the rising. In the following year, the emperor appointed some younger men to high posts and increased educational opportunities. Fighting broke out between Ethiopia and the Somali Republic in 1961, 1964, and 1967 because of a disputed border between the two countries.

—Hibberd V. B. Kline, Jr.; Vera L. Zolberg

FINLAND

Official name: Republic of Finland
Area: 130,119 square miles
Population: (1967 est.) 4,664,000
Capital: Helsinki (Pop., 1965 est., urban area, 651,988)
Language: Finnish, Swedish
Religion: Protestantism
Currency unit: Mark
National holiday: Independence day, December 6

Finland is a republic in northern Europe. It is bounded on the north by Norway, on the east by the Soviet Union, on the south by the Gulf of Finland, and on the west by the Gulf of Bothnia and Sweden. The Åland Islands, between the Baltic Sea and the Gulf of Bothnia, are Finnish.

THE LAND. The name Finland means "land of fens and marshes," and much of Finland is quite low and swampy. Ten percent of the land area is occupied by about 50,000 lakes, most of which are concentrated in the central third of the country. The southwestern third of Finland lies on a low coastal plain. Elevations rise to above 1,000 feet only in the northern third of the country where densely forested uplands extend into the barren Lapland region of the far north.

About one-third of Finland lies north of the Arctic Circle, but the sea moderates the climate, especially in the south. Finland has long, cold winters and short, warm summers. Snow covers the ground for from four months of the year in the south to almost eight months in parts of the north. Rainfall averages about 30 inches in the southwest and decreases generally toward the north.

THE PEOPLE. Finland is rather sparsely populated. Population is concentrated in the southwestern third of the country, especially along the coast near Finland's largest cities, which include Helsinki, the capital, Turku, and Tampere.

The majority of the people speak Finnish, a language related to Estonian and Hungarian. Swedish is a second language, spoken by fewer than 10 percent of the people. Most Finns are

UNITED NATIONS

ETHIOPIAN COPTIC PRIESTS celebrating the Feast of the Timkat in Addis Ababa.

Lutheran, but there are Orthodox Christian, Jewish, and Roman Catholic, as well as other Protestant groups.

The semi-nomadic Lapps of the far north make up about 5 percent of the population. They remain generally isolated from Finnish life.

ECONOMY. Finland's economy is based on the exploitation of its rich forest and mineral resources, especially copper. Almost two-thirds of the country is forested, and deposits of copper, nickel, lead, zinc, and iron are mined. Abundant water is available for power.

Manufacturing contributed 28 percent to the national product in 1965, with wood and paper products the principal manufactured goods. Copper smelting and iron and steel production are also important. Shipbuilding and shipping are valuable industries, and the Finnish fleet in 1966 totaled over 1 million gross registered tons.

Agriculture is of decreasing importance in Finland, but in the mid-1960s agriculture and forestry together em-

ployed approximately 30 percent of the labor force and contributed about 20 percent to the net domestic product. Only about 8 percent of the land is under cultivation, and farming is confined almost entirely to the south. Dairying is the main activity, and such hardy crops as hay, fodder, and cereals are grown. Minks and foxes are raised for their fur, and coastal fishing is prosperous.

The Finnish economy depends heavily on foreign trade, which increased sharply in value during the 1950s and 1960s. In 1966 exports earned $1,505 million and imports cost $1,726 million. Much of the trade deficit is made up by shipping and other invisible items.

Finland's exports include paper and wood pulp, timber and wood products, machinery, and transportation equipment. The major imports are heavy machinery and vehicles, finished consumer goods, fuels, chemicals, and foodstuffs. Most of Finland's trade is with Great Britain, West Germany, the Soviet Union, and Sweden.

GOVERNMENT. Finland is a republic, with a president as head of state. Executive power is wielded by a prime minister and cabinet responsible to the parliament. Members of the parliament, which has one house, are popularly elected to four-year terms.

HELEN BUTTERFIELD

FINLAND IN WINTER. The midwinter sun shines only six hours a day in Finland.

Finland is a member of the United Nations and the Nordic Council, an association of the Scandinavian nations.

HISTORY. Finland contains archeological evidence of human settlement as early as the Stone Age, over 50,000 years ago. Modern Finland was settled by people who migrated from the eastern Baltic region in about 100 AD. For many centuries they lived in a tribal society based on hunting, trapping, and fur trading.

In the 1100s Sweden conquered the Finnish tribes and converted them to Christianity. The Finns absorbed a great deal of Western culture through Swedish influence and with Sweden adopted Lutheranism in the 1500s. For most of the 600 years that Sweden controlled Finland, the Swedes and the Russians competed for control of the Baltic region, and Finland was often their battleground.

Finally, in 1808, during the Napoleonic wars, Sweden lost Finland to Russia. Emperor Alexander of Russia made Finland an autonomous grand duchy and allowed it to govern itself. The Finns enjoyed a great deal of autonomy throughout the 1800s. Beginning in 1894, however, rising Russian nationalism resulted in the loss of Finnish home rule and threatened Finnish national identity.

Independence. Finland took advantage of the turmoil caused in Russia by the 1917 revolutions and proclaimed its independence. In January 1918 civil war broke out in Finland between the communists and socialists, called the Reds, and conservative factions, called the Whites. Aided by German troops, the Whites won and established a republic.

Occasional fighting with Russia over territorial issues continued through 1919, but in 1920 the Soviet government ceded to Finland an ice-free port. Finland joined the League of Na-

tions in 1920 and in 1921 was given sovereignty over the Åland Islands, which were to retain an autonomous government.

In the 1920s and 1930s the Finns labored to establish a stable society, and the country passed advanced social and economic reform legislation. But the young republic had difficulty in striking a balance between the extremes of the right and left. During the 1930s several attempted right-wing coups shook the government, and in 1937 a socialist coalition government came to power and banned extreme rightist organizations.

In the 1930s the Soviet Union put forth claims to Finnish territory, and in 1939 Soviet armies invaded Finland. The Finns put up a strong resistance, but in 1940 they were forced to surrender about 16,000 square miles of territory in southern Finland.

Between 1941 and 1944, during World War II, Finland renewed the struggle with the Soviet Union. But under the peace settlement it lost more territory and was forced to pay heavy reparations.

A 1947 peace treaty confirmed the reparations debt, which Finland paid by 1952, and limited the size of the Finnish army. In 1948 the Soviet Union and Finland signed a long-term mutual assistance treaty.

During the 1950s and 1960s Finland's foreign policy was strongly influenced by the powerful presence of the Soviet Union, and Finland was able to make few decisions fully independent of Soviet pressures. The Soviet Union also influenced Finnish domestic affairs.

During the postwar era, while trying to maintain the security of its borders, Finland concentrated on expanding its economy. A socialist coalition won elections in 1966 and initiated projects designed to improve Finland's economic situation.

FRANCE

Official name: French Republic
Area: 211,206 square miles
Population: (1966 est.) 49,400,000
Capital: Paris (Pop., 1962, urban area, 7,369-387)
Language: French
Religion: Roman Catholicism
Currency unit: Franc
National holiday: Bastille day, July 14

France, the largest country in western Europe, is bounded on the north by the English Channel, Belgium, and Luxembourg; on the northeast by West Germany; on the east by Switzerland and Italy; on the south by the Mediterranean Sea and Spain; and on the west by the Bay of Biscay, an arm of the Atlantic Ocean. Corsica, an island lying about 100 miles southeast of the Mediterranean coast, is also part of France.

France occupies a central position in western Europe and for centuries has played an important role in European affairs. Its intellectual and cultural life have been outstanding and have had a major influence on other countries.

THE LAND. The surface of France is quite varied. The interior consists largely of plains and low plateaus and includes the Northern French Lowlands, the Breton Massif, the Aquitaine Basin, the Rhone-Saône valley, and the Mediterranean plain. With the exception of the Massif Central, an extensive highland area in the south central part of France, the upland and mountain regions are found on or near the borders of the country.

The Alps, in the southeast, separate France from Italy. The Jura and Vosges mountains in the east run along France's boundaries with Switzerland and Germany. The Pyrenees form France's boundary with Spain in the south, and in the north the Ardennes cross the border with Belgium.

France's major rivers are the Seine, the Loire, the Garonne, and the Rhone. The Rhine River forms part of the eastern border with Germany.

Climate. Most of France has a maritime climate, with cool winters and mild summers. The southern coast has a typical Mediterranean climate, with hot, dry summers and mild, rainier winters. The greatest seasonal variations in temperature occur in the east and in the highland areas.

THE PEOPLE. France has one of Europe's most homogeneous populations. There is a strong feeling of cultural unity, and France has been troubled very little by minority unrest.

French is the universal language, and more than 95 percent of the people are Roman Catholic. Breton, Flemish, German, Catalan, and Basque are spoken in the border areas by relatively few people. The only substantial linguistic minority is the German-speaking population in Alsace.

In the early 1960s there were hundreds of thousands of foreign workers employed in French industry. Algerians formed the largest single group. Other large groups were from Italy, Portugal, and Spain.

Long comparatively stable, France's population increased between 1958 and 1964 at an annual rate of 1.3 percent, somewhat above the European average. France's population is fairly evenly distributed throughout the country. Only a few areas, such as the high Alps and parts of the infertile Landes district, near the Spanish border, are sparsely populated, and only a few industrial areas are densely settled.

Paris, the capital, is by far the largest city. Other major cities, with the 1962 populations of their urban areas, include the industrial city of Lyon, 885,944; France's principal seaport, Marseille, 807,500; the seaport and industrial center of Bordeaux, 462,171; the manufacturing and marketing center of Toulouse, 329,044; and Nice, 310,063.

ECONOMY. France's economy moved ahead briskly during the late 1950s and early 1960s, sharing fully in the remarkable economic resurgence of western Europe. Membership in the European Coal and Steel Community and the European Economic Community, the EEC or Common Market, has given a tremendous impetus to French industrial and agricultural growth.

Part of this economic growth has been the result of the revamping of much of the nation's transportation and communications system, and heavy investments in the modernization of French mines and factories during the early and middle 1950s.

Strong governmental direction of the economy under a series of formal development plans also contributed greatly to France's economic growth. The plans involve close cooperation between government and private business and have been successful in channeling resources and balancing economic growth. The fifth plan covered the period 1966–1970.

Natural Resources. France's mineral endowment is varied and, by European standards, moderately rich. There are major deposits of iron ore in Lorraine and bauxite, from which aluminum is made, in the southeast. France leads Europe in the production of these minerals. There are many coal fields scattered throughout the country, but mining them is expensive and much of the coal is of modest quality.

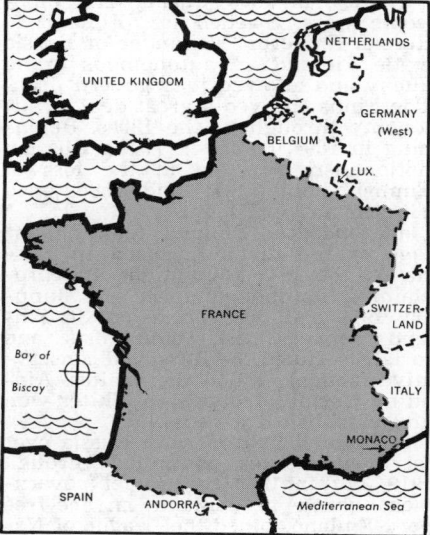

TRANS WORLD AIRLINES

EIFFEL TOWER, in Paris' Champs de Mars, is for many a symbol of Paris and France.

Securing adequate coal, particularly coke, has long been a problem of the French economy. However, the country has benefited by the rapid development in the late 1950s and the 1960s of huge French-controlled North African oil and natural gas deposits. Other mineral resources of importance are lignite sulfur, and potash.

The abundant water power of the Alps, Pyrenees, and Massif Central place France second in Europe in developed hydroelectric capacity. The country's forests and coastal fisheries also yield substantial harvests. In 1964 France ranked third in Europe in lumber production and in 1965 ranked sixth in fish catch.

Agriculture. France leads Europe in agricultural production and exports more farm products than any other European country. France has several natural features that have contributed to its success in agriculture. It has large tracts of fertile soils; in fact, one half of the European Economic Community's farmland is in France. France is also fortunate in having a climate well suited for the production of a variety of crops.

Although one-fifth of France's labor force is in agriculture, which is high for so important an industrial nation, French agriculture is highly mechanized. Great increases in the use of fertilizers, improved farm practices, and progress in consolidating fragmented individual holdings have further raised productivity and made farming more efficient, particularly in northern France. The extension of irrigation works in the dry-summer Mediterranean region have greatly increased production there.

France produced 14,270 thousand metric tons of wheat in 1965, by far the most wheat of any European country, and it ranks high in the production of meat, milk, oats, and barley. France vies with Italy as the world's leading wine maker, producing 1.8 million gallons in 1965. Other important agricultural items include corn, sugar beets, cheese, butter, and a great variety of fruits and vegetables.

Industry. France is one of the world's most important industrial nations, and French industry produces many different products. In 1965 France ranked second in Europe in the production of cement and radio and television receivers, and third in the production of iron and steel, paper, synthetic rubber, and motor vehicles. France is Europe's leading primary aluminum producer, and ranks high in the production of textiles, in shipbuilding, and in coke manufacture.

France's manufacturing is concentrated in five major industrial regions: Le Nord, Paris, Lorraine, Alsace, and Lyon–St. Étienne. The region of Le Nord, situated along the Belgian border in the midst of France's extensive coal fields, is the country's leading textile-producing area. Metal manufacture, metal fabrication, and chemical production are also important industries in Le Nord. The region's major urban center is Lille; others are Tourcoing, Roubaix, and Valenciennes.

Paris and its suburbs form France's most important industrial district. The city's large reservoir of highly skilled workers, concentrated market with high buying capacity, and position as France's government and chief cultural center have led to the development of a great variety of industries.

Especially important there are those industries characterized by their small consumption of raw materials and their high value, producing such items as scientific instruments and machine tools. Paris is the major center of the important French automotive industry and of a host of enterprises specializing in luxury articles such as jewelry, fine furniture, and perfumes—items often called "Paris goods." Paris is also world renowned for the manufacture of women's clothing.

Lorraine's manufacturing is concentrated along the Moselle valley from Nancy, its chief city, in the south to Thionville, in the north, where it extends west to include Longwy, near the Luxembourg border. The district

is the site of Europe's leading iron mines and produces more than three-fourths of France's iron and steel. Some coal is brought from eastern Lorraine, but most of it is imported from nearby West Germany. Chemicals, particularly fertilizers, are also important.

Alsace is a leading textile district. The French side of the Rhine valley houses most Alsatian industry. Mulhouse is the leading manufacturing city in the south, Strasbourg in the north. The cotton textile industry, however, is scattered throughout the hilly Vosges country in central and western Alsace. The fertilizer industry, based on large potash deposits near Mulhouse, is also important.

The Lyon–St. Étienne district, which possesses coal and metals, is located at the juncture of the Rhone and Saône rivers. It produces textiles and chemicals, particularly fertilizers, are also steel and metal fabrication.

Other manufacturing centers outside the five major industrial regions are Marseille, Toulouse, Grenoble, Bordeaux, Nantes, Clermont-Ferrand, and Le Havre.

Transportation. France has an excellent transportation network. There are about 25,000 miles of railroad track, about a fifth of which is electrified. The road network is about 500,000 miles long and extends to all parts of the country. Air transportation is also highly developed, and Paris' Orly and Le Bourget airports are among Europe's busiest.

Navigable inland waterways are vital to France's economy, and there are more than 3,000 miles of both navigable rivers and canals. French flag vessels carry two-thirds of the goods entering and leaving French ports, and at the beginning of 1963 the French merchant fleet included 5,260,000 gross registered tons.

Trade. In 1966 France's exports were valued at $10,898 million and its imports cost $11,875 million. France's major exports include steel, chemicals, perfumes, transportation equipment, foodstuffs, pottery and glassware, natural and synthetic rubber, and textiles.

The principal imports include petroleum products and fuels, ores, raw textiles, and machine tools.

France's principal trading partners are West Germany, Belgium, Luxembourg, Italy, Algeria, the Netherlands, Switzerland, Britain, and the United States. About two-fifths of France's foreign trade is with its European Economic Community partners. France has made a determined effort to develop trade with Eastern Europe, the Soviet Union, Communist China, and the developing countries of Asia, Africa, and Latin America.

GOVERNMENT. France is a democratic republic. The head of state and chief executive is the president, who is directly elected to a seven-year term. The president appoints a prime minister and council of ministers, or cabinet, as well as all other civil and military officials.

The constitution grants the president the right to dissolve the powerful lower house of the legislature, the National Assembly, after conferring with the prime minister, and the right to call new elections. In the event of a national emergency, the president may assume all executive and legislative powers.

Legislative authority is vested in the parliament, which consists of the National Assembly and the Senate. The stronger of the two houses is the National Assembly, whose 487 deputies are popularly elected to four-year terms. The 274 members of the Senate are elected by regional and city electoral colleges to nine-year terms.

France was once master of a vast overseas empire. In 1958, under the constitution of the Fifth Republic, French territories were offered the choice of becoming independent, becoming overseas departments of France, or keeping their dependent status.

In 1966 the overseas departments of France were Martinique, Guadeloupe, Réunion, and Guiana. French dependencies included New Caledonia, French Polynesia, the French Territory of the Afars and Issas formerly

FRENCH EMBASSY PRESS AND INFORMATION DIVISION

THE LAND AND THE PEOPLE. The grape harvest in the Champagne country *(left)* and the peaceful Normandy countryside *(above)* reflect traditional aspects of French life today.

French Somaliland), the Comoro Archipelago, Saint-Pierre and Miquelon, the Southern and Antarctic Territories, and the Wallis and Futuna Islands.

France is a member of the French Community, a loose confederation of French overseas territories and former colonies, and the European Communities. It is also a member of the United Nations and the North Atlantic Treaty Organization (NATO).

HISTORY. France, which was known in ancient times as Gaul, was inhabited by Celtic tribes when Julius Caesar led his Roman legions into the region in 58 BC. By 51 BC Caesar had brought all of Gaul under his control. The Romans introduced the Latin language, and, later, Christianity to the Gauls.

For over 200 years the region was prosperous, and had a distinctive Gallo-Roman culture. By the 200s AD, however, Gaul was beset by political and economic upheavals as the Roman Empire began to disintegrate. The Gallo-Romans could not prevent the infiltration of Teutonic tribes, and in the 400s Visigoths, Franks, and Burgundians established themselves in various parts of Gaul.

The Merovingians. In the late 400s the Franks set out to conquer all of Gaul. They were led by Clovis I, the first of the Merovingian kings, who ruled from 481 to 511. By the end of the 400s Clovis had succeeded in conquering Gaul and western Germany. By converting to Christianity, and forcing his army to do the same, Clovis won the support of the Christian Celts. Nonetheless, Clovis was unable to create a permanently unified state, and his sons divided his lands among themselves after his death.

During the 500s and 600s rival Merovingian rulers quarreled with each other, and the high degree of civilization that the Gauls enjoyed under the Romans drastically declined. The Merovingians were weakened by civil war and were led by ineffectual leaders, called *rois fainéants,* or do-nothing kings.

In the 600s the Carolingians, who were the royal stewards of the Merovingians, assumed most of the royal authority. In 732 the Carolingian, Charles Martel, thwarted Muslim invaders at Tours—halting the Muslim threat to France and enhancing the prestige of his house. But Charles did not depose the Merovingians, who continued as nominal rulers of the Franks until 751, when Charles' son, Pepin the Short, seized the throne.

The Carolingians. Pepin's son, Charlemagne, or Charles the Great, who ruled from 768 to 814, won control of most of western Europe. He created a powerful empire, which he administered efficiently. Charlemagne was a patron of learning, and scholars from all of western Europe came to his capital, Aachen. Charlemagne cooperated closely with the Church, and in 800 Pope Leo III crowned him emperor of the Romans. His coronation marked the birth of the Holy Roman Empire.

The strength of the Carolingian empire was dependent upon the genius of Charlemagne. His son, Louis the

FRENCH EMBASSY PRESS AND INFORMATION DIVISION

AUTOMOBILES drying under infrared lights. Autos are a major French export.

Pious (r.814–840), was incapable of maintaining a strong hold over the kingdom. The centralized administration collapsed, and Louis' three sons struggled among themselves for supremacy. In 843 they finally settled their differences and signed the Treaty of Verdun, which divided the Carolingian empire into three parts.

The eastern region, Germany, was awarded to Louis the German; the western region, France, went to Charles the Bald; and the middle strip, which included northern Italy and Alsace-Lorraine, was given to Lothair I, who also retained the title of Holy Roman Emperor. The partition of 843 marked the beginnings of modern France and Germany.

Throughout the Middle Ages France remained a separate kingdom, except for the period from 884 to 887, when Charles the Fat briefly reunited the Carolingian empire. Carolingian rule declined rapidly in the 800s and 900s. New barbarian invasions shook Europe, and political power fell into the hands of feudal lords. Economic life shrank and became centered on the self-sufficient manor.

The Capetians. The Carolingian dynasty died out in 987, and the powerful nobles chose Hugh Capet as king. Hugh Capet reigned from 987 to 996, and the Capetian kings—Hugh and his descendants—brought authority and prestige to the French crown. The Capetian kings of the 900s and 1000s had limited power and did not even control the royal domain of the Île de France, a narrow strip of land running from just north of Paris to just south of Orléans.

The Capetians gradually extended their domain and built a strong monarchy. Louis VI (the Fat; r.1108–1137), coerced the feudal lords who owed him allegiance into accepting his sovereignty and organized his domain into administrative districts (*prévôtés*) and appointed royal officers (*prévôts*) to govern them. The *prévôts* were loyal to the throne and effectively executed the king's will.

Unfortunately, Louis VI's son, Louis VII (r.1137–1180), lacked his father's political wisdom. King Henry

II of England had acquired by inheritance, diplomacy, and marriage the "Angevin empire," consisting of the huge counties and duchies of Normandy, Poitou, Guyenne, Gascony, Anjou, Maine, and Touraine. Before his death Louis VI had arranged the marriage of his son to Eleanor of Aquitaine to assure France Eleanor's duchy of Aquitaine.

Finding Eleanor incompatible, Louis asked the pope to dissolve the marriage. Henry seized the opportunity to add Aquitaine to his Angevin empire and married Eleanor shortly after Louis received an annulment. The Angevin empire then surrounded the Île de France.

Louis VII's son, Philip Augustus (r.1180–1223), was determined to regain the territory lost to England and unify all of France with himself as absolute monarch. Philip succeeded in wresting control of Normandy, Anjou, Maine, Poitou, and Touraine from the English between 1202 and 1204.

To carry royal power to his newly acquired territories, Philip replaced the feudal *prévôts* with larger administrative districts (*bailliages*) governed by royal agents (*baillis*). After a crusade against the Albigensians (1208–1213), the French crown acquired the huge fiefs of the counts of Toulouse in the south.

During the reign of Louis IX (r.1226–1270) the royal court began to evolve into a central bureaucracy. Louis established a high court of justice, known as the *parlement,* and reorganized the royal treasury into a more workable body of government.

Under Philip IV (the Fair; r.1285–1314) the crown developed new sources of revenue from indirect taxes on commerce, money payments from nobles in place of military service, and taxation of the clergy. Philip proposed this last measure without securing papal approval, thus defying a papal bull of 1296 that prohibited rulers from levying taxes on the clergy.

A bitter feud ensued between the French monarch and Pope Boniface VIII, and in 1302 Boniface promulgated the most emphatic declaration of papal supremacy in the Middle Ages in the bull, *Unam sanctam.* Philip then summoned an assembly of the Estates General, which was made up of the nobility, clergy, and bourgeoisie (the middle class of the towns), to secure their support for his ecclesiastical policies. With their backing, the French monarch determined to limit papal interference.

At the death of Boniface in 1305, Philip effected the election of a French prelate as pope. This pope, Clement V, was induced by Philip to establish his residence at Avignon, on the border of France. For over 70 years—an era called the "Babylonian Captivity"—the popes reigned from Avignon under the supervision of the French monarchs.

The Valois Kings. The Capetian line expired in 1328, and the throne passed to one of Philip's nephews, Philip VI (r.1328–1350), who was the first of the Valois dynasty. Under the Valois royal power continued to grow, despite some major setbacks.

In 1337 the right of Philip VI to the throne was challenged by his distant cousin, Edward III of England. This led to a long, complex dynastic conflict from 1337 to 1453 known as the Hundred Years' War. During this war the French crown also faced a revolt of French peasants, the *Jacquerie* of 1358; a Parisian insurrection; and bitter civil strife among powerful French nobles, particularly between those of Armagnac and Burgundy.

In 1420 Henry V of England, who had defeated the French at Agincourt in 1415, forced the Valois king, Charles VI, to disown his own son and make Henry the heir to the French throne. However, the dauphin, as the French heir to the throne was known, fought back. With the help of Joan of Arc, who escorted him to Reims, where in 1429 he was crowned Charles VII (r.1422–1461), he managed to drive the English out of all of France except Calais by 1453.

During the Hundred Years' War the French kings had begun to create a more effective army by placing it under royal control, supporting it with royal funds, and selecting its officers. They also obtained a special direct tax on land, called the *taille*, which they did not give up at the end of the conflict.

Louis XI (r.1461–1483) inherited a monarchy that had almost absolute power and that was no longer threatened by foreign intervention. Louis destroyed the power of the remaining feudal lords and brought most of present-day France under royal control. Louis continued to reinforce the strength of the monarchy, and sought ways to ally the throne with the growing middle class. He appointed advisers from among the bourgeoisie and paid them generously for their support.

Louis XI's son, Charles VIII (r. 1483–1498), introduced a French policy of expansion abroad with campaigns in Italy. Although they were unsuccessful, they succeeded in stimulating French interest in Renaissance culture. Charles' cousin, Francis I (r.1515–1547), continued the Italian campaigns and initiated French support of German Protestants as a means of weakening the rival Hapsburg dynasty, which controlled Spain, the Holy Roman Empire, and the Lowlands (present-day Belgium and the Netherlands).

Henry II (r.1547–1559) won a foothold in Lorraine by seizing the bishoprics of Toul, Metz, and Verdun from the Holy Roman Emperor Charles V. The French also captured Calais, the last English possession in France, and ended the Italian wars.

Religious Conflict. After Henry's death, his three sons ruled France in succession—Francis II (r.1559–1560), Charles IX (r.1560–1574), and Henry III (r.1574–1589). During most of that period, the queen mother, Catherine de Médicis, dominated French political life.

Catherine and her sons were unable to maintain royal control in the face of Calvinism, rivalry between the powerful Catholic Guise and Protestant Bourbon families, and the intervention of Hapsburg Spain in French affairs.

The Huguenots, as the French Calvinists were called, created the greatest problems for the three Medici monarchs. During their reigns the royal army was intermittently engaged in a fierce civil war with Huguenot forces.

The struggle reached its bloodiest point in 1572, when Catherine incited Parisian Catholics against a large assemblage of Huguenots gathered in the capital to attend the wedding of Margaret of Valois, Catherine's daughter, and the Huguenot, Henry of Bourbon, King of Navarre. The Massacre of St. Bartholomew's Day ensued, resulting in the death of many Protestants.

The leadership of the Huguenots fell to Henry of Navarre, who had successfully escaped the massacre, and when the Valois line ended in 1589 amid the confusion of civil and religious strife, Henry returned to Paris to ascend the throne as Henry IV (r.1589–1610), the first of France's Bourbon kings.

Bourbon Rule. The Bourbons made France a relatively centralized state and a world power. Henry IV took several steps to bring order to divided France. He became a Roman Catholic to consolidate his position as king, but in 1598 he issued the Edict of Nantes, which gave the Huguenots religious rights and political guarantees. He defeated or bought off rebellious nobles and rebuilt the economy.

After initial difficulties, his successor, Louis XIII (r.1610–1643), was able to continue the expansion of royal power by delegating authority to Cardinal Richelieu. Richelieu, an important force from 1624 to 1642, crushed rebellious Huguenots while allowing them religious privileges; forced the nobles to demolish fortifications that did not protect the frontiers; developed the technique of sending out royal inspectors, or *intendants*, to supervise local administration; and ruthlessly suppressed conspiracies against the regime.

Outside France, the cardinal intervened in Germany's religious conflict, the Thirty Years' War, on the side of the Protestant princes to prevent the consolidation of Hapsburg power.

After Richelieu's death in 1642, Cardinal Mazarin carried on his work, surviving a series of revolts—called the *Fronde*—by the nobility and *parlements*, who sought greater participation in government.

Mazarin also brought the Thirty Years' War to an end in 1648 with the Peace of Westphalia. This settlement strengthened the French foothold in Lorraine and won France most of Alsace. Although the Austrian Hapsburgs had conceded defeat, the Spanish Hapsburgs continued to fight until 1659, when they yielded some territories in the Pyrenees and the Lowlands.

Louis XIV. With the death of Mazarin in 1661, Louis XIV (r.1643–1715) began to rule France personally. By that time France was already the most unified,

FRENCH EMBASSY PRESS AND INFORMATION DIVISION

FISHING AND CHEESE MAKING have long been important. Brittany's fishermen (*left*) continue to sail the oceans, and the cheese makers near Rouen (*above*) still produce Camembert.

TRANS WORLD AIRLINES

MONT-SAINT-MICHEL rises on a rock-island base between Britanny and Normandy.

most populous, and wealthiest state in Europe. Louis, known as "the Sun King," further strengthened the power of the monarchy and reinforced French hegemony in Europe.

Louis excluded the great nobles from his councils in favor of reliable middle class officials, domesticated the troublesome aristocracy in his splendid palace at Versailles, silenced opposition from the *parlements*, used *intendants* to enforce his will in the provinces, and avoided convening the Estates-General.

Jean Baptiste Colbert, his controller general of finance, encouraged the development of industry with favors and protection; the Marquis de Louvois, minister of war, reorganized the army; and the Marquis de Vauban, a military engineer, improved military fortifications. In North America, French explorers and soldiers built an empire extending from the St. Lawrence River and the Great Lakes to the mouth of the Mississippi River on the Gulf of Mexico.

The work of modernizing France was only half-completed, however. The tax system remained riddled with exemptions and inequities; internal customs barriers still impeded commerce outside of central France; and underneath the royal superstructure lay a confusion of local administrative organs, courts, and laws inherited from the past.

Louis, moreover, weakened French economic life when he revoked the Edict of Nantes in 1685, suppressing the remaining Protestant rights. This led to the emigration of thousands of Huguenots, large numbers of whom were merchants, manufacturers, and craftsmen.

Finally, Louis' wars, inspired primarily by a desire for glory, drained French resources and made his reign unpopular. As a result of the first three wars (War of Devolution, 1667–1668; Dutch War, 1672–1678; and War of the League of Augsburg, 1688–1697) France acquired bits of the Spanish Netherlands, the Franche-Comté, in east-central France, and Alsace. After the War of the Spanish Suc-

cession (1701–1714), however, waged against a Grand Alliance of European powers, France had to recognize English claims to Newfoundland, Nova Scotia, and Hudson Bay territory in North America; and although one of Louis' grandsons became Philip V of Spain, the Spanish and French were thrones never to be united.

Decline of the Monarchy. In the 1700s the French monarchy began to lose its power and prestige. Louis XV (1715–1774) preferred private pleasure to the tasks of government. French intellectuals of the Enlightenment, a contemporary philosophic movement characterized by its emphasis on the idea of universal human progress, campaigned for social and political reform.

Although their ideas influenced large numbers of the bourgeoisie and many European monarchs, including Catherine the Great of Russia and Frederick of Prussia, the most famous "enlightened despots" of the period, Louis XV chose to ignore them. Ministers quarreled, necessary reforms were defeated, and the *parlements* repeatedly challenged royal authority on behalf of vested interests.

France also became involved in several new wars. The War of the Polish Succession (1733–1735) assured France of eventual acquisition of the rest of Lorraine, but the War of the Austrian Succession (1740–1748) ended in stalemate. Finally, the Seven Years' War (1756–1763), fought after a "diplomatic revolution" in which France became allied with its old rival, Hapsburg Austria, resulted in the loss of French Canada to the British.

Louis XVI (r.1774–1792) was a well-intentioned ruler, but he, too, lacked determination. Early in his reign he was faced with the problem of the public debt, swelled by war costs and aid to the American rebels against England. The antiquated tax system could not provide enough funds to balance the budget, and the nation faced bankruptcy.

A series of reform ministers who saw the need to tax the upper classes were dismissed. Finally, as the crisis mounted, a program was proposed that would force the aristocracy to assume their share of the tax burden. They rebelled, maintaining that the Estates-General alone had the authority to approve new taxes. In 1789, hopeful of consolidating their position, the aristocracy compelled the king to summon the Estates-General for the first time in 175 years.

The Revolution. The aristocratic rebellion finally sparked the French Revolution. The middle-class representatives of the third estate took over the Estates-General and renamed it the National Constituent Assembly. They then destroyed the remnants of feudalism, swept away antiquated laws and local institutions, guaranteed certain basic civil rights, and created a constitutional monarchy with a fairly democratic legislative assembly.

The revolutionaries antagonized many Frenchmen when they seized church property to gain revenue and proceeded to turn the church into a

government department with elected priests paid by the state and virtually detached from Rome. The revolution also produced economic disorder and high prices, which kept the country unsettled. Even more serious for the new constitutional monarchy was the public distrust of Louis XVI and his queen, Marie Antoinette.

Even before the constitution went into effect in the autumn of 1791, the royal family had tried to escape the country. The leaders of the legislative assembly became convinced that reactionary European rulers were allying against them and on Apr. 20, 1792 they declared war on Austria, inaugurating the wars of the French Revolution, which were to last until 1815. When it became clear that the king and queen sympathized with the enemy, the monarchy was overthrown by a Parisian insurrection on August 10.

The First Republic. On Sept. 21, 1792, a new revolutionary assembly, the National Convention, announced the establishment of the First Republic. The convention delegates, elected by universal manhood suffrage, were republicans and they proceeded to draft a republican constitution. In the convention, the radical Jacobin party, which was allied with the Parisian populace, gradually defeated the moderate Girondists.

A reign of terror occurred in 1793–1794, when the Jacobin leaders of the convention formed a Committee of Public Safety to conduct the government. Faced with foreign invasion, serious threats of counterrevolution, and grave economic problems, the committee created a "revolutionary government" designed to crush its enemies and prepare the way for the establishment of a democratic republic.

This revolutionary government, led by Maximilien de Robespierre, featured a centralized dictatorship, a single party, a police regime, a dictated economy, and attempts at mass propaganda. Thousands of Girondists and counterrevolutionaries, as well as Louis XVI and Marie Antoinette, were executed.

To win the war—which had expanded by the spring of 1793 to include Prussia, Sardinia, Britain, the Dutch Republic, and Spain—the government drafted the entire able-bodied male population. With the largest army ever organized in Europe, the French Republic turned the tide of war in its favor.

The Directory. In July 1794 Robespierre was overthrown by the more moderate members of the convention. A reaction against the terror followed, culminating in 1795 in the establishment of a conservative republic called the Directory, because executive authority was shared by five directors.

Under the Directory (1795–1799), France experienced ineffective and unstable government at home, but enjoyed marked military success abroad. France won control over Belgium, the Rhineland, and much of Italy. In 1799 Napoleon Bonaparte, the Republic's most successful general, overthrew the Directory and proclaimed himself consul. In 1802 he made himself consul for life, and in 1804, emperor. Each change was approved by the people in a plebiscite.

Napoleonic Era. Within France Napoleon created a political system that was an amalgam of the old monarchy and the Revolution. He made himself a hereditary, divine-right ruler and formed a new aristocracy composed of those who served the state well. He made peace with the Roman Catholic Church in 1801 in a concordat with the pope, although he did not return the clergy's confiscated lands.

Napoleon issued a new civil law code, usually known as the Code Napoléon, which assured all citizens equality under the law. He introduced a tax system that was more efficient and equitable than that of the Old Regime and instituted administrative reforms that gave France a highly organized and centralized bureaucracy.

Abroad, France absorbed Belgium, Holland, the Rhineland, and part of Italy. Napoleon set up puppet states in western Germany, Switzerland, Italy, and Poland, and forced Austria, Prussia, and Russia into an alliance. However, failure to crush Britain either militarily or economically, a costly war in Spain, and a disastrous campaign in Russia led in 1814 to Napoleon's defeat by a European coalition. Napoleon's attempt to regain control—known as the Hundred Days—ended in his final defeat at Waterloo, Belgium, in 1815.

Restoration. Under the terms of the peace agreement concluded at the Congress of Vienna in 1815, France's territory was reduced to what it had been in 1792 and the Bourbons were restored to the French throne. The Bourbons could not restore the Old Regime, however, and in 1814 Louis XVIII (r.1814–1824) issued the Constitutional Charter to win the support of the bourgeoisie and the peasants. It guaranteed basic liberties and created a constitutional monarchy modeled on the British system.

The king headed a chamber of peers whom he appointed and a chamber of deputies chosen by a small electorate. The "ultra-royalists" in the chamber of deputies, who opposed the liberalism of the king, were not discouraged, for their leader was the count of Artois, the brother of Louis and heir to the throne. When he succeeded Louis as Charles X (r.1824–1830), he immediately made it clear that he wished to reestablish the prerevolutionary order.

Charles chose reactionary ministers, granted indemnities to the nobles whose lands had been confiscated during the revolution, and entrusted public education to the clergy. The chamber, dominated by the liberal bourgeoisie, tried to stop the king's actions.

Charles dissolved the chamber and called for new elections, but the majority of the electorate failed to support his policies. He retaliated by promulgating the July Ordinances, which restricted the freedom of the press, reduced the size of the electorate, and again dissolved the chamber of deputies.

Fearing that the ordinances were a prelude to a coup d'état, liberal intellectuals incited the Parisians to revolt in the July Revolution of 1830. Charles abdicated, and a constitutional monarchy was established. A cousin of the deposed ruler, Louis Philippe, duke of Orléans, became the new king.

The July Monarchy. To the disappointment of the republicans, the liberal middle class, and the workers, the "July Monarchy," as Louis' reign was called, proved to be as opposed to social and economic reforms as the previous regime. At first Louis Philippe mollified the republicans and liberals by upholding the Constitutional Charter of 1814 and extending the right to vote.

But the revolution had merely shifted the power from one small group to another—the upper middle class, or *haute bourgeoisie*, had replaced the nobility. Like their aristocratic predecessors, the bourgeoisie refused to widen voting privileges, and they used their newly acquired power to develop industries and businesses for their own material gains.

Many groups opposed the "July Monarchy." The "Legitimists" wanted Charles X or his grandson, the duke of Bordeaux, restored to the throne, and the republicans wanted universal suffrage and a republic. The workers demanded better working conditions and a voice in the government.

The workers joined with the republicans, both groups believing that only a radical change in the country's political structure could bring about improved social conditions. On Feb. 22, 1848, rioting broke out in Paris, and two days later Louis abdicated. Although the liberals were willing to place Louis' grandson on the throne, the republicans demanded a republic.

The Second Republic. A provisional government headed by the poet Alphonse de Lamartine and the journalist Louis Blanc was established. Blanc, strongly in favor of social reform, established National Workshops to provide jobs for the unemployed. He was unable to provide enough work for everyone, however, and in the ensuing dissension dissolved the workshops. The closing of the workshops was followed by rioting, which was finally suppressed by the army.

In November 1848 an assembly completed the drafting of a new constitution, which provided for a legislature of one house and a president with strong powers to be elected by universal suffrage. In December 1848 the first presidential election under the Second Republic was held. The vote made Louis Napoleon, a nephew of Napoleon Bonaparte, president, and revealed that the country as a whole, especially the French peasantry, was much more conservative than the vocal Paris populace.

Second Empire. Louis Napoleon overthrew the republic in 1851 and established an empire the following year, becoming Emperor Napoleon III. Under the Second Empire France enjoyed rapid economic growth, but in the 1860s Louis Napoleon's free trade policies and meddling in Italian affairs brought about opposition.

TRANS WORLD AIRLINES

THE ARC DE TRIOMPHE, in Paris, covers the tomb of France's "unknown soldier."

To gain popularity, Napoleon liberalized his regime and initiated an aggressive foreign policy. But his indecisiveness and military ineptness resulted in a series of national humiliations. Napoleon III was also incapable of halting the rising power of Prussia.

On July 19, 1870, with French international prestige and military strength at its lowest point, the Prussian Chancellor Otto von Bismarck provoked Napoleon into a disastrous conflict, the Franco-Prussian War. When news reached Paris on Sept. 2, 1870, that Napoleon III had surrendered to the Germans at Sedan, the Parisians demanded a republic be proclaimed.

The Third Republic. On Sept. 4, 1870, the Third Republic was born. A provisional government of national defense raised an army to try to prevent the Germans from occupying the city of Paris, but the Parisians were defeated after a four-month siege. Under the terms of the peace treaty negotiated between Bismarck and Adolphe Thiers, the head of the National Assembly, France was forced to cede Alsace and part of Lorraine to Germany and to pay a huge indemnity.

Before the treaty was signed the Third Republic was confronted by an insurrection in Paris, which evolved into a civil war. Unwilling to concede defeat to the Prussians, the Parisians drove the French government troops out of the capital in March 1871 and formed their own municipal regime—the Paris Commune. Civil war raged for two months until the supporters of the National Assembly managed to suppress the commune.

Although the Third Republic started badly, it survived until 1940. The republic, headed by Thiers, was provisional at first since a majority of deputies in the National Assembly favored a monarchy. But the monarchists were divided between supporters of the Bourbon and Orleans lines, and gradually the voters turned to conservative republican candidates. By 1879, when Jules Grévy was chosen president, the republicans controlled all branches of government.

During the Third Republic there was a rapid change in cabinets—more than 50 before World War I. Since presidents did not call elections when ministries were voted out, deputies were not afraid to overthrow a cabinet. More important, France did not develop large, disciplined political parties such as those in Britain. Instead, after a century of ideological conflict, there was a multitude of small parties.

This system, which continued into the Fourth Republic, was not as unstable as it seemed, however. Changing ministries were composed of many of the same men who represented coalitions of center parties. Also, behind the shifting ministries stood the Napoleonic administrative structure, with its centralized bureaucracy.

The republic weathered a number of crises—such as a threatened coup in 1889 and the Dreyfus Affair in the late 1890s. In 1894 Alfred Dreyfus, a Jewish army officer, was convicted of treason. Later evidence pointed to his innocence, but the army refused to reopen the case. Monarchists, conservatives, and militarists opposed reopening the case, wishing not only to stand behind the army but to disgrace the republic. The country was bitterly divided.

In 1898 the case was reopened, and the following year Dreyfus was pardoned. In 1906 he was fully exonerated. Thus the Dreyfus Affair ultimately discredited the monarchists and strengthened the republic.

The Third Republic proved politically radical but socially conservative. Republicans led by Jules Ferry restricted the role of the church in education, and the schools were to turn out loyal republicans. An anticlerical movement culminated in the absolute separation of church and state in 1905, ending Napoleon's 1801 concordat with the Roman Catholic Church.

In social welfare legislation, however the republic lagged behind Germany and Britain. The Radical Socialists, who held the balance of power in the chamber before World War I, proved radical in name only.

France had a large conservative bloc of voters composed of peasants and small merchants. The working class was still too small and divided to exert any real pressure on the government, and the workers did not give united support to the Socialists, who spoke for them in the chamber.

Industry expanded, but not as rapidly as in other nations, and the population barely increased at all. Yet French trade grew considerably as a result of extensive colonial expansion in Africa and Southeast Asia (Indochina). By 1914 France's colonial empire was second only to Britain's.

To protect its colonial interests and to secure its position against Germany, France strengthened its army and navy, formed an alliance with Russia in 1894, and entered the Entente Cordiale with Britain in 1904. Rather than risk losing a vital ally, France supported Russia in the Balkan crisis that precipitated World War I.

World War I. In August 1914 German troops drove westward through Belgium to invade France, and soon most of Europe was involved in the conflict.

Britain supported France, and the United States entered the conflict on their side in 1917. For four years most of the fighting on the western front was done in northeastern France, costing the lives of over 1 million French soldiers and untold physical damage.

Although the Allies eventually defeated Germany, France still faced a powerful German state, and after the 1917 Bolshevik Revolution Russia was lost as an ally. Under the terms of the Treaty of Versailles (1919) France was granted a 15-year occupation of the Rhineland, which was to be permanently demilitarized.

Germany was disarmed, and France was given Alsace-Lorraine. France also received the coal mines of the Saar for the duration of the 15-year occupation, large war reparations, and some former German colonies. The period from 1919 to 1925 was marked by labor unrest and serious inflation, and French foreign policy was based on a tough line against Germany. France occupied the Ruhr in 1923 to force reparation payments from Germany, and in 1921 formed an alliance with Poland.

Interwar France. From 1925 to 1932 France pursued a more conciliatory German policy, although France allied itself with the nations of the Little Entente—Czechoslovakia, Romania, and Yugoslavia. The Locarno treaties of 1925, guaranteeing the Versailles frontiers and providing for arbitration of disputes, seemed to ensure European stability. At home, prosperity obscured the need for social legislation, although a modest social security system was approved. The world economic depression of the 1930s and the rise of Adolf Hitler in Germany ended this quiet interlude.

Unemployment, growing insecurity, and a succession of ineffective ministries gave rise to extreme right-wing groups, who were as militant, antirepublican, and antidemocratic as their prototypes in Italy and Germany. In 1934, when the government was alleged to be involved in a financial scandal, the rightists staged antiparliamentary riots.

In response to the right-wing threat, the Socialist, Radical Socialist, and Communist parties formed a political

bloc, known as the Popular Front, which came to power in 1936. The Popular Front's premier, Léon Blum, promised moderate reforms well within a capitalistic economic system.

Blum won parliamentary approval to establish collective bargaining, a 40-hour work week, paid vacations, closer government control over national financial affairs, nationalization of the arms industry, and cultural programs for the lower classes. But Blum's government lasted only a year, and in 1938 France returned to economic and social conservatism under Premier Edouard Daladier.

With its finances exhausted, lacking British support, preoccupied with internal politics, and with an influential right-wing sympathetic to Germany's Nazi dictator, Adolph Hitler and Italy's Fascist dictator, Benito Mussolini, France avoided taking action against the growing aggressiveness of Nazi Germany.

France failed to halt German rearmament in 1935, remilitarization of the Rhineland in 1936, or the annexation of Austria and the dismemberment of Czechoslovakia in 1938. A Nazi-Soviet nonaggression pact in 1939 nullified an undeveloped alliance with the Soviet Union and left France without a powerful ally on Germany's east.

World War II. In 1939 World War II began with Germany's attack on Poland. France was economically stagnant, politically divided, and militarily unprepared. In May 1940 France collapsed before the German *blitzkrieg*, and on June 22 an armistice was signed with the Nazis.

Northwestern France was occupied by the Germans. In the southeast the Germans set up a puppet government headed by Marshal Henri-Philippe Pétain, which was known as the Vichy regime after the town that was its capital.

Gen. Charles de Gaulle and a handful of Frenchmen escaped to London and formed the French Committee of National Liberation (the Free French). At first the committee functioned to recruit Frenchmen to continue the fight against Germany, but eventually it took the form of a provisional government ready to take control of France after the defeat of Germany.

FRENCH EMBASSY PRESS AND INFORMATION DIVISION

NUCLEAR POWER PLANT, at Chinon, illustrates France's industrial and technological progress.

After four years of German occupation and government by the Vichy regime, France was liberated in August 1944 by Allied forces, which included contingents of the Free French under General de Gaulle. During the immediate post-liberation period De Gaulle presided over a provisional government, but he resigned in 1946 because of communist and socialist opposition to a constitution providing for a strong executive.

After the resignation of De Gaulle, a coalition of communists, socialists, and members of the MRP (the Catholic Popular Republican Movement) carried through various social reforms and nationalized the country's most important power, transportation, and banking facilities.

The Fourth Republic. Soon after the establishment of the Fourth Republic in 1946, however, the coalition broke up over ideological differences and Cold War tensions. Power once again was given to the center parties—the Socialists, the MRP, and the Radicals, and France once more returned to social and economic conservatism.

During the late 1940s France was beset by inflation, strikes, and foreign exchange problems. Nevertheless, the French economy was modernized and production increased with the help of U.S. aid under the Marshall Plan, which was inaugurated in 1947.

The most serious problem facing the Fourth Republic was the struggle to maintain the French colonial empire. France waged a losing war in Indochina from 1946 to 1954, when it was forced to withdraw. A few months later France was engaged in a costly war against nationalists in Algeria, where there were many French settlers.

Finally, weakened by the old pattern of changing ministries, the Fourth Republic was destroyed in 1958 by an attempted coup led by French soldiers and settlers in Algeria determined to forestall an agreement with the nationalists.

The Fifth Republic. De Gaulle returned to power as head of France's Fifth Republic, which placed extensive powers in the hands of the president, and in 1962 he recognized Algerian independence. Meanwhile, France had granted independence to most of its other African dependencies.

During the first decade of the Fifth Republic France enjoyed stability and prosperity, and played an ambitious role in foreign affairs. De Gaulle worked to build France into a major power free from the constraint or influence of other nations, particularly the United States, and foreign policy was directed toward that end.

France developed its own nuclear atomic force and refused to participate in an international atomic test-ban treaty in 1960. It recognized Communist China in 1964, and in 1966 withdrew all French troops from allied command and ordered NATO headquarters, military bases, and troops from France. Despite reduced support in presidential elections held in 1965 and in legislative elections in 1967, De Gaulle retained control of France's future.

—James A. Leith

UNITED NATIONS
GABONESE FISHERMEN on the beach near Libreville, the capital of the West African country.

GABON

Official name: Gabon Republic
Area: 103,346 square miles
Population: (1966 est.) 468,000
Capital: Libreville (Pop. 1964, urban area, 45,909)
Language: French, African languages
Religion: Christianity, Islam, traditional religions
Currency unit: Franc CFA (African Financial Community)
National holiday: August 17

Gabon, a republic in west Africa, is bordered on the north by Spanish Equatorial Guinea (Río Muni) and Cameroon, on the east and south by the Congo (Brazzaville), and on the west by the Atlantic Ocean. Gabon was a French territory until 1960, when it received its independence.

THE LAND. Most of Gabon is covered by wet tropical forests. Inland from a coastal plain is the edge of the African Plateau, called the Crystal Mountains in the north and the Mayombé Mountains in the south. In the southeast is the Batéké Plateau, a region of grasslands. Gabon's principal river is the Ogooué. The climate throughout the country is hot and humid.

THE PEOPLE. There are many different tribal groups in Gabon, most of which are Bantu-speaking. The Fang, who migrated from the north in the 1800s, form the largest group. There are also peoples of the Eschira, Okande, and Adouma tribes.

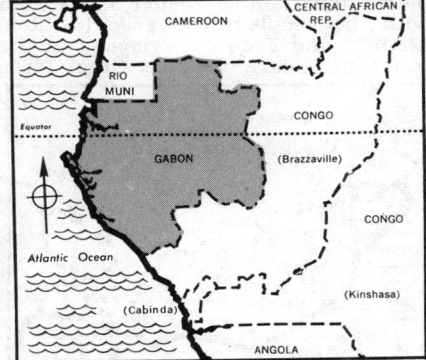

Gabon is thinly populated. Most of the people live in rural areas, and the major city is the capital, Libreville. Port Gentil is Gabon's major port.

ECONOMY. The economy of Gabon is based largely on mining and forestry, although most of the people are engaged in subsistence farming. Manioc, corn, and bananas are the country's main crops.

Gabon is rich in minerals. The country has some of the world's largest deposits of manganese and iron ore. In 1965 Gabon produced over 637,000 metric tons of manganese ore, about 11 percent of the world total. Uranium, petroleum, and natural gas are also produced. Gabon's forest areas provide wood products of great value.

In 1966 exports earned $100 million and imports cost $66 million. Gabon exports wood and wood products and minerals, and imports foodstuffs and manufactured goods. Gabon is a member of a tariff union with the countries of the Central African Republic, Chad, and the Congo (Brazzaville).

GOVERNMENT. Gabon has a presidential system of government. Executive power is vested in a president popularly elected to a seven-year term. Legislative power rests with a unicameral National Assembly. The assembly has 47 members elected by universal suffrage to five-year terms.

Gabon is a member of the United Nations and of the Organization of African Unity (OAU).

HISTORY. Little is known of the early history of the Gabon area. In the 1400s Portuguese explorers established trade relations with the Loango kingdom. The original trade in gold dust, ivory, palm oil, and wood soon gave way to slaving. Several European countries joined in the slave trade, but France became predominant.

French Rule. Slave trading was abolished in the early 1800s, and in 1849 France established a center for freed slaves at Libreville. In 1899 France began granting concessions to private companies to develop the region. Company abuses led to depopulation, depletion of resources, and loss of capital. In 1910 Gabon became part of French Equatorial Africa.

Political activities before World War II were confined mainly to groups in Libreville, religious cults, and Fang tribal societies. After the war, France liberalized its colonial system, and in 1946 created the French Union. Gabon was permitted to establish territorial assemblies and to elect deputies to the French National Assembly. Jean-Hilaire Aubame, representing the northern Fang people, was elected to the French assembly.

Self-Rule. France granted Gabon internal self-government in 1957. Leon M'Ba, representing the southern Fang and other groups in his party, the Gabonese Democratic Bloc (BDG), became prime minister of a coalition government that included Aubame's Gabonese Social and Democratic Union (UDSG).

Gabon became a member of the French Community in 1958, but broke its ties with French Equatorial Africa, from which it had long desired to secede because of its own wealth.

Gabon became independent on Aug. 17, 1960, and M'Ba was elected president. Early in 1964 a military coup threatened the regime, but the French intervened in support of M'Ba. In elections held in April 1964 M'Ba's party won a majority of seats in the National Assembly, and M'Ba continued as president until his death in 1967. He was succeeded by Bernard-Albert Bongo, a political associate.

—Hibberd V. B. Kline, Jr.;
Vera L. Zolberg

GAMBIA

Official name: The Gambia
Area: 4,361 square miles
Population: (1966 est.) 336,000
Capital: Bathurst (Pop. 1964, urban area, 42,104)
Language: English, African languages
Religion: Islam, traditional religions
Currency unit: Pound
National holiday: Independence day, February 18

The Gambia, a small independent nation in West Africa, is bordered on the north, east, and south by Senegal, and on the west by the Atlantic Ocean. The Gambia received its independence in 1965 after a century and a half of British control.

THE LAND. The Gambia is dominated by the Gambia River, which flows through the narrow country from east to west for a distance of over 200 miles. Mangrove swamps line the river for about 150 miles inland from the ocean. Beyond the swamps the land is grassy with patches of sandy soil. Sandstone plateaus cover the region farthest from the river.

The Gambia receives about 40 inches of rain a year. The rainy season lasts from June to October.

THE PEOPLE. Several different peoples live in the Gambia. Among the larger groups are the Mandingo, Wolof, and Fulani, most of whom are Muslims.

The Gambia's major city, Bathurst, is on St. Mary's Island at the mouth of the Gambia River.

ECONOMY. The Gambia's economy depends on agriculture. The main crop is peanuts, and in 1964–1965 the Gambia produced about 114,000 metric

UNITED NATIONS

GAMBIA'S PRIME MINISTER, Dawda Jawara, addresses villagers during an election campaign.

tons of peanuts. The people grow sorghum and rice for local consumption. The Gambia has few mineral deposits and little industry. Livestock grazing is hindered by the prevalence of disease caused by the tsetse fly.

In 1965 the Gambia's imports cost $16 million and its exports earned $14 million. Peanuts accounted for about 95 percent of the value of exports. The Gambia imports rice, wheat, sugar, petroleum products, motor vehicles, and manufactured goods.

GOVERNMENT. The Gambia has a parliamentary system of government. The British Queen is head of state and is represented by a governor-general, who serves as nominal chief executive. Actual executive powers rest with a prime minister and cabinet responsible to the legislature, the House of Representatives. The legislature has 32 popularly elected members and 4 members elected by local chiefs.

The Gambia is a member of the United Nations and the Organization of African Unity (OAU).

HISTORY. Little is known about the early history of the Gambia. A Carthaginian, Hanno, may have sailed up the Gambia River in the 500s BC. During the 900s AD, the Gambia region was probably a distant outpost of the empires of Ghana and Mali.

In the 1400s the Portuguese explored the Gambia region and traded with the people there, as did Dutch, English, and French merchants in the following years. Between the 1500s

and the 1700s, slaves from the area were transported to America.

By the 1700s the British and French had established trading posts and forts at the mouth of the Gambia River. British and French merchants competed vigorously throughout the 1700s for control of trade with the Gambia, but in 1783 the Gambia was awarded to Britain by treaty.

British Rule. Throughout the 1800s British merchants trading on the Gambia River resisted proposals that the Gambia should become part of French-controlled Senegal. The Gambia was ruled from the British Crown Colony of Sierra Leone until 1843, when the Gambia was made a crown colony. The two colonies once again were administered jointly for a brief period, from 1866 to 1888, but after 1888 the Gambia remained a separate entity.

In 1889 Britain and France agreed on the present boundaries of the Gambia, which Britain had been acquiring piece by piece from tribal chiefs since the early 1800s.

After World War II Britain faced the problem of Senegalese demands for the Gambia. Senegal wanted the Gambia in order to round out its own boundaries and to eliminate smuggling between the two countries. The Gambians had mixed feelings about union with Senegal. They realized that their country could not be economically successful, but there were significant differences in language and culture between the two countries.

Self-Rule. Out of the differences of opinion created by possible unification with Senegal, Dawda Jawara formed the Progressive People's Party, which won elections held in 1960 and 1962.

In 1963 the Gambia became self-governing with Jawara as prime minister. He led the Gambia to independence in February 1965, without the issue of its future relations with Senegal having been resolved.

—Hibberd V. B. Kline, Jr.;
Robert I. Rotberg

GERMANY

WEST GERMANY

Official name: Federal Republic of Germany
Area: 95,743 square miles (excluding West Berlin: 186 square miles)
Population: (1966 est.) 57,458,000 (excluding West Berlin: 2,191,000)
Capital: Bonn (Pop., 1965 est., 141,700)
Language: German
Religion: Protestant, Roman Catholic
Currency unit: Deutsche Mark

EAST GERMANY

Official name: German Democratic Republic
Area: 41,661 square miles (excluding East Berlin: 156 square miles)
Population: (1966 est.) 15,988,000 (excluding East Berlin)
Capital: East Berlin (Pop., 1966 est., 1,079,000)
Language: German
Religion: Protestantism, Roman Catholicism
Currency unit: Mark

Germany is a divided nation in north-central Europe. German territory is bounded on the north by the North Sea, Denmark, and the Baltic Sea; on the east by Poland and Czechoslovakia; on the south by Austria, Liechtenstein, and Switzerland; and on the west by France, Luxembourg, Belgium, and the Netherlands.

After World War II Germany was divided among the four major Allied powers—Britain, France, the United States, and the Soviet Union. Its capital city, Berlin, was also partitioned into four zones. Each zone was occupied by one of the Allied powers. Pre-World War II territories of Germany lying east of the Oder and Neisse rivers were placed under Polish administration. East Prussia, a separate territory on the east coast of the Baltic, was annexed by the Soviet Union.

In 1949 the Soviet zone was established as the German Democratic Republic, with the eastern sector of Berlin as its capital, and the other Allies merged their three zones into the Federal Republic of Germany. The line separating East Germany, as the communist sector is called, from West Germany, the noncommunist sector, runs an irregular course south from Lubeck, on the Baltic Sea, to Adorf, on the Czechoslovakian border.

THE LAND. The political division of Germany is arbitrary, for East and West Germany form a geographical unit containing two distinct and strikingly different regions—northern Germany, low and flat, and southern Germany, hilly and of complex relief. The North German Plain, south of a low, sandy northern coastline, is low and dotted with swamps and lakes especially in the northeast. Toward the interior are hummocks and low hills.

The elevation begins to rise in central Germany, the *Mittelland,* a region of uplands with plateaus and low mountains broken by broad river valleys. These uplands rise into the Bohemian forest, the Black Forest, and the Bavarian Plateau until, near the southern border, the Alps reach almost 10,000 feet.

Several major European rivers cross Germany. The Rhine, with its tributaries, including the Main and the Moselle; the Ems; the Weser; and the Elbe all flow through central Germany into the North Sea. The Oder crosses eastern Germany and empties into the Baltic. The Danube and the Inn drain southern Germany and flow toward the Black Sea.

Germany's climate is temperate. Warm ocean currents moderate the cold of the far north, and high elevations counteract warmer tendencies toward the south. Winter temperatures average below 20°F in the south and about 30°F in the north. Summer temperatures average in the mid-60s throughout the country. Rainfall is moderate, averaging about 30 inches for the country as a whole and generally decreasing toward the south.

THE PEOPLE. The population of both Germanys is quite homogeneous. German is the universal language. A majority of the people are Protestant, with Lutherans forming the largest community. Roman Catholicism ranks second. There are no major minority groups. A large Jewish community that lived in Germany before World War II was destroyed by the Nazi regime.

During the 1950s and early 1960s, West Germany received a steady flow of refugees from East Germany. The western population was also swollen by an influx of foreign workers, mostly from southern Europe, who were attracted by West Germany's manpower shortage. As a result of the migrations, West Germany, in 1965 was one of the most crowded nations in Europe.

West Germany is highly urbanized, but with many small cities rather than a few large metropolitan centers. The largest cities are Hamburg, in the north, and Munich, in the south. Divided Berlin is the largest city in all Germany.

GERMAN INFORMATION CENTER
GERMANY'S LANDSCAPE includes the mountains of Bavaria *(left),* whose peaks tower over high valleys, and the rolling banks of the Rhine River *(above),* which hold terraced vineyards.

GERMAN INFORMATION CENTER

ASSEMBLY LINE turning out auto parts reflects Germany's highly industrialized economy.

The East German population density is much lower, in part because of a steady migration to the west. In the 1950s and 1960s urbanization was rapid, but East Germany's largest cities, Dresden and Leipzig, are smaller than many West German cities.

ECONOMY. Both East and West Germany are prosperous countries, although West Germany is by far the wealthier of the two. Germany's prosperity is based on a long tradition of industry and on a highly skilled, well-disciplined, and industrious labor force. Industry makes the greatest contribution to the German economy.

The economies of both Germanys expanded rapidly during the 1950s and 1960s. In West Germany, the expansion consisted of rebuilding and developing industries destroyed in World War II, to become the leading industrial nation in Europe. In East Germany, the expansion consisted largely of developing new industries, to become the most industrialized of the east European countries other than the Soviet Union. Both Germanys concentrate on heavy industry.

Germany has some excellent farmland, especially in the river valleys of the *Mittelland,* but agriculture is of much less importance than industry in both East and West. It contributes a greater proportion of the East German national product than the West German.

International trade is of more importance in the economy of West Germany than in that of East Germany. West Germany is fully integrated into the western European economy through the Common Market. East Germany's economy is tied to that of other communist-dominated eastern European countries through their economic alliance, the Council for Mutual Economic Cooperation (COMECON).

West Germany. West Germany's principal natural resource is high-grade hard coal. There are also de-

LOOK MAGAZINE

MUNICH PARADERS celebrate *Oktoberfest,* a traditional Bavarian festival held in autumn.

posits of petroleum, potash, iron, copper, and zinc, and water power is abundant. The leading West German industries are iron and steel production, mining, chemical manufacture, machinery and vehicle production, shipbuilding, and power production. The older light industries of textile weaving, brewing, food processing, and precision tool manufacture still prosper, however.

West German industry is concentrated in the Saar and the Ruhr regions near the western border, on the northern plain, and in the middle Rhine valley.

West Germany is Western Europe's leading producer of rye and potatoes. Wheat, barley, and sugar beets are also important crops. Tobacco, nuts, and fruits—especially wine grapes—are grown in the lower Rhine valley. Dairy cattle and other livestock, particularly pigs, are important.

West Germany is the second-ranking trading nation in the world. In 1966 its exports earned over $20,000 million and its imports cost just over $18,000 million. Machinery and equipment, automobiles, and chemicals are the leading exports, and foodstuffs and raw materials are imported. Most West German trade is with other Western European countries and the United States.

East Germany. East Germany's main natural resource is lignite, of which it is the world's leading producer. Uranium, cobalt, iron, copper, potash, and zinc are also available, and water power is abundant. All East German industry is nationalized, and the state has concentrated on developing heavy industry. Iron and steel production, mining, machinery and vehicle production, chemical manufacture, shipbuilding, and power production are the main industries.

All East German agriculture is collectivized. Wheat, rye, barley, sugar beets, and potatoes are the leading crops. Livestock, especially pigs, are raised, and dairying is also important to the economy.

East Germany has a generally favorable balance of trade. In 1966 both exports and imports were valued at about $3,000 million. Machinery and vehicles, textiles, and chemicals are the leading exports, and foodstuffs and raw materials are imported. Most East German trade is with other communist-dominated Eastern European countries, particularly the Soviet Union.

GOVERNMENT. The Federal Republic of Germany is a democracy; the German Democratic Republic is a totalitarian state.

West Germany. West Germany is a federal union of 10 *lander,* or states. The city of West Berlin has close political ties with West Germany. A president is head of state. Actual executive power rests with a chancellor, or prime minister, who is elected by the *Bundestag,* the larger house of the legislature. He and the cabinet he leads are responsible to the legislature.

Members of the *Bundestag* are popularly elected to four-year terms. Members of the *Bundesrat,* the smaller, less powerful upper house, are chosen by the governments of the individual *lander* for indefinite terms. Representatives of West Berlin sit as members of the West German legislature.

The Federal Republic is a member of the European Communities and the North Atlantic Treaty Organization (NATO).

East Germany. Political life in the German Democratic Republic is dominated by the East German Communist party, officially called the Socialist Unity Party. The politburo, or political bureau, of its central committee determines national policy, and the first secretary of the party is usually the key figure in the government.

The East German constitution provides for a popularly elected legislature. Candidates for the legislature are nominated under party control. The legislature chooses a council of state to act for it between its short sessions, and the chairman of the council serves as head of state. Actual executive power rests with a council of ministers, or cabinet, and its chairman, who is equivalent to a prime minister.

Most noncommunist countries do not recognize the Democratic Republic. It is a member of the Soviet-controlled Warsaw Pact, a military grouping of east European states.

HISTORY. Political division is not new to Germany. With no major natural boundaries save the Alps, the territory has been open to invasion from east, north, and west. In ancient times there were many small, tribal states, all subject to easy conquest. Among the earliest settlers were the Teutons, a Germanic people.

The territory was divided among several Teutonic tribes—the Franks, the Saxons, and the Thuringians—led by elective kings. Beginning in the 200s AD, other Germanic peoples from the east settled in the area—notably the Goths and the Burgundians. The Romans made several unsuccessful attempts to conquer the Germanic tribes, but no single ruler gained control of the entire region until the 300s, when the Huns swept across the land.

Both the Huns and the Vandals, who followed soon after, were migratory, warlike peoples whose main goal was conquest, and their rule over the settled tribes was brief. It was only the Franks, who settled in the Rhine valley in the late 300s, who attempted to unite permanently the Germanic peoples.

Frankish Kingdom. The Franks expanded westward from the Rhine into Gaul, driving out the Roman legions stationed there. They adopted Christianity and won the support of the popes, whose power by the 500s was greater than that of the Roman emperors. They defeated the other Germanic tribes and in 732 they fought off a Muslim invasion of Europe.

The Franks reached the height of their power under Charles the Great, or Charlemagne, who became king in 768. Under Charlemagne, the Franks controlled a vast territory ranging from Central Italy on the south to the Baltic Sea on the north and from the Pyrenees on the west to the Elbe River on the east. Charlemagne accepted the role of protector of the popes, and in 800 he was crowned emperor in Rome, an act that laid the religious and political foundations for the later Holy Roman Empire.

The unity Charlemagne achieved did not long survive him. Several decades of disunity followed his death in 814, and in 843 the Treaty of Verdun divided his territories into three parts. The eastern, predominantly Teuton, portion, between the Rhine and the Elbe Rivers, went to Louis the German, and became the core of modern Germany.

The Saxons. The tribal loyalties and ambitions born before Charlemagne's time had not been forgotten. Each major tribal unit had formed a country, and the dukes and princes who led them vied for control of the German throne. By the early 900s one

Teuton clan, the Saxons, had emerged dominant. Its first ruler, Henry the Fowler, extended German territory to the Oder River and defended it against attacks from Magyar and Slavic peoples to the south.

A Saxon king, Otto I, in 962 was given the crown of Italy and became the first Holy Roman Emperor as a reward for aiding the pope. The Holy Roman Empire revived, at least in name, the old Roman Empire and gave to Germany the empire's prestige as well as the support of the papacy. As Holy Roman Emperor, Otto gained control over the German dukes and princes, who were willing to support a prestigious empire that was growing in size and power.

By about 1030, the Holy Roman Empire was a prosperous feudal nation with thriving towns and vigorous trade. Henry III, who became emperor in 1039, probably held more actual power than any other. He brought all of the mightiest princes—his rivals for power—into submission and he maintained tight control of the church, introducing many needed reforms.

Henry was the last emperor with such power, however. After his death in 1056 a regent ruled for his young heir, and the period of the regency was fatal for the strength of the German throne. Both the church and the nobility had become dissatisfied with their lack of power. By the 1070s the pope and the emperor were in open conflict over the distribution of political and religious power. The local princes sided with the papacy to reduce the strength of the emperor.

The conflict continued into the mid-1200s, and although both emperors and popes won victories, the final result of the struggle was a great loss of power for both. The empire disintegrated into a state of anarchy in the 1250s. For a 20-year period known

as the "Great Interregnum" no one man ruled Germany, although many tried. Moreover, as each faction grew in power—the princes, the dukes, the bishops, and the towns—a tradition of disunity was firmly established, and it became even harder to consolidate political power.

It was only in 1273, at the insistence of Pope Gregory X, who feared the growing power of France, that the German princes elected one of their number to be Holy Roman Emperor. Their choice was Rudolf of the House of Hapsburg in Austria, which was then a minor princely house. Rudolf took steps to insure the continuance on the throne of members of his family, and later Hapsburg emperors became powerful.

The Hapsburgs. During the Middle Ages, the Hapsburg emperors added to the territory under their control, but the unification of the German states did not follow the Hapsburg

GERMAN INFORMATION CENTER

DUISBURG, GERMANY, where the Rhine and Ruhr rivers join, has Europe's larger river harbor.

rise to power. The German emperor was an elected king by tradition and by a law enacted in 1356. As he could rule only with the consent of the princes who elected him, the German emperor constantly had to make concessions to them, and he was unable to rule as firmly as a hereditary monarch could.

Because of the weakness of the central government, the German states were less an empire than a federation dominated by the stronger states. Nearly constant competition for power kept the German states in turmoil from the 1300s to the 1800s, but the Hapsburg family remained the dominant power through the 1700s. An important factor in German decentralization was the growth in importance and size of the German towns during the Middle Ages.

Administrative and economic policies initiated during the 1100s had encouraged the development of the towns. By the middle of the 1300s, these policies, coupled with a renewed interest in the arts and an expanding economy, had transformed many towns into "free cities"—large, autonomous units free from the control of local princes. From the middle of the 1200s to the middle of the 1400s, the influence of German cities rivaled that of German princes.

Despite the fragmentation of the Holy Roman Empire, it reached the height of its power and size in the early 1500s under Emperor Charles V, who, by inheritance and marriage, ruled Spain, Portugal, Belgium, and the Netherlands as well as the German states. It was during his reign, however, that religious controversy flared, contributing to the final disintegration of the empire. In 1517 Martin Luther, an Augustinian monk, called for reforms in the Roman Catholic Church.

Reformation. The Lutheran "reformation" attracted many more radical social, political, and religious reformers, and they became a threat to both the church and the empire. Charles V led a diet, or council, at Worms in 1521 to try Luther. The council banned the spread of any new doctrines. The reformers continued, however, encouraged by power-seeking princes, who adopted their reforms as a means of opposing the emperor.

The progress of the Reformation was speeded by Charles' involvement in a series of wars with France. In Germany, disputes among the proliferating Protestant sects and between Protestants and Roman Catholics led to a series of religious wars, which were ended in 1555 by the Peace of Augsburg.

The peace settlement marked the final collapse of the emperor's real power. It granted to each prince within the empire the right to determine the religion of his subjects. In 1556 Charles abdicated, leaving his Spanish possessions to his son Philip, and his German dominions to his brother, Ferdinand.

The Peace of Augsburg had not finally settled the religious disputes, and it had only aggravated Germany's political confusion. In 1618 fighting began again in the war that was to earn the name of the Thirty Years' War. At first the war was confined to the Roman Catholic–Protestant conflict, but almost immediately the old issues of prince versus emperor, and federation versus empire, were renewed.

The war spread and eventually involved most of continental Europe as well as England and Sweden. The Peace of Westphalia, which settled the war in 1648, formalized German disunity by giving the local princes more power than the emperor. Each of the 300 separate German states received the right to conduct its own diplomacy, determine the religion of its people, and vote on the emperor's rights to collect taxes, raise an army, or conduct foreign policy.

Germany's enemies, notably France, gained from German fragmentation, which greatly diminished its international power. Between the mid-1600s and mid-1700s, France led Europe, and the only real power left to the Holy Roman Empire was that which its Hapsburg emperors derived from their own vast personal territories. Austria continued as leader and protector of the German states, defending them, for instance, from the onslaught of the Ottoman Turks in the 1600s.

Rise of Prussia. During the latter half of the 1600s, however, Prussia, known then as Brandenburg, began to grow from a small duchy into the most powerful state in Germany. Prussia's ruling Hohenzollern house increased the territory within its domain and, at the same time, established an efficient, centralized administration to control it. The army, officered by the nobility, became the central institution of the state.

Decisive in Prussia's ascendency to power within Germany was the succession to the throne in 1740 of Frederick II, called the Great, a man of driving force and shrewd statesmanship. Immediately upon assuming the throne he invaded Silesia, a large and wealthy Austrian territory.

The wars precipitated by the invasion of Silesia engulfed most of Europe for 15 of the next 23 years. Finally, in 1763, Prussia won the disputed Silesian territory, which doubled Prussia's population and natural resources. Germany was then polarized between northern Germany, dominated by Prussia, and southern Germany, led by Austria.

Prussia's rapid rise to power had been due in large part to Frederick the Great, and after his death in 1786, the system he had built could not function effectively. Thus in 1806, when the French armies of Napoleon were conquering Europe, Prussia offered little resistance and fell to Napoleon after the Battle of Jena.

Napoleonic Era. By 1806 Napoleon controlled most of the German states, which he organized into the Confederation of the Rhine, and he persuaded the Austrian emperor, Francis I, formally to dissolve the Holy Roman Empire. In 1809 Austria itself yielded to the French, and Napoleon's troops occupied all of Germany.

The French occupation ended in 1813, however, after Austria reluctantly joined forces with Prussia and Russia in a war of liberation that pushed Napoleon's armies west of the Rhine. But the fairly brief French occupation had wrought changes in Germany more significant than the formal dissolution of the Holy Roman Empire.

Germany was still a loose collection of states, but the Napoleonic Confederation of the Rhine had reduced their number and the Congress of Vienna, held in 1815 after Napoleon's defeat, accepted the reduction by creating the Germanic Confederation, a loose grouping of 38 independent German states.

Prussia, represented at Vienna by the liberal statesman Baron Heinrich Stein, had pressed for a more unified Germany, but the congress encouraged the autonomy of the states as sought by the Austrian foreign minister, Prince Klemens von Metternich. Metternich's leadership led to tightened monarchial control over the social, political, and economic life of Austria. This "Metternich system" dominated the south German states.

In Prussia, too, the movement for reform—which before 1815 had resulted in tax and administrative reforms and the abolition of serfdom—began to lag as reactionary forces triumphed over liberalism throughout Germany.

The Napoleonic wars had awakened democratic and nationalistic movements that the German governments

LUFTHANSA

HARBOR OF BREMEN, an important port of entry and the principal seat of German import and export trade. Once a free port, Bremen joined the German Customs Union in 1888.

felt must be repressed. Under the leadership of Austria's Metternich, the German states imposed tight controls on all civil liberties, especially on the activities of the universities. These controls only spurred the liberals and nationalists, and in 1848 they rebelled against Metternich's reactionary government.

Risings of 1848. Inspired by a similar revolution in Paris, large numbers of Austrians, mostly in Vienna, organized and demanded a constitution. Metternich fled Austria, and the emperor granted a constitution and abdicated in December 1848.

The rebellion had spread from Vienna to the Hapsburg's Hungarian and Slavic subject peoples, who demanded the establishment of independent Slavic and Magyar states. The Slavs organized a Pan-Slav Congress to lead their nationalistic movement. A new Austrian emperor, Francis Joseph I, concentrated on crushing the rebellions in Hungary and the Slavic areas, ignoring the more peaceful rebellion among the Germans.

The rebellious Germans were demanding not only political and social liberties, but the political union of Germany. Most German states elected liberal local governments, which in turn elected liberal representatives to a national assembly which met in Frankfurt in May 1848 to establish a republic. In 1849 the assembly drafted a democratic constitution for a unified German state and elected Prussia's ruler, Frederick William IV, emperor of the new nation.

Some of the states opposed the new organization, however, and Austria, which with Russia's help had quelled the Hungarian and Slavic revolutions in early 1849, refused to join the unification movement, which would have forced it to give up its non-German territories.

Frederick William IV, unwilling to accept the throne from an elected assembly, refused the imperial crown, and by 1850 the old constitution of the Germanic Confederation had been readopted and the unification and reform efforts of the assembly had failed. Austria was once more able to impose a superficial calm on Germany after putting down the 1848 rebellions, but it could not stem the movement for unification.

Unification. In 1844 Prussia had encouraged unification by organizing a customs union, the *Zollverein,* among more than half the German states, excluding Austria. The unification efforts gathered strength after 1862 under the leadership of Otto von Bismarck, Prussia's chief minister, who followed a stern policy of "blood and iron" in leading Germany to European dominance.

Bismarck centralized and strengthened Prussia's government and pressed the development of the army and expansion into new territory. Prussia annexed the two predominantly German duchies of Schleswig and Holstein, which Denmark claimed. Austria aided Prussia to drive out the Danes, but Bismarck's subsequent attempt to control Holstein angered Austria, and war between the two was only narrowly averted.

War did break out between them for seven weeks in 1866 after the Diet of Frankfurt, at which Bismarck had pressed for federal reform. In the Seven Weeks' War Prussian forces easily defeated Austria, and in 1867 a constitution was adopted for a new confederation excluding Austria and several south German states.

Constitutionally a federal state, the new North German Confederation was actually under Prussian control. Austria, having lost control of Germany, was forced to admit Hungary as an equal partner in a dual monarchy, and Austrian history diverged from that of Germany.

German Empire. Prussia quickly became the greatest power in Europe and roundly defeated France in 1870–1871 in a war over dynastic claims to the throne of Spain. Prussia forced France to accept a harsh and humiliating settlement—France ceded the industrially rich territories of Alsace and Lorraine, paid a large indemnity, and supported a German army of occupation.

Now the leader of all Europe, Bismarck also succeeded in 1871 in bringing the south German states except Austria into the North German Confederation. He became the first chancellor of this German Empire.

The new Prussian state was a curious mixture of democratic and authoritarian institutions. Advanced social welfare laws existed side-by-side with legislation curbing the Roman Catholic Church and suppressing the socialists. Both the central government and the 25 states comprising the union had monarchial forms of government.

Each state enjoyed a large degree of autonomy, although the federal government, or *Reich,* was empowered to administer a common communications system, maintain an army, and conduct foreign affairs. In addition to the *Kaiser,* or emperor, the federal government had a legislature with two houses—the *Bundesrat,* where the states received representation, and the *Reichstag,* where the people were represented through a system of universal manhood suffrage.

The economic growth of the new empire was astounding. In 1860, for example, German steel production did not even equal that of France; by 1900 it exceeded that of both England and France combined. By 1900, moreover, German naval power rivaled that of Great Britain, the traditional "mistress of the sea."

Germany's political prestige also grew, a result not only of its strengthened economic and military position but also of the capable leadership of the "iron chancellor." Bismarck consolidated Germany's continental position by arranging alliances in 1882 with Austria-Hungary and Italy, in the Triple Alliance, and in 1887 with Russia.

Bismarck fell from power in 1890, when the young emperor, William II, who opposed his authoritarian measures and his diplomatic techniques, decided to conduct German diplomacy personally.

Under William, Germany followed a policy of aggressive imperialism

which divided Europe into two opposing camps—pro-German and anti-German. William antagonized Britain by enlarging the German navy, enraged his ally Russia by competing with it for territory in the Near East, and made no attempt to improve relations with France, which had been poor since the acquisition of Alsace-Lorraine.

German aggressiveness drew France and Britain, traditional enemies, closer together. In the Entente Cordiale of 1904 the two settled several long-standing disputes and united in opposition to Germany. In 1905 William tested the Entente by openly urging independence for the French protectorate of Morocco.

The Entente proved solid, and in 1906 France and Britain led the Algeciras Conference of European powers, which berated Germany for its insult to France. In 1907 Russia, Germany's former ally, entered the British-French alliance, forming the Triple Entente. In 1911 Germany precipitated a second "Moroccan Crisis" and was again rebuked.

World War I. The European powers were able to settle the incidents of 1905 and 1911 peacefully, but crisis followed crisis in the Balkan region. Bulgaria and Turkey, having lost territory in Balkan wars in 1912 and 1913, joined Germany, Austria-Hungary, and Italy to form the alliance of Central Powers in opposition to the Triple Entente.

In 1914 a crisis caused by the assassination of Archduke Francis Ferdinand, heir to the Austrian throne, led to World War I. Bosnia, where the assassination occurred, was an Austrian territory, but as the assassin was Serbian, and as Serbia had led Pan-Slav activity in Bosnia, Austria threatened reprisals against Serbia. Germany supported Austria and Russia backed Serbia.

Both sides misjudged the seriousness of the situation, and the war that resulted involved the allies of Germany and Russia and eventually all of Europe as well as the United States, Japan, and the Middle East. Germany had predicted that the war would be short, and had based its military strategy on that prediction. But the war lasted four years, and Germany was unable to maintain the strength of its forces.

In 1918, with defeat imminent, rebellions broke out in the German territories, resulting in the abdication of the emperor and the declaration of a German republic. The peace settlements exacted huge reparations payments; confiscated German overseas possessions and non-German-speaking European territories, including Alsace and Lorraine; and disarmed the country.

Weimar Republic. A republic was formally established in July 1919, when the Weimar Constitution was adopted. The new German state faced difficulties from its establishment, especially in dealing with the humiliation of the dictated peace and in bearing the heavy burden of reparations, which led to inflation and a currency collapse.

The lack of a tradition of unity

and of parliamentary democracy provided a shaky foundation for the new government, made more unstable by attacks from communists on the extreme left and authoritarian nationalists on the extreme right.

In 1929, just as the government had begun to solve its economic and political problems and had begun to be reintegrated into Europe by joining the League of Nations, the worldwide economic depression struck. Unemployment rose and with it came widespread resentment against the existing German government. The heavy victories of extremist parties in elections held in 1930 reflected the growing popular discontent.

On the left, the communists scored heavily, and on the right, Adolf Hitler's National Socialist, or Nazi, party, gained enough seats to become the second largest party in the *Reichstag*. In 1932 elections, the Nazis became the largest single party in the *Reichstag*, and in 1933 Adolf Hitler was appointed chancellor.

Nazi Era. Hitler came to power partly by heading a highly organized political party, but also because the brand of nationalism that he preached was attractive to the Germans—humiliated by defeat in the war, impoverished by the depression, and fearful for their property in the face of communism.

He promised to create a revitalized, strengthened Germany—a Germany stronger than the First Reich, the Holy Roman Empire, or the Second Reich, Bismarck's empire. He assured Germans that they were capable of greatness because they were descended from the strong, pure, "Aryan race" of Teutons, and he directed their hostility toward the Jews and non-Germans, especially the Slavs.

Although the Nazi Party received only 44 percent of the vote in elections held in late 1933, Hitler proclaimed that the elections had made him the spokesman of all Germany. The *Reichstag* granted him dictatorial powers and suspended the constitution. Germany was transformed from a federal state into a highly centralized state. The office of president

GERMAN INFORMATION CENTER

EAST BERLIN lies beyond the Brandenburg Gate, divided by a wall from the city's western half.

was abolished, and Hitler assumed all powers of state.

Economic policy was determined by the central government, and unemployment was reduced by public works projects and massive rearmament. All opposition parties were banned and strict censorship was imposed. The legal system was reorganized to place the needs of the state above accepted standards of justice, and concentration camps were opened to imprison Hitler's "convicted" political opponents.

The camps came to be used primarily for the imprisonment and murder of Jews, as anti-Semitism became an increasingly important part of the Nazi program. Jews were forbidden to teach, hold office, attend universities, or engage in many businesses, and non-Jews were ordered to ostracize them and to boycott Jewish businesses. Between 1935 and 1945 Hitler's regime killed some 6 million European Jews.

At the basis of Hitler's foreign pol-

icy was hostility to the conditions imposed on Germany by the Versailles treaty system that ended World War I. In 1933 Germany ended its membership in the League of Nations. Hitler abrogated German agreements to remain neutral, and in 1935 began openly to rearm the country.

In 1936 and 1937 Germany entered into treaties with Japan and Italy. Italy, led by the Fascist dictator Benito Mussolini, became an especially close ally, forming one half of the "Rome-Berlin Axis." One common feature of these treaties was their declaration of opposition to communism, but in 1939 Hitler entered a nonaggression pact with the communist government of the Soviet Union.

Hitler also refused to obey the territorial limits set by the Versailles settlement. Using the desire to unite all German-speaking peoples as an excuse, Hitler annexed Austria in 1938 and in 1939 he took part of Czechoslovakia. The World War I allies did not strongly object to his actions, hoping to appease him and prevent a second world conflict.

World War II. Until 1939 Hitler had gained territory and allies bloodlessly, but in that summer he demanded that the Free City of Danzig, within Poland's borders, be "restored" to the Reich. When he was refused, Germany invaded Poland and occupied Danzig. Britain and France, bound by treaty to protect Poland and realizing that Hitler could not be appeased, declared war on Germany on Sept. 3, 1939.

The major German offensive against the west began in 1940, when German troops overran the neutral states of Denmark, Norway, the Netherlands, and Belgium, and invaded France. In June, 1941 German armies broke the nonaggression pact and invaded the Soviet Union.

In December 1941 the United States entered the war against Hitler, and in 1942 Soviet troops began a counteroffensive. Before the tide turned in favor of the Allies, Hitler controlled

U.S. ARMY

NÜRNBERG COURTROOM was the scene of German war crimes trials held after World War II.

by conquest or alliances almost all of continental Europe as far east as Moscow and territories in North Africa and the Middle East.

The main Allied counteroffensive began in June 1944, when British, Canadian, and U.S. troops landed on the beaches of Normandy. By September 1944 the Allies had reached the German border. When Soviet troops reached the outskirts of Berlin from the east in May 1945 and the fall of the city seemed imminent, Hitler committed suicide. The Germans surrendered, and the war was over.

Occupation. The leaders of the four major allied nations met at Potsdam, Germany, in July 1945 and agreed to partition Germany into four zones of occupation. The Soviet Union occupied the portion east of the Elbe River and the United States, Britain, and France divided the territory to the west.

Portions of Germany east of the Oder and Neisse rivers were placed under the administration of Poland, which was dominated by the Soviet Union. The Allies also divided Berlin into four occupation zones and established the Allied Control Council to coordinate the occupation.

The Soviets did not cooperate with the other members of the council, and in 1948, after several policy disputes with the Soviet Union, France, Britain, and the United States merged their sectors and gave the new zone a large measure of self-government.

Later in the same year, elections were held in western Germany and a federal constitution was agreed upon. The Soviet Union responded in October 1949 by establishing the Soviet zone of occupation as the German Democratic Republic.

Germany was thus divided again. The Soviet Union tried to force the Allies to leave Berlin and to allow unification on Soviet terms by blockading Berlin in 1949, but a massive airlift broke the blockade.

Britain, France, and the United States maintained nominal control over West Germany until 1955, when the Federal Republic of Germany became fully sovereign. In 1955 the Soviet Union recognized the sovereignty of the German Democratic Republic, in the east.

Divided Germany. In the early 1950s both Germanys concentrated on repairing the destruction wrought by the war, and both worked to develop and expand their industry. By the mid-1960s West Germany had become one of the world's leading industrial nations. Its political recovery paralleled its economic recovery.

Under the leadership of Konrad Adenauer and his Christian Democratic party, West Germany became integrated into Western Europe as a staunch ally of the west. A resurgence of extreme right-wing nationalism in the mid-1960s disturbed the government and led in 1966 to the formation of an alliance of the Christian Democrats and their traditional opponents, the Social Democrats. Willy Brandt, leader of the Social Democratic party, joined the cabinet led by the Christian Democratic chancellor, Kurt Kiesinger.

East Germany made somewhat slower progress in rebuilding its economy. Although it had become relatively prosperous by the early 1960s, the general standard of living of its people remained low. It became fully integrated into the economy of the Soviet bloc and its industry became a vital factor in the economies of other Soviet-bloc states.

Despite its progress, the East German regime remained dependent on the Soviet Union for its existence as a sovereign state. In 1953, for example, Soviet troops and tanks were required to put down an antigovernment rising in East Berlin.

East Germany demonstrated some independence of Soviet policies, however. Both Wilhelm Pieck, a German communist leader who was president of East Germany until his death in 1960, and party secretary Walter Ulbricht, who in 1960 formally assumed the additional duties of chief executive, refused, for example, to follow the program of "de-Stalinization" of Soviet Premier Nikita Khrushchev in the late 1950s.

West Germany refused to recognize the existence of East Germany and refused to give up its support of West Berlin. The western half of the city, whose economic progress made a striking contrast to the rather drab eastern sector, became a showcase of western prosperity, and an important escape point for Germans fleeing the eastern zone. In 1961 the East Germans built a wall separating the two sectors to stem the flow of refugees.

The wall emphasized the depth of the postwar political division of Germany. No way was found to achieve reunification of the country, as neither side could agree to the conditions for negotiations demanded by the other.

—George Kren

GHANA

Official name: Republic of Ghana
Area: 92,099 square miles
Population: (1966) 7,945,000
Capital: Accra (Pop. 1964, urban area, 557,-348)
Language: English, African languages
Religion: Christianity, Islam, traditional religions
Currency unit: Cedi
National holiday: Independence day, March 6

Ghana, a republic in western Africa, is bordered on the north by Upper Volta, on the east by Togo, on the south by the Gulf of Guinea, an arm of the Atlantic Ocean, and on the west by the Ivory Coast and Upper Volta. Ghana was formed in 1957 by the union of the former British colonies of the Gold Coast and Ashanti, the British protectorate of the Northern Territories, and British Togoland.

THE LAND. Grasslands and forests occupy much of Ghana's land. The Volta River and its principal tributaries, the Black Volta, White Volta, and Oti, drain all of northern Ghana and about half of the south. Extensive grassy plains and isolated hills are typical of the Volta Basin landscape. The south and west of Ghana is hilly and forested.

In the southeast the Volta River flows between the Akwapim Hills and the Togo Mountains. At that point there is a large dam and power plant, at Akosombo. The climate throughout the country is tropical.

THE PEOPLE. Many Ghanaians are Akan-speaking people, mainly Fanti along the coast and Ashanti further inland. The Ga people, who are related by culture and language to the Ashanti, live around the city of Accra. In the north are the Moshi-Dagomba people.

UNITED NATIONS

GHANAIAN TRIBAL CHIEF attending a ceremony marking the inauguration of a fellow chief.

UNITED NATIONS

GHANAIAN STUDENTS in the library of the Institute of Public Administration, at Achimeta.

Most Ghanaians are farmers. Ghana's major cities include the capital, Accra; Kumasi; and the ports of Tema and Takoradi.

ECONOMY. Ghana's economy depends heavily on agriculture. Ghana is a major producer of cacao, and in 1965 Ghana produced over 415,000 metric tons of cacao. Yams, rice, cassava, and grains are basic food crops. Tropical wood and wood products from forests in south and west are important to Ghana's economy.

Ghana also has rich mineral deposits. In 1965 Ghana produced almost 2.3 million carats of diamonds, about 288,-000 metric tons of manganese ore, more than 760,000 troy ounces of gold, and 309,000 metric tons of bauxite, from which aluminum is made. Ghanaian industry has developed gradually since the time of independence and is centered around Accra and the nearby port of Tema.

In 1966 Ghana's imports cost $352 million and its exports earned $244 million. The major exports are cacao, gold, diamonds, manganese, timber, and aluminum. Ghana imports manufactured goods, machinery, food, and chemicals. The country's major trading partners are Britain, the United States, and western Europe.

GOVERNMENT. In 1966 a military coup overthrew Ghana's government and a 12-member National Liberation Council took power. Before the coup executive power was vested in a president and a cabinet responsible to the legislature. The president was elected to a five-year term by members of the legislature. Legislative power was held by the National Assembly, which consisted of 104 directly elected members and 10 specially elected women members.

Ghana is a member of the United Nations, the Commonwealth of Nations, and the Organization of African Unity (OAU).

HISTORY. Ghana is named after a medieval empire in western Africa. In 1471 Portuguese explorers encountered the Fanti people, who were then migrating southward. In the years that followed several European countries engaged in trade for gold, ivory, and slaves supplied by the Ashanti through Fanti middlemen.

British Rule. The British and the Ashanti waged wars throughout the 1800s. In 1874 the British finally achieved victory and formed the coastal area of Ghana into the Gold Coast Colony. In 1896 Britain exiled the Ashanti king, Prempeh I, and in 1901 the British established the Colony of Ashanti, which included the interior region north of the Gold Coast Colony.

In the same year, 1901, the Northern Territories, the region north of Ashanti, became a British protectorate. The German colony of Western Togoland became a British mandate under the League of Nations after World War I, and was administered together with the Gold Coast.

In the 1920s railroads were built and cocoa became an important export. A new class of educated Africans formed trade unions, professional associations, and cultural groups, and began to contest the power of traditional chiefs, through whom Britain administered the country.

After World War II, Ashanti representatives were given seats in the colony's legislative council, which had been established at the beginning of colonial rule, and in 1946 the council acquired an African majority.

In 1947 Dr. J. B. Danquah organized a nationalist movement, the United Gold Coast Convention (UGCC). Kwame Nkrumah broke away from UGCC in 1949 and founded the Convention People's Party (CPP). Riots broke out in 1950 in support of Ghanaian independence, and Nkrumah was arrested for his role in the disturbances.

Nkrumah's party won elections held in 1951, and he was released to become a member of the government. In 1952 he became prime minister. Although the CPP won elections held in 1954 and 1956, newly formed regional parties challenged its power. Several of these parties merged into the National Liberation Movement, which called for a federation of regions rather than a unitary state.

Independence. In March 1957 the Gold Coast, Ashanti, the Northern Territories, and British Togoland became independent as the nation of Ghana. Ghana became a republic in July 1960, and Nkrumah was elected president. Nkrumah became a leader in Pan-African affairs.

The CPP remained dominant, but strong political opposition developed. The regime became increasingly authoritarian, and its opponents resorted to plotting and an attempted assassination of the president.

In January 1964 Nkrumah acquired dictatorial powers. He ran the country into debt, and his regime was accused of corruption. While on a trip to Communist China and North Vietnam in February 1966, the National Liberation Council, headed by Lt. Gen. J. A. Ankrah, overthrew Nkrumah's government. Nkrumah found asylum in Guinea, where he was named honorary president.

Ankrah pledged his government to revive the economy and to repay the external debts built up by the Nkrumah government. Ankrah proposed a new constitution that would eventually return Ghana to a two-party system.

—Hibberd V. B. Kline, Jr.;
Vera Zolberg

GREECE

Official name: Kingdom of Greece
Area: 50,944 square miles
Population: (1966 est.) 8,614,000
Capital: Athens (Pop., 1961, urban area, 1,852,700)
Language: Greek
Religion: Orthodox Christianity
Currency unit: Drachma
National holiday: Independence day, March 25

Greece, the southernmost state of the Balkan peninsula, is a mountainous country with many small peninsulas that jut out into the Mediterranean Sea. Almost one-fifth of the total land area consists of islands, the largest of which are Crete, Rhodes, Lesbos, Chios, and Sámos. Mainland Greece is bordered on the northwest by Albania, on the north by Yugoslavia and Bulgaria, and on the northeast by Turkey. To the east is the Aegean Sea; to the west, the Ionian Sea; and to the south, the open Mediterranean.

THE LAND. The surface of Greece is mainly rough and hilly, and there is very little flat land. The rugged Pindus Mountains dominate the landscape of western mainland Greece from the northern border to the southern coast. Plains are few and lie mostly along the eastern coast. They are isolated by

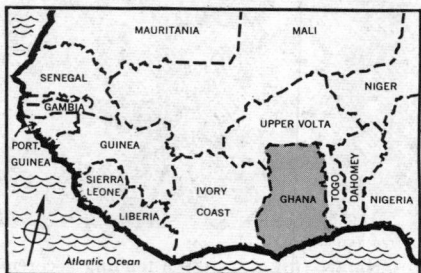

intervening highlands. Rivers are short and usually dry in summer.

The climate varies from region to region. In general, the south and east have hot, dry summers, and mild, moist, windy winters. In the north and west winters are rather cold, summers are hot, and rainfall is more abundant than in the south and east.

West of the mainland are the Ionian Islands. To the east, in the Aegean, are the Cyclades, Sporades, Dodecanese, and other island groups.

THE PEOPLE. Almost the entire population of the country is Greek, but there are small minorities of Bulgarians, Turks, Slavs, and Albanians in the border areas.

Population is densest along the eastern coast, in the Athens region, in the major towns of Macedonia in the north, and on a few of the islands. The southern Peloponnesus and the more mountainous interior are sparsely populated. Greece has traditionally had a high rate of emigration, and Greeks have settled throughout the world.

ECONOMY. Greece is not a prosperous country. Agriculture, which employed about half the labor force in 1961, is the mainstay of the economy, despite the fact that less than 30 percent of the land is suitable for cultivation.

The country has a variety of minerals, including iron and iron pyrites, lignite, lead, zinc, bauxite, emery, chromium, manganese, and oil. They are present only in very small amounts, however, and facilities are lacking to exploit them fully. Supplies of lignite and oil are inadequate for fuel needs, and, despite impressive gains in hydroelectric production during the early 1960s, energy shortages persist.

Greece's generally poor soils are suitable for only a limited variety of crops. In the south and along the coasts, the most important crops are olives and grapes. Some cotton and tobacco also are grown. In the interior and the northeast, grains and tobacco predominate. In the rugged but wet northwest, sheep and goat-herding are the main occupations, and corn is raised extensively.

In 1966 Greece's imports cost more than $1,000 million and its exports earned only slightly more than $406 million. The expenditures of tourists in Greece, more than $100 million in 1964, and the remittances of Greeks abroad partially offset the large deficit. The chief exports are tobacco, fruits,

cotton, wine, olives and olive oil, and mineral ores. The main imports are machinery and vehicles, lumber, textiles, manufactured consumer goods, foodstuffs, chemicals, and petroleum. Greece's leading trading partner is West Germany, followed by the United States and Britain.

GOVERNMENT. Greece is a constitutional monarchy. Under the 1952 constitution the king was empowered to appoint a premier, or prime minister, for an indefinite term. The premier and his cabinet were responsible to a popularly elected unicameral parliament. The constitutional system was overthrown in 1967, however, and a military government took power.

HISTORY. Modern Greece has roots in the Classical Greek civilization that flourished on the Hellenic peninsula in ancient times. Between about 800 BC and 300 BC, the Greeks developed a culture that laid the foundation for much of later Western civilization.

In 338 BC Greece was conquered by its northern neighbor, Macedonia, and Greek culture was spread throughout Macedonia's vast Middle Eastern and Mediterranean empire, which eventually came under the control of Rome. Rome, too, absorbed many Greek artistic and intellectual achievements.

In 285 AD the Roman Empire was divided, and Greece became part of the eastern section, ruled from Byzantium. In 330 Byzantium, renamed Constantinople, became the capital of all that remained of the Roman Empire. As a part of this Byzantine Empire, the Greeks were still the cultural and intellectual leaders of the eastern Mediterranean.

While western Europe struggled with the disorder produced by barbarian invasions, the Orthodox Christian, Graeco-Roman civilization of the eastern empire maintained its stability. Greek cultural influence was dependent on Byzantine political strength, however, and the eastern empire was unable to withstand the

onslaught of a new power in Asia Minor, the Ottoman Turks.

In the 1000s, the Turks began to attack the Byzantine Empire. Over a period of 400 years they conquered Byzantine territory bit by bit, until in 1453 they captured Constantinople itself.

Ottoman Rule. The Greeks did not fare badly under the Ottomans. They enjoyed some self-government, and Greeks in Constantinople, called Phanariots, filled many high positions in the Ottoman administration. The Turks did not force the Greek Christians to convert to Islam, although those who did enjoyed a higher status in the Muslim society.

For the most part, the Ottoman government ignored Greeks living outside Asia Minor, and in many cases neglected them. What remained of Classical Greek culture decayed, and the people of Greece sank into poverty.

The Greeks were far from content under Turkish rule, however. In the 1700s those who still lived in the Hellenic peninsula began to develop a feeling of national pride and a desire for independence. Moreover, in the 1700s the Ottoman government began to loosen control over its more distant territories.

The Greek economy, exhausted since Roman times, began to revive, and Greek trade, industry, and shipping expanded. At the same time self-government began to develop on the local level. The spirit of nationalism swept Europe in the early 1800s, and Greek nationalism took the form of a desire for full freedom from Turkey and included the goal of uniting all Greek-speaking people into one nation.

Independence. The Greek struggle for independence began in 1821, when Alexander Ypsilanti, a leader of a secret revolutionary organization, *Hetairia Philiké*, or Society of Friends, led a revolt in the Phanariot-governed principalities of Moravia and Wallachia, part of present-day Romania.

LUFTHANSA
ACROPOLIS OF ATHENS, site of the Parthenon and other masterpieces of classical Greek art.

Ypsilanti had hoped for aid from neighboring Russia, but he received no support and was defeated. Uprisings also broke out in the south of Greece, however, and continued despite severe Turkish reprisals.

By 1822 the rebellion was country-wide, and the Greeks declared their independence. Over the next few years Greek guerrilla forces won control of much of their territory from the Ottoman Turks. In 1825, however, Turkey gained the support of Egypt, nominally a part of the Ottoman Empire. The untrained Greek guerrillas could not stand up against the power and organization of the Turkish-Egyptian army, and the Greeks steadily lost the land they had won.

The rebels would have met total defeat if they had not received help in 1827 from Britain, France, and Russia. All three had interests in the Balkans, and all opposed Turkish domination of the region. The European nations agreed to join in finding or forcing a solution to the war. They tried to impose an armistice and urged Turkey to grant independence to Greece.

When the Turks refused, the European powers ordered a blockade to enforce a truce and to prevent the Turkish forces from receiving supplies. In enforcing the blockade, ships from Britain, Russia, and France destroyed most of the Egyptian fleet when it tried to bring troops and supplies into the port of Navarino in October 1827.

In 1828 Russia declared war on Turkey, and by so doing aided the Greeks. Although the war grew out of a Russo-Turkish territorial dispute, Russia also saw an advantage in weakening Tur-key by driving the Turks from Greece.

Russia defeated Turkey in August 1829, and the Treaty of Adrianople, which ended the war, contained a provision granting independence to Greece. Turkey agreed to accept the London Protocol of March 1829, in which the three European powers decided that Greece—which then included only the Peloponnesus, the Cyclades, and Central Greece—would be an autonomous state under a king to be chosen from among the royal families of Europe.

The Greeks, however, already had a government. In 1827 they had chosen an assembly and elected a president, Ioannes Kapodistrias. He was assassinated in 1831, however, and Greece then accepted the powers' choice of a Bavarian prince, Otto, as king.

A New Nation. The new state faced great problems. Many Greeks wished to continue fighting to liberate territory that was inhabited by Greeks but not governed by Greece. The economy, severely damaged by the revolution, was weak—there was little manufacturing and agricultural techniques were old-fashioned and inefficient. A sense of local pride hindered administration by a national government.

Otto's attempts to solve these problems led to a highly centralized, bureaucratic government that was too clumsy to be effective and too complex for the people to deal with. In addition, the European powers still had great influence in Greek politics.

In 1843 two political factions, one supported by the British and one by the Russians, rebelled against the king. The rebels demanded a constitution

NATIONAL TOURIST ORGANIZATION OF GREECE
GREEK BOYS WHITEWASHING THE STREETS in Mykonos, one of the Cyclades islands.

and an elected assembly. Otto agreed to these demands and established a constitutional monarchy. The new system worked almost as poorly as absolute rule had, and in 1862 Otto was deposed.

In the following year a Danish prince was named king as George I of Greece (r.1863–1913). The Greeks had selected another leader, but accepted the powers' choice of George when Britain gave Greece the Ionian Islands, which had been a British protectorate.

George's attempts to transform Greece into a country governed by the most advanced parliamentary institutions were only partly successful. The Greeks' lack of education and their inexperience with parliamentary government resulted in a rapid turnover of governments.

The first leader to have any success in establishing an efficient Greek government was Eleutherios Venizelos, who became prime minister in 1910. Venizelos won a strong majority in parliament in 1911 and passed a revised constitution that allowed for more stable parliamentary government.

Venizelos reorganized and simplified the bureaucracy and reduced the power of the army in government affairs. During his first years in office the educational system was broadened and large estates were divided among small farmers.

Expansion. During the reign of George I, Greece made many additions to its territory. The European powers exerted great efforts to prevent this expansion from resulting in a clash with Turkey that could lead to a general European war. In 1881 the powers forced Turkey to yield most of Epirus and Thessaly to Greece as part of the settlement of the Russo-Turkish War of 1877.

In 1896 Greece, trying to aid a rebellion in Crete against Turkish rule, did go to war against Turkey, and was soundly defeated. But Britain, France, and Russia forced Turkey to evacuate Crete, which was then occupied by the

NATIONAL TOURIST ORGANIZATION OF GREECE
THESSALY'S CRAGGY PEAKS shelter many Christian monasteries, such as this one at Meteora.

three powers and by Italy. Crete successfully rebelled in 1905, and in 1908 declared its union with Greece. The European alliance withdrew its forces the following year.

Greece entered another territorial war before World War I. In the spring of 1912 Premier Venizelos made an alliance with Bulgaria, and in the following fall Greece and Bulgaria—with its ally, Serbia—declared war on Turkey over conflicting territorial claims. Greece and its allies won this First Balkan War, and in 1913, by the Treaty of London, Turkey gave up its claims to Crete and ceded Macedonia to the Balkan allies.

Another Balkan War in the summer of 1913, fought by Greece, Serbia, and Romania against Bulgaria, determined which state would receive what part of the territory. By the Treaty of Bucharest, Greece gained part of Macedonia and another section of Epirus.

In World War I, Premier Venizelos urged Greek intervention on the side of the Allies (Britain, Russia, and France). King Constantine, who had come to the throne after his father's death in 1913, preferred to remain neutral. It was not until 1917, after an Allied ultimatum forced Constantine to yield the throne to his son, Alexander, that Greece entered the war against Germany.

Greek troops fought primarily in the Balkans, and at the end of the war the Treaty of Sèvres gave Greece eastern Thrace, the Turkish islands in the Aegean, and a mandate to occupy a part of Turkey's mainland. Turkish nationalists opposed the treaty, however, and in 1920 a Greek army invaded Turkey, only to meet disastrous defeat in 1922. King Constantine, who had regained the throne after Alexander's death in 1920, was forced to abdicate again.

Search for Stability. Constantine's son became king as George II, but his government was forced out of office in 1923 by a powerful faction that favored a republican form of government. In 1924 this faction formed a revolutionary government that proclaimed Greece a republic. The republic was a failure. The leaders of the new government could not agree on policy, and after a rapid succession of governments, George II was restored to the throne in 1935.

Greece's extreme political instability left the nation helpless in the face of serious problems. The greatest difficulties were economic. Weak industry, unproductive agriculture, and an extremely high birth rate kept the people in poverty. The world economic depression of the 1930s was particularly severe for Greece because of its dependence on exporting such costly items as wine and olive oil.

In 1936 King George appointed Gen. Ioannes Metaxas as premier after a parliamentary election gave no party a majority. Metaxas dissolved the parliament and made himself dictator. His fascist-like regimentation of society was unpopular, but he relieved some of the country's economic problems.

World War II ended the Metaxas dictatorship, but brought enormous economic, social, and political prob-

lems. The Greeks successfully fought off an Italian invasion attempt in 1940, but in 1941 German forces conquered the country and occupied it until 1944.

During the war George Papandreou, a leader of the Greek parliament, formed a government-in-exile. After the war, however, his government remained in office for only three months, in 1945. Its rivals for power were two opposing political organizations formed during the war.

A communist-led resistance group had political and economic control of the countryside, and a right-wing royalist faction dominated parliament. An election in 1946 restored the monarchy, but by the time King George returned a few weeks later, a civil war had broken out between the right and the left.

Greece's desperate political and economic troubles inflamed the war, which continued with support from

NATIONAL TOURIST ORGANIZATION OF GREECE
GREEK FISHERMEN REPAIRING THEIR NETS on Thasos, an island in the northern Aegean Sea.

Yugoslavia for the communist guerrillas and with U.S. aid for the government forces. In 1947 Yugoslavia withdrew military assistance from the rebels and the United States gave large-scale financial and military aid to the country under the Truman Doctrine. By 1949 Greek government troops were able to subdue the rebels.

King Paul took the throne after his brother George's death in 1947. He built a constitutional monarchy that was able to maintain a fairly stable government despite occasional political clashes. When he died in 1964, his son succeeded him as Constantine II.

Contemporary Greece. Between 1963 and 1967, Greece endured almost continual government crises. No one party succeeded in winning a majority in parliament, and premiers were forced to rely on weak coalition cabinets. George Papandreou, head of the Center Union party, led coalition cabinets

in 1963, 1964, and 1965, when he resigned in a dispute with the king.

The caretaker premiers who followed had to rely on Papandreou for much of their support. In March 1967 Papandreou withdrew the support of the Center Union from the government, causing its fall.

King Constantine appointed Panayotis Canellopoulos, leader of the conservative National Radical Union party, premier. Canellopoulos, a personal and political rival of Papandreou, formed a one-party cabinet and dissolved parliament in April 1967 to permit his government to last until scheduled elections could be held in May. But in April a group of army officers led a coup that took power from the civilian authorities.

The military leaders of the coup maintained that their takeover had saved the country from a leftist rebellion planned by Andreas Papandreou,

son of George Papandreou. Many prominent political leaders were imprisoned, and intellectual and cultural life was subjected to censorship.

The colonels stated that their purpose was to "purify" Greek government and society—they hoped to restore the country to "traditional morality" and to revive the spirit of nationalism. They suspended many civil liberties and imposed direct government control over the politically and socially important Greek Orthodox Church.

In November 1967 King Constantine attempted to overthrow the junta, but he failed and went into exile. The colonels strengthened their hold on the army by purging officers believed loyal to the king, and in 1968 won diplomatic recognition for their government from the United States and other countries.

—George Kren

GUATEMALA

Official name: Republic of Guatemala
Area: 42,042 square miles
Population: (1966 est.) 4,575,000
Capital: Guatemala City (Pop., 1964 est., 577,100)
Language: Spanish
Religion: Roman Catholicism
Currency unit: Quetzal
National holiday: Independence day, September 15

Guatemala, the largest republic in Central America, is bordered on the west and north by Mexico; on the east by British Honduras, the Gulf of Honduras (an arm of the Caribbean Sea) and Honduras; and on the south by El Salvador and the Pacific Ocean.

THE LAND. Guatemala is a mountainous land. The Central American Cordillera, which lies roughly parallel to the Pacific coast, includes the highest peak in Central America, the volcanic Mt. Tajumulco, 13,812 feet above sea level.

A narrow plain borders the Pacific coast. Inland from the plain are the central highlands, which include about

a fifth of the country's land area. In the southeast are the Caribbean lowlands. In the north is the Petén district, a sparsely settled forest region containing about a third of the country's area.

The Caribbean lowlands are hot and rainy. The Pacific coast has dry winters and wet summers. The central highlands have a cool, dry climate.

THE PEOPLE. More than half of Guatemala's people are of American Indian stock, descendants of the Mayas, and about 30 percent are *ladino*, or mestizo, of mixed Indian and European background. A small minority, perhaps 10 percent of the population, claims unmixed European descent. Most of the people live in the highlands, where Guatemala City is located.

The population is increasing at a very rapid rate, estimated at more than 3 percent a year between 1958 and 1967. This rapid rate of increase places heavy strains on the economy, for more and more goods, more housing, and more jobs must be provided every year.

ECONOMY. Guatemala is an agricultural country, and in 1966 agriculture contributed 28 percent to the national product. Approximately 60 percent of the population is directly dependent

on agriculture for its livelihood, and three crops—coffee, cotton, and bananas—contributed more than 60 percent of total export earnings in the mid-1960s.

Agriculture is concentrated in the central highland valleys and the narrow coastal plains. The main commercial crops are coffee, cotton, sugarcane, and bananas. The major food crops include corn, rice, wheat, and beans. Livestock include cattle, sheep, and pigs.

Forests cover about 40 percent of the country's land, and forest resources are increasingly exploited. The country's mineral resources include antimony, chromium, lead, and zinc, but only salt is produced in appreciable quantities.

Industry became the most rapidly growing part of Guatemala's economy in the mid-1960s, and by 1965 industry contributed 16 percent of the national product. The most rapidly growing industries include chemicals and textiles. Food processing is also important to the country.

In 1965 Guatemala's exports earned $187 million and imports cost $229 million. Coffee is the most important export, representing more than 40 percent of 1965 earnings. Cotton, meat, sugar, bananas, chicle, and essential oils such as citronella are also valuable exports. Manufactured goods are of growing importance. Imports include foodstuffs, petroleum products, machinery and vehicles, and manufactured goods.

Guatemala is a member of the Central American Common Market, and the country's trade increasingly has been directed to fellow market members, especially El Salvador. In 1965 about 20 percent of Guatemala's trade was within the market area, but the United States remained the country's

most important trading partner, taking 37 percent of exports and supplying 43 percent of imports.

GOVERNMENT. Guatemala has a long tradition of political upheaval and of dictatorial rule. The country's third constitution in 20 years was promulgated in 1965.

The 1965 constitution vested executive powers in a president and vice-president. Legislative powers rest with the Congress, which has but one house of 55 members. The president, vice-president, and congressmen are popularly elected to four-year terms of office. If no presidential candidate wins a majority of votes, the Congress chooses the president.

Guatemala is a member of the United Nations and the Organization of American States (OAS). The country has engaged in a long-standing dispute with Britain over British Honduras, which is claimed by Guatemala.

HISTORY. Long before the Spanish conquest of Central America in the 1500s, most of present-day Guatemala was part of the great Mayan civilization, which flourished in the area between 300 and 800 AD. Mayan civilization had declined as a result of internal dissension, and in 1524 Spanish forces led by Pedro de Alvarado conquered the area.

The region became part of the Spanish colonial captaincy-general of Guatemala, which included much of Central America. In 1543 the capital of the captaincy was established at Antigua, a city near present-day Guatemala City. Antigua was destroyed by an earthquake in 1773, and soon after Guatemala City became the capital.

Independence. On Sept. 15, 1821, following Mexico's successful independence struggle, Guatemala was peacefully separated from Spain and joined to the Mexican Empire of Augustín de

PAN AMERICAN AIRWAYS

OPEN AIR MARKET in the plaza of Chichicastenango, a village in Guatemala.

Iturbide. Quickly dissatisfied with Mexican control, Guatemala joined El Salvador, Honduras, Costa Rica, Nicaragua, and Chiapas (now part of Mexico) in the United Provinces of Central America. The United Provinces were torn by internal conflicts, and in 1838 the federal system collapsed.

Guatemala became a sovereign state in 1839 under the leadership of Rafael Carrera, who remained the country's strong man until his death in 1865. Carrera had the complete support of the Indians, and his conservative policies won the support of the upper classes and the army. He made Guatemala a republic in 1847, and in 1851 he was elected president. He assumed the presidency for life in 1854. Conservatives remained in power until a liberal revolt in 1871.

Guatemala was ruled by a liberal dictator, Justo Rufino Barrios, from 1873 to 1885. His administration was characterized by great progress in railroad construction, educational reforms, and encouragement of foreign investment. In an attempt to reestablish the Central American Federation under his leadership, he launched a war against Guatemala's neighbors and was killed in battle.

Manuel Estrada Cabrera gained control of the country in 1898. During his administration, the United Fruit Company, a U.S. firm, entered Guatemala and began to play an influential role in Guatemalan politics. Estrada Cabrera was toppled from power in 1920.

Jorge Ubico Castañeda ruled Guatemala from 1931 to 1944. He led the country through the world economic depression of the 1930s, but his despotic rule provoked widespread dissatisfaction. He was removed from power by the military, which attempted to replace him with Federico Ponce.

PAN AMERICAN AIRWAYS

LAKE ATITLAN, in southwestern Guatemala, lies at an elevation of about 4,700 feet.

PAN AMERICAN AIRWAYS

THE CATHEDRAL OF SAN JOSÉ in Antigua, a city that was once the capital of Guatemala.

But student riots and a general strike forced the military to allow free elections and grant a new constitution.

Modern Guatemala. The "revolutions" of Oct. 20, 1944 raised the hopes of many Guatemalans for a new era of social reform. Serious inequalities in the distribution of wealth and income plagued the country. A small number of wealthy people had controlled economic and political life, and the mass of the people had little land and lived in poverty.

Dr. Juan José Arévelo was overwhelmingly elected president, and he launched a program that included support for trade unions and the introduction of social security programs. Although opposition from the privileged minority threatened his administration, he became one of the few presidents to complete his term of office. In 1951 he was peacefully succeeded by Col. Jacobo Arbenz Guzmán.

Arbenz attempted to continue the reforms. He initiated an extensive land reform program and restricted the activities of the United Fruit Company. His administration was charged with being communist dominated, and in 1954 an armed force led by Col. Carlos Castillo Armas and supported by the United States invaded Guatemala from Honduras and toppled Arbenz.

Castillo Armas took control and promulgated a new constitution in 1956. Castillo Armas was assassinated in 1957, and in 1958 Gen. Miguel Ydígoras Fuentes became president. Attempts at moderate reform won Ydígoras the enmity of the conservatives, who thought he was going too far, and of the left, which felt he was not going far enough.

In 1963 the military overthrew Ydígoras and Col. Enrique Peralta Azurdía was placed in power. Peralta's administration abrogated the 1956 constitution. Considerable economic growth was achieved under Peralta's rule, and in 1964, bowing to popular pressure, a constituent assembly was convened to draw up a new constitution. The new basic law, promulgated in 1965, outlawed communist and other totalitarian groups.

Elections were held in 1966, but the military split into two major factions and a civilian candidate, Julio César Méndez Montenegro, led the *Partido Revolucionario* (PR—Revolutionary Party) to victory. The PR won 30 of the 55 seats in Congress, and since no candidate had won a majority of votes in the presidential contest, the Congress elected Méndez president.

Inaugurated on July 1, 1966, Méndez moved to further economic diversification and to expand social development programs. He took the lead in promoting the further integration of the Central American nations through the Central American Common Market.
—George W. Carey; Jerome Fischman

GUINEA

Official name: Republic of Guinea
Area: 94,909 square miles
Population: (1966 est.) 3,608,000
Capital: Conakry (Pop., 1964 est., urban area, 175,000)
Language: French, African languages
Religion: Islam, traditional religions
Currency unit: Franc
National holiday: Independence day, October 2

Guinea, a republic in western Africa, is bounded on the north by Portuguese Guinea, Senegal, and Mali, on the east by Mali and the Ivory Coast, on the south by Liberia and Sierra Leone, and on the west by the Atlantic Ocean. Guinea was a territory of France until 1958, when it declared its independence.

THE LAND. The landscape of Guinea is varied. There is a wide, rainy coastal plain, but further inland the land is drier and has elevations of more than 3,000 feet above sea level. In the central part of the country is the mountain region of Fouta Djallon. From the mountains the land descends to the east into the drainage basins of the Senegal and Niger rivers. There are grasslands and forests in the east.

Temperatures vary throughout the country. In the coastal region temperatures average about 80°F. The Fouta

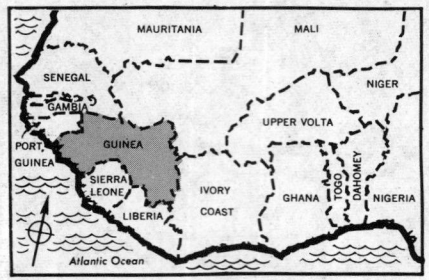

Djallon is relatively cool. Temperatures range over 80°F in the region north and east of the Fouta Djallon.

THE PEOPLE. There are many different ethnic groups in Guinea. The larger groups are the Fulani, Malinke, and Susu. A majority of the people are Muslim.

Most of the people live in rural areas. Guinea's largest city is the capital, Conakry, situated on Tombo Island off the mainland of Guinea. Conakry is also Guinea's major port.

ECONOMY. Guinea's economy depends largely on agriculture. Bananas, coffee, palm products, and peanuts are the chief cash crops. The basic food crops are manioc, fruits, millet, and rice.

Mining, especially of bauxite, is increasing in importance in Guinea. The country has abundant hydroelectric power, which is used in processing bauxite into alumina, enriched bauxite. In 1965 almost 2 million metric tons of bauxite were produced, more than six times the amount produced at the time of independence in 1958. Diamonds and iron ore are also mined.

In 1964 Guinea's imports cost $49 million and its exports earned $43 million. Guinea's main imports are petroleum products, cement, and sugar. The chief exports are bauxite and alumina, iron ore, diamonds, bananas, and palm kernels.

GOVERNMENT. Guinea has a presidential system of government. Executive power is vested in a president, who is popularly elected to a seven-year term. Legislative power rests with a 75–member National Assembly. Assembly members are popularly elected to five-year terms.

Guinea is a member of the United Nations and the Organization of African Unity (OAU).

HISTORY. Little is known of the early history of Guinea. Beginning in the 1400s the peoples of Guinea were in regular commercial contact with European sailors and merchants. They also had connections of long standing with trade across the Sahara.

Islam penetrated what is now Guinea, and many of the Fulani of upper Guinea became Muslims. In the early 1700s Muslims in the Fouta Djallon region revolted against their pagan rulers and created a state of their own.

The French began to acquire portions of Guinea in the 1800s. The indigenous peoples fought against these acquisitions, but they were largely unsuccessful. Samori ibn Ture, a warrior who assembled his own army and ruled much of upper Guinea, fought a frequently victorious guerrilla war against the French in the 1880s and 1890s. By 1898, however, French armies had forced Samori into exile.

French Rule. In 1895 Guinea became a part of French West Africa, and was subject to direct rule from France. In the Muslim area of Fouta Djallon, however, France initiated a system of indirect rule. Schools and hospitals were provided in both the coastal and interior areas.

The peoples of the coastal region, particularly those of Conakry, became thoroughly acquainted with French culture. A railway was built which linked Conakry to Kankan, in upper Guinea, by 1925. The railway thus made possible the export of tropical products.

In 1946 Guinea became a territory within the French Union, but Guinea was the only French territory that refused to join the newly formed French Community in 1958. In October 1958, under the leadership of Sékou Touré, claimed as a descendant of Samori and a prominent trade unionist, Guinea became independent.

Independence. At the time of independence, France withdrew financial and administrative help, causing a serious crisis in Guinea. In July 1961 Guinea joined with Ghana and Mali to found a short-lived union.

Even after the breakup of the union, Guinea continued to follow a pan-African policy. In 1966, after the overthrow of Ghana's government, Touré named former Ghanaian president Kwame Nkrumah honorary president of Guinea.

—Hibberd V. B. Kline, Jr.;
Robert I. Rotberg

GUYANA

Official name: Guyana
Area: 83,000 square miles
Population: (1966 est.) 665,000
Capital: Georgetown (Pop. 1960, urban area, 148,391)
Language: English
Religion: Hinduism, Christianity, Islam
Currency unit: Dollar
National holiday: Independence day, May 26

Guyana, a small country on the northeast coast of South America, is bounded on the north by the Atlantic Ocean, on the east by Surinam (Dutch Guiana), on the south and southwest by Brazil, and on the west by Venezuela. Guyana received its independence from Britain in 1966, after more than 150 years as the colony of British Guiana.

THE LAND. Guyana's land surface consists of a low coastal plain that rises gradually into the heavily faulted Guiana Highlands. The coastal plain varies between 10 and 40 miles in width. Although it represents only 3.5 percent of Guyana's total land area, it is the home of 90 percent of the population. The coastal plain is the only area suitable for agriculture, and the country's two main crops, sugarcane and rice, are raised there.

South of the coastal plain is an inland forest region, which covers 86 percent of Guyana. The inland forest contains great quantities of commercially valuable wood, but transportation is poor and the region has remained largely unexploited. Guyana also has about 8,000 square miles of grassland savannas, located primarily in the southwestern interior and off the northeast coast.

Guyana has four major rivers—the Essequibo, Demerara, Berbice, and Courantyne—as well as a number of small rivers, but they are generally navigable only from about 40 to 100 miles upstream. Further inland the irregularity of the highland terrain creates numerous falls and rapids, which have hindered access to the interior.

Guyana has a humid tropical climate. The coastal plain is cooled by the northeast trade winds and has an average temperature of 80°F, but the savannas and inland forest have somewhat higher temperatures. Annual rainfall ranges from about 80 inches on the coast to about 100 inches in the interior. The coast has two rainy seasons, from April to August and from November to January.

THE PEOPLE. About 50 percent of the population is descended from East Indian laborers who came to work on the sugar plantations in the mid-1800s. About 31 percent is descended from Negro slaves. Twelve percent is mixed. The remainder consists of indigenous Indians (Amerindians), Chinese, and Portuguese and other Europeans.

The diversity of Guyana's people is reflected in their religious beliefs. Some 30 percent of the population is Hindu, 15 percent Muslim, 35 percent Protestant, and 15 percent Roman Catholic.

ECONOMY. The economy of Guyana is based on agriculture and mining. The chief agricultural product is sugar, which constitutes about one-fourth of Guyana's exports. Rice has become an important crop and in 1965 made up about 14 percent of the country's exports. Coconuts, coffee, cocoa, citrus, and other fruits are grown largely for domestic consumption.

Guyana's most important mineral is bauxite, from which aluminum is made. In 1966, 3,348 million metric tons of bauxite were produced. Manganese has been discovered in the northwest, at Matthews Ridge, and large-scale mining operations began in 1960. Small amounts of gold and diamonds are also mined.

In 1965 Guyana's exports were valued at $97 million and its imports cost $104 million. Major exports are sugar, bauxite, rice, fish, uncut diamonds, manganese ore, rum, and wood. Principal imports are foodstuffs, petroleum products, textiles, iron and steel products, machinery, transportation equipment, and chemicals. Guyana trades primarily with Britain, Canada, the United States, and Trinidad and Tobago.

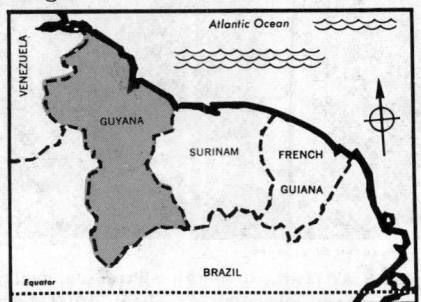

GOVERNMENT. Guyana has a parliamentary system of government. The British monarch is the head of state and is represented in Guyana by a governor-general. Executive power is exercised by a prime minister and cabinet. The prime minister is normally the leader of the majority party in the legislature.

Legislative power is vested in the unicameral House of Assembly, whose 53 members are elected directly under a system of proportional representation.

Guyana is a member of the Commonwealth of Nations and the United Nations.

HISTORY. The Guyana coast was one of the first parts of South America to be discovered by Europeans. There was no immediate attempt at colonization, but the legend of the golden land of El Dorado and tales of fabulous riches to be found further inland led to the exploration of the interior by Sir Walter Raleigh, who led expeditions in 1595 and 1617.

During the 1600s the Dutch, French, and English established small settlements along the coast. For 200 years different parts of the Guianas passed back and forth among the three powers, and it was not until the Congress of Vienna in 1814–1815 that the Guianas were formally divided into British, French, and Dutch areas.

British Rule. The economy of British Guiana was based on sugar, which was raised on large plantations worked by Negro slaves. During the early 1800s there was a great deal of unrest among the slaves, partly fostered by abolitionists in England. Slavery was abolished in 1833, and the economy suffered when the former slaves drifted off into the unsettled backlands and established themselves as small farmers.

Efforts were made to find an alternative labor force, and East Indians were eventually brought to work on the sugar plantations under a system of indentured labor. By 1883 they constituted one-fourth of the population. Sugar production rose in step with East Indian immigration, but friction began to develop among groups of different backgrounds.

The British kept the colony under tight political control and allowed only a few wealthy Guyanese to have some voice in its government. Serious discontent, however, did not become evident until the 1900s. There was some minor labor unrest as a result of the world economic depression of the 1930s, but it did not reach major proportions until after World War II.

In 1949 Cheddi Jagan, of East Indian origin, established the People's Progressive Party (PPP) to work for social and economic reforms, and to achieve self-government. Britain granted the colony a constitution providing for a good deal of autonomy in 1953. The PPP won elections held in April 1953 under the new constitution, but in October Britain suspended the constitution, charging the PPP was under strong communist influence.

In 1955 the PPP split along ethnic lines. Forbes Burnham led most of the Negro members into a new party, the People's National Congress (PNC).

New elections were held in 1961 under a new constitution, and the PPP returned to power. But communal violence and fear of Jagan's left-wing connections led the British to intervene once more.

Independence. Elections were held under a system of proportional representation in 1964, and the People's National Congress, with the support of a small conservative party, the United Force, gained control of the government. Britain granted Guyana independence on May 26, 1966, and Forbes Burnham became the country's first prime minister.

—David Bushnell; Kempton E. Webb

HAITI

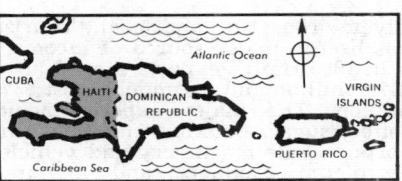

Official name: Republic of Haiti
Area: 10,714 square miles
Population: (1966 est.) 4,485,000
Capital: Port-au-Prince (Pop., 1960 est., 240,000)
Language: French, Creole
Religion: Roman Catholicism
Currency unit: Gourde
National holiday: Independence day, January 1

The Republic of Haiti occupies the western third of the island of Hispaniola in the Greater Antilles. The Dominican Republic occupies the eastern two-thirds of the island. Hispaniola is bounded by the Atlantic Ocean on the north and by the Caribbean Sea on the south. Cuba lies to the west, and Puerto Rico to the east.

THE LAND. Haiti is a mountainous country. The principal ranges are the Massif du Nord, in the north; the Montagnes Noires, in the center; the Montagnes du Trou d'Eau, the Chaine des Matheux, and the Massif de la Selle, all in the southeast; and the Massif de la Hotte, in the south.

Between the mountains is a system of plains and valleys. Among the most important are the Cul-de-Sac in the south, where Port-au-Prince is situated, the Plaine du Nord in the northeast, the Plaine de l'Artibonite in the center, and the Plaine Centrale in the east. Haiti's most important river is the Artibonite.

Haiti has a tropical climate, but temperatures are modified by altitude, rainfall, and sea winds.

THE PEOPLE. Haiti's people are mainly of African Negro origin, but about 10 percent of the population is mulatto, of mixed African and European background. The mulattoes dominated Haitian political, economic, and social life for many years.

Most of the people live in the mountain valleys, but transportation facilities through the mountains are poor and the cities lie along the coasts.

ECONOMY. Agriculture is the main source of income, and most of the people are poor farmers who work very small plots of land in the mountain valleys. The leading cash crops are coffee, cacao, and sugarcane. Sisal, essential oils, and castor beans are also important export crops. Cotton, bananas, tobacco, fruits, and rice are grown as well.

Manufacturing industries produce cotton textiles, soap and pharmaceuticals, sisal rope and plastics, furniture and building materials, foodstuffs, and molasses and rum.

Bauxite is mined for export, and there are deposits of other minerals, including copper, manganese, gold,

LOOK MAGAZINE

MARDI GRAS IN HAITI. The pre-Lenten festival is celebrated with costumes, masks, and floats.

silver, iron, tin, and coal. Tourism has been a major source of income.

In 1965 Haiti's exports earned about $37.5 million and its imports cost $37.7 million. The major exports include coffee, sugar, bauxite, and sisal. Imports include machinery and vehicles, petroleum products, and manufactured goods.

A major barrier to economic development is the increasing pressure of people on the land. Only about one-third of the country's land can be cultivated, and it is estimated that there are some 1,500 persons per square mile in the agricultural areas. Although the government instituted programs to encourage industrial development and increase agricultural production, Haiti in the mid-1960s remained one of the world's most underdeveloped nations.

GOVERNMENT. Haiti has a long tradition of political instability and of dictatorial rule. The country is formally a republic headed by a president. In 1961 Dr. François Duvalier was elected to a six-year term of office, and in 1964 had himself proclaimed president for life. A legislature with one house of 58 deputies was also elected to a six-year term in 1961. Haiti is a member of the United Nations and of the Organization of American States (OAS).

HISTORY. Christopher Columbus discovered the island of Hispaniola in 1492 during his first voyage to the New World. The peaceful Arawak Indian inhabitants called the island Haiti, "land of mountains," but Columbus named it Española, which later became Hispaniola.

Columbus described the Arawak in a letter to the Spanish monarchs as "timid, full of fear, and lovable." Nonetheless, the Indians were soon subjected to severe exploitation by Spanish colonists, and by the end of the 1500s the Arawak had been almost completely exterminated.

Although Spain claimed the entire island, Spanish settlements were concentrated in the east, and French and English pirates were able to establish themselves on the western coast. The French eventually drove out the English, and in 1697 Spain ceded the western end of the island to France, which called it St. Dominique.

French Rule. The French established sugar and tobacco plantations, importing slaves to work the land. They gradually succeeded in building a flourishing colony in which many mulattoes prospered and became slaveholders themselves. But social class rivalry was intense, and the slaves were kept in the worst possible conditions.

In 1791, sparked by the French Revolution in Europe, civil war broke out in Haiti. Toussaint L'Ouverture, a former slave, led the Negroes in a victorious revolt. He forced the French to abolish slavery in 1793, and in 1801 became head of an autonomous government. He successfully expelled Spanish and British forces that attempted to intervene, but in a struggle to achieve complete independence from the French he was captured and sent to prison in France, where he died.

Independence. Jean Jacques Dessalines, another former slave, assumed leadership of the struggle and ultimately led a Negro army to victory. Independence was declared on Jan. 1, 1804, and Dessalines proclaimed himself governor-general for life. He was later crowned Emperor Jacques I. His despotic rule over a war-ravaged country ended with his murder in 1806.

Two states emerged in Haiti following Dessalines death, and there began a struggle for power between Henri Christophe, in the north, and Alexandre Pétion, in the south. Christophe ruled as a benevolent despot from 1811 to 1820, and the north made considerable economic progress. Pétion's rule in the south during the same period had disastrous results.

North and south were reunited in 1820 under the rule of Jean Pierre Boyer, who had succeeded Pétion in the south in 1818 and then extended his rule to the north when Christophe committed suicide. Boyer ruled ineffectively until 1843, when he was exiled. At that time the inhabitants of Santo Domingo, in the eastern part of the island, broke away and established the Dominican Republic.

U.S. Intervention. The next 70 years were marked by almost constant misrule, misery, and revolution. Dictators rapidly succeeded each other, and Haiti fell into a state of chaos. In 1915 U.S. marines landed in Haiti. The U.S. occupation was ordered by Pres. Woodrow Wilson, who feared that Haiti's political and economic breakdown and recurring violence would spread throughout the Caribbean.

Although considerable progress was made during the occupation, Haitians expressed continued resentment of foreign interference. Under Pres. Herbert Hoover, a U.S. commission met with leading Haitian citizens to discuss withdrawal of U.S. troops; by 1934, under the administration of Pres. Franklin Roosevelt, evacuation of the marines was completed.

Modern Haiti. Following the end of the U.S. occupation, several enlightened mulatto leaders ruled Haiti. In 1946, however, the Negroes revolted and restored leadership to the "authentique," the Negro. The government changed hands many times during the next several years, and disorder and misery increased. Then, in September 1957 François Duvalier, a physician, was elected president.

"Papa Doc," as Duvalier became known, established an oppressive dictatorship. Duvalier's rule rested in large part on his secret police, popularly called the *tonton macoute* (Haitian Creole for "bogeyman").

Duvalier became involved in disputes with the United States, which led to the withdrawal of U.S. aid in 1963, and with his neighbor, the Dominican Republic. Relations with the Dominican Republic improved in 1966, after the election of Joaquín Balaguer as that country's president. Duvalier also came into conflict with the Roman Catholic Church, but relations with the church improved in 1966, when a Haitian was inaugurated archbishop.

—George W. Carey; Jerome Fischman

HONDURAS

Official name: Republic of Honduras
Area: 43,277 square miles
Population: (1967 est.) 2,445,000
Capital: Tegucigalpa (Pop., 1965 est., 170,-500)
Language: Spanish
Religion: Roman Catholicism
Currency unit: Lempira
National holiday: Independence day, September 15

Honduras, the second largest of the Central American republics, is bounded on the north by the Caribbean Sea; on the east by Nicaragua; on the south by the Gulf of Fonseca, an arm of the Pacific Ocean, and El Salvador; and on the west by Guatemala. Honduras includes the Bay Islands, or Islas de la Bahía, which lie off the north coast.

THE LAND. Honduras is a mountainous country. The Central American Andes dominate the landscape, running from northwest to southeast. The highlands are cut through by fertile river valleys, the largest of which is the valley of the Río Ulúa.

A fertile, well-watered plain stretches inland from the Caribbean coast. The plain is narrow in the west, near the border with Guatemala, and broad in the east, along the border with Nicaragua. The eastern part of the plain is known as the Mosquito Coast. There is another, smaller lowland region along the Pacific coast.

The Caribbean lowlands have a hot, humid tropical climate. The Pacific coastal region has wet summers and dry winters. The uplands have a pleasant, temperate climate.

THE PEOPLE. Most Hondurans are mestizo, of mixed Indian and European origin. There are some Indians, whites, and Negroes.

The population of Honduras is increasing at a very rapid rate, estimated at 3.3 percent a year between 1958 and 1964. This rapid rate of growth places heavy strains on the economy, for more food, housing, and jobs must be found each year.

ECONOMY. Honduras is an agricultural land. In the mid-1960s, two out of every three working people were employed in agriculture and agriculture contributed one half the national product. The chief crops raised for export are bananas, coffee, and cotton. Bananas are the country's most valuable export, and in 1965, 917,000 metric

tons of bananas were produced. Sugarcane, corn, sorghum, beans, and rice are grown for local food needs.

Honduras has rich forest resources, and lumbering is an important economic activity. The country also has considerable mineral resources, including gold, silver, lead, and zinc. But there is little manufacturing, and the major products of Honduran industry are consumer goods, such as clothing.

A government development plan covering the years 1965–1969 was designed to diversify the economy. A program of road building to provide links between the various parts of the country was begun, and Honduras began to tap the rich hydroelectric power potential offered by its rivers.

In 1965 Honduras' exports earned $129 million and imports cost $122 million. Exports consist almost entirely of agricultural products and raw materials. The major exports are bananas, coffee, cotton, wood, and minerals. Imports consist largely of manufactured goods, machinery and transportation equipment, chemicals, and foodstuffs.

Honduras is a member of the Central American Common Market (CACM), and its foreign trade is increasingly with fellow market members, especially El Salvador. Nonetheless, the United States remains the country's major trading partner, buying almost 60 percent of exports and providing over 45 percent of imports in 1965.

GOVERNMENT. Honduras is officially a republic with democratic institutions. But there is a strong tradition of political instability and of military interference with constitutional processes.

Constitutional government was overthrown by the military in 1963, and a junta composed of military men took power. A 64-member constituent assembly was elected in 1965, and it chose as president of Honduras the leader of the junta.

HISTORY. Christopher Columbus reached the area of Honduras in 1502, on his final voyage to the New World. But it was not until 1524 that the first Spanish colony was established. The American Indian inhabitants fiercely resisted the Spanish conquest, and the Indian chief Lempira is regarded as a national hero for his bravery in the struggle against the Spanish.

In 1539 Honduras was included in Spain's captaincy-general of Guatemala. Silver was discovered in the 1570s, and an influx or prospectors led to the founding of Tegucigalpa.

Independence. Following Mexico's achievement of independence in 1821, the Central American region proclaimed its independence of Spanish rule. The area was annexed to Augustín de Iturbide's Mexican empire, but after Iturbide's fall in 1823 it regained its freedom. Honduras then formed part of the United Provinces of Central America, which also included Costa Rica, El Salvador, Guatemala, and Nicaragua.

By the late 1830s the federation was divided by bitter rivalries among its members, as well as by divisions within the member states. In 1838 Honduras withdrew to become a separate nation, and in 1841 Francisco Ferrara became the country's first constitutional president.

During the later 1800s and early 1900s, Honduras struggled to remain independent in the face of threats posed by its neighbors, particularly Guatemala and Nicaragua. Rafael Carrera, dictator of Guatemala from 1838 to 1865, unseated liberal regimes in Honduras, and in 1885 Justo Rufino Barrios of Guatemala unsuccessfully attempted to restore the Central American federation by force.

In 1841 Britain gained control of the Bay Islands, withdrawing only in 1859. From 1871 to 1874 Honduras was at war with Guatemala and El Salvador, and in 1906 Honduras and El Salvador fought Guatemala.

By 1912 the troubled political situation led Pres. William Howard Taft to send troops to protect U.S. business interests in the country, mainly the United Fruit Company. U.S. forces intervened again in 1919 and in 1924.

Modern Honduras. Honduras achieved a measure of stability under the rule of Tiburcio Carías Andino, who ruled from 1933 to 1948. During that period economic progress was made, roads were built, and schools and hospitals were opened.

In 1948 Carías Andino gave the presidency to Juan Marval Gálvez, who permitted the organization of trade unions, a free press, and open political debate. He retired in 1954, a year marked by a 10-week strike against the United Fruit Company.

Elections were held in 1954. No candidate won a majority of the votes, and Julio Lozano Díaz assumed the presidency. He was overthrown in 1956 by a bloodless coup, and an army-supported junta took power.

The junta held elections for a constituent assembly in 1957. The assembly drafted a new constitution and chose Dr. Ramón Villeda Morales president. Villeda brought Honduras into the Central American Common Market and worked to raise the standard of living of the people.

In 1963 the military toppled the Villeda government and a junta again took power. Col. Oswaldo López Arellano, leader of the junta, called for the election of a new constituent assembly in 1965, and the assembly elected him president.

—George W. Carey; Jerome Fischman

HUNGARY

Official name: Hungarian People's Republic
Area: 35,919 square miles
Population: (1967 est.) 10,212,000
Capital: Budapest (Pop., 1965 est., 1,944,000)
Language: Hungarian
Religion: Roman Catholicism, Protestantism
Currency unit: Forint
National holiday: Anniversary of the liberation, April 4

The Hungarian People's Republic, a nation in central Europe, occupies the middle basin of the Danube River. It is bounded on the north by Czechoslovakia, on the northeast by the Soviet Union, on the east by Romania, on the south by Yugoslavia, and on the west by Austria.

THE LAND. Most of Hungary is flat land less than 600 feet in elevation. The lowlands fall into two main areas, the Lesser Hungarian Plain and the

Greater Hungarian Plain, divided by the Central Hungarian Uplands.

In the northwest lies the fertile, triangular Lesser Hungarian Plain, drained by tributaries of the Danube.

The Greater Hungarian Plain occupies the southeastern half of the country and is crossed on the west by the Danube. West of the Danube, the Greater Hungarian Plain is characterized by rolling land that rises gradually towards the south, culminating in the Mecsek uplands in the southernmost part of Hungary. East of the Danube the plain is almost completely level, drained toward the south by tributaries of the Danube, and dotted with lakes.

The central uplands consist of several ranges of hills and low mountains. West of the Danube, in the region known as Transdanubia, are the mineral-rich Bakony and Vértes ranges. East of the Danube, in the north-central part of the country, are the higher, heavily forested, Börzsöny, Cserhát, Mátra, and Bükk ranges, which reach a height of over 3,000 feet near the northern border.

The Danube, Hungary's largest river, forms part of the boundary between Hungary and Czechoslovakia and cuts through the Hungarian upland. The Danube's two most important tributaries in Hungary are the Drava in the south and the Tisza in the east. Lake Balaton, along the southwestern edge of the central uplands, is Hungary's largest lake.

Hungary's climate varies from region to region. For the country as a whole, summer temperatures average 71°F and winter temperatures average 31°F. About 25 inches of rain falls each year. The greater plain tends to be hotter and drier, and the uplands somewhat colder and wetter than the average.

THE PEOPLE. Over 95 percent of the population is Magyar, or Hungarian. The Hungarian, or Magyar, language is similar to Estonian and Finnish, and is unrelated to any of the languages spoken in neighboring countries. About two-thirds of the people are Roman Catholic, and most of the rest are Protestant. There are small minorities of Germans, Slovaks, Serbs and Croats, and Romanians.

About 40 percent of the people are urban-dwellers and half of these live in the capital, Budapest, which is the political, cultural, economic, and intellectual center of the country. Other important cities are Miskolc, an industrial center in the northeast, Debrecen, an eastern university town, Pécs, near the center of an important southern mining district, and Szeged, a southeastern city known for its textiles and food products and especially for its strong paprika.

ECONOMY. The Hungarian economy, traditionally based on agriculture and light industry, became industrialized under the communist regime that took power in 1947. Industrialization was based largely on development of the country's natural resources.

Natural Resources. Bauxite, found mainly in the western part of the central upland, is the most important mineral, and Hungary is one of the world's largest producers, mining over 1.4 million metric tons in 1966. Uranium is mined in the southwest, and there are deposits of iron ore and manganese.

Coal is Hungary's prime source of energy, but the reserves are mostly of low quality, consisting largely of brown coal and lignite. A dam on the middle Tisza River is the major hydroelectric installation. There is oil in the southwest, and some natural gas is produced.

Agriculture. Hungary's soil is quite rich and is especially suitable for raising grains. Corn, the leading crop, and wheat, barley, and rye represent about half of the total crop acreage. Potatoes, sugar beets, sunflowers, and tobacco are the main industrial crops. Warm summers enable Hungary to produce table and wine grapes, fruit, and vegetables. Almost all agriculture is collectivized.

Industry. In 1966 industry contributed over half of the national product. Under the communist regime, there has been a distinct shift from light to heavy industrial production, and by 1960 heavy industry accounted for two-thirds of the value of output and nearly two-thirds of industrial employment.

Iron, steel, chemicals, heavy construction machinery, railroad equipment, and small ships are the main products of heavy industry. Light industries still prosper and produce wool, cotton, and synthetic textiles, and flour and sugar. Budapest is Hungary's major industrial center.

Trade. Hungary generally has a favorable balance of trade. In 1966 exports earned nearly $1,600 million and imports cost just over $1,500 million. Raw materials, farm products, processed food, and some machinery are exported, and raw materials, textiles, and machinery are imported.

Hungary is integrated into the economy of the Soviet bloc through COMECON, the Council of Mutual Economic Assistance, an association of communist countries. Most of Hungary's trade is with other East European countries, but it also trades with Western Europe and Britain.

GOVERNMENT. Political activity in Hungary is dominated by the country's Communist party, officially called the Hungarian Socialist Workers Party. The political bureau, or politburo, of its central committee determines national policy, and its first secretary is usually the key figure in the government.

The Hungarian constitution places supreme governmental power in a one-house legislature, the National Assembly. All candidates for assembly seats are sponsored by the Communist party, and all legislation is proposed by the party.

The assembly elects a presidential council to act for it between sessions, and to serve collectively as head of state. Actual executive power rests with a cabinet, the council of ministers, appointed by the assembly with party approval. The council is led by a prime minister.

Hungary is a member of the United Nations and of the Warsaw Pact, a Soviet-led military alliance of eastern European communist states.

HISTORY. The Hungarian plains and the Danube valley lie along a major ancient European migration route and offered good settlement sites for early European peoples. The territory, known to the Romans as Pannonia, was inhabited by a succession of Germanic and Slavic tribes and by the Huns between about 1000 BC and the 800s AD. In the late 800s the Magyars, a people from the Ural Mountains, arrived on the Pannonian plains and conquered and mixed with the Slavic peoples settled there.

The Magyars were a semi-nomadic and warlike people. Under their leader, Prince Árpád, they expanded their territory at the expense of nearby Germanic and Slavic kingdoms. In 955 they were defeated by the Germans, and the Magyars, by then a mixture of Magyar, Slavic, and Germanic peoples, retreated to territory in the Danube basin and settled into an agricultural way of life.

The Hungarian Kingdom. By the end of the 900s the Magyars had developed a stable government and a well-organized feudal society. In 997 Stephen, a descendant of Árpád, became Hungary's first king. Stephen established strong ties with western, rather than eastern, Europe and with the Roman Catholic Church.

During Stephen's reign, the Magyars became Christian. Stephen began what was to be a long struggle to weaken the great nobles and centralize Hungary's government. During Stephen's reign, Hungary's territory was greatly expanded.

Several decades of dynastic warfare followed Stephen's death in 1038, but order was restored in 1077, when Ladislas, also of Árpád's line, became king. For the next 150 years Hungary's territory grew, its prosperity increased, and its ties with the west strengthened.

Hungary was unable to resolve the conflict between the king and the nobles, however. The nobles' feuds and rebellions against the king threatened the stability of the nation and left the country unprotected, as the nobles were responsible for its defense.

In 1241 Mongol armies swept across Hungary, meeting little opposition. The destruction they wrought was repaired, but by the end of the 1200s no solution had been found to the dispute between the king and the nobles. Their rivalries for power permitted a foreigner, Charles of Anjou, to take the throne in 1308.

Hungary's new rulers also held thrones in other countries, and as a result of the foreign involvements of Charles and his descendants during the 1300s and early 1400s Hungary became increasingly active in the diplomatic affairs of Western Europe.

Hunyadi. In the early 1400s the Ottoman Turks posed a threat to Europe, and Hungary assumed the role of protector of the west. Between 1437 and 1456 Hungarian armies led by a powerful nobleman, János Hunyadi, blocked attempted Turkish invasions of Europe.

Hunyadi's son, Matthias, became king of Hungary in 1458 and led the country to its peak of greatness. He broke the power of the great nobles, organized an efficient centralized administration, and introduced the art and learning of the Renaissance into Hungary.

In an attempt to become leader of a united central Europe that could crush the Ottoman Turks, Matthias conquered territory in Bohemia, where he was named king, and in Silesia, Moravia, and Austria. At his death in 1490 Hungary was the most powerful state in western Europe. Matthias' successors were weak men. They lost most of his political and territorial gains, and they took no action against the Turks.

Ottoman Era. In the early 1500s the Turks began to move toward Hungary, and in 1526 they overwhelmed the country. Although the Turks were the nominal overlords of all Hungary, in fact the country was divided in three parts.

Northern and western Hungary was ruled by the Hapsburgs of Austria, who succeeded to the throne of Hungary in 1526. In the northeast, the principality of Transylvania grew so powerful that it was independent in all but name. The Turks controlled central Hungary.

Throughout the country there was turmoil. The Magyars resented Austrian and Turkish rule; Hungary's Slavic peoples resented the Austrians, the Turks, and the Magyars; and the Magyar nobility was split between those who had gained power by supporting the Turks and those who fought against the Turks and the pro-Turkish Magyars.

To these frictions was added religious strife arising from the Protestant Reformation. The Hungarians were unable to resolve their differences or to throw off Turkish rule.

Austrian Rule. In 1686 Austria's armies drove the Turks out of the region, and Austria assumed complete rule over the Magyar and Slavic peoples of Hungary. Austria did little to rebuild the country, which was still laboring under an outmoded feudal structure and which had been ravaged by years of warfare. Austrian rule at first was harsh and autocratic, and was unpopular with all Hungarians.

The Austrian rulers of the latter half of the 1700s were more liberal, however. They improved the economy and expanded the educational system, which in turn stimulated efforts for more radical reforms. Organizations were formed by democratic, progressive nationalists, and in the late 1700s and early 1800s, inspired by the French Revolution, they led demands for social, economic, and governmental reforms.

The Austrian emperor, with the support of the conservative Hungarian nobility, refused the demands and harshly repressed the movement. Repression only intensified the revolutionary spirit. In 1848, when liberal, democratic rebellions were breaking out all over Europe, Hungarian nationalistic reformers led an uprising against the Austrian Empire and demanded independence as a democratic state. The emperor yielded, the Hungarian nobles fled, and a republican government was established.

The new regime abolished the country's feudal, social, and economic organization, but the republic was short-lived. In 1849, under orders from a new emperor, Austrian and Russian troops crushed the republic, and Hungary once more became a subject state. The old order could not be restored by force, however, and Hungary remained the most independent of all of Austria's territories.

The Dual Monarchy. After 1848 Austria steadily lost power to Prussia, and in 1867 Prussia organized a union of German states that excluded Austria. The Hungarians took that opportunity to demand independence. In the same year, 1867, Austria and Hungary arrived at a compromise by which the Dual Monarchy of Austria-Hungary was formed.

The two states shared control of foreign policy, finance, and defense. Hungary, however, was a self-governing state that ruled Slavic subjects as well as Magyars. The Slavs resented Magyar rule, which was no better than Austrian rule had been.

Austria-Hungary had joined the series of alliances creating the Central powers, and in 1914 entered World War I. In 1918 Hungary went down to defeat with its allies. When defeat was imminent, a rebellion broke out in Hungary, and in November 1918 a republic was proclaimed. But in 1919 the Communist party assumed control. Communist rule was overthrown at the end of 1919 by monarchists, who chose Admiral Miklós Horthy as regent in 1920.

The Regency. In June 1920 the Hungarian government signed the Treaty of Trianon, which officially ended World War I for Hungary and which stripped Hungary of much of its territory and power. Under the treaty, Hungary ceded almost three-quarters of its land and two-thirds of its population to Austria, Romania, and the new states of Czechoslovakia and Yugoslavia. In 1921 Hungary's king, who attempted to return, was exiled.

The regency remained in power throughout the 1920s and 1930s. It was a conservative and authoritarian government, and all efforts at reform were stifled. Hungarian foreign policy was based on opposition to the Treaty of Trianon, and the government sought to recover the lands and peoples lost under the treaty.

HUNGARIAN RISING OF 1956. Citizens of Budapest rally on a tank in front of the Parliament building situated in the main square of the nation's capital and largest city.

The regency was bitterly hostile to the "Little Entente" of the new Slavic states and to their western patron, France. It was equally hostile to the Soviet Union, because of the brief but violent and destructive communist dictatorship of 1919.

The government of the regency thus was attracted by the political and territorial aims of Adolf Hitler of Germany and Benito Mussolini of Italy. Despite strong opposition within Hungary from monarchists, communists, and democratic liberals, right-wing nationalists prevailed in the government. In 1934 Hungary entered a political and economic alliance with Italy and Austria and moved closer to the National Socialist (Nazi) government of Germany.

In 1939 and 1940 Adolf Hitler restored to Hungary parts of its former territories in Romania and Czechoslovakia. In November 1940 Hungary formally allied itself with the Axis powers, although Hungarians did not fight in the war at first.

The Germans used the country as a base to delay Soviet advances into Central Europe, and in 1944 took direct control of the government. In the winter of 1944–1945 Soviet troops invaded and occupied Hungary, and when the war ended they were in firm control of the country.

Communist Rule. After the war a Control Commission of representatives of the Allied nations directed Hungary's government. The Soviets used their position on the commission to assist Hungary's minority Communist party to come to power. In 1948 a communist dictatorship with close ties to the Soviet Union was established under the leadership of Mátyás Rakosi. The Communist regime did not enjoy wide support and used repression and terrorism to stay in power. Communist efforts to transform the basis of Hungary's economy from feudalistic agriculture to state-owned heavy industry were inefficient and seriously damaged the country's economic life.

Economic, political, and social grievances fanned Hungarian nationalism and desire for independence from Soviet control. After the death of the Soviet dictator Joseph Stalin in 1953, the Hungarian Communist party split between advocates of continuing tight controls over all aspects of life and those seeking a more moderate, national course.

In October 1956 demonstrations against the government erupted and led to a popular rising. The revolution had wide support, even from the communist prime minister, Imre Nagy, but it was crushed by Soviet troops and tanks.

Janos Kadár became prime minister and first secretary of the Communist party. In 1958, after a secret trial, Nagy was executed. The Hungarian Communist party, which had disintegrated during the revolution, was completely reorganized.

The methods used by Kadár to consolidate power were repressive, but when the government's position was more secure Kadár began to relax controls and allowed an increasing measure of freedom. Under Kadár's administration economic programs were reorganized to achieve greater efficiency and a better balance between agriculture and industry.

Some free enterprise was permitted, consumers and producers were given a greater voice in the economy, and trade with noncommunist countries was expanded. The general standard of living rose, and by the mid-1960s Kadár's regime was among the least repressive of the governments of Eastern Europe.

In 1965 Kadár relinquished the role of prime minister to Gyula Kállai, although Kadár retained the more powerful post of first secretary of the Communist party. Jenö Fock became prime minister after elections held in 1967, which were the first in which "opposition" candidates were allowed to participate.

—Robert F. Byrnes; George Kish

UNITED NATIONS

HYDRO-ELECTRIC POWER STATION for the Sog and Laxa river project in Iceland.

ICELAND

Official name: Republic of Iceland
Area: 39,768 square miles
Population: (1966 est.) 195,000
Capital: Reykjavik (Pop., 1965 est., urban area, 89,400)
Language: Icelandic
Religion: Lutheranism
Currency unit: Krona
National holiday: Anniversary of the establishment of the republic, June 17

Iceland is an island republic in the North Atlantic Ocean, less than 200 miles southeast of Greenland. The Arctic Circle just touches the northern tips of Iceland.

THE LAND. Iceland is a forbidding land, with a rugged, barren terrain. The island is quite mountainous, with a central core of highlands rising above 5,000 feet. Glaciers cover large areas, and many swift rivers rush down from the glaciers.

Iceland is of volcanic origin, and some volcanoes are still active. Hot springs are common in the volcanic areas. In the early 1960s two new volcanic islands rose in Iceland's coastal waters.

The island's northerly climate is moderated by a section of the Gulf Stream that warms its coasts. Average temperatures range between 30°F and 52°F throughout the year. Almost 50 inches of rain a year falls in the southern lowlands. The mountains are much wetter, but the far north receives only an average of 15 inches.

THE PEOPLE. Iceland is rather sparsely settled, but its population is growing rapidly. In the mid-1960s it had one of the highest birthrates in Europe, almost 25 per 1,000 inhabitants. The interior of the island is almost entirely uninhabited, and most of the people live along the coast, especially in the southwest around Reykjavik, where almost 40 percent of Icelanders live.

Iceland's population is quite homogeneous. Almost all the people are Scandinavian in origin, and Icelandic, a Scandinavian tongue, is the universal language. Over 95 percent of the population is Lutheran.

ECONOMY. Despite its barrenness, Iceland is a moderately prosperous country with an economy based almost entirely on fishing and trade. The chief natural resources are its rushing rivers, which provide hydroelectric power, its thermal springs, and its geographic position near rich fishing banks and along a major route between Europe and North America.

Less than 1 percent of the land is cultivated, and only hay, root crops, and other hardy crops can be grown. Grazing land is available and dairying is of some importance.

Fishing and related activities make the greatest single contribution to the Icelandic economy. Cod and herring, from coastal waters and from the Grand Banks near Canada, are the chief catches. Fishing and fish processing constitute the bulk of Iceland's industrial activity. Salted, dried, frozen, and canned fish, and fish meal and oils are the country's main products.

During the 1950s and 1960s Iceland investigated other resources and developed new industries, in an effort to end its economic dependence on a single commodity. Major new industries, supported largely by private investment, included a huge aluminum plant and a vast power project in southwestern Iceland.

Other newer industries include textile milling, book production, chemical manufacture, and shipbuilding. Many of the farms, businesses, and industries in Iceland are organized in cooperatives.

Trade is vital to the Icelandic economy. In 1966 exports earned $141 million and imports cost $159 million. Fresh and processed fish and fish products accounted for over 90 percent of the country's exports in the mid-1960s. Raw materials, foodstuffs, machinery, manufactured goods, petroleum products, and ships must be imported. Most of Iceland's trade is with Great Britain, the United States, West Germany, the Soviet Union, and the Scandinavian countries.

GOVERNMENT. Iceland is a republic, with a president as head of state. Actual executive power rests with a prime minister and cabinet responsible to the legislature. Members of the bicameral legislature, the *Althing,* are popularly elected. The Althing chooses one-third of its members to sit as an upper house; the remaining two-thirds forms the lower, more powerful, house.

Iceland is a member of the United Nations, the North Atlantic Treaty Organization (NATO), the Council of Europe, and the Nordic Council.

HISTORY. Iceland was settled in the late 800s by Norwegian Vikings. Immigration increased through the 900s, with settlers coming from the British Isles as well as from Norway. By the end of the 900s, the descendants of these first settlers had established their own system of representative government, with a constitution, a court system, and the Althing.

The yearly Althing, the meeting of chieftains and popular representatives, soon became the social and cultural center of Icelandic life, as well as the country's legislature and supreme court. In 1000 the Althing adopted Christianity as the religion for the entire country. During the 900s and 1000s, Vikings from Iceland made many voyages of exploration. They discovered and settled Greenland and visited North America.

Dissension among the Icelanders during the early 1200s led to the breakdown of government, and in 1262 Iceland joined with Norway and submitted to the rule of the Norwegian king. Although the island remained nominally self-governing, government under Norwegian rule was centralized and by the mid-1300s Iceland was ruled by an absolute monarch. In 1387, when Denmark and Norway were united, Iceland came under the rule of the Danish crown.

Danish Rule. Between the 1300s and the 1700s the island was struck by many natural disasters, including volcanic eruptions, plague, and floods. Denmark did little to alleviate the resulting famine and poverty. Moreover, during the 1600s and 1700s, trade monopolies and other commercial regulations served Danish rather than Icelandic interests.

In the early 1800s, when Iceland had begun to recover from the effects of the natural disasters, a spirit of nationalism spread through the island and led to demands for independence. The first step toward increased autonomy was the restoration of power to the Althing in 1843.

In 1854 Denmark relaxed its trade restrictions and Iceland's economy began to improve. In 1874 Iceland was granted a new constitution, which provided for Icelandic self-government under the supervision of a Danish minister. The island became completely self-governing in 1904.

Independence. After World War I Iceland demanded the self-determination that had been granted to other nations by the Treaty of Versailles. In 1918 a Danish-Icelandic treaty recognized Iceland's independence within a personal union with the Danish crown, and Denmark remained responsible for Iceland's foreign affairs and defense.

During the 1920s and 1930s Iceland was generally isolated from the rest of the world. During World War II, however, Iceland was of great strategic importance as an Allied air and naval base. After its occupation by Germany in 1940, Denmark was unable to handle Icelandic affairs, and in 1944 Iceland proclaimed itself a sovereign republic.

During the 1940s and 1950s Iceland concentrated on expanding and balancing its economy. The island began to participate more fully in world affairs, and it became increasingly dependent on international trade agreements and defense pacts. It was also an important link on international air travel routes as well as being a strategically important NATO base manned by the United States.

In 1951 the United States agreed to manage Iceland's defense, as Iceland has no military establishment, but domestic and international political conflicts led to the withdrawal of most U.S. troops in the early 1960s.

In 1958 Iceland extended the limits of its territorial waters from four miles to 12 miles, leading to international protests from fishing nations. In 1961 Britain, most affected by the new limits, agreed to recognize them.

Economic expansion began to flag in the mid-1960s, and elections held in 1966 reflected an increase in the strength of the left-wing Progressive and Social Democratic parties.

INDIA

Official name: Republic of India
Area: 1,175,579 square miles (excluding Kashmir)
Population: (1967 est.) 511,115,000 (excluding Kashmir)
Capital: New Delhi (Pop., 1966 est., 314,400)
Language: Hindi, English
Religion: Hinduism, Islam, Christianity
Currency unit: Rupee
National holiday: Anniversary of the proclamation of the republic, January 26

The Republic of India occupies most of the southern appendage of the Eurasian land mass known as the subcontinent of India. The country is bounded on the north by Nepal, Sikkim, Bhutan, and China; on the east by Burma, East Pakistan, and the Bay of Bengal; on the south by the Indian Ocean; and on the west by the Arabian Sea and West Pakistan.

Before it became independent in 1947, India was part of British India, which included most of the subcontinent. In 1947 the subcontinent was divided. Predominantly Muslim areas in the north became the nation of Pakistan, and the bulk of the subcontinent, predominantly Hindu, became the nation of India.

A number of semiautonomous princely states in the subcontinent were given the freedom to join either Pakistan or India. The Hindu ruler of predominantly Muslim Kashmir, one of the largest and richest of the states, acceded to India. Pakistan protested the act and insisted that the people of Kashmir be allowed to express their view in a plebiscite. India refused, and warfare broke out.

The United Nations arranged a cease fire, but the status of Kashmir, partly occupied by Pakistani forces and partly incorporated into India, remained a sore point in Indian-Pakistani relations. In 1964 Indian Kashmir had an estimated population of 3,729,000.

THE LAND. India, approximately one-third the size of the United States, stretches about 2,000 miles from north to south. It has three major land regions: the Himalayas and associated mountain ranges in the north, the Indus-Ganges-Brahmaputra plain in north-central India, and the Deccan Plateau in the south.

Land Regions. The Himalayas extend from east to west for 1,500 miles, broken only by gaps produced by the Indus and Brahmaputra rivers. The mountains range from 150 to 200 miles in width, from north to south. In many places the mountain system consists of three parallel ranges.

The Great Himalayas are the northernmost chain and the highest, with many peaks exceeding 20,000 feet

above sea level. The Lesser Himalayas are the middle range, with the highest elevations averaging 12,000 to 15,000 feet. The third and southernmost range, the Outer Himalayas, overlooks the Gangetic plain. Average elevations in the Outer Himalayas are 3,000 to 4,000 feet.

The Indus-Ganges-Brahmaputra Plain, which lies between the Himalayas and the Deccan Plateau, is formed by hundreds of feet of fine sediment laid down by three rivers and is one of the largest alluvial plains in the world. Two of these rivers, the Indus and the Brahmaputra, originate on the northern side of the Himalayas. The Ganges, the third river, originates on the southern side of the Himalayas. It flows directly eastward and joins the Brahmaputra.

The Deccan Plateau, which forms the triangle-shaped peninsular portion of the Indian subcontinent, is bounded by the Vindhya-Satpura mountains in the north. Running southwest to northeast for about 800 miles, they rise from 1,500 to over 4,000 feet.

The plateau tilts eastward toward the Bay of Bengal. It is bounded along the Arabian Sea coast by the Western Ghats and along the Bay of Bengal by the Eastern Ghats. The Western Ghats rise abruptly to elevations of 3,000 feet with some peaks reaching 4,700 feet. Near the southern tip of the peninsula, the Western Ghats have peaks of over 8,000 feet.

The Eastern Ghats have an average height of 1,500 to 2,000 feet. The inner areas of the plateau average 1,000 to 3,000 feet in elevation, with some hills rising to 4,000 feet.

The northern edge of the plateau is drained by a series of rivers flowing northward to the Gangetic plain. The Narbada-Tapti river system in the northwestern portion of the plateau drains westward into the Gulf of Cambay. The major rivers of the plateau rise on the eastern flanks of the Western Ghats, flow eastward across the plateau, and drain into the Bay of Bengal. The largest of these rivers are the Godavari, Krishna, and the Cauvery.

Climate. The Himalayas shield the Indian subcontinent from the main body of the Eurasian land mass. As a result, the climate of the subcontinent is unique. In winter, high pressure systems in the Punjab region produce winds that move down the Gangetic plain into the Bay of Bengal. Winters are generally dry in most of the subcontinent.

During March, April, and May, there is little air movement and the subcontinent begins to heat up, creating low pressure conditions in the north. By the end of May or the beginning of June, the summer monsoons arrive, bringing rain into the Ganges valley.

Rainfall varies considerably. On the Ganges-Brahmaputra Delta, in the Khasi and Chittagong hills, Assam, the southern zone of the Himalayas, and along the Malabar coast, the total may exceed 80 inches a year. In the northeastern portions of the Deccan, along the southeast coast, and in parts of the Western Ghats and the Punjab, the total ranges from 40 to 80 inches. In Kathiawar and the western half of the Deccan, the annual rainfall is 20 to 40 inches.

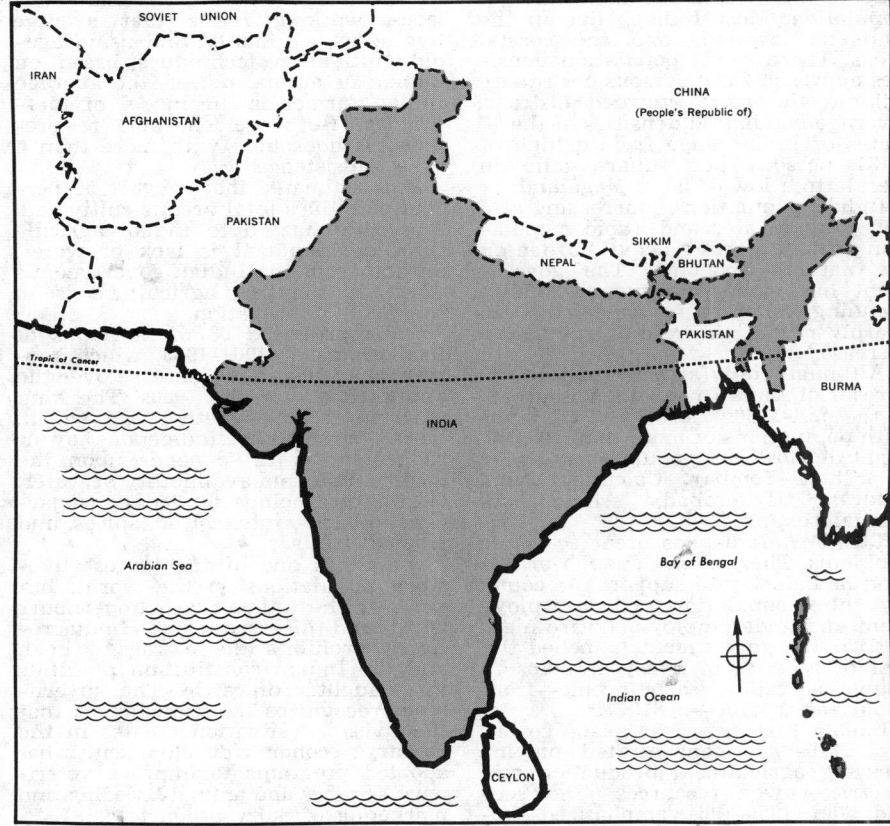

In the southern half of the country, temperatures are tropical and vary little from month to month. In northern India, however, the annual range is considerable. In January the average temperature in the north may be 30°F lower than in the south.

THE PEOPLE. India has a varied population. The majority of Indians, however, belong to either Indo-Aryan or Dravidian language groups. The tall, light-skinned people who live mainly in northern India speak Indo-Aryan languages. The people of southern India mostly speak Dravidian languages. Tribal people such as the Khasis, Nagas, Bhils, and Santals, who live in the Himalaya regions, speak a number of languages, many of which are neither Indo-Aryan nor Dravidian.

Fourteen major languages are spoken in India, and these are broken up into hundreds of dialects. The Indo-Aryan languages include Hindi, Urdu, Assamese, Bengali, Gujarati, Kashmiri, Marathi, Oriya, Panjabi, and Rajasthani. The main Dravidian languages are Kannada, Malayalam, Tamil, and Telugu. Hindi is the official national language although English is still used in government and is the common means of communication among educated Indians.

The vast majority of Indians are Hindus, but India has one of the world's largest Muslim communities. In addition, there are about 10 million Christians, 7.5 million adherents of Sikhism, and 2 million followers of Jainism.

India is second only to China in population. In 1965 the average population density was 413 persons per square mile, but there is great geographic variation in the distribution of population. Most Indians live in the Gangetic lowlands and the coastal areas. There, rural population densities approach 2,000 persons per square mile in the more crowded districts. Average population densities of the 17 states of India range from a high of 1,131 persons per square mile in Kerala to a low of 58 in Nagaland.

India's population is increasing at a very rapid rate, and rapid population growth places a heavy burden on the nation's economy. The government has embarked upon a family planning program in an attempt to sharply reduce the rate of population increase.

Although only approximately 30 percent of India's population is urban, in the mid-1960s there were 110 cities with populations of more than 100,000. Eight of those had populations of over 1 million—Bombay, Calcutta, Delhi, Madras, Hyderabad, Ahmedabad, Bangalore, and Kanpur.

ECONOMY. India has great economic problems. There is not enough arable land or industry to support the country's huge population, and unemployment and underemployment are high. In 1951 the government launched the first of a series of five-year plans to double per capita yearly income—from about $55 to $100—by 1977.

India's first five-year plan, covering 1951-1956, concentrated on increasing agricultural production and electric power resources. The second plan, 1956-1961, emphasized rap-

UNITED NATIONS

BOATS ON THE GANGES RIVER, at Banaras, in northern India.

id industrialization through the development of heavy industry. The third plan, 1961-1966, provided for expansion of both food and industrial production, and gave special attention to family planning and population control. The fourth plan emphasized the same objectives as the third plan.

Natural Resources. India has most of the mineral resources required for industrial expansion. It has one of the largest high-grade iron ore reserves in the world as well as large deposits of coal. Among the more common industrial raw materials, the most serious deficiencies appear to be petroleum, lead, zinc, nitrogen, sulphur, and phosphates.

Agriculture. About 70 percent of India's working population is engaged in agriculture. Living in small villages, working farms that average two acres per family, and using age-old cultivation techniques based on human or animal power, the average Indian farmer is the model of inefficiency. He is seldom able to provide his household with more than a bare subsistence.

It is estimated that roughly 50 percent of India's total area is cultivated. The chief hazard to Indian agricultural development is lack of water, and much of the Indian government's effort to improve agriculture is in the field of irrigation.

India produced 93 million tons of food grains in 1964-1965, which represents a substantial increase over the annual levels of the 1950s. The kind of grain grown—whether rice, wheat, barley, corn, or the indigenous jowar, raggee, or bajra—depends upon the local climate and availability of water. Cash crops include tea, coffee, sugarcane, tobacco, jute, cotton, spices, and tropical fruits.

India has one of the largest livestock populations in the world, but most of the animals are undernourished and diseased. The Hindu religion prohibits the eating of beef, and the Indian constitution prohibits the slaughter of cattle. The government recognizes the impediment that the livestock situation creates in the country's economic development. It has adopted programs to improve veterinary services and animal breeding and marketing of dairy products.

Industry. As of 1964 industrial production contributed less than one-fifth of the domestic product. The Indian government is seeking ways to develop manufacturing and increase its role in the economy.

Manufacturing in India can be divided into two groups. The first group consists of handicraft industries organized on a household or guild basis. They are small, producing light consumer goods and utilizing traditional techniques. The second group is made up of modern factory industries.

The chief industry is the manufacture of cotton and silk textiles, but the Tata iron and steel mills are the largest in Asia. India is also an important producer of chemical fertilizers, sulfuric acid, drugs and pharmaceuticals, dyestuffs, and plastics. There is also an expanding automotive industry.

In 1964 India had an installed electric generating capacity of 8.4 million kilowatts, and this capacity is increasing quite rapidly with government construction of large-scale hydroelectric plants.

Trade. Since India achieved independence in 1947 imports have exceeded exports. In 1966 India's imports cost $2,751 million and its exports earned only $1,608 million. India's leading exports are jute products, cotton piece goods, tanned hides and skins, tea, iron ore, pepper, nuts, and tobacco. The chief imports include food grains, machinery, mineral oils, motor vehicles, and chemicals. India's major trading partners are the United States and Britain.

GOVERNMENT. India is a democratic republic and has a parliamentary system of government. The head of state is the president. He is elected to a five-year term by the members of the national and the state legislatures. Effective executive power is exercised by a prime minister, who is normally the leader of the majority political party.

Parliament consists of two houses, the *Rajya Sabha* (Council of States) and the *Lok Sabha* (House of the People). The Council of States consists of up to 250 members, who are indirectly elected to six-year terms. The House of the People may have up to 525 members. Of these, 500 may be direct-

VILLAGE CHIEFS of Faridabad township meet to plan for community development.

ly elected to five-year terms by universal suffrage from territorial constituencies in the states; up to 25 representatives of the Union Territories may be chosen according to laws passed by parliament.

Unlike the Council of States, which is a permanent body, the House of the People can be dissolved by the president, and new elections called, if the prime minister loses the support of a majority in parliament.

The organization of India's 17 state governments is similar to that of the federal government. Each has a legislature and an administration headed by a governor, who is appointed by the president.

In emergency situations the federal government has extraordinary power over the states. Parliament can, under special circumstances, take over the power of the state legislatures. India also has ten Union Territories, governed by the president through an administrator appointed by him.

India is a member of the Commonwealth of Nations and the United Nations. It has played a prominent role in international affairs as a leader of the nonaligned nations—those countries seeking to avoid identification with either of the world's two great power blocks, the Eastern, or communist, group of states led by the Soviet Union, and the Western, or noncommunist nations, led by the United States.

HISTORY. Evidence of the first permanent village settlements in India, dating from about 3000 BC, is found in the hilly areas of southern Baluchistan. Some time after the appearance of these settlements a great urban civilization developed in the Indus Valley, which lasted from about 2500 to 1500 BC. It is probable that this civilization was related to the great river valley civilization that had already appeared in Mesopotamia, but there is little evidence of direct borrowing.

An extraordinary cultural uniformity is observable in Indus civilization throughout its thousand years of history, suggesting some form of strong, central political control. The Indus people had a system of writing, but the script has not been deciphered and very little is known of their beliefs or ideas.

The Indus civilization was apparently destroyed by invaders in about 1500 BC. Nothing certain is known of these invaders, but they may have been a group of the Aryans, a wandering, pastoral people. Between 2000 and 1500 BC, the Aryans spread from their homeland, which may have been in southern Russia, to Europe, Mesopotamia, and India. Aryan migrations into India probably extended over several centuries after about 1500 BC.

The Aryans spoke an Indo-European language from which classical Sanskrit and the modern languages of northern India, such as Hindi, Bengali, Marathi, and Gujarati, are descended. The Aryans gradually advanced from northeastern India through the Punjab, down into the Gangetic plain. By 900 BC they had probably begun to penetrate the Deccan Plateau.

During this long period of expansion the Aryans subjugated the native inhabitants, whom they referred to contemptuously as *dàsas* (dark spirits). These people were a dark-skinned race who may have been related to the Indus Valley people or to the Dravidians, the people of southern India.

The conquest of new lands and contact with the original inhabitants led to profound changes in the Aryan way of life. The Aryan tribes settled in permanent communities and began to cultivate the land. By the 600s BC the tribal communities were being absorbed into small kingdoms, which had hereditary monarchs and capital cities.

Changes also took place in the Aryan religion. The relatively simple rites and ceremonies of the *Rigveda,* the most ancient of the Aryan religious texts, gave way to elaborate sacrificial rituals that exalted the role of the Brahmans, or priestly class. At the same time use of magic and the worship of various deities not known in the earliest Vedic traditions became part of the religion of the Aryans.

These two movements—emphasis on the importance of the Brahmanic priesthood and absorption of religious practices from many sources—transformed the older Aryan cult into Hinduism, the religious structure that colored the later history of India.

The First Empires (600 BC–AD 300). By the 600s BC a number of small kingdoms had appeared in northern India, the most important of which were Kosala, between the Ganges and the Nepal mountains, and Magadha, south of the Ganges in modern Bihar. In the 500s BC this area of the Gangetic plain also produced Buddhism and Jainism, two great religions that denied the authority of the old Vedic scriptures and the supremacy of the Brahmanic priesthood.

By the beginning of the 300s BC Magadha, ruled by the Nandas, had become the dominant power in the Gangetic plain. In about 322 BC the Nanda dynasty was overthrown by a young adventurer, Chandragupta Maurya, who ruled until about 298 BC. Chandragupta embarked on a policy of conquest that brought under his control most of northern India, including part of modern Afghanistan, and much of southern India.

The Maurya empire was ruled from the splendid capital of Pataliputra (modern Patna). Asoka (r.273–232 BC), Chandragupta's grandson, extended the empire by conquering Kalinga, the coastal region of modern Orissa and Andhra Pradesh. After that acquisition, however, he turned his back on territorial expansion and sought to make Buddhist ethics the guiding force for a kingdom of righteousness.

On rock walls and pillars all over the kingdom he had engraved the principles of conduct that his people were to follow. In these edicts he emphasized honesty, obedience to parents and teachers, religious toleration, and service to others.

Asoka's espousal of Buddhism helped its spread throughout India and Ceylon. The beginning of the Buddhist shrines that were to provide many of the great masterpieces of Indian art date from Asoka's reign. Neither at that time nor later did the majority of the Indian people become Buddhists, but for 500 or 600 years Buddhism tended to be the religion of kings and merchants. In addition to its effect on artistic creativity, Buddhism made important contributions to philosophy.

The Mauryan empire disintegrated soon after Asoka's death in 232 BC, when foreign invaders entered from the northwest. Among the invaders of the Mauryan empire were the people known as Sakas, or Scythians, whose kingdoms were first established by the generals of Alexander the Great in Bactria, and the Kushan, a Central Asian people.

Of all the invaders the Kushans were the most influential. They established a strong kingdom in northern India in the first century AD that lasted for nearly 200 years. Their greatest king, Kanishka (r.c.78–c.110 AD), supported Buddhism, and during his reign missionaries carried Buddhism to Central Asia. From there it was eventually transmitted to China and other parts of East Asia.

In most of southern India Mauryan control had probably never been very strong, and in the extreme south three kingdoms—the Chola, the Pandya, and the Chera—had existed independently during Asoka's reign. These three kingdoms, with periods of decay and obscurity, continued to exist up to the 1100s AD. Following the disintegration of the Mauryan empire, the history of southern India tended to be quite separate from that of the north. From the first century BC to about 200 AD, most of Deccan was controlled by the Satavahanas, who ruled from Andhra Pradesh.

Guptas and Rajputs (300–1200 AD). After the downfall of the Kushan no empire developed in northern India until the 300s, when the Guptas, a family from the Magadha region (modern Bihar), built up a powerful new kingdom. Under Samudragupta (r.c.330–c.375) and his son Chandragupta II (r.c.375–c.413), the dynasty's power spread all over northern India. The principal cities of the empire were Pataliputra and Ujjain.

The Gupta period was an age of great activity in literature, the fine arts, religion, science, and philosophy. Its intellectual and artistic accomplishments reflected a prosperity and state of material well-being perhaps never again matched in India's history. During this golden age, Buddhism and Jainism remained important, but Hinduism, which had developed its characteristic social laws and devotional rituals, had become dominant.

The intellectual and religious achievements of the Gupta age remained the great heritage of Indian civilization during the centuries of invasions and political unrest that followed its decline at the end of the 300s. A Central Asian people, the Huns, invaded northern India in the 400s, and while their empire was short-lived, it destroyed the power of the Guptas.

Attempts were made in the following century, notably by Harsha (r.606–647) to recreate a single political authority in northern India, but none of these efforts was particularly successful. By the 800s northern India was split up into many kingdoms ruled by Rajputs, who claimed to trace their origins to the ancient ruling families of Rajasthan, but who may have been descendants of invaders who were accepted into Hinduism as members of the warrior class.

The greatest of the Rajput kingdoms was that of the Pratiharas. The Pratiharas and the other Rajput kings were almost always at war with one another. While this may have prevented them from uniting against enemies, it did lead to the growth of a martial spirit and an emphasis on heroic action that helped to preserve the society when it was later threatened.

Developments in Southern India. During the period of Gupta and Rajput ascendancy in northern India, southern India was controlled by various regional kingdoms. The Chalukyas, who ruled from Badami in the western Deccan, were dominant from about 600 to 750 AD. Their major enemies were the Pallavas, whose capital was Kanchipuram. The Pallavas ruled from the 300s until the end of the 700s, when they were overthrown by the Chola kings of Tanjore.

The Cholas maintained control of all the territory south of the Tungabhadra River from about 850 to 1200, when they were superseded by the revived power of the Pandyas at Madura. The later Chalukya of the Deccan were also destroyed during the 1100s, and their kingdom was divided among the Hoysalas of Mysore, the Yadavas of Devagiri (modern Daulatabad), and the Kakatiyas of Warangal.

The southern kingdoms were the centers of cultural and religious movements of great importance. Most of the rulers were great builders, and they adorned their kingdoms with magnificent temples and palaces. The Pallavas were responsible for the series of rock–carved temples at Mamallapuram and the great temple complex at Kanchipuram. The Cholas built numerous temples, of which the most famous is that at Tanjore, and decorated them with stone and bronze sculpture.

A religious movement of great vitality underlay this outburst of temple building. Out of the synthesis of Aryan and Dravidian cultures had come a new Hindu devotional sect that emphasized the worship of three great deities, Brahma, Siva, and Vishnu.

This new movement, aided by the support of kings, brought to an end the flourishing Buddhist and Jain communities of southern India.

Muslim Dominance (1200–1700). The first impact of Islam on India came in 712, when Arab control was established over Sind, the lower Indus Valley. The Rajput kings of northern India prevented their further expansion. The next Islamic intrusion came not from the Muslims of the Middle East, but from Afghan Turks who had established their power at Ghazni (now part of Afghanistan).

The Ghaznavids made numerous raids into India throughout the 1000s, but actually ruled only the territory west of Lahore. A change came when a new dynasty of Afghan Turks from Ghor defeated a confederacy of Rajput kings in 1192 at Taraori. The Indian defeat was probably due not only to internal divisions among the Rajput kings, but to the superior military techniques of the Turks as well.

The Turks established a sultanate at Delhi and from there gradually extended their control over all northern India. Under Ala-ud-din Khalji (r.1296–1316), the Turks conquered southern India. This new empire, the greatest in India since that of the Mauryas, began to disintegrate under the Tughluq dynasty, which came to power after Ala-ud-din's death.

This process of disintegration was hastened by the invasion of Tamerlane in 1398. He made no attempt to establish his authority, but his raids weakened the control of the sultanate in northern India.

By 1500 the Delhi sultanate held only parts of the Punjab and the Gangetic plain. But permanent changes had been effected in the pattern of Indian civilization by 300 years of Muslim occupation. A large Muslim minority had been created, and Islamic ideas and values had begun to influence Indian life. This influence was never very great as far as the masses of the people were concerned, and orthodox Hinduism remained quite unchanged.

A new group of invaders entered India in 1526, led by Babur, a Turkish chieftain who had founded a kingdom at Kabul after having been driven out of his homeland in Turkistan. Because one of his remote ancestors was the Mongol conqueror Genghis Khan, his family came to be referred to as Mughals, or Moguls. He defeated the Delhi sultan at Panipat in 1526, and made himself master of the Gangetic plain up to Patna.

On his death in 1530 he was succeeded by his son Humayun, who was driven out of India in 1540 by Sher Shah, an Afghan chieftain. Humayun recovered Delhi in 1555, but he died the following year. He was succeeded by his son Akbar (r.1556–1605), the real founder of the Mughal empire. Akbar pursued an aggressive policy of expansion that brought all of northern India under his control.

Akbar's reign is one of the most vital in Indian history, for he initiated policies that had a lasting influence. At the very beginning of the conquests, the Muslims had been faced with the problem of the proper treatment of the Hindus. A compromise had been effected that allowed them to practice their religion, but they were subjected to discriminatory taxes and laws and many rulers showed their orthodoxy by destroying Hindu temples.

Akbar enunciated a policy of universal toleration, the most obvious sign of which was the abolition of the *jizya*, the discriminatory tax. Some of the highest officers in the army were Hindus, and Akbar made marriage alliances among the Rajputs. His interest in Hindu culture led to a synthesis of Indian and Islamic artistic forms, which in turn created a new flowering in music, literature, painting, and architecture.

His support of an eclectic religion, the Din-i-Ilahi, which drew upon Hindu metaphysics, lent credence to the charge made by orthodox Muslims that he had abandoned Islam. Akbar also instituted far-reaching administrative reforms. One of the most important of these was the expansion of the revenue system initiated by Sher Shah. Akbar ordered a careful survey of all cultivated land and reformed the system of taxation.

Akbar's successors, Jahangir (r.1605–1627) and Shah Jahan (r.1628–1658), continued his policy of consolidation and expansion. During Shah Jahan's reign the Muslim kingdoms of the Deccan were brought under imperial control. Shah Jahan was also a great builder. The Taj Mahal and the Pearl Mosque at Agra, and the palace and Great Mosque at Delhi, are among the great monuments of his reign.

Shah Jahan's son, Aurangzeb, (r.1658–1707) reversed the religious policy initiated by Akbar. As a devout Muslim he looked with disfavor on the growing power and prosperity of the Hindus, and as a statesman he probably questioned the possibility of holding the empire together without the loyalty of a Muslim ruling class. The discriminatory taxes were reimposed on the Hindus, the building of new temples was forbidden, and an attempt was made to replace Hindu government officials with Muslims.

Aurangzeb also embarked on a policy of territorial expansion that brought all of India, except the extreme southern tip, under Mughul control. For 20 years he battled the Marathas of southern India under their great leader Sivaji.

Aurangzeb's vast empire began to crumble within a generation of his death. Rebellions broke out everywhere in the Mughul empire, and a series of weak successors to the throne were unable to control the administration effectively. In 1739 northern India was invaded by Nadir Shah of Persia. By 1750 the empire was reduced to the territory around Delhi, and regional kingdoms had been established throughout India.

Western Dominance and Unification. The Marathas were the most important of the regional powers that emerged from the wreckage of the Mughul empire. By 1760 they controlled all of central India and much of the south. Their expansion was checked in 1761 with their defeat at Panipat by a combined Mughul and Afghan army, and further halted in

GEOPHYSICAL GLOBE

ROTHSTEIN/LOOK

AFGHANISTAN

ALBANIA

ALGERIA

ANDORRA

ARGENTINA

AUSTRALIA

AUSTRIA

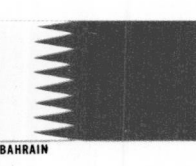

BAHRAIN

BARBADOS

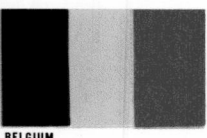

BELGIUM

BHUTAN

BOLIVIA

BOTSWANA

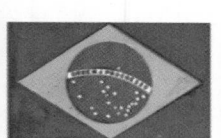

BRAZIL

BULGARIA

BURMA

BURUNDI

CAMBODIA

CAMEROON

CANADA

CENTRAL AFRICAN REPUBLIC

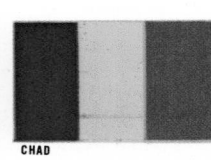
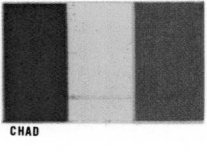

CEYLON

CHAD

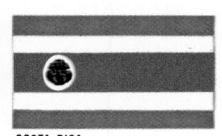

CHILE

CHINA Communist

CHINA Nationalist

COLOMBIA

CONGO Brazzaville

CONGO KINSHASA

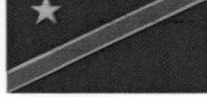

COSTA RICA

CUBA

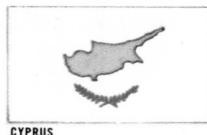

CYPRUS

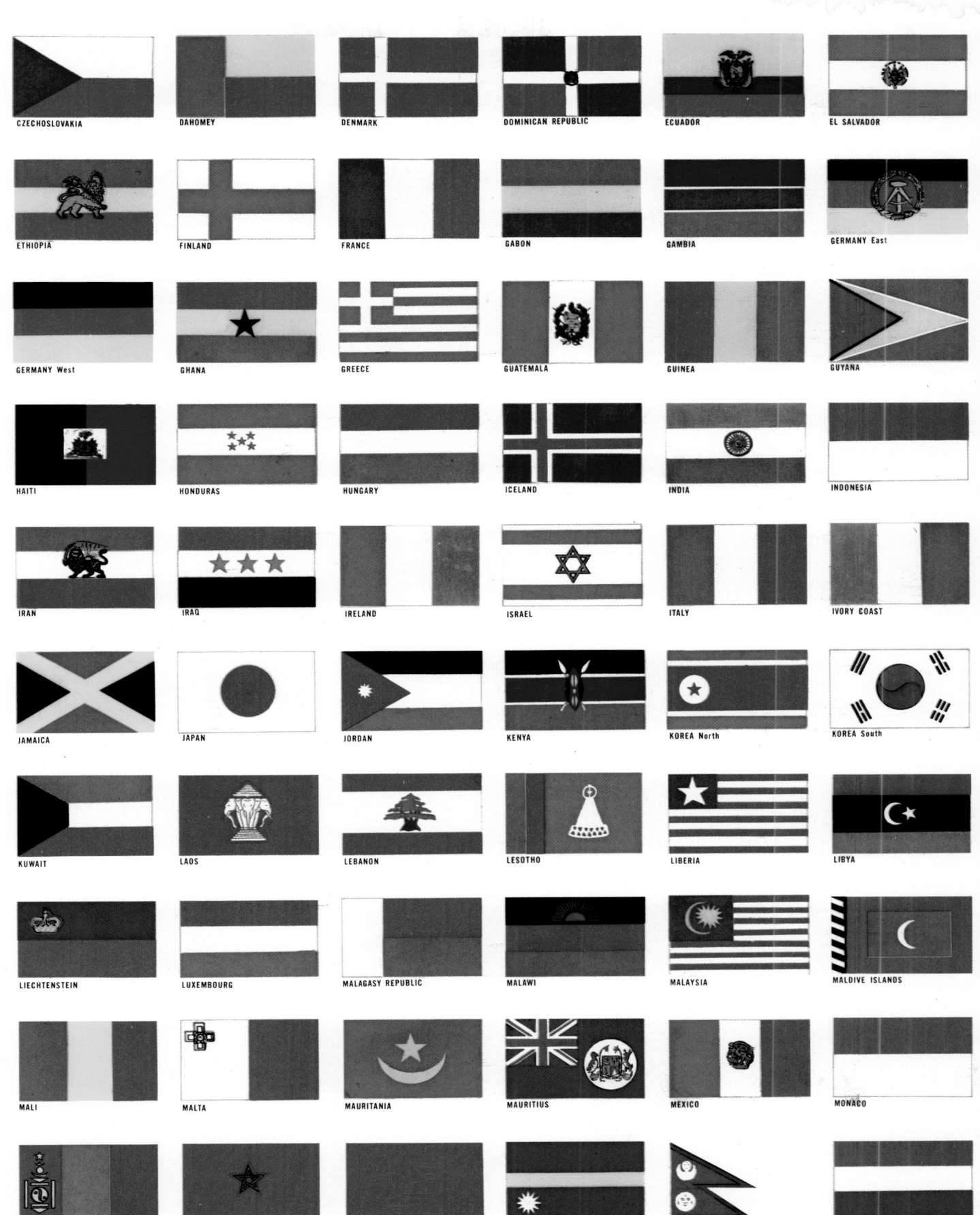

CZECHOSLOVAKIA DAHOMEY DENMARK DOMINICAN REPUBLIC ECUADOR EL SALVADOR

ETHIOPIA FINLAND FRANCE GABON GAMBIA GERMANY East

GERMANY West GHANA GREECE GUATEMALA GUINEA GUYANA

HAITI HONDURAS HUNGARY ICELAND INDIA INDONESIA

IRAN IRAQ IRELAND ISRAEL ITALY IVORY COAST

JAMAICA JAPAN JORDAN KENYA KOREA North KOREA South

KUWAIT LAOS LEBANON LESOTHO LIBERIA LIBYA

LIECHTENSTEIN LUXEMBOURG MALAGASY REPUBLIC MALAWI MALAYSIA MALDIVE ISLANDS

MALI MALTA MAURITANIA MAURITIUS MEXICO MONACO

MONGOLIA MOROCCO MUSCAT & OMAN NAURU NEPAL NETHERLANDS

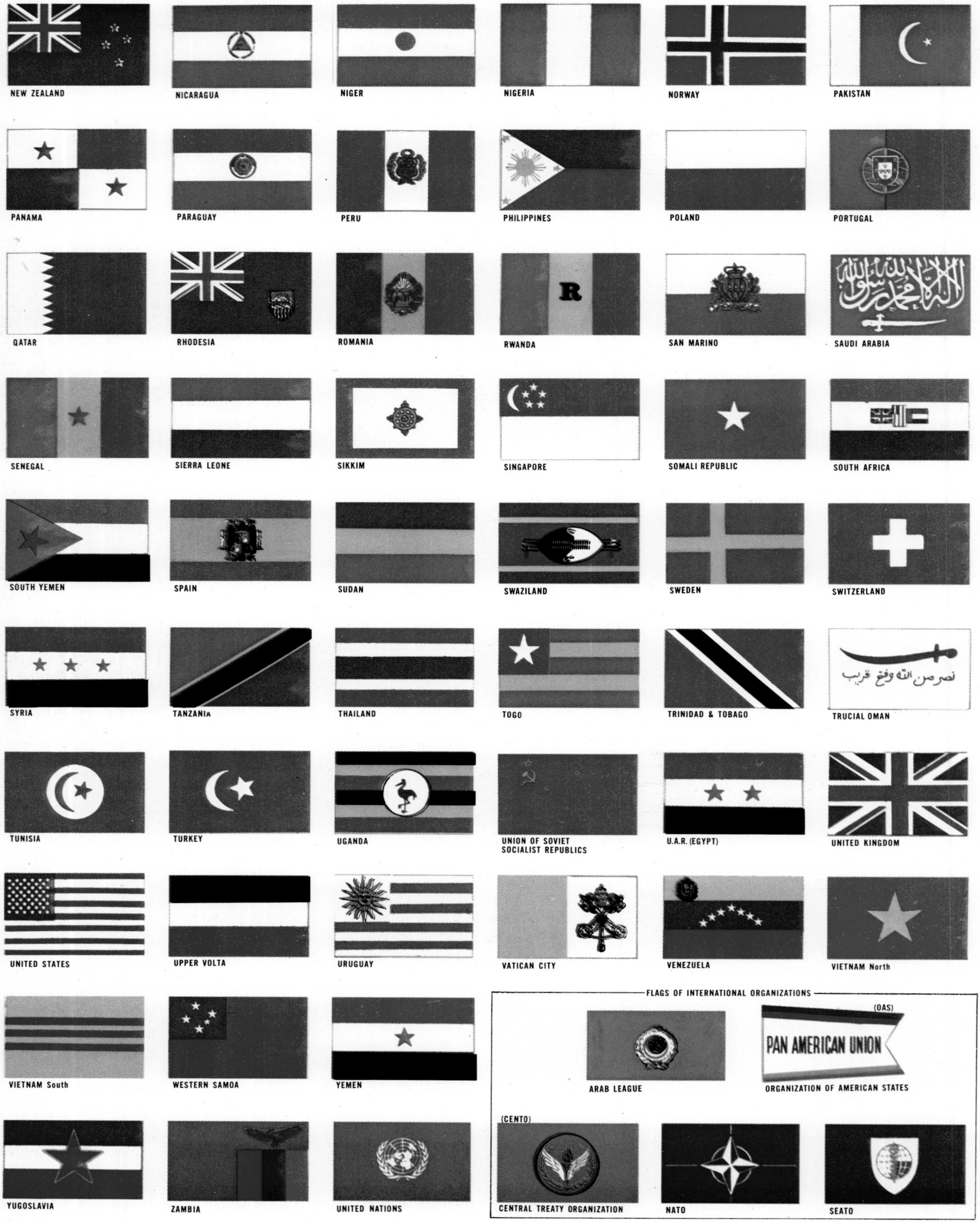

NEW ZEALAND

NICARAGUA

NIGER

NIGERIA

NORWAY

PAKISTAN

PANAMA

PARAGUAY

PERU

PHILIPPINES

POLAND

PORTUGAL

QATAR

RHODESIA

ROMANIA

RWANDA

SAN MARINO

SAUDI ARABIA

SENEGAL

SIERRA LEONE

SIKKIM

SINGAPORE

SOMALI REPUBLIC

SOUTH AFRICA

SOUTH YEMEN

SPAIN

SUDAN

SWAZILAND

SWEDEN

SWITZERLAND

SYRIA

TANZANIA

THAILAND

TOGO

TRINIDAD & TOBAGO

TRUCIAL OMAN

TUNISIA

TURKEY

UGANDA

UNION OF SOVIET
SOCIALIST REPUBLICS

U.A.R. (EGYPT)

UNITED KINGDOM

UNITED STATES

UPPER VOLTA

URUGUAY

VATICAN CITY

VENEZUELA

VIETNAM North

VIETNAM South

WESTERN SAMOA

YEMEN

─── FLAGS OF INTERNATIONAL ORGANIZATIONS ───

ARAB LEAGUE

(OAS)

PAN AMERICAN UNION

ORGANIZATION OF AMERICAN STATES

(CENTO)

CENTRAL TREATY ORGANIZATION

NATO

SEATO

YUGOSLAVIA

ZAMBIA

UNITED NATIONS

the 1780s by the rising power of the English East India company.

The English had been in India since 1600 as traders, but the company be- came important as a political power only after the decline of Mughul pow- er. In 1757 the company interfered in a succession dispute over the throne of Bengal. By 1765 the company was in effective control of Bengal's resources, which it used to pay for the cost of expansion. By 1820 it was the para- mount power in India, and within the next 30 years all of India was brought under its control.

From 1784 on the British govern- ment had a decisive voice in the selec- tion of the chief officials of the company. In 1857 an uprising, gener- ally known as the Great Mutiny, oc- curred in northern India. It was instigated by the company's Indian soldiers but was abetted by other groups in the population who had spe- cial grievances against the new power, such as rulers who had been dispos- sessed of their lands.

The rebellion was crushed, and the company lost its power to rule. A new administration was created, directly responsible to the British crown.

The new administration directly ruled Bengal, Bombay, Madras, the Punjab, and the United Provinces (modern Uttar Pradesh). Indirect con- trol was exercised over the remaining two-fifths of the territory through 600 Indian princes. Although these rulers had internal autonomy, they had no control over their relations with other states. Overall supervision was exercised by a governor-general through his representatives in the in- dividual states.

The political unity achieved in the 1800s was made possible by a number of factors. The development of mod- ern communications and transporta- tion brought all India under the immediate control of the central gov- ernment through telegraphs, railways, and steamships.

Improved communications also made possible the strategic location of the army. Although smaller than that of previous empires, it had the advantage of modern techniques and the new forms of discipline developed in Eu- rope in the 1700s and 1800s.

Although all army officers were Brit- ish, many enlisted men were Indian. An efficient civil service was also cre- ated for the first time. A uniform legal system introduced Western ideas and methods of jurisprudence. Finally, En- glish was the language used not only in administration but in higher educa- tion. Colleges and universities gave Indians a common means of communi- cation as well as a common knowledge of Western thought.

The Rise of Nationalism. The emer- gence of a nationalist movement in the late 1800s was the direct result of po- litical unification. Educated Indians became aware simultaneously of the Western tradition of political freedom, the dependent state of their own coun- try, and the glory of their own past history. The nationalist movement had its for- mal beginnings in 1885 with the found- ing of the Indian National Congress by Allan Octavian Hume and a small group of Indian intellectuals.

The Congress at first asked only for a measure of representative govern- ment that would allow Indians to share with the British the administra- tion of the country. This moderate demand was rejected by a radical group in the Congress, led by Bal Gangadhar Tilak, who argued that freedom was not something to be given to the Indians but for the Indians to take as their birthright.

The nationalist movement, with its demands for responsible government and a larger degree of independence, was complicated by Hindu-Muslim re- lations. Muslim leaders argued that re- sponsible government based on direct popular representation would mean that Muslims, who constituted 25 per- cent of the population, would be a permanent minority ruled by Hindus. This led to the founding in 1906 of the Muslim League to look after Muslim interests.

The British responded to the de- mands of the nationalists in 1909 through the Morley-Minto Reforms. They allowed the direct election of a number of Indians to provincial legis- latures under a restricted property franchise and gave the Muslims sepa- rate electorates to ensure them ade- quate representation. The Indian National Congress denounced this as an attempt by the British to continue their hold over India by turning one religion against another.

The next response to nationalist demands came in 1919, when a new constitution, known as the Montagu- Chelmsford Reforms, increased the power of the elected representatives in the provinces and widened the fran- chise. Indian political leaders were disappointed with the constitution, for they felt the British had, through the control of finance, kept all the impor- tant sources of power in their own hands.

The Indian National Congress, un- der the leadership of Mohandas K. Gandhi, passed a resolution in 1920 condemning the new system of gov- ernment and began a campaign of non- violent noncooperation. This became the characteristic method of the Con- gress in its struggle against the British from that time on.

Gandhi's great achievement was making the demand for independence a mass movement through the use of terminology and symbols drawn from traditional Indian religion and culture rather than from Western political thought. His chief lieutenant was Jawaharlal Nehru, who appealed to the intellectuals of India as well as to the country's masses.

Gandhi's successful use of tradition- al religious symbols and cu- ltural terms tended to alienate the Muslims, who increasingly argued that when freedom came, provision should be made for the Muslims to control their own destinies. Muhammad Ali Jinnah emerged as the leader of the Muslims.

The Government of India Act of 1935 granted Indians a further mea- sure of responsible government, but it failed to satisfy the nationalists. On the outbreak of World War II in 1939, the Congress leaders who had been elected to major political offices in elections held in 1937 resigned their posts on the grounds that India had been drawn into the war by Britain without their consent. They started a campaign in 1942 demanding that the British quit India at once, and the Con- gress leaders, including Gandhi and Nehru, were jailed for the duration of the war.

In 1945 a new Labor government in Britain entered into negotiations with the leaders of the Congress and the Muslim League. Jinnah insisted that Nehru's demands for British with- drawal and the election of a constitu- ent assembly to decide the future of the country would leave the Muslims without any protection against the Hindu majority.

Jinnah's demand for some form of separate homeland for the Muslims was rejected by the Congress leaders until 1947, when outbreaks of violence between Hindus and Muslims, and growing support for Jinnah from all sections of the Muslim population, con- vinced the Congress that the creation of a separate Muslim state was the only solution to the problem.

Independence. On Aug. 15, 1947 Brit- ish rule ended in India. A Muslim state, Pakistan, was formed from terri- tories in the west and east, with Jin- nah as governor-general and Liaqat Ali Khan as prime minister. The re- mainder of British India became the Dominion of India, and the new state inherited British India's organization and international obligations and rights. Nehru became prime minister and Lord Mountbatten was made gov- ernor-general.

With partition, violence flared along the border, particularly between West Pakistan and the Indian part of Pun- jab, as Hindus fled to India and Mus- lims to Pakistan. Estimates of the number killed in two months of blood- shed are as high as half a million. The two governments finally succeeded in stopping both the riots and killings.

The bitterness of the communal struggle led on Jan. 30, 1948, to the assassination of Gandhi by a member of a Hindu extremist organization. Nehru then became leader of the new India.

Many issues remained, and combined with the memory of violence on both sides and dislike by most Indians of the fact of partition, have strained re- lations between the two countries. These issues include such things as the use of the water of the Indus river system for irrigation, payment of com- pensation for property left behind by refugees, and, above all, disputes over Kashmir.

The Indian states, which had treaty relations with the British crown but were not part of British India, were given the right to join either India or Pakistan in 1947. Most of the states made their decisions on the basis of geographical contiguity, but Kashmir, one of the largest, refused to make a decision. Its ruler, Maharaja Hari Singh, was a Hindu, with a reputation for bad relations with his subjects, most of whom were Muslim.

When the maharaja refused to make any commitment about the state's fu- ture, Muslim tribesmen from the Pakistan side of the border invaded

his territory and moved toward the capital of Srinagar. The maharaja called for Indian help, but the government said they could not take action unless he agreed to join India.

The maharaja agreed to accede to India and the Indian army entered Kashmir. At the end of 1947 India appealed to the United Nations on the grounds that Pakistan had invaded Kashmir. On Jan. 1, 1949, a cease-fire was arranged by the United Nations along the lines occupied by both sides, and general agreement was given for holding the plebiscite to determine the wishes of the people of Kashmir. The plebiscite was not held because of the inability of India and Pakistan to agree on prior conditions.

On Jan. 26, 1950, India adopted a new constitution by which it became a sovereign republic but remained a member of the Commonwealth of Nations. Universal suffrage created an electorate of 176 million, about one-half of whom voted in the first election, which was held in 1952.

In 1952 and in elections in 1957 and 1962, the Indian National Congress won a majority of seats in the national legislature. Jawaharlal Nehru, as head of the Congress party, remained prime minister until his death in 1964.

Contemporary India. Relations with China became of crucial importance in 1959, when the Peking government asserted direct control over Tibet. The Indian government attempted, without success, to get the Chinese to accept the existing Indian-Chinese borders as defined during the era of British rule, and there was an increasing number of incidents along the remote Himalayan frontier.

In October 1962 the Chinese began what the Indians regarded as unprovoked aggression by sending troops into areas of Ladakh and the North-East Frontier Agency, which China claimed had been acknowledged as its territory in the 1800s. Indian troops were forced to withdraw in a number of strategic areas.

Although China refused to negotiate, it withdrew its troops to the approximate positions held before the October movements. India began to expand its defense forces, and accepted military aid from both the Western countries and the Soviet Union.

Relations between Pakistan and India worsened during this period as Pakistan agreed to negotiate a treaty with China in May 1962. The treaty defined a part of the frontier west of the Karakorum Pass held by Pakistan but claimed by India.

A new quarrel broke out in April 1965 over the boundaries between the two in the Rann of Kutch, a desolate territory on the western coast. India insisted that the boundaries established in the early 1900s by the British were binding. Pakistan asserted that they should be redefined since the existence of two independent countries altered the situation. Fighting broke out, but a truce was arranged in June 1965.

At the end of August 1965 fighting again erupted between the two nations, this time along the border between Indian- and Pakistani-controlled Kashmir. The intervention of the UN Security Council brought about a cease fire in September.

In January 1966 Lal Bahadur Shastri, India's prime minister since the death of Nehru in 1964, and Pres. Ayub Khan of Pakistan, at the invitation of Soviet Premier Aleksei Kosygin, went to Tashkent, in the Soviet Union, to settle the Kashmir problem.

The outcome of the conference was the Tashkent Agreement, a pledge taken by both Pakistan and India to move their troops back to positions held before the fighting. Several hours after he signed the agreement, Prime Minister Shastri died.

Indira Gandhi, the daughter of Nehru and an important figure in the Congress party, succeeded Shastri as prime minister. In elections held in February 1967 Mrs. Gandhi's party barely won the majority necessary to keep her in office. The elections revealed that the power of the Congress party, although still the largest party in India, was dwindling. The Communist party, the second ranking party in India, gained a substantial number of seats in parliament.

In May 1967 India reaffirmed its status as a secular state with the election of a Muslim, Zakir Husain, to the presidency. He succeeded Pres. Sarvepalli Radhakrishnan, who had declined to seek another term.

—Ainslie T. Embree; M. G. Inaba

INDONESIA

Official name: Republic of Indonesia
Area: 575,896 square miles (excluding West Irian, 159,376 square miles)
Population: (1966 est.) 107,000,000 (excluding West Irian, 800,000)
Capital: Djakarta (Pop. 1965 est., 3,500,000)
Language: Bahasa Indonesian
Religion: Islam
Currency unit: Rupiah
National holiday: Independence day, August 17

The Republic of Indonesia, a southeast Asian island nation, occupies the Malay Archipelago. It lies between Asia and Australia and separates the Indian Ocean from the Pacific Ocean. The archipelago is separated from the Asian mainland, to the north, by the Strait of Malacca and the South China Sea. In the northeast the Sulu Sea and the Celebes Sea lie between Indonesia and the Philippines. The Pacific Ocean lies to the east. On the south, the Arafura and Timor seas separate Indonesia from Australia. The Indian Ocean is to the southwest of Indonesia.

Indonesia consists of over 3,000 islands and stretches some 3,000 miles from east to west and some 1,500 miles from north to south across the equator.

The islands are divided into three main groups—the Greater Sundas, in the west; the Lesser Sundas, in the south; and the Moluccas, in the east. The Greater Sundas include Indonesia's largest and most important islands—Java, Sumatra, Kalimantan (Borneo), Bali, and Sulawesi (Celebes). The western part of New Guinea, West Irian, is also part of Indonesia. The islands are separated by many seas and straits, some of which, like the Java Sea, are shallow and studded with reefs; but others, like the Banda Sea, are quite deep.

THE LAND. A typical Indonesian island consists of a core of high mountains and hills ringed by coastal plains. The islands are divided into three geologic regions. The largest islands, in the northwestern portion of the archipelago, are outcroppings of the Sunda Shelf, a submerged extension of the continent of Asia. The southeastern islands are part of the Sahul Shelf, the continental shelf of Australia and New Guinea.

Between these two stable geologic regions lies a third region still in formation. It is marked by a semicircular band of some 300 volcanoes, of which 60 are considered active.

Indonesia has an equatorial climate moderated by the influence of the sea. Temperatures are high, but not excessively so, and stable throughout the year, usually ranging between 75°F and 90°F. Rainfall is generally heavy, between 40 and 100 inches a year.

THE PEOPLE. Indonesia is one of the world's most populous nations and in 1966 ranked fifth among the nations in population. Almost two-thirds of the people live on Java, which accounts for only one-tenth of the country's area. Population is extremely dense near Djakarta, the capital. The two next largest Indonesian cities are also on Java—Surabaja, the leading port, and Bandung, a cultural and educational center. Parts of Sumatra and Bali are also heavily populated, but elsewhere population is sparse.

Most Indonesians are Malays, but the population is divided into many ethnic and cultural groups that speak numerous dialects. Approximately 90

percent of Indonesians are Muslim, and most of the rest are Hindu, Christian, and Buddhist. There are Chinese and Arab minorities.

ECONOMY. Although it is extremely rich in natural resources, Indonesia is a poor country, largely as a result of economic mismanagement and political instability. The largest reserves of petroleum in the Far East are in Sumatra, Borneo, Java, and Ceram, and in 1966 Indonesia produced over 23 million metric tons of oil. Indonesia is also a leading world producer of tin, mining nearly 13,000 metric tons in 1966. Tin deposits are found mostly on three small islands—Bangka, Belitung (Billiton), and Singkep. There is also bauxite on Bintan, sulfur and manganese on Java, nickel on Celebes, and low-grade coal in Sumatra, Java, and Borneo. In addition to their rich resources, the islands are covered by valuable forests, which provide teak, sandalwood, bamboo, resins, camphor, and oils.

Most of Indonesia's resources are undeveloped, however, and agriculture is the mainstay of the economy. The equatorial climate permits year-round farming. Agricultural products raised primarily for export include cinchona, rubber, coffee, tea, copra, palm oil, kapok, sisal, tobacco, sugar, cocoa, indigo, and pepper and other spices. The basic food crops include rice, corn, sweet potatoes, peanuts, soybeans, bananas, manioc, and a variety of vegetables.

Mining and food processing are the major industries. Manufacturing is limited largely to handicrafts and the production of some light consumer goods, mostly in factories on Java.

Indonesia's economy traditionally relies heavily on the earnings of exports. In the late 1950s and early 1960s the country's international trade was damaged by its political instability, and although the trade balance remained favorable, the value of exports declined steadily.

In 1966 imports cost $583 million and exports earned $679 million. Rubber, petroleum, tin, copra, tea, coffee, and forest products are the chief exports. Textiles, machinery, foodstuffs, chemicals, and iron and steel are imported. Malaysia, Singapore, the United States, Britain, Japan, West Germany, Mainland China, Australia, and the Soviet Union are the country's major trading partners. Indonesia relies heavily on foreign financial aid.

GOVERNMENT. Although Indonesia's independence constitution of 1950 established a parliamentary form of government, representative institutions functioned effectively for only a brief period in the mid-1950s.

The constitutional system provides for a president as chief of state and vests executive power in a prime minister and cabinet responsible to a popularly elected legislature of one house. For the first few years of independence the president was the dominant figure in the government and he appointed the parliament until 1955, when the first parliamentary elections were held.

Political instability led to the dissolution of the parliament in 1960, and a new governmental system called "Guided Democracy" was introduced. This system was based on a 1945 pre-independence constitution that gave the president great power. The president again appointed members of the parliament, which was made part of a larger body, the People's Consultative Assembly, which was also appointed by the president.

"Guided Democracy" ended in 1966, when a military government took power. The military established a 5-man presidium, or governing council, at the head of a large cabinet and retained the People's Consultative Assembly. In 1967 the congress appointed the leader of the military group as acting president to serve until elections could be held. Indonesia is a member of the United Nations.

HISTORY. Indonesia has been inhabited since prehistoric times, and remains of one of the earliest forms of man have been found on Java. By the 100s BC, Malay people had developed on the islands of the archipelago simple societies based on fishing, agriculture, and seafaring. In the 100s AD Indian peoples began to come to the islands, first as traders and then as settlers. The Malays were strongly influenced by Indian culture. By the 500s and 600s many small Indian-Malayan Buddhist and Hindu kingdoms had been established on the islands, and there developed a variety of cultures and societies. They built up a vigorous trade with nearby island and mainland states, and with India and China.

Early Kingdoms. The first of these kingdoms to achieve significance beyond its own island territory was Srivijaya, on Sumatra. It developed a high Buddhist culture and an advanced civilization, and by the 800s it controlled an empire that included part of the Malay peninsula as well as most of the Indonesian islands.

In the 1100s internal conflicts and threats of attack from the mainland weakened Srivijayan control over the islands, and a new kingdom centered at Majapahit, on Java, gained power. After leading a defense of the islands against an attack by the Mongols in the late 1200s, the Javanese kingdom became the dominant influence in the archipelago.

In the 1300s and 1400s Muslim Arabs began to settle in Indonesia, and by the late 1400s Islamic influence had weakened the older Hindu and Buddhist kingdoms, so that by the early 1500s there was no single powerful state governing Indonesia. In the 1400s and 1500s European traders began visiting the islands, attracted by the fame of the spices, woods, and other goods of the "East Indies" and the "Spice Islands," as Indonesia was called.

European Control. The Portuguese were the first Europeans to establish trading posts in the islands. By the mid-1500s they held military control over most of the islands, and they attempted to convert the islanders to Christianity. The islanders were unable to drive out the conquerors, but they did resist them. Islam spread rapidly through the islands as one weapon against the Europeans.

Portugal held a virtual monopoly of the islands' trade by 1580, when Spain acquired the Portuguese crown. Spain's European rivals, especially England and the Netherlands, redoubled their efforts to break the monopoly after 1580. The Dutch won out with the assistance of Muslim islanders, and they gained a foothold on the islands. In 1602 the Dutch formed the East India Company, and during the 1600s it drove out the Portuguese and other European traders and soon subdued the islanders. The Dutch trading center of Batavia, on western Java, grew into a prosperous center for the rich trade of the islands. The Dutch were joined in the 1700s by Chinese immigrants, whose plantations first developed the islands' agricultural potential and who began investing in the colony's business.

Dutch Rule. In 1798 the Netherlands government took direct control of the colony from the East India company. The company's government had grown corrupt and inefficient, and the Netherlands needed the islands as a naval base during the Napoleonic wars. Moreover, the colony had proved even richer than expected. In the early 1800s the French and the British briefly occupied the Netherlands East Indies, but the Dutch resumed control in 1816.

During the 1800s the Dutch reaped great riches from the colony through a system of state-regulated privately owned plantations. The Europeans' concentration on producing export crops to the exclusion of subsistence crops led to frequent famines and to the misuse and depletion of the islands' resources.

Although the Dutch encouraged and educated some islanders and did not prohibit them from owning their own

PAN AMERICAN AIRWAYS

INDONESIAN RICE TERRACES climb the hillsides to increase the amount of usable farmland.

businesses or farms, the majority of Indonesians were illiterate, poor, and powerless. And although colonial regulations protected native workers from mistreatment, most of them were severely exploited.

In the early 1900s Indonesian nationalist movements grew out of the resentment of colonial inequities. Led by Dutch-educated Indonesian intellectuals, the movements grew rapidly. In 1916 these groups succeeded in obtaining from the Dutch a *Volksraad*, or people's council, in which Indonesians could participate. The council had little authority, however, and did not satisfy the nationalists.

As the nationalists grew stronger and more active in the 1920s and 1930s, they met with repression. Their leaders were jailed and the colony's limited social welfare and educational programs were curtailed.

In 1942, during World War II, Japanese forces invaded Indonesia, quickly crushed the Dutch defenses, and occupied the islands. The Japanese encouraged Indonesian nationalism by allowing the Indonesians to participate in the occupation government. One government leader, Achmed Sukarno, had founded the National Indonesian Party, one of the country's major nationalist organizations.

Indonesian leaders who opposed the Japanese established a government-in-exile in Australia. There they outlined a plan for a gradual postwar separation of Indonesia from the Netherlands.

In 1945, three days after the Japanese surrender, Sukarno and Muhammad Hatta, another nationalist leader, proclaimed the independence of the Republic of Indonesia.

Independence. Several years of political conflict and warfare followed, with Sukarno's government fighting not only the Dutch, who attempted to reestablish their control, but more conservative nationalist groups as well. In 1949 the Netherlands yielded sovereignty over the islands.

An independent federal union was established, loosely united with the Netherlands. Dissatisfaction with this organization led in 1950 to the abolition of the centralized Republic of Indonesia, which included all the islands.

The new country was faced from the start with the problem of unifying a large number of islands with a variety of cultures and no tradition of unity. It tried to solve this problem with a strong central government. Between 1950 and 1955, Sukarno, the nation's first president, held great power, appointing all local officials and all members of parliament.

The country held its first elections in 1955 for both a parliament and a constituent assembly, which was to draft a permanent constitution. Of Indonesia's 29 political parties, the communists emerged from the elections as one of the four strongest, along with two Muslim parties and Sukarno's Nationalist party.

The army objected to the influence of the communists on the government, and in 1958 army officers on Sumatra rebelled, sparking an uprising that spread to Sulawesi and many smaller islands. The rebellions were not quelled until 1961.

Between 1957 and 1959 Dutch property was seized and all Dutch businesses and Dutch citizens were harassed, and all Dutch citizens were ordered out of Indonesia. The resulting economic crisis compounded the problems created by the rebellion and left the government very weak. Moreover, the constituent assembly was unable to agree on plans for a new constitution. In 1959 it was dissolved and a government reorganization was begun.

By 1960 the country was under a system that Sukarno called "Guided Democracy"—a government, parliamentary in form, but with an executive so powerful that popular participation was effectively stifled—but dissension among the islanders did not end. Conflicts with the Dutch also continued, with Indonesia demanding sovereignty over the Netherlands New Guinea colony, called West Irian by the Indonesians. In 1963 the Netherlands agreed to surrender the territory.

Contemporary Indonesia. In 1963 a new, more violent dispute erupted out of the opposition of the Sukarno government to the establishment of the nearby Federation of Malaysia, formed by the union of four former British colonial areas—Malaya, Singapore, Sarawak, and Sabah (North Borneo). A "Crush Malaysia" campaign soon became the prime concern of the Indonesian government. Border fighting was frequent, and in 1965 Indonesia announced its withdrawal from the United Nations after Malaysia was admitted to membership.

Hostility to Malaysia was one aspect of Sukarno's general opposition to all European involvement in southeast Asia. In 1965 Indonesia nationalized all foreign-owned businesses in the country, and although it officially remained neutral in foreign affairs, the government strengthened its ties with Communist China as its opposition to western nations stiffened.

Indonesia's Communist party grew in power, and in October 1965 attempted to seize the government. The coup attempt was crushed by the army, and thousands of Indonesian communists were killed in the aftermath. Many thousands of Indonesia's Chinese residents were murdered or driven from their homes. Some of Sukarno's top aides were convicted of complicity in the communist plot.

The army took control of the government in 1966, and Lieutenant General Suharto became prime minister. Sukarno retained the post of president until March 1967, when the People's Consultative Assembly dismissed him and appointed Suharto acting president until elections could be held.

The military government concentrated on rebuilding the economy, ravaged by years of violence and political upheavals. It reestablished normal relations with western nations and relations with Communist China deteriorated. It established friendly diplomatic relations with Malaysia and resumed Indonesia's membership in the United Nations.

—Thomas E. Ennis; M. G. Inaba

IRAN

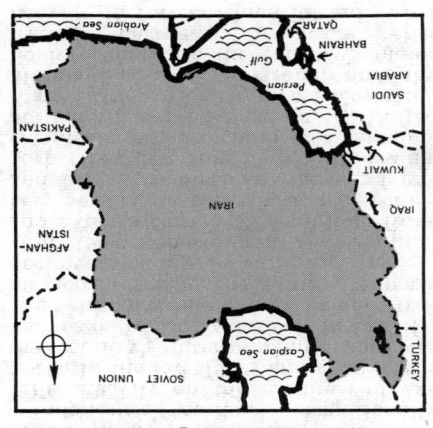

Official name: Empire of Iran
Area: 636,296 square miles
Population: (1966 est.) 25,500,000
Capital: Teheran (Pop. 1963 est., 2,317,000)
Language: Persian
Religion: Islam
Currency unit: Rial
National holiday: Birthday of the shah, October 26

Iran, an oil-rich nation in the Middle East, is bounded on the north by the Soviet Union, on the east by Afghanistan and Pakistan, on the west by Iraq and Turkey, and on the south by the Gulf of Oman and the Persian Gulf.

THE LAND. Central Iran lies on a great plateau which has an average elevation of 4,000 feet above sea level. It contains two barren, salty deserts—the Dasht-i-Kavir and the Dasht-i-Lut. West and south of the plateau are the rugged Zagros Mountains, and to the north the Elburz range rises to over 18,000 feet above sea level. Narrow, fertile lowlands skirt the country's seacoasts.

Iran's climate varies from region to region. Rainfall averages only 12 inches a year for the country as a whole, but the plateau receives less than 5 inches and the mountains and northern coasts may receive as much as 40 inches annually. In the central deserts summer temperatures rise above 115°F., but the mountain areas are cooler both in summer and in winter.

THE PEOPLE. Population is concentrated on the lower mountain slopes and in the coastal regions. Ancient Iran was settled by tribes that migrated into the region from Europe. The country's population also includes Arabs, Jews, Armenians, and nomadic Kurds, Baluchi, Turkoman, and Bakhtiari.

ECONOMY. The wealth of Iran is derived from oil, but farming and herding are the occupations of most Iranians. The bulk of the cultivated land is in the moist northwest, where wheat and barley are the leading crops. Corn, rice, sugar beets, tea, tobacco, and fruits are also raised. Cotton thrives on the edges of the plateau, and goats, sheep, and camels are grazed in semi-desert areas. Fishing prospers on the Caspian coast.

Industry increased in economic importance in the 1950s and 1960s. Most of Iran's industries process agricul-

...tural products, producing cotton and wool textiles, dried fruits, cigarettes, vegetable oils, and leather. Carpet weaving is an ancient craft that is still important.

Revenues from oil production and refining constitute the largest single portion of Iran's national income. A government-owned company and several international companies pump the oil. In 1966 production totaled more than 100 million metric tons.

GOVERNMENT. Iran is a constitutional monarchy, with a shah, or king, as hereditary head of state. A prime minister appointed by the shah acts as chief executive, and with his cabinet is responsible to the lower house of parliament.

Members of the Majles, or National Assembly, the lower and more powerful house of parliament, are popularly elected to a normal term of four years. The upper house is the Senate, one-half of which is elected and one-half appointed by the shah to a two-year term. Although the shah is subject to the will of parliament, he does have constitutional authority to dissolve parliament and assume absolute control of the country in times of emergency.

Iran is a member of the United Nations and of the Central Treaty Organization (CENTO).

HISTORY. The modern history of the Middle East began in Iran in 1908, when the region's first oil was found there. In ancient times, too, Iran—or Persia—was important as the core of the great Persian Empire, which ruled the entire Near East in the 500s and 400s BC. Alexander the Great conquered the empire in the 300s BC, and his successors were defeated by Parthians in the 200s BC. It was not until the 200s AD that Persians regained control of their land, under the Sassanian dynasty.

Sassanids ruled until 641, when they were overthrown by Arab armies that converted the Persians to Islam. Seljuk Turks replaced the Arabs as rulers in the 1000s, and they in turn were overthrown by the Mongols in the 1200s. When the Mongol empire disintegrated in the 1500s, Persians united the country.

Under Nadir Shah, who ruled in the 1700s, the Persians drove out invading Afghans and went on to conquer Afghanistan and part of India. Civil war followed Nadir Shah's death in 1747 and caused the loss of all the newly conquered territory. The Qajar faction emerged dominant from the civil wars and founded a dynasty that ruled until the 1920s.

Although Persia remained sovereign during the 1800s and early 1900s, it was subject to the competing economic and political influences of Russia and Britain. In 1905 a rebellion broke out among Persians who objected to the weak shah's dependence on these foreign states, and in 1906 the shah yielded to the rebel's demands for a constitution and an elected assembly.

Riza Shah. Foreign interference increased after the discovery of oil in 1908, and in 1921 Riza Pahlavi, an army officer, led a coup that drove the pro-British shah into exile. In 1923 Pahlavi became prime minister, and in 1925 the Majles proclaimed him shah.

Riza Shah began the modernization of Persia. During his reign, communications, education, and industry were expanded and the judiciary, military, and all of society began to be reordered on a western pattern. Britain retained its influence only as operator of the Iranian oil fields.

During World War II Iran declared itself neutral, but Britain and Russia occupied the country. In 1941 the Allies forced Riza Shah to yield the throne to his son, Muhammad Riza.

Contemporary Iran. After the war a strong Iranian nationalist movement developed, with the ending of foreign control as its primary goal. Muhammad Mossadegh, a leader of the nationalists, became prime minister in 1951 and ruled as a dictator. During Mossadegh's ministry the British-owned oil fields were nationalized. Iran was unable to market the oil without foreign help, however, and the country faced financial ruin. In 1953 the shah removed Mossadegh from office and had him arrested. Oil production began again in 1954 under the direction of British, U.S., French, and Dutch companies that shared the profits with Iran. Oil revenues were spent on programs of social and economic reform, and during the 1950s and 1960s the pace of industrialization and modernization was speeded. By 1967 Iran was able to end U.S. economic aid programs, although U.S. military assistance continued. In 1967 Iran climaxed a two-year celebration of its 2,500 years as a nation with the official coronation of Muhammad Riza.

—Sergio Barzanti; Alexander Melamid

IRAQ

Official name: Republic of Iraq
Area: 173,258 square miles
Population: (1966 est.) 8,338,000
Capital: Baghdad (Pop., 1965, 1,745,328)
Language: Arabic
Religion: Islam
Currency unit: dinar
National holiday: Anniversary of the revolution and the establishment of the republic, July 14

Iraq, an Arab republic in the Middle East, lies in the valleys of the Tigris and Euphrates rivers. It is bordered on the north by Turkey, on the east by Iran, on the south by Kuwait, Saudi Arabia, and a neutral zone jointly administered with Saudi Arabia, and on the west by Syria and Jordan.

THE LAND. The high Zagros Mountains rim Iraq on the north and east. The western and southwestern regions are desert. Central Iraq consists of a "lower plain," in the southern part of the Tigris-Euphrates valley, and an "upper plain," a rolling, hilly region in the northeast of the country. About 5 inches of rain falls yearly on the lower plain, and the upper plain receives about 15 inches of rain a year. The rest of the country is quite dry. Summer temperatures in Iraq's desert areas often climb above 120°F, but averages for the country as a whole range from about 50°F in winter to 95°F in summer.

THE PEOPLE. The population is concentrated in the river valleys. Most Iraqis are Arab, but the population also includes a large Kurdish minority in the northeast. Bedouin tribes live in the southwest.

ECONOMY. Iraq's economy is based on oil production and agriculture. Oil is the most valuable resource, and almost no other minerals are mined. The country's rivers provide water for irrigation. Farmers in the fertile central plain grow barley, wheat, rice, tobacco, cotton, and dates. Sheep are raised on the upper plain and on the fringes

Map labels: TURKEY • U.S.S.R. • Caspian Sea • SYRIA • LEBANON • ISRAEL • Mediterranean Sea • JORDAN • U.A.R. • IRAQ • IRAN • SAUDI ARABIA • KUWAIT • Persian Gulf

PAN AMERICAN AIRWAYS

ISFAHAN, IRAN, is famed for its royal mosque, built by Shah Abbas I in the 1500s.

Other great empires—Babylonia, Assyria, and Persia—followed Sumer in the "fertile crescent" between the Tigris and the Euphrates rivers.

In 750 AD, Arab Muslims conquered the region and converted the people to Islam. Arab rule continued until 1258, when Mongol armies devastated the country. Iraq made little recovery under the Ottoman Turks, who took power in 1638 and ruled the area until World War I.

After the war Britain received a League of Nations mandate over Iraq. In 1921 Iraqis chose as king Emir Faisal of the Arabian province of Hejaz, and in 1924 the country was proclaimed a constitutional monarchy. **Independence.** In 1932 the League of Nations recognized Iraq's sovereignty by admitting it as a full member. Faisal died in 1933 and was succeeded by his son Ghazi, who reigned until his death in 1939. Ghazi's young son and heir, Faisal II, was a minor, and a regent ruled in his name.

Iraq's modern history has been turbulent. In the 1930s minority groups rebelled against the new government, and nationalists fought against the presence of British personnel and troops. During 1941 a pro-Nazi group briefly controlled the government, but it was overthrown, and Iraq supported the Allies in World War II.

Faisal II came of age in 1953, but in 1958 army officers led by Gen. Abdel Karim Qasim overthrew the government, assassinated King Faisal, and proclaimed Iraq a republic. Qasim became premier, but was killed in February 1963 during another coup, in which Abdel Salaam Arif took power.

Contemporary Iraq. After the unsuccessful attempt to form a federation with the United Arab Republic (U.A.R.) and Syria, Arif in November 1963 split with the pan-Arab leaders in power in the U.A.R. and Syria. In the following year a new constitution took effect that favored a close alliance, but not a merger, with the U.A.R.

Arif died in an accident in 1966, and his brother, Abdel Rahman Arif, became president. Several attempted coups in 1965 and 1966 resulted in a series of governmental reorganizations, but the army remained in control.

A major domestic problem between 1961 and 1966 was a rebellion among the Kurds, who wanted to establish an independent Kurdish state. A 1966 settlement granted the Kurds self-government within their own region.

Abroad, Iraq participated in the 1948-1949 and 1967 Arab wars against Israel, and the republic tended to follow the policy of the U.A.R. in international affairs.

Iraq made gradual social progress in the 1950s and 1960s. Oil revenues financed the expansion of educational and health services, the improvement of communications and transportation facilities, and agricultural reforms. The country as a whole, however, did not undergo a swift modernization or radical westernization, and most Iraqis continued to live according to ancient customs.

—Sergio Barzanti; Alexander Melamid

GOVERNMENT. A provisional constitution adopted in 1964 provided for a president as head of state and a premier, or prime minister, appointed by the president as chief executive. The constitution also provided for a popularly elected legislature.

HISTORY. Modern Iraq is the site of ancient Mesopotamia, "the land between the rivers," where the oldest known civilization—that of the Sumerians—flourished in about 3000 BC.

of the desert. Large-scale irrigation and flood control programs were undertaken in the 1950s and 1960s to create more usable farm land.

Oil production began in 1927 and by the mid-1960s remained Iraq's only major industry. Over 68 million metric tons of oil were pumped in 1966. The richest fields are at Kirkuk, Mosul, and Basra. The government owns one oil company, but the largest firms are internationally owned and pay royalty fees to Iraq. Iraq's other industries are mostly small in scale, producing building materials, textiles, carpets, cigarettes, dried fruits, and leather goods.

The country's chief export is oil, which accounted for all but a small portion of the $882 million earned by exports in 1965. Barley, dates, wool, and cotton are also exported. Imports, which cost $450 million in 1965, include foodstuffs, machinery, iron, and steel.

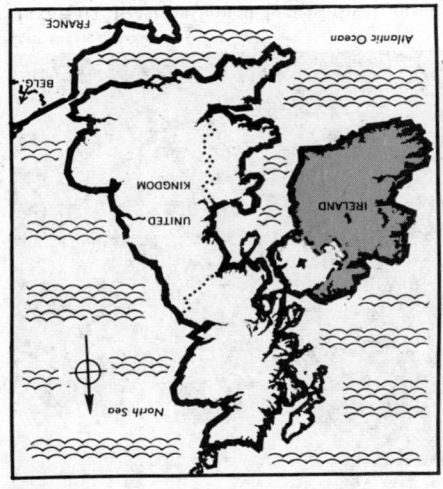

BAGHDAD, IRAQ, has many large mosques.

UNITED NATIONS

IRELAND

Official name: Republic of Ireland (Irish Republic)
Area: 27,135 square miles
Population: (1966 est.) 2,884,000
Capital: Dublin (Pop. 1966, urban area, 647,-336)
Language: Irish, English
Religion: Roman Catholicism
Currency unit: Pound
National holiday: St. Patrick's Day, March 17

The Republic of Ireland, or Eire, is an independent country that occupies the southwestern five-sixths of the island of Ireland, one of the two main British Isles. The northeastern sixth of the island makes up Northern Ireland, which is part of the United Kingdom. The North Atlantic lies to the west and south, and the Irish Sea to the east, separating Ireland from Britain.

THE LAND. Ireland is an old, low, glaciated plateau with few elevations above 2,000 feet. There is a central plain, opening more widely on the east, fringed by higher and more rugged land, especially in the north and southwest. Drainage is a problem, and much of Ireland is covered by odd-shaped lakes, marshes, and peat bogs.

The combination of damp, acid soils, a very damp climate, and uncertain drainage has restricted forest growth and greatly limited the variety of agriculture. More than a third of Ireland is classified as moor and heath, although there are sizable tracts of excellent grassland suitable for raising livestock.

The climate is dominated by maritime influences. Winters are mild, and summers are quite cool. The humidity is high, rain is abundant and frequent, and it is often cloudy or foggy. Dublin has a temperature range of only 20°F, with August averaging 62°F and January 42°F.

THE PEOPLE. The Irish people are culturally quite homogeneous. Irish, a Celtic Indo-European language related to Gaelic, is the official first language and is spoken in the southern and western coastal regions of Cork, Kerry, Mayo, and Donegal. English, however, is universally spoken, and official documents are printed in English and Irish. About 94 percent of the population is Roman Catholic. Most of the remainder is Anglican or Protestant.

Ireland's population declined steadily from the late 1840s until the 1960s. In the 1840s potato diseases began to attack the country's principal crop, and famine precipitated a flood of emigrants to North America and other areas. A high rate of celibacy and a low birth rate contributed to the decline in population, a trend reversed only in the 1960s.

Dublin, the capital, is by far the largest city, and one-fifth of the entire population of Eire resides in the Dublin area.

ECONOMY. Ireland is predominantly agricultural. In the mid-1960s farmers constituted more than one-third of

the labor force and agricultural products made up more than half of the total value of exports. Most farms are small, less than 30 acres in size.

The economies of the industrial, agriculturally deficient British and the nearby, largely agricultural Irish have become highly complementary, and the Irish economy has been geared toward meat and dairy exports to Britain. Recent developments, however, are changing this. The Irish are emphasizing raising wheat and sugar beets in an attempt to reduce imports, and the country is making an intensive effort to industrialize.

Ireland's exports in 1966 were valued at $680 million, and its imports at $1,044 million. Tourism and the remittances of Irish abroad help to fill the gap. Exports consist chiefly of agricultural products. Major exports include livestock, meat, dairy products, eggs, beer, stout, and Irish whiskey. The principal imports are machinery, electrical goods, textiles, coal, vehicles, grain, mineral oils, and fats.

Ireland's leading trading partner is Britain, which in 1965 received about 70 percent of exports and provided about 50 percent of imports. Ireland also exports to the Benelux countries and West Germany and imports from the United States, West Germany, France, and the Netherlands.

GOVERNMENT. Ireland is a republic. The head of state is the president, who is elected to a term of seven years. Executive powers are wielded by a prime minister, who is usually the leader of the majority party in the House of Representatives. He is appointed to a five-year term by the president, on the recommendation of the House of Representatives.

Legislative power is vested in the Parliament, which includes the House of Representatives, elected on the basis of proportional representation, and the Senate, which is partly elected and partly appointed by the prime minister.

HISTORY. In the 300s BC, the Celts crossed from Europe to Ireland and easily defeated the indigenous population. The Celts divided the country into a number of small kingdoms. Ireland lived in isolation until the 400s AD, when St. Patrick landed on the island to spread Christianity among the generally pagan populace. Christianity quickly took hold, and a brilliant scholarly tradition was begun at newly founded monasteries, which became widely known centers of learning and culture.

In the 800s the island was invaded by the Northmen, or Vikings, who raided the land periodically. They were not defeated until 1014, when a great Irish king, Brian Boru, routed them at Clontarf, near Dublin.

In 1167, King Henry II of England invaded Ireland upon the invitation of a deposed Irish king, Dermot MacMurrough. The Irish were defeated, and in 1171 Henry established his personal rule over the country.

English Rule. In time, England relaxed its attention was almost totally given to the Hundred Years' War (1338-1453) with France and to the internal Wars of the Roses (1455-1485). A considerable degree of autonomy had gradually been obtained by the local aristocracy, and the era is known as the period of "aristocratic home rule." Direct English control was actually reduced to an area around Dublin known as the Pale.

It was not until 1494, under the first of the Tudors, Henry VII, that English power was reestablished throughout the island. During the Tudor dynasty, the major issues that were to poison relations between the two countries—religion, land ownership, and home rule—began to arise. Henry VIII broke with the papacy in 1534 and attempted to eradicate Roman Catholicism from Ireland.

Mary I, Henry's daughter, tried to force the assimilation of the Irish by confiscating the lands of the Irish lords who refused to conform and distributing them to English settlers. Elizabeth I continued this system,

IRISH TOURIST OFFICE

ASHFORD CASTLE, in County Mayo, stands on the northeastern shore of Lough Corrib.

which came to be known as "plantation," and excluded the Irish from any significant role in the administration. A great rebellion—known as the "Tyrone Wars"—finally broke out in Ulster. As its leaders became two of the most celebrated Irish heroes—Hugh O'Neill, earl of Tyrone, and Hugh O'Donnell. After a series of victories, they were finally defeated in 1601 by the English at Kinsale.

Under England's Stuart king, James I, Scottish settlers were given lands in Ulster. As a result, a new rebellion started in 1641, when the Ulstermen massacred many of the usurpers of their lands. Terrible revenge was taken in 1649 by England's Puritan dictator, Oliver Cromwell. The population of the town of Drogheda in eastern Ireland was slaughtered, and most of the land still remaining in Irish hands was confiscated.

Conditions were better under Charles II, and they improved greatly under James II, who was a Roman Catholic. The Glorious Revolution of 1688, however, soon removed him from the throne, and he was finally defeated on Irish soil at the battle of the Boyne in 1690.

Eventually the Penal Laws—a series of laws first formulated under James I that sought to reduce the power of the Irish—were made more stringent, and economic measures ruinous to the Irish nation were enacted. Tension mounted steadily.

It was only in 1798, however, that a major revolution, led by Wolfe Tone, was attempted. The effort failed, and England then deprived Ireland of its own parliament. In 1800 Ireland was united to England and allowed representation in the English Parliament.

The Period of Union. A great disaster, the "potato famine," struck the island in 1845, causing about 1 million deaths in a few years. A massive emigration then began, directed chiefly to the United States.

Emigrants living in the United States founded the Fenian Society to continue the struggle against Britain. In 1873 the Home Rule League was formed in Ireland. Its outstanding figure was Charles Stewart Parnell, a brilliant and extremely popular leader.

Later, a more active movement, the Sinn Féin, came to the fore. On Easter Monday, 1916, in the middle of World War I, several hundred of its members rose in Dublin, but the rebellion was put down by British troops. In the following years, another organization, the IRA (Irish Republican Army) harassed the British.

Free State and Republic. After the war, the Sinn Féin triumphed in elections held in 1918, winning most of the Irish seats in the British Parliament. These candidates refused to go to England, however, and instead set up their own parliament in Dublin, declaring Ireland an independent republic.

A period of political upheaval followed, during which the British tried to maintain order by pouring troops into the country. But in 1922 Britain recognized the Irish Free State and granted it dominion status. The six counties of Ulster, predominantly northern, Protestant, chose to remain part of the United Kingdom. The new situation provoked profound and violent dissension among the Irish.

Under Prime Minister (later president) Eamon de Valera, a new constitution was promulgated in 1937, whereby the sovereign country of Ireland, or Eire, was proclaimed. In 1948 the last ties with the British Commonwealth were cut and Ireland proclaimed itself a republic on Apr. 18, 1949. Eamon de Valera again became prime minister in 1951, as a result of the republic's first general elections. Ireland became a member of the United Nations in 1955.

De Valera lost to John A. Costello in 1954, but became prime minister again in 1957. In 1959 he resigned to become president, and Sean Lemass was appointed prime minister. Lemass was re-appointed in 1961 and 1965. De Valera was reelected president in 1966, but Lemass retired in favor of Finance Minister Jack Lynch.

—Sergio Barzanti

ISRAEL

Official name: State of Israel
Area: 7,992 square miles
Population: (1967 est.) 2,669,000
Capital: Jerusalem (Pop., 1965 est., 191,700)
Currency unit: Pound
Religion: Judaism, Christianity, Islam
Language: Hebrew and Arabic
National holiday: Independence day, May 15

Israel, a republic established in 1948 in the land of ancient Palestine, lies on the eastern coast of the Mediterranean Sea. A bitter war between Israel and the Arab states of the Middle East accompanied the proclamation of the State of Israel in 1948. The boundaries set in 1948–1949 by truce agreements left the new state bordered on the north by Lebanon, on the east by Syria and Jordan, on the south by the Gulf of Aqaba, on the southwest by the Sinai region of the United Arab Republic (U.A.R.), and on the west by the Mediterranean Sea and the Gaza Strip, a small area once part of Palestine under U.A.R. administration.

Israel's 1948–1949 boundaries were disputed by the Arab states and defended by Israel until 1967, when a new Arab-Israeli war erupted. In the 1967 campaign Israeli forces occupied the Gaza Strip and the Sinai Peninsula and that part of Jordan lying west of the Jordan River, including all of the ancient city of Jerusalem, which had been divided between Israel and Jordan.

THE LAND. Israel is a small, irregularly shaped country with a varied landscape. A narrow, fertile plain borders the Mediterranean. In central Israel, the hilly Judaean plateau rises east of the coastal plain. In the north rise the highlands of Galilee, a region of rolling hills and rich valleys. Near Israel's eastern border the land drops sharply into the valley of the Jordan River. The wedge-shaped, barren Negev desert, in the south, occupies more than half of Israel's land area. The Jordan, Israel's principal river, flows along the northeastern border into Israel's largest freshwater lake,

the Sea of Galilee, and on into the Dead Sea. Smaller streams thread the northern and central portions of the country, but only dry river beds are found in the southern regions.

The southern desert receives almost no rain, but rainfall in the northern and central areas averages 20 inches a year, most of it falling during the winter and spring. In the desert, average summer daytime temperatures average 65°F. Temperatures climb to about 100°F and winter temperatures average 80°F in summer and 45°F in winter along the coast and in the hills

THE PEOPLE. Between 1948, when Israel became a state, and 1966 more than 1 million Jews poured into this new land. In 1948 Israel's population of about 1.5 million included only about 655,000 Jews, who were living largely as pioneers. By 1966 the total had reached more than 2.6 million, of which over 2.3 million were Jews. The remainder consists mostly of Christian and Muslim Arabs. During and after the 1948–1949 Arab-Israeli war, most Arabs fled Israel and took refuge in neighboring Arab states.

Population is concentrated in the more fertile and temperate northern and central regions of Israel. The two largest cities, Haifa and Tel Aviv-Jaffa, are on the coast. Jerusalem, the capital, lies in the center of the Judaean Hills.

ECONOMY. The people of Israel have worked hard to meet the challenge of a harsh land. In an area that a few decades ago had only a subsistence agriculture, Israelis have developed manufacturing industries and have increased agricultural production to feed an expanding population and to export produce.

Israel's desert lands hold a great variety of mineral resources. Potash and salts are obtained from the Dead Sea, and stone is quarried in the southern Negev, and copper is mined in the center of the country. Israel has some oil and natural gas, but not enough to meet its needs.

Agriculture. Although agriculture occupies only one-sixth of the population, the land is intensively cultivated. In areas that once were swamps or deserts, farmers use every available piece of land and every drop of water to raise their crops. About one-third of the cultivated land is irrigated. Citrus fruit, grown on the coastal plain, is the most important farm product and is one of Israel's principal exports. Grains, tobacco, grapes, olives, and other fruits are grown in Galilee. Farmers on the fringes of the Negev raise cotton and dates. Nomadic herdsmen graze goats and sheep in the Negev, and dairy farming prospers in the north and on the plain.

Industry. Manufacturing contributes 25 percent of Israel's income. The refining of domestic oil and of crude oil shipped to Haifa is the country's most important heavy industry. Others include chemical production, metal processing, and machinery manufacturing. Israelis work in many light industries, including diamond polishing, textile weaving, glass making, food processing, and wine making.

Many industries and farms are operated as cooperatives or collectives. Most of Israel's factory, farm, and office workers belong to Histadrut, the leading national labor union, which provides a wide variety of social and economic services.

Trade. Israel exports fruit, machinery, textiles, chemicals, and building materials. The value of these exports in 1966 was over $475 million. The country imported over $810 million worth of raw materials, food, machinery, and other goods in 1966.

Most of Israel's trade is with the United States and western European countries. Grants and loans from the United States, reparations payments from West Germany, technical aid from the United Nations, and contributions from private groups and individuals around the world help to support the Israeli economy.

GOVERNMENT. Israel is a parliamentary democracy. The chief of state is a president, who is elected every five years by the parliament, or knesset. With the advice of the knesset, the president appoints a prime minister to act as chief executive. The prime minister and the cabinet he chooses are responsible to the parliament.

Members of the knesset, which has one house, are popularly elected to a normal term of four years. Participation in government is open to all Israeli citizens, including non-Jews. Israel is a member of the United Nations.

HISTORY. Although the state of Israel is new, the land is ancient. In about 2000 BC wandering tribes of Hebrews appeared in "Canaan," later called Palestine. Perhaps 500 years later a group of Hebrews was conquered and enslaved by the Egyptians. After 1200 BC Hebrews once again inhabited Palestine and developed a society based on herding and agriculture. Over the next 1,000 years there developed the Hebrew culture and religion that produced the Hebrew bible, the Old Testament; gave root to Christianity; and contributed its part to the foundation of Western civilization.

Despite the strength and importance of their culture, the Jews were never powerful militarily or politically. In the 900s BC the Hebrew kingdom split in two—the kingdom of Israel in the north and the kingdom of Judah (the source of the word Jew) in the south. By 586 BC both kingdoms had been conquered and most Jews were in exile in Babylonia. Fifty years later Babylon fell and the Jews were permitted to return to Palestine.

Those who returned settled in southern Palestine and rebuilt Jerusalem. They were free from foreign domination only briefly, however. Palestine became in turn a province of Persia (538–332 BC), of Alexander (332–323 BC), of Egypt (323–198 BC), and of the Syrian Seleucid dynasty (198–168 BC).

The Jews were able to maintain their own society and culture, however, and it was during the period

after the Babylonian captivity that the Hebrew bible was compiled from earlier and contemporary writings.

In 168 BC the Jews successfully rebelled against the Seleucids, only to be subjugated in 63 BC by the Romans. In 70 AD the Jews tried to throw off Roman rule, but they were crushed and their capital city, Jerusalem, was destroyed.

The Diaspora. Many Jews left Palestine and scattered throughout the world in what was called the *diaspora*, or the dispersion. Palestine remained in the hands of the Romans and their successors, the Byzantines, until the 600s. Then, the armies of a new religion, Islam, made Palestine part of a vast Arab empire.

Four hundred years later, the Seljuk Turks conquered Palestine but were soon challenged by the Christian Crusaders, who penetrated the country. Finally, Egypt drove out the crusaders and held Palestine until it became a part of the Ottoman Turkish empire in the 1500s. Palestine remained Turkish until the end of World War I.

Many of the dispersed Jews had never been completely accepted into the societies in which they had settled. Often they were victims of prejudice and persecution, but they maintained their religion, their culture, and the hope that they would one day return to Palestine, or "Zion."

Zionism. During the 1800s a Zionist, or nationalist, movement arose, and small groups of Jews returned to Palestine as pioneers. The first Zionist Congress was held in 1897 at Basel, Switzerland, under the leadership of Theodore Herzl, an Austrian Jew.

The congress greatly strengthened the efforts of the early idealistic pioneers and formulated the Basel Program, which called for the settlement of Jews in Palestine and the creation of a homeland there for the Jewish people. Zionism as an international, mass movement included both religious idealists and political nationalists, and it won the support of many non-Jews.

The Zionists tried to persuade Turkey to allow mass settlement of Jews in Palestine, but the request was refused. In 1917, during World War I, Britain's foreign secretary, Arthur Balfour, publicly announced Britain's support for the Zionist program. This "Balfour Declaration" pledged to facilitate "the establishment in Palestine of a national home for the Jewish people" without injuring the non-Jewish population already there.

British Mandate. The Zionists were well organized. They established organizations to encourage immigration, handle finances, set up political structures, and plan agricultural and industrial development. The Jewish community developed alongside the traditional Arab society, but Jewish immigration and land purchases and the pioneer spirit of the Jews encountered Arab resistance.

The British sought to appease the Arabs by restricting Jewish activity. Finally, in 1939-1940, they drastically limited Jewish immigration and land purchases to keep Jews a minority in Palestine. The Arabs were not satisfied, however.

During World War II the Palestinian Arab leader, the Mufti of Jerusalem, cooperated with the Germans. The Jews supported the British in the war, and a Jewish brigade fought in the Middle East and in Europe. Jews did defy the British effort to close Palestine to refugees from Nazi countries, and many Jews entered Palestine despite British opposition.

Opinion in the non-Arab world began to turn against Britain. By the end of the war the deadlock over Palestine was complete. Britain, unable to find a solution satisfactory to all sides, submitted the dilemma to the United Nations in February 1947.

Statehood. In November 1947 the UN voted to terminate the British mandate and to partition Palestine into an Arab state, a Jewish state, and a multinational enclave in Jerusalem. The British left Palestine by May 15, 1948, and an Israeli government immediately took power, and was soon recognized by most non-Arab states.

Desultory fighting had broken out in Palestine immediately after the UN partition resolution, and on the heels of the British withdrawal the Arab states of the Middle East, united in the Arab League, invaded Israel. The Israelis drove the invaders out, and in 1949 the UN negotiated separate armistice agreements between Israel and the Arab states. But no final peace treaty was signed, and a formal state of war continued.

The Arabs refused to recognize Israel and employed tactics of encirclement, noncommunication, economic boycott, and border harassment. Several times this tension hardened into widespread conflict. When Egypt began a military buildup on Israel's frontier in 1956, Israel invaded Egyptian territory. The Israelis were defeating Arab forces when the UN forced them to withdraw.

The Suez Canal had been closed to Israeli shipping and remained closed. In 1967 the United Arab Republic announced the blockade of the Gulf of Aqaba, Israel's only outlet to the south, and other Arab states threatened Israel's borders. Fighting broke out, and Israel quickly routed the Arab armies.

Israel opened the Gulf of Aqaba, encamped on the east bank of the Suez Canal, and occupied Jordan's part of Jerusalem and the land west of the Jordan River, as well as the Syrian heights, which had dominated Israel's northern border. The UN again arranged a ceasefire, but was still unable to achieve a permanent solution to the conflict between the Arab states and Israel.
—Oscar Janowsky; Alexander Melamid

ITALY

Official name: Italian Republic
Area: 116,304 square miles
Population: (1966 est.) 51,962,000
Capital: Rome (Pop, 1965 est.) 2,484,737)
Language: Italian
Religion: Roman Catholicism
Currency unit: Lira
National holiday: Anniversary of the republic, June 2

Italy, a republic in southern Europe, is bounded on the north by Switzerland and Austria; on the east by Yugoslavia and the Adriatic and Ionian seas; on the south by the Mediterranean Sea; on the southwest by the Tyrrhenian Sea; and on the north-west by the Ligurian Sea and France. The country is a boot-shaped peninsula measuring about 750 miles in length and averaging about 125 miles in width. Its territory includes two large islands—Sicily, lying just off the toe of the boot, and Sardinia, lying 130 miles off the southwest coast—as well as a number of smaller islands. Of these the most important are Elba, Capri, Ischia, Capraia, Gignlio, and the Lipari Islands. Although Italy was not politically unified until 1870, it has since been Roman

ISRAEL'S HEBREW UNIVERSITY is situated in Jerusalem, the nation's capital.
W. BRAUN

times made important contributions to the cultural and intellectual life of Europe.

THE LAND. Much of Italy is hilly or mountainous, and the amount of land suitable for agriculture is limited. The Alps run along the entire northern border. In the northeast they curve south to form the Apennines, which extend down through the peninsula into the toe of the boot and across to Sicily. The only sizable plain is the valley of the Po River, in the north, although there are coastal plains and numerous interior basins. Italy's major rivers are the Po, the Adige, the Arno, and the Tiber. Many shorter streams originate in the Apennines and flow toward the Adriatic or Tyrrhenian coasts.

Italy's climate is varied. The north has a continental climate, with warm summers and cold winters, which are often accompanied by heavy snowfall in the more mountainous regions. Southern Italy has a typically Mediterranean climate, with hot, dry summers and mild, rainy winters.

Rainfall varies, generally decreasing toward the southeast. The north averages over 30 inches a year, but parts of Apulia, at the heel of the boot, receive less than 15 inches.

THE PEOPLE. The country is densely settled. Overpopulation has long plagued Italy and has led to a heavy outflow of Italians to the rest of Europe and to many other parts of the world. The Italian birthrate is no longer one of the highest in Europe, and the rate of population increase, counting emigration, is less than 1 percent a year. This modest rate of increase is manageable for the present-day Italian economy.

Italian is the nearly universal language. There are a few small linguistic minority groups, the largest being the German-speaking population of the South Tyrol, in the north along the Austrian border. More than 99 percent of the people are at least nominally Roman Catholic.

Italy is traditionally urban, and over half of the population lives in cities and towns. According to 1964 estimates four cities—Rome, Milan, Turin, and Naples—had more than 1 million inhabitants and 30 other Italian cities had populations of more than 100,000.

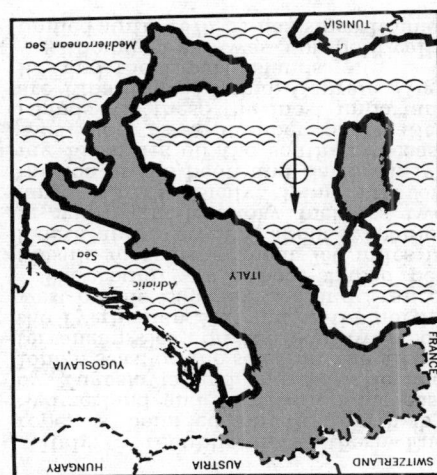

Natural Resources. Italy is poor in natural resources. Sulfur and mercury are mined in quantity and large amounts of limestone and marble are quarried. Aside from these, and modest deposits of coal, petroleum, and natural gas, there are no major minerals. The shortage of fuels has led Italy to tap the large water power resources of the Alpine zone, and in 1964 the country led Western Europe in installed hydroelectric capacity.

Agriculture. Agriculture employs about one-fourth of the labor force, although increasing numbers of farm workers are being absorbed by industry. In recent years production has improved with land consolidation, increased mechanization, and improved agricultural methods.

The Po Valley, which has an extensive irrigation system, raises all the nation's rice, most of its wheat, and three-fourths of its corn. Yields per acre compare favorably with those of northwestern Europe and rank among the world's highest. The region also supports large numbers of cattle and produces substantial quantities of wine.

Southern Italy grows a variety of vegetables, fruit, and nuts. Among the most important of these are olives, peas, beans, grapes, citrus fruits, and almonds. Livestock is also raised in the south, but sheep and goats are more numerous than cattle.

ECONOMY. Before the mid-1950s, the Italian economy was largely dependent on agriculture and tourism. Although both are still important, their relative weight in the economy has declined in the wake of industrial expansion in the mid-1950s and early 1960s. A rapid growth of industry accompanied Italy's participation in the European Economic Community, and the gross domestic product almost tripled between 1953 and 1965.

An important factor in the Italian economy is the tremendous difference in the standard of living between the north and south. The north is highly industrialized and has the country's most fertile farmland, which is the most intensively cultivated in southern Europe. The south is heavily populated and suffers chronically from high unemployment. It is much poorer and far less developed, having little industry and small, inefficient farms. In 1950 the government established the Fund for the South, an ambitious program for land reclamation and industrial development. In 1967 the government initiated a five-year program for economic development that included a $524 million yearly allotment for the industrialization of the south.

Industry. The government plays an important role in Italian industry. Three state-owned holding companies—the Industrial Reconstruction Institute, the National Hydrocarbons Agency, and the National Power Authority—control a major part of the country's industrial capital. Government holdings are heavily concentrated in iron and steel, engineering, telecommunications, shipbuilding, shipping, petroleum, gas, and electric power.

Most of Italy's industry is concentrated in the northwestern part of the Po Valley, particularly in the triangle formed by the cities of Milan, Turin, and Genoa. Textiles, refined and fabricated metals, machinery, vehicles, and electrical equipment are the most important manufactures. Food processing, based on the varied harvest of the region, is also a major industry.

Trade. Italy's exports in 1966 earned $8,031 million and its imports cost $8,571 million. Italy's main exports are textiles, vehicles, electrical equipment, machinery, chemicals, fruits and vegetables, and wine. Principal imports include iron and steel, petroleum, coal, chemicals, foodstuffs, timber and paper products, and raw cotton and wool.

The nation's most important trading partners are West Germany, the United States, France, the Benelux countries, Britain, and Switzerland.

Government. Italy is a democratic republic with a parliamentary form of government. The chief of state is the president, who is elected to a seven-year term by the legislature. The president has the power to dissolve the legislature and call for new elections. He also nominates the prime

TRANS WORLD AIRLINES

FLORENCE'S PONTE VECCHIO, on the Arno River, is crowded with jewelry and leather shops.

minister, who must be approved by the legislature.

The prime minister chooses the ministers who form his cabinet from among the members of the legislature. The prime minister and cabinet are responsible to the legislature.

The legislature, or parliament, consists of the 630-member Chamber of Deputies and the 315-member Senate. Both chambers are directly elected on the basis of proportional representation. The Senate also includes 5 lifetime members and former presidents of the republic. Legislation may originate in either house and must be passed by a majority of both.

Italy belongs to the European Economic Community, the North Atlantic Treaty Organization (NATO), and the United Nations.

HISTORY. Italy has been inhabited since very early times, and traces of Paleolithic and Neolithic cultures have been found throughout the peninsula. In about 2000 BC a group of people closely related to the ancient Greeks entered Italy from the north and gradually established themselves throughout the peninsula.

Approximately 1,100 years later the Etruscans came from Asia Minor, settled in north-central Italy, and subjugated the local inhabitants. In the 700s and 600s BC the Greeks colonized parts of southern Italy and Sicily. They dominated the area to such an extent that it was known as *Magna Graecia*, or Greater Greece.

In 388 BC Rome, an insignificant city-state that until 100 years earlier had been dominated by the Etruscans, gained control of the surrounding area of Latium. By 270 BC the Romans had conquered all of Italy, and the history of Italy from the 200s BC to the 400s AD is largely the history of Rome and the Roman Empire.

In the 400s Italy was invaded by peoples from central and eastern Europe, including the Visigoths, Ostrogoths, Heruli, and Huns. In 476 the last Roman emperor in the west, Romulus Augustus, was deposed by Odoacer, a Heruli chieftain. Odoacer ruled until 493, when he was killed by Theodoric, king of the Ostrogoths. Theodoric established a kingdom that lasted until 553, when Italy was conquered by the emperor of the east, who ruled from Byzantium.

The Byzantines were unable to defend Italy, and in 568 it was invaded by the Lombards. The Lombards gained control of most of the peninsula except Rome, Ravenna, and Naples. Furthermore, in 726 Pope Gregory II, who had quarreled with the Byzantine emperor over ecclesiastical matters, declared Rome independent.

Rome's independence was continually threatened by the Lombards, and the popes began to turn to the Carolingian kings of the Franks for help. In 756 Pepin subdued the Lombards and forced them to cede part of central Italy to Pope Stephen II, creating the nucleus of the Papal States. Pepin's son Charlemagne deposed the last Lombard king in 774, and in 800 Charlemagne was crowned Emperor of the Romans by Pope Leo III. Italy was ruled by the Franks until 887, when the Carolingian empire disintegrated.

A century of turmoil followed, during which Muslims established themselves in southern Italy and Sicily. Order was restored in 962 with the coronation by Pope John XII of Otto I of Saxony as emperor of Italy and Germany. This union of Italy and Germany marked the beginning of the Holy Roman Empire.

The German emperors, who were mainly concerned with domestic affairs, rarely visited Italy, and the northern and central parts of the country were ruled by warring feudal lords. In the south the Normans wrested Sicily from the Muslims and Apulia and Calabria, at the tip of the peninsula, from the Byzantines. The Normans established the Kingdom of the Two Sicilies.

City-states. During the 900s cities began to develop, particularly in north-central Italy, and by the 1000s and 1100s they had become independent communes. The Italian cities prospered as a result of the Crusades and increased trade with the Muslim world. Venice and other cities in the north became Europe's market places and banking centers.

Strong rivalries existed between these cities and prevented even partial national unification. By the end of the 1200s Italy was divided into several hundred city-states. In the 1300s and 1400s several republics, such as Genoa and Venice, and the ruling princes of a number of other cities, including the Medici of Florence, the Visconti and Sforza of Milan, and the Este of Ferrara, grew extremely rich and powerful.

There was constant warfare among the city-states, and Italy became prey to its more powerful neighbors. But the era of the city-states saw the development of the Renaissance, and the intellectual and artistic works of the Italian Renaissance remain even today as a symbol of cultural greatness.

Foreign Domination. The descent of Charles VIII of France into Italy in 1494 began the Italian Wars, which arose over rival French and Spanish claims to the throne of the Kingdom of Naples. The wars did not end until 1559, when the Treaty of Cateau-Cambrésis was signed. The treaty recognized Spanish supremacy in Italy, and marked the end of independence for most of the Italian states.

The wars of the Spanish Succession (1701-1713) and of the Polish Succession (1733-1735) increased foreign domination of Italy. At the end of the War of the Austrian Succession, which lasted from 1740 to 1748, the only independent states left were the declining republics of Venice, Genoa, and Lucca; the Papal States; and the Kingdom of Sardinia, established in 1720 under the house of Savoy.

Although divided and under foreign domination, Italy during the 1700s enjoyed enlightened rule. The rulers of Italy, inspired by the principles of rationalism, which emphasized the idea of universal human progress, embarked on a program of government reform.

By about 1790, however, the French Revolution had caused a reactionary government. Nonetheless, many Italians had become familiar with progressive ideas, and when the French emperor, Napoleon Bonaparte, won Lombardy from the Austrians in 1796, a movement for independence and unity developed and spread throughout the peninsula of Italy.

Under the protection of Napoleon several republics were created. In 1799 Napoleon was driven out of Italy by Russian and Austrian armies of the Second Coalition, formed the previous year between Russia, Britain, Austria, Portugal, and the Ottoman Empire. But Napoleon returned in 1801 and was crowned king of Italy in 1805.

The government of Napoleon was one of enlightened despotism. Although the Italians had little political freedom, many economic, administrative, and educational reforms were carried out.

The Napoleonic empire collapsed in 1814, and the Congress of Vienna, which met to redraw the map of Europe, restored the old regimes in Italy. Austrian influence was dominant in the peninsula. By and large the restoration was reactionary, and most of Napoleon's reforms were repealed.

Risorgimento. Many Italians, especially those of the middle class who had benefited the most under Napoleonic government, realized how advantageous a strong central government could be. This realization, the memory of the earlier reform governments of the 1700s, the recent republican experiments, and a growing feeling of nationalism, all contributed to the development of the *risorgimento*, or resurgence, and the desire for a united and independent Italy.

Some of the more daring patriots joined secret societies, whose aim was to overthrow the existing governments. The most important of these societies was the Carbonari. The Carbonari staged a revolution in Naples in 1820 which overthrew the monarchy there and set up a constitutional government. But Austrian troops defeated the rebels the following year.

The Carbonari also led a number of less successful revolutions—in Piedmont in 1821 and in Modena, Parma, and the Papal States in 1831-1832. Soon after the failure of these uprisings the Carbonari began to decline. It was largely replaced by Giovine Italia, Young Italy, founded in 1831 by Giuseppe Mazzini, a former member of the Carbonari.

Mazzini believed that God's will was an independent Italy that would take the lead in the spiritual and political regeneration of Europe. During the 1840s and 1850s Mazzini incited numerous revolts throughout Italy, all of which were unsuccessful.

Unification. Italian unification was finally brought about by Count Camillo Benso di Cavour, prime minister of the Kingdom of Sardinia. Cavour understood that foreign aid was needed to free Italy from Austrian domination. In 1838 Cavour met

Italy's international prestige, and acquisition of colonies was necessary to Italy's international prestige, and the acquisition of colonies was necessary to 1900s many Italians felt that the acquisition of colonies was necessary to

Expansion. In the late 1800s and early 1900s many Italians felt that the acquisition of colonies was necessary to Italy's international prestige, and the army and navy were strengthened.

This program was continued and expanded by the Left, which held power from 1876 to 1891. The right to vote was extended, elementary education was made compulsory, administrative and legal reforms were instituted, and the army and navy were strengthened.

The Kingdom of Italy was a constitutional monarchy with a parliamentary form of government. The two major political forces were the Right, which was conservative, and the Left, which was radical. From 1860 to 1876 the government was controlled mainly by the Right. A highly centralized government was about establishing national armed forces, restoring the country's finances, modernizing the transportation system, encouraging industry, and improving agriculture.

Nonetheless, the Kingdom of Italy, excluding Rome, was proclaimed in 1861 under Victor Emmanuel, the king of Sardinia. In 1870 French troops were withdrawn from Rome when war broke out between France and Prussia, and the Papal States and Rome were added to the new kingdom.

In May 1860 Giuseppe Garibaldi, a nationalist leader, landed in Sicily with 1,000 volunteers. By September he had won not only Sicily but Naples as well. Sardinian troops then marched into the Papal States, but France intervened on behalf of the pope.

War broke out in 1859 and the Austrians were defeated, but the Sardinians gained only Lombardy. Meanwhile, however, Tuscany, Modena, Parma, and Romagna had declared their independence and formed provisional governments. Under the sanction of Napoleon III plebiscites were held in March 1860 and the four states voted for union with Sardinia.

secretly with Napoleon III of France at Plombières and promised him Nice and Savoy in return for military assistance against the Austrians.

THE ROMAN COLOSSEUM, as seen through the Arch of Titus.

ITALIAN STATE TOURIST OFFICE

World War I broke out in July 1914 and Italy proclaimed its neutrality in the conflict, which ranged the Central Powers, led by Germany and Austria-Hungary, against the Allied Powers, led by Britain, France, and Russia. Italy maintained that it was not bound by the terms of the Triple Alliance insomuch as Austria was an aggressor.

Within Italy feelings were divided as to whether the country should remain neutral throughout the course of the conflict. Many Italians felt that they should not let the war end without trying to secure territory in the Balkans and firmly establish the border with Austria, which was open to question.

To secure these ends Italy began negotiations with Austria. The Austrians proved evasive, and on Apr. 26, 1915 Italy concluded the secret Treaty of London with the Allies. In the event of Allied victory, the treaty promised Italy Trentino, the south Tyrol, Istria, Gorizia, Gradisca, and the city of Trieste, some of the Dalmatian Islands, sovereignty over the Dodecanese Islands, part of Germany's African colonies, and the seaport of Adalia on the coast of Asia Minor.

Italy declared war on Austria-Hungary in May 1915 and in August 1916 declared war on Germany. Italian troops fought the Austrians and Germans along the northern frontier for four years with varying degrees of success. In 1918 they held firm against a major offensive launched in June and in November won a decisive victory at Vittorio Veneto.

Fascism. At the 1919 Versailles Peace Conference which ended the war, Italy won little of what it had been content, together with postwar social and political unrest, contributed to the development of an extreme nationalistic movement, Fascism, led by Benito Mussolini. Fascism was embraced primarily by discontented members of the lower middle class. On Oct. 28, 1922 the Fascists staged a march on Rome. King Victor Emmanuel III, rather than use the military to put down the revolt, asked Mussolini to form a government. Mussolini was named prime minister and gradually created a dictatorial regime. Parliament became his puppet, and in 1938 the lower house, the Chamber of Deputies, was replaced by the Chamber of Fasces and Corporations, whose members were appointed by the Fascist party.

Fascist foreign policy was imperialistic. In defiance of the League of Nations, Mussolini invaded Ethiopia in October 1935, and following the conquest of Ethiopia, Victor Emmanuel assumed the title of emperor of Ethiopia. In 1937 Italy withdrew from the League of Nations, and in 1939 Italy conquered Albania and Victor Emmanuel was named its king.

Mussolini also supported fascist movements abroad. He aided Gen. Francisco Franco in the Spanish Civil War of 1936–1939 and supported Adolf Hitler in Germany's annexation of Austria and Czechoslovakia. Finally, on May 22, 1939, he concluded an alliance with Germany, establishing the Rome-Berlin Axis.

World War II. Following the outbreak of World War II in September 1939, Mussolini declared Italy's neutrality. But in June 1940, when France was on the verge of defeat, he invaded southern France, bringing Italy into the war. The Italian troops were ill-prepared and were soon demoralized by disaster after disaster. General discontent grew as the war continued, and German troops moved into Italy. On July 25, 1943 the king dismissed Mussolini as head of the government, a new government was formed by Marshal Pietro Badoglio. The Allies invaded Sicily in July and August 1943, and in September Italy surrendered, Mussolini proclaimed a ''social republic'' in the German-controlled north, which lasted until the country was completely liberated in 1945.

On May 9, 1946 Victor Emmanuel abdicated in favor of his son, who became King Humbert II. But the monarchy had lost its popularity as a result of its cooperation with Mussolini, and a referendum held in June made Italy a republic. A new constitution was adopted in 1947, and in 1948 Luigi Einaudi became president.

Republic. Italy soon developed three major political parties—the Christian Democrats, led by Alcide de Gasperi; the Socialists, led by Pietro Nenni; and the Communists, led by Palmiro Togliatti. From 1945 to 1953 the government was headed by Prime Minister Alcide de Gasperi.

De Gasperi developed programs for the reconstruction of war-torn Italy and cooperated closely with other nations of western Europe and the United States. Italy joined the United Nations in 1955 and in 1957 became a founding member of the European Economic Community.

De Gasperi's government fell in 1953, and a succession of Christian Democrats headed right-center coalition governments until 1962. In 1962 to strengthen the government, Christian Democrats joined with the Socialists to form a coalition known as the ''opening to the left.''

In October 1967 parliament approved renegotiation of the Concordat of 1929, which determined Italy's relations with the Vatican, in answer to popular demand for less church involvement in state affairs. Under the terms of the Concordat, Roman Catholic religious doctrines are taught in public schools and marriage is governed by church law, which effectively forbids divorce in Italy.

—Sergio Barzanti

IVORY COAST

Official name: Republic of Ivory Coast
Area: 124,504 square miles
Population: (1966 est.) 3,920,000
Capital: Abidjan (Pop., 1963 est., urban area, 250,800)
Language: French, African languages
Religion: Traditional religions, Islam, Christianity
Currency unit: Franc CFA (African Financial Community)
National holiday: First Monday in August

The Ivory Coast, a republic in western Africa, is bordered on the north by Mali and Upper Volta, on the east by Ghana, on the south by the Atlantic Ocean, and on the west by Liberia and Guinea. The Ivory Coast was a territory of France until 1960, when it received its independence.

THE LAND. The surface of the Ivory Coast is relatively flat. There are plantations along the eastern part of the country's coast, beyond which are tropical rain forests. There are forests along the western part of the coast. North of the forest is a savanna region. There are mountains in the west and northwest with elevations above 5,000 feet.

Three almost parallel rivers flow from north to south—the Sassandra in the west, the Bandama, and the Comoé in the east. The Cavalla River flows along part of the Ivory Coast's western border.

The Ivory Coast has a hot, tropical climate. The coastal region receives an average of about 80 inches of rain each year, and the northern part of the country receives an average of about 50 inches yearly.

THE PEOPLE. There are many ethnic groups in the Ivory Coast. The most important are the Baule, Senufo, Agni, and Kru. Most of the people are farmers. The Ivory Coast's largest city and major port is Abidjan, the country's capital.

ECONOMY. The Ivory Coast's economic life depends heavily on agriculture. The country's most important crops are coffee, cacao, pineapples, and bananas. Although most of the Ivory Coast's land is undeveloped, in 1964-1965 the country was the world's third largest producer of coffee and the fourth largest producer of cacao. Large quantities of bananas and pineapples are also produced.

The basic food crops are yams, manioc, and rice.

The Ivory Coast is becoming an important fishing country; in 1965 the catch was 58,500 metric tons. The Ivory Coast is also breeding cattle resistant to disease carried by the tsetse fly.

The Ivory Coast has rich forest resources, and wood and wood products are valuable exports. There are deposits of diamonds and manganese in the country. Although the Ivory Coast is not highly industrialized, light industry has been developing.

In 1966 imports cost $265 million and exports earned $310 million. The country's major imports are machinery, petroleum products, and consumer goods. Exports include coffee, cacao, bananas, timber, and pineapple. The Ivory Coast in 1959 joined with Da-homey, Upper Volta, and Niger, and in 1966 with Togo, for mutual economic cooperation.

GOVERNMENT. The Ivory Coast has a presidential system of government. Executive powers are vested in a president, who is popularly elected to a five-year term. Legislative power is held by an 85-member National Assembly. Assembly members are elected by universal suffrage to five-year terms.

The Ivory Coast is a member of the United Nations and the Organization of African Unity (OAU).

HISTORY. The important Muslim city of Kong in the north of the present-day Ivory Coast dates from the 1000s as a caravan trade center. African kingdoms in the southeast of the country date from the time of the expansion of Ashanti people from present-day Ghana in the 1700s and 1800s.

French Rule. France had contacts with the Ivory Coast in the 1600s and 1700s. In 1893 France established the Ivory Coast Colony, and in 1904 the colony was made a part of the Federation of French West Africa. But the total conquest of the area was not completed until the end of World War I.

There was little freedom of political expression for Africans until after World War II. At that time Felix Houphouët-Boigny founded the Ivory Coast Democratic Party (PDCI), a local section of the African Democratic Rally. The PDCI rapidly became the dominant political force in the country. In 1946 the colony became a territory within the French Union. With support from French communists and the French administration, Houphouët-Boigny was elected to the French National Assembly.

He gained fame in the assembly for his law abolishing forced labor. France then attempted to suppress the PDCI, and as a result many regional parties sprang up. In 1950 Houphouët-Boigny broke with the communists and adopted a pro-French policy. He rebuilt his party, benefiting from prosperity created by a coffee boom and from French aid.

Independence. From 1956 to 1959 Houphouët-Boigny was a member of successive French administrations. In 1958 his country voted overwhelmingly to become an autonomous member of the French Community.

The Ivory Coast became independent on Aug. 7, 1960, and Houphouët-Boigny was unanimously elected president of the republic. All opposition parties were silenced, and the PDCI became the country's sole legal political party.

—Hibberd V. B. Kline, Jr.; Vera L. Zolberg

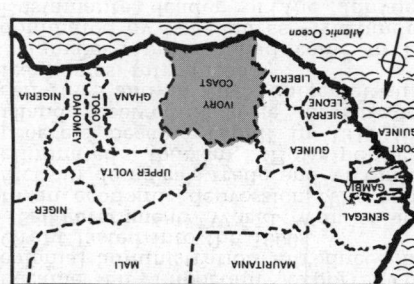

JAMAICA

Official name: Jamaica
Area: 4,411 square miles
Population: (1966 est.) 1,839,000
Capital: Kingston (Pop., 1960, urban area, 376,520)
Language: English
Religion: Anglicanism, Protestantism, Roman Catholicism
Currency unit: Pound
National holiday: First Monday in August

Jamaica, an island nation in the West Indies, lies 90 miles south of Cuba in the Caribbean Sea. Jamaica received its independence in 1962 after more than 300 years of British control.

THE LAND. Jamaica is a mountainous island. A central mountain axis runs from west to east, reaching elevations above 7,000 feet in the east. There is a narrow coastal plain in the north and a wider coastal plain in the south, where Kingston, the capital and chief port, is located.

The climate varies with elevation. Temperatures throughout the year average in the low 80's° F in the plains, but it is much cooler in the mountain areas. The mountains also affect the distribution of rain. The slopes facing northeast receive the heaviest rainfall, about 200 inches a year. The southern coast is blocked off from rain-bearing winds and receives little rain.

THE PEOPLE. Most Jamaicans are of African and of mixed African and European descent. There are also people of Chinese, East Indian, European, and Near Eastern origins.

Jamaica is a densely populated island. In the cultivable areas, there is an average of more than 2,000 people per square mile. Many Jamaicans migrated to other countries, particularly to the United States and Britain, in search of work. Immigration restrictions, however, have reduced the possibilities of employment abroad. Thus the country's growing population, which constantly must find more jobs for its growing population, increased at the rate of almost 2 percent a year between 1958 and 1965.

ECONOMY. Agriculture and mining are the mainstays of the Jamaican economy, and they form the basis for the island's developing industry. The country has rich soils and produces valuable tropical crops, and Jamaica is one of the world's major sources of bauxite, from which aluminum is made. The island also earns a great deal of money from tourism, and resorts such as Montego Bay, on the northwest coast, are popular.

The most valuable export crops are sugarcane and bananas. In 1965 the island produced 497,000 metric tons of sugar and 318,000 metric tons of bananas. Sweet potatoes, rice, and corn are important food crops. Other crops include coffee, citrus fruit, cacao, ginger, pimento, cassava, and tobacco.

Jamaica's mineral resources include gypsum as well as bauxite, but baux-ite is the most valuable product of the island. In 1966 bauxite production exceeded 9.2 million metric tons.

Industry is based on processing agricultural and mineral products. Sugar and sugar products—rum and molasses. Jamaica trades mainly with Britain, the United States, and Canada.

GOVERNMENT. Jamaica has a parliamentary system of government patterned on that of Great Britain. The head of state is the British monarch, who is represented by a governor-general. Executive powers are wielded by a prime minister and cabinet responsible to the parliament. The prime minister is normally the leader of the majority party in the parliament.

The parliament has two houses, a 21-member Senate and a 53-member House of Representatives. Senators are appointed by the governor-general—13 on the advice of the prime minister and 8 on the advice of the leader of the opposition party. House members are popularly elected to a term of five years.

Jamaica is a member of the United Nations and the Commonwealth of Nations.

HISTORY. Christopher Columbus claimed Jamaica for Spain in 1494, during his second voyage to the New World. The island, called Xaymaca by its Arawak Indian inhabitants, became a Spanish colony in 1509. Under Spanish rule, the Arawak were exterminated and slaves were brought from Africa to provide labor for the colony.

Britain captured Jamaica in 1655. During the British conquest, many of the slaves fled to the mountains, where they developed a distinct culture. Known as Maroons, they successfully fought off the British for more than 100 years. Jamaica had become a haven for pirates, but piracy was suppressed after 1670, when British control was officially recognized in the Treaty of Madrid.

British Rule. Jamaica became a prosperous colony, thriving as the major slave market of the Western Hemisphere and as a producer of tropical produce, especially sugar and coffee. The slave trade was abolished in 1807, and slavery itself was ended in 1838, after a serious slave revolt. Before the island could recover from the loss of slave labor, Britain in 1846 removed its protective colonial tariff and the plantation economy was ruined.

Economic hardship and misgovernment combined in 1865 to provoke a Negro rising at Morant Bay. The rebellion quickly spread throughout the island and was suppressed only after a bitter struggle marked by violent excesses by both sides.

In 1866 Jamaica was made a crown colony and Sir John Peter Grant was sent from Britain as governor. He initiated political, economic, and social reforms and introduced the cultivation of bananas, which soon became an important export. The colonial administration introduced by Grant lasted into the 1900s.

Self-government. World War II led to an economic depression. The conflict cut Jamaica's trade and virtually eliminated tourism. But political progress became rapid. In 1944 the island received a large measure of self-rule, and in 1945 universal suffrage was introduced.

Jamaican politics had come to be dominated by two figures—Alexander Bustamante, leader of the Jamaica Labor Party, and Norman Manley, leader of the People's National Party. Both parties rested on trade-union support. Bustamante won elections held in 1945 and in 1949, but Manley was victorious in 1955.

In 1958 Manley brought Jamaica into the Federation of the West Indies, which united several British Caribbean and West Indian Territories. Jamaicans voted in 1961 to withdraw from the federation, and in 1962 general elections were held in Jamaica. **Independence.** Bustamante was returned to power in April, and on Aug. 6, 1962 he led the island to independence. Although no longer led by Bustamante, the Jamaica Labor Party was again victorious in elections held in 1967.

—George Carey; Jerome Fischman

JAPAN

Official name: Japan
Area: 142,727 square miles
Population: (1967 est.) 99,920,000
Capital: Tokyo (Pop. 1965, urban area, 10,869,800)
Language: Japanese
Religion: Buddhism, Shintoism
Currency unit: Yen
National holiday: Birthday of the emperor, April 29

Japan, an island nation in the northwest Pacific Ocean, is separated from the Soviet Union and Korea on the Asian mainland by the Sea of Okhotsk, to the north, and by the Sea of Japan and the Korea Strait, to the west. The Soviet island of Sakhalin lies 26 miles north of Japan, and the Soviet Kuril Islands lie 10 miles to the northeast. The East China Sea separates Japan from Mainland China on the southwest.

THE LAND. The Japanese archipelago consists of over 3,000 islands and extends 1,400 miles from northeast to southwest. But 98 percent of the area lies within the four major islands of Honshu (87,300 square miles); Hokkaido (30,300 square miles); Kyushu (16,200 square miles); and Shikoku (7,200 square miles).

Most of the country is mountainous, with only about 15 percent of the land sufficiently level for cultivation. The country's limited plains areas are concentrated on Honshu. Many of the mountains are folded ranges upthrust from the Pacific floor. Japan is crossed by seven principal volcanic chains containing 192 major volcanoes, 58 of which are active. An average of four seismic shocks a day are recorded. Volcanic masses produce the highest peaks in the country. Mt. Fuji, a dormant volcano on Honshu, has an elevation of 12,389 feet. Associated with this intense vulcanism are thousands of natural springs.

All of Japan's rivers are short and swift with greatly varying water levels. Only three rivers exceed 200 miles in length—the Shinano and the Tone on Honshu, and the Ishikari on Hokkaido. The Inland Sea, bounded by Honshu, Shikoku, and Kyushu, serves Japan as a major waterway. It is about 250 miles long and is connected with the Pacific Ocean by the Kii and Bungo Straits and with the East China Sea by the Shimonoseki Strait.

The coastline of the Sea of Japan has few indentations and consequently has few good harbors. The western and southern Kyushu coasts, however, are remarkably indented and have many offshore islands. The southern coast of Honshu contains Japan's most important harbors and ports, such as Tokyo, Yokohama, Nagoya, Osaka, and Kobe. Three famous bays—Sagami, Suruga, and Ise—lie between Tokyo Bay and the Inland Sea.

Climate. Japan's climate, subtropical in the south and cooler in the north, is generally mild and pleasant. The average mean January temperature is 45°F in southern Kyushu and 14°F in Hokkaido. August is usually the hottest month of the year, with a mean of 81°F in the south and 69°F in the north.

Western Hokkaido, eastern Honshu, and the Inland Sea region receive 40 to 60 inches of rain a year. In central Honshu and along the Sea of Japan 100 to 120 inches of rain is not uncommon. In most parts of the country maximum precipitation occurs in early summer.

THE PEOPLE. The Japanese are a Mongoloid people with an admixture of Malay and Caucasoid stocks. The only large minority group consists of about 600,000 Koreans. There are small groups of Chinese and Europeans. Japanese is the national language, and Buddhism and Shintoism, the latter indigenous to Japan, the principal religions. There are about 700,000 Christians, mostly members

of various Protestant denominations.

With a population about half that of the United States in a land smaller than California, Japan in 1967 had a population density of almost 700 people per square mile. Because the country is mountainous and largely unsuitable for agriculture, the number of people per square mile of arable land was close to 5,000. The Japanese, however, have succeeded in reducing population growth to the lowest rate of any Asian nation—1 percent a year between 1958 and 1965. The 1965 census listed seven urban areas with populations of over 1 million. All are industrial centers on the island of Honshu—Kitakyushu (1,042,388); Kobe (1,216,666); Kyoto (1,365,007); Nagoya (1,935,430); and Tokyo (10,869,800).

ECONOMY. Japan's rate of economic growth since the end of World War II has been extraordinary. The economy expanded at an average annual rate of about 11 percent between 1947 and 1952. Although growth slowed down for a few years when postwar reconstruction was completed and the Korean War (1950-1953) ended, the average annual rate of increase was about 10 percent from 1955 to the mid-1960s.

In 1966 Japan's gross national product reached $97.3 billion, the fifth largest in the world. Per capita income is by far the highest of any Asian country, although still low by West European standards.

Natural Resources. Japan has a large variety of mineral resources but the deposits are small and inadequate for Japan's advanced level of industrial development. Coal is the main mineral resource, but most of it is of low grade and unfit for coking. Coking coal has to be imported, as do other basic industrial materials such as oil and bauxite, from which aluminum is made.

Minerals in which domestic production is sufficient are lead, zinc, arsenic, bismuth, pyrite, sulfur, limestone, gypsum, barite, silica, feldspar, and dolomite. Vanadium, chromium, molybdenum, tungsten, titanium, tin, manganese, mercury, antimony, and iron ore are also produced, but large imports are still required to meet the economy's needs.

Japan's mountainous terrain and abundant rainfall help make the country the fourth largest producer of hydroelectricity in the world. Japan also has rich forests and coastal fisheries.

Agriculture. The position of agriculture has been declining steadily since World War II. It contributed 21 percent to the gross domestic product in 1953 and only 12 percent in 1965. In 1965 about one-quarter of the labor force was employed in agriculture, but only about 20 percent of the farm households in Japan were entirely dependent on agriculture for their income.

The average Japanese farm of about 2.5 acres is intensively cultivated. Such techniques as fertilizers, irrigation, multiple cropping, and terracing place Japan's crop yields per acre among the highest in the world.

About half the cultivated land is used for the production of paddy rice, the staple of the Japanese diet. Barley, wheat, potatoes, pulses, vegetables, and fruits are also grown. Since World War II Japan's silk industry has become less important, and in the mid-1960s there were only about 432,000 acres of mulberry orchards. Livestock raising is limited by the lack of land, but some cattle, pigs, and poultry are raised.

Fishing. Fish ranks second to rice in the Japanese diet and is the principal source of protein. Japan's fish catch in 1965 reached almost 7 million metric tons, the second largest in the world. Japanese coastal waters contain a great variety of fish because of the mixing of two major ocean currents off the coast, the warm Kuro Shio from the south and the cold Oya Shio from the north.

The sardine catch leads in both volume and value, although herring and mackerel are important in northern waters. In addition to coastal fishing, Japan has a large fleet which goes to distant fishing grounds in the north and south Pacific.

The Japanese government has promoted a shallow sea culture of raising fish (chiefly prawn, sea bream, and yellowtail), which led to a 25 percent rise in total fish production between 1961 and 1964. Fish production in Japan not only provides a major food item but is also important for oil, meal, and fertilizer.

Forestry. About two-thirds of Japan is covered by productive forests, which are the source of building materials, fuel, paper, and other articles. The forests are also important in stabilizing the soils and the water runoff in this mountainous country. Oak, laurel, and bamboo grow in southern Japan. A mixed forest including maple, ash, birch, cypress, and pine is found in central Japan. And conifers such as spruce, fir, and hemlock grow in mountain areas in northern Japan.

Industry. Despite its limited natural resource base, Japan is one of the world's major industrial nations. From the end of World War II until 1959, Japan was engaged in reconstructing and reorganizing its war-devastated industries. By 1960 the emphasis was on expanding heavy industry.

In the mid-1960s improvements in technology and production, rather than expansion, were emphasized. The petrochemical and electronics industries, in particular, began to create new products for industry and for the consumer.

In 1966 Japan ranked first in world production of rayon and acetate fabrics. It ranked second as a producer of zinc, woolen fabrics, synthetic rubber, jute yarn, plastics, resins, and tires. Japan ranked third in the production of cement, aluminum, iron alloys, and crude steel; fourth in the production of cotton fabrics; and fifth in refined and smelter copper.

Japan is also a major producer of automobiles, ships, cameras, sewing machines, electric generators, machinery for textile production, aircraft, precision machinery, and chemicals.

An important development since World War II has been Japan's rise as a producer of electronic equipment such as television sets, transistors, transistor radios, tape recorders, and computers. Over 73 percent of Japan's electrical-machinery exports consists of electronic products.

Japan in 1965 ranked fourth in the world in electric energy production. Installed capacity (kw) in 1965 was 41 million kilowatts (kw), about 40 percent of which was hydroelectric. Three-quarters of Japan's waterpower potential had been developed by the mid-1960s and many large hydroelectric installations had been built. Because of the small size of Japan's rivers, most of the stations have small capacities and are the "run-of-stream" type, which is based upon natural flow rather than impounded water. The greatest concentration of hydroelectric stations is found in central and northern Honshu.

Since the mid-1950s thermoelectric power has been emphasized, and in 1962 more power was produced by this means than by water resources. The generation of electric power through nuclear energy has begun in Japan, with 2 million kwh produced in 1964. Atomic power output by 1980 is estimated at 8 million kwh.

Trade. Deficient in arable land and natural resources, Japan is heavily dependent upon foreign trade. In 1966 it was the world's sixth largest trading nation, with imports costing $9.5 billion and exports earning $9.7 billion.

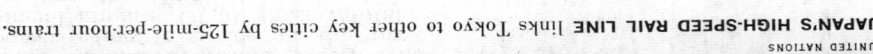

UNITED NATIONS

JAPAN'S HIGH-SPEED RAIL LINE links Tokyo to other key cities by 125-mile-per-hour trains.

Raw materials, foodstuffs, and fuel are Japan's principal imports, es-pecially cereals, sugar, raw cotton and wool, iron ore, bauxite, copper ore, coking coal, crude rubber, and crude petroleum. Almost all of Ja-pan's exports are manufactured goods, such as textiles, particularly cotton and synthetic fabrics, radios, iron and steel and other metal products, automobiles, radios, textile and leath-er machinery, ships, and scientific instruments.

Japan's most important trading partner is the United States, which in 1965 accounted for about 30 percent of both exports and imports. Canada and Australia are other important trading partners.

GOVERNMENT. Japan is a constitu-tional monarchy with a parliamentary system of government. The emperor is the symbol of the state, and execu-tive power is wielded by a prime minister and cabinet responsible to the legislature, the Diet. The prime minister, chosen by the Diet from among its members, appoints the cabinet ministers, at least half of whom must be members of the Diet. The Diet is composed of the House of Representatives, whose 486 mem-bers are elected to four-year terms, and the House of Councillors, with 250 members elected to six-year terms. One hundred Councillors are elected by the nation at large, and the other 150 members are elected from constituencies.

Japan is a member of the United Nations.

HISTORY. Although the first inhabi-tants of Japan were ancestors of the modern Ainu, a Caucasoid people, archeological evidence indicates that most of the early Japanese were Mongoloid invaders from Korea, who first appeared in Japan in about 200 AD. They brought with them a bronze and iron civilization and founded the Japanese state.

Early Japan was ruled by numer-ous clans, one of which, the Yamato, gained supremacy by the 200s or 300s. From the Yamato descended the Jap-anese royal family, although the Japa-nese tradition maintains that the Sun Goddess of the Yamato chiefs is the progenitor of the imperial family.

Chinese Influence. Contact with the advanced civilization of China, which began in about 550 with the introduc-tion of Buddhism into Japan, revolu-tionized Japanese culture. Eager to learn from their powerful neighbor, the Yamato sent an official embassy to China in 607, a practice which lasted until the 800s. Japanese scholars returning from the embassies helped introduce Chinese ideas and institu-tions into Japan.

For the first time the Yamato chief conceived of himself as an emperor as well as Shinto high priest. A com-plex centralized administration in the Chinese manner was established and Chinese-style cities were built. Nara was built as the capital in 710. It was replaced by Kyoto in 794. Less suc-cessfully imitated by the Japanese were China's provincial administra-tion and land distribution systems, which were strongly opposed by the clans.

Such cultural borrowings as Bud-dhism and Buddhist art were the most enduring. Attempts to adapt the Chinese writing system to the Japa-nese language were largely unsuccess-ful and made writing unnecessarily difficult. After 200 years of imitation a native Japanese culture began to emerge, and in 838 the last Japanese embassy was sent to China.

A brilliant Japanese court life de-veloped which came to be dominated by the Fujiwara family. The Fuji-wara gained control over the imperial family through intermarriage, and from about 850 on its head acted either as regent or as civil dictator. While the Fujiwara dominated the court in the 900s and 1000s, real power came to reside in the pro-vincial knights. Of all these military families, the Minamoto emerged the most powerful in 1185. Its chief, Yoritomo, settled in Kamakura and gave himself the title of shogun, or generalissimo.

Kamakura Era. By appointing its men as estate managers throughout the country, the Kamakura group was able to control both peasants and court nobles, whose incomes came from the Kamakura-managed estates. Kamakura became the only real cen-tral government in Japan, and the institution of the shogunate lasted until 1867.

Upon Yoritomo's death, the Hojo family assumed power, ruling through a puppet shogun from the Fujiwara family and then from the royal family.

By the late 1200s the Kamakura system had begun to disintegrate, al-though Kamakura soldiers were able to repel Mongol invasions ordered by Kublai Khan in 1274 and 1281. The Japanese were aided by a typhoon called *kamikaze*, or divine wind, which was supposed to protect the land from foreign invaders.

The Kamakura system collapsed as loyalties to the chief lessened and as increasing numbers of knights de-creased the number of lucrative positions available. Daigo II, a retired emperor, led a revolt against Kamakura, beginning a 200-year period of political disorganiza-tion. During this period of political collapse, however, commerce and manufacturing prospered and trade with China expanded.

From China Japan imported South-east Asian and Indian products as well as Chinese goods, and by the 1500s Japan was exporting not only raw materials but manufactured products as swords and fans. The East China Sea trade was soon domi-nated by Japanese sailors.

Political reunification came in the late 1500s when Oda Nobunaga, a feudal lord, seized Kyoto in 1568 and became ruler of central Japan. His successor, Hideyoshi, assumed power in 1582 and reunited the entire coun-try. He attempted an invasion of Korea in 1592, but was repulsed by Chinese forces. Hideyoshi was suc-ceeded in 1598 by Tokugawa Ieyasu, who took the title of shogun in 1603.

Tokugawa Era. Tokugawa and his suc-cessors created a political system which remained unchanged for 250

ACTOR YAMASHINA SHIOJURO as a samurai.

FLETCHER FUND

years. The price of stability and peace, however, was an oppressive and reactionary government. To achieve social stability, four classes were created—warrior-administrator, peasant, artisan, and merchant. Mem-bers of the aristocracy of warriors were called *samurai*, and their em-blem was a long and a short sword worn at the side.

While repressive domestically, the Tokugawa were even more extreme in their foreign relations, which had become important with the arrival of Europeans in the Far East. The first Europeans to reach Japan were Portuguese sailors who landed in 1542, and in 1549-1551 St. Francis Xavier, a Jesuit missionary, introduced Chris-tianity to Japan.

Japanese officials, regarding Chris-tianity as a political menace associated with European expansion in east Asia, banned all Christian missionaries in 1587. The Spanish and Portuguese were expelled, and in 1638 Japanese construction of oceangoing vessels was also prohibited. But Chinese merchants were allowed to trade at Nagasaki and the Dutch were permitted to maintain a trading post on a small island in Nagasaki harbor.

By the 1800s the isolation of Japan had become anachronistic, and in 1853 U.S. Commodore Matthew C. Perry arrived in Tokyo Bay with a letter from Pres. Millard Fillmore asking for the establishment of trade rela-tions. For the first time in 600 years the emperor was asked his opinion. Although the emperor wanted no foreigners in Japan, the Tokugawa had no choice but to sign a trade treaty when Perry returned in 1854. In 1858 a full commercial treaty with the United States was signed, and similar agreements with European countries followed. Foreign businesses were established in Yokohama, which soon became a major world port.

Meiji Restoration. The Tokugawa re-gime lost national confidence by ne-gotiating a treaty with a foreign country, and in 1867 the new shogun voluntarily surrendered control of the country to the emperor. This return to royal rule was called the Meiji Restoration, and in 1868 the capital was moved to Tokyo.

A period of rapid modernization followed the emperor's return to power. Although a constitution establishing a Diet with two houses was promulgated in 1889, the electorate was small (universal manhood suffrage was not introduced until 1925) and government was carried on by a small, competent group of oligarchs. Japanese students, sent abroad to study Western science and government, returned home to create a modern army, navy, and civil service. Aware that rapid modernization required a technically competent citizenry, the government set up a system of universal education in which technical skills useful to the government were taught. Both the schools and a conscript army employed techniques of political indoctrination, glorifying military prowess and the Japanese nation. Thus a nationalistic, technically skillful population was created. The government controlled public utilities and to some degree directed business and industry, which expanded rapidly due to the combination of Western technology and cheap labor. With a strong army and navy, and a large industrial complex, Japan was ready to test itself as a world military power.

Expansionism. A quarrel with China over Korea provoked the Sino-Japanese war of 1894–1895, which was easily won by Japan. In 1902 Japan signed a Treaty of Alliance with Britain, confirming its newly achieved international status. Clashes of interest with Russia over Korea and Manchuria finally produced the Russo-Japanese war of 1904–1905, a war won by the Japanese after a series of stunning victories on land and on sea. Korea was annexed in 1910.

In 1914 Japan, as Britain's ally, declared war on Germany in World War 1. Seeking to take advantage of the situation, Japan in 1915 presented China the Twenty-one Demands, calculated practically to transform China into a Japanese protectorate. But China's territorial integrity was preserved by decisions made at the Washington Conference of 1922. Japan agreed to give up its wartime territorial acquisitions and to limit its navy, in return for the promise that no Anglo-American naval bases would be built east of Singapore or west of Hawaii. Japanese-American relations deteriorated, however, after the United States moved to exclude Japanese immigrants in 1924.

The democratic, progressive elements which had grown up in Japan in the 1920s were gradually eliminated by the military, and a policy of armed expansionism was shaped. This aggressive posture was aggravated by the world economic depression of the 1930s, which proved disastrous to Japan's foreign trade. To maintain its economy and large population, Japan was desperately in need of foreign markets where it could obtain supplies and sell its exports. With the depression, Japan became subject to the will of other nations' tariff policies. By the 1930s many Japanese, especially the militarists, were eager to engage in a policy of colonial expansion to obtain sources of raw materials and markets. This culminated in the invasion of Manchuria in 1931. Full-scale war with China started in 1937. Meanwhile, in 1936, Japan had signed with Germany the Anti-Comintern Pact. Finally, in 1940, the Rome-Berlin-Tokyo Axis was established. To break the economic blockade set up by the Western nations, especially the United States, in protest against Japanese aggression, Japan attacked without warning at Pearl Harbor on Dec. 7, 1941.

After many important initial Japanese successes, the United States and its allies counterattacked. By 1943 Japan was in retreat. Yet Japan did not surrender until Aug. 14, 1945, after the United States dropped the world's first atomic bombs on the Japanese cities of Hiroshima and Nagasaki.

Japan was occupied by U.S. forces under the command of Gen. Douglas MacArthur and attempts at a thorough democratization of the country were started. Emperor Hirohito disclaimed his divinity, and in 1946 suffrage was extended to women and a new constitution was promulgated.

Contemporary Japan. Economic recovery was slow after the destruction wrought by the war. But the rapidly changing international situation provoked sharp modifications in U.S. policy in regard to Japan. The dismantling of large financial-industrial groups was discontinued in 1948 and reparations from capital equipment were almost abandoned.

The real turning point came with the outbreak of the Korean War (1950–1953). Japan enjoyed great benefits from its strategic position and its industries were given a tremendous push by the "special procurements" for U.S. armed forces. By the end of 1951, Japanese industrial production was equivalent to that of prewar years.

Important political advantages also derived to Japan from the new situation: it regained its independence following the signature of a peace treaty at San Francisco on Sept. 8, 1951. On the same day the United States concluded a security pact with Japan.

Since the peace treaty, Japan has been ruled by conservative governments which have maintained friendly relations with the West. The Liberal Democratic Party (LDP) and the Japan Socialist Party (JSP) came to dominate Japanese politics. Eisaku Sato of the LDP became prime minister in 1964, and the LDP received almost 49 percent of the vote in the 1967 legislative elections. Together with a 5 percent independent vote, the LDP held a majority in the House of Representatives.

In November 1967 Prime Minister Sato and U.S. Pres. Lyndon B. Johnson met in Washington and discussed the status of the Bonin and Ryukyu Islands, under U.S. administration since 1945. The United States agreed to consider the early return of the Bonin Islands to Japan and announced that the status of the Ryukyu Islands would be reviewed.

—Sergio Barzanti; M. G. Inaba

JORDAN

Official name: Hashemite Kingdom of Jordan
Area: 37,737 square miles
Population: (1966 est.) 2,040,000
Capital: Amman (Pop. 1966 est. 330,000)
Language: Arabic
Religion: Islam
Currency unit: Dinar
National holiday: Independence day, May 25

The Hashemite Kingdom of Jordan is bordered on the north by Syria, on the east and south by Saudi Arabia, and on the west by Israel. Jordan has a short coastline on the Gulf of Aqaba, at the extreme southern tip of the country.

THE LAND. Most of Jordan is barren land. Almost the entire eastern half of the country is desert, partly covered by salt or lava. In the west a hilly region separates the desert from a wide, deep gorge that runs the length of the country. The Jordan River flows through the northern part of this gorge, from the Sea of Galilee into the salty Dead Sea. South of the Dead Sea the gorge is a dry river bed, the Wadi al Araba. West of the Jordan River is the fertile Judaean Hill region, which was seized from Palestine in 1948 and occupied by Israel in 1967.

In the western uplands, Jordan's climate is mild, with average temperatures of from 45°F to 76°F and from 15 to 25 inches of rainfall a year. Almost no rain falls in the desert, where summer temperatures rise above 120°F.

THE PEOPLE. Almost the entire Jordanian population is Arab. In 1965 it included more than 688,000 Arab refugees who had fled Palestine during the 1948–1949 Arab-Israeli war. Population is densest in the north-western hills and valleys.

ECONOMY. Jordan is a very poor, arid country, with little surface water, infertile soils, and few exploitable resources. Potash and phosphates, mined around the Dead Sea, are its most important minerals. Some marble, gypsum, manganese, and ceramic clays are also mined, and there are untapped reserves of copper, iron, sulfur, and silicon.

Only about 10 percent of Jordan's land is suitable for cultivation, and any part of that was being farmed in the 1960s. The best growing regions are in the moist northwest, but even there some irrigation is necessary. Barley and wheat are the main crops. Beans, tobacco, and citrus and other fruits grow in the Jordan valley, and grapes, dates, figs, olives, and nuts are raised in the drier areas. Goats, sheep, camels, and horses are raised.

Natural phosphates, vegetables, and fruits are the most important of Jordan's exports, which were valued at $36 million in 1966. The country imported $187 million worth of goods in 1966, primarily foodstuffs, petroleum, pharmaceuticals, textiles, and machinery. Most trade is with the United States, Britain, West Germany, and the Arab states. The United Nations contribute heavily to the support of the Jordanian economy.

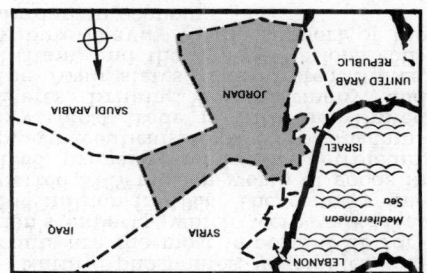

GOVERNMENT. Jordan is a constitutional monarchy. The hereditary head of state is a king who wields great authority over all branches of government. He appoints the prime minister and other members of the cabinet and may dismiss them at will. The ministers are also responsible to the lower house of the National Assembly, the House of Representatives, which is elected every four years by male citizens. Members of the upper house, the Senate, are appointed by the king.

Jordan is a member of the United Nations and the Arab League.

HISTORY. The area of Jordan is believed to have been inhabited since prehistoric times, and it was part of the land of the ancient Hebrews. As a part of Syria, the region was occupied by a succession of Middle Eastern empires. The last was the Ottoman Empire, which controlled the country from the 1500s into the 1900s.

After World War I Jordan became part of a new Syrian kingdom, which came under French control. In 1922 the League of Nations gave Britain a mandate over Palestine and Transjordan, as the territory between the Jordan River and Saudi Arabia was called. In 1923 Transjordan gained semi-independent status within the mandate area.

Emir Abdullah ibn Hussein, an Arabian ruler, governed with British advice. He was the first of the Hashemite ("of Hashem," or "Hussein") dynasty. For the next 20 years the country moved toward independence with British assistance. Transjordanian troops aided the Allies in World War II, and a treaty signed in 1946 with Britain established Transjordan's sovereignty. Britain retained great influence, however.

In 1948–1949 Transjordan participated in the Arab war against the newly proclaimed state of Israel. Abdullah annexed a portion of Palestine just west of the Jordan River and changed the country's name from Transjordan, "across the Jordan," to Jordan.

Contemporary Jordan. King Abdullah was assassinated in 1951, and his son and heir, Talal, was judged incompetent. Talal's son, Hussein, came to the throne in 1952. Hussein sought British aid in meeting the country's pressing economic and social problems. But the presence in the country of a large number of Palestinian refugees demanding renewed war with Israel to allow them to return to their homes led to political instability. Anti-Western riots in 1955 and 1956 forced the departure from the country of all British personnel and an

end to British assistance. In 1957 and 1958 King Hussein himself barely avoided being deposed during a government upheaval. In the early 1960s Jordan's domestic politics remained relatively calm, but the monarchy's position was precarious. Pan-Arab sentiment fostered by the United Arab Republic (Egypt) looked to the establishment of a republic and a resumption of the Arab-Israeli war.

In 1967 the Arab-Israeli conflict again broke into open warfare, and Israeli forces swept through Jordan's defenses. When the conflict ended, the west bank of the Jordan River was occupied by Israel, and Jordan was faced with economic ruin.

—Alexander Melamid; Charles Issawi

KENYA

Official name: Republic of Kenya
Area: 224,960 square miles
Population: (1967 est.) 9,948,000
Capital: Nairobi (Pop. 1962, urban area, 314,760)
Language: English, Swahili and other African languages
Religion: Traditional religions, Christianity, Islam
Currency unit: Shilling
National holiday: Independence day, December 12

Kenya, a republic in eastern Africa, is bordered on the north by Sudan and Ethiopia, on the east by the Somali Republic and the Indian Ocean, on the south by Tanzania, and on the west by Uganda.

Kenya received its independence from Britain in 1963.

THE LAND. Kenya has a varied landscape. The land is low in both northern and eastern Kenya behind the coast. Except for the area around Mombasa, the eastern and northern regions are too dry for intensive settlement. Lake Rudolf extends into northern Kenya. In the southeastern part of the country the land is flat and dry. There is a highland region in the west and southwest.

The highland terrain is extremely varied. The Rift Valley cuts through the highlands. There are also lakes and volcanic peaks, including Mt. Kenya, which has an elevation of over 17,000 feet. Lake Victoria borders Kenya's southwestern corner. The highland region receives abundant and reliable rainfall, and temperatures are moderate.

THE PEOPLE. Africans make up about 97 percent of Kenya's population, and Europeans, Asians, and Arabs account for the remaining 3 percent. Kenya's people belong to many different tribes. The largest tribes are the Kikuyu, Luo, Baluhya, Masai, and Kamba. The Kikuyu people have played an important role in Kenya's political history.

Kenya's largest city is its capital, Nairobi. Mombasa, on the Indian Ocean, is the country's major port.

ECONOMY. Kenya's economy is based largely on agriculture. The highlands have become the mainstay of the country's economy. Many crops are grown on European-owned plantations, including coffee, tea, and sisal.

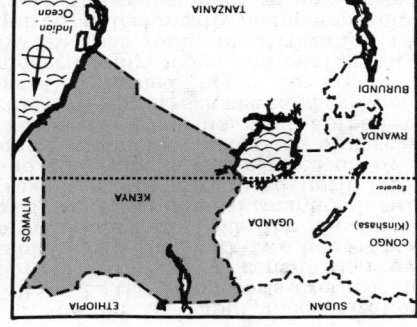

Kenya is the world's largest producer of pyrethrum, a vegetable ingredient used in certain insecticides. In 1964–1965 about 6,000 tons of pyrethrum were produced. The staples of the country, produced by Africans and Europeans, include corn, wheat, vegetables, dairy products, and meat.

Although Kenya is apparently not well-endowed with mineral resources, the country is a major producer of soda ash. The Kenyan government has made efforts to develop the country's industry and has encouraged tourism, based largely on safaris from Nairobi to see the country's varied wildlife.

In 1966 imports cost $315 million and exports earned $168 million. Kenya's main imports are machinery, petroleum, food, and fabrics. Exports include coffee, tea, sisal, pyrethrum, and petroleum products. The country's main trading partners are Britain, the United States, West Germany, the Netherlands, and Japan.

With a well-built seaport at Mombasa and connecting railroads and roads, Kenya is the principal handler of Uganda's trade. Kenya, Uganda, and Tanzania cooperate closely in the fields of communications, technical services, trade, and economic development.

GOVERNMENT. Kenya has a presidential system of government. Executive power is held by a president, who is popularly elected to a five-year term. Legislative power is vested in a 175-member House of Representatives. House members are popularly elected to five-year terms.

Kenya is a member of the United Nations, the Organization of African Unity (OAU), and the Commonwealth of Nations.

HISTORY. Starting in the 700s the peoples of present-day Kenya traded with the Arabs, mainly for slaves. By the 1600s Turks and Portuguese had joined the trade, but in the early 1800s Britain outlawed slaving.

British Rule. In 1887 the Sultan of Zanzibar, who had nominal control of the region, granted the British East African Company control over all of present-day Kenya in return for a fixed sum of money. Britain declared the area a protectorate in 1895. In the same year Britain began building a railroad from Mombasa to Uganda, with the aid of Indian laborers. To make the railroad pay for itself by transporting agricultural products, the British government encouraged Europeans to settle and farm in Kenya by offering long-term land leases in the highlands. Britain set up reserves in

of land for Africans south and north of the highlands.

Britain established a legislative council in the region in 1907. In 1920 all but the coastal region became a crown colony. The coastal area became the Kenya Protectorate.

Nationalism. In 1938 the highland region, which became known as the "white highlands," was officially closed for settlement to all but Europeans. The European community came to dominate political affairs. Meanwhile, the African population, especially the Kikuyu people, was increasing and crowding the reserves. Many Africans were forced to seek work in the new cities. Although an African was nominated to the legislative council in 1944, power remained in the hands of the white settlers and unrest grew among the Africans. Educated Kikuyu, such as Harry Thuku and Jomo Kenyatta created African political organizations in the 1940s.

Starting in 1952 the Man Mau, a movement of militant Kikuyu trying to gain independence for Kenya, terrorized the country. Britain declared a state of emergency. In the years of terrorism, 13 Europeans and 19 Asians were killed, but 9,597 Africans were killed, 7,811 of whom were listed as Man Mau. Kenyatta was imprisoned and exiled as presumed leader of the Man Mau. The Man Mau danger came to an end in 1956.

After the Man Mau uprising, British policy in Kenya changed. In 1957 Britain permitted a limited number of Africans to vote for the first time, and in 1960 Britain promised that Kenya would be an independent country ruled by Africans. Constitutional changes gave more representation to Africans and ended white-settler power. Britain opened the highlands to African settlement and provided African farmers with loans to buy land.

With liberalization, new political parties emerged. The Kenya African National Union (KANU), made up of the larger ethnic groups—the Kikuyu, Luo, and Kamba peoples—favored a centralized government. The Kenya African Democratic Union (KADU), representing the many smaller groups, favored regional autonomy.

Independence. In June 1963 Britain granted Kenya internal self-government. Kenya became fully independent within the Commonwealth of Nations on Dec. 12, 1963, with Kenyatta, leader of KANU, as prime minister. One year later Kenya became a republic and Kenyatta became the country's first president. In 1964 the leaders of KADU dissolved their party, leaving Kenya a one-party state. In 1966 the Senate was dissolved and all Senate members were given seats in the House of Representatives.

—Hibberd V. B. Kline, Jr.;
Vera L. Zolberg

KOREA

SOUTH KOREA

Official name: Republic of Korea
Population: (1967 est.) 29,784,000
Area: 38,004 square miles
Capital: Seoul (Pop. 1966, 3,800,000)
Language: Korean
Religion: Buddhism, Ch'ondogyo, Christianity
Currency unit: Won
National holiday: Independence day, August 15

NORTH KOREA

Official name: Democratic People's Republic of Korea
Population: (1966 est.) 12,400,000
Area: 46,568 square miles
Capital: Pyongyang (Pop. 1960 est. 653,100)
Language: Korean
Religion: Buddhism, Ch'ondogyo, Christianity
Currency unit: Won

Korea is a divided nation occupying the Korean Peninsula in northeastern Asia. The peninsula was divided at the end of World War II at the 38th parallel, a division reaffirmed in 1953 after a ceasefire ended the Korean conflict. The Democratic People's Republic of Korea, or North Korea, occupies the northern half of the peninsula, and the Republic of Korea, or South Korea, occupies the southern half.

North Korea is bounded on the north by China and the Soviet Union, on the east by the Sea of Japan, and on the south by South Korea, and on the west by Korea Bay. South Korea is bounded on the north by North Korea, on the east by the Sea of Japan, on the south by the Korea Strait, which separates the peninsula from Japan, and on the west by the Yellow Sea.

THE LAND. Mountains dominate the Korean peninsula, especially in the north, where branches of China's Chang-pai range rise over the northern border. In the northeast the Taebaek Mountains rise sharply from the east coast to over 8,300 feet.

The Taebaeks extend south along the eastern coast, but they do not rise over 5,600 feet in the south. From the Taebaek range, spurs radiate to the west and southwest, gradually descending into highlands that extend almost to the Yellow Sea coast.

Many narrow, winding rivers thread Korea's hills. The Yalu and the Tumen mark North Korea's northern border. Farther south the major navigable streams are the Ch'ongch'on, the Han, and the Tae-dong. Almost all of these drain south

Map: CHINA · SOVIET UNION · KOREA (North, People's Republic of) · KOREA (South) · JAPAN · Sea of Japan

or west. The southern and western coasts are deeply indented and dotted with islands.

The South Korean climate is temperate, with mild winters and hot summers. In the north, the winters are long and severe. Average yearly rainfall ranges from 60 inches along the southwestern coast to 25 inches in the northern interior.

THE PEOPLE. Almost all of the people of the Korean Peninsula are Korean. They speak Korean, and the rate of literacy is very high. Although there are slight regional variations in language and culture, the only significant minority is a small number of Chinese. Korean religions include Buddhism, Confucianism, Christianity, Shamanism, and Ch'ondogyo, a religion that originated in Korea.

South Korea is much more densely populated than North Korea. In 1966 the South Korean population was over 29 million, and the North Korean population was about 12.4 million. Population is concentrated on the western and southern coasts. Seoul, the south's capital and largest city, and Pyongyang, the north's capital and only large city, are both in the west. Pusan, South Korea's second largest city and most important port, is on the southern coast.

ECONOMY. Both North and South Korea have expanding economies. The north is by far the richer in natural resources, with deposits of iron ore, copper, lead, zinc, pyrites, tungsten, graphite, coal, and magnesite. Water power is abundant and there are many acres of forests. A northern climate and the rough terrain limit agriculture, although rice, barley, maize, sorghum, and wheat are grown. Fishing is important, as is forestry.

The main manufactures are steel, chemicals, cement, and machinery. Agriculture is collectivized, and industry is nationalized. Almost all North Korean trade is with the Soviet Union and Communist China.

South Korea has only a small share of the peninsula's mineral resources, although some iron, coal, tungsten, copper, graphite, and kaolin are extracted. It does have most of the peninsula's cultivable land, however. Agriculture is the mainstay of the South Korean economy, contributing over 40 percent of the national product in 1965. Rice is the main crop. Barley, wheat, cotton, fruits, vegetables, and mulberry trees are also cultivated. Fishing thrives, and forestry is also important, but many forests have been depleted.

UNITED NATIONS

KENYA'S PORT CITY OF MOMBASA

There are few heavy industries in South Korea, but light industry grew rapidly in the 1950s and early 1960s. Textiles, processed foods, clothing, paper, and other consumer items are the leading products. South Korea relies heavily on U.S. technical and financial aid to develop and support its economy, and from 1946 through 1966 U.S. nonmilitary aid totaled more than $4,348 million.

South Korea has a very unfavorable balance of trade. In 1966, for example, imports cost $716 million and exports earned only $250 million. Silk textiles, fish, and tungsten and iron ores are the leading exports. Chemicals, cereal grains, sugar, raw cotton, petroleum, textile yarns, transportation equipment, and machinery are imported. Japan, Hong Kong, and the United States are Korea's chief trading partners.

GOVERNMENT. Both North and South Korea have highly centralized governments led by strong executives. In North Korea the Communist party, officially called the Korean Workers Party, dominates political life. Its central political committee determines national policy and its chairman is usually the key figure in North Korea's government.

A constitution adopted in 1948 vests supreme power in a popularly elected legislature, the Supreme People's Assembly, but the party nominates all candidates for the assembly. The assembly elects a presidium, or governing council, to act for it between its short sessions. The president of the presidium is head of state. The assembly elects a premier and cabinet, officially responsible to it.

South Korea's 1962 constitution established a republican form of government. The president, popularly elected every four years, is the central figure in the government and wields strong executive power. He presides over an appointed administrative cabinet that includes a prime minister, who serves as the assistant to the president. A popularly elected legislature of one house exercises legislative power.

HISTORY. Korea was settled more than 3,000 years ago, probably by peoples from Manchuria or northern China. They lived by hunting, fishing, and herding, and over many centuries developed a culture unique to the peninsula. Although many legends exist about civilizations that grew up in the Korean Peninsula in the 2000s and 1000s BC, the first known state of any significance was the kingdom of Wiman Choson, which was founded in the 190s BC. It was destroyed in the 100s BC by the Chinese and replaced by four Chinese colonies. Only one of these, Lolang, or Nangnang, in the northwest, survived Korean rebellions. Lolang grew prosperous on trade with China and Japan and became the source of Chinese influence on the peninsula.

By the end of the 300s AD native Korean kingdoms had developed—Koguryo in the north, Paekche in the southwest, and Silla in the southeast. Koguryo destroyed Lolang and tried to conquer the other two Korean kingdoms, which united and successfully resisted Koguryo. Silla grew in power under the strong leadership of a political and military elite, and in the 600s, with aid from China, it conquered Paekche and Koguryo. Silla ruled a unified peninsula for almost 250 years, a period considered the golden age of Buddhism. The government was efficiently run, society was well organized and peaceful, trade prospered, the arts flourished, and Buddhist culture and learning took firm root. By the 800s, however, Silla's kingdom began to collapse and society was divided into three warring factions—king, aristocracy, and peasantry.

Disorder led in 935 to the establishment of a new dynasty, the Koryo, from whose name Korea is derived. The Koryo restored order by establishing a centralized, bureaucratic government. The new government did nothing to remedy the inequitable division of land and power that had split Korean society, however, and civil disorders continued.

A military group seized power in the 1100s, but it also broke up into factions, and Koryo became too weak to defend itself. In the 1250s it surrendered to invading Mongol armies. Korea suffered greatly under the Mongols, but by the late 1300s it was independent again, under the Yi dynasty.

Yi Dynasty. The Yi dynasty was founded by an army general, who gave the kingdom its ancient name, Choson. Once more the central government was reorganized.

The era of the Yi dynasty is considered the golden age of Confucianism in Korea. Confucian emphasis on learning produced an elite of scholars and was responsible in the 1400s for the development of an alphabet for the Korean language. The Korean alphabet eventually was blended with the Chinese writing system. Confucian ethics served to widen the divisions within the traditional social and economic order, and factionalism severely weakened the country.

In the 1590s Japanese troops invaded Korea on the way to attack China, and defending Chinese troops were sent into Korea. Before both armies withdrew, Korea had been devastated. It had barely begun to recover when, in the 1620s and 1630s, it was overrun by Manchu armies that conquered all of China and established the Ch'ing dynasty in China. The Yi remained in power, but they had little left to rule. Poverty and disorder reigned, and the country was totally dependent on China for support and protection.

New Influences. The total destruction of the old social and economic orders and the weakness of traditional values left Korea open to new influences. Christian missionaries began to visit the country in the 1600s, and by 1800 they had won many converts and had introduced "Western learning" and ideals into the peninsula. Also by the middle 1800s, a new middle class of craftsmen and merchants had replaced the old feudal landlords as the dominant and most prosperous group in society. Trade with Japan thrived, and the appearance of trading ships from Western nations in the 1800s promised even greater prosperity for the merchants.

The Korean government tried unsuccessfully to maintain traditional society by repressing "Western learning" and banning foreign trade. Moreover, by the mid-1800s China had lost much of its power and was unable to serve as Korea's protector or as its agent in foreign affairs. By the late 1800s Korea was open to many foreign influences and was forced into involvement in world affairs.

Foreign Rivalries. Japan and China vied for political, commercial, and diplomatic control of Korea. To back its position, China invited the United States, Britain, Germany, Italy, France, and Russia to enter into trade and diplomatic relations with Korea, and in the 1800s Korea became a diplomatic battleground for the world's great powers. The government was sharply divided into rival factions and extremely unstable.

In protest against domestic disorder and international interference in Korea, there developed a conservative and antiforeign, nationalistic religious movement called Tonghak, or "Eastern learning," which was later called Ch'ondogyo. In 1894 it led a rebellion to demand the withdrawal of all foreigners from the country.

The government requested aid from China in quelling the rebellion. Japan then sent troops into Korea to "protect" Japanese interests, precipitating a Sino-Japanese war that ended in 1895 in victory for Japan. Japan forced China to relinquish all claims to Korea, and promised to "guarantee" Korean sovereignty.

Russia, with interests and influence in Korea second only to those of China, challenged Japanese dominance over Korean affairs. Russo-Japanese rivalry led to war between the two in 1904. The treaty ending the war in 1905 recognized Japan's dominant position in Korea, and in 1910 Japan annexed Korea, making it a colony.

UNITED NATIONS

SOUTH KOREAN FARMER. Agriculture is the mainstay of South Korea's economy.

Japanese Rule. Korea was ruled despotically, and Japan was concerned only with economic exploitation of the land and the people. The Japanese developed the country's industries and resources by using forced labor, they gave the best land and jobs to Japanese, and they tried to impose Japanese culture on the people of Korea.

Japan's rule was bitterly resented, and an independence movement soon developed. Although the independence movement was able to do little against the leaders it developed dealt with the World War II Allies who were fighting Japan—China, Britain, the United States, and the Soviet Union.

Divided Land. In 1945 Soviet and U.S. troops liberated the peninsula from the Japanese. To facilitate acceptance of the Japanese surrender and to prepare the country for independence, the two agreed to divide their authority in Korea at the 38th parallel. U.S. and Soviet representatives could not agree on the formation of a provisional government for a reunited country, or on the withdrawal of their troops, and the matter was turned over to the United Nations.

In 1947 the United Nations called for elections in Korea under UN supervision. But when elections were held in 1948, UN observers were not permitted in the northern zone. In the south, a constituent assembly was elected and a constitution adopted. Syngman Rhee, a leader of the independence movement, was elected president.

In the northern zone a government was established on the Soviet pattern. It was dominated by a newly formed Communist party. In China, the Chinese Communist party had just won a long civil war and established a communist government there that greatly influenced the affairs of North Korea.

The division of the country added to the difficulties it faced in recovering from years of war and colonial rule, and Korea became a focus of the worldwide confrontation between the United States and the Soviet Union. In 1949, feeling that South Korea could stand on its own, the United States withdrew most of its troops from the southern zone. In 1950 North Korean troops invaded South Korea, and the United Nations Security Council was called into immediate session. When fighting continued even after a UN call for a ceasefire, the UN asked for an international armed force.

The United States, later followed by 15 other nations, immediately sent troops to South Korea. The U.S.-UN troops drove the North Koreans back, only to face an attack by Chinese Communist troops. Negotiations for an armistice began in 1951 and continued, along with the fighting, until July 1953, when fighting was formally stopped and a ceasefire line was set at the 38th parallel. The 38th parallel remained heavily armed and guarded.

Contemporary Korea. While dealing with continuing military threats, both Koreas devoted their energies to developing strong governments and rebuilding their economies. In the north both the government and the economy were centralized under the control of the Communist party, and North Korea repaired the damages of the war and continued to develop its heavy industry.

North Korea received friendly relations with both the Soviet Union and Communist China, but it remained cut off from the noncommunist world.

The south, with fewer resources, made slower economic progress. It received support from the United Nations, the United States and other Western nations in improving its agriculture and developing light industries. But inexperience with democracy made political stability difficult to achieve under the south's democratic constitution. President Rhee assumed strong powers and was accused of governing autocratically and undemocratically.

In 1960 Rhee won a fourth presidential term in elections that his opponents charged were dishonest. Antigovernment riots broke out, and Rhee resigned, leaving a caretaker government in power.

In 1961 a military group seized power and established a dictatorship, led by Gen. Chung Hee Park. Voters elected a constituent assembly that drafted a new constitution in 1962, and in elections held in 1963 Park was elected president.

South Korean politics remained turbulent, but in 1967 Park was reelected with a minimum of disorder. Strengthening its ties with the noncommunist world, Park's government established official relations with Japan in 1965, and sent troops to aid the U.S. and South Vietnamese forces in South Vietnam.

Korea again became a focus of world attention in 1968, when North Korea seized a U.S. intelligence ship, claiming it had violated North Korea's territorial waters.

—Thomas E. Ennis; M. G. Inaba

KUWAIT

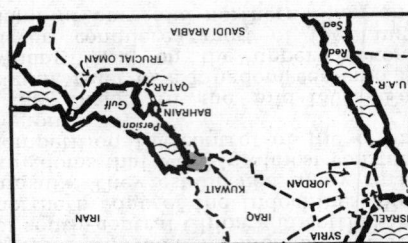

Official name: State of Kuwait
Area: 6,178 square miles
Population: (1966 est.) 491,000
Capital: Kuwait (Pop., 1965, 99,609)
Language: Arabic
Religion: Islam
Currency unit: Dinar
National holiday: National day, February 25

Kuwait is an oil-rich Arab sheikhdom on the west coast of the Persian Gulf. It is bordered on the north and west by Iraq, on the east by the Persian Gulf, and on the south by Saudi Arabia and a neutral zone jointly administered with Saudi Arabia.

THE LAND AND PEOPLE. Kuwait's surface is level desert broken only by a single ridge of hills and a few small oases. The climate is extremely hot, and almost no rain falls.

Native Kuwaitis are Arabs but there are large minorities of Indians, Iranians, and non-Kuwaiti Arabs, as well as European and U.S. oil workers. The largest cities—Kuwait, the capital, and Al Ahmadi, the oil port—are on the coast.

ECONOMY. Oil is Kuwait's only important natural resource. An estimated one-fifth of the world's proved oil reserves lie beneath Kuwait's land and off its coasts. Water, however, is scarce. Water is imported and seawater is desalted. Most of the land is not suitable for cultivation, but fruits and vegetables are grown in oases, and in the 1950s and 1960s large areas of desert were irrigated to provide more farmland.

Kuwait's major industry is oil. In 1966 the tiny country was the world's fifth largest producer of crude oil, pumping over 114 million metric tons. In 1965-1966 taxes and royalties paid by the foreign operating companies that exploit the oil totaled more than $500 million.

Much of the oil money is used to finance social welfare programs and economic development projects. By the mid-1960s Kuwait's industries included chemical production, food canning, and the manufacture of building materials.

Kuwait's major export is oil, but processed foods, leather goods, building materials, and other manufactures are also exported. Imports include vehicles, foodstuffs, and raw materials.

GOVERNMENT. Kuwait is a constitutional monarchy in which the ruler, a sheikh, exercises great power. The sheikh appoints a council of ministers and a prime minister, a national assembly elected every four years by male citizens proposes legislation for the sheikh's approval and may override his veto.

Kuwait is a member of the Arab League and the United Nations.

HISTORY. Kuwait was first settled in the early 1700s by Arab peoples from the interior of Arabia. It grew prosperous as a trading center and a pearl fishery. Attacks from Saudi Arabia in the late 1700s impoverished the country, but by the end of the 1800s the economy had recovered.

In 1899, after attempts by the Ottoman Empire to annex Kuwait, the country signed a treaty of protection with Britain. By that treaty and a later agreement, Britain assumed responsibility for Kuwait's foreign affairs and defense.

The beginnings of full-scale oil production in 1946 radically changed the way of life of the people of Kuwait. Within 20 years the country had become a wealthy welfare state.

Kuwait gained full independence in June 1961, when the 1899 protective treaty with Britain was canceled and replaced by a treaty of friendship. Within the month, Iraq announced its intention of annexing Kuwait, which it claimed as Iraqi territory. British troops were sent to protect Kuwait, and later an international force of the

Arab League replaced the British troops. Arab League forces remained in Kuwait until the threat from Iraq ended in 1962. The dispute was not finally settled until 1963, however, when new leaders seized power in Iraq.

Since 1962 the Kuwait Fund for Arab Economic Development has been a major source of funds for development projects in other Arab lands, and in 1967, after renewed Arab-Israeli hostilities caused severe economic problems in many Arab states, Kuwait increased its aid to these Arab lands.

—Charles Issawi; Alexander Melamid

LAOS

Official name: Kingdom of Laos
Area: 91,429 square miles
Population: (1966 est.) 2,700,000
Capital: Vientiane (Pop., 1962 est., urban area, 162,297)
Currency unit: Kip
Language: Lao, French
Religion: Buddhism
National holiday: Constitution day, May 11

THE LAND. Laos is a long, narrow country, broader in the north and with a southern panhandle that narrows to little more than 50 miles in width. In the northern region sandstone and limestone plateaus are deeply etched by the Mekong River and its tributaries. In the center of this region is a low-land area where the Mekong meets the Ou and Seng rivers.

The country has its highest elevation, over 9,000 feet, in the Plain of Jars, east of the Mekong. In the south the Mekong forms most of the western boundary. East of its broad, low valley rise the foothills of the Annam mountains. At the southern tip of the country is the high Bolovens Plateau.

Laos has a tropical climate, with high humidity and year-round temperatures averaging between 80°F and 90°F. There are some regional variations. On the lowlands frost is unknown and rainfall is just sufficient for rice growing. In the uplands temperatures may be considerably lower and rainfall higher. Monsoons occur from May to October.

THE PEOPLE. About half the people of Laos are Lao, a branch of the Tai people of southern China, who speak Lao. There are various other peoples who have their origins in present-day China, such as the Miao, and there is a small group of Kra, the aboriginal inhabitants of Laos. Most Laotians are Buddhist.

Laos is sparsely populated. Ninety percent of the population lives in rural areas, and there is no large metropolis. Vientiane, the administrative capital, is the largest city. Luang Prabang, the royal capital, ranks second, with a much smaller population.

ECONOMY. Laos is a poor country with an underdeveloped economy and an unskilled, largely illiterate labor force. It is thought to have deposits of iron ore, manganese, gold, coal, and copper, but these have not been explored. Tin, gypsum, salt, and limestone are mined in small amounts. Almost all of the country is forested with potentially valuable timber, and the soil is very rich, especially in the valleys of the Mekong River and its tributaries.

Subsistence agriculture dominates the economy. In the lowlands the major crop is paddy rice, but yields are very low, only 500 to 600 pounds per acre. In areas where irrigation is not possible, upland rice, corn, and sweet potatoes are produced.

Vegetables, spices, and some fruits, including bananas, mangoes, and pineapples, are grown throughout the country. Cotton is widely raised, and there is some commercial tobacco farming around Vientiane.

Many upland tribes still follow the "slash and burn" form of farming. These farmers clear the forest by cutting down the smaller trees and burning the refuse. In the fields thus cleared, they plant a variety of crops for a few seasons and then abandon the field to the forest to start over again within a certain radius of the village has been exploited, the people migrate to a new area.

Foreign trade is of little importance in the economy, and the balance of trade is very poor. Exports earned in 1965 $33 million and imports cost $1 million. The main exports are tin, coffee, soy beans, leather, and forest products such as wood, cardamom, benzoin, and lac. Petroleum, manufactured goods, and foodstuffs are imported. Laos relies heavily on technical and financial aid from abroad.

GOVERNMENT. Laos is a constitutional monarchy with a king as head of state. A council of ministers, headed by a prime minister, is responsible to a popularly elected legislature to house. Laos is a member of the United Nations.

HISTORY. The aboriginal Kha people of Laos were joined in the mid-1200s AD by the Lao, one tribe of the Tai peoples who fled the Mongol invasion of south-central China and settled the northern edge of the Indochinese Peninsula. They established many small kingdoms that were in almost constant competition for control of the entire region.

Lan Chang. In the mid-1300s Fa-Ngum, ruler of a kingdom centered in Muang Swa, on the upper Mekong River, conquered most of the kingdoms of Laos and northern Siam and united them in the empire of Lan Chang, or Lan Xang, the "Land of a Million Elephants." The culture and religion of Laos, transmitted through tribes south of Laos, heavily influenced Lao culture. Fa-Ngum adopted Buddhism and made his capital a center of Buddhist culture.

His son, Sam Sene Tai, consolidated the kingdom and established an efficient administration. By the late 1300s Lan Chang was a powerful, peaceful kingdom that had grown prosperous as a producer of forest products and as a center of trade in Southeast Asia.

During the 1500s attacks by two powerful neighbors of Laos—Annam, to its east, and Siam ('Thailand'), to its west—weakened Lan Chang and lowered its prestige. During this period the Lao capital was moved south, to Vientiane, and Muang Swa was made a temple city and renamed Luang Prabang.

Civil Strife. In the late 1500s Laos was torn by violent dynastic struggles that left it poverty stricken and defenseless against tribal rebellions and attacks by Annam and Siam. By the early 1700s, this civil strife had split Laos into two rival states, one ruled from Luang Prabang and the other from Vientiane.

Neither state could regain the former power, prosperity, and prestige that the unified kingdom had enjoyed, and each sought the aid of Siam, Annam, and Burma in conquering the other. As a result, Laos continued to be torn by conflict throughout the 1700s, and by the early 1800s Siam had conquered both kingdoms and had annexed Laos.

During the 1800s European explorers, traders, and missionaries began to visit Laos. Although Laos itself, with few riches and no access to the sea, held little attraction for the Europeans, competition was keen among the European states for control of all the territory in Southeast Asia.

French Control. By the late 1800s only Siam, which included Laos, separated British Burma from French Cambodia. The British wanted Siam to remain independent, and the French wanted to gain control of Siam. In 1893, in an effort to hold off French conquest, Siam ceded to France all its territory east of the Mekong, which included most of Laos. In 1904 most of the remainder of present-day Laos became French.

France governed Laos as part of French Indochina, which also included Cambodia and the Vietnamese regions of Annam, Cochin China, and Tonkin. Unlike the rest of French Indochina, Laos did not resist French rule. The Lao had seen so much war that a peaceful conquest did not affect them, and the French did not much to improve conditions.

The French imposed peace on the warlike Lao tribes and kingdoms, and they allowed Lao leaders to participate in the government. They modernized the government, abolished slavery, and brought education and medical care to the Lao. The French also attempted to develop the country's natural resources and improve its economy, but the world economic depression of the 1930s hindered any real economic progress.

Japan occupied all of Indochina from 1941 to 1945, during World War II, and during the Japanese occupation, Lao nationalism began to grow. A "Free Laos" government was organized and it took over when the Japanese withdrew. After the war the French made an unsuccessful attempt to reestablish their control. In 1947 the Lao adopted a constitution establishing a monarchy and a parliament, and in 1949 Laos became an independent state within the French Union.

Opposition to the French was quite violent elsewhere in Indochina. In Vietnam open war, supported by communist forces, was raging against the French, and in 1953 the communist-supported Vietminh forces of Vietnam invaded Laos. In 1954 the French gave up the struggle in Vietnam.

Independence. A peace conference held at Geneva later in 1954 officially ended the war and recognized Laos as a sovereign state. Lao independence and neutrality were guaranteed by all the participants in the Geneva Accords, including the United States, France, the Soviet Union, and Communist China.

Political and economic chaos reigned in Laos between 1954 and 1960, as the governments that came to power were too unstable to deal with the many factions within Laos or to repair the social and economic damage of years of warfare. In addition, communists from Vietnam recruited and organized a rebel army, the Lao People's Liberation Army, originally called the Pathet Lao.

In 1960 a conflict between neutralist and anticommunist politicians caused a government crisis that precipitated a civil war between the Pathet Lao and government forces. Fighting continued even after a ceasefire was arranged in 1961. In 1962 an international conference at Geneva established a coalition government for Laos consisting of pro-Western, neutralist, and procommunist factions. A neutralist, Souvanna Phouma, became premier. The coalition soon disintegrated, however, leaving Souvanna Phouma as sole executive. Fighting erupted again, with the Pathet Lao in control of most of northern Laos. The Laotian People's Liberation Army received heavy support from Communist China and North Vietnam.

In 1964 the Laotian government began receiving military aid from the United States, and the fighting remained stalemated. Political disputes within Laos further worsened the condition of the country.

In addition to its own internal conflicts, Laos became involved in renewed warfare in neighboring Vietnam. U.S. and Vietnamese planes bombed Lao territory used by the North Vietnamese for supply, transport, and invasion bases.

In 1967 Lao government troops engaged in direct combat with North Vietnamese forces for control of a range of hills in northeastern Laos. In elections held in 1967, Souvanna Phouma's government was reelected, but the Lao Patriotic Front, the political arm of the Pathet Lao, boycotted the elections.

—Thomas E. Ennis; M. G. Inaba

LEBANON

Official name: Republic of Lebanon
Area: 4,015 square miles
Population: (1966 est.) 2,460,000
Capital: Beirut (Pop., 1964 est., 700,000)
Language: Arabic
Religion: Christianity, Islam
Currency unit: Pound
National holiday: Independence day, Nov. 22

(Map: Mediterranean Sea, CYPRUS, LEBANON, SYRIA, IRAQ, JORDAN, SAUDI ARABIA, UNITED ARAB REPUBLIC, ISRAEL)

Lebanon is an independent republic at the eastern end of the Mediterranean Sea. It is bordered on the north and the east by Syria, on the south by Israel, and on the west by the Mediterranean.

THE LAND. Mountains cover more than half of Lebanon. The Lebanon Mountains chain extends along the eastern country, and the Sharqi, or Anti-Lebanon, chain runs through the center of the country. Between the coast and the Lebanon Mountains lies a narrow, fertile plain on border. A fertile plateau, the Bekaa, lies between the Lebanon Mountains and the Sharqi plateau. Lebanon's major river, the Litani, flows through the Bekaa.

Lebanon's climate is mild and moist. Average temperatures range from 50°F in winter to 80°F in summer, and yearly rainfall averages between 30 and 50 inches.

THE PEOPLE. The Lebanese people are largely Arab. Approximately half the population is Christian and half is Muslim. There are many separate sects within each community. The largest are the Maronite Christians and the Sunni Muslims.

The population is concentrated in port cities along the coast, especially Beirut, Tripoli, and Sidon. Heavy emigration, primarily to North and South America, has characterized the Lebanese population since the 1860s, and there are almost as many Lebanese living abroad as in Lebanon. Many emigrants maintain economic and social ties with Lebanon and contribute to the country's economic and cultural life.

ECONOMY. Lebanon's economy is more diversified than that of many other Middle Eastern nations. Agriculture, industry, and trade are all important. The country has no major exploitable mineral resources except for some deposits of iron ore.

Agriculture occupies about half of the labor force and in 1965 contributed approximately 17 percent to the country's national product. The leading crops are grains, tobacco, olives, and citrus and other fruits. Sheep, pastured in the mountains, and timber forests, in central Lebanon, are also of economic importance.

International trade and finance are vital to the Lebanese economy. They contributed about one-third of the country's income during the early 1960s. Lebanon is a leading banking center, and Lebanese ports handle a large share of the trade passing through the eastern Mediterranean. In 1965 Lebanese exports earned $85 million and imports cost $482 million. The main exports are agricultural products and the major imports include machinery and vehicles, textiles, and manufactured consumer goods.

GOVERNMENT. Lebanon is a republic in which power is divided between Christians and Muslims. A Christian president, elected by a unicameral parliament, is head of state. A prime minister, who is a Muslim, and a cabinet are responsible to the parliament. Members of parliament are popularly elected under a system of confessional representation by which each religious group elects a number of representatives in proportion to its membership. Lebanon is a member of the United Nations and the Arab League.

HISTORY. Lebanon is an ancient land. In its forests grew the Cedars of Lebanon mentioned in the Old Testament, and its excellent ports have made it a vital trading center since ancient times. Before 2000 BC the area was the home of the Canaanites, or Phoenicians, who were the leading traders of the ancient world, and in the 800s BC it was conquered by the Assyrians.

Lebanon's history has been closely associated with that of Syria, but Lebanon was set apart by the strong influence of Christianity. Because of its proximity to Palestine, Phoenicia was the site of some of the earliest Christian communities, and by the 300s AD it was entirely Christian. A small group of Lebanese Christians escaped Muslim armies that conquered and converted most of Syria-Lebanon in the 600s AD. Their descendants became the Maronites—Arab Christians affiliated with the Roman Catholic Church.

Ottoman Era. In the 1500s the Ottoman Empire conquered both Lebanon and Syria, but Lebanon was allowed a great deal of autonomy. This relative freedom and the country's commercial importance placed Lebanon in an advantageous position that it maintained through the 1800s. In addition, the presence of a large number of British and French missionary schools and colleges made it a center for Arab intellectual development in the 1800s.

During the period of Ottoman rule, Lebanese Christian and Muslim communities expanded, and the two occasionally came into conflict. In 1860 a revolt by Christian peasants against Muslim overlords touched off widespread religious strife, eventually leading to civil war. Britain and France-

intervened and forced Turkey to give Lebanon an autonomous government that divided power between the Christians and the Muslims.

Independence. After the defeat of the Ottoman Empire in World War I, France received a League of Nations mandate over Lebanon. In 1926 the French created a republican government, but the Lebanese demanded complete independence. In 1941, following Germany's defeat of France in World War II, a free Lebanese government proclaimed the country's independence of the German-controlled Vichy French administration. A treaty recognizing Lebanon's sovereignty was signed in 1943 by Lebanon and the free French government. In 1945 Lebanon was admitted to the United Nations as an independent nation and it also joined the Arab League. All foreign troops had left the country by 1946, and in 1947 parliamentary elections were held.

A high rate of literacy, experience with representative government, and continuing vigorous trade made the early republic stable and prosperous. During the 1950s and 1960s Lebanon strengthened its economy and expanded social welfare and development programs.

Lebanon followed a moderate course in foreign affairs and came into conflict with more extreme pan-Arab nationalist groups in neighboring states. In 1958 the Lebanese government accused the United Arab Republic (Egypt) of inciting a widespread rebellion. Civil war was ended only with the landing of U.S. troops. Relations with Syria, too, became tense during conflicts over trade policies and border defenses.

In general, however, Lebanon attempted to maintain strict neutrality in conflicts among the Arab states. Although Lebanon lent diplomatic and economic support to the Arab side in the Arab-Israeli war of 1967, it did not become deeply involved and was not seriously harmed by the conflict.

—Sara Gilbert; Charles Issawi

LESOTHO

Official name: Kingdom of Lesotho
Area: 11,716 square miles
Population: (1966 est.) 860,000
Capital: Maseru (Pop., 1966, urban area, 18,000)
Language: English, Sesotho
Religion: Christianity, traditional religions
Currency: South African rand
National holiday: Independence day, October 4

Lesotho, a republic in southern Africa, lies entirely within the borders of the Republic of South Africa. Lesotho, formerly known as Basutoland, received its independence from Britain in 1966.

THE LAND. The Drakensberg Mountains occupy most of Lesotho. The mountains reach elevations of about 11,000 feet above sea level, but they have areas of grassland and alpine pasture. Lowlands, in the west, occupy about one-quarter of Lesotho. The Orange River and its tributaries flow through the country. Rainfall averages about 28 inches a year.

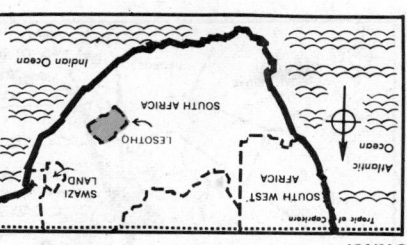

THE PEOPLE. Almost the entire population is made up of Africans of the Basuto tribe. Most of the people live in the lowlands. About 70 percent of the people are Christian. Many thousands of Basutos are employed in the Republic of South Africa because Lesotho cannot support its population. Lesotho's major city is its capital, Maseru.

ECONOMY. Lesotho's economy is based on subsistence agriculture, livestock raising, and the earnings of workers employed in South Africa. The chief crops are corn, beans, sorghum, peas, and wheat. Cattle, sheep, and goats are raised throughout the country, and hides, wool, and mohair are produced. There are only a few small industries in the country. Mineral deposits, except for diamonds, have not been discovered. In 1967 one of the world's largest diamonds, more than 600 carats, was found in Lesotho.

In 1965 imports cost about $24.5 million. Lesotho imports food, machinery, manufactured goods, and petroleum products. Exports include wool and mohair, diamonds, and foodstuffs. Most of Lesotho's trade is with the Republic of South Africa, with which Lesotho has a customs union. Lesotho receives financial aid from Britain.

GOVERNMENT. Lesotho has a parliamentary system of government. The head of state is the king. The prime minister, appointed by the king, holds actual executive power. The prime minister is ordinarily the leader of the majority party in the National Assembly.

Legislative powers are held by a parliament, consisting of a Senate and National Assembly. The Senate is composed of 22 tribal chiefs and 11 members nominated by the king. The 60 members of the National Assembly are popularly elected to five-year terms.

Lesotho is a member of the Commonwealth of Nations and the United Nations.

HISTORY. The Basuto nation emerged in the early 1800s from the union of Sotho and other Bantu-speaking peoples under the leadership of a northern chief, Moshesh. Moshesh had successfully defended these peoples from raiding Zulu and Matebele bands.

The newly organized nation ran into conflict with the Boers, Dutch farmers migrating northward from the Orange Free State. The conflicts led Moshesh to sign a treaty of friendship with the British governor of Cape Colony. In 1868 Britain declared a protectorate over present-day Lesotho to prevent seizure of the country by the neighboring Orange Free State.

British Rule. In 1871, a year after the death of Moshesh, the British gave control of Basutoland to Cape Colony. Between 1880 and 1882 Cape Colony troops waged the Gun Wars, a series of military campaigns, to disarm Basutoland's inhabitants who had rebelled against Cape Colony rule. The effort failed, and Cape Colony abandoned the territory. In 1884 Basutoland became a British High Commission Territory.

The British administered the territory through a resident commissioner who rarely acted contrary to the wishes of the paramount chief. Basuto traditional law endured under British rule.

Basutoland's economic affairs were tied to South Africa, and until 1948 Britain assumed that South Africa would eventually incorporate Basutoland. Union with South Africa was unacceptable to Basutoland, however, because of South Africa's policy of apartheid, or rigid separation of the races.

Nationalism. In the 1950s the Basutoland African Congress, an African nationalist organization, campaigned for Basutoland's independence. The Congress also sought support from Britain and the United Nations to lessen Basutoland's economic dependence on South Africa.

In 1964 Britain abolished the High Commission, and appointed a representative to Basutoland. On Oct. 4, 1966 Basutoland became an independent member of the Commonwealth. The new nation, renamed Lesotho, was led by the Basuto paramount chief, Moshoeshoe II. In 1967 the king accepted the role of a constitutional monarch, and Prime Minister Leabua Jonathon acquired greater executive powers.

—Hibberd V. B. Kline, Jr.; Gary A. Weissman

LIBERIA

Official name: Republic of Liberia
Area: 43,000 square miles
Population: (1966 est.) 1,090,000
Capital: Monrovia (Pop., 1962, 80,992)
Language: English, African languages
Religion: Christianity, Islam, traditional religions
Currency unit: U.S. Dollar
National holiday: Independence day, July 26

Liberia, a republic in western Africa, is bordered on the north by Guinea, on the east by the Ivory Coast, on the south by the Atlantic Ocean, and on the west by Sierra Leone. Liberia declared itself a sovereign nation in 1847.

THE LAND. Most of Liberia is occupied by hills and low uplands. The country has a rocky coastline, beyond which are swampy plains. In the north, along the border with Guinea, are the grass-covered Nimba Mountains, with elevations of about 4,500 feet. The Lofa, St. Paul, St. John, and Cess rivers flow through the country. Liberia is one of the rainiest areas in western Africa. The rainy season extends from May through October. Rainfall averages more than 140 inches a year in the coastal region and over 100 inches a year in the interior of the country.

THE PEOPLE. There are two distinct population groups in Liberia—the Americo-Liberians, descended from Negroes brought to Liberia from the United States during the 1800s, and the tribal peoples, who form the majority of Liberia's people. Liberia's indigenous tribes include the Kru, Mandingo, Gola, Vai, and Kissi.

The major cities of Liberia are Monrovia, Buchanan, and Harper, all of which are ports.

ECONOMY. Liberia's economy is based on subsistence agriculture, mining, and rubber growing. The people raise cassava, rice, palm fruit, and bananas for local consumption. Liberia exported only palm oil products, coffee, and cassava until 1926, when the Firestone Rubber Company established rubber plantations in Liberia and loaned the government capital for development. In the 1960s other private companies established rubber plantations in Liberia, and in 1965 over 52.6 million tons of rubber were exported.

Liberia is a major producer of iron ore, and in 1965 over 10 million metric tons of ore were exported. There are iron ore deposits in the Bomi Hills, some 45 miles northwest of Monrovia, in the Nimba Mountains, and in other places.

In the 1950s a railroad built from Monrovia to the ore deposits at Bomi Hills made possible the export of high-grade iron ore. Ore mined in the Nimba Mountains travels by rail to Buchanan for export.

Liberia also has deposits of many other minerals, including gold, diamonds, and lead.

In 1965 Liberia's imports cost $104.5 million and exports earned over $130 million. Liberia's main imports are food, fuels, and machinery. The main exports are iron ore and natural rubber. Most trade is conducted with the United States, West Germany, Britain, and Italy. Liberia receives economic assistance from the United States.

GOVERNMENT. Liberia has a presidential system of government. Executive power is held by a president, who is popularly elected to an initial eight-year term and is eligible for reelection to four-year terms. Legislative powers rest with a Senate and a House of Representatives. The Senate is composed of 18 members elected by universal suffrage to six-year terms. The house has 52 members popularly elected to four-year terms.

Liberia is a member of the United Nations and the Organization of African Unity.

HISTORY. Europeans began establishing trading posts in Liberia in the 1400s. In 1822 the American Colonization Society began to settle freed slaves from the United States in Liberia. Malaria killed most of the original colonizers, but several new groups followed. They negotiated treaties with the native tribes, until consolidation of the land was completed in 1838.

Agents of the American Colonization Society administered the region until July 26, 1847, when Liberia declared its independence. Most world powers quickly recognized the new nation's independence, but the United States withheld recognition until 1862. Liberia established a government modeled after that of the United States.

In the early 1900s Liberia was faced with a financial crisis when the world-market price for its coffee dropped. Liberia sought the aid of foreign countries. In 1926 the Firestone Rubber Company leased large land areas from Liberia which provided the country with an important source of revenue. In the 1930s a League of Nations study of labor conditions uncovered widespread forced labor which resulted in the resignation of Liberia's president, Charles D. B. King.

During World War II U.S. soldiers built the first roads into the interior, and in 1948 the first modern port opened at Monrovia, built with U.S. money.

William V. S. Tubman was elected president in 1943 for an eight-year term. Tubman was re-elected in 1951, 1955, 1959, 1963, and 1967 without much opposition to his True Whig Party, the governing party in Liberia for over 100 years.

Tubman ended the Firestone company's monopoly by inaugurating an open-door policy to international investment, thus beginning the development of the country's rich resources of iron ore. Tubman has also had some success in bringing tribal Liberians into the modern economy.

—Hibberd V. B. Kline, Jr.; Vera L. Zolberg

LIBYA

Official name: Kingdom of Libya
Area: 679,362 square miles
Population: (1967 est.) 1,738,000
Capitals: Tripoli (Pop., 1964, 213,506); Benghazi (Pop., 1964, 137,295)
Language: Arabic
Religion: Islam
Currency unit: Pound
National holiday: Independence day, December 24

Libya, a kingdom in northern Africa, is bordered on the north by the Mediterranean Sea, on the east by the United Arab Republic (Egypt) and Sudan, on the south by Chad and Niger, and on the west by Algeria and Tunisia. Libya is made up of three historic regions—Tripolitania in the northwest, Cyrenaica in the northeast, and the Fezzan in the southwest.

THE LAND. Libya is almost entirely desert. Less than 2 percent of the land is cultivated, and less than 1 percent is forested.

The Gulf of Sidra (Sirte) divides Libya's Mediterranean coast into two major segments, northern Tripolitania in the west and northern Cyrenaica in the east. There are oases in the coastal region separated from each other by sand dunes and salt marshes. There are highlands beyond the coast, including the Jabal Nafusah in Tripolitania and the Al Jabal al Akhdar in Cyrenaica.

The Sahara has many landscapes, three of which are important in Libya—upland bare rock surfaces, as in the Hammadah al Hamra in southern Tripolitania; gravel-covered plains, as in the Sarir Tibasti in the south; and areas of extensive sand dunes, as in the Idehan Marzuq in the Fezzan and the Sand Sea of Calanscio of northeastern Cyrenaica.

There are a few oases in southern and eastern Libya. Oases are more common in the southwestern Fezzan, where they are usually formed by springs and wells in valleys and at the foot of escarpments.

Libya does not have any year-round rivers, but there are dry water routes in many parts of the country. There are deep, salty lakes in Libya, the largest of which is Arrashia, in Cyrenaica. Rainfall averages about 14 inches a year along the Mediterranean coast. There is virtually no rainfall in the desert regions.

THE PEOPLE. Most of the people in Libya are Arabic-speaking Muslims of mixed Arab and Berber origin. There are also some Berber-speaking peoples in northern Libya and in the desert region. Italians form the largest European community in Libya.

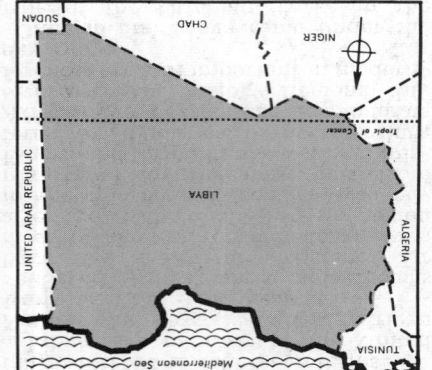

UNITED NATIONS

THE LIBYAN DESERT is being held back by the planting of thatch grass from Tunisia.

Libya is one of Africa's least densely populated countries. Only at oases in the Sahara and near the borders of the Mediterranean Sea is permanent human habitation possible. Many of the people are nomads, who must move about in the desert in search of grazing land for their flocks. Most of the cities and towns are concentrated in the coastal region. Libya's largest cities are Tripoli and Benghazi.

ECONOMY. The modern economy of Libya is based on oil production. The traditional economy is based on dates and other produce of the coast and oases, flocks and herds raised by the nomads, the catch of Mediterranean fishermen, and the handicrafts of urban dwellers.

Since 1959 economic life has been almost completely altered by the production of petroleum, particularly from the Zelten and Dahra fields, both of which have pipelines leading to the Gulf of Sidra. In 1966 Libya produced more than 72 million metric tons of petroleum.

The majority of the population is engaged in subsistence farming. Barley, date palms, citrus fruits, and peanuts are grown, mostly in the coastal region, where there is sufficient rainfall for crops. Date palms are also grown in the desert oases. Sheep, camels, and goats are raised by nomads, mainly in Cyrenaica.

Libya's industry centers on the production and processing of its oil and its agricultural products. There are canneries in Tripolitania that process fish caught in the coastal waters.

In 1966 Libya's imports cost $405 million and exports earned $995 million. The country's main imports are petroleum, iron and steel, and machinery. Although Libya's chief export is petroleum, hides and skins, peanuts, and fruits are also exported. Most trade is conducted with France, West Germany, Italy, the Netherlands, and Britain.

GOVERNMENT. Libya is a constitutional monarchy. The king is head of state and executive power is vested in him. The king appoints a prime minister, who serves as head of government.

Legislative power is exercised by the king in conjunction with a parliament. Parliament consists of the Senate, with 24 members appointed by the king to eight-year terms, and the House of Representatives, in which there is one deputy for every 20,000 inhabitants. House members are popularly elected to four-year terms.

Libya is a member of the United Nations, the Organization of African Unity, and the Arab League.

HISTORY. Libya's three main regions have had a separate existence for most of the country's history. Even after the Arab conquest of the region in the mid-600s, Cyrenaica was administered for the most part from Egypt, and Tripolitania was administered by dynasties in northwestern Africa. The Fezzan has also had its own distinctive history. Regional differences are still important in modern-day Libya.

Ottoman Era. Libya came under the rule of the Ottoman Turks in the 1500s. For over a century, from 1711 to 1835, a local dynasty, the Qaramanli, controlled Tripoli. In the early 1800s the United States fought against the bey, or governor, of Tripoli, whose pirates were raiding U.S. ships. European nations united to eliminate piracy in the Barbary States—Tripoli plus Algiers and Tunis to the west—thus cutting off one of the major sources of government revenue. The Qaramanli regime declined, and the Ottoman government reestablished direct control of Tripoli in 1835.

Italian Rule. In the mid-1800s a Muslim leader, Muhammad bin Ali al-Sanusi, created the Sanusian religious brotherhood, which soon became the most important social and political force in Cyrenaica and the Fezzan. In 1911 Italy wrested control of Libya from the Ottoman Empire after a short war and the Sanusiya served as the local point of resistance to Italian colonialism.

During World War II major battles were fought in Libya. The North African campaigns virtually wiped out the Italian colonial settlements, and after the war a defeated Italy was stripped of its colonies. A deadlock over which major power should assume trusteeship for Libya led to the decision to give the former colony complete independence.

Independence. The Sanusiya had cooperated with the Allied powers in fighting the Axis, and it was the strongest political force in Libya. The Sanusian chief, Idris, grandson of the order's founder, became king when Libya attained independence in December 1951. From 1951 to 1963 Libya was a federal state composed of its three regions. In 1963 Libya became a unified state.

—Hibberd V. B. Kline, Jr.;
L. Carl Brown

LIECHTENSTEIN

Official name: Principality of Liechtenstein
Area: 61 square miles
Population: (1965 est.) 19,000
Capital: Vaduz (Pop., 1961 est.) 3,514
Language: Alemannic
Religion: Roman Catholicism
Currency unit: Swiss franc
National holiday: January 23

Liechtenstein is a very small independent principality located on the border between Austria and Switzerland. It extends no more than 16 miles from north to south and 7 miles from east to west.

THE LAND. The Alps dominate the country's landscape in the east, rising to over 8,000 feet. Western Liechtenstein lies in the valley of the Rhine River, which flows along the country's western border. Winters are long and cold, but summers are mild.

THE PEOPLE. Liechtenstein's population is concentrated in the Rhine Valley, where Vaduz, the capital and only large town, is located. The people speak Alemannic, a Germanic dialect. More than 90 percent of the population is Roman Catholic. During the 1950s and 1960s large numbers of foreign workers, mostly from southern Europe, swelled the population.

ECONOMY. Liechtenstein's economy was once based almost entirely on agriculture, but by the mid-1900s industry had become the main source of income. Cattle, dairy foods, corn, fruit, and potatoes are the leading farm products.

Liechtenstein's hydroelectric power resources, good transportation facilities, and skilled labor force combine to attract industry. Liechtenstein's major manufactured products include precision instruments, small machine parts, pharmaceuticals, and false teeth. Textiles, ceramics, leather goods, and processed foods are also produced.

A large portion of the country's income consists of registration fees paid by foreign companies which incorporate in the principality because of its favorable tax policies. The sale of postage stamps to collectors also contributes to the economy, as does tourism, which increased greatly during the 1950s and 1960s.

Liechtenstein has a favorable balance of trade, as its exports earn a great deal and it must import only a few items. It trades heavily with western Europe and the United States, and it has a customs union with Switzerland.

GOVERNMENT. Liechtenstein is a constitutional monarchy ruled by a prince of the house of Liechtenstein. A head of government, an assistant head, and two councilors, all appointed by the prince, are responsible to a 15-member, popularly elected parliament. Switzerland represents the country's interests abroad.

HISTORY. In ancient times, Liechtenstein's territory was part of the Roman province of Rhaetia. During the 1300s and 1400s the Holy Roman Empire's county of Vaduz and barony of Schellenburg were united under a single count, and by 1712 this feudal state had come into the possession of the Liechtenstein family.

In 1719 the Holy Roman Emperor granted the fief to the family as the Principality of Liechtenstein, and at the dissolution of the Holy Roman Empire in 1806 it became fully independent. Since then, to secure protection, diplomatic representation, and trade advantages, it has become associated with a succession of other states, including those of the Flemish Confederation, the German Confederation, and Austria-Hungary.

In 1919, after Austria-Hungary's defeat in World War I, Switzerland agreed to represent Liechtenstein abroad. In 1921 Liechtenstein established a democratic form of government, adopted Swiss currency, and entrusted postal and telecommunica-

...tions services to Switzerland. In 1924 the two countries formed a customs union.

Liechtenstein avoided involvement in World War II. The country concentrated on developing its economy, and by the mid-1960s its people enjoyed a high level of prosperity. During the 1960s Liechtenstein began to meet formally with other small European states to discuss matters of mutual concern.

—Sergio Barzanti

LUXEMBOURG

Official name: Grand Duchy of Luxembourg
Area: 998 square miles
Population: (1966 est.) 335,000
Capital: Luxembourg (Pop., 1965 est., 78,721)
Language: Letzeburgesch (Luxembourgish), French, German
Religion: Roman Catholicism
Currency unit: Franc
National holiday: Grand Duke's birthday, June 23

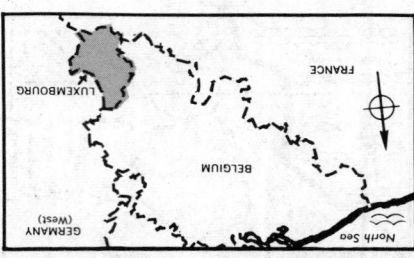

Luxembourg, one of the smallest countries of Europe, is bordered on the north and west by Belgium, on the east by West Germany, and on the south by France.

In 1922 Luxembourg and Belgium formed an economic union that abolished the customs frontier between them. The union was dissolved in 1940, but was reestablished in 1945. In 1948 a customs union went into effect among Luxembourg, Belgium, and the Netherlands, which is known as the Benelux Customs Union. Full economic union of the three countries has existed since 1960.

THE LAND. The southern third of Luxembourg is part of the Lorraine Plateau and consists of rolling plains. The northern two-thirds of the country is part of the Ardennes and is hilly and wooded. Its principal river is the Sauer.

Luxembourg has a cool, temperate, rainy climate. Winters are mild and summers cool, with summer temperatures averaging 60°F. Precipitation averages about 30 inches a year.

THE PEOPLE. Luxembourgers are a mixture of nationalities—primarily French, Dutch, German, and Belgian. The official languages are French and German, but Letzeburgesch, a Germanic national language. More than 95 percent of the people are Roman Catholic. The only important urban center is the capital, Luxembourg.

ECONOMY. The mainstay of Luxembourg's economy is the iron and steel industry. There are large iron ore deposits in southwestern Luxembourg, and there is coal nearby in Germany. This combination has made Luxembourg one of western Europe's major iron and steel producers. Other important industries include distilling and tanning.

About one-fifth of the labor force is employed in agriculture, which is sparsely settled, in the hilly, northern two-thirds of the country. Livestock is raised, and the principal crops are potatoes, wheat, barley, and wine grapes. Domestic production meets most of Luxembourg's food needs.

The iron and steel industry provides about 85 percent of Luxembourg's exports. Major imports include fuels, motor vehicles and parts, machinery, and a variety of manufactured goods. Luxembourg's major trading partners are Belgium, West Germany, France, and the Netherlands.

GOVERNMENT. Luxembourg is a constitutional monarchy with a grand duke as chief of state. Executive power is exercised by the grand duke and the Council of Government. The council, or cabinet, is headed by a minister of state, or prime minister.

Legislative power rests with the Chamber of Deputies, which is directly elected to a term of five years. The Council of State, an advisory body of elder statesmen appointed by the grand duke, deliberates on proposed legislation and expresses its opinion on other matters referred to it, but its decisions can be overruled by the Chamber of Deputies.

In addition to being part of Benelux, Luxembourg is a member of the European Economic Community, the United Nations, and the North Atlantic Treaty Organization (NATO).

HISTORY. The name Luxembourg is derived from the castle of Lützelburg, the seat of Count Siegfried I, under whose sway several lands were united in the 900s. The size of the country gradually increased under a series of able rulers. In 1308 Count Henry of Luxembourg became Holy Roman Emperor. In 1354 his grandson, Emperor Charles IV, expanded Luxembourg's territories considerably and made it a duchy.

Luxembourg was conquered by Philip the Good of Burgundy in 1443. Philip II of Spain received it from Charles V as part of the Low Countries. Luxembourg was conquered by Louis XIV and ruled by France until 1697, when it was restored to Spain. It was ruled by Austria from 1714 until 1795, when it again came under French rule. Luxembourg was annexed to the French Republic and subsequently became a part of the Napoleonic empire. At the Congress of Vienna (1814-1815) Luxembourg was made a grand duchy, ruled by William I, who was also king of the newly created Kingdom of the Netherlands.

Luxembourg was associated with Belgium when it seceded from the Netherlands in 1830, but in 1839 part of the country merged with Belgium and the rest remained an independent grand duchy under the personal rule of the Netherlands' king.

Lacking economic ties with the Netherlands, Luxembourg became associated with the German states, and in 1866, upon dissolution of the German Confederation, Luxembourg was neutralized, and the crown passed to Grand Duke Adolphe of Nassau.

Modern Luxembourg. Luxembourg was invaded by the Germans in 1914, at the outbreak of World War I, and it remained under German occupation throughout the war. Luxembourg's neutrality was violated again in World War II, when German troops occupied the Low Countries in 1940. Grand Duchess Charlotte and the cabinet carried on a government-in-exile in London and Montreal, Canada. The country was liberated in 1944.

In 1945 Luxembourg became one of the charter members of the United Nations. In 1949 the country abandoned its traditional position of neutrality and became a member of the North Atlantic Treaty Organization (NATO). Luxembourg and five other European countries formed the European Coal and Steel Community in 1952, and in 1958 the country became a member of the European Common Market and Euratom.

In 1964 Grand Duchess Charlotte, who had reigned since 1919, abdicated in favor of her son, Grand Duke Jean.

—Sergio Barzanti

MADAGASCAR

Official name: Malagasy Republic
Area: 226,658 square miles
Population: (1966 est.) 6,200,000
Capital: Tananarive (Pop., 1965 est., 321,654)
Language: Malagasy, French
Religion: Christianity, traditional religions
Currency unit: Franc (African Financial Community)
National holiday: Proclamation of the republic, October 14.

The Malagasy Republic is an island nation in the Indian Ocean, some 240 miles off the southeastern coast of Africa. Its territory consists of the large island of Madagascar and several small, adjacent islands. Madagascar received its independence from France in 1960.

THE LAND. Madagascar is about 1,000 miles long and 360 miles at its greatest width. Most of the island is dominated by a great interior highland, which has an average elevation of about 4,000 feet above sea level. The highlands contain deep canyons and volcanic mountains, with elevations as high as about 9,400 feet. Steep cliffs border the highlands, especially in the east. The island's major rivers are the Mangoky, Betsiboka, and Mania.

Easterly winds, which blow all the year on the eastern cliffs, bring heavy rains to eastern Madagascar, but it is dry to the west of the cliffs and in the south.

THE PEOPLE. Madagascar's indigenous population is made up of 18 different ethnic groups. The largest is the Hova, or Merina, who live mainly in the central highlands and are important in the political life of the country. The Betsileo people also live in the central highlands. Other important groups include the Betsimisaraka, in east-central Madagascar; the Sakalava, in the western part of the island; and the Bara, a

pastoral people who live in southern Madagascar.

The country's largest city is its capital, Tananarive, which is situated in the highlands.

ECONOMY. The economy of Malagasy has suffered because of its isolation. Madagascar's economy is based on agriculture. Coffee, vanilla, rice, sugar, and cloves are the principal crops. Although mineral resources are not well developed, Madagascar is a major producer of graphite. The island also has deposits of mica. There is little industry.

In 1967 Madagascar's imports cost $145 million and its exports earned $104 million. The country's major imports include manufactured goods, especially textiles and iron and steel, machinery, petroleum products, and food. Major exports include coffee, vanilla, sugar and tobacco. Most trade is conducted with France, West Germany, and the United States. Malagasy receives economic assistance from France.

GOVERNMENT. Madagascar has a presidential system of government. Executive power rests with a president, elected by universal suffrage to a seven-year term.

Legislative powers are held by a 107-member National Assembly and a 54-member Senate. Assembly members are popularly elected to five-year terms. In the Senate, 36 members are elected by provincial electoral colleges and 18 members are appointed by the president. Senators serve six-year terms.

The Malagasy Republic is a member of the United Nations and the Organization of African Unity.

HISTORY. Arab traders established small, feudal principalities along the Madagascar coast as early as the 1000s or 1100s. In the 1500s and 1600s Dutch, French, and British merchants established trading and supply posts on the island as part of their routes to India. Buccaneers established a short-lived republic on the island in the 1700s.

During the 1500s and 1600s the indigenous peoples were involved in civil wars. Confederations and military commands were established on the island, but most collapsed because of internal strains or the rebellion of subjugated peoples. In the central plateau, however, the Hova people gradually expanded the area under their control.

In the early 1800s a Hova king, Radama I, brought European advisers to his court, welcomed missionaries, and instituted education in the Malagasy language. Later rulers played the British and the French off against each other. In 1890 French claims to Madagascar were recognized by Britain, and in 1896 Madagascar became a French colony. France abolished the Hova monarchy and exiled the Queen. By 1904 the French had established their control over the entire island.

Modern Madagascar. Short-lived nationalist movements emerged briefly during World War I and again in the 1920s. In 1947 discontent over land confiscation and the periodic imposition of involuntary labor led to a serious revolt. France suppressed the revolt and took steps to develop Madagascar's economy, but at the same time it prohibited political activity.

In 1956 France changed its policy and permitted political activity in all French African colonies. Of the several political parties that emerged in Madagascar, the nationalist Social Democratic Party (PSD) won most local elections.

In October 1958, under the leadership of Philibert Tsiranana, Madagascar became an autonomous republic within the French Community. Tsiranana became head of a provisional government formed in 1958, and in May 1959 he was elected president. In June 1960 the country became independent as the Malagasy Republic. Tsiranana was reelected president in 1965.

—Hibberd V. B. Kline, Jr.; Gary A. Weissman

MALAWI

Official name: Republic of Malawi
Area: 46,066 square miles
Population: (1966 est.) 4,035,000
Capital: Zomba (Pop., 1966, 19,000)
Language: English, African languages
Religion: Christianity, Islam
Currency unit: Pound
National holiday: Independence day, July 6

Malawi, a republic in southern Africa, is bordered on the north and northeast by Tanzania, on the southeast, south, and southwest by Mozambique, and on the west by Zambia. Malawi, formerly called Nyasaland, received its independence from Britain in 1964.

THE LAND. Most of Malawi is occupied by mountains and plateaus. Because of its rugged terrain, Malawi has been described as "Switzerland without snow." The Great Rift Valley runs through Malawi in a north-south line. Lake Nyasa, or Malawi, which stretches along the eastern border, lies in the valley. The Shire River, the lake's outlet, flows southward into Mozambique.

West of the lake the land climbs steeply to a plateau with elevations between 4,000 and 7,000 feet. The Shire Highlands are south of Lake Malawi. East of the Shire is Mt. Mlanje, which has an elevation of about 9,800 feet.

The lake region of Malawi has a generally hot, humid climate. Temperatures vary with differences in altitude.

THE PEOPLE. Most of Malawi's people are Bantu-speaking. The largest groups, the Nyanja and Yao, live mainly near Lake Malawi. The Nyanja are descendants of early inhabitants of Malawi. There are also communities of Europeans and Asians.

Zomba, in southern Malawi, and Lilongwe and Blantyre, in the central part of the country, are Malawi's largest cities.

ECONOMY. The economy of Malawi is based on agriculture. Malawi's resources cannot support its population, and many workers find employment in nearby countries. Basic food crops include corn, millet, cassava, peanuts, and rice. Commercial crops include cotton, tobacco, and tea.

There is no mining or manufacturing of any significance in the country. The Shire Highlands is the key economic region of the country. In 1963 construction was begun on a hydroelectric plant on the Shire River.

Malawi's landlocked position and its limited transportation system have slowed economic development.

In 1966 Malawi's imports cost $75.8 million and its exports earned $48.6 million. The major imports are manufactured goods, especially textiles and iron and steel, chemicals, petroleum products, and machinery. Exports include cotton, tobacco, tea, and peanuts. Most of Malawi's trade is with Britain and Rhodesia. Malawi receives economic aid from Britain.

GOVERNMENT. Malawi has a presidential system of government. Executive power is held by a president, who is elected to a five-year term. Legislative power is held by a National Assembly elected to a five-year term. Fifty of the assembly's members are elected by universal suffrage, and five are appointed by the president.

Malawi is a member of the United Nations, the Commonwealth of Nations, and the Organization of African Unity.

HISTORY. Malawi owes its name to the Malawi, or Maravi, people who entered the area in the 1500s. Portuguese explorers in the mid-1500s believed them to be the rulers of a vast empire. The western shore of Lake Malawi became a popular route for Bantu-speaking immigrants entering central Africa from the north, and by the 1800s the area's dense population made it a favorite target for Arab slave-raiders.

European interest in present-day Malawi originated in the 1870s, after the explorations of David Livingstone and other Scottish missionaries who were anxious to put an end to the slave trade. In 1889 missionary pressure for governmental action against the Arab slave traders and the threat of Portuguese occupation led Britain to declare the area the British Central Africa Protectorate. Cecil Rhodes' British South Africa Company financed the region's administration in the early years of the protectorate, but a dispute over political control led the British government to accept complete responsibility for the territory. In 1907 the name of the area was changed to Nyasaland.

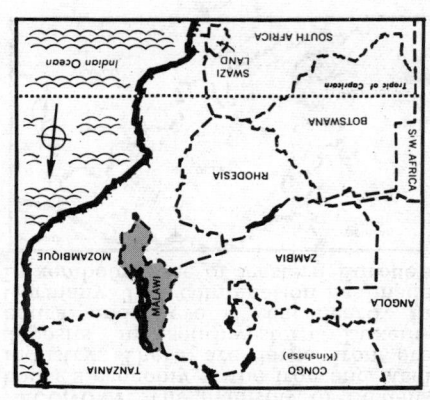

Nationalism. African nationalist movements developed early in Nyasaland, organized by politically conscious laborers returning from work in the mines of Northern Rhodesia (present-day Zambia), Southern Rhodesia, and South Africa. Because of resentment of British colonial policies and fear of federation with the Rhodesias, nationalists formed the Nyasaland African Congress in 1944.

In 1951 the Congress leadership demanded self-government for Nyasaland. Two years later, however, Britain joined the two Rhodesias and Nyasaland into the Federation of Rhodesia and Nyasaland.

The nationalists, under the leadership of Dr. Hastings Banda, attracted wide support denouncing the federation. Britain finally agreed to an African elected majority in the Nyasaland legislative council, and in elections held in 1961 Dr. Banda's Malawi Congress Party won an impressive victory.

Independence. Britain formally dissolved the federation in 1963, and on July 6, 1964 the country became independent with Banda as its prime minister.

In 1966 Malawi became a republic, and Banda became the first president. In 1967 Malawi signed a trade agreement with South Africa, despite South Africa's policy of apartheid and the opposition of other African countries.

—Hibberd V. B. Kline, Jr.; Gary A. Weissman

MALAYSIA

Official name: Malaysia
Area: 128,400 square miles
Population: (1966 est.) 9,725,000
Capital: Kuala Lumpur (Pop., 1963, 1,258,894)
Language: Malay, Chinese
Religion: Islam, Buddhism
Currency unit: Dollar
National holiday: National day, August 31

Malaysia, a federal state in Southeast Asia formed in 1963, includes Malaya, on the southern end of the Malay peninsula, and Sabah, on the island of Borneo. Singapore was a member of the federation between 1963 and 1965. West Malaysia, on the Malay Peninsula, and East Malaysia, on Borneo, lie more than 400 miles apart, separated by the South China Sea.

West Malaysia is bordered on the north by Thailand, on the east by the South China Sea, on the south, across the narrow Johore Straits, by Singapore, and on the west by the Strait of Malacca. East Malaysia is bordered on the north by the South China Sea, on the east by the Sulu Sea, on the south by Indonesia, and on the west by Indonesia and the South China Sea. The British protectorate of Brunei forms an enclave in Sarawak.

THE LAND. West Malaysia consists of a narrow interior core of low, jungle-covered mountains rimmed by swampy coastal plains. East Malaysia has a mountainous interior and mineral-rich coastal plains. East Malaysia has a narrow border of swampy coastal plains. Small islands lie off the coasts of both West and East Malaysia. Of the many rivers that thread Malaysia, the most important are the Pahang, in West Malaysia, and the Rajang, in East Malaysia.

The Malaysian climate is equatorial. The year-round temperature averages 80°F., and an annual average of 100 inches of rain falls on the country as a whole.

THE PEOPLE. The Malaysian population is quite varied. Just under half of the people are Muslim Malays, who speak Malay. Slightly more than one-third are Chinese. The Chinese are primarily urban; the Malays are predominantly rural. Indians and Pakistanis make up about 10 percent of the population, and the remainder consists of a variety of native islanders, mostly in east Malaysia.

Population is concentrated in the coastal regions. It is densest in the western half of West Malaysia, where the country's largest cities are located—Kuala Lumpur, the federation's capital; Ipoh, and Georgetown, a port city on Penang Island in the Malacca Strait. Malaysia's population is growing at a rapid rate, estimated at 3 percent a year between 1958 and 1965.

ECONOMY. Malaysia has a prosperous and growing economy, due largely to its wealth of natural resources, especially rubber and tin. Malaysia is the world's leading producer of natural rubber, with an output of almost 1 million metric tons in 1965. Most rubber comes from West Malaysia. Malaysia's abundance of high-grade tin ore, concentrated on the west coast of the Malay peninsula, has made it the world's largest producer of tin, mining 70,000 metric tons in 1966. Forests cover more than 75 percent of Malaysian territory and are one of the country's most valuable resources, supplying timber, palm oil, pepper, hemp, and coconut products. Bauxite, iron ore, and petroleum are also found in Malaysia.

Rubber processing and tin smelting are the country's major industries. In an effort to lessen its economic dependence on two commodities—rubber and tin—which fluctuate sharply in value, the government in the mid-1960s encouraged the development of diversified manufacturing industries. Very little of Malaysia's cultivable land is devoted to subsistence crops. Rice paddies, concentrated in the coastal lowlands, account for most of the farmland, and the country's farmers raise less than half of the rice they need. Fish, the other staple of the Malaysian diet, are abundant off the coasts.

Malaysia has a favorable balance of trade, with West Malaysia making a much larger contribution to the country's trade than East Malaysia. In 1966 imports cost about $1.1 billion, of which West Malaysia accounted for $860 million, and exports earned nearly $1.3 billion, of which West Malaysia accounted for more than $1 billion. Rubber and tin represent about half the value of exports, which also include timber and other forest products. Foodstuffs (mainly rice), textiles, and machinery are imported. Britain, the United States, Singapore, and Japan are Malaysia's chief trading partners.

GOVERNMENT. Malaysia is a constitutional monarchy. The Paramount Ruler, or king, is elected to a five-year term by the sultans of the states of West Malaysia. He serves as chief of state and as Muslim religious leader. Actual executive power is wielded by the federation's prime minister and cabinet, who are responsible to a parliament.

The Senate, the upper house of parliament, is partly elected by the state legislatures and partly appointed by the king. The larger, more powerful House of Representatives is popularly elected. Parliament shares legislative power with the state legislatures.

Each member state has a parliamentary government, with a legislature of one house. The member states of the federation are quite powerful. Malaysia is a member of the United Nations and of the Commonwealth of Nations.

HISTORY. The territory of present-day Malaysia was inhabited in ancient times by Malay peoples who lived in many small coastal kingdoms and whose economies were based on fishing, farming, and trading. From the 800s to the 1200s they were controlled by the Sumatran Buddhist Srivijayan empire, and in the 1300s by the Javanese Hindu kingdom of Majapahit.

In about 1400 a Malay ruler founded the state of Malacca, on the western coast of the peninsula. Its capital, the port city of Malacca in the center of the eastern shore of the Strait of Malacca, soon became the most important trading center in Southeast Asia. During the 1400s Arab traders and missionaries converted the ruler and the people of Malacca to Islam. The state became a center for the spread of Islam throughout the area. Malacca's port attracted European nations that were establishing colonies in Southern Asia in the late 1400s. In 1511 Malacca fell to the Portuguese, but in 1641 the Portuguese were ousted by the Dutch. The Europeans did not develop the territory or attempt to bring all of Malaya under their authority. Malacca gradually declined in importance except as a stopping-off point on the sea route between Asia and Europe.

British Role. In 1795 Britain took Malacca from the Dutch. In 1826 it was consolidated with the British settlements at Penang, at the northern end of the Strait of Malacca, and with Singapore, at the southern end of the peninsula, to form the Colony of the Straits Settlements.

In the mid-1800s an English adventurer, James Brooke, gained control of Sarawak in northwest Borneo. In

1881 a British chartered company took over what is now Sabah in north Borneo. Thus an arc of British influence developed across the northern edge of the island world at the same time that Dutch influence was slowly growing in what is now Indonesia. The Dutch and the British formally apportioned sovereignty over the island world by treaties in 1824 and 1891.

After the opening of the Suez Canal in 1869, Southeast Asian trade became more profitable and important, and competition increased among European states for territory in the region. Also in the late 1800s the wealth of Malaya's tin mines was realized, and the tin industry there grew prosperous and attracted the interest of the British.

By 1914 Britain had concluded treaties making protectorates of the sultanates on the Malay peninsula. Once the British presence guaranteed their security, Chinese miners poured into Malaya. These workers formed the nucleus of the states' large Chinese minority.

Malaya soon was the world's leading producer and exporter of tin. In the early 1900s the British also developed rubber plantations on the peninsula. The rubber industry was manned largely by Indian labor, and the Malay states soon ranked as the world's leading producer of rubber. By the 1920s, with a well-ordered government under British administration and a prosperous economy run by Chinese and Indian labor, Malaya was economically, politically, and socially unique in Southeast Asia. The great alien immigration that had left the native Malays and their sultans a bare majority in their own land inhibited the development of nationalist movements.

Malayan nationalism was finally awakened during World War II, when the country was occupied by Japanese forces. Under Japanese direction the Malayans were largely self-governing, and a desire for full independence followed liberation from the Japanese.

In 1948, after two years of an unsatisfactory trial union, the protected Malay states were united to form the Federation of Malaya. In June 1948 guerrilla fighting broke out, instigated by Chinese communists with the support of part of the Malayan Chinese population. Rivalries and conflicts between the Chinese and the Malays within the federation government helped to keep the war going. With the aid of British troops, the federation government gradually defeated the guerrillas.

Independence. In 1957 Malaya was granted full independence under a constitution that attempted to balance carefully the power of the Chinese and the Malay portions of the population.

In 1961 the self-governing British colony of Singapore proposed union with Malaya as a step to ensure its economic position. Malaya agreed on condition that the British colonies on Borneo, with their predominantly Malay population, be admitted to the union to balance Singapore's heavily Chinese population.

In 1963 the union took place, creating the Federation of Malaysia, with Tunku Abdul Rahman as leader of the new state. The inclusion of the Borneo states aroused the opposition of two neighboring states, Indonesia and the Philippines. Each claimed territory in East Malaysia.

The Philippines suspended diplomatic relations, and in 1963 Indonesia began a "Crush Malaysia" campaign. The campaign led to open fighting between 1964 and 1966, when the fall from power of Indonesia's President Sukarno ended Indonesia's opposition to the federation.

Nor did the inclusion of the Borneo states of Sabah and Sarawak balance the power of Singapore's Chinese to the satisfaction of the Malays. In 1965 Singapore reluctantly withdrew from the federation.

—M. G. Inaba

MALDIVE ISLANDS

Official name: Maldive Islands
Area: 115 square miles
Population: (1966 est.) 101,000
Capital: Male (Pop., 1965, 11,202)
Language: Maldivian
Religion: Islam
Currency unit: Rupee

The Maldive Islands is an independent island nation occupying an archipelago about 400 miles southwest of Ceylon. The archipelago lies between the Arabian Sea and the Indian Ocean.

THE LAND AND PEOPLE. The country is formed of some 2,000 islands grouped into 12 distinct atolls, or island groups. Most of the islands are very small and low-lying, and only about 220 are inhabited.

The Maldivians are an amalgam of peoples from Ceylon, India, Southeast Asia, the Middle East, and Africa. They speak a language similar to Elu, or old Sinhalese, the language of ancient Ceylon. Almost all the people are Muslim. Population is densest near the center of the group, on Male Atoll, which is the site of the capital and largest city, Male.

ECONOMY. The economy of the Maldive Islands is based on fishing and diving. Fishing is the main activity, and dried bonito, called Maldive fish, is the country's chief product. Coconuts are processed for their oil, fibers, and other products.

Dried fish and coconut products are exported. The country relies heavily on rice and other necessities must be imported. The country relies heavily on foreign assistance, primarily from Britain.

GOVERNMENT. The Maldive Islands is a constitutional monarchy. A sultan, or king, is elected for life. The popularly elected legislature, the Majlis, has one house. A prime minister appointed by the sultan with the consent of the Majlis heads the government. The country is a member of the Commonwealth of Nations and the United Nations.

HISTORY. The Maldive's have been inhabited by peoples of the Indian Ocean region for many centuries. They had strong ties with the island of Ceylon and were long required to pay tribute to the kings of Kandy, in Ceylon. During the 1500s the islands were under the nominal control of Portugal, and during the 1600s they were under Dutch rule.

Britain made Ceylon a crown colony in 1789 and assumed indirect authority over the Maldive Islands. In 1887 the islands became a British protectorate. During World War II, Britain built an important air base on Gan Island, in the southern Addu Atoll.

The 1950s were years of great unrest for the islands. In 1953 the national assembly abolished the sultanate and proclaimed a republic, but in 1954 an insurrection resulted in the restoration of the sultanate. British attempts to reactivate its air base on Gan led to clashes between those opposing and those favoring the British presence in the islands. Moreover, the government was unable to deal with the islands' severe food shortage.

Discontent led in 1959 to an insurrection in Suvadiva, south of Male. A rebel leader declared Suvadiva a republic and requested aid from Britain. Britain granted the aid, arousing strong anti-British feeling in Male. In 1960 the Suvadiva rebellion ended and the British were allowed to reopen their air base.

During the early 1960s the Maldivian government and Britain negotiated the islands' future, and in 1965 a treaty between Britain and the Maldive Islands granted full sovereignty to the country. Britain was allowed to retain control of the Gan Island base and agreed to provide financial and technical aid to relieve the new nation's pressing economic problems.

—Sara D. Gilbert

MALI

Official name: Republic of Mali
Area: 463,950 square miles
Population: (1967 est.) 4,745,000
Capital: Bamako (Pop., 1965 est., urban area, 165,000)
Language: French, African languages
Religion: Islam
Currency unit: Franc
National holiday: Independence day, September 22

Mali, a republic in western Africa, is bordered on the north by Algeria, on the east by Niger, on the southeast by Upper Volta, on the south by the Ivory Coast and Guinea, and on the west by Senegal and Mauritania. Mali, long a French territory known as the Soudan, was joined with Senegal from 1959 until 1960 as the Mali Federation. It declared its independence in 1960.

THE LAND. Most of Mali is flat, with areas of low plateaus. The vast desert wasteland of the Sahara occupies the northern third of the country. In the northeast is a mountain region.

The Niger River flows through southern Mali, and the Senegal River flows from southwestern Mali. The desert region is hot and dry, but the southern part of the country is cooler.

THE PEOPLE. There are many different ethnic groups in Mali. The largest include the Mandingo (including the Bambara, who number over 1 million), Sarakolle, Fula (Fulani), and Malinke. Tuareg live in the desert region. Most of Mali's people are Muslim.

The country's largest cities are Bamako, Mopti, Ségou, and Tombouctou ('Timbuktu'). All are near the Niger River or its tributaries.

ECONOMY. The economy of Mali is based on agriculture. Millet, rice, and corn are the basic food crops. The principal commercial crops are peanuts and cotton. Fish from the Niger River are an important export. Cattle, sheep, and goats are raised, mainly in central and northern Mali.

The Niger River valley is the most productive region in Mali. There is a large irrigation project on the upper part of the river, and the land near the lower Niger is fertile.

There is little mining, although there are deposits of salt, bauxite, phosphates, manganese, zinc, copper, and gold. There is also little industry, and the country's industrial development is hampered by the country's inaccessibility.

In 1965 imports cost $43 million and exports earned $16 million. Major imports include manufactured goods—especially textiles, iron and steel, and machinery—and sugar. Peanuts, live animals and hides, raw cotton, and fish are Mali's major exports. Most trade is conducted with neighboring countries and with France and the Soviet Union.

GOVERNMENT. Mali has a presidential system of government. Executive power is vested in a president, who is elected to a five-year term. Legislative power is held by the National Assembly. The 80 members of the assembly are elected by universal suffrage to five-year terms.

Mali is a member of the United Nations and the Organization of African Unity (OAU).

HISTORY. In the early 1200s Sundiata, a powerful leader of a group of Mandingo people, defeated Sumanguru, ruler of the Susu people, and created the Mali empire. By the 1300s this empire stretched from the Gambia River to what is now the northwestern border of Nigeria. The people of Mali traded gold from the upper Niger and Senegal River regions for the salt of the Sahara. In the early 1300s, the old kingdom of Mali's most illustrious ruler, Musa, extended the empire from Niger to the southern Sahara. In the late 1400s the ruler of old Mali was over-thrown by the king of the new state of Songhai. The Songhai kings governed the vast area once loyal to Musa until 1591, when a Moroccan army crossed the Sahara and defeated the Songhai. The Moroccan army was not strong enough to control the entire empire, and the territory broke up into smaller city-states.

During the 1800s two Muslim reformers, Ahmadu Lobo and Al-hajj Umar, created Islamic theocracies in the region. The creation of the Islamic states was one phase of a wave of religious revivalism that swept tropical Africa south of the Sahara.

French Rule. France at that time was extending its colonial rule southward from northern Africa, and Al-hajj Umar's state clashed with French forces. By 1880 France had emerged victorious, and in 1895 France formed the colony of the Sudan, which it administered as part of French West Africa. In 1946 this area became a territory, and in 1958 this area became an autonomous member of the French Community.

In 1959 France joined the Soudan with Senegal to form the Mali Federation, and in June 1960 the federation became an autonomous member of the French Community. Two months later Senegal withdrew from the federation, and on Sept. 22, 1960, the former Soudan withdrew from the French Community and proclaimed itself the Republic of Mali.

Independence. Modibo Keita became the first president of the new republic. In 1963 relations with Senegal were normalized, and work was begun to rehabilitate the railroad linking Mali to the port of Dakar, in Senegal.

—Hibberd V. B. Kline, Jr.;
Robert I. Rotberg

MALTA

Official name: Malta
Area: 122 square miles
Population: (1967 est) 319,000
Capital: Valletta (Pop, 1965 est, 17,679)
Language: Maltese, English
Religion: Roman Catholicism
Currency unit: Pound
National holiday: Independence day, September 21

Malta is an island nation in the Mediterranean Sea about 60 miles south of Sicily. The country includes the islands of Malta, Comino, and Gozo, and two uninhabited islands.

THE LAND. The Maltese islands are rather flat and consist of limestone rock sparsely covered with a thin layer of soil. There are few trees and no rivers or lakes.

The climate is semitropical, with mild winters and hot summers. An average of 20 inches of rain a year falls on the islands, but the amount varies greatly from year to year.

THE PEOPLE. The Maltese are a Mediterranean people who speak a Semitic language. The population is almost entirely Roman Catholic. Malta's population density is extremely high—about 2,600 persons per square mile in 1967. Emigration, especially since the end of World War II, has been high and directed mainly to Australia, Britain, and Canada.

ECONOMY. Malta is in the process of developing its economy. Its only resources are its people, its geographic location, and the limestone of its rocks.

Agriculture contributed only about 3 percent to the country's domestic product in 1965. Potatoes, tomatoes, grapes, and wheat are the leading crops. Fishing is important.

Industrialization began on Malta in the early 1960s. Manufactures, which accounted for 19 percent of the domestic product in 1965, included textiles, rubber products, and gloves. Processed farm products, especially wine, are also important. Construction and ship repair are Malta's most valuable industries. The main dockyard was long an important British naval installation.

Malta's imports cost about $98 million in 1965 and exports earned only about $24 million. The leading exports are textiles, and cut flowers. The leading imports are foodstuffs, machinery, textiles, and consumer goods.

GOVERNMENT. Malta is a parliamentary democracy. The head of state is the British monarch, who is represented by a governor-general. Executive power is exercised by a prime minister and cabinet responsible to parliament. The popularly elected parliament has one house.

Malta is a member of the Commonwealth of Nations and the United Nations.

HISTORY. Malta, called Melita in ancient times, and its small sister island, Gozo, were inhabited in prehistoric times by people whose great stone monuments are still in existence. An important refuge for ships following Mediterranean trade routes, the islands were visited by early Phoenicians and Greeks, and in the 200s bc they passed under Carthaginian rule. Malta became a Roman possession in 216 bc. During the first century ad the Maltese adopted Christianity.

After the dissolution of the Roman Empire, Malta passed successively to the Byzantine Empire, the Arabs, the Kingdom of Aragon, and then to the united kingdoms of Aragon and Castile. In the early 1500s the Holy Roman emperor received Malta from Spain by inheritance, and in 1530 he granted it to the Order of the Hospital of St. John of Jerusalem.

The knights, who served as protectors of religious pilgrims, regarded Malta as an outpost for the defense of Christianity. They withstood attacks by the Muslim Turks, including a long siege in 1565. The island under the knights was supported and protected by the nations of Europe, and it grew prosperous from Mediterranean trade. The military strength and effectiveness of the order declined during the 1600s and 1700s, and in 1798 Napoleon Bonaparte of France occupied Malta. Two years later, with the aid of the Maltese, a British force drove out the French, and the Maltese requested permanent British protection. In 1814 Malta became a British crown colony and a vital British naval base.

British Rule. The islanders had partial self-government during the 1800s. They were self-governing during the 1920s and 1930s, but two issues sharp-

ly divided the island—the choice of Maltese or Italian as an official language and church-state relations. The conflict grew so bitter that Malta's home rule was abolished in 1936.

During World War II, Malta had great strategic value. It withstood heavy German and Italian air bombardments and was a base for the Anglo-U.S. invasion of Sicily in 1943. In 1942 Britain awarded the George Cross to the Maltese people for their bravery during the bombardments.

Independence. After the war the country worked to achieve sufficient internal self-government, which it received in 1962. Maltese and English were made the official languages, and Roman Catholicism was declared the official religion of Malta. In 1964 the British granted the country full independence.

Malta concentrated its economy on expanding its dependence on the British naval base, which had been its major source of income and which was being closed down. In 1966 a serious Anglo-Maltese conflict arose when Britain announced plans to withdraw its defense forces from the island, but a compromise was reached.

—Charles Nowell

MAURITANIA

Official name: Islamic Republic of Mauritania
Area: 397,955 square miles
Population: (1966 est.) 1,070,000
Capital: Nouakchott (Pop., 1965 est., 15,000)
Language: Arabic
Religion: Islam
Currency unit: Franc
National holiday: Independence day, November 28th

THE LAND. Mauritania, a republic in western Africa, is bounded on the north by Algeria, on the east by Mali, on the south by Senegal, and on the west by the Atlantic Ocean and the Spanish Sahara. Mauritania received its independence from France in 1960.

About two-thirds of Mauritania is desert. In the west long lines of sand dunes are separated by broad lowlands. In the north and east rocky desert surfaces are common. There is cultivated land in the southwest, near the Senegal River, which flows along the country's southwestern border. The climate of Mauritania is generally hot and dry.

THE PEOPLE. Most Mauritanians are nomadic Moors, people of mixed Berber and Arab stock. Negro Muslims live in southern Mauritania, mainly near the Senegal River, and Tuareg people live in the central part of the country. Mauritania's largest cities are Kaédi, Fort Gourand, Port Étienne, and Nouakchott, the capital.

ECONOMY. Mauritania's economy is based on livestock breeding and agriculture. Sheep, cattle, goats, and camels are raised, mainly in central and northern Mauritania. The only considerable area of cultivated land is in the Chemama, the Mauritanian part of the Senegal River valley. The basic foodcrops are millet, dates, rice, and corn. Acacia trees, the source of gum arabic, are grown in the central part of the country. Fish from the

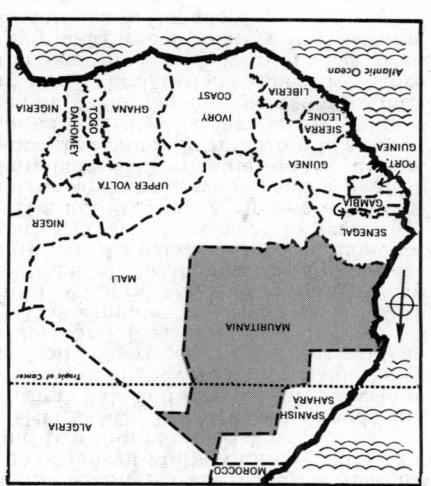

Senegal River also provide an important source of income.

There is an extremely rich deposit of iron ore at Fort Gourand, in western Mauritania. In 1963, to export the ore, a 400-mile railroad was built linking Fort Gourand with Port Étienne, on the Atlantic Ocean. Valuable copper and oil deposits have also been discovered.

In 1964 imports cost $15.7 million and exports cost $45.8 million. The country's major imports are manufactured goods, machinery, and food stuffs. Major exports include animals, fish, iron ore, copper, and gum arabic. Most trade is conducted with France, the Congo (Brazzaville), the United States, and West Germany.

GOVERNMENT. Mauritania has a presidential system of government. Executive power is held by a president, who is popularly elected to a five-year term. Legislative power is held by a 40-member National Assembly. Assembly members are elected by universal suffrage to five-year terms. Mauritania is a member of the United Nations and the Organization of African Unity. Mauritania has strong ties with Morocco, based on common backgrounds in religion and language, but relations between the two countries have been complicated by Moroccan claims to Mauritania.

HISTORY. In about the 800s a confederation of nomadic Berbers entered Mauritania from the north and forced the existing Negro population southward. The Berbers adopted Islam in the 900s, but retained many of their traditional beliefs. In the 1000s they united to form the Almoravids (al-Murabitun), which quickly became a powerful religious and political force. The Almoravids overran Morocco, western Algeria, and Muslim Spain. Their leaders founded the famous city of Marrakech, in Morocco, and established a dynasty which lasted almost 100 years. A branch of the Almoravids went south and conquered the empire of Ghana in 1076. Starting in the 1300s nomadic Arabs migrated into Mauritania, and the region gradually became Arabized.

In the 1800s the French established their control over areas to the north, Morocco and Algeria, and to the south, Senegal and present-day Mali. In the early 1900s, France began to occupy Mauritania. In 1903 it became a French protectorate, and in 1920 a colony, part of French West Africa. But effective French control over the country was not achieved until 1934.

In 1946 Mauritania became a territory in the newly formed French Union, and in 1958 an autonomous member of the French community. On Nov. 28, 1960, France granted the country its independence. In 1961 Mokhtar Ould Daddah became Mauritania's first president, and in 1966 he was reelected president.

—Hibberd V. B. Kline, Jr.

MAURITIUS

Official name: Mauritius
Area: 790 square miles
Population: (1967 est.) 774,000
Capital: Port Louis (Pop., 1965 est., urban area, 129,700)
Religion: Hinduism, Islam, Christianity
Language: English, French, Creole
Currency unit: Rupee

Mauritius is an island nation in the Indian Ocean, about 500 miles east of the island of Madagascar. The country's territory includes the island of Mauritius, Rodrigues Island, and the smaller islands of the Agalega and Cargados Carajos archipelago.

THE LAND. The islands of Mauritius are volcanic in origin, and Rodrigues rises sharply from the sea. On Mauritius, a 2,200-foot central plateau is rimmed by rocky mountains. Many rivers and streams flow down from the mountains. Rodrigues is mountainous and barren except for some fertile valleys. The Agalega islands are low and fertile, and the Cargados Carajos islands are little more than rocky reefs.

The country's climate is semitropical, with hot summers, cool winters, and high humidity. Rainfall is heavy—from 50 to 200 inches a year on all the islands. Cyclones are a frequent danger, especially between December and April.

THE PEOPLE. The population density of Mauritius is very high—almost 1,000 persons per square mile on Mauritius and Rodrigues in 1966. The population continued to grow rapidly in the 1950s and 1960s, at a rate of 3 percent a year. Malaria, which once decimated the population in the late 1940s, was eliminated in the late 1940s, and population growth soared. In the 1960s family-planning measures were introduced in an effort to reverse the trend.

The people of Mauritius are of varied origins, and the population is rather sharply divided along ethnic lines. Between 65 and 70 percent of the population is Indo-Mauritian, of Indian background; under 5 percent is Sino-Mauritian, of Chinese descent; and about 30 percent, called the "general population," is of European, African, and mixed origins.

English is the official language, but Creole, a French dialect, is the common tongue. Chinese, Hindi, French, and Arabic are also spoken. Slightly less than half the population is Hindu, about 30 percent is Christian, and some 15 percent is Muslim.

ECONOMY. Mauritius depends almost completely on sugar. During the early 1960s efforts were undertaken to diversify the economy, because of the dangers of a single-crop economy. The island has valuable forest resources, but exploitation of the forests was not begun until the mid-1960s.

The chief crop is sugarcane, grown on over 90 percent of Mauritius' cultivated land in 1965. Tea is the only other important crop, but in the early 1960s, under a program of agricultural diversification, increased acreage was devoted to tobacco, food crops, and livestock, including dairy cattle. Fish catches are abundant.

Sugarcane processing is the leading industry, with sugar and molasses the principal products. Related industries include making fiber bags for the sugar. Newer industries include cigarette-making, tea production, soap manufacture, brewing, and brick-making.

In 1966 exports earned almost $71 million and imports cost just under $70 million. Sugar accounted for almost 90 percent of exports in 1965, although the percentage declined from the previous year as tea, tobacco, and other goods gained in importance. Foodstuffs, fuels, fats, chemicals, and other manufactured goods must be imported. Mauritius relies on British aid to implement its economic development projects.

GOVERNMENT. Mauritius has a parliamentary form of government, with the British monarch as head of state. Actual executive power is wielded by a prime minister and a cabinet responsible to a popularly elected legislature.

HISTORY. Mauritius has been known for many centuries to Arab and Malay sailors, who probably first saw it for shelter before 1000. Portuguese sailors landed on the island in the 1500s, but they did not establish settlements. The Dutch, who named the island Mauritius for their ruler, Prince Maurice, attempted to establish a colony but failed. No successful settlement was made until 1715, when the French East India Company claimed the island for France and renamed it Ile de France. The French began sugar cultivation, using slave labor, and the colony grew prosperous.

In 1767 the French government took control from the company and made the island a naval base for use in France's struggle with Britain for control of India, and in 1814 the Treaty of Paris, which ended the Anglo-French wars, awarded the island to Britain.

British Rule. The island, renamed Mauritius, was Britain's main source of sugar during the 1800s. Few Britons settled there, however, and French cultural influence remained strong. In 1833 Britain abolished slavery on the sugar plantations. The indentured workers, mostly from India, were brought to Mauritius to work the sugar plantations.

The economy grew increasingly dependent on sugar, which was subject to damage by cyclones and drought and to sharp fluctuations in world market prices.

Independence. After 1886 limited home rule was granted to Mauritius. The islands moved gradually toward fuller self-government, led most frequently by the Indo-Mauritians, who had become the dominant political force on the island.

Seewoosagur Ramgoolam, a leader of the independence movement, was elected the country's first premier after self-government was granted in 1964. In 1967 the Legislative Assembly, dominated by his party, voted to request full independence from Britain. Britain agreed to grant Mauritius its independence effective Mar. 12, 1968.

—Sara D. Gilbert

MEXICO

Official name: United States of Mexico
Area: 761,604 square miles
Population: (1967 est.) 45,671,000
Capital: Mexico City (Pop., 1966 est., 3,287,334)
Language: Spanish
Religion: Roman Catholicism
Currency unit: Peso
National holiday: Independence day, September 16

THE LAND. The physical geography of Mexico is very complex, partly due to the fact that it is formed by both North American and Central American land structures. North American landforms end in the volcanic region south of Mexico City. The mountains of Oaxaca, which lie west of the isthmus of Tehuantepec, together with all the highlands to the south are Central American.

Eastern Mexico, north of Oaxaca, consists of a coastal plain. This plain is broad near the U.S. border, where it forms a continuation of the Texas Gulf coastal plain, but narrows sharply south of Veracruz, ending with Mt. San Martin, the beginning of the Tabasco coastal lowlands and marshes. West of the coastal plain are the eroded valleys and peaks of the Sierra Madre Oriental, whose elevations exceed 13,000 feet above sea level. The Sierra Madre Oriental forms the eastern border of the Central Plateau, which is subdivided into a northern and southern region by the Zacatecas. The southern region of the Central Plateau contains Mexico City and most of the country's people.

The Sierra Madre Occidental forms a barrier of chasms, and arid pocket valleys between the central plateau and the narrow Pacific coastal plain. These mountains are so rugged that in Jalisco the land plunges 5,000 feet into the Pacific within a distance of only 275 miles. Only one pass through this range is used extensively for transportation, and Guadalajara, Mexico's second largest city, is located at that strategic point. A cordillera of volcanic mountains runs from east to west across Mexico south of Mexico City. Peaks like Popocatepetl, over 17,880 feet, and Iztaccihuatl, over 17,340 feet, are scenically striking, but form a barrier that isolates the southern plateau region from the Balsas Valley to the south.

The Sierra Madre del Sur, to the southwest, forms a barrier between the Balsas Valley and the very narrow Pacific coastal plain. This range runs eastward into Oaxaca and forms a tangled mountain knot west of the Isthmus of Tehuantepec.

The Central American portion of Mexico includes the Tabasco lowlands, the limestone plateau of the Yucatan Peninsula, and the mountain system of Chiapas, which extends into Mexico from northwestern Guatemala.

The peninsula of southern California is an extension of the coastal range of California and lies across the Gulf of California from northern Mexico.

Climate. As the surface of Mexico is complex, so is the climate, which varies with altitude and wind pattern. Mountain slopes facing the prevailing winds receive more rainfall than the leeward slopes. The highlands are cooler and have less variation in temperature than the lowlands.

Along the western coast of the peninsula of lower California are cold, upwelling Pacific waters which chill the air masses passing over them, inhibiting rainfall. Thus, much of the north and northwest of Mexico is desert. The eastern coastal plain, on the other hand, receives much moisture south of Tamaulipas, where the trade winds encounter the Sierra Madre Oriental.

THE PEOPLE. Approximately 75 percent of the people of Mexico are mestizo, of mixed European and Indian ancestry. About 10 percent of the population are of European descent—primarily Spanish. The remaining 15 percent of the Mexican population is Indian.

Spanish is the official language, but more than 2 million Mexicans speak Indian languages. These fall into more than 30 major linguistic groups and range from Nahuatl, or Aztec, and Otomi, which are spoken by large groups of people, to tribal languages spoken by only a few family groups.

The overall Mexican population density of 57 people per square mile is not great, but more than 50 percent of the people live within the Central Plateau, which represents only 14 percent of the national territory. Mexico's population is increasing at a very rapid rate, 3.4 percent a year between 1958 and 1965. But the economy has been developing fast enough to absorb the increase.

The country's capital, Mexico City, is one of the world's major urban centers. Unlike most major cities in the Western Hemisphere, it is located inland, with no river access to the ocean.

This also is true of Mexico's largest cities, including Guadalajara, which had a 1966 estimated population of 1,105,900; Monterrey, 849,700; Ciudad Juárez, 415,600; and Puebla, 349,500. Tampico and Veracruz, located on the Gulf of Mexico, are the principal seaports. Mazatlán is the most important seaport on the Pacific coast.

ECONOMY. Mexico has an expanding economy. Between 1960 and 1965 the gross domestic product rose at an annual average rate of 6 percent. While the economy as a whole has been developing steadily, this rise is largely due to the increasingly important role played by industry.

Natural Resources. Mexico is rich in natural resources. It is one of the world's leading producers of silver and ranks high in the production of antimony, graphite, sulfur, mercury, lead, zinc, copper, and gold. The country also mines quantities of iron ore, cadmium, molybdenum, tungsten, manganese, arsenic, and bismuth. Mexico has an abundance of coal, oil, and natural gas. Production of natural gas increased over 50 percent between 1960 and 1966.

Agriculture. About half of Mexico's labor force is engaged in agriculture, which contributed 17 percent of the gross domestic product in 1965. Agricultural production has been increasing rapidly and more than doubled between 1953 and 1965. This increased production is largely the result of government irrigation projects. A major share of Mexican farming is devoted to the production of basic food crops such as corn, wheat, beans, and rice. Commercial crops, which are also important, include sugarcane, cotton, coffee, and henequen, a fiber plant.

Industry. The growth of industry has been steady. The contribution made by industry to the gross domestic product rose from 27 percent in 1950 to 32 percent in 1965. In recent years the government has made a concerted effort to develop the manufacture of chemicals, synthetic fibers, plastics, industrial machinery, and automobiles. In spite of major advances in these areas, Mexico's most important industries are textiles, food processing, and beverages. The country also produces cement, iron and steel, and a variety of consumer goods.

About 40 percent of Mexico's industry is concentrated in the area around Mexico City, and Monterrey and Guadalajara are also important industrial centers.

Trade. In 1966 Mexico's exports earned $1,222 million and its imports cost $1,605 million. Mexico usually imports more than it exports, but tourism helps to make up the gap. The country's chief exports include cotton, sugar, coffee, fish, wheat, and metals. Principal imports are chemicals, machinery, appliances, and transportation equipment. Approximately half of Mexico's trade is with the United States.

GOVERNMENT. Mexico is a federal republic composed of 29 states, 2 territories, and a Federal District, in which the capital, Mexico City, is located. The head of state and chief executive is the president, who is directly elected by popular vote to a six-year term. He may not serve more than one term. The president is assisted by a cabinet appointed by him. Legislative power is vested in the Congress, which consists of the Senate and the Chamber of Deputies. The Senate has 60 members, who are elected to six-year terms. The members of the Chamber of Deputies are directly elected to three-year terms. Senators and deputies may not serve two consecutive terms.

Mexico is a member of the United Nations and the Organization of American States (OAS).

HISTORY. Before Columbus discovered the New World in 1492, Mexico was the site of the greatest Indian civilizations on the North American continent.

The civilization of the Mayas, which was at its height from about 300 BC to 800 AD, was centered in Guatemala and southern Mexico. The Mayas built great cities and were skilled at astronomy and mathematics. They also developed a calendar that was probably more accurate than the one used in Europe at the time, and they had a well-developed system of writing.

In the 800s the Mayas, for unknown reasons, abandoned their cities and reestablished themselves in the Yucatán peninsula. Gradually, however, the Mayas became weakened by attacks made on them from the north by the Toltec Indians of the Central Plateau. By the 1400s Mayan civilization was in decline.

The Toltecs, whose capital was in the Valley of Mexico in the Central Plateau, were subjugated in the early 1400s by the Aztecs, whose original homeland is unknown.

The Aztecs built an empire ruled from their capital, Tenochtitlán, founded in 1325 near the site of present-day Mexico City. Nearly invincible, Tenochtitlán was constructed upon a group of islands in the middle of Lake Texcoco and connected to the mainland by a series of causeways of

In 1517-1518 the Spanish governor of Cuba sent two expeditions to investigate rumors of the existence of

MEXICAN GOVERNMENT TOURIST DEPARTMENT

UNIVERSITY OF MEXICO LIBRARY. The library's murals show themes from Mexico's past.

mainland civilizations rich in gold. Both expeditions retreated to Cuba after brief and bloody encounters with the Indians. In 1518-1519 Hernán Cortés, undaunted by the failures of his predecessors, undertook the conquest of Mexico with fewer than 600 men.

The conquest of the Aztec empire was accomplished primarily by the skillful use of horses and guns, which terrified the Indians who had never seen them before. In addition, the Indians believed that the light-skinned, bearded Spaniards riding on horses were gods, and Cortés was allowed to enter Tenochtitlán. He captured Montezuma, the Aztec emperor, and by the mid-1500s all Mexico had been subdued.

Spanish Rule. Following the Spanish conquest, the Indians were reduced to the level of slaves. They were forced to work in the mines or on the estates of the Spaniards. Gold and silver were taken from the land with unceasing zeal.

In 1535 Mexico City became the capital of the viceroyalty of New Spain, which included a large part of Central America as well as Mexico. The immediate subordinates of its governor, or viceroy, were the peninsulares, Spaniards born in Spain. Native-born Spaniards, known as Creoles, were not permitted to hold high government office.

During the colonial period the Creoles grew to resent the privileged position of the peninsulares. Discontent also surged among the rapidly growing population of mestizos, those of mixed Spanish and Indian parentage. The successful American and French revolutions of the late 1700s further increased native resentment of Spanish injustice and exploitation.

In 1808 Napoleon Bonaparte of France conquered Spain and imprisoned Spain's king, Ferdinand VII, thus leaving Mexico without a legitimate ruler.

Struggle for Independence. On Sept. 16, 1810 a Creole priest in the town of Dolores, Miguel Hidalgo y Costilla, issued the famous "Cry of Dolores," in which he denounced the injustices of the Spanish government and cried out for social reform. With Indian support, Hidalgo and his followers were able to dominate southern Mexico.

The Creoles would not support Hidalgo's social revolution, which threatened their own position, and without Creole support the revolt could not succeed. Hidalgo was defeated and executed. The struggle was renewed by another priest, José María Morelos, a mestizo, but he too was eventually defeated and exe-cuted, in 1815.

Hope for independence lay dor-mant until 1820, when Ferdinand VII, who had been restored to the Spanish throne after Napoleon's armies were expelled from Spain, was forced by internal pressures to approve a new liberal constitution. Mexican Creoles feared that the liberal reforms would weaken their position in Mexico and they aligned themselves with the struggle for independence.

Independence. In 1821 Gen. Augustín de Iturbide led another revolution. He declared Mexico independent and established himself as emperor Au-gustín I. In 1823 he was overthrown by Antonio López de Santa Anna, another ambitious general, who pro-claimed a republic. Santa Anna re-mained the dominant political figure in the new republic until 1855. For most of those years he was either president or dictator, although he was intermittently overthrown.

In 1836 the territory of Texas, which had been settled largely by people from the United States, de-clared its independence. Santa Anna attempted to prevent the secession, but after an initial victory at the Alamo he was decisively defeated at the battle of San Jacinto, in April 1836. The United States annexed Texas in 1845, which angered the Mexicans, who had never recognized Texan independence.

War broke out between Mexico and the United States in 1846. Mexico was defeated, and under the terms of the Treaty of Guadalupe Hidalgo (1848) Mexico was forced to cede a large section of land north of the Rio Grande to the United States. The land lost included New Mexico and Cali-fornia, as well as Texas. In 1853 Santa Anna, short of government funds, sold the Mesilla Valley to the United States in the Gadsden Pur-chase. This final loss of territory gravely insulted the Mexicans.

Revolution and Reform. Shortly after-ward, bands of guerrillas gathered in the mountains and stormed the capital, demanding liberal reforms. Led by Juan Alvarez and Benito Juárez, the rebels declared their in-tention to institute many reforms for the good of the people of Mexico. They planned to assert civilian con-trol over the church and the military; to eliminate sharp class distinctions by breaking up large estates and dis-tributing land among the peasants; and to unite the country to prevent further losses to the United States.

In 1855 Santa Anna was overthrown by the rebels and Alvarez became acting president. Various edicts out-lining the reforms were issued from Mexico City, and in 1857 a new con-stitution, which provided for a more liberal and democratic government, was adopted. The Liberals were staunchly opposed by the army, the

church, and the upper classes. The ultimate result was civil war lasting from 1858 to 1860, when Benito Juárez led his Liberal forces to a costly victory.

During the war Mexico had become deeply indebted to Spain, Britain, and France. In 1861 Juárez, faced with national bankruptcy, suspended pay-ment on these debts. A combined army of French, Spanish, and British troops invaded Mexico in December 1861 to force payment. Napoleon III of France seized this opportunity to conquer the country. A Mexican vic-tory at the battle of Puebla in May 1862 only temporarily halted the French advance, and with reinforce-ments the French won control in 1863. In 1864 Napoleon declared Maxi-milian, an Austrian prince, Emperor of Mexico. In 1867, under diplomatic pressure from the United States, which objected to French interven-tion, France withdrew its troops. Maximilian, under the erroneous im-pression that he had popular support, refused to leave the country and was captured and shot. Juárez returned as president and held office until 1872.

Díaz Era. Juárez and his successor, Sebastián Lerdo de Tejada, attempted to enact liberal reforms, but in 1876 the government was overthrown by Porfirio Díaz, who ruled as dictator from 1876 to 1911. Under his rule the upper class again enjoyed pros-perity, foreign investments multi-plied, and the government budget was balanced. The Indians and the growing working class were neglected, however. The slogan, "Mexico, mother of foreigners, stepmother of Mexi-cans," expressed the growing popular resentment.

Discontent with Díaz's rule cul-minated in revolution in 1910. In an interview with a U.S. news corre-spondent, Díaz expressed the view that Mexico was prepared for a demo-cratic election. Although his com-ments were intended to be read only in the United States, translations of his statement reached northern Mexico, challenged Díaz to hold free elections, and Díaz was forced to up-hold the declaration he had made. The elections were rigged, however, and Madero was imprisoned after his defeat by Díaz. Resentment surged throughout the country, and the peo-ple revolted. In the north, Francisco ("Pancho") Villa and Pascual Orozco led armies of peasants in rebellion. In the south, Emiliano Zapata and an army of Indians raided large estates. In May 1911 Díaz was forced to flee from the country.

Civil Strife. Francisco Madero became the popularly acclaimed president in November 1911. His term of office brought some extension of democratic institutions, but no sorely needed economic and social reforms. The Indians and workers remained dis-satisfied and once again revolted. In 1913 Madero unwisely enlisted the support of Gen. Victoriano Huerta, who betrayed Madero and had him assassinated.

Huerta ruled as dictator until 1914, when revolutionary movements erupted throughout Mexico. Venus-

tiano Carranza, Alvaro Obregón, and Pancho Villa led the revolutionary movements in the north. In the south, an army of peasants was again led by Emiliano Zapata. Huerta's army was defeated and he fled to the United States.

Peace was not restored to Mexico, however, for the victorious troops then fought among themselves for control of the government. Villa and Zapata seized Mexico City, while Carranza and Obregón held Vera Cruz. With promises of extensive liberal reforms, the Obregón forces triumphed and a liberal constitution was drawn up.

Reform Era. The constitution protected labor, limited church authority, and provided for the division of large estates into the ancient Indian com-munal land system, known as the ejido. The constitution was not im-plemented, however, and when Car-ranza tried to choose his own successor, he was overthrown by Ob-regón. In September 1920 Obregón was elected president, and during his four-year term a modest, but solid, program of reforms was initiated.

In 1924 Gen. Plutarco Elías Calles was elected president. Disputes with the church and with foreign investors plagued his administration. In 1928 Obregón was again elected, but was assassinated before taking office. From 1928 to 1934 a series of puppet presidents, controlled by Calles, ruled Mexico. During this period the strongly reformist Partido Nacional Revolu-cionario (PNR), or National Revolu-tionary Party, was formed and came to dominate Mexican politics.

In elections held in 1934, the PNR candidate, Lázaro Cárdenas, was elected to the presidency. Under the Cárdenas administration, reforms de-manded during the revolution were enacted. Millions of acres of land were distributed to the ejidos and schools, hospitals, and roads were constructed. In 1938 both the U.S. and British oil industries were national-ized.

Contemporary Mexico. In 1940 Manuel Avila Camacho was elected president. Although Camacho made no innova-tions during his own term of office, he consolidated the gains that had already been made. In 1942, after German submarines had sunk Mexi-can tankers, Mexico declared war on the Axis. Mexico contributed strategic raw materials to the war effort. Mexicans enlisted in the United States armed forces, and a squadron of the Mexican air force was sent to the Pacific. In 1945 Mexico became a charter member of the United Na-tions.

Postwar administrations basically followed the domestic policies of President Camacho and focused on increasing food production and de-veloping transportation. Pres. Adolfo Ruiz Cortines (1952–1958) greatly ex-tended Mexico's farmland through irrigation projects. Under Adolfo López Mateos (1958–1964) Mexico's educational system was expanded. In 1964 Gustavo Díaz Ordaz was elected president. During his admin-istration, on Oct. 28, 1967, Mexico

MONACO

Official name: Principality of Monaco
Area: 368 acres
Population: (1966 est.) 23,000
Capital: Monaco
Language: French
Religion: Roman Catholicism
Currency unit: French franc
National holiday: November 19

Monaco is a tiny principality on the French Riviera. It is bounded on the north, east, and west by France and on the south by the Mediterranean Sea.

THE LAND AND PEOPLE. Monaco is set into steep cliffs surrounding an excellent harbor. Its climate is mild and rather dry.

There are three sections in the principality—Monte Carlo, La Condamine, and Monaco-Ville, which lies atop a rocky promontory jutting into the Mediterranean.

A majority of the people are from other European countries, and in the mid-1960s only slightly more than one-tenth of the people were native Monégasques. French is the official language, and Roman Catholicism the predominant religion.

ECONOMY. Tourists, attracted by Monaco's scenery, beach resorts, and gambling casino, are the major source of Monaco's income. The sale of postage stamps to collectors is important, and the country also has light industries producing pharmaceuticals, precision tools, and luxury consumer items.

Monaco has no income tax, and it long served the wealthy as a refuge from taxes.

GOVERNMENT. Monaco is governed by a prince, who is assisted by a small appointed cabinet. An elected council shares legislative power with the prince. France is responsible for Monaco's foreign affairs and defense, but the principality maintains consulates and missions throughout the world.

HISTORY. The ancient Phoenicians, Greeks, Carthaginians, and Romans all used Monaco's harbor. In the 600s and 700s Monaco was occupied by the Lombards, who built a fortress on its rocky promontory. In the 800s the fortress fell to the Saracens.

Monaco became part of the Holy Roman Empire, and in the 900s Monaco was granted to a leading family of Genoa, which later took the name

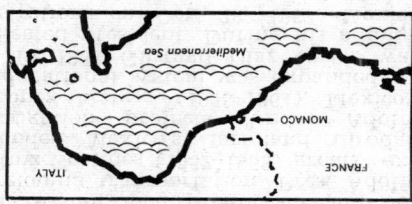

of Grimaldi. The Grimaldis did not exercise their rights over the territory until the late 1200s, when they were driven from Genoa as a result of political feuds.

The tiny state was in constant danger of being overwhelmed by its larger neighbors. With its fortress and its excellent harbor and port facilities, Monaco was coveted by Genoa, Savoy, Florence, France, and Spain. Monaco managed to maintain its independence, however, and in 1512 the right of the Grimaldis to rule Monaco was formally acknowledged by the king of France.

After the French Revolution, in 1793 France annexed the principality. The sovereignty of the Grimaldis was restored in 1814, and in 1815 the Treaty of Vienna made Monaco a protectorate of the Kingdom of Sardinia. In 1861 the principality once more came under the protection of France. In 1911 Monaco adopted a constitution ending the absolute rule of the princes.

During the early 1900s, the principality developed into a fashionable resort, well-known for its gambling casino. In the mid-1900s Monaco moved to broaden and modernize its economy by developing light industry. Prince Rainier III, who took the throne in 1949, married a U.S. actress, Grace Kelly, in 1956.

—Sergio Barzanti

MONGOLIA

Official name: Mongolian People's Republic
Area: 604,249 square miles
Population: (1966 est.) 1,140,000
Capital: Ulan Bator (Pop., 1962 est., 195,300)
Language: Mongolian
Religion: Buddhism
Currency unit: Tugrik
National holiday: People's revolution day, July 11

Mongolia is both a geographical region and a nation. The region, in east-central Asia, lies between Siberia and northern China. It is divided between Inner Mongolia, south of the Gobi, part of China, and Outer Mongolia, an independent nation officially called the Mongolian People's Republic.

The Mongolian People's Republic is bounded on the north by the Soviet Union and on the east, south, and west by Communist China.

THE LAND. Much of Mongolia occupies the grassy, rolling Mongolian Plain, which ranges in elevation from 3,000 to 6,000 feet. Mountains in the north and west rise to between 5,000 and 11,000 feet. Along the southwestern border tower the Altai range mountains, over 12,000 feet. In the south and southeast, the Mongolian Plain slopes into the barren desert of the Gobi Depression, which extends into Inner Mongolia.

All of Mongolia's principal rivers flow northward, toward the Soviet Union. They include the Selenga and the Orkhon, which empty into Lake Baykal, and the Kerulen, an important tributary of the Amur River.

Mongolia's climate is generally dry and is characterized by long, cold winters and short, cool summers. Pre-cipitation increases from south to north, ranging from less than 5 inches to 15 inches a year.

THE PEOPLE. The population is almost entirely Mongol, divided into a number of groups, of which the Khalkha is by far the largest. They use an alphabet similar to the Russian. There are minorities of other Mongols, and some Russians and Chinese. Lamaist Buddhism is the dominant religion, but its practice has been restricted since the 1930s.

Over half of the population is rural, and was semi-nomadic. Population is concentrated in the northern half of the country. About 25 percent of the people live in Ulan Bator, the capital, in east central Mongolia.

ECONOMY. Livestock herding, the mainstay of the country's economy. But by the mid-1900s settled agriculture had increased and industrialization had begun, and an increasing proportion of the population was sedentary.

The country's huge herds of sheep, goats, cattle, horses, and camels provide most necessities, including food, clothing, shelter, and transport, as well as goods for export. The principal crops are grain, potatoes, and some vegetables. Agriculture is collectivized.

Mongolia mines coal, copper, gold, iron, and petroleum. The country's considerable hydroelectric capacity is being developed, and manufactures include building materials, textiles, and processed foodstuffs.

Mongolia exports farm and animal products and some metal ores. Consumer goods, raw materials, and machinery are imported. Mongolian trade is primarily with communist countries, especially with the Soviet Union.

GOVERNMENT. Although Mongolia is constitutionally a republic in which supreme power is vested in a popularly elected assembly, the Khural, political power actually rests with the country's Communist party, officially called the Mongolian People's Revolutionary Party.

The party proposes all candidates for the Khural, and its political bureau, or politburo, sets national policy. The party first secretary is the key figure in the government. The chief of the presidium, a council elected by the Khural to govern between its short sessions, serves as a collective head of state.

Mongolia is a member of the United Nations and the Council for Mutual Economic Assistance (COMECON), a Soviet-led economic alliance of communist states.

HISTORY. The early Mongols were divided into many rival nomadic tribes. They lived by herding and raiding neighboring tribes and states, and by the beginning of the 1200s, the Mongols held the territory all around the Gobi.

Expansion. The first leader to unite the Mongol tribes was Timujin, who in 1206 became Genghis Khan, the "very mighty king." He led the Mongols in the conquest of northern China, eastern Russia, and the Islamic lands of the Near East. The Mon-

gol's small but skilled mounted army conquered quickly, and the Mongols destroyed much of the conquered lands.

After Genghis Khan's death in 1227 his son, Ogotai, led the Mongols across Hungary and Poland as far west as Vienna. Ogotai's death in 1241 forced the Mongols to retreat to elect a new khan. Kublai Khan, their choice, conquered all of China and Korea and controlled much of Southeast Asia. The Mongols proved less skillful at governing than at conquering, however, and in eastern Europe and the Middle East effective Mongol rule ended as soon as the Mongol armies were withdrawn. In China, where the Mongols had established the Yuan dynasty, government corruption eroded Mongol authority and scattered revolts broke out in the Chinese provinces.

Decline. After Kublai Khan's death in 1294 the empire was divided, with the East Asian portion coming under the Mongol-Chinese Chin dynasty. In the late 1300s, under Tamerlane, a second Mongol empire briefly ruled western Asia. But Mongol power and influence had declined greatly, and the Mongols were gradually pushed back to the Mongolian Plain.

In the 1500s Lamaist Buddhism spread to Mongolia and soon became a powerful force. Buddhist monasteries came to hold much of the land, and a large proportion of the male population became monks.

In the 1600s Inner Mongolia came under the control of the Manchus, who conquered China in 1644 and established the Ching dynasty. Despite Mongol resistance, the Manchus had conquered almost all of Outer Mongolia by the 1680s, and Mongolia became a province of China. In the early 1700s Russia began to exert a strong influence on northwestern Mongolia.

Apart from its contacts with China and Russia, during the 1700s and 1800s Mongolia remained isolated from the outside world. Mongolians came to resent their Chinese administrators, who governed the region as though it was a colony, and Chinese settlers, who appropriated grazing land for farm use.

Autonomy. Manchu power had declined by the early 1900s and Japan and Russia agreed to share influence in Mongolia, with Japan controlling eastern Inner Mongolia and Russia dominating Outer Mongolia. In 1911 a revolution in China overthrew the Manchu dynasty and the people of Outer Mongolia, with Russian support, toppled the Chinese provincial government and proclaimed the autonomy of Outer Mongolia. The Mongolians chose a lama, the *hutukhtu*, or "Living Buddha," as nominal ruler. The country was far from independent, however. China did not recognize Mongolia's autonomy, and it remained under the protection of Russia. In 1919, during the upheaval accompanying the fall of the monarchy in Russia, China resumed rule over Mongolia. By 1921 Soviet troops had occupied Outer Mongolia, however, and in 1924, when the reigning hutukhtu died, Mongolia became the

Mongolian People's Republic, the first state to follow the communist pattern of government established in Russia. During the 1920s and 1930s the government promoted radical and rapid economic and social change. The economic power of the Chinese in Mongolia was destroyed, and the power of the Buddhist lamas and the monks was crushed. All opposition to government programs was suppressed.

Inner Mongolia had remained a Chinese province, and in the 1930s it was occupied by Japanese forces. Japanese occupation posed a threat to the Mongolian People's Republic, and in 1939 Soviet and Mongol troops drove the Japanese from the border area.

The Mongolian People's Republic participated briefly in World War II. In 1945, as part of the war settlement, the people of Outer Mongolia voted in a referendum to be independent of China, and in 1946 China, under Chiang Kai-shek, recognized Outer Mongolia's independence. In 1950, after a communist government had been established in China, the Chinese communists and the Soviets agreed to guarantee the independence of the Mongolian People's Republic.

In the late 1950s Mongolia began to expand its diplomatic and commercial contacts with the west, and in 1961 Mongolia became a member of the United Nations. In the early 1960s, when a split developed between Communist China and the Soviet Union, Mongolia sided with the Soviets. In 1966 Mongolia and the Soviet Union reaffirmed their close relations in elaborate ceremonies accompanying the signing of a 20-year treaty of friendship, protection, and aid.

—Thomas E. Ennis; M. G. Inaba

MOROCCO

Official name: **Kingdom of Morocco**
Area: (1967 est.) **171,835 square miles**
Population: (1967 est.) **14,140,000**
Capital: Rabat (Pop., 1965 est., 355,000)
Language: Arabic
Religion: Islam
Currency unit: Dirham
National holiday: Independence day, March 3

Morocco, a kingdom in northern Africa, is bounded on the north by the Mediterranean Sea, on the east by Algeria, on the south by Spanish Sahara, and on the west by the Atlantic Ocean. Between 1912 and 1956 Morocco was divided into a French zone, two Spanish zones, and the international zone of Tanger ('Tangier'). In 1956 Morocco became a sovereign state.

THE LAND. The western end of the Atlas Mountain system dominates Morocco. In the north the Rif Atlas runs parallel to the Mediterranean

CHINA (People's Republic of)

MONGOLIA

SOVIET UNION

Sea. The Middle Atlas, which has elevations of over 10,900 feet, and the Grand Atlas, which has elevations of over 13,600 feet, run through central Morocco. The Anti-Atlas, in the southwest, borders the desert region of the Sahara, which stretches along eastern and southern Morocco.

The Moroccan Meseta, or plateau, lies on the Atlantic side of the Grand Atlas and Middle Atlas. It is irrigated in places, as at Marrakech, and crossed by rivers leading into lowland plains. The Moulouya River and valley are east of the Middle Atlas. The Grand Atlas and the Middle Atlas intercept rain-bearing winds, which bring moisture to the north and west, and cause hot, desert conditions in the south and near-desert conditions in the east.

THE PEOPLE. The Moroccans are descended from Berber-speaking peoples, possibly the original inhabitants of the area, and from later Arab settlers. Most of the people are Muslim. There is a small Jewish population in the country, and there are small communities of Europeans, mainly French and Spanish.

Morocco's major cities include Rabat, the capital; Casablanca, an industrial and commercial center and port; Fes ('Fez'); Marrakech; and Tanger ('Tangier').

ECONOMY. The economy of Morocco is based primarily on agriculture. The basic food crops are wheat and barley, wine grapes, citrus fruits, and vegetables. With the aid of foreign capital, particularly from France, Morocco has become an important source of seasonal fruits and vegetables for Western Europe. Large irrigation projects have been developed to increase agricultural production. Sheep and goats are raised in the mountains.

Morocco has deposits of several minerals. Phosphate rock, used in the production of fertilizers, is the most important, and in 1965 over 9.8 million metric tons of phosphate rock were produced. Iron ore, manganese, cobalt, and zinc are also mined. There are a number of small industries in the country. Cement, superphosphates, Moroccan leather, flour, sugar, and other products are produced.

In 1966 imports cost $477 million and exports earned $429 million. The major imports are petroleum products, food, manufactured goods, especially iron and steel and textiles, and machinery. Exports include live animals, fish, fruit, vegetables, phosphates and fertilizers, iron ore, and leather. Most trade is conducted with France, West Germany, the United States, and Spain.

GOVERNMENT. Morocco's 1962 constitution vested executive powers in the king, the head of state, and legislative power in the popularly elected House of Representatives and the House of Counsellors, elected by local authorities and various interest groups. In June 1965 the king took all executive and legislative powers. Morocco is a member of the United Nations, the Organization of African Unity, and the Arab League.

HISTORY. The earliest known inhabitants of present-day Morocco were Berber-speaking peoples. In the 1200s

MOROCCO'S ISLAMIC HERITAGE is reflected in architecture and the dress of the people.

PAN AMERICAN AIRWAYS

BC Phoenicians landed on the Moroccan coast and established trading posts in the region. In the 100s AD Rome established a province in northwestern Morocco. Roman domination came to an end in the 400s with the invasion of the Vandals.

In the early 700s Muslim armies invaded Morocco, and the Berber-speaking peoples gradually adopted Islam. In the late 700s most of the country united under Idris, a member of the 'Alid family. His son established the city of Fez.

In 1056 Berber-speaking tribes formed a powerful religious and political force, the Almoravids. The Almoravids founded the city of Marrakech in 1062, and established a dynasty which ruled Morocco until 1147. The Almohads, another Berber confederation, defeated the Almoravids, and established a dynasty which lasted until 1269. The Marinid dynasty succeeded the Almohads.

In 1544 Morocco came under the rule of another 'Alid dynasty, the Sa'dis, and in 1664 yet another branch of the 'Alid, the Filalis, or Alawites, assumed control.

European Control. Although only about seven miles from Europe, Morocco did not come under European rule until the 1900s. In the early 1900s Britain, Spain, France, and Germany competed for control of Morocco. In

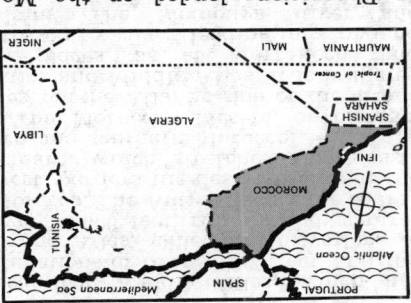

1912 the Moroccan sultan was forced to sign the Treaty of Fez with France, and most of Morocco became a French protectorate. In the same year Spain obtained control of a region in the north and one in the south. In 1923 the city of Tangier became an international zone.

From 1912 to 1925 Louis Lyautey ruled French Morocco as resident-general. He brought security to most of the country and established good relations with the Moroccans, based on respect for the monarchy and the traditional Moroccan way of life.

In 1921 a leader in the Rif Mountains, Abd al-Krim led a rising against the Spanish, and then fought a combined Spanish and French force. He was defeated in 1926. After 1925 the government of French Morocco was more centralized and the European population in Morocco steadily increased.

Nationalism. Moroccan nationalism began to develop in the late 1920s. In 1927 France placed Muhammad bin Yusuf (Muhammad V) on the throne, believing he would act favorably to France. The French assumption appeared valid when in 1930 Muhammad signed the Berber Dahir, which downgraded the importance of Islamic law. After that, however, Muhammad responded to the appeals of the nationalists.

By the time of World War II he was cautiously cooperating with them while maintaining favorable relations with France. In 1953 France forced Muhammad to abdicate in order to end his nationalist activity. He went into exile, but as a result nationalist disturbances intensified. In 1955 France accepted the necessity of dealing with Muhammad, and he returned to Morocco in triumph.

Independence. Negotiations quickly led to independence for French Morocco, achieved on Mar. 2, 1956. By agreements in April 1956 and April 1958 the Spanish zones were granted independence, and in October 1956 Tangier was incorporated into Morocco.

Muhammad V died in 1961, and his son Hasan II succeeded him. In 1962, with the adoption of its first constitution, Morocco became a constitutional monarchy. In June 1965 Hasan took over all executive and legislative powers because of opposition he faced in parliament from the major political parties.

—Hibberd V. B. Kline, Jr.;
L. Carl Brown

MUSCAT and OMAN

Official name: Sultanate of Muscat and Oman and Dependencies
Area: 82,000 square miles
Population: (1966 est.) 565,000
Capital: Muscat (Pop., 1960 est., urban area, 6,208)
Language: Arabic
Religion: Islam
Currency unit: Persian Gulf Indian rupee

Muscat and Oman, an Arab sultanate in the southeastern corner of the Arabian peninsula, occupies a strategic position at the mouth of the Persian Gulf. The country is bordered on the northwest by the Trucial Coast, on the north by the Gulf of Oman, on the east and south by the Arabian Sea, and on the southwest by South Yemen. The borders of Muscat and Oman are largely undefined, and some are disputed.

THE LAND. A narrow plain skirts the country's 1,000-mile coastline. The northwestern portion of the plain, the Batinah, is quite fertile. Rugged mountains rise sharply to nearly 10,000 feet above the plain. In the interior is a low, barren plateau, the eastern end of the vast Rub al Khali, or "Empty Quarter," of the Arabian Peninsula. The climate throughout the country is hot and dry.

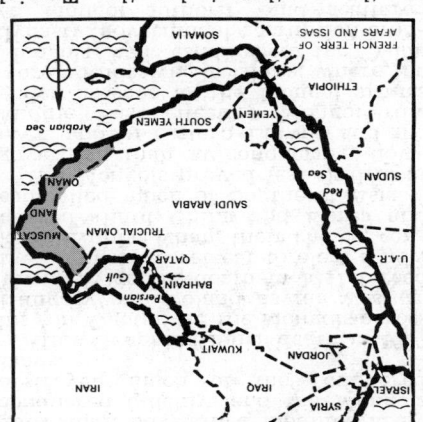

THE PEOPLE. The native people are Arab, but there are Indian, Iranian, and Negro minorities. Population is concentrated in three main regions—Muscat, on the northeast; Oman, in the mountains; and Dhofar, on the Arabian Sea coast.

ECONOMY. Muscat and Oman's economic life is based on farming, herding, and trading. The major mineral resource is oil, which was discovered in 1964 in sufficient quantities for production. Dates, grown on the Batinah and in mountain valleys, are the leading crop. Coconuts, cereals, and citrus fruits are also grown. Large herds of camels are raised in the interior, and there is good fishing off the coast. There is little industry.

Trade is important. The main port is Matrah, on the Gulf of Oman. Dates are the chief export, with India, Pakistan, and the Persian Gulf states the leading markets. Foodstuffs, cement, textiles, and vehicles are imported, primarily from Britain, India, and Pakistan.

GOVERNMENT. Muscat and Oman is ruled by the sultan of Muscat. The province of Oman has some autonomy under its own ruler, but Muscat has sovereignty over the region.

HISTORY. Arab peoples have inhabited Muscat and Oman for many centuries. Because of its strategic position at the mouth of the Persian Gulf, the land attracted conquerors seeking control of the gulf. In 1508 the Portuguese occupied Muscat, and during the following century they competed for control of the region with the Ottoman Turks, who had captured several areas.

By 1650 the native Arabs had driven out both the Portuguese and the Turks. Arab control was not secure, however, until 1737, when the Ahmad Ibn Said dynasty fought off a Persian invasion.

During the 1700s and 1800s the sultanate extended its control over parts of southern Iran and eastern Africa. In the later 1800s, however, internal political disputes divided the region between coastal Muscat and interior Oman. The power of both declined, and foreign territories were lost.

In 1891 Muscat granted special privileges to Britain in return for British protection. Close ties with Britain were reaffirmed several times in the 1900s by treaties of friendship. British-led troops helped put down a rebellion in the interior. Following this conflict, the United Nations acknowledged Muscat's sovereignty over Oman.

The traditional way of life of the people of the country faced new challenges in the late 1960s as the exploitation of oil resources brought increased prosperity and drew world attention to Muscat and Oman.

—Charles Issawi; Alexander Melamid

NAURU

Official name: Nauru
Language: Nauruan
Religion: Christianity
Capital: Nauru
Population: (1966) 6,056
Area: 8 square miles

THE LAND AND PEOPLE. Nauru, a small, isolated coral island in the South Pacific Ocean, is located about 30 miles south of the equator, northeast of the Solomon Islands. It was made a UN Trust Territory in 1947 and placed under the joint control of Britain, Australia, and New Zealand, with Australia as administrator. The trustees granted Nauru its independence Jan. 31, 1968.

Nauru is ringed by coral reefs. The island consists of a narrow coastal plain encircling an upland region, most of which is occupied by phosphate-bearing rock. The climate is hot and humid throughout the year.

Native Nauruans are a mixture of Micronesian and Polynesian stocks. Most are Christian. Chinese and European foreign workers and managers make up about half the population.

ECONOMY. The island's economy is almost totally dependent on phosphate mining, although coconuts and other fruits and a few vegetables are raised on the coastal plain. The production of phosphates is Nauru's chief industry, and the island is one of the world's leading producers of phosphate rock, mining over 1.7 million metric tons in 1964–1965.

The mining and export of the rock is managed by Britain, Australia, and New Zealand, under Nauruan and UN supervision. Royalties and other fees are paid to the Nauruans. As a result, the islanders have one of the highest standards of living in the world, pay no taxes, and enjoy free education and medical services.

Phosphates are the only exports, and food, machinery, and consumer goods are imported. Most trade is with Australia, New Zealand, and Britain. In the early 1960s efforts began to diversify the economy in preparation for the predicted depletion of the phosphate deposits in the 1990s.

GOVERNMENT. Nauru's government is headed by a president, who is chosen by a popularly elected legislative assembly from among its members.

HISTORY. Nauru was discovered in 1798 by a British explorer, but for over a century it remained a beachcomber's refuge and a minor source of copra. In 1888 possession passed to Germany.

In 1900 Nauru was found to be rich in phosphate rock, the basis of a fertilizer then coming into extensive use in Australia and New Zealand. By agreement with the Germans, phosphate mining was undertaken by an Australian-based British company.

After World War I, in 1919, Nauru was made a League of Nations mandate entrusted to Britain, but Australia administered economic and political affairs. Phosphate production was shared by Australia, New Zealand, and Britain. Occupied by the Japanese in World War II, the island was reoccupied in 1945 by Australian troops. Following the war it became a UN Trust Territory under joint Australian, British, and New Zealand authority, but with Australia administering the three. In 1964, as exhaustion of the phosphate rock was foreseen, Australian and Nauruan officials discussed relocating the islanders, but the Nauruans wished to remain on Nauru. In 1966 the UN General Assembly recommended that the trustee nations make the island habitable again when the phosphate was depleted by replacing all soil that had been removed with the rock. The UN also recommended independence for Nauru, and the island became an independent nation on Jan. 31, 1968.

NEPAL

Official name: Kingdom of Nepal
Area: 54,360 square miles
Population: (1966 est.) 10,294,000
Capital: Katmandu (Pop., 1961, 122,507)
Language: Nepali
Religion: Hinduism and Buddhism
Currency: Rupee
National holiday: National day, February 18

Nepal is a small Kingdom in South Asia. It is a landlocked country bounded on the north by the Tibet region of China and on the east, south, and west by India.

THE LAND. Nepal can be divided into three distinct geographical regions, each extending east to west. The Great Himalayas dominate the northern region, an area of spectacular alpine scenery with many of the world's tallest mountains. There are eight peaks with elevations of over 26,000 feet, and Mt. Everest, on the Nepal-Tibet border, with an elevation of 29,028 feet, is the tallest mountain in the world. Elevations in the northern region generally exceed 20,000 feet, and the lower portions of this region are forested. The climate is extremely cold and rather dry.

The second region, in central Nepal, is also mountainous. Elevations range from 4,500 in the valley bottoms to 10,000 feet. Most of the lower slopes and valleys are cultivated. The most important part of the central region is the Katmandu Valley, the heart of the country. Only 18 by 15 miles in area and surrounded by high mountains, it contains Nepal's main towns—Katmandu, the capital, Patan, and Bhadgeon. The valley is well-watered, receiving about 58 inches of precipitation annually, and has a moderate climate.

The third region, called the terai, is a narrow belt 10 to 20 miles wide next to the Indian border. Much of the terai is heavily wooded. Its climate is hot and humid, with rainfall averaging 60 inches a year. Winters can be quite pleasant, however. Many rivers flow from the Himalayas through Nepal, including the Kosi, the Trisuli, the Baghmati, the Gandak, and the Karnali.

THE PEOPLE. Nepal's population is concentrated in the central region, especially the Katmandu Valley, and in the southern region, the terai. The north is sparsely populated. The Nepalese are descendants of Mongols and peoples of northern India. They are traditionally divided along tribal lines, with the Gurkha the dominant group. The minority Newar and Sherpa peoples are Mongol-Tibetan. The Nepalese speak Nepali and a variety of hill dialects. Buddhism and Hinduism are the major religions.

ECONOMY. The Nepalese economy is based on agriculture, but the country is rich in natural resources. Nepal's mineral resources include deposits of copper, iron, sulfur, coal, hematite, and bauxite. But in the 1960s they remained virtually untapped because of Nepal's isolation and lack of transportation facilities.

There are many acres of valuable forests, especially in the south, where the hardwood sal tree is the most valuable commercial timber. Because of its many rapid rivers, Nepal has a large hydroelectric potential.

The country's best farmland is in the south, where farmers grow rice, jute, mustard, tobacco, wheat, linseed, and some sugarcane. The south produces a surplus of cereal grains. The majority of farmers in the central region eke out a subsistence existence by intensively cultivating small, terraced plots of irrigated land.

Rice is grown in the warm season and wheat and vegetables in the dry, cool months. Corn, millet, and legumes are grown on the hillsides. A few cows are kept for milk.

Herding is the main activity of the Sherpa in the north, who graze sheep, goats, and yaks on the Himalayan slopes. Wheat and barley are grown in the valley bottoms of the north.

An important source of income and foreign exchange traditionally has been the service of Gurkha soldiers in the British and Indian armies.

Nepal relies on financial and technical assistance from many nations and from the UN for development.

Nepal's international trade is limited. The main exports are rice, jute, wool, timber, linseed, and hides. Textiles, fuels, medicines, footwear, and industrial raw materials are imported. Most trade is with India.

GOVERNMENT. Nepal is a constitutional monarchy, with a king as chief executive and head of state. The king appoints a council of ministers to advise him and he chooses a council of ministers from among the members of the Panchayat, the legislative assembly. Most members of the Panchayat are elected to five-year terms by local and regional panchayats, and some are appointed by the king.

Nepal is a member of the United Nations.

HISTORY. The earliest inhabitants of the Katmandu Valley were the Newars, who lived under a tribal form of government and developed a religion and customs representing a blend of Buddhism and Hinduism. In the first centuries AD the valley came under the rule of Indian kings, who consolidated Indian influence in Nepal in the form of the Hindu religion and culture and monarchial government.

When the last of the dynasty of Indian kings, the Malla, began to weaken in the 1400s, the country returned to tribal government. In the 1500s a western Nepalese principality, Gurkha, gained strength under the Shah dynasty, whose most famous ruler, Prithvi Narayan, conquered the Katmandu Valley in 1769 and created the modern Nepalese state.

Expansionism. Combining fierce military ambition with an unusual talent for administration, Prithvi Narayan extended his rule eastward to Darjeeling, now in India, and his descendants expanded Nepalese hegemony to the east as far as Kashmir and to the south into present-day India. Nepalese expansion to the east and to the south brought conflicts with Tibet and India. Two Nepalese invasions of Tibet, in 1788 and 1791, brought retaliation from China, which had gained suzerainty over Tibet. A Chinese army crossed the Himalayas and approached the Katmandu Valley. Nepal was forced to withdraw from Tibet and to pay tribute to China. The payments ceased in 1908.

Nepalese expansionism turned southward and confronted the British, who were extending their control of India northward in the Ganges Valley. The Nepalese refused to negotiate with the British and permitted frequent raids into the Indian plains.

The British were able to subdue the Nepalese marauders and reach a settlement with Nepal in 1816, in the Treaty of Sagauli. The treaty established Nepal's boundary with India and gave Britain a deciding influence in Nepalese foreign relations. Gurkha soldiers began to be used by British armies.

Rana Rule. Struggles for power in the early 1800s weakened Nepal and in 1846 resulted in the establishment of rule by the prime ministers, the Ranas. This pattern of government continued until 1951. Rana rule, supported by the army and the British in India, was marked by conspiracies and assassinations within the extended Rana family and the isolation of Nepal from modernizing influences.

In the 1900s in India Nepalese intellectuals began to aspire to advancement for their country, and this led to a movement supported by the titular ruler, King Tribhuvana, to unseat the Ranas. After India achieved independence in 1950, the Nepalese National Congress, modeled on the Indian Congress party, led a reform drive which was backed by the new government in India.

The Ranas responded with legislative concessions in 1950, but revolts broke out and with Indian encouragement King Tribhuvana was able to end Rana power in 1951. The political and administrative turmoil accompanying the downfall of the Ranas lasted for 8 years, while the country was held together by the newly found power of the king. Tribhuvana died in 1955 and was succeeded by his son, Mahendra.

Contemporary Nepal. King Mahendra experimented unsuccessfully with various political leaders and party coalitions in the 1950s. But none seemed able to unify the country or introduce needed reforms. Meanwhile, Chinese power was increasing in Tibet, and the security in Nepal, as well as India, was threatened. In 1959 the king promulgated a new constitution giving himself supreme executive powers but also providing for a legislature.

In an unprecedented election in 1959, 43 percent of the electorate voted, a considerable achievement in a country of hundreds of semi-isolated village settlements. B. P. Koirala, of the Nepalese Congress, took office as prime minister with a program calling for land reform, more efficient administration, and the development of a more active foreign policy.

King Mahendra overthrew the Koirala government at the end of 1960 and introduced direct royal rule. The king's action did not lead to dictatorship, but rather to a new delegation of authority to village councils in what the King called "democracy from below" and to a resurgence of popular support for the monarch.

The King attracted a progressive body of supporters in the government with a program directed toward modernization of the still largely traditional society and economy. He also pursued an active policy in foreign relations, including a state visit to the United States in 1967.

—Charles H. Heimsath; M. G. Inaba

NETHERLANDS

Official name: Kingdom of the Netherlands
Area: 12,990 square miles
Population: (1967 est.) 12,597,000
Capital: Amsterdam (Pop. 1965 est., 864,900)
Language: Dutch
Religion: Protestantism, Roman Catholicism
Currency unit: Guilder
National holiday: Birthday of the queen, April 30

The Netherlands, a small nation in western Europe, is bounded on the north and west by the North Sea, on the east by West Germany, and on the south by Belgium. The Frisian Islands separate the mainland from the open sea in the north.

In 1948 a customs union went into effect linking Belgium, Luxembourg, and the Netherlands, which is known as the Benelux Customs Union. Full economic union of the three countries has existed since 1960.

THE LAND. The Netherlands consists mostly of low plains, although there are some hilly sections in the east. Much of the land along the coast lies below sea level. It is protected by dikes and kept dry by drainage and pumping systems. The Dutch have a much higher percentage of reclaimed land than any nation in Europe, and systematic land reclamation continues. The climate is maritime, with cool summers, mild winters, and high humidity. Rainfall is ample and reliable.

THE PEOPLE. The Netherlands is one of the most densely settled of the world's developed nations, with some 970 people per square mile. The population in the western half of the country. The largest city in the Netherlands is Amsterdam. Other major cities include Rotterdam, The Hague, Utrecht, Eindhoven, and Haarlem.

The population is homogeneous. There are no large ethnic minorities, although religious differences have been the basis of past friction. About 40 percent of the population is Roman Catholic, and 40 percent is Protestant. Most of the rest profess no religion. Dutch is the universal language.

ECONOMY. The Netherlands is located along the heavily trafficked North Sea coast, and commerce is a mainstay of the Dutch economy. The Dutch merchant fleet is one of Europe's largest, and Rotterdam is the continent's leading port.

The mineral resources of the Netherlands are limited. There is some coal in the extreme south, in Limburg, and there are deposits of good ceramic clays. In 1960 Europe's largest natural gas field was discovered in the northeastern province of Groningen. Most land in the Netherlands is suited for agriculture, and about 70 percent of the land is used for crops or grazing. Dutch agriculture uses intensive and highly efficient methods, and yields per acre and per animal are among the highest in the world. Industry has expanded greatly since 1950, and by the mid-1960s about 40 percent of the labor force was engaged in manufacturing. Major industrial products include steel and other finished metals, transportation equipment, machinery, chemicals, refined

petroleum, radios, textiles, ships, and a wide variety of processed foodstuffs. The chief industrial cities are Rotterdam, Amsterdam, Utrecht, Eindhoven, Limburg, and Groningen.

In 1967 exports earned U.S. $7,288 million, and imports cost $8,338 million. About 70 percent of the Netherlands' exports consist of industrial products, and 25 percent consist of agricultural produce and foodstuffs. Industrial exports chiefly include chemicals, refined petroleum, metal and electrical goods, and textiles. Major imports are industrial raw materials, which make up about one third of the total; foodstuffs; fuels; and a variety of consumer goods.

The Netherlands' chief trading partners are West Germany, Belgium, Luxembourg, the United States, Britain, and France.

GOVERNMENT. The Netherlands is a constitutional monarchy. The sovereign is head of state, but executive power is exercised by a prime minister and cabinet. The prime minister must normally be able to command a majority of votes in the legislature.

Legislative power is held by the States-General, which consists of two houses. The upper house is called the First Chamber, and its members are chosen by provincial legislatures for six-year terms. Members of the lower house, the Second Chamber, are directly elected and serve four-year terms.

The Netherlands is a member of the European Communities, the United Nations, and the North Atlantic Treaty Organization (NATO).

Surinam, or Dutch Guiana, and the Netherlands Antilles are the remains of a once vast overseas empire controlled by the Dutch.

HISTORY. When Roman legions led by Julius Caesar first advanced into the Netherlands in 57 BC, the area was inhabited by Celtic and Germanic tribes. The region south of the Rhine became a part of the Roman Empire, and remained so until 400 AD, when the Netherlands came under the control of the Franks. The Netherlands were part of Charlemagne's empire from 800 to 843. After the breakup of the empire, they emerged as a group of duchies, most often under the control of German princes. After 1384 they were ruled by the dukes of Burgundy. Mary of Burgundy married the future Holy Roman Emperor Maximilian I in 1477, and in 1493 the Netherlands became part of the Holy Roman Em-

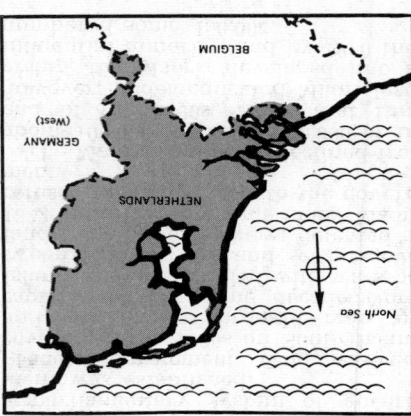

pire. After the resignation of Emperor Charles V in 1555, the empire was divided, and the Netherlands passed to Philip II of Spain.

During the second half of the 1600s, many of the Dutch accepted Calvinism. Philip, a devout Roman Catholic, saw the suppression of Protestantism as a paramount goal and introduced the Inquisition into the Netherlands. Religious persecution intensified the existing conflict between the Dutch and Spaniards. In addition to religious freedom, the Dutch desired economic independence and self-government, and they strongly resented foreign rule.

Independence. In 1579 the seven northern provinces formed the Union of Utrecht, and two years later they proclaimed their independence. A bloody civil war was fought until 1609, when a twelve-year truce was signed. Under the leadership of William of Orange the Dutch Netherlands thus achieved their de facto independence.

At the end of the truce, Spain resumed the war, but the Dutch were more than able to hold their own, and in 1648 the Treaty of Westphalia formally recognized the independence of the United Netherlands. The southern provinces continued to be ruled by Spain and then by Austria until the end of the 1700s.

During the 1600s the Dutch nation reached its political and cultural height. The Dutch established a colonial empire, and for a brief time the Netherlands was the leading commercial power in Europe. Dutch supremacy was broken by a series of wars with England (1652-1654; 1665-1667), which soon reduced the Netherlands to the status of a second-rate power.

During the second half of the 1600s, the Dutch were also engaged in trying to stem the expansionist tendencies of France under King Louis XIV. Although successful, they were never able to recover from the strain of the effort, and after the War of the Spanish Succession (1702-1713) the Dutch economy declined.

In 1795 the Netherlands were conquered by France and made into the puppet state of the Batavian Republic. In 1810 the Dutch were incorporated into the Napoleonic empire. After the defeat of Napoleon, the Congress of Vienna (1814-1815) restored independence to the Netherlands.

Union. The Congress of Vienna also joined the Austrian and former Spanish provinces with the Dutch Netherlands, which was intended to serve as a bulwark against future French expansion. But the union between Belgium and Holland was short-lived.

Holland was Germanic in orientation, Calvinistic in religion, and favored a policy of free trade, whereas Belgium was French in orientation, predominantly Roman Catholic, and sought high tariffs to protect its growing industry. In 1830 a revolution broke out in Belgium which eventually resulted in the separation of the two countries.

Modern Netherlands. The Netherlands remained neutral in World War I, but was invaded by the Germans during

World War II. It suffered greatly during the German occupation. Queen Wilhelmina escaped to London, where she led a government in exile. After the liberation in 1944 she was restored to her throne. In 1948, after a reign of 50 years, she abdicated in favor of her daughter, Juliana.

During the postwar period, the Netherlands lost a large portion of its colonial possessions. A nationalist rebellion broke out in Indonesia in 1945, and in 1949 the Dutch granted the country its independence. In 1954 the American colonies of Dutch Guiana and the Netherlands Antilles gained internal self-government, but they remained in the kingdom as equal partners of the Netherlands. In 1962 Netherlands New Guinea (West Irian) was transferred to Indonesia.

The Netherlands has played a prominent role in bringing about closer ties among the countries of Western Europe. In 1967 the Netherlands met with Belgium and Luxembourg to discuss extending the integration between their countries beyond the field of economics, hoping thus to encourage closer cooperation between France, West Germany, and Italy, the other members of the West European Community.

—George M. Kren

NEW ZEALAND

Official name: New Zealand
Area: 103,740 square miles
Population: (1967 est.) 2,726,000
Capital: Wellington (Pop., 1966, urban area, 167,844)
Language: English
Religion: Anglicanism, Protestantism, Roman Catholicism
Currency: Dollar
National holiday: New Zealand day, February 6

New Zealand, an independent nation in the South Pacific Ocean, lies some 1,200 miles southeast of Australia, from which it is separated by the Tasman Sea. New Zealand is made up of two main islands, North Island and South Island, and several smaller islands, including Stewart Island and the Chatham Islands.

THE LAND. New Zealand is a relatively mountainous country. The South Island contains several areas of level land at fairly low elevations, notably the Canterbury and Southland plains. The eastern part of South Island. Cook, in the west-central part of South Island, is Mount Cook, the highest peak, reaching an elevation of 12,349 feet above sea level. The Southern Alps extend along the length of South Island, and there are 28 peaks with elevations over 10,000 feet.

Cook Strait separates North Island from South Island. North Island has four volcanic peaks with elevations of over 6,000 feet, the highest of which is Ruapehu, with an elevation of 9,175 feet. Among the larger lowland regions of North Island are the Waikato-Thames Plain and the Manawatu-Horowhenua Coastal Plain. There are many rivers on the islands, including the Waikato, Wanganui, and the Rangitaiki on North Island, and the Waitaki, Oreti, and Clutha on South Island.

THE PEOPLE. Over 90 percent of New Zealanders are of British descent. There are also small numbers of Europeans of other origins. The Maori, a people of Polynesian stock, migrated to the Pacific islands beginning in the 900s. In 1965 Maoris made up over 7 percent of the population.

New Zealand has a rapidly growing population, and between 1958 and 1965 the rate of population growth was 2.1 percent a year. About two-thirds of the people live on North Island. The New Zealanders are largely urban dwellers, and two cities, Auckland and Wellington, with their suburbs, accounted for over 25 percent of the population in 1965.

ECONOMY. New Zealand is primarily an agricultural country. At one time all of North Island and most of South Island were forested. In the 1800s European settlers cleared large areas to establish farms, and today only about 20 percent of New Zealand is forested. In many places the removal of natural cover resulted in erosion or the growth of tussock grasses.

Agriculture. The country's mild climate and its grasslands provide excellent conditions for pastoral industries. Sheep are raised in most parts of the country, and in 1965 there were more than 53.7 million sheep in New Zealand.

Sheep on South Island are raised primarily for their wool, and sheep on North Island are raised for wool and mutton. On South Island sheep are grazed on large ranges in the mountainous central region. There are two sheep-rearing regions on North Island, one extending along the entire east coast and the other running from Auckland to Wanganui.

Dairying is also an important agricultural industry in New Zealand. Most of the dairying is confined to North Island, in the areas north and south of Auckland, and in the southwestern corner of the island. The principal products are butter and cheese. Although the sheep and dairy industries dominate New Zealand agriculture, many other products and crops are produced in significant quantities. In the eastern and southern coastal regions of South Island, wheat, oats, barley, and turnips are grown. Fruits and vegetables are grown mainly on North Island and in the northern tip of South Island.

Mining and Manufacturing. New Zealand is not an important mining country, but enough coal is mined to meet local needs in most years and some gold is produced. Because of a lack of major mineral resources and a limited home market, New Zealand has not developed a great number of manufacturing industries.

Aside from the processing of agricultural products, such as butter and cheese making, canning and freezing vegetables, and leather and wool preparation, most manufacturing is based on imported raw materials. Auckland is the principal manufacturing center, with automobile assembly, woodworking, textile, brewing, and light engineering plants. Christchurch has automobile assembly plants.

Trade. In 1967 imports cost over U.S. $955 million and exports earned over $933 million. The major imports are petroleum, textile yarn and fabrics, iron and steel, and machinery. The major exports are meat, dairy products, and wool. Most trade is conducted with Britain, the United States, Australia, Canada, and Japan.

GOVERNMENT. New Zealand has a parliamentary system of government. The head of state is the British Queen, who is represented in New Zealand by a governor-general. Actual executive power is vested in a prime minister and cabinet responsible to the legislature. Legislative power is held by an 80-member House of Representatives. House members are popularly elected to three-year terms.

New Zealand is a member of the United Nations and the Commonwealth of Nations. It is also a member of the Southeast Asia Treaty Organization (SEATO); the Tripartite Security Treaty (ANZUS), with Australia and the United States; and ANZAM, a defense agreement with Australia and Britain.

HISTORY. The Maori migrated to New Zealand between the 900s and 1300s. In 1642 the Dutch navigator Abel Tasman sighted the islands of New Zealand, but they were not visited by Europeans again until 1769, when Capt. James Cook accurately charted the coasts.

Only after European settlement in Australia in the late 1700s and early 1800s did Europeans develop an interest in New Zealand. From the 1790s to the 1840s Europeans exploited New Zealand's timber, seals, whales, and flax and established a port of call at the Bay of Islands, on North Island.

Missionaries worked among the Maoris, while Britain sought to maintain order on the islands and stimulate trade without assuming governmental responsibility. Perhaps 2,000 Europeans then lived in New Zealand.

British Rule. In 1840 settlement began in earnest. In that year the British signed the Treaty of Waitangi with the Maoris. By this treaty Britain extended its sovereignty over New Zealand and promised protection of Maori land rights and equality in a biracial society. In 1841 New Zealand became a crown colony.

In quick succession, settlements were made at Wellington, Auckland, and at Nelson, Dunedin, and Christchurch on South Island. The British settlers intended to develop an economy based on crop production, but sheep grazing and wool production proved more feasible and profitable. South Island was dominant until about 1910. There were few Maoris there and the land was reasonably accessible. North Island had many Maoris and was heavily wooded. In 1852 Britain granted New Zealand a constitution providing for a loose federation of six provinces, and in 1856 a parliamentary system of government was established.

Federal Government. Gold was discovered in the 1860s on South Island, and gold rushes brought men and capital. In that same decade North Island was preoccupied with wars between Maori tribes and settlers over land. The Maoris were defeated in 1872 and after that time many Maoris refused to cooperate with the government.

The Maori population declined from about 100,000 in 1840 to 40,000 at the end of the 1800s. After that time, however, the Maoris developed into an influential minority, and by 1960 they numbered some 150,000.

PAN AMERICAN AIRWAYS

NEW ZEALAND'S SOUTH ISLAND is mountainous, and many of the mountains extend to the sea.

Aside from problems arising from conflicts between the central and provincial governments and relations with the Maori, New Zealand concerned itself with social and economic development. The effective power for this development rested with the provinces. In 1876, seeking to effect a national development program, Sir Julius Vogel, the prime minister, dissolved the provinces.

Centralization. Vogel's development program included borrowing funds in Britain, railroad construction, encouraging immigration, and opening up land for individual purchase to encourage diversified agricultural production. The program was not entirely successful, however. Borrowing became difficult, the railroad system was left incomplete, immigrants could not acquire closely held lands, and economic diversification did not materialize.

New Zealand stagnated in the 1880s and people left the island. Technological changes solved New Zealand's problems, however, as the introduction of refrigerated shipping made possible the export of meat and dairy products to Britain. This development diversified pastoral exports and triggered a rapid growth of dairying on North Island.

In 1891 the Liberal party, supported by small farmers and city workers, came to power. Prime Minister Richard Seddon launched a program of social and economic experimentation. The government introduced land reforms, compulsory labor arbitration, and social services. Trade unions grew in importance. Reforms, along with technological changes and improved export prices, provided a system which benefited the common man, farmers in particular. In 1907 Britain granted New Zealand dominion status.

Dominion. Seddon had died in 1906, and in 1912 the Liberal party was defeated. Between 1912 and 1935 a more conservative government, supported mainly by North Island farmers, remained in office almost constantly.

The power of the farmers confirmed New Zealand's role as a supplier of dairy products, meat, and wool to which it was also politically and culturally loyal. New Zealand soldiers aided the British in World War I. After the war, land industries predominated, and factories chiefly processed farm produce.

Politically important in the years from 1916 to 1935 was the rise of the Labor party, supported by a growing industrial working class. In 1931 the Labor party's strength provoked Seddon's followers and the farmer party to form a coalition. But in 1935 Labor came to office and held power continuously for 14 years.

The world economic depression of the 1930s had hit New Zealand hard. The Labor government arranged guaranteed prices for farmers, and took control of exports and imports, emphasized the redistribution of income, elaborated a social security system, and promoted factory industry. It tries to balance the economy. In effect, the government sought to socialize the means of production rather than national income.

Contemporary New Zealand. In 1939 New Zealand entered World War II, collaborating with the United States in the Pacific and with Britain in Europe and Africa. After the war New Zealand continued to collaborate with the United States in defense and political affairs.

In 1949 the National party, emphasizing a program of private enterprise, defeated Labor, and Sydney Holland became prime minister. The National party further advanced the social welfare policies introduced by the Labor government.

Holland retired in September 1957, and Keith Holyoake became prime minister. Three months later elections were held and the Labor party, led by Walter Nash, was victorious. But in 1960 the National party, led by Holyoake, was returned to power and was reelected in 1963 and 1966.

—David A. Smith

NICARAGUA

Official name: Republic of Nicaragua
Area: 50,000 square miles
Population: (1966 est.) 1,715,000
Capital: Managua (Pop., 1965 est., 262,000)
Language: Spanish
Religion: Roman Catholicism
Currency unit: Córdoba
National holiday: Independence day, September 15

Nicaragua, the largest of the Central American republics, is bounded on the north by Honduras, on the east by the Caribbean Sea, on the south by Costa Rica, and on the west by the Pacific Ocean.

THE LAND. Most of Nicaragua is occupied by the Central American cordillera of the Andes, which extends in a north-south direction through the center of the country. The cordillera separates the wide Caribbean coastal plain, known as the Mosquito Coast, from a narrow Pacific coastal plain.

A long, narrow depression runs diagonally across Nicaragua from the Gulf of Fonseca in the northwest into Costa Rica. This depression contains two large lakes, Lake Nicaragua and Lake Managua. Lake Nicaragua, about 100 miles long and 45 miles wide, is one of the largest bodies of fresh water in Central America.

The mountains to the west of the depression are actively volcanic, and eruptions and earthquakes are a constant hazard in the area.

Nicaragua has a hot climate. Temperatures seldom drop below 75°F., although it is generally cooler in the central mountain region. Rainfall is moderate on the Pacific coast and in the mountains. It is extremely heavy, however, along the Caribbean coast, where some places receive as much as 200 inches a year.

THE PEOPLE. Over 70 percent of the people of Nicaragua are mestizo, of mixed Indian and European ancestry. About 15 percent are of European descent. The remainder of the population is composed of the indigenous Mosquito Indians and Negroes from the West Indies.

Much of Nicaragua is thinly settled. The Mosquito Indians and most of the Negroes live in the Caribbean coastal plain. The bulk of the population is concentrated along the Pacific coast and in the area around Lake Nicaragua and Lake Managua. It is in this area that Nicaragua's three largest cities—Managua, León, and Granada—are located.

ECONOMY. Nicaragua is predominantly an agricultural nation, although the government has been attempting to diversify the economy.

Nicaragua is rich in minerals. Mining is confined mainly to gold, silver, and copper, but there are deposits of iron, bauxite, antimony, tungsten, mercury, and manganese.

About half of Nicaragua is covered with forests, and timber, including mahogany, pine, cedar, rosewood, and balsa, is an important forest product. Rubber is also an important forest product.

Agriculture. Agriculture employs about 60 percent of the labor force. A major share of the country's crops are raised in the west, where extensive tracts of fertile soil are ideal for mechanized farming, but a large percentage of Nicaragua's arable land is not cultivated.

Corn, beans, rice, and sugarcane are raised for domestic consumption. Cotton, coffee, and sesame are the leading commercial crops. Tobacco, cacao, and fruits are grown, and cattle are important in the west.

Industry. Nicaraguan industry is almost entirely limited to food processing and the manufacture of a few consumer items for local consumption. The largest industry is sugar refining. Factories produce cement, insecticides, cigarettes, soap, liquor, and clothing.

Trade. Nicaragua's exports in 1967 earned $146 million and imports cost $204 million. Major exports are cotton, coffee, copper, oilseeds (cotton and sesame), meat, and timber. Principal imports include machinery, transportation equipment, chemicals, textiles, and foodstuffs. Most of Nicaragua's trade is with the United States, Japan, and West Germany.

GOVERNMENT. Nicaragua is a republic. The head of state and chief executive is the president, who is directly elected to a four-year term. Congress consists of the Senate and the Chamber of Deputies, whose members are directly elected to four-year terms on the basis of proportional represen-

MEXICO
GUATEMALA
BRITISH HONDURAS
HONDURAS
EL SALVADOR
NICARAGUA
COSTA RICA
Caribbean Sea
Pacific Ocean

tation. In addition, all former presidents are appointed to the Senate as members for life.

Nicaragua is a member of the United Nations and the Organization of American States (OAS).

HISTORY. Nicaragua was discovered in 1502 by Christopher Columbus on his last voyage to the New World, but it was not explored until 1522, when Gil González Dávila led an expedition from Panama. In 1524 the Spanish founded the cities of León and Granada in the western lowlands, and except for sporadic raids by English pirates during the latter half of the 1600s, the colonial period in Nicaragua was peaceful.

Independence from Spain was won in 1821, but Nicaragua was annexed to the Mexican Empire. When the Mexican Empire collapsed in 1823, Nicaragua joined the United Provinces of Central America, which included El Salvador, Honduras, Guatemala, and Costa Rica. In 1838 Nicaragua left the United Provinces and declared itself independent.

Sovereignty. As a sovereign nation, Nicaragua suffered from intense rivalry between Liberals, centered in León, and Conservatives, in Granada, who battled for political control of the country. In 1856, when the Conservatives gained power and attempted to establish a strong and stable government, the Liberals invited an adventurer from the United States, William Walker, to help oust the Conservative administration.

With a following of approximately 60 men, Walker managed to capture control of Nicaragua and install himself as president. The U.S. financier, Cornelius Vanderbilt, who feared that a steamship monopoly he held would be restricted by Walker and the Liberals, took an active role in Nicaragua's politics. Vanderbilt helped organize an invading army recruited in neighboring countries, and after only one year in office, Walker was forced to flee. In 1860 he was captured in Honduras and executed. Following Walker's death, tension between Liberals and Conservatives was temporarily abated and Nicaragua enjoyed peace and prosperity under several consecutive Conservative administrations.

Zelaya Era. A revolution by Liberal forces in 1893 brought José Santos Zelaya to power. Zelaya moved the capital from León to Managua, promoted railroad construction, brought the Indians of the east coast under the government's jurisdiction, and promoted agricultural development. Zelaya also involved Nicaragua in revolutions in neighboring Central American countries.

In 1909 Zelaya executed two U.S. engineers, whom he maintained were implicated in a plot to overthrow his government. The United States severed diplomatic relations with Nicaragua, weakening the prestige of the Zelaya administration. The Conservatives rebelled, forcing Zelaya to resign.

U.S. Intervention. For several years political and economic conditions in Nicaragua were in a chaotic state. In 1912 the United States sent marines to restore order at the request of provisional Pres. Adolfo Díaz. In the same year Díaz was elected president, and in 1914 Nicaragua signed the Bryan-Chamorro Treaty with the United States. The treaty gave the United States the right to construct a trans-isthmian canal through Nicaragua and to establish military bases on both coasts. Except for a brief period in 1925, the U.S. marines remained in the country until 1933.

Contemporary Nicaragua. In 1936 Gen. Anastasio Somoza, commander of the U.S.-trained National Guard, established himself in the presidency and assumed dictatorial powers. His administration was characterized by economic development and political repression. During World War II Somoza actively cooperated with the United States.

In 1947 Leonardo Argüello was elected president, but Somoza had him removed from office. Victor Manuel Roman y Reyes was then selected by a constituent assembly to occupy the presidency. Roman y Reyes died in May 1950, at which time Somoza again became president. Somoza was assassinated in September 1956, and his son, Luis Somoza Debayle, was appointed acting president for the duration of his father's term. The following year he was elected president.

Luis Somoza's administration, contrary to expectations, proved to be less oppressive than that of his father. Civil liberties, freedom of the press, and political opposition were permitted.

In 1963 René Schick Gutiérrez was elected president. Schick died in 1966, and Congress elected Lorenzo Guerrero Gutiérrez to finish his term. In 1967 Gen. Anastasio Somoza Debayle, the brother of Luis Somoza, was elected president.
—George W. Carey; Jerome Fischman

NIGER

Official name: Republic of Niger
Capital: Niamey (Pop, 40,172)
Population: (1967 est.) 3,546,000
Area: 489,000 square miles
Language: French, African languages
Religion: Islam, traditional religions
Currency unit: Franc CFA (African Financial Community)
National holiday: Proclamation of the republic, December 18

Niger, a republic in western Africa, is bounded on the north by Algeria and Libya, on the east by Chad, on the south by Nigeria and Dahomey, and on the west by Upper Volta and Mali. Niger was granted its independence from France in 1960.

THE LAND. Most of Niger is flat. In the north there is desert and in the east there are scrubby and grassy lowlands. In north-central Niger a great mass of volcanic mountains known as the Aïr (Azbine) rise to elevations of almost 6,000 feet. Lake Chad lies at the southeastern corner of Niger. The Niger River flows through southwestern Niger.

Niger's climate is hot and dry. Half of Niger receives less than four inches of rain each year. Rainfall averages about 20 inches a year near the border with Nigeria.

THE PEOPLE. There are four main ethnic groups in Niger—the Hausa, Djerma, Fulani (Fula), and Tuareg. The greatest concentration of people is in the southern part of the country, especially near the Niger River. Most of the people are Muslim. Niger's largest cities are Niamey, the capital, and Zinder.

ECONOMY. The economy of Niger is based on agriculture. The basic food crops are millet, sorghum, rice, beans, and wheat, and the main commercial crops are peanuts, cotton, and tobacco. Most of the cultivated land is near the border with Nigeria. Cattle, sheep, and goats are raised in most parts of the country.

Tin and tungsten are mined in the Aïr Mountains. There are also small deposits of salt, oil, and copper. The country's industry is poorly developed.

In 1965 imports cost $38 million and exports earned $25 million. The main imports include sugar, petroleum products, machinery, and manufactured goods, especially textiles. Niger's major exports are live animals, peanuts, and peanut oil, and vegetables. Most trade is conducted with France, Nigeria, the Ivory Coast, and the Netherlands. Niger has close economic ties with Dahomey, the Ivory Coast, Togo, and Upper Volta.

GOVERNMENT. Niger has a presidential system of government. Executive power is held by a president, who is popularly elected to a five-year term. Legislative power rests with a 50-member National Assembly, which is also popularly elected every five years.

Niger is a member of the United Nations and the Organization of African Unity (OAU).

HISTORY. Much of what is now western Niger was part of the Songhai empire, which flourished from the 1400s to the late 1500s, when it was conquered by a Moroccan army. During the same period, the city-states of the Hausa people in southern Niger maintained their independence from foreign domination. In the north the nomadic Tuareg roamed the arid fringe of the Sahara. All of these peoples traded with North Africa, and the city of Zinder was a center for trade caravans.

In the early 1800s the Hausa region was engulfed in a revolution. Usuman dan Fodio, a Fulani Muslim cleric,

proclaimed a holy war against the Hausa ruling class of Gobir, one of the more important city-states. He voiced long-existing religious and social complaints of the subjects of the Hausa rulers.

The war lasted from 1804 to 1810, by which time nearly all the Hausa states had come under Fulani rule. In time, all of southern Niger and northern Nigeria owed allegiance to Fulani overlords.

French Rule. The power of the Fulani rulers, and of the Tuareg, was broken by the French, whose army conquered what is now Niger between 1890 and 1914. Beginning in 1895 Niger was administered as part of French West Africa. After World War II Niger became a territory within the French Union.

In 1958 the Niger Progressive Party, led by Hamani Diori, won an overwhelming majority of seats in the territorial assembly. In that year Niger became an autonomous member of the French Community. The assembly soon dissolved all opposition parties.

Independence. On Aug. 3, 1960, Niger became independent and Diori became president. There has been organized opposition from outside the country to Diori's one-party system, and several attempts to overthrow his government have been made. Nonetheless, Diori was re-elected president in 1965.

—Hibberd V. B. Kline, Jr.
Robert I. Rotberg

NIGERIA

Official name: Republic of Nigeria
Area: 356,669 square miles
Population: (1966 est.) 58,600,000
Capital: Lagos (Pop., 1963, 665,246)
Language: English, African languages
Religion: Islam, traditional religions
Currency unit: Pound
National holiday: Independence day, October 1

Nigeria, a republic in western Africa, is bounded on the north by Niger, on the east by Chad and Cameroon, on the south by the Gulf of Guinea, an arm of the Atlantic Ocean, and on the west by Dahomey. Nigeria was granted its independence by Britain in 1960.

THE LAND. Most of Nigeria is occupied by plains or low rolling hills. There are tropical forests and mangrove swamps along the coast. The Niger River, which flows through south-central Nigeria, forms a large delta where it reaches the ocean. There are grassy savannas in central Nigeria, north of the junction of the Niger and Benue rivers. In the north-central part of the country is the Bauchi Plateau, which has an elevation of almost 6,000 feet above sea level. There is grassland and desert in the far north. The Adamawa Mountains are in the southwest. The climate of Nigeria is hot and humid. Some areas in the south receive as much as 150 inches of rain each year.

THE PEOPLE. Nigeria is one of the most populous countries in Africa. There are four main ethnic groups in Nigeria—the Yoruba, Ibo, Hausa, and Fulani (Fula). The Fulani and Hausa peoples are predominantly Muslim and are concentrated in northern Nigeria. The Yoruba live mainly in the west, and the Ibo in the east.

The country's largest cities include Lagos, the national capital, which is on an island off the southwestern coast; Ibadan and Ogbomosho, in the southwestern coast; and Kano, in the north.

ECONOMY. Nigeria's economy is based largely on agriculture. Peanuts, oil palm products, cacao, cotton, and rubber are the leading commercial crops. The basic food crops include yams and corn. Nigeria has rich forest resources, and timber is exported. Fish from the Niger River provide an additional source of food. Cattle are raised mainly in the northern part of the country.

Nigeria also has vast mineral resources. There are vast petroleum deposits, mainly in the Niger delta, and in 1966 over 1.7 million metric tons of petroleum were produced. There are also reserves of natural gas, coal, tin, and columbite.

Nigerian industry developed greatly after independence was achieved in 1960. Textiles, cement, plywood and timber, and automobiles are produced.

A large dam has been planned for the Niger River to provide the country with hydroelectric power. The transportation system is well developed, and railroads link Port Harcourt, Kano, and Nguru.

In 1966 exports earned $792 million and imports cost $718 million. The main exports are cacao, palm products, peanuts and peanut oil, rubber, crude petroleum, and tin. Major imports include machinery, iron and steel, fabrics, cereals, and chemicals. Most trade is with Britain, West Germany, the Netherlands, and the United States.

GOVERNMENT. The 1963 constitution of Nigeria provided for a federal government and governments for the country's four regions—Eastern, Western, and Mid-Western.

Federal legislative power was held by a House of Representatives and a Senate. House members were popularly elected from the regions. The Senate members were appointed from the regions. The federal legislature elected a president to serve as head of state. Executive power was wielded by a prime minister and cabinet.

Each region had its own legislature consisting of a popularly elected House of Assembly and a House of Chiefs. The people elected a governor, who appointed a provincial prime minister. Executive power was exercised by the prime minister.

In 1966 the constitution was suspended and a military council took executive and legislative powers. The four regions were abolished, and in their place the council established 12 states.

Nigeria is a member of the Commonwealth of Nations, the Organization of African Unity (OAU), and the United Nations.

HISTORY. The many peoples of Nigeria have a rich heritage. In about the 1100s the Yoruba people settled in western Nigeria, and in the north Hausa people established agricultural states. In the 1200s the Hausa were converted to Islam by the Fulani people, who came from eastern Africa. In the early 1800s a Fulani leader, Usuman dan Fodio, conquered the Hausa city-states and replaced the Hausa dynasties with Fulani emirs.

Portuguese traders came to Nigeria in 1472, and Portugal and other European countries shared in the lucrative slave trade that developed. The British penetrated the area beginning in 1807 to halt the slave trade. Lagos was occupied by Britain in 1861, and the United Africa Company, later known as the Royal Niger Company, opened the Niger Valley to trade. In 1885 the Oil Rivers Protectorate was set up in the coastal region.

British Rule. The British government took over direct administration of the protectorate in 1891, and by 1893 the addition of a region beyond the coast formed the Niger Coast protectorate. In 1900 it became the protectorate of Southern Nigeria. In the same year the territory of the Royal Niger Company became the protectorate of Northern Nigeria. In 1903 the emirates of the north came under British control.

The protectorates were united in 1914, and after World War I the former German colony of Cameroon was added as a mandate under the League of Nations. In 1939 southern Nigeria was divided into the Eastern and Western provinces.

Nigerians had begun to seek greater freedom before World War I, but nationalist movements were to be regional. Most prominent were the Northern Peoples' Congress (NPC) led by Sir Ahmadu Bello, the Action Group in the Western region led by Chief Obafemi Awolowo, and the National Council of Nigeria and Cameroons (NCNC) led by Dr. Nnamdi Azikiwe. After World War II regional legislatures and elections were introduced.

In 1954 the first national elections were held, and the NPC and NCNC obtained the most votes. Eastern and western Nigeria became self-governing in 1957, but the north, which was less developed, did not achieve self-government until 1959.

Independence. On Oct. 1, 1960 Nigeria became an independent nation. In 1961 a UN plebiscite was held in the British Cameroons, and the North-

Map labels: ALGERIA, MALI, NIGER, CHAD, NIGERIA, CAMEROON, Atlantic Ocean, UPPER VOLTA, DAHOMEY, TOGO, GHANA

ern Cameroons voted to become part of Nigeria, which then consisted of three regions—Eastern, Western, and Northern Nigeria. On Oct. 1, 1963 Nigeria became a republic and Azikiwe was elected president by the federal Parliament. Abubakar Tafawa Balewa became prime minister. In the same year, the Mid-Western region was formed.

In January 1966 there was a military coup and Balewa was assassinated. Gen. Johnson Aguyi-Ironsi became head of state. In July 1966 Aguyi-Ironsi was assassinated and Yakubu Gowon of the Northern region became head of state.

In May 1967 Eastern Nigeria voted to secede and declared itself the Republic of Biafra. Gowon took full power as head of the national government. He proclaimed a state of emergency and moved to end the secession by force.

—Hibberd V. B. Kline, Jr.;
Vera L. Zolberg

NORWAY

Official name: Kingdom of Norway
Area: 125,182 square miles
Population: (1967 est.) 3,784,000
Capital: Oslo (Pop., 1965 est., 483,196)
Language: Norwegian
Religion: Lutheranism
Currency unit: Krone
National holiday: Constitution day, May 17

Norway, a kingdom in northern Europe, occupies the entire western side of the Scandinavian Peninsula. It is bounded on the north by the Arctic Ocean, on the east by Sweden, on the northeast by the Soviet Union and Finland, on the south by the Skagerrak and the North Sea, and on the west by the Norwegian Sea, an arm of the North Atlantic Ocean.

THE LAND. Norway is a long, narrow country described as being "all mountains and sea." It is almost totally devoid of plains. Most of the terrain is rugged and mountainous, but there is a high, hilly plateau region in the center of the country.

A mountainous ridge follows the border with Sweden. It rises to about 8,000 feet in the south-central region, and steep slopes plunge into the Skagerrak along the coast.

Norway's long coastline is penetrated by almost innumerable deep, sheltered, navigable inlets, or fjords, and is protected from the open sea by a fringe of islands. Many lakes lie scattered throughout Norway, and many rivers and streams rush down from the mountains.

More than one-third of the country lies north of the Arctic Circle, and two arctic islands, Jan Mayen and Spitsbergen (Svalbard), are part of Norway.

Norway's climate is varied. The south has a temperate marine climate, with cool summers, mild winters, and much cloudiness. The warm North Atlantic drift keeps the entire coast ice-free all the year. In the north and in the higher elevations the climate is colder and more severe. Precipitation is plentiful, particularly in the mountains.

THE PEOPLE. Norway has one of Europe's smallest populations, and in 1966 there were about 30 persons per square mile. The population is increasing very slowly, less than 1 percent a year between 1958 and 1965.

The interior and the northern two-thirds of the country are sparsely inhabited, and most of the people live along the southern coast, where Norway's main cities, Oslo, Bergen, and Trondheim, are located.

Almost all of the people are Norwegian. Norwegian is the universal language and Evangelical Lutheranism is the established religion. In the far north there is a minority of about 20,000 semi-nomadic Lapps, who have their own language and culture. There is also a small Finnish minority in the north.

ECONOMY. Norway's economy traditionally was based upon merchant shipping, fishing, forestry, and agriculture. In the 1900s the country began to expand its industry by developing and utilizing its natural resources.

Norway's most valuable resource is its enormous water power, which is easy and inexpensive to harness for electricity. Norway also has a modest endowment of minerals, including pyrites and some iron, copper, zinc, molybdenum, and nickel. Forests cover about one-quarter of the land and provide the basis for important wood pulp and paper industries.

Commercial fishing, though of less importance than formerly, still prospers, and forestry is important in the economy.

Merchant shipping, always important to Norway's economy, contributed about one-eighth of the national product in 1965. Norway has one of the world's largest merchant fleets, over 16 million gross registered tons in 1966. Income from the fleet accounts for about one-third of the country's foreign exchange earnings.

Agriculture. Less than 5 percent of Norway's land is cultivable, and in 1965 agriculture contributed only 9 percent to the domestic product. But agriculture employed about 20 percent of the labor force and met a large part of the country's food requirements. The major emphasis is on livestock raising and dairying. Hardy grains, potatoes, and some fruits and vegetables are also grown.

Manufacturing. Norwegian industry received a tremendous boost in the 1950s and 1960s from the rapid development of hydroelectric power, which almost doubled in output between 1957 and 1965. In 1965 manufacturing contributed 27 percent of the national product. Among the newer industries made possible by cheap and abundant electricity are the electrometallurgical and electrochemical industries. Major industrial products include ships, machinery, and vehicles. Lumber and pulp and paper mills are also important, and fish processing plants produce some of Norway's major exports.

Trade. Earnings from shipping and tourism help to make up for Norway's poor balance of international trade. In 1966 imports cost $2,746 million and exports earned only $1,736 million.

Major imports are ships and boats, machinery, petroleum products, textiles, and foodstuffs. Metals and ores, pulp and paper, and fish and fish products are the leading exports. Sweden, Britain, West Germany, the United States, and Denmark are Norway's major trading partners.

GOVERNMENT. Norway is a constitutional monarchy, with a king as head of state. Actual executive power is wielded by a prime minister and cabinet responsible to the parliament. The parliament, called the Storting, is popularly elected every four years. It elects one-quarter of its members to sit as an upper house, the Lagting. The remainder of the Storting is called the Odelsting. Most legislative actions are taken by the united Storting.

Norway is a member of the United Nations, the Council of Europe, the North Atlantic Treaty Organization (NATO), and the Nordic Council, an association of the Scandinavian nations—Norway, Sweden, Denmark, Finland, and Iceland.

HISTORY. Archeological evidence indicates that man lived in Norway as early as 8,000 years ago. Beginning about 7,000 years ago, a variety of wandering tribes from the north and south appeared in Scandinavia. Germanic tribes, the main forebears of the present Norwegian people, had established themselves in the land by about 500 BC.

For the next 1,000 years, during the eras of the Roman Empire and the barbarian migrations, tribal groups in Norway shifted and resettled, competing for dominance over the entire region.

During the 800s AD the tribal communities were gradually united, and Harald Fairhair (Harald Haarfager) became Norway's first king. The united tribes began to expand their territory, and from the late 800s through the early 1000s, Norwegian Vikings explored the shores of Britain, Ireland, the Faroe Islands, Iceland, Greenland, and probably North America.

During several brief intervals in the late 900s and early 1000s the country was under Danish rule, but Norwegian kings always regained control, and by the mid-1000s the monarchy was quite strong.

Early Kingdom. Through the efforts of King Olaf Tryggvesson and King Olaf Haraldsson in the late 900s and early 1000s Christianity was introduced into Norway. As the church gained influence, it challenged royal power and was supported by members of the growing land-owning aristocracy. Civil wars filled the period between the mid-1100s and the mid-1200s, but the strength of the monarchy was maintained, and the 1200s marked the high point of Norwegian power and prosperity. Between 1217 and 1263, during the reign of King Haakon IV, Norwegian art and literature flourished, and King Magnus VI sponsored a codification of law for the entire country in the 1270s.

This era of greatness was short-lived, however. In the mid-1300s the Black Death killed half of Norway's population and crippled the country. The merchants of the German Hanseatic League gained a firm grip on Norwegian economic life. Moreover, the Norwegian royal succession became entangled with that of Sweden and Denmark.

In 1380 King Olaf V, the last of Harold Fairhair's dynasty, became king of both Norway and Denmark. When he died in 1387, his mother, Queen Margaret of Denmark, combined the thrones of both kingdoms. In 1397 Sweden was added to form the Kalmar Union, which was dominated by Denmark.

Norway was the weakest member, and its territory, prestige, and autonomy declined steadily in the 1400s. The union was frequently torn by internal struggles, and in 1523 Sweden broke away.

Danish Union. Norway remained linked with Denmark, as part of a kingdom ruled and administered by Danes. With Denmark, Norway became Lutheran in 1536. Norway shared Danish wars, including a series of territorial and dynastic struggles with Sweden between the 1560s and the 1720s.

The Norwegians did enjoy some economic benefits from Danish rule, however, between 1588 and 1648. King Christian IV reformed the administration of Norway and initiated the development of Norwegian resources. Absolutists who ruled Denmark-Norway after 1660 stimulated Norway's economy by expanding exports and founding new towns.

Modest but steady economic growth continued through the 1700s and helped to lay the basis for the development of a Norwegian national consciousness. In 1807 Denmark granted Norwegian requests for a national assembly, during the Napoleonic wars, in which Norway's sufferings stimulated Norwegian nationalism. In 1814 Sweden, which had opposed Napoleon and had won a victory over Denmark, forced Denmark to cede Norway.

Swedish Union. The Norwegians rose in protest and refused to recognize Swedish rule. They convened a national assembly, which adopted a liberal constitution in May 1814, and they elected the Danish prince Christian Frederick as their king.

The crown prince of Sweden invaded the country and succeeded to the Norwegian throne, however. Nevertheless, the Norwegians, by their resistance, secured a great deal of autonomy before they would accept union with Sweden. Norway was granted an elected *Storting* and was proclaimed indivisible and independent; it was joined in personal union with the Swedish crown. The *Storting* ratified the union in 1815.

During the 1800s Norway underwent a national renaissance. Scholarly and scientific activities widened, and arts and letters flourished. The economy of Norway-Sweden improved steadily during the 1800s.

As their strength increased, Norwegian liberal intellectuals grew restless under rather arbitrary kings. Sweden granted concessions, including a system of free education, complete religious freedom, expansion of voting rights, and, in 1864, a new liberal constitution.

The reform movement accelerated in Norway after the passage of the constitution. In the late 1880s a parliamentary system of government was introduced, based on universal manhood suffrage. In the 1890s Norwegian demands for complete independence grew, led by Johan Sverdrup. The economies of both countries were booming, with Norway's merchant fleet as the basis of the prosperity.

Renewed Independence. As Norway's international trade expanded, the Norwegian *Storting* requested permission to handle Norway's consular affairs under its own flag. When the Swedish king refused, the Norwegian *Storting* declared Norway independent in June 1905. Norway elected the Danish prince Charles to be king as Haakon VII. Sweden accepted Norway's declaration of independence in October 1905.

Norway was well prepared for independence by its material progress, political activism and social reforms of the late 1800s. Democratic reform continued in Norway after independence. The royal veto over the *Storting* was abolished, the vote was extended to women, and social welfare programs were initiated.

Norway remained neutral in World War 1, but its vital merchant fleet was severely damaged. After the war the nation suffered an economic depression which was intensified by the world economic depression of the 1930s.

Economic and social reforms initiated during the 1920s and 1930s included the formation of cooperative enterprises, the institution of national collective bargaining, and the expansion of social welfare legislation under the leadership of Liberal, Labor, and left-wing farmers' party governments. A Labor government elected in 1935 was successful in ending Norway's economic crisis by expanding government participation in the economy.

In 1940, during World War II, Germany invaded Norway, and despite many stiff Norwegian resistance Nazi troops conquered and occupied the country. The Germans governed Norway through a puppet minister, Vidkun Quisling. The exiled King Haakon rallied resistance to the Germans, and the Norwegian home front played a prominent part in Norway's liberation from the Germans in 1945.

The nation had suffered severe economic damage during the war, and a Labor government elected in 1945 instituted an austerity program which, by the early 1950s, had restored many of the losses.

Contemporary Norway. Norway participated actively in postwar international affairs. In 1945 it became a charter member of the United Nations and a signer. Trygve Lie became the first secretary general of the UN. In 1948-1949, when its neighbors pressed for a Scandinavian defense union, Norway joined NATO, but it encouraged the social, economic, and cultural unity of the Scandinavian nations and in 1952 joined the newly formed Nordic Council.

Sharing a common border with the Soviet Union, Norway has had to be circumspect in its foreign policy during the era of the Cold War between the Soviet Union and the United States, but it remained anti-Communist in domestic politics and tended to be pro-Western in international

NORWAY'S LANDSCAPE is dominated by mountains stretching the length of the country.

NORWEGIAN INFORMATION SERVICE

foreign affairs. In 1957 King Haakon died and was succeeded by his son, Olav V.

During the 1950s and 1960s Norway concentrated on expanding and modernizing its economy and developing its natural resources, particularly its water power. The growth of industry was not rapid enough to support Norway's broad social welfare programs, and in the early 1960s the economy began to falter. The Labor government, which had introduced most of the social welfare programs during nearly 30 years in power, bore the brunt of popular dissatisfaction. In 1965 Labor was voted out of office and was replaced by a coalition of more conservative parties. In its first years in office the coalition government tried to stabilize the economy. In 1967, to strengthen its international economic position, Norway applied for admission to the European Common Market.

PAKISTAN

Official name: Islamic Republic of Pakistan
Area: 365,529 square miles (excluding Jammu and Kashmir)
Population: (1967 est.) 107,258,000 (excluding Jammu and Kashmir)
Capital: Islamabad; interim capital: Rawalpindi (Pop., 1961, 340,175)
Language: Bengali, Urdu, English
Religion: Islam, Hinduism
Currency unit: Rupee
National holiday: Pakistan day, March 23

Pakistan, a republic in South Asia, was created in 1947 from predominantly Muslim regions of British India. It consists of two distinct geographic parts, East Pakistan and West Pakistan, separated by nearly 1,000 miles of Indian territory. West Pakistan, centered on the Indus River Valley, has an area of more than 310,000 square miles, and East Pakistan, in the Ganges River delta, has an area of approximately 55,000 square miles. West Pakistan is bounded on the north by Afghanistan and China, on the east by India, on the south by the Arabian Sea, and on the west by Iran. East Pakistan is bordered on the north, east, and west by India, on the southeast by Burma, and on the south by the Bay of Bengal. There are boundary disputes with India, and both Pakistan and India claim Kashmir, a region at the northern tip of the Indian subcontinent, and each has occupied a portion of it.

THE LAND. The two regions of Pakistan are quite dissimilar. Most of East Pakistan, the smaller region, is low, level, and swampy, and is drained by the Ganges and the Brahmaputra rivers. The only upland areas are found along the margins of the Khasi hills in the northeast and in the Chittagong hills in the northeast.

East Pakistan has a subtropical climate, with rainfall averaging between 70 and 90 inches a year and as much as 200 inches falling annually in the northeast. Temperatures remain in the 80s°F.

West Pakistan can be divided into five separate geographic regions. Baluchistan, in the southwest, is an arid region of mountains and valleys.

The Makran Coast forms a narrow corridor connecting the Indus valley with Iran. The Northwest Frontier is a subhumid mountain and hill region whose many mountain passes, including the Khyber Pass, historically have been the gateways to the Indian subcontinent.

Punjab, in the upper Indus valley, is the traditional economic, political, and cultural heart of Pakistan. Sind, a desert region, occupies the lower Indus Valley and the southeastern corner of the country.

The mighty Indus River and its many tributaries flow through the eastern part of the region and empty into the Arabian Sea. In contrast with the east, West Pakistan is arid, with an average annual rainfall of about 20 inches. Temperatures vary widely between cold winters and hot summers.

THE PEOPLE. The population is not evenly divided between East and West Pakistan. Although it occupies almost 85 percent of the nation's total territory, West Pakistan has less than 50 percent of the population. The country's two largest cities, Karachi and Lahore, are in West Pakistan, however.

Pakistanis are varied in background and language. Urdu is the national language of West Pakistan and Bengali the language of East Pakistan, but a number of regional languages are also spoken, especially in West Pakistan. About 90 percent of Pakistanis are Muslims, and about 10 percent are Hindus. Most Hindus live in East Pakistan.

ECONOMY. Faced with the dual problem of modernizing its economy and building a separate economic system from one formerly joined with India, Pakistan has made economic progress, especially in the 1960s. Despite the initiation of major industrialization, in the mid-1960s agriculture remained the dominant factor in the economy.

Industrial development has been hindered by the country's scarcity of natural resources. Its limited supplies of minerals are concentrated mainly in West Pakistan and include modest deposits of chromite, low-grade coal, oil, iron ore, limestone, gypsum, and rock salt. Large reserves of natural gas discovered in the early 1960s in both East and West Pakistan constitute an important resource for industry.

Pakistan's soil suffers from a high salt content and aridity in the west and poor drainage in the east. The Indus Valley is fertile, however, and productive when irrigated.

Agriculture. In the mid-1960s agriculture contributed about half of the domestic product and occupied over two-thirds of the labor force. Pakistan's major food crops are rice, grown in the east, and wheat, grown in the west. Other crops include millet, corn, and barley.

The principal commercial crops are jute, cotton, tea, sugarcane, and tobacco, all of which are valuable as exports and as industrial raw materials. Livestock-raising is important, especially in the west, and oxen, buffalo, sheep, and goats are raised.

Most Pakistani farmers cultivate small plots of land. Traditional agricultural methods are primitive and inefficient, and the improvement of irrigation, farming techniques, and the quality of crops is a major goal.

Manufacturing. In the mid-1960s manufacturing and mining contributed about 11 percent to the domestic product. In 1952 the government established the Pakistan Industrial Development Corporation to expand the production of cotton textiles, processed jute, refined sugar, cigarettes, cement, paper, fertilizers, chemicals, and steel.

An indicator of Pakistan's industrialization is the production of electricity, which rose from 129 million kilowatt hours (kwh) in 1948 to 950 million kwh in 1957, and quadrupled between 1957 and 1966, when 3.9 billion kwh were produced. In 1967 the giant Mangla Dam, one of a series in Pakistan's hydroelectric-irrigation development projects, was opened on the Jhelum River.

Trade. Rapid expansion of exports in the 1950s and 1960s did little to improve Pakistan's unfavorable balance of trade, for imports expanded even more than exports. In 1966 imports cost more than $900 million and exports earned $601 million.

Jute and cotton, dependent on weather and subject to sharp fluctuations in world-market prices, are the leading exports. Hides, tea, and wool are also exported. The major imports are wheat, iron and steel, machinery, and consumer goods. Most trade is with Britain, The United States, West Germany, Japan, and India.

GOVERNMENT. Under its 1962 constitution Pakistan is a federal republic led by a strong executive, the president. Legislative power is vested in a National Assembly. East Pakistan and West Pakistan each has a powerful provincial assembly and is administered by an appointed governor. The president and the members of the national legislature are elected by a body of some 120,000 popularly elected local officials called "basic democrats." Pakistan is a member of the United Nations, the Central Treaty Organization (CENTO), and the Southeast Asia Treaty Organization (SEATO), and the Commonwealth of Nations.

HISTORY. Although Pakistan shared India's history until 1947, its existence as a separate Muslim state is rooted in the early history of northern India. Islam began to influence northern India in the early 600s, when Muslim sailors from Arabia visited the coast of Sind, at the mouth of the Indus. Muslim conquerors ruled Sind from the 600s, and spread Islam there. In the 1000s Muslims from Afghanistan began extending their rule over territory in northwest India and until the 1800s Afghans, Turks, Arabs, and finally the Mughals (or Moguls), ruled all or part of northern India, establishing many small kingdoms and princely states that at times were unified into empires. In addition to their religion, the Muslims brought Persian and Arabic art, literature, learning, and customs, to produce a way of life different from that of Hindu India to the south.

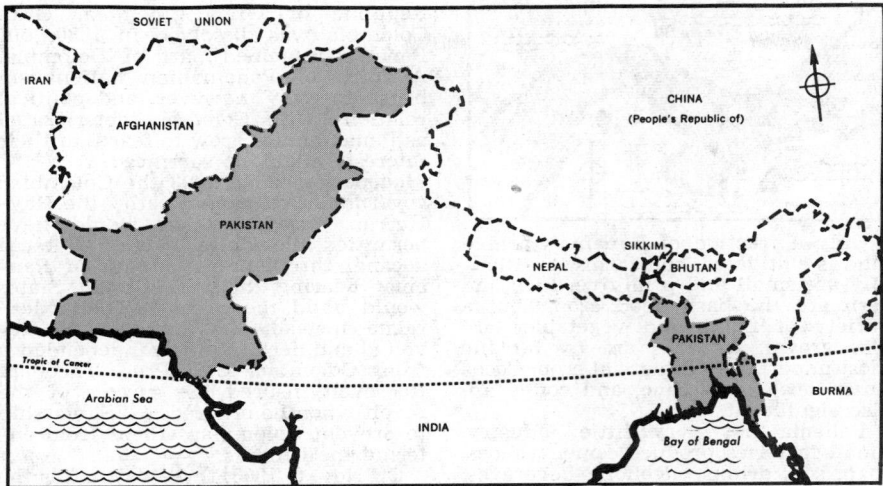

Britain began extending its influence over India in the 1700s. By the early 1900s the British controlled most of the Muslim territories, and by the mid-1800s, with the addition of Punjab and Sind, the British were in firm command of all of India.

In the late 1800s, when Indian leaders began to demand a stronger voice in their country's government, Muslims made up about one-quarter of India's population. The Indian National Congress, formed in 1885 to work for gradual measures of self-government, spoke for all of India and included prominent Muslims. Its composition, however, was predominantly Hindu.

Muslim Autonomy. The positive movement toward autonomy for Indian Muslims began soon after the Indian nationalist movement was organized, and in part as a result of its organization. Sir Sayyid Ahmad Khan and other Muslim leaders argued that there was a distinct Muslim "nation" in India which should not be submerged in the Hindu majority as, they contended, would happen if the British left the country and fully representative government was introduced.

While urging Muslims to advance their relatively backward condition through education and commerce, Sir Sayyid recommended that they not participate in the activities of the Indian National Congress. Muslim fears of Hindu domination deepened at the turn of the century, when a strong movement developed in India for the revival of Hinduism and the creation of a nation based essentially on Hindu traditions and culture.

Muslim League. In 1906 Muslims founded the All India Muslim League to press for special protection and advantages for Muslims. Although its overall goal, self-government for India, was the same as that of the National Congress, the two organizations could not agree on a plan for dividing power and protecting Muslim interests.

In 1909 the British responded to Indian demands for self-government by permitting the election of members of the legislative council. The reforms satisfied the Muslims' plea for representation by providing separate electorates for them. But the limited franchise and weak powers of the legislature were a bitter disappointment to both Hindu and Muslim nationalists.

After World War I Mohandas K. Gandhi assumed the leadership of the Congress with a program designed in part to unify India's Hindus and Muslims for a great struggle to overthrow British rule. Gandhi and many leading Hindu members of the Congress argued that Muslim fears of Hindu domination were groundless and a result of British efforts to divide and rule.

Rioting between Hindus and Muslims in the 1920s and 1930s as well as continued sponsorship of a Hindu revival widened the split within the nationalist movement. The final blow to unity came in 1937, when the Congress gained control of most provincial legislatures popularly elected on a broadened franchise. The Muslim League believed that the policies of these Congress majorities discriminated against Muslims.

It was after 1937 that Muhammad Ali Jinnah, a former Indian Congress leader and advocate of Hindu-Muslim unity, began a drive for the creation of a separate Muslim state. By 1940, under Jinnah's leadership, the Muslim League resolved that a Muslim state should be created when India was given independence.

In 1946 negotiations took place for a transfer of power to Indians, but the Congress and the League could not agree on terms for establishing an interim government, or for drafting a constitution for the new state. The British had strongly supported a unified India, but they had also sponsored separate religious electorates and encouraged Muslim ambitions.

Partition. In 1947, when the Hindu-Muslim stalemate could not be broken, Britain acquiesced in Muslim demands for a separate state. It was to consist of all contiguous areas with Muslim majorities in British India. Bengal and the Punjab were divided and the princely states adjacent to Pakistan were to be given the choice of joining one or the other of the new states.

On Aug. 15, 1947 Pakistan was created an independent nation within the British Commonwealth. Muhammad Ali Jinnah became Pakistan's first governor-general.

Partition created serious problems for both India and Pakistan. Communal rioting, especially in the Punjab, killed thousands. The economies of the two countries were disrupted by the migration of millions of Muslims to Pakistan and millions of Hindus to India.

More lasting internal problems plagued the government of Pakistan. Separation of Muslim majority areas from India implied the creation of a state governed according to Islamic principles, but many Pakistanis urged that traditional religious ideals could not determine the policies of a modern state. Split on this fundamental issue, the government of the new state had a difficult start.

The cultural difference between the eastern and western parts of the new state also caused much antagonism and sharpened struggles for political power. In addition, Pakistani political leadership faltered after the death in 1948 of Jinnah and the assassination in 1951 of Liaqat Ali Khan, Pakistan's first prime minister. Delays in formulating a constitution extended the period of governmental instability.

The Republic. A republican constitution was finally adopted in 1956. But years of political turmoil had severely weakened the economy, and the decentralized federal system established by the constitution could do little to solve the country's economic problems.

Relations with India, bitter after decades of religious conflict, grew especially hostile in the mid-1950s over the issue of Kashmir. India gained control of the bulk of Kashmir, but the region has a Muslim majority, and Pakistan argued that Kashmir should be made part of the Muslim state. This dispute worsened Pakistan's internal political and economic situation.

In 1958 a group of military leaders under Gen. Muhammad Ayub Khan took control of the government. They revoked the constitution, dissolved the legislatures, banned political parties, and imposed martial law. Ayub assumed the title of president, and in 1960 he was elected in an indirect vote under his own system of "basic democracies." Under this system locally elected officials choose national leaders.

The government took firm control of economic activity and initiated modernization programs which improved the economy. In 1962 a new constitution was adopted, and martial law was gradually lifted and civil rights restored. In 1965 President Ayub Khan won re-election by a large majority. The country's economy continued to improve in the mid-1960s under government development programs using aid from abroad.

In 1965 the dispute over Kashmir again broke into open warfare. Bitter fighting lasted three weeks, until a stalemate was reached. At an international conference at Tashkent, in the Soviet Union, an Indian-Pakistani truce was signed, but no lasting solution to the dispute was achieved.

—M. G. Inaba

PANAMA

Official name: Republic of Panama
Area: 29,762 square miles (including the Canal Zone)
Population: (1967 est.) 1,329,000 (excluding the Canal Zone)
Capital: Panamá (Pop., 1966 est., 343,700)
Language: Spanish
Religion: Roman Catholicism
Currency unit: Balboa
National holiday: Independence day, November 3

Panama, a Central American republic situated on the Isthmus of Panama, is bounded on the north by the Caribbean Sea, on the east by Colombia, on the south by the Pacific Ocean, and on the west by Costa Rica. The Panama Canal cuts through the country at its narrowest point. The canal runs through the Canal Zone, a strip of land 5 miles wide on each side of the canal, leased to the United States by the Panamanian government in 1903.

THE LAND. Panama's land surface is mostly hilly and mountainous. The highest mountains rise in the west, near the Costa Rican border, and are volcanic. The highest peak is Chiriquí Volcano, 11,410 feet above sea level. These mountains gradually slope down toward a hilly central lowland, which separates them from jungle-covered highlands in the east. It is through this lowland that the Panama Canal runs.

The only other significant lowlands are plains along the Caribbean and Pacific coasts. The Caribbean plain, along the north coast, is extremely rainy. Tropical evergreen rain forests predominate. The Pacific plain, along the south coast, has a wet and a dry season, producing semi-deciduous forest mingled with savanna.

Panama's climate varies with elevation. The lowlands have a tropical climate, with an average annual temperature of about 80°F. Temperatures in the mountains range from 50°F to 66°F.

THE PEOPLE. The people of Panama are largely mestizo, of mixed European and Indian parentage, but there are small groups of whites, Negroes, and Indians. The overwhelming majority of the population is Roman Catholic. Spanish is the national language, although English is widely understood.

Colón, near the northern end of the canal, and Panamá, at its southern end, are the country's major seaports and urban centers. Outlying areas are sparsely settled, especially the region east of the Canal Zone.

ECONOMY. The economy of Panama is largely based on providing goods and services for the Canal Zone. In recent years the government has sought to lessen Panama's dependence on the canal and diversify the economy by increasing agricultural production and expanding industry.

Panama has rich natural resources, but they are mostly unexploited. Only small quantities of gold, silver, and manganese are mined. Limestone is quarried and it supplies the cement industry. Panama also has valuable timber and an abundance of fish in its coastal waters.

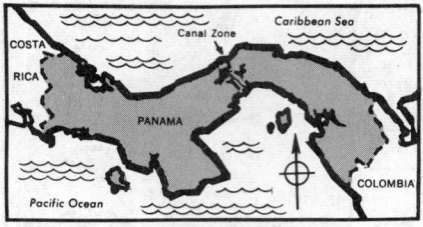

Only a fraction of Panama's arable land is cultivated, and farms traditionally are small and primitive. Rice and corn are the basic food crops, but a variety of fruits and vegetables are also grown. Bananas are by far the most important commercial crop. Coconuts, cacao, sugarcane, and coffee are also significant.

Panama has very little industry. Small factories produce cement, shoes, soap, soft drinks, alcoholic beverages, furniture, and clothing. There is also some food processing and a variety of home handicraft industries. In 1961 a large oil refinery was built near Colón.

Trade. In 1966 Panama's exports were valued at $89 million and imports at $215 million. Most of the gap is made up by income from the Canal Zone and fees from the registry under the Panamanian flag of vessels of world shippers.

Panama's chief exports are bananas, petroleum products, fish—especially shrimp—sugar, and coffee. Principal imports include petroleum, machinery, motor vehicles, textiles, chemicals, and foodstuffs. The bulk of Panama's trade is with the United States.

GOVERNMENT. Panama is a democratic republic. The president, who is directly elected to a term of four years, is the head of state and chief executive. Legislative power is vested in the National Assembly, whose members are directly elected to four-year terms.

Panama is a member of the United Nations and the Organization of American States (OAS).

HISTORY. Panama was discovered in 1501 by Rodrigo de Bastidas. In 1502 Christopher Columbus explored the Caribbean coast and claimed the territory for Spain. Further explorations led to the establishment of settlements along the Caribbean coast. In 1513 Vasco Núñez de Balboa crossed the isthmus and discovered the Pacific Ocean, thereby putting the western coast within Spanish reach.

In 1519 the small village of Panamá, on the Pacific coast, was made the capital of the isthmus. The Spanish explorer Francisco Pizarro used Panama as the base for expeditions to Peru in 1531. The cities of Nombre de Dios and, later, Portobelo became the ports through which gold and silver were shipped to Spain.

During the late 1600s and the 1700s Spain entered a period of political and economic decline and the importance of Panama began to wane. In 1751 Panama lost its autonomy and became part of the viceroyalty of New Granada, which included present-day Colombia.

In 1821 Panama gained independence from Spain and joined with Colombia, Ecuador, and Venezuela to form the

Republic of Gran Colombia. Gran Colombia was dissolved in 1830, but Panama remained part of Colombia. A spirit of Panamanian nationalism began to grow, however, and political relations with Colombia deteriorated as Panamanians grew to fear that their interests might be sacrificed.

Independence. In 1903 the Colombian government refused to ratify the Hay-Herrán Treaty, which would have permitted the United States to build a canal through the Isthmus of Panama. Fearing that the United States would build the canal through Nicaragua instead, the Panamanians revolted and declared their independence from Colombia. U.S. Pres. Theodore Roosevelt insured the success of the revolt when he ordered a U.S. warship to prevent Colombian troops from entering the isthmus.

On Nov. 6, 1903, three days after the revolution began, the United States recognized an independent Panamanian government. Panama's newly formed government leased the Canal Zone to the United States in perpetuity for a payment of $10 million and an annual payment of $250,000.

Panama became prosperous as a result of the Panama Canal, but political unrest developed during the world economic depression of the 1930s. Panama sided with the Allies in World War II and in 1945 became a charter member of the United Nations.

Contemporary Panama. During the mid-1950s opposition to U.S. sovereignty over the Canal Zone began to grow. In November 1959 anti-United States demonstrations broke out in Panamá and Colón. Tension was further increased by Washington's announcement of its interest in constructing a new sea level canal in another part of Central America.

In January 1964 Panamanian students led violent anti-United States riots, which resulted in the breaking off of diplomatic relations between the United States and Panama. Diplomatic relations were resumed in April 1964, and the two countries agreed to negotiate their differences.

In June 1967 the negotiators drafted a new treaty, which provided for Panamanian sovereignty over the Canal Zone and a joint board to govern the canal itself.

—George W. Carey; Jerome Fischman

BOAC

PANAMA'S SAN BLAS ISLANDS, lying in the Atlantic, are peopled by American Indians.

PARAGUAY

Official name: Republic of Paraguay
Area: 157,047 square miles
Population: (1967 est.) 2,161,000
Capital: Asunción (Pop., 1962, 305,160)
Language: Spanish, Guaraní
Religion: Roman Catholicism
Currency unit: Guaraní
National holiday: Independence day, May 14

Paraguay, a small landlocked republic in South America, is bounded on the north by Bolivia, on the east by Brazil, and on the south and west by Argentina.

THE LAND. The Paraguay River, which flows down from Brazil and joins the Paraná River in the southwestern corner, at the Argentine border, divides Paraguay into two contrasting regions. The western region, or Chaco Boreal, is a hot, parched wasteland, partially covered with scrub forest. The eastern region consists of fertile plains, grasslands, and dense forests.

In the extreme east is the heavily forested Paraná Plateau, which ranges in altitude from 1,000 to 2,000 feet above sea level. In the northern part of the plateau the forests give way to grasslands or savannas. West of the plateau are rolling, grassy plains.

Climate. Because of its location within the interior of the continent, Paraguay experiences wider temperature fluctuations than almost any other part of South America. Summer temperatures average about 80°F, but temperatures over 100°F are fairly common. Winter temperatures average 55°F.

Annual rainfall varies, although it is generally quite dry in the west and becomes progressively wetter towards the east. The average annual rainfall at Asunción, on the Paraguay River, is 62 inches, but near the Brazilian border it increases to about 80 inches.

THE PEOPLE. The overwhelming majority of the people are of mixed Guaraní Indian and Spanish ancestry. Although the admixture of Spanish blood in the population is small, there are few pureblooded Indians left in Paraguay and they mostly inhabit the remoter regions of the Chaco. There are also small numbers of foreigners who have settled in agricultural communities. They include Germans, Japanese, Italians, Brazilians, Argentines, and Canadian Mennonites.

The official language is Spanish but Guaraní is spoken almost universally. Most Paraguayans belong to the Roman Catholic Church.

About 96 percent of the people live in the eastern region, which represents 40 percent of the national territory, and about 75 percent of the people live within 100 miles of the capital of Asunción. Most of the country's economic activity is also located within the same radius.

ECONOMY. Paraguay's economy is based on agriculture and forestry, and these activities account for almost all the country's exports.

Paraguay has deposits of manganese, iron, copper, kaolin, mica, talc, and bauxite, but the only two minerals mined are limestone and salt. The country's most important natural re-

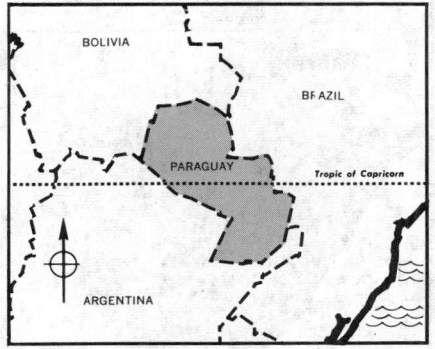

source is its forests, which yield valuable hardwoods and a variety of other products. Two of the most important forest products are tannin, used in tanning, dyeing, making ink, and medicine, and yerba maté from which a tea-like beverage is made.

Agriculture. Although 70 percent of the people are engaged in agriculture, only a fraction of Paraguay's arable land is cultivated. Farming methods are primitive and most farmers raise only enough to feed their own families.

Food crops include manioc, corn, sugarcane, sweet potatoes, rice, and citrus and other fruits. The country's most important commercial crops are cotton, tobacco, coffee, and oilseeds.

Cattle have long been an important source of income, and meat products are Paraguay's most valuable export. Cattle are raised chiefly in the area between the Paraguay and Paraná rivers, in Concepción near the northwestern border, and in the Chaco.

Industry. Paraguay is one of the least industrialized countries in South America. The nation's few industries are limited to the processing of its agricultural products and the manufacture of a small number of consumer goods and construction materials such as soap, matches, glass, cement, and bricks.

Trade. Paraguay's exports in 1966 earned $49.4 million and imports cost $49.5 million. The major exports are meat, woods, tobacco, cotton, tannin, and coffee. Imports include machinery, wheat, iron and steel products, transportation equipment, fuel oil, and chemicals.

Paraguay exports primarily to Argentina, the United States, Britain, the Netherlands, and Spain. Most imports come from the United States, Argentina, West Germany, and Britain.

GOVERNMENT. Paraguay is a republic. The head of state and chief executive is the president, who is directly elected to a term of five years. He is assisted by a cabinet, which he appoints.

The legislative branch of government consists of the House of Representatives, with 60 members, and the Senate, with 30 members.

Paraguay is a member of the United Nations and the Organization of American States (OAS).

HISTORY. Paraguay was discovered in 1524 by Alejo García, a Portuguese explorer. Two years later Sebastian Cabot explored the Paraná and Paraguay rivers for Spain, and in 1537 a permanent Spanish settlement was made at Asunción, on the Paraguay River.

Spanish Rule. In 1609 the Jesuits arrived in Paraguay to convert the Guaraní Indians. The Jesuits were highly successful in their missionary work and they founded more than 30 *reducciones*, which were self-sufficient, autonomous mission communities. Between 150,000 and 200,000 Indians lived and worked within this system.

The Jesuits were not popular with the Spanish colonists, who wanted the Indians to work for them and who resented the competition from mission agricultural produce. In 1767 Spain expelled the Jesuits from South America, and the *reducciones* collapsed.

In 1776 Paraguay was incorporated into the newly formed Viceroyalty of Río de la Plata, which included present-day Argentina and was governed from Buenos Aires. In 1810 the Argentinians rebelled against Spain and set up a junta, or government council, at Buenos Aires. Paraguayans refused to recognize this government, but the following year they threw off Spanish rule and established a junta of their own at Asunción.

Independence. In 1814 one of the members of the junta, Jose Gaspar Rodríguez de Francia, took over the government and became president. Francia exercised strong autocratic control, aided both by an internal spy network and by the superstitious reverence that he managed to inspire in the common people. He followed a policy of political isolation, which protected Paraguay from outside influences and encouraged economic self-sufficiency.

Francia died in 1840, and in 1844, after a brief period of transition, his nephew, Carlos Antonio López, became president. López made education free and compulsory, built roads, and loosened Francia's policy of isolation. But whereas Francia had been personally honest, López and his family profiteered at the nation's expense. When López died in 1862 his son Francisco Solano López immediately became president.

The central feature of the regime of Francisco Solano López was the War of the Triple Alliance, which pitted Paraguay against Argentina, Brazil, and Uruguay. In 1864 López attacked Brazil, ostensibly because of Brazil's interference in the affairs of Uruguay. Also at stake was López's ambition to expand Paraguayan influence and territory at the expense of Argentina and Brazil, with whom Paraguay had long-standing territorial disputes.

In 1865 the conflict expanded into a general war. Paraguay was victorious at first, but the overwhelmingly superior resources of the allies assured Paraguay's eventual defeat. In 1870 López was killed and the war ended. The devastation from the war was tremendous. Paraguay's population had fallen from approximately 1 million to about 220,000, of whom fewer than 30,000 were adult males. Paraguay also lost some territory, but rivalry between Argentina and Brazil prevented Paraguay's complete dismemberment.

Modern Paraguay. Recovery was slow and political conditions were unstable. Between 1870 and 1932 Paraguay had 29 presidents. Nonetheless, Paraguay made some economic progress in these years. Foreign capital and enterprise, much of it from Argentina, assisted the nation's development, and a number of small immigrant colonies were established.

In 1932 Paraguay fought a war with Bolivia over the Gran Chaco, a semi-wasteland lying between the two countries. Paraguay, with the benefit of superior leadership and shorter lines of communication, defeated Bolivia. A truce was declared in 1935, and under the treaty signed in 1938 Paraguay gained possession of three-fourths of the disputed territory.

Gen. José Félix Estigarribia, the commander of Paraguay's forces during the Chaco War, became president in 1939. He was killed in an airplane accident and was succeeded by Higinio Morínigo. General Morínigo soon evolved a strong dictatorship, but was forced out of office by a revolt in 1948.

In 1954, following a series of short-lived governments, the army under Gen. Alfredo Stroessner took over the government. Running without opposition, Stroessner was elected to the presidency later that year. Stroessner was reelected in 1958, 1963, and 1968.

Stroessner established a rigid dictatorship. Over the years his rule became less harsh, however, and he gave the country stability and relative prosperity. In 1968 opposition candidates were permitted to enter the presidential race, although Stroessner easily won a third term.

—David Bushnell; Kempton E. Webb

PERU

Official name: Republic of Peru
Area: 496,224 square miles
Population: (1967 est.) 12,385,000
Capital: Lima (Pop., 1961, urban area, 1,436,-231)
Language: Spanish, Indian languages
Religion: Roman Catholicism
Currency: Sol
National holiday: Independence day, July 28

Peru, a republic on the west coast of South America, is bounded on the north by Ecuador and Colombia, on the east by Brazil and Bolivia, on the south by Chile, and on the west by the Pacific Ocean.

THE LAND. Peru is a country of striking diversity. Within its borders are humid tropical lowlands, in the east; ice covered peaks, in the Andes; and rainless coastal desert, in the west. The country has three main geographic regions: the coastal desert, or costa; the Andean highlands, or sierra; and the eastern Andean slopes and Amazon lowlands, or montaña.

The coastal zone extends from Ecuador to Chile and is generally less than 30 miles wide. It is extremely dry. Winds blowing in from the ocean are chilled by the cold Peru, or Humboldt, Current and yield no moisture. The only oases are the valleys of 50 or 60 seasonal rivers that drain the western slopes of the Andes. These rivers flow from June to November and provide water for irrigation.

The Andean highlands consist of a broad altiplano, or plateau, which lies between 10,000 and 15,000 feet above sea level, and is surmounted by moun-

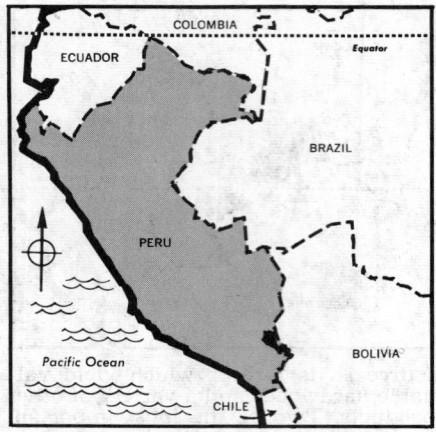

tain peaks. The grassland vegetation of the altiplano, known as puna, provides good pasturage for livestock, and the mountain valleys contain Peru's most fertile land.

The montaña is part of the Amazon Basin and is covered with tropical forest and jungle. Although it constitutes 60 percent of the nation's territory, it is very thinly populated. Development of the area has been impeded by its physical isolation.

Climate varies from region to region. The climate on the coast is dry and temperate. Temperatures in the sierra vary with altitude from temperate to frigid and most of the area is fairly dry. The montaña is hot and humid, with temperatures in the 70°sF and 80°sF, and rainfall often exceeds 100 inches a year.

THE PEOPLE. About half of the population is Indian and most of the remainder is mestizo, of mixed Indian and Spanish ancestry. About 10 percent is of European origin. Spanish is the official language but it is spoken by only about half of the population. The Andean Indians speak either Quechua or Aymara, and the Amazon tribes of the montaña have their own Indian languages. Roman Catholicism is the state religion.

Peru's principal city is Lima, the capital, which is the largest and most important city on the Pacific coast of South America. Other major urban centers, with their 1961 census populations, include Arequipa, 135,358; Callao, 155,953; and Trujillo, 100,130.

ECONOMY. Peru's economy is based largely on agriculture and mining, and the Peruvian Andes are rich in minerals. Although the country has deposits of a wide variety of minerals, copper, iron, zinc, and lead are the mainstays of the mining industry. There are important oil fields in the northwest.

Fish abound in Peru's offshore waters. In 1965 the country's fish catch of almost 7.5 thousand metric tons was the world's largest, and fish meal is a leading export.

The forests of the montaña cover more than half the country's territory. Although still largely unexploited, they produce valuable quantities of cedar, mahogany, and other tropical hardwoods as well as rubber, leche caspi (used in making chewing gum), jute, and a variety of medicinal plants.

Agriculture. Agriculture employs approximately half the labor force and is the backbone of the Peruvian economy. It contributed 20 percent of the gross domestic product in 1964. But there is a lack of well-watered arable land and farming methods are often inefficient. As a result, Peru cannot raise enough food for its own use and foodstuffs must be imported.

Potatoes and corn are the major food crops and are raised in the sierra, which has 60 percent of the country's cultivated land. Large quantities of rice and beans are also grown. The leading commercial crops are sugarcane and cotton, which are grown in the coastal valleys and in the montaña. The montaña also produces coffee, tobacco, cacao, fruit, and nuts.

Peru has very few cattle, and meat and dairy products must be imported. Sheep, vicuñas, and alpacas are raised in the southern Andes and their wool exported.

Industry. Peruvian industry is limited largely to the processing of agricultural products, smelting and refining, and the manufacture of a variety of domestic consumer goods. The most important of these include textiles, beverages, footwear, leather goods, construction materials, paper and cardboard, chemicals, pharmaceuticals, and synthetic fertilizer.

Trade. In 1966 Peruvian exports earned $774 million and imports cost $833 million. The country's major exports are fish meal, cotton, sugar, iron ore, copper, lead, zinc, and silver. Principal imports include machinery, transport equipment, foodstuffs, chemicals, and pharmaceuticals. Major trade partners are the United States, West Germany, Japan, and Britain.

GOVERNMENT. Peru is a republic. The head of state and chief executive is the president, who is directly elected along with two vice-presidents to a six-year term. The president cannot serve consecutive terms. Legislative power is vested in the Senate and Chamber of Deputies. Members of both houses, whose numbers vary, are also elected to six-year terms.

Peru is a member of the United Nations and the Organization of American States (OAS).

HISTORY. Before Christopher Columbus reached the New World in 1492, Peru was the center of a great American Indian civilization, that of the Inca. In about 1200 the Incas began to move out from their original homeland in the southern Peruvian Andes and subjugate neighboring Indian peoples living in the highlands and on the coast.

By the late 1400s the Incas had established an empire that stretched along the western coast of South America from Ecuador to Chile. This vast empire was joined together by an intricate network of roads and was ruled from the city of Cuzco, high in the Andes of southern Peru.

In 1531 a small army of Spaniards led by Francisco Pizarro invaded Peru. Despite their small numbers the Spanish easily conquered the Incas, who were weakened and divided by civil war and terrified by the guns and horses of the Spaniards. By 1533 Cuzco had fallen.

Spanish Rule. In 1542 the Spaniards transformed what had been the Inca empire into the Viceroyalty of Peru, ruled from Lima, which Pizarro had founded in 1535. Rich deposits of precious metals, particularly silver, made Peru for many years the most prized of Spain's American colonies.

In the 1700s Peru's importance was diminished by the creation of the viceroyalties of New Granada, in 1717, and Río de la Plata, in 1776. Internal tranquility was shaken by a number of Indian uprisings, the most serious being that of Tupac Amaru, between 1780 and 1783. Nevertheless, during the first years of the 1800s when Spain's other South American colonies were seeking independence, Peru remained a loyalist stronghold.

It was not until 1820, when the Argentine leader José de San Martín, who had already defeated the Spaniards in Chile, landed with an Argentine-Chilean army of liberation, that the Peruvian struggle for independence began in earnest. San Martín captured Lima and a year later, on July 28, 1821, declared Peru independent. But Spain's power was not finally broken until December 1824, when the forces of Simón Bolívar, who had replaced San Martín, routed the Spanish at the battle of Ayacucho. The independence of Peru marked the end of Spain's empire in South America.

Independence. For nearly 20 years after gaining independence, Peru was controlled by a succession of military dictators, or *caudillos*, including Luis José Orbegosa, who drew Peru into a short-lived confederation with Bolivia from 1836 to 1839.

In 1845 the presidency was assumed by Gen. Ramón Castilla, who, except for a brief interval from 1851 to 1854, ruled the country until 1862. Castilla brought about the abolition of Negro slavery and a reduction in the special privileges of the church, developed Peru's guano and nitrate sources, and provided the country a large measure of stability.

The 10 years following Castilla's regime were marked by a growing public debt, political corruption, and internal disorder, all of which were intensified in 1865–1866 by a brief war with Spain, which sought redress for the mistreatment of Spanish citizens in Peru. Chile, Ecuador, and Bolivia came to the aid of Peru, and the Spanish ultimately withdrew.

Dissatisfaction with the military in Peruvian politics increased. As a result, in 1872 Manuel Pardo, a civilian, who represented a coalition of landed aristocrats and financial and commercial interests, was elected president. Pardo aided higher education, sought to reduce the size and influence of the army, and tried to improve the economy. He was hindered in his efforts by a decline in the important guano industry, which was only partially offset by increased nitrate production in the southern coastal province of Tarapacá.

Through an alliance that Pardo had made with Bolivia in 1873, Peru became involved in the War of the Pacific, from 1879 to 1883, which resulted from a dispute between Bolivia and Chile over the Atacama nitrate fields. Chile was victorious and under the terms of the peace treaty Peru was forced to yield its nitrate province of Tarapacá as well as to permit Chilean occupation of the adjoining provinces of Arica and Tacna. Peru was left bankrupt and exhausted.

Modern Peru. Peru did not fully recover until the early 1900s. Progress was especially notable during the second administration of Augusto B. Leguía y Salcedo, which stretched from 1919 to 1930. Leguía managed to bolster the economy by securing foreign loans and investments. He also built large-scale public works.

Leguía was relatively popular until 1930, when the world economic depression cut off the inflow of foreign capital and reduced the earnings of Peruvian exports. He was then overthrown by Col. Luis Sánchez Cerro, who remained in power until 1933, when he was assassinated. Under his successor, Oscar Benavides, in office until 1939, Peru gradually recovered from the depression.

Nevertheless, the Indian population of the Andean region received little direct benefit from the progress that had taken place. Control of Peruvian society remained in the hands of a small, wealthy minority and protest movements arose. One of these was the *Alianza Popular Revolucionaria Americana* (APRA—American Popular Revolutionary Alliance) founded by Victor Raúl Haya de la Torre.

APRA's original program was Indianist, socialistic, and extremely hostile to foreign capital. During the 1930s, APRA became the strongest political movement in Peru, but it was distrusted by the military and repeatedly frustrated in its efforts to gain power even though it gradually became more conservative.

The moderately leftist and prodemocratic *Partido de Acción Popular* (PAP—Popular Action Party), founded and led by Fernando Belaúnde Terry, ultimately had more success. Belaúnde was elected president in 1963 and sponsored agrarian reforms and supported other measures beneficial to the Indians, while seeking to effect a larger degree of popular participation in government. He also put special emphasis on the development of the *montaña*. But Belaúnde was hampered by the high cost of his programs and by his inability to obtain solid support from the Congress.
—David Bushnell: Kempton E. Webb

PHILIPPINES

Official name: Republic of the Philippines
Area: 116,000 square miles
Population: (1967 est.) 34,656,000
Capital: Quezon City (Pop., 1965 est., 482,-400)
Language: Filipino, English, Spanish, indigenous languages
Religion: Roman Catholicism
Currency unit: Peso
National holiday: Independence day, June 12

The Philippines is an independent island nation in the Pacific Ocean, some 450 miles off the southeastern coast of China. The country's nearest neighbors are Taiwan, about 65 miles to the north, and Indonesia, approximately 150 miles to the south. The Philippines received its independence from the United States in 1946.

THE LAND. There are more than 7,000 islands within the Philippine archipelago, but the 11 largest islands account for 94 percent of the country's total land area. The largest islands are Luzon (40,420 square miles) and Mindanao (36,537 square miles). Each of the remaining islands is less than 6,000 square miles in area.

Most of the islands are hilly or mountainous with only limited areas of level land. In the northern half of Luzon, the principal island, there are several mountain ranges running from north to south. The Sierra Madre range runs parallel to the northeastern coast, and the Central Cordillera forms the spine of the island. Between the two ranges is the Cagayan Plain, one of the two sizable lowlands on Luzon.

The other major lowland is the Central Plain, between the Central Cordillera and the Zambales Mountains, in western Luzon. Most of southeastern Luzon is made up of discontinuous mountains and volcanoes, including Mt. Mayon, which reaches an elevation of over 8,200 feet. Manila Bay juts into southwestern Luzon.

The Philippines has a warm, even temperature the year round. Average monthly temperatures at sea level range from 76°F to 84°F. Although it is cooler at higher altitudes, temperatures below 60°F rarely occur. Typhoons strike the Philippines every year. Most of the Philippines receives at least 60 inches of rain a year, and some regions, up to 125 inches.

THE PEOPLE. Most people in the Philippines are of Malay stock, but there are also people of Chinese, American, and Spanish origin. The Philippines has a rapidly growing population, and between 1958 and 1965 the rate of increase was 3.3 percent a year.

The population is unevenly distributed. Luzon, Cebu, Negros, Bohul, Leyte, and Panay are the most heavily populated islands. The largest city is Manila, on Luzon, which had a 1965 population estimated at 1,356,000.

ECONOMY. The economy of the Philippines is based on agriculture, and almost 60 percent of the labor force is dependent upon agriculture for its livelihood. About one-third of the land is arable, and about three-quarters of that is devoted to domestic food crops.

Rice occupies almost one-half of the cropped land. Corn and coconuts are also important crops. Other crops of some significance include root crops, fruits, nuts, sugarcane, abaca, tobacco, ramie, kapok, and rubber.

The yields per acre in the Philippines are among the lowest in Asia. The low productivity of Philippine agriculture stems largely from poor farm management, inadequate use of fertilizers, poor seeds, and lack of incentive on the part of the farmers, many of whom are tenant farmers.

The number of persons engaged in fishing is second only to the number in agriculture. Fish ranks second to rice in the Filipino diet, and fishing is becoming an increasingly important industry. In 1965 the fish catch exceeded 685,000 metric tons.

Forests cover about 40 percent of the country and are among the most important resources of the Philippines. *Luan*, commonly called Philippine mahogany, is one of the most important commercial woods. There are vast pine forests in the high mountains of northern Luzon.

Various minerals are mined in the Philippines, including gold, iron ore, copper, and chromite. The country lacks adequate supplies of mineral fuels, although some coal is mined on the islands of Cebu and Mindanao.

Before independence in 1946, industry was confined largely to processing agricultural products. Since independence, the government has promoted industrialization. A number of consumer goods industries have been established or expanded and some heavy industry has been established. There are iron and steel works, oil refineries, and assembly plants for automobiles and trucks.

In 1966 imports cost $957 million and exports earned $838 million. The main imports are machinery, cereals, transportation equipment, iron and steel products, and petroleum. The major exports are copra, sugar, wood, copper, and iron ore. Most trade is conducted with the United States and Japan. The Philippines receives economic aid from the United States.

GOVERNMENT. The Philippines has a presidential system of government. Executive power is vested in a president, who is popularly elected to a four-year term. Legislative power is held by a congress consisting of a Senate and House of Representatives. Senators are popularly elected to six-year terms, and members of the House are popularly elected to four-year terms.

The Philippines is a member of the United Nations and the Southeast Asia Treaty Organization (SEATO). In 1966 agreement was reached on the formation of a Southeast Asian regional association with Malaysia, Indonesia, and Thailand.

HISTORY. Ferdinand Magellan visited the Philippines in 1521 and claimed the islands for Spain. In 1571 Miguel López de Legazpe, a Spanish soldier, established the first Spanish settlement in the Philippines. Legazpe extended Spanish control over Cebu, Leyte, Mindanao, Panay, and central Luzon. In 1571 he took possession of Manila and made it the capital of the territory.

Long before the Spanish conquest, the Philippines traded with China. Later, Spanish galleons brought silver to Manila from the port of Acapulco, in Mexico, to trade with the Chinese for luxury goods, and Manila became an important trading center.

Under Spanish rule, Christianity and Western legal concepts and customs were introduced into the Philippines, and a centralized government was established. In the 1800s resentment against Spanish rule grew, and by the end of the 1800s the Filipinos had staged a number of revolts.

In 1896 José Rizal, a leading Filipino patriot, was executed for his part in uprisings that broke out in that year. His death spurred the revolutionary movement. Spain promised to grant Filipino representation in Madrid and to permit wider autonomy for the islands. Spain failed to keep these promises, however, and the Filipinos, led by Gen. Francisco Makabulas, offered strong resistance to Spanish rule.

U.S. Rule. In April 1898 the United States declared war on Spain, after the U.S. battleship *Maine* was destroyed in Havana harbor, in Cuba, which was also under Spanish rule. By that time the Filipinos were battling hard against the Spanish in the Philippines. In August 1898 U.S. forces occupied Manila, and in the Treaty of Paris, signed on Dec. 10, 1898, Spain ceded the Philippines to the United States for $20 million.

In 1899 a war of insurrection against the United States was led by Emilio Aguinaldo, head of the anti-Spanish rebellion of 1896. The United States put down the rising, and in 1901 Aguinaldo was captured.

Between the summer of 1900 and the summer of 1901 the islands were administered by a military governor and the Taft Commission, established by Pres. William McKinley and headed by William Howard Taft. In July 1901 this system became a civil government, headed by Taft. Plans were made to establish a legislature, to be made up of an elected assembly, or lower house. In 1907 the first elections were held for the assembly.

In 1934 Pres. Franklin D. Roosevelt signed the Tydings-McDuffie Act, stipulating that independence was to be granted the Philippines in 1946. Under the terms of the act, the Philippines in 1935 became a self-governing Commonwealth headed by an elected president, and Manuel Quezon was chosen the first president.

On Dec. 7, 1941 Japanese forces struck the islands, and on Jan. 2, 1942 Manila was occupied by the Japanese. Valiant defensive battles were fought on Bataan peninsula and Corregidor, an island in Manila Bay, but the Philippines were forced to surrender in May 1942.

Japan established a puppet government in the Philippines, in which many Filipinos served. Quezon established a government-in-exile in Washington, D.C., and Americans and Filipinos organized a large-scale guerrilla movement to fight the Japanese in the Philippines.

After the Japanese invasion in 1941, many landlords fled to Manila. During the war, the Japanese started a reign of terror, supported by some of the landlords who arrested peasant leaders and union organizers and turned them over to the Japanese for execution.

Early in the war the peasant farmers struck back by creating an army, the Hukbalahap, commonly called Huk, led by Luis Taruc. The Huks rallied the rural population and killed some 25,000 Japanese and their Filipino supporters.

On Oct. 20, 1944 U.S. troops, supported by Filipino guerrillas, landed on the island of Leyte, and on Feb. 23, 1945, after a fierce three-week battle, the Allied forces took Manila.

Independence. On July 4, 1946 the Philippine Islands became independent and Manuel Roxas became president. The new government faced the problem of rebuilding the country's war-ravaged economy. Another problem facing the new government was the rebellion of the Huk, which became a communist-dominated group.

Under the leadership of Pres. Ramón Magsaysay, who was elected in 1953, the Huk rebellion was suppressed. In 1957 Magsaysay was killed in a plane crash and was succeeded by Carlos García. In 1961 Diosdado Macapagal became president. He was defeated by Ferdinand Marcos in 1965. In 1967 there was a resurgence of Huk strength in central Luzon, and Huks staged attacks against government forces.

—Thomas E. Ennis; M. G. Inaba

POLAND

Official name: Polish People's Republic
Area: 120,665 square miles
Population: (1967 est.) 31,944,000
Capital: Warsaw (Pop., 1965 est., 1,249,100)
Language: Polish
Religion: Roman Catholicism
Currency unit: Zloty
National holiday: National liberation day, July 22

Poland, a communist-controlled nation in Eastern Europe, is bounded on the north by the Baltic Sea, on the east by the Soviet Union, on the south by Czechoslovakia, and on the west by East Germany.

Following World War II Poland underwent major territorial changes. In 1945, as a result of the Potsdam Agreement among the leading Allied Powers—Britain, the Soviet Union, and the United States—the country lost nearly 45 percent of its territory, in the east, to the Soviet Union. In compensation Poland was given German lands east of the Oder and Neisse rivers. Permanent determination of the German-Polish frontier, however, was to be decided by a future peace treaty.

THE LAND. The greatest part of Poland is level to rolling lowland, although there are local variations in relief. In the north, near the Baltic coast, the soil is sandy, and sand dunes, some of which are several hundred feet high, dominate the landscape. To the south of the coastal zone a belt of low hills studded with lakes stretches from west to east across the country.

Central Poland is a flat plain and the only noticeable relief features are deeply cut river valleys. The Vistula, Poland's largest and longest river, crosses the eastern part of this plain and flows north to the Baltic. The Warta and the Noteć rivers cross the plain in the west to join the Oder, which flows north along the western border. South of the central plains, low plateaus and rolling hills stretch from the upper course of the Oder eastward to the Polish-Soviet frontier.

Southern Poland is mountainous. To the west lies the Sudeten Range, to the east, the Carpathian Mountains. The two mountain systems are separated by the uppermost valley of the

Oder River, which is known as the Moravian Gate.

Most of Poland has a distinctly continental climate, characterized by wide yearly temperature variation. Winters are cold and snowy, and summers are warm and dry.

THE PEOPLE. Before World War II Poland was a state with substantial minorities—Byelorussians, Germans, Jews, and Ukrainians. After World War II it became largely homogeneous.

The former religious and linguistic minorities were either exterminated during the wartime German occupation, or were forced to leave Poland after 1945. The Byelorussians and Ukrainians had been concentrated in the eastern regions annexed by the Soviet Union. The population is now nearly all Polish-speaking and Roman Catholic, although there are small Greek Orthodox and Protestant communities.

Warsaw, Poland's capital, suffered greater destruction during World War II than almost any other city in Europe. Warsaw had more than 1 million people in 1939, but in 1945 it had only about 20,000 inhabitants living in bombed-out ruins.

Other major cities include Łódź, which is primarily industrial, and Kraków, which was untouched by the war and is full of monuments to Poland's past. Gdańsk (Danzig), at the mouth of the Vistula, on the Baltic, is Poland's first port for freight traffic. Nearby Gdynia specializes in passenger traffic.

ECONOMY. Before World War II Poland was primarily an agricultural country. As a result of the Potsdam Agreement in 1945, however, Poland gained industrial areas in Silesia in the west and lost farmland in the east, and thus emerged with the resources for a more balanced economy.

The government has made intensive efforts to industrialize the country, and economic development has been fairly steady. But despite overall gains the standard of living remained relatively low, and in the mid-1960s serious shortages remained in areas such as housing and quality consumer goods.

Natural Resources. Coal is Poland's most valuable mineral resource, and its major source of energy. Polish coal deposits, located largely in Upper and Lower Silesia, the middle and upper valley of the Oder River, are the third largest in Europe. In 1965

EASTFOTO

CRACOW, POLAND, served as the capital of that nation from 1320 to 1609. Seen in the picture above is the former Royal Castle, the *Wawel*, now the city residence of the president.

Poland was the world's fifth largest coal producer.

Upper Silesia's coal deposits are the most extensive, but are short on coking coal, necessary for steel making. Lower Silesia (the middle Oder valley) produces high-grade coking coal. Poland has little iron ore but possesses large deposits of sulfur, lead, zinc, rock salt, and copper, as well as some nickel, gold, and arsenic.

Agriculture. Polish agriculture differs fundamentally from that in most other communist-controlled countries, for little land is collectivized. Nearly nine-tenths of Poland's agricultural land is privately cultivated. Farms are generally small, averaging between 8 and 30 acres. Animal power is still widely used in farming, although agricultural machinery is being produced in increasing quantities.

The government has encouraged the raising of livestock, with an emphasis on pigs and sheep. Poland produces enough meat to fill domestic needs, and meat and meat products are important exports.

Rye is the principal crop, but large quantities of wheat, barley, and oats are also grown. Potatoes are grown for food, fodder, and the making of alcohol.

Industry. Industry expanded greatly following World War II and in 1965 contributed 51 percent of the gross domestic product. Poland's largest industrial center is located in Upper Silesia, near the country's major coal deposits.

Although occupying only a small area, Upper Silesia had six cities with more than 100,000 people in the mid-1960s. The largest, Katowice, is one of Europe's principal industrial centers. Iron and steel, heavy machinery, and chemicals are the main products of Upper Silesian industry. Fifty miles to the east of Katowice is Poland's newest steel center, Nowa Huta, which is supplied with coal from Silesia and iron ore from the Soviet Union.

A second, smaller industrial center is in Lower Silesia, around the cities of Wrocław, Walbrzych, and Jelenia Góra. This area contains mostly light industry and produces some consumer goods. Łódź, in central Poland, is the nation's leading textile center. Poznań, in the west, and Warsaw account for a substantial portion of the output of machinery, cars and trucks, and chemicals. The city of Szczecin, at the mouth of the Oder, is Poland's leading shipbuilding center.

Trade. In 1967 Poland's exports earned $2,640 million and its imports cost $2,521 million. Poland's chief exports include coal, meat, and ships. Principal imports are petroleum, cotton, iron ore, wheat, and metalworking machinery. Poland trades mainly with the Soviet Union, Czechoslovakia, and East Germany.

GOVERNMENT. The Polish Communist party, officially known as the Polish United Worker's Party, dominates political life. The politburo, or political bureau, of the party's central committee determines national policy and the party's first secretary is usually the most powerful figure in the government.

Under the constitution supreme authority is vested in the *Sejm*, or parliament. Members of the Sejm are directly elected to four-year terms. The Sejm elects the 15-member Council of State, which exercises legislative functions and acts as a collective head of state, and the Council of Ministers, which performs executive functions.

Poland is a member of the United Nations and the Warsaw Pact, a military alliance of Communist states headed by the Soviet Union.

HISTORY. The Poles were originally one of several Slavic tribes that settled between the Oder and Vistula rivers before the 700s. During the 900s they joined with neighboring peoples to fight off a series of invasions by Germanic tribes and became unified under the Piast dynasty.

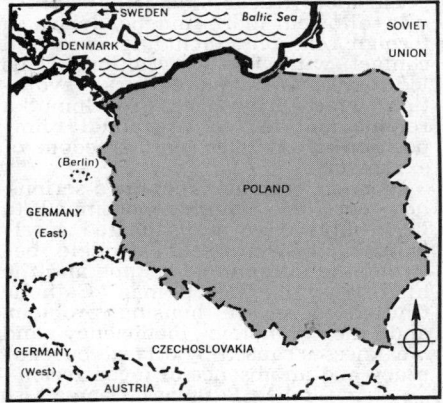

In 966 one of the early Piast rulers, Prince Mieszko accepted Christianity. Mieszko's successors expanded Polish domains, especially to the east. In 1138, with the death of Boleslav III, Poland entered a period of political disintegration that was worsened by attacks from the Mongols.

Under Casimir the Great (r. 1333–1370), however, Poland revived. Casimir strengthened the central government, consolidated Polish territory, developed agriculture, and constructed roads and bridges. In 1364 he founded the University of Kraków, one of the oldest institutions of higher learning in Eastern Europe.

On the death of Casimir in 1370 the Piast dynasty died out and the crown passed to Louis I of Hungary, Casimir's nephew. Louis was succeeded by his daughter Jadwiga, who in 1386 married Ladislas Jagello of Lithuania. Under the Jagellons, cultural activity reached a peak and Poland greatly extended its territory, which by the mid-1500s stretched from the Baltic to the Black Sea.

The Jagellon dynasty ended in 1572 with the death of Sigismund Augustus, and for 200 years the succession to the Polish throne was contested by the various ruling houses of Europe. The succession was further complicated by the fact that the king was elected by the Polish parliament, which was composed of the nobility.

Any noble could block any measure by his one vote. This practice, known as the *liberum veto*, not only made the election of a new monarch extraordinarily difficult, but almost paralyzed the central government.

Partition. In 1764 a pro-Russian Polish nobleman, Stanislas Poniatowski, was made king through pressure exerted by Russia. This interference by Russia was resented by the Polish nobles, who rebelled in 1768. Russian troops crushed the rebellion, but Prussia and Austria feared that Russia would absorb Poland to their disadvantage. As a result, in 1772, the three countries agreed to partition Poland. Russia, Prussia, and Austria annexed territories adjoining them, and Poland lost approximately one-third of its land.

Alarmed, the Poles sought to strengthen their government and institute various reforms. Russia, however, invaded Poland again in 1793 and the country was once more partitioned, with Russia and Prussia each annexing more land. A third partition by Russia, Prussia, and Austria took place in 1795, and Poland was wiped off the map.

In 1807 Napoleon I of France created the Grand Duchy of Warsaw out of the Polish territories that had been annexed by Prussia. Although nominally independent, the Grand Duchy was really a puppet state. After Napoleon's defeat, the Congress of Vienna, held in 1814–1815, divided the Grand Duchy among Russia, Prussia, and Austria. Thousands of Polish intellectuals left the country for other nations in Western Europe, where they kept the spirit of Polish nationalism alive.

Life for Poles in the three territories varied. In Russian Poland, despite some persecution, Poles took part in Russian national life. In Austrian Poland, the Poles gained important political privileges and frequently held posts in the Austrian government service. In Prussian Poland, the Poles were politically oppressed but became strong economically.

Throughout the 1800s, however, all Poles sought to rid themselves of foreign rule. Uprisings in Russian Poland took place in 1830 and 1863 but were brutally crushed.

Independence. At the turn of the century the movement for independence gained momentum. In 1917, during World War I, Polish political leaders from Austria and Russia formed the Polish National Committee in Paris, which was recognized by the Allies as the spokesman for Polish independence. When U.S. Pres. Woodrow Wilson enunciated his Fourteen Points in 1918, he called for an independent Poland. Meanwhile, inside Poland, a group was organized under the leadership of Józef Piłsudski, a Polish officer.

The Central Powers were defeated in 1918, and Piłsudski established an independent Polish government in Warsaw. Under the terms of the Treaty of Versailles in 1919, Poland regained most of Polish territory from Prussia and much of Upper Silesia. The region around the Lithuanian city of Vilna, which both countries claimed, was granted to Lithuania in 1920 but seized by Poland in 1922.

Poland gained access to the sea through the Polish Corridor, a narrow strip of land that cut through Germany to the port of Danzig, which was made a free city under the supervision of the League of Nations. Poland's claim to territories in the east, however, soon resulted in a clash with the Soviet Union.

The Allies had suggested a border between Poland and the Soviet Union based on ethnic lines, with the non-Polish territories in the east going to the Soviet Union. This suggested border, known as the Curzon Line, was rejected by the Poles, and in 1920 fighting broke out between Poland and the Soviet Union. A peace treaty signed at Riga in 1921 made Poland's frontier much the same as it had been before the partition in 1795.

Interwar Era. In 1921 Poland adopted a democratic constitution that provided for a parliamentary form of government. The new republic, lacking a strong executive and subject to the conflicting demands of many different political parties, was unable to deal effectively with the myriad problems caused by bringing together territories that had been parts of other states for more than 100 years, and large minorities of other nationalities, including Ukrainians, Byelorussians, and Germans.

In 1926 Józef Piłsudski headed a military coup that overthrew the existing government and established himself as dictator. On his death in 1935 a group of army colonels continued the dictatorship.

World War II. The rise to power of Adolf Hitler in Germany, the disintegration of the League of Nations, and the collapse of the various efforts within Europe to establish regional security arrangements led, on Sept. 1, 1939, to World War II. The war began with a German invasion of Poland from the west, and two weeks later the Soviet Union invaded from the east. The Poles fought bravely, but were quickly overwhelmed. A government-in-exile was established in London, and Polish units fought with the Allies throughout the war.

In April 1943 the Soviet government broke relations with the Polish government in London, and in July 1944 created the Polish Committee of National Liberation on conquered Polish territory. In January 1945 the Soviet Union reorganized the committee as the government of Poland.

British and U.S. efforts to ensure the active participation of democratic groups in this government and to guarantee free elections in Poland were unsuccessful, and after controlled elections in January 1947 a communist government was firmly in power.

Communist Rule. The history of Poland under Communism followed that of the other states of Eastern Europe, with the destruction of rival political groups, the purge of the Communist party itself, rapid industrialization, forced collectivization of agriculture, a mass indoctrination effort, and complete control of the army and internal security police by the Soviet Union.

This pattern was broken in the summer of 1956, however, when riots for "bread and freedom" in Poznań sparked a successful revolt against Soviet rule. Władysław Gomułka, a former head of the Polish Communist party who had been ousted in 1948 and later imprisoned for opposing certain Stalinist policies, was made first secretary of the party. Stefan Cardinal Wyszyński, the ranking Roman Catholic churchman, was released from detention.

All Poland united to resist Soviet pressure, and Gomułka was able to win a wide measure of freedom for his country to allow it to pursue a Polish rather than a Soviet "road to socialism." The Polish army was placed under Polish officers, and the terms of Polish-Soviet trade were revised in Poland's favor. Collectivization was almost completely abandoned, industry was decentralized to some degree, and more attention was given to the production of consumer goods.

Most important, the Poles were given more freedom, and the country was allowed more independence in foreign relations, including increased contact with Western nations. This led to an artistic and cultural revolution, which frightened the Gomułka regime and led to a gradual reimposition of controls over freedom of expression.

Poland's problems remained serious, however. The country continued to be troubled by a disaffected intellectual class, a bitter struggle between the Communist regime and the hierarchy of the Roman Catholic Church, a severe housing problem, and the economic inefficiency and weaknesses caused by a large bureaucracy and an absence of incentives.

—Robert F. Byrnes; George Kish

PORTUGAL

Official name: Republic of Portugal
Area: 35,510 square miles
Population: (1966 est.) 9,335,000
Capital: Lisbon (Pop., 1965, 822,000)
Language: Portuguese
Religion: Roman Catholicism
Currency unit: Escudo
National holiday: Day of Portugal, June 10

Portugal, a republic occupying the western part of Europe's Iberian peninsula, is bounded on the north and east by Spain and on the south and west by the Atlantic Ocean. The Madeira islands and the Azores, lying respectively, about 1,000 and 750 miles to the southeast in the Atlantic Ocean, are administered as integral parts of Portugal.

THE LAND. Portugal has three major geographic regions. In the northeast the western fringe of the high tablelands of central Spain produces a fairly rugged terrain. Narrow mountain ranges rise to elevations of more than 3,000 feet above sea level and extend almost to the Atlantic. In the west is a broad coastal plain, which widens toward the south. The southeast is covered by low, rolling hills, mostly under 650 feet in elevation.

Portugal's principal rivers are the Duoro in the north; the Tagus, which divides the country almost equally into northern and southern regions; and the Guadiana in the southeast. The wide, protected mouth of the Tagus gives the city of Lisbon one of the world's finest natural harbors.

Portugal has a temperate maritime climate. Winters are generally mild, except in the highland areas where they are cold and snowy. Summers are warm in the north and hot in the south. North of the Tagus rainfall is abundant, averaging nearly 30 inches annually, but it decreases toward the southeast and is less than 20 inches along the southern coast.

THE PEOPLE. Portugal has no significant minority groups. Portuguese is the universal language, and the overwhelming majority of the people are Roman Catholic.

The population is concentrated in the north along the coast from the region of Setúbal to the Spanish border, and is especially dense in the lower Tagus and the lower and middle Duoro river valleys. The country is sparsely settled south of the Tagus and along the entire eastern border.

Portugal has the highest birth rate in Europe next to Iceland. Substantial emigration, however, keeps the average net population increase down to about 0.7 percent a year.

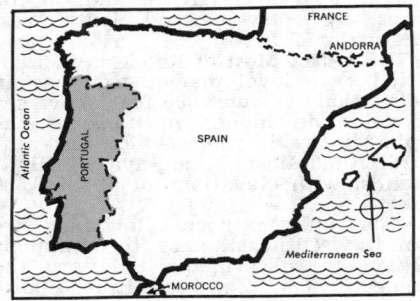

Portugal's population is mostly rural and in the mid-1960s there were only two cities with more than 100,000 inhabitants—Lisbon and Porto, the second largest city, at the mouth of the Duoro River.

ECONOMY. Portugal is one of Europe's poorest countries. In 1965 annual per capita income was estimated at $340. The economy is improving, however, and the country's gross domestic product rose at an annual average of 6.2 percent between 1960 and 1965.

Natural Resources. Portugal has few important mineral resources. The most important mineral mined is wolframite, from which tungsten is produced. Some coal, copper, iron, pyrites, tin, lead, and kaolin—a fine white clay used for ceramics—are also mined.

Approximately 25 percent of Portugal is forested and forest products constitute one of the country's major exports. Portugal ordinarily supplies 50 percent of the world's cork. Other important forest products include turpentine, rosin, and timber.

Fish, particularly tuna and sardines, are an important source of income. In 1965 Portugal's fish catch amounted to 554,000 metric tons and fish constituted the country's leading export.

Agriculture. Portugal is an agricultural country, and in 1965, 42 percent of the labor force was engaged in agriculture, one of the highest percentages in Europe. Portugal's major agricultural product is wine, and the country is known for its port and Madeira.

Fruits and nuts, produced in the south, are also important exports and include oranges, lemons, figs, grapes, and almonds. Olives are grown throughout the country and rice, the principal cereal crop, is raised in the Tagus river valley.

Industry. Industry is largely undeveloped, although in the mid-1960s improvements in the transportation system, increased hydroelectric capacity, and foreign loans spurred hopes for more rapid industrialization.

Portugal's most important industries are textiles and food processing. Also manufactured are tile, tobacco, glass, pottery, and cement. Heavy industry is almost nonexistent, although a steel mill opened in 1961 at Seixal, near Lisbon.

Trade. In 1966 Portugal's exports earned $620 million and imports cost $1,023 million. The deficit is largely made up by tourism, emigrant's remittances, and earnings from Portugal's overseas provinces.

Portugal's major exports include fish, wine, agricultural produce, and cork. Principal imports are manufactured goods, machinery, transportation equipment, coal, petroleum, chemicals, and cotton and other raw fibers.

The country's chief trading partners are West Germany, Britain, the United States, and France.

GOVERNMENT. Portugal is officially a corporative republic but it has had a dictatorship since 1932, when Dr. António de Oliveira Salazar became premier and concentrated power in his own hands.

Under the constitution, the president is elected to a seven-year term by an electoral college composed of members

CASA DE PORTUGAL

PORTUGUESE BOAT, with painted prow.

of the National Assembly, the Corporative Chamber, and representatives from overseas legislatures. The president appoints the premier and a cabinet, which are responsible to him.

The legislature consists of the National Assembly, whose 130 members are directly elected to four-year terms. There is also an advisory group, the Corporative Chamber, which is made up of representatives from various commercial, industrial, religious, and cultural groups.

Following World War II the status of Portugal's overseas possessions was changed from "colonies" to "provinces." The Portuguese overseas provinces are the Cape Verde Islands, Portuguese Guinea, St. Tome and the Principe Islands, Angola, Mozambique, Portuguese Timor, and Macao.

Portugal is a member of the United Nations and the North Atlantic Treaty Organization (NATO).

HISTORY. The history of Portugal is inseparable from that of Spain until the 1000s. In 1055 Ferdinand I of León and Castile began to reconquer from the Muslims, or Moors, the northern part of present-day Portugal and organize it as a country. In 1094 Ferdinand granted the Country of Portugal to Henry of Burgundy, who had distinguished himself in the campaign against the Muslims.

Afonso Henriques of the Burgundian dynasty became count in 1128 and declared Portugal independent of Castile. In 1143, in the Treaty of Zamora, Castile formally recognized Portuguese independence, and Afonso Henriques was proclaimed king.

Afonso continued to push the Muslims southward, and in 1147 he captured Lisbon and established a frontier on the Tagus River. Afonso's immediate successors, Sancho I, Afonso II, and Sancho II, extended Portugal to its present boundaries, which were attained in 1249.

Avís Dynasty. Afonso's direct descendants reigned until 1385, when John I of Avís seized the throne and successfully defended Portugal against Castilian invasion. During the 1400s the Portuguese kingdom consolidated its power and began to expand overseas.

Under the direction of Prince Henry the Navigator (1394–1460), the third son of King John I, Portugal discovered and colonized the Madeira Islands, the Azores, and the Cape Verde Islands, and explored far down the west coast of Africa.

John II (r.1481–1495) further advanced Portuguese exploration, and in 1488 Bartholomeu Dias reached the Cape of Good Hope. During the reign of Manuel I (r.1495–1521) the Portuguese sailed to India, discovered Brazil, and began to establish a vast empire through the acquisition of territories in the East Indies and Southeast Asia.

During the 1500s the Eastern trade brought great profits for a time, but holding such extensive territories proved difficult and eventually the empire proved a disastrous drain. Reckless spending, persecution of the Jews, who were prominent in banking and finance, and the introduction of the Inquisition further weakened the small kingdom.

Bragança Dynasty. In 1580 the Portuguese throne fell vacant and was seized by Philip II of Spain. Philip and his son and grandson ruled for 60 years, during which time Portugal was little more than a conquered province. The kingdom regained its independence in 1640, when the Portuguese revolted and elected John of Bragança to the throne, but most of Portugal's Eastern empire had been lost to the Dutch and the English.

The 1700s brought a revived prosperity, largely due to the trade and newly discovered wealth of Brazil. In the mid-1700s the country was ruled by the Marquis of Pombal, a powerful minister of Joseph Emanuel (r.1750–1777).

Although he was often ruthless, Pombal sought to strengthen the monarchy, develop trade and agriculture, and reorganize the army and navy. He also attempted to break the power of the church and nobility in order to weaken class differences. The Braganças proved unable to cope with the international problems raised by the French Revolution of 1789, and in 1807 the country was conquered by Napoleon I of France.

The Braganças fled to Brazil and did not return until 1822, seven years after Napoleon's final defeat at the battle of Waterloo. In the same year Brazil declared its independence and Portugal was beset by a series of political and constitutional struggles that lasted until the mid-1800s.

The reigns of Peter V (r.1853–1861) and Louis I (r.1861–1889) brought some measure of political calm. Portugal attempted to balance the budget and reduce poverty, but little progress was made and discontent with the monarchy grew.

The reign of Carlos I (r.1889–1908) brought no improvement. The king was financially extravagant and licentious. Popular discontent increased and Carlos was assassinated in 1908. His son Manuel II was also financially irresponsible and following an insurrection in Lisbon in 1910, he was forced to flee the country. Portuguese leaders immediately proclaimed a republic but political conditions remained extremely chaotic and a total of 18 revolutions took place during the next 16 years.

Republic. During World War I Portugal fought on the side of the Allies, but the government was continually threatened by pro-German factions, which made several attempts to seize power.

In 1926 a junta of military officers, headed by Gen. António Oscar de Fragoso Carmona, seized power. In 1928, unable to handle economic problems, the generals appointed a professor of economics, António de Oliveira Salazar, finance minister. In 1932 Salazar became premier, or prime minister, and soon established a dictatorship. Although he did not assume the presidency, he arranged for the successive election of figureheads while firmly holding power himself.

Portugal remained neutral in World War II, but provided Britain with raw materials from its African possessions and the right to establish a military base in the Azores. In 1946 Portugal attempted to join the United Nations, but the Soviet Union vetoed its proposed membership and the country did not gain admittance until 1955.

During the late 1950s and in the 1960s Portugal was troubled by problems with its overseas possessions. In 1961 India seized Portugal's Indian territories of Goa, Damão, and Diu, and nationalist rebellions broke out in the African territories of Angola, Mozambique, and Portuguese Guinea. Despite increasingly open internal opposition, as well, Salazar remained at the center of power in the Portuguese government.

—Charles E. Nowell

QATAR

Official name: Sheikhdom of Qatar
Area: 8,500 square miles
Population: (1966 est.) 71,000
Capital: Doha (Pop., 1963 est., 45,000)
Language: Arabic
Religion: Islam
Currency unit: Qatar/Dubai dinar

Qatar, an oil-rich Arab sheikhdom, occupies the Qatar Peninsula on the southern shore of the Persian Gulf, which borders the country on the north, east, and west. To the south are Saudi Arabia and Trucial Oman. The land boundaries are undefined.

THE LAND AND PEOPLE. The Qatar Peninsula is a low plain, thinly covered with sand. The climate is hot and dry, and rainfall is less than 4 inches a year. The people of Qatar are of Arab stock. The population also includes Arabs from neighboring states and European and U.S. oil workers.

ECONOMY. Oil is Qatar's only natural resource, and the country has almost no cultivable land. Fishing, pearl diving, and the herding of goats and camels, the main means of livelihood before the discovery of oil, continue to contribute to the economy of Qatar.

Oil production, begun in 1949, is the country's only industry. In 1966 the wells at Dukhan, in western Qatar, and those off the coasts produced almost 14 million metric tons of oil. Foreign companies operate the fields and pay large royalty fees to Qatar's sheikh, who spends much of the in-

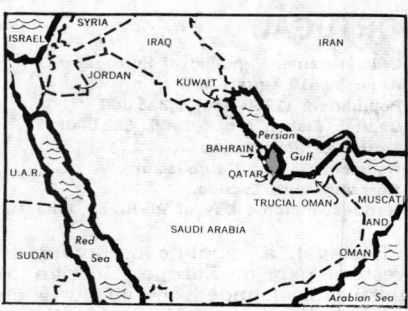

come on social and economic development programs.

In addition to oil, Qatar exports some pearls. Food, machinery, textiles, as well as raw materials must be imported.

GOVERNMENT. Qatar is under the absolute rule of a hereditary sheikh. By treaty, Britain manages Qatar's foreign relations and provides for its defense.

HISTORY. Qatar has been inhabited by Arab peoples for many centuries. The sheikhs of Qatar were compelled to pay tribute to sheikhs of Bahrain for protection and support until 1872. In 1868 Qatar entered into the first of a series of treaties with Britain, which was then building a strong position in the Persian Gulf. Between 1872 and 1914, however, the Ottoman Turks maintained a fort in Qatar and controlled the country.

In a treaty signed in 1916 Qatar's sheikhs granted Britain special diplomatic and commercial rights in return for protection. The discovery of oil in 1939 brought wealth and international importance to the sheikhdom, and since World War II Britain has encouraged the development of Qatar's independence.

—Charles Issawi; Alexander Melamid

RHODESIA

Official name: Rhodesia
Area: 150,333 square miles
Population: (1967 est.) 4,530,000
Capital: Salisbury (Pop., 1965 est., urban area, 325,000)
Language: English, African languages
Religion: Anglicanism, Presbyterianism, Roman Catholicism, traditional religions
Currency unit: Pound

Rhodesia is a British dependency in southern Africa that proclaimed its independence in 1965. The Rhodesian unilateral declaration of independence (UDI) was considered unconstitutional by Britain. Rhodesia is bordered on the north by Zambia, on the east by Mozambique, on the south by South Africa, and on the west by Botswana and South West Africa.

THE LAND. Most of Rhodesia is occupied by a level plateau that has an elevation of over 3,000 feet above sea level. The higher portions of the plateau are in the east. In east-central Rhodesia are the Inyanga Highlands, with elevations of about 8,500 feet.

The only extensive lowlands are in the southeast, near the Limpopo River and its principal tributary, the Shashi. The Zambezi River flows along part of the northern border, and many other rivers flow through the country. Kariba Lake is in north-western Rhodesia.

The lowlands are hot and dry, but temperatures on the plateau above 3,500 feet are moderate. Rainfall is confined to the period from October to April.

THE PEOPLE. About 95 percent of the people are of African origin, and about 5 percent are of European background. Most of the Europeans are of British or South African origin.

The Africans are mostly Bantu-speaking, and mainly of the Shona (Mashona) tribe in the east and the Ndebele (Matabele) in the southwest. The Ndebele are related to the Zulu people of South Africa. Many of the Africans are Christians.

The major cities are Salisbury, the capital, and Bulawayo.

ECONOMY. Agriculture is important in the Rhodesian economy. The basic crops are corn and grains. The major commercial crops are tobacco and sugar, which are grown mainly on European-owned farms. Cattle and sheep are raised in most parts of the country.

Rhodesia has rich mineral resources, particularly gold, asbestos, and chromium ore. Industry is more highly developed than in most African countries, and a wide range of products is manufactured.

In 1965, after Rhodesia declared its independence, Britain called for economic sanctions against Rhodesia, and British trade with Rhodesia was virtually cut off. Soon after, the UN Security Council requested member countries to impose economic sanctions on Rhodesia. Most member nations, including the United States, joined the embargo.

In 1965, before sanctions were imposed, imports cost $335 million and exports earned $442 million. In 1966 imports cost $236 million and exports earned $293 million. The country's major exports are tobacco, asbestos, gold, and chromium ore. The major imports are machinery, transportation equipment, textiles, iron and steel products, and fertilizers.

GOVERNMENT. The 1961 Rhodesian constitution provided for a parliamentary system of government. The British queen was head of state, and nominal executive power was vested in her representative, the governor-general.

Actual executive power was held by a prime minister and cabinet responsible to the legislature. Legisla-

tive power was held by a 65-member Legislative Assembly popularly elected every five years. Fifteen seats in the assembly were reserved for Rhodesian Africans.

After independence was declared, the new government replaced the governor-general with an "officer administering the government," but kept the general framework of the 1961 constitution.

HISTORY. In about 1000 AD Bantu-speaking tribes from central Africa drove off the aboriginal Bushmen living in the region of present-day Rhodesia. They established trade relations with Arabs of the eastern coast of Africa and, through them, with Indian sea traders.

The Bantu-speaking people founded the Zimbabwe civilization, which left imposing stone ruins. In the 1400s another Bantu-speaking people, the Shona, expelled or absorbed their predecessors and built the Monomotapa empire, which was based on gold mining.

In the 1600s Portuguese from Mozambique ravaged the African states in the Zambezi valley, and the Monomotapa empire collapsed. The Portuguese imposed their overlordship on the Shona, and destroyed the trade between Africa and India. By the 1800s the power of the Portuguese had declined, and in the early 1800s the Matabele subjugated the Shona.

British Control. Matabeleland lay in the path of British expansion northward from Cape Colony in South Africa, and in 1888 the Matabele king accepted British protection over the area. He also granted to Cecil Rhodes, for whom Rhodesia is named, a monopoly over mining rights for his British South Africa Company. Rhodes then organized the white occupation of the territory. The Matabele rebelled in 1893 but were defeated.

The company administered Southern Rhodesia until 1923, when the white settlers voted for autonomy under British rule and Southern Rhodesia became a crown colony. Southern Rhodesian whites persistently pressed for confederation with Northern Rhodesia (now Zambia) and Nyasaland (now Malawi). Because Southern Rhodesia was under white-settler control, Africans in Northern Rhodesia and Nyasaland vehemently protested against any such association.

Nonetheless, in 1953 Britain established the Federation of Rhodesia and Nyasaland, but on Dec. 31, 1963 the federation was dissolved. Northern Rhodesia and Nyasaland became independent, and Southern Rhodesia remained under British control as the self-governing colony of Rhodesia.

UDI. The Rhodesian government pressed for independence, but Britain refused, insisting on assurances of adequate representation for the country's African majority. Despite Britain's position, Prime Minister Ian Smith declared Rhodesia independent on Nov. 11, 1965. Britain declared the act illegal and refused to recognize Smith's government.

—Hibberd V. B. Kline, Jr.; Gary A. Weissman

ROMANIA

Official name: Social Republic of Romania
Area: 91,699 square miles
Population: (1967 est.) 19,287,000
Capital: Bucharest (Pop., 1965 est., urban area, 1,382,000)
Language: Romanian
Religion: Orthodox Christianity, Roman Catholicism, Protestantism, Judaism
Currency unit: Leu
National holiday: Liberation day, August 23

Romania, a communist-controlled country in southeastern Europe, is bordered on the north and northeast by the Soviet Union, on the east by the Black Sea, on the south by Bulgaria, and on the west by Yugoslavia and Hungary.

THE LAND. The land surface of Romania is dominated by the great arc-shaped mountain system formed by the Carpathians and the Transylvanian Alps. The Carpathians run from the northwest to the southeast, where they meet the Transylvanian Alps. The Transylvanian Alps run across the country from the southeast to the southwest, ending at the Danube River.

West and north of these mountains lies Transylvania. This triangular plateau is drained by the Mures and Somes rivers, which flow northeast toward Hungary. The Transylvanian plateau is separated from the Hungarian plain by the low Bihor Mountains. Beyond the Bihor, Romania controls a long, narrow strip of the Hungarian plain.

The region between the Carpathians and the Prut River, which forms the border with the Soviet Union, is known as Moldavia. The area between the Transylvanian Alps and the Danube is Walachia. Between the Danube and the Black Sea lies the Romanian portion of the Dobruja Plateau.

The Danube is Romania's largest river, although for much of its course it forms the border with Bulgaria and Yugoslavia. The Oltul and Siret, which cross the lowlands of Walachia and Moldavia, are the Danube's most important tributaries.

Most of Romania has a continental climate with hot, dry summers and cold, windy, snowy winters.

THE PEOPLE. Romanians represent about 86 percent of the total population. Approximately 9 percent of the population is Hungarian and 2 percent is German. Other small minority groups include Ukrainians, Gypsies, Russians, and Yugoslavs (Serbs and Croatians). The minorities are concentrated in western and west-central Romania.

The Romanian language, which is derived from Latin, belongs to the Romance group. Its vocabulary, however, contains substantial borrowings from the Slavic languages.

The population is predominantly rural, and only about 30 percent of the people live in urban areas.

Bucharest, the capital, is the country's political, artistic, and intellectual center. It is a large sprawling metropolis and contains only a few relics of its long history. The second largest city is Cluj, in Transylvania.

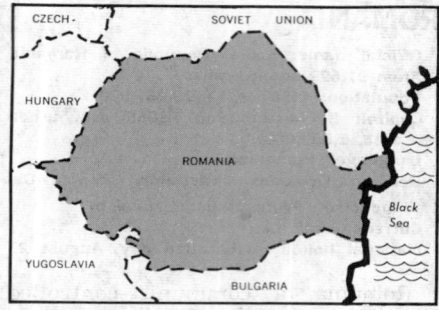

Timisoara, in the southwest, and Brasov, in eastern Transylvania, are important regional trade centers. Ploesti is the oil center of Walachia. Iasi, in Moldavia, is known for its university.

ECONOMY. Before World War II Romania was largely an agricultural nation, but under the communist regime great emphasis has been placed on industrial development.

Natural Resources. Oil is Romania's most important resource, and in 1966 Romania ranked second among European oil producers, producing more than 12.8 million metric tons. The principal oil fields are located along the southern and eastern flanks of the main mountain system, in Walachia and Moldavia.

Romania also has major deposits of natural gas near its oil fields and in Transylvania. The production of natural gas has been growing rapidly and it doubled between 1957 and 1964. In 1966 Romania produced 18,612 million cubic meters of natural gas, making it the fourth largest producer in the world. In addition, Romania mines iron, manganese, gold, silver, and uranium.

Agriculture. Most of Romanian agriculture is collectivized. In 1961 more than 84 percent of the country's cultivated land was controlled by collective and state farms. Cereals are the country's major crops. The most widely grown cereal is corn, which is used for both food and animal feed. Wheat ranks second and together with maize accounts for two-thirds of the country's crop acreage.

Potatoes, fodder, crops, and sunflowers—an important source of vegetable oil—are also grown. The best farmland is in Moldavia and Walachia. Little livestock is raised, although some sheep are pastured in the central uplands.

Industry. Although Romanian industrialization has been rapid, it has been directed toward the development of heavy industry rather than the production of consumer goods. In 1966 Romania produced almost 3.7 million metric tons of steel, almost ten times as much as in 1948.

Substantial progress has also been made in the production of iron, machinery, and chemicals, as well as in nonferrous metallurgy. Textiles and food processing are the most important light industries.

The country's chief industrial centers are Bucharest, Ploesti, Brasov, Timisoara, Resita, and Hunedoara.

Trade. In 1966 Romanian exports earned $1,186 million and imports cost $1,213 million. The country's chief exports include electric motors, petroleum products, window glass, wood products, ball bearings, and transformers. Major imports include automobiles, iron ore, finished rolled metal, coking coal and industrial coke, and industrial equipment.

About one-third of Romania's trade is with the Soviet Union. Other important trading partners are West Germany, Czechoslovakia, East Germany, Italy, and France.

GOVERNMENT. Political life in Romania is dominated by the Romanian Communist Party, and the party's leading role is written into the constitution. Under the constitution the Grand National Assembly, is the supreme organ of state. Its 465 members are popularly elected to four-year terms.

The assembly meets for only a few days a year, however, and when not in session its functions are carried out by the Council of State, which is elected by the assembly from among its members. The president of the council is Romania's chief of state. The assembly also appoints a council of ministers to carry out executive functions.

Romania is a member of the United Nations and the Warsaw Pact, a military alliance of communist countries headed by the Soviet Union.

HISTORY. During the 300s BC, what is now Romania was settled by the Dacians, a people related to the Thracians in Greece. In about 60 BC the Dacians were united by Burebistas. The Roman Emperor Trajan conquered the Dacian kingdom in 105–106 AD and in 107 made it a Roman province. Roman rule lasted until 271, when the Emperor Aurelian, who was faced with the threat of barbarian invasions and various problems within the empire, withdrew Roman troops together with a substantial part of the population.

For the following 700 years Romania was swept by successive waves of barbarian invaders, including the Visigoths, Huns, Lombards, Avars, Slavs, and Magyars. These invasions all but obliterated the original Dacian population.

During the 1200s two principalities, Moldavia and Walachia, emerged. The principalities were prevented from gaining power, however, by the strength of their neighbors, Poland, Hungary, and the Ottoman Empire. By the 1500s the Moldavian and Walachian princes were reduced to paying heavy tribute to the Ottoman Turks.

For a brief period during the late 1500s, Michael the Brave of Walachia succeeded in defeating the Turks and uniting the two principalities. But on his death in 1601 the Turks regained control of the area. Early in the 1700s Moldavia and Walachia allied themselves with Peter the Great of Russia in his campaign against the Turks, but the joint effort failed.

Phanariot Rule. The Turks appointed Phanariots, wealthy Byzantine Greeks, to the thrones of Moldavia and Walachia. The Ottoman sultan usually sold the throne to the highest bidder, and the Phanariot princes sought to

THE UNITED NATIONS
WHEAT HARVEST on a Romanian collective.

extort enough money from the populace to show a profit over their original investment. The Phanariot period was one of misery for the Romanians.

From 1802 to 1812, as the result of wars between the Russians and Turks, the principalities were occupied by the Russians. The Peace of Bucharest in 1812 restored Ottoman control, but the Moldavian province of Bessarabia remained in Russian hands.

In 1821 revolts against the Phanariots took place in Moldavia and Walachia. Although the revolts failed, the Turks replaced the Greeks with native princes. In 1829, as a result of the Russo-Turkish War of 1828–1829, the Russians once again occupied the principalities.

Autonomy. Russia withdrew in 1834, and Moldavia and Walachia were granted autonomy under Ottoman suzerainty. During the following 14 years the principalities made progress in education, agriculture, and trade.

In 1848 Romanian intellectuals staged revolutions in Moldavia and Walachia to secure social and political reforms. The revolt in Moldavia was quickly put down, but in Walachia the rebels established a republic. The Russians and Turks both intervened to suppress the republican government, and the princes were restored under an arrangement whereby they were elected to seven-year terms of office.

After the Crimean War (1854–1856), in which Russia was defeated by the British, French, Sardinians, and Turks, it was decided that a commission would determine the future status of the principalities. Elections were held in 1857, and Moldavia and Walachia voted for union under one prince. But the Convention of Paris, held in 1858, decided that the principalities were to have a central control commission but separate legislatures and separate princes. Both Moldavia and Walachia then elected the same prince, Alexander Cuza.

In 1861 the principalities succeeded in having their union recognized by the Turks and the European powers, and in 1862 they established a single legislature and cabinet. Cuza, however, proved to be unpopular and in 1866 he was forced to abdicate.

Independence. Cuza was replaced by Charles of Hohenzollern-Sigmaringen, who reigned as Carol I. After the Russo-Turkish War of 1877–1878, in which Romania sided with Russia, the Turks were forced to recognize Romanian independence, which was recognized internationally by the Treaty of Berlin in 1878. In 1881 Carol became Romania's first king.

In the years following independence Romania was governed by a conservative and authoritarian landowning class that allied the country and its economic and political development with Germany and Austria-Hungary. Nonetheless, the desire to gain Transylvania and Bukovina from Austria-Hungary led Romania to enter World War I on the side of the Allies in 1916.

Romania emerged from the war having gained not only those two territories but also Bessarabia, from the Soviet Union, and eastern Banat, from Austria-Hungary, which had a large Magyar (Hungarian) population.

In the postwar period the government remained conservative and authoritarian. In the 1930s the world economic depression brought financial hardship to the Romanians and especially to the peasantry. Dissatisfaction was expressed politically and the Romanian Communist Party and the strongly pro-German fascist Iron Guard grew in strength.

Dictatorship. In 1938 several factors, including a mounting agricultural crisis and a need to control the power of the Iron Guard in the face of increasing pressure from Nazi Germany, led King Carol II to establish a royal dictatorship. Nonetheless, in 1940 Germany and Italy forced King Carol to cede Transylvania to Hungary and southern Dobruja to Bulgaria in an agreement known as the Vienna Award. The Romanians were outraged and the king was forced to abdicate.

Carol was succeeded by his son Michael, and the government was taken over by Gen. Ion Antonescu, the former prime minister under Carol, who had strong Iron Guard leanings and who continued to maintain a dictatorship.

During World War II Romania was occupied by the Germans and participated in Germany's campaign against the Soviet Union. In August 1944 King Michael overthrew Antonescu's dictatorship and entered the war on the side of the Allies. Romania restored Bessarabia and Bukovina to the Soviet Union, which in turn nullified the Vienna Award.

Communist Rule. Following World War II, despite the presence of an Allied Control Council in the country, the Soviet Union managed to take control of Romania. King Michael abdicated in December 1947 and Romania was proclaimed a People's Republic. By 1952 nationalist communist leaders had been replaced by pro-Soviet Romanian communists.

A constitution modeled after that of the Soviet Union was adopted, and Georghe Georghiu-Dej, the first secretary of the Communist party, became president of the State Council. Under the communist regime agriculture was collectivized and forced industrialization took place. Georghiu-Dej died in 1965 and was succeeded as first secretary by Nicholai Ceausescu.

In the mid-1960s Romania began to take an international position that was increasingly independent from that of the Soviet Union. The government refused to cooperate fully with the Soviet-dominated Council of Mutual Economic Assistance (COMECON), and Romania increased its trade with Western Europe.

Romania also proclaimed its intention to pursue its own industrialization policies, abolished Russian as a required language in the schools, and revived many national traditions. In 1967 Ceausescu also became the head of state.

—Robert J. Byrnes; George Kish

RWANDA

Official name: Republic of Rwanda
Area: 10,169 square miles
Population: (1967 est.) 3,306,000
Capital: Kigali (Pop., 1959, urban area, 4,273)
Language: Kinyarwanda, French
Religion: Roman Catholicism, traditional religions
Currency unit: Franc
National holiday: Independence day, July 1

Rwanda, a landlocked republic in eastern Africa, is bordered on the north by Uganda, on the east by Tanzania, on the south by Burundi, and on the west by the Congo (Kinshasa). Rwanda was joined with present-day Burundi as Ruanda-Urundi until 1962, when it received its independence from Belgium.

THE LAND. Rwanda is composed mainly of hills and uplands. A continuous chain of mountains with elevations above 6,500 feet runs along Rwanda's western border. An eroded plateau slopes eastward from the mountains. In the north there are active volcanoes in the Virunga Mountains, which reach an elevation of over 14,700 feet. The Kagera River drains Rwanda's plateau. Lake Kivu is in western Rwanda.

There are two wet and two dry seasons each year. In most places between 40 and 60 inches of rain falls during the wet seasons.

THE PEOPLE. There are three ethnic groups in Rwanda—the Hutu, the Tusi ("Watusi"), and the Twa. About 86 percent of the people are Hutu, 13 percent are Tusi, and about 1 percent are Twa. Until recently the Hutu, traditionally farmers, were dominated by the Tusi under a feudal system. The Twa people, pygmy forest-dwellers, are probably descendants of Rwanda's original inhabitants.

Rwanda had a population density of over 300 persons per square mile in 1965, and population pressure on

the land is great. The rate of population growth is high, 3.1 percent a year between 1958 and 1965.

There are few towns or cities in the country, and the largest urban center is Kigali, the capital.

ECONOMY. Rwanda's economy is based on agriculture. The basic food crops are beans, corn, and sweet potatoes, and the basic cash crop is coffee. Cattle are numerous and are a symbol of both wealth and social position.

Soil erosion and drought are constant problems throughout the country. Belgium instituted a ten-year economic development plan in 1952, and new drought-resistant crops were introduced.

Although Rwanda has deposits of cassiterite, tungsten, and other minerals, the country's resources have not been fully developed, and there is little industry.

In 1965 exports earned about $13.6 million and imports cost about $18 million. Rwanda's main exports are coffee, tin, and tungsten. Imports include foodstuffs, textiles, machinery, chemicals, and petroleum products. Most trade is conducted with Belgium, Luxembourg, the United States, Uganda, and West Germany.

GOVERNMENT. Rwanda has a presidential system of government. Executive power is held by a president, who is popularly elected to a four-year term. The president is assisted by a council of ministers, equivalent to a cabinet. Legislative power is held by the 47-member National Assembly. Assembly members are popularly elected to four-year terms.

Rwanda is a member of the United Nations and the Organization of African Unity.

HISTORY. The Tusi people, who probably came from Ethiopia, invaded Rwanda in the 1500s. They established themselves as a ruling aristocracy, headed by a mwami, or king, over the agricultural Hutu people of the region.

In 1894 the first European, Graf von Goetzen, a German, reached the kingdom, and in 1899 Germany established a protectorate over the region. Germany administered the area as part of German East Africa until World War I. After the war the former protectorate became a mandate of Belgium under the League of Nations. Belgium administered the region jointly with present-day Burundi as Ruanda-Urundi. In 1946 the area became a UN trust territory.

Belgium permitted little African political activity and until the 1950s supported traditional Tusi rule over the Hutu majority. At that time Africans organized political parties along ethnic lines, and the Party of the Hutu Emancipation Movement (PARMEHUTU), composed mainly of Hutu people, opposed the Tusi-dominated National Rwandan Union (UNAR). Tension between the Hutu and the Tusi led to civil war in 1959. The Hutu ended Tusi dominance, and large numbers of Tusi fled to neighboring countries.

In elections held in 1961 PARMEHUTU won an overwhelming victory. The Belgium trusteeship was ended on June 28, 1962, and Rwanda was declared an independent republic on

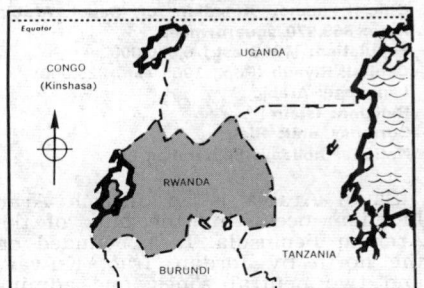

July 1, 1962. Grégoire Kayibanda of PARMEHUTU became president.

Kayibanda initiated a policy of reconciliation and appointed Tusi ministers to his cabinet. But in 1963 fighting again broke out between Tusi and Hutu. Many Tusi were massacred, and many fled the country. Kayibanda was reelected in 1965.

—Hibberd V. B. Kline, Jr.;
Vera L. Zolberg

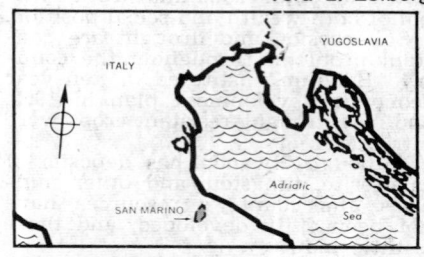

SAN MARINO

Official name: Republic of San Marino
Area: 23.6 square miles
Population: (1966 est.) 18,000
Capital: San Marino (Pop. est., urban area, 3,817)
Language: Italian
Religion: Roman Catholicism
Currency unit: Italian lira
National holiday: Anniversary of the foundation of San Marino, September 3

San Marino is a tiny republic in the north of the Italian Peninsula and is entirely surrounded by Italy.
THE LAND. San Marino consists almost entirely of one mountain, the three-peaked Mt. Titano, which rises over 2,700 feet. Several rivers rush down the mountain. The most important rivers are the Fumicello and the San Marino.

San Marino's climate is mild, with rather cold winters and warm summers. Rainfall is moderate.
THE PEOPLE. Almost all of San Marino's population is of Italian descent. Roman Catholicism is the religion of all but a few, and the people speak Italian.

Most of the population is concentrated in 12 towns lying around the base and on the peaks of Mt. Titano. The largest town, Borg Maggiore, is on one peak of the mountain. The capital, San Marino, is on the highest peak.
ECONOMY. San Marino is a moderately prosperous country. Its chief natural resources are building stone, which is quarried, farm and pasture land, and magnificent scenery, which attracts many tourists.

Farming is the main occupation. Grapes and wheat are the leading crops, and dairying is important. San Marino's industries produce textiles, paper, leather goods, pottery, bricks, cement, wine, and candy. Tourism and the sale of postage stamps contribute heavily to the country's income. San Marino has a customs union with Italy and uses Italian currency.

San Marino's international trade is modest, and is almost entirely with Italy. It exports building materials, foodstuffs, wine, and hides, and imports manufactured consumer items.

GOVERNMENT. San Marino is a republic. Legislative power is vested in a 60-member assembly, the Grand and General Council, which is popularly elected every five years.

Twice yearly the council appoints from among its members two regents who, with the Council of State, or cabinet, wield executive power. San Marino is represented diplomatically abroad by Italy.
HISTORY. According to tradition, San Marino was founded in the 300s AD by Marinus, a Christian stonemason from Dalmatia who was fleeing from religious persecution. Marinus is said to have been later made a saint, San Marino. The earliest document definitely establishing San Marino's existence as an independent commune, however, is dated 885. San Marino was apparently self-governing at that time.

San Marino's rugged terrain and its political and economic insignificance protected it from destruction by medieval invaders of Italy and helped to keep it generally aloof from violent political and religious feuds that disrupted Italy during the 1200s and 1300s.

In the 1400s and 1500s San Marino avoided incorporation into the Papal States and was able to expand its territory somewhat. In the 1500s it was controlled for a brief period by the powerful Italian Borgia family, but in 1549 Pope Paul III proclaimed its sovereignty.

When Napoleon I of France conquered Italy in the late 1700s, he spared the tiny republic. When the many states of Italy were united in 1861, San Marino did not join the new nation. In 1862 it entered a customs union with Italy, and in 1879 San Marino and Italy signed a treaty of friendship.

San Marino entered World War I as an ally of Italy, and in the 1930s, when Benito Mussolini led the fascist government of Italy, San Marino adopted a fascist form of government. In World War II, it proclaimed its neutrality and was a haven for refugees, but it was bombed by Allied planes and suffered damage from ground fighting.

After the war, in the late 1940s, a communist-socialist coalition government was elected and held power until 1957, when the more conservative Christian Democratic party took control. Elections held in 1964 gave the Christian Democrats a majority in the assembly.

—Charles Nowell

SAUDI ARABIA

Official name: Kingdom of Saudi Arabia
Area: 869,970 square miles
Population: (1966 est.) 6,870,000
Capital: Riyadh (Pop., 1965 est., 225,000)
Language: Arabic
Religion: Islam
Currency unit: Rial
National holiday: September 23

Saudi Arabia is an oil-rich Arab kingdom occupying the bulk of the Arabian Peninsula. It is bounded on the north by Jordan, Iraq, Kuwait, and two neutral zones, one admin-

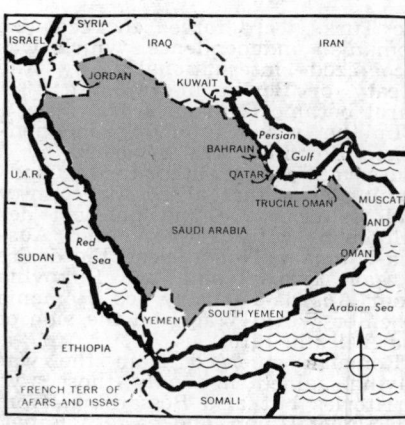

istered jointly with Iraq and one shared with Kuwait. It is bordered on the east by the Persian (or Arabian) Gulf, Trucial Oman, and Muscat and Oman; on the south by Muscat and Oman, South Yemen, and Yemen; and on the west by Yemen and the Red Sea. Many of the boundaries are not demarcated.
THE LAND. Most of the surface of Saudi Arabia is barren. A narrow, infertile plain, the Tihama, lies along the western coast. To its east the Hejaz mountains, in the north, and the Asir mountains, in the south, rise sharply to 11,000 feet. These treeless, sandstone and lava mountains slope into an interior plateau, which consists of two desert regions—An Nafud, in the north, and the Rub al-Khali, in the south.

The interior plain occupies about 90 percent of the country's area and is largely uninhabited. Along Saudi Arabia's eastern border rolling coastal plains slope into the Persian Gulf.

Saudi Arabia has no rivers—only wadis, dry river beds where rainfall may collect. Underground water is tapped by wells.

The climate is hot and dry. Summer daytime temperatures often climb to over 125°F in most of the country, but nights, especially in the desert, can be quite cold. In the mountains and along the eastern coast the average year-round temperature is more moderate, 80°F. Rainfall is rare, and the deserts may go for years without any rain.
THE PEOPLE. Almost all Saudi Arabians are Arabic-speaking Muslims. Population is clustered around its few oases, watered by underground springs, where such large towns as Mecca, Jidda, Riyadh, Hofuf, and Medina developed.

Nomadic Bedouin tribesmen have long roamed the deserts. Government programs have been directed toward settling the nomads in areas where irrigation can make sedentary life possible.
ECONOMY. Saudi Arabia's wealth is based on oil. Oil is the country's most important natural resource, and oil production is the major industry. Oil operations are centered in the eastern part of the country. The principal refinery is on the east coast, at Ras Tanura. Saudi Arabia produced 7 percent of the world's oil in 1967 and is believed to have 10 percent of the world's oil reserves.

Income from fees, taxes, and royalties paid by the foreign companies that hold exploitation rights exceeded $800 million in 1967. Oil revenues are used to provide free education and health care for Saudi Arabians, government expenses, and domestic improvements including industrialization and agricultural expansion and modernization.

Most of the people of the country live as farmers or herders. The country's only major crops are grains, citrus fruits, and dates, which are grown in oases. Sheep, goats, and camels graze in the deserts. There is some pearl diving and fishing along the coasts. Money spent in the country by Muslim pilgrims to the holy cities of Mecca and Medina is the second most important source of Saudi Arabia's income.

Saudi Arabia's prosperous international trade is based on oil. In 1963-1964 imports cost $282 million and exports earned $1,175 million. Oil is the main export. Foodstuffs, building materials, textiles and clothing, machinery, and chemicals are imported. Saudi Arabia sells oil throughout the world, but Japan is the largest single customer. The United States, Western European countries, and other Middle Eastern states are the kingdom's main sources of imports.

GOVERNMENT. Saudi Arabia is an absolute monarchy with a king who serves as political and religious leader of the country. The king appoints a cabinet and an assembly, but he may overrule them. Saudi Arabia is a member of the United Nations and the Arab League.

HISTORY. Saudi Arabia became a nation in 1926, but Arabia has been inhabited since ancient times by Arab herdsmen and traders and was the site of several ancient kingdoms. Muhammad, the prophet, was born in the trading city of Mecca in 570 AD, and the city became an important center of the Muslim religion.

During the century following Muhammad's death in 632 Muslim armies conquered North Africa and the entire Middle East and Muslim power extended into Spain. Religious disputes and competition for power soon brought disorder to Arabia, however. It was divided into two major sheikhdoms—Nejd in the interior of the peninsula and the Hejaz in the west—and many petty states.

Parts of Saudi Arabia were conquered in the 1200s by the Egyptians and in the 1500s by the Ottoman Turks. The conquerors were most interested in the Hejaz, because of the importance of controlling the Muslim holy city of Mecca, its capital.

Wahhabis. In Nejd in the 1700s a Muslim sect whose goal was to reform and purify Islam was founded by Muhammad Ibn Abd al-Wahhab. His followers, the Wahhabis, allied with Muhammad ibn Saud, a ruler of part of Nejd.

Saud's successors carried Wahhabism to the Persian Gulf and by 1806 had conquered the Hejaz from the Sharifs, the rulers of Mecca who controlled the Hejaz. But Saud's Wahhabis were driven back into the interior of Nejd by Turkish and Egyptian

SAUDI ARABIAN PUBLIC RELATIONS BUREAU

SAUDI. ARABIA'S PROPHET'S MOSQUE, a Muslim shrine, is in the city of Medina.

troops. In Nejd they lost power to the rival sheikhdom of al-Rashid.

Nearly 100 years later, in 1902, Saud's descendant, Abd al-Aziz Al Saud, conquered Nejd's capital, Riyadh, from the Rashids. By 1913 he had defeated the Rashids and had driven the Ottomans from most of central Arabia.

In 1916 Saud's rival for power, Sharif Hussein of Mecca, led a pan-Arab revolt against the Turks that carried his sons to the thrones of the new Arab states of Iraq and Transjordan (present-day Jordan). After World War I uneasy relations between the Husseins and the Saudis led to warfare in 1924. The Saudis captured the Hejaz and forced out the Husseins.

In 1926 Abd al-Aziz united Nejd and the Hejaz and two small dependencies, Asir and Hasa, into a Wahhabist state. He proclaimed himself king of the entire region, which he named Saudi Arabia in 1932.

Modern Saudi Arabia. Under Abd al-Aziz the modernization of Arabia began, and the discovery of oil in 1938 greatly speeded up the process by providing a source of income for the government. Large-scale oil production began in 1945, after World War II. Oil revenues made possible social changes which promised to affect radically Saudi Arabian life, but the country maintained internal political and social stability.

Abd al-Aziz' son, Saud, succeeded him as king in 1953, but in 1964 he was replaced by his half-brother, Faisal.

The United Arab Repubiic (U.A.R.), led by Gamal Abdel Nasser, favored rapid, radical social reform in the Arab states, and thus came into conflict with the traditionalist, conservative royal House of Saud. The U.A.R. and Saudi Arabia became the principal rivals for the leadership of the Arab world. In 1966 King Faisal formed the Islamic Alliance with the leaders of Jordan and Iran to counter the U.A.R.'s influence. In a civil war that erupted in Yemen in 1962, Saudi

Arabia and the U.A.R. supported and supplied opposing factions, but Nasser and Faisal agreed in 1967 to withdraw their aid and support from the contending Yemen factions.

Saudi Arabia did unite with its Arab rivals in opposing the state of Israel, however. Faisal supported President Nasser's blockade of the Gulf of Aqaba in 1967 but did not participate directly in the resulting Arab-Israeli war.

—Charles Issawi; Alexander Melamid

SENEGAL

Official name: Republic of Senegal
Area: 75,750 square miles
Population: (1966 est.) 3,580,000
Capital: Dakar (Pop., 1961 est., urban area, 374,700)
Language: French, African languages
Religion: Islam, Christianity, traditional religions
Currency unit: Franc CFA (African Financial Community)
National holiday: Independence day, April 4

Senegal, a republic in western Africa, is bordered on the north by Mauritania, on the east by Mali, on the south by the Republic of Guinea and Portuguese Guinea, and on the west by the Atlantic Ocean. The Gambia, a small, independent nation, forms an enclave in Senegal, stretching inland from the Atlantic coast. Senegal proclaimed its independence from France in 1960.

THE LAND. Senegal is occupied mostly by lowlands with elevations below 650 feet, and sandy plains are typical of most parts of the country. Senegal lies largely in Africa's Sahelian zone, a region of sparse grass and spiny trees.

There are plateaus in the southeast with elevations up to about 1,640 feet, and swamps and tropical rain forests in the southwest. The Cape Vert Peninsula, Senegal's westernmost point, protrudes into the Atlantic Ocean.

Four major rivers flow through the country—the Sénégal in the north, the Gambia and Saloum in central Senegal, and the Casamance in the south.

Temperatures are moderate in most parts of the country. Some regions in southern Senegal receive as much as 60 inches of rain each year. The peninsula receives about 24 inches a year.

THE PEOPLE. There are many tribal groups in Senegal. The largest groups are the Wolof; the Fula, or Peul; the Serer; the Mandingo; and the Tukulor. Most of the people are Muslims. There is a small number of non-Africans, who are mainly Europeans, Syrians, and Lebanese.

Dakar, located on the peninsula, is Senegal's largest city. Other large cities are Kaolack, Saint Louis, and Thiès.

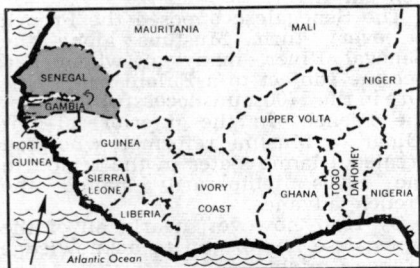

ECONOMY. The economy of Senegal is based on agriculture. The basic food crops are millet, sorghum, and rice. Peanuts are the main commercial crop, and in 1965 over 1.1 million metric tons of peanuts were produced. Fishing is also important in the Senegalese economy.

Senegal has rich phosphate deposits, and in 1965 over 1 million metric tons of phosphate were produced. Industry is centered in Dakar and is well developed. Peanuts, phosphates, and fish are processed for export.

In 1966 imports cost $161 million and exports earned $149 million. The main imports are textiles, machinery, and foodstuffs. The leading exports are peanuts, peanut oil, and phosphates. Most trade is conducted with France, Cambodia, West Germany, and the United States. Senegal receives economic aid from France.

GOVERNMENT. Senegal has a presidential system of government. Executive power is held by a president, who is popularly elected to a four-year term. Legislative power is held by an 80-member National Assembly. Assembly members are also popularly elected to four-year terms.

Senegal is a member of the United Nations and the Organization of African Unity.

HISTORY. Between about the 400s and 200s BC the peoples of what is now Senegal traded by sea with the Carthaginians. During the next millennium they traded with the merchants of ancient Ghana and Mali.

Portuguese sailors visited the shores of Senegal during the 1400s, and beginning in the 1500s French, Dutch, and British merchants came to the region. In the late 1600s the French established settlements at Saint Louis and on Gorée Island, near the Cape Vert Peninsula.

Under a succession of energetic colonial governors, the French tried to transform Senegal into a profitable outpost of their empire. But few Frenchmen could be induced to settle there, and wars with Britain over control of the area were costly. Britain conquered Senegal in the 1750s and administered the area in union with the Gambia as the Crown Colony of Senegambia.

French Rule. By the 1800s France had gradually reestablished its control over most of the country. Only at that time did the French alter the indigenous way of life. From 1854 to 1865, under the aggressive governor Louis Léon César Faidherbe, the French subjugated the people living between Saint Louis and Gorée Island, and successfully asserted their authority over the peoples living on both banks of the Sénégal River.

The Senegalese opposed the French at every turn. Muslims along the Sénégal River, many of whom had become subject to a Fulani-ruled empire in the 1700s, unsuccessfully fought the French. In the interior, al-hajj 'Umar, a Muslim reformer who had created Islamic states in the region in the 1800s, temporarily halted the French advance.

By 1890, however, nearly all of the Senegalese had begun to acknowledge France's might.

In 1904 Dakar became the capital of French West Africa. The more important schools and hospitals of French West Africa were located there, and Senegal's coastal region became the most westernized part of French West Africa.

In 1946 Senegal became a territory within the French Union. In elections held in 1951 and 1957 Léopold Senghor, a French-educated poet, led the Senegalese Progressive Union to victory. In 1958 Senegal became an autonomous member of the French Community.

Independence. In 1959 France joined Senegal with present-day Mali to form the Mali Federation, which became an autonomous member of the French Community in June 1960. On Aug. 20, 1960 Senegal withdrew from the federation and proclaimed its independence. Senghor became Senegal's first president, governing the country together with the prime minister, Mamadou Dia.

In 1962, after an unsuccessful attempt by the prime minister to overthrow Senghor, the country adopted a new constitution providing for a strong presidential system of government. In 1963 relations with Mali were normalized.

—Hibberd V. B. Kline, Jr.; Robert I. Rotberg

SIERRA LEONE

Official name: Sierra Leone
Area: 27,699 square miles
Population: (1967 est.) 2,439,000
Capital: Freetown (Pop., 1966 est., 148,000)
Language: English, African languages
Religion: Islam, Christianity, traditional religions
Currency: Leone
National holiday: Independence day, April 27

Sierra Leone, a republic in western Africa, is bordered on the north by Guinea, on the east by Liberia, and on the south and west by the Atlantic Ocean. Sierra Leone received its independence from Britain in 1961.

THE LAND. Sierra Leone has a varied landscape. In the northwest a mountainous peninsula extends into the Atlantic Ocean. Inland from the peninsula and in other places along the coast there are swampy plains. Further inland the plains rise to plateaus.

There are forests and grasslands in the north and east. In the northeast are the Loma Mountains, with a peak elevation of over 6,390 feet. Many rivers flow through the country, including the Rokel and the Moa.

Sierra Leone has a tropical climate, and the peninsula is one of the rainiest parts of western Africa, receiving about 145 inches of rain each year.

THE PEOPLE. There are some 20 tribal groups in Sierra Leone, the largest of which are the Mende and the Temne. The Mende live mainly in the south and the Temne live in the north. There are also several thousand Creoles, descendants of freed slaves who came to Sierra Leone in the 1700s and 1800s.

The Creoles live mainly in and near Freetown, the country's capital and largest city. Bo, Kenema, and Makeni are also major urban centers.

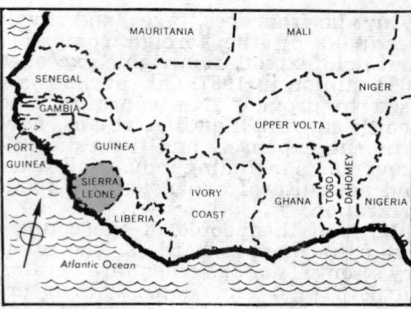

ECONOMY. The economy of Sierra Leone is based on agriculture. The basic food crops are rice and cassava. Palm kernels, cacao, kola nuts, ginger, and coffee are important commercial crops. Fishing is also an important source of income for the people along the coast.

Sierra Leone has rich mineral resources, and the country is one of the world's major producers of diamonds, which are dug from river gravels. Iron ore, another important export, is shipped from the port of Pepel, near Freetown. There are also deposits of chromium ore and bauxite, from which aluminum is made.

In 1966 imports cost $100 million and exports earned $83 million. The principal imports are foodstuffs, petroleum products, textiles, and machinery. The major exports are diamonds, iron ore, and coffee. Most trade is conducted with Britain, the Netherlands, West Germany, and Japan.

GOVERNMENT. Sierra Leone's 1961 independence constitution provided for a parliamentary system of government with the British queen as head of state, represented by a governor-general. Actual executive power was vested in a prime minister responsible to the legislature.

Legislative power was held by the House of Representatives, which consisted of 62 popularly elected members and 12 paramount chiefs chosen by the tribal chiefs. All legislators were elected to five-year terms.

In March 1967 the military seized control of the government, and an eight-man National Reformation Council assumed executive and legislative powers.

Sierra Leone is a member of the United Nations, the Commonwealth of Nations, and the Organization of African Unity.

HISTORY. The Portuguese explorer Pedro da Cintra visited Sierra Leone in 1462 and gave the area its name, which means Lion Mountain. The course of Sierra Leone's modern history was affected by the proclamation in 1772 by Britain's Lord Chief Justice William Mansfield that slavery was never acknowledged by law; consequently, slaves held in England were set free.

In London and in other British cities freed slaves found it difficult to obtain employment, and they constituted a source of embarrassment to the British government. The government gave its support to a plan of a private company, the Society for the Abolition of Slavery, to ship the freed slaves to Africa.

In 1788 the first shipload of freed slaves settled in present-day Sierra Leone. First by purchase and later by force, they acquired land and built villages near what later became Freetown. In 1791 the Sierra Leone Company began administering the settlement. New groups of freed slaves came to Sierra Leone from Nova Scotia and Jamaica.

British Rule. In 1808 the coastal area became a British crown colony. The colony grew in wealth and importance, new settlements were made along the coast, and the settlers began to increase their trade contacts with the tribes of the interior. The settlers also took more and more tribal land. In the early 1800s the number of settlers was increased by the addition of slaves freed at sea by a British patrol stationed in Freetown.

In 1896, in a move to prevent French territorial expansion, the British government established a protectorate over the interior. The two regions—the colony and the protectorate—were administered separately until 1924. British administrative policy during the 1930s and 1940s helped to integrate the peoples of the protectorate with those of the colony. It also worked to eliminate the antagonism between the descendants of the settlers, the Creoles, and the Africans of the interior.

At first the peoples of the coast felt superior because of their higher educational attainments, but the growth of indigenous political movements reversed this. In 1951 Milton Margai, a Mende physician from the protectorate, led the Sierra Leone People's Party to an important electoral victory over the combined opposition of the parties loyal to two Creoles, Dr. H. C. Bankole-Bright and I. T. A. Wallace-Johnson.

Independence. Margai strengthened his position in elections in 1957, and when Sierra Leone became independent on Apr. 27, 1961, he became the first prime minister. Milton Margai

died in 1964, and his half-brother, Albert Margai, who had been finance minister, became prime minister.

In March 1967 elections were held for the House of Representatives in the midst of criticism caused by Albert Margai's attempts to establish a one-party state. The elections were contested by two main parties—Margai's Sierra Leone People's Party and the All People's Congress led by Siaka Stevens.

On the basis of early election returns, the governor-general appointed Stevens prime minister. Disturbances broke out almost immediately. The military seized control of the government and established a National Reformation Council headed by Lt. Col. Andrew Juxon-Smith to run the country.　—Hibberd V. B. Kline, Jr.; Robert I. Rotberg

SIKKIM

Official name: Sikkim
Area: 2,744 square miles
Population: (1966 est.) 180,000
Capital: Gangtok (Pop., 1961 est., 6,848)
Language: Lepcha, Nepali, English
Religion: Buddhism, Hinduism
Currency: Indian rupee

Sikkim is a small principality in South Asia lying high in the Himalayas. It is a protectorate of India. Sikkim is bordered on the north by the Tibet region of China, on the east by Bhutan, on the south by India, and on the west by Nepal. The small country lies astride important routes over the Himalayas connecting Tibet and India.

THE LAND. Sikkim is a mountainous country. The Singalila Range rises on its western border, and the Chola Range rises on the east. Between these border mountains there is a succession of ranges and valleys generally trending north to south.

Elevation increases toward the north, with the highest peak, Kanchenjunga, rising to 28,168 feet in the northwestern corner of the country. At least three other peaks are known to be over 20,000 feet. The Natu La and the Jelip La over the Chola Range are important passes to and from Tibet. The Tista River flows south from the Himalayas across Sikkim.

Sikkim's climate varies with elevation. In the lower regions of the south, temperatures are subtropical; in the central valleys and plateaus, they are moderate; and in the high regions of the north, they are arctic. The line of perpetual snow is reached at about 17,000 feet. Precipitation is abundant, with an annual average of 137 inches of rainfall at Gangtok, the capital, in the center of the country.

THE PEOPLE. Sikkim's population consists of three main elements—Nepalese, Bhotias, and Lepcha. The Nepalese, who constitute a majority, are concentrated in the higher altitudes. The Bhotias, of Tibetan extraction, live mainly in the central plateaus. The Lepcha, believed to be Sikkim's earliest inhabitants, are found in the lower valleys.

The Nepalese are Hindu, but although they are in the majority,

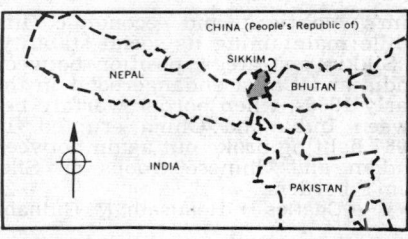

Lamaist Buddhism, the religion of the Bhotia and the Lepcha, is the official religion.

ECONOMY. Farming and herding are the major occupations in Sikkim. Livestock is grazed on summer pastures on the plateaus at elevations of between 12,000 and 15,000 feet. Corn, millet, fruit, legumes, and potatoes are raised on terraced fields near the center of the country at elevations of from 4,500 to 6,500 feet. At lower elevations in the southern valleys rice is grown wherever irrigation is possible.

There is no modern industry in the country. Cottage industries produce items such as clothing and household utensils and supply most of the peoples' requirements. There is some trade across the Indian border exchanging manufactured items for potatoes, fruit, and various other agricultural products.

In the 1960s, with aid from India, Sikkim began to improve its transportation system and to modernize its economy.

GOVERNMENT. Sikkim, a protectorate of India, is ruled by a hereditary maharajah with the advice of an Indian official. Also advising the maharajah is a state council. Two-thirds of the council members are elected, with representation divided proportionally among Sikkim's three ethnic groups. India is responsible for Sikkim's foreign affairs, defense, and communications.

HISTORY. Sikkim has been inhabited for many centuries, but little is known of its early history. It was long used as a trade route between India and Tibet, and because of its strategic position it has been ruled by Nepal, Tibet, and China. Its Lepcha people became Buddhists in the 1500s, and its ruling dynasty was founded in the 1600s.

Britain extended its influence from India into Sikkim in the 1800s, during wars against Nepal and Tibet. In 1890 Britain made Sikkim a protectorate, and responsibility passed to India in 1947, when India became independent. A treaty signed in 1950 reaffirmed Sikkim's status as a protectorate.

The British encouraged Nepalese to settle in Sikkim, and by the mid-1900s the Nepalese were in the majority. Their demands for a larger share in the government of the country became Sikkim's major political problem. They were granted a majority of the seats on the advisory council in 1960 and their voting rights were expanded in 1961.

Maharajah Gyalsay Palden Thondup Namgyal, who had married an American, came to the throne in 1963. He concentrated on modernizing Sik-

UNITED NATIONS

SIERRA LEONE WORKERS panning for alluvial diamonds along a river bank.

kim's political and economic life while maintaining its social stability.

Sikkim's strategic position between India and China endangered it in the early 1960s, when border warfare between India and China erupted. In 1967 fighting broke out again between Indian and Chinese troops on Sikkim's borders.

—Charles H. Heimsath; M. G. Inaba

SINGAPORE

Official name: Republic of Singapore
Area: 224 square miles
Population: (1967 est.) 1,956,000
Capital: Singapore (Pop., 1967 est., 1,956,-000)
Language: Malay, Chinese, Tamil, English
Religion: Islam, Christianity, Buddhism, Hinduism
Currency unit: Dollar
National holiday: August 9

Singapore is a small island republic lying off the southern tip of the Malay Peninsula in Southeast Asia. It became a sovereign state in 1965 after two years as part of the nation of Malaysia. Before joining Malaysia, it had been a British possession for some 150 years.

Singapore is separated from West Malaysia on the north, east, and west by the narrow Johore Strait. To the south, the Riao Islands of Indonesia lie across the Singapore Strait.

THE LAND. The nation of Singapore consists of the large island of Singapore and some 40 low-lying islets within 10 miles of its eastern and southern shores. On Singapore Island, a coastal plain surrounds a central plateau that has a peak of 581 feet. Once swampland and jungle, most of the island has been cleared for farming and building.

Singapore's climate is hot and humid. The average year-round temperature is about 81°F and an average of 96 inches of rain falls each year.

THE PEOPLE. Singapore is very densely populated, with over 7,500 persons per square mile in 1965, and the rate of population growth is high, 3 percent a year between 1958 and 1966. Approximately two-thirds of the people live in the capital and largest city, Singapore, on the southern coast of Singapore Island.

The people are of many backgrounds. About three-quarters of Singapore's people are of Chinese descent. Malays and Indonesians make up some 14 percent, about 8 percent are of Indian and Pakistani origins, and there are small groups of Europeans and people of mixed ethnic backgrounds.

Malay is the national language, and Malay, Chinese, English, and Tamil, an Indian language, are official languages. Many Chinese adhere to Confucianism, Taoism, and Buddhism. Most of the Malays and Pakistanis are Muslim, the Indians are largely Hindu and Sikh, and there are many Christians.

ECONOMY. Singapore's prosperity is based on its location on important sea routes between the Indian Ocean, the South China Sea, and the Pacific, and on its large, industrious popula-

tion. Singapore is the commercial and financial center of Southeast Asia, and a large share of the region's trade passes through its large, excellent harbor.

There is little agricultural land, but in the 1960s the government initiated agricultural development programs and reclamation projects to create new farmland. Rubber is the chief crop, and coconuts, vegetables, fruits, and tobacco are raised. Dairying is important, and pigs and chickens are raised for domestic use and export.

Industry. Singapore's industry traditionally has been based on processing Southeast Asia's natural products, especially tin, rubber, spices, copra, coffee, and timber. These industries still prospered in the 1960s, as did Singapore's important shipyards.

In the 1960s the government encouraged the development of new industries to broaden the base of the economy. Hydroelectric power stations, iron and steel mills, an oil refinery, chemical plants, textile mills, clothing factories, and dairy processing plants were among the new facilities opened in the 1960s. Many of them are located in a large industrial park at Jurong, west of Singapore city.

Trade. Commerce, especially transshipment trade, remained the major factor in Singapore's economy, however, as the country processed Asian goods for export and distributed imports to Asian market centers.

In 1966 Singapore's imports were valued at $1,328 million, and its exports were valued at $1,102 million. Over half of the totals were transshipped goods. Rubber, petroleum products, tin, wood products, spices, and some finished goods are exported. Machinery and vehicles, foodstuffs, and finished consumer goods are the main imports.

Malaysia, Indonesia, Japan, Britain, the United States, and Communist China are Singapore's principal trading partners.

GOVERNMENT. Singapore is a republic with a parliamentary system of government. The head of state is the president, who is chosen by a popularly elected legislature, or parliament. Executive powers are exercised by a cabinet, headed by a prime minister, responsible to the parliament. The parliament has one house with 51 members elected under a system of compulsory universal suffrage.

Singapore is a member of the United Nations and the Commonwealth of Nations.

HISTORY. Singapore had become an important commercial center by the 1100s AD. In 1377 Singapore city was

destroyed by Java, and it lost its trading importance. In 1819 Sir Stamford Raffles, an agent of the British East India Company, established a trading post on the island. Commerce flourished, and in 1824 the British bought Singapore and the adjacent islands.

British Rule. In 1826 Britain established the "Straits Settlements," combining Singapore with two former rival trading centers, Malacca and Penang. In 1867, as their prosperity and importance increased, the settlements were raised to the status of a crown colony.

The opening of the Suez Canal in 1869 and the development of steamships increased Europe's trade with the Far East, and further bolstered Singapore's prosperity. In the late 1800s profitable tin smelting and rubber processing were added to the island's trading activities.

In the 1920s the British established a major naval base at Singapore, and in the 1930s an air base. In 1942, during World War II, Japan captured Singapore and occupied it until the British recaptured it in 1945. In 1946 Singapore was separated from Penang and Malacca and made a separate crown colony.

In the 1950s Singapore moved toward self-government, and in 1959 it was granted full internal autonomy. The major political force in the country became the largely Chinese People's Action Party.

Independence. In 1963 Singapore joined the new nation of Malaysia, formed of Malaya, Sabah (North Borneo), and Sarawak. Singapore's dominant economic position and its Chinese majority led to friction between it and Malaysia's federal government. As a result, in 1965 Singapore reluctantly withdrew from the federation and became a sovereign state.

The nation concentrated on expanding its economy and on maintaining a policy of friendly relations with Malaysia and its other Asian neighbors. In 1967 it joined with Malaysia, Indonesia, Thailand, and the Philippines to form the Association of Southeast Asian Nations (ASEAN), an organization for economic, social, and political cooperation.

—Sara D. Gilbert; M. G. Inaba

SOMALI REPUBLIC

Official name: Somali Republic
Area: 246,201 square miles
Population: (1966 est.) 2,580,000
Capital: Mogadiscio (Pop., 1966 est., 170,000)
Language: Somali
Religion: Islam
Currency unit: Shilling
National holiday: July 1

The Somali Republic, an independent country in eastern Africa, is bordered on the north by the French Territory of the Afars and Issas (French Somaliland) and the Gulf of Aden, on the east by the Indian Ocean, on the south by Kenya, and on the west by Ethiopia. The Somali Republic was formed in July 1960 by a union of the former Italian Somalia Protectorate and British Somaliland.

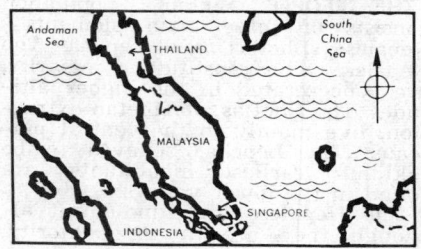

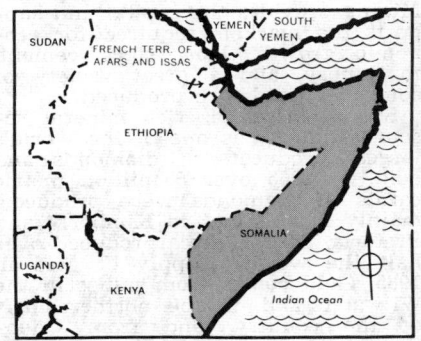

THE LAND. Most of the Somali Republic is occupied by a featureless, high plain. In some places, especially in the north, high limestone cliffs border the plain. Near the eastern coast the plain is sandy, and gives way inland to low hills and ridges.

In the northeastern part of the country, the Somali Peninsula juts into the Indian Ocean. Near the peninsula are the Carcar Mountains, which have an average elevation of 3,000 feet. The country's main rivers are the Giuba (Juba) and the Shabali (Scebeli).

Although the southwestern part of the country receives about 20 inches of rain each year, semiarid and arid conditions prevail in most of the Somali Republic. The northern part of the country receives less than 10 inches of rain each year.

THE PEOPLE. The Somali Republic has a relatively homogeneous population. Most of the inhabitants are Somali, a people of mixed Ethiopian, Arab, and Indian ancestry. Bantu-speaking people live in the southern part of the country.

The Somali Republic's largest city is its capital, Mogadiscio (Mogadishu), which is on the Indian Ocean.

ECONOMY. The Somali Republic's economy is based on herding, and camels, sheep, and goats are raised in most parts of the country.

The basic food crops are corn and sorghum, and the main cash crop is bananas, which are grown mainly on irrigated plantations in the southern part of the country. In 1965, 140,000 metric tons of bananas were produced. Sugarcane and a variety of fruits are also grown.

Although there are small canneries and leather tanneries, industry is poorly developed. The Somali Republic has deposits of iron ore, gypsum, beryl, and columbite, but mineral deposits have not been fully exploited. A five-year plan was begun in 1963 to develop transportation, communications, agriculture, and industry.

In 1965 imports cost about $49.5 million and exports earned about $33.2 million. The main imports are rice, petroleum products, textiles, and machinery. The main exports are bananas, live animals, and hides and skins. Most trade is conducted with Italy, the Soviet Union, and Kenya.

GOVERNMENT. The Somali Republic has a parliamentary system of government. Legislative power rests with the 122-member National Assembly. Assembly members are directly elected under a system of universal adult suffrage to five-year terms. The head of state is the president, who is elected by the assembly to a six-year term. Executive powers are exercised by a prime minister responsible to the legislature.

The Somali Republic is a member of the United Nations and the Organization of African Unity.

HISTORY. In about the 900s the Galla people, who were originally from Ethiopia, migrated into what is now the Somali Republic and pushed the indigenous agricultural Bantu-speaking peoples southward. Between the 1200s and 1300s the Somali peoples displaced the Galla.

Arabs and Persians made settlements on the northern coast between the 800s and 1500s, and helped make Islam the dominant religion. In the early 1800s the sultan of Zanzibar obtained control of the southern part of the country.

The Protectorates. Egyptians occupied the area of the Somali Republic between 1874 and 1885. The Egyptian occupation was ended when Britain established a protectorate over the northern part of the country. Under the terms of agreement made with the sultan of Zanzibar, Italy established the Protectorate of Somalia in the south in 1889.

Between 1900 and 1920 both the British and the Italians fought a rebellion led by a Muslim religious leader, Sayyid Muhammad Abdulla Hassan, whom they called the "Mad Mullah."

In the 1920s and 1930s the fascist government of Italy maintained firm control of the south and encouraged settlement by Italian colonists. Italy used the region as a staging base to attack Ethiopia in 1934. After World War II broke out, Britain took over the administration of the Italian protectorate in 1941.

Postwar politics centered on reuniting the Somali people. Haja Muhammad Hussein, leader of the Somali Youth League (SYL), a nationalist movement he had founded in 1943, called for unification of the two protectorates under a single UN trusteeship.

In 1949, however, the UN General Assembly voted to return southern Somalia to Italy as a trusteeship for a ten-year period so that Italy could prepare the region for independence. In 1956 elections were held in the Italian trust area, and Abdullaha Issa of the SYL became the first prime minister of Somalia.

In 1954 a British-Ethiopian agreement granted the Haud area of Ogaden in the western part of the country to Ethiopia, but the Somali people retained the right to graze their cattle on the land. A legislative council was created in British Somaliland in 1957, and on June 26, 1960 Britain granted the former protectorate its independence.

Independence. On July 1, 1960, after the Italian trusteeship had ended, the Italian and British regions were united to form the Somali Republic. Aden Abdullah Osman was elected president by the parliament, and he appointed Abdi Rashid Shermarke prime minister.

At the time of independence Ethiopia withdrew the rights of the Somali to graze cattle in Ogaden. Both the Somali Republic and Ethiopia claimed the area, and fighting broke out in 1963. Fighting also broke out with Kenya over disputed land.

Members of all political parties united in the Somali National Congress to deal with the territorial claims of the Somali Republic to land in Ethiopia, northern Kenya, and French Somaliland (the present-day French Territory of the Afars and Issas). In 1964 a new government was formed, and Hussein became prime minister.

Border fighting with Kenya broke out again in 1966 and 1967. In July 1967 the National Assembly elected Shermarke president, and he appointed Muhammad Ibrahim Egal prime minister.

—Hibberd V. B. Kline, Jr.;
Vera L. Zolberg

SOUTH AFRICA

Official name: Republic of South Africa
Area: 471,445 square miles
Population: (1967 est.) 18,733,000
Capital: Pretoria (Pop., 1960 est., urban area, 422,600)
Language: English, Afrikaans, Bantu languages
Religion: Protestantism, Roman Catholicism, traditional African religions
Currency: Rand
National holiday: May 31, Republic day

The Republic of South Africa, an independent country in southernmost Africa, is bordered on the north by South West Africa, Botswana, and Rhodesia; on the east by Mozambique, Swaziland, and the Indian Ocean; on the south by the Indian Ocean; and on the west by the Atlantic Ocean. Walvis Bay, located on the Atlantic coast of South West Africa, is a part of South Africa. Lesotho lies completely within the borders of South Africa.

SOUTH AFRICAN RAILWAYS
SOUTH AFRICA'S CAPE TOWN is the country's second largest city and its chief port.

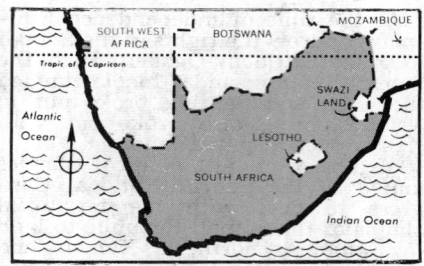

Between 1910 and 1961 South Africa was a union of four provinces—Cape Province in the west, Orange Free State in the central part of the country, Transvaal in the northeast, and Natal in the east. On May 13, 1961 South Africa withdrew from the British Commonwealth because its policy of apartheid, the rigid separation of the races, was unacceptable to other Commonwealth countries. On May 31, 1961 South Africa became a republic.

In 1963 the government established the Transkei, an area near Port Elizabeth in South Africa, as a partially self-governing homeland, or "Bantustan," for Negro Africans.

THE LAND. Most of South Africa is occupied by a plateau, which slopes inward from its rim. The most striking feature of the landscape is the Great Escarpment, which borders the plateau in an almost unbroken line running southward from the northeastern corner of the country, rounding the southern coast, and continuing northward on the western side of the country. The upper edge of the escarpment is over 5,000 feet above sea level.

South Africa's highest point is in the east, where the Drakensberg, a mountainous region, reaches an elevation of over 11,400 feet above sea level.

Between the oceans and the foot of the Great Escarpment is a coastal zone about 100 miles wide. This region consists of greatly eroded, steplike landforms cut by streams and valleys, especially in the wetter, eastern side of the country. In the south these steps give way to long, low mountains known as the Cape Ranges, some of which reach the sea in peninsulas.

Cape Agulhas, the southernmost point of Africa, separates the Atlantic Ocean on its west from the Indian Ocean on its east. The most famous point on the Atlantic coast is the Cape of Good Hope.

Most of the plateau is drained by the Orange River and its principal tributary, the Vaal. Both rivers flow westward from the Great Escarpment. The Augrabies Falls are at the head of a deep canyon leading to the Atlantic Ocean at the point where the Orange River leaves the surface of the plateau. The northern half of the Transvaal is drained by the Limpopo River, which forms the border with Rhodesia.

Climate. Rainfall in South Africa is much heavier on the east coast and on some parts of the Cape Ranges than on the plateau surface. Half of the country receives less than 20 inches of rain a year, and water-supply problems are common, particularly in the west.

The climate is moderate in most parts of the country. Northern and eastern Transvaal are tropically hot, but most of South Africa has cool winters with occasional frost.

THE PEOPLE. The South African population is legally divided into four distinct groups—"Bantu," or Negro; white; "Colored," those of mixed origins; and Asian. In mid-1967 Negro Africans made up 68 percent of the South African population; whites, 19 percent; Coloreds, 10 percent; and Asians, 3 percent.

Most of the Negro Africans are Bantu-speaking peoples. Among the main tribal groups are the Xhosa, Zulu, and Sotho. About two-thirds of the Negro Africans live either on farms owned by whites or on reserves established by the government.

A majority of the whites are Afrikaners, Afrikaans-speaking people descended from Dutch, German, and French Huguenot settlers. Most of the remainder of the whites are of British descent. The Coloreds are descended largely from the indigenous Hottentots, Malays, and white settlers. The Asians are largely of Indian origin.

The major cities of South Africa include Johannesburg, in the Transvaal, a major commercial center and industrial city; Cape Town, in Cape Province, South Africa's legislative capital and major port; Durban, in Natal, the Indian Ocean outlet for the Transvaal and the center of the English-speaking and Indian business communities; Pretoria, in the Transvaal, South Africa's administrative capital and major industrial center; and Port Elizabeth, in Cape Province, an industrial city and port.

ECONOMY. South Africa has the most highly developed industrial economy of any African country. Economic development has been made possible largely by South Africa's rich mineral resources, especially diamonds and gold.

Negro African labor plays an essential part in South Africa's growing economy. Although Negro Africans form the bulk of unskilled labor in industry, agriculture, and mining, they are generally barred from the skilled labor force. The whites are the most economically prosperous group in South Africa. Although Coloreds and Asians are economically better off than the Negro Africans, they are not as prosperous as the whites.

Agriculture. Between 1945 and 1964 over 40 percent of the population was engaged in agricultural occupations. Agriculture employs a considerable proportion of Afrikaners and most Negro Africans. Crop production, however, is restricted by limited rainfall and poor soil in most parts of the country.

The basic food crop of the Negro African population is corn. Fruits, especially citrus and grapes, are the most important commercial crops and are grown mainly in the region inland from Cape Town. Cattle and sheep are raised, and wool and hides are important exports.

Mining and Manufacturing. Manufacturing developed rapidly after World War II, and in 1965 it accounted for 22 percent of the national product.

Mining provides the capital and supports the markets required for economic growth. Iron, steel, cement, machinery, and a great variety of consumer goods are produced.

South Africa has rich mineral resources, and it is one of the world's largest producers of diamonds and gold. In 1965 over 5 million metric carats of diamonds were produced, mainly from mines in Kimberly and Pretoria. South Africa produced over half the world's supply of gold in 1965. Gold comes from mines in the Witwatersrand, in the northern part of the country, and from Odendaalsrus, in central South Africa. Waste materials at the gold mines are reprocessed to yield uranium.

South Africa also has vast resources of coal and iron ore. The shortage of petroleum products is partially relieved by a coal distillation process yielding liquid fuels.

Trade. In 1966 South Africa's imports cost $2,300 million and its exports earned $1,700 million. The leading imports are iron and steel, machinery, petroleum and petroleum products, textiles, plastics, coffee, and tea. The leading exports are diamonds, gold, fruits, and wool.

Most of South Africa's trade is with Britain, the United States, West Germany, and Japan. In 1967 South Africa signed a trade agreement with Malawi, its first with an African country. But its share in the developing African market is jeopardized by its racial policies, which are unacceptable to most African nations and to many other nations.

GOVERNMENT. South Africa is ruled by a white minority. The right to vote is limited to whites over 18 years of age. In Cape Province Coloreds and Asians over 21 years of age with certain educational and income or property qualifications have limited voting rights. In the Transvaal and Orange Free State, Coloreds and Asians cannot vote. Members of parliament must be white.

South Africa has a parliamentary system of government. Nominal executive power is held by a president, who serves as head of state. The president is elected to a seven-year term by an electoral college. Actual executive power is held by a prime minister and cabinet responsible to the legislature.

Legislative power is held by a parliament with two houses—the Senate and the House of Assembly. There are 54 members in the Senate, 43 of whom are elected by an electoral college made up of members of parliament and members of councils in the provinces and in South West Africa. One senator is appointed by the president to watch over the interests of the Coloreds of Cape Province. Ten are appointed by the president to represent the interests of nonwhites. All senators serve five-year terms.

There are 170 members in the House of Assembly, who serve five-year terms. Of these, 160 are elected to represent whites, six to represent South West Africa, and four to represent the Coloreds of Cape Province.

South Africa is a member of the United Nations.

HISTORY. Bantu-speaking peoples from northern Africa came to South Africa in the 1400s or 1500s, destroying or intermarrying with the indigenous Hottentots.

In the 1480s a Portuguese explorer, Bartholomeu Dias, rounded the Cape of Good Hope. But permanent European settlements were not made in South Africa until 1652, when the Dutch East India Company founded Cape Town as a supply base for voyages to the East Indies. The base developed into the Cape Colony, composed of Dutch settlers who supplied food for passing ships. Because cash crops would not grow well in the poor soil, the farmers, called Boers, turned to hunting and cattle raising.

Pushing eastward, the Boers repeatedly clashed with the Bantu-speaking peoples over grazing land, water, and cattle thefts. By the end of the 1700s, Boer pressure on the Bantu-speaking peoples' already crowded land gave rise to a powerful military organization led by Chaka, chief of a Bantu-speaking clan called Zulu. In the early 1800s Zulu forces made widespread destructive attacks on the Europeans and on other African peoples in southern Africa.

British-Boer Conflict. The British seized control of the colony in 1795. They stimulated the economy and extended the government to the frontier. Britain abolished slavery in 1834, and in 1836 it returned to the Bantu-speaking peoples territory captured from them by the Boers.

The Boers, irritated by the liberal racial policies and the new legal institutions of the British, undertook a mass migration to the east known as the Great Trek. During the migration, the Boers destroyed the Zulu forces.

To deny the Boers access to the sea, the British annexed the seaport city of Natal in 1844. The Boers then journeyed to the north and founded the republics of the Transvaal and the Orange Free State, which Britain recognized as independent states in the 1850s.

The discovery of diamonds in 1867 and gold in 1886 in the two republics attracted many English-speaking immigrants. British and Afrikaner businessmen cooperated in Cape Colony, but the discovery of gold only strained relations between Britain and the Transvaal. The Transvaal refused to enter into any political or economic union with Britain's colonies.

In 1895 the Cape Colony's prime minister, Cecil Rhodes, supported the Jameson Raid, an attempt to overthrow the Transvaal's president, Paul Kruger, and install an English-speaking government. The raid turned the political conflict into an ethnic conflict between Afrikaners and Englishmen. In 1899 the dispute erupted into the Boer, or South African, War, which the British won.

By 1902 Britain had conquered the Afrikaner republics, but granted them self-government in 1906. On May 31, 1910 the British colonies of Cape Colony and Natal were united with the former republics to form an independent Union of South Africa. At that time reserves of land were marked off for occupation by the Bantu-speaking peoples.

The Union. During World War I South Africa fought with Britain against Germany. Led by two Afrikaners, Jan Christiaan Smuts and Louis Botha, South African forces captured the German colony of South West Africa. In 1919 Smuts became South Africa's first prime minister.

After World War I a steady price for gold and cheap labor enabled the country to industrialize. Taxes, drought, and overcrowding on government-created reserves had driven many young Negro Africans off the land in search of jobs. Racial segregation was extended into industry, and labor agitation became a punishable crime.

In the 1920s the National Party, formed by conservative Afrikaners, came to power. The party extended racial segregation beyond the industrial color bar. Apartheid legislation came to include residential segregation, prohibitions against individual ownership of land by Negro Africans, restriction of movement, segregated churches, separate and unequal educational facilities, and denial of the vote to Negro Africans.

In 1952 the African National Congress, an African association formed in 1912 to protest racial discrimination, organized boycotts and demonstrations to protest the racial laws. The government retaliated by jailing some 10,000 participants and by enacting a law declaring government critics "subversive."

In 1960 South African police fired into a crowd of nonwhites demonstrating against racial policies in Sharpeville, some 30 miles south of Johannesburg. World opinion rallied against South Africa, but the government turned a deaf ear. In 1961 Albert Luthuli, a Zulu chief, received the Nobel Peace Prize for advocating peaceful methods for resolving South Africa's racial problems.

The Republic. On May 31, 1961 South Africa withdrew from the British Commonwealth and became a republic. In 1962 South Africa withdrew its delegation to the United Nations when the General Assembly voted economic sanctions against South Africa because of its racial policies. But heavy British and U.S. investments in South Africa blocked the effective application of sanctions.

In 1963 South Africa created the Transkei, an all-African Bantustan, or homeland, with a government separate from, but not independent of, the republic. Chief Kaizer Mantanzima became chief minister of the Transkei.

On Sept. 6, 1966 a white South African assassinated Prime Minister Hendrik Verwoerd. He was succeeded by Balthasar Vorster, as firm a supporter of apartheid as his predecessor had been.

In October 1966 the UN General Assembly voted to end South Africa's mandate to govern South West Africa because it had failed to fulfill its obligations. Vorster declared the resolution illegal and announced South Africa's intention to continue administering South West Africa.

Renewed protests against South Africa's administration of South West Africa came in 1968, when a number of South West African nationalists were tried and given long prison terms by South African courts.
—Hibberd V. B. Kline, Jr.;
Gary A. Weissman

SOUTH YEMEN

Official name: People's Republic of South Yemen
Area: (1967 est.) 112,000 square miles
Population: (1967 est.) 1,000,000
Capital: Medina as-Shaab
Language: Arabic
Religion: Islam
Currency unit: Dinar

The People's Republic of South Yemen is an Arab state in the southwestern Arabian Peninsula. It was created in 1967 from the former British colony of Aden and the protectorates of South Arabia, a group of 20 sheikhdoms and sultanates, most of which had been united in the British-protected Federation of South Arabia between 1959 and 1967.

South Yemen is bordered on the north and west by Yemen and the Rub al Khali desert of Saudi Arabia, on the east by the sultanate of Muscat and Oman, and on the south by the Gulf of Aden and the Indian Ocean. Socotra, an island in the Indian Ocean off the northeast coast of the Somali Republic, is part of South Yemen, as are Kamaran, an island off the coast of Yemen in the southern Red Sea, and Perim, an island in the Bab al Mandab strait.

The status of the Kuria Muria Islands, off the southern coast of Muscat and Oman, is disputed. Britain wants the islands to go to Muscat and Oman, and South Yemen claims them for itself.

THE LAND AND PEOPLE. Rugged mountains rise in western South Yemen, but most of the region is a high rolling desert plateau on which almost no rain falls.

The country's population, composed almost entirely of Muslim Arabs, is concentrated along the coast, especially in Aden, the largest city.

ECONOMY. Herding and farming are the principal occupations of South Yemen's people. Cotton, grains, and fruits are raised, and sheep and goats are grazed on the fringes of the desert. There is some fishing along the coast. Soap and cigarette manufacturing, oilseed production, and salt refining are important.

The port city of Aden is the principal commercial center for the lower Arabian Peninsula. It has a large oil refinery and oil storage facilities, and is a major Arabian port for oil exporting

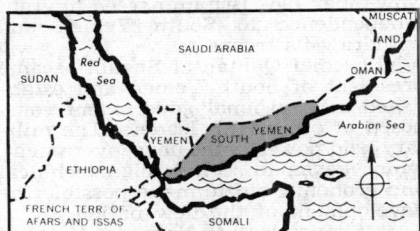

LOOK MAGAZINE

VAST GRAIN FIELDS of the Soviet Ukraine are part of the European-West Siberian Plain.

and ship refueling. Income from this transit trade is vital to the economy of South Yemen. Trade in South Yemen's own goods is small.

GOVERNMENT. A provisional government, composed of South Yemen's National Liberation Front, controls the affairs of the republic, which is divided for administrative purposes into six governorates.

HISTORY. For centuries, the former sheikhdoms that now make up South Yemen were controlled by Egyptians, Turks, and Yemenis before being ruled by independent sultans. The port of Aden has been an important and prosperous trading center since ancient times.

Ottoman Turks captured the port in 1538, when Aden's importance was already in decline, due to the establishment of trade routes around the Cape of Good Hope. In 1839 the British East India Company seized the port for use as a coaling station for ships traveling between Bombay and Suez. With the opening of the Suez Canal in 1869, Aden once again became a major port.

During the 1800s the British, eager to keep peace in the area, signed agreements promising to protect the neighboring sheikhdoms.

In 1959 six of the protected sheikhdoms established a federation, which by 1965 included 16 sheikhdoms and Aden. Yemen's independence was in part achieved by the efforts of Arab nationalist groups that were active in the area in the 1960s. In 1964 Britain promised independence to the federation by 1968, but as the independence date approached violence in the region increased and Britain was reluctant to withdraw.

Yemen intensified warfare along the border, hoping to gain control of the territory, and two nationalist groups—the National Liberation Front (NFL) and the Front for the Liberation of Occupied South Yemen—engaged in anti-British terrorism and competed for control of the protectorate. The NFL won out over its rival, and in November 1967 Britain agreed to grant independence to South Yemen and withdraw its troops.

NFL chief Qahtan al-Shaabi became president of South Yemen and established a provisional government composed of other NFL leaders. The military held power in the new government, which began to seek foreign technical and economic aid to make possible the development of the new nation.
—Charles Issawi; Alexander Melamid

SOVIET UNION

Official name: Union of Soviet Socialist Republics
Area: 8,649,534 square miles
Population: (1966 est.) 233,105,000
Capital: Moscow (Pop., 1965 est., urban area, 6,423,000)
Language: Russian
Religion: Orthodox Christianity, Islam
Currency unit: Ruble
National holiday: Anniversary of the revolution, November 7

The Union of Soviet Socialist Republics, the world's largest sovereign state, is bounded on the north by the Arctic Ocean; on the east by the Pacific Ocean; on the south by North Korea, the Mongolian People's Republic, China, Afghanistan, Iran, the Caspian Sea, Turkey, and the Black Sea; and on the west by Romania, Hungary, Czechoslovakia, Poland, the Baltic Sea, Finland, and Norway.

The country is sometimes referred to by its initials, U.S.S.R., but more often by a short form, the Soviet Union. Before the seizure of power by communists in 1917, the country was called Russia. The term Russia now properly applies only to one part of the Soviet Union, the Russian Soviet Federated Socialist Republic (R.S.F.S.R.).

THE LAND

The Soviet Union covers one-sixth of the land surface of the earth and extends over two continents, occupying much of eastern Europe and all of northern Asia. A natural boundary between the European and Asian parts of the country is formed by the Ural Mountains, the Ural River, and the Caspian Sea.

PHYSICAL REGIONS. The Soviet Union may be divided into five major land regions: the European-West Siberian Plain, the Central Siberian Plateau, Eastern Siberia, the Soviet Far East, and Soviet Central Asia.

European–West Siberian Plain. The dominant physical feature of the Soviet Union is the great plain that extends from the European border into Siberia, broken only by the Ural Mountains. The great majority of the Soviet People live within the confines of this plain.

The European part of the plain is far from uniform, and consists of rolling plains, low hills, wide river valleys, and coastal lowlands. The Siberian part is a nearly level plain, stretching unbroken for some 1,200 miles east from the Urals to the Yenisey River and nearly the same distance northward to the shores of the Arctic Ocean.

Central Siberian Plateau. East of the Yenisey lies the Central Siberian Plateau, which extends to the Lena River. Varying in elevation from 600 to 3,000 feet, the plateau is covered almost entirely by forest. It is sparsely settled, and its few inhabitants are mostly miners, hunters, and trappers.

Eastern Siberia. Beyond the Lena, stretching eastward to the Pacific Ocean and the Bering Strait, is Eastern Siberia. Vast mountain chains, comparable in length to the Appalachians, divide this area into subregions, most of which are drained by rivers that flow into the Arctic Ocean. The mountains and valleys of Eastern Siberia are the most remote, least inhabited, and the least known part of the Soviet Union.

Soviet Far East. The Soviet Far East, separated from the Central Siberian Plateau and Eastern Siberia by the Stanovoy and Yablonovvy Mountains, is the Soviet Union's link with China, Japan, and the Pacific Ocean. The Amur River, which drains into the Pacific Ocean north of Japan, is the region's major waterway. Its valley and that of its tributary, the Ussuri, are the most heavily settled areas of the region.

Soviet Central Asia. East of the Caspian Sea and south of Siberia is Soviet Central Asia. In the north it consists of a plateau; in the center and south, lowlands. The few rivers that cross it either drain into salty, brackish lakes such as Lake Aral and Lake Balkhash, or disappear into desert sands.

MOUNTAIN SYSTEMS. The mountains of the Soviet Union vary greatly in size, elevation, and characteristic features. The Ural Mountains are for the most part a low, worn-down range. They are among the most highly mineralized parts of the earth, and one of the principal centers of Soviet mining and manufacturing.

Most of the uplands of the European parts of the Soviet Union are not really mountains. The sole exception is a small segment of the Carpathians, near the western border, which became part of the Soviet Union after World War II.

Caucasus. In the southwest the Caucasus Mountains, a major physical feature of the Soviet Union, run some 700 miles from the Black Sea to the Caspian Sea. They form the traditional boundary between European Russia and the countries of the Near East. Early in the 1800s, the Russian Empire extended its rule south of the Caucasus and conquered what is now known as the Trans-Caucasus, or Transcaucasia.

The northern part of Transcaucasia is composed of two lowlands: that of the Rion River in the west, which drains into the Black Sea; and that of the Kura and Araks rivers in the east, which drains into the Caspian. The southernmost part of Transcaucasia consists of dry, desert mountains, and is generally known as the Little Caucasus.

Eastern Ranges. From the eastern shores of the Caspian Sea to eastern Siberia the borders of the Soviet Union are dominated by a series of mountain systems. Farthest west are the Kopet Dagh Mountains and the foothills of the Hindu Kush chain, which separate the Soviet Union from Iran and Afghanistan. Beyond the valley of the Amu River, which flows into Lake Aral, lie the Pamir Plateau and the Alai Mountains.

The mountains north of the Pamir and Alai form the boundary between the Soviet Union and China. The principal components of this complex range are the Tien Shan, Ala Tau, Tarbagatay, Altai, and Sayan mountains. The Sayan Mountains lie in southern Siberia and overlook the deepest lake in the world, Lake Baykal.

VEGETATION ZONES. The combined result of the influences of surface features, climate, and soils on the land of the Soviet Union is several different vegetation zones, which extend in a general east-west direction across Soviet territory.

Tundra. In the far north, along the shores of the Arctic Ocean, on the Arctic islands, and inland for a distance varying from 100 to 400 miles is the tundra zone. This is an arctic desert, where low year-round temperatures inhibit the growth and variety of vegetation.

During the short growing season, which seldom exceeds three months, the tundra is covered with moss, lichens, scattered clumps of wild flowers, and, along the southern, warmer edge of the zone, small, bushy plants and dwarf trees. During the greater part of the year, however, the tundra is an empty, storm-swept place, covered with snow and ice.

Taiga. South of the tundra and stretching across the entire width of the Soviet Union is the northern forest zone, or taiga. The taiga is composed mostly of coniferous evergreen trees—pine, fir, and larch—interspersed with clumps of birches.

Mixed Forest. South of the taiga, in the European part of the Soviet Union, is a triangle-shaped mixed-forest zone with its points located near the cities of Leningrad in the northwest, Kiev in the southwest, and Perm, in the Urals. Oak, beech, birch, pine, and fir trees predominate in this region, but there are sizable natural clearings along the rivers.

Much of the original mixed forest has long since been cut, and substantial areas are under the plough. Moscow, Leningrad, and Kiev, the three largest Soviet cities, are located within this zone, as are some of the leading Soviet industrial areas and the bulk of the population.

Steppe. South of the mixed forest is the grassland zone, or steppe. This area is covered with black earth, one of the most fertile soils known to man. Virtually all of the steppe in the European part of the Soviet Union and in western Siberia is now under cultivation.

Along the southern edge of the steppe rainfall gradually becomes more scarce and the soils have less organic content. This transition zone south of the steppe is known as the dry steppe or "semidesert." In this zone irrigation is essential for the successful growing of crops; otherwise only grazing can be carried on.

Desert. The southernmost of the great vegetation zones is the desert region of Soviet Central Asia. Annual rainfall there is usually only 3 to 8 inches, but a long growing season, over six months, the longest in the Soviet Union, can guarantee rich harvests of certain crops, such as cotton, fruit, and vegetables, if water for irrigation is available.

Farms and settlements cling closely to rivers, irrigation canals, or artesian wells. The adjacent mountains provide good grazing during the spring, summer, and early fall.

Subtropical. The one exception to the great vegetation zones that cross the Soviet Union is a small area, lying along the westernmost flanks of the Great Caucasus overlooking the Black Sea, which the Soviets call the "subtropical zone." There a narrow coastal strip and the adjacent low hillsides sheltered by the Caucasus range are favored by mild winters and usually heavy rainfall.

CLIMATE. The greater part of Soviet territory is too distant from the sea, or faces too cold a sea, to enjoy the moderating effect that large bodies of water have on climate. With the exception of a few coastal areas on the Black Sea and on the Caspian, the greatest part of the Soviet Union has a continental climate, characterized by extremes of temperature and rainfall.

Winter temperatures throughout most of the Soviet Union are well below freezing, but it is coldest in the northeast. Siberia, the coldest part of the country, has average January temperatures of $-20°F$, and northeastern Siberia has January averages that run as low as $-50°$ to $-60°F$.

Summers, on the other hand, are likely to be warm, except in the far north. Some of the highest summer temperatures on earth have been recorded in Soviet Central Asia.

Rainfall ranges from an annual average of 70 to 80 inches in the western Caucasus to less than 8 inches in Soviet Central Asia.

One important consequence of climatic extremes is the soils characteristic of the Soviet Union. Over 40 percent of the area of the Soviet Union is covered by permafrost, or permanently frozen soil, which varies in depth from one foot to several hundred feet and thaws only a few inches during the summer months. Agriculture, as well as road and railroad building, can be carried out only with extreme difficulty and at great expense on this permanently frozen ground.

THE PEOPLE

ETHNIC GROUPS. The Soviet Union is a multinational state, and the 1959 census listed 108 separate groups. Nearly three-fourths of the population of the Soviet Union is part of the East Slavic language group, however.

Slavs. The Slavic group has three major subdivisions—Russian, Ukrainian, and Belorussian (White Russian). The Russians, who number about 114 million according to the 1959 census, are the largest Slavic subgroup, as well as the country's largest national group. They are represented in every region of the Soviet Union, and Russian is the official language of the Soviet Union.

The Ukrainians (37.3 million) are the second largest subgroup and second in size among all national groups. They inhabit the southern European part of the Soviet Union, and have a separate historical and cultural heritage. The third group, the Belorussians (7 million), live north of the Ukrainians.

Western Borders. Along the shores of the Baltic are the Estonians, Latvians, and Lithuanians, often referred to as the Baltic peoples. The Lithuanians (2.3 million) and the Latvians (1.4 million) speak languages of the Indo-European group. The Estonians (969,

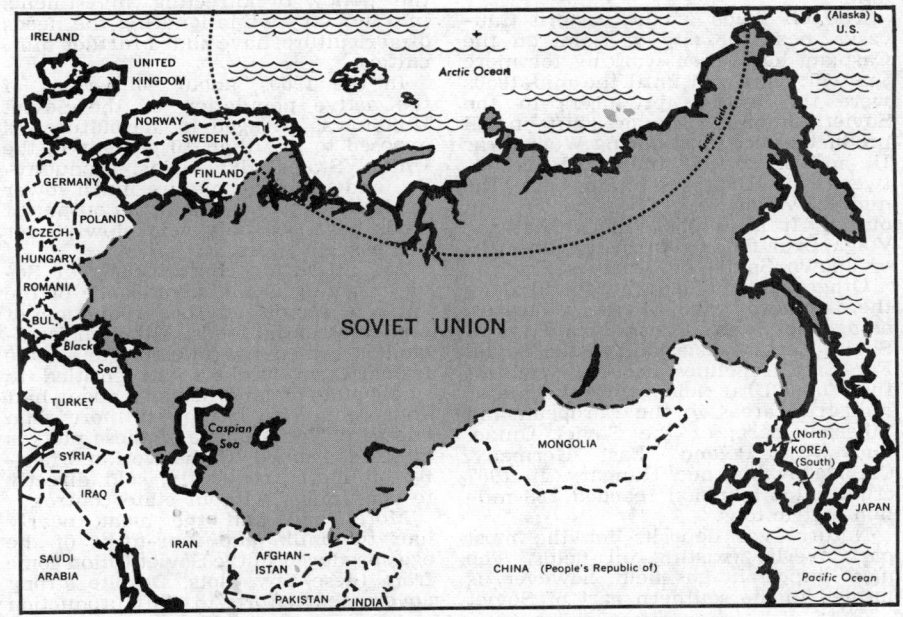

000), who live farthest north of the three Baltic peoples, speak a language of the Finno-Ugric group, which is closely related to Finnish.

Along the southwestern boundary of the Soviet Union live the Moldavians (2.2 million), who are closely related to the Romanians and speak Romanian. In the Middle Volga Valley there are the Chuvash (1.5 million), who speak a Turkic language, and the Mordovians (1.3 million), who speak a Finno-Ugric language; as well as the Tatars (5 million), who speak Asian languages, and Bashkirs (989,000), who speak a Turkic language.

Caucasus and Central Asia. The peoples of the Caucasus are the most diverse within the Soviet Union. The three major groups in this area are the Georgians (2.7 million), Armenians (2.8 million), and Azerbaijanis (2.9 million). There are also about 25 other minority groups, ranging in size from 268,000 to less than 4,000 people.

The peoples of Soviet Central Asia are, for the most part, Turkic and fall into four major groups. The Uzbeks (6 million) live in the central part of the region; the Kazakhs (3.6 million) are concentrated in the north; and the Turkmenians (1 million) live in the mountains and valleys of the east. The Tajiks (1.4 million), who speak a language related to Persian, live near the border with Afghanistan.

Eastern Region. Siberia has a small but diverse native population. Except for the Yakuts, a Turkic-speaking people of the Lena valley in eastern Siberia, who number about 230,000, none of the surviving native groups of Siberia has a population of over 25,-000, and some number less than 1,000.

Koreans are found in the Soviet Far East, and Buryats, related to the Mongols of neighboring Mongolia, live in southern Siberia.

Jews. In the Soviet Union, Jews are listed as a separate national group, and the census of 1959 listed 2.3 million Soviet citizens as Jews, a decrease of nearly one-half since the previous census in 1939. The decrease was largely a result of the persecution of Jews in German-occupied parts of the Soviet Union in World War II.

DISTRIBUTION. Owing to climate and geography, the distribution of population is very uneven in the Soviet Union. The majority of the people live within the European part of the country, but there has been a marked increase in the population east of the Urals and the Caspian Sea. Between 1939 and 1959, for example, Western Siberia increased its population by 34 percent and Soviet Central Asia by 30 percent.

There has also been a substantial migration from the countryside to the cities. Still, about 50 percent of the people live in nonurban areas, a much larger proportion than is found in most of Western Europe and North America.

According to 1966 estimates, the Soviet Union had 187 cities with populations of over 100,000 and 28 cities of over 500,000. Eight cities—Moscow, Leningrad, Kiev, Tashkent, Gorky, Baku, Novosibirsk, and Kharkov—had more than one million inhabitants.

ECONOMY

In the 50 years following the Russian Revolution, the Soviet Union made significant economic progress, changing from an agricultural to an industrial nation with a gross output second only to that of the United States. Soviet gains, however, were made by concentrating on heavy industry at the expense of consumer goods, services, and agriculture.

In the first half of the 1960s, economic growth began to lag. In 1965 the government initiated a reform program designed to make the economy less rigid and more efficient. Industrial management was decentralized, and emphasis was shifted from output to profits. Economic problems remained, however. Agricultural production is often insufficient for domestic needs, there is an acute housing shortage, and consumer goods remain in short supply.

NATURAL RESOURCES. The Soviet Union is extremely rich in natural resources. Most metals and minerals are produced in such quantities that imports from abroad are of minor importance.

There are large deposits of iron ore, copper, lead, zinc, nickel, chrome, manganese, bauxite, and mercury. The Soviet Union produces substantial quantities of gold, and following the discovery of a large deposit of diamonds in Siberia the country became one of the world's leading diamond producers.

Fuels. The Soviet Union also has abundant fuel resources. Coal is the major fuel used in Soviet transportation, homes, and factories, and in 1967 coal production amounted to 595 million metric tons. The Donets basin, in the southern European part of the Soviet Union, is first in coal production and has the largest reserves.

The Kuznetsk basin of southern Siberia is second in production, eastern Siberia is third, and the Karaganda area of Soviet Central Asia is fourth. Other important coal deposits are in the Urals and in the Moscow area.

The oil fields of the eastern Caucasus, near the city of Baku on the Caspian, have been working for more than 75 years and until the mid-1950s were the leading producers in the Soviet Union. A major shift in oil production occurred during World War II, and after 1954 the oil fields between the Ural Mountains and the middle Volga River became first in output. It is now estimated that the Volga-Ural fields represent four-fifths of known Soviet oil reserves.

Other major oil fields are found along the northern edge of the Caucasus, along the Soviet-Polish boundary, in Soviet Central Asia, and in the Soviet Far East. Pipelines not only connect the Volga-Ural fields with the major industrial areas in the European and Siberian parts of the Soviet Union, but with Poland, East Germany, Czechoslovakia, and Hungary. In 1967 crude oil production reached 288 million metric tons.

Natural gas deposits for the most part overlie existing oil fields. The most important gas field, however, is located in the southern part of Soviet

Central Asia. It is now being tapped to pipe natural gas to the great industrial centers.

Hydroelectric power is a relatively unimportant energy source in the Soviet Union, for most of the available sites for hydroelectric development are far removed from major cities and industrial areas. The most spectacular hydroelectric project is on the Volga River, where five dams have transformed the Volga into a series of enormous reservoirs. In the mid-1960s larger projects were under construction in Siberia on the Yenisey River and its tributary, the Angara.

AGRICULTURE. Use of arable land in the Soviet Union is severely limited by cold in the north and drought in the south. As a result, fully tillable farmland is confined to an area known as the Fertile Triangle, with its corners in Leningrad on the Baltic Sea, Odessa on the Black Sea, and the lowland of Western Siberia.

Soviet cropland equals the combined sown areas of the United States and Canada. The northerly location of the country (the bulk of the Fertile Triangle lies north of the U.S.-Canadian boundary), however, results in a shorter growing season, and the distances separating Soviet cropland from warm seas are reflected in limited and undependable rainfall.

These severe handicaps are responsible for the low yields that have characterized Soviet agriculture. They have not been compensated for by the extension of cropland into areas of marginal rainfall, nor by attempts to develop varieties of plants that could mature quickly in areas farther north, where growing seasons are very short.

Collectivization. To these environmental difficulties the Soviet system added man-made ones. The fact that virtually all cultivable land is under either collective or state farms has deprived the Soviet farmer of the incentive present when men work on land they own. The reluctance of the Soviet government to offer farm workers sufficient rewards for their labor, and the policy of directing investments into industry while ignoring the needs of agriculture, have added further difficulties.

In the 1960s, about 40 percent of the active population of the Soviet Union was engaged in agriculture, as opposed to less than 10 percent in the United States. But yields, productivity, and farm income are much lower in the Soviet Union, and the output of foods has risen only very slowly over the past 40 years.

An interesting characteristic of Soviet farming is the significance of the "private sector" in the production of certain essential foods. Although farmland is owned by collective and state farms, farm workers are entitled to small plots of land, usually about half an acre in size but never more than one acre. The produce of these plots is either consumed by the worker's family or, more frequently, sold directly to consumers, without state control.

More than half the meat, nearly half the milk, and four-fifths of the eggs produced in the Soviet Union come from these tiny plots. Despite strong government efforts to shift production

LOOK MAGAZINE

HEAVY INDUSTRY, symbolized by these Volgograd smokestacks, is vital to the Soviet economy.

to the collective and state farms, the "private sector" continues to play a vital role in Soviet food production.

Products. Grains, the leading crop of Soviet farms, include wheat, rye, and barley. The Soviet Union grows virtually all the cotton it needs, exports considerable amounts of flax, and produces part of the hemp its industry consumes. Sugar beets and oilseeds—sunflower, rapeseed, and castor beans—are among the leading industrial crops.

Soviet livestock suffered severe losses during the drive for collectivization (1929–1933), when nearly half the cattle and two-thirds of the hogs in the country were destroyed by farmers unwilling to turn over their animals to collective ownership.

The livestock levels of 1929 were not regained until 1956, and further growth, with the exception of hogs, has been very slow. The output of meat, milk, eggs, and other dairy products remains well below that of the United States and Western Europe.

INDUSTRY. Iron and steel production is a general indicator of industrial strength, and since 1945 the Soviet Union has ranked next to the United States as the world's largest producer of pig iron and steel. In 1967 the Soviet Union produced more than 102 million metric tons of crude steel and almost 75 million metric tons of pig iron.

Two regions, the Ukraine and the Urals, account for more than four fifths of the iron and more than three-fourths of the steel produced. The Ukraine has iron ore, good coking coal, limestone, and ferroalloys available within a small area, and until the 1950s it led in ferrous metallurgy.

The vast iron deposits of the Urals have caused the region to surpass the Ukraine although coking coal must be imported from other parts of the Soviet Union. During the mid-1960s a third major center of iron and steel production was being built in Siberia, where coal and iron are both locally available.

Major Centers. Before the Revolution of 1917, Russian industry was concentrated in the European part of the country. St. Petersburg (renamed Leningrad in 1924) and Moscow were among the leading centers of light industry. Heavy industry was concentrated in the Ukraine.

The temporary loss of much of Russia's industrial capacity during World War I and the civil war that followed led to efforts to decentralize industry and develop new centers further removed from the vulnerable western borders of the Soviet Union. One of the tasks of planning the Soviet economy after 1927 was the establishment of new industrial areas far away from the former manufacturing centers.

Four major regions dominate Soviet industry. The Central Industrial Region, in the Moscow area, contains the country's most valuable industries. This region produces electrical equipment, ball bearings, engines, and automobiles, as well as a number of consumer goods including textiles, shoes, clothing, processed foods, and household articles.

The Ukraine is noted for iron and steel, heavy machinery, and chemicals. It is a less concentrated area than the Central Industrial Region, and consists of four distinct subregions: the Dnepr valley, the Donets basin, the shores of the Sea of Azov, and the area surrounding the city of Kharkov.

The Ural industrial region owes its present large-scale development to Soviet planning, although small-scale industry has been in operation there for over 100 years. In addition to iron and steel, the Urals are important for the production of petroleum and its byproducts, heavy machinery, and chemicals.

The fourth major industrial center, also largely a creation of the Soviet government, is spread out across the edges of the Siberian lowland and adjacent river valleys near the Soviet-Chinese border. Large resources of coal and a variety of metals have given rise to substantial metallurgical, chemical, and machine industries in the area.

Smaller Centers. In accordance with its policy of industrial decentralization, the Soviet government has developed other, smaller industrial centers to lessen the dependence of its farflung territories on the major industrial areas and thereby reduce the burden on its transportation system. Some of the more important smaller industrial centers are located in Transcaucasia, Soviet Central Asia, and the Soviet Far East.

In each of these centers an attempt was made to provide for the needs of the surrounding area. Thus steel pipes are made in Transcaucasia, cotton machinery in Central Asia, and ships in the Far East. Each center also manufactures a variety of consumer goods.

TRADE. In 1966 the Soviet Union's exports earned $8,841 million and its imports cost $7,913 million. Major exports include petroleum, coal, timber, iron ore, industrial equipment, and iron and steel. Principal imports are ships, wheat, sugar, clothing, metal ores, and industrial machinery.

The Soviet Union carries on most of its trade with East Germany, Czechoslovakia, Poland, Bulgaria, Hungary, Romania, Cuba, and Britain.

GOVERNMENT

The Communist Party of the Soviet Union (CPSU) dominates political life. The presidium, formerly the politburo, or political bureau, of the party's central committee determines national policy, and the party's first secretary is the most powerful figure in the government.

Formally, the highest authority in the Soviet Union is the national legislature, the Supreme Soviet. It has two houses, the Soviet of the Union, elected on the basis of population, and the Soviet of Nationalities, elected on the basis of territorial units. The two houses have equal powers and the members of both are directly elected to four-year terms.

The Supreme Soviet elects a presidium to act as the supreme state authority between its relatively short sessions. The chairman of the presidium serves as head of state. The Supreme Soviet also appoints a council of ministers, or cabinet, which is the highest executive and administrative organ of the government.

The Soviet Union is a member of the United Nations and the Warsaw Pact, a military alliance of East European communist countries.

HISTORY

Archeological evidence indicates that various societies existed in European Russia before there were written records. The earliest Slavic inhabitants probably arrived there from an unknown point of origin several hundred years before the birth of Christ.

Slowly their language, as well as some of their political organization and social customs, became dominant. Their settlements tended to concentrate in the south, near the Black Sea, and along the river systems that stretch inland from the Baltic and Black seas.

The river routes made it possible for groups of Scandinavian, or "Varangian," warriors and traders to move through the same regions. From this composite of Slavs, Scandinavians, and remnants of earlier populations the oldest Russian state emerged during the 800s AD.

KIEVAN RUSSIA. The oldest Slavic state, known as Kiev Rus', was a confederation of Slavic-dominated principalities. Its two most important cities, Kiev and Novgorod, were located along the major river trade routes, and the Kievan principalities contained a mixture of merchants, peasants, and warrior-politicians.

The sources of Kievan power and wealth, and of Kiev's social and political structure, were agrarian as well as commercial. This duality made for complex patterns of political administration, which included a hereditary prince and his warrior-administrator retinue, or *druzhina*; an elected city council, or *veche*, which often acted as a check on the prince and reflected the interests of wealthy merchants; and village assemblies in the agrarian areas.

In the 900s Orthodox Christianity was introduced into Kievan Russia from the Byzantine Empire. Like other cultural importations from Byzantium and the Balkan Peninsula, eastern Christianity made a deep and lasting impression on Russia.

The most severe problems of Kievan society were political and military. Much of the princely administrative system was gradually rendered ineffective by strife among claimants to the princely thrones within the confederation. The final blow came from without, however. Mongols swept into Europe from the east in the 1200s, and in 1240 Kiev fell to them.

RISE OF MOSCOW. The era which succeeded that of Kiev Rus' is often called the Appanage Period because of the subdivision of the country into a large number of tiny principalities, or appanages. In the 1300s and 1400s, however, certain appanage princes were able to reverse the process of frequent subdivision of their principalities and increase their holdings by purchase, marriage, or conquest.

Among the most aggressive and skillful of the appanage princes were those who ruled Moscow, or Muscovy. The first of these was Ivan I (r.1325–1340). By the time of Ivan's death Moscow had secured important advantages over its neighbors. Ivan I granted administrative posts to the boyars, or great nobles, loyal to him, and he encouraged the growth of agriculture, which was the basis of the region's economy.

Ivan III (r.1462–1505). Under Prince Ivan III, called "the Great," the ambitions of Moscow and of its ruling house began to be fulfilled. Moscow succeeded in establishing its sovereign authority over important independent principalities in central European Russia, as well as over "frontier" territories to the east and north.

The most important challenge to Muscovite expansion was the flourishing commercial principality of Novgorod. Nevertheless, the principality fell easily under Muscovite pressure. After Novgorod's defeat in 1478, the incorporation into Muscovy of other independent but minor principalities presented no difficulty.

By the early 1500s Muscovy had grown to many times its original size and this increase in area was more than matched by an increase in power and prestige. Muscovite expansion tended to resolve problems of Mongol domination. With larger territories under their command the princes of Moscow were better able to resist Mongol demands and began to strive to throw off Mongol control.

As Moscow grew strong, the Mongol political system became weakened by internal division and dissension. After the 1400s Mongol settlements to the south and east of the expanding boundaries of Moscow were more a source of irritation, as a source of armed raids, than a threat to Muscovite independence.

Muscovite expansion to the north and west brought the state into conflict with the Baltic countries of Europe, especially Poland, Lithuania, and Sweden. Moreover, by the early 1500s serious internal problems beset the Muscovite state.

To ensure continued support from their boyar warriors and administrators, the Muscovite princes often rewarded them with special privileges and large grants of land. As a result, the power of the boyars increased and some members of this Muscovite aristocracy began to challenge the authority of the sovereign prince himself.

Muscovite Russia. Ivan IV (r.1533–1584), wishing to continue the expansionist policies of his predecessors and determined to preserve and increase sovereign authority, met these problems aggressively.

Ivan IV, sometimes called "the Terrible," was one of the most brutal and bloody figures in Russian history. Taking for himself the titles of *tsar* (caesar) and autocrat, he proceeded to attempt to acquire dominions befitting a tsar, or emperor, and to wield the absolute political power of an autocrat.

During the first years of Ivan IV's reign, the young tsar undertook reforms generally regarded as enlightened and necessary. Muscovy was a patchwork of formerly independent principalities and separate local units of varying independence, and the Muscovite state was badly in need of administrative reorganization and legal reform.

Among Ivan's measures were a codification of laws (*Sudebnik* of 1550) and a reorganization of local administration. In 1549 Ivan ordered the convocation of the first national assembly, or *Zemski Sobor*.

During the 1550s Ivan also became deeply involved in wars of territorial expansion. At first Muscovite military power was concentrated against a fragment of the old Mongol empire, the Khanate of Kazan on the middle Volga River. This campaign, however, invited conflicts with other khanates at Astrakhan and in the Crimea.

A much more serious campaign began in 1557 at the opposite corner of the Muscovite state against the inhabitants of the eastern Baltic region. Although weak, they blocked Russian access to the Baltic Sea and northern Europe. This conflict gradually ex-

panded until Ivan IV's armies were involved in an exhausting war with the large and powerful states of Poland and Sweden.

Centralization. At the same time the tsar's policies of expansion and domestic reform ran into mounting opposition, particularly from the boyars, who felt themselves threatened by administrative reforms and who bore the burden of the military campaigns. This political struggle came to a crisis in the early 1560s, when Ivan IV renounced the throne and retired to a monastery. Ivan returned only after the boyars and the church agreed to meet certain of his demands.

The victorious tsar then organized the central territories of Muscovy as a separate administrative unit subservient to his will. Using hand-picked men, called *oprichniks*, Ivan began to punish "evildoers" as he saw fit. It soon became clear that he intended to classify as an "evildoer" anyone who stood in his way or objected to his policies of expansion and creating a centralized state.

A virtual reign of terror was unleashed against the boyars, and Muscovy was plunged into near civil war. Crushing most opposition, Ivan IV became far more powerful than any previous Muscovite prince.

Theodore I (r.1584–1598), Ivan IV's successor, was too weak to master the legacy of power and antagonism bequeathed him by his father, and real authority began to fall into the hands of court favorites. When Theodore died, the ancient Muscovite dynasty died with him.

Time of Troubles. The church, boyars, petty nobility, and merchants then had to establish and support a new ruler and a new dynasty, or else find a way of administering Russian society without the autocracy. During the years immediately following the death of Theodore, both alternatives were tried, without success.

The failure of these efforts, each occurring amidst a background of increasing domestic strife, foreign wars and, finally, Polish invasion, is known as the Time of Troubles (1598–1613). Poland was eventually defeated, and peasant uprisings and other social disorders were suppressed. The Time of Troubles finally ended in 1613 with the accession to the throne of the new Romanov dynasty.

ROMANOVS. Physically exhausted and verging on economic ruin, Russian society only slowly regained the international independence and domestic order that had characterized it in the early days of Ivan IV. The first Romanovs were unable to claim the prestige and authority of the earlier rulers of Moscow.

Nevertheless, Tsar Michael Romanov (r.1613–1645) and his successor, Alexis (r.1645–1676), managed to reassert and extend centralized autocratic authority, and to restore some measure of prosperity. They also recovered possessions, such as Smolensk and Novgorod, which had been lost to Poland and Sweden.

Serfdom. Change was not accomplished without sacrifices, however, and by the 1600s the institution of serfdom had become central to the functioning of the state. Exploitation of the large areas of land granted by the tsars to their royal servitors since the early days of Muscovite expansion was feasible only through the use of serf labor.

A community of interest between the warrior landowners and the tsar known as the *pomiestie* system developed. The noble landowner became responsible not only for providing soldiers and military leadership during time of war, but also for administering the land under his control.

Gradually the landowner became the immediate representative of authority over the peasant who worked the land. To insure social stability and to placate an increasingly demanding nobility, the state made it legally more difficult for the peasant to escape bondage to land and lord.

Renewed Expansion. By the mid-1600s Russia had largely regained the territory it had lost during the Time of Troubles. It had also renewed the policy of relentless expansion, which brought it into conflict with the Ottoman Empire in the south and with Poland and Sweden in the west.

Some government leaders, including, perhaps, Tsar Alexis himself, recognized that to continue this process of expansion Russia had to be able to draw on all its resources and to make use of Western organization and technology. It was Peter the Great, however, who initiated an era of rapid modernization and reform.

Peter the Great (r.1689–1725). Peter's reign inaugurated the Imperial period of Russian history. One of Peter's major goals was to modernize Russia as quickly as possible. He made the church subordinate to the state, reorganized the central government and provincial administration, and introduced a new military and civil service based on merit. Peter also required the nobility to serve the state, undertook tax and financial reforms, and developed trade and industry.

Following the acquisition of the eastern Baltic coastlands from Sweden in 1703, Peter built a new capital, St. Petersburg, on the Gulf of Finland. He called it Russia's "window to the West."

In carrying out his reforms, Peter continued the process of concentrating state power in royal hands. In addition, Peter fought the Poles and the Turks and became deeply involved in European diplomacy. By the end of his reign, in 1725, it was clear that Russia had become a major power in Europe, and that old Muscovy had been shaken to its foundations and transformed into the Russian Empire.

Early Empire. Certain of Peter's reforms were more permanent than others. For example, the apparatus of government administration he established remained largely intact under the tsars of the 1700s. Under the unremitting pressure of the nobility, however, the requirements of noble service and of merit competition were abandoned.

The nobles were given greater and finally absolute authority over their serfs, while owing fewer and fewer

LOOK MAGAZINE

ANCIENT SAMARKAND, in Soviet Central Asia, came under Russian rule in the 1800s.

obligations to the state. Finally, in 1762, the nobility was freed entirely from compulsory state service, although it still remained a ruling class because of its control over the peasantry and the tsar's dependence on it for political support.

The emergence of the nobility from the service position it had occupied under Peter was partly due to the weakness or indifference of his successors. Lax leadership allowed groups such as the Guards' Regiments in St. Petersburg, which were composed exclusively of nobles, to gain power. During the reign of the powerful, brilliant Catherine II, "the Great," (r. 1762–1796) the nobles suffered no loss of power. Catherine, who had come to the throne through a coup d'etat, needed their political backing and administrative talents. On the other hand, public office and thus public power came to be held by a group of individuals drawn from an increasingly smaller professionalized reservoir of nobles and civil servants.

The bureaucracy continued to be dominated by the nobility, but many nobles settled into a life of apathy and indolence on their estates. As a result, in the 1800s men of various classes, or *raznochintsi*, began to fill the lower ranks of the administration, and the direct authority and influence of the nobility was gradually reduced.

Imperial Expansion. In the mid-1700s Russia's former great enemies to the west and south, Poland and Turkey, became increasingly impotent because of growing Russian power and their own internal weaknesses. By the end of Catherine the Great's reign in 1796, Russian control of the Ukraine had been consolidated, and areas north of the Black Sea that had been protectorates of the Ottoman Empire had been added to the Russian state.

All of Siberia to the Pacific Ocean and more and more of Central Asia had also been incorporated into the Russian Empire, which had become by far the largest land state in the world. Most important, however,

Russian expansion brought with it direct and constant contact with the great European powers—France, Britain, Austria, and Prussia.

Contact with the powers resulted in Russian involvement in major European wars of the 1700s and Russian participation between 1772 and 1795 in the partitions of Poland. Thus, the Russian Empire found it difficult to escape involvement in the wars of the French Revolution and the Napoleonic wars (1789–1815).

Alexander I (r.1801–1825). In 1812, despite efforts by Alexander I to hold Russia aloof from the Napoleonic struggle in the west, Napoleon invaded Russia. After heroic resistance and great suffering, the Russian armies forced the French to retreat, and Russia joined Austria and Prussia in a coalition which helped defeat Napoleon in 1813–1814.

As a result of these events Russia rose to new heights of European importance. The conclusion of the Napoleonic wars also left the Russian tsar in control of additional territories bordering the empire, including Finland and Bessarabia.

Before his accession to the throne, and during the first years of his reign, Alexander discussed the possibility of undertaking extensive reforms, including the easing or abolition of serfdom and the drawing up of a constitution for the empire. In spite of the fact that Alexander surrounded himself with individuals favorable to his ideas, the projects themselves were never effectively realized.

When real reform failed to materialize, a protest movement was formed by educated Russians. By the mid-1800s demands for radical social and economic reform had grown into a chorus of opposition to the government.

Nicholas I (r.1825–1855). Unfortunately, Alexander's successor, Nicholas I, was naturally conservative and did not favor reform. Furthermore, his accession to the throne was immediately followed by the Decembrist Revolt, an attempted seizure of the government by a group of liberal and re-formed-minded officers and nobles. The rising made Nicholas determined to dominate not only the actions, but the thoughts, of his subjects.

The government attempted to pro-tect society from "radical" political and social influences, and it viewed most proposals for change with great suspicion. This policy was disastrous for Russia. It not only allowed severe problems to go unsolved, but it stifled Russia intellectually, technologically, and economically at a time when Europe was being transformed by the profound changes resulting from the industrial and the French revo-lutions.

The foreign policies of Nicholas I were easily as conservative as his domestic ones. Nevertheless, he was drawn into a major conflict with Britain, France, and the Ottoman Em-pire in the Crimean War (1853–1856). Russia was defeated in the conflict, and the defeat of Russian armies, on Russian soil, by countries supplying their troops by sea over many thou-sands of miles was a disaster.

Reform. On Nicholas' death in 1855 the new tsar, Alexander II (r.1855–1881), realized, as did everyone else, that the time for talking of reforms had passed and the time for action had come. Critics of the regime considered the continued existence of serfdom the central problem, and in 1861 the serfs were freed. The first reform had been undertaken.

Other reforms encouraged economic growth and social change, which were seen as essential to Russia's survival in the modern European world. They included reforms in state finance, in local government, in the judicial sys-tem, and in military administration. But the inertia of a tradition-bound society, combined with the conserva-tism of the landed nobility and the government bureaucracy, prevented rapid social change.

As a result, liberal critics were not stilled by Alexander's reforms, and they became increasingly frustrated and isolated from society as a whole. After the 1860s their dissatisfaction was manifested by the formation of groups dedicated to overthrowing the autocracy. In 1881 one of these groups assassinated Alexander II, hoping thereby to touch off a revolution.

Alexander III (r.1881–1894). Although Alexander III succeeded in crushing his father's assassins, the revolutionary movement continued to grow. It grew not only inside Russia, but also among the many Russian émigrés in West-ern Europe.

Alexander III determined to meet the problems of Russian society with force and more thorough bureaucratic control. But even Konstantin Pobe-donostsev, the extremely reactionary adviser of Alexander, could not pre-vent industrialization and urbaniza-tion and the social changes that ac-companied them.

Consequently, in the 1880s govern-ment policy became ambivalent. The ministry of finance promoted rapid change, while the ministry of the interior remained extremely conserv-ative. At the same time Russia's position in international affairs was delicate, and in contrast to its most powerful European neighbors, Russia became politically and militarily weaker.

Nicholas II (r.1894–1917). The stage was set for a social and political crisis of unprecedented dimensions when the able and determined Alexan-der III was succeeded by the weak and indecisive Nicholas II. Nicholas pursued the same domestic policies as his predecessor, and continued his conservatism and repression. But the policies evoked only greater protest and unrest, spurred by an agricultural crisis. It was a disaster in foreign af-fairs, however, that touched off Rus-sia's first modern revolution.

War and Revolution (1904–1905). Con-flicting interests of Russia and Japan in East Asia led to war between Russia and a recently strengthened and Westernized Japan. The conflict broke out in February 1904, and the Russians experienced a series of hu-miliating defeats on land and sea. In September 1905, through the mediation of U.S. Pres. Theodore Roosevelt, a peace settlement was reached at Ports-mouth, New Hampshire.

The domestic repercussions of this war were serious. In addition to the burdensome and unimaginative rule of Nicholas II, basic changes taking place in the social and economic struc-ture of Russia produced a revolu-tionary spirit. By 1902–1903 the whole country was in ferment. The disas-trous war with Japan reinforced and encouraged widespread dissatisfaction, and during 1904 a broadly based rev-olutionary movement emerged.

A series of peaceful meetings, pro-tests, and discussions erupted into violence in January 1905, when Im-perial troops opened fire on a crowd of unarmed workers trying to present a petition of grievances to the tsar. This incident, known as "Bloody Sunday," fanned the fires of revolution. The Revolution of 1905, as it is known, spread widely in the cities and coun-tryside, and even to some units of the armed forces.

The tsar offered minor concessions, but they failed to stem the tide. By the autumn of 1905 peasant riots and seizure of their landlords' estates, to-gether with a general strike, virtually paralyzed the government. With the situation out of control, Nicholas II called in Count Sergei Witte.

Witte pointed out the two alterna-tives facing the tsar—military dictator-ship or extensive reform. Reluctantly Nicholas chose reform and issued the October Manifesto, which promised basic civil liberties and the convo-cation of a national assembly, the Duma.

The Duma (1906–1917). The Duma did not have full parliamentary pow-ers, and its members were chosen by indirect and unequal suffrage. More-over, in theory and to a considerable extent in practice, the tsar retained complete sovereignty over the country.

Despite their restricted nature, the first two Dumas elected proved to be so critical of the government that the tsar dissolved them. In 1906 Nicholas dismissed Count Witte as prime minister and appointed Peter A. Stolypin, who promptly revised the electoral laws to weight the franchise even more heavily in favor of the propertied classes.

As a result, the third Duma, elected in 1907, and the fourth Duma, chosen in 1912, were able to last out their normal terms of five years in a state of uneasy truce with the government. Duma deputies on the right supported the tsar and his policies, and liberal leaders and parties of the center tried to work within the Duma.

The liberals and moderates worked to achieve necessary reform and to extend gradually the Duma's authority and influence so that it might become a representative parliament like those of the Western democracies. The few deputies of the extreme left, primarily Social Democrats (Marxists), contin-ued to oppose the government whole-heartedly.

In 1907 the continued restlessness of the peasantry, caused by land hun-ger and general economic hardship, led Prime Minister Stolypin to in-troduce agrarian reforms. He sought to break up the traditional peasant commune, under which land was owned collectively, and to encourage individual peasant proprietors.

It was hoped that if the peasants became property owners they would have a stake in the existing social order and develop a less revolution-ary attitude. The transfer of land belonging to the state and to the nobles into peasant hands was also stepped up. World War I interrupted these re-forms before their full impact could be measured.

World War I. In 1914 the Austrian Archduke Francis Ferdinand was as-sassinated at Sarajevo, in present-day Yugoslavia, by Bosnian terrorists. Serbia, faced with a sweeping ultima-tum from Austria-Hungary, turned to Russia for help. The Russians de-cided to back Serbia, although many Russian leaders realized that Russia was ill-prepared for war and might not be able to withstand the strain on its resources.

Russia's leader hoped the war would be short and victorious, and that they would receive substantial territorial gains in the Balkans. These hopes were to be bitterly disappointed, and the war soon proved disastrous for the Russians as German and Austro-Hungarian armies battered Russia's western areas.

Losses in men and equipment were high, mismanagement of supplies and of the general war effort was com-mon, and morale sagged badly, both at the front and at home. By 1916 the economy as a whole had begun to col-lapse, and there were severe food and fuel shortages in the cities.

The situation was complicated by a general disintegration in leadership at the upper level. Gregory Rasputin, a charlatan "holy man," had acquired considerable influence over the Em-press Alexandra as a result of his success on several occasions in pre-venting her only son, the heir to the throne, from dying of hemophilia.

In 1915 Nicholas II decided to go to the front to take personal com-mand of the armies. Rasputin, through his hold on Alexandra, began to have a strong influence on the appointment of ministers and the formation of government policy. Although Rasputin was murdered in 1916 by a group of patriotic noblemen, the weakness, inefficiency, and political ineptitude of the government persisted.

REVOLUTION. The situation became critical in March 1917. Quite unexpectedly food riots, coupled with strikes, lockouts, and general labor unrest, led to a mass demonstration in the capital, St. Petersburg (Petrograd), against which the government proved powerless. Within one week the tsar had been toppled from the throne.

With the collapse of the government there was no legally constituted authority, but two centers of power sprang up. One was the Provisional Government, a temporary committee formed by members of the Duma to rule until elections could be held for a constituent assembly. The other was the Petrograd Soviet (Council) of Workers' and Soldiers' Deputies, the revival of an institution which had existed briefly during the Revolution of 1905.

Provisional Government and Soviet. The Soviet was more representative of the Russian people than the Provisional Government. The Soviet fell at first under the domination of doctrinaire socialists, primarily Mensheviks (moderate Marxists) and Social Revolutionaries (agrarian socialists). At that time the extreme wing of the Marxists in Russia, the Bolsheviks, constituted only a tiny minority of the Soviet.

A compromise between the Soviet and the Provisional Government was reached, and the Soviet agreed to let the Provisional Government run the basic governmental system, provided civil liberties and other democratic guarantees were maintained. The Soviet retained control over certain services, such as communications, and exerted a strong influence in the army. The resulting "dual power" system provided a rather shaky government for a society wracked by revolution and war.

Moreover, there were a number of basic social and economic issues on which the Provisional Government and the Soviet disagreed. The leaders of the Provisional Government wanted to continue the war until victory could be achieved. The leaders of the Soviet, however, wanted a rapid end to the war and opposed annexations of territory by the victors.

For the masses of the Russian people the key issues were the ending of the war, the distribution of land, and better living conditions. The general population wanted immediate peace and instant reform. V. I. Lenin, leader of the Bolshevik, or extremist, faction of the Russian Marxists, stepped into this breach.

Bolsheviks. Taking advantage of the basic desires as well as the growing radicalism of the masses, Lenin propounded the slogan, "Peace, Land, and Bread," and saw that the Soviet might be the means by which his Bolshevik party could seize power. As a result, after an abortive popular uprising in the summer of 1917, Lenin began to lay plans to overthrow the Provisional Government, which had become a coalition of liberals and moderate socialists.

Overcoming the opposition of some of his own comrades in the party, Lenin, with the brilliant assistance of Lev Trotsky, seized power in Petrograd on Oct. 25–26, 1917, and shortly thereafter in most of Russia. This "October Revolution," which became the November Revolution when the Russian calendar was changed, easily overthrew the existing moderate regime and instituted sweeping changes in Russia.

SOVIET UNION. After the Bolshevik seizure of power, Lenin turned to the tasks of consolidating the authority of his government and meeting the basic demands of the people. He called for peace and nationalized all land, although permitting the peasants to use the acreage they had seized during the revolution. Lenin also decreed the separation of church and state, and nationalized major industries and banks.

Lenin also promulgated a new, "socialist," constitution for the Russian Soviet Federated Socalist Republic (R.S.F.S.R.). He encouraged the formation of separate but closely allied socialist republics under Bolshevik control in non-Russian areas of the former tsarist empire, and between 1922 and 1924 these were joined to the R.S.F.S.R. to form the Union of Soviet Socialist Republics (U.S.S.R.).

Dictatorship. Lenin suppressed opposition parties and ended freedom of expression. He also dissolved the Constituent Assembly, which he had allowed to be elected in November 1917, when it convened with the Bolsheviks in a minority, and established the Cheka, the forerunner of the secret police, to ferret out and punish "counter-revolutionaries."

Despite considerable opposition not only within the Bolshevik party but throughout the country, Lenin finally forced through his policy of obtaining peace for Russia. On Mar. 3, 1918 the war with Germany and Austria-Hungary was ended by the Treaty of Brest-Litovsk.

Under the terms of the treaty of Brest-Litovsk Russia suffered heavy territorial and economic losses. The treaty outraged many patriotic Russians and contributed to the outbreak of civil war between Bolshevik supporters (Reds) and those opposed to the new Soviet government (Whites). The treaty also helped lead to intervention in Russia by U.S. and Allied troops.

The Western Powers, furious at what they considered Russia's betrayal of the common cause against German militarism, and desperately anxious to reestablish an eastern front against Germany, sent small forces to northern Russia and Siberia and money, supplies, and advisers to various anti-Bolshevik forces.

After the end of World War I, in November 1918, the Allies continued a half-hearted intervention in the hope of overthrowing the Bolshevik regime. But by the end of 1920 the Soviet government had succeeded in defeating its internal and external foes, although the country was exhausted, near starvation, and demoralized.

Ruthlessly putting down peasant protests and disorders, as well as a serious popular uprising at the city and naval base of Kronstadt, Lenin made it clear that the Bolsheviks would not tolerate opposition from the people. In addition, at the Tenth Party Congress in 1921, Lenin crushed dissent within the party itself, making it clear that the leadership would not tolerate opposition from the rank and file. Thus the foundation was laid for the Communist party's dictatorship over Russia.

NEP. Lenin began reconstruction of the devastated country by launching the New Economic Policy, or NEP, under which some of the controls and centralization that had characterized the previous period of wartime communism were abandoned.

Considered a temporary expedient from the start, the NEP did not solve the problem of how to increase Russia's productive forces and build an economy firm enough to support the socialist society envisaged by the com-

UNITED PRESS INTERNATIONAL

PORTRAIT OF V. I. LENIN, who led the 1917 Bolshevik Revolution, overlooks modern Moscow.

munist leaders. By 1927, however, the economy had been restored to its 1913 level and Soviet leaders were faced with the problem of establishing new goals.

This situation was complicated by a power struggle within the Communist party following Lenin's death in 1924. Joseph Stalin, the general secretary of the party, emerged victorious, first defeating Lev Trotsky and his "Left" supporters, and then the so-called Right opposition. Stalin established one-man rule over both the party and the country.

Stalinism. After expelling Trotsky from the party's politburo, Stalin adopted Trotsky's domestic policy, which called for rapid and extensive industrialization. To achieve this, the First Five-Year Plan was begun in 1928, and completed ahead of schedule in 1932. But to obtain the labor and capital for industrialization, Stalin found it necessary to control the peasants. This he accomplished by forcing them onto state-owned collective farms.

Massive peasant resistance bordered on civil war, and an estimated 5 to 10 million peasants were killed, died of starvation, or were exiled to Siberia and Central Asia. But by 1933 Stalin had won out. He also directed the energies of the Russian people toward the goal of industrialization.

Stalin established complete party control over every aspect of private and public life and instituted a rigid totalitarian regime, known as "Stalinism." At the cost not only of lives but of an almost total loss of freedom, Soviet society thus achieved remarkable industrial growth during the decade of the 1930s.

Fearing that critics of his program were springing up within the party, Stalin began a "great purge" in 1936, starting with former party colleagues and rivals. The elimination of alleged "traitors to the party" soon spread to all levels of the party and to people in all walks of Soviet life.

No one was immune from the purge, and many thousands were arrested, imprisoned, exiled to slave labor camps, or executed. The blood bath finally ended in 1938, but by then terror had become a major ingredient of Soviet daily life under the Stalinist regime.

Foreign Policy. During the 1920s Soviet foreign policy had been directed toward gaining recognition and support for the new Soviet state and preventing the possibility of Western intervention in Russia, such as had occurred during the revolution. Soviet leaders also founded and directed an organization of Communist parties throughout the world, the Third, or Communist, International (Comintern, 1919–1943).

The Comintern was designed to coordinate and assist the development of the proletarian revolution in other countries, but it had little success. During the 1930s the Comintern de-emphasized its promotion of revolution and urged Communist parties in Europe to cooperate with socialist and moderate parties in antifascist coalitions known as "popular fronts" or "united fronts."

In foreign policy the Soviet Union proposed disarmament and the formation of alliances against Adolf Hitler's Nazi Germany and Benito Mussolini's Fascist Italy. But Stalin finally became disillusioned with the "appeasement" policies of France and England and embarked on a bold and dangerous gamble in power politics.

In August 1939, ignoring communist ideology, which decried fascism, and the anguished protests of millions of communists and Soviet sympathizers around the world, Stalin signed a non-aggression pact with Hitler. In so doing he bought time and some territory in Eastern Europe, but he also permitted Hitler to conquer Poland and France, which meant that by June 1941 Hitler was able to launch a major offensive against the Soviet Union.

World War II. After sweeping initial successes, facilitated by Stalin's unwillingness to believe that Hitler would attack and by inadequate Soviet preparations, the Nazi armies were checked before Moscow and Leningrad (formerly Petrograd) in the late fall of 1941. The Soviet Union's allies, Britain and the United States, furnished considerable aid to the Soviet Union, and all three nations subscribed to general war aims set forth in the Atlantic Charter.

The Soviet armies continued to bear the brunt of the fighting, and Stalin pressed the United States and Britain to open a "second front" in Europe. Despite the considerable successes of the Germans in 1942, the Soviet forces remained intact and inflicted a major defeat on the Nazi armies in the last months of 1942 at the battle of Stalingrad, the present-day city of Volgograd.

From that time on Soviet troops began to push the Germans back, a process assisted by the British-U.S. landing in France in June 1944. Attacked on two fronts, the Germans surrendered in May 1945. The Soviet Union attacked Japan on Aug. 8, 1945 and completely occupied Manchuria after token Japanese resistance.

Cold War. After victory the Soviet Union faced two major problems: reconstruction and its relationship with its Western allies. Despite attempts in a series of wartime conferences to work out cooperative arrangements for the postwar period, friction soon arose between the Western powers and the Soviet Union, marking the beginning of the "cold war."

The chief issues were Germany and Eastern Europe. The Soviet Union, which had agreed to joint four-power occupation of Germany, began to extract unilateral reparations to assist its own reconstruction effort. As a result, Germany soon became divided into a pro-Allied West Germany and a Soviet-dominated East Germany.

In Eastern Europe the Soviet Union, whose armies had liberated much of the area from German domination, exerted pressure to insure the emergence of pro-Soviet governments despite Soviet promises at the Yalta Conference—held by representatives of Britain, the United States, and the Soviet Union in February 1945—that free elections would be held in those countries.

LOOK MAGAZINE

MOSCOW, viewed from the Kremlin, reflects the Russian past and the Soviet present.

Between 1946 and 1948 one country after another in Eastern Europe came under Soviet domination over the protests of the Western nations, who were powerless, short of starting a new war, to reverse this trend. Hostility between the West and the Soviet Union was carried into the United Nations.

Stalin clearly intended to extend Soviet domination as far west into Europe as possible, assuming that by doing so he not only ensured the security of the Soviet Union, but aided the spread of "socialist" revolutions in the world. The opportunity for Soviet expansion in Western Europe arose through the disorder left by the war and the large Communist parties that existed in France and Italy.

The United States instituted the Marshall Plan, a massive aid program that permitted Western Europe to recover political and economic stability and avert the threat of communist engulfment. It also launched programs of military aid to West European nations, as well as to Greece and Turkey. The Western powers thus embarked on a policy of "containment," to limit Soviet expansion and support anticommunist governments.

Iron Curtain. At home Stalin launched a renewed program of industrialization and totalitarianism. The mild freedom of thought and activity that had been permitted during the war was ended, and strict adherence to anti-Western and nationalistic dogma was demanded in all areas of Soviet life.

To prevent Soviet and East European peoples from comparing themselves with the West and to keep out Western influences, Stalin drew an "iron curtain" between Western and Eastern Europe, cutting off all contacts and normal interchange. At the same time he forced the Soviet people to make even greater sacrifices to rebuild the country and further advance the process of industrialization.

Post–Stalin Era. When Stalin died in 1953 there was a change in Soviet foreign and domestic policy. At home the new leaders were anxious to eliminate the worst abuses of Stalinism without undermining their own control. After a brief power struggle, Nikita S. Khrushchev emerged as the strongest figure, and soon began a daring experiment in "de-Stalinization."

Blaming the evils of the Soviet system on Stalin personally, Khrushchev attempted to reduce substantially the use of terror and to increase material incentives to achieve higher economic performance. To do this meant encouraging initiative, providing a higher standard of living, and permitting a slightly wider range for intellectual and artistic creativity.

Khrushchev was deposed in 1964, largely because of the personal and arbitrary nature of his rule, but his successors, Leonid Brezhnev and Aleksei Kosygin, followed the same basic policies. To a considerable degree these have been successful. The first Soviet space vehicle (*Sputnik*) was launched in 1957, followed by other pioneering Soviet efforts in space. Housing and living conditions improved, and Soviet artists and intellectuals were given somewhat less restricted opportunities for creative work.

Problems, of course, remained. The economy continued to be sluggish, partly because of the difficulties involved in central planning for such a huge, complex, industrialized society. Agricultural productivity remained low, and the commitment to communism of many citizens, particularly young people, was formalistic or nonexistent.

Peaceful Coexistence. In foreign policy, the Soviet leaders accepted the realities of the nuclear age and espoused a policy of "peaceful coexistence." Realizing that the Soviet Union and the United States each had the nuclear capability to destroy one another, they decided that the contest between "capitalism" and "communism" must take place on nonmilitary grounds.

The new approach to the East-West struggle led to serious problems for the Soviet Union within the communist camp. Relaxation of Stalinist controls had ended direct Soviet power over the communist governments it had established in Eastern Europe. Many of those governments chose to act independently of the Soviet Union, and by 1968 Romania had become the prime example of open opposition to Soviet policies.

A more critical divison arose between the Soviet Union and China, where a communist regime had won little power in 1949 with Soviet aid. The Chinese communist leaders sought to continue and intensify the worldwide struggle between East and West. The Chinese moved to replace the Soviet Union as leader of the world communist movement, and pursued a policy of denouncing Soviet "revisionism" and "appeasement."

—George Kish; Don Karl Rowney; John M. Thompson

SPAIN

Official name: The Spanish State
Area: 194,885 square miles
Population: (1967 est.) 32,140,000
Capital: Madrid (Pop., 1964 est., 2,558,583)
Language: Spanish
Religion: Roman Catholicism
Currency unit: Peseta
National holiday: Spanish labor day, July 18

Spain occupies the bulk of the Iberian Peninsula in southwestern Europe. It is bounded on the north by the Bay of Biscay and France, on the east and southeast by the Mediterranean Sea, on the south by the Strait of Gibraltar, and on the west by Portugal and the Atlantic Ocean.

The Canary Islands, which lie in the Atlantic about 800 miles off the southwest coast, and the Balearic Islands, in the Mediterranean just off the east coast, are also part of Spain.

THE LAND. Most of Spain consists of a high tableland, the Meseta, which has an average elevation of more than 2,500 feet above sea level. Most of the Meseta is flat, but it has many hilly and mountainous areas.

The principal mountain ranges of the Meseta are the Sierra de Gata, the Sierra de Gredos, and the Sierra de Guadarrama, to the west and north of Madrid; the Sierra Morena in the south-central area; and the Cantabrian Mountains in the north.

Northeastern Spain is dominated by the rugged Pyrenees, which run along the border with France, isolating the Iberian Peninsula from the rest of Europe.

There is a relatively narrow coastal plain in the east, along the Mediterranean, which widens substantially only in the lower Ebro River valley. This plain is broken in many places by mountains that extend to the sea. In southwestern Andalusia, along the Atlantic shore, the coastal plain is fairly wide.

Spain's major rivers are the Ebro, the Duero, the Tagus, the Guadiana, and the Guadalquivir. The Guadalquivir is the only river navigable for any significant distance.

Climate. The climate of Spain is varied. The southern and eastern coasts have a Mediterranean climate, with long, hot, dry summers and short, cool, moderately rainy winters.

The interior has a continental climate, with very hot summers and cold winters. It is generally quite dry. Galicia and the northern coast have a maritime climate, by far the rainiest in Spain. The higher elevations experience cooler summers and much colder winters.

THE PEOPLE. The Spanish people tend to reflect strong regional differences due to the country's historical development and to the mountainous terrain, which helps isolate one part of the country from another.

The official language is Castilian Spanish, which is generally understood throughout the country. Numerous regional dialects are spoken, however, including Galician in the northwest and Andalusian in the south. Catalan, spoken in the northeast, and Basque, spoken in the mountains of the north, differ greatly from Castilian.

The state religion is Roman Catholicism, and more than 99 percent of the population is at least nominally Roman Catholic. There are small minorities of Jews, Muslims, and Protestants.

Spain has one of the highest birth rates and lowest death rates in Europe, but substantial emigration has kept the average annual increase in population low. From 1958 to 1966 the annual rate of increase was only 0.8 percent, slightly under the average for Western Europe. The population density in 1966 was about 165 persons per square mile, lower than in most European countries.

Spain's principal city is the capital, Madrid, located almost at the geographic center of the country. Spain's second largest city is the Mediterranean port of Barcelona. Other major cities are Valencia, Seville, Zaragoza, and Bilbao.

ECONOMY. The Spanish economy is one of the least developed in Western Europe. Nonetheless, substantial improvement has taken place since 1959, when the government instituted a vigorous economic program, which included devaluation of the peseta, liberalization of trade restrictions, and promotion of foreign investment.

Foreign investment greatly increased following the relaxation of government restrictions. In addition, there has been a phenomenal rise in income from tourism, which reached more than $1,000 million in 1965, and a large gain in remittances from Spaniards working in many booming, but labor-short, Western Europe countries.

In 1964 the government initiated a four-year economic and social development plan to raise the gross national product by 6 percent. This plan was successful, and in 1968 a second plan, emphasizing agricultural development, went into effect.

Natural Resources. Spain's mineral resources compare favorably with those of the rest of southern Europe, but fuels, including high-grade coal, petroleum, and natural gas, are in short supply.

Spain has large deposits of mercury and in 1965 led in world production with 3,100 metric tons. Spain has long been a major producer and exporter of iron ore, and lead, zinc, tungsten, and copper are also mined.

Agriculture. Spain is traditionally an agricultural nation, and about 35 percent of the labor force is engaged in farming. As a result of the country's varied climate, Spanish agriculture is quite diversified.

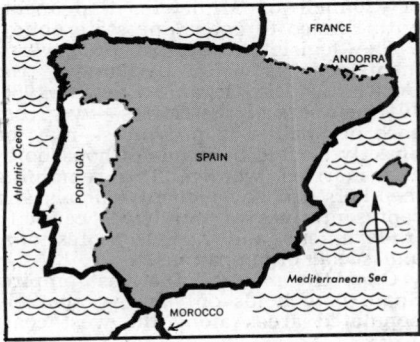

The Mediterranean coast specializes in olives, grapes, and almonds. Valencia and areas further south produce oranges in abundance. Rice is raised in a number of irrigated coastal areas. Wheat and barley are grown in the Meseta, which also provides pasturage for Merino sheep and goats. Galicia and Asturias produce corn, potatoes, and apples. Cattle are also raised in these regions.

Cork is gathered from cork oaks, which are planted throughout the country in hilly areas unsuited to the raising of other crops. Spain generally leads the world in cork production.

Industry. Spanish industry has been growing steadily and in 1964 it contributed 30 percent to the gross domestic product. But it is still largely undeveloped and is unable to meet domestic requirements.

Of the few industrial areas, the port of Barcelona, in the northeast, is by far the most important and most diversified. Its chief industries include textiles, chemicals, iron and steel, metal working, vehicle production and assembly, and printing and publishing.

The Bilbao-Santander district in the north and Avilés and Oviedo further west have developed sizable iron and steel industries. Ship building, zinc smelting, and chemical production are important in the coastal part of this area. Murcia and Cartagena in the southeast form Spain's only other true industrial district, although some manufacturing takes place in nearly all of the larger cities.

Trade. In 1967 Spain's imports cost $3,462 million and its exports earned $1,384 million. The country's principal exports are oranges, nuts, fresh and dried fish, vegetables, wine, textiles, olive oil, and cork. The chief imports include machinery, foodstuffs, chemicals, manufactured goods, and petroleum. Spain's major trading partners are the United States, West Germany, France, and Britain.

GOVERNMENT. Although Spain officially became a monarchy in 1947, no king sits on the throne. In actual fact Spain is a dictatorship led by Gen. Francisco Franco, who is head of state and chief of government as well as commander in chief of the armed forces.

An Organic Law approved by popular referendum in December 1966 allows General Franco to lighten his load if he so wishes by appointing a prime minister as chief of government from a list of three nominees selected by the Council of the Realm. In addition to the Council of the Realm, which is an advisory body, there is a cabinet, or Council of Ministers, that meets with Franco to determine state policy.

The legislative branch of government consists of a parliament, the Cortes. By the Organic Law of 1966, 104 members of the Cortes—two from each of Spain's 52 provinces—may be directly elected by heads of households and married women. The remaining members are government officials and representatives of municipal councils, trade unions, and various professional and social organizations.

Once the master of a vast empire, Spain now holds only a few sparsely populated areas along the west coast of Africa, including the overseas provinces of Ifni, the Spanish Sahara, and Fernando Póo and Río Muni, which form Equatorial Guinea. In Morocco, the tiny enclaves of the Peñón de Alhucemas, Ceuta, Chafarinas, Melilla, and the Peñón de Vélez are under Spanish sovereignty.

Spain is a member of the United Nations.

HISTORY. Spain was peopled in prehistoric times by primitive Basques and Iberians. In about 900 BC Celts began entering the peninsula from the north.

The Phoenicians began founding trading colonies on the southeastern coast in about 800 BC, and the Greeks followed suit from about 500 BC. The Phoenician city of Carthage, in North Africa, acquired control over southern Spain during the 200s BC. In 202 BC Rome defeated Carthage in the Second Punic War and subsequently undertook the conquest of Spain. By the beginning of the first century AD, Roman control over the peninsula was complete.

Under Roman rule classical civilization entered Spain, which soon became one of the most Romanized provinces of the empire. Spain made significant contributions to Latin literature and produced one of Rome's greatest emperors, Trajan. Spain was also one of the first parts of the empire to accept Christianity.

In 409 AD Spain was overrun by the Vandals, who were in turn driven out by the Visigoths. In 419 the Visigoths established a kingdom that included Spain and southern France. They contributed little to Spain culturally, and put up little resistance when Arab and Berber Muslims from North Africa invaded the country in 711. The Muslims, or Moors as they were called, ruled most of Spain from Córdoba, which became the center of a brilliant civilization.

Reconquest. A small Christian nucleus survived the Muslim invasions in the Asturian Mountains, which in 722 became the kingdom of Asturias. The establishment of this kingdom marked the beginning of the Reconquest, the 800 year struggle of the Christians to rid Iberia of the Muslims.

In addition to Asturias, which evolved into the kingdom of León in the 1000s, there arose the Christian kingdoms of Aragon and Navarre, the county of Catalonia, and the county—later the kingdom—of Castile. Each of these medieval Christian states had its own body of law and feudal customs. Each also had a *côrtes*, or representative assembly.

For 300 years these kingdoms waged unsuccessful wars with the Caliphate of Córdoba, the ruling power of Muslim Spain. In the 1000s civil war among the Muslims shattered the unity of the caliphate. Its disintegration aided the Reconquest, and by 1300 the Christians had reduced the Muslim hold to a narrow strip in southern Spain known as the kingdom of Granada.

Aragon and Catalonia had merged in the 1100s, and Castile and León had done the same in the 1200s. But Portugal separated from Castile in 1143 and became an independent kingdom. Further unification of Christian Spain

SPANISH NATIONAL TOURIST DEPT.

VEJER DE LA FRONTERA, in Cadiz, Spain, is an old city with narrow winding streets.

was brought about by the marriage in 1469 of Ferdinand of Aragon (r. 1479–1516) and Queen Isabella of Castile (r. 1474–1504).

In 1478 they supported the Inquisition, whose ecclesiastical courts sought out the thousands of converted Jews and Muslims living in Spain, whose allegiance to Roman Catholicism was doubted.

In 1492 Ferdinand and Isabella conquered Granada, the last Muslim stronghold, and to completely unify the country they expelled the remaining Jews and Muslims. In the same year Christopher Columbus discovered the New World and claimed it for Spain, thus opening up vast new territories for colonization.

The Hapsburgs. Joanna, the daughter of Ferdinand and Isabella, married Philip of Hapsburg, the heir to the Holy Roman Empire and to much of northern Europe. Their son, Charles I of Spain (r. 1516–1556), became the Holy Roman Emperor Charles V in 1519.

Charles encouraged Spanish colonial expansion, and during his reign Spain gained control of most of Middle America and northwestern South America. In his role as emperor, however, he embroiled Spain in a series of wars against France. A devout Roman Catholic, he made an unsuccessful attempt to defeat Lutheranism in Germany and engaged in a long struggle against the Muslims of North Africa.

Philip II. Charles' son, Philip II (r. 1556–1598), did not succeed to the Holy Roman Empire, but he did inherit Spain, the New World possessions, Franche-Comté, Milan, Naples, and the Netherlands. As staunch a Roman Catholic as his father, Philip's foreign policy was often largely the result of his religious feelings.

Philip was determined to suppress Protestantism among his subjects in the Netherlands, but his attempts failed and the Netherlands declared their independence from Spain in 1581. His greatest failure, however, was his attempt to conquer England, which was not only Protestant but also Spain's rival for control of the seas.

In 1588 Philip launched the Spanish Armada against the English. The Armada was largely destroyed, and its destruction marked the beginning of the end of Spanish sea power. Philip's only notable success in foreign affairs was the acquisition of Portugal in 1580.

Decline and Renewal. Spain declined rapidly in the 1600s, partially as a result of mediocre and indolent kings, who left governing to inferior ministers. The country grew poorer, government revenue proved insufficient despite heavy gold imports from Spain's American colonies, and the population declined. The Dutch and English crippled Spanish trade on the seas, and Portugal regained its independence in 1640.

The nation was at its weakest when Charles II (r. 1665–1700) died without heirs and the throne passed to Philip V (r. 1700–1746) of the French Bourbon line. Under the Bourbons, Spain underwent a revival in the 1700s. Trade and industry grew, the population increased, colonial administration improved, and the Spanish army and navy regained some of their former strength. These gains, however, were swept away during the Napoleonic era.

Spain in the 1800s. In 1807 Napoleon I of France seized the Spanish throne for his brother Joseph, and the Spanish monarch, Ferdinand VII, was forced to abdicate. The Spanish carried on guerrilla warfare against the French, and in 1813, aided by the British, they finally drove Napoleon's troops from the peninsula.

In 1814 Ferdinand VII was restored to the throne, but Spain had been seriously weakened. The mainland American colonies, which had proclaimed their independence during Ferdinand's reign, were completely lost by 1825, and a family quarrel among Spanish Bourbons over the throne led to a fierce civil war, the Carlist struggle, that raged from 1834 to 1839.

The reign of Isabella II, who had come to the throne in 1833 as an infant, was marked by political unrest and internal disorder. In addition, she was personally unpopular and in 1868 was forced to abdicate.

After an experiment with an imported Italian monarch, Amadeo I (r. 1871–1873), a republic was established in 1873. The following year, however, Isabella's son, Alfonso XII (r. 1875–1885), came of age and was recalled to the throne.

Alfonso XII died in 1885 and was succeeded by Alfonso XIII (r. 1885–1931), who was born after his father's death. In 1898 Spain fought a disastrous war with the United States, the Spanish-American War. It lost Cuba, Puerto Rico, the Philippines, and Guam, reducing Spain's colonial empire to a few minor holdings in Africa.

Instability. Spain was neutral in World War I, but the wartime demand for goods led to an expansion of Spanish industry. In the postwar period, when the demand for goods and munitions ceased, Spain suffered labor problems and political instability. The country was also burdened with the financial and miltary problem of putting down uprisings in Spanish Morocco, where a Spanish zone had been established in the early 1900s.

In 1921 a military disaster in Morocco seriously threatened the monarchy. The political situation grew steadily worse, and in 1923 Gen. Miguel Primo de Rivera seized power with the king's consent and established a dictatorship. Primo de Rivera resigned in 1930, and the republicans took advantage of the overwhelming majority they had won in parliamentary elections in 1931 to proclaim a republic.

The Second Spanish Republic, which attempted liberal reforms, was unpopular with the Roman Catholic Church and the aristocracy. General dissatisfaction with the republic increased as the world economic depression of the 1930s began to affect Spain.

The army, the monarchists, the landowning aristocracy, and the church were united in their opposition to the republic. The republic was supported, on the other hand, by the socialists, communists, republicans, and various liberal groups.

Civil War. Following a republican victory in elections held in 1936, violence broke out and the army, led by Gen. José Sanjurjo, rose against the government. General Sanjurjo was killed in an airplane crash, and Gen. Francisco Franco assumed leadership of the rebels.

Soon after the outbreak of the hostilities foreign nations began to intervene. The Loyalists, as the supporters of the government were called, were aided by sympathizers in the United States and other countries as well as by the Soviet Union. Franco, however, received large-scale aid from Nazi Germany and Fascist Italy, and by 1939 the Loyalists were defeated.

Franco set up a dictatorship and governed with the title "El Caudillo," or "the leader," aided by the Falangists, the Spanish equivalent of the Italian Fascists.

Contemporary Spain. Although openly favorable to the Axis powers in World War II, Franco remained neutral. In 1947 Franco promulgated the Law of Succession, which restored the monarchy by providing for the election of a king by a Regency Council after his death.

In 1953, during the Cold War, the United States changed its previously unfavorable attitude toward Franco's government and obtained military bases in Spain in return for $226 million in financial aid. In 1955 Spain became a member of the United Nations.

During the mid-1960s Franco's government began to show signs of political liberalization, and in 1966 a new constitution was adopted. The new constitution provided for the appointment of a prime minister and the direct election of two members of parliament from each province. A greater measure of freedom of religion was granted non-Roman Catholics, and less stringent censorship regulations and labor restrictions were decreed.

In December 1967 Spain's claim to the British colony of Gibraltar, an issue that had severely strained relations between the two countries during the mid-1960s, came before the UN General Assembly. The assembly called for talks between Britain and Spain to arrange for the decolonization of the area.

—Charles E. Nowell

SUDAN

Official name: Republic of Sudan
Area: 967,499 square miles
Population: (1967 est.) 14,355,000
Capital: Khartoum (Pop., 1964 est., 173,500)
Language: Arabic, African languages
Religion: Islam, Christianity, traditional religions
Currency unit: Pound
National holiday: Independence day, January 1

Sudan, a republic in northern Africa, is bordered on the north by the United Arab Republic (Egypt); on the east by the Red Sea and Ethiopia; on the south by Kenya, Uganda, and the Congo (Kinshasa); and on the west by the Central African Republic, Chad, and Libya. Between 1899 and 1953 Sudan was ruled jointly by Britain and Egypt as a condominium. From 1954 to 1956, Sudan was self-governing, and on Jan. 1, 1956 it became independent.

THE LAND. Sudan, the largest country in Africa, has a varied landscape. Most of northern Sudan is occupied by the desert region of the Sahara. The Nile River flows north through central Sudan, creating a fertile region. The river's two main branches, the Blue Nile and the White Nile, meet at Khartoum, and then the great, single river flows northward into the United Arab Republic.

In west-central Sudan the Marra mountains reach elevations above 10,000 feet. East of the Marra Mountains is the Kordofan Plateau. In central Sudan the Nuba Mountains reach elevations of over 4,300 feet. South of Khartoum, in east-central Sudan, there are tropical savanna lands.

In the south there are tropical rain forests, and in the extreme southern part of the country the White Nile

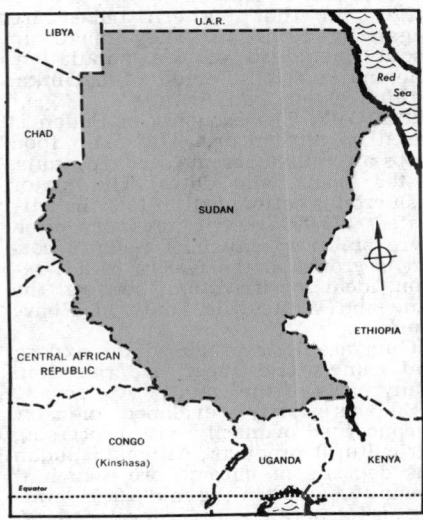

LOOK

SUDAN'S PEOPLE include many different ethnic groups, among them the Dogon.

overflows to create a swampy region called the *Sudd.* The Atbara River, a tributary of the Nile, flows through eastern Sudan.

Rainfall averages only about four inches a year in east-central Sudan, and the Red Sea coast is arid and hot. It is relatively rainy in the western mountain region, and the south has a hot and humid tropical climate.

THE PEOPLE. There are two distinct groups of people in Sudan: Muslims in the northern provinces of Kassala, Khartoum, Blue Nile, Kordofan, Darfur, and Northern; and Negro tribes in the southern provinces of Upper Nile, Bahr el Ghazal, and Equatoria.

Most of the Muslims, who make up the majority of Sudan's population, are Arabic-speaking. They are divided into great tribal groups including the Jaaliin, Shaiqiyya, and Kababish. The more important non-Arabic-speaking peoples in northern Sudan are the Beja, who live near the Red Sea; the Nubians, along the Nile from Dongola to the Egyptian border; the Negroid Nuba, in southern Kordofan; and the Negroid Fur in Darfur.

Most of the southern tribes are pagan or Christian. They make up about one third of the population. The major tribes include the Dinka, Shilluk, Nuer, and Azande.

ECONOMY. The economy of Sudan is based on agriculture. The main food crops are millet, sesame seeds, peanuts, castor beans, and dates. The major cash crop is cotton, and in 1965 an estimated 163,000 metric tons of cotton were produced. Much of Sudan's cotton is grown in the Gezira, a flat region, ideal for irrigation, between the Blue and White Nile South of Khartoum.

Gum arabic is produced for export, and camels and sheep are raised in many parts of the country.

Sudan's poorly developed industry is concerned primarily with processing agricultural products. Although Sudan has deposits of chrome ore, which it began to export in the mid-1960s, mining is generally underdeveloped. A

ten-year development program was begun in 1960 to improve transportation facilities and build irrigation systems and dams.

In 1966 imports cost $217 million and exports earned $205 million. The major imports are petroleum products, textiles, machinery, and foodstuffs. The major exports are cotton, sesame seed, and gum arabic. Most trade is conducted with Britain, West Germany, and Italy.

GOVERNMENT. In 1956 a transitional constitution was adopted. The constitution was reinstated in 1965, after a period of military rule that began in 1958. The constitution vests executive power in a five member Supreme Council of State, headed by a president.

Legislative power is held by a Constituent Assembly whose members are popularly elected. The assembly elects a prime minister, who appoints a cabinet. Cabinet members are responsible to the legislature.

Sudan is a member of the United Nations, the Organization of African Unity, and the Arab League.

HISTORY. Sudan's history has always been closely linked with Egypt. In about 3000 B.C. the pharaohs of ancient Egypt sent expeditions into Sudan to raid for slaves, and by about 2000 BC Egypt had extended its rule into Sudan. The region of present-day Sudan came to be called Kush. The power of Egypt began to decline after about 2000 BC.

A Nubian from Napata, in north-central Sudan, proclaimed himself king of Kush in 750 BC. He gained control of Egypt and established a Sudanese dynasty, which lasted until 661 BC, when the Assyrians conquered Egypt. After that time, Egyptian civilization in Sudan declined.

The kingdom of Kush reestablished itself as an independent state and survived until about 350 AD, at which time it was destroyed by the kingdom of Axum, in northern Ethiopia. After that, Negro peoples from the south began to migrate into northern Sudan. Beginning in the 500s the peoples of Northern Sudan became Christians, and two Christian dynasties, Maqurra and Alwa, were established.

In the late 1200s the Mamluks, a Muslim dynasty in Egypt, destroyed Maqurra. Arabs began migrating into northern Sudan, and many of the people were converted to Islam. Alwa survived until the early 1500s, at which time a Negro tribe called the Funj established the powerful Muslim state of Sennar. Until its decline some 300 years later, the Funj dynasty provided much of Sudan with unity and security.

Egyptian conquest of Sudan began in 1820, and Sennar was overrun by Egyptian armies. At the junction of the White and Blue Niles, Egypt created a military and administrative center, Khartoum, which became the capital of Egyptian Sudan. Egyptian rule lasted until 1885. In that year a Sudanese, Muhammad Ahmad al-Mahdi, captured Khartoum after a four year religious and political struggle against Egyptian rule.

Condominium. Sudan remained under the control of Muhammad Ahmad's successor until an Anglo-Egyptian force conquered Sudan in 1896–1898.

Sudan became a condominium ruled jointly by Britain and Egypt in 1899, but in fact Britain controlled Sudan. The period of British rule was considered by many a model of good colonial administration, achieving security and economic development.

Although nationalist movements emerged in the 1920s, they became important only during World War II. The nationalist movement was strongly marked by rivalry between two major Muslim religious brotherhoods, the Khatmiya and the Ansar. The Khatmiya, led by Sayyid Ali al-Mirghani, favored union with Egypt. The Ansar, led by Sayyid Abd al-Rahman al-Mahdi, a posthumous son of Muhammad Ahmad al-Mahdi, took a more pro-British stand and favored complete independence.

In 1953 Egypt and Britain signed an agreement granting Sudan self-government, and soon all sides were able to agree on complete independence for Sudan. A parliament was established in January 1954, and the National Unionist Party (NUP), which represented a more secular policy than the brotherhoods, formed the first cabinet. On Jan. 1, 1956 Sudan became an independent republic.

Independence. The Umma Party, mainly the Ansar, and the People's Democratic Party, largely the Khatmiya, formed a coalition, and in July 1956 the National Unionist Party was forced from power. Political instability followed, and in 1958 parliamentary government was ended by a bloodless coup led by Lt. Gen. Ibrahim Abboud. In 1964 demonstrations against the military forced Abboud's resignation and a return to civilian rule.

Elections held in 1965 gave the NUP and the Umma Party a majority in the assembly. The two formed a coalition government with Muhammad Ahmad Mahjoub as prime minister. The three southern provinces did not vote in the elections. They had gone into rebellion against the Muslim-Arab north in 1963.

Early in 1968 the Constituent Assembly was dissolved, and a draft constitution abandoned. New elections were called for April, and prospects brightened for the participation of the Southern provinces.

—L. Carl Brown;
Hibberd V. B. Kline, Jr.

SWAZILAND

Official name: Swaziland
Area: 6,704 square miles
Population: (1966 est.) 375,000
Capital: Mbabane (Pop., 1962 est., urban area, 8,390)
Language: Swazi, English
Religion: Traditional religions, Christianity
Currency unit: South African rand

Swaziland, a country in southeastern Africa, is bordered on the north, south, and west by the Republic of South Africa, and on the east by Mozambique. Britain granted Swaziland internal self-government in 1967 and agreed to full independence effective Sept. 6, 1968.

THE LAND. Swaziland has three well-defined veld, or grassland, regions—the highveld, middleveld, and lowveld.

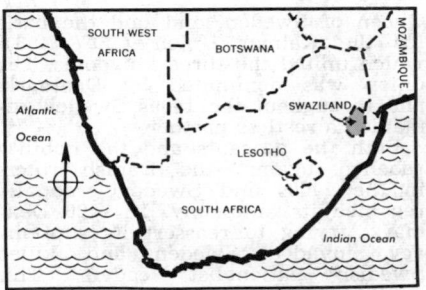

The highveld, in western Swaziland, is mountainous and has an average elevation of 3,500 feet. To the east is the middleveld, with an average elevation of 2,000 feet. The lowveld, in eastern Swaziland, has average elevations of 1,000 feet. The Lebombo, a plateau region, is in the extreme eastern part of the country.

The Great Escarpment, a geological feature of southern Africa that rises some 6,000 feet above the plain, runs through Swaziland.

The highveld is humid and receives between 40 and 90 inches of rain each year. The climate in the middleveld and Lebombo plateau is subtropical and drier, receiving between 30 and 45 inches of rain each year. The lowveld receives between 20 and 30 inches of rain each year.

THE PEOPLE. Most of the people of Swaziland belong to the Bantu-speaking Swazi tribe. The Swazi have traditionally been a pastoral people. There is also a small number of Bantu-speaking Zulu people in southern Swaziland.

About 2.5 percent of the people are of European origin, mainly Afrikaans-speaking in southern Swaziland and English or Afrikaans-speaking in the north. There is a small community of people of mixed European and African descent.

There are only two large cities in Swaziland—Mbabane, the capital, and Manzini, formerly known as Bremersdorp, the country's commercial center.

ECONOMY. Swaziland's economy is based on agriculture. The country has rich mineral and forest resources and fertile soils. In recent years the Swazi have become successful farmers. The basic food crops are corn and sorghum. The chief cash crops are cotton and tobacco. Sugar cane, citrus, rice, and other fruits and vegetables are grown in irrigated areas.

Cattle are raised in most parts of the country. The Swazi have traditionally valued the cattle as a symbol of social status and only in recent years have cattle acquired economic importance. Forestry, mainly in the highveld, is of growing importance to the economy.

Swaziland's mineral resources include large deposits of iron ore and asbestos. There are also deposits of coal, gold, tin, barytes, and pyrophyllite. Iron ore mined at Ngwenya, in western Swaziland, is carried by rail to the port of Lourenço Marques, in Mozambique, for export. There is little manufacturing apart from the processing of minerals and agricultural products.

Swaziland's main imports are textiles, machinery, and petroleum products. The leading exports are iron ore, asbestos, and sugar. Most trade is conducted with South Africa, Britain, and Japan.

Swaziland has close economic ties with South Africa, and many Swazis find work in South Africa. Customs duties for Swaziland are collected by South Africa, and Swaziland receives a fixed percentage of South Africa's customs revenue each year. Swaziland also uses South African currency.

GOVERNMENT. Swaziland has a parliamentary system of government. The king, or Ngwenyama, of Swaziland is head of state. Actual executive power is held by a prime minister and cabinet responsible to the legislature.

Legislative power is held by a parliament made up of a 30-member House of Assembly and a 12-member Senate. Twenty-four of the House members are popularly elected, and six are appointed by the king. Six members of the Senate are elected by the House of Assembly, and six are appointed by the king.

HISTORY. In the mid-1700s a group of tribal peoples in southern Africa, the Ngoni, broke away from the main body of Bantu-speaking peoples. They came into conflict with another group of Bantu-speaking people, the Zulu, and by the early 1800s the Zulu had forced them northward into present-day Swaziland.

A Ngoni chief, Sobhuza, founded the Swazi nation by fusing several Ngoni clans with some Sotho-speaking people they had conquered. Sobhuza's son Mswati, from whom the Swazi derive their name, extended Swazi power and prestige among neighboring Bantu-speaking peoples.

European Influence. Europeans began to settle in the area in the 1800s, and the Swazi ruler granted them many land concessions. Both the British colony of Natal, in present-day South Africa, and the Afrikaner, or Boer, Republic of the Transvaal, also in present-day South Africa, claimed Swaziland. In 1890 a compromise was reached, and a provisional government was established composed of representatives of the Swazi, the British, and the Transvaal Afrikaners.

To appease the Afrikaners, the British ceded administration of Swaziland to the Transvaal in 1894, despite Swazi protests. In the Boer, or South African, War (1899–1902) the British conquered the Transvaal, and assumed control of Swaziland. In 1907 the British High Commissioner for South Africa took over the administration of Swaziland.

The rise of nationalism in the 1940s and 1950s threatened the Swazi aristocracy and the white community, both of whom feared the loss of power and privilege. In 1960 these groups jointly requested Britain to grant a constitution that would in effect preserve the status quo. A British-sponsored constitution promulgated in 1964 did not satisfy traditionalists, nationalists, or the white minority.

Independence. Traditionalist forces, led by the Swazi paramount chief Sobhuza II, formed the Imbokodvo Party, which won a majority of seats in the legislative council in Swaziland's first elections in 1964. In April 1967, Britain granted Swaziland internal self-government, and promised independence not later than 1969.

The Imbokodvo won elections held in April 1967, and Sobhuza II became king of Swaziland. Prince Makhosini Diamini, his cousin, became prime minister. In July 1967 the king asked Britain to speed independence, and Britain agreed to grant full independence effective Sept. 6, 1968.

—Hibberd V. B. Kline, Jr.;
Gary A. Weissman

SWEDEN

Official name: Kingdom of Sweden
Area: 173,666 square miles
Population: (1967 est.) 7,869,000
Capital: Stockholm (Pop., 1965 est., urban area, 1,179,340)
Language: Swedish
Religion: Lutheranism
Currency unit: Krona
National holiday: Birthday of the king

Sweden, a kingdom in northern Europe, occupies the eastern half of the Scandinavian peninsula. It is bordered on the north by Norway and Finland; on the east by Finland, the Gulf of Bothnia and the Baltic Sea; on the south by the Baltic Sea; and on the west by the Kattegat and the Skagerrak, arms of the North Sea, and Norway. Gotland and Öland islands in the Baltic are part of Sweden.

THE LAND. Sweden may be divided into two geographic regions—the Norrland, the northern two thirds of the country, and the south. Part of the Norrland lies north of the Arctic Circle. In western Norrland the Kjölen Mountains, the backbone of the Scandinavian peninsula, rise to nearly 7,000 feet. The Northern Plateau occupies the center, and in the east there is a relatively narrow coastal plain. The main rivers of the region drain eastward into the Gulf of Bothnia.

The southern third of Sweden includes the broad, level Central Lowland and the Skåne, a flat plain in the extreme south. These two regions are separated by a rough upland zone, the Småland plateau, which has many rivers and includes Sweden's largest lakes, Vänern and Vättern.

Each region has a distinct climate. The Norrland is subarctic, with long, cold winters and short, cool summers. The severity of the climate increases to the north and in the higher elevations. Southern Sweden has much milder winters and slightly warmer, although still cool, summers. The country as a whole is rather dry, receiving only about 20 inches of rainfall a year, most of it concentrated in the south.

THE PEOPLE. The Swedish people are ethnically and culturally homogeneous. Swedish is the universal language, and the dominant religion is Lutheranism. There are small minorities of Lapps and Finns in the north.

Although Sweden is one of Europe's largest countries in area, its population density—44 persons per square mile in 1965—is one of Europe's lowest. With one of the lowest rates of increase in the world, 0.6 percent a year between 1958 and 1965, the population is growing very slowly. Although fairly large numbers of im-

migrants from the Baltic states arrived in Sweden after World War II, the net gains from migration are negligible.

Most Swedes live in the southern third of the country, especially in the central lowland and the Skåne. The Småland plateau and the Baltic Coast are rather thinly populated, and the northern interior is sparsely settled. Sweden's major cities include Stockholm, the capital, on the southeast coast; Göteborg, on the southwest coast; and Malmö, at the southern tip of Sweden.

ECONOMY. Sweden has a highly industrialized economy based upon rich natural resources. All of Norrland and much of the south are heavily forested, and the dense timber stands make Sweden's forestry output one of Europe's largest. Sweden's many swift rivers and streams are harnessed for electricity, and electrical production increased steadily during the 1950s and 1960s, reaching a total of 50,640 million kilowatt hours in 1966.

Sweden's most important mineral resources are its exceptionally large deposits of high quality iron ore. There are also modest reserves of lead, zinc, manganese, tungstun, sulfur, copper, gold, silver, and uranium.

Agriculture. Due to poor climate, poor soil, and rough topography, only about 7 percent of the land can be cultivated, most of it in the south, and agriculture employs only about 14 percent of the labor force. Nevertheless, efficient farming techniques produce high yields per acre.

Dairying is the main agricultural activity, and dairy products account for about half of farm revenue. Oats, wheat, rye, barley, and potatoes are the main crops. Commercial fishing prospers and provides important export products.

Manufacturing and Shipping. Manufacturing is the most important part of the Swedish economy. Industry, which expanded greatly after World War I, is modern and diverse. Although there is some iron and steel production, metal working, and shipbuilding, emphasis has been placed on producing electrical machinery, vehicles, furniture, scientific instruments, paper, porcelain, and glass.

Merchant shipping makes an important contribution to the economy. Sweden's merchant fleet in 1966 totalled 4.4 million gross registered tons. The earnings of the fleet help to offset Sweden's unfavorable balance of trade.

Trade. In 1967 imports cost more than $4,700 million and exports earned over $4,500 million. The leading imports are machinery and transportation equipment, petroleum products, iron and steel products, and foodstuffs. The major exports are machinery, lumber and wood pulp, iron and steel, paper and cardboard, sawed timber, and ships. Most Swedish trade is with West Germany, Britain, the United States, Denmark, Norway, and the Netherlands.

GOVERNMENT. Sweden is a constitutional monarchy, with a king as head of state. Actual executive power is exercised by a prime minister and cabinet responsible to the legislature, the *Riksdag*.

The *Riksdag* consists of two houses with equal powers. One eighth of the Upper Chamber is elected indirectly each year and the entire Lower Chamber is elected directly to a normal term of four years. Under a planned constitutional reform, the *Riksdag* is to become a unicameral body by 1971.

Sweden is a member of the United Nations and the Nordic Council, an association of Scandinavian states.

HISTORY. In about 1000 BC Germanic peoples related to modern-day Swedes appeared in the land. The settlers remained divided into numerous small bands and kingdoms until about 600 AD, when two large tribal groups became dominant—the Goths, on the shores of Lake Vättern, and the Svear, around Lake Mälaren, near Stockholm.

As other Scandinavian Vikings, or adventurers, sailed westward between 800 and 1050, Sweden's Vikings thrust eastward along European river systems. In the 1100s they established colonies on the eastern shore of the Baltic and governed territory between the Baltic and the Black Sea.

Although the kingdoms of Gothia and Svealand were united in the early 800s, competition for power continued between the Goths and the Svear. Nevertheless, by the end of the 1100s a unified Swedish state had emerged in which Svear, or Swedish, influence tended to prevail.

Christianity spread to Sweden in the 800s, and by 1000 the Church was a powerful influence. During the 1100s Christianity was an important part of the culture the Swedes carried to the Finnish peoples of the territories they conquered.

The 1200s and early 1300s were turbulent, as a newly formed land-owning aristocracy challenged the political and economic dominance of a powerful middle class of townsmen and merchants. Contacts with the German merchants of the Hanseatic League introduced strong German influence into Sweden in the 1300s, and in 1363, a member of the German family of Mecklenburg took the Swedish throne.

Kalmar Union. When opposition to the king arose, the nobility in 1388 called on Margaret, Queen of Denmark and Norway, to intervene. She became

Queen of Sweden, and laid the basis for the Kalmar Union (1397–1483), which united the three kingdoms. The union was dominated by Denmark, and throughout the 1400s Sweden remained a restless partner.

Both the peasants and the nobility rebelled against the Danish rulers in the 1400s and Sweden gradually regained its autonomy. In 1520 Denmark, trying to reassert its supremacy, invaded Sweden and killed Swedish nationalist leaders. This sparked a nationalist revolt led by Gustavus Vasa, a young nobleman.

Vasa Kings. Sweden succeeded in breaking away from the Kalmar Union, and in 1523 Gustavus became the first king of the House of Vasa. He had the strong support of the merchants and townsmen, and one of his first acts was to end the German Hanseatic League's monopoly of trade in the Baltic area. During his rule, too, the Reformation came to Sweden, and by the mid-1500s Lutheranism was the dominant religion.

Under generally able kings of the house of Vasa, Sweden developed a prosperous economy, and a position of prestige and power in the world. In 1630 the intervention of King Gustavus II Adolphus on the side of Protestantism in the religious-political conflict of the Thirty Years' War was decisive in making Protestantism dominant in northern Europe and in bringing the fighting to an end.

Sweden spent most of the rest of the 1600s and the early 1700s in wars of conquest against Poland, Russia, and Denmark. Sweden's greatest soldier-king, Charles XII, died in 1718, and Russia soon won from Sweden most of the territory conquered from Poland and Denmark in the preceding century.

The country returned briefly to constitutional government, but absolutism was restored in 1772 under Gustavus III, who feared that Sweden would come totally under the control of Prussia. At first he ruled as an "enlightened despot," introducing progressive and liberal measures, but in the 1780s his rule grew more repressive.

Gustavus invaded Russian Finland in an unsuccessful attempt to regain dominance in the Baltic. However, he succeeded in making Sweden dominant in Scandinavia by defeating the Danes and briefly uniting Denmark and Sweden before his assassination in 1792.

Turmoil followed the death of Gustavus. His successor, Gustavus IV, lost Sweden's Finnish provinces in still another war with Russia in 1808, and he was forced by the dissatisfied nobility to abdicate in 1809 in favor of Charles XIII. In 1809 a new constitution was adopted giving great power to the aristocracy.

Reforms and Growth. In 1812 Sweden joined the coalition against Napoleonic France, and the end of the Napoleonic era brought major territorial changes. In 1814 Sweden acquired control of Norway from Denmark and the two states were joined in a personal union under the Swedish king. A change of dynasty also came about. In 1818 Jean Baptiste Bernadotte, on of Napoleon's marshalls, who had been

THE AMERICAN SWEDISH NEWS EXCHANGE

SWEDISH CASTLE, dating from the 100s.

chosen crown prince in 1810 in an effort to prevent Napoleon from conquering the country by force, succeeded to the throne as Charles XIV John.

Bernadotte's tendency toward arbitrary rule stimulated liberal reform movements. Under his successor, Oscar I, the Liberals made some headway toward universal education and the limitation of royal power. Under Oscar's successor, Charles XV, they achieved electoral reforms and finally, in 1864, a Liberal constitution establishing parliamentary government.

During the later 1800s Sweden underwent rapid industrialization, especially after 1872, when Oscar II came to the throne and initiated programs that made Sweden a commercial and industrial state. The social upheaval that accompanied rapid industrialization resulted in progressive social welfare and suffrage legislation, the growth of trade unionism, and the development of the cooperative movement.

Prosperity and political reform affected Norway, too, and by the 1890s Norwegian nationalism was a major force. In 1905, in a dispute over consular service, Norway proclaimed its independence, which Sweden accepted late in the year.

Modern Sweden. Political and social progress continued in the 1900s. Under Gustavus V, who came to the throne in 1907, universal suffrage and a system of proportional representation were introduced. In 1914 Sweden's Socialist Party won about one-third of the seats in the lower house of the parliament, and the pace of social legislation accelerated.

Sweden managed to stay neutral in World War I and suffered little from it. During the 1920s and 1930s under continuing Socialist direction, prosperity continued. Sweden successfully combatted the world economic depression of the 1930s by heavily involving the government in the economy and introducing unemployment insurance legislation.

When Adolf Hitler's Nazi party came to power in Germany in the 1930s, Sweden armed itself but maintained its neutrality. Its neutrality was severely tested in 1939, when Finland was invaded by the Soviet Union, and later in 1940, during World War II, when Denmark and Norway were attacked and occupied by German forces. Sweden was forced to make some concessions to Germany, but it also gave asylum to refugees.

After the war Sweden's economy continued to expand and its standard of living rose to one of the highest levels in Europe. Prosperity and a successful combination of socialism and individualism combined to produce a stable society that was at the same time dynamic and liberal.

Sweden participated actively in the international organizations of the postwar world and used its historic position of neutrality to work for international peace. Swedish troops served with UN peacekeeping forces throughout the world, and a Swede, Dag Hammarskjöld, served as Secretary General of the UN from 1953 until 1961, when he was killed while on a peacekeeping mission to the Congo (Kinshasa).

SWITZERLAND

Official name: Swiss Confederation
Population: (1966 est.) 5,999,000
Area: 15,941 square miles
Capital: Bern (Pop., 1965 est. urban area, 247,300)
Language: French, German, Italian, Romansh
Religion: Protestantism, Roman Catholicism
Currency unit: Franc
National holiday: Anniversary of the founding of the Swiss Confederation, August 1

Switzerland, a small, landlocked country in western Europe, is bounded on the north by West Germany, on the east by Austria and Liechtenstein, on the south by Italy, and on the west by France.

The Swiss have achieved a remarkable internal cohesiveness in spite of a rugged physical environment, a long history of decentralized government, and considerable cultural and linguistic diversity.

THE LAND. Switzerland has three major physical regions: the Jura Mountains in the northwest, the central Swiss Plateau, and the Alps, which cover the southern three-fifths of the country.

Switzerland has many lakes, of which Lake Geneva is the largest. The principal rivers are the Rhine and the Rhône, which have their headwaters high in the Swiss Alps only a few miles from one another.

Switzerland's climate is humid, with mild to cool summers and mostly cold winters. Winters increase in severity with altitude, and the more rugged parts of the Alps are very cold and snowy. In the south and along Lake Geneva the climate is much milder.

THE PEOPLE. The Swiss are descended from several different ethnic groups. Rhaetic and Celtic tribes who lived in Switzerland in Roman times were overwhelmed by the Germanic Alemanni and Burgundians in the 400s. Roman culture and the Latin language

remained strongest in the south. These ethnic differences have remained and are expressed linguistically.

Switzerland has four official languages—French, German, Italian, and Romansh—and most Swiss have at least a working knowledge of more than one language. According to the 1960 census, German is the principal language of 69.3 percent of the population, French of 18.9 percent, and Italian of 9.5 percent. About 60,000 Swiss concentrated in the southeastern canton of Graubünden speak Romansh, a language derived from Latin.

Slightly more than half of the population is Protestant, and slightly less than half is Roman Catholic. Protestants predominate in the cities and Roman Catholics in the rural areas.

The annual natural rate of population growth between 1958 and 1965 was about 1.9 percent, almost exactly the European average. But substantial immigration gave Switzerland a net annual population growth rate of 2.1 percent, the highest in Western Europe. The highest population density is found on the Swiss Plateau, in an east-west band from Zurich to Geneva, and in the Rhine corridor.

Switzerland in 1966 had six cities with urban area populations of more than 100,000. These included Zurich, 651,600; Basel, 345,300; Geneva, 285,200; Bern, 247,300; Lausanne, 202,100; and Lucerne, 140,400.

ECONOMY. Switzerland has few natural resources, and agriculture is limited by the rugged terrain. But the Swiss have developed a prosperous economy based on the manufacture of high quality, low bulk goods that involve a high degree of skilled workmanship, such as watches and clocks. These goods enjoy an excellent reputation and have a steady market abroad.

The economy has also been aided by the country's political stability and policy of strict neutrality, which have made it a great international banking and insurance center. Switzerland also derives large revenues from international transit traffic, mainly between West Germany and Italy, and from tourism.

Natural Resources. Switzerland has no important mineral deposits other than salt and stone. But the country's rivers provide an excellent source of hydroelectric power, which the Swiss have developed to compensate for the lack of fuels. In 1965 Switzerland had an installed hydroelectric capacity of 8.1 million kilowatts.

Agriculture. Agriculture employs about 11 percent of the labor force. It is efficient but production does not meet domestic requirements.

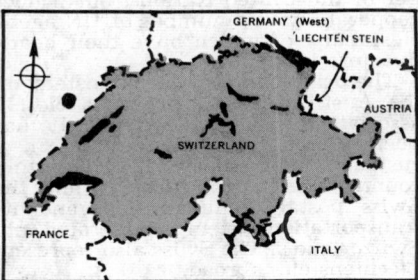

FIECHTER

AROSA, SWITZERLAND. The historic church of Arosa is more than 500 years old.

The raising of livestock, particularly dairy cattle, is the most important agricultural activity. The major crops are wheat and potatoes, which are grown in the central plateau.

Industry. Swiss industry must import a large part of its raw materials and most of its products are exported. The most important industries produce textiles, chemicals, dyestuffs, inks, pharmaceuticals, clocks and watches, and precision machinery. Printing is also important.

Trade. In 1967 Swiss exports earned $3,502 million and imports cost $4,118 million. The country's chief exports are watches and clocks, medicines and pharmaceuticals, chemicals, dyestuffs, textiles, and machinery. Major imports include foodstuffs, machinery, iron and steel, motor vehicles, raw fibers, and petroleum.

Switzerland conducts the bulk of its trade with West Germany, France, Italy, the United States, and Britain.

GOVERNMENT. Switzerland is a federal republic of 22 cantons, which are roughly equivalent to provinces or states. The executive branch of government consists of the Federal Council, composed of seven ministers who head various administrative departments.

The head of state is the president, who is elected to a one-year term from among the members of the Federal Council by the legislature. The president has comparatively little power and cannot serve consecutive terms.

Legislative power is vested in the Coucil of States and the National Council. The Council of States has 44 members, two from each canton, and their terms of membership and means of election are determined by each canton. The National Council has 200 members directly elected to four-year terms. Women have the right to vote in only four cantons, where they may participate in local elections.

Neutral Switzerland is not a member of the United Nations, but it does cooperate with a number of UN agencies, many of which have their headquarters in Geneva.

The principality of Liechtenstein, on the Austrian-Swiss border, is closely associated with Switzerland. It has been united with Switzerland in a customs union since 1924. The tiny country uses Swiss currency and the Swiss postal administration, and its transportation system is integrated into Switzerland's. The Swiss also represent Liechtenstein abroad.

HISTORY. The earliest recorded inhabitants of present-day Switzerland were a number of Celtic tribes, among them the Helvetii, who had at an earlier time probably subjected the Rhaeti, who also lived in the area. In the first century BC these tribes were defeated by the Romans under Julius Caesar, and Switzerland became Roman territory.

During the 400s AD, when Roman power began to decline, the area was conquered by the Alamanni, the Burgundians, and Franks. By the early 800s Switzerland had become part of Charlemagne's empire, although it was divided under Charlemagne's successors.

Independence. During the 1200s the area around Lake Lucerne came under the rule of the Swabian Hapsburg family. In 1921 the Swiss communities, or cantons, of Schwyz, Uri, and Unterwalden entered into a defensive league, or confederation, against the Hapsburgs, whose rule was oppressive. The Hapsburgs were decisively defeated in 1315 at the battle of Morgarten, and the cantons gained their independence.

By 1513 the confederation had expanded to include 13 cantons, and Switzerland became an important military power. Swiss expansionism, however, was permanently checked by Francis I of France, who won a crushing victory over the Swiss at Marignano in 1515.

In the 1500s the Reformation, led by Ulrich Zwingli in Zurich and John Calvin in Geneva, provoked civil war between Roman Catholic and Protestant cantons and seriously weakened the league. Switzerland remained neutral throughout the Thirty Years War, but was able to gain international recognition of its independence and neutrality in 1648 at the Peace of Westphalia, which ended the conflict.

For 100 years following the Peace of Westphalia, Switzerland was in a decline, which came to an end in the mid-1700s with the growth of industry and an intellectual renaissance. In 1798, during the French Revolutionary Wars, the confederation was replaced by the French-sponsored Helvetic Republic, which had a strong central government and abolished the sovereignty of the cantons.

Neutrality. In 1815 the Congress of Vienna, which redrew the map of Europe after Napoleon's defeat, reaffirmed Switzerland's independence and perpetual neutrality. It also drew up

a federal plan for the cantons that granted them a large degree of individual autonomy. In 1848 a new constitution was adopted which strengthened the central government. It was revised in 1874 to strengthen central authority even further.

In the 1800s and 1900s Switzerland's neutrality led many international organizations to choose the country as the site of their headquarters. The country stayed neutral, although heavily armed, throughout both world wars.

Contemporary Switzerland. In 1946, to maintain is neutrality, Switzerland decided not to join the United Nations, although it participates in the work of some of the organizations specialized agencies. Many international conferences are held in Switzerland, and the Atomic Test-Ban Treaty of 1963 was agreed upon at Geneva.

Postwar prosperity, especially in the 1950s and 1960s, led to an influx of foreign workers into labor-short Switzerland. By the mid-1960s the number of foreign workers exceeded 14 percent of the total population.

Reaction against the presence of so many foreign workers, strongest in the financial and industrial center of Zurich, led the Swiss government in 1967 to announce a referendum to determine whether or not to limit constitutionally the number of foreign workers to a smaller percentage of the total population.

—Sergio Barzanti

SYRIA

Official name: Syrian Arab Republic
Area: 71,498 square miles
Population: (1966 est.) 5,400,000
Capital: Damascus (Pop., 1964 est., 562,907)
Language: Arabic
Religion: Islam
Currency unit: Pound
National holiday: Independence day, April 17

The Syrian Arab Republic, a Middle Eastern state, is bounded by Turkey on the north, Iraq on the east, Jordan on the south, and Lebanon, Israel, and the Mediterranean Sea on the west. The present country of Syria was created after World War I out of a larger, historical region which included present-day Jordan, Lebanon, and Israel.

THE LAND. A narrow, fertile plain follows Syria's Mediterranean coast. To its east the rugged Alawite and the Anti-Lebanon mountains rise to over 9,000 feet on the northwestern border.

The Orontes River waters a fertile valley east of the mountains, and in northern and northeastern Syria are the rolling plains and rich valley of the Euphrates River. In central Syria, arid, rolling hills give way to the barren Syrian Desert, which occupies the southeastern corner of the country.

Syria's coastal climate is mild and rather moist, with about 30 inches of rainfall each year along the coast. Central and eastern Syria are quite dry, with extremely hot summers and cold winters.

THE PEOPLE. Most Syrians are Muslim Arabs, but the population also includes Kurds, Druze, and Armenians. Population is densest in the temperate, fertile western part of the country. Damascus, the capital and largest city, lies in the southwest near the Lebanese border.

ECONOMY. The Syrian economy is based on agriculture. The country has few natural resources other than the fertile soil of its coastal areas and river valleys. Asphalt and gypsum are mined, and oil deposits do exist, but by the mid-1960s oil production was only in the early stages.

Agriculture. Farming is the occupation of most Syrians, and agriculture contributed over one-third of the gross domestic product in the mid-1960s. About one-third of the country's land is cultivated, and one-third is suitable for pasturage. Most farmland is in the west and north, and much of it requires irrigation. A land redistribution program in the 1950s and 1960s created many small farms from large estates.

The leading farm crops are cotton, wheat, and barley. Corn and other grains, dates, olives, sugar beets, and tobacco are also raised, and wool and silk are important commodities. Large herds of goats and sheep are grazed on the central plains.

Industry. The processing of agricultural products is Syria's most important industry. Textiles, leather products, dried fruits, and wines are the leading manufactures. Gypsum and asphalt are processed. Many industrial, commercial, and financial enterprises were nationalized in the 1960s.

Trade. International trade is important in the Syrian economy, and the country's chief port, Latakia, is a major Middle Eastern commercial center. Syria collects fees and taxes on oil from Iraq carried to the Mediterranean by pipeline across Syria. In 1967 exports earned $155 million and imports cost $264 million. Cotton, grains, and other farm products are the chief exports, and machinery, industrial raw materials, clothing, and other consumer items are imported.

Most trading activity is controlled by the government. Lebanon, France, the Soviet Union, the United States, and West Germany are Syria's leading trading partners.

GOVERNMENT. Syria has a republican form of government that is dominated by the military. Traditionally there is an appointed president, who serves as head of state, and a prime minister, who functions as chief executive.

Syria is a member of the United Nations and the Arab League.

HISTORY. The modern nation of Syria has roots in the ancient region of Syria, which was the site of some of the world's earliest civilizations. Syria was the center of the prosperous trade routes used by the great nations of the ancient world.

Located between the Tigris-Euphrates Valley and the Nile Valley, it was often the object of rivalry between the powerful nations that grew up in both valleys. Trade and war between the civilizations to the north and south of Syria brought many different peoples and cultures to the area.

Between 2000 BC and 333 BC, the Akkadians, the Sumerians, the Amorites, the Hittites, the Egyptians, the Assyrians, and the Persians succes-

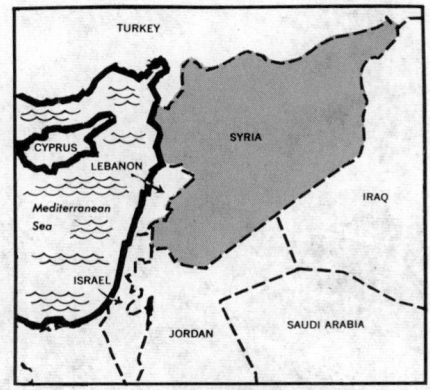

sively occupied the Syrian region. During that time three groups, the Hebrews, the Aramaeans, and the Canaanites, made permanent settlements in the land.

In 333 BC Alexander the Great conquered Syria from the Persian empire. After his death, Syria went to one of his generals, Seleucus, who founded the Seleucid dynasty that ruled Syria (including modern Israel, Lebanon, and Jordan) until the Romans conquered the region in 64 BC.

Syria was one of the first Roman provinces to accept Christianity, in the first century AD, and Syria's language, Aramaic, was the language of the early Christians, most of whom lived within what was then western Syria.

In the 630s Muslim Arab armies conquered the region. Islam replaced Christianity, Arabic replaced Aramaic, and Syria became an Arab country. The city of Damascus became the center of a great Arab empire and Syria's prosperity increased.

As the Arab empire weakened, however, Syria entered a decline. Ruled by outsiders, it suffered neglect. The Christian crusades against the Muslim Middle East in the 1000s, 1100s, and 1200s did great damage to Syria and its economy, and the invasions of Mongols and Tatars from the north and east in the 1200s and 1300s left Syria weak and impoverished.

Ottoman Rule. In 1516 the Ottoman Turks conquered Syria and made it part of their empire. Under the Ottoman Turks Syria remained peaceful, but neglect and poor government caused the economy and cultural life to decline further, especially in the 1700s, when the disintegration of the empire brought anarchy to Syria.

The opening of the Suez Canal in 1869 also hurt the country by taking away much of the trade between the Mediterranean and the Indian Ocean that had previously passed through Syria. Some economic improvements were made in the later 1800s, but the country remained largely undeveloped.

Nationalism. In the late 1800s Syria began to feel the impact of the spirit of nationalism that had been growing in Europe. Syria became a center for an Arab cultural revival and for Arab nationalism, and Syrians demanded self-government.

When the Ottoman Empire entered World War I on the side of Germany, Syria cooperated with the Allies. In

return, Britain supported Syrian Arab nationalism and aided a 1916 Arab uprising against the Ottoman government.

At the end of the war in 1918 French troops tried to occupy the country, but Faysal ibn-Husayn, a leader of the nationalist rebellion, proclaimed Syria's sovereignty. A Syrian National Congress was called, and in 1920 Faysal was proclaimed king. France, which had received a League of Nations mandate over Syria, deposed Faysal later in 1920 and set up its own government.

Syrian discontent with French rule led in 1925 to a two-year rebellion, which the French put down harshly. Discontent grew. In 1930 the French proposed a constitution that would have made the country a republic but would not have granted complete independence. The Syrians rejected it.

Independence. In World War II the Vichy French government of Syria was driven out in 1941 by British and Free French forces. Syria was formally declared an independent republic, although British and French troops did not withdraw until after the war, in 1946.

In 1943 Shukri al-Kuwatly was elected the first president of the republic, and in 1945 Syria entered the United Nations and joined other Arab states in forming the Arab League.

Turmoil marked the first two decades of the republic, and the military became the dominant factor in political life. In 1949 an army officer, Husni al-Zaim, ousted the civilian government. More coups followed, and from 1949 to 1954 the government was dominated by Col. Adib Shishakly, who ruled behind the official presidency of Hashim al-Atasi. In 1954 Shishakly was forced into exile, and the next year Kuwatly again became president.

In 1958 Syria merged with Egypt to form the United Arab Republic (U.A.R.), with Egypt's Gamal Abdel Nasser as president. In 1961 the Cairo government imposed an unpopular socialist program on the Syrian part of the U.A.R., and Syria withdrew from the union.

Contemporary Syria. Political instability increased. In March 1963 a military coup overthrew the government and a new cabinet was appointed. The new cabinet was dominated by Baathists, members of the pan-Arab Baath party, which advocated a strongly socialist and pan-Arab program. In 1966 a new military coup brought Nureddin al-Atassi to power.

Syria's frequent changes of government in the 1950s and 1960s hampered the country's economic development, and also affected its foreign relations. Most of the Baathist governments tended to be anti-Western. Syria's only consistent foreign policy, however, one shared with its Arab neighbors, was hostility toward the state of Israel.

In June 1967 Arab-Israeli warfare broke out anew, and Syrian forces were beaten by Israeli troops. Israel occupied the southwestern tip of Syria, along the Israeli border, including the heights overlooking the Sea of Galilee.
—Charles Issawi;
Alexander Melamid

TANZANIA

Official name: United Republic of Tanzania
Area: 362,820 square miles
Population: (1966 est.) 11,833,000
Capital: Dar es Salaam (Pop., 1965 est., 190,200)
Language: Swahili, Arabic, English
Religion: Traditional religions, Islam, Christianity
Currency unit: Shilling
National holiday: Union day, April 26

Tanzania, a republic in eastern Africa, was formed in 1964 by the merger of the mainland nation of Tanganyika and the offshore island nation of Zanzibar. Britain had granted independence to Tanganyika in 1961 and to Zanzibar in 1963.

Mainland Tanzania is bordered on the north by Uganda and Kenya; on the east by the Indian Ocean; on the south by Mozambique, Malawi, and Zambia; and on the west by the Congo (Kinshasa), Burundi, and Rwanda. The Indian Ocean islands of Zanzibar and Pemba, the former republic of Zanzibar, lie some 20 miles east of the mainland.

THE LAND. Tanganyika is by far the larger part of the republic, with an area of some 361,800 square miles. Zanzibar, which includes Zanzibar and Pemba islands, has an area of 1,020 square miles.

Tanganyika is occupied mainly by a plateau with an elevation of between 2,000 and 4,000 feet above sea level. Much of the plateau surface is semi-arid. There are mountain masses in the northeast and southwest.

The highest point, located near the border with Kenya, is Mt. Kilimanjaro, which reaches an elevation of about 19,340 feet. There is an extensive lowland in the north, which is partly occupied by Lake Victoria. A narrow plain extends along most of the coast.

The coastal plain is hot and humid, and the plateau is hot and drier. The Rufiji River flows through central Tanganyika.

Zanzibar and Pemba are low-lying coral islands with many inlets. There are mangrove swamps on the islands. The islands' temperatures are high from December to March and lower between June and October. Heavy rains fall in April and May, and there are light rains in November and December.

THE PEOPLE. Over 96 percent of Tanzania's population lives on the mainland, and the country's largest cities, Dar es Salaam and Mwanza, are in Tanganyika. Tanganyika's people include members of some 120 tribes, most of which are Bantu-speaking. The largest tribe is the Sukuma. There are also groups of Arabs, Europeans, and people of Indian and Pakistani origin.

Zanzibar and Pemba also have many different peoples, including Shirazis, descendants of ancient Persians, Africans from the mainland, Arabs, Asians, and people from the Comoro Islands.

ECONOMY. The economy of Tanzania is based on agriculture. The basic food crops are rice, corn, and sorghum.

UNITED NATIONS
CATTLE SALE held in northern Tanzania.

In Tanganyika, cotton, coffee, and sisal, a fiber used in rope, are the most important commercial crops. Tanganyika is one of the most significant producers of sisal in the world, and in 1964, production totaled 241,600 metric tons.

Sisal and coffee are generally grown on mountain slopes, and cotton is produced mainly in the lowlands near Lake Victoria. Most of the plantations are owned by Europeans, but Africans also grow coffee on small plots. Cattle are raised in most parts of the mainland.

Large quantities of cloves are grown on plantations in Zanzibar and Pemba. Coconuts are also an important commercial crop. Fishing is significant in the islands' economy.

Industry in Tanzania consists mainly of food processing. Mineral resources are considerable on the mainland, but they are widely distributed and transportation costs are high. Diamonds are mined, and there are also deposits of lead, gold, and iron ore.

In 1964 Tanzania instituted a Five Year Plan for Economic and Social Development to expand industry and develop land for agriculture. In 1967

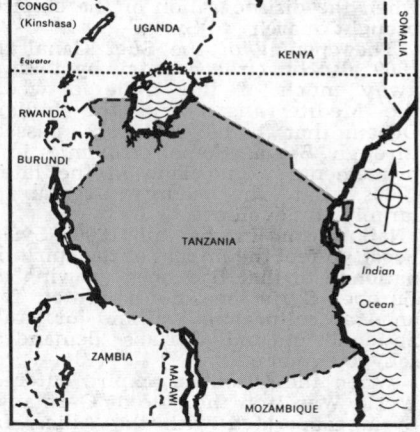

the government nationalized banks and much of the country's industry.

In 1966 imports cost $178 million and exports earned $235 million. The major imports are petroleum products, textiles, and machinery. The major exports are sisal, coffee, cotton, and cloves. Most trade is conducted with Britain, Hong Kong, West Germany, Japan, and India.

GOVERNMENT. Tanzania has a presidential system of government. Executive power is vested in a president, who is popularly elected to a five-year term. The president is assisted by two vice presidents. The First Vice President is responsible for the administration of Zanzibar, and the Second Vice President assists in the administration of Tanganyika.

Legislative power is held by a 204-member National Assembly, with 107 members popularly elected and 77 appointed by the president. There are also three commissioners from districts in Zanzibar, and 17 commissioners from districts in Tanganyika.

Tanzania is a member of the United Nations, the Organization of African Unity (OAU), and the Commonwealth of Nations.

HISTORY. The 1964 union of Tanganyika and Zanzibar merged the histories of two separate regions in eastern Africa.

Zanzibar. Arabs began colonizing Zanzibar in the 700s. Portuguese arrived in the late 1500s and brought the area under Portuguese rule. Arabs from Oman broke Portugal's control of the islands in about 1700, and established a sultanate. The Arabs developed a prosperous slave market and they encouraged clove plantations.

In the 1800s Britain gained control of the islands and ended the slave trade. In 1890 Britain formally established a protectorate over Zanzibar. The sultan remained as nominal ruler, however, and until 1956 the islands were ruled primarily by Arabs under British supervision.

Two political parties were formed in the 1950s—the Zanzibar Nationalist Party (ZNP), representing the Arabs, and the Afro-Shirazi Party (ASP), representing mainly the African population and some Shirazi. In 1957 the ASP split, and the Zanzibar and Pemba Peoples' Party (ZPPP) was formed.

On June 24, 1963, Zanzibar became self-governing, and elections were held in July. Although the African-dominated ASP won the largest number of the votes, the government was controlled by a coalition of the ZNP and ZPPP.

Zanzibar received its independence on Dec. 9, 1963, and Sheikh Muhammad Shamte became prime minister of the coalition government. The opposition, consisting largely of Africans, staged a bloody coup against Arab rule on Jan. 12, 1964. The Sultan was overthrown and a republic proclaimed. Sheikh Adeid Amani Karume, leader of the ASP, became president.

Tanganyika. In the 700s Arabs also established settlements in the coastal region of Tanganyika. The Portuguese settled in the region in the late 1400s. The Arabs developed a prosperous slave trade in the interior, which flourished until the 1800s, when it was checked by Christian missionaries led by David Livingstone.

Germany began colonizing the area in 1884, and in 1890 the region became part of German East Africa. After World War I Tanganyika became a British mandate under the League of Nations, and in 1946 it became a UN trust territory. Nationalism grew in the 1950s, and in 1954 Julius Nyerere formed a nationalist political party, the Tanganyika African National Union (TANU). TANU candidates were victorious in the first elections for a legislative council held in 1958.

In 1959 Britain took steps to establish internal self-government for Tanganyika, and Neyerere was named Chief Minister. In May 1961 Tanganyika became autonomous and Nyerere became prime minister. Tanganyika became an independent member of the Commonwealth of Nations on Dec. 9, 1961, and a republic one year later with Nyerere as president.

United Republic. A union of Tanganyika and Zanzibar was announced on Apr. 26, 1964, and the two countries took the name Tanzania. Nyerere became the first president of the new nation and Karume became First Vice President.

In 1967 Nyerere announced the government's intention of placing the country's means of production under the control of the workers and farmers, and many businesses were nationalized.

—Hibberd V. B. Kline, Jr.;
Vera L. Zolberg

THAILAND

Official name: Kingdom of Thailand
Area: 198,450 square miles
Population: (1967 est.) 32,680,000
Capital: Bangkok (Pop., 1963 est., urban area, 1,608,305)
Language: Thai
Religion: Buddhism
Currency unit: Baht
National holiday: King's birthday

Thailand, called Siam until 1939, is a kingdom in Southeast Asia. It is bounded on the north by Burma and Laos, on the east by Laos and Cambodia, on the south by the Gulf of Siam and Malaysia, and on the west by the Andaman Sea and Burma.

THE LAND. Thailand has several distinct land regions. The north-south trending Bilauktaung mountain range follows the border with Burma. It extends southward across the Kra Isthmus into peninsular Thailand, forming the backbone of the Malay Peninsula.

In northwestern Thailand, a deeply dissected upland area with an elevation of 600 to 3,000 feet above sea level, lies between the Salween and the Mekong river basins. This rugged region forms an obstacle to communications. It contains the major tributaries of the Mae Nam Chao Phraya, the principal river system of the country.

The basin of the Chao Phraya, which contains the fertile Bangkok Plain, is the core region of Thailand.

The basin has an inverted U-shaped outline, with the Dawna and the Bilauktaung mountain ranges on the west, the uplands of the hilly Shan Plateau on the north, and the Phetchabun Mountains on the east.

The Phetchabun Mountains form the western margin of the Khorat Plateau, a rolling basin with elevations generally below 700 feet. Rising in the Khorat Plateau is the Mun River, the chief Thai tributary of the Mekong River. The Dang Raek scarp establishes the southern boundary of the Khorat Plateau, and between this scarp and the Cardamon Mountains on the Gulf of Siam coast, a narrow lowland connects the Tonle Sap basin of Cambodia with the delta of the Chao Phraya.

Climate. Thailand lies within the monsoon area of Southeast Asia, but due to the "rain shadow" effect of the surrounding mountains, annual precipitation is limited in the lowlands.

Much of the delta receives less than 60 inches of rain a year and some areas close to the base of the mountains receive less than 40 inches. Moreover, there is considerable variability in rainfall from year to year. The peninsular portion of the country is wetter, and receives rain during both the southwest and northeast monsoons. The dry season is short and yearly variations small.

Thailand is in the tropical zone, and temperatures are generally above 50°F in the lowlands, although it is slightly cooler at higher elevations. The coolest months are December and January, and the hottest period is February through May.

THE PEOPLE. Almost all of Thailand's people are Thai, related to the people of Laos and eastern Burma. They speak Thai, and most are Buddhists. The largest minority group is Chinese.

Compared with most Southeast Asian countries, Thailand, with a population density of about 175 people per square mile in 1967, is rather thinly settled. Its population is growing at a rapid rate, however, averaging 3 percent a year between 1958 and 1965.

Population is concentrated in the river valleys, especially that of the Chao Phraya. Bangkok (Krung Thep), the capital and largest city, is located near the mouth of the Chao Phraya.

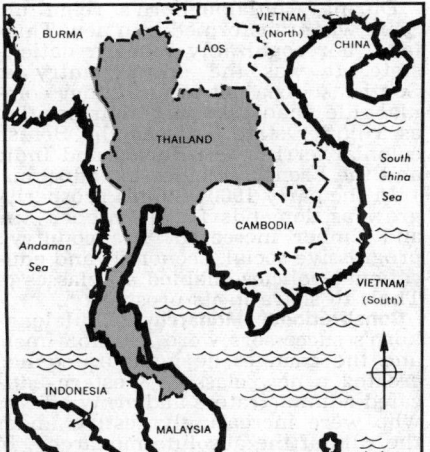

ECONOMY. Thailand is a relatively prosperous country. Agriculture is the basis of economic life, but industry increased in the 1950s and 1960s based largely on exploitation of Thailand's rich natural resources.

One of Thailand's most valuable resources is timber. More than half of the country is covered by forests. Tropical evergreen rainforests in the mountains contain a great variety of hardwoods and dense monsoon forests contain teak, of which Thailand is one of the world's leading producers. There is an abundance of fish in the waters off Thailand's long coast and in its rivers.

The country also has a rich variety of minerals. Tin is the most important, and in 1966 Thailand was the world's third greatest producer of tin, with over 17,000 metric tons. Other minerals include tungsten, manganese, and gold, and there are precious and semiprecious gems.

Thailand has a considerable waterpower potential, but it lacks well developed supplies of fuel, although there are deposits of lignite, bituminous coal, and petroleum. Wood and charcoal from the forests remained the chief fuels in the mid-1960s.

Agriculture. One of Thailand's richest resources is its soil. Agriculture contributed one-third of the gross domestic product in 1965 and occupied the majority of the work force. Most Thai farms are small and individually owned. In the rich Bangkok rice region, however, farms are larger, and there are a number of estates cultivated by tenant farmers.

Rice is central to Thai prosperity, and in the mid-1960s about 90 percent of the cultivated land was planted in rice. Three-fourths of Thailand's rice area is in the Bangkok plain, where terrain, soil, and moisture are most suitable for paddy rice. Thai rice is of excellent quality, and its price is controlled by the government to make it highly competitive in the world's rice market.

Other agricultural activities include rubber production, both on large estates and on small holdings. Some short-staple cotton is produced on the peninsula in the northern sections of the central plain. Other crops include tobacco, sugarcane, corn, cassava, peanuts, soybeans, coconuts, sesame, castor beans, silk, and peppers.

Industry. Forestry, mining, and related operations are the country's leading nonagricultural activities, and industry is limited. In 1965 it contributed only 15 percent of the gross domestic product. Aside from the processing of natural resources and agricultural products, there is little manufacturing.

The leading industrial establishments include rubber factories, sawmills, textile mills, and cement, glass, and plywood factories. In the early 1960s the country's first large tin-smelting plant began operations.

Government efforts to stimulate industrialization in the 1950s and 1960s received financial and technical aid from abroad, especially from the United States. The development of hydroelectric power resources, which began in the early 1960s with the construction of several huge dams, was expected to spur industrialization.

Trade. Thailand's international trade depends primarily on the country's farms, forests, and mines. In 1966 exports earned $694 million and imports cost $1,166 million. Rice, rubber, tin, and teak are the major exports. Fuels and manufactured goods are the major imports.

The major markets for Thai rice are Malaysia, Indonesia, and Hong Kong. Much of the rubber and tin are exported to Malaysia and Singapore for processing and re-export. Thai imports come chiefly from Japan, the United States, and Britain.

GOVERNMENT. Thailand is a constitutional monarchy with a king as head of state. An appointed prime minister and a cabinet hold executive power. The parliament, which exercised legislative power, was dissolved in 1958, and the constitution was revoked by the ruling military-supported government.

A constituent assembly was appointed in 1959 to draft a new constitution. But in the 1960s the government operated under an interim constitution, which placed great power in the office of prime minister.

Thailand is a member of the United Nations and the Southeast Asia Treaty Organization (SEATO).

HISTORY. The Thai have a long history, and people speaking closely related dialects of the Thai language have been living throughout the hilly region of southern China and northern Southeast Asia since nearly the beginning of recorded history. Modern Thailand has its origins in a state created by small warbands of Thai-speaking people who moved down into the lowlands of the Chao Phraya Valley in the 1200s.

In the late 1200s, under their first important kingdom, Sukhot'ai, the Thai conquered most of the area of present-day Thailand from Mon and Khmer peoples. They accepted the Theravada Buddhism of their Mon subjects, and they adopted the political system of the Khmer rulers whom they displaced.

Between the 1300s and the 1700s, the Thai ruled from a capital located at Ayut'ia, about 75 miles north of modern Bangkok. The Thai state, like others in Southeast Asia at that time, had no real boundaries. The king ruled his palace-city and its surrounding area directly.

The king exercised some control over most of the Chao Phraya plain through semiautonomous noble-officials. If the king was powerful, he exacted tribute from more distant vassals in Malaya, Cambodia, Laos, and northern Thailand. Wars were common and were generally fought to enforce claims to tribute or to capture new subjects rather than to acquire territory.

Chakri Dynasty. In the 1500s the Burmans overran the kingdom and sacked Ayut'ia. The Thai recovered, only to suffer another crushing defeat by Burma in 1767. A powerful Thai revival led to the founding of a strong, new dynasty, the Chakri, in 1782. The Chakri kings established their capital

UNITED NATIONS

A WOMAN SPINS silk into thread, which will then be woven into Thailand's famous silk.

at the port city of Bangkok, and it was from there that Thailand—called Siam by Westerners—faced the might of European imperialism in the 1800s.

The Chakri kings, unlike their Burman, Vietnamese, and Chinese counterparts, were actively interested in commerce and aware of what was happening in the world outside. In 1855 King Mongkut willingly signed a treaty with the British opening Siam to international trade, and he took the first steps to modernize and westernize the monarchy.

Mongkut's son, Chulalongkorn, ruled from 1868 to 1910. He carefully steered the country toward modernization while avoiding the dangers presented by European imperialists and Siamese reactionaries.

Slowly but steadily Chulalongkorn abolished slavery, replaced the traditional forced labor with money taxes, drawn in part from rapidly rising exports of rice and teak, and reorganized the administration with the help of European advisors. He was obliged to yield control of large vassal areas to the British and French, but at the same time he greatly extended the area effectively ruled by Bangkok.

During Chulalongkorn's reign old Siam was transformed into new Thailand, a recognizably modern nation-state. It was the only country in Southeast Asia not to fall under colonial rule, thanks in part to its position as a buffer state between the British colonial territory in Burma and India and the French colonies in Indochina.

In the early 1900s Siam's prosperity grew as demands for its rubber, tin, and timber increased. The country's progressive social, economic, and educational policies enabled all classes of Thais to share in its prosperity.

Constitutional Monarchy. Chulalongkorn's successors were less able men, and the changes he inaugurated had created a new class of Western-educated administrators and army officers who were increasingly restive under the rule of the absolute monarchy. In

1932 a small group of civilians and officers seized power in a bloodless coup.

The Chakris were reduced to the status of constitutional monarchs. The king was apparently ready to yield what he considered archaic absolute powers, and his willingness contributed to the stability of the constitutional system despite frequent changes of administration.

Following Chulalongkorn's "survival diplomacy," the Thais joined Japan as a passive ally during World War II to avoid invasion and occupation. When Japan's defeat became inevitable, Thailand quietly let it be known that it supported the Allies. After 1945 Thailand was actively pro-Western and in 1954 was a founding member of SEATO, although it also attempted to maintain informal, friendly contacts with Communist China.

Contemporary Thailand. In the decades after the war Thailand concentrated on industrializing and modernizing its economy and on protecting itself from the military conflicts that raged in Southeast Asia. Several coups d'etat did not weaken political stability, and although the governments were more autocratic than democratic they were not oppressive.

The threat of rebellion by Communist-supported guerrillas in the late 1950s led in 1958 to a suspension of the parliament and the constitution. There was a tightening of executive control, and, in the rebellious areas, an increase in military strength and an expansion of social and economic programs.

Thailand permitted U.S. planes participating in the Vietnamese War to use airstrips in Thailand, and in 1967 the Thai announced plans to send combat troops to aid South Vietnamese and U.S. forces in the war.

—M. G. Inaba

TOGO

Official name: Republic of Togo
Area: 21,620 square miles
Population: (1967 est.) 1,724,000
Capital: Lomé (Pop., 1962 est., urban area, 90,000)
Language: French, African languages
Religion: Traditional religions, Christianity
Currency unit: Franc CFA (African Financial Community)
National holiday: Independence day, April 27

Togo, a republic in western Africa, is bordered on the north by Upper Volta; on the east by Dahomey; on the south by the Gulf of Guinea, an arm of the Atlantic Ocean; and on the west by Ghana.

After World War I Togo was divided by Britain and France into separate League of Nations mandates, and after 1946 they were administered as separate UN trust territories. In 1957 the British territory became part of Ghana, and in 1960 the French territory received its independence.

THE LAND. Grasslands occupy most of Togo. There is a sandy coast, behind which are lagoons. Inland from the lagoons is the Terre de Barre, a low, clay plain which rises to a sandy plateau. The Togo Atakora mountains cross the center of the country. The Mono and Ogou rivers flow through Togo. The climate is hot and humid.

THE PEOPLE. There are many different ethnic groups in Togo. The largest groups are the Ewe and the Adja-Watyi in the south and the Kabrai-Losso in the north. Lomé, the capital, is Togo's largest city.

ECONOMY. The economy of Togo is based on agriculture. Yams, rice, corn, millet, and sorghum, grown mainly in the interior, are the main food crops. Cacao and coffee are the leading commercial crops. Palm products, such as copra and palm oil, are important, and the peoples near the coast and the lagoons prepare copra and coconut oil. Palm oil, cacao, and coffee are produced in the Terre de Barre region.

Togo has rich phosphate deposits, and in 1965, 974,000 metric tons of phosphate were produced. There is little industry. In 1966 the government instituted a Five-Year Development Plan to promote the growth of agriculture and industry.

In 1966 imports cost $47 million and exports earned $36 million. The main imports are machinery, foodstuffs, textiles, and petroleum products. The major exports are phosphate, coffee, and cacao. Most trade is conducted with France, West Germany, and Japan.

GOVERNMENT. Until January 1967 Togo had a presidential system of government. Executive power was vested in a president, who was popularly elected to a five-year term. Legislative power was held by a 52-member National Assembly, also popularly elected every five years. The legislature was dissolved in 1967 and a new government was established, composed of eight civilians and four military men, headed by a president.

Togo is a member of the United Nations and the Organization of African Unity (OAU).

HISTORY. Between about the 1200s and the 1800s many African tribal kingdoms established their rule over the area of present-day Togo. In the 1400s Portugal developed trade relations with the Ewe. By the mid-1890s Germany had established a protectorate over Togo. After World War I the German protectorate was divided into separate British and French mandates under the League of Nations. In 1946 the mandates became UN trust territories.

Britain administered its trust territory along with the Gold Coast colony. In 1956 British Togoland voted to join the Gold Coast, which became the independent nation of Ghana in 1957.

After World War II France established a locally elected territorial assembly in French Togoland. In 1956 French Togoland obtained internal self-government from France, and Nicolas Grunitzky, of the Togolese Progressive Party, became the country's first prime minister. Grunitzky's party lost elections held in 1958, and his brother-in-law, Sylvanus Olympio, leader of the Committee for Togolese Unity party, became prime minister.

Independence. On April 27, 1960 Togo became independent, and Olympio became president. On Jan. 13, 1963 Olympio was assassinated, and in May, Grunitzky was elected president. Grunitzky was ousted in January 1967 after a bloodless coup led by Lt. Col. Étienne Eyadema.

Eyadema suspended the constitution, dissolved the National Assembly, and formed a Committee of National Reconciliation. In April 1967 Eyadema assumed the position of president.

　　　　　　—Hibberd V. B. Kline, Jr.;
　　　　　　　　　　Vera L. Zolberg

TRINIDAD AND TOBAGO

Official name: Trinidad and Tobago
Area: 1,980 square miles
Population: (1966 est.) 995,000
Capital: Port-of-Spain (Pop., 1960 est., 93,-954)
Language: English
Religion: Roman Catholicism, other Christian, Hinduism, Islam
Currency unit: Dollar
National holiday: Independence day, August 31

Trinidad and Tobago, an independent island country in the West Indies, lies off the eastern coast of South America between the Caribbean Sea and the Atlantic Ocean. Venezuela, on the South American mainland, is only 7 miles from Trinidad.

The country consists of two islands, Trinidad, the second largest island in the West Indies, 1,864 square miles in area, and Tobago, some 20 miles northeast of Trinidad, 116 square miles in area. Some tiny islets lie off the coast.

THE LAND. Trinidad is crossed by three mountain ranges—the Central, Southern, and Northern ranges. The mountains rise to a peak of more than 3,000 feet and are separated by lowlands. Tropical forests cover about one-half of Trinidad. There are many small streams, and the east-central coast is swampy.

Tobago's terrain is rugged. A central core of volcanic hills rises over 1,800 feet and drops sharply to the sea in the northeast. Except for some isolated coastal plains, flat land is limited to the southwestern tip of Tobago.

The climate of the islands is tropical with temperatures averaging 77°F throughout the year. Rainfall ranges from about 120 inches a year on Tobago and in northern Trinidad to about 50 inches a year in southwestern Trinidad.

THE PEOPLE. Most of Trinidad and Tobago's people are of African descent. About one-third of the population is of East Indian origin and 14

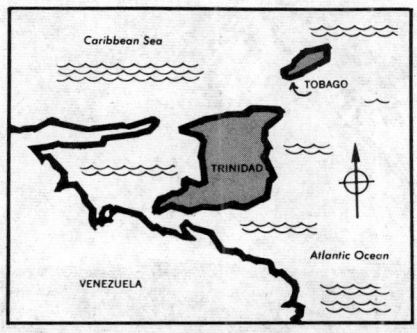

percent is mulatto, of mixed European and African origins. There are also people of Chinese, European, and Near Eastern background.

English is the official language, but a dialect combining English with French, Spanish, and other tongues is widely spoken.

About 90 percent of the country's population lives on Trinidad. The population grew at the rapid rate of 3.1 percent between 1958 and 1965.

ECONOMY. Trinidad and Tobago has a moderately prosperous economy based on international trade, tourism, and on the exploitation of its rich natural resources, especially petroleum and asphalt.

Agriculture. Arable land is limited in Trinidad and Tobago, but agriculture employs about one-fifth of the labor force and provides important exports.

Sugarcane is the most important commercial crop and is grown in western Trinidad. Cocoa, second in importance, is raised mainly on Tobago and in the wetter regions of Trinidad. Coffee, citrus fruits, and bananas are also raised for export, and limited quantities of fruits and vegetables are grown for local consumption.

Industry. Industry is of prime importance in the economy, and the processing of petroleum is the leading industrial activity. The major oil producing areas are in Trinidad's Southern Range and off its western coast.

The processing of asphalt extracted from Pitch Lake at La Brea, one of the world's largest sources of natural asphalt, is also important, as is the quarrying of building stone. Other significant manufactures are rum, cement, chemicals, paper products, and metal goods.

Trade. In 1967 exports earned $438 million and imports cost $403 million. The principal imports are crude petroleum, foodstuffs, machinery, transportation equipment, and iron and steel. Petroleum products, sugar, fruit, and cocoa are the main exports.

The country's main trading partners are Britain and the United States. Tourism is important, and in the mid-1960s it was one of the country's major sources of income.

GOVERNMENT. Trinidad and Tobago has a parliamentary system of government. The head of state is the British monarch, who is represented by a governor-general. Actual executive powers are wielded by a prime minister and cabinet responsible to the legislature, which consists of an appointed Senate and a popularly elected House of Representatives.

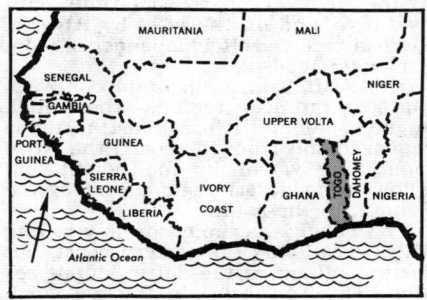

TRINIDAD AND TOBAGO TOURIST BOARD

TRINIDAD SURF breaks on a sandy beach.

Trinidad and Tobago is a member of the United Nations, the Commonwealth of Nations, and the Organization of American States (OAS).

HISTORY. Both Trinidad and Tobago were visited by Christopher Columbus on his third voyage to the New World in 1498. Trinidad was at that time inhabited by Arawak Indians. Tobago was uninhabited when Dutch settlers arrived in 1632.

Trinidad was settled by Spain, which made it a colony in about 1550. The island was subject to constant raids by French, Dutch, and British privateers, and the Spanish maintained their control only with difficulty. Cocoa crop failures in the early 1700s led to the abandonment of most settlements on the island.

The colony revived after 1783, when the Spanish government invited Roman Catholics from other countries to settle in Trinidad. Many Frenchmen moved to the island, bringing with them sugarcane, cotton, coffee, and new types of cocoa. Plantation agriculture prospered, based on the labor of slaves imported from Africa.

British Rule. In 1798 Britain captured Trinidad and its control was recognized in 1802 by the Treaty of Amiens. The treaty gave Tobago to France, but the French ceded the island to Britain in 1814. The sugar and cocoa industries prospered and were expanded under British colonial rule.

In the 1830s the slaves were freed, and a critical labor shortage in the second half of the 1800s led to contract workers being brought from India. Oil was discovered in the early 1900s and soon played a key role in the economy.

The islands had been made a single colony in 1889, and they began to move toward independence in 1925, when popular representatives were first elected to the governing council. Popular participation in government gradually increased. In 1958 the colony entered the Federation of the West Indies, which united a number of Britain's West Indian and Caribbean colonies, but it withdrew in 1961 when Jamaica left the federation.

Independence. In 1962, a year after complete internal self-government had been granted, Trinidad and Tobago became an independent country. The new nation concentrated on improving its economy by encouraging foreign investment and by diversifying its activities.

Trinidad and Tobago was admitted to the Organization of American States in 1967. It thus became the second English-speaking member state in the organization.

—George W. Carey; Jerome Fischman

TRUCIAL OMAN

Official name: Trucial States
Area: 32,300 square miles
Population: (1966 est.) 130,000
Language: Arabic
Religion: Islam
Currency unit: Qatar/Dubai dinar, Bahrain dinar

The Trucial Oman, often referred to as the Trucial Coast, is an association of seven independent sheikhdoms on the southern coast of the Persian Gulf. The Trucial Oman is bordered on the north by Qatar, on the east by Muscat and Oman, on the south by Muscat and Oman and Saudi Arabia, and on the west by Saudi Arabia.

Abu Dhabi, Dubai, Sharjah, Ajman, Umm al Qaiwain, Ras al Khaimah, and Fujairah make up the association, whose name derives from a series of truces signed with Britain in the 1800s.

THE LAND AND PEOPLE. Flat, hot, and dry except for the humid coast, the region is mainly barren desert dotted with a few oases. Rainfall averages only three inches a year.

The native population of the Trucial Oman is entirely Arab and Muslim. Dubai, capital of Dubai state, is the major port and the principal city.

ECONOMY. Nomadic grazing of livestock, pearl diving, fishing, trading, and date-farming, were once the only means of livelihood in the states. They became of secondary importance after 1958, when the production of oil became the mainstay of the economy. The principal oil fields lie within the sheikhdom of Abu-Dhabi, which gains the greatest income from them in the form of royalty fees and taxes collected from foreign oil companies for exploitation rights.

Of the seven sheikhdoms, Abu Dhabi has the most prosperous trade because of its oil exports. Dubai, however, with its good port, has long done a brisk transshipment trade and is the chief commercial center for the region. It has also recently struck oil.

The states export hides, dates, pearls, and fish products and import machinery, foodstuffs, and manufactured items. Most trade is with neighboring countries and with Britain, Japan, and India.

GOVERNMENT. Each sheikhdom is governed by an absolute ruler, a sheikh. Britain is responsible for defense and foreign affairs of the states.

HISTORY. For centuries the sheikhs of the region now known as the Trucial Oman battled for control of the territory. In the 1500s, when Portugal controlled the Persian Gulf, the sheikhs turned to piracy and the slave trade. By the 1700s their ships ranged over the entire Persian Gulf and into the Arabian Sea. They waged undeclared war against the British East India Company, the principal trader in the area.

At the beginning of the 1800s the company and Britain suppressed the piracy, and in 1820 they signed a treaty of peace with the sheikhdoms. By later agreements the sheikhs promised to abandon slaving and piracy, turned control of their foreign affairs and defense over to Britain, and granted the British exclusive trading privileges.

Until the 1950s the sheikhdoms experienced little internal or external strife. The discovery of oil in the 1950s, however, and the wealth and influx of foreigners that oil production brought to the states disrupted the traditional society. In the 1960s programs were initiated to use oil revenues for health care, education, and technological improvements.

In the 1950s and 1960s border disputes with neighboring states were frequent. In 1967, when Aden and the South Arabian sheikhdoms became independent as South Yemen, there were discussions of incorporating the Trucial sheikhdoms into the new state.

—Charles Issawi; Alexander Melamid

TUNISIA

Official name: Republic of Tunisia
Area: 63,379 square miles
Population: (1966 est.) 4,460,000
Capital: Tunis (Pop., 1964 est., urban area, 662,000)
Language: Arabic
Religion: Islam
Currency unit: Dinar
National holiday: Independence day, June 1

Tunisia, a republic in northern Africa, is bounded on the north and east by the Mediterranean Sea, on the south by Libya, and on the west by Algeria. Tunisia received its independence from France in 1956.

THE LAND. Tunisia has four contrasting geographical regions—the Sahel, or plains, along the east coast; a steppe region inland from the coast; the Atlas mountain system in the north; and a low-lying desert region, part of the Sahara, in the south.

The Sahel is occupied by low rolling hills. Paralleling the eastern coast, but further inland, is the flatter steppe region. The Tell Atlas in the far north

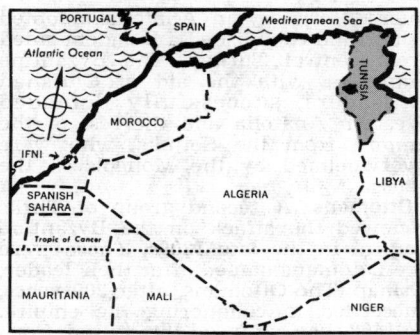

is separated from the Saharan Atlas, or High Tell, by the Medjerda River valley. The Tell Atlas extends to the coast in Cape Blanc, and the Saharan Atlas extends to the coast in Cape Bon.

South of the mountains is the Shott el Jerid, a salt lake close to sea level, which receives some streams from the mountains. In the southwest, along the boundary with Algeria, lies part of the Great Eastern Erg, a major sand area of the Sahara.

In the northern part of the country winters are mild and rainy and summers are hot and dry. South of the Shott el Jerid the climate is hot and dry with less than 4 inches of rain a year.

THE PEOPLE. Most of Tunisia's people are Muslim, and are descended from indigenous Berber-speaking peoples and later Arab immigrants. There are small communities of Jews and Europeans, mainly French, Italian, and Maltese. There are nomadic Berber tribes in the desert region.

Tunis, the capital, is the country's largest city and principal port. Bizerte, Sfax, Sousse, and Gabès are also important seaports. Qairouan is an historic Muslim holy city.

ECONOMY. The economy of Tunisia is based on agriculture. The main crops are wheat, barley, and olives. Tunisia is one of the world's largest producers of olive oil, and in 1965 about 105,000 metric tons of olive oil were produced. Figs and citrus fruits are also grown, as are wine grapes. Nomads raise sheep, goats, cattle, and camels.

Tunisia has rich phosphate and iron ore deposits, and in 1965 produced more than 3 million metric tons of phosphate rock and 609,000 metric tons of iron ore. There are also deposits of lead and silver. Industry has developed since the time of independence in 1956. Most factories process the country's agricultural and mineral products.

In 1966 imports cost $249 million and exports earned $140 million. The major imports are lumber, petroleum, textiles, iron and steel, and machinery. The major exports are fruits, phosphates, iron ore, and olive oil. Most trade is conducted with France, Indonesia, the United States, and Italy.

GOVERNMENT. Tunisia has a presidential system of government. Executive power is vested in a president, who is popularly elected to a five-year term. Legislative power is held by the National Assembly, which is also popularly elected every five years.

Tunisia is a member of the United Nations, the Arab League, and the Organization of African Unity.

HISTORY. In 814 BC the Phoenicians founded the city of Carthage, near the site of present-day Tunis. In 146 BC Rome destroyed Carthage and Tunisia came under Roman domination. Roman rule ended in the 400s AD with invasions by the Vandals. In the 500s the region came under Byzantine rule.

A decisive break in Tunisian history occurred with the arrival of Muslim Arabs in the mid-600s. Although the native Berber-speaking peoples were the most Romanized and Christianized people of northwestern Africa, Tunisia became part of the Arab-Muslim world.

Tunisia shared the fortunes of the dynasties that arose in northern Africa and Spain. In the early 800s the Aghlabids gained control of Tunisia. The Fatimids controlled much of Tunisia in the 900s, and in the 1100s a Morocco-based dynasty, the Almohad, gained control of the region. In 1228 the Almohads were succeeded by the Hafsids, who controlled Tunisia until the early 1500s, when the Ottoman Turks began a series of invasions.

By 1574 Tunisia had become part of the Ottoman Empire, but it was soon able to achieve a considerable measure of self-rule. In 1705 an Ottoman Turkish ruler of Tunisia, owing allegiance to the sultan, established the Husayn Dynasty, which lasted until the monarchy was abolished in 1957.

The Tunisian government attempted internal reforms and westernization early in the 1800s. But Tunisia soon fell victim to foreign indebtedness and increasing European interference. In 1881, after a brief military campaign, France established a protectorate over Tunisia.

French Control. Although large numbers of French and other Europeans settled in the country, native institutions were left largely intact. Tunisians learned technical skills from the French and benefited from the country's economic growth without being overwhelmed in the process.

Nationalism developed rapidly after World War I, and the Tunisian struggle for independence came to be personified by Habib Bourguiba, who organized the nationalist Neo-Destour party in 1934. The Neo-Destour itself grew out of an earlier, more traditional party, the Destour, or Constitution.

After a long period of intermittent negotiations and armed struggle, France agreed to grant Tunisia internal self-government in 1954. On Mar. 20, 1956 France granted Tunisia complete independence, and in 1957 Tunisia became a republic with Bourguiba as president.

Independence. Tunisia, since its independence, has made impressive domestic reforms in education and economic development. Diplomatically, the period from 1956 until neighboring Algeria won its independence from France in 1962 placed Tunisia in the delicate position of attempting to maintain necessary relations with France while supporting the Algerian independence movement.

Fighting erupted in Tunisia between the French and the Tunisian supporters of the Algerians, and in 1958 France bombed the Tunisian border city of Sakiet-Sidi-Youssef. In 1961 Tunisia demanded the removal of troops France had maintained in Bizerte after independence.

The Tunisian demand for the withdrawal of the troops further strained French-Tunisian relations. In 1963, after months of fighting, France withdrew its troops. In 1964 Tunisia nationalized French holdings in Tunisia, and France ended its technical and economic assistance.

In 1965 relations between Tunisia and the United Arab Republic (U.A.R.) became strained when Bourguiba suggested a reconciliation between the Arab states and Israel, and in 1966 diplomatic relations were broken off with the U.A.R. In 1967 diplomatic relations were resumed after Tunisia pledged its full support to the Arab states in renewed warfare with Israel.

—L. Carl Brown; Hibberd V. B. Kline, Jr.

TURKEY

Official name: Republic of Turkey
Area: 301,382 square miles
Population: (1967 est.) 33,823,000
Capital: Ankara (Pop., 1965 est., urban area, 902,218)
Language: Turkish
Religion: Islam
Currency unit: Lira
National holiday: Republic Day, October 29

Turkey is a republic located both in Asia and Europe. Most of the country lies in Asia Minor, or Anatolia. The small European portion, called Thrace, is on the Balkan peninsula. The republic was formed in 1923 from the Turkish region which for centuries had been the core of the Ottoman Empire.

Turkey is bordered on the north by Bulgaria, the Black Sea, and the Soviet Union; on the east by Iran; on the south by Iraq, Syria, and the Mediterranean Sea; and on the west by the Aegean Sea and Greece.

THE LAND. Thrace consists of rolling plains bounded by uplands in the north and a mountainous coastline in the south. It is separated from Anatolia by a small sea—the Sea of Marmara—and two straits—the Bosporus in the east and the Dardanelles in the west.

In Asian Turkey the Pontic Mountains rising over 11,000 feet, follow the shores of the Black Sea. The Taurus mountain range on the southern coast rises to a peak of over 11,500 feet above the Mediterranean. Narrow, fertile plains separate both ranges from the sea.

Between the mountain ranges is the Anatolian Plateau, with an average elevation of 3,000 feet. Toward the west the plain breaks into a series of fertile river valleys separated by low ridges. In the east the plateau merges with the Pontic and Taurus mountains in the rugged highland of Armenia, where Mt. Ararat, Turkey's highest point, rises to 16,946 feet. Turkey's largest lakes—Van, in the east and Tuzi, in the west—are saltwater lakes.

Many rivers flow from Turkey's highlands towards the long coastline. The longest is the Kizil, which rises

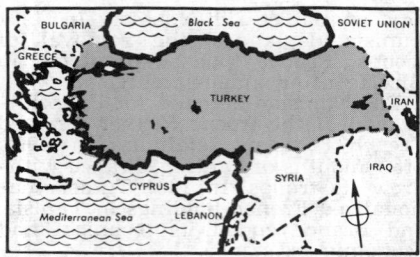

in the eastern highlands and flows west and north to empty into the Black Sea. Other important rivers are the Firat, or Euphrates, which rises in Turkey and flows south, the Seyhan in central Anatolia, and the Sakarya in the northwest.

Climate. Thrace and coastal Anatolia have a mild, moist climate. Temperatures range from 40° to 80°F, and rainfall averages 20 to 40 inches annually. Most rain falls in the winter.

In the dry Anatolian Plateau only 10 to 20 inches of rain falls a year, and temperatures are hotter in summer and colder in winter than on the coasts. The inland mountains have a colder climate and are often snow-covered.

THE PEOPLE. Most Turks are Turkish —related to peoples of Central Asia. They speak Turkish. Over 98 percent of the population is Muslim. The largest minority group is the Kurds, a seminomadic people who inhabit the eastern highlands. There are also small Greek and Armenian minorities.

Most Turks live in small towns encircling the Anatolian Plateau. The interior of the plateau is quite sparsely settled. The densest population is in northwestern Anatolia and eastern Thrace, where Istanbul, the country's largest city is located. The capital, Ankara, is in central Anatolia.

ECONOMY. Throughout history the area which is now Turkey has been famous for its agricultural and mineral products. Turkey's economy is still based heavily on agriculture, but industrialization began in the 1950s.

Turkey's wide variety of known minerals include rich deposits of coal and chrome and fairly large reserves of oil, zinc, copper, iron, and lead. Turkey also has abundant waterpower resources, which were under development in the 1960s.

Agriculture. Farming and herding were the occupations of over two-thirds of the people in the mid-1960s, and in 1965 agriculture contributed 36 percent of the gross domestic product. Some one-third of the land area is cultivated, and over one-third is used for pasture. Sheep, goats, cattle, and other livestock are grazed on the Anatolian plain and in the eastern highlands.

Cereals, especially wheat, are the major farm crops. Cotton and sugar beets are also important, and legumes, citrus and other fruits, and nuts are raised. Tobacco is the most important commercial crop. Most farms are small, and agricultural methods are generally outmoded and inefficient.

Evergreen forests cover some 13 percent of the country's area, and forestry is important. There is some fishing off the coasts.

Industry. Although Turkey's industry expanded greatly in the 1950s and early 1960s, by 1965 it contributed only 18 percent of the gross domestic product and consisted primarily of the processing of agricultural products. Textile weaving is the leading industry. Refined sugar, flour, paper, tobacco products, dried fruits, oils, canned foods, cement, and iron and steel and chrome products are among Turkey's leading manufactured products.

Trade. Turkey has a generally unfavorable balance of trade. In 1967 exports earned $522 million and imports cost $691 million. The chief exports are agricultural products, especially grain, tobacco, cotton, and sugar. Metal ores are also exported. Machinery and motor vehicles, fuels, manufactured consumer goods, and industrial raw materials are the main imports.

Most Turkish trade is carried on with the United States, Britain, West Germany, Italy, Belgium, and Czechoslovakia.

GOVERNMENT. Turkey is a republic. A 1961 constitution vested legislative power in the Grand National Assembly, a popularly elected legislature of two houses. The assembly elects a president from among its members to a 7-year term as head of state. A prime minister appointed by the president and responsible to the assembly is chief executive.

Turkey is a member of the United Nations, the North Atlantic Treaty Organization (NATO), and the Central Treaty Organization (CENTO).

HISTORY. Although the Turks did not appear there until the Middle Ages, the region called Turkey has been inhabited since ancient times. The history of the land extends back nearly 4,000 years to the civilization of the Hittites.

After conquests by Persians, Greeks, and Romans, Turkey became in the 200s AD the core of the eastern half of the Roman Empire. In 330 AD Byzantium (later called Constantinople, the modern Istanbul) became the capital of the Byzantine Empire, the successor to the Roman empire.

In the 900s the first Turks, the Seljuks, migrated into Asia Minor from Central Asia. In the 1000s they con-

quered territory in Anatolia, adopted Islam, and established a kingdom ruled from central Turkey. The Byzantine emperors, with the aid of Christian Crusaders, successfully defended Western Anatolia and the rest of the empire from the Seljuks, who were overwhelmed by the Mongols in the 1200s.

Ottomans. A second group of Turks renewed the attack on the Byzantine empire in the late 1200s. These were the Ottomans named after their leader, Osman. The Ottomans, after 200 years, succeeded in conquering the empire. In 1453 they captured the capital, Constantinople.

From Constantinople the Ottomans ruled a mighty empire which, at its height under Sulayman the Magnificent, who ruled from 1520 to 1566, was probably the most powerful in the world. It stretched from Austria in the north to the Indian Ocean in the south, and from Persia (Iran) in the east to Algeria in the west.

The Ottoman Empire in the 1500s was not only the largest and the most powerful state in the world, but the most efficiently governed as well. Its society was ordered along a feudalistic pattern, and its leaders combined political power with religious influence. The Ottoman Empire had an administrative bureaucracy, a court system, taxation methods, and an army and navy that were excellent even by modern standards.

Decline. The 300 years following Suleiman's reign, however, witnessed an almost uninterrupted decline. A disastrous defeat by the armies of the Holy Roman Empire in 1571 ended Ottoman world military supremacy and put the once-conquering Turkish armies on the defensive. Governmental administration collapsed under weak sultans and bureaucratic corruption, and military discipline crumbled.

Local authorities gradually assumed power, and by the 1800s many provinces were independent in fact, if not in name. In addition, France, Britain, Austria, and Russia conquered parts of the empire, and the Balkan provinces rebelled, leaving Turkey only Thrace of its once considerable European possessions. The Ottoman Em-

TURKISH INFORMATION SERVICE

DOLMABAHÇE SQUARE on the Bosphorus in Istanbul, showing the Mosque with its minarets.

pire in the 1800s had become the "Sick Man of Europe."

Toward the end of the 1800s progress was made in reforming the government and restoring order. The era also saw the beginning of a cultural and literary revival. In 1876 Sultan Abd-al-Hamid II took the throne and a liberal constitution was proclained.

The Sultan soon ended the reform efforts, however. He revoked the constitution, abused his subjects, especially the minority nationalities, and took Turkey into wars that resulted in disastrous losses.

Young Turks. In the discontent caused by his failures and abuses, a revolutionary party was formed, the Committee of Union and Progress, or the "Young Turks." The party hoped to restore Turkish power by Westernizing the country and by expanding Turkish territory.

In 1908, with the support of the army, the young Turks forced Abd-al-Hamid to grant a new constitution and parliamentary government. In 1909 he was deposed and replaced by his brother.

Soon, however, the Young Turks divided into factions. Moreover, in trying to regain lost territories they lost still more. As each of their projects failed, their government grew more despotic. By 1913 a military wing of the party assumed power by a coup-d'etat.

Under this government Turkey entered World War I on the side of Germany and suffered terrible losses. When the war ended in 1918, the country was occupied by troops from many Allied countries and was threatened with partition among the Allied states. All that remained of the Ottoman Empire was Anatolia and Thrace, and the Young Turk government fled into exile.

In 1920 a nationalist party organized an unofficial Turkish government under Mustafa Kemal to drive out the Allied occupation forces. Kemal, with the support of the majority of Turks, organized an army and by 1923 had forced the Allies to leave and to recognize Turkey's sovereignty over Asia Minor and eastern Thrace in the Treaty of Lausanne.

The Republic. In October 1923 Turkey was proclaimed a republic, with an elected legislature and with Kemal as president. The political and religious authority of the old sultanate and the caliphate were abolished.

Kemal, who was later given the surname "Atatürk," or "father of the Turks," radically reformed Turkish government, economy, and society, turning its medieval Islamic social and political structure into that of a modern, Western-style nation. At Atatürk's death in 1938 his prime minister, Ismet Inönü, became the president and continued the Westernization program.

Turkey did not participate in World War II, but it favored the Allies. After the war it pursued a pro-Western policy, joining the North Atlantic Treaty Organization. Turkey was aided in its fight against expanding Communist influence by U.S. economic aid under the Truman Doctrine and Marshall Plan.

In 1950 the Democratic Party took power from Inönü's Republican People's Party government. The Democratic government faced rising discontent at home. Economic expansion and modernization had proceeded rapidly, and in 1950 severe inflation threatened the economy. The government responded with unpopular financial restrictions. Unrest was met with repression, which the people, especially Turkey's new educated class, resented.

Contemporary Turkey. In 1960 a military group seized power and placed Gen. Cemal Gürsel at the head of a provisional government. In 1961 a new constitution was written, establishing a second republic.

Inönü became prime minister, and Gürsel remained as president. The government instituted reforms and initiated ambitious economic development programs, which were designed to develop natural resources, modernize agriculture, and expand industry at a moderate pace.

Inönü's government fell in 1965. The Justice party won elections held in 1965, and Süleyman Demiral became prime minister. The legislature elected Gen. Cevdet Sunay president in 1966 when President Gürsel became ill.

In 1967 Turkey threatened war with Greece over the status of the Turkish minority on the island-nation of Cyprus. The crisis was one in a series that had arisen between the two states since 1963, when fighting erupted on Cyprus between Greek and Turkish Cypriots. UN emissaries and a U.S. negotiator prevented open fighting and arranged a temporary settlement of the dispute.

—Charles Issawi; Alexander Melamid

UGANDA

Official name: Republic of Uganda
Area: 91,134 square miles
Population: (1966 est.) 7,934,000
Capital: Kampala (Pop., 1959 est., urban area, 123,300)
Language: English, Luganda and other African languages
Religion: Christianity, Islam, traditional religions
Currency unit: Shilling
National holiday: Independence day, October 9

Uganda, a republic in eastern Africa, is bounded on the north by Sudan, on the east by Kenya, on the south by Tanzania and Rwanda, and on the west by the Congo (Kinshasa). Uganda received its independence from Britain in 1962.

THE LAND. Most of Uganda is occupied by a plateau with elevations between 3,000 and 6,000 feet above sea level. The Ruwenzori Mountains run along the western border, reaching an elevation of more than 16,760 feet in the Margherita Peak. In the east Mount Elgon reaches an elevation of almost 14,180 feet.

Lake Victoria is at the southeastern corner of Uganda. Lakes Edward and Albert are in western Uganda, and Lake Kyoga is in central Uganda. The Albert Nile and the Victoria Nile are among the many rivers flowing through Uganda.

Uganda has a tropical climate. In the northeast rainfall averages about 20 inches a year, but in the southwest and west it averages between 50 and 60 inches a year.

THE PEOPLE. There are many tribal groups in Uganda, most of which are Bantu-speaking. The largest Bantu-speaking tribe is the Baganda. Other large groups include the Iteso, the Banyankole, and the Basoga. There are also peoples of Nilotic and Nilo-Hamitic stock, and small communities of Asians and Europeans.

Uganda's largest cities include Kampala, the capital; Entebbe; and Jinja. All three are near Lake Victoria.

ECONOMY. Uganda's economy is based on agriculture. The basic food crops are corn, beans, and cassava, and the main cash crops are cotton and coffee. Tobacco, sugarcane, and tea are also grown. Cattle are raised in many parts of the country, and fish from Uganda's lakes are important to the economy.

Uganda has rich copper deposits, and in 1965, 17,200 metric tons of copper were produced. There are also deposits of apatite, beryl, and bismuth, although production of these minerals is limited.

Most industry is engaged in the processing of Uganda's mineral and agricultural products. The Owen Falls hydroelectric plant, near Lake Victoria, supplies most of the country's electricity, and industry is concentrated in the Owen Falls region. The government instituted a five-year development plan in 1962, and at its completion in 1966 a new five-year plan began.

In 1966 imports cost $119 million and exports earned $188 million. The major imports are textiles, petroleum products, iron and steel, and machinery. The main exports are coffee, cotton, and copper. Most trade is conducted with Britain, the United States, Belgium, and Luxembourg. Uganda has close economic ties with Kenya and Tanzania.

GOVERNMENT. In 1967 a new constitution was promulgated in Uganda. Legislative powers are vested in a National Assembly, which is popularly elected every five years. Executive power is vested in a president, who is elected by the legislature to a five-year term.

Uganda is a member of the United Nations, the Organization of African Unity (OAU), and the Commonwealth of Nations.

HISTORY. Between the 1400s and 1600s various peoples established kingdoms in present-day Uganda. In the 1600s the Buganda kingdom became powerful and conquered many of the existing states.

James Augustus Grant and John Hanning Speke explored the source of the Nile in 1862 and established trade relations between Britain and Mutesa I, the *kabaka*, or king, of Buganda. Protestant and Roman Catholic missionaries followed, as well as Muslims, who were in contact with neighboring regions. In the 1880s, Mutesa's successor, Mwanga, attempted to stop the spread of Christianity in the area, and many Christians were killed in a widespread persecution.

British Rule. In 1888 the Imperial British East Africa Company concluded a treaty with Buganda, and the kingdom came under company administration. The company withdrew from Uganda because of economic difficulties, and in 1894 Britain established a protectorate over the region. By 1896 the protectorate included all of present-day Uganda.

In 1900 the Buganda regent signed the Uganda Agreement with Britain, which established administrative arrangements that endured until Uganda achieved self-government in 1962. The kabaka, or king, with his *lukiko,* or assembly, was recognized as the ruler of Uganda as long as he cooperated with Britain. Four regions were marked out—the Eastern, Western, Northern, and Buganda regions. The Buganda region occupied south-central Uganda.

Britain established a legislative council following World War I, and African members were appointed to the council after World War II. In 1953 Buganda demanded independence from the rest of Uganda because of fears of being forced into federation with the British protectorate of Kenya and Tanganyika, and thereby coming under the control of Kenya's white-settler community. In the same year, Kabaka Edward Mutesa II was exiled after refusing to nominate Buganda members to the legislative council.

In March 1961 elections were held for representatives to the legislative council and a majority of seats was won by the largely Roman Catholic, Democratic Party (DP). Buganda boycotted the election. In September 1961 a constitutional conference was held in London, and an agreement was reached granting Uganda self-government in March 1962. Differences between Buganda and the legislative council were settled, and Buganda stopped threatening to secede.

Independence. In 1961 Milton Obote of the Uganda People's Congress (UPC) formed an alliance with the Kabaka Yekka, a Buganda party which supported the kabaka. In April 1962 elections were held for a new parliament established by the 1961 London conference.

A coalition government composed of the UPC and the Kabaka Yekka came to power with Obote as prime minister. On Oct. 9, 1962 Uganda became independent, with Obote as prime minister and the king of Buganda, Edward Mutesa II, as president.

In 1966 Obote took full control of the government, suspended the constitution, and ousted President Mutesa. Obote assumed the position of president. Fighting broke out in Buganda, protesting Obote's seizure of the government, but the rising was quickly suppressed and the kabaka fled the country. A new constitution was promulgated in 1967.

—Hibberd V. B. Kline, Jr.; Vera L. Zolberg

UNITED ARAB REPUBLIC (EGYPT)

Official name: United Arab Republic
Area: 386,100 square miles
Population: (1966 est.) 30,147,000
Capital: Cairo (Pop., 1962 est., 3,518,200)
Language: Arabic
Religion: Islam
Currency unit: Pound
National holiday: National day, July 23

The United Arab Republic (U.A.R.) is an independent country in northern Africa formerly known as Egypt. In 1958 Egypt and Syria joined to form the U.A.R. Syria withdrew from the Union in 1961, but Egypt continued to use the name United Arab Republic. The country is a major center of Arab culture and a leading force in the movement for unity in the Arab world.

The United Arab Republic is bordered on the north by the Mediterranean Sea; on the east by Israel and the Red Sea; on the south by Sudan; and on the west by Libya. In 1967, during the Arab-Israeli war, Israel occupied the Gaza Strip and almost all of the Sinai region of the United Arab Republic.

THE LAND. The United Arab Republic consists of two main regions, which are divided by the Suez Canal. East of the canal is the Sinai Peninsula, a rugged desert country with only a few oases. The region west of the canal is occupied mainly by desert.

The Nile River flows northward through the western region. The fertile valley formed by the river is between 2 and 10 miles wide. In the north the valley widens into a delta through which the Nile reaches the Mediterranean Sea. The desert begins at the edge of the valley. The flow of the Nile is regulated by several dams to provide a maximum of water for irrigation.

The Western Desert, west of the Nile, contains a few oases, including El Faiyum in the northern part of

the country. The Qattara Depression, Africa's lowest point, is in the north. The Eastern Desert, east of the Nile, is rugged and contains no important oases.

Summers in the U.A.R. are very hot and dry, and winters are warm and dry. A little winter rain falls in the area of Alexandria, in the north.

THE PEOPLE. The population of the U.A.R. is concentrated in the Nile valley and its delta. The country has a high rate of population growth, and between 1958 and 1965 the population grew at a rate of 2.6 percent a year.

Most Egyptians are descended from Hamitic-speaking peoples who inhabited the Nile valley in ancient times with some mixture of Arab stock from the time of the Muslim conquest in the 600s. Over 90 percent of the people are Muslim, and the Egyptians speak Arabic. Most of the remaining people are Copts, Egyptian Christians. Nomadic herdsmen, or Bedouin, roam the desert regions in search of food and water for their livestock.

Cairo, the capital, lies at the junction of the Nile valley and delta. Alexandria, the main port, had a population of over 1.5 million in the mid–1960s. Other large cities are Port Said, Tanta, and Aswan.

ECONOMY. The economy of the United Arab Republic depends on agriculture. In recent years industry, which is under government control, has been expanded.

Agriculture. Between 1945 and 1964 agriculture was the occupation of 57 percent of the labor force. In ancient times, barley and wheat were the main crops. With improvements in irrigation techniques, sugar and cotton have largely replaced them as the major crops. In 1965 over 4 million metric tons of sugar and 504,000 metric tons of cotton were produced. Rice and corn are also grown.

The Nile River irrigates about 7 million acres of land. The Aswan Dam on the Nile River provides water for irrigation as well as hydroelectric power.

Manufacturing and Mining. The main industries process the cotton grown in the country. Modern textile and chemical plants have been established in many towns, especially in and near Tanta, near the Mediterranean Sea. Armament industries have also been founded. Tourism provides additional income. The United Arab Republic received revenues from the operation of the Suez Canal. In 1967, as a result of the Arab-Israeli war, all shipping through the canal was stopped.

Petroleum is produced in the Sinai Peninsula and on the western shore of the Red Sea. In 1966, 6.2 million metric tons of petroleum were produced, but production was insufficient for domestic needs. Iron ore is mined in the southern part of the country, and is converted into steel in a plant near Cairo. Some copper is also mined.

Trade. In 1967 imports cost over $754 million and exports earned $567 million. The main imports are cereals, petroleum, and machinery. The major exports are cotton and textiles. Most trade is conducted with the Soviet Union, West Germany, and Czechoslovakia. The United Arab Republic has received large-scale economic assistance from the Soviet Union, the United States, and other countries.

GOVERNMENT. The United Arab Republic has a presidential system of government. The president is nominated by the legislature and approved by popular vote. He is elected to a six-year term. The president appoints a cabinet, headed by a prime minister, which is responsible to the legislature.

Legislative power is vested in a National Assembly, with 350 popularly-elected members and 10 additional members appointed by the president. Members serve five-year terms. The United Arab Republic is a one-party state, the Arab Socialist Union being the only recognized party in the country.

The United Arab Republic is a member of the United Nations, the Arab League, and the Organization of African Unity (OAU).

HISTORY. Civilization has existed in Egypt for over 7,000 years. Successive Egyptian dynasties ruled until foreign invaders overran the country. The first of these invasions occurred in 945 BC, when a Libyan prince, Sheshonk, seized control of Egypt. Libyans ruled Egypt until the late 700s BC, when an Ethiopian dynasty took power. In about 670 BC Assyrians established control over the country, only to be conquered by Persians in 525 BC.

In 332 BC Alexander the Great of Macedonia conquered Egypt and brought the country into his empire. At Alexander's death in 323 BC, one of his generals, Ptolemy, took control of Egypt and founded the Ptolemaic dynasty. Egyptian culture and politics became infused with the Greek tradition, or Hellenized. Egypt prospered under the Ptolemies—academies were built and trade was encouraged.

In 30 BC Egypt, weakened by internal conflicts, fell to the powerful forces of Rome. During the Roman occupation, probably in about the 300s AD, Christianity spread to Egypt, and the Coptic Church, the church of the Christian Egyptians, was established.

Islam. Egypt remained under Roman authority until 639 AD. In that year, Arab-speaking Muslims conquered Egypt. Since that time, Egypt has been closely identified with the Islamic world. The Muslims converted most of the Egyptian people, and Egypt became a major part of early Muslim empires.

In 969 a Muslim dynasty, the Fatimid, established its control over Egypt and made Cairo its capital. In the 1100s Christian Crusaders threatened the Muslim empire. Saladin, a Syrian officer, came to the aid of the Muslim rulers, repulsed the Christian troops, and in 1169 founded the Ayyubid dynasty.

In 1250 the slave guards of the Ayyubids, the Mamluks, seized control of the country and ruled it until 1517. In that year the Ottoman Turks defeated the Mamluks and absorbed Egypt into the Ottoman Empire. But the Ottoman Turks maintained only

LUFTHANSA
MERCHANTS display wares on a Cairo street.

loose control over Egypt, and they left the Mamluks most of their former political power.

European Influence. In 1798 Napoleon I of France invaded Egypt, but French rule was short-lived. In 1801 British and Ottoman forces expelled the French. In 1805 an Albanian Muslim soldier, Muhammad Ali, seized power and established a dynasty that lasted until 1952. Although Muhammad Ali and his successors did much to Westernize Egypt, their attempts were only partially successful.

In 1869 the Suez Canal was opened. The canal, built by the French Suez Canal Company, which obtained operations rights for 99 years, shortened the routes between Europe and the East, and increased Britain's interest in Egypt.

In 1876 Egypt, near bankruptcy from enormous expenditures from efforts to westernize the country, was forced to accept French and English financial advisors. In 1882, after a brief Egyptian nationalist uprising led by Ahmad Arabi, British troops occupied Egypt. Between 1883 and 1907 Sir Evelyn Baring (Lord Cromer) exercised chief responsibility for Egypt, and did much to develop the country economically.

In 1914 Britain declared a protectorate over Egypt. Egyptians resented British rule and called for independence. In 1922 Britain gave Egypt limited independence, but continued to control defense, foreign policy, and other important matters. On Aug. 26, 1936 Britain and Egypt signed a treaty whereby Britain withdrew its troops from all regions except the Suez Canal zone.

In the same year, 1936, King Faruq succeeded to the throne. In 1945 Egypt and six other Arab nations formed the Arab League to promote unity among member nations. In 1948 Egypt and the other Arab nations fought an unsuccessful war against the newly created state of Israel. Israel drove the invaders out, and the United Nations negotiated separate armistice agreements between the Arab states and Israel, but no final peace treaty was signed. Egypt obtained control of the Gaza Strip,

UNITED NATIONS
ON THE NILE, a camel turns a waterwheel.

a small area on the Mediterranean Sea once part of Palestine.

Republic. After the Arab-Israeli clash Egypt, troubled with the causes for failure in the war, a corrupt regime, and social unrest, fell into political turmoil. In 1952 an army group called the Free Officers seized control of the government and forced the king to abdicate.

Gen. Muhammad Najib (Naguib) became prime minister. In June 1953 Egypt became a republic, and Najib became president. In 1954 Lt. Col. Gamal Abdel Nasser, a leader of the military revolt, ousted Najib and assumed the position of president.

In 1956 the United States withdrew offers of a loan for the building of a high dam at Aswan. Because of the withdrawal of the loan offer, Nasser nationalized the Suez Canal and announced his intention to use canal revenues to build the dam. Nasser also accepted large-scale Soviet aid for the project. A dispute over free access to the canal arose after nationalization, and a new conflict erupted. British, French, and Israeli forces attacked in October 1955, and after a brief but intensive struggle, both sides accepted a UN cease-fire.

U.A.R. On Feb. 1, 1958 Egypt, in an effort to build Arab unity, joined with Syria to form the United Arab Republic. The following month, the U.A.R. joined with the Kingdom of Yemen to form the United Arab States. In September 1961 Syria withdrew from the U.A.R., and three months later Egypt ended its tie with Yemen. In 1962 the United Arab Republic supported republican forces in Yemen fighting against Yemeni royalist forces.

In 1967 The United Arab Republic blockaded the Gulf of Aqaba, cutting off Israel's outlet to the Red Sea. On June 5 fighting erupted between the Arab states and Israel, and the Israeli army again defeated the Arab forces. Israel opened the Gulf of Aqaba, occupied the Sinai Peninsula and the Gaza Strip, and seized control of the east bank of the Suez Canal. The United Nations again arranged a ceasefire, but a permanent solution to the conflict was not achieved.

—L. Carl Brown; Alexander Melamid

UNITED KINGDOM

Official name: United Kingdom of Great Britain and Northern Ireland
Area: 94,220 square miles
Population: (1967 est.) 55,068,000
Capital: London (Pop., 1965 est., urban area, 7,948,300)
Language: English
Religion: Anglicanism, Protestantism, Roman Catholicism
Currency unit: Pound
National holiday: Queen's birthday

The United Kingdom of Great Britain and Northern Ireland, usually referred to as Great Britain or Britain, lies on the British Isles, off the northwest coast of continental Europe.

The major island, Great Britain, includes England, in the south and east, Wales, in the west, and Scotland, in the north. It is separated from France on the south by the English Channel and the strait of Dover, and from northern Europe on the east by the North Sea. The Norwegian Sea, an arm of the North Atlantic Ocean, lies to the north.

Great Britain is separated from the other large island of the group, Ireland, by St. George's Channel, the Irish Sea, and the North Channel. Northern Ireland, part of the United Kingdom, shares the island with the independent Republic of Ireland.

Most of the islands near Great Britain, including the Hebrides, Shetland, and Orkney groups off Scotland and the Isle of Wight off England, are British. The Channel Islands in the English Channel and the Isle of Man in the Irish Sea are British dependencies.

THE LAND. A complex geological structure gives the British Isles a varied topography despite their limited size. On Great Britain a moderately high highland region arches northward from the Cambrian Mountains in southwestern Wales and the Cotswold hills in western England. It extends through the Pennine Mountains in north-central England and the Cheviot Hills, the Southern Uplands, and the Grampian Mountains of Scotland to the Scottish Highlands, where the island's and the nation's highest peak, Ben Nevis, rises to 4,406 feet.

Most of England is occupied by low plains. In central England the Midlands occupy the basins of the Mersey and the Trent rivers between the Cotswold to the south and the Pennines to the north. In the south and east the lowlands are called the Downs and Fens. The Central Lowland, in Scotland between the Southern Upland and the Highlands, is the only major lowland outside of England.

Narrow plains skirt the deeply indented coasts of Wales, northern England, and southern Scotland, but the highlands of northern Scotland drop sharply into the sea. The northern and western sections of Northern Ireland are rolling uplands, levelling off in the south and east.

The most important of Britain's rivers are the Thames and the Severn in England and the Tweed and the Clyde in Scotland. Most British lakes are in the "Lake District" of northwestern England and in the Scottish highlands, which are also marked by long, narrow fjord-like inlets. Britain's largest lake, Lough Neagh, lies in the center of Northern Ireland.

Climate. Britain has a temperate maritime climate. The cold temperatures usual for the islands' northerly location are moderated by the warm Gulf Stream flowing just west of the islands, and by warm winds off the Atlantic Ocean. As a result, winters are generally mild and summers cool, with few temperature extremes. Average temperatures for the country as a whole are about 40°F in winter and 60°F in summer.

Rainfall is moderate to heavy, ranging from 20 inches a year in the southeast to 120 inches on the west coast, and averages about 40 inches a year for the country as a whole. Cloudiness is the rule, with southeastern England having the most sunshine, about 6 hours a day in summer.

THE PEOPLE. Britain is one of the world's most densely settled countries, with a density of 582 persons per square mile in 1966. The bulk of the country's population lives in England and Wales, which had a density of 824 persons per square mile in 1966. Settlement is sparser towards the north and west.

Britain is also a highly urbanized nation, and most Britons live in cities or suburbs. In 1967 there were six cities with urban areas of over 1 million people. The metropolitan area of London, the capital, has the largest population, with more than 8 million people in 1967.

Between 1958 and 1966 the population grew at the slow rate of 0.7 percent a year, and the country limits immigration.

Britain's population is quite homogeneous. Most Britons are descendants of Celtic, Scandinavian, French, and Germanic peoples who had settled in the islands by the 1000s.

English is the universal language, although the Celtic languages of Welsh and Gaelic are spoken in the north and west. The Church of England (Anglican) is the established church and the dominant religion, but other Protestant denominations and Roman Catholicism are also important.

The few ethnic minority groups of any significance are made up of immigrants from member nations of the British Commonwealth of Nations. Most prominent are people from the West Indies and from India and Pakistan.

ECONOMY. The British economy, once the most stable and prosperous in the world, faced serious difficulties in the mid-1900s. Its earlier prosperity was based on commerce, made possible by its strategic maritime location, and upon mineral resources which provided an excellent base for the early development of industry.

Britain's natural resources include abundant fields of excellent coal and rich iron ore deposits, mostly in the Pennines, as well as quantities of limestone, gravel, chalk, and fine clays. There are also small deposits of zinc, tin, and lead, and bauxite is mined in northern Ireland. With the depletion over the years of the coal and iron ore deposits, and lacking petroleum, natural gas, and water-power resources, Britain was at a disadvantage by the mid-1900s.

Agriculture. The soils of Britain's lowlands and river valleys, especially in eastern England and northern Ireland, are quite fertile, but limited in quantity. The highlands are generally unsuitable for farming, but they provide excellent grazing land.

In the mid-1960s about 30 percent of Britain's land area was used for farming. In 1965, however, agriculture contributed only some 3 percent of the gross domestic product and occupied a very small proportion of the labor force.

A great variety of crops are raised. Wheat and barley are important, and fruits, vegetables, and other grains are also raised. Dairy farming prospers, particularly in Wales, Northern Ireland, the Scottish lowlands, and western England. Large herds of sheep are grazed in the Highlands and the Midlands, and pigs, poultry and beef cattle are important throughout the country.

Fishing contributed less than 1 percent of the gross domestic product in the mid-1960s, but it provides an important item in the British diet and is vital to the economies of Scotland and the northern islands.

Industry. Britain is a highly industrialized nation, and in 1965 manufacturing contributed 36 percent of the gross domestic product, one of the highest percentages in the world. British industry, originally based upon its coal, its iron, and its wool, was forced to shift in the mid-1900s to keep pace with modern technology and to meet the varied demands of modern markets. Heavy industry remained central to British industry, however.

Iron and steel working, metal finishing, chemical production, shipbuilding, and the manufacture of machinery, machine tools, and vehicles are the most important activities. Textiles, both wool and the newer synthetics, are an important element in British industry.

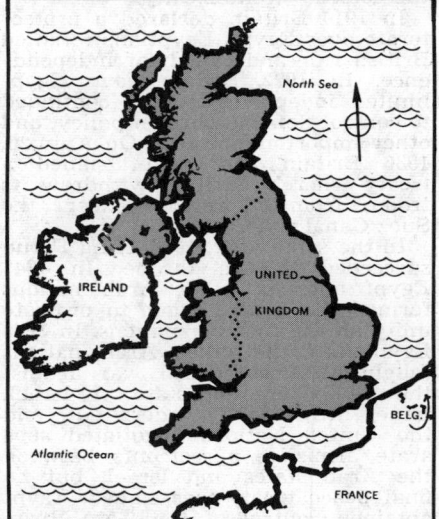

BRITISH TRAVEL ASSOCIATION

GREAT BRITAIN'S HOUSES OF PARLIAMENT lie on the banks of the Thames River in London.

The centers of British heavy industry are in the Midlands, in southern Wales, in the Scottish lowlands, and, to a lesser extent, in coastal northern Ireland and on the northern English coast. Greater London is the center of British light industry, including paper making, printing, food processing, and the production of finished consumer foods. It is also the commercial and financial center of the country.

The British government plays an active role in the economy, stimulating and regulating agriculture and industry and providing broad social services for the British people. The government owns and operates in whole or in part the country's rail and air transport systems, its coal and steel industries, and its radio, television, and telecommunications networks.

The government exercises controls over wages and prices in most areas of the economy, but in the 1950s and 1960s it was unable to control a series of recessions and inflationary booms. Late in 1967 the government was forced to devalue the pound from $2.80 to $2.40.

Trade. International trade is vital to Britain's economy, and Britain for many years was the world's first-ranking trading nation. In the 1950s an increasingly poor balance of trade developed. Once trade imbalances had been made up by "invisible items," including foreign investment and shipping, but by the 1950s income

from invisible items had declined greatly.

In 1967 Britain's exports earned $17,248 million and its imports cost $13,847 million. Foodstuffs constitute the largest single import classification, and fuels, industrial raw materials, and finished and semi-finished consumer goods are also imported. Machinery, vehicles, and scientific instruments are the leading exports, and textiles, chemicals, metals, and other manufactured goods are also important.

The United States, Canada, Australia, West Germany, France, the Netherlands, and the Scandinavian countries are Britain's major trading partners. As a leading member of the Commonwealth of Nations, Britain has many special trade arrangements with other Commonwealth nations.

GOVERNMENT. Britain is a constitutional monarchy with a parliamentary system of government. The British queen is head of state. Actual executive power is wielded by a prime minister and cabinet responsible to the legislature, the Parliament. Parliament has two houses—a popularly elected lower house, the House of Commons, and the less powerful, hereditary and appointive upper house, the House of Lords.

Britain does not have a single written constitution; rather, its government is based upon a series of documents, judicial decisions, and traditions that have the force of law.

These define the civil rights of British citizens and outline the powers of the organs of government.

Commonwealth and Empire. Britain is the central member of the Commonwealth of Nations, a group of nations all of which were once colonies of Britain and all of which recognize the British monarch as the symbolic head of the Commonwealth. The Commonwealth nations hold frequent meetings to discuss mutual problems, and member nations provide financial, technical, and often military aid to one another.

By 1968 Britain's once vast colonial empire had shrunk greatly. During the two decades following World War II, most of Britain's African and Asian colonial territories won their independence, as did many colonial areas in the western hemisphere. Moreover, Britain began withdrawing from the Middle East, where it had established many protectorates, particularly in the Persian Gulf area.

Britain still held a considerable number of territories, however, although most were internally self-governing. In Europe, the empire included the Channel Islands, the Isle of Man, and Gibraltar. In Asia and the Pacific, Hong Kong, the Indian Ocean Territories, Fiji, the Gilbert and Ellice Islands, and other small areas remained British. In the western hemisphere, Britain retained Bermuda, British Honduras, and a number of West Indian Islands.

International Relations. Britain is a member of the United Nations, the North Atlantic Treaty Organization (NATO), the European Free Trade Association (EFTA), the Central Treaty Organization (CENTO), and the Southeast Asia Treaty Organization (SEATO).

Britain also has special treaty relations with a number of countries, such as the Trucial Oman, under which Britain is responsible for the defense and foreign relations of those countries.

HISTORY. The British Isles have been inhabited since prehistoric times. In about 600 BC Celtic peoples from the mainland of Europe began to settle on the island. They were divided into two groups: Gaels and Britons. The Gaels arrived first and settled in the north and west. The Britons occupied the south and east.

The Roman emperor Julius Caesar invaded the British Isles in 55 BC and found Gaels and Britons living in informal communities whose economies were based on agriculture, metalworking, and trading. But the Romans did not seriously attempt to conquer the Celts until 43 AD, when the emperor Claudius led a military expedition to the islands and occupied part of present-day England.

The Romans established settlements, founded cities, built roads and forts, and eventually extended Roman civil and military administration up to the present-day Scottish border. There the emperor Hadrian had a wall built in the 120s.

Many Celtic tribes remained outside of Roman control in present-day Ireland, Wales, and Scotland, and they, along with such non-Celtic peoples as the Picts in Scotland, were a constant threat to the Romans. Present-day England, however, inhabited by Britons, was Roman, and from the 40s AD to the 300s its history is part of the history of the Roman empire.

As England shared in Rome's greatness, it shared in its decline. After more than 100 years of attempted invasions from the north, in 367 the Picts and the Scots breached Hadrian's wall. Within the next 50 years Rome withdrew its troops from Britain to defend the empire in other areas. With the departure of the Roman troops, the cities, laws, prosperity, and culture that had been associated with Roman rule degenerated and in many cases disappeared.

The departure of the Romans left Britain subject to foreign invasions. From about 450 to 600 successive waves of invaders from northern Germany—Jutes, Angles, and Saxons—conquered the Celts or forced them to retreat to the western areas of the island, into Cornwall and Wales.

The various tribes of Anglo-Saxon invaders eventually created a number of kingdoms in the various parts of the island each had settled. The most important kingdoms were Northumbria, in the northeast; Mercia, in the Midlands; and Wessex, stretching from London westward to the Severn River. The other kingdoms included East Anglia, Essex, Kent, and Sussex in the south and east.

In the 600s all the Anglo-Saxon kingdoms were converted to Christianity through the influence of a missionary from Rome, Augustine, who baptized Ethelbert, king of Kent, and in 601 became the first archbishop of Canterbury. With the conversion of the Anglo-Saxons, English Christianity changed from the variety preserved by the Celts into the form of Rome.

Monastic life flourished in England and produced notable figures like the Venerable Bede (673–735), a monk at Jarrow, who wrote a history of the English people. Through the work of the monasteries, the Germanic Anglo-Saxon tongue became a written language, English. Church structure developed early, and religious leaders often exerted great influence, especially in Mercia and Wessex.

Rivalries among the kingdoms prevented any real unity for many centuries. Mercia, under Offa II (r. 757–796), and Wessex, led by Egbert of Wessex (r.802–839), underwent marked political development and extended their boundaries westward. By the early 800s a unique English social and political structure had taken shape, and the once warlike, semi-nomadic Anglo-Saxons had become a settled, agricultural people, enjoying peace and stability. Protected only by an army of untrained farmers, however, they were prey to more warlike peoples.

A people the Anglo-Saxons called "Danes," the inhabitants of present-day Denmark, Sweden, and Norway, began raiding the east coast of Britain in 787. In the 850s the Danes began a systematic conquest of the island, and by 870 all of the Anglo-

Saxon kingdoms except Wessex had surrendered.

Wessex, led by King Alfred the Great (r.871–899), successfully resisted, and in 878 Alfred made a treaty with the Danes that divided England along a line running from London northwest to the Irish Sea. The area northeast of the line remained in Danish hands and was called the "Danelaw." The area southwest of the line was an enlarged kingdom of Wessex.

Alfred created in Wessex a strong political and cultural unit, and in 955 his grandson was able to conquer the Danelaw. Alfred's descendants ceased to be kings merely of Wessex and became the first kings of all England.

Unity did not bring security, however, and in about 980 the Danes renewed their raids. The reign of Ethelred the Redeless, or Unready, from 978 to 1016, was troubled by Danish invasions. In an attempt to buy off the Danes, Ethelred resorted to direct taxation of his subjects by instituting the Danegeld. The tribute paid from the Danegeld did not satisfy the Danes, and by 1017 they had defeated the English in battle.

Ethelred and his son both died in 1016 and the Witan, responsible for choosing a new king, was forced to name the Danish king, Canute, king of England (r.1017–1035). Canute ruled England, Denmark, and Norway, and established an orderly system of government in each. His two sons lacked his ability, however, and in 1042 the Witan chose one of Alfred's descendants, Edward "the Confessor," as king (r.1042–1066).

During Edward's reign, two groups competed for power. One was led by Godwin, the earl of Wessex, and his son Harold, whose family controlled not only Wessex but other earldoms as well. Their rivals were Normans, the descendants of a group of marauding Northmen, who in 910 had settled opposite England's south coast on the French peninsula that came to be called Normandy. They had built a strong, well organized duchy by the 1000s. The Norman faction was led by William, duke of Normandy.

Edward the Confessor favored the Normans, and he was said to have promised the English throne to William. It was also claimed that Harold himself had sworn to support William's succession to the throne. But when Edward died in 1066 the Witan chose Harold as king (r. January–October, 1066).

Norman Conquest. William of Normandy immediately made plans to take by force the throne that he claimed was rightfully his. In his efforts he had the valuable support of the pope and the aid of Harold's brother, Tostig, and of Harold Hardrada, the king of Norway, whose army united with Tostig against Harold.

Harold was forced to go to the north to meet the Norwegian threat, and at the Battle of Stamford Bridge in September 1066 Harold was victorious and both Hardrada and Tostig lost their lives.

Immediately following this victory, however, William of Normandy landed on the south coast of England. Harold rushed his army southward

BRITISH TRAVEL ASSOCIATION

DOVER CASTLE in Kent is built around what is believed to be Britain's oldest building.

and attacked the invaders at Hastings on October 14. By the end of the day, Harold was dead and William, "the Conqueror," triumphant.

He pressed on with his army to London, where the Witan submitted and recognized him as king. For several years William had to suppress English revolts against the Normans, but he had acquired the crown of England, perhaps by right, as he asserted, but certainly by conquest.

The Norman conquest of England did not involve a replacement of all things English with all things Norman. William retained the Anglo-Saxon divisions of the kingdom and the offices and practices associated with them. The Danegeld, the English courts and laws, their army, and, for a time, the Witan, remained as well.

William. Gradually, William replaced England's informal democracy with more rigid institutions. The Witan became the *curia regis*, or king's court, a council of lay and clerical nobles who advised and assisted the king.

Feudalism also was introduced into England as a result of the Norman conquest, when the lands and offices of dispossessed, rebel Anglo-Saxons were granted to loyal Normans in return for their accepting military and other duties. The oaths by which William bound these tenants to him were the legal framework for a feudal structure of government that had in it elements of both Anglo-Saxon and Norman custom, yet was itself unique.

By 1085 William's rule over England was firm. His Norman followers held lands throughout the kingdom and acknowledged him as their feudal overlord; his castles were built at strategic points to protect the land from internal and external violence. The thoroughness and efficiency of William's rule is illustrated by the "Domesday" survey of 1086, in which the king's officials compiled a complete report, chiefly for tax purposes, of property ownership throughout England.

In religious matters, William worked to make the church in England conform to the standards of the papacy while preventing papal influence in England from becoming superior to his own.

Most importantly, William's conquest of England bound the island, through Normandy, to Latin Christendom and turned it away from those ties it had had with Scandinavian lands, peoples, and customs.

Henry I (r.1100–1135). When William died in 1087 he left the kingdom of England to his second son, William Rufus (William II, r.1087–1100), who lacked his father's wisdom and ruled oppressively. Another of the Conqueror's sons, Henry I, who followed William II to the throne, showed something of his father's skill and energy in government.

Because some disputed his right to the throne, Henry's first acts as king were bids for popular favor. One of the most significant was his issuance of a charter promising to remedy many grievances the people had held against his predecessor. By this limiting of the king's own powers, his charter provided a precedent for later demands upon royal prerogatives.

Henry also made legal and administrative reforms. He developed further the *curia regis*, and began the practice of sending itinerant justices of the king's court throughout the land. The creation of these circuit courts added royal justice to the decrees of local and clerical courts.

Henry II (r.1154–1189). Many of the gains in the direction of an ordered royal government were lost when dynastic disputes followed Henry I's death in 1135. The king left no direct male heir, and the nobles' rivalry for power brought near anarchy between 1135 and 1154. In 1154 Henry I's grandson, Henry of Anjou, gained the throne as Henry II.

Through inheritance and marriage, Henry controlled nearly all of southwestern France and was thus lord of not only England, but of continental territories far larger than those directly controlled by the actual king of France. Ireland, too, came at least nominally under the English king's authority when in 1154 Pope Adrian IV allowed Henry to extend his kingdom there.

Henry II strengthened the position of the monarchy, which had been weakened during the dynastic struggle. He reestablished royal preeminence by using powers that his predecessors had only rarely or poorly exercised and in making their application regular and normal. By defining royal rights, he strengthened the position of the king over the barons, and he employed his additional powers in continually making improvements in the machinery of government.

Henry II also carried forward the legal reforms of Henry I. He strengthened the powers of the *curia regis*, he regularized the procedure by which the itinerant justices acted, and he extended the use of the sworn testimony of "jurors" to help in arresting criminals. It is largely due to Henry II that English common law, not Roman law, and trial by jury, not trial by inquisition, became the English legal tradition.

To have his courts and his law prevail over the private courts of feudal barons and over the independent courts of the church, Henry issued the Constitutions of Clarendon in 1164 and other royal edicts to make royal law common to the whole land and superior to law of other courts. By weakening church courts, however, these reforms brought Henry into conflict with his archbishop of Canterbury, Thomas Becket.

Four of Henry's knights murdered Becket in 1170, and Becket was immediately regarded as a martyred saint. Henry was forced to make a public act of penance and to accept the church's view of the role of church courts.

Richard I (r.1189–1199). Henry was succeeded by his son Richard. Richard I, "the Lionhearted", was great in legend, but of little importance in fact as far as England was concerned. Throughout almost all of his reign he was engaged in the Third Crusade, which kept him out of the country.

The absence of a king did not cause the degeneration of royal power, largely as a result of Henry II's reforms and the work of Hubert Walter, Archbishop of Canterbury.

By the 1100s English society was well settled into its particular pattern of feudalism. Differing from continental feudalism, the English manorial system led more to internal peace than to internal conflict, for, with armed castles required to be licensed by the king and thus few in number, the noblemen of England were more gentlemen landowners than warriors. Feudal duties to higher lords, including the king, were fulfilled more often through the courts of law than on the battlefield.

Serfs, bound to the land of their lord's manor, kept the agricultural economy running. Each manor-town was largely self-sufficient, and its land was rich enough to support its inhabitants without a need for trade.

At the end of the 1100s, the towns began to grow in size and significance, and the free townsmen began to gain importance. Both towns and townsmen were encouraged in their rise by Hubert Walter. He granted town charters which gave an extraordinary degree of self-government to the towns.

John (r.1199–1216). John, upon the death of his brother, came to the throne full of ambition and talent. He wanted to press forward the claims of the crown against both the church and the nobility, but his efforts failed, largely because he both inherited and created many formidable enemies.

During John's reign England lost its continental Angevin possessions, including Normandy, to France. Moreover, John's attempts to control the nomination of the archbishop of Canterbury failed, and in 1213 he had to humble himself before the pope and acknowledge that England was a papal fief.

In his attempt to extend royal power at the expense of the barons, especially in the dispensing of justice and the levying of taxes, John was brought to heel by a revolt of the barons. In 1215, at Runnymede, the discontented nobles forced him to grant a long and detailed charter, which came to be known as the Great Charter, or *Magna Carta*.

The charter was not a comprehensive grant of liberties to all of John's subjects. It dealt very specifically with certain complaints that the influential classes in England raised with the policies of Henry II and John. Most of its clauses were meant to apply only to barons, clergymen, wealthy townsmen, or freemen. Few were of general application or referred to the majority of Englishmen, the serfs.

The charter's most significant aspect, the requirement that the king must act according to laws or customs that he could not set aside at will, was modeled on the charter granted by Henry I. John's charter's significance lay in the fact that the king's subjects demanded the grant as their right. The nobles' demand for control over the king was a first step away from absolutism. The significance of the charter increased in later years as it came to be regarded as protecting the rights of all Englishmen.

Henry III (1216-1272). The nobility increased its control over the monarchy during the reign of Henry III, who came to the throne as a child in 1216. Later, Henry, a pious man and a patron of the arts, to the disgust of many of his English subjects, filled his court with foreigners and dismissed Englishmen who had served him well. As a result, many of the English nobility and clergy banded together against him.

In 1258 Henry was forced to accept an agreement, the Provisions of Oxford, which established a permanent committee of barons to control the king's government. By 1264, however, this settlement had broken down, and the quarrel between Henry and his nobles degenerated into civil war in which the barons, led by Simon de Montfort, Henry's brother-in-law, defeated Henry.

To gain broad support for their government, the baronial council of government, organized and dominated by de Montfort, called for a "Model Parliament" in 1265. The Model Parliament was to be attended by two knights elected from each shire and, for the first time, two representatives from each city and borough.

Under such a strong threat to their power, however, the king and the more conservative barons rallied, and late in 1265 the king's forces led by his son and heir, Prince Edward, defeated the barons in battle and killed Montfort. The baronial rebellion and experiment with government ended. All charters granted were annulled.

Edward I (r.1272-1307). Edward became king while in the Holy Land on a crusade. On his return in 1274, he determined to bring order to the kingdom by extending the power of the crown. Moreover, Edward saw that the gathering of a parliament bringing together the greater clergy, the nobility, and representatives of the towns could serve his purposes in extending royal authority.

For Edward, the gathering of the higher clergy, the nobility, and the representatives of counties and boroughs in parliament was an enlarged *curia regis*, or council of advisors. Through it he could discover the outstanding abuses that existed in the kingdom, and at the same time, it could effectively announce royal policy and influence public opinion. Moreover, Parliament could be most useful in opening to the king new sources of revenue beyond the limited and inadequate income that the crown derived from its traditional source, fixed feudal dues.

Edward needed new sources of money and support because of his ambitious foreign and domestic policies. While he was making inroads in the power of the barons and the church in England, he was at war with France on the continent to defend one of his French territories. Even more aggressive and costly were wars he waged in Wales and Scotland.

Wales had for centuries been a troublesome and occasionally threatening land on the western frontier of the English kingdom. In the early 1200s Wales had been united under Llewelyn the Great (r. 1194-1240) and

BRITISH TRAVEL ASSOCIATION

ROYAL GUARDSMAN, one of the Queen's personal escorts, stands duty at Whitehall.

started to take advantage of the rifts existing among English political factions.

In the late 1200s Edward I decided that the peace of England required the conquest of Wales, and by 1284 he had conquered the kingdom. Although Welsh laws, customs, and language survived, independent Wales ceased to exist, and Edward's castles dominated the land. In 1301 Edward proclaimed his son and heir the "Prince of Wales."

Edward had less success in Scotland, the kingdom to the north. Scotland, like Wales, had had a troubled domestic history, and for centuries had been a threat to England. After the death in 1286 of its king, Alexander III, Scotland found itself without a ruler and prey to the evils arising from a disputed succession to the throne. Edward I was called in to choose a king, and in 1292 he declared John Baliol king of Scotland. Taking advantage of his position, Edward then made extensive demands on the Scots.

To resist the king's aggression, the Scots made a military alliance with the king of France. John Baliol, William Wallace, and Robert Bruce led Scotland in wars against English domination, which continued for over 30 years and did not end until 1328, when King Edward III recognized Bruce's title to the Scottish crown.

Edward II (r.1307-1327). Although Edward had strengthened the position of the monarchy, his failures in other fields left it open to attack on other fronts. Thus, although he left his son Edward II the benefits of advancements in the laws and institutions of the realm, he also left a drained treasury, an exhausting war in Scot-

land, and a host of enemies at home and abroad. Edward II was not the man to take advantage of the benefits or overcome the difficulties or take full advantage of the benefits of his position.

In Edward II's reign, the barons sought with some success to supervise royal policy through a commission known as the Lord's Ordainers. When, in 1327, Edward, surrounded by plots and conspiracy, was deposed and murdered, it was Parliament that named his successor, proclaiming his 15-year-old son King Edward III.

Edward III (r.1327-1377). The young king came to the throne during a turbulent period in England's social and political development. During the 1200s and early 1300s English cultural and economic life had quickened most dramatically, and the speed of the resulting social change was increased by a long series of wars and a major epidemic during the 1300s.

English cities and towns, which had grown into thriving centers of trade, had developed a particularly active commerce in cloth with the Low Countries—Belgium, the Netherlands, and Luxembourg.

In part to insure the continuation of this commerce and to foil the attempts of the French king to interrupt it, Edward III in 1337 began a conflict with the French that lasted so long it earned the name, the Hundred Years' War. The French alliance with the Scots in their war against England also encouraged Edward III to go to war against France. He used the pretext that, as a descendant of Philip II of France, he had a valid claim to the crown of France.

Britain enjoyed early victories, and the Treaty of Brétigny in 1360 brought the first phase of the long war to an end. By it, England received the port of Calais, protection for its cloth trade, title to a large section of southwestern France, and promise of ransom for the heir to the French throne, whom the English had captured.

France had been ravaged by the war, and England also suffered, both from financial exhaustion and from the violent onset in 1348 of the plague known as the Black Death. The plague killed perhaps one-third of the English population.

By causing a manpower shortage that broke the traditional bonds of the serf to the land and the manor, the Black Death hastened the process of social change. Feudalism began to disintegrate and the position of the towns and of a newly formed middle class was strengthened. Aided by the collapse of feudal loyalties and by the new spirit of nationalism inspired by the wars with France, the English monarchy in the late 1300s was able to centralize its power at the expense of the local lords and clergy.

The new social order not only increased the power of the monarchy and its local representatives, the justices of the peace; it also enhanced the status of the representatives of the expanding middle class in Parliament, and it was during the mid-1300s that the practice developed of having Parliament divide into two groups, one body of nobles and higher clergy and one of knights of the shire and townsmen.

Between 1339 and 1349 the knights and burgesses began to be designated as the "Commons," because they had by custom established a common meeting place, a common clerk, and had begun electing a common speaker to speak for them before the king.

The continuing wars with France also strengthened Parliament, as the growth of parliamentary power depended primarily on the control of taxation, and Edward III was continually in need of funds to wage the war. He asked Parliament to take on the burden of levying taxes, and Parliament consented to grant the funds in return for the king's remedying grievances or giving additional privileges sought by Commons.

By the end of Edward's reign, Parliament's power was great. Not only had the nobles succeeded in increasing their control over finance, but they had also secured an important role in formulating legislation, and had even exerted occasional pressures to control executive policy.

Richard II (r.1377–1399). Edward was succeeded in 1377 by his grandson, Richard, still a minor. As Richard II, he came to a troubled throne. In the wars with France, the English had suffered many defeats and, by 1375 had been driven from all but a few coastal points on the continent.

In England, the burdens of war and taxation added to the discontent the lower classes felt in the era's rapid social changes and economic instability and led in 1381 to a briefly successful "Peasants' Revolt."

Richard responded to foreign failures and domestic unrest by arbitrary, absolute rule which made many enemies who rallied behind Richard's cousin, Henry of Lancaster, in 1399 and forced Richard to abdicate.

Henry IV (r.1399–1413). Parliament's proclamation of Henry of Lancaster as King Henry IV marked a great step in Parliament's growth. Henry reigned as a frankly constitutional monarch. By putting down several attempted rebellions and invasions, Henry passed on to his son Henry V a kingdom more secure than the one he had taken, and it looked as though stability had returned to England.

Henry V (r.1413–1422). Henry V was able to pursue the long war with France with remarkable success. By his victories and by his marriage to the daughter of the king of France, Henry became heir to the French throne in 1420. But two years later, he unexpectedly died, and left only an infant son, Henry VI. Both France and England were ruled by regents, and under these circumstances, both kingdoms deteriorated.

Henry VI (r.1422–1461). France recovered first. It improved its military position, and between 1429 and 1431 the tide of battle turned against the English. The French heir won his claim to the French throne against the young English king's, and bit by bit the French won back the English Continental territories.

England's reverses on the Continent had repercussions at home. Unfavorable terms accepted after England's losses caused the House of Commons to raise treason charges against the king's ministers. A brief rebellion by landed gentry followed and weakened Henry VI's shaky hold on the throne. In 1455 the weakness of the monarchy caused rivalries among contenders for the throne to erupt into civil war.

Henry VI's Lancastrian followers opposed the supporters of other descendants of Edward III, who were led by Richard of York, Henry's cousin. The conflicts that arose between the two houses were known collectively as the War of the Roses, because the traditional badge worn by Lancastrians was the red rose, and the Yorkists' badge was the white rose.

Bloody civil war between the houses dragged on for 30 years with the leaders of each faction claiming the right by inheritance to be king, but an end seemed to be in sight in 1461. Richard of York had been killed the year before, but his son, Edward, defeated the Lancastrians in 1461.

York. Edward of York was proclaimed king as Edward IV (r. 1461–1483). His reign and that of his brother, Richard III (1483–1485), were marked by continuing warfare and violence. Many powerful groups in England, including Yorkists, turned to Henry Tudor, earl of Richmond. Henry had only a remote claim to the throne as a Lancastrian, but he had resided safely in France during the dynastic wars. Henry invaded England in 1485 and defeated Richard III's army. As a result of Richard's death in the battle, Henry gained the crown as Henry VII.

Henry VII (r.1485–1509). Henry had come to the throne through military victory and parliamentary consent; hereditary right had played little part. He sought to make his throne secure for himself and his descendants and to bring peace and order back to England. To achieve both ends, in 1486 he united the formerly warring houses by marrying Elizabeth of York, the eldest daughter of Edward IV, and founded the Tudor dynasty.

Under the Tudors, England entered one of its greatest eras. Under Henry's guidance, the first royal navy was built, and the Cabots explored the coasts of North America, preparing the way for English colonies there.

Henry VIII (r.1509–1547). Henry VII's son, Henry VIII (r.1509–1547), had the ambition and talent to make the most of the powerful Tudor position his father had established. In the early part of his reign Henry VIII led England into participation in the diplomatic and military affairs of Europe. From 1515 to 1529, Thomas Wolsey, lord chancellor, was his brilliant adviser and agent in foreign affairs.

But Wolsey ultimately failed the king in the matter that after 1527 became Henry's chief concern—his desire to divorce his wife, Catherine of Aragon, who had failed to bear him a male heir. At the outset, Henry attempted to obtain a divorce through the papal courts at Rome, but this attempt failed in 1529.

Henry resented the church for reasons other than its refusal to grant him a divorce. That an outsider, like the pope, should exercise independent power within the realm of England was unpleasant to Henry. His predecessors had tried for centuries to limit church authority. Henry VII had come close to subordinating the nobility to the monarchy, but the church remained, with its courts, laws, taxes, and massive properties. Henry's divorce would provide the occasion for a sweeping reform of the relations between the monarchy and the church.

By 1533 Henry had an English court declare his marriage to Catherine invalid, and he had married Anne Boleyn. In 1534 Henry passed an Act of Supremacy, making himself and his successors head of the church in England, and declared all appeals to Rome illegal.

Although at the time that Henry defied the church, the Protestant Reformation was sweeping Europe, the

BRITISH TRAVEL ASSOCIATION

BUCKLAND-IN-THE-MOOR. A thatched cottage in the Dart Valley near southern Dartmoor.

impetus for England's "reformation" was more political than religious. The Anglican Church differed little from Roman Catholicism, except that Henry, not the pope, was its head.

Henry's marriage to Anne Boleyn did not serve his dynastic purposes. In 1533 she bore him a daughter, Elizabeth, but no son. In 1536 he had Anne executed, and he married Jane Seymour, who died in 1537 while giving birth to a son, Edward. Two other wives preceded Henry's sixth, Catherine Parr, who survived him.

Edward VI (r.1547–1553). Henry's actions had made religion a vital issue in English politics, and its importance increased after Henry's death. Henry was succeeded by his 10-year-old son, Edward VI, whose policies were determined by the Duke of Somerset and the Duke of Northumberland, both of whom worked to make the English church more Protestant.

Mary (r.1553–1558). After Edward VI's death, however, the crown passed to Mary, the devoutly Roman Catholic daughter of Henry VIII and Catherine of Aragon. Mary tried unsuccessfully to restore Roman Catholicism in England. She married Philip II of Spain, heir to the Holy Roman Empire, but their marriage was unpopular because of English fears of intervention and domination by Roman Catholic Spain.

Mary's persecution of Protestants earned her the name "Bloody Mary," although in her insistence on a single national religion she was in company with every other European ruler in the 1500s. Her death brought her half-sister, Elizabeth, to the throne.

Elizabeth (r.1558–1603). Elizabeth combined the Tudor qualities of determination and practicality most happily. She saw the importance of bringing order and peace to the realm, and with the help of talented advisors she found means and developed policies to do so with remarkable success.

In the area of religion, Elizabeth moved cautiously, not making a decision until Parliament did. By the Act of Supremacy (1559) and Uniformity (1563), passed by Parliament, she achieved a broad religious settlement that was moderate enough to satisfy the great majority of her subjects.

Elizabeth increased royal power by gaining widespread popular support through insuring the welfare of the people. Elizabeth initiated a program of national regulation of economic and social affairs unprecedented in Europe. Currency was stabilized, and industry was stimulated by grants of patents and monopolies. The "poor laws" provided relief for the disabled and the indigent, and the Statute of Apprentices regulated the hours and conditions of labor. Laws against religious dissent were enforced only when it threatened the peace of the realm.

The economic vitality of the kingdom found expression in the formation, near the end of Elizabeth's reign, of a number of trading companies—the most famous of which was the East India Company—that established commercial relations and

trading outposts in many parts of the world.

Elizabeth also used the English institutions of government to her, and England's, benefit. Under the Tudors the privy council, consisting of the monarch's personal advisors, usually led Parliament, which passed into law many of the measures initiated by the council. The centralizing of these institutions, together with the elimination of older ones associated with feudalism or Roman Catholicism, made the English machinery of government more efficient.

Elizabeth's government brought England international prestige, as well. By successfully facing a series of crises brought on by the Spanish king and other Roman Catholic leaders determined to restore Roman Catholicism in England, Elizabeth gained new respect for her country.

Moreover, in Elizabeth's reign English sailors broke the Spanish monopoly of trade with the New World and established England as a leading maritime nation. They plundered Spanish galleons, raided Spanish colonial outposts, and seized Spanish treasure. These exploits increased Englishmen's national pride and their awareness of the importance of the sea to England's world position.

England's maritime supremacy led Philip II of Spain to build a great Armada in 1586 to destroy the English fleet and to make possible the conquest of England. Faced with this great crisis, the English navy defeated the Spanish Armada in 1588, and thus opened the way for the further expansion of trade and, eventually, for the building of an empire.

James I (r.1603–1625). Elizabeth had never married, and upon her death in 1603, the crown passed to James VI of Scotland, son of her cousin, Mary of Scotland. James became the first of the Stuart kings, as James I of England. Although the crowns of England and Scotland were united in one person, the kingdoms remained separate.

Religion was one of the first issues confronting James. Dissatisfaction with the vagueness and breadth of Elizabeth's church settlement had increased in the late 1500s, and many hoped that further changes could be made in the law to eliminate vestiges of Roman Catholicism in the Church of England. The term "Puritan" came to be applied to those who were thus dissatisfied.

These Puritans turned first to Parliament for church reform, but with little effect. James, himself an Anglican, was unwilling to commit himself on the issue and gave the Puritans little more than permission to make a new translation of the Bible. The king's stubbornness was one cause for the departure of some Puritans to America, where they established a colony—the second English colony in the New World. "Jamestown," a settlement of James' followers in Virginia, had been the first.

Roman Catholics, too, were unhappy over James' refusal to revoke the Elizabethan anti-Roman Catholic laws. In 1605 they formed a conspir-

acy called the "Gunpowder Plot," designed to blow up Parliament. When the plot was exposed, it inspired strong anti-Roman Catholic feeling in the general public, and resulted in further restrictions on Roman Catholics.

James was also unsuccessful in dealing with Parliament, and during his reign the conflicts between king and commons over religion, foreign policy, and economic affairs grew increasingly sharp. The central issue of James' reign was the extent of royal authority.

James held to the "divine right" theory of kingship—royal authority came from God and the king was above the law. James' ineptitude in handling the institutions of government caused the Commons to become equally rigid in asserting the rights of subjects and in fixing constitutional limits upon the arbitrary use of royal power.

Unable to deal with Parliament, James ruled without it almost continuously from 1611 to 1621. Parliament's hostility toward James impelled it to develop powerful procedures and strong leaders capable of initiating and carrying through policies. The conflicts between the king and the Commons grew still sharper during the reign of James' son, Charles I.

Charles I (r.1625–1649). Charles' economic and governmental policies hardened and enlarged opposition to the king. Charles, after dissolving two Parliaments which opposed his arbitrary rule, was forced by Parliament in 1628 to grant the Petition of Right, a document which declared illegal certain royal taxes, such as forced loans, and practices, such as arbitrary imprisonment. Charles had had to reconvene Parliament and grant its demands because he needed Parliamentary approval to finance English involvement in the Thirty Years' War, a European religious and political conflict which had begun in 1618.

When Parliament continued to refuse funds, Charles ruled without it between 1628 and 1640, resorting to makeshift methods of taxation and dictatorial behavior, which alienated the populace. In 1640, when the additional expense of a war with Scotland forced Charles to reconvene Parliament, the members were ready to challenge the king.

They passed measure after measure eliminating institutions that Charles had used to maintain his absolute rule. Two of his advisors were executed. In 1641 the House of Commons formulated a program called the "Grand Remonstrance," that would have created a limited parliamentary monarchy in England and would have modified the episcopal organization of the church.

In 1642, a few months after the Commons had passed the Remonstrance, Charles accused the Parliamentary leaders of treason and tried personally to arrest them. Unsuccessful, he left London, and it was clear that more than votes would be needed to settle the conflict between king and Parliament.

BRITISH TRAVEL ASSOCIATION

EDINBURGH, SCOTLAND, with Ed Castle *(left)* and the Sir Walter Scott Memorial *(right)*.

In 1642 civil war began between the royalists, called "Cavaliers," who supported the king, and the Parliamentarians, called "Roundheads." The Cavaliers were generally Anglican nobles or gentry; the Roundheads were mostly Puritan burghers and townsmen who wanted to abolish the episcopacy.

Led by Oliver Cromwell, the Puritans and their allies, the Scots, won many important early victories, and in 1646 Charles surrendered to the Scots, who handed him over to the Parliamentarians in 1647. The victors, however, then quarreled among themselves as to what forms of government should replace the old form.

Charles took advantage of these disagreements and made an alliance with his former opponents, the Scots. A second civil war broke out in 1648, and again Cromwell and the Parliamentarians were victorious. They decided that, to achieve any permanent victory, they must execute Charles.

Commonwealth. Charles I was tried and beheaded early in 1649. The monarchy and the House of Lords were abolished and England was declared to be a commonwealth. An executive council led by Cromwell ran the government, and Cromwell discovered how difficult it was to rule with Parliament.

Between 1649 and 1653 under the Commonwealth, and then between 1653 and 1658 under a similar government called the Protectorate, Cromwell had as much difficulty with Parliament as Charles had had, and several times he found it necessary to dismiss Parliament.

Cromwell's revolutionary government made little progress with constitutional experiments it had planned. One of the few benefits of the commonwealth was the needed support it gave to Puritan colonists in America. In Scotland and Ireland, however, its excessive zeal only alienated the populations and made future union more difficult.

Charles II (r.1660–1685). After Cromwell's death in 1658 the Protectorate was too weak to survive, and in 1660 Charles I's son took the throne as Charles II. Religion continued to be the central issue, and in the 1670s Parliament passed a series of laws directed against Catholic and Protestant dissenters.

Much of the parliamentary debate centered on a bill that would have excluded Charles' brother, James, from the throne because he was a Roman Catholic. During this debate the labels "Whig" and "Tory" came into use, and the attitudes associated with them developed.

Whig designated one favoring religious toleration and the exclusion of James, that is, asserting Parliamentary control over the succession. Tory designated one favoring an intolerant and exclusive Anglican church policy and the hereditary right of kingship, even if it should involve bringing a Roman Catholic to the throne.

James II (r.1685–1688). The issue of religion and royal succession arose again in the 1680s and led to the firm establishment of a constitutionally limited monarchy in England.

James II followed his brother to the throne in 1685, and most Englishmen were willing to be loyal to him, accepting his declaration that he would defend the Anglican church and keep his own Roman Catholic loyalties a purely private matter. By 1688, however, James' actions, such as giving Roman Catholics high positions in his council and in the army and his harshness toward Anglican opponents, had caused many men to contemplate acting against him.

The birth of a son to James' wife in June 1688 brought this discontent to a head, for in the absence of a son, the throne would have gone to James' daughter, Mary. Mary, a staunch Protestant, was married to William of Orange, head of the Dutch state and leader of the Protestant forces in Europe against Roman Catholic Louis XIV of France. Thus Mary's succession and the future of Protestantism in England seemed doubtful.

In June 1688 a small group of both Whigs and Tories invited William of Orange to invade England, and William and an army landed in England in November 1688. Finding little support in England against this challenge, James II fled to France.

William of Orange (r.1689–1702). A specially convened Parliament declared the throne vacant and offered it to William and Mary, with William acting as king. In making its offer, Parliament made it clear that it and the law were above the king's will.

In accepting a Declaration of Rights along with the crown, the new sovereigns accepted constitutional limitations upon their royal authority, which were written into the Bill of Rights. The absolutist theory of "divine right" was dead. The king ruled by grace of legally constituted popular representatives who could remove his authority as well as grant it.

The events of the "Glorious Revolution" were confirmed in a number of statutes. By them, the king could not suspend acts of Parliament, and was required to convene Parliament annually. In addition, Roman Catholics were excluded from the throne, but limited toleration was granted to Protestant dissenters.

As king, William had to deal with unrest in Scotland and Ireland. Scotland, though still officially ruled by the English king, was more loyal to the deposed James II than to England, and William only barely managed to maintain his position there. Roman Catholic Ireland, still smarting from harsh treatment under Cromwell, was more rebellious, and the Protestant king responded with severity.

As soon as the political situation in England was stabilized, William brought England into the League of Augsburg, an alliance that united both Protestant and Roman Catholic Europe against the territorial aggression of Louis XIV of France. War began in 1689 and continued with brief interludes of peace until 1713.

Anne (r.1702–1714). Despite strong allies and Parliament's vigorous support of the war, England and its allies did not begin to win until William's successor, Mary's sister Anne, appointed John Churchill, first duke of Marlborough, as commander of the armed forces. His brilliant victories resulted in the defeat of Louis XIV's policies and led to the Treaty of Utrecht in 1713.

The terms of the treaty laid the groundwork for the expansion of England's empire. By the treaty,

England received as colonies Gibraltar and Minorca in the Mediterranean and the Hudson Bay Region and Newfoundland in Canada. In addition Britain gained trading rights with Spanish colonies and a monopoly of the slave trade in Europe for the next 30 years.

At the head of this embryonic empire was the newly formed "United Kingdom." Scotland and England had been formally joined in 1707 into "Great Britain." All of the British Isles were under the control of the British monarch, although Ireland's membership in the union was in little more than name. The Irish still resisted British rule that was no more than a military occupation.

None of Queen Anne's children outlived her, and upon her death the Parliamentary rules concerning the succession operated, thus excluding from the throne the Roman Catholic Stuarts.

House of Hanover. The next in line was the head of the German state of Hanover, a descendant of James I. He ascended the throne of England as George I (r.1714–1727). Because George I and his son, George II (r. 1727–1760), spoke poor English, had little knowledge of British politics, and were more interested in the affairs of their German state, Britain's development into a nation governed by ministers advanced rapidly during their reigns.

Cabinet government had gradually developed from the monarchs' custom of using members of the privy council as their active agents in Parliament. Because it was expedient to have a united cabinet, supported by the majority in the House of Commons, the kings found it necessary to consider Parliament's desires when choosing a cabinet. The Georges were often absent from cabinet meetings, allowing the ministers great autonomy, and this custom hardened into a precedent.

Both Georges employed the political genius of their advisor, Sir Robert Walpole, in making the difficult machinery of government work. Walpole was the first man in British history to warrant the designation of prime minister. Walpole's policies gave England political stability, and his reforms of fiscal and commercial regulations stimulated internal industry, shipping, and foreign trade. Moreover, he had refused to let England become involved in European conflicts.

In 1739, however, the House of Commons forced Walpole to declare war on Spain to protect British mercantile interests from Spain's interference with British ships. The "War of Jenkins' Ear," as it was called, went badly for England at first, and Walpole, opposed to the war, resigned in 1742.

As the conflict continued, England gradually became involved in a general European struggle known as the War of the Austrian Succession (1740–1748). The war had imperial and commercial overtones, as Europe's overseas colonies and international trading privileges were at stake.

Hostilities stopped in 1748, only to resume in 1756, as the Seven Years' War, which was more directly between England and France, the leading European powers. An important part of the conflict stemmed from colonial and commercial rivalries in North America and in India.

Britain's victory in the war, directed by the war minister William Pitt, made England the most powerful nation in Europe and the foremost colonial and commercial power in the world. By the Peace of Paris of 1763 England received most French possessions in North America east of the Mississippi and increased trading power in India.

George III (r.1760–1820). George II's successor, George III, played a stronger personal role in politics than had his predecessors. But neither his ministers nor the policies he and they pursued were particularly successful. An important failure was the loss of the prosperous American colonies.

George III's attempts to strengthen the ties between England and the colonies and extend his own influence through repressive legislation ended in 1775 with the outbreak of the American War of Independence. Britain recognized the independence of the colonies in 1782, and signed the Treaty of Paris in 1783, formally ending the United States' colonial status.

George's policies were more successful after 1783, when he named Pitt's son, William Pitt "the Younger," as prime minister. Pitt's genius for finance led to fruitful economic reforms, and he did much to eliminate governmental corruption. Above all, he organized a massive war effort against the government established in France after the French Revolution of 1789, and later against the French empire under Napoleon in the early 1800s.

The war machine that Pitt created contributed to the final defeat of Napoleon in 1815 and Pitt's diplomacy helped lay the international foundations for peace, which prevailed in Europe for the next 100 years.

In 1800, to strengthen England's strategic position, Pitt brought about the incorporation of Ireland into the "United Kingdom" as an equal partner. The union was doomed from the first, for Pitt had promised some religious freedom for Irish Roman Catholics, but the king forbade him to keep the promise, and in 1801 the union was repealed.

Ireland was not the only discontented part of the United Kingdom. All Britons were restless as the pace of social change accelerated. During the 1700s and 1800s agricultural production in England increased as the result of improved techniques, fertilizers, and land management. Increased agricultural output was needed to support the population that had grown enormously in George III's reign and continued to grow rapidly after 1820.

New farm methods reduced the number of laborers needed to produce the extra food, however, and an increasing portion of the enlarged population moved from the farms into the cities. What in 1750 had been a predominantly rural society was 100 years later an increasingly urban society in which half the population lived in towns.

MINISTRY OF PUBLIC BUILDINGS AND WORKS

THE HOUSE OF LORDS. The throne is reserved for the Queen at each opening session.

Simultaneously with this urbanization, rapid technological innovation and invention caused an "industrial revolution." The significance of this so-called revolution, actually a complex and protracted evolution, lay in the chain reaction of events that it set off in economic, political, social, and cultural life.

These developments, together with the difficult shift from war to peace in 1815, led to considerable social unrest. Fearing a revolution similar to that in France in 1789, political leaders introduced legislation that made criticism of the government dangerous and radical agitation impossible.

Moreover, the people were unsure of the strength of the government, for after 1811 George III was completely insane. His son served as prince regent until George III's death in 1820, when he became king George IV.

George IV (r.1820–1830). By that time, however, Parliament, not the king, actually ruled. It formulated policy that merely required the king's approval, which was seldom withheld. The Tory, or conservative, faction, in power for nearly 30 years at the beginning of the 1800s, was responsible for many of the restrictive laws passed at that time. Some fairly liberal Tories, however, felt that public protests of injustice had validity and responded by passing legislation reforming labor, criminal, and religious toleration laws.

The Tories refused to reform electoral laws, however, which, written centuries before the radical population shifts and class changes forced by the Industrial Revolution, deprived many citizens of representation. The Tories lost the 1830 election on this issue of election reform, and the new Whig, or liberal, majority in the House of Commons gave priority to the issue, and began a gradual reform of the electoral system.

Victoria (r.1837–1901). Reform was achieved in other areas, as well. For the remainder of the 1800s both Whig and Tory cabinets under Queen Victoria passed masses of legislation that radically changed the structure of English society.

Slavery in the colonies was abolished in 1833. Factory acts limited working hours and set standards for conditions and wages, while other laws regulated trade unions. Poor laws established national relief programs. As the century drew to a close, Parliament overhauled the judiciary and the educational systems and established a public health system.

During Victoria's reign, especially in the 1850s and 1860s, many Englishmen felt that their constitution and their society, adjusted by these legislative changes, had reached a perfect balance that insured peace at home and abroad and guaranteed continued prosperity. England seemed to be at a peak of power and progress, and the interruption of European peace during the Crimean War (1854–1856) into which England blundered did little to shake the prevailing optimism.

BRITISH INFORMATION SERVICE

NUMBER 10 DOWNING STREET, the official residence of the prime minister of Britain.

Industry and trade had made Britain the world's most prosperous state. It became the leading political power after the 1850s, when it acquired colonies all over the world. Benjamin Disraeli, who became prime minister in 1868, was the guiding light of English imperialism.

In 1875, to enlarge the empire, he acquired on his own a controlling interest in the Suez Canal Company and turned it over to England. By the end of the century Britain had colonies or commercial interests in the Far East, the Middle East, and Africa, in addition to its older colonies in North America and the Caribbean.

But Britain's imperial role brought the country into conflicts with other colonial powers. All the major European countries were establishing colonies in Africa and Asia, and Britain sought to compete. It became involved in a series of crises and conflicts over colonial territories, from the Afghan and Zulu wars of the late 1870s through the South African, or Boer War of 1899–1902.

By the end of the 1800s the optimism and confidence that had marked the mid-1800s had waned considerably in Britain. In addition to conflicts abroad, industry at home ceased to enjoy the unquestioned superiority it had once held over other nations, and agriculture began to suffer from foreign competition.

Edward VII (1901–1910). In the early years of the 1900s, during the reign of Queen Victoria's son, Edward VII, two Liberal governments passed radical social welfare legislation, including old age pensions and national unemployment and medical insurance.

In 1909 the Liberals in the House of Commons introduced a radical "people's budget" designed to put the burden of taxes on the rich. By refusing to pass the bill, the House of

Lords lost its dominant position in the government.

George V (1910–1936). In 1910, the year that George V came to the throne, the House of Commons passed a law limiting the power of the Lords over the Commons on all issues.

Ireland remained a problem. In 1912 the introduction of a series of bills that would have provided home rule for Ireland led to a crisis between the government and the people of Protestant Ulster, who declared their intention to resist home rule. A showdown was prevented only by the outbreak of war in Europe in 1914.

A series of international crises involving the great powers after 1900 had encouraged Britain to make alliances with France (1904) and Russia (1907) to counteract the Triple Alliance of Germany, Austria-Hungary, and Italy. A dispute between Austria-Hungary and Serbia in the summer of 1914 led to the outbreak of World War I. Britain declared war on Germany on August 4, 1914.

The war was costly for England and resulted in a staggering loss of men before it ended in November 1918. The war also severely damaged the British economy and drained industrial resources. As a result, Britain lost its preeminent world economic position to newly industrialized nations that had suffered less during the war, notably the United States.

British international political power declined as well, as the nation's colonial empire began to disintegrate. At a conference in 1926, Britain and its domains agreed to form an association in which no member should have subordinate status—the British Commonwealth of Nations. The era of British imperial power was drawing to a close. The Commonwealth agreement was formalized in 1931 by the Statute of Westminster.

The United Kingdom itself lost one of its members when Ireland rebelled in 1920. In 1922 it became the Irish Free State, and only Ulster, in the north, remained British.

Britain's main problems in the 1900s were economic. Neither the coalition Liberal-Conservative governments, nor the first governments of the newly formed socialistic Labor Party, nor the Conservative governments in power between 1918 and 1931, succeeded in improving England's poor economic situation.

The economy never fully recovered after World War I, and unemployment spread. As Britain lost colonies and fell behind in manufacturing, its trade also declined. The worldwide economic depression of the 1930s worsened Britain's situation.

George VI (1936–1952). In 1936 Edward VIII came to the throne and abdicated in less than a year. He was succeeded by his brother George VI. A national coalition government of Conservatives, Liberals, and Laborites, formed in 1931, held power throughout the 1930s.

The government's attempts to cope with the depression extended Britain's broad social welfare programs and introduced great control by the government over industry and trade. Little progress was made, however, and the depression's cure was left largely to time.

Inactivity marked the coalition's foreign policy. Britain had entered the "collective security" agreements of the League of Nations and the Locarno Pact in the 1920s, but, in a policy of appeasement, failed to stand by these agreements when confronted by the aggressive foreign policies of Fascist Italy and Nazi Germany.

The policy of appeasement reached its peak in 1938 when Prime Minister Neville Chamberlain consented to Nazi occupation of the Sudeten German region of Czechoslovakia in meetings with Adolf Hitler at Munich. In March 1939 Hitler repudiated the Munich agreements by annexing the remainder of Czechoslovakia.

World War II. Realizing the failure of Chamberlain's appeasement policy, the British and French governments reaffirmed their guarantee of the independence of Poland. By the end of the summer, however, Hitler invaded Poland, and on Sept. 3, 1939 Britain and France declared war on Germany.

Within nine months Holland, Belgium, and France had fallen, and Britain stood virtually alone against the Germans. In May 1940 Winston Churchill succeeded Chamberlain as prime minister, and, at the head of a coalition government, provided vigorous leadership in the resistance to German air attacks in 1940 and 1941.

Churchill led Britain into alliances with the Soviet Union and the United States which brought about the defeat of Italy in 1943 and of Germany in 1945. After the war Britain took on a large measure of responsibility in the making of the peace and in the subsequent formation of the United Nations. In July 1945 a general election replaced Churchill with a Labor government led by Clement Attlee.

Contemporary Britain. Labor took advantage of its first clear majority over all other parties and carried through a sweeping program of economic reform before it fell in 1951. It greatly expanded programs of national insurance; it created the National Health Service, which provided low cost medical care; and it nationalized the Bank of England, the coal industry, and the railroads, among others.

The great cost of World War II to Britain had worsened its already critical economic situation. The national debt had tripled during the war, and the domestic economy was drastically dislocated. It was essential that Britain regain its all-important overseas markets and increase trade by 50 percent above prewar levels to get the country back on a sound economic basis.

In 1949 the pound sterling was devalued, to stimulate exports and industry. Rationing of food, fuel, and other consumer goods imposed during the war continued into the 1950s.

The economy remained the central problem of Conservative governments that held power from 1951 through 1963 under Churchill, Anthony Eden, Harold MacMillan, and Alec Douglas-Home. The difficulty in the early 1950s lay in expanding the domestic economy without incurring greater balance-of-payments deficits by too heavy reliance on foreign nations.

George VI died in 1952, and his daughter, Elizabeth, came to the throne as Elizabeth II. In the late 1950s inflation became a problem, and the government was forced to reimpose many unpopular economic restrictions. Losses in local elections followed, and in 1964, the Conservative government gave way to a Labor cabinet led by Harold Wilson.

Labor's efforts to restore economic balance met with little early success. Wilson's government imposed tight controls on wages and prices, reduced private spending abroad, reduced overseas defense commitments, nationalized the steel industry, and accelerated the pace of granting independence to remaining British dependencies in Asia, Africa, and the Caribbean.

A major problem for Britain and the Commonwealth arose in 1965, when the southern African colony of Rhodesia declared itself independent after refusing to yield to British demands that it grant popular representation to its black African citizens as a condition for independence.

To improve its international status as well as its economy, Britain made several attempts in the 1960s to join the European Economic Community, the Common Market, formed in 1957. Due largely to the opposition of Pres. Charles de Gaulle of France, it was refused admission.

In November 1967, after a series of monetary crises, Britain again devalued its currency, forcing a monetary reshuffling in many countries of the world. The devaluation was followed by new austerity measures at home. It was hoped that the move would stimulate the domestic economy and help create an era of stability and prosperity. The immediate result, however, was the defeat of Labor candidates in a series of by-elections held in 1968.   —Dudley W. R. Bahlman

UNITED STATES

Official name: United States of America
Area: 3,615,211 square miles
Population: (1967 est.) 199,118,000
Capital: Washington (Pop., 1965, urban area, 2,413,000)
Language: English
Religion: Protestantism, Roman Catholicism, Judaism
Currency unit: Dollar
National holiday: Independence day, July 4

The United States of America occupies the central portion of the North American continent and the continent's northwest corner, as well as a small archipelago in the mid-Pacific Ocean. Of the country's 50 states, 48 are conterminous, that is, they share the central portion of the continent. The remaining continental state, Alaska, is separated from the conterminous United States by Canada. The Pacific islands of Hawaii, some 2,000 miles off the west coast, form the 50th state. The conterminous United States is bordered on the north by Canada, on the east by the Atlantic Ocean, on the south by the Gulf of Mexico and Mexico, and on the west by the Pacific Ocean.

Alaska is bordered on the north by the Arctic Ocean; on the east by Canada; on the south by the Gulf of Alaska; and on the west by the Bering Sea, the Bearing Strait—which separates Alaska from the Soviet Union—and the Chukchi Sea. The island state of Hawaii is surrounded by the Pacific Ocean.

THE LAND. The United States is the world's fourth largest nation in area and contains a great variety of landscapes and climates. Its three segments—the conterminous states, Alaska, and Hawaii—are topographically distinct.

The conterminous United States extends some 3,000 miles from east to west and 1,500 miles from north to south and contains five major regions.

Regions. In the east, the Atlantic and Gulf coastal region consists mainly of a wide, fertile plain. The northeastern shoreline is rocky.

Between 100 and 200 miles inland the plain rises into a region of rolling hills, called the Piedmont, the foothills of the Appalachian Mountains. The Appalachians extend from just north of the southern coast across the northern border and contain rounded, forested mountains generally below 4,000 feet in elevation.

West of the mountains, across the Appalachian Plateau, is a vast interior plains region which includes the prairies of the Central Lowlands and the high plains of the continent's Great Plains. The prairies are generally flat and range from 1,000 to 1,500 feet in elevation. The land slopes toward the center into the valley of the Mississippi River. In the north it slopes toward the basin of the Great Lakes, and in the south it rises slightly in the Ozark hills.

To the west, the plains rise gradually in elevation into the high plains, which reach elevations of nearly 5,000 feet in the foothills of the Rocky Mountains. This rugged mountain range stretches the entire length of the continent, with elevations reaching over 14,000 feet. Along its ridge lies the Continental Divide, the watershed dividing westward and eastward flowing rivers.

West of the Rockies is a series of ranges, plateaus, and basins. There, the Great Basin contains the country's deserts—the Mojave in the southwest and the Great Salt Lake and Black Rock deserts to the north.

Within the basin is Death Valley, 280 feet below sea level, and the lowest point on the continent. The high, steep Sierra Nevada and Cascade ranges form the western boundary of this rugged region.

A narrow, fertile valley separates these mountains from those of the Coastal Range, which runs the length of the west coast and in places drops sharply into the Pacific Ocean.

Lakes and Rivers. Of the country's many lakes, the five huge freshwater Great Lakes in the north-central region, the Great Salt Lake in the west, Lake Pontchartrain and Lake Okeechobee in the south, and Iliamna Lake in Alaska are the largest.

COUNTRIES OF THE WORLD

The conterminous United States has many mighty rivers. In the east the Hudson, the Delaware, the Potomac, and the Savannah are among the many that flow into the Atlantic Ocean.

In the center, the 2,470-mile long Mississippi, with its many branches, including the Tennessee, the Ohio, the Missouri, and the Arkansas, drains the entire plains region. The Rio Grande flows southeast from the Rockies and forms part of the country's southern border.

In the west the Colorado, the Snake, and the Columbia are the most important rivers that flow westward from the mountains.

Coastlines. The western coastline of the conterminous United States is generally straight, but there are several inlets that provide good harbors, notably at San Francisco, in California, and in northwestern Washington.

The Atlantic and Gulf coasts are lower and deeply indented. In the south the shore tends to be silted or swampy, and the extreme north is rocky. The major inlets include the Delaware and Chesapeake bays in the east and Tampa and Mobile bays in the south.

The coastline of Alaska is deeply indented and fringed with islands. The islands of the Aleutian Archipelago stretch westward from the mainland. Lowlands lie along most of the coast, and include a tundra region above the Arctic Circle.

The barren, rugged Alaskan Range follows the state's southern border. Mt. McKinley, the highest point in North America, rises 20,320 feet in the Alaskan Range. The Brooks Range rises to about 8,000 feet in the north. The long Yukon River flows through an interior basin.

Hawaii consists of several large islands and many islets and reefs. The islands are volcanic in origin and consist generally of a mountainous core ringed by narrow coastal lowlands.

Climate. Although all but the Arctic northern third of Alaska lies within the temperate zone, the U.S. climate varies quite sharply from region to region. The north tends to be colder than the south, and the interior and the east coast are subject to greater extremes in climate than the rest of the country.

The Atlantic coast generally receives adequate rainfall, and has hot to mild summers and mild to cold winters. The central plains region is

quite dry and has very cold winters and very hot summers.

The western mountains are damp with generally moderate temperatures, but the higher regions are colder and the deserts south and west of the Rockies are hot and dry. The west coast has moderate rainfall, mild winters and warm to hot summers.

Alaska's climate ranges from mild and damp on the southern coast to warm summers and cold winters in the interior, and to the arctic climate of the north. Hawaii's climate is mild, with moderate rainfall and little seasonal variation in temperature.

THE PEOPLE. With more than 200 million people in 1968, the United States has the fourth largest population in the world. Between 1960 and 1966 the population grew at the rate of 1.4 percent a year. Population density was about 55 persons per square mile in the mid-1960s, although the mountains and arid regions in the interior are rather sparsely settled.

Distribution. The east coast, particularly the Middle Atlantic region, is the most densely populated part of the United States. It contains eight of the country's largest cities, including New York, the largest city in the country, with some 12 million people living in its urban area in the mid-1960s.

Major cities in other regions include Los Angeles, California, on the west coast; Chicago, Illinois, in the interior; Denver, Colorado, in the western mountains; and Dallas, Texas, in the southwest.

The country underwent rapid urbanization in the mid-1900s, and in 1960 nearly 70 percent of the population was classified as urban.

Origins. The United States is a land of immigrants, and Americans, as the people of the United States call themselves, represent a variety of ethnic backgrounds. The overwhelming majority of the people are of European descent, but there are also large groups from other parts of the world.

By the mid-1900s most ethnic differences had become all but unidentifiable, but some groups remained separate from the dominant culture. These include large numbers of American Indians; people of Chinese and Japanese origin; Negroes, who comprise about one-tenth of the total population; and Spanish-speaking people of Mexican and Caribbean origin.

Language and Religion. English is the dominant language, although first-generation immigrants often continue to speak their native tongues. Most of the world's religions are represented in the United States.

The many Protestant sects have the most adherents. Roman Catholics are second in number, and Jews third. There are also Orthodox Christians and Muslims, and Latter Day Saints, members of an indigenous religious community popularly known as Mormons.

ECONOMY. The United States is the richest of the world's major nations, and its people enjoy a high standard of living. The prosperity of the United States is based primarily on industry. The country's size and economic and political unity have been basic to its economic growth, derived from the exploitation of abundant natural resources, including rich soils and a large variety of minerals.

The United States is a leading world producers of aluminum, copper, iron ore, uranium, sulfur, phosphates, potash, and molybdenum. Its energy resources include petroleum, natural gas, and coal, and much of its waterpower potential is exploited, especially on the Columbia, Colorado, and Tennessee rivers.

Agriculture. The relative importance of agriculture in the U.S. economy decreased steadily in the 1900s as the value of manufactures rose. The number of farms and the number of persons employed in agriculture dropped sharply. In 1965 agriculture contributed only 4 percent of the gross domestic product and employed only about 7 percent of the labor force.

Nevertheless, the country is one of the world's most important agricultural producers, and the output of farm

SANTA FE RAILWAY

SIERRA NEVADA PEAKS, capped by snow, are seen in Yosemite National Park in California.

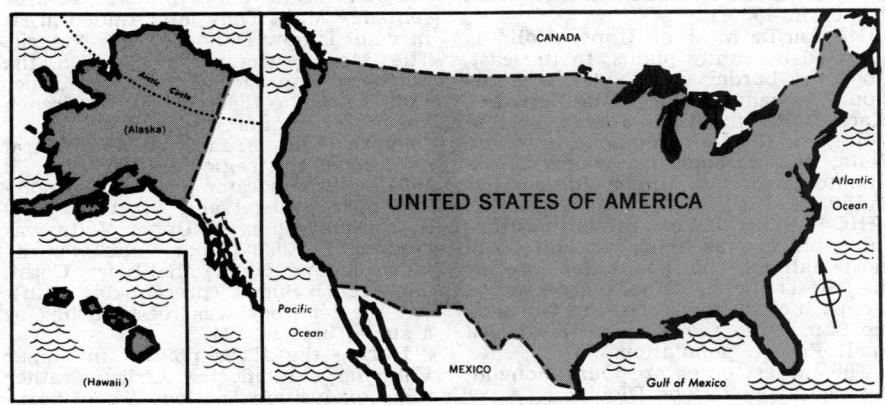

CANADA

UNITED STATES OF AMERICA

Arctic Circle

(Alaska)

(Hawaii)

Pacific Ocean

Atlantic Ocean

MEXICO

Gulf of Mexico

products increased greatly between the 1940s and 1960s. Improvements in agricultural technology have enabled the country to produce sufficient food for domestic needs and large surpluses for export.

The United States is the world's leading grower of corn and oats and one of the world's leading producers of wheat and other grains. In the mid-1960s the country also led the world in the production of tobacco and cotton. Other major crops are sugarcane and sugar beets; oranges, apples, grapes, peaches, and other fruits; and potatoes, beans, cabbage, lettuce, and other vegetables.

Livestock, especially cattle, hogs, and poultry, are raised in large numbers, and dairying is an important activity.

Crops vary from region to region. East coast farms concentrate on raising fruits and vegetables and poultry. Cotton, sugarcane, and tobacco are raised mostly in the south. The central plains contain vast grain-growing areas, and in the north-central region dairy cattle are raised and fruits and vegetables are grown.

In the more arid regions of the west and southwest, cattle-raising is a major activity, and large-scale irrigation systems make it possible to produce large quantities of vegetables. Fruits and vegetables are raised in the moister valleys of the far west.

Forestry and Fishing. About one-third of the country is forested with a variety of hard and soft woods, and forestry and the production of wood and paper products are important activities.

Fishing thrives in inland lakes and rivers and along the coasts, especially in the Gulf of Mexico and off the northwestern coast.

Industry. The leading factor in the country's economy is industry, and in 1965 manufacturing contributed about one-third of the gross domestic product. Metal processing, especially iron and steel making, and the production of machinery and transportation equipment from those metals are basic industries.

Chemicals, petroleum products, lumber and wood products, building materials, fine instruments, textiles, foodstuffs, furniture, clothing, and household appliances are also major industrial products. The construction and transportation and communications industries are also important in the economy, contributing 5 and 6 percent respectively to the 1965 gross domestic product.

Trade. The United States is the world's most prosperous trading nation. In 1967 its exports earned over $31,000 million and its imports cost almost $27,000 million.

Machinery and vehicles, foodstuffs, industrial raw materials, chemicals, and manufactured consumer goods are the leading exports. Raw materials, foodstuffs, machinery and vehicles, fuels, and clothing are among the larger imports.

The United States trades with most of the world's countries, but its major trading partners are Canada, Britain, and the western European countries. In addition to trade, U.S. businesses and industries have extensive invest-

ments abroad, especially in Western Europe, Latin America, and the Middle East.

The United States has military bases and commitments throughout the world, and the government gives financial and technical aid to the developing nations. These programs require heavy expenditures and in the mid-1960s created problems in the balance of payments, despite the country's favorable trade balance.

GOVERNMENT. The United States is a federal republic. The chief executive and head of state is the president, who is popularly elected to a four-year term of office.

Legislative power is exercised by a popularly elected Congress, which consists of two houses—the Senate and the House of Representatives. The Senate has 100 members, two from each state, elected to six-year terms. Members of the House of Representatives, elected from each state on a population basis, serve two-year terms.

Each of the 50 states has a governor and a legislature elected according to its state constitution.

U.S. overseas territories include the Commonwealth of Puerto Rico, the Virgin Islands, and a number of small islands in the Caribbean; Guam, American Samoa, and other islands in the Pacific; and the Canal Zone, which cuts through the Isthmus of Panama in Central America.

The United States is a member of the United Nations, the Organization of American States (OAS), the North Atlantic Treaty Organization (NATO), and the Southeast Asia Treaty Organization (SEATO).

—Sara D. Gilbert

UPPER VOLTA

Official name: Republic of Upper Volta
Area: 105,870 square miles
Population: (1967 est.) 5,054,000
Capital: Ouagadougou (Pop., 1961 est., 59,100)
Language: French, African languages
Religion: Traditional religions, Islam, Christianity
Currency unit: Franc CFA (African Financial Community)
National holiday: Republic day, December 11

Upper Volta, a republic in western Africa, is bounded on the north and west by Mali, on the east by Niger, and on the south by Dahomey, Togo, Ghana, and the Ivory Coast. Upper Volta received its independence from France in 1960.

THE LAND. Most of Upper Volta is occupied by sandy plains. In the east, along the border with Niger, is a region of swamps. The Volta Noire, or Black Volta, the Volta Rouge, or Red Volta, and the Volta Blanche, or White Volta, flow through the country. The climate in most of Upper Volta is hot and dry.

THE PEOPLE. There are many different tribal groups in Upper Volta. Almost half of the population are of the Mossi tribe. Other large tribal groups include the Bobo, the Gurunsi, the Samo, and the Marka. There is a small French population.

The largest cities are Ouagadougou, the capital, and Bobo Dioulasso.

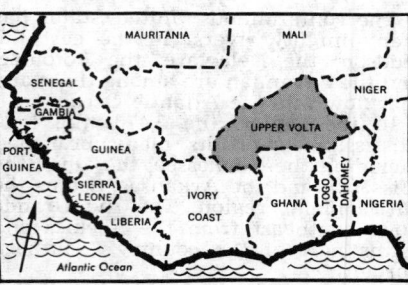

ECONOMY. The economy of Upper Volta is based on agriculture. The basic food crops are millet and sorghum. Peanuts and cotton are also grown. Cattle, sheep, and goats are raised in most parts of the country.

Industry is poorly developed. There are deposits of manganese, bauxite, and gold, but mining is basically undeveloped. Many of the people work outside the country, mostly in Ghana and the Ivory Coast. A railroad connects Ouagadougou with the Ivory Coast port of Abidjan.

In 1964 imports cost $40 million and exports earned $11 million. The main imports are foodstuffs, textiles, and machinery. The major exports are live animals, and hides and skins. Most trade is conducted with Ghana, the Ivory Coast, and France. Upper Volta is a member of an economic union with Dahomey, the Ivory Coast, Niger, and Togo.

GOVERNMENT. Until 1966 Upper Volta had a presidential system of government. Executive power was vested in a president, popularly elected to a five-year term. Legislative power rested with a National Assembly, which was also popularly elected every five years.

In January 1966 the government was overthrown, and a provisional government made up of a Council of Ministers and a consultative committee was established.

Upper Volta is a member of the United Nations and the Organization of African Unity (OAU).

History. In about 1000 AD the Mossi people migrated into Upper Volta and established two principal kingdoms—Ouagadougou and Yatenga. The kingdoms competed with the Dagomba and Mamprussi peoples to the south for primacy in the area. In about 1300 the Mossi came into conflict with the warriors of the ancient empires of Mali and Songhai.

In the 1400s and 1500s Mossi armies raided areas beyond Timbuktu, in present-day Mali. They later raided areas in what is now Dahomey and Nigeria. The Mossi successfully guarded the northern approach routes to Upper Volta until the 1800s, when the French began to conquer the area.

French Rule. France gained control over most the region in 1896, and in 1904 the area became part of the colony of Upper Senegal and Niger. In 1919 a separate colony of Upper Volta was created. In 1932 Upper Volta was divided among Niger, the Ivory Coast, and French Sudan (present-day Mali), but the territory was reestablished as a single unit in 1947.

During the 1950s politics in Upper Volta largely reflected African, rather than exclusively national, considerations. At that time a local branch of the African Democratic Rally (RDA), an African regional organization with headquarters in the Ivory Coast, had many followers in Upper Volta. In the late 1950s, however, the Upper Volta branch of the RDA began to take up national issues and joined with a smaller reform group to form the Voltaic Democratic Union (VDU).

Independence. In August 1960 Upper Volta became an independent country, and Maurice Yaméogo, leader of the VDU, became president. In January 1966 Lt. Col. Sangoulé Lamizana ousted Yaméogo, suspended the constitution, and established a provisional government.

—Hibberd V. B. Kline, Jr.;
Robert I. Rotberg

URUGUAY

Official name: Oriental Republic of Uruguay
Area: 72,173 square miles
Population: (1967 est.) 2,783,000
Capital: Montevideo (Pop., 1963, 1,158,632)
Language: Spanish
Religion: Roman Catholicism
Currency unit: Peso
National holiday: Independence day, August 25

Uruguay, a small republic on the east coast of South America, is bounded on the north and east by Brazil, on the south by the Atlantic Ocean, and on the west by Argentina.

THE LAND. Most of Uruguay consists of low, gently rolling plains. There are two long ranges of hills known as *cuchillas*, or "knives"—the Cuchilla de Haedo in the west and the Cuchilla Grande in the east. The eastern coast is edged by tidal lakes, lagoons, and sand dunes. The southern coast is characterized by wide, sandy beaches.

The climate of Uruguay is subtropical. The summers are warm and winter temperatures are generally above freezing. Rainfall is fairly evenly distributed throughout the year and averages about 35 inches.

THE PEOPLE. The people of Uruguay are mostly of Italian and Spanish descent. The native Churrúa Indians were almost completely driven out during the Spanish colonial period, and today less than 10 percent of the population can be classified as Indian or mestizo. Spanish is the official language and Roman Catholicism the principal religion.

Uruguay's population increased at an annual rate of 1.4 percent between 1958 and 1965, one of the lowest rates in Latin America. Uruguay has no sparsely populated areas but approximately 45 percent of the people live in the capital, Montevideo.

THE ECONOMY. Uruguay has almost no natural resources other than its fertile land, and the economy is based on agriculture. About 70 percent of the country's land is devoted to the raising of cattle and sheep, and almost 90 percent of exports consist of wool, hides, meat, and various meat products.

About 11 percent of the total land area is under cultivation. Wheat is the principal crop but rice, oats, corn, and barley are grown in large quantities. Sunflower seeds and linseed are also major crops.

WIDE WORLD

MONTEVIDEO, URUGUAY. Shoppers examine fresh produce in one of the open air markets.

Uruguay's industry is largely undeveloped, and consists for the most part of meat packing, food processing, and the manufacture of a few domestic consumer goods. Manufactured products include textiles, glass, rubber, paper, cement, ceramics, beverages, and tobacco.

Trade. In 1967 Uruguay's exports earned $150 million and imports cost $169 million. Principal exports are wool, meat, and hides. Major imports include motor vehicles and parts, machinery, chemicals and pharmaceuticals, raw cotton, and paper.

Uruguay's exports go primarily to the United States, Britain, the Netherlands, West Germany, Italy, and Spain. Most imports come from the United States, West Germany, Britain, Brazil, and Venezuela.

GOVERNMENT. Uruguay is a republic. The chief executive and head of state is the president, who is directly elected to a five-year term. Legislative power is vested in the General Assembly, which consists of the 31-member Senate and the 99-member Chamber of Deputies. Senators and deputies are directly elected on the basis of proportional representation to five-year terms.

Uruguay is a member of the United Nations and the Organization of American States (OAS).

HISTORY. Uruguay was discovered by the Spanish navigator Juan Díaz de Solís in 1516 and further explored in 1520 by the Portuguese captain, Ferdinand Magellan. It was not colonized until 1680, however, when Portugal built a fort at Colonia. During the 1700s the area's location between Brazil and what is now Argentina made it a bone of contention between the Portuguese and Spanish empires.

Spain had a better legal title to Uruguay than Portugal, however. Furthermore, Uruguay was too close to the Spanish military and administrative center of Buenos Aires for Spain to allow it to remain in hostile hands. In 1776 Spain incorporated Uruguay into the newly formed Viceroyalty of Río de la Plata, and in 1777 seized control of the Portuguese settlement at Colonia.

In 1810 Argentina began its struggle for independence from Spain, and in 1811 Uruguay followed suit under the leadership of José Gervasio Artigas. Artigas favored the formation of a loose confederation with Argentina, but Argentina was unwilling to accept this solution.

A complex struggle soon developed among the forces of Artigas, Argentina, and Spain, as well as Portugal, which took advantage of the general confusion to revive its earlier claim to the country. The Portuguese were successful, and when Brazil gained its independence in 1822 Uruguay became a Brazilian province.

Independence. In 1825 a new group of Uruguayan revolutionists rose up against Brazil and declared Uruguay annexed to Argentina. The result was a war between Argentina and Brazil which ended in a military stalemate. In 1828 British mediation brought about a peace treaty, which provided for Uruguay's independence.

Independence did not mark the end of foreign intervention in Uruguayan affairs. Uruguay soon developed two political parties, the Blancos and the Colorados, and Argentina, Brazil, and Paraguay frequently intervened in the struggles for power between the two parties. In 1865 a five-year war broke out, in which Uruguay was allied with Argentina and Brazil against Paraguay.

During the last two decades of the 1800s, Uruguay began to achieve a degree of stability. Educational facilities were expanded, agricultural production increased, and large-scale immigration took place.

Batlle Era. It was not until the early 1900s, however, under the Colorado leader José Batlle y Ordóñez, that Uruguay made major social and economic progress. Batlle twice served as president (1903–1907, 1911–1915) and exerted a strong influence over the country until his death in 1929.

Batlle helped make Uruguay a model of democratic government and encouraged such social and economic reforms as workers' accident compensation, and a minimum wage. He also initiated government enterprises in banking, meat-packing, and other areas.

Contemporary Uruguay. Some democratic procedures were suspended during the world economic depression of the 1930s under the administration of Gabriel Terra (1931–1938), but constitutional procedures were reinstated later in the 1930s. In 1942 Uuruguay broke diplomatic relations with the Axis powers and in February 1945 declared war on them. Later that year Uruguay became a charter member of the United Nations.

In 1951 Uruguay adopted a new constitution, which replaced the president with a nine-member executive council. In the late 1950s the country began to suffer from serious economic difficulties caused in part by a decline in foreign trade and the heavy financial burden of extensive social welfare programs.

The executive council proved unable to provide the leadership necessary to deal effectively with these and other problems, and in November 1966 a new constitution reinstating the presidential system was approved in a referendum.

Oscar Gestido was elected president in November 1966. Gestido initiated an austerity program and he took strong fiscal measures, which slowly began to improve the country's economic situation. Gestido died suddenly in December 1967 and was succeeded by the vice president, Jorge Pacheco Areco.

—David Bushnell; Kempton E. Webb

VATICAN CITY

Official name: State of the Vatican City
Area: 109 acres
Population: (1964 est.) 1,000
Language: Italian, Latin
Religion: Roman Catholicism
Currency unit: Lira
National holiday: Celebration of the coronation of the Holy Father

The Vatican City, located in Rome, Italy, is the world's smallest sovereign state. It is the seat of the central administration of the Roman Catholic Church and the residence of the supreme pontiff, or pope. The term "the Vatican" is frequently used to refer to both the central administration of the church and the government of the Vatican City.

Vatican City lies on the west bank of the Tiber River. It includes St. Peter's Basilica, St. Peter's Square, the Vatican palaces, Belvedere Park, and the Vatican Gardens.

The Vatican also exercises extraterritorial sovereignty over a dozen buildings and some territory in or near Rome, including the basilicas of

AIR FRANCE

VATICAN CITY LANDMARK is St. Peter's Basilica, with a dome designed by Michelangelo.

St. Mary Major, St. John Lateran, and St. Paul without the Walls; the pope's summer residence at Castel Gandolfo; and the Vatican radio station at Santa Maria di Galeria.

The Vatican population consists of clergy of all nations, the Vatican guard, and a number of lay personnel in the service of the Vatican.

GOVERNMENT. The Vatican is ruled by the pope, who has absolute power. He delegates much of the actual administration of the Vatican to the Pontifical Commission for the State of the Vatican City. The commission has five members and is headed by a governor.

The Vatican's diplomatic relations with foreign countries are carried on by the Secretariat of State, and the Vatican maintains diplomatic relations with about 60 countries. The pope is pledged to neutrality in political disputes between governments except when his mediation is requested by both sides. The Vatican also has a permanent observer at the United Nations.

HISTORY. The traditional seat of the papacy has always been Rome. Throughout the Middle Ages the popes controlled not only the city of Rome but large territories in central Italy, the Papal States. The popes lost most of the territory that formed the Papal States during the Italian struggle for unification in the 1850s and 1860s.

In 1849 a Roman Republic was declared, and France, intervening on behalf of the pope, sent troops to Rome. The Kingdom of Italy was formed in 1861, and in 1870, when French troops were withdrawn on the outbreak of the Franco-Prussian War, Rome was added to the new kingdom.

In 1871 the Italian government passed the Law of Guarantees granting the papacy full sovereignty over Vatican City and an annual income from the Italian treasury. The pope refused the offer. But the 1929 Lateran Treaties restored relations between the papacy and the Italian government.

The treaties recognized the sovereignty of the papacy within Vatican City, regulated the status of the church in Italy, and arranged for an indemnity to be paid to the papacy as compensation for the loss of the Papal States. In 1947 the terms of the Lateran Treaties were incorporated into the constitution of the Italian Republic.

—Sergio Barzanti

VENEZUELA

Official name: Republic of Venezuela
Area: 352,144 square miles
Population: (1967 est.) 9,352,000
Capital: Caracas (Pop., 1965 est., urban area, 1,674,728)
Language: Spanish
Religion: Roman Catholicism
Currency unit: Bolívar
National holiday: Independence day, July 5

Venezuela, a republic on the northern coast of South America, is bounded on the north by the Caribbean Sea, on the east by Guyana, on the south by Brazil and Colombia, and on the west by Colombia. Seventy-two small offshore islands are also part of Venezuela. The largest of these is Margarita Island, which is famous for its pearl fisheries.

THE LAND. Venezuela has four major geographic regions—the northern highlands, the Maracaibo lowlands, the Orinoco *llanos*, or plains, and the Guiana highlands. The northern highlands, part of the Andes mountain system, extend from the Colombian border in the southwest to the Paria peninsula in the northeastern part of the country.

The mountainous highland area has five subdivisions: the Sierra de Perijá in the extreme west; the Sierra Nevada de Mérida in the southwest; the Segovia highlands, which run eastward from the Sierra Nevada de Mérida along the coast; the central highlands, which run parallel to the coast; and the northeastern highlands in the Araya and Paria peninsulas.

Although the northern highlands cover only about 12 percent of Venezuela's land area, they contain three-fifths of the population and constitute the economic, political, and cultural core of the country.

The Maracaibo lowlands lie to the northwest of the northern highlands. In the center of this area is Lake Maracaibo, which has an area of 6,300 square miles and is the largest lake in South America.

The Orinoco *llanos* extend from the northern highlands south to the Orinoco River. This region is a rolling savanna, or grassland, dotted with a few scattered trees and bushes, and crossed by the numerous streams that feed the Orinoco. These streams swell enormously during the rainy season, and large areas in the *llanos* are flooded for almost half the year.

The Guiana highlands lie to the south of the Orinoco and cover roughly half of the country's territory. This area is a high, jungle-covered tableland with elevations ranging between 3,000 and 6,000 feet above sea level. It is not easily accessible and parts of the area have not been thoroughly explored.

The country's major river is the Orinoco, which rises in the south and flows northeast for about 1,500 miles before emptying into the Atlantic Ocean. The Orinoco and its many tributaries provide Venezuela with excellent water transportation routes.

Climate. Venezuela lies entirely within the tropics, but its climate varies widely according to altitude. The lowlands are hot and humid, and Maracaibo has an annual average temperature of 86°F, the highest registered in South America. The capital, Caracas, in the central highlands at an altitude of about 3,000 feet, has an annual average temperature of 71°F. Temperatures become cooler as the elevation increases.

Venezuela has a wet summer season from May to November and a dry winter season from December through April. Rainfall is generally heavier at higher altitudes. It ranges from about 17 inches a year at Maracaibo on the coast to over 70 inches at Mérida in the northern highlands.

THE PEOPLE. About 70 percent of Venezuela's population is mestizo, of mixed Indian and European descent. Pure-blooded Indians are few in number and live in the more remote parts of the Guiana highlands, the Orinoco delta, and the western Maracaibo lowlands. Europeans constitute about 20 percent of the population and are mainly concentrated in the larger cities. Negroes and mulattos, who make up about 7 percent of the population, live largely along the coast.

Spanish is the official language and Roman Catholicism the predominant religion.

In 1968 an estimated 74 percent of Venezuela's population was urban. Major cities include Caracas, Maracaibo, Barquisimeto, and Valencia.

ECONOMY. The Venezuelan economy depends heavily on petroleum, which in 1966 contributed about 20 percent to the gross national product and ac-counted for over 90 percent of exports. In recent years, however, the government has made an attempt to diversify the economy by expanding industry and strengthening agriculture through agrarian reform measures.

Natural Resources. Venezuela's most important natural resource is its petroleum deposits, most of which are located in the Maracaibo lowlands. In 1965 Venezuela produced 182.4 million metric tons of petroleum, making it the third largest producer in the world.

The country also has extremely valuable iron ore deposits at El Pao and Cerro Bolívar in the Guiana highlands. Iron ore ranks as the second largest export. In 1965 production amounted to 10.8 million metric tons. Gold, diamonds, natural gas, asbestos, bauxite, sulfur, copper, gypsum, limestone, and salt are also mined.

Agriculture. Agriculture employed about 32 percent of the labor force in 1964, and agricultural production increased 34 percent between 1960 and 1966. The major crops are sugarcane, corn, bananas, and rice. Coffee and cacao are important commercial crops. Beans, sesame, cotton, casava, sisal, potatoes, and tobacco are also raised in large quantities.

Cattle are raised in the Orinoco *llanos,* but are generally of poor quality. The government has been working to improve the breed and to better grazing conditions. In 1966 Venezuela had more than 6.5 million head of cattle.

Industry. Venezuelan industry has expanded rapidly since World War II. Major industries include cotton and wool textiles, leather goods, cement, petrochemicals, and automobile assembly. Other important industries are food processing, meat packing, construction materials, fats and oils, tires, automobile parts, soap, matches, and liquor.

During the mid-1960s plans were underway for the development of a major industrial center at Santo Tomé de Guayana in the Orinoco delta. Although formerly sparsely populated, this area has great potential value because of its access to nearby iron ore deposits and abundant hydroelectric power resources.

Trade. In 1966 Venezuela's exports earned $2,713 million and imports cost $1,188 million. Major exports include petroleum, iron ore, coffee, and cocoa. Principal imports are industrial raw materials, machinery, transportation equipment, construction materials, foodstuffs, and a variety of consumer goods.

Venezuela exports primarily to the United States, the Netherlands Antilles, Canada, and Britain. Imports come mainly from the United States, West Germany, Canada, Britain, Japan, and Italy.

GOVERNMENT. Venezuela is a republic. The head of state and chief executive is the president, who is popularly elected to a five-year term. Legislative power is vested in the Congress, which consists of the Senate and the Chamber of Deputies.

Two senators are elected from each of Venezuela's 20 states and from its Federal District, Caracas. Additional senators are appointed to represent minorities. There is one seat in the Chamber of Deputies for every 50,000 inhabitants. Both senators and deputies are elected to five-year terms.

Venezuela is a member of the United Nations and the Organization of American States (OAS).

HISTORY. Venezuela was discovered in 1498 by Christopher Columbus on his third voyage to the New World. The first permanent settlement was made by Spain about 1520 at Cumaná, on the Caribbean coast. In 1528 Charles I of Spain (Charles V of the Holy Roman Empire) granted a contract to settle Venezuela to the Welser mercantile firm of Augsburg, Germany. The Welsers were ruthless administrators, and in 1556 the contract was cancelled.

In 1526 the original colony of Venezuela was placed under the jurisdiction of the Audiencia of Santo Domingo. Later it was included in the Viceroyalty of New Granada (Colombia). In 1777 Venezuela became the Captaincy-General of the United Provinces of Venezuela, and in 1786 the Audiencia of Caracas was created. In the last half of the 1700s Venezuela became prosperous from plantation agriculture and a flourishing cattle industry.

Struggle for Independence. In 1806 a Venezuelan patriot, Francisco de Miranda, and a group of volunteers attempted to free the country from Spain. But most Venezuelans remained loyal to Spain, and the attempt failed. In 1808 Napoleon Bonaparte of France deposed Spain's King Ferdinand VII and placed his brother Joseph Bonaparte on the throne. In 1810 a successful revolt took place at Caracas, which deposed the Spanish captain-general of Venezuela and installed a junta, or ruling council.

In 1811 Venezuela declared its independence from Spain, but for several years control passed back and forth between Venezuelan patriots and forces loyal to Spain. Leadership of the struggle for independence passed to Simón Bolívar.

In 1819 Bolívar defeated the Spanish at the battle of Boyacá in what is now Colombia. He subsequently formed the Republic of Gran Colombia, which included present-day Venezuela, Colombia, Panama, and Ecuador. In 1821 Bolívar virtually

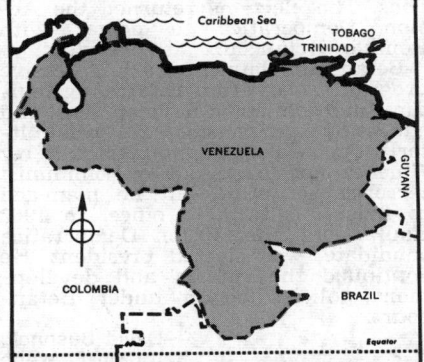

CREOLE PETROLEUM CORP.

VENEZUELA'S OIL INDUSTRY, one of the world's largest, centers around Lake Maracaibo.

VIETNAM

NORTH VIETNAM

Official name: Democratic People's Republic of Vietnam
Area: 61,294 square miles
Populaion: (1967 est.) 20,100,000
Capital: Hanoi (Pop., 1960 est., urban area, 643,600)
Language: Vietnamese
Religion: Buddhism, Roman Catholicism
Currency unit: Dong

SOUTH VIETNAM

Official name: Republic of Vietnam
Area: 65,949 square miles
Population: (1967 est.) 16,973,000
Capital: Saigon (Pop., 1964 est., 1,370,600)
Language: Vietnamese
Religion: Buddhism, Roman Catholicism
Currency unit: Piastre
National holiday: Anniversary of the revolution, November 1

completed the struggle for independence with a decisive victory at the battle of Carabobo.

Independence. In 1830, under the leadership of Gen. José Antonio Paéz, Venezuela seceded from the republic of Gran Colombia. Páez, an outstanding military leader during the struggle for independence, governed Venezuela from 1830 to 1846. He gave the country stability without resorting to oppression, but those who benefited most were mainly the members of a small elite of the educated and well-to-do.

During the 1850s and 1860s the government was often dictatorial, and the political scene was marked by confusion and instability. Nonetheless, a few constructive measures were undertaken, including the abolition of slavery in 1854.

In 1870 Antonio Guzmán Blanco seized power and ruled the country for 18 years. During his dictatorship there was relative peace, and although corrupt and autocratic, Guzmán Blanco did much to extend public education and to stimulate economic development. In 1889 he lost control, and the country entered a new period of turmoil.

During 1895–1896 Venezuela engaged in a dispute with Britain over its border with British Guiana, the present-day nation of Guyana. In 1902–1903 the country was blockaded by Britain, Germany, and Italy as the result of financial claims of their citizens against the Venezuelan government. The United States intervened to promote a settlement.

In 1909 domestic peace returned following the seizure of the presidency by Juan Vicente Gómez, who ruled the country with a heavy hand for 26 years. Gómez encouraged the rapid growth of the petroleum industry through liberal concessions to British and U.S. companies, but he used the oil revenues for personal gain, military expenses, and showy public works rather than for education, public welfare, or development.

Reform and Reaction. Gómez died in 1935 and his immediate successors gradually dismantled the apparatus of dictatorship and devoted attention to social and labor legislation. Nevertheless, many Venezuelans were dissatisfied with the pace of change. In 1945 a popular rising brought the leftist Acción Democrática party, led by Rómulo Betancourt, to power.

The new regime's most notable achievement was an agreement with the oil companies which stipulated that half their profits were to go to the Venezuelan government, which hoped to use this income for a far-reaching program of social betterment. Presidential elections were held in 1947 and Rómulo Gallegos, the Acción Democrática candidate, was elected.

In 1948 the government was overthrown by the army, which set up a military junta. In 1952, after an interlude of confusion, Marcos Pérez Jiménez was made provisional president. He soon established a new military dictatorship that was in many ways a repetition of the Gómez regime.

Public opposition to the dictatorship was strong, and in 1958 Pérez Jiménez was forced to resign. A brief provisional government restored political liberty, increased the government's share of oil industry profits, and in December 1958 held free elections. The elections returned the Acción Democrática to power with Rómulo Betancourt as president.

Betancourt launched an aggressive program of agrarian reform, agricultural and industrial development, and educational expansion. He was bitterly opposed by supporters of Pérez Jiménez and harassed by communist terrorist activities, but he managed to finish his term of office. In 1963 Raúl Leoni, the Acción Democrática candidate, was elected president. He continued the reform and development policies begun under Betancourt.

—David Bushnell;
Kempton E. Webb

Vietnam is a divided country on the east coast of the Indochinese peninsula in Southeast Asia. The Peoples' Democratic Republic of Vietnam, or North Vietnam, a communist-dominated state, lies north of a demarcation line set in 1954 at the 17th parallel and the Republic of Vietnam, or South Vietnam, lies to the south.

North Vietnam is bounded on the north by Communist China; on the east by the Gulf of Tonkin, an arm of the South China Sea; on the south by the Republic of Vietnam; and on the west by Laos. South Vietnam is bounded on the north by North Vietnam, on the east by the South China Sea, on the south by the South China Sea and the Gulf of Siam, and on the west by Cambodia and Laos.

A union of three small kingdoms in eastern Indochina—Tonkin in the north, Annam in the center, and Cochin China in the south—Vietnam was a French colony until 1945. After proclaiming its independence in 1945, Vietnam was torn by warfare.

Until 1953 France and the Viet Minh, a communist-led nationalist movement, fought for control of the country. After the French defeat in 1954 Vietnam was divided.

In the south, communist-led uprisings and infiltration from the north continued, however, and the United States aided the South Vietnamese government in its efforts to defeat the insurgents. Fighting intensified until by the mid-1960s a full-scale air, ground, and sea war was being waged in Vietnam.

THE LAND. North and South Vietnam share a narrow, S-shaped strip of territory, which consists of two river deltas—the Red and the Mekong—and a connecting mountain range—the Annam Cordillera. The 1954 division gave the two Vietnams almost equal areas.

Lying entirely within the tropics, all the lowlands of Vietnam have warm, moist, frost-free weather. The total amount of rainfall and the maximum period of rainfall depend upon exposure to the northeast and southwest monsoons.

From mid-September to March, the northeast monsoons bring cool weather to the Red delta area, rain to the entire east coast, and sunny skies to the Mekong delta. From June to September, the southwest monsoons bring high humidity and rain to all Vietnam. From July to November the country is subjected to irregular and sometimes damaging typhoons.

North Vietnam. The core of North Vietnam is the Red River delta, in the east. It is the compound delta of the Red, the Black, and other lesser rivers, most of which originate in adjacent China and Laos. The delta has many levels because of the uneven sedimentation in each of the component rivers.

The Red River surmounts the delta on a raised bed and has several distributaries, which branch out about 70 miles inland. The delta is the only major lowland in North Vietnam, but there are a few smaller, isolated delta lowlands along the coastal fringe.

Mountains and highlands trending northwest to southeast dominate the landscape throughout the western two-thirds of the country. In central Tonkin rocky, deeply incised mountains rise steeply to more than 10,000 feet.

Lower ranges include the Thai Hills in the western corner of the country, the hilly North Vietnamese Midlands north of the delta, and a deeply dissected high plateau south of the Red River. Further south, along the western border, the northern edge of the Annam Cordillera attains elevations of 8,000 feet in places and drops sharply to the sea.

North Vietnam's climate is tropical monsoon, with temperatures averaging between 60° and 80°F. Between September and April the weather is cool and rather dry. In the monsoon season, from June to September, temperatures are high, rain is heavy, and typhoons are a threat.

South Vietnam. South of the 17th parallel, the Annam Cordillera and its foothills form a central massif known as the Southern Mountain Plateau. It occupies some two-thirds of South Vietnam's area and leaves room for only a few small, enclosed coastal plains. The south's only major lowland lies in the poorly drained, swampy delta of the Mekong River at the southern tip of the country.

The climate of South Vietnam is warm and humid, with temperatures ranging from about 60°F to about 90°F in Saigon. During the monsoon season, from June to September, about 80 inches of rain fall in the south, and typhoons are a danger. From September through to April, the weather is drier and cooler, except along the central coast, where rainfall is heavy throughout the year.

THE PEOPLE. Almost all of the people of both North and South Vietnam are Vietnamese, descended from Mongol and Indonesian peoples. They speak Vietnamese. The major religions are Roman Catholicism and Buddhism.

The largest minority group consists of *Montagnards*, the aboriginal people of the country, of Malay-Indonesian or Mon stock, who lead semi-nomadic lives in the mountains. There are also minorities of Chinese, Cham, Indian, and Malay peoples.

North Vietnam. In North Vietnam the population is concentrated in the Red River delta. In 1965 the density for the country as a whole was about 312 persons per square mile. The highlands are only sparsely settled. All the north's major towns and its only large cities—Hanoi, the capital, and Haiphong, the major port—are located in the delta.

South Vietnam. In South Vietnam the overall population density was about 244 persons per square mile in 1965. The most densely settled area is in the Mekong delta region, especially around Saigon, the capital and largest city. The coastal fringe is thinly settled, and the hills have a very sparse population.

After 1954 the south's population was swollen by an influx of refugees, especially Roman Catholics from the north. The influx created housing and employment problems.

ECONOMY. The economies of both North and South Vietnam were in a state of disarray in the 1950s and 1960s due to war in the country. In normal times, the economies of both are agricultural, with rice production the leading activity.

North Vietnam. In the north, the major rice-growing area is located in the Red River delta, where the population density averages over 1,200 persons per square mile. The north cannot produce sufficient rice to feed its people despite the high productivity of the Red River delta region. Sugarcane, corn, and cotton are also important crops, and tea, coffee, tobacco, castor oil seeds, and silk are produced. Most agriculture is collectivized.

The mountains of the north are heavily forested and contain some minerals. Coal, tin, and tungsten are mined. Some industries were developed in the 1950s, chiefly in Hanoi and Haiphong. They included shipbuilding and iron and steel working.

No trade statistics are available for North Vietnam, but it is assumed that most of the country's foreign trade consists of importing necessary supplies and war materials from Communist China and the Soviet Union.

South Vietnam. Before the war, South Vietnam had an economy based almost wholly on agriculture. Rice was grown in the Mekong delta, and other crops included sweet potatoes, peanuts, tea, and corn. There was also some rubber raised on delta

UNITED NATIONS

VIETNAMESE SCENE, unmarred by years of war, is the tranquil Gulf of Nhatrang.

plantations, but the plantations became inoperative as the intensity of the war increased in the late 1950s and the 1960s.

The country has little industry. Saigon is the chief commercial and transportation center.

With exports almost nonexistent, South Vietnam had a trade deficit exceeding $300 million in 1965, and the gap was widening between exports and imports. The economy was almost entirely dependent on U.S. aid.

GOVERNMENT. North Vietnam's government is democratic in form but controlled in fact by the Lao Dong, or Workers, Party of Vietnam, the North Vietnamese communist party. The constitution adopted in 1960 vests supreme governmental authority in the popularly elected National Assembly, which chooses a standing committee to act for it between its short sessions.

The assembly also elects a president as head of state. The president appoints the prime minister and other cabinet members.

The Worker's Party nominates all candidates for the National Assembly, and government leaders are usually top officers of the party. The political bureau, or politburo, of the party's central committee determines national policy.

By a constitution adopted in 1967 South Vietnam is a republic. Executive power is wielded by a popularly-elected president as chief of state and a prime minister appointed by the president. Legislative power is exercised by a popularly elected assembly of two houses. Because of the war and several political upheavals in the 1960s, power is concentrated in the military.

HISTORY. Vietnam has been inhabited for many centuries, but little is known of its early history. It is thought to have been settled by people moving northward and westward from elsewhere in Indochina and from the neighboring islands, and by people moving southward from China.

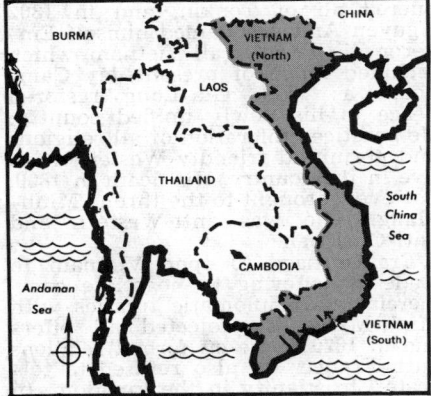

By about 500 BC a kingdom had been established by these Viet peoples, as they called themselves. It extended from present-day North Vietnam across the modern southern Chinese province of Kwangtung. In the 200s BC the Viet began to feel the cultural influence of China, and their kingdom was conquered by generals of the disintegrating Ch'in dynasty of China.

Chinese Rule. These Chinese ruled until 111 BC, when armies of China's Han dynasty, the successor to the Ch'in, conquered Vietnam and annexed it to China. It remained Chinese for about 1,000 years.

During this period, despite rule by Chinese, incorporation into the Chinese economy, and the imposition of Chinese language, customs, and religion, the Vietnamese retained much of their own culture. Several rebellions were attempted against the Chinese, but they were crushed.

The T'ang dynasty came to power in China in 618, and one of its first steps was to make its border areas secure by imposing stricter controls over the non-Chinese population and tying them closer to China. When Vietnam had come under the complete control of China's central government, it was called the "Pacified South," or *An-Nam.*

The T'ang government, unpopular because of its success in subduing the Viet, was even more disliked in the late 700s, when it was unable to prevent the Indochinese kingdom of Champa, south and west of Annam, from conquering large pieces of Vietnamese territory. Vietnamese resentment increased in the late 800s when T'ai peoples from the northwest invaded Tonkin and conquered Hanoi, the capital and central city.

Independence. In 907 the T'ang dynasty collapsed, and in the chaos the Vietnamese successfully rebelled. In 939 a rebel leader, Ngo Quyen, founded a Vietnamese dynasty that by 940 had regained control of all the territory from the 17th parallel to the southern Chinese province of Yünnan. China never recognized Annam's independence, and the country remained under nominal Chinese control.

The early Vietnamese rulers had little success in strengthening the power of the throne over the country's many petty chieftains and separate tribes, and between 939 and 1009 the ruling dynasty changed three times. The first strong dynasty was the Li, which ruled between 1009 and 1225.

During the Li era, the Vietnamese launched a successful drive to regain territory from the Chams of Champa. In 1471, after the Chams had been severely weakened by civil war, the Vietnamese were able to conquer the entire Champa kingdom and extend their Annamese empire across Cochin and into present-day Cambodia. Annam had become a great power in Southeast Asia, but its era of unity, power, prestige, and peace, was short.

Dissension. The 1500s were years of political upheaval that in 1620 erupted into civil war between two powerful families—the Trinh in the north, or Tonkin, and the Nguyen in the

LOOK MAGAZINE

VIETNAMESE WORKERS unloading rice.

south, or Annam. Each supported and controlled rival dynasties.

Civil war continued with a few peaceful interludes for almost 200 years. The country was in fact split into two kingdoms, with neither side able to gain a foothold on the territory of the other.

While the Vietnamese were fighting each other during the 1700s, Europeans began establishing colonies in Southeast Asia. Missionaries, explorers, and merchants arrived in Vietnam from Britain, France, Holland, Portugal, and Spain. Despite their internal warfare, the Vietnamese successfully prevented any of the foreigners from establishing colonies. But Roman Catholic missionaries, most of whom were French, were successful in converting and influencing many people.

Unification. One of the missionaries, Pigneau de Behaine, had become a close advisor of Nguyen Anh, the emperor of Annam. Through him in 1787 the emperor first requested French aid in conquering all of Vietnam. French volunteer sailors and soldiers helped reorganize and train the Annamese army. They helped Nguyen Anh put down a rebellion in Annam and then assisted him in a successful attack upon Tonkin.

By 1802 the Annamese had conquered all of Tonkin, and in 1802 Nguyen Anh proclaimed himself Emperor Gia-Long of all Vietnam, which included much of present-day Cambodia as well. Gia-Long restored peace to his newly unified country. He practiced toleration of all religions and permitted friendly Westerners to live in the country. His death in 1820, however, brought to the throne Minh-Mang, who was anti-Western and anti-Christian.

France tried to open Vietnam to trade by offering to negotiate commercial and diplomatic treaties with Minh-Mang. He rejected all offers and in 1826 broke off formal relations with France. He also refused to tolerate Christianity in the kingdom. In

the 1830s he ordered the persecution of Christians, and some Western missionaries were killed.

Minh-Mang's successor, Thieu-Tri, practiced even harsher persecution of the missionaries and merchants, most of whom were French. By the 1840s France held a strong position in Southeast Asia, and it was no longer willing to have its citizens undergo such treatment. France began to press Thieu-Tri to change his policies, but the persecution of Christians—Vietnamese as well as Europeans—increased. It worsened under Thieu-Tri's successor, Tu-Duc.

In 1851, when a French missionary was put to death, French ships bombarded Vietnamese coastal forts. In 1856 another French missionary was killed, and in 1857 a Spanish bishop was executed. Vietnam refused to apologize or grant restitution. In response, France joined Spain in attacking Vietnam in 1858.

French Conquest. France's emperor, Napoleon III, had been looking for a means of getting Vietnamese territory, and this seemed a good opportunity. In 1859 French forces occupied Saigon, in the south. By 1861 France controlled Cochin China and most of the Mekong delta. In 1862 Tu-Duc signed a treaty ceding the southern region to France, and France used the area as a base for French expansion into the rest of Indochina.

Meanwhile, Annam and Tonkin were in chaos. Tu-Duc had lost control of his kingdom, which was in rebellion and which both France and China were trying to seize. Tu-Duc placed Vietnam under Chinese protection in the 1870s, but in the 1880s French armies conquered Tonkin. In 1884 the Treaty of Hué placed all Vietnam under French protection by giving France the right to maintain troops in the country.

China protested that Vietnam was part of the Chinese empire and that no treaty signed without Chinese approval was valid. France responded by sending more troops into Vietnam. The Chinese also sent troops, but China was not actually prepared to fight France. By 1887 France had established its control over the region and united Cambodia, Cochin China, Annam, and Tonkin into the colony of French Indochina.

By the 1890s the French colonial government had put down the many rebellions raging throughout the country and had established itself as master of the area. The French established rubber, tea, and coffee plantations and opened forestry operations.

Rebellions were frequent. In the 1920s France granted the Vietnamese a partially elected council to advise the colonial governor-general. Vietnamese representation was not effective, however, and in 1930–1931 more violent rebellions occurred. They were put down quite harshly. Opposition to French rule grew and Vietnamese nationalist groups were organized.

World War II. In 1940, after the outbreak of World War II, Japan invaded and occupied Vietnam, and took control of the colony from the Vichy-French regime. The Japanese permitted Vietnamese leaders to participate more fully in the government than the French had allowed, and although the Japanese exploited the country economically, they gave the people greater freedom than the French had.

During the war, a communist-led movement had gained power in Vietnam. The Viet Minh, as it was called, led by Ho Chi Minh, was the first anti-Japanese guerrilla force in Vietnam. In March 1945, near the end of the war, Japan declared Vietnam independent.

In August 1945 Ho's forces seized Hanoi and demanded the abdication of the emperor, Bao Dai. In September Ho proclaimed the independence of the "Democratic Republic of Vietnam." A struggle for power followed between the Viet Minh, non-communist Vietnamese, and French forces, which had returned to Vietnam in October.

Division. In December 1946 full-scale war broke out between French soldiers and Viet Minh forces. The people tended to support the Viet Minh. Communist countries aided the rebels, especially after 1949 when a communist regime came to power in China. The United States became involved in the struggle in 1950, when the United States declared support of Vietnamese independence, under Bao Dai.

Finally, in 1954, at the battle of Dien Bien Phu, the French suffered a shattering defeat and decided to withdraw. The 1954 Geneva Conference, which arranged for a ceasefire, provisionally divided Vietnam into northern and southern sectors at the 17th parallel. The unification of Vietnam was to be achieved by general elections to be held in July 1956 in both sectors under international supervision. In the north, the "Democratic Republic of Vietnam" was led by its president, Ho Chi Minh, and was dominated by the Communist party.

In the south, Ngo Dinh Diem, a Roman Catholic who was prime minister under Emperor Bao Dai, took over the government when Bao Dai left the country in 1954. As the result of a referendum held in 1955, a republic was established in South Vietnam, with Diem as president.

Diem's government proved unable to solve South Vietnam's problems. Political power was concentrated in Diem's family, and his brother, Ngo Dinh Nhu organized a secret police force to enforce Diem's policies. Hostility toward the increasingly repressive regime aided the organization of Communist-supported rebels, the Vietcong, who opened guerrilla activity in the late 1950s. In December 1960 the communists created the National Liberation Front of South Vietnam.

Vietnam War. The United States, committed to supporting the Diem regime, sent military and political advisors to train the South Vietnamese army and assist the government. Little headway was made against either the insurgents or the country's pressing social and economic problems, due in part to widespread corruption in the government. The elections for a constituent assembly

required by the 1954 Geneva agreements were not held.

Resentment against the government increased, especially among Buddhist leaders, who believed the government discriminated against Buddhists. Anti-government riots, led by the Buddhists, broke out in Saigon and Hué, and several Buddhist monks and nuns burned themselves to death in protest. Finally, in November 1963, a military group seized power. During the coup, Diem and his brother were killed.

After 1963 the war intensified as the United States poured more and more men, arms, and equipment into the country. U.S. forces expanded their role in the war from training and advising to actual combat in the early 1960s. Also assisting the South Vietnamese army were Australian, Filipino, Korean, New Zealand, and Thai forces. Air raids began carrying the war to the north in 1965.

Between 1963 and 1965 several military groups seized power in the south. In 1966, under U.S. pressure, an election was held in the south to choose a constituent assembly. A constitution was drafted, and in 1967 a president and a parliament were elected. Nguyen Van Thieu, leader of the ruling military junta, became president.

No end to the war was in sight, despite growing world pressure for a negotiated settlement. The governments of North Vietnam and South Vietnam, the National Liberation Front, and the United States were unable to find common ground on which to begin negotiations.

—Thomas E. Ennis; George Inaba

WESTERN SAMOA

Official name: The Independent State of Western Samoa
Area: 1,097 square miles
Population: (1967 est.) 135,000
Capital: Apia (Pop., 1961, urban area, 21,700)
Language: Samoan, English
Religion: Protestantism, Roman Catholicism
Currency unit: Tala

Western Samoa, an island republic in the South Pacific Ocean, lies some 1,600 miles northeast of New Zealand. A former German protectorate, Western Samoa was administered by New Zealand as a League of Nations mandate from 1920 to 1946, and as a UN trust territory from 1946 to 1962. In 1962 Western Samoa received its independence.

THE LAND. Western Samoa is made up of two large islands, Savai'i (660 square miles) and Upolu (430 square miles), and several small islands, including Manono and Apolima. The islands are volcanic in origin and are almost entirely surrounded by coral reefs. Mountains form the core of the two major islands, reaching an elevation of 3,608 feet in Upolu and 6,094 feet in Savai'i.

Western Samoa has a tropical climate. Temperatures average about 80°F, and yearly rainfall is 112 inches.

THE PEOPLE. Most of the people of Western Samoa are of Polynesian stock, and most are Christian. About 70 percent of the people live on

Upolu, and about 28 percent live on Savai'i. Apia, on Upolu, is the largest city and the commercial center of the islands.

Western Samoa has a rapidly growing population, with a rate of increase of almost 3 percent a year between 1958 and 1965.

ECONOMY. The economy of Western Samoa is based on agriculture. The basic food crops are taro, yams, breadfruit, and papaya. Fish are also important in the diet of the people, and poultry and pigs are raised. Cocoa, coconuts, and bananas are grown for export. The islands have few mineral resources, and there is little industry.

In 1965 imports cost about $9 million and exports earned about $6 million. The major imports are food, wood, textiles, and machinery. The major exports are bananas, cocoa, and copra. Most trade is conducted with New Zealand, the Netherlands, Australia, and Britain.

GOVERNMENT. The constitution of Western Samoa provides for a head of state, known as *O le Ao o le Malo*, elected by the legislature to a five-year term. Executive power is exercised by a cabinet, headed by a prime minister responsible to the legislature.

Legislative powers are held by the Legislative Assembly. In the assembly, 45 members are elected by the chiefs of clans, and two members are popularly elected to a three-year term. New Zealand represents Western Samoa in foreign affairs.

HISTORY. Western Samoa was discovered in 1722 by a Dutchman, Jacob Roggeveen. The islands were later visited by other explorers, but European penetration did not begin until 1830, initiated by British missionaries. British, U.S., and German traders came to the islands in the following years.

Foreign Interests. The British were interested in the islands as a place for missionary work, trade, and the development of plantations. U.S. interest centered on trade and the control of the exceptional harbor at Pago Pago, in present-day American Samoa. The Germans came first to trade and then developed the largest plantation interests.

New Zealand also held an interest in the political fate of the islands, but the Samoans were able politicians and were bent upon retaining their independence.

The last three decades of the 1800s saw periodic clashes arising from efforts of the three great powers to "settle" the Samoan question. Much of the time they assumed that Samoa would be independent, but with one of the powers exercising a dominant political influence in the islands. The United States, firmly in control of Pago Pago, was most consistently concerned with Samoan independence. Germany and Britain favored an agreement to leave a single power in control.

By an international agreement in 1900, the islands were divided. Germany gained control of present-day Western Samoa, and granted Britain territories elsewhere in the Pacific. The United States annexed Eastern

Samoa. From 1900 to World War I Western Samoa was a German colony.

New Zealanders occupied the islands early in the war, and in 1920 began to administer the islands as a League of Nations mandate. In 1946 Western Samoa became a UN trust territory under New Zealand administration. The Samoans had continuously sought independence, and in 1959 Western Samoa became self-governing.

Independence. In 1961 a plebiscite was held under UN supervision, and the people voted overwhelmingly for independence. On Jan. 1, 1962 Western Samoa became the first independent Polynesian state of modern times, but close ties were maintained with New Zealand. Fiame Mataʻafa Faumuina Mulinuʻu II, the first prime minister, retained his position in elections held in 1964 and 1967.

YEMEN

Official name: Yemen Arab Republic
Area: 75,000 square miles
Population: (1965 est.) 5,000,000
Capital: Sana (Pop., 1956 est., 60,000)
Language: Arabic
Religion: Islam
Currency unit: Riyal
National holiday: Proclamation of the republic, September 26

The Yemen Arab Republic lies in the southwestern corner of the Arabian peninsula on the coast of the Red Sea. It is bordered on the north and east by Saudi Arabia, on the south by South Yemen, and on the west by the Red Sea. The eastern boundary is undefined.

THE LAND. East of a narrow coastal plain, rugged mountains rise to over 12,000 feet, towering above a high central plateau. The eastern border is also mountainous, and desert land lies at the northern border.

In the desert and along the coastal plain less than 10 inches of rain fall a year and temperatures rise to over 130°F. A more temperate climate prevails in the mountains and the central plateau, where an average of 12 inches of rain fall a year and average temperatures range from 60°F to 80°F.

THE PEOPLE. The Yemeni are Arab Muslims of the Sunni and the Shiʻi sects. Population is concentrated on the coast and on the central plateau, where the capital, Sana, is located.

ECONOMY. Yemen's economy is based on agriculture. There are no known important mineral resources.

Farming, the chief occupation, prospers on carefully terraced mountainsides and in irrigated fields in the central plateau. Qat, a mild narcotic shrub, cotton, and coffee are the most important crops. Yemeni farmers also raise grains, citrus fruits, vegetables, and tobacco. Herders graze sheep, goats, camels, and horses in the more barren regions.

The tanning of hides and the working of leather are important crafts, and Yemen manufactures some soap and glass, but it has no large-scale industries. Yemen receives financial and technical aid from such countries as the Soviet Union, Communist China, and the United States.

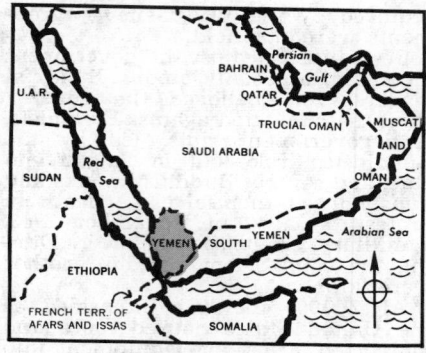

Trade is traditionally important in the economy, and the port facilities at Al Hudaydah were modernized in 1961. Civil war in the mid-1960s disrupted almost all commercial activity, however, and the country became dependent on foreign aid for nearly all necessities. Traditional exports include coffee, qat, cotton, hides, salt, and fruit.

GOVERNMENT. Yemen's government is republican in form, with actual power concentrated in the military. A president is chief executive and he appoints a prime minister and cabinet responsible to him.

Yemen is a member of the United Nations and the Arab League.

HISTORY. During the first 1,000 years before our era, several states, of which the best known was the Sabean, or Sheban, developed in Yemen. A high degree of economic prosperity earned the country the name of *Arabia Felix* among the Greeks and Romans.

Yemen's prosperity was based on an elaborate system of irrigation and the export of frankincense, precious jewels, and spices. Yemen also controlled a large part of the trade between India and the Mediterranean.

In the first centuries of the Christian era prosperity declined as the India-Mediterranean trade moved along new routes, and the irrigation works broke down. The cultural level also fell.

Early in the 500s Christian Ethiopians crossed the Red Sea and conquered the country. Later in the 500s Persian invaders conquered Yemen.

Yemen was converted to Islam in the 600s and formed part of the Islamic empires ruled successively from Medina, Damascus, and Baghdad. During the 500s and 600s Yemen's prosperity and culture deteriorated further. A revival came under the Zaydi imams, a family of political-religious leaders. In the 800s they founded a dynasty that ruled Yemen until 1962.

In the 1500s and 1600s Portugal and the Ottoman Turks competed for control of Yemen, but their invading forces were driven off. During the next 200 years the country suffered a cultural and economic relapse caused by its isolation and the diversion of trade routes around Africa.

In 1872 the Ottoman Turks succeeded in making Yemen part of their empire, but Yemeni resistance continued in the highlands until World War I. The Ottomans were forced to withdraw in 1918, at the end of World War I, leaving Yemen independent under the Zaydi ruler, the Imam Yahya.

The imam closed the country to outsiders, and although Yemen joined the Arab League in 1945 and the United Nations in 1947, it had almost no contact with the rest of the world. In 1948 Yahya was killed during an attempted revolution, and his son, Ahmad, succeeded him.

Ahmad gradually allowed foreign diplomats into Yemen. In 1958 Yemen and the United Arab Republic (U.A.R.) formed a federation, the United Arab States. By early 1962 the union had been abolished, however.

In September 1962 Ahmad died, and a week later the government of his son Imam Muhammad al-Badr, was overthrown by Yemeni army officers led by Abdullah al-Sallal.

The rebels declared Yemen a republic, with Sallal as president, and a constitution was drafted. After the revolution, civil war raged between the royalist forces of the deposed imam and republican army troops. The war involved the rest of the Middle East. The U.A.R. sent arms and troops to aid the republicans, and Jordan and Saudi Arabia provided the royalists with arms and money.

On November 5, 1967, a republican military coup ousted President al-Sallal, and Abdul Rahman al-Iryani became provisional president. At the end of November the U.A.R. pulled its troops out of Yemen after reaching an agreement with Saudi Arabia. The Egyptian withdrawal, however, was accompanied by a Soviet announcement that its aid to the Yemen Republic would continue. Saudi Arabian assistance to Yemeni royalists also continued.

—Charles Issawi; Alexander Melamid

YUGOSLAVIA

Official name: Socialist Federal Republic of Yugoslavia
Area: 98,766 square miles
Population: (1967 est.) 19,958,000
Capital: Belgrade (Pop., 1961 est., 585,200)
Language: Serbo-Croatian, Slovenian, Macedonian
Religion: Orthodox Christianity, Roman Catholicism, Islam
Currency unit: Dinar
National holiday: Proclamation of the republic, November 29

Yugoslavia, a nation at the western edge of the Balkan peninsula in southeastern Europe, is bounded on the north by Austria and Hungary, on the east by Romania and Bulgaria, on the south by Greece and Albania, and on the west by the Adriatic Sea and Italy.

The country is a federal union of six republics: Slovenia in the northwest; Croatia in the north; Serbia in the east; Bosnia-Herzegovina in the center; Macedonia in the southeast; and Montenegro in the south. There are also two autonomous provinces, Vojvodina in the north, and Kosovo-Metohija in the south.

THE LAND. Yugoslavia has three major geographic regions: the coastal plain, the mountains, and the interior lowlands.

Coastal Plain. Traditionally called Dalmatia, the coastal plain is a narrow band of territory extending along the Adriatic Sea. The coastline is irregular and lined with many offshore islands.

Mountains. Mountains cover about two-thirds of Yugoslavia. In the extreme northwest, along the border with Austria and Italy, are the Julian Alps, which contain the country's highest peak, the Triglav, 9,393 feet.

To the southeast of the Julian Alps are the Dinaric Alps, which run parallel to the coast southward to the Albanian border. The Dinaric Alps rise sharply from the shores of the Adriatic and, except in the far northwest, present a serious barrier to travel inland. The central portion of this range consists largely of a dry limestone plateau. Water quickly disappears underground and the surface is pockmarked with many large and small depressions.

Further inland the Dinaric Alps are less rugged and are composed of more resistant rock. Water is retained in valleys, and rivers are formed. The rivers of this inner region—the Kupa, the Vrbas, the Bosna, and the Drina—flow north into the Sava, a tributary of the Danube River.

Interior Lowlands. The Sava River valley forms the center of the Slovenian-Croatian hills. These hills grade eastward into the plains of northern Yugoslavia, where the Danube and its tributaries form a wide lowland, the Vojvodina. This area has rich soil and is Yugoslavia's chief food-producing region.

South of the Vojvodina in Serbia is the valley of the Morava River, the country's second major agricultural region. To the south, the Vardar valley separates Serbia from Macedonia, the southernmost region of the country. Much of Macedonia's land is eroded and not fit for cultivation, but agriculture is carried on wherever the soil is deep enough.

Climate. Yugoslavia has a varied climate. The Adriatic coast has a mild climate with cool, rainy winters and hot, dry summers. The northwest and the Dinaric Alps have warm summers and cold winters. The northeast has a continental climate with seasonal extremes of heat and cold.

THE PEOPLE. Yugoslavia is a multinational state. The great majority of its people, however, are of the group known as South Slavs. According to the 1961 census they consisted of 7.8 million Serbs, 4.3 million Croatians, 1.6 million Slovenes, 1 million Macedonians, and 500,000 Montenegrins. The largest minorities were Albanians (915,000), Hungarians (500,000), and Turks (183,000).

There is as much religious as ethnic diversity among Yugoslavs. About 41 percent of the population is Orthodox Christian, 32 percent is Roman Catholic, 12 percent is Muslim, and 1 percent is Protestant.

The majority of the population speaks Serbo-Croatian, a South Slavic language written in the Cyrillic alphabet by the Serbs and in the Latin alphabet by the Croatians. The Slovenes and Macedonians speak South Slavic languages of their own.

The country's principal city is the capital, Belgrade. Other large cities include Zagreb, the capital of Croatia and an important industrial center; Skopje, the capital of Macedonia; Sarajevo, the capital of Bosnia-Herzegovina and a major commercial center; and Ljubljana, the capital of Slovenia and a transportation center.

ECONOMY. Before World War II the Yugoslav economy was based on agriculture and mining. During the postwar period, however, the role played by industry increased greatly under the direction of the Yugoslav Communist party, which had come to power during the war.

Economic growth in the 1950s and early 1960s was rapid, and the gross domestic product more than doubled between 1953 and 1965. But the economy has been troubled by an unfavorable balance of payments caused by the necessity of importing large quantities of foodstuffs and industrial raw materials.

Natural Resources. Yugoslavia is well endowed with minerals and has important deposits of copper, zinc, lead, iron ore, bauxite, mercury, and chromite as well as some magnesite, asbestos, and pyrites. In 1965 copper production was 62,600 metric tons and zinc production 67,000 metric tons.

Yugoslavia's most important energy resource is petroleum. Production in 1965 amounted to more than 2 million metric tons. Coal reserves are mostly low-grade, but Yugoslavia's rivers have a high hydroelectric power potential.

In the mid-1960s hydroelectric plants existed on most of the major rivers or were under construction. In the 1960s plans went into effect for the construction of a huge hydroelectric project on the Danube. In 1965 Yugoslavia had an installed electric capacity of 3.7 million kilowatts (kw), of which hydroelectric plants represented 2.3 million kw.

Agriculture. After a brief and not very successful experiment with collectivization in the immediate postwar period, Yugoslavia returned to a system of private landownership. Collective farms do exist, particularly in the north, but about 80 percent of the country's arable land is privately owned.

Private holdings tend to be small, averaging less than 25 acres, and thus are not well suited to modern farming methods. This fact, coupled with recurrent droughts, has kept agricul-

UNITED NATIONS
YUGOSLAVIA'S DALMATIAN COAST

tural production low, and during the mid-1960s foodstuffs had to be imported.

Cereal grains, particularly corn and wheat, are planted on most of the land. Other major crops include potatoes, sugar beets, and hemp. Feed crops are gaining in importance. Tobacco, which is raised in Macedonia, is a leading export crop. Wine grapes are grown on the Adriatic coast and fruit is raised in Croatia and Serbia.

The raising of livestock and poultry is important, and meat is one of Yugoslavia's most valuable exports.

Industry. Yugoslav industry was largely underdeveloped before World War II, but it expanded rapidly during the 1950s and early 1960s. By 1965 industry contributed 38 percent to the gross domestic product.

Growth has been greatest in heavy industry, and major increases have been made in the production of iron, steel, and chemicals. Other industries produce ships, machinery, textiles, foodstuffs, construction materials, leather, paper, rubber, tobacco, and beverages.

Yugoslavia has a thriving handicraft industry, and textiles, leather, wood, and metal goods are made in many parts of the country.

Trade. In 1967 Yugoslavia's exports earned $1,252 million and imports cost $1,707 million. Major exports are live animals, machinery and transportation equipment, minerals, chemicals, beverages and tobacco, and textiles. Principal imports are cereal grains, industrial raw materials, chemicals, coal, manufactured goods, and machinery and transportation equipment. Yugoslavia's major trading partners include the Soviet Union, Italy, East and West Germany, the United States, Britain, and Poland.

Government. Yugoslavia is officially a republic. Political life is controlled by the country's Communist party, however, which is officially called the League of Communists of Yugoslavia (LCY). Key government posts are

filled by league members and the league's central committee determines government policy.

Under a constitution adopted in 1963, the head of state and chief executive is a president, who is elected by majority vote of the federal legislature to a four-year term. He may not serve more than two consecutive terms, but this restriction does not apply to Pres. Josip Broz Tito.

Legislative power is vested in the Federal Assembly, which consists of five chambers: the Federal Chamber, the Economic Chamber, the Chamber of Education and Culture, the Chamber of Social Welfare and Public Health, and the Organizational-Political Chamber. Each chamber has 120 members, who serve four-year terms. The Federal Chamber consists of an additional 70 members who represent Yugoslavia's six republics and two autonomous provinces. They make up a Chamber of Nationalities.

Members of the Federal Chamber are directly elected by popular vote but members of the other chambers are indirectly elected by various social, economic, and professional groups.

The executive organ of the Federal Assembly is the Federal Executive Council, whose chief function is to carry out the Assembly's policies. It is headed by a president, who is a member of the Federal Assembly, nominated by the president of the republic, and elected by the Federal Assembly.

Yugoslavia is a member of the United Nations.

HISTORY. In the 500s the South Slavs, or "Yugo Slavs," migrated into the Balkan peninsula from territories to the east. During the Middle Ages the histories of the various tribes that composed the South Slavs began to diverge.

The Slovenes in the northwest became part of the Frankish empire in the 700s and were under German rule until 1918. The Croatians in the north had an independent kingdom until they came under Hungarian domination in 1102.

The Serbs in the east were part of the Byzantine empire until the 1100s, when they established a kingdom which reached its height in the 1300s under Stephen Dushan. It remained independent until 1389, when it was absorbed by the Ottoman Empire. By 1500 not only Serbia, but also Macedonia, Bosnia, Herzegovina, and Montenegro had fallen to the Ottoman Turks. After the Ottoman defeat of Hungary in 1520, most of Slovenia and Croatia were added to the Ottoman Empire.

Independence and Unity. During the 1800s, with the decline of the Ottoman Empire, the South Slavs began to agitate for independence. In 1878 the Treaty of Berlin, which settled the Russo-Turkish War of 1877–1878, guaranteed the independence of Serbia and Montenegro.

These two small states, influenced by the doctrine of Pan-Slavism, or Slavic unity, enlisted the support of Russia, the most powerful Slavic state, in the struggle for complete South Slav independence and unity.

In October 1908 Austria announced the annexation of Bosnia and Herzegovina, two Slav provinces that Serbia had hoped to bring under Serbian authority. To resist the encroachments of the Ottoman and Austrian empires, a Balkan League was organized in the spring of 1912. Balkan Wars broke out in 1912 and 1913, and Serbia conquered much of Macedonia from Turkey.

In 1914 World War I was precipitated by the assassination at Sarajevo, the capital of Bosnia, of Franz Ferdinand, heir to the Austro-Hungarian throne, by a Bosnian nationalist. The defeat of Austria-Hungary and of Ottoman Turkey in the war and the sympathy of the Allies, particularly of the United States, helped the South Slavs to gain full independence.

In November 1918 Montenegro declared itself united with Serbia, and on December 1, 1918, the Kingdom of the Serbs, Croats, and Slovenes was proclaimed. King Peter of Serbia became king under the regency of Prince Alexander. In January 1921 a new constitution providing for a centralized government was proclaimed. In August, King Peter died and was succeeded by Alexander.

Internal Dissension. Success in bringing all Yugoslavs into the new kingdom was soon overshadowed by the enormous problems facing the new state. The Yugoslavs had been ruled for hundreds of years by empires with varying cultures, and they not only had different traditions but different religions. The Yugoslavs who had been under Austria-Hungary were Roman Catholic, whereas those ruled by the Turks were either Orthodox Christian or Muslim.

National and religious diversity presented a serious difficulty, particularly because the 1921 constitution reflected the centralistic wishes of the Serbs, who dominated the new state. The kingdom of Serbia was the nucleus of Yugoslavia, whose army and bureaucracy were generally dominated by Serbia. This, combined with Serbian insensitiveness to the feelings of the other groups, especially the Croatians, led to animosity and friction.

In 1929 King Alexander established a dictatorship, and changed the name of the country to Yugoslavia. Alexander was assassinated by a Macedonian revolutionary associated with Croatian extremists while on a visit to France in 1934. The 11-year-old Peter II became king under the regency of his cousin, Prince Paul, who continued the dictatorship until August 26, 1939, when Yugoslavia returned to democratic government. A federal system was to be established, and Croatians were to enjoy full cultural and economic freedom. But a week later Yugoslavia found itself engulfed in World War II.

After 1934 the Yugoslav government had drifted steadily into a pro-German position. On Mar. 25, 1941 Prince Paul endorsed the Tri-Partite Pact of Germany, Japan, and Italy. Two days later Prince Paul was overthrown by a military coup led by pro-Allied Serbs, and the young Peter was declared king.

World War II. Following the coup, on April 6, Germany invaded Yugoslavia. King Peter fled the country and set up a government in exile in London. Pro-German puppet states were established in Croatia and Serbia, and the rest of the country was divided among Germany, Italy, Hungary, Italian-ruled Albania, and Bulgaria.

Yugoslavia became one of the bloodiest battlefields of the war. Between 1941 and 1945, 1.7 million Yugoslavs, or more than 10 percent of the population, lost their lives. This toll was caused not only by guerrilla fighting against the occupying armies, but also by a bitter civil war that developed between the resistance forces themselves.

Early in the war Col. Draža Mihajlović, a Serbian army officer, organized patriot guerrilla bands known as the Chetniks. The initial Chetnik fighting brought brutal German reprisals, and Mihajlović decided to proceed with caution. The government-in-exile in London promoted him to general and made him commander in chief of the resistance forces.

After German armies invaded the Soviet Union in June 1941, the Partisans were organized by the head of Yugoslavia's Communist party, Josip Broz, who was generally known as Tito.

In 1943 the Allies, who had recognized the Chetniks as the official Yugoslav resistance movement, concluded that Tito's group was doing most of the actual fighting, and threw their support to the Partisans. With the help of the Allies, Tito and the Partisans gained control of Yugoslavia.

Communist Control. Elections were held in November 1945, but they were controlled by the communists and resulted in the election of a constituent assembly composed mostly of communists or pro-Tito elements. On Nov. 29, 1945 the assembly proclaimed the Federal People's Republic of Yugoslavia. In 1946 General Mihajlović was sentenced to death and executed on charges of collaboration with the Germans.

During the immediate postwar period Yugoslavia was a firm supporter of the Soviet Union. In 1948, however, Premier Joseph Stalin of the Soviet Union, who had been disturbed by Tito's independence in foreign and domestic policy, broke with Yugoslavia. The other communist-controlled states of Eastern Europe followed the lead of the Soviet Union and severed all political and economic ties with Yugoslavia.

Following its break with the other communist countries, Yugoslav leaders began to reevaluate their economic policies. Central controls were somewhat relaxed, and in the early 1950s workers' councils were established in industrial plants to give workers greater responsibility. Municipal and district producers' councils were also formed to give workers an even larger role in decision making. Collectivized agriculture was abandoned in favor of private ownership, and the federal constitution was revised in 1953 to provide for less control by the central government.

After 1948 Yugoslav foreign policy also underwent a change. Inasmuch as the communist countries had broken economic as well as political ties with Yugoslavia, the country was forced to direct its foreign trade to the West and to neutral countries. Yugoslavia began to receive economic and military assistance from the United States and formed political, cultural, and economic ties with the countries of Western Europe.

Western economic aid, technical advice, and cultural exchanges helped keep Yugoslavia independent of the Soviet Union. At the same time Tito steered a middle course in international affairs, supporting the Soviet Union whenever it relaxed its hostility toward Yugoslavia.

Soviet-Yugoslav relations improved after the death of Joseph Stalin in 1953, and remained good until Soviet suppression of the Hungarian Revolution in 1956. In the 1960s, however, Soviet-Yugoslav relations were again strengthened.

—Robert F. Byrnes; George Kish

ZAMBIA

Official name: Republic of Zambia
Area: 290,586 square miles
Population: (1967 est.) 3,947,000
Capital: Lusaka (Pop., 1965 est., urban area, 138,300)
Language: English, African languages
Religion: Traditional religions, Christianity
Currency unit: Kwacha
National holiday: Independence day, October 24

Zambia, a republic in southern Africa, is bordered on the north by the Congo (Kinshasa) and Tanzania; on the east by Malawi; on the south by Mozambique, Rhodesia, Botswana, and South West Africa; and on the west by Angola.

In 1953 Britain joined Zambia, formerly known as Northern Rhodesia, with Southern Rhodesia and present-day Malawi, the former Nyasaland, to form the Federation of Rhodesia and Nyasaland. In 1963 the federation was dissolved, and in 1964 Britain granted Zambia its independence.

THE LAND. Most of Zambia is occupied by a high plain, with elevations between 3,000 and 4,000 feet above sea level. In the east are the Muchinga Mountains, with a peak of over 6,000 feet. The Abercorn Highlands are in the far north of the country.

The Zambezi River flows along the border with Rhodesia, and the Luangwa and Kafue rivers, tributaries of the Zambezi, flow through Zambia. Along the Zambezi River is Victoria Falls, where the river plunges more than 300 feet into a deep canyon. Kariba Lake, formed by the Kariba Dam on the Zambezi River, is one of the largest man-made lakes in the world, covering about 2,000 square miles.

In the northeast is the Chambeshi River, which flows into a swampy region near Lake Bangeweulu. Lakes Mweru and Tanganyika lie along the northern border.

Zambia has a subtropical climate. The country receives between 25 and 30 inches of rain a year.

THE PEOPLE. Most of the people in Zambia are Bantu-speaking Africans. About 2 percent of the population is European. Most Europeans live in the north-central part of the country. There are also some Asians and people of mixed origins.

ECONOMY. The Zambian economy depends heavily on copper mining. Although some 70 percent of the population is engaged in farming, in 1965 agriculture contributed only 10 percent of the gross domestic product, and mining contributed over 5 percent. The basic food crops are corn, cassava, and millet. Tobacco, peanuts, and cotton are also grown.

Zambia is one of world's largest producers of copper, and in 1967 617,000 metric tons of copper were produced. Most copper is mined in the "Copper Belt," in north-central Zambia. The Kariba Dam provides most of the hydroelectric power for smelting and refining the copper. Zinc, lead, and cobalt are also mined. In 1967 a four-year development plan was instituted to develop industry and agriculture.

In 1966 imports cost $345 million and exports earned $691 million. The main imports are textiles, petroleum products, iron and steel, and machinery. The major exports are copper, zinc, and tobacco. Most trade is conducted with Britain, West Germany, Rhodesia, and Japan.

In 1965, when the white minority government of Rhodesia declared Rhodesia's independence from Britain, the UN Security Council requested that member nations impose economic sanctions against Rhodesia. Since that time, Zambia has made efforts to reduce its dependence on Rhodesian products.

GOVERNMENT. Zambia has a presidential system of government. Executive power is vested in a president, who is popularly elected to a five-year term. The president appoints a vice-president. Legislative power rests with the 75-member National Assembly. Assembly members are popularly elected to five-year terms.

Zambia is a member of the United Nations, the Commonwealth of Nations, and Organization of African Unity (OAU).

HISTORY. Little is known of the early history of Zambia. In the early 1800s, Mulambwa, chief of one Bantu-speaking tribe, the Lozi, built a powerful state in Barotseland, in the northwestern part of the country.

RHODESIA NATIONAL TOURIST BOARD

ZAMBIA'S KARIBA LAKE, fed by the Zambezi River, is part of a modern resort area.

In the 1830s the Lozi state crumbled before the Kololo, a military band composed of different Bantu-speaking clans. In the 1860s, however, the Lozi reestablished their dominance in Barotseland. By the late 1800s, under the Lozi ruler Lewanika, Lozi authority in the region was acknowledged by neighboring peoples.

In the mid-1800s Europeans began to settle in present-day Zambia, and in 1890 Cecil Rhodes' British South Africa Company obtained a monopoly over rights from Lewanika. In 1891 Rhodes divided the region north of the Zambezi River into three protectorates—Nyasaland, Northeastern Rhodesia, and Northwestern Rhodesia (which included Barotseland). In 1911 the company joined Northeastern and Northwestern Rhodesia to form Northern Rhodesia.

Control of the region by the British South Africa Company ended in 1923, and the British government took over the administration of Northern Rhodesia. Southern Rhodesia, however, became self-governing, and white-settler governments came to power there. Thus when representatives of the Southern Rhodesian government and the white settlers of Northern Rhodesia, at a meeting in Victoria Falls in 1936, decided to work for the union of the two countries, the Africans of Northern Rhodesia were outraged. Nonetheless, in 1953 Britain established the Federation of Rhodesia and Nyasaland.

Opposition from African nationalists in Northern Rhodesia and Nyasaland led Britain to dissolve the federation in December 1963. In parliamentary elections held in Rhodesia in January 1964, the United National Independence Party led by Kenneth Kaunda won a majority of the seats. On Oct. 24, 1964, Britain granted Northern Rhodesia its independence, and the country adopted the name Zambia. Kaunda became the first president.

—Hibberd V. B. Kline, Jr.; Gary A. Weissman

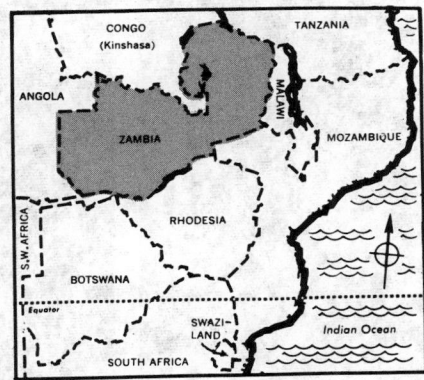

COLONIES AND DEPENDENCIES

ANGOLA

Status: Overseas province of Portugal
Area: 481,351 square miles
Population: (1966 est.) 5,225,000
Capital: Luanda (Pop., 1960, urban area, 224,540)

Angola, on the southwestern coast of Africa, consists of two sections, Angola proper and Cabinda. Angola proper is bounded on the north by the Congo (Kinshasa), on the east by the Congo (Kinshasa) and Zambia, on the south by South West Africa, and on the west by the Atlantic Ocean.

The smaller Cabinda region, about 2,800 square miles in area, is an enclave separated from Angola proper by the Congo (Kinshasa). It is bounded on the north by the Congo (Brazzaville) and on the west by the Atlantic Ocean.

THE LAND. Most of Angola lies on a deeply dissected plateau with an average elevation of 4,000 feet. A narrow coastal plain skirts the plateau on the west, and in the east a higher plateau rises to 7,000 feet. Low-lying Cabinda is covered by dense tropical jungle.

Much of the interior of Angola is heavily forested. Some portions of the east are swampy, and the Moçâmedes Desert lies in the southwest. Many rivers rush from the plateau toward the borders.

Angola's climate is varied. Cabinda and the coastal and northern regions are tropical, with high heat and humidity. The south and southeast are generally drier. The lower areas are hot, and the higher regions cool.

THE PEOPLE. The overwhelming majority of the people are Bantu-speaking Africans of many tribal groups, including the Bakongo, Kimbundu, Ovimbundu, and Chokwe. About 4 percent of the population is European, and there is a small group of mixed African and European origin.

The official language is Portuguese, but a number of African languages are spoken. The illiteracy rate is extremely high among both Africans and Europeans. Roman Catholicism is the predominant religion, but many Africans are members of Protestant groups, and many follow traditional religions.

ECONOMY. Angola is a rich land. There are diamonds, oil, copper, manganese, iron, gold, and other minerals, and the hydroelectric potential is considerable. Farming is the chief economic activity of most of the people, however.

The basic food crops are manioc, corn, rice, and vegetables. Coffee, cotton, sisal, and sugarcane are the major cash crops and are raised on plantations. The country's forests yield palm products and timber, and there is fishing off the coasts.

Mining is Angola's major industrial activity. An oil refinery was opened in the 1960s. Among the many smaller industries are food processing and the manufacture of building materials. Large-scale industry awaits the development of the country's hydroelectric capacity, which was begun in the 1960s.

Angola's trade is prosperous and growing. In 1966 imports cost $209 million, and exports earned $221 million. Coffee, gold, iron ore, fish products, corn, sisal, and oil are the chief exports. Machinery and vehicles, textiles, drugs, and manufactured goods are imported. Most trade is with Britain, the United States, West Germany, and Portugal.

GOVERNMENT. Angola is officially a province of Portugal. The administration is headed by an appointed governor-general, who wields both executive and legislative powers. He is responsible to the Overseas Ministry in metropolitan Portugal.

An elected Legislative Council and an elected Economic and Social Council advise the governor-general and have limited authority in local matters. Angola elects representatives to the Portuguese National Assembly, in Lisbon.

HISTORY. Angola was part of the large, advanced Bantu-speaking kingdom of the Congo when it was visited in 1482 by the Portuguese explorer Diogo Caõ. Friendly relations were established, and Portugal sent missionaries, traders, and settlers to the territory in the 1500s. Although portions of the territory later came under direct Portuguese administration when the Congo kingdom began to disintegrate, Portugal did little to develop or exploit the region's resources.

During the 1600s the Portuguese defeated Dutch attempts to win control of Angola, and in the 1700s and 1800s Angola was a major source of slaves for Portugal's Brazil colony. In 1878 slaving was prohibited and replaced by a system of contract labor. Under the contract system, men over 18 who were employed fewer than six months a year could be forced to work. In practice, women and young children were frequently drafted to meet labor needs.

Portugal's title to Angola was affirmed and the colony's boundaries set in 1885 and 1886. Colonial development was largely in private hands until the 1930s, when the government encouraged Portuguese to settle there.

The government initiated full exploitation of the area's resources and imposed centralized control by breaking the power of local chiefs. Portugal's official policy was to incorporate Angola into the culture, society, and economy of European Portugal.

Nationalism. Although some political participation was permitted Angolans after 1951, when Angola was declared an overseas province, the government failed to meet the education, health, and welfare needs of the majority of the people, and concentrated on exploiting the land. This neglect spurred the growth of a nationalist movement, and in 1961 an insurrection broke out in Cabinda and northern Angola.

Portugal moved to suppress the revolt by military force, but guerrilla warfare continued in the north and

ANGOLA. Fort São Miguel *(left)* is located in Luanda, the capital. Illiteracy is high and many Angolan children still do not attend school.

SECRETARIADO NACIONAL DA INFORMACAO

LOOK MAGAZINE

nationalist leaders established a government-in-exile and demanded independence.

Portugal's administration in Angola came under criticism in the United Nations, and self-determination for Angola's people has been urged. No grounds for discussion of the problem could be agreed upon that satisfied Portugal and Angolan nationalist leaders, however.

In the 1960s the Portuguese government initiated programs to broaden the economy by developing industry and to improve the education and social condition of the Angolans while keeping the territory part of Portugal. Rich oil finds in 1966 held out the prospect of greater funds for Angolan development, but guerrilla warfare continued.

—Hibberd V. B. Kline, Jr.; John E. Oliver; Vera L. Zolberg

ANTIGUA

Status: State in association with Britain.
Area: 170 square miles
Population: (1966 est.) 60,000
Capital: St. John City (Pop., 1960, 21,595)

Antigua, one of the Leeward Islands of the Lesser Antilles chain, between the Caribbean Sea and the Atlantic Ocean, lies northeast of the island of Montserrat. The territory includes two smaller nearby islands, Barbuda and Redonda.

THE LAND AND PEOPLE. The island's terrain is rolling to hilly, and the climate is warm. About 45 inches of rain falls each year. Most of the people are of mixed European and African descent, and they speak English.

ECONOMY. Antigua's economy is based on the raising of sugarcane and cotton. Fruits, corn, and vegetables are grown for domestic consumption. Droughts are frequent.

Efforts were underway in the mid-1960s to expand industry beyond the processing of sugar and cotton, and an oil refinery was built in 1966. Tourism became of increasing importance to the economy in the 1960s.

Trade is limited. Imports of necessities, supplied largely by Britain and the United States, far outweigh exports of cotton and sugar, which go mainly to Britain.

GOVERNMENT. Antigua is self-governing. An appointed governor is the nominal chief executive. Actual executive powers are wielded by an executive council responsible to a small elected assembly.

HISTORY. Antigua was discovered by Christopher Columbus in 1493. It was first colonized by the British in 1632, with competition from French and Dutch settlers. Plantations were established, and slaves were imported from West Africa to work them in the 1700s. The slaves were freed in 1838.

In 1871 Antigua was included in the colony of the federated Leeward Islands. This federation was replaced in 1958 by the Federation of the West Indies, an internally self-governing British dependency disbanded in 1962. In 1967 Antigua became self-governing and with St. Christopher (St. Kitts), Nevis, and Anguilla formed the West Indies Associated States.

HEYER
BERMUDA. Tourists enjoy the scenery while riding in an open carriage.

BAHAMAS

Status: British colony
Area: 4,403 square miles
Population: (1967 est.) 144,000
Capital: Nassau (Pop., 1964, 80,907)

The Bahamas form an archipelago in the Atlantic Ocean off the southeastern tip of Florida.

THE LAND AND PEOPLE. The 22 islands and 650 islets of the archipelago have low, rocky, flat, or rolling terrain and are ringed with coral reefs. The climate is warm throughout the year. About 50 inches of rain falls each year. Three-quarters of the people are Negro, and the rest are of European or mixed descent. The people are English speaking.

ECONOMY. Tourism is the prime factor in the economy, but agriculture is also significant on most of the islands. Bananas, citrus fruits, and vegetables are grown. Forestry and salt production are important and, with food processing, constitute the only industrial activities.

In the 1960s government programs sought to persuade businesses to make their headquarters on the islands. The poor balance of trade caused by the need to import necessities is partially offset by the expenditures of tourists.

GOVERNMENT. The Bahamas have internal self-government under a prime minister and cabinet responsible to a popularly elected legislative assembly. An appointed administrator represents Britain.

HISTORY. The Bahamas were discovered in 1492 by Christopher Columbus, but the first settlements were made by the English in the 1600s. Plantations were established, and Negro slaves were imported. The islands became a British colony in 1783 and retained that status until 1964, when self-government was granted. In 1967 the islands' first Negro prime minister took office and began to move the colony toward greater independence from Britain.

—George Carey; Jerome Fischman

BERMUDA

Status: British crown colony
Area: 20 square miles
Population: (1967 est.) 50,000
Capital: Hamilton (Pop., 1965, 3,000)

Bermuda, an archipelago of 20 islands and numerous islets in the Atlantic Ocean, lies some 600 miles east of the United States.

THE LAND AND PEOPLE. The coral-rimmed islands of Bermuda are rather flat and heavily forested. The climate is warm and humid throughout the year. Most of the people are of mixed African and European descent. There are groups of Europeans and a large number of U.S. military personnel.

ECONOMY. Bermuda's economy is based on tourism. U.S. military bases also contribute to the islands' income. Some fruits and vegetables are raised, and there is some fishing, but most foodstuffs must be imported. Pharmaceuticals and perfume essences are among the islands' few manufactures.

Favorable taxation policies encourage many foreign-owned corporations to make Bermuda their headquarters. Most of the islands' trade is with the United States and Canada, which supply foodstuffs, clothing, and other necessities.

GOVERNMENT. An appointed governor administers the colony with the advice of an executive council. The legislature, which consists of one popularly elected house and one appointed house, has considerable control over local affairs.

HISTORY. Bermuda was discovered in 1503 by a Spaniard, Juan de Bermudez, but no settlement was made until after British colonists were shipwrecked there in 1609. Under a royal charter, colonization increased through the 1600s. Plantations were opened, and Africans were brought as slaves to work them. They soon constituted the bulk of the population.

In the 1900s the islands became a popular resort for the wealthy. An aristocratic form of government with suffrage limited to property owners continued until 1963, when universal adult suffrage was introduced. In the mid-1960s pressure grew for increased independence from Britain.

BRITISH ANTARCTIC TERRITORY

Status: British colony
Area: 2,040 square miles (excluding Graham Land)
Population: No permanent population

The British Antarctic Territory consists of the South Orkney and the South Shetland islands, in the south Atlantic Ocean off the southern tip of South America, Graham Land, on the Antarctic peninsula, and Coatsland and Caird coast, along the Antarctic's Weddell coast.

The islands are rocky and barren, and the mainland is ice-covered and barren. The climate is cold and dry. There are no permanent inhabitants. Sealing and whaling are the colony's chief economic activities. The colony is the site of scientific research stations. It is administered by the governor of the nearby Falkland Islands colony.

The islands and Graham Land were discovered in the 1820s by British explorers and sealers. The other mainland territory was charted in the early 1900s by British explorers. The British Antarctic territory was part of the Falkland Island colony until 1962, when the two were separated.

BRITISH HONDURAS

Status: British colony
Area: 361 square miles
Population: (1967 est.) 113,000
Capital: Belize (Pop., 1964, urban area, 45,-572)

British Honduras lies on the eastern coast of Central America. It is bounded on the north by Mexico, on the east by the Caribbean Sea, on the south by the Gulf of Honduras and Guatemala, and on the west by Guatemala.

THE LAND AND PEOPLE. British Honduras has a varied landscape. The northern and coastal lowlands are swampy, and the Maya Mountain range dominates the south. Much of the land is covered by dense jungle. The climate is tropical, with high heat and humidity throughout the year.

Negroes, Maya and Carib Indians, and people of mixed origins form the bulk of the population. There are also small groups of East Indian and European origins. English is the official language, but Spanish, Maya, and Carib are spoken.

ECONOMY. Farming and forestry are the main economic activities. Sugarcane, citrus fruits, bananas, rice, coconuts, cacao, vegetables, and nuts are grown commercially, and livestock is raised. The forests yield pine, mahogany, cedar, and rosewood. There are sawmills, sugar refineries, distilleries, and other plants for the processing of farm products. Boatbuilding and handicrafts are also important in the economy.

British Honduras has a poor balance of trade. In 1965, for example, exports earned $12 million and imports cost $24 million. Sugar and sugar products, citrus fruits, and lumber are the main exports. Manufactured goods, machinery, foodstuffs, and fuels are imported. The United States, Britain, and the islands of the West Indies are the principal trading partners.

GOVERNMENT. British Honduras' government is headed by an appointed governor, whose powers are limited by a popularly elected legislative assembly.

HISTORY. British Honduras was a site of early Mayan civilization. It was crossed by the Spanish conqueror, Hernan Cortes, in the 1500s and was first settled by British privateers in the early 1700s. In the late 1700s British colonists settled the interior and established plantations using slave labor, and in 1789 Honduras became a British colony.

The colony was governed from Jamaica until the 1880s, when a separate administration was established. During the 1900s the government concentrated on developing the economy of the colony. Popular participation in government was broadened with the goal of eventual independence, and in 1964 full internal self-government was achieved.

—George Carey; Jerome Fischman

BRITISH INDIAN OCEAN TERRITORY

Status: British colony
Area: 30 square miles.
Population: (1966 est.) 2,000

The British Indian Ocean Territory consists of scattered islands in the Indian Ocean lying from 500 to 2,000 miles off the eastern coast of Africa. The colony was formed in 1965 from former dependencies of Seychelles and Mauritius. It consists of the Chagos Archipelago, the Farquhar group, Desroches Island, and the Aldabra islands.

The colony's chief importance is its strategic location, and there is a military base at Diego Garcia, in the Chagos group.

THE LAND AND PEOPLE. Most of the islands are very small. They are volcanic in origin and are mountainous and forested. They have a tropical monsoon climate.

The population is of varied origins, and includes Africans, Indians, Chinese, Europeans, and people of mixed background. French, English, and a variety of other languages are spoken in the territory.

ECONOMY. The colony's economy is based primarily on fishing and agriculture. Coconuts, cinnamon, and vanilla are the main agricultural products. Coffee and some fruits and vegetables are raised and sugarcane is grown in the Chagos group. The only industries are coconut processing and fish salting. The colony imports food, clothing, and consumer goods, and exports fish, coconuts, and spices. Most trade is with Britain and neighboring islands.

GOVERNMENT. The colony is administered by an appointed commissioner, who is also governor of Britain's Seychelles colony.

HISTORY. The islands of the territory were uninhabited and visited only by Malay and Arab sailors until the 1500s, when the Portuguese landed on the western islands of the Farquhar, Desroches, and Aldabra islands. The islands, important in the spice trade, were controlled at various times by Portugal, the Netherlands, and France. In the early 1800s they became British possessions.

The islands were part of the Crown Colony of Mauritius until 1903, when those near the Seychelles were made part of that colony. In 1965 the British government bought the Chagos group from Mauritius and created the territory. In 1967 Britain and the United States agreed to use the islands jointly for military bases.

BRITISH SOLOMON ISLANDS

Status: British protectorate
Area: 11,500 square miles
Population: (1966 est.) 141,000
Capital: Honaira (Pop., 1956 est., 6,700)

The British Solomon Islands, a dozen large islands and many islets, extend for over 900 miles in the South Pacific Ocean, some 300 miles east of New Guinea.

THE LAND AND PEOPLE. The islands are mountainous, rugged, and rimmed by coral reefs. The climate is warm and rainfall is heavy.

Melanesian, Polynesian, and Micronesian people make up the bulk of the population, and there is a small group of Europeans. English is the official language, but pidgin English is more widely spoken.

ECONOMY. The islands' forests have a rich, but untapped, potential and there are deposits of gold, which are only partially exploited. Most of the people live by subsistence farming and fishing. Coconuts are the chief commercial crop. There is little manufacturing.

Coconut products and timber are the chief exports, and manufactured goods are imported. Britain, Japan, and Australia are the islands' major trading partners.

GOVERNMENT. The Solomon Islands are administered by Britain's Western Pacific High Commission. The high commissioner has the assistance of the Solomon Islands executive council, which is responsible to the partially elected Solomon Islands legislative assembly. Local government officials are popularly elected.

HISTORY. Little is known of the islands before their discovery by the Spanish in 1567. They were soon lost to Europeans again, and were authoritatively relocated by the French only in 1792. They served Europeans as a source of copra and labor until the 1890s, when the British established a protectorate. In the 1900s British settlers established plantations, Christian missions, and trading posts.

The islands, especially Guadalcanal in the southwest, were the scene of fierce fighting between Japanese and

Allied troops in World War II. In the decades after the war Britain concentrated on raising the islanders' standard of living and expanding the economy by developing natural resources.

BRITISH VIRGIN ISLANDS

Status: British colony
Area: 59 square miles
Population: (1966 est.) 9,000
Capital: Roadtown (Pop., 1960, 891)

The British Virgin Islands lie at the northern end of the Leeward Islands group of the Lesser Antilles, between the Caribbean Sea and the Atlantic Ocean. The group includes three large and several smaller islands and some 30 islets.

THE LAND AND PEOPLE. The islands are generally low-lying, with interior hills. The climate is warm throughout the year and rather dry. The population is almost entirely of African descent and speaks English.

ECONOMY. Fishing, cattle raising, and farming are the major economic activities. The few light industries include a distillery and boatyards. Tourism makes a substantial contribution to the economy, and remittances of islanders who work in the United States and nearby U.S. Virgin Islands help to offset a poor trade balance.

Cattle, fish, and farm products are the only exports, and most necessities are imported. The United States is the islands' chief trading partner.

GOVERNMENT. The British Virgin Islands are administered by an appointed governor with the advice of an executive council and a partly elected legislative council.

HISTORY. The islands were discovered in 1493 by Christopher Columbus. They served primarily as a base for pirates until the early 1700s, when English planters settled on the larger islands. Slaves imported to work the plantations soon became the islands' principal inhabitants.

The islands became a colony in 1774 and were governed as part of the Territory of the Leeward Islands until 1956, when they became a dependency of the Leeward Islands colony. In the 1960s the British Virgin Islands became a separate colony. In the 1950s and early 1960s migration to Britain was heavy, and the British government concentrated on improving social and economic conditions in the islands.

BRUNEI

Status: British-protected state
Area: 2,225 square miles
Population: (1966 est.) 104,000
Capital: Brunei Municipal (Pop., 1960, 9,702)

Brunei, a sultanate on the island of Borneo, is bordered on the north by the South China Sea and on the east, south, and west by the East Malaysian state of Sarawak.

The western and coastal regions of Brunei are swampy, and there is a rugged, hilly region in the east. The climate is tropical, with high heat and humidity throughout the year. Malays

BOAC

BRUNEI. The modern section of the capital city is dominated by the great mosque built in 1958.

and Chinese form the bulk of the population, and there are several smaller groups of Borneo native peoples. Islam is the official religion and Malay the official language.

Brunei has rich oil deposits, and oil production and refining constitute the major economic activity. Rubber and rice are grown, and forest products are produced. Brunei's chief export is oil, and its main imports are foodstuffs, raw materials, and machinery.

Brunei's government is headed by a sultan, who rules with the assistance of a council and a British commissioner, and with the advice of an elected legislative assembly. Britain is responsible for Brunei's foreign affairs and defense.

Once the center of a powerful island empire, Brunei signed a treaty of protection with Britain in 1888 as a defense against piracy. Oil was discovered in 1929, and Brunei's importance increased. In 1959 the sultan issued a constitution that introduced limited democracy.

In 1963, when the federation of Malaysia was formed, Brunei was the only British Malay dependency in the area not to join. In 1967 Sultan Omar Ali Saifuddin abdicated after 17 years on the throne, and was succeeded by his son, Pengiran Muda Mahkota Hassanal Bolkiah.

CAPE VERDE ISLANDS

Status: Overseas province of Portugal
Area: 1,557 square miles
Population: (1965 est.) 232,000
Capital: Praia (Pop., 1960, urban area, 13,-142)

The Cape Verde Islands lie in the Atlantic Ocean some 275 miles west of Senegal, on the African mainland. There are 10 islands and several islets in the group.

THE LAND AND PEOPLE. The islands are volcanic in origin and are mountainous, rocky, and barren. The climate is extremely hot and dry. The majority of the islands' population is of mixed African and Portuguese descent. About one-third is African, and a very small proportion is European.

Portuguese is the official language, but a creole dialect of Portuguese and other languages is widely spoken. Roman Catholicism is the predominant religion.

ECONOMY. The islands have no exploitable mineral resources, and their soil is generally too dry and poor to support vegetation. Bananas, coffee, nuts, oil seeds, and corn are raised, and some salt is produced. Fish are abundant off the coasts and some livestock is grazed. The islands have several good ports, and the refueling of ships is the main economic activity.

Trade is limited. In 1965 imports cost $8 million and exports earned $11 million. Coffee, fish, banana, and nuts are exported, and foodstuffs, textiles, and building materials are imported. Most trade is with mainland Portugal.

GOVERNMENT. The Cape Verde Islands are administered as a province of Portugal and elect representatives to the Portuguese National Assembly. Local government is in the hands of an appointed governor-general, who is advised by a small, partly elected legislative council.

HISTORY. The Cape Verde Islands were uninhabited when they were discovered in 1456 by the Portuguese. The Portuguese began to settle the islands in the late 1400s and early 1500s, and African slaves began to be imported. In 1587 a governor was appointed for the colony, and in the 1600s and 1700s settlers from Spain, Italy, and Britain joined the Portuguese on the islands. The colony thrived on plantation agriculture and trading.

In 1951 the colony was made an overseas province of Portugal, and in 1961 the islanders received full Portuguese citizenship.

CAYMAN ISLANDS

Status: British colony
Area: 100 square miles
Population: (1966 est.) 9,000
Capital: Georgetown (Pop., 1960, 2,573)

The Cayman Islands—Grand Cayman, Little Cayman, and Cayman Brac—lie in the Caribbean Sea some 100 miles northwest of Jamaica and about 100 miles south of Cuba.

CHANNEL ISLANDS. This view of the Isle of Jersey shows St. Orgueil Castle.

Low, rocky, and coral-rimmed, the islands have densely-forested interiors. The climate is tropical, with high heat and humidity throughout the year. The population includes people of European, African, and mixed origins.

Coconuts and sisal are the only significant crops, and seafaring, boatbuilding, ropemaking, and tourism are the major sources of income.

The islands are governed by an appointed administrator, a partially elected legislative assembly, and an executive council chosen by the assembly.

Discovered by Christopher Columbus in 1503, the islands were uninhabited until the 1700s, when British from Jamaica settled them. They were governed as part of Jamaica until Jamaica became independent in 1962, when the Caymans were placed under a separate administration.

CHANNEL ISLANDS

Status: Dependency of the British crown
Area: 75 square miles
Population: (1966 est.) 115,000
Capital: Jersey—St. Helier; Guernsey—St. Peter Port

The Channel Islands lie in the English Channel 10 to 35 miles off the western coast of France. They include Jersey, Guernsey, and six small dependencies of Guernsey—Alderney, Brechou, Little Sark, Great Sark, Herm, Jethou, and Lihou.

THE LAND AND PEOPLE. The Channel Islands consist mainly of rolling plains. Their climate is rather damp and mild, with an average temperature in the 60°s F.

The population is of French and British origin. French is the official language in Jersey, and English is the official language in Guernsey.

ECONOMY. The islands have excellent farm and pasture land, and agriculture and dairying are the main economic activities. Jersey cattle are raised on Jersey, and Guernsey cattle on Guern-

sey and its dependencies. Jersey farmers grow flowers, potatoes, tomatoes, and other vegetables, and Guernsey farms produce fruits, tomatoes, and flowers. There is some stone quarrying on the islands.

Tourism is a major source of income. Almost all trade is with Britain. The islands export farm products and import fuels, foodstuffs, and machinery.

GOVERNMENT. Each island is administered by an appointed bailiff responsible to a popularly elected assembly. An appointed governor represents the British crown.

HISTORY. The Channel Islands were part of the French duchy of Normandy during the Middle Ages. After the Norman conquest of England in 1066, the islands were ruled with England and Normandy. England gradually lost all of mainland Normandy, and by the 1500s the Channel Islands remained the British crown's sole Norman possessions.

In 1940, during World War II, the islands were occupied by German forces. The Germans deported many of the islanders and built extensive fortifications. The islands were liberated in 1945.

CHRISTMAS ISLAND

Status: Territory of Australia
Area: 52 square miles
Population: (1960 est.) 3,000

Christmas Island lies in the Indian Ocean some 200 miles south of the Indonesian island of Java. It is hilly, rocky, and rather barren. The climate is warm and dry. The island's small population is mostly Chinese and Malayan origins.

Phosphate rock is the island's only important resource, and the extraction of phosphate is the only economic activity.

The island is under the direct authority of the Australian government, which appoints a representative to administer local affairs.

Christmas Island was uninhabited when it was discovered in the 1600s by British sailors. In 1888 Britain formally annexed it and governed the island through the Colony of the Straits Settlements between 1889 and 1900, when it was incorporated into Singapore.

Phosphate extraction was begun in the early 1900s, using Chinese and Malay labor. In 1948 Australia and New Zealand bought out the private company that had mined the phosphate and agreed to joint operation of the phosphate work. In 1958 Britain transferred sovereignty over the island to Australia.

COCOS ISLANDS

Status: Territory of Australia
Area: 5.4 square miles
Population: (1966 est.) 1,000

The Cocos, or Keeling, Islands, in the Indian Ocean some 500 miles southwest of the Indonesian island of Java, consist of 27 small coral islands forming two atolls. The islands are low-lying and rather flat, with a warm climate and moderate rainfall. About

two-thirds of the population is of Malayan descent, and about one-third is European.

The cultivation of coconuts is the mainstay of the islands' economy, and the production of copra and coconut oil is the islands' only industry.

The islands are administered by an appointed representative of the Australian government.

Discovered in 1609 by Capt. William Keeling of the British East India Company, the islands remained uninhabited until 1826, when British and Malay settlements were established. Britain annexed the islands in 1857.

The Cocos Islands were governed through the colony of Ceylon between 1878 and 1882, when responsibility for them was placed with the Colony of the Straits Settlements. They were incorporated into the colony of Singapore in 1903 and were made an Australian territory in 1955.

COMORO ISLANDS

Status: Overseas territory of France
Area: 838 square miles
Population: (1965 est.) 220,000
Capital: Moroni (Pop., 1966, urban area, 11,515)

The Comoro Islands lie in the Mozambique Channel between the eastern coast of Africa and the island of Madagascar. The territory consists of four main islands—Mayotte, the southernmost, is 144 square miles, Anjouan is 164 square miles, Mohéli is 112 square miles, and Grande Comore, the northernmost, is 443 square miles.

THE LAND AND PEOPLE. The islands are of volcanic origin and consist of mountainous or deeply dissected plateau cores ringed by very narrow coastal plains. Coral reefs surround the islands. The climate is tropical.

Most of the people of the Comoro Islands are a mixture of Arab and African stocks, but there are Arabs, Indians, and Europeans. The language is Malagasy, which is spoken on Madagascar, and Islam is the predominant religion.

ECONOMY. The islands have almost no mineral resources, but their soil is very rich, and agriculture is the mainstay of the economy. Rice, corn, vegetables, and fruits are raised for local consumption. The chief commercial crops are vanilla, spices, coffee, sisal, and coconuts. Industry is limited to the processing of the agricultural products of the islands.

The Comoras trade mainly with France, Madagascar (the Malagasy Republic), and the United States. They export copra, vanilla, and spices. Imports consist primarily of foodstuffs, textiles, and metals.

GOVERNMENT. Executive power in the territory is wielded by an appointed high commissioner and by an appointed government council, which is responsible to a popularly elected territorial assembly. The islanders also elect two representatives to the French National Assembly.

HISTORY. The Comoro Islands have been known since ancient times and were conquered by Arabs in the 600s. In the 1500s they were visited by the

Portuguese, French, and Dutch, and the French established a settlement. In the 1800s the Arab kingdoms on the islands were attacked by Malagasy armies from Madagascar, and years of warfare followed. By the 1900s the rulers of the islands had ceded authority to France.

The French expanded agricultural production by opening plantations. In 1912 the islands were joined with Madagascar into a single French colony. In 1946 their status was changed to that of an overseas territory, and they were granted internal autonomy. In the 1960s a nationalist organization demanding complete independence caused unrest in the islands. The majority of the people were thought to favor no more than loose ties with France, which was responsible for economic and social improvements on the islands.

COOK ISLANDS

Status: Self-governing country in free association with New Zealand
Area: 90 square miles
Population: (1966 est.) 19,000

The Cook Islands, in the South Pacific Ocean some 2,000 miles northeast of New Zealand, consist of the Northern Group of seven islands and the Southern Group of eight islands. The Northern Group consists of low-lying, barren, coral atolls; the islands of the Southern Group are higher and fertile. The climate is hot and dry, and the islands are subject to hurricanes.

Population is concentrated on the Southern Group. Most Cook Islanders are Maori Polynesians, and there is a small group of Europeans.

Agriculture is the mainstay of the economy, with citrus fruits, bananas, pineapples, tomatoes, and coconuts the main commercial crops.

The islands have internal self-government under a prime minister responsible to an elected legislative assembly. New Zealand manages foreign affairs and defense.

The islands were discovered in 1773 by a Briton, James Cook. Britain made the islands a protectorate in 1888 and attached them to New Zealand in 1901.

British and New Zealander colonists established plantations on the islands, which were governed as a New Zealand territory until 1965, when they were granted internal self-government.

DOMINICA

Status: State in association with Britain
Area: 290 square miles
Population: (1966 est.) 68,000
Capital: Roseau (Pop., 1960, 10,417)

Dominica is one of the Windward Islands of the Lesser Antilles, lying between the Caribbean Sea and the Atlantic Ocean. It has a rugged, mountainous terrain. The climate is hot throughout the year, and rainfall is heavy.

Dominica's population is of mixed African, European, and Carib Indian descent. The people speak English and a Creole dialect.

The economy is agricultural. Bananas, limes and other citrus fruits, cacao, vanilla, and coconuts are the chief crops. The only industries process farm products and manufacture straw goods. Exports of bananas, copra, and lime juice are outweighed by imports of foodstuffs, machinery, and other necessities, and most of the limited trade is with Britain, the United States, and the other islands of the West Indies.

The island has internal self-government, with a council of ministers responsible to an elected assembly. An appointed administrator represents Britain.

The island was inhabited by Indians when discovered by Chistopher Columbus in the 1490s. Between the 1600s and the 1800s it was settled by colonists from several European countries. They developed plantations worked by imported African slave labor. In 1814 the island became British, and it was governed as part of the Leeward Islands until 1940, when it became a separate colony. In 1967 Dominica gained self-government as a state in association with Britain, and it joined the West Indies Associated States.

EQUATORIAL GUINEA

Status: (1966) Self-governing territory of Spain.
Area: 10,830 square miles
Population: (1966 est.) 272,000
Capital: Santa Isabel (Pop., 1960, 37,237)

Equatorial Guinea, formerly known as Spanish Guinea, consists of two provinces—Río Muni and Fernando Póo. Río Muni, on the west African mainland and adjacent islands, is bounded on the north by Cameroon, on the east and south by Gabon, and on the west by the Gulf of Guinea, an arm of the Atlantic Ocean. Fernando Póo occupies two islands and several islets in the Gulf of Guinea. Fernando Póo, the larger island, is about 20 miles northwest of Río Muni; Annobón, the smaller, is some 370 miles southwest of the mainland province.

THE LAND. In Río Muni, a coastal plain fives way some 12 miles inland to a higher, rolling plateau, which rises in the east to a hilly region. Fernando Póo consists of two volcanoes separated by a narrow valley. Its coastline is steep except in the southwest, where there is an excellent harbor at San Carlos. Annobón is also volcanic in origin, and has a rugged terrain.

The climate of the territory is tropical, with high heat and humidity throughout the year.

THE PEOPLE. Most of the people of Fernando Póo are descended from the islands' native people, the Bubes. There are also Europeans and other Africans. Most of Río Muni's population is part of the Fang people. There are people of other African tribal groups and a small number of Europeans. Río Muni's population is nearly triple Fernando Póo's.

Catholicism is the predominant religion, although there are some Protestants, Muslims, and people who have

held to traditional religions. Spanish is the official language, but a number of African languages are spoken.

ECONOMY. Equatorial Guinea's economy is chiefly agricultural, and its mineral resources remained largely unexplored and unexploited in the mid-1960s. The main products are cacao, grown in Fernando Póo, and coffee, timber, and forest products from Río Muni. There is little manufacturing.

Most of Equatorial Guinea's products are exported to Spain, which furnishes needed imports, although West Germany, Britain, and the United States purchase some items.

GOVERNMENT. Equatorial Guinea became self-governing in 1963. Executive power is vested in an Executive Council, which is chosen by a popularly elected legislature. The Spanish government is represented by a commissioner general and retains final authority in most matters.

HISTORY. Little is known of the history of the region before it was visited by Europeans. The islands of Fernando Póo and the nearby mainland were discovered in the 1470s by the Portuguese, and they remained Portuguese until 1778, when they were ceded to Spain. Possession of the mainland was disputed until 1900, when the Treaty of Paris granted Río Muni to Spain. Spanish settlers established plantations using African laborers.

In the 1950s and 1960s Spain's goal was the improvement of the welfare of the people, the expansion of the economy, and the incorporation of the territory into the Spanish nation.

After the granting of internal self-government in 1963, however, various political groups developed, some favoring independence or incorporation into Cameroon, same favoring separation of Fernando Póo and Río Muni, and some favoring the maintenance of the system introduced in 1963. In 1967 Spain and Equatorial Guinea convened a constitutional conference to plan the territory's future.

—Hibberd V. B. Kline, Jr.;
Vera L. Zolberg

FAEROE ISLANDS

Status: Self-governing national community within the Danish kingdom
Area: 540 square miles
Population: (1966 est.) 37,000
Capital: Thorshavn (Pop., 1964, 7,447)

The Faeroe Islands, in the North Atlantic Ocean midway between Norway and Iceland, lie some 250 miles north of Scotland. They consist of 17 islands separated by narrow channels.

THE LAND AND PEOPLE. The islands are generally low-lying and grass-covered, with interior hills and many lakes. The climate is mild and damp. The people are descended from early Scandinavian settlers, and speak Faeroese, a dialect of Old Norse, although Danish is also spoken.

ECONOMY. Fishing and whaling are the major economic activities of the islands. Sheepherding is the most important agricultural occupation. The processing of fish and wood-working are the islands' main industries. Fish constitute the bulk of the islands' exports, which are shipped largely to Britain, Italy, and Brazil. Necessities are imported from Denmark and Britain.

GOVERNMENT. The Faeroe Islands have internal self-government under a popularly elected assembly, which chooses an administrative council. The islands also send representatives to the Danish legislature.

HISTORY. The Faeroe Islands were settled in the 900s AD by Viking navigators from Norway, and they became part of the kingdom of Norway. In 1390, the islands came under Danish control.

During World War II Denmark was occupied by German forces, and the Faeroes were occupied by Britain. A nationalist movement developed, and after the war the Faeroes demanded independence. In 1948 they were granted autonomy within the Danish kingdom and were permitted to use their own currency and flag. In the 1950s and the 1960s the islands concentrated on improving their economy by modernizing the fishing fleet and expanding fish processing facilities.

FALKLAND ISLANDS

Status: British crown colony
Area: 4,618 square miles
Population: (1966 est.) 2,000
Capital: Stanley (Pop., 1962, 1,074)

The Falkland Islands lie in the South Atlantic Ocean off the southeastern coast of Argentina. They consist of East Falkland and West Falkland, which are separated by the Falkland Strait, and many smaller islands.

The islands are hilly and grass-covered, and their climate is cool and rainy. Almost all of the population is of British origin. Sheep raising is the chief economic activity, and sealing and whaling are important. The colony's only industries process sheep, seal, and whale carcasses and hides for export to Britain.

The colony is administered by an appointed governor and a small elected council. Its two dependencies, South Georgia and South Sandwich islands to its east, house whaling, sealing, and meteorological stations.

A British explorer first sighted the islands in 1592. In the 1760s France settled East Falkland and later ceded it to Spain. Britain occupied West Falkland. All the settlements soon were abandoned, and in the 1820s Argentina colonized the islands. In the 1830s Britain occupied both islands, but Argentina continued to claim them.

FIJI ISLANDS

Status: British colony
Area: 7,015 square miles
Population: (1967 est.) 490,000
Capital: Suva (Pop., 1965 est., 60,000)

The Fiji Islands, consisting of two large islands, Viti Levu and Vanua Levu, many islets, and numerous atolls, lie in the South Pacific Ocean about 1,000 miles north of New Zealand.

THE LAND AND PEOPLE. The islands are coral-rimmed and consist primarily of densely forested volcanic mountains deeply etched by rapid rivers. The climate is tropical, with high year-round heat and humidity.

Nearly three-quarters of the people live on Viti Levu. The population is divided between Fijians, a Melanesian people, and people of East Indian origin. There are small groups of Europeans and Chinese. English is the official language.

ECONOMY. The islands have good forest resources, some gold deposits, and rich farmland in river deltas. Agriculture is the mainstay of the economy, with fruits, sugarcane, coconuts, cacao, and rice the chief commercial crops.

Forestry, gold mining, and the processing of agricultural products are the chief industries. There is some boat building and repair.

Agricultural products are the main exports, and manufactured goods, fuels, and equipment are imported. Britain, Australia, and Japan are the islands' major trading partners.

GOVERNMENT. The islands are internally self-governing under an executive council that is responsible to a partially elected legislature, in which the Fijian and Indian groups are represented proportionately. An appointed governor represents the British crown.

HISTORY. Little is known of the islands before they were discovered in the 1600s by the Dutch. They were virtually ignored by Europeans until the 1700s, when traders came in search of sandalwood, coconut products, and other exotic goods. The traders were followed by Christian missionaries, who converted many of the islanders.

Tribal warfare raged on the islands in the mid-1800s, and in 1874 the tribal chiefs ceded power to Britain. Plantations were established in the late 1800s, and East Indian laborers were imported to work them. The islands' economy prospered on farming and forestry. The East Indians soon grew to be a majority of the population, and disputes between the Indians and Melanesians continued into the mid-1900s. In 1966 a constitution came into effect that divided representation between them in an effort to settle the ethnic conflict.

FRENCH GUIANA

Status: Overseas department of France
Area: 35,135 square miles
Population: (1966 est.) 37,000
Capital: Cayenne (Pop., 1961, urban area, 18,235)

French Guiana, on the northeastern coast of South America, is bordered on the north by the Atlantic Ocean, on the east and south by Brazil, and on the west by Surinam (Dutch Guiana).

THE LAND. A narrow, low, swampy plain, the Terres Basses ("the Lowlands") skirts the coast. The interior, the Terres Hautes ("the Uplands"), is an eroded granite plateau. Dense rain forest almost completely covers the country, and many rivers flow from the interior. The climate is tropical, with high temperatures throughout the year and abundant rainfall.

THE PEOPLE. Most of the population is of mixed African and European descent, but groups of Negroes and American Indians inhabit the interior. About half the population lives in Cayenne, the capital and major port.

ECONOMY. Guiana is rich in bauxite, and there are deposits of gold, manganese, nickel, copper, and molybdenum. The forests contain valuable wood. Farmland is limited, but cassava, corn, breadfruit, and sugarcane are grown, and cattle, goats, hogs, and poultry are raised. Efforts to expand and diversify agriculture were underway in the 1960s. River and offshore fishing is profitable. Mining and logging are the major industries. There are paper mills, sawmills, and food processing plants. Other industries were being started in the mid-1960s, as exploitation began of the country's excellent hydroelectric potential. There are numerous scientific research stations in the country, including an international space research installation. French Guiana's exports consist largely of minerals and lumber. Exports are far outweighed by imports, mostly foodstuffs and manufactures. Most trade is with France.

GOVERNMENT. Guiana is administered by an appointed prefect with the advice of a popularly elected assembly. The department elects representatives to the French National Assembly.

HISTORY. Guiana has been inhabited for many hundreds of years by American Indians. Christoper Columbus sighted the Guiana coast in 1498, and rumors of fabulous treasures in the interior attracted adventurers from all parts of Europe in the 1500s. In the early 1600s Frenchmen established a settlement at present-day Cayenne and gained trading rights to a large part of the interior.

French possession was reaffirmed in 1814, when the boundaries of Guiana were set. In 1848 full French citizenship and universal suffrage were granted to the inhabitants. In the mid-1800s France established prison colonies in Guiana. The most notorious was on Devil's Island, a small island off the coast. In 1945 the prison colonies were abolished, and in 1946 Guiana was made an overseas department of France.

During the 1950s and 1960s Guiana concentrated on expanding its economy and improving the standard of living of its people.

—David Bushnell

FRENCH POLYNESIA

Status: Overseas territory of France
Area: 1,544 square miles
Population: (1966 est.) 90,000
Capital: Papeete, Tahiti (Pop., 1960 est., 16,000)

French Polynesia, in the South Pacific Ocean, consists of 130 islands divided into 5 archipelagos.

THE LAND. The Society, Marquesas, Gambier, and Austral groups are of volcanic origin and consist of rugged, mountainous cores encircled by narrow coastal plains and ringed by coral reefs. The Tuamotu Archipelago and Clipperton Island, attached to the Austral group, are low-lying, barren, coral atolls. The climate is hot, humid, and windy throughout the year.

THE PEOPLE. Most of the islanders are Maori Polynesians. There are some Asians and a few Europeans. Population is concentrated in the Society Islands, especially on Tahiti, near the center of the territory.

ECONOMY. Agriculture and the mining of phosphates are the main economic activities of the islands. The phosphates are found on the Tuamotu atoll. The soil of the islands is very rich, and coconuts, vanilla, coffee, tropical fruits, and vegetables are raised. There is some fishing, and mother-of-pearl shells are collected.

The processing of phosphates, coconuts, and foodstuffs are the main industries. The islands' limited trade consists of the export of phosphates, copra, and vanilla to France, New Zealand, and Japan, and the import of manufactured goods, foodstuffs, and fuels from France and the United States.

GOVERNMENT. The islands are administered by an appointed governor and by a government council chosen by a popularly elected legislature. The islanders elect representatives to the French National Assembly.

HISTORY. The scattered islands of French Polynesia have been inhabited for many centuries by Polynesian peoples. They were discovered by Europeans during the 1500s, 1600s, and 1700s. European traders and missionaries came to the islands, and in the early 1800s the islands placed themselves under French protection. By 1880 all the islands of the group had become French colonies.

French settlers expanded agriculture and took responsibility for the health and education of the islanders. In 1946 Polynesia was made an overseas territory of France, and in 1958 the islanders voted to retain their territorial status.

FRENCH SOUTHERN AND ANTARCTIC TERRITORIES

Status: Overseas territory of France
Area: 2,918 square miles
Population: No permanent population

The French Southern and Antarctic Territories consist of the Crozet and Kerguelen archipelagos, Ile Amsterdam, and Ile St. Paul, all in the Indian Ocean, and Terre Adélie, a region on the Indian Ocean coast of Antarctica.

The territory is barren and frigid. The only inhabitants are members of the French scientific research teams, and St. Paul is totally uninhabited. The territories are under the authority of an appointed administrator and council which sits in Paris.

St. Paul was discovered by Portuguese seamen and Amsterdam by Ferdinand Magellan in the 1500s. Frenchmen discovered the Crozet and Kerguelen archipelagos in the 1700s, and a Frenchman, Dumont D'Urville, explored Terre Adélie in the 1840s.

FRENCH GOVERNMENT TOURIST OFFICE

TAHITI, the largest and most famous of French Polynesia's more than 100 islands.

The territories remained uninhabited through the mid-1900s, although France opened research stations in Terre Adélie in 1947 and on Amsterdam in 1950.

FRENCH TERRITORY OF THE AFARS AND THE ISSAS

Status: Overseas territory of France
Area: 8,494 square miles
Population: (1961 est.) 81,200
Capital: Djibouti (Pop., 1963 est., urban area, 43,200)

The French Territory of the Afars and the Issas, formerly French Somaliland, is bordered on the north by Ethiopia and the Red Sea; on the east by the Bab al Mandab strait, the Gulf of Tadjoura, an inlet of the Gulf of Aden, and the Somali Republic; and on the south and west by Ethiopia.

THE LAND. Most of the territory is desert. The interior is a low, rolling desert basin. North of the Gulf of Tadjoura, the Mabla and Gouda mountains rise to a peak of just under 6,000 feet. Their slopes hold the territory's only forests. The coastline is low and flat except along the southern shore of the Tadjoura gulf, which is steep. The climate is hot and dry.

THE PEOPLE. The original inhabitants of the region are Issa Somalis and the Hamitic Afar people. There are now large minorities of Arabs and Europeans. Almost all the people are Muslim, and they speak French, Afar, Arabic, and Somali. Most of the Issas and Afars are semi-nomadic, and the only cities are along the coast.

ECONOMY. The territory's strategic location at the mouth of the Red Sea insures its economic importance. Its only known mineral resource is salt, which remained largely unexploited in the mid-1960s. Herding, especially of goats, is the chief activity of the people. Some farming is possible with irrigation near the coast, and vegetables, melons, and dates are the main crops. Shipbuilding and construction are the only industries.

Trade is the mainstay of the economy. A modern port at Djibouti, the capital, is an important refueling, storage, and distribution point for Red Sea and Indian Ocean commerce. Most of the country's own small trade consists of the importing of necessities from France.

GOVERNMENT. Territorial administration is under the direction of the Head of the Territory, appointed by the French government. He is assisted by a government council chosen by a popularly elected territorial assembly, which has authority over local matters. The territory elects two representatives to the French National Assembly.

HISTORY. The region has been inhabited for many years by the semi-nomadic Issas and Afars. In 1862 Afar chiefs ceded power to the French government, and by 1869, several French trading settlements and ports that had been established on the coast were prosperous.

Treaties signed in the 1880s with the Afars and the Issas extended French authority, and in 1896 the territory became known as the colony of French Somaliland. Djibouti rapidly became an important port and refueling station, and in the early 1900s a railroad was built between it and the capital of Ethiopia.

In 1946 the colony was made an overseas territory, and in 1956 it was granted internal self-government. In the 1950s and 1960s France initiated programs to improve education and welfare in the territory and to broaden its economy. In 1967, acting on a request by the territorial assembly, the French National Assembly changed the name French Somaliland to the more accurate French Territory of the Afars and the Issas. In a 1967 referendum the people voted to remain under French control. The Issas, however, generally favored independence whereas the Afars opposed it. Ethiopia and the Somali Republic challenged the fairness of the vote, and rioting broke out after the election.

—Hibberd V. B. Kline, Jr.;
Vera L. Zolberg

GIBRALTAR

Status: British crown colony
Area: 2.3 square miles
Population: (1966 est.) 25,000
Capital: Gibraltar (Pop., 1964 est., 24,836)

Gibraltar, occupying a small peninsula on the southern coast of Spain, is bordered on the north by Spain, on the east by the Alboran Sea, an arm of the Mediterranean, and on the south and west by the Strait of Gibraltar.

THE LAND AND PEOPLE. The flat sandy terrain of the northern part of Gibraltar gives way in the south to the 1,400 foot Rock of Gibraltar, which overlooks the sea. The limestone rock is filled with caves, and shrubs grow on its surface. Gibraltar's climate is warm and rather dry.

Most of the population is of Italian, Portuguese, Maltese, and Spanish origins. There is a large group of British government and military personnel and many non-resident Spanish workers who commute to the colony daily. English is the official language, and Spanish is widely spoken.

ECONOMY. Gibraltar has no natural resources and no useable farmland, and the colony depends heavily on tourism, transit trade, and its excellent harbor and drydock facilities. A British naval base contributes heavily to the economy.

GOVERNMENT. The colony is administered by an appointed governor, who is also the commander of the military base. He is assisted by a partially elected executive council and a partially elected legislative council.

HISTORY. Because of its strategic location and fortress-like defenses, Gibraltar has been important since ancient times. It was occupied by Carthaginians, Romans, and Visigoths before being captured in 711 by Muslim forces under the general Tariq, for whom the rock was named Jabal Tariq (Tariq's Mountain), or Gibraltar.

Spain conquered the rock in 1462 and held it until 1704, when a joint Dutch-British force captured it. By the Treaty of Utrecht in 1713 Britain gained title of Gibraltar, which it made into a fortress and naval base.

In the 1960s Spain intensified efforts to regain possession of the rock, but in a 1967 referendum Gibraltar's residents voted to remain a British colony rather than join Spain.

GILBERT AND ELLICE ISLANDS

Status: British colony
Area: 342 square miles
Population: (1967 est.) 56,000
Capital: Tarawa (Pop., 1965, 7,911)

The Gilbert and Ellice Islands colony consists of 35 islands scattered across more than 2 million square miles of the South Pacific Ocean. It includes the 16 Gilbert, nine Ellice, three Line, and six Phoenix islands, and Ocean Island. Two additional Phoenix islands, Canton and Enderbury, and five other Line islands are under separate administrations.

THE LAND AND PEOPLE. All but one of the islands are low-lying, coral atolls. The exception, Ocean Island, is of volcanic origin with a rather rugged, mountainous terrain. The islands' climate is hot and humid year-round, with rainfall ranging from 40 to 120 inches annually.

The people of the Gilbert Islands are Micronesian; Ellice islanders are Polynesian. The Phoenix Islands are uninhabited, and the Line group and Ocean Island are peopled by Gilbert and Ellice islanders, Chinese, and Europeans. Population is concentrated on Ocean Island and in the Gilberts.

ECONOMY. Ocean Island has rich deposits of lime phosphate, and phosphate mining is the primary source of income. Coconuts grow on the other islands, and copra production is important.

GOVERNMENT. The colony is governed by an appointed commissioner with the aid of appointed islanders, who administer the affairs of each island.

HISTORY. Many of the islands have been inhabited for centuries by Polynesian and Micronesian peoples. The first Europeans to sight them may have been Spanish sailors in the 1500s, but it is certain that most were discovered in the late 1700s and early 1800s by British seamen.

Britain proclaimed the Gilbert and Ellice islands a protectorate in 1888, and added Ocean Island in 1900. At the request of the islanders, they annexed them as a colony in 1916. The other islands were added to the colony between 1916 and 1938. British settlers established copra plantations, and the British government has used the islands as cable stations, ports, and radar stations.

The Gilbert Islands were the scene of heavy fighting in World War II. After the war, efforts were made to expand the economy of the islands, extend self-government, and relieve population pressure on the crowded islands.

GREENLAND

Status: Province of Denmark
Area: 840,003 square miles
Population (1966 est.) 41,000
Capital: Godthab (Pop., 1960, 3,179)

Greenland, the world's largest island, lies off the northwestern coast of North America. It is bounded on the north by the Arctic Ocean, on the east by the Greenland Sea, on the south by the Atlantic Ocean, and on the west by Davis Strait and Baffin Bay.

THE LAND. Greenland consists of a high interior plateau rimmed with mountains. The coastline is irregular and deeply indented. Most of the island lies north of the Arctic Circle and is covered with thick ice. Vegetation is limited to the southern coastlines. The climate is quite cold and dry throughout the year. The southwestern coast has the most moderate climate.

THE PEOPLE. The island is very thinly populated, and most of the people live on the southwestern coast. Native Greenlanders, who form the bulk of the population, are Eskimo or of Eskimo-Danish descent. There is also a large group of Danish settlers, scientists, and administrators. Greenlandic, an Eskimo dialect, is the official language, but Danish is also widely spoken on the island.

ECONOMY. The island's mineral resources are largely unexplored, but Greenland is the world's leading source of cryolite, used in glassmaking and aluminum processing, and it has deposits of lead, zinc, uranium, molybdenum, and coal. Fishing and sealing are the main occupations of the people. Sheep herding is important, and there is some farming. Mining and fish processing are the only important industries. The island is also the site of military bases and scientific research stations.

The island's trade balance is poor, with exports earning $13 million in 1965 and imports costing $34 million. Cryolite, fur, and fish products are exported, and foodstuffs, textiles, machinery, and fuels are imported. Most trade is with Denmark.

GOVERNMENT. Greenland is a province of Denmark and is administered by an appointed commissioner and a popularly elected national council. Greenlanders send two representatives to the Danish parliament.

HISTORY. Inhabited for many hundreds of years by Eskimos, Greenland was settled in the 900s AD by Scandinavians under Eric the Red. In 1261 the Greenlanders yielded their independence to the Norwegian crown. European settlements slowly died out, and by the 1500s had completely disappeared. In the 1700s a new colonization was undertaken, principally by Danes, and by the Treaty of Kiel in 1814 the island formally became a Danish colony.

It remained relatively undeveloped until World War II, when Denmark was occupied by German forces. Greenland remained free and was used by Allied forces for important military bases. After the war, Denmark expanded health, welfare, and educational programs for the islanders and began to develop the economy. In 1951 the United States and Denmark agreed to jointly defend the island, and U.S. and NATO military bases and observation posts were established there. In 1953 Greenland became a province of Denmark. Military operations and meteorological research expanded rapidly during the 1960s.

—Sergio Barzanti

GRENADA

Status: State in association with Britain
Area: 133 square miles
Population: (1966 est.) 97,000
Capital: St. George's (Pop., 1960, 7,303)

Grenada is one of the Windward Islands of the Lesser Antilles, which lie between the Caribbean Sea and the Atlantic Ocean. It has a mountainous terrain. The climate is hot throughout the year and rainfall is heavy. The population is of mixed African, European, and Carib Indian origin.

Grenada's economy is based on agriculture. Cocoa, nutmegs, mace, and bananas are the chief crops. Processing these products constitutes the only industry. There is limited trade with Britain and the United States, which supply the island with textiles, flour, and equipment.

Grenada has internal self-government under a council of ministers responsible to an elected legislative assembly. An appointed administrator represents Britain.

The island was inhabited by Indians when discovered by Christopher Columbus in the 1490s. Colonists from several European countries settled in Grenada in the 1600s and 1700s. They established plantations worked by slaves brought from Africa. In 1814 the island became British.

Grenada was governed as a unit with the other Windward Island colonies until 1967, when it gained self-government as a state in association with Britain.

GUADELOUPE

Status: Overseas department of France
Area: 686 square miles
Population: (1967 est.) 320,000
Capital: Pointe-à-Pitre (Pop., 1954, urban area, 26,160)

Guadeloupe is one of the Windward Islands of the Lesser Antilles, which lie between the Caribbean Sea and the Atlantic Ocean.

Guadeloupe consists of two adjacent islands, Basse-Terre and Grande-Terre, and four smaller islands to the east.

Basse-Terre is mountainous, with rugged terrain and a steep shoreline. Grande-Terre is low and rocky with a deeply indented coast. The climate is warm and humid throughout the year. Annual rainfall ranges from less than 40 inches on the easternmost island to nearly 400 inches on Basse-Terre's highest elevations. The population, mostly of mixed African and European origin, is growing rapidly.

The economy is based on agriculture. Sugarcane and bananas are the main commercial crops. Sugar refining and distilling are the only important industries. Most of the islands' limited trade is with France and nearby French islands.

The department is administered by an appointed prefect with the assistance of a popularly elected assembly. Guadeloupe is represented in the French National Assembly.

Guadeloupe was discovered by Christopher Columbus in 1493 and first settled in 1635 by Frenchmen. In 1674 France annexed the islands and developed plantation agriculture, employing slaves imported from Africa. Slavery was abolished in the early 1800s and universal suffrage introduced in 1848. In 1946 Guadeloupe was made an overseas department of France.

HONG KONG

Status: British crown colony
Area: 398 square miles
Population: (1966 est.) 3,732,000
Capital: Victoria (Pop., 1961, urban area, 674,962)

Hong Kong is situated on the South China Coast 80 miles southeast of the Chinese city of Canton. It is bordered on the north by China, on the east and south by the South China Sea, and on the west by China's Pearl River. The colony includes the island of Hong Kong and Stonecutters Island, and on the Chinese mainland, Kowloon and the New Territories. Victoria Channel separates the two most important parts of the colony, Kowloon and the capital and port city of Victoria on tiny Hong Kong island.

THE LAND AND PEOPLE. The colony consists almost entirely of urban areas and hilly or swampy wasteland. It has a monsoon subtropical climate, with long, hot, and humid summers. Three-fourths of the annual rainfall of 85 inches falls between June and August, when the southwest monsoons prevail. Winters are temperate and very dry.

Chinese comprise 99 percent of Hong Kong's population. There are small Malay and British groups. Most of the Chinese are from adjacent areas of south China, and many settled in the colony after the 1949 Communist takeover of the Chinese mainland. The colony is densely populated—over 9,300 people per square mile in 1966 —and population pressure is accentuated by the fact that so much of the land is hilly and unusable for food production or habitation.

ECONOMY. Commerce, finance, and industry are the bases of the colony's economy. There is virtually no agriculture, although reclamation projects were begun in the 1960s to increase farmland. The original basis for the economy of the colony was its port and entrepot function. It has the best harbor facilities between Shanghai and Singapore, and it serves as a distribution point for most of Southeast Asia.

With government encouragement, entrepreneurs who fled China in 1949 used their technical skill and capital to make manufacturing an important part of the economy. Textile weaving is the major industry. Shipbuilding and iron and steel working are important, and many small industries developed, so that by the beginning of the 1960s about 40 percent of the goods shipped from Hong Kong were manufactured there.

Although the colony has a rather poor balance of trade, with exports earning $1,527 million in 1967 and imports costing $1,818 million, the deficit is made up by earnings from tourism and shipping. Chief exports are manufactured goods and textiles. Foodstuffs, raw materials, and equipment are imported. Hong Kong's principal trading partners are the countries of Southeast Asia, China, Britain, the United States, and Japan.

GOVERNMENT. An appointed governor and executive council administer the colony. They are assisted by an appointed legislative council including members of the colony's ethnic and interest groups.

HISTORY. Hong Kong was a part of China until the rocky island was ceded to Britain "in perpetuity" in 1842. It rapidly grew in importance as the best port for Western trade with China. In 1860 the colony was extended to include Kowloon and Stonecutters Island, and in 1898 the New Territories were leased from China for 99 years. The Chinese revolution of the 1920s and the Sino-Japanese war of the 1930s increased Hong Kong's importance as a safe and stable port for Asian trade.

In 1941, during World War II, the colony fell to Japanese forces after a stiff resistance, but Britain reoccupied it in 1945. Long an outpost of British colonial conservatism, the character of the colony changed after the Chinese Communists took power on the mainland in 1949 and many thousands of Chinese fled to the colony. Although this immigration greatly increased the prosperity of Hong Kong, the nearness of the Communist regime posed a constant threat to the colony.

In the mid-1960s China's Communist government increased its pressure on Britain by inciting riots and terrorism in the colony.

—Thomas E. Ennis; George Inaba

IFNI

Status: Overseas territory of Spain
Area: 579 square miles
Population: (1964 est.) 52,000
Capital: Sidi-Ifni (Pop., 1960, 12,751)

Ifni, a Spanish enclave in the northwestern coast of Africa, is bounded on the north, east and south by Morocco and on the west by the Atlantic Ocean.

THE LAND AND PEOPLE. Ifni is arid and mountainous. The climate is dry, with moderate temperatures. The population consists almost entirely of Berber-speaking Muslims.

PAN AMERICAN
HONG KONG, on the south China coast, has one of the finest natural harbors in the world.

ECONOMY. Ifni is a poor country. The people subsist on farming and herding. Barley, corn, wheat, and some fruits are grown, and goats, sheep, cows, and camels are raised. Industry is limited to handcrafting such items as carpets, furniture, and jewelry. Ifni's limited trade consists of importing necessities from Spain.

GOVERNMENT. Ifni's administration is in the hands of an appointed governor-general responsible to the government of Spain.

HISTORY. Ifni has been inhabited for many centuries by semi-nomadic Berber-speaking peoples. It was a part of Morocco until 1860, when Morocco ceded the territory to Spain after a Spanish military victory over Morocco.

In 1912 international treaties reaffirmed Spain's possession of Ifni, but Spain did not occupy the enclave until 1934. Spain then established schools and hospitals, built roads, and initiated agricultural improvement projects in the province.

Morocco, after it became independent in 1956, claimed sovereignty over Ifni, and in the 1950s and 1960s Ifni was attacked several times by Moroccan forces. In 1966 the UN General Assembly formally requested Spain to cede Ifni to Morocco, but no action was taken.
—L. Carl Brown;
Hibberd V. B. Kline, Jr.

ISLE OF MAN

Status: Dependency of the British crown
Area: 227 square miles
Population: (1966 est.) 50,000
Capital: Douglas (Pop., 1961, 18,821)

The Isle of Man is a large, rugged island in the Irish Sea between England and Northern Ireland.

THE LAND AND PEOPLE. The Isle of Man consists of a mountainous core that rises to a peak of 2,034 feet, rimmed on the north and east by a narrow coastal plain. In the west, it drops sharply to the sea. The climate is rather warm and dry due to the warm Gulf Stream flowing around it.

The people are of English and Scandinavian origin, with a strong Celtic strain. Manx, a Celtic language, was traditionally the language of Man, but its use declined in the mid-1900s as English became dominant.

ECONOMY. Agriculture is the mainstay of the economy, with oats, wheat, and barley the chief crops. Livestock, especially sheep, are herded. Stone quarrying is the main industry, and wool is woven. Tourism is of some importance. The island's limited trade is entirely with the other British Isles.

GOVERNMENT. The Isle of Man has an ancient traditional form of democracy, and is almost completely independent of the British government. Executive power is wielded by the Court of Tynwald, which consists of a governor appointed to represent the crown; the island's bishop; its "First Deemster," or chief judge; the attorney general; two appointees; and five members elected by the House of Keys, the legislature. The House is popularly elected.

HISTORY. The Isle of Man was settled by Celts in the first centuries AD and remained independent until it was conquered by the Danes in the 800s. In 1266 Denmark ceded it to Scotland, and in 1399 the British crown gained possession.

By the 1400s it had developed its own culture, different from that of the other British Isles, and its people continued in their traditional ways of life. Periodic demands were made in the 1800s and 1900s for independence, but no serious negotiations were undertaken.

MACAO

Status: Overseas province of Portugal
Area: 6 square miles
Population: (1965 est.) 280,000
Capital: Macao (Pop., 1960, 161,252)

Macao, on the Macao peninsula of eastern China, is bounded on the north and west by China, on the east by the mouth of China's Pearl River, and on the south by the mouth of the Hsi River. The province consists of the city of Macao and the islands of Taipa and Colôane in the Pearl River.

The province is hilly. Macao is almost completely urban, but the islands are densely forested. The climate is rather hot and humid. With the exception of a small group of Portuguese and others, the population is Chinese.

Macao's excellent harbor and its many light industries that specialize in finishing Chinese goods are the backbone of the economy. Although there is some fishing, there is almost no agriculture and most food must be imported. Most of the province's exports originate in China. Tourism adds to the earnings derived from trade.

Macao is administered by an appointed governor and is represented in the Portuguese National Assembly.

Portugal made its first settlement on Macao in the 1550s, with Chinese permission. Although China revoked its permission when Portugal began treating Macao as a possession, the Portuguese refused to leave and the dispute continued into the 1800s. In 1833 Portugal made Macao an overseas province. In 1849 it convinced China to make Macao a free port, and in 1887 China ceded Macao to Portugal without defining the boundaries.

Macao prospered in the early 1900s. After the Communist regime gained power in China in 1949, the province's fortune declined somewhat as trade with China decreased and as refugees from China flooded the tiny enclave. By the mid-1960s Portugal held little but formal power in Macao. After Chinese-incited rioting in 1967, provincial leaders yielded to China's demands for control over the province and agreed to ban activities of anti-Communist Chinese groups.

MARTINIQUE

Status: Overseas department of France
Area: 425 square miles
Population: (1967 est.) 330,000
Capital: Port-de-France (Pop., 1954, urban area, 60,648)

Martinique is one of the islands of the Lesser Antilles, which lie between the Caribbean Sea and the Atlantic Ocean. It is of volcanic origin, with a generally hilly to mountainous terrain. The climate is warm and humid throughout the year. Annual rainfall ranges from less than 40 inches on the southern coast to nearly 200 inches on the mountains. The population is of mixed African, European, and Carib Indian descent.

Agriculture, especially the cultivation of bananas, sugarcane, and pineapples, is the mainstay of the economy. The processing of agricultural products constitutes the islands' main industry, and agricultural products make up the bulk of exports. Most trade is with France.

Martinique is administered by an appointed prefect with the assistance of a popularly elected legislative council. The island is represented in the French National Assembly.

Martinique was discovered by Christopher Columbus in 1502. It was first settled in 1635 by Frenchmen, and was annexed by France in 1674. Plantations were established, and Africans were brought to the island as slaves. Slavery was abolished in the 1800s and universal suffrage introduced in 1848. In 1946 the island was made an overseas department of France.

BRITISH TRAVEL ASSOCIATION
ISLE OF MAN. The famous lighthouse is at Douglas, the capital city and chief port.

MONTSERRAT

Status: British colony
Area: 38 square miles
Population: (1966 est.) 14,000
Capital: Plymouth (Pop., 1960, 1,911)

Montserrat is one of the Leeward Islands of the Lesser Antilles, which lie between the Caribbean Sea and the Atlantic Ocean. Montserrat is situated between the islands of Nevis and Guadeloupe.

The island consists of a rocky, forested, mountainous spine flanked on the east and west by coastal lowlands. The climate is warm throughout the year, and rainfall is abundant. Most of the population is of mixed African and European origin.

Cotton is the mainstay of the economy. Some sugarcane is raised for rum, and fruits and vegetables are grown. Cotton ginning and rum making are the only important industries, although there is some tourism. The trade balance is poor with imports of necessities outweighing exports of cotton and sugar. Most trade is with Britain and the United States.

The colony is administered by an appointed governor with the advice of a partly-elected legislative council.

The island was discovered by Columbus in 1493 and settled by Irish colonists in 1632. It formally became a British colony in 1783 and was governed as a unit with other British West Indian territories until 1962, when it received its own administration.

MOZAMBIQUE

Status: Overseas province of Portugal
Area: 302,328 square miles
Population: (1966 est.) 7,040,000
Capital: Lourenço Marques (Pop., 1960, 177,-929)

Mozambique, on the eastern coast of Africa, is bounded on the north by Tanzania, on the east by the Mozambique Channel and the Indian Ocean, on the south by Swaziland and South Africa, and on the west by Rhodesia, Zambia, and Mali.

THE LAND. Most of the long, irregularly shaped land consists of a flat or rolling plateau, ranging from 800 to 2,000 feet in elevation. In the east a narrow lowland skirts a coast, and in the west a zone of high plateaus and mountains reaches a peak of nearly 8,000 feet. The most important of the country's many rivers are the Zambezi, which crosses central Mozambique, and the Limpopo, in the south.

The climate is hot and humid along the coast, especially in the north. Temperatures are moderate in the interior, which is also drier.

THE PEOPLE. About 98 percent of Mozambique's population is African. Europeans comprise about 1.5 percent, and the remainder is of Chinese, Indian and Pakistani, and mixed background. Most of the Africans belong to a variety of Bantu-speaking tribes.

Portuguese is the official language, but many African languages are more commonly spoken. Most of the people follow traditional religions, but there are large numbers of Muslims and Roman Catholics.

ECONOMY. Mozambique is a very poor land, with a primarily agricultural economy. Its mineral resources have not been fully exploited, although some coal, bismuth, bauxite, and other minerals are mined. The forests that cover some 90 percent of the land remained uncut, and Mozambique's vast hydroelectric power potential was virtually unexploited in the mid-1960s.

Farming is especially productive in the river valleys and in the north, where sugarcane, cotton, corn, copra, tea, sisal, manioc, fruits, and vegetables are raised, mostly on large, European-owned commercial plantations. Cashew nuts grow wild and are picked for sale. Restrictions imposed by the government on food crops until 1961 severely damaged Mozambique's traditional agriculture, but recovery had begun by the mid-1960s.

Industry is limited to the processing of agricultural products, the milling of cotton textiles, and the manufacture of such items as rope, soap, cement, and leather goods. An important contribution to the economy is made by money earned by Mozambique laborers hired to work in the mines of neighboring Rhodesia and South Africa.

Mozambique has a very poor balance of trade. In 1966 imports cost $208 million and exports earned only $112 million. Nuts, cotton, sisal, sugar, and copra are among the leading exports, and machinery, vehicles, fuels, and industrial raw materials are among the imports. The bulk of the country's overseas trade is with metropolitan Portugal.

GOVERNMENT. Mozambique is constitutionally a province of Portugal. Its government is administered by a governor-general appointed by the Portuguese cabinet, and he is advised by an economic and social council representing various interest groups, such as business and labor. Limited legislative power is vested in a small elected legislative council, and Mozambique elects members to the Portuguese National Assembly. Tribal leaders unofficially retain considerable local authority.

HISTORY. Mozambique has been inhabited for many centuries by Bantu-speaking peoples. Between the 900s and 1300s sophisticated city states, such as Sofala, developed on the basis of iron and gold exports to Asia and the Arab world. When the Portuguese, the first Europeans to reach the region, arrived in the early 1500s, Arab trading colonies had been established along the coast. In the 1530s the Portuguese sacked the coastal trading cities and broke the trade network established with Africa and India. The Portuguese established a monopoly over sea trade and explored the interior.

Unsuccessful in their search for gold and silver, the Portuguese turned to the slave trade for revenue. The slave trade had been carried on before the arrival of the Europeans, but the Portuguese expanded it, and it soon became the colony's most profitable enterprise.

Soldier-settlers, called *prazeros*, established petty chieftainships in the interior. They seized African villages, which they converted into peasant colonies and ruled independently of Portuguese authority. Slavery was legally abolished in 1878, but the labor situation scarcely changed. *Prazeros* kept their slaves, but referred to them as "contractual laborers." Local officials cooperated with the *prazeros* by declaring unemployed Africans vagrants and thus eligible to be forced into contracts requiring them to work for the Europeans.

In the 1930s Portugal tightened its control over its colonies. The government took over the exploitation of the colonies' resources.

In 1951 Mozambique's status was changed to that of an overseas province, and in 1961 Portugal granted its African inhabitants full Portuguese citizenship, with an announced goal of integrating all the country's overseas provinces into Portuguese national life. Although some reforms were initiated in 1961 to improve the welfare and education of the Africans, little progress was made. Forced labor continued in many places, and African political rights were limited. Poverty, illiteracy, and disease remained common.

In the 1960s, the United Nations and many countries, and some groups within Mozambique increased pressure on Portugal to improve conditions in the colony and to grant Mozambique self-determination. In the 1960s, with support from other African states, a Mozambique nationalist liberation organization developed and in 1964 began a rebellion against Portugal. Guerrilla warfare, concentrated in the north, continued through the 1960s despite an increase in Portuguese military strength in Mozambique.

—Hibberd V. B. Kline, Jr.;
Robert I. Rotberg

NETHERLANDS ANTILLES

Status: Autonomous part of the kingdom of the Netherlands
Area: 371 square miles
Population: (1967 est.) 212,000
Capital: Willemstad, Curaçao (Pop., 1966, 343,700)

The Netherlands Antilles consists of six islands in the Caribbean Sea. The islands of Arbua, Bonaire, and Curaçao lie off the northwest coast of Venezuela, on the South American mainland. They are part of the Leeward Islands. Saba, St. Eustacious, and St. Maarten, which is shared with France, are in the Windwards, some 200 miles east of Puerto Rico.

THE LAND. The larger islands, in the Leeward group, are generally flat, except for a mountainous region on northern Bonaire, and arid or semiarid. The small Windward Islands are mountainous, rather moist, and densely forested. Temperatures on all the islands average in the 80°s F. throughout the year.

THE PEOPLE. The people of the Netherlands Antilles are of varied origins. Negroes and people of mixed background predominate on Curaçao and Bonaire. The population of Aruba is of Carib Indian and European descent, and the Windward Islands are populated primarily by Europeans and Negroes.

Roman Catholicism is the predominant religion on the Leeward Islands; Protestantism on the Windward Islands. Dutch is the official language, but Papiamento, a dialect combining Dutch, Spanish, and African and Indian tongues, is spoken.

ECONOMY. The islands have no important mineral deposits, and the larger islands have poor soils. Fruits, sugarcane, and some vegetables are raised on the eastern islands, and there is fishing off the coasts.

The mainstays of the economy, however, are the income derived from tourism and the operation of two large oil refineries on Curaçao and Aruba that process crude oil shipped from Venezuela. These refineries are the only important industries, although the government is attempting to attract other businesses to the islands. In 1966 exports earned $592 million and imports cost $616 million. Oil is exported to Western Europe and North America, and foodstuffs, machinery, textiles, and other necessities are imported, mostly from the Netherlands and Caribbean nations.

GOVERNMENT. The Netherlands Antilles is administered by an appointed governor and council, whose powers are limited by a popularly elected legislature. Each island has authority over local matters and the administration is headed by an appointed lieutenant governor.

HISTORY. The islands of the Netherlands Antilles were discovered in the late 1400s and early 1500s by Spanish navigators. They were successively occupied and claimed by Spain, Portugal, Britain, and the Netherlands. They were formally ceded to the Dutch in 1815 by the Treaty of Paris.

From the first, Curaçao was the most important island, and in the 1700s and 1800s it was a center for the Caribbean slave trade. The island declined in importance when slaving was abolished in the 1860s, but its status rose again after 1916, when the Royal Dutch Shell Company built a refinery there.

In 1954 the islands' status was changed from that of a colony to that of a self-governing region within the kingdom of the Netherlands. In the 1950s and 1960s economic expansion became the main concern of the islands' government.

NEW CALEDONIA

Status: French overseas territory
Area: 7,336 square miles
Population: (1966 est.) 93,000
Capital: Nouméa (Pop., 1960 est., 30,000)

New Caledonia is an island in the South Pacific Ocean about 1,115 miles east of Australia. The nearby Loyalty Islands, the Isle of Pines, and the Huan and Chesterfield archipelagos are dependencies of New Caledonia.

THE LAND AND PEOPLE. New Caledonia has an area of 6,530 square miles and consists of rather high, rugged, forested mountain cores. There are fertile valleys and a plains area in the west. The island is encircled by coral reefs. The Isle of Pines and the three Loyalty Islands

are coral and filled with caverns. Huan and Chesterfield are low-lying atolls. The climate is mild throughout the year.

The population is divided almost evenly between the Australo-Melanesian aboriginal people of New Caledonia and people of European origin. There are also groups of temporary workers from Asian lands.

ECONOMY. New Caledonia is rich in minerals, especially nickel, chrome, iron, and manganese, and mining is the chief source of income. There are also abundant, well developed hydroelectric power resources.

The territory of New Caledonia also has rich farmlands. Coffee and coconuts are the chief commercial crops, and rice, fruits, and vegetables are grown for local food needs. There are also large numbers of cattle, pigs, and other livestock. Metal processing is the chief industry, and the processing of agricultural products is also important. The island's trade is profitable, based on the export of nickel and other metals.

GOVERNMENT. The territory is administered by an appointed high commissioner and a government council. There is a popularly elected territorial assembly, and the islands are represented in the French National Assembly.

HISTORY. New Caledonia has been inhabited by Melanesian peoples for many centuries. In 1768 a French navigator was the first European to visit New Caledonia, which was named in 1774 by an English sailor.

Between the 1790s and 1820s the French explored the islands, and in 1844 France claimed them. In 1853 they became a French colony. Mines and plantations were opened in the late 1800s and early 1900s. In 1946 the colony was made an overseas territory of France, and in 1958 the islands' assembly voted to retain territorial status.

NEW GUINEA

Status: UN trust territory under Australian administration
Area: 92,159 square miles
Population: (1966 est.) 1,582,000

The trust territory of New Guinea consists of the northeastern quarter of the Southwest Pacific island of New Guinea, the islands of the nearby Bismarck Archipelago, Bougainville and Buka islands, and some 600 smaller nearby islands. The islands lie just north of Australia.

The mainland territory is bordered on the north by the Bismarck Sea, on the east by the Solomon Sea, on the south by the Territory of Papua, and on the west by the Indonesian region of West Irian.

THE LAND AND PEOPLE. The surface of northeastern New Guinea rises sharply from a swampy interior lowland to peaks of over 14,500 feet. Some of the mountains are active volcanoes. Many of the islands are encircled by coral reefs.

The climate of New Guinea is hot throughout the year and humid at lower elevations. Rainfall ranges from 45 inches to 245 inches a year.

AUSTRALIAN NEWS AND INFORMATION BUREAU

NEW GUINEA. Outrigger canoes under sail.

Indigenous Melanesian peoples form a majority of the territory's population, and there are groups of Australians, Europeans, and Asians. The population is concentrated in northeastern New Guinea and on the larger islands of New Britain and New Ireland.

ECONOMY. Although there are petroleum deposits in the territory, agriculture is the mainstay of the economy. Most farms are owned by the New Guineans and islanders. Copra, rubber, coffee, and cocoa are the chief commercial crops. Sisal, spices, hemp, tobacco, sugarcane, tobacco, and other crops are also raised for export.

Food production is insufficient for local needs. Industry is limited to the processing of agricultural products.

GOVERNMENT. Australia administers the trust territory as a unit with the Australian territory of Papua, in southeastern New Guinea. An appointed commissioner manages the territory with the assistance of local commissioners and with the advice of a partially elected legislative assembly.

HISTORY. New Guinea and the adjacent islands have long been inhabited by Melanesians. Spanish and Dutch sailors visited them in the 1600s, but no European settlement was made until 1828, when the Dutch occupied western New Guinea.

After a German company began trading in eastern New Guinea, Queensland, Australia, annexed the territory in 1882 without British approval. In 1884 Britain established a protectorate over southeastern New Guinea and Germany established a protectorate over North East New Guinea.

In 1914, at the beginning of World War I, Australian troops occupied German New Guinea. In 1921, after Germany had been defeated in the war, the League of Nations gave Australia a mandate over the German territory. In 1945, after World War II, the territory was made a UN trusteeship under Australian administration.

In the 1950s and 1960s Australia initiated projects to develop the territory's natural resources and improve agriculture. Popular participation in government was expanded, and in 1964 an elected assembly was introduced.

NEW HEBRIDES

Status: Condominium of Britain and France
Area: 5,700 square miles
Population: (1966 est.) 70,000
Capital: Vila (Pop., 1962 est., 3,700)

The New Hebrides, a chain of approximately 80 islands, extends across the southwestern Pacific for some 400 miles.

THE LAND AND PEOPLE. The islands are of volcanic origin and have rugged, mountainous interiors rimmed by low coastal plains. The climate is hot and humid throughout the year. Most of the islanders are Melanesian, and there are people of British and French origin.

ECONOMY. The economy is agricultural, with coconut palms and coffee the chief commercial crops. Yams, bananas, and manioc are grown for local consumption. Large herds of cattle are raised, and there is considerable fishing. Industry is limited to the processing of farm products, hides, and fish.

GOVERNMENT. The islands are governed jointly by Britain and France through the French governor of New Caledonia and the British governor of Fiji, each of whom is represented in the islands by a commissioner.

HISTORY. The New Hebrides have been inhabited for many centuries by Melanesian peoples. European planters and traders began visiting the islands after their discovery in 1606 by the Spanish.

By the mid-1800s British and French settlers outnumbered other Europeans, and in 1887 the two nations formed a joint commission to protect their mutual interests. In 1906 the condominium was established. In the mid-1900s projects were undertaken to modernize and expand the islands' economy and to improve the health and welfare of the islanders.

NIUE

Status: Territory of New Zealand
Area: 100 square miles
Population: (1967 est.) 5,000

Niue, an island of the Cook Archipelago in the South Pacific Ocean, is so far from the other islands of the group that it is administered separately.

Niue is a low-lying, rather barren, coral island with a hot, dry climate. Hurricanes are frequent. The population is overwhelmingly Polynesian, but there are a few Europeans and New Zealanders.

Coconuts, sweet potatoes, and bananas are the major crops, and industry is limited to the processing of agricultural products.

The island is administered by an appointed commissioner with the advice of an appointed council of islanders.

Niue was inhabited by Polynesian peoples when it was discovered in the 1770s by the British. With the other Cook Islands, it became a British protectorate in 1888 and was made part of New Zealand in 1901. The island received its own administration in 1903.

NORFOLK ISLAND

Status: Territory of Australia
Area: 14 square miles
Population: (1966 est.) 1,000

Norfolk Island lies in the South Pacific Ocean about 600 miles east of Australia. It is hilly and covered with lush vegetation. The climate is mild throughout the year. Most of the people are of British descent.

Norfolk has fertile soil and valuable forests. Citrus fruits, vegetables, bananas, and beans are raised commercially, and forestry is of increasing importance. Tourism is a major source of income.

The island is governed by an appointed administrator with the assistance of an appointed council of islanders.

Norfolk Island was discovered in 1774, and in the late 1700s and early 1800s it served as a British penal colony. In 1856 descendants of mutineers from the British ship *Bounty* migrated to Norfolk from Pitcairn island.

Norfolk was administered as part of the colony of New South Wales, in Australia, until 1913, when it was placed under the authority of the Australian Minister of Territories. The island's economy expanded in the mid-1900s with the encouragement of tourism and the development of Norfolk's natural resources.

PAPUA

Status: Territory of Australia
Area: 86,099 square miles
Population: (1966 est.) 601,000
Capital: Port Moresby (Pop., 1965 est., 42,000)

The Papua Territory consists of the southeastern quarter of the South Pacific island of New Guinea, or Papua proper, and the Trobriand, Woodlark, D'Entrecasteaux, and Louisiade archipelagos lying off the east coast of New Guinea.

Papua proper is bordered on the north by the Territory of New Guinea and the Solomon Sea, on the east and south by the Coral Sea, and on the west by the Indonesian region of West Irian.

THE LAND AND PEOPLE. The interior and eastern tip of Papua proper are extremely mountainous, but there are lowlands in the south and west. There are many rivers. The islands are also mountainous, and coral reefs ring Papua and most of the islands.

Indigenous Melanesian peoples form the bulk of the population. There are also Europeans and Asians.

ECONOMY. The economy of the territory is based on agriculture, and coconuts, cacao, coffee, and rubber are the chief commercial crops. There is also commercial forestry and fishing. Most industries process the territory's agricultural products, but light manufacturing was developing in the 1960s.

GOVERNMENT. Papua forms an administrative unit with the territory of New Guinea and is governed by an appointed commissioner with the advice of a partially elected assembly and elected local councils.

HISTORY. New Guinea and the adjacent islands were inhabited by Melanesian peoples when they were first visited by the Spanish and Dutch in the 1600s. No settlement was made until 1828, when the Dutch occupied the western half of New Guinea. In 1882, after a German company had begun trading in eastern New Guinea, Queensland, Australia occupied Papua without British approval, but in 1884 Britain made southeastern New Guinea a protectorate, as British New Guinea. Australia was given sovereignty over the area in 1905.

New Guinea was occupied by Japanese forces in the 1940s, during World War II. After the war, economic development projects were begun. Forestry and fishing were developed, and new industries were started. Popular participation in government also increased, and in 1964 a representative assembly was introduced.

PITCAIRN ISLAND

Status: British colony
Area: 1.9 square miles
Population: (1966) 92

Pitcairn, a small, isolated island in the southeastern Pacific, is of volcanic origin and mountainous. The climate is warm throughout the year. The people are of mixed British and Polynesian origin.

Subsistence agriculture and fishing are the main economic activities. Fruit and handcrafts are sold to passing ships.

The governor of Fiji has authority over the island, but actual administration is in the hands of a small island council.

Discovered in 1767 by a French explorer, the island remained uninhabited until 1790, when mutineers from the British ship *Bounty* settled there with a few Tahitian men and women. In 1856, when over-crowding became a problem, the islanders were moved to Norfolk Island, but in the 1860s some of them returned to Pitcairn. Three tiny uninhabited adjacent islands were annexed in 1902.

In 1959 responsibility for the island was shifted from the Western Pacific High Commissioner to the governor of Fiji. In the 1960s emigration outpaced natural growth, and the population began to decrease.

PORTUGUESE GUINEA

Status: Overseas province of Portugal
Area: 13,948 square miles
Population: (1966 est.) 529,000
Capital: Bissau (Pop., 1950, urban area, 18,309)

Portuguese Guinea lies on the western coast of Africa. It is bounded on the north by Senegal, on the east and south by Guinea, and on the west by the Atlantic Ocean.

THE LAND. Portuguese Guinea consists of a mainland, with a deeply indented coast, and a number of offshore islands, including those of the Bijagos archipelago. Most of the province consists of low coastal plain, much of which is swampy. In the east is a higher, drier savanna region.

There are many rivers and streams, and the Cacheu, Mansoa, Geba, and Crubal rivers have large deltas. The climate is characterized by high temperatures and extreme humidity.

THE PEOPLE. Most of the population is African, and there are small groups of Portuguese and mulattoes, people of mixed African and European origin. The Africans are members of many tribal groups, including the Balante, Mandyako, and Malinke.

Many languages are spoken, including Portuguese and African languages, but a Creole patois is the most commonly understood tongue. Roman Catholicism, Islam, and traditional religions are all represented.

ECONOMY. Portuguese Guinea is an agricultural land, and the standard of living is very low. The country's forests are exploited for their timber. The main commercial crops are palm kernals and peanuts raised on European-owned plantations. Basic food crops include rice, millet, coconuts, manioc, beans, and bananas. There is little industry.

Almost all of the province's limited trade is with Portugal. Peanuts and palm kernels are the chief exports, and machinery and consumer goods are imported.

GOVERNMENT. Constitutionally a province of Portugal, Portuguese Guinea is administered by a governor-general appointed by the Portuguese national government.

A cabinet assists the governor in his executive functions, and a small, partly elected legislative council advises him as well. Tribal chieftains unofficially exercise authority in the localities.

HISTORY. Portuguese sailors were the first Europeans to visit present-day Portuguese Guinea, in 1446, and Portugal established trading posts and ports at the mouth of the rivers and on the Bijagos islands. In the late 1400s the region was made a dependency of the nearby Portuguese colony of Cape Verde Islands. From the late 1500s through the mid-1800s the colony prospered from the slave trade.

Portugal occupied only coastal portions of the territory, and sent very few permanent settlers. In the 1800s Portuguese claims to the region were disputed by Britain and France. In the late 1800s agreement was reached on the division of west-central Africa among the European powers, and Portuguese control of the area was formally recognized.

Portuguese attempts to control the interior led to rebellions among the Africans, angered by Portugal's participation in the slave trade. The rebellions were put down by 1915, and Portuguese settlers expanded their plantations in the colony. In the 1930s colonial administration was centralized.

In 1951 the colony was made an overseas province. Portugal did little to develop the economy and virtually ignored the education, health, and general welfare needs of the African population. Forced labor, under the "contract labor" system, remained the rule. In 1961 Portugal did, however, formally grant full Portuguese citizenship to African Guineans.

With encouragment from neighboring African states, a national liberation movement developed in the early 1960s and in 1961 began a rebellion for independence. By the mid-1960s the rebel leaders claimed control over most of the country and its people, and the Portuguese armed forces had been unable to quell the uprising.

In 1968 Portugal's president, Americo Rodrigues Thomas, visited Portuguese Guinea to reaffirm Portuguese sovereignty in the face of the widespread rebellion.

—Hibberd V. B. Kline, Jr.;
Robert I. Rotberg

PORTUGUESE TIMOR

Status: Overseas province of Portugal
Area: 146 square miles
Population: (1966 est.) 560,000
Capital: Dili (Pop., 1960, 52,158)

Portuguese Timor consists of the eastern half of the Southeast Asian island of Timor in the Malay Archipelago, several smaller islands, and an enclave, Ocussi-Ambeno, on the Savu Sea coast of the western half of Timor island, surrounded by Indonesian Timor.

Portuguese Timor proper is bounded on the north by the Ambai Strait, on the east by the Wetar Strait, on the south by the Timor Sea, and on the west by Indonesian Timor.

THE LAND AND PEOPLE. A central spine of mountains in Timor proper is flanked by coastal plains. The climate in the coastal areas is hot and humid. The climate in the mountains is moderate and rainfall is heavy most of the year.

The bulk of the varied population is native to the island and similar to Indonesian and Melanesian peoples. There are also Chinese, Arabs, Africans, Europeans, and people of mixed origins.

ECONOMY. Despite the availability of rich forest and agricultural resources, the main economic activity is subsistence farming. Coffee, copra, and rubber grown for exports are shipped to Portugal. Manufactured items are imported from Japan and Hong Kong.

GOVERNMENT. An appointed governor administers the province. Representatives are elected to the Portuguese National Assembly.

HISTORY. Timor was inhabited for many centuries by island peoples before Portugal established its first settlement there in the 1500s. The Dutch disputed the Portuguese presence on Timor, and a boundary dividing the island between the two countries was not established until 1850. Disputes continued into the 1900s, however.

In the 1940s, during World War II, Timor was occupied by Japan, but Portugal regained control in 1945. In the 1960s Portugal introduced economic and social development projects.

RÉUNION

Status: Department of France
Area: 969 square miles
Population: (1967 est.) 418,000
Capital: Saint-Denis (Pop., 1961, 65,614)

Réunion is a mountainous tropical island in the Indian ocean, east of Madagascar and southwest of Mauritius. Its population is of Indian, French, Chinese, Southeast Asian, and African origins. The island is densely populated, and the rate of population growth is extremely high.

The island's economy is based on the cultivation and processing of sugarcane and making perfume essences. Most foodstuffs must be imported. Trade is mainly with France.

Government is in the hands of an appointed prefect and a popularly elected council. The island sends representatives to the French National Assembly.

Réunion was uninhabited when it was discovered in 1528 by the Portuguese. The first settlers were Frenchmen who arrived in the early 1600s, and in the late 1600s France claimed it as Bourbon Island. Immigration increased rapidly from France, Africa, and Asia, and the island's plantations prospered. Its name was changed to Réunion in 1793. In 1946 it became a department of France.

FRENCH EMBASSY PRESS & INFORMATION DIV.

RÉUNION'S CAPITAL, Saint-Denis, lies on the north coast of the French Indian Ocean island.

ST. HELENA

Status: British colony
Area: 121 square miles
Population: (1965 est.) 5,815
Capital: Jamestown (Pop., 1958 est., 1,600)

St. Helena and its two dependencies, Ascension and Tristan de Cunha, are islands in the Atlantic Ocean off the west coast of Africa. Ascension, the northernmost of the three, lies about 1,000 miles off the coast of Angola. St. Helena is about 600 miles to the southeast, and the Tristan de Cunha group lies approximately 1,000 miles southwest of St. Helena.

All the islands are mountainous. St. Helena is inhabited by descendents of Portuguese, British, and Dutch settlers. Its economy is agricultural, with flax the main crop. Rope-making is the island's only industry. Most trade is with Britain and South Africa.

St. Helena's two dependencies are only sparsely inhabited. Ascension is important as a cable station and satellite and missile tracking station. Of the four islands of the Tristan De Cunha group, only Tristan de Cunha is inhabited. Its people are descendants of early British settlers. Catching, canning, and freezing crayfish is the basis of the island's economy.

An appointed governor, aided by a partially elected council, administers the islands from St. Helena.

HISTORY. St. Helena was uninhabited when discovered by the Portuguese in 1502. The British and the Dutch both claimed it until 1673, when the British gained possession of it. St. Helena was the site of the French emperor Napoleon I's exile between 1815 and 1821.

Ascension was discovered by the Portuguese in 1501, but it remained uninhabited until a British garrison was placed on the island in 1816 to guard Napoleon on St. Helena. During the 1800s it was an important port on the sea route around Africa. During World War II it was the site of a vital airbase.

Tristan de Cunha was also first settled by soldiers of a British garrison established in 1816. Its inhabitants thrived on the crayfish industry until 1961, when a volcano on the island erupted and devastated the community. After temporary relocation in Britain, the islanders returned in 1963 and rebuilt their homes and factories.

ST. KITTS-NEVIS-ANGUILLA

Status: State in association with Britain
Area: 3,435 square miles
Population: (1966 est.) 58,000
Capital: Basse-Terre (Pop., 1960, 15,726)

St. Kitts-Nevis-Anguilla, three islands in the Leeward Islands of the Lesser Antilles, lie between the Caribbean Sea and the Atlantic Ocean. St. Kitts (St. Christopher) and Nevis are adjacent. Anguilla lies some 50 miles to their north, beyond several French and Dutch islands.

THE LAND AND PEOPLE. St. Kitts and Nevis have mountainous, rugged interiors rimmed by lowlands or bluffs. Coral-rimmed Anguilla is generally flat and low-lying. The climate is warm throughout the year, and about 55 inches of rain falls each year. The people are mostly of mixed African and European descent.

THE ECONOMY. The cultivation of sugarcane and cotton is the mainstay of the economy. Plantation agriculture predominates on St. Kitts, but small farms are the rule on the other islands. Sugar refining and cotton processing are the only important industries. Tourism was of increasing importance in the 1960s.

The islands' limited trade consists of exporting sugar, molasses, and cotton and importing foodstuffs and other necessities. Britain and the United States are the islands' major trading partners.

GOVERNMENT. The islands are self-governing, with an appointed governor as nominal chief executive. Actual powers are wielded by an executive council responsible to a small, popularly elected legislative assembly.

HISTORY. The islands were discovered in 1493 by Christopher Columbus. In 1623 St. Kitts was the site of the first British settlement in the West Indies, and Nevis was settled in 1628. St. Kitts was shared with France until 1783, when the three islands became British possessions. In 1871 the islands were made part of the federated Leeward Islands colony, which in 1958 joined the Federation of the West Indies.

The federation was dissolved in 1962, and in 1967 St. Kitts-Nevis-Anguilla became a single self-governing state in association with Britain. Anguilla proclaimed its independence in 1967 but was prevented from breaking away.

ST. LUCIA

Status: State in association with Britain
Area: 238 square miles
Population: (1966 est.) 5,000
Capital: Castries (Pop., 1960, 4,353)

St. Lucia is one of the Windward Islands of the Lesser Antilles chain, which lies between the Caribbean Sea and the Atlantic Ocean. It has a rugged, mountainous terrain. The climate is hot throughout the year, and rainfall is abundant. The population is of mixed African, European, and Indian origin.

Agriculture is the mainstay of the economy, and bananas, copra, cocoa, and spices are the chief commercial crops. Processing these crops constitutes the islands' industry. The bulk of exports go to Britain, the United States, and nearby islands. Imports are fertilizer, fuels, machinery, and other manufactured goods.

St. Lucia has internal self-government under a council of ministers responsible to an elected assembly. An administrator represents Britain.

St. Lucia was inhabited by Indians when it was discovered by Europeans in the late 1400s. It was settled in the 1600s by colonists from several European countries. They established plantations worked by slaves brought from Africa in the 1700s. St. Lucia became a British colony in 1814 and gained self-government in 1967.

ST. PIERRE AND MIQUELON

Status: Overseas territory of France
Area: 93 square miles
Population: (1966 est.) 6,000
Capital: St. Pierre

St. Pierre and Miquelon consists of three islands and several islets in the Atlantic Ocean off the southern coast of Newfoundland, Canada.

The islands' terrain is generally rocky and hilly, with many swamps and peat bogs. The climate is cold and damp. The islands are peopled by the descendants of early French settlers.

Fishing is the mainstay of the economy, and cod is the most important catch. Fish processing is the main industry. Fish and fish products constitute the bulk of exports, and most necessities must be imported. The islands trade mainly with France, the United States, and Canada.

An appointed administrator governs the territory with the assistance of a popularly elected council. The islands send representatives to the French National Assembly.

The islands were probably first discovered in the 1000s, but the first permanent settlement was made by Frenchmen in 1604. In 1713 the islands were ceded to Britain, and the small group of settlers was deported. France regained possession in 1783, and the colony grew slowly. In 1946 the islands were made an overseas territory, and in a referendum in 1958 the inhabitants voted to retain that status.

ST. VINCENT

Status: State in association with Britain
Area: 150 square miles
Population: (1966 est.) 90,000
Capital: Kingstown (Pop., 1960, 2,339)

St. Vincent is one of the Windward Islands of the Lesser Antilles, which lie between the Caribbean Sea and the Atlantic Ocean. It consists of a heavily forested spine of mountains flanked by coastal plains. The climate is hot throughout the year and rainfall is abundant. The people are of mixed African, European, and Indian origin.

The economy is based on agriculture. Bananas, arrowroot, copra, cotton, fruits, spices, and yams are the chief crops. Processing of these crops is the main industrial activity, but development of harbor and fishing facilities was undertaken in the 1960s. Exports of farm products are outweighed by imports of foodstuffs, raw materials, and machinery.

St. Vincent has internal self government under a council of ministers responsible to an elected assembly. An appointed administrator represents Britain.

Inhabited by Indians when discovered by Christopher Columbus in the 1490s, St. Vincent was settled in the 1600s by Europeans from several countries. They established plantations worked by slaves brought from Africa. The island became a British colony in 1814 and was governed with the other Windward Islands until 1967, when it gained self-government.

SÃO TOMÉ AND PRINCIPE

Status: Overseas province of Portugal
Area: 372 square miles
Population: (1964 est.) 59,000
Capital: São Tomé (Pop., 1960, 5,714)

The islands of São Tomé and Principe and their offshore islets lie some 124 miles off western Africa in the Gulf of Guinea, an arm of the Atlantic Ocean.

THE LAND AND PEOPLE. The islands are volcanic in origin and consist of a hilly, forested interior ringed by a wide, flat, coastal plain. The climate is extremely hot. The humidity is high, and rainfall is heavy.

São Tomé, the southern island, has nearly 15 times as many inhabitants as the slightly smaller Principe. Most of the permanent population is descended from Portuguese and African settlers, but in the mid-1900s temporary workers from other Portuguese provinces in Africa outnumbered the native population. Portuguese is the major language, and Roman Catholicism the religion of most of the people.

ECONOMY. The island province has a rather prosperous economy based primarily on the cultivation of cacao. Copra, coffee, and palm trees are also important commercial crops. Industry is limited to the processing of agricultural products.

The standard of living of the islanders is quite high in comparison with the low levels of most of Portuguese Africa. Because of poor working conditions on the plantations, however, labor must be imported.

The province's trade is balanced. In 1965, for example, exports earned $5 million and imports cost $5 million. Cacao, palm and coconut products, and coffee are exported. Food, textiles, and other necessities are imported. The Netherlands, the United States, Britain, and Portugal are the main markets, and imports come largely from Portugal and Portuguese provinces in Africa.

GOVERNMENT. An appointed governor administers the province, which sends representatives to the Portuguese National Assembly.

HISTORY. The islands were discovered by the Portuguese in the 1470s and in 1522 were made a Portuguese colony. Emigrants from Portugal and people from western Africa settled the islands, and cocoa plantations prospered.

In 1951 the colony was incorporated into the Portuguese nation as an overseas province. In 1966 Portugal arrested and imprisoned a group of island nationalists for anti-government activities.

SEYCHELLES

Status: British crown colony
Area: 156 square miles
Population: (1965 est.) 48,000
Capital: Port Victoria, Mahé (Pop., 1960, urban area, 10,504)

The Seychelles Archipelago consists of about 90 islands and islets in the Indian Ocean, some 1,000 miles east of Africa. The largest is Mahé. Others include Silhouette, Praslin, La Digue, and Curieuse.

THE LAND. Most of the smaller islands are coral, barren, and uninhabitable. The large ones consist of a mountainous, forested interior ringed by a low, flat coastal plain. The climate is warm, with heavy rainfall.

THE PEOPLE. Population is clustered on Mahé and the other large islands. Most of the people are descendants of early French and African settlers. There are also people of British, Chinese, and Indian origin. The rate of population growth is rapid, about 3 percent a year between 1958 and 1966.

English and a Creole dialect are spoken. Roman Catholicism is the predominant religion.

ECONOMY. The islands are poor. Although large plantations produce coconuts, palms, and spices, most of the islanders subsist by farming small plots and fishing. Projects were undertaken in the 1960s to diversify agriculture and to expand fishing into a commercial activity.

The colony's industries process coconuts, palm kernels, and spices. A U.S. satellite tracking station established on the islands in the early 1960s contributes to the economy.

Exports of copra and other coconut products and spices are far outweighed by imports of foodstuffs, clothing, and other necessities. Most of the limited trade is with Indian Ocean coastal nations.

GOVERNMENT. An appointed governor administers the colony with the advice of a partly elected legislative council.

HISTORY. The Seychelles were uninhabited when discovered by the Portuguese in the early 1500s. They were not settled until the mid-1700s, when the French established communities on the islands and claimed them for France.

Britain received the islands in 1814 by the Treaty of Paris and administered them with the Mauritius colony until 1888, when the two were separated. In 1903 Seychelles became a crown colony.

In the mid-1900s popular participation in government was gradually increased. Political parties developed in the 1960s and concerned themselves mainly with improving the islands' economy.

SOUTH WEST AFRICA

Status: Territory administered by South Africa
Area: 318,259 square miles
Population: (1966 est.) 584,000
Capital: Windhoek (Pop., 1960, 36,051)

South West Africa is a large territory in southwestern Africa bounded on the north by Angola and Zambia, on the east by Zambia, Botswana, and South Africa, on the south by South Africa, and on the west by the Atlantic Ocean.

The status of South West Africa is disputed, for although the League of Nations mandated it to South Africa in 1920, The United Nations did not reaffirm the mandate and the United Nations does not recognize the authority that South Africa exercises over South West Africa.

THE LAND. A strip of low desert borders the Atlantic coast. The interior is a rugged, arid region of plains interspersed with mountains ranging from 3,000 to 6,500 feet in elevation. In the eastern third of the territory is the sand and limestone Kalahari Desert.

The climate is warm and very dry. There is little rainfall except for occasional, extremely heavy downpours in the central region.

THE PEOPLE. The vast majority of the population is African, belonging to a variety of tribal groups. There is a white minority and a small group of people of mixed origin. The Negro Africans speak a variety of African languages, and the whites speak English, German, and Afrikaans. Protestantism and traditional religions predominate.

The country is very sparsely populated, with only 2.6 persons per square mile in 1965. Most of the white population lives in the south, and Negro Africans are concentrated in the north.

ECONOMY. The territory's most valuable resource is diamonds. Other minerals that are mined include copper, lead, manganese, and zinc. Most of the people live by grazing goats, cattle, and sheep—especially the valuable karakul breed. Fishing is important on the coast.

Mining is the major industry, and the processing of fish, karakul skins, and meat is also important. Diamonds and other minerals and fish are exported, and foodstuffs and other necessities are imported through South Africa.

GOVERNMENT. An administrator appointed by South Africa directs the government with the advice of a legislative assembly elected by suffrage limited to whites. The white voters of the territory also send representatives to South Africa's national legislature.

The Apartheid, or segregation, laws of South Africa extend to South West Africa and restrict nonwhite South West Africans from significant participation in the control of the territory's government, economy, or social life.

HISTORY. South West Africa has been inhabited for many centuries. Its earliest known inhabitants were Khoisan peoples, the Bushmen, Bergdama, and Nama (Hottentot) peoples. In the 1500s they were joined by Bantu-speaking peoples—the agricultural Ovambo and the pastoral Herero groups.

Europeans first came to South West Africa in the 1700s. In 1884 Germany, which had established a port and trading colonies in the area, proclaimed it a German protectorate. In the early 1900s the Germans put down a series of uprisings by killing some 100,000 of the Africans.

In 1915, during World War I, South African troops conquered South West Africa. After Germany's defeat in the war, the League of Nations made South West Africa a mandate under the administration of South Africa. After the United Nations was formed in 1945 it reviewed the status of all mandated territories, but South Africa did not recognize UN authority and did not submit South West Africa for review.

In the 1950s and 1960s South Africa gradually incorporated South West Africa's administration into that of its own, and the territory became a part of South Africa in all but name.

A case brought before the international Court of Justice in 1962 by Ethiopia and Liberia charging a violation of South Africa's mandate was ruled invalid in 1966 because the plaintiff nations had no legal standing in the matter.

In 1966 the United Nations, which had officially terminated the mandate and had repeatedly censured South Africa for its handling of the territory, established a committee to study the problem of the territory's native population and to recommend a means by which it could achieve self-determination.

In 1967 South Africa placed on trial several African nationalists for terrorist activities in South West Africa. The trial was protested as invalid, but the terrorists were convicted in 1968.

—Hibberd V. B. Kline, Jr.;
Gary Weissmann

SPANISH SAHARA

Status: Overseas province of Spain
Area: 102,702 square miles
Population: (1964 est.) 48,000
Capital: El Alún (Pop., 1961 est., 5,500)

Spanish Sahara lies on the northwestern coast of Africa. It is bounded on the north by Morocco, on the east by Algeria and Mauritania, on the south by Mauritania, and on the west by the Atlantic Ocean.

THE LAND AND PEOPLE. The province is almost entirely desert or semidesert, and the climate is hot and dry. The people include Spanish, Arab, Berber, and some Negro groups.

Spanish Sahara is sparsely populated, with fewer than 1 person per square mile in 1966. The population is concentrated near the coast, although nomads roam parts of the interior.

ECONOMY. Spanish Sahara is rich in phosphates, which were first mined in the 1960s, and there are oil, iron, and other mineral deposits which remained unexploited. But in the mid-1960s fishing was the mainstay of the economy. Goats, sheep, and camels are raised, but there is almost no farming.

The chief industry is fish processing, and dried fish and other fish products are the major exports. Phosphates are also exported. Most trade is with Spain.

GOVERNMENT. Spanish Sahara is administered as a province of Spain by an appointed governor-general.

HISTORY. The region has been inhabited for many centuries. Spain established a port at Tarfaya on the coast in 1884 and in 1886 claimed a large region of the interior as a protectorate. Spanish claims were disputed by France.

In 1912 Spanish territory was defined in treaties which also divided Morocco into French and Spanish protectorates. In addition to the Spanish Sahara, it included southern Morocco and the enclave of Ifni, which was the capital of the entire region, called Spanish West Africa.

Morocco became independent in 1956, and the capital was moved to El Aiún, on the coast. In 1958 Spain ceded Tarfaya to Morocco.

Morocco and Mauritania both claim Spanish Sahara, and in 1966 the United Nations requested Spain, Morocco, and Mauritania to arrange for a referendum to permit the people of the territory to decide their future. No action was taken. In 1966 Spain established a commission to begin the social and economic development of the province.
—L. Carl Brown;
Hibberd V. B. Kline, Jr.

SURINAM

Status: Autonomous part of the Kingdom of the Netherlands
Area: 16,533 square miles
Population: (1966 est.) 350,000
Capital: Paramaribo (Pop., 1964, 110,876)

Surinam, or Dutch Guiana, is situated on the northeastern coast of South America. It is bordered on the north by the Atlantic Ocean, on the east by French Guiana, on the south by Brazil, and on the west by Guyana.

THE LAND AND PEOPLE. Surinam has a flat, narrow, fertile coastal plain and a hilly, forested interior, from which flow many rivers. The climate is warm and damp.

The population is of varied origins, but most of the people are of Indian, Indonesian, African, and mixed origins. There are some American Indians (Amerindians), Chinese, and Europeans. The population is growing at an extremely rapid rate, 4.4 percent a year between 1958 and 1965.

Dutch and Sranantongo, a local language, are the chief languages. Religious life is as diverse as the people, and there are Hindus, Muslims, Protestants, and Roman Catholics.

ECONOMY. Surinam has rich deposits of bauxite, from which aluminum is made, and excellent timber resources. Farming is important, and rice, sugar, cacao, fruits, and coffee are raised. Mining and forestry are the only important industries.

Exploitation of the country's hydroelectric resources was begun in the mid-1960s to prepare the way for the development of other industries, made necessary to keep pace with the rapid growth of population.

Surinam's balance of trade is poor. In 1965, for example, imports cost $95 million, and exports earned $58 million. Bauxite, timber, and fruits are exported, and foodstuffs, raw materials, textiles, and consumer goods are imported. The United States, the Netherlands, and Canada are Surinam's chief trading partners.

GOVERNMENT. Surinam is internally self-governing. The queen of the Netherlands appoints a governor, who functions as head of state. Executive power is exercised by a council of ministers, headed by a minister president, equivalent to a prime minister. The council is responsible to a popularly elected legislature, the Staten.

HISTORY. Surinam was first visited in the 1500s by Spaniards in search of gold. They abandoned the territory, and in the 1600s and 1700s it changed hands among Britain, the Netherlands, and France.

In 1815 the area was ceded to the Netherlands by the Treaty of Paris. The Dutch established plantations and began extensive mining and timber operations in the late 1800s and early 1900s, when they brought Indian and Indonesian laborers to Surinam.

During the 1900s Surinam gained an increasing measure of popular government, and in 1954 it became a self governing part of the Kingdom of the Netherlands. Surinam faced severe economic and social problems because of its rapid rate of population growth and the variety of ethnic groups comprising its population. In the 1950s and 1960s the government concentrated on expanding industry and improving agriculture.

SVALBARD AND JAN MAYEN ISLANDS

Status: Territory under Norwegian sovereignty
Area: 24,101 square miles
Population: (1965 est.) 3,000

The Svalbard Archipelago and Jan Mayen Island lie well above the Arctic Circle.

THE LAND AND PEOPLE. Jan Mayen, some 300 miles north of Iceland in the Greenland Sea, is rocky, mountainous, and barren. Tundra predominates on the eight islands and many islets of the Svalbard Archipelago. The climate is very cold and rather dry.

The Svalbard islands are sparsely populated by Norwegian and Soviet workers who mine the islands' rich coal deposits. Jan Mayen has no permanent population and serves only as the site of a Norwegian weather station.

NORWEGIAN EMBASSY INFORMATION SERVICE
SVALBARD. Coal mining is the key activity.

GOVERNMENT. The Svalbard islands are governed by an administrator appointed by the Swedish government, and the Soviet Union has jurisdiction over the mining areas. The manager of the Jan Mayen meteorological station has police power over that island.

HISTORY. Jan Mayen was discovered in the early 1600s by Henry Hudson and was rediscovered in 1611 by a Dutch whaler, Jan May. It was visited only by sealers and whalers until 1921, when Norway established a weather station on the island. In 1929 Norway gained sovereignty.

The Svalbard group was discovered by Norwegians in the 1100s and rediscovered in the 1500s by the Dutch. In the 1600s whale-hunting attracted sailors from the Netherlands, Britain, and Norway, and all three claimed the islands. The dispute ended in the 1700s when whaling declined. Russian and Norwegian fur trappers hunted on the islands through the 1800s.

Coal was discovered in the early 1900s, and possession of the islands was again disputed. A 1920 treaty gave sovereignty to Norway, and Norway ceded some mineral rights to the Soviet Union. In 1925 the islands were incorporated into the Norwegian state. In the 1960s French, Norwegian, Soviet, and U.S. prospectors began searching for oil.

TOKELAU ISLANDS

Status: Territory of New Zealand
Area: 3.8 square miles
Population: (1966 est.) 2,000

The Tokelau Islands lie in the South Pacific Ocean north of Western Samoa. They consist of three coral atolls—Atafu, Nukunono, and Fakaofo. The climate is hot and very wet, and hurricanes are frequent. The people are Polynesian.

Subsistence farming, fishing, and the production of copra are the only economic activities. The islands are under the authority of an appointed official with headquarters on Western Samoa. Local administration is by appointed islanders.

The Tokelau Islands were visited by the French in the 1760s, and in the 1800s Britain made them part of its Gilbert and Ellice Islands colony. New Zealand was given authority over the Tokelau Islands in 1925, and they were incorporated into New Zealand in 1949.

TONGA

Status: British protectorate
Area: 270 square miles
Population: (1966 est.) 77,000
Capital: Nuku'alofa (Pop., 1965, 9,202)

The Tonga, or Friendly, Islands lie in the South Pacific Ocean about 400 miles east of Fiji. They include about 150 small islands which form three major groups—Tongatapu, the largest, in the south; Ha'apai; and Vava'u, in the north.

THE LAND AND PEOPLE. Some of the Tonga Islands are volcanic in origin and have a mountainous, rugged terrain. Others are coral formations and are flat and low. Coral reefs ring most of the islands of the group. The climate is mild throughout the year and rainfall is moderate.

Tongans, a Polynesian people, make up about 99 percent of the population, and there are small groups of Europeans and other islanders. Tonga, a Polynesian language, and English are spoken, and most of the people are Protestant.

ECONOMY. The Tongan economy is based on agriculture. Coconuts, bananas, melons, and pineapples are the main commercial crops, and taros, yams, fruits, and corn are grown for local consumption. Pigs and cattle are raised, and there is some fishing.

With no mineral resources other than a small quantity of building stone, and no important fuel resources, the islands' only industry is copra production. Tonga exports copra and fruit and imports foodstuffs, fuels, and machinery. New Zealand, Japan, and Britain are its major trading partners.

GOVERNMENT. Tonga is a constitutional monarchy with a hereditary king as chief of state. An administrative council assists the king and is responsible to a popularly elected legislative assembly.

Tonga is under the protection of Britain, which is responsible for foreign affairs and defense. Britain is represented in the islands by a commissioner.

HISTORY. Traditional Tongan history extends back to the 900s, at the least, when it is said the first Tongan ruling dynasty was founded. Europeans reached the islands in the 1600s, and in the late 1700s European ships began to visit Tonga. In the 1820s European Christian missionaries arrived on the islands, and by the mid-1800s most of the islanders were Christian.

The islands, governed by petty chieftains, were not united into a single kingdom until 1845, when the king of Ha'apai won the thrones of Vava'u and Tongatapu as well. The king granted a democratic constitution in 1875. In 1900 Tonga and Britain signed a treaty of friendship, and the islands became a British protectorate.

Under a new treaty ratified in 1959 Tonga received greater local autonomy, and in 1965 Britain further relaxed its authority over Tongan affairs. In December 1965 King Taufa'ahau Tupou IV took the throne, after the death of his mother, Queen Charlotte.

TURKS AND CAICOS ISLANDS

Status: British colony
Area: 166 square miles
Population: (1966 est.) 6,000
Capital: Grand Turk (Pop., 1960, 2,339)

The Turks and Caicos Islands, numerous small islands of the Bahama Archipelago, lie in the Atlantic Ocean about 100 miles north of the island of Hispaniola.

Low, rocky, and generally barren, the islands have a hot, dry climate broken by frequent hurricanes. Only about six of the islands are permanently inhabited. The population is mainly of African origin with some people of European and mixed background.

Salt is the islands' only important resource, and salt-raking is the only industry. Crayfish, conch, and other fish are caught, but there is little agriculture. The United States maintains a guided missile base and a tracking station on Grand Turk island. Trade is limited to the export of salt and fish and the import of foodstuffs, clothing, and other necessities.

Administration is in the hands of an appointed governor and an executive council responsible to an elected legislative assembly.

Discovered by Spain in the 1500s, the islands remained uninhabited until the 1600s, when Bermudians opened the salt-raking industry. France and Spain tried unsuccessfully to occupy the islands in the 1700s and 1800s, and in 1873 the islands were incorporated into the British colony of Jamaica. When Jamaica became independent in 1962, the islands were made a separate colony.

WALLIS AND FUTUNA ISLANDS

Status: Overseas territory of France
Area: 77 square miles
Population: (1966 est.) 8,000
Capital: Mata Utu

The Wallis and Futuna islands lie in the South Pacific Ocean about 800 miles north of New Zealand. They consist of 21 islands in the Wallis Archipelago and two islands in the Futuna group.

The islands of both groups are volcanic in origin, mountainous, densely forested, and ringed by coral reefs. The climate is hot and very wet. Most of the people are Polynesians, but there are a few Europeans.

The economy of the islands is based on agriculture, and coconuts are the chief commercial crop. Yams, bananas, taros, and melons are grown for local consumption. Pigs and chickens are raised, and there is some fishing. Copra production is the only industry.

The islands are governed by an appointed administrator with the advice of a partially elected executive council and a popularly elected assembly. The islands are represented in the French National Assembly.

The islands were first settled by people from the Tonga Islands. The Futuna group was discovered in the 1600s by the Dutch, and the Wallis group in the 1700s by the British. French Roman Catholics opened missions on the islands in the 1800s, and in the 1880s France made the islands a protectorate, at the islanders' request.

The islands served as an Allied base during World War II. In 1959 the islanders voted in a referendum to change their status from that of a protectorate to that of a territory. The islands officially became an overseas territory in 1961.

NATURAL FEATURES

ABERDARE, a mountain range of southeastern Africa, in western Kenya. It has an average elevation of 10,000 feet and peaks of 13,000 feet.

ACONCAGUA, a South American mountain in the Andes chain situated on the Chile-Argentina border. Aconcagua is the highest mountain in the western hemisphere, rising to an altitude of 22,834 feet above sea level.

ADEN, GULF OF, an arm of the Indian Ocean, bounded on the north by Arabia and on the south by Africa's Somali coast. The gulf is 550 miles long and connects with the Red Sea to the west through the Mandeb Strait.

ADRIATIC SEA, an arm of the Mediterranean Sea lying between Italy on the southwest and Yugoslavia and Albania on the northeast. The Adriatic is about 500 miles long and 100 miles wide. To the south, the Strait of Otranto links it with the Ionian Sea.

AEGEAN SEA, an arm of the Mediterranean Sea between Greece and Turkey. The Aegean is about 400 miles long and 200 miles wide, and flows into the Sea of Crete in the south. It contains a great many dry, rocky islands, including those in the Cyclades, Sporades, and Dodecanese groups.

AFRICA, the second largest of the world's continents, with an area of more than 11.6 million square miles. It had a 1965 population of 310 million. Africa is separated from Europe, to the north, by the Mediterranean Sea and from Asia, to the east, by the Red Sea and the Gulf of Aden. The Atlantic Ocean lies to its west and the Indian Ocean to its east.

Moderately high mountains rim the coasts of the continent. The northern and southern interiors are mostly desert or semi-desert. The central portion is hilly and covered by dense tropical vegetation. Central Africa is threaded by rivers and contains several large lakes.

AGUSAN, a river on the Philippine island of Mindanao. The river valley, about 150 miles long, has a moderate, tropcal climate and rich soils that produce fruits, corn, hemp, and tobacco.

AHAGGAR, a mountainous plateau in northern Africa, in the Sahara region of southern Algeria. It is a barren volcanic rock mass with peaks rising to 10,000 feet.

AIR, or Azbine, a mountainous region of Africa, in the southern Sahara in the Republic of Niger. It reaches a peak of over 6,000 feet. Its valleys are fertile and produce fruits and grains.

ÅLAND, a group of more than 300 small islands at the southern end of the Gulf of Bothnia off the southwestern coast of Finland. Most of the islands, which belong to Finland, are uninhabited.

ALBERT, a lake in east-central Africa, on the border between the Congo (Kinshasa) and Uganda. The lake is 100 miles long and 25 miles wide, and lies at an altitude of about 2,000 feet. The Semliki River enters it in the southwest, and the Victoria Nile enters in the northeast. The Albert Nile flows from the northern end of the lake.

ALIA, a mountain range of Soviet Central Asia, extending westwards from the Tien Shan through Khirgizia, and into Tadzhikistan. The average elevation is about 16,000 feet, and its peak is over 19,000 feet.

ALPS, an extensive and complex mountain system in central Europe, extending from southeastern France east through southwestern Austria, and south into western Yugoslavia. Mountains of a crystalline formation in the center of the range are flanked on the north and south by limestone. High, rugged, and dotted with glaciers, the range is narrow in the west and widens toward the east.

A variety of regional names are applied to the Alps. Some of the more important sections are the Maritime Alps, in France; the Dolomites and Pennines, in northern Italy; the Dinaric Alps, in Yugoslavia; and the Leopontines, in Switzerland.

Alpine pastures support dairy industries, and the valleys produce grains, wine grapes, and vegetables. Some of Europe's major rivers flow from the Alps, including the Rhine, the Rhône, and the Po, and Alpine water power is a valuable resource for European industry.

ALTAI, a mountain range in western Mongolia and northwestern China. Its highest peaks rise above 15,000 feet. The Irtysh and the Ob rivers of Central Asia rise in the Altai.

ALTIPLANO, in Spanish a high flat area or plain, usually used to refer to a high South American plateau in Peru and Bolivia. The plateau ranges from 12,000 to 15,000 feet above sea level and has a gently rolling surface. The eastern edge, or montaña zone, is deeply cut by rivers. Its climate is cool and dry. The Altiplano was the heartland of the American Indian empire of the Incas which flourished in the 1300s and 1400s.

AMAZON, a South American river, the largest river in the world in terms of volume and catchment area. It extends 3,900 miles across Brazil and Peru, and its tributaries form a basin of some 2.7 million square miles in central South America. Its basin includes the floodplain, or *varzea*, which is fertile after rains between November and May, and the unflooded areas, or *terra firme*, which have sterile soils.

AMU, or Jahun, a river of south-central Asia that rises in the Pamir mountains. It flows 1,500 miles through the Hindu Kush, along the northern border of Afghanistan, and into the Soviet Union, where it empties into the Aral Sea.

AMUR, a river of northeastern Asia marking part of the boundary between China and the Soviet Union. It is formed by the Argun and the Shilka rivers. The Amur flows eastward for about 1,800 miles and then turns northeastward before emptying into the Tatar Strait. The Ussuri and the Sungari are its major tributaries.

ANATOLIA, or Asia Minor, a peninsula of western Asia, lying west of an indefinite line between the Gulf of Alexandretta (Iskenderun) and the Black Sea. It is bounded on the west by the Aegean Sea and on the south by the Mediterranean. It is part of Turkey.

ANDAMAN, a sea to the east of the Bay of Bengal, an arm of the Indian Ocean. It is bounded on the west by the Andaman and Nicobar islands and on the east by the Malay Peninsula.

ANDES, a massive mountain system of western South America. The Andes stretch for more than 4,000 miles in a great crescent from northeastern Venezuela westward and then southward to the southernmost tip of the continent. Elevations range generally from 10,000 to 20,000 feet, but there are several peaks over 20,000 feet.

The system consists largely of ranges that merge and separate in a wide variety of structures that are folded, faulted, and, in parts, made up of volcanic elements.

In places, the Andes are separated from the Pacific coast by coastal ranges. Their foothills to the east across the altiplano, or high plain, include the Occidental, Central, and Oriental ranges. Further east, the piedmont includes the lower hills of the montaña that are part of the yungas, or the slope into the interior lowlands.

UNITED NATIONS

ANDES HIGHWAY twisting through the South American chain near La Paz, Bolivia.

ANGARA, a river in southeastern Siberia, in the eastern Soviet Union. It flows for some 1,100 miles from Lake Baykal north-northwest and then west, and joins the Yenisey River near the city of Yeniseysk.

ANGEL FALLS, the highest waterfall in the world, located in southeastern Venezuela on a tributary of the Caroni River. Actually a series of falls, it drops a total of 3,212 feet, and its highest fall is 2,650 feet.

ANNAM CORDILLERA, a mountain range of Southeast Asia. It extends northwest to southeast along the central portion of the border between Laos and Vietnam. The peaks are between 5,000 and 9,000 feet high.

ANTARCTICA, the continent surrounding the South Pole, about 5.5 million square miles in area. It is washed by the Atlantic, Pacific, and Indian oceans. From a mountainous interior, it slopes toward the coast. Antarctica is ice-covered, and very cold and dry.

ANTILLES, a large archipelago between North and South America lying partly in the Caribbean Sea and partly in the Atlantic Ocean. The Greater Antilles, at the northwestern end of the curving chain, includes the large islands of Cuba, Jamaica, Hispaniola, and Puerto Rico.

The Lesser Antilles, the southern and eastern portions of the archipelago, includes the many small islands off the coast of Venezuela in the south and the islands of the Windward and Leeward groups in the east. Many of the Antilles are volcanic in origin, and most are mountainous.

APENNINES, a mountain range that forms the backbone of peninsular Italy. The Apennines extend in a long arch from the Ligurian Alps in northwestern Italy to Calabria in the south. Elevations range from 6,000 feet to just under 10,000 feet. Pastures and forests cover the upper slopes, and fruits and grains are grown in the valleys.

AQABA, GULF OF, an extension of the Red Sea lying between the Sinai Peninsula and the Arabian Peninsula. The gulf is 100 miles long and from 5 to 17 miles wide.

ARABIA, a large peninsula in southwestern Asia, separated from the bulk of the continent in the northeast by the Persian Gulf and the Gulf of Oman. High mountains along the western and southern boundaries are separated from the Red Sea on the west and the Gulf of Aden on the south by narrow coastal plains. The central Arabian Plateau slopes gently eastward into the Persian Gulf basin.

Most of the land is desert or semi-desert with few perennial rivers, and the climate is generally hot and dry. In its oases dates, grains, indigo, and cotton are grown, and the peninsula has rich petroleum deposits.

ARABIAN SEA, an arm of the Indian Ocean lying between the Indian subcontinent and the Arabian Peninsula.

NEW ZEALAND INFORMATION SERVICE

ANTARCTICA is the icy home of these emperor penguins guarding their young.

ARAFURA SEA, a sea between Australia and southeastern Indonesia, with an area of about 280,000 square miles.

ARAKAN, a mountain range in western Burma with a peak of over 10,000 feet, but with elevations averaging about 6,000 feet. The coastal plain to its west, along the Bay of Bengal, is known as the Arakan Coast.

ARAL SEA, a lake in Soviet west-central Asia in the Kazakh and Uzbek republics. It lies in a desert region 175 miles east of the Caspian Sea. Some 240 miles long and 175 miles wide, the slightly saline Aral Sea is fed by two large rivers, the Amu and the Syr, but it has no outlet.

ARARAT, a mountain in eastern Turkey near the border with Iran. Of volcanic origin, Ararat consists of two peaks, Great Ararat, about 17,000 feet, and Little Ararat, about 13,000 feet. Great Ararat is the legendary landing place of Noah's Ark.

ARAVALLI, a mountain range in northwestern India, extending about 350 miles in southern and central Rajasthan state. The range has an average elevation of 2,000 feet and peaks of over 5,000 feet.

ARCTIC OCEAN, a large body of water surrounding the North Pole, north of the Arctic Circle. It has an area of more than 5 million square miles. The many arms of the Arctic Ocean include the Barents Sea and the Norwegian Sea north of Europe; the Laptev Sea and the East Siberian Sea above the Soviet Union; the Beaufort Sea northwest of Canada; and the Greenland Sea near Greenland.

ARDENNES, a forested plateau in northern France, southeastern Belgium, and northwestern Luxembourg, south and east of a bend in the Meuse River.

ARGONNE, a forested plateau in northeastern France, south of the Ardennes and west of the Meuse River.

ARNO, a river in Italy that rises in the Apennines in central Italy, passes through Florence, and flows about 150 miles west to empty into the Ligurian Sea near Pisa. It is navigable but subject to sudden flooding.

ASAMA, an active volcano in Japan, on Honshu Island, about 100 miles northwest of Tokyo. It is one of Japan's largest volcanoes, rising more than 8,300 feet.

ASIA, the largest of the continents, with an area of 17 million square miles and a population of about 2 billion in the mid-1960s. It lies west of the Pacific, north of the Indian Ocean, south of the Arctic Ocean, and east of a line that generally follows the Ural Mountains, the Caspian Sea, the Dardanelles, the west coast of Anatolia, and the Red Sea.

The Himalayas and their foothills form the east-west backbone of the continent. Lowlands and plateaus lie north and south of the Himalayan mountain system.

ATACAMA, a desert region of South America that extends for about 600 miles southward from the southernmost point of Peru through Atacama Province in Chile. It lies between the Pacific coastal range on the west and the Andean piedmont on the east. The desert proper, with an elevation of about 2,000 feet, is a series of dry salt basins rich in nitrates, and is so dry that in some places rainfall has never been recorded.

ATBARA, a river in northeastern Africa. It rises in northern Ethiopia and flows northward for about 500 miles to enter the Nile at Atbara, in Sudan.

ATHABASCA, a lake of west-central Canada, lying in northeastern Alberta and northwestern Saskatchewan provinces at the edge of the Canadian Shield. It has an area of nearly 3,000 square miles. The Athabasca River flows into it in the southwest, and the Great Slave River flows out of it in the northwest.

ATLANTIC, one of the world's major oceans, with an area of about 32 million square miles. The Atlantic separates Europe and Africa from North and South America. The North Atlantic Ocean lies between North America and Europe; the South Atlantic Ocean lies between South America and Africa.

ATLAS MOUNTAINS, a 1,500-mile-long mountain system of North Africa, extending from the southwest coast of Morocco westward to Cape Bon on the northeast coast of Tunisia. The Atlas system includes the Anti-Atlas in the southwest; the Grand, or High, Atlas in central Morocco; and the Saharan Atlas stretching across northern Algeria. The Grand Atlas includes Toubkal, 13,661 feet, the highest peak in the Atlas system.

AWASH, a river of northeastern Africa. It rises in central Ethiopia and follows a twisting course for about 500 miles through the Great Rift Valley and into the western Somali Republic, where it disappears into the arid Danakil Depression.

AZORES, a group of small volcanic islands belonging to Portugal and lying in the Atlantic Ocean about 750 miles west of mainland Portugal.

BAFFIN BAY, an inlet of the Arctic Ocean located between Canada's Arctic archipelago and Greenland. The bay is deep and dotted with icebergs brought down from the Arctic Ocean by the Labrador Current.

BAJA CALIFORNIA, a long, narrow peninsula in western Mexico south of California. The Pacific Ocean is to its west, and the Gulf of California to the east separates it from the rest of Mexico. Mountain ridges occupy the eastern and central portions of the peninsula. Most of the land is desert or arid plains.

BALATON, a lake in western Hungary located between the Danube and the Drava rivers. It has an outlet to the Danube. About 250 square miles in area, it is the largest lake in Central Europe.

BALEARIC ISLANDS, a group of five large islands and 12 islets in the Mediterranean Sea belonging to Spain. Mallorca is the largest, and Minorca, Cabrera, Ibiza, and Formentera are the other large islands of the group. Mountain scenery and the islands' warm, dry, climate foster a thriving tourist industry.

BALKAN MOUNTAINS, a range of mountains in Bulgaria with elevations under 8,000 feet. They extend from the Iron Gate on the Danube River to the Black Sea.

BALKAN PENINSULA, Western Europe's southeastern coast, washed by the Adriatic and Ionian seas on the west, the Mediterranean on the south, and the Aegean and the Black seas on the east. The Balkan states, the countries on or adjacent to the peninsula, are Albania, Bulgaria, Greece, Romania, and Yugoslavia. The European portion of Turkey is also part of the Balkans.

The peninsula is mountainous and contains the southern Carpathian Mountains, the Dinaric Alps, and the Balkan, Rhodope, and Pindus ranges.

BALKHASH, a salt lake in the southeastern part of the Soviet Union's Kazakh republic. It lies between the Kazakh Hills on the north and the Sary-Ishikotrau Desert on the south at an altitude of about 1,110 feet. Lake Balkhash is 375 miles long and from 15 to 55 miles wide, and has an average depth of 20 feet. There is no outlet.

BALTIC SEA, an arm of the North Atlantic Ocean separating the Scandinavian Peninsula and Finland from the rest of continental Europe. It flows into the North Sea to the west through the Kattegat and Skagerrak straits.

The Baltic is a vital link with the open ocean for the nations surrounding it, although most of it is icebound for part of the winter. The Baltic has two large branches—the Gulf of Bothnia in the north and the Gulf of Finland in the east.

BANDA SEA, in Southeast Asia, lies northwest of the Arafura Sea and east of the Flores Sea. The Banda Sea is surrounded by Indonesian islands and is dotted with islands, including the Banda group.

BANGWEULU, a lake in north Zambia in south-central Africa. About 60 miles long and 25 miles wide, the lake is shallow and surrounded by extensive swamps, and it appears to be drying up.

BARENTS SEA, a shallow arm of the Arctic Ocean north of Norway and the Soviet Union. It lies between Novaya Zemlya and Spitzbergen.

BAYKAL, a large lake in Soviet Central Asia, just north of Mongolia. It is the deepest lake in the world, with a maximum depth of 5,315 feet. It lies about 1,500 feet above sea level and measures nearly 400 miles in length and 50 miles in width. More than 300 rivers, including the Selenge, feed Lake Baykal, but the Angara River is its only outlet.

BEAUFORT SEA, a part of the Arctic Ocean. It lies northeast of Alaska, northwest of Canada, and west of Banks Island.

BENGAL, BAY OF, an arm of the Indian Ocean between India and Burma.

BERING SEA, the northernmost portion of the Pacific Ocean. It is bounded by Siberia on the west and northwest, by Alaska on the east and northeast, and by the Aleutian Islands on the south.

The Siberian Anadyr and the Alaskan Yukon and Kuskokwim rivers flow into the sea, which is connected with the Chukchi Sea and the Arctic Ocean to the north through the Bering Strait. Whaling, fishing, and sealhunting are major activities.

BHIMA, an Indian river in the northern Deccan. It rises in the Western Ghats near Bombay and flows southeast for about 400 miles to join the Kistna River.

BIÉ, a plateau in central Angola, in West Africa, with an average elevation of 6,000 feet. The outstanding physical characteristic of Angola, it is also one of the main watersheds of the continent, separating the headwaters of the Congo River drainage system in the north from the Zambezi River system in the south.

BIHOR, a mountain massif of Transylvania, in west-central Romania. It is a dissected plateau with an average elevation of 5,000 feet but rising above 6,000 feet in places. It is forested and contains mineral deposits.

BILAUKTAUNG, a mountain range of Southeast Asia running north-south along the central portion of the Thailand-Burma border. Elevations range between 2,000 and 5,000 feet.

BISCAY, BAY OF, an inlet of the Atlantic Ocean, bounded by France on the north and east and by Spain on the south.

BIWA, a Japanese lake on Honshu Island just northeast of Kyoto. About 480 square miles in area, it is the largest lake in Japan. The lake is drained by the Yodo River.

BLACK FOREST, a mountainous region in southwestern Germany. The mountains reach a peak of nearly 5,000 feet and are thickly forested. They contain the sources of the Danube and Neckar rivers.

BLACK SEA, a large inland sea in eastern Europe lying north of Asian Turkey, west and south of the Soviet Union, and east of Romania, Bulgaria, and European Turkey. About 170,000 square miles in area, it receives the Danube, the Dnester, the Dnepr, and other major rivers. The Sea of Azov, a small arm of the Black Sea, lies to the north. The Bosporus, the Sea of Marmara, and the Dardanelles link the Black Sea with the Aegean.

BOHEMIAN FOREST, a mountainous region in southeastern Germany and western Czechoslovakia. It has a peak of over 4,700 feet and is densely forested.

BORNEO, or Kalimantan, an island in Southeast Asia lying between the South China Sea on the north and west, the Java Sea on the south, and the Makassar Strait, Celebes Sea, and Sulu Sea on the east. It straddles the equator. The island, about 290,000 square miles in area, is the third largest in the world.

Rugged mountains rising above 13,000 feet occupy most of Borneo. It is rich in oil and other minerals and is heavily forested. Indonesia, Malaysia, and Brunei share the island.

BOSPORUS, a strait between European and Asian Turkey. It joins the Sea of Marmara with the Black Sea.

BOTHNIA, GULF OF, the northern arm of the Baltic Sea. It lies between Sweden on the west and Finland on the east.

BRAHMAPUTRA, or Tsangpo, or Jumna, a river on the Indian subcontinent that rises in the Kailas Mountains of southwestern Tibet. As the Tsangpo, it flows through Tibet for about 700 miles before turning sharply southward to flow for 1,100 miles to the Bay of Bengal. Its southern course is navigable for 800 miles and it waters a vast valley.

BRITISH ISLES, an island group of western Europe lying between the Atlantic Ocean and the North Sea. It includes the two large islands of Britain and Ireland and many smaller adjacent islands.

CAGAYAN, a river on the Philippine island of Luzon. It rises in the eastern mountains and flows north for about 250 miles into the Babuyan Channel, an arm of the Philippine

Sea. The 50-mile-wide Cagayan Valley is the island's richest forest and farming region.

CAMEROON MOUNTAIN, in west-central Africa near the Atlantic coast of Cameroon. It is of volcanic origin and is over 13,300 feet high.

CAMPECHE BAY, a broad inlet of the Gulf of Mexico on Mexico's curving southeastern coast. The Yucatan Peninsula is to the east.

CANARY ISLANDS, an archipelago in the Atlantic Ocean, off the northwestern coast of Africa, belonging to Spain. The seven islands and three islets of the archipelago are of volcanic origin, and are rocky and mountainous. They have a warm, dry climate.

CANTABRIAN MOUNTAINS, or Cordillera Cantabrica, a mountain range in northern Spain. The mountains lie parallel to the Bay of Biscay coast. Elevations range between 5,000 and 8,000 feet.

CAPE AGULHAS, the southernmost point of Africa. It is some 100 miles east of the Cape of Good Hope, in the Republic of South Africa.

CAPE BLANC, the northernmost point of Africa. It projects into the Mediterranean Sea from the north coast of Tunisia.

CAPE BON, a headland in North Africa at the northeastern tip of Tunisia. It is a part of the Atlas mountain system. Cape Bon projects into the Strait of Sicily, in the Mediterranean Sea.

CAPE COMORIN, the southern tip of the Indian subcontinent. It projects into the Laccadive Sea, an arm of the Indian Ocean.

CAPE GARDAFUI, the tip of the eastern horn of Africa, located in Somalia. The cape forms an impressive headland almost 1,000 feet high.

CAPE HORN, the southernmost point of South America, part of the Wollaston Island group south of Tierra del Fuego. It is a rock rising to an altitude of 1,390 feet above sea level.

CAPE OF GOOD HOPE, a point of land near the southern tip of Africa, on the southwest coast of the Republic of South Africa.

CAPE YORK PENINSULA, the northernmost point of Australia, east of the Gulf of Carpentaria and west of the Great Barrier Reef in the Coral Sea. It ends in Cape York, in Torres Strait.

CARIBBEAN SEA, a body of water between North and South America at the western edge of the Atlantic Ocean. On the north and east it is ringed by the islands of the Greater and Lesser Antilles. The Caribbean Sea is over 1 million square miles in area and has an average depth of more than 8,000 feet.

CAROLINE ISLANDS, an archipelago in the western Pacific Ocean lying east of the Philippines. The archipelago consists of nearly 1,000 small islands and coral reefs. The chief island of the group is Caroline Island, and the archipelago includes the Palau Islands, also called the Western Carolines.

CARPATHIANS, a mountain system of central and eastern Europe extending more than 1,000 miles through Czechoslovakia, Hungary, Poland, Romania, and the Soviet Union. Although a continuation of the Alps, the Carpathians are more rounded and lower than the Alps; the highest peak is less than 9,000 feet.

The Carpathians are usually divided into four groups—the Western, Central, and Eastern Carpathians, and the Transylvanian Alps. They are rich in minerals and contain the sources of many rivers, including the Vistula and the Dnestr.

CARPENTARIA, GULF OF, an inlet of the Arafura Sea in northern Australia. It lies between Arnhemland, on the west, and Cape York Peninsula on the east.

CASPIAN SEA, a large lake located between the Soviet Union and Iran, at the border of Europe and Asia. The world's largest saltwater lake, it is 759 miles long and from 140 to 300 miles wide. There are no outlets, but the Ural, Volga, Kuma, Terek, and Atrek rivers flow into the Caspian.

The Soviet Union uses the Caspian as an inland water route and as a source of fish, including salmon, herring, sturgeon, and carp.

CAUCASUS MOUNTAINS, an extensive mountain range in the Soviet Union, forming part of the boundary between Europe and Asia. The Caucasus lie between the Sea of Azov and the Black Sea on the west and the Caspian Sea on the east.

The Greater Caucasus, in the north, is about 750 miles long and has average elevations of between 10,000 and 12,000 feet with peaks over 18,000 feet. Volcanic in origin, this chain has hot springs and occasional earthquakes.

The lower Surami Range to the south is the link between the Greater Caucasus and the Lesser Caucasus, a mountain system formed in Asia Minor by the northern ranges of the Armenian Highland.

CEVENNES, a mountain range in southeastern France with an average elevation of 3,000 feet. The mountains contain the sources of many French rivers, including the Loire and the Ardèche.

CHAD, a lake in north-central Africa, located at the junction of the boundaries of Chad, Niger, and Nigeria. Lake Chad contains fresh water and is fed by the Chari, Logone, and Komadugu rivers.

CH'ANGPAI, a Chinese mountain range in southern Manchuria. It extends along the China-Korea border and has a peak of over 9,000 feet.

CHAO PHRAYA, the principal river of Thailand, formed from the Ping, the Yom, and the Nan, which rise in the northern mountains and then merge at Nakhon Sawan. The river's total length is about 750 miles from the mountains to its mouth on the Gulf of Siam.

CHARI, or Shari, a river rising in the Central African Republic and flowing northwest for about 1,400 miles to Lake Chad, where it forms an extensive delta.

CHEJU, a mountainous island off the southern coast of Korea, in the Korea Strait.

CHERSKI, a mountain range in northeastern Siberia, in the eastern Soviet Union. The range is about 600 miles long and has a peak above 10,000 feet.

CHIH-LI, or Po Hai, a gulf on the eastern coast of China. It is an arm of the Yellow Sea, and is partially enclosed by the Liaotung and Shantung peninsulas.

CHU, or Pearl, a river on the east China coast, one channel in the Si River delta. The important Chinese city of Canton is situated on its banks, and the British island colony of Hong Kong lies in its broad estuary.

CLYDE, a river in Scotland, flowing from South Lanarkshire in the Southern Uplands through the Scottish Lowland, past Glasgow, and into the Firth of Clyde. Its valley, Clydeside, is one of Britain's leading industrial districts.

COLORADO, a river 550 miles long in southeastern South America. It rises in the Andes near the Chilean border and flows southeast across southcentral Agentina to the Atlantic Ocean.

COMO, a lake in northern Italy, about 20 miles north of Milan, in Lombardy. There are many resorts around the lake, and Como is the largest town on its shores.

CONGO, a river in central Africa. With its tributaries, it is one of the world's longest rivers, about 2,900 miles, and it drains a basin about 1.6 million square miles in area. The Lualaba, its main headstream, rises on the Katanga Plateau in the Congo (Kinshasa) and flows northward to join the Luapula and Lukuga rivers.

Before turning to the west at Kisaugani (Stanleyville), where it becomes the Congo proper, the river crosses the 60-mile stretch of the Stanley Falls. About 350 miles from its mouth, it widens to form Stanley Pool, where Brazzaville and Kinshasa (Léopoldville) are located, the end of the inland navigation route. The Congo then falls some 850 feet over Livingstone Falls, which lead into the river's estuary.

CONSTANCE, or Boden, a lake bordering Germany, Austria, and Switzerland. It is fed largely by the Upper Rhine.

UNITED ARAB REPUBLIC TOURIST OFFICE

THE NILE, the world's longest river, flows for more than 4,000 miles through northeastern Africa to the Mediterranean Sea.

VENEZUELA MINISTRY OF DEVELOPMENT

ANGEL FALLS, the world's highest waterfall, in Venezuela, has a drop of more than 3,200 ft.

FPG

MT. EVEREST, the world's highest mountain, rises more than 29,000 feet in the Himalayas.

DALIA CARMEL

DEAD SEA, almost 1,300 feet below sea level, is the world's lowest land point. It lies on the border of Israel and Jordan.

CORAL SEA, a western arm of the South Pacific Ocean lying between Australia, New Guinea, and the Melanesian islands. It is dotted with small islands and coral atolls.

COROMANDEL, the southeastern coast of India extending from the eastern end of Palk Strait, separating India and Ceylon, north to the mouth of the Krishna River. The important city of Madras lies at about the center of the coast, which lacks good natural harbors.

CRIMEA, a peninsula in the southern part of the Ukrainian republic, in the southwestern Soviet Union. It extends 120 miles into the Black Sea and measures about 200 miles from west to east. The narrow Perekop Isthmus connects it with the mainland.

The Crimea can be divided into four distinct geographical regions: the level and dry northern steppe; the Crimean Mountains on the southern coast, with peaks above 5,000 feet; the subtropical Black Sea coast at the foot of the steep Crimean Mountains; and the arid, mineral-rich Kerch Peninsula.

CRYSTAL, a West African mountain massif lying inland from the coastal plain of Gabon. Elevations are generally under 5,000 feet.

CUNENE, a river of southwestern Africa that rises in central Angola. It flows south and then west for 700 miles and has many rapids and cataracts. The Cunene forms part of the boundary between Angola and South West Africa.

CUQUENÁN, or Kukenan, a waterfall in eastern Venezuela on a tributary of the Arabopó River. Dropping some 2,000 feet, it is one of the world's highest waterfalls.

DANUBE, a major river of central and southeastern Europe. It rises in the Black Forest of southwestern Germany and flows for some 1,750 miles through or along the borders of eight countries before emptying into the Black Sea in northeastern Romania. Its major tributaries include the Drava, the Sava, and the Prut.

DARDANELLES, a strait separating parts of European and Asian Turkey. It links the Aegean Sea and the Sea of Marmara.

DEAD SEA, a salt lake, about 450 square miles in area, on the Israel-Jordan border at the southern end of the Jordan River. Lying 1,296 feet below sea level, its shores and surface are at the lowest known point of land on earth. It is saltier than sea water and contains many other minerals as well.

DHAULAGIRI, a Himalayan peak in Nepal with an elevation of 26,810 feet. It is the fifth highest mountain in the world.

DIU, an island in the Gulf of Cambay off India's west coast. A former Portuguese enclave, it was occupied by India in 1961.

DNEPR, a major river of the western Soviet Union. It rises near Smolensk and flows southwest and south for over 1,400 miles, emptying into the Black Sea. Its tributaries include the Sozh, Desna, and Berezina rivers.

The entire course of the Dnepr is navigable, and it is an important source of hydroelectric power. Connected by canals to the Dvina, Niemen, and Vistula rivers, it forms part of a continuous waterway from the Black Sea to the Baltic Sea.

DOGGER BANK, a submerged sand bank beneath the North Sea, about 60 miles east of Britain. It is an important fishing zone.

DON, a major river of the western Soviet Union. It rises in the Central Russian Upland, southwest of Moscow. It flows southeastward until it nears Volgograd (Stalingrad), and then flows southwest and west for a total of over 1,200 miles before emptying into the Sea of Azov.

Tributaries of the Don include the Donets, Medveditsa, Sal, and Manych rivers. Seagoing ships can travel as far as Rostov, the principal port, near the mouth of the river, and the entire course is navigable by smaller vessels.

DONEGAL BAY, an inlet of the Atlantic Ocean on the northwest coast of Ireland at the mouth of the Eask River.

DRAKE PASSAGE, a channel separating the southern tip of South America from Antarctica, joining the Pacific and the Atlantic oceans.

DRAKENSBERG, a mountain range of southern Africa extending some 700 miles southwest to northeast in the Republic of South Africa. Elevations reach 10,000 feet.

DRAVA, or Drau, a river of eastern Europe, about 450 miles long, that rises in southern Austria. It flows east through Yugoslavia to the border with Hungary, and then turns southeast to join the Danube River in northeastern Yugoslavia.

DRINA, a river of central Yugoslavia, formed by the confluence of the Tava and Piva rivers. Flowing generally northward for about 200 miles, it joins the Sava River about 50 miles west of Belgrade.

DUERO, a river that rises in north central Spain. It flows west for nearly 500 miles, emptying into the Atlantic Ocean at Porto, Portugal.

DVINA, two rivers in Europe. The Western, or Southern, Dvina rises in the western Soviet Union and flows about 650 miles to the Gulf of Riga, on the Baltic. The Northern Dvina is formed by the confluence of the Vychegda and Sukhona rivers in the northern part of the Soviet Union's Russian republic. It flows generally northwest for over 540 miles to its outlet into the Gulf of Dvina, at Archangelsk.

EAST CHINA SEA, an arm of the western Pacific Ocean off the east coast of China. It lies between the Yellow Sea on the west and the Ryukyu Islands on the east.

EAST INDIES, a general term for the Malay Peninsula, the Malay Archipelago, Indochina, India, and Indonesia.

EAST SIBERIAN SEA, a part of the Arctic Ocean. It lies north of eastern Siberia, in the Soviet Union, east of the New Siberian Islands, and west of Wrangel Island.

EBRO, a river of northeastern Spain that rises in the Cantabrian Mountains and flows eastward for about 500 miles to the Mediterranean Sea at Cape Tortosa. It is partly navigable and an important source of water for irrigation.

EDWARD, a lake in East Africa, in the western part of the Great Rift Valley, located on the Uganda-Congo (Kinshasa) border. It lies southwest of Lake George and is about 800 square miles in area.

ELBA, an Italian island in the Tyrrhenian Sea between Corsica and the Italian mainland. It is mountainous and rich in minerals.

ELBE, or Labe, a river in central Europe. Over 700 miles long, it rises on the Poland-Czechoslovakia border in the Erg Gebirge range and flows north-northwest through Czechoslovakia and Germany, forming part of the boundary between East and West Germany.

Near Hamburg, numerous channels of the Elbe unite to form a 60-mile estuary that empties into the North Sea near Cuxhaven. The Elbe is partly navigable and is linked with the Rhine and Oder rivers by several canals.

ELBRUS, a mountain peak in the Caucasus, in the northern part of the Soviet Union's Georgian republic. It has an elevation of 18,481 feet and is the highest peak in Europe.

ELBURZ, a mountain range in northern Iran separating the Caspian Sea from the Iranian Plateau. A 650-mile-long crescent-shaped chain, it consists of several steep, parallel ranges whose summits often reach above 13,000 feet. Mt. Demavend, nearly 19,000 feet, is the highest peak.

ENGLISH CHANNEL, a body of water between Britain and France that joins the Atlantic Ocean and the North Sea. It is less than 20 miles wide at its narrowest point, the Strait of Dover, between Dover, in Britain, and Calais, in France.

ETHIOPIAN HIGHLANDS, an extensive upland region of eastern Africa, lying mainly in Ethiopia. It rises sharply from surrounding lowlands and has an average elevation of between 10,000 and 13,000 feet.

The region is divided into two parts by the Great Rift Valley. To the northwest the region is broken by very deep, steep-sided valleys through which flow many rivers, including the Blue Nile. To the southeast of the Rift Valley, the highlands are flatter and less rugged.

EUPHRATES, a river in southwest Asia that rises in eastern Turkey. It flows southeast for over 1,700 miles through Syria and Iraq to the Persian Gulf. The river is formed by two headstreams, the Kara and the Murat, and about 120 miles from the Persian Gulf, the Euphrates joins the Tigris River to form the Shatt al-Arab.

Syria and Iraq depend on the Euphrates for water for irrigation, and ancient peoples built a complex system of canals that allowed the Tigris and Euphrates plain to support great civilizations.

EUROPE, a continent with an area of about 4 million square miles and a population of some 620 million people in the mid-1960s. It is bounded on the north by the Arctic Ocean, on the east by the Ural Mountains, on the south by the Mediterranean Sea, and on the west by the Atlantic Ocean.

The continent is customarily divided into Western Europe—those nations from Germany and Austria westward —and Eastern Europe—the lands from Poland and Czechoslovakia eastward.

EYRE, a lake in south-central Australia, some 200 miles north of the Eyre Peninsula. It is the largest lake in Australia. Eyre is a salt lake in an arid region. Its size varies with the season, but its normal area is about 2,700 square miles.

FINLAND, GULF OF, a shallow eastern arm of the Baltic Sea, about 260 miles long and varying in width from 40 to 85 miles. It is bordered by Finland on the north and the Soviet Union's Estonian republic on the south. The gulf receives the waters of lakes Ladoga and Onega as well as other streams.

FOUTA DJALLON, a mountainous region with a peak of about 5,000 feet, forming the western edge of the Guinea Highlands in Guinea, West Africa.

FRANZ JOSEF LAND, a group of some 85 islands in the Arctic Ocean, east of Spitzbergen and north of Novaya Zemlya. The islands are part of the Soviet Union. They include Aleksandra Land, George Land, and Graham Bell Island. The northernmost land in the Eastern Hemisphere, the islands are almost completely covered by glaciers.

FRISIAN ISLANDS, a series of low barrier beaches that jut into the North Sea. They belong to the Netherlands, West Germany, and Denmark.

FUJI, a Japanese volcanic peak on central Honshu Island. The single peak rises nearly 12,400 feet from the surrounding plain. It last erupted in the 1600s and is now considered dead.

FUNDY, BAY OF, an inlet of the Atlantic Ocean between Nova Scotia and New Brunswick, Canada. It is about 180 miles long and from 30 to 50 miles wide. It divides into Chignecto Bay and Minas Channel. At the narrow entrance to Chignecto Bay tides sometimes vary more than 50 feet.

GALILEE, SEA OF, or Lake Tiberias, a freshwater lake in northeastern Israel at the border with Syria. It is more than 680 feet below sea level and is fed and drained by the Jordan River.

GAMBIA, a river in West Africa, about 450 miles long, that rises in Guinea. It flows northwest through Senegal and then west to the Atlantic Ocean through the country of Gambia.

GANGES, a river of northern India that rises in the Himalayas and flows south and east for more than 1,550 miles to the Bay of Bengal, off the coast of East Pakistan. It is heavily used for transportation, and provides power for industries and water for irrigation. The Gangetic Plain is a plateau formed by the river in northern India. The Ganges is a sacred river for Hindus.

The major southern tributaries of the Ganges are the Son and the Jumna. The major northern tributaries are the Gumti, the Kusi, the Gogra, and the Gandak. The Ganges is joined by the Brahmaputra (Jumna) River about 100 miles from its mouth to form the Padma. The delta is the largest in the world.

At its mouth, the river breaks into several major channels: the Meghna, the Tetulia, the Madhumata, the Baleswar, and the Hooghly (Bhagirathi). There are swampy jungles, called Sundarbans, along the coast.

GARDA, a lake in northern Italy, about 300 square miles in area. Its mild climate and majestic scenery make it an important tourist center.

GARONNE, a river in Western Europe that rises in the Spanish Pyrenees and flows northwest through France for 400 miles. The Garonne flows through Toulouse and past Bordeaux to join the Dordogne and form the Gironde River before emptying into the Bay of Biscay.

GASPÉ, a peninsula of eastern Canada, between the St. Lawrence River on the west, the Gaspé Passage on the north, and the Gulf of St. Lawrence on the east. The Notre Dame Mountains in the interior are ringed by a low and often rocky coastal plain.

GENEVA, or Leman, a crescent-shaped lake on the border of France and Switzerland.

GERSOPPA, a waterfall in southwestern India, on the Sharivari River. With a drop of 830 feet, it is the highest known waterfall in Asia. The falls are used to provide hydroelectric power for the region.

GHATS, two mountain ranges on India's southern coasts. The Eastern Ghats run parallel to the Bay of Bengal for about 500 miles south from the Mahanadi River and have an average elevation of 1,800 feet. The Western Ghats run parallel to the Arabian

TURIZM VE TANITMA BAKANLIĞI

EUPHRATES RIVER carved this gorge in its upper course near Malatya, eastern Turkey.

Sea and have an average elevation of 4,000 feet. Both ranges are heavily forested.

GIBSON DESERT, an arid area in western Australia. It has a rolling, sandy surface.

GOBI, a desert region in southern Mongolia and north-central China, about 500,000 square miles in area. It lies in a depression of the Mongolian Plateau ringed with mountains and steppes. The Gobi is covered by scrub grass that is suitable in some areas for grazing.

GODAVARI, a river in central India that rises in the Western Ghats and flows eastward for 900 miles to the Bay of Bengal. It is navigable in the east and is vital for irrigation in the region. Hindus consider it a sacred river.

GODWIN AUSTIN, or K2, a mountain in the Karakorum Range in northeastern Pakistan. The second highest mountain in the world, it has an elevation of 28,250 feet.

GOTLAND, an island in the Baltic Sea about 55 miles off the southeastern coast of Sweden. Gotland is a province of Sweden. Sheepherding and fishing are the main economic activities.

GRAN CHACO, a lowland region of south-central South America, divided among Argentina, Bolivia, and Paraguay. Much of the region is arid, but there are swampy areas and the climate is quite hot. It is barren and sparsely populated.

GRAND BANKS, a submerged plateau in the Atlantic Ocean southeast of Newfoundland, about 300 miles long, 200 miles wide, and from 120 to 600 feet deep. Most of the area is crossed by the cold Labrador Current, but the warm Gulf Stream passes along the eastern part. The mixing of the two currents makes the Grand Banks rich in marine life and a major cod-fishing region.

GREAT AUSTRALIAN BIGHT, a wide, cresent-shaped bay of the Indian Ocean on the south coast of Australia.

GREAT BARRIER REEF, a coral reef off the coast of northeastern Australia and southeastern New Guinea at the edge of the continental shelf. It protects the coastline, and forms a channel that contains many small coral islets.

GREAT BEAR, a lake in northwestern Canada, drained by the Great Bear River, a tributary of the Mackenzie. It is Canada's largest lake, with an area of 12,275 square miles.

GREAT DIVIDING RANGE, a mountain chain bordering the eastern coast of Australia. The mountains are generally below 5,000 feet, but Mt. Kosciusko, in the south, rises more than 7,300 feet. Among the foothills of the range are the Australian Alps, the Snowy Mountains, and the New England, Calliope, Drummond, Connors, Clark, and Gregory ranges.

GREAT RIFT VALLEY, a depression in southwestern Asia and northeastern Africa, formed by a downfaulting of the earth's crust. The depression consists of two rifts—the Main, or Eastern Rift, and the Western Rift.

The Main Rift extends for roughly 4,000 miles from southern Turkey, in southwestern Asia, to Mozambique, in southeastern Africa. The Western Rift extends 1,100 miles from southern Sudan to Malawi, where it joins the Main Rift. The rift valleys vary in width from 30 miles in the south to 250 miles toward the north.

The floor of the depression lies below sea level in the northernmost area, but rises to over 6,000 feet in Kenya. Many lakes and seas are located in the valleys outlined by the Great Rift.

GREAT SANDY DESERT, an arid region in northwestern Australia between the King Leopold Ranges on the northeast and the Hamersley Ranges on the southwest. It contains salt marshes and some scrub vegetation.

GREAT SLAVE, a lake in west-central Canada, over 10,500 square miles in area. It is fed by the Great Slave and Hay rivers and drained by the Mackenzie River.

GREAT VICTORIA DESERT, an arid region in southwestern Australia, north of the Nullarbor Plain. It has a sandy surface broken by salt marshes.

GREENLAND, the largest island in the world, 840,000 square miles in area. A dependency and former colony of Denmark, it lies northeast of North America and is washed by the North Atlantic and Arctic oceans and by the Greenland Sea. About three-quarters of its area lies above the Arctic Circle, and almost seven-eighths of Greenland is covered by ice.

GREENLAND SEA, a part of the Arctic Ocean east of Greenland, west of the Barents Sea, and north of the Norwegian Sea, of which it is generally considered an extension.

GUADALQUIVIR, a river in southwestern Spain that flows for over 350 miles, passing Córdoba and Seville, to enter the Atlantic Ocean in the Gulf of Cádiz.

GUAYAQUIL, GULF OF, an inlet of the Pacific Ocean in Ecuador, in northwestern South America. It is dotted with islands and has several good harbors.

GUIANA HIGHLANDS, an area of northeastern South America, extending from central Venezuela across northern Brazil and through southern Guyana and Surinam to French Guiana. It is the central portion of Guiana—a region bounded by the Orinoco, Negro, and Amazon rivers and the Atlantic Ocean.

GUINEA, GULF OF, a great inlet of the Atlantic Ocean in West Africa. Generally accepted as extending from Senegal to Angola, it includes the bights of Benin and Biafra. The adjacent mainland is known as the Guinea Coast.

HAINAN, a large Chinese island lying about 15 miles south of the mainland. The island is mountainous, thickly forested, and rich in minerals.

HARI, a river that rises in the mountains of central Afghanistan and flows for about 650 miles, ending in the Kara Kum desert. The Hari flows west through the Herat Valley and then north along the Iranian border into the Soviet Union.

HEBRIDES, a group of British islands lying in the Atlantic Ocean off the northwestern coast of Scotland. The islands have an area of about 2,900 square miles and are divided into the Inner Hebrides and the Outer Hebrides, separated by a strait, the Little Minch.

HELMAND, a river in southwestern Afghanistan that rises in the central mountains and flows west for about 650 miles, emptying into Lake Helmand on the border with Iran. The Helmand river is being developed for navigation, irrigation, and power production.

HIGHLANDS OF SCOTLAND, or the Northern Highlands, a mountainous region in the north of Scotland. Most of the highlands are part of a hilly, rocky plateau, but there are some high ranges. The hills are broken by val-leys, and there are many lochs, or lakes. Sheepherding is the main economic activity.

HIMALAYAS, a mountain system in southeastern Asia containing the world's highest peaks. The range extends for about 1,600 miles from Kashmir in the west to Assam in the east. It forms an arc separating the subcontinent of India from the rest of Asia.

The system may be divided into three sections—the Greater Himalayas in the north, the Lesser Himalayas in the center, and the Outer Himalayas in the south. The Greater Himalayas contain Mt. Everest, 29,028 feet, the highest peak in the world.

The Himalayas contain the sources of several of Asia's important rivers, including the Ganges, the Tsangpo-Brahmaputra system, and the Sutlej.

HINDU KUSH, a mountain range in northeastern Afghanistan that extends for about 500 miles along the border with West Pakistan as far as Kashmir. The mountains form a barrier between the Soviet Union and Afghanistan, Pakistan, and Kashmir. The highest peak is Tirich Mir, more than 25,000 feet above sea level. The Hindu Kush is also a watershed between the Amu and Indus river systems.

HISPANIOLA, a large island of the Greater Antilles between the Caribbean Sea and the Atlantic Ocean. Its two mountain ranges are separated by a deep valley and ringed by narrow coastal plains. The climate is tropical and the vegetation is lush. Hispaniola is shared by Haiti and the Dominican Republic.

HONDURAS, GULF OF, an outlet of the Caribbean Sea touching British Honduras, Guatemala, and Honduras. It is dotted with coral islands and atolls.

HUDSON BAY, an inland sea in east-central Canada at the center of the Canadian Shield lowland. Over 475,-000 square miles in area, it receives the Churchill, Nelson, Nottaway, and other rivers. Its major arms are the Fox Basin in the north and St. James Bay in the south. It joins the Labrador Sea, an arm of the North Atlantic, through Hudson Strait.

HWANG, or Yellow, river, the second longest river of China. The Hwang rises in the Kunlun Mountains of northwestern China and flows in a generally easterly direction for 2,700 miles, emptying into the Gulf of Chihli. Its tributaries include the Fen, Huai, and Wei rivers. The Hwang is navigable for most of its course. The river has been the cause of numerous floods.

IBERIA, a peninsula in the southwestern corner of Europe, between the Mediterranean Sea and the Atlantic Ocean, occupied by Spain and Portugal. It is ringed with mountains, with the Pyrenees and the Cantabrian Mountains on the north, the Sierra da Estrella on the west, and the Cordillera Penibética on the southeast.

PAN AMERICAN AIRWAYS

IGUASSÚ FALLS, a series of cataracts along part of the Brazil-Argentina border.

The interior is also mountainous, with the Sierra Morena and Sierra de Guadarrama the most important chains. The major rivers crossing the peninsula are the Duero, the Tejo (Tagus), the Guadiana, the Ebro, and the Guadalquivir.

IGUASSÚ FALLS, a great waterfall on the Brazil-Argentina border. It is on the Iguassú River, 14 miles upstream from its confluence with the Upper Paraná River. Iguassú Falls, a 2.5-mile-wide series of cataracts, has a vertical drop of about 215 feet.

IJSSEL MEER, formerly the Zuider Zee, an inlet of the North Sea within the Netherlands. Flooding joined the former lake to the sea, but diking and draining in the 1950s and the 1960s separated the two again to reclaim over 500,000 acres for farmland.

ILI, a river in northwestern Sinkiang province, in western China. It rises in the Tien Shan range and flows west for 800 miles through a fertile valley to Lake Balkhash, in the Soviet Union.

INDIAN OCEAN, the third largest body of water in the world, more than 28 million square miles in area. It is bounded by Africa on the west, Asia on the north, Australia and the Australasian Islands on the east, and Antarctica on the south. The meridian of longitude at 20° East separates the Indian and Atlantic oceans.

The Indian Ocean's greatest depth is over 24,000 feet, in the Java Trench, but the average depth is 13,000 feet, exceeding that of the Atlantic. Several large rivers feed the ocean, including the Indus, Ganges, Irrawaddy, and, through the Persian Gulf, the Tigris-Euphrates of Asia, and the Zambezi and Limpopo of Africa. The Arabian Sea and the Bay of Bengal are its two major arms.

INDOCHINA, a general name for the peninsula of Southeast Asia occupied by Vietnam, Laos, Cambodia, Thailand, Burma, and the mainland portion of Malaysia. French Indochina was a French colony that included present-day Cambodia, Laos, and Vietnam.

INDUS, one of the major rivers of South Asia. Rising on the northern slopes of the Kailas range of southwestern Tibet, it flows northwest into Kashmir, then southwest through central Pakistan to the Arabian Sea—a total of more than 1,800 miles. Its major tributaries include the Chenab, the Sutlej, the Jhelum, and the Ravi. The Indus has a wide delta known as "the Mouths of the Indus," flowing into the Arabian Sea.

INLAND SEA, a shallow inlet of the Pacific Ocean between the Japanese islands of Honshu, on the north, and Shikoku and Kyushu, on the south. It is separated from the open sea by the Kii Strait on the southeast, the Bungo Strait on the south, and the Shimonoseki Strait on the west.

INN, a European river that is a major tributary of the Danube. It rises in Switzerland and flows 320 miles through northwestern Austria and southeastern Germany to join the Danube at Passau.

IONIAN SEA, a portion of the Mediterranean Sea between Italy and Greece, connected to the Adriatic Sea through the Strait of Otranto. It contains many rocky islets and islands, including Corfu, Paxos, Leukas, and Ithaca.

IRISH SEA, an arm of the Atlantic Ocean between the western coast of England and the eastern coast of Ireland. It is connected with the Atlantic Ocean through North Channel on the north and St. George's Channel on the south.

IRON GATE, a two-mile-long gorge cut by the Danube River through the southwestern Transylvanian Alps on the border of Romania and Yugoslavia.

IRRAWADDY, a major river of Burma that rises in Tibet and flows for more than 1,300 miles to empty into the Gulf of Martaban of the Bay of Bengal near Rangoon. The delta of the Irrawaddy is about 150 miles long. The river's chief tributaries are the Nmai and the Chindwin.

IRTYSH, a major river of northeastern Asia. It is over 2,200 miles long and a major tributary of the Ob River. Rising in the northern part of China's Sinkiang province, the river flows westward and is known as the Kara Irtysh until it enters Lake Zaysan in the Soviet Union's Kazakh republic. It then travels north and northwest through the Altai Mountains and the western Kulunda Steppe into the Russian republic, meeting the Ob at Khanty-Mansiysk.

ISLANDS. Greenland, 840,000 square miles in area, is the world's largest island. Lying partly in the Arctic Ocean and partly in the Atlantic, it is adjacent to the fifth largest island, Baffin, 183,810 square miles, which lies north of Hudson Bay.

The world's second and third largest islands lie at the western edge of the Pacific. New Guinea, 317,000 square miles, is separated from Australia, to its south, by the Arafura Sea and the Coral Sea. To its west is Borneo, 287,400 square miles, washed by the South China, Sulu, Celebes, and Java seas.

Madagascar, 229,812 square miles, is the world's fourth largest island. It lies in the Indian Ocean and is separated from East Africa by the Mozambique Channel.

JAPAN, SEA OF, an arm of the western Pacific Ocean between Japan and the East Asian mainland. About 400,000 square miles in area, it is linked with the East China Sea on the south through the Korea Strait, between the Japanese island of Kyushu and Korea, and with the Sea of Okhotsk on the north through the Tatar Strait and La Perouse Strait.

JORDAN, a river in the Middle East that rises in four headstreams in the anti-Lebanon Mountains of Syria. It flows south for some 200 miles in Israel and Jordan through the Sea of Galilee and into the Dead Sea. The Yarmuk River is the principal tributary of the Jordan, whose course lies in the Great Rift Valley.

JOS, a plateau region in West Africa, in the center of the Northern Region of Nigeria. Rising steeply from the valley of the Benoué River, the plateau has an average elevation of 4,000 feet, with a maximum height of nearly 6,000 feet near the town of Jos. The plateau contains important mineral deposits.

JUNGFRAU, a mountain in the Bernese Alps, in southwestern Switzerland. Rising over 13,600 feet, it is one of Europe's highest mountains.

JURA, a mountain range along the French-Swiss border north of Geneva. It is a spur of the western Alps, and has a peak of over 5,500 feet.

JUTLAND, or Jylland, a peninsula in northern Europe extending north from Germany. It lies between the North Sea on the west and the Baltic on the east and is separated from Scandinavia by the Skagerrak.

Jutland is low-lying, with a flat to rolling surface and an irregular coastline. Part of it is occupied by the Danish mainland and part by the West German state of Schleswig-Holstein.

KAILAS, a mountain range of southwestern Tibet with a peak of more than 23,000 feet. The Range is the source of the Indus, Sutlej, and Brahmaputra rivers.

KALAHARI, a desert of southern Africa. It extends southward from Lake Ngami through central Botswana into northern South Africa as far as the Orange River, and westward from eastern Botswana into South West Africa.

KAMCHATKA, a peninsula in northeastern Siberia, in the Soviet Union. It is 750 miles long and from 80 to 300 miles wide, and divides the Bering Sea and the Pacific Ocean on the east from the Sea of Okhotsk on the west. Two tall, volcanic mountain ranges run the length of the peninsula and enclose a central valley, which is drained by the Kamchatka River.

KANCHENJUNGA, a mountain in the Himalayas on the Nepal-Sikkim border. With one of its three peaks rising to 28,165 feet, it is the third highest mountain in the world.

KARAKORAM, a mountain range lying along the northern borders of West Pakistan and Kashmir. It extends eastward into China's Tibet region and along the southern border of Sinkiang. It lies between the Hindu Kush and the Kunlun Mountains.

The Karakoram range includes many peaks above 22,000 feet. The Karakoram Pass, the chief route between Kashmir, in northern India, and China, lies at an elevation of nearly 18,300 feet.

KARIBA, a man-made lake, 165 miles long, in southeastern Africa. It was formed by the Kariba Dam on the Zambezi River, between Zambia and Rhodesia.

KARROO, a tableland region in South Africa, west and northwest of the Drakensberg Mountains. It is divided into three parts: the North Karroo, a desert area south of the Orange River; the Great, or Central, Karroo, a dry area between the North Karroo and the Swartberg; and the Little, or Southern, Karroo, in places a fertile area, south of the Swartberg along the southern coast of South Africa.

KARUN, a 450-mile-long river in western Asia. It rises west of Isfahan, in Iran, and has cut large gorges through the Zagros Mountains. It flows south and west, joining the Shatt-al-Srab near the north end of Abadan Island in the Persian Gulf.

KASAI, a 1,200-mile-long African river, rising in northeastern Angola. It flows east and north to form part of the Angola-Congo (Kinshasa) boundary, and then northwest to the Congo River near Brazzaville. It is the main southern tributary of the Congo River.

KATHIAWAR, a peninsula on India's western coast, northwest of the Gulf of Cambay and southeast of the Gulf of Kutch.

KATTEGAT, a strait between Sweden on the east and the Danish Jutland Peninsula on the west. It connects the Baltic Sea to the Skagerrak and the North Sea.

KENYA HIGHLANDS, a mountainous region of East Africa, running west to southwest in Kenya. The mountains are largely of volcanic origin, and include Mt. Kenya, over 17,000 feet, the second-highest mountain in Africa. The region is cut by the Great Rift Valley.

KERULEN, a river of northeastern Mongolia. It flows about 800 miles across the Mongolian Plateau and empties into Lake Hulun.

KHASI HILLS, uplands of west-central Assam, in northeastern India, east of the Brahmaputra River. The highest elevation in the Khasi Hills is over 6,400 feet.

KHINGAN, a mountain system of northeastern China. The system forms an inverted V, with the fertile Manchurian Plain lying between the two flanks.

The western flank is the Greater Khingan Range, which runs northeast to southwest through north-central Inner Mongolia and averages 3,000 to 5,000 feet. The eastern flank is the Lesser Khingan Range, which runs northwest to southeast near the northeastern border of Heilungkiang and the Soviet Union. The highest peak is over 3,500 feet.

KILIMANJARO, the highest mountain in Africa, located in East Africa on the border of Kenya and Tanzania. Kibo, the site of relatively recent volcanic activity, is the highest peak at 19,340 feet. It is covered by glaciers. Mawenzi, the other major peak, is 17,500 feet and has no glaciers.

KING LEOPOLD RANGES, a mountain system in northwestern Australia. It lies at the southwestern edge of the Kimberley Plateau and has elevations generally below 3,000 feet.

KISTNA, or Krishna, an Indian river that rises in the Western Ghats and flows eastward for about 800 miles to the Bay of Bengal.

KIVU, an African lake lying on the border of the Congo (Kinshasa) and Rwanda, in the western portion of the Great Rift Valley. It is about 1,000 square miles in area.

KJÖLEN, a Scandinavian mountain range extending along the border between northeastern Norway and northwestern Sweden. The highest peak is Kebnekaise, 6,965 feet.

KLONDIKE, a region south of the Ogilvie Mountains in the Yukon Territory of northwestern Canada. Gold was found there in 1896.

KOKO, or Tsinghai, a large lake in northeastern Tsinghai Province, in northern China. It lies south of the Nan Shan range and north of the eastern end of the Kunlun Mountains.

KOLYMA, a mountain range in the eastern Soviet Union, in northeastern Siberia. The mountains contain rich deposits of gold, mined in the Kolyma Gold Fields. The range has a peak of nearly 7,300 feet and is the source of the 1,500-mile-long Kolyma River.

KOREA BAY, the northeastern arm of the Yellow Sea, in East Asia. It lies between the Korean Peninsula, on the northeast, and China's Liaotung Peninsula, on the northwest.

KRA, ISTHMUS OF, the narrow section of the Malay Peninsula, occupied by Burma and Thailand. The Gulf of Siam is to the east and the Andaman Sea is to the west.

KRIMML, a waterfall on the Krimml River in west-central Austria. It is the highest waterfall in Europe, with a total drop of 1,250 feet.

KUNLUN MOUNTAINS, a range on the northern edge of Tibet, just south of the Takla Makan and the Astin Tagh ranges. The highest peak, Ulugh Maz Tagh, is over 25,000 feet. The Kunlun range contains the sources of the Yellow, the Yangtze, and the Mekong rivers.

KURIL ISLANDS, an archipelago of 32 islands in northeastern Asia, belonging to the Soviet Union. They extend northeast-southwest for some 730 miles between the Japanese island of Hokkaido and the Soviet Kamchatka Peninsula. The islands separate the Sea of Okhotsk from the Pacific Ocean and are separated from the Kamchatka Peninsula by the Kuril Strait.

KUTCH, GULF OF, or Cutch, an inlet of the Arabian Sea north of India's Kathiawar Peninsula and south of the Rann of Kutch, a salt marsh in west-central India.

KYOGA, a 1,000-square-mile lake in East Africa, in south-central Uganda. The Victoria Nile flows through the lake.

LACCADIVE SEA, an arm of the Arabian Sea between the southwestern coast of India and the Laccadive, Minicoy, Amindivi, and Maldive islands.

LADOGA, the largest lake in Europe, covering some 7,000 square miles. It lies 40 miles northeast of Leningrad, in the northwestern Soviet Union. Once divided between Finland and Russia, it is now wholly within the Soviet Union, about 20 miles southeast of the border with Finland.

LAGOA DOS PATOS, a tidal lagoon on the southeastern coast of Brazil. This "Lake of the Ducks" is about 30 miles wide and 150 miles long. It is linked with the Atlantic Ocean by a narrow, shallow opening at Rio Grande. The lagoon is separated from the ocean by an offshore sand bar, from 5 to 20 miles wide.

LAKE DISTRICT, a hilly region of northwestern England, in eastern Lancashire. A portion of Lombardy, in north-central Italy, is sometimes called the "Italian Lake District."

LAKES. The largest lake in the world is the 143,550-square-mile saltwater Caspian Sea, on the border of the Soviet Union and Iran. Second in size is North America's Lake Superior, 31,800 square miles, which is the world's largest freshwater lake.

Lake Victoria, in eastern Africa, ranks third, with an area of 26,828 square miles. The saltwater Aral Sea, in southwestern Soviet Asia, is the world's fourth largest lake, with an area of 25,300 square miles. Lake Huron, 23,000 square miles, in North America, ranks fifth.

The world's deepest lake is Lake Baykal, in the western Soviet Union, which has a depth of 5,315 feet. The largest lake wholly within Europe is Lake Ladoga, about 7,000 square miles in area, in the northwestern Soviet Union. Latin America's largest lake is Lake Nicaragua, 2,972 square miles, in central Nicaragua. In Australia, the largest is the saltwater Lake Eyre, whose area varies with the seasons and averages 3,700 square miles.

LAPLAND, an area of about 150,000 square miles within the Arctic Circle. It extends across northern Norway, Sweden, and Finland and into the Kola Peninsula of the northwestern Soviet Union.

Lapland is mountainous in the west and is largely forest or tundra further east. It is sparsely populated by about 35,000 Lapps, a nomadic people who subsist by fishing and reindeer herding.

LAPTEV SEA, a part of the Arctic Ocean along the northern coast of Siberia, in the Soviet Union. It lies between the Taymyr Peninsula and the New Siberian Islands. Vil'katskiy Strait links it with the Kara Sea on the west and Laptev Strait connects it with the East Siberian Sea on the east.

LAURENTIAN HIGHLANDS, a low, rounded mountain range in the southeastern part of Canada's Quebec Province. The highlands lie between the northern coast of the St. Lawrence river and the southern edge of the Canadian Shield. The highest point in the range is Mt. Tremblant, 3,130 feet.

LEBANON MOUNTAINS, a 100-mile-long range, extending almost the length of Lebanon parallel to the Mediterranean coast. The highest mountains are to the north. They include Qurnat as Sawda, 10,130 feet, the highest peak. East of northern Lebanon are the Anti-Lebanon Mountains, running along the Lebanese-Syrian border.

LENA, the longest river in the Soviet Union, 2,650 miles. It rises near Lake Baykal, in Siberia, and flows north and northeast to Yakutsk. There it turns and flows northwest and then north into the Laptev Sea. The Vitim, Alden, Olekema, and Vilyuy rivers are its major tributaries.

LEOPOLD II, an African lake in the western part of the Congo (Kinshasa), lying in the lowest part of the interior Congo depression. The lake varies in area from about 900 square miles in the dry season to about 3,200 square miles in the wet season.

LIAO, a 700-mile-long river of Eastern Asia, in southern Manchuria. It rises in the Greater Khingan Mountains and flows northeast and then southwest to the Gulf of Chihli (Po Hai), an arm of the Yellow Sea.

LIGURIAN SEA, an arm of the western Mediterranean between northern Corsica and the Italian Riviera. The inner portion of the Ligurian Sea is called the Gulf of Genoa.

LIMPOPO, a 1,000-mile-long river of southeastern Africa. It rises in the Witwatersrand area of South Africa and flows northwest to the Botswana border. It continues northeast along the Botswana border, turns east at the Rhodesian border, and then flows southeast through Mozambique to the Indian Ocean. Its major tributary is the Olifants River, which joins the Limpopo in Mozambique.

LIONS, GULF OF, a bay of the Mediterranean Sea on the southern coast of France. It extends from the eastern side of the Rhône delta to the coast of Spain.

LIPARI ISLANDS, a group of small volcanic islands in the southeastern Tyrrhenian Sea, off the northeastern tip of Sicily.

LITANI, a river of southern Lebanon. About 95 miles long, it rises near Baalbek and flows southwest along the eastern side of the Lebanon Mountains, turning west to empty into the Mediterranean north of Tyre.

LLANOS, a low-lying plains region of South America, in eastern Colombia and the Orinoco basin of central Venezuela.

LOFOTEN ISLANDS, a Norwegian island group in the Norwegian Sea, off the northwestern coast of the mainland.

LOGONE, an African river that rises in the highlands of the Central African Republic and flows north to Lake Chad. It meets the Chari river at Fort Lamy, and forms part of the boundary between northeastern Cameroon and Chad.

LOIRE, the longest river of France. It rises in the Cévennes Mountains in the southeast, flows northwest and west for about 625 miles, and empties into the Bay of Biscay through a wide estuary at St. Nazaire.

LOLLAND, or Laaland, one of the three main islands of Denmark. It lies southwest of Zealand, or Sjaelland, and just north of the German coast. With Falster Island it forms a Danish county.

LUANGWA, a 400-mile-long river of southeastern Africa. It rises in the Muchinga Mountains of northeastern Zambia and flows southwest to join the Zambezi River on the western border of Mozambique.

LUCERNE, a roughly cross-shaped lake in central Switzerland, bounded by the cantons of Lucerne, Unterwalden, Uri, and Schwyz.

MACDONNELL RANGES, a highland in central Australia with elevations reaching 5,000 feet. It is generally arid and barren.

MACKENZIE, a major North American river that flows for 1,200 miles through northwestern Canada, just east of the Mackenzie Mountains. The Mackenzie proper originates in Great Slave Lake, but the lake's major feeder stream, the Great Slave River, which is formed from the Peace and Atha-

AUSTRALIAN NEWS & INFORMATION BUREAU
MACDONNELL RANGES of central Australia.

basca rivers, is generally considered part of the Mackenzie. The entire Mackenzie system flows for some 2,500 miles before emptying into the Beaufort Sea, an arm of the Arctic Ocean.

MADAGASCAR, one of the largest islands in the world, lying in the Indian Ocean some 250 miles across the Mozambique Channel from Africa's southeast coast. It consists of a mountainous core ringed with coastal lowlands and swamps. It has an area of about 230,000 square miles, and is occupied by the Malagasy Republic.

MADEIRA, an archipelago with two large islands and several islets in the Atlantic Ocean, some 350 miles east of North Africa. The islands belong to Portugal. They are mountainous and noted for their fine scenery and mild climate. Sugarcane is grown and wine is produced.

MADEIRA, a river in central South America formed from the union on the Bolivia-Brazil border of the Beni and the Mamore rivers, which rise in Bolivia. The Madeira flows for over 1,500 miles north and east to join the Amazon east of Manaus.

MAGDALENA, a South American river that flows northward for some 1,000 miles through Colombia. It lies between the massive Cordillera Central, to the west, and the Cordillera Oriental, to the east. It is joined near its mouth by the Cauca.

MAGGIORE, a lake, about 80 square miles in area, in the Alpine region of northern Italy and southern Switzerland. Its mild climate and scenic beauty attract many tourists.

MAIN, a river in central Germany that rises in Bavaria and flows westward for some 300 miles through Wurzburg and Frankfurt to the Rhine, at Mainz.

MAKALU, a mountain in the Himalayas on the border between Nepal and the Tibet region of China. It is the fourth highest mountain in the world, with an elevation of 27,824 feet.

MAKARIKARI, a large salt basin in arid northeastern Botswana, in south-central Africa. Although usually dry, it may receive the overflow of water from Lake Ngami during the wet season. There are brine deposits of commerical importance in the north.

MALABAR COAST, India's southwestern coast, lying between the Western Ghats and the Arabian Sea.

MALAY ARCHIPELAGO, the world's largest island group, extending east from the Malay Peninsula. The archipelago is bounded on the north by the South China Sea, on the east by the Pacific Ocean, and on the south and west by the Indian Ocean. It includes the islands of the Philippines, Indonesia, and the Federation of Malaysia, which are separated by many straits and small seas.

MALAY PENINSULA, a projection of mainland Southeast Asia between the Andaman Sea, on the west, and the Gulf of Siam, an arm of the South China Sea, on the east. It is occupied by Burma, Thailand, and West Malaysia. The peninsula is heavily forested and hilly and is rich in minerals.

MANAGUA, a lake in Central America, the northernmost of Nicaragua's two major lakes.

MANILA BAY, an inlet of the South China Sea on the southwestern coast of Luzon Island, in the Philippines. It is one of the best natural harbors in eastern Asia.

MANNAR, GULF OF, an inlet of the Indian Ocean between Ceylon and southern India. It is connected to the Bay of Bengal by Palk Strait.

MARACAIBO, a brackish lagoon, 130 miles long and 75 miles wide, in northwestern Venezuela. It is a major South American petroleum-producing area. Petroleum was discovered there in the early 1900s and many oil wells are located around the eastern shore and in the middle of the lake.

MARAJÓ, a large South American island, located at the eastern end of the Amazon River and forming a part of the Amazon delta. It is about 150 miles long and 100 miles wide. The western half is covered mostly with tropical rainforest, and the eastern half is grassland, which is flooded during the rainy season. Beef cattle are grazed, and rubber, timber, and medicinal plants are extracted.

MARIAS ISLANDS, an archipelago of four small mountainous islands in the Pacific Ocean off Mexico's eastern coast.

MARITSA, a river of eastern Europe that rises in the Rhodope mountains of western Bulgaria. It flows eastward and then south for about 300 miles along the boundary of Greece and Turkey and empties into the Aegean Sea.

MARMARA, an inland sea, some 175 miles long and up to 50 miles wide, separating European Turkey from Asian Turkey. It is linked with the Aegean Sea by the Dardanelles and with the Black Sea by the Bosporus. The city of Istanbul is located on its northeastern shore.

MARNE, a river that rises in eastern France and flows north and west for about 325 miles through a rich agricultural region. It empties into the Seine at Charenton.

MARRA, an African mountain range in western Sudan that rises to a peak of more than 10,000 feet, at Mt. Marra.

MASAI STEPPE, an African plateau region of volcanic origin, in southwestern Kenya near the Zambian border. A dry pasture area, it is used by semi-nomadic peoples for cattle grazing.

MASSIF CENTRAL, a high mountainous plateau occupying all of southwestern France. It contains the headwaters of many important rivers.

MEDITERRANEAN, the largest inland sea in the world, 2,400 miles long and up to 1,000 miles wide. It separates the continents of Europe to the north, Asia to the east, and Africa to the south. The Mediterranean is linked with the Atlantic Ocean by the Strait of Gibralter and with the Red Sea by the Suez Canal.

The irregularly-shaped sea is divided into two deep basins by the Italian Peninsula, the island of Sicily, and a submarine ridge joining Sicily and Tunisia. There are islands in each basin. The western basin, connected to the Black Sea by the Bosporus and Dardanelles, has two northern extensions—the Adriatic and Aegean seas.

Among the several rivers feeding the Mediterranean are the Rhône, Po, and Nile. The climate of the Mediterranean Basin consists of hot, dry summers and warm, wet winters.

MEKONG, a major river of eastern Asia rising in the Himalayas, in eastern Tibet. It follows a twisting, generally southeasterly course for 2,600 miles before emptying into the South China Sea through a wide delta at the southern tip of Indochina.

The Mekong's major tributaries include the Mun, the Hou, the Khong, the Srepok, and the Chinit. The Tonle Sap, a large lake in west central Cambodia, serves as a reservoir for the Mekong's flood waters.

The river marks parts of the Burma-China, Burma-Laos, and Thailand-Laos borders. It is navigable to north-central Laos and has a fertile valley and delta.

MENDERES, the name of three rivers of Asia Minor, the most notable being the Büyük Meander. This river, rising in western Turkey and flowing southwest and west into the Aegean Sea, is about 250 miles long. Its wandering course has given us the term, meander.

MEUSE, a river that rises in northeastern France and flows into Belgium, where it is joined by the Sambre at Namur. The Sambre-Meuse valley is underlain by rich coal deposits and is Belgium's most important industrial district. In the Netherlands, the Meuse becomes the Maas. It turns west near Nijmegen, and enters the North Sea south of Dordrecht.

MORAVA, a 260-mile-long river in Yugoslavia. It rises north of Skopje and flows northward to join the Danube near Smederevo.

MOSELLE, a major river of France and Germany. Rising in the French Vosges Mountains, it flows north through the Lorraine industrial district of northeastern France, enters Germany, and joins the Rhine River at Koblenz.

MOSKVA, a river of the Moscow region of the Soviet Union. Rising in the Smolensk-Moscow Upland, west of the city of Moscow, it flows for some 300 miles to join the river Oka after passing through the city. Navigable below Moscow, it is connected to the Volga River by canal.

MOSQUITO COAST, the eastern, Caribbean, coast of Nicaragua and Honduras, in Central America. It is named for the indigenous Mosquito Indians.

MOULOUYA, a North African river. It rises in the Atlas Mountains in Morocco and flows northeastward for some 300 miles to the Mediterranean Sea.

MOUNTAINS. Mt. Everest, 29,028 feet, and the world's next four highest mountains—Godwin Austin, Kanchinjunga, Makalu, and Dhaulagiri, each more than 26,000 feet in elevation—all lie in the Himalayas, in Southern Asia. The highest peaks on each of the other continents are much lower.

South America's highest peak, Aconcagua, rises 22,834 feet. North America's Mt. McKinley is 20,320 feet. Kilimanjaro, in Africa, rises 19,340 feet, and El'brus, in Europe, is 18,481 feet. The Antarctic's highest known point, the Vinson Massif, is about 16,860 feet in elevation. Australia's highest mountain, Kosciusko, rises only 7,316 feet.

MT. COMMUNISM, a mountain in the Pamir range in the southeastern part of the Soviet Union's Tadzhik republic. Formerly called Garmo Peak, and later Stalin Peak, it is the highest mountain in the Soviet Union, rising more than 24,500 feet.

MT. EVEREST, the world's highest mountain. It rises 29,028 feet in the Himalayas on the border between Nepal and Tibet in south-central Asia.

MURRAY-DARLING, Australia's principal river system. The Murray rises near Mt. Kosciusko, in southeastern Australia and flows westward to its mouth at Encounter Bay, off the Indian Ocean on the south Australian coast.

The Darling, among whose headstreams are the Barwon and Macquarie rivers, flows westward and southward from northern New South Wales to

Wentwork, where it joins the Murray. The Murray-Darling watercourse, 2,310 miles long, is used extensively for irrigation.

MWERU, a lake in central Africa on the border between the Congo (Kinshasa) and Zambia, and some 100 miles west of the southern tip of Lake Tanganyika.

NAN, a mountain range in north-central China at the northern end of the Tibetan Plateau. Its peaks range from 18,000 to over 20,000 feet above sea level. The range is cut by deep valleys.

NEGEV, a semi-desert region in southern Israel. The Negev contains copper, potash, phosphate, and oil deposits. Limited agriculture is carried on with water brought by pipeline from the north.

NEVA, a river in the western Soviet Union that flows from Lake Ladoga westward into the Gulf of Finland. Although only 45 miles long, the Neva is an important part of the North Russian canal system, which allows large ships to reach Leningrad.

NEW GUINEA, the world's second largest island, lying in the southwest Pacific Ocean, north of Australia. The island, with an area of 317,000 square miles, has a mountainous interior and swampy coastlines. New Guinea has extensive mangrove and sandalwood forests and contains deposits of gold, oil, cobalt, and nickel.

Politically New Guinea is divided into three parts—West Irian, a part of Indonesia; the Trust Territory of New Guinea, a UN trust administered by Australia; and the Territory of Papua, an Australian territory.

NICARAGUA, the largest lake in Central America, with an area of 3,060 square miles. It is located in southwestern Nicaragua.

NIGER, a major river in West Africa, rising in southeastern Guinea and flowing northeast into Mali and then southeast into the Republic of Niger and Nigeria. The river flows for some 2,600 miles and empties into the Gulf of Guinea. About 80 miles from its mouth, the Niger forms an extensive delta.

NILE, the longest river in Africa and in the world. Its course can be traced from the Kagera River headwaters in northern Tanzania to the Mediterranean Sea, a distance of 4,145 miles.

The Nile is formed by the joining of the White Nile and the Blue Nile at Khartoum, in Sudan. The White Nile flows north from Tanzania into Uganda and Sudan, where it is joined by its major tributaries, the Ghazal and the Sobat, before joining the Blue Nile. The Nile proper continues north through the United Arab Republic (Egypt) and forms an extensive delta north of Cairo.

NIMBA, a range of mountains in West Africa, in northern Liberia and southern Guinea. The Nimba Mountains contain rich iron ore deposits.

NORTH AMERICA, a continent in the northern half of the western hemisphere, with an area of more than 9.4 million square miles and a population of over 300 million in the mid-1960s.

North America extends from islands north of the Arctic Circle to the Isthmus of Panama, near the equator. It is bounded on the west by the Pacific Ocean, on the east by the Atlantic Ocean, and it includes the West Indies islands in the Caribbean Sea. High mountains dominate the western part of the continent, vast plains cover most of its central portion, and lower mountains and coastal plains mark the eastern coast.

NORTH CHANNEL, a strait between the Irish Sea and North Atlantic Ocean. It separates Scotland from Northern Ireland.

NORTH SEA, an arm of the North Atlantic Ocean, separating Britain from the northwestern European mainland.

NORWEGIAN SEA, a body of water off the western coast of Norway between the North Atlantic and the Arctic oceans.

NOVAYA ZEMLYA, an archipelago in the Arctic Ocean between the Barents Sea on the west and the Kara Sea on the east. It is composed of two large islands, separated by Matochkin Shar Strait, and several small islands. The archipelago is part of the Soviet Union.

NUBIAN DESERT, a desert area in northeastern Sudan, lying between the Nile River and the Red Sea.

NYASA, the third largest lake in Africa, located on the border of Tanzania, Malawi, and Mozambique. The lake has a surface area of over 11,000 square miles and a mountainous shoreline. Its only outlet is the Shire River, a tributary of the Zambezi River.

OB, a river in the Soviet Union, over 2,000 miles long. The Ob rises in the Altai Mountains of western Siberia. It flows northwest to join the Irtysh River and then north into the Gulf of Ob, an inlet of the Kara Sea.

ODER, a river in central Europe, over 500 miles long. It rises in Silesia, flows north through western Poland, is joined by the Neisse River, and continues north to the Baltic Sea. The Oder forms a major part of the border between East Germany and Poland.

OKAVANGO, a river of southwestern Africa, some 1,000 miles long. The Okavango rises in central Angola and flows generally southeast, forming part of the border between South West Africa and Angola. It empties into Okavango Basin, a marsh in northern Botswana.

OKHOTSK, SEA OF, a western arm of the North Pacific Ocean off the eastern coast of the Siberian region of the Soviet Union. It is bounded on the east by the Kamchatka Peninsula

and the Kuril Islands, and on the southwest by Sakhalin and Hokkaido islands. It joins the Sea of Japan, to the southwest, through the Tatar and the Soya, or La Perouse, straits.

OLYMPUS, or Olimbus, a mountain range in Greece, near the coast of Thessaly. Mt. Olympus, 9,550 feet, the highest point in the range and in Greece, was thought in ancient times to be the home of the gods.

OMAN, GULF OF, an arm of the Arabian Sea between Arabia and Iran. It is linked with the Persian Gulf by the Strait of Hormuz.

ONEGA, the second largest lake in Europe, lying in the northwestern Soviet Union. Onega has a surface area of over 3,500 square miles. Its outlet is the Svir River, which flows into Lake Ladoga, Europe's largest lake.

ORANGE, a river of southern Africa, rising in northeastern Basutoland and flowing 1,300 miles in a generally westward direction to the Atlantic Ocean. The river forms part of the boundary between South West Africa and South Africa.

ORDOS, a desert region of Inner Mongolia. It lies within the great bend of the Hwang Ho (Yellow River).

ORE, or Erz, a mountain range in eastern Germany and northwestern Czechoslovakia with a peak of just over 4,000 feet.

ORIENT, a general term for Asia and especially eastern Asia. The region known as the Orient, or East, is divided into three sections—the Near East, including the countries at the eastern end of the Mediterranean Sea, northeastern Africa, and the Arabian peninsula; the Middle East, including the southern Asian countries from Iraq to Burma, and sometimes including the Near East; and the Far East, including China, Korea, Japan, the Malay Peninsula, and the Malay archipelago.

ORINOCO, a river of South America that flows for about 1,500 miles from the Parima Mountains of Venezuela west and then north along the Venezuela-Colombia border, and then northeast to the Atlantic Ocean. The Orinoco forms a wide delta in northeastern Venezuela.

ORKNEY ISLANDS, a Scottish archipelago, lying off the northeastern coast of Scotland and separated from it by Pentland Firth. The largest island is Pomona, locally known as the Mainland. South of Pomona lies a treacherous bay, the Scapa Flow.

ORONTES, a 246-mile-long river in western Syria. It rises in northeastern Lebanon and flows north to the Turkish border, where it turns and flows west to the Mediterranean Sea.

PACIFIC OCEAN, the largest of the oceans, almost 64 million square miles in area. It lies between the American continents, Australia, the Malay Archi-

NATURAL FEATURES

pelago, and Asia, and extends from the Arctic Circle to the Antarctic Region. Between the Arctic and the equator it is known as the North Pacific; from the equator to the Antarctic it is called the South Pacific.

PAMIR, a mountain range in the southern Soviet Union, lying along the borders of Pakistan, Kashmir, and China, north of the Hindu Kush and Karakorum ranges. Peaks in the Pamirs rise over 25,000 feet above sea level.

PAMPAS, grassy treeless plains of South America. They extend some 1,000 miles through east-central Argentina from the lower Paraná River south to the Colorado River.

PANAMA, ISTHMUS OF, a narrow neck of land in southern Central America separating the Caribbean Sea from the Gulf of Panama, an arm of the Pacific Ocean. It is occupied by Panama and by the Panama Canal Zone, the U.S.-controlled site of a canal across the isthmus.

PARAGUAY, a river of South America, rising in southwestern Brazil and flowing generally south for some 1,500 miles. The Paraguay forms parts of the boundaries between Brazil and Bolivia, Brazil and Paraguay, and Paraguay and Argentina before it empties into the Paraná River in the southwestern corner of Paraguay.

PARANÁ, the second longest river in South America. Formed by the junction of the Grande and Paranaíba rivers in south-central Brazil, it flows generally southwest for some 2,500 miles.

The river forms part of the boundary between Brazil and Paraguay and all of the boundary between Paraguay and Argentina. It joins the Paraguay River in the southwestern corner of Paraguay, and flows south through Argentina to the Río de la Plata.

PARIA, GULF OF, an arm of the Atlantic Ocean lying between the northeast coast of Venezuela and the west coast of Trinidad. The Paria peninsula of Venezuela is on the north.

PAROPAMISUS, a mountain range of western Asia, in northwest Afghanistan near the western end of the Hindu Kush.

PATAGONIA, a barren tableland of southern South America lying between the Andes and the Atlantic Ocean. It extends south of the Negro River to the Strait of Magellan.

PAULO AFONSO FALLS, a series of three waterfalls in eastern Brazil, with a height of over 270 feet. They form the principal cataract along the São Francisco River.

PELOPONNESOS, a peninsula and province of southern Greece, connected with the mainland by the narrow Isthmus of Corinth. The Peloponnesos is the site of ancient Corinth and Sparta.

PENNER, two rivers in south-central India, both of which rise in the hills of Mysore state. The Northern Penner flows east for about 350 miles, emptying into the Bay of Bengal near Nellore. The Southern Penner flows southeast for about 245 miles into the Bay of Bengal near Cuddalore.

PERSIAN GULF, a shallow extension of the Arabian Sea, bounded by the Trucial Coast, Qatar, Saudi Arabia, Kuwait, Iraq, and Iran. It is some 550 miles long and is connected with the Gulf of Oman to the southeast. The Persian Gulf is important for pearl fishing and petroleum.

PESCADORES, or P'enghu, a group of Chinese islands lying in the Formosa Strait between the China mainland and Taiwan.

PINDUS, a mountain range in southeastern Europe that begins in central Albania and extends generally southeast through central Greece.

PLATA, RÍO DE LA, an estuary in the southeast coast of South America. It forms part of the border between Uruguay and Argentina, stretching some 250 miles from the Atlantic Ocean to the mouths of the Paraná and Uruguay rivers.

POYANG, a lake in southeastern China, the second largest in the country. It lies in Kiangsi province in the basin of the Yangtze River, which feeds it.

PRUT, a river of eastern Europe that rises in the Carpathian Mountains of the southwestern Soviet Union and flows generally southeast for some 520 miles. The Prut forms part of the border between the Soviet Union and Romania and joins the Danube about 75 miles from the Black Sea.

PYRENEES, a European mountain range extending some 270 miles along the entire Spanish-French border, from the Bay of Biscay to the south coast of the Gulf of Lions. The highest peak is Pico de Aneto, 11,168 feet.

QATTARA DEPRESSION, a low area of northern Africa, in the northwestern United Arab Republic (Egypt). Its lowest point is 436 feet below sea level.

RED, or Hong, a principal river of North Vietnam. It rises in Yünnan, in China, as the Yüan and flows about 500 miles southeast into the Gulf of Tonkin, an arm of the South China Sea. Its chief tributaries are the Da (Black), the Gam, and the Lo rivers. The lower valley forms the economic, political, and cultural center of North Vietnam.

RED RIVER OF THE NORTH, a river of North America. It rises in the northeastern corner of South Dakota and flows north into Canada 350 miles to the south end of Lake Winnipeg.

RED SEA, an inland sea between northeastern Africa and the Arabian Peninsula, part of the Great Rift Valley system. It is about 1,450 miles long

SPANISH NATIONAL TOURIST OFFICE

THE PYRENEES form a mountain barrier on the boundary between France and Spain.

and less than 250 miles wide, and its greatest depth is more than 7,250 feet.

Two arms of the Red Sea, the Gulf of Aqaba and the Gulf of Suez, lie to the north. The sea is connected to the Mediterranean by the Suez Canal and to the Gulf of Aden through the strait of Bab el Mandeb. An ancient trade route, it assumed new importance with the opening of the Suez Canal in 1869.

RHINE, a west European river that rises in the Swiss Alps and flows north and west, forming parts of the boundaries of Liechtenstein, Switzerland, France, and Germany. In Germany it crosses a rich, densely populated, and highly industrialized region before turning west into the Netherlands, where it divides into two branches, the Nederrijn and the Waal, which empty into the North Sea near Rotterdam.

The Rhine is over 800 miles long, and its major tributaries include the Neckar, Main, Ruhr, Lippe, and Moselle rivers. It is navigable for most of its course, and is connected by canal with other major European river systems.

RHÔNE, a west European river that flows some 500 miles through Switzerland and France. It rises in the Swiss Alps, passes through Lake Geneva and crosses into France. Joined at Lyon by the Saône River, it turns south and empties into the Mediterranean Sea west of Marseilles. Its large delta around Marseilles, called the Camargue, is the center of French rice-growing and processing.

RIVERS. The world's longest river is Africa's 4,145-mile-long Nile. Second in length, but greater in volume, is the Amazon, which flows for 3,900 miles in South America. The Mississippi-Missouri-Red Rock river system is the third largest, extending for a total of 3,860 miles in North America.

The Ob-Irtysh waterway, in western Asia, is 3,460 miles long and ranks fourth. The Yangtze, flowing for 3,400 miles in eastern Asia, is the world's fifth longest river. Europe's longest river is the Volga, which follows a curving course for 2,290 miles in east-central Europe. The Murray-Darling waterway, 2,310 miles, is Australia's longest river. The Antarctic continent has no rivers.

RIVIERA, a Mediterranean seacoast in southern France and northwestern Italy. Its blue water and white beaches have made it one of the world's most popular resort areas.

ROSS SEA, an arm of the Pacific Ocean extending into Antarctica between Victoria Land and Marie Byrd Land. McMurdo Sound is an inlet of Ross Sea in the coast of Victoria Land.

RUB AL KHALI, or Empty Quarter, a desert region, with an area of some 300,000 square miles, in the southern half of the Arabian Peninsula. It contains no known vegetation or sources of water and is uninhabited.

RUDOLF, an African lake in northwestern Kenya in the Great Rift Valley. It has an area of about 2,400 square miles, and is fed by the Omo River.

RUFIJI, an African river that rises in the plateau of south-central Tanzania. It flows northeast and east to empty into the Indian Ocean through a wide delta.

RUWENZORI, an African mountain massif between lakes Albert and Edward on the Uganda-Congo border. The highest nonvolcanic peak in Africa, its highest part, Mt. Stanley, consists of two summits—Mt. Margherita and Mt. Alexandria—both over 16,700 feet. The Ruwenzori is generally accepted as being the "Mountains of the Moon" of the ancient geographers.

SABARMATI, a river of western India that rises in the Aravalli Mountains. It flows southward through a rich agricultural region for about 200 miles to the Gulf of Cambay.

SAHARA, a desert region of North Africa extending about 3,000 miles from west to east and 1,000 miles from north to south. It is the world's largest desert, and its relief is extremely varied.

The Sahara includes high, deeply dissected plateaus, such as the Tibesti, Ahaggar, and Aïr, the summits of which may attain 10,000 feet, and depressions, such as the Bodélé, or Chad, which are less than 500 feet above sea level. The landscape includes both sandy desert, or erg, and stony desert, or reg.

Rainfall averages less than 10 inches a year, and the only permanent rivers are the Nile and Niger. Inhabited largely by nomadic peoples, the desert has rich mineral deposits.

SAKHALIN, an island about 550 miles long and 30 miles wide, located in the Sea of Okhotsk, an arm of the Pacific Ocean. It lies off the eastern coast of the Siberian region of the Soviet Union, of which it is a part. Sakhalin is separated from the mainland by the Tatar Strait and from the Japanese island of Hokkaido by the Soya, or La Perouse, Strait. Two parallel mountain ranges on the island are divided by a central valley through which the Tym and Poronai rivers flow.

SALWEEN, a major Asian river that rises in the Thanglha Mountains of Tibet. It flows east and south for about 1,750 miles through China and Burma to empty into the Gulf of Martaban, an arm of the Andaman Sea.

SANAGHA, a river of southwestern Africa that rises in Cameroon and flows southeast to join the Congo river below its confluence with the Ubangi River.

SÃO FRANCISCO, a South American river that flows northward from the highlands of east-central Brazil to the arid northeast, and then eastward to the Atlantic Ocean. It is partially navigable, but broken by rapids.

SATPURA, a mountain range in west-central India, between the Narbada and the Tapti rivers, with an average elevation of about 3,000 feet. The mountains are forested and contain manganese and copper.

SAVA, a river of northern Yugoslavia that rises in the Karawanken Alps on the Italian-Yugoslav border. It flows eastward for some 450 miles to join the Danube at Belgrade. The Drina, the Boma, and the Verbas rivers are its main tributaries.

SAYAN, a mountain range of the Soviet Union that lies to the east of the Altai, in the southern part of the Irkutsk region. It has a peak of over 11,000 feet. The lower slopes of the mountains are forested and contain important deposits of iron ore, gold, silver, mercury, and graphite.

SCANDINAVIA, a peninsula of northwestern Europe washed by the Arctic Ocean on the north, the Norwegian Sea on the west, the North Sea, Skagerrak and Kattegat straits on the south, and the Baltic Sea and Gulf of Bothnia on the southeast. Western Scandinavia is mountainous; lowlands occupy the east. Much of it lies above the Arctic Circle, and the climate is cold. It is shared by Norway, Sweden, and Finland.

SCHELDE, a Belgian river that rises in northern France. It flows north and west for some 250 miles to empty into the North Sea through a broad estuary near the port of Antwerp.

SCILLY ISLANDS, a group of about 140 British islands in the Atlantic Ocean off the Land's End cape in southwestern Britain. Once a pirates' haven, today they are important for vegetable and flower growing.

SEINE, a river of northern France that rises in the highlands northwest of Dijon. It flows through Troyes and Paris and empties into the English Channel through a broad estuary.

SEISTAN, a marshy area of western Asia south of the Plateau of Iran. It is on the Iran-Afghanistan border and includes Lake Helmand.

SELENGE, an Asian river that rises in northwestern Mongolia and flows northeast for about 750 miles into the Soviet Union's Lake Baykal. Its principal tributary is the 300-mile-long Orkhon, which joins it near Mongolia's northern border.

SÉNÉGAL, a river of western Africa, formed by the joining of the Bafing and Bakoy rivers in western Mali. It flows in a generally northwest direction, forming the boundary between Mauritania and Senegal, and empties into the Atlantic Ocean. Including the Bafing, the Sénégal River is over 1,000 miles long.

SEVERNAYA ZEMLYA, or Northern Land, a group of Arctic islands lying to the north of Cape Chelyuskin on the Taimyr Peninsula of the Soviet Union. The group consists of three main islands, and many smaller ones, and covers an area of over 13,000 square miles. They divide the Laptev Sea from the Kara Sea and are separated from the mainland by Vilkitski Strait.

SEVERN, a river of southeastern Britain that rises in east-central Wales, flows northeast into England, then east and south into the Bristol Channel through a broad estuary.

SHANNON, a river in Ireland that rises in the north and flows southward for 250 miles. It drains the north-central, central, and southwestern parts of the island, and enters the Atlantic Ocean through a long and deep estuary.

SHETLAND ISLANDS, a British archipelago in the Atlantic Ocean northeast of the Orkney Islands. The Shetlands have an area of about 550 square miles. Livestock herding and fishing are the principal occupations.

SI, a river about 1,000 miles long in southern China. Formed by the Hungshui and the Yu, it enters the South China Sea near Canton.

SIAM, GULF OF, an arm of the South China Sea on the southeast coast of Thailand. It lies between the Malay peninsula on the southwest and Cambodia and Vietnam on the northeast.

SICILY, the largest island of the Mediterranean. A part of Italy, it is separated from the southwestern tip of the mainland by the narrow Strait of Messina. Most of Sicily is mountainous and rugged, and the climate is dry and mild. The island produces olives and has deposits of sulfur, petroleum, and natural gas.

SIDRA, GULF OF, an inlet of the Mediterranean Sea on the coast of northern Libya.

SIERRA MADRE, three high mountain ranges that dominate the landscape of Mexico. The Sierra Madre Oriental runs from north to south in central

Mexico. The Sierra Madre Occidental lies in the west, and the Sierra Madre del Sur is in the southwest.

All three ranges have peaks between 12,000 and 15,000 feet, and they converge in south-central Mexico. The lower slopes are densely forested, and the mountains are rich in minerals.

SINAI, a triangular peninsula that forms the easternmost portion of the United Arab Republic (Egypt). It extends southward from a 150-mile-long Mediterranean coast for over 200 miles to the northern tip of the Red Sea. Two extensions of the Red Sea—the Gulf of Suez and the Gulf of Aqaba—form the western and eastern boundaries of the peninsula.

This dry, barren land, inhabited by nomads, is considered a part of Asia rather than Africa. The extensive central plateau of El-Tih rises to the south and culminates in Mt. Katherina, over 8,000 feet high. Nearby is Musa Mountain, thought by many to be the Mount Sinai of the Old Testament. Sinai is a source of crude oil, iron, and manganese. The peninsula was occupied by Israeli forces in 1967.

SITTANG, a river of east-central Burma. It rises in the central mountains and flows southward for about 350 miles to the Gulf of Martaban.

SIWALIK, a mountain range of north-central India, in the foothills of the Himalayas. The average elevation is 2,500 feet. It is an important source of forest products and contains some copper.

SKAGERRAK, a strait between Norway and Denmark, about 150 miles long and 80 miles wide. It leads into the North Sea in the southwest and the Kattegat in the northeast, and forms an important link in the North Sea-Baltic waterway.

SOBAEK, a mountain range in Korea extending from the east-central coast to the southwestern tip of the peninsula.

SOCOTRA, an island in the Indian Ocean about 120 miles east of Africa's Cape Guardafui and 220 miles south of the coast of Arabia. About 1,380 square miles in area, it consists largely of a barren plateau with mountains rising to 4,500 feet.

SOMME, a river that rises in north-central France and flows westward for 150 miles to the English Channel.

SOUTH AMERICA, a continent in the southern half of the western hemisphere, with an area of nearly 7 million square miles and a 1967 population of about 175 million. It is bordered on the north by the Caribbean Sea, on the east by the Atlantic Ocean, on the south by the Drake Passage, which separates it from Antarctica, and on the west by the Pacific Ocean.

High mountains of the Andes system tower over a narrow coastal plain in the west. The interior consists of lowlands that are densely forested in the north and swampy or arid in the south. Highlands dominate the east.

SOUTH CHINA SEA, a body of water between southeastern China and Indochina on the west, and the Philippine and Indonesian islands on the east and south. About 1.3 million square miles in area, it is the world's largest sea.

SUDETES, a mountain system in east-central Europe extending about 200 miles along the German-Czechoslovakian and the Polish-Czechoslovakian borders. Elevations are less than 5,300 feet.

SULAIMAN, a mountain range in central West Pakistan between the Indus valley and northeastern Baluchistan. It has a peak over 11,000 feet, and its most important passes are the Bolan and the Gumal, both of which lie at about 6,000 feet.

SUNGARI, the chief river of Manchuria, in northeastern China. It rises near Korea and flows north and west for 800 miles to join the Amur on the China-Soviet Union border. The Nonni is its most important tributary.

SUTHERLAND, a waterfall in southwestern New Zealand. The fifth highest in the world, it falls 1,904 feet.

SYR, an Asian river extending 1,500 miles from headwaters in the Tien Mountains to the Aral Sea of the Soviet Union. In its upper course, the river flows through deep gorges and is called Naryn. The river is navigable for 850 miles in its lower course and, flowing through an arid and semi-arid area, is used extensively for irrigation.

TAEBAEK, a mountain range in Korea running parallel to the eastern coast of the peninsula.

TAGUS, or Tejo, a major river of the Iberian Peninsula that rises in Spain's eastern mountains, flows west across Spain, and forms a small section of the border with Portugal before turning southwest to enter the Atlantic through a broad estuary at Lisbon. Nearly 600 miles long, it is the longest river on the Iberian peninsula.

TAKLA MAKAN, a desert region near the western border of China, north of Tibet and the Himalayas. It lies in the basin of the Tarim River.

TANA, an East African river that rises near Mt. Kenya in south-central Kenya. It flows in a great arc for some 500 miles to the Indian Ocean at Formosa Bay.

TANGANYIKA, an African lake on the border of Tanganyika and the Congo (Kinshasa). Long and narrow, it has an area of over 12,500 square miles, and its depth of some 4,700 feet makes it one of the world's deepest lakes.

TAPA, a mountain range of west-central China, with peaks to about 9,500 feet. The Yangtze River cuts spectacular gorges through the mountains.

TARANTO, GULF OF, an inlet of the Mediterranean Sea on the southeastern coast of Italy.

TASMANIA, an island off the southeastern coast of Australia, lying between the Indian Ocean and the Tasman Sea. Tasmania, about 180 miles by 190 miles, is geologically a continuation of the Australian continent. A high central plateau is surrounded by forested mountains in the west and agricultural lands in the north and southeast.

TEHUANTEPEC, GULF OF, an inlet of the Pacific Ocean on the coast of the Isthmus of Tehuantepec, in southwestern Mexico. Its irregular coastline is backed by steep mountains.

THAMES, a river about 200 miles long in southern Britain. It rises in Gloucestershire, flows east into the densely settled fertile English Lowlands, through London, and empties into the North Sea.

THANGLHA, a mountain range in the Tibet region of China. It lies north of the Himalayas and south of the Kunlun Mountains.

IRISH TOURIST BOARD
IRELAND'S SHANNON RIVER, some 250 miles long, flows past St. John's Castle in Limerick.

THAR, a desert on the Indian subcontinent between the Aravalli Mountains and the Indus River.

TIBER, a river of central Italy, about 250 miles long. It rises in the central Apennines, flows south through Umbria and northern Latium, turns southwest through Rome, and enters the Tyrrhenian Sea at Ostia.

TIBESTI, a high mountain range in the central Sahara of northern Africa. Situated in northern Chad and in Libya, the massif is approximately 250 miles in diameter. Its rugged peaks, of volcanic origin, reach their highest point in Koussi Volcano, over 11,000 feet.

TIERRA DEL FUEGO, a group of islands at the southern tip of South America. They lie south of the Strait of Magellan and extend to Cape Horn, a headland on the southernmost island. They are divided between Chile and Argentina.

TIGRIS, a river of southwestern Asia that rises in two headstreams in the Taurus Mountains of eastern Turkey. After forming a small part of the Turkish-Syrian border, the river flows southeastward through Iraq for over 1,100 miles until it joins the Euphrates River at Qurna, to form the combined river of Shatt al-Arab. The Tigris has several tributaries, including the Great Zab, the Little Zab, and the Diyala.

TIMOR, an island of the lesser Sunda group lying across the Timor Sea from northeastern Australia. It consists of a mountainous core rimmed with lowlands. Timor is divided between Portugal and Indonesia.

TISZA, a river of eastern Europe that rises in the Carpathian Mountains in the Soviet Union's Ukrainian republic. It flows west and south for about 850 miles on a tortuous, meandering course to join the Danube River about 30 miles north of Belgrade, in Yugoslavia.

TITICACA, a lake in South America on the border of Peru and Bolivia. It lies more than 12,500 feet above sea level in the altiplano of the central Andes. Lake Titicaca is about 110 miles long, 35 miles wide, and 700 feet deep.

TONLE SAP, a lake in Southeast Asia, in west central Cambodia. Literally "Great Lake," its area varies between 1,000 and 9,500 square miles according to the season.

TORRES STRAIT, a channel between northeastern Australia and southeastern New Guinea. It links the Arafura Sea to the west with the Coral Sea to the east.

TROODOS, or Olympus, a mountain range of west-central Cyprus. It contains deposits of copper pyrites, chrome ore, and asbestos. The highest point is Mt. Troodos, over 6,400 feet.

TSINLING, a mountain range of central China, running from east to west between the Han and the Wei rivers.

SATOUR

THE VAAL RIVER OF SOUTH AFRICA flows through the Transvaal into the Cape Province.

The mountains rise to about 11,000 feet and are the traditional dividing line between north and south China.

TUGELA, a series of waterfalls in eastern South Africa on the Tugela River. The world's second highest waterfalls, they drop a total of 3,110 feet.

TUMEN, a 220-mile-long Asian river that rises in northeastern Korea and forms part of the border of China and Korea. It flows generally northeast, turning sharply southeast at the tip of Korea to flow into the Sea of Japan.

TUNGTING, a large, shallow lake in southeastern China. Fed by the Yuan, Lin, and Tzu rivers, it also serves as a reservoir for the Yangtze River during the high water season. Its area varies with the season from 2,000 square miles to 4,000 square miles. The basin is a rich agricultural region.

TUZ, a salt lake of western Asia, in central Turkey. It lies at an altitude of 3,100 feet and at times is dry.

TYRRHENIAN SEA, an arm of the Mediterranean Sea. It lies between Italy on the east, Corsica and Sardinia on the west, and Sicily on the south.

UBANGI, a river of central Africa, formed in the northern Congo (Kinshasa) by the joining of the Bomi and Uele rivers. It flows generally southwest for about 700 miles to the Congo River. The Ubangi forms part of the boundaries between the Congo (Kinshasa) and the Central African Republic, and the Congo (Kinshasa) and the Congo (Brazzaville).

UNGAVA, a bay on the northern coast of Quebec, Canada, between the Ungava Peninsula, on the west, and Labrador, on the east.

URAL, a river in the west-central Soviet Union. It rises in the southern Ural Mountains and flows southwest, and south again, emptying into the Caspian Sea. The river is about 1,500 miles long.

URAL MOUNTAINS, a mountain system in the Soviet Union that extends from the Arctic Ocean to the Ural River, forming the geographic boundary between Europe and Asia. The Urals can be divided into three sections—the Northern Urals, which contain the highest peaks; the Central Urals, which are gently rounded and are crossed by rail lines; and the Southern Urals, which are formed by a series of parallel ridges.

URUGUAY, a 980-mile-long river of southeastern South America. It rises in the Serra do Mar of southern Brazil and flows west, southwest, and then south into the Río de la Plata.

VAAL, a river in South Africa. It rises in the Transvaal and flows generally west for about 700 miles before joining the Orange River in northern Cape Province.

VAN, a large salt lake of western Asia, in eastern Turkey near the border of Iran. It has an area of some 1,425 square miles and lies at an altitude of 5,260 feet.

VANCOUVER, a Canadian island lying off the southwestern coast of British Columbia. It is separated from the Canadian mainland by the Strait of Georgia and Queen Charlotte Sound. The Juan de Fuca Strait separates Vancouver from Washington in the United States.

VÄNERN, a Scandinavian lake in southwestern Sweden. It has an area of 2,141 square miles.

VÄTTERN, a Scandinavian lake in southern Sweden, east of Lake Vänern. It has an area of 733 square miles and is connected to the Baltic through the Göta Canal.

VENEZUELA, GULF OF, an inlet of the Caribbean Sea on the north coast of South America. It lies between the Paraguana Peninsula of Venezuela, on the east and the Guajira Peninsula of Colombia, on the west, and extends south as Lake Maracaibo.

VERKHOYANSK, a mountain range of the eastern Soviet Union, in northeastern Siberia, east of the Lena River valley and west of the Cherskiy range. The mountains have a peak of nearly 8,000 feet and contain deposits of zinc, lead, coal, and other minerals.

VESUVIUS, an active volcano in Italy, lying on the eastern shore of the Bay of Naples. Vesuvius is about 4,000 feet above sea level, but its exact height varies with each eruption.

VICTORIA, a lake in east-central Africa, the world's second largest lake. Lake Victoria is bounded by Uganda on the northwest and north, Kenya on the east, and Tanzania on the southeast, south, and southwest. The lake, which is about 250 miles long and 200 miles wide, is the major source of the Nile River.

VICTORIA FALLS, a waterfall in southern Africa on the Zambezi River between Zambia and Rhodesia. The falls are about 350 feet high.

VINDHYA, a mountain range in central India that runs from southwest to northeast and separates the Ganges basin from the Deccan Plateau. The highest peaks are about 5,000 feet. The Narbada River flows along the southern foot of the range.

VINSON MASSIF, the highest Antarctic peak, 16,864 feet above sea level. It is in the Ellsworth Mountains near the Filchner Ice Shelf at the head of the Weddell Sea.

VISTULA, or Wista, a river in Poland, over 650 miles long. The Vistula rises in the southwest, near the border with Czechoslovakia, and flows northeast in an arc as far as Warsaw. At Warsaw it turns west and then flows north into the Baltic Sea.

VOLGA, the longest river of the Soviet Union and of Europe, 2,290 miles. It rises in the Kalinin Region of the northwestern Soviet Union and follows a winding course to the Caspian Sea. The Volga flows first east and southeast to Kazan and then generally south to Astrakhan, where it forms an extensive delta.

Under the Greater Volga Scheme, dams have been built on the river for flood control, irrigation, and the generation of power. A comprehensive series of canals joins the Volga to the Baltic and Black Sea river systems.

VOLTA, a river of western Africa, some 900 miles long. The Volta, which empties into the Gulf of Guinea, is formed by the joining of the Black Volta and the White Volta in central Ghana.

The Black Volta rises in southwestern Upper Volta and flows northeast and then south, forming parts of the Ghana-Upper Volta and Ghana-Ivory Coast borders. The White Volta rises in central Upper Volta and flows generally south.

WATERFALLS. Two of the world's highest waterfalls, measured by their total drop, are in Venezuela, in South America. The world's highest fall, 3,212-foot Angel Falls, and the fourth highest, 2,000-foot Cuqenán, are in southeastern Venezuela.

Tugela, in South Africa, 3,110 feet, is the second highest waterfall, and the 2,425-foot Yosemite waterfall in North America is the world's third highest. The fifth highest waterfall is Sutherland, in New Zealand, which drops 1,904 feet.

Europe's highest waterfall, 1,250 feet, is the Krimml in Austria. Asia's highest known fall is only 830 feet high—the Gersoppa Falls on the Shanan River in southwestern India.

WEDDELL SEA, an arm of the South Atlantic Ocean extending into Antarctica between the Antarctic Peninsula, and Princess Martha Coast in Coats Land.

WESER, a West German river, formed by the confluence of the Fulda and Werra rivers in central Germany. It flows generally north for nearly 300 miles across the North German Plain and empties into the North Sea at Bremerhaven.

WEST INDIES, a group of islands in the western hemisphere, lying between southeastern North America and northern South America, and enclosing the Caribbean Sea. The group is divided into the Greater Antilles (Cuba, Hispaniola, Jamaica, and Puerto Rico), the Lesser Antilles (the Virgin, Leeward, and Windward islands, including Trinidad, Tobago, and Barbados), and the Bahama Islands.

WIGHT, a British island and county in the English Channel off the southern coast of Britain. It is a resort center.

WINNIPEG, a lake in south-central Canada, north of Winnipeg, Manitoba. It is nearly 9,400 square miles in area and is fed by the Winnipeg and Red Rivers from the south. It is drained to the north by the Nelson River.

WITWATERSRAND, a region in eastern South Africa that consists of a 150-mile-long ridge where several industrial cities, including Johannesburg, Germiston, and Krugersdorp, are located. It has the most productive gold field in the world, and also yields manganese and coal.

WORLD. The world has an area of 196,940,000 square miles. Slightly less than 30 percent of that is land and slightly more than 70 percent is water. The land area is divided into seven continents—Asia, the largest; Africa; North America; South America; Europe; Australia; and Antarctica, the smallest. The world's largest island, Greenland, lies partly in the Arctic Ocean and partly in the North Atlantic Ocean.

More than 90 percent of the world's water area is made up of four oceans—the Pacific, the largest; the Atlantic; the Indian; and the Arctic. There are also smaller bodies of intercontinental water, or seas. The largest are the South China Sea and the Caribbean Sea. The largest inland body of water is the Caspian Sea, lying partly in Europe and partly in Asia.

The lowest and highest points on the earth's land surface are both in Asia. The lowest point, 1,296 feet below sea level, is on the shores of the Dead Sea, in western Asia. The highest point, 29,028 feet, is at the top of Mt. Everest, the highest mountain, in south-central Asia.

The world's longest river, the Nile, flows for 4,145 miles in northern Africa. The river with the greatest volume is the Amazon, in South America. The highest waterfall in the world is also in South America—Angel Falls, with a total drop of 3,212 feet.

YALU, a river that rises in northeastern Korea and forms the western part of the Korea-China border. It flows for 300 miles, emptying into Korea Bay.

YANA, a river in Siberia, in the northeastern Soviet Union. Three main headstreams rise in the Verkhoyansk Mountains, and the river flows northward for about 750 miles to the Laptev Sea.

YANGTZE, one of the principal rivers of China and of the world. It rises in Tibet and follows a twisting course for 3,400 miles before it empties into the East China Sea. The portion east of its rugged gorges—about one-sixth of its length—is navigable by ocean vessels.

The tributaries of the Yangtze include the Kialing, the Yalung, the Chinsha, the Wu, and the Han. It flows through rich farmland, and over one-tenth of the world's population lives in its basin.

YELLOW SEA, a shallow arm of the Pacific Ocean between the Chinese mainland and the Korean peninsula.

YENISEY, a major river of the Soviet Union located in central Russia. It is formed from two rivers, the Greater Yenisey, rising in the Sayan Mountains of Mongolia, and the Lesser Yenisey, rising in the Siberian highlands. They meet at Kyzyl to form the Yenisey proper.

Major tributaries of the Yenisey include the Lower Tunguska, Stony Tunguska, Angara, and Abakan rivers. The Yenisey empties into the Yenisey Gulf of the Kara Sea.

YUCATAN, a large peninsula off Mexico's southeastern coast. It lies between Campeche Bay and the Caribbean Sea and is separated from Cuba, to the northeast, by the Yucatan Channel. The terrain is low and barren and consists largely of swamps and semidesert.

ZAGROS, a mountain range in southwestern Iran that forms the western and southern borders of the Iranian plateau. The range is about 1,000 miles long and rises to a height of 15,000 feet.

ZAMBEZI, a river in southern Africa that rises in eastern Angola. It flows southeast, then northeast, and turns southeast again over the Cohorabasa Rapids in Mozambique before entering the Mozambique Channel. The Zambezi follows the boundary between Zambia and Rhodesia, and forms the Victoria Falls near Livingston, in Zambia. Its tributaries include the Kabompo, Cuando, Kafue, and Luangwa rivers.

CITIES OF THE WORLD

ABADAN, in southwestern Iran, situated on the northern end of Abadan Island, at the head of the Persian Gulf. Pipelines link the city with oil fields to the north, and Abadan is a major oil refining and shipping center of the Middle East. Pop., 1963 est., 302,200.

ABIDJAN, in West Africa, the capital of the Ivory Coast. The city is located on the Ebrie Lagoon, which is connected to the Gulf of Guinea by the Vridi Canal. Abidjan has modern port facilities and is the terminus of a highway network and a railroad from Ouagadougou, in neighboring Upper Volta. Pop., 1963 est., 250,800.

ACAJUTLA, a seaport on the Pacific coast of El Salvador, located about 50 miles southwest of San Salvador. The city is connected by railroad and highway to all parts of the country. New harbor facilities were constructed between 1956 and 1961, making Acajutla one of the most modern ports in Central America. The city also has oil refineries and a large fertilizer plant. Pop., 1965 est., 15,000.

ACCRA, on the northwestern coast of Africa, the capital of Ghana. The city lies on the Gulf of Guinea and is a seaport. Accra has an international airport and is linked by railroad to the cacao-growing districts of Ghana's interior. The University of Ghana is in Accra. Pop., 1966 est., urban area, 600,200.

ADANA, in southern Turkey, on the Seyhan River about 30 miles inland from the Mediterranean Sea. The city is the commercial and industrial center of the surrounding Cilician Plain. The manufacture of cotton textiles is the chief industry. Pop., 1965, 290,515.

ADDIS ABABA, in northern Africa, the capital and largest city of Ethiopia. It is situated in a hilly region in the central part of the country. Addis Ababa is the country's chief commercial, industrial, and educational center. Its industries produce cement, cigarettes, metal and leather goods, and soap. Ethiopia's first university, Haile Selassie I University, was founded at Addis Ababa in 1961. Pop., 1965 est., 560,000.

ADELAIDE, the capital of South Australia, located on the Torrens River about seven miles inland from the Gulf of St. Vincent. The city has knitting mills, food processing plants, and automobile works. It is the seat of the University of Adelaide. Pop., 1966, urban area, 726,930.

ADEN, in South Yemen, located on southern Arabia's Aden Peninsula, which extends into the Gulf of Aden. Situated along the important shipping lane between the Mediterranean Sea and the Indian Ocean, Aden is a leading port. Light industries produce textiles, cigarettes, soap, and metal utensils. Pop., 1964 est., urban area, 225,000.

AGANA, the capital of Guam, an island territory of the United States in the West Pacific Ocean. Agana is located on the island's west coast, on Agana Bay, about eight miles northeast of Apra Harbor. Pop., 1960, urban area, 1,642.

AGRA, in northern India, on the Jumna River in Uttar Pradesh State. One of the oldest cities in India, Agra is famous as the site of the Taj Mahal, the Red Fort, and other historic monuments. It is an important agricultural trading center and is well known for gold and silver inlay work. Pop., 1966 est., urban area, 579,600.

AHMADABAD, in northwestern India, on the Sabarmati River. It is the capital of Gujarat State. Ahmadabad is a major commercial and industrial center noted for the manufacture of cotton textiles. Metal-working is an important handicraft. Pop., 1966 est., urban area, 1,381,300.

AHMADNAGAR, in west central India, in Maharashtra State, 65 miles northeast of Poona. It is a district capital and an important market town. Pop., 1966, 126,353.

AHVAZ, in southwestern Iran, the capital of Khuzistan Province. Ahvaz is the commercial and transportation center of an oil producing area. It is connected by rail to ports on the Persian Gulf. Pipelines that carry oil to refineries at Abadan also pass through the city. Pop., 1963 est., 155,100.

AIÚN, the capital of the province of Spanish Sahara in Spanish West Africa. It is located on the El Hamra River, about 35 miles from the Atlantic Ocean. Aiún's economy is based on coastal fishing and nomadic grazing in the desert. Pop., 1961 est., 5,500.

AJMER, in northwestern India, in Rajasthan State, 84 miles southwest of Jaipur. Ajmer is an important trade center, especially for salt, and has a thriving cotton textile industry. It is noted for its historic monuments and its educational institutions, including Mayo Rajkumar College, which was founded in 1875. Pop., 1966, 249,699.

AKITA, the capital of Japan's Akita Prefecture, at the mouth of the Omono River near the northwest coast of Honshu. The chief industries include oil refining and the manufacture of textiles. Bronze, silver, and gold ornamental articles are also produced. Pop., 1965, 216,607.

AKYAB, the capital of the Arakan Division of Burma, located at the mouth of the Kaladan River on the Bay of Bengal. Akyab is one of Burma's chief seaports and exports much of the rice grown in the surrounding area. Pop., 1953, 42,329.

ALBERTVILLE, in the Congo (Kinshasa), located in Katanga Province on the western shore of Lake Tanganyika. It is a port and is connected by rail to Kabalo and the Congo River transport system. There is steamer service between Albertville and Kigoma, Tanganyika, on the eastern shore of the lake. Pop., 1958 est., 29,500.

ALEPPO, in northwestern Syria, an important trading center that is connected by rail with major cities in Turkey and Iraq. There is some light manufacturing, and local factories produce soap, carpets, textiles, and vegetable oils. Pop., 1965 est., 599,700.

ALEXANDRIA, situated west of the Rosetta mouth of the Nile River on the Mediterranean Sea, the principal seaport and second largest city of the United Arab Republic (Egypt). The city has an eastern and a western harbor, but the western harbor is deeper and handles most maritime traffic. Raw cotton is the main export.

UNITED NATIONS

ABIDJAN, the capital of the Ivory Coast, is one of West Africa's most modern cities.

Alexandria was founded by Alexander the Great in 332 BC and became an important port and intellectual center. It was famous for its lighthouse, which was one of the seven wonders of the ancient world; its library; and its school of medicine. Pop., 1966, 1,800,951.

AL FAYYUM, in the United Arab Republic (Egypt), west of the Nile River and about 70 miles southwest of Cairo. It is a provincial capital and a commercial center. Pop., 1963 est., 121,100.

ALGIERS, the capital of Algeria, the major Mediterranean port on the northwest coast of Africa. The city's port facilities handle such exports as wool, fruit and vegetables, and wine, most of which are sent to France. Local industries produce cement, metal products, shoes, and perfume. Tourism is also important. Pop., 1966, 943,142.

ALIGARH, in Uttar Pradesh State in north central India, on the upper Ganges plain. Aligarh is an important trade center for the agricultural produce of the surrounding area, including grain and sugarcane. Its chief industries are butter production and cotton processing. The city is also the seat of Aligarh Muslim University. Pop., 1966, 208,167.

ALLAHABAD, in Uttar Pradesh State in northern India, at the confluence of the Ganges and Jumna rivers. The city is a shipping and trade center for local agricultural produce, especially sugarcane and cotton. Allahabad is also a holy city for Hindus. It was built in 1583 by the Mughal emperor Akbar the Great and has many historic monuments. Pop., 1966 est., urban area, 483,200.

ALLEPPEY, a seaport on the west coast of India, in Kerala State. The city is a center for the manufacture of coir, or coconut fiber, products. Coir, copra, coconuts, pepper, ginger, and cardamoms are the port's major exports. Pop., 1966 est., 150,700.

ALMA ATA, in Soviet Central Asia, the capital of the Kazakh Soviet Socialist Republic of the Soviet Union. Founded in 1855 as a military post, the city developed as a trading and transportation center. Alma Ata is the hub of a large fruit-growing area. The principal industries include fruit and vegetable canning and textile manufacture. Pop., 1966 est., 634,000.

AMBALA, in northern India, the capital of Punjab State. The city is a railroad junction and trade center for the surrounding area. Pop., 1966 est., urban area, 197,600.

AMMAN, the capital of Jordan, in the northwestern part of the country about 25 miles northeast of the Dead Sea. Amman is Jordan's chief industrial and commercial center and the hub of a rail and highway network. Industries include food processing and the manufacture of textiles, leather goods, cement, and tiles. Pop., 1966 est., 330,000.

AMOY, a seaport in southeastern China, located on a small island off the coast of Fukien Province. The city has an excellent harbor and was a major Chinese port until 1949, when it was blockaded by Nationalist Chinese forces based on nearby Quemoy Island. Pop., 1953, 224,300.

AMRAVATI, in central India, the capital of the Berar Division and Amravati District of Maharashtra State. The city is a cotton trading center and has cotton gins and oilseed mills. Pop., 1966 est., 156,600.

AMRITSAR, in northeastern India, the capital of Amritsar District in Punjab State. The city is an important commercial and manufacturing center. The principal industry is textiles. Amritsar is the site of the Golden Temple, the major shrine of the Sikh religion. Pop., 1966 est., urban area, 432,000.

AMSTERDAM, the capital and largest city of the Netherlands, located in the province of North Holland. The city lies at the junction of the Amstel and IJ rivers near the IJsselmeer (formerly the Zuider Zee) and is connected by canal with the North Sea and the Rhine River.

Amsterdam is the commercial and industrial center of the Netherlands and one of its busiest ports. The most important manufactures include iron and steel, machinery, chemicals, paper, printed matter, and beer. Amsterdam also is a center of the diamond-cutting industry. Pop., 1965 est., 864,900.

ANKARA, the capital and second largest city of Turkey, located on the central Anatolian plateau on the Ankara River. The city is almost completely modern and is an important commercial and industrial center.

Ankara markets and processes agricultural products of the surrounding region and is famous for the production of Angora goat wool, or mohair. Other manufactures include beer, cement, textiles, leather goods, and tile. Pop., 1965, urban area, 902,216.

ANNABA, a port on the northeast coast of Algeria, near the border with Tunisia, about 260 miles east of Algiers. Annaba was formerly called Bône. Manufactures include tobacco and olive oil. Exports include phosphates and iron ore. Pop., 1966, urban area, 168,790.

ANSHAN, located in the Chinese province of Liaoning in southern Manchuria. The city, which lies near large coal and iron ore deposits, is China's largest producer of iron and steel. Pop., 1957 est., 805,000.

ANTUNG, a seaport on the northeast coast of China, situated at the mouth of the Yalu River in Liaoning Province. The chief export is timber, which is floated down the Yalu from the interior. Antung's industries include soybean processing and the manufacture of silk and synthetic fibers, matches, and paper pulp. Pop., 1953 est., 360,000.

ANTWERP, the second largest city in Belgium and the country's chief port. It is located on the Schelde River about 50 miles inland from the North Sea. Antwerp has one of the world's largest harbors and is among the busiest ports in Europe.

Antwerp's major industries include shipbuilding, metallurgy, brewing, distilling, lacemaking, sugar refining, and diamond cutting. The city has many historic buildings and art treasures. Pop., 1965 est., urban area, 657,500.

APARRI, a seaport in the Philippines, located in Cagayan Province on the northern end of Luzon Island, at the mouth of the Cagayan River. The city lies at the head of the fertile Cagayan valley and exports its agricultural produce, including tobacco, corn, and rice. Fishing and lumbering are also important. Pop., 1960, urban area, 33,500.

APIA, the capital, largest city, and chief port of Western Samoa, in the northwest South Pacific Ocean. Apia is located on the north coast of the island of Upolu, the largest and south-

NETHERLANDS INFORMATION SERVICE
AMSTERDAM'S CANALS accommodate houseboats and the barges that carry commercial traffic.

ernmost of the Marianas Archipelago. Apia is a commercial center. Chief exports are copra, bananas, and cocoa. Pop., 1961, urban area, 21,699.

AQABA, in southwestern Jordan, situated at the southern end of the great valley Wadi el'Araba on the Gulf of Aqaba. Known in ancient times as Elath, it commanded the caravan trade route from Egypt to Arabia. Jordan's only seaport, Aqaba began to be developed in 1952, when new harbor facilities were installed. Pop., 1965 est., 10,560.

ARAD, in western Romania, the capital of Arad District. The city is situated on the Mures River at the junction of the Hungarian lowland and the Transylvanian highlands. Arad is a commercial and industrial center that manufactures transport equipment, furniture, leather goods, machinery, and flour. Pop., 1965 est., urban area, 125,800.

ARKHANGEL'SK, a seaport on the northeastern coast of the Soviet Union, at the mouth of the Dvina River on the Gulf of Dvina, an inlet of the White Sea. Due to its northern location, Arkhangel'sk is blocked by ice for six months of the year, although it is kept open longer by ice-breakers. The port has numerous sawmills, and timber is its chief export. Railroads connect the city with Moscow and Leningrad. Pop., 1966 est., 308,000.

ASAHIGAWA, located on Hokkaido Island, Japan. It lies on the Ishikari River in the central part of the island in the midst of an important rice-growing region. Asahigawa is a major railroad junction and served as the headquarters of the Japanese army during World War II. Pop., 1965, 245,246.

ASHKHABAD, in the southwestern Soviet Union, the capital of the Turkmen Soviet Socialist Republic. Located near the Iranian border in the Akhal-Tekinsk Oasis, the city is a major commercial center on the Trans-Caspian Railroad. Ashkhabad is joined by oil pipeline to Krasnovodsk on the Caspian Sea. Pop., 1966 est., 230,000.

ASMARA, the capital of Eritrea, a province of Ethiopia, in East Africa. The city is the trade center of an agricultural region that produces fruit, vegetables, coffee, and oilseeds. Asmara is a modern city that has numerous attractive public and private buildings. It is connected by rail to the port of Massawa, 40 miles to the northeast on the Red Sea, and by highway to other Ethiopian cities. Pop., 1964 est., 131,800.

ASUNCIÓN, the capital of Paraguay, a port on the Paraguay River about 630 miles north of Buenos Aires. It is the country's political, economic, and cultural center. It is connected to Buenos Aires by air and rail and to other American capitals by air.

Paraguay has no seacoast and Asunción's river port handles most of the country's trade. Asunción has few

industries and they consist for the most part of food processing and the manufacture of consumer goods. Pop., 1962, 306,160.

ASWAN, the capital of Aswan province, United Arab Republic (Egypt), located on the east bank of the Nile River about 550 miles south of Cairo. The city is the site of Aswan and Aswan High dams and the southern terminus of the U.A.R.'s main railroad. Aswan's dry, mild climate makes it a popular tourist resort during the winter months. Pop., 1967 est., 30,000.

ASYUT, the largest city in Upper Egypt, the capital of Asyut Province, the United Arab Republic. Occupying the site of ancient Lycopolis, Asyut lies on the left bank of the Nile River about 235 miles south of Cairo. The city is well known for its handicrafts, especially pottery, carved ivory, and wood inlay work. Pop., 1963 est., 137,000.

ATHENS, the capital and largest city of Greece, located on the Attic plain about five miles inland from its port of Piraeus on the Saronic Gulf. Named after the classical Greek goddess of wisdom, Athens was an important city in ancient Greece. The flat-topped hill of the Acropolis, which overlooks the city, contains the ruins of some of the most beautiful buildings of ancient Greece.

Modern Athens is the center of Greece's political, cultural, and economic life. It is also the manufacturing center of the country. The products of its wide variety of industries include ships, flour, alcoholic beverages, and textiles. Athens is one of the busiest ports on the Mediterranean Sea and lies on major railway and airline routes. Pop., 1961, urban area, 1,852,709.

AUCKLAND, the largest city and chief port of New Zealand, located on North Island between the harbors of Waitemata and Manukau. The major exports of the port are dairy products, hides, wool, timber, and gold. Auckland is New Zealand's largest indus-

trial center, and it produces ships, refined sugar, chemicals, shoes, ammunition, and processed foods. It is the site of the University of Auckland and the Auckland War Memorial Museum, noted for its Maori collection. Pop., 1966, urban area, 547,915.

AYUTHIA, in northern Thailand, located on an island in the lower Chao Phraya River about 40 miles north of Bangkok. The city serves as the trade center for the forest and agricultural products of the surrounding area, notably rice and teak. Ayuthia was the capital of the country from 1350 to 1767 and has many ruins of historic interest. Pop., 1960, 32,368.

AZ ZAHRAN, or Dhahran, a city of east-central Saudi Arabia, situated about five miles west of the Persian Gulf. It is an international air center, developed in the late 1930s as the headquarters of an oil company. The city, which has a plant for the removal of hydrogen sulfide from oil, is linked by pipeline to Saudi Arabian oil fields. Pop., 1961 est., 12,500.

BAALBEK, in eastern Lebanon, located in the Bika valley, about 35 miles north of Damascus. Known in ancient times as Heliopolis, the city is on the old route from Beirut to Homs that has been followed by modern roads and railroads. Baalbek is noted for its Hellenistic and Roman ruins. The city is visited by many tourists.

BACOLOD, the capital of Negros Occidental Province, the Philippines, located on the northwest coast of Negros Island. The city lies in the center of the most important sugar-producing region of the Philippines and its economy is based on the processing and exporting of this commodity. Bacolod is also the site of the University of Negros Occidental. Pop., 1965 est., 142,000.

BAGDAD, the capital and largest city of Iraq, located on the banks of the Tigris River, in the east central part of the country. The city is the intellectual, commercial, and indus-

UNITED NATIONS

ASUNCIÓN, capital and chief port of Paraguay, is on the east bank of the Paraguay River.

BANGKOK, the capital of Thailand, is an important transportation and administrative center.

UNITED NATIONS

trial center of Iraq. The chief industry is oil refining, but factories manufacture a variety of products, including shoes, clothing, and cement.

Bagdad was founded in 762 AD by Caliph al-Mansur. It was the capital of the Islamic world and a brilliant cultural center until 1258, when it was destroyed by the Mongols. Pop., 1965, 1,745,328.

BAKU, the capital of the Azerbaizhan Soviet Socialist Republic in the southwestern Soviet Union, situated on the western shore of the Caspian Sea. Located in the center of an extensive oilfield, it has large oil refineries and distribution pipelines. The city also has a variety of industries that produce ships, flour, tobacco, chemicals, tires, machinery, and shoes. Baku is one of the Soviet Union's largest cities and a major port. Pop., 1966 est., urban area, 1,164,000.

BAMAKO, the capital of Mali Republic in western Africa, situated on the Niger River, in the southwestern part of the country. It serves as the trade center for the surrounding area and exports peanuts, cotton, and tobacco. Bamako is connected to Dakar in Senegal by rail and has an international airport. Pop., 1965 est., urban area, 165,000.

BANARAS, in India, one of the most sacred Hindu holy cities, located on the banks of the Ganges River in southeastern Uttar Pradesh state. Hindu pilgrims from all over India come to wash away their sins in the waters of the Ganges at Banaras, which is reputedly the oldest city in India.

A cultural center, the city is the seat of Banaras Hindu University and Banaras Sanskrit College. Banaras' numerous handicraft industries produce brocades, saris, shawls, gold and silver jewelry, and brassware. Pop., 1966 est., urban area, 561,400.

BANDUNG, the capital of West Java Province, Indonesia, located on the island of Java, about 75 miles southeast of Djakarta. The city is an important resort because of its cool climate. It is the site of many medical and educational institutions, including the Pasteur Institute and Padjajaran University. Bandung industries produce textiles, rubber goods, chemicals, quinine, and machinery. Nearby Malabar radio station is one of the most powerful in the world. Pop., 1961, 972,566.

BANGALORE, the captial of Mysore State in southeastern India, located on the Deccan Plateau, about 180 miles west of Madras. The city serves as a trade center for the surrounding agricultural area and is an important railroad junction. Bangalore has modern factories, including a large aircraft assembly plant, as well as numerous handicraft industries. It is also an educational center and the site of the Indian Institute of Science. Pop., 1966 est., 124,200.

BANGKOK, the largest city and capital of Thailand, located on the Chao Pharaya River about 20 miles inland from its mouth on the Gulf of Siam. The city is Thailand's major port and handles almost all the country's foreign trade. Bangkok is an important rail center and has one of the most modern airports in Southeast Asia.

Bangkok is the headquarters of the Southeast Asia Treaty Organization (SEATO), and many Far Eastern divisions of UN specialized agencies are located in the city. Pop., 1963 est., 1,608,300.

BANGUI, the capital of the Central African Republic, located on the Ubangi River near the western border. The city is the country's major port and handles almost all foreign trade. Bangui is linked by road with Chad and Cameroon and has an international airport. Local industry consists for the most part of food processing and the manufacture of a few consumer goods. Pop., 1964, urban area, 126,602.

BARCELONA, on the northeast coast of Spain, the capital of Catalonia Province and the second largest city in the country. Barcelona is Spain's leading manufacturing center and its largest port. The major industries produce textiles, chemicals, machin-

ery, precision instruments, paper, and printed matter. Barcelona is connected by rail with other Spanish cities. Pop., 1965 est., 1,696,800.

BAREILLY, in north-central India, located in Uttar Pradesh state on the Ramganga River, about 130 miles east of Delhi. The city is an important railroad junction and serves as a trade center for the sugarcane, corn, rice, wheat, and barley grown in the surrounding area. Pop., 1966 est., urban area, 307,400.

BARODA, in western India, one of the leading cities of Gujarat State. It is situated on the Viswamitra River, about 245 miles north of Bombay. Baroda is a transportation center and serves as the market for the surrounding agricultural region. Its most important industries produce dyes, textiles, chemicals, rubber goods, and machinery. The city is the seat of Baroda University. Pop., 1966 est., 339,800.

BASEL, in northern Switzerland, situated on the Rhine River near the French and German borders. It is the second largest city in Switzerland and a major port handling a large portion of the landlocked country's foreign trade. Basel is also an important railroad junction and travel center. The chief local industries produce dyes, chemicals, silk ribbons, gloves, paper, and beer. Pop., 1966 est., 212,200.

BASRA, in northern Iraq, a port on the Shatt-al-Arab, about 60 miles inland from the Persian Gulf. The city handles most of the trade of Iraq, and exports include dates, wool, hides, and oil. Basra is connected by oil pipeline to Fao on the Persian Gulf and by rail to Bagdad. Pop., 1965, 313,327.

BASSEIN, the leading port of Burma, located on the Bassein River, which flows from the Irawaddy River to the Bay of Bengal. It lies in a major rice-growing region, and rice is its chief export. Pop., 1953, 77,900.

BASSE-TERRE, the captial of St. Kitts Island and the St. Kitts-Nevis territory in the Leeward Island colony, British West Indies. The city lies on the southwest coast. Pop., 1960 est., 15,700.

BATA, on the west coast of Africa, is the capital of Río Muni, an overseas province of Spain. The city lies on the Gulf of Guinea about 125 miles north of the equator. The major export of Bata is timber, which is floated down rivers from the interior. Pop., 1960, 27,024.

BATHURST, the capital of Gambia, on the west coast of Africa, located on St. Mary's Island at the mouth of the Gambia River. The city's major industry is the processing of peanuts, which are Gambia's chief export. Bathurst is linked with other parts of the country by road and has an international airport. Pop., 1965 est., 29,800.

BATUMI, in the southwestern Soviet Union, the capital of the Adzhar Autonomous Soviet Socialist Republic, which is within the Georgian S.S.R. The city lies on the east coast of the Black Sea near the Turkish border. It is connected by rail and oil pipeline to Baku and Tiflis. Oil refining is the major industry and oil is the chief export. Pop., 1966 est., 98,000.

BEERSHEBA, in central Israel, located about 50 miles southwest of Jerusalem, at the northern edge of the Negev Desert. Founded in Biblical times, Beersheba is being developed as the administrative and industrial center of the Negev District. It is linked by rail to Tel Aviv and by road to Elath on the Red Sea. Beersheba is the site of the Negev Institute for Arid Research. Pop., 1965, 65,200.

BEIRA, a seaport on the southeastern coast of Mozambique, Africa, located at the mouth of the Pungwe River. The port is one of the busiest on the east coast of Africa and has railroad connections with Zambia, Malawi, and Rhodesia. Major exports include grain, cotton, sugar, and tobacco. Pop., 1960, 40,000.

BEIRUT, the capital of Lebanon, located on the eastern shore of the Mediterranean Sea, about 75 miles west of Damascus, Syria. Long an important center for east-west trade, Beirut is a busy port and transportation center. It lies on the Cairo-Isstanbul-Bagdad railway, is the hub of a good road network, and has an international airport. Beirut is also a banking and educational center. It is the site of several universities, including the American University of Beirut. Pop., 1964 est., 700,000.

BELÉM, the capital of Pará State, Brazil, located on the Pará River, about 90 miles inland from the Atlantic Ocean. The city lies at the mouth of the Amazon River system and is a transshipment point for Amazon River traffic. It is linked by high-way with the capital of Brasilia. Belém's industries produce ships, soap, beer, cement, and forest products. Pop., 1966 est., 471,000.

BELGRADE, the capital of Yugoslavia, located on the Danube River, about 50 miles from the Romanian border. The city is an active port and a transportation and industrial center. Belgrade industries produce automobiles, farm machinery, airplanes, electrical equipment, paper, textiles, and processed foods. It is the seat of the University of Belgrade and has many museums. Pop., 1961, 585,234.

BELFAST, the capital of Northern Ireland, located on the east coast, at the mouth of the Lagan River. The city is Northern Ireland's leading port and manufacturing center. Belfast industries produce linen and other textiles, ships, aircraft, processed foods, tobacco, and whiskey. Many educational institutions are located in Belfast, including Queen's University. Pop., 1965 est., 406,800.

BELIZE, the capital, largest city, and chief port of British Honduras. It is located at the mouth of the Belize River, on the Caribbean Sea, in northeastern Central America. Belize is a trading center and exports chicle, lumber, coconuts, and bananas. Pop., 1964 est., urban area, 45,600.

BELO HORIZONTE, in southeastern Brazil, the capital of Minas Gerais State. The first planned city in South America. It was inaugurated in 1897. Belo Horizonte processes the iron ore, manganese, gold, and precious stones mined in the state. Other industries include food processing, meat packing, and the manufacture of textiles. The city has several universities and is the educational center of Minas Gerais. Pop., 1966 est., 929,000.

BENGAZI, one of Libya's two capitals and the capital of Cyrenaica Province, situated on the shore of the Gulf of Sidra on the Mediterranean Sea. The city is a transportation and tourist center and serves as a market for the agricultural produce of the Jebel-el-Akhdar region. Local industries include brewing, food processing, and the manufacture of bricks and cement. Pop., 1964, 137,294.

BERGEN, the second largest city in Norway, lying at the head of By Fiord on the Atlantic coast. The city is an important trade center for fish and has flour mills, distilleries, iron foundries, textile mills, and paper, glass, and furniture factories. Norway's largest and most important city in the 1800s, Bergen is now a major cultural center. It is the site of the University of Bergen. Pop., 1965 est., 117,300.

BERLIN, in East Germany, located on the Spree River, about 165 miles southeast of Hamburg. Berlin was the capital of Germany until the end of World War II, when it was divided into four zones and occupied by the United States, France, Britain, and the Soviet Union.

In 1949 the U.S., British, and French zones became West Berlin and the Soviet zone became East Berlin. East Berlin is the capital of East Germany and West Berlin has close ties with West Germany. Although partition caused its importance to decline, Berlin is a financial, commercial, and manufacturing center. Pop., West Berlin, 1966 est., 2,190,600; East Berlin, 1965 est., 1,073,600.

BERN, the capital of Switzerland and of Bern canton, located in the west-central part of the country, on the Aare River. The city has some light industry and is a cultural, educational, banking, and commercial center. The older sections contain some excellent examples of medieval architecture. Pop., 1966 est., 165,900.

BETHLEHEM, in western Jordan, located about five miles southwest of Jerusalem. Bethlehem was the birthplace of Jesus and is mentioned often in the Bible. The Church of the Nativity, built by Emperor Constantine in 330 AD, occupies the reputed site of the stable where Jesus was born. The major business is the sale of souvenirs to tourists and pilgrims. Pop., 1961, 22,453.

BHAVNAGAR, in northwestern India, located in Gujarat State, on the Gulf of Cambay. The city is the most important seaport on the Kathiawar Peninsula. Industries include the manufacture of silk and cotton textiles, metal goods, and bricks and tile. Pop., 1966 est., 192,000.

BHOPAL, in central India, the capital of Madhya Pradesh State. The city is a major commercial and transportation center. After Hyderabad, Bhopal is the most important Muslim city in India. Pop., 1966 est., urban area, 287,300.

BHUBANESWAR, in northeastern India, the capital of Orissa State. The city serves as a trade center for rice produced in the surrounding agricultural

GERMAN INFORMATION CENTER

BERLIN is divided into East Berlin and the larger and more prosperous enclave of West Berlin.

region. Bhubaneswar is well known as the site of a large group of Hindu temples built between 700 and 1100 AD. Pop., 1961, 38,211.

BIALYSTOK, the capital of Bialystok Province, Poland, about 100 miles northeast of Warsaw. Bialystok is an important railroad junction and textile manufacturing center. Pop., 1965 est., 137,800.

BIKANER, in northwestern India, located about 250 miles west of New Delhi. Bikaner is an important trade center and is famous for the manufacture of wool rugs and carpets. It is the site of Anup Sanskrit Library, which contains one of the world's major collections of Sanskrit manuscripts. Pop., 1966 est., 168,500.

BIRMINGHAM, in south-central England, located in Warwickshire with suburbs extending into parts of Staffordshire and Worcestershire. The second largest city in England, Birmingham is one of the world's leading industrial centers. The city specializes in the manufacture of motor vehicles and electrical products and is a major center of the hardware industry. The production of iron, steel, and nonferrous metals is also important. Pop., 1965 est., urban area, 2,392,600.

BISSAU, on the west coast of Africa, the capital and chief port of Portuguese Guinea. The major exports are peanuts and copra. The city is linked by rivers to communities in the interior and has an airport. Pop., 1965 est., 25,000.

BIZERTE, in northern Tunisia, a port on the Mediterranean Sea. It has an inner harbor that is connected to an outer one by canal. The city is strongly fortified and has naval and air bases. Exports include grapes, olives, iron, lead, and zinc. Bizerte has large oil refineries. Pop., 1956, 44,721.

BLOEMFONTEIN, the capital of Orange Free State Province in the Republic of South Africa, located in the central part of the country. The city is primarily a market center for the agricultural produce of the surrounding area. It is also a transportation hub and the educational center of the Orange Free State. The highest court in South Africa is located at Bloemfontein. Pop., 1960, urban area, 145,273.

BOBO-DIOULASSO, in southwestern Upper Volta, West Africa. The second largest city in Upper Volta, Bobo-Dioulasso serves as a trade center for local agricultural products. It has an airport and is on the railroad that runs from Ouagadougou, the capital, to Abidjan, Ivory Coast. Pop., 1960 est., 45,000.

BOGOTÁ, the capital of Colombia, located in the central part of the country. The city is the political, economic, and cultural center of Colombia. Light industries produce a variety of consumer goods for domestic consumption. Bogotá is the seat of the National

PAN AMERICAN

BRASILIA, inaugurated as the capital of Brazil in 1960, is a model of modern urban design.

University and has a number of other educational institutions. Pop., 1964, 1,697,311.

BOLOGNA, in north-central Italy, at the foot of the Apennine Mountains, about 50 miles north of Florence. Bologna is the capital of the political region of Emilia-Romagna. The city is an industrial, commercial, and educational center. Manufactures include machinery, chemicals, paper, glass, and plastics. Bologna is also a tourist center and an important agricultural market. Pop., 1965 est., urban area, 481,527.

BOMBAY, the largest city in India and the capital of Maharashtra State, located on the west coast of the subcontinent. The city is a major commercial, financial, and industrial center. As a port Bombay ranks second only to Calcutta. Its major industries produce cotton textiles, chemicals, drugs, refined oil, processed foods, and motion pictures. Bombay has many educational institutions, including the University of Bombay. Pop., 1966 est., 4,784,000.

BONN, the capital of West Germany, situated on the Rhine River, about 20 miles northeast of Cologne. Long an educational and cultural center, the city is noted for its architecture, its museums, and its university. After it became the West German capital in 1949 Bonn expanded rapidly. The city's industries produce electrical equipment, chemicals, pharmaceuticals, and precision instruments. Pop., 1965 est., 141,700.

BORDEAUX, in southwestern France, located on the Garonne River. The city is an important seaport and a leading commercial and cultural center. Its principal industries are oil refining, shipbuilding, and food processing. It produces and exports wines, liqueurs, pharmaceuticals, and dyes. The history of Bordeaux dates

back to Roman times, and in old sections there are Roman ruins and medieval buildings. Pop., 1962, urban area, 462,171.

BRAILA, in southeastern Romania, located in Walachia, on the Danube River. The city is an important trade center for grain. Its industries produce paper, flour, cement, paint, furniture, and hardware. Pop., 1965 est., urban area, 127,000.

BRASILIA, the capital of Brazil, located in the interior of the country, about 600 miles northwest of Rio de Janeiro. Brasilia is a planned city which was built in the late 1950s and inaugurated as the capital in April 1960. It was designed by Lúcio Costa and Oscar Niemeyer. The city is linked by highway to Belo Horizonte and Belém and has an airport. Pop., 1965 est., 200,000.

BRATISLAVA, the capital of Slovakia Province, Czechoslovakia, on the Danube River, near the borders with Hungary and Austria. The city is a railroad junction and a major river port. Oil pipelines connect Bratislava with the Ukraine and oil refining is an important industry. The city also produces chemicals, machinery, and cloth. Pop., 1965 est., 268,500.

BRAZZAVILLE, the capital and largest city of the Congo (Brazzaville), on the Congo River directly opposite Kinshasa (formerly Léopoldville). Brazzaville is an important river port and the country's commercial and educational center. Major industries include food processing and the manufacture of furniture, cigarettes, soap, and bricks. Pop., 1962, 136,200.

BREMEN, the capital of the West German state of Bremen, located on the Weser River, about 40 miles inland from the North Sea. The city is one of West Germany's largest ports and handles much of its foreign trade.

EGYPTIAN STATE TOURIST ADMINISTRATION

CAIRO, the capital of the United Arab Republic, is an old city with many new sections.

Shipbuilding is the major industry, but oil refining and the manufacture of textiles are also important. Pop., 1965 est., 592,400.

BRIDGETOWN, the capital, largest city, and chief port of Barbados, an island nation in the West Indies. The city is located on the southwest coast of the island, on Carlisle Bay. Bridgetown is a railroad terminus and the financial, commercial, and tourist center of Barbados. Exports include sugar, molasses, and rum. Pop., 1960, 11,452.

BRISBANE, the capital and principal port of Queensland, Australia, on the Brisbane River, 14 miles from Moreton Bay. The city is an important industrial center, manufacturing steel, automobiles, munitions, and electrical appliances. Exports include wool, meat, hides, sugar, and dairy products. Brisbane is the seat of the University of Queensland. Pop., 1966, urban area, 719,140.

BRISTOL, a port on the west coast of Britain, located at the junction of the Avon and Frome rivers, near the Bristol Channel. The city is one of Britain's most important ports. The leading industry is shipbuilding, but automobile and aircraft assembly, food processing, and printing are also important. Bristol is an ancient city and has many historic buildings. It is the seat of several fine secondary schools and of Bristol University. Pop., 1965 est., 430,000.

BROKEN HILL, in central Zambia, southern Africa, about 70 miles north of Lusaka, the capital. Broken Hill is located in an important mining center that produces lead, zinc, and vanadium. It is the site of the discovery of the fossil skull of prehistoric Rhodesian Man. Pop., 1963 est., 44,600.

BRUNEI, capital of Brunei, a sultanate under British protection on the northwest coast of Borneo. The city is located on Brunei Bay, an inlet of the South China Sea. It exports rubber, petroleum, and wood. Pop., 1960, 9,702.

BRNO, or Brünn (German), in south central Czechoslovakia, located about 115 miles southeast of Prague. Brno is the second largest city in Czechoslovakia and an important industrial center. Its chief manufactures include iron and steel, textiles, machinery, chemicals, and automobiles. Pop., 1965 est., 328,500.

BRUSSELS, the capital and largest city of Belgium, located near the center of the country, on the Senne River. Brussels is an important administrative, financial, and cultural center. It is the headquarters of both the European Economic Community and the European Atomic Energy Commission and is often the site of international conferences. The city manufactures chemicals, furniture, clothing, and soap. Brussels is famous for its lace and carpets. Pop., 1965 est., urban area, 1,695,900.

BUCHAREST, the capital and largest city of Romania, located in central Walachia, on the Dimbovita River. The city is the country's commercial, industrial, and cultural center. Its industries produce machinery, munitions, aircraft, textiles, clothing, chemicals, and processed foods. Bucharest is known for its parks, churches, and many cultural and educational institutions. Pop., 1965 est., urban area, 1,382,200.

BUDAPEST, the capital and largest city of Hungary, on the Danube River in the north-central part of the country. Hungary's largest industrial center, Budapest produces iron and steel, textiles, furniture, shoes, drugs, machinery, refined oil, and processed foods. The city is also the cultural and educational center of Hungary and has several museums and libraries. It is the seat of the University of Budapest. Pop., 1965 est., 1,944,000.

BUENOS AIRES, the capital of Argentina and the largest city in Latin America, located on the Rio de la Plata, about 170 miles inland from the Atlantic Ocean. The city is the financial, commercial, and industrial center of Argentina. The chief industries are meat packing, tanning, flour milling, and the manufactures of textiles and chemicals. Buenos Aires has one of the world's largest and busiest ports and is an important rail and air center. The city has many libraries, museums, and theaters. It is the seat of the University of Buenos Aires, one of the leading universities of Latin America. Pop., 1960 est., urban area, 7,000,000.

BUJUMBURA, the capital of Burundi, in east-central Africa, located at the northern end of Lake Tanganyika. The city, which was formerly called Usumbura, is an important lake port and trade center for agricultural produce from the surrounding region. Pop., 1965 est., 71,000.

BULAWAYO, the second largest city in Rhodesia and the capital of Rhodesia's Bulawayo Province, in Matabeleland. The city is an important railroad junction and commercial and industrial center. Bulawayo manufactures iron and steel, soap, clothing, and processed foods. It is the site of the National Museum of Rhodesia, a mining school, and a meteorological station. Pop., 1965 est., 226,000.

BURGAS, a seaport in eastern Bulgaria, located on the Gulf of Burgas, an inlet of the Black Sea. The city's major exports are grain and tobacco. Industries produce ships, metalware, machinery, cotton textiles, and processed foods. Burgas is a popular summer resort. Pop., 1965 est., 105,700.

CAIRO, the capital of the United Arab Republic (Egypt) and the largest city in Africa, at the head of the Nile Delta. It is an important transportation, commercial, and industrial center. Manufactures include iron and steel, textiles, and chemicals. Al-Ahzar University, founded in 970 AD, is the world's oldest and largest center of Islamic scholarship. The ancient pyramids are nearby. Pop., 1966, 4,196,998.

CALCUTTA, the largest city in India, on the east bank of the Hooghly River, a tributary of the Ganges, about 80 miles north of the Bay of Bengal. It is the capital of West Bengal State. Calcutta is one of the world's busiest ports. Exports include jute products, animal hides, and tea; manufactured articles are imported. From 1833 to 1912, Calcutta was the capital of British India. Pop., 1966 est., urban area, 4,703,400.

CALGARY, in southern Alberta, Canada, at the junction of the Bow and Elbow rivers, in the foothills of the Rocky Mountains. Calgary is the center of Alberta's cattle and oil industries. Manufactures include iron and steel products and cement. Pop., 1965 est., urban area, 323,000.

CAMBRIDGE, in eastern England, on the Cam River, about 50 miles north of London. It is the home of Cambridge University and contains many medieval and Renaissance churches. Pop., 1966 est., 99,800.

CANBERRA, the capital of Australia, in the Australian Capital Territory, in the southeastern corner of New South Wales. A model city, Canberra was founded in 1913 and became the seat of government in 1927. The Australian National University is located there. Pop., 1966, urban area, 95,913.

CANTERBURY, in southeastern England, on the Stour River, about 55 miles southeast of London. The cathedral of Canterbury is the seat of the Church of England's ranking prelate, the Archbishop of Canterbury. The city has many other churches and buildings of historic interest. Pop., 1966 est., 32,800.

CANTON, in southern China, on the Pearl River, about 80 miles from the South China Sea. It is the capital of Kwangtung Province and an important commercial and industrial center. A major river port, Canton was first visited by Europeans in the 1500s and until 1842 was the only Chinese port open to foreign trade. Pop., 1957 est., 1,840,000.

CAPE TOWN, the legislative capital of the Republic of South Africa and the capital of Cape Province. Cape Town is located on the southwestern shore of Table Bay, near the southern tip of Africa. It is an important manufacturing center and port. Exports include gold and other minerals. Pop., 1960, urban orea, 807,211.

CARACAS, the capital and largest city of Venezuela, in a mountain basin more than 3,000 feet above sea level. It is linked by superhighway with nearby La Guaira, its port on the Caribbean. Earnings from the nation's oil industry have financed extensive development. The Central University occupies a modern campus covering 307 acres in the city. Caracas is the birthplace of Simón Bolívar, South American patriot. Pop., 1966 est., urban area, 1,764,300.

CARDIFF, the capital and largest city of Wales, on the Taff River, near Bristol Channel in western Britain. Cardiff is the cultural and educational center of Wales. Its major industries include coal mining and processing, iron and steel manufacture, and ship repairing. Pop., 1965 est., 260,200.

CASABLANCA, the largest city in Morocco, on the Atlantic coast of North Africa. One of the world's largest artificial ports, Casablanca handles most of Morocco's passenger traffic and foreign trade. Phosphates are the city's chief export. Industries include textile, cement, and glass manufacture. Pop., 1965 est., 1,085,000.

CASTRIES, the capital, largest city, and chief port of St. Lucia, one of the Windward Islands of the British West Indies. Castries is located on the northwest coast of the island and has a fine, landlocked harbor. Chief exports are bananas, cocoa, copra, and coconut oil. Castries is also the tourist center of the island of St. Lucia. Pop., 1960, 4,353.

CAWNPORE, on the Ganges River in northern India. It is a district capital, railroad junction, and the most important industrial center in the state of Uttar Pradesh. Cawnpore processes grain, wool, cotton, and leather and manufactures textiles and machinery. Pop., 1966 est., urban area, 1,112,800.

CAYENNE, the capital of French Guiana, on the northeast coast of South America. It lies on an island near the mouth of the Cayenne River and is French Guiana's largest city and principal port. Nearby Devil's Island was the site of a French penal colony from 1851 to 1945. Exports include tropical woods, sugar, coffee, spices, and gold. Its most famous product is Cayenne pepper. Pop., 1961, 18,615.

ČESKÉ BUDĚJOVICE, in western Czechoslovakia, on the Vltava River, about 75 miles south of Prague. It is also known by its German name, Budweis. České Budějovice has manufacturing plants, lumber and paper mills, and breweries. Pop., 1962 est., 65,900.

CEUTA, a Spanish enclave on the coast of Morocco, administered by Spain as part of the Province of Cádiz. It is located on a low, narrow peninsula and guards the eastern entrance to the Strait of Gibraltar. Ceuta has extensive harbor facilities. Pop., 1966 est., 81,700.

CHAMPERICO, on the Pacific coast of southwestern Guatemala. It is a railroad terminus and port. Exports include coffee, lumber, and sugar. Pop., 1950, 982.

CHANDIGARH, in northern India, near the Ghaggar River, at the foot of the Himalayas. It is a Union Territory and the joint capital of Punjab and Haryana states. Chandigarh was designed by the Swiss architect, Le Corbusier. Construction was begun in 1950 and the city was inaugurated as the capital of Punjab state on Oct. 7, 1953. It is a model of modern city planning. Pop., 1961, 119,881.

CHANGCHUN, in northeastern China, on the west bank of the Itung River, about 175 miles northeast of Mukden. It is the capital of Kirin Province in Manchuria. An important industrial center, Changchun's manufactures include motor vehicles, locomotives, and machinery. Pop., 1957 est., 975,000.

CHANGSHA, in south-central China, on the east bank of the Hsiang River, 45 miles south of Tungting Lake. It is the capital of Hunan Province. Changsha is an important marketing and transportation center. Pop., 1957 est., 703,000.

CHANKIANG, a port in southeastern China, on the east side of the Luichow Peninsula, about 270 miles west of Hong Kong. A former French treaty port, it was restored to China in 1946. Pop., 1953, 166,000.

CHARLOTTE AMALIE, the capital, largest city, and chief port of the Virgin Islands of the United States. The city is located on the south-central coast of St. Thomas Island, about 40 miles east of Puerto Rico. It was formerly called St. Thomas. The city is the chief commercial and tourist center of the Virgin Islands. Pop., 1960, 12,880.

CHENGTEH, in northeastern China, on the Luan River in Hopeh Province, about 110 miles northeast of Peking. It is also called Jehol. The city is enclosed by walls and was once the summer residence of the Ch'ing (Manchu) emperors of China. It is an important commercial center. Pop., 1953, 92,900.

CHENGTU, in west-central China, on the Min River, a branch of the Yangtze, about 170 miles northwest of Chungking. It is the capital of Szechwan Province and one of China's oldest cities. Once a capital of imperial China, Chengtu is an agricultural and commercial center. Pop., 1957 est., 1,107,000.

LOOK MAGAZINE

CARACAS, Venezuela's capital, is a city of modern highways and high-rise apartment houses.

GERMAN INFORMATION CENTER

COLOGNE, in West Germany, is a cathedral city situated on both banks of the Rhine River.

CHIANG MAI, the largest city in northern Thailand and the capital of Chiang Mai Province. It is located on the upper course of the Ping River, about 80 miles east of the Burma border. Chiang Mai is a railroad terminus and commercial center. Pop., 1960, 65,736.

CHIBA, on Honshu Island, Japan, on the eastern shore of Tokyo Bay. It is the capital of Chiba prefecture and a manufacturing center. Pop., 1965, urban area, 332,118.

CHINCHOW, in northeastern China, at the head of the Gulf of Chihli, about 130 miles southwest of Mukden. It is a railroad junction and an industrial center. Pop., 1953, 352,200.

CHINNAMPO, on the west coast of North Korea, at the mouth of the Taedong River. It is about 25 miles southwest of the capital, Pyongyang. Chinnampo is an industrial center and Pyongyang's port. The city's exports include iron and coal. Pop., 1955, 82,162.

CHITTAGONG, in East Pakistan, near the mouth of the Karnaphuli River. It is a district capital and the chief port of East Pakistan. Exports include rice, tea, cotton, jute, and hides. Pop., 1961, 364,205.

CHONGJIN, on the northeastern coast of North Korea, about 140 miles southwest of the Soviet city of Vladivostok. It is an industrial center and port. Exports include iron and textiles. Pop., 1944, 184,301.

CHRISTCHURCH, in New Zealand, near the east coast of South Island. Its port is Lyttelton. Christchurch is New Zealand's largest city and South Island's commercial and industrial center. It is the chief market for grain, dairy products, timber, and coal from the nearby Canterbury Plains. The city has fertilizer plants, tanneries, woolen mills, meat-freezing plants, and iron foundries. Pop., 1966, urban area, 246,773.

COCHIN, on India's Malabar coast, about 120 mile west of Madurai in Kerala state. A major naval station, port, and railroad terminus, Cochin serves much of India's southwest coast. Pop., 1961 est., urban area, 300,000.

COIMBATORE, in southern India, on the Noyil River, about 280 miles southwest of Madras. Important products are cotton yarn and cloth, hides, and coffee. Pop., 1966 est., 333,500.

COLOGNE, or Köln, in western West Germany, on both banks of the Rhine River in the state of North Rhine-Westphalia. The Rhineland's most important industrial center, Cologne manufactures motor vehicles, railroad cars, diesel engines, machinery, and textiles. It is a busy river port and has extensive shipyards. It is also a leading cultural and educational center. Cologne Cathedral is the city's most famous landmark. Pop., 1965 est., 854,500.

COLOMB BÉCHAR, in western Algeria, about 300 miles southwest of Oran, near the border with Morocco. It is a railroad terminus and a coal mining center. Pop., 1954, urban area, 43,250.

COLOMBO, the capital, largest city, and chief port of Ceylon. It is located at the mouth of the Kelani River on the island's southwestern coast. Colombo exports most of Ceylon's tea, coconut products, cotton, and rubber. It was settled in 1517 by the Portuguese and named in honor of Christopher Columbus. Pop., 1963, 510,947.

COMODORO RIVADAVIA, in southern Argentina, on the Gulf of San Jorge (Atlantic Ocean), about 900 miles southwest of Buenos Aires. It is Argentina's chief petroleum refining center and oil port. Pop., 1960, 35,966.

CONAKRY, the capital of Guinea in West Africa. It is located on the small island of Tombo and is joined to the mainland by a bridge. Conakry is Guinea's largest city, chief port, and commercial and industrial center. Its deepwater harbor is one of West Africa's finest. Exports include bauxite and iron ore. Pop., 1964 est., urban area, 175,000.

CONCEPCIÓN, in south-central Chile, on the banks of the Bío Bío River. Concepción is one of Chile's largest cities and an industrial center. Its port, Talcuhuano, lies nearby to the northwest. Concepción, which was founded in the mid-1500s, has been struck by several destructive earthquakes. Pop., 1965 est., 174,200.

COPÁN, in western Honduras, on the Copán River, near the border with Guatemala. It is a tourist center for the nearby ruins of the Mayan city of Copán. Pop., 1950, 977.

COPENHAGEN, or København, the capital and largest city of Denmark, lying on Zealand and Amager islands. An important industrial center, the city produces ships, machinery, and chemicals. It has an excellent natural harbor and is a major European port. The city's Kastrup Airport is the busiest in northern Europe. Copenhagen's Tivoli Gardens, founded in 1843, is a famous amusement center. The city is the seat of Copenhagen University. Pop., 1965, urban area, 1,377,608.

CÓRDOBA, or Cordova, a city of south-central Spain, situated on the Guadalquivir River at the foot of the Sierra Morena. The city is an industrial, commercial, and tourist center. The manufacture of leather goods, traditionally Córdoba's most important industry, has been surpassed by textile mills, distilleries, and heavy industries. The city also serves as the market center for an area that produces wheat and corn.

Once a center of Arab power, Córdoba shows strong Muslim influence in its architecture. Notable are the Cathedral of Córdoba, formerly a mosque, and the Alcázar, or citadel. Pop., 1965 est., 214,300.

CORINTO, on the Pacific coast of Nicaragua, at the southeastern end of Aserradores Island. It is joined to the mainland by a bridge. Corinto is Nicaragua's main port of entry. Exports include coffee, sugar, timber, and hides. Pop., 1950, 4,765.

COTONOU, on the Atlantic coast of Dahomey, in West Africa, on a thin strip of land between the Gulf of Guinea and Lake Nakoué. It is Dahomey's largest city, chief commercial center, and main port, with a modern, deepwater harbor. Exports include palm kernels and palm oil. Pop., 1964, 109,328.

CURITIBA, in southern Brazil, on a plateau near the Iguaçu River, about 65 miles west of Paranaguá, its port on the Atlantic Ocean. Curitiba is the capital of the state of Paraná and an important transportation, trade, and industrial center. The city's products include timber, coffee, bananas, and sugar. Pop., 1966 est., 582,000.

CUSCO, in southern Peru, about 350 miles southeast of Lima. It lies at an altitude of about 11,000 feet above sea level in the Andes. Cusco, the capital of the Inca Empire, was captured by the Spanish in 1533. The city's Inca ruins and Spanish colonial buildings attract many tourists. Cusco is also a commercial center. Pop., 1961, 79,857.

CUTTACK, in northeastern India, on the south bank of the Mahanadi River. It is about 60 miles inland from the Bay of Bengal and 220 miles southwest of Calcutta. Cuttack is a district capital in the state of Orissa. It manufactures ice, cigarettes, and shoes. Pop., 1966 est., 169,700.

CZESTOCHOWA, in south-central Poland, on the left bank of the Warta River, about 125 miles southwest of Warsaw. It is a railroad junction and a major industrial center, producing iron, steel, and textiles. Czestochowa is an important religious center. Pop., 1965 est., 175,200.

DACCA, the capital of East Pakistan, lies between the Meghna and Ganges rivers. The city is a trade and processing center for the surrounding agricultural area, and is noted for the production of gold and silver jewelry, carved shells, and jute. It is the seat of the University of Dacca. Pop., 1961, 556,712.

DAKAR, the capital and chief seaport of Senegal, located on the Cape Verde Peninsula on Africa's west coast. The city, which has a strategic location and an excellent harbor is a transportation center with important air, rail, and shipping facilities.

Dakar's diversified industries produce canned fish, refined sugar, chocolate, vinegar, rope, and textiles. The city is the seat of the University of Dakar, the Pasteur Institute, and the Institut Français d'Afrique Noire. Pop., 1961 est., urban area, 374,700.

DAMASCUS, or Dimashaq, the capital and largest city of Syria, situated in the southwestern part of the country on the Barada River. The city is an oasis that has been continuously inhabited since biblical times. Modern Damascus is a major Middle Eastern administrative, communications, commercial, and industrial center. Its products include cement, glass, textiles, and sugar.

Damascus was a noted market place on the caravan route as early as the 600s AD. The city retains its citadel, bazaars, Roman gates, and historic churches. Damascus is the seat of the Syrian University and Damascus College. Pop., 1965 est., 599,700.

DAR ES SALAAM, the capital of Tanzania, is a major seaport of East Africa. Its harbor is on a bay, linked by a narrow channel to the Indian Ocean. The city is an administrative, transportation, and economic center. Among its exports are coffee, copra, peanuts, gold, diamonds, and tin. Dar es Salaam's industries produce furniture, pharmaceuticals, and processed foods. Pop., est. 1965, 190,200.

DAVAO, a port in the Philippines, is situated in the southeastern part of Mindanao Island at the mouth of the Davao River. The city's major industries process the abaca (Manila hemp) grown in the surrounding area. Pop., 1965 est., 269,300.

DEBRECEN, a marketing center in eastern Hungary, situated on the East Hungarian Plain. It lies in an agricultural region that grows grain and raises livestock. Debrecen's major industries produce processed foods and agricultural machinery. Pop., 1965 est., 147,000.

DEHRA DUN, a commercial and administrative center of northern India, situated in the Himalayan foothills, about 150 miles northeast of Delhi. Dehra Dun is a trade center for the surrounding agricultural area and a popular resort. A military institute and college of forestry are located in the city. Pop., 1966 est., urban area, 162,800.

DELHI. See *New Delhi.*

DILI, the capital of Portuguese Timor, situated on northeastern Timor, an island at the eastern end of the Indonesian chain. Dili lies in an area that trades in coffee, cocoa, hides, and shells. Pop., 1960, 52,158.

DJIBOUTI, the capital of the French Territory of the Afars and Issas (French Somaliland), an East African port, located on the Gulf of Tadjoura. Djibouti is the terminal of a railway from Addis Ababa, Ethiopia, and its exports are mainly Ethiopian products. These include coffee, hides, and skins, and oilseeds. Pop., 1963 est., urban area, 43,200.

DNEPRODZERZHINSK, an industrial city of the western Soviet Union, situated on the Dnieper River. Nearby iron and coal deposits and electric power from the river, combine to make the city a major iron and steel center. Pop., 1966 est., 219,000.

DNEPROPETROVSK, an administrative, commercial, and railroad center of the western Soviet Union, located on the Dnieper River near the head of the rapids. The city is an important manufacturer of steel and metal products. It is also a trade center for the surrounding wheat growing area. Pop., 1966 est., 790,000.

DOHA, the capital and chief port of Qatar, located on the east side of the Qatar Peninsula on the Persian Gulf. Since the discovery of oil in Qatar in the 1940s, Doha has become an important commercial center, with oil as its chief export. Pop., 1963 est., 45,000.

DOUALA, the main seaport of Cameroon, situated on the west coast of Africa on the Gulf of Guinea. Douola serves as a port for aluminum refined at nearby Edea and for agricultural products raised in the interior. Pop., 1965 est., urban area, 200,000.

DOUGLAS, the capital of the Isle of Man, an island in the Irish Sea. Douglas is a seaport and resort town with some commerce and industry. Pop., 1961, 18,821.

DRESDEN, an East German industrial city situated on the Elbe River. Its manufactures include chemicals, machinery, optical instruments, and glass. It is also an important river port. The city's buildings include some excellent examples of Baroque architecture. Pop., 1965 est., 504,900.

DUBLIN, the capital, largest city, and chief port of the Republic of Ireland, located on Ireland's east coast at the mouth of the Liffey River.

Dublin is a major transportation, commercial, and administrative center. Its industries include brewing and distilling, flour milling, and textile weaving. The city is Ireland's cultural and educational center, containing a large university, a cathedral, and many museums and libraries. Pop., 1966, urban area, 125,790.

LOOK MAGAZINE

DUBLIN, Ireland's capital and chief seaport, has retained much of its traditional character.

ITALIAN GOVERNMENT TOURIST OFFICE

FLORENCE, with the city's famous Ponte Vecchio, or Old Bridge, spanning the Arno River.

DURBAN, a major seaport and tourist resort on the east coast of South Africa. The city, which lies on Natal Bay in the Indian Ocean, has a subtropical climate and excellent beaches. Its chief exports are coal, manganese, and other minerals. Durban's industries produce machinery, furniture, textiles, glass, paper, and processed foods. Pop., 1960, urban area, 681,492.

DURRËS, Albania's chief seaport, situated on the Adriatic Sea, about 20 miles west of Tiranë, to which it is joined by rail. Its products include flour, cigarettes, clothing, and soap. An ancient settlement, known as Epidamnus, was founded on the site of Durrës by Greeks from Corcyra (Corfu) and Corinth in the 600s BC. Pop., 1960, 39,946.

DUSHANBE, in the south-central Soviet Union, the capital of the Tadzhik Soviet Socialist Republic. The city is an important market area for the surrounding agricultural district and a growing industrial center. Pop., 1966 est., 323,000.

DÜSSELDORF, the capital of the West German state of North Rhine-Westphalia, situated on the Rhine north of Cologne. One of the largest and most industrialized cities of the Rhineland, Düsseldorf manufactures iron and steel, chemicals, textiles, and glass. The city has a large harbor and an excellent railway system. Pop., 1965, 700,080.

EAST LONDON, in southeastern Cape Province, South Africa. It is located at the mouth of the Buffalo River on the Indian Ocean, about 540 miles east of Capetown. East London is an important industrial, agricultural, and fishing center. Exports include wool and citrus fruit. Pop., 1960, urban area, 116,056.

EDEA, in western Cameroon, West Africa. The city is on the Sanaga River, about 40 miles southeast of Douala. An aluminum smelter was completed at Edea in 1956.

EDINBURGH, the capital of Scotland and the seat of Midlothian county. It is located on the south shore of the Firth of Forth (North Sea) in southeastern Scotland. Edinburgh is primarily a residential and administrative city. It is noted for its cultural and educational activities and historic buildings. The chief industry is printing. Breweries and distilleries are also important. Pop., 1965 est., 476,400.

EDMONTON, the capital and largest city of Alberta, Canada. The North Saskatchewan River flows through the city, which is in the south-central part of the province. Edmonton lies in a region of coal mines and gas and oil wells. It is the headquarters of Canada's oil industry and the transportation center of the Canadian Northwest. Pop., 1965 est., urban area, 385,000.

ELATH, port city at the southern tip of Israel, at the head of the Gulf of Aqaba. It was founded in 1948 and is connected to northern ports by an oil pipeline and a road. Pop., 1965 est., 9,700.

ELBASAN, in east-central Albania, on the Shkumbi River, about 20 miles southeast of Tiranë, the capital. Elbasan is a market center for olives, tobacco, and fruit. Manufactures include textiles and leather. Pop., 1960, 29,787.

EL FASHER, in western Sudan, about 500 miles southwest of Khartoum, the capital. El Fasher is a market center situated on an ancient caravan route. Pop., 1956, 26,161.

ENTEBBE, in Uganda, East Africa, on a peninsula on the north shore of Lake Victoria, about 20 miles southwest of Kampala, the capital. Entebbe was the capital of Uganda until 1960. It is a commercial center. Pop., 1959, 10,941.

ENUGU, capital of the former Eastern Region of Nigeria in West Africa. It is located in a coal mining region about 50 miles east of the Niger River. Enuga was proclaimed the capital of the break-away state of Biafra in 1967, when the Eastern Region attempted to secede from Nigeria. Pop., 1963, 138,457.

ERZURUM, in northeastern Turkey, about 450 miles east of Ankara. It lies in the mountains of Turkish Armenia and is the capital of Erzurum Province. The city is an important military, commercial, and rail center. Pop., 1965, 106,301.

ESSEN, in western West Germany, located between the Ruhr and Lippe rivers in the state of North Rhine-Westphalia. An industrial city in a region of coal and iron fields, Essen manufactures steel, locomotives, and machinery. Other products include textiles, glass, and chemicals. Essen is also an important railroad junction. Pop., 1965 est., 726,800.

ESZTERGOM, in northern Hungary, about 25 miles northwest of Budapest. It is located on the Danube River and is a river port and railroad terminus. Manufactures include woolen textiles, machinery, and lumber. Pop., 1963 est., 24,700.

FAMAGUSTA, in the eastern Mediterranean Sea, on the east coast of Cyprus, about 40 miles east of Nicosia. It is a district capital and port. Pop., 1967 est., 39,000.

FÈS, in northern Morocco, North Africa, about 150 miles northeast of Casablanca. Fès is an historic city and a major Muslim religious center. It is also an important commercial city. Pop., 1965 est., 235,000.

FLORENCE, in central Italy, on the bank of the Arno River, in the western Apennines. It is the capital of Tuscany and a center of commerce and light industry. One of the world's foremost art centers, Florence attracts many tourists. Handicrafts include textiles, pottery, jewelry, and leather goods. A flood in 1966 damaged many art treasures and buildings. Pop., 1965 est., urban area, 454,900.

FOOCHOW, a port on the southeast coast of China, near the mouth of the Min River, at the northern end of Formosa Strait. It is the capital of Fukien Province. Foochow is a port and an industrial center. Manufactures include chemicals and textiles. Pop., 1957 est., 616,000.

FORTALEZA, on the northeast coast of Brazil, about 270 miles northwest of Natal. Fortaleza is the capital of the state of Ceará and an educational center. The city manufactures textiles and processes agricultural products. Coffee, sugar, and cotton are shipped from is port. Pop., 1966 est., 486,000.

FORT–DE–FRANCE, the capital and largest city of Martinique, French West Indies. Located on the Bay of Fort-de-France, on the southwest coast of the island, the city has a large, landlocked harbor. Exports include sugar, rum, and bananas. Pop., 1954, urban area, 60,648.

FORT–LAMY, the capital of Chad, in north-central Africa, about 70 miles south of Lake Chad. It is the largest city and chief transportation, industrial, and commercial center of Chad. Pop., 1964 est., urban area, 99,000.

FRANKFURT AM MAIN, in central West Germany, on the north bank of the Main River, about 100 miles southeast of Cologne. A leading industrial city, Frankfurt manufactures machinery, electrical equipment, and chemicals. The city is a commercial and financial center and its location makes it the transportation hub of West Germany. Frankfurt is also an educational and cultural center. Pop., 1965 est., 690,900.

FREDERICTON, the capital of New Brunswick, Canada. It lies on the Saint John River, about 85 miles from the Bay of Fundy. Fredericton is situated in a hunting and fishing region. Manufactures include lumber products, textiles, and leather goods. Pop., 1966, 22,460.

FREETOWN, the capital and chief port of Sierra Leone in West Africa. It is located on the estuary of the Sierra Leone River and has an excellent natural harbor. Freetown is the transportation and commercial center of Sierra Leone. Exports include minerals and palm kernels and oil. Pop., 1966 est., 148,000.

FRUNZE, capital of the Kirghiz republic in the Central Asia region of the Soviet Union. Frunze is about 300 miles northeast of Tashkent. Manufactures include machinery and textiles. Pop., 1966 est., 380,000.

FUKUOKA, on the northwest coast of Kyushu Island, Japan. The island's largest city, Fukuoka is a port and an industrial center. Manufactures include paper, textiles, and machinery. Pop., 1965, urban area, 749,808.

FUKUSHIMA, on the island of Honshu, Japan, about 160 miles north of Tokyo. Fukushima is a railroad junction and a leading commercial center. Pop., 1965, urban area, 173,678.

GABERONES, the capital of Botswana, situated in south-central Africa in an arid cattle-grazing region. Water is provided by a dam on a nearby branch of the Limpopo River. Pop., 1965 est., 4,200.

GANGTOK, the capital of Sikkim, situated about 30 miles northeast of Darjeeling, India. The city is a commercial center on the trade route between India and Tibet. Pop., 1961, 6,848.

GDAŃSK, formerly Danzig, a Polish seaport situated on the Baltic Sea, on the delta of the Wista (Vistula) River. Gdańsk, which was settled by the 900s, was a port city in the Hanseatic League in the late 1300s. Later it became part of Poland, and in the late 1700s it became part of Prussia. Following World War I, it became the Free City of Danzig, under the League of Nations. Early in World War II the Germans captured Danzig,

SWISS NATIONAL TOURIST OFFICE

GENEVA, a center of international business, lies on the shores of scenic Lake Geneva.

holding it until 1945. Following the war, the city was returned to Poland.

The port of Gdańsk handles coal, lumber, and grain. Products of the city's varied industries include ships, processed foods, and chemicals. Pop., 1965 est., 319,400.

GDYNIA, a port and naval base in Poland, lying on the Baltic Sea. Before 1924 Gdynia was a small fishing village. It was developed as a port to compete with the Free City of Danzig (Gdańsk). Gdynia's modern facilities ship coal, coke, lumber, chemicals, and food products. Pop., 1965 est., 165,000.

GENEVA, or Genève, the capital of Geneva canton in southwestern Switzerland, located on the Rhône River at the southern end of Lake Geneva. The city serves as the headquarters for a number of international organizations. Its industries include tourism and the manufacture of clocks, jewelry, precision tools, surgical and optical equipment, leather goods, and textiles.

Geneva is an ancient city that became important during the Reformation. It is an intellectual and cultural center with many schools, museums, libraries, and old buildings. Pop., 1966 est., 174,500.

GENOA, or Genova, a port in northwestern Italy on the Gulf of Genoa in the Mediterranean Sea. It is the capital of the province of Genoa and the region of Liguria. Genoa's exports include foodstuffs, marble, and silk. Among the many products of the city's industries are steel, metal goods, and cement. Pop., 1965 est., 845,400.

GEORGETOWN, capital and chief city of the British Cayman Islands, located on Grand Cayman Island, about 200 miles northwest of Jamaica. Pop., 1960, 2,573.

GEORGETOWN, the capital, largest city, and chief port of Guyana, on the northeastern coast of South America.

Georgetown is located at the mouth of the Demerara River, on the Atlantic Ocean. It is a railroad terminus and Guyana's communications and transportation center. Chief exports are sugar, bauxite, and rice. Pop., 1960, urban area, 148,391.

GERMISTON, a city in South Africa situated about 10 miles east of Johannesburg. Germiston is an important gold-refining center with excellent air and rail facilities. Pop., 1960, urban area, 214,393.

GIFU, a Japanese city in central Honshu, lying on the Nagara River. It is the capital of Gifu prefecture and an educational and manufacturing center. Its products include paper goods and textiles. Pop., 1965, 358,190.

GLASGOW, a port and industrial city of west-central Scotland, lying on the Clyde River. Glasgow is the largest city in Scotland, and the third largest in the British Isles. Its principal industries are shipping and shipbuilding, followed by the production of chemicals, bricks, glass, and textiles. Pop., 1965 est., 1,013,000.

GORKI, formerly Nizhni-Novgorod, a river port in the Soviet Union, the capital of Gorki Oblast. The city lies at the confluence of the Volga and Oka rivers, about 250 miles east of Moscow. Its port handles foodstuffs, building materials, and manufactured goods. Gorki's industries produce automobiles, aircraft, and refrigeration equipment. Pop., 1966 est., 1,100,000.

GÖTEBORG, or Gothenburg, the capital of the Swedish province of Göteborg och Bohus, in southwestern Sweden on an estuary of the Göta River. The city, which has access to the North Sea, is Sweden's most important seaport and the center of an excellent canal and rail system. Shipping and shipbuilding are the leading industries, followed by the manufacture of machinery, automobiles, and electrical equipment. Pop., 1966 est., urban area, 615,900.

GRANADA, the capital of the province of Granada, situated in southern Spain on the Genil River. The city is the commercial and industrial center for the region. Its chief industries are food processing, brewing and distilling, chemical production, and leather and metal handcrafting. Granada is the site of the Alhambra, an ancient Muslim fortress and palace, and other Muslim and Renaissance buildings. Pop., 1965 est., 158,000.

GRENOBLE, a commercial and industrial center of southeastern France, and the capital of Isère Province. The city lies on the Isère River, near the Grande Chartreuse range of the Alps. In 1968 the winter Olympics were held in Grenoble. The city is famous for the manufacture of gloves. Other products include cement, paper, and chemicals. Grenoble is the seat of the University of Grenoble. Pop., 1962, urban area, 233,243.

GROZNY, a city in the Soviet Union, the capital of the Chechen-Ingush Autonomous Soviet Republic. Grozny lies in the Caucaucus on a tributary of the Terek River. The city is an important producer of petroleum and a manufacturer of mining machinery and chemicals. Pop., 1966 est., 319,000.

GUADALAJARA, the second largest city in Mexico and capital of the state of Jalisco, located about 380 miles northwest of Mexico City. Guadalajara is the commercial center for a rich agricultural and mining region and is an important rail and highway hub. Its industries produce flour, textiles, leather goods, pottery, and glassware. Pop., 1966 est., 1,105,900.

GUATEMALA CITY, the capital and largest city of Guatemala, in Central America. It is located in the central highlands, at an altitude of about 5,000 feet, about 75 miles from the Pacific Ocean. It is the commercial, cultural, educational, financial, and political center of the country. Manufactures include textiles, soap, cement, and furniture. Guatemala City is a transportation, communications, and tourist center. Pop., 1964 est., 577,100.

THE HAGUE, or 's Gravenhage, the seat of the Netherlands' legislature and royal residence, and the capital of the province of South Holland. The Hague lies near the country's west coast. It is the site of many international conferences and the headquarters of several international organizations. The Hague is mainly a residential city. Pop., 1965 est., 596,700.

HAIFA, Israel's major port and an important industrial center. The city is situated in northern Israel, at the foot of Mt. Carmel, on the Bay of Acre in the Mediterranean Sea. Among its many industries are flour and textile mills, foundries, cement works, and an oil refinery. The Haifa Institute of Technology is in the city. Pop., 1965 est., 596,700.

HAIPHONG, the chief port of North Vietnam, situated on the Gulf of Tonkin about 60 miles east of Hanoi. The harbor must be constantly dredged to prevent silt deposits. There are auto, rail, and canal routes from Haiphong to the interior. The city has several heavy industries, including shipbuilding. In the mid-1960s, during the Vietnamese War, Haiphong harbor was subject to U.S. bombing raids. Pop., 1960, urban area, 369,248.

HAKODATE, a Japanese seaport on the southwestern coast of Hokaido. It has a railroad and a ferry terminus, in addition to its shipping facilities. The city lies in an important dairying region. Pop., 1965, 243,418.

HALIFAX, a seaport in southeastern Canada, the capital of Nova Scotia, located on the Atlantic Coast. The port is ice-free throughout the year, making Halifax an important winter terminal for trans-Atlantic shipping. The city is a rail, fishing, and commercial center. Its industries include shipbuilding, food processing, and the manufacture of clothing and furniture. Pop. 1961, urban area, 369,248.

HAMBURG, the capital of the West German state of Hamburg, situated at the confluence of the Elbe, Alster,

and Bille rivers, near the North Sea. Hamburg is Germany's largest seaport and an important industrial center. Shipping and shipbuilding are the city's major industries, followed by the manufacture of machinery, textiles, and beer. Hamburg also has important food processing industries. Pop., 1965 est., 1,857,000.

HAMILTON, capital and chief port of the Bermuda islands in the western Atlantic Ocean, about 600 miles east of North Carolina. The city lies in the center of a popular resort area. Pop., 1965 est., 3,000.

HANGCHOW, a port in east-central China, the capital of Chekiang province. It lies at the southern end of the Grand Canal, on Hangchow Bay in the East China Sea. The city, which was founded in about 2200 BC, is now highly industrialized. It is famous for the production of silk and tea. Pop., 1957 est., 784,000.

HANNOVER, in northern West Germany, on the Leine River, about 80 miles south of Hamburg. Hannover is the capital of the state of Lower Saxony. The city is a railroad junction and an industrial and commercial center. Manufactures include machinery, chemicals, textiles, tobacco, and glass. Hannover is an important educational and cultural center. Pop., 1965 est., 559,000.

HANOI, the capital of North Vietnam, situated on the Red River delta. Until 1946, Hanoi was the capital of French Indochina. The city, which lies in the middle of a rich agricultural region, is an important commercial and industrial center. Pop 1960, urban area, 643,576.

HARBIN, the capital of the Chinese province of Heilungkiang, situated in the northeast on the Sungari River. Harbin, which is located near the center of Manchuria, is an important commercial and transportation center for a large part of the region. Pop., 1957 est., 1,552,000.

HAVANA, capital and chief commercial city of Cuba, located on the island's northwestern coast. Havana is Cuba's major port and exports the island's chief commercial crops, sugar and tobacco. Cigars, cigarettes, consumer goods, and heavy machinery are manufactured in the city.

Havana is also Cuba's cultural center and has universities, libraries, and museums. Until Fidel Castro came to power in Cuba in 1959, Havana was a popular resort. Pop., 1965 est., urban area, 1,543,900.

HELSINKI, the capital and largest city of Finland. It is situated on the southern coast, on the Gulf of Finland. Helsinki is a major seaport and the country's chief trading center.

Shipbuilding is Helsinki's leading industry. The production of textiles, foodstuffs, paper and wood products, and ceramics is also important. Helsinki is an educational center with a university and several colleges. Pop., 1965 est., urban area, 652,000.

GERMAN INFORMATION CENTER

HAMBURG, in West Germany, has an architectural mixture of modern and historic buildings.

HIMEJI, an industrial center of Japan, situated on the southeastern coast of Honshu, on the Inland Sea. The city's industries produce iron and steel, textiles, and matches. Pop., 1965, 367,807.

HIROSHIMA, a Japanese seaport, the capital of Hiroshima Prefecture, lying on the Inland Sea. The city is an important industrial, commercial, and cultural center for the surrounding farming and fishing area. Hiroshima was the target of an atom bomb attack near the end of World War II. The city, which was almost completely destroyed, has been largely rebuilt. Pop., 1965, 504,245.

HOMS, a city in western Syria, lying on the Orontes River. Homs is the marketing center for the surrounding fruit-producing area, and an important road and rail junction. Pop., 1965 est., 189,900.

HONIARA, capital of the British Solomon Islands, located on the northern coast of Guadalcanal, east of New Guinea. Pop., 1964 est., 4,300.

HOWRAH, an industrial city in northeastern India, situated on the Hooghly River, opposite Calcutta. The city's rail, docking, and warehousing facilities also serve Calcutta. Howrah's industries produce rope and twine, textiles, and iron and steel. Pop., 1966 est., 554,700.

HUBLI, a city in southwestern India, situated about 300 miles southeast of Bombay. Hubli is a rail junction, commercial center, and military base. Milling and ginning cotton and the production of textiles are its most important industries. Pop., 1966 est., 193,600.

HUE, a South Vietnamese port on the Hue River, near the South China Sea. The city was once the capital of the Vietnamese empire in Indochina, and of the French colonial state of Annam. In 1968 Hue became a major battleground of the Vietnamese War. Pop., 1964 est., 103,600.

HYDERABAD, in south-central India, the capital of Andhra Pradesh, situated on the Musi River. Until 1956, Hyderabad was a separate state. The city is noted for the production of pottery, paper, textiles, and rugs. Pop., 1966 est., urban area, 1,316,000.

IASI, in northeastern Romania, on the Bahluiu River. The city is a commercial center and railroad junction. The most important industry is the manufacture of textiles. Iasi has several historic churches and cultural and educational institutions. Pop., 1965 est., 159,600.

IBADAN, the largest city in Nigeria and the capital of the former Western Province, in the southwest part of the country. The city lies in a rich agricultural region that produces cacao, cotton, yams, and corn, and its industries process these products. Ibadan is connected by rail to Lagos on the Gulf of Guinea and has an airport. Pop., 1963, 627,379.

PAN AMERICAN AIRWAYS

ISFAHAN, IRAN, a city famous for its magnificent mosques with their colored tile domes.

ICHANG, a walled port on the Yangtze River in Hupeh Province, China. The city lies at the head of the Yangtze Gorges region and is the transshipment point for river boats coming upstream from Shanghai and Hangchow. Pop., 1948 est., 81,000.

ILOILO, a port on the southeast coast of Panay Island, the Phillipines. The city is the capital of Iloilo Province and a leading port and commercial center. The chief export is sugar. Iloilo is also an important educational center and is the site of Central Phillipines University and the University of San Augustin. Pop., 1965 est., 180,900.

IMPHAL, the capital of the Union Territory of Manipur in northeastern India. The city is situated on the Imphal Plain, about 400 miles northeast of Calcutta. Imphal is a transportation center and serves as a market for the rice, sugarcane, fruit, mustard, and tobacco grown in the surrounding region. Pop., 1961, 67,717.

INDORE, in northwestern India, located in Madhya Pradesh State, about 320 miles northeast of Bombay. The city serves as a market for the surrounding agricultural region and has a number of cotton mills. Pop., 1966 est., 439,800.

IRKUTSK, capital of the Irkutsk Region in Soviet Asia. The city is located on the Angara River, about 45 miles from the southwest shore of Lake Baikal. Irkutsk is one of the major cities of Eastern Siberia and a main station on the Trans-Siberian Railway It lies in the midst of a gold-mining area and is a commercial, industrial, and educational center. Pop., 1966 est., 409,000.

ISFAHAN, the major city of central Iran, about 200 miles south of Tehran, located on the Zaindah River. The city is famous for its magnificent architecture, particularly its mosques, which are decorated with brilliantly colored tile. Most of the city's finest buildings were constructed during the reign of Shah Abbas the Great (r. 1586–1628). Isfahan is the center of the Iranian textile industry and is known for its metalwork. Pop., 1963 est., 339,900.

ISKENDERUN, a seaport in southern Turkey, on the southeastern shore of the Gulf of Iskenderun, an inlet of the Mediterranean Sea. The city is Turkey's major port on the Mediterranean and a market for the crops and livestock raised in the surrounding agricultural area. Pop., 1965, 69,300.

ISLAMABAD, the capital of Pakistan, situated on the Potwar Plateau in West Pakistan, about eight miles northeast of Rawalpindi. Still under construction, the city is scheduled for completion in 1976. The interim capital is Rawalpindi but the legislature meets in Dacca, East Pakistan.

ISTANBUL, the largest city in Turkey, located on the banks of the Bosporus at its entrance to the Sea of Marmara. One of the Mediterranean's busiest ports, Istanbul is Turkey's principal transportation, commercial, and industrial center. Its manufactures include processed foods, tobacco, leather goods, cement, glass, and soap.

The city was the capital of the Byzantine and Ottoman empires and has many historic buildings. The most famous of these is Hagia Sophia, a fourth century church that is now a museum, whose dome dominates the city. In 1968 plans were announced for building a bridge across the Bosphorus, joining Europe and Asia. Pop., 1965, urban area, 1,750,642.

IZMIR, a seaport in western Turkey, located at the southern end of the Gulf of Izmir on the Aegean Sea. Formerly called Smyrna, the city is Turkey's second largest port and a major transportation center. Izmir's industries concentrate on processing the agricultural products shipped from its port. Pop., 1965, urban area, 417,411.

JABALPUR, in central India, near the Narbada River, about 150 miles northeast of Nagpur. Jabalpur is an important manufacturing and commercial center. It is located on the Bombay-Calcutta railroad line. Pop., 1966 est., urban area, 425,700.

JAIPUR, in northern India, about 140 miles west of Agra. Jaipur is the capital of the state of Rajasthan. The city is a commercial center. Manufactures include textiles and jewelry. Pop., 1966 est., 463,300.

JAMESTOWN, the capital and port of St. Helena, a British colonial island in the South Atlantic Ocean. The island is located about 1,200 miles west of Africa and 1,800 miles east of Brazil. Its chief export is flax.

JAMSHEDPUR, in northeastern India, about 140 miles west of Calcutta. Jamshedpur is an important industrial city in the state of Bihar. The steel center of India, Jamshedpur also manufactures metal products and machinery. It is situated on the Bombay-Calcutta railroad line. Pop., 1966 est., 386,600.

JERUSALEM, one of the great religious centers of the world and the capital of Israel. Jerusalem is located in the Judean Hills of central Palestine, about 35 miles from the Mediterranean Sea and about 15 miles west of the north end of the Dead Sea. The Old City of Jerusalem, occupied by Jordan in 1948, contains most of the holy places, while the New City is the religious, economic, and administrative center of Israel. During the brief Arab-Israeli war of June 1967, Israeli troops captured the Old City. Pop., 1965 est., 191,700.

JESSELTON, a port in Malaysia, on the northwest coast of the island of Borneo. It is the capital of the state of Sabah. Pop., 1960, 21,719.

JINJA, in East Africa, on the north shore of Lake Victoria in Uganda. The city is an important copper smelting center. Pop., 1959, 29,741.

JODHPUR, in western India, about 300 miles southwest of Delhi. Jodhpur is a walled city in the state of Rajasthan. It is a railroad junction and trade center for locally produced grain. Pop., 1966 est., 248,200.

JOHANNESBURG, the largest city in the Republic of South Africa, in southern Transvaal Province, about 30 miles southwest of Pretoria. Johannesburg is situated on a plateau more than 5,700 feet above sea level. It is the industrial and commercial center of South Africa. Gold mining is the chief industry. Pop., 1960, urban area, 1,152,525.

JOLO, a port in the Philippines, on the northwest coast of Jolo Island in the Sulu Archipelago, about 600 miles south of Manila. Jolo is the capital of Sulu Province. Exports include coconuts and hemp. Pop., 1960, 33,259.

JOS, in the former Northern Region of Nigeria, West Africa. It is about 150 miles south of Kano and is a tin-mining center. Pop., 1963, 90,402.

LUFTHANSA AIRLINES
JERUSALEM, a major world religious center, is sacred to Christians, Jews, and Muslims.

JUDDAH, in Saudi Arabia, a port on the Red Sea about 45 miles west of Mecca. Juddah is a walled city and the chief port for pilgrims to Mecca. Pop., 1965 est., 194,000.

JULLUNDUR, in northern India, south of the Himalayan foothills and about 80 miles east of Lahore. Jullundur is a district capital in the state of Punjab. The city processes agricultural products and is an important railroad junction. Pop., 1966 est., urban area, 298,700.

KABUL, the capital of Afghanistan, situated on the Kabul River about 50 miles from the Pakistani border. The city is a commercial center, and its industries produce wool cloth, leather, furniture, and glass. It is the seat of Kabul University and other educational institutions. Pop., 1965, urban area, 438,854.

KADUNA, the capital of the former Northern Region of Nigeria. It is situated in north-central Nigeria on the Kaduna River. It is a transportation and distribution center for the surrounding agricultural area. Kaduna's main industry is the production of textiles. Pop., 1963, 149,910.

KAGOSHIMA, a Japanese port, situated on southern Kyushu on Kagoshima Bay. The city is the capital of Kagoshima Prefecture. It is noted for the production of fine pottery known as Satsuma ware. Its other products include textiles, glass, wood, and bamboo goods. Pop., 1965. 328,446.

KAIFENG, the capital of Honan Province in east-central China, situated in the Hwang Ho valley. The city was the capital of China from the 900s to the 1100s AD. It is now a commercial center that produces silk and flour. Pop., 1953, 299,100.

KALGAN, or Changkiakow, a communications center of northern China, about 100 miles northwest of Peking. Originally a caravan terminus, the city is now a rail and highway hub. Pop., 1953, 229,300.

KALININ, a river port in the western Soviet Union, situated on the Volga River about 100 miles northwest of Moscow. The city is the capital of the Kalinin Region. Kalinin, formerly known as Tver, was founded in the 1200s. It is a commercial and industrial center that manufactures iron and steel products, transportation equipment, and textiles. Pop., 1966 est., 311,000.

KALININGRAD, formerly Königsberg, a port in the western Soviet Union, situated on the Pregel River and connected with the Bay of Danzig (Gdańsk) by canal. An industrial and commercial center, its manufactures include machinery, transportation equipment, iron and steel products, chemicals, and cement.

Kaliningrad, which was founded in the 1200s, was once part of East Prussia. Following World War II it became part of the Soviet Union under the agreement reached at the 1945 Potsdam Conference. Pop., 1966 est., 261,000.

KAMAKURA, a Japanese resort and historic city, situated on Honshu Island on Sagami Bay. The city was a capital of Japan from the late 1100s to the early 1300s. Kamakura is widely known for its large statue of Buddha. Pop., 1965, 118,329.

KAMPALA, the capital of Uganda and the province of Buganda, situated in east-central Africa, near the equator. The city is a trade and transportation center for the surrounding region, which produces coffee, tea, sugarcane, cotton, tobacco, and livestock. The city also has small industries. It is the seat of the University of East Africa. Pop. 1959, urban area, 123,332.

KANDAHAR, the capital of Kandahar Province in southeastern Afghanistan. The city is a trading center for fruit and tobacco grown in the surrounding agricultural area. It is also noted for the production of silk and felt.

Kandahar is an ancient walled city, reputedly founded by Alexander the Great. In the 1700s it was made the capital of Afghanistan by Ahmad Shah, whose imposing tomb is one of the city's most impressive sights. Pop., 1966 est., 121,200.

KANDY, the capital of Ceylon's Central Province, situated on the Mahaweli River among the mountains and lakes of the central highlands. The capital of the former Kingdom of Kandy, the city contains many temples, mosques, palaces, and crypts. Pop., 1963 est., 67,800.

KANO, in northern Nigeria, the capital of Kano Province. The city, with its international airport and railroad, is the major marketing center for agricultural products of the region. It is also Nigeria's leading manufacturing center. Its products include soap, metalware, leather goods, and peanut and cotton oils. Pop., 1963, 295,432.

KARACHI, the largest city and most important port of Pakistan, situated in West Pakistan on the Arabian Sea and the delta of the Indus River. The city has excellent air, rail, and shipping facilities. Its industries produce textiles, chemicals, transportation equipment, cigarettes, and cement. Printing is also an important industry in Karachi, as is movie-making. Pop., 1961, 1,912,598.

KARAGANDA, a city in the southwest-central Soviet Union, situated near the Nura River in the Kazakh Hills. The city lies in the center of the important Karaganda coal basin, and mining is its main industry. The city's manufactures include iron and steel, cement, and mining equipment. Pop., 1966 est., 489,000.

KATAMANDU, the capital of Nepal in South Asia, situated in the Valley of Nepal in the foothills of the Himalaya. The city, located on an ancient trade route, is a marketing center for rice, fruit, vegetables, and livestock raised in the area. Katmandu has some small industries and is the seat of several educational institutions. Pop., 1961, 122,507.

KATOWICE, or Kattowitz, the capital of the Polish province of Katowice, situated about 40 miles west of Kraków. The city is an important coal-mining center with iron and steel industries. Pop., 1965 est., 286,300.

KAUNAS, a river port in the western Soviet Union in the Lithuanian Soviet Socialist Republic, situated at the confluence of the Neman and Vilia rivers. In the 1920s and 1930s Kaunas served as the capital of Lithuania. The city is an important trade and communications center. It handles agricultural produce, livestock, and textiles, and its industries produce metal goods. Pop., 1966 est., 804,000.

KAZAN, in the eastern European Soviet Union, the capital of the Tatar Autonomous Soviet Socialist Republic. The city lies on a tributary of the Volga River and is one of the most important commercial and industrial centers of the mid-Volga area. Its industries produce soap, chemicals, textiles, leather goods, and metal products.

Kazan, which was founded in 1437 near the site of an older settlement, has suffered from invasions and revolutions. Its old buildings include a kremlin (walled fortress), cathedral, mosques, and a monastery. The city is the seat of Kazan University. Pop., 1966 est., 804,000.

KHABAROVSK, a city in the eastern Soviet Union. The city lies on the Amur River. Once an agricultural and fur trading center, Khabarovsk is now a transportation center on the Trans-Siberian Railroad and an industrial city with oil refineries. Pop., 1966 est., 420,000.

KHARKOV, a city in the southwestern Soviet Union. The city, which lies on a tributary of the Donets River, near the Donbas coal and iron region, is an industrial center and a rail and air junction. Its manufactures include mining, transportation, and electrical equipment. Kharkov is the seat of the Institute of People's Education. Pop., 1966 est., 1,092,000.

KHARTOUM, the capital of Sudan, in northern Africa, situated near the junction of the White Nile and the Blue Nile. Khartoum is the communication, commercial, financial, and educational center of Sudan. It contains modern stores and boulevards, as well as a bazaar and several mosques and churches. Pop., 1964 est., 173,500.

KIEV, a city in the western Soviet Union, the capital of the Ukranian Soviet Socialist Republic. It is situated on the Dnepr River about 450 miles southwest of Moscow. Kiev is a commercial, industrial, and transportation center. Its industries produce electric motors, agricultural machines, radio and telephone equipment, and cables.

Kiev was the capital of a Russian principality in the 800s, and the first seat of the Russian Orthodox Church. It is an educational and cultural center, with museums and a national library. Pop., 1966 est., 1,367,000.

KIGALI, the capital of Rwanda, situated about 135 miles south of the equator in central Africa. It lies in a poor agricultural area, where coffee is the leading cash crop. Pop., 1959 est., urban area, 4,200.

KIMBERLEY, a city in central South Africa, one of the major diamond centers of the world. Founded after the discovery of diamonds in 1870, the city's main industries are mining, cutting, and polishing diamonds. Pop., 1960, urban area, 79,031.

KINGSTON, the capital and chief port of Jamaica, located on the southeastern coast of the island in the western Caribbean Sea. It exports Jamaica's rum, sugar, molasses, bananas, bauxite, and alumina. Pop., 1960, urban area, 376,520.

KINGSTOWN, capital and seaport of St. Vincent island, one of the British Windward Islands, located on the southern coast, in the eastern Caribbean Sea. Pop., 1960, 4,308.

KINSHASA, formerly Léopoldville, the capital and largest city of the Republic of the Congo, situated in west-central Africa on the Congo River. Kinshasa is the cultural, administrative, financial, commercial, and transportation center of the country. Its industries manufacture chemicals, textiles, processed foods, ships, and metal products. It is the seat of Louvanium University. Pop., 1966 est., 507,900.

KIRIN, or Chilin, a city in the Manchurian region of eastern China, on the Sungari River. The city is a trade center for tobacco and lumber, and there is an important chemical industry. Pop., 1957 est., 568,000.

KIRKUK, an oil center in northeastern Iraq. Before the discovery of oil in the 1920s, the city was a market for sheep raised in the surrounding area. Kirkuk is connected by oil pipeline with Baniyas, Syria, and Tripoli, Lebanon. Pop., 1965, urban area, 176,148.

UNITED NATIONS
KATMANDU'S SINGHA DARBAR, a 1,500 room palace, now the seat of the Nepal government.

KISANGANI, formerly Stanleyville, a city in the northeastern Congo (Kinshasa), situated on the Congo River near Stanley Falls. A river port and a rail and air transportation center, it serves as a market for local cotton, rice, and fish. It has textile, pharmaceutical, and printing industries. Pop., 1966, 149,887.

KISHINEV, in the southwestern Soviet Union, the capital of the Moldavian Soviet Socialist Republic and the former capital of Bessarabia. Kishinev lies on a tributary of the Dnestr River. It is a commercial center for the surrounding agricultural area. Pop., 1966 est., 289,000.

KLAIPEDA, or Memel, a seaport of the western Soviet Union, situated on the Baltic Sea at the mouth of the Niemen River. The city, which was founded in the 1200s, has been held by Sweden, Russia, Prussia, and Germany. It is a commercial and manufacturing center. Klaipeda's exports include wood and wood products, iron products, and chemicals. Pop., 1966 est., 125,000.

KOCHI, a Japanese seaport on Shikoku Island. Fishing and shipping are important industries, and the city manufactures textiles, chemicals, and paper products. Pop., 1965, 217,889.

KOKURA, a Japanese seaport on Kyushu Island. It is a transportation, commercial, and industrial center that produces machinery and heavy cotton cloth. Pop., 1960, 286,476.

KOLHAPUR, a city in west-central India, about 180 miles southeast of Bombay. Kolhapur is a trade, education, and motion picture center. The Mahalaxmi Temple in Kolhapur is a famous religious sanctuary. Pop., 1966 est., 214,400.

KOMSOMOLSK, a city in the eastern Soviet Union, situated on the Amur River. It was established in 1932 on the site of a small village by volunteers of the Young Communist League (Komsomol). The city is an industrial center with good rail connections. Its industries include steelworks, shipyards, and oil refineries. Pop., 1966 est., 207,000.

KOŠICE, a city in southeastern Czechoslovakia, situated on the Hernad River near the Hungarian border. It is a market center with industries that produce wine, woolens, and tobacco. At various times in its history, Košice has been part of Hungary. Pop., 1965 est., 102,000.

KOZHIKODE, formerly Calicut, a port of India, lying on the southwestern coast. It is a trade center for coconut palms grown in the region. Other exports include rubber, lumber, and spices. Pop., 1966 est., urban area, 296,500.

KRAKÓW, or Cracow, a city in southern Poland on the Vistula (Wista) River. It is a rail and commercial center that manufactures machinery, construction materials, chemicals, paper, and

THE UNITED NATIONS

LAHORE, in West Pakistan, is a city of mosques and minarets, Mughal forts, and royal tombs.

clothing. The city is also a cultural and educational center with medieval buildings, a Gothic cathedral, a castle, and a university. Pop., 1965 est., 516,600.

KRASNOVODSK in the southern Soviet Union, a seaport on the Caspian Sea. The city is an important gateway to central Asia, to which it is linked by rail. Its imports include oil, grain and timber, and its exports include cotton and fruit. Pop., 1956 est., 38,000.

KUALA LUMPUR, the capital of Malaysia, situated on the western part of the Malay Peninsula, about 200 miles northwest of Singapore. It is a transportation center with industries based on rubber and tin production. Pop., 1957, 316,230.

KUCHING, the capital of Sarawak, situated on the northwestern coast of Borneo. The city is a port with steamer service to Singapore. Pop., 1960, 50,579.

KUMAMOTO, a city in Japan on Kyushu Island, situated on the Shira River. It is a tourist resort, with a feudal castle, and an educational center. Pop., 1965, 407,052.

KUMASI, a city of central Ghana, the former seat of the Ashanti tribal chiefs. It is a commercial center with good transportation facilities. Cacao, wood products, and bauxite are shipped from Kumasi. Pop., 1965, 230,500.

KUNMING, a city in southwestern China, situated about 380 miles southwest of Chungking. Kunming is a distribution center for, and the capital of, Yünnan Province. Its principal exports are tin and copper goods and spices and herbs. The city is also a tourist resort. Pop., 1957 est., 880,000.

KURUME, a Japanese city on Kyushu Island, about 50 miles northeast of Nagasaki. The city is a distribution center for the surrounding agricultural area, and is noted for its cotton textiles. Pop., 1965, 158,974.

KUWAIT CITY, or Al Kuwait, the capital of Kuwait and a port, located at the northwestern end of the Persian Gulf. The city's main export is oil, but pearls, horses, and woollens are also important. Pop., 1965, 99,609.

KUYBYSHEV, formerly Samara, a city in the central European Soviet Union, situated at the confluence of the Volga and Samara rivers. The city is a distribution and trade center for grains, and its industries produce machinery, transportation equipment, and electrical goods. Pop., 1966 est., 969,000.

KWEIYANG, a transportation center of southwestern China, located on the route between Kunming and Chungking. Kweiyang is both an agricultural and an industrial city, whose products include grains, tobacco, and tea. Textiles, chemicals, and lacquerware are also produced in Kweiyang. Pop., 1957 est., 504,000.

KYOTO, the former capital of Japan, situated on west-central Honshu Island. Kyoto is a cultural and artistic center, known for its handicraft industries. There are many temples and shrines in the city, and parts of the old imperial palace are preserved. Kyoto's industries produce chemicals and electrical goods. Pop., 1965, 1,365,-007.

LADYSMITH, in Natal Province, Republic of South Africa, about 200 miles northwest of Durban. The city is a railroad junction and a shipping center for the livestock raised in the surrounding area. It is the site of a famous siege of the British by Transvaal troops during the Boer War. Pop., 1960, 23,000.

LAGOS, the capital and major port of Nigeria, located on the mainland and on islands in Lagos Lagoon, off the Gulf of Guinea. Its modern harbor handles much trade, including exports of rubber, cacao, peanuts, and hardwood. Lagos is connected by road and rail to other Nigerian cities and is served by an international airport. Pop., 1963, 665,246.

LAHORE, capital of the province of West Pakistan in Pakistan, located in the Punjab about 270 miles northwest of New Delhi, India. The second largest city in Pakistan, Lahore is an important railroad junction and industrial center. It also serves as the market for the agricultural produce raised in the surrounding area. Lahore has many cultural and educational institutions and is the site of Punjab University. Pop., 1961, 1,296,477.

LAMBARÉNÉ, in Gabon, West Africa, located in the western part of the country on the Ogooué River. The city serves as a trade center for the surrounding agricultural area. It is the site of a hospital and medical center founded in 1913 by Dr. Albert Schweitzer.

LANCHOW, capital of Kansu Province in northwestern China, located on the Hwang Ho, near the Great Wall. The city lies on the medieval caravan route known as the Silk Road and because of its position near the border was known as the Gateway to China. Modern Lanchow is an important industrial center that produces machinery, refined petroleum, and chemicals. It is also a major railroad junction. Pop., 1957 est., 699,000.

LA PAZ, the chief capital and largest city of Bolivia, in west-central South America. Situated at an altitude of more than 11,000 feet on the high plateau of western Bolivia, La Paz is the highest capital and major city in the world. It is the industrial, commercial, political, and cultural center of Bolivia, although Sucre is the legal capital. Manufactures include textiles, cement, glass, and furniture. Pop., 1965 est., 360,300.

LASHIO, in northeastern Burma, on the Shan Plateau, about 130 miles northeast of Mandalay. The city is a trade center and the northeastern terminus of the railroad from Mandalay. Lashio was formerly an important point on the old Burma Road. Pop., 1956, 5,869.

LATAKIA, seaport in western Syria and capital of Latakia Province, located on the Mediterranean Sea about 110 miles north of Beirut. An ancient city, Latakia reached a height of prosperity during the Crusades and then declined until the 1700s, when it became the center of an important tobacco-raising district. The port's main exports are tobacco, silk, and sponges. Pop., 1963 est., 75,400.

LEEDS, in north-central England, on the Aire River, about 165 miles northwest of London. Leeds is an industrial city located near coal and iron mines. It is the center of England's wool industry. Manufactures include textiles and clothing, iron and steel, machinery, chemicals, and leather goods. The city is an important cultural and educational center. Pop., 1965 est., urban area, 1,726,200.

LE HAVRE, an important seaport on the northern coast of France at the mouth of the Seine River on the English Channel. Le Havre handles imports and exports for Paris and northwestern France, trading primarily with North America and northern Europe. The city's industries include shipbuilding and the manufacture of machinery, electrical equipment, and chemical products. Le Havre also has an important oil-refinery. Pop., 1962, urban area, 222,565.

LEIPZIG, an East German city on the Pleisse River at its junction with the Elster and the Parthe. It is a major commercial and industrial center, manufacturing vehicles and machinery, chemicals, steel, and textiles. It lies at the junction of many rail, road, and river transportation routes, and it is an important river port. Leipzig has many colleges and museums and is a leading German cultural center. Pop., 1965 est., 594,700.

LENINGRAD, the second largest city in the Soviet Union, located at the mouth of the Neva River on the Gulf of Finland, an inlet of the Baltic Sea.

The city was known as St. Petersburg until 1914 and as Petrograd until 1924. Leningrad is a major industrial center. Its industries produce electrical equipment, precision tools, machinery, chemicals, textiles, and paper. It is also an important shipbuilding center. The city has many cultural and educational institutions, including the Hermitage art museum and the University of Leningrad.

Leningrad was founded in 1703 by Peter the Great. It was the capital of Russia from 1713 until 1918 and was the place where the Russian Revolution began in 1917. Pop., 1965 est., urban area, 3,665,000.

LIBREVILLE, capital of Gabon in West Africa, located 30 miles north of the equator on the Atlantic Ocean. It is Gabon's largest city and a major port. Hardwoods are Libreville's leading exports. Pop., 1964, 45,909.

LIÈGE, capital of Liège Province, Belgium, in the eastern part of the country, on the Meuse River. Surrounded by a coal-mining region. Liège is an important industrial center. Its chief manufactures are steel, firearms, crystal, and glass. Liège has a number of historic buildings, a notable art museum, and a university. Pop., 1965 est., urban area, 452,700.

LIEPAYA, seaport and second largest city in Latvia, located on an isthmus between Lake Liepaya and the Baltic Sea. The city is a naval base and industrial center. Its chief manufactures are steel, chemicals, machinery, ships, and processed foods. Pop., 1966 est., 84,000.

LIKASI, the former Jadotville, in Katanga Province, southeastern Congo (Kinshasa), West Africa. The city is located about 60 miles northwest of Lubumbashi and is an important copper smelting center. Pop., 1966 est., 102,200.

LIMA, capital and largest city of Peru, on the Rimac River, about 8 miles inland from the Pacific Ocean and its port, Callao. The city is the political and cultural center of Peru. Founded in 1535 by Francisco Pizarro, Lima retains many buildings from its colonial past and is one of the most picturesque capitals of South America. It is connected by rail and road to Callao and other cities in Peru. Pop., 1961, urban area, 1,436,231.

LIMASSOL, a seaport on the south coast of Cyprus, located on Akrotiri Bay. The city exports the wine, barley, and livestock of the surrounding area and minerals from the interior. Local industries produce alcoholic beverages, perfumes, and cigarettes. Pop., 1960, 43,593.

LISBON, the capital and largest city of Portugal, located at the mouth of the Tagus River on the Atlantic Ocean. It is Portugal's leading port and exports the country's fish, olive oil, and wine. Lisbon contains most of the country's industry and produces ships, refined oil, textiles, chemicals, processed foods, and tile. The city has

BRANIFF AIRWAYS
LA PAZ, in western Bolivia, is the world's highest capital, over 11,000 feet above sea level.

THE UNITED NATIONS

LOMÉ, the capital of Togo, is a commercial center and seaport with busy outdoor markets.

many beautiful churches and a number of interesting Muslim and Renaissance buildings. Pop., 1965 est., 822,000.

LIVERPOOL, the second largest seaport in Britain, situated on the Mersey River, near the Irish Sea. The city's economy is based on shipping and warehouse storage, especially of cotton, wool, tobacco, and grain. Liverpool is a rail center and is connected with Manchester and its industrial region by the deep-water Manchester Ship Canal. Its industries produce flour, refined sugar, candy, soap, and glass. Pop., 1965 est., urban area, 1,381,100.

LJUBLJANA, the capital of Slovenia, Yugoslavia, located on the Sava River. The city lies in a rich agricultural region for which it serves as a trade center. It is also an important railroad junction. Ljubljana's industries produce textiles, machinery, and paper. Pop., 1961, 134,169.

LOBITO, the principal port of Angola, in southwestern Africa, located on the Atlantic Ocean about 24 miles north of Benguela. The city is the terminus of a railroad from the Katanga copper mines in the Congo and copper is one of its major exports. Lobito also exports Angola's sisal, cotton, corn, and iron ore. It is linked by air to other cities in Africa and Europe. Pop., 1960, 50,164.

LÓDŹ, the second largest city of Poland, about 75 miles southwest of Warsaw, in the central part of the country. It is an important industrial center and produces textiles, machinery, electrical equipment, paper, and processed foods. Pop., 1965 est., 742,900.

LOMÉ, in West Africa, the capital and major seaport of Togo, located on the Gulf of Guinea. The city is the chief commercial and industrial center of the country. Its port exports phosphate, cacao, coffee, copra, timber,

and palm oil. Lomé is connected by rail with the cities of the interior. Pop., 1966 est., 86,400.

LONDON, the capital of Britain and one of the world's largest cities, located on the Thames River about 40 miles from the North Sea. London is Britain's major port and commercial center. Its industries produce mostly finished consumer goods, including clothing, metal and electrical goods, chemicals, processed foods, plastics, and cigarettes. London is also a major center for banking, insurance, publishing, and printing.

A city since Roman times, London has many points of historical interest and its fine educational institutions, libraries, and museums make it an important cultural and intellectual center. London is joined to other parts of Britain and the world by an excellent network of land, sea, and air transportation. Pop., 1965 est., urban area, 7,948,300.

LOURENÇO MARQUES, the capital and largest city of Mozambique, Africa, located on an inlet of the Indian Ocean, near the country's southern border. Rail connections with Transvaal and Natal, South Africa, and a modern harbor make the city a leading port and an outlet for South African products. Major exports are coal, cotton, hardwoods, meat, and hides. Pop., 1960, urban area, 177,929.

LUANDA, seaport on the west central coast of Africa, capital of Angola. The city is Angola's major industrial center and produces soap, tobacco, and wood veneer. There is also a large oil refinery. Luanda's chief exports are coffee, sugar, cotton, fish, and diamonds. It is linked to Malange and Casengo in the interior by rail and is served by an airport. Pop., 1960, urban area, 224,540.

LUANG PRABANG, in Laos, situated on the Mekong River, about 130 miles north of the capital of Vientiane. Located at the last navigable point

on the river, the city serves as a trade center for the rice, teakwood, and other forest products of the surrounding area. Pop., 1962 est., 25,000.

LUBLIN, in eastern Poland, on the Bystryzca River, about 105 miles southwest of Warsaw. The city is a railroad junction and a trade center for the grain, potatoes, flax, and hemp raised in the surrounding area. Lublin's industries produce agricultural machinery, aircraft, trucks, and textiles. Pop., 1965 est., 202,900.

LUBUMBASHI, formerly Elisabethville, in Katanga, the Congo (Kinshasa), located near the border with Zambia. The city is a transportation and industrial center. Katanga is rich in copper, which is smelted in Lubumbashi. Other industries include printing, brewing, and the manufacture of textiles, flour, and vegetable oil. Pop., 1966 est., 507,900.

LUCKNOW, the capital of Uttar Pradesh state, India, located on the Gumti River, about 270 miles southeast of Delhi. The city is an important railroad junction and industrial center. It also serves as a market for the grain, sugarcane, mangoes, and oilseeds produced in the surrounding area. Lucknow handicraft industries produce metal goods, pottery, and embroidered muslins. Pop., 1966 est., urban area. 740,400.

LUSAKA, the capital of Zambia, in south-central Africa, located in the south-central part of the country. The city lies in an agricultural region near a mining district that produces copper, gold, and bismuth. Lusaka is the hub of an extensive road and rail network that links it to the Congo, Rhodesia, and Malawi. Pop., 1965 est., 138,000.

LUXEMBOURG, capital of Luxembourg, located in the south-central part of the country. The city is an important financial center and the headquarters of the European Coal and Steel Community. Luxembourg's industries produce iron and steel, textiles, leather goods, machinery, and processed foods. Pop., 1965 est., 78,700.

LVOV, formerly Lwów, in the Ukrainian Soviet Socialist Republic of the Soviet Union, near the Polish border. Formerly part of Poland, the city has a long history and was once one of the great trade centers of medieval Europe. It is now an important railroad junction and commercial center. Its major industries produce textiles, machinery, and refined oil. Pop., 1966 est., 502,000.

LYON, the third largest city in France, situated at the confluence of the Saône and Rhône rivers, in the southeastern part of the country. Lyon is second only to Paris as a commercial and industrial center.

The leading industry of Lyon is the manufacture of silk textiles, but the city also produces chemicals, drugs, dyes, and electrical machinery. A stock exchange and international banks make it a financial center, and yearly international trade fairs are held in the city. Over 2,000 years old, Lyon has many points of historical interest. Pop., 1962, urban area, 885,944.

MADRAS, a port on the southeastern coast of India, about 640 miles southeast of Bombay. Madras is the capital of Madras State and one of India's largest cities. It is a transportation and commercial center. Exports include cotton, coffee, tea, rice, and tobacco. Pop., 1966 est., 1,896,100.

MADRID, the capital and largest city of Spain. The city is located in the region of New Castile, at the geographical center of the Iberian Peninsula. Madrid is situated on a plateau, at an altitude of about 2,150 feet above sea level. It is Spain's leading administrative, financial, and cultural center. It is also among the nation's chief educational and tourist centers. Manufactures include machinery, leather goods, and paper. Pop., 1965 est., urban area, 2,599,300.

MADURA, in southern India, on the Vaigai River, about 265 miles southwest of Madras. Madura is a district capital in the state of Madras and an important industrial and commercial center. The chief manufacture is textiles. Exports include rice and tobacco. Pop., 1966 est., 458,400.

MAGNITOGORSK, in the Ural Mountains of the Soviet Union, on the left bank of the Ural River, about 800 miles east of Moscow. Magnitogorsk is a leading Soviet steel center. Mining machinery is also manufactured. Pop., 1966 est., 352,000.

MAIDUGURI, in West Africa, in the northeastern part of the former Northern Region of Nigeria. It is about 315 miles east of Kano. Maiduguri is a transportation center. Pop., 1963, 139,-965.

MAKASAR, a port in Southeast Asia, on the island of Celebes in Indonesia. It is one of Indonesia's largest cities and the capital of the province of South Sulawesi. Exports include coffee, copra, rice, and spices. Pop., 1961, 384,159.

MALACCA, a Southeast Asian port, capital of the state of Malacca in Malaysia. The city is located on the southwest coast of the Malay Peninsula, about 125 miles northwest of Singapore. Exports include rubber and tin. Pop., 1957, 69,848.

MALE, the capital of the Indian Ocean nation of Maldive Islands, situated on Male atoll. The town processes and exports local fish and coconuts. Pop., 1965, 11,202.

MANAGUA, capital and largest city of Nicaragua, situated in the west on the southern shore of Lake Managua. It lies on the main rail and road transportation routes and is the economic and cultural center of the country. It has food-processing plants, textile mills, pharmaceutical factories, and other industries. The city has been severely damaged by earthquakes several times. Pop., 1965 est., 262,000.

MANAMA, the capital and principal town of the sheikhdom of Bahrain, situated on the northern coast of Bahrain Island, on the Persian Gulf. Refining and exporting the sheikhdom's petroleum are the port city's main industries, and there is some boatbuilding and fishing. Pop., 1959, urban area, 61,726.

MANCHESTER, in northwestern England, on the Irwell River in Lancashire, about 30 miles northeast of Liverpool. Manchester, Britain's leading manufacturing center, is among the world's chief producers of cotton goods. Other products include aircraft, motor vehicles, machinery, chemicals, and rubber goods. Manchester is a railroad junction and an ocean port, linked to the Irish Sea by the deepwater Manchester Ship Canal. Pop., 1965 est., urban area, 2,457,300.

MANDALAY, in Southeast Asia, on the left bank of the Irrawaddy River in central Burma, about 350 miles north of Rangoon, the capital. Mandalay is an important religious and cultural center. The leading industry is silk weaving. Pop., 1958 est., 195,300.

MANGALORE, a port on the southwest coast of India, at the mouth of the Netravati River, about 190 miles west of Bangalore. Mangalore is a district capital in the state of Mysore. The city is a railroad terminus and shipping center. Exports include coffee, pepper, and tea. Pop., 1966 est., 198,600.

MANILA, the largest city, chief port, and administrative center of the Philippines. It lies on Luzon Island on Manila Bay. The city is a transportation, manufacturing, and educational center. Its products include coconut oil, sugar, rice, textiles, and transportation equipment. Pop., 1965 est., 1,356,00.

MARRAKECH, in west-central Morocco, on the western slopes of the Grand Atlas Mountains in North Africa. Marrakech is one of the largest cities of Morocco and a major Muslim religious center. Manufactures include wool, flour, carpets and leather goods. Pop., 1965 est., 255,000.

MARSEILLE, in southeastern France, the greatest port on the Mediterranean Sea. It is located on the Gulf of Lions, about 25 miles east of the mouth of the Rhône River. It is the capital of the department of Bouches-du-Rhône and a leading European industrial center. Manufactures include motor vehicles, machinery, sugar, textiles, and olive oil. Pop., 1962, urban area, 807,499.

MASERU, the capital of Lesotho, in southern Africa. The city is located near the western border with South Africa, at an altitude of more than 5,000 feet above sea level. Maseru is the nation's transportation center. Exports include wool, mohair, and hides. Workers for South African mines are recruited in Maseru. Pop., 1966, urban area, 18,000.

MASHHAD, in northeastern Iran, near the border with the Soviet Union, about 440 miles east of Tehran, the capital. Mashhad is an important holy city and a leading commercial and transportation center. Manufactures include cotton, wool, and leather. Pop., 1963 est., 312,200.

MATADI, in the extreme western Congo (Kinshasa), near the mouth of the Congo River, at the border with Angola. Matadi is the chief port of the Congo and exports agricultural and forest products. Pop., 1958 est., 59,000.

MATHURA, in northern India, on the right bank of the Jumna River, about 30 miles northwest of Agra. Mathura is an important religious and cultural center. Manufactures include cotton and paper. Pop., 1966 est., urban area, 135,700.

MBABANE, the capital and chief town of Swaziland, in southeastern Africa. Mbabane is located about 95 miles southwest of Lourenço Marques, the

THE UNITED NATIONS
RUSH HOUR IN MANILA, the administrative center and chief port of the Philippines.

SAUDI ARABIAN PUBLIC RELATIONS BUREAU

MECCA, in Saudia Arabia, is Islam's holiest shrine and a city of modern parks and avenues.

capital of Portuguese Mozambique, with which it is linked by rail. Exports from Mbabane include iron ore and asbestos. Pop., 1962 est., urban area, 8,400.

MECCA, the chief holy city of the Muslim world. It is located in a valley in west-central Saudi Arabia, about 45 miles east of Juddah, its port on the Red Sea. Mecca is the birthplace of Muhammad and contains the Kaaba, chief shrine of Islam, which is visited by many thousands of pilgrims each year. The city is also the capital of the province of Hejaz and a commercial center. Pop., 1965 est., 185,000.

MEDELLÍN, in Colombia, in a mountain valley at an altitude of about 5,000 feet above sea level, about 150 miles northwest of Bogotá. Medellín is the capital of the department of Antioquia and the second largest city of Colombia. Medellín is an educational center and the nation's chief industrial city. It manufactures steel, textiles, chemicals, sugar, and paper. Pop., 1964, 772,887.

MEDINA, in northwestern Saudi Arabia, about 100 miles from the Red Sea coast. It is second only to Mecca as a Muslim holy city. The Great Mosque in Medina contains the tomb of Muhammad and is annually visited by many thousands of pilgrims. The city is located in a fertile oasis and is a market center for agricultural products. Pop., 1963 est., 72,000.

MEERUT, in northern India, on a branch of the Ganges River, about 35 miles northeast of Delhi. It is a district capital in the state of Uttar Pradesh and a trade and transportation center. Manufactures include steel, chemicals, sugar, and soap. Pop., 1966 est., urban area, 311,100.

MELBOURNE, the capital, largest city, and chief port of Victoria, Australia. Melbourne is located at the mouth of the Yarra River on Port Phillip Bay, in southeastern Australia. The city is an important railroad terminus and one of Australia's leading commercial centers. Manufactures include aircraft, motor vehicles, textiles, and processed foods. Pop., 1966, urban area, 2,228,511.

MELILLA, a Spanish enclave on the north coast of Morocco, administered by Spain as part of the province of Málaga. The city is situated about 30 miles west of the border with Algeria. Melilla is an important fishing port. It exports iron ore and lead. Pop., 1966 est., 77,900.

MEXICO CITY, the capital of Mexico, located in the southern part of the Central Plateau. Mexico City is one of the oldest cities in North America. In 1325 the Aztecs built their capital, Tenochtitlán, on the site. Today one of the largest cities in the Western Hemisphere, Mexico City is a major cultural, commercial, and industrial center. Its fine buildings and sites of historical interest, beautiful location, and pleasant climate attract many tourists. Pop., 1966 est., 3,287,300.

MILAN, in northern Italy, located between the foothills of the Alps and the Po River, near the border with Switzerland. Milan is the second largest city in Italy and the nation's leading industrial and commercial center. Manufactures include aircraft, motor vehicles, heavy machinery, chemicals, and textiles. Pop., 1965 est., urban area, 1,669,500.

MINSK, in the far western Soviet Union, the capital of the Byelorussian Soviet Socialist Republic. The city is located on a branch of the Berezina River, about 470 miles southwest of Moscow and about 150 miles east of the border with Poland. Minsk is Byelorussia's leading industrial, cultural, and transportation center. Manufactures include trucks, tractors, and radios. Pop., 1966 est., 739,000.

MISKOLC, in northeastern Hungary, on the Sajó River, about 85 miles northeast of Budapest. Miskolc is an important industrial city and trade center. Manufactures include iron and steel, motor vehicles, textiles, and lumber. Pop., 1965 est., 169,000.

MOGADISCIO, the capital and chief port of Somalia, in eastern Africa. It is located on the Indian Ocean, about 700 miles southeast of Addis Ababa, the capital of Ethiopia. Mogadiscio exports bananas and hides. Pop., 1966 est., 170,000.

MOKPO, a port in southwestern South Korea, on the Yellow Sea, about 190 miles south of Seoul. Mokpo's industries include fishing and food processing. Pop., 1965, est., 157,400.

MOMBASA, the chief port of Kenya, off the coast of eastern Africa. Mombasa is located on a small island in the Indian Ocean and is linked to the mainland by a causeway, a bridge, and ferries. The city exports coffee, cotton, tea, sugar, and other agricultural products. Pop., 1962, urban area, 179,575.

MONROVIA, the capital, largest city, and chief port of Liberia in West Africa. Monrovia is located on Cape Montserrado, near the mouth of the Saint Paul River, on the Atlantic Ocean. The city is the commercial, educational, and cultural center of Liberia. Exports include rubber, iron ore, gold, and coffee. The city was named for U. S. Pres. James Monroe. Pop., 1962, 80,992.

MONTE CARLO, a commune in the principality of Monaco. It is located on the French Riviera, nine miles from Nice, France. Monte Carlo is a famous resort. Pop., 1965, 9,038.

MONTEVIDEO, the capital, largest city, and chief port of Uruguay. It is located on the north shore of the Rio de la Plata, about 135 miles southeast of Buenos Aires, Argentina. Montevideo is the industrial, commercial, and cultural center of Uruguay. The city's leading industry is meat packing. Chief exports are wool, meat, and hides. Pop., 1963, 1,158,632.

MONTREAL, the largest city in Canada. It is located on the island of Montreal, at the confluence of the Ottawa and St. Lawrence rivers, in southern Quebec. Montreal is situated at the entrance to the St. Lawrence Seaway. Although the city is about 1,000 miles from the Atlantic Ocean, it is one of the world's largest inland ports.

It is Canada's industrial, financial, and transportation center. Manufactures include aircraft, iron and steel, oil, chemicals, electrical equipment, processed foods, and clothing. Pop., 1966, urban area, 2,436,817.

MORADABAD, in northern India, on the right bank of the Ramganga River, about 90 miles east of Delhi. Moradabad is a district capital in the state of Uttar Pradesh and an important trade and transportation center. Pop., 1966 est., urban area, 207,800.

MORONI, the capital of the Comoro Islands, a French possession at the north entrance to the Mozambique Channel. Moroni is located on the east coast of Grande Comore Island. The town is the chief port. Pop., 1966 est., urban area, 11,500.

MOSCOW, the capital and largest city of the Soviet Union. It is located on both banks of the Moscow River, about 400 miles southeast of Leningrad. Moscow is the Soviet Union's industrial, political, and transportation center. Manufactures include motor vehicles, machinery, electrical equipment, chemicals, textiles, and steel.

Moscow is the headquarters of the Communist Party of the Soviet Union and the administrative and cultural center of the nation. Landmarks include the Kremlin, Red Square, and St. Basil's Cathedral. Pop., 1966 est., urban area, 6,463,000.

MOSHI, in eastern Africa, on the southern slope of Mt. Kilimanjaro in northeastern Tanzania. Moshi is a trading center in an agricultural region. Pop., 1957, 13,726.

MOSUL, in Iraq, on the west bank of the Tigris River, about 220 miles northwest of Bagdad, the capital. Mosul is situated in an oil producing region and is Iraq's oil center. The ruins of ancient Nineveh are nearby. Pop., 1965, urban area, 315,157.

MOULMEIN, a port in Southeast Asia, situated at the mouth of the Salween River in lower Burma, on the Gulf of Martaban. Moulmein is a district capital and commercial center. Exports include tea and rice. Pop., 1958 est., 108,000.

MUNICH, or München, capital of the state of Bavaria and the third largest city in West Germany. Munich is situated on the Isar River, about 25 miles north of the Bavarian Alps in southeastern West Germany. The city is an important industrial, commercial, and transportation center.

In addition to beer, for which the city is famous, Munich manufactures vehicles, machinery, chemicals, and textiles. The city is also a major cultural, educational, and tourist center. Pop., 1965 est., 1,210,500.

MURMANSK, the Soviet Union's chief port on the Arctic Ocean. The city is located on the Kola Peninsula in the far north, on the east bank of the Tuloma River, about 35 miles from the Barents Sea. It is the largest city north of the Arctic Ocean and the only large Soviet ice-free port.

Murmansk is a naval and fishing center and is linked by railroad to Leningrad, which is about 625 miles to the south. Exports include fish, lumber, and minerals. Pop., 1966 est., 279,000.

MURORAN, in northern Japan, situated on the southwest coast of Hokkaido Island, at the entrance to Uchiura Bay. Muroran is a naval base and an iron and steel center. Coal is the chief export. Pop., 1965, urban area, 161,252.

MUSCAT, capital of Muscat and Oman, a country in the southeastern part of the Arabian Peninsula. The city is located on Muscat Bay, an arm of the Gulf of Oman, at the entrance to the Persian Gulf. Pop., 1960 est., urban area, 6,200.

UNITED NATIONS
MOSCOW CITIZENS shop in GUM, the largest department store in the Soviet Union's capital.

NACALA, a seaport of northern Mozambique in southeastern Africa. Its deep natural harbor was improved during a six-year plan ending in 1958. The port's subsequent growth reflects development of the hinterland for agriculture and utilization of local deposits of graphite, copper, and chrome ores. It is the coastal terminus of a rail line to Lake Nyasa.

NAGASAKI, a seaport on the northwest coast of Kyushu Island, Japan. Opened to foreign trade in 1568, it has had the longest contact with the Western world of any Japanese city. A large steel rolling mill and nearby coal fields have made it an important shipbuilding center and coaling station. Almost half of the city was destroyed on Aug. 9, 1945 by the second U. S. atomic bomb used in warfare. Pop., 1965, 405,479.

NAGOYA, the third largest city of Japan, located on the south coast of Honshu Island at the head of Ise Bay. A major port, industrial and rail center, the city produces pottery and porcelain, textiles, machine tools, automobiles, and chemicals. It is the site of Nagoya University. Pop., 1965, 1,935,430.

NAGPUR, a city in Maharashtra state, India, 420 miles northeast of Bombay. An important rail center, the city also has many cotton and woolen mills and an important hand-weaving industry. The city is the site of Nagpur University. Pop., 1966 est., urban area, 799,700.

NAHA, a seaport and the capital of the U.S.-controlled Ryukyu Islands, located on the southeast coast of Okinawa Island. The city was the capital of the Okinawa Prefecture of Japan until the island was captured by the United States in 1945. Its manufactures include lacquerware and textiles. Pop., 1965 est., 226,000.

NAIROBI, the capital and largest city of Kenya, in east Africa. It is the focus of several rail lines which carry coffee, cotton, tea, and sisal from parts of Kenya and Uganda to the Indian Ocean port of Mombasa. Principal industries include meat packing, flour milling, and the manufacture of furniture, soap, chemicals, foodstuffs, and paper products. Pop., 1962, urban area, 314,760.

NANCHANG, the capital of Kiangsi Province, China. It is on the Kan River, southwest of Poyang Lake. Located at the junction of two rail lines, the city is the commercial center of a rich agricultural area. Its industries include cotton milling, food processing, and the manufacture of machine tools, farm implements, paper, and matches. Pop., 1957 est., 508,000.

NANKING, the capital of Kiangsu Province, China. It is on the Yangtze River, which seagoing vessels can navigate to the city. Rail lines connect it to Peking and Shanghai. Traditional industries include the manufacture of silk and cotton cloth and a firm, durable cotton fabric called Nankeen. Since communist rule began in 1949, heavy industrial and chemical plants have been established.

An important cultural and educational center, Nanking is the site of scientific research institutes and several institutions of higher learning, including Nanking University. It was the capital of China during the Nationalist period, which ended in 1949. Pop., 1957 est., 1,419,000.

NAPLES, or Napoli, a major seaport in Italy on the Bay of Naples, off the Tyrrhenian Sea. It is 10 miles northwest of Mount Vesuvius. The third largest city in Italy, it is an industrial center and important for the manufacture of ships, engines, textiles, glass, gloves, wine, and machinery.

Naples was founded several hundred years before the birth of Christ. Many relics from the ruins of Pompeii are in the National Museum. Naples has medieval and Renaissance buildings, as well as a university, libraries, and museums. Pop., 1965 est., 1,228,100.

NARA, a Japanese city, within 50 miles of Kyoto and Osaka. It was the first capital of Japan, from 710 to 784. During the Nara Period, Japanese culture began to develop independently of the earlier Chinese domination. The city is the site of the Nara National Museum. Pop., 1965, 160,641.

NAZARETH, an ancient town of northern Israel, southwest of the Sea of Galilee (Lake Tiberias). Although the site of the boyhood of Jesus, it was not recognized as significant until about 600 AD. Tourism is the major source of income. Pop., 1965 est., 29,100.

NDOLA, a town of western Zambia, in south-central Africa. Located in the copperbelt, it is a mining and refining center. The city is linked by rail to the capital, Lusaka, to the south. Pop., 1965 est., urban area, 100,000.

NEICHIANG, a city in Szechwan Province, China. It is on a rail line between Chungking and Chengtu. Neichiang is a commercial center. Pop., 1953, 190,200.

NEW DELHI, the capital of India, situated in the north-central part of the country on the Jumna River. New Delhi lies adjacent to Delhi, or Old Delhi. Together the cities form a trade, transportation, and industrial center. Manufactures include textiles, clothing, metal products, chemicals, and handicrafts of gold, silver, ivory, and wood. Old Delhi is the seat of the University of Delhi.

The site of Old and New Delhi has been inhabited since about 400 BC. The present city of New Delhi was designed and constructed as an administrative center. The seat of government was transferred from Calcutta to Delhi in 1912 and to New Delhi in 1931. Pop., 1966 est., New Delhi, 314,400; Delhi, 2,440,500.

NIAMEY, the capital of the Republic of Niger in West Africa. An inland port on the Niger River, it is a market center for the agricultural products of the region. Pop., 1962 est., 40,172.

NICE, an ancient city in southern France on the Mediterranean Sea near the Italian border. The Maritime Alps lie to the north, and the city's beautiful location and climate make it a world-renowned resort. The tourist trade is the city's chief industry but also important are the manufacture of perfume oils, soap, clothing, and the preparation of olive oil. Flowers and olive trees are cultivated, and there is an important trade in cut flowers. Pop., 1962, urban area, 310,063.

NICOSIA, the capital of Cyprus, an island in the eastern Mediterranean Sea near Turkey. It is a commercial center of the Messaori Plain, which produces wheat, wine, olive oil, almonds, citrus fruits, and livestock. Textiles, leather, machine tools, and cigarettes are manufactured in the city. Pop., 1964 est., urban area, 103,000.

NINGPO, or Ninghsien, a seaport of China, south of Hangchow Bay in the East China Sea. An important fishing center, the city manufactures furniture, lace, and straw products and exports cotton, drugs, tea, and fish. Pop., 1953, 237,500.

FRENCH GOVERNMENT TOURIST OFFICE

NICE, a resort city, lies on the curving Mediterranean seacoast of the French Riviera.

NIS, a city of eastern Yugoslavia, on the Morava River, some 120 miles southeast of Belgrade. A commercial center, the city has rail connections with the major cities of the country. Its manufactures include furniture, liquor, cigarettes, leather, and textiles. Pop., 1961, 81,073.

NOUAKCHOTT, capital of the Islamic Republic of Mauritania, in West Africa. Lying four miles from the Atlantic Ocean, it is a market center with limited port facilities. Pop., 1965 est., 15,000.

NOUMÉA, seaport and capital of New Caledonia, an overseas territory of the French Community, in the Southwest Pacific Ocean. An attractive city with a pleasant climate, Noméa attracts many tourists. It is the site of the French Research Institute of Oceania and headquarters of the six-nation South Pacific Commission. The principal industry is nickel smelting. Pop., 1963, 34,990.

NOVI SAD, a city in northeastern Yugoslavia, on the Danube River about 45 miles northwest of Belgrade. An important Danube port and rail center, it is the market for agricultural products of the region, and manufactures machinery, pottery, textiles, and chemicals. The city is the chief Serbian religious and cultural center. Pop., 1961, 102,469.

NOVOSIBIRSK, capital of the Novosibirsk Oblast, U.S.S.R. It is some 1700 miles east of Moscow. The largest city in Siberia, it is on the Ob River, at the point where it is crossed by the Trans-Siberian Railroad. It has long been an agricultural center.

With iron and coal sources nearby, the city's industrial capacity was increased when many industrial plants were moved there from threatened areas of western Russia in World War II. It manufactures steel, automobiles, machinery, ships, textiles, plastics, and foodstuffs. It is also a cultural center with a branch of the Academy of Sciences, a university, and ballet, opera, and dramatic theaters. Pop., 1966 est., 1,049,00.

NUKU' ALOFA, seaport and capital of Tonga, a British protectorate in the Southwest Pacific. It is located on the north coast of Tongatabu Island. Pop., 1956, 9,202.

NURNBERG, or Nuremberg, in southern West Germany, on the Pegnitz River, about 90 miles northwest of Munich. Nurnberg is an industrial and transportation center. Manufactures include machines, chemicals, textiles, electrical equipment, and beer. It is a center of German culture and history. Pop., 1965 est., 472,000.

ODESSA, a city in the southwestern Soviet Union, situated on the Black Sea near the mouth of the Dnestr River. The city is one of the major seaports of the Soviet Union. Its excellent harbor handles a variety of exports, including grain, wood, wool, and foodstuffs. Imports include coal, cotton, and tea. Odessa manufactures such products as machinery, clothing, housewares, and processed foods. Pop., 1966 est., 753,000.

OKAYAMA, a Japanese port, situated on Honshu Island on the Inland Sea. The city is a rail center. Fishing and the manufacture of cotton textiles, chemicals, and porcelain are important industries. Pop., 1965, 291,825.

OMUTA, a Japanese port, situated on Kyushu Island on Shimabara Bay. The city's industries, which produce coke, steel, zinc, and fertilizers, use coal from the nearby Miike deposits. Pop., 1965, 193,875.

ONITSHA, a Nigerian city in the former Eastern Region, situated on the Niger River, about 130 miles from its mouth. Onitsha is an industrial city, lying in the middle of a coal and oil producing region. Pop., 1963, 163,032.

ORADEA, or Oradea Mare, a city of northwestern Romania, situated on the Koros River near the Hungarian border. Oradea is a communications and trading center for an area that produces wine, grain, fruit, and livestock. Pop., 1965 est., urban area, 124,100.

ORAN, a port of northwestern Algeria, situated on the Mediterranean Sea. The city, originally a small market town, was founded by the Moors and has been held by the Spanish, Turks, and French. In 1791 it was destroyed by an earthquake. Oran is a commercial center. The city exports minerals and agricultural products. Pop., 1966, urban area, 328,257.

OSAKA, a Japanese port, situated on the southwestern coast of Honshu Island. Osaka is one of the most important industrial and commercial centers of Japan. Its industries produce a wide variety of goods, including cotton textiles, automobiles, and chemicals. Osaka is also an educational center. Pop., 1965, 3,156,222.

OSHOGBO, a Nigerian city in the former Western Region. The city, which lies on a railroad, is a trading center in a region that produces lead and zinc, cocoa, and tobacco. Pop., 1963, 208,966.

OSLO, the capital of Norway, lying at the northern end of Oslo Fjord, near the Skaggerak straits. The largest city in Norway, Oslo is also the country's principal port and its adminstrative, commercial, and industrial center. Industrial activities include shipbuilding and the manufacture of textiles, paper products, and chemicals. The city has many historic sites and cultural institutions, and is the seat of the University of Oslo. Pop., 1965 est., 483,200.

OSTRAVA, formerly Moravska Ostrava, a city in north-central Czechoslovakia, situated on the Ostravice River near its confluence with the Oder River. Ostrava is strategically located at the Moravian Gate. The city is the center of an important coal-mining region, and its industries produce iron and steel, and iron and steel products. Pop., 1965 est., 262,100.

OTARU, a Japanese port, situated on the west coast of Hokkaido Island. The city's protected harbor and large piers are used in the shipping and storing of coal from the nearby Ishikari fields. Pop., 1965, 196,771.

OTTAWA, the capital of Canada, situated in southeastern Ontario Province on the Ottawa River, about 100 miles west of Montreal. The city is primarily an administrative center, but there are some industries. The manufacture of wood, pulp, and paper products is most important. Hydroelectric power is supplied by Chaudière Falls on the Ottawa River. Pop., 1965 est., urban area, 482,000.

OUAGADOUGOU, the capital and leading city of Upper Volta in West Africa. It is connected by rail with Abidjan, an Atlantic port in the Ivory Coast. Ouagadougou is the trade center for the surrounding agricultural region. Its main exports are peanuts, cotton, and animal hides. Pop., 1961, 59,126.

OUJDA, a city in northeastern Morocco, situated near the Algerian border. It is a rail and commercial center for the nearby mining and agricultural regions. It exports lead and zinc, grains, citrus fruits, and wool and hides. Pop., 1965 est., 130,000.

OXFORD, a city in central England, situated on the Thames River. Oxford is the seat of Oxford University, which was founded in the 1100s. The city was the meeting place of some of the earliest English parliaments. Oxford's industries include the production of automobiles and printing and publishing. Pop., 1965 est., 109,300.

PADANG, an Indonesian port, situated on the west coast of the island of Sumatra. The city is an export center for coal, rice, tobacco, tea, palm oil, and rubber. Padang is noted for the manufacture of textiles. Pop., 1961, 143,699.

PAGO PAGO, the capital of American Samoa, situated on Tutuila Island in the South Pacific Ocean. The city is a seaport and air transportation center, with an important fishing industry. Pop., 1960, 1,251.

PALEMBANG, a river port of Indonesia, situated in southeastern Sumatra on the Moesi River. It is the most important trade center and the largest city of Sumatra. Palembang, which has important oil refineries, exports oil and petroleum products, rubber, coffee, spices, and coal. Pop., 1961, 474,971.

PALERMO, an Italian port, the capital of the province of Palermo and the region of Sicily, situated on the northern coast of Sicily. The city has shipyards and warehouses, and its industries produce wine, chemicals, textiles, and steel. Palermo, which is thought to be over 2,500 years old, has many historical and architectural monuments. Pop., 1965 est., 628,100.

PANAMA CITY, the capital of Panama, situated at the Pacific end of the Panama Canal. The city is a transportation and commercial center with an important tourist industry. Its manufactures include food products and clothing. Panama City is the seat of two universities. Pop., 1966 est., 343,700.

PANJIM, a port of west-central India, the capital of the former Portuguese territory of Goa. The port handles fish, rice, and other agricultural products. Pop., 1950, 31,950.

PAPEETE, the capital of French Polynesia, a seaport situated on Tahiti Island in the east-central Pacific Ocean. The city exports mother-of-pearl, copra, sugar, and rum. Pop., 1962, urban area, 27,786.

PARAMARIBO, the capital of Surinam, a Netherlands territory situated in northeastern South America. The city is a port that has good rail and road connections with the interior. Its exports include bauxite, gold, sugar, and rice. Pop., 1964, 110,867.

PARIS, the capital of France and of the Seine department, situated in east-central France on the Seine River. The city is the administrative and commercial center of France, and one of the cultural and intellectual centers of the world. Its collections of art and architecture are outstanding, and its excellent educational facilities attract students from all over the world.

Among the best known points of interest in Paris are the Louvre, Notre Dame Cathedral, the Opera, and the Eiffel Tower. Paris is also an industrial city that produces machinery, electronic equipment, and a variety of luxury consumer goods. Pop., 1962, urban area, 7,369,387.

PATNA, a city in northeastern India, the capital of Bihar state, situated on the Ganges River. It was formerly known as Pataliputra. It is a transportation and trade center for a rich agricultural region that produces grains, oilseeds, and sugarcane. The city is considered sacred by the Sikhs, and is the seat of two universities.

Patna is an ancient city. It served as the capital of the Magadha kingdom in about 500 BC and remained important until about 300 AD. The city was restored in about 1500 AD under the Mughal emperors. Pop., 1966 est., 406,500.

ITALIAN STATE TOURIST OFFICE
CATHEDRAL OF PALERMO, on the Italian island of Sicily, was built in the 1100s and 1200s.

FRENCH EMBASSY PRESS & INFORMATION DIV.

POINTE-A-PITRE, capital of Guadeloupe, is a seaport at the mouth of the Salee River.

PÉCS, or Fünfkirchen, a city in southern Hungary, situated on the slopes of the Mecsek Hills. The city, which lies in a coal mining area, is a rail and industrial center that transports coal to other industrial regions. Its industries produce textiles, clothing, and leather goods. Pécs is the seat of the University of Poszony. Pop., 1965 est., 135,000.

PEKING, or Peiping, the capital of Communist China, situated in northeastern China at the northern end of the Grand Canal. The city is an air and rail center, with links throughout China and connections with the Soviet Union and Korea. Its major industries produce steel, transportation equipment, agricultural machinery, and textiles. Peking serves as a trade center for the grain, fruit, and cotton raised in the surrounding area.

Peking is an ancient walled city, probably founded earlier than 1000 BC. It is composed of the Inner City in the north, the Outer City in the south, and recently annexed suburban areas. Pop., 1957 est., 4,010,000.

PERM, formerly Molotov, a city in the west-central Soviet Union, lying on the Kama River west of the Ural Mountains. Perm is an important industrial, commercial, and cultural center, as well as a river port and rail junction. Its manufactures include lumber products, steel, and agricultural machinery. Pop., 1966 est., 785,000.

PERTH, the capital of the Australian state of Western Australia, situated on an estuary of the Swan River, about 10 miles from its mouth. The city is the commercial, financial, and cultural center of the state. Its manufactures include cement, textiles, automobiles, furniture, fertilizer, and munitions. Pop., 1966, urban area, 499,494.

PESHAWAR, a city in West Pakistan, strategically situated near the entrance to the Khyber Pass. The city serves as a gateway to Afghanistan and central Asia. Peshawar, a road and rail junction, is the trade center for a region that produces grain, oilseed, cotton, and sugarcane. Pop., 1961, 218,691.

PHNOM PENH, the capital of Cambodia, situated at the junction of the Tonle Sap and Mekong rivers about 130 miles northwest of Saigon. Phnom Penh is a rail center and a river port. It has an important fishing industry and produces handicrafts of silver, leather, and wood. The city also has a soft-drink factory. Pop., 1962, urban area, 403,500.

PIETERMARITZBURG, a city in east-central South Africa, the capital of Natal Province. It is an administrative and commercial center, serving an area that produces grain, citrus fruits, and wattle. Pietermaritzburg is a rail junction and an industrial city with tanneries and shoe, furniture, and carpet factories. Pop., 1960, urban area, 128,589.

PIRAEUS, a port in southeastern Greece, situated on the Saronic Gulf of the Aegean Sea. Piraeus, which serves as the port for Athens, is Greece's leading port and industrial city. Its manufactures include chemicals, fertilizers, soap, drugs, flour, machinery, and jute. Pop., 1961, 183,957.

PLOIEȘTI, a city in south-central Romania. Ploiești, with its extensive pipelines, refineries, and storage tanks, is the center of Romania's petroleum industry. The city's manufactures include petroleum products, glass, paper, rubber, furniture, hardware, and textiles. Pop., 1965 est., 177,300.

PLOVDIV, a city in south-central Bulgaria on the Maritsa River. It lies in a fertile lowland and serves as a market center for livestock, tobacco, grain, and grapes and wine. Plovdiv's manufactures include textiles, soap, furniture, flour, and sugar. Pop., 1965 est., 220,600.

PLYMOUTH, the capital of Montserrat, one of the British Leeward Islands in the eastern Caribbean Sea. The city exports some of the agricultural products of the island. Pop., 1960, 1,911.

PLZEŇ, or Pilsen, a city in western Czechoslovakia about 50 miles southwest of Prague. Nearby coal and iron ore deposits supply the city's enormous metallurgical works. Plzeň is famous for the production of beer. Its other manufactures include machinery, hardware, chemicals, paper, and clothing. Pop., 1965 est., 140,200.

POINTE-A-PITRE, the capital and chief city of Guadeloupe, in the West Indies. The city is a seaport that exports food products, especially sugar, rum, cacoa, coffee, and bananas. Pop., 1954, urban area, 26,160.

POONA, a city in west-central India, situated about 80 miles southeast of Bombay. The city is an educational and commercial center with rice, sugar, and cotton mills; distilleries; and metal works. Poona is the summer residence of the governor of Bombay. Pop., 1966 est., urban area, 810,500.

PORT-AU-PRINCE, the capital and chief port of Haiti, situated on the west coast of Hispaniola, on the Caribbean Sea. The chief exports of Port-au-Prince are coffee, bananas, rum, sugar, and sisal. Pop., 1960 est., 240,000.

PORT ELIZABETH, a port in South Africa, situated on the country's southeastern coast, on the Indian Ocean. Port Elizabeth is a transportation center with a well-equipped harbor and several rail and air lines. Its principal exports are hides and fruit. Fishing, food processing, and the production of textiles, glass, soap, chemicals, furniture, and machinery are the main industries. Pop., 1960, urban area, 290,693.

PORT HARCOURT, a port in southeastern Nigeria, situated near the mouth of the Bonny River. It is an industrial city with important petroleum refineries. The city's exports include coal and palm oil. Pop., 1963, 179,563.

PORT LOUIS, the capital and chief port of Mauritius, an island in the Indian Ocean about 500 miles east of Madagascar. Sugar, the main crop and export of Mauritius, is shipped from Port Louis. Pop., 1965 est., urban area, 129,700.

PORT MORESBY, the capital of the Australian territory of Papua, in the South Pacific Ocean. Port Moresby lies on the southeastern coast of Papua Island. It is a commercial center that exports copra, rubber, and wood products. Pop., 1966, urban area, 42,133.

PORTO, or Oporto, the second largest city of Portugal, situated on the Atlantic coast at the mouth of the Douro River. Porto is known for the export of port wine. Its industries produce beverages, textiles, clothing, and pottery. Pop., 1965 est., 319,300.

PORTO–NOVO, the capital of Dahomey, situated on the southern coast of western Africa, on the Gulf of Guinea. Porto-Novo is a seaport that exports palm products and cotton. Pop., 1964, 69,500.

PORT SAID, a port of the United Arab Republic, situated at the northern end of the Suez Canal. It lies on a narrow strip of land between the Mediterranean Sea and Lake Manzala. Port Said is primarily a fueling stop for ships passing through the canal, although there is some industry. Pop., 1966, 282,876.

PORT SUDAN, a port of northeastern Sudan, situated on the Red Sea. The city has rail connections with most of Sudan's cities. Its main exports include cotton and cotton seed and gum arabic. Pop., 1963 est., 56,000.

PORT VICTORIA, capital of the Seychelles, a British Crown Colony occupying an archipelago in the Indian Ocean. The city lies on Mahe Island. Its port is the base for a fishing fleet and exports the islands' cinnamon, vanilla, and coconut products. Pop., 1960, urban area, 10,504.

POTSDAM, an East German city on the Havel River adjacent to Berlin. It has pharmaceutical, precision instrument, and textile industries, and it is the site of several historically important buildings and monuments. Pop., 1965 est., 110,100.

POZNAN, a city in west-central Poland, situated on the Warta River. Poznan is an important railway junction with industries that produce transportation equipment, agricultural machinery, and furniture. Pop., 1965 est., 436,000.

PRAGUE, or Praha, the capital of Czechoslovakia, situated in the west-central part of the country on the Vltava (Moldau) River. The city is the seat of the central Bohemian regional government, as well as an educational center and a transportation hub. Its manufactures include hydraulic and electrical equipment, chemicals, and textiles. Prague has many historic monuments representing Romanesque, Gothic, Italian Renaissance, and Baroque styles. Pop., 1965 est., 1,023,000.

PRAIA, the capital of the Cape Verde Islands, which lie in the Atlantic Ocean, about 500 miles west of Africa. Praia, situated on São Tiago Island, is a seaport that exports citrus fruits, sugarcane, coffee, and castor beans. Fishing is an important industry. Pop., 1960, urban area, 13,142.

PRETORIA, the administrative capital of South Africa and the capital of Transvaal Province, situated on the Apies River about 40 miles northeast of Johannesburg. Pretoria, a transportation, industrial, and political center, is also the seat of two universities. Its manufactures include steel, chemicals, ceramics, glassware, processed foods, and tobacco. Pop., 1960, urban area, 422,590.

CEDOK

IN PRAGUE, the Neo-Renaissance National Theatre viewed from the Vltava (Moldau) River.

PUERTO BARRIOS, a port in eastern Guatemala, situated on the Caribbean Sea. Its exports include bananas and other fruits, chicle, and wood. Pop., 1964, 22,242.

PYONGYANG, the capital of North Korea, situated on the Taedong River in the western part of the country. The city lies in a productive agricultural area and is close to important coal mines. Pop., 1960 est., 653,100.

QUEBEC, capital of Quebec Province, Canada, situated near the southeastern corner of the province on the St. Lawrence River. Part of the city, Upper Town, lies on a high bluff called Cape Diamond, and Lower Town is built around the waterfront. The capital of the French colony in Canada in the 1600s and 1700s, Quebec remains the cultural and political center of French Canada.

The city has an excellent harbor and port facilities accessible to ocean-going vessels, and it serves as a distribution point for much of eastern Canada. Its industries include paper milling, shipbuilding, tanning, brewing, and tobacco processing. Pop., 1965 est., urban area, 392,000.

QUE QUE, a recently developed industrial town of Rhodesia, located about 100 miles southwest of Salisbury. It lies on an extensive deposit of iron ore, of which production for export began in 1962. The ore is also utilized for local iron and steel manufacturing. Pop., 1963 est., 17,700.

QUETTA, a city in West Pakistan, the capital of the Quetta division in the Baluchistan region. It controls access to the important Bolan Pass over the Sulaiman Mountains and is a center for trade with Iran and Afghanistan. Fruit is grown and chromite is mined in the surrounding area. Pop., 1961, 106,633.

QUEZON CITY, the official capital of the Philippine Islands, situated on Luzon Island, 10 miles northeast of Manila. Quezon City is primarily a residential area and the site of the national university, however, and most government offices are located in Manila. Pop., 1965 est., 482,400.

QUITO, the capital and second largest city of Ecuador, located on a 9,350-foot plateau in the Andes at a point near the equator. An important city in the empire of the Inca Indians, it still has a large Indian population. Quito is primarily an administrative center, and its industry is limited to textile milling. Pop., 1965 est., 401,800.

RABAT, the capital of Morocco, situated on the south bank of the Bou Regneg, near its mouth on the Atlantic Ocean. Local handicraft industries produce leather goods, baskets, tapestries, and embroidered cloth. The city is the site of Mohammed V University. Pop., 1965 est., 355,000.

RAMPUR, in northern India, located in Uttar Pradesh state on the Kosi River, about 115 miles east of Delhi. The city is the capital of Rampur District and a commercial center. Rampur is known for its library, which houses a collection of rare Oriental manuscripts. It is also the site of an Arabic college. Pop., 1966 est., 136,000.

RANCHI, in northeastern India, a district capital in Bihar State. It is a commercial and administrative center. A radium institute, two mental hospitals, and several colleges are located in the city. Pop., 1966 est., urban area, 158,100.

RANGOON, the capital of Burma, on the Rangoon River, 21 miles from the Bay of Bengal. It is Burma's largest city and chief port. Rice and teakwood are the major exports. Local industries produce silk and cotton textiles and pottery. There are also shipyards and sawmills. The city is modern in appearance and has many cultural and educational institutions, including the University of Rangoon. The skyline is dominated by the 368-

foot-high Shwe Dagon Pagoda, which is covered with gold leaf and reputedly over 2,000 years old. Pop., 1957 est., 821,800.

RAWALPINDI, in western Pakistan, situated on the Potwar plateau, near the Himalayan foothills. The city is an industrial center and has an oil refinery, a steel mill, a locomotive works, and chemical plants. In 1949 Rawalpindi was made the interim federal capital pending the completion of a new capital at Islamabad, eight miles away. Pop., 1961, 340,175.

RECIFE, capital of Pernambuco State, Brazil, located at the mouths of the Capibaribe and Beberibe rivers on the Atlantic Ocean. It is the third largest city in Brazil. The city's economy is based on processing and exporting the agricultural products of the interior, including coffee, cotton, sugar, and hides. A rail and road network links Recife with other parts of Brazil. The city has two universities and many fine churches, some of which date from the colonial period. Pop., 1966 est., 1,010,000.

REGINA, the capital of Saskatchewan Province, in west-central Canada, located about 100 miles north of the U.S. border. The city has excellent railway connections and is the distribution center for a large area. Industries include automobile assembly, oil refining, printing, woodworking, bookbinding, meat packing, and the manufacture of dry batteries. Pop., 1965 est., 126,000.

REYKJAVÍK, the capital of Iceland, located on the southwestern coast of the country. It is the country's leading seaport and only major city. Reykjavík has a large fishing industry, busy shipyards, and publishing houses. It is the site of the University of Reykjavík. Pop., 1965 est., 89,400.

REZA'IYEH, also known as Urmia, capital of the administrative province of western Azerbaijan in northwestern Iran, located on the west bank of Lake Urmia. It is situated in a fruit and tobacco growing area. Pop., 1956 est., 67,605.

RIGA, the capital and largest city of the Latvian Soviet Socialist Republic of the Soviet Union. The city lies on the Dvina River, about eight miles inland from the Gulf of Riga on the Baltic Sea. It is a major Baltic port and Latvia's leading industrial and cultural center. Local industries produce machinery, chemicals, textiles, wood products, cameras, and construction materials. Pop., 1966, 668,000.

RIO DE JANEIRO, the second largest city in Brazil, located on Guanabara Bay, on the Atlantic Ocean. It served as the capital of the country from 1763 to 1960. Rio de Janeiro is Brazil's cultural center and a major port, ranking second only to São Paulo. There are three universities and several museums. Local industries produce domestic consumer goods, including shoes, clothing, furniture, drugs, and processed foods. Pop., 1966 est., 3,909,000.

RIYADH, the capital of Saudi Arabia, located in the east-central part of the country on the Nejd Plateau. An ancient oasis settlement, Riyadh serves as a trade center for the dates, vegetables, and grain produced in the surrounding area. After the city became the capital in 1953, it was greatly modernized. Riyadh is connected by rail to Ad Dammam on the Persian Gulf. Pop., 1965 est., 225,000.

ROAD TOWN, capital of the British Virgin Islands, located on Tortola Island. It is situated in the central part of the island on the Caribbean coast. Pop., 1960, 891.

ROME, the capital of Italy, located in the west-central part of the country, on the Tiber River, 17 miles inland from the Tyrrhenian Sea. Rome has been a major center of civilization for over 2,000 years. It was the capital of the Roman Empire and retained its importance during the Middle Ages as the seat of the papacy. In the 1500s and 1600s Rome became the center of the Italian Renaissance, and many magnificent palaces and churches, decorated with beautiful sculpture and paintings, were built.

Modern Rome is an important commercial, financial, and transportation center. Its industries include leathercrafting, metalworking, distilling, food processing, printing, and publishing. The city attracts many tourists and is an international center for the arts. Pop., 1965 est., 2,484,000.

ROSEAU, the capital and largest city of Dominica in the Windward Islands group of the Lesser Antilles. The city is located in the southwestern part of the island on the Caribbean Sea. Primarily a port, Roseau exports the island's limes, lime juice, bananas, and copra. Pop., 1960, 10,417.

ROTTERDAM, the second largest city in the Netherlands, on the New Maas River, an outlet of the Rhine River, near the North Sea. The centers of Pernis, Botlek, and Europoort to the west are also part of the port. With easy access to both the North Sea and Rhine River, Rotterdam is one of the busiest ports in Europe. Shipping and shipbuilding are Rotterdam's leading industries, but chemicals, sugar, furniture, refined petroleum, lumber, and processed foods are also produced. Pop., 1965 est., 731,315.

RUSE, the largest city in northern Bulgaria, located on the Danube River, about 40 miles south of Bucharest. The city is Bulgaria's largest port on the Danube and an important transportation center. Ruse's major industries produce textiles, leather, processed foods, refined petroleum, and agricultural implements. Pop., 1965 est., 128,000.

SAGA, the capital of the Japanese prefecture of Saga, on northwestern Kyushu island. It is a distribution point for coal mined and rice grown in the surrounding area, and it has textile and ceramics industries. Pop., 1965, 134,575.

SAIGON, the capital of South Vietnam, situated on the Saigon River near the country's southeastern coast. It is the commercial and political center of the country, and with its industrial suburb, Cholon, it is South Vietnam's major port and industrial complex. The leading industries include shipbuilding, distilling, and food processing. Pop., 1965 est., 1,485,-300.

SAINT-DENIS, the capital and chief town of Réunion, an Overseas Department of France, on Réunion Island in the Indian Ocean, some 400 miles east of Madagascar. The town's industries process local sugar, distill rum, and produce perfume essences. Pop., 1961, 65,614.

ST. GEORGE'S, the capital and principal town of Grenada, a British-associated island state in the Caribbean Sea. The town, on the island's southwestern coast, has a deep natural harbor and exports locally grown cocoa, bananas, and spices. Pop., 1960, 7,303.

PAN AMERICAN

ST. GEORGE'S, a seaport, trading center, and the capital of Grenada, British West Indies.

PAN AMERICAN

SANTIAGO, Chile, lies in a valley between the Andes Mountains and the Pacific coastal range.

ST. JOHN CITY, the capital of Antigua, a British-associated island state in the Caribbean Sea. It is a port that exports sugar cane and cotton and imports petroleum to be refined on the island. Pop., 1960, 21,595.

SAINT JOHN'S, the capital of Newfoundland province, Canada, located on the southeastern coast of Newfoundland Island. It is a seaport with an excellent harbor that is the center of a large fishing fleet. Fish processing and fish-oil refining are the main industries, and margarine, soap, paints, and fishing and marine equipment are manufactured. Pop., 1966, urban area, 101,161.

SAINT-LOUIS, a coastal town in northern Senegal, in West Africa, situated on an island at the mouth of the Sénégal River. The site of the first permanent French settlement in Africa, it served as the capital of French West Africa in the 1800s and was the capital of Senegal until 1958. It exports hides and peanuts from the surrounding area and is connected by rail with Dakar. Pop., 1961 est., 48,800.

SAKAI, a Japanese industrial center on Honshu Island, located on Osaka Bay. Textile, chemical, and electronics manufacturing are its major industries. Pop., 1965, 466,412.

SALEM, a city in southeastern India, in Madras state, located in the Cauvery River basin. Iron and manganese are mined in the surrounding area, and the city has mineral-processing and textile-milling industries. It is on a rail route and is a regional trade center. Pop., 1966 est., 274,100.

SALISBURY, the capital of Rhodesia, located in the northeastern part of the country. Surrounded by a rich gold-mining region, it is a transportation and commercial center for southeastern Africa. Tobacco processing is its major industry. Pop., 1965 est., urban area, 325,000.

SALVADOR, a port and industrial city on the eastern coast of Brazil. It processes and exports sugar, cotton, cacao, and tobacco grown in the surrounding region, and it manufactures textiles and cigars. It is the oldest city in Brazil and for 200 years was the capital of the Portuguese colony there. Pop., 1966 est., 832,000.

SALZBURG, a resort city in Austria, situated on the Salzach River at the foot of the Alps. The city is a noted music center, and its manufactures include musical instruments. Salzburg is also a rail junction between Munich and Vienna. Pop., 1965 est., 115,700.

SAMARKAND, an ancient city of Soviet Asia, located in the Central Uzbek Soviet Socialist Republic, on the slopes of the Alai mountains. Samarkand is one of the oldest cities in the world, and it still prospers on commerce and light industry, especially the weaving of cotton and silk textiles. Pop., 1966 est., 240,000.

SAN'A, the capital of Yemen, located in a high mountain valley in southwestern Arabia. It lies in the center of a rich irrigated agricultural region that produces fruits and coffee, and it is the cultural and commercial center for the area. Pop., 1965 est., 60,000.

SAN JOSÉ, the capital and largest city of Costa Rica, situated on the Rio Grande near the center of the country. It is on international air and rail routes and is the commercial center for a coffee-growing region. It produces furniture and textiles. Pop., 1965 est., urban area, 339,100.

SAN SALVADOR, the capital and largest city of El Salvador, situated in the mountains in the west-central portion of the country. It is a commercial center for locally grown coffee, sugar, tobacco, and rubber. The city is subject to severe earthquakes and has frequently been badly damaged. Pop., 1963 est., 281,100.

SANTA ISABEL, the capital of Equatorial Guinea, a Spanish overseas province, located on the island of Fernando Póo off the western coast of Africa. It is a seaport that exports cacao and coffee raised on local plantations. Pop., 1960, 37,237.

SANTIAGO, the capital of Chile, situated in a high valley near the center of the country. In addition to being the political, cultural, and commercial heart of Chile, it manufactures iron and steel, chemicals, textiles, paper, and other products. Pop., 1965 est., urban area, 2,248,400.

SANTO DOMINGO, the capital and largest city of the Dominican Republic. Its refineries and distilleries process locally grown sugar. The city has textile mills and is the chief port of the country. Founded in 1492, it has been continuously inhabited longer than any other city in the western hemisphere. Pop., 1966 est., 560,600.

SANTO TOMÉ DE GUAYANA, a city in northeastern Venezuela at the junction of the Caroni and Orinoco rivers. The city is a planned grouping of four small neighboring towns. Its industries are concerned with processing and shipping iron ore mined in the region. Pop., 1965 est., 75,000.

SÃO PAULO, capital of São Paulo state in southeastern Brazil. It is the commercial and industrial center of Brazil, with oil refineries, chemical plants, and factories manufacturing heavy machinery, vehicles, pharmaceuticals, electrical devices, and textiles. Pop., 1966 est., 4,098,000.

SÃO TOME, capital and port city of the Portuguese overseas province of São Tome and Principe. It lies on the island of São Tome in the Gulf of Guinea some 125 miles off Africa's west coast. It processes and exports cacao, coffee, and coconuts raised on the island. Pop., 1960, 5,714.

SAPELE, an industrial town in the former Western Region of Nigeria, on the Benins River. It is the site of a large lumber mill and plywood plant which process local timber. The city also processes locally grown rubber. Pop., 1963, 61,007.

SAPPORO, the capital of the Japanese island of Hokkaido, located in the southwestern portion of the island. It is a cultural center, and it has food, hemp, and rubber processing industries. Pop., 1965, 794,908.

SARAJEVO, the capital of the Yugoslavian constituent republic of Bosnia and Herzegovina. Sarajevo is an industrial and commercial center that manufactures textiles, electrical equipment, metal goods, and carpets, and serves as the shipping point for locally mined minerals. It is a Muslim cultural center. Pop., 1961, 143,117.

SARATOV, the capital of the Saratov Region in the southeastern Soviet Union, situated on the Volga River. It is a major river port, shipping local minerals and farm products. Industries include an oil refinery, shipyard, and plants producing precision instruments, chemicals, and machinery. Pop., 1966 est., 699,000.

SATU–MARE, a city of northwestern Romania, situated on the Somesul River. The market center for an agricultural region, it also has industries manufacturing mining and farming equipment, machinery, and textiles. Pop., 1963 est., 63,700.

SEKONDI–TAKORADI, coastal towns of southern Ghana joined into a single municipality in the 1940s. Fishing is important, and fish-processing plants and sawmills are the main industries. The towns' ports ship cacao, timber, and minerals. Pop., 1966 est., urban area, 181,000.

SENDAI, the capital of Miyagi prefecture, Japan, on northern Honshu Island. It is an industrial city, manufacturing silk textiles, machinery, chemicals, and metal products. It lies on the Sendai Plain, a rich agricultural region. Pop., 1965, 480,925.

SEOUL, the capital of the Republic of Korea (South Korea), situated near the Han River in the northwestern corner of the country. The cultural and economic center of South Korea, it is the site of several colleges, and its industries include flour mills, rail yards, and textile mills. It is on international air routes and is connected by rail with its port, Inchon. Pop., 1966 est., 3,800,000.

SEVASTOPOL, a Black Sea port on the Crimean peninsula in the southern Ukraine region of the Soviet Union. It is the site of an important naval base, and its industries include shipbuilding and food processing. Pop., 1966 est., 200,000.

SEVILLA, or Seville, a city of southwestern Spain, situated on the Guadalquivir River. Sevilla is a river port that handles iron, lead, and food products. It is also a transportation, marketing, and industrial center. Its manufactures include munitions, machine tools, and pottery.

Sevilla, which was founded by the Phoenicians and has been held by Romans, Vandals, Visigoths, and Moors, is noted for its architecture and art treasures. Pop., 1965 est., 474,100.

SFAX, a Mediterranean seaport on the eastern coast of Tunisia. The site of ancient Phoenician and Roman trading colonies, today it processes and exports olives and dates raised in the region and phosphates mined nearby. Pop., 1956, 65,645.

SHANGHAI, a port city on the eastern coast of China, near the mouth of the Yangtze River. It is the largest city in China and is a major East Asian industrial and commercial center. It manufactures machinery, ships, aircraft, weapons, textiles, iron and steel, books, and other products. It lost its former importance in foreign trade after the Communist takeover in 1949. Pop., 1957 est., 6,900,000.

UNITED NATIONS

SEOUL, capital of South Korea, is a busy commercial city with a rapidly growing population.

SHILLONG, the capital of Assam state, in northeastern India. Situated high in the Khasi Hills, it has a mild climate and is a popular vacation and health resort. Pop., 1966 est., urban area, 125,800.

SHIMONOSEKI, a seaport at the southwestern tip of Japan's Honshu island, situated on the Shimonoseki Strait at the western end of the Inland Sea. In addition to its port facilities, it has shipyards and chemical, metal-working, and engineering industries. Pop., 1965, 254,376.

SHIRAZ, capital of Fars Province, in southwestern Iran. It is a commercial center for fruits, silk, and tobacco grown in the surrounding region, and it produces wine, carpets, and silk textiles. Founded in the 600s, it served as the country's capital several times before the 1900s, and it became a center for Persian culture and learning. Pop., 1963, 229,761.

SHIZUOKA, capital of Shizuoka prefecture on Japan's Honshu island, situated on Suruga Bay. It is a commercial center for an orange- and tea-growing region, and its industries produce lacquerware, paper, and textiles. Pop., 1965, 367,705.

SHKODER, a town in northwestern Albania, near the southern end of Lake Scutari. It is the commercial center for a rich agricultural region and has food-processing industries. An ancient fortified city, it was colonized by the Romans in the 100s AD, and was conquered and reconquered by many nations until the 1900s. Pop., 1960, 43,234.

SHOLAPUR, a south-central Indian city in Maharashtra state. Situated in a cotton-growing region, it has important textile mills. Pop., 1966 est., 3,695,800.

SIBIU, a city in the Transylvanian region of central Romania. It is a commercial center for the surrounding agricultural region. Sibiu's industries produce chemicals, textiles, and farm machinery. The former capital of Transylvania, it remains an important cultural center. Pop., 1965, urban area, 104,434.

SIDI–IFNI, the capital of Ifni, a small Spanish overseas territory on the northwest coast of Africa. It is a port with limited trade and a small fishing industry. Pop., 1960, 12,751.

SINING, capital of Tsinghai province in western China, situated on the Sining River. Located on a main route to Tibet, it is a trading center for timber, wool,. and hides. Pop., 1957 est., 300,000.

SKOPJE, capital of the Macedonian region of southeastern Yugoslavia, situated on the Vardar River. It is a trade center for minerals mined in the region. Much of the town was demolished in a severe earthquake in 1963, but it was later rebuilt. Pop., 1961, 165,529.

SOFIA, the capital and largest city of Bulgaria, situated in the western foothills of the Balkan Mountains. It is the economic center of the country, with industries producing machinery, electrical equipment, textiles, and processed foods. Sofia is the home of the country's main educational institutions. It lies on the site of the ancient Roman city of Sardica. Pop., 1965 est., 793,300.

SOOCHOW, a port city in eastern China, on the Grand Canal in Kiangsu province. Soochow manufactures textiles and produces many handcrafted items. Threaded by canals, it is known as the Venice of China. Pop., 1957 est., 633,000.

SOPRON, an ancient town in western Hungary near the border with Austria. Sopron has a long history as a cultural center and produces wines and textiles. Pop., 1963 est., 43,400.

SOUSSE, a Mediterranean port on the east coast of Tunisia. Situated on the site of an ancient Carthaginian city that was occupied by the Romans, today the city serves primarily as a shipping point for local minerals and farm products. Pop., 1965, 48,185.

SPLIT, an ancient seaport on the Adriatic coast of the Dalmatian region of Yugoslavia. In addition to its harbor facilities, it has shipyards and chemical, cement, and metal processing plants. It lies on major transportation routes and is a commercial and tourist center. The city was founded by the Roman emperor Diocletian and contains ancient ruins and historic monuments. Pop., 1961, 99,462.

SPRINGS, a town in the Transvaal region of South Africa. It is the commercial center for a region where coal, gold, and uranium are mined. Pop., 1960, urban area, 141,943.

SRINIGAR, capital of the state of Kashmir in northwestern India. It is situated on the Jhelum River in the Vale of Kashmir. Srinigar produces silk and woolen textiles, carpets, and wood and metal handcrafts. It is also a major resort. Pop., 1961, urban area, 295,084.

STANLEY, capital and chief city of the Falkland Islands, a British crown colony in the South Atlantic Ocean. It is located on the northeast coast of East Falkland Island. Possessing a good harbor, Stanley handles almost all the colony's trade. Pop., 1962, 1,074.

STOCKHOLM, the capital and largest city of Sweden. It is situated in the southeast, on Malaren Lake near the Baltic Sea. The city is Sweden's chief port and its industries include shipyards, food-processing plants, chemical and machinery factories, and paper and textile mills. It is an important commercial and financial center, and its many schools, museums, libraries and theaters give it great cultural importance as well. Pop., 1966 est., urban area, 1,247,300.

STUTTGART, in southern West Germany, on the Neckar River, about 95 miles south of Frankfurt. Stuttgart is the capital of the state of Baden-Württemberg. Manufactures

include motor vehicles, textiles, chemicals, and machinery. It is an educational and cultural center with a flourishing publishing industry. Pop., 1965 est., 632,800.

SUBOTICA, an ancient town in northeastern Yugoslavia. It is a market center for the surrounding grain-growing region. The city's manufactures include chemicals, textiles, machinery, and processed food. Pop., 1961, 74,832.

SUCRE, the official capital of Bolivia, situated in a high Andean valley in the south-central part of the country. Although Sucre is the site of the national university and many government buildings, La Paz is the working capital. Sucre is important mainly as a commercial center for an agricultural and mining region. Pop., 1965 est., 58,400.

SUDBURY, a city of southeastern Ontario, Canada. It is in the center of a region where rich nickel deposits as well as copper, lead, zinc, and silver are mined. Metal-processing is the city's main industry. Other important manufactures include machinery, bricks, and lumber. Pop., 1961, urban area, 110,694.

SUEZ, or El Suweis, a seaport of the United Arab Republic (Egypt) situated at the southern end of the Suez Canal, at the head of the Gulf of Suez. The port is a refueling station and a center for petroleum trade. The city has a large oil refinery and chemical fertilizer plants. Pop., 1966, 264,025.

SUKARNAPURA, capital of the Indonesian province of West Irian (the western half of the island of New Guinea) north of Australia. Located on the northern coast, the city has an excellent harbor. A university is also located in the city. Pop., 1961 est., 14,500.

SURABAJA, a seaport on the eastern coast of the Indonesian island of Java. It exports rubber, oil, sugar, spices, tobacco, and other local goods, and Surabaja has shipyards, oil refineries,

textile mills, rubber processing plants, and chemical factories. Pop., 1961, 1,007,945.

SURAT, a small city in Gujarat state in western India, situated on the Gulf of Cambay. A center of early European colonial and commercial activity in India, today the city is a small port with some light industries producing paper and textiles. Pop., 1966 est., 348,300.

SUVA, the capital of the British South Pacific colony of Fiji, situated on Viti Levu Island. It is a port of call on international shipping routes, and it processes and exports island products including fruits, sugar, coconuts, cacao, and timber. Pop., 1966 est., 54,900.

SVERDLOVSK, the capital of the Sverdlovsk region of the Soviet Union, situated just east of the Ural Mountains. It is the center of a region rich in copper, gold, and iron. The city's major industries include metal processing and the manufacture of heavy machinery and precision instruments. Pop., 1966 est., 940,000.

SWATOW, a seaport in Kwangtung province in southeastern China. It exports citrus fruits, tea, and tobacco grown in the surrounding region. Pop., 1953, 280,400.

SYDNEY, the capital of New South Wales, on the southeastern coast of Australia. It is the country's largest city and chief industrial and commercial center. Industrial facilities include metal-processing plants, textile mills, automobile and chemical factories, and a sugar refinery. It has a deep natural harbor and an excellent port that ships such products as coal, timber, grain, and wool. Sydney is the site of several colleges and of the national art and history museums. Pop., 1966, 2,444,735.

SYDNEY, an industrial city of Nova Scotia, Canada, on the eastern coast of Cape Breton Island. Coal mining is Sydney's main industry, and it also has steel mills, shipyards, chemical factories and metal-working plants. Pop., 1966, 32,767.

SZCZECIN, the capital of Szczecin department in northwestern Poland, situated at the mouth of the Oder River. It is a leading Baltic port and has shipyards, iron foundries, and other industrial facilities. Founded in the Middle Ages, it has been administered by several European nations, including Sweden, Prussia, France, and Germany. Pop., 1965 est., 310,000.

SZEGED, a city in southeastern Hungary, on the Tisza River. It is a river port and an important commercial center. Industries include boat building, textile milling, and tobacco processing. Pop., 1965 est., 115,000.

TABRIZ, a city in northwestern Iran, situated near the border with the Soviet Union. It is an ancient city that has repeatedly suffered damage from earthquakes. Tabriz is a com-

BRITISH EUROPEAN AIRWAYS
STOCKHOLM is often called the "Venice of the North" because of its many waterways.

mercial center for an area that produces rice, tobacco, and fruits. Its manufactures include rugs, leather goods, and cotton thread. Pop., 1963 est., 387,800.

TAEGU, a city of South Korea, situated in the south-central part of the Korean peninsula. Taegu is a rail and commercial center where silk is manufactured. Pop., 1965 est., 811,400.

TAIPEI, the capital of Nationalist China, situated at the northern end of Taiwan (Formosa). The city is a commercial and industrial center with good transportation facilities. Its manufactures include processed foods, chemicals, and metal products. Taipei is the seat of the National Taiwan University. Pop., 1965 est., 1,135,500.

TAIYÜAN, a city of east-central China, situated on the Fen River, about 250 miles southwest of Peking. Taiyüan is an industrial and rail center, lying near important coal fields. Its industries produce iron and steel, agricultural equipment, and chemicals. The city also has machine shops and oil refineries. Pop., 1957 est., 1,020,000.

TAKAMATSU, a Japanese port situated on the northeastern coast of Shikoku Island. The city is a rail center and the main port in the trade between Shikoku and Honshu islands. Pop., 1965, 243,444.

TALLINN, the capital of the Estonian Soviet Socialist Republic, in the northwestern Soviet Union. It is a leading port, situated on the southern coast of the Gulf of Finland, opposite Helsinki. Tallinn is a commercial and industrial center that manufactures textiles, glass, paper, furniture, and mining equipment. Pop., 1966 est., 335,000.

TANGIER, a port of northern Morocco, strategically situated on the Atlantic coast, just west of the Strait of Gibraltar. The city is a transportation center that exports cork, hides, and food products. Tourism and the production of leather goods, pottery, and rugs are important industries. Pop., 1965 est., 110,000.

TANJORE, or Thanjavor, a city in southeastern India. It is an agricultural, commercial, and rail center in an area that grows rice, tobacco, and sugarcane. Tanjore's industries produce jewelry, carpets, and embroidered handicrafts. Pop., 1966 est., 116,700.

TANNARIVE, the capital of the Malagasy Republic, situated on the east-central part of Madagascar Island. The city is an administrative and commercial center, connected by rail to the port of Tamatave. Pop., 1965 est., 321,700.

TANTA, a city in the northern United Arab Republic (Egypt), about 50 miles north of Cairo. Tanta is an important transportation and manufacturing center. Its products include cotton goods, sugar, and soap. Pop., 1963 est., 215,400.

TARAWA, capital of the Gilbert and Ellice Islands, a British colony in the central Pacific Ocean. It is located on an atoll eight square miles in area and is the colony's major port of entry and commercial center. Exports include copra, phosphates, and pearl shell. During World War II Tarawa was occupied by the Japanese. It was captured by the United States in November 1943. Pop., 1966 est., 8,700.

TASHKENT, a city in the southwest-central Soviet Union, the capital of the Uzbek Soviet Socialist Republic. Tashkent, an oasis settlement, lies on a small tributary of the Syr Darya. The city has good rail facilities and is an industrial and commercial center.

Textiles, leather goods, metal products, and farm machinery are manufactured, and cotton and grain are traded. Tashkent is also the focus of cultural and educational activities in central Soviet Asia. Pop., 1966 est., 1,127,000.

TBILSI, or Tiflis, a city in the southwestern Soviet Union, capital of the Georgian Soviet Socialist Republic. The city, which lies on the Kura River, is a resort with thermal springs. It is also an agricultural and economic center. Tbilsi's industries produce textiles and clothing, wood products, and industrial equipment. Pop., 1966 est., 823,000.

TEHRAN, or Teheran, the capital of Iran, situated in the north, about 70 miles from the Caspian Sea. The city is the cultural, industrial and transportation center of Iran. Manufactures include cotton, glass, metal products, construction materials, and automobile parts. Pop., 1963 est., 2,317,100.

TEL AVIV, a port in Israel, situated on the Mediterranean Sea. The city, which includes the ancient port of Jaffa, is the industrial and commercial center of Israel. Its industries include woodworking, textile milling, food processing, and the manufacture of chemicals and tobacco products. Tel Aviv supports several theaters, an orchestra, and a university. Pop., 1965 est., 392,100.

THESSALONÍKI, or Salonika, a seaport in northeastern Greece, situated on the Gulf of Thessaloníki. It is an important trading center and an industrial city that manufactures cotton, silk, and wool textiles; leather goods; and carpets. Pop., 1961, urban area, 378,444.

THORSHAVN, the capital and chief city of the Faroe Islands of Denmark. It is located on Stömö Island, the largest of the Faroes, about 190 miles northwest of the Shetland Islands. The chief industry is fishing and the primary export is fish. Pop., 1960, 7,447.

TIENTSIN, or Tienching, a port of northeastern China, situated at the junction of the Pei River and the Grand Canal, about 80 miles southeast of Peking. Tientsin is a commercial center that handles much of the import-export trade of the surrounding region. It is also the seat of several institutions of higher education. Pop., 1957 est., 3,220,000.

TIMIŞOARA, a city in western Romania, situated on the Béga Canal, near the Hungarian border. The city is a communications and rail center with an extensive grain and lumber trade. Pop., 1965 est., urban area, 170,800.

TIRANË, or Tirana, the capital of Albania. Tiranë is served by Durrës, an Adriatic seaport some 20 miles to the west. The city is a commercial and industrial center in an agricultural region noted for the production of olives. Tiranë's manufactures include building materials, metal products, and textiles. Tiranë is the seat of a university, a science institute, and several museums. Pop., 1964 est., 157,000.

UNITED NATIONS

TEHRAN, capital of Iran, is one of the largest and most modern cities of the Middle East.

CONSULATE GENERAL OF JAPAN N.Y.

TOKYO at night is ablaze with one of the world's greatest concentrations of neon signs.

TIRUCHIRAPPALLI, formerly Trichinopoly, a city in southeastern India, situated on the Cauvery River about 200 miles southwest of Madras. The city is a trade and transportation center in a region that produces rice, millet, sugar, cotton, and oilseed. Manufactures include textiles and cement. Pop., 1966 est., 266,400.

TOKYO, the capital of Japan and one of the largest cities in the world, situated on Honshu Island, on Tokyo Bay. The city is the administrative, economic, and industrial center of Japan. Its manufactures include automobiles, airplane parts, electrical equipment, machine tools, and chemicals.

It is served by an excellent port, national and private railroads, an international airport, an extensive highway system, and a rapid transit system. Tokyo is also Japan's cultural, educational, and religious center. It is the seat of Tokyo University and has many museums, theaters, and religious shrines. Pop., 1965, urban area, 10,869,800.

TORONTO, the capital of Ontario in south east-central Canada, on Lake Ontario. Toronto is the second largest city in Canada and one of the busiest of the Great Lakes ports. It is a financial, commercial, and industrial center with railroad shops and metalworks. Meat-packing, printing and publishing, and shipbuilding are important industries. Pop., 1965 est., urban area, 2,066,000.

TOULOUSE, a city in southern France on the Garonne River. Industries include food and beverage processing, flour milling, textile and shoe manufacturing and airplane production. Toulouse is also a market for the agricultural products of the surrounding region. The University of Toulouse dates from the 1200s. Pop., 1962, urban area, 329,044.

TOURS, in the Loire Valley of France, about 130 miles southwest of Paris. The city's manufactures include textile products, chemicals, leather goods, pottery, and printed matter. Tours is the commercial center for the surrounding agricultural region, handling products such as wine, grain, and dried fruit. Tours was the capital of a Roman province in France and the site of a decisive battle in 732 AD, when the Franks defeated an invading Arab army. Pop., 1962, urban area, 151,359.

TOYAMA, a Japanese port situated on Honshu Island, on the Sea of Japan. The city is an industrial and market center in a rice-growing region. Manufactures include textiles and drugs. Pop., 1965, 239,810.

TRIESTE, a port in northeastern Italy, situated on the Adriatic Sea, near the border with Yugoslavia. Trieste serves as a port for Czechoslovakia, Austria, Hungary, Yugoslavia, and Italy. Following World War II the city was made part of a free territory, but in the 1950s it was returned to Italy. The main industry is shipbuilding. Pop., 1965 est., 280,500.

TRIPOLI, a port in Lebanon, situated on the Mediterranean Sea, about 40 miles northeast of Beirut. The city has rail connections with Beirut and Syria, and is the terminus of an oil pipeline from Iraq. The principal industries are oil refining, sponge fishing, and the manufacture of soap. Pop., 1964 est., 127,600.

TRIPOLI, with Bengasi the capital of Libya, situated in northwestern Libya on the Mediterranean Sea. The city is a transportation and trading center for an agricultural region. Its industries produce armaments, tobacco products, and salt. Pop., 1964, 213,506.

TRIVANDRUM, a port in southwestern India, situated on the Indian Ocean. The city is a religious and educational center. It lies near a forest area that produces teak, bamboo, and ebony. Pop., 1966 est., urban area, 358,000.

TSINAN, or Chinan, a city of eastern China, the capital of Shantung Province. The city is a railroad junction and an industrial center. Its most important manufactures are silk and cotton textiles. Pop., 1957 est., 862,000.

TSINGTAO, a port in northeastern China, situated on the Yellow Sea at the southern end of the Shantung Peninsula. The port is one of the largest in China. Tsingtao's manufactures include textiles and processed foods. Pop., 1957 est., 1,121,000.

TSITSIHAR, or Chichihar, a city of northeastern China, situated on the Nonni River, about 175 miles northwest of Harbin. The city is a rail junction and river port, with trade in grain and other agricultural products. Pop., 1957 est., 668,000.

TUNIS, the capital of Tunisia, situated in the northeastern part of the country between the Lake of Tunis and the Sedjoumi salt flat. Tunis is connected to the Mediterranean Sea by a channel. The city is the major commercial, industrial, and transportation center of the country. Its products include processed foods, soap, chemicals, and perfume. Pop., 1964 est., urban area, 662,000.

TURIN, or Torino, the capital of the Italian province of Torino, situated on the Po River in northwestern Italy. Turin, with Milan and Genoa, forms the industrial triangle of northern Italy. The principal manufactures include iron and steel, machinery, tools, automobiles, and textiles. The city is the seat of the University of Turin, founded in the 1400s. Pop., 1965 est., 1,111,700.

UFA, capital of the Bashkir Soviet Socialist Republic of the Soviet Union, in the southern Ural Mountains, at the confluence of the Belaya and Ufa rivers. The city has important oil, chemical, metallurgical, coal, and steel industries. A state university and a branch of the Academy of Sciences are also located there. Pop., 1966 est., 683,000.

UJJAIN, a city in Madhya Pradesh state, India. The city has important flour milling and textile industries. Vikram University, with about 30,000 students, is located there. Ujjain is one of the seven sacred Hindu cities and an important pilgrimage center. Pop., 1966 est., 151,800.

ULAN BATOR, capital of the Mongolian People's Republic, located on the Tuula River. It is connected by the Trans-Mongolian railroad and by air service with the Soviet Union and China. Ulan Bator contains a state university and the major Buddhist monastery in the country. The city's industries produce woolen textiles, leather goods, and processed sheep and goat skins. Pop., 1962 est., 195,300.

ULAN—UDE, in the Soviet Union, capital of the Buryat Autonomous Soviet Socialist Republic, at the confluence of the Uda and Selenge rivers near Lake Baykal. Manufactures include building materials, leather goods, and textiles. Coal is mined nearby. The city is a junction for a railroad line connecting the Trans-Siberian railroad with the frontier between the Soviet Union and Mongolia. Pop., 1966 est., 220,000.

UMTALI, in east central Rhodesia, on the Mozambique border. It is the eastern gateway to Rhodesia on the railway connecting the port of Beira, Mozambique, with Salisbury, the capital of Rhodesia. A large oil refinery is located nearby. Pop., 1963 est., 39,600.

VADUZ, capital of the European principality of Liechtenstein, situated on the banks of the Rhine River. As the country's chief city, it is primarily an administrative center. Tourism is important. Pop., 1961 est., 3,514.

VALENCIA, capital of Valencia province in eastern Spain, situated on the Turia River near the Mediterranean. It is Spain's third largest city and an important commercial and industrial city. It manufactures chemicals, textiles, and furniture and processes grains, fruits, tobacco, and vegetables grown nearby. Pop., 1965 est., 501,800.

VALLETTA, the capital and largest city of the Republic of Malta, situated on the northeastern coast of Malta island. Valletta has two deep natural harbors. Shipbuilding and ship repair are the main industries. Pop., 1965 est., 25,000.

VANCOUVER, a port city in southwestern British Columbia, Canada, situated opposite Vancouver Island on the Strait of Georgia, an arm of the Pacific Ocean. It is Canada's third largest city and the leading Canadian Pacific port, shipping grain, fish, lumber, and metals. Industrial facilities include shipyards, lumber mills, metal works, and food-processing plants. Pop., 1965 est., urban area, 850,000.

VARNA, a Black Sea port of northeastern Bulgaria. It exports grains, dairy products, and cattle. Industrial facilities include shipyards, textile mills, and metal-processing plants. Pop., 1965 est., 177,400.

VENICE, the capital of the province of Venezia, in northeastern Italy. Occupying more than 100 islets in a lagoon off the Adriatic Sea, the city is built on a foundation of sunken piles and is connected with the mainland by bridges. Transportation within the city is by boat along numerous canals.

Venice is noted for its outstanding architecture in a variety of styles, and it has long been an artistic center for Italy and the world. The city's chief source of income is tourism; its few light industries produce glass, jewelry, textiles, furniture, and handicrafts. Pop., 1965 est., 362,000.

VENTSPILS, a Baltic port at the mouth of the Venta River on the west coast of Latvia in the Soviet Union. It exports timber and agricultural products. Pop., 1959 est., 27,400.

VEREENIGING, an industrial city located on the Vaal River in southern Transvaal, Republic of South Africa. The city is situated in an important coal-mining region and produces iron, steel, and machinery. In 1902 British and Boer representatives met in Vereeniging to discuss terms for ending the Boer War. Pop., 1960, 78,835.

VICTORIA, capital of the province of British Columbia, Canada, situated at the southern tip of Vancouver island, just off the mainland. Victoria is a major port that ships lumber, pulp, cement, fish, and fruit. It also serves as a base for a large deep-sea fishing fleet. Industrial facilities include lumber and paper mills, fish canneries, and plants that turn out furniture, machinery, and building supplies. Pop., 1961, urban area, 154,152.

VIENNA, or Wien, the capital of Austria, located in the northeastern part of the country on the Danube River. Vienna is Austria's major commercial and industrial city, producing chemicals, textiles, machinery, and food products. As capital of the Austrian Empire, Vienna was for centuries a European cultural center. With its state university, technical schools, and music, drama, and fine arts academies, Vienna is still an important intellectual center. Pop., 1965 est., 1,640,100.

VIENTIANE, in Southeast Asia, the administrative capital of Laos, on the Mekong River near the border with Thailand. The city is a commercial center, dealing in textiles and wood products. River and air service connects Vientiane and other Laotian cities, and there is also air service to Saigon, in South Vietnam. Pop., 1962 est., urban area, 162,300.

VILA, a port and the capital of the New Hebrides, a group of islands located about 1,000 miles east of Australia and administered by Britain and France. Vila is situated on the south coast of Efate Island. Exports include coffee, copra, and wool. Pop., 1948 est., 800.

VILNIUS, capital of the constituent republic of Lithuania in the Soviet Union, on the Neris River. An important commercial city since the 1300s, Vilnius has been fought over by many nations, including Poland and the Soviet Union. It is an important railway junction and produces textiles and leather goods. Pop., 1966 est., 305,000.

VLADIVOSTOK, a port on the Sea of Japan, in southeastern Siberia in the Soviet Union. It is the most important Soviet port on the Pacific Ocean and is kept open in the winter by icebreakers. The city is the terminus of the Moscow-Vladivostok airline. Fishing fleets are based in Vladivostok, and the city's industries include fish canning, shipbuilding, and mineral refining. The city is also a Soviet naval base. Pop., 1966 est., 379,000.

VLONË, a seaport on the southwestern coast of Albania. Inhabited since antiquity because of its fine harbor, Vlonë exports petroleum and agricultural products. Pop., 1960, 41,285.

VOLGOGRAD, from 1925 to 1961 called Stalingrad, an industrial city on the Volga River in the southwestern Soviet Union, about 280 miles northwest of the Caspian Sea. The city's industries produce agricultural machinery, ships, aluminum, chemicals, refined oil, and food products. Volgograd is an important river port and railway center. The Battle of Stalingrad in 1942 saw Russian troops decisively defeat German armies. Pop., 1966 est., 720,000.

VOLTA REDONDA, an industrial city on the Paraíba River in southeastern Brazil, about 70 miles northwest of Rio de Janeiro. Latin America's leading iron and steel manufacturing center, Volta Redonda was built in 1947 along the railroad and highways linking Rio de Janeiro and São Paulo. Located near raw materials, markets, transportation facilities, and labor supplies, the city's industrial plants produce rails, plates, and structural steel. Pop., 1960 est., urban area, 135,000.

IN VENICE, the main thoroughfare is the Grand Canal, and many people travel by gondola.

UNITED NATIONS
MARKET IN YAOUNDE, the capital of Cameroon, displays colorful fabric used for clothing.

WAKAYAMA, port in Japan, on the south coast of Honshu Island. The city lies near the mouth of the Kino River, about 35 miles southwest of Osaka. Wakayama is a prefectural capital and the southernmost part of Osaka's industrial region. Textiles are a major manufacture. Pop., 1965, urban area, 328,657.

WARSAW, the capital and largest city of Poland. It is located on both banks of the Vistula River, in the east-central part of the country, about 30 miles east of Berlin. Warsaw is the commercial, political, educational, and cultural center of Poland. Manufactures include machinery, chemicals, textiles and clothing, and food products. Warsaw is a river port and the communications and transportation center of Poland. Pop., 1965 est., 1,249,100.

WELLINGTON, the capital of New Zealand. It is located at the southwestern tip of North Island, overlooking Cook Strait. Wellington has a large harbor and is one of New Zealand's busiest ports. It is a railroad terminus and an industrial center, manufacturing automobiles, chemicals, and textiles. Pop., 1966, 167,844.

WIESBADEN, in central West Germany, at the southern foot of the Taunus Mountains, about 20 miles west of Frankfurt. Wiesbaden is the capital of the state of Hesse and an important tourist resort. Industries include printing and publishing and boat-building. Pop., 1965 est., 261,100.

WILLEMSTAD, the capital, largest city, and chief port of the Netherlands Antilles. It is located on the southwest coast of the island of Curaçao. Willemstad has a fine harbor and is a world center of oil refining. Pop., 1960, urban area, 94,133.

WINDHOEK, the capital of the territory of South West Africa. It is located on a plateau at an altitude of about 5,400 feet, some 250 miles east of Walvis Bay. Windhoek is a commercial and distributing center and is linked by railroad to South Africa. Pop., 1960, 36,051.

WINNIPEG, the capital and chief city of Manitoba, Canada. It is located at the junction of the Assiniboine and Red rivers in central Canada, about 65 miles north of the border with the United States. Winnipeg is the railroad and grain market center of Canada. It is also a financial, commercial, and industrial center. Manufactures include motor vehicles, meat products, and clothing. Pop., 1965 est., urban area, 490,000.

WONSAN, a port on the east coast of North Korea. It is a commercial and transportation center with a fine natural harbor. Fishing is a major industry and exports include fish, rice, and soybeans. Pop., 1944, 112,952.

WROCLAW, in southern Poland, on both banks of the Oder River, about 190 miles southwest of Warsaw. Wroclaw, formerly called Breslau, is a river port and railroad junction. Manufactures include machinery, chemicals, textiles, and food. The city is a cultural center. Pop., 1965, est., 471,300.

WUHAN, in east-central China, at the confluence of the Han and Yangtze rivers. It consists of three cities, Hankow, Hanyang, and Wuchang, and is the capital of Hupeh Province. Wuhan is an industrial, administrative, and transportation center. Manufactures include iron and steel, and textiles. Pop., 1957 est., 2,146,000.

YAMAGATA, in Japan, on the Mogami River, in the north-central part of Honshu Island, about 180 miles north of Tokyo. Yamagata is a commercial and resort center situated in an agricultural region. Pop., 1965, urban area, 193,737.

YAOUNDE, the capital of Cameroon in West Africa. It is located in the west-central part of the country, about 130 miles east of Douala, its port on the Atlantic Ocean. Yaounde is Cameroon's commercial and educational center. It is also a transportation center and market for the region. Pop., 1965 est., 101,000.

YEREVAN, in the southwestern Soviet Union, near the border with Turkey, at the foot of Mount Ararat. Yerevan is the capital of the Armenian Soviet Socialist Republic. The city is an industrial, commercial, and cultural center. Manufactures include machinery, chemicals, textiles, clothing, and furniture. Pop., 1966 est., 643,000.

ZAGREB, in northern Yugoslavia, near the Sava River, about 230 miles northwest of Belgrade. Zagreb is the second largest city in Yugoslavia and the nation's commercial and financial center. Is is the capital and cultural and educational center of Croatia. Manufactures include machinery, textiles, and paper. Pop., 1961, 430,802.

ZAMBOANGA, a port in the southern Philippines, at the southwestern tip of Mindanao Island, about 550 miles south of Manila. Zamboanga is a commercial and tourist center located in a fertile agricultural region. Pop., 1965 est., urban area, 158,000.

ZANZIBAR, the capital and chief port of the island of Zanzibar, in Tanzania, off the southeastern coast of Africa. The city is located on the west coast of the island, about 45 miles north of Dar es Salaam, the capital of Tanzania. Exports include cloves, citrus fruit, and copra. Pop., 1958, 57,923.

ZAPOROZHYE, in the far western Soviet Union, on the Dnepr River in the Ukrainian Soviet Socialist Republic. Zaporozhye is a river port, railroad junction, and industrial center. Manufactures include iron and steel, aluminum, machinery, and chemicals. Pop., 1966 est., 571,000.

ZARIA, in the former Northern Region of Nigeria, in West Africa. It is a rail junction and market center in an agricultural region producing cotton and tobacco. Pop., 1963, 166,170.

ZHDANOV, in the southwestern Soviet Union, on the northern shore of the Sea of Azov in the Ukraine. Zhdanov is a port, railroad terminus, and steel center. Exports include iron and steel, machinery, chemicals, coal, and grain. Pop., 1966 est., 373,000.

ZOMBA, the capital of Malawi, about 70 miles south of Lake Nyasa, in southeastern Africa. Zomba is a transportation and market center in an agricultural region producing cotton and tobacco. Pop., 1966, 19,000.

ZURICH, in Switzerland, at the mouth of the Limmat River, on the northern shore of Lake Zurich. It is the capital of the canton of Zurich and the largest city in Switzerland. The city is the industrial, commercial, and financial center of the country. Manufactures include machinery, textiles, radios, and paper. The city is also a leading cultural, educational, and tourist center. Pop., 1966 est., urban area, 435,000.

BIBLIOGRAPHY

GENERAL

LANGER, WILLIAM L. *An Encyclopedia of World History* (rev.). Houghton Mifflin Co., 1957.

PALMER, R. R. (ed.). *Atlas of World History.* Rand McNally & Co., 1957.

STEINBERG, S. H. (ed.). *The Statesman's Year-Book.* St. Martin's Press (annual).

UNITED NATIONS, *Demographic Yearbook* N. Y. (annual).

UNITED NATIONS, *Statistical Yearbook* N. Y. (annual).

AFRICA

BARBOUR, NEVILL (ed.). *A Survey of North West Africa.* Oxford University Press, 1959.

FAGE, J. D. *An Atlas of African History.* Edwin Arnold Ltd., 1966.

JUNOD, VIOLAINE I., and IDRIAN N. RESNICK (eds.). *The Handbook of Africa.* New York University Press, 1963.

KITCHEN, HELEN (ed.). *A Handbook of African Affairs.* Frederick A. Praeger, 1964.

MARSH, Z. A. and G. KINGSNORTH. *An Introduction to the History of East Africa* (2nd ed.). Cambridge University Press, 1961.

MOORE, CLARK D., and ANN DUNBAR (eds.). *Africa Yesterday and Today.* Bantam Books, 1968.

OLIVER, ROLAND and J. D. FAGE. *A Short History of Africa.* New York University Press, 1963.

ROTBERG, ROBERT I. *A Political History of Tropical Africa.* Harcourt, Brace, & World, Inc. 1965.

WALKER, ERIC A. *A History of Southern Africa.* Longmans, Green & Co., 1965.

WARD, W. E. F. *A History of Africa* (2 vols.). George Allen & Unwin Ltd., 1966.

ASIA

BOSWORTH, C. E. *The Islamic Dynasties.* Aldine Publishing Co., 1967.

BROCKELMANN, CARL. *History of the Islamic Peoples.* Routledge & Kegan Paul Ltd., 1950.

DURDIN, TILLMANN. *Southeast Asia.* Atheneum, 1966.

FAIRBANK, JOHN K., EDWIN O. REISCHAUER, and ALBERT M. CRAIG. *East Asia—The Modern Transformation.* Houghton Mifflin Co., 1965.

FAIRBANK, JOHN K., and EDWIN O. REISCHAUER. *East Asia—The Great Tradition.* Houghton Mifflin Co., 1958.

GOODRICH, L. CARRINGTON. *A Short History of the Chinese People* (3d ed.). Harper & Row, 1963.

HALL, D. G. E. *A History of South-East Asia* (2nd ed.). St. Martin's Press, 1964.

HAY, RUPERT. *Persian Gulf States.* Middle East Institute, 1959.

HERRMANN, ALBERT. *An Historical Atlas of China.* Aldine Publishing Co., 1966.

JANOWSKY, OSCAR I. *Foundations of Israel.* D. Van Nostrand Co., Inc., 1959.

LENCZOWSKI, GEORGE. *The Middle East in World Affairs* (3rd ed.). Cornell University Press, 1962.

LEWIS, BERNARD. *The Arabs in History.* Hillary House, 1966.

MORELAND, W. H., and ATUL CHANDRA CHATTERJEE. *A Short History of India.* Longmans, Green & Co., 1947.

ONORATO, MICHAEL P. *Historical Atlas of the Far East in Modern Times.* Denoyer-Geppert, 1967.

SHARABI, H. B. *Governments and Politics of the Middle East in the Twentieth Century.* D. Van Nostrand Co., Inc., 1962.

SPEAR, PERCIVAL. *A History of India* (vol. 2). Penguin Books, Inc., 1965.

THAPAR, ROMILA. *A History of India* (vol. 1). Penguin Books, Inc., 1965.

WINT, GUY (ed.). *Asia—A Handbook.* Frederick A. Praeger, 1967.

AUSTRALIA AND OCEANIA

ALLEN, JACK, and A. E. HOWLAND. *Pacific Islands and Antarctica.* Prentice-Hall, Inc., 1965.

ORD, I. G. *Atlas of the South-West Pacific.* Tri-Ocean Books, 1967.

SHAW, A. G. L. *Short History of Australia.* Frederick A. Praeger, 1967.

STAMP. L. DUDLEY. *Australia and New Zealand* (9th ed.). John Wiley & Sons, Inc., 1965.

GRATTEN, C. HARTLEY. *The Southwest Pacific to 1900.* University of Michigan Press, 1963.

EUROPE

ADAMS, ARTHUR, and others. *Atlas of Russian and East European History.* Frederick A. Praeger, 1966.

ATKINSON, WILLIAM C. *A History of Spain and Portugal.* Penguin Books, Inc., 1960.

BAYERSCHMIDT, CARL F., and E. J. FRIIS (eds.). *Scandinavian Studies.* University of Washington Press, 1965.

CHARQUES, RICHARD D. *A Short History of Russia.* E. P. Dutton & Co., 1958.

CHEW, ALLEN F. *An Atlas of Russian History.* Yale University Press, 1967.

COBBAN, ALFRED. *History of Modern France.* (rev. ed., 3 vol.). Penguin Books, 1961-1963.

DANIELS, ROBERT V. *Russia.* Prentice-Hall, Inc., 1964.

DILL, MARSHALL, JR. *Germany—A Modern History.* University of Michigan Press, 1961.

DMYTRYSHYN, BASIL. *The U.S.S.R.: A Concise History.* Charles Scribner's Sons, 1965.

DUNLOP, JOHN K. *Short History of Germany.* Dufour Editions, 1966.

EYCK, F. GUNTHER. *The Benelux Countries.* D. Van Nostrand Co., 1959.

GOTTMANN, JEAN. *A Geography of Europe* (3rd ed.). Holt, Rinehart, & Winston, Inc., 1954.

GRINDROD, MURIEL. *Italy.* Oxford University Press, 1964.

HOFFMAN, GEORGE W. and others. *Geography of Europe* (2nd ed.). Ronald Press Co., 1963.

HOLBORN, HAJO. *History of Modern Germany.* (3 vols.). Alfred A. Knopf, Inc., 1958-1968.

LIVERMORE, HAROLD. *A History of Spain.* Grove Press, Inc., 1960.

LIVERMORE, HAROLD. *A New History of Portugal.* Cambridge University Press, 1966.

LOPEZ, ROBERT. *The Birth of Europe.* M. Evans & Co., 1967.

PALMER, R. R., and JOEL COLTON. *A History of the Modern World* (3rd ed.). Alfred A. Knopf, Inc., 1966.

PETERS, D. J. *Short History of France.* Pergamon Press, 1967.

RIASANOVSKY, NICHOLAS V. *History of Russia.* Oxford University Press, 1963.

SHABAD, THEODORE. *Geography of the U.S.S.R.* Columbia University Press, 1963.

STAVRIANOS, LEFTEN S. *Balkans Since 1453.* Holt, Rinehart, & Winston, Inc., 1958.

TREVELYAN, G. M. *History of England* (3 vols.). Doubleday-Anchor, 1952.

TREVELYAN, JANET P. *Short History of the Italian People From the Barbarian Invasion to the Present Day.* Pitman Publishing Corp., 1956.

WOLFF, ROBERT L. *The Balkans in Our Time.* W. W. Norton & Co., 1967.

WUORINEN, JOHN H. *Scandinavia.* Prentice-Hall, Inc., 1965.

NORTH AMERICA

CREIGHTON, DONALD G. *Story of Canada.* Houghton Mifflin Co., 1960.

McHENRY, J. P. *Short History of Mexico.* Doubleday & Co., 1962.

McINNIS, EDGAR. *Canada, A Political and Social History.* Holt, Rinehart & Winston, Inc., 1959.

MORTON, W. L. *The Kingdom of Canada.* Bobbs-Merrill Co., 1963.

PARKES, HENRY B. *History of Mexico* (rev.). Houghton Mifflin Co., 1960.

RODRIGUEZ, MARIO. *Central America.* Prentice-Hall, Inc., 1965.

WEST, ROBERT C., and J. P. AUGELLI. *Middle America: Its Lands and Peoples.* Prentice-Hall, 1966.

WILGUS, CURTIS A. (ed.). *Caribbean: The Central American Area.* University of Florida Press, 1968.

SOUTH AMERICA

BELLO, JOSÉ MARIA. *A History of Modern Brazil.* Stanford University Press, 1966.

FAGG, JOHN EDWIN. *Latin America—A General History.* Macmillan Co., 1968.

HERRING, HUBERT. *A History of Latin America.* Alfred A. Knopf, Inc., 1961.

LEVENE, RICARDO. *A History of Argentina.* Russell & Russell, 1963.

MORÓN, GUILLERMO. *History of Venezuela.* Roy Publishers.

ROBINSON, HARRY. *Latin America—A Geographical Survey.* Frederick A. Praeger, 1967.

The pages of the Atlas have been given special numbers to make this volume of even greater usefulness. Thus, Atlas page 3 (Atlas-3) is equivalent to page 2383 and Atlas page 64 (Atlas-64) is equivalent to page 2444.

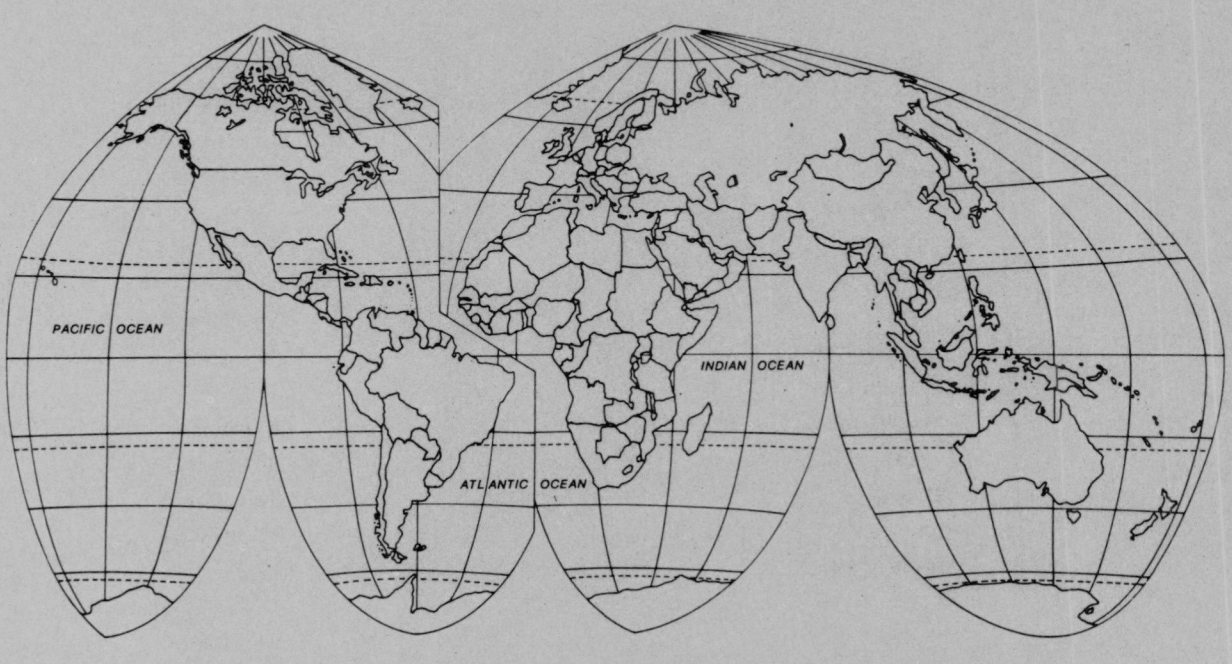

Afghanistan	28	Burundi	39	El Salvador	55
Africa	34-35	Cambodia	30	Ethiopia	34-35
Albania	18	Cameroon	35, 37	Europe	8-9
Algeria	12, 37	Canada	58-59	Finland	14-15
Andorra	23	Central African Republic	35, 38	France	22-23
Antarctica	5	Ceylon	29	Gabon	38
Argentina	45; 46-47	Chad	34-35	Gambia	36
Asia	26-27	Chile	45, 46-47	Germany	16
Australia	42-43	China	32-33	Ghana	36-37
Austria	17	Colombia	52-53	Greece	9, 19
Bahrain	25	Congo (Brazzaville)	38	Guatemala	55
Barbados	57	Congo (Kinshasa)	38-39	Guinea	36
Belgium	22	Costa Rica	52, 55	Guyana	44
Bhutan	29	Cuba	56-57	Haiti	57
Bolivia	44-45; 51	Cyprus	26	Honduras	55
Botswana	40	Czechoslovakia	9, 16-17	Hungary	18-19
Brazil	48-49	Dahomey	37	Iceland	14
Britain	10-11	Denmark	15	India	28-29
Bulgaria	19	Dominican Republic	57	Indonesia	30-31
Burma	29	Ecuador	50	Iran	25, 28

Iraq	25	Polar Map of the World	4-5
Ireland	10-11	Portugal	12
Israel	24	Qatar	25
Italy	13	Rhodesia	41
Ivory Coast	36	Romania	19
Jamaica	56	Rwanda	39
Japan	33	San Marino	13
Jordan	24, 25	Saudi Arabia	25
Kenya	39	Senegal	36
Korea	33	Sierra Leone	36
Kuwait	25	Sikkim	29
Laos	30	Singapore	30
Lebanon	24	Somali Republic	25, 35
Lesotho	40-41	South Africa	40-41
Liberia	36	South America	44-45
Libya	34	South Yemen	25
Liechtenstein	17	Soviet Union	20-21, 26-27
Luxembourg	22	Spain	12
Madagascar (Malagasy		Sudan	34-35
Republic)	41	Swaziland	41
Malawi	39	Sweden	14-15
Malaysia	30	Switzerland	17
Maldive Islands	28	Syria	25
Mali	36-37	Taiwan (Formosa)	33
Malta	13	Tanzania	39
Mauritania	36	Thailand	30
Mexico	54-55	Togo	37
Monaco	23	Trinidad and Tobago	53, 57
Mongolia	32-33	Trucial Oman	25
Morocco	12	Tunisia	13
Muscat and Oman	25	Turkey	26
Nauru	6	Uganda	39
Nepal	29	United Arab Republic	
Netherlands	22	(Egypt)	24, 26
New Zealand	6	United Kingdom	10-11
Nicaragua	55	United States	64
Niger	37	Upper Volta	36-37
Nigeria	37	Uruguay	45
North America	64	Vatican City	13
Norway	14-15	Venezuela	52-53
Pakistan	28-29	Vietnam	30
Panama	52	Western Samoa	6
Paraguay	45	World	6-7
Peru	50-51	Yemen	25
Philippines	31	Yugoslavia	18-19
Poland	8-9	Zambia	38-39

PARALLELS OF LATITUDE

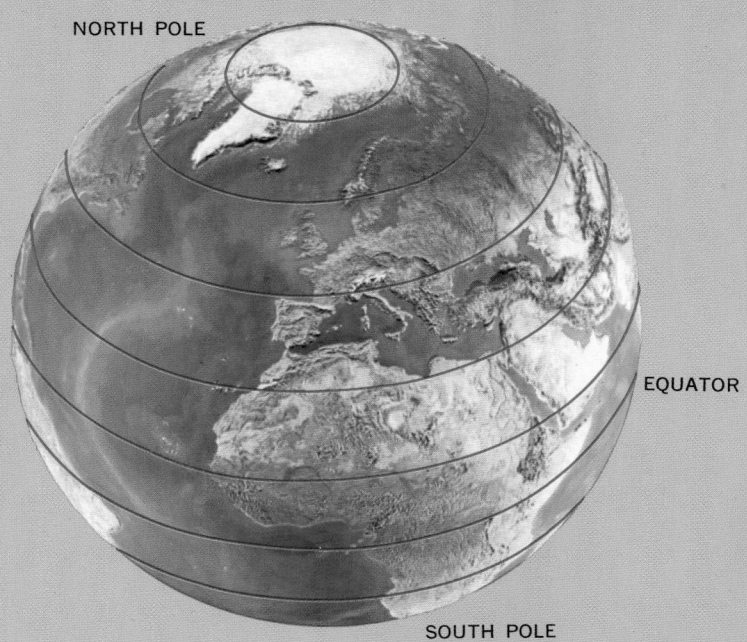

NORTH POLE

EQUATOR

SOUTH POLE

MERIDIANS OF LONGITUDE

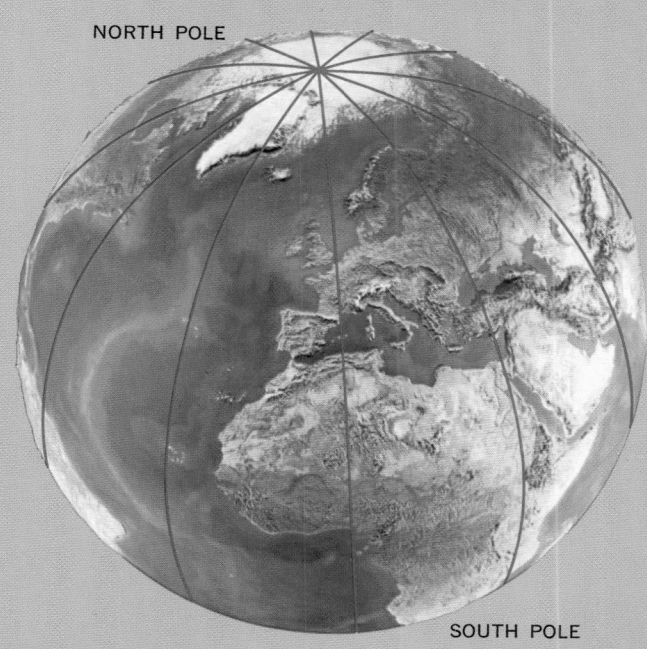

NORTH POLE

SOUTH POLE

LATITUDE AND LONGITUDE

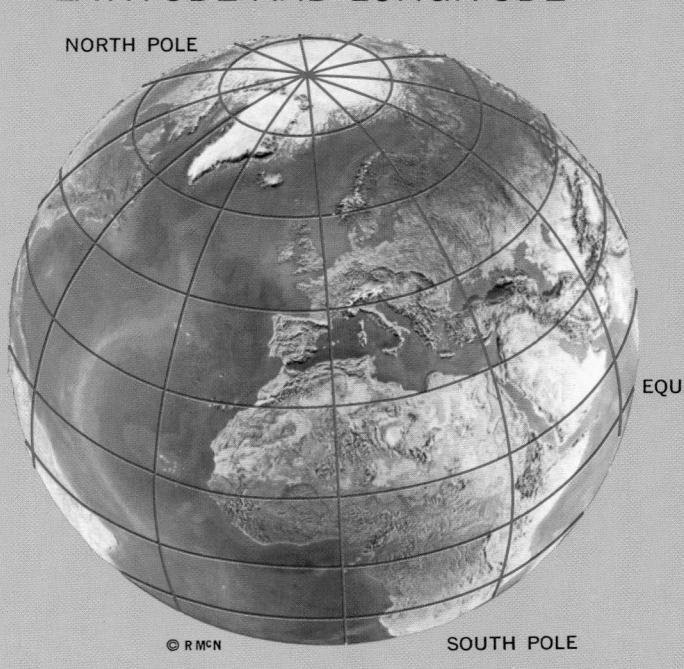

NORTH POLE

© R McN

EQUATOR

SOUTH POLE

The indexing system used on these maps is based upon the conventional pattern of parallels and meridians used to indicate latitude and longitude. Place names in the index are followed by a key letter and number. The key letter is placed between corresponding degree numbers of latitude in the vertical borders of the map and the key number is placed between corresponding degree numbers of longitude in the horizontal borders of the map. The intersection of the parallels and meridians thus identified forms a confining ''box'' in which the given place appears.

MAP PROJECTIONS

A map projection is merely an orderly system of parallels and meridians on which a flat map can be drawn. There are hundreds of projections, but no one represents the earth's spherical surface without some distortion. The distortion is relatively small for most practical purposes when a small part of the sphere is projected. For larger areas, a sacrifice of some property is necessary.

Most projections are designed to preserve on the flat map some particular property of the sphere. By varying the systematic arrangement or spacing of the latitude and longitude lines, a projection may be made either equal-area or conformal. Although most projections are derived from mathematical formulas, some are easier to visualize if thought of as projected upon a plane, or upon a cone or cylinder which is then unrolled into a plane surface. Thus, many projections are classified as plane (azimuthal), conic, or cylindrical.

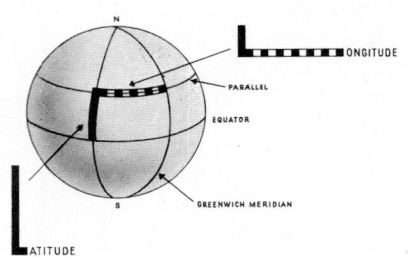

SIMPLE CONIC PROJECTIONS

A perspective projection on a tangent cone with the origin point at the center of the globe. At the parallel of tangency, all elements of the map are true angles, distances, shapes, areas. Away from the tangent parallel, distances increase rapidly, giving bad distortion of shapes and areas.

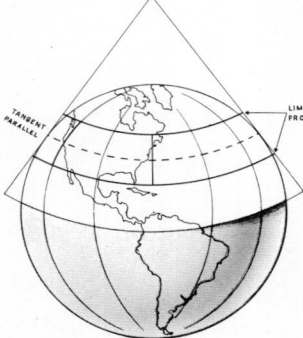

EARTH PROJECTED UPON
A TANGENT CONE

CONE CUT FROM BASE TO APEX

CONE DEVELOPED INTO
A PLANE SURFACE

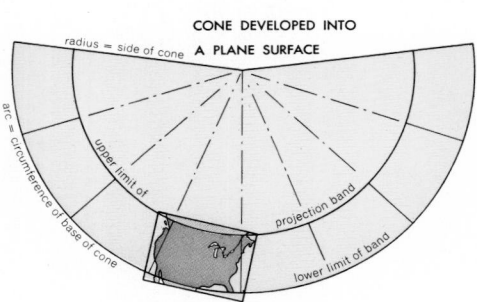

MODIFIED CONIC PROJECTION

EARTH PROJECTED UPON AN INTERSECTING CONE

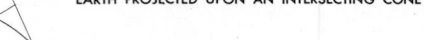
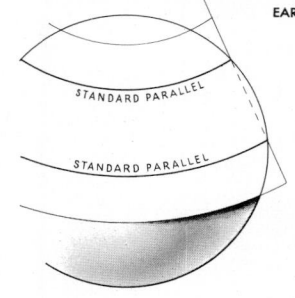

This modification of the conic has two standard parallels, or lines of intersection. It is not an equal-area projection, the space being reduced in size between the standard parallels and progressively enlarged beyond the standard parallels. Careful selection of the standard parallels provides however, good representation for areas of limited latitudinal extent.

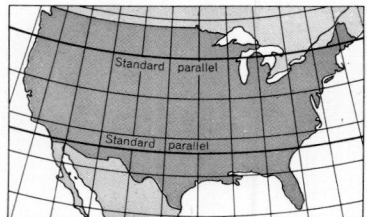

CONIC PROJECTION WITH TWO STANDARD PARALLELS

BONNE PROJECTION
An equal-area modification of the conic principle. Distances are true along all parallels and the central meridian; but away from it, increasing obliqueness of intersections and longitudinal distances, with their attendant distortion of shapes, limits the satisfactory area.

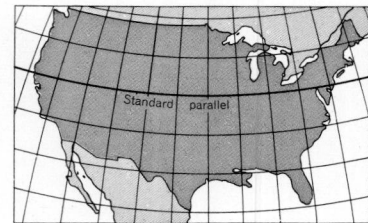

POLYCONIC PROJECTION

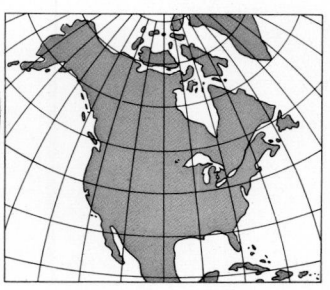

This variation is not equal-area. Parallels are nonconcentric circles truly divided. Distances along the straight central meridian are also true, but along the curving meridians are increasingly exaggerated. Representation is good near the central meridian, but away from it there is marked distortion.

EARTH CONSIDERED AS FORMED
BY BASES OF CONES

DEVELOPMENT OF THE CONICAL BASES

POLYCONIC PROJECTION

TYPICAL PLANE PROJECTIONS

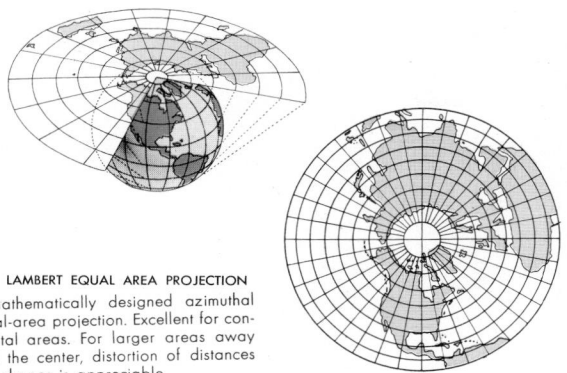

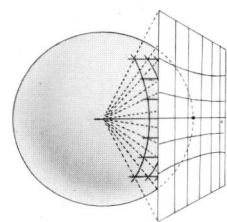

LAMBERT EQUAL AREA PROJECTION

A mathematically designed azimuthal equal-area projection. Excellent for continental areas. For larger areas away from the center, distortion of distances and shapes is appreciable.

GNOMONIC PROJECTION

A geometric or perspective projection on a tangent plane with the origin point at the center of the globe. Shapes and distances rapidly become increasingly distorted away from the center of the projection. Important in navigation, because all straight lines are great circles.

CYLINDRICAL PROJECTIONS

EARTH PROJECTED UPON A CYLINDER

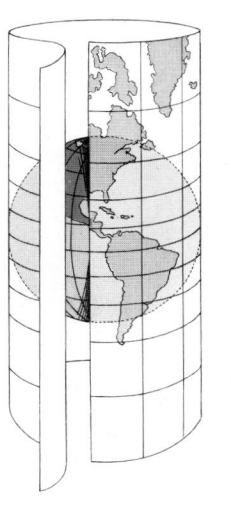

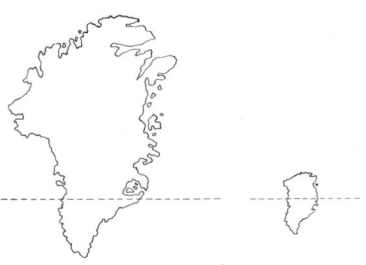

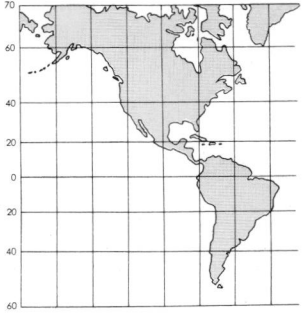

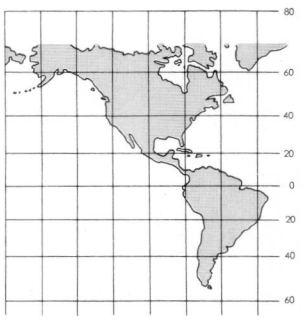

PERSPECTIVE PROJECTION

A perspective projection on a tangent cylinder. Because of rapidly increasing distortion away from the line of tangency and the lack of any special advantage, it is rarely used.

Note the increasing distortion of Greenland (above left) compared to an equal area projection (above right).

MERCATOR CONFORMAL PROJECTION

Mercator's modification increases the longitudinal distances in the same proportion as latitudinal distances are increased. Thus, at any point shapes are true, but areas become increasingly exaggerated. Of value in navigation, because a line connecting any two points gives the true direction between them.

MILLER PROJECTION

This recent modification is neither conformal nor equal-area. Whereas shapes are less accurate than on the Mercator, the exaggeration of areas has been reduced somewhat.

EQUAL AREA PROJECTIONS OF THE WORLD

The earth's surface peeled like the skin from an orange.

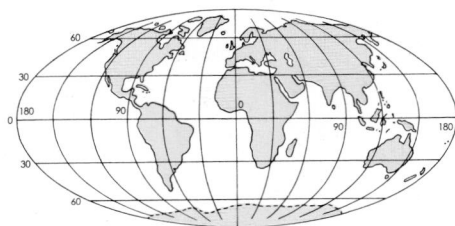

MOLLWEIDE'S HOMOLOGRAPHIC PROJECTION

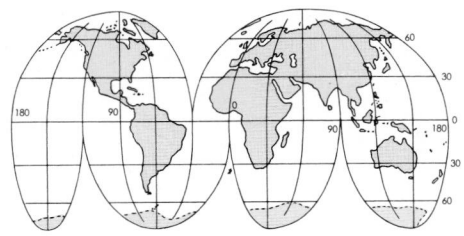

GOODE'S INTERRUPTED HOMOLOGRAPHIC PROJECTION

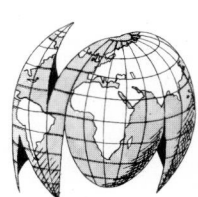

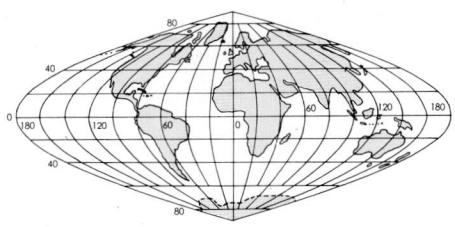

SINUSOIDAL PROJECTION

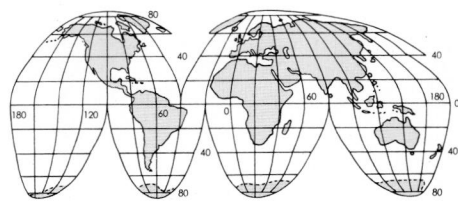

GOODE'S INTERRUPTED HOMOLOSINE PROJECTION

Although each of these projections is equal-area, differences in the spacing and arrangement of latitude and longitude lines result in differences in the distribution and relative degree of the shape and distance distortion within each grid. On the homolographic, there is no uniformity in scale. It is different on each parallel and each meridian. On the sinusoidal, only distances along all latitudes and the central meridian are true. The homolosine combines the homolographic, for areas poleward of 40°, with the sinusoidal. The principle of interruption permits each continent in turn the advantage of being in the center of the projection, resulting in better shapes.

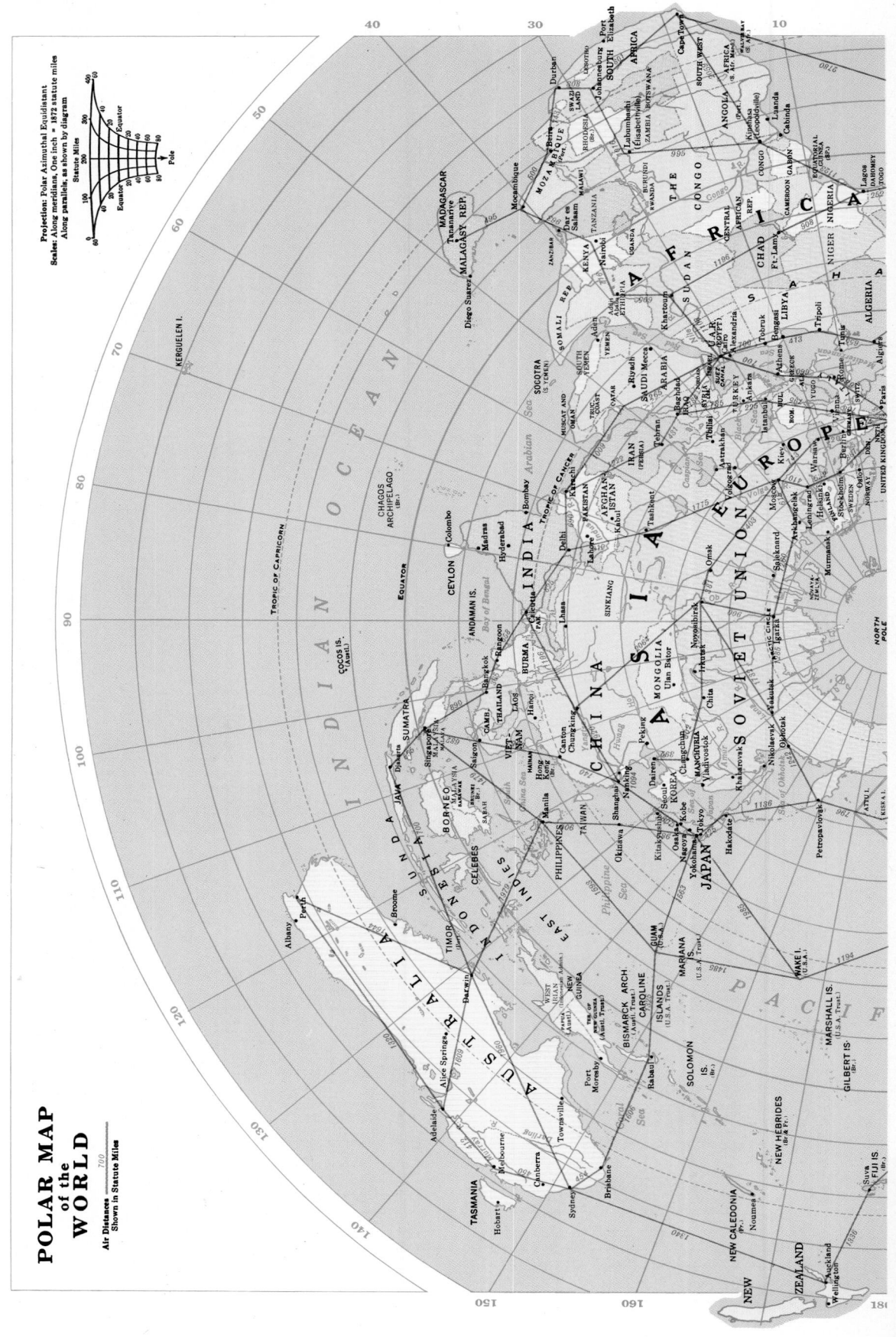

POLAR MAP of the WORLD

Air Distances ———700——— Shown in Statute Miles

Projection: Polar Azimuthal Equidistant
Scales: Along meridians, One inch = 1872 statute miles
Along parallels, as shown by diagram

Statute Miles
Equator
Pole

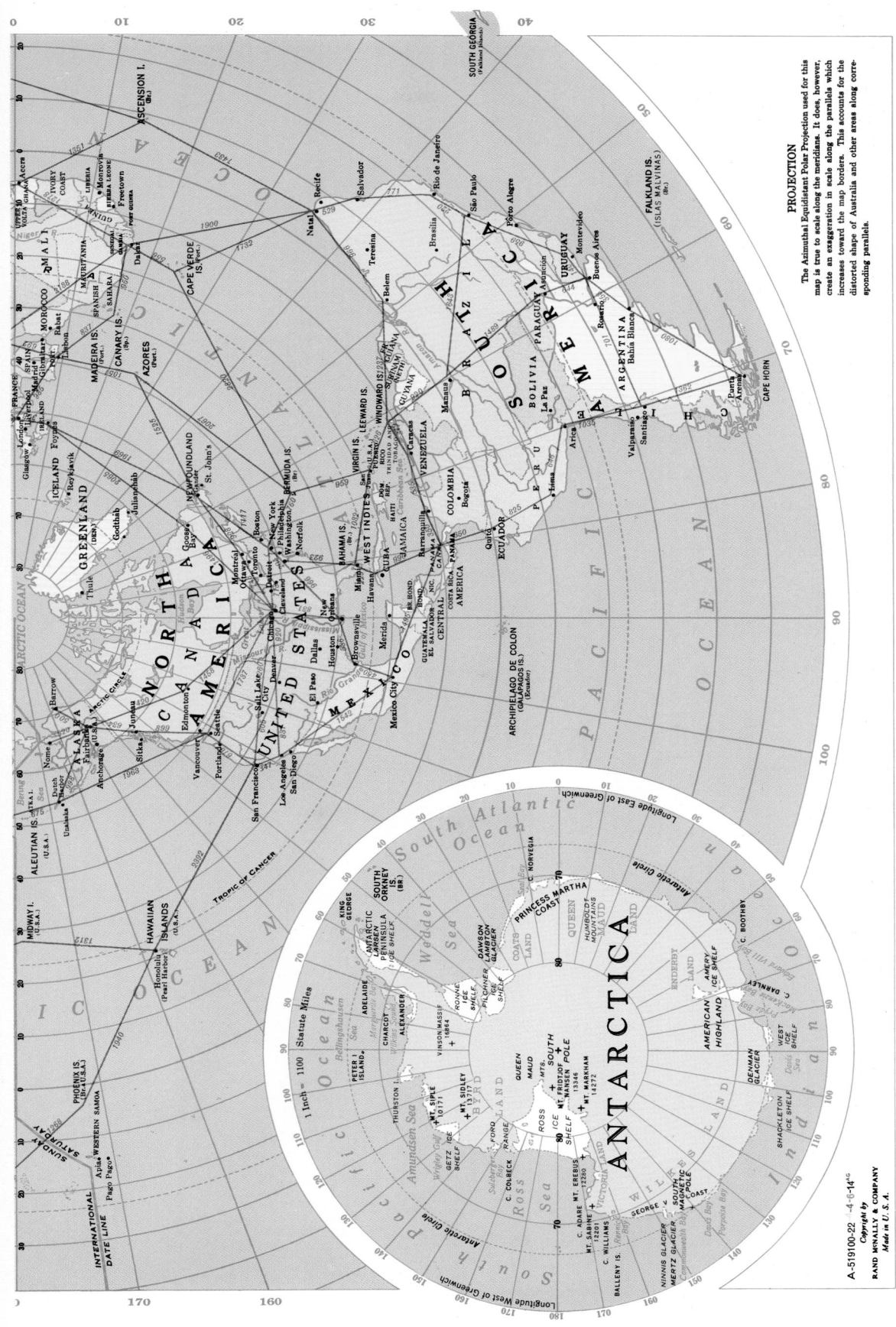

A-519100-22·4·6·14⁴⁶
Copyright by
RAND McNALLY & COMPANY
Made in U. S. A.

PROJECTION

The Azimuthal Equidistant Projection used for this map is true to scale along the meridians. It does, however, create an exaggeration in scale along the parallels which increases toward the map borders. This accounts for the distorted shape of Australia and other areas along corresponding parallels.

THE WORLD

Afars & Issas F23
Afghanistan . . . . D 1
Albania D22
Andorra *D21
Angola G21
Argentina I16
Australia . . . . H 5
Austria C22
Azores D19
Bahama Islands E15
Barbados F17
Belgium C21
Bermuda D16
Bhutan . . . . E 3
Bolivia H16
Botswana H22
Brazil G17
British Honduras E15
Brunei . . . . *F 4
Bulgaria D22
Burma . . . . E 3
Burundi G23
Cambodia . . . . F 3
Cameroon F21
Canada C13
Canary Islands E19
Cape Verde Islands E19
Central African
  Republic F22
Ceylon . . . . F 2
Chad E22
Chile I16
China . . . . D 4
Colombia F19
Congo (Brazzaville) G22
Congo, (The Democratic
  Republic of the
  Congo) G22
Costa Rica F15
Cuba E15
Cyprus *D23
Czechoslovakia C21
Dahomey *F21
Denmark C21
Dominican Republic E16
Ecuador G15
Egypt, see U.A.R.
El Salvador F15
Equatorial Guinea F21
Ethiopia F23
Faeroe Islands B20
Falkland Islands J17
Finland B22
Formosa, see Taiwan
France C21
French Guiana F17
Gabon G21
Gambia F19
Germany C21
Ghana F20
Greece D22
Greenland A17
Guadeloupe E16
Guatemala F14
Guinea F20
Haiti E16
Honduras F15
Hong Kong . . . . *E 4
Hungary C22
Iceland B19
Ifni *E20
India . . . . E 2
Indonesia . . . . G 4
Iran D24
Iraq D23
Ireland C20
Israel D23
Italy D21
Ivory Coast *F20
Jamaica E15
Japan . . . . D 6
Jordan D23
Kenya F23
Korea . . . . D 5
Kuwait E24
Laos . . . . E 3
Lebanon D23

A-510000-22 -4-5-18^AG
COSMO SERIES WORLD
Copyright by
RAND McNALLY & COMPANY
Made in U.S.A.

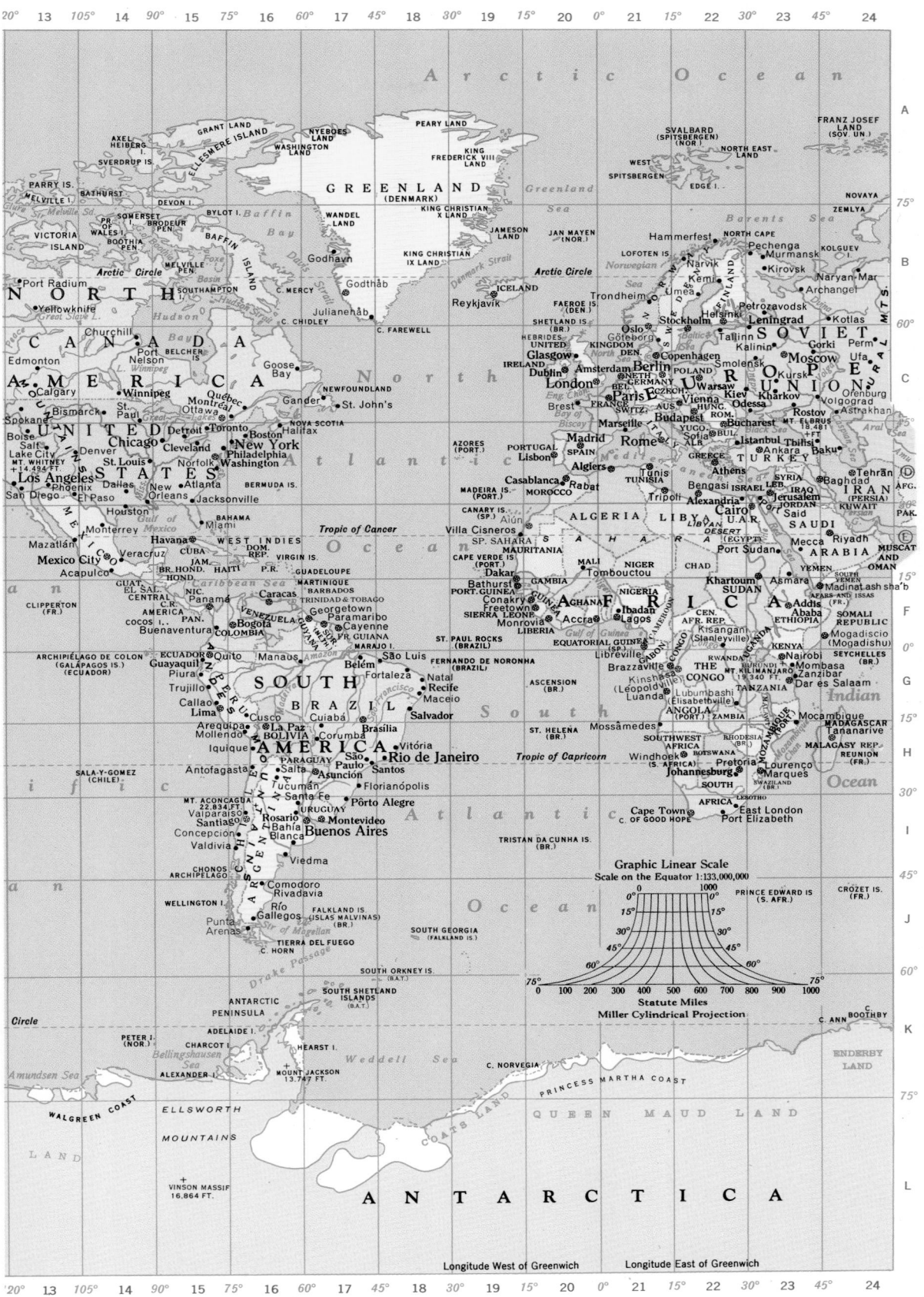

Lesotho H22
Liberia F20
Libya E22
Liechtenstein *C21
Luxembourg *C21
Macao . . . . *E 4
Malagasy Republic H24
Malawi G23
Malaysia . . . . F 4
Mali E20
Martinique F16
Mauritania E19
Mauritius H24
Mexico E14
Mongolia . . . . C 3
Morocco D20
Mozambique H23
Muscat & Oman E24
Nauru . . . . G 8
Nepal . . . . E 2
Netherlands C21
New Caledonia . . . . H 8
New Hebrides . . . . H 8
New Zealand . . . . I 8
Nicaragua F15
Niger E21
Nigeria F21
Norway B21
Pakistan . . . . E 1, E 3
Panama F15
Papua . . . . G 6
Paraguay H17
Peru G15
Philippines . . . . F 5
Poland C22
Portugal D20
Portuguese Guinea F19
Puerto Rico E16
Qatar *E24
Rhodesia H22
Romania C22
Rwanda G22
San Marino *D21
Saudi Arabia E23
Senegal *E19
Sierra Leone F20
Singapore . . . . F 3
Somali Republic F24
South Africa H22
South Yemen E24
South West Africa H22
Soviet Union . . . . B 3
Spain D20
Spanish Sahara E20
Sudan F22
Surinam F17
Swaziland H23
Sweden B22
Switzerland C21
Syria D23
Taiwan (Formosa) . . . . . . E 5
Tanzania G23
Thailand . . . . E 3
Togo *F21
Trinidad & Tobago F17
Trucial Coast *E24
Tunisia D21
Turkey D23
Uganda F23
United Arab Republic
  (Egypt) E22
United Kingdom C20
United States D14
Upper Volta *E20
Uruguay I17
Vatican City *D21
Venezuela F16
Vietnam . . . . E 4
Virgin Islands E16
Western Samoa . . . . G 9
West Indies E16
West Irian . . . . G 6
Yemen E23
Yugoslavia D22
Zambia G22

* Not shown on map. Index key denotes approximate location.

WESTERN EUROPE
⊛ **Capitals**

Amsterdam, Neth......E 9
Belgrade, Yugo........G12
Berlin, Ger., E........E10
Bern, Switz..........F 9
Bonn, Ger., W........E 9
Brussels, Bel.........E 8
Bucharest, Rom.......G13
Budapest, Hung.......F11
Copenhagen, Den......D10
Dublin, Ire..........E 6
Helsinki, Fin.........C12
London, Eng..........E 7
Oslo, Nor............D10
Paris, Fr............F 8
Prague, Czech........E10
Reykjavík, Ice........C 3
Sofia, Bulg..........G12
Stockholm, Swe.......D11
The Hague, Neth......E 8
Vienna, Aus..........F11
Warsaw, Pol..........E12

Physical Features

Adriatic, sea..........G11
Aegean, sea..........H13
Alps, mts............F 9
Apennines, mts.......G10
Balearic, is..........H 8
Balkan, mts..........G12
Baltic, sea..........D11
Barents, sea.........A13
Biscay, bay..........G 7
Black, sea...........G14
Blanc, mtn..........F 9
Bosporus, strait.....G13
Bothnia, gulf........C12
Brenner, pass........F10
Cantabrian, mts......G 6
Carpathians, mts.....F12
Channel, is..........F 7
Cheviot, hills.......E 7
Clear, cape..........E 6
Corsica, isl.........G 9
Crete, isl...........H12
Crete, sea...........H12
Cyclades, is.........H12
Danube, riv..........G13
Dardanelles, strait...G13
Denmark, strait......B 3
Dinaric Alps, mts.....G11
Dnepr, riv...........F14
Dnestr, riv..........F13
Douro, riv...........G 6
Drin, riv............G12
Drina, riv...........G11
Ebro, riv............G 7
Elba, isl............G10
Elbe, riv............E10
English, chan.........E 7
Etna, mtn...........H10
Faeroe, is...........C 6
Faxafloi, bay........C 3
Finland, gulf........C13
Firth of Forth, chan...D 7
Galdhöppigen, mtn....C 9
Gibraltar, strait.....H 6
Gotland, isl.........D11
Grampians, mts.......D 7
Guadalquivir, riv.....H 6
Guadarrama, mts......G 7
Guadiana, riv........H 6
Hardangerfjord, fjord..D 8
Hardangervidda, plat..C 9
Hebrides, is.........D 6
Inari, lake..........B13
Ionian, sea..........H11
Irish, sea...........E 6
Jan Mayen, isl.......A 6
Karkinitskiy, bay....F14
Kattegat, chan.......D10
Kemijoki, riv........B13
Kola, pen...........B15
Ladoga, lake.........C14

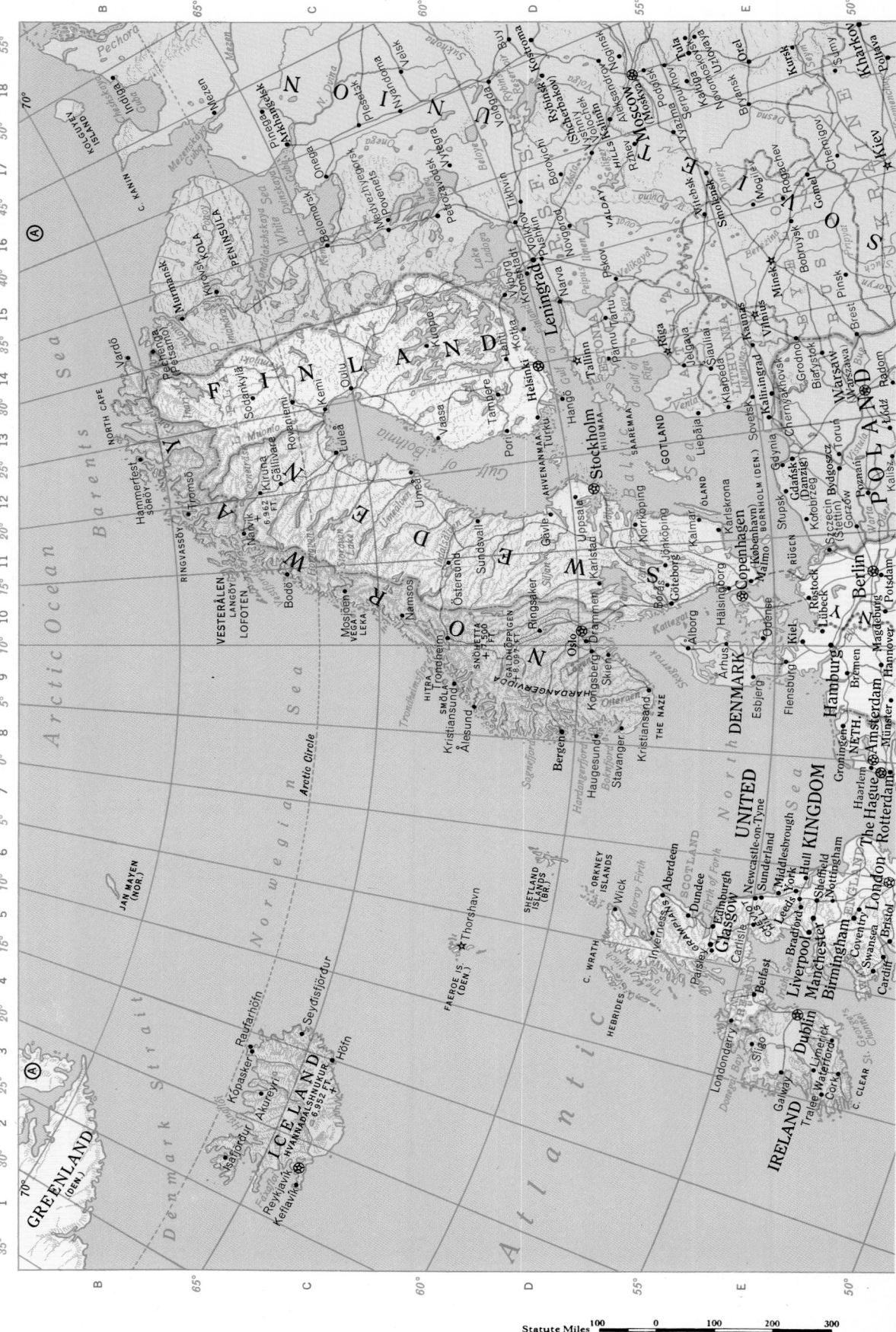

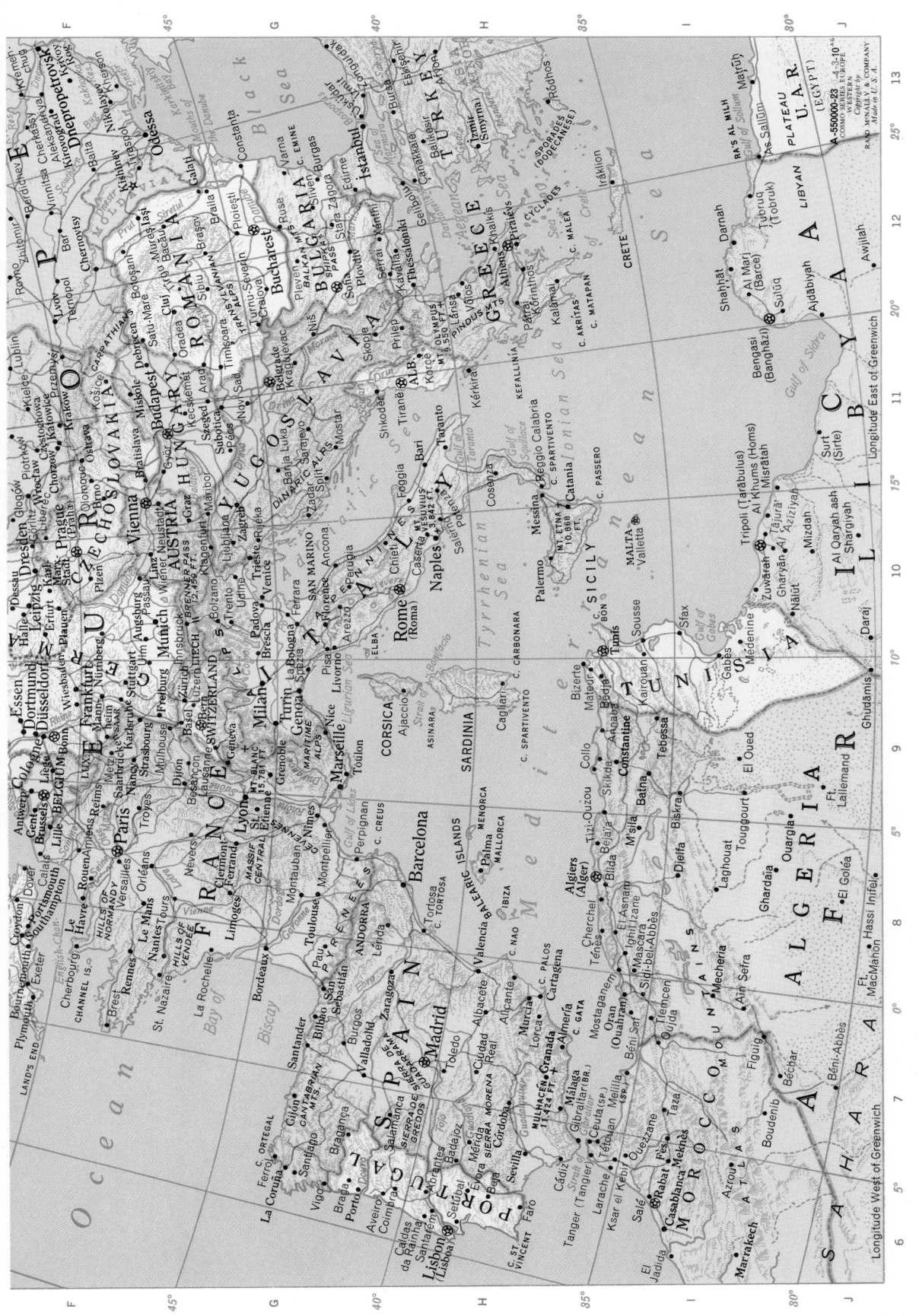

Lågen, riv . . . . D 9
Land's End, cape . . . . . . E 6
Ligurian, sea . . . . G 9
Lions, gulf . . . . G 8
Lofoten, is B10
Loire, riv . . . . E 7
Mälaren, lake D11
Mallorca, isl . . . . H 8
Malta, isl H10
Maritime Alps, mts . . . . . G 9
Maritsa, riv G13
Marmara, sea G13
Marne, riv . . . . F 8
Massif Central, mts . . . . F 8
Matapan, cape H12
Mediterranean, sea H10
Menderes, riv H13
Menorca, isl . . . . H 8
Morava, riv G12
Moray, firth . . . . D 7
Morena, mts . . . . H 6
Mulhacén, mtn . . . . H 7
Muonio, riv B12
Muresul, riv F12
Normandy, hills . . . . F 7
North, cape A13
North, sea . . . . D 8
Northern Dvina, riv C16
Norwegian, sea . . . . B 7
Oder, riv E11
Olympus, mtn G12
Onega, lake C15
Onega, riv C15
Orkney, is . . . . D 7
Otteraen, riv . . . . H 7
Palos, cape . . . . H 7
Passero, cape H11
Peipus, lake D13
Pindus, mts H12
Po, riv G10
Pripyat, riv E13
Pskov, lake D13
Pyrenees, mts . . . . G 8
Rhine, riv . . . . E 9
Rhône, riv . . . . F 8
Riga, gulf D12
Rybinsk, res D15
St. George's, chan . . . . . E 6
St. Vincent, cape . . . . . . H 6
Saone, riv . . . . F 8
Sardinia, isl . . . . G 9
Scutari, lake G11
Seine, riv . . . . F 8
Shetland, is . . . . C 7
Shipka, pass G13
Sicily, isl H10
Skagerrak, chan . . . . D 9
Somme, riv . . . . E 8
Spartivento, cape . . . . . . H 9
Spartivento, cape H11
Sporades
   (Dodecanese), is H13
Squillace, gulf H11
Storavan, lake B11
Tajo, riv . . . . H 6
Tanaelv, riv B13
Taranto, gulf G11
Tevere, riv G10
The Minch, strait . . . . . . D 6
The Naze, cape . . . . D 9
Tornetrask, lake B12
Transylvanian Alps, mts . . F12
Tyrrhenian, sea H10
Umeälven, riv C11
Vänern, lake D10
Vardar, riv G12
Vattern, lake D10
Vesterålen, is B10
Vestfjorden, fjord B10
Vesuvius, mtn G10
Vienne, riv . . . . F 8
Vistula, riv E11
Warta, riv E11
Weser, riv . . . . E 9
Western Dvina, riv D14
White, sea B15
Wrath, cape . . . . D 6

Conic Projection
SCALE 1:16,000,000   1 Inch = 252 Statute Miles

UNITED KINGDOM
ENGLAND
Principal Cities

Pop.—Thousands

Pop.	City	Ref
144	Birkenhead	D 5
1,116	Birmingham	D 6
105	Blackburn	D 5
151	Blackpool	D 5
160	Bolton	D 5
151	Bournemouth	E 6
297	Bradford	D 6
163	Brighton	E 6
434	Bristol	E 5
80	Burnley	D 5
96	Cambridge	D 7
314	Coventry	D 6
17	Cowes	E 6
84	Darlington	C 6
132	Derby	D 6
87	Doncaster	D 6
110	Enfield	k12
103	Gateshead	C 6
97	Grimsby	D 6
96	Halifax	D 6
132	Huddersfield	D 6
301	Hull (Kingston-upon-Hull)	D 6
119	Ipswich	D 7
514	Leeds	D 6
270	Leicester	D 6
740	Liverpool	D 5
7,973	London	E 6, k12
136	Luton	E 6
655	Manchester	D 5
158	Middlesbrough	C 6
263	Newcastle-on-Tyne	C 6
105	Northampton	D 6
120	Norwich	D 7
315	Nottingham	D 6
114	Oldham	D 5
107	Oxford	D 6
210	Plymouth	E 4
94	Poole	E 5
225	Portsmouth	E 6
112	Preston	D 5
122	Reading	E 6
86	Rochdale	D 5
153	Salford	D 5
495	Sheffield	D 6
84	Slough	E 6, k11
207	Southampton	E 6
166	Southend-on-Sea	E 7
109	South Shields	C 6
143	Stockport	D 5
266	Stoke-on-Trent	D 5
191	Sunderland	C 6
96	Swindon	E 6
103	Wallasey	D 5
121	Walsall	D 6
98	West Bromwich	D 6
150	Wolverhampton	D 5
67	Worcester	D 5
80	Worthing	E 6
104	York	D 6

WALES
Principal Cities

Pop.—Thousands

Pop.	City	Ref
39	Aberdare	E 5
10	Aberystwyth	D 4
15	Bangor	D 4
9	Caernarvon	D 4
261	Cardiff	E 5
13	Carmarthen	E 4
8	Denbigh	D 5
10	Holyhead	D 4
17	Llandudno	D 5
59	Merthyr Tydfil	E 5
13	Milford Haven	E 4
31	Neath	E 5
14	Pembroke	E 4
100	Rhondda	E 5
21	Rhyl	D 5
170	Swansea	E 4
36	Wrexham	D 5

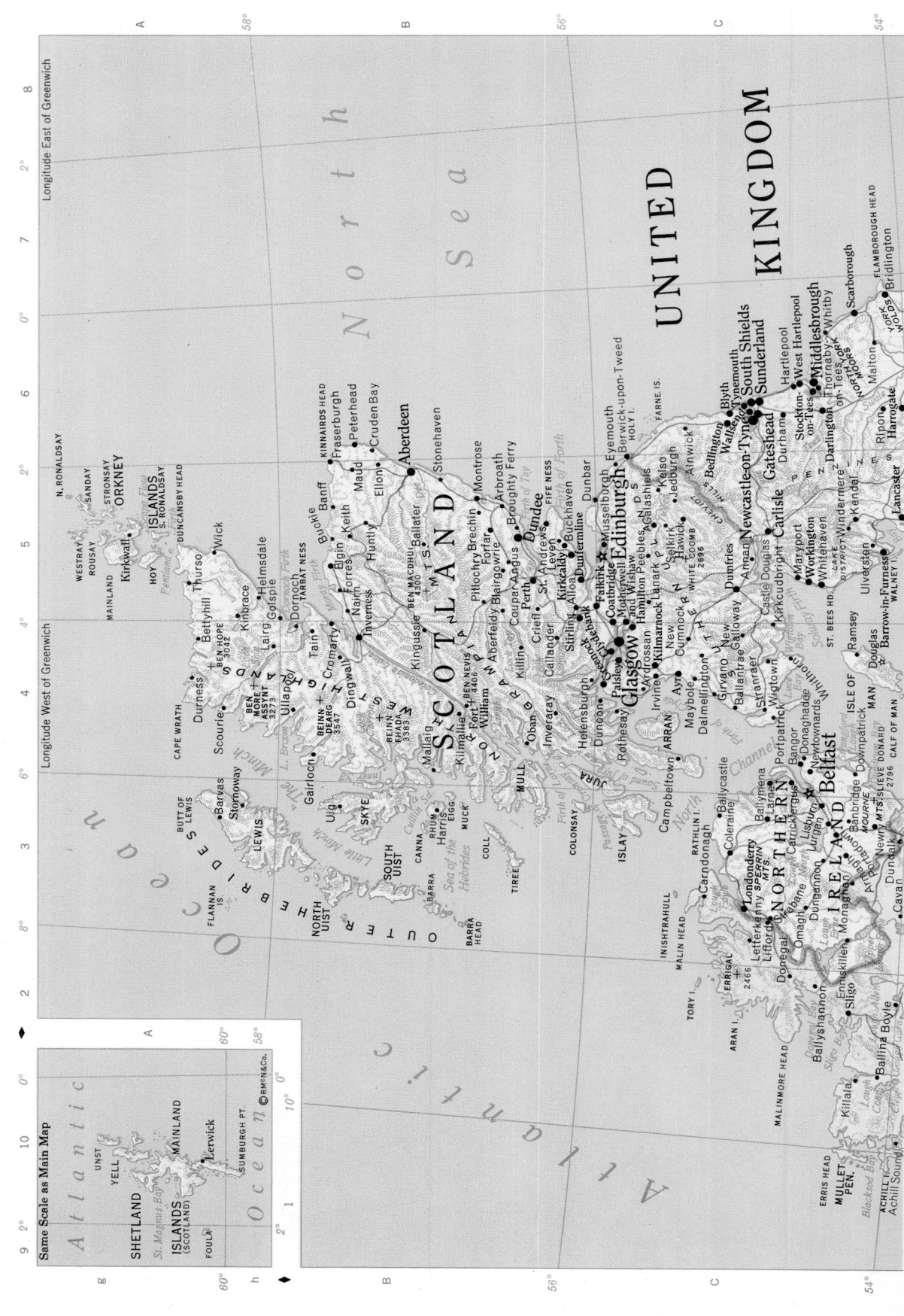

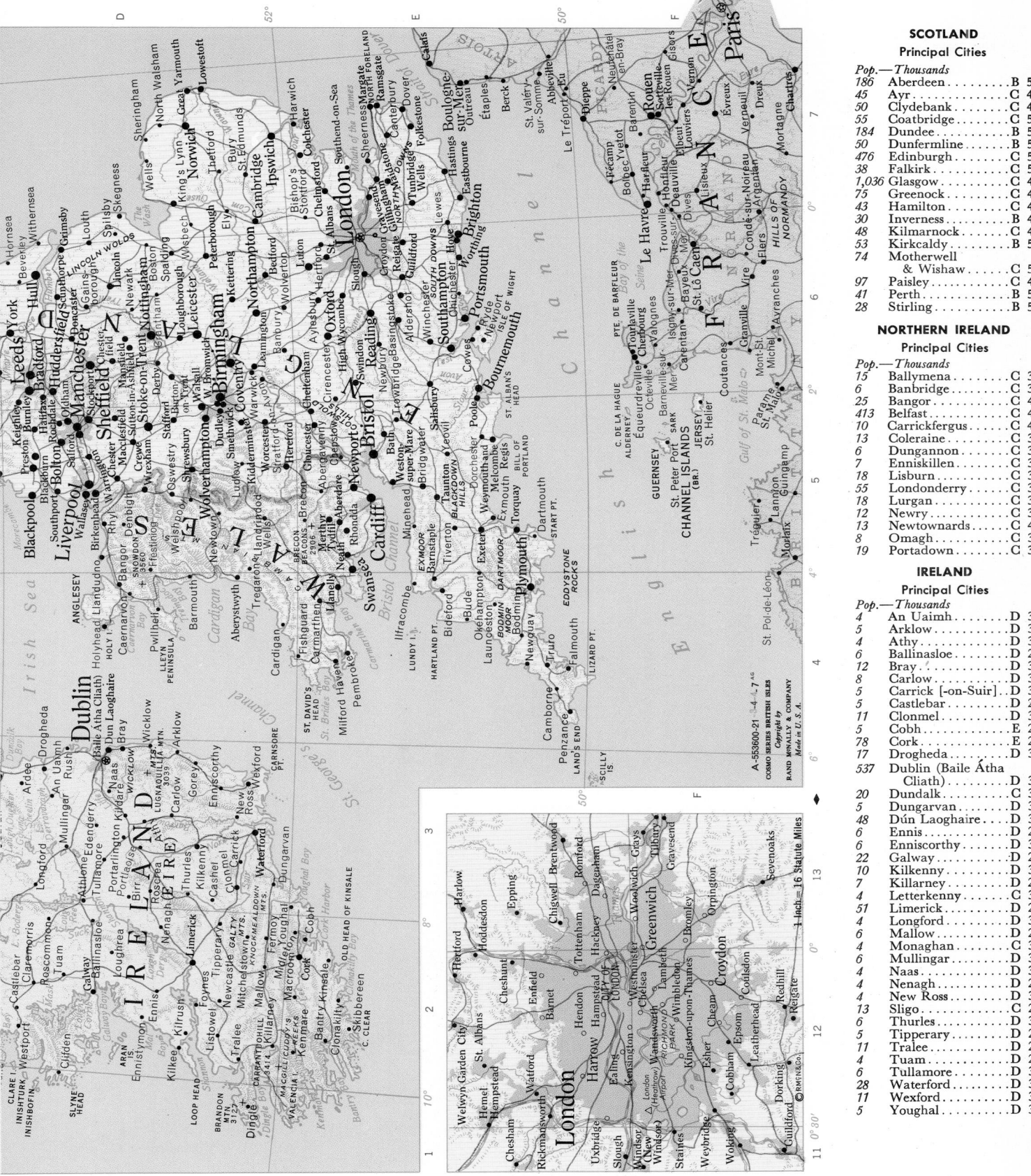

SCOTLAND
Principal Cities

Pop.—Thousands

186	Aberdeen	B 5
45	Ayr	C 4
50	Clydebank	C 4
55	Coatbridge	C 5
184	Dundee	B 5
50	Dunfermline	B 5
476	Edinburgh	C 5
38	Falkirk	C 5
1,036	Glasgow	C 4
75	Greenock	C 4
43	Hamilton	C 4
30	Inverness	B 4
48	Kilmarnock	C 4
53	Kirkcaldy	B 5
74	Motherwell & Wishaw	C 5
97	Paisley	C 4
41	Perth	B 5
28	Stirling	B 5

NORTHERN IRELAND
Principal Cities

Pop.—Thousands

15	Ballymena	C 3
6	Banbridge	C 3
25	Bangor	C 4
413	Belfast	C 4
10	Carrickfergus	C 4
13	Coleraine	C 3
6	Dungannon	C 3
7	Enniskillen	C 3
18	Lisburn	C 3
55	Londonderry	C 3
18	Lurgan	C 3
12	Newry	C 3
13	Newtownards	C 4
8	Omagh	C 3
19	Portadown	C 3

IRELAND
Principal Cities

Pop.—Thousands

4	An Uaimh	D 3
5	Arklow	D 3
4	Athy	D 3
6	Ballinasloe	D 2
12	Bray	D 3
8	Carlow	D 3
5	Carrick [-on-Suir]	D 3
5	Castlebar	D 2
11	Clonmel	D 3
5	Cobh	E 2
78	Cork	E 2
17	Drogheda	D 3
537	Dublin (Baile Átha Cliath)	D 3
20	Dundalk	C 3
5	Dungarvan	D 3
48	Dún Laoghaire	D 3
6	Ennis	D 2
6	Enniscorthy	D 2
22	Galway	D 2
10	Kilkenny	D 3
7	Killarney	D 2
4	Letterkenny	C 3
51	Limerick	D 2
4	Longford	D 3
6	Mallow	D 2
4	Monaghan	C 3
6	Mullingar	D 3
4	Naas	D 3
4	Nenagh	D 2
4	New Ross	D 3
13	Sligo	C 2
6	Thurles	D 3
5	Tipperary	D 3
11	Tralee	D 2
4	Tuam	D 2
6	Tullamore	D 3
28	Waterford	D 3
11	Wexford	D 3
5	Youghal	D 3

Conic Projection
SCALE 1:4,000,000   1 Inch = 63 Statute Miles

**WESTERN
MEDITERRANEAN**

✪ Capitals

Andorra, And . . . . C 7
Lisbon, Port . . . . E 2
Madrid, Sp . . . . D 5
Rome, It D13

Physical Features

Adige, riv B12
Adour, riv . . . . C 6
Adriatic, sea B13
Alboran, isl . . . . G 5
Alps, mts B11
Amaro, mtn C14
Aneto, mtn . . . . C 7
Apennines, mts C13
Arno, riv C12
Asinara, isl D11
Atlas Saharien, mts . . . . H 6
Baïse, riv . . . . C 7
Balearic, is . . . . E 8
Belle, isl . . . . A 5
Biscay, bay . . . . B 5
Blanc, cape F11
Blanc, mtn B10
Bon, cape F12
Bonifacio, strait D11
Bosna, riv B16
Brač, isl C15
Cantabrian, mts . . . . C 3
Caprara, pt D11
Capri, isl D14
Carbonara, cape E11
Carvoeiro, cape . . . . E 2
Cévennes, mts . . . . C 8
Cher, riv . . . . A 8
Chergul, salt lake . . . . . . G 7
Cinto, mtn C11
Columbretes, isl . . . . E 7
Corno, mtn C13
Corse, cape C11
Corsica, isl C11
Côtes du Nivernais, hills . A 8
Danube, riv B16
D'Hyères, is C10
Dinaric Alps, mts B15
Djerba, isl H12
Djerid, salt lake H11
D'Oléron, isl . . . . B 6
Dordogne, riv . . . . B 7
Douro, riv . . . . D 2
Drava, riv B15
Dugi Otok, isl C14
Durance, riv . . . . C 9
D'Yeu, isl . . . . A 5
Ebro, riv . . . . D 6
Écrins, mtn B10
Egadi, is F13
Elba, isl C12
Espichel, cape . . . . E 2
Etna, mtn F14
Ferrat, cape . . . . G 6
Finisterre, cape . . . . C 2
Formentera, isl . . . . E 7
Gabès, gulf G12
Garonne, riv . . . . C 7
Gata, cape . . . . F 6
Genoa, gulf C11
Gibraltar, strait . . . . G 3
Giglio, isl C12
Grand Atlas, mts . . . . I 3
Grand Erg Oriental,
   sand dunes H10
Gredos, mtn . . . . D 4
Grossglockner, mtn A13
Guadalquivir, riv . . . . . . F 4
Guadarrama, mts . . . . D 5
Guadiana, riv . . . . E 4
Hammamet, gulf F12
Hauts, plat . . . . H 6
Hodna, salt lake . . . . G 9

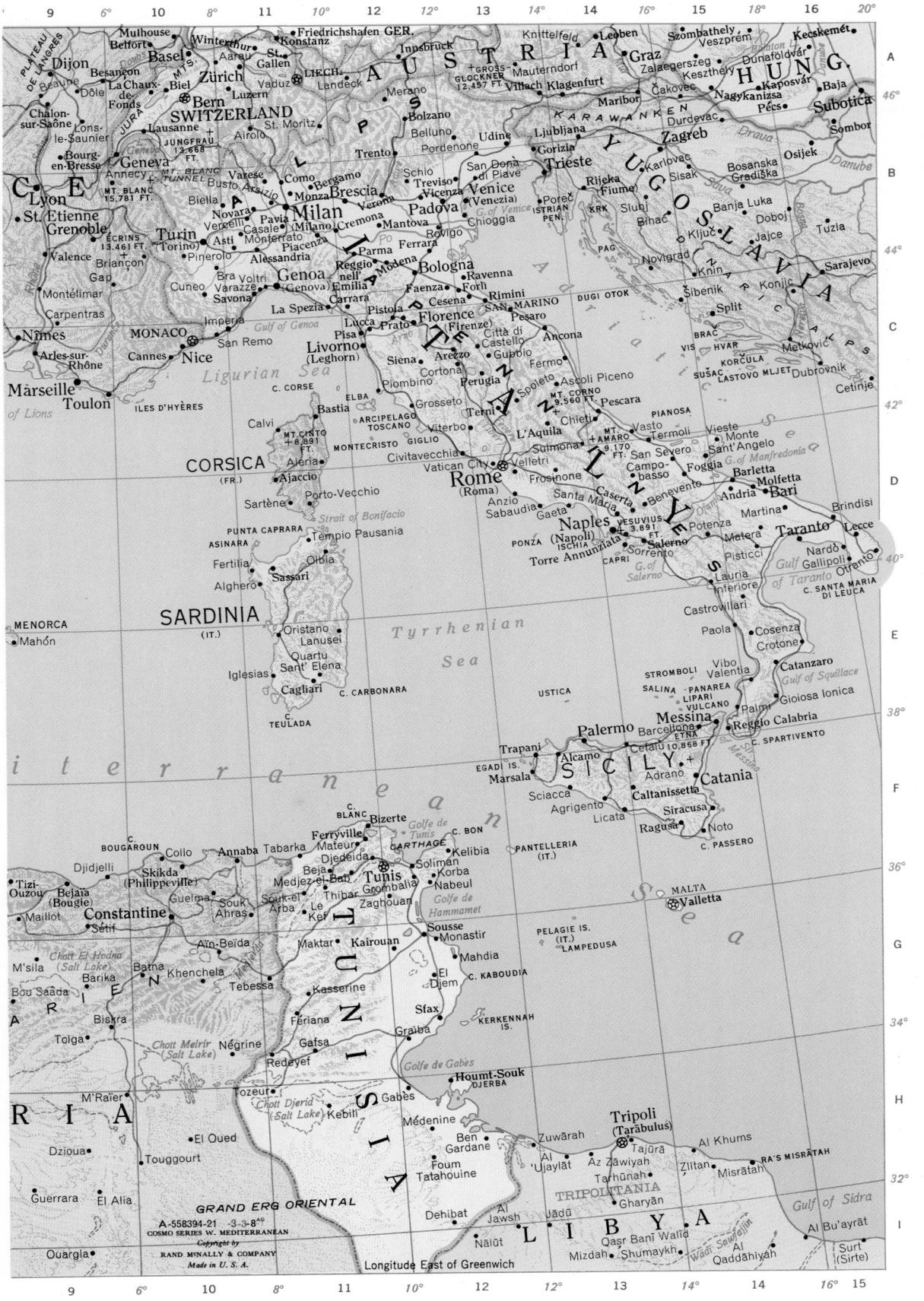

Hvar, isl C15
Ibiza, isl . . . . E 7
Ischia, isl D13
Istrian, pen B13
Júcar, riv . . . . E 6
Jungfrau, mtn A10
Jura, mts A10
Kaboudia, cape G12
Karawanken, mts A14
Kerkennah, is G12
Korčula, isl C15
Krk, isl B14
Langres, plat . . . . A 9
Lastovo Mljet, isl C15
Ligurian, sea C10
Lions, gulf . . . . C 8
Lipari, isl E14
Loire, riv . . . . A 6
Lot, riv . . . . B 7
Mallorca, isl . . . . E 8
Malta, isl F14
Manfredonia, gulf D15
Massif Central, mts . . . . . B 8
Mediterranean, sea . . . . . E 7
Melrir, salt lake G10
Menorca, isl . . . . D 9
Messina, strait F14
Michichaco, cape . . . . C 5
Misrâtah, cape H14
Mljet, isl C15
Montecristo, isl C12
Morena, mts . . . . E 4
Moulouya, riv . . . . H 5
Mur, riv A14
Nao, cape . . . . E 7
Neretva, riv C15
Noirmoutier, isl . . . . A 5
Ofanto, riv D14
Ortegal, cape . . . . C 3
Pag, isl B14
Palos, cape . . . . F 6
Panarea, isl E14
Pantelleria, isl F13
Passero, cape F14
Pelagie, is G13
Pianosa, isl C14
Po, riv B12
Ponza, isl D13
Pyrenees, mts . . . . C 6
Ré, isl . . . . A 6
Rhône, riv . . . . B 9
St. Vincent, cape . . . . F 2
Salerno, gulf D14
Salina, isl E14
Salinas, cape . . . . E 8
Santa Maria di Leuca,
    cape E16
Saône, riv . . . . A 9
Sardinia, isl D11
Sava, riv B15
Sebou, riv . . . . G 4
Sidra, gulf I14
Spartel, cape . . . . G 4
Spartivento, cape F15
Squillace, gulf E15
Stromboli, isl E14
Sušac, isl C15
Taranto, gulf D15
Tejo (Tagus), riv . . . . E 3
Ténès, cape . . . . F 7
Teulada, cape E11
Tevere (Tiber), riv C13
The Landes, heath . . . . . . B 6
Tortosa, cape . . . . D 7
Toscano, is C12
Tres Forcas, cape . . . . G 5
Tunis, gulf F12
Tyrrhenian, sea E12
Ustica, isl E13
Vendee, hills . . . . A 6
Venice, gulf B13
Vesuvius, mtn D14
Vienne, riv . . . . A 7
Vis, isl C15
Vulcano, isl E14

Lambert Conformal Conic Projection

SCALE 1 : 8,000,000   1 Inch = 126 Statute Miles

NORWAY
Principal Cities

Pop.—Thousands

Pop.	City	Ref.
19	Ålesund	F 2
11	Arendal	H 3
5	Askim	p29
116	Bergen	G 1
13	Bodø	D 6
31	Drammen	H 4, p28
14	Fredrikstad	H 4, p28
8	Gjøvik	G 4
10	Halden	G 4
14	Hamar	G 4
27	Haugesund	H 1
14	Horten	H 4, p28
10	Kongsberg	H 3, p27
5	Kragerö	H 3
17	Kristiansund	F 2
11	Larvik	H 4, p28
6	Lillehammer	G 4
11	Lilleström	H 4, p29
21	Moss	H 4, p28
13	Narvik	C 7
8	Notodden	H 3
5	Odda	G 2
477	Oslo	H 4, p28
11	Porsgrunn	p27
6	Rjukan	H 3
7	Sandefjord	p28
13	Sarpsborg	p29
16	Skien	H 3, p27
53	Stavanger	H 1
12	Tönsberg	H 4, p28
12	Tromsö	C 8
59	Trondheim	F 4

SWEDEN
Principal Cities

Pop.—Thousands

Pop.	City	Ref.
18	Alingsås	I 5
13	Angelholm	I 5
16	Arvika	H 5
14	Boden	E 9
67	Borås	I 5
27	Borlänge	G 6
13	Enköping	H 7, t35
59	Eskilstuna	H 7, t34
16	Fagersta	G 6
14	Falköping	H 5
19	Falun	G 6
15	Finspång	u33
6	Gällivare	D 9
55	Gävle	G 7
405	Göteborg	I 4
39	Halmstad	I 5
77	Hälsingborg	I 5
17	Härnösand	F 8
14	Hässleholm	I 5
14	Huskvarna	I 6
51	Jönköping	I 6
36	Karlskoga	H 6
33	Karlskrona	I 6
43	Karlstad	H 5
19	Katrineholm	H 7, u34
19	Kiruna	D 9
18	Köping	H 6, t33
26	Kristianstad	I 6
29	Landskrona	J 5
29	Lidingö	H 8, t36
17	Lidköping	H 5
65	Linköping	H 6
12	Ludvika	G 6
31	Luleå	E10
40	Lund	J 5
229	Malmö	J 5
27	Mölndal	I 5
27	Motala	H 6
18	Nässjö	I 6
2	Njurunda	F 7
91	Norrköping	H 7, u34
24	Nyköping	H 7, u34
75	Örebro	H 6, t33
13	Oskarshamn	I 7

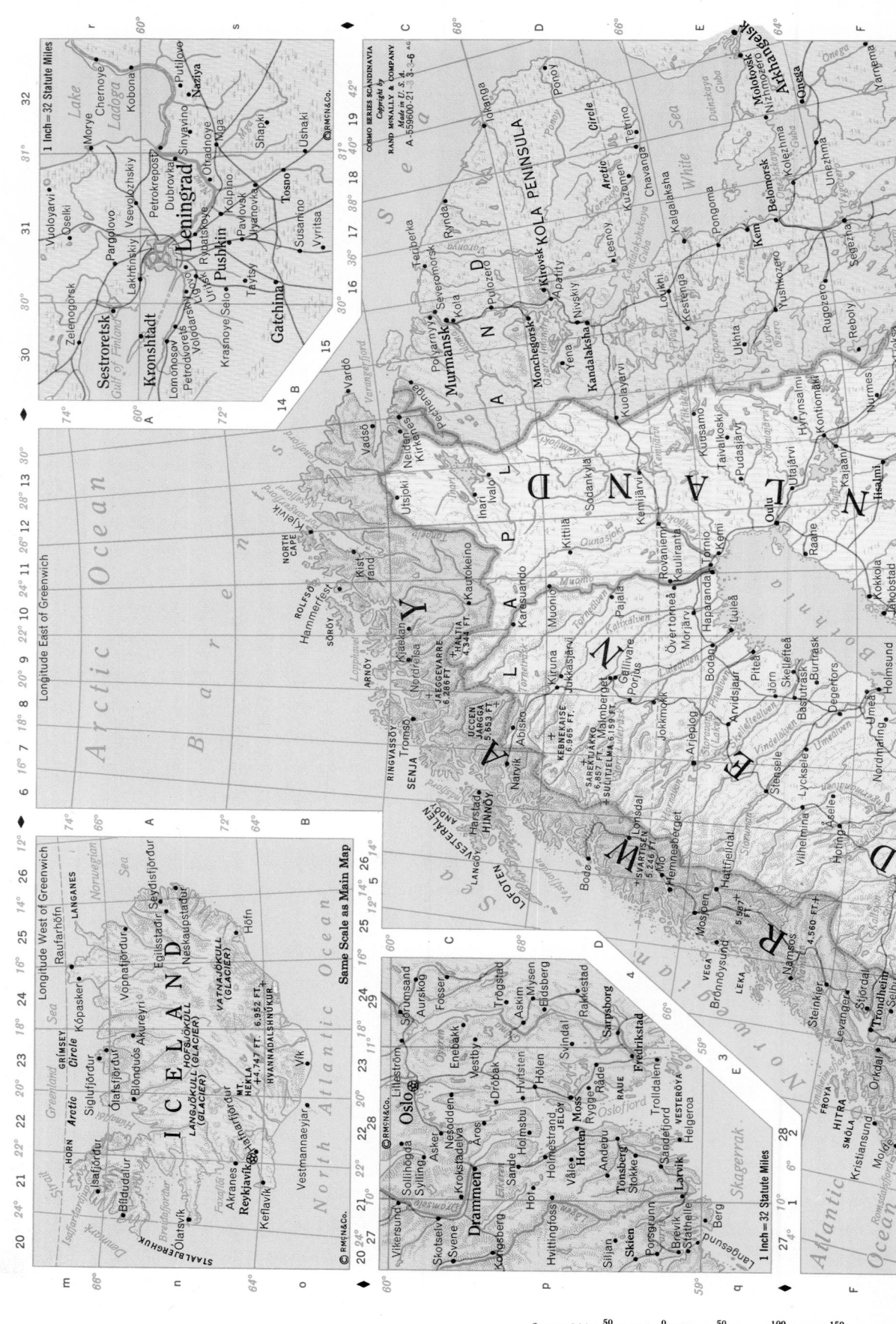

COSMO SERIES SCANDINAVIA
Copyright by
RAND McNALLY & COMPANY
Made in U.S.A.
A-559600-21-3-6
©RM'N&Co.

Statute Miles 50 0 50 100 150

Kilometers 50 0 50 100 200

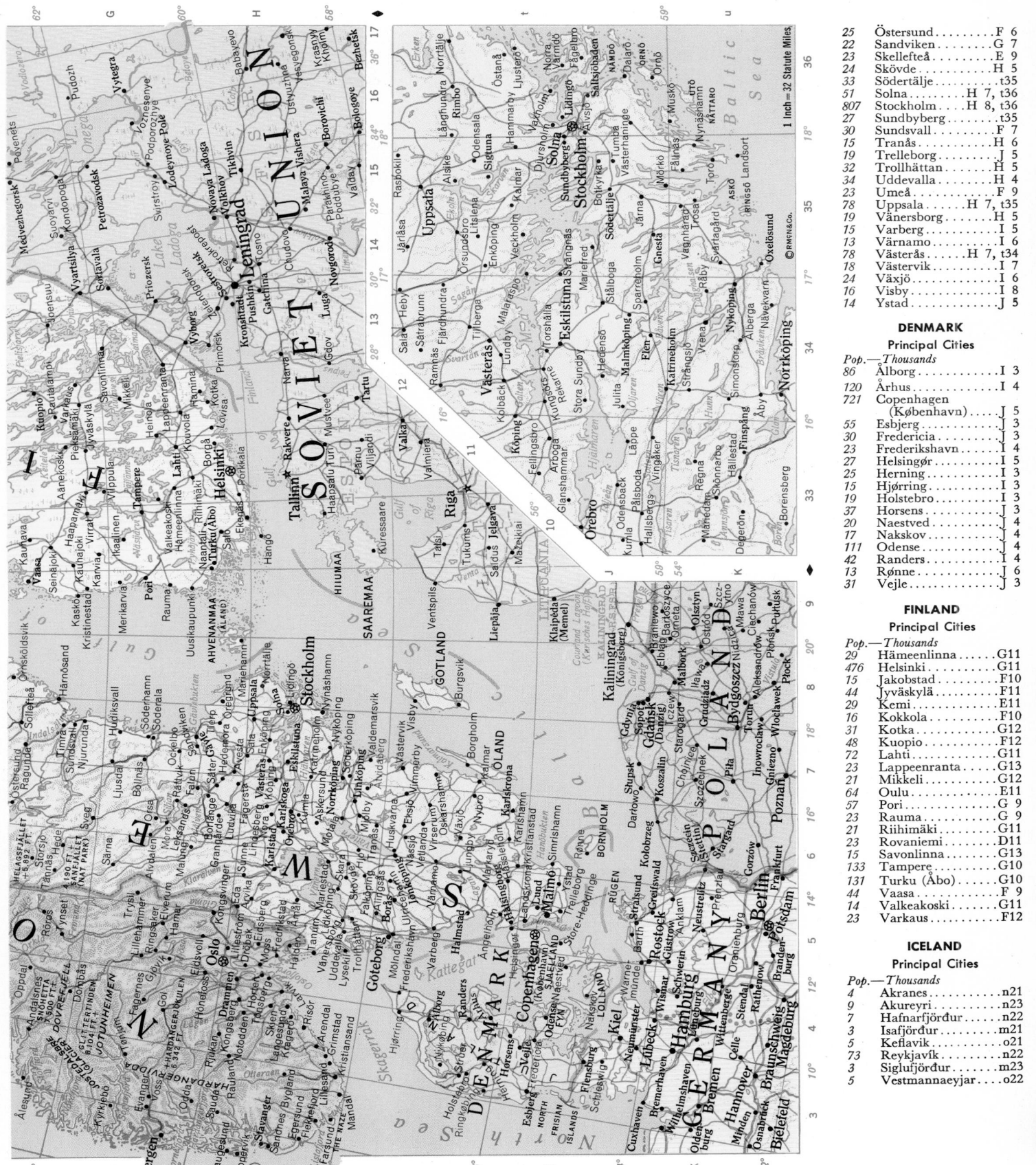

25	Östersund	F 6
22	Sandviken	G 7
23	Skellefteå	E 9
24	Skövde	H 5
33	Södertälje	t35
51	Solna	H 7, t36
807	Stockholm	H 8, t36
27	Sundbyberg	t35
30	Sundsvall	F 7
15	Tranås	H 6
19	Trelleborg	J 5
32	Trollhättan	H 5
34	Uddevalla	H 4
23	Umeå	F 9
78	Uppsala	H 7, t35
19	Vänersborg	H 5
15	Varberg	I 5
13	Värnamo	I 6
78	Västerås	H 7, t34
18	Västervik	I 7
24	Växjö	I 6
16	Visby	I 8
14	Ystad	J 5

DENMARK
Principal Cities
Pop.—Thousands

86	Ålborg	I 3
120	Århus	I 4
721	Copenhagen (København)	J 5
55	Esbjerg	J 3
30	Fredericia	J 3
23	Frederikshavn	I 4
27	Helsingør	I 5
25	Herning	I 3
15	Hjørring	I 3
19	Holstebro	I 3
37	Horsens	J 3
20	Naestved	J 4
17	Nakskov	J 4
111	Odense	J 4
42	Randers	I 4
13	Rønne	I 6
31	Vejle	J 3

FINLAND
Principal Cities
Pop.—Thousands

29	Hämeenlinna	G11
476	Helsinki	G11
15	Jakobstad	F10
44	Jyväskylä	F11
29	Kemi	E11
16	Kokkola	F10
31	Kotka	G12
48	Kuopio	F12
72	Lahti	G11
23	Lappeenranta	G13
21	Mikkeli	G12
64	Oulu	E11
57	Pori	G 9
23	Rauma	G 9
21	Riihimäki	G11
23	Rovaniemi	D11
15	Savonlinna	G13
133	Tampere	G10
131	Turku (Åbo)	G10
44	Vaasa	F 9
14	Valkeakoski	G11
23	Varkaus	F12

ICELAND
Principal Cities
Pop.—Thousands

4	Akranes	n21
9	Akureyri	n23
7	Hafnarfjörður	n22
3	Isafjörður	m21
5	Keflavik	o21
73	Reykjavík	n22
3	Siglufjörður	m23
5	Vestmannaeyjar	o22

Conic Projection

SCALE 1:8,000,000   1 Inch = 126 Statute Miles

GERMANY †
Principal Cities

Pop.—Thousands

178	Aachen	C 3
211	Augsburg	D 5
1,072	Berlin, East	†B 6
2,197	Berlin, West	B 6
170	Bielefeld	B 4
356	Bochum	C 3
141	Bonn	C 3
90	Brandenburg [an der Havel]	†B 6
235	Braunschweig	B 5
596	Bremen	B 4
146	Bremerhaven (Wesermünde)	B 4
139	Darmstadt	D 4
96	Dessau	†C 6
657	Dortmund	C 3
504	Dresden	†C 6
487	Duisburg	C 3
698	Düsseldorf	C 3
190	Erfurt	†C 5
725	Essen	C 3
97	Flensburg	A 4
683	Frankfurt [am Main]	C 4
154	Freiburg [im Briesgau]	D 3
96	Fürth	D 5
371	Gelsenkirchen	C 3
107	Gera	†C 6
89	Görlitz	†C 7
203	Hagen [in Westfalen]	C 3
274	Halle [an der Saale]	†C 6
1,854	Hamburg	B 5
553	Hannover	B 4
125	Heidelberg	D 4
99	Hildesheim	B 4
84	Jena	†C 5
86	Kaiserslautern	D 3
294	Karl-Marx-Stadt (Chemnitz)	†C 6
253	Karlsruhe	D 4
215	Kassel	C 4
270	Kiel	A 5
102	Koblenz	C 3
857	Köln (Cologne)	C 3
222	Krefeld	C 3
595	Leipzig	†C 6
240	Lübeck	B 5
176	Ludwigshafen [am Rhein]	D 4
265	Magdeburg	†B 5
144	Mainz	D 4
328	Mannheim	D 4
154	Mönchengladbach	C 3
191	Mülheim [an der Ruhr]	C 3
1,215	München (Munich)	D 5
196	Münster [in Westfalen]	C 3
472	Nürnberg (Nüremberg)	D 5
259	Oberhausen	C 3
117	Offenbach [am Main]	C 4
129	Oldenburg	B 4
143	Osnabrück	B 4
81	Plauen	†C 6
110	Potsdam	†B 6
128	Recklinghausen	C 3
125	Regensburg	D 6
134	Remscheid	C 3
179	Rostock	†A 6
134	Saarbrücken	D 3
117	Salzgitter	B 5
91	Schwerin	†B 5
175	Solingen	C 3
629	Stuttgart	D 4
86	Trier	D 3
93	Ulm	D 4
64	Weimar	†C 5
260	Wiesbaden	C 4
101	Wilhelmshaven	B 4
422	Wuppertal	C 3
122	Wurzburg	D 4
129	Zwickau	†C 6

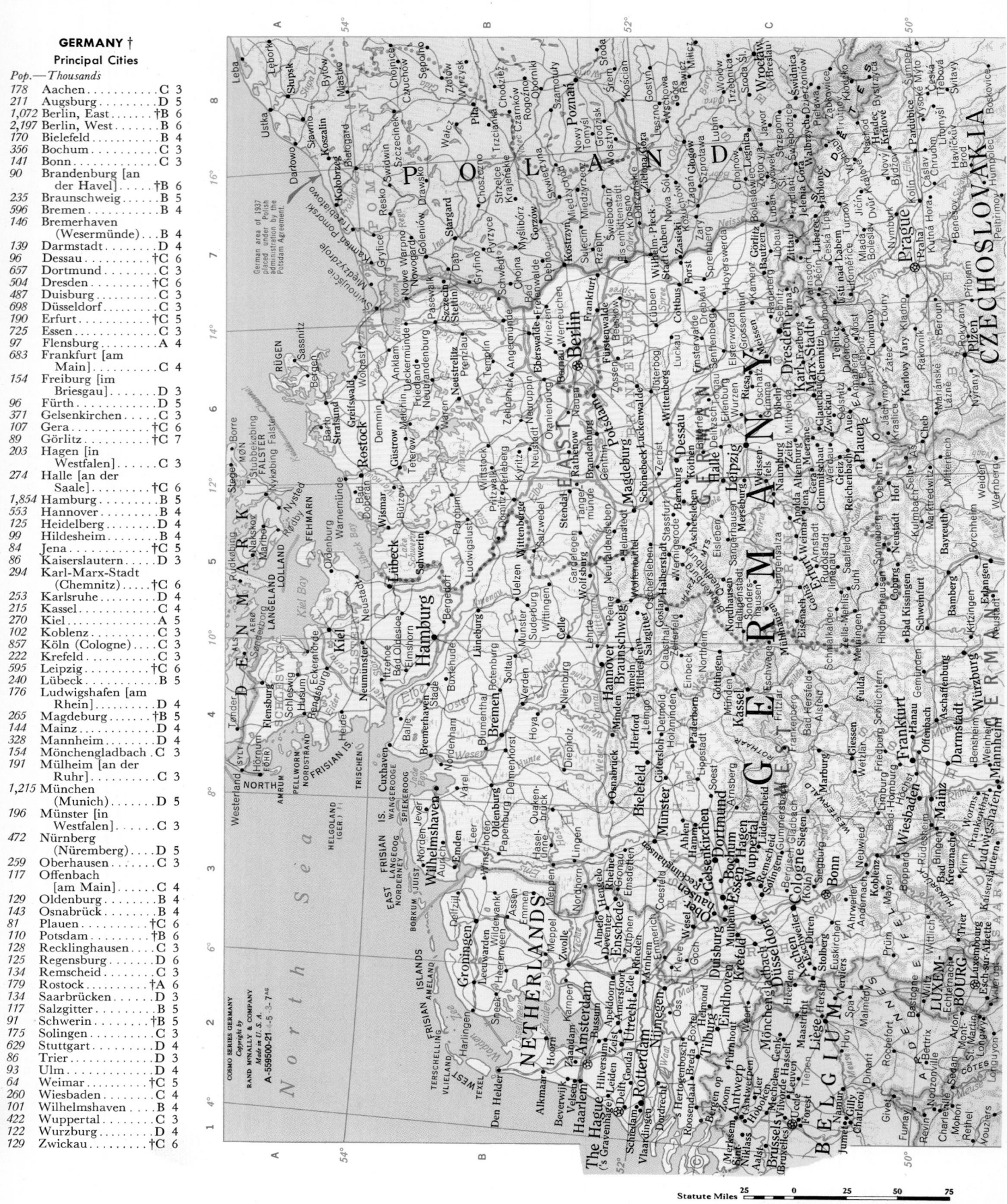

COSMO SERIES GERMANY
Copyright by
RAND McNALLY & COMPANY
Made in U.S.A.
A-559500-21 -5 -3 -7⁴⁰

Statute Miles   25   0   25   50   75

Kilometers   25   0   25   50   100

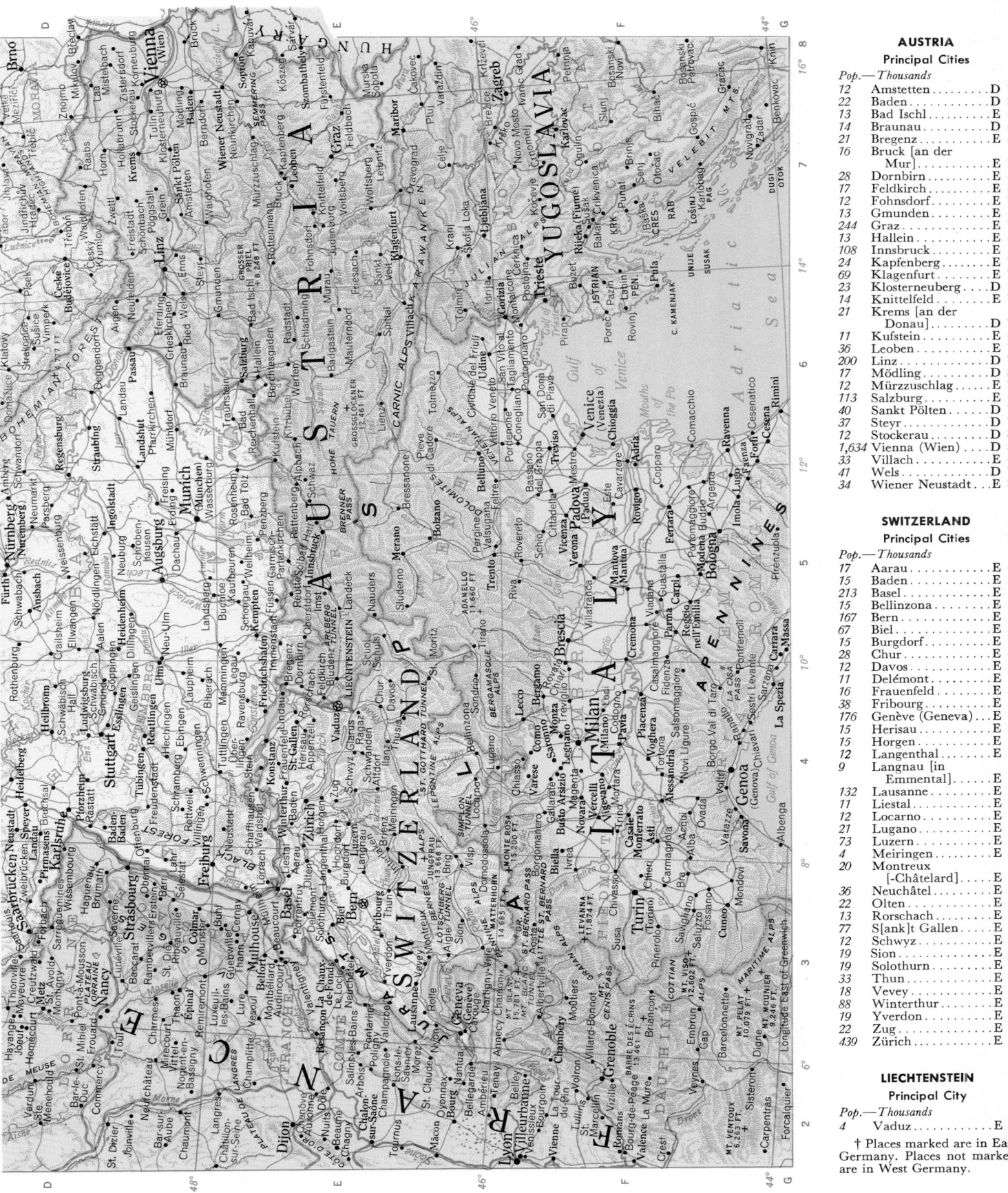

AUSTRIA
Principal Cities

Pop.—Thousands

12	Amstetten	D 7
22	Baden	D 8
13	Bad Ischl	E 6
14	Braunau	D 6
21	Bregenz	E 4
16	Bruck [an der Mur]	E 7
28	Dornbirn	E 4
17	Feldkirch	E 4
12	Fohnsdorf	E 7
13	Gmunden	E 6
244	Graz	E 7
13	Hallein	E 6
108	Innsbruck	E 5
24	Kapfenberg	E 7
69	Klagenfurt	E 7
23	Klosterneuberg	D 8
14	Knittelfeld	E 7
21	Krems [an der Donau]	D 7
11	Kufstein	E 6
36	Leoben	E 7
200	Linz	D 7
17	Mödling	D 8
12	Mürzzuschlag	E 7
113	Salzburg	E 6
40	Sankt Pölten	D 7
37	Steyr	D 7
12	Stockerau	D 8
1,634	Vienna (Wien)	D 8
33	Villach	E 6
41	Wels	D 7
34	Wiener Neustadt	E 8

SWITZERLAND
Principal Cities

Pop.—Thousands

17	Aarau	E 4
15	Baden	E 4
213	Basel	E 3
15	Bellinzona	E 4
167	Bern	E 3
67	Biel	E 3
15	Burgdorf	E 3
28	Chur	E 4
12	Davos	E 4
11	Delémont	E 3
16	Frauenfeld	E 4
38	Fribourg	E 3
176	Genève (Geneva)	E 3
15	Herisau	E 4
15	Horgen	E 4
12	Langenthal	E 3
9	Langnau [in Emmental]	E 3
132	Lausanne	E 3
11	Liestal	E 3
12	Locarno	E 4
21	Lugano	E 4
73	Luzern	E 4
4	Meiringen	E 4
20	Montreux [-Châtelard]	E 3
36	Neuchâtel	E 3
22	Olten	E 3
13	Rorschach	E 4
77	S[ank]t Gallen	E 4
12	Schwyz	E 4
19	Sion	E 3
19	Solothurn	E 3
33	Thun	E 3
18	Vevey	E 3
88	Winterthur	E 4
19	Yverdon	E 3
22	Zug	E 4
439	Zürich	E 4

LIECHTENSTEIN
Principal City

Pop.—Thousands

4	Vaduz	E 4

† Places marked are in East Germany. Places not marked are in West Germany.

ALBANIA
Principal Cities
Pop.— Thousands

30	Elbasan	E 5
40	Korcë	E 5
43	Shkodër	D 4
153	Tiranë	E 4

BULGARIA
Principal Cities
Pop.— Thousands

25	Asenovgrad	E 7
22	Blagoevgrad (Gorna Dzhumaya)	D 6
73	Burgas	D 8
15	Chirpan	D 7
34	Dimitrovgrad	D 7
38	Gabrovo	D 7
31	Kazanlŭk	D 7
39	Khaskovo	E 7
21	Kŭrdzhali	E 7
25	Kyustendil	D 6
23	Lom	D 7
18	Lovech	D 7
15	Nova Zagora	D 8
39	Pazardzhik	D 7
60	Pernik	D 6
16	Petrich	E 6
58	Pleven	D 7
185	Plovdiv	D 7
18	Razgrad	D 8
110	Ruse	D 7
17	Samokov	D 6
42	Shumen	D 8
20	Silistra	C 8
46	Sliven	D 8
695	Sofia (Sofiya)	D 6
25	Stanke Dimitrov (Dupnitsa)	D 6
55	Stara Zagora	D 7
18	Svishtov	D 7
43	Tolbukhin (Dobrich)	D 8
25	Tŭrnovo	D 7
145	Varna (Stalin)	D 8
24	Vidin	C 6
27	Vratsa	D 6
42	Yambol	D 8

HUNGARY
Principal Cities
Pop.— Thousands

30	Baja	B 4
43	Békéscsaba	B 5
1,900	Budapest	B 4
30	Cegléd	B 4
140	Debrecen	B 5
31	Dunaujváros	B 4
39	Eger	B 5
25	Esztergom	B 4
29	Gyöngyös	B 4
75	Győr (Raab)	B 3
27	Hajdúböszörmény	B 5
40	Hódmezővásárhely	B 5
47	Kaposvár	B 4
49	Kecskemét	B 4
23	Kiskunfélegyháza	B 4
30	Makó	B 5
160	Miskolc	A 5
34	Nagykanizsa	B 3
42	Nyíregyháza	B 5
27	Orosháza	B 5
34	Ózd	A 5
25	Pápa	B 3
127	Pécs	B 4
32	Salgótarján	A 4
43	Sopron	B 3
107	Szeged	B 5
61	Székesfehérvár	B 4
25	Szentes	B 5
51	Szolnok	B 5
58	Szombathely	B 3
57	Tatabánya	B 4
25	Vác	B 4
25	Veszprém	B 3

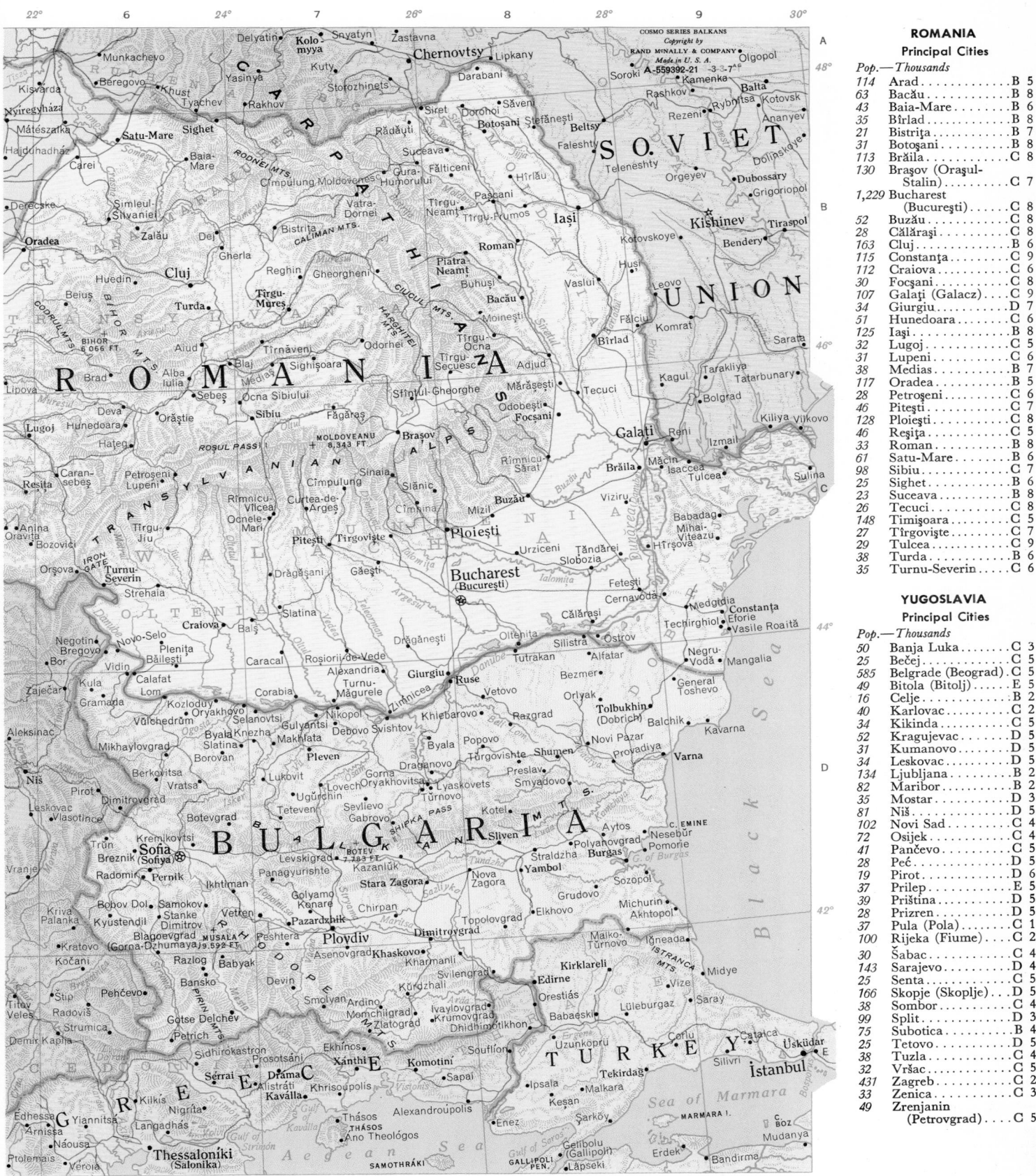

ROMANIA
Principal Cities
Pop.—Thousands

Pop.	City	Ref.
114	Arad	B 5
63	Bacău	B 8
43	Baia-Mare	B 6
35	Bîrlad	B 8
21	Bistrița	B 7
31	Botoșani	B 8
113	Brăila	C 8
130	Brașov (Orașul-Stalin)	C 7
1,229	Bucharest (București)	C 8
52	Buzău	C 8
28	Călărași	C 8
163	Cluj	B 6
115	Constanța	C 9
112	Craiova	C 6
30	Focșani	C 8
107	Galați (Galacz)	C 9
34	Giurgiu	D 7
51	Hunedoara	C 6
125	Iași	B 8
32	Lugoj	C 5
31	Lupeni	C 6
38	Medias	B 7
117	Oradea	B 5
28	Petroșeni	C 6
46	Pitești	C 7
128	Ploiești	C 5
46	Reșița	C 5
33	Roman	B 8
61	Satu-Mare	B 6
98	Sibiu	C 7
25	Sighet	B 6
23	Suceava	B 8
26	Tecuci	C 8
148	Timișoara	C 5
27	Tîrgoviște	C 7
29	Tulcea	C 9
38	Turda	B 6
35	Turnu-Severin	C 6

YUGOSLAVIA
Principal Cities
Pop.—Thousands

Pop.	City	Ref.
50	Banja Luka	C 3
25	Bečej	C 5
585	Belgrade (Beograd)	C 5
49	Bitola (Bitolj)	E 5
16	Celje	B 2
40	Karlovac	C 2
34	Kikinda	C 5
52	Kragujevac	D 5
31	Kumanovo	D 5
34	Leskovac	D 5
134	Ljubljana	B 2
82	Maribor	B 2
35	Mostar	D 3
81	Niš	D 5
102	Novi Sad	C 4
72	Osijek	C 4
41	Pančevo	C 5
28	Peć	D 5
19	Pirot	D 6
37	Prilep	E 5
39	Priština	D 5
28	Prizren	D 5
37	Pula (Pola)	C 1
100	Rijeka (Fiume)	C 2
30	Šabac	C 4
143	Sarajevo	D 4
25	Senta	C 5
166	Skopje (Skoplje)	D 5
38	Sombor	C 4
99	Split	D 3
75	Subotica	B 4
25	Tetovo	D 5
38	Tuzla	C 4
32	Vršac	C 5
431	Zagreb	C 2
33	Zenica	C 3
49	Zrenjanin (Petrovgrad)	C 5

Conic Projection
SCALE 1:4,000,000   1 Inch = 63 Statute Miles

WESTERN SOVIET UNION
Principal Cities

Pop.—Thousands

32	Akhtyrka...........F10
66	Artemovsk.....G12, q21
64	Balashikha........D11
68	Balashov..........F14
18	Balta.............H 7
64	Baranovichi........E 5
72	Bataysk..........H12
92	Belgorod..........F11
73	Beltsy............H 6
57	Berdichev.........G 7
108	Bobruysk..........E 7
29	Borislav..........G 4
57	Borisoglebsk......F13
65	Borisov...........D 7
44	Borovichi.........B 9
82	Brest.............E 4
249	Bryansk..........E10
142	Cheboksary......C16
124	Cherepovets......B11
103	Cherkassy........G 9
113	Chernigov.........F 8
152	Chernovtsy........G 5
74	Daugavpils (Dvinsk)D 6
207	Dneprodzerzhinsk..G10
738	Dnepropetrovsk...G10
774	Donetsk.......H11, q20
180	Dzerzhinsk.......C14
105	Elektrostal.......n18
106	Engels...........F16
37	Gatchina..........B 8
199	Gomel............E 8
1,042	Gorki (Gorkiy)..C15
309	Gorlovka.....G12, q21
88	Grodno............E 4
59	Gus-Khrustalnyy...D13
368	Ivanovo..........C13
192	Kadiyevka....G12, q21
292	Kalinin..........C10
238	Kaliningrad (Königsberg)....D 3
157	Kaluga...........D11
40	Kamenets-Podolskiy.......G 6
62	Kamensk-Shakhtinskiy....G13
65	Kamyshin.........F15
247	Kaunas...........D 4
107	Kerch............I11
1,006	Kharkov.........G11
192	Kherson..........H 9
51	Khimki...........n17
72	Khmelnitskiy......G 6
1,248	Kiev............F 8
91	Kineshma.........C14
142	Kirovograd.......G 9
254	Kishinev.........H 7
105	Klaipēda (Memel).D 3
60	Klin.............C11
42	Klintsy..........E 9
125	Kolomna....D12, n18
110	Kommunarsk .G12, q21
56	Konotop..........F 9
94	Konstantinovka....q20
193	Kostroma........C13
105	Kovrov...........C13
126	Kramatorsk...G11, q20
368	Krasnodar.......I12
98	Krasnyy Luch....q21
40	Krasnyy Sulin.....H13
100	Kremenchug.......G 9
448	Krivoy Rog......H 9
40	Kronshtadt........B 7
59	Kropotkin........I13
233	Kursk...........F11
64	Kuznetsk........E16
3,180	Leningrad.......B 8
77	Liepāja..........C 3
205	Lipetsk..........E12
314	Lugansk.....G12, q22
69	Lutsk............F 5
469	Lvov.............G 5
100	Lyubertsy........n17
381	Makeyevka...G11, q20
104	Melitopol........H10
85	Michurinsk.......E13
644	Minsk............E 6

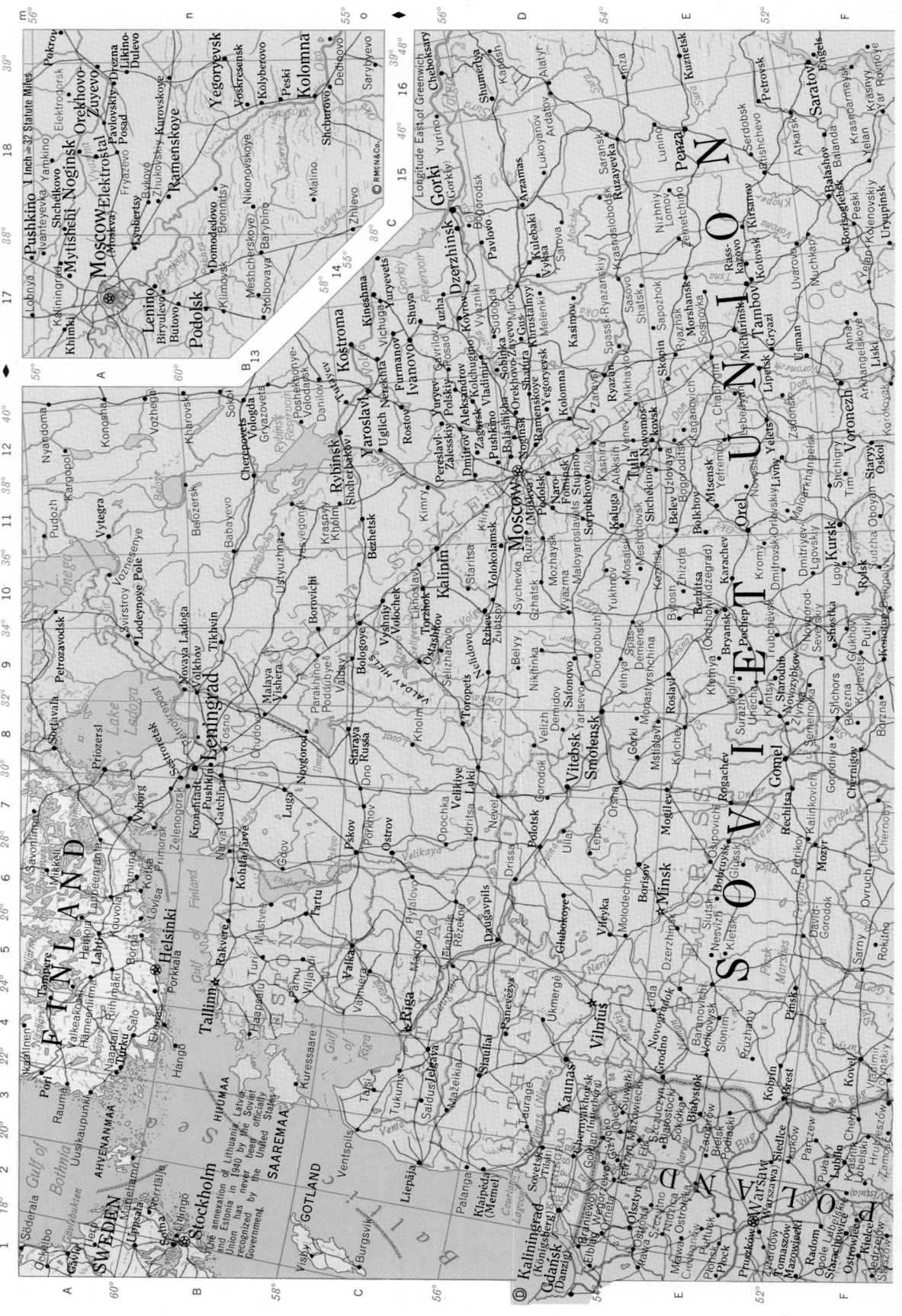

Statute Miles 50 0 50 100 150
Kilometers 50 0 50 100 200

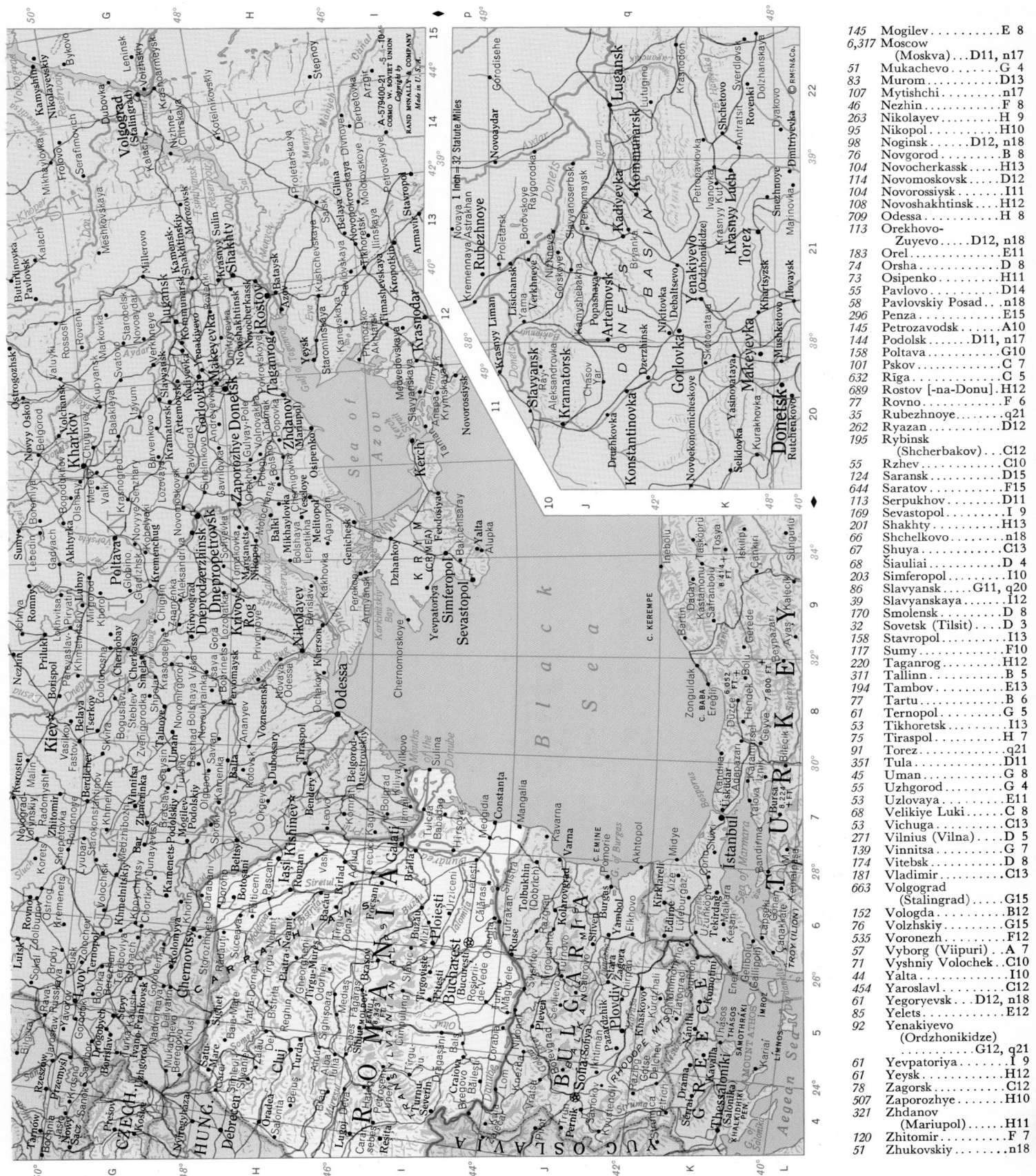

145	Mogilev	E 8
6,317	Moscow (Moskva)	D11, n17
51	Mukachevo	G 4
83	Murom	D13
107	Mytishchi	n17
46	Nezhin	F 8
263	Nikolayev	H 9
95	Nikopol	H10
98	Noginsk	D12, n18
76	Novgorod	B 8
104	Novocherkassk	H13
114	Novomoskovsk	D12
104	Novorossiysk	I11
108	Novoshakhtinsk	H12
709	Odessa	H 8
113	Orekhovo-Zuyevo	D12, n18
183	Orel	E11
74	Orsha	D 8
73	Osipenko	H11
55	Pavlovo	D14
58	Pavlovskiy Posad	n18
296	Penza	E15
145	Petrozavodsk	A10
144	Podolsk	D11, n17
158	Poltava	G10
101	Pskov	C 7
632	Riga	C 5
689	Rostov [-na-Donu]	H12
77	Rovno	F 6
35	Rubezhnoye	q21
262	Ryazan	D12
195	Rybinsk (Shcherbakov)	C12
55	Rzhev	C10
124	Saransk	D15
644	Saratov	F15
113	Serpukhov	D11
169	Sevastopol	I 9
201	Shakhty	H13
66	Shchelkovo	n18
67	Shuya	C13
68	Šiauliai	D 4
203	Simferopol	I10
86	Slavyansk	G11, q20
39	Slavyanskaya	I12
170	Smolensk	D 8
32	Sovetsk (Tilsit)	D 3
158	Stavropol	I13
117	Sumy	F10
220	Taganrog	H12
311	Tallinn	B 5
194	Tambov	E13
77	Tartu	B 6
61	Ternopol	G 5
53	Tikhoretsk	I13
75	Tiraspol	H 7
91	Torez	q21
351	Tula	D11
45	Uman	G 7
55	Uzhgorod	G 4
53	Uzlovaya	E11
68	Velikiye Luki	C 8
53	Vichuga	C13
271	Vilnius (Vilna)	D 5
139	Vinnitsa	G 7
174	Vitebsk	D 8
181	Vladimir	C13
663	Volgograd (Stalingrad)	G15
152	Vologda	B12
76	Volzhskiy	G15
535	Voronezh	F12
57	Vyborg (Viipuri)	A 7
71	Vyshniy Volochek	C10
44	Yalta	I10
454	Yaroslavl	C12
61	Yegoryevsk	D12, n18
85	Yelets	E12
92	Yenakiyevo (Ordzhonikidze)	G12, q21
61	Yevpatoriya	I 9
61	Yeysk	H12
78	Zagorsk	C12
507	Zaporozhye	H10
321	Zhdanov (Mariupol)	H11
120	Zhitomir	F 7
51	Zhukovskiy	n18

Conic Projection

SCALE 1:8,000,000   1 Inch = 126 Statute Miles

FRANCE
Principal Cities

Pop.—Thousands

Pop.	City	Ref.
68	Aix -èn-Provence	F 6
41	Alès	E 6
105	Amiens	C 5
115	Angers	D 3
48	Angoulême	E 4
82	Argenteuil	C 5, g10
82	Asnières	C5 g10
71	Aubervilliers	g10
48	Aulnay-sous-Bois	g11
73	Avignon	F 6
48	Belfort	D 7
96	Besancon	D 7
250	Bordeaux	E 3
107	Boulogne-Billancourt	C 5, g 9
49	Boulogne [-sur-Mer]	B 4
61	Bourges	D 5
136	Brest	C 1
40	Brive [-la-Gaillarde]	E 4
91	Caen	C 3
70	Calais	B 4
58	Cannes	F 7
41	Carcassonne	F 5
42	Châlons-sur-Marne	C 6
44	Chalon-sur-Saône	D 6
58	Champigny-sur-Marne	g11
45	Châteauroux	D 4
37	Cherbourg	C 3
48	Clamart	g10
128	Clermont-Ferrand	E 5
56	Clichy	g10
52	Colmar	C 7
77	Colombes	g10
59	Courbevoie	g10
136	Dijon	D 6
48	Douai	B 5
66	Drancy	g10
37	Fontenay [-sous-Bois]	g10
157	Grenoble	E 6
52	Issy	g10
53	Ivry-sur-Seine	g10
67	La Rochelle	D 3
184	Le Havre	C 4
132	Le Mans	C 4
43	Lens	B 5
62	Levallois Perret	g10
193	Lille	B 5
118	Limoges	E 4
61	Lorient	D 2
529	Lyon	E 6
51	Maisons-Alfort	g10
778	Marseille	F 6
103	Metz	C 7
55	Montluçon	D 5
119	Montpellier	F 5
92	Montreuil [-sous-Bois]	C5 g10
45	Montrouge	g10
109	Mulhouse	D 7
129	Nancy	C 7
83	Nanterre	g 9
240	Nantes	D 3
73	Neuilly -sur-Seine	g11
293	Nice	F 7
100	Nîmes	F 6
84	Orléans	D 4
46	Pantin	g10
2,790	Paris	C 5, g10
60	Pau	F 3
39	Périgueux	E 4
83	Perpignan	F 5
62	Poitiers	D 4
40	Puteaux	g 9
134	Reims	C 6
152	Rennes	C 3
52	Roanne	D 6
113	Roubaix	B 5
121	Rouen	C 4
43	St. Brieuc	C 2
94	St. Denis	C 5, g10
201	St. Étienne	E 6

Statute Miles 25 0 25 50 75

Kilometers 25 0 25 50 100

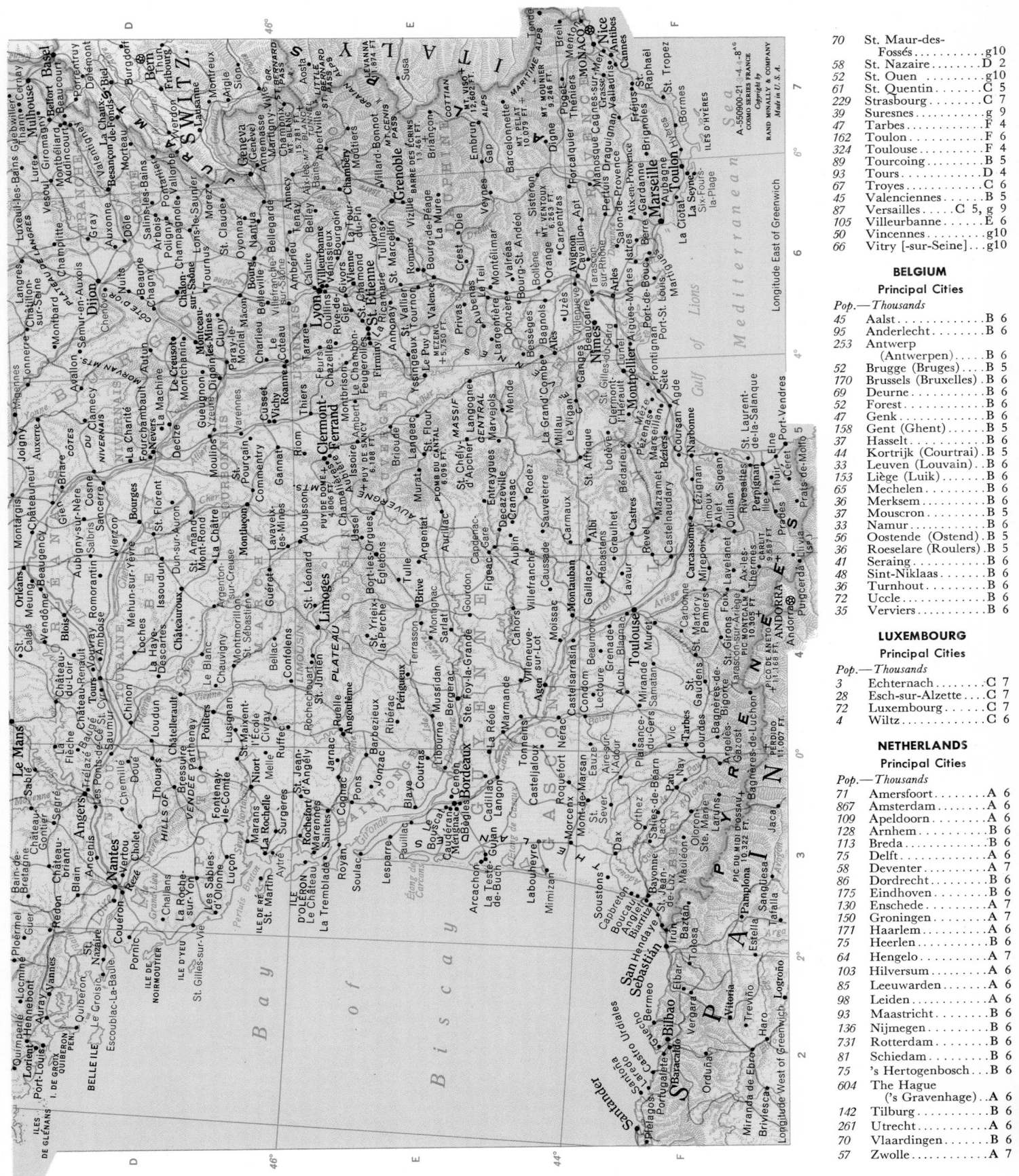

70	St. Maur-des-Fossés	g10
58	St. Nazaire	D 2
52	St. Ouen	g10
61	St. Quentin	C 5
229	Strasbourg	C 7
39	Suresnes	g 9
47	Tarbes	F 4
162	Toulon	F 6
324	Toulouse	F 4
89	Tourcoing	B 5
93	Tours	D 4
67	Troyes	C 6
45	Valenciennes	C 5
87	Versailles	C 5, g 9
105	Villeurbanne	E 6
50	Vincennes	g10
66	Vitry [-sur-Seine]	g10

BELGIUM

Principal Cities

Pop.—Thousands

45	Aalst	B 6
95	Anderlecht	B 6
253	Antwerp (Antwerpen)	B 6
52	Brugge (Bruges)	B 5
170	Brussels (Bruxelles)	B 6
69	Deurne	B 6
52	Forest	B 6
47	Genk	B 6
158	Gent (Ghent)	B 5
37	Hasselt	B 6
44	Kortrijk (Courtrai)	B 5
33	Leuven (Louvain)	B 6
153	Liège (Luik)	B 6
65	Mechelen	B 6
36	Merksem	B 6
37	Mouscron	B 5
33	Namur	B 6
56	Oostende (Ostend)	B 5
36	Roeselare (Roulers)	B 5
41	Seraing	B 6
48	Sint-Niklaas	B 6
36	Turnhout	B 6
72	Uccle	B 6
35	Verviers	B 6

LUXEMBOURG

Principal Cities

Pop.—Thousands

3	Echternach	C 7
28	Esch-sur-Alzette	C 7
72	Luxembourg	C 7
4	Wiltz	C 6

NETHERLANDS

Principal Cities

Pop.—Thousands

71	Amersfoort	A 6
867	Amsterdam	A 6
109	Apeldoorn	A 6
128	Arnhem	B 6
113	Breda	B 6
75	Delft	A 6
58	Deventer	A 7
86	Dordrecht	B 6
175	Eindhoven	B 6
130	Enschede	A 7
150	Groningen	A 7
171	Haarlem	A 6
75	Heerlen	B 6
64	Hengelo	A 7
103	Hilversum	A 6
85	Leeuwarden	A 6
98	Leiden	A 6
93	Maastricht	B 6
136	Nijmegen	B 6
731	Rotterdam	B 6
81	Schiedam	B 6
75	's Hertogenbosch	B 6
604	The Hague ('s Gravenhage)	A 6
142	Tilburg	B 6
261	Utrecht	A 6
70	Vlaardingen	B 6
57	Zwolle	A 7

Conic Projection

SCALE 1:4,000,000   1 Inch = 63 Statute Miles

ISRAEL
Principal Cities

Pop.—Thousands

Pop.	City	
28	Acre	g 5, B 3
15	Afula	B 3
52	Beersheba	h 5, C 2
11	Beit Shan	B 3
3	Binyamina	B 2
52	Bnei Braq	B 2
4	Daliyat el Karmil	B 3
7	Elath (Eilat)	E 2
7	El Yehūdiya	B 2
3	Er Rāma	B 3
8	Et Taiyiba	C 3
27	Hadera	g 5, B 2
191	Haifa	g 5, B 2
30	Herzliya	g 5, B 2
55	Holon	B 2
176	Jerusalem	h 5, C 3
16	Kfar Ata	B 3
19	Kfar Sava	B 2
21	Lod (Lydda)	h 5, C 2
28	Migdal Ashqelon	C 2
16	Nahariya	A 3
46	Nathanya	B 2
26	Nazareth	g 5, B 3
8	Pardess Hanna	B 2
59	Petah Tiqva	B 2
96	Ramat Gan	B 2
24	Ramle	C 2
30	Rehovot	C 2
30	Rishon le-Zion	C 2
12	Safad	g 5, B 3
8	Shfaram	B 3
330	Tel Aviv-Yafo	g 5, B 2
22	Tiberias	g 5, B 3
11	Tirat Carmel	B 2
8	Ummel Fahm	B 3
6	Yavne	C 2
2	Yavneel	B 3
4	Zikhron Ya'aqov	B 2

JORDAN
Principal Cities

Pop.—Thousands

Pop.	City	
5	'Ajlūn	B 3
9	Al'Aqabah (Aqaba)	k 5, E 3
7	Al Karak	h 5, C 3
38	Al Khalīl (Hebron)	h 5, C 3
225	'Ammān	h 5, C 3
10	Arīhā (Jericho)	C 3
16	As Salt	g 5, B 3
5	At Tafīlah	h 5, D 3
22	Bayt Lahm (Bethlehem)	h 5, C 3
45	Irbid	g 5, B 3
14	Janīn	B 3
60	Jerusalem	h 5, C 3
7	Ma'ān	h 5, D 3
11	Ma'dābā	C 3
46	Nābulus	g 5, B 3
15	Rām Allāh	C 3
21	Tūl Karm	B 3

LEBANON
Principal Cities

Pop.—Thousands

Pop.	City	
10	Baalbek	f 6
3	Batroun	f 5
400	Beirut (Beyrouth)	g 5
6	Hermel	f 6
3	Qana	A 3
20	Saida (Sidon)	g 5
115	Tarabulus [esh Sham] (Tripoli)	f 5
3	Tibnine	A 3
10	Tyre (Sur)	g 5, A 3
30	Zahle	g 5

PALESTINE (GAZA STRIP)
(Egyptian administration)
Principal Cities

Pop.—Thousands

Pop.	City	
100	Ghazzah (Gaza)	h 5, C 2
10	Khān Yūnis	h 5, C 2

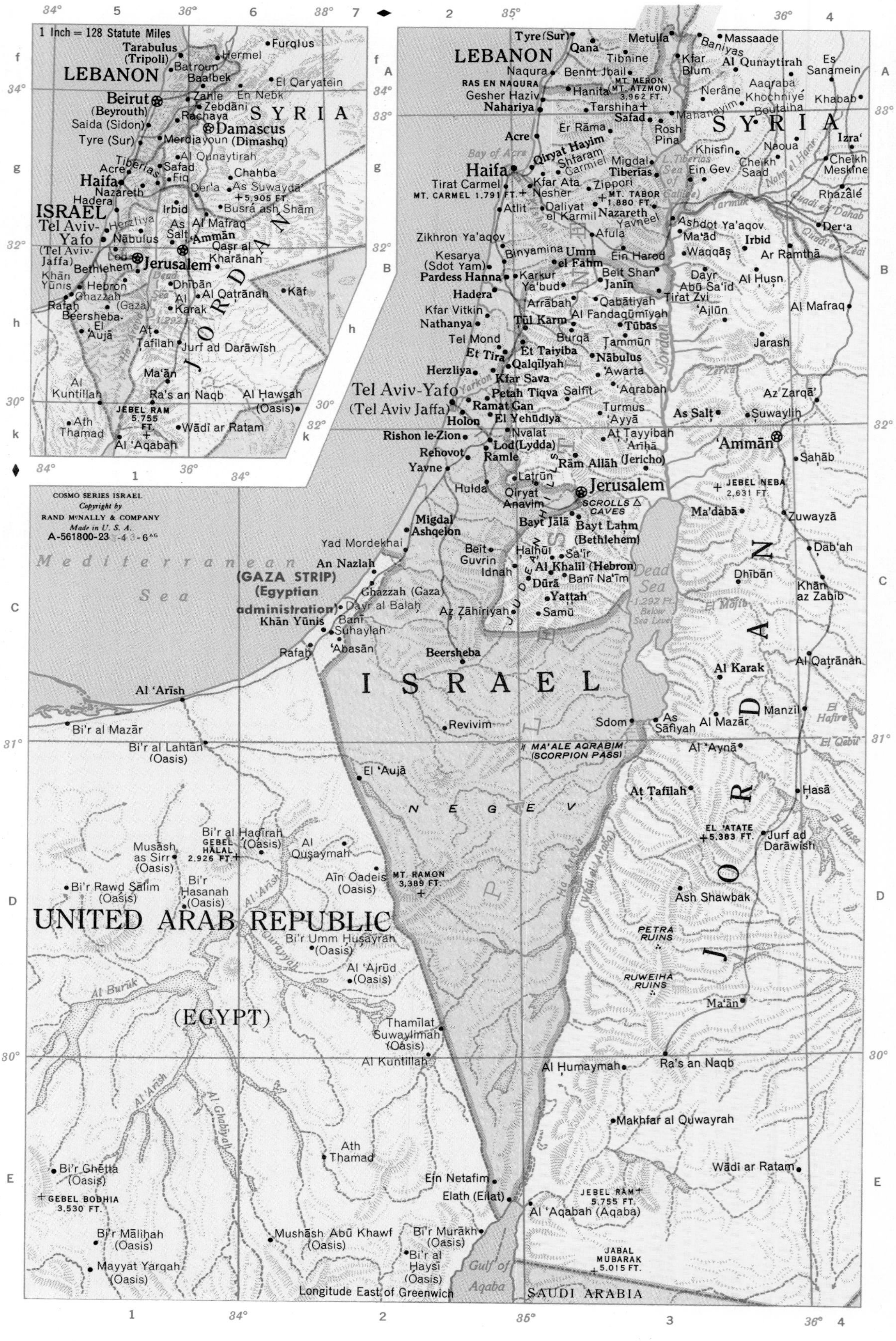

1 Inch = 128 Statute Miles

COSMO SERIES ISRAEL
Copyright by
RAND McNALLY & COMPANY
Made in U.S.A.
A-561800-23 -4-3-6 AG

Lambert Conformal Conic Projection
SCALE 1 : 2,000,000 1 Inch = 32 Statute Miles

Statute Miles
Kilometers

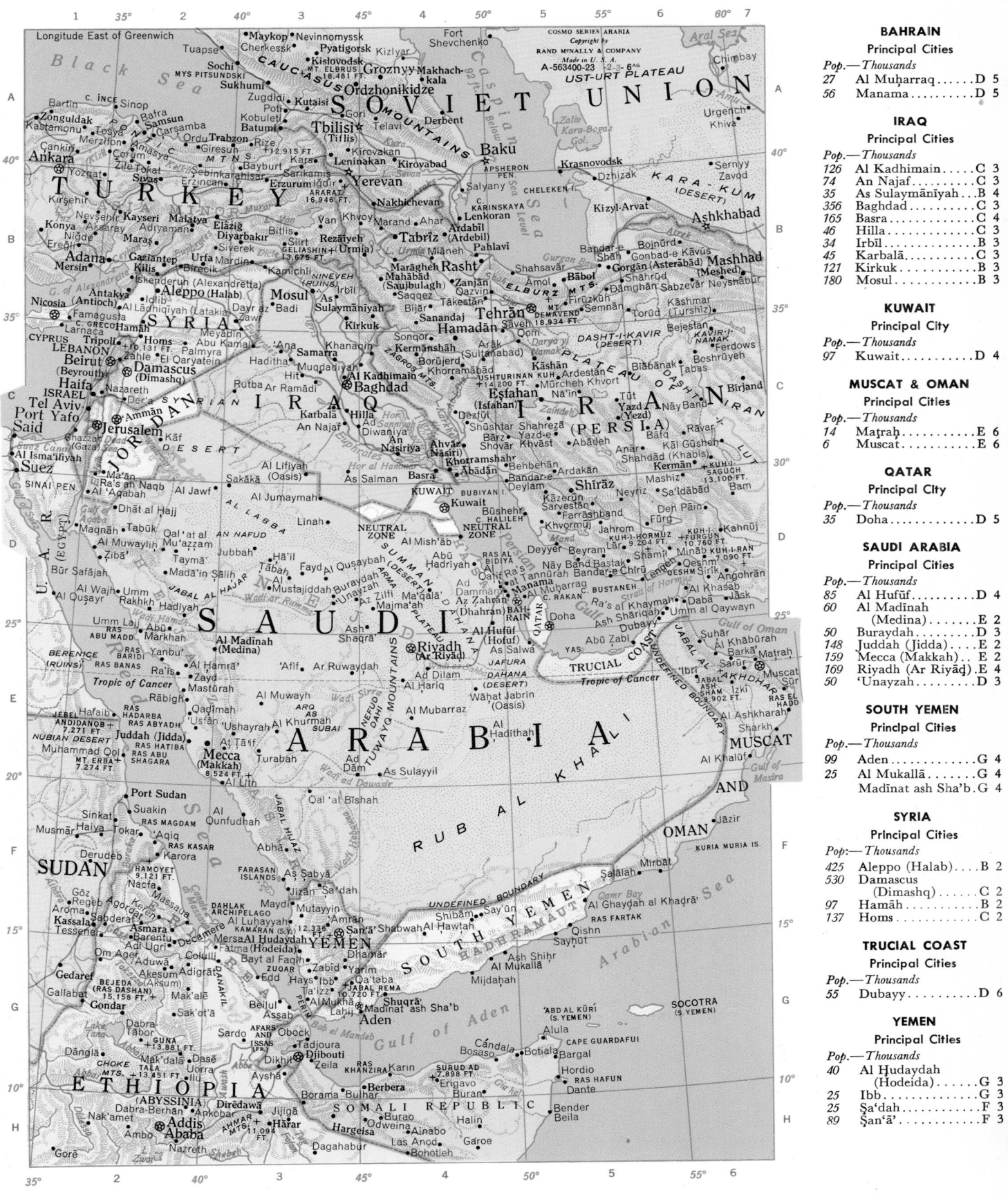

COSMO SERIES ARABIA
Copyright by
RAND McNALLY & COMPANY
Made in U.S.A.
A-563400-23 2-3- 6 AG

BAHRAIN
Principal Cities
Pop.—Thousands

27	Al Muḥarraq	D 5
56	Manama	D 5

IRAQ
Principal Cities
Pop.—Thousands

126	Al Kadhimain	C 3
74	An Najaf	C 3
35	As Sulaymānīyah	B 4
356	Baghdad	C 3
165	Basra	C 4
46	Hilla	C 3
34	Irbīl	B 3
45	Karbalā	C 3
121	Kirkuk	B 3
180	Mosul	B 3

KUWAIT
Principal City
Pop.—Thousands

97	Kuwait	D 4

MUSCAT & OMAN
Principal Cities
Pop.—Thousands

14	Maṭraḥ	E 6
6	Muscat	E 6

QATAR
Principal City
Pop.—Thousands

35	Doha	D 5

SAUDI ARABIA
Principal Cities
Pop.—Thousands

85	Al Hufūf	D 4
60	Al Madīnah (Medina)	E 2
50	Buraydah	D 3
148	Juddah (Jidda)	E 2
159	Mecca (Makkah)	E 2
169	Riyadh (Ar Riyāḍ)	E 4
50	'Unayzah	D 3

SOUTH YEMEN
Principal Cities
Pop.—Thousands

99	Aden	G 4
25	Al Mukallā	G 4
	Madīnat ash Sha'b	G 4

SYRIA
Principal Cities
Pop.—Thousands

425	Aleppo (Halab)	B 2
530	Damascus (Dimashq)	C 2
97	Hamāh	B 2
137	Homs	C 2

TRUCIAL COAST
Principal Cities
Pop.—Thousands

55	Dubayy	D 6

YEMEN
Principal Cities
Pop.—Thousands

40	Al Hudaydah (Hodeida)	G 3
25	Ibb	G 3
25	Ṣa'dah	F 3
89	Ṣan'ā'	F 3

Lambert Conformal Conic Projection
SCALE 1:18,500,000 1 Inch = 290 Statute Miles

Statute Miles
Kilometers

ASIA
⊗ Capitals †

Baghdad, Iraq . . . . F 7
Bangkok, Thai H13
Brunei, Bru I14
Colombo, Cey I10
Dacca, Pak G12
Hanoi, Viet., N G13
Islamabad, Pak F10
Kuala Lumpur, Mala I13
Macao, Macao G14
Madīnat ash Sha'b,
  S. Yem . . . . H 7
New Delhi, India G10
Peking, China F14
Phnom Penh, Camb H13
Pyŏngyang, Kor., N F15
Quezon City, Phil H15
Rangoon, Bur H12
Saigon, Viet., S H13
Seoul, Kor., S F15
Singapore, Singapore I13
Taipei, Taiwan G15
Tōkyō, Jap F16
Ulan Bator, Mong E13
Victoria, Hong Kong G14
Vientiane, Laos H13

† For capital cities of Indonesia, Portuguese Timor, Singapore and West Irian see map of Southeastern Asia; for Nepal and Sikkim see map of South Central Asia.

Physical Features

Aden, gulf . . . . H 7
Aldan, riv D16
Altai, mts E11
Altyn Tagh, mts F11
Amu Darya, riv . . . . E 9
Amur, riv D16
Anadyr, range C20
Andaman, is H12
Angara, riv D13
Arabian, sea . . . . H 9
Arafura, sea J16
Aral, sea . . . . E 8
Balkhash, lake E10
Banda, sea J15
Baykal, lake D13
Bengal, bay H11
Black, sea . . . . E 6
Bonin (Ogasawara), is . . . G17
Borneo, isl I14
Buru, isl J15
Caspian, sea . . . . E 8
Celebes, isl I15
Celebes, sea I15
Ceram, isl J15
Ceylon, isl I11
Chelyuskin, cape B14
Cherskiy, mts C16
Comorin, cape I10
Cyprus, isl . . . . F 6
Deccan, plat H10
Demavend, mtn . . . . F 8
Dzhugdzhur, mts D16
East China, sea F15
Eastern Ghats, mts H10
East Siberian, sea B19
Elburz, mts . . . . F 7
Euphrates, riv . . . . F 7
Everest, mtn G11
Formosa, strait G14
Franz Josef Land, is . . . . A 9
Ganges, riv G10
Gobi, des E13
Godavari, riv H10
Grand, canal F14
Greater Khingan, mts . . . E14
Gydan, mts C18
Hainan, isl H14
Himalaya, mts F10
Hindu Kush, mts . . . . . . F 9
Hokkaidō, isl E17
Honshū, isl F17
Hwang Ho, riv F14
Indian, des G10
Indus, riv . . . . G 9
Iran, plat . . . . F 8
Irrawaddy, riv H12
Irtysh, riv D10

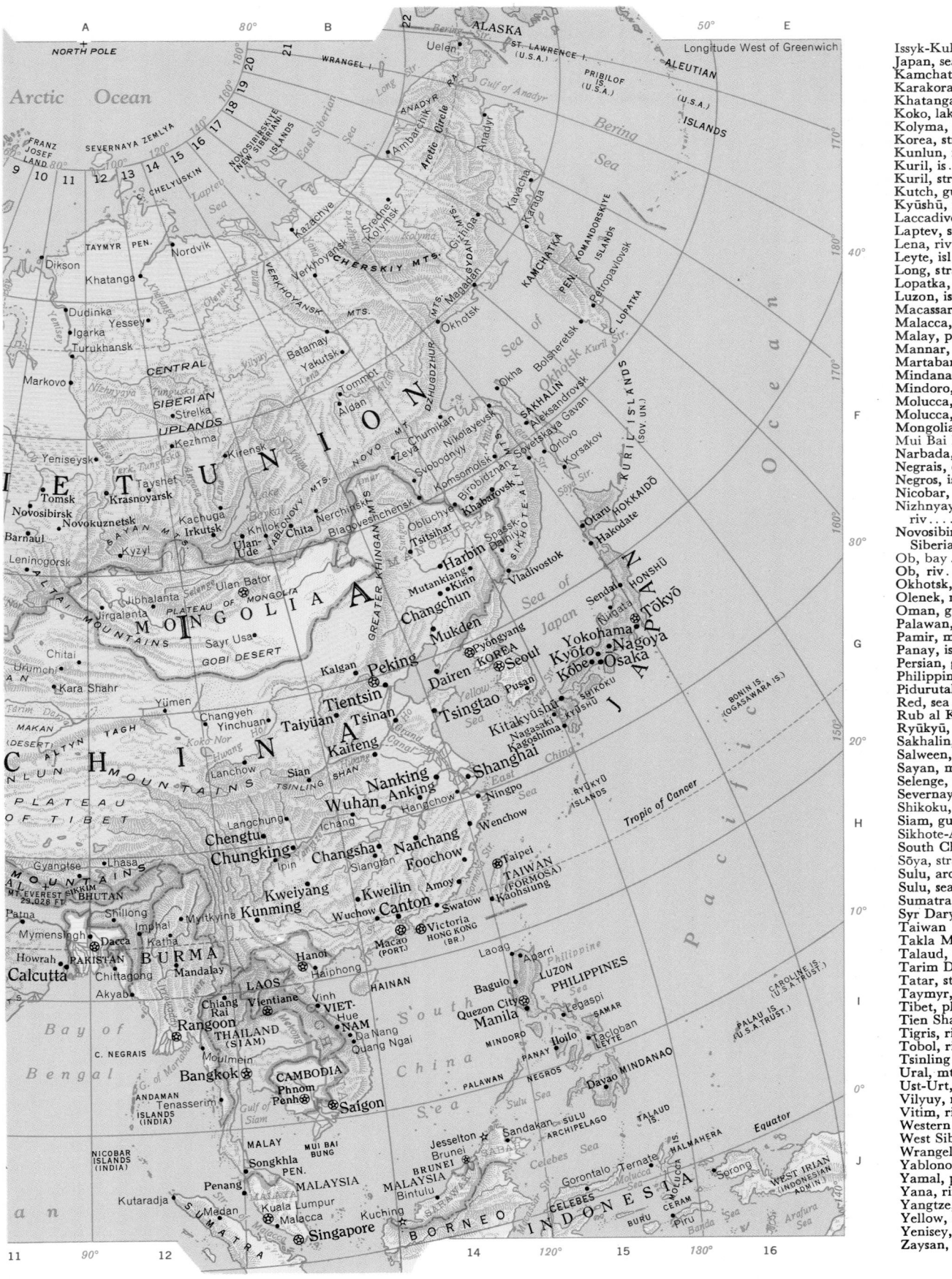

Issyk-Kul, lake E10
Japan, sea E16
Kamchatka, pen D18
Karakoram, range F10
Khatanga, riv B13
Koko, lake F12
Kolyma, riv C18
Korea, strait F15
Kunlun, mts F11
Kuril, is E18
Kuril, strait D18
Kutch, gulf . . . . G 9
Kyūshū, isl F16
Laccadive, is H10
Laptev, sea B15
Lena, riv C15
Leyte, isl H15
Long, strait B20
Lopatka, cape D18
Luzon, isl H15
Macassar, strait I14
Malacca, strait I13
Malay, pen I13
Mannar, gulf I10
Martaban, gulf H12
Mindanao, isl I15
Mindoro, isl H14
Molucca, is J15
Molucca, sea I15
Mongolia, plat E13
Mui Bai Bung, pt I13
Narbada, riv G10
Negrais, cape H12
Negros, isl H15
Nicobar, is I12
Nizhnyaya Tunguska,
  riv C12
Novosibirskiye (New
  Siberian), is B16
Ob, bay C10
Ob, riv D11
Okhotsk, sea D17
Olenek, riv C14
Oman, gulf . . . . G 8
Palawan, isl H14
Pamir, mts F10
Panay, isl H15
Persian, gulf . . . . G 8
Philippine, sea H15
Pidurutalagal, mtn I11
Red, sea . . . . G 6
Rub al Khali, des . . . . G 8
Ryūkyū, is G15
Sakhalin, isl D17
Salween, riv H12
Sayan, mts D12
Selenge, riv E13
Severnaya Zemlya, is A12
Shikoku, isl F16
Siam, gulf H13
Sikhote-Alin, mts E16
South China, sea H14
Sōya, strait E17
Sulu, arch I15
Sulu, sea I14
Sumatra, isl I12
Syr Darya, riv . . . . E 9
Taiwan (Formosa), isl . . . G15
Takla Makan, des F11
Talaud, is I15
Tarim Darya, riv E11
Tatar, strait D17
Taymyr, pen B12
Tibet, plat F11
Tien Shan, mts E10
Tigris, riv . . . . F 7
Tobol, riv . . . . D 9
Tsinling Shan, mts F13
Ural, mts . . . . D 8
Ust-Urt, plat . . . . E 8
Vilyuy, riv C14
Vitim, riv D14
Western Ghats, mts H10
West Siberian, lowland . . . D10
Wrangel, isl B21
Yablonovy, mts D14
Yamal, pen B10
Yana, riv C16
Yangtze, riv G13
Yellow, sea F15
Yenisey, riv C11
Zaysan, lake E11

Lambert Azimuthal Equal Area Projection

SCALE 1:42,000,000   1 Inch = 663 Statute Miles

SOUTH CENTRAL ASIA

AFGHANISTAN
Principal Cities

Pop.—Thousands

30	Andkhui	A 4
25	Baghlan	A 4
30	Ghazni	B 4
100	Herat	B 3
25	Jalalabad	B 5
275	Kabul	B 4
100	Kandahar	B 4
30	Maimana	A 3
70	Mazar-i-Sharif	A 4
30	Tāshkurghan	A 4

BHUTAN
Principal Cities

Pop.—Thousands

	Paro	C 8
	Punakha	C 8
	Thimbu	C 8

BURMA
Principal Cities

Pop.—Thousands

42	Akyab	D 9
78	Bassein	E 9
23	Bogale	E10
24	Chauk	D 9
62	Henzada	E10
27	Insein	E10
195	Mandalay	D10
25	Meiktila	D10
34	Mergui	F10
26	Monywa	D10
108	Moulmein	E10
20	Mudon	E10
37	Myingyan	D10
31	Pakokku	D10
47	Pegu	E10
37	Prome	E10
22	Pyinmana	E10
822	Rangoon	E10
18	Shwebo	D10
40	Tavoy	F10
38	Thaton	E10
32	Toungoo	E10
13	Ye	E10

CEYLON
Principal Cities

Pop.—Thousands

511	Colombo	G 6
56	Galle	G 7
77	Jaffna	G 7
57	Kandy	G 7
28	Matara	G 7

INDIA
Principal Cities

Pop.—Thousands

462	Agra	C 6
1,150	Ahmadabad (Ahmedabad)	D 5
231	Ajmer	C 5
185	Aligarh	C 6
412	Allahabad	C 7
376	Amritsar	B 5
471	Banaras	C 7
905	Bangalore	F 6
254	Bareilly	C 6
295	Baroda	D 5
171	Bhavnagar	D 5
185	Bhopal	D 6
151	Bikaner	C 5
4,152	Bombay	E 5
2,927	Calcutta	D 8
286	Coimbatore	F 6
146	Cuttack	D 8
2,062	Delhi	C 6
151	Gaya	D 7
180	Gorakhpur	C 7
187	Guntur	E 7
301	Gwalior	C 6
513	Howrah	D 8
171	Hubli	E 6
931	Hyderabad	E 6
395	Indore	D 6
295	Jabalpur	D 6
403	Jaipur	C 6
292	Jamshedpur	D 8

The boundary between India and Pakistan through the disputed state of Jammu and Kashmir follows the cease-fire line of 1949.

A-569200-21 6- 6- 6 ᴬᴳ
COSMO SERIES SO. ASIA
Copyright by
RAND McNALLY & COMPANY
Made in U.S.A.

Longitude East of Greenwich

Statute Miles 100   0   100   200   300
Kilometers 100   0   100   200   300   400

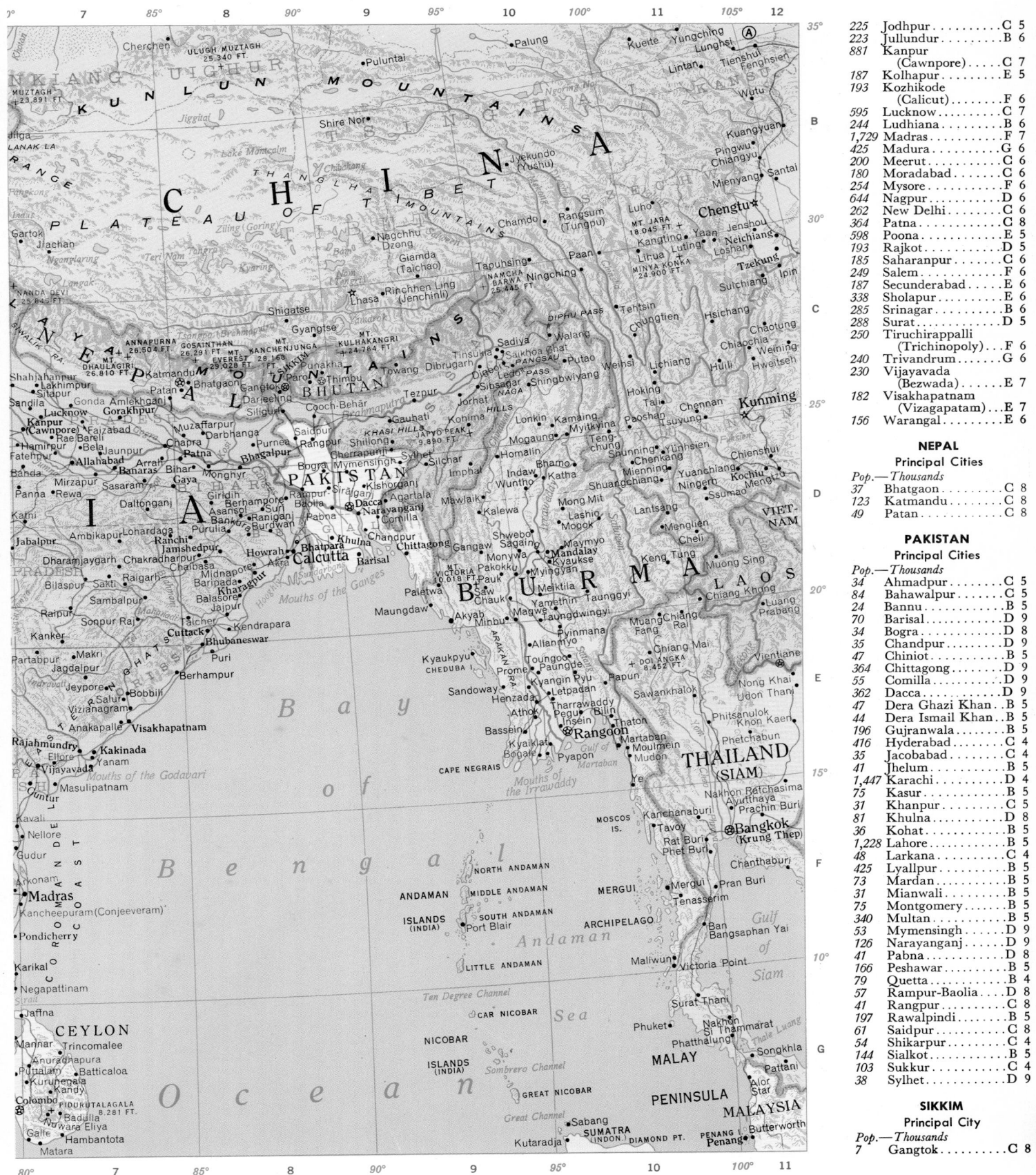

225	Jodhpur	C 5
223	Jullundur	B 6
881	Kanpur (Cawnpore)	C 7
187	Kolhapur	E 5
193	Kozhikode (Calicut)	F 6
595	Lucknow	C 7
244	Ludhiana	B 6
1,729	Madras	F 7
425	Madura	G 6
200	Meerut	C 6
180	Moradabad	C 6
254	Mysore	F 6
644	Nagpur	D 6
262	New Delhi	C 6
364	Patna	C 8
598	Poona	E 5
193	Rajkot	D 5
185	Saharanpur	C 6
249	Salem	F 6
187	Secunderabad	E 6
338	Sholapur	E 6
285	Srinagar	B 6
288	Surat	D 5
250	Tiruchirappalli (Trichinopoly)	F 6
240	Trivandrum	G 6
230	Vijayavada (Bezwada)	E 7
182	Visakhapatnam (Vizagapatam)	E 7
156	Warangal	E 6

NEPAL
Principal Cities

Pop.—Thousands
37	Bhatgaon	C 8
123	Katmandu	C 8
49	Patan	C 8

PAKISTAN
Principal Cities

Pop.—Thousands
34	Ahmadpur	C 5
84	Bahawalpur	C 5
24	Bannu	B 5
70	Barisal	D 9
34	Bogra	D 8
35	Chandpur	D 9
47	Chiniot	B 5
364	Chittagong	D 9
55	Comilla	D 9
362	Dacca	D 9
47	Dera Ghazi Khan	B 5
44	Dera Ismail Khan	B 5
196	Gujranwala	B 5
416	Hyderabad	C 4
35	Jacobabad	C 4
41	Jhelum	B 5
1,447	Karachi	D 4
75	Kasur	B 5
31	Khanpur	C 5
81	Khulna	D 9
36	Kohat	B 5
1,228	Lahore	B 5
48	Larkana	C 4
425	Lyallpur	B 5
73	Mardan	B 5
31	Mianwali	B 5
75	Montgomery	B 5
340	Multan	B 5
53	Mymensingh	D 9
126	Narayanganj	D 9
41	Pabna	D 9
166	Peshawar	B 5
79	Quetta	B 4
57	Rampur-Baolia	D 9
41	Rangpur	C 8
197	Rawalpindi	B 5
61	Saidpur	C 8
54	Shikarpur	C 4
144	Sialkot	B 5
103	Sukkur	C 4
38	Sylhet	D 9

SIKKIM
Principal City

Pop.—Thousands
7	Gangtok	C 8

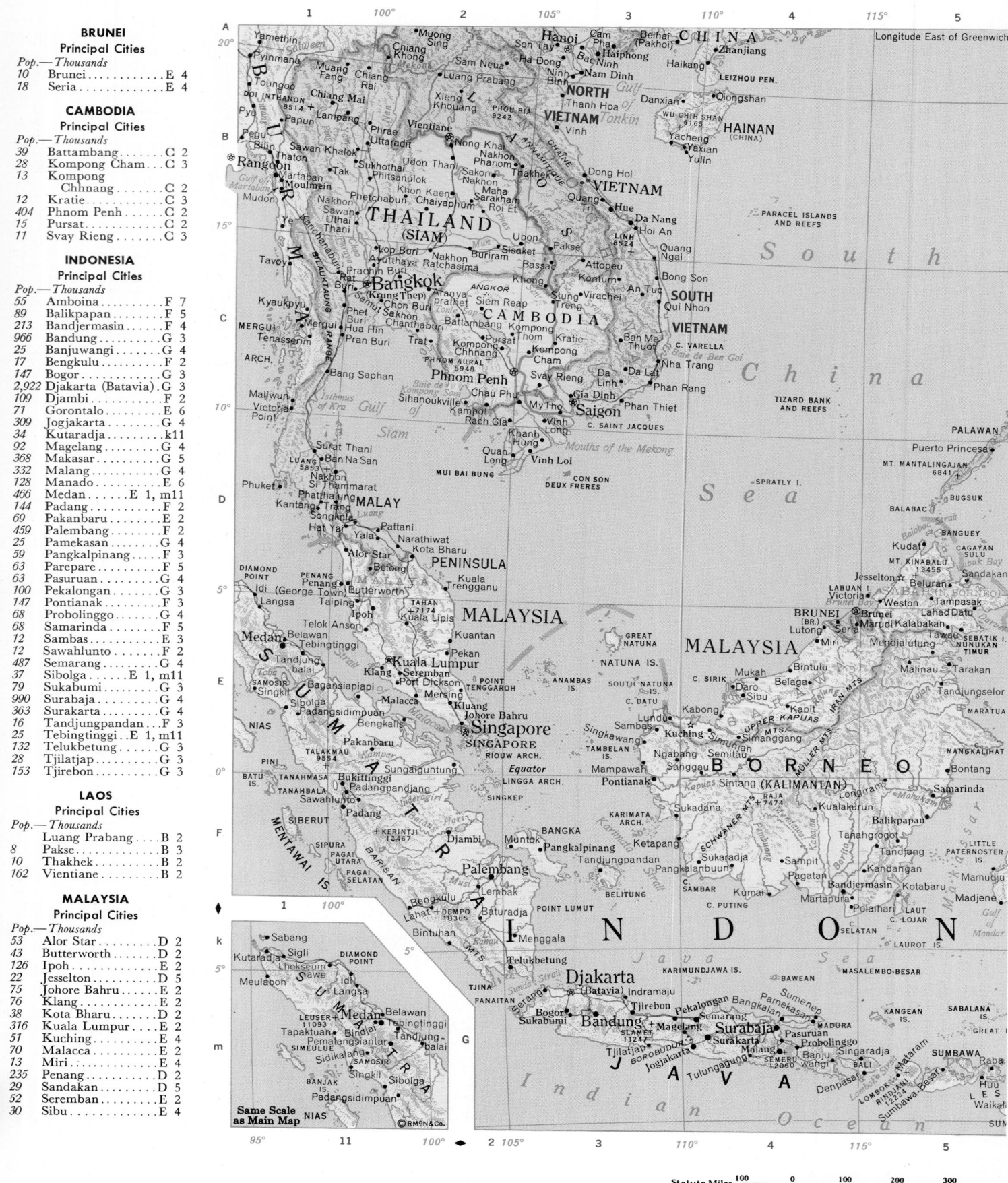

BRUNEI
Principal Cities

Pop.—Thousands

10	Brunei	E 4
18	Seria	E 4

CAMBODIA
Principal Cities

Pop.—Thousands

39	Battambang	C 2
28	Kompong Cham	C 3
13	Kompong Chhnang	C 2
12	Kratie	C 3
404	Phnom Penh	C 2
15	Pursat	C 2
11	Svay Rieng	C 3

INDONESIA
Principal Cities

Pop.—Thousands

55	Amboina	F 7
89	Balikpapan	F 5
213	Bandjermasin	F 4
966	Bandung	G 3
25	Banjuwangi	G 4
17	Bengkulu	F 2
147	Bogor	G 3
2,922	Djakarta (Batavia)	G 3
109	Djambi	F 2
71	Gorontalo	E 6
309	Jogjakarta	G 4
34	Kutaradja	k11
92	Magelang	G 4
368	Makasar	G 5
332	Malang	G 4
128	Manado	E 6
466	Medan	E 1, m11
144	Padang	F 2
69	Pakanbaru	E 2
459	Palembang	F 2
25	Pamekasan	G 4
59	Pangkalpinang	F 3
63	Parepare	F 5
63	Pasuruan	G 4
100	Pekalongan	G 3
147	Pontianak	F 3
68	Probolinggo	G 4
68	Samarinda	F 5
12	Sambas	E 3
12	Sawahlunto	F 2
487	Semarang	G 3
37	Sibolga	E 1, m11
79	Sukabumi	G 3
990	Surabaja	G 4
363	Surakarta	G 4
16	Tandjungpandan	F 3
25	Tebingtinggi	E 1, m11
132	Telukbetung	G 3
28	Tjilatjap	G 3
153	Tjirebon	G 3

LAOS
Principal Cities

Pop.—Thousands

	Luang Prabang	B 2
8	Pakse	B 3
10	Thakhek	B 2
162	Vientiane	B 2

MALAYSIA
Principal Cities

Pop.—Thousands

53	Alor Star	D 2
43	Butterworth	D 2
126	Ipoh	E 2
22	Jesselton	D 5
75	Johore Bahru	E 2
76	Klang	E 2
38	Kota Bharu	D 2
316	Kuala Lumpur	E 2
51	Kuching	E 4
70	Malacca	E 2
13	Miri	E 4
235	Penang	D 2
29	Sandakan	D 5
52	Seremban	E 2
30	Sibu	E 4

Longitude East of Greenwich

Same Scale as Main Map

©RMN&Co.

Statute Miles
Kilometers

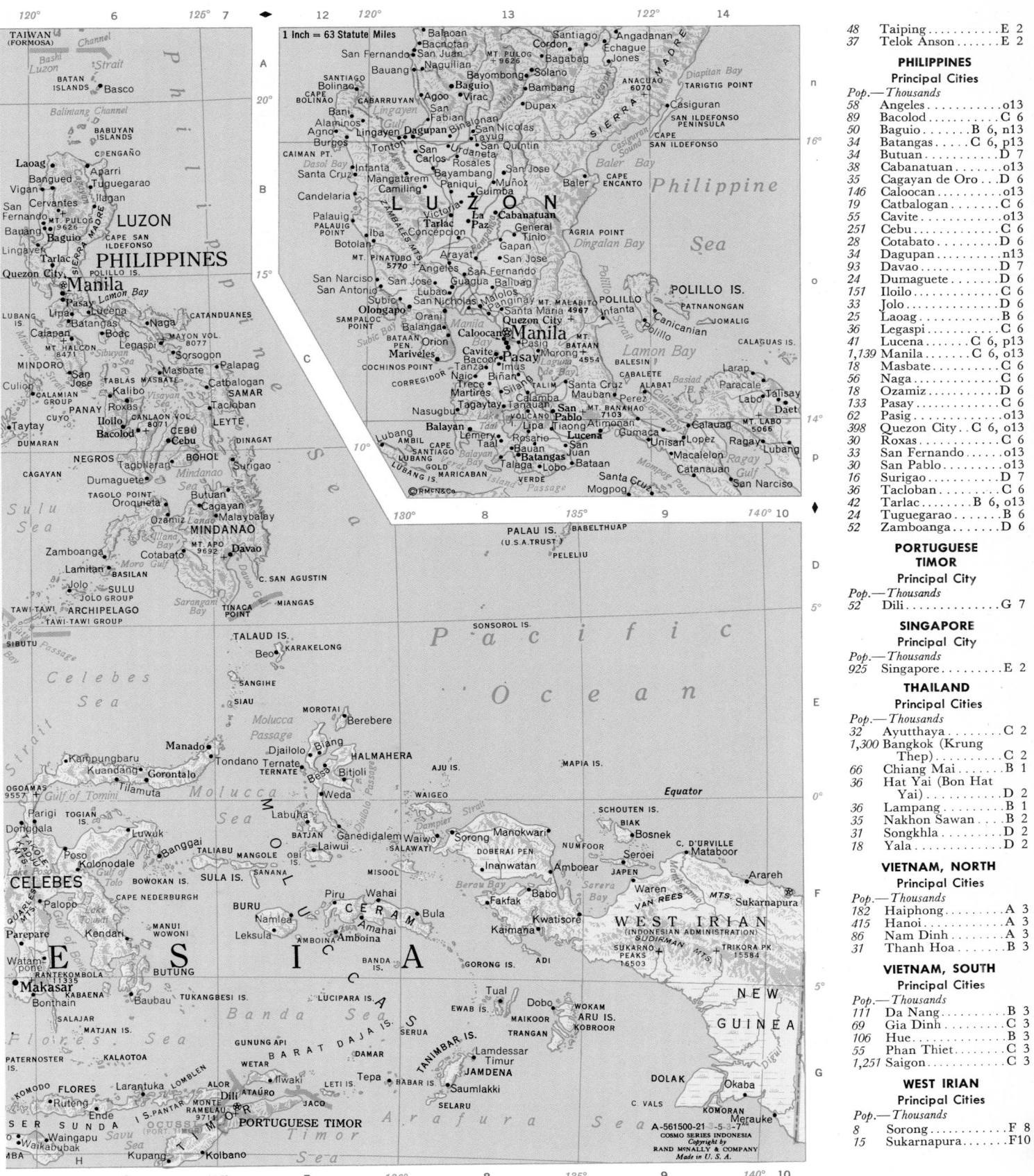

| 48 | Taiping | E 2 |
| 37 | Telok Anson | E 2 |

PHILIPPINES
Principal Cities

Pop.—Thousands

58	Angeles	o13
89	Bacolod	C 6
50	Baguio	B 6, n13
34	Batangas	C 6, p13
34	Butuan	D 7
38	Cabanatuan	o13
35	Cagayan de Oro	D 6
146	Caloocan	o13
19	Catbalogan	C 6
55	Cavite	o13
251	Cebu	C 6
28	Cotabato	D 6
34	Dagupan	n13
93	Davao	D 7
24	Dumaguete	D 6
151	Iloilo	C 6
33	Jolo	D 6
25	Laoag	B 6
36	Legaspi	C 6
41	Lucena	C 6, p13
1,139	Manila	C 6, o13
18	Masbate	C 6
56	Naga	C 6
18	Ozamiz	D 6
133	Pasay	C 6
62	Pasig	o13
398	Quezon City	C 6, o13
30	Roxas	C 6
33	San Fernando	o13
30	San Pablo	o13
16	Surigao	D 7
36	Tacloban	C 6
42	Tarlac	B 6, o13
24	Tuguegarao	B 6
52	Zamboanga	D 6

PORTUGUESE TIMOR
Principal City

Pop.—Thousands

| 52 | Dili | G 7 |

SINGAPORE
Principal City

Pop.—Thousands

| 925 | Singapore | E 2 |

THAILAND
Principal Cities

Pop.—Thousands

32	Ayutthaya	C 2
1,300	Bangkok (Krung Thep)	C 2
66	Chiang Mai	B 1
36	Hat Yai (Bon Hat Yai)	D 2
36	Lampang	B 1
35	Nakhon Sawan	B 2
31	Songkhla	D 2
18	Yala	D 2

VIETNAM, NORTH
Principal Cities

Pop.—Thousands

182	Haiphong	A 3
415	Hanoi	A 3
86	Nam Dinh	A 3
31	Thanh Hoa	B 3

VIETNAM, SOUTH
Principal Cities

Pop.—Thousands

111	Da Nang	B 3
69	Gia Dinh	C 3
106	Hue	B 3
55	Phan Thiet	C 3
1,251	Saigon	C 3

WEST IRIAN
Principal Cities

Pop.—Thousands

| 8 | Sorong | F 8 |
| 15 | Sukarnapura | F10 |

Polyconic Projection
SCALE 1:16,000,000 1 Inch = 252 Statute Miles

CHINA
Principal Cities

Pop.—Thousands

Pop.	City	Ref.
224	Amoy	G 8
805	Anshan	C 9
360	Antung	C 9
1,840	Canton	G 7
297	Changchow	E 8
975	Changchun (Hsinking)	C10
703	Changsha	F 7
166	Chankiang	G 7
766	Chengchow	E 7
1,107	Chengtu	E 5
352	Chinchow	C 9
208	Chinkiang	E 8
1,800	Chungking	F 6
950	Dairen (Talien)	D 9
616	Foochow	F 8
985	Fushun	C 9
189	Fusin	C 9
784	Hangchow	E 9
1,814	Harbin	B10
235	Hengyang	F 7
304	Hofei	E 8
314	Huhehot (Kweisui)	C 7
178	Ipin	F 5
299	Kaifeng	E 7
229	Kalgan (Changkiakow)	C 7
146	Kiamusze	B11
568	Kirin (Chilin)	C10
160	Kochiu	G 5
880	Kunming	F 5
145	Kweilin	F 7
504	Kweiyang	F 6
699	Lanchow	D 5
171	Loyang	E 7
159	Luichow	G 6
2,411	Mukden (Shenyang)	C 9
151	Mutankiang	C10
508	Nanchang	F 8
165	Nanchung	E 6
1,419	Nanking	E 8
264	Nanning	G 6
190	Neichiang	F 5
238	Ningpo (Ninghsien)	F 9
265	Paoting (Tsingyüan)	D 8
400	Paotow	C 7
3,500	Peking (Peiping)	D 8
253	Pengpu	E 8
449	Penki	C 9
6,900	Shanghai	E 9
1,310	Sian (Hsian)	E 6
184	Siangtan	F 7
171	Sinsiang	D 7
663	Soochow	E 9
676	Süchow	E 8
280	Swatow	G 8
1,020	Taiyüan	D 7
229	Tatung	C 7
2,850	Tientsin	D 8
862	Tsinan (Chinan)	D 8
1,121	Tsingtao	D 9
668	Tsitsihar	B 9
291	Tzekung	F 5
275	Urumchi	C 2
149	Weifang	D 8
45	Weihai	D 9
202	Wenchow	F 9
2,146	Wuhan	E 7
242	Wuhu	E 8
613	Wusih	E 9

MONGOLIA
Principal Cities

Pop.—Thousands

Pop.	City	Ref.
11	Choibalsan	B 7
5	Jibhalanta (Uliassutai)	B 4
5	Öndör Haan (Chechenhan)	B 7
195	Ulan Bator (Urga)	B 6

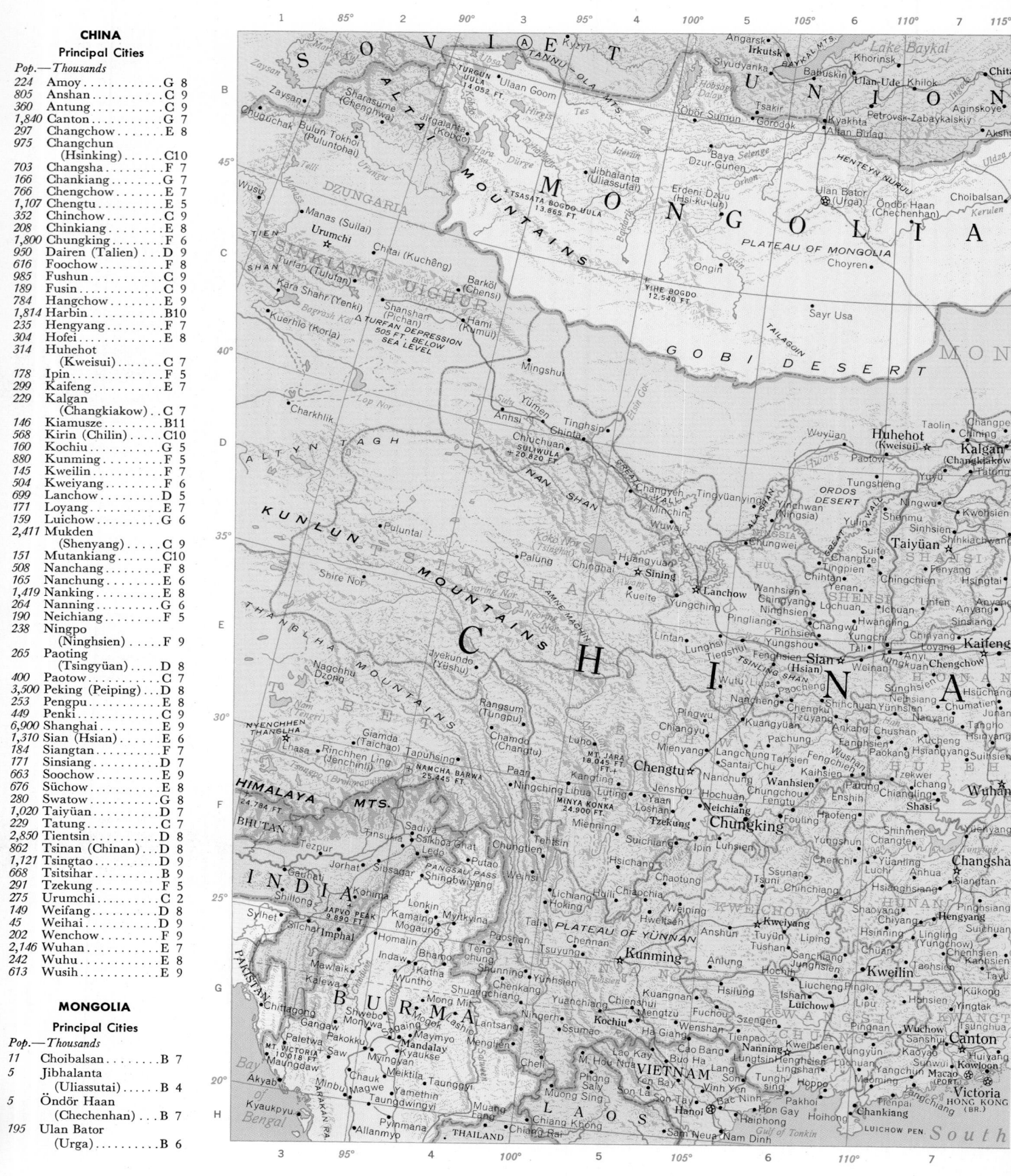

Statute Miles 100 0 100 200 300
Kilometers 100 0 100 200 300 400

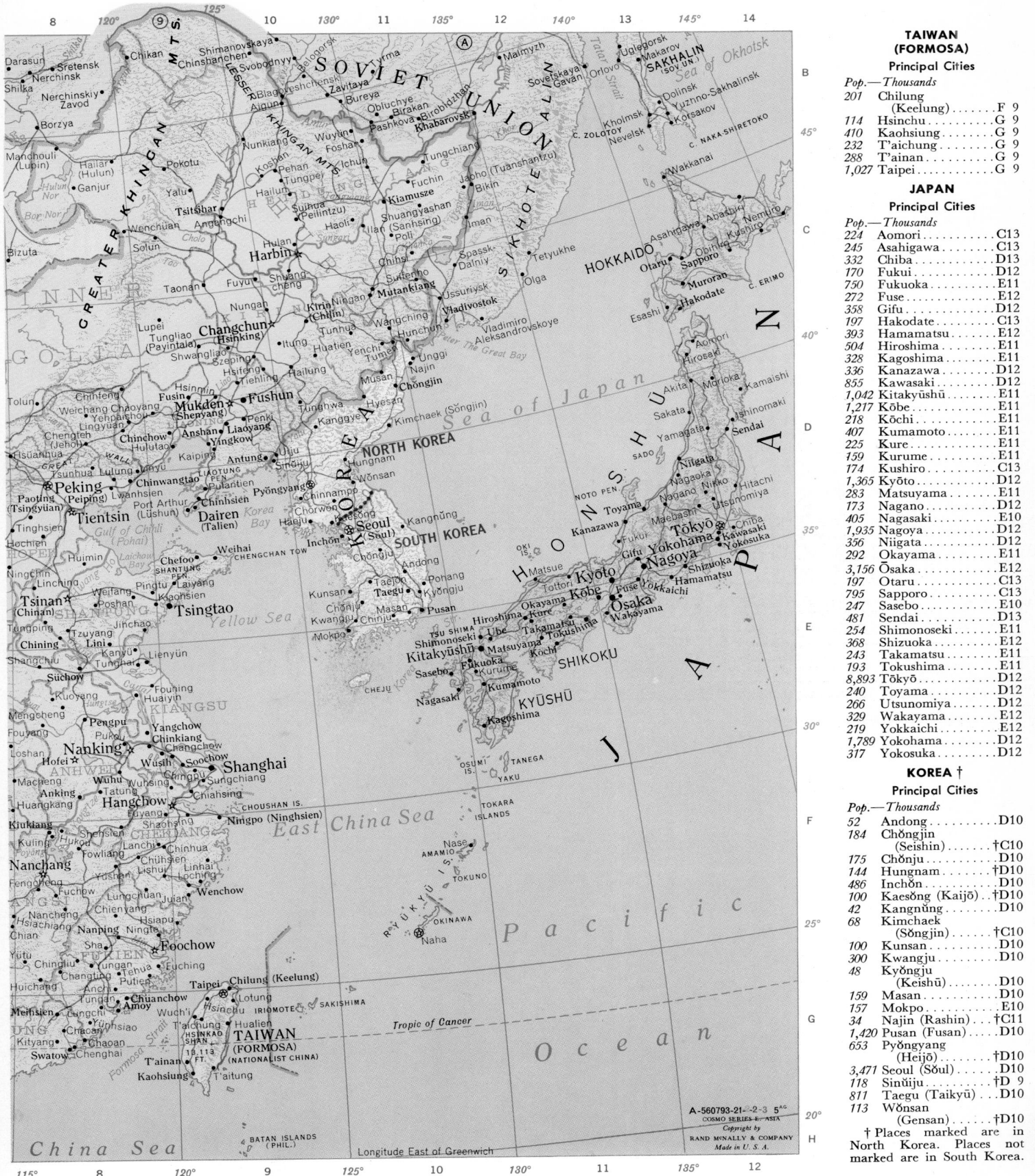

TAIWAN (FORMOSA)
Principal Cities
Pop.—Thousands

201	Chilung (Keelung)	F 9
114	Hsinchu	G 9
410	Kaohsiung	G 9
232	T'aichung	G 9
288	T'ainan	G 9
1,027	Taipei	G 9

JAPAN
Principal Cities
Pop.—Thousands

224	Aomori	C13
245	Asahigawa	C13
332	Chiba	D13
170	Fukui	D12
750	Fukuoka	E11
272	Fuse	E12
358	Gifu	D12
197	Hakodate	C13
393	Hamamatsu	E12
504	Hiroshima	E11
328	Kagoshima	E11
336	Kanazawa	D12
855	Kawasaki	D12
1,042	Kitakyūshū	E11
1,217	Kōbe	E11
218	Kōchi	E11
407	Kumamoto	E11
225	Kure	E11
159	Kurume	E11
174	Kushiro	C13
1,365	Kyōto	D12
283	Matsuyama	E11
173	Nagano	D12
405	Nagasaki	E10
1,935	Nagoya	D12
356	Niigata	D12
292	Okayama	E11
3,156	Ōsaka	E12
197	Otaru	C13
795	Sapporo	C13
247	Sasebo	E10
481	Sendai	D13
254	Shimonoseki	E11
368	Shizuoka	E12
243	Takamatsu	E11
193	Tokushima	E11
8,893	Tōkyō	D12
240	Toyama	D12
266	Utsunomiya	D12
329	Wakayama	E12
219	Yokkaichi	E12
1,789	Yokohama	D12
317	Yokosuka	D12

KOREA †
Principal Cities
Pop.—Thousands

52	Andong	D10
184	Chŏngjin (Seishin)	†C10
175	Chŏnju	D10
144	Hungnam	†D10
486	Inchŏn	D10
100	Kaesŏng (Kaijō)	†D10
42	Kangnŭng	D10
68	Kimchaek (Sŏngjin)	†C10
100	Kunsan	D10
300	Kwangju	D10
48	Kyŏngju (Keishū)	D10
159	Masan	D10
157	Mokpo	E10
34	Najin (Rashin)	†C11
1,420	Pusan (Fusan)	D10
653	Pyŏngyang (Heijō)	†D10
3,471	Seoul (Sŏul)	D10
118	Sinŭiju	†D 9
811	Taegu (Taikyū)	D10
113	Wŏnsan (Gensan)	†D10

† Places marked are in North Korea. Places not marked are in South Korea.

Polyconic Projection
SCALE 1:16,000,000 1 Inch = 252 Statute Miles

AFRICA
⊗ Capitals

Abidjan, I.C............F 5
Accra, Ghana...........F 5
Addis Ababa, Eth.......F 9
Aiún, Sp. Sah..........D 4
Bamako, Mali...........E 5
Bangui, Cen. Afr. Rep..F 7
Bata, Equat. Gui.......F 6
Bathurst, Gam..........E 4
Bissau, Port. Gui......E 4
Brazzaville, Congo.....G 7
Bujumbura, Burundi.....G 8
Cape Town, S. Afr......J 7
Conakry, Guinea........F 4
Dakar, Sen.............E 4
Dar es Salaam, Tan.....G 9
Djibouti, Afaras & Issas.E10
Fort-Lamy, Chad........E 7
Freetown, S.L..........F 4
Gaberones, Botswana....I 8
Kampala, Ug............F 9
Khartoum, Sud..........E 9
Kigali, Rwanda.........G 9
Kinshasa, Congo,
  The..................G 7
Lagos, Nig.............F 6
Libreville, Gabon......F 6
Lomé, Togo.............F 6
Lourenço Marques, Moz..I 9
Luanda, Ang............G 7
Lusaka, Zambia.........H 8
Maseru, Lesotho........I 8
Mbabane, Swaz..........I 9
Mogadiscio, Som........F10
Monrovia, Lib..........F 4
Nairobi, Ken...........G 9
Niamey, Niger..........E 6
Nouakchott, Maur.......E 4
Ouagadougou, Upper
  Volta................E 5
Porto-Novo, Dah........F 6
Pretoria, S. Afr.......I 8
Santa Isabel, Equat. Gui.F 6
Salisbury, Rhodesia....H 9
Tananarive, Malag......H10
Windhoek, S. W. Afr....I 7
Yaoundé, Cam...........F 7
Zomba, Malawi..........H 9

Physical Features

Aden, gulf.............E10
Agulhas, cape..........J 7
Ahaggar, mts...........D 6
Albert, lake...........F 9
Ascension, isl.........G 4
Aswān High, dam........D 9
Atlas, mts.............C 5
Azores, is.............C 3
Batu, mtn..............F 9
Bíjagós (Bissagos), is.E 4
Blanc, cape............D 4
Blue Nile, riv.........E 9
Bodélé, depression.....E 7
Brandberg, mtn.........I 7
Cape Verde, is.........E 3
Chad, lake.............E 7
Chari, riv.............E 7
Chech, sand dunes......D 5

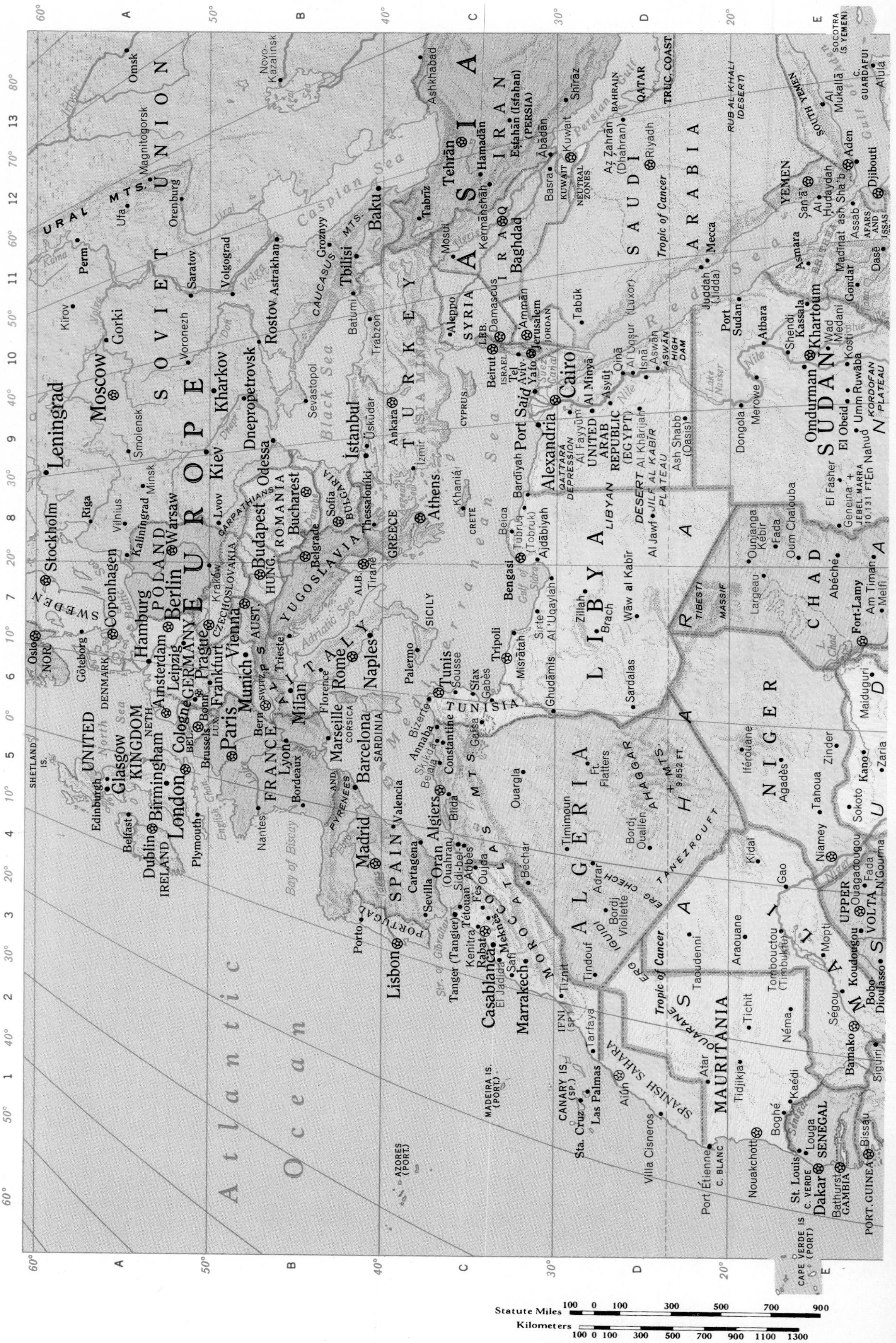

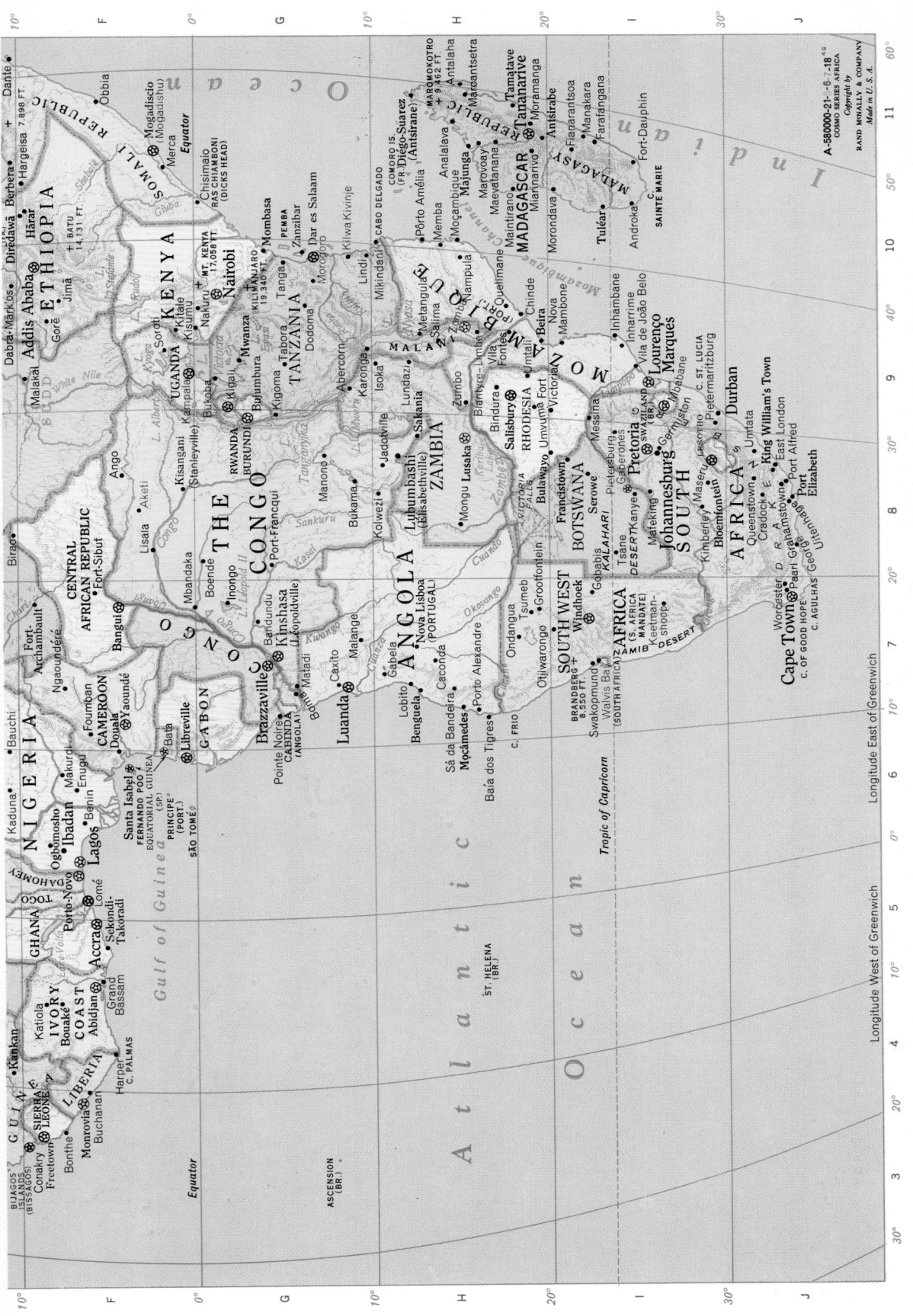

Sinusoidal Projection
SCALE 1:36,313,000   1 Inch = 565 Statute Miles

Chiamboni, cape G10
Congo, riv . . . . G 7
Cuando, riv . . . . H 8
Cuanza, riv . . . . G 7
Cunene, riv . . . . H 7
Delgado, cape H10
Drakensberg, mts . . . . . . J 8
Eyasi, lake . . . . G 9
Fernando Póo, isl . . . . . . F 6
Frio, cape . . . . H 7
Gibraltar, strait . . . . . . C 5
Giuba, riv F10
Good Hope, cape . . . . . . J 7
Guardafui, cape E11
Guinea, gulf . . . . F 6
Iguidi, sand dunes . . . . . D 5
Jilf al Kabīr, plat . . . . . . D 8
Kalahari, des . . . . I 8
Kasai, riv . . . . G 8
Kenya, mtn . . . . F 9
Kilimanjaro, mtn . . . . . . G 9
Kordofan, plat . . . . E 9
Kwango, riv . . . . G 7
Kyoga, lake . . . . F 9
Léopold II, lake . . . . G 7
Libyan, des . . . . D 8
Limpopo, riv . . . . I 9
Madagascar, isl H10
Madeira, is . . . . C 4
Maromokotro, mtn H10
Marrah, mtn . . . . E 8
Mediterranean, sea . . . . C 7
Mozambique, chan H10
Mweru, lake . . . . G 8
Namib, des . . . . I 8
Niger, riv . . . . E 6
Nile, riv . . . . D 9
Nyasa, lake . . . . H 9
Okovango, riv . . . . H 7
Orange, riv . . . . I 7
Ouarane, sand dunes . . . . D 4
Palmas, cape . . . . F 5
Pemba, isl G10
Qattara, depression . . . . D 8
Red, sea . . . . D 9
Ruaha, riv . . . . G 9
Rudolf, lake . . . . F 9
Rufiji, riv . . . . G 9
Sahara, des . . . . D 5
Ste. Marie, cape I10
St. Helena, isl . . . . H 5
St. Lucia, cape . . . . I 9
Sankuru, riv . . . . G 8
Sénégal, riv . . . . E 4
Shabelē, riv F10
Sidra, gulf . . . . C 7
Socotra, isl E11
Stefanie, lake . . . . F 9
Sudd, swamp . . . . F 8
Suez, canal . . . . C 9
Tana, lake . . . . E 9
Tanezrouft, des . . . . D 6
Tanganyika, lake . . . . . . G 8
Tibesti, plat . . . . D 7
Ubangi, riv . . . . F 7
Verde, cape . . . . E 4
Victoria, falls . . . . H 8
Victoria, lake . . . . G 9
Volta, riv . . . . F 5
White Nile, riv . . . . F 9
Zambezi, riv . . . . H 8

DAHOMEY
Principal Cities
Pop.—Thousands
19	Abomey	E 5
109	Cotonou	E 5
5	Kandi	D 5
14	Ouidah	E 5
70	Porto-Novo	E 5

GAMBIA
Principal City
Pop.—Thousands
29	Bathurst	D 1

GHANA
Principal Cities
Pop.—Thousands
338	Accra	E 4
41	Cape Coast	E 4
17	Keta	E 5
35	Koforidua	E 4
181	Kumasi	E 4
20	Nsawam	E 4
23	Obuasi	E 4
20	Oda	E 4
123	Sekondi-Takoradi	F 4
40	Tamale	E 4
14	Tarkwa	E 4
15	Tema	E 5
25	Winneba	E 4
16	Yendi	E 4

GUINEA
Principal Cities
Pop.—Thousands
6	Boké	D 2
43	Conakry	E 2
3	Gaoual	D 2
29	Kankan	D 3
25	Kindia	D 2
6	Kouroussa	D 2
13	Labé	D 2
9	Mamou	D 2
11	N'Zérékoré	E 3
13	Siguiri	D 3

IVORY COAST
Principal Cities
Pop.—Thousands
180	Abidjan	E 4
13	Agboville	E 4
45	Bouaké	E 3
8	Katiola	E 3
17	Man	E 3
4	Mankono	E 3
3	Odienné	E 3

LIBERIA
Principal City
Pop.—Thousands
81	Monrovia	E 2

MALI
Principal Cities
Pop.—Thousands
135	Bamako	D 3
7	Gao	C 5
7	Goundam	C 4
29	Kayes	D 2
13	Mopti	D 4
6	Nioro	C 3
8	San	D 4
28	Ségou	D 3
14	Sikasso	D 3
8	Tombouctou	C 4

MAURITANIA
Principal Cities
Pop.—Thousands
10	Atar	B 2
9	Kaédi	C 2
12	Nouakchott	C 1
3	Selibaby	C 2
4	Tidjikja	C 2

NIGER
Principal Cities
Pop.—Thousands
5	Agadès	C 6

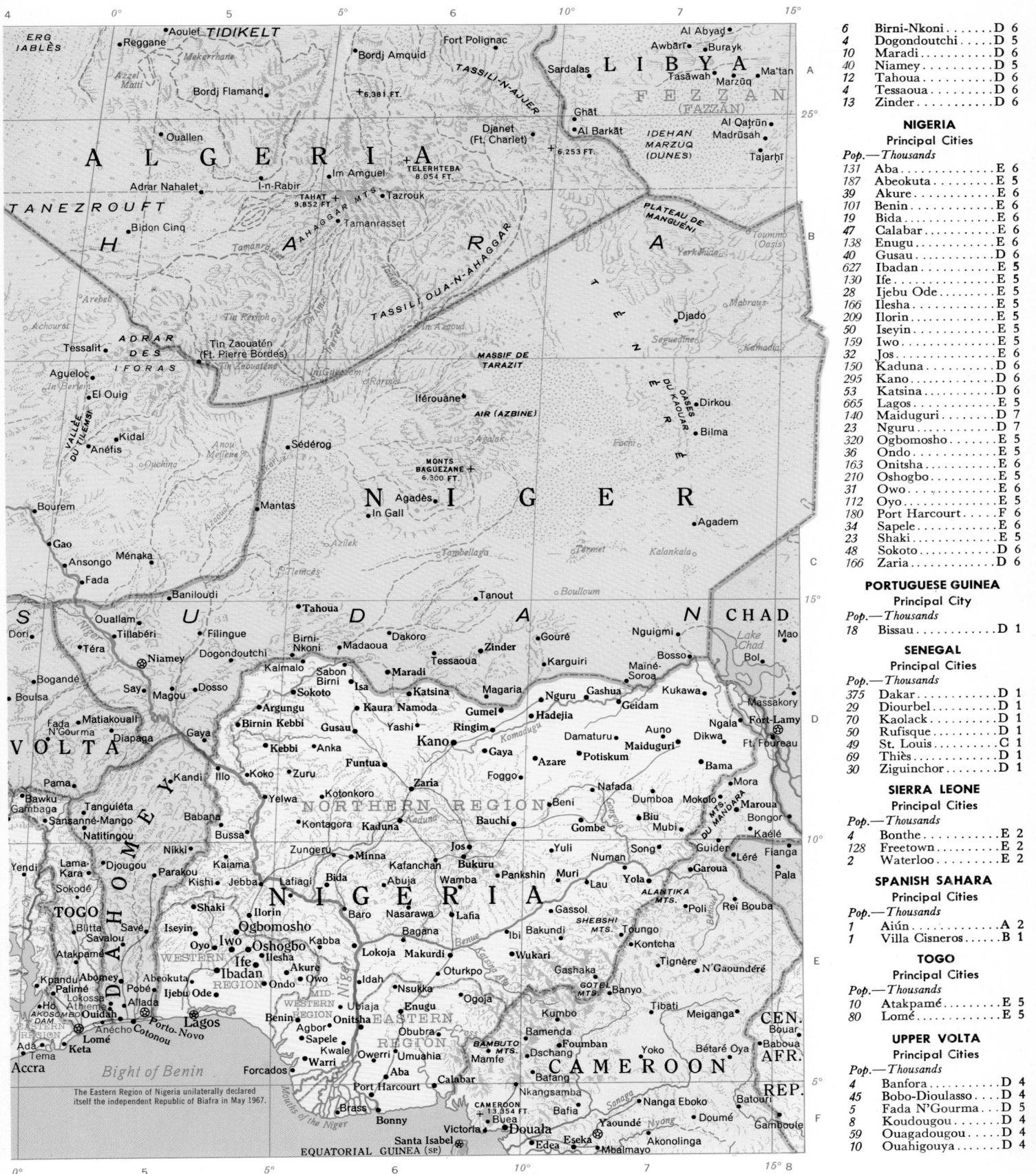

6	Birni-Nkoni	D 6
4	Dogondoutchi	D 5
10	Maradi	D 6
40	Niamey	D 5
12	Tahoua	D 6
4	Tessaoua	D 6
13	Zinder	D 6

NIGERIA
Principal Cities
Pop.—Thousands

131	Aba	E 6
187	Abeokuta	E 5
39	Akure	E 6
101	Benin	E 6
19	Bida	E 6
47	Calabar	E 6
138	Enugu	E 6
40	Gusau	D 6
627	Ibadan	E 5
130	Ife	E 5
28	Ijebu Ode	E 5
166	Ilesha	E 5
209	Ilorin	E 5
50	Iseyin	E 5
159	Iwo	E 5
32	Jos	E 6
150	Kaduna	D 6
295	Kano	D 6
53	Katsina	D 6
665	Lagos	E 5
140	Maiduguri	D 7
23	Nguru	D 7
320	Ogbomosho	E 5
36	Ondo	E 5
163	Onitsha	E 6
210	Oshogbo	E 5
31	Owo	E 6
112	Oyo	E 5
180	Port Harcourt	F 6
34	Sapele	E 6
23	Shaki	E 5
48	Sokoto	D 6
166	Zaria	D 6

PORTUGUESE GUINEA
Principal City
Pop.—Thousands

| 18 | Bissau | D 1 |

SENEGAL
Principal Cities
Pop.—Thousands

375	Dakar	D 1
29	Diourbel	D 1
70	Kaolack	D 1
50	Rufisque	D 1
49	St. Louis	C 1
69	Thiès	D 1
30	Ziguinchor	D 1

SIERRA LEONE
Principal Cities
Pop.—Thousands

4	Bonthe	E 2
128	Freetown	E 2
2	Waterloo	E 2

SPANISH SAHARA
Principal Cities
Pop.—Thousands

| 1 | Aiún | A 2 |
| 1 | Villa Cisneros | B 1 |

TOGO
Principal Cities
Pop.—Thousands

| 10 | Atakpamé | E 5 |
| 80 | Lomé | E 5 |

UPPER VOLTA
Principal Cities
Pop.—Thousands

4	Banfora	D 4
45	Bobo-Dioulasso	D 4
5	Fada N'Gourma	D 5
8	Koudougou	D 4
59	Ouagadougou	D 4
10	Ouahigouya	D 4

The Eastern Region of Nigeria unilaterally declared itself the independent Republic of Biafra in May 1967.

Sinusoidal Projection
SCALE 1: 11,400,000   1 Inch = 180 Statute Miles

ANGOLA
Principal Cities
Pop.—Thousands

23	Benguela	D 1
5	Caconda	D 2
9	Caxito	C 1
5	Gabela	D 1
50	Lobito	D 1
225	Luanda	C 1
13	Malange	C 2
7	Moçâmedes	E 1
39	Nova Lisboa	D 2
14	Sá da Bandeira	D 2
4	São Salvador	C 1
12	Silva Porto	D 2
4	Vila Luso	D 2
4	Vila Robert Williams	D 2
5	Vila Teixeira da Silva	D 2

BURUNDI
Principal Cities
Pop.—Thousands

50	Bujumbura	B 4
3	Kitega	B 5

CONGO (BRAZZAVILLE)
Principal Cities
Pop.—Thousands

	Abala	B 2
134	Brazzaville	B 2
13	Dolisie	B 1
	Ewo	B 1
	Makoua	A 2
	Pangala	B 1
80	Pointe Noire	B 1
	Zanaga	B 1

CONGO, THE (DEMOCRATIC REPUBLIC OF THE CONGO)
Principal Cities
Pop.—Thousands

4	Aba	A 5
12	Aketi	A 3
30	Albertville	C 4
41	Bakwanga	C 3
5	Bandundu	B 2
32	Boma	C 1
34	Bukavu	B 4
5	Bunia	A 5
11	Buta	A 3
10	Isiro	A 4
75	Jadotville	D 4
32	Kamina	C 4
11	Kikwit	C 2
14	Kindu [-Port Empain]	B 4
403	Kinshasa (Léopoldville)	B 2
15	Kipushi	D 4
127	Kisangani (Stanleyville)	A 4
48	Kolwezi	D 4
8	Lubudi	C 4
115	Luluabourg	C 3
184	Lubumbashi (Élizabethville)	D 4
10	Lusambo	B 3
20	Manono	C 4
59	Matadi	C 1
38	Mbandaka	A 2
4	Port-Francqui	B 3
12	Sakania	D 4
11	Shinkolobwe	C 4
12	Thysville	C 1
6	Tshikapa	C 3
13	Yangambi	A 3

KENYA
Principal Cities
Pop.—Thousands

20	Eldoret	A 6
8	Kericho	B 6
24	Kisumu	B 5
9	Kitale	B 5
180	Mombasa	B 6
267	Nairobi	B 6
38	Nakuru	B 6

Statute Miles 50 25 0 50 100 150 200 250

Kilometers 50 0 50 100 150 200 250 300

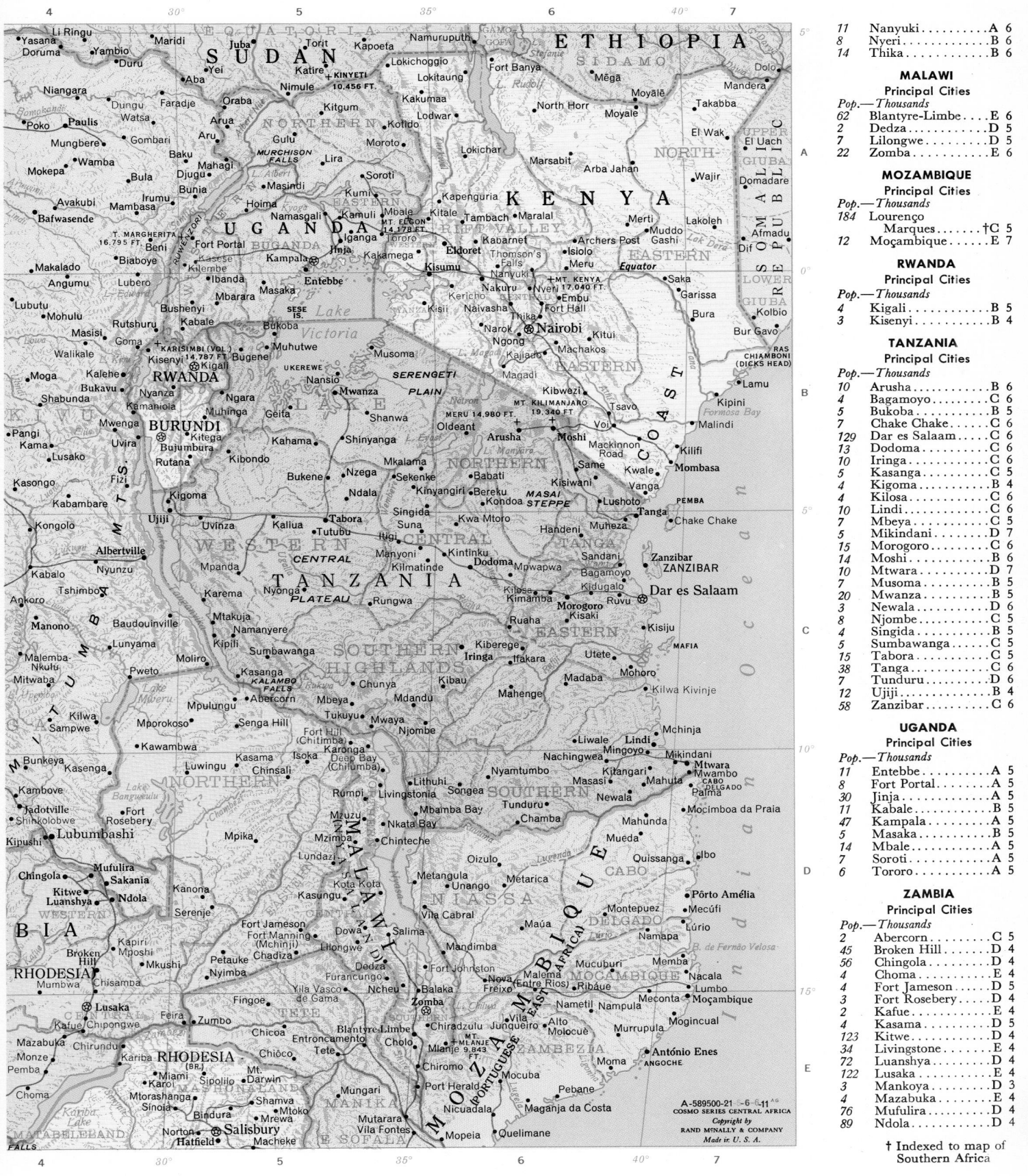

11	Nanyuki	A 6
8	Nyeri	B 6
14	Thika	B 6

MALAWI
Principal Cities
Pop.—Thousands

62	Blantyre-Limbe	E 6
2	Dedza	D 5
7	Lilongwe	D 5
22	Zomba	E 6

MOZAMBIQUE
Principal Cities
Pop.—Thousands

184	Lourenço Marques	†C 5
12	Moçambique	E 7

RWANDA
Principal Cities
Pop.—Thousands

4	Kigali	B 5
3	Kisenyi	B 4

TANZANIA
Principal Cities
Pop.—Thousands

10	Arusha	B 6
4	Bagamoyo	C 6
5	Bukoba	B 5
7	Chake Chake	C 6
129	Dar es Salaam	C 6
13	Dodoma	C 6
10	Iringa	C 6
5	Kasanga	C 5
4	Kigoma	B 4
4	Kilosa	C 6
10	Lindi	C 6
7	Mbeya	C 5
5	Mikindani	D 7
15	Morogoro	C 6
14	Moshi	B 6
10	Mtwara	D 7
7	Musoma	B 5
20	Mwanza	B 5
3	Newala	D 6
8	Njombe	C 5
4	Singida	B 5
5	Sumbawanga	C 5
15	Tabora	C 5
38	Tanga	C 6
7	Tunduru	D 6
12	Ujiji	B 4
58	Zanzibar	C 6

UGANDA
Principal Cities
Pop.—Thousands

11	Entebbe	A 5
8	Fort Portal	A 5
30	Jinja	A 5
11	Kabale	B 5
47	Kampala	A 5
5	Masaka	B 5
14	Mbale	A 5
7	Soroti	A 5
6	Tororo	A 5

ZAMBIA
Principal Cities
Pop.—Thousands

2	Abercorn	C 5
45	Broken Hill	D 4
56	Chingola	D 4
4	Choma	E 4
4	Fort Jameson	D 5
3	Fort Rosebery	D 4
2	Kafue	E 4
4	Kasama	D 5
123	Kitwe	D 4
34	Livingstone	E 4
72	Luanshya	D 4
122	Lusaka	E 4
3	Mankoya	D 3
4	Mazabuka	E 4
76	Mufulira	D 4
89	Ndola	D 4

† Indexed to map of
Southern Africa

BOTSWANA
Principal Cities
Pop.—Thousands

10	Francistown	B 4
10	Gaberones	B 4
34	Kanye	B 4
18	Mochudi	B 4
30	Molepolole	B 4
34	Serowe	B 4

LESOTHO
Principal City
Pop.—Thousands

9	Maseru	C 4

MALAGASY REPUBLIC
Principal Cities
Pop.—Thousands

5	Ambalavao	h 9
12	Ambositra	h 9
12	Antalaha	f10
23	Antsirabe	g 9
3	Belo	g 8
3	Betroka	h 9
30	Diégo-Suarez (Antsirane)	f 9
10	Farafangana	h 9
36	Fianarantsoa	h 9
11	Fort-Dauphin	h 9
7	Hellville	f 9
3	Maevatanana	g 9
4	Mahanoro	h 9
3	Maintirano	g 8
34	Majunga	g 9
12	Manakara	h 9
3	Mananara	h 9
16	Mananjary	h 9
5	Maroantsetra	g 9
14	Marovoay	g 9
6	Moramanga	g 9
11	Morondava	h 8
4	Port Bergé	g 9
40	Tamatave	g 9
270	Tananarive	g 9
34	Tuléar	h 8

RHODESIA
Principal Cities
Pop.—Thousands

214	Bulawayo	B 4
32	Gwelo	A 4
18	Que Que	A 4
220	Salisbury	A 5
40	Umtali	A 5
20	Wankie	A 4

SOUTH AFRICA
Principal Cities
Pop.—Thousands

11	Aliwal North	D 4
11	Barberton	C 5
16	Beaufort West	D 3
24	Bethlehem	C 4
113	Bloemfontein	C 4
78	Brakpan	C 4
5	Bredasdorp	D 3
7	Burgersdorp	D 4
5	Calvinia	D 2
508	Cape Town	D 2
4	Carnarvon	D 3
4	Carolina	C 5
6	Christiana	C 4
5	Colesberg	D 4
19	Cradock	D 4
14	De Aar	D 3
4	Dordrecht	D 4
4	Douglas	C 3
11	Dundee	C 5
560	Durban	C 5
114	East London	D 4
7	Empangeni	C 5
17	Ermelo	C 5
9	Estcourt	C 4
8	Ficksburg	C 4
10	Fort Beaufort	D 4
15	George	D 3

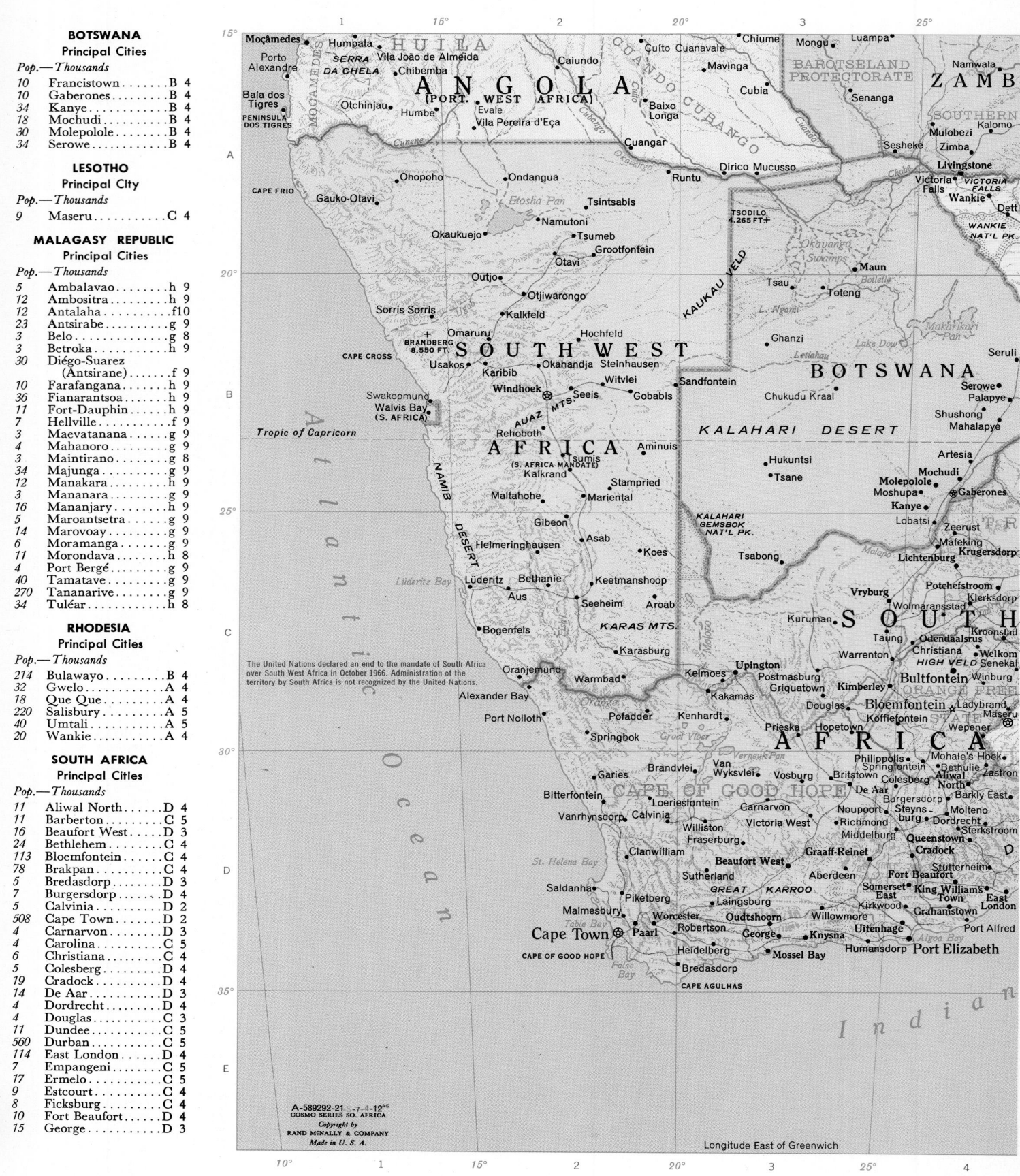

The United Nations declared an end to the mandate of South Africa over South West Africa in October 1966. Administration of the territory by South Africa is not recognized by the United Nations.

A-589292-21 -7-4-12^AG
COSMO SERIES SO. AFRICA
Copyright by
RAND McNALLY & COMPANY
Made in U. S. A.

Longitude East of Greenwich

Statute Miles 50 25 0 50 100 150 200 250
Kilometers 50 0 50 100 150 200 250 300

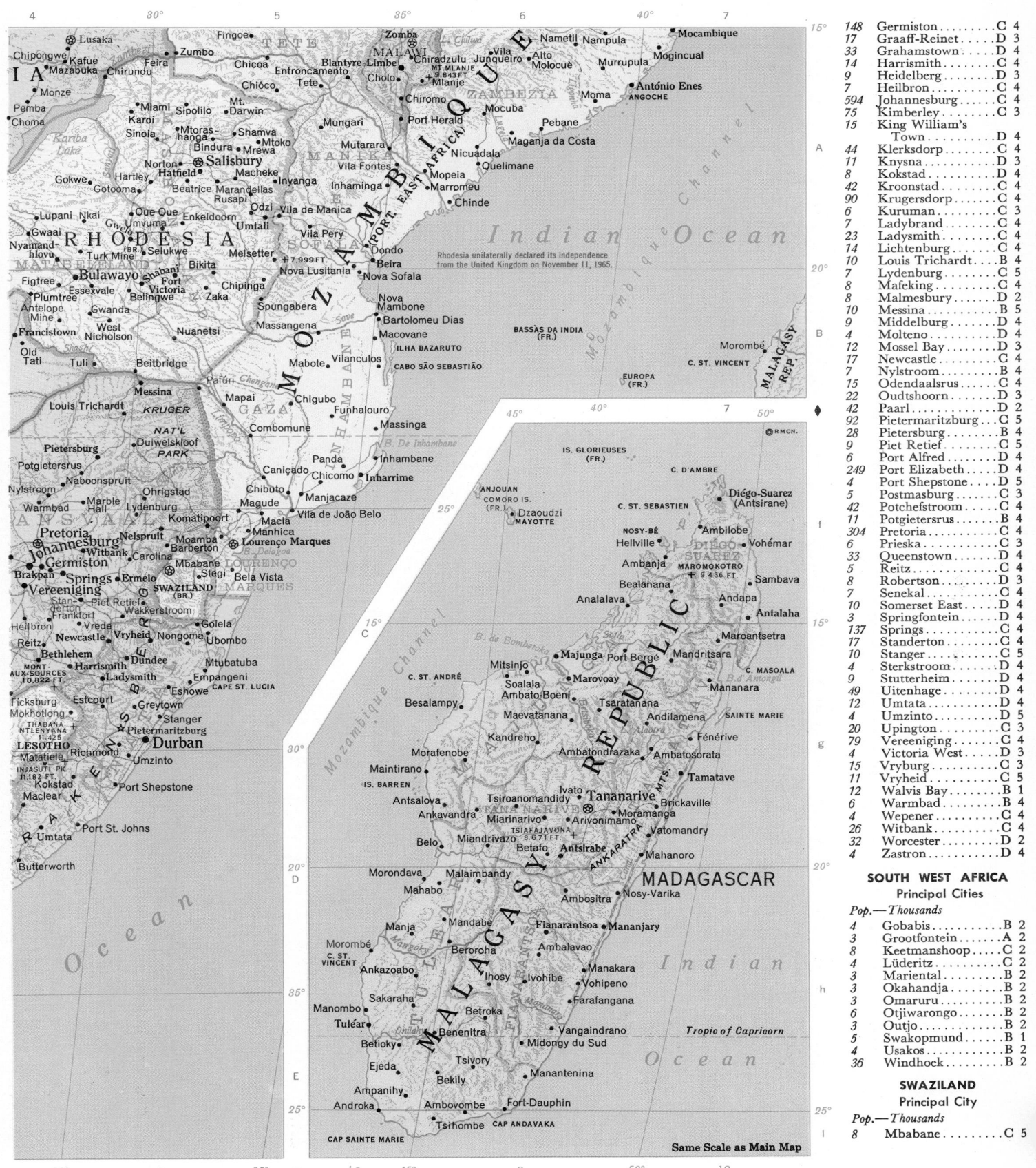

148	Germiston	C 4
17	Graaff-Reinet	D 3
33	Grahamstown	D 4
14	Harrismith	C 4
9	Heidelberg	D 3
7	Heilbron	C 4
594	Johannesburg	C 4
75	Kimberley	C 3
15	King William's Town	D 4
44	Klerksdorp	C 4
11	Knysna	D 3
8	Kokstad	C 4
42	Kroonstad	C 4
90	Krugersdorp	C 4
6	Kuruman	C 3
7	Ladybrand	C 4
23	Ladysmith	C 4
14	Lichtenburg	C 4
10	Louis Trichardt	B 4
7	Lydenburg	C 5
8	Mafeking	C 4
8	Malmesbury	D 2
10	Messina	B 5
9	Middelburg	C 4
4	Molteno	D 4
12	Mossel Bay	D 3
17	Newcastle	C 4
7	Nylstroom	B 4
15	Odendaalsrus	C 4
22	Oudtshoorn	D 3
42	Paarl	D 2
92	Pietermaritzburg	C 4
28	Pietersburg	B 4
9	Piet Retief	C 5
6	Port Alfred	D 4
249	Port Elizabeth	D 4
5	Port Shepstone	C 5
42	Postmasburg	C 3
11	Potchefstroom	C 4
11	Potgietersrus	B 4
304	Pretoria	C 4
6	Prieska	C 3
33	Queenstown	D 4
5	Reitz	C 4
8	Robertson	D 3
7	Senekal	C 4
10	Somerset East	D 4
3	Springfontein	C 4
137	Springs	C 4
17	Standerton	C 4
10	Stanger	C 5
4	Sterkstroom	D 4
9	Stutterheim	D 4
49	Uitenhage	D 4
12	Umtata	D 4
4	Umzinto	D 5
20	Upington	C 3
79	Vereeniging	C 4
15	Victoria West	D 3
15	Vryburg	C 3
11	Vryheid	C 5
12	Walvis Bay	B 1
6	Warmbad	B 4
4	Wepener	C 4
26	Witbank	C 4
32	Worcester	D 2
4	Zastron	D 4

SOUTH WEST AFRICA
Principal Cities

Pop.—Thousands

4	Gobabis	B 2
3	Grootfontein	A 2
8	Keetmanshoop	C 2
4	Lüderitz	C 2
3	Mariental	B 2
3	Okahandja	B 2
3	Omaruru	B 2
6	Otjiwarongo	B 2
3	Outjo	B 2
5	Swakopmund	B 1
4	Usakos	B 2
36	Windhoek	B 2

SWAZILAND
Principal City

Pop.—Thousands

8	Mbabane	C 5

Rhodesia unilaterally declared its independence from the United Kingdom on November 11, 1965.

Same Scale as Main Map

Sinusoidal Projection
SCALE 1: 11,400,000   1 Inch = 180 Statute Miles

AUSTRALIA
⊗ Capital

Canberra . . . . G 8

Physical Features

Arafura, sea . . . . B 5
Banks, isl . . . . B 7
Blue Mud, bay . . . . B 6
Cape York, pen . . . . B 7
Carpentaria, gulf . . . . B 6
Coral, sea . . . . C 9
D'Entrecasteaux, is k13
D'Entrecasteaux, pt . . . . F 2
Encounter, bay . . . . G 6
Eyre, pen . . . . F 6
Flinders, range . . . . F 6
Gairdner, lake . . . . F 6
Geographe, chan . . . . . . D 1
Gibson, des . . . . D 3
Hamersley, range . . . . . . D 2
Jacquinot, bay k13
Joseph Bonaparte, gulf . . . B 4
King Leopold, ranges . . . . . C 4
Macdonnell, ranges . . . . . D 5
Neales, riv . . . . E 6
Nullarbor, plain . . . . F 4
Owen Stanley, range k12
Papua, gulf k11
Port Phillip, bay . . . . G 7
Princess Charlotte, bay . . B 7
Sir Edward Pellew Group,
  is . . . . C 6
Spencer, gulf . . . . F 6
Swain, reefs . . . . D 9
Tasman, sea . . . . G 9
Thursday, isl . . . . B 7
Torrens, lake . . . . F 6
Torres, strait . . . . A 7
Van Diemen, gulf . . . . . . B 5
Wellesley, isl . . . . C 6

Principal Cities

Pop.—Thousands

20 Adelaide . . . . F 6
12 Albany . . . . F 2
25 Albury . . . . G 8
6 Alice Springs . . . . D 5
8 Ararat . . . . G 7, n14
14 Armidale . . . . F 9
7 Bairnsdale . . . . . . G 8, n15
42 Ballarat . . . . . . G 7, n14
2 Barcaldine . . . . D 8
17 Bathurst . . . . F 8
4 Bega . . . . G 8, n15
31 Bendigo . . . . G 7
2 Blackall . . . . D 8
1 Bombala . . . . . G 8, n15
6 Boulder . . . . F 3
3 Bourke . . . . F 8
5 Bowen . . . . C 8
1 Brewarrina . . . . E 8
644 Brisbane . . . . E 9
30 Broken Hill . . . . F 7
1 Broome . . . . C 3
15 Bunbury . . . . F 2
24 Bundaberg . . . . D 9
15 Burnie o15
3 Busselton . . . . F 2
26 Cairns . . . . C 8
86 Canberra . . . . G 8
2 Carnarvon . . . . D 1
35 Cessnock . . . . F 9
5 Charleville . . . . E 8
8 Charters Towers . . . . D 8
2 Clermont . . . . D 8
2 Cloncurry . . . . D 7
8 Collie . . . . F 2
3 Condobolin . . . . F 8
3 Coolgardie . . . . F 3
9 Cooma . . . . G 8
2 Coonamble . . . . F 8
3 Cunnamulla . . . . E 8
8 Dalby . . . . E 9
16 Darwin . . . . B 5
6 Deniliquin . . . . G 7
1 Derby . . . . C 3
14 Devonport o15
1 Dirranbandi . . . . . . E 8
15 Dubbo . . . . F 8
7 Echuca . . . . G 7

Map of Australia. Scale: Statute Miles 100 0 100 200 300; Kilometers 100 0 100 200 300 400. Longitude East of Greenwich.

A-590200-21-2-3-2-9 AG
COSMO SERIES AUSTRALIA
Copyright by
RAND McNALLY & COMPANY
Made in U.S.A.

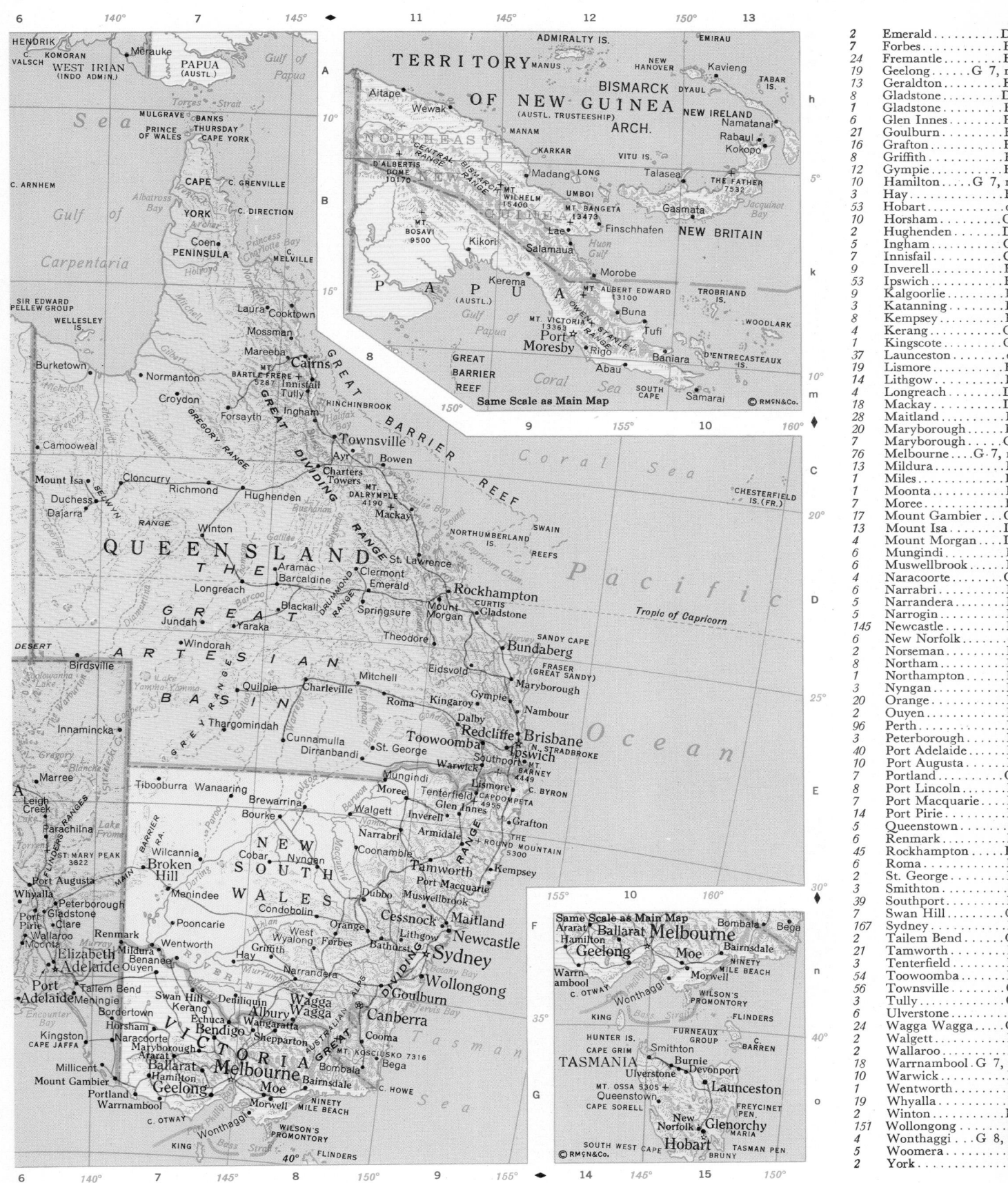

2	Emerald	D 8
7	Forbes	F 8
24	Fremantle	F 2
19	Geelong	G 7, n14
13	Geraldton	E 1
8	Gladstone	D 9
1	Gladstone	F 6
6	Glen Innes	E 9
21	Goulburn	F 8
16	Grafton	E 9
8	Griffith	F 8
12	Gympie	E 9
10	Hamilton	G 7, n14
3	Hay	F 7
53	Hobart	o15
10	Horsham	G 7
2	Hughenden	D 7
5	Ingham	C 8
7	Innisfail	C 8
9	Inverell	E 9
53	Ipswich	E 9
9	Kalgoorlie	F 3
3	Katanning	F 2
8	Kempsey	F 9
4	Kerang	G 7
1	Kingscote	G 6
37	Launceston	o15
19	Lismore	E 9
14	Lithgow	F 9
4	Longreach	D 7
18	Mackay	D 8
28	Maitland	F 9
20	Maryborough	E 9
7	Maryborough	G 7
76	Melbourne	G 7, n14
13	Mildura	F 7
1	Miles	E 9
1	Moonta	F 6
7	Moree	E 8
17	Mount Gambier	G 7
13	Mount Isa	D 6
4	Mount Morgan	D 9
6	Mungindi	E 8
6	Muswellbrook	F 9
4	Naracoorte	G 7
6	Narrabri	F 8
5	Narrandera	F 8
5	Narrogin	F 2
145	Newcastle	F 9
6	New Norfolk	o15
2	Norseman	F 3
8	Northam	F 2
1	Northampton	E 1
3	Nyngan	F 8
20	Orange	F 8
2	Ouyen	G 7
96	Perth	F 2
3	Peterborough	F 6
40	Port Adelaide	F 6
10	Port Augusta	F 6
7	Portland	G 7
8	Port Lincoln	F 6
7	Port Macquarie	F 9
14	Port Pirie	F 6
5	Queenstown	o15
6	Renmark	F 7
45	Rockhampton	D 9
6	Roma	E 8
2	St. George	E 8
3	Smithton	o15
39	Southport	E 9
7	Swan Hill	G 7
167	Sydney	F 9
2	Tailem Bend	G 6
21	Tamworth	F 9
2	Tenterfield	E 9
54	Toowoomba	E 9
56	Townsville	C 8
3	Tully	C 8
6	Ulverstone	o15
24	Wagga Wagga	G 8
2	Walgett	F 8
2	Wallaroo	F 6
18	Warrnambool	G 7, n14
10	Warwick	E 9
1	Wentworth	F 7
19	Whyalla	F 6
2	Winton	D 7
151	Wollongong	F 9
4	Wonthaggi	G 8, n15
5	Woomera	F 6
2	York	F 2

Lambert Azimuthal Equal Area Projection
SCALE 1:16,000,000   1 Inch = 252 Statute Miles

SOUTH AMERICA
⊗ Capitals †

Asunción, Par . . . . F 5
Belize, Br. Hond . . . . B 2
Bogotá, Col . . . . C 3
Brasília, Braz . . . . E 6
Buenos Aires, Arg . . . . . . G 5
Caracas, Ven . . . . B 4
Cayenne, Fr. Gu . . . . C 5
Georgetown, Guy . . . . . . C 5
Guatemala, Guat . . . . B 1
Havana, Cuba . . . . A 2
Kingston, Jam . . . . B 3
La Paz, Bol . . . . E 4
Lima, Peru . . . . E 3
Managua, Nic . . . . B 2
Montevideo, Ur . . . . G 5
Nassau, Ba. Is . . . . A 3
Panamá, Pan . . . . C 3
Paramaribo, Sur . . . . C 5
Port-au-Prince, Hai . . . . . B 3
Port-of-Spain, Trin . . . . . B 4
Quito, Ec . . . . D 3
San José, C.R . . . . C 2
San Juan, P.R . . . . B 4
San Salvador, Sal . . . . . . B 2
Santiago, Chile . . . . G 5
Santo Domingo, Dom.
   Rep . . . . B 4
Sucre, Bol . . . . E 4
Tegucigalpa, Hond . . . . . B 2

† For capital city of Mexico
see map of Mexico.

Physical Features

Aconcagua, mtn . . . . G 4
Amazonas (Amazon), riv . D 5
Andes, mts . . . . D 3, H 3
Andros, isl . . . . A 3
Angamos, pt . . . . F 3
Araguaia, riv . . . . D 6
Atrato, riv . . . . C 3
Bascuñán, cape . . . . F 3
Bermejo, riv . . . . F 5
Branco, riv . . . . C 4
Brazilian, highlands . . . . . E 5
Caquetá, riv . . . . D 4
Caribbean, sea . . . . B 3
Caroní, riv . . . . C 4
Catoche, cape . . . . A 2
Cauca, riv . . . . C 3
Chico, riv . . . . H 4
Chiloé, isl . . . . H 3
Chimborazo, vol . . . . D 3
Chonos, arch . . . . H 3
Chubut, riv . . . . H 4
Colón (Galápagos), arch . C 1
Colorado, riv . . . . G 4
Corrientes, cape . . . . C 3
Corumiquara, pt . . . . D 7
Cuba, isl . . . . A 2
Curaçao, isl . . . . B 4
Cuyuni, riv . . . . C 5
Desengaño, cape . . . . . . H 4
Devils, isl . . . . C 5
Dos Bahías, cape . . . . . . H 4
Essequibo, riv . . . . C 5
Falkland (Islas Malvinas),
   is . . . . I 4
Fernando de Noronha,
   isl . . . . D 7
Fitz Roy, mtn . . . . H 3
Frio, cape . . . . F 6
Gallinas, pt . . . . B 3
Gracias a Dios, cape . . . . B 2
Gran Chaco, plain . . . . . . F 4
Greater Antilles, is . . . . . B 3
Guaporé, riv . . . . E 4
Guaviare, riv . . . . C 3
Guayaquil, gulf . . . . D 1
Honduras, gulf . . . . B 2
Horn, cape . . . . I 4
Huascarán, mtn . . . . D 3
Içá, riv . . . . D 4
Isabela, isl . . . . D 1
Isle of Pines, isl . . . . A 2
Jamaica, isl . . . . B 3
Japurá, riv . . . . D 4
Jari, riv . . . . D 5
Javari, riv . . . . D 3
Jequitinhonha, riv . . . . . . E 6

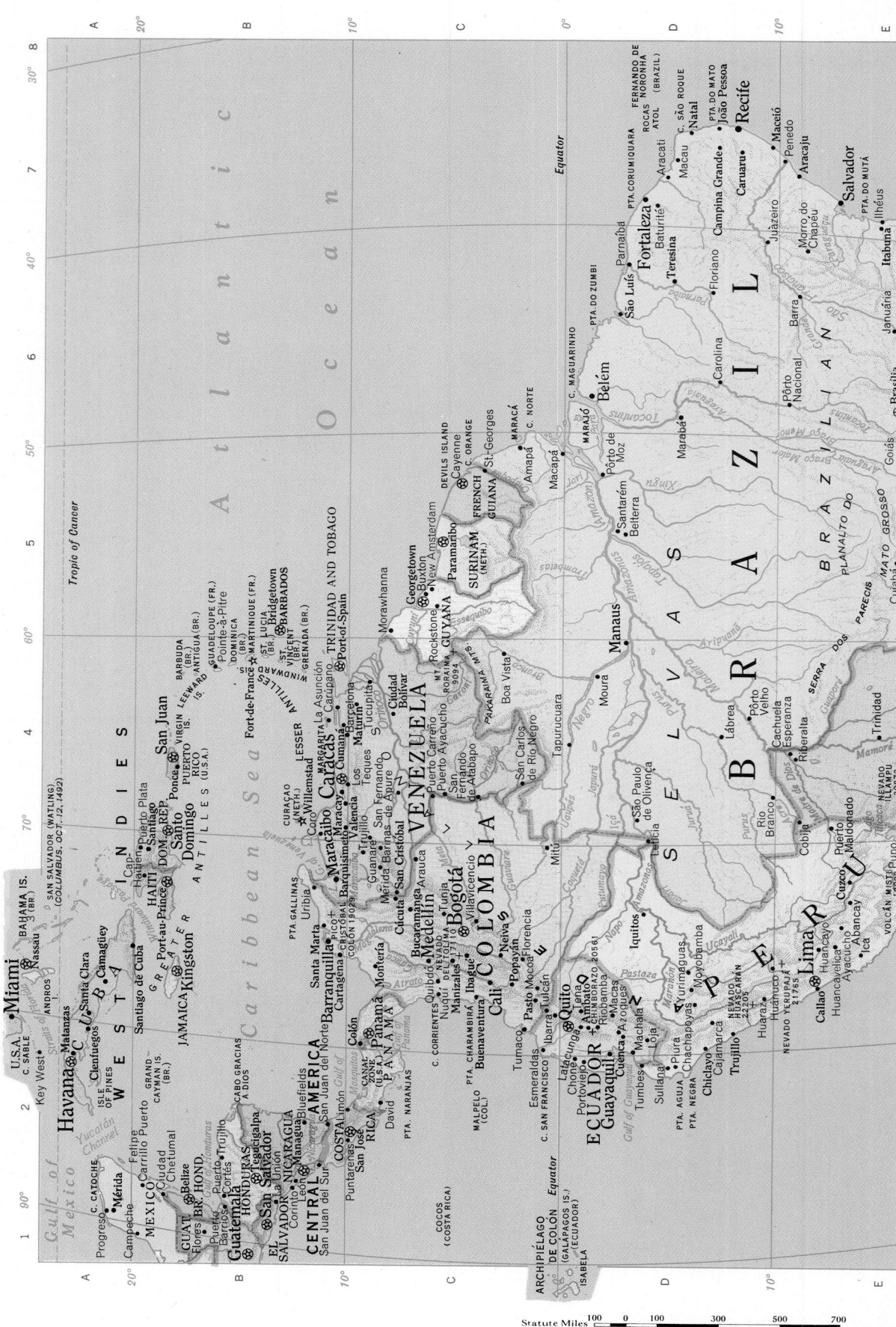

Statute Miles 100 0 100   300   500   700

Kilometers 100 0 100 300   500 700 900   1100

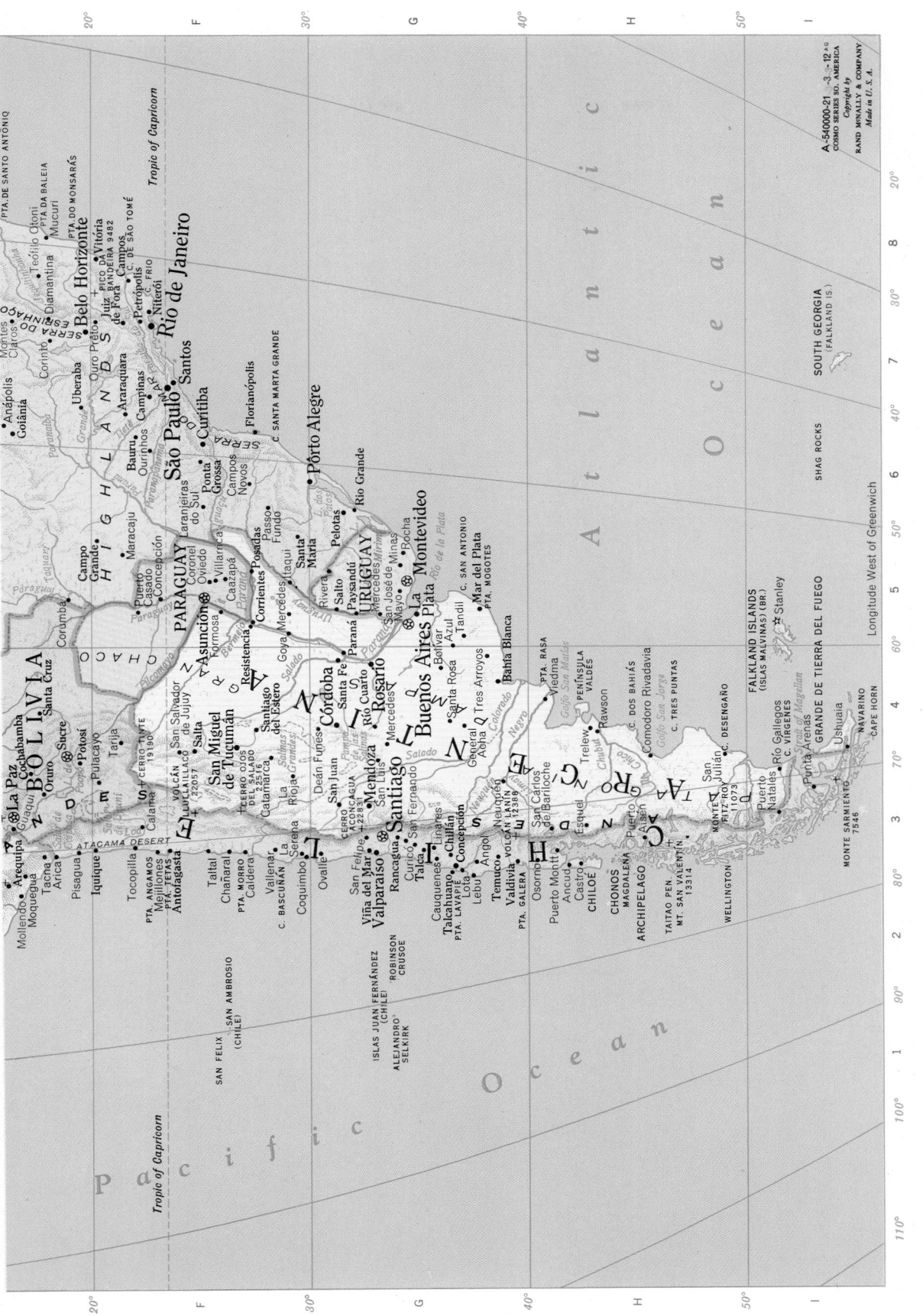

Juan Fernández, is......G 3
Juruá, riv..........D 4
Lavapie, pt..........G 3
Lesser Antilles, is......B 4
Limay, riv..........G 4
Loa, riv..........F 4
Llanos, plains..........C 4
Llullaillaco, vol........F 4
Madeira, riv..........D 4
Madre de Dios, riv......E 4
Magdalena, riv........C 3
Magellan, strait........I 4
Mamoré, riv..........E 4
Maracá, isl..........C 5
Maracaibo, lake........C 3
Marajó, isl..........D 6
Marañón, riv..........D 4
Margarita, isl..........B 4
Mato, pt..........D 7
Mato Grosso, plat......E 5
Meta, riv..........C 3
Mexico, gulf..........A 2
Mirim, lake..........G 5
Misti, vol..........E 3
Mogotes, pt..........G 5
Monsarás, pt..........E 7
Mosquitos, gulf........C 2
Mutá, pt..........E 7
Napo, riv..........D 3
Negro, riv..........D 4
Negro, riv..........G 4
Negra, pt..........D 2
Nicaragua, lake........B 2
Oiapoque, riv..........C 5
Orange, cape..........C 5
Orinoco, riv..........C 4
Pakaraima, mts........C 4
Pampa de las Salinas,
    salt flats..........G 4
Panama, gulf..........C 3
Pará, riv..........D 6
Paraguay, riv..........F 6
Paraíba, riv..........F 6
Paraná, riv..........F 4
Paranapanema, riv......F 5
Parecis, mts..........E 5
Parnaíba, riv..........D 6
Patos, lake..........G 5
Pilcomayo, riv..........F 4
Plata, riv..........G 5
Poopó, lake..........E 4
Puerto Rico, isl........B 4
Purus, riv..........D 3
Putumayo, riv..........D 3
Robinson Crusoe, isl......G 3
Rocas, is..........D 7
Rosa, pt..........H 4
Salado, riv..........F 4
Salinas Grandes, salt
    flats..........F 4
San Ambrosio, isl......F 3
San Antonio, cape......G 5
San Felix, isl..........F 2
San Francisco, cape......C 4
San Jorge, gulf........H 4
San Matías, gulf........H 4
San Valentín, mtn......H 3
São Francisco, riv......E 6
São Roque, cape........D 7
São Tomé, cape........F 6
Taitao, pen..........H 3
Tapajós, riv..........D 5
Taquari, riv..........E 5
Tetas, pt..........F 4
Tierra del Fuego, isl....I 4
Tietê, riv..........F 6
Titicaca, lake..........E 4
Tocantins, riv..........D 6
Tres Puntas, cape......H 4
Trombetas, riv..........D 5
Uaupés, riv..........D 3
Ucayali, riv..........D 3
Uruguay, riv..........G 5
Uyuni, salt lake........F 4
Valdés, pen..........H 4
Venezuela, gulf........B 3
Vírgenes, cape........I 4
Wellington, isl........H 3
Xingú, riv..........D 5
Yerupaja, mtn..........E 3
Yucatán, chan..........A 2
Zumbi, pt..........D 6

Sinusoidal Projection
SCALE 1 : 29,465,000   1 Inch = 465 Statute Miles

CENTRAL AND SOUTHERN ARGENTINA AND CHILE

SOUTHERN ARGENTINA
Principal Cities
Pop.—Thousands

Pop.	City	Ref.
6	Adolfo Alsina	B 4
12	Alta Gracia	A 4
8	Arrecifes	g 6
275	Avellaneda	A 5, g 7
9	Ayacucho	B 5
29	Azul	B 5
136	Bahía Blanca	B 4
15	Balcarce	B 5
10	Baradero	f 6
16	Bell Ville	A 4
2	Bernasconi	B 4
14	Bolívar	B 4
16	Bragado	B 4, g 6
2,967	Buenos Aires	A 5, g 7
6	Cañuelas	B 5, g 7
8	Carlos Casares	B 4
5	Carmen de Patagones	C 4
11	Casilda	A 4
13	Chacabuco	A 4, g 6
9	Chascomús	B 5
23	Chivilcoy	A 4, g 6
8	Colón	A 5
26	Comodoro Rivadavia	D 3
31	Concepción del Uruguay	A 5
64	Concordia	A 5
580	Córdoba	A 4
4	Coronel Brandsen	B 5, g 7
7	Coronel Dorrego	B 4
13	Coronel Pringles	B 4
11	Coronel Suárez	B 4
16	Cruz del Eje	A 4
14	Deán Funes	A 4
14	Dolores	B 5
6	Esquel	C 2
5	General Acha	B 4
4	General Belgrano	B 5
7	General Madariaga	B 5
11	General Pico	B 4
5	General Viamonte	B 4
5	Gonzáles Chaves	B 4
24	Gualeguay	A 5
37	Gualeguaychú	A 5
4	Henderson	B 4
8	Juárez	B 5
36	Junín	A 4
5	Justo Daract	A 3
9	Laboulaye	A 4
15	La Paz	A 5
295	La Plata	A 5, g 8
9	Las Flores	B 5
13	Lincoln	A 4
8	Lobería	B 5
8	Lobos	B 5, g 7
19	Luján	g 7
5	Maipú	B 5
10	Marcos Juárez	A 4
203	Mar del Plata	B 5
109	Mendoza	A 3
17	Mercedes	A 5, g 7
26	Mercedes	A 3
11	Monte Caseros	A 5
18	Necochea	B 5
7	Neuquén	B 3
12	Nogoyá	A 5
14	Nueve de Julio	B 4
24	Olavarría	B 4
110	Paraná	A 4
14	Pehuajo	B 4
32	Pergamino	A 4
5	Quequén	B 5
24	Rafaela	A 4
5	Rauch	B 5
70	Río Cuarto	A 4
6	Río Gallegos	E 3
11	Río Tercero	A 4
7	Rojas	A 4
595	Rosario	A 4
11	Rosario Tala	A 5
11	Rufino	A 4
8	Saladillo	B 5
4	San Antonio Oeste	C 4

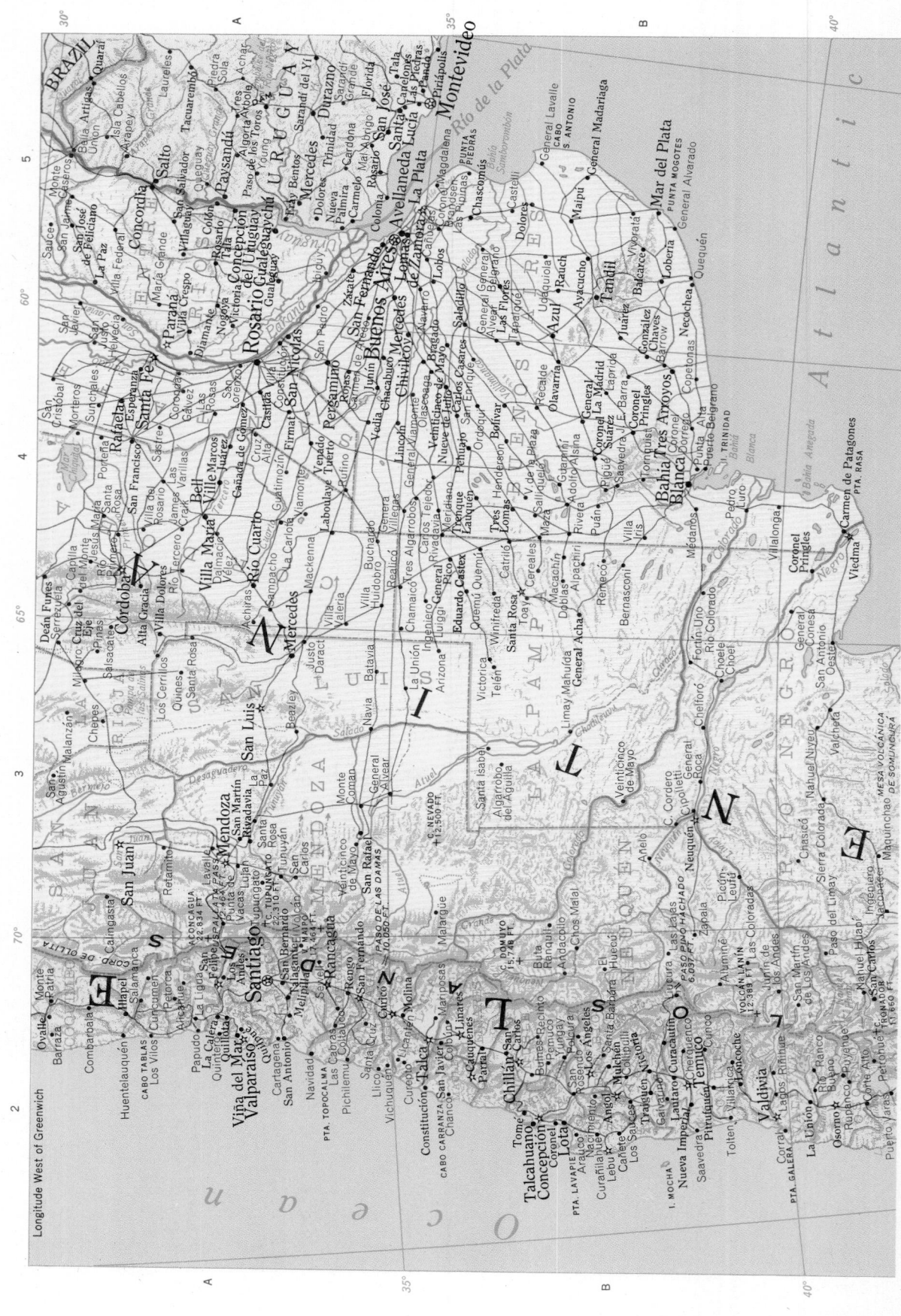

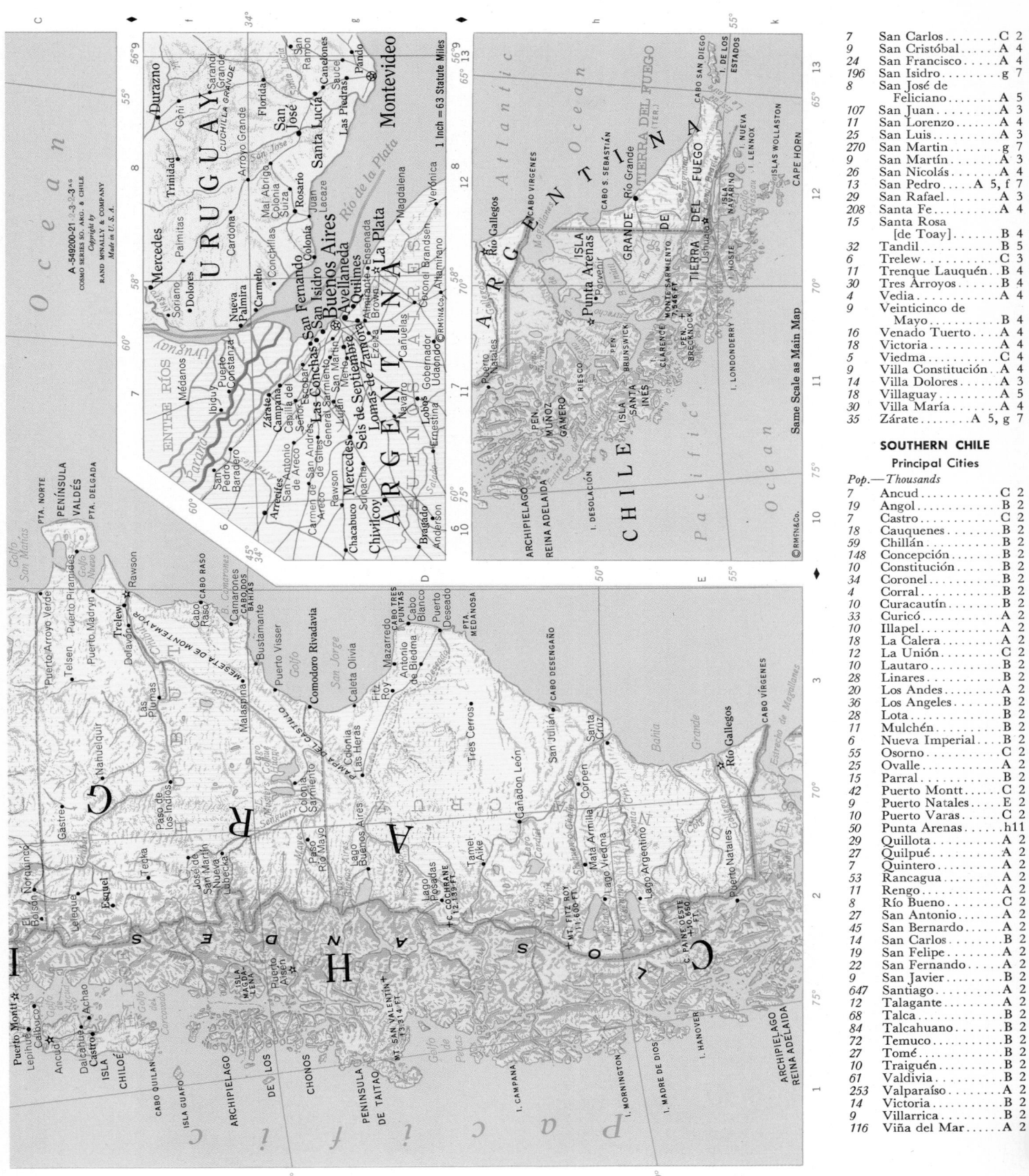

7	San Carlos	C 2
9	San Cristóbal	A 4
24	San Francisco	A 4
196	San Isidro	g 7
8	San José de Feliciano	A 5
107	San Juan	A 3
11	San Lorenzo	A 4
25	San Luis	A 3
270	San Martín	g 7
9	San Martín	A 3
26	San Nicolás	A 4
13	San Pedro	A 5, f 7
29	San Rafael	A 3
208	Santa Fe	A 4
15	Santa Rosa [de Toay]	B 4
32	Tandil	B 5
6	Trelew	C 3
11	Trenque Lauquén	B 4
30	Tres Arroyos	B 4
4	Vedia	A 4
9	Veinticinco de Mayo	B 4
16	Venado Tuerto	A 4
18	Victoria	A 4
5	Viedma	C 4
9	Villa Constitución	A 4
14	Villa Dolores	A 3
18	Villaguay	A 5
30	Villa María	A 4
35	Zárate	A 5, g 7

SOUTHERN CHILE
Principal Cities
Pop.—Thousands

7	Ancud	C 2
19	Angol	B 2
7	Castro	C 2
18	Cauquenes	B 2
59	Chillán	B 2
148	Concepción	B 2
10	Constitución	B 2
34	Coronel	B 2
4	Corral	B 2
10	Curacautín	B 2
33	Curicó	A 2
10	Illapel	A 2
18	La Calera	A 2
12	La Unión	C 2
10	Lautaro	B 2
28	Linares	B 2
20	Los Andes	A 2
36	Los Angeles	B 2
28	Lota	B 2
11	Mulchén	B 2
6	Nueva Imperial	B 2
55	Osorno	C 2
25	Ovalle	A 2
15	Parral	B 2
42	Puerto Montt	C 2
9	Puerto Natales	E 2
10	Puerto Varas	C 2
50	Punta Arenas	h 11
29	Quillota	A 2
27	Quilpué	A 2
7	Quintero	A 2
53	Rancagua	A 2
11	Rengo	A 2
8	Río Bueno	C 2
27	San Antonio	A 2
45	San Bernardo	A 2
14	San Carlos	B 2
19	San Felipe	A 2
22	San Fernando	A 2
9	San Javier	B 2
647	Santiago	A 2
12	Talagante	A 2
68	Talca	B 2
84	Talcahuano	B 2
72	Temuco	B 2
27	Tomé	B 2
10	Traiguén	B 2
61	Valdivia	C 2
253	Valparaíso	A 2
14	Victoria	B 2
9	Villarrica	B 2
116	Viña del Mar	A 2

Oblique Conic Conformal Projection
SCALE 1:8,000,000   1 Inch = 126 Statute Miles

BRAZIL
Principal Cities
Pop.—Thousands

38 Alagoinhas........E 5
34 Alegrete..........p11
49 Anápolis..........F 3
113 Aracaju...........E 5
54 Araçatuba.........G 2
36 Araguari..........F 3
58 Araraquara........G 3
24 Araras............G 3
24 Araxá.............F 3
30 Assis.............G 2
20 Avaré.............G 3
48 Bagé..............q12
42 Barbacena.........G 4
29 Barra do Piraí....G 4
47 Barra Mansa.......G 4
40 Barretos..........G 3
85 Bauru.............G 3
18 Bebedouro.........G 3
360 Belém (Pará)......C 3
643 Belo Horizonte....F 4
47 Blumenau......H 3, p13
34 Botucatú..........G 3
27 Bragança Paulista.G 3
150 Brasília..........F 3
16 Brusque.......H 3, p13
39 Cachoeira do Sul...q12
39 Cachoeiro do
      Itapemirim......G 4
116 Campina Grande..D 5
180 Campinas..........G 3
64 Campo Grande....G 2
91 Campos............G 4
22 Caratinga.........F 4
18 Caràzinho.........p12
64 Caruaru...........D 5
21 Cataguases........G 4
37 Catanduva.........G 3
19 Caxias............C 4
61 Caxias do Sul......p12
29 Conselheiro
      Lafaiete........G 4
37 Corumbá...........F 1
28 Crato.............D 5
33 Cruz Alta.........p12
27 Cruzeiro..........G 4
43 Cuiabá............F 1
345 Curitiba..........H 3
22 Curvelo...........F 4
42 Divinópolis.......G 4
15 Dom Pedrito.......q12
25 Erechim......H 2, p12
16 Estância..........E 5
62 Feira de Santana...E 5
74 Florianópolis..H 3, p13
19 Formiga...........G 3
355 Fortaleza.........C 5
47 França............G 3
34 Garanhuns.........D 5
18 Garça.............G 3
19 Goiana............D 6
133 Goiânia...........F 3
70 Governador
      Valadares.......F 4
38 Guaratinguetá.....G 3
46 Ilhéus............E 5
54 Itabuna...........E 5
39 Itajaí.......H 3, p13
31 Itajubá...........G 3
29 Itapetininga......G 3
23 Itu...............G 3
34 Jaboatão..........D 6
20 Jaboticabal.......G 3
31 Jaú...............G 3
40 Jequié............E 4
136 João Pessoa
      (Paraíba)......D 6
44 Joinville.....H 3, p13
21 Juàzeiro..........D 4
53 Juàzeiro do Norte..D 5
125 Juiz de Fora......G 4
80 Jundiaí...........G 3
35 Lajes........H 2, p12
24 Lavras............G 3
45 Limeira...........G 3
21 Limoeiro..........D 5
32 Lins..............G 3
38 Livramento........q11
74 Londrina..........G 2

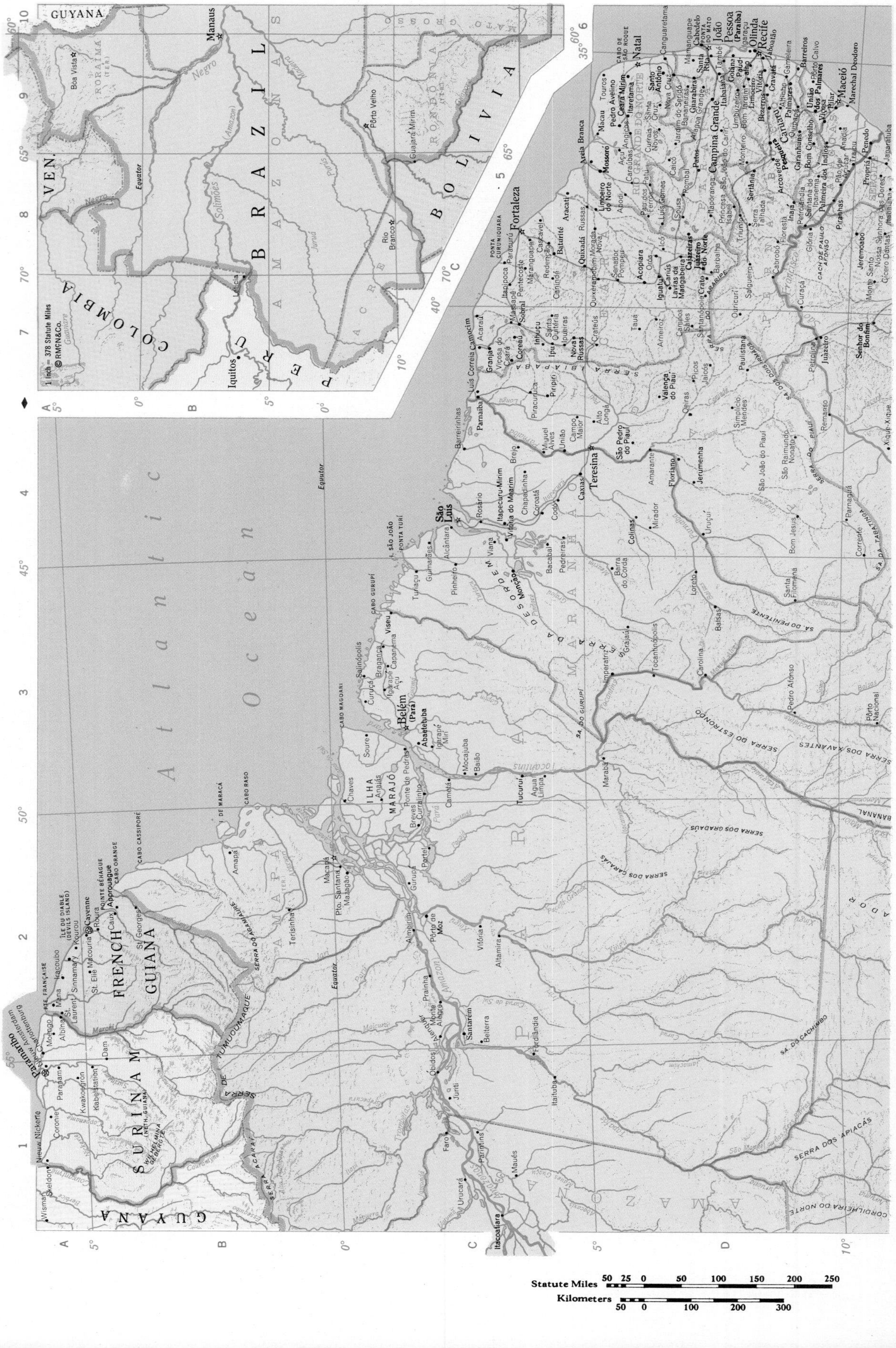

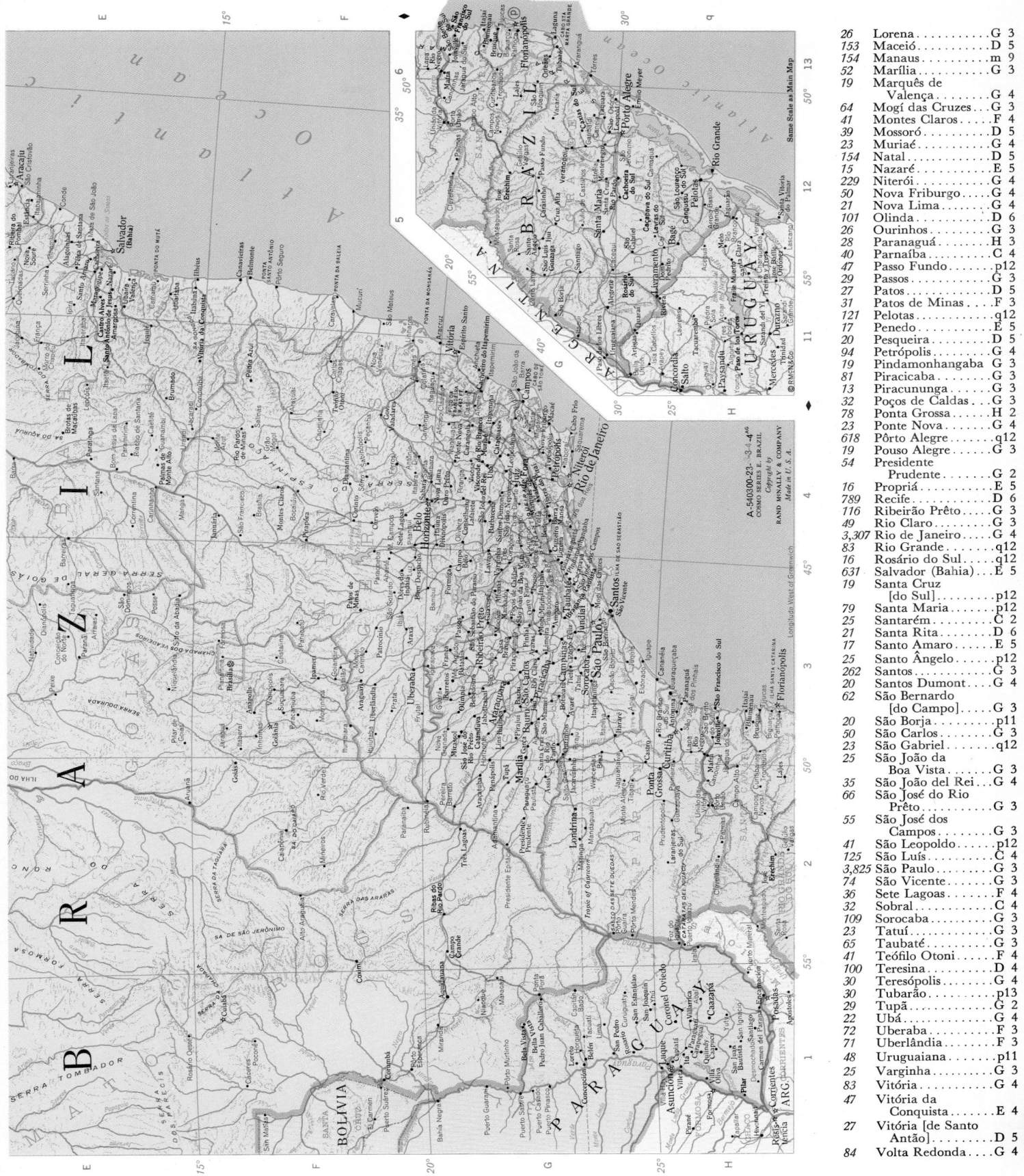

26	Lorena	G 3
153	Maceió	D 5
154	Manaus	m 9
52	Marília	G 3
19	Marquês de Valença	G 4
64	Mogí das Cruzes	G 3
41	Montes Claros	F 4
39	Mossoró	D 5
23	Muriaé	G 4
154	Natal	D 5
15	Nazaré	E 5
229	Niterói	G 4
50	Nova Friburgo	G 4
21	Nova Lima	G 4
101	Olinda	D 6
26	Ourinhos	G 3
28	Paranaguá	H 3
40	Parnaíba	C 4
47	Passo Fundo	p12
29	Passos	G 3
27	Patos	D 5
31	Patos de Minas	F 3
121	Pelotas	q12
17	Penedo	E 5
20	Pesqueira	D 5
94	Petrópolis	G 4
19	Pindamonhangaba	G 3
81	Piracicaba	G 3
13	Piracununga	G 3
32	Poços de Caldas	G 3
78	Ponta Grossa	H 2
23	Ponte Nova	G 4
618	Pôrto Alegre	q12
19	Pouso Alegre	G 3
54	Presidente Prudente	G 2
16	Propriá	E 5
789	Recife	D 6
116	Ribeirão Prêto	G 3
49	Rio Claro	G 3
3,307	Rio de Janeiro	G 4
83	Rio Grande	q12
16	Rosário do Sul	q12
631	Salvador (Bahia)	E 5
19	Santa Cruz [do Sul]	p12
79	Santa Maria	p12
25	Santarém	C 2
21	Santa Rita	D 6
17	Santo Amaro	E 5
25	Santo Ângelo	p12
262	Santos	G 3
20	Santos Dumont	G 4
62	São Bernardo [do Campo]	G 3
20	São Borja	p11
50	São Carlos	G 3
23	São Gabriel	q12
25	São João da Boa Vista	G 3
35	São João del Rei	G 4
66	São José do Rio Prêto	G 3
55	São José dos Campos	G 3
41	São Leopoldo	p12
125	São Luís	C 4
3,825	São Paulo	G 3
74	São Vicente	G 3
36	Sete Lagoas	F 4
32	Sobral	C 4
109	Sorocaba	G 3
23	Tatuí	G 3
65	Taubaté	G 3
41	Teófilo Otoni	F 4
100	Teresina	D 4
30	Teresópolis	G 4
30	Tubarão	p13
29	Tupã	G 2
22	Ubá	G 4
72	Uberaba	F 3
71	Uberlândia	F 3
48	Uruguaiana	p11
25	Varginha	G 3
83	Vitória	G 4
47	Vitória da Conquista	E 4
27	Vitória [de Santo Antão]	D 5
84	Volta Redonda	G 4

Oblique Conic Conformal Projection
SCALE 1:12,000,000   1 Inch = 189 Statute Miles

ECUADOR
Principal Cities

Pop.—Thousands

7	Alausí	B 2
53	Ambato	B 2
8	Azogues	B 2
16	Babahoyo	B 2
9	Bahía de Caráquez	B 1
7	Balzar	B 2
4	Baños	B 2
5	Calceta	B 1
5	Cañar	B 2
5	Cariamanga	B 2
4	Catacocha	B 2
8	Cayambe	A 2
3	Celica	B 2
13	Chone	B 1
60	Cuenca	B 2
7	Daule	A 2
33	Esmeraldas	A 2
2	Girón	B 2
3	Gualaceo	B 2
10	Guaranda	B 2
511	Guayaquil	B 2
26	Ibarra	A 2
13	Jipijapa	B 1
15	Latacunga	B 2
27	Loja	B 2
5	Macará	B 2
4	Machachi	B 2
29	Machala	B 2
34	Manta	B 1
5	Montecristi	B 1
9	Otavalo	A 2
13	Pasaje	B 2
3	Píllaro	B 2
32	Portoviejo	B 1
3	Pujilí	B 2
355	Quito	B 2
42	Riobamba	B 2
4	Rocafuerte	B 1
3	Salcedo	B 2
5	Salinas	B 1
7	San Gabriel	A 2
4	Santa Ana	B 1
4	Santa Elena	B 1
9	Santa Rosa	B 2
1	Sigsig	B 2
16	Tulcán	A 2
6	Vinces	B 2
3	Yaguachi	B 2
9	Zaruma	B 2

PERU
Principal Cities

Pop.—Thousands

9	Abancay	D 3
2	Acobamba	D 3
2	Acomayo	D 3
2	Andahuaylas	D 3
2	Andamarca	D 3
2	Anta	D 3
2	Antabamba	D 3
157	Arequipa	E 3
4	Ascope	C 2
2	Ayabaca	B 2
24	Ayacucho	D 3
8	Ayaviri	D 3
5	Azángaro	D 3
3	Cabana	C 2
11	Cajabamba	C 2
23	Cajamarca	C 2
3	Cajatámbo	D 2
3	Calca	D 3
161	Callao	D 2
5	Camaná	E 3
7	Cañete	D 2
2	Caraz	C 2
2	Carhuaz	C 2
5	Casma	C 2
3	Castilla	C 1
9	Catacaos	C 1
6	Celendín	C 2
6	Cerro de Pasco	D 2
7	Chachapoyas	C 2
3	Chalhuanca	D 3
3	Chancay	D 2
8	Chepén	C 2
87	Chiclayo	C 2

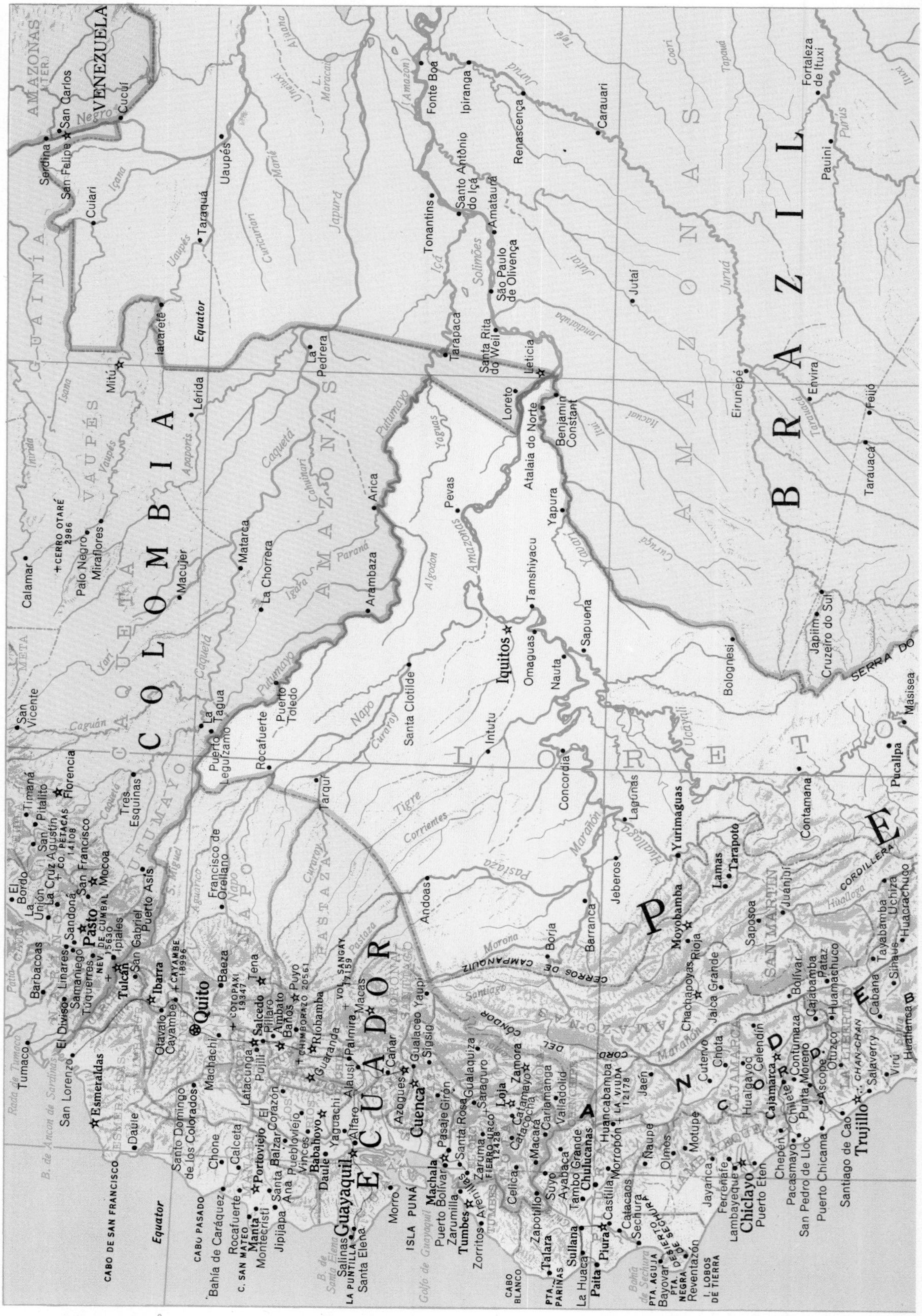

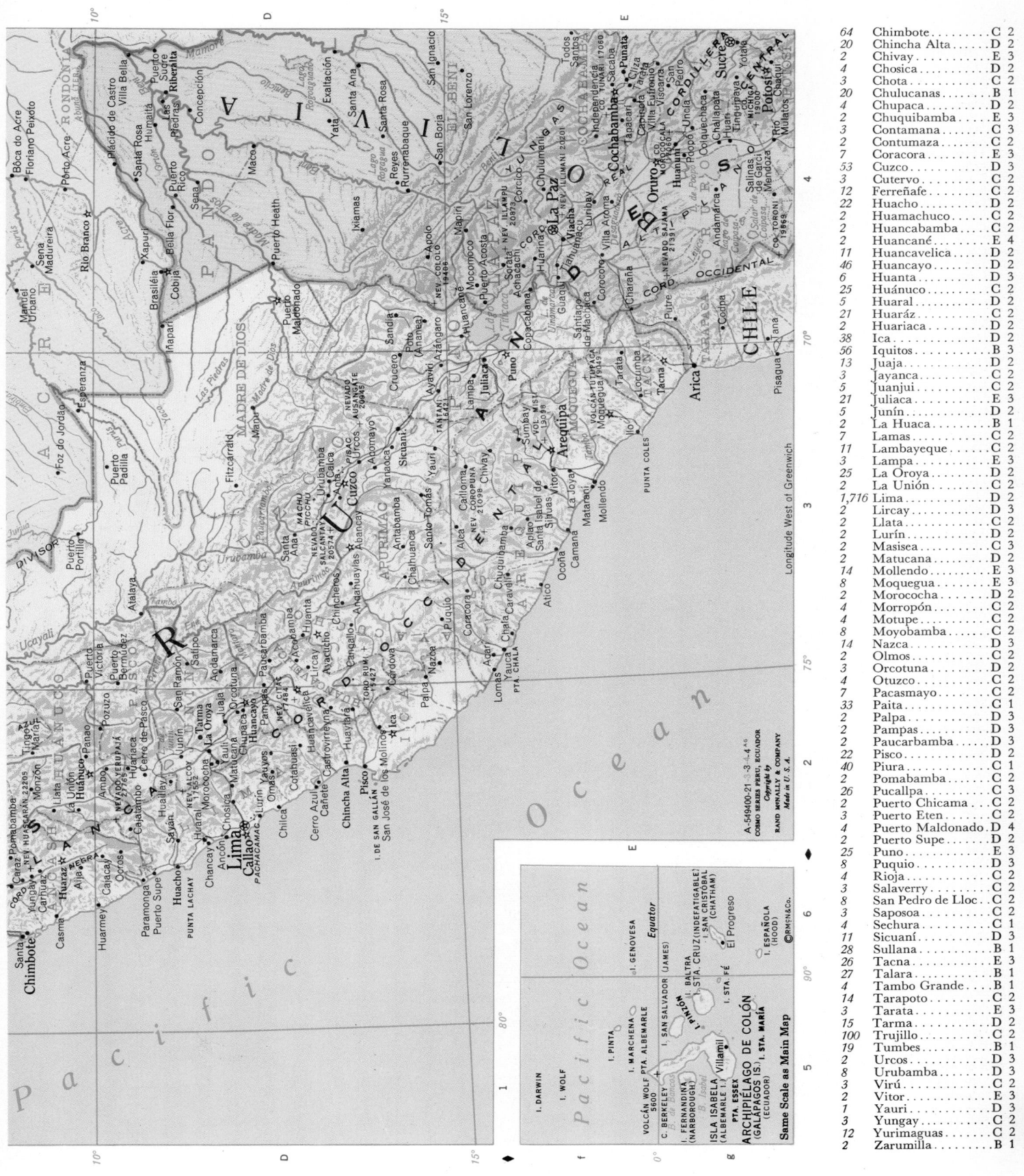

Oblique Conic Conformal Projection
SCALE 1:8,000,000   1 Inch = 126 Statute Miles

64	Chimbote	C 2
20	Chincha Alta	D 2
2	Chivay	E 3
4	Chosica	D 2
3	Chota	C 2
20	Chulucanas	B 1
4	Chupaca	D 2
2	Chuquibamba	E 3
3	Contamana	C 3
2	Contumaza	C 2
7	Coracora	E 3
53	Cuzco	D 3
3	Cutervo	C 2
12	Ferreñafe	C 2
22	Huacho	D 2
2	Huamachuco	C 2
2	Huancabamba	C 2
2	Huancané	E 4
11	Huancavelica	D 2
46	Huancayo	D 2
6	Huanta	D 3
25	Huánuco	C 2
5	Huaral	D 2
21	Huaráz	C 2
2	Huariaca	C 2
38	Ica	D 2
56	Iquitos	B 3
13	Juaja	D 2
3	Jayanca	C 2
5	Juanjui	C 2
21	Juliaca	E 3
5	Junín	D 2
2	La Huaca	B 1
7	Lamas	C 2
11	Lambayeque	C 2
3	Lampa	E 3
25	La Oroya	D 2
2	La Unión	C 2
1,716	Lima	D 2
2	Lircay	D 3
2	Llata	C 2
2	Lurín	D 2
2	Masisea	C 3
2	Matucana	D 2
14	Mollendo	E 3
8	Moquegua	E 3
2	Morococha	D 2
3	Morropón	C 2
4	Motupe	C 2
8	Moyobamba	C 2
14	Nazca	D 3
2	Olmos	C 2
3	Orcotuna	D 2
4	Otuzco	C 2
7	Pacasmayo	C 2
33	Paita	C 1
2	Palpa	D 3
2	Pampas	D 3
2	Paucarbamba	D 3
22	Pisco	D 2
40	Piura	C 1
2	Pomabamba	C 2
26	Pucallpa	C 3
2	Puerto Chicama	C 2
3	Puerto Eten	C 2
4	Puerto Maldonado	D 4
2	Puerto Supe	C 2
25	Puno	E 3
8	Puquio	D 3
4	Rioja	C 2
3	Salaverry	C 2
8	San Pedro de Lloc	C 2
3	Saposoa	C 2
4	Sechura	C 1
11	Sicuaní	D 3
28	Sullana	B 1
26	Tacna	E 3
27	Talara	B 1
4	Tambo Grande	B 1
14	Tarapoto	C 2
3	Tarata	E 3
15	Tarma	D 2
100	Trujillo	C 2
19	Tumbes	B 1
2	Urcos	D 3
8	Urubamba	D 3
3	Virú	C 2
2	Vitor	E 3
1	Yauri	D 3
3	Yungay	C 2
12	Yurimaguas	C 2
2	Zarumilla	B 1

COLOMBIA
Principal Cities

Pop.—Thousands

8	Aguadas	B 2
8	Anserma	B 2
12	Arjona	A 2
78	Armenia	C 2
10	Armero	C 3
25	Barrancabermeja	B 3
498	Barranquilla	A 3
28	Bello	B 2
1,697	Bogotá	B 3
230	Bucaramanga	B 3
57	Buenaventura	C 2
48	Buga	C 2
11	Caicedonia	C 2
16	Calarcá	C 2
638	Cali	C 2
242	Cartagena	A 2
49	Cartago	C 2
12	Chaparral	C 2
10	Chiquinquirá	B 3
24	Ciénaga	A 3
130	Cúcuta	B 3
8	Duitama	B 3
10	El Banco	B 3
10	El Carmen de Bolívar	B 2
9	Espinal	C 3
13	Facatativá	B 3
49	Girardot	C 3
16	Honda	B 3
90	Ibagué	C 2
12	Ipiales	C 2
15	La Dorada	B 3
12	Líbano	C 3
17	Magangué	B 2
222	Manizales	B 2
773	Medellín	B 2
9	Mompós	B 3
39	Montería	B 2
66	Neiva	C 2
15	Ocaña	B 3
83	Palmira	C 2
16	Pamplona	B 3
68	Pasto	C 2
121	Pereira	C 2
55	Popayán	C 2
9	Puerto Berrío	B 3
9	Puerto Tejada	C 2
43	Quibdó	B 2
14	Sabanalarga	A 3
10	San Gil	B 3
48	Santa Marta	A 3
17	Sevilla	C 2
22	Sincelejo	B 2
12	Socorro	B 3
14	Sogamoso	B 3
20	Soledad	A 3
11	Sonsón	B 2
29	Tuluá	C 2
13	Tumaco	C 2
69	Tunja	B 3
10	Turbaco	A 2
9	Valledupar	A 3
30	Villavicencio	C 3
10	Yarumal	B 2
13	Zipaquirá	B 3

NETHERLANDS ANTILLES
Principal City

Pop.—Thousands

44	Willemstad	A 4

PANAMA
Principal Cities

Pop.—Thousands

9	Chitré	B 1
60	Colon	B 1
23	David	B 1
319	Panamá	B 2

TRINADAD & TOBAGO
Principal Cities

Pop.—Thousands

94	Port-of-Spain	A 5
40	San Fernando	A 5

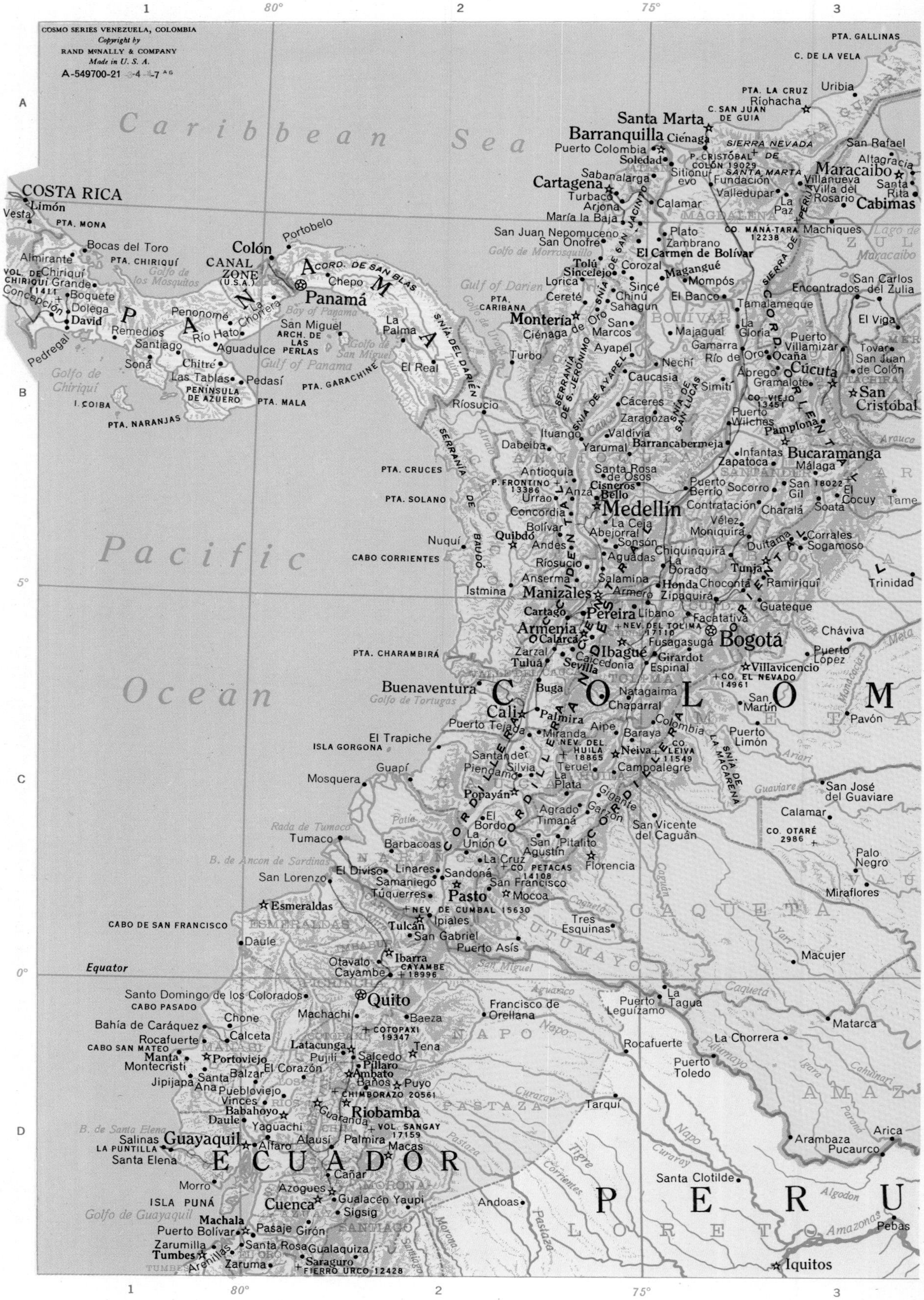

COSMO SERIES VENEZUELA, COLOMBIA
Copyright by
RAND McNALLY & COMPANY
Made in U.S.A.
A-549700-21

VENEZUELA
Principal Cities

Pop.—Thousands

Pop.	City	Ref.
32	Acarigua	B 4
14	Altagracia	A 3
14	Altagracia de Orituco	B 4
27	Anaco	*B 5
35	Antímano	*A 4
11	Araure	*B 4
41	Barcelona	A 5
26	Barinas	B 3
197	Barquisimeto	A 4
42	Baruta	*A 4
10	Boconó	*B 3
93	Cabimas	A 3
14	Cagua	*A 4
15	Calabozo	B 4
14	Cantaura	B 5
787	Caracas	A 4
19	Caripito	A 5
22	Carora	A 3
38	Carúpano	A 5
62	Chacao	*A 4
10	Chivacoa	*A 4
56	Ciudad Bolívar	B 5
45	Coro	A 4
72	Cumaná	A 5
97	El Recreo	*A 4
42	El Tigre	B 5
15	El Tocuyo	B 4
106	El Valle	*A 4
9	El Viga	B 3
10	Encontrados	B 3
11	Guacara	*A 4
17	Guanare	B 4
14	Guarenas	*A 4
11	Guatire	*A 4
11	Güiria	A 5
20	La Guaira	A 4
68	Lagunillas	*A 3
62	La Vega	*A 4
23	La Victoria	A 4
44	Los Dos Caminos	*A 4
35	Los Teques	A 4
14	Machiques	A 3
73	Maiquetía	A 4
433	Maracaibo	A 3
134	Maracay	A 4
53	Maturín	B 5
13	Mene Grande	*B 3
40	Merida	B 3
14	Ocumare del Tuy	A 4
11	Palo Negro	*A 4
75	Petare	*A 4
21	Porlamar	A 5
51	Puerto Cabello	A 4
55	Puerto la Cruz	A 5
16	Punta Cardón	*A 3
42	Punto Fijo	A 3
10	Rosario	*A 4
12	Rubio	*B 3
15	San Antonio del Táchira	*B 3
12	San Carlos	B 4
14	San Carlos del Zulia	B 3
96	San Cristóbal	B 3
28	San Felipe	A 4
32	San Felix	*B 5
22	San Fernando de Apure	B 4
26	San Juan de los Morros	B 4
12	Santa Rita	A 3
75	Santo Tomé de Guayana	B 5
19	Trujillo	B 3
10	Tucupita	B 5
12	Upata	B 5
161	Valencia	A 4
45	Valera	B 3
24	Valle de la Pascua	B 4
20	Villa de Cura	A 4
10	Zaraza	B 4

* Not shown on map. Index key denotes approximate location.

Oblique Conic Conformal Projection
SCALE 1:8,000,000 1 Inch = 126 Statute Miles

EL SALVADOR
Principal Cities
Pop.—Thousands

13	Ahuachapán........	E 7
11	La Unión........	E 7
40	San Miguel......	E 7
256	San Salvador......	E 7
73	Santa Ana........	E 7
15	San Vicente........	E 7
24	Sonsonate........	E 7

GUATEMALA
Principal Cities
Pop.—Thousands

11	Antigua Guatemala.....	E 6
9	Chiquimula.......	E 7
7	Comalapa........	E 6
3	Gualán........	D 7
573	Guatemala........	E 6
7	Jalapa........	E 6
5	Jutiapa........	E 7
11	Mazatenango.......	E 6
15	Puerto Barrios.....D 7
28	Quezaltenango......	E 6
9	Retalhuleu........	E 6
3	San José........	E 6
8	Zacapa........	E 7

HONDURAS
Principal Cities
Pop.—Thousands

4	Catacamas........	E 7
11	Choluteca........	E 7
8	Comayagua........	E 7
6	Danlí........	E 7
25	La Ceiba........	D 7
17	Puerto Cortés.....	D 7
59	San Pedro Sula....	D 7
134	Tegucigalpa......	E 7

MEXICO
Principal Cities
Pop.—Thousands

26	Acámbaro....C 4, m13
49	Acapulco [de Juárez].........D 5
127	Aguascalientes ....C 4, m12
20	Apatzingán [de la Constitución]...n12
31	Atlixco........n14
64	Azcapotzalco..h 9, n14
44	Campeche........D 6
59	Celaya........m13
150	Chihuahua......B 3
20	Ciudad Acuña......B 4
23	Ciudad Mante.....C 5
24	Ciudad de Valles.....C 5, m14
31	Ciudad Guzmán....D 4, n12
262	Ciudad Juárez....A 3
68	Ciudad Obregón....B 3
51	Ciudad Victoria....C 5
37	Coatzacoalcos (Puerto Mexico).D 6
44	Colima........D 4, n12
47	Córdoba..........n15
55	Coyoacán.....h 9, n14
37	Cuernavaca....D 5, n14
85	Culiacán........C 3
97	Durango........C 4
43	Ensenada........A 1
36	Fresnillo........C 4
61	Gómez Palacio....B 4
737	Guadalajara..C 4, m12
28	Guanajuato...C 4, m13
35	Guaymas........B 2
103	Gustavo A. Madero..h 9
96	Hermosillo......B 2
41	Hidalgo del Parral..B 3
27	Iguala........D 5, n14

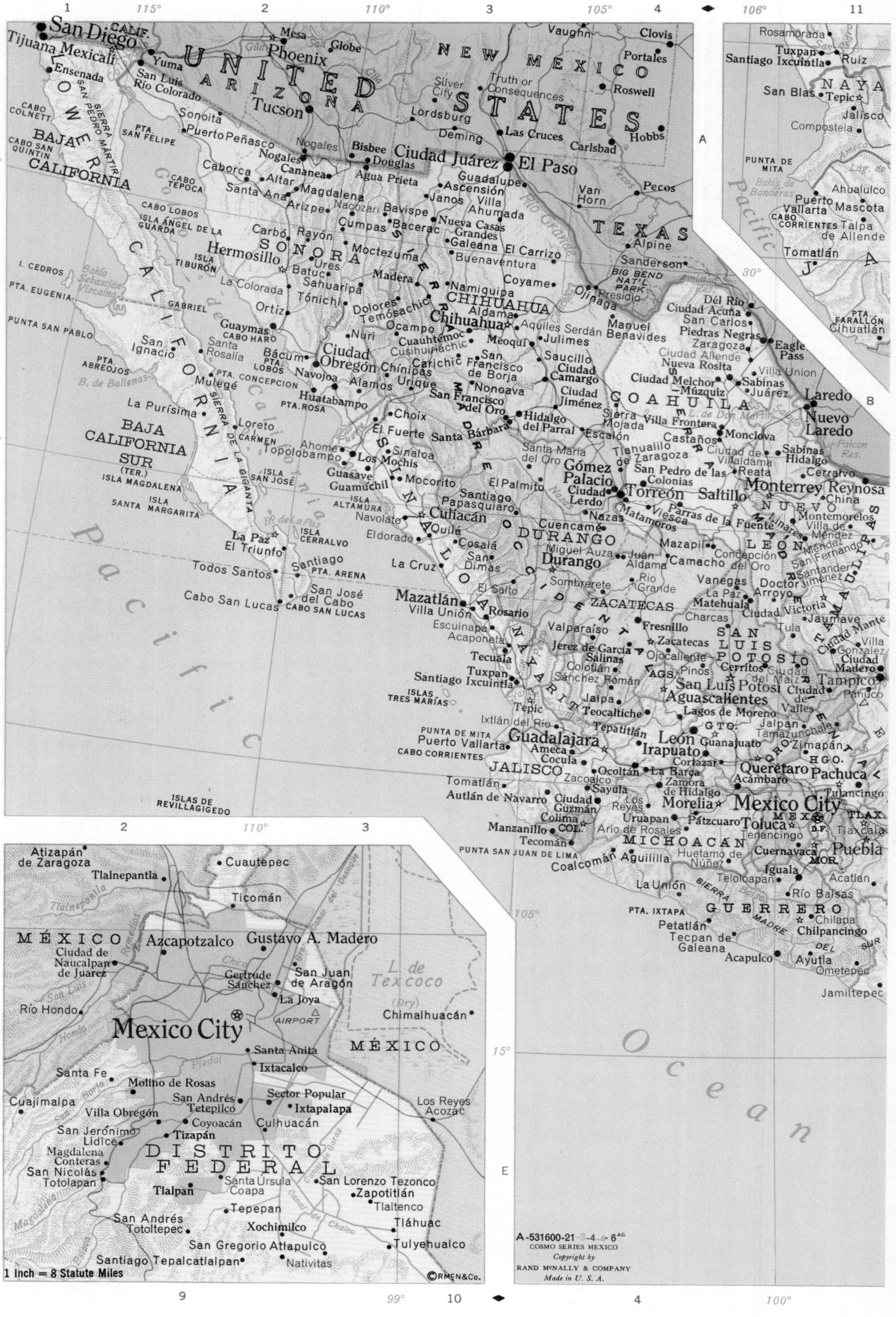

A-531600-21-3-4-6 AG
COSMO SERIES MEXICO
Copyright by
RAND McNALLY & COMPANY
Made in U.S.A.

1 Inch = 8 Statute Miles

©RMcN&Co.

Statute Miles 50 25 0   50   100   150   200   250
Kilometers   50   100   200   300

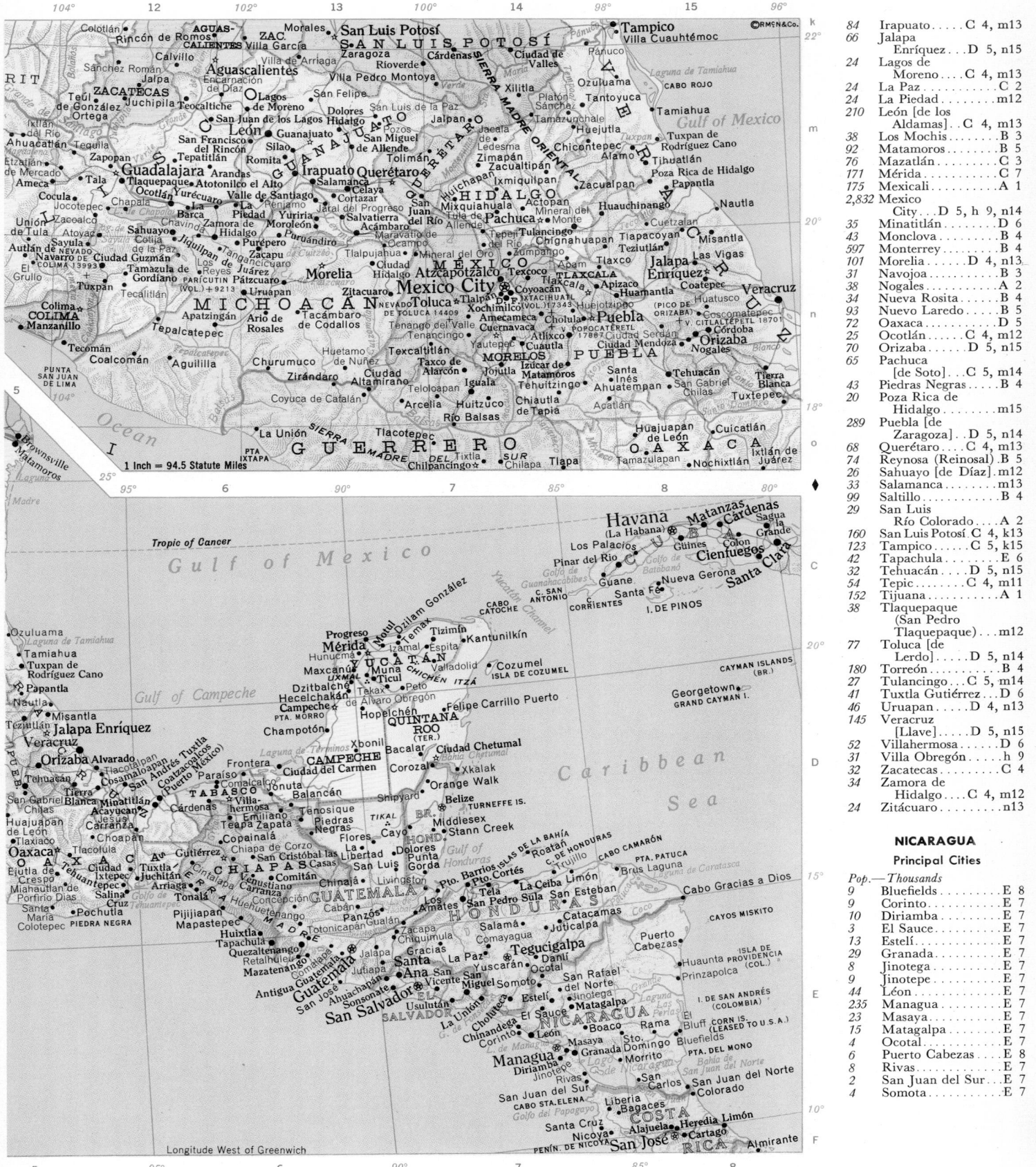

Oblique Conic Conformal Projection
SCALE 1:12,000 000 1 Inch = 189 Statute Miles

84	Irapuato	C 4, m13
66	Jalapa Enríquez	D 5, n15
24	Lagos de Moreno	C 4, m13
24	La Paz	C 2
24	La Piedad	m12
210	León [de los Aldamas]	C 4, m13
38	Los Mochis	B 3
92	Matamoros	B 5
76	Mazatlán	C 3
171	Mérida	C 7
175	Mexicali	A 1
2,832	Mexico City	D 5, h 9, n14
35	Minatitlán	D 6
43	Monclova	B 4
597	Monterrey	B 4
101	Morelia	D 4, n13
31	Navojoa	B 3
38	Nogales	A 2
34	Nueva Rosita	B 4
93	Nuevo Laredo	B 5
72	Oaxaca	D 5
25	Ocotlán	C 4, m12
70	Orizaba	D 5, n15
65	Pachuca [de Soto]	C 5, n14
43	Piedras Negras	B 4
20	Poza Rica de Hidalgo	m15
289	Puebla [de Zaragoza]	D 5, n14
68	Querétaro	C 4, m13
74	Reynosa (Reinosa)	B 5
26	Sahuayo [de Díaz]	m12
33	Salamanca	m13
99	Saltillo	B 4
29	San Luis Río Colorado	A 2
160	San Luis Potosí	C 4, k13
123	Tampico	C 5, k15
42	Tapachula	E 6
32	Tehuacán	D 5, n15
54	Tepic	C 4, m11
152	Tijuana	A 1
38	Tlaquepaque (San Pedro Tlaquepaque)	m12
77	Toluca [de Lerdo]	D 5, n14
180	Torreón	B 4
27	Tulancingo	C 5, n14
41	Tuxtla Gutiérrez	D 6
46	Uruapan	D 4, n13
145	Veracruz [Llave]	D 5, n15
52	Villahermosa	D 6
31	Villa Obregón	h 9
32	Zacatecas	C 4
34	Zamora de Hidalgo	C 4, m12
24	Zitácuaro	n13

NICARAGUA

Principal Cities

Pop.—Thousands

9	Bluefields	E 8
9	Corinto	E 7
10	Diriamba	E 7
3	El Sauce	E 7
13	Estelí	E 7
29	Granada	E 7
8	Jinotega	E 7
9	Jinotepe	E 7
44	León	E 7
235	Managua	E 7
23	Masaya	E 7
15	Matagalpa	E 7
4	Ocotal	E 7
6	Puerto Cabezas	E 8
8	Rivas	E 7
2	San Juan del Sur	E 7
4	Somota	E 7

BAHAMAS
Principal Cities
Pop.—Thousands
1	Matthew Town	D 7
6	Nassau	B 5, m17

Pop.—Hundreds
5	Governors Harbour	B 5
5	Old Bight	B 6
6	West End	A 4

BARBADOS
Principal Cities
Pop.—Thousands
1	Bathsheba	J15
11	Bridgetown	J15

BERMUDA
Principal Cities
Pop.—Thousands
3	Hamilton	p20
2	St. George	o20

BRITISH WEST INDIES
Principal Cities
Pop.—Thousands
16	Basseterre	H13
4	Castries	J14
4	Kingstown	J14
10	Roseau	I14
7	St. George's	J14
21	St. John's	H14

CUBA
Principal Cities
Pop.—Thousands
20	Artemisa	C 2
25	Banes	D 6
12	Baracoa	D 6
26	Bayamo	D 5
26	Caibarién	C 4
150	Camagüey	D 5
14	Camajuaní	C 4
55	Cárdenas	C 3
47	Ciego de Avila	D 4
70	Cienfuegos	C 3
16	Colón	C 3
13	Cruces	C 3
29	Florida	D 4
8	Fomento	C 4
8	Gibara	D 5
55	Guanabacoa	C 2
18	Guanajay	C 2
82	Guantánamo	D 6
36	Güines	C 2
16	Güira de Melena	C 2
978	Havana	C 2
80	Holguín	D 5
13	Jovellanos	C 3
52	Manzanillo	D 5
325	Marianao	D 2
80	Matanzas	C 3
22	Morón	C 4
7	Niquero	D 5
15	Nuevitas	D 5
33	Palma Soriano	D 5
6	Palmira	C 3
52	Pinar del Río	C 2
31	Placetas	C 4
10	Puerto Padre	D 5
31	Regla	C 2
12	Remedios	C 4
8	Sagua de Tánamo	D 6
31	Sagua la Grande	C 3
20	San Antonio de los Baños	C 2
47	Sancti-Spíritus	D 4
12	San Luis	D 6
110	Santa Clara	C 4
212	Santiago de Cuba	D 6
20	Trinidad	D 4
28	Victoria de las Tunas	D 5

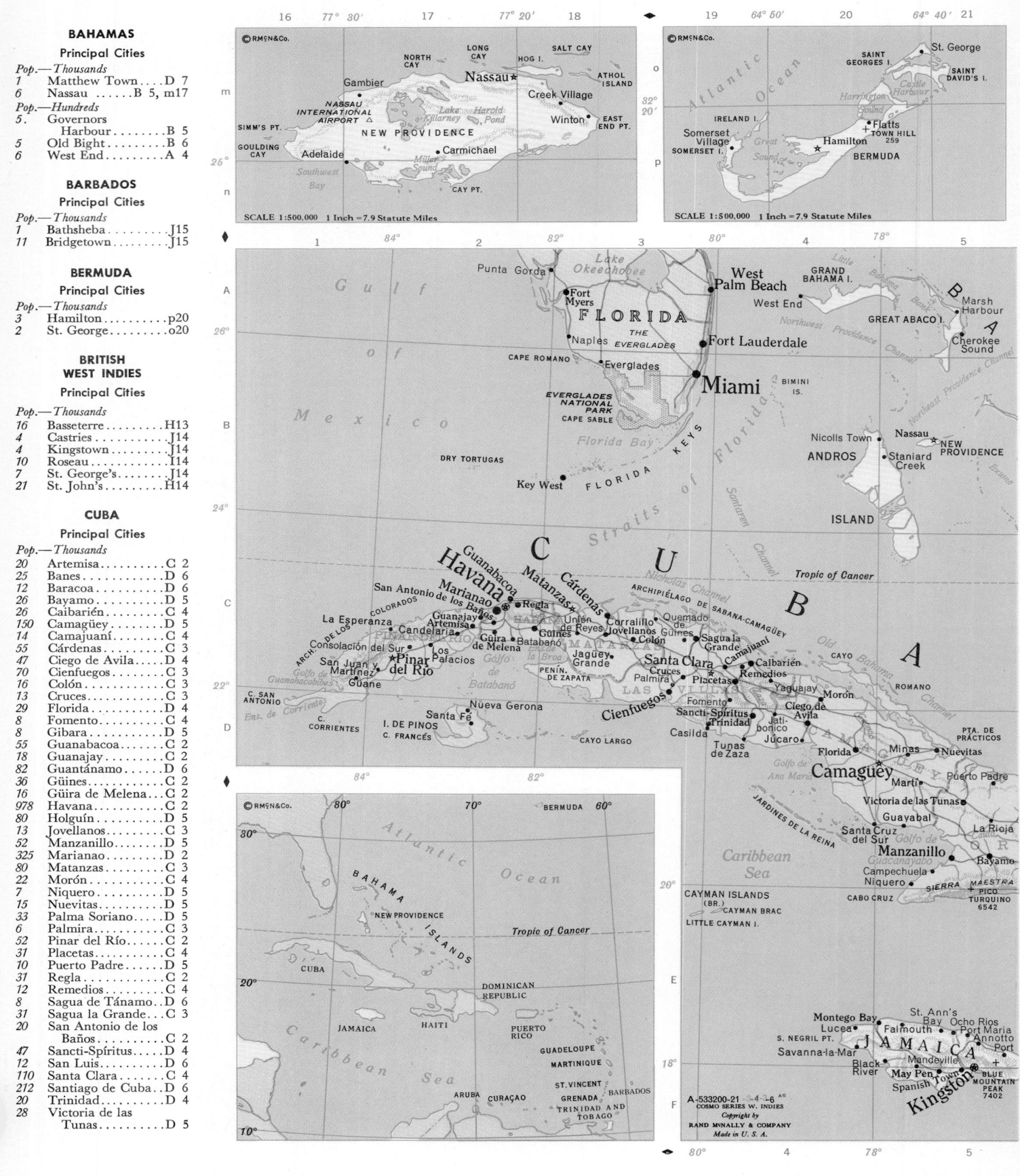

Statute Miles 25 0 25 75 125

Kilometers 25 0 25 75 125 175

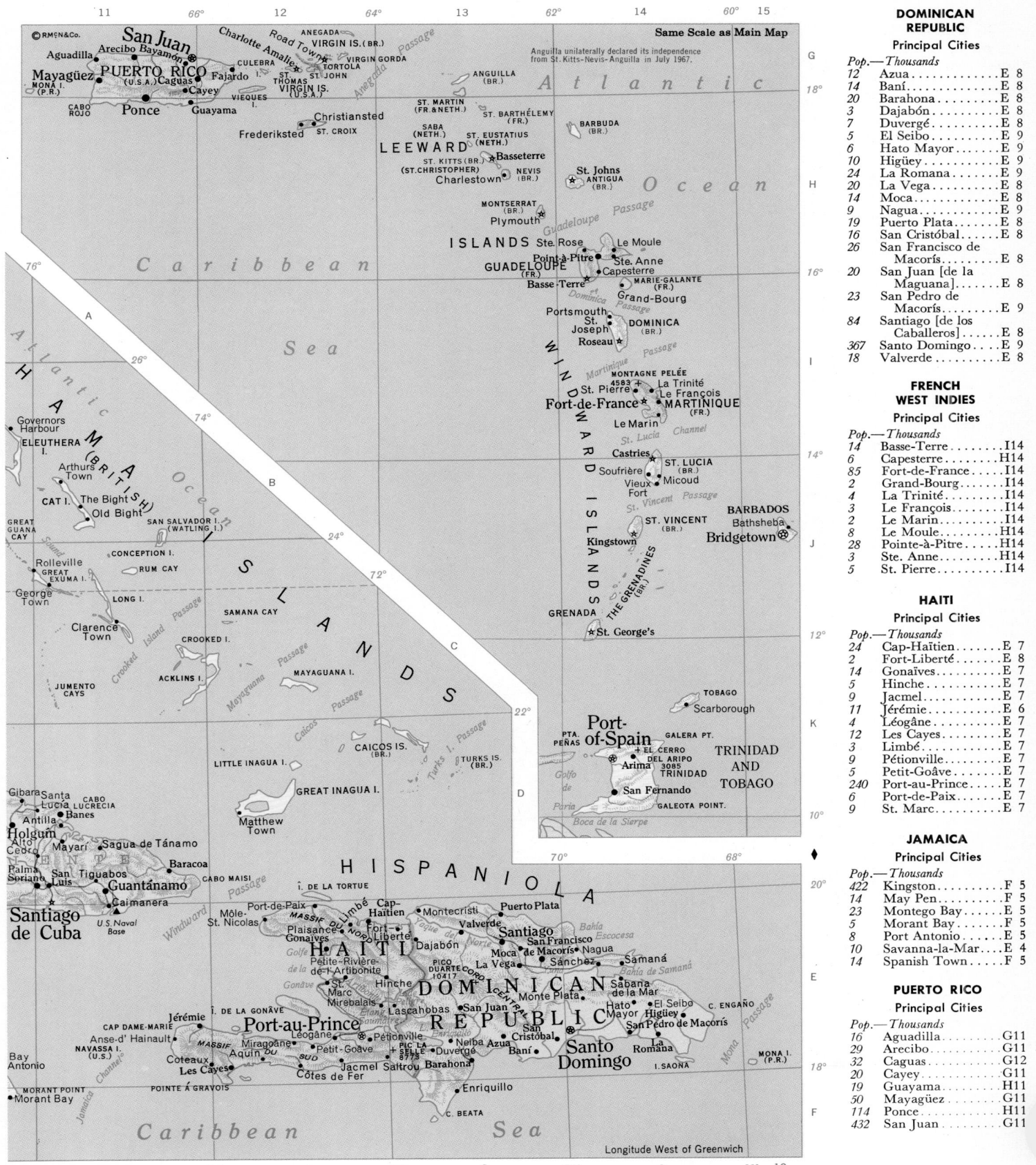

DOMINICAN REPUBLIC
Principal Cities
Pop.—Thousands

12	Azua	E 8
14	Baní	E 8
20	Barahona	E 8
3	Dajabón	E 8
7	Duvergé	E 8
5	El Seibo	E 9
6	Hato Mayor	E 9
10	Higüey	E 9
24	La Romana	E 9
20	La Vega	E 8
14	Moca	E 8
9	Nagua	E 9
19	Puerto Plata	E 8
16	San Cristóbal	E 8
26	San Francisco de Macorís	E 8
20	San Juan [de la Maguana]	E 8
23	San Pedro de Macorís	E 9
84	Santiago [de los Caballeros]	E 8
367	Santo Domingo	E 9
18	Valverde	E 8

FRENCH WEST INDIES
Principal Cities
Pop.—Thousands

14	Basse-Terre	I14
6	Capesterre	H14
85	Fort-de-France	I14
2	Grand-Bourg	I14
4	La Trinité	I14
3	Le François	I14
2	Le Marin	I14
8	Le Moule	H14
28	Pointe-à-Pitre	H14
3	Ste. Anne	H14
5	St. Pierre	I14

HAITI
Principal Cities
Pop.—Thousands

24	Cap-Haïtien	E 7
2	Fort-Liberté	E 8
14	Gonaïves	E 7
5	Hinche	E 7
9	Jacmel	E 7
11	Jérémie	E 6
4	Léogâne	E 7
12	Les Cayes	E 7
3	Limbé	E 7
9	Pétionville	E 7
5	Petit-Goâve	E 7
240	Port-au-Prince	E 7
6	Port-de-Paix	E 7
9	St. Marc	E 7

JAMAICA
Principal Cities
Pop.—Thousands

422	Kingston	F 5
14	May Pen	F 5
23	Montego Bay	E 5
5	Morant Bay	F 5
8	Port Antonio	E 5
10	Savanna-la-Mar	E 4
14	Spanish Town	F 5

PUERTO RICO
Principal Cities
Pop.—Thousands

16	Aguadilla	G11
29	Arecibo	G11
32	Caguas	G12
20	Cayey	G11
19	Guayama	H11
50	Mayagüez	G11
114	Ponce	H11
432	San Juan	G11

Oblique Conic Conformal Projection
SCALE 1:6,000,000 1 Inch = 95 Statute Miles

CANADA
Physical Features

Albanel, lake	F19
Albany, riv	F16
Amadjuak, lake	C19
Amundsen, gulf	B 8
Arctic, ocean	k27
Aston, cape	B20
Athabasca, lake	E12
Athabasca, riv	E11
Atlantic, ocean	I20
Attawapiskat, riv	F16
Baffin, bay	n35, B19
Baffin, isl	n34, B19
Banks, isl	B 9
Barrow, strait	n31, B14
Beaufort, sea	B 4
Belle Isle, strait	F22
Black, lake	E12
Bonavista, bay	G23
Boothia, gulf	B15
Boothia, pen	B14
Breton, cape	G21
Brodeur, pen	B16
Bylot, isl	n35, B18
Caniapiscau	E20
Chidley, cape	D21
Churchill, riv	E14
Coast, mts	E 7
Cree, lake	E12
Cree, riv	E12
Cumberland, sound	C20
Davis, strait	B21
Dease, strait	C12
Devon, isl	m32, A15
Dolphin and Union, strait	C10
Dubawnt, lake	D13
Eau-Claire, lake	E18
Ellesmere, isl	k33, A16
Erie, lake	H17
Feuilles, riv	E19
Fort George, riv	F18
Foxe, pen	C18
Foxe, basin	C17
Foxe, channel	C17
Franklin, mts	C 8
Fundy, bay	H20
Garry, lake	C13
Goodhope, mtn	F 9
Great Bear, lake	C 9
Great Slave, lake	D11
Grizzly Bear, mts	C 9
Hamilton, inlet	F22
Hay, riv	E10
Hayes, riv	E15
Hazen, strait	m28, A11
Hecate, strait	F 7
Henrietta Maria, cape	E17
Home, bay	C20
Hopes Advance, cape	D20
Horn, mts	D10
Hudson, bay	D16
Hudson, strait	D19
Hunt, mtn	D 8
Huron, lake	G17
Island, lake	F15
James, bay	F17
James Ross, strait	B14
Keele, peak	D 7
Kellett, cape	B 8
Lake of the Woods, lake	G15
Lancaster, sound	n33, B16
Larch, riv	E19
Liard, riv	E 8
Liverpool, bay	B 7
Logan, mts	D 5
Mackenzie, bay	C 6
Mackenzie, mts	C 7
Mackenzie, riv	C 8
Maclean, strait	m29, A12
Manitoba, lake	F14
Manitoulin, isl	G17
McClintock, channel	B13
Melville, isl	m29, A10
Melville, lake	F21
Mercy, cape	C21
Michikamau, lake	F21
Minto, lake	E18
Mistassini, lake	F18
Nass, riv	E 8

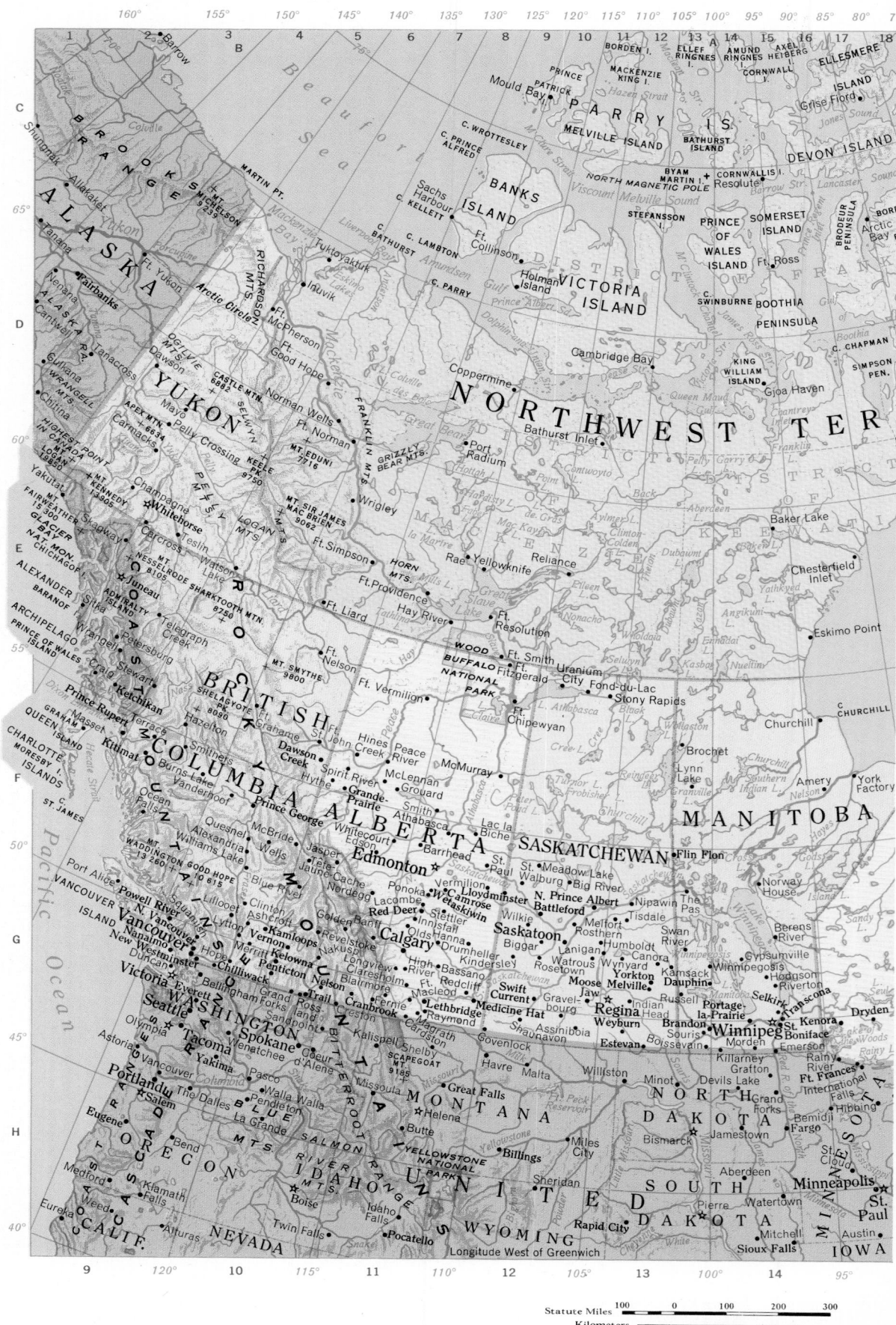

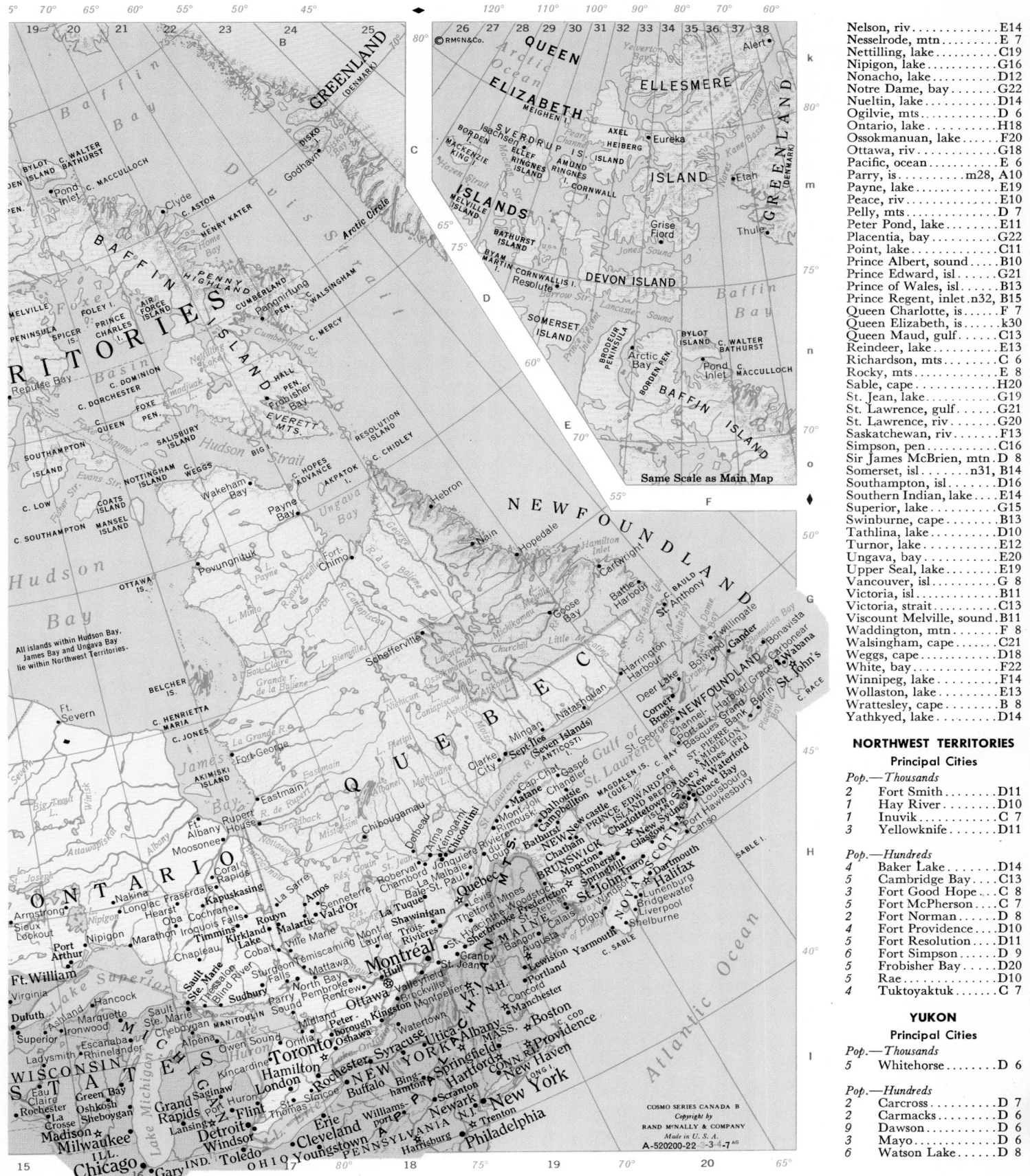

Nelson, riv............E14
Nesselrode, mtn........E 7
Nettilling, lake........C19
Nipigon, lake..........G16
Nonacho, lake.........D12
Notre Dame, bay......G22
Nueltin, lake..........D14
Ogilvie, mts...........D 6
Ontario, lake..........H18
Ossokmanuan, lake.....F20
Ottawa, riv...........G18
Pacific, ocean.........E 6
Parry, is...........m28, A10
Payne, lake...........E19
Peace, riv............E10
Pelly, mts.............D 7
Peter Pond, lake.......E11
Placentia, bay.........G22
Point, lake............C11
Prince Albert, sound.....B10
Prince Edward, isl.....D20
Prince of Wales, isl......B13
Prince Regent, inlet.n32, B15
Queen Charlotte, is.....F 7
Queen Elizabeth, is......k30
Queen Maud, gulf......C13
Reindeer, lake.........E13
Richardson, mts........C 6
Rocky, mts...........E 8
Sable, cape...........H20
St. Jean, lake.........G19
St. Lawrence, gulf......G21
St. Lawrence, riv.......G20
Saskatchewan, riv.......F13
Simpson, pen..........C16
Sir James McBrien, mtn..D 8
Somerset, isl.......n31, B14
Southampton, isl........D16
Southern Indian, lake....E14
Superior, lake.........G15
Swinburne, cape........B13
Tathlina, lake.........D10
Turnor, lake..........E12
Ungava, bay..........E20
Upper Seal, lake.......E19
Vancouver, isl.........G 8
Victoria, isl..........B11
Victoria, strait........C13
Viscount Melville, sound..B11
Waddington, mtn.......F 8
Walsingham, cape......C21
Weggs, cape..........D18
White, bay............F22
Winnipeg, lake........F14
Wollaston, lake........E13
Wrattesley, cape.......B 8
Yathkyed, lake........D14

NORTHWEST TERRITORIES

Principal Cities

Pop.—Thousands
2   Fort Smith.......D11
1   Hay River.......D10
1   Inuvik..........C 7
3   Yellowknife......D11

Pop.—Hundreds
4   Baker Lake......D14
5   Cambridge Bay....C13
3   Fort Good Hope...C 8
5   Fort McPherson...C 7
2   Fort Norman.....D 8
4   Fort Providence...D10
5   Fort Resolution...D11
6   Fort Simpson....D 9
5   Frobisher Bay....D20
5   Rae............D10
4   Tuktoyaktuk.....C 7

YUKON

Principal Cities

Pop.—Thousands
5   Whitehorse.......D 6

Pop.—Hundreds
2   Carcross........D 7
2   Carmacks........D 6
9   Dawson..........D 6
3   Mayo...........D 6
6   Watson Lake.....D 8

COSMO SERIES CANADA B
Copyright by
RAND McNALLY & COMPANY
Made in U. S. A.
A-520200-22 -3-4-7 AG

Lambert Conformal Conic Projection
SCALE 1 : 17,638,000   1 Inch = 277 Statute Miles

WESTERN
UNITED STATES
Principal Cities
Pop.—Thousands

23	Aberdeen, S. Dak..	A 8
90	Abilene, Tex.....	D 8
22	Alamogordo, N. Mex....	D 6
201	Albuquerque, N. Mex........	C 6
138	Amarillo, Tex.....	C 8
44	Anchorage, Alsk...	F 4
14	Arkansas City, Kans........	C 8
12	Artesia, N. Mex...	D 7
187	Austin, Tex.......	D 8
57	Bakersfield, Calif..	C 4
28	Bartlesville, Okla...	C 8
35	Bellingham, Wash...	A 3
111	Berkeley, Calif....	C 3
31	Big Spring, Tex....	D 7
53	Billings, Mont....	A 6
31	Bismarck, N. Dak...	A 7
72	Boise, Idaho......	B 4
38	Boulder, Colo.....	C 6
29	Bremerton, Wash...	A 3
12	Brigham City, Utah.	B 5
48	Brownsville, Tex...	E 8
28	Butte, Mont......	A 5
26	Carlsbad, N. Mex...	D 7
5	Carson City, Nev...	C 4
39	Casper, Wyo.....	B 6
44	Cheyenne, Wyo....	B 6
24	Clovis, N. Mex....	D 7
14	Coeur d'Alene, Idaho........	A 4
17	Coffeyville, Kans..	C 8
70	Colorado Springs, Colo........	C 7
168	Corpus Christi, Tex........	E 8
21	Corvallis, Oreg...	B 3
56	Council Bluffs, Iowa........	B 8
680	Dallas, Tex....	D 8
494	Denver, Colo.....	C 7
277	El Paso, Tex.....	D 6
18	Emporia, Kans....	C 8
39	Enid, Okla.......	C 8
51	Eugene, Oreg.....	B 3
40	Everett, Wash.....	A 3
13	Fairbanks, Alsk....	E 4
50	Fargo, N. Dak....	A 8
24	Farmington, N. Mex........	C 6
14	Fergus Falls, Minn.	A 8
25	Flagstaff, Ariz....	C 5
25	Fort Collins, Colo..	B 6
356	Fort Worth, Tex...	D 8
20	Fremont, Nebr....	B 8
134	Fresno, Calif....	C 4
123	Glendale, Calif....	D 4
38	Grand Forks, N. Dak........	A 8
26	Grand Island, Nebr.........B	B 8
19	Grand Junction, Colo..........	C 6
55	Great Falls, Mont..	A 5
26	Greeley, Colo....	B 7
41	Harlingen, Tex....	E 8
21	Hastings, Nebr....	B 8
20	Helena, Mont....	A 5
26	Hilo, Haw. Is.....	F 7
26	Hobbs, N. Mex....	D 7
294	Honolulu, Haw. Is........F	6, F 7
938	Houston, Tex.....	E 8
14	Huron, S. Dak....	B 8
38	Hutchinson, Kans...	C 8
36	Idaho Falls, Idaho.	B 5
7	Juneau, Alsk......	F 5
28	Kailua, Haw. Is....	F 6
14	Kearney, Nebr....	B 8
6	Ketchikan, Alsk....	F 5
17	Klamath Falls, Oreg..........	B 3
18	Laramie, Wyo.....	B 6
61	Laredo, Tex.....	E 8
29	Las Cruces, N. Mex........	D 6

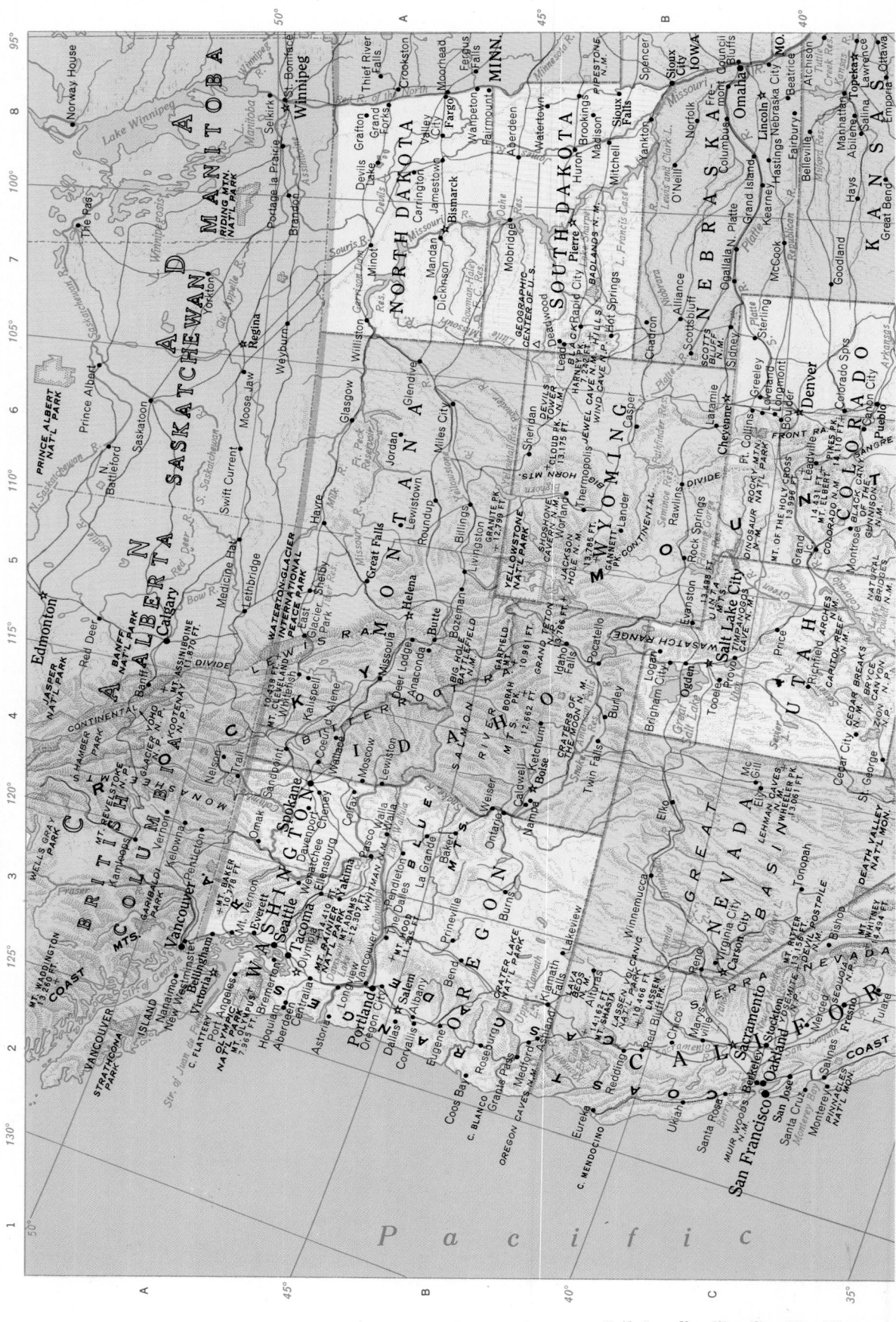

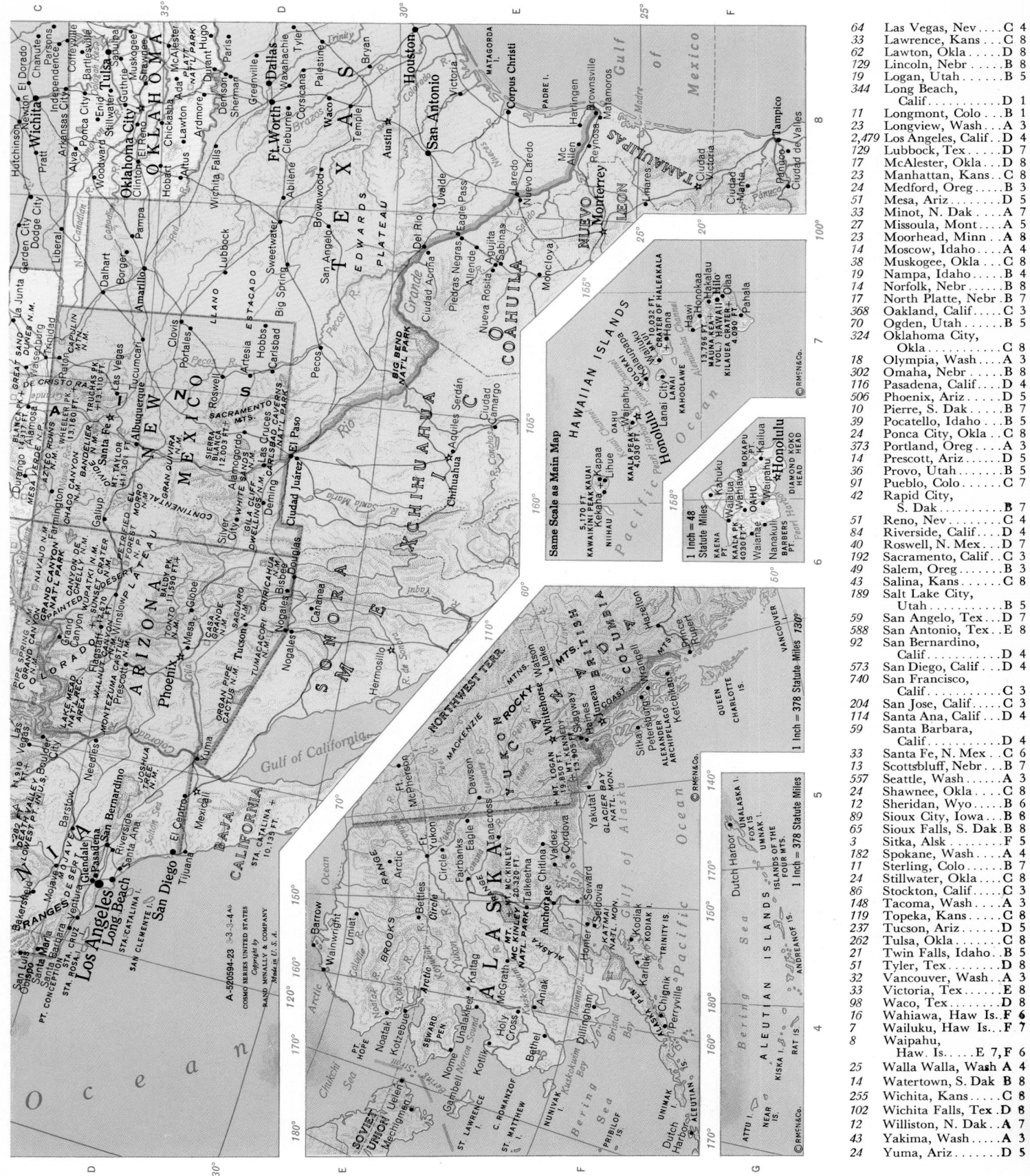

Lambert Conformal Conic Projection
SCALE 1:12,000,000 1 Inch = 189 Statute Miles

64	Las Vegas, Nev	C 4
33	Lawrence, Kans	C 8
62	Lawton, Okla	D 8
129	Lincoln, Nebr	B 8
19	Logan, Utah	B 5
344	Long Beach, Calif	D 1
11	Longmont, Colo	B 1
23	Longview, Wash	A 3
2,479	Los Angeles, Calif	D 4
129	Lubbock, Tex	D 7
17	McAlester, Okla	D 8
23	Manhattan, Kans	C 8
24	Medford, Oreg	B 3
51	Mesa, Ariz	D 5
33	Minot, N. Dak	A 7
27	Missoula, Mont	A 4
23	Moorhead, Minn	A 8
14	Moscow, Idaho	A 4
38	Muskogee, Okla	C 8
19	Nampa, Idaho	B 4
14	Norfolk, Nebr	B 8
17	North Platte, Nebr	B 7
368	Oakland, Calif	C 3
70	Ogden, Utah	B 5
324	Oklahoma City, Okla	C 8
18	Olympia, Wash	A 3
302	Omaha, Nebr	B 8
116	Pasadena, Calif	D 4
506	Phoenix, Ariz	D 5
10	Pierre, S. Dak	B 7
39	Pocatello, Idaho	B 5
24	Ponca City, Okla	C 8
373	Portland, Oreg	A 3
14	Prescott, Ariz	D 5
36	Provo, Utah	B 5
91	Pueblo, Colo	C 7
42	Rapid City, S. Dak	B 7
51	Reno, Nev	C 4
84	Riverside, Calif	D 4
40	Roswell, N. Mex	D 7
192	Sacramento, Calif	C 3
49	Salem, Oreg	B 3
43	Salina, Kans	C 8
189	Salt Lake City, Utah	B 5
59	San Angelo, Tex	D 7
588	San Antonio, Tex	E 8
92	San Bernardino, Calif	D 4
573	San Diego, Calif	D 4
740	San Francisco, Calif	C 3
204	San Jose, Calif	C 3
114	Santa Ana, Calif	D 4
59	Santa Barbara, Calif	D 4
33	Santa Fe, N. Mex	C 6
13	Scottsbluff, Nebr	B 8
557	Seattle, Wash	A 3
24	Shawnee, Okla	C 8
12	Sheridan, Wyo	B 6
89	Sioux City, Iowa	B 8
65	Sioux Falls, S. Dak	B 8
3	Sitka, Alsk	F 5
182	Spokane, Wash	A 4
11	Sterling, Colo	B 7
24	Stillwater, Okla	C 8
86	Stockton, Calif	C 3
148	Tacoma, Wash	A 3
119	Topeka, Kans	C 8
237	Tucson, Ariz	D 5
262	Tulsa, Okla	C 8
21	Twin Falls, Idaho	B 5
51	Tyler, Tex	D 8
32	Vancouver, Wash	A 3
33	Victoria, Tex	E 8
98	Waco, Tex	D 8
16	Wahiawa, Haw Is	F 6
7	Wailuku, Haw Is	F 7
8	Waipahu, Haw. Is	E 7, F 6
25	Walla Walla, Wash	A 4
14	Watertown, S. Dak	B 8
255	Wichita, Kans	C 8
102	Wichita Falls, Tex	D 8
12	Williston, N. Dak	A 7
43	Yakima, Wash	A 3
24	Yuma, Ariz	D 5

EASTERN UNITED STATES
Principal Cities

Pop.—Thousands

Pop.	City	Ref.
290	Akron, Ohio	C 3
56	Albany, Ga.	E 3
130	Albany, N.Y.	C 5
40	Alexandria, La.	E 1
91	Alexandria, Va.	D 4
108	Allentown, Pa.	C 4
69	Altoona, Pa.	C 4
41	Anderson, S.C.	E 3
23	Annapolis, Md.	D 4
60	Asheville, N.C.	D 3
41	Athens, Ga.	E 3
487	Atlanta, Ga.	E 3
60	Atlantic City, N.J.	D 5
71	Augusta, Ga.	E 3
22	Augusta, Maine	C 6
939	Baltimore, Md.	D 4
39	Bangor, Maine	C 6
152	Baton Rouge, La.	E 1
119	Beaumont, Tex.	E 1
19	Biddeford, Maine	C 5
44	Biloxi, Miss.	E 2
69	Binghamton, N.Y.	C 4
341	Birmingham, Ala.	E 2
697	Boston, Mass.	C 5
157	Bridgeport, Conn.	C 5
533	Buffalo, N.Y.	C 4
114	Canton, Ohio	C 3
104	Cedar Rapids, Iowa	C 1
76	Charleston, S.C.	E 4
86	Charleston, W. Va.	D 3
202	Charlotte, N.C.	D 3
130	Chattanooga, Tenn.	D 2
64	Chester, Pa.	D 4
3,550	Chicago, Ill.	C 2
503	Cincinnati, Ohio	D 3
812	Cleveland, Ohio	C 3
97	Columbia, S.C.	E 3
117	Columbus, Ga.	E 3
471	Columbus, Ohio	D 3
29	Concord, N.H.	C 5
60	Covington, Ky.	D 3
89	Davenport, Iowa	C 1
262	Dayton, Ohio	D 3
78	Decatur, Ill.	D 2
207	Des Moines, Iowa	C 1
1,670	Detroit, Mich.	C 3
7	Dover, Del.	D 4
57	Dubuque, Iowa	C 1
107	Duluth, Minn.	B 1
78	Durham, N.C.	D 4
82	East St. Louis, Ill.	D 1
138	Erie, Pa.	C 4
79	Evanston, Ill.	C 2
142	Evansville, Ind.	D 2
100	Fall River, Mass.	C 5
197	Flint, Mich.	C 3
84	Fort Lauderdale, Fla.	F 3
64	Fort Smith, Ark.	D 1
162	Fort Wayne, Ind.	C 2
18	Frankfort, Ky.	D 3
67	Galveston, Tex.	E 1
178	Gary, Ind.	C 2
177	Grand Rapids, Mich.	C 2
63	Green Bay, Wis.	C 2
120	Greensboro, N.C.	D 4
42	Greenville, Miss.	E 1
66	Greenville, S.C.	E 3
80	Harrisburg, Pa.	C 4
162	Hartford, Conn.	C 5
62	High Point, N.C.	D 4
84	Huntington, W. Va.	D 3
124	Huntsville, Ala.	E 2
476	Indianapolis, Ind.	D 2
144	Jackson, Miss.	E 1
34	Jackson, Tenn.	D 2
201	Jacksonville, Fla.	E 3
28	Jefferson City, Mo.	D 1
276	Jersey City, N.J.	C 5
31	Johnson City, Tenn.	D 3
82	Kalamazoo, Mich.	C 2
122	Kansas City, Kans.	D 1
476	Kansas City, Mo.	D 1

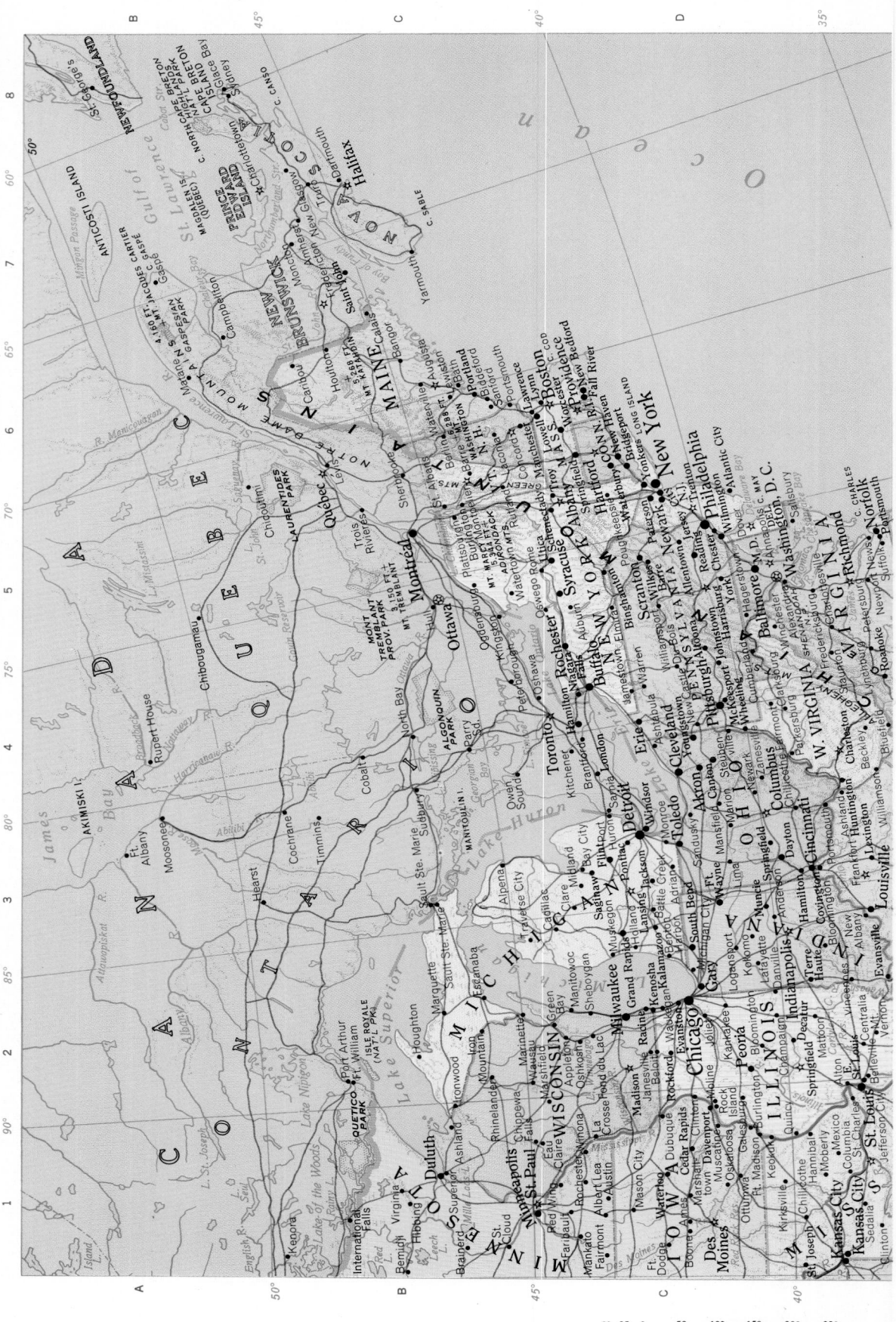

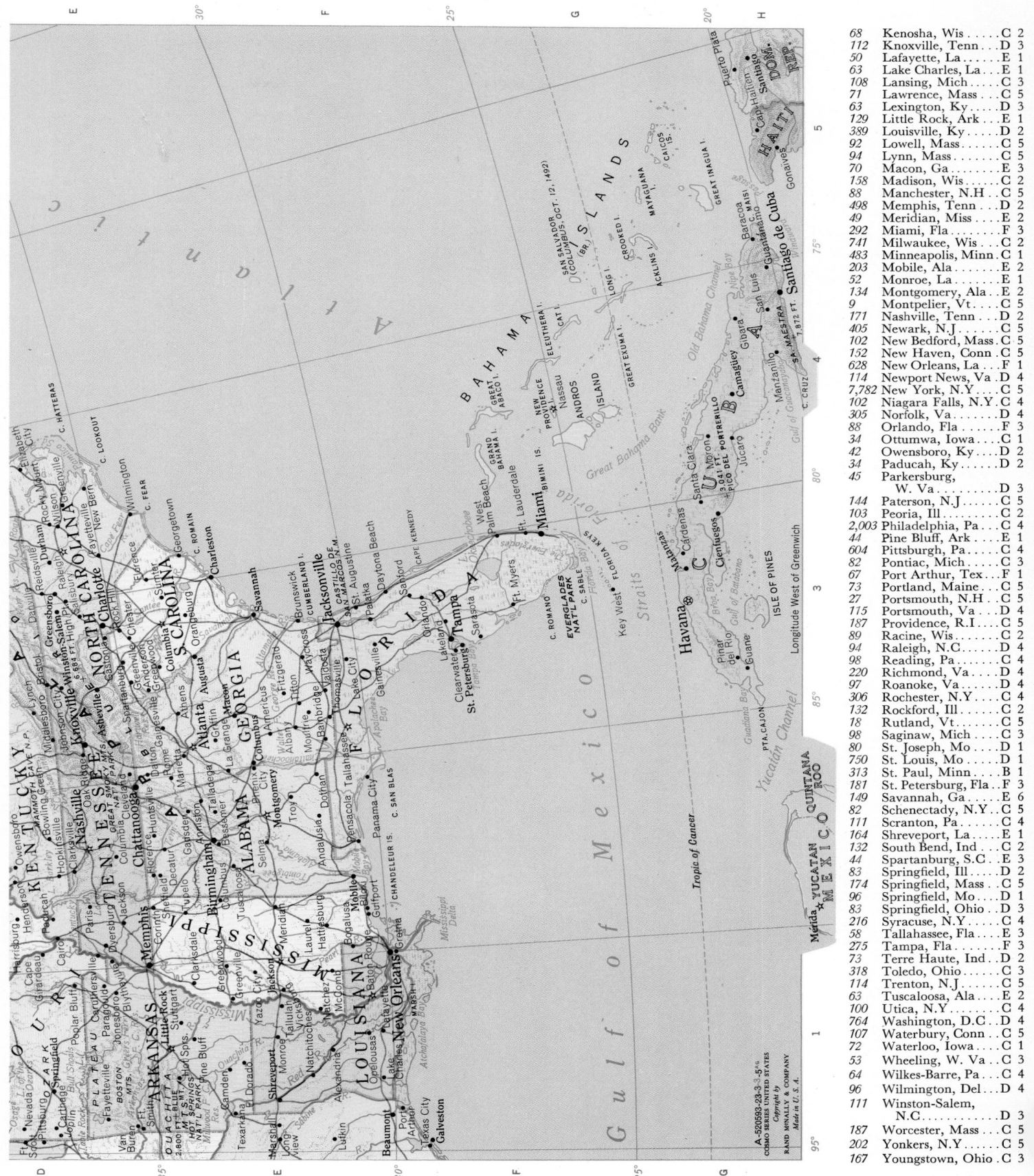

Lambert Conformal Conic Projection
SCALE 1:12,000,000   1 Inch = 189 Statute Miles

68	Kenosha, Wis	C 2
112	Knoxville, Tenn	D 3
50	Lafayette, La	E 1
63	Lake Charles, La	E 1
108	Lansing, Mich	C 3
71	Lawrence, Mass	C 5
63	Lexington, Ky	D 3
129	Little Rock, Ark	E 1
389	Louisville, Ky	D 2
92	Lowell, Mass	C 5
94	Lynn, Mass	C 5
70	Macon, Ga	E 3
158	Madison, Wis	C 2
88	Manchester, N.H.	C 5
498	Memphis, Tenn	D 2
49	Meridian, Miss	E 2
292	Miami, Fla	F 3
741	Milwaukee, Wis	C 2
483	Minneapolis, Minn	C 1
203	Mobile, Ala	E 2
52	Monroe, La	E 1
134	Montgomery, Ala	E 2
9	Montpelier, Vt	C 5
171	Nashville, Tenn	D 2
405	Newark, N.J.	C 5
102	New Bedford, Mass	C 5
152	New Haven, Conn	C 5
628	New Orleans, La	F 1
114	Newport News, Va	D 4
7,782	New York, N.Y.	C 5
102	Niagara Falls, N.Y.	C 4
305	Norfolk, Va	D 4
88	Orlando, Fla	F 3
34	Ottumwa, Iowa	C 1
42	Owensboro, Ky	D 2
34	Paducah, Ky	D 2
45	Parkersburg, W. Va	D 3
144	Paterson, N.J.	C 5
103	Peoria, Ill	C 2
2,003	Philadelphia, Pa	C 4
44	Pine Bluff, Ark	E 1
604	Pittsburgh, Pa	C 4
82	Pontiac, Mich	C 3
67	Port Arthur, Tex	F 1
73	Portland, Maine	C 5
27	Portsmouth, N.H.	C 5
115	Portsmouth, Va	D 4
187	Providence, R.I.	C 5
89	Racine, Wis	C 2
94	Raleigh, N.C.	D 4
98	Reading, Pa	C 4
220	Richmond, Va	D 4
97	Roanoke, Va	D 4
306	Rochester, N.Y.	C 4
132	Rockford, Ill	C 2
18	Rutland, Vt	C 5
98	Saginaw, Mich	C 3
80	St. Joseph, Mo	D 1
750	St. Louis, Mo	D 1
313	St. Paul, Minn	B 1
181	St. Petersburg, Fla	F 3
149	Savannah, Ga	E 6
82	Schenectady, N.Y.	C 5
111	Scranton, Pa	C 4
164	Shreveport, La	E 1
132	South Bend, Ind	C 2
44	Spartanburg, S.C.	E 3
83	Springfield, Ill	D 2
174	Springfield, Mass	C 5
96	Springfield, Mo	D 1
83	Springfield, Ohio	D 3
216	Syracuse, N.Y.	C 4
58	Tallahassee, Fla	E 3
275	Tampa, Fla	F 3
73	Terre Haute, Ind	D 2
318	Toledo, Ohio	C 3
114	Trenton, N.J.	C 4
63	Tuscaloosa, Ala	E 2
100	Utica, N.Y.	C 4
764	Washington, D.C.	D 4
107	Waterbury, Conn	C 5
72	Waterloo, Iowa	C 1
53	Wheeling, W. Va	C 3
64	Wilkes-Barre, Pa	C 4
96	Wilmington, Del	D 4
111	Winston-Salem, N.C.	D 3
187	Worcester, Mass	C 5
202	Yonkers, N.Y.	C 5
167	Youngstown, Ohio	C 3

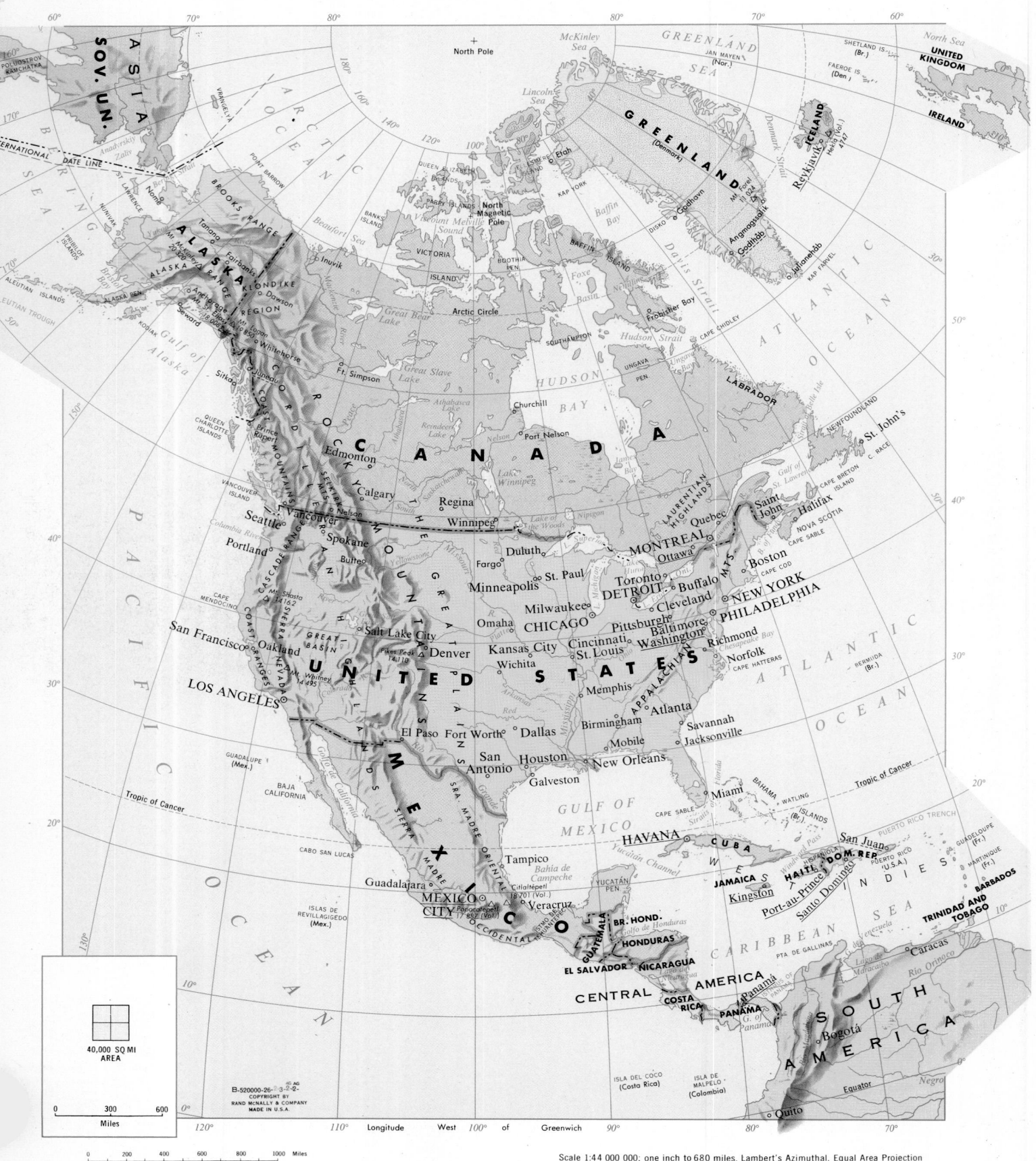

Scale 1:44 000 000; one inch to 680 miles. Lambert's Azimuthal, Equal Area Projection
Elevations and depressions are given in feet

40,000 SQ MI
AREA

0   300   600
Miles

0   200   400   600   800   1000   Miles
0   400   800   1200   1600   Kilometers

B-520000-26-2-3-2-2-
COPYRIGHT BY
RAND McNALLY & COMPANY
MADE IN U.S.A.

VOLUME TWENTY SEVEN

INDEX

How To Use the Index   2446

Abbreviations   2446

Index   2447

INDEX

A

Aa (lava) 479a
Aalto, Alvar 189a, 1101c
Aardvark 13a
Aaron 1450a
Abacá 1648a
Abacus (arch.) 75a
Abacus (math instr.) 1236a
Abadan, Iran 2344a
Abaddon 1430b
Abalone 13a
Abandonment (law) 849a
Abbas I (the Great) 189a
Abbey, Edwin tab 108, 189a
Abbot, The (Scott) 1393a
Abbotsford 1393a
Abbott, Grace 189a
Abbott, Jacob 189a, tab 1474
Abbott, Lyman 189a
Abboud, Ibrahim 2266c
Abbreviations biblical 1450a
  dictionary of 1338–1340
ABC Powers 2064b
Abd-al-Hamid II, Sultan (Turkey) see Abdul-Hamid II
Abd al-Krim 2222b
Abd al-Quadir 2088a
Abd al-Wahhad, Muhammad 2247a
Abd-ar-Rahman 2086a
Abdication 849a
Abdiel 1422b
Abduction 849a
Abduction of Rebecca (paint.) tab 112
Abdul-Aziz ibn-Saud see Ibn-Saud, Abdul-Aziz
Abdul-Hamid II 2279a
  abdication 849a
  biography 189a
Abdullah ibn-Husein 189a
A Becket, Thomas see Becket, Thomas à
Abel 1450b
Abel, Niels Henrik 1506c
Abélard, Pierre 1377b, 1754c
  biography 189a
Abenteuerliche Simplicissimus, Der 1383c
Aberdare Mountains 2325a
Aberrations (optics) 1908b
Abidjan, Ivory Coast 2197a, 2344a
Abigail 1450b
Abilene Christian College 701
Abilene, Texas 1995c
Ablation 479a
Abner 1450b
Abney level (instrument) 479a
Abnormal psychology 1951c
Abo, Finland see Turku
Abolitionists 1022c–1023a, 2038b
Abomey 2141a
Aborigines 2092a, 2092c
Aborigines, Australian see Australian aborigines
Abort (astronautics) 1778a
Abou ben Adhem (poem) 1393a
Abraham 1450b, 1628c
Abrasion 479a
Abrasives 1192a
Abscissa 1602b
Absalom 1450b
Absalom and Achitophel (satire) 1362c, tab 1468
Absaroka Mountains 1987c
Abscissa 1602b
Absentee ballot 849a
Absentee ownership 583c
Absolute (philos.) 1620b
Absolute atmosphere 479a
Absolute scale see Kelvin scale
Absolute time 479a
Absolute value (math.) 1533a, 1601a
Absolute zero 1898c, 1916b, 1920a
Absolutism (philos.) 1620b
Absorption (physics) 1904a, 1916b
Absorption (plants) 1646a–1646b
Absorptivity (physics) 1916b
Abu Hanifah tab 1465
Abukir, Battle of 1398c
Abyssal (oceanog.) 479a
Abyssal deposits 479a

Abyssal region (oceanog.) 1865c
Abyssinia see Ethiopia
A.C. see Alternating current
Acacia 1648a
Académie Française see French Academy
Acadia 2114c
  see also Nova Scotia
Acajutla, El Salvador 2344a
Acanthus 1648a
A cappella 172b
  motets 160c
A capriccio 172b
Accelerando (accelerato) (music) 172b
Acceleration (physics) 1875a, 1916b
Accelerators (particle) 1912a
  research 1912c
Accent (music) 172b
Accessory (law) 849b
Accessory notes (music) 172b
Accidentals (music) 172b
Accidents 954a
Acción Democrática party (Venezuela) 2298a
Accius, Lucius 1354a, 1355b
Accompaniment (music) 172b
Accordions 172b
Accounting 583b
  auditing 584c
  career 377a
Accounts 583a
Accra, Ghana 2163c–2164a, 2344a
Accretion 479a
Acetals 1220a
Acetate 1208c
Acetate fabrics (Japan) 2199c
Acetic acid 1817b, 1821c
  vinegar 1845b
Acetobacter 1845b
Acetylcholine 928a
Acetylene 1819c
Acetylene gas 1210b
Achaen League 994a
Achates 1422b
Achene fruit 1646b
Acheron 1422b
  Charon 1428c
  Hades 1433c
Acheson, Dean Gooderham tab 796, 2078a
Acheson, Edward Goodrich 1192b
Achilles 1350c, 1422b
Achitophel 1461a
Achromabacter 1845c
Achromatic lenses 1909a
Acid soil 751c, 749b
Acidic rocks 479a
Acids 1816c
Acinar cells 926a
Acis 1432c
  Polyphemus 1444a
Acne 918c
Aconcagua, Mt. 2089b, 2121b, 2325a
Aconite 1648a
Acorn Agricultural and Mechanical College 678
Acoustical Engineering 1192c
Acoustics 1870a, 1894c, 1916b
  acoustical engineering 1192c
  beat 1916b
  diffraction 1917c
  harmonic 1918b
  music 172b
  spectrum 1919c
Acquisition (astronautics) 1778a
Acre, Palestine, Crusades 984b
Acre (unit) tab 1500
Acrisius 1429c
Acromegaly 940a
Acropolis (Athens) il 2165
  sculpture 113c
Acrostics 1393a
  biblical 1450b
Acrylics 1209a
Acrylonitrile 1209a
Act (legis.) 849b
Act of God 849b
Act of Supremacy (England, 1534) 815c, 2287c, 2288a
Act school (psych.) 1948a
Actaeon 1422c
ACTH 925c, 926a
Actinium 1809b, 1830
  atomic weight tab 1805
Actinomycetales 1844b

Actinomycosis tab 946
Action Group (Nigeria) 2229c
Actium (sea battle) 994a
Activated charcoal 1200c
Acton, 1st Baron (John Emerich Edward Dalberg) 189b
Actors (career) 374a
Actors' Equity Association 1742a
Actresses (career) 374a
Acts of the Apostles 1450b
Actuaries 385c, 583c
Acute angles 1601b
Acute bronchitis 940c
Acute triangles 1607c
Ad libitum (music) 172c
Ad valorem tax 583c
Adagio (music) 172b
Adam 1450c
  Lilith 1438b
Adam, Adolphe tab 171c
Adam, Robert 189b
  furniture 1098b
Adam Bede (nov.) 1368a, 1393b
Adam Brothers (arch.) 78b
Adam de la Halle tab 171b, 1377c
Adamawa Mountains 2229a
Adams, Brooks 189b
Adams, Charles Francis (1807–1886) 189b, tab 800, 881a
Adams, Charles Francis (1835–1915) 189b
Adams, Charles Francis (1866–1954) tab 796
Adams, Franklin Pierce 189b
Adams, Grantley 2097c
Adams, Henry 189b, 965b, 1375b
  autobiography 1402a
Adams, Herbert 124a, tab 125
Adams, Isaac 148a
Adams, John 189b, tab 798–799, 964c
  administration 2032
  administration, events paralleling tab 1061
  appointments 852b
  Cabinet tab 795
  Declaration of Independence tab 803
  election and inauguration tab 800
  Federalist Party 878c
Adams, John (astron.) 1759c
Adams, John Couch 189c
Adams, John Quincy 189c, tab 798–799
  administration 2036b
  administration, events paralleling tab 1062
  Cabinet tab 795
  Democratic Party 873a
  election and inauguration tab 800
Adams, Samuel 190a
  Declaration of Independence tab 803
  presidential candidate tab 800
Adams, Will (Anjin Sama) 190a
Adams, William T. see Optic, Oliver
Adams State College of Colorado 659
Adamson Act 2064a
Adana, Turkey 2344a
Adaptation 1927c
  racial 1927b
Adar Oes Iforas Mountains 2214c
Addams, Jane 190a
Adder see Viper
Adding machines 1236a
  operators 387a
Addinsell, Richard 169b
Addis Ababa, Ethiopia 2145c, 2146a, 2344a–2344b
Addison, Joseph 162c, 1167b, 1358a, 1363b, tab 1469
  biography 190a
  Roger de Coverley 1400a
  Spectator 1417c
Addison's disease 940a
Addition 1515c, 1601a
  algebra 1532b
  algorithms 1518c
  facts tab 1513a
  fractions 1527a
  history 1509c
  justification of the process, tab 1516
  mechanics 1873c
Addition reactions (chem.) 1823b
Address, forms of tab 1119

Ade, George 190a
Adelaide, Australia 2093a, 2344b
Adelard of Bath 1503c
Adelphi 1355b
Adelphi University 683
Aden, Gulf of 2325a
Aden, South Yemen 2253c, 2344b, map Atlas-25
Adenauer, Konrad 2163a
  biography 190a
Adenine 1840c, 1854b
Adenosine diphosphate (ADP) 1825c
Adenosine triphosphate (ATP) 927c, 1825c
  body requirements 919c
ADH see Antidiuretic hormone
Adhesives 1192c
Adiabatic process 1916b
Adiabatic rate 479a
Adige River 2194a
Adirondack Mountains 1990b, 2016a
Adirondack Murray see Murray, William H. H.
Adirondack State Park 895c
Adjectives 1305b
  uses of 1303c
Adkins Case (law) 833a
Adler, Alfred 190a, 1947a, 1958a
Adler, Cyrus 190b
Adler, Felix 190b
Admetus 1422c
Administrative agencies 849b
Administrative law 849c
Administrative services 576–577
Administrator (law) 849c
Admirable Crichton (play) 1369c, 1393b
Admirable Doctor see Bacon, Roger
Admiralty law 849c
Admission Day Arizona 841b
  California 842b
Adobe 479a
Adolphe (nov.) 1381a
Adolphe of Nassau, Grand Duke 2211c
Adonais (poem, Shelley) 1393c, 1402a, 1461a
Adonis 1422c
Adoption (law) 849c
Adoration of the Christ Child (paint.) tab 109
Adoration of the Mystic Lamb (paint., Van Eyck) 248b
Adoration of the Magi (paint., Bosch) tab 111
Adoration of the Magi (paint., Botticelli) tab 110, tab 113
Adoration of the Magi (paint., Pisano) 121a
Adoration of the Magi (paint., Rubens) tab 109
Adoration of the Magi (paint., Da Vinci) tab 110
Adoration of the Shepherds (paint., El Greco) tab 112
Adoration of the Shepherds (paint., van der Goes) tab 110
Adorra la Vella, Andorra 2088a
Adoula, Cyrille 2135b
ADP see Adenosine diphosphate
Adreanoff Island 2016a
Adrenal cortex 925c, 926a
  Addison's disease 940a
Adrenal glands 924a, 926a
Adrenal medulla 926a, 939a
Adrenalin (epinephrine) 926a, 939a
Adrenocorticotrophic hormone see ACTH
Adrian IV (pope) 190b, 2285b
Adrian College 675
Adrianople, Treaty of 2166b
Adriatic Sea 2325a
Adua, Battle of 2146b
Adult education 634c
  public school registrations 636a
Advancement of Learning (tract) 1362a
Advection 479a
Adventures of Peregrine Pickle see Peregrine Pickle
Adverbs 1308b
  use of 1303c

Advertising 583a
  bait advertising 584c
  careers 375a, 377a
  layout 596b
  magazines 1167c
  restrictions 849c
Advisory opinion (law) 849c
A.E. (pseud.) *see* Russell, George William
Aedes aegypti 1843a
Aeetes 1424c, 1433b
Aegean Age 973c
Aegean Sea 2325a
Aegeus 1448a
Aegina, Temple of 116a
Aegir 1422c
Aegis 1422c
Aegisthus 1422c
  Clytemnestra 1429b
Aeife 1428c
Aeneas 1422c
Aeneid (Vergil) 1000b, 1357a, 1393c, 1422b
  Aeneas 1422c
  Amazons 1424a
  Dido 1430c
  translations 1360a
Aenesidemus 1615b
Aeolus 1423a
Aeon *see* Timrod, Henry
Aerating roots 1644b
Aeration, zone of 520c
Aerial roots 1644b
Aerial stems 1644b
Aerology 479a
Aeronautical engineering 1154b
Aeronautics 1154b–1159c
  engineers 379c
  technicians 380a
  see also Airplanes
  see also Astronautics
Aeroplanes *see* Airplanes
Aerostatics *see* Airships
Aerovanes 474c
Aeschines *tab* 1464
Aeschylus 1352b, *tab* 1464
  Agamemnon 1423b
  biography 190b
  Prometheus Bound 1414a
Aesculapius *see* Asclepius
Aesir 1423a
Aesop 190c, 1351b
Aesop's Fables 1393c
  King Log and King Stork 1437b
Aëtius, Flavius 190c
Affection (psych.) 1948c
Affidavit 850a
Affluent (rivers) 479a
Affonso *see* Alfonso
Afghan Wars 2291b
Afghanistan 2085–2086, 2189b
  agriculture 2085b
  economy 2085b
  flag *il* 2182
  foreign interference 2085c–2086a
  geography 2085a
  government 2085b
  history 2085c–2086a
  people of 2085a
  pomegranates 1688b
  religion 2085c
  rugs 1110c
A. F. of L. *see* American Federation of Labor
Afonso II (Portugal) 2241c
Afonso *see* Alfonso
Afreet 1423b
Africa 2325a
  aardvark 13a
  antelope 14a
  anthropology 1924b
  ass 14b
  avocet 14c
  baboon 14c
  Belgium's empire in 2099a
  body mutilation 1930c
  catfish 20b
  chameleon 20c
  cheetah 21a
  civet cat 22a
  cobra 22a
  coffee 729b
  colonization 865c
  coot 23a
  cuckoo 25a
  deer 25b
  dog 25c
  duck 26a
  eagle 26b
  economic geography 771c–772b
  elephant 33a
  flamingo 33c
  flycatcher 34b
  fox 34c
  gazelle 35b

  giraffe 35c
  gnu 35c
  guinea fowl 37b
  hake 37c
  hare 38a
  hedgehog 38b
  herring 39a
  historical outline *tab* 1029, *tab* 1030
  horse 39b
  hyena 40a
  ibis 40b
  Italy in 2196b
  kingfisher 41a
  kudu 41c
  lion 20a
  lizard 43a
  loon 43c
  lovebird 44a
  lynx 44b
  map *Atlas*-34
  map, central *Atlas*-38
  map, southern *Atlas*-40
  map, western *Atlas*-36
  mole 46a
  races 1927a
  sculpture 124b
  wild game 1867b
African Culture Region 769b–769c
African Democratic Rally (RDA) 2295a
African languages 1337c
African National Congress 2253b
African sleeping sickness 1848c
Afrikaans (lang.) 1337a
Afro-Shirazi Party (ASP) 2272c
Afterglow 479b
Aftershock (earthquakes) 279b
Aga Khan I 190c
Aga Khan II 190c
Aga Khan III 190c, 892a
Aga Khan IV 190c
Aga Mohammed Khan *see* Agha Mohammed Khan
Agalega Islands 2216c
Agamemnon 1423b
  Aegisthus 1422c
  Clytemnestra 1429b
Agamemnon (Aeschylus) 1352b
Agana, Guam 2344b
Aganippe 1423b
Agassiz, Alexander 190c
Agassiz, Jean Louis Rodolphe 190c
Agate 479b
Agate (print.) 150b
Agate (pseud.) *see* Reid, Whitelaw
Agate line (print.) 150b
Agave *see* Century plant
Age of Bronze (sculp., Rodin) 123a
Agee, James 190c
Agency (law) 821c, 850b
Agenor 1428a
Agent (law) 821c, 822a, 850b
Ageratum 1648a
Agesander 117c
Agesilaus II 191a
Agglomerate (volcanoes) 479b
Agglutinate (volcanoes) 479b
Aggradation (rivers) 479b
Aggregate (rocks) 479b
Agha Mohammed Khan 191a
Agincourt, battle at 994a
Agitato (mus.) 172c
Aglaius *see* Timrod, Henry
Agnes Grey (bk.) 1367c
Agnes Scott College 661
Agonic 479b
Agnosticism 1620b
Agora 970c
Agostino di Duccio *tab* 125
Agouti 13a
Agra, India 2344b
  Taj Mahal 78a
Agram, Yugos. *see* Zagreb
Agranulocytosis 940a
Agrarian Reform Act 2079a
Agribusiness 584a
Agricola (Rom. gen.) 191a
Agricola (Georg Bauer) 452a, 1798b
Agricultural Adjustment Administration 2073a
Agricultural chemistry 722a
Agricultural Cooperative Extension Service 629c, 635c
Agricultural economics 584a
Agricultural engineering 722a
  careers 379c
Agricultural Marketing Bill 2071b
Agricultural Research Administration 850b

Agricultural revolution 987a
  American 720c
Agricultural science 722b
Agricultural and Technological College of North Carolina 688
Agriculture 719–748, 2263c–2264a, 2317b
  Afghanistan 2085b
  agronomy 749a
  Alabama 1974a, 1974b
  Albania 2086b
  Alaska 1975a
  Algeria 2087c–2088b
  American Samoa 2000a
  ancient civilization 972c
  Andorra 2088c
  Angola 2306a
  Argentina 2089c
  Arizona 1975c
  Arkansas 1976a, 1976b
  Australia 2092a
  Austria 2095a
  Babylonia 996c
  bacteria 1846a
  Bahamas 2307b
  Bahrain 2096c
  Barbados 2097a, 2097b
  Belgium 2098b
  Bhutan 2099b
  Bolivia 2100b
  Botswana 2101b
  Brazil 2102a, 2103a
  British Honduras 2308a
  British Soloman Islands 2308c
  British Virgin Islands 2309a
  Bulgaria 2105b, 2106b
  Burma 2107a
  Burundi 2108b
  California 1977a
  Cambodia 2108c
  Cameroon 2110a
  Canada 2110c, 2112a–2112b, 2114b
  careers 380c, 381b
  Cayman Islands 2310a
  Central African Republic 2119b
  Ceylon 2119c
  Chad 2120c
  Channel Islands 2310a
  Chile 2121c
  China 2123, 2124a, 2125a–2125b
  Colombia 2132c
  Colorado 1977b
  Comoro Islands 2310c
  Congo (Brazzaville) 2134a
  Congo (Kinshasa) 2134c
  Connecticut 1978a
  contour strip cropping 1999
  Cook Islands 2311a
  Costa Rica 2135a
  Cuba 2136c
  Cyprus 2138a
  Czechoslovakia 2139a
  Dahomey 2140c
  Denmark 2141b
  Dominica 2311b
  Dominican Republic 2142c
  Ecuador 2143c–2144b
  El Salvador 2145a–2145b
  employment 381a
  Equatorial Guinea 2311c
  Ethiopia 2146a, 2146b
  farm machinery 1251a
  fertilizers 733a
  Fiji Islands 2312b
  Finland 2147a
  Florida 1979b
  France 2148c–2149a
  French Guiana 2312b–2312c
  French Polynesia 2313a
  French Territory of the Afars and the Issas 2313b
  Gambia 2156a–2156b
  Georgia 1979c
  Germany 2158a, 2158b
  Ghana 2164a
  glossary 722–748
  Great Britain 2282c, 2290c
  Greece 2165b–2165b
  Grenada 2314c
  Guadaloupe 2315a
  Guam 2001a
  Guatemala 2168a–2168b
  Guinea 2170a
  Guyana 2170b, 2170c
  Haiti 2171c, 2172a
  Hawaii 1980b
  Hungary 774, 2174a
  Idaho 1980c 1981
  Ifni 2316a
  Illinois 1981b
  India 2178b
  Indiana 1981c
  Indonesia 770, 2187a
  industrialization 987a
  Iowa 1982b
  Iran 2188c–2189a
  Iraq 2189c–2190a
  Ireland 2190c–2191a
  irrigation 740a
  Isle of Man 2316b
  Israel 2192b
  Italy 2194b–2194c
  Ivory Coast 2197a

  Jamaica 2197c–2198a
  Japan 2199b
  Jordan 2201c
  Kansas 1982c
  Kentucky 1983b
  Kenya 2202b
  Korea 2203c, 2204c
  Kuwait 2205c
  Laos 2206b
  Lebanon 2207b
  Lesotho 2208b
  Liberia 2209a
  Libya 2210a
  Liechtenstein 2210c
  Louisiana 1984b
  Luxembourg 2211b
  Madagascar 2212a
  Maine 1984b
  Malawi 2212b–2212c
  Malaysia 2213b
  Mali 2215a
  Malta 2215c
  Martinique 2316c
  Maryland 1985a
  Massachusetts 1985b
  Mauritania 2216a
  Mauritius 2217a
  Mexico 2218a
  Michigan 1986a
  Minnesota 1986b
  Mississippi 1987a
  Missouri 1987b
  Mongolia 2220c
  Montana 1988a
  Montserrat 2317c
  Morocco 2221c
  Mozambique 2317b
  Muscat and Oman 2222c
  Nebraska 1988c
  Nepal 2223c
  Netherlands 2224c
  Netherlands Antilles 2318a
  Nevada 1988c
  New Caledonia 2318b
  New Guinea 2318c
  New Hampshire 1989b
  New Hebrides 2319a
  New Jersey 1989c
  New Mexico 1990a
  New York 1990c
  New Zealand 2226a–2226b
  Nicaragua 2227c
  Niger 2228c
  Nigeria 2229b
  Niue 2319a
  North Carolina 1991b
  North Dakota 1991c
  Norway 2230b
  Ohio 1992a
  Oklahoma 1992b
  Oregon 1993a
  origins 719a
  Pakistan 2232b–2232c
  Panama 2234b
  Papua 2319b
  Paraguay 2235b
  Pennsylvania 1993c
  Peru 2236b, 2236c
  Pitcairn Island 2319c
  Poland 2239a, 2239b
  Portugal 2241b
  Portuguese Guinea 2320a
  Portuguese Timor 2320b
  Philippines 2207c
  prehistoric 1928c
  primitive 1933c, 1934a
  Puerto Rico 2002b
  Réunion 2320c
  Rhode Island 1994a
  Rhodesia 2243a
  Romania 2244a, 2245a
  Rwanda 2245c
  St. Helena 2321a
  St. Kitts-Nevis-Anguilla, 2321b
  St. Lucia 2321b
  St. Vincent 2321c
  San Marino 2241b
  Saudi Arabia 2247a
  Senegal 2248a
  Seychelles 2322b
  Sierra Leone 2248c
  Sikkim 2249c
  Singapore 2250c
  Somali Republic 2251a
  South Africa 2252b
  South Carolina 1994b
  South Dakota 1994c
  South Yemen 2253c
  Sudan 2266a
  Surinam 2323b
  Swaziland 2267a
  Sweden 2269a
  Switzerland 2269c–2270a
  Syria 2271a
  Taiwan 2125c
  Thailand 2273c
  Tennessee 1995b
  Texas 1995c
  Togo 2275a
  Tokelau Islands 2324a
  Tonga 2324b
  Trinidad and Tobago 2275c
  Tunisia 2277a
  Turkey 2278a

Uganda 2279c
United Arab Republic 2280c
U.S.S.R. 2256c–2257a
U.S. 1968b–1969a, 2293c–2294a
Upper Volta 2294b
Uruguay 2295a
Venezuela 2297b
Vermont 1997a
Vietnam 2299b–2299c
Virgin Islands 2004b
Virginia 1997c
Utah 1996b
Wallis and Futuna Islands 2324c
Washington 1998a
West Virginia, 1998c
Western Samoa 2301c
Wisconsin 1999a–1999b
Wyoming 1999c
Yemen 2302a
Yugoslavia 2303b–2303c
Zambia 2305b
Agriculture, Department of 850b, 888c
  bureaus 858b
  Cabinet members *tab* 797
  Commodity Credit Corporation 867a
  education 629c
  establishment *tab* 797
Agrimony 1648a–1648b
Agrippa, Marcus Vipsanius (63–12 BC) 191a
Agronomy 749–754
  defined 1638a
  history 749a
Aguinaldo, Emilio 2060b, 2238b
Aguirre Cedra, Pedro 2122c
Aguiyi-Ironsi, Gen. Johnson 2230a
Agusan River 2325a
Ah, Wilderness! (play) 1394a
Ahab 1450c
Ahaggar Mountains 2087c
Ahaggar Plateau 2325a
Ahasuerus 1450c
Ahidjo, Ahmadou 2110b
Ahimsa 1624c
Ahithophel 1451a
Ahmad, Iman 2302c
Ahmad al-Mahdi, Muhammad 2266b, 2266c
Ahmad Ibn Said (dynasty) 2223a
Ahmadabad, India 2344b
Ahmadnagar, India 2344c
Ahmadu Lobo 2215b
Ahmed Fuad Pasha *see* Fuad I
Ahmes 1501b, 1556c
Ahomadegbé, Justin 2141a
Ahmedabad, India 2178a
A horizon *see* Soil profile
Ahura Mazda *see* Ormazd
Ahvaz, Iran 2344c
Ahvenanmaa Islands *see* Aland Islands
Aida (opera) 167b
Aiken, Conrad 191a
Ainsworth, William Harrison
  Tower of London 1404c
Ainu 978b, 1925c
Air
  see Atmosphere
  see also Air pollution
  see also Air pressure
Air (mus.) 172c
Air Force (U.S.) 850c
  careers 388c
  education 629c
Air mass 475c, 477a, 479b
Air (Azbine) Mountains 2228b, 2228c, 2325a
Air pollution 777a, 958b, 1230a
Air pressure 468c
  barometer 468c
Air sickness 942c
Airborne infections 955a
Air-breathing missiles 1779a
Air conditioning careers 379c, 380a, 386a
Airglow 1778a
Air mail
  Roosevelt, F. D. 1156b
  subsidy 909c
Airplanes 1155b
  aeronautical engineering 1154c
  commercial 1156a, 1157a
  etiquette in 1116a
  mechanics of flight 1159c
  World War II 1156b
Airships 1154c
  blimps 1155a
  rigid 1155a
  semirigid 1155a
Airy, Sir George Biddell 191a
Aiún, Spanish West Africa 2344c

Aissa Saved (nov.) 1371c
Aitken, Robert *tab* 125, 1167b
Aix-la-Chapelle, Congress of (1821) 874c
Aix-la-Chapelle, Treaty of (1748) 2026c
Ajax (myth.) 1423b
Ajax the Less 1423b
Ajmer, India 2344c
Akbar 2180b–2180c
  biography 191a
Akee 1648b
Akeley, Carl Ethan 191a
A Kempis, Thomas *see* Thomas à Kempis
Akhenaten *see* Ikhnaton
Akerman, Amos *tab* 796
Akita, Japan 2344c
Akosombo, Ghana 2163c
Akron, Ohio 1992a, 2005a
  rubber 1277c
Akron, University of 690
Aksakov, Sergei 1389c
Akyab, Burma 2344c
Al Ahmadi, Kuwait 2205c
Al Fayyum, United Arab Republic 2345a
Al Kuwait, Kuwait 2360c
Al Hudaydah, Yemen 2302b
Al Manamah, Bahrain 2096c
Ala Mountains 2124a
Ala Tau Mountains 2255a
Alabama 1974
  admission to U.S. 2035b
  agriculture 1974a, 1974b
  capital punishment 860b
  census (1960) 1970
  climate 1974a
  colleges of 654
  commercial law 826
  congressional apportionment *tab* 853
  Dutchman's pipe vine 1665c
  economy 1974b
  flag 2010
  geography 1974a
  government 1974b
  holidays 841–842
  labor legislation 832c
  people of 1974a–1974b
  public school enrollment *tab* 646
  public school expenditures *tab* 644
  secession 2043c
  student enrollment *tab* 645
Alabama (cruiser) 994a
Alabama (ship) 2053c
  Civil War 2049
Alabama Claims 853c, 994a–994b
  treaty 2053c
Alabama, University of 654
Alabama Agricultural and Mechanical College 654
Alabama River 2012a
Alabaster 1212a
Aladdin 1423c
Alai Mountains 2255a
Aland Islands 2146b, 2147c, 2325a
Alarcón, Pedro Antonio de 1392b
Alarcón y Mendoza, Juan Ruiz de 1392a
Alaric I 191a
Alashan Desert 2123c, 2124a
Alaska 998c, 1974–1975
  agriculture 1975a
  apportionment 853
  capital punishment 860a
  census (1960) 1970
  colleges of 655
  commercial law 826
  congressmen at large 855a
  deer 25b
  economy 1975a
  electoral votes 876c
  employment age 832a
  Eskimos 1975a
  flag 2010
  geography 1974c–1975a
  ginseng species 1669b
  government 1975a
  history 2056a, 2062c
  holidays 841–842
  hummingbird 39c
  Indians 1975a
  larch 1675a
  merganser 45c
  octopus 48b
  otter 49a
  people of 1975a
  poplar trees 1688b
  ptarmigan 53b
  public school enrollment *tab* 646
  public school expenditures *tab* 644

  spruce trees 1694b
  robin 54c
  sandpipers 55b
  sea lions 56c–57a
  statehood 194a
  student enrollment *tab* 645
  woodpeckers 68a–68b
  yellowlegs 68b–68c
Alaska, University of 655
Alaska Methodist University 655
Alaska Purchase 903b, 2053a
Alaska Range 2019b
Ala-ud-din Khalji 2180b
Alaungpaya 2107b
Alba, Duke of *see* Alva, Duke of
Alba Madonna *tab* 113
Albanese (lang.) 1334a
Albani, Francesco 107
Albania 1015b, 2086–2087
  agriculture 2086b
  communism 2086b, 2087b
  economy 2086b
  flag 2182
  geography 2086a
  government 2086b
  history 2086c–2087b
  Italian occupation (1939) 1028a
  language 1334a
  people of 2086b
  religion 2086b
Albanian Democratic Front 2086c
Albany, Georgia 1979c
Albany, New York 1990c, 2005a
  founding 654b, 2024b
Albany Congress (1754) 2026b
Albany State College 661
Albatross 13a
Albedo 479c
Albedo (astron.) 1793a
Albee, Edward 191b, 1377a
Albemarle, Duke of
  North Carolina 2025b
Albemarle, N.C. 2025b
Albéniz, Isaac 169b, *tab* 172a
  biography 191b
Alberich 1423c
Albert, Lake 2134c, 2279b, 2325b
Albers, Josef 191b
Albert I (Belg. k.)
  biography 191b
Albert (Eng. pr. consort) 191b
Albert National Park Congo (Kinshasa) 896a
Albert Nile (river) 2279b
Alberti, Leon Battista 76c, 1386b
  biography 191c
Albertinelli, Mariotto *tab* 106
Albertus Magnus College 659
Albertus Magnus 1755b, 1798b
  biography 191c
Albertville, Congo (Kinshasa) 2344c
Albigenses 985b, 994b
Albigensian Crusade 994b
Albinism 940a
Albion 1423c
Albion College 675
Albite 453b
Albizu Campos, Pedro 2003a
Albright College 694
Albumen 1172b
Albumin 921c, 922c, 1824b
Albuquerque, Affonso de 191c
Albuquerque, New Mexico 1990a–1990b, 2005a
Albuquerque, University of 683
Alcaeus 974b, 1351c, *tab* 1464
  biography 191c
Alcamenes 116c
Alcaptonuria 1856a
Alceste (opera, Gluck) 163b
Alcestis 1423c
Alchemy 1755a, 1798a
Alcibiades 191c
Alcman 1351c, *tab* 1464
Alcmene 1423c
Alcock, Sir John William 191c, 1156a
Alcoforado, Mariana 1388c
Alcohol 1192c, 1820c
  fuel 1137b
  thermometers 469b
Alcoholic beverages 723b, 1933c
  yeast 748c, 1847b
Alcoholics Anonymous 1742a
Alcoholism 959c
Alcon, R. *see* Brontë, Emily
Alcott, Amos Bronson 1373c, *tab* 1474
  biography 191c

Alcott, Louisa May 192a, *tab* 1477
  Little Women 1409b
  novels 1409b
Alcuin 192a, *tab* 1465
Alcyone 1444c
Aldabra Islands 2308b, 2308c
Aldebaran (star) *tab* 1786
Aldehyde 1821c
Alden, Isabella Macdonald
  pseudonym 1462c
Alden, John 192a, 1019a
Alder 1648b
Aldermen 850c
  forms of address *tab* 1119
Aldermen, Board of 850c, 857c
Alderney Island 2310a
Alderson-Broaddus 706
Aldhelm 192a
Aldington, Richard 192a, 1371b, *tab* 1480
Aldosterone 926a
Aldrich, Nelson W. 192a
Aldrich, Thomas Bailey *tab* 1477
  Marjorie Daw 1410b
Ale 724a
Aleardi, Aleardo 1387b
Alecto 1423c
Alectryon 1423c
Aleichem, Sholem 192a
Alemán Valdés, Miguel 192a
Alembert, Jean le Rond d' 1380b
Alencar, José Martiniano de 1393b
Aleppo, Syria 2344c
Alessandri Palma, Arturo 192b, 2122b, 2122c
Aleutian Islands 998c, 2016a, 2019c
  sea lions 56c–57a
Aleutian low 479c
Alewife 13a–13b
Alexander, Grover Cleveland 192c
Alexander, John White *tab* 108
Alexander, Joshua W. *tab* 797
Alexander, King
  (Greece) 2167a
  (Serbia) 2304b
  (Yugoslavia) 2304b
Alexander I (Bulg. pr.)
  abdication 849a
Alexander I Czar (Russia) 192b, 1014b, 2147b, 2259c
Alexander II Czar (Russia) 192b, 987c, 2260a
  nihilism 894a
Alexander III Czar (Russia) 192b, 2260a
Alexander III, King (Scotland) 2286b
Alexander III (Macedonian k.)
  see Alexander the Great
Alexander John I (Rum. pr.) *see* Cuza, Alexandru Ioan
Alexander and Diogenes (sculp.) 122c
Alexander the Great 192b, 1003a, 1003c, 1015b, 1017a, 1018a, 2085c, 2179c, 2189a, 2271b, 2281a
  battle at Arbela 995b
  Lysippus 117a
  wars of *tab* 1071
Alexander Nevski 192c
Alexander Severus 193a
Alexander's Feast (poem) 1362c
Alexandria, Egypt 1003c–1005a
  ancient library at 779a–779b, 994b–994c, 1503c
  ancient museum 1753a
  Arab conquest of (641) 994b
  lighthouse 1167a
  painting 84b
  sculpture 117b
Alexandria, United Arab Republic 2280c, 2344c–2345a
Alexandrian Age 1394a
Alexis (Gr. au.) 1353a
Alexius Comnenus *see* Alexius I
Alexius I (Grand Comnenus) (c. 1180–1222) 193a, 1001c
Alexis I Mikhailovich, Czar (Russia) 193a
Alfalfa 724a, 1648b–1648c
Alfaro, Eloy 2144b–2144c
Alfieri, Vittorio 1387b, *tab* 1471
  biography 193a
Alfonso I (Naples k., Sicily k.) *see* Alfonso V (Aragon k.)
Alfonso V (Alfonso the Magnanimous), (Aragon k.) 193a

Alfonso X (Alfonso the Wise),
(Castile and León k.) 193a
literature 1391a
Alfonso XII (Sp. k.) 193a
Alfonso XIII (Sp. k.) 2265a
abdication 849a
biography 193a
Alfred the Great (Eng. k.) 193a
English literature 1358a
writings *tab* 1465
Alfred the Great, King (Wessex)
2284b
Alfred University 684
Alfven, Hugo 172b
Algae 1639a–1640a, 1847c, 1859c
blue-green 1639c–1640a
brown 1640a
green 1639c
red 1640a
Algardi, Alessandro 193b
Algebra 1532–1555
algebraic expressions 1534c
Boolean 1507a, 1601c
coefficients 1602b
completing the square 1548b
definition 1601a
discriminants 1603a
equations 1603b
expressions 1534c, 1535a
factors 1536c
fractions 1538b
graphs 1553a
history of 1504a, 1506b
inequalities 1544a
letters, use of 1534b
numbers, types of 1532a
postulates 1532b
problems 1543a
radicals 1607a
set notation 1540c
sentences 1540b
square roots 1546b
Algebraic equations 1603b
Algebraic expressions 1534c, 1535a
Alger, Horatio 193b, *tab* 1477
Alger, Russell Alexander 193b, *tab* 796
Algeria 995b, 997c, 2087–2088
agriculture 2087c–2088a
Algerian War 863, *tab* 1077
anthropology 1924c
cedar trees 1657b
economy 2087c–2088a
flag 2182
French conquest of 997c
geography 2087b
government 2088a
history 2088a
independence of 2155a
map 2087
occupation by France 2088a
people of 2087c
religion 2088a
Algiers, Algeria 2087b, 2087c, 2345a
il 2087
Algology 1638a
Algonquin Indians manito 1439a
Algorithms 1519c, 1601a
Euclidean 1525b
Al-hajj Umar 2215b
Alhambra 76a
architecture 78a
gates of 1096b
Alhazen 1754b
Ali, Mehemet *see* Mehemet Ali
Ali al-Sanusi, Muhammad bin
2210b
Ali Baba 1423c
Ali Jinnah
Moslem League 892a
Ali Khan, Liaqat 2185c, 2233c
Ali Pasha 1014a
Alia Mountains 2325b
Alias (law) 851a
Alid dynasty 2222a
Alidade (instrument) 479c
Alibi (law) 851a
Alice's Adventures in Wonderland
(bk.) 1367c, 1394a
Cheshire Cat 1399a
Alicyclic compounds 1819c
Alien and Sedition Acts 2032b
censorship 861c
Aliens 851a
citizenship 864a
immigration 883b
naturalization 892c
Aligarh, India 2345a
Alighieri, Dante *see* Dante
Aliphatic compounds 1820a
Alkali 1193b
glass 133a
see also Bases
Alkali flat 479c
Alkali metals 1809b
Alkalies 1193b

Alkaline earth metals 1809b
Alkaline soil 752b
Alkanes 1820b
Alkenes 1819b, 1820b
Alkyl halides *see* Haloalkanes
Alkynes 1820b
All Fools' Day *see* April Fools'
Day
All India Muslim League 2233a,
2233b
All for Love 1362c
All Saints' Day *see* Allhallows
Alla breve 172c
Allah 981c, 983a, 1634a
see also Islam
Allahabad, India 2345a
All-American Canal 904c
Allan-a-Dale 1423c
Allegheny College 694
Allegheny Mountains 1984c
Allegheny River 2013a, 2019c
Allegory 1315a, 1394b
Allegri, Gregorio *tab* 171b, 193b
Allegretto 172c
Allegro 172c
Allegro con brio 172c
Alleles 1850c, 1852a
Allemande (dance) 182a
Allen, Ethan 193b, 2028a
Allen, Florence E. 193c
Allen, Grant 193c
pseudonym *tab* 1463c
Allen, Hervey 193c, *tab* 1480
Allen, James Lane 1375a, *tab* 1478,
biography 193c
Allenby, Edmund Hynman
(1st Viscount Allenby) 193c,
1002b, 1017b
Allentown, Pennsylvania 1014c,
1993b, 2005a
Alleppey, India 2345a
Allergy 940a
hay fever 942a
serum sickness 945b
Allhallows (All Saints' Day)
1423c
Louisiana 842c
Alliance College 694
Alliance for Progress 2080a, 2135c
Allibone, Samuel Austin *tab* 1475
Alligator *see* Crocodile
Alligator pear *see* Avocado
Allison, William Boyd 193c
Alliteration 1315c, 1394b
Allori, Alessandro *tab* 107
All-or-none law (physiol.) 939b
Allotropic 479c
Allotropic forms 1803a
Alloys 1193b
major 1194a
steel 1212c
tin 1225a
All-Russian Congress of Soviets
851a
1918 meeting 857a
All-Saints' Day *see* Allhallows
Allspice 1648c
Allston, Washington 193c, *tab* 108
All-Union Congress of Soviets 851a
Alluvial fan 479c
Alluvium 479c
Alma College 676
Alma Ata, U.S.S.R. 2345a
Almagest (treatise) *tab* 1464,
1503a, 1756c
Almayer's Folly (nov.) 1370a
Almeida-Garrett, Visconde de 1388c
Almira (opera) 162b
Almond 1648c
Almoravids 2216b, 2222a
Almqvist, Karl J. L. 193c, *tab* 1473
Alpaca 13b
Alpha Centauri *tab* 1786
Alpha particles 1912a, 1916b
Alphabet 1295a
evolution *tab* 1294
first written 1018a
inventors 973a
Korea 977c
Latin 1354a
prehistoric 142a
principal alphabets with En-
glish equivalents *tab* 1295
Alpheus (myth) 1424c
Alphonso *see* Alfonso
Alpides (mountains) 379c
Alpine (mountains) 479c
Alpine glaciers 449a
Alps 2210b, 2325b
antelope 14a

Austria 2094
edelweiss 1665c–1666a
France 2148a, 2148b
Germany 2157b
Italy 2194a
Romania 2243c
Switzerland 2269b
Yugoslavia 2303a
Aloe 1648c
Alsace 2148a, 2149b, 2153c, 2154b,
2161b, 2161c
Alsace-Lorraine attempted Ger-
manization of 994c
Franco-Prussian War 994c
Al-Sallal, Abdullah 2302c
Alströmer, Jonas 193c
Altai Mountains 2123c, 2220b,
2255a, 2325b
Altair (star) *tab* 1786
Altamira Cave (Sp.) 971a
Altar of John the Baptist (paint.)
tab 109
Altar of Peace (Rome) 118b
Altar of the Portinari Family
(paint.) *tab* 110
Altarpieces 73a
Altdorfer, Albrecht *tab* 107, 136b
biography 193b
Alte Pinakothek (Munich) *tab* 111
Alternating current 1882b
generators 1139a, 1885a
inductance 1918b
motors 1142b
rectification 1919c
transformers 1147a, 1886a
Alternation of generations, 1641c–
1642a
Altgeld, John Peter 2058c
Althing 851b, 2176b, 2176c
Altimeter 479c
Altiplano 2325c
Altitude 479c
respiration 922a
Altitude sickness 940a
Alto (music) 172c
Altocumulus clouds 470c
Alton Locke (nov.) 1367c
Altoona, Pennsylvania 1993b
Altostratus clouds 470c
Al'ud 155b
Alumina 1194b, 1200a
glass 133a
Aluminum 762a, 1193a, 1194b, 1830,
2110a
Arkansas 1976b
atomic weight *tab* 1805
bauxite 453c
conductivity 1882a
electrovalence 1809a
Jamaica 2197c
Japan 2199c
qualities 1194c
soil 751c
Surinam 2323b
U.S. 2293c
Aluminum oxide 1192b
hardness 1192b
Alundum 1194b
Alva, Duke of (Duke of Alba)
194a
Alvarado, California 744c
Alvarado, Pedro de 2145b, 2168c
biography 194a
Alvarez, Juan 2219a
Alveolar consonants 1294c
Alveoli 922a
emphysema 941c
Alverno College 707
Alves, Antonio de Castro 1393a
Alyssum 1648c
Amadeo I, King (Spain) 2265a
Amadeo, Giovanni Antonio 194a
Amadis de Gaula (poem) 1391b
Amado, Jorge 1393c
Amalgamation 584a
Amalthea 1424a
Amami Island 2003b, 2003c
Amanullah, King 194a, 2086a
Amaranth family 1648c
Amarillo, Texas 1995c
Amarna Letters *tab* 1463
Amaryllis 1648c–1649a
Amaterasu 979a
Amateur Athletic Union of the
United States 1703a
Amateur Softball Association of
America 1742a
Amati (It. family) 194a
Amati, Andrea 194a
Amati, Antonio 194a
Amati, Geronimo (1556–1630) 194a
Amati, Geronimo (1649–1740) 194a
Amati, Nicolò 194a

Amazing Marriage, The 1368a
Amazon River 2100a, 2102a, 2132b,
2325c
angelfish 13c
herring 39a
piranha 51c
sea cows 55b
tanager birds 62a
waterlily 1699a
weasels 66c
Amazons (myth) 1424a
sculpture 117a
Ambala, India 2345a
Ambassador Bridge *tab* 1197
Ambassadors 851b
forms of address *tab* 1119
at large 855a
Amber 1881a
Amber glass 133c
Amberger, Christopher *tab* 107
Amberjack (fish) *il* 1717
Ambrose (St.) *tab* 1464
biography 194a
music 158a, *tab* 171b
Ambyite dynasty 1005a
Ameba *see* Amoeba
Amen, Temple of 1003c
Amendment (law) 851b
Amendments (U.S. Constitution)
see Bill of Rights (U.S.)
see Constitution (U.S.)—
Amendments
Amenhotep I (Egy. k.) 194a
Amenhotep II (Egy. k.) 194a
Amenhotep III (Egy. k.) 194a
Amenhotep IV *see* Ikhnaton
Amenophis IV (Egy. k.) 1003c
America history 2021–2022
name origin 2022c
see also Central America
see also Latin America
see also North America
see also South America
see also United States
American Academy of Arts and
Letters 1742c
American Academy of Political and
Social Sciences 1745b
American architecture 78b, *il* 79
American art furniture 1099b–
1101b
glassware 134c, 135
painting 103c, *tab* 107–109
pottery 128b, 129, *tab* 130–132,
131c
printing 146a
sculpture 123c–124b, *tab* 125
American Association for the Ad-
vancement of Science 1745c
American Association of Engineers
1742c
American Association of University
Professors 1746a
American Association of University
Women 1746a
American Astronomical Society
1742c
American Automobile Association
1742c
American Bankers Association
1742c
American Bar Association 1742c
American Bible Society 1742b
American Chemical Society 1743a
American Civil Liberties Union
1743b
American Civil War *see* Civil War
(U.S.)
American College of Surgeons
1745c
American Colonization Society
2209a–2209b
American Culture Region 768b–769a
American Daily Advertiser 1171a
American elm 1985a, 1988a, 1991b
il 1664
American Expeditionary Forces
(World War I) 1025c, 2065c,
2066a
American Falls 2020c
American Farm Bureau Federation
1743c
American Farmer (journal) 719c
American Federation of Arts 1742c
American Federation of Labor
(AFL) 838b, 1742b, 2057a
adult education 637b
see also C.I.O.
American Federation of Musicians
1745a
American Geographical Society
1744a

American history *tab* 1052–1070, 2021–2082
  Civil War 2045–2051a
  conscription 868b
  parallel outlines *tab* 1060–1071
  protectorates 902c
  Secession 2043b
  social progress *tab* 1061–1070
  Spanish-American War 2060a
  Westward expansion 2022b
  woman suffrage 914a
  World War I 2064c
  see also Colonial America
American holly 1978a
American Indians *see* Indians, American
American Institute of Architects 1742b
American International College 673
American Legion 1742b
American Library Association 1744c
American literature 1370–1377, 1467–1481
  colonial period 1372a
  Imagist school 1376a
  Revolutionary period 1372b
  twentieth century 1375b
American Mathematical Society 1744c
American Medical Association 1744c
American Music 169c–171b
  composers *tab* 172c
  folk music 170c
American National Red Cross 2065c
American Newspaper Publishers Association 1745a
American Numismatic Society 1745a
American Nurses Association 1745a
American Olympic Association 1703b
American Osteopathic Association 1745b
American Party 851c
  Know-Nothing Party 887c
American pasqueflower 1994b
American Philatelic Society 1745b
American Philosophical Society 1724b
American Physical Society 1745b
American Popular Revolutionary Alliance (APRA) (Peru) 2237b
American Portraits 1397b
American Prison Association 1742b
American Radio Relay League 1745b
American Revolution 830a, 987a, 1002c, *tab* 1073, 2028a, 2029
  battles 2029
  Canada 2115a
  Congress 786b
  events 2029
  fiat money 592b
American River 2013c
American Rocket Society 1767c, 1768b
American saddle horse 739b
American Samoa 2000
  agriculture 2000a
  economy 2000a
  climate 2000a
  geography 2000a
  government 794b, 2000a–2000b
  history 2000b
  people of 2000a
American School of Classical Studies
  archeological excavations 970c
American Society for the Prevention of Cruelty to Animals 1742c
American Society of Civil Engineers 1201b
American Society of Mechanical Engineers 1215b
American steam locomotive 1178b
American Sunbathing Association 1745c
American Telephone and Telegraph Company 1184c
American Tobacco Company
  trust busting 2062a
American University 660
American Woman Suffrage Association 914b
Americium 1830
  atomic weight *tab* 1805
Amerigo Vespucci *see* Vespucci, Amerigo
Ames, James Barr 194a
Ames, Joseph Sweetman 194a
Amethyst 1220c
Amfortas 1442c
Amherst, Jeffrey (Baron) 194b
Amherst College 673

Amici, Giovanni Battista 194b
Amici prism 1909a
Amicis, Edmondo de *see* De Amicis, Edmondo
Amiens, Treaty of 2276a
Amiens Cathedral 76c, 120a, 985a
Amino, Leo *tab* 125
Amino acids 919b, 920c, 921a, 1824b, 1825b, 1840b
  genetics 1855a
  RNA *tab* 1855
Amman, Jordan 2201c, 2345a
Ammanati, Bartolommeo 122b, *tab* 125
Ammeters 1916b, 1918a
Ammonia
  chemical bonding 1810a
  fertilizers 733a
  heat capacity 1899b
  refrigeration 1902b
Ammonium carbonate 1817c
Ammonium hydroxide 1817b
Ammonium nitrate 1207c
Amnesia 1957a
Amnesty 851c
Amnesty Act (U.S.) 2053c
Amo Chu River 2099b
Amoeba 13b, 1848a
Amoebic dysentery 1848a
Amon 1622b
Amontons, Guillaume 194b
Amorphous 479c
Amorphous solids 1871a
Amortization 584a
Amos 1451a
Amoy, China 2345b
Ampère, André Marie 194b, 1882c
Amperes 1882c, 1916b
Ampersand 150b
Amphibole 453b, 479c
  asbestos 1195c
Amphion 157a, 1424a
Amplification 1894c
  telephone 1889a
Amplitude 1916b
Amravati, India 2345b
Amritsar, India 2345b
Amsterdam, Netherlands 2224c, 2225a, 2345b
Amu River 2255a, 2325c
Amulius 1446a
Amundsen, Roald 194b
Amur River 2220b, 2254c, 2325c
Amygdale 479c
Amylase 920b
Amyot, Jacques 1378b, *tab* 1466
An Lu-shan 2127b
An mein Volk (manifesto) 1014b
Ana 1394c
Anabasis (hist.) 1353b, 1394c
Anabatic 479a
Anaconda *see* Boa
Anacreon 1351c, 1352a, *tab* 1464
  anacreontics 1394c
  biography 194b
Anacreontics (poems) 1394c
Anacrusis 1394c
Analemma 480a
Analgesics 1274a
Analog computers 1243a
Analysis (math.) 1601a
Analytical chemistry 1800c, 1827–1828
Analytical dynamics 1507b
Analytic geometry 1504b, 1590–1593
  coordinate systems 1590a
  definition 1601a
  introduction 1590a
Analytic trigonometry 1581a
Analytic psychology 1957c
Ananias 1451a
Anapest 1394c
Anarchism 851c, 904c
Anastasius I (E. Rom. emp.) 194c
Anatolia peninsula 2325c
Anatolian rugs 1110c
Anatomy *il* (1613–1620
  careers 390c
  defined 1637b–1637c
  see also Physiology
Anatomy Lesson (paint.) *tab* 111
Anatomy of Melancholy (treatise) 1346c, 1461c, *tab* 1467
Anaxagoras 1557b, 1613c
  biography 194c
Anaxandrides 1353a
Anaximander 1612c, 1751a
  biography 194c
Anaximenes 1613a, 1751a
  biography 194c

Ancestors (nov., Freytag) *tab* 1475
Ancestor worship ancient China 1623a
Anchises 1424a
Anchor ice 479c
Anchovy 13b
Anchorage, Alaska 1975a
Ancient Mariner *see* Rime of the Ancient Mariner
Ancyrean inscription 994c–995a
Andalusian horse 739b
Andaman Islanders
  firemaking 1929c
  shelter 1930a
Andaman Sea 2325c
Andante 172c
Andantino 172c
Andean Indians 2236b
Anderson, Indiana 1981c
Anderson, Carl David 194c
Anderson, Clinton P. *tab* 797
Anderson, Elbert 1022c
Andersen, Hans Christian 194c, *tab* 1474, *il* 207
  Ugly Duckling 428b–431b
Anderson, Marian 194c
Anderson, Maxwell 195a, *tab* 1480
Anderson, Robert 2044a
Anderson, Robert B. *tab* 796
Anderson, Sherwood 195a, *tab* 1480
Anderson College 665
Anderson Ranch Dam 1206
Andersonville (nov.) 995a
Andersonville prison 994
  mortality rate 994a
Andes Mountains 2089b, 2121b, 2132a, 2143c, 2236a, 2236b, 2236c, 2325c
  alder 1648b
  alpaca 13b
  avocet 14c
  hawkweed 1670c
  vultures 64a–65b
Andesite 479c
Andocides 1353b
Andocides 195a
Andorra 2088
  agriculture 2088c
  de Gaulle visit 2088c
  economy 2088c
  flag 2182
  geography 2088b
  government 2088c
  history 2088c
  people of 2088c
  religion 2088c
André, John 195a, 2029
Andrée, Salomon August 195a
Andreev, Leonid N. 1390a, *tab* 1480
  biography 195a
Andreoli, Giorgio 127a, *tab* 130
Andrew (Eng. pr.) 243c
Andrew (St.) 1451b, 1630c
Andrews, Elisha Benjamin 195b
Andrews, Roy Chapman 195b
Andrews University 676
Andreyev, Leonid *see* Andreev, Leonid
Andria (play) 1355b
Androcles (Androclus) 1424a,
Androcles and the Lion (fable) 444c, 1424a
Androgens 926a
Andromache 1424a
Andromaque (play) 1379a
Andromeda (galaxy) 1787a, *tab* 1785
Andromeda (myth) 1424a
  Perseus 1444a
Andronicus, Lucius Livius *see* Livius Andronicus
Andronicus of Rhodes 195b
Andros, Sir Edmund 2025a, 2027a
  biography 195b
Andvari 1424a
Anemia 920b, 940a,
  Rh Factor 923a
  sickle cell anemia 1856c, 945b
Anemograph 480a
Anemometer 474b, 480a
Anemone 1649a
Anerio, Felice *tab* 171b
Aneroid barometer 469a
Anet Chateau 122b
Aneurysm 940b
Angara River 2326a
Angel Falls 2326a, *il* 2330
Angelfish 13b–13c
Angelico, Fra *tab* 106
  biography 195b
  Deposition *tab* 110
  Virgin and Child *tab* 109

Angell, James R. 195b, 1948b
Angell, Norman 195b
  original name 1461a
Angelo State College 701
Angevin *see* Anjou
Angiosperms 1642c–1643b
Angkor, Cambodia 2109a, *il* 2109
Angle of repose 480a
Angles (math.) 1601a
  geomery 1562b
  trigonometry 1582b
Anglican Church *see* Church of England
Angling (fishing) 1703b, *il* 1715
Anglo-Frisian (lang.) 1337b
Anglo-Saxon (lang.) *see* Old English
Anglo-Saxon Chronicles 1358c, 1395a
Angola 2134a, 2241c, 2306–2307
  agriculture 2306a
  ass 14b
  economy 2306b
  gazelle 35
  geography 2306a
  government 2306b
  history 2306c–2307a
  map *Atlas*-38
  people of 2306a–2306b
  religion 2206b
Angora goat 738c
Angra Mainyu (deity) 1627b
Ångström, Anders Jonas 195b
Angstrom units 1903c
Anguilla Island 2321
Angular unconformity 480a
Anh, Nguyen 2300b
Anhydrous 480a
Aniline rocket fuels 1766c
Animal fats 1821c
Animal glues 1211c
Animal husbandry 721b, 1933c, 1934a
Animal Kingdom (bk. Cuvier) *tab* 1471
Animal psychology 1951a
Animal waxes 1227a
Animals 13a–68c, 766c, 1859
  Assyrian sculpture 115c
  bacteria 1846a
  diet 1825b
  diseases 1842a
  domestic 1867c
  early agricultural 719a
  fats and oils 732a
  furs 738a, 1209b
  geological time *tab* 456–457
  leather 1209b
  preservation of 1867b
  public health 957c
  space experiments 951a
  transport 1934b
  see also names of animals
  see also Zoology
Animate energy 480a
Animism 1622a
Anions 1809a, 1827b
  ions 1808c
Anise 1649a
Anisotropic 480a
Anjou (Fr. family) 195b
Anjouan Island 2310c
Ankara, Turkey 2277c, 2345b
Ankrah, Lt. Gen. J. A. 2164c
Ann Arbor, Michigan 1985c
Anna Comnena 195c
Anna Karenina (nov.) 1389c, 1395a, *tab* 1476
Anna Maria College 673
Annaba, Algeria 2345c
Annales (epic Ennius) 1355a
Annales (epic Livy) 1357c
Annales (epic Tacitus) 1358a
Annales Cambriae (chronicle) 1395b
Annam 2206c
Annam Cordillera 2206a, 2298c, 2299a, 2326a
Annapolis, Maryland 1984c, 2005a
  see also United States Naval Academy
Annapolis Convention 786c, 2030b
Annapolis Royal, Nova Scotia 2026c
Anne (Eng. pr.) 243c
Anne, Queen (England) 195c, 1020b
  reign of 2289c–2290a
Anne of Austria 195c
Anne of Cleves 195c
Annexation Manifesto 2115c

Annhurst College 659
Annobón Island 2311b
Announcers 378b
Annual plants 1644c
Annual report 584a
Annual rings 1644c
Annuals (bot.) 1934a
Annuities 584a
Annular drainage pattern 480b
Annular eclipse 1794b
Annulment 875b
Annunciation (paint.) *tab* 110
Annunzio, Gabriele d' *see* D' Annunzio, Gabriele
Ann Veronica (nov.) 1370a
Anodes 1131c, 1274a, 1284a, 1886c
Anomalistic month 1795b
Anomalistic year 1797c
Anomaly 480b
Anopheles mosquito 957b, 1848c
Anorthite *see* Feldspar
Anouilh, Jean 195c
Anselm (St.) 195c
Ansermet, Ernest 196a
Anshan, China 2345c
Anspacher, Louis Kaufman 196a
Ant 13c
Ant and the Grasshopper, The (fable) 442c
Ant lion 14a
Antaea 1426c
Antaeus 1424a
Antarctic *see* Antarctica
Antarctic Circle 480b
Antarctica 1652a, 2326a
  beech 1652a
  map *Atlas*-5
  mouse 46c
  penguin 50b
  sea lions 56c–57a
Anteater 13b–14a
Antecedent river 480b
Antelope 14a
Antennas (radio) 1176a
Anthemius 76a
Anthems 172c
Anther (flower) 1645c
Anthology 1395a
  Greek 1354b, *tab* 1464
Anthony, Mark *see* Mark Antony
Anthony, Susan Brownell 196a, 914a
Anthony (Anthony the Great) (St.) 196a
Anthracite coal 480b, 1202a, 1136c
  U.S. 1967a
Anthrax *tab* 946
Anthropogeography 480b
Anthropology 1923-1937
  bibliography 1937c
  careers 390c
  cultural 1929a
  literary works 1348b
  physical 1923c
  relationship to other fields 1923a
  see also Man
Antibiotics 1273c, 1845c
Antibodies 922c, 925a, 1849b
Anticipations (nov.) 1370a
Anticlimax (lit.) 1315b
Anticlinal theory 480b
Anticlines 451a, 480c
Anticlinorium 480c
Anti-Comintern Pact 1028a, 2201b
Anticosti Island 2110c
Anticyclone 480c
Antidiuretic hormone 925c
Antietam, Battle of 2048b, 2049
Anti-Fascist Peoples Freedom League (AFPFL) (Burma) 2107c, 2108a
Anti-Federalist Party 851c
  Third Parties 910c
Antigens 922c, 1849b
Antigone (myth) 1424b
Antigonus I 196a
Antigua, Guatemala 2168c, *il* 2169
Antigua (island) 2307a
Antihistamines 1274c
Antilles Archipelago 2326a
Antilogarithms 1596b, 1604c
Anti-Masonic Party 851c
Antimony 1830
  atomic weight *tab* 1805
  Mexico 2218a
  Nicaragua 2227c
Antinomy (philos.) 1620b
Antioch College 690

Antiochus III (the Great) (Syr. k.) 196a
Antiochus IV (Antiochus Epiphanes) (Syr. k.) 196a
  Jerusalem 1455c
Antioxidants 732b
Antipater (Macedonian gen.) 196a
Antipater (procurator of Judea) 237b
Antipator 1015b
Antiphanes 1353a
Antiphon 1353b, *tab* 1464
Antipodes 480c
Anti-poverty program 2082b
Antiquary, The (nov.) 1366a
Antiquitates (treatise, Varro) 1356a
Anti-Semitism 2162a, 2162b
Antisthenes 1614a
Antithesis 1315b
Antitoxins 1849b
Antitrades (winds) 480c
Antitrigonometric functions 1607c
Antitrust laws 584b
Antoinette, Marie *see* Marie Antoinette
Antonescu, Ion 2245a
Antoninus, Marcus Aurelius (Rom. emp. 161–180)
  see Marcus Aurelius
Antoninus, Marcus Aurelius (Rom. emp. 188–217)
  see Caracalla
Antoninus Pius 196a
Antony, Marc *see* Mark Antony
Antung, China 2345c
Antwerp, Belgium 2098a, 2098b, 2345c
  cathedral 76c
  printing 144a
Anubis 1424b
Anvil (anat.) 937a, 1894b
Anxiety 1957c
Anzengruber, Ludwig *tab* 1477
Aorist (gram.) 1297a
Aorta 923b, 924a
Apap 1430b
Aparri, Philippines 2345c
Apartments 1091a
Apassionato (mus.) 172c
Apatite *tab* 1192b
Ape 14a
  classification 1923c
Apelles 196b
Apennine Tunnel 1226c, 1226
Apennines (mountains) 2326a
Aphanitic (rocks) 480c
Aphasia 940b
Aphelion 480c, 1763c, 1778a, 1783b
Aphids 14a–14b
Aphorism 1315b, 1395a
Aphrodite 1424b, 1449a, 1628a
  Paris 1442c
Aphrodite of Cnidus (sculp.) 117a
Apia, Western Samoa 2301b, 2345c–2346a
Apiculture 724b
Apis 1424b
Apithy, Sourou-Migan 2141a
Apocalypse 1451b
Apocalyptic literature 1451b
Apocrypha (Bib.) 1450a, 1451c
Apogee 480c, 1778a, 1793b
Apolima Island 2301b
Apollinaire, Guillaume 196b
Apollo 1424b, 1434a, 1444b, 1628a
  Hyacinthus 1435b
  Midas 1440a
  music 157a
Apollo, Project *see* Project Apollo
Apollo Belvedere 117b
Apollodorus 84a
Apollodorus of Damascus 196b
Apollonius of Perga 1502c, 1504b
  biography 196b
Apollonius of Rhodes 196b, 1354a, *tab* 1464
Apollos 1451c
Apollyon 1424b, 1451c
Apologia pro Vita Sua (treatise) 1366b
Apostles' Creed 1631b
Apostrophe (figure of speech) 1315a
Apostrophe (punct.) 1314b
Apothecaries' system *tab* 1500
Apoxyomenos (sculp.) 117a

Appalachian Mountains 1961b–1962a, 1979c, 1989a, 1995a, 1997b, 2016a, 2019a, 2111a, 2292c
  azaleas 1650b
  erosion 448a
  Lily-of-the-Valley 1676a
Appalachian Piedmont (U.S.) 1961c
Appalachian Ridge 1989b, 1993b, 1998b
Appalachian State Teachers College 688
Appalachian Zone (U.S.) 1961b–1962a
Apparel *see* Clothing
Apparent time 480c
Appeal (law) 851c, 852a
Appellate courts 827a
  jurisdiction 792a
Appendicitis 940b
Appian (Gr. au.) *tab* 1464
Appius Claudius *see* Claudius, Appius
Apple blossom 1975c, 1985c
Apples 1649
  Spain 2264a
  U.S. 2294a
  Vermont 1997a
  Virginia 1997c
  Washington 1998a
  West Virginia 1998c
Appleseed, Johnny 221b, 1436c, 1461a
Applied mathematics 1601b
Applied physics 1869c
Appoggiatura 172c
Appointment (public officials) 852a
Appomattox Court House, Battle of 2049, 2050c
Apportionment 852c
  Congress 853
Appreciation (property) 584b
Apprenticeship 616b
  Colonial America 829a
Appropriation 852c
Apricot 1649a
Apse (arch.) 75c
Apsides 1793b
Apuleius, Lucius 196c, *tab* 1464
  Golden Ass 1405a
Aqaba, Jordan 2346a
Aqaba, Gulf of 2193c, 2201c, 2281c, 2326a
Aquaplaning 1703c
Aquatint 138c
Aqueducts 1195b
Aqueous 480c
Aquiclude (rocks) 480c
Aquifer (rocks) 480c
Aquifuge (rocks) 480c
Aquilo (myth) 1427b
Aquinas, Thomas 985a, 1612a, 1615c, 1616a
  biography 196c
  nickname 1461a
  Summa 1347b, 1755c
Aquinas College 676
Ara Pacis (sculp.) 118b
Arab League 2206a, 2208a
  flag *il* 2184
  Jordan River reclamation project 995b
  members 995b
  purpose of 995b
Arab-Berber Culture Region 769b
Arabesque (mus.) 173a
Arabi, Ahmad 2281b
Arabia 995a, 2326a
  baboon 14c
  badger 15a
  earliest known inhabitants 995a
  gazelle 35b
  lion 20a
  literature *tab* 1465
  music 155b
  pottery *tab* 130
  Roman Empire 995a
Arabian Nights (bk.) 1395a
  Aladdin 1423c
  Ali Baba 1423c
  Barmecide Feast 1396c
  roc 1446a
  Sindbad 1447b
Arabian Peninsula 2222c
  goat 36a
Arabian Sea 2326a
Arabs Islam 1632c
  mathematics 1503b
Arachne 1424c
Arad, Romania 2346a

Arafura Sea 2326b
Arago, Dominique François 196c
Arakan Mountains 2326b
Araks River 2254c
Aral, Lake 2254c, 2255a
Aral Sea 2326b
Aramis 1396a
Ararat, Mt. 1451c, 2277c, 2326b
Araucanian Indians 2121b, 2122a
Araucaria family 1649a–1649b
Arawak Indians 2003a, 2097a, 2137b, 2172a, 2276a
Arbeau, Thoinot 182a
Arbela 995b
  battle at 995b, 1002c
Arbitrage 584b
Arbitration 853b, 584b
Arbor vitae 1649b
Arbua Island 2317a
Arbuckle Mountains 1992b
Arbuthnot, John 196c
Arbutus 1649b
Arc (math.) 1603a
Arc, Joan of, *see* Joan of Arc
Arc de Triomphe (Paris) *il* 2153
  sculpture 122c
Arc furnaces 1248a
Arc welding 1287c
Arcadelt, Jacob *tab* 161b
Arcadia *see* Nova Scotia
Arcadia (myth) 1424c
Arcadia (poem, Sidney) 1346a, 1360c, *tab* 1466
Arcadius, Emperor 999c
Arce, Gaspar Núñez de, *see* Núñez de Arce, Gaspar
Arcesilaus 1615b
Arch 73a, 1196b
  furniture 1094a
  structural mechanics 1190c
Arch dams 1206c
Archaeology 967–971
  careers 390c
  excavating 968a
  origin of 968c
  prehistoric 1927c
  technology 1124b
Archaic art (Gr.) 114b, 116a
Archaism (lit.) 1395b
Archeology *see* Archaeology
Archeozoic era 458a
Archer, Frederick Scott 1172b
Archery 1703b
Arches *see* Arch
Archilochus 1351b
Archimedes 975a, 1215c, 1502c, 1753b
  biography 196c
Archipelago 480c
Archipenko, Alexander 124b, *tab* 125
  biography 196c
Architectural orders 75a
Architecture 71a, 72a, 73–82
  careers 373b
  civil engineering 1201b
  draftsmen 373c
  history 73c
  middle ages 985a
Architrave 75a
Arctic
  evening primrose 1666c
  goose 36b
  phalarope 50c–51a
  plover 52a–52b
  porcupine 52b–52c
  saxifrage 1692a
  swan 61b–61c
  terns 63a
  walrus 65c
  whales 66c–67a
  wolves 67b
  willow 1699c
Arctic air mass 480c
Arctic Circle 480c
Arctic Ocean 2326b
Arctic Pack (ice floes) 480c
Arcturus (star) *tab* 1786
  temperature 1789a
Arcus 1428a
Ardashir I (Persian k.) 981c
Arden, Forest of 1395b
Ardennes Mountains 2148a
Ardennes Plateau 2326b
Are (meas.) *tab* 1500
Area 1601b
  postulates 1573b
  weights and measures *tab* 1500

Arellano, Oswaldo López 2173b
Arenaceous (rocks) 480c
Arensky, Anton 169a, tab 172a
Areopagitica (bk.) 861a, 1347c
Arequipa, Peru 2236b
Ares (myth) 1424c, 1439a, 1628a
Arête (mountain ridge) 480c
Arethusa 1424c
Aretino, Guido see Guido d' Arezzo
Aretino, Pietro 197a, 1387a
Aretino, Spinello, tab 106
Arévelo, Juan José 2169b
Arezzo, Guido d' see Guido d' Arezzo
Arezzo, Ristoro d' see Ristoro d' Arezzo
Argand, Aimé 197a
Argand, Jean Robert 1140b
Argentina 2064b, 2089–2091, 2235c, 2236a
  agriculture 2089c
  anteater 13c
  boa 17c
  eagle 26b
  economy 2089c–2090b
  flag il 2182
  geography 2089a
  government 2090a
  history 2090a–2091a
  immigration 2021c
  Indians 2090a
  industry 2089a
  map 2089, Atlas 45–47
  nighthawk 47c
  pampas grass 1684a
  plover 52a–52b
  people of 2089b
  petunias 1686a
  rabbit 53c
  religion 2090b, 2090c–2091a
  sloth 58c
  soapberry 1693b–1693c
  stork 60b–60c
  trade 2089a–2090a
  trogons 64a–64b
  vultures 65a–65b
  war with Brazil 2295c
  war with Paraguay 2235c
  World War I 2090c
  World War II 2090c
Argillaceous (rocks) 481a
Arginine 1856c
Argo (ship) 1424c
Argon 1808b, 1830
  atmosphere 468a
  atomic structure 1807b
  atomic weight tab 1805
  electrons 1807a
Argonauts 1424c
Argonne Forest, Battle of 995b, 2066b
Argonne Plateau 2326b
Argote y Góngora, Luis de see Góngora y Argote
Argument (composition) 1319a
Argus 1424c
Argyll, 8th Earl of (Archibald Campbell) 197a
Aria (mus.) 160c, 161c, 173a
Ariadne 1425a
Arianism 995c
  condemned 1016c
  Nicaea, Council of 871b
Arianna (opera) 161c
Arid 481a
Ariel 1425a
  Shakespeare 1395b, 1418b
Ariel (biog., Maurois) 1347a, 1382c
Arif, Abdel Rahman 2190b
Arif Abdel Salaam 2190b
Arioso (mus.) 173a
Ariosto, Ludovico 1386c, tab 1466
  biography 197a
Arista, Mariano 2039c
Aristarchus 1311c
Aristarchus of Samos 197a, 1503a
Aristarchus of Samothrace 197a
Aristides 197a
Arıstippus 1614a, 1615b
  biography 197a
Aristocracy 784c
Aristophanes 1352c, 1353a, tab 1464
  biography 197a
Aristotle 974c, tab 1464, 1638a, 1798a, 1975
  biography 197b
  medieval reaction to 1755b
  meteorology 468a
  philosophy 1614c
  Poetics 1353c
  science 1752b
  universe 1752c

Aristotle Contemplating the Bust of Plato (paint.) tab 112
Aristotelian method 1798b
Aristoxenus 157b
Arithmetic 1507b, 1508–1531
  addition 1601a
  basic operations 1515c
  definition 1601c
  division 1603a
  fractions 1526a
  mixed numbers 1605a
  multiplication 1605a
  number congruence 1530c
  percent 1530b
  proportions 1530a
  ratio 1530a
  short cuts 1531b
  subtraction 1607b
Arithmetic mean 1604c
Arithmetic progression 1607a
Arithmetic series 1607b
Arius 197c, 995c
Arizona 1975b–1975c
  agriculture 1975c
  capital punishment 860b
  census (1960) 1970
  climate 1975b
  colleges of 655
  commercial law 826
  congressional apportionment tab 853
  economy 1975c
  geography 1975b
  government 1975c
  holidays 841–842
  Indians 1975c
  initiative and referendum 884c
  lizard 43a
  Meteor Crater 1784b
  peccary 50a
  people of 1975c
  public school enrollment, tab 646
  public school expenditures, tab 644
  recall 904b
  saguaro 1691b
  student enrollment tab 645
  tanager birds 62a
Arizona, University of 655
Arizona State University 655
Arkansas 1975–1976
  agriculture 1976a, 1976b
  capital punishment 860b
  census (1960) 1970
  climate 1976a
  colleges of 655
  commercial law 826
  congressional apportionment tab 853
  divorce 875b
  economy 1976a–1976b
  geography 1975c
  government 1976b
  holidays 841–842
  Hot Springs National Park 896a
  initiative and referendum 884c
  kingbird 41a
  people of 1976a
  public school enrollment tab 646
  public school expenditures tab 644
  secession 2045a
  student enrollment tab 645
Arkansas, University of 655
Arkansas Agricultural & Mechanical College 655
Arkansas College 655
Arkansas Polytechnic College 655
Arkansas River 1962a, 1977b, 1982c, 2011a, 2015b, 2015c, 2016a, 2016b, 2018c, 2293a
  length of 2020b
Arkansas State University 655
Arkansas Valley 1976a
Arkose 481a
Arkhangel'sk, U.S.S.R. 2346a
Arkwright, Richard 197c, 1281c
Arlberg Tunnel 1226
Arles, France
  St. Trophine, Church of 119a
Armadillo 14b
Armageddon 1451c
Armagnac 723c
Armaments, limitations 854a
Armas, Carlos Castillo 2169b
Armatures (elec.) 1885b
Armed Forces, careers 388c
Armenian (lang.) 1334a
Armide (opera) 163c
Arminius, Hermann 197c
Arminius, Jacobus 197c
Armistice Day see Veterans Day
Armory Show (1913) 104c, 124b

Armour, Philip D. 524b
Armour Meat Packing Company 2057c
Armstrong, Edwin H. 1152a
Armstrong, James tab 800
Armstrong, John tab 795
Armstrong, (Daniel) Louis ("Satch-mo") 197c
Armstrong, William George 197c
Army (U.S.) aircraft 1157b
  careers 388c
  education 629c
  forms of address tab 1119
  National Guard 892b
  space programs 1769a
Army, Department of the 913a
Army of Virginia 2048b
Army of the Potomac 2045b, 2048b, 2050a
Arnauld, Antoine 197c
Arndt, Ernst Moritz 198a, tab 1471
Arne, Thomas Augustine tab 171c
Arnica 1649b
Arnim, Achim von tab 1472
Arno River 2194a, 2194b, 2194c, 2326c.
Arnold, Benedict 198a, 2028a, 2115a
Arnold, Edwin tab 1477
Arnold, Henry Harley ("Hap") 198a
Arnold, John 1162b
Arnold, Matthew 1366b, tab 1476
  biography 198a
  essay 1402c
  literary criticism 1400b
  Sohrab and Rustum 1417c
Arnold, Samuel 169c
Arnold, Thomas 198a, 1016b, tab 1473
Arnstadt, Germany
  Bach, J. S. 163a
Aromatic compounds 1820a
Arosa, Switzerland 2270
Arosemena Gómez, Otto 2144c
Arosemena Monroy, Carlos Julio 2144c
Arouet, François Marie see Voltaire
Arp, Jean 1853, tab 109, tab 125
Arpeggio 173a
Arquello, Leonardo 2228b
Arraignment 854a
Arrashia Lake 2209c
Arrest (law) 854b
Arrhenius, Svante August 1799b, 1817b, 1839c
  biography 198a
Arrian (Flavius Arrianus) 198b
Arrondissements 873b
Arrowhead 1649c
Arrowrock Dam 1206c
Arrowroot 1649c
  St. Vincent 2321c
Arrows 1703c
Arroyo (stream bed) 481a
Arsenic 1830
  atomic weight tab 1805
Ars Magna (treatise) 1503a
Arson 854b
Art 71–186
  architecture 71–82
  Buddhist 2200b
  careers 374c
  ceramics 126–132
  furniture 1093–1102
  galleries tab 106–113
  glassware 133–135
  graphic arts 136–141
  history of 963c
  kindergarten 399c
  painting 82–113, tab 106–113
  primitive culture 1937c
  sculpture 113–125
  see also under the names of specific branches of art, such as Painting
Art Institute of Chicago, famous paintings tab 110
Art nouveau, furniture 1101b
Art Poetique, L' (treatise, Boileau-Despreaux) 1379c
Artaxerxes I 198b, 1451c
Artaxerxes II 198b, 1451c
Artaxerxes III 198b
Artemis 1425a, 1444b, 1447a, 1628a
  Iphigenia 1435c
  see also Diana (myth)
Artemisia 198b
Arteries 924a
  aneurysm 940b
  arteriosclerosis 940b
  pulmonary embolism 945b

Arterioles 924a
Arteriosclerosis 940b
  aneurysm 940b
Artesian water 481a
Artesian wells 1195b
Artevelde, Jacob van 198b
Artful Dodger 1395b
Arthritis 940b
Arthropods diseases 957a
Arthur (leg.) 1425a
  Avalon 1426b
  Camelot 1428b
  Excalibur 1431b
  Idylls of the King 1406b
  Lancelot 1437c
  Merlin 1439b
Arthur, Chester Alan 198b, tab 798–799, 849b
  administration 2056a
  administration, events parallelling tab 1066
  cabinet tab 796–797
  election and inauguration tab 801
Arthurian legend 1395b
  cycle 1400b
  Morte d'Arthur 1411a
  Round Table 1446a
Arthur's Pass, tunnel 1226
Artibonite River 2171c
Artichoke 1649c
Article (law) 854b
Articles of Confederation 786b, 854b, 2030a
  signers 806b
  text 804–806
Articulation (music) 173a
Artificial insemination
  animal breeding 725c
  livestock 721b
Artificial languages 1338b
Artigas, José Gervasio 2295c
Artist's Father (paint., Dürer) tab 111
Artois, Comte d' see Charles X (Fr. k.)
Arts careers 373c
Arts and crafts movement 1105b
Artsibashev, Mikhail 1390a
Arum family 1649c
Aryan languages see Indo-Iranian languages
Aryans 980b
As You Like It (play) 1395c
  Arden 1395b
  Rosalind 1416a
Asahi Tokyo (news.) tab 1170c
Asahigawa, Japan 2346a
Asama Volcano 2326c
Asbestos 481a, 1195c, 1208a
  Cyprus 2138a
Asbury, Francis 198b
Asbury College 669
Ascanius 1425b
Ascenders (print.) 150b
Ascension Island 2321a
Asch, Sholem 198a
Ascham, Roger 198c
Ascheim-Zondek Test 926c
Asclepius 1425c
Asclepiades of Bithynia 198c
Ascorbic acid see Vitamin C
Ascospores 1856a
Aseptic canning 736c
Asgard 1425c
Ash 481a, 1649c–1650a
Ashanti 2164b, 2164c
Ashburton, 1st Baron see Baring, Alexander
Asheville, North Carolina 1991a
Asheville-Biltmore College 688
Ashford Castle 2191b
Ashkhabad, U.S.S.R. 2346a
Ashoka see Asoka
Ashokan Dam 1206
Ashland, Kentucky 1983b, 1998b
Ashland College 690
Ashurbanipal 198c
Asia 2326c
  albatross 13a
  ancient civilizations 976a
  antelope 14a
  badger 15a
  buffalo 18b
  carp 19b
  cattle 20b
  chamois 21a
  coal 1202b
  cobra 22a 22b

cod 22c
cony 23a
cuckoo 25a
deer 25b
dog 25c
economic geography 772b–773b
eider 33a
flycatcher 34b
gibbon 35b–35c
goldeneye 36a
goldfinch 36b
goose 36b
history outline *tab* 1027–1030
horseshoe crab 39c
hyena 40a
leech 42c
lion 20a
lizard 43a
loon 20a
lynx 44b
map *Atlas*-26–27
tiger 20a
wildcat 19c
Asia Minor 2325c
ass 14b
gazelle 35b
goat 36a
hamster 38a
history outline *tab* 1032–1033
locust 43c
Asiatic cholera 956c
Asir Mountains 2246c
Asmara, Ethiopia 2146a–2146b, 2346a
Asoka 198c, 2179c
Asparagus 1650a
Aspdin, Joseph 1189c, 1199c
Aspen 1650a, *il* 1664
Asphalt 481a
properties of 1870c
varnishes 1227a
Asphodel 1650a
Aspinwall, Panama *see* Colón, Panama
Aspirin 1274a
Asquith, Herbert Henry 198c
Ass 14b–14c
Ass in the Lion's Skin 444a
Assault and battery 854c
Assay 481a
Assaying 1230c
Assembly 854c
Assembly, Right of *see* Right of assembly
Assembly-line 1232a
Assemblyman forms of address *tab* 1119
Assessment 584b
Assessor (gov.) 854c
Assets 584b
Assignment (law) 854c
Assimilation (plants) 1647a
Assimilation (rocks) 481a
Assisi, Francis of *see* Francis of Assisi
Assize 854c
Association of ideas (psych.) 1949c
Association of Southeast Asian Nations (ASEAN) 2250c
Association of University Evening Colleges 635b
Associations
athletic 1703a
social, fraternal and scientific 1742–1746
Assonance 1315c
Assumpsit (law) 855a
Assumption College 673
Assumption of the Virgin (paint., El Greco) *tab* 110
Assur (anc. deity) 1623a
Assurbanipal *see* Ashurbanipal
Assyria 1018b, 1451c
archaeology 969a
architecture 74b
civilization 973c
furniture 1093b
history outline *tab* 1027–1028
music 155c
pottery *tab* 130
printing 142b
religion 1623a
rulers of *tab* 1078
sculpture 113a, 115b
weather forecasting 468a
Astarte 1424b, 1425c
Astatine 1830
atomic weight *tab* 1805
Aster 1650a
Asteroid 481a, 1780a, 1781a, 1783c, 1793b
Bode's law *tab* 1781
meteors 1784a
Asthma 940b

Asti spumante 723c
Astigmatism 940c, 1299b
lenses 1908b
Astin Tagh (mountain) 2123c
Aston, Francis William 198c
Astor, John Jacob (1763–1848) 198c
Astrée (bk.) 1378c
Astronautics 1763–1779
astronomical instruments 1792c
beginnings of scientific 1764b
bibliography 1779c
early history 1763a
future expectations 1777b
glossary 1778–1779
manned flight *tab* 1770, 1770a
photos from *Faith 7 il* 1773
planetary and lunar probes 1771a, *tab* 1772
rockets 1764a
satellites, artificial 1769b
scope 1763a
Astronauts 1763a, *tab* 1770
gravitational problems 949a
Astronomia Nova (tract) 1763b
Astronomical instruments 1790–1793
Astronomical units 1780c, 1793b
Astronomy 1780–1797
Babylonia 972c
bibliography 1797c
Bode's law 1780c
careers in 390a
expanding universe 1787b
galaxies 1785b
glossary 1793–1797
history of 1756b, 1759b, 1763b
instruments 1790c
Kepler's laws 1781a
Mesopotamia 1751a
solar system 1790a
Astrophel (pseud.) 1461a
Asturian Mountains 2264b
Astyanax 1425c
Asunción, Paraguay 2235a, 2235b, 2346b
Aswan, United Arab Republic 2280c, 2346a
Aswan Dam 1206, 2280c, 2281c
Asylums 1954b
Asynchronous motor 1142c
Asyut, United Arab Republic 2346b
At large (gov.) 855a
Atacama Desert 2121b, 2326c
Atahualpa 199a
Atalanta 1425c
Meleager 1439b
Atalanta in Calydon (poem) 1369a, 1425c
Ataractis *see* Tranquilizers
Atasi, Hashim al– 2271c
Atatürk *see* Kemal, Mustafa
Atbara River 2266a, 2326c
Ate (myth) 1425c
Athabasca, Lake 2326c
Athalie (play) 1379b
Athanasius (St.) 199a, *tab* 1464
Atharva-Veda 1420b
Athena (Gr. myth) 1425c, 1628a
Pallas 1442b
see also Minerva (Rom. myth.)
Athena Parthenos (sculp., Phidias) 116c
Athena Parthenos, Temple of *see* Parthenon, The
Athenian Mercury (journ.) 1167b
Athenodorus 117c
Athens, Greece 974b, 2164c–2165a, 2346b
acropolis *il* 2165
archaeology 970c
education 613b
pottery 83c
voting 855c
Athens College 654
Atherton, Gertrude *tab* 1478
Athletics *see* Sports
Athos (myth) 1396a
Atitlan (lake) *il* 2169
Atkinson (Justin) **Brooks** 199a
Atlanta, Georgia 1979c, 2005a–2005b
Civil War 2050b
Atlantic Charter 990a, 996a
Atlantic Christian College 688
Atlantic City, New Jersey 1989c
Atlantic Coastal Plain (U.S.) 1961c
Atlantic Ocean 2326c
auk 14c
bass 15b
by-the-wind sailor 18c
conch 22c
crab 23c

duck 26b
frigate bird 34c
gallinule 35a
hake 37c
horseshoe crab 39c
lamprey 42a
ling 43a
lobster 43b
marlin 44c
menhaden 45b
petrel 50c
salmon 55a–55b
sandpipers 55b
sea cows 55b
seals 55b
shad 57a–57b
sharks 57b
smelt 59a
squeteague 59c
sturgeon 60c
swordfish 61c–62a
tarpons 62b–62c
terns 63a
tuna 64b
Atlantic salmon *il* 1717
Atlantic Union College 673
Atlantis (leg.) 1426a
Atlas (maps) 2379–2344
Atlas (myth) 1426a
Atlas (rocket) fuels 1766b
Atlas Mountains 2087b, 2221b–2221c, 2326c
Atli 1426b
Atmosphere 481a–481b, 762–765
composition 468a
condensation 763c
evaporation 763c
fronts 764a
gases 1840b
high pressure centers 764a
ionosphere 763b
Jupiter 1783a
Mars 1783a
meteorology 468a
origin of life 1840a
oxidizing 1840a
ozonosphere 763a–763b
photosynthesis 1861b
precipitation 764a–764c
reducing atmosphere 1840a
regional climate 765a
stratosphere 763a
temperature 468b
thermal balance 763b–763c
troposphere 763a
Venus 1782c
wind patterns 763c–764a
see also Air pollution
Atmospheric drag 1769b
Atoll 481
Atom *see* Atoms
Atom smashers *see* Particle accelerators
Atomic bomb 2076c
dropped on Japan 2201b
Atomic energy
conservation 775c
Atomic Energy Commission
education 630a
Atomic number 1806a, elements 1830–1838
Atomic hypothesis (Dalton) 1779a
Atomic piles *see* Nuclear reactor
Atomic rockets 1767b
Atomic structure 1803c
nuclear physics 1911b
Atomic Test-Ban Treaty (1963) 2270c
Atomic theory 1803c
Greece 1751b
Atomic volume 1808a
Atomic weight *tab* 1805, 1806a
elements 1830–1838
Atomism (philos.) 1615b
glossary 1620b
Atoms 1803a, 1881b
nuclear physics 1911b
semiconductors 1891a
Aton (anc. deity) 1622c
Atonement, Day of (Judaism) *see* Yom Kippur
ATP *see* Adenosine triphosphate
Atrioventricular node 923c
Atropos 1426b, 1432a
Attachment (law) 855a
Attainability of the Heavenly Bodies, The (bk.) 1765a
Attainder (law) 855a
Attalus I (Soter) 117b
biography 199a
Attalus II (Philadelphia) 199a
Attalus, Stoa of 970c
Attic Bee (pseud.) 1461a
Attic Muse *see* Xenophon
Attic Nights (bk.) 1358b

Attila 199a
nickname *tab* 1463b
Attius, Lucius *see* Accius, Lucius
Attlee, Clement 199a, 2292a
Attorney 855a
Attorney general 790c, 855b
Attraction (elec.) magnets 1883c
static electricity 1881b
Aubame, Jean-Hilaire 2156a
Auber, Daniel François 166c, *tab* 170c
Aubigné, Théodore Agrippa d' 1378b
Auburn, Maine 1984b
Auburn University 654
Aubusson
upholstery 1097c
Aucassin and Nicolette (bk.) 1396a, *tab* 1465
Auckland, New Zealand 2226b, 2226c, 2346b–2346c
Auction 584c
Auden, Wystan Hugh 199b, 1371c
Audion 1889a
Auditing 584c
career 377a
Audition *see* Hearing
Auditory nerve 937c
Audubon, John James 51a, *tab* 1472
biography 199b
Audubon Society, National 1742c
Aue, Hartmann von *see* Hartmann von Aue
Auer, Leopold 199c
Auerbach, Berthold 1385a, *tab* 1475
biography 199c
Auenbrugger von Auenbrug, Leopold 199c
Augean Stables 1426b
Augen (minerals) 481b
Augier, Emile 1381c, *tab* 1476
Augite 453b
Augmentation (mus.) 173a
Augrabies Falls 2252a
Augsburg, Diet of 874a
Augsburg, League of 2289c
Augsburg, Peace of 2160a–2160b
Augsburg College 677
Augusta, Georgia 1979c
Augusta, Maine 2005a
Augustan Age 1396a
Augustana College 663, 669
Augustín I 2219a
Augustine (missionary) 2284a
Augustine, Saint *tab* 161b, 965c, *tab* 1465
biography 199c
City of God 1356a
hymn 158a
Augustine, Saint (Archbishop of Canterbury) 199c
Augustus, Octavius, Emperor (Rome) 975c, 994a
age of 976b
Ancyrean inscription 994c–995a
biography 199c
census 862a
Augustus, Romulus, Emperor (Rome) 2195a
Auk 14b–14c
Auld Lang Syne (song) 1364b, 1396a
Auld Licht Idylls (bk.) 1369c
Auld Reekie 1396a
Aulin, Tor 168b, *tab* 172b
Aurangzeb 2180c
Aurelian, Emperor 200a, 2244b
Aurelius, Marcus *see* Marcus Aurelius
Aureole 481
Auricles 923a
Aurignacian Venuses 1928b
Aurora 481b–481c
Aurora (myth) 1426b, 1431a
Aurora (polar lights) *see* Aurora polaris
Aurora australis 1793b
Aurora borealis 468b, 1793b
Aurora College 663
Aurora Leigh (poem) 1368c, 1396a
Aurora polaris 757c, 1793b
Aurora 7 (spacecraft) *tab* 1770
Aurungzebe (emp.) 199c–200a
Ausable River 2016a
Ausonius *tab* 1464
Austen, Jane 1366a, *tab* 1472
biography 200a

Emma 1402b
Pride and Prejudice 1413c
Sense and Sensibility 1416c
Auster 1426b
Austin, Alfred 1413b
Austin, Warren R. United Nations *tab* 797
Austin, Texas 1995b–1995c, 2005b
Austin College 701
Austin Peay State University 700
Austral Islands 2312c–2313a
Australia 878c, 2091a–2094a
  acacia 1648a
  agriculture 2092a
  animal life 2091c–2092a
  animal preserves 896a
  avocet 14c
  baobab 1651b
  bat 15b
  beech 1652a
  bird of paradise 17a
  black widow 17b
  bluegrass 1653c
  canberra 875a
  cattle 20c
  caucus 860b
  in Christmas Island 2310c
  climate 2091c
  in Cocos Islands 2310b–2310c
  Commonwealth status 1000c
  convict system 2092c, 2093a
  Country Party 2093a
  crocodile 24b
  cycad 1660b
  daisy 1660c
  deer 25b
  dog 25c
  duckbill 26
  economic geography 771a
  economy 2092a
  eggplant 1666a
  emu 33b
  eucalyptus 1666b
  Eucumbene Dam *il* 2091
  euonymus 1666b
  everlasting plants 1666c
  flag *il* 2182
  flycatcher 34b
  fowl 34b
  frigate bird 34c
  geography 2091a–2092a
  goose 36b
  gull 37b
  hare 38a
  history 2092c–2094a
  ibis 40b
  immigration 883c
  kangaroo 40c
  koala 41b
  Labor Party 2093b
  ladybeetle 42a
  lizard 43a
  loon 43c
  loosestrife species 1677a
  lovebird 44a
  lungfish 44a
  lyrebird 44b
  magpie 44c
  map *Atlas*-42–43
  mining 2092b
  mouse 46c
  myrtle species 1681a–1681b
  in Nauru 2223b
  nettle 1681a
  in New Guinea 1650b, 2318b–2318c
  in Norfolk Island 2319b
  olive trees 1682c
  opossum 48b–48c
  oriole 48c
  in Papua 2319b–2319c
  parrot 49c
  penguin 50b
  pelican 50b
  people of 2092a
  pigeon 51b
  pitcher plant 1687b
  plant life 2091c
  polypody species 1688a
  poppy 1688b
  quail 53c
  religion 2091a
  rhododendron 1690a
  robin 54c
  saltbush 1691c
  screwpine 1692a
  sea cows 55b
  sea lions 56c–57a
  sheep 57b–57c
  shrews 57c–58a
  snipe 59a
  SEATO 1021a
  squirrels 59c–60a
  stilts 60b
  sundew 1695a
  swan 61b–61c
  teal ducks 62c
  termites 63a
  trade 2092b
  transportation 2092b
  trout 64b
  wool 748b
  wallaby 65b–65c
  wombats 67c
  World War I 2093b–2093c
  World War II 2094a
Australian aborigines 1924a, 2092a, 2092c
  adaptation 1927b
  cooking 1933a
  messages 1935b
  tools 1928a
  water transport 1934c
Australian Alps 2091b
Australian ballot 855c, 856a
Australian Colonies Government Act 2093a
Australoids 1924a, 1925c
  migrations 1925b
Australopithecines 1924a
Australopithecus 1924a
Austria *tab* 1052, *tab* 1054, *tab* 1056, 2094–2096, 2139b–2140a, 2175a
  agriculture 2095a
  Alps *il* 2094
  architecture 77c, 78a
  cheese *tab* 731b
  Christian Socialist Party 2095c–2096b
  climate 2094c
  Congress of Vienna 1023c
  Dual Monarchy 999a, 2175a
  economy 2094c–2095a
  flag *il* 2182
  geography 2094b–2094c
  German seizure (1938) 1015a
  government 2095a
  history 2095a–2096b
  Holy Alliance 1010a–1010b
  in Hungary 2174c–2175a
  industry 2094c–2095a
  maps 2094, *Atlas*-17
  Pragmatic Sanction 1019a
  people of 2094c
  religion 2094b, 2094c
  rocket engines 1768a
  Social Democratic Party 2095c–2096b
  Swiss War *tab* 1072
  Triple Alliance (1882) 1022c, 1025a
  union with Germany 2096a–2096b
  World War I 1024c–1025c, 2064c, 2066c, 2095b–2095c, 2161c, 2175a
  World War II 1028c, 2096b, 2154c, 2162c
  in Yugoslavia 2304b
Austria-Hungary World War I 2291c
Austrian Alps *il* 2094
Austrian Hyena (pseud.) *see* Haynau, J. J. von
Austrian State Treaty 2096b
Austrian Succession, War of 1019c, *tab* 1073, 2026c, 2290b
  causes of 1019a
  results of 1021b
Austric languages *tab* 1336
Autecology 1859a
Authentic cadence 173a
Author's alterations 150b
Authors' League of America 1742a
Author's proof 150b
Autobiography 1396a
Autoclave 1196a
Autocracy 784c
Autocrat of the Breakfast Table (essays) 1374a, 1396a, 1461a
Autogiro *see* Gyroplane
Automatic control systems 1231a
Automatic pistols 1255a
Automation 584c, 1230a, 1231c
  dairy industry 731b
Automobiles 1154a, 1986a
  air pollution 777a
  brakes 1235b
  carburetors 1240a
  electrical system 1131b
  history 1169b
  tunnels 1226c
Automotive industry 1169c, 1232a
  assembly line 1232a
  careers 386c
  mass production 1232a
Autonomic nervous system 918c, 924a, 938c
Autonomy (gov.) 855b
Autosomes 1852a
Autotransformer 1147c
Autotrophic organisms 1841b
Autumn 1797a
Autumnal equinox 1794c
  harvest moon 1794c
Autun, France
  cathedral 119b
Auxiliary notes (mus.) 173a
Auxin 1645a, 1647c
Avalanche 481c
Avalon (myth) 1426b
Ave Maria (music) 173a
Avebury, Baron *see* Lubbock, Sir John
Avenue at Middelharnis (paint.) *tab* 111
Average (math.) 1604c
Avernus, Lake 1426b
Averroës (ibn-Rushd) 200a, *tab* 1465
Avery, O. T. 1853c
Aves *see* Birds
Avesta (rel. writ.) 1627b
Avestan (lang.) 1334a
Aviation 1155c
Avicenna (ibn-Sina) *tab* 1465, 1754a
  biography 200a
Avignon, France 985c, 2150c
Avila College 679
Avilés, Spain 2264a
Avocado 1650a–1650b
Avocat Pierre Patelin, L' 1378a, *tab* 1467
Avocet 14c
Avogadro, Amadeo 1871c, 1916b
  biography 200a
Avogadro's hypothesis 1802a, 1828a
Avogadro's law 1871c, 1872b
Avogadro's number 1811b, 1916b
Avoirdupois system (wts.) *tab* 1500
Avon, Swan of *see* Shakespeare, William
Awash River 2146a, 2326c–2327a
Awolowo, Obafemi 2229c
Axes
  prehistoric 1928c
Axils (plant) 1645b
Axiology 623a, 1611b
Axiomatics 1501c
Axioms 1601c
  algebra 1532b
  geometry 1559a
Axis (geog.) 481c, 1601c
Axons 939a
Axum, Kingdom of 2266b
Ayacucho, Peru 2100c
Ayacucho, Battle of 2237a
Ayala, Ramón Pérez de *see* Pérez de Ayala, Ramón
Ayer, A. J. 1619a
Ayrer, Jacob *tab* 1467
Ayrshire Bard *see* Burns, Robert
Ayub Khan 2186b, 2233c
Ayuthia, Thailand 2274a, 2346b
Ayyubid dynasty 2281a
Az Zahran, Saudi Arabia 2346c
Azalea 1650b
  soil 751c
Azana, Emperor 2146b
Azbine Mountains 2325a
Azeglio, Marchese d' (Massimo Taparelli) 1387b
Azimuth 1795a
Azonal soils 481c, 762a–762b
Azores (islands) 2241a, 2327a
  canary 19a
  seamounts 463a
Azorín *see* Ruiz, José Martínez
Aztec Indians 64a, 971b, 2218b, 2218c
  civilization 2021a
Azikiwe, Nnamdi 2229c–2230a
Azul (bk., Darío) 1393b
Azurdia, Enrique Peralta 2169b
Azusa Pacific College 656

B

B. e. v. 1917c
B horizon *see* Soil profile
Ba (rel.) 1426b
Baal 1426b, 1451c
Baalbek, Lebanon 2346c
Baath Party (Syria) 2271c
Bab Ballads (poems) 1396b
Babbage, Charles 200b, 1236b
Babbitt (nov.) 1375c, 1396b
Babbitt, Isaac 200b
Babbitt metal *tab* 1193, 1225a
Babcock, Orville E. 2054c
Baboon 14c
Babrius 1394a
Babur 200b, 2085c, 2180b
Baby bonds 584c
Babylon 996c–997a, 1003c, 1451c
  Hanging Gardens 997a
  law 813c
  sculpture 113a
  Tower of Babel 997a, 1451c
Babylonia 972b, 996a–996b, 1003c, 2192c
  agriculture 996c
  Alexander the Great conquest of 995b
  architecture 74a
  Chaldea 1452b
  clay tablet 779
  climate 996b
  cuneiform writing system, 997a, 1295c
  furniture 1093b
  Hammurabi's code 813b
  history outline *tab* 1027–1028
  Jewish exiles in 1017a, 1451c
  literature outline *tab* 1463
  mathematics 1501c, 1751a
  music 155c
  numbers 1510b
  religion 1622c
  sculpture 113a, 115b
  topography 996b–996c
Baby's-breath 1650b
Bacchelli, Riccardo 1388a
Bacchus *see* Dionysus (myth)
Bacchus and Ariadne (paint., Titian) *tab* 111
Bacchylides 1351c, *tab* 1464
Baccio della Porta *see* Bartolommeo, Fra
Bach, Johann Sebastian 162a, 163a, *tab* 171c
  biography 200b
Bach, Karl P. E. *tab* 171c
Bache, Benjamin Franklin 145a
Bachelor's button *see* Cornflower
Bacillary dysentery 956c
Bacilli 1843b, 1845c
  spores 1844a
Back margin (print.) 150b
Back to Methuselah (play) 1370a
Backbone Mountain 1984c
Backed-up (print.) 150b
Backing (print.) 150b
Backing (winds) 481c
Backset beds 481c
Backset eddy (oceans) 481c
Bacolod, Philippines 2346c
Bacon, Francis 986c, 1361c, *tab* 1466, 1798b
  agronomy 749b
  biography 200b

essay 1402c
New Atlantis, The 1426a
Novum Organum 1348a
  philosophy 1616a
Bacon, Henry 200c
Bacon, Nathaniel *see* Bacon's
  Rebellion
Bacon, Robert *tab* 796
Bacon, Roger *tab* 1465, 1616a, 1798b
  biography 200c
  explosives 1207b
  nickname 1461a
Bacon's Rebellion 997b, 2026c
Bacteria 1640c, 1843b
  agriculture 1846a
  classification 1844b
  control of 1844b
  decay 1860c
  food poisoning 956a
  genetics 1853c
  industrial uses 1845b
  infections 954b, 955b
  movement 1843c
  nitrogen-fixing 1646c, 1862b
  sewage 1846a
  water 1845c
Bacteriology 1638a
Bacteriophage 1843b
Bactrian 727a
Badarians 969a
Baden history 875c
Baden-Powell 1st Baron (Robert
  Stephenson Smyth) 200c
Badger 15a
Badger, George 947, *tab* 795
Badlands 481c, 1991b, 2016, *il* 2017
  South Dakota 2016b
Badminton 1704b
Badoglio, Pietro 200c, 2196c
Baedeker, Karl 201a
Baekeland, Leo Hendrik plastics
  1219a
Baeyer, Adolf von 201a
Báez, Buenaventura 2143a
Baffin, William 201a
Baffin Bay 2327a
Baffin Island 2110c
Baffin Land
  goose 36b
Bagasse 1136c, 1282a
Bagatelle (mus.) 173c
Bagdad, Iraq 2189c, 2190a, 2346c–
  2347a
Bagehot, Walter *tab* 1476
Baghdad Pact 1000b
Baghmati River 2223c
Bagirmi 2121a
Bagpipe 173a
Bahamas 2307
  croton 1660a
  eel 26c
  flamingo 33c
  frigate bird 34c
  lobster 43c
  map *Atlas-56*
Bahr, Hermann *tab* 1479
Bahrain 2096–2097
  agriculture 2096c
  climate 2096c
  economy 2096c
  flag *il* 2182
  geography 2096c
  government 2096c
  history 2097a
  map 2096, *Atlas-25*
  people of 2096c
  religion 2096c
Baif, Jean Antoine de 1378b
Baikal, Lake 2220b
Bail (law) 855c
Bailey, Harry (lit.) 1360a
Bailey, Liberty H. 201a
Baily, Francis 1793b
Baily's beads 1793b
Bainbridge, William 201a
Bait (fishing) *il* 1717
Baja California (peninsula) 2327a
  frigate bird 34c, *see also* Lower
  (Baja) California
Bajada 482a
Bajazet (play) 1379a
Bajazid I (Bayasid) (Ottoman
  sultan) 204a
Bakelite *tab* 1219a
Baker, Newton Diehl 201a, *tab* 796
Baker, Ray Stannard *tab* 1480,
  pseudonym 1462b
Baker, Sir Samuel White 201a
Baker Island 2001
Baker tent 1710b
Baker University 668
Bakewell, Robert 719c

Bakhuisen, Ludolf *tab* 107
Bakony Mountains 2173c
Bakst, Léon 184a
Baku, U.S.S.R. 1110c, 2347a, 2256a
Bakunin, Mikhail A. 201a, 851c
Balaam 1451c
Balaguer, Joaquín 2143b, 2172b
Balakirev, Mili 169a, *tab* 172b
Balaklava, Battle of 997c
Balalaika 173a
Balance (design) 1103a
Balance (physics) 1874b
Balance (physiol.) 937b
Balance sheet 584c
Balance of trade 584c
Balanchine, George 201b
Balaton, Lake 2173c, 2327a
Balboa, Vasco Núñez de 2023b,
  2234b
  biography 201b
Bald-cypress 1650b, 1983c
Bald-cypress family 1650b–1650c
Balder 1426a
Balder Dead (poem) 1426c
Baldness 918b
Baldovinetti, Alessio *tab* 106
Baldung, Hans *tab* 106, 140c
Baldwin, Abraham U.S. Constitu-
  tion 809c
Baldwin, Henry Supreme Court *tab*
  802a
Baldwin, James 1375c, 1377a
Baldwin, Matthias W. 201b
Baldwin, Robert 2115c–2116a
Baldwin, Stanley 863a
  biography 201b
Baldwin I, Emperor (Byzantine
  Empire) 999c, 1002b
Baldwin-Wallace College 690
Baldy Smith *see* Smith, William
  Farrar
Balearic Islands 2263b, 2327a
Balewa, Abubakar Tafawa 2230a
Balfe, Michael William 201c, *tab*
  172a
Balfour, Arthur James 201c, 1001a,
  2193b
Balfour Declaration 2193b
Balfour Report 875b
Bali 2186c
Baliol, John de (1249–1315) 201c
Balk (sports)
  baseball 1706a
  squash rackets 1733b
Balka (dog) 951b
Balkan Mountains 2105a, 2327a
Balkan Peninsula 2327a
Balkan Wars 1015b, *tab* 1075, 2106a
Balkhash, Lake 2254c, 2327a
Ball, Thomas *tab* 125
Ball bearings 1234a
Ball State University 666
Ballad of Reading Gaol 1368b
Ballads 173b, 1396b
  Scottish and English 1343c
  secular music 171a
Ballet 173b, 182a
  modern 183c
Ballinger, Richard *tab* 797
  Pinchot, G. 2062c
Ballistite 1766c, 1778c
Ballo in Maschera, Un (opera)
  167b
Balloons airplanes 1154c
Ballot 855c, 856a
  voting machine 1284c
  see also Elections
Ball's Bluff, Battle of 2049
Balm 1650c
Balmaceda, José Manuel 2122b
Balm-of-Giliad *see* Poplar
Balmung 1426c
Balor 1426c
Balsa 1650c
Balsam 1650c
Balsam fir *see* Fir
Balsas Valley 2217c
Baltic languages 1334b, *tab* 1334
Baltic Sea 2238c, 2239a, 2240a,
  2327a–2327b
Baltimore, Lord *see* Calvert,
  George
Baltimore, 2nd Baron *see* Calvert,
  Cecilius
Baltimore, Maryland 2005b
  public health 960c
  tunnels 1226
Baltimore and Ohio Railroad
  tunnel 1179a

Baltimore oriole 1984c
Balzac, Guez de *tab* 1467
Balzac, Honoré de *il* 207, 1381a,
  tab 1474
  biography 201c
  Père Goriot 1412c
Bamako, Mali 2214c–2215a
Bamberg, Germany printing 143c
  statute of Conrad III 120c
Bamboo 1650c
Ban de Benoic 1437c
Banana 1650c–1651a
  Bahamas 2307b
  British Honduras 2308a
  Cameroon 2110a
  Cape Verde Islands 2309c
  Colombia 2132c
  Cook Islands 2311a
  Dominica 2311b
  Dominican Republic 2142c
  Ecuador 2144a
  Grenada 2314c
  Guadeloupe 2315a
  Guatemala 2168b
  Guinea 2170a
  Honduras 2172c–2173a
  Indonesia 2187a
  Ivory Coast 2197a
  Jamaica 2197a, 2198a
  Liberia 2209a
  Martinique 2316c
  Niue 2319a
  Norfolk Island 2319b
  Panama 2234b
  Portuguese Guinea 2320a
  Puerto Rico 2002c
  St. Lucia 2321b
  St. Vincent 2321c
  Somali Republic 2251a
  Tonga 2324b
  Trinidad and Tobago 2275c
  Venezuela 2297b
  Wallis and Futuna Islands 2324c
  Western Samoa 2301c
Banana family 1651a
Banaras, India *il* 2178, 2347a
Banat 2245a
Bancroft, George 201c, *tab* 795,
  tab 1474
Band (rocks) 482a
Band spectra 1906a
Banda, Hastings 2213a
Banda Sea 2327b
Bandama River 2197a
Bandaranaike, S. W. R. D. 2120b
Bandello, Matteo 1386c
Bandinelli, Baccio 122b, *tab* 125
  biography 202a
Bandung, Indonesia 2186c, 2347a
Baneberry 1651a
Banff National Park 2020b
Bangalore, India 2178a, 2347b
Bangeweulu, Lake 2305a, 2327b
Bangka Island 2187a
Bangkok, Thailand 981b, 2273a,
  2273b, 2274b, 2347b
Bangs, John Kendrick
  nickname 1462b
Bangui, Central African Republic
  2119a, 2347b
Banjo 155b, 173c
Bank (fin.) *see* Banking, Banks
Bank (rivers) 482a
Bank note 585a
Bank examiner 585a
Bank for International Settlements
  2072a
Bank Holiday 585a
  Roosevelt, F. D. 2072c
Bank of England 2292a
Bank of the United States, Second
  2035b, 2037b
Banker and His Wife (paint.) *tab*
  112
Bankhead, William B. *tab* 802b
Banking 529a
  career guidance 375c
  checks 821b
  clerks 375c
  Federal Reserve System 879a
  tellers 375c
Banking Act (1933) 704a, 2073c–
  2074a
Bankole-Bright, H. C. 2249a
Bankruptcy 856b
  insolvency 885b
Banks 584c
  clearinghouse 587c
  FDIC 878b
  Federal Credit Administration
  878a
  wildcat 2038a
Banks, Joseph 202a

Banks, Nathaniel Prentiss 202a
  Civil War 2048a
  House of Representatives *tab*
  802b
  Vice-presidential candidate *tab*
  801
Bannerman, Helen 425b
Bannockburn, Battle of 1020a,
  1427c
Banque Générale 1016b–1016c
Banquet of Officers of St. George
  tab 111
Banquo 1396c
Banshee 1426c
Banting, Frederick Grant 202a
Bantock, Granville 169b, *tab* 172b
Bantu languages 1333a, 1337c
Banyan tree *see* Fig
Baobab 1651a
Bao-Dai, Emperor 849a, 2301a
Bar (meteorology) 482a
Bar (mus.) 173c
Bar (sand) 482a
Barabbas 1452a
Barat College 663
Baratynski, Evgeni 1389b
Barbados 2097
  agriculture 2097a, 2097b
  climate 2097a
  Commonwealth status 1000c
  economy 2097a–2097b
  flag *il* 2182
  geography 2097a
  government 2097b
  history 2097b–2097c
  map *Atlas-57*
  people of 2097a
  religion 2097a
  slavery 2097b–2097c
  World War I 2097c
Barbados Labor Party (BLP) 2097c
Barbara Frietchie (poem) 1396c
Barbarelli, Giorgio *see* Giorgione, Il
Barbarians Rome 982a
Barbarossa, Frederick *see* Fred-
  erick I (Holy Rom. emp.)
Barbary States 997c, 2210b
  slavery 997c
Barber, E. A. 128c
Barber, Samuel *tab* 170b, 172c
  biography 202a
Barberini, Francesco 1386c
Barberry 1651b
Barberry family 1651b
Barber-Scotia College 688
Barbirolli, John 202a
Barbiturates 1273c
Barbizon School (art) 86a
Barbour, James *tab* 795
Barbour, John 1360a
Barbour, Philip P.
  House of Representatives *tab*
  802b
  Supreme Court *tab* 802a
Barbusse, Henri 1382c, *tab* 1480
Barca, Pedro Calderón de la
  see Calderón de la Barca,
  Pedro
Barcarolle (mus.) 173c
Barcelona, Spain 2263c, 2264a,
  2347b–2347c
Barchan (sand dune) 482a
Barchester Towers (nov.) *tab* 1475
Barclay de Tolly, Mikhail 202a
Bard College 684
Bard of Avon *see* Shakespeare
Bard of Rydal Mount *see* Words-
  worth, William
Bardeen, John 1283a, 1890c
Bardi, Giovanni 161b
Bards Middle Ages 159a
Bareilly, India 2347c
Baren 141a
Barents Sea 2327b
Barham, Richard H.
  pen name 1462b
Baring, Alexander 202b
Baring, Evelyn 2281b
Baritone 173c
Barium 1830
  atomic weight *tab* 1805
Barium Oxide
  glass 133a
Barker, Wharton *tab* 801
Barkhan *see* Barchan
Barkis (lit.) 1396c
Barkley, Alben 202b

Barlach, Ernst 123b, *tab* 125
  biography 202b
Barley 724b, 1651b, *il* 1661
  Algeria 2087c
  Argentina 2089c
  Great Britain 2282c
  Ifni 2316a
  India 2178b
  Iran 2188c
  Iraq 2189c
  Isle of Man 2316b
  Japan 2199b
  Jordan 2201c
  Libya 2210a
  Montana 1988a
  Morocco 2221c
  North Dakota 1991c
  Oklahoma 1992b
  Pakistan 2232b
  Poland 2239b
  Spain 2264a
  Sweden 2268a
  Syria 2271a
  Tunisia 2277a
  U.S.S.R. 2257a
  U.A.R. 2280c
  Uruguay 2295a
Barlow, Joel 202b
Barmecide Feast 1396c
Barmecides (Persian family) 982a
Barnabas 1452a
Barnacle 15a
Barnard, Edward Emerson 202b,
  1793b
Barnard, George Grey *tab* 125
  sculpture *tab* 124a
Barnard, Henry 615b, 622c
Barnard College 684
Barnard's star 1793b
Barnburners 856b
  Free-Soil Party 881a
Barneveldt, Jan van Olden 202b
Barnum, Phineas Taylor 202b
Baroda, India 2347c
Baroja, Pio 1392b
Barometer 468c, 482a
  invention 468a
Barometric pressure 468c
Baron forms of address *tab* 1120
Baroness forms of address *tab*
  1120
Baroque art sculpture 114b, 122b
Barr body 1852c
Barrack-Room Ballads 1396c
Barracuda *il* 1717
Barrage 482a
Barranca 482a
Barranco (valley) 482b
Barranquilla, Colombia 2132c
Barrel distortion 1908c
Barrès, Maurice 1382c, *tab* 1479
Barrett, Elizabeth *see* Browning,
  Elizabeth Barrett
Barretts of Wimpole Street, The
  (play) 1396c, 1368c
Barrias, Louis *tab* 125
Barrie, James Matthew 1369c, *il*
  207, *tab* 1479
  biography 202b
  M'Connachie 1462c
—Works
  Admirable Crichton 1393c
  Little Minister, The 1409b
  Quality Street 1414b
  Sentimental Tommy 1417a
  Tommy and Grizel 1419a
Barrier reef 482b
Barrington College 698
Barrios, Justo Rufino 2169a, 2173b
Barron, Robert 1264b
Barrow, Errol 2097c
Barry, Charles 202c
Barry, John 202c
Barry, William *tab* 795
Barry College 661
Barry, Comtesse du, *see* Du Barry
Barrymore, Ethel 202c
Barrymore, John 202c
Barrymore, Lionel 202c
Bars (geol.) 449c
Barter (trade) 585a
  primitive culture 1937b
Bartered Bride, The (opera) 164c
Barth, Karl 203a
Bartholdi, Frédéric 203a
Bartholomew, Saint 1452a
Bartholomew, Saint, Massacre of,
  997c, 1010c
Bartlett, Josiah *tab* 803
Bartlett, Paul Wayland *tab* 125
  sculpture 124a

Bartók, Béla 169c, *tab* 172b
  biography 203a
Bartolommeo, Fra *tab* 106, 1850
  biography 203a
Bartolommeo Colleoni (sculp.)
  121c
Barton, Clara 203a
Bartram, John 203b
Baruch (bib.) 1452a
Baruch, Bernard M. 203b
  War Industries Board 2066a
Barye, Antoine Louis 122c, *tab* 125
Baryon 1916a
Barysphere *see* Earth structure
Basaiti, Marco *tab* 106
Basal conglomerate (rocks) 482b
Basalt (rocks) 450c, 482b
Base (math.) algebra 1534c
Base level 482b
Base line 482b
Baseball 1704b
  abbreviations 1707a
  grounds 1705c
  indoor 1732c
  materials 1705b
  terms 1706a
Basel, Switzerland 2072a, 2269c,
  2347c
Basement complex (rocks) 482b
Bases (chem.) 1816c
Basic (rocks) 482b
Basil, Saint 203b
Basili, Giovanni *tab* 1467
Basilica (arch.) 75c
Basilisk (cockatrice) 1426c
Basin 482b–482c
Basin flooding 482c
Baskerville, John 144c
Basket of Apples (paint.) *tab* 110
Basketball 1707a
Basle, Switzerland *see* Basel
Basophils 922b
Basque languages 1337c
Basques (people)
  anthropology 1927a
Basra, Iraq 2190a, 2347c
Bass (fish) 15b, *il* 1717
  angling 1703c
Bass (mus.) 173c
Bassano, Jacopo 203b
Bassein, Burma 2347a
Basse-Terre, St. Kitts-Nevis-
  Anguilla 2321a, 2347c
Basse-Terre Island 2315a
Bassetto, Corno di *see* Shaw,
  George Bernard
Bassett, Richard U.S. Constitution
  809c
Bassoon 173c
Basswood 1676a, *see also* Linden
Bastard title (print.) 150b
Bastidas, Rodrigo de 2234b
Bastille, The 998a
Basuto tribe 2208b
Basutoland 2208a, 2208c
  see also Lesotho
Basutoland African Congress 2208c
Bat 15b–15c
  sound 1894b
Bata, Spanish Guinea 2347c
Bataan Peninsula 2238b
Batavian Republic 2225b
Bates, Edward *tab* 796
Bates, Herbert Ernest 1371c
Bates College 671
Bateson, William 203b
Batholith (rocks) 450c, 455a, 482c
Bath-sheba 1452a
Bathurst, Gambia 2156a, 2347c–
  2348a
Bathyal *see* Ocean depth zones
Bathyal region (oceanog.) 1865c
Bathysphere (vehicle) 482c
Batista, Fulgencio, 874a, 2079c,
  2137c
Batlle y Ordóñez, José 2296a
Baton (mus.) 173c
Baton Rouge, Louisiana, 1983c,
  2018c, 2005b–2005c
Battani, al- 203c
Battenberg, House of 203c
Batter (print.) 150b
Batteries automobile 1131b
  chemical cells 1883a
  electric 1131c
Battle Hymn of the Republic
  (poem) 1397a

Battle of the Books (satire) 1363a
Battle of the Gods and Giants
  (sculp.) 117c
Battle of the Kegs (poem) 1372b
Battles (history) *see under the
  latter part of the name, such
  as* Agincourt, Battle of
  decisive historical 1002c–1003a
  *see also under the names of
  individual battles, such as*
  Waterloo, Battle of
Batumi, U.S.S.R. 2348a
Baucis 1426c
Baudelaire, Charles 203c, 1381b,
  tab 1476
Baudouin I, King (Belgium) 203c
Bauer, Andrew 148a
Bauer, Georg *see* Agricola
Baum, Lyman Frank 203c
Baumes Act 882a
Baumgarten, Alexander G. 203c
Baunsgaard, Hilmar 2142b
Bauxite 482c, 1192b, 1194b
  Arkansas *il* 1975, 1976b
  France 2148b
  French Guiana 2312c
  Ghana 2164a
  Great Britain 2282c
  Guinea 2170a
  Guyana 2170c
  Haiti 2171c
  Hungary 2174a
  Indonesia 2187a
  Jamaica 2197a
  Mozambique 2317b
  Nepal 2223c
  Nicaragua 2227c
  Surinam 2323b
  U.S.S.R. 2256b
  U.S. 1967a
  Upper Volta 2294c
  Venezuela 2297b
  Yugoslavia 2303b
Bavaria, Germany *il* 2157
  Congress of Vienna 1023c
Bavarian Succession, War of 1021b
Bax, Arnold 169b, *tab* 172b
Baxter, Richard *tab* 1468
Bay (geog.) 482c
Bay of (geog.) *see under the
  latter part of the name, such
  as* Bengal, Bay of
Bay City, Michigan 1985c
Bay Islands (Islas de la Bahía)
  2172c, 2173b
Bay State Psalm Book 145a
Bayard, Pierre Terrail 203c
Bayard, Thomas F. 203c, *tab* 796
Bayazid I *see* Bajazet I
Bayberry 1651b
Bayberry family 1651b–1651c
Bayeux Tapestry 1009a
Baykal, Lake 2255a, 2327b
Bayle, Pierre 1380a, *tab* 1468
  biography 204a
Baylor University 701
Baymouth bar 482c
Bayou 482c
Bayreuth, Germany
  music 167a
  pottery *tab* 131
Bay-rum tree *see* Myrtle
Bayrut, Lebanon *see* Beirut
Bazaine, Achille François 204a
Bazán, Emilia Pardo *see* Pardo
  Bazán
Beach, Chester *tab* 125
Beach (geog.) 482c
  raised 512b
Beaconsfield, Lord 877a
Beaded drainage 483a
Beadle, George Wells 1856a, 1858c
Beagle, H.M.S. (ship) 461c
Beal, William James 721a
Beans 1651c
  Mexico 2218a
  Michigan 1986a
  Niger 2228c
  Norfolk Island 2319b
  Peru 2236c
  Portuguese Guinea 2320a
  Rwanda 2245c
  Sudan 2266a
  Uganda 2279c
  U.S. 2294a
  Venezuela 2297b
  Wyoming 1999c
Bear (animal) *see* Bears
Bear (fin.) 585a
Bear grass 1651c, *il* 1661
Bear Mountain Bridge, New York
  1197
Bear Mountain State Park 2018

Beard, Charles A. 204a
Beardsley, Aubrey Vincent 204a
Bearings 1234a
Bears 15c, *il* 30
  black, Asia 15c
  black, North America 15c
  grizzly, Rocky Mountains 15c
  Kodiak, Alaska 15c
  Malayan sun, Southeast Asia
  15c
  sloth, Ceylon 15c
Beat (acoustics) 1916b
Beaton, Cecil 204a
Beatrice (lit.) 1386a
Beatty, David 204a
Beau Brummell *see* Brummell,
  George Bryan
Beauchamp, Katherine *see* Mans-
  field, Katherine
Beauchamp, Pierre 183a
Beauchamp's Career (nov.) 1368a
Beaufort, Francis 474b
Beaufort Sea 2327b
Beaufort Wind Scale 483a
Beaumarchais, Pierre A. C. de 204a,
  1380b, *tab* 1470
Beaumont, Francis 204b, 1361c, *tab*
  1467
Beaumont, William 204b
Beaumont, Texas 1995c
Beauneveu, André *tab* 106
Beauregard, Pierre Gustave 204b,
  2045b
Beauvais, France
  upholstery 1097c
Beauvais Cathedral 76c
Beauvoir, Simone de 1383, *tab* 1481
Beaux, Cecilia *tab* 108
Beaver 15c–16a
Beaver College 694
Beaver Falls, Pennsylvania 130a
Beaver State *see* Oregon
Beaverbrook, 1st Baron 204b
Bebel, August 204b
Becerra, Gasparo *tab* 125
Becher, Johann Joachim 1798c
Bechuanaland *see* Botswana
Bechuanaland Democratic Party
  2101c
Becket, St. Thomas à 204b, 2285b
Beckman, Max *tab* 109
Becky Sharp 1397a, 1420a
Becque, Henri 1381c, *tab* 1477
Becquerel, Antoine Henri 204b,
  1914a
Bed (rocks) 483a
Bed load (rivers) 483a
Bedbug 15a
Bedding plane (rocks) 483a
Bede 1358c, *tab* 1465, 2284a
  biography 204c
Bedford, Gunning, Jr. 809c
Bed in Summer (poem) 414a
Bedivere 1426c
Bedlam (asylum) 1954b
Bedrock 483a, 750a
Bedroom 1109a
Bedroom at Arles (paint.) *tab* 110
Bedsores 940c
Bedstraw 1651c
Bee *il* 29, 16a–16c, 724b
Beebe, (Charles) William 204c
Beech 1651c–1652a
Beech family 1652a
Beecham, Thomas 204c
Beecher, Henry Ward 204c
Beecher, Lyman 204c
Beelzebub 1426c, 1430b, 1452a
Beer 723b, 724a
Beerbohm, Max 205a
Beersheba, Israel 1452a, 2348a
Bees *see* Bee
Beeswax 724b
Beet 1652a
Beet sugar *see* Sugar beets
Beethoven, Ludwig Van 164c, *tab*
  172a
  biography 205a
Beetle 16c
Begas, Reinhold *tab* 125
Beggars, The (paint., Brueghel)
  il 97
Beggar's Opera, The 1363b
Begonia 1652a
Behaine, Pigneau de 2300b
Behavior 1942b, 1947a
  conditioning 1949b

Behaviorist school (psych.) 1948b
Beheaded stream 483a
Behistun Rock (inscription) 997a
Behring, Emil Adolf von 205a
Behrman, Samuel 205a
Being and Nothingness (bk.) 1382c
Beira, Mozambique 2348a
Beirut, Lebanon 2207b, 2348b
Bel *see* Baal
Bel and the Dragon (Bib.) 1452a
Belalcázar, Sebastián de 2144b
Belasco, David 205a
Belaúnde Terry, Fernando 2237b
Belém, Brazil 2348a–2348b
Belfast, Ireland 2348c
Belgrade, Yugoslavia 2302c, 2303b
Belgium 2098–2099
  African empire 2099a
  agriculture 2098b
  Benelux customs union 998b
  cheese *tab* 731b
  in the Congo 2135a
  Congress of Vienna 1023c
  economy 2098b
  European Common Market 877b
  flag *il* 2182
  geography 2098a
  government 2098b
  history 2098c–2099b
  map 2098, *Atlas-22*
  people of 2098a
  printing 144a
  proportional representation 902a
  religion 2098a, 2098c
  in Rwanda 2245a
  World War I 2099a
  World War II 1028a, 2099a,
    2162c, 2292a
Belgian Congo 2099a
  parks 896a
  see also Congo (Kinshasa)
Belgrade, Yugoslavia 2348b
Belhaven College 678
Belial 1426c
Belidor, Bernard Forest de 1190c
Belisarius 205a
Belitung (Billiton) **Island** 2187a
Belize, British Honduras 2308a,
    2348b
Belknap, William *tab* 796
  scandals 2054c
Bell, Acton *see* Brontë, Anne
Bell-the-Cat *see* Douglas, Archibald
Bell, Alexander Graham 205b, 1151c,
    1183c
Bell, Charles 205b, 1947c
Bell, Clive 205b
Bell, Currer *see* Brontë, Charlotte
Bell, Ellis *see* Brontë, Emily
Bell, Henry 205b
Bell, John (Amer. states.) 205b,
    tab 795
  Constitutional Union Party 870b
  House of Representatives *tab*
    802b
  presidental candidate *tab* 801,
    2043b
Belladonna 1652a–1652b
Belladonna lily *see* Amaryllis
Bellamy, Edward 1375b
  biography 205b
  Looking Backward 908a, 1409c
**Bellarmine, Roberto Francesco
    Romolo,** Saint 205b
Bellarmine College 669
Bellay, Joachim du 1378b
Belle Fourche River 2016b
Belle Isle, Strait of 2023c
Belleau, Remi 1378a
Belleau Wood, battle of 2066b
Bellechose, Henri *tab* 106
Belleek ware 130a
Bellerophon 1426c
Belles-lettres 1397a
Bellini, Gentile *tab* 106
  biography 205b
  *Procession in Piazza of San
    Marco tab* 112
Bellini, Giovanni *tab* 106
  biography 205b
  Madonna of the Two Trees tab
    112
  St. Francis in Ecstasy tab 111
Bellini, Jacopo *tab* 106
  biography 205b
Bellini, Vincenzo 166c, *tab* 171c
  biography 205c
Bellman, Karl Mikael *tab* 1470
Bello, Ahmadu 2229c
Belloc, Hilaire 205c, 1371a
Bellona 1427a

Bellotti, Bernardo *tab* 107
Bellow, Saul 205c
Bellows, George *tab* 109
  biography 205c
  Emma and Her Children tab
    110
Bells (mus.) 173c
  percussion 177a
Bell's palsy 940c
Bell Telephone System transistors
    1890b
Belmont, Missouri, Battle of 2049
Belmont Abbey College 688
Belmont College 700
Belmonte und Konstanze (opera)
    164b
Belo Horizonte, Brazil 2102b, 2348b
Beloit College 707
Belshazzar 1452a
Belshazzar (oratorio, Handel) 163a
Baluchistan rugs 1110c
Beluchistan *see* Baluchistan
Bemidji State College 677
Bembo, Pietro 1386c, *tab* 1466
Ben (mountain) 483a
Ben Bella, Ahmed 2088b
  biography 205c
Ben Day 150b
Ben Hur (nov., Wallace) 1397a,
    tab 1476
Ben Nevis, Scotland 1019
Benavente y Martínez, Jacinto
    1392c, *tab* 1479
  biography 205c
Benavides, Oscar 2237b
Bench mark 483a
Benchley, Robert Charles 205c
Benda, Julien 1382a
Bends, The (disease) *see* Decompression sickness
Benedict, Julius *tab* 172a
Benedict of Nursia *see* Benedict,
    Saint
Benedict, Saint 998a–998b
  biography 206a
  monasticism 982c
Benedict XIII, Pope 205c, 1001a
Benedict XIV, Pope 205c
Benedict XV, Pope 206a
Benedict College 698
Benedictine order 998a–998b
Benedictine Rule 982c
Benefit of clergy 856b
Benelux 998b
Benelux Customs Union 2098a,
    2211a, 2224c
Benes, Eduard 206a, 2140a
Benét, Stephen Vincent 206a, 1376b,
    tab 1481
Beneventum Trajan's arch 118b
Bengal, Bay of 2177c, 2327b
Bengali (lang.) 1334a
Bengazi, Libya 2210a, 2348b–2348c
Benghazi, Libya *see* Bengazi
Ben-Gurion, David 206a
Beni River 2100a
Benign tumors 945c
Benjamin 1452a
Benjamin, Judah Philip 206a
Benjamin Franklin Bridge 1197
Bennett, Arnold 1370b, *tab* 1479
  biography 206a
Bennett, Edwin 129a
Bennett, Floyd 1156a
Bennett, James (potter) 129a
Bennett, James Gordon (1795–
    1872) 1171a
Bennett, James Gordon, II 206b
  polo 1727c
Bennett, Richard 2118a
Bennett College 688
Bennington, Vermont
  pottery 129c
Bennington, Battle of 2028a
  holiday 842b
Bennington College 704
Benoit, Pierre 1382c
Benson, Allan L. presidential candidate *tab* 801
Benson, Ezra *tab* 797
Benson, Frank *tab* 108
Bentham, Jeremy *tab* 1470
  biography 206b
  philosophy 1618b
Benthic *see* Ocean depth zones
Benthic existence 1866a
Benthos 465c
Bentivogio, Cardinal, (painting,
    Van Dyck) *tab* 110

Bentley, Richard *tab* 1469
Benton, Thomas Hart (Amer.
    states.) *tab* 1472
  biography 206b
  nickname 1462c
Benton, Thomas Hart (Amer. art.)
    tab 109
  biography 206b
Bentonites 1201c
Benue River 2229a
Benz, Karl 1169b
Benzene 1820a
  coal tar 1203a
Benzoic acid 1821c
Benzol *see* Benzene
Beowulf (epic) 1397a, 1343b, 1344a,
    1358b, 1421b, *tab* 1465
Beowulf (lit. char.) 1427a
Béranger, Pierre Jean de 1380c,
    tab 1472
Bérard, Christian *tab* 109
Berber rugs 1109c
Berbers (people) anthropology
    1925b
Berbice River 2170c
Berea College 669
Berceuse (mus.) 173c
Bérénice (play) 1379a
Berenson, Bernard 206b
Berg, Alban 168a, 172
  biography 206b
Berg wind 483a
Bergama rugs 1110c
Bergamot 1652b
Bergen, Norway 2230b, 2348c
Berger, Victor Louis 908b
Bergerac, Cyrano de *see* Cyrano
    de Bergerac, Savinien de
Bergh, Henry 206b
Bergman, (Ernst) Ingmar 206c
Bergman, Tobern Olaf 1798c
Bergschrund (glaciers) 483a
Bergson, Henri 1348c, 1382a, *tab*
    1479
  biography 206c
  philosophy 1619c
Beriberi 920b, 940c
Bering, Vitus 206c
Bering Sea 2019c, 2327b
  albatross 13a
  auk 14c
  jurisdiction, controversy over
    998c
Berkeley, George *tab* 1469
  biography 206c
  philosophy 1617a
Berkeley, William 997b
  biography 206c
Berkelium 1830
  atomic weight *tab* 1805
Berkshire Hills 1985a
Berlin, Irving 206c
Berlin, Germany 2157a, 2157c,
    2158c, 2348c
  State Library *tab* 1463
Berlin, Treaty of (1878) 2106a,
    2245a, 2304a
Berlin blockade 2163c
Berlin Conference on African Affairs (1884) 2134a–2135a
Berlin wall 2163b
Berliner, Emile 1171b
Berlioz, (Louis) Hector 166b, 171c
  biography 206c
Berm 483b
Bermuda 2307–2308
  economy 2307c
  geography 2307c
  government 2307c
  history 2307c–2308a
  lilies 1675c
  lobster 43c
  map *Atlas-56*
  onions 1682c
  oyster 49b–49c
  people of 2307c
  slavery 2307c
Bermudez, Juan de 2307c
Bern, Switzerland 2269b, 2269c,
    2348c
Bernadette of Lourdes 209a
Bernadotte, Jean Baptiste 2268c–
    2269a
Bernard, Claude 1200b, 1381b
Bernard of Clairvaux (Saint) 209a,
    1377b
Bernardin de Saint-Pierre 209a,
    1380b, 1412b, *tab* 1470
Berne, Switzerland *see* Bern
Bernhardt, Sarah 209a
Berni, Francesco 1386c

Bernini, Giovanni Lorenzo *tab* 125
  biography 209a
  sculpture 122c
Bernoulli family 1506c
Bernoulli's principle 1154b
Bernstein, Henri *tab* 1480
Bernstein, Leonard 170b, *tab* 172c,
    il 371
  biography 209a
Berrien, John *tab* 795
Berries 1646a
  farms 381a
Berry College 661
Berthollet, Claude Louis de 209a
Bertillon, Alphonse 209a
Berylliosis 940c
Beryllium 1808a, 1809b, 1830
  atomic weight *tab* 1805
  electrons 1807a
Berzelius, Jöns Jakob 209b, 1225b,
    1799a
Besier, Rudolf 1371b, 1396c
Bessarabia 2245a
Bessemer, Henry 209b, 1189b
Bessemer converter 1261c
Bessemer process 1261b
Best Friend of Charleston (locomotive) 1178a
Bestiaries 1445c
Beta particles 1804c, 1916c
Bétancourt, Romulo 2143b, 2298b
Betatrons 1919b
Bethany 1452a
Bethany College 668, 706
Bethany Nazarene College 692
Bethel 1452a
Bethel College 668, 700
Bethel College and Seminary 677
Bethlehem, Jordan 1452a, 2348c
Bethlehem, Pennsylvania 1993b,
    2005a
Bethmann-Hollweg, Theobald von
    209b
Bethune-Cookman College 661
Betsiboka River, 2211c
Better Homes & Gardens (magazine) 1167b
Betterton process 1213c
Bettis, Valerie 184c
Betts process 1213c
Bevan, Aneurin 209b
Bevatrons 1919b
Bevel (print.) 150b
Beveling (geology) 483b
Beverly, Robert *tab* 1469
Bevin, E. J. 1208c
Bevin, Ernest 209b
Bewick, Thomas 140c
Beyle, Marie Henri *see* Stendhal
Beyrouth, Lebanon *see* Beirut
    Lebanon
Bhadgeon, Nepal 2223c
Bhagavad-Gita (rel. lit.) 1437b,
    1624c
  Mahabharata 1410a
Bhakara Dam *tab* 1206
Bhartrihari 209b
Bhavabhuti 209b
Bhavnagar, India 2348c
Bhima River, 2327b
Bhopal, India 2348c
Bhubaneswar, India 2348c–2349a
Bhutan 2099
  agriculture 2099b
  climate 2099b
  communism 2099c
  economy 2099b–2099c
  flag *il* 2182
  geography 2099b
  government 2099b
  history 2099c
  map 2099, *Atlas-29*
  people of 2099b
  religion 2099b
Bialystok, Poland 2349a
Bibb, George M. *tab* 795
Bible
  dictionary of 1450–1461
  Gutenberg 142c, 143b
  influence on civilization 1347b
  King James Version 1362a
  law 814c
  Phoenician territory, references
    1018b
  place in literature 1345a
  polyglot 144b
  translations 1360a
  weights, measures, distances
    tab 1460–1461
Bible paper 150b
Bibliography 1397a

Bibulus, Marcus 209b
Bicetre 1954b
Bickerstaff, Isaac (pseud.) 1461b
Bid (fin.) 585a
Bidault, Georges 209b
Biddle, Francis *tab* 796
Biddle, John 209c
Bidwell, John *tab* 801
Bié Plateau 2327b
Bienville, Sieur de (Jean Baptiste Lemoyne) 209c
Bierce, Ambrose 209c, *tab* 1478
    pseudonym 1462b
Bierstadt, Albert 104b, *tab* 108
Bifrost 1427b
Big Brother and Big Sister Federation 1743a
Big Sioux River 2018c
Bigamy 856c
Bighorn 16c
Bighorn Mountains 2020b
Bight (geog.) 483b
Biglow, Hosea 1397b
    pseudonym 1461b
Biglow Papers (satire) 1397b
Bigonia family 1652b
Biha, Léopold 2108b
Bihar, India 2179c
Bihari (lang.) 1334a
Bihor Mountains 2243c, 2327b
Bijagos Archipelago 2319c
Bikaner, India 2349c
Bikini (atoll) 2004a
Bilac, Olavo 1393b
Bilauktaung Mountains 2273b, 2327b
Bilbao, Spain 2263c, 2264a
Bile 921a
    cholangitis 941a
    jaundice 942b
Bile ducts 921b
Bile salts 920c
Bill (legis.) 849b, 856c
Bill of attainder 855a
Bill of exchange (law) 585b, 820c
Bill of Rights (Eng.) 856c
Bill of Rights (U.S.) 787b, 857a, 2031a
    censorship 861c
    civil rights 864c
    text 810
Billings, Josh *see* Shaw, Henry Wheeler
Billings, Montana 2005c
Bimetallic thermometer 469b
Bimetallism 585b, 2057c
Bimini (is.) 2023a
Bin El Ouidane Dam *tab* 1206
Binary form (mus.) 173c
Binary stars 1790c
Binary system (math.) 1505b, 1512b, 1605b
Bindings (print.) 150c
Binding edge (print.) 150c
Binet, Alfred 621b
Binet-Simon scale 1950b
Binghamton, New York 1990c
Binomials (math.) 1601c
    algebra 1535b
    multiplying 1537a
Bioastronautics *see* Space biology
Bío-Bío River 2121b
Biochemistry 1800c, 1825a
Bioclimatology 483b
Biogeography 483b
Biography definition 1397b
    dictionary of 189–368
    literary 1347a
    modern American 1377a
Biola College 656
Biological oceanography *see* Marine biology
Biological relationships 1859–1868
    food chains 1861c
Biological sciences
    careers 381b
Biologicals 1274a
Biology biological relationships 1859
    chemistry 1825a
    conservation 1867a
    influence on philosophy 1619b
    life, origin of 1839a
    science, history of 1761c
    space biology 949–953
Biomes 1863a
Bion (Gr. poet) 209c, *tab* 1464
Bion (pseud.) *see* Southey, Robert
Bionomial method 1638b
Biosphere 765–766
    animal kingdom 766c

    defined 483b
    man 766c
    plant world 766b–766c
Biostratigraphy 483b
Biota 483b
Biotic community 1859b
Biotic potential 1859b
Biotic succession 1860a
Biotin 919
Biotite 453b
Bipropellant system 1766b
Birch 1652c
    white 1989a
Birch family 1652c
Birch, Samuel 1556c
Birch bark 1934c
Bird of paradise 17a
Birds diseases 1843a
    see also under names of individual birds, such as Bluebird
Birgitta, Saint *tab* 1466
Birmingham, Alabama 1974b, 2005c
Birmingham, England 2349c
Birmingham-Southern College 654
Birney, James G. 889c, 2039b
    presidential candidate *tab* 800
Birnweed 1652b–1652c
Birth of Christ (paint.) *tab* 113
Birth of Venus (paint.) *tab* 110
Birth rate 1859b
Birth trauma 1958a
Birthwort family 1652c
Biscay, Bay of 2327c
Bise (winds) 483b
Bishops' Bible 1362a
Bismarck, Otto von 987c, 2153c, 2161a, 2161b
    biography 209c
Bismark, North Dakota 1991b, 2005c, 2018c
Bismarck Archipelago 2318b
Bismuth 1830
    atomic weight *tab* 1805
    Mozambique 2317b
Bison 17a
Bissau, Portuguese Guinea 2319c, 2349a
Bissell, Wilson *tab* 796
Bitter, Karl *tab* 125
Bitterroot 1652c–1653a, 1987c
Bittersweet 1652c
Bituminous coal 483b, 1136c, 1202a
Bivar, Ruy Díaz de *see* Cid, El
Biwa, Lake 2327c
Bizerte, Tunisia 2277a, 2349a
Bizet, Georges 168a, 171c
    biography 209c
    Carmen 155a, 1398c
Bjorkander, Niels 168c
Björnson, Björnstjerne 210a, *tab* 1477
Black (color) 1904a
Black, Hugo 210a
    Supreme Court *tab* 802a
Black, James *tab* 801
Black, Jeremiah *tab* 796
Black, Joseph 1760a, 1798c
Black Beauty (bk.) 1397c
Black Book of Carmarthen (poem) 1395c
Black crappie *il* 1717
Black Death 2286c
Black duck 17a
Black Dwarf, The (nov.) 1366a
Black earth (soils) 483b
Black Forest (mountains) 2327c
Black glass 133c
Black grouper *il* 1717
Black Hawk (Amer. Ind. chief) 210a, 2037c
Black Hills 1961a, 1994b, 2016b
Black Hills National Park 2016b
Black Hills spruce 1994b
Black Hills State College 699
Black Jack (nickname) 1461b
Black letter (print.) 150c
Black market 585c
Black Mesa 1992b
Black Mountain, Kentucky 1983b
Black pepper 744a
Black Prince, The 875c
Black River 2016a, 2299a
Black sands 1222c
Black Sea 2240a, 2327c
    perch 50b
    sturgeon 60c
Black soil 750a

Black tea 745c
Black Volta River 2163c
Black widow 17a–17b
Blackberry 1653a
Blackbird 17a
Blackbody 483b
Blackburn College 663
Black-eyed Susan 1653a, 1984c
Black-figured painting 83c
Black-figured ware 126b
Blackhaw 1653a
Blackhead (disease) 746c
Blackmail 857c
Blackmore, Richard D. 1367c, *tab* 1476
    biography 210a
    Lorna Doone 1409c
    nickname 1462c
Blackstone, William 210a, 1364a, *tab* 1470
Blackwell, Elizabeth 210b
Bladder 925b
Bladderwort 1653a
Bladderwort family 1653a
Bladelin Altarpiece, The (paint.) *tab* 110
Blades microliths 1928c
    prehistoric 1928a
Bladud 1427b
Blagonravov, Anatoli 1765b, 1768b
Blaine, James Gillespie *tab* 796
    biography 210b
    epithet *tab* 1463b
    House of Representatives *tab* 802b
    presidential candidate *tab* 208, 2056a
Blair, Francis P., Jr. *tab* 801
Blair, John Supreme Court *tab* 802a
    U.S. Constitution 809c
Blair, Montgomery *tab* 796
Blake, Robert 210b
Blake, William 1345a, 1364b, *tab* 1471
    biography 201b
    The Piper 416c
    graphic arts 140c
    painting 107
Blakelock, Ralph *tab* 108
Blakey, William 1234b
Blanc, Louis 210b, 908a, 987c, 2153b
Blanc, Mont tunnel 1226
Blanchard, Thomas 1169a
Blanchefleur 1428c
Blanco y Erenas, Ramón 2060b
Blancos party (Uruguay) 2295c
Bland-Allison Act 2055b
Blank verse 1345b, 1397c
Blantyre, Malawi 2212b
Blarney Stone 1427b
Blasco-Ibáñez, Vicente *tab* 1479
    biography 210b
    Four Horsemen of the Apocalypse 1404b
Blashfield, Edwin *tab* 108
Blast furnaces 1256a
Blasting gelatin 1766c
Blastomycosis *tab* 946
Blatchford, Samuel Supreme Court *tab* 802a
Bleak House (nov.) 1366c, 1397c
Bleed (print.) 150c
Bleeding heart *see* Dutchman's-breeches
Blenheim, Battle of 998c–999a, 1002c
Blennerhassett, Harman 210c
Blériot, Louis 210c
Blessed Damozel, The (poem) 1369a
Bligh, William 210c, 1398a, 1654b, 2092c
Blighted ovum 926c
Blimps 1154c, 1155c
Blind valley 483b
Blindness 928c, 959b
    Social Security benefits 837c
Bliss, Arthur 169b, *tab* 172b
Bliss, Cornelius *tab* 797
Blister copper 1205a
Blithedale Romance, The (nov.) 1397c
    Brook Farm 1398a
Blitzstein, Marc 170b
Blizzard 483b
Bloc 857b
Bloch, Ernest 170c, *tab* 172c
    biography 210c

Block diagram 483b
Block lava *see* Aa
Block mountains 483b
Blockade 857b
Block books 140c
Block City (poem) 414b
Block prints 140c
    Japanese 141a
Blocks kindergarten 398c, 407a
Blodek, Wilhelm 169a, *tab* 172a
Bloembergen, N. 1910a
Bloemfontein, South Africa 2349a
Blok, Alexander 1390b
Blood 922b
    agranulocytosis 940a
    anemia 940a
    arteries 924a
    capillaries 924b
    components 922b
    embolus 941c
    hematoma 942a
    hemophilia 942a
    leukemia 942b
    polycythemia vera 945a
    purpura 945b
    Rh factor 922c
    shock 945b
    sickle cell anemia 945b
    stroke 945c
    thrombophlebitis 945c
    thrombosis 945c
    transfusions 922c
    veins 924b
    see also circulatory system
Blood cells 922b
Blood clots 922b
    embolus 941c
    hemophilia 942a
    sickle cell anemia 945b
    thrombophlebitis 945c
    thrombosis 945c
Blood factors 922c
Blood groups 922c
    heredity 1858a
Blood platelets 922b
Blood poisoning 954b
Blood pressure 924a
Blood proteins 922b
Bloodroot 1653a–1653b
Bloody Mary *see* Mary I (Eng. q.)
Bloomer, Amelia Jenks 210c
Bloomfield College 682
Bloomington, Illinois 1981b
Bloomsburg State College 694
Blouet, Paul
    pseudonym 1462c
Blount, William
    U.S. Constitution 809c
Blow, John 210c
Blowout 483b
Blücher, Gebhard Leberecht von 210c, 1024a
    nickname 1462c
Blue 1104b, 1907c
    color vision 928c
Blue baby 940c
Blue Boy, The (paint.) *tab* 112
Blue chip 585c
Blue gas 1210b
Blue glass 133c
Blue hen chicken 1978a
Blue jay *see* Jay
Blue laws
    colonial New Haven 2025a
Blue marlin *il* 1717
Blue Mountain College 678
Blue Mountains 2091b, 2097c
Blue mud (oceans) 483c
Blue Ridge (mountains) 1979c, 1991a, 1993b, 1994a, 1994b, 1994c, 1997b, 1998b, 2016a
Blue Ridge Parkway 896c
Blue spruce 1977a, 1996a
Blue Vase, The (paint. Cézanne) *tab* 112
Bluebeard 1427b
Bluebell 1653b
Blueberries 751c, 1653b
Bluebird 17b, 1987a, 1990b
    mountain 1980c, 1988b
Blue Bird, The (Maeterlinck) 1394b, 1397c
Bluebonnet 1995b
Bluefield State College 706
Bluefin tuna *il* 1717
Bluefish 17b, *il* 1717
Bluegill *il* 1717
Bluegrass 1653c
Bluegrass region 2016b

Blue-green algae 1842b, 1847c
Blue-sky laws 585c, 816b, 857b
Bluetooth, Harold 2142a
Bluff (cliffs) 483c
Bluff Hal see Henry VIII (Eng. king)
Bluffton College 690
Blum, Léon 210c, 857b, 2154c
Blume, Peter tab 109
Bly, Nellie see Cochrane, Elizabeth
Boa 17c
Boadicea 211a
Board of (gov.) 857b
  see under the latter part of the name, such as Regents, Board of
Boaz 1459b
Bobadil 1009a
Bobbin 1286a
Bobbitt, Franklin 638c
Bobby Shaftoe (nursery rhyme) 409a
Bobo Dioulasso, Upper Volta 2294b, 2349a
Bobolink 17c
Bobwhite 17c–18a
Boccaccio, Giovanni il 208, 1346a, 1386a, tab 1466
  biography 211a
  Decameron 1401a
Boccherini, Luigi 211a, tab 171c
Boccioni, Umberto tab 125
Bock, Hieronymus 1638a
Bocklin, Arnold tab 108
Bode, Johann Elert 211a, 1780c
Boden, Lake 2328c
Bode's law 1780c, tab 1781
Bodhidharma 211a
Bodleian Library tab 1463
Bodmer, J. J. 1384a, tab 1469
Bodoni, Giambattista 144c, 211a
Body (anat.)
  see Anatomy, Physiology
Body painting 1930b
Body temperature 918c
Body type (print.) 150c
Body wave (earthquakes) 483c
Boehme, Jacob tab 1467
Boer War (South African War) (1899–1902) tab 1075, 2267b, 2291b
Boerhaave, Hermann 1761c
Boethius, Anicius Manlius Severinus tab 171b, tab 1465, 1503b
  biography 211a
  De Musica 157c
Bog 483c
Boganda, Barthelemy 2119b
Bogaz 483c
Boghaz-Keui (Turk.) 970b
Bogle 1427b
Bogotá, Colombia 2132a, 2132b–2132c, 2349a–2349b
  Pan American Conference of 1948 1000b, 1017c
Bohemia 999a, 2138c, 2139b–2140a
  glass 134a, tab 135
  music 168c, 172a
  Thirty Years' War 999a
  waxwings 66c–66c
  see also Czechoslovakia
Bohemian Forest 2138c
Bohemian Forest Mountains 2327c
Bohemian language see Czechoslovak (lang.)
Bohm, Max tab 108
Bohorok (winds) 483c
Bohr, Niels 211a, 1803c, 1870a, 1904a
Bohul, Philippine Islands 2237c
Boiardo, Matteo M. 1386c, tab 1466
Boieldieu, François Adrien 166c, tab 171c
Boii people 999a
Boileau-Despréaux, Nicolas 1379c, tab 1468
Boiler 1234b
Boiling point 1815c, 1828, 1916c, 1898b
  elements 1830–1838
  temperature scales 1920a
Boine, Giovanni 1388a
Boise, Idaho 1980c, 2005c
Boise River 2005c
Boito, Arrigo 167b, tab 172a, 211b
Bojer, Johan tab 1480
Bok, Edward
  biography 211b
Bokassa, Jean Bedel 2119b

Bokhara rugs 1110c, 1111a
Bol, Ferdinand tab 107
Bolas 1929c
Bold face (print.) 150c
Bolero (dance) 173c, 182a
Boleslav III 2240a
Boleyn, Anne 1022c, 2287c
  biography 211b
Bolingbroke, 1st Viscount (Henry St. John) 211b
Bolívar, Simón 1017c, 2100c, 2133a, 2144b, 2237a, 2297c–2298a
  biography 211b
  nickname 1462b
Bolivia 2090b, 2100–2101, 2236a
  agriculture 2100b
  anteater 14a
  avocet 14c
  chinchilla 21b
  coca 1658c
  economy 2100b–2100c
  established church 877b
  flag il 2182
  geography 2100a
  government 2100c
  history 2100c–2101a
  League of Nations 1012c
  map 2100, Atlas-51
  mining 2100a
  people of 2100a–2100b
  religion 2100a
  Spanish rule 2100c
  war with Chile 2122b
  war with Paraguay 2236a
  World War I 2101a
Bolkiah, Pengiran Muda Mahkota Hassanal 2309b
Boll weevil see Weevil
Bolm, Adolph 184a
Bologna, Giovanni da 122b, tab 125
Bologna, Italy 2349b
Bolshevik Revolution (1917) 2154b, 2261a–2261b
Bolsheviks 858a
Bolson 483c
Bolts 1252b
Boltzmann, Ludwig 211b
Boltzmann's constant 1872b
Bolyai, János 1506a, 1566b, 1558a, 1580c
Bomb (volcanic) 483c
Bombay, India 980c, 2178a, 2349b
Bomi Hills 2209a
Bonaire Island 2317a
Bonaparte, Charles (Amer. states.) tab 796
Bonaparte, Charles Louis Napoleon see Napoleon III
Bonaparte, François Charles Joseph see Napoleon II
Bonaparte, Joseph 211b, 2297c
Bonaparte, Louis 211c
Bonaparte, Lucien 211c
Bonaparte, Napoleon see Napoleon I
Bonaparte, Napoleon Joseph Charles Paul
  nickname tab 1463a
Bonaventura 211c, tab 1463b
Bonbax family 1653c
Bonds 585c
  blue-sky laws 857b
  convertible 589b
  coupon 589c
  odd lot 599c
  par value 600b
  sinking fund 603c
Bone china 128a
Bonefish il 1717
Bones 917b
  osteochondritis 945a
  osteomalacia 945a
  Paget's disease 945a
Bonheur, Rosa tab 108, 211c
Boneset 1653c
Bongo, Bernard-Albert 2156a
Boniface VIII, Pope 211c, 2150c
Bonin Islands 2000, 2201b
Bonington, Richard tab 108
Bonito il 1717
Bonivard, François de 1365a
  Chillon 1399a
Bonn, Germany 2157a, 2349b
Bonnard, Pierre tab 108, 212a
Bonneville, Lake 2018a
Bonneville Dam 2017a
Bonney, William H. 212b
Bonnie Prince Charlie see Stuart, Charles Edward
Bonocini, Giovanni Battista tab 171c
Bontempelli, Massimo 1388a

Bony pike see Gar
Book of Common Prayer, The 1632a
Book of the Dead tab 1463, 1622c
Book of German Poetry 1383c
Book of Kings (Firdausi) tab 1465
Book of Martyrs (Foxe) tab 1466
Book of Mormon 1348a
Book publishing 1160a
Book of Songs (Goethe) tab 1474
Book of Stones 451c
Book of True Love (Ruiz) tab 1466
Bookbinding 1234c
Bookkeeping 586a
  account 583a
  careers 386c
  ledger 596b
Books
  best sellers tab 1160
  binding 150c
  cases 1107b
  children 400c
  influence on life 1347a
  jackets 151c
  paper 1950c
  photoengraving 148b
  printing 142
  woodcuts 140c
Boole, George 1507a, 1601c
Boolean algebra 1506a
Boom (bus.) 586a
Boomerangs origin 1929c
Boone, Daniel 212a
Boonsborough Turnpike Road 1180a
Booster (rocketry) 1778b
  sustainer 1779c
Bootes Cluster (galaxies) tab 1785
Booth, Edwin 212a
Booth, John Wilkes 212a, 963c–964a, 2051a
Booth, William 212a
Bora (winds) 483c
Borage 1653c
Borah Peak 1980c
Borax glassmaking 133b
Bordeaux, France 2148b–2149b, 2349b
Borden, Robert 2117c–2118a
Bore (waves) 483c
Boreal forest 483c, 1863c
Boreas 1427b
Borghese, Pauline statue of 122c
Borgia, Cesare 212a
Borgia, Lucrezia 212a
Borgia, Rodrigo see Alexander VI
Borgia family 2246b
Boris, Emperor 2105c
Boris Godunov (play, Pushkin) 1389b
Borglum, Gutzon tab 125
  biography 212b
Borglum, Solon Hannibal tab 125
Borie, Adolph tab 796
Borne, Ludwig 1384c, tab 1473
Bornea 2327c
Borneo 2187a
  anthropology 1924a
  orangutan 48c
  rhinoceros 54c
Bornholm Island 2141a
Bornu 2121a
Borodin, Aleksandr 169a, tab 172a
  biography 212b
Boron, Robert de 1395c
Boron 1808a, 1831
  atomic weight tab 1805
  electrons 1807a
  ions 1809b
  oxide 133a
Boron Carbide
  hardness tab 1192b
Borough 858a
Borrow, George tab 1474
Boru, Brian see Brian
Börzsöny Mountains 2173c
Bors, Sir (lit. char.) 1427b
Bosanquet, Bernard 1618b
Boscán, Juan 1466
Bosch, Hieronymus (Jerome Bosch) tab 106
  Adoration of the Magi tab 111
  biography 212b
Bosch, Juan 2143b
Bosna River 2303a
Bosnia 2161c
Bosporus (strait) 2277c, 2327c
Boss (rocks) 483c
Bossi, M. E. 167c
Bossuet, Jacques 1379c, tab 1468
Boston, Massachusetts, 1985a–1985b, 2005c
  American Revolution 2029

founding 2024b
  Public Library tab 1463
  temperature 477a
Boston, State College at 673
Boston College 673
Boston Common 895b
Boston ivy 1653c
Boston Massacre 2027b
Boston Mountains 1976a
Boston News Letter 1170c
Boston Port Bill 2027c
Boston Public Library tab 1463
  architecture 78c
Boston Symphony Orchestra establishment 170a
Boston Tea Party 2027c
Boston University 673
Boswell, James 212b, tab 1470
  Johnson, Samuel 1363c, 1397b, 1409a
  nickname 1461b
Botany 1637–1639
  areas covered by 1637a–1638a
  fruits 737c
  hydroponics 739c
  photosynthesis 1861a
  plant breeding 726a
  see also Plants
Botany Bay 2092c
Botfly 18a
Botha, Louis 212b, 2253b
Bothnia, Gulf of 2327c
Bothwell, James Hepburn 1020b
Botsford, G. W. 1002c
Botswana 2101
  agriculture 2101b
  cattle 2101b
  climate 2101b
  Commonwealth status 1000c
  economy 2101b–2101c
  flag il 2182
  geography 2101b
  government 2101c
  history 2101c
  map 2101, Atlas-40
  people of 2101b
  religion 2101b
Botta, Carlo G. tab 1471
Böttger, Johann Friedrich 127c
Botticelli, Sandro 96, tab 106
  Adoration of the Magi tab 133
  biography 212b
  Primavera il 96
  Uffizi Gallery tab 110
Bottom, Nick 1397c
Bottom land see Floodplain
Bottomset beds 483c
Botulism 736c, 940c, 956b
  bacteria 1845a
Bouchard, Henri 129
Bouchardat, Guy 1221c
Boucher, François 85a, tab 107, 212b
Bouchardon, Edme tab 108
Boudin, Eugène tab 108
Boudinot, Elias Continental Congress tab 802b
Bougainville, Louis Antoine de 212b
Bougainville Island 2318b
Bougainvillea 1653c
Bouillon, Godefroy de see Godefroy de Bouillon
Boulder, Colorado proportional representation 902b
Boulder clay 483c
Boulder Dam see Hoover Dam
Boulle, André Charles 1097b
Boumedienne, Houari 2088b
Bouncing bet 1654a
Boundary Peak 1988b
Bounty 909c
Bounty (ship) 1654b, 2319b, 2319c
Bourbon, House of 212c
Bourbon Island 2320c
Bourbon kings 2151c–2152c, 2153a
Bourdaloue, Louis 1379c, tab 1468
Bourdelle, Antoine 123b, tab 125
Bourdichon, Jean tab 106
Boureshes, France
  World War I 2066c
Bourgeois French literature 1378a
Bourgeois, Léon 1012b–1013c
Bourget, Paul 1382c, tab 1478
Bourguiba, Habib 2277b, 2277c
Bourinot, Arthur S. tab 1480
Bouts, Dirk tab 106
  Prophet Elijah, The tab 109
Boutwell, George tab 796
Boveri, T. 1851b
Bow, England
  pottery tab 131

Bow (archery) 1703c
Bowditch, Nathaniel 212c
Bowdoin College 671
Bowen, Elizabeth 212c, 1371c, tab 1481
Bowen's Reaction Series (minerals) 483c–484a
Bowie State College 672
Bowing (mus.) 173c
Bowling 1707c
  scoring 1708a
Bowling Green State University 690
Box 1654a
Box canyon 484a
Box elder see Maple
Box head (print.) 150c
Boxer Rebellion 904a, 2129c
  reparations 905b
Boxing 1708b
  defense 1709a
  offense 1708c
Boy Who Cried Wolf, The (fable) see Shepherd Boy, The
Boyce, William tab 171c
Boycott 586a
  direct boycott 591a
  secondary boycott 603a
Boyd Lynn
  House of Representatives tab 802b
Boyer, Jean Pierre 2172b
Boyle, Robert 1798c, 1800b, 1871b
  biography 212c
  gases 1828a
Boyle's law 1801c, 1802a, 1871b, 1872b
Boyne, Battle of 2191c
Boy with a Goose (sculp.) 117c
Boy Scouts of America 1743
Boys' Clubs of America 1743a
Boz see Dickens, Charles
Bozzy see Boswell, James
Brace (punct.) 1314a
Brachman, Robert tab 109
Brackets 1314a
Brackish (waters) 484a
Bradbury, William B. 169c
Braddock, Edward 212c
Bradford, Gamaliel 1397b
Bradford, William (1590–1657) 1018b, 1018c, 1019a, tab 1467, 2024b
  American literature 1372a
  biography 212c
Bradford, William (Amer. jurist) tab 795
Bradley, Francis Herbert 1618b
Bradley, Joseph B.
  Supreme Court tab 802a
Bradley, Omar N. 212c
Bradley University 663
Bradstreet, Anne 1372a, tab 1468
Bradstreet, Simon 827b
Brady, Diamond Jim 212c
Brady, Mathew B. 212c, 1172b
Bragança dynasty 2242a
Bragg, Braxton 213a
Bragg, William Henry 213a, 1800a
Bragg, William Lawrence 1800a
Bragi 1427b
Brahe, Tycho 213a, 1125a, tab 1466, 1757a
Brahma 1427a, 1437b
Brahmans 980b, 1624b
Brahmaputra River 2099b, 2177a–2177b, 2232a, 2327c
Brahms, Johannes 167b, tab 172a
  biography 213a
Braided stream 484a
Braila, Romania 2349c
Braille, Louis 213a
Brain 938a
  aphasia 940b
  breathing 922b
  cerebral palsy 941a
  chorea 941a
  epilepsy 941c
  hydrocephalus 942b
  learning 1949b
  mental deficiency 1953a
  neurology 1952b
  optic nerve 928b
  physiological psychology 1950c
  stroke 945c
Brake 1235b
Braken 1654a
Bramante, Donato d'Agnolo 76c, 213a
Bramlette, T. E. tab 801
Bran (myth) 1427b

Branch, John tab 795
Branch (bus.) 586a
Branco, Camillo Castello 1388c
Brancusi, Constantin 123b, tab 125, 213a
Brand name 586a
Brandeis, Louis Dembitz 213a
  Supreme Court tab 802a
Brandeis University 673
Brandenberger, Jacques Edwin 1199b
Brandenburg Gate il 2162
  architecture 77c
Brandes, Georg 1478
Brandt, Willy 2163a
Brandy 723c
Brandy Station, Battle of 2049
Brandywine, Battle of 2029
Brandywine Creek 2015c
Brangwyn, Frank tab 108
Brannan, Charles F. tab 797
Brant, Sebastian 1383b, tab 1466
Brantôme, Seigneur de (Pierre de Bourdeilles) 1378c
Braque, Georges 86c, 103b, tab 108
  biography 213b
Brash ice 484a
Brasilia, Brazil 2102a, 2102c, 2349c
Brasov, Romania 2244a
Brass tab 1193, 1195c
  furniture 1097b
Brass instruments (mus.) 173c
Brasstown Bald Mountain 1979c
Bratislava, Czechoslovakia 2139a, 2349c
Brattain, Walter H. 1283a, 1890c
Braun, Karl 1240c
Braun, Wernher von see Von Braun, Wernher
Braxton, Carter
  Declaration of Independence tab 803
Brazil 2064b, 2090b, 2102–2104
  agriculture 2102a, 2103a
  agrimony 1648a–1648b
  airlines 2103a
  anteater 14a
  bigonias 1652b
  bougainvillea 1653c
  coffee 729a, 1659a
  duck 26a
  economy 2102c–2103b
  flag il 2182
  frigate bird 34c
  geography 2102a–2102b
  government 2103b
  history 2103b–2104c
  Indians 1930c, 2102c, 2103c
  literature 1393b
  map 2102, Atlas-48
  menhaden 45b
  oranges 1682c–1683a
  pampas grass 1684a
  passion-flowers 1684c
  people of 2102b–2102c
  piranha 51c
  plover 52a–52b
  religion 2102a, 2104a
  rubber trees 1690c
  sage 1691b
  slavery 2102c, 2103c, 2104a
  tapir mammals 62b
  tarpons 62b–62c
  toucan 64a
  war with Argentina 2295c
  war with Paraguay 2235c
  World War II 2104b
Brazil nut 1654a
Brazil nut family 1654a
Brazing 1235c
  flux 1209b
Brazos River 1995c, 2016b
  length of 2020b
Brazza, Pierre Savorgnan de 2134a
Brazzaville, Congo 2119b, 2133c, 2134a, 2349c
Bread and Ale, Assize of 855a
Breadfruit 1654a–1654b
Bread-Winners, The (nov.) 1375b
Break (mus.) 173c
Breaker (waves) 484a
Breakfast room 1108b
Breakwater see Jetty
Brearly, David
  U.S. Constitution 809c
Breastbone see Sternum
Breast stroke 1733c
Breathing 922a
  regulation 922a
  see also Respiration
Breccia (rocks) 450a, 484a
Brechou Island 2310a
Brecht, Bertolt 1385c

Breckenridge, H. tab 108
Breckinridge, John C. tab 795
  presidential candidate tab 801, 2043b
  vice-presidency tab 800
Breeders (nuclear reactors) 1829b
Breeding animal 725a
  plant 726a
  swine 745b
Breeze 514a
  sea 514a
Breitinger, J. J. 1384a
Breitmann, Hans see Leland, Charles Godfrey
Bremen, Germany 2349c–2350a
  free city status 1009c
  Hanseatic League 1009b–1009c
Bremer, Fredrika 1474
Bremersdorp, Swaziland 2267a
Brennan, William J., Jr.
  Supreme Court tab 802a
Brenau College 662
Brentano, Clemens tab 1472
Brentano, Elizabeth 1461b
Brescia College 670
Breshkovsky, Catherine 213c
Brest-Litovsk, Treaty of 1025c, 2261c
  terms 999a–999b
Brétigny, Treaty of 2286c
Breton, Jules tab 108
Breton (lang.) 1336c
Bretón de los Herreros, Manuel tab 1474
Bretton Woods Agreements 536a
Breuer, Josef 1954c
Breuer, Marcel 81c, 1101c
  biography 213c
Breughel, Pieter (the Elder) (1525–1569) tab 107
  Beggars, The il 89
  biography 214c
  Imperial Gallery tab 113
Breve (punct.) 1314c
Breviary 158a
Brewer, David J.
  Supreme Court tab 802a
Brewster, Benjamin tab 796
Brewster, David 213c
Brewster's angle 1905c
Brezhnev, Leonid I. 213c, 2263a
Brian (Brian Boru) 213c, 760c, 2191a
Briand, Aristide 213c
Briand-Kellogg Pact 854a, 880c
Briar Cliff College 667
Briar Creek, Battle of 2029
Briarcliff College 684
Briareus 1427c
Brice's Cross Roads, Battle of 2049
Bricklayers careers 376b
Bricks 132b, 1196a
  making of 128b
Bridal wreath 1654b
Bride of Lammermoor (nov.) 1366a
Bridge, Frank 172b
Bridge (mus.) 174a
Bridge of Sighs (poem) 1365b
Bridgeport, Connecticut 1978a
Bridgeport, University of 659
Bridges, Robert 213c
  nickname 1462a
  Poet Laureate 1413b
Bridges 1196b
  famous 1197
  first iron 1189b
  movable 1198a
  see also under the names of individual bridges, such as George Washington Bridge
Bridgetown, Barbados 2097a, 2350a
Bridgewater, State College at 673
Bridgewater College 704
Bridgman, Percy Williams 1869b
Brie tab 731b
Brief (public speaking) 1328b
Brieux, Eugène 1382b, tab 1479
Briggs, Henry 1596a, 1604b
Brigham Young University 703
Bright, John
  biography 213c
Brightness 1907a
Brindisi (mus.) 174a
Brisbane, Arthur 908a
Brisbane, Australia 2350a
Briseis 1422c
Bristletail 18a
Bristol, England 2350a
  ceramics 128a
  pottery tab 131

Bristow, Benjamin tab 796
Bristow, George F. 170a
Bristowe Tragedie (poem) 1364a
Britain see Great Britain
Britannia Bridge 1196c
Britannic languages 1336a
British Antarctic Territory 2308
British Cameroons see Cameroons, British
British Central Africa Protectorate 2212c
British Columbia, Canada il 2112
  dogwoods 1665b
  pelican 50a–50b
  skunks 58b
British Commonwealth of Nations 868a, 877a
  dominion 875b
British East African Company 2202c
British East India Company see East India Company
British Guiana 2059a
British Honduras 2308
  agriculture 2308a
  anteater 13c
  economy 2308a–2308b
  geography 2308a
  government 2308b
  history 2308b
  people of 2308a
  turkey 64c
British Imperial System (meas.) tab 1500
British Indian Ocean Territory 2308
British Institution of Civil Engineers 1201b
British Isles 2327c
  see Great Britain
  see Ireland
  see Wales
British Museum tab 1463
  archeology 970c
  architecture 77c
British North America see Canada
British Solomon Islands 2308–2309
  agriculture 2308c
  economy 2308c
  geography 2308c
  government 2308c
  history 2308c–2309a
  people of 2308c
  World War II 2308c–2309a
British South Africa Company 2212c, 2243b, 2305c
British thermal unit 1899c
British Virgin Islands 2309
  slavery 2309a
Brittany, France il 2151
Britten, Benjamin 169b, tab 172b
  biography 214a
Brno, Czechoslovakia 2139a, 2350b
Broad jump 1738a
Broadcasting 1152a
Brobdingnag 1398a, 1405b
Broccoli see Mustard
Brock, Isaac 2034b
Brockton, Massachusetts 1985b
Brodel 484a
Broilers (zool.) 728a
Broken Hill, Zambia 2350a
  anthropology 1924c
Brokers 586a
  careers 389c
Bromellin 734c
Bromfield, Louis tab 1480
Bromine 1831
  atomic weight tab 1805
Bronchi (anat.) 922a
Bronchial asthma 940c
Bronchiectasis 940c
Bronchitis 940c
  emphysema 941c
Bronsted, Johannes Nicolaus 1817a
Brontë, Anne 1367c
  pseudonym 1461b
Brontë, Charlotte 1367c, tab 1475
  biography 214a
  Jane Eyre 1407a
  pseudonym 1461b
Brontë, Emily 1367c, tab 1475
  biography 214a
  pseudonyms 1461a
  Wuthering Heights 1421b
Bronx-Whitestone Bridge 1197
Bronze tab 1193, 1198a
  first use of 767b
Bronze Age 967b, tab 1027, 1124b, 1427c

anthropology 1929a
Crete 970c
Bronzing (print.) 150b
Bronzino, Il tab 107
Brook, Alexander tab 109
Brook 484a
Brook Farm 1373b, 1398a
Blithedale Romance 1397c
Brook Kerith, The (nov.) 1369c
Brooke, Arthur 1416a
Brooke, James 2213c
Brooke, Rupert 1371a, tab 1480
Brookhaven National Laboratory
synchrotron 1912c
Brooklyn-Battery Tunnel 1226c
Brooklyn Bridge 1191a, 1197a, 2056a
Brooks, Van Wyck 214a
works 1377a
Brooks, John A. tab 801
Brook trout il 1717
Broom, Jacob
U.S. Constitution 809c
Broom 1654b
Broom corn 1654b–1654c
Brothers Karamazov, The (nov.)
tab 1476
Brouwer, Adriaen tab 107
Brown, Aaron tab 796
Brown, Arthur 1156a
Brown, B. Gratz
presidential candidate tab 801
Brown, Charles B. 1372c, tab 1472
Brown, Charles Farrar tab 1477
pseudonym tab 1463c
Brown, George 2116a
Brown, Henry B. Supreme Court
tab 802a
Brown, Henry Kirke tab 125
Brown, Jacob 2034c
Brown, John 214a, 2043a
Brown, Walter F. tab 796
Brown coal see Lignite
Brown pelican 1983c
Brown thrasher 18a, 1979c
Brown trout il 1717
Brown University 698, 1993
Brown v. Topeka (law case) 2078c
Brown Westhead ware tab 132
Browne, Sir Thomas 214a, 1362a,
tab 1467
Religio Medici 1347a
Brownell, Herbert, Jr. tab 796
Brownie (Scot. folklore) 1427c
Browning, Elizabeth Barrett 1358a
1368c, tab 1475
Aurora Leigh 1396a
Barretts of Wimpole Street
1396c
biography 214a
Euripides 1352c
Sonnets from the Portuguese
1417c
Browning, Orville H. tab 797
Browning, Robert 1358a, 1368c, tab
1475, il 208
Barretts of Wimpole Street
1396c
biography 214b
Ring and the Book, The 1415b
Year's at the Spring, The 416c
Brownlee Dam 1205c
Brownsville, Texas 1995c
Broz, Josip see Tito
Bruce, Robert VIII see Robert I
(Scot. k.)
Bruce and the Spider (leg.) 1427c
Brucellosis tab 946, 957c
Bruch, Max 167c, tab 172
Bruckner, Anton 167b, tab 172a
biography 214c
Brueghel see Breughel
Bruei Municipal, Brunei, 2309a
Bruges, Belgium 2098c
printing 144a
Brummell, George Bryan (Beau
Brummell) 214c
nickname 1461a
Brun, Charles 1182c
Bruneau, Alfred 168b
Brunei 2309
map, *Atlas-39*
Brunei, Brunei 2350a
Brunelleschi, Filippo 76c, tab 125,
214c
Brunetière, Ferdinand 1382a, tab
1478
Brunfels, Otto 1638a
Brunhild 1427c
Bruni, Leonardo
tomb of 121c
Brünn, Czechoslovakia see Brno
Brunnehild see Brunhild

Bruno, Giordano 214c, 1387a
Bruno of Cologne 214c
Brunswick, Duke of 1007c
Brush, George de F. tab 108
Brussels, Belgium 2098a, 2098b,
2350b
Brussels sprouts see Mustard
Brut (Brutus) (leg. k.) 1428a
Brut, The (poem, Layamon) 1359c
Arthur 1425b
Brut, The (poem, Wace) 1428a
Brutus, Marcus Junius 214c
Shakespeare 1407c
Bruyère, Jean de La see La Bruy-
ère, Jean de
Bryan, William Jennings 906b
biography 214c
Cabinet tab 796
Democratic Party 873a
Populist Party 900a
presidential candidate tab 801,
2059b, 2060c, 2062b
World War I 2065a
Bryan-Chamorro Treaty 2228b
Bryant, William Cullen 1374b, tab
1473
biography 215a
Thanatopsis 1418c
Brynhild see Brunhild
Bryn Mawr College 694
Bryophyta see Liverworts
see Mosses
BTU see British thermal unit
Bubble chamber 1914b
Buber, Martin 215a
Buccaneers 999b
Buccina 157c
Buchanan, James tab 795, tab 798–
799
administration 2042b-2044a
biography 215a
cabinet tab 796-797
election and inauguration tab
800
events paralleling administra-
tion tab 1064
land bills 888b
nicknames 1462c
Buchanan, Robert W. tab 1477
pseudonym 1462c
Buchanan, Liberia 2209a
Bucharest, Romania 2243c, 2244a,
2350c
Bucharest, Peace of (1812) 2244
Bucharest, Treaty of 2167a
Buck, Dudley 170a, tab 172c
Buck, Pearl S. 215a, tab 1480
Bucket shop (fin.) 586b
Buckeye 1991c
Bucknell University 694
Buckner, Simon B.
vice-presidential candidate tab
801
Buckthorn, 1654c
Buckthorn family 1654c
Buckwheat 1654c
Bucolics (Vergil) see Eclogues
(Vergil)
Bud scales (plant) 1645a
Budapest, Hungary 2173b, 2174a,
2350b
World War II 1028c
Buddenbrooks (nov.) 1385b
Buddha (Gautama Buddha) 980b,
1627a, 1667a
biography 258c
Buddhism 977c, 1624c, 2127b
Burmese monks il 2107
China 976b
India 980b
Japan 1628a
lamaist 1021c
nonresistance 894b
sacred tree of 1667a
Budget 858a, 586b
household 1089b
preparing 1089c
recreation expenses 1090a
Budget, Bureau of the 791a, 858c
Budget Act (1921) 870c
Buds (plant) 1644a
axillary 1644c
lateral 1644c
terminal 1644c
Buell, Don Carlos 1020c, 2045c
Buen Retiro, Spain
pottery tab 131
Buena Vista, Battle of 2040a
Buena Vista College 667
Buenos Aires, Argentina 2089a,
2090a, 2235c, 2350b–2350c
Pan American Conference
(1910) 1017c
Buerger's disease 941a

Buffalo il 17, 18a–18b
Buffalo Bill see Cody, William F.
Buffalo, New York 1990c, 2006a
flour milling 1255c
government 864c
Buffer solutions 1817c
Bufflehead 18b
Buffon, Georges de 1380b, tab
1470
Buganda (kingdom) 2279c–2280a
Building and loan association 603a
Building codes 1198c
Building Construction 73a, 1198b
career guidance 376b
Building materials 1189
brick 1196a
cement 1199c
clay 1201b
concrete 1203c
granite 1211c
limestone 1214a
sandstone 1223a
Buildings schools 617c
Bujumbura, Burundi 2108a, 2350c
Buka Island 2318b
Bukk Mountains 2173c
Bukovina 2245a
Bulawayo, Rhodesia 2350c
Bulbourethral gland 926b
Bulbs (plant) 1644a
Bulfinch, Charles 78c
Bulganin, Nikolai A. 215a
Bulgaria 1015b, 2105–2106, 2167a
agriculture 2105b, 2106b
Cominform 866a
communism 2105b–2105c, 2106a-
2106b
Crusades 1002a
economy 2105a–2105b
established church 877b
flag il 2182
geography 2105a
government 2105b–2105c
history 2105a–2106b
map 2105, *Atlas-18*
people of 2105a
refugee resettlement (World
War I) 1013b
religion 2105a, 2105c
U.S.S.R. 2106a–2106b
World War I 1025a, 2066c, 2106a,
2161c
World War II 2106a
Bulgarian language 1334b
Bulk modulus 484a
Bull, John 171a, tab 171c
Bull, Ole 167b, 172a
Bull (fin.) 586b
Bull (zool.) 727b
Bull market (econ.) 586b
Bull Moose Party 858b
Bull Run, First Battle of 2045b,
2049
Bull Run, Second Battle of 2048b,
2049
Bull Shoals Dam 1206
Bullhead (fish) il 1717
Bulrush 1654c–1655a
Bülow, Prince Bernhard Von 215b
Bulwer-Lytton, Edward George
1367b, tab 1474
Last Days of Pompeii 1408c
Bulwer-Lytton, Edward Robert 1369b,
tab 1477
pseudonym 1462c
Bumper, Project see Project
Bumper
Buna-N (rubber) 1222b
Buna-S (rubber) 1222a
Bunchberry 1655a
Bunche, Ralph J. 215b
Bungo Strait 2198c
Bunin, Ivan 215b, 1390a
Bunion 941a
Bunker Hill, Battle of 2029, 2027c
Bunsen, Robert Wilhelm 215b,
1799a
Bunting 18b
Bunting v. Oregon 834c
Bunyan, John tab 1468
biography 215c
Pilgrim's Progress 1362c, 1394b,
1413a
Bunyan, Paul 1442c
Buonarroti, Michelangelo see Mi-
chelangelo
Buoninsegna, Duccio di see Duccio
di Buoninsegna
Burbank, Luther 215c
Burchfield, Charles 104, tab 109
Burchfield, Charles tab 109, 104c
Burckhardt, Jacob 1938b
Burden (mus.) 174a

Burdock 1655a
Bureau (U.S. gov.) 858b
*for individual bureaus see un-
der the latter part of the
name, such as* Labor Stan-
dards, Bureau of
Bureaucracy 858c
Burebistas 2244b
Burgas, Bulgaria 2105a, 2350c
Bürger, Gottfried 1411b
Burgess 858c
Burghers of Calais (sculp.) 123a
Burgkmair, Hans tab 106
Burglary 858c
larceny 888c
Burgomaster 858c
Burgos, Sp. cathedral 76c
Burgoyne, John 215c, 1002c
American Revolution 2028b
Burgundians 2159a
Burgundy 998
painting 167a
seized by France 999b–999c
Burgundy (wine) 723c
Burial at Ornans, The (paint.) tab
112
Burin 139c, 140b
Burke, Edmund 215c, 1364a, tab
1470
Burlador de Sevilla, El (play)
1392a
Burleigh, 1st Baron see Cecil,
William
Burleigh, Henry 171a
Burleson, Albert S. tab 796
Burma 2106–2108, 2206c
agriculture 2107a
body mutilation 1930c
civilization 981a
climate 2106c
economy 2107a
elephant 33a
flag il 2182
geography 2106b–2106c
government 2107a–2108a
history 2107a–2108a
map 2106, *Atlas-29*
people of 2106c
religion 2106b
skimmer birds 58b
teak 1696b
World War II 1028c, 2107c
Burnham, Forbes 2171a–2171b
Burne-Jones, Edward 215c, tab 108
Burnett, Frances Eliza 215c
Burney, Fanny 1364a
Burnham, Daniel Hudson 215c,
1820c
Burnham, James 1348c
Burning bush see Euonymus
Burns, Robert 1364b, tab 1471, il
208
Auld Lang Syne 1396a
biography 216a
Catullus 1356b
Cotter's Saturday Night 1400a
nickname 1461a
Tam O' Shanter 1418b
Burnside, Ambrose Everett 2048b
Burr, Aaron 2033c
biography 216a
electoral votes 2032c
presidential candidate tab 800
Burrinjuck Dam 1206
Burritt, Elihu 1461b
Burro see Ass
Burroughs, John 216a, tab 1477
Bursa (physiol.) 941a
Bursitis 941a
Burslem ware tab 132
Burt, William 1188a
Burton, Harold H.
Supreme Court tab 802a
Burton, Richard Francis
Arabian Nights 1395a
biography 216b
Burton, Robert tab 1467
Anatomy of Melancholy 1346c
biography 216b
pseudonym 1461c
Burundi 2108
agriculture 2108b
climate 2108a
economy 2108b
flag il 2182
geography 2108a
government 2108b
history 2108b
map 2108, *Atlas-38*
people of 2108b
religion 2108a
World War I 2108b
Bush 484b

Bushel *tab* 1500
Bushman language 1337c
Bushmaster *see* Pit viper
Bushmen 1924c
  anthropology 1925b, 1927a
  art 83a
  cooking 1933a
Bushnell, David 1182c
Bushnell, Horace *tab* 1474
Bushnell Park (Conn.) 895c
Business 523–606
  computers 569–575
  corporations 822b
  economic control 876a
  educational programs 637a
  nineteenth century 523c
  twentieth century 525b
  see also Industry
Business administration
  careers 376c
Business cycles 586b
  boom 586a
  deflation 590b
  inflation 594c
Business law 858c
  states of U.S. 826
  U.S. 816b
Business organization 524c
Busoni, Ferruccio 167c, 172a
Bustamante, Alexander 2198b
Butane 1210c

Butaprene *see* Buna-S
Butler, Benjamin Franklin 2048a, *tab* 795
  presidential candidate *tab* 801
Butler, Joseph (Bishop Butler) *tab* 1469
Butler, Nicholas Murray 216b
  vice-presidential candidate *tab* 801
Butler, Pierce
  Supreme Court *tab* 802a
Butler, Samuel (1612–1680) *tab* 1468
  Hudibras 1362c
Butler, Samuel (1835–1902) 1367c
  biography 216b
  Erewhon 1402c
  Way of All Flesh, The 1420c
Butler, William O. *tab* 800
Butler University 666
Butte (mountains) 484b
Butte, Montana 2006a
Buttercup 1655c
Buttercup family 1655a
Butterfly 18b–18c
  monarch *il* 8
Butterfly-bush 1655a
Butterfly-flower 1655a–1655b
Butterfly weed *see* Milkweed

Butternut *see* Walnut
Butterwort 1655b
Buttery, The (painting, Pieter de Hooch) 109
Buttonwood *see* Plane-tree family
Butyl rubber 1222a
Buxtehude, Dietrich 162a, 163a, *tab* 171c, 216b
Buying
  marketing 560–564
Buying in (fin.) 586c
Buys Ballot's Law 484b
  see also Cyclone
Buzzard *see* Vulture
Bye, baby bunting (nursery rhyme) 408c
By-election 858c
Byelinski, Vissarion 1389b
Bykovsky, Valery *tab* 1770
Bylaw 859a
Byrd, Richard Evelyn (1888–1957)
  airplanes 1156a
  biography 216b
Byrd, William (1540–1623) 161a, *tab* 171c
Byrd, William (1674–1744) 1372a, *tab* 1469
Byrnes, James F. *tab* 796, 2077b
  Supreme Court *tab* 802a

Byrns, Joseph W.
  House of Representatives *tab* 802b
Byron, Lord (George Gordon) 1365a, *tab* 1473
  biography 216b
  Bounty mutiny 1398a
By-the-wind sailor 18c–19a
Byzantine architecture 75b, 76a
  Mohammedan architecture 78a
Byzantine art 71c
  colors 1103c
  glass *tab* 135
  painting 84c
  sculpture 114b, 118c
Byzantine Empire, 999c–1000a, 2105c
  beginning of 999c–1000a
  end of 1000a
  fall of 984b
  history 983a
  history outline *tab* 1035–1040, *tab* 1042, *tab* 1044
Byzantines 2195a
Byzantium
  ancient city *see* Constantinople-ancient
  capital of the Roman Empire 983a, 2165b

C

C horizon *see* Soil profile
C.g.s. system 1873b
  impulse 1880a
Caamaño Deñó, Francisco 2143b
Caatinga (vegetation) 484b
Caballero, Fernán 1392b
Caballo Dam 2020a
Cabbage *see* Mustard
Cabell, James Branch *tab* 1480
Cabinet (government) 859a
Cabinet (Eng.) 859a
Cabinet (Fr.) 859c
Cabinet (U.S.) 2031a, 790c, 859b
  forms of address *tab* 1119
  officers *tab* 795–797
  presidential succession 795
  salary 795
  secretaries of 907b
Cabinets (furniture) French 1095b
  German 1096b
  Spanish 1096c
Cable, George Washington 1374c, *tab* 1478
Cables 1235c
  armorless 1184c
  coaxial 1184c
  first undersea telephone 1184c
  telephone 1184c
  transatlantic 1184c
Cabot, John 2023a, 2113b, 2287c
  biography 216c
Cabot, Sebastian 216c, 2235b
Cabral, Donald Reid 2143b
Cabral, Pedro Alvares 2103c
Cabrera, Manuel Estrada 2169a
Cabrini, Francis Xavier (St.) 216c
Cacao 726b, 1655b, 2103c
  Cameroon 2110a
  Colombia 2132c
  Dominica 2311b
  Dominican Republic 2142c
  Ecuador 2144a
  Equatorial Guinea 2311c
  Fiji Islands 2312b
  Ghana 2164a
  Haiti 2171c
  Ivory Coast 2197a
  Nicaragua 2227c
  Nigeria 2229b
  Panama 2234b
  Papua 2319b
  Peru 2236c
  Sao Tomé and Principe 2322a
  Sierra Leone 2248c
  Surinam 2323b
  Togo 2275a
  Venezuela 2297b
  see also Cocoa
Caccini, Giulio *tab* 171b
Cáceres, Ramón 2143a

Cacheu River 2320a
Cachucha 174a
Cactus family 1655b
Cactus wren 1975b
Cacus (myth) 1428a
Cadastral survey 484b
Cadence (mus.) 174a
Cadence (verse) 1404b
Cadenza 174a
Cadets (Russ. pol. party) 860a
Caddisfly 19a
Cade, Jack 1000a
Cade's Rebellion 1000a
Cadillac, Antoine de la Mothe 216c
Cadiz, Spain 2264
  dance 182a
Cadman, Charles Wakefield 170b, *tab* 172c
Cadmium *tab* 1831
  atomic weight *tab* 1805
Cadmus 1428a
Caduceus 1428a
Caecilius Statius 1355b
Caedmon 1358c, *tab* 1465
Caesar, Gaius Julius 994a, 2098c, 2150a, 2225a, 2270b
  biography 216c
  British Isles invaded by 2283c
  Commentaries tab 1464
  dictator 873c
  Latin literature 1356a
Caesura 1398a
Cagayan River 2327c–2328a
Cagliari, Paolo *see* Veronese, Paul
Caiaphas 1452a
Caicos Islands 2324
Cain (Bib.) 1365a, 1452a
Cain Killing Abel (paint., Bellini) *tab* 112
Cairo, Illinois 2019c
Cairo, United Arab Republic 2280b, 2280c, 2350c
  climate 477a
  mosques 78a
Cairo Conference 2076b
Caisson disease *see* Decompression sickness
Cajuns 1983c
Cakes and Ale (nov.) 1371a
Calabash tree 1655b–1655c
Calais, France 2151a, 2151b
  Hundred Years' War 2286c
Calcareous 484b
Calcareous soil 752a
Calceolaria 1655c
Calciferol *see* Vitamin D₂
Calcimine 1199a
Calcite (mineral) 453a, 484b
  hardness *tab* 1192b
  light 1905c

Calcium 463b, 1831
  atomic weight *tab* 1805
  body requirements 919c
  bone 917c
  chemical bonding 1809c
  in plants 1646b
  soil 751c, 752a
Calcium carbonate
  soil 752a, 753a
Calcium chloride
  chemical bonding 1809c
Calcium cyclamate 745a
Calcium hydroxide 1214a, 1817b
Calcium oxide fertilizers 753a
Calculating machines 1236a
  operators 387a
  see also Computers
Calculus 1594–1595
  applications 1595c
  basic concepts 1594a
  definition 1602a
  history 1504b
Calculus of variations 1505a
Calcutta, India 980c, 2178a, 2350c
Calder, Alexander (1898–   ) 123c, *tab* 125, 217a
Calder, Alexander Stirling (1870–1945) 124b
Caldera 451c, 484b
Calderón de la Barca, Pedro 1392a, *tab* 1467
  biography 217a
Caldwell, Erskine 217b
Caldwell College for Women 682
Caleb Williams, The Adventures of (nov.) 1366a
Calendars
  ancient civilizations 972b
  months 1795b
  systems 758a–758b
  years 1797a
Calendula *see* Pot-marigold
Calf (animal) 727b
Calgary, Canada 2350c
Calhoun, John Caldwell 2034b, 2036b, *tab* 795
  biography 217b
  election and inauguration *tab* 800
Caliban 1398b, 1418b
Caliban upon Setebos (poem) 1398b
Caliche 484b
Calicut, India 2360a
California 1976–1977
  agriculture 1977a
  almonds 1648c
  architecture 1105c
  artichokes 1649c
  bighorn 16c
  budget system 858b
  capital punishment 860b
  census (1960) 1970
  Chinese residents 883b

  Christmas berry 1658a
  cinnamon 1658b
  climate 1976c
  colleges of 656–659
  commercial law 826
  Compromise of 1850 2041a
  congressional apportionment *tab* 853
  cotton 730c
  dogwoods 1665b
  Drake, Sir Francis 2023a
  economy 1977a
  electoral votes 876c
  forests 896a
  fruit 738a
  gecko 35b
  geography 1976b–1976c
  ginseng 1669b
  Gold Rush 2040b
  goose 36b
  government 1977a
  governor's salary 881b
  grapes 739a
  grouse 37a
  holidays 841–842
  ice plant 1673a
  initiative and referendum 884c
  labor legislation 832c, 833c, 834b
  ladybeetle 42a
  lamprey 42a
  laurel 1675a
  loganberry 1676c
  loon 43c
  loquats 1677a
  magpie 44c
  Mexican War 2040a
  oak 1682a–1682b
  octopus 48b
  ostrich farms 49a
  otter 49a
  pampas grass 1684a
  people of 1976c–1977a
  peppertrees 1686a
  pine trees 1686c
  pitcher plant 1687b
  plum trees 1687c
  poison ivy 1688a
  poplar trees 1688b
  poppy 1688c
  privets 1689a
  public school enrollment *tab* 646
  public school expenditures *tab* 644
  recall 904c
  sea lions 56c–57a
  sequoia trees 1692b–1692c
  snowplant 1693b
  spruce trees 1694b
  squeteague 59c
  student enrollment *tab* 645
  swallow 61a
  vegetables 747a
  vultures 65a–65b
  walnut trees 1699a
  whales 66c–67a
  woodpeckers 68a–68b
  yellowthroats 68c

California, University of 629a
  Berkeley Campus 656
  Davis Campus 656
  Los Angeles Campus 656
  Riverside Campus 656
  Santa Barbara Campus 656
California Institute of Technology 656
California Institute of the Arts 656
California Lutheran College 656
California redwood 1976b
California State College 694
California State College at San Bernardino 656
California State Polytechnic College 656
  Kellogg Campus 656
California valley quail 1976b
California white sea bass il 1717
Californium 1831
  atomic weight tab 1805
Caligula, Gaius Caesar 217b
Calks 1199a
Call (fin.) 586c
  see also Put (fin.)
Call of the Wild (nov.) 1398b
Calla lily 1655c
Callao, Peru 2236b
Calles, Plutarco Elías 2219c
Callesto (satellite) 1783b
Calligraphy Chinese 978a
Callimachus 1354a, tab 1464
Callinus 1351b
Calliope 1428a
Callisto 1428a
Callot, Jacques tab 107, 136b
Caloric theory (heat) 1760a, 1897c
Calories
  heat 1899a, 1916c
  fats and oils 732b
  nutrition 955
Calotype 1172a
Caltrop 1655c–1656a
Caltrop family 1656a
Calumet see Hopkinson, Francis
Calvary (Bib.) see Golgotha
Calvert, Cecilius 217c, 2024c
Calvert, Edward 140c
Calvert, George 217c, 1016a
Calvert, Leonard 2024c
Calvin, D. Leigh tab 801
Calvin, John 986b, 2270b, tab 1466
  biography 217c
  literary style 1378b
Calvin College 676
Calvinism 1632a
Calving (glaciers) 484b
Calvisius, Sethus tab 171b
Calydonian boar 1428a
  Meleager 1439b
Calypso (myth) 1428a
Calyx (flower) 1645c
Cam 1236c
Camacho, Manuel Avila 2219c
Camaguey, Cuba 2136c
Cambert, Robert tab 171c
Cambium 1643c
Cambodia 2108–2109
  agriculture 2108c
  economy 2108c
  climate 2108c
  flag il 2182
  geography 2108b–2108c
  government 2108c–2109a
  history 981b, 2109a–2109b
  map 2109, Atlas-30
  people of 2108c
  religion 2108b
  sculpture 1146, 124c
  World War II, 2109b
Cambrian Mountains 2282a
Cambrian Period tab 456, 484c
Cambridge, England 2350c
  University library tab 1463
Cambridge, Massachusetts
  library tab 1463
  printing 145a
Cambridge University
  Baskerville, John 144c
  library tab 1463
  representatives, House of Commons 867c
Cambyses, King (Persia) 995a
  biography 218a
Cambyses (play, Preston) 1360c
Camden, Battle of 2029
Camel 19a, 727a
  Ifni 2316a
  Libya 2210a
  Mauritania 2216a
  Mongolia 2220c
  Qatar 2242b

Saudi Arabia 2247a
  Somali Republic 2251a
  Spanish Sahara 2323a
  transportation 1934b
  Tunisia 2277a
  Yemen 2302a
Camellia 1656a, 1974a
  soil 751c
Camelot 1428b
Camembert cheese tab 731b
Camera obscura 1171c
Cameras 1161b, 1237a
  accessories 1238b
  history of 1171c
  motion picture 1161b
Cameron, David tab 108
Cameron, George Frederick 1390c
Cameron, James tab 796
Cameron, Simon tab 796
Cameroon 2109–2110, 2229c–2230a
  agriculture 2110a
  climate 2109c
  economy 2110a
  flag il 2182
  geography 2109c
  government 2110a
  history 2110a–2110b
  map 2110, Atlas-35
  people of 2109c
  religion 2109c
Cameroon Mountain 2328a
Camoëns, Luis Vaz de 218a, 1388b, tab 1466
Camomile 1656a
Campana, Dino 1388a
Campanella, Tommaso 1387a, tab 1467
Campbell, Alexander 218a
Campbell, George tab 795
Campbell, James tab 796
Campbell, John Archibald tab 802c
Campbell, Robert see MacGregor, Robert
Campbell, Thomas 1365b, tab 1472
Campbell, William Wilfred 1390c
Campbell Hill 1992a
Campbellsville College 670
Campeche Bay 2328a
Campfires 1710c
Camphor 1199a, 1821b
Campin, Robert tab 106, tab 111
Camping 1709–1712
  tents 1709c
Campos grasslands 484c
Campus Martius (Rome)
  Altar of Peace 118b
Camus, Albert 1383a, tab 1481, 1620a
  biography 218a
Cana, Galilee 1452a
Canaan 1452a, 1628c
Canaanites 1017a
Canada 2110–2119
  agriculture 2110c, 2112a–2112b, 2114b
  American Revolution 2115a
  arbor vitae 1649b
  badger 15a
  barberry 1651b
  birch 1652c
  bluebird 17b
  bluegrass 1653c
  bobolink 17c
  bobwhite 17c
  boston ivy 1653c
  bunting 18b
  candytuft 1656a
  cat 19c
  census 862b
  cheese tab 731b
  chickadee 21a
  chimney swift 21b
  chipmunk 21c
  climate 2111a–2111b
  Commonwealth status 1000c
  coot 23a
  daisy 1660c
  deer 25b
  dobsonfly 25b
  douglas fir 1665c
  economy 2112a–2112c
  elder trees 1666a
  Eskimos 2111b
  Expo '67 2118c
  fir trees 1667a–1667b
  flag 2111, 2118c, il 2182
  fox 34c
  geography 2110b, 2110c–2111b
  goldeneye 36a
  goldfinch 36a
  goose 36b
  government 862b, 878b, 2022a, 2112c–2119a
  grackle 36c
  grouse 37a

history tab 1061–1070, 2113a–2119a
  immigration 883b
  Indians 2111b, 2113c, 2114a, 2114c
  ivy 1673c
  jay 40b
  junco 40b
  kittiwake 41b
  Korean War 2118b
  lavender 1675a
  licorice 1675c
  literature 1390–1391
  locoweed 1676c
  lynx 44b, 1859c
  map 2111, Atlas 58–59
  maple trees 1678a–1678b
  melon 1679a
  merganser 45c
  NATO 1016c
  Niagara Falls 2019b
  nighthawk 47c
  oriole 48c
  oswego tea 1683b
  pelican 50a–50b
  people of 2111b–2112a
  pike 51b
  pine trees 1686c
  pintail duck 51c
  pit-viper 51c–52a
  plum trees 1687c
  pokeweeds 1688a
  poplar trees 1688b
  prairie dog 53a
  provinces of 2110c
  rabbit 53c
  raccoon 53c–54a
  religion 2110b, 2111c, 2114a, 2115a, 2117a
  robin 54c
  shrews 57c–58a
  shrike birds 58a
  skunks 58b
  snipe 59a
  sparrows 59a–59b
  spiraea 59a
  squirrels 59c–60a
  sticklebacks 60a
  stork 60b–60c
  Suez Canal crisis 2118b
  swallow 61a
  tanager bird 62a
  teal ducks 62c
  tent caterpillars 62c–63a
  turkey 64c
  U.S. relations with 2115b, 2116a, 2116b, 2116c, 2117c, 2118b, 2118c, 2119a
  vultures 65a–65b
  waterlily 1699a
  waxwings 66b–66c
  weasels 66c
  wheat 1699b–1699c
  wolves 67b
  woodcocks 67c–68a
  World War I 2117c
  World War II 2118b, 2163a
  wrens 68b
  yellowthroats 68c
Canadian National Railroad 2112c
Canadian Pacific Railroad 2022b, 2112c, 2116c
Canadian River 2016b
Canadian Shield 759c, 1961a
Canadien, Le (newspaper) 1391b
Canal Zone
  government 794b
Canaletto, Antonio tab 107
Canals 397b, 484c, 1153a, 1160b
  first in U.S. 1160c
  see also under names of individual canals, such as Panama Canal
Canary 19a
Canary Islands 2263b, 2328a
  canary 19a
  cineraria plants 1658b
  horehounds 1672c
  onions 1682c
  foxglove 1667c
Canaveral Peninsula 2016c
Canberra, Australia 875a, 2091a, 2351a
Cancer 941a
Cancer, Tropic of see Tropic of Cancer
Cancioneiros 1388b
Candidate 860a
Candidiasis tab 946
Candle see Candles
Candlenut 1980a
Candlepins (game) 1708a
Candles 1140b
  units 1907a
Candolle, Augustin de 1638c
Candytuft 1656a
Cane furniture 1098b

Cane sugar see Sugarcane
Canellopoulos, Panayotis 2167c
Canisius College 684
Cankerworm 19a–19b
Canna 1656a
Cannae 1000a
Cannae, Battle of 1000a
Cannel coal 1202a
Canning 736c, 1239a
  seafood 734b
Cannizzaro, Stanislao 1799c
Cannons 1254b
Cano, Alonso tab 125
Canoes 1934c, 1712a
  carrying 1712b
  paddling 1712b
  racing 1713a
  sailing 1713a
Canon (Bib.) 1450a
Canon (music) 174a
Canon and Patron Saints (paint.) tab 111
Canon of Medicine (treatise) 1754a
Canon law 860a
Canopy 1094a
Canova, Antonio 122c, tab 125
  biography 218a
Cantabile (music) 174a
Cantabrian Mountains 2328a
Cantaloupe see Melon
Cantata 160c, 174a
Cantemir, Antiokh 1389a
Canterbury, England 2351a
  cathedral 76c
Canterbury Bell, see Bellflower
Canterbury Tales 1398b, 1360a
Canticles (Bib.) see Song of Songs
Canticles (music) 174a
Cantigny, France
  World War I 2066b
Cantilever bridges 1191a, 1196b
Cantiones sacrae 160a
Canto 174a
Canton, China 2128b, 2128c–2129a, 2351a
Canton, Ohio 1992a
Canton Island 2000c
Cantons (gov.) 860a, 873b
Cantor, Georg 1507a
Cantor (music) 174a
  Hebrew music 156b
Cantos (poems, Pound) 1376b
Cantus (mus.) see Chant
Cantus firmus 160a, 174a
Canty, Tom 1414a
Canute, King (England) 1428b, 2142a, 2284b
Canute II 218a
Canvasback see Duck
Canyon 484c
  submarine 517a
Canyonlands National Park 1996
Canzone 162a, 174a
Caõ, Diogo 2306c
Cap rock 484c
Capacitance (elec.) 1886b, 1916c
Capacitors 1916c
Cape (geography) 484c
  for individual capes see under full name such as Cape of Good Hope
Cape Agulhas 2252a, 2328a
Cape Blanc 2328a
Cape Bon 2328a
Cape Canaveral 2016c
Cape Breton Island 2023a, 2110c
Cape Cod 2016b–2016c
Cape Cod Canal 2016c
Cape Colony 2208c
Cape Comorin 2328a
Cape Gardafui 2328a
Cape of Good Hope 2252a, 2328a
Cape Hatteras 2016c
Cape Horn 2328a
Cape Kennedy, Florida 1979b, 2016c
Cape Range 2252a
Cape Town, South Africa 2251, 2252b, 2351a
Cape Verde Islands 2241c, 2242a, 2309, 2328a
Cape York Peninsula 2328a
Cape-Jasmine see Gardenia
Capek, Karel M. tab 1480
Capella (star) tab 1786

Capellmeister *see* Kapellmeister
Capen House (Mass.)
  architecture 78b
Capentaria, Gulf of 2091b, 2328b
Caper 1656b
Caper family 1656b
Capernaum 1452a
Capet, Hugh *see* Hugh Capet
Capetians 984a, 1000b, 2150b–2150c
Capillaries 924b
  purpura 945b
Capillary action 1802c, 1871a
Capillary fringe 484c
Capital (fin.) 586c
  asset 586c
  capitalization 587a
  gain 586c
  loss 586c
Capital letters 150c
Capital punishment 860a
Capital University 690
Capitalism 587a, 988a
  nationalization 892c
Capitol (Wash., D.C.)
  architecture 78c
Capo di Monte, Italy
  pottery *tab* 131
Capoids 1925c, 1927a
Caporetto, Battle of 1025c
Capraia Island 2193c
Capri Island 2193c
Capriccio 174a
Capricorn, Tropic of *see* Tropic of
  Capricorn
Caps (print.) 150c
Captain Brassbound's Conversion
  (play) 1370a
Captains Courageous (novel) 1398c
Captions 150c
Capuana, Luigi 1387c
Car *see* Automobiles
Caracalla
  biography 218a
  law 815a
  sculpture of 118a
Caracas, Venezuela 2296c, 2351a
Caracci (Carracci) (It. family)
  218c
Caracci, Agostino 218c, *tab* 107
Caracci, Annibale 218c, *tab* 107
Caracci, Lodovico 218c
Caravaggio, Michelangelo da *tab*
  107, 218b
  Cheat, The tab 110
  Entombment, The tab 112
Caravans 1934c
Caraway 1656b
Carbanion 1823a
Carbohydrates 919b, 1824a, 1825a
Carboloy
  alloys *tab* 1193
Carbon 1808a, 1818a, 1821a, 1831
  atomic weight *tab* 1805, 1806a
  electrons 1807a
  in plants 1646b
  ions 1809b
  properties 1871a
Carbon dioxide 1811a
  chemical bonding 1810a
  lungs 925b
  phases 1872c
  photosynthesis 1861b
  plants 749c
  radiocarbon dating 454c
  respiration 922a
  space biology 953a
Carbon-14 454c, 484c
Carbon monoxide
  chemical bonding 1810a
  public health 958b
Carbon tetrachloride
  chemical bonding 1810a
Carbonari (society) 2195c
Carbonate of lime *see* Calcium
  carbonate
Carbonation 484c
Carbonek Castle 1428b
Carbonic acid 1817b
Carboniferous period *see* Mississippian period; Pennsylva-
  nian period
Carbonium ion 1823a
Carborundum 1192b
Carboxylic acid 1821b
  anhydrides 1821c
  halides 1821c
Carburetors 1136b, 1240a
Carchemish 970b
Carchemish, Battle of 1003c
  Nebuchadnezzar 1458b
Card Player (paint., Chardin) *tab*
  110

Cardamom 1656b
Cardamon Mountains 2273b
Cardano, Geronimo (Jerome Car-
  dan) 1503a
  biography 218b
Cardarelli, Vincenzo 1388a
Cárdenas, Lázaro 2219
Cardiff, Wales 2351a
Cardinal 19b, 1981a, 1981c, 1983a,
  1990c, 1991c, 1997a, 1998b
Cardinal flower *see* Lobelia
Cardinal numbers 1508c
Cardinal points 484c
Cardinal Stritch College 707
Cardinals (rel.)
  forms of address *tab* 1119
Cardozo, Benjamin Nathan 218b,
  tab 802a
Carducci, Giosuè 218b, 1387c, *tab*
  1477
Career guidance 317–390
  clerical occupations 386c
  education 609a
  etiquette 1115b
  job requirements 373b
  politics 392
Carey, Henry *tab* 171c, *tab* 1469
Carey Act 904b
Cargados Carajos Islands 2216c
Cargo ships 1180b
Carías Andino, Tiburcio 2173b
Carib Indians 2137b, 2314c 2317b
Caribbean Sea 2328b
Cariboo Mountains 2020b
Caribou *see* Reindeer
  conch 22c
Carillons 174a
Carissimi, Giacomo 160c, 161c, *tab*
  171b
Carl, William Crane 168b
Carla (hurricane) 478a
Carleton, Guy 815c, 2115a
Carleton, Mark A. 747b
Carleton College 677
Carlisle, John Griffin *tab* 796, *tab*
  802b
Carloadings 587a
Carlos (Spanish kings)
  see Charles
Carlos de Bourbon, Don *see*
  Charles III (Sp. k.)
Carlos I, King (Portugal) 2242a
Carlsen, Emil *tab* 108
Carlyle, Thomas 965b, 1358a, 1366a,
  tab 1473
  biography 218b
  Herr Teufelsdröckh tab 1463b
Carman, (William) Bliss 1390c,
  1395a, *tab* 1479
Carmel, Mount 1452a
Carmen (opera, Bizet) 155a, 168a,
  1398c
Carmen (nov., Mérimée) 1381b,
  1398c
Carmen Sylva *see* Elizabeth,
  Queen (Romania)
Carnap, Rudolph 1619a
Carnation
  scarlet 1991c
  see also Pink
Carnauba wax 1227a
Carneades 1615b
Carnegie, Andrew 524b
  biography 218b
Carnegie Institute of Technology
  695
Carnivores 1860c
Carnot, Nicolas Léonard Sadi 218c,
  1916c
Carnot cycle 1916c
Carob *see* Locust
Carol I, King (Romania) 2244c,
  2245a
Caroll II, King (Romania) 2245a
  abdication 849a
Carol (music) *see* Carols
Carolina jessamine 1994a
Carolina wren 1994a
Carolinas, The
  see North Carolina
  see South Carolina
Caroline Islands 2003c, 2328b
  government 794b
Carolingian dynasty 1000a–1000b,
  1016a
Carolingians, 984a, 1000a–1000b,
  2150a–2150b
  feudalism 983c
  founder 983b
Carols (music) 174a

Carothers, Wallace 1208c
Carp 19b, *il* 1717
Carpaccio, Vittore *tab* 106, *tab* 112
Carpathian Mountains 2138c, 2238c,
  2254c, 2328b
Carpeaux, Jean Baptiste 122c, *tab*
  125
Carpels (flower) 1645c
Carpenter, John Alden 170b, 172c
Carpenter, M. Scott *tab* 1770
Carpenters
  career 376b
Carpetbag government 1019b
Carpets 1110c
  tufting 1283c
Carpio, Lope Félix de Vega *see*
  Vega, Lope de
Carquinez Bridge 1197
Carra, Carlo *tab* 109
Carracci *see* Caracci
Carranza, Venustiano 2064b, 2219b–
  2219c
Carrel, Alexis 218c
Carrera, Rafael 2169a, 2173b
Carrière, Eugène *tab* 108
Carriers (med.) 955b
Carrillo, Braulio 2136a
Carroll, Charles 219a
  Declaration of Independence
  tab 803
Carroll, Daniel 809c
Carroll, George W. *tab* 801
Carroll, Lewis 1367c, *tab* 1477
  biography 237c
Carroll College 680, 707
Carrot 1656b
Carrot family 1656c
Car sickness 942c
Cars *see* Automobiles
Carson, Christopher (Kit Carson)
  219c
Carson City, Nevada 1988b, 2006a
Carson-Newman College 700
Cartage 587a
Cartagena, Colombia 2132c, 2133a
Cartagena, Spain 2264a
Cartago, Costa Rica 2136a
Cartels 539a, 587a
Carter, Henry *see* Leslie, Frank
Carteret, George 2025a
Cartesian coordinates 1553c, 1602a
Carthage 1000c, 1016b, *tab* 1032–
  1034
  founded 997c
  rivalry with Rome 1000b
  Second Punic War 1000a
Carthage College 707
Cartier, Jacques 219a, 2023b, 2113c
Cartilage 917b
Cartography 484c–485a
Carton, Sidney 1398c, 1418a
Cartoonists 375a
Cartridge brass 1196a
Cartridges 1254c
Cartwright, Edmund 219a, 1286c
Caruso, Enrico 219a
Carver, George Washington 219a
Carver, John 219b, 1019a, 2024b
Cary, Joyce 1371c, *tab* 1481
Cary, Samuel F. *tab* 801
Caryopsis fruit 1646a
Casa Guidi Windows (poem) 1368c
Casabianca (poem) 1398c
Casablanca, Morocco 2221c, 2351a
Casals, Pablo 219b
Casamance River 2247c
Casanova, Giovanni Jacopo 219b
Casas, Bartolomé de las *see* Las
  Casas, Bartolomé de
Casaubon, Isaac *tab* 1467
Cascade (waters) 485a
Cascade College 693
Cascade Mountains 1976c, 1992c,
  1998a, 2292c
Cascade Range 2016c, 2019b
Cascade Tunnel 1179b
Cascades 2019a
  see also Waterfalls
Cascara Sagrada *see* Buckthorn
Case (gram.) 1297a, 1304b
Case (print.) 149c
Case Institute of Technology 690
Casein 727a, 731c, 1211c
  plastics 1219
Casella, Alfredo 168a, *tab* 172a
Casgrain, Raymond 1391a
Cash 587a
Cash on delivery (C.O.D.) 587b

Cashew 1656c
Cashmere rugs 1110c
Casimir the Great 2240a
Caslon, William 144c
Casona, Alejandro 1392c
Caspian Sea 2328b
  sturgeon 60c
Cass, Lewis 2040c, *tab* 795, *tab*
  796
  presidential candidate *tab* 800
Cassander 219b
Cassation 860b
Cassandra 1428b
Cassatt, Mary *tab* 108, 219b
Cassava 1656c
  Central African Republic 2119b
  French Guiana 2312c
  Liberia 2209a
  Sierra Leone 2248c
  Thailand 2273c
  Uganda 2279c
  Venezuela 2297b
  Zambia 2305b
Cassegrain, Guillaume N. 1791a
Cassiopeia 1428b
Cassiterite 453c, 1224c
Cassius Longinus, Gaius 219b
Cast (ind.) *see* Casting
Cast iron *tab* 1193
  bridges 1196c
Castagno, Andrea del *tab* 106
Castaneda, Jorge Ubico 2169a
Castanets 174a
Caste (social)
  see Caste system
Caste system 1936a, 1944c
  India 612b, 980b, 1624b
Castelfranco, Giorgione da *see*
  Giorgione, Il
Castello Branco, Humberto 2104c
Castelnuovo-Tedesco, Mario 168a,
  tab 172a
Castelvecchio Bridge 1196c
Castiglione, Baldassare 1386b
Castilla, Ramón 2237a
Casting (ind.)
  metal 1267b
Castle of Indolence, The (poem)
  1363b
Castle of Otranto, The (nov.)
  1364a
Castle Rackrent (nov.) 1398c
Castlereagh, Lord 1023c
Castleton State College 704
Castor and Pollux 1428b
Castor ware 126c
Castor-oil plant 1656c–1657a
Castries, St. Lucia 2321b, 2351a
Castro, Eugenio de 1388c
Castro, Fidel 2079b
  biography 219b
Castro, Rosalia de 1392b
Castro, Salvador Castañeda 2145b–
  2145c
Castro Ruz, Raúl 2137c
Castro y Bellvis, Guillén de 1392a
Casts (ind.) *see* Casting
Cat 19b–19c
Cat of Losanne 1428b
Cataclastic (rocks) 485a
Catalan (dialect) 1335b
Catalonian Fresco (paint.) *tab* 110
Catalpa 1657a
Catalysts 1812a
Cataracts (eye) 928c
Cataracts (geog.) 485a, 941a
  see also Waterfalls
Catastrophism 485a
Catawba College 688
Catazone (rocks) 485a
Catbird 20a–20b
Catboats 1728b
Catch (music) 174a
Catchment basin 485a
Cateau-Cambrésis, Treaty of 2195b
Caterpillars 20b, 1862b
Catfish 20b
Cathedral school 613c
Cathedrals
  glass 134a
  Gothic 76c
  see also under names of indi-
  vidual cathedrals
Cather, Willa Sibert 1346c, *tab*
  1480
  biography 219c
Catherine (Eng. q.) *see* Catherine
  of Aragon
  see Catherine of Valois

Catherine of Aragon (Eng. q.) 219c, 2287c, 2288a
Catherine the Great *see* Catherine II (Russ. emp.)
Catherine de Médicis 219c, 997c, 2151b
furniture 1095b
Catherine (St.) 219c
Catherine II (Catherine the Great) 219c, 2152b, 2259b
Catherine Archipelago *see* Aleutian Islands
Catherine Spalding College 670
Cathode *see* Cathodes
Cathode luminescence 1906b
Cathode-ray tubes 1240b
Cathode rays 1886c
Cathodes 1131c, 1284a, 1886c
Catholic Church *see* Roman Catholic Church
Catholic Legion of Decency 1168c
Catholic Popular Republican Movement (MRP) 2155a
Catholic University of America 660
Catholicus *see* Newman, John Henry
Catiline, Lucius (Rom. pol.) 219c
conspiracy of 1001a
Cations 1808c, 1809a, 1827b
Catkins 1643a
Catlin, George 104b
Catnip 1657a
Cato (pseud.) *see* Hamilton, Alexander
Cato, Marcus Porcius (Cato the Censor) (the Elder) 1355b, *tab* 1464
biography 219c
Cato, Marcus Porcius (the Younger) 220a
Cato (drama) 1363b
Catron, John *tab* 802a
Cats-paw (winds) 485a
Catskill Mountains 1990c, 2016a
Catskill pipeline 1195b
Catt, Carrie Chapman 914b
biography 220a
Cattail 1657a–1657b
Cattle 20b–20c, 727b
Arizona 1975c
Argentina 2089c
Australia 2092a, 2093b
Botswana 2101b
breeds 727b
British Virgin Islands 2309a
California 1977a
Chad 2120c
Channel Islands 2310a
Colombia 2132c
Colorado 1977b
dairy industry 727b
Delaware 1978c
Denmark 2141b
diseases 727c
Georgia 1980a
Hawaii 1980b
Idaho 1980c
Ifni 2316a
India 2178b
Iowa 1982b
Italy 2194c
Ivory Coast 2197a
manure analysis *tab* 752c
Mauritania 2216a
Mississippi 1987a
Mongolia 2220c
Montana 1988a
Nebraska 1988b
Nevada 1988c
New Caledonia 2318b
New Mexico 1990a
New Zealand 2226b
Nicaragua 2227a
Niger 2228c
Ohio 1992a
Oklahoma 1992b
Oregon 1993a
Paraguay 2235b
Rhodesia 2243a
Rwanda 2245c
South Africa 2252b–2252c
South Dakota 1994c
South West Africa 2322c
Spain 2264a
Swaziland 2267a
Switzerland 2270a
Tanzania 2272b
Tennessee 1995b
Texas 1995c
Tunisia 2277a
Turkey 2278a
Uganda 2279c
undulant fever 958a
U.S.S.R. 2257a
U.S. 1968b, 1969a, 2294a
Upper Volta 2294b
Uruguay 2295a

Vermont 1997a
Virgin Islands 2004b
West Virginia 1998c
wholesale cuts of beef 735c
Wyoming 1999c
Catullus, Gaius Valerius 1356b, *tab* 1464
biography 220a
Cauca River 2132a–2132b
Caucasian languages 1337c
Caucasoids 1925c
Ainu 1925c
migrations 1925b
Caucasus Mountains 2254c, 2328c
Caucus 860b
Cauliflower *see* Mustard
Caustic soda *see* Sodium hydroxide
Cauvery River 2177c
Cavalcanti, Guido 1385c, 1386a
Cavalieri, Emilio del 161c, *tab* 171b
Cavalieri's principle 1578b
Cavalla River 2197a
Cavalleria Rusticana (opera) 167c, 1387c
Cavalli, Pietro Francesco *tab* 106, *tab* 171b, 1387a, *tab* 1467
Cavatina 174a
Caves 485a, 1389a
archeology 971a
Cave painting 82b, 1928b
Caveat emptor 587b
Caveat venditor 587b
Cavell, Edith 220a
Cavendish, Henry 220a, 1215c, 1798c
Cavern 485a
Cavitation 485a, 1897a, 1917a
Cavities (teeth) 959b
Cavour, (Count) **Camillo Benso di** 220a, 987c, 2195c
Cavy *see* Guinea pig
Cawnpore, India 2351b
Caxton, William 144a, 1360a
biography 220b
Morte d' Arthur 1411a
Cay (island) 485a
Cayenne, French Guiana 2312b, 2351b
Cayley, George 1155b, 1158a
Cayman *see* Crocodile
Cayman Islands 2309–2310
C.C.C. *see* Civilian Conservation Corps
C.C.N.Y. *see* College of the City of New York
Ceausescu, Nicholai 2245a
Cebu, Philippines 2237c, 2238a
Cecil, Edgar Algernon Robert 220b
Cecil, Robert 1012b
Cecil, William (1st Baron Burleigh) 220b
Cecilia (St.) 220b
Cecrops 1428b
Cedar 1657b
Cedar Creek, Battle of 2049
Cedar Crest College 695
Cedar Rapids, Iowa 1982b
Cedars of Lebanon 1018b, 2207c
Cedilla (punct.) 1314c
Ceiba (fiber) *see* Kapok
Celaeno 1444c
Celebrezze, Anthony J. *tab* 797
Celandine 1657b
Celebes 2187a
Celery 1657b
Celesta (mus.) 174a
Celeste (mus.) 174a
Celestial equator 1793c
Celestial mechanics 1781b
Celestial poles 1793c, 1796c
Celestial sphere 485a, 1793c
latitude 1795a
longitude 1795a
nodes 1795c
Celestina, La (nov.) 1391b
Celestine III (pope) 220b
Celestine V (pope, St.) 220b
Celiac disease 941a
Cell *see* Cells
Cellini, Benvenuto 122a, *tab* 125, 1386c
autobiography 1396a, *tab* 1466
biography 220b
Cello *see* Violoncello
Cellophane 1199b
Cells (bio.) 917a, 1842a
cambium layer 1644c
energy production 921c
phloem layer 1644c

plant 1643b–1643c
turgid 1646b
xylem layer 1644c
Cells (elec.) chemical 1883a
Celluloid 1218c
Cellulose 1199c, 1824b
cellophane 1199b
synthetic textiles 1208c
Cellulose acetate *tab* 1219a
Cellulose nitrate *tab* 1219
Celsius, Anders 220b, 1920a
Celsius scale *see* Centigrade scale
Celso Barbosa, José 2003a
Celtic languages *tab* 1334, 1335c
influence on English 1321b
Celts 1019c, 1358b, 2191a
Cembalo 174a
Cement 450a, 1199c, 1889b
manufacture 1200a
world production 1200b
Cementation (minerals) 485a
Cenci, The (drama) 1365b
Cenozoic era 458a
Censors (Rom. gov.) 860c
Censorship 860c–862a
church 861a
Census 862a
United States (1960) 1970–1973
Census, Bureau of the 862b
Centare (unit) *tab* 1500
Centaur (rocket) 1766c
Centaurs 116b, 1428b
Centenary College of Louisiana 671
Center of gravity 1879a, 1917a
Center Hill Dam 1206
Centigrade scale 1898b, 1920a
Centigram *tab* 1500, 1873b
Centiliter *tab* 1500
Centimeter *tab* 1500, 1873b
Centipede 20c
Central Africa Federation 878c
Central African Republic 2119
agriculture 2119b
economy 2119b
flag *il* 2182
geography 2119a–2119b
government 2119b
history 2119b
map 2119, *Atlas*-35
people of 2119b
religion 2119a
Central America
agouti 13a
anteater 13c
archeology 971a
armadillo 14b
catbird 20a
crocodile 24c
duck 26a
eagle 26b
gallinule 35a
gull 37b
ibis 40b
immigration 883b
pottery 180b
Central American Andes 2172c, 2227b
Central American Common Market 2135c, 2136b, 2168b, 2169c, 2173b
Central American Cordillera 2168a
Central College 667
Central Connecticut State College 660
Central Cordillera 2237c
Central Intelligence Agency 862b
Central Lowlands and Plains (U.S.) 1962a–1962b
Central Methodist College 679
Central Michigan University 676
Central Missouri State College 679
Central nervous system 938a
Central Park (N.Y.) 895c
Olmsted, Frederick Law 775b
Central Plains (U.S.) 1992b
Central Siberian Plateau 2254c
Central State College 690, 693
Central Treaty Organization (CENTO) members 1000b
Central Washington State College 705
Centralization (gov.) 862b
Centre College of Kentucky 670
Centrifugal force 485a, 1804a, 1876a
Centrifugal pumps 1275b
Centripetal force 1804a, 1876a
Centromere 1851c
Centrosphere *see* Earth structure
Century plant 1657b–1657c
Cepheid variable 1786b
Ceram 2187

Ceramics 126–132, 1200b
development of 126b
glassware 133a
industrial 132c
materials 126a
see also Pottery
Ceramic engineers 379c
Cerebellum 938a
Cerberus 1428b
Hades 1433c
Cerebral cortex 928a, 938a
Cerebral palsy 941a
Cerebrum 938a
Ceres (asteroid) 1783c
Ceres (myth) 1428b, 1430a
Cerium 1831
atomic weight *tab* 1805
Cerro de Punta Mountains 2202a
Certificate 587b
Certified checks 587b
Certified public accountants 377a
Certiorari 862c
Cervantes Saavedra, Miguel de *il* 208, 1391c, *tab* 1467
biography 220c
Don Quixote 1401c
Cervera y Topete, Pascual 2060a
Cervix 926c
Cesalpino, Andrea 1638a
Cesium 1831, 1886c
atomic weight *tab* 1805
Ceské Budejovice, Czechoslovakia 2351b
Céspedes, Carlos Manuel de 2137b
Cess River 2208c
Cesti, Marcantonio *tab* 171b
Ceuta, Morocco 2351b
Cevennes Mountains 2328b
Ceylon 2214b–2214c, 2119–2120
agriculture 2119c
Buddhism 980c
cardamom 1656b
cinnamon 1658b
climate 2119c
Commonwealth status 1000c
ebony 1665c
economy 2119c–2120a
flag *il* 2182
geography 2119c
government 2120a
history 2120a–2120c
kapok 1674b
magpie 44c
map, *Atlas*-29
nux vomica 1682a
peafowl 50a
people of 2119c
pit-viper 51c–52a
religion 2119c
tea 745c
Cezanne, Paul 86c, *tab* 108
Basket of Apples *tab* 110
biography 220c
Blue Vase tab 112
Chabrier, Alexis Emmanuel 168b, *tab* 171c
biography 220c
Chaco War 2236a
Chaconne (mus.) 174a
Chad 2119b, 2120–2121
agriculture 2120c
climate 2120c
economy 2120c
flag *il* 2182
geography 2120c
government 2120c–2121a
history 2121a
map 2121, *Atlas*-34–35
people of 2120c
religion 2120c, 2121a
World War II 2121a
Chad, Lake 2120c, 2228b, 2328b
anthropology 1924b
Chad Progressive Party 2121a
Chadron State College 681
Chadwick, George Whitefield 170a, 1095c
Chafin, Eugene *tab* 801
Chagall, Marc 103c, *tab* 109
biography 221a
Chagos Archipelago 2308b, 2308c
Chain 485a
Chain reactions 1829a
Chain stores 587c
Chaine des Cardamomes 2108c
Chaine des Matheux Montains 2171b
Chairs 1094c
Chippendale 1098a
Cromwell 1097b
Egyptian 1093b
Flemish 1095a
Gothic 1094a
upholstered 1096c

Chaka (Zulu chief) 2253a
Chakri dynasty 2274a–2274b
Chalcedon, Council of 1631b
Chalcedony (minerals) 485b
Chalcopyrite 453c
Chaldea 973a, 1452b
  art 74a
Chaley, Joseph 1197a
Chaliapin, Feodor Ivanovitch 221a
Chalk (minerals) 485b
Challenger, H.M.S. (ship) 462a
Chalons, Battle of 1002c
Chalukyas, the 2180a
Chalybia 1212b
Chamber (gov.) 862c
Chamber music 160a, 174a
Chamber of Deputies 862c
Chamber of Commerce 587c
  U.S. 1743a
Chamberlain, Joseph 221a, 860b
Chamberlain, (Arthur) Neville
  863a, 1013c, 2292a
  biography 221a
Chamberlin, Thomas Chrowder
  454a
Chambers, B. J. tab 801
Chambeshi River 2305a
Chameleon 20c–21a
Chaminade, Cécile 168b
Chaminade College of Honolulu
  663
Chamisso, Adelbert von tab 1472
Chamois 21a
Champagne (wine) 723b
Champaign, Illinois 1981b
Champerico, Guatemala 2351b
Champion, Richard 128a
Champion Hill, Battle of 2050a
Champlain, Samuel de 221b, 2113c
Champlain, Lake 1996c, 2016c,
  2018a, 2018b
Champlain Valley 1996b
Champollion, Jean François 221b,
  969a
Chamson, André 1382c
Chancellor (gov.) 862c
Chancellor of the Exchequer 862c
Chancellorsville, Battle of 2048c
Chancery, Court of 863a
Chancroid tab 946
Chandigarh, India 2351b
Chandler, William tab 796
Chandler, Zachariah tab 797
Chandragupta 2179c
Ch'ang-an, China 978a
Changchun, China 2351c
Changeling 1428c
Changkiakow, China 2358b
Changkiang, China 2351c
Changsha, China 2351c
Channel (waters) 485b
Channel bass il 1717
Channel cat (fish) il 1717
Channel Islands 2282a, 2283c,
  2310, 2382a
  cattle 20c
  Home Office 882a
Channing, William Ellery 221b, tab
  1472
Ch'anpai Mountains 2328b
Chanson (mus.) 159b, 174a
Chanson de Roland, La 1377c, 1398c
  Roland 1446a
Chansons de geste 1377b, 1398c,
  1428c
  Italian literature 1385c
Chant 158a, 174a
  Anglican 162a
  see also Gregorian chant
Chanticleer 1428c
Chantilly, France 127a
Chao Phraya River 2328c
Chaos 1428c
Chapais, Thomas 1391b
Chaparral (bird) 1989c
Chaparral (shrub) 485b, 1863b,
  1864a
Chapeau de Paille (paint.) tab 111
Chapin, Roy Dikeman tab 797
Chaplin, Charles Spencer
  biography 221b
Chapman, George tab 1467
Chapman, John see Appleseed,
  Johnny
Chapman, Oscar L. tab 797
Chapman College 656
Chapu, Henri tab 125
Chapultepec, Act of 1000b
Character disorders 1954a

Characters (mus.) 174a
Charcoal 1136c, 1200c
Charcot, Jean Martin 1954c
Chard see Beet
Chardin, Jean Baptiste 85a, tab
  107
  biography 221c
  Card Player tab 110
Chardonnet, Hilaire de 1208c
Charge of the Light Brigade, The
  (poem) 997c, 1399a
Chari River 2328c
Charioteer (sculp.) 116a
Charis 1428c
Charites (myth) 1433c
Charlemagne 983b, 1000b, 1010b,
  1430c, 2088c, 2095a, 2098c,
  2150a, 2159a, 2195a, 2225a,
  2270b
  biography 221c
  chansons de geste 1398c
  Roland 1446a
Charleroi, Belgium 2098a
Charles (Eng. pr.) 243c
Charles (Ger. kings) see Charles
  (Holy Rom. emperors)
Charles I (Austrian emp.) abdi-
  cation 849a
Charles I, King (England) 1016c
  beheaded 1009a, 1020b, 2289a
  biography 221c
  portrait by Van Dyck tab 112
  reign of 2288c–2289a
Charles II, King (England) 997b,
  1020b, 1362c, 2191b
  biography 222a
  cabinet 859a
  Connecticut 785a
  nicknames 1462c
  Penn, William 2025c
  reign of 2289b
  Rye House Plot 1019b
Charles II (Fr. k.) see Charles
  the Fat
Charles V (Fr. k.)
  biography 222a
Charles VI (Fr. k.) 2151a
Charles VII (Fr. k.) 222a, 985c,
  2151a
Charles VIII (Fr. k.) 2151a–2151b,
  2195b
Charles IX (Fr. k.) 997c, 2151b
  Carolina 2025b
Charles X (Fr. k.) 222a, 2153a–
  2153b
Charles I, Emperor (Holy Rom.
  emp.) see Charlemagne
Charles IV, Emperor (Holy Rom.
  emp.) 2139b, 2211b
Charles V, Emperor (Holy Rom.
  emp.) 2098c, 2151b, 2160a,
  2225b, 2264c, 2297a, 2297c
  biography 222a
Charles VI, Emperor (Holy Rom.
  emp.) 1019a, 1021b
Charles III (Hung. k.) see Charles
  VI (Holy Rom. emp.)
Charles IV (Hung. k.) see Charles
  I (Austrian emp.)
Charles XIV (Nor. k.) see Charles
  XIV John (Swed. and Nor.
  k.)
Charles XV (Nor. k.) see Charles
  XV (Swed. and Nor. k.)
Charles I, King (Spain) 2297a
  see also Charles V (Holy Rom.
  emp.)
Charles II, King (Spain) 1021a,
  2265a
Charles X Gustavus (Swed. k.)
  222b
Charles XII, King (Sweden) 222b,
  2268c
  nickname 1462c
Charles XIII, King (Sweden) 2268c
Charles XIV, King (Sweden and
  Norway) 222b
Charles XIV, King (Sweden) 2269a
Charles XV, King (Sweden) 2269a
Charles of Anjou, King (Hungary)
  2174a
Charles the Bald, King 2150c
Charles Edward (Eng. pr.) see
  Stuart, Charles Edward
Charles the Fat, King 2150b
Charles Francis Joseph see Charles
  I (Austrian emp.)
Charles the Great see Charle-
  magne
Charles of Luxemburg see Charles
  IV (Holy Rom. emp.)
Charles Martel, King 222b, 2150a
Charles d'Orléans (Charles of
  Orleans) 1378a, tab 1466

Charles the Well-Beloved see
  Charles VI (Fr. k.)
Charles the Wise see Charles V
  (Fr. k.)
Charles, Jacques Alexandre César
  1154c, 1871b
Charles, Lake (Louisiana) 1983c
Charles's law 1802a, 1871b, 1872b
Charles Mound, Illinois 1981a
Charles River 2005c
Charleston, South Carolina 1994b
  American Revolution 2028c, 2029
  founding 2025c
Charleston, West Virginia 1998b,
  2006a
Charlotte (Grand Duchess of
  Lux.) 875c, 2211c
Charlotte, Queen (Tonga) 2324c
Charlotte, North Carolina 1991a
Charlotte Amalie, Virgin Islands
  2204b, 2351c
Charon 1428c
Charonton, Engverrand tab 106
Charpentier, Gustave 222b
Charter 863a
Charter of Barbados 2097b
Charter of Labor 863b
Charters, W. W. 638c
Chartist movement 1000b–1000c
Chartres Cathedral
  architecture 76c
  sculpture 120a
Charybdis (myth) 1428c
Chase (print.) 150c
Chase, Salmon Portland tab 796,
  2050b
  biography 222c
  Johnson, Andrew 2052b
  Supreme Court tab 802c
Chase, Samuel tab 802a
  biography 222c
  Declaration of Independence
  tab 803
Chase, William tab 108
Chasm 485c
Chassériau, Théodore tab 108
Château Steen (paint.) tab 111
Chateaubriand, François René de
  222c, 1380c, tab 1471
Chatham College 695
Chatham Island 2225c
Chattahoochee River 1974a
Chattanooga, Tennessee 1995a,
  2006a
Chattanooga, Battle of 2049
Chattanooga, University of 700
Chattels 863b
  mortgage 892a
  replevin 906a
Chatterton, Thomas 222c, 1364a
Chatterton (play) 1381a
Chaucer, Geoffrey 1345b, 1358a,
  1359c, tab 1466
  biography 222c
  Canterbury Tales 1398b
  Troilus and Cressida 1419b
Chausson, Ernest 168b, 171c
Chautemps, Camille 857b
Chavannes, Puvis de see Puvis de
  Chavannes, Pierre
Chávez, Carlos tab 172c
Cheaka Mountain 1974a
Cheap money 587c
Cheat, The (paint.) tab 110
Checkers 1713a
Checkoff 587c
Checks (fin.) 587c, 821b
Checks and Balances (gov.) 863c
Cheddar cheese tab 731b
Cheese tab 731b
  bacteria 1845b
  Vermont 1997a
  Wisconsin 1999a
Cheetah 21a
Cheju Island 2328c
Cheka 863c
Chekhov, Anton Pavlovich il 207,
  1390a, tab 1479
  biography 222c
Chelsea, England
  pottery tab 131
Chelating agents 734c
Chemical bonding 1809b
Chemical cells (elec.) 1883a
Chemical cycles (ecology) 1862a
Chemical elements see Elements
  (chem.)
Chemical energy
  conversion chart 1130
Chemical engineering 1200c
  careers 379c
Chemical equations 1810c

Chemical formulas 1810b
Chemical fuels 1778b
  liquid propellants 1779a
  solid propellants 1779c
Chemical kinetics 1800c
Chemical oceanography 461a, 463b
Chemical technology 380a
Chemical thermodynamics 1800c
Chemical weathering 447a
Chemical weathering 485b
Chemicals
  bacteria 1845b
  food poisoning 956b
  petrochemicals 1216c
  plants 1646b
  public health 958b
  soil 753a
Chemistry 1798–1800, 1869c
  analytical 1827a
  agricultural 722a
  bibliography 1829c
  branches of 1800b
  careers 390a
  development of 1761a
  elements 1830–1838
  history of 1798a
  inorganic 1801–1828
  nineteenth century 1799a
  nuclear 1828c
  organic 1799b, 1800c, 1818–1827
  quantitative 1798c
  periodic law 1807c
  physical 1828
  polarized light 1906a
  twentieth century 1800a
Chemoreceptors 922a
Chemosphere 485b
Chengteh, China 2351c
Chénier, André de 1008a, 1380b,
  tab 1471
  biography 223a
Ch'en Tu-Hsiu 223a
Cheops see Khufu
Chera Kingdom 2179c
Cherimoya see Custard-apple
Chernozem (soil) 485b, 743a
Chernushka (dog) 951b
Cherokee Indians 2037c
Cherokee rose 1979c
Cherokee Strip Day 842b
Cherry 1657c
Cherry Creek 2006c
Cherski Mountains 2328c
Chert (minerals) 485b
Cherubini, Maria Luigi 166c, tab
  171c, 223a
Chesapeake (ship) 2033b
Chesapeake Bay 1984c, 2019c
  mackerel 44b
  shoreline 448c
Chesapeake Bay Bridge 1197, 1984
Chesapeake Bay Tunnel tab 1226
Cheshire Cat 1399a
Cheshire Cheese (club) 1363c
Chess 1713b
Chesterfield, 4th Earl of
  letters tab 1469
Chesterfield Archipelago 2318a,
  2318b
Chesterton, Gilbert Keith 1370b,
  tab 1480
Chestnut 1657c
  tannin 1209c
Chestnut Hill College 695
Chestnut soil 485b
Chevalier, Charles 1269b
Cheves, Langdon
  House of Representatives tab
  802b
Cheviot Hills 2282a
Cheyenne, Wyoming 1999b, 2006a
Cheyenne River 2016b, 2018c
Cheyney State College 695
Chiabrera, Gabriello 1387a
Chiang Kai-shek 223a, 2130b,
  2130c–2131a, 2131b, 2131c,
  2221b
Chiang Kuo 2131c
Chiang Mai, Thailand 2352a
Chianti 723c
Chiapas Mountains 2217c
Chiarini, Giuseppe 1387c
Chiba, Japan 2352a
Chicago, Illinois 1981b, 2006a–
  2006b, 2293b
  architecture 81b
  libraries tab 1463
  meat packing 735b
  power tab 1132b
Chicago, The University of
  college 663
  library tab 1463
  nuclear chemistry 1829a

Chicago Drainage Canal 1189c, 1244b
Chicago News *tab* 1171
Chicago Public Library *tab* 1463
Chicago Sanitary and Ship Canal 1967c
Chicago Sun-Times *tab* 1171
Chicago Tribune *tab* 1171
Chichicastenango, Guatemala 2168
Chichihar, China 2375c
Chickadee 21a, 1984a, 1985a
Chickamauga, Battle of 2049
Chickamauga, Rock of (nickname) *see* Thomas, George Henry
Chicken pox *tab* 946
Chickens 728a
  creeper fowl 1857b
  egg production 732a
Chickweed 1657c
Chico State College 656
Chicopee, Massachusetts 1985b
Chicory 728a, 1657c–1658a
Chief executives (U.S.) *see* Presidents (U.S.)
Chief Justice (U.S.) 791c, 802a
  forms of address *tab* 1119
  impeachment 884a
  list of *tab* 802a
Chieftains 1936c
Chigger *see* Jigger
Chigoe *see* Jigger
Chihli, Gulf of 2124b, 2328c
Chilblains 941a
Child, Francis J. 1396b
Child labor
  American colonies 829b
  apprenticing 829a
  England 830b
  U.S. laws 831c
Child psychology 383b, 1951c
Child welfare careers 379a
Childbirth 959a
  maternal mortality 958c
Childe Harold's Pilgrimage (poem) 1365a
Children
  development 397–444
  educational toys 406–407
  health problems 959b
  penmanship 1301b
  reading 1299a
  sense games 423
  Social Security Act 837c
  songs for 418–424
  speech 1298a, 1298b
  spelling 1302c
Children of Ler (myth) 1428c
Children's Bureau 908b
Children's court *see* Juvenile court
Children's Crusade 1002b
Children's literature 400b
  fables 442–444
  Mother Goose Rhymes 408–412
  poems 412–417
  stories 425–442
Child's Garden of Verses (poetry) 414a, 1368b, 1399a
Chile 2100c, 2121–2122, 2237a–2237b
  ABC Powers 2064b
  agriculture 2121c
  butterfly-flowers 1655a–1655b
  chinchilla 21b
  climate 2121b
  economy 2121b–2122a
  flag *il* 2182
  geography 2121b
  government 2122a
  history 2122a–2122c
  Indians 2121b, 2122a
  League of Nations 1012c
  map 2121, *Atlas* 44–47
  minerals 2121b–2121c
  osprey 48c–49a
  people of 2121b
  peppertrees 1686a
  religion 2121b
  salpiglossis 1691b–1691c
  shelter 1930a
  woodpeckers 68a–68b
  World War I 2122b
  World War II 2122c
Chilin, China 2359c
Chillon Castle 1399a
Chimaera (Chimera) (myth) 1429a
Chimborazo (volcano) 2143c
Chimes 174a
Chimney swift 21b
Chimpanzees 21b
  anthropology 1923c
Ch'in dynasty 2221a, 2126c–2127a
Ch'in Ling Mountains 2124a
China 1015b, 2099c, 2123–2131
  agriculture 2123, 2124a, 2125a–2125b

anthropology 1924a
area 2123b
arrowhead plants 1649c
badger 15a
boston ivy 1653c
Ch'ing dynasty 2126c–2127a, 2128a–2128b, 2128c, 2129a, 2130b
Chou dynasty 2126a–2126b
cinnamon 1658b
citron 1658b
climate 2124b–2124c
cormorant 23b
culture region 770a–770b
cycad 1660b
cypress 1660c
Dutchman's-breeches 1665c
education 612a
flag *il* 2182
gardenia 1668b
geography 2123b–2124c
ginseng 1669b
government 2125c–2126a
Great Wall 2126c, 2127b
guava 1670c
Han dynasty 2127a
hemlock 1671b
Hsia dynasty 2126a
influence on Japan 978b, 2200a–2200b
jasmine 1673c
jujube 1674a
Korean War 1010c–1012b
lacquer tree 1674c
League of Nations 1012c, 1013c
lotus 1677a
lowlands 2124a–2124b
madder species 1677b
magnolia 1677b
map 2124, *Atlas* 32–33
mathematics 1505b
millet 1679c
Ming dynasty 2127c–2128a
missionaries to 2128a, 2128b, 2128c, 2129a
Mongolia 2221a, 2221b
mulberry 1680b–1680c
mustard 1680a–1681a
narcissus 1681b
natural resources 2125b
oranges 1682c–1683a
pigword species 1667a
people of 2125a
philosophers of 2126b–2126c
philosophy 977a
porcupine 52b–52c
potatoes 1688c
praying mantis 53a
purslane 1689b
rebellions 2128c
regions 2123c
religion 1623a, 2125a
rhubarb 1690a
rivers 2124b
rocketry, early 1764a
roses 1690b
Shang dynasty 2126a
sheep 57b–57c
sericulture 1223b
Sui dynasty 2127b
Sung dynasty 2127c
swift birds 61c
tallow tree 1695c
T'ang dynasty 2127b–2127c
tree of heaven 1697a
tulip tree 1697c
tung tree 1697c
uplands 2123c–2124a
Vietnam 2300a, 2300b
war with Japan 2130c
Western influence 2128b–2128c
willows 1699c
wistaria 1699c–1700a
World War I 2130a
World War II 2130c
Yin dynasty 2126a
Yüan dynasty 2127c
see also Chinese language
see also Chinese literature
—**Arts**
glass *tab* 135
music 155a
paper 142a
porcelain 126c, *tab* 130–131
pottery 1220c
sculpture 114b
—**Economy** 2125a–2125c
coal 1202b
lend-lease 889b
reparations 905b
—**History** 2126a–2131b
ancient 976a
Boxer Rebellion 2129c
naval conference 2069a
open-door policy 2060b
Sino-Japanese War (1894–1895) *tab* 1075
Sino-Japanese War (1937–1945) *tab* 1076
China, Communist 868a, 877c, 2099c, 2263a
  agriculture 2123, 2124a, 2125a–2125b

Cuba 2137a
economy 2125a–2125c
geography 2123b–2124c
government 2125c–2126a
history 2126a–2131b
India 2186a
industry 2125b
people of 2125a
recognized by France 2155a
rice 742b
trade 2125c
China, Nationalist 2123
  economy 2125c
  extraterritoriality 877c
  geography 2124c–2125a
  government 2126c
  history 2131b–2131c
  people of 2125a
  see also Nationalist Party (China)
China (ceramics) *see* Porcelain
China Democratic Party 2131c
Chinaberry 1658a
Chinan, China 2375b
China's Sorrow *see* Hwang Ho (river)
Chinch bug 21b
Chinchilla 21b
Chinchow, China 2352a
Chinese (lang.) *see* Chinese language
Chinese (people)
  California 883b
  immigration (U.S.) 883c
Chinese cabbage *see* Mustard
Chinese Exclusion Act 883b, 2056a
Chinese Gordon *see* Gordon, Charles George
Chinese language 1333a
  writing 977b
Chinese literature *tab* 1463–1464
  poetry 978a
Chinese rugs 1110c
Ch'ing dynasty 1015b, 2128a–2128b, 2128c, 2129a, 2130b, 2204b, 2221a
Chinnampo, North Korea 2352a
Chios 2164c
Chinook (winds) 485b
Chinook salmon *il* 1717
Chipmunk 21c
Chippendale, Thomas
  biography 223b
  furniture 1097c, 1098a
Chirico, Giorgio de 103b, *tab* 109
Chiriquí Volcano 2234a
Chiron 1429a
Chiropractors (career) 381c
Chittagong, Pakistan 2352a
Chittagong Hills 2177c
Chivalry, Age of
  music 159b
Chlamydomonas 1847c
Chlorella 1847c
Chlorine 463b, 1193b, 1199b, 1822a, 1831
  atomic weight *tab* 1805
  bacteria control 1844c
  body requirements 919c
  chemical bonding 1809c
  electrovalence 1809a
  hydrochloric acid 1212a
Chlorite 454a
Chlorophyll 461a
  photosynthesis 1861b
Chloroplasts 1842a
  plant 1643c
Chocano, José Santos 1393b
Chocolate 726b
  see also Cacao
Choephorae, The (play) 1352b
Choice of Hercules (paint.) *tab* 111
Choir 156a, 174a
Choir organ 174b
Chola kingdom 2179c, 2180a
Chola Range 2249b
Cholangitis 941a
Cholera *tab* 946
  bacteria 1845b
Cholesterol 732c, 1824c
Choline *tab* 919
Chomo-lungma *see* Everest, Mount
Ch'ondogyo movement 2204c
Ch'ongch'on River 2203b–2203c
Chongjin, North Korea 2352a
Chopin, Frédéric 166a, *tab* 172a
  biography 223b
Chopping tools (prehistoric) 1928a
Choragus 157a
Choral 160b, 162a, 174b

Chorale 174b
Chord (math.) 1571b
Chord (music) 174b
  acoustics 1896c
  polyphony 161b
Chorea 941a
Chorister 174b
Chorus 174b
  Greek music 157a
Chosen *see* Korea
Chou Dynasty 1220c, 2126a
Chou-En-lai 223b
Choukoutien, China
  anthropology 1924a
Chrétien de Troyes 223b, 1377c, 1395c
Christ *see* Jesus Christ
Christ (poem, Cynewulf) 1358c
Christ and Angel Musicians (paint.) *tab* 109
Christ Appearing to His Mother (paint.) *tab* 112
Christ Entering Jerusalem (paint.) 83b
Christabel (poem) 1364c
Christchurch, New Zealand 2226b, 2226c, 2352a
Christensen, Bernhard 168c
Christensen, P. P. *tab* 801
Christian II, King (Denmark, Norway, Sweden) 223b
Christian IV, King (Denmark, Norway, Sweden) 223b, 2231a
Christian X, King (Denmark) 2142b
Christian, Fletcher 1398a
Christian Brothers 614c
Christian Brothers College 700
Christian Democratic Party
  Chile 2122c
  Italy 2196c
  San Marino 2246b
  West Germany 2163a
Christian Frederick, King (Norway) 2231a
Christian Socialist Party
  Austria 2095c–2096b
Christianity *tab* 1034–1040, *tab* 1042, *tab* 1044, *tab* 1046, *tab* 1048, *tab* 1050, 1630a
  Albania 2086b
  benefit of clergy 856b
  current challenges to 1632c
  drama, early 1360c
  education 613c
  established church 877b
  Messiah 1629b
  Middle Ages 982b, 985a, 1360a
  painting 84b
  philosophy 1615c
  religious shrines 1017
  Roman Empire 976b, 1016c
  sculpture 118c
  see also names of Christian churches, such as Roman Catholic Church
  see also headings starting Church
  see also names of sects, such as Huguenots
Christina River 2015c
Christmas 842c
  Knecht Ruprecht 1437c
  Kriss Kringle 1437b
  St. Nicholas 1446c
Christmas berry 1658a
Christmas Carol (nov., Dickens) 1399a
Christmas Island 2310
Christmas rose *see* Hellebore
Christophe, Henri 2172b
Christus, Petrus *tab* 106
Chromatic aberration (optics) 1908c
Chromatic scale 157b, 174b
Chromatic signs 174b
Chrome 1209c
  New Caledonia 2318b
  Turkey 2278a
  U.S.S.R. 2256b
Chromite
  Cuba 2136c
  Pakistan 2232b
  Philippines 2238a
  Yugoslavia 2303b
Chromium 1831
  alloys 1193a
  architecture 82a
  atomic weight *tab* 1805
Chromium oxide
  glass 133c
Chromoplasts
  plants 1643c

Chromosomes 1841a, 1842a, 1851b, 1855c
  meiosis 1851c
  mitosis 1851c
  plant 1643b
  sex-linkage 1852a
  X chromosome 1852c
  Y chromosome 1853a
Chromosphere 1793c
Chronicles, Book of 1452b
Chronicles of England, Scotland and Ireland 1361a
Chronometers 1162b
Chrysanthemum 1658a
Chrysostom tab 1464
Chu River 2328c
Chu Yüan-chang 2127c
Chuang-tse 1623c
Chubb, Jeremiah 1264b
Chukchi 1930a
Chulalongkorn, King (Siam) 2274b
Chungyang Mountains 2124c, 2125c
Church, Frederic Edwin tab 108
Church, William 147a
Church see under names of individual churches
Church and State 1631a
  established church 877b
  kings 887b
Church architecture 75c
Church censorship 861a
Church College of Hawaii 663
Church of England (Anglican Church) 909b
  established 2288a
Church of Jesus Christ of Latter Day Saints see Mormons
Church music 157c, 160b, 162a
  England 171c
  hymns 1344b
Church of San Francesco (Assisi)
  Giotto painting il 87
Churchill, John 2289c
  see also Marlborough, 1st Duke of
Churchill, Winston (American author)
  Crisis, The 1400a
  Crossing, The 1400b
Churchill, Winston Leonard Spencer (British statesman) 963c, tab 1480, 2292a
  Atlantic Charter meeting 996a
  biography 223a
  Iron curtain 886b
  United Nations 990a
  World War II 1028b, 2076b, 2292a
Churrigueresque architecture 77a
Chute (waters) 485b
Chu Teh 223c
CIA see Central Intelligence Agency
Cibber, Colley 1413b
Cicada 21c–22a
Cienaga 485b
Cicero 976a, 1354b, 1355c, 1464, 1615b
  biography 223c
  De Republica 1353c
  epithet 1462a
Cid, El (hero) 1391a, 1399a
  biography 224a
Cid, Le (play, Corneille) 1379a, 1399a
  derivation 1392a
Cid, Poem of the tab 1465
Cierva, Juan de la 1159a
Cilia 926c, 1849a
Ciliophora 1849a
Cimabue, Giovanni tab 106
  biography 224a
  Madonna Enthroned tab 110
Cima da Conegliano tab 106
Cimarron River 2016b
Cimarosa, Domenico tab 171c
Cimon 224a
Cinchona 1658a, 1658b
  Indonesia 2187a
Cincinnati, Ohio 1992a, 2006b, 2019c
  government 793c, 864b
  power tab 1132c
  proportional representation 902b
  public library tab 1463
Cincinnati, University of 691
Cincinnatus, Lucius Quinctius
  biography 224a
Cinder cone (volcanoes) 485c
Cineraria 1658b
Cinderella 1429a
  wallflower popularity 1422a
Cinematography 1161a
Cinna (drama) 1379a

Cinna, Lucius Cornelius 224a
Cinnamon 744b, 1658a
Cino da Pistoja 1386a
Cintra, Pedro da 2248c
C.I.O. 838b, 1743b
  adult education 637a
  see also A. F. of L.
Circe 1344a, 1429a
  Scylla 1447a
Circles 1571b
  conic section 1602c
  definition 1592c
  measurement 1582b
  regular 1574c
Circuit Court of Appeals 792c
Circuits, Electric see Electric circuits
Circulation (bus.) 587c
Circulatory system 922b, 923a
  Buerger's disease 941a
  Harvey, William 1759b
  Raynaud's disease 945b
  shock 945b
  varicose veins 945c
  see also Blood
Circumcision 1930c
Circumference 1602b
Circumflex 1314c
Circumpolar stars 1793c
Cirenaica see Cyrenaica
Cirque (rocks) 485c, 449b
Cirrhosis of the liver 941a
Cirrocumulus clouds 470c
Cirrostratus clouds 470c
Cirrus clouds 470c
Cislunar space 1779a
Cismone River 1196b
Cistrons 1855c
Citadel, The 698
Cities see City
Citizen King see Louis Philippe
Citizenship 863c–864a
  Fourteenth Amendment 787b, 810c, 2051c
  naturalization 892c
Citrine 1220c
Citron 1658c
Citrus fruits
  Arizona 1975c
  Israel 2192b, 2192c
  Libya 2210a
  Morocco 2221c
City 864a
  transportation 1153c
City College (N. Y.) see College of the City of New York
City of God (rel. lit.)
  Latin sources 1356a
City planning 864b
  careers 389a
City government 793c, 864a
  comptroller 870c
  council 870a
  home rule 882a
City managers 864b
City-states (Greece) 974a
  education 613a
City University of New York—City College 684
City University of New York—Hunter College 684
City University of New York—Queens College 684
Ciudad Juaréz, Mexico 2218a
Ciudad Trujillo, Dominican Republic see Santo Domingo
Civet cat 22a
Civil death 864b
Civil engineering 1201a
  careers 379c, 380b
  sanitary engineering 1223a
Civil law 815b, 864b
Civil Liberties Union 1743b
Civl procedure 825c
Civil rights 864c
  Eisenhower, D. 2078b
  Truman, H. S. 2078a
Civil Rights Act (1964) 864c
  Johnson, Lyndon B. 2082a
Civil Rights Bill (1865) 2051c
Civil Service 864c, 865a, 2056b
  National Reform League 2056a
  Reform 2054a
Civil Service Commission (U.S.) 791a, 865a, 866b
Civil War (England) 1009a, 1016c
  background 2288c–2289a
  Cavaliers 1019b, 2289a
  Roundheads 1019b, 2289a
  see also English Civil War
Civil War, Spanish see Spanish Civil War

Civil War (U.S.) 963b, 994a, 995a, tab 1075, 2045–2051a
  battles 2049
  Canada in 2116a
  causes 2045
  events 2049
  Hampton Roads Conference 1009a–1009b
  literature 1372c
  memorials 896a
  neutrality 893c
  Reconstruction 1019b
  results 2051a
  see also under the names of the battles, such as Gettysburg, Battle of
Civil Works Administration 2073b
Civilian Conservation Corps 868c, 888c, 2073b
Civilizations
  agriculture 719a
  ancient 972–976
  Burmese 981a
  Chinese 976a
  Greek 973b
  Indian 980a
  Japanese 978b
  Mayan 2021a
  medieval European 984c–985
  Persian 981c
  Roman 976a
  Turkish 982c
Civitali, Matteo tab 125
Claflin University 698
Clam 22a
Claremont Men's College 656
Clarendon, Assize of 855a
Clarendon, Constitutions of 2285b
Claret 723c
Clarinets 157b, 174b, 1896b
Clarion State College 695
Clarissa Harlowe (nov.) 1363c
Clark, Abraham tab 803
Clark, Champ
  House of Representatives tab 802b
Clark, Francis Edward 1743a
Clark, George Rogers 224a
Clark, John Maurice 539c
Clark, Thomas C.
  Cabinet tab 796
  Supreme Court tab 802a
Clark, William 1014a, 2033b
  biography 224a
Clark College 662
Clark University 673
Clarke, John Hessin
  Supreme Court tab 802a
Clarke College 667
Clarkson Institute of Technology 684
Class (social) 1945a, 1946b
  rise of middle and lower 987b
Classes (plant) 1639a
Classic architecture
  see Greek architecture
  see Roman architecture
Classic art 71b
  see also Greek art
  see also Roman art
Classicism 1399a
  French literature 1378c–1379
  French painting 85a
  interior decoration 1102a
  neoclassicism 122b
Classics 1399a
Clastic rock 485c
Claude Lorrain tab 107
  biography 300b
  Evening tab 110
Claudel, Paul 1382b
Claudian 224b, tab 1464
Claudius, Appius (Caecus) 1002c, 1354c
Claudius I, Emperor (Rome) 2283c
  biography 224b
Clauses 1309a
Clausewitz, Karl von 224b
Clausius, Rudolf Julius Emanuel 224b
Claviarium 161b
Clavecin 161b
Clavichords 161b
Clavicle 917c
Clay, Henry tab 795, 2034b, 2036a
  agriculture 719c
  biography 224b
  Compromise of 1850 2041a
  House of Representatives tab 802b
  nickname 1462c, tab 1463a
  presidential candidate tab 800, 2039b

Whig Party 914a
Clay, Lucius Dubignon
  biography 224b
Clay 450a, 485c 1201b
  kaolin 1201b
  kindergarten 400a
  products 132a
  red 512b
  soil 752b
  types 1201b
Clayton, John (English scientist) 1140b
Clayton, John Middleton tab 79c
Clayton Act 539b, 885a, 879c, 906c
Clearinghouse 587c
Cleavage (geol.) 453a, 485c
Cleavers (prehistoric) 1928a
Clef (music) 158b, 174b
Cleft palate 941a
Cleisbotham, Jedediah 1461c
Cleisthenes 974a
Clematis 1658b
Clemenceau, Georges Eugène Benjamin
  biography 224b
Clemenceau, Georges 1023a
Clemens, Samuel see Twain, Mark
Clement V, Pope 2150c
Clementi, Muzio tab 171c
Clemson University 698
Cleopatra 224c, 994a, 1005a
Cléopâtre (tragedy, Jodelle) tab 1466
Clergymen (career) 379a
Clerk-Maxwell, James see Maxwell, James Clerk
Clermont, Council of 1001c, 1002a
Clermont-Ferrand, France 2149b
Cleveland (Stephen) Grover 784a, tab 798–799, 906b
  administration, first tab 1066, 2056b–2057b
  administration, second tab 1067, 2058b–2059b
  biography 225a
  cabinet tab 796–797
  Democratic Party 873a
  election and inauguration tab 801
Cleveland, Ohio 619b, 1992a, 2006b
  proportional representation 902b
  public library tab 1463
Cleveland Rocket Society 1767c
Cleveland State University 691
Cliburn, Van
  biography 225a
Cliff (rocks) 485c
Clifford, Nathan tab 795
  Supreme Court tab 802a
Clifton, New Jersey 1989c
Climate 455a, 477a, 485c–486a
  erosion 761b–761c
  regional 765
  world regions tab 764
Climatic Zone
  see Frigid zone
  see Temperate zone
  see Torrid zone
Climatologists 390b
Climatology 486a
Climax (lit.) 1315b
Climax (plants) 486a
Climax community 1860b
Climograph (weather) 486a
Clines (anthropology) 1927a
Clingmans Dome 1995a
Clinical psychology 1952b
  careers 383a
Clinometer (instrument) 486a
Clinton, De Witt
  biography 225b
Clinton, George tab 800, 2034a
Clinton, Henry 2028
Clio (myth) 1429b
Clipperton Island 2313a
Chlorite (minerals) 485b
Clive, Robert
  biography 225b
Clocks 1162a
Clodion tab 107
Cloister and the Hearth, The (nov.) 1367c, 1399b
Close, Upton (pseud.) see Hall, Josef W.
Closed circuits 1917a
Closed shop 588a
Close-encounter theories 1784c
Close harmony 174b
Closure rules 865a
Cloth see Textiles

Clothing
camping 1711b
home management 1088c
prehistoric 1928b
primitive 1930b
see also Fashion
Clothing industry 1241b
wool 748b
Clotho 1432a, 1429b
Cloud chamber 1914a, 1917a
Cloud seeding 475a
Cloudburst 486a
Cloudiness 486a
Clouds 470b, 486a
formation of 473b
rainmaking 475a
types 470c
Clouds, The (comedy, Aristophanes) 1353a
Clouet, François *tab* 107
Dauphin of France tab 109
Clouet, Jean (1485–1545) *tab* 106, *tab* 110
Clove tree 1658c
Clover 728b, 1658b–1658c
red 1996b
Cloves 744b
Clovis I, King (Gaul) 983b, 1016a, 2150a
biography 225b
Club moss 1642a, 1658c
Clubfoot 941a
Cluj, Romania 2243c
Clutches
automobile 1242a
Clutha River 2225c
Clutterbuck, Cuthbert 1461c
Clyde River 2282a, 2328c
Clymer, George *tab* 803, 148a, 809c
Clytemnestra 1429b
Aegisthus 1422c
Clytie 1429b
Cnut *see* Canute
Coacervates 1841a
Coal 486a, 762a, 450b, 459b, 1201c
Alabama 1974b
Arkansas 1976b
Australia 2092b
bituminous 483b, 1202a
Brazil 2103a
Canada 2112a
China 2125b
coke 1203b
Colorado 1977b
energy 1129a, 1130a
France 2148b, 2148c
fuel 1136c
Germany 2158a
Great Britain 2282c
Greenland 2314b
Hungary 2174a
Illinois 1981b
Indiana 1981c
Jan Mayen Island 2324a
Japan 2199a
Kentucky 1983b
Korea, South 2203c
Laos 2206b
Mongolia 2220c
Mozambique 2317b
Nepal 2223c
North Dakota 1991c
Oklahoma 1992b
Pakistan 2232b
Pennsylvania 1993c
Poland 2239a–2239b
Portugal 2241b
production 1202c
South Africa 2252c
Spain 2263c
Svalbard Archipelago 2324a
Swaziland 2267a
Tennessee 1995b
Turkey 2278a
U.S.S.R. 2256b, 2257a
U.S. 1967a, 2293c
Utah 1996b
varieties 1201c
Virginia 1997c
West Virginia 1998c
world reserves 1202a
Yugoslavia 2303b
Coal gas 1210b
Coal measures 486a
Coal mining
strike 2061a
Coal tar 1203c
Coalbrookdale, England 1196c
Coalport ware *tab* 132
Coast 486a
Coast Mountains 2016c
Coast Ranges 1976c, 2019a, 2019c
Coast rhododendron 1997c
Coastal plain 486a
Coastline 486a

Coates, Eric 169b
Coaxial cable
telephone 1184b
television 1152a
Cobalt 1193a, 1831
atomic weight *tab* 1805
Congo (Kinshasa) 2134c
Cuba 2136c
ferromagnetism 1884b
Germany 2158b
Morocco 2221c
Cobalt oxide
glassmaking 133c
Cobb, Howell *tab* 796, *tab* 802b
Cobb, Tyrus R. (Ty Cobb) 225b
Cobble *see* Wentworth grade scale
Cobia *il* 1717
Cobra 22a–22b
Coca 1658c–1659b
Cocci (biol.) 1843b
Coccidioidomycosis *tab* 946
Cochabamba, Bolivia 2100a, 2100b
Cochin, India 2352b
Cochlea 937a, 1894b
Cochrane, Elizabeth 1461b
Cockatoo *see* Parrot
Cockatrice *see* Basilisk
Cockle *see* Clam
Cockroach 22b
Cockroft, J. Douglas 1912b
Cockroft-Walton accelerator 1912b
Cockscomb 1659a
Cocktail Party, The (play) 1376b
Cocoa 726b
American Samoa 2000a
Grenada 2314c
Indonesia 2187a
New Guinea 2318c
St. Lucia 2321b
Trinidad and Tobago 2275c
Western Samoa 2301c
see also Cacao
Cocoa butter 726c
Coconut oil 728c
Coconut palm 728b
Coconuts 728c
British Indian Ocean Territory 2308b
British Solomon Islands 2308c
Cayman Islands 2310a
Ceylon 2119c, 2120a
Cocoas Islands 2310c
Comoro Islands 2310c
Cook Islands 2311a
Dominica 2311b
Fiji Islands 2312b
French Polynesia 2313a
Gilbert and Ellice Islands 2314a
Maldive Islands 2214b
Muscat and Oman 2222c
New Caledonia 2318b
New Hebrides 2319a
Niue 2319a
Panama 2234b
Papua 2319b
Philippines 2237c
Portuguese Guinea 2320a
Seychelles 2322b
Singapore 2250b
Tanzania 2272b
Thailand 2273c
Tonga 2324b
Wallis and Futuna Islands 2324c
Western Samoa 2301c
Cocos Islands 2310
Cocteau, Jean 225b, 1382b, *tab* 1480
Cocytus 1433c
Cod 22b–22c
Cod, Cape *see* Cape Cod
Coda (music) 174b
Codes (law) 865b
Code of Laws (Abu Hanifah) *tab* 1465
Code Napoléon 865b, 2153a
Cody, William F. 225c
Coe College 667
Coefficients (math.) 1602b
Coffee 728a, 1659a, 2100b
American Samoa 2000a
Angola 2306b
Brazil 2102c, 2103a, 2103b, 2104b
British Indian Ocean Territory 2308b
Burundi 2108b
Cameroon 2110a
Cape Verde Islands 2309c
Central African Republic 2119b
chicory 728b
Colombia 2132c, 2133c
Comoro Islands 2310c
Cuba 2136c
Dominican Republic 2142c
Ecuador 2144a
Equatorial Guinea 2311c
Ethiopia 2146b

French Polynesia 2313a
growing 728c
Guatemala 2168b
Guinea 2170a
Haiti 2171c
Honduras 2172c
India 2178b
Indonesia 2187a
instant 729a
Ivory Coast 2197a
Jamaica 2198a
Kenya 2202b
Liberia 2209a
Madagascar 2212a
New Caledonia 2318b
New Guinea 2318c
New Hebrides 2319a
Nicaragua 2227b
Panama 2234b
Paraguay 2235b
Peru 2236c
Portuguese Timor 2320b
processing 729a
Puerto Rico 2002c
Rwanda 2245c
Sao Tomé and Principe 2322a
Sierra Leone 2248c
Surinam 2323b
Tanzania 2272b
Togo 2275a
Trinidad and Tobago 2275c
Uganda 2279c
Venezuela 2297b
Vietnam 2299b
Yemen 2302a
Coffee houses 728c
Coffeetree *see* Kentucky coffee-tree
Cofferdam 1242b
Cognac 723c
Cognates (Germanic) 1297c
Cohan, George M. 225c
Cohen, Paul 1507c
Coherent light 1918c
Coil springs 1281c
Coimbatore, India 2352b
Coinage 588a, 865b
archeology 967c
Coir 728c
Coke (coal) 486b, 1203b
Pennsylvania 1993b
Coke, Edward 225c
Coke, Thomas 719c
Coker College 698
Col (mountains) 486b
Cola di Renzi *see* Rienzi
Colbert, Jean Baptiste 225c, 1102b, 2114a, 2152a
Colby, Bainbridge *tab* 796
Colby College 672
Cold front 477a
Cold Harbor, Battle of 2049, 2050b
Cold pole 486b
Cold sores *tab* 946
Cold War 995b, 2262b–2262c
France 2155a
Norway 2231c–2232a
Spain 2265b
Cold wave 486b
Colds *tab* 946
incubation period 955a
Cole, King *see* King Cole
Cole, Thomas 104b, tab 108
biography 225c
Cole, Timothy 140c, 148b
Coleridge, Samuel Taylor 1364c, *tab* 1472, 1618b
Ancient Mariner, The Rime of the 1394c
biography 225c
epigram 1402b
Kubla Khan 1408b
lake poets 1408c
Schiller 1351a
Coleridge-Taylor, Samuel 169b
Colette, Sidonie Gabrielle 226a, 1382c
Colfax, Schuyler 226a, 1001b
House of Representatives *tab* 802b
scandals 2054b
vice-presidency *tab* 801
Colgate University 684
Coligny, Gaspard de 226a
Coligny, Gaspard de Chatillon 997c, 1010c
Colines, Simon de 144a
Colitis 941a
Collagen 1825b
Collamer, Jacob *tab* 796
Collateral 588a
Collective bargaining 588a, 839a
Collective unconscious 1958a
Collectivism 588a

College of Charleston 699
College of Emporia 668
College of Great Falls 680
College of the Holy Cross 674
College of the Holy Names 656
College of Idaho 663
College Misericordia 695
College of Mount St. Joseph on the Ohio 691
College of Mount Saint Vincent 684
College of New Rochelle 684
College of Notre Dame 656
College of Notre Dame of Maryland 672
College of Our Lady of the Elms 674
College of Saint Benedict 677
College of St. Catherine 677
College of St. Elizabeth 682
College of St. Francis 663
College of St. Mary of the Springs 691
College of Saint Rose 684
College of St. Scholastica 677
College of Saint Teresa 677
College of St. Thomas 677
College of Southern Utah 703
College of Steubenville 691
College of William and Mary 704
College of Wooster 691
Colleges 627b, 628b, 654–708
adult education 635a
evening 635a
Collenchyma tissue 1643c
Collins, Michael 226a
Collins, (William) Wilkie 1367c, *tab* 1476
Moonstone, The 1411a
Collins, William 1364a
Collision hypothesis 454a
Collodion 1172b
Colloid 486b, 1816a, 1841a
Colloid chemistry 1800c
Colloquialisms 1321c
Colloquies (Erasmus) *tab* 1466
Collotype 150a, 1174a
Colluvium 486b
Colman, Norman J. *tab* 797
Coloane Island 2316b
Cologne, West Germany 2352b
cathedral of 76c
printing 143c
Colomb Béchar, Algeria 2352b
Colombe, Michel 122b, *tab* 125
Colombia 2132–2133, 2234c
agriculture 2132c
climate 2132b
coffee trees 1659a
economy 2132c
flag *il* 2182
geography 2132a–2132b
government 2132c
history 2132c–2133c
Indians 2132b
map 2133, *Atlas*-52–53
Panama Canal 2061b
people of 2132b–2132c
Negroes 2132b
religion 2132a, 2133b
Colombian coffee 729a
Colombo, Ceylon 2119c, 2352b
Colon (punct.) 1312c
Colón, Panama 2234a, 2234c
Colonial America *tab* 1060, 2024
agriculture 719c
architecture 78b
censorship 861b
charter colonies 863a
education 615c
explosives 1207b
furniture 1100b, 1099c
government 785–786
interior decoration 1105c, 1108b
labor 827b
law 815c
literature 1372a
music 169c, 171a
Navigation Acts 2027a
newspapers 1171a, 1170c
painting 103c
printing 145a
Thirteen Colonies 2024a
union of 786b
Colonna, Vittoria 1386c, *tab* 1466
Colony (geog.) 865b
Color 1103–1104, 1905b, 1907b
additive process 1907c
definition 1917b
etching 137c
incandescence and luminescence 1906a

in history 1102b
interior decoration 1106b
light 1904a
paints and inks 1907c
printing 149a, 1907c
subtractive process 1907c
theories of 1103c
Color blindness
heredity 1852c
Color photography 1172c
Color television 1187b
Color vision 928c
Colorado 1977
admitted to U.S. 2055a
agriculture 1977b
capital punishment 860b
census (1960) 1970
climate 1977a
colleges of 659
commercial law 826
congressional apportionment
tab 853
economy 1977b
flag il 2010
geography 1977a–1977b
government 793b, 1977c
holidays 841–842
initiative and referendum 884c
national forests 896a
people of 1977b
public school enrollment tab
646
public school expenditures tab
644
recall 904b
student enrollment tab 645
Colorado, University of 659
Colorado College 659
Colorado Desert 1976c
Colorado River 1975b, 2005b, 2017a,
2017c, 2020c, 2293c, 2328c
aqueduct 1195b, 1226c
Grand Canyon 448a
length of 2020b
reclamation 904c
Colorado School of Mines 659
Colorado Springs, Colorado 1977b
Colorado State College 659
Colorado State University 659
Colorado tick fever tab 946
Colorados Party (Uruguay) 2295c
Coloratura 158c, 174b
Colorimetry 1827c
Colquitt, A. H. tab 801
Colt, Samuel 226a
Colum, Padraic 1370c
Columbia College of Columbia University 684
Columbia Dam 2017a
Columbia, District of see District
of Columbia
Columbia Plateau 1992c
Columbia River 1992c, 1997, 2005c,
2013c, 2017e, 2020c 2111a,
2293a
basin 904c
length of 2020b
smelt 59a
Columbia Union College 672
Columbian Exposition (Chicago,
1893) Mac Monnies, Frederick
124a
Columbia, South Carolina 1994a,
1994b, 2006b
Columbine 1659a–1659b
Columbus, Bartholomew 2142c
Columbus, Christopher 64c, 226a,
779a, 1695c, 1964b, 2003a, 2004c,
2135c, 2137b, 2143a, 2172a, 2173a,
2198a, 2228a, 2234c, 2236c,
2264c, 2297c, 2312c, 2316c
biography 226a
islands discovered by 2307a,
2307b, 2309a, 2310a, 2311b,
2312c, 2314c, 2315a, 2316c,
2317a, 2321b, 2321c
San Salvador 2023a
Columbus Day 842c
Columbus, Georgia 1979c
Columbus, Ohio 1991c, 1992a,
2006c
Columbus, New Mexico 2064b
Columnar jointing (rocks) 486b
Columns (arch.) 75a
Coma (optics) 1908b
Coma cluster (galaxies) 1787a,
tab 1785
Combattimento di Tancredi e Clorinda, Il (opera) 161c
Combination (bus.) 588b
(math.) 1602b
Combination locks 1264c
Combine (machinery) 1251c
Combustion gases 1768a

Comédie Humaine (nov.) 1381b,
tab 1474
Comedy 1399b
Greek 194c–195a, 1352c–1353a
Come, Lasses and Lads (song)
418
Comenius, John Amos 615a
Comets 1783c
definition 1793c
Halley's 1759b
tail 1784a
Comines (Commines), Philippe de
1378a, tab 1466
Cominform 865c, 866a
Comintern 2262
Comma 1313a, 1318a
Commager, Henry Steele 1377a
biography 226b
Command economy 528c, 588b
Commentaries (Caesar) 1356a, tab
1464
Commentaries on the Laws of
England (bk.) tab 1470
Commerce definition 588b, 866a
ICC 886b
legal contracts 819b
restraint of trade 906c
Commerce, Department of 866a
bureaus 858c, 866b
census 862b
education 630a
establishment tab 797
secretaries of tab 797
Weather Bureau 477c
Commerce and Labor, Department
of 2062a
Commercial arbitration 588c
Commercial art careers 374c
Commercial banks 529b
Commercial law see Business law
Commercial paper (negotiable instruments) 588b
Commercial Revolution 986a
Commissary store (Company
store) 588c
Commission (govt.) 866b
Commission Government 864a
Commission of European Economic
Cooperation 1015c
Committee on Industrial Organization see C.I.O.
Committee of Public Safety
(France) 2152c
Committees 866b
parliamentary 843b
Commodity Credit Corporation
850b, 867a
Commodity exchange 588b
futures 593a
stock ticker 1182a
Common carriers 867a
Common denominator 1602b
Common factor (common divisor) 1602b
Common law 815b, 867a
beginning of 2285b
Common logarithms 1604b
Common loon 1986a
Common Market 877b, 2099a, 2292b
Common plea (law) 867b
Common Sense (pamphlet) 1348a,
1372c
Common stock 545c
Commons, House of see House
of Commons
Commonwealth (govt.) 867c
Commonwealth of Nations 1000c–
1001b, 2092c, 2110b, 2112c,
2283c
members 1000c
resignations from 1000c
Commune (govt.) 868a
Communications 1151–1188
FCC 878b
history 1151a
primitive 1935a
radio 1174c
careers 377c
telegraph 1182c
telephone 1183c
Communications Satellite Corporation 1163a
Communications satellites 1162b,
1769c
types 1163a
Communism 784c, 868a, 988c, 1618c
Albania 2086b, 2087b
All-Union Congress of Soviets
851a
Bhutan 2099c
Bolsheviks 858a
Bulgaria 2105b–2105c, 21^6a–
2106b

China 2125c–2126a
Cominform 865c
Cuba 2136b, 2137a–2138a
Czechoslovakia 2139a, 2140a–
2140b
dictator 874a
Finland 2147b
France 2154c
Germany, East 2158c
Greece 2167b
Hungary 2174a–2174b, 2175a,
2175b–2175c
Indonesia 2188b
Italy 2196c
Ivory Coast 2197b
Laos 2207a
Manchuria 980a
North Korea 2204a, 2205a, 2205b
Poland 2238a, 2239b, 2239c, 2240c
red 904c
Romania 2243a, 2244a, 2244b,
2245a–2245b
San Marino 2246b
Thai'and 2274c
Vietnam 2301a
Yugoslavia 2303b, 2303c–2304a,
2304c–2305a
see also China, Communist,
Soviet Union
Communism Mountain 2337c
Communist China see China, Communist
Communist Control Act 2078b
Comunist Manifesto 908a
Communist Party of Cuba 2137a–
2137b
Communist Party of the Soviet
Union (CPSU) 2257c
Community (ecology) 1859a
Community Colleges 627c
Commutators (elec.) 1885a
Commutator-type motors 1885b
Como, Lake 2328c
Comodoro Rivadavia, Argentina
2352b
Comoé River 2197a
Comoro Islands 2310–2311
lemur 42c
Compact of the Pilgrims 1018b–
1018c
Compaction 486b
Company of New France 2114a
Company of One Hundred Associates 2114a
Company store see Commissary
store
Company union 588c
Comparative psychology 1951a
Compartment closure 865b
Compass (instrument) 486b, 1163b,
1883c
Compensated dollar 589a
Compensation (fin.) 868a
Competence 486b
Competition (bus.) 525a, 539c, 589a
Complaint (law) 868b
Compleat Angler, The (bk.) 1347a,
1362a, 1399b, tab 1467
Complementarity (math.) trigonometry 1584c
Complementary angles 1601b
Complementary colors 1907c
Complex (rocks) 486b
Complex numbers 1548a
Composite cone (volcanoes) 486b
Composite numbers 1523b
Composition (arts) 1316a
music 174c
writing 1316–1320
Composition (print.) 151a
Compound fracture 917c
Compressors 1242b
Compromise of 1850 2041a
Compton, Arthur Holly 226b
Comptroller (govt.) 870b
Comptroller of the Currency 870c
Computers 1236b, 1243a, 1289c
and business 569–575
careers 387b
data processing 1163a
data transmission 1164a
digital 1243a
transistors 1890c
weather forecasting 478b
Comstock, Anthony 226b
Comte, Auguste 1381b, tab 1474
biography 226b
sociology 1938a
Cosmus (masque) 1362b, 1399c,
1410b
Conakry, Guinea 2169c, 2170a,
2170b, 2352b–2352c
Conant, James Bryant 226c
Conation 1949a

Concave lenses 1908a, 1918c
Concepción, Chile 2121b, 2121c,
2352c
Concepción, Paraguay 2235b
Conception Island see Grenada
Concert 174c
Concert, The (paint., Giorgione)
tab 110
Concert, The (paint., Ter Borch)
tab 109
Concertina 174c
Concertmeister 174c
Concerto 174b, 174c
Conch 22c
Conchobor 1429b
Concord, New Hampshire 1989a,
2006c
Concord, Battle of (Mass.) 2027c
Concord College 706
Concordant pluton (rocks) 486b
Concordat of 1929 2196c
Concordia College 677
Concordia Teachers College 681
Concrete 1189c, 1203c
architecture 73b, 82b
bridges 1197a
Concretion (rocks) 486b
Condensation 470a, 763c, 764a–764c
definitions 486b, 1917b
matter, properties of 1872c
meteorology 473a
Condensers 1244a
Condensers (elec.) 1916c
Condillac, Etienne de tab 1470
Conditioned responses 1949b
Condor see Vulture
Conductance (elec.) 1882c
Conduction 486c
heat 1900a
Conduction bands 1891b
Conductivity (elec.) 1814a, 1882a
Conductor (mus.) 174c
Conductors (elec.) 1381c, 1890a
metals 1882c
Cone of depression 486c
Cone sheet 486c
Cone shell 22c–23a
Conegliano, Cima da see Cima da
Conegliano
Cones (anat.) 928b
Cones (geom.) 1602b
Coney Island of the Mind, A
(poems) 1376b
Confederacy (U.S.) 2043c
Confederate Memorial Day 842a
Confederate States of America
Great Britain and 994a
Hampton Roads Conference
1009a–1009b
Confederation (gov.) 878b
Confederation of the Rhine 2160c
Confessio Amantis (allegory)
1360a
Confessions of a Young Man
(nov.) 1369c
Confessions of an English Opium
Eater (prose) 1365c, 1399c
Confidence level (probability)
1597b
Conflict of laws 868b
Confluence (waters) 486c
Conformable 486c
Confucianism 977a, 1623a, 2126b–
2126c, 2127a, 2127b, 2129b
Confucius 612a, 977a, tab 1463,
1623a, 2126b–2126c
biography 226b
Congaree River 2006b
Conglomerate (rocks) 450a, 486c
Congo (Brazzaville) 2119b, 2133c–
2134b
agriculture 2134a
bamboo 1650c
climate 2133c
economy 2134a
flag il 2182
geography 2133c
government 2134a
history 2134a–2134b
map 2134, Atlas-38
peafowl 50a
people of 2134a
religion 2133c
slavery 2134a
World War II 2134b
Congo (Kinshasa) 2134–2135
agriculture 2134c
bamboo 1650c
economy 2134b–2135a
flag il 2182
geography 2134b–2134c

government 2135a
history 2135a–2135b
map 2134, *Atlas*-38–39
peafowl 50a
people of 2134b
religion 2134b, 2135a
United Nations 993c
Congo River 2133c, 2134c, 2328c
crocodile 24b
Congoids 1925c 1927a
Capoids 1927a
Congress (U.S.) 787b
apportionment *tab* 853
closure rules 865a
committees 866b
Constitution, U.S. 806c–807a
forms of address *tab* 1119
House of Representatives 788a
leaders 888c
qualifications for membership 810c
Senate 788a
sessions 789b
state representation *tab* 853
Supreme Court 869b
Congress of *see under the latter part of the name, such as* Vienna, Congress of
Congress of Industrial Organizations *see* C. I. O.
Congress of Vienna (1815) 2098c, 2153a, 2160c, 2195c, 2211b, 2225b, 2240a, 2270b
Congressional Government (bk., Wilson) 2063a
Congreve, William (artillerist) 1764b
Congrever, William (author) 226c, *tab* 1469
Congreve rockets 1764b
Congruence 1564b, 1602c
Conic sections 1592b, 1602c
Conidia 1856a
Conifers ecology 1863c
Conjugations (gram.) 1296c, 1308c
use of 1303c
verb "to be" 1306–1307
Conkling, Roscoe 2055c
Connate water 486c
Connaught, Duke of (Arthur William Patrick Albert) 226c
Connecticut 1977–1978
agriculture 1978a
capital punishment 860b
climate 1978a
colleges of 659–660
colonial government 785a
colonial history 2025a
commercial law 826
congressional apportionment *tab* 853
divorce 875b
economy 1978a
flag *il* 2010
geography 1977c–1978a
government 1978a
holidays 841–842
labor legislation 833c
people of 1978a
public school enrollment *tab* 646
public school expenditures *tab* 644
student enrollment *tab* 645
Connecticut, University of 660
Connecticut College 660
Connecticut River 1977a, 1985a, 1996b, 2008a
Connective tissue 919a
Connor, John *tab* 797
Connor, Ralph 1390c, *tab* 1479
pseudonym 1461c
Conquest of Granada (play) 1362c
Conrad III (Ger. k.) statue 120c
Conrad, Charles (Amer. jur.) *tab* 796
Conrad, Charles (astronaut) 951c
Conrad, Joseph 1370a, *tab* 1478
biography 227a
Nigger of the Narcissus 1411b
Rescue, The 1415a
Typhoon 1419c
Youth 1421c
Conscience 1957c
Conscientious objectors 894c
Conscious Lovers, The (play) 1363b
Consciousness 1947b
Conscription (mil.) 868b
Conselheiro, Antônio 2104b
Consequent stream 486c
Conservation 775–777, 868c, 1867a
Roosevelt, T. 2062b
soil 381b
Conservation of Matter and of Energy, Law of 1801b

Conservative Party (Canada) 2116a, 2116c, 2117b, 2117c, 2118b, 2118c
Consideration (contract) 818c
Consideration of the Justifying Values of a Public Park, A (treatise) 775b
Consolations of Philosophy (bk., Boethius) 1358c
Consols (consolidated annuities) 589a
Consonants 1294b, *tab* 1294c
development 1336a
Con sordino 174c
Consortium 589a
Conspiracy (pol.) 868c
Constable, John 86a, *tab* 108
biography 227a
Salisbury Cathedral tab 113
Stoke-By-Nayland tab 110
Valley Farm tab 111
Constance, Council of 1001a
Constance, Lake 2328c
Constant, Benjamin 1381a, *tab* 1471
Constant (math.) 1603a
algebra 1534b
Constantine I, King (Greece)
biography 227a
abdication 849a
Constantine II, King (Greece) 2167b–2167c
Constantine I (Constantine the Great), Emperor (Rome)
biography 227a
Christianity 1631b
Constantinople 983a, 999c–1000a, 2165b, 2165c
Byzantine architecture 75c, 78a
Byzantine art 119a
Crusades 984b
fall of (1453) 1000a, 1001c
glass *tab* 135
Middle Ages 976c
Sancta Sophia 75c
see also Istanbul
Constellations 1793c
zodiac 1797c
Constitution (frigate) 2034c
Constitution (gov.) 868c–870b
initiative and referendum 884c
Constitution (U.S.)
adoption of 2030c
amendments 861c
articles 787a
censorship 861c
citizenship 863c
copyright 870c
development of 786c
Federalist 1372c
preamble 806c
ratification 787a, 809c
signers 809c
text 806–811
veto 912a
—**Amendments** 787a, 810–811, 851b
XII 2033a
XIII 2051a
XIV 863c, 2051c
XV 2053b
XVI 2062c
XVII 2062c
XVIII 812c, 2068b
XIX 2068b
XX ("Lame Duck") 888a, 2072b
XXIV 899c
XXV 899c
civil rights 864c
compensation 868b
minority rights 892a
passage 792c, 809b, 851b
text 810–811
see also Bill of Rights (U.S.)
Constitution of 1791 (France) 1006c
Constitution of the Year III (France) 1006c
Constitutional Convention 786c, 2030b
Constitutional law 869a
amendments 851b
Constitutional monarchy 881b
Consitutional Union Party 870b, 2043b
Construction (gram.) *see* Syntax
Construction engineering 1204b
equipment 1244a
materials and structures 1189–1227
Consul (pol.) 870b
forms of address *tab* 1119
Consumer 589a
Consumers Price Index 530c, 589c
Consumption (med.) *see* Tuberculosis
Contact condensers 1244a
Contact infections 955a

Contact metamorphism 486c
Contemporaneous deformation (rocks) 486c
Contempt (law) 870b
Continent defined 486c *see also* Continents
Continental air mass 486c
Continental Association 2027c
Continental climate 486c
Continental Congress 2029
presidents of *tab* 802b
Continental Congress, First 2027c
boycott 2026c
Declaration of Rights 786b
Continental Congress, Second 2027c
Declaration of Independence 2026c
Continental Divide 1977b, 1987c, 1989c, 2017a
defined 486c
Continental drift 759c
defined 486c
Continental glaciers 449a, 487a
Continental shelf 462b, 487a, 1866a
Continental slope 487a
Continents 759c–761a
characteristics of 759c–761a
formation of 455a
Contingent liabilities 596c
Continuous feldspar series *see* Bowen's reaction series
Continuous spectrum 1906b
Contour strip cropping 1999
Contraband 870b
Contrabass 174c
Contracts 817b, 818b
discharging of 820a
illegal 819a
interpretation of 819c
quasi 824a
Contralto 174c
Controller (gov.) *see* Comptroller
Convection 1900b
defined 487a
Convenience goods 589a
Convention People's Party (CPP) 2164b, 2164c
Converse College 699
Conversion hysteria 1954a
Convertible bonds 589b
Convex lenses 1908a, 1918c
Conveyor belts automotive 1266b
Convicts colonial America 828c
Conway Cabal 2029
Conwright, S. C., Mrs.
see Schreiner, Olive
Cony 23a
Cook, James 227a, 1654b, 1964b, 2092c, 2226c, 2311a
oceanography 461c
Cook, Islands 2311, 2319a
Cook, Mount 2225c
Cook Strait 2225c
Cooke, John Esten *tab* 1477
Cooking primitive 1933a
outdoors 1711a
Cookworthy, William 127c, *tab* 131
Coolidge, Calvin *tab* 798–799, 849b, 906b
administrations 2069c–2071b
administrations, events paralleling *tab* 1068
biography 227a
cabinet *tab* 796–797
election and inauguration *tab* 801
Coolidge, William David 1140c, 1241a, 1290b
Coolidge tube 1241a, 1290b
Coon, C. S. 1925c
Cooper, Anthony Ashley (1621-1683) *see* Shaftesbury, 1st Earl of
Cooper, J. Gordon 951b, *tab* 1770
space photographs *il* 1773
Cooper, James Fenimore 1373a, 1473
biography 227b
Last of the Mohicans 1408c
Leatherstocking Tales 1409a
pseudonym 1462b
Cooper, Peter 227b
presidential candidate *tab* 801, 881c
Cooper Union 684
Co-operative banks 878a
Cooperative Commonwealth Federation 2118b
Coordinates (math.) 1581a
Cartesian 1602a
polar 1606b
Coot 23a
Copán, Honduras 2352c
Copeland china 128a
Copenhagen, Denmark 2141a, 2352c
pottery *tab* 131

Copernicus, Nikolaus 1348a, 1756b, 1794c
biography 227b
Copland, Aaron 170b, *tab* 172c
biography 227c
Copley, John Singleton 104a, *tab* 107
biography 227c
Coppée, François *tab* 1478
Copper 761c–762a, 1204c, 1832
alloys 1193a
Angola 2306b
Arizona 1988a
atomic weight *tab* 1805
Australia 2092b
brass 1195c
bronze 1198a
chalcopyrite 453c
Chile 2121c
conductance 1890a
conductivity 1882a, 1900b
Congo (Kinshasa) 2134c
crystal structure 1870c
Cuba 2136c
Cyprus 2138a
electrochemistry 1814a
engravings 139b
first use of 767b
French Guiana 2312c
Germany 2158b
Korea, North 2203c
Korea, South 2203c
Laos 2206b
Mauritania 2216b
Mexico 2218a
Mongolia 2220c
Montana 1988a
Nepal 2223c
Nevada 1988c
New Mexico 1990a
Nicaragua 2227c
Peru 2236b
Philippines 2238a
Poland 2239b
Portugal 2241b
pyrite 453c
South West Africa 2322c
Spain 2263c
Sweden 2268a
Turkey 2278a
Uganda 2279c
U.S.S.R. 2256b
U.A.R. 2280c
U.S. 2293c
Utah 1996b
Venezuela 2297b
Yugoslavia 2303b
Zambia 2305b
Copper oxide rectifiers 1890b
Copper-base alloys 1194a
Copperheads (snakes) 1711c
see also Pit Viper
Coppin State College 672
Copra 728c
American Samoa 2000a
Cocos Islands 2310c
Gilbert and Ellice Islands 2314a
Indonesia 2187a
Mozambique 2317b
New Guinea 2318c
Portuguese Timor 2320b
St. Lucia 2321b
St. Vincent 2321c
Sao Tomé and Principe 2322a
Tokelau Islands 2324a
Wallis and Futuna Islands 2324c
Coprolites 455c
defined 487a
Coptic Church *il* 2146, 2281a
music 158c
Copy editors 388a
Copyright 870c
Coques, Gonzales *tab* 107
Coquina 23a
minerals 487a
Coral 23b, 450a, 450b
defined 487b
Coral islands 450b
Coral reefs 463a, 487b
origin of 461c
Coral Sea 2331
Coral snake *il* 32
Corday, Charlotte biography 227c
Corded lava *see* Pahoehoe
Cordelia (lit.) 1408c, 1437b
Cordillera (mountains) 487b
Cordillera Cantabrica (mountains) 2328a
Cordillera Central (mountains) 2132a, 2135b, 2142c
Cordillera de Guanacaste (mountains) 2135b
Cordillera Occidental (mountains) 2132a, 2143c
Cordillera Oriental (mountains) 2132a, 2143c

Cordillera Septentrional 2142c
Cordillera de Talamanca (mountains) 2135b
Cordite 1766c, 1778a
Cordoba (Cordova), Hernandez de (d. 1518) 2023b
Cordoba, Argentina 2089b
Cordova, Spain 2352c
mosque of 78a
Core (earth) defined 487b
see also Earth structure
Core tools 1927c
Corelli, Arcangelo tab 171b
biography 227c
Corelli, Marie 1461c
Coreopsis 1659c
Corinth, Mississippi 1020c
Corinthian order 75a
Corinto, Nicaragua 2352c
Coriolis, Gaspard Gustave de 1778a
Coriolis effect 1778b
Coriolis force 465a, 473c
defined 487b
Cork 1205b
Portugal 2241b
Spain 2264a
Cormac, King 1432b
Cormorant 23b
Corms (plant) 1644c
Corn 729b, 1659b
Alabama 2174b
Albania 2086b
Argentina 2089c
Bulgaria 2105b
Cape Verde Islands 2309c
Comoro Islands 2310c
farms 381a
farm machinery 1251c
French Guiana 2312c
Georgia 1979c
Greece 2165a
growing conditions 729c
Guam 2001a
Hungary 2174a
hybrid 721a
Ifni 2316a
India 2178b
Indiana 1981c
Iowa 1982b
Italy 2194b–2194c
Kansas 1982c
Kentucky 1983b
Mali 2215a
Maryland 1985a
Mauritania 2216a
Mexico 2218a
Michigan 1986a
Minnesota 1986b
Mississippi 1987a
Mozambique 2317b
Nebraska 1988b
North Carolina 1991b
Ohio 1992a
Pakistan 2232b
Panama 2234b
Paraguay 2235b
Pennsylvania 1993c
per-acre yield 721b
Peru 2236c
Philippines 2237c
Rhodesia 2243a
Romania 2244a
Rwanda 2245c
Sikkim 2249c
South Africa 2252b–2252c
South Carolina 1994b
South Dakota 1994c
Spain 2264a
Swaziland 2267a
Syria 2271a
Tanzania 2272a
Tennessee 1995b
Thailand 2273c
Togo 2275a
Uganda 2279c
U.A.R. 2280c
U.S. 1963b, 1968b–1968c, 2294a
Uruguay 2295a
varieties 729c
Venezuela 2297b
Vietnam 2299b
Virginia 1997c
West Virginia 1998c
yield 754a
Yugoslavia 2303b
Zambia 2305b
Corn belt climate 487c
Corn Islands 2000
Cornborer 23b
Cornea 928b
Corneille, Pierre 1379a, tab 1467
Andromeda 1424a
biography 227c
Cornel see Dogwood
Cornelia 227c
Cornelius (Bib.) 1452b
Cornelius, Peter von tab 172a
biography 227c

Cornelius Van Der Geest (paint.) tab 111
Cornell, Katharine 228a
Cornell College 667, 684
Cornets 174c
Cornflower 1659b
Cornices Greek 75a
interior decoration 1105a
Corning Glass Works (N.Y.) 135a
Cornish (lang.) 1336a
Cornucopia 1424a
Cornwall, Barry see Procter, Bryan W.
Cornwallis, Charles (1st Marquis Cornwallis) 228a, 2030a
American Revolution 2028c
Corolla (flowers) 1645c
Corollary (math.) 1559a
Coromandel 2331a
Corona 487c
Coronado, Francisco Vásquez de 228a, 1964b, 2023b
Coronado, Juan Vásquez de 2136a
Coronation of the Virgin (paint.) tab 110
Coroner 870c
Coroner's jury 887c
Corot, Jean Baptiste Camille 86a, tab 108
Interrupted Reading tab 110
biography 228a
Ville D'Avray tab 112
Corporations 524c
dissolving of 822c
legal powers 818b, 822b
Corporative State 870c
Corpus Christi, Texas 1995c
Corpus Iuris 1001a
Corpus Juris Civilis 815a, 983a
Corpus luteum 926b
Corrasion 487c
Correggio, Antonio Allegri da tab 107, tab 112
biography 228a
Nativity tab 110
Corregidor Island 2238b
Correlation 487c
Correspondence see Letter writing
Correspondence (geometry) 1561a
Correspondence schools 636b
Corrie see Cirque
Corrosion (rocks) 487c
Corsair, The (poem) 1365a
Corsica sheep 57b–57c
Cort, Henry 1189b
Cortelyou, George tab 796, 797
Cortereal, Gaspar 2023a
Cortereal, Miguel 2023a
Cortés, Hernán 2023b, 2218c, 2308b
biography 228a
Corticosteroids 926a
Cortines, Adolfo Ruiz 2219c
Cortisone 925c, 926a, 1824c
Corundum 1194b
Corwin, Thomas tab 796
Cosby, William 1171a
Cosecants 1607c
Cosgrave, William Thomas 228b
Cosines 1583a, tab 1589, 1607c
law of 1587b
Cosmic dust 1786c
Cosmic rays 952a, 1917b
defined 487c
Cosmogony 454a, 1611a
defined 487c
Cosmology 1611a
defined 488a
Cosmonauts 1763a, tab 1770
Cosmos II 1662
Cosmotrons 1919b
Cossa, Francesco tab 106
Cossacks dance 108a
Cost 589c
Cost accountants 377a
Cost of living 589c
Cost plus 589c
Costa, Lorenzo tab 106
Costa Rica 2135–2136
agriculture 2135c
cinchona 1658a–1658b
climate 2135b
economy 2135c
flag il 2182
geography 2135b
government 2135c
history 2135c–2136a
map 2135, Atlas-44
people of 2135c
religion 2135b
Costa e Silva, Artur da 2104c
Costeau, Jean 1246c

Costello, John A. 2191c
Costume see Clothing; Fashion
Cotangents 1607c
Cotapaxi (volcano) 2143c
Côte d'Azur see Riviera
Cotillion 174c
Cotman, John tab 108
Cotonou, Dahomey 2140c, 2141a, 2352c
Cottage cheese tab 731b
Cotter's Saturday Night (poem) 1400a
idyl 1406b
Cotton 720a, 730, 1659b
Alabama 1974a, 1974b
Albania 2086b
Angola 2306b
Antigua 2307a
Arizona 1975c
Arkansas 1976b
Cameroon 2110a
Central African Republic 2119b
Chad 2120c
Colombia 2132c
farms 381b
farm machinery 1252a
fiber crops 733c
Georgia 1979c
growing conditions 730a
Guatemala 2168b
harvest 930b
Honduras 2172c
India 2178b, 2178c
Iraq 2189c
Louisiana 1984a
Malawi 2212c
Mali 2215a
Mississippi 1986, 1987b
Montserrat 2317a
Mozambique 2317b
New Mexico 1990a
Nicaragua 2227c
Niger 2228c
Nigeria 2229b
North Carolina 1991b
Oklahoma 1992b
Pakistan 2232b
Paraguay 2235b
Peru 2236c
Rhode Island 1994a
St. Vincent 2321c
South Carolina 1994b
South Yemen 2253c
Sudan 2266a
Swaziland 2267a
Syria 2271a
Tanzania 2272b
Tennessee 1995b
Texas 1995c
Thailand 2273c
Turkey 2278a
Uganda 2279c
U.S.S.R. 2257a
U.A.R. (Egypt) 2280c
U.S. 1966b, 1968c, 2294a
Upper Volta 2294c
Venezuela 2297b
Vietnam 2299b
Yemen 2302a
Zambia 2305b
Cotton belt climate 488a
Cotton gin 720a, 2032a
Cotton picker (machine) 1252a
Cottonmouth see Pit viper
Cottonmouth moccasin 1711c
Cottonwood 1982b, 1999b
see also Poplar
Cotyledon 1642c
Coucy, Chatelain de tab 171b
Cougar see Cat
Cougar Dam tab 1206
Coughlin, Rev. Charles E. 2074b
Coulee 488a
Coulomb, Charles Augustin de 1190b, 1760b, 1882c
biography 228b
Coulomb 1882c
Coulomb force 1911b
Council (gov.) 871a
Council of Constance 985c
Council of Europe 872a, 2230c
Council for Mutual Economic Co-operation (COMECON) 2158a
Council of National Defense 2065c
Council of Nicaea see Nicaea, Council of
Council of Trent 871b
Counseling psychology 383b
Countdown 1778c
Counterattack (poem) 1371a
Counterglow 1794c
Counterpoint 159a, 160a, 174c
Counter-Reformation 1632b, 2114a
Counter-trade winds see Anti-trades
Countess forms of address tab 1120

Count of Monte Cristo (nov.) 1400a
Country Party (Australia) 2093c, 2094a
Country rock 488a
Counts, George S. 612a
County 871c
political organization 793c
County boroughs 871c
County government (U.S.) boards 857c
political party organization tab 393
Coup d'état 871c
Couperin, François 228b
Couplets (lit.) 1400a
development 1345b
Couplings 1244c
Coupons 589c
Courante 174c
dance 182a
Courantyne River 2170c
Courbet, Gustave 86a, tab 102
biography 228b
Burial at Ornans tab 112
Hunting Scene tab 110
Courier 1B (satellite) tab 1163
Courts appeals 792c
district 792b, 875a
equity 863a
Orphans' Court 894c
probate 901c
states 793b
Court schools 614b
Courtship of Miles Standish (poem) 1400a
Cousin, Victor tab 1473
Cousins, James Gould tab 1481
Cousteau, J. Y. tab 1481
Coustou, Guillaume tab 125
Coustou, Nicolas tab 125
Couture, Thomas tab 108
Covalence 1810a
Covalent bonds 1809c, 1818a
Cove (geog.) 488a
Cover crops 730c
Coverdale, Miles 228b
Covered bridges 1196b
Coverley, Roger de see Roger de Coverley
Covert, Bernard 169c
Coward, Noel 169b, 1371b, tab 1480
biography 228b
Cowbird 23b–23c
Cowboy music 171a
Cowles, Gardner 228b
Cowley, Abraham 228c, tab 1468
essay 1402c
poetic style 1394c
Cowpea 1659c
Cowpens, Battle of 2029
Cowper, William 1364a, tab 1470
biography 228c
John Gilpin 1407b
Cowper's gland see Bulbourethral
Cowpox incubation 955a
smallpox 1849a
Cowrie 23b–23c
Cows 727b
see also Cattle
Cowslip 1659c
Cox, Jacob D. tab 797
Cox, James M. 2068b
candidacy, presidential tab 801
Cox, Kenyon tab 108
Cox, Samuel S. tab 1463b
Coxey's Army 2058c
Coyote 23c
Coypel, Antoine tab 107
Coysevox, Antoine tab 125
Crab 23c
Crabbe, George 1364b, tab 1471
Crabgrass 1659c
Cracow, Poland 2360a–2360b
Cracking process 1273b
Craddock, Charles E. see Murfree, Mary N.
Cradle (art instr.) 139a
Craft unions 589c
Crag 488a
Cragie, Andrew 1273c
Cram, Ralph Adams 81a
Cranach, Lucas tab 106, 140c
biography 228c
Cranberries 1659c
Massachusetts 1985b

Crane 23c–24a
Crane, Hart 228c
Crane, Ichabod 1400a
Crane, Stephen 1375b, *tab* 1480
  biography 228c
  Red Badge of Courage 1415a
Cranfill, James R. *tab* 801
Cranford (nov.) 1400a
Cranial nerves 938a
Cranmer, Thomas 228c
Crape myrtle 1659c
Crapsey, J. F. *tab* 108
Crassus, Marcus Licinius 228c
Crater Lake 451c, 2017a
Crater Lake National Park 2017a
Craters 488a
  lunar 1784b
Crates 1353a
Cratinus 1353c
Crawford, Francis Marion *tab* 1478
Crawford, George *tab* 796
Crawford, Thomas 123c
Crawford, Warner *tab* 125
Crawford, William Harris *tab* 795, *tab* 800, 2036a
Crawl (swimming) 1734a
Crawley, Rawdon 1400a
Crayfish 24a
Crayon, Geoffrey *see* Irving, Washington
Cream cheese *tab* 731b
Creasy, Edward 1002c
Creation, The (mus., Haydn) 164b
Creative writing 1319b
Creativity tests 621b
Credi, Lorenzo di *tab* 106
  biography 228c
Credit bills of 856c
Credit banks 878a
Crédit Mobilier of America 1001b–1001c, 2054b
Creeft, José de 124b, *tab* 125
Creek 488a
Creep 488a
Creeper fowl 1857b
Creighton University 681
Cremazie, Octave 1391b
Cremona (mus.) 174c
Creoles 1983c, 2218c–2219a, 2248c
Creon 1424c
  Oedipus 1441c
Creosote-bush 1659c
Crescendo 174c
Crescent moon 1796a
Cress 1660a
Creston, Paul 170b
Creswell, John *tab* 796
Cretaceous period *tab* 457, 458a, 488a
Crete 2164c, 2166c–2167a
  archaeology 970c
  candytuft plants 1656a
  civilization 973c
  painting 83b
Cretinism 941b, 1953a
Creusa 1429b
Crevasse (glaciers) 488a
Crèvecoeur, John de 1372c
Crichton, James 1393b, 1461c
Crick, Francis Harry Compton 1854b, 1858c
Cricket 24a–24b
Cricket (sport) 1713c
Cricket on the Hearth (story) 1400a
Crime 813a
  primitive society 813b
  see also Criminal law
Crimea Peninsula 2331
Crimean War (1853–1856) *tab* 1074, 2244c, 2260a, 2291a
  battle of Balaklava 997c
Criminal law 813a, 872a
  procedure 826b
  tort 910c
Criollo 726b
Crisis, The (nov.) 1400b
Crisp, Charles F. *tab* 802b
Cristae 937b
Critical and Historical Dictionary *tab* 1468
Critical angle (optics) 1909a
Critical Art of Poetry 1384a
Critical point (phys.) 1872c
Critical temperature 1828b, 1900a
Critique of Judgment 1384a
Critique of Practical Reason 1384a
Critique of Pure Reason 1384a
Critius 116b
Crittenden, John Jordan 229a, *tab* 795, *tab* 796

Crivelli, Carlo *tab* 106
Croaker and Company 1461c
Croatia 2304a, 2304c
Croce, Benedetto 229a, 1387c, 1618b
Crockett, David 229a
Crocodile 24b
Crocodile tears 1429b
Crocus 1660a
Croesus, King (Lydia) 1015a, 1429b
  biography 229a
Croft, William *tab* 171c
Cro-Magnon Man art 71b
  culture 1928b
Crome, John *tab* 107
Crompton, Samuel 229a, 1281c
Cromwell, Oliver 229a, 1009a, 1016c, 1019b, 2191b
  Commonwealth government 2289a–2289b
  death of 1020b, 2289b
  nickname 1462c
Cromwell, Thomas 229b
Cronica general (bk.) 1391a
Cronus 1429b
Crookes, Sir William 229b, 1240c
Crookes tube 1290b
Crops alfalfa 724a
  barley 724b
  cover crops 730c
  fiber crops 733c
  specialty farms 381b
Crop yield 754a
Croquet (game) 1714a
Crosby, Fanny 1461c
Cross, Charles F. 1208c
Cross-country runs 1737b
Cross-cut saws 1288c
Crossing, The (nov.) 1400b
Cross-lamination 488a
Crossover (genetics) 1853b
Cross-pollination 1645c
Crothers, Rachel *tab* 1480
Croton 1660a
Croton Dam 1190a
Crowds (soc.) 1940a
Crow 24c
Crow Island School 618a
Crown (gov.) 872a
Crown Mountain 2004b
Crowninshield, W. Benjamin *tab* 795
Crozet Archipelago 2313a
Crubal River 2320a
Crucifixion, The (paint., El Greco) *tab* 111
Crucifixion, The (paint., Rubens) *tab* 109
Crude oil 488a
Cruden, Alexander 1461a
Cruikshank, George 229c
Crusades 54b, 984a, 1001c–1002b, 1017b, *tab* 1040–1043, *tab* 1072, 1672a, 2193a, 2285b
  Albigensian 994b
  beginning of 1001c–1002a
  first 984a, 1002a
  number of 1002b
Crust (earth's) 488a
  see also Earth structure; Lithosphere
Cruz, Juana Inez de la 1393a
Cryogenic fluids 1902c
Cryogenics 1902c, 1917b
Cryolite 1194b
  Greenland 2314b
Cryopaedeia (bk.) 1353b
Cryptococcosis *tab* 946
Cryptocrystalline 488a
Cryptorchism 941b
Cryptozoic eon 488a–488b
Crystalline rock 488b
Crystalline wax 1227a
Crystallization 488b
Crystalloblastic 488b
  see also Metamorphic facies
Crystalloid 488b
Crystal lattice 452a, 1891b
Crystal Mountains 2155b, 2331a
Crystals 488b, 1828b
  faces 452b
  formation of 1828c
  minerals 452a
Crystal rectifiers 1890b
Crystal structure 1870c
  elements 1830–1838
  structure 1870c
Cserhát Mountains 2173c
Cuba 794c, 2060b, 2136–2138
  agriculture 2136c
  coffee trees 1659a
  communism 2136b, 2137a–2138a

Communist China and 2137a
  economy 2136c–2137a
  Eisenhower, Dwight 2079b
  flag *il* 2182
  geography 2136b–2136c
  government 2137a–2137b
  history 2137b–2138a
  Indians 2137b
  Kennedy, J. F. 2080b–2081a
  López filibustering expedition to 1006a
  map Atlas-56–57
  palms 1684a
  people of 2136c
  religion 2136b
  slavery 2137b
  Spanish-American War 2060a
  sugar cane 1694c–1695a
  tanager birds 62a
  U.S.S.R. and 2137a, 2138a
  U.S. 2042a, 2062a
  U.S. and 2136b, 2136c, 2137a, 2137b–2138a
  woodpeckers 68a–68b
Cubeb *see* Pepper
Cubic centimeter *tab* 1500
Cubic foot *tab* 1500
Cubic inch *tab* 1500
Cubic meter *tab* 1500
Cubic millimeter *tab* 1500
Cubic yard *tab* 1500
Cubism 86c, 103b
Cuchulain (leg. char.) 1429b
Cuckoo 25a
Cucumber 1660a
Cuesta (ridges) 488b
Cueva, de la Garoza, Juan de la 1392a
Cugnot, Nicholas 1169a
Cui, César 169a, *tab* 172b
Culain 1429b
Cullen, Countee *tab* 1481
Culprit Fay, The (poem) *tab* 1473
Cultivators 1251b
Cultural anthropology 1923a, 1929–1937
  careers 390c
  languages 1333c–1337
Cultural geography 767–770
  African Region 769b–769c
  American Region 768b–769a
  Dry-World Region 769a–769b
  elements of 767–768
  European Region 768a–768b
  Oriental Region 769c–770c
  Pacific Region 770c
Culture 1929b, 1940c
  food in 767c
  individuals and 1942b
  prehistoric 1927c
  regions, U.S. 1965a–1965b
  tools in 767c
  transportation in 767c
Culture of Cities, The (bk.) 1348b
Culver-Stockton College 679
Cumaean sibyl 1447a
Cumberland Mountains 2016a
Cumberland River 2012a, 2019b
Cummings, Edward Estlin (E. E. Cummings) 229c
Cummings, Homer S., *tab* 796
Cumulonimbus clouds 473a
Cumulus clouds 473a
Cunard, Sir Samuel 229c
Cuneiform 972c
Cuneiform writing system 997
Cunen River 2331a
Cunha, Eclides da 1393c
Cunningham, C. E. *tab* 801
Cupid 1429c, 1431b
  Psyche 1445b
Cupid and Psyche (statue) 122c
Cuquenán Waterfall 2331a
Curaçao Island 2317a
Curel, François de 1382b
Curie, Marie 229c, 1800a
Curie, Pierre 229c, 1800a
Curing process 735c
Curitiba, Brazil 2352c
Curium 1832
  atomic weight *tab* 1805
Curleuse Island 2322a
Curly locks (nursery rhyme) 408c
Currant 1660a–1660b
Currency *see* Money
Current meter (instrument) 488b
Currents (electric) *see* Electric currents
Currents (ocean) 461a, 465a, 1866b
  defined 488b
  see also Ocean Current
Curriculum 611a, 617b, 638–643
  changing the 642c
  direction of 643a

elementary school 641b
  kindergarten 398b
  language 619b, 1329a
  secondary school 641c
Currier and Ives Prints 149b
Curry, John Steuart *tab* 109
Cursive writing 1302a
Curtis, Benjamin R. *tab* 802a
Curtis, Charles A. *tab* 801
Curtis, George Ticknor 229c
Curtis, George William *tab* 1476
  nickname 1462b
Curtiss, Glenn 1157a
Curtiss, Glenn Hammond 229c
  airplanes 1155c
Curulё chair 1093c
Curve (geom.) 1603a
Curwood, Mt. 1985c
Curzon Line 2240b
Cusco, Peru *see* Cuzco, Peru
Cushing, Caleb *tab* 796
Cushing, William Supreme Court *tab* 802a
Cushite people 1003a
Custard-apple 1660b
Custard-apple family 1660b
Custer, George Armstrong 230a
Cutebra Island 2002a
Cuttack, India 2353a
Cutthroat trout *il* 1717
Cuttlefish 25a
Cuvier, Baron Georges Leopold C. F. D. 230a, *tab* 1471
Cuyahoga River 2006b
Cuyp, Aalbert *tab* 107
Cuza, Alexander 2244c
Cuzco, Peru 2236c, 2353a
Cyaxeres, King (Media) 1016a
Cybele 1429c, 1445c
Cybernetics 1245a, 1917b
Cycads 1642b, 1660b
Cyclades 2165a
Cyclamen 1660b–1660c
Cycle (lit.) 1400b
Cycle (phys.) 1917b
Cycle of erosion *see* Geographical cycle
Cyclohexysulfamic acid 745a
Cyclic populations 1859c
Cyclic school (poetry) 1351a
Cyclone defined 488b
  tropical 519a
Cyclopes 1429c
Cyclotrons 1804b, 1912b, 1919b
  first builder 1912b
Cylinder (geom.) 1603a
Cylinder lock 1264b
Cylinder press 151a
Cymbals (mus.) 174c
Cymric (lang.) *see* Welsh language
Cynewulf 1358c, *tab* 1465
Cynicism (philos.) 975a, 1614a, 1615b
Cypress 1660c
  bald 1983c
Cypress family 1660c
Cyprus 2138, 2279b
  agriculture 2138a
  cedar trees 1657b
  Commonwealth status 1000c
  copper 1204c
  economy 2138a
  flag *il* 2182
  geography 2138a
  government 2138b
  history 2138b
  language 1295c
  people of 2138a
  religion 2138a
  United Nations 993c
  World War I 2138b
Cyrano de Bergerac, Savinien de 230a
  play 1400b, *tab* 1479
Cyrenaica 2209b, 2210a
Cyrenaics (philos.) 1614a, 1615b
Cyrillic alphabet 1296a, 1334a
Cyrus the Great, King (Persia) 230a, 997a, 1015a, 1452b
  allows Jewish exiles to return home 1017a
  Croesus 1429b
Cyrus the Younger 230a
Cystic fibrosis 941b
Cystocele 941b
Cysts (amoeba) 1848a
Cytogenetics 1857a
Cytology 725a, 1643b
  defined 1637c–1638a
  see also Cells (bio.)

Cytoplasm 1842a, 1851b
  heredity 1858a
  plant 1643b
Cytosine 1854b
Czardas (dance) 174c, 182a
Czech (lang.) 1334a
Czechoslovak (lang.) 1334a

Czechoslovakia 999a, 2095c, 2138–2140
  agriculture 2139a
  climate 2138c
  Cominform 866a
  communism 2139a, 2140a–2140b
  economy 2139a
  flag il 2183
  geography 2138c

government 2139a–2139b
  Hapsburg rule 2139b–2140a
  history 2139b–2140b
  industry 2139a
  Little Entente 1014c–1015a
  map 2138, Atlas-9
  music 154c, tab 172a
  people of 2138c–2139a
  religion 2138c, 2139b, 2139c

Sudeten Germans in 2292a
  trade 2139a
  U.S.S.R. and 2140a–2140b
  World War I 988c, 2139c
  World War II 2140a, 2154c, 2162c
Czechs (tribe) 999a
Czerny, Karl 230a
Czestochowa, Poland 2353a
Czolgosz, Leon 2060c

D

D' (in names) *see also under latter part of name, such as* Alembert, Jean le Rond d'
Da capo (mus.) 174c
Da Ponte, Lorenzo 164b, 230c
Da *see also under latter part of name, such as* Gama, Vasco da
Dacca, Pakistan 2353a
Dacian Wars tab 1072
Dacite (rocks) 488b
Dacko, David 2119b
Dacron 1824c
Dactyl 1400b
Daddy longlegs *see* Harvestman
Dado (arch.) 1105a
Daedalus 1429c
  Minos 1440a
Daffodil *see* Narcissus
Dagger (print.) 151a
Daghestan rugs 1110c
Dagon 1452b
Daguerre, Louis Jacques Mandé 1172a
Daguerrotypes 1172a
Dahl, Carl 1272a
Dahlia 1660c, il 1663
Dahlstjerna, Gunno tab 1469
Dahn, Felix tab 1477
Dahomey 2140–2141
  agriculture 2140c
  climate 2140b
  economy 2140c
  flag il 2183
  geography 2140b
  government 2140c
  history 2141a
  map 2140, Atlas-37
  people of 2140b–2140c
  religion 2140b
  slavery 2141a
Daigo II, Emperor (Japan) 2200b
Dail Eireann 870a
Daily Advertiser, The 1171a
Daily Bread (poem) 1371a
Daimler, Gottlieb 1169b, 1170b
Daingerfield, Elliott tab 108
Dairy industry 381a, 721b, 727b, 731b
  artificial insemination 725c
Dairy products 731b
  Alabama 2174b
  Denmark 2141b
  Great Britain 2282c
  Maryland 1985a
  Massachusetts 1985b
  Michigan 1986a
  Minnesota 1986b
  Mississippi 1987a
  Montana 1988a
  New Hampshire 1989b
  New Jersey 1989c
  New York 1990c
  Oregon 1993a
  Pennsylvania 1993c
  San Marino 2246a
  Sweden 2268a
  Switzerland 2270a
  U.S.S.R. 2257a
  U.S. 1968b, 1968c, 2294a
  Vermont 1997a
  Virginia 1997c
  Washington 1998a
  West Virginia 1998c
  Wisconsin 1999a
Daisy 1660c
Daisy family 1660c–1661a
Daisy Miller (nov.) 1369b, 1400c
Dakar, Senegal 2247a, 2353a
Dakota Wesleyan University 699
Dal (river) *see* Dal River
Dalai Lama 979b, 2099c

Dali, Salvador tab 108
Dalin, Olaf von tab 1470
Dallas, Alexander tab 795
Dallas, George Mifflin tab 800, 2039b
  events during vice-presidency tab 1063
Dallas, Texas 1995c, 2006c, 2293b
Dallas, University of 701
Dalles 488b
Dallin, Cyrus E. 125
Dalmatia 2303a
Dalmatian Islands 2196b
Dalou, Jules tab 125
Dalton, John 1760b, 1799a, 1871b
  gases 1828a
Dalton, Massachusetts 618c
Dalton Plan 618c
Dalton's law 1802a, 1871c
Dam *see* Dams
Damages (law) 872a
Damascus, Syria 1452b, 2270c, 2271b, 2353a
Dame aux Camelias (nov.) tab 1476
Damocles 1429c
Damon 1429c
Damrosch, Frank Heino 170b
Damrosch, Leopold 170a
Damrosch, Walter 170b, 172b, 1410a
Dams 488b, 1205c, 1997, 2280c, 2305a, 2305b
  flood control 1255a
  noted modern tab 1206
  structural mechanics 1190c
  see also under names of individual dams, such as Grand Coulee Dam
Damselfly 25a–25b
Dan (Bib.) 1452b
Dana, Charles Anderson 230b, 908a
Dana, James Dwight 230b
Dana, Richard Henry, Jr. 230b, 1373b, tab 1475
  Two Years Before The Mast 1419c
Dana College 681
Danae (myth) 1429c
  Perseus 1444a
Danae (paint., Correggio) tab 112
Danae (paint., Rembrandt) tab 110
Danaides 1429c
Danaus 1429c
Danbury State College 660
Dance 180–184
  ballet 182a
  career guidance 374a
  modern 184a
  primitive 180a
  Renaissance 182c
Dandelion 1665a
Danforth, Charles 1281c
Dangling participle 1316c
Danican, François Philidor tab 171c
Daniel (Bib.) 1452c
  Susanna 1460b
Daniel, Peter V. Supreme Court tab 802a
Daniel, William tab 801
Daniel Deronda (nov.) 1368a
Daniell, John F. 1814b
Daniell cell 1814b
Daniels, Josephus tab 796
Danish language 1336a
  classification 1333b
  cognates tab 1297c
Danish West Indies *see* Virgin Islands
Dannecker, Johann von 122c, tab 125
D'Annunzio, Gabriele 230b, 1387c, tab 1479
Danquah, Dr. J. B. 2164b
Dante (Dante Alighieri) il 208, 1386a, tab 1466

biography 230c
Divine Comedy 1346a, 1401b
Dante and Virgil (paint.) tab 112
Danton, Georges Jacques 230c, 1007b, 1007c, 1008a, 1008c
Danu 1429c
Danube River 2094b, 2094c, 2105a, 2138c, 2157b, 2173b, 2173c, 2243c, 2303a, 2331a
Danzig (Gdańsk, Poland) 2162c, 2240b, 2355a–2355b
  established as Free City 1023a
Daphne (myth) 1429c
Daphnis and Chloe (Gr. lit.) tab 1464
Dar es Salaam, Tanzania 2272a, 2353a
Darcy's Law defined 488b
Dardanelles 2277c, 2331a
Dare, Virginia 230c, 2023c
Daret, Jacques tab 106
Dargomyzhsky, Aleksandr tab 172a
Darien, Manchuria 1015b
Darien, Panama settlement 2023a
Darío, Félix Rubén 230c, 1392c, 1393b
Darius I, King (the Great) (Persia) 995b, 997a, 1021c
  biography 231a
Darius III, King (Persia) 231a
Darjeeling, India 2224a
Dark Ages *see* Middle Ages
Dark Continent *see* Africa
Dark Forest, The (nov.) 1371c
Darling Downs 2091b
Darnay, Charles 1418a
Darnley, Henry Stewart 1020b
Darrow, Clarence S. 231a
D'Arsonval galvanometer 1248b
D'Artagnan 1400c
Dartmouth College 682
Darwin, Charles Robert 461c, 721c, 965b, 1348a, 1366c, tab 1475, 1638c
  biography 231a
  evolution 1762a, 1839c, 1858b
  influence on philosophy 1619c
  Origin of Species 1411c
Das Kapital (bk.) 908a, 1348a, 1385a
Dash (punct.) 1313c
Dasheen *see* Taro
Dasht-i-Kavir Desert 2188c
Dasht-i-Lut Desert 2188c
Data processing machines 620b
Data processing systems 1163c
Data transmission 1164a
  telephone 1185a
Dates French Territory of the Afars and the Issas 2313b
  Iraq 2189c
  Libya 2210a
  Mauritania 2216a
  Muscat and Oman 2222c
  Saudi Arabia 2247a
  Sudan 2266a
  Syria 2271a
  Trucial Oman 2276b
Datum level 488c
Dauberval 183c
Daubigny, Charles François 86a, tab 108
Daudet, Alphonse 231a, 1382a, tab 1477
Daugherty, Harry M. tab 796, 2068c
Daughter element 488c
Daughters of the American Revolution 1742
Daughters of Leucippus (paint.) tab 111
Daumier, Honoré 86b, tab 108
  biography 231a
  lithography 141c
Dauphin of France (paint.) tab 109
Davao, Philippines 2353b

Davenant, Sir William 231b
Davenport, Iowa 1981b, 1982b
David, King (Israel) 1017a, 1452c
  biography 231b
David I, King (Scotland) 1020a
David, Félicien César tab 171
  biography 231b
David, Ferdinand tab 172a
David, Gheerardt tab 106
  Birth of Christ tab 113
  National Gallery (London) tab 111
David, Jacques Louis 85a, tab 107
  biography 231c
  Madame Récamier tab 112
David, Pierre Jean tab 125
David, Mt. 1993b
David Balfour (nov.) 1400c
David Copperfield (nov.) 1366c, 1400c
  Barkis 1396c
  Uriah Heep 1405b
David Harum (nov.) 1401a
David Lipscomb College 700
Davidson, Joe tab 125
Davidson, John tab 1478
Davidson College 688
Davies, Arthur Bowen tab 108
Dávila, Gil González 2228a
Davis, Charles H. tab 108
Davis, David presidential candidate tab 801
  Supreme Court tab 802a
Davis, Dwight F. tab 796
Davis, Emma Lu tab 125
Davis, Henry G. tab 801
Davis, James J. tab 797
Davis, Jefferson 231c
  birthday observance 842a
  cabinet position tab 796
  Confederacy 2043c
Davis, John (navigator) (John Davys) 232a
Davis, John William (statesman) 789c, 2070b
  biography 231c
  presidential candidate tab 801
Davis, Richard Harding 232a
  Gallegher and Other Stories 1404b
Davis, Stuart tab 109
Davis and Elkins College 706
Davitt, Michael 232a
Davy, Sir Humphry 1171c, 1194c
  biography 232a
  fuel cell 1137c
Davys, John *see* Davis, John (navigator)
Dawes, Charles Gates 1023b, 2070b, 2072a
  biography 232a
  vice-presidency tab 801
Dawes Commission 1023b
Dawes Plan 905c, 1002b, 2070c
Dawna Mountains 2273b
Day, J. Edward tab 796
Day, Matthew 145a
Day, Stephen 145a
Day, William R. tab 796
  Supreme Court tab 802a
Day 1794a
Day of Atonement (Judaism) *see* Yom Kippur
Day of Doom, The (poem) 1372a, tab 1468
Daylight Saving Time local option 890b
Dayton, Jonathan House of Representatives tab 802b
  U.S. Constitution 809c
Dayton, William L. tab 800
Dayton, Ohio 1992a
  government 864b

Dayton, University of 691
D.C. (elec.) *see* Direct current
DDT 741b, 775b, 957c, 1858c
De (in names) *see also under latter part of name, such as* Vega, Lope de
De Amicis, Edmondo 232a, 1387c, *tab* 1478
De Facie in Orbe Lunae (treatise) 1763a
De Forest, Lee 232c, 1152a, 1889a
  vacuum tubes 1284a
De Gaspari, Alcide 2196c
De Gaulle, Charles 232c, 2088b, 2118c, 2155a, 2292b
  visits Andorra 2088c
  World War II 2154c–2155a
De Kooning, Willem *tab* 109
  biography 232c
De Koven, Henry Louis Reginald 170a
  biography 233a
De la littérature (essay) 1380c
De la Mare, Walter 233a
De la Roche, Mazo 1390c
De la Salle, Sieur 2114b
De La Warr, 3rd Baron (1577–1618) 2024a
De l'Allemagne (essay) 1380c
De Lesseps, Ferdinand *see* Lesseps
De Moivre, Abraham 1506c
De Morgan, William Frend *tab* 1477
De Musica (bks., Boethius) 157c
De Plantis (Cesalpino) 1638a
De Profundis (prose, Wilde) 1368b
De Quincy, Thomas 1365c, *tab* 1473
  biography 233c
  Confessions of an English Opium Eater 1399c
De Re Rustica (treatise) 1355b
De Republica (bk., Cicero) 1353c, 1356a
De Rerum Natura (book) 1346a, 1356b
De Sanctis, Francesco 1387c
De Soto, Hernando 234a, 1964b, 2023b
De Valera, Eamon 234a, 2191c
De Vries, Hugo 234b
De Witt, Jan 234b
Dead Sea 1453a, 2192b, 2331a
Deafness 937b, 959b
Deakin, Alfred 2093b
Deane, Silas 232a
Dear Brutus (play) 1369c
Dearborn, Henry *tab* 795
Death customs and rites 1937b
  ancient Egypt 1622c
Death instinct 1957b
Death rate 1859b
Death Valley 2292c
Debating 1328
  parliamentary law 844b
Debenture 590a
Debenture bonds 590a
Debit 590a
Deborah 1453a
Debrecen, Hungary 2174a, 2353b
Debris 488c
Debs, Eugene Victor 232b, 885a, 908b
  presidential candidate *tab* 801, 2063a
Debussy, Claude Achille *tab* 168b, *tab* 172a
  biography 232b
Debye, Peter Joseph Wilhelm 1800a
Décades Da Asia (bk.) 1388c
Decagon 1606b
Decagram *tab* 1500
Decahedron 1606c
Decaliter *tab* 1500
Decameron, The (tales) 1386b, 1401a, *tab* 1466
Decameter *tab* 1500
Decane 1820b
Decastere *tab* 1500
Decatur, Stephen 232b
Decatur, Illinois 1981b
Deccan Plateau people 980c
Decemvirate (commission) 1002c
Decentralization (gov.) 862b
Deciduous forests 1864a
Deciduous plants 1645a
Deciduous teeth 920b
Decigram *tab* 1500, 1873b
Deciliter *tab* 1500
Decimal system 1605b
  Hindu-Arabic 1511a
Decimeter *tab* 1500

Decistere *tab* 1500
Decius 1447a
Deck the Halls (song) 418
Deckle edge 151a
Declaration (law) 872b
Declaration of Independence (U.S.) 1014c, 2012c, 2022a, 2027c
  signers *tab* 803
  text 802–803
Declaration of Rights (England) 2289c
Declaratory judgment 872b
Declensions 1297a
Declination 488c
Decline and Fall of the Roman Empire (bk.) 1401a
Decline of the West (bk.) 1348c
Decomposition (geol.) 447a
Decompression sickness 941b, 1226a
Decoration Day *see* Memorial Day
Decree 872b
Dedekind, Richard 1507b
Deduction (philos.) 1616b, 1620b
Deed (law) 825a, 872b, 907a
Deeds of the Kings of England (bk.) 1425a
Deep (oceans) 488c
Deer 25b, 1860c
  ecology 1816c
Deere, John 720b
Deerfield, Massachusetts Indian massacre 2026c
Deerslayer, The (nov.) 1409a
Defendant 872b
Defenders' Day 842b
Defense, Department of 872b
  Air Force 850c
  bureaus 858c
  education 629c
  establishment *tab* 797
  secretaries of *tab* 797
Defense mechanisms 1957c
Defense of Poetry (essay, Shelley) 1365b
Defiance College 691
Deflation (econ.) 590b
Deflation (erosion) 488c
Defoe, Daniel 1346a, 1363a, *tab* 1469
  biography 232b
  Robinson Crusoe 1415c
Deformation primitive culture 1930c
Deformation (rocks) 488c
  see also Diastrophism
Degas, Edgar 86b, *tab* 108
  biography 232c
  Impressionism 1406c
  Tub, The il 92
Degradation 488c
Degree-day 488c
Dehmel, Richard *tab* 1479
Dehra Dun, India 2353c
Dehydration food preservation 737b
Deianira 1430a, 1434c
Deidamia (opera) 162c
Deirdre 1430a
Deirdre of the Sorrows (drama) 1430a
Deism 1620b
Dekker, Thomas 232c, *tab* 1467
Del (in names) *see also under latter part of name, such as* Castagno, Andrea del
Delacroix, Eugène 85c, *tab* 108
  biography 233a
  Abduction of Rebecca il 112
Delambre, Jean Baptiste Joseph 233a
Deland, Margaretta W. *tab* 1478
Delano, Columbus *tab* 797
Delaroche, Hippolyte Paul *tab* 108
Delaunay, Robert *tab* 109
Delavigne, Casimir *tab* 1473
Delaware 1978
  agriculture 1978b, 1978c
  amendment process 851c
  appointment 852b
  capital punishment 860a
  census (1960) 1970
  climate 1978c
  colleges of 660
  colonial history 2024c
  commercial law 826
  congressional apportionment *tab* 853
  congressmen at large 855a
  county 871c
  economy 1978b–1978c
  electoral votes 876c
  flag *il* 2010
  geography 1978b

government 1978c
  legal holidays 841–842
  people of 1978b
  public school enrollment *tab* 646
  public school expenditures *tab* 644
  referendum 884c
  student enrollment *tab* 645
  U.S. Constitution 809c
Delaware, University of 660
Delaware River 1978a, 1978c, 1989b, 2005a, 2012c, 2015b, 2015c, 2017b, 2293a
Delaware River Aqueduct 1226c
Delaware State College 660
Delaware Water Gap 2017b
Delcassé, Théophile 233b
Del credere agency 872c
Deledda, Grazia 1387c, *tab* 1480
Delegate 872c
Delftware 126c
Delhi, India 980c, 2178a, 2180b, 2180c, 2353b
  see also New Delhi, India
Delibes, Leo *tab* 171c
  biography 233c
Delilah 1453a
  Samson 1459c
Delius, Frederick 169b, *tab* 172b
  biography 233b
Dell (geog.) 488c
Della (in names) *see under latter part of name, such as* Robbia, Luca della
Dello-Joio, Norman 170b
Delphi, Greece legend 1430a
Del rey abajo ninguno (play) 1392a
Delta State College 678
Deltas 449a, 488c
  see also Bottomset beds
Demand (econ.) 590b
Dementia praecox 1953a
Demerara River 2170c
Demeter 1428b, 1430a, 1628a
DeMille, Agnes 184c
DeMille, Cecil 233b
Demiral, Süleyman 2279b
Demiurgos 1752b
Democracy 784c
  ancient Greece 974a
  early American 2022a
Democracy and Education (bk.) 622c
Democracy in America (bk.) *tab* 1474
Democratic Labor Party (Barbados) 2097c
Democratic Party (DP) 2280a
Democratic Party (Turkey) 2279b
Democratic Party (Uganda) 2280a
Democratic Party (U.S.) 872c
  Barnburners 856b
  Republican Party 906a
  rise of 2036b
  third parties 910c
Democratic-Republican Party 872c, 873a, 906a
Democritus 233c, 1557c, 1615b, 1751b, 1798a
  nickname 1462b
  philosophy 1613c
Democritus Junior *see* Burton, Robert
Demosthenes 233c, 1353c, *tab* 1464
Dempsey, Jack 233c
Demurrer 873b
Demuth, Charles *tab* 109
Denby, Edwin *tab* 796, 2068c
Dendrites 939a
Dendritic drainage pattern (rivers) 488c
Dendrochronology 488c
Deneb (star) *tab* 1786
Dengue fever 946
Denishawn Company 184b
Denison University 691
Denmark 2141–2142
  agriculture 2141b
  ceramics *tab* 131, *tab* 132
  cheese *tab* 731b
  climate 2141b
  Congress of Vienna 1023c
  economy 2141b–2141c
  in Faeroe Islands 2311c–2312a
  flag *il* 2183
  geography 2141b
  government 2141c
  in Greenland 2314b–2314c
  history 2142a–2142b
  in Iceland 2176c
  map 2141, *Atlas*-15
  musicians *tab* 172a
  nightingale 47c–48a

Norway and 2230c–2231a
  people of 2141b
  raids on the British Isles 2284a
  religion 2141a, 2142a
  in the Virgin Islands 2004c
  World War I 2142b
  World War II 1028a, 2142b, 2162c
Dennison (ship) 1180b
Dennison, William *tab* 796
Denny, Frederick *tab* 1463a
D'Enrecasteaux Archipelago 2319b
Density (phys.) 1880b, 1917b
  defined 488c–489a
Density (population) 1859b
Density current 489a
Densmore, James 1188a
Dental consonants 1294c
Dentine 920b
Dentistry, career guidance 381c
  cavities 959b
  dental hygienists 383c
  laboratory technicians 384a
  public health 959b
Denudation 489a
Denver, Colorado 1977a, 1977b, 2006c, 2007, 2293b
  government 864b
Denver, University of 659
Deoxyribonucleic acid (DNA) 1841a, 1842a, 1853b, 1855a
  bacteria 1844a
Deoxyribose 1854b
Department (gov.) 873b
Department of (gov.) *see under latter part of name, such as* Agriculture, Department of
Department stores 590b
DePaul University 663, 666
Dependency (gov.) 873b
Dependent Pension Act 2058a
Deportation 873c
Deposition (geology) 455a, 489a
Deposition (law) 873c
Deposition (paint., Fra Angelico) *tab* 110
Deposition of Christ (paint., Rembrandt) *tab* 111
Deprès, Josquin *see* Josquin des Prés
Depression (econ.) 590c
Depression (geology) 489a
Depression (psych.) 1953c
Depression of 1837 Canada 2115b–2115c
Depression of 1929 U.S. 903a, 2071c
Depression of 1930s Australia 2093c–2094a
  Barbados 2097c
  Brazil 2104b
  Canada 2118a
  Czechoslovakia 2140a
  New Zealand 2227a
  Norway 2231c
  Panama 2234c
  Sweden 2269a
Depth psychology Freud S. 1957b
  Jung, Carl 1958a
Depths of the Sea, The (bk.) 462a
Deputy 873c
Derain, André *tab* 108
Derbend rugs 1110c
Derby, George Horatio pseudonyms *tab* 1463a
Derby, England ceramics 127c, *tab* 131–132
Dermatitis 941b
Dermis 918a
Dern, George H. *tab* 796
Derzhavin, Gabriel 1389a
Desalinization 489a, 1245b
Desargues, Gérard 234a, 1505a
Descant 174c
Descartes, René 234a, 986c, 1379a, *tab* 1467, 1616c
  analytic geometry 1504b, 1590a
  coordinate system 1553c
  topology 1599a
Descenders (print.) 151a
Description (writing) 1318c
Desdemona 1401a
Desert Land Act 904b
Desert pavement 489b
Deserted Village, The (poem) 1363c, 1401a
Deserts 489a, 1865a
  Angola 2306a
  Arizona 1975
  California 1976c
  Chile 2121b

Ethiopia 2146a
Jordan 2201c
Kuwait 2205c
Libya 2209b, 2209c
Mali 2214c
Mauritania 2216a
Mongolia 2220b
Pakistan 2232b
China 2123c–2124a, 2124b, 2124c
erosion 447c
Iran 2188c
Israel 2192a, 2192b
Saudi Arabia 2246c
shelter 1930a
soils 743a
South Yemen 2253c
Sudan 2265c
Syria 2270c
Tunisia 2276c
U. A. R. (Egypt) 2280b–2280c
U.S. 1963b, 2292c
U.S.S.R. 2255b
Yemen 2302a
see also under names of individual deserts, such as Sahara
Desiccation 489b
Desiderio da Settignano 121c, tab 125
Design painting 82a
Designers fashion 375a
Deskey, Donald 1102a
Des Moines, Iowa 1982a, 1982b, 2007a
government 864a
Des Moines River 2007a
Desmoulins, Camille 234a, 1008a
Desoxyribonucleic acid see Deoxyribonucleic acid
Despiau, Charles tab 125
Despotism 784c
Des Prés, Josquin see Josquin des Prés
Desroches Island 2308b, 2308c
Dessalines, Jean Jacques 234a, 2172b
Destouches, Philippe tab 1469
Destour Party (Tunisia) 2277b
Destruct (astronautics) 1778b
Destructive interference (light) 1905a
Detergents 1224a
Determinants (math.) 1505b
Determinism (philos.) 1620b
Detritus 489b
Detroit-Canada Tunnel 1226
Detroit Free Press tab 1171
Detroit Institute of Technology 676
Detroit, Michigan 1985c, 1986a, 2007a
War of 1812 2034b
Detroit News tab 1171
Detroit River 2007a
Detroit, University of 676
Dett, Nathaniel 170b, 171a
Deucalian 1430a
Deuterium 1806a
atomic weight 1806a
Deuteronomy (Bib.) 1453a
Deutsches Requiem (cantata) 167b
Deutschland see Germany
Deutschland Uber Alles (song) tab 1474
Deva 1430b
Devaluation 590c
Devens, Charles tab 796
Devereux, Penelope 1461a
Devereux, Robert (1567–1601) see Essex, 2nd Earl of
Deviated septum 941b
Devil 1430b
Mephistopheles 1439b
Satan 1459c
Devil (print.) 151a
Deville, Henri Sainte-Claire 1195a
Devils Island 2312c
Devil's-paintbrush see Hawkweed
Devils Tower National Monument 2016b
Devolution 873c
Devonian Period tab 456, 489b
Dew 473b, 489b
Dew point 470a, 489b–489c
Dewar, Sir James 234b, 1917b
Dewar vessel 1917b
Dewberry see Blackberry
Dewey, Charles M. tab 108
Dewey, George 234b
Spanish-American War 2060b
Dewey, Thomas E. 234b, 2077c
presidential candidate tab 801
Republican Party 906b

Dewey, John 622c, 623c, 624a, 1948b
biography 234b
philosophy 1619a
Dew-point hygrometer 470a
Dexter, Samuel tab 795
Dextrose 744b
Dhahran, Saudi Arabia 2346c
Dhaulagiri Peak 2331a
Dhu, Roderick 1401a, 1408c
Di (in names) see under latter part of name, such as Credi, Lorenzo di
Dia, Mamadou 2248b
Diabetes insipidus 941b
Diabetes mellitus 926a, 941b
Diablo cojuelo, El (nov.) 1391c
Diablo Dam 1206
Diacritical marks 1314b
Diadumenos (sculp.) 116c
Diaeresis 1314c
Diaghiley, Sergei P. 184a, 234c
Dial, The (periodical) 1373c
Dialectic (philos.) 1620c
Dialectical materialism 1618c
Dialogues (bk., Lucian) 1354a
Dialysis 489c
Diamini Prince Makhosini 2267c
Diamond (baseball) 1704b
Diamonds 489c
Angola 2306b
Brazil 2103a
Central African Republic 2119b
Congo (Kinshasa) 2134c
crystal structure 1870c
etching 138a
Ghana 2164a
hardness 453a, tab 1192b
Ivory Coast 2197a
Lesotho 2208b
Liberia 2209a
Sierra Leone 2248c
South Africa 2252b
South West Africa 2322c
Tanzania 2272b
U.S.S.R. 2256b
Venezuela 2297b
Diana (myth.) 1425a, 1430b, 1438c, 1453a
see also Artemis
Diana (Sp. poem) 1391b
Diana and Her Nymphs (paint., Domenichino) tab 112
Diana of the Crossways (nov.) 1368a, 1401a
Diana of the Fountain (sculp.) 122b
Diane de Poitiers 1095b
Diapason (mus.) 174c
Diaper rash 941b
Diaphantine analysis 1603a
Diaphragm (anat.) 921a, 922a
Diaphragm cell 1199b
Diarmait 1430b
Diary of Samuel Pepys see Pepy's Diary
Dias, Antonio Gonçalves see Gonçalves Dias
Dias, Bartholomeu 234c, 2242a, 2253a
Diaspora 1629c
Diaspore clay 1201c
Diastole 923b
Diastrophism 450b, 451a, 455a
defined 489c
Diatomaceous earth (diatomite) 450b, 1847c
explosives 1766c
Diatomaceous ooze 489c
Diatoms 450b, 465b, 1847c
Diatonic (mus.) 157b, 174c
Diavolo, Fra see Fra Diavolo
Díaz, Adolfo 2228b
Diaz, Armando 234c
Díaz, Julio Lozano 2173b
Díaz, Porfirio 234c, 2219b
Diaz de Bivar, Ruy see Cid, El
Diaz de La Peña, Narcisse 86a, tab 108
Díaz Ordaz, Gustavo 2219c–2220a
Diazo process (duplicating) 1164c
Dice tab 1219a
probability 1597c
Dichroic materials 1905c
Dickens, Charles 1346c, 1366c, tab 1475
biography 234c
pen name 1461b

—Novels
Bleak House 1397c
Christmas Carol 1399a
Cricket on the Hearth 1400b
David Copperfield 1400c
Dombey and Son 1401b
Great Expectations 1405a
Hard Times 1405b
Nicholas Nickleby 1411b
Old Curiosity Shop 1411c
Oliver Twist 1411c
Pickwick Papers 1412c
Tale of Two Cities 1418a
Dickerson, Mahlon tab 795
Dickinson, Don tab 796
Dickinson, Emily 1374c, tab 1477
biography 237c
Dickinson, Jacob M. tab 796
Dickinson, John 2030a
nickname tab 1463
U.S. Constitution 809c
Dickinson College 695
Dickinson State College 690
Dickory, dickory, dock (nursery rhyme) 408a
Dicotyledons 1638a, 1642c, 1643a–1643b
Dictator (ancient Rome) 873c
Dictatorship 784c, 881b
censorship 862a
Middle Ages 985c
modern 873c, 988c
Dictionary abbreviations 1338–1340
biblical names 1450–1461
biographical 189–368
economics and business 583–606
governmental and legal 849–914
how to use 1321a
legal procedure 817–827
literary allusions 1393–1421
music terms 172–179
mythology, legend and folklore 1421–1449
printer's terms 150–153
sobriquets and pseudonyms 1461–1463
Dictionary (Olafsson) tab 1467
Dictionary of the English Language (Johnson) 1363c
Diderot, Denis 1380b, tab 1470
biography 237a
Didjero-Doo Man 1937c
Dido (leg. q.) 1430b
Dido, Queen (Carthage) 1000b
Dido and Aeneas (opera, Purcell) 161c
Didot, Firmin 145a
Didot, François 144c
Didot, Pierre 145a
Die casting 1267b
Die cutting 150b
Diederich, Hunt tab 125
Diefenbaker, John 2118c
Diem, Ngo Dinh 318b, 2301a, 2301b
Dien Bien Phu, Battle of 2301a
Dies 1246a
Diesel, Rudolf 237a, 1132a
Diesel engines 1132a
locomotives 1178c
submarines 1182a
Diet
public health 955c
Diet (gov.) 874a
Dietitians (career) 384a
Dietrich von Bern see Theodoric (the Great)
Difenbaker, John George 237a
Differential calculus 1504b, 1602a
Differential psychology 1951b
Differential weathering 489c
Diffraction (phys.) 1905b, 1917c
Diffusion 1917c
Digestion plants, 1646c
Digestive system 920b
disorders 956a
higher animals 1825b
intestines 920c
mouth 920b
phases of digestion 920c
stomach 920b
Diggs, Thomas 1282c
Digital computers 1236b, 1243a
Dihedral angle 1601b
Dijon, France sculpture 120b
Dikes (geol.) 450c, 489c
Dili, Portuguese Timor 2320b, 2353b
Dill 1665a
Dillard University 671
Diller, a dollar (nursery rhyme) 411a
Dillon, C. Douglas tab 796
Dillon, George 1381c

Dimashaq, Syria 2353a
Dimension (art) 82a
Dimeter 1401a
Diminished chord 174c
Diminishing returns 590c
Diminuendo 174c
Dinaric Alps 2303a
Dinesen, Isak 237a
Dingley Tariff Bill 2059b
Dingo see Dog
Din-i-Ilahi (religion) 2180c
Dining room 1107c, 1108a
Dinoflagellates 465b
Dinosaur 490a
Dinwiddie, Robert 237a
Diocletian 237b
George, Saint 1446b
sculpture 118c
Diodes p-n junction diode 1890b
tunnel 1890c
Diodorus Siculus Historical Library 1354a
Diogenes 237b, 1614a
Diomedes 1430c
Dion Chrysostomus tab 1464
Dione 1430c
Dionysus (Bacchus) (myth.) 1352b, 1430c
Midas 1440a
Dionysius the Elder 237b
Damocles 1429c
Dionysius of Halicarnassus 237b, 1002c
Diophantus 1503b
Diori, Hamani 2229a
Diorite (rock) 490a
Dioscorides 1638a
Dioscuri see Castor and Pollux
Dip (geol.) 490a
Diphtheria tab 946
Diploid 1850b
Diplomatic service 874a
Dirce 117c
Direct current 1882b
generators 1138b, 1885a
motors 1141c
rectifiers 1919c
transmission 1133b
Directional gyro 1163c
Director (bus.) 591a
Dirge 174c
Dirigibles 1154c
Dis (myth.) 1430c, 1444c
Disarmament United Nations 993c
Disarmament Commission (U. N.) 993c
Disasters deaths in U.S. annually 954b
hurricanes 475b
Discharge (waters) 490a
Disconformity (rocks) 490a–490b
Discontinuity (geology) 490b
see also Earth structure
Discord (mus.) 174c
Discordant pluton (rocks) 490b
Discount 591a
Discourse of the Campaign of Igor (epic) 1389a
Discourse on Method (Descartes) 1504b
Discourses on Two New Sciences (Galileo) 1758a
Discourses by Way of Essays (Bacon) 1402a
Discovery, Age of 986a
Discriminant (math.) 1603a
Discrimination economic 591b
employment 836c
labor unions 839a
Discus Thrower (Discobolos) (sculp., Myron) 116b
Discus throwing 1739a
Diseases 940–945
bacterial 1845a
cattle 727c
control 955b
eye 928c
fungal 1847a
fur farming 738b
glossary of 940–945
goats 739a
immunity 1849a
infectious 954c, tab 946–948
mental illness 1953a
nutritional 920a
protozoan 1848c
rickettsial 1846c
viruses 1842c
yeast 1847c

see also under the names of various diseases, such as Measles
Dishonor (banking) 591b
Dishwasher 1260b
Disintegration (geol.) 447b
see also Mechanical weathering
Disk springs 1282c
Disney, Walt 237b
Disneyland 237b
Dispersed harmony 174c
Dispersion (light) 1904b, 1917c
Displaced persons 884a, 1003a
relief agencies 905b
Display type (print.) 151a
Display workers (careers) 375a
Disraeli, Benjamin 237b, *tab* 1474
nickname 1461c
Dissection 490b
Dissociation (psych.) 1957a
Dissociation of affect 1953b
Dissolution 874c
Dissonance (mus.) 174c
Distillation 1933b
Distortion (optics) 1908c
Distributary (geog.) 449a, 490b
Distribution (econ.) 591b
District 875a
District courts 792b, 875a
District of Columbia capital punishment 860b
colleges of 660–661
commercial law *tab* 826
government 875a
labor legislation 832c
legal holidays 841–842
public school enrollment *tab* 646
public school expenditures *tab* 644
student enrollment *tab* 645
see also Washington, D.C.
District of Columbia Teachers College 660
Dithyramb 1352b
Dittersdorf, Karl von *tab* 171c
Diu Island 2331b
Diurnal range 490b
Divertimento 174c
Divide (ridge) 490c
Dividends (fin.) 591b
Dividends (math.) 1603a
Divine Comedy, The (poem) 985a, 1346a, 1386a, 1401b, *tab* 1466
Divine Fire, The (nov.) 1370b
Divine Right of Kings 887b
Diving (sport) 1246b, 1734a
Diving bell 1246b
Divisi (mus.) 174c
Division (math.) 1517c
algebra 1534a
algorithm 1521a
definition 1603a
fractions 1529a
Division of labor 603c–604a, 1935a, 1943b
Divisor (math.) 1603a
Divorce 875b
decree 872b
Nevada 1988c
U.S. 1941c
Dix, Dorothy Lynde 1954b
Dix, John A. *tab* 796
Dix, Otto *tab* 109
Dixie (song) 1401b
Dixon, Jeremiah 2025a
Dizziness 937b
Dizzy (nickname) *see* Disraeli, Benjamin
Djakarta, Indonesia 2186b, 2186c
Djibouti, French Territory of the Afars and the Issas 2313b, 2313c, 2353c
DNA *see* Deoxyribonucleic acid
Dnepr River 2331b
Dneprodzerzhinsk, Soviet Union 2353c
Dnepropetrovsk, Soviet Union 2353c
Doak, William N. *tab* 797
Doane College 681
Dobbin, James C. *tab* 796
Döbereiner, Johann Wolfgang 237c, 1799c
Dobruja 2245a
Dobson (Henry) Auston 1369b, *tab* 1477
Dobsonfly 25b
Dock 1665a
Doctor Faustus (Marlow) 1360c, 1403c, 1432b

Doctor Jekyll and Mr. Hyde (nov.) 1368b, 1401c
Doctor Zhivago (nov.) 1390b
Dodder 1665a–1665b
Dodecagon 1606c
Dodecahedron 1606c
Dodecanese Islands 2165a–2196b
Dodge, Mary Mapes *tab* 1477
Dodgson, Charles L. *see* Carroll, Lewis
Dog in the Manger (fable) 443a
Dog and the Shadow, The (fable) 442c
Dogbane 1665b
Dogbane family 1665b
Doge Leonardo Loredano (paint.) *tab* 111
Dogfish 25c
Dogger Bank 2331b
Dogs 25c
anthropology 1934a
hearing 1894a
Dog tent 1709c
Dogtooth violet 1665b
Dogwood 1665b
flowering 1987a, 1990c, 1997c
Dogwood family 1665b
Doha, Qatar 2242b, 2353c
Dohnanyi, Ernst von 169c, *tab* 172b
Dolci, Carlo *tab* 107
Doldrums 490c
Dole, Sanford Ballard 237c, 2060b
Dolinen 490c
Dollfuss, Engelbert 237c, 2096a
Dolls 398c, 406c
Doll's House, A (play) 1401b
Dolly Varden trout *il* 1717
Dolomite 450b, 490c
Dolores, Mexico 2218c
Dolphins 25c–26a, *il* 1717
Dom João, Prince Regent 2103c
Dombey and Son (nov.) 1367a, 1401b
Dome (arch.) 73a
Dome (geology) 490c
Domenichino *tab* 107
Diana and Her Nymphs tab 112
biography 237c
Domesday Book 862b
Domesday survey of 1086 2285a
Domestic cat 19c
Dominant (mus.) 175a
Dominant traits 1850b
Dominic, Saint 985b, 998b, 1755b
biography 237c
Dominica 2311
Dominican College 707
Dominican College of San Rafael 656
Dominican Republic 2142–2143, 2172b
agriculture 2142c
climate 2142c
economy 2142c–2143a
formerly Santo Domingo 2054c, 2061c
flag *il* 2183
geography 2142c
government 2143a
history 2143a–2143b
map 2143, *Atlas*-57
1965 uprising 2082c
people of 2142c
religion 2142c
see also Hispaniola
Dominican Revolutionary Party 2143b
Dominicans
science, history of 1755b
Dominion (gov.) 875b
Dominion of New England 2027a
Don Carlos (opera, Verdi) 167b
Don Carlos (play, Schiller) 1384b
Don Giovanni (opera, Mozart) 164b, 1401c
Don Juan (Byron) 1365a, 1401c
Don Juan (lit. char.) 1401b
creation 1392a
Don Quixote (nov.) 1391c, 1401c, *tab* 1467
Don River 2331b
Don Roderigo Vazquez (paint.) *tab* 111
Don Sebastian Martinez (paint.) *tab* 112
Donaldson, Jesse M. *tab* 796
Donatello 121b, *tab* 125
biography 237c
Donatello (lit. char.) 1401b
Donaudy, Stefano 168a
Dondi, Giovanni de 1162a

Donegal Bay 2331b
Donelson, A. J. *tab* 800
Donizetti, Gaetano 166c, *tab* 171c
biography 238a
Donkey *see* Ass
Donne, John 1362b, *tab* 1467
biography 238a
Donnelly, Ignatius *tab* 801
Donor and St. John the Baptist (paint.) *tab* 111
Dooley, Mr. (pseud.) *see* Dunne, Finley Peter
Doolittle, Hilda 1371b, *tab* 1480
biography 238a
Dopants 1917c
Doping (phys.) 1917c
Doppler, Christian Johann 1794a, 1894a
Doppler effect 1794a, 1894a
astronomy 1790c
Doppler shift 1787b
astronomy 1790c
Dorat, Claude 1378b
Doré, Paul Gustave 238a
Dorians 83c, 973c
Doric order (arch.) 75a
sculpture 116a
Dornberger, Walter 1768b
Dorr, Thomas 238a
Doryphoros (sculp.) 116c
Dos Passos, John 1375c, *tab* 1480
biography 238a
Dost, Mohammed Khan 238b
Dostoevski, Feodor 1389c, *tab* 1476
biography 238b
Dou, Gerard *tab* 107
Douala, Cameroon 2109c, 2353c
Douay Bible 1460c
Double argument formulas (math.) 1585b
Double bar (mus.) 175a
Double bass (mus.) 175a
Double flat (mus.) 175a
Double jeopardy 875c
Double leaded (print.) 151a
Double octave 175a
Double sharp 175a
Double stars 1790b
discovery of 1759b
Double time (mus.) 174c
Double-base powders 1766c, 1767a, 1778c
Dougherty, Paul *tab* 108
Doughty, Thomas 104b, *tab* 108
Douglas, Alfred Bruce 238b
Douglas, Archibald 1461b
Douglas, Gavin 1360a
Douglas, Alaska 2008c
Douglas fir 1665c, 1992c
Douglas, Isle of Man 2316a, 2353c
Douglas, John Sholto *see* Queensbury, 8th Marquis of
Douglas, L. C. *tab* 1480
Douglas, Stephen Arnold 238b
Kansas-Nebraska Bill 2041c
nickname 1462b
presidential candidate *tab* 801, 2043a
Douglas, William O. Supreme Court *tab* 802a
Douglas-Home, Alec 2292a
Douglas Island 2008c
Douglass College of Rutgers University 682
Doulton pottery 128a, *tab* 132
Doumergue, Gaston 238c
Doumic, René *tab* 1479
Douw, Gerard *see* Dou, Gerard
Dove *see* Pigeon
Dove prism 1909b
Dover, Delaware 1978a, 2007a
Dover, New Hampshire
founding 2024c
Dover Castle 2284
Dow, Gerard *see* Dou, Gerard
Dow, Neal *tab* 801
Dowland, John 161a, *tab* 171c
Down (upland) 490c
Down beat (mus.) 175a
Down by the Station (song) 419
Downing, Jack *see* Smith, Seba
Doxology 175a
Doyle, Sir Arthur Conan 1370a, *tab* 1479
biography 238c
Sherlock Holmes 1417a
Draco 238c
Draft (mil.) *see* Conscription
Draft riots 868c
Draftsmen 373c

Drag 1154b
Drag (geol.) 491a
Dragonfly 26a
Dragons 1430c
Drainage basin 491a
Drainage canals 1160b
Drake, Francis American explorations 2023b
biography 238c
Lost Colony 2023c
Drake, Joseph Rodman 1461c, *tab* 1473
Drake Passage 2331b
Drake University 667
Drakensberg Mountains 2208a, 2331b
Dram *tab* 1500
Drama 1401c
American 1376c
English 1360b
French classic 1379a
French 18th century 1380b
German 1384
Greek, ancient 1352b
Italian 1387a
Russian 1389c
Spanish 1391c
Drau River 2331b
Draughts (game) 1713a
Drava River 2173c, 2331b
Dravidian languages *tab* 1336
classification 1333a
Dravidians 980b, 1624b
India 981a
Drawing
career guidance 374c
etching 137a
photoengraving 149a
Drawing room 1094b
Dream of St. Ursula (paint.) *tab* 112
Drebbel, Cornelis 1182c
Dred Scott Decision 792b, 2042b
Dredging 491a, 1246c
Dreiser, Theodore 1375c, *tab* 1480
biography 238c
Dresden, Germany 2158a, 2353c
Dresden china 127c, *tab* 131
Dresden Gallery tab 110
Dress *see* Clothing
Drew, John, Jr. 239a
Drew University 682
Drexel Institute of Technology 695
Dreyfus, Alfred 239a, 2154a
Dreyfus Affair 2154a
Drift 491a
see also Continental drift
Drift-ice 491a
Drilling (mining) 1269c
petroleum 1217c
Drills (tools) 1266a
Drina River 2303a, 2331b
Drinkwater, John 239a, *tab* 1480
Dripstone (minerals) 491a
Driskill Mountain 1983c
Drives (psych.) 1949a
Drizzle 473b
Droch *see* Bridges, Robert
Drogheda, Ireland 2191b
Dromedary 727a
see also Camel
Drone (mus.) 175a
Dropsy *see* Edema
Drosophila genetics 1853a
Drossing 1216a
Droste-Hulsoff, Annette von 1385a
Drought 491a
Drown 491a
Drug Label Act 2062c
Drugs pharmaceutical industry 1273c
psychology 1958b
Drumlins 449b, 491b
Drummond, Henry 239a
Drummond, W. H. 1390c, *tab* 1478
Drums (mus.) 175a
Drupes 1646a
Drury College 679
Drusus, Nero Claudius 239a
Dry 491b
Dry cells (elec.) 1131c, 1883a
Dry farming 491b
Dry hole 491b
Dry ice 1899c
Dry measure, U. S. system *tab* 1500
Dry offset printing 1174a
Dry point (art) 138a

Dry snow 491b
Dry valley 491b
Dryads 1430c
Dryden, John 1358a, 1362c, *tab* 1468
  biography 239b
  Poet Laureate 1413b
Dryer 1260a
Dryopithecines 1923c
Dry-World Culture Region 769a–769b
Du Barry, Comtesse (Marie Jean Becu) 239b
Du Bellay, Joachim *see* Bellay, Joachim du
Du Maurier, Daphne 239c
Du Maurier, George 239c, *tab* 1477
  Peter Ibbetson 1412c
  Trilby 1419b
Du Pont (family) 240a
Du Pont, Eleuthère Irénée 240a
Du Pont, Victor Marie 240a
Du Pont de Nemours, Pierre Samuel 240a
Du Pont de Nemours & Company 1199b, 1978b, 2015c
Duane, William *tab* 795
Dublin, Ireland 2190b, 2190c, 2191b, 2191c, 2353c
Dubois, François Théodore 168b
Dubois, Paul *tab* 125
Dubos, René 1845c
Dubuffet, Jean 109
Dubuque, Iowa 1982c
  schools 625c
Dubuque, University of 667
Duccio di Buoninsegna 106
Duchamp, Marcel *tab* 109, 239b
Duchamp-Villon, Raymond *tab* 125
Duchesne College of the Sacred Heart 681
Duchess forms of address *tab* 1120
Duchess of Malfi, The (drama) 1361c
Duchy 875c
Duckbill 26b
Duckpins 1708a
Ducks 26a–26b, 731c
Ductile minerals 453a
Dudevant, Baroness *see* Sand, George
Dudgeon, Richard 1169a
Dudley, John 1022c

Dudley, Robert (Earl of Leicester) 296a
Due process of law 875c
Duero River 2263b, 2331b
Duesbury, William *tab* 131
Duet 175a
Dufay, Guillaume *tab* 171b
Dufaycolor process 1173a
Dufy, Raoul *tab* 108, *tab* 109
  biography 239b
Duisberg, Germany 2159
Dukas, Paul *tab* 172a
  biography 239b
Duke forms of address *tab* 1120
Duke of *see under the latter part of the name, such as* Windsor, Duke of
Duke University 688
Dulcimers 155c
Dulles, John Foster *tab* 796
  biography 239b
Duluth, Minnesota 1986, 1986b, 1999a
Dumas, Alexandre (1802–1870) (pere) *il* 208, 1381a, *tab* 1474
  biography 239c
  Count of Monte Cristo 1400a
  Three Musketeers 1418c
Dumas, Alexandre (1824–1895) (fils) 239c, *tab* 1476
Dumas, Jean Baptiste André 239c
Dumbarton Oaks 876a
Dummy (print.) 151a
Dumping (econ.) 591b
Dun *see* Downs
Dunbar, Paul Laurence 239c, *tab* 1480
Dunbarton College of Holy Cross 660
Duncan (lit.) 1401c, 1409c
Duncan, Isadora 183c, 184b
Duncan, Norman *tab* 1480
Duncan I, King (Scotland) 1020a
Dunciad, The (poem) 1363a
Dunedin, New Zealand 2226c
Dunes (geog.) 447c, 491c
  longitudinal 505b
  parabolic 509c
  transverse 518c
Dunkirk World War II evacuation of 1028b
Dunne, Finley Peter pseudonym 1461c

Dunoyer de Segonzac, André *tab* 109
Duns Scotus, John 240b
Dunsany, 18th Baron (Edward John Plunkett) 240a, *tab* 1480
Dunstable, John 160c, *tab* 171b
Dunstan, Saint 240a
Dunster, Henry 145a
Duodecimal system 1512c, 1605b
Duoro River 2241a, 2241b
Dupin, Amandine *see* Sand, George
Duplicating machines 1164b
Duplication (art) 136a
Dupré, Jules 86a, *tab* 108
  biography 240b
Duquesne University 695
Dura-Europos 969c
Duralumin *tab* 1193
Durand, Asher Brown 104b, *tab* 108
Durand, Peter 1239b
Durant, Will *tab* 1481
Durante, Francesco *tab* 171c
Durban, South Africa 2252b, 2354a
Dürer, Albrecht *tab* 106, 143c
  Artists Father tab 111
  biography 240b
  etching 136b
  Madonna of the Cut Pear tab 113
  Kaiser Friedrich Museum *tab* 109
  woodcuts 140c
Duress (law) 820a
Durham, Earl of 1001a
Durham, North Carolina 1991a
Durkheim, Emile 1622a
Durkin, Martin *tab* 797
Durrani, Ahmad 2085c
Durrell, Lawrence 240a
Durrës, Albania 2354a
Duruy, Victor *tab* 1475
D'Urville, Dumont 2313a
Duse, Eleanora 240b
Dushan, Stephen 2304a
Dushanbe, Soviet Union 2354a
Düsseldorf, Germany 2354a
Dust 491c
Dust, ground (art) 138c
Dust bowl 491c
Dust storm 491c
Dust devil 491c

Dutch art architecture 77c, 78a
  ceramics 126c, *tab* 130
  furniture 1095c, 1096a
  painting *tab* 106–1098
Dutch East India Company *see* East India Company
Dutch elm disease 1666a
Dutch Guiana 2225c *see also* Surinam
Dutch language classification 1333b
  cognates *tab* 1297b
Dutch New Guinea *see* Netherlands New Guinea
Dutch War (1672–1678) 2152a
Dutchman's-breeches 1665c
Dutchman's pipe 1665c
Dutra, Enrico Gaspar 2104c
Duval, Gabriel Supreme Court *tab* 802a
Duvalier, François 2172a, 2172b
Duveneck, Frank *tab* 108
Dvina River 2331b
Dvořák, Anton 168c, *tab* 172a
  biography 240b
Dwarf banana *il* 1661
Dwarfism 941c
Dwarfs (myth) 1430c
Dwellings *see* Housing
Dwight, John 128a
Dwight, Timothy 1372b
Dyadic number system 1605b
Dyer's Case 876a
Dyes 1247b
Dye-transfer process (duplicating) 1164c
Dying Gaul, The (sculp.) 117b
Dykstra, Clarence A. 240b
Dynamic compressors 1242c
Dynamics (mus.) 175a
Dynamics (phys.) 1870a, 1875b
Dynamite 1207c
  Nobel, A. 1766c
Dynasts, The (play) 1368a
Dyne 491c
Dynesecond 1880a
D'Youville College 684
Dysentery amebic *tab* 946
  bacillary *tab* 946
Dysprosium 1832
  atomic weight *tab* 1805

E

E. I. Du Pont de Nemours & Co. *see* Du Pont de Nemours & Company
Eadmund II, King (England) *see* Edmund, King (England)
Eads, James 1197a
Eads, James Buchanan 240c
Eads Bridge 1197, 1224b
Eagle Mountain 1986b
Eagles 26b
Eakins, Thomas 104b, *tab* 108
  biography 240c
Eames, Charles 1102a
Eardrums 1894b
Earhart, Amelia 1156a
  biography 240c
Earl forms of address *tab* 1120
Earle, Thomas *tab* 800
Earlham College 666
Early, Jubal Anderson 240c
Early American architecture 78b, 1100b
Early American furniture 1108b
Early Bird (satellite) 1162b, *tab* 1163, 1163a
Earnshaw, Thomas 1162b
Ears 937a
  health 959b
  hearing 1894a
Earth 757–759
  animal kingdom 766c
  atmosphere 762–765
  biosphere 765–766
  climate 764–765a

composition 757b
condensation 763c
continental drift 759c
continents 759c–761a
crust of 757b
defined 491c–492a
earthquakes 761a
evaporation 763c
geologic time 759b
history 758c–759b
hydrologic cycle 765a–765b
hydrosphere 765
International Date Line 758b–758c
ionosphere 763b
landforms 761a–761c
latitude 758c
lithosphere 759–762
longitude 758c
man 766c
mineral deposits 761c–762a
ocean basins 759c
oceans 765b–765c
origin 758c–759a
ozonosphere 763a–763b
plant world 766b–766c
precipitation 764a–764c
shape of 757a–757b
size of 757a–757b
soils 762a–762c
stratosphere 763a
structure 492b–492c
thermal balance 763b–763c
time 758a–758b
time zones 758b
troposphere 763a
volcanoes 761a
wind patterns 763c–764a
Earth (planet) 447a, 1780b, *tab* 1782, 1783a
  age 454b
  albedo 1793c
  atmosphere 1840a

Bode's law *tab* 1781
comets 1784a
distance from sun 1780c
eclipse 1794a
light 1793a
Meteor Crater 1784b
meteors 1784b
orbit 1771c
origin 454a
planetary probes 1771b
rocks 449c
tides 464c
Venus 1782c
Earth dams 1205c
Earth sciences 447–520, 1869c
  careers 390b
Earthenware 128a, *tab* 130–131
  manufacture 1220c
Earthflow 492a
Earthlight 1794a
Earthly Paradise, The (epic) 1369a
Earthquakes 451c, 492a, 761a
  seismograph 1778b
Earth-sun relationships 757b–758c
Earthworms 26c, 1862c
Earwigs 26c
East, Edward Murray 721a
East African Federation 878c
East Anglia, Kingdom of 2284a
East Carolina College 688
East Central State College 693
East Chicago, Indiana 1981c, 2007c
East China Sea 2331b–2331c
East Germany *see* Germany, East
East India Company, British 864c–865a, 2099c, 2128b, 2288a–2288b
  charter 863b
  Dutch 2023b, 2120b, 2187c, 2253a

East Indies 2331c
  badger 15a
  deer 25b
  eagle 26b
  flying lemur 34b
  gibbon 35b–35c
  horseshoe crab 39c
  marten 45a
East Liverpool, Ohio
  pottery 129a, 130a
East London, South Africa 2354a
East Lynne (nov.) 1401c
East Prussia 2157a
East River 2018b
East Siberian Sea 2331c
East Stroudsburg State College 695
East Tennessee State University 700
East Texas Baptist College 701
East Texas State University 702
Easter Monday 842a
Eastern Baptist College 695
Eastern Desert 2280c
Eastern Empire *see* Byzantine Empire
Eastern Ghats 2177b
Eastern goldfinch 1982a, 1989b
Eastern Illinois University 664
Eastern Island 2001b
Eastern Kentucky University 670
Eastern Mennonite College 704
Eastern Michigan University 676
Eastern Montana College 680
Eastern Nazarene College 674
Eastern New Mexico University 683
Eastern Oregon College 693

Eastern Roman Empire *see* Byzantine Empire
Eastern Samoa *see* American Samoa
Eastern Washington State College 705
Eastlake, Charles Locke 240c
Eastman, George 241a, 1172b
Easton, Pennsylvania 1993b, 2005a
Eaton, John H. *tab* 795
Ebb current 492c
Ebers, Georg Moritz 241a, *tab* 1477
Ebert, Friedrich 241a
Ebner-Eschenbach, Marie von 1385a
Ebony 1665c
Ebony family 1665c
Ebro River 2331c
Eça de Queiroz, José María 1388c
Ecclesiastes (Bib.) 1453a
Ecclesiastical History of Britain (bk., Bede) 1358c
Ecclesiastical History of New England (bk.) 1372b
Ecclesiastical Polity (bk.) *tab* 1466
Ecclesiasticus (Bib.) 1453a
Echegaray, José 1392b, *tab* 1477
Echeverría, Esteban 1393a
Echinus 75a
Echo (myth) 1431a
Echo (sound) 175a, 1893b, 1917c
Echo I 1163a
Echo II 1163a
Echo chamber 1917c
Eck, Johann 241a
Eckener, Hugo 241a
Eckert, J. Presper, Jr. 1243b
Eckhart, Meister 241a, 1383b, *tab* 1465
Eclampsia 941b
Eclectic teaching 623a
Eclecticism 77c, 1102a
  architecture 78c
  furniture 1101a
Eclipses 1794a
Ecliptic 1794b
Ecliptic year 1797c
Eclogue 1402a
Eclogues (Bucolics) (Vergil) 1354a, 1356c, *tab* 1464
Ecology 492c, 1859a
  defined 1638a
  niche 1860c
Econometrics 591c
Economic Advisers, Council of 876a
Economic Co-operation Administration (ECA) 1016a
Economic geography 771–775
  Africa 771c–772b
  Asia 772b–773b
  Australia 771a
  Europe 773b–774c
  North America 774c–775c
  South America 771a–771c
Economic and Social Council (UN) 991b
Economic control 876a
Economic Co-operation Administration 876b
Economic geology 447a, 458–459
Economics 523–606
  books that influenced 1348a
  career guidance 390c
  definition 591c
  effect of technology 1125c
  types of economies 528b
ECOSOC *see* Economic and Social Council
Ecosystems 1859a, 1860b
Ectopic pregnancy 927a
Ecuador 2133a, 2143–2144, 2234c
  agriculture 2143c–2144b
  economy 2144a–2144b
  flag *il* 2183
  frigate bird 34c
  geography 2143c–2144a
  government 2144b
  history 2144b–2144c
  Indians 2144a, 2144b
  League of Nations 1012c
  map 2144, *Atlas*-50
  Negroes 2144a
  people of 2144a
  religion 2143c, 2144b
  tapir mammals 62b
Eczema 941b
Edam cheese *tab* 731c
Edaphology 492c
Eddas (epics) 1402a, *tab* 1465
Eddies 465a
Eddington, Arthur Stanley 241a, 1348b
Eddy, Mary Baker 241b

Eddystone Lighthouse 1167a, 1201b
Edea, Cameroon 2354a
Edelweiss 1665c–1666a
Edema 924c, 941b
Eden, Anthony 241b, 2292a
Eden, Garden of 1453b
Edgewood College 707
Edgeworth, Maria 1366a, *tab* 1471
  Castle Rackrent 1398c, *tab* 1471
Edict of Nantes 909b, 1016c, 2151c, 2152a
  rescinded 1010c
  terms of 1016c
Edinboro State College 695
Edinburgh, Scotland 2289a, 2354b
  epithet 1396a
  temperature 477a
Edirne, Turkey *see* Adrianople
Edison, Charles *tab* 796
Edison, Thomas A. 241b, 307c, 1181a
  battery, electric 1132a
  cell 1883b
  incandescent lamp 1140c
  nickname *tab* 1463c
  phonograph 1171b
  stockticker 1182a
  telegraph 1183a
Edison cells 1883b
Edition (print.) 151a
Edition binderies (print.) 150c
Editors 388a
Edmonton, Canada 2354b
Edmund (Eadmund II), King (England) 241c
  nickname 1462b
Edmunds Act 2056a
Education 609–716
  career guidance 371c
  compulsory attendance laws 832a
  curriculum 638–643
  educational structure 625–637
  federal government 629a
  history of 612–621
  introduction to 609–611
  kindergarten 397–444
  philosophies of 622–624
  reading 1300c
  technology 1127a
  U.S. 615c
  writing 1301b
Education, Board of 857c
  local 634b
  state 631a
Education, Office of 630b
  grants 630c
Education of Henry Adams (bk.) 1375b, 1402a
Education Sentimentale, L' (bk.) 1381c
Educational psychology 383b, 1951c
Educational television 619a
Educational toys 406–407
Edward (the Aetheling) 1020a
Edward (the Black Prince) 242b
Edward, Prince (England) 243c
Edward (the Confessor), King (England) 241c, 2284b–2284c
Edward I, King (England) 1020a
  biography 241c
  reign of 2286b–2286c
Edward II, King (England) 241c
  reign of 2286b–2286c
Edward III, King (England) 2286b, 2287b
  biography 242a
  reign of 2286c–2287a
Edward IV, King (England) 242a, 2287b
Edward V, King (England) 242a
Edward VI, King (England) 242a, 2288a
Edward VII, King (England) 242a
  reign of 2291b–2291c
Edward VIII, King (England) abdication 2291c
  see also Windsor, Duke of
Edward, Lake 2134c, 2279b, 2331c
Edwards, Jonathan 242b, 1372b, *tab* 1469
Eels 26c–33a
Eena, Meena, Mina, Mo (nursery rhyme) 411a
Effluent 492c
Efts 47c
Egal, Muhammad Ibrahim 2251c
Egbert (the Great), King (West Saxony) 242b
Egbert of Wessex 2284a
Eggleston, Edward 1374c
Eggplant 1666a
Eggs, chicken 728a
  goose 739a
  Guinea fowl 739b

  pheasant 741c
  pigeon 742a
  production 732a
  turkey 746c
Eggs (ova) (bio.) genetics 1851b
  meiosis 1851c
Egmont (drama) 1384b
Ego 1957b
Egoist, The (nov.) 1368a, 1402a
  Patterne, Sir Willoughby 1412b
Egrets *see* Herons
Egypt 995b, 1003a–1006a
  Ambyite rule 1005a
  British rule 1005a–1006a
  cat 19c
  cobra 22b
  Fatamid rule 1005a
  hollyhock 1672a
  ibis 40b
  Israel and 2193c
  lotus 1677a
  madder 1677b
  melon 1679a
  mongoose 46b
  oldest monument in 1003a
  papyrus 1684b
  Sudan and 2266b–2266c
  Suez crisis of 1957–1958, 995b
  World War II 1028a–1028b
  see also United Arab Republic
Egypt (ancient) 972b, 1003a–1005a, 2281a
  archeology 968c, 969a
  architecture 74a
  art 74a, 1003b
  biblical 1453b
  calendar system of 758a
  color 1103b
  dance 181a
  dynastic rule in 1003a–1005a
  furniture 180
  geometry 1556c
  glass *tab* 135
  as Greek state 1003c–1005a
  history *tab* 1027
  history outline *tab* 1027, *tab* 1032, *tab* 1034
  kings of *tab* 1078
  language 1295c, 1296a
  law 813c
  literature 1003b, *tab* 1463
  madder dye 1677b
  mathematics 1501a, 1751a
  music 155c
  numbers 1509c, 1510a
  painting 83a, 84a
  pottery *tab* 130
  religion 1622b, 2281a
  Roman rule 1005a
  sculpture 113a, 114c–115b
  see also United Arab Republic
Egyptian Quarantine Board 960c
Ehrenburg, Ilya 242b
Ehrlich, Paul 242b, 1273c
Eichendorff, Joseph von 1384c, *tab* 1473
Eichmann, Adolf 242b
Eider 33a
Eiffel, Alexandre 242c
Eiffel Tower 2148c
Eighth (mus.) 175a
Einaudi, Luigi 2196c
Eindhoven, Netherlands 2224c, 2225a
Einstein, Albert astronomy 1759c
  biography 242c
  nuclear fusion 1919a
  quantum theory 1904a, 1909c
  relativity, theory of 1870a
Einsteinium 1832
  atomic weight *tab* 1805
Erie *see* Ireland
Eisenhower, Dwight D. *tab* 798–799
  administration 2078a–2080a
  Atoms for Peace 993c
  biography 242c
  cabinet *tab* 796–797
  events paralleling administration *tab* 1070
Eisenhower Doctrine 880c
Eisenlohr, August 1556c
Eisner, Kurt 243a
Ejecta (volcanoes) 492c
Ekaterinburg, Soviet Union *see* Sverdlovsk
Ekkehard 1383a, *tab* 1465
Ekman transport 465a
El Aaiún, Spanish Sahara 2323a
El Caney, Battle of 2060a
El Capitan Dam 1206
El Fasher, Sudan 2354c
El Greco *tab* 107
  Adoration of the Shepherds *tab* 112
  Assumption of the Virgin *tab* 110
  biography 264b

  famous paintings *tab* 111
El Hamad *see* Syrian Desert
El Paso, Texas 1995c, 2007a–2007b
El Salvador 2144–2145, 2168b, 2173b
  agriculture 2145a–2145b
  climate 2145a
  economy 2145a–2145b
  flag *il* 2183
  geography 2144c–2145a
  government 2145b
  history 2145b–2145c
  Indians 2145a
  map 2145, *Atlas*-54
  people of 2145a
  religion 2144c
Elaine (leg.) 1431a
Elastic energy conversion chart 1130
Elath, Israel 2354b
Elba Island 1024a, 2193c, 2331c
Elbasan, Albania 2354b
Elbe River 2138c, 2331c
Elbert, Mount 1977b, 2019a
Elbro River 2263b
Elbrus Mountain 2331c
Elburz Mountains 2188c, 2331c
Elder 1666a
Eleanor of Aquitaine 2150c
Eleatics (philos.) 1613b
Elecampane 1666a
Election Day 842c
Elections 876c
  by-election 858c
  caucus 860b
  Congress 807a
  Constitution (U.S.) 810b
  initiative and referendum 884b
  nomination 894a
  plural voting 899b
  primary 900c–901a
  recall 904a
  senators 787c
  voting machine 1284c
  see also Electoral College; Suffrage
Electoral College 789c, 876c
  establishment 2030c
Electra (myth) 1431a, 1444c
Electric arc furnace 1262a
Electric cell invention 1183a
Electric circuits 1886b, 1917a
Electric currents 1869a, 1881c, 1890a
  conductivity 1814a
  magnetic field 1884a
  production of 1882c
  transistors 1890b
  types 1882b
Electric elevators 1166a
Electric energy 1129a, 1129c
Electric fields 1881c
Electric furnace 1248a
Electric generators 1885a
Electric heating 1258c
Electric motors 1885b
Electric power transmission 1132c
Electric transit 1165a
Electrical appliances 1259a
  servicemen 386a
Electrical charge 1869a
Electrical energy conversion chart 1130
Electrical engineering 1134a
  career guidance 379c
Electrical measuring instruments 1248b
Electrical resistance measurement 1898c
Electricians career guidance 376c
Electricity 1870a
  electric current 1881c
  electricity and magnetism 1881–1890
  generators 1138b, 1885a
  lightning 1141b
  motors 1885b
  science, history of 1760b
  semiconductors 1890a
  static electricity 1881a
  transformers 1885c
  units of measure 1882c
Electrochemical cells 1814b
Electrochemistry 1761b, 1800c, 1814a
Electrocution capital punishment 860b
Electrodes 1814c, 1882b
  chemical cells 1883b
Electroencephalograph 1951a
Electroluminescent 1906b, 1917c
Electroluminescent lamps 1141a
Electrolysis 1814c
Electrolytes 1131c, 1138a, 1814c, 1882b

chemical cells 1883a
Electrolytic process 1214c
Electromagnetic induction see Induction, Electromagnetic
Electromagnetic radiation masers 1909b
Electromagnetism light waves 1903b
Electromagnets 1884b
Electrometer 1248
Electromotive force 1882c, 1917c
Electromotive series 1814c
Electron see Electrons
Electron cloud (phys.) 1806a
Electron microscope 1249a, 1889c
Electron volt 1912c, 1917c
Electron-beam welding 1288a
Electronic computers agriculture 722c
astronomy 1792c
Electronic emission 1886c
Electronic engineering 1165c
Electronic welding 1889c
Electronics 1886–1890
astronomy 1792c
careers 380b
educational uses 620b
industry 1249b, 1889c
lasers 1910b
masers 1909b
Electrons 1803c, 1804b, 1881b
conductance 1882a
definition 1917c
discovery of 1886c
insulators 1891b
orbits 1806a
quantum numbers 1806c
Electrophilic substitution 1823b
Electroplating 1250a, 1815a
Electroscope 1249a
Electroslag welding 1288a
Electrostatic printing 1174b
Electrotyping 148b, 151a
Electrovalence 1809a
Electrovalent bonding see Ionic bonding
Elefin fibers 1209a
Elegiac meter 1350c, 1351a
Elegy 1402a
Latin literature 1357b
Elegy Written in a Country Churchyard (poem) 1351a, 1364a, 1402a
Elementary schools 625c
adult education 636a
buildings 618a
curriculum tab 638, 641b, 642a
organization 626c
Elementary and Secondary Education Act (1965) 2082a
Elements (chem.) 1803a, 1830–1838
chain reactions 1829a
defined 492c
methods of analysis 1827b
periodic law 1807c
periodic system 1799c
soil 750c
symbols 1803b
valence 1809a
Elements (bk., Euclid) 1502c, 1558a, 1604a
Elene (story) 1358c
Elephant Butte Dam 2020a
Elephantiasis 941b
Elephants 33a–33b
Elephant's ear see Begonia
Eleusis, Greece 1628a
Elevation 492c
Elevation of the Cross (paint.) tab 111
Elevator 1166a
safety devices 1166a
Elf 1431a
Elgar, Sir Edward 169b, tab 172a
biography 243a
Elgon, Mount 2279a
Eli 1453b
Elia see Lamb, Charles
Elijah (Bib.) 1453b
Elimination reactions (chem.) 1823c
Eliot, Charles William 243a
Eliot, George 1368a, 1362a, tab 1476
biography 243a
—Novels
Adam Bede 1393b
Mill on the Floss 1410c
Romola 1416a
Silas Marner 1417b
Eliot, John 243a
nickname 1461a
Eliot, Thomas Stearns (T. S. Eliot) 243b, 1348c, 1376a, tab 1480

Elisha (Bib.) 1453b
Elissa see Dido
Elizabeth, Queen (Romania) pen name 1461b
Elisabethville, Congo (Kinshasa) 2134c, 2362c
Elizabeth of York 2287b
Elizabeth I, Queen (England) 243b, 995c–996a, 2191b
birth of 2288a
death of 1020b
Elizabethan Age 1402a
epithet tab 1463c
music 161a
reign of 2288a–2288b
Elizabeth II, Queen (England) 2292b
biography 243
Elizabeth City State College 688
Elizabeth Islands 2016c
Elizabethan Age 986b, 1402a, 1405a
furniture 1097a
Shakespeare 1361b
Elizabethtown College 695
Elkins, Stephen tab 796
Elkins Act 2062a
Elks (zool.) ecology 1867c
see also Deer
Ellery, William Declaration of Independence tab 803
Ellesmere Island 2110c
Ellice Islands see Gilbert and Ellice Islands Colony
Elliott, Charles L. tab 108
Elliott, John (paint.) tab 108
Ellipse 1592c
conic section 1602c
Ellipsoid 1603b
Elliptic geometry 1580c
Ellis, Henry Havelock 243c
Ellison, Ralph 1375c
Ellmaker, Amos tab 800
Ellsworth, Lincoln 244a
Ellsworth, Oliver 244a
presidential candidate tab 800
Supreme Court tab 802a
Elm 1666a
American 1985a, 1988a, 1991b
Elm family 1666a
Elmhurst College 664
Elmira College 684
Elon College 689
Elsa (leg.) Lohengrin 1438b
Eluviation 492c
zone of 520c
Eluvium 492c
Ely, Eugene 1157a
Elyria, Ohio 1992a
Elysium 1431a
Elzevir (family) 144a
E. m. f. see Electromotive force
Em (print.) 151a
Emancipation Day (Puerto Rico) 841b
Emancipation Proclamation 2048b
Emanuel (the Great), King (Portugal) 244a
Embargo 876c
Embargo Act (U.S.) 2033c
Embarkation for Cythera (paint.) tab 112
Embezzlement 876c
Embolus 941c
Embossing 150b, 151a
Embryo (bio.) 1857b
Embryo (seed) 1646a
Emer 1431a
Emergence 492c
Emergency Banking Law 2072c
Emerson, Ralph Waldo 1373b, tab 1474
biography 244a
essays 1402c
Emerson College 674
Emmanuel College 674
Emigration 883b
Emile (nov.) 1380a
Eminent domain 876c
Eminent Victorians (bk.) 1397b
Emission (elec.) 1886c
Emissivity 1906c
Emma (nov.) 1366a, 1402b
Emma and Her Children (paint.) tab 110
Emmet, Robert 244b
Emmett, Daniel Decatur 1401b
Emory and Henry College 704
Emory University 662
Emotions 1942c, 1948c
Empedocles 244b, 1613b, 1798a

Emperor Jones, The (play) 1402b
Emphysema, Pulmonary 941c
Empire 877a
Empire City see New York, New York
Empire Style 1102b
American furniture 1101a
furniture 1099a
Empiricism 1617a, 1620c
Employees Compensation Commission 2064a
Employer's liability 877a
Employment see Career guidance
Employment see Labor
Employment agencies 836c
public 840a
Employment Security, Bureau of 908b
Empty Quarter Desert 2340a
Ems River 2157b
Emus 33b
En (print.) 151a
Enabling act 877a
Enamel 1216b
ceramics 132c
Enamel (teeth) 920b
Enceladus 1433b
Encke, Johann Franz 244b
Encore 175a
Encyclopedists 1617c
End moraines 449b
Endecott, John 2024b
Enderbury Island 2000
Endicott, John 244b, 827b
Endicott, William tab 796
Endive see Chicory
Endocrine glands 925b
Endocrine system 939a
Endocrines (drugs) 1273c
Endogamy 1936c
Endogenetic (rocks) 492c
Endorsement (law) 821a
Endosperm (seed) 1642c, 1646a
Endothermic reaction 1811c
End-rhyme 1415a
Endymion (myth) 1431a
Endymion (poem, Keats) 1365a
Energy 757c–758a, 1129–1150, 1877b
conversion 1130b
conversion chart 1130
definition 1918a
ecology 1860b, 1861a
heat 1897b
inanimate 503a
incandescence 1906a
kinds 1801a
incandescence 1906a
science, history of 1761a
solar 1861a
sources 1924a, 1841c
units of 1899a
Enesco, Georges 244b
Engagement etiquette 1117a
Engels, Friedrich 244b
philosophy 1618c
socialism 908a
Engineering 1869c
career guidance 379b
polarized light 1906a
Engines 1901a
aircooled 1136a
internal-combustion 1153a
liquid-cooled 1136a
England
anthropology 1924a
budget system 858a
canon law 860a
cheese tab 731b
child labor 830b
common law 867a
Congreve rockets 1764b
early agriculture 719a
immigration 883c
labor 827a, 829a
law 813a, 815b, 816a, 855a
parks 895a
printing 144c
railroads 1176c
see also English literature; United Kingdom
—Arts
architecture 76b, 77a
church music 161c
dance 181c
furniture 1096c, 1097c
Gothic architecture 76c
interior decoration 1102c
music 160c, 161a, tab 171b
painters tab 107–109
painting 85c, 86a
pottery 127c, tab 130–132
—Government 881b
appointment 852b
appropriations 853a

Cabinet 859a
chancery 863a
citizenship 863c
committees 866c
commonwealth 867c
constitution 869c
county 871c
crown 872a
eminent domain 876c
Home Office 882a
House of Commons 867b
House of Lords 890c–891a
king 887b
legislation 889b
local government 890b
mercantilism 986c
offices 894c
Prime Minister 901a
Privy Council 871a
rulers of tab 1078
social insurance 837a
socialism 908a
woman suffrage 914b
see also Parliament (England)
—History tab 1042, tab 1044, tab 1046
American explorations 2023
American Revolution 2028a
benefit of clergy 856b
Bill of Rights 856c
explorations tab 1060
Hundred Years' War 1359c
king 887b
Navigation Acts 2027a
New World 2023c
Norman Conquest 1358c
People's Charter 863b
Reform Bills 987b
Reformation 1632a
rise of nationalism 985c
rulers of tab 1078
subsidy 909b
Trent Affair 2045b
England, Bank of see Bank of England
England, Church of see Church of England
English (lang.) see English language
English, William H. tab 801
English Bards and Scotch Reviewers (poem) 1365a
English Channel 2282a, 2331c
English Civil War 904a, 987a, tab 1073
English language 1296c, 1297b
alphabet, origin of 1295a
consonants 1294c
correct usage 1320–1322
derivatives tab 1297c
development 1337c
etymology 1297c
relationship to other languages 1297b
English literature 1358–1371, tab 1465–1481
Age of Criticism 1362c
drama 1360c
Imagist school 1371a
Poet Laureate 1413b
Romanticism 1364b
twentieth century 1369b
Victorian Age 1366a
English and Scottish Popular Ballads (Child) 1396b
English-Dutch wars 999b
English-French wars 999b
English-Speaking Union 1743c
Engraving 139b, 1250b
graphic arts 136a
gravure method 149c
woodcuts 139c
Engstrom, Elmer 1126a
Enharmonic 157b, 175a
Enisei (river) see Yenisei
Eniwetok (atoll) 2000
Enlightenment, Age of 1617c
Enlightenment 2152b
Ennius, Quintus 1354a, 1355a, tab 1464
biography 244b
Enoch 1453c
Enoch Arden (poem) 1368c, 1402b
Enos (chimpanzee) 1770b
Enriquillo, Lake 2142c
Ensemble (mus.) 175a
Ensor, James tab 109
biography 244c
Entablature 75a
Entebbe, Uganda 2279c, 2354b
Entente Cordiale 2154c, 2161c
Enthalpy 1918a
Entombment, The (paint., Caravaggio) tab 112
Entombment, The (paint., Matsys) tab 109

Entombment, The (paint., Raphael) *tab* 112
Entombment, The (paint., Titian) *tab* 111
Entomologists 390c
Entr'acte (mus.) 175a
Entrenched meander (streams) 492c
Entrepreneur 591c
Entropy 1918a
Enugu, Nigeria 2354b–2354c
Enver Pasha 244c
Environment 1859a
  space biology 951c
Environmental resistance 1859c
Enzymes 919c, 1825b
  intestines 920c
  mouth 920b
  stomach 920c
Eocene Epoch *tab* 457, 458a, 492c
Eolian 492c
Eon 492c
Eos 1426b, 1431a
Eosinophils 922b
E P T A *see* Expanded Program of Technical Assistance
Epaminondas 244c
Epée, Charles Michel de l' 244c
Epeiric seas 494a
Epeirogenesis 455a
Epeirogeny 494a
Ephemeral stream 494a
  see also Intermittent stream
Ephesus Diana 1453c
Ephialtes 1021c
Ephraim 1453c
Epic poetry 1343b, 1344a, 1350c, 1402b
  Aeneid, The 1422c
  Beowulf 1427a
  chanson de geste 1398c
  Iliad, The 1406c
  Mahabharata 1410a
  Odyssey, The 1411b
  Paradise Lost 1412a
  Ramayana 1414c
Epicenter 494a
Epicontinental 494a
Epicontinental sea 494a
Epictetus 244c, 976b, 1354a, *tab* 1464, 1615b
Epicureanism 975a, 1615b
Epicurus 1615b
  biography 244c
  language 1293b
  Lucretius 1346a
Epicycle 1794c
Epidermis animals 918a
Epidote (mineral) 494a
Epigene 494a
Epigram 1315b, 1351b, 1354b
  definition 1402b
  Roman literature 1357c
Epigrams (poems, martial) *tab* 1464
Epilepsy 941c
Epimetheus 1442b
Epinephrine *see* Adrenalin
Epinay, Louise 244c
Epiphytes 1859c
Episode (mus.) 175a
Epistemology 623a, 1611a, 1617a
Epistle to the Ephesians (Bib.) 1453c
Epistle to the Galatians (Bib.) 1454a
Epistle to the Hebrews (Bib.) 1454b
Epistle of Jude (Bib.) 1456b
Epistle of Paul to the Colossians (Bib.) 1452b
Epistle to Philemon (Bib.) 1459a
Epistle to the Phillippians (Bib.) 1459a
Epistle to the Romans (Bib.) 1459b
Epistle to Titus (Bib.) 1460b
Epistles (poems, Horace) 1354a, 1357b
Epistles to the Corinthians (Bib.) 1452b
Epistles to the Thessalonians (Bib.) 1460b
Epithalamium 1402b
Epithalamium (poem, Spenser) 1402c
Epochs (geol.) 455b
  defined 494c
Epolene 1188c
Epoxy *tab* 1219
Epping Forest 895b
Epstein, Rabbi Isidore 612c
Epstein, Jacob *tab* 125

biography 244c
  sculpture 123b
Epworth League *see* National Conference of Methodist Youth
Equal temperament scale (mus.) 1896c
Equality (math.) 1603b
Equations 1603b
  checking 1541a
  chemical 1810c
  graphing 1554a
  quadratic 1544c
  simultaneous 1550b
  solving first-degree 1541a
Equator 494a, 758a, 1794b
  bat 15c
  thermal 517c
Equator, Celestial *see* Celestial equator 1321c
Equatorial Guinea 2311
Equestrian statues 118c
Equiangular triangles 1607c
Equilateral (math.) 1603c
Equilateral triangles 1607c
Equilibrium *see* Balance
Equinox 1793c
  definition 1794c
  procession 1796c
Equity 816c, 826a, 863a, 877c
Eras (geol.) 455b, 494a
Erasistratus 247a
Erasmus, Desiderius 986b, *tab* 1466
  biography 247a
  Holbein's portrait *tab* 112
Erato 1431a
Eratosthenes 779a, *tab* 1464, 1502c
  biography 247a
  Sieve of 1523c, *il* 1523c
Erbium 1832
  atomic weight *tab* 1805
Ercilla y Zúñiga, Alonso de 1393a, *tab* 1466
Erckmann, Emile *tab* 1476
Erebus (myth) 1431a
Erechtheum (Athens) 75a
Erewhon (nov.) 1402c
Erg (deserts) 494a
Ergosterol 1824c
Ergot 742c
Erhard, Ludwig 247a
Eric the Red 247b, 2314c
Ericson, Leif 2023a
  map based on voyage of 780
  biography 247b
Ericsson, John 247b
Erie, Pennsylvania 1993b
Erie, Lake 2017b, 2017c, 2018a, 2115b
Erie Canal 1153a, 1160c, 1189c, 1967c, 2035b, 2115b
Erin *see* Ireland
Erinyes 1431a
Eris 1431a
Eritrea 2146c, 2196b
Erlking 1431b
Ermine *see* Weasel
Ernani (opera) 167b
Ernst, Max *tab* 109, 247b
Eroica (mus.) 164c
Eros (myth) 1431b
  see also Cupid
Eros (psych.) 1957b
Erosion 447c, 455a, 494a, 743c
  cover crops 730c
  glacial 761b
  headward 500c
  in humid climates 761b–761c
  sheet 514a
  splash 515c
Erratics (geol.) 449b, 494a
Erskine College 699
Eruption 494a
Erythroblastosis fetalis 922c
Erythrocytes *see* Red blood cells
Erz Mountains 2138c, 2338c
Erzurum, Turkey 2354c
Esaki, Leo 1890c
Esarhaddon 247b
Esau 1453c
Escalator 1166b
Escalator (moving walk) 1170c
Escape velocity 1778c
Escarpment (cliff) 494a
Escorial (Madrid) 77c
Eschenbach, Wolfram von *see* Wolfram von Eschenbach
Escriche, Ernesto *tab* 172c
Escrow 877c
Esker (glacial drift) 494a
Eskers 449b
Eskimo language 1337c
  classification 1333a

Eskimos adaptation 1927b
  Alaska 1975a
  body mutilation 1930c
  Canada 2111b
  cooking 1933a
  family 1941a
  Greenland 2314c
  hunting 1933c
Esnault-Pelterie, Robert 1763a, 1768c
  rocket engines 1767c
Esophagus 920b
  heartburn 942a
Espanca, Florbela 1389a
Esperanto (lang.) 1338b
Espionage Act 2065c
Espla, Oscar *tab* 172c
Espronceda, José de *tab* 1475
Espy, James P. 247b
Essay 1347b, 1402c
Essay on Criticism (Pope) 1363c
Essay on Man 1363a, 1403a, 1611c
Essays (Bacon) 1362a
Essays (Montaigne) 1402c
Essays in Criticism (Arnold) 1402c
Essays of Elia 1347b, 1365b, 1403a
Essen, West Germany 2354c
Essenes 1629c
Essequibo River 2170c
Essex, 2nd Earl of (Robert Devereux) 247a
Essex, Kingdom of 2284b
Established church 877b
Estaing, Charles Hector d' 247b
Estate (law) 824b
Estate system (soc.) 1945a
Estate tax 591c
Estaunié, Edouard 1382c
Este family 2195b
Esterhazy (family)
  Haydn, F. J. 164c
Esther (Bib.) 1453c
Esther (play) 1379b
Esther Waters (nov.) 1369c
Esthetics 1611c
Estienne, Henri 144a
Estienne, Robert 144a
Estigarribia, José Félix 2236b
Estimate, Board of 857c
Estimate, Board of 857c
Estrada Cabrera, Manuel 2169a
Estrada Palma, Tomás 2137c
Estradiol 1824c
Estrogen 926b
Estuary (tidal bay) 494b
Esztergom, Hungary 2354c
Etching 136a, 1250c
  aquatint 138c
  color 137c
  dry point 138a
  paper 137c
  printing 137b
  soft-ground etching 138b
Eteocles 1424b, 1431b
Eternal City *see* Rome, Italy
Ethelbert, King (England) 247b, 2284b
Ethelred II, King (England) 247b, 2284b
Ethelwulf 247c
Etheridge, George *tab* 1468
Ethers 1820c
Ethics 1611c
  Confucius 1623c
Ethics (bk., Spinoza) 1616c
Ethiology 1929b
Ethiopia 2145–2146
  agriculture 2146a, 2146b
  ass 14b
  baboon 14c
  coffee trees 1659a
  economy 2146b
  flag *il* 2183
  geography 2145c–2146a
  goat 36a
  government 2146b
  history 2146b–2146c
  Italian invasion 1013c, 1028a, 2196c
  and Italy *tab* 1076
  League of Nations 1013c
  map 2145, *Atlas*-34-35
  people of 2146a
  religion 2145c, 2146a, 2146b
  teal ducks 62c
Ethiopian Highlands 2331c–2322a
Ethnographic present 1929b
Ethnography 1929b
Ethnology 1951a *see also* Cultural anthropology
Ethyl alcohol 1825a
  rocket fuels 1766b
Ethyl cellulose *tab* 1219

Ethylene-propylene rubbers 1222b
Etienne Chevalier and St. Stephen (paint.) *tab* 110
Etiquette 812a, 1112–1120
  dance 1113b
  dinner 1113a, 1114a
  employment 1115b
  engagement 1117a
  funeral 1116c
  home 1112a
  making introductions 1114c
  theater 1113a
  travel 1116a
  wedding 1117b
Etranger, L' (nov., Camus) 1612a
Etruria pottery *tab* 131
Etruscan language 1337c
Etruscans 975b, 2195a
  architecture 73c
  sculpture 113a
Ettrick Shepherd *see* Hogg, James
Etty, William *tab* 108
Etudes (mus.) 175a
Etymology 1297b, 1321b
Etzel 1431b
Eubacteriales 1844b
Eucalyptus 1666b
Eucaryotic cells 1842a
Eucken, Rudolf Christoph 247c
Euclid 975a, 1502c, 1558a, 1615b
  algorithm 1525b
  biography 247c
  geometry 1604a
Euclidean geometry 1604a
Eudoxus (of Cnidus) 1557c, 1752b
  biography 247c
Eucumbene Dam *il* 2091
Eugene, Prince (Savoy) 998c
Eugene, Oregon 1992c
Eugène (drama, Jodelle) *tab* 1466
Eugénie, Empress (France) 247c
Euglena 1847c
Euler, Leonhard 1505a, 1603c
  biography 247c
  topology 1599a
Eulogy 1327c
Eumaeus 1431b
Eumenes, King 117c
Eumenides (myth) 1431b
Eumenides, The (play) 1352b
Eunuchoidism 941c
Euonymus 1666b
Euphemism 1315b
Euphony 175a
Euphorbia 1666b
Euphotic zone (ocean.) 1865c
Euphrates River 1453c, 2189c, 2270c, 2278a, 2332a
Euphrosyne 1431b
Euphues (nov.) 1360c, *tab* 1466
Eupolis 1353a
Eurasia
  avocet 14c
  badger 15a
  bunting 18b
  coot 23a
  cuckoo 25a
  deer 25b
  duck 26a
  eagle 26b
  flamingo 33c
  fox 34c
  goat 36a
  grouse 37b
  hare 38a
  ibis 40b
  kingfisher 41a
  lemming 42c
  magpie 44c
  merganser 45c
  mockingbird 46a
  mole 46a
  see also Asia, Europe
Eureka College 664
Euridice (opera) 161c
Euripides 1352c, *tab* 1464
  Alcestis 1423c
  Andromache 1424a
  biography 247c–248a
  Hippolytus 1435a
Europa (myth) 1431b
Europa (satellite) 1783b
Europe
  antelope 14a
  anthropology 1925a
  archeology 971a
  beaver 15c
  bison 17a
  carp 19b
  cattle 20b
  chamois 21a
  chickadee 21a
  clam 22a

cockroach 22b
conch 22c
cony 23a
coot 23a
cornborer 23b
cricket 24b
crow 24c
cultural influence on the New World 2022b
economic geography 773b–774c
eels 26c
eider 33a
elephant 33a
flycatcher 34b
gallinule 35a
goldeneye 36a
goldfinch 36b
goose 36b
grosbeak 37a
hamster 38a
hare 38a
hedgehog 38b
heron 38c
historical outline *tab* 1027–1030
hornet 39a
immigration 883b
lamprey 42a
languages of 1330–1337
limpet 43a
ling 43a
lion 20a
lobster 43b
lynx 44b
map *Atlas-8, Atlas-14*
marten 45a
merganser 45b
modern history 986
printing 143c
see also under the names of individual countries, such as France
European Coal and Steel Community 2099a, 2148b, 2211c
European Culture Region 768a–768b
European Economic Community 2099a, 2148b *see also* Common Market
European Monetary Agreement (1950) 2099a
European Recovery Program (ERP) 2077c
enacted 1015c–1016a
European Secret Army Organization (OAS) 2088b
Europium 1832
atomic weight *tab* 1805
Eurus 1431b
Eurydice (myth) 1431b
Orpheus 1442a
Eurystheus 1431b

Eusden, Laurence 1413b
Eusebius of Caesarea (Greek hist.) 248a
Eustachio, Bartolommeo 248a
Eustasy 494b
Eustis, William *tab* 795
Eutaw Springs, Battle of 2029
Euterpe 1431b
Eutrophic waters 1866b
Evangeline (poem) 1403a
Evans, Arthur 970c
Evans, Catherine 1283c
Evans, Herbert McLean 248a
Evans, Mary Ann *see* Eliot, George
Evans, Maurice 248a
Evans, Oliver 1169a
Evans, Robley D. 248a
nickname 1462a
Evansville, Indiana 1981c, 2019c
Evansville, University of 666
Evaporation 470a, 494b
in the atmosphere 763c
matter, properties of 1872c
refrigeration 1902a
Evaporite (rock) 494b
Evapotranspiration 494b
Evarts, William Maxwell 248a, *tab* 796
Eve (Bib.) 1453c
Eve of St. Agnes (poem) 1403b
Evelina (nov.) 1364a
Evelyn, John 248b, *tab* 1468
Evelyn Inness (nov.) 1369c
Evening (paint., Claude Lorrain) *tab* 110
Evening colleges 635a
Evening primrose 1666c
Evening-primrose family 1666c
Everest, Mt. 2223b, 2337c
height 462b
Everett, Edward *tab* 796, 870b
biography 248b
Vice-presidential candidate *tab* 801
Everett, Washington 1998a, 2020a
Everglade (swamp) 494b
Everglades National Park 2017b
Evergreens 1642c
Everlasting 1666c
Every Man in His Humour (play) 1361c
Everyman (play) 1360c, 1411a
Evgeni Onegin (verse nov.) 1389b
Evidence (law) 827b, 856b
Evil eye 1431b

Evolution early organisms 1841b
genes 1858a
life, origin of 1839a
Ewell, Richard Stoddert 248b
Ewing, Thomas *tab* 795, *tab* 797
Examiner, The (journal) 1167b, 1365c
Excalibur 1431b
Excess profits tax 592a
Exchange 592a
see also Commerce; Stock exchange
Excise tax 592a, 877b, 910b
Exclamation point 1312b
Exclusive agency 592a
Execution (law) 877b
Executive Department (U.S.) 789b
establishment of various departments *tab* 797
state government 793a
Executor (law) 877c
Exemption (law) 877c
Exercise (mus.) 175a
Exfoliation 494b
Exiles (play) 1371b
Existentialism 1619c
education 624c
French literature 1382c
Existentialism (bk., Sartre) 1348c
Exobiology 949a
Exocrine glands 925b
cystic fibrosis 941b
Exodus (Bib.) 1453c
Exogamy 1936c
Exogenetic (rock) 494b
Exophthalmos 941c
Exothermic reaction 1811c
Exotic river 494b
Expanded Program of Technical Assistance 992c
Expanding universe 1787b
Expedition of Humphrey Clinker (nov.) 1363c
Expense 592a
Experience and Education (bk., Dewey) 624a
Experiment in Autobiography (bk.) 1370b
Experimental psychology 1947c
Experimentalism (philos.) 623c
Explementary angles 1601b
Exploits of Brigadier Gerard, The (bk.) 1370a
Exploration *tab* 1060
America 2023a

see also under the names of individual explorers, such as Columbus, Christopher
Exploration of Planetary Space by Means of Reaction-powered Equipment (treatise) 1764c
Explorer I (satellite) 952b, 1769b
Explosion crater 494b
Explosives 1207
history 1207b
Nobel, A. 1766c
Explosives (gram.) 1294c
Expo '67 2118c
Exponential series 1607b
Exponents (math.) 1603c
algebra 1534c
Exports Administrative Board 2065c
Exposition (writ.) 1318c
Ex post facto 877c
Expounder of the Constitution *see* Webster, Daniel
Expression (mus.) 175a
Expressionism 86c
Extemporize (mus.) 175a
Exterior angle 1601b
External ear 937a
Exterritoriality 877c
Extradition 877c
Extratropical cyclone 494b
Extraversion 1958a
Extravaganza (mus.) 175a
Extrusion 1195a
Extrusive rock 494c
Eyadema, Etienne, 2275b
Eyck, Hubert van 248b
Eyck, Jan van *tab* 106
biography 248b
Man With the Pink tab 109
National Gallery, London *tab* 111
Virgin and Child With Chancellor Rolin tab 112
Eyelashes 918b
Eyes 928b
cataract 941a
disorders and diseases 928c
exophthalmos 941c
glaucoma 942a
health 959b
light sensitivity 1906c
see also Vision
Eyre, Lake 2091b, 2332a
Eyuk 970b
Ezekiel 1453c
Ezra and Nehemiah (Bib.) 1453c

F

FAO *see* Food and Agriculture Organization
Fabian Society 908a
Fabius (Quintus Fabius Maximus) (d. 203) 248c
Fables 1422b, 1315a
Greek 1351b
Fontaine 1379b, *tab* 1468
Fabliaux 1377c
Fabriano, Gentile da *see* Gentile da Fabriano
Fabric (rocks) 494c
Fabrics *see* Textiles
Facies 494c
mechanical 506c
see also Metamorphic facies
Facsimile telegraph systems 1183b
Factor (merchant) 592a
Factorial (math.) 1603c
Factoring (math.) algebra 1536c
complete 1538a
Faculae (astron.) 1794c
Faenza, Italy 127a
Faerie Queene, The (poem) 1360c, 1403b, *tab* 1466
Faeroe Islands 2141a, 2141c, 2142a, 2311–2312
Fafnir 1431b
Faggi, Alfeo *tab* 125
Fagin (lit.) 1403b
Faguet, Emile *tab* 1478

Fahlberg, Constantin 745a
Fahrenheit, Gabriel Daniel 1125a, 1760a, 1920a
biography 248c
thermometers 469b
Fahrenheit scale 1898b, 1920a
Faidherbe, Louis Léon César, 2248a
Faïence ware 126c
Fair Employment Practices Commission 878a
Fair Labor Standards Act (Federal Wage and Hour Law) 831b, 832a, 833a, 835b, 912c
Fair Oaks, Battle of *see* Seven Pines, Battle of
Fairbanks, Alaska 1975a
Fairbanks, Charles Warren vice-presidency *tab* 801
Fairchild, Charles *tab* 796
Fairfax, Edward 1407b
Fairfield, Cecily *see* West, Rebecca
Fairfield University 660
Fairhair, Harold (Harald Haarfagar), King (Norway) 2230c, 2231a
Fairies 1431c
Fairleigh Dickinson University 682
Fairmount Park (Philadelphia) 895c
Fairmont State College 706
Fairy *see* Fairies
Fairy Tales (Andersen) *tab* 1474
Faisal, Ghazi 2190a–2190b
Faisal, King (Saudi Arabia) 2247b–2247c
Faisal I (Feisal I), Emir, King (Iraq) 248c, 2190a, 2190b

Faisal II, King (Iraq) 2190b
Faith 7 (spacecraft) *tab* 1770
Falcon 33b
Falcon Dam 2020a
Falguière, Alexander *tab* 125
Falkenhayn, Erich von 248c
Falkirk, Battle of 1020a
Falkland Current 765c
Falkland Islands 2312
Falkner, William *see* Faulkner, William
Fall (season) *see* Autumn
Fall, Albert Bacon *tab* 797, 2068c
Fall line defined 494c
Fall River, Massachusetts 1985b
Falla, Manuel de 169b, *tab* 172c
biography 248c
Fallen Timbers, Battle of 2032a
Fallersleben, Hoffmann von *see* Hoffmann, August Heinrich
Fallières, Clément Armand 248c
Fallopian tubes 926c
Fallopio, Gabriello 248c
Falls (geog.) *see* Waterfalls
False imprisonment 878a
False pretenses (law) 878a
Falsetto 175a
Falstaff, Sir John (lit.) 1403b
Falstaff (opera, Verdi) 167b
Famagusta, Cyprus 2354c
Familiar Studies of Men and Books (essays) 1368b
Family (plant) 1639a
Family (soc.) 817b, 1936a, 1941a
China 977a

social stratification 1944b
Family Circle (magazine) circulation 1167a
Family of Charles IV (paint.) *tab* 111
Fancies (mus.) 161a
Fandango 175a, 182a
Fanfani, Amintore 248c
Fanfare 175b
Fa-Ngum 2206b–2206c
Fantasia (mus.) 162a, 175b
Fantin-Latour, Ignace *tab* 108
biography 249a
Farabi, al- 249a
Faraday, Michael 1760c, 1799b
generator 1138b
biography 249a
magnets 1884c
Farce 1403b
Far East butterfly 18c
civilizations 976a
Far from the Madding Crowd (nov.) 1368a
Farewell Address (Washington) 1403c, 2032a
Fargo, North Dakota 1986b, 1991c, 2007b
Faridabad, India *il* 2179a
Farigoule, Louis *see* Romains, Jules
Farley, James A. *tab* 796
Farley, John Murphy 249b
Farm Credit Administration 878a
Farm machinery 1251a

Farman, Henri 1155c
Farmer in the Dell (song) 420
Farming see Agriculture
Farmington State College 672
Farnese, Alessandro (1468–1549) see Paul III, Pope
Farnese, Alexander 995c
Farnese Bull (sculp.) 117c
Farnsworth, Philo 1152a
Faroes (islands) see Faeroe Islands
Farouk I, King (Egypt) 249b, 1006a, 2281b
Farquhar, George tab 1469
Farquhar Islands 2308b, 2308c
Farragut, David Glasgow 249b
  New Orleans 2048a
Farrar, Geraldine 249b
Farrell, Edelmiro 2090c
Farrell, James 249b, 1375c
Farruca (dance) 182a
Farsightedness 941c, 1299b
Faruq, King (Egypt) see Farouk I, King (Egypt)
Farwell, Arthur 170c
Fascism 784c, 878a
  Charter of Labor 863b
  Italy 2196b–2196c
Fashion careers 375a
  see also Clothing
Fashoda, Sudan 1005c
Fasilidas, Emperor 2146b
Fast Day 842a
Fast ice 494c
Fasteners 1252a, 1290a
Fat see Fats
Fata Morgana (mirage) 1432a
Fatamid dynasty 1005a
Fates (myth) 1432a
Father of his Country see Cicero; Washington, George
Father of History see Herodotus
Father of Medicine see Hippocrates
Fathers and Sons (nov.) 894a, 1403c
Fathom 494c
Fatima 1427b, 1432a
Fatimid dynasty 2281a
Fatimids 2277b
Fats 919b
Fats and oils 732a
Fatty acids 920c
Faulkner, William 249c, 1375c, tab 1481
Fault (rocks) 451a, 494c
  hinge 501a
  rotary 513a
  synthetic 517b
  wrench 520c
Fault block (rocks) 494c
Fault scarp (rocks) 494c
Faun (myth) 1432a
Fauna 494c
  paleontology 458a
Faunal and floral succession, Law of 455c
Faun's Mask (sculp.) 122a
Faunus 1432a
Fauré, Gabriel 1249c, 168b, tab 172a
Faust (leg.) 1403c, 1432a
Faust (Goethe) 1346a, 1403c, 1432b, tab 1471
Faust, Johann 249c
Favonius 1449c
Favrile glass 134a
Fawkes, Guy 250a
Fayetteville, North Carolina 1991a
Fayetteville State College 689
Faysal, King (Syria) 2271c
FBI see Federal Bureau of Investigation
FCC see Federal Communications Commission
Featherbedding 592b
Feathering (rowing) 1730b
Federal Bureau of Investigation 878b
Federal Communications Commission 878b
Federal Credit Unions 908b
Federal Deposit Insurance Corporation 529c, 878b, 2074a
Federal Emergency Relief Administration 905a, 2073b
Federal Extension Service 629c
Federal Farm Board 878a, 2071b
Federal government 878b
Federal Home Loan Board 878c

Federal Housing Administration 883a
Federal Land Banks 878a
Federal Mediation and Conciliation Service 891c
Federal Power Commission 878c
Federal Reserve Bank Act 2063b
Federal Reserve System 529, 530a, 791a, 857c, 879a, 2063c
  criticism of 532a
  establishment 530a
Federal Security Agency 849c, 862b, 879a, 908b, 2078b
  bureaus 879b
Federal Trade Commission 791a, 849c, 866b, 879c
Federal Trade Commission Act 2063c
Federal Wage and Hour Law see Fair Labor Standards Act
Federalist, The (essays) 1348a, 1372c, 2030c
Federalist Party 873a, 878c, 2031b
Federation 878b
Federation of French Equatorial Africa 2110b, 2119b, 2121a
Federation of French West Africa 2141a
Federation of the West Indies 2097c, 2198b, 2307a
Feet bunion 941a
  clubfoot 941c
  flat feet 941c
Feininger, Lyonel tab 108
  biography 250a
Feisal see Faisal, Faysal
Feldspar 453b, 494c–495a
  carbon dioxide 447a
  glass making 133b
  hardness tab 1192
Felix Holt (nov.) 1368a
Felony 880a
Felsenmeer (rocks) 497a
Felsite 450c, 497a
Felt 1208a
Female genetics 1852b
Femmes Savantes, Les (play) 1379b
Femur (anat.) 917c
Fen (marsh) 497a
Fénelon, François de Salignac de La Mothe 1379c, tab 1469
Fennel 1666c
Fenrir 1432b
Feoktistov, Konstantin tab 1770
Ferber, Edna 250a
Fer-de-lance see Pit viper
Ferdinand, Archduke (Austria) see Francis Ferdinand
Ferdinand, Prince 2106a
Ferdinand I, Emperor (Holy Roman Empire), King (Hungary) 250a
Ferdinand II, Emperor (Holy Roman Empire), King (Hungary) 250a
Ferdinand II, King (Aragon) see Ferdinand V, King (Spain)
Ferdinand I, King (Austria) see Ferdinand I, Emperor (Holy Roman Empire)
Ferdinand II, King (Austria) see Ferdinand II, Emperor (Holy Roman Empire)
Ferdinand I, King (Bulgaria) abdication 849a
Ferdinand I, King (Castile and León) 2241c
Ferdinand V, King (Castile and León) 250b, 985c
  Isabella I 282a
Ferdinand III, King (Naples) see Ferdinand V, King (Spain)
Ferdinand II, King (Spain) 2264c
Ferdinand V, King (Spain) 1009a
Ferdinand VII, King (Spain) 2090a, 2122a, 2133a, 2173a, 2218c, 2219a, 2221c, 2222a, 2265a, 2297c
Ferdinand II, King (Two Sicilies) 250a
Ferlinghetti, Lawrence 1376b
Fermat number 1603c
Fermat, Pierre de 250b, 1505a
Fermata (mus.) 175b
Fermentation 1193a, 1239a, 1933b
  bacteria 1845b
  food preservation 736c, 737b
Fermi, Enrico 250b, 1829a
Fermium 1832
  atomic weight tab 1805
Fern allies 1641c–1642b

Fernández de Lizardi, José Joaquín 1393a
Fernando Pó Island 2311b
Ferns 1641c–1642b
  tree 1641c
Ferrara, Francisco 2173a
Ferrara, Italy 2195b
Ferrari, Lodovico 1388b, 1504a
Ferreira, Antonio 1388b
Ferrel's Law 497a
Ferrero, Guglielmo 2050b
Ferromagnesian (minerals) 497a
Ferromagnetism 1884b
Ferrous alloys 1194a
Ferry, Jules 497a
Fertility (soil) 750c
Fertilizer grade 753b
Fertilizer ratio 753b
Fertilizers 497a, 721c, 733a
  chemical tab 753, 753a
  natural 752a, tab 752c
  organic tab 753
  potash 1220b
  sulfuric acid 1224c
Fès, Morocco 2354c
Fessenden, William Pitt tab 796, 2050b
Festin de Pierre, Le (prose) 1379b
Festus, Porcius 815a
Fetch 497a
Feuchtwanger, Lion tab 1480
Feudalism 888a, 1006a–1006b, 1020a, 2285a, 2285c
  decline of 2286c
  education 614a
  England 1358c
  estate system 1945a
  Middle Ages 983c, 1006a–1006b
  origin of 1006a
  Roman Empire 1006a
  weakness of 1006b
Feuillet, Octave tab 1476
Few, William 809c
Fez, Treaty of 2222b
Fezzan 2210a, 2210b
Fezzan Desert 2209c
Fiard (valley) 497a
Fiat money 592b
Fiber crops 733c
Fibers, structural 1208a
Fibers, synthetic 1208a
  cellulose fibers 1208c
  chemical fibers 1208c
Fibich, Zedenko 169a, tab 172a
Fibonacci, Leonardo 1503c, 1504a, 1603c
Fibonacci sequence 1603c
Fibrinogen 921c, 922c
Fibroin 1824b
Fibroma 941c
Ficthe, Johann Gottlieb 1384c, tab 1471
  biography 250b
Fiction 1404a
  stream of conciousness 1418a
Fictions (law) 880a
Fidelio (opera) 164c
Field capacity 497a
Field, Cyrus West 250c
Field, David Dudley 250c, 865b, 900b
Field Code 865b
Field, Eugene 1374c, tab 1478
  Rock-a-by-Lady 415c
  Wynken, Blynken and Nod 416a
Field hockey 1725b
Field, Stephen J. Supreme Court tab 802a
Field rheostat 1142a
Fielding, Henry 1346a, 1363c, tab 1469
  biography 250c
  Joseph Andrews 1407c, 1412a
  Tom Jones 1419a
Fields, W. C. 251a
Fiesole, Giovanni da see Angelico, Fra
Fiesole, Mino da 121c, tab 125
Fife (mus.) 175b
Fifteen Decisive Battles of the World (Creasy) 1002c
Fifth (mus.) 175b
Fig 1667a
Fighting Bob see Evans, Robley D. D.
Fighting Temeraire (paint.) tab 111
Figueres, José 2136a
Figure (mus.) 175b
Figure skating 1729c
Figures of speech 1314–1315

allegory 1315a
alliteration 1315c
antithesis 1315b
apostrophe 1315a
assonance 1315c
climax 1315b
epigram 1315b
euphemism 1315b
hyperbole 1315c
irony 1315c
metaphor 1314c
metonymy 1315a
onomatopoeia 1315c
personification 1315a
rhyme 1315c
simile 1314b
synecdoche 1315b
vision 1315a
Figwort 1667a
Figwort family 1667a
Fiji Islands 2283c, 2312
Filali dynasty 2222a
Filament (flower) 1645c
Filarete 251a
Filariasis tab 946
Filbert see Hazel
Filibuster 880a
  defined 1006a
Filicaja, Vicenzo da tab 1468
Filippino Lippi see Lippi, Filippino
Filippo Lippi see Lippi, Fra Filippo
Fill 497a
Fillet (print.) 151a
Fillmore, Millard 251a, 849b, tab 798–799, 2200c
  administration 2041b
  cabinet tab 796–797
  election and inauguration tab 800
  events paralleling administration tab 1064
  vice-presidency 2040c
Film 1237a
  cinematography 1161b
  motion picture 1238a
Filters (optical) 1907c
Filth-borne infections 956c
Finance 541–546
Financial statement 592b
Finck, Heinrich 160c, tab 171b
Finale (mus.) 175b
Finch 33b
  purple 1989a
Finch college 684
Finding Moses (paint.) tab 110
Fine (law) 880a
Fine arts 71–186
  architecture 73–82
  dance 180–184
  divisions of 72a
  graphic arts 136–141
  introduction to 71–73
  music 154–179
  painting 82–113
  printing 142–153
  sculpture 113–125
Finger Lakes 2017b–2017c
Finiguerra, Tommaso 149c
Finland 2146–2147
  agriculture 2147a
  architecture 78a
  climate 2146c
  communism 2147b
  duchy 875c
  economy 2147a
  established church 877b
  flag il 2183
  geography 2146c
  government 2147a–2147b
  history 2147b–2147c
  Kalevala 1408a
  map 2147, Atlas-14–15
  music 168c
  music 168c, tab 172b
  national anthem 138c
  people of 2146c–2147a
  religion 2146c, 2147a, 2147b
  war debts 2072a
  World War I 988c
  World War II 1028b, 2147c
Finland, Gulf of 2332a
Finlay, Carlos 2137c
Finley, James 1191a, 1197a
Finn, Mac Cumal 1432b
Finno-Ugric languages 1333a, tab 1335
Finns (people) anthropology 1927a
Finsen, Niels Ryberg 251a
Fiqueiredo, Fidelino de 1389a
Fir 1667a–1667b
  Douglas 1992c
Firat River 2278a

Firdausi *tab* 1465
Fire communications 1151a
  primitive culture 1929c
Fire detection 1253a
Fire insurance 595a
Fire prevention 1254a
Firearms 1254b
Fireclay 1201c
Fireballs 1795b
Firefly 33b
Firemen (career) 389a
Fires *see* Fire
Firestone, Harvey 251a
Firestone Rubber Company 2209a,
  2209b
Fireweed 1667b
Fireworks 1764a, 1765b
Firn snow 497a
First aid camping 1711b
First Balkan War 2167a
First Crusade 1002a–1002b
First Republic 2152c
Firth (waters) 497a
Firth of *see under the latter part
  of the name, such as Forth,
  Firth of*
Fischart, Johann 1383c, *tab* 1466
**Fischer von Erlach, Johann Bern-
  hard** 251a, 2095
Fish *il* 1717
  commercial 733c
  as food 733c
  see also Fisheries; Fishing
Fish, Hamilton 251a, *tab* 796
Fish Magic (paint.) *il* 93
Fisher *see* Marten
Fisher, Irving 531b
Fisher, John Arbuthnot 251b
Fisher, Walter *tab* 797
Fisheries 734a
  conservation 1868a
Fish gorge 1933c
Fishing Alabama 1974b
  Alaska 1975a
  Angola 2306b
  Bermuda 2307c
  British Indian Ocean Territory
    2308b
  British Solomon Islands 2308c
  British Virgin Islands 2309a
  Canada 2112b, 2113b, 2115b
  Connecticut 1978a
  Delaware 1978b
  Faeroe Islands 2311c
  French Polynesia 2313a
  Gabon *il* 2155
  Great Britain 2282c
  Greenland 2314b
  Guam 2001a
  Iceland 2176b, 2177a
  Iran 2188c
  Ivory Coast 2197a
  Japan 2199b
  Korea, South 2203c
  Labrador 2112b
  Louisiana 1984a
  Macao 2316c
  Maine 1984b
  Maldive Islands 2214b
  Massachusetts 1985b
  Michigan 1986a
  Mississippi 1987a
  Netherlands Antilles 2318a
  New Jersey 1989c
  New York 1990c
  Newfoundland 2112b
  Norway 2230b
  Oregon 1993a
  Papua 2319b
  Pennsylvania 1993c
  Peru 2236b
  Philippines 2237c–2238a
  Pitcairn Island 2319c
  Portugal 2241b
  primitive culture 1933c
  Puerto Rico 2002c
  Qatar 2242b
  St. Pierre and Miquelon 2321c
  Senegal 2248a
  Seychelles 2322b
  Sierra Leone 2248c
  South Carolina 1994b
  South Yemen 2253c
  Spanish Sahara 2323a
  sport 1703b
  Sweden 2268a
  Tanzania 2272b
  Texas 1995c
  Tokelau Islands 2324a
  Trucial Oman 2276b
  U.S. 1969a, 2294b
  Virginia 1997a
  Washington 1998a
  Western Samoa 2301c
Fisk, Clinton B. presidential candi-
  date *tab* 801
Fisk, James (Jim Fisk) 251b, 524a

Fiske, John 251b, *tab* 1478
Fisk University 700
Fissile 497a
Fission (nuclear) 1143c, 1828c
Fissure (rocks) 497a
Fistula 941c
Fitch, Clyde *tab* 1479
Fitch, John 251b
Fitchburg, Massachusetts 1985b
Fitchburg, State College at 674
FitzGerald, Edward 251b, 982b,
  1369b, *tab* 1475
  Rubaiyat 1416b
Fitzgerald, F. Scott 251b, 1375c
Fitzsimons, Thomas 809c
Fitzwater, Matilda 1438c
Five Classics (Chinese lit.) *tab*
  1463
Five Forks, Battle of 2049, 2050c
Five-Power Treaty 2069a
Five Year Plan (U.S.S.R.) 880a,
  898a
Fixation (psych.) 1957b
Fjord (waters) 497a–497b, 2230a
Flag *see* Flags
Flag Day 842a
Flagella bacteria 1843c
  flagellates 1848b
Flagellates 1848b
Flags
  semaphore 1151a
  U.S. *il* 2010
  world *il* 2182–2184
Flagstad, Kirsten 251c
Flake tools 1928c
Flamenco dances 182a
Flaming Gorge Dam *tab* 1206
Flamingo 33c
Flanders *see headings beginning
  Flemish*
Flannagan, John B. 124b, *tab* 125
Flash method (teaching) 1299c
Flat (mus.) 175b
Flat feet 941c
Flatfish 33c
Flatiron (rocks) 497b
Flaubert, Gustave 1381c, *tab* 1476
  biography 251c
Flax 733c, 1667b
  linen 1214a
  North Dakota 1991c
  St. Helena 2321a
Flaxman, John 122c, *tab* 125
  biography 251c
Flea 33c–34a
Fléchier, Valentin 1379c
Fleming, Sir Alexander 251c
  penicillin 1845c
Fleming, Sir John Ambrose 251c
  vacuum tubes 1284a
  valves 1886c
Fleming, Sandford 252a
Fleming valve 1284a, 1886c
Flemish art *tab* 107
  furniture 1095c, 1096a
Flemish language 1337a
Flemming, Arthur S. *tab* 797
Fletcher, Benjamin 2026a
Fletcher, John (Eng. au.) 1361c,
  tab 1467
Fletcher, John Gould (Amer.
  poet) 1376a
Fleurs du Mal (poems) 1381c
Fleury, André Hercule de 252a
Flexner, Simon 258a
Flexography printing 1174a
Fliegende Holländer Der *see Fly-
  ing Dutchman, The*
Flies control of 957b
  public health 957a
Flint (rock) 497b
Flint, Michigan 1985c
Floating (swimming) 1733b
Flocculate 497b
Flocculi 1794c
Flodden Field, Battle of 1006b,
  1020b
Floe, ice 497b
Flood control 1255a
Flood current 497b
Floodplains 448a, 497b
Floods 455b
  dams 1205c, 1206c
Flora (bio.) 497b
  paleontology 458a
Flora (myth) 1432b
  festival 1439a
Floralia 1439a
Florence, Italy 2194b–2194c, 2195b,
  2354c

  architecture 76c
  bridges 1196c
  Renaissance 986a
  see also Florentine art
Florence State College 654
Florentine art 986a
  painting 106–107
  pottery *tab* 130
  sculpture 114a, 121a
Flores, Juan José 2144b
Florida 1979
  acquired from Spain 1964c
  agriculture 1979b
  architecture 1105c
  armadillo 14b
  arrowroots 1649c
  butterfly 18c
  capital punishment 860b
  census (1960) 1970
  cinnamon 1658b
  climate 1979a–1979b
  cod 22b
  colleges of 661
  commercial law 826
  congressional apportionment
    tab 853
  coquina 23a
  crocodile 24b
  croton 1660c
  cycad 1660b
  discovery 2023b
  economy 1979b
  flag *il* 2010
  flamingo 33c
  fruit industry 738a
  geography 1979a–1979b
  government 793b, 1979b
  holidays 841–842
  ibis 40b
  labor legislation 832c
  lignum vitae 1675c
  lime 1676
  lobster 43c
  mahogany 1677c
  Mahogany trees 1677c
  opossum 48b–48c
  palms 1683c–1684a
  people of 1979b
  peppertrees 1686a
  phoebe 51a
  pit-viper 51c–52a
  public school enrollment *tab*
    646
  public school expenditures *tab*
    644
  purchase 903b, 2035c
  sea cows 55b
  secession 2043c
  sedge 1692b
  sisal 1693a
  student enrollment *tab* 645
  sunfish 61a
  taro 1696a
  vegetables 747a
**Florida Agricultural and Mechan-
  ical University** 661
Florida Memorial College 661
Florida Southern College 661
Florida State University 661
Florida, University of 661
Florio, John 1402c
Flotation 1271c
Flotow, Friedrich von *tab* 171c,
  biography 258a
Flounder *il* 1717
  see also Flatfish
Flour milling 1255b
Flow *see* Deformation
Flowering dogwood 1987a, 1990c,
  1997a
Flowers 1645c–1646a
  parts of 1645c
  pollination 1645c–1646a
  *see also under names of indi-
    vidual kinds of flowers, such
    as Orchids*
Floyd, John *tab* 796
  presidential candidate *tab* 800
Floyd, William *tab* 803
Fluidram *tab* 1500
Fluidounce *tab* 1500
Fluke 34a
Fluorescence 1906b, 1918a
Fluorescent lights 1140c–1141a,
  1890a, 1906a
Fluorides teeth 959b
Fluorine 1808a, 1832
  atomic weight *tab* 1805
  electrons 1807a, 1808c
  ions 1809b
  oxidizer 1779b
Fluorite hardness *tab* 1192b
Flush (biog.) 1371b
Flutes (arch.) 75a
Flutes (mus.) 157b, 175b
Fluvial cycle 497b
Flux 1209b
  glassmaking 133a

Fluxmeter 1249a
Fly 34a
  see also Flies
Flycatcher 34b
Flying buttress 76c
Flying Dutchman (Fliegende Hol-
  länder) (opera) 166c, 1432b
Flying Dutchman (ship) 1432b
Flying fish 34b
Flying lemur 34b
F.O.B. *see* Free On Board
Focal point (optics) 1908a
Foch, Ferdinand 258a
  World War I 2066b
Fock, Jenö 2175c
Focus (earthquakes) 497b
Fodio, Usuman dan 2229c
Foehn (wind) 497b
Foerster, Joseph Bohuslav 168c
Fog 473b
  defined 497b–497c
Fogazzaro, Antonio 1387c, *tab* 1478
Fokine, Michel 183c, 184a
Fold (rocks) 451a, 497c
  tight 518b
Folger, Charles *tab* 796
Foliation 497c
Folic acid *tab* 919
Folio (print.) 151a
Folk dances 181b
Folklore definition 1421c
  dictionary of 1421–1449
  see also Mythology
Folk music 154c, 157c, 422–423
  American 170c
  Middle Ages 159a
Folkunga Fountain 123b
Follicle-stimulating hormone 926b
Folsom, Marion B. *tab* 797
Fomors 1432b
Foncha, John Ngu 2110b
Fonseca, Manoel Deodoro da 2104a–
  2104b
Fonseca, Gulf of 2227b
Font (print.) 151a
Fontaine, Jean de la *see* La
  Fontaine, Jean de
Fontainebleau, Forest of
  Barbizon School 86a
Fontana, Domenico 252a
Fontana Dam 1206
Fontane, Theodor *tab* 1476
Fontanne, Lynn 252b
Fontbonne College 679
Fontenelle, Bernard le Bovier de
  252b, 1380a
Fonteyn, Dame Margot 252b
Fonvisin, Denis 1389a
Foochow, China 2354c
Food 719–748
  bacteria 1845a
  camping 1711b
  canning 1239a
  in cultures 767c
  ecology 1861d
  fish 733c
  frozen 737b
  kindergarten 402c
  plant storage 1646c
  preparation 1087c
  primitive 1933a
  seafood 733c
  space travel 952c–953a
Food Additives 734c
Food Administration Board 2065c–
  2066a
Food and Agriculture Organization
  (FAO) (UN) 750b, 993a
Food chains (bio.) 1861c
Food engineering 735a
Food manufacturing 735b
  fruit products 736a
  meat packing 735b
  poultry products 735c
  vegetable products 736a
Food poisoning 941c, 956a
  botulism 940c, 956b
  prevention 956b
Food preservation 736c
  curing 735c
Fool Errant, The (nov.) 1370c
Fool's gold *see* Pyrite
Foolscap (print.) 151b
Foot (anat.) *see* Feet
Foot (measure) *tab* 1500
Foot (music) 175b
Foot (poetry) 1404a
Football 1714b
  penalties 1723c
  rules 1723a
Foot-candle (unit) 1907a

Foote, Andrew Hull 2045c
Foote, Arthur 170b, *tab* 172c
Foot line (print.) 151b
Foothills 497c
Footnotes 151b
Foppa, Vincenzo *tab* 106
Fouquet, Jean 253a
Foraker Act (1900) 2003a, 2060b
Foraminifera 1848a
Foraminiferal ooze 497c
Forastero 726b
Forbes-Robertson, Sir Johnston 252c
Force (phys.) 1873a
  definition 1918a
Ford, Henry 252c
Ford, John *tab* 1467
Ford, Paul Leiscester 1375a
Ford (waters) 497c
Fordham College 685
Fore edge (print.) 151b
Foreshock (earthquakes) 497c
Foreshore (waters) 497c
Foreign Children (poem) 414a
Foreign exchange 592c
Foreign exchange rate 592c
Foreign languages
  study of 1330–1333
  teaching of 619b
Foreign Ministers, Council of 880b
Foreign policy 880b
Foreign Service 389a
Forester, Cecil Scott *tab* 1481
Forest Lovers, The (nov.) 1370c
Forestry 1265b
  Alabama 1974b
  Austria 2095a
  Bahamas 2307b
  Canada 2112b
  defined 1638a
  Finland 2147a
  Gabon 2155c
  Guatemala 2168b
  Honduras 2173a
  Ivory Coast 2197a
  Japan 2199b–2199c
  Korea, North 2203c
  Laos 2206b
  Lebanon 2207c
  Nicaragua 2227c
  Nigeria 2229b
  Norway 2230b
  Papua 2319b
  Paraguay 2235a–2235b
  Peru 2236b
  Philippines 2238a
Forests 1863b
  Angola 2306b
  British Honduras 2308a
  British Solomon Islands 2308c
  Brunei 2309b
  California 1976c, 1977a
  Colorado 1977b
  Connecticut 1978a
  conservation 775c
  Equatorial Guinea 2311c
  Fiji Islands 2312b
  Florida 1979b
  Georgia 1979c
  Idaho 1980c
  Kentucky 1983b
  lumber and timber industry 1265b
  Maine 1984b
  Minnesota 1986b
  Mississippi 1987a
  Mozambique 2317b
  Norfolk Island 2319b
  North Carolina 1991a
  Oregon 1992c
  Portugal 2241b
  Portuguese Guinea 2320a
  Portuguese Timor 2320b
  Surinam 2323b
  Swaziland 2267a
  Sweden 2268a
  Thailand 2273c
  Turkey 2278a
  U.S. 1963b–1963c, 1969a, 2294a
Forge, The (paint.) *tab* 111
Forget-me-not 1667b–1667c, 1974c
Forgery 880c
Forgetting 1950a
Forge welding 1287b
Forging (metal.) 1268a
Form (print.) 151b
Format 151b
Formations (geol.) 455b
Formic acid 1821b
Formosa (Taiwan)
  see China, Nationalist; Taiwan
Forms of address *tab* 1119
Formulas (math.) 1604a
Forrest, Nathan B. 252c, 2050a
Forrestal, James V. *tab* 796, *tab* 797

Forsaken Merman, The (poem) 1440a
Forseti 1432b
Forster, E. M. 252c, *tab* 1480
Forsyte Saga (novels) 1370b, 1404a, 1410c
Forsyth, Alexander 1254c
Forsyth, John *tab* 795
Forsythia 1667c
Fort Christina founding 2024c
Fort Donelson, Tennessee 2045c, 2049
Fort Fisher, Battle of 2049
Fort Garry 2116c
Fort Gourand, Mauritania 2216a, 2216b
Fort Hays, Kansas 668
Fort Henry, Tennessee 2045c
Fort Lauderdale, Florida 1979b
Fort Leavenworth, Kansas 629c
Fort Lewis College 659
Fort Smith, Arkansas 1976a
Fort Moultrie 2028a
Fort, Paul *tab* 1480
Fort Peck Dam 1205c, 1206
Fort Orange 2024c
Fort Pickens 2044a
Fort Pillow, Tennessee 2049
Fort Sumter 2044c
Fort Valley State College 662
Fort Wayne, Indiana 1981c
Fort Worth, Texas 1995c, 2007b
Fort Wright College of the Holy Names 706
Fortaleza, Brazil 2354c
Fort-de-France, Martinique 2354c
Fortissimo 175b
Fort-Lamy, Chad 2120c, 2355a
Fortas, Abe 954a
Forte (mus.) 175b
Forth Bridge, Firth of 1197, 1197a
Fortuna 1432b
Fortunate Isles *see* Canary Islands
Fortunatus, Venantius *tab* 1465
Fortunes of Nigel (nov.) 1365c
Fortuny y Carbo, Mariano *tab* 108
Forum (Fora) 976a
Forum, Roman 971a
  sculpture 118c
Forward, Walter *tab* 795
Forwarding (bookbinding) 151b
For Whom The Bell Tolls (nov.) 1375c
Forzando (mus.) 175b
Foscari, Francesco 252c
Foscolo, Ugo 252c, 1387b
Fosse (glaciers) 497c
Fossil fuels 450c, 455c, 459b
  defined 497c
Fossils 455c
  anthropology 1924a
  defined 497c
Foster, Benjamin *tab* 108
Foster, Charles *tab* 796
Foster, John Watson 253a, *tab* 796
Foster, Rev. P. 1338b
Foster, Stephen Collins 169c, *tab* 172c, 1374b, *tab* 1476
  biography 253a
Foster, William Z. presidental candidate *tab* 800
Foucault, Jean B. L. 253a, 497c
Foucault pendulum (instrument) 497c–498a
Fouche, Joseph 907b
Fouls (basketball) 1707b
Foundry form (print.) 151b
Foundry proof (print.) 151b
Fountain of Energy (sculp.) 124a
Fountain of Youth 1432b, 2023a
Fouque, F. de la Motte *see* La Motte-Fouque, F. de
Fouquet, Jean *tab* 106
Four Apostles (paint.) *tab* 111
Four Books, The (Chinese lit.) *tab* 1464
Fourdrinier Brothers 148b, 1272a
Four-H Clubs 1744a
Four Horseman of the Apocalypse (nov.) 1404b
Fourier, François Marie Charles *tab* 1472
  biography 253a
Four o'clock (bot.) 1667c
  genetics 1851a
Four o'clock family 1667c
Four Oxen and the Lion (fable) 443c
Four Power Treaty (1921) 2069a

Fourteen Points 874c, 2066c
1440 World Map 780
Four Vedas (lit.) 1420b
Fourth (mus.) 175b
Fourth of July *see* Independence Day (U.S.)
Fouta Djallon Mountains 2169c, 2332a
Fowl 34b–34c
  see also Poultry
Fowler, Henry H. *tab* 796
Fox 34c
Fox, Charles James 253b
Fox, George 253b
Fox, John William, Jr. *tab* 1479
Fox and the Cat, The (fable) 442b
Fox and the Crow, The (fable) 442a
Fox and the Grapes, The (fable) 442c
Fox and the Lion, The (fable) 442a
Fox and the Stork, The (fable) 442b
Fox Island 2016a
Foxe, John *tab* 1466
  biography 253b
Foxglove 1667c
F. P. A. *see* Adams, Franklin Pierce
Fra Angelico *see* Angelico, Fra
Fra Diavolo 253b
Fra Elbertus *see* Hubbard, Elbert
Fractional-horsepower motors 1143c
Fractionation 1273a
Fractions 1526a, 1604a
  addition 1527a
  algebra 1538b
  division 1529a, 1539b
  equality 1526c
  multiplication 1527c, 1539a
  signs of 1538c
  subtraction 1528c
Fractures (geol.) 453a
Fractures (medical) 917c
Fracture (minerals) 498a
Fragments of Ancient Poetry (bk.) 1364a
Fragonard, Jean Honoré 85a, *tab* 107
  biography 253b
  Romance of Love and Youth *tab* 111
Fragoso Carmona, António Oscar de 2242b
Framingham, State College at 674
Francaix, Jean *tab* 172a
France, Anatole 1382c, *tab* 1478
  biography 253b
France 2148–2155
  abolishes monarchy 1006c, 1007c
  agriculture 2148c–2149a
  anchovy 13b
  anthropology 1925a
  Benelux customs union 998b
  bloc 857b
  the Bourbons 2151c
  in Cambodia 2109a–2109b
  Canada and 2113a, 2113c–2114c, 2116a
  the Capetians 2150b–2150c
  the Carolingians 2150a–2150b
  in Central African Republic 2119b
  in Chad 2121a
  cheese *tab* 731b
  in China 2129a, 2129c
  citizenship 863c
  climate 2148a, 2148c
  Cold War 2155a
  communism 2154c
  in Comoro Islands 2310c–2311a
  in Congo (Brazzaville) 2134a–2134b
  Congress of Vienna 1023c
  constitution of 2149c
  Constitution of 1791 1006c, 1008b
  Constitution of the Year III 1006c, 1008b
  Crimean War 997c
  in Dahomey 2141a
  the Directory 1006c, 1008b, 2152c–2153a
  economy 2148b–2149c
  in Egypt 2281b
  English-French wars 999b
  established church 877
  European Common Market 877b
  feudalism 1006b, 1007b
  Fifth Republic 2149c, 2155a
  flag *il* 2183
  flax 1667b
  Fourth Republic 2155a
  Franco-Prussian War 994c, 1024c

  in French Guiana 2312b–2312c
  in French Polynesia 2312c–2313a
  in French Southern and Antarctic Territories 2313a–2313b
  in French Territory of the Afars and the Issas 2312b–2313c
  in Futuna Islands 2324c
  in Gabon 2155c–2156a
  geography 2148a
  in Guadaloupe 2315a
  in Guinea 2170a–2170b
  in Guyana 2171a
  in Haiti 2172a
  Hundred Years War 994a, 2286c
  industry 2149a–2149b
  in Ivory Coast 2197b
  in Laos 2206c–2207a
  lavender industry 1675a
  League of Nations 1012c
  in Lebanon 2208a
  Louisiana Territory purchased from 1964b–1964c
  in Madagascar 2212a–2212b
  in Mali 2215b
  map 2148, *Atlas-22–23*
  marigolds 1678b–1678c
  in Martinique 2316c
  in Mauritania 2216b–2216c
  in Mauritius 2217a
  the Merovingians 2150a
  Mississippi Bubble scheme 1016b–1016c
  Napoleonic Era 2153a
  natural resources 2148b–2148c
  in New Caledonia 2318a–2318b
  in New Hebrides 2319a
  in Niger 2229a
  nuclear power 2155a
  occupation of Algeria 2088a
  occupation of Germany 2163a
  people of 2148a–2148b
  purslane 1689b
  recognizes Communist China 2155a
  religion 2148a, 2150a, 2151b–2151c
  in Réunion 2320c
  rocket engines 1767c
  in St. Pierre and Miquelon 2321c
  SEATO 1021a
  Second Empire 2153b–2153c
  Second Republic 2153b
  in Senegal 2248a–2248b
  Seven Years' War 2290b
  social insurance 837a
  Third Republic 2153c–2154a
  trade 2149b–2149c
  transportation 2149b
  Triple Alliance (1717) 1022c
  in Tunisia 2277b–2277c
  in Upper Volta 2294c–2295a
  the Valois kings 2150c–2151b
  in Vietnam 2300c–2301a
  in the Virgin Islands 2004c
  in Wallis Islands 2324c
  War of the Spanish Succession 998c–999a
  wines 723c
  World War I 995b, 1015c, 1024c–1025c, 2154a–2154b
  World War II 1025c–1028c, 2154c–2155a, 2162c, 2292a
  see also French language; French literature
  —Arts
  architecture 76c, 77b, 78a
  ballet 182c
  cave art 971a
  ceramics 126c, 127b, 130–132
  dance 182a
  furniture 1095a, 1097b, 1099a
  glass *tab* 135
  interior decoration 1102b
  music 154c, 166a, 168a, *tab* 171b
  painting *tab* 106–109
  printing 144a
  Romanticism 85c
  sculpture 119, 120a, 122b, *tab* 125
  see also French literature
  —Government 881b, 2149c–2150a
  budget system 858b
  bureaus 858b
  cabinet 859c
  commune 868a
  constitution 869c
  Council of Ministers 872c
  Council of State 871a
  Court of Cassation 860b
  departments 873b
  interpellation 886b
  kings *tab* 1078
  legislation 889b
  parliament 894a
  premier 901a
  presidency 875a
  —History *tab* 1036–1058, 2150a–2155a
  civil wars *tab* 1073

colonies in Americas 2023b
Cominform 866a
coup d'état 871c
explorations *tab* 1060
Hundred Years' War 1359c
kings *tab* 1078
mercantilism 986c
nationalism, rise of 985c
naval conference 2069a
subsidy 909b
reparations 905b
see also French Revolution
France (ship) 1180c
Francesca, Piero della *tab* 106
Portrait of the Duke of Urbino *tab* 110
Francesca da Rimini 253b
Francesco di Giorgio 253c
Franchetti, Alberto 167c
Francia (It. art.) *tab* 106
Francia, José Gaspar Rodríguez de 2235c
Francis, David R., *tab* 797
Francis Ferdinand, Archduke 1024c, 2095b, 2161c
Francis Ferdinand (Franz Ferdinand) 253c
Francis I, Emperor (Austria) 1021b, 2160c
see also Francis II, Emperor (Holy Roman Empire)
Francis I, Emperor (Holy Roman Empire) 253c
Francis I, King (France) 2113c, 2151b, 2270b
biography 253c
furniture 1095b
tomb 122b
Francis I, King (Hungary) *see* Francis II (Holy Roman Empire)
Francis II, Emperor (Holy Roman Empire) 2095b
biography 253c
Francis II, King (France) 2151b
Francis III (Duke of Lorraine) *see* Francis I, Emperor (Holy Roman Empire)
Francis Joseph I, Emperor (Austria) 2161a
biography 253c
Francis, Saint 998b
Francis of Assisi, Saint 254a, 985b
writings 1386a
Francis of Sales (François de Sales), Saint 254a, *tab* 1467
Francis (of Assisi), Saint *see* Francis of Assisi
Francis (of Sales), Saint *see* Francis of Sales
Francis Xavier, Saint 366c, 2200c
Francium 1832
atomic weight *tab* 1805
Franciscans
science 1755a
Franck, César Auguste 168c, *tab* 171c
biography 254a
Franco, Francisco 874a, 988c, 2196c, 2264a, 2265b
biography 254a
Franco of Cologne *tab* 171b
François *see* Francis
Franconium 1808b
Franco-Prussian War 994c, 1023a, 1024c, *tab* 1075, 2153c
Frank, Bruno 1101c
Frankenstein (nov.) 1365b, 1404b
Frankenthal Germany
pottery *tab* 131
Frankfort, Kentucky 1983a, 2007b
Frankfurt am Main, West Germany 2355a
Frankfurter, Felix Supreme Court *tab* 802a
Frankie and Johnnie (ballad) 1396b
Frankland, Edward 1761b
Franklin, Benjamin 874a
biography 254a
constitution 809c, 2030b
Declaration of Independence *tab* 803
lightning 1881a
nicknames *tab* 1463a
oceanography 461c
Poor Richard's Almanac 1413c
printing 144c, 145a
weather 468a
writing 1167b, 1321c, 1372c, *tab* 1469
Franklin College 666
Franklin, Sir John 254b
Franklin and Marshall College 695
Franks 983b, 1019b, 2159a

Franks (tribe) 1000a–1000b
Franz (Ger. form of Francis) *see* Francis
Franz Ferdinand, Prince 2304b
see also Francis Ferdinand
Franz Josef *see* Francis Joseph I
Franz Josef Land *see* Fridtjof Nansen Land
Franz Josef Land Islands 2332a
Franzen, Franz Mikael *tab* 1472
Frasch, Herman 1224a
Fraser, James Earle *tab* 125
Fraser River 2111a
Fraternal twins 1857a
Fraternities 1938c
Fraud 820a, 881a
Fraunhofer, Joseph von 254b
Fraunhofer lines 1906b
astronomy 1789b
Frazee, John *tab* 125
Frazer, Sir James George 254b, 1622a
Frechette, Louis 1391b
Frederick Barbarossa *see* Frederick I, Emperor (Holy Roman Empire)
Frederick the Great *see* Frederick II, King (Prussia)
Frederick of Prussia 2152b
Frederick I (Barbarossa), Emperor (Holy Roman Empire)
biography 254b
Frederick I, King (Germany) *see* Frederick I (Barbarossa), Emperor (Holy Roman Empire)
Frederick I, King (Sicily) *see* Frederick II, Emperor (Holy Roman Empire)
Frederick II, King (Germany) 2160c *see* Frederick II, Emperor (Holy Roman Empire)
Frederick II, Emperor (Holy Roman Empire) 254c
patronage 1385c
Frederick II (the Great), King (Prussia) 254c, 965b
nickname 1462a
Frederick William, Elector (Brandenburg) 254c
nickname 1462b
Frederick William I, King (Prussia) 254c
Frederick William III, King (Prussia) 254c, 1014b
Frederick William IV, Emperor 2161a
Fredericksburg, Battle of 2048b, 2049
Frederiction, Canada 2355b
Fredonia, New York natural gas 1210a
Free association (psych.) 1957a
Free coinage 592c
Free enterprise 523b
Free on board 592c
Free Soil Party 881a, 906a, 2040c
date formed 2040b
Liberty Party 889c
Free trade 593a
Free verse 1404b
Free water 498a
Freedmen's Bureau 2051c
Freedom of assembly *see* Right of assembly
Freedom of petition *see* Right of petition
Freedom 7 (spacecraft) *tab* 1770
Freedom of the press 810a, 860c, 861b, 1171a
Freedom of religion 810a
Freedom of speech 810a
influence of literature 1347c
Freeman, Mary E. Wilkins *tab* 1478
Freeman, Orville *tab* 797
Freemasons 1744a
Scottish Rite 1744a
Free-radical reaction *see* Homolytic fission
Freesia 1667c
Freetown, Sierra Leone 2248b, 2249a, 2355a
Freezers 1260a
Freezing point 1803a, 1815c, 1898b, 1918a
temperature scales 1920a
Frei Montalva, Eduardo 2122c
Freiburg, Germany cathedral 76c
Freight 593a
Freiligrath, H. Ferdinand *tab* 1475
Freischütz, Der (opera) 165b
Frelinghuysen, Frederick (1753–1804) 255a

Frelinghuysen, Frederick Theodore (1817–1885) *tab* 796
Frelinghuysen, Theodore *tab* 800
Fremiet, Emmanuel *tab* 125
Frémont, John C. 2040a
biography 255a
nickname *tab* 1463a
presidential candidate *tab* 800, 906a, 2042b
French, Alice 1374c
pseudonym *tab* 1463b
French, Daniel Chester 123c–124a, *tab* 125, 255a
French, John Denton Pinkstone 255c
French (lang.) *see* French language
French Academy of Inscriptions and Letters excavations 969c
French Academy founding 1378c
French art *see* France — Arts
French Broad River 2020c
French Committee of National Liberation (Free French) 2154c
French East India Company 2217a
French Equatorial Africa 2155c
French Guiana 2312
French history *see* France—History
French and Indian War *tab* 1073, 2026c
French language 1295a, 1296c, 1297a, 1331a, 1335c
English derivatives *tab* 1297c
Norman conquest 1358c
punctuation 1312c, 1314c
French literature 1377–1383, 1465–1481
Age of Enlightenment 1380a
chanson de geste 1398c
Classical Age 1378c
influence on Canadian 1391a
influence on Spanish 1392b
realism 1381b
romanticism 1380c
French Polynesia 2312–2313
French Revolution 963b, 987a, 1006c–1008c, 2152b–2152c, 2290c
beginning of 1006c
causes of 1007a
Committee of Public Safety 1006c, 1007c–1008a
conscription 868b
end of 1006c–1007a
effects of 1007a
Girondists and 1008a, 1008b–1008c, 1010c
Jacobins 1010c
Reign of Terror 1006c, 1007c–1008a, 1008c
September Massacres 1007c, 1008a
storming of the Bastille 998a
wars of *tab* 1074
French Revolution (bk., Carlyle) 1366a
French Somaliland *see* French Territory of the Afars and the Issas
French Southern and Antarctic Territories 2313
French Territory of the Afars and the Issas 2313
French Union 869c, 2156a
French West Africa 2170b
Freneau, Philip 255a, 1372b
Frenssen, Gustav *tab* 1479
Frequency 1918a
Frequency-modulation (FM) telegraph 1183b
Fresco 73a
Frescoes Aegean 83b
Frescobaldi, Girolamo *tab* 171b
Fresh water 498a
habitat 1866b
Freshet (waters) 498a
Fresnel, Augustin Jean 255b, 1761a
Fresno State College 657
Freud, Sigmund 1348b, 1947a, 1957a
biography 255b
psychoanalysis 1957a
Frey (Freyr) 1432c
Freya (Freyja) 1432c
Freytag, Gustav 1385a, *tab* 1475
biography 255b
Friable (rocks) 498a
Friant Dam 1206
Friar Rush 1432c
Friar Tuck 1432c
Fricatives 1294c
Frick, Henry Clay 255b, 524c
Frick Gallery (New York) *tab* 111
Friction 1876c, 1918a
coefficient of 1876c
Friedrich *see* Frederick
Friendly Islands *see* Tonga Islands

Friends University 668
Friendship 7 (spacecraft) *tab* 1770
Frieze 75a
interior decoration 1105a
Frigate bird *il* 28, 34c
Frigga 1432c
Frigid climate 498a
Frigid zone 498a
Friml, Rudolf 168c
Fringing reef 498a
Frisian Islands 2224c, 2332a
Frisian (lang.) 1337c
Frissell, Mount 1977c
Frit 127a, 130a
Fritillary 1667c–1668a
Froberger, Johann 162a, *tab* 171c
Frobisher, Martin 255c, 2023b
Fröding, Gustaf *tab* 1479
Froebel, Friedrich 255c
Froelich, John 721a
Frog 34c–35a
Frog test 926c
Froissart, Jean 1378a, *tab* 1466
biography 255c
Froment, Nicholas *tab* 106
Fromm, Erich 255c
Frondizi, Dr. Arturo 2091a
Frontenac, Count de (Louis de Buade) 255c
Fronds 1641c
Front (air masses) 498a
Frontier in American History (bk.) 1348c
Fronts 764a
meteor. 477a
Frost, Robert 1344a, 1376a, *tab* 1480
biography 255c
Frost 473b
defined 498a
Frost heaving 498a
Frost line 498a
Frostbite 941c
Frostburg State College 672
Froude, James Anthony 1366c, *tab* 1475
Frozen assets 593a
Frozen foods 737b
Fruits 737c, 1646a
aggregate 1646a
Albania 2086b
American Samoa 2000a
Bahamas 2307b
British Honduras 2308a
California 1977a
Cook Islands 2311a
Delaware 1978c
Dominica 2311b
dry 1646a
farming 381b
Fiji Islands 2312b
fleshy 1646a
Florida 1979b
food manufacturing 736a
French Polynesia 2313a
Georgia 1979c
Great Britain 2282c
Hawaii 1980b
Ifni 2316a
industry 737c
multiple 1646a
Montserrat 2317a
Mozambique 2317b
Netherlands Antilles 2318a
New Caledonia 2318b
Norfolk Island 2319b
Oregon 1993a
Portugal 2241b
St. Vincent 2321c
Saudi Arabia 2247a
Sikkim 2249c
simple 1646a
Singapore 2250b
South Africa 2252b–2252c
South Yemen 2253c
Spain 2264a
structural differences in 1646a
Surinam 2323b
Swaziland 2267a
Tonga 2324b
Trinidad and Tobago 2275c
Tunisia 2277a
U.S. 1968c, 2294a
Yemen 2302a
Yugoslavia 2303b
see also under names of individual fruits
Fruit fly 35a
Frunze, Soviet Union 2355a
Frustrum of a cone 1602b
Fry, William Henry 170a
Frye, William Pierce 256a
FSH *see* Follicle-stimulating hormone

Fuad I, King (Egypt) 1005c–1006a
Fuchs, Leonhard 1638a
Fuchsia 1668a
Fuegian Indians cooking 1933a
Fuel Administration Board 2066a
Fuel cells 1137c, 1883b
Fuel injection 1136b
Fuel oil 1137a
Fuel systems rockets 1766b
Fuels 1136c
  liquid 1137a
  rockets 1765a, 1766b
  solid 1136c
Fuentes, Gen. Miguel Ydigoras 2169b
Fugue (mus.) 162a, 175b
Fuji, Mt. 2198b
Fuji Volcano 2332a
Fujiwara family 2200b
Fukien Massif (mountains) 2124a
Fukuoka, Japan 2355a
Fukushima, Japan 2355a
Fulham, Eng. pottery *tab* 130
Full score (mus.) 175b
Fuller, George *tab* 108

Fuller, Margaret 1373c, *tab* 1475
  biography 256a
Fuller, Melville Weston 256a
  Supreme Court *tab* 802a
Fuller, Thomas *tab* 1467
Fuller's earth 498b, 1201c, 1209b
Fullerton, California State College at 657
Fulper ware *tab* 132
Fulton, Robert 256a, 1182c
Fumarole 498b
Fumitory 1668a
Fumitory family 1668a
Funan, Kingdom of 2109a
Functional diseases psychology 1952b
Functional group (chem.) 1820b
Functionalism (arch.) 82b
Functional school (psych.) 1948a
Functions (math.) 1604a
  inverses of 1586b
  trigonometry 1583a
Fundamental (mus.) 175b
Fundamental Orders of Connecticut 2025a, 2026b
Funds 593a

Fundy, Bay of 2332a–2332b
Funerals etiquette 1116c
Fünfkirchen, Hungary 2368b
Fungi 1640a–1641a, 1846c, 1860c
  bacteria 1640c
  decay 1860c
  diseases 1847a
  diseases, incubation of 955b
  genetics 1856a
  gibberellins 738c
  lichens 1640c–1641a
  reproduction of 1847a
  slime molds 1640c
  uses of 1847b
  yeast 748c
Fungicides 741c
Fumicello River 2246a
Funnel cloud *see* Tornado; Water spout
Funston, Frederick 256a
Fur *see* Furs
Fur farming 738a
Fur trade Canada 2112b, 2113b, 2114b
  Finland 2147a
Furens Dam 1205c
Furetière, Antoine 1378c

Furies 1431a
Furlong *tab* 1500
Furman University 698
Furnaces 1256a
Furniture 73b, 1093–1102
  interior decoration 1102–1111
  manufacturing 1256a
  Renaissance 1094c
  Twentieth Century 1101b
  wood finishing 1288a
Furnivall, Frederick 256a
Furnivals ware *tab* 132
Furs 738a, 1209b
Furstenberg, Germany pottery *tab* 131
Furtwängler, Adolf 256a
Furze *see* Gorse
Fusion (metal) 1287c
  alloys 1193c
Fusion (nuclear) 1143c, 1829a
Fust, Johann 143b
Futuna Islands *see* Wallis and Futuna Islands
Future (fin.) 593a
Futures market 588c
Fyn Island 2141a

G

Gabbro 450c, 498b
Gabo, Naum 123b, *tab* 125
Gaberones, Botswana 2101b, 2355a
Gabès, Tunisia 2277a
Gabon 2119b, 2155b–2156a
  economy 2155c
  flag *il* 2183
  geography 2155b
  government 2155c
  history 2155c–2156a
  map 2155, *Atlas*-35
  people of 2155b–2155c
  religion 2155b, 2156a
  slavery 2155c
Gabonese Democratic Bloc (BDG) 2156a
Gabonese Social and Democratic Union (UDSG) 2156a
Gabriel (Bib.) 1432c, 1454a
Gabriel, Jacques (1630–1686) 256b
Gabriel, Jacques (1667–1742) 256b
Gabriel, Jacques Ange (1698–1782) 256b
Gabrieli, Andrea 162a, *tab* 171b
Gabrieli, Giovanni 162a, *tab* 171b
Gabrilowitsch, Ossip 256b
Gad 1454a
Gaddi, Agnolo 256b
Gaddi, Gaddo 256b
Gaddi, Taddeo *tab* 106
  biography 256b
Gade, Jacob 168c
Gade, Niels Wilhelm 168b, *tab* 172a
Gadolinium 1832
  atomic weight *tab* 1805
Gadsden, James 256b, 2042a
Gadsden, Alabama 1974b
Gadsden Purchase 1964c, 2042a, 2219a
  acres 903b
Gaea 1432c
Gaelic language 1335c
  alphabet *tab* 1295
Gagarin, Yuri A. 256b, 951b, 1770c, *tab* 1770
Gage, Lyman J. *tab* 796
Gage, Thomas American Revolution 256b, 2028a
Gaillard, David Du Bose 256b
Gaillarde (dance) 182a
Gaillardia 1668a
Gaillon Chateau 122b
Gainsborough, Thomas *tab* 107, 1103b
  biography 256c
  Blue Boy 112
  Mrs. Siddons *tab* 111
Gaínza, Gabino 2136a
Gaitán, Jorge E. 2133c
Gaius Caesar
  see Caligula, Gaius Caesar
Gaius (Rom. jur.) 256c

Gal 498b
Galactic latitude 1795a
Galactic longitude 1795b
Galactosemia 1856b
Galahad 1432c
  Morte d' Arthur 1411a
  Siege Perilous 1447b
Galapagos Islands 2143c
  finch 33b
  flamingo 33c
  penguin 50b
  sea lions 56c–57a
  tortoises 63c–64a
Galatea (myth) 1432c
  Polyphemus 1444c
  Pygmalion 1445b
Galaxies 1785b, *tab* 1785, 1787
  Magellanic clouds 1795b
  population of 1786c
Galba, Servius Sulpicius 256c
Galcit fuels 1778c
Galdós, Benito Pérez
  see Pérez Galdós, Benito
Gale (wind) 498b
Gale, Zona *tab* 1480
Galen 256c, *tab* 1464, 1753a
Galena 453c, 498b
Galilee 1454a
Galilee, Sea of 2192b, 2332b
Galileo (Galileo Galilei) 498b, 1190b, 1387a, *tab* 1467, 1504c, 1757b, 1798b
  biography 256c
  Jupiter 1763c, 1783b
  thermometer 468a
Gall, Franz Joseph 257a
Galla (people) 1935c
Galland, Antoine 1395a
Gallatin, Albert 257a, *tab* 795
Gallatin River 2018c
Gallaudet, Thomas Hopkins 257a
Gallaudet College 661
Gallbladder 921b
Galle, Johann Gottfried 257a
Gallegher and Other Stories (Davis) 1404b
Gallegos, Rómulo 2298b
Galley (print) 151b
Galli-Curci, Amelita 257a
Gallic War *tab* 1072
Gallieni, Joseph Simon 257b
Gallinule 35a
Gallipoli campaign (World War I) 1025a
Gallium 1832
  atomic weight *tab* 1805
Gallon *tab* 1500
Galloway, Joseph 2027c
Galofalo (whirlpool) *see* Charybdis
Galois, Evariste 257b, 1506c
Galop (dance) 175b
Galsworthy, John 1370b, *tab* 1479
  biography 257b
  Forsyte Saga 1404a
  Justice 1408a

  Modern Comedy 1410c
  on W. H. Hudson 1414b
  pseudonym *tab* 1463c
Galton, Sir Francis 257b, 1506c
Galuppi, Baldassare *tab* 171c
Galván, Ignacio Rodríguez 1393a
Galvani, Luigi (Aloiso Galvani) 257b
Galvanometer 1248b, 1918a
Galveston, Texas 1995c, 2007b–2007c
  hurricane 475b
Gálvez, Juan Marval 2173c
Gama, José Basílio da 1393a
Gama, Vasco da 257b
Gambetta, Léon 257c
Gambia 2156a–2156c
  agriculture 2156a–2156b
  Commonwealth status 1000c
  economy 2156a–2156b
  flag *il* 2183
  geography 2156a
  government 2156b
  history 2156b–2156c
  map 2156, *Atlas*-36
  people of 2156a
  religion 2156a
  slavery 2156c
Gambia River 2156a–2156c, 2215a, 2247c, 2332b
Gambier Islands 2312c–2313a
Gambling mathematics 1505a
  Nevada 1988c
Game reserves 896a
Games 1703–1740
  for kindergarten 403a
  primitive 1937a
  singing games 418–424
Gametes 1850b
Gamma globulin 922c, 1825b
Gamma rays 1918a
Gammer Gurton's Needle (play) 1360c
Gamow, George 1787c
Gamut 158c
Gan Island 2214c
Gandak River 2223c
Gandhi (Shrimati) **Indira** 257c, 2186b
Gandhi, Mohandas Karamchand (Mahatma Gandhi) 965a, 981a, 1624c, 2185b, 2185c, 2233b
  biography 257c
  nonreistance 894b
Ganelon 1432c
Ganges River 2177b, 2178, 2232a, 2332b
  religion 980c
Ganglia 938a
Gangrene 941c
Ganktok, Sikkim 2249b, 2355a
Gangue 498b
Gannon College 695
Gannett Peak 1999b
Ganswindt, Hermann 1764c
Ganymede (myth) 1432c

Ganymede (satellite) 1783b
Gap (geog.) 498b
Gar 35b
Garber, Daniel *tab* 108
Garbo, Greta 257c
García, Alejo 2235b
García, Carlos 2233c
García, Manuel 257c
García Iñiguez, Calixto 257c, 2137b
García Moreno, Gabriel 2144b
García-Godoy, Héctor 2143b
Garcilaso de la Vega *tab* 1466
Garda, Lake 2332b
Garden Clubs National Council of State 1744a
Garden of Eden *see* Eden, Garden of
Gardenia 1668b
Gardening *see* Horticulture
Gardiner, Samuel Rawson 258a
Gardner, James *tab* 797
Gareth 1432c
Garfield, Harry Augustus 2066a
Garfield, James Abram *tab* 798–799, 906b
  administration 2055c
  assassination 2055c
  biography 258a
  cabinet *tab* 796–797
  election and inauguration *tab* 801
  events paralleling administration *tab* 1066
Garfield, James R. *tab* 797
Gargallo, Pablo *tab* 125
Gargantua 1378b
Garibaldi, Giuseppe 258a, 2196a
Garland, Augustus H. *tab* 796
Garland, Hamlin 1374c, *tab* 1479
Garlic 1668b
Garm 1432c
Garment industry *see* Clothing industry
Garmo Peak 2337c
Garneau, François Xavier 1391b
Garner, John Nance 258b
  House of Representatives *tab* 802b
  vice-presidency *tab* 801
Garnet (mineral) 453c, 498b
Garnier, Robert 1378c
Garnishment (law) 881a
Garonne River 2148a, 2332b
Garrett, Visconde de Almeida *see* Almeida-Garrett, Visconde de
Garrick, David 258b, 1363b
Garrison, Lindley M. *tab* 796
Garrison, William Lloyd 258b, 2037c
Garrison Dam 1206
Garrod, A. E. 1855c
Garrotin (dance) 182a
Garshin, Vsevolod *tab* 1478
Gary, James A. *tab* 796

Gary, Indiana 1981c, 2007c
Gas 762a
  Canada 2112a
  marsh 506b
Gas, Natural *see* Natural gas
Gas turbines 1148c
Gases 1801b, 1828a, 1871b
  commercial 1201a
  conductance 1882b
  heat 1899c
  kinetic theory 1872a
  scientific laws 1871b
Gaskell, Elizabeth C. S. *tab* 1475
  Cranford 1400a
Gasoline 1137a, 1210b, 1216c
  lead 1213c
Gasoline engines 1134b
Gaspé Peninsula 2332b
Gastric juices 920c
Gas welding 1287c
Gat (geog.) 498c
Gates, Horatio 258c, 2028b
Gates, Sir Thomas 2024a
Gates, Thomas S., Jr. *tab* 797
Gath 1454a
Gathas (rel. verses) 1627b
Gatt *see* General Agreement on Tariffs and Trade
Gattamelata (sculp.) 121b
Gaudier-Brzeska, Henri *tab* 125
Gauguin, Paul 86c, *tab* 108
  biography 258c
  Maternity il 90
Gaul 1377b, 2150a
Gauls (people) *tab* 1071
  Italian invasion *tab* 1071
Gauss, Karl Freidrich 1506a, 1558a, 1566b, 1580c, 1764a
  biography 258c
  number congruence 1530c
Gautama Buddha *see* Buddha
Gautier, Theophile 258c, 1381b, *tab* 1475
Gavazzeni, Gianandrea *tab* 172a
Gavotte 175b, 182a
Gawain 1432a
  Morte d' Arthur 1411a
  Gawain and the Green Knight (poem) 1432c
Gay, John 258c, 1363b, *tab* 1469
Gay-Lussac, Joseph Louis 258c
  gases 1828a, 1871b
Gay-Lussac's law 1871c
Gaza 1454a
Gaza Strip 2192a, 2280b, 2281b, 2281b-2281c
  map *Atlas*-24
Gazelle 35b
Gdańsk (Danzig), Poland 2239a, 2355a-2355b
Gdynia, Poland 2239a, 2355b
Ge (myth) *see* Gaea
Geanticline 498c *see also* Fold
Gears 1257a, 1280c
Geba River 2320a
Geber (Jabir) 258c
Gecko 35b
Geddes, Sir Auckland Campbell 259a
Geertgen van Haarlem *tab* 106
  St. John Baptist in Wilderness *tab* 110
Geese 36b-36c, 739a
Gegenschein 1794c
Gehrig, Lou 259a
Geibel, Emanuel *tab* 1475
Geiger, Hans 1914a
Geiger counter 1914c
Geiger-Muller counter 1249a, 1275c
Geijer, Erik Gustaf *tab* 1472
Gelatin 738c, 1824b
Gelber, Jack 1377a
Gellert, C. F. *tab* 1470
Gellius, Aulus 1358b
Gell-Mann, Murray 1916a
Gelon 259a
Gem 460a, 498c
Gemara 1525a
Gemini *see* Castor and Pollux
Gemini, Project *see* Project Gemini
Gemini 5 951b, 1138a
  fuel cell 1138a
Gemini 7 951c
Gems *see* Gem
Gender 1304b
Gene (bio.) *see* Genes
Genealogy 1923c
Genera Plantarum (Jussieu) 1638c
General Agreement on Tariffs and Trade 993a

General Assembly (UN) 990c
General Beadle State College 699
General Introduction to Psychoanalysis (Freud) 1348c
General Magazine 1167b
General paresis 1954a
General psychology 1948b
General store 593a
Generations, alternation of 1641c-1642a
Generators 1885a
  automobiles 1131b
  electric 1138b
Genes 1841a, 1850a
  and development 1857b
  evolution 1858a
  internal structure 1855b
  Mendel, G. J. 1850b
Genesee River 2013c
Genesis (Bib.) 1454a
Genet, Edmond Charles 2031c
Genetic code 1855a
Genetic psychology 1951a
Genetics 1850-1858
  breeding, animal 725a
  careers 390c
  defined 1638a
  Mendel, G. J. 1850a
  progress 1858c
Geneva, Switzerland 2269c, 2270c, 2355b
Geneva, Lake 2269b, 2332b
Geneva Bible 1362b
Geneva College 695
Geneva Conference (1954) 2301a
Genevieve, Saint 259a
Genghis Khan 979c, 1021a, 1021c, 2085c, 2220c, 2221a
  biography 259b
Genghis rugs 1110c
Génie du Christianisme, Le (bk.) 1380c
Genii (genius) (myth) 1433a
Genius 1952c
  sociology 1938b
Genoa, Italy 2194c, 2355b
  medieval map-making in 779c
  Republic of 2195b
Genocide 881a, 913c
Genoveva (opera) 166a
Genseric 259a
Gentian 1668b-1668c
Gentian family 1668c
Gentile da Fabriano *tab* 106, 259a
Gentile, Giovanni 259a
Gentleman's Magazine 1167b
Genus 1638b, 1639a
Geo 498c
Geocentric orbit 1779a
Geocentric system 1794c
Geochemical cycle 498c
Geochemistry 1800c
Geode (minerals) 498c
Geodesy 498c
Geoffrey of Monmouth 1359c, 1436a, *tab* 1465
  Arthurian legend 1395c
  History of the Kings of Britain 1425a
Geoffroy, Etiene François (1672-1731) 1798c
Geographical cycle 498c
Geography 498c
  geographic societies 1744
  U.S. 1961-1969
  see also Cultural geography; Economic geography; Physical geography
Geography (Ptolemy) 779a-779b
Geoid 498c
Geologic column 455b
Geologic erosion 499a
Geologic time 454c, *tab* 456-457, 498c-499a, 759b
  chart 455b
  divisions 455a
Geological oceanography 461a, 462b
Geology 447-459, 499a
  careers 390b
  dating methods 454b
  economic geology 459
  fossils 455c
  historical geology 454a
  mineralogy 451c
  paleontology 458a
  physical geology 447a
  structural 516c
Geometric mean 1604c
Geometric progression 1607a
Geometric series 1607b
Geometry 1556-1580
  absolute value 1601a

  analytic 1590-1593
  congruence 1602c
  constructions 1578c
  definition 1604a
  history of 1501c, 1504b
  logic 1559a
  numbers 1525a
  Pythagoreans 1752a
  rise of non-Euclidean 1505c
  topology 1507a, 1607b
Geomorphic cycle 499a
Geomorphology 499a
Geophysics 447a
  careers 390b
George I, King (England) 259b, 2290a-2290b
George I, King (Greece) 259c, 2166c
George II, King (England) 259b, 2290a-2290b
George II, King (Greece) 259c, 2167a-2167b
  abdication 849a
George III, King (England) 259b
  American Revolution and 2290c
  insanity 2291a
  reign of 2290c-2291a
George IV, King (England) 259b
George V, King (England) 259b
  reign of 2291c
George VI, King (England) 259c
  death of 2292b
  reign of 2291a, 2291c-2292b
George, Saint 1446b
  biography 259a
  Donatello's statue 121b
George, Henry 907c
  biography 259c
George, Stefan 1385b, *tab* 1479
George, Lake 2016a
George Fox College 693
George Peabody College for Teachers 700
George Washington Bridge 1191a, 1197a
George Washington University, The 661
George Williams College 664
Georgetown, Cayman Islands 2309c, 2355b
Georgetown, Guyana 2170b, 2355b-2355c
Georgetown, Malaysia 2213b
Georgetown University 661
Georgetown College 670
Georghiu-Dej, Georghe 2245a
Georgia 1979-1980
  agriculture 1979c
  capital punishment 860b
  census (1960) 1970
  Civil War 995
  climate 1979c
  colleges 661-663
  colonial history 2026a
  commercial law *tab* 826
  congressional apportionment *tab* 853
  Dutchman's pipe vine 1665c
  economy 1979c-1980a
  flag *il* 2010
  geography 1979c
  government 1980a
  grouse 37a
  hickory trees 1672a
  legal holidays 841-842
  people of 1979c
  public school enrollment *tab* 646
  public school expenditures *tab* 644
  restored to Union 2053b
  secession 2043c
  student enrollment *tab* 645
  tea trees 1696b
  U.S. Constitution 809c
  voting age 912c
Georgia College at Milledgeville 663
Georgia Southern College 662
Georgia Southwestern College 662
Georgia State College 662
Georgia Institute of Technology 662
Georgia, University of 662
Georgian Court College 682
Georgian Style (arch.) 78b
Georgics (poems) 1354, *tab* 1464
Georgie Porgie (nursery rhyme) 409b
Geosphere 499a
Geophysics 499a
Geostrophic 499a
Geosyncline 499a
Geothermal gradient 499a
Geotropism plants 1647a-1647b

Geranium 1668c
Gerbert *see* Sylvester II, Pope
Gerhardt, Paul 1383c, *tab* 1467
Geriatrics 960a
Géricault, Jean Louis 259c
Gericault, (Jean) Theodore *tab* 108
Gerin-Lajoie, Antoine 1391a
German art *see* Germany—Arts
German, Edward 169b
German East Africa 2273a
German history *see* Germany—History
German language 1295a, 1296c, 1337a
  classification 1333b
  cognates *tab* 1297b
  punctuation 1314c
  study of 1331a
German literature 1383-1385
  Faust 1432a
  outline 1465-1481
German measles *tab* 946
  pregnancy 959a
Germania (Tacitus) 1358a
Germanic languages 1297b, 1333b, *tab* 1334, 1336
Germanicus Caesar 259c
Germanium 1832, 1890a, 1892b
  atomic weight *tab* 1805
Germanium transistors 1890b
Germantown, Battle of 2029
Germany 2157-2163
  absentee voting 849a
  agriculture 2158a, 2158b
  anthropology 1925a
  Anti-Comintern Pact (1936) 1028a
  Austria's union with 2096a-2096b
  ballot 855c
  censorship 862a
  cheese *tab* 731b
  civil service 865a
  climate 2157b
  coal 1202b
  Crusades 1002b
  Czechoslovakia occupied by 2140a
  Denmark occupied by 2142b
  dictatorship 873c
  division of 2163a-2163b
  economic control 876b
  economics 988a
  economy 2158a-2158c
  established church 877b
  feudalism 1006b
  flags *il* 2183
  Franco-Prussian War 994c, 1024c
  Frankish Kingdom 2159a
  geography 2157b
  government 2158c-2159a
  government planning 899a
  the Hapsburgs 2159c-2160a
  history 2159a-2163b
  Jews 2157c, 2162a, 2162b
  Kiaochow Bay seized by 2129b
  League of Nations 1012c, 1013c, 1015a
  labor legislation 830c
  law 815b
  map 2157, *Atlas*-16-17
  Nazi Era 2162a-2162c
  nonaggression pact with Soviet Union 2162c
  occupation of 2163a
  occupation of Iceland 2176c
  people of 2157c-2158a
  printing 143c
  Reformation 2160a-2160b
  Reich 905a
  religion 2157b, 2157c, 2159a, 2160a-2160b, 2161b
  reparations debt (World War I) 1023b
  risings of 1848 2161a
  rockets 1764c, 1765a, 1768b
  in Romania 2245a
  in Rwanda 2245c
  the Saxons 2159a-2159c
  seizes Austria (1938) 1015a
  social insurance 837a
  Treaty of Brest-Litovsk 999a-999b
  Triple Alliance (1882) 1022c, 1025a
  unification 2161a-2161b
  V-2 rocket 1765c
  Weimar Republic 2161c-2162a
  wine 723c
  workmen's compensation 835c
  World War I 995b, 999a-999b, 1015c, 1017b, 1024c-1025c, 2095b-2095c, 2099a, 2154b, 2161c, 2291c
  World War II 1025c-1028c, 2099a,

2154c–2155a, 2162c, 2163a
see also German language;
German Literature
—Arts
architecture 77b
furniture 1096b
glassware *tab* 135
Gothic cathedrals 76c
music 154c, 160c, 168a, *tab* 171b
painting *tab* 106–109
pottery *tab* 130–131
sculpture 120b, 122b, *tab* 125
—History *tab* 1038–1050, *tab* 1056, *tab* 1058
emperors of *tab* 1078
Gestapo 907b
mercantilism 986c
reparations 905b
Versailles Treaty 854a
World War I 2064c
Germany, East
communism 2158c
economy 2158b–2158c
flag *il* 2183
government 2158c–2159a
religion 2157a
Soviet Union and 2163b
Germany, West
decentralization 862c
economy 2158a–2158b
European Common Market 877b
flag *il* 2183
government 878b, 2158c
NATO 1016c
religion 2157a
Germination 1647b–1647c
Germiston, South Africa 2355c
Germs *see* Bacteria
Gerome, Jean Leon *tab* 108
Gerontology 960a
Gerry, Elbridge 259c, 881a, 2032b
Declaration of Independence *tab* 803
Gerrymander 852c, 881a
Gershwin, George 170b, *tab* 172c
biography 260a
Gersoppa Waterfall 2332b
Gerund 1306a
Geryon 1433a
Gesneria family 1668c–1669a
Gessner, Salomon *tab* 1470
Gest, Morris 260a
Gestalt psychology 1948b
learning 1950a
Gestapo 881a
Gestido, Oscar 2296a
Gettysburg, Pennsylvania 1008b
Gettysburg, Battle of 963b, 1002c–1003a, 2048c, 2049
Gettysburg Address 1404b
Gettysburg College 695
Geysers 499a
Ghana 2163c–2164c, 2170b
agriculture 2164a
cocoa 726c
Commonwealth status 1000c
economy 2164a
flag *il* 2153
geography 2163c
government 2164a
history 2164a–2164b
map 2164, *Atlas-36–37*
people of 2163c–2164a
religion 2163c
slavery 2164b
Ghats (mountains) 2332b–2332c
Ghazzali 260a
Ghengis Khan *see* Gengis Khan
Ghent, Justus Van *tab* 106
Ghent, Belgium 2098a, 2098b
Ghent, Treaty of 2035
Ghibelline family 1009a
Ghiberti, Lorenzo 144a, 121b *tab* 125
biography 260a
Ghirlandaio, Domenico 260a
Ghost (folklore) 1433a
Ghoul (folklore) 1433b
G I Bills 912a
G. I. Bill of Rights *see* Servicemen's Readjustment Act
Gia-Long, Emperor (Vietnam) 2300c
Giacosa, Giuseppe 1387c, *tab* 1478
Giacometti, Alberto *tab* 125
Giantism 942a
Giant (folklore) 1443b
Giaour, The (story) 1365a
Gibberellic acid 738c
Gibbon 35b–35c
classification 1923c

Gibbon, Edward 994c, 1364a, *tab* 1470
biography 260a
Decline and Fall of the Roman Empire 1401a
Gibbons, Grinling *tab* 125
Gibbons, James 260a
Gibbons, Orlando 161a, *tab* 171c
Gibbs, Josiah Willard 260b, 1127b, 1507b
Gibbs, Sir Phillip 1371a
Gibraltar 2265c, 2283c, 2313, 2314
Gibraltar, Strait of Pillars of Hercules 1434c
Gibson, Wilfrid 1371a
Gibson Desert 2332c
Gide, André 260b, 1382c, *tab* 1479
Gideon (Bib.) 1454b
Gideons (organ.) 1454
Gielgud, Sir John 260b
Gieseking, Walter 260b
Giffard, Henri 1154c
Gifford, Robert S. *tab* 108
Gifu, Japan 2355c
Gigawatt 1920b
Gigli, Beniamino 260b
Giglio Island 2193c
Gigue *see* Jig
Gil Blas (nov.) 1380b, *tab* 1469
Gila monster *il* 32, 43a, *see also* Lizard
Gilbert, Sir Humphrey 260b
Gilbert, Joseph Henry 749c, 753a
Gilbert, William 260c, 1759c, 1798b, 1881a
Gilbert, Sir William Schwenck 169b, 1369b, *tab* 1477
Bab Ballads 1396b
biography 260c
operas 1404c
Gilbert and Ellice Islands 2283c, 2314
Gilbreth, Frank B. 1261a
Gildersleeve, Basil Lanneau 260c
Gilead 1454c
Gilgal 1454b
Gill, Eric *tab* 125
Gill (meas.) *tab* 1500
Gillett, F. H. House of Representatives *tab* 802b
Gillette, William Hooker 260c, 1417b
Gillyflower *see* Stock; Wallflower
Gilman, Nicholas U. S. Constitution 809c
Gilmer, Thomas *tab* 795
Gilpin, Charles 1402b
Gilpin, Henry *tab* 795
Gilson, Etienne 260c
Gin (beverage) 724a
Ginastera, Alberto *tab* 172c
Ginger 744b, 1669a
Ginger family 1669a
Gingerbread Boy (story) 427a
Ginkgo 1642b, 1669a
Ginsberg, Allen 260c, 1376b
Ginseng 1669a–1669b
Ginseng family 1669b
Gintl, Wilhelm 1183a
Gioberti, Vincenzo 1387b
Giono, Jean *tab* 1481
Giordano, Luca 260c
Giordano, Umberto 167c, 168a
Giorgione, Il (Giorgione da Castelfranco) *tab* 106
biography 261a
Pastoral Symphony *tab* 112
Sleeping Venus *tab* 110
Giorno, Il (poem, Parini) 1387a, *tab* 1470
Giotto *tab* 106
biography 261a
St. Francis Breaks With His Father *il* 87
sculpture 121a
Giotto's Tower 76c, 121a
Giovine Italia (society) 2195c
Gypsy Girl (paint.) *tab* 112
Gipsy Madonna (paint.) *tab* 113
Giraffe 35c
Giralda Tower (Spain) 78a
Girard College (Philadelphia) architecture 78c
Girardon, François 122c, *tab* 125
Giraudoux, Jean 261a, 1382b
Gird (organ.) 1768a
Girls and boys, come out to play (nursery rhyme) 409c
Girl Reading a Letter (paint.) *tab* 109
Girl Scouts 1744a

Girondists 1008a, 1008b–1008c, 1010c, 2152c
Gissing, George 1368b, *tab* 1478
Giuba River 2251a
Giusti, Giuseppe 1387b
Glacial 449a
Glacial milk 449a
Glacial period 499a
Glaciation 449a, 455a
Glacier National Park 2020b
Glaciers 449a, 499a–499b, 761b, 2110c
hanging 500b–500c
Iceland 2176a
kinds of 449a
rock 513a
salt 513b
Glackens, William James *tab* 108
Glades 499b
Gladiolus *il* 1663, 1669b
Gladstone, William Ewart 261a, 863a
Glagolitic script 1334a
Glasgow, Ellen *tab* 1480
Glasgow, Scotland 2355c
Glass Carter 261b, *tab* 796
Glass 449b, 133–135, 1210c, 1890a
architecture 82a
ceramics 132c
characteristics *tab* 1211
chemical composition 1211a
colors 133c
heat transfer 1901a
history of 134a
products *tab* 1211
properties of 1870c
Glass fibers 1209a
Glassboro State College 682
Glassmaking 134a
Glassware 133–135
Glass wool 1208b
Glauber, Johann Rudolf 261b, 1798b
Glaucoma 928c, 942a
Glaucus (myth) 1426c, 1433b
Scylla 1447a
Glazes (ceramics) 120b, 131c
Glazunov, Alexander 169a, *tab* 172b, 184a
Gleaners, The (paint.) *tab* 112
Glee (mus.) 175b
Glei (soil) 499b
Gleipnir 1433b
Glen Canyon Dam *tab* 1206, 1975b
Glenn, John H., Jr. 261b, 1770b, *tab* 1770, 2080c
Glens 499b
Glenville State College 706
Gliders 1155b
Gliere, Reinhold 169b, *tab* 172b
Glinka, Mikhail 169a, *tab* 172a, 261b
Glissando (mus.) 175b
Globigerina ooze 499b
Globin 1824b
Glockenspiel 175b
Glomerulonephritis 942a
Glomerulus 925b
Glorieux, Le (comedy) *tab* 1469
Glorious Revolution 987a, 2191b–2191c
Glossitis 942a
Glottis 1284b
Glover, Jose 145a
Gloxinia 1669b
Glucagon 926a
Gluck, Christoph Willibald von *tab* 171c
biography 261b
Glucose 927b, 1824a, 1825b
photosynthesis 1861a
Glue 1211c
casein 727a
gelatin 738c
Glycerin explosives 1207c
Glycerol 920c
Glycogen 921a, 927b, 1824a, 1825b
Glycon 261b
Glycolysis 1825b
Gneiss (rocks) 450c, 453c, 499b
Gnome 1433b
Gnosticism 1008c–1009a
G. N. P. *see* Gross national product
Gnu 35c
Goat 36a
Goat Island, California *see* Yerba Buena Island
Goats 738c
diseases 739a
French Territory of the Afars and the Issas 2313b
Greece 2165a
Ifni 2316a
Libya 2210a

Mauritania 2216a
Mongolia 2220c
Nepal 2223c
Niger 2228c
Pakistan 2232b
Qatar 2242b
Saudi Arabia 2247a
Somali Republic 2251a
South West Africa 2322c
South Yemen 2253c
Spanish Sahara 2323a
Tunisia 2277a
Turkey 2278a
undulant fever 958a
Upper Volta 2294c
Yemen 2302a
Gobelin (fam.) 261b
Gobi Desert 2124a, 2332c
Goblin 1433b
Godard, Benjamin *tab* 171c
Godavari River 2177c, 2332c
Goddard, John 1099c
Goddard, Robert H. 1765a, 1767c, 1768b
Goddard College 704
Godfrey of Bouillon *see* Godefroy de Bouillon
Godefroy de Bouillon (Godfrey of Bouillon) 261b, 1002b, 1407b
Godetia 1669c
Godiva 261c, 1433b
Godowsky, Leopold 261c, 1173a
Godoy, Manuel de 261c
Godthab, Greenland 2314a
Godunov, Boris, Emperor (Russia) 261c
Godwin (Earl of Wessex) 261c, 2284c
Godwin, Francis 1763b
Godwin, William 261c, 1366a
Godwin, Mary (1797–1851) *see* Shelley, Mary
Godwin Austin (mountain) 2332c
Goebbels, Joseph Paul 261c, 886b
Göring Hermann 263b
Goes, Hugo van der *tab* 106
Adoration of the Shepherds *tab* 110
biography 262a
Goethals, George W. 262a, 2061c
Goetzen, Graf von 2245c
Goethe, Johann Wolfgang von *il* 208, 1384a, *tab* 1471
biography 262a
Faust 1346a, 1403c
Goff, Nathan Jr., *tab* 796
Gog and Magog (Bib.) 1454b
Gog and Magog (statues) 1404c
Gogh, Vincent van *see* Van Gogh
Gogol, Nikolai Vasilevich 1389c, *tab* 1475
biography 262b
Goidelic languages *see* Gaelic languages
Goiter 942a
Gola tribe 2209a
Gold 460b, 1832
Alaska 1975a
Angola 2306c
atomic weight *tab* 1805
Australia 2092b, 2093a
Brazil 2103b, 2103c
British Solomon Islands 2308c
coinage 865c
conductivity 1882a
Congo (Kinshasa) 2134c
Fiji Islands 2312b
Ghana 2164a
Laos 2206b
Liberia 2209a
Mexico 2218a
Mongolia 2220c
Montana 1988a
New Zealand 2226a
Nicaragua 2227c
Panama 2234a
Philippines 2238a
pyrite 453c
Rhodesia 2243a
Romania 2244a
South Africa 2252b, 2252c
South Dakota 1994c
Swaziland 2267a
Sweden 2268a
Tanzania 2272b
Thailand 2273c
U.S.S.R. 2256b
Upper Volta 2294c
Utah 1996b
Venezuela 2297c
Gold Bug, The (tale) 1404c
Gold Coast *see* Ghana
Gold Coast Colony 2164b *see also* Ghana

Gold exchange standard 593b
Gold standard 536a
Goldbach, Christian 1524b
Goldberg, Arthur J. 262b
  labor department *tab* 797
  Supreme Court *tab* 802a
  United Nations *tab* 797
Golden Age 1405a, 1433b
Golden Ass (stories) 1405a, *tab* 1464
Golden Fleece 1424c, 1433b
  Jason 1436b
Golden Gate (strait) 2017c
Golden Gate Bridge 1191a, 1197a
Golden Mean 975a, 1615a
Golden poppy 1976b
Golden section (geom.) 1604a
Golden Treasury of Songs and Lyrics (anthology) 1395a
Golden-bell see Forsythia
Golden-chain see Laburnum
Goldeneye 36a
Goldenrod 1669c, 1983a, 1988a
Goldfinch 36a–36b
  Eastern 1982a, 1989b
  willow 1997c
Goldmark, Karl 168a, *tab* 172a
Goldoni, Carlo 262b, 1387a, *tab* 1470
Gold Rush 2040b
Goldsmith, Oliver 262b, 1346a, 1363c, *tab* 1470
  Deserted Village 1401a
  She Stoops to conquer 1417a
  Vicar of Wakefield 1420b
Gold Standard Act 2060c
Goldwater, Barry 262c, 2082a
Goldwyn, Samuel 262c
Golf 1724a
Golgotha 1454b
Goliards 159a
Goliath 1454b
Gollwitzer, Helmut *tab* 1481
Golovlev Family, The (nov.) 1389c
Gómez, José 2137c
Gómez Juan Vicente 874a, 2298a–2298b
Gómez y Báez, Máximo 262c, 2137b
Gomorrah 1460a
Gompers, Samuel 262c
  A. F. of L. 2057a
Gomulka, Wladyslaw 2240c
Gonçalves Dias, Antonio 1393a
Goncharov, Ivan 1389c
Goncourt, Edmond de 262c, *tab* 1476
Goncourt, Jules de 262c, 1382a, *tab* 1477
Gondwanaland 2091a
Goneril 1405a, 1408b
Gong (mus.) 175b
Góngora y Argote, Luis de 1391c
Goniometer 452a
Gonococcus 1845a
Gonorrhea *tab* 946, 958c
Gonzaga University 706
Gonzalez, Julio *tab* 125
Good, James W. *tab* 796
Good Counsel College 685
Good Friday states celebrating 841c
Good Gray Poet see Whitman, Walt
Good Hope, Cape of
  Flying Dutchman 1432b
Good Neighbor Policy 1017c, 2022b
Good Tempars Prohibition Party 901c
Good Will 593b
Goodhue, Bertram Grosvenor 81a
Goodman, Benny 263a
Goodrich, Benjamin F. 263a
Goodrich, Samuel G. *tab* 1473
  pseudonym 1462c
Goodyear, Charles 263a, 1276c
Goose see Geese
Goose with the Golden Eggs (fable) 444a
Gooseberry 1669c
Goosefoot family 1669c
Goossens, Eugene *tab* 172b
Gopher 36c
Gorboduc (tragedy) 1360c
  blank verse 1397c
Gordian knot 1433c
Gordon, Charles George 263a, 1005a
  death of 1005b
  nickname 1461c
Gordon, Charles W. see Connor, Ralph
Gordon, Lou 1156a
Gordon College 674
Gore, Howard M. *tab* 797

Goree Island 2248a
Gorgas, William Crawford 263a, 388c
Gorges 499b
Gorgias 1614a
Gorgons 1443c
  Medusa 1439a
Gorgonzola cheese *tab* 731b
Gorham, Nathaniel *tab* 802b, 809c
Gorham State College 672
Gorilla 36c
  anthropology 1923c
Gorini, Gino *tab* 172a
Gorky, Arshile *tab* 109
Gorky, Maxim 263b, 1390a, *tab* 1479
Gorky, Soviet Union 2256a, 2355c
Gorse 1669c–1670a
Gorton, John 2094a
Goshen, Egypt 1454b
Goshen College 666
Gosnold, Bartholomew 263b
Gospel Book (Otfried) rel. verses 1383a, *tab* 1465
Gossart, Jan see Mabuse, Jan
Gosse, Sir Edmund 263b, 1369c, *tab* 1478
Gossec, François *tab* 171c
Göteborg, Sweden 2355c–2356a
Gothenburg, Sweden see Göteborg, Sweden
Gothia, Kingdom of 2268b
Gothic period (art) 72a
  architecture 76b, 985a
  furniture design 1094a
  sculpture 114b, 120
Gothic language 1336b
Gothic type (print.) 151b
Goths 2159a
Gotland Island 2332c
Gotterdämmerung, Die (opera) 167a
Gottfried von Strassburg *tab* 171b, 1383b, *tab* 1465
  biography 263b
Gottschalk, Louis Moreau 170a
Gottsched, Johann Christoph 1384a, *tab* 1469
Gottwald, Klement 2140a
Gotunns 1433b
Götz Van Berlichingen (play) 1384b
Gouda cheese *tab* 731b
Gouda Mountains 2313b
Goucher College 672
Goudimel, Claude *tab* 171b
Goudy, Bertha 146c
Goudy, Frederick W. 146b
Goujon, Jean 122b, *tab* 125
  biography 263b
Goulart, João 2104c
Gould, Benjamin Apthorp 263b
Gould, George Jay 263b, 1629a
Gould, Jay 263b, 524a
Gould, Morton 170b
Gounod, Charles François 168a, *tab* 171c
  biography 263b
Gourd family 1670a
Gournay, Sieur de 596a
Gout 940b, 942a
Government 783–914
  anarchism 851c
  bibliography 914
  budget 532a
  bureaucracy 858c
  and business 526b
  cabinet 859a
  careers 389a
  censorship 860c
  centralization 862b
  city manager form 864b
  commission form 864a
  checks and balances 863c
  Commonwealth 867c
  constitutions 868c
  county 871c
  crown 872a
  decentralization 862b
  dictatorship 873c
  dictionary of terms 849–914
  economic control 876a
  education 629a
  eminent domain 876c
  forms 784c, 881a
  local, U.S. 890a
  mandate 891a
  mayor-council form 864a
  nihilism 893c
  parliamentary 896b
  party government 896c–897a
  planning 898a
  public utility 903b
  revolutionary 906c
  theory of 783–785
  totalitarian 910c
  U.S. 785–811
  see also under the names of

individual countries
Government bonds 593b
Government of India Act (1935) 2185b
Governor 881b
  form of address *tab* 1119
Governor-General (Canada) forms of address 1119
Gower, John 1360a, *tab* 1466
Gowon, Yakubu 2230a
Goya y Lucientes, Francisco José de 85b, *tab* 107, *tab* 111
  biography 263c
  Don Sebastian Martinez tab 112
  Marquesa de Pontejos tab 113
Goyen, Jan van *tab* 107
Gozo Island 2215b
Gozzi, Carlo 1387a, *tab* 1470
Gozzoli, Benozzo *tab* 106
GR-S (rubber) see Buna-S
Graaf, Regnier de 263c
Grabbe, Christian D. *tab* 1474
Graben 499b
Gracchus, Gaius Sempronius 263c
Gracchus, Tiberius Sempronius 263c
Grace notes 175b
Graces (myth) 1433c
Graceland College 667
Grackle 36c
Gradation (geol.) 455a, defined 499b
Grade scale see Wentworth grade scale
Graded bedding 499b
Graded shore line 499b
Graded stream 499b
Gradual (mus.) 158c
Graham, Martha 184c
  biography 263c
Graham, William (Amer. pol.) *tab* 796
Graham, Rev. William F. (Billy Graham) 263c
Grahame, Kenneth 263c
Graham's law 1802a
Grain see names of cereal plants, such as Wheat
Grain (meas.) *tab* 1500
Grain (print.) 151b
Grainger, Percy 169b
  biography 264a
Grainne 1430b
Gram *tab* 1500, 1873b
Grammar 1303–1311
  composition and writing 1316–1320
  correct English 1320–1322
  figures of speech 1314–1315
  parts of speech 1304a
  public speaking 1326–1328
  punctuation 1311–1314
  sentence analysis 1308c
  words and phrases often misused 1322–1325
Grampian Mountains 2282a
Gran Chaco Lowlands 2332c–2333a
Gran Colombia 2144b, 2133a
Granada, kingdom of 1009a, 2022c
Granada, Nicaragua 2227c, 2228a
Granada, Spain 2356a
  furniture 1096b
Granados, Enrique 169b, *tab* 172c
Granados, Federico Tinoco 2136a
Grand Assize 855a
Grand Banks Plateau 2333a
Grand Calumet River 2007c
Grand Canal (China) 1160c
Grand Canyon 759b, *il* 2009, 2017c
Grand Canyon National Park 2017c
Grand Coulee Dam 888c, 1190a, 1205c, 1206, 1997, 2017a
Grand Dixence Dam *tab* 1206
Grand Duchy of Warsaw 2240a
Grand jury 886c
Grand Lama see Dalai Lama
Grand mal 941c
Grand Pré, Nova Scotia
  Evangeline 1403a
Grand Rapids, Michigan 1985c
Grand River 2011b
Grand Teton Mountains 1999
Grand Teton National Park 2020b
Grand Turk, Turks and Caicos Islands 2324a
Grande Comore Island 2310c
Grande-Terre Island 2315a
Granduca Madonna (paint.) *tab* 110
Granger, Francis *tab* 795
Granite 450c, 453b, 499c, 1211c
Granite Peak 1987c

Grant, Duncan *tab* 109
Grant, James Augustus 2280a
Grant, John Peter 2198a
Grant, Ulysses Simpson 264a, *tab* 798–799, 2143a
  administration of 2053–2055a
  Cabinet *tab* 796–797
  Civil War 2045c, 2050
  election and inauguration *tab* 801
  events paralleling administration *tab* 1065–1066
  Liberal Republican Party 889c
  nickname *tab* 1463c
  Republican Party 960a
  at Shiloh 1020c
Grantee (law) 825a
Grantor (law) 825a
Granule (rock) 499c
Granville-Barker, Harley 1371c
Grape family 1670a
Grape hyacinth 1670b
Grapefruit 1670a–1670b
Grapes 739a, 1670a
  Greece 2165a
  Oregon 1992c
Graphic arts 73a, 136–141
  aquatint 138c
  engraving 139b
  lithography 141a
  mezzotint 139a
  printing 142–153
  woodcuts 139c
Graphite (carbon) 499c
  crystal structure 1870c
  Korea, South 2203c
  Madagascar 2212a
  Mexico 2218a
Graphs 1604b
  algebra 1553a
  equations 1555c
  first-degree equations 1554a
  inequalities 1555c
  two variables 1554b
Graptolite (organism) 499c
Grass, Gunther 264a
Grass family 1670b
Grasse, François J. P. de 2030a
Grasshopper *il* 29
Grasslands 499c 1865a
Grassman, Hermann Günther 1507b
Gratianus, Emperor 999a
Gratings (optics) 1905b
Grattan, Henry 264a
Grau San Martin, Dr. Ramón 2137c
Graubunden (Grisons) (canton)
  Switzerland
  language 1335c
Graun, Karl Heinrich *tab* 171c
Gravel 499c, 752b
Gravenhage, 's, Netherlands 2356b
Graves, Morris *tab* 109
Graves, Robert 264a
Gravimeter 1217c
Gravimetric analysis 1827c
Gravitation 499c
Gravitational energy
  conversion chart 1130
Gravitational potential energy 1877c
Gravitational theory 499c
Gravity 499c, 949a, 1876a
  acceleration of 1916a
  celestial mechanics 1781b
  center of 1879a, 1917a
  Newton 1763c
  planets 1782a
  solar 1780a
  specific 515c
Gravity dams 1205c
Gravity irrigation 740a
Gravity meter 460a
Gravure printing 149c, 1174a
Gray, Elisha 264a
Gray, George 264b
Gray, Horace
  Supreme Court *tab* 802a
Gray, Robert 264b
Gray, Stephen 264b
Gray, Thomas 264b, 1364a, *tab* 1470
  Elegy Written in a Country Churchyard 1402a
Gray see also Grey
Gray matter 938a
Grayson, David
  see Baker, Ray Stannard
Graywacke (sandstone) 499c
Grazzini, Antonio 1386c
Great apes 1923c
Great Australian Bight 2333a
Great Barrier Reef 2091b, 2333a
  gull 37b
Great Bear Lake 2333a

Great Britain 1010b
abolish Pelagic sealing 998c
absentee voting 849a
Act of Supremacy 2287c, 2288a
Alabama claims dispute 994a–994b
in Antigua 2307c
archeology 971a
asters 1650a
balance-of-payments deficits 2292b
in Bahamas 2307b
Battle of Hastings 1009, 1009c–1010a, 1020a
beginning of seapower 996a
Benelux customs union 998b
Bering Sea controversy 998c
in Bermuda 2307c–2308a
Black Death 2286c
Board of Education 857c
Board of Trade 857b
borough 858a
in Botswana 2101c
in British Antarctic Territory 2308a
in British Honduras 2308a–2308b
in British Solomon Islands 2308c–2309a
in British Indian Ocean Territory 2308a–2308b
in British Virgin Islands 2309a
in Brunei 2309a–2309b
in Burma 2107b–2107c
Cade's Rebellion 1000a
in Caicos Islands 2324b–2324c
Canada and 2112c–2113a, 2113b, 2114c–2116a, 2118c
cattle 20c
in Cayman Islands 2309c–2310a
censorship 861a
in Channel Islands 2310a–2310b
Chartist movement 1000b–1000c
chickadee 21a
in China 2128b–2129a, 2129c
cicada 21c
civil service 865a
Civil War 1009a, 1016c, 1020b, 2288c–2289a
coal 1202b
Commonwealth 1009a, 1020b, 2289a–2289b
Confederate States of America and 994a
Congress of Vienna 1023c
coot 23a
copyright laws 870c
Crimean War 997c
curia regis 2285a, 2285b, 2286a
in Cyprus 2138c
Declaration of Rights 2289c
diplomatic service 874b
Domesday survey of 1086, 2285a
in Dominica 2311a–2311b
economy 2292a–2292b
in Egypt 2281b
in Ellice Islands 2341a–2314b
elm trees 1666a
in Falkland Islands 2312a
feudalism 1006b, 2285a, 2285c
in Fiji Islands 2312a–2312b
freedom of speech 861b
gallinule 35a
in Ghana 2164b–2164c
in Gibraltar 2313c–2314a
in Gilbert Islands 2314a–2314b
goldenrod 1669c
government 881b
government planning 899a
in Grenada 2314c
in Guyana 2171a–2171b
House of Lords 852a
Iceland and 2177a
in India 2177a, 2185a–2186a
in Iran 2189b
in Hong Kong 2315a–2315c
Hundred Years War 994a, 2286c
industry 2291b, 2292b
Invincible Armada attack on 995c–996a
in Isle of Man 2316a–2316b
in Jamaica 2197c, 2198a–2198b
in Kenya 2202c–2203a
kinglet 41a
kittiwake 41b
in Kuwait 2205c–2206a
League of Nations 1012c, 1013c
in Lesotho 2208c
limpet 43a
in Malaysia 2213c–2214a
in the Maldive Islands 2214c
in Malta 2215–2216a
maritime power 2288b
in Mauritius 2217a–2217b
in Montserrat 2317c
mouse 46c
mullet 47a
in Muscat and Oman 2223a
National Health Service 2292a
nationalizes steel industry (1964) 2292b
in Nauru 2223b
in New Hebrides 2319a

in New Zealand 2226a–2226b
newt 47c
in Nigeria 2229c
nightingale 47c–48a
oak 1682a–1682b
occupation of Germany 2163b
oriole 48c
in Pakistan 2233a–2233c
Palestine Mandate 1017b, 1017c
in Pitcairn Island 2319c
in Qatar 2242c
as papal fief 2285c
Peasants' Revolt 2287a
phalarope 50c–51a
pheasant 51a
plover 52a–52b
ptarmigan 53b
puffin 53b
Reformation 1015a, 2287c–2288a
Revolution of 1688, 1020b, 2289c
in Rhodesia 2243a–2243b
Rhodesian crisis (1965) 2292b
robin 54c
Roman Empire 1019c
roses 1690b
in St. Helena 2321a
in St. Kitts-Nevis-Anguilla 2321a–2321b
in St. Lucia 2321b
in St. Vincent 2321c
Seven Years' War 2290b
in Seychelles 2322a–2322b
in Sierra Leone 2294a
in Sikkim 2249c
in Singapore 2250c
in South Yemen 2254a
sterling devaluation 2292a 2292b
in South Africa 2253a
in Sudan 2266c
swallow 61a
titmouse 63b
in Tobago 2276a–2276b
in Tonga 2324a–2324b
trade 2291b
Triple Alliance (1668, 1717) 1022c
in Turks Islands 2324b–2324c
in Uganda 2280a
union with Scotland (1707) 1020b
vetch 1680b
in the Virgin Islands 2004c
walnut trees 1698c
War of the Roses 2287b
weights and measures *tab* 1500
woman suffrage 914b
workmen's compensation 835c
World War I 1015c, 1024c–1025c, 2154b, 2291c
World War II 1025c–1028c, 2162c, 2163a
on Zionism 2193b
see also England; Scotland; United Kingdom; Wales.
—**History** *tab* 1036–1059
naval conferences 2072a, 2069a
Great Charter
see Magna Charta
Great Commoner
see Pitt, William (the Elder)
Great Divide *see* Continental Divide
Great Dividing Range 2333a
Great Elector
see Frederick William (Brandenburg elector)
Great Expectations (nov.) 1367a, 1405a
Great Falls, the 2019c
Great Falls, Montana 2007c, 2018c
Great Indian Desert *see* Thar Desert
Great Interregnum 2159c
Great Lakes 1985c, 1999a, 2006a, 2007a, 2110c, 2017c, 2292c
cod 22c
formation of 1961b
Great Lakes-St. Lawrence Seaway, 1967c
Great Northern Railroad tunnel, 1179b
Great Plains 1991b, 1995c, 2017c–2018a
Great Pyramid of Cheops
see Cheops, Pyramid of
Great Rebellion (Eng.)
see English Civil War
Great Rift (astron.) 1787a
Great Rift Valley 2145c–2146a, 2212b, 2333a
Great Russian (lang.)
see Russian language
Great Saint Bernard Pass
see Saint Bernard Pass
Great Salt Lake 1866c 2018a, 2292c
Great Salt Lake Desert 1996a
Great Sandy Desert 2333a
see also Rub al Khali
Great Sark Island 2310a
Great Schism 985c

Great Sea
see Mediterranean Sea
Great Slave Lake 2333a
grackle 36c
Great Swan Island 2003c
Great Victoria Desert 2333a
Great Wall of China 977a, *il* 2126
Greater Antilles Islands 2171b
Greater Khingan Mountains 2124a
Greater Magellanic cloud 1795b
Greater New Orleans Bridge *tab* 1197
Greater Sundas Islands 2186c
Grebe 37a
Grece, El
see El Greco
Greco-Roman War *tab* 1071
Greece 1015b, 2164c–2167c
agriculture 2165a–2165b
anchovy 13b
ancient 2165b–2165c
climate 2165a
communism 2167b
Cyprus controversy 2138b
dictator 874a
economy 2165a–2165b
established church 877b
flag *il* 2183
geography 2164c–2165a
government 2165b
history 2165b–2167c
history outline *tab* 1053–1057
map 2165, *Atlas-9*
people of 2165a
refugee resettlement (World War I) 1013b
religion 2164c, 2165b, 2167c
Turkey and 2165c–2167a
World War I 1025a, 2167a
World War II 2167a–2167b
—**Ancient** 963a
Achaean League 994a
agronomy 749a
archeology 970c
Battle of Marathon 1015b–1015c
city-state 974a
civilization 973b
color 1103c
dance 181a
defeat at Syracuse (413 BC) 1002c
education 613a
execution of prisoners in 1688a
furniture 1093c
glass *tab* 135
Helots 1010a
history *tab* 1030–1033
ivy symbolism in 1673c
mathematics 1501c
music 156b, 157a
musical instruments 157b
numbers 1510b, 1524c
Peloponnesian War 1021c
philosophy 1612–1615
religion 1628a
Roman conquest of 994a
science 1751a
slavery 964c, 1010a
see also Greek architecture; Greek art; Greek literature
Greek Anthology (poems) 1354b, 1395a, *tab* 1464
Greek Architecture 74c, 974c
orders 75a
Greek Art painting 72c, 83c, 84a
pottery 126b, *tab* 130
sculpture 113a, 114a, 116–117
Greek fire 1207b
Greek language 1293b, 1297c, 1334c, 1350b
alphabet 1294, *tab* 1295, 1296a
English derivatives *tab* 1297c
tenses 1297a
Greek Literature 974b, 1350–1354
classicism 1399a
drama 974b
lyric poetry 1344b
oratory 1353b
outline *tab* 1463–1464
poetry 1343a
prose 1353a
Greek mythology 1628a
see also names of individual gods and goddesses
Greek philosophy 1353c, 1612–1615
Greek Revival Architecture 77c
U.S. 78c
Greek War of Independence (1821–1829) *tab* 1074
Greeley, Horace 264b, 908a
irrigation 740a
Liberal Republican Party 889c
presidential candidate *tab* 801, 2054a
Greely, Adolphus 264c
Green (river) *see* Green River
Green Helmet, The (play) 1370c
Green, John Richard 1366c, *tab* 1477
Green, Julian 1382c

Green Mansions (nov.) 1405a
Green sands 1223a
Green, T. H. 1618b
Green tea 745c
Green, Valentine *tab* 107
Green, William 264c
Green 1104b, 1907c
Green
color vision 928c
Green Bay, Wisconsin 1999a
Green Mountains 1996c, 2016a
Greenaway, Kate
Under the Window 413c
Greenback Party 881c
Greenback-Labor Party 881c
Greenbacks (money) 593b
fiat money 592b
Greene, Graham 264c, 1371c
Greene, Nathanael 264c, 2028c, 2029
Green, Robert 1360c
Greenhouse effect 499c
Greenhouses 1901a
Greenland 2141a, 2141c, 2142a, 2142b, 2176c, 2231a, 2314, 2333b
eagle 26b
ling 43a
loon 43c
musk ox 47a–47b
osprey 48c–49a
Greenland Sea 2333a
Greenough, Horatio 123c, *tab* 125
Greensboro, North Carolina 1991a
Civil War 2050c
Greensboro College 689
Greenville, South Carolina 1994b
Greenville College 664
Greenville Treaty 2032a
Greenwich, England 1797b
Greenwich Mean Time (GMT) 1797b
defined 499c
Greenwich time *see* Greenwich Mean Time
Geenwich meridian 758b
Gregor, William 1225b
Gregorian chant 158b, 175c
Gregory I, Saint, Pope 983a, *tab* 1165
biography 264c
music 158b *tab* 171b
Gregory II, Pope 2195a
Gregory VII, Saint, Pope 265a
Crusades 984c
Gregory X, Pope 2159c
Gregory XII, Pope 1001a
Gregory, Lady Augusta 265a, 1369c
Gregory, John *tab* 125
Gregory, Thomas W. *tab* 796
Grenchenberg Tunnel 1226
Grenada 2314
allspice 1648c
Grendel 1344a 1397a, 1433c
Grenoble, France 2149b, 2356a
Grenville, Sir Richard 265a
Grès de Flandres 128b
Gresham, Sir Thomas 265a
Gresham, Walter Quinton *tab* 196
Gresham's law 593c
Gresset, Louis *tab* 1470
Gretchaninov, Aleksandr T. 169b, *tab* 172a
Grétry, André *tab* 171c
Greuze, Jean Baptiste *tab* 107
Grévy, François Paul Jules 265b
Grevy, Jules 2153c
Grew, Nehemiah 265b
Grey, Sir Edward 265b, 1012b
Grey, Lady Jane 265b, 1022c
Grey, Zane 265b
Grey *see also* Gray
Greylock, Mount 1985a
Griboyedov, Aleksander 1389a
Grieg, Edvard 168b, *tab* 172a
biography 265b
Grier, Robert C.
Supreme Court *tab* 802a
Griffes, Charles T. *tab* 172c
Griffin 1433c
Griffin, Cyrus *tab* 802b
Griffith, Arthur 265b
Griffith, David 265c
Griggs, John W. *tab* 796
Grijalva, Juan de 2023c
Grile, Dod
see Bierce, Ambrose
Grillparzer, Franz 265c, 1385a, *tab* 1473

Grimm Brothers 265c, 813c, 1405a, *tab* 1473
—Fairy Tales
Hansel and Gretel 431b–433a
Grimm, Jakob 265c
Grimm, Wilhelm 265c
Grimaldi family 2220a–2220b
Grimmelshausen, H. S. Christoffel von 1383c, *tab* 1468
Grimm's Fairy Tales 1405a
Grinders (tools) 1266a
Grinding wheels 1192a
Grinnell College 667
Grippe, Peter 124b, *tab* 125
Gris, Juan *tab* 109
biography 265c
Grissom, Virgil I. *tab* 1770
Grisons (canton), Switzerland *see* Graubunden
Griswold, Roger *tab* 795
Groin (coastline) 499c
Gromyko, Andrei Andreyevich 265c
Groningen, Netherlands 2225a
Gronouski, John A. *tab* 796
Groot, Huig de
see Grotius, Hugo
Grooves (rocks) 499c–500a
Gropius, Walter 81c
biography 266a
Gropper, William *tab* 109
Gros, Antoine Jean *tab* 108
Grosbeck, W. S. *tab* 801
Gross, Chaim *tab* 125
Gross national product 593c
cyclical changes 532c
Grosseteste, Robert 1755a
Grosz, George *tab* 109
biography 266a
Grote, George 266a
Groton, Connecticut 1978a
Grottos 500a
Grotius, Hugo 266a, *tab* 1467
Grouchy, Emmanuel de 266a
Ground moraines 449b
Ground pines *see* Clubmoss
Ground waves (radio) 1175a
Ground-ivy 1670b–1670c
Groundnut *see* Peanut
Groundwater 448b, 500a
Group (time) 500a
Group insurance 595a
Groups (soc.) 1938b
characteristics 1939a
Grouse 37a–37b
ruffled 1993a
Grove, Sir George 266b
Grove, Sir William 1137c
Groves 500a
Grow, Galusha A. *tab* 802b
Growing season 500a
Grozny, Soviet Union 2356a
Grün, Hans
see Baldung, Hans
Grunitzky, Nicolas 2275b
Gruber, Max von 266b
Grundy, Felix *tab* 795
Grundy, Mrs. 1405a
Grünewald, Matthias *tab* 107
biography 266b
Grus (rocks) 500a
Gryphius, Andreas 1383c, *tab* 1468
Guadalajara, Mexico 2217b, 2218a, 2356a
Guadalcanal, Battle of 1028c
Guadalcanal Island 2308c
Guadaloupe 2315

slavery 2315a
Guadalquivir River 2263b, 2333b
Guadalupe Hidalgo, Treaty of (1848) 2040a, 2219a
Guadiana River 2241a, 2263b
Guaiacum *see* Lignum vitae
Gualterus 159a
Guam 2001, 2060a
agriculture 2001a
climate 2001a
economy 2001a
geography 2001a
government 794b, 2001a
history 2001a–2001b
people of 2001a
World War II 1028c, 2001b
Guanine 1854b
Guano 500a
Guantanamo Bay 2136b–2137c
Guaraní Indians 2235a
Guaranty 881c
Guard cells (plant) 1645b
Guardi, Francesco *tab* 107
Guardia, Calderon 2136a, 2136b
Guardia, Tomás 2136a
Guardian (journ.) 1167b
Guardian (law) 881c, 913c
Guards (print.) 151b
Guarini, Giovanni Battista 1387a
Guarnieri, Camargo *tab* 172c
Guatemala 2136a, 2168a–2169c, 2173b
agriculture 2168a–2168b
climate 2168a
economy 2168a–2168c
flag *il* 2183
geography 2168a
government 2168c
history 2168c–2169c
Indians 2168a, 2168c, 2169a
industry 2168b
League of Nations 1012c
map 2168, *Atlas*-55
people of 2168a
pine trees 1686c
religion 2168a
swordtail 62a
tanagar birds 62a
titmouse 63b
trogons 64a–64b
turkey 64c
Guatemala City, Guatemala 2168a, 2168c, 2356a
Guava 1670c
Guayaquil, Ecuador 2144a, 2144b
Guayas River 2144a
Guayule 1221b, 1670c
Gudrun 1433c
Gudrunlied (epic) 1383b
Guelph family 1009a
Guelphs 1009a
Guenther, J. C. *tab* 1469
Guericke, Otto von 266b, 1125a
Guernsey cattle 727b
Guernsey Island 2310a
Guerra, Gregorio de Matos 1393a
Guerra Junqueiro, Abilio Manuel 1388c
Guerrazzi, Francesco 1387b
Guerrero Gutiérrez, Lorenzo 2228b
Guerriere (ship) 2034c
Guest, Edgar *tab* 1480
biography 266b
Guevara, Ernesto "Che" 2104c, 2138a
Guevara, Luis Velez de
see Velez de Guevara
Guggenheim, Daniel 266b
Guggenheim, Simon 266c
Guggenheim Aeronautical Laboratory 1778c

Guggenheim Museum *il* 79
Guiana dog 25c
Guiana, British *see* Guyana
Guiana, Dutch *see* Surinam
Guiana, French
see French Guiana
Guiana Highlands 2333b
Guicciardini, Francesco 1386c, *tab* 1466
Guided Democracy 2187b, 2188b
Guided missiles 1257b
Guido d'Arezzo 158b, *tab* 171b
biography 266c
Guido, José Maria 2091a
Guido Reni *see* Reni, Guido
Guilds minstrels 159a
Guilford College 689
Guilford Courthouse, Battle of 2028c, 2029
Guillaume, Charles Edouard 266c, 1162b
Guillaume de Lorris *tab* 1465
Guillaume de Machaut *tab* 171b
Guillements 1312c
Guillen, Nicholas 1393c
Guillotin, Joseph Ignace 266c
Guillotine closure 865b
Guilmant, Felix Alexandre 168b, *tab* 171c
Guinea 2169c–2170b
agriculture 2170a
climate 2169c–2170a
economy 2170a
flag *il* 2183
geography 2169c–2170a
government 2170a
history 2170a–2170b
map 2170, *Atlas*-36–37
people of 2170a
religion 2169c, 2170a
Guinea, Portuguese *see* Portuguese Guinea
Guinea, Spanish *see* Spanish Guinea
Guinea fowl 37b, 739b
Guinea pig 37b
Guiness, Sir Alec 266c
Guinevere 1433c
Lancelot 1437c
Guion, David 170b
Guise, 1st Duke of (Claude de Lorraine) 266c
Guise, 2nd Duke of (François de Lorraine) 266c
Guise, 3rd Duke of (Henry I of Lorraine) 266c
Guise, 5th Duke of (Henry II of Lorraine) 266c
Guise family 1010c
Guitars 155b, 159c, 175c
Guiteau, Charles J. 2055c
Guiterman, Arthur 1376b
Guizot, François Pierre Guillaume 267a, 1381b, *tab* 1473
Gulches 500a
Gulf of (geog.) *see under the latter part of the name, such as Mexico, Gulf of*
Gulf Coast gallinule 35a
Gulf states bunting 18b
Gulf Stream 500a, 765c
eels 26c
Gulfs 500a
Gull 37b
Gullberg, Hjalmar *tab* 1480
Gulliver's Travels (bk.) 436b, 1363a, 1407b

Brobdingnag 1398a
Yahoo 1421c
Gully 500a
Gumbo (soil) 500a
Gumbotil (soil) 500a
Gun wars 2208c
Guncotton 1207c
Nobel, A. 1766c
Gunnar 1433c
Gunny *see* Jute
Gunpowder 1207b
Guns *il* 1719–1722
Gunter, Edmund 1282c
Gunther 1433c
Gunther, John 267a, *tab* 1481
Guppy 37b–37c
Guptas 2179c–2180a
Gürsel, Cemal 2279b
Gustavus Adolphus College 677
Gustavus II (Gustavus Adolphus), King (Sweden) 267a, 2268c
nickname 1162b
Gustavus IV, King (Sweden) 2268c
Gustavus V, King (Sweden) 267a, 2269a
Gut (waters) 500a
Gutenberg, Johann 267a
printing 142a, 143a
Guthrie, A. B. *tab* 1481
Guthrie, James *tab* 796
Gutta-percha *see* Rubber
Gutters (print.) 151b
Gutzkow, Karl F. 1384c
Guy Mannering (nov.) 1366a
Guyana 2170b–2171b
agriculture 2170b, 2170c
climate 2170c
Commonwealth status 1000c
economy 2170c, 2171a
flag *il* 2183
geography 2170b–2170c
government 2171a
history 2171a–2171b
map 2170, *Atlas*-44
people of 2170c
religion 2170b, 2170c
slavery 2170c, 2171a
Guyot, Arnold Henry 267a
Guyots defined 500a
see also Tablemounts
Guzmán, Jacobo Arbenz 2169b
Guzmán Blanco, Antonio 2298a
Gwinnett, Button Declaration of Independence *tab* 803
Gwynedd-Mercy College 695
Gymnosperms 1642c
Gynecology careers 382b
Gypsite 1212a
Gypsophila *see* Baby's Breath
Gypsum 454a, 500b, 1212a
Bhutan 2099b
hardness *tab* 1192
Jamaica 2197a
New Mexico 1990a
Oklahoma 1992b
Pakistan 2232b
soil 752a
Somali Republic 2251a
Gypsies dances 182a
Gypsy (lang.) 1334a
Gyre (oceans) 500b
Gyrocompass 1163c, 1257c
Gyroplane (Autogiro) 1159a
Gyroscope 1257c
Gyrosyn compass 1163c

H

H. M. S. Pinafore (operetta) *see* Pinafore
Haakon IV, King (Norway) 2231a
Haakon VII, King (Norway) 267b, 2231b, 2231c
Ha'apai Islands 2324a
Haar (fog) 500b
Haarlem, Netherlands 2224c
Ruysdael's landscape *tab* 111

Haarlem Museum (Netherlands) *tab* 111
Habakkuk 1454b
Habana, Cuba *see* Havana, Cuba
Habeas corpus 789a, 881c
Haber process 1812c
Habit (geol.) 452c
Habitat defined 500b
marine 1865c
Habitual criminals 882a
Hackberry 1670c
Hackly 500b
Hadal zone (oceans) 500b
see also Ocean depth zones

Hadassah 1744a
Haddock 37c
Haden, Francis *tab* 108, 136c
Hades 1433c, 1444c
Hadley, Henry Kimball 170a, *tab* 172c
Hadrian, Emperor (Roman Empire) 267b, 2283c
Haeckel, Ernst Heinrich 267b, 1842a
Hafiz 267b, *tab* 1466
Hafnium 1833
atomic weight *tab* 1805
Hafsids 2277b
Hagar 1454b

Hagedorn, Friedrich von *tab* 1469
Hagemann, Richard 170b
Hagen 1433c
Hagen, Walter 267b
Haggai 1454b
Haggard, Sir Henry Rider 267b
Hague, The, Netherlands 2224c, 2356b
language association 1338c
peace conference 913b
United Nations 992a
World Court 914b
Hague Conference 853c

Hague Tribunal *see* Permanent International Court of Arbitration
Hahn, Reynoldo 168b
Hahn, Ulrich 160b, *tab* 171b
Haifa, Israel 2192b, 2356b
Hail 473b
Hail and Fairwell (bk.) 1369c
Haile Selassie I, Emperor (Ethiopia) 267c, 2146c
Hainan Island 2123b, 2124c, 2333b
Haiphong, North Vietnam 2299b, 2356b
Hair 918a
  humidity 469c
  hirsutism 942b
Hair hygrometer 469c
Hair line (print.) 151b
Haiti 2171b–2172b
  agriculture 2171c, 2172a
  climate 2171c
  in Dominican Republic 2143a
  economy 2171c–2172a
  flag *il* 2183
  geography 2171b–2171c
  government 2172a
  history 2172a–2172b
  Indians 2172a
  map 2171, *Atlas-57*
  people of 2171c
  religion 2171b, 2172b
  slavery 2172a
Hake 37c–38a
Hakluyt, Richard 267c, *tab* 1467
Hakodate, Japan 2356b
Haldane, Richard Burdon 267c, 268a
Hale, Edward Everett 268a, *tab* 1476
  Man Without a Country 1410a
Hale, George Ellery 268a
Hale, John P. *tab* 800
Hale, Nathan 268a
Hale telescope 1791b
Halévy, Jacques François Fromental Elie 166c, *tab* 171c
  biography 268a
Halévy, Ludovic 268a, 1381c, *tab* 1477
Half-life 500b, 1918b
Half note 175c
Half rest (mus.) 175c
Half title (print.) 150b
Half tone (print.) 148b, 149a, 151b, 1173c
Halffter, Rodolfo *tab* 172c
Haliburton, Thomas Chandler 1390c, *tab* 1463b, *tab* 1474
Halicarnassus 117a
Halifax, Canada 2356b
Halite (mineral) 454a, 500b
Hall, Charles Martin 268a, 1195a
Hall, Edwin H. 1892a
Hall, Granville Stanley 268b
Hall, James N. (au.) 1398a
Hall, John H. 1229c
Hall, Josef W. 1461b
Hall, Nathan K. *tab* 796
Hall, Lyman *tab* 803
Hall, Robert N. 1890c, 1911a
Hall, Thomas W. 1179b
Hall effect 1892a
Hall process 1195a
Hallam, Arthur Henry 268b
  In Memoriam 1406c
Hallam, Henry 268b, 1002c, *tab* 1472
Halleck, Fitz-Greene 1461c, *tab* 1473
Halleck, Henry Wager 268b, 2045c
Haller, Albrecht von 268b, 1384a, *tab* 1470
Hallermund, A. von Platen 1384c
Halley, Edmund 268b, 1758b, 1759b
Hallgrimsson, Jonas *tab* 1475
Hallowe'en 1423c, 1433c
Halmyrolysis (rocks) 500b
Halo (weather) 500b
Haloalkanes 1820c
Halogens 500b, 1809b, 1820b
Halomorphic (soil) 500b
Hals, Frans *tab* 107, *tab* 111–113
  biography 268c
  Hille Bobbe *tab* 110
Halvorsen, Johan 168b
Halyard 1728b
Ham (Bib.) 1454b
Hamadan, Iran 1016a
Hamburg, Germany 2157c, 2356b–2356c
  free city status 1009c
  Hanseatic League 1009b–1009c
Hamburgische Dramaturgie (drama) 1355b, 1384a
Hamilcar Barca 268c

Hamilton, Alexander 268c, 873a, 1372c, *tab* 1471, 2031b
  Burr, Aaron 2033c
  Cabinet 859b
  Constitution 786c, 809c, 2030b
  Federalist, The 1348a
  Federalist Party 878c
  pseudonym 1461b
  Secretary of the Treasury *tab* 795
  theory of government 862c
  Zenger trial 1171a
Hamilton, Paul *tab* 795
Hamilton, William Gerard *tab* 1463b
Hamilton, William Rowan 1507b, 1601a
Hamilton, Bermuda 2307c, 2356c
Hamilton, Ohio 1992a
  proportional representation 902b
Hamilton College 685
Hamito-Semitic languages 1333a, *tab* 1335
Hamlet (play, Shakespeare) 1405b
  Gravedigger Scene *il* 207
Hamlin, Hannibal 268c, *tab* 801
Hamline University 677
Hammada (plateau) 500b
Hammarskjöld, Dag 269a, 992b, 2269b
Hammer (anat.) 937a, 1894b
Hammer throw 1739a
Hammerstein, Oscar, 2nd. 269a
Hammond, Indiana 1981c, 2007c
Hammond, John Hayes, Jr. 269a
Hammurabi 269a, 972c, *tab* 1463
  code of 813b
  Shamash 1623a
Hamp, Pierre 1382c
Hampden-Sydney College 704
Hampton, Wade 269a
Hampton Roads Conference 1009a–1009b
Hampton, Virginia 1997c
Hampton Institute 704
Hamster 38a
Hamsun, Knut *tab* 1479
Han Dynasty 977b, 2127a, 2300a
Han River 2203b–2203c
Hanaman, Franz 1140c
Hancock, John 269a 1020c
  Continental Congress *tab* 802b
  Declaration of Independence *tab* 803
  presidential candidate *tab* 800
Hancock, Winfield Scott 296b
  presidential candidate *tab* 801, 2055c
Hand, (Billings) **Learned** 269b
Hand axes 1928a
Hand cheese *tab* 731b
Handball 184c
Handel, Georg Friedrich 162b, *tab* 171c
  biography 269b
Handel and Haydn Society 169c
Handwriting 1301–1302
  curriculum 641c
  cursive 1302a
  development in children 1301b
  manuscript 1302a
Handy, William C. 269b
Hangchow, China 2356c
Hangest, Hélène de 127b
Hanging (capital punishment) 860b
Hanging Gardens of Babylon 997a
Hanging glaciers 500b–500c
Hanging indention 151c
Hanging Rock, Battle of 2029
Hanging valley 500c
Hanley, J. Frank *tab* 801
Hanna, Marcus A. 269b, 2062a
Hannah (Bib.) 1454b
Hannibal 269c, 1016b
  battle of Cannae 1000a
Hanno 2156b
Hannover, Germany 2356c
Hanoi, North Vietnam 2298a, 2299b, 2301a, 2356c
Hanover College 666
Hanover family 2290a–2291a
Hansberry, Lorraine 1377a
Hanseatic League 1009b–1009c
Hansel and Gretel (story) 431b–433a
Hans in Luck (story) 453c–436b
Hanson, Howard *tab* 172c
  biography 269c
Hanson, John 269c, *tab* 802b
Haploid 1850b
Happy Thought (poem) 414c

Hapsburg dynasty 2151b
Hapsburg family 999a, 999c, 1023c, 2095a–2095b, 2098c, 2139b–2140c, 2151c, 2211b
Hapsburgs
  Germany 2159c–2160a
  in Spain 2264c
  Switzerland and 2270b
Haraldsson, Olaf, King (Norway) 2231a
Harappa, Pakisan 969c
Harbin, China 2356c
Harbor 1166b
Hard Times (bk.) 1366a, 1405b
Hard water 500c, 1285b
Hard money 593c
Hardenberg, Friedrich von *tab* 1472
  pseudoynm 1462c
Hardening of the arteries *see* Arteriosclerosis
Hardie, Keir 908a
Hardin-Simmons University 702
Harding, Chester *tab* 108
Harding, Warren Gamaliel 269c, *tab* 798–799, 906b
  administration 2068c–2069c
  Cabinet *tab* 796–797
  election and inauguration *tab* 801
  events paralleling administration *tab* 1068
Harding College 655
Hardness scale 500c
Hardpan (soils) 500c
Hardy, Arthur S. *tab* 1478
Hardy, Thomas 269c, 1368a, *tab* 1477
  Return of the Native 1415a
  Tess of the D'Urbervilles 1418b
  Wessex Tales 1421a
Hardy-Weinberg law 1858a
Hare 38a
Hare, Thomas 902a
Hare and the Tortoise (fable) 442c
Harebell *see* Bluebell
Harelip 942a
Hares and the Frogs, The (fable) 443a
Hargreaves, James 270a, 1281c
Haring, Wilhelm *tab* 1474
Hari Singh, Maharaja 2185c, 2186a
Hari River 2333b
Hariri *tab* 1465
Harker ware *tab* 132
Harlan, James *tab* 797
Harlan, John M. *tab* 802a
Harlem Heights, Battle of 2029
Harlingen, Texas 1995c
Harmar, Josiah 2032a
Harmattan (wind) 500c
Harmensen, Jacob *see* Arminius, Jacobus
Harmodius and Aristogiton (sculp.) 116b
Harmon, Judson *tab* 796
Harmonic 1918b
Harmonic mean 1604c
Harmonic modulation 175c
Harmonic progression 1607a
Harmonic series 1607b
Harmonics 175c, 1896c
Harmonium 177c
Harmony (mus.) 154a, 160a, 175c
Haroeris 460a
Harold Hardrada, King (Norway) 2284c
Harold II, King (England) 1010a, 1358c, 2284c
Harp 159c, 175c
  Egypt 155c
  Hebrew music 155c
Harper, Robert G. *tab* 800
Harper, Liberia 2209a
Harper's Ferry, West Virginia 1998
  Brown, John 2043a
Harpies 1433c
Harpsichord 161b
Harpur College 685
Harriman, (William) **Averill** *tab* 797
Harriman, Edward H. 270a
Harriman, Mary 1744a
Harris, Joel Chandler 270a, 1374c, *tab* 1478
  Uncle Remus 1419c, *tab* 1463c
Harris, Roy 170b, *tab* 172c
Harris, William Torrey 270a
Harris process 1213c
Harris Teacher's College 679

Harrisburg, Pennsylvania 1993a, 1993b, 2008a
Harrison, Benjamin (1726–1791)
  Declaration of Independence *tab* 803
Harrison, Benjamin (1833-1901) *tab* 798–799, 906b
  administration 2057b–2958b
  biography 270a
  Cabinet *tab* 796–797
  election and inaugration 784a, *tab* 801
  events paralleling administration *tab* 1066
Harrison, John 1162b
Harrison, L. Birge *tab* 108
Harrison, Robert H. *tab* 800, *tab* 802
Harrison, William Henry *tab* 798-799, 873a
  administration 2039a
  biography 270a
  Cabinet *tab* 795
  election and inauguration *tab* 800, 2038c
  events paralleling administration *tab* 1063
  nickname *tab* 1463b
  presidential defeat 2038a
  Whig Party 914a
Harsha 2180a
Hart, James *tab* 108
Hart, John *tab* 803
Hart, Moss 270b
Hart, William *tab* 108
Harte, Bret 270b, 1374c, *tab* 1477
Hartford, Connecticut 1977c, 1978a, 2008a
  founding 2025a
  voltage *tab* 1132b
Hartford Convention 2035a
Hartford, University of 660
Hartford Wits 1372b
Hartley, Marsden *tab* 108
Hartmann, Karl Robert Eduard *tab* 1478
Hartmann van Aue 1383b
Hartwick College 685
Harun-al-Rashid 270b, *tab* 1465
Harvard, John 270b
Harvard, Mt. 2019a
Harvard College 674
Harvard University 144c
  library *tab* 1463
Harvey Mudd College 657
Harvest Home (song) 419
Harvest moon 1794c
Harvesters 1251b
Harvestman 38a–38b
Harvey, William 270b
  blood 1759a, 1798b
Harz Mountains canary 19a
Hasan Ibn-al-Sabbah 982b
Hassam, Childe 104c, *tab* 108
Hassan, Sayyid Muhammad Abdulla 2251b
Hasan II 2222b
Hasdrubal 270b, 1016b
Hashemite dynasty 2202a
Hasler, Hans Leo *tab* 171b
Hasse, Johann Adolph *tab* 171c
Hastings, Thomas 169c
Hastings, Warren 270c
Hastings, Battle of 1002c, 1009c–1010a, 1020a
Hastings College 681
Hathaway, Ann 203a, 1361a
Hats (millinery) felt 1208a
  primitive 1930c
Hatshepsut, Queen (Egypt) 270c, 1003c
Hatto II 1440c
Hatton, Frank *tab* 796
Hattosas 970b
Hauff, Wilhelm *tab* 1474
Hauptmann, Gerhart *il* 207, 1385b, *tab* 1479
  biography 270c
Havana, Cuba 2136b, 2136c, 2238b, 2356c
  Pan American Conference (1928) 1017c
Havelock, Henry 270c
Haverford College 696
Haverhill, Massachusetts 1985b
Hawaii 1980, 2293a
  agriculture 1980b
  albatross 13a
  American history 2058a, 2060b
  apportionment 853
  arrowroots 1649c
  capital punishment 860c
  census (1960) 1970
  climate 1980b

colleges 663
commercial law 826
congressmen at large 855a
coreopsis 1659b
deer 25b
economy 1980b
flag *il* 2010
geography 1980a–1980b
goose 36b
government 1980b
legal holidays 841–842
mesquite 1679a–1679b
mongoose 46b
myrtle species 1681a–1681b
Pearl Harbor attack 1028b
people 1980b
pineapples 1686c–1687a
public school enrollment *tab* 646
public school expenditures *tab* 644
seamounts 463a
student enrollment *tab* 645
sugar cane 1694c–1695a
taro 1696a
teal ducks 62c
volcanoes 2018b
Hawaii, University of 663
Hawaiian goose 1980a
Hawaiian Islands Bird Reservation 13a
Hawaiian phase *see* Volcanoes
Hawk 38b
Hawkins, Sir John 270c
Hawkweed 1670c
Hawley-Smoot Tariff Act *see* Smoot-Hawley Tariff Act
Hawthorne 1671a, 1987a
Hawthorne, Charles W. *tab* 108
Hawthorne, Nathaniel *il* 208, 1346c, 1373c, *tab* 1474
   biography 270c
   Brook Farm 1398c
   Blithdale Romance 1397c
   House of the Seven Gables 1405c
   Marble Faun 1410a
   Scarlet Letter 1416b
   Tanglewood Tales 1418b
   Twice-Told Tales 1419c
   Wonder Book 1421b
Hay, John 270c, *tab* 796, 1375b
   open door policy 2060b
Hay
   Illinois 1981b
   Indiana 1981c
   Iowa 1982b
   Kansas 1982c
   Kentucky 1983b
   Missouri 1987b
   South Dakota 1994c
   U. S. 1968b–1968c
   see also names of hay crops, such as Alfalfa
Hay fever 942a
Haya de la Torre, Victor Raúl 2237b
Hayakawa 1348c
Hay-Bunau Varilla Treaty 2061
Haydn, Franz Joseph 164a, *tab* 177c
   biography 271a
Hayes, Carlton J. H. 1007b
Hayes, H. K. 721a
Hayes, Helen 271a
Hayes, Max S. *tab* 801
Hayes, Patrick Joseph 271a
Hayes, Rutherford B. *tab* 798–799, 906b, 1019b
   administration 2055
   events paralleling administration *tab* 1066
   biography 271a
   Cabinet *tab* 796–797
   election and inauguration *tab* 801
Hay-Herrán Treaty 2061b, 2234c
Haynau, J. J. von 1461a
Hayne, Paul Hamilton *tab* 1477
Hayne, Robert Young 271a
Haynes, Elwood 271a
Hay-Pauncefote Treaty 2061b .
Hays, Will H. 271b, *tab* 796
Hayward, California State College at 657
Haywood, John *tab* 1466
Haze 500c
Hazel 1671a
Hazleton, Pennsylvania 1993b
Hazlitt, William 271b, 1365b, *tab* 1472
H. D. *see* Doolittle, Hilda
Heading (print.) 151b
Headlands 500c
Head-voice (mus.) 175c
Headwall (cliff) 500c
Headward erosion 500c
Headwater 500c

Health labor legislation 835b
   see also Mental health; Public health
Health, Board of 857c
Health, Education and Welfare, Department of 2078b
   establishment *tab* 797
   Public Health Service 960c
   secretaries of *tab* 797
Hearing (law) 882a
Hearing (physiol.) 937a, 1894a
   speech defects 1298c
Hearn, Lafcadio 271b
Hearst, William Randolph 271b
Heart circulatory system 923a
   heart beats 923b
   muscle 927a
Heart of Midlothian (nov.) 1366a
Heart of the Matter (bk.)1371c
Heartburn 942a
Heat 1861a, 1896–1903
   asbestos 1195c
   calorie 1916c
   conduction 1900a
   convection 1900b
   conversion chart 1130
   definition 1897b, 1918c
   radiation 1900c
Heat capacity 1899a
Heat Considered as a mode of Motion (bk.) 1366c
Heat cramp 918a
Heat of fusion 1899c
Heat engines 1901a
Heat gradient *see* Geothermal gradient
Heat lightning 1141b
Heat of reaction 1813a
Heat stroke 918a
Heat of sublimation 1899c
Heat transfer 1897b
   applications of 1901a
   mechanisms 1900a
Heath, Sir Robert
   North Carolina 2025b
   South Carolina 2025b
Heath family 1671a
Heath hen *see* Grouse
Heathcliffe 1421c
Heather 1671a
Heaths 500c
Heating 1258b
Heavy water 1806a
Hebbel, Friedrich 1385a, *tab* 1475
Hebe 1434a
Hebrew (lang.) alphabet *tab* 1295, 1296a
Hebrew literature *tab* 1463–1464
Hebrew University *il* 2193
Hebrews
   ancient civilization 973a
   education 612c
   history outline *tab* 1029, *tab* 1030
   music 155c
   religion 1628c
   see also Jews
Hebrides Islands 2282a, 2333b
Hebron (Bib.) 1454b
Hecate 1434a
Hectare *tab* 1500
Hectogram *tab* 1500
Hectoliter *tab* 1500
Hectometer *tab* 1500
Hector 1434a
Hecuba 1434a
Hedgehog 38b
Hedgehog cactus *il* 1661
Hedin, Sven Anders 271b, *tab* 1479
Hedonism 1615b, 1620c
Heep, Uriah 1405a
Hegel, Georg Wilhem Freidrich 271b, 965c. 1384c, *tab* 1471
   dialectic 1620c
   philosophy 1618a
Hegenberger, Albert F. 1156a
Hegira 1632c
Heidegger, Martin 271b, 1620a
Heidelberg College 691
Heidelberg man 1925a
Heidenstam, Karl von *tab* 1479
Heifer 727b
Height to paper (print.) 151b
Heimdall 1434a
Heimskringla (saga)*tab* 1465
Heine, Heinrich *il* 208, 1348c, *tab* 1474
   biography 271c
   Catullus 1356b
Heinrich, Anton 170a
Heisenberg, Werner Karl von 271c, 1915c

Hejaz Mountains 2246c
Hel (Hela) 1434a
Helen of Troy 1434a
Helena, Montana 1987c, 2008a
Helena Fourment (paint.) *tab* 111
Helenus 1424a
Helias 1437b, 1438c
Helicopter 1159b
Heliocentric orbit 1779a
Heliocentric system 1794c
Heliodorus 271c
Helios 1424b, 1434a
Heliotrope *il* 1663, 1671a–1671b
Helis 1437b
Helium 1808b, 1833
   alpha particles 1916c
   atomic structure 1807b, 1911b
   atomic weight *tab* 1805
   boiling point *tab* 1902
   electrons 1806c
   heat capacity 1899a
   ionization 1808b
   sun 1782b
   Texas 1995c
Hell Gate Bridge New York 1197
Hellbox (print.) 151b
Helle (myth) 1424c
Hellebore 1671b
Hellen (myth) 1434b
Hellenistic period 974c, 975a
   literature 1353c
   mathematics 1502c
   painting 84a
   physics 1753b
   science 1753a
   sculpture 116a, 117a
Hellespont *see* Dardanelles
Hellman, Lillian 1481
Hells Canyon 1980c, 2020c
Helmand River 2333b
Helmholtz, Hermann Ludwig Ferdinand von 271c, 1761a
Helmont, Jan Baptista van 1125a, 1798b
Helots 1010a
Helsinki, Finland 2146c 2356c
Helvétius, Claude Adrien 271c
Hemanitics 1273c
Hemans, Felicia D. 1365b, *tab* 1473
   Casabianca 1398c
Hematite (iron oxide) 453c, 501a
   Nepal 2223c
Hematoma 942a
Hemingway, Ernest 271c, 1375c *tab* 1481
Hemlock 1671b, 1993a
   Western 1997c
Hemmestvelt, Torjus 1731b
Hemoglobin 919c, 922a, 942a, 1825b, 1856c
Hemorrhages purpura 945b
Hemorrhoids 942a
Hemp 1671b–1671c
   fiber crops 733c
Henderson, Arthur 908a
Henderson, David Bremner *tab* 802b
Henderson State College 655
Hendon, Miles 1414a
Hendricks, Thomas Andrews 2056b
   presidential candidate *tab* 801, 2054a
Hendrix College 655
Henequen fiber crops 733c; *see also* Century plant
Henley, William Ernest 1368b, *tab* 1478
Hennepin, Louis 271c
Henri, Robert *tab* 108
Henriques, Afonso 2241c
Henry, kings (Germany) *see* Henry, emperors (Holy Roman Empire)
Henry, Prince (Portugal) *see* Henry the Navigator
Henry I, King (England) 272a
   judicial reforms 2285b
   reign of 2285a–2285b
Henry II, King (England) 272a, 2150b–2150c, 2151b, 2191a, 2285c
   assize 855a
   legal reforms 2285b
   reign of 2285b
Henry III, King (England) 272a
   reign of 2286a
Henry IV, King (England) 272a, 867b
   reign of 2287a
Henry V, King (England) 272a, 994a, 2151a
   reign of 2287a

Henry VI, King (England) 272a, 1000a
   reign of 2287a–2287b
Henry VII, King (England) 272b, 1020a, 2113b, 2191b
   American exploration 2023a
   reign of 2287b–2287c
Henry VIII, King (England) 272b, 2191b
   law 815c
   nickname 1461b
   at Flodden Field 1020b
   reign of 2287c–2288a
Henry I, King (France) 272b
Henry II, King (France) 272b
   furniture 1095b
   tomb 122b
Henry III, King (France) 272b, 2151b, 2159b
Henry IV, King (France) 272c, 1010c, 1016c, 2113c, 2151b–2151c
Henry VII, King (France) 985c
Henry IV, Emperor (Holy Roman Empire) 272c
Henry V, emperor (Holy Roman Empire) 272c
Henry III (play, Dumas) *tab* 1474
Henry IV (play, Shakespeare) 1405b
   Falstaff 1403b
Henry V (play, Shakespeare) 1405b
Henry, John (Amer. pol.) *tab* 800
Henry, John (leg.) 1436c
Henry, Joseph 273a, 1183a
Henry, O.
   see Porter, William Sydney
Henry, Patrick 273a, 1372c, *tab* 1470, 2026b, 2030c
Henry of Burgundy 2241c
Henry Esmond (nov.) 1367b, 1405c
Henry the Fowler 2159b
Henry the Lion (Duke of Saxony) 272c
Henry of Luxembourg, Count 2211b
Henry of Navarre *see* Henry IV, King (France)
Henry the Navigator 273a, 2241c
Henry II ware 127b
Hens 746b
   egg production 732a
Henshaw, David *tab* 795
Henty, George Alfred 273a
Hepatic vein 924c
Hepatica 1671c
Hepatitis
   infectious *tab* 946
   serum *tab* 946
Hepburn Act 886b, 2062a
Hephaestus 1434b, 1449a
Hepplewhite, George 1098b
Heptagon 1606b
Heptahedron 1606c
Heptameron (tales) *tab* 1466
Heptameter 1405c
Heptane 1820b
Hepworth, Barbara *tab* 125
Hera 1434b, 1437a, 1628a
Heracles *see* Hercules
Heracles and Hydra (paint.) *tab* 110
Heraclitus 273a, 1613a
Herb Christopher *see* Baneberry
Herbaceous stems 1644b, 1644c
Herbart, Johann Friedrich 1618b
Herbert, George 273b
Herbert, Hilary *tab* 796
Herbert, Victor 170a, *tab* 172c
   biography 273b
Herbicides 741c
Herbivores 1860c
   energy 1861c
Herculaneum 84b
Herculano, Alexandre 1388c
Hercules (constellation) 1793b
Hercules (Heracles) (myth) 1434b
   Augean Stables 1426c
   Pillars of 1434c
Hercules Cluster (galaxies) *tab* 1785
Herder, Johann Gottfried von 273b, 1384a, *tab* 1470
Heredia y Campuzano, José María de 1381c, *tab* 1478
Heredity
   cytoplasmic inheritance 1850a, 1857c
   see also Genetics
Hereford cattle 719c
Heresy Middle Ages 985b
Here We Go Round the Mulberry Bush (song) 420
Hering-Breur reflex 922a

Herkimer, Nicholas 2028b
Herm Island 2310a
Hermes 1434c. 1439b
  music 157a
Hermione 1454c
Hermit thrush 1996b
Hermitage (Leningrad) *tab* 110
Hermod 1423a, 1426b
Hermon, Mount 1454b
Hernia 942b
Hero (Heron) (Gr. sci.) 273b, 1234b
  boiler 1234b
Hero (myth) 1434c
Hero and Leander (epic) *tab* 1464
Hero of our Times, A (nov.) 1389b
Herod (Herod the Great) 273b, 1454c
Herod Antipas 237b
  John the Baptist 1456a
Herod the Great *see* Herod
Herodes, Atticus 273b
Herodians 1629c
Herodias 1454c
  John the Baptist 1456a
Herodotus 237b, 963a, 965a, 974c, 1015c, *tab* 1464
  fossils 455c
  literary style 1353a
  sobriquet 1462a
Heroes, The (bk.) 1368a
Heroes and Hero Worship (bk.) 1366a
Herold, Louis Joseph 166c, *tab* 171c
Hero-myth 1421b
Herons 38c
Héroult, Paul 1195a, 1262b
Herrera, Fernando de *tab* 1467
Herrera, Francisco de (the Elder) *tab* 107
Herreros, Manuel Bretón de los *see* Bretón de los Herreros
Herrick, Robert (Eng. poet) 237b, 1362b, *tab* 1467
Herring 38c–39a
Herriot, Edouard 273c
Herschel, John 1171c
Herschel, John Frederick William 273c
Herschel, William 273c, 1759b
Hersey, John 273c, *tab* 1481
Herter, Christian A. 273c, *tab* 796
Hertz, Heinrich Rudolph 273c
Hertz, Henrik *tab* 1474
Hertzen, Alexander *tab* 1475
Hertzsprung, Ejnar 1790a
Hervieu, Paul *tab* 1478
Herzl, Theodor 273c, 2193a
Herzog, Emile *see* Maurois, Andre
Herzog, Maurice *tab* 1481
Hesdin, Jacquemart de *tab* 106
Hesiod 273c, 1357a, *tab* 1463
Hesione 1438a
Hesperides (myth) 1434c
Hesperides (poems) 1362b
Hess, Germain Henri 1811b
Hess, Law of 1811b
Hess, Rudolf 274a
Hess, Victor Franz 274a
Hess, Hermann 274a
Hesselius, Gustavus *tab* 107
Hestia 1435a, 1449a
Hetairia Philiké (Greek organization) 2165c
Heterocyclic compounds 1819c
Heteropolar generator 1138b
Heterotrophic organisms 1841b
Heterozygote 1850c
Heureaux, Ulises 2143a
Hevea braziliensis (tree) 1276c
Hewes, Joseph Declaration of Independence *tab* 803
Hewlett, Maurice 1370c
Hexachords 158c
Hexagon 1606b
Hexahedron 1606c
Hexameter (poetry) 1405c, 1344b
Hexane 1802b
Hey! diddle, diddle (nursery rhyme) 410c
Heyse, Paul von *il* 208, 1385a, *tab* 1477
Heyward, Thomas, Jr. Declaration of Independence *tab* 803
Hezekiah, King (Judah) 1454c
H. H. (pseud.) *see* Jackson, Helen Hunt
Hiawatha (poem) 1405c
Hibernians in America, Ancient Order of 1744a

Hibiscus 1671c 1980a
Hickety, pickety, my black hen (nursery rhyme) 408c
Hickory 1671c–1672a
Hicks, Elias 274a
Hicks, Granville 1377a
Hicks, William 1005b
Hidalgo y Costilla, Miguel 2218c
Hideyoshi 2200b
Hieratic 1501b
Hieroglyphics 972b, 969a
Hieronymus Holzchuer (paint.) *tab* 109
Higelac 1427a
Higginson, Thomas Wentworth 274a
High (air mass) *see* Anticyclone
High Jump 1737c
High pressure centers 764a
High Point, North Carolina 1991a
High Point College 689
High Point Mountains 1989b
High school 617a, 626b
  adult education 636a
  buildings 618a
  curriculum *tab* 638, 642a
  dropouts 609a
  first public in U. S. 616b
  future 618c
  organization 626c
  parliamentary procedure 846–848
Higher education 627b
  student enrollment *tab* 645
High-fidelity 1181b
Highland Dawn (poems) 1371a
Highland fling 181c
Highlands of Scotland 2333b–2333c
Highways 1179c
Highway engineering 1166c
Hilary of Poitiers 158a, *tab* 171b
Hilbert, David 1507c, 1558a
Hildebrand, Adolf von 122c, *tab* 125
Hildebrand *see* Gregory VII, Saint, Pope
Hildebrandslied (saga) 1383a
Hilkiah 1454c
Hill, Ambrose Powell Civil War 2048a
Hill, Edward B. *tab* 172c
Hill, James J. 524a
Hill, James Jerome 274a
Hille Bobbe (paint.) *tab* 110
Hilliard, Nicholas *tab* 107
Hillocks (hills) 501a
Hillquit, Morris 908b
Hills 501a
Hillsdale College 676
Himalayas (mountains) 2099b, 2123c, 2177a–2177c, 2223a, 2223b, 2223c, 2333c
  goose 36b
  rabbit 53c
  robin 54c
Himeji, Japan 2357a
Himmler, Heinrich 274a
  Gestapo 881a
Hind and the Panther, The (poem) 1362c
Hindemith, Paul 168a, *tab* 172a
  biography 274a
Hindenburg, Paul von 274b
  World War I 2066c
Hindi (lang.) 1334a
Hindu-Arabic numeration system 1510c
Hindu Kush Mountains 2255a, 2333c
Hinduism 612b, 1623c
  compared to Buddhism 1627a
  Kama 1437a
Hindus
  architecture 78a
  Dravidian languages *tab* 1336
  music 155b
  numbers 1509c
Hinge fault 501a
Hinterland 501a
Hipparchus 274b, 1503a, 1753a, 1796
  zodiac 1797c
Hippias of Elis 1614a
Hippity hop (nursery rhyme) 408c
Hippocrates 274b, 974c, 1557c, 1753a
  sobriquet 1462b
Hippodamia 1428b
Hippolyte 1435a
Hippolytus 1435a
Hippomenes 1435a
Hipponax 1351b
Hippopotamus *il* 38, 39a
Hippur, library at 997a
Hiram, King (Tyre) 1081b, 1454c

Hiram College 691
Hiring halls 882a
Hirohito, Emperor (Japan) 274b, 2201b
Hiroshige 141a
  biography 274b
Hiroshima, Japan 2201b, 2357a
  atomic bombing of 1028c, 1914c, 2076c
Hirsutism 942b
Hisgen, Thomas L. *tab* 801
Hispania *see* Spain
Hispaniola Island 2171b, 2172a, 2333c
  see also Dominican Republic; Haiti
Hiss, Alger 2078c
Hissarlik, Asia Minor
  archaeology 970c
Histoire de la Litterature Anglaise (bk.) 1381b
Histology 1643c
  defined 1637c
Histoplasmosis *tab* 946
Historiae (bk., Tacitus) 1358a
Historical geology 454–458, 447a
Historical Library (bk.) 1354a
History 967–1080
  art 963c
  ancient civilization 972–976
  acheology 967–971
  bibliography 1081b–1082
  careers in 390c
  causes 965b
  chronological history of the world *tab* 1027–1059
  decisive battles of 1002c–1003a
  defined 963a
  forms of 963a–964b
  interpretation of 965a–965b
  judging 965b–965c
  to justify slavery 964c
  literary works 1348c, 1377b
  of map-making 779a–780c
  Marxism 1618c
  Middle Ages 982–986
  Modern European 986–989
  notable wars *tab* 1071–1077
  Oriental 976–982
  outline of *tab* 1027–1070, *tab* 1463–1481
  perspectives 964c–965a
  philosophy of 963a, 965c
  problems of 965a–965c
  recording fact in 963b–963c
  science 963c–964a
  technical 964a–964b
  uses of 964b–965a
  see also under individual countries
History of England (bk., Hume) 1364a
History of England (bk., Macaulay) 1366b
History of Frederick the Great (bk., Carlyle) 1366a
History of New York from the Beginning of the World to the End of the Dutch Dynasty (bk.) 1462b
History of Plimouth Plantation (bk., Bradford) 1018c–1019a, 1372a
History of Rome (bk., Livy) *tab* 1464
History of the Britons (bk., Nennius) 1395b
  Arthur 1425a
History of the Dividing Line (bk.) 1372a
History of the Jewish War (bk.) *tab* 1464
History of the Kings of Britain (bk., Geoffrey of Monmouth) 1395c
History of the Kings of Britain (bk., Nennius) 1425a
History of the United States (bk., Bancroft) *tab* 1474
Hitchcock, Ethan A. *tab* 797
Hitchcock, Frank H. *tab* 796
Hitler, Adolf 964c, 988c, 1023b–1023c, 2096a, 2096b, 2140a, 2154b, 2154c, 2162a–2163a, 2175b, 2196c, 2240b, 2262b, 2269b, 2292a
  biography 274b
  censorship 862a
  centralization 862c
  enabling act 877a
  Mein Kampf 1348c
  Nazi Party 893c
  World War II 1028a–1028c, 2076a
Hittite (lang.) 1333b
Hittites 970a
Hives 942a
H. M. S. (in names of ships) *see under the latter part of the names, such as* Challenger, H. M. S.

Hoar, Ebenezer *tab* 796
Hoare, Samuel 981a
Hobart College 685
Hobbema, Meyndert *tab* 107
  Avenue at Middelharnis tab 111
  La Ferme au Soleil tab 113
Hobbes, Thomas 274c, 623b, 1616b
Hobby, Oveta Culp *tab* 797, 2078b
Hobgoblin 1435a
Hobson, Richmond Pearson 274c
Hoccleve, Thomas 1360a
Ho Chi Minh 274c, 2301a
Höchst, Germany pottery *tab* 131
Hockey 1725a
Hoder 1423a, 1426b, 1438c
Hodges, Luther *tab* 797
Hodgkin's disease 942b
Hodler, Ferdinand *tab* 108
Hoe invention 719a
Hoe, Richard March 247c
Hoenir 1423a
Hofer, André (Swiss paint.) *tab* 108
Hofer, Andreas (Tyrolese patriot) 274c
Hoff, Jacobus Henricus van't *see* Van't Hoff
Hoffa, James 274c
Hoffman, August Heinrich (Hoffmann von Fallersleben) *tab* 1474
Hoffman, Malvina 124a, *tab* 125
Hoffmann, Ernst Theodor *tab* 1472
Hoffmann, Hans 275a
Hofmannsthal, Hugo von 275a
Hofstadter, Robert 1915b
Hofstra University 685
Hog *see* Hogs; Swine
Hogarth, William *tab* 107
  biography 274c
  Shrimp Girl tab 111
Hogarth Press 1371b
Hogback (rocks) 501a
Hogg, James *tab* 1472
  nickname 1462a
Hogs 2294a
  Great Britain 2282c
  Illinois 1981b
  Indiana 1981c
  Iowa 1982b
  Minnesota 1986b
  Nebraska 1988b
  New Caledonia 2318b
  Ohio 1992a
  Poland 2239b
  Soviet Union 2257a
  Tennessee 1995b
  U. S. 1968b
  Wallis and Futuna Islands 2324c
  West Virginia 1998a
  Western Samoa 2310c
  Wyoming 1999c
Hohenstaufen, House of 274a, 984c
Hohenzöllern, House of 274a, 2160b–2160c
Hohmann, Walter 1765a, 1771b
  transfer ellipse 1778c
Hohmann-A orbit 1771b
Hohusai, Katsushika 274a
Hojo family 2200b
Hokkaido Island 2198b, 2198c
Hokku 978c
Hokusai 141a
Holbein, Hans (the Elder) *tab* 106
Holbein, Hans (the Younger) *tab* 107, *tab* 111, 140c
  biography 274a
  Jane Seymour tab 113
  Portrait of Erasmus tab 112
Holberg, Ludvig 274a, *tab* 1469
Hold (mus.) 175c
Holderlin, Friedrich *tab* 1471
Holding company 594a
Hole (elec.) 1918b
Holger 1435a
Holinshed, Raphael 274a
Holland *see* Dutch art; Dutch language; Netherlands
Holland, John Phillip submarines 1182c
Holland, Sydney 2227b
Holland, The (submarine) 1182c
Holland Tunnel 1226c
Hollerith, Herman 1236b, 1243a
Hollins College 704
Holly 1672a
Hollyhock 1672a
Hollywood, California 2011b
Hollywood, Florida 1979b
Holm, Hanya 184c
Holman-Hunt, William *tab* 108

Holmes, Oliver Wendell (1809–1894) *il* 208, 1374a, *tab* 1475
  Autocrat of the Breakfast Table 1396a
  biography 274b
  pen name 1461a
Holmes, Oliver Wendell (1841–1935) 274b
  Supreme Court *tab* 802a
Holmes, Sherlock *see* Sherlock Holmes
Holmium 1833
  atomic weight *tab* 1805
Holst, Gustav *tab* 172b
Holstein (duchy) 2161a
Holstein-Friesian cattle 727c
Holston River 2020c
Holt, Harold 2094a
Holt, Joseph *tab* 796
Holy Alliance 1010a–1010b, 2035c
Holy Face, The (paint.) *il* 93
Holy Family (paint., Michelangelo) *tab* 110
Holy Family College 696, 707
Holy Family with Saint Francis (paint.) *tab* 112
Holy Ghost 1454c
Holy Grail 1435a
Holy Land *see* Palestine
Holy Living (bk.) *tab* 1468
Holy Roman Empire 984a, 2094b, 2095a–2095b, 2098c, 2195b, 2225a–2225b, 2278c
  birth of 2150a
  diets 874a
  emperors *tab* 1078
  foundations for 2159a
  influence of 1010b
Holyoake, Keith 2227b
Holyoke, Massachusetts 1985b
Holz, Arno 1385b, *tab* 1479
Home, Earl of 274b
Home economics 1085–1091
  bibliography 1091c
  career guidance 379b
Home Loan Bank Board 878c
Home Office (Eng.) 882a
Home of the Heron, The (paint.) *tab* 110
Home Owners' Loan Act 883a
Home Owners' Loan Corporation 882c, 881a
Home rule 882a, 864a
Home Rule League 2191c
Homer 274b, 974b, 1343a, *tab* 1463
  epic poetry 1350c
  Iliad, The 1406c
  Odyssey 1411b
Homer, Sidney 1368b
Homer, Winslow 104b, *tab* 108
  biography 274b
  Maine Coast tab 112
Homer-Laughlin ware *tab* 132
Homestead, Pennsylvania
  steel strike 2058b
Homestead Act 888b
Home Sweet Home (song) *tab* 1473
Homicides 882b
  U.S. 959c
Hominidae 1923c, 1924a
Homo (genus) 1923c, 1924a
Homo erectus 1924a
  Neanderthals 1925a
Homo habilis 1924c
Homo sapiens 1924b, 1925a
  Europe 1925a
  Neanderthals 1925a
  races 1925b
Homocline (rocks) 501a
Homolytic fission 1822c
Homophony 175c
Homopycnal inflow (waters) 501a
Homoseismal line 501a
Homozygote 501a
Homs, Syria 2357a
Honaira, British Solomon Islands 2308c, 2357a
Honduras 1006a, 2172c–2173b
  agriculture 2172c–2173a
  climate 2172c
  economy 2172c–2173a
  flag *il* 2183
  geography 2172c
  government 2173a
  history 2173a–2173b
  independence 2173a–2173b
  Indians 2172c, 2173a
  League of Nations 1012c
  map 2172, *Atlas*-55
  people of 2172c
  religion 2172c
  sloth 58c
  smilax 1693a
  World War I 1025a

Honduras, Gulf of 2333c
Honegger, Arthur 168b, *tab* 172a
  biography 274c
Honey 724a
Honey locust *see* Locust
Honeybee *see* Bee
Honeydew melon *see* Melon
Honeysuckle 1672a
Honeysuckle family 1672b
Hong Kong 2128c, 2283c, 2315
  climate 2315a
  economy 2315b
  geography 2315a–2315b
  government 2315b–2315c
  history 2315c
  people of 2315a–2315b
  World War II 1028b
Hong River 2339c
Honolulu, Hawaii 1980a, 2008a–2008b
Honorious, Emperor 999c
Honorius, Flavius 274c
Honshu Island 2198b, 2198c, 2199a
Hooch, Pieter de *tab* 107
  Buttery, The tab 109
  Court of Dutch House tab 111
Hood, John Bell 2050b
Hood, Thomas 274, 1365b, *tab* 1474
Hood College 672
Hood, Mount 451b, 1992c, 2019a
Hoof-and-mouth disease 1843a
Hook (cape) 501a
Hooke's Law 501a
Hooked rugs 1109c
Hooker, Joseph 275c, 2048c
Hooker, Richard *tab* 1466
Hooker, Thomas 275c
Hooker telescope 1791b
Hooks (geol.) 449a
Hookworm 39a, *tab* 946
Hooper, William Declaration of Independence *tab* 803
Hoosac Tunnel 1179a, 1226, 1244b
Hoosier Poet *see* Riley, James Whitcomb
Hoosier State *see* Indiana
Hoover Dam 1221a
Hoover, Herbert Clark 275c, *tab* 798–799, 906b, 2068c, 2172b
  administration 2071b–2072b
  cabinet *tab* 796–797
  Commerce Department *tab* 797
  commission 882b
  election and inauguration *tab* 801
  events paralleling administration *tab* 1068
  food administration 2066a
  Republican Party 906a
Hoover Commission 791b, 849c, 882b
Hoover Dam 888b, 1206c, 1975b
  reclamation 904c
Hop 1672b
Hope College 676
Hopkins, Harry L. 276b, *tab* 797, 2073b
Hopkins, Samuel 897a
Hopkins, Stephen Declaration of Independence *tab* 803
Hopkinson, Francis 169c, *tab* 172c, 1372b
  biography 276a
  Declaration of Independence *tab* 803
  nickname 1461b
Hopkinson, Joseph 169c, *tab* 172
Hopper, Edward 104c, 109, 276a
Hoppner, John *tab* 107
  Lady Beauchamp tab 112
Horace (Quintus Horatius Flaccus) 276a, 1354a, 1357b, *tab* 1464
Horace (drama) 1379a
Horeb, Mount *see* Sinai, Mount
Horehound 1672b
Horizon 501a
Horizon system (astron.) 1795a
Hormones 922b, 925c
  plants 1647c
Horn (mountains) 501a
Hornbeam 1672b
Hornet 39a–39b
Hornblende (mineral) 453b, 501a
Hornbooks 616a
Horned beetle *il* 29
Hornfels (silicate) 501a
Horns (mus.) 154b, 173c, 175c, 1896b
Horowitz, Norman 1841b
Horowitz, Vladimir 276a
Horse *see* Horses

Horse chestnut 1672b–1672c
Horse latitudes 501a
Horsepower 1878c
Horseradish 1672c
Horses 39b, 739b, 1983b
  manure analysis *tab* 752c
  Mongolia 2220c
  transportation 1152c
  Yemen 2302a
Horse's Mouth, The (nov.) 1371c
Horseshoe crab 39b–39c
Horseshoe pitching 1726b
Horsetail 1672c
Horsetails 1642a–1642b
Horst (rock.) 501b
Horthy, Admiral Miklos 2175a
Horthy, Nicholas 873c
Horticulture 1638a
Horus (anc. deity) 1435b, 1622b
Hosea 1454c
Hosmer, Harriet *tab* 125
Hot embossing (print.) 151c
Hot springs 501b
Hot Springs National Park 896a
Hot-air heating 1258c
Hot china 130a
Hot-dip method 1267a
Hotel china 130a
Hotels etiquette 1116b
Hottentot (language) 1337c
Hottentots anthropology 1927b
Hot-water systems (heating) 1258c
Houdini, Harry 276a
Houdon, Jean Antoine 122c, *tab* 125
  biography 276a
Houghton College 685
Houphouët-Boigny, Felix 2197b
Hourglass 1162a
Housatonic River 1977c
House, Edward M. 276a
House of Burgesses (Virginia) 2026b
House of Commons (Great Britain) 867b
  appropriations 853a
  closure rules 856b
  committees 866c
  division 875a
  no confidence, vote of 894a
House of Fame (poem, Chaucer) 1360a
House of Lords (Great Britain) 852a 890c–891a
House of Representatives (U.S.) 787b, 806c
  apportionment 852c
  closure rules 865a
  committees 866b
  duties and qualifications of members 810c
  impeachment 884a
  quorum 904a
  Speakers 908c, *tab* 802b
House of the Seven Gables (nov.) 1405c
House spider 39c
Houseflies life span 957a
Household appliances 1259a
Housing 882b–883a
  apartments 1691a
  interior decoration 1102a
  Japanese 978c
  primitive 1930a
Housing and Home Finance Agency 883a
Housing and Urban Development, Department of *tab* 797, 883a
Housman, Alfred Edward 276a, 1370c, *tab* 1479
  Shropshire Lad 1417b
Houston, David F. *tab* 796, *tab* 797
Houston, Sam 276a
Houston, Texas 1995c, 2008b
Houston, University of 702
Houten, C. J. van 726c
Hovey, Richard *tab* 1479
Hovhaness, Alan 170c
Howadji *see* Curtis, George William
Howard, Henry (Earl of Surrey) (1517–1547) 1360b, *tab* 1466
  blank verse 1397c
Howard, Oliver Otis 276b
Howard, Sidney Coe 276b, *tab* 1480
Howard Payne College 702
Howard University 661
Howe, Elias 276b, 1241b, 1279a, 2040c
Howe, Julia Ward 276b, 1374c, *tab* 1476
  Battle Hymn of the Republic 1397a
Howe, Richard 276b

Howe, Timothy *tab* 796
Howe, William 276b, 2028a
Howells, William Dean 276b, 1375a, *tab* 1477
Howland Island 2001
Howrah, India 2357a
Hoxha, Enver 2087b
Hoxie, Vinnie Ream 276b
Hoyle, Edmond 276c
Hoyle, Fred 1787c
Hoysalas, the 2180a
Hroswitha *tab* 1465
Hrothgar 1427a
Hsi River 2124a
Hsia dynasty 976c, 2126a
Hsi-ling-shi 1223b
Hsuan T'ung Emperor (China) *see* Pu-yi, Henry
Hsüntzu 2126b, 2126c
Huan Archipelago 2318a, 2318b
Huang-ti, Emperor (China) 1223b
Huang River 2124b
Hubay, Jeno 169c
Hubbard, Elbert 276c
  pseudonym 1462a
Hubbard, Samuel *tab* 796
Hubble classification 1787b
Hubble parameter 1787c
Hubli, India 2357a
Hucbald *tab* 171b
Huch, Ricarda *tab* 1480
Huckleberry 1672c
Huckleberry Finn (nov.) 1405c, 1419a
Hudibras (poem) 1362c, *tab* 1468
Hudson, Henry 276c, 2023b, 2324a
Hudson William Henry 276c
  Green Mansions 1405a
  Purple Land 1414b
Hudson Bay 2110c, 2111b, 2114c, 2333c
  explorations 2023c
  yellowlegs 68b–68c
Hudson River 1989b, 1990b, 2005a, 2012b, 2018a, 2293a
  exploration 2023c
Hudson River School (art) 104b
Hudson's Bay Company 863b, 2116c
Hüe, Georges 168b
Hue, South Vietnam 2357a
Hué, Treaty of 2300c
Huerta, Victoriano 2062c, 2064a, 2219b
Huet, Paul *tab* 108
Hugh Capet, King 2150b
Hughes, Charles Evans 276c, *tab* 796, 2068c
  censorship 862a
  martial law 891b
  minimum wage laws 833a
  presidential candidate *tab* 801, 2065b
  Supreme Court *tab* 802a
Hughes, Langston 276c
Hughes, Thomas *tab* 1476
  Tom Brown's School Days 1418c
Hughes, William Morris 2093c
Hugin 1441b
Hugo, Victor Marie *il* 208, 1380c, 1382a, *tab* 1474
  biography 276c
  Les Miserables 1409a
  Notre-Dame de Paris 1411b
Huguenots 909b, 1010b–1010c, 2151b, 2152a
  emigration of 1010c, 1016c
  St. Bartholomew Day massacre 997c, 1010c
  in South Carolina 1010c
Huizinga, Johan 279a
Hukbalahap army 2238b, 2238c
Hull, Cordell 279a, *tab* 796
Hull, Isaac 729a
Hull, William 2034b
Hulme, T. E. 1348c
Human engineering 1951b
Humayun 2180b
Humbert I, King (Italy) 279a
Humbert II, King (Italy) 2196c
Humboldt, Alexander von 279a, *tab* 1471
Humboldt, Karl Wilhelm von 279a
Humboldt Current 2236a
Humboldt State College 657
Hume, Allan Octavian 2185a
Hume, David 279a, 1364a, *tab* 1470
  philosophy 1617
Humery, Konrad 143b
Humidity 469c, 501b
  units 470a
Humming bird 39c

Hummock 501b
Humperdinck, Engelbert 169a, tab 172a
  biography 279b
Humphrey Clinker (nov.) see Expedition of Humphrey Clinker
Humphrey, Doris 184c
Humphrey, George M. tab 796
Humphrey, Hubert Horatio, Jr. 279b, 2082a
Humphreys Peak 1975b
Humpty Dumpty (poem) 410c, 1435b
Humus 150b
Hunchback of Notre Dame (nov.) see Notre-Dame de Paris (nov.)
Hundred Years War 994a, tab 1072, 2151a, 2191a, 2286c
Hundredweight 1500
Hundreiser, Emil tab 125
Hunedora, Romania 2244a
Hungarian Rhapsodies (mus.) 166b
Hungarian Socialist Workers Party 2174a–2174b
Hungary 873c, 2095c, 2139b–2140a, 2173b–2175c
  agriculture 774, 2174a
  Austrian rule 2174c–2175a
  climate 2173c
  Cominform 866a
  Crusades 1002a
  communism 2174a–2174b, 2175a, 2175b–2175c
  constitution 2174b
  Dual Monarchy 999a, 2175a
  economy 2174a
  flag il 2183
  geography 2173b–2173c
  government 2174a–2174b
  history 2174b–2175c
  industry 2174a
  language 2173c
  map 2173, Atlas 18–19
  music 169c, tab 172a
  natural resources 2174a
  Ottoman Era 2174c
  people of 2173c–2174a
  refugee resettlement (World War I) 1013a
  religion 2173b, 2173a, 2174c
  revolution of 1956, 2175c
  trade 2174a
  World War I 2175a
  World War II 1028c, 2175b
Huns 2159a
Hunt, Leigh 279b, 1365c, tab 1472
  Abou Ben Adhem 1393a
  Bleak House 1397c
Hunt, Richard Morris 279b
Hunt, Walter 1278c
Hunt, Ward Supreme Court tab 802a
Hunt, William H. tab 796
Hunt, William Morris tab 108, 279b

Hunter, John 279c
Hunter, M. A. 1225b
Hunter, R. M. T. tab 802b
Hunter Mountains 2091b
Hunters in the Snow (paint.) tab 113
Hunting il 1719, 1933b
  divsion of labor 1935c
Hunting Scene (paint., Courbet) tab 110
Huntingdon College 654, 666
Huntington, Anna Hyatt tab 125
Huntington, Daniel tab 108
Huntington, Samuel Continental Congress tab 802b
  Declaration of Indepedence tab 803
  presidential candidate tab 800
Huntington, West Virigina 1983b, 1998b
Huntington Gallery, California tab 112
Huntsville, Alabama 1974b
Hunyadi, János 279c, 2174c
Hurdles (sport) 1737c
Hurley, Edward N. 2066a
Hurley, Patrick J. tab 796
Huron, Lake 1985c, 2017c, 2018a
Huron College 699
Hurricanes 475a, 501b
  forecasting 478b
  see also Meterology
Husain, Zakir 2186b
Husbandry 1933c
Huss, John 279c, 985c, 2139b
Hussein, Abdullah ibn, Emir (Jordan) 2202a
Hussein, Haja Muhammad 2251b
Hussein, King (Jordan) 2202a, 2202b
Hussein, Sharif 2247b
Husserl, Edmund 1620b
Hussey, Obed 720b
Hutchinson, Anne 279c
Hutchinson, R. C. tab 1481
Hutchinson, Thomas 279c
Hutten, Ulrich von tab 1466
Huts 1930a
Hutten, Ulrich von 1383c
Huxley, Aldous 280a, 1371c
Huxley, Julian Sorell 280a, 1370b
Huxley, Thomas Henry 280a, 1366c, tab 1476
Huygens, Christian 280b, 1125a
  pendulum 1162a
Huygen's principle 501b
Huysmans, Cornelis 280b
Huysmans, Jacob 280b
Huysmans, Jan Baptist 280b
Huysmans, Joris Karl 280b, 1382a
Hwang Hai see Yellow Sea

Hwang Ho (river) 759b, 2123c, 2124b, 2333c
Hyacinth 1672c
Hyacinthus 1435b
Hyades (astron.) 1787a
Hyades (myth) 1435b
Hyatt, John Wesley 1218c
Hybrid systems (astronautics) 1767b
Hyde, Arthur M. tab 797
Hyde, Douglas 280b
Hyde Park (London) free speech 861b
Hyderabad, India 2178a, 2357a
Hydra 39c–40a
Hydra (myth) 1435b
Hydra Cluster (galaxies) tab 1785
Hydrangea 1673a
Hydrated lime see Calcium hydroxide
Hydraulic cement 1199c
Hydraulic elevator 1166a
Hydraulic gradient 501b
Hydraulic lime 1214a
Hydraulic organ 157c, 161a
Hydraulic turbines 1148b
Hydriotaphia (prose) see Urn-Burial
Hydrocephalus 942b
Hydrochloric acid 902c, 1212a, 1817b
Hydroelectric power
  Austria 2095c
  Canada 2112a
  Cameroon 2110a
  El Salvador 2145a
  Guinea 2170a
  Iceland 2176b
  Japan 2199b, 2199c
  Liechtenstein 2210c
  Nepal 2223c
  New Caledonia 2318b
  Nigeria 2229b
  Pakistan 2232c
  Portugal 2241b
  Soviet Union 2256c
  Thailand 2273c–2274a
  Uganda 2279c
  U.S. 2293c
  Yugoslavia 2303b
  Zambia 2305b
  see also Water power
Hydrofoils 1180b
Hydrogen 1806a, 1833
  acid-base reaction 1817b
  airship 1154c
  atomic structure 1911b
  atomic weight tab 1805
  boiling point tab 1902
  chemical bonding 1810a
  discoverer 1798c
  electron cloud 1806a
  electron displacement 1822b
  isotopes 1806a
  in plants 1646b

  rockets 1766c, 1767b
  sun 1782b
Hydrogen bond 1816c
Hydrogen chloride 1212a
Hydrogen cyanide 1840c
Hydrogen-helium cycle 1915a
Hydrogenation 732b
Hygrograph 470a, 501b
Hydrography 501b
Hydrologic cycle 501b, 765a
Hydrologists 390b
Hydrology 501b
Hydrolysis 501b, 1817c
Hydrometallurgy 1215c
Hydronephrosis 942b
Hydrophobia see Rabies
Hydroponics 739c
Hydrosphere 501b, 765
  hydrologic cycle 765a–765b
  oceans 765b–765c
Hydrothermal 501b
Hydrotropism plants 1647b
Hyena 40a
Hygiene see Mental health; Public health
Hygrometer 469c, 501b
Hygroscopic water 501c
Hyksos 208b, 1003b
Hymen (myth) 1435b
Hymn 158a, 175c
Hymnody 158a
Hymns to the Night (Novalis) tab 1472
Hypabyssal (rocks) 501c
Hypatia (Gr. philos.) 280c
Hypatia (nov.) 1367c, 1406a
Hyperbola (math.) 1592c
  conic section 1602c
Hyperbole (lit.) 1315c
Hyperbolic geometry 1508c
Hyperboloid 1604b
Hypergolic fuels 1766c
Hyperpycnal inflow 501c
Hyperion 1435b
Hypermnestra (myth) 1435b
Hyperthyroidism 942b
Hyphae 1846c
Hyphen 1314b
Hypnosis 1954c
  Freud, Sigmund 1957a
Hypodermis 919a
Hypogene 501c
Hypogonadism 942b
Hypophysis see Pituitary gland
Hypopycnal inflow 501c
Hypothalamus 938c
Hysteria (psych.) 1954c
Hysteresis 501c

I

I.C.C. see Interstate Commerce Commission
I Love Little Pussy (nursery rhyme) 408c
I.Q. see Intelligence quotient
I.W.W. see International Workers of the World
Iambic meters 1351a
Iambic pentameter
  blank verse 1397c
Iamblichus 1354a
Iambus 1351a, 1406a
Iapetus 1435b
Iarbas 1430c
Iasi, Romania 2244a, 2357a
Iatrochemistry 1798b
Ibadan, Nigeria 2229b, 2357a
Ibañez, Carlos 2122c
Ibáñez, Vicente Blasco see Blasco-Ibáñez, Vicente
Ibarbourou, Juana de 235c
Ibarra (Sp. printer) 144b
Iberian Peninsula 2333c–2334a
  see also Portugal; Spain
Ibert, Jacques tab 172a

  biography 280c
Iberville, Sieur d' 280c
Ibis 40a
Ibn Ezra 280c
Ibn Saud, King Abdul Aziz, (Arabia) 280c, 995a
Ibn-al-Haytham see Alhazen
Ibn-Rushd see Averroes
Ibn-Sina see Avicenna
Ibsen, Henrik il 208, tab 1476
  biography 280c
  Doll's House 1401b
  Peer Gynt 1421b
Ibycus 1351c, tab 1464
Icarus 1435b
  Daedalus 1429c
ICBM see Intercontinental Ballistics Missile
Ice 501b
  crystal structure 1870c
  glaciers 449a
  pack 509b
Ice age see Glacial Period; Pleistocene Epoch
Ice cap 501c
Ice cap climate 501c
Ice floes 501c
Ice hockey 1725c
  skating 1729b
Ice Plant 1673a
Ice sheet 501c

Ice skating 1729b
Icebergs 501c, 2111b
Iceboating 1726c
Icebox 1260a
Iceland 2142a, 2142b, 2176a–2177a, 2231a
  Althing 851b
  auk 14c
  climate 2176a
  eagle 26b
  economy 2176b
  eider 33a
  flag il 2183
  geography 2176a
  goldeneye 36a
  government 2176b
  history 2176b–2177a
  independence 2176c
  industry 2176b
  kittiwake 41b
  language 1336a
  map Atlas-14
  loon 43c
  merganser 45c
  people of 2176a
  poppy 1688b
  puffin 53b
  religion 2176a, 2176c
  rugs 1109c
  World War II 2176c
  wrens 68b
Icelandic low 501c
Ichabod (poem) 1374a

Ichabod Crane 1409a
Ichang, China 2357b
Ichor 1435b
Ickes Harold tab 797, 2073b
Iconel alloys tab 1193
Iconoscope 1152a
Icosahedron 1606c
Ictinus 280a, 373b
Id 1957b
Ida, Mount 1435b
Idaho 1980–1981
  agriculture 1980c, 1981
  capital punishment 860b
  census (1960) 1970
  climate 1980c
  colleges 663
  commercial law tab 826
  congressional apportionment tab 853
  divorce 875b
  economy 1980a
  flag il 2010
  geography 1980c
  government 1981a
  holidays 841–842
  initiative and referendum 884c
  mock oranges 1630a–1680b
  national forests 896a
  people of 1980c
  public school enrollment tab 646
  public school expenditures tab 644

recall 904b
statehood 2058a
student enrollment *tab* 645
student enrollment *tab* 645
Idaho State University 663
Idealism (philosophy) 1618b
arts 1406a
education 623b
Identical twins 1856a
Identity (math.) 1603b
trigonometry 1584a
Ideograms 1296a
Ideographs Japan 978b
Idioms 1316b
Idiopathic epilepsy 941c
Idiot, The (pseud.) *see* Bangs, John
Kendrick
Idiots 1952c
Idler, The (essay) 1363b
Ido (lang.) 1338c
Idomeneo (opera) 164b
Idomeneus 1435b
Idris 2222a
Idris, King (Libya) 2210b
Idyl (idyll) 1406b
Idylls (poems, Theocritus) 1354a
Idylls of the King (poems, Tenny-
son) 1368c. 1406b
blank verse 1397c
Holy Grail 1435a
Ieyasu, Tokugawa 2200b
Ifni 2315–2316
Ignatius, Saint 280a
Ignatius of Loyola, Saint *see* Loyo-
la, Ignatius de
Igneous rocks 449c, 450c, 503a
dating 454c
Ignition (automobile) 1131b
Igraine 1435c
Iguana 40a–40b
Iguassú Falls 2334a
Ijssel Meer Inlet 2334a
Ijssel (lake) *see* Yssel
Ikhnaton (Amenhotep IV) King
(Egypt) 83b, 1622c
arts 115a
biography 280a
Il Penseroso (poem) 1362b, 1406c
Ile Amsterdam 2313a
Ile de France *see* Mauritius
Ile St. Paul 2313a
Ili River 2334a
Iliad (epic) 1343a, 1350c, 1406c, *tab*
1463
Achilles 1422b
Greek education 613a
Iliamna Lake 2018a, 2292c
Ilium *see* Troy (anc. city)
Illía, Arturo 2091a
Illinois 1981
agriculture 1981b
budget system 858b
capital punishment 860b
census (1960) 1970, 1971
climate 1981b
colleges 663–665
commercial law *tab* 826
congressional apportionment
tab 853
economy 1981b
electoral votes 876c
flag *il* 2010
geography 1981a–1981b
government 1981b
holidays 841–842
home rule 882b
labor legislation 832c
people of 1981c
proportional representation
902b
public school enrollment *tab* 646
public school expenditures *tab*
644
statehood 2030b, 2035b
student enrollment *tab* 645
Illinois, University of *tab* 1463
—**Chicago Circle** 664
Illinois College 664
Illinois Institute of Technology 664
Illinois River 2018c
Illinois State University 664
Illinois Teachers College Chicago-
North 664
Illinois Teachers College Chicago-
South 664
Illinois Waterway 1967c
Illinois Wesleyan University 664
Illite 503a
Illuminance 1907a
Illumination *see* Lighting
Illustrators (career) 375a
Illuviation 503a
Illyrian (language) 1334a

ILO *see* International Labor Or-
ganization
Iloilo, Philippines 2357b
Ilmenite 503a
Image (optics) 1918b
Images Old and New (poem) 1371b
Imaginary Conversations (poem)
1365c
Imaginary numbers 1548a, 1605b
Imagist School (lit.) 1371a, 1376a
Imbecile 1952c
Imbokodvo Party (Swaziland)
2267b–2267c
IMF *see* International Monetary
Fund
Imhotep 373b
Imitation (mus.) 175c
Imitation of Christ (bk.) 1347b, *tab*
1466
Immaculata College 696
Immaculate Conception (paint.,
Murillo) *tab* 109
Immaculate Heart College 657
Immermann, K. L. 1384c, *tab* 1474
Immigration 883b, 2021c
Immigration, Bureau of
establishment 2062a
labor 840b
Immigration Act (1924) 2070a
Immunization 1849b
tetanus 954b
Immunology 1849a
Impact area (astronautics) 1778c
Imphal, India 2357b
Impeachment 884a
U. S. Senate 788b
Impedance (elec.) 1886b, 1918b
Imperial Fora (Rome) 971a
Imperial Gallery (Vienna) *tab* 113
Imperial Valley 2018a
Imperial War Conference (1917)
2117c–2118a
Imperialism 884a
Impermeable rock 503a
Importance of Being Earnest (play)
1368b
Imports 594a
Imposition (print.) 147c, 151c
Impresario (mus.) 175c
Impressionism (art) 86b, 1406c
forerunners 86a
influence on American art 104c
Impromptu (mus.) 1891c
Improper fractions 1604a
Improprieties (lang.) 1321c
Improvisation (mus.) 175c
Impulse (phys.) 1880a
Impulse turbines 1148b, 1150a
In Catilinam (Cicero) 1001a
In the Days of the Comet (bk.)
1370a
In Flanders Fields (poem) 1390c
In Memoriam (poem, Tennyson)
1368c, 1406c
In personam (law) 885a
In rem (law) 885a
In situ 503a
Inanimate energy 503a
Inauguration Day 841a
Inbreeding 1936b
Inca Indians 1695b, 2021a, 2090a,
2100c, 2122a, 2144b, 2236c
Incandescence 1886c, 1906a
Incandescent lamps 1140c
Incarnate Word College 702
Inch *tab* 1500
Incised meander 503a
Incline (optics) 1909b
Income 594a
Income Tax 534b, 910b
amendment passed 2062c
Incorruptible, The *see* Robespierre
Increasing return 594b
Incubation (diseases) 955a
Incus *see* Anvil (anat.)
Ind Valley 981a
Indehiscent fruit 164a
Indention (print.) 151c
Indentured labor
Colonial America 828a, 829a
Independence Day (U.S.) 842b
Independent Assortment, Law of
1851a
Independent Labor Party 908a
Indeterminate sentence 884b
Index number (econ.) 594b
India 2099c, 2120c, 2177a–2186b
acacia 1648a
agriculture 2178b
ass 14b

badger 15a
balsam 1650c
bamboo 1650c
camellias 1656a
cardamon 1656b
cattle 20b, 2178b
chinaberry 1658a
citron 1658b
climate 2177c–2178a
cobra 22b
Commonwealth status 1000c
Communist China and 2186a
crocodile 24b
culture region 770a
dill 1665a
dog 25c
ebony 1665c
economy 2178a–2178c
eggplant 1666a
elephant 33a
figs 1667a
first empires (600BC–AD300)
2179b–2179c
flag *il* 2183
gazelle 35b
geography 2177a–2178a
government 2178c–2179a
Guptas 2179c–2180a
hibiscus 1671c
history 2179a–2186b
independence 2185c–2186a
indigo 1673a
industry 2178c
jimson weeds 1674a
lion 20a
loosestrife species 1677a
lotus 1677a
mahogany 1677c
map 2177, *Atlas*-28–29
millet 1679c
mongoose 46b
Muslim dominance (1200–1700)
2180b–2181c
natural resources 2178b
nux vomica 1682a
Pakistan and 2232c, 2233c
peafowl 50a
people of 2178a
pomegranates 1688b
purslane 1689b
Rajputs 2180a, 2180c
religion 2177a, 2178a, 2179b,
2180a–2180b, 2185b
rhinoceros 54c
rice 742a
rise of nationalism 2185a–2185c
robin 54c
rubber trees 1690c
safflower 1691a–1691b
sandalwood 1691c
Sikkim and 2249c
size of 2177a
skimmer birds 58b
soil 751a
stork 60b–60c
sugar 744b, 1694c–1695a
tamarind 1695c–1696a
taro 1696a
tea 745c
tea tree 1696a–1696b
teak 1696b
temples 2180a–2180b, 2180c
thrushes 63a
tiber 20a
trade 2178c
tupelo 1697c
walnut trees 1698c
World War II 2185b–2185c
wrens 68b
see also Kashmir; Portuguese
India
—**Culture** 980a
architecture 78a
caste system 1945a
division of labor 1935c
education 612b
literature outline *tab* 1463–1464
Mahabharata 1410a
mathematics 1503b
music 155b
pottery *tab* 130
racial types 981a
Ramayana 1414c
religion 1623a
sculpture 114b
Vedas 1420b
—**History** 2179a–2186b
Moslem League 892a
see also Pakistan
—**Pakistan Conflict** 2177a, 2185c–
2186c
India paper (print.) 151c
Indian, American *see* Indians,
American
Indian corn *see* Corn
Indian Desert *see* Thar Desert
Indian Day 842b
Indian hemp 1673a
Indian National Congress 2233a,
2233b

Indian Ocean 2211c, 2334a
cuttlefish 25a
frigate bird 34c
nautilus 47b–47c
sea cows 55b
tortoises 63c–64a
tuna 64b
Indian paintbrush 1999b
Indian pipe 1673a
Indian summer 503a
Indian tobacco *see* Lobelia
Indian turnip *see* Jack-in-the-
pulpit
Indiana 1981–1982
agriculture 1981c
capital punishment 860b
census (1960) 1971
climate 1981c
colleges 665–667
commercial law *tab* 826
congressional apportionment
tab 853
economy 1981c
flag *il* 2010
geography 1981c
government 1981c–1982a
holidays 841–842
labor legislation 832c, 833b
people of 1981c
public school enrollment *tab*
646
public school expenditures *tab*
644
statehood 2030b, 2035b
student enrollment *tab* 645
Indiana Central College 666
Indiana Institute of Technology
666
Indiana Northern University 666
Indiana State University 666
Indiana University 666
Indiana University of Pennsylvania
696
Indianapolis, Indiana 1981c, 2008b
2008b
Indians 963b, 1660b, 1683b, 1690b,
1695b
American 997b
Andean 2236b
Araucanian 2121b, 2122a
Arawak 2003a, 2097a, 2137b,
2172a, 2198a, 2276a
Argentina 2090a
Aztec 64a, 2218b, 2218c
Bolivia 2100a–2100b, 2100c
Brazil 2102c, 2103c
calendar system of 758a
Canada 2111b, 2112c, 2114a, 2114c
Carib 2137b, 2314c, 2317c
Chile 2121b, 2122a
Colombia 2132b
Cuba 2137b
Ecuador 2144a, 2144b
El Salvador 2145a
Grenada 2314c
Guatemala 2168a, 2168c, 2169a
Guaraní 2235a, 2235c
Haiti 2172a
Honduras 2172c, 2173a
Inca 2100c, 2122a, 2144b, 2236c
Jamaica 2198a
Maya 64b, 758a, 2168a, 2168c,
2218b
Mexico 2218b–2218c
Mosquito 2227b–2227c
Netherlands Antilles 2317c
Nicaragua 2227b–2227c
Panama 2234a, 2234c
Paraguay 2235a, 2235c
Peru 2236b, 2236c, 2237a
Puerto Rico 2003a
pumpkin cultivation 1689a
St. Lucia 2321b
Toltec 2218b
Trinidad and Tobago 2276a
Tupi 62a
U.S. 1963b, 1964a, 2293c
Indians, American 997b, 1925b,
2021a
adaptation 1927b
agriculture 719b
Alaska 1975a
Arizona 1975c
body mutilation 1930c
cooking 1933a
corn cultivation 1659b
languages 1337c
music 170c
New Mexico 1990a
Penn, William 2025c
tobacco 746a
tools 1928a
U.S. history 2037c
*see also under the names of in-
dividual tribes, such as* Iro-
quois Indians
Indic languages 1334a
Indictment (law) 884b
bill of 856c
Indigo 1673a

Indium 1833
  atomic weight *tab* 1805
Individualism 594c
Individual psychology 1958a
Indochina 2129a
Indochina Peninsula 2334a
Indo-Chinese languages *tab* 1336
Indo-European languages 1296a,
  1333–1337, *tab* 1334
  classification 1333a
Indo-Iranian languages 1333c, *tab*
  1334
Indonesia 2186b–2188b, 2225c
  agriculture 770, 2187a
  climate 2186c
  communism 2188b
  Communist China and 2188b
  economy 2186c–2187a
  flag *il* 2183
  geography 2186c
  government 2187a–2187b
  history 2187b–2188b
  independence 2188a–2188b
  map 2186, *Atlas*-30–31
  number of islands of 2186c
  people of 2186c
  porcupine 52b–52c
  religion 2186b, 2186c, 2187c
  rubber production 1221b
  screwpines 1692a
  World War II 2188a
Indore, India 2357b
Indra 1435c, 1624a
Inductance (elec.) 1886b, 1918b
Induction, electromagnetic 1130c,
  1884c
Induction heating 1248a
Induction motors 1885c
Induction (philos.) 1616a, 1620c
Induction, magnetic 1884a
Induction welding 1287c
Inductor alternators 1139b
Inductors 1918b
Indurated 503a
Indus River 2177a, 2177b, 2185c,
  2232a, 2232b, 2334b
Industrial arbitration 594c
Industrial chemistry 1800c
Industrial control 1260c
Industrial design careers 375b
Industrial engineering 1261a
  careers 379c, 380b
Industrial psychology 383b
Industrial Reconstruction Institute
  2194c
Industrial Revolution 906c, 987a,
  1125b, 1129a, 1229a, 2291a
  education 615b
Industrial unions 594c
Industry 1123–1290
  education 609a
  electronics 1889c
  pensions 897c
  progress outline *tab* 1061–1070
Indy, Vincent d' *tab* 172a, 1099b
  biography 280a
Inertia (phys.) 1804a, 1873b, 1918b
  Newton 1763c
Infanta Margarita (paint., Velas-
  quez) *tab* 112, *tab* 113
Infanta Maria Theresa (paint.,
  Velasquez) *tab* 110, *tab* 111
Infant mortality 958c
Infants 884b
  law 818a
  speech 1298a
  see also Children
Infections
  air-borne 955a
  death rates (U.S.) 954b
  filth-borne 956c
Infectious diseases *tab* 946–948,
  tab 954c
  control 955b
  treatment 955b
Infeld, Leopold 1348b
Inferiority complex 1958a
Inferiors (print.) 151c
Infiltration rate 503c
Infinite sequence (math.) 1607a
Infinitive 1306a, 1307c
Infinity (optics) 1918b
Inflation 530c, 594c
Inflation Bill (1874) 2054b
Inflection (lang.) 1296b 1303c
Inflection (mus.) 175c
Influent stream 503a
Influenza *tab* 947
  incubation 955a
Information (law) 884b
Infrared light 1903b
Infrared process (duplicating)
  1164c

Inge, William Motter (Amer. play-
  wright) 280b
Inge, William Ralph (Eng. clergy-
  man) 280b
Ingemann, B. S. *tab* 1473
Ingersoll, Jared 809c
Ingersoll, Robert Green 280b
  Blaine, James G. *tab* 1463a
Ingham, Samuel *tab* 795
Ingres, Jean Auguste Dominique
  85c, *tab* 108
  biography 280b
  Comtesse d' Haussonville tab
  111
  La Source *tab* 112
Inheritance tax 591c, 594c
Initiation rites 1939a
Initiative (law) 884b, 889b
Injection lasers 1890c
Injunction (law) 863a, 884c
Inks colors 1907c
Inlaid furniture 1096b, 1098c
Inland Sea 2334b
Inland Waterways Corporation 868c
Inlet 503a
Inlier 503a
Inman, Henry *tab* 108, 280b
Inn River 2157b, 2334b
Innate ideas 1620c
Inner ear 937a
Inness, George (1825–1894) 104b,
  tab 108
  biography 280c
  Home of the Heron tab 110
Inness, George (1854–1926) 280c
Innocent III, Pope 280c, 985b
Innocent III, Pope 994b
Innocents Abroad (bk., Twain)
  1406c
Ino 1424c
Inönü, Ismet 2297a
Inorganic chemistry 1800b, 1801–
  1828
  historical development 1818a
  qualitative analysis 1827b
Inorganic reactions 1822c
Inositol *tab* 919
Inquest 885a
Inquisition 985b
  Netherlands 2225b
  Portugal 2242a
  Spain 2264c
Insanity law 818a, 885a, 1953a
Insect control 1868c
Insecticides 740, 1868c
  pollution 776b
  public health 958a
Insects
  geological time *tab* 456–457
Insequent stream 503a
Inserts (print.) 151c
Inside form (print.) 151c
Insight learning 1950a
Insolation 503a
Insolvency 885b
Installment selling 594c
Instinct 1951b
**Institution of Mechanical Engi-
  neers** 1201b
Institutes of the Christian Religion
  (Calvin) *tab* 1466
Institutio Oratoria (bk.) 1357c
Institutions (soc.) 1940b, 1936a
Instrumental conditioning 1949b
Instrumentalism (philos.) 1619
Instrumentation 1261a
Instrumentation (bus.) careers
  380b
Instrumentation (sci.) 1125a
Instruments, musical *see* Musical
  instruments
Insulated stream 503a–503b
Insulators (elec.) 1881c, 1890a,
  1891b
Insulin 926a, 1824b, 1825b
  diabetes mellitus 941b
Insurance 594c
  brokers 389c
  careers 389c
Intaglio 113a, 140a, 151c, 1174a
Integers 1532a, 1604b
Integral calculus 1504b, 1602a
**Integrated Revolutionary Organiza-
  tions** (ORI) 2137a
Integration Eisenhower, Dwight
  2078b
Integument 1642a
Intelligence (psych.) 1950b
Intelligence quotient 621b, 1950b
  classification 1952c
Intelligence tests 621a, 1950b

Inter-American Conferences *see*
  Pan-American Conferences
Interatrial septum 923c
**Intercollegiate Association of
  Amateur Athletes of America**
  1703a
Intercontinental Ballistics Missile
  1257b
Interest (fin.) 595a
  laws in U.S. *tab* 826
Interference (light) 1905a
Interfluve 503a
Intergalactic space 1779a
Interglacial period 503b
Interior 503b
Interior, Department of the 885b
  bureaus 858c, 885b
  Cabinet members *tab* 797
  divisions 875b
  establishment *tab* 797
Interior angle 1601
Interior decoration 73b, 1102–1111
  American styles 1105c
  apartments 1091b
  bedroom 1109a
  careers 375b
  classical influence 1102a
  color 1103b
  dining room 1107c, 1108c
  French styles 1102b
  furniture 1093–1102
  little rooms 1108a
  living room 1106c
  necessary elements 1103c
  pictures 1111a
  planning 1105a
  relation to arts 1102c
  rugs 1109c
Interjections (grammar) 1308c
  use 1303c
Interlude (mus.) 175c
Intermezzo 175c
Intermittent stream 503b
Intermontane 503b
Internal-combustion engines 1134b,
  1153a, 1901c
  agriculture 721a
  automobiles 1169b
  cam 1236c
  cylinders 1135b
**Internal Macedonian Revolutionary
  Organization** (IMRO) 2106a
Internal Revenue 877b, 885b
Internal Revenue, Bureau of 911a
**International American Conference
  on War and Peace** 1000b
**International Atomic Energy
  Agency** 992c, 993c
**International Auxiliary Language
  Association** 1338c
**International Bank of Reconstruc-
  tion and Development** 993a
**International Business Machines
  Corporation** 1243b
  typewriter 1188b
**International Civil Aviation Or-
  ganization** 993a
International Court of Justice 886a,
  914b, 992a
International date line 503b, 758b–
  758c
**International Development Asso-
  ciation** 933a
International economics 534c
International Finance Corporation
  993a
International Labor Organization
  840b, 992c, 1013c
International law 885c–886b
  mediation 891c
**International Maritime Consultative
  Organization** 993a
International Monetary Fund 536a,
  993a
International operations 565–568
International Public Health Office
  960c
**International Society of Christian
  Endeavor** 1743a
**International Telecommunication
  Union** 993a, 1174c
International Telegraph Union
  1174c
International trade 595a
International Workers of the World
  910a
Interpellation (law) 886b
Interplanetary space 1779a
Interprovincial Conference (1887)
  2117a
Interrogation (figure of speech)
  1315b
Interrogation point (punct.) *see*
  Question mark

Interrupted Reading (paint.) *tab*
  110
Interrupted stream 503b
Interstate Commerce Act 886b,
  2056b
  rebate 526c
Interstate Commerce Commission
  527a, 791a, 866b, 886b
  Cleveland, Grover 2056c
Interstellar space 1779a
Interstice 503b
Interstitial water 503b
Intertidal zone 1866a
Intertype (print.) 147a, 151c
Interval (mus.) 175c
Interstate (law) 886b
Intertype 1174b
Intestines 920c
  colitis 941a
  obstruction 942b
  regional enteritis 945b
  ulcers 945c
Intimations of Immortality (poem)
  1364c, 1406c
Intonation (mus.) 175c
Intoxication legal phases 818a
Intramontane 503b
Intratelluric 503b
Intrazonal soil 503b
Introduction (mus.) 175c
Introversion 1958a
Intrusive rock 503b
Intuition (philos.) 1620c
Inventions patents 897a
Inventory (bus.) 595b
Inverse logarithms *see* Antilogar-
  ithms
Inverse operation (math.) 1604b
Inverse square law 1907a
Inversion 503b
Inversion (mus.) 175c
Inverted images 1909a
**Investigation into the Laws of
  Thought** (bk.) 1507a
Investment 595b
Investment bank 529b, 595b
Invictus (poem) 1368b
Invincible Armada 995c–996a, 1002c,
  2288b
Invoice (fin.) 595b
Involutional melancholia 1953c
Io (myth.) 1435c
Io (satellite) 1783b
Ioannina (prov.) *see* Yanina
Iobates 1426c
Iodine 1833
  atomic weight *tab* 1805
  body requirement 919c
  oxidation-reduction reactions
  1812b
Iodix acid 1813b
Ion *see* Ions
Iona College 685
Ionian Islands 2165a, 2166c
Ionian Sea 2334b
Ionesco, Eugene 281c
Ionia 974a
Ionians 83c
Ionic bonding 1809c
Ionic orders (arch.) 75c
Ionic school (sculp.) 116a
Ionization 1808b
Ionosphere 468b, 503b, 763b
Ions 468b, 1918b
  negative 1808c
  positive 1808c
  radicals 1811c
  size 1809b
Iowa 1982
  admission to Union 2040c
  agriculture 1982b
  capital punishment 860b
  census (1960) 1971
  climate 1982a
  colleges 667–668
  commercial law 826
  congressional apportionment
  tab 853
  economy 1982b
  flag *il* 2010
  geography 1982a
  government 1982b
  holidays 841–842
  labor legislation 832c
  people of 1982b
  public school enrollment *tab* 646
  public school expenditures
  tab 644
  student enrollment *tab* 645
Iowa, The University of
  College of Liberal Arts 667

Iowa City, Iowa tractors 721a
Iowa State University of Science and Technology 667
Iowa Wesleyan College 667
Ipecac 958b
Iphigéne (play) 1379a
Iphigenia (myth) 1435c
Iphigènie en Aulide (opera) 163c
Iphigènie en Tauride (opera) 163c
Iphitus 1434c
Ippolitov-Ivanov, Mikhail 169b
Ipoh, Malaysia 2213b
Iran 2097a, 2188c–2189c
  agriculture 2188c–2189a
  ass 14b
  CENTO 1000b
  cheetah 21a
  climate 2188c
  economy 2188c–2189a
  flag *il* 2183
  geography 2188c
  government 2189a–2189b
  industry 2188c–2189a
  map 2188c, *Atlas-26*
  melon 1679a
  people of 2188c
  religion 2188c
  walnut trees 1698c
  World War II 2189b
  see also Persia
Iranian language 1334a
Iranians (people) 982b
Iraq 995b, 2189c–2190b, 2205c–2206a
  agriculture 2189c–2190a
  area 2189c
  climate 2189c
  economy 2189c–2190a
  flag *il* 2183
  geography 2189c
  government 2190a
  history 2190a–2190b
  independence 2190a–2190b
  map 2189c, *Atlas-25*
  people of 2189c
  religion 2189c
  World War II 2190b
  see also Assyria; Babylonia; Mesopotamia
Iredell, James presidential candidate *tab* 800
  Supreme Court *tab* 802a
Ireland 2190b–2191c, 2282a, 2283c
  agriculture 2190c–2191a
  ancient name 1402c
  area 2190b
  climate 2190c
  economy 2190c–2191a
  emigration 2190c, 2191c
  flag *il* 2183
  geography 2190c
  government 870a, 2191a
  history 2191a–2191c
  independence 2291c
  industry 2283c
  map 2190c, *Atlas-10–11*
  merganser 45c
  people of 2190c
  ptarmigan 53b
  religion 2190b, 2190c, 2191a
  resigns from Commonwealth of Nations 1000c
  shamrocks 1692c
—**Arts**
  dances 181c
  folklore of 1431c
  music 154c
Ireland, Northern
  House of Lords 891a
Irene, Empress (Byzantine Empire) 281c
Iridium 1833
  atomic weight *tab* 1805
Irigoyen, Hipólito 2090c
Iris (anat.) 928c
Iris (myth) 1435c
Iris (plant) 1673a–1673b, 1994c
Iris family 1673b
Irish Free State *see* Ireland
Irish language 1335c
Irish moss 1673b
Irish Republican Army (IRA) 2191c
Irish Sea 2334b
Irkutsk, Soviet Union 1020c, 2357b
Iron 1212b, 1833
  atomic weight *tab* 1805
  body requirements 919c
  conductivity 1882a
  magnetism 1884b
  mineral colors 452c
  production 1261b
  rise of industry 524b

soil 751c
  see also Iron ore; Steel; *and headings beginning* Ferro
Iron (appliance) 1260a
Iron, Perchloride of 137a
Iron, Ralph (pseud.) *see* Schreiner, Olive
Iron Age 1124b, 1212b, 1435c, 1929a
Iron bridges 1196c
Iron Curtain 886b
Iron Duke *see* Wellington, 1st Duke of
Iron Gate Gorge 2334b
Iron ore 1212b
  Alabama 1974b
  Alaska 1975a
  Angola 2306b
  Australia 2092b
  Austria 2095a
  Belgium 2098b
  Brazil 2103a
  Chile 2121c
  China 2125b
  Cuba 2136c
  Cyprus 2138a
  France 2148b
  Gabon 2155c
  Germany 2158b
  Great Britain 2282c
  hematite 453c
  Hong Kong 2315b
  India 2178c
  Indiana 1981c
  Korea, North 2203c
  Korea, South 2203c
  Laos 2206b
  Lebanon 2207b
  Liberia 2209a
  limonite 453c
  Luxembourg 2211a–2211b
  Mauritania 2216b
  Michigan 1986a
  Minnesota 1986b
  Missouri 1987b
  Mongolia 2220c
  Morocco 2221c
  Nepal 2223c
  Nevada 1988c
  New Caledonia 2318b
  Nicaragua 2227c
  Pakistan 2232b
  Pennsylvania 1993b
  Peru 2236b
  Philippines 2238a
  in plants 1646b
  Poland 2239b
  Portugal 2241b
  Romania 2244a
  Sierra Leone 2248c
  Somali Republic 2251a
  South Africa 2252c
  Soviet Union 2256b, 2257a
  Spain 2263c
  Spanish Sahara 2323a
  Swaziland 2267a
  Sweden 2268a
  Turkey 2278a
  U.A.R. 2280c
  U.S. 1967a–1967b, 2293b
  Utah 1996b
  Venezuela 2297b
  Wyoming 1999c
  Yugoslavia 2303b
Iron oxide glass 133c
Ironside (nickname) *see* Edmund, King (England)
Ironweed 1673c
Ironwood 2107a
Irony 1315c
Iroquois Indians 786b, 2113c
Irradiance 1907a
Irrational numbers 1546c, 1547b, 1605b
Irrigation 740a
Irritability plants 1647a
Irruptions (population) 1859c
Irtysh River 2334b
Irving Sir Henry 1417b
Irving, Washington *il* 208, 1373a, *tab* 1473
  biography 281c
  Legend of Sleepy Hollow 1409a
  pseudonyms 1461c, 1462b
  Rip Van Winkle 1415c
  Sketch Book 1417c
Isaac (Bib.) 1454c
Isaac, Heinrich 160c
Isaacs, Jorge 1393a
Isabel (is.) *see* Ysabel
Isabella I, Queen (Spain) 282, 985c, 1009a, 2022c, 2264c

Isabella II, Queen (Spain) 2265a
Isabella Brant (paint.) *tab* 111, *tab* 113
Isaeus *tab* 1464
Isaiah 1454c
Ischia Island 2193c
Ise Bay 2198c
Iseult *see* Isolde
Isfahan, Iran 982b, 2189a–2189b, 2357b–2357c
Isfahan rugs 1110c
Isherwood, Christopher 282a, 2044a
Ishikari River 2198c
Ishmael 1455a
Ishtar 1436a, 1623a
Isidore of Seville 282a
Isis 976b, 1436a, 1622b
Iskenderun, Turkey 2357c
Islam 981c, 1005a, 1632c, 2085c, 2281a–2281b
  Algeria 2087c
  history of science 1754a
  Middle Ages 983a
  religious shrines 1017
  spread of 995a, 997c
  see also Moslems (Muslims)
Islamabad, Pakistan 2232a, 2357c
Island *see* Islands
Island, The (poem) 1398a
Island Gunnarsholmi (songs) *tab* 1475
Islands 503b, 2334b–2334c
Isle of *see under the latter part of the name, such as* Man, Isle of
Islets of Langerhans 926a
Ismail Pasha 282a, 1005a
Isobar 503c
Isocrates 282a, 1353b, *tab* 1464
Isodorus 76a
Isogonic line 503c
Isolde 1435c
Isomers 1819a
Isomorphism 1828c
Isoprene 1221c, 1824c
Isosceles (math.) 1604b
Isosceles triangles 1607c
Isoseismic line 503c
Isostacy 503c
Isostatic compensation 503c
Isothermal process 1918c
Isothermal region *see* Stratosphere
Isotopes 1806a, 1828c
  dating 454c
  uranium 1911c
Isotropic 503c
Israel 2192a–2193c
  agriculture 2192b
  anthropology 1925b
  climate 2192a
  during Crusades 1017b
  economy 2192b–2192c
  Egypt and *see* U.A.R. and flag *il* 2183
  geography 2192a–2192b
  government 2192b
  history 2192b–2193c
  independence (1948) 1017c
  map 2192, *Atlas-24*
  people of 2192b
  religion 2192a, 2192b, 2192c
  Suez crisis (1957–1958) 995b
  trade 2192c
  U.A.R. and 2190b, 2192a, 2192b, 2193c
  see also Palestine
—**Ancient** 1017a–1017b, 1455a
  northern kingdom 1017a
  Roman conquest 1017a–1017b
  rulers *tab* 1079
  southern kingdom 1017a
Israelites 1017a
Israels, Joseph *tab* 108
Issa, Abdullah 2251b
Issue (law) 886b
Istanbul, Turkey 982c, 2278a, 2278b, 2357c
  see also Constantinople
Isthmus 503c
Isthmus of Panama 2234c
It Is Never Too Late To Mend (bk.) 1367c
Italia (airship) 1155a
Italian East Africa 2146c
Italian language 1335c

English derivatives *tab* 1297c
  study 1331a
Italian Liberation, War of *tab* 1074
Italian literature *tab* 1466–1471
Italian Somaliland 2146c
Italians Argentina 2021c
Italic languages *tab* 1334, 1335a
Italic type (print.) 151c
Italy 2095c, 2193c–2196c
  agriculture 2194b–2194c
  Anti-Comintern Pact (1936), 1028a
  anchovy 13b
  archeology 970c
  cheese *tab* 731b
  chestnuts 1657c
  wine 723c
  city-states 2195b
  climate 2194a
  cod 22c
  communism 866a, 2196c
  conch 22c
  economy 2194b–2194c
  Ethiopian invasion 1013c, 1028a, *tab* 1076
  fascism 2196b–2196c
  feudalism 1006b
  flag *il* 2183
  foreign domination 2195b–2195c
  geography 2194a
  government 2194c–2195a
  hazel trees 1671a
  history 2195a–2196c
  industry 2194c
  League of Nations 1012c, 1013c
  in Libya 2210b
  map 2194, *Atlas-13*
  Middle Ages 1009a
  millet 1679c
  natural resources 2194b
  people of 2194a
  religion 2193, 2194a, 2196c
  Renaissance 2195b
  risorgimento 2195c
  trade 2194c
  Triple Alliance (1882) 1022c, 1025a
  unification 2195c–2196a
  woodbine 1700a
  World War I 1024c–1025c, 2161c, 2196b, 2291c
  World War II 1025c–1028c, 2196c
  see also Italian language; Italian literature
—**Arts**
  architecture 77b, 78a
  ceramics 126c, 127a, *tab* 130–131
  dance 182a
  furniture 1094c
  glass *tab* 135
  music 167c, *tab* 171b
  opera 161b
  painting *tab* 107–109
  sculpture *tab* 125
—**Government** 2194c–2195a
  citizenship 863c
  communism 866a, 2196c
  constitution 869c
  corporative state 870c
  dictatorship 862c, 872c, 873c
  economic control 876b
  European Common Market 877b
  fascism 863b, 878a, 2196b–2196c
  labor legislation 830c
  relation to church 877b
—**History** *tab* 1041, *tab* 1055, *tab* 1057, 2195a–2196c
  Ethiopian War 1013c, 1028a, *tab* 1076
  kings *tab* 1078
  mercantilism 986c
  relation to Church *tab* 1036–1039, *tab* 1042, *tab* 1044, *tab* 1050
Ithaca College 685
Ithaca (is.) 1436a
Ithunn 1436a
Ito, Hirobumi 282a
Iturbide, Augustín de 282b, 2136a, 2145b, 2168c–2169a, 2173a, 2219a
Iuka, Battle of 2049
Ivan I, Czar (Emperor) (Russia) 2258a
Ivan III (Ivan the Great) *see* Ivan III Vasilevich
Ivan III Vasilevich, Czar (Emperor) (Russia) 282b, 2258a–2258b
Ivan IV (Ivan the Terrible) *see* Ivan IV Vasilevich
Ivan IV Vasilevich, Czar (Emperor) (Russia) 282b, 2258b–2258c
Ivanhoe (bk.) 1365c, 1407a
  Allan-a-Dale 1423c
  Friar Tuck 1432c

Rebecca 1415a
Rowena 1416b
Ives, Burl 282b
Ives, Charles tab 172c
  biography 282b
Ives, Frederic Eugene 148c
  biography 282b
Ivory
  Congo 2135a

sculpture 119a
Ivory Coast 2197a–2197b
  agriculture 2197a
  climate 2197a
  communism 2197b
  economy 2197a–2197b
  flag il 2183
  geography 2197a
  government 2197b
  history 2197b

independence 2197b
map 2196, Atlas-36
people of 2197a
religion 2197a
**Ivory Coast Democratic Party
  (PDCI)** 2197b
Ivy 1673c
Iwo Jima, Battle of 1028c
Ixion 1436a

Izaak Walton League of America
  1744b
Izalco, El Salvador il 2145
Izanagi 1627c
Izanami 1627c
Izmir, Turkey 2357c
Iztaccihuatl, Mt. 2217c
Izvestia tab 1170c

J

Jabalpur, India 2357c–2358a
Jabberwock 1407a
Jabir see Geber
Jack be nimble (nursery rhyme)
  409a
Jack and the Beanstalk (story)
  1436a
Jack the Giant Killer (story) 1436a
Jack and Jill (nursery rhyme)
  1436a
Jack Spratt (nursery rhyme) 410a
Jackal see Dog
Jack-in-the-pulpit 1673c
Jackson, Andrew 282c, tab 798–799
  administration 2036c–2038a
  Cabinet tab 795
  centralization 862c
  Democratic Party 873a
  election and inauguration
    tab 800
  events paralleling administra-
    tion tab 1063
  holiday 841b
  New Orleans, Battle of 2035a
  Seminoles 2035c
  sobriquet 1462c
Jackson, Helen Hunt 1374c
  pseudonym 1426b
  Ramona 1414c
Jackson, Howell E.
  Supreme Court tab 802a
Jackson, Robert H. tab 796, tab 802a
Jackson, Shirley 1376a
Jackson, Thomas J. (Stonewall)
  282c
  Civil War 2045b, 2048a
  death of 2048c
  origin of nickname tab 1463b
Jackson, William
  U. S. Constitution 809c
Jackson, Michigan 1985c
Jackson, Mississippi 1986b, 2008b
Jackson College 674
Jackson State College 678
Jacksonville, Florida 1979b, 2008b–
  2008c
Jacksonville, Mississippi 1968c
Jacksonville State University 654
Jacob (Bib.) 1455b
  Esau 1453c
Jacobean Period furniture 1097a
Jacobi, Karl Gustav Jakob 1507b,
  1601a
Jacobin Party (France) 2152c
Jacobins 1010c
Jacobs, Charles B. 1192b
Jacquard, Joseph Marie 282c, 1280c,
  1286c, 1287a
Jacques I, Emperor (Haiti) 2172c
Jadwiga, Queen (Hungary) 2240a
Jael 1455b
Jaffa, Israel 1456b, 2192b
Jagan, Cheddi 2171a, 2171b
Jagello, Ladislas 2240a
Jaguar 19c–20a
Jahan, Shah see Shah Jahan
Jahangir 2180c
Jahn, Friedrich Ludwig 283a
Jahun River 2325c
Jaipur, India 2358a
Jalisco, Mexico 2217b
Jamaica 2097c, 2197c–2198b
  agriculture 2197c–2198a
  akee trees 1648b
  allspice 1648c
  climate 2197c
  Commonwealth status 1000c
  economy 2197c
  English capture of 999b
  flag il 2183

geography 2197c
government 2198a
history 2198a–2198b
independence 2198b
Indians 2198a
map Atlas-56–57
minerals 453c
mongoose 46b
people of 2197c
religion 2197c
slavery 2198a
smilax 1693a
World War II 2198b
Jamaica Labor Party 2198b
James (the Apostle) 1455b
James I, King (England) 283a,
  1020b, 2191b, 2191c
  divine right theory 2288c
  reign of 2288b–2288c
James I, King (Scotland) 1020a
  King's Quair 1360a
James II, King (England) 283a,
  1020b, 2191b
  reign of 2289b–2289c
James IV, King (Scotland) 1006b,
  1020a–1020b
James V, King (Scotland) 1020b
James VI, King (Scotland) see
  James I, King (England)
James VII, King (Scotland) 1020b
James, Henry 283b, 1369b, 1375a,
  tab 1478
  Daisy Miller 1400c
James, Jesse 283b
James, Thomas tab 796
James, William 283b, 623c, 1375b,
  tab 1478, 1612a, 1947c, 1948a
  philosophy 1619a
James River 1991b, 2013c
Jameson, Leander Starr 283b
Jamestown, St. Helena 2321a, 2358a
Jamestown, Virginia 2288b
  colonial history 2024a
Jamestown College 690
Jamestown Festival Park 1997
Jammes, Francis 1382c, tab 1479
Jamshedpur, India 2358a
Jamshid (myth) 1463a
Jan Arnolfini and his Wife (paint.)
  tab 111
Jan Mayen Island 2230a, 2323 2324
Janáček, Leoš 110c
  biography 283c
Jandaia il 28
Jane Eyre (bk.) 1367c, 1407a
  Rochester, Edward Fairfax
    1416a
Janet, Théodore 1954c
Jansen, Cornelis 283c
Jansenist Movement
  influence of French literature
    1378c–1379
Janssen, Zacharias 1269b
Janus (myth) 1436b, 1628b
Jansz, Willem 2092c
Japan 2198b–2201b
  agriculture 2199b
  Ainu 1925c
  architecture 78a
  beans 1651c
  boston ivy 1653c
  cabinet government 860a
  in Cambodia 2109b
  camellias 1656a
  cherry trees 1657c
  Chinese influence 978b, 2200a–
    2200b
  chipmunk 21c
  chysanthemums 1658a
  cinnamon 1658b
  climate 2198c
  coot 23b
  coral 23b
  cormorant 23b
  cycad 1660b
  domestic cat 19c
  duck 26a

Dutchman's breeches 1665c
economy 2199a–2200a
exterritoriality 877c
figwort species 1667a
fishing 2199b
flag il 2183
forestry 2199b–2199c
gains control of Korea 2129a
geography 2198b–2198c
government 979a, 2200a
hemlock 1671b
history 978b, tab 1059, 2200a
  2201b
in Indonesia 2188a
industry 2199c
invades Taiwan 2129a
jasmine 1673c
Kamakura Era 2200b
in Korea 2204c–2205a
lacquer tree 1674
in Laos 2207a
laurel 1675a
lilies 1675c
in Malaysia 2214a
Manchuria invasion (1931)
  1012c–1013a, 1013c, 2130b–2130c
Manchuria invasion (1936) 1028c
mandate 891a
map 2198, Atlas-33
maple trees 1678a–1678b
Meiji Restoration 2200c–2201a
Mongolia and 2221a, 2221b
in Muscat and Oman 2223a
music 155a
natural resources 2199a–2199b
in Nauru 2223b
paper 137c
pelagic sealing, abolition 998c
people of 2198c–2199a
persimmon 1686a
in the Philippines 2238b
pit-viper 51c–52a
pottery tab 130
plum trees 1687a
privets 1689a
quince 1689b–1689c
rabbit 53c
rat 54a–54b
religion 1627c, 2198b, 2198c–
  2199a, 2200a, 2200c
rice production 742b
roses 1690b
rubber (synthetic) 2199c
rush plants 1691a
salamanders 54c–55a
sea lions 56c–57a
sculpture 114b
secret police 907b
sericulture 1223b
shipyards 773
in Singapore 2250c
snipe 59a
tea tree 1696a–1696b
Tokugawa Era 2200b–2200c
trade 2199c–2200a
tunnels 1226a
in Vietnam 2300c–2301a
war with China 2130c
waxwings 66b–66c
wistaria 1700a
World War I 2201a
World War II 1016b, 1028a–1028c,
  2188a, 2201b
see also Japanese language
—**History** 978b, tab 1059, 2200a–
  2201b
  armaments, limitation of 854a,
    2069a
  censorship 862a
  Chinese influence 978b, 2200a–
    2200b
  Chinese–Japanese War (1894)
    tab 1075
  Chinese–Japanese War (1937)
    tab 1076
  Korea 977c, 2129a, 2204c–2205a
  London Conference 2072a
  Perry's treaty 2042b
  reparations 905b
  Russo-Japanese War tab 1075
  World War II 2076b
Japan, Sea of 2334c

Japan current 503c
Japan Socialist Party (JSP) 2201b
Japan wax 1227a
Japanese language 978b, 1337c
Japanese prints 136a, 141a
Japheth 1435b, 1455b
Japonica 1673c
Jardine, William M. tab 797
Jarnefelt, Edvard Armas tab 172b
Jarvis Island 2001
Jasmin, Jacques 1462b
Jamine 1673c–1674a
Jason (myth) 1424c, 1436b
  Medea 1439a
Jasper National Park 2020b
Jaspers, Karl 283c
Jaundice 924b
Java, Indonesia 2186c, 2187a, 2187b,
  2187c
  anthropology 1924a
  cardamom 1656b
  coffee trees 1659a
  dog 25c
  kapok 1674b
  maple trees 1678a–1678b
  music 155a
  peafowl 50a
  rhinoceros 54c
  rubber trees 1690c
  sculpture 114b, 124c
  sugar cane 1694c–1695a
  trogons 64a–64b
Javelin throw 1739a
Jawara, Dawda 2156c
Jaxartes River see Syr River
Jay 40b
Jay, John 283c, tab 795
  Continental Congress tab 802b
  Federalist, The 1372c, 2030c
  Federalist Party 878c
  presidential candidate tab 800
  Supreme Court tab 802a
  treaty with England 2031c
Jean, Grand Duke (Luxembourg)
  2211c
Jean, Sir James 1348b
Jeanne d' Arc see Joan of Arc
Jeanne Hebuterne (paint.) il 93
Jeans, Sir James Hopwood 283c
Jebel Ighoud
  anthropology 1924c
Jeffers, (John) Robinson 283c
Jefferson, Thomas 284a, tab 798–
  799, 873a, 874a, 964c, 2031
  administration 2032c–2034a
  agriculture 720a
  appointments 852b
  architecture 78c, 1100a
  birthday 841c
  Cabinet tab 795, 859b
  Declaration of Independence
    tab 803
  Democratic Party 872c
  election and inauguration
    tab 800
  events paralleling administra-
    tion tab 1061
  literary works tab 1471
  foreign policy 880b
  Republican Party 2031b
  sobriquet tab 1463a
  theory of government 862c
  Vice-President 2032a
Jefferson City, Missouri 1987a,
  2008c, 2019a
Jefferson River 2018c
Jeffreys, George 284a
Jehovah 1455b
Jehu 1455b
Jelenia Góra, Poland 2239c
Jellicoe, John Rushworth 284a
Jellyfish see Medusa
Jelobensky, Valery Viktorovich 169b
Jen (rel.) 1623b

Jena, Germany
  glass *tab* 135
Jena, Battle of 2160c
Jenghiz Khan *see* Genghis Khan
Jenkins, Charles J.
  presidential candidate *tab* 801
Jenkins' Ear, War of 2290b
Jenks, Jeremiah Whipple 284a
Jenner, Edward 284b, 1849a
Jennewein, Carl *tab* 125
Jensen, Johannes V. *tab* 1480
Jenson, Nicholas 144a
Jephthah (Bib.) 1455b
Jephtha (oratorio) 163a
Jerablus, Syria archeology 970b
Jeremiah (prophet) 1455c
Jeremiah (Bib. bk.) *tab* 1463
Jericho (Bib.) 1455c
Jerimoth Hill 1993c
Jeroboam 1455c
Jerome, King (Westphalia)
  see Bonaparte, Jerome
Jerome, Saint 284b, *tab* 1464
  El Greco's portrait *tab* 111
Jerome of Prague 284b
Jersey cattle 20c, 727b
Jersey City, New Jersey 1989c
  censorship 862a
  government 864b
  porcelain 129b
Jersey City State College 682
Jersey Islands 2310a
Jerusalem (city) 2192a, 2192c,
  2193a–2193b, 2358a
  Babylonian capture of 1017a
  Crusades and 1001c–1002b
  history 1455c
  medieval map-making 779c
  Temple at 1018b
Jerusalem, kingdom of 1017b
  Crusades 984c
  Jerusalem artichokes 1649c
Jerusalem delivered (poem) 1386c,
  1407b, *tab* 1467
Jespersen, Otto 1338c
Jessamine Carolina 1994a
Jesse (Bib.) 1455c
Jesselton, Malaysia 2358a
Jesuits 614c, 1632b, 2235c
Jesus Christ 284b, 1455c, 1630a
  Saint Peter 1458c
Jet planes 1156c
Jet stream (meteor.) 474a, 503c,
  763a
Jethou Island 2310a
Jethro 1455c
Jetstar (plane) 1158a
Jettison 595b, 1778c
Jetty 503c
Jeu de la Feuillée (drama) 1377c
Jeu de Robin et Marion (drama)
  1377c
Jevons, William Stanley 284b
Jew of Malta (drama) 1360c
Jewell, Marshall *tab* 796
Jewelry repairmen 386b
  see also Gems
Jewelweed 1674a
Jewett, Sarah Orne 1374c, *tab* 1478
Jewish Antiquities (hist.) *tab* 1464
Jewish law 813c, 814a
Jews 1455a, 2192–2193c
  Babylonian exile 1017a
  culture of 2192a
  the diaspora 2193a
  Germany 2157c
  in Germany 2162a, 2162b
  immigration 884a
  kings *tab* 1079
  law of 813c–814a
  religious shrines 1017
  Roman War *tab* 1072
  Soviet Union 2256a
  in Spain 2264c
  Spanish language 1335b
  World War II 913c
  Zionism 2193a–2193b
  see also Hebrews; Judaism
Jhelum River 2232c
Jig (dance) 175c, 181c
Jigger 957c
Jigs and fixtures 1264a
Jiménez, Mario Echandi 2136b
Jiménez de Quesada, Gonzalo 2133a
Jimmu (Jimmu Tenno), Emperor
  (Japan) 978b
Jimson weed 1674a
Jingle Bells (song) 418
Jinja, Uganda 2279c, 2358a
Jinnah, Muhammad Ali 284b, 2233b,
  2233c
Jinni 1436c

Joab, 1455c
Joan of Arc 284c, 965b, 985c, 2151a
  sobriquet 1462c
  victory at Orleans 1002c
Job (Bib. char.) 1455c
  Satan 1430b
Job, Book of (Bib.) *tab* 1464, 1456a
Job press (print.) 151c
Jobber 595c
Jobs *see* Career guidance; Labor
Jocasta 1436c
Jodelle, Etienne 1378b, *tab* 1466
Jodhpur, India 2358a
Jodrell Bank, England 1796c
Joel 1456a
Joe-Pye weed 1674a
Joffre, Joseph Jacques Césaire 284c
Johannesburg, South Africa 2252b,
  2358a
Johansen, John *tab* 108
Johansson, Lars *tab* 1468
John, King (England) 285a, 2285c
John II, King (France) 285a
John III, Sobieski, King (Poland)
  285b
John II, King (Portugal) 2242a
John Baliol, King (Scotland)
  1020a, 2286b
John XII, Pope 2195b
John XXIII, Antipope 1001a
John XXIII, Pope 284c
John, Augustus *tab* 108
  biography 284c
John the Apostle, Saint 1456a
John of Austria 1013c–1014a
John of Avis 2241c
John the Baptist, Saint 1456a,
  1630a
John of Bragança (Portugal) 2242a
John of the Cross, Saint 1392a
John the Divine *see* John the
  Apostle, Saint
John of Gaunt 285a, 875c
  Chaucer 1359c
John Brown University 655
John Brown's Body (poem) 1376b
John Carroll University 691
John Gilpin (poem) 1407b
John Halifax, Gentleman (bk.)
  1376c, 1407c
Johns Hopkins University 672
  graduate school founding 1127c
Johnson, Andrew 285b, *tab* 798–799,
  849b
  administration 2051b–2053a
  amnesty 851c
  apprenticeship 829b
  election and inauguration
    tab 801
  events paralleling administra-
    tion *tab* 1065
  impeachment 884a, 2052b
  Republican Party 906a
Johnson, Benjamin F. (pseud.)
  see Riley, James Whitcomb
Johnson, Cave *tab* 795
Johnson, Eastman *tab* 108
Johnson, Esther 1363a, *tab* 1463b
Johnson, Herschel V. (1812–1880)
  tab 801
Johnson, Herschel V. (1894–   )
  United Nations *tab* 797
Johnson, Hiram Warren 285b,
  tab 801
Johnson, Hugh Samuel 2073a
Johnson, James Weldon 285b
Johnson, Louis A. *tab* 797
Johnson, Lyndon Baines 285b, *tab*
  798, *tab* 1070, 2003c, 2118c,
  2143b, 2201b
  administration 2081c–2082
  cabinet *tab* 796–797
  foreign policy 2082c
Johnson, Marmaduke 145a
Johnson, Reverdy *tab* 796
Johnson, Richard M. *tab* 800
Johnson, S. (Amer. pol.) *tab* 800
Johnson, Samuel 144c, 1363b,
  tab 1470
  biography 285c
  Boswell, James 1397b, 1409a,
    1461b
  Juvenal 1358a
  Rambler, The 1414c
  Rasselas 1414c
  sobriquet 1462b
Johnson, Thomas *tab* 802a
Johnson, Walter 285c
Johnson, William Samuel
  Supreme Court *tab* 802a
  U.S. Constitution 809c
Johnson Act 884a
Johnson C. Smith University 689

Johnson State College 704
Johnson ware 128a, *tab* 132
Johnston, Albert Sidney 2045a
Johnston, Sir Harry 48b
Johnston, Joseph Eggleston 285c,
  2045b, 2048a, 2050b
Johnston, Mary 1375a, *tab* 1480
  To Have and To Hold 1418c
Johnston Island 2001
Johnstown, Pennsylvania 1993b
Joint (geol.) 503c
Joint (physiol.) arthritis 940b
Joints (physiol.) arthritis 940b
Joint-stock company 822c
Joinville, Jean de 285c, 1378a,
  tab 1465
Jókai, Maurus 285c
Jokhang Lamasery 979b
Joliet, Louis *see* Jolliet, Louis
Jolliet, Louis 286a, 2114b
Jolo, Philippines 2358a
Jommielli, Nicola *tab* 171c
Jonah 1456a
Jonathan 1456a
Jonathon, Leabua 2208c
Jones, Donald F. 721a
Jones, Ernest *tab* 1481
Jones, Henry Arthur 268a, 1369c,
  tab 1478
Jones, Inigo 77b
  biography 286a
Jones, Jesse *tab* 797
Jones, John Paul 286a
Jones, John W. House of Repre-
  sentatives *tab* 802b
Jones, LeRoi 1377a
Jones, Robert Tyre 286a
Jones, William *tab* 795
Jones Act (1917) 2003c
Jongkind, Johann *tab* 108
Jongleur de Notre Dame (opera)
  159a
Jongleurs 159a, 1398c
Jonquil *see* Narcissus
Jonson, Ben 286a, 1361c, *tab* 1467
  Masque 1410b
  Shakespeare 1396b
Joppa *see* Jaffa
Jordaens, Jakob *tab* 107
  biography 286b
Jordan, (Marie Ennemond) Camille
  1600b
Jordan 995b, 2193c, 2201c–2202b
  agriculture 2201c
  Arab-Israeli conflict 2202b
  climate 2201c
  economy 2201c
  flag *il* 2183
  geography 2201c
  government 2202a
  history 2202a–2202b
  map 2202, *Atlas*-24
  people of 2201c
  religion 2201c
  Suez crisis (1957–1958) 995b
  World War II 2202a
Jordan curve theorem 1600b
Jordan River 1456b, 2014b, 2192a,
  2201c, 2202a, 2334c
  Arab League reclamation pro-
    ject 995b
Jormungand 1436c
Jos, Nigeria 2358a
Jos Plateau 2334c
Joseph (husband of Mary) 1456b
Joseph (son of Jacob) 1456b
Joseph II, Emperor (Holy Roman
  Empire) 286b
Joseph, King (Spain and Naples)
  see Bonaparte, Joseph
Joseph of Arimathaea, Saint 1436c,
  1456b
Joseph Andrews (nov.) 1363c, 1407c
  Pamela 1412a
Joseph Ferdinand, Prince (Bavaria)
  1021a
Josephus, Flavius 286b, 1354a, *tab*
  1464
Joshua (biblical) 1003c, 1456b
Joshua (mus.) 163a
Joshua Tree National Monument
  2019a
Josiah 1456b
Josquin des Prés 160a, *tab* 171b,
  233c
Jotham 1456b
Jotunn 1437a
Joubert, Petrus Jacobus 286b
Joule, Sir James Prescott 286c,
  1761a, 1870b, 1802b
  heat 1898a
Joule's law 1871c, 1872b
Joule-Thomson effect 1802b

Journal (bookkeeping) 595c
Journal des Savants 1167b
Journal of the Plague Year (Defoe)
  1363b
Journal to Stella (Swift) 1363a
Journalism newspapers 1170c
Jove *see* Jupiter (myth)
Joyce, James 286c, 1348c, 1371b, *tab*
  1480
Juan de Fuca Strait 2020a
Juana *see* Cuba
Juárez, Benito 286c, 2219a, 2219b
Judaean Hills 2192b
Judah (son of Jacob) 1456b
Judah, Kingdom of 1017a
  Israel 1455a
  kings of *tab* 1079
Judaism 1628c
  education 612c
  historical 1628c
  Messiah 1629b
  post-exilic period 1629b
  Roman Empire 976b
Judas (disciple) 1456b
Judas Iscariot 1456b, 1630c
Judas Maccabaeus 300c
Judas Maccabaeus (mus.) 163a
Judas tree *see* Redbud
Juddah, Saudi Arabia 2358b
Jude the Obscure (nov.) 1368a
Judea 1456b
  Israel 1455a
  kings of *tab* 1079
Judges forms of address *tab* 1119
Judges, The Book of (Bib.) 1456b
Judgment (law) 886b
Judgment of Paris (paint.) *tab* 111
Judicial councils 886c
Judicial Departments (U.S.) 791c
  Disrict Courts 792b
  State government 793b
Judicial review 886c
Judiciary state governments 817a
  U.S. Constitution 808c
Judith (Bib.) 1456b
Judith (poem, Cynewulf) 1358c
Judson College 645
Jugendstill furniture 1101b
Juggernaut 1437a
Jugtown ware *tab* 132
Jugurtha 286c, 1356b
Jugurtha Before the Consul (paint.)
  tab 109
Jugurthine War *tab* 1071
Jujitsu 1740a
Jujube 1674a
Jules, Mervin *tab* 109
Julian, George W. *tab* 800, *tab* 801
Julian Alps 2303a
Julian the Apostate 287a
Juliana, Queen (Netherlands) 2225c
Juliana (poem, Cynewulf) 1358c
Julius II, Pope 287a
  Raphael's portrait *tab* 110
  tomb 122a
Julius Caesar *see* Caesar, Julius
Julius Caesar (play, Shakespeare)
  1407c
  Portia 1413c
Jullundur, India 2358b
Jumna River 2327c
Jumping (sport) 1737c–1738b
Junco 40b–40c
Junction diode 1918c
Junction transistors 1890b, 1892b
June bug 40c
June Bug (plane) 1155c
Juneau, Alaska 1974c, 2008c
Juneau, Mt. 2008c
Jung, Carl Gustav 287a, 1348b,
  1947a, 1957c
Jungfrau (mountain) 2334c
Jungle 503c
Jungle, The (bk.) 1348c, 1375c
Jungle Books (Kipling) 1408a
Juniata College 696
Junior college 627c
Junior high school 626a
  curriculum 641c, 642b
  organization 627a
Junior Leagues of America 1744b
Juniper 1647a–1674b
Junkers, Hugo 1136a
Juno 1434b, 1437a
Junqueiro, Abilio Manuel Guerra
  see Guerra Junqueiro
Jupiter (myth) 1437a, 1449c
Jupiter (planet) 1783a, *tab* 1782
  albedo 1793b

atmosphere 1840b
Bode's law *tab* 1781
moons 1782a
size of 757a
Jupiter (rocket) 1769a
Jura Mountains 2148a, 2269b, 2334c
Jurassic Period *tab* 457, 458a, 503c
Jury 886c
Jussieu, Antoine de 1638c

Just, Alexander A. 1140c
Justice (play) 1408a
Justice, Department of 887a
attorney-general 855b
bureaus 858c
cabinet members *tab* 795–796
divisions 887a
education 630b
establishment *tab* 797
Justice Party (Turkey) 2279b

Justice of the Peace 887a
Justicialismo 2090c
Justify (print.) 151c
Justin the Martyr, Saint 287a
Justin Martyr *tab* 1464
Justinian I (Justinian the Great)
287a, 938a
Roman Law 815a
Santa Sophia 75c

Jute 1276c, 1674b
Pakistan 2232b
Jutland, Battle of 1025b
Jutland Peninsula 2334c
Juvenal 287a, 1358a, *tab* 1464
Juvenile court 887b
Juvenile water 504a
Juxon-Smith, Andrew 2249b
Jylland Peninsula 2334c

K

K2 (mountain) 2332c,
see also Godwin Austen
Kabaka Yekka Party (Buganda)
2280a
Kabalevsky, Dmitri 169b, *tab* 172b
Kabistan rugs 1110c
Kabul, Afghanistan 2085a, 2358b
Kabul Kingdom 2180b
Kadár, Janos 2175c
Kaduna, Nigeria 2358b
Kaédi, Mauritania 2216a
Kafir corn *see* Sorghum
Kafka, Franz 287b, 1385c, *tab* 1480
Kafue River 2305a
Kagera River 2245b
Kagoshima, Japan 2358b
Kahoolawe Island 1980b
Kaifeng, China 978a, 2358b
Kai-fung-fu, China 1764a
Kailas Mountains 2334c
Kaisarish rugs 1110c
Kaiser Friedrich Museum (Berlin)
Kaiser, Georg 1385c, *tab* 1480
tab 109–110
Kakatiyas, the 2180a
Kala Azar 1848c
Kalahari Desert 2101b, 2322c, 2334c
Kalakaua, David 287b
Kalamazoo, Michigan 617a, 902b,
1985c
Kalamazoo College 676
Kale *see* Mustard
Kalevala (poems) 1408a
Kalgan, China 2358b
Kalidasa *tab* 1464
Kalimantan (Borneo) 2186c
Kalimantan Island 2327c
Kalinin, Soviet Union 2358c
Kaliningrad, Soviet Union 2358c
Kallai, Gyula 2175c
Kalmar Castle (Sweden) 2269a
Kalmar Union (1397–1483) 2268b–
2268c, 2231a
Kalsomine
see Calcimine
Kama (myth) 1437a
Kamakaura, Japan 2358c
Kamakura Era 2200b
Kamchatka, Sea of *see* Bering Sea
Kamchatka Peninsula 2334c–2335a
Kame 504a
Kame terrace 504a
Kamehameha Day 842a
Kamikaze 2200b
Kampala, Uganda 2280b, 2279c,
2358c
Kanat 504a
Kanawah River 2019c, 1968a
Kanchenjunga Mountain 2335a
Kanchipuram, India 2180a
Kandahar, Afghanistan 2358c–
2359a
Kandinsky, Vasili 287b, 103b,
tab 109
Kandy, Ceylon 980c, 2359a
Kandy, Kingdom of 2120b
Kane, Elisha Kent 287b
Kane, Saul
see Sassoon, Siegfried
Kanem Empire 2121a
Kang Te, Emperor (China)
see Pu-yi, Henry
K'ang Yu-wei 2129b
Kangaroo 40c
Kangaroo closure 865b
Kanishka, King (India) 2179c

Kanjera, Kenya 1924c
Kankan, Guinea 2170b
Kanmon Tunnel *tab* 1226
Kano, Eitoku 287c
Kano, Masanobu 287b
Kano, Morinobu 287c
Kano, Motonobu 287b
Kano, Nigeria 2229b, 2359a
Kanpur, India 2178a
Kansas 1982–1983
admission to the Union 2042c–
2043a
agriculture 1982c
capital punishment 860b
census (1960) 1971
climate 1982c
colleges of 668–669
commercial law *tab* 826
congressional apportionment
tab 853
economy 1982c–1983a
flag *il* 2010
geography 1982c
government 793a, 1983a
legal holidays 841–842
people of 1982c
public school enrollment *tab* 646
public school expenditures
tab 644
recall 904b
student enrollment *tab* 645
sunflowers 1695b
Kansas, University of 669
Kansas City, Kansas 1982c, 2019a
Kansas City, Missouri 1987b, 2008c,
2019a
flour milling 1285c
government 864b
Kansas City Art Institute 679
Kansas-Nebraska Bill 2041c
Kansas River 2008c, 2015b
Kansas State College of Pittsburg
669
**Kansas State Teachers College of
Emporia** 669
Kansas State University 669
Kansas Wesleyan University 669
Kant, Immanuel 287c, 1384a,
tab 1470, 1784c
matter 1760c
nebular hypothesis 454a
philosophy 1617c, 1618a
Kantor, MacKinlay 995a
Kaolack, Senegal 2247c
Kaolin 1201b, 1213a
discovery *tab* 131
hotel china 130a
Korea, South 2203c
porcelain 127c
Kaolinite 454a, 504a
Kapellmeister (Capellmeister)
174a
Handel, G.F. 162c
Kapodistrias, Ioannes 2166b
Kapok 1213a, 1674b
Karachi, Pakistan 2232b, 2359a
Karaganda, Soviet Union 2359a
Karaj Dam *tab* 1206
Karaman rugs 1110c
Karamzin, Nikolai 1389a
Karatepe, Turkey 970b
Karbagh rugs 1110c
Karfiol, Bernard *tab* 109
Kariba Dam 1221a, 2305a, 2305b
Kariba, Lake 2243a, 2305a, 2335a
Karkoram Mountains 2335a
Karl (kings) *see* Charles
Karl Franz Josef *see* Charles I,
Emperor (Austria)
Karma 1624b
Kármán, Theodore von 1768c
Karnak, Egypt 74a
Karnali River 2223c
Károlyi, Mihály (1875–1955) 287c

Karroo (tableland) 2335a
Karsavina, Tamara 184a
Karsh, Yousuf 287c
Karst topography 504a
Karume, Adeid Amani 2272c, 2273a
Kasai River 2134c, 2335a
Kashan rugs 1110c
Kashgar rugs 1110c
Kashmir 981a, 2177a, 2185c, 2186a,
2186b, 2232a, 2233c
goat 36a
plebiscite 899b
Kastrioti, Gjergj 2087a
Kasubian (lang.) 1334a
Katabatic wind 504a
Katahdin, Mount 1984b
Kathiawar Peninsula 2335a
Kathleen ni Houlihan (play) 1370c
Katkov, Mikhail 1389b
Katmandu, Nepal 2223b, 2223c,
2359a
Katmandu Valley 2223c, 2224a
Katowice, Poland 2239b, 2359b
Katsura, Taro 287c
Kattegat Strait 2335a
Kattowitz, Poland 2359b
Katydid 40c–41a
Katzenbach, Nicholas de B. *tab* 796
Kauai Island 1980b
Kauffman, Angelica 1098b
Kaufman, George 287c
Kaunas, Soviet Union 2359b
Kaunda, Kenneth 2305c
Kaunitz, Wenzel Anton 287c
Kay, John 1286c
Kay, Sir 1437a
Kayibanda, Grégoire 2246a
Kazak rugs 1110c
Kazan, Alfred 1377a
Kazan, Soviet Union 2359b
Kazantzakis, Nikos 288a, *tab* 1481
Kean, Edmund 288a
Kearney, Stephen 2039c
Kearney State College 681
Kearsarge (ship) 1610b
Keats, John 288a, 1365b, *tab* 1473
Adonais 1393c, 1461a
Eve of Saint Agnes 245b
example of poetry 1345c
writing style 1321a
Keble, John 288a
Keel 1279
Keeling, William 2310c
Keeling Islands 2310
Keene State College 682
Keifer, Joseph W. *tab* 802b
**Kekule von Stradonitz, Friedrich
August** 1761c, 1799b
Keller, Friedrich 1272a
Keller, Gottfried 1385c, *tab* 1476
Keller, Helen Adams 288a
Kellgren, Johan Henrik *tab* 1471
Kellogg, Frank Billings 288b, *tab* 796
Kelly, Grace 2220b
Kelly, Oakley 1156a
Kelly, William 1261b
Kemal, Mustafa 2279a
Kelmscott Press 146a
Kelpie (myth) 1437a
Kelvin, Lord (William Thomson)
288b, 1920a, 1802b
Kelvin scale 1893c, 1920a
Kemal Atatürk 288b
Kempis, Thomas à
see Thomas à Kempis
Kendall, Amos *tab* 795
Kenesaw Mountain, Battle of 2050b
Kenilworth (bk.) 1408a
Kennan, George Frost 288b
Kennebec River 2005b

Kennedy, John Fitzgerald 288b,
610b, *tab* 798–799, 2080a–2081c,
2138a
assassination 2081c
cabinet *tab* 796–797
election 2079c
events paralleling administration *tab* 1070
Kennedy, John Pendleton *tab* 796,
tab 1473
Kennedy, Robert Francis 288c,
tab 796
Kenny, Sister Elizabeth 288c
Kenosha, Wisconsin 1999a
Kensett, John Frederick 104b,
tab 108
Kensico Dam 1190a, 1206c
Kensington, Minnesota archeology
971a
Kent, Rockwell 288c, *tab* 109
Kent, Kingdom of 2284a
Kent State University 691
Kentucky 1983
admission to Union 2032a
agriculture 1983b
bluegrass 1653c
capital punishment 860b
census (1960) 1971
climate 1983b
colleges 669–671
commercial law *tab* 826
commonwealth 867c
congressional apportionment
tab 853
Constitutional Union Party 870b
crayfish 24a
economy 1983b
flag *il* 2010
geography 1983a–1983b
government 1983b
legal holidays 841–842
musk ox 47a–47b
people of 1983b
public school enrollment *tab* 646
public school expenditures *tab*
644
student enrollment *tab* 645
voting age 912c
Kentucky, University of 670
Kentucky coffee tree 1674b
Kentucky Derby 2011b
Kentucky River 2007b, 2019c
Kentucky State College 670
Kentucky and Virginia Resolutions
2032c
Kentucky Wesleyan College 670
Keyna 2202b–2203b
agriculture 2202b
anthropology 1924c
ass 14b
baboon 14c
Commonwealth status 1000c
economy 2202b–2202c
flag *il* 2183
geography 2202b
government 2202c
history 2202c–2203b
independence 2203b
map 2202, *Atlas*-39
nationalism 2203a
people of 2202b
religion 2203b
slavery 2202c
Kenya, Mt. 2202b
Kenya African Democratic Union
(KADU) 2203a
Kenya African National Union
(KANU) 2203a
Kenya Highlands 2335a
Kenyapithecus 1923c
Kenyatta, Jomo 2203a
Kenyon College 691
Kepler, Johannes 288c, 1504b, 1757a,
1763b, 1781a
epicycle 1794b
Kepler's laws 1781a

Keratin 1824b
Kerem, (mus.) 155c
Kerenski, Aleksandr F. 289a
Kerguelen Archipelago 2313a
Kerl, Johann Kasper *tab* 171c
Kermanshah rugs 1110c
Kern (print.) 151c
Kern, Jerome 289a
Kerner, Andreas Justinus *tab* 1473
Kerosene 1137a, 1213a
  racket fuels 1764c, 1766b
Kerouac, Jack 1376b
Kerr, John 1761a
Kerr, Michael C. *tab* 802b
Kerulen River 2220b, 2335a
Ketones 1821b
Ketosis 942b
Kettering, Charles Franklin 289a
Kettle 504a
Kettle holes 449b
Kettledrums 176a
Keuka College 685
Key 504a
Key (mus.) 176a
Key, David Mc K. *tab* 796, 2055b
Key, Ellen *tab* 1478
Key, Francis Scott 289a, *tab* 1472
  Star Spangled Banner 1352b
Keyboards (mus.) 176a
  instruments with 171a
Keynes, John Maynard 289a, 532b
Keynesian economics 533a
Keynotes (mus.) 176a
Keyplate (print.) 151c
Keypunch operators 387c
Keyserling, Count Hermann 289b
Khabarovsk, Soviet Union 2359b
Khachaturian, Aram 169b, 172b
Khafre (sculp.) 114c, 115a
Khalifa dynasty 2097a
Khama, Seretse 2101c
Khanbaliq, China 979c
Kharhov, Soviet Union 2256a,
  2257b, 2359b
Khartoum, Sudan 2359c, 2265c,
  2266b
Khasi Hills 2177c, 2335b
Khayr-ad-Din 2088a
Khayyam, Omar *see* Omar Khay-
  yam
Kheraskov, Mikhail M. 289b
Khingan Mountains 2124a, 2335b
Khorsabad (anc. city) 74b
  sculpture 113a
Khowarizmi, al- 1503c
Khrushchev, Nikita S. 289b, 2163b,
  2263a
  Cuba 2081a
  Eisenhower, Dwight 2079b
  Kennedy, John F. 2080b
Khufu *see* Cheops
Khyber Pass 2232b
Kiachow Bay 2129b
Kidd, William 289b
Kidnaping 849a, 887b
Kidnapped (bk.) 1408b
  David Balfour 1400c
Kidneys 925a
  glomerulonephritis 942a
  hydronephrosis 924b
  nephrosis 945a
  uremia 945c
Kieft, William *tab* 1463c
Kiel, Treaty of 2314c
Kierkegaard, Sören 289b, 1619c,
  1620a
Kieselguhr *see* Diatomaceous earth
Kiesinger, Kurt 2163a
Kiev, Soviet Union 2256a, 2258a,
  2359c
Kigali, Rwanda 2245b, 2359c
Kii Straight 2198c
Kilauea (volcano) 1980a
Kilimanjaro, Mt. 2272a, 2335b
Kilmer, Joyce *tab* 1480
Kilns 1264a
Kilogram *tab* 1500
Kiloliter *tab* 1500
Kilometer *tab* 1500a, 1873b
Kilowatt 1920b
Kim (nov.) 1408b
Kimba, Evariste 2135b
Kimberly, South Africa 2252c, 2359c
Kindergarten 397–444
  activities 397–398a
  art 399c
  bibliography 400c
  curriculum 398b
  fables 442–444
  food for children 402c

group interests 403a
health and hygiene 402c, 404a
in home 404a
language development 399b
literature 400b
modern methods 397–444
Mother Goose rhymes 408–412
musical training 401a
parent-teacher relationships
  403c
poetry and poems 400c
science 400a
sense games 423a
songs and singing games 418–424
stories 400c
toys 398c, 406
  educational 406–407
Kinematics 1870a, 1875b
Kinescope 1240b
Kinetic energy 1877c, 1897b, 1918a
  conversion chart 1130
Kinetic molecular theory 1801b
Kinetic theory of gases 1872a
King, Charles D. B. 2209b
King, Horatio *tab* 796
King, (William Lyon) Mackenzie
  289b, 2118a, 2118b
King, Martin Luther 289b, 2082b
King, William Rufus *tab* 800, 809c
King College 700
King (mus. instr.) 155a
King (ruler) 887b, 1937a
  forms of address *tab* 1120
King Cole 1437a
King George's War 1921b, 2026c
King Henry VI (play, Shakespeare)
  1000a
King James Bible 283a, 1362a, 1450–
  1461
King Lear (play, Shakespeare)
  1408B
  Goneril and Regan 1405a
  Celtic legend 1438b
King Leopold Ranges 2335b
King Log and King Stork (fable)
  1437b
King Mackeral *il* 1717
King of France (song) 421
King of the Golden River (story)
  1366b
King William's War 2026c
Kingbird 41a
Kingdom 887c, *see also under the
  name of individual kingdoms,
  such as* Funan, Kingdom of
Kingfisher 41a
Kinglet 41a–41b
Kingmaker, The *see* Warwick, 1st
  Earl of
Kingman Reef 2001
Kings, Book of 1456c
King's Company (actors) 1361c
Kings' Mountain, Battle of 2028c
Kings Peak 1996a
King's Quair, The (poems) 1360a
King's College 696
Kingsley, Charles 1367c, *tab* 1476
  Hypatia 1406a
  Water Babies 1420c
  Westward Ho! 1421a
Kingston, Jamaica 2197c, 2359c
Kingstown, St. Vincent 2359c
Kinkajou 41b
Kinsey, Alfred C. 1348b
Kinshasa, Congo (Kinshasa) 2134a,
  2359c
Kinship 1936a, 1941a
Kipling, Rudyard 289c, 1370c,
  tab 1479
—Writings
  Barrack-Room Ballads 1396c
  Captains Courageous 1398c
  Jungle Books 1408a
  Kim 1408b
  Plain Tales from The Hills 1413a
  Puck of Pook's Hill 1414a
  Rewards and Fairies 1415b
  Stalky and Co. 1418a
  Wee Willie Winkie 1421a
Kipps (drama) 1371b
Kirchner, Ernst Ludwig 289c
Kirchoff, Gustav Robert 289c, 1799a,
  1906c
Kirchoff's law 1906c
Kirchner, Leon 170c, *tab* 172c
Kirchner, Ludwig *tab* 109
Kirin, China 2359c
Kirkpatrick, D. *tab* 801
Kirkpatrick, George R. *tab* 801
Kirkuk, Iraq 2190a, 2359c
Kirkwood, Samuel J. *tab* 797
Kisangani, Congo (Kinshasa)
  2134c, 2360a

Kishinev, Soviet Union 2360a
Kisling, Moise *tab* 109
Kiss, The (sculp.) 123a
Kissi tribe 2209a
Kissimmee River 2019c
Kistna River 2335b
Kit (pseud.) *see* North, Christo-
  pher
Kitakyushu, Japan 2199a
Kitchen home management 1088a
Kitchen Cabinet (hist.) 2037a
Kitchen God, Festival of the 2387a
Kitchener, Horatio Herbert 289c,
  1005b
Kite 41b
Kithara 157b
Kittatinny Ridge 2017b
Kittiwake 41b
Ki-tze 977c
Kivu, Lake 2134c, 2245b, 2335b
Kiwanis International 1744b
Kiwi 41b
Kizil River 2277c–2278a
Kierulf, Halfdan *tab* 173a
Kjölen Mountains 2267c, 2335b
Klaipeda, Soviet Union 2360a
  see also Memel
Klamath Mountains 1976b, 1922c
Klaproth, Martin H. 1225b
Klaus, Josef 2096b
Klavier 161b
Klee, Paul 103b, *tab* 108
  biography 290a
  Fish Magic il 101
Klein, Felix 1580c
Kleist, Edwald C. von 1384a, *tab* 1470
Kleist, Heinrich von *tab* 1472
Klinger, Max *tab* 125
Klingsor 1473b
Klippe 504a
Klondike 2335b
Klopstock, Friedrich 290a, 1384a,
  tab 1470
Knecht Ruprecht 1437b
Knickerbocker, Diedrich *see* Irving,
  Washington
Knickerbocker Trust Company
  2062b
Knighthood 614c
  forms of address *tab* 1120
Knight of the Swan (leg.) 1437b
Knights of Columbus 1744b
Knights of Labor 838a, 2057a
Knights of Pythias 1744b
Knob 504b
Knoll 504b
Knoop, F. 1192b
Knoop scale 1192b
Knossos, Crete 83c
  palace 83b
Knot 504b
Knowles ware *tab* 132
Know-Nothing Party 887c, 906a
  American Party 851c
  Constitutional Union Party 870b
Knox, Frank *tab* 796, *tab* 801
Knox, Henry 290a, 2031a, *tab* 795
Knox, John 290a, 986b
Knox, Philander 290a, *tab* 796
Knox College 657
Knoxville, Tennessee 1995a, 2011a
Knoxville College 700
Knut *see* Canute
Koala 41b–41c
Kobe, Japan 2198c, 2199a
Köbenhaven, Denmark 2352c
Kobold 1437b
Koch, Robert 290b, 1223b, 1845a
Kochi, Japan 2360a
Kodachrome film 1173a
Kodály, Zoltán 169c, *tab* 172b
  biography 290b
Koestler, Arthur 290b
Koguryo Kingdom 2204a
Köhler, Wolfgang 1948b
Kohlrabi *see* Mustard
Koirala, B. P. 2224b
Kokiu 155a
Koko, Lake 2335b
Kokoschka, Oskar 290b
Kokura, Japan 2360a
Kolbe, Georg 123b, *tab* 125
Kolhapur, India 2360a
Kollowitz Kathë 290b
Köln, Germany 2352c
  see also Cologne, Germany
Koltsov, Aleksyey 1389b, *tab* 1475
Kolyma Mountains 2335b
Komarov, Vladimir *tab* 1770

Komensky, Jan Amos *see* Comenius
Komodo Island
  lizard 43a
  loon 43c
Komsomolsk, Soviet Union 2360a
Komura, Jutaro 290b
Kong, Ivory Coast 2197b
König, Friedrich 148a
Königin von Saba, Die (opera) 168a
Königsberg, Soviet Union 2358c
Kootenay National Park 2020b
Kopet Dagh Mountains 2255a
Kopit, Arthur 1377a
Koran 981c, 982a, 1408b, *tab* 1465,
  1634a
Korana (people)
  anthropology 1927b
Korea 977b, 2127c, 2129a, 2203b–
  2205b
  agriculture 2203c, 2204c
  climate 2203c
  economy 2203c–2204a
  geography 2203b–2203c
  government 2204a
  history 2204a–2205b
  independence of 2129b
  Japan gains control of 2129a
  map 2203, *Atlas*-33
  people of 2203c
  religion 2203b, 2203c, 2204b
  Yi dynasty 2204b
Korea, North
  agriculture 2203c
  climate 2203c
  communism 2204a, 2205a, 2205b
  economy 2203c
  flag *il* 2183
  map 2203, *Atlas*-33
  religion 2203b
Korea, South
  agriculture 2203c, 2204c
  climate 2203c
  economy 2203c–2204a
  flag *il* 2183
  map 2203, *Atlas*-33
  religion 2203b
  United Nations 993b
Korea Bay 2335b
Korean language 1337c
Korean War 1010c–1012b, *tab* 1077,
  2078a, 2131a, 2201b, 2205a
  air supremacy 1021a–1021b
  armistice 1012b, 2078b
  beginning of 1010c
  Canada 2118b
  communist troop strength 1012a
  helicopter 1159b
  Inchon landing 1010c
Korean Workers Party 2204a
Kornberg, Arthur 1854c, 1858c
Körner, Theodor *tab* 1473
Korngold, Erich 168a
Korolenko, Vladimir 1390a
Korzeniowski, T. J. K. *see* Conrad,
  Joseph
Koryo dynasty 2204b
Kosala Kingdom 2179b
Kosciusko, Thaddeus 290c
Kosciusko, Mount 2091b
Kosi River 2223c
Košice, Czechoslovakia 2360a
Kossuth, Louis 290c
Kosygin, Aleksei N. 290c, 2186b,
  2263a
Koto 155a
Kotzebue, August von *tab* 1471
Kouilou River 2133c
Koussevitzky, Serge 290c
Kozhikode, India 2360a
Kra, Isthmus of 2335b, 2273a
Kraepelin, Emil 1954a
Krafft-Ebing, Richard von 291a
Krag, Jens Otto 2142b
Kraków, Poland 2239a, 2360a–2360b
Kraków, University of 2240a
Krasnovodsk, Soviet Union 2360a
Krebs, Arthur 1155a
Krebs cycle 921c, 927b
Kreis, Henry *tab* 125
Kreisler, Fritz 291a
Krenek, Ernst 168a, *tab* 172a
Kreuzfahrer, Die (opera) 165c
Kriemhild 1437b
Krimml Waterfall 2335c
Krishna 1437b
Krishna Menon, V. K. 291a
Krishna River 2177c, 2337b
Kriss Kringle 1437b
Kroll, Leon *tab* 109
Kroll, W. A. 1225b

Kroll-Betterton process 1213c
Kromdraai, Africa anthropology 1924b
Kronstadt, Soviet Union 2261c
Kropotkin, Pëtr A. 291a
Kru tribe 2209a
Krueger, Maynard *tab* 801
Krug, Julius A. *tab* 797
Kruger, Stephanus Johannes Paulus 291a, 896a, 2253a
Krupp, Alfred (1812–1887) 291a
Krupp, Alfred (1907–) 291b
Krupp, Friedrich (1787–1826) 291a
Krupp, Friedrich Alfred (1854–1902) 291a
Krylov, Ivan 1389a, *tab* 1471
Krypton 1808b, 1833
    atomic structure 1807b
    atomic weight *tab* 1805
    electrons 1807a
Kshatriyas 980b
Kuala Lumpur, Malaysia 2213a, 2213b, 2360b
Kubitschek, Juscelino 2104c

Kubla Khan (poem) 1364c, 1408b
    alliteration 1394b
Kublai Khan 291b, 980a, 1021c, 2200b, 2221a, 2127c
Kuching, Sarawak 2360b
Kudu 41c
Kudzu 1674b
Kuhn, Walt *tab* 108
Kuhnau, Johann *tab* 171c
Kukenan Waterfall 2331a
Ku Klux Klan 887c, 2053b
Kuka, Frantisek 291b
Külpe, O. 1948a
Kumasi, Ghana 2164a, 2360b
Kumquat 1674b
Kunamoto, Japan 2360b
Kundry 1437c
Kunlun Mountain 2123c, 2127a, 2335c
Kuniyoshi, Yasuo *tab* 109
    biography 291b
Kunming, China 2360b
Kuomintang (KMT) party (China) 2130a, 2130b–2130c, 2131c *see also* Nationalist Party (China)

Kupa River 2303a
Kupffer cells 921a
Kuprin, Alexander 1390a
Kura River 2254c
Kurdish rugs 1110c
Kurdistan rugs 1110c
Kuria Muria Islands 2253c
Kuril Islands 2335c
Kurka, Robert 170c
Kuro Shio (current) *see* Japan Current; Kuroshio
Kurobegawa Dam *tab* 1206
Kuroki, Tamemoto 291b
Kuroshio 504b
    see also Japan Current
Kurume, Japan 2360b
Kush, Kingdom of 2266b
Kutch, Gulf of 2335c
Kutuzov, Mikhail 291b
Kutztown State College 696
Kuwait 995b, 2205b–2206a
    agriculture 2205c
    economy 2205c
    flag *il* 2183

    geography 2205c
    government 2205c
    history 2205c–2206a
    independence 2205c
    Indians in 2205c
    map 2205, *Atlas-25*
    people of 2205c
    religion 2205b
Kuwait City, Kuwait 2360c
Kuwait Fund for Arab Economic Development 2206a
Kuwatly, Shukri, Earl 2271c
Kuybyshev, Soviet Union 2360c
Kwangchow Bay 2129c
Kwangtung (prov.), China anthropology 1924b
Kwashiorkor 920b
Kweiyang, China 2360c
Kyd, Thomas 291b, 1360c
Kymatology 504b
Kyoga, Lake 2279a, 2335c
Kyoto, Japan 2199a, 2200a, 2200b, 2360c
Kyrenia Mountains 2138a
Kyushu Island 2198b, 2198c

L

La Belle Jardinière (paint.) *tab* 112
La Brea, Trinidad 2275c
La Bruyère, Jean de 291c, 1379c, *tab* 1468
La Digue Island 2322a
La Farge, John *tab* 108, 134a
    biography 291c
La Farge, Oliver 291c
La Ferme au Soleil (paint.) *tab* 113
La Follette, Robert Marion (1855–1925) 292a
    presidential candidate *tab* 801, 2070b
    Progressive Party 901c
La Fontaine, Jean de 292a, 1379b, *tab* 1468
    Aesop's Fables 1394a
La Guardia, Fiorello 292a
La Grange College 662
La Kermesse (paint.) *tab* 112
La Motte-Fouqué, F. de *tab* 1472
La Mouthe (cave) 971a
La Noue, François de 1378c
La Paz, Bolivia 2100b, 2100c, 2361a
La Pérouse, Count de 293b
La Rochefoucauld, François de 293c, 1379c, *tab* 1468
La Salle, Antoine de (1388–1462) 1378a
La Salle, René Robert de 293c
La Sierra College 657
La Source (paint.) *tab* 112
La Tour, Georges de 294a
La Tour, Maurice Quentin de *tab* 107
La Verne College 657
Laaland Island 2336b
Laban 1456c
Labe River 2331c
Labiche, Eugène 1381c, *tab* 1475
Labiodental consonants 1294c
Labor 595c
    construction industry 1189c
    educational programs 637a
    struggle for jobs 609b
—History
    Cleveland, Grover 2056c
    Hayes, Rutherford B. 2055b
    injunctions 885a
    Roosevelt, Theodore 2061a
Labor, Department of 887c–888a
    bureaus 832c, 840a, 858c, 888a
    establishment *tab* 797, 866b, 2062c
    secretaries *tab* 797
Labor Day 842b
Labor, Division of *see* Division of labor
Labor economics 596a
    employment 528a
Labor legislation 826–841
    homeworkers 833b
    injunctions 839b
    New Deal 839a
    safety 835b

    Social Security act 836c
    Taft-Hartley Law 831c
    unemployment compensation 837a
    wages 833–834
    working hours 832a
    workmen's compensation 835c
Labor Management Relations Act *see* Taft-Hartley Act
Labor Party (Australia) 2093b, 2094a
Labor Party (New Zealand) 2227a
Labor Standards, Bureau of 467a
Labor unions 596a
    adult education 637b
    A. F. of L. 838b
    A. F. of L.-C.I.O. 838c
    C.I.O. 838b
    hiring halls 882a
    history 838a
Labrador
    black duck 17a
    explorers 2023a
    fishing 2112b
    yellowlegs 68b–68c
Labrador current 504b, 765c
Labradorite (min.) 453b
Laburnum 1674c
Labyrinth (myth) 1437c
Lac bug *see* Scale insect
Laccadive Sea 2335c
Laccolith 450c, 504b
Lace Maker, The (paint.) *tab* 112
Lacewing 41c
Lachaise, Gaston 124a, *tab* 125
    biography 291c
Lachesis 1432a, 1437c
Lackland, John *see* John, King (England)
Lacordaire, Jean Baptiste Henri 1381b
Lacquers 1213b, 1216b
Lacquer tree 1674c
Lacrima christi 723c
Lacrosse 1727a
Lactic acid 731c, 927b, 1825b
Lactose 744b
Lacustrine 504b
Ladder system (educ.) 617a
Ladd-Franklin theory 928c
Ladies' Home Journal (magazine) 1167b
Ladin (lang.) 1335c
Ladislas, King (Hungary) 2174b
Ladoga, Lake 2335c
Ladon (myth.) 1437c
Ladrone Islands *see* Marianas
Ladu 540b
Lady (title) *tab* 1120
Lady Beauchamp (paint.) *tab* 112
Lady Godiva *see* Godiva
Lady Governors of St. Elizabeth's (paint.) *tab* 111
Lady Hamilton (paint.) *tab* 111
Lady of the Lake (leg.) 1437c
Lady of the Lake (poem) 1365a, 1408c
    Roderick Dhu 1401a

Lady or the Tiger, The (story) 1408c
Lady Washing Her Hands (paint.) *tab* 110
Lady Windermere's Fan (play) 1368b, 1408c
Lady's slipper 1674c
Ladybeetle 41c–42a
Ladybird, Ladybird (nursery rhyme) 92c, 410c
Ladycliff College 685
Ladysmith, South Africa 2360c
Laertes (Eng. lit.) 1405b
Laertes (Gr. lit.) 1437c
Lafayette, Marie Madeleine de 1379c, *tab* 1468
Lafayette, Marquis de 291c
    American Revolution 2030a
    French Revolution 998a
Lafayette College 696
Lafayette, Louisiana 1983c
Lafitte, Jean 292a
Lafontaine, Louis H. 2116a
Lagash, Sumeria 74b
Lager beer 724a
Lagerkvist, Pär 292a, *tab* 1481
Lagerlöf, Selma 292a, *tab* 1479
Lagoon 449a, 504b
Lagos, Nigeria 2229a, 2229b, 2229c, 2360c
Lagos Dos Patos (lagoon) 2335c
Lagrange, Joseph Louis 1505a, 1507b, 1601a
Lahore, Pakistan 2232b, 2361
Laika (dog) 951a
Laissez-faire 596a, 987a
Laius 1441b
Lajos (Hungarian kings) *see* Louis, kings (Hungary)
Lake Erie College 691
Lake Forest College 664
Lake District 2335c
Lake poets 1408c
Lake School (lit.) 1364c
Lake trout *il* 1717
Lake of the Woods 2018b
Lakeland College 707
Lakes 504c, 1866c, 2335c–2336a
    erosion 448b
Lakes (geog.) *see also under the names of individual lakes, such as* Erie, Lake
Lalande, Joseph Jérôme Lefrançais de 292c
Lalla Rookh (poem) 1365b
L'Allegro (poem) 1345c, 1362b, 1406c, 1408c
    Handel, G. F. 163a
Lalo, Edouard *tab* 171c
    biography 292b
Lamaism 979a
    lamaseries 979b
    Mongolia 979c
Lamar, Joseph R.
    Supreme Court *tab* 802a
Lamar, Lucius *tab* 797
    Supreme Court *tab* 802a
Lamar State College of Technology 702

Lamarck, Jean Baptiste de 292b, 1762a
Lamartine, Alphonse de 292b, 1380c, *tab* 1473, 2153b
Lamb, Charles 292b, 1347b, 1365b, *tab* 1472
    Essays of Elia 1403a
    pseudonym 1462a
Lamb, Henry *tab* 109
Lamb, Mary 1365b
Lambaréné, Gabon 2361a
Lambda-zero 1916a
Lambert, Constant *tab* 172b
Lambert, Johann Heinrich 292c
Lambeth, England
    ceramics *tab* 130
Lamb's-quarters 1674c
Lambton, John George *see* Durham, Earl of
Lambuth College 700
Lame Duck Amendment 888a, 2072b
Lamennais, Félicité Robert de 1381b
Lamentations (Bib.) 1456c
Lamina (plant) 1645a
Laminar flow 504c
Lamizana, Sangoulé 2295a
Lamlam, Mt. 2001a
Lamont, Daniel Scott *tab* 796
Lamont, Robert Patterson *tab* 797
Lampblack 1213b
Lampman, Archibald 1390c
Lamprey 42a
Lamps 1140c
Lan Chang 2206b–2206c
Lanai Island 1980b
Lancaster, Pennsylvania 1993b
Lancelot 42a–42b
Lancelot 1437c
    Morte d' Arthur 1411a
Lanchow, China 2361a
Lancret, Nicholas *tab* 107
Land 596b
    conservation 775a
    public 888a
Land breeze 504c
Land iguana *il* 32
Land Ordinance (1785) 888b
Land reclamation 754c, 904b
Lander College 699
Landforms 761–761c
Landing of Marie de Médicis at Marseille (paint.) *tab* 112
Landis, Kensaw Mountain 292c
Landlocked 504c
Landlocked salmon *il* 1717
Landlord 596b
Landon, Alfred M.
    presidential candidate *tab* 801, 2074b
    Republican Party 906b
Landor, Walter Savage 292c, 1365c, *tab* 1472
    Bleak House 1397c
Landowska, Wanda 292c

Landreth, Ira *tab* 801
Landscape 504c
Landseer, Sir Edwin Henry *tab* 108
Landslides 447b
Landslide 504c
Landtag (Germany) 874a
Lane, Edward William 1395a
Lane, Franklin K. *tab* 797
Lane, John 720b
Lane, Joseph *tab* 801
Lane, Ralph Norman Angell *see* Angell, Norman
Lane, Sir Ralph 2023c
Lane College 700
Lang, Andrew 292c, 1366c
Langdon, John *tab* 800
    U.S. Constitution 809c
Langland, William 293a, 1360a
    Piers Plowman 1413a
Langley, Samuel Pierpont 293a, 1155b
Langmuir, Irving 293a, 1140c, 1800a
Langston University 693
Langton, Stephen 293a
Language 1293–1340
    abbreviations 1338–1340
    alphabet 1295a
    anthropology 1935a
    culture 1941c, 1942a
    extension of 1935b
    kindergarten 399b
    learning 1298
    misused words 1322–1325
    origin 1293b
    public speaking 1326–1328
    semantics 1298b
    sounds 1293c–1295a
    voiced and unvoiced sounds 1294b
    vowels 1294b
Language in Action (bk.) 1348c
Languages classification 1333–1338
    etymology *tab* 1296
    evolution of alphabet *tab* 1294
    foreign 1329–1333
    inflections 1296a
    principal alphabets *tab* 1295
    relation of English to others 1297b
    teaching of 619b
    see also under the names of individual languages, such as French language
Languedoc Canal 1225c
Lanier, Sidney 293a, 1374b, *tab* 1478
Lanolin 1227b
Lansdowne, 5th Marquis of 293b
Lansing, Robert 293b, *tab* 796, 2065a
Lansing, Michigan 1985c, 2011b–2011c
Lanson, Gustave 1382a
Lanston, Tolbert 147a
Lanthanum 1809b, 1833
    atomic weight *tab* 1805
Lao Tzu 2126b
Laocoön (myth) 1438a
Laocoön (sculp.) 117c
Laokoon (essay) 1384c
Laomedon 1438a
Laos 2206a–2207b
    agriculture 2206b
    climate 2206a
    communism 2207a
    economy 2206a–2206b
    flag *il* 2183
    geography 2206a
    government 2206b
    history 981b, 2206b–2207a
    independence 2207a
    Kennedy, John F. 2080b
    map 2206, *Atlas*-30
    people of 2206a
    religion 2206a, 2206c
    World War II 2207a
Lao-tse 293b, *tab* 1463, 1623c
Lapies 504c–505a
Lapilli 505a
Lapithae 116b, 1438a
Laplace, Pierre Simon de 293c, 454a, 1506c, 1760b, 1784c
Lapland 2146c, 2336a
Lapps adaptation 1927b
    anthropology 1927a
Lapse rate 505a
Laptev Sea 2335a
Laramie Mountains 2020b
Larceny 888c
Larch 1674c–1675a
Lardner, Ring 293c, 1376a
Laredo, Texas 1995c
Lares 1438a

Large intestine 920a
Largemouth black bass *il* 1717
Larghetto (mus.) 176a
Largillière, Nicolas *tab* 107
Largo (mus.) 176a
Lark 42b
Lark bunting 1977a
Larkspur 1675a
Larreta, Enrique 1393b
Larsson, Carl *tab* 108
Larsson, Lars-Erik 168c
Larynx
    music 176a
    speech sounds 1293c–1294a
Las Casas, Bartolomé de *tab* 1466
Las Vegas, Nevada 1988c, 2011a
LaSalle College 696
Lasca, Il *see* Grazzini, Antonio
Lasers (phys.) 1910–1911, 1918c
    injection 1890c
    technical uses 1910c
Lashio, Burma 2361a
Laski, Harold J. 293c
Lassale, Ferdinand 294a
Lassen Peak 1976c
Lasso, Orlando di 160a, *tab* 171b
Lasswitz, Kurt 1764c
Last (shoe) 1280b
Last Days of Pompeii (bk.) 1408c
Last of the Mohicans (bk.) 1408c
    Leatherstocking Tales 1409a
Last of the Tribunes *see* Rienzi
Last of the Troubadours *see* Jasmin, Jacques
Latakia, Syria 2271a, 2361a
Late Stone Age *see* Neolithic Age
Laterial lisp 1298c
Lateran Treaties 2296b–2296c
Lateranus, Lucius Sextius 1014c
Laterite 505a
Latex 1221b, 1276c, 1278a
Lathes 1265c
Latimer, Hugh 294a, *tab* 1466
Latin America
    censorship 862a
    history outline *tab* 1061–1070
    literature 1393
    music *tab* 172c
Latin language 1293c, 1295a, *tab* 1297b, 1335a
    alphabet *tab* 1294, 1296a
    classification 1333a
    Italian literature 1385b–1386a
    study 1330c
    tenses 1297a
Latin literature 976b, 1354–1358, *tab* 1464–1465
    classicism 1399a
Latin Quarter (Paris) *see* Left Bank
Latini, Brunetto 294a, 1386a
Latinus 1438b
Latitude 758c, 1795a
Latitudes horse 501a
Lateral imbalance (vision) 1299b
Latona *see* Leto
Latosolic soils 743a
Latosols 762b
Latrobe, Benjamin Henry 78c
    biography 294a
Latvia language 1334a
    League of Nations 1012c
Laube, Heinrich 1384c, *tab* 1475
Laud William 294a
Laue, Max von 1918c
Laue pattern (phys.) 1918c
Laughing jackass *see* Kingfisher
Laughing Philosopher *see* Democritus
Launch pad 1778c
Laura (lit. char.) 1386a
Laurel 1675a
    mountain 1993
Laurel family 1675a
Laurens, Henri (art.) *tab* 125
Laurens, Henry (states.) 294a
    Continental Congress *tab* 802b
Laurent, Robert *tab* 125
Laurentian Highlands 2336a
Laurier, Sir Wilfrid 294b
Laurier, Wilfrid 2117b–2117c
Lausanne, Switzerland 2269c
Lausanne, Treaty of 2279a
Lautrec, Henri Toulouse *see* Toulouse-Lautrec
Lava 450c, 505a
    pillow 511a
Lavender 1675a
Lavender's Blue (song) 422
Lavinia (myth) 1423a, 1438b

Lavoisier, Antoine Laurent 294b, 1008a, 1760a, 1761a, 1798c
    sulfur 1224a
Law, Andrew Bonar 294b
Law, John 294c, 1016b–1016c
Law 783, 812–817
    Anglo-American law 815b
    Babylonian law 813c, 972c
    bibliography 914
    business law 858c
    career guidance 384c
    codification 816b
    common law 815b
    constitutional law 869a
    Egyptian law 813c
    equity 816c, 862a
    forms of address *tab* 1119
    Jewish law 813c
    legal procedure 817–827
    martial law 891b
    military law 891c
    primitive culture 1937a
    private law 901b
    prize law 901c
    public opinion 812c
    Roman law 814a
    suits 909c
    see also Legislation
Law of cross-cutting relationships 505a
Law merchant 888c
Law of superposition 505a
Law of the Twelve Tables (Roman Republic) 1002c
Lawes, Henry *tab* 171c
Lawes, Sir John Bennet 749c, 753a
Lawes, William *tab* 171c
Lawn tennis 1734b
Lawrence of Arabia *see* Lawrence, Thomas Edward
Lawrence, David Herbert (D. H. Lawrence) 294c, 1371c, *tab* 1480
Lawrence, Ernest O. 1912b
Lawrence, Sir Thomas *tab* 108
    Pinkie tab 112
Lawrence, Thomas Edward (Lawrence of Arabia) 294c
    Odyssey translation 1351a
Lawrence, Massachusetts 524a, 1985b
Lawrence University 707
Lawrencium 1833
    atomic weight *tab* 1805
Lawrie, Lee 125
Laws *see* Law
Lawson, Ernest *tab* 108
Lawton, Henry Ware 2060a
Lawton, Oklahoma 1992b
Lay of Hildebrand (poem) *tab* 1465
Lay of the Honeysuckle (poem) 1377c
Lay of the Last Minstrel (poem) 1365a
Lay of Walther of Aquitaine (poem) *tab* 1465
Layamon 1395c, 1425b
    Brut, The 1359c
Layard, Sir Austen Henry 969a
Layouts (print.) advertising 151c, 596b
    careers 375a
Lays of Ancient Rome (poem) 1366b, 1396c, 1409a
Layson Island teal ducks 62c
Lazarillo de Tormes, El (bk.) 1391b, *tab* 1466
Lazarus 1456c
Lazarus, Emma 295a
Le Bel, Joseph Achille 1761c
Le Brun, Charles *tab* 107, 1095c
    biography 295a
Le Châtelier, Henri Louis 1799b, 1812b
Le Corbusier 295a, 1101c
Le Galliene, Eva 295c
Le Havre, France 2149b, 2361b
Le Moyne College 685, 700
Le Nain Antoine *tab* 107
Le Nain, Louis *tab* 107
Le Nain, Mathieu *tab* 107
Lesage, Alain René 297a, 1379c, 1380b, *tab* 1469
Leaching (soil) 505a, 750a
Leacock, Stephen 1390b
Lead (metal) 505a, 1213b, 1833
    atomic weight *tab* 1805
    Australia 2092b
    galena 453c
    Great Britain 2282c
    Greenland 2314b
    Korea, North 2203c
    Liberia 2209a
    Mexico 2218a

Missouri 1987b
Montana 1988a
ores 1213c
Peru 2236b
Poland 2239b
Portugal 2241b
radioactive decay 454b
South West Africa 2322c
Soviet Union 2256b
Spain 2263c
Sweden 2268a
Tanzania 2272b
Turkey 2278a
Utah 1996b
Yugoslavia 2303b
Lead mold (print.) 151c
Lead wool 1208b
Lead-acid cells 1883a
    batteries 1131c
Lead-base alloys 1194a
Leaders (print.) 151c
Leading note (mus.) 176a
Lead-uranium ratio 505a
Leaf (bot.) *see* Leaves
Leaf scar (plant) 1645b
Leaf springs 1281c
Leaflets (plant) 1645a
Leafhopper 42b–42c
League of Augsburg, War of the 2026c
League of Communists of Yugoslavia (LYC) 2303c
League of Nations 880b, 988c, 1012b–1013c, 1015a, 1017b, 1025c, 2068a, 2095c, 2096a, 2118a, 2146c, 2162a, 2240b, 2292a
    Article X 854c, 2068a
    beginning of 1012c
    commissions 1013b
    covenant 907a, 1012c
    end of 1012c, 1013c
    established 1023a
    mandate 891a
    membership 1012c–1013a
    Public Health Organization 1013b
    Refugee Settlement Commission 1013b
    resignations from 1012c
    success of 1013b–1013c
    United Nations 990a
    United States 2072a
    withdrawals from 1028a
    World Court 914b
Leah 1456c
Leakey, Lewis S.B. 1124c, 1924c
Lean ore 505a
Leander 1434c
Leap year 1797b
Lear (leg. k.) 1437a
Lear, Edward 295a
    Owl and the Pussy-Cat 413c
Learning 1949a
    memory 1950a
    reading 1299a–1301a
    speaking 1298–1299
    spelling 1302c–1303c
    writing 1301–1302
    see also Education
Lease 889a
Leather 1209b
Leatherstocking Tales (bks.) 1409a
Leaves (plant) 1644c–1654c
    arrangement of 1645b
    bud scales 1645a
    form of 1645a
    internal structure 1645b–1645c
    lamina 1645a
    longevity 1645a–1645b
    petoile 1645a
    spines 1645a
    veins 1645a
    venation 1645a
Leaves of Grass (poem) 1374c, 1404b
Lebanon 995b, 2207b–2208a
    agriculture 2207b
    cedar trees 1018b
    climate 2207b
    economy 2207b–2207c
    emigration 2207b
    flag *il* 2183
    geography 2207b
    government 2207b
    history 2207c–2208a
    independence 2208a
    industry 2207b
    map 2207, *Atlas*-24–25
    in Ottoman Empire 2207c–2208a
    Ottoman Era 2207c–2208a
    people of 2207b
    religion 2207c–2207c
    trade 2207b, 2208a
Lebanon Mountains 1456c, 2207b

Lebanon Valley College 696
Leblanc, Nicholas 1212a
Leblanc process 1212a
Lechic language 1334a
Lecky, William Edward 295a
Leconte de Lisle 1381c, *tab* 1475
Lectern Bible 146b
Lecture 1327c
Leda 1438b
Lederberg, Joshua 1854a, 1858c
Ledger 596b
Ledger lines (mus.) 176a
Lee 505a
Lee, Ann 1462c
Lee, Charles 295a, *tab* 795, 2029
Lee, Edmund 1150b
Lee, Francis Lightfoot 295a, *tab* 803
Lee, Harper 1375c
Lee, Henry 295b, *tab* 800
　nickname 1462b
Lee, Manfred *tab* 1463a
Lee, Richard Henry 295b, *tab* 802b, *tab* 803
Lee, Robert E. 295b, 2050a
　birthday 841a
　Brown, John 2043a
　Civil War 2045a, 2048a
　home 78c
　surrender 2050c
Leech 42c
Leeds, England 2361b, *tab* 132
Lee-Jackson Day 841a
Leek, 1675b
Leeuwenhoek, Anton van 295b, 1269b
Leeward 505a
Leeward Islands 2307a, 2309a, 2311b, 2317c
Legal procedure 817–827
Legal tender 889a
Legare, Hugh Swinton *tab* 795, 1474
Legato (mus.) 176a
Legazpe, Miguel López de 2238a
Legend of Montrose, The (bk.) 1365c
Legend of Sleepy Hollow (story) 1409a
　Ichabod Crane 1400a
Legende of Goode Women (poem) 1360a
Legendre, Adrien Marie 1506c, 1566b
Legends 1421–1449, 1422a
　see also Folklore, Mythology
Legends (print.) 151c
Léger, Fernand 103b, *tab* 108
　biography 295b
Leghorn chickens 932a
Legislation 889a
　initiative 884b
　referendum 884b
　see also Law
Legislative department 793a
Legislature 889b
Legree, Simon 1419c
Lequía y Salcedo, Augusto B. 2237b
Legumes 1646a, 1934a
　nitrogen 1862b
　soil 751c
Lehar, Franz 295c
Lehigh River 2005a
Lehigh University 696
Lehman, Herbert H. 295c
Lehmann, Liza 169b, 1416b
Lehmbruck, Wilhelm *tab* 125
　biography 295c
Lehr (glassmaking) 133b
Leibl, Wilhelm *tab* 108
Leibniz (Leibnitz), Gottfried Wilhelm von 295c, 1243a, 1383c, *tab* 1468, 1504b, 1616c
　calculus 1602a
　topology 1507a
Leicester, Earl of (c. 1208–1265)
　see Montfort, Simon de
Leicester, Earl of (c. 1532–1588)
　see Dudley, Robert
Leif Ericson see Ericson, Leif
Leipzig, Germany 2158a, 2361b
　Bach, J. S. 163b
Leipzig, Battle of 1014b
Leishmaniasis *tab* 947
Leitmotif (leitmotiv) 167a, 176a
Leland, Charles Godfrey (pseudonym) 1461b
Lely, Sir Peter 296a, *tab* 107
LEM see Lunar Excursion Module
Le Moyne, Jean Baptiste see Bienville, Sieur de
Leman, Lake 2332b

Lemass, Sean 2191c
Lemaitre, Jules 1382a, *tab* 1478
Lemke, William presidential candidate *tab* 801
Lemma (geom.) 1559a
Lemming 42c
Lemnos 1438b
Lemoine, François *tab* 107
Lemon 1675b
Lempira (Indian chief) 2173a
Lemur 42c
Lemus, José María 2145c
Lena River 2336a
Lenau, Nikolaus 1385a, *tab* 1474
Lenbach, Franz von *tab* 108
Lend-lease 889b
Lend-Lease Act
　Roosevelt, Franklin D. 2076b
L'Enfant, Pierre Charles 296a
Length *tab* 1500
　biblical measures *tab* 1460–1461
　physics 1869a
Lenin, Nikolay see Lenin, V. I.
Lenin, V. I. 296a, 988c, 1390b, 1618c, 2261b–2262a
　Bolshevik 858a
　Cominform 865c
　see also Soviet Union
Lenin (ship) 1167c
Lenin State Library (Moscow) *tab* 1463
Leningrad, Soviet Union 2256a, 2257b, 2262b, 2361b–2361c
　National Public Library *tab* 1463
Lenoir, J. J. Etienne 1169b
Lenoir Rhyne College 689
Lenormand, Henri René 1382b
Lenotre, André 296b
Lenox ware (pottery) *tab* 132
Lens (anat.) 928b
Lens (optics) 1908a, 1918c
Lenticular 505a
Lentil 1675b
Lentilli, Leo *tab* 125
Leo I (Leo the Great), Saint, Pope 296b, 983a
Leo III, Pope 2150a, 2195b
Leo X, Pope 296b
Leo XIII, Pope 296b
Leofric 1433c
Leominster, Massachusetts 1985b
León, Nicaragua 2227c, 2228a
Leonard Wood Memorial for the Eradication of Leprosy 1744c
Leonardo da Pisa see Fibonacci, Leonardo
Leonardo da Vinci see Vinci, Leonardo da
Leoncavallo, Ruggiero 167c, *tab* 172a
　biography 296b
Leone, Sierra Leone 2248b
Leoni, Raúl 2298b
Leonidas, King (Sparta) 296b, 1021c
Leonine rhyme 1415b
Leopard see Cat
Leopard (English frigate) 2033b
Leopardi, Giacoma 1387b, *tab* 1474
Leopold I, Emperor 2095
Leopold I, King 2098c, 2099a
Leopold II King 2099a, 2135a
Leopold II, King (Belgium) 296c
Leopold III, King 2099a
Leopold III, King (Belgium) 296c
Leopold II, Lake 2336a
Léopoldville, Congo (Kinshasa) 2134c, 2359c
Lepanto (Chesterton) 1014a
Lepanto, Battle of 1013c–1014a
Lepidus, Marcus Aemilius 296c
Leprechaun 1438c
Leprosy *tab* 947, 1744c
Lepton 1916a
Leptospirosis *tab* 947
Ler (myth) see Lir
Lerdo de Tejada, Sebastián 2219b
Lermontov, Mikhail Y. 297a, 1389b, *tab* 1475
Lesbos 2164c
Les Baux, France 1194b
Les Miserables (bk.) 1382a, 1409a
Lescaze, William 81c, 82c
Lesley College 674
Leslie, Frank 1462b
Lesotho 2208a–2208c
　agriculture 2208b
　Commonwealth status 1000c
　economy 2208b

flag *il* 2183
　geography 2208a
　government 2208b
　history 2208b–2208c
　industry 2208b
　map 2208, *Atlas-40–41*
　nationalism 2208c
　people of 2208b
　religion 2208a, 2208b
Lesseps, Ferdinand de 297a
Lesser Antilles 2004a
Leser Khingan Mountains 2124a
Lesser Magellanic Cloud 1795b
Lesser Sundas Islands 2186c
Lessing, Gotthold E. 297a, 1355b, 1384a, *tab* 1470
　Laokoon 1438a
Lesueur, Jean François 171c
Leszczynski, Stanislas
　see Stanislas I
Let (sports)
　squash 1733b
　tennis 1735a
Lethe (myth) 1438b
　Hades 1433c
Leto 1438b
Letter of advice 596c
Letters de cachet 998a
Letter of credit 596c
Letter writing forms of address *tab* 1119
Letterpress printing 142a, 151c, 1173c
Letters from an American Farmer (essays) 1372c
Letters from Paris (journal) *tab* 1473
Lettish language 1334c
Lettuce 1675b–1675c
Letvia see Latvia
Leucippus 297a, 1613c, 1751b, 1798a
Leucocytes see White blood cells
Leucoplasts plant 1643c
Leukemia 942b
Leutze, Emanuel *tab* 108
　biography 297a
Levant, Oscar 297a
Levee 505a
Levees 448a
Level 505a
Lever Act 2065c
Levering, Joshua presidential candidate *tab* 801
Leverrier, Urbain Jean Joseph 297b, 1759c
Levertin, Oskar Ivar *tab* 1479
Levi (Bib.) 1456c
Levi, Carlo 1388b
Leviathan of Literature see Johnson, Samuel
Leviticus (Bib. bk.) 1456c
Lewanika, Chief 2305c
Lewes, George Henry 297b
Lewin, Kurt 1948b
Lewis, Cecil Day 297b, 1371c
Lewis, Francis *tab* 803
Lewis, Gilbert Newton 1800a
Lewis, John L. 297b, 831b
Lewis, Matthew Gregory (Monk Lewis) 1462c
Lewis, Meriwether 297b, 1014a, 2033b
Lewis, Sinclair 297b, 1375c, *tab* 1480
　Babbitt 1396b
　Main Street 1410a
Lewis, William 1171c
Lewis, Wyndham *tab* 109
Lewis College 664
Lewis and Clark College 693
Lewis and Clark Expedition 1014a–1014b
Lewiston, Maine 1984b
Lexington, Kentucky 1983b
Lexington, Battle of 2027c, 2029b
Leyden, Lucas van see Lucas van Leyden
Leyte (Philippine Islands) 2237c, 2238a, 2238b
Lezghian rugs 1110c
Lhasa, Tibet 1022b
　lamasery 979b
Li (rel.) 1623b
Li Dynasty 2300a
Li Hung-chang 297c
Li Po 978a
Li Tzu-ch'eng 2128a
Li Yüan 2127b
Li Yüan-hung 2130b
Liabilities 544a, 596c
Lianas (bot.) 1859c
Liang Chi'-ch'ao 2130a

Liao River 2124a, 2336a
Liaotung, Gulf of 2124a
Libau, Latvia see Liepaja
Libel 889b
Libellant (law) 898a
Liber Abaci (bk.) 1503c
Liberal arts 628b
Liberal Democratic Party (LDP) (Japan) 2201b
Liberal Party (Canada) 2116a, 2116c, 2117b, 2118a, 2118b, 2118c
Liberal Party (England) 860b
Liberal Party (New Zealand) 2227a
Liberal Party (Puerto Rico) 2003a
Liberal Republican party 889c, 906a
Liberation, War of (1813–1814) 1014b
Liberator, The see Bolívar, Simón
Liberator, The (journal) 2037a
Liberia 2208c–2209b
　agriculture 2209a
　economy 2209a
　flag *il* 2183
　geography 2208c
　government 2209b
　history 2209a–2209b
　independence 2209b
　map 2209, *Atlas-36*
　people of 2209a
　religion 2208c
　rubber production 1221b
　World War I 1025a
　Wold War II 2209b
Liberty Bell 7 (spacecraft) *tab* 1770
Liberty bonds 2065b
Liberty League 2074b
Liberty party 889c
　Free-Soil Party 881a
Liberty Tubes (tunnel, Pittsburgh) 1226
Libido 1957b
Libraries *tab* 1463
　adult education 637c
　careers 379b
　home 1106c
　see also under names of individual libraries, such as Boston Public Library
Library of Congress *tab* 1463
Libration (astron.) 1795c
Libretto 176a
Libreville, Gabon 2155b–2155c, 2361c
Libya 995b, 997c, 2196b, 2209b–2210b
　agriculture 2210a
　economy 2210a
　flag *il* 2183
　geography 2209b–2209c
　government 2210a
　history 2210a–2210b
　independence 2210b
　industry 2210a
　map 2209, *Atlas-34*
　people of 2209c–2210a
　religion 2209b, 2210b
　World War II 2210b
Lice 957c
Licenses 889c
Lichen planus (disease) 924c
Lichens 1640c–1641a, 1847c, 1848a
　ecology 1859c
Lichenology 1638a
Licinian Rogations 1014c
Lick Observatory telescope 1791b
Licking River 2019c
Licorice 1675c
Lie, Jonas *tab* 108, *tab* 1477
Lie, Trygve 297c, 992b, 2231c
Liebermann, Max *tab* 108
Liebig, Justus von 749c, 752a, 1799b
Liebknecht, Wilhelm Philipp Martin 297c
Liechtenstein 2210b–2211a
　agriculture 2210c
　economy 2210c
　flag *il* 2183
　geography 2210b–2210c
　government 2110c
　history 2210c–2211a
　map 2210, *Atlas-17*
　people of 2210c
　religion 2110b
　Switzerland and 2270a
Liechenstein family 2210c
Lied (mus.) 176a
Liège, Belgium 2098a, 2361c
Lien (law) 889c
Liepaya, Latvia 2361c
Lieurance, Thurlow 170c
Lietuva see Lithuania

Lieutenant governor
forms of address *tab* 1119
Lif and Lifthrasir 1445c
Life origins 461a, 1839–1841
Life (mag.) circulation 1167b
Life of Cowley (bk.) 1397b
Life for the Czar, A (opera) 169a
Life and Death of Jason (poem) 1369a
Life instinct 1757b
Life insurance 595a
Life on the Mississippi (bk.) 1409a
Life of St. John the Baptist (paint.) *tab* 1110
Life of Samuel Johnson, The (bk.) 1363b, 1397b, 1409a, *tab* 1470
Life space (psych.) 1948b
Life zones (geog.) 1865b
Life-support system 1778c
Ligature (mus.) 176a
Light 1902–1909
aberration 1793a
absorption 1904a, 1916b
albedo 1793a
color 1907b
diffraction 1905b, 1917c
diffusion 1917c
dispersion 1904b, 1917c
electroluminescence 1917c
fluorescence 1918a
incandescence 1906a
interference 1905a
luminescence 1906a
Neo-Platonic theory 1755a
polarization 1905c
quantum theory 1903c
reflection 1904a
transmission 1904a
refraction 1904b, 1919c
semiconductors 1891c
units 1906c
velocity 1904a
wave theory 1903b
see also Optics
Light waves 1903b
Light year 505b, 1786a, 1795a
Light-Horse Harry *see* Lee, Henry
Lighthouses 1167a
Lighting 1139c, 1890a, 1906a
automobiles 1131c
electric circuits 1886b
electronics 1890a
interior decoration 1104c, 1105a
Lightning 457b, 1141b, 1881a, 1882b
casualties in U.S. 475c
Lignite 505b, 1136c, 1202a
Germany 2158b
North Dakota 1991c
Lignum vitae 1675c
Ligurian languages 1335c
Ligurian Sea 2336a
Lihou Island 2310a
Likasi, Congo (Kinshasa) 2361c
Like terms (math.) 1535b
Lilac 1675c, 1989a
Liliencron, Detlev von *tab* 1478
Lilienthal, David 297c
Lilith 1438b
Liliuokalani, Lydia Kamekeha 297c
Lille, France 2149a
Lilliput 1405b
Lilly, Willim pseudonym *tab* 1463c
Lilongwe, Malawi 2212b
Lily 1675c–1676a
Sego 1996a
Lily family 1676a
Lily-of-the-valley 1676a
Lima, Ohio 1992a
Lima, Peru 2236a, 2236b, 2237a, 2361c
Pan American Conference (1938) 1017c
Limassol, Cyprus 2361c
Limb 505b
Limburg, Netherlands 2224c, 2225a
Limburger cheese *tab* 731b
Lime 505b, 1676a
brick 1196a
portland cement 1200a
Lime (chem.) 1214a
fertilizer 753c
glass 133a
Limerick (lit.) 1409b
Limestone 450b, 505b, 1214a
Alabama 1974b
Bhutan 2099b
Florida 1979b
Great Britain 2282c
Italy 2194b
Pakistan 2232b
Soviet Union 2257a
U.S. 1967b
West Virginia 1998c
Limestone College 699

Limitations, Statute of 890a
Limited company 597a
Limnetic zone 1866c
Limoges, France
pottery *tab* 132
Limón, José 184c
Limonite 453c, 505b
Limnology 505b
Limpet 42c–43a
Limpopo River 2101b, 2242c, 2317a, 2252a, 2336a–2336b
Lin Piao 298b
Lin Yutang 298c
Lincoln, Abraham 297c, *tab* 798–799, 963c–964a, 2015a
administration 2044a–2051a
events paralleling *tab* 1065
Cabinet *tab* 796–797
Civil War 2045–2051a
death 2051a
election and inauguration *tab* 801
Emancipation Proclamation 2048b
Gettysburg Address 1404b
Hampton Roads Conference and 1009a–1009b
Republican Party 906a
slavery views 2044b
sobriquets 1461a, 1462a, *tab* 1463a
Lincoln, Benjamin presidential candidate *tab* 800
Lincoln, Levi *tab* 795
Lincoln, Mary Todd 298a
Lincoln, Robert Todd *tab* 796
Lincoln, Nebraska 1988a, 1988b, 2011a
Lincoln Memorial (Washington, D.C.)
French, Daniel Chester 124a
Lincoln Memorial University 700
Lincoln Tunnel (New York–New Jersey) 1226c
Lincoln University 679, 696
Lind, Jenny 298a
nickname *tab* 1463c
Lindbergh, Charles A. 298a, 1156a
kidnapping 388c, 887b
Lindemann, Ferdinand 1502c
Linden 1676a
Linden family 1676a
Lindenthal, Gustav 1190c
Lindenwood College 679
Lindsay, Howard 298b
Lindsay, (Nicholas) Vachel 298b, 1376a, *tab* 1480
Lindsey, Benjamin Barr 298c
Line (math.) 1604b
Line drawing 151c
Line engraving 1173c
Line of force 1881c
Line spectra 1906a
Linear accelerators 1912c, 1919b
Linear functions 1591b
Linfield College 693
Linen 1214a
Ling 43a
Linguistics 1935a
Linkoping, Sweden
fountain 123b
Linnaeus, Carolus (Karl von Linné) 298b; *tab* 1470, 1638b, 1761c
Linné, Karl von *see* Linnaeus, Carolus
Linoleic acid 732b
Linotype 147a, 151c, 1171a, 1174b
Linseed oil 732c
Lintels 73a
Linton, Ralph 1946a
Lion *see* Cat
Lion Mountain 2248c
Lion Hunt, The (paint.) *tab* 111
Lion and the Mouse, The (fable) 443b
Lion of the North *see* Gustavus II
Lion's Share, The (fable) 444a
Lions International 1744c
Lions, Gulf of 2336b
Lipari Island 2193c, 2336b
Lipchitz, Jacques 123b, *tab* 125
Lipoma 942c
Lippi, Flippino *tab* 106
biography 298c
Lippi, Fra Filippo *tab* 106
biography 298c
Adoration of the Christ Child *tab* 109
Coronation of the Virgin *tab* 110
Lippmann, Gabriel 298c

Lippmann, Walter 298c
Liquefaction 1899c
Liquid petroleum gas 1137c
Liquidation 597a
Liquid-fuel rockets 1765a
fuel systems 1766b
Liquid fuels 1765a, 1766b
Liquid oxygen 1137b, 1903a
rockets 1766b
Liquid propellants 1779a
Liquids 1802b, 1880b, 1828b
capillary action 1871a
conductance 1882b
heat 1899c
measure *tab* 1500
properties 1871a
surface tension 1871a
viscosity 1871b
Liquor
Eighteenth Amendment 811b
local option 890b
Twenty-first Amendment 811c
Lir 1438b
Lisbon, Portugal 2241a, 2241b, 2241c, 2242a, 2361c–2362a
Lisle, Leconte de *see* Leconte de Lisle
Lisle, Rouget de *see* Rouget de Lisle
Lisping 1298c
Lister, Joseph 298c
Liszt, Franz 166b, *tab* 172a
biography 299a
Litani River 2207b, 2336b
Litany 176a
Litchi 1676a–1676b
Liter *tab* 1500
Literacy Test Act 2064a
Literal factor (math.) 1535b
Literary agents 388b
Literary allusions dictionary 1393–1421
Literary criticism 1377a, 1400b
Literature 1343–1498
age of criticism 1362c
American 1371–1377
Canadian 1390–1391
censorship 860c
dictionary of literary allusions 1393–1421
dictionary of mythology, legend and folklore 1421–1449
English 1358–1371
French 1377b–1383a
German 1383–1385
Greek 1350–1354
heroes and heroines 1346b
historial outline *tab* 1027–1059
history 1350–1395
humor 1346b
Italian 1385–1388
kindergarten 400b
Latin American 1393
libraries, great *tab* 1463
Middle Ages 985a
outline of world literature *tab* 1463–1481
philosophy 1611c
poetry 1343–1346
Portuguese 1338b–1339a
prose 1346a
realism 1415a
Russian 1389–1390
Spanish 1391–1392
see also under the names of specific literatures, such as American literature; French literature
Lithification 505b
Lithium 1808a, 1809b, 1818b, 1833
atomic weight *tab* 1805
electrons 1807a
Lithography 141a, 149a, 151c, 1174a
transfer 141b
Lithology 505b
Lithosols 505b
Lithosphere 505b, 759–762
continental drift 759c
continents 759c–761a
earthquakes 761a
landforms 761a–761c
mineral deposits 761c–762a
ocean basins 759c
soils 762a–762c
volcanoes 761a

Little Dorrit (nov.) 1366c
Little drops of water (nursery rhyme) 410b
Little Entente 1014c–1015a, 2154b, 2175b
members 1014c
Little Flowers of Saint Francis (bk.) 1386a
Little Giant *see* Douglas, Stephen Arnold
Little Golden Hood (story) 434a–435b
Little Jack Horner (nursery rhyme) 408c
Little John 1438b
Little Land, The (poem) 414a
Little Mac *see* McClellan, George B.
Little Men (nov.) 1373c, 1409b
Little Mermaid (fairytale) 1440a
Little Minister, The (nov.) 1369c, 1409b
Little Miss Muffet (nursery rhyme) 409a
Little Phil *see* Sheridan, Philip Henry
Little Pine Tree, The (story) 425b
Little Red Hen, The (story) 424
Little Red Riding Hood (story) 1438b
Little Rock, Arkansas 1975c, 1976a, 2011a–2011b
school integration 2078c
Little Rock University 655
Little Russian (lang.)
see Ukranian language
Little Sark Island 2310a
Little Swan Island 2003c
Little Tommy Tucker (nursery rhyme) 409c
Littlepage, Cornelius
see Cooper, James Fenimore
Littleton, Sir Thomas 299a
Little Women (nov.) 1373c, 1409b
Littoral 505b
Liu Pang 2127a
Live oak 1979c
Live-forever *see* Orpine
Liver 920c, 927b
cirrhosis 941a
Liverpool, England 2362a
pottery *tab* 130
Liverpool Range 2091b
Liverworts 1641c
Lives of the Caesars (biography) 1358b, *tab* 1464
Lives of the Poets (biography) 1363c
Livestock
Alabama 1974b
American Samoa 2000a
Arkansas 1976b
artificial insemination 721b
California 1977a
farming careers 381a
Guam 2001a
Isle of Man 2316b
Kansas 1982c
Kentucky 1983b
Maine 1984b
meat packing 735b
Michigan 1986a
Missouri 1987b
Montana 1988a
New Caledonia 2318b
public health 957c
Romania 2244a
Sikkim 2249c
South Dakota 1994b
Soviet Union 2257a
Switzerland 2270a
Trucial Oman 2276b
Turkey 2278a
U.S. 1968b, 2294a
Virginia 1997c
Yugoslavia 2303c
Living Room 1106c
Livingston, Brock
Supreme Court *tab* 802a
Livingston, Edward *tab* 795
Livingston, Philip *tab* 803
Livingston, Robert R. 299a
Livingston, William 809c
Livingston College 689
Livingston State College 654
Livingstone, David 299a, 2212c, 2273a
Livius Andronicus 1354c, *tab* 1464
Livy 299a, 963a, 965c, 1357c
History of Rome tab 1464
Lizard 43a–43b
Ljubljana, Yugoslavia 2303b, 2362a

Llama 43b
Llano 505b, 2336b
Llewellyn, Richard *tab* 1481
Llewelyn the Great, Prince (Wales) 2286b
Lloyd George, David 299a, 1023a
Lloyd, Henry Demarest 525b
Lloyd's Register (list) 597a
Llyr *see* Lir
LOX (fuel) *see* Liquid oxygen
Load 505b
Loam 505b
Loango Kingdom 2155c
Loans 597a
Lobachevsky, Nikolai 1506a, 1558a, 1580c
Lobby (govt.) 890a
Lobelia 1676b
Lobito, Angola 2362a
Lobster 43b
  processing 734b
Local government 890a
  charters 863b
  city 864a
  county board 857c
  home rule 882a
  mayor 891c
  political divisions 793c
  political party organization *tab* 393
  public health 960c
  school boards 634b
  school districts 633b
Local Government Act (England) 871c
Localisms (lang.) 1321c
Local option 890b
Locarno Conference purpose of 1015a
Locarno treaties (1925) 2154b, 2292a
Loch 505b
Lochinvar 1409b
Lochner, Stephan *tab* 106
Lock Haven State College 696
Locke, David *tab* 1477
  pseudonym 1462c
Locke, John 299b, 623b, *tab* 1468, 1617a, 2022b
Lockhart, John Gibson 299b
Lockjaw *see* Tetanus
Lockout 597a
Locks 1264b
Locks (canal) 1160c
Lockup (print.) 148a
Lockyer, Sir Joseph Norman 299b
Locomotives 1178a
  U.S. history 2038a
Locoweed 1676c
Locust 43c, 1676c
Lode 505b
Lodestone 1881a
Lodge, Henry Cabot (1850–1924) 299b
Lodge, Henry Cabot, Jr. 299b, 2079c
  United Nations *tab* 797
Lodge, Sir Oliver Joseph 299c
Lódz, Poland 2239a, 2239c, 2362a
Loeb, Jacques 299c
Loeffler, Charles Martin 170b, 172c
Loess 447c, 505b
Loetschberg tunnel 1226
Loewe, Johann Carl *tab* 172a
Lofa River 2208c
Lofoten Islands 2336b
Logan, J. H. 1676c
Logan, John Alexander
  nickname 1461b
  Vice-presidential candidate *tab* 801
Logania family 1676c
Logan's Cross Roads, Battle of *see* Mill Springs, Battle of
Logaoedic poetry 1351b
Logarithms 1504c, 1596a, 1603b, 1604b
  slide rule 1596c
  table *tab* 1600
Logan, Friedrich von *tab* 1467
Loganberry 1676c
Logic 1557b, 1611b
  principles of 1559a
  symbolic 1598a
Logical empiricism 1619a
Logical positivism 1618c
Logone River 2336b
Logotype 151c
Logroscino, Nicola 171c
Logwood 1676c
Lohengrin (knight) 1438b
Lohengrin (opera) 167a

Lohenstein, Daniel Casper von *tab* 1468
Loire River 2148a, 2336b
Loki 1438c
Lolang Kingdom 2204a
Lolland Island 2141a, 2336b
Lollards 1015a, 1360a
Loma Mountains 2248b
Lomax, Louis 299c
Lombard Street (London) 597a
Lombards 2195a
Lombroso, Cesare 299c
Lomé, Togo 2274c, 2275a, 2362a–2362b
Lomonosov, Mikhail 1389a, *tab* 1470, 1799a
London, Jack 299c, 1375a, *tab* 1480
  Call of the Wild 1398b
London (poem) 1358a, 1363b
London, England 2282a, 2283a, 2362b
  borough 858a
  population of 2282b
  World War II air bombings 1028b
—**Landmarks**
  British Museum *tab* 1463
  Lombard Street 597a
London, Tower of 1022c
London, Treaty of (1841) 1005a
London, Treaty of (1915) 1025a, 2196b
London Bridge (song) 420
London Company 2024a
London Conference (1930) 2072a
London Daily Express *tab* 1170c
London Daily Mail *tab* 1170c
London Daily Mirror *tab* 1170c
London Protocol (March 1829) 2166b
London Stock Exchange 604c
London Spy (journ.) 1167b
London Times (news.) 148a
Lone Star State *see* Texas
Long, Crawford Williamson 299c
Long, Huey P. 299c, 2074b
Long, John D. *tab* 796
Long (wt.) *tab* 1500
Long Beach, California 1976c, 2011b
Long Beach, California State College at 657
Long haul 597b
Long Island 1990b, 2018b
  goldfinch 36b
Long Island, Battle of 2029
Long Island Railroad 1165b
Long Island University
  C.W. Post College 685
  Conolly College 685
  Southampton College 685
Long John Silver 1419b
Long ton *tab* 1500
Longfellow, Henry Wadsworth *il* 208, 1374a, *tab* 1474
  biography 300a
  Courtship of Miles Standish 1400a
  Evangeline 1403a
  Hiawatha 1405c
  Tales of a Wayside Inn 1418a
Longhi, Pietro *tab* 107
Longinus *tab* 1464
Longitude 758c, 1795a
Longitudinal dunes 505b
Longitudinal valley 505c
Longshore bars 449a
Longshore current 505c
Longstreet, James 300a, 2048c
Longview Bridge 1197
Longworth, Nicholas House of Representatives *tab* 802b
Longwood College 705
Longwy, France 2149a
Lönnrot, Elias 1408a
Look (magazine)
  circulation 1167b
  xograph 1188b
Looking Backward (nov.) 908a, 1375b, 1409c
Looms 1286a, 1287a
Loon 43c
Loosestrife family 1677a
Lope de Vega
  see Vega, Lope de
Lopes, Fernao 1388b
López, Alfonso 2133b
López, Carlos Antonio 2235c
López, Francisco Solano 2235c
López Mateos, Adolfo 2219c

López de Mendoza, Iñigo *see* Mendoza, Iñigo López de
López, Narciso 1006a, 2137b
Lopoukowa, Mlle. 184a
Loquat 1677a
Lorain, Ohio 1992a
Loras College 668
Lorca, Federico García 300a, 1392c
Lord Heathfield (paint.) *tab* 111
Lord Jim (nov.) 1370a
Lord Philip Wharton (paint.) *tab* 113
Lords (noblemen) 890c
Lords, House of *see* House of Lords
Lorelei (myth) 1438c
Lorenzetti, Ambrogio *tab* 106
  biography 300a
Lorenzetti, Pietro *tab* 106
  biography 300a
Lorenzini, Carlo 300a
Lorenzo, Fiorenzo di *tab* 106
Lorenzo the Magnificent
  see Medici, Lorenzo de
Lorenzo, Monaco 300a
Loretto Heights College 659
Lorna Doone (nov.) 1367c, 1409c
Lorrain, Claude
  see Claude Lorrain
Lorraine 2148a, 2149a–2149b, 2151c, 2152b, 2153c, 2154b, 2161b, 2161c
Lorris, Guillaume de
  see Guillaume de Lorris
Lortzing, Gustave *tab* 172a
Los Angeles, California 1976c, 2011b, 2293b
  public library *tab* 1463
  recall 904b
Los Angeles, California State College at 657
Los Angeles Herald Examiner (newspaper) *tab* 1171
Los Angeles Mountains 1976c
Los Angeles Times (newspaper) *tab* 1171
Lost Colony
  see Roanoke Island
Lost Generation 1375c
Lost Tribes of Israel 1455a
Lost river 505c
Lot (Bib.) 1456c
Lot (Arthurian leg.) 1438c
Lothair I, Emperor (Holy Roman Empire) 1023a
Lothair I, King 2150c
Loti, Pierre 1382c, *tab* 1478
Lotophagi 1438c
Lotti, Antonio *tab* 171c
Lotto, Lorenzo *tab* 107
Lotus *il* 1662, 1677a
Loubet, Emile 300b
Lough Neagh 2282b
Louis (Bavarian kings) *see* Ludwig
Louis, Saint *see* Louis IX, King (France)
Louis I, Emperor (Holy Roman Empire) 1023a, 2150a–2150b
Louis I, King (France) *see* Louis I, Emperor (Holy Roman empire)
Louis I, King (Germany) *see* Louis I, Emperor (Holy Roman empire)
Louis I, King (Hungary) 2240a
Louis I, King (Portugal) 2242a
Louis I de Bourbon, Prince 1010c
Louis II, King (Germany) 2150c, 2159a
Louis VI, King (France) 2150b, 2150c
Louis VII, King (France) 2150b–2150c
Louis IX, King (France) (Saint Louis) 300b, 2150c
Louis XI, King (France) 985c, 2151a
  seizes Burgundy 999c
Louis XII, King (France) 300b
Louis XIII, King (France) 300b, 2151c
Louis XIV, King (France) 300b, 998a, 999a, 1016c, 1022c, 2113c, 2114a, 2151c–2152a, 2211b, 2225b, 2289c
  dance 182c
  mercantilism 986c
  patron of arts 1379a
  Versailles 1102b
Louis XV, King (France) 300c, 998a, 1007a, 1021b, 2152b

Louis XVI, King (France) 300c, 998a, 2152b–2152c
  executed 1006c, 1008a, 1008c
  imprisoned 1007b
  printing 144c–145a
  summons (States General 1007a–1007b
  veto 912a
Louis XVII, King (France) 300c
Louis XVIII, King (France) 300c, 2153a
Louis, Joe 301a
Louis Bonaparte *see* Bonaparte, Louis
Louis Napoleon
  see Napoleon III
Louis Philippe, King (France) 301a, 2153b
  nickname 1461c
Louis XIV (furniture style) 1097b
Louis XV (furniture style) 1097c
Louis XVI (furniture style) 1097c
Louisburg, Nova Scotia 2026c
Louisiade Archipelago 2319b
Louisiana 1983–1984
  agriculture 1984b
  budget system 858b
  capital punishment 860b
  census (1960) 1971
  climate 1983c
  code 865b
  colleges 671
  colonization 2023c
  commercial law *tab* 826
  congressional apportionment *tab* 853
  economy 1983c–1984c
  flag *il* 2010
  geography 1983c
  government 1984a
  holidays 841–842
  magnolia 1677b–1677c
  people of 1983c
  public school enrollment *tab* 646
  public school expenditures *tab* 644
  recall 904b
  restored to Union 2053c
  secession 2043c
  statehood 2035b
  student enrollment *tab* 645
  water thrushes 66b
Louisiana College 671
Louisiana Polytechnic Institute 671
Louisiana Purchase 1014b, 2033a
  acres 903b
Louisiana State University & Agricultural & Mechanical College 671
Louisiana State University in New Orleans 671
Louisville, Kentucky 1983b, 2011b, 2019c
Louisville, University of 670
Lounsbury, Thomas R. *tab* 1477
Lourenço Marques, Mozambique 2267a, 2317a, 2362b
Louse 43c–44a, 1393c
  see also Lice
L'Ouverture, Toussaint
  see Toussaint L'Ouverture
Louvois, Marquis de 2152a
Louvre *tab* 112, 1111a
Lovanium University 2135a
Love 1941a
Lovebird 44a
Lovelace, Richard *tab* 1468
Lover, Samuel *tab* 1474
Lovett, Robert A. *tab* 797
Low, Juliette Gordon 301a
Low, Will H. *tab* 108
Low 505c
Low brass 1196a
Low Countries
  historical outline *tab* 1058
  see also Belgium; Luxembourg; Netherlands
Low water 505c
Lowell, Abbott Lawrence 301a
Lowell, Amy 301b, *tab* 1480
  Imagists 1376a
Lowell, Francis Cabot 523c
Lowell, James Russell 301b, 1374a, *tab* 1476
  Biglow Papers 1397b
  pseudonym 1461b
  Vision of Sir Launfal 1420c
Lowell, Percival 301b
Lowell, Robert 301b
Lowell, Massachusetts 524a, 1985b
  government 864b
Lowell, State College at 674
Lowell Technological Institute 674

Lower (Baja) California 1976c
Lower case (print.) 150c, 153a
Lower Paleolithic Age 1928a
Lowery, Thomas Martin 1817a
Lowes, John L. 1377a
Lowestoft, England pottery *tab* 131
Low-to-paper (print.) 151c
Loyalties (play) 1370b
Loyalty Islands 2318a
Loyola, Ignatius de, Saint 301b, 1632b
Loyola College 672
Loyola University 664, 671
Loyola University of Los Angeles 657
Luanda, Angola 2306a, 2362b
Luang Prabang, Laos 2206a, 2206c, 2362b–2362c
Luangwa River 2305a, 2336b
Lubbock, Sir John 301c
Lubbock, Texas 1995c
Lübeck, Germany free city status 1009c
    Hanseatic League 1009b–1009c
Lübke, Heinrich 301c
Lublin, Poland 2362c
Lubricants 1214b
Lubumbashi, Congo (Kinshasa) 2134c, 2362c
Lucalox lamps 1141a
Lucan *Pharsalia* 1357c, *tab* 1464
Lucas van Leyden *tab* 107, 139c
    biography 301c
Lucca, Italy sculpture 121c
Lucca, Republic of 2195b
Luce, Claire Boothe 301c
Luce, Henry R. 301c
Lucerne, Switzerland 2269c
Lucerne, Lake 2270b, 2336b
Lucian *tab* 1464
    Dialogues 1354a
    moon 1763b
Lucifer 1438c, 1430b
Lucilius, Gaius 1355c
Lucite 1824c
Luck of Barry Lyndon (nov.) 1367b
Lucknow, India 2362c
Lucretius 301c, 1354b, 1356b, *tab* 1464
    De Rerum Natura 1346a
    language 1293b

Lucullus, Lucius Licinius 301c
Ludendorff, Erich F. W. 302a
Ludlow typograph 147b, 1174b
Ludwig (German name for Louis) see Louis
Ludwig, Emil 302a, 1385c, *tab* 1480
Ludwig, Otto 1385a, *tab* 1475
Ludwig II, King (Bavaria)
    Wagner, Richard 167a
Ludwigsburg, Germany pottery *tab* 131
Luffa see Vegetable sponge
Lug (Lugh) 1438c
Luini, Bernardino *tab* 106
Luke, Saint 1456c, 1631a
Luks, George *tab* 108
Lullaby 176a
Lully, Giovanni 161c, *tab* 171c
Lully, Jean Baptiste 302a
Lumber 1264c
    Canada 2115b
    production 1264a
Lumen (unit) 1906c
Lumière, Auguste M. L. 302a
Lumière, Louis Jean 302a
Lumière process 1173a
Luminance 1907a
Luminescence 1906a
Luminosity stars 1788c, 1790a
Luminosity curve 1906c
Luminous units 1906c
Lumumba, Patrice 2135a–2135b
Luna (myth) 1438c, 1447a
Lunacy 1954b
Lunar day 505c
Lunar eclipse 1794a
Lunar Excursion Module 1778a
Lunar month 505c
Lundy's Lane, Battle of 2034c
Lungfish 44a
Lungs 922a
    circulatory system 924c
    emphysema 941c
    pleurisy 945a
    pulmonary embolism 945b
    silicosis 945c
Lunik I *tab* 1772
Lunik II *tab* 1772
Lunt, Alfred 302a
Lupine 1677a

Lupus erythematosus 942c
Lurton, Horace H. *tab* 802a
Lusaka, Zambia 2305a, 2362c
Lusatian (lang.)
    see Wendish (lang.)
Lusiad (epic) *tab* 1466
Lusitania (ship) 2065a
Luster 505c
    minerals 453a
Lute 155b, 159c
Luteotrophic hormone 926b
Lutetium 1834
    atomic weight *tab* 1805
Luther, Martin 171b, 874a, 986b, *tab* 1466, 1612b, 2160a
    biography 302a
    education 614c
    language 1337b
    literature 1383b
    music 160b
    Nicaea, Council of 871b
Luther College 668
Lutheranism 1632a
Luthuli, Albert 2253b
Lutrin, Le (poem) 1379c
Luxembourg 2098a, 2098b, 2099b, 2211a–2211c, 2362c
    agriculture 2211b
    Benelux customs union 998b
    climate 2211a
    duchy 875c
    economy 2211a–2211b
    European Common Market 877b
    flag *il* 2183
    geography 2211a
    government 2211b
    history 2211b–2211c
    map 2211a, *Atlas*-22
    people of 2211a
    religion 2211a
    World War I 2211c
    World War II 2211c
Luya Mountains 2124a
Luzon (Philippine Islands) 2237c, 2238a, 2238c
Lvov, Soviet Union 2362c
Lyautey, Louis 2362c
Lycidas (poem) 1409c, 1362b
Lycomedes
    Theseus 1448b
Lycoming College 696
Lycurgus 302c
Lydgate, Charles 302c

Lydgate, John style of verse 1360a
Lydia (ancient) 1015a
Lyly, John 1360c, *tab* 1466
Lymph glands
    Hodgkin's disease 942b
    lymphosarcoma 942c
Lymph nodes 924c
Lymphatic system 924c
Lymphocytes 922b
Lymphogranuloma venereum *tab* 947
Lymphosarcoma 942c
Lymph vessels 924c
Lynch, Jack 2191c
Lynch, Thomas, Jr. Declaration of Independence *tab* 803
Lynch law 891a
Lynchburg, Virginia 1997c
Lynchburg College 705
Lynx 44a–44b
Lyon, Corneille de *tab* 107
Lyon, James 169c
Lyon, Mary 1852c
Lyon, France 2148b, 2149b, 2362c–2363a, 2363c
    commune 868a
Lyonesse (poem) 1369a
Lyre 155c, 157a, 176a
Lyre and Sword (poems) *tab* 1473
Lyrebird 44b
Lyrical Ballads (bk. of poems) 1364c, 1394c
Lyric poetry 1409c, 1351b
    beginnings 1344a
    French 1380c
    Greek 974b
    growth of 1345b
    ode 1411b
    Portuguese 1388b
Lysander 302c
Lysias 1353b, *tab* 1464
Lysimachus 302c
Lysimeter 505c
Lysippus 117a, 302c
Lysogenic bacteria 1844b
Lytton, Bulwer (English family)
    see Bulwer-Lytton

M

M.H.D. see Magnetohyrodynamics
Ma Chu River 2099b
Maar 505c
Maartens, Maarten 1462a
Maas, Nicolaas *tab* 107
Mass River see Meuse River
Mabla Mountains 2313b
Mabuse, Jan (Jan Gossart) *tab* 106
    biography 303a
Mac (in names) see also Mc
Macadam roads 1179c
Macalester College 677
MacAlpin, Kenneth, King of Scots 1019c–1020a
Macao 2129a, 2241c, 2316
Macao, Macao 2316b
Macapagal, Diosdado 2238c
MacArthur, Douglas 303a, 2131a, 2201b
    dismissed from command 1012a
    Korean War 1010c–1012c
    World War II 1028c
Macaulay, Thomas Babington 303a, 1366b, *tab* 1474
    Lays of Ancient Rome 1396c, 1409a
Macbeth, King (Scotland) 303a, 1020a
Macbeth (play, Shakespeare) 1020a, 1409c
    Banquo 1396c
    Duncan 1401c
Maccabees 303b, 1456c
Maccabees, The (frat. organ.) 1744c
Macchia 505c

Macchiavelli see Machiavelli
MacDonald, James Ramsay 304a
    socialism 908a
Macdonald, Sir John Alexander 304a
Macdonald, John A. 2116c, 2117a, 2117b
MacDonnell Ranges 2091b, 2336b
Macdonough, Thomas 2034c
MacDowell, Edward 170a, *tab* 172c
    biography 304a
Macduff (lit. char.) 1409c
Mace (spice) 744b
Macedonia 994a, 2165a, 2165b
    ancient territorial limits 1015a–1015b
Maceo, Antonio 2137b
MacGregor, Robert (Rob Roy) 304a
Mach, Ernst 1619a
Mach number 1918c
Machado, Gerardo 2137c
Machado de Assiz, Joaquim 1393c
Machaut, Guillaume de
    see Guillaume de Machaut
Machen, W. B. *tab* 801
Machiavelli, Niccolò 304b, 1386b, *tab* 1466
Machine tools 1229c, 1265c
Machines 1228–1290
    simple machines 1280c
    calculating 1236a
    evolution of 1228a
    energy 1878a
    industrial control 1260c
    printing 146c
Macintosh, Charles 1276c
MacIver, Loren *tab* 109
Mack, Connie 304b
Mackail, J. W. 1352a
Mackay Mary see Corelli, Marie

Mackenzie, Alexander 304b, 1390a, 2116c
MacKenzie, William Lyon 304b, 2115c
MacKenzie River 2336b–2336c
Mackeral 44b
Mackinac Straits Bridge 1197
MacLeish, Archibald 304c
MacLennan, Hugh 1390c
MacLeod, C. M. 1853c
Macleod, Fiona see Sharp, William
MacLeod, John James Rickard 304c
MacMahon, Marie Edme P. M. de 304c
MacMillan, Donald Baxter 304c
Macmillan, Harold 304c, 2292a
MacMonnies, Frederick 124a, *tab* 125
MacMurrough, Dermot, King (Ireland) 2191a
MacMurray College 664
MacNamara, Robert 304c
MacNeice, F. L. 1371c
MacNeil, Hermon *tab* 125
Macon, Nathaniel *tab* 800
    House of Representatives *tab* 802b
Macon, Georgia 1979c
MacOrlan, Pierre 1382c
Macpherson, James 305a, 1364a, *tab* 1470
    Ossian 1441c
    Fingal 1432b
Macquarie, Lachlan 2029c
Macready, John A. 1156a
Macroanalysis (chem.) 1827a
Macroeconomics 597b, 529a, 534a
Macromolecules 1824c
MacVeagh, Franklin *tab* 796
Mad Anthony see Wayne, Anthony

Madagascar (Malagasy Republic) 2211c–2212b
    agriculture 2212a
    economy 2212a
    flag *il* 2183
    geography 2211c
    government 2212a
    history 2212a–2212b
    independence 2211c
    map *Atlas*-41
    people of 2211c–2212a
    religion 2211c
Madagascar Island 2336c
    bamboo 1650c
    banana species 1651a
    baobab 1651a
    boa 17c
    chameleon 20c
    coffee trees 1659a
    crocodile 24b
    eagle 26b
    frigate bird 34c
    ginger 1669a
    guinea fowl 37b
    ibis 40b
    lemur 42c
    lovebird 44a
    papyrus 1684b
    periwinkle 1686a
    squirrels 59c–60a
    swine 61c
    see also Madagascar (Malagasy Republic)
Madame Bovary (nov.) 1381c, *tab* 1476
Madame Charpentier and Children (paint.) *tab* 112
Madame Récamier (paint.) *tab* 112
Madame How and Lady Why (bk.) 1368a
Madder 1677b
Madder family 1677b
Madiera Archipelago 2336c

Madeira Islands 2241a, 2242a
  canary 19a
Madeira River 2336c
Madeira wine 2241b
Madeleine, Church of the (Paris)
  architecture 77c
Madero, Francisco 305a, 2062c,
  2219b
Madison, Dolley 305b
Madison, James 305a, *tab* 798–799
  administration 2034a–2035b
  administration, events paral-
    lelling *tab* 1062
  Cabinet *tab* 795
  Constitution 809c
  Constitutional Convention 2030b
  Democratic Party 873a
  election and inauguration
    tab 800
  Federalist, The 1348a, 1372c
  Federalist Party 878c
Madison, Wisconsin 1998c, 1999a,
  2011c
Madison River 2018c
Madman of the North *see* Charles
  XII, King (Sweden)
Madonna College 676, 705
Madonna and Child (paint., Lippi)
  tab 154
Madonna and Child (paint., Man-
  tegna) *tab* 109
Madonna and Child (paint. Mat-
  sys) *tab* 110
Madonna di Foligno (paint., Ra-
  phael) *tab* 112
Madonna Enthroned (paint., Cima-
  bue) *tab* 110
Madonna in Glory with Six Saints
  (paint.) *tab* 112
Madonna of the Candelabra (paint.,
  Raphael) *tab* 109
Madonna of the Cut Pear (paint.)
  tab 113
Madonna of the Goldfinch (paint.,
  Dürer) *tab* 109
Madonna of the Goldfinch (paint.,
  Raphael) *tab* 110
Madonna of the Harpies (paint.)
  tab 110
Madonna of the Meadow (paint.)
  tab 113
Madonna of the Rocks
  National Gallery *tab* 111
  Louvre *il* 89, *tab* 112
Madonna of the Two Trees (paint.)
  tab 112
Madonna with Cherries (paint.)
  tab 113
Madonna Mountain 1996c
Madras, India 2178a, 2363a
Madrid, Spain 2263b, 2263c, 2363a
  National Library *tab* 1463
Madrid, Treaty of 2198a
Madrigal 161a, 176a
Madroña 1677b
Madroño 1677b
Madura, India 2363a
Mae Nam Chao Phraya River 2273b
Maecenas, Gaius Cilnius 305b
  Vergil 1356c
Maeterlinck, Maurice *il* 207, 1382b,
  tab 1479
  biography 305b
  Blue Bird 1394b, 1397c
Maffei, Francesco Scipione di
  1387a, *tab* 1469
Maga, Hubert 2141a
Magadha Kingdom 2179b
Magazine Mountain 1976a
Magazines 1167b, 1365b
  careers 388b
  circulation 1167b
  letterpress printing 142a
  photoengraving 148b
Magdalenian Period
  cave paintings 1928b
Magdalena River 2132a–2132b, 2336c
Magellan, Ferdinand 305b, 2001a,
  2004a, 2023b, 2238a, 2295b,
  2313a
Magellanic clouds 1795b
Maggiore, Lake 2336c
Maggots public health 957b
Magi 1627c
Magic primitive religion 1622a
Magic Mountain (bk.) 1346c, 1385b
Magic square 1604c
Magma 455a, 505c
Magmatic differentiation 505c–506a
Magna Charta 863a, 898a, 984b
  assize 854c
  terms of 2285c
Magnesia glassmaking 133a

Magnesium 463b, 1194a, 1214c,
  1808b, 1834
  atomic weight *tab* 1805
  chemical bonding 1809c
  electrovalence 1809a
  electrons 1807a
  limestone 1214a
  in plants 1646b
  soil 751c
Magnesium oxide chemical bonding 1809c
Magnet *see* Magnets
Magnetic circuits 1886b
Magnetic compass 1163b
Magnetic declination 506a
Magnetic fields 1883c
  fusion reactions 1829a
  lines of force 1884a
Magnetic moment 1915b
Magnetic pole 506a
Magnetic storm 506a
Magnetic tape recorder 1181a
Magnetism 1870a, 1881–1890
  ferromagnetism 1884b
  history of 1769b
  magnetic fields 1883c
Magnetite 453a, 506a
Magnetohydrodynamics 1130c,
  1141b, 1918c
Magnetometer 460a, 506a, 1217c
Magnets 1883c, 1884a
  permanent 1884c
Magnifying glass 1908b
Magnitogorsk, Soviet Union 2363a
Magnitudes (astron.) 1788b
Magnolia 1677b–1677c, 1986c
Magnolia family 1677c
Magnus VI, King (Norway) 2231a
Magog *see* Gog and Magog
Magoudi (mus.) 155b
Magpie 44b–44c
Magsaysay, Ramón 2238c
Magyars 2173c, 2174b
  invasion of Germany 983c
Mahabharata (epic) 1344a, 1410a
Mahan, Alfred Thayer 305b, 965b
Mahayana Buddhism 1627b
Mahé Island 2322b
Mahendra, King (Nepal) 2224b
Mahjoub, Muhammad Ahmad 2266c
Mahler Gustav 167c, *tab* 172a
  biography 305b
Mahogany 1677c
  furniture 1097b
Mahogany family 1677c
Mahomet *see* Mohammed, Mu-
  hammad
Mahrattas (people) 980c
Maia 1438c
Maid Marian 1438c
Maid of Orleans *see* Joan of Arc
Maidenhair tree *see* Ginkgo
Maids of Honor (paint.) *tab* 111
Maiduguri, Nigeria 2363a
Maillol, Aristide 123b, *tab* 125
  biography 305b
Mail-order houses 597b
Maiman, T. H. 1910c
Maimonides 305b
Main River 2157b, 2336c
Main Street (nov.) 1375c, 1410a
Maine, Sir Henry 813c
Maine 1984
  admission to U.S. 2035b
  agriculture 1984b
  capital punishment 860a
  census (1960) 1971
  climate 1984b
  cod 22b
  colleges 671–672
  commercial law *tab* 826
  congressional apportionment
    tab 853
  council 871a
  economy 1984b
  flag *il* 2010
  gentian 1668b
  geography 1984a–1984b
  government 793b, 1984b
  governor 881b
  holidays 841–842
  initiative and referendum 884c
  Missouri Compromise 2035c
  oyster 49b–49c
  people of 1984b
  public school enrollments
    tab 646
  public school expenditures
    tab 644
  puffin 53b
  student enrollment *tab* 645
  sunfish 61a
  Webster-Ashburton Treaty
    2039a

Maine (ship) 2060a, 2238b
Maine, University of 672
Maine Coast (paint., Homer)
  tab 112
Mainitchi Tokyo *tab* 1170c
Maintenon, Françoise d'Aubigné
  305b
Mainz, Germany
  Cathedral 76b
  printing 143a
Maize *see* Corn
Maitland, Frederick W. 815a
Maitland, Lester J. 1156a
Maitland, Thomas *see* Buchanan,
  Robert W.
Maître Pierre Patelin (play)
  see Avocat Pierre Patelin, L'
Maiano, Benedetto da 121c, *tab* 125
Majapahit Kingdom 2187c, 2213c
Majolica pottery 126c
Major (mus.) 176a
  scale 176a
Majoram 1678c
Majorca ceramics 126c
Makabulas, Francisco 2238b
Makalu Mountain 2337a
Makamat (prose) 1465
Makarikari Basin 2337a
Makarios, Archbishop 2138b
Makasar, Indonesia 2363a
Makers of Canada (bk.) 1390b
Make-up (print.) 147c, 153a
Malabar Coast 2337a
Malacca, Malaysia 2363a
Malachi 1457a
Malagasy Republic *see* Madagascar
Malamud, Bernard 305c, 1375c
Malaprop, Mrs. 1410a
Malären, Lake 2268b
Malaria *tab* 947, 957b, 1848c
  genes 1858b
  Liberia 2209b
  Mauritius 2216c
Malawi 2212b–2213a
  agriculture 2212b–2212c
  climate 2212b
  Commonwealth status 1000c
  economy 2212b–2212c
  flag *il* 2183
  geography 2212b
  government 2212c
  history 2212c–2213a
  independence 2213a
  map 2212, *Atlas*-39
  nationalism 2213a
  people of 2212b
  religion 2212b, 2212c
Malawi, Lake 2212b, 2212c
Malawi Congress Party 2213a
Malay Archipelago 2337a
Malay culture region 770c
Malay Peninsula *see* Malaysia
Malaya 2188b
  badger 15a
  bamboo 1650c
  cassava 1656c
  crocodile 24b
  cuckoo 25a
  dog 25c
  eagle 26b
  elephant 33a
  flying lemur 34b
  guava 1670c
  hare 38a
  kapok 1674b
  marten 45a
  nuthatch 48a
  oranges 1682c–1683a
  pit-viper 51c–52a
  rubber trees 1690c
  sandalwood 1691c
  tapir mammals 62b
  taro 1696a
  teak 1696b
  trogons 64a–64b
  World War II 1028c
  see also Malaysia
Malaya, Federation of 2214a
  history 981c
  see also Malaysia
Malayan War *tab* 1077
Malayo-Polynesian languages
  see Austronesian languages
Malaysia 2188b, 2213–2214
  agriculture 2213b
  climate 2213b
  Commonwealth status 1000c
  cooking 1933a
  economy 2213b–2213c
  flag *il* 2183
  geography 2213a–2213b
  government 2213c
  history 2213c–2214b
  independence 2214a–2214b
  Indians in 2213b
  map 2213, *Atlas*-30

Maine (ship) — people of 2213b
  religion 2213a, 2213c
  rubber production 1221b
  World War II 2214a
Malbone, Edward *tab* 108
Malcolm II, King (Scotland) 1019c
Malcolm III, King (Scotland) 1020a
Maldarelli, Oronzio *tab* 125
Maldive Islands 2214
  economy 2214b
  flag *il* 2183
  geography 2214b
  government 2214b
  history 2214b–2214c
  map *Atlas*-28
  people of 2214b
  religion 2214b
  World War II 2214c
Male, Maldive Islands 2214b, 2363c
Malebranche *tab* 1468
Malenkov, Georgi 305c
Males
  genetics 1852b
  life expectancy (U.S.) 954a
  chromosome 1852c
Malevich, Kazimir 305c
Malgaran rugs 1110c
Malherbe, François de 1378c,
  tab 1467
Mali 2170b, 2214–2215, 2215a
  agriculture 2215a
  economy 2215a
  flag *il* 2183
  geography 2214c
  government 2215a
  history 2215a–2215b
  map 2215, *Atlas*-36–37
  people of 2214c–2215a
  religion 2214c, 2215b
Mali Federation 2248b
Malignant tumors 945c
Malipiero, Gian Francesco 168a,
  tab 172a
Malla dynasty 2224a
Mallard 44c
Mallarmé, Stéphane 305c, 1382a,
  tab 1478
Malleable minerals 453a
Mallee 506a
Malleus *see* Hammer (anat.)
Malloney, Joseph F. presidential
  candidate *tab* 801
Mallow 1677c
Mallow family 1677c
Malmesbury, William of *see* Wil-
  liam of Malmesbury
Malnutrition 955c
Malocclusion 920b
Malone College 691
Malory, Sir Thomas 305c, 1395c,
  1425b, *tab* 1466, 1411a, 1360b
Malpighi, Marcello 305c
Malraux, André 305c, *tab* 1480
Malt 724c
Malta 2215–2216
  agriculture 2215c
  climate 2215b
  Commonwealth status 1000c
  economy 2215c
  emigration 2215b
  flag *il* 2183
  geography 2215b
  government 2215c
  history 2215c–2216a,
  independence 2216a
  map *Atlas*-13
  people of 2215b
  religion 2215b, 2216a
  World War II 1028b, 2216a
Malthus, Thomas Robert 305c
Malvern, England
  pottery *tab* 130
Malvern Hill, Battle of 2048b
Mamallapuram, India 2180a
Mamelukes control of Egypt 1005a
Mammals diet 1825b
Mammon 1438c
Mammoth *see* Elephant
Man 766c
Man (anthropology) 1923a
  earliest ancestors 1923c
Man (biology) 1862a
  classification 1923c
Man (philosophy) 1612a
Man of Destiny *see* Napoleon I
Man, Isle of 2282a, 2283c, 2316
  domestic cat 19c
  Home Office 882a
  language 1336a
Man and Nature (bk., Perkins)
  775b
Man of Property (nov.) 1404a

Man and Superman (play) 1370a, 1410a
Man with Red Turban (paint.) *tab* 111
Man with the Glove (paint.) *tab* 112
Man with the Hoe (poem) 1376a
Man with the Pink (paint.) *tab* 109
Man Without a Country (story) 1410a, *tab* 1476
Managed currency *see* Compensated dollar
Management science 547a
Managerial economics 597b
Managerial Revolution, The (bk.) 1348c
Managua, Lake 2227b, 2227c, 2337a
Managua, Nicaragua 2227b, 2227c, 2228a
Manama, Bahrain 2363b
Manannan 1438c
Manas River 2099b
Manassas, Battle of *see* Bull Run, First Battle of
Manasseh 1457a
Manatee *see* Sea cow
Manchester, England 2363b
Manchester, New Hampshire 1989a
  schools 625c
Manchester College 666
Manchu (Ch'ing) Dynasty 978b, 1021c, 2221a
  overthrown 1022a
Manchukuo 2130c
  see also Manchuria
Manchuria 1015a, 2123c, 2127c, 2201a, 2201b
  beans 1651c
  civilization 980a
  climate 2124b
  ginseng 1669b
  Japanese invasion (1931) 1012c–1013a, 1013c, 2130b–2130c
  Japanese invasion (1936) 1028a
  treaty with Soviet Union (1945) 1015b
Manchurian Plain 2124a
Manchus (people) 980a, 2128a, 2221a
Mandalay, Burma 2106c, 2363b
Mandamus (law) 891a
Mandate 891a
Mandeville, Sir John *tab* 1466
Mandingo tribe 2209
Mandolin 155b, 176a
Mandolin Player (paint., Ter Borch) *tab* 109
Mandrake 1677c–1678a
Mandrill *see* Baboon
Manes (myth) 1438c
Manet, Edouard 86b, *tab* 108
  biography 306a
  impressionism 1406c
  Olympia tab 112
  Woman With A Parrot tab 112
Manetho 1003a
Mangalore, India 2363b
Manganese 1834
  alloys 1193a
  Angola 2306b
  atomic weight *tab* 1805
  Brazil 2103a
  Cuba 2136c
  French Guiana 2312c
  Gabon 2155c
  Ghana 2164a, 2170c
  glassmaking 133c
  Ivory Coast 2197a
  Laos 2206b
  Montana 1988a
  Morocco 2221c
  New Caledonia 2318b
  Nicaragua 2227c
  Panama 2234a
  Romania 2244a
  South West Africa 2322c
  Soviet Union 2256b
  Sweden 2268a
  Thailand 2273c
  Upper Volta 2294c
Manganese bronze 1196a
Mangel-wurzel *see* Beet
Mangla Dam 2232c
Mango 1678a
Mangoky River 2211c
Mangrove 1678a
  tannin 1209c
Mangrove swamp 506b
Mangum, W. P. presidential candidate *tab* 800
Manhattan purchase 2024b
Manhattan College 685
Manhattanville College 685
Mania River 2211c
Manic-depressive psychosis 1953c

Manioc *see* Cassava
Manfred (poem) 1365a
Manila, Phillipines 2237c, 2238b, 2363b
Manila Bay 2237c, 2238b, 2337a
Manila Bay, Battle of 2060a
Manila hemp *see* Abacá
Manitoba
  tanager birds 62a
Manitou (Manito) 1439a
Mankato State College 677
Manley, Norman 2198b
Manly, Charles 1155c
Mann, Horace 306a, 615b, 622c
Mann, Thomas 306a, 1385b, *tab* 1480
  Magic Mountain 1346c
Mann-Elkins Act 2062c
Manner, Gulf of 2337a
Mannes, Leopold D. 1173a
Manning, Daniel *tab* 796
Man-of-war *see* Portuguese man-of-war
Manon Lescaut (nov.) 1380b, *tab* 1469
Manono Island 2301b
Manpower Commission 840b
Manpower Development and Training Act 609c
Mansart, François 306a
Mansfield, Katherine 306a, 1371c, 1462c, *tab* 1480
Mansfield, William 2248c
Mansfield, Mt. 1996c
Mansfield Park (nov.) 1366a
Mansfield State College 696
Manship, Paul *tab* 125
  Dancer and Gazelles 124a
Manslaughter 891b
Mansoa River 2320a
Manta *see* Ray
Mantanzima, Kaizer 2253b
Mantegna, Andrea *tab* 106, 139c
  biography 306b
  Madonna and Child tab 109
Mantissa 1596a, 1604c
Mantle 506b
Mantuan Swan *see* Vergil
Manu 1439a
Manual (mus.) 176a
Manuel I, King (Portugal) 2242a
Manuel II, King (Portugal) 2242a
  abdication 849a
Manuel, Juan 1391a
Manufacturing 555–559
  Alabama 1974b
  Alaska 1975a
  American Samoa 2000a
  Arizona 1975c
  Australia 2092a
  Belgium 2098b
  Bolivia 2100b
  Brazil 2102b
  California 1977a
  Canada 2112b
  Ceylon 2119c
  Colombia 2132c
  Colorado 1977b
  Connecticut 1978a
  Costa Rica 2135c
  Cuba 2137a
  Delaware 1978b
  Denmark 2142b–2141c
  division of labor 1935c
  Finland 2147a
  Florida 1979b
  France 2149a–2149b
  Georgia 1979c
  Great Britain 2282c
  Guam 2001a
  Hawaii 1980b
  Hong Kong 2315b
  Idaho 1980c
  Illinois 1981b
  India 2178c
  Indiana 1981c
  Indonesia 2187a
  Iowa 1982b
  Israel 2192b
  Italy 2194c
  Japan 2199c
  Kansas 1982c
  Kentucky 1983b
  Korea, North 2203c
  Louisiana 1984a
  Maine 1984b
  Maryland 1985a
  Massachusetts 1985b
  Michigan 1986a
  Minnesota 1986b
  Mississippi 1987a
  Missouri 1987b
  Mozambique 2317b
  Nebraska 1988b
  Nevada 1989a
  New Hampshire 1989b

New Jersey 1989c
New Mexico 1990a
New York 1990c
New Zealand 2226b
North Carolina 1991a
North Dakota 1991c
Norway 2230b
Ohio 1992a
Oklahoma 1992b
Pakistan 2232c
Pennsylvania 1993b
Portugal 2241b
Puerto Rico 2002c
Rhode Island 1994a
South Africa 2252b–2252c
South Carolina 1994b
South Dakota 1994c
South Yemen 2253c
Soviet Union 2257b–2257c
Sweden 2268a
Swizerland 2269c
Syria 2271a
Tennessee 1995a–1995b
Texas 1995c
U.A.R. 2280c
U.S. 1969a–1969b, 2294a
Uruguay 2295b
Utah 1996b
Venezuela 2297b
Vermont 1997a
Virginia 1997c
Washington 1998a
West Virginia 1998c
Wisconsin 1999a
Wyoming 1999c
Manure 749b, 752c
  analysis *tab* 752c
Manuscript writing (handwriting) 1302a
Manuscripts 142a
Manutius, Aldus (Aldo Manuzio) 144a, 1311c
  biography 306b
Manx
  domestic cat 19c
Manx language 1336a
Manzanita 1678a
Manzini, Swaziland 2267a
Manzoni, Alessandro 306b, 1387b, *tab* 1473
Mao Tse-tung 306b, 2130b, 2130c, 2131a
Maori 2226a, 2226c–2227a
Map *see* Maps
Maple 1678a–1678b
  red 1993
  sugar 1990b, 1996b, 1998b, 1999c
Maple syrup
  New Hampshire 1989b
  Vermont 1997a
Maps *Atlas* 1–63, 779–780
  ancient 779a–779b
  azimuthal projection 780b–780c
  conic projection 780b
  cylindrical projection 780a–780b
  four-color 1600b
  homolographic projection 780c
  interrupted homolosine projection 780c
  latitude 779b
  longitude 779b
  Middle Ages 779b–779c
  modern 779c
  projections 780. *Atlas*-2–3
  Renaissance 779c
  sinusoidal projection 780c
Maquis 506b, 1864a
Mar del Plata, Argentina 2089b
Maracaibo, Lake 771, 2297a, 2337a
Marajo Island 2337a
Marash, Turkey
  archeology 970b
Marat, Jean Paul 306b, 1007b, 1008c
Marathas, the 2180c
Marathas Kingdom 2180c
Marathi language 1334a
Marathon, Battle of 1002c, 1015b–1015c
  casualties 1015c
  results of 1015b–1015c
Marathons 1737b
Marble 451a, 506b, 1215b
  Italy 2194b
Marble Faun, The (nov.) 1410a
  faun 1432a
  Donatello 1401b
Marblehead ware *tab* 132
Marc, Franz *tab* 108
Marcato (mus.) 176a
Marceau, Marcel 306c
Marcello, Benedetto *tab* 171c
Marcellus, Pope Palestrina 160a
March (mus.) 176a
March King *see* Sousa, John Philip
Marchioness forms of address *tab* 1120
Marcks, Gerhard *tab* 125

Marco Polo *see* Polo, Marco
Marconi, Guglielmo 306c, 1151c
Marcos, Ferdinand 2238c
Marcus Aurelius 306c, 976b, 1354a, *tab* 1464, 1615b
  statue of 118c
Marcus Aurelius Antoninus Bassinus, Emperor (Rome), *see* Caracalla
Marcus, Siegfried 1169b
Marcy, William Learned 307a, *tab* 795, *tab* 796
Marcy, Mt. 1990b
Mardi Gras 2012b
  Haiti *il* 2172
Marduk 1623a
Marées, Hans von *tab* 108
Margai, Albert 2249b
Margai, Milton 2249a
Margaret, Queen (Denmark, Norway, Sweden) 307a, 2231a, 2268b
Margaret of Anjou 307a
Margaret of Navarre 307a, *tab* 1466
Margaret of Orleans *see* Margaret of Navarre
Margaret of Valois (1492–1549) 2151b, *see also* Margaret of Navarre
Margaret of Valois (Margaret of France) (1553–1615) 1378c
Marggraf, Andreas 744c
Margin (fin.) 597b
Marginal productivity theory of wages 597c
Marginal utility 597c
Margins (print.) 153a
Margraves 875c
Marguerite *see* Daisy
Maria (name) *see also* Marie; Mary
Maria (tale) 1393b
Maria Theresa, Empress (Austria-Hungary) 307a, 1021b, 2095
  pragmatic sanction 1019a
Marian College 666
Marian College of Fond du Lac 708
Marianas Archipelago 2001a
Marianas Islands 2203c
  government 794b
Marianas trench 462b
Marias Islands 2337a
Marie (name) *see also* Maria; Mary
Marie, Queen (Romania) 307a
Marie Antoinette, Queen (France) 307a, 1007c, 2152c
  Gluck, C. 163c
  guillotined 1008a
Marie de France (poetess) 1377c, *tab* 1465
Marie de Médicis 307a
  Rubens portrait *tab* 111
Marie Louise, Empress (France) 307b
Marie Louise of Parma (paint.) *tab* 111
Marietta College 691
Marigold 1678b
Marimbas 179c
Marin, John *tab* 108
Marin, John Cheri 307b
Marine 506b
Marine biology 461a, 465a
  chemical nutrients 1866a
Marine climate 506b
Marine Corps (U.S.) Navy 893c
Marine ecology 467b, 1865c
Marine engineering 1167c
Marine geology *see* Geological oceanography
Marine Hospital Service 960c
Marine insurance 595a
Marine signaling 1168a
Marine technology 461a, 467c
Mariner (spacecraft) 1889b
  Venus 1782c
Mariner II (spacecraft) *tab* 1772
Mariner's magnetic compass 1163c
Marini, Giambattista 1387a
Marini, Marino *tab* 125
Marinid dynasty 2222a
Marinus 2246b
Marion, Francis 307b
Mariposa lily 1678c
Maris, Jacob *tab* 108
Maritain, Jacques 307b, *tab* 1481
Maritime 506b
Maritime climate 506b
Maritsa River 2105a, 2337a–2337b
Marius, Gaius 307b

Marivaux, Pierre 1380b
Marjorie Daw (story) 1410b
Mark (Arthurian leg.) 1439a
Mark, Saint 1457a
Mark Antony 196b, 994a, 1005a
  dictator 873c
Market 597c–598a
Market economy 528c, 598a
Market Gardner see Blackmore,
  Richard D.
Marketing 560–564, 598b
Marketing research (market an-
  alysis) 598a
  careers 377c
Markham, Edwin il 207, 1376a, tab
  1478
  biography 307b
Marl 506b, 749b, 753a
Marlborough, 1st Duke of (John
  Churchill) 223c
Marlborough, Duke of at Blenheim
  998c–999a
Marlin 44c, il 1717
Marlowe, Christopher 307c, 1360c,
  tab 1466
  blank verse 1397c
  Doctor Faustus 1403c
  metre 1345b
Marmalade-plum 1691c
Marmara, Sea of 2337b
Marmion (poem) 1006b, 1410b,
  1365a
  Lochinvar 1409b
Marmoset 44c–45a
Marmot 45a
Marne, Battle of the 1003a, 1015c,
  1025b, 2066b
Marne River 2337b
  World War I 1015c
Maro, Publius Vergilius see Vergil
Maronites 2207c
Marot, Clément 1378b, tab 1466
Marquand, John Phillips 307c, tab
  1480
Marquee (tent) 1710a
Marquesa de Pontejos (paint.)
  tab 113
Marquesas Islands 2312c–2313a
Marquetry 1096a
Marquette, Jacques 307c, 2114b
Marquette University 708
Marquina, Eduardo 1392c
Marquis forms of address tab
  1120
Marra Mountains 2265c, 2337b
Marrakech, Morocco 2216b, 2221c,
  2222a, 2363b–2363c
Marriage 1936b, 1941b
  bigamy 856c
  citizenship 864a
  legal phases 818a, 819b
Marriage a la Mode (play) 1362b
Marriage at Cana (paint.) tab 112
Marrillac College 679
Marryat, Frederick 307c, tab 1473
Mars (planet) 757a, 1781a, tab
  1782, 1783a
  albedo 1793b
  atmosphere 1840a
  Bode's law tab 1781
  life 1783a, 1841a
  photographs 1152b
Mars (myth) 1439a, 1424c, 1628b
Mars I (spacecraft) tab 1772
Marschall Vorwarts see Blücher,
  Gebhart Lebrecht von
Marschner, Heinrich tab 172a
Marseille, France 2148b, 2149b,
  2363c
  Children's Crusade 1002b
Marseillaise, La (song) 1380c,
  tab 1471
Marseillaise (statue) 122c
Marsh 506b
  salt 513b
  tidal 518a
Marsh, George Perkins 775b
Marsh, Reginald tab 109
  biography 307c
Marsh gas 506b
Marsh havester 720b
Marsh marigold 1678c
Marshall, George C. 307c, tab 796,
  2077b, 2130c
Marshall, James tab 796
Marshall, John 307c, tab 795, 1014c,
  tab 1471, 2032b
  appointments 852b
  Burr, Aaron 2033c
  Supreme Court 792b, tab 802a,
  2032c
  vice-presidential candidate
  tab 800

Marshall, Thomas Riley Vice-presi-
  dency tab 801
Marshall Islands 2003c
  government 794b
Marshall Plan 867b, 998b, 2140b,
  2142b, 2155a, 2262c, 2279a
  enacted 1015c–1016a
  expenditures 1016a
  purpose of 1015c–1016a
Marshall University 707
Marshmallow 1678c
Marsigli, Luigi F. 461c
Marsin, Marshal 998c
Marsuppini, Carlo 121c
Marsyas (myth) 157a
Marsyas (sculpt.) 116b
Martel, Charles see Charles Martel
Marten 45a
Martha (Bib.) 1457a
Martha's Vineyard 2016c
  grouse 37b
Marti, José 307c, 1393b
Martial 308a
Martial (Rom. au.) 1357c, 1402b,
  tab 1464
Martial law 891b
Martin, Henri tab 1475
Martin, Homer Dodge tab 108
Martin, Joseph W., Jr. tab 802b
Martin, Josiah 2025b
Martin Chuzzlewit (nov.) 1366c
Martineau, Harriet tab 1474
Martínez, Maximiliano Hernández
  2145b
Martínez Ruiz, José see Ruiz,
  José Martínez
Martínez Sierra, Gregorio 1392c
Martini, Simone tab 106
  Annunciation, The tab 110
Martinique 2316
Martinu, Bohuslav tab 172b
Martucci, Giuseppe 167c, tab 172a
Martyrdom of St. Bartholomew
  (paint.) tab 111
Marvel, Ik see Mitchell, Donald
Marvell, Andrew 308a, tab 1468
Marx, Karl 308a, 987c, 1938a
  class system 1945a
  Das Kapital 1348a, 1385a
  dialectical materialism 1618c
  historical interpretation and
  965b
  socialism 908a
Marxists 2261a–2261b
Mary (name) see also Maria;
  Marie
Mary (Queen of Scots) 308b, 1019,
  2288b
  executed 995c, 1020b
  imprisoned 1020b
Mary (Virgin Mary) 1457a
Mary of Burgundy 2225a
Mary Magdalene 1456c
Mary I, Queen (England) 308a,
  2191b
  Moro painting tab 111
  persecution of Protestants 2288a
  reign of 2288a
Mary II, Queen (England) 308a,
  1020b, 2289c
Mary Baldwin College 705
Mary had a little lamb (nursery
  rhyme) 409a
Mary Hardin-Baylor College 702
Mary Leszczynski 1021b
Mary Manse College 691
Mary Stuart see Mary (Queen of
  Scots)
Mary Tudor see Mary I, Queen
  (England)
Mary Washington College 705
Marycrest College 668
Marygrove College 676
Maryhurst College 694
Maryland 1984–1985
  agriculture 1985a
  black-eyed susans 1653a
  budget system 858b
  capital punishment 860b
  climate 1984c–1985a
  colleges 672–673
  commercial law tab 826
  congressional apportionment
  tab 853
  congressmen at large 855a
  Constitution (U.S.) 809c
  convicts 828c
  economy 1985a
  flag il 2010
  geography 1984c–1985a
  government 1985a
  history, colonial 2024c
  holidays 841–842
  labor legislation 833b

Mason and Dixon boundary
  line 1016a
  people of 1985
  public school enrollments
  tab 646
  public school expenditures
  tab 644
  student enrollment tab 645
  white oak 1984c
  workmen's compensation 835c
Maryland, University of 629c, 672
Maryland Day 841b
Maryland State College (division
  of University of Maryland)
  672
Marymount College 657, 669, 685
Marymount Manhattan College 686
Maryville College 700
Maryville College of the Sacred
  Heart 679
Marywood College 696
Masaccio tab 106
  biography 308b
Masai Steppe 2337b
Masaryk, Thomas G. 308b, 2139c,
  2140a
Mascagni, Pietro 167c, tab 172a,
  1387c
  biography 308b
Mascarene Islands
  boa 17c
  papyrus 1684b
Mascaron, Jules de 1379c
Masefield, John 308b, 1371a, tab 1480
  Poet Laureate 1413b
Masers 1909–1910, 1918c
Maseru, Lesotho 2208a, 2363c
Mashhad, Iran 2363c
Mask (drama) see Masque
Masked Ball, A see Ballo in Mas-
  chera, Un
Masolino da Panicale tab 106
Mason, Charles 2025a
Mason, Daniel Gregory 172c
Mason, John (1586-1635) 2024c
Mason John Young tab 795
Mason, Lowell 169c, 172c
Mason, William 170a, tab 172c
Mason and Dixon's Line 1016a,
  2025a
Masons (frat. organ.) 1744a
  Anti-Masonic Party 851c
  Eastern Star 1743c
Masque (drama) 1410b
  dance 182c
Mass (phys.) 1801a, 1869a, 1873b
  definition 1919a
Mass (rel.) 176a
Mass Action, Law of 1812b
Mass production 1229c
  automobiles 1169c
Mass ratio rockets 1765b
Mass spectograph 1827c
Massachusetts 1985
  agriculture 1985a
  appointment 852b
  budget system 858b
  capital punishment 860b
  census (1960) 1971
  climate 1985b
  colleges 673–675
  commercial law tab 826
  committees 866c
  commonwealth 867c
  congressional apportionment
  tab 853
  Constitution (U.S.) 809c
  divorce 875b
  economy 1985b
  flag il 2010
  geography 1985a–1985b
  government 793a, 1985c
  governor 881b
  history, colonial 2024a
  holidays 841–842
  labor legislation 832b, 833b, 840a
  law 815c
  people 1985b
  public health 960c
  public school enrollments
  tab 646
  public school expenditures
  tab 644
  Shay's Rebellion 1020b
  student enrollment tab 645
Massachusetts, University of (Amherst) 674
Massachusetts, University of (Boston) 674
Massachusetts Ballot 856a
Massachusetts Bay Colony 2024b
  labor legislation 827b
  printing 145a
Massachusetts Institute of Technology (MIT) 674

Massacre of St. Bartholomew's
  Day 2151b
Massamba- Debat, Alphonse 2134b
Massasoit (Ind. chief) 308b
Massenet, Jules 308c, tab 172a
Massif 506b
Massif Central (plateau) 2337b
Massif de la Hotte (mountains)
  2171b
Massif du Nord (mountains) 2171b
Massif de la Salle (mountains)
  2171b
Massillon, Jean 1379c, tab 1469
Massinger, Philip 1361c, tab 1467
Massive, Mt. 2019a
Masson, André tab 109
Masson, Frédéric tab 1478
Mass-wasting 506b
Mastodon see Elephant
Master of Ballantrae, The (stories)
  1368b
Master Humphrey's Clock (periodi-
  cal) 1411c
Master William Blair (paint.)
  tab 112
Masters, Edgar Lee 308c, 1376a,
  tab 1479
  Spoon River Anthology 1417c
Mastersinger see Meistersinger
Masthead (naut.) 153a
Mastigophora 1848a
Matadi, Congo (Kinshasa) 2363c
Mata-Utu, Wallis and Futuna Is-
  lands 2324c
Matchett, Charles H. presidential
  candidate tab 801
Matchlock (firearm) 1254c
Maté see Holly
Materia Medica (book, Bock) 1638a
Material handling 1266b
Mathematical analysis 1507b
Mathematical Principles of Natural
  Philosophy (Newton) 1758b,
  1763c
Mathematics 1501–1608
  advanced 1596–1600
  applied 1601b
  bibliography 1608
  calculus 1594–1595, 1602a
  careers 385a
  data processing systems 1163c
  definition 1604c
  equations 1603b
  geometry 1556–1580
  glossary 1601–1607
  logarithms 1604b
  mechanics 1873c
  modern 1506b
  programming 548c
  pure 1601a
  signs and symbols 1604c, tab
  1605a
  statistics 1506c, 1607b
  topology 1506c
Mathematics, History of 1501a
  Seventeenth Century 1504b
  Eighteenth Century 1505a
  Egypt 1751a
  Islam 1754a
  Mesopotamia 1751a
  Non-Euclidean geometry 1506a
  origins 1501a
  Pythagoras 1613a
Mathematike Syntaxis (Ptolemy)
  779a–779b
Mather, Cotton 308c, 1372b, tab
  1469
Mather, Increase 308c
Matheson, Johann tab 171c
Mathura, India 2363c
Mating system 725b
Matisse, Henri 86c, 103b, tab 108
  biography 308c
Mátra Mountains 2173c
Matrah, Muscat and Oman 2222c
Matrix (print.) 153a
Matsu 2131c
Matsya 1449a
Matsys, Quentin tab 106
  Banker and his Wife tab 112
  biography 308c
  Entombment tab 109
  Madonna and Child tab 110
Matta, Sebastian Antonio tab 109
Matter (phys.) 1869a, 1870–1873
  kinetic molecular theory 1801b
  phase changes 1899b
  plasma 1919b
  properties of 1202b
Matter (print.) 153a
Matterhorn 506b
Matthew (Bib.) 1457a

Matthews, Stanley *tab* 802a
Matthews Ridge, Guyana 2170c
Matthias (Bib.) 1457a
Matthias, King (Hungary) 2174c
Mau Mau 2203a
Mauchly, John W. 1243b
Maud (poem) 1368c
Maugham, (William) **Somerset** 309a, 1371a, *tab* 1480
Maui Island 1980b
Mauna Kea (volcano) 1980a, 2018b
Mauna Loa (volcano) 1980a
Maupassant, **Guy de** 309a, 1381c, *tab* 1478
Maurer, James A. *tab* 801
Mauriac, François 1382c, *tab* 1480
Maurice Prince (Netherlands) 2217a
Mauritania 2216, 2323b
  agriculture 2216a
  climate 2216a
  economy 2216a–2216b
  flag *il* 2183
  geography 2216a
  government 2216b
  history 2216b–2216c
  map 2216, *Atlas*-36
  people of 2216a
  religion 2216a, 2216b
Mauritius 2216–2217
  agriculture 2217a
  climate 2216c
  Commonwealth status 1000c
  economy 2217a
  flag *il* 2183
  geography 2216c
  government 2217a
  history 2217a–2217b
  independence 2217b
  people of 2216c
  religion 2216c
Mauritius Island 2216c
Maurois, André 309a, 1347a, 1382c, 1462c, *tab* 1480
Maury, **Matthew Fontaine** 309a, 461c
Maurya, Chandragupta 2179b–2179c
Maurya empire 2179b–2179c
Mausoleum at Halicarnassus
  sculpture 117a
Mausolus statue of 117a
Mauve, Anton *tab* 108
Mauvoisin Dam 1206c
Maxim, Hiram P. 1169b
Maximian, Emperor (Rome) throne 119a
Maximilian, **Emperor (Mexico)** 309a, 2219b, 2225
Maximilian I, **Emperor (Holy Roman Empire)** 309a
Maximilian III Joseph, Elector (Bavaria) 1021b
Maximus Planudes (monk) 1394a
Maxwell, **James Clerk** 309b, 1761a, 1801b
  color photography 1172c
Maxwell (unit) 1884a
May (month) origin of name 1438c
May beetle *see* June bug
May Day 1439a
Maya (rel.) 1624c
Maya Indians 64b, 2168a, 2168c, 2218b
  calendar system of 758a
  see also Mayan Civilization
Maya Mountains 2308a
Mayagüez 2002b
Mayan civilization 971b, 2021a
  pottery *tab* 130
  sculpture 124b
  see also Maya Indians
Mayapple 1678c
Mayer, Julius Robert 1761a
Mayer ware *tab* 132
Mayflower (bot.) *see* Arbutus
Mayflower (ship) 1018, 2024a
  passenger list 1018c–1019a
Mayflower Compact 2026b
Mayfly 45a–45b
Mayhem 891c
Maynard, Horace *tab* 796
Mayo, Charles Horace 309b
Mayo, Elton 526a
Mayo, **William James** 309b
Mayombé Mountains 2155b
Mayon, Mt. 2237c
Mayor 864c, 891c
  forms of address *tab* 1119
Mayotte Islands 2310c
Mayow, John 1798c
Mayville State College 690
Mazama, Mt. 2017a

Mazarin, Cardinal 2151c
Mazarin, Jules 309b
Mazurka 176b, 182a
Mazatlán, Mexico 2218a
Mazzini, **Giuseppe** 309b, 1387b, 2195c
M'Ba, Leon 2156a
Mbabane, Swaziland 2266c, 2267a, 2363c–2364a
Mc (in names) *see also* Mac
McAdam, John Loudon 303a, 1152c, 1179c
McAdoo, **William Gibbs** 303a, *tab* 796, 2066a, 2070b
McBurney, Charles 303b
McCall's (magazine)
  circulation 1167b
McCarthy, Joseph R. 2078c
McCarthy, Mary 303b
McCarty, M. 1853c
McClellan, George B. 303b
  Civil War 2045b, 2048a
  presidential candidate *tab* 801, 2050b
  nickname 1462b
McClelland, Robert *tab* 797
McCloskey, John 303c
McCone, John A. 862b
McCormack, John *tab* 802b
McCormick, **Cyrus Hall** 303a, 720b, 2037c
McCormick, Vance 2066a
McCrae, John 1390c
McCrary, George *tab* 796
McCullers, Carson 303c, *tab* 1481
McCulloch, Hugh *tab* 796
McDowell, Franklin D. *tab* 1481
McDowell, Irvin 2045b, 2048a
McElroy, Neil H. *tab* 797, 1769b
McFee, Henry *tab* 109
McGranery, James P. *tab* 796
McGrath, J. Howard *tab* 796
McGraw, John 304a
McGuffey, William Holmes 304b
McGuire, Matthew *tab* 801
McHenry, James *tab* 795, 809c
McKay, Douglas *tab* 797
McKay Method (shoes) 1280a
McKean, Thomas
  Continental Congress *tab* 802b
  Declaration of Independence *tab* 803
McKee, P. G. 1303a
McKenna, Joseph *tab* 796
  Supreme Court *tab* 802a
McKim, Charles Follen 304b
McKim, Mead and White 78c
McKinley, John Supreme Court *tab* 802a
McKinley, **William** 304b, *tab* 798–799, 2238b
  administration 2059b–2061a
  assassination 2060c
  Cabinet *tab* 796–797
  election and inauguration *tab* 801
  events paralleling administration *tab* 1067
McKinley, Mount 1974c, 2019a, 2019b, 2293a
McKinley Tariff Act 2057b
McLane, Louis *tab* 795
McLean, John
  Supreme Court *tab* 802a
McMurry College 702
McNamara, Robert *tab* 797
McNary, Charles *tab* 801
McNeese State College 671
M'Connachie 1462c
McPherson College 669
McReynolds, James C. *tab* 796
  Supreme Court *tab* 802a
McVeagh, Wayne *tab* 796
Mead, Margaret 309b
Mead, Lake 1221a, 1975b
Meade, **George Gordon** 309b, 2048c, 2050a
Meadow 506b
Meadowlark 1999b
  Western 1982b, 1987c, 1988a, 1991b, 1992c
Meakin ware 128a, *tab* 132
Mean (math.) 1604c
Mean sea level 506c
Mean sun 1795b
Meander 506b
Meander River *see* Menderes River
Meany, (William) **George** 309b, 838c

Measles immunization 1849c

Measure (mus.) 176b
Measures *tab* 1500
  Biblical *tab* 1460–1461
  electricity 1882c
  mechanics 1873a
  telemetry 1183b
Meat sheep 742c
Meat Inspection Act 956b
Meat packing 735b
  industry beginnings 524a
  by products 735c
Mecca, Saudi Arabia 982a, 2247a, 2364a
  Mohammed 1634a
Mechanic (career) 385c
Mechanical engineering 1215b
  careers 379c, 380c
  marine engineering 1167c
Mechanical weathering 447b, 506c
Mechanics (phys.) 1869c, 1870a, 1873–1880
  friction 1876c
  vectors 1873c
Mecklenburg Declaration of Independence 2025b
  anniversary 842a
Medaille College 686
Medea 1439a
  Jason 1424a
Medellín, Colombia 2364a
Medes 969c, 1016a, 1457a
Media (ancient) 1016a
  kings *tab* 1078
  see also Medes
Median (math.) 1605a
Mediant (mus.) 176b
Mediation 891c
Medicare 2082b
Medici, Caterina de' *see* Catherine de Médicis
Medici, **Giuliano de'**
  Michelangelo 122a
Medici, **Ippolito de'**
  Titian portrait *tab* 110
Medici, **Lorenzo de'** (Lorenzo the Magnificent) 309c, *tab* 1466
  Michelangelo 122a
  patronage 1386b
Medici, Maria de' *see* Marie de Médicis
Medici family 2195b
Medici Palace 77b
Medicine 960a
  ancient Greece 1753a
  Babylonia 972c
  careers 382c
  cryogenic fluids 1903a
  diseases 940–945
  genetics 1850–1858
  immunization 1849b
  neurology 1952b
  physiology 917–945
  psychiatry 1952a
  Seventeenth Century 1759a
  ultrasonics 1897b
Medicine Bow Mountains 2020b
Medicine men 1937b
Médicis, Catherine de
  see Catherine de Médicis
Médicis, Marie de
  see Marie de Médicis
Medieval Period *see* Middle Ages
Medina, Vicente 1392b
Medina Sidonia, Duke of 995c–996a
Medina, Saudi Arabia 2364a
Medina as-Shaab, South Yemen 2253a
Meditations (poems) 1380c
Meditations (Marcus Aurelius) 976b
Mediterranean climate 506c
Mediterranean forests 1864a
Mediterranean Sea 2337b
  biblical name 1454b
  cod 22b
  coral 23b
  cuttlefish 25a
  hake 37c
  hamster 38a
  lobster 43c
  loon 43c
  marten 45a
  octopus 48b
Mediumship 1952a
Medjerda River 2277a
Medlar 1679a
Medley 176b
Medtner, Nikolaus 169b
Medulla, adrenal *see* Adrenal medulla
Medulla oblongata 938a
Medusa 45b
Medusa (myth) 1439a
  Perseus 1424a

Meer, Jan van der
  see Vermeer, Jan
Meerut, India 2364a
Meganthropus 1924a
Megawatt 1920b
Mehemet Ali (Mohammed Ali) 309c, 1005a
Méhul, Etienne 166c, *tab* 171c
Meighen, Arthur 2118a
Meiji Restoration 2200c–2201a
Meilhac, Henri 1381c, *tab* 1477
Mein Kampf (bk., Hitler) 1348c
Meiosis 1851c, 1853b
Meissen, Heinrich von *tab* 171b
Meissen, Germany
  pottery *tab* 131
Meistergesang 156b, 1383b
Meistersinger 159b, *tab* 171b, *tab* 176b, 1410b
Meistersinger von Nürnberg, Die (opera) 159c, 167a, 1410b
Mekong River 2108b, 2108c, 2206a, 2273a, 2298c, 2299a, 2337b
Melbourne, Australia 2092a, 2093a, 2364a–2364b
Melamine *tab* 1219
Melanchthon, Philipp 1383c, *tab* 1466
Melanesians
  anthropology 1927b
Melanin
  melanoma 942c
Melanoma 942c
Melba, Nellie 309c
Melchers, Gari *tab* 108
Melchior, Lauritz 309c
Melchizedek 1457b
Meleager 1439c
Melilla, Morocco 2364b
Melita 1457b, 2215c
Mell, Max 1385b
Mellon, Andrew William *tab* 796, 2070a
Mellon Plan 2070a
Melo, Francisco Manuel de 1388c
Melodeon 177c
Melodrama 176b, 1410b
Melody 154a, 176b
Melon 1679a
Melos frescoes 83c
Melozzo da Forli *tab* 106
  Sixtus IV tab 112
Melpomene 1439c
Melt 506c
Melting point 1918a
  elements 1830–1838
Meltwater 506c
Melusina 1439c
Melville, Herman 67a, 309c, *tab* 1476
  Moby Dick 1373b
Memel, Soviet Union 2360a
Memling, Hans *tab* 106
  biography 309c
  Christ and Angel Musicians tab 109
  Madonna tab 112
  Seven Joys of the Virgin tab 111
  Virgin and Donor tab 113, *tab* 1857
Memnon 1439b
Memoirs Relating to the State of the Royal Navy (Pepys) 1362c
Memorabilia (Xenophon) 1353b, 1397b
Memorial Day (Decoration Day) 842a
Memory 1949c
Memphis, Tennessee 1995a, 2011c, 2018c
Memphis State University 701
Men Against the Sea (bk.) 1398a
Men of the Old Stone Age (bk.) 1356b
Menaechmus 1504b
Menai, Wales
  bridge 1191a
Menander 309c, 1353a
  Caecilius 1355b
Mencius 310a, 977a, *tab* 1464, 1623b, 2126b
Mencken, Henry Louis 310a
Mendel, **Gregor Johann** 310a, 721a, 1850a
Mendeleev, **Dimitri I.** 310a, 1761b, 1799c, 1808a
Mendelevium 1834
  atomic weight *tab* 1805
Mendelssohn, Erich 81c
Mendelssohn, **Felix** 165c, *tab* 172a
  biography 310a

Menderes River 2337b
Mendes-France, Pierre 310a
Mendoza, Diego Hurtado de *tab* 1466
Mendoza, Iñigo López de 1391b, *tab* 1466
Mendoza, Pedro de 2090a
Menelaus 1439b
    Helen of Troy 1434a
Menelik II 310a
Menes 1003a
Mengs, Anton Raphael *tab* 107
Meng-tse
    see Mencius
Menhaden 45b
Meniere's disease 942a
Meningitis yeast 1847c
Mennin, Peter 170c
Menotti, Gian-Carlo 170b, *tab* 172c
    biography 310a
Mensheviks 858a, 2261a
Menstruation 926a
Mensural notation 160b
Mental deficiency 1952c
Mental health 959b
Mental hygiene 1958b
Mental illness 1952b
    character disorders 1954a
    neuroses 1954a
    psychoses 1953a
Mentelin, Johann 143c
Menteur, Le (drama) 1379a
Mentor (myth) 1439b
Menuhin, Yehudi 310b
Menzel, Adolf *tab* 108
Menzies, Robert Gordon 2094a
Mephistopheles 1403c, 1430b, 1439b
Meray, Charles 1507b
Mercalli intensity scale 506c
Mercantilism 598b, 986c, 2021c
Mercaptans *see* Thioalcohols
Mercator, Gerardus 310b, 780a–780b, 2022c
Mercer University 662
Merchandising 598b
    careers 389b
Merchant of Venice (play) 1410b
    Portia 1413c
    Shylock 1417b
Mercia, Kingdom of 2284v
Mercie, Antonin *tab* 125
Mercier, Honoré 2117a
Mercury (chem.) 1834, 2263c
    atomic weight *tab* 1805
    barometers 468c
    electrovalences 1809a
    Italy 2194b
    Mexico 2218a
    Nicaragua 2227a
    Soviet Union 2256b
    thermometers 469b, 1898b
    Yugoslavia 2303b
Mercury (myth) 1434c, 1439b
Mercury (planet)   757a,   1759c, 1782c, *tab* 1782
    albedo 1793c
    atmosphere 1840a
    Bode's law *tab* 1781
    speed of orbit 1771b
Mercury, Project
    see Project Mercury
Mercury cell 1131c, 1199b
Mercury lamps 1141a
Mercury vapor lamps 1890a
Mercury-Atlas IV 1770a
Mercury-Atlas V 1770a
Mercy College of Detroit 676
Mercyhurst College 696
Meredith, Edwin Thomas *tab* 797
Meredith, George 310b, 1368a, *tab* 1476
    Diana of the Crossways 1401a
    Egoist, The 1402a
    Ordeal of Richard Feverel 1411c
Meredith, Owen
    see Bulwer-Lytton, Edward Robert
Meredith, William *tab* 796
Meredith College 689
Merezhkovski, Dmitri 1390a
Merganser 45b–45c
Mergenthaler, Ottmar 147a
Merger 598b
Meriden, Connecticut 1978a
Meridians time measurement 1797c
Meridian telescopes 1791c
Mérimée, Prosper 310b, 1381b, *tab* 1474
    Carmen 1398c
Merino sheep 742c
Meristem 1643c
Meristematic zone (plant) 1647c
Merlin 1439b

Mermaids 1439c
Meroe, Africa
    Iron Age 1929a
Merope Pleiades 1444c
Merovingians 1061a, 2150a
Merrimac (ship) 2049
Merrimack College 674
Merrimack River 2006c
Merry Monarch
    see Charles II, King (England)
Mersey River 2282a
Mersey Tunnel 1226c
Meryon, Charles 136c
Mesa 506c
Mesa Verde National Park 2020b
Mesabi Range 2018b
Mesdag, Hendrik *tab* 108
Meshed rugs 1110c
Mesilla Valley 2219a
Mesmer, Franz (Friedrich Mesmer) 310b, 1954c
Mesmerism 1954c
Mesolithic Age 1928b
Mesons 1915c, 1919a
Mesophyll (plant) 1645b
Mesopotamia 2179a, 2190a
    archeology 969a
    furniture 1093b
    mathematics 1751a
Mesothermal 506c
Mesozoic Era 458a, 506c
Mesquite 1679a–1679b
Messiaen, Olivier *tab* 172a
Messiah 1457b, 1629b
Messiah, The (oratorio, Handel) 163a
Mestrovič, Ivan 124b, *tab* 125
Messiah College 696
Metabolism 920c
Metallic bonding 1813c
Metallic yarns 1209a
Metalloids 1809b, 1810b
Metallurgy alchemy 1798a
    careers 380a
    prehistoric 1929a
Metals 1189b, 1809a
    agriculture 719b
    alloys 1193b
    anthropology 1929a
    brazing 1235c
    conductance 1882a
    crystal structure 1870c
    eletroplating 1250a
    heat 1789a
    nonferrous 1215c
    semiconductors 1890a
    soldering 1281b
Metal coating 1267a
Metal shaping 1267b
Metamorphic facies 506c
Metamorphic rocks 450c, 449c, 506b
Metaphor 1314c
Metaphysics 1611a
Metasomatism 506c
Metastasio (Pietro Trapassi) 1387a, *tab* 1469
Metastasis 506c
Metate 1933b
Metaurus, Battle of the 1002c, 1016a, 1016b
Metaurus River 1016b
Metaxas, Ioannes 2167a
Metcalf, Victor H. *tab* 796, *tab* 797
Metcalf, Willard *tab* 108
Metempsychosis 1945a
Meteor 507a
Meteoric water 507a
Meteorite 507a, 1784a, 1795b
Meteoroid 1784a
Meteorology 468–478, 507a, 1869c
    careers 390b
Meteors 1784a, 1795b
Meter (meas.) *tab* 1500
Meter (mus.) 176b
Meter (poetry) 1410b
Methane 507a
    boiling point *tab* 1902
    molecule 1818c
Methanol 1193a
Method of components (phys.) 1874b
Methods engineering 1269a
Methuselah 1457c
Methyl alcohol 1823a
Metonymy 1315a
Metre *see* Meter
Metric system *tab* 1500, 1873b
Metric ton *tab* 1500
Metronome 176b
Metternich, Klemens Wenzel von 310c, 1023c, 2059b, 2160c, 2161a

Mettur Dam 1206
Metzner, Franz *tab* 124
Metzu, Gabriel *tab* 107
Meunier, Constantin *tab* 125
M. e. v. 1917c
Meuse River 2098a, 2337c
Mexico 2217–2220
    agouti 13a
    agriculture 2218a
    anteater 14a
    armadillo 14b
    badger 15a
    bear grass 1651c
    bluebird 17b
    boa 17c
    brown thrasher 18a
    bufflehead 18b
    bunting 18b
    calceolaria 1655c
    catbird 20a
    climate 2217c
    creosote-bush 1659c
    cuckoo 25a
    cycad 1660b
    dock weeds 1665a
    dogwoods 1665b
    duck 26a
    eagle 26b
    economy 2218a
    euphorbia 1666c
    flag *il* 2183
    Gadsden Purchase 2042a
    gar 35b
    geography 2217b–2217c
    goldfinch 36b
    government 2218b
    grackle 36c
    guayule 1670c
    hare 38a
    history 2218b–2220a
    independence 2219a
    Indians 2218b–2218c
    industry 2218a
    junco 40b
    kingfisher 41a
    ladybeetle 42a
    licorice 1675c
    lime 1676a
    lizard 43a
    locoweed 1676c
    loon 43c
    lynx 44b
    madroña 1677b
    map 2217, *Atlas*-54–55
    mesquite 1679a–1679b
    natural resources 2218a
    in Nicaragua 2228a
    night-blooming cereus 1681a
    orchid species 1683a
    oriole 48c
    owl 49a–49b
    peccary 50a
    painting *tab* 108
    pelican 50a–50b
    people of 2217c–2218a
    peppertrees 1686a
    phoebe 51a
    pit-viper 51c–52a
    poison hemlock 1687c–1688a
    pottery *tab* 130
    purslane 1689b
    prairie dog 53a
    rabbit 53c
    religion 2217b
    robin 54c
    quail 53c
    sagebrush 1691b
    salamanders 54c–55a
    sandpipers 55b
    sapodilla 1619c
    shrike birds 58a
    smilax 1693a
    soapberry 1693b–1693c
    swallow 61a
    swordtail 62a
    tanager birds 62a
    tapir mammals 62b
    teal ducks 62c
    trade 2218a
    tuberose 1697b
    turkey 64c
    vultures 65a–65b
    war with U.S. 2219a
    whales 66c–67a
    woodpeckers 68a–68b
    wolves 67b
    World War II 2219c
    yellowthroats 68c
    zinnia 1700c
Mexico, University of 2218b–2218c
Mexico City, Mexico 875a, 2217b, 2218a, 2218b, 2218c, 2364b
    Pan American Conference (1901) 1017c
Mexican War (1846–1848) *tab* 1074, 2039b
Mexico, Gulf of
    conch 22c
    loon 43c
    oyster 49b–49c
    shrimp 58a

tortoises 63c–64a
    yellowlegs 68b–68c
Mey, Cornelius 2024b
Meyer, Adolf 1958c
Meyer, Conrad Ferdinand *tab* 1476
Meyer, George von Lengerke tab 796
Meyer, Julius Lothar 1800a
Meyerbeer, Giacomo 166c, *tab* 172a
    biography 310c
Meyers, Jacob 1284c
Meyers Ballot Machine 1284c
Mezzo-soprano 176b
Mhos 1882c
Miami, Florida 1979b, 2011c
Miami, University of 661, 691
Miami River 2011c
Mica 453a, 507a
Micah (prophet) 1457a
Micah Clarke (bk.) 1370a
Mice 46c
Michael (archangel) 1457c
Michael, King (Romania) 849a
Michael the Brave 2244b
Michal (Bib.) 1457c
Michaud, Jean François *tab* 1471
Michel, Claude
    see Clodion
Michel, Georges *tab* 108
Michelangelo 122a, *tab* 125, 964c, 2296
    biography 310c
    Holy Family tab 110
    literature 1386c
    painting 106
Michelet, Jules 965b, 1331a, *tab* 1474
Michelson, Albert Abraham 311a, 1904a
Michigan 1985–1986
    agriculture 1986a
    capital punishment 860a
    census (1960) 1971
    climate 1985c
    colleges 675–677
    commercial law *tab* 826
    congressional apportionment *tab* 853
    economy 1985c–1986a
    flag *il* 2010
    geography 1985c
    government 793a, 1986a
    holidays 841–842
    initiative and referendum 884c
    labor legislation 836c
    people of 1985c
    recall 904b
    public school enrollment *tab* 646
    public school expenditures *tab* 644
    statehood 2030b
    student enrollment *tab* 645
Michigan, Lake 1985c, 2006a, 2017c, 2018a, 2018b–2018c
Michigan, University of 676
Michigan State University 676
Michigan Technological University 676
Michigan Territory 2034b
Mickiewicz, Adam 311a
Micombero, Michel 2108b
Microamperes 1916b
Microanalysis 1827a
Microbiology 1842–1849
    careers 390c
    defined 1638a
Microcysts 1844b
Microeconomics 529a, 537a, 598b
Microelectronics 1249c
Microliths 1928c
Micronesia anthropology 1927b
Microorganisms 1842a
Microscopes 1269
    electron 1889c
Microseism 507a
Microwaves
    communications satellites 1162c
    masers 1918c
    telephone 1184b
Midas 1440a
Middle Ages 982–986, 998b, 1009a
    art 72b
    Christian philosophy 1615c
    devil 1430b
    duchies 875c
    education 613c
    feudalism 983c, 1006a–1006b
    law 815a
    map-making 779b–779c
    mathematics 1503b
    Scholasticism 985a
    weapon makers in 1655c–1656a

—Arts 71b, 72b, 73a
  architecture 76b, 985a
  French literature 1377b
  music 157c, 158
  Spanish literature 1391a
Middle ear 937a
Middle East 980a
Middle English 1359c
Middle Paleolithic Age 1928a
Middle Stone Age *see* Mesolithic
  Age
Middle Tennessee State University
  701
Middlebury College 704
Middleman (bus.) 598b
Middlemarch (bk.) 1368a
Middleton, Arthur *tab* 803
Middletown, Ohio 1992a
Middletown, Henry
  Continental Congress *tab* 802b
Midgard 1440a
Midge 45c
Mid-Hudson Bridge 1197
Midianites 1458a
Midland, Texas 1995c
Midland Lutheran College 681
Midnight sun 507a, 1795b
Midocean ridge 507a
Midsummer Night's Dream (play)
  1410c
  fairies 1432a
  Mendelssohn, Felix 165c
  Nick Bottom 1397c
  Oberon 1441a
  Puck 1445b
Midway, Battle of 1003a, 1016b,
  1028c, 2001c
Midway Island 2001
  government 794b
  World War II 2001c
Midwestern University 702
Mies van der Rohe, Ludwig 81c
  biography 311a
  furniture 1101c
Mieszko, Prince 2240a
Mifflin, Thomas
  Constitution (U.S.) 809c
  Continental Congress *tab* 802b
Migmatite 507a
Mignard, Pierre *tab* 107
Mignonette 1679b
Migrations 1925b
  in cultures 767c
  Europeans to Americans 2021b
Mihai *see* Michael, King
  (Romania)
Mihajlović, Draža 2304c
Mikado (Jap. title) 979a
Mikado, The (operetta) 1369b
Mikhail (Russian form of Michael)
  see Michael
Mikoyan, Anastas I. 311a
Milan (1854–1901) (Serbia)
  abdication 849a
Milan, Italy 2194a, 2194c, 2195b,
  2364b
Milan Cathedral 76c
Mile 507a, *tab* 1500
Milesian School (philos.) 1612b
Miletus (ancient city) 974a
  philosophy 1612b
  science 1751a
Milhaud, Darius 92b, *tab* 172a
  biography 311a
Military forms of address *tab* 1119
  pensions 897b
Military law 891c
Militia 891c
Milk 727c
  breast feeding 959a
  casein 727a
  cheese *tab* 731b
  dairy industry 731b
  goats 738c
  pasteurization 956b, 1844c
Milkweed 1679b
Milkweed family 1679c
Milkwort 1679c
Milky Way 1785b, 1787a
  dimensions 1786a
  radio stars 1796c
Mill, Henry 1187c
Mill, John Stuart 311a, 623b, 1366b,
  tab 1475
  laissez-faire 596a
  woman suffrage 914b
  philosophy 1618b
Mill, The (paint., Ruysdael)
  tab 109
Mill on the Floss (nov.) 1368a,
  1410c
Mill Springs, Battle of 2049
Millais, Sir John Everett *tab* 108

  biography 311b
Millay, Edna St. Vincent 311b,
  1376b, *tab* 1480
  Baudelaire 1381c
Mill-boy of the Slashes
  see Clay, Henry
Miller, Arthur 311b, 1376c
Miller, Edgar *tab* 125
Miller, Henry 311b
Miller, Joaquin (Cincinnatus
  Heine Miller) 1462c, *tab* 1477
Miller, Samuel F.
  Supreme Court *tab* 802a
Miller, Stanley L. 1840c
Miller, William Henry Harrison
  tab 796
Millerand, Alexandre 311b
Millersville 696
Milles, Carl 123b, 124b, *tab* 125
Millet, Jean François (1814–1875)
  86a, *tab* 108
  biography 311b
  Gleaners, The tab 112
Millet 1679c
  Chad 2120c
  Mali 2215a
  Mauritania 2216a
  Niger 2228c
  Pakistan 2232b
  Portuguese Guinea 2320a
  Senegal 2248a
  Sikkim 2249c
  Sudan 2266a
  Togo 2275a
  Upper Volta 2294c
  Zambia 2305b
Milliampere 1916b
Millibar 507a
Milligan College 701
Milligram *tab* 1500, 1873b
Millikan, Robert Andrews 311c
Millikin University 664
Milliliter *tab* 1500
Millimeter *tab* 1500, 1873b
Millinery *see* Hats
Milling machines 1265c
Mills, Clark *tab* 125
  biography 311c
Mills, Ogden L. *tab* 796
Mills Bill 2057b
Mills College 657
Mills College of Education 686
Millsaps College 678
Milne, A. A. 311c
Milo (island) *see* Melos
Milo of Crotona (sculp.) 122c
Miltiades 311c, 1015c
Milton, John *il* 207, 1358a, 1362b,
  tab 1467
  biography 311c
  censorship 861a
—Works *Comus* 1399c
  Il Penseroso 1406c
  L' Allegro 1408c
  Lycidas 1409c
  Paradise Lost 1412a
  Paradise Regained 1412b
Milton, John (Amer. pol.)
  presidential candidate *tab* 800
Milwaukee, Wisconsin 1999a, 2011c-
  2012a
Mimeograph 1164b
Mimir 1440a
Mimnermus of Colophon 1351b
Mimosa 1679c–1680a
Mimung 1449a
Minaean people 995a
Mind 1947a
  see also Psychology
Mindanao (Philippine Islands)
  2237c 2238a
Mineptah, King (Egypt) 1003c
Mineral energy 1129a
Mineral wood 1208b
Mineralogy 447a, 451–454, 507a
Mineraloids 452b
Minerals 447a, 451c, 452a, 460b, 507a
  body requirements 919c
  Bolivia 2100c
  Botswana 2101b
  Brazil 2102c–2103a
  Burma 2107a
  Canada 2112a
  Chile 2121b–2121c
  China 2125b
  cleavage 453a
  color 452c
  crystal structure 452a
  deposits 460a
  Cuba 2136c
  Czechoslovakia 2139a
  Dominican Republic 2142a
  El Salvador 2145a

  Finland 2147a
  France 2148b–2148c
  Gabon 2155c
  Georgia 1979c
  Ghana 2164a
  Greece 2165a
  Haiti 2171c–2172a
  hardness 453a
  Honduras 2173a
  Hungary 2173c, 2174a
  Idaho 1980c
  Identification 452c
  Indiana 1981c
  Israel 2192b
  Jamaica 2197a
  Japan 2199a
  Korea, North 2203c
  Korea, South 2203c
  Liberia 2209a
  Louisiana 1983c
  luster 453a
  Madagascar 2212a
  magnetism 453a
  Mississippi 1987a
  Montana 1988a
  Morocco 2221c
  Mozambique 2317b
  Muscat and Oman 2222c
  Nepal 2223c
  New Caledonia 2318b
  New Mexico 1990a
  Nicaragua 2227c
  Nigeria 2229b
  Peru 2236b
  Philippines 2238a
  Poland 2239a–2239b
  Rhodesia 2243b
  Sierra Leone 2248c
  rock-forming 453b
  specific gravity 453a
  Swaziland 2267a
  tenacity 453a
  Texas 1995c
  U.S. 1966c–1967a, 1967b
  West Virginia 1998c
  Wyoming 1999c
  see also under names of indi-
  vidual minerals
Minerva (myth) 1426a, 1440a
  see also Athena
Ming Dynasty 978b, 1674c, 2127c–
  2128a
Minh-Mang, Emperor (Vietnam)
  2300b–2300c
Miniatures (art) 84c
Minié, Claude Etienne 1255a
Minim (meas.) *tab* 1500
Minimum wage 598c, 833a, 834a,
  835b, 912c
Mining 460a, 1269c, 2089c
  Alaska 1975a
  Angola 2306b
  Australia 2092b, 2093a
  Bolivia 2100a
  Cameroon 2110a
  Canada 2112b
  Chile 2121c
  Colorado 1977b
  Delaware 1978b
  Florida 1979b
  France 2148b
  French Guiana 2312c
  French Polynesia 2313a
  Gilbert and Ellice Islands 2314a
  Greenland 2314b
  Guiena 2170a
  Guyana 2170a, 2170c
  Indonesia 2187a
  Jamaica 2197c–2198a
  Jordan 2201c
  Massachusetts 1985b
  Mexico 2218a
  Minnesota 1986b
  Missouri 1987b
  Mongolia 2220c
  Montana 1988a
  Nauru 2223a, 2223b
  Nebraska 1988b
  Nevada 1988c
  New Caledonia 2318b
  New York 1990c
  New Zealand 2226b
  Nicaragua 2227c
  North Dakota 1991c
  Ohio 1992a
  Oklahoma 1992b
  Oregon 1993a
  Peru 2236b
  Pennsylvania 1993c
  Philippines 2238a
  Puerto Rico 2002c
  Rhodesia 2243a, 2243b
  South Africa 2252b–2252c
  South Carolina 1994b
  South Dakota 1994c
  South West Africa 2322c
  Tennessee 1995b
  U.A.R. 2280c
  Utah 1996b
  Vermont 1997a
  Virginia 1997c

  Washington 1998a
  West Virginia 1998c
Mining engineering careers 380a
Minister (diplomatic) forms of
  address *tab* 1119
Minks fur farming 738a
Minna von Barnhelm (drama) 1384a
Minnelied 159b
Minneapolis, Minnesota 1986b
  2012a, 2018c
Minnesang 1383b
Minnesinger 159b, *tab* 171b, 1410c
Minnesota 1986
  admission to Union 2042c
  agriculture 1986b
  capital punishment 860a
  census (1960) 1971
  climate 1986b
  colleges 677–678
  comercial law *tab* 826
  congressional apportionment
  tab 853
  economy 1986b
  flag *il* 2010
  flour milling 1255c
  gentian 1668b
  geography 1986a–1986b
  government 1986c
  holidays 841–842
  housing 882c
  people of 1986b
  public school enrollments
  tab 646
  public school expenditures
  tab 644
  student enrollment *tab* 645
Minnesota River 2018c
Minnesota, University of 629a, 678
Minnow 45c
Minoan Civilization art 116a
Minor (mus.) 176b
  scale 176b
Minorities 891c–892a
  educational problems 610a
  political rights 892a
Minos (myth) 1440a
Minot, George Richards 311a
Minot State College 690
Minotaur 1440b
Minsk, Soviet Union 2364b
Minstrels Middle Ages 159a
Mint 1680a
Mint family 1680a
Minton, Sherman *tab* 802a
Minton ware 128a, *tab* 132
Minturnae (ancient city) arche-
  ology 970
Minuet 176b, 182a, 183a
Minuit, Peter 312a, 2024b
Minute 507a
Minute Men 2028a
Miocene Epoch *tab* 457, 458, 507b
  anthropology 1923c
Mirabeau, Comte de 312a, 1007b,
  tab 1471
Miracle of St. Ildefonso (paint.) *tab*
  113
Miracle of St. Mark (paint.) *tab* 112
Miracle plays 159a, 1360c, 1410c,
  tab 1466
Mirage 507b
Miranda, Francisco de 2297c
Miriam 1458a
Miró, Gabriel 1392c
Miró, Joan 103b, *tab* 109
  biography 312a
Mirrors 1904b
  lasers 1910c
Misanthrope, Le (play) 1379b
Miscarriages 926c
Misdemeanor 880a, 892a
Mishnah 1629c
Miskolc, Hungary 2174a, 2364b
Misrepresentation (law) 820a
Missa 176b
Misses Beckford, The (paint.)
  tab 112
Missiles 1779a
  guided missiles 1257b
Missionaries
  British Isles 2284a
  to China 2128a, 2128b, 2128c,
  2129a
  in the Congo 2135a
  Fiji Islands 2312b
  Korea 2204b
  in Lebanon 2007a–2208a
  Malawi 2212c
  Malaysi 2213c
  New Zealand 2226c
  in Paraguay 2235c
  Tanzania 2273a
  Tonga 2324b

Uganda 2280a
Vietnam 2300b, 2300c
Western Samoa 2301c
Mississippi 1677b–1677c, 1986–1987
 admission to U.S. 2035b
 agriculture 1987a
 capital punishment 860b
 census (1960) 1971
 climate 1986c
 colleges 678–679
 commercial law *tab* 826
 congressional apportionment
   tab 853
 cotton 730c, 1986, 1987b
 economy 1987a
 flag *il* 2010
 gar 35b
 geography 1986c
 government 1987a
 governor 881b
 holidays 841–842
 kite 41b
 people of 1987a
 physicians 960b
 public school enrollments
   tab 646
 public school expenditures
   tab 644
 schools 627b
 student enrollment *tab* 645
Mississippi, University of 678
Mississippi Alluvial Plain 1976a
Mississippi Bubble scheme 1016b–
  1016c
Mississippi College 678
Mississippi River 759b, 1962a, 1975c,
  1979c, 1981a, 1982a, 1983b, 1983c,
  1986b, 1986c, 1987a, 1987b, 1994c,
  1999a, 2005c, 2011c, 2012a, 2012b,
  2013c, 2016a, 2018c, 2019c, 2020a,
  2018c, 2293a
 discovery 2023b
 length of 2020a
 mussels 47b
 sunfish 61a
 valley 448a
Mississippi River delta 2018c
Mississippi State College for
  Women 678
Mississippian period *tab* 456, 507b
Missouri 1987
 admission to U.S. 2035b
 agriculture 1987b
 bunting 18b
 capital punishment 860b
 census (1960) 1971
 charter 863b
 climate 1987b
 colleges 679–680
 commercial law *tab* 826
 congressional apportionment
   tab 853
 economy 1987b
 flag *il* 2010
 geography 1987a–1987b
 government 1987b
 holidays 841–842
 home rule 882b
 initiative and referendum 884c
 osage-orange 1683b
 people of 1987b
 public school expenditures
   tab 644
 public school enrollments
   tab 646
 student enrollment *tab* 645
Missouri, University of (Columbia)
  679
Missouri, University of (Kansas
  City) 679
Missouri, University of (St. Louis)
  679
Missouri (battleship) 1028c
Missouri Compromise 2035c, 2041c
  Texas 2039f
Missouri Plateau 1991b
Missouri River 1962a, 1982a, 1987b,
  1988a, 1991b, 1994b, 2005c, 2007c,
  2008a, 2008c, 2012c, 2013, 2018c–
  2019a, 2293a
 basin 904c
 length of 2020a
Missouri Valley College 679
Mist 473b, 507b
Mr. Britling Sees It Through (story)
  1370a
Mistletoe 1680a, 1922a
Mistral 507b
Mistral, Gabriela 1393c, *tab* 1480
Mistress Mary (nursery rhyme)
  410a
Mitchell, Donald *tab* 1476
 pseudonym 1462c
Mitchell, James P. *tab* 797
Mitchell, Margaret 312a, *tab* 1481
Mitchell, Silas Weir 1375a
Mitchell, William DeWitt *tab* 796
Mitchell, Mt. 1991a, 2016a, 2019a

Mite 45c–46a
Mitford, Mary 1366a
Mithra (Mithras) 1440b, 1624a
Mithridate (play) 1379a
Mithridates 312a
Mithridatic Wars *tab* 1071
Mithraism 976b
Mitochondria physiology 921c
Mitochondria (plant) 1643c
Mitosis 1851c
Mitra (ancient deity) *see* Mithra
Mitre, Bartolomé 2090b
Mitropoulos, Dimitri 312a
Mitzpah 1458a
M.k.s. system 1873c
Mlanje, Mt. 2212b
Mnemosyne 1440b
Moa River 2248b
Moab 1458a
Moallakat (poems) *tab* 1465
Mobile, Alabama 1974a, 1974b,
  2012a
Mobile River 1974a, 2012a
Mobutu, Joseph 2135b
Moby Dick (nov.) 67a, 1373b
Moçambes Desert 2306a
Moccasin *see* Pit viper
Mocedades del Cid (drama) 1392a
Mock orange 1680a–1680b
Mock title (print.) 150b
Mockingbird 46a, 1975c, 1979a,
  1986c, 1994c, 1995b
Mode (mus.) 176b
 Greek 157b
 Gregorian 158b
Model T Ford 1170a
Modern architecture 78a, *il* 79–80,
  81a
Modern art 72a
 furniture 1101b
 interior decoration 1102b, 1106a
 painting 86c, *il* 90–94, 103c
 sculpture 114b, 123a
Modern Athens (sobriquet)
  see Edinburgh, Scotland
Modern Comedy, The (novels)
  1404a, 1410c
Modern dance 184a
Modernism (lit.) 1393b
Modern Painters (treatise, Ruskin)
  1366b
Modern Man in Search of a Soul
  (bk.) 1348b
Modern Times (movie) 862a
Modern typefaces (moderns) 153a
Modibo, Keita 2215b
Modigliani, Amedeo *tab* 108
 biography 312c
 Jeanne Hebuterne il 93
Modred 1440b
Modulated light recording 1181c
Modulation (mus.) 154b, 176b
Moe, Jörgen *tab* 1475
Moebius, A. F. 1600a
Moffat Tunnel *tab* 1226
Mogadiscio, Somali Republic
  2250c, 2251a, 2364b–2364c
Mohammed 981c, 983, 1632c, 2247a
 biography 312a
 music 155b
Mohammed Ali *see* Mehemet Ali
Mohammedans *see* Islam
Mohawk River 1990b, 2005a, 2016a
Mohawk River Valley 1990b
Mohéli Island 2310c
Mohendyo Daro 969c
Moho 507b
Mohole 507b
Mohs, Friedrich 453a, 1192b
Mohs' scale 453a, 507b, 1192b
Moholy-Nagy, Laszlo 123b, *tab* 125
Moirai 1432a, 1440b
Moissac, France sculpture 119b
Mojave Desert 1976c, 2019a
Mokhtar Ould Daddah 2216c
Mokpo, South Korea 2364c
Molar solution 1815b
Molasses 1282a, 2097a
Molasses Act 2027b
Mold (bio.) 1846
 slime 1640c
Moldavia 2244b, 2244c
Mole (animal) 46a
Mole (unit) 1899a
Molecular biology 722c
Molecular Energy 1897b
Molecules 1803a, 1881b, 1909c
 activation level 1811c
 heat 1897b
 lasers 1960c

Molière *il* 207, 1346b, *tab* 1468
 biography 312b
Molina, Tirso de *see* Tirso de
  Molina
Moline, Illinois 1981b, 1982b
Moll Flanders (nov.) 1363b
Molnár, Ferenc 312c
Molniya 1 (satellite) *tab* 1163
Molniya 2 (satellite) *tab* 1163
Moloch 1440b
Molokai Island 1980a–1980b
Molopo River 2101b
Molotov, Vyacheslav M. 312c
Molotov, Soviet Union 2368a
Moltke, Count Helmuth von 312c
Molto (mus.) 176b
Moluccas Islands 2186c
 nutmeg 1682a
Molybdenum 1834
 alloys 1193a
 atomic weight *tab* 1805
 Colorado 1977b
 French Guiana 2312c
 Greenland 2314b
 U.S. 2293c
Mombasa, Kenya 2202b, 2364c
Momentum 1879b, 1919a
Mommsen, Theodor *tab* 1475
Momus 1440b
Mona Lisa (paint.) *tab* 112
Monaco 2220
 economy 2220a
 flag *il* 2183
 geography 2220a
 government 2220a
 history 2220a–2220b
 map 2220, *Atlas*-23
 people of 2220a
 religion 2220a
Monaco, Monaco 2220a
Monads 1617a
Monadnock 507b
Monarch butterfly *il* 8
Monarchy 784c
Monasteries education 613c
Monastery, The (nov.) 1365c
Monasticism 982c
 Benedictine rule for 998b
 see also names of monasteries
Monaulos (mus.) 157c
Monck, George 312c
Monday's Child (nursery rhyme)
  411a
Mondrian, Piet 103b, *tab* 109, 1853
 biography 312c
Monet, Claude 86b, *tab* 108, 1406c
 biography 312c
Money 529a, 598c
 legal tender 889a
Mongkut, King (Siam) 2274b
Mongol Empire China 978b
Mongolia 2123c, 2127c, 2220–2221
 agriculture 2220c
 ass 14b
 climate 2220b
 communism 2220c
 economy 2220c
 flag *il* 2183
 gazelle 35b
 geography 2220b–2220c
 government 2220c
 history 979c, 2220c–2221b
 horse 39b
 map 2221, *Atlas* 32–33
 people of 2220c
 pheasant 51a
 polecat 52b
 religion 2220b, 2220c, 2221a
 World War II 2221b
Mongolian People's Revolutionary
  Party 2220c
Mongolism (med.) 1953a
Mongoloids 1924b, 1925c
 Capoids 1927a
 migrations 1925b
Mongols 2107b
 houses 1930a
 see also Mongolia
Mongoose 46a–46b
Monitor (ship) 2049
Monk, George *see* Monck, George
Monkey 46b
 anthropology 1923c
Monkshood *see* Aconite
Monmouth, Duke of (James Scott)
  313a, 1019b
 Dryden 1362c
Monmouth, Geoffrey of *see*
  Geoffrey of Monmouth
Monmouth, Battle of 2028c, 2029
Monmouth College 664,682
Monocacy, Battle of 2049
Monocline 451a, 507b

Monocotyledons 1638a–1638b, 1642c–
  1643a
Monocytes 922b
Monody 176b
Monogamy 1941b
Monomotapa empire 2243b
Monongahela River 1968a, 2013a,
  2019c
Mono Lake salt 1866c
Monomer 1219c
Monometallism 585b
Monomials 1535b
 dividing 1535c
 multiplying 1535b
Monopoly 539a, 599a
 Sherman Antitrust Act 2057c
Monopropellant system 1766c
Monopsony 599a
Monorail 1165b
Monosaccharides 1824a, 1825b
Monotheism 1613b, 1622b
 Judaism 1629a
Monotone 176b
Monotype 1174b
Monotype (print.) 147a, 153a
Monroe, James 313a, *tab* 798–799
 administration 2035b–2036b
 administration, events parallel-
   ing *tab* 1062
 Cabinet *tab* 795
 Democratic Party 873a
 election and inauguration *tab*
   800
 veto 912a
Monroe, Louisiana 1983c
Monroe Doctrine 880b, 2022a, 2035c,
  2059a
 international law 886a
 Roosevelt Corollary 2061c
Monrovia, Liberia 2208c–2209b,
  2364c
Monsieur Beaucaire (nov.) 1411a
Monsigny, Pierre Alexandre *tab*
  171c
Monsoon forests 1864b
Monsoons 474a, 507b, 2106c
 Hong Kong 2315a
 Laos 2206a
Montagnes Noires (mountains)
  2171b
Montagnes du Trou d'Eau (moun-
  tains) 2171b
Montagu, Charles (Halifax, 1st
  Earl of) 313a
Montagu, Elizabeth Robinson 313a
Montagu, Lady Mary Wortley 313b
Montagu-Chelmsford Reforms 2185b
Montaigne, Michel E. de 313b, 1347b,
  1378b, *tab* 1466
 essay 1402c
Montale, Eugenio 1388a
Montalvo, García Rodrigues de
  1391b
Montana 1987–1988
 agriculture 1988a
 bittersweet 1652c–1653a
 capital punishment 860b
 census (1960) 1972
 climate 1987c
 colleges 680–681
 commercial law *tab* 826
 congressional apportionment
   tab 853
 economy 1988a
 flag *il* 2010
 geography 1987c
 government 1988a
 holidays 841–842
 initiative and referendum 884c
 labor legislation 836c
 national forests 896a
 people 1987c–1988a
 public school enrollments *tab*
   646
 public school expenditures *tab*
   644
 statehood 2058a
 student enrollment *tab* 645
 swan 61b–61c
 workmen's compensation 835c
Montana, University of 680
Montana College of Mineral
  Science & Technology 680
Montana State University 680
Montane forests 1863c
Montañés, Juan *tab* 125
Mont Blanc Tunnel *tab* 1226, 1226c
Montcalm de Saint-Véran, Marquis
  Louis Joseph de 313b
 Plains of Abraham 2027a, 2114c
Mont Cenis Tunnel 1226
Montclair State College 682
Montdidier, France World War I
  2066b
Monte Carlo, Monaco 2364c

Monte Cassino monastery 998b
Montemayor (Montemór), Jorge de
  1388b, 1391b
Montemezzi, Italo 167c
Montenegro, Julio César Méndez
  2169c
Monterrey, Mexico 2218a
  Mexican War 2040a
Montes, Ismael 2101a
Montesquieu, Baron de 1007a
Montesquieu, Baron de la Brède
  et de (Charles de Secondat)
  313b, 1380b tab 1469
Montessori, Maria 313c
Monteverde (Monteverdi), Claudio
  161c, tab 171b, 1387a, tab 1467
  biography 313c
Montevideo, Uruguay 2295a, 2364c
  Pan American Conference
  (1933) 1017c
Montezuma 313c, 2218c
Montfort, Simon de 313c, 994b,
  2286a
Montgolfier, Jacques 313c
Montgolfier Brothers 1154c
Montgomery, Bernard 1028b
Montgomery, Bernard L. 313c
Montgomery, James tab 1472
Montgomery, Lucy M. 1390c
Montgomery, Richard 2115a
Montgomery, Alabama 1974a,
  1974b, 2012a, 2082b
Months 1795b
Monti, Vincenzo 1387b
Monticelli, Adolphe tab 108
Monticello architecture 78c
Montluc, Blaise de 1378c
Montpelier, Vermont 1996b, 2012a
Montreal, Canada 2020c, 2111b,
  2113c, 2114a, 2115a, 2364c
  American Revolution 2029
  discovery 2023b
  voltage tab 1132b
Mont-Saint-Michel 2152a
Mont-Saint-Michel and Chartres
  (bk.) 1375a
Montserrat 2317
Monumental City see Baltimore,
  Maryland
Monuments see National monu-
  ments
  see also under individual monu-
  ments, such as Washington
  Monument
Mood (gram.) 1306–1307
Moody, William Henry tab 796, tab
  802a
Moody, William Vaughn 314a, tab
  1479
Moon 507c, 1780a
  apogee 1743b
  craters 1784b
  early literature 1763a
  eclipse 1794a
  harvest moon 1794c
  libration 1795a
  lunar probes 1771a, tab 1772
  phases 1796a
Moon and Sixpence, The (nov.)
  1371a
Moonstone, The (nov.) 1411a, 1367c
  tab 1476
Moor (geog.) 507c
Moore, Alfred tab 802a
Moore, Clement C. Night Before
  Christmas 416c
Moore, Douglas tab 172c
Moore, Francis 1169a
Moore, Frank 1372c
Moore, George 314a, 1369c, tab 1478
Moore, Henry 123b, tab 125
  biography 314a
Moore, James 2025c
Moore, Marianne 314a
Moore, Thomas il 208, 1365b,
  tab 1472
  biography 314a
  nicknames 1461a, 1462a
  poetic style 1394c
Moore and Company (Eng.) pot-
  tery tab 80
Moorhead, Minnesota 1991c, 1986b
Moorhead, North Dakota 2007b
Moorhead State College 678
Moorman, Edgar V. tab 801
Moors (people) Spain 2022c
Moose see Deer
Moose, Loyal Order of 1745a
Mopti, Mali 2215a
Moradabad, India 2364c
Moraes Barros, Predente José de
  2104b

Moraine 507c
  glaciers 449b
Morales, Luis de tab 107
Morales, Dr. Ramón Villeda 2173b
Moral Essays (Seneca) 1357c
Morality 812a
Morality plays 1360c, 1411a
  Scandinavian tab 1466
Moran, Edward tab 108
Moran, Thomas 104b, tab 108
Morand, Paul 1382c, tab 1480
Moratín, Leondro Fernández de
  1392b
Morava River 2105a, 2138c, 2303a,
  2337c
Moravia, Alberto 1388b
Moravia 2138c, 2139b–2140a, 2165c
Moravian College 696
Moravian Gate 2239a
Moravians (rel.) pacifism 894c
Moravska Ostrava, Czechoslovakia
  2367a
Morazan, Francisco 2136a
Morbidity statistics 955a
Mordecai 1458a
More, Sir Anthony see Moro, An-
  tonio
More, Hannah 314a, tab 1470
More, Sir Thomas 314a, 1022c, tab
  1466
  Holbein portrait tab 111
  Utopia 1360b, 1420a
Moreau, Gabriel tab 107
Moreau, Gustav tab 108
Morehead State University 670
Morehouse College 662
Morel mushroom il 1661
Morelos, José María 2219a
Moretto, Il tab 107
Morgan, Arthur E. 910b
Morgan, Daniel 2028c
Morgan, John Hunt 314a
Morgan, John Pierpont (1837–1913)
  314b, 524a
Morgan, John Pierpont (1867–1943)
  314b
Morgan, Thomas Hunt 1858c
Morgan, William 851c
Morgan, William de see De Morgan,
  William Frend
Morgan le Fay 1432a, 1440b
Morgan horse 739c
Morgan State College 672
Morgante Maggiore (poem) 1386c
Morgenthau, Henry 314b, tab 796
Morgenthau, Henry, Jr. tab 796
Mörike, Eduard tab 1474
Morínigo, Higinio 2236a
Morisot, Berthe tab 108
Morley, Christopher 314b, tab 1480
Morley, John 314c, tab 1477
Morley, Thomas 161a, tab 171b
Morley-Minto Reforms 2185b
Mormons
  polygamy 2056a
Morning sickness 942c
Morning Star of the Reformation
  see Wycliffe, John
Morning-glory see Bindweed
Morning-glory family 1680b
Morningside College 668
Moro, Antonio tab 107
  Queen Mary tab 111
  Utrecht Canons As Pilgrims
  tab 110
Morocco 995b, 997c, 2161c, 2221–
  2222
  agriculture 2221b
  anthropology 1924c
  cedar trees 1657b
  economy 2221c
  flag il 2183
  geography 2221b–2221c
  government 2221c
  history 2221c–2222b
  independence 2222b
  map 2222, Atlas-34
  nationalism 2222b
  people of 2221c
  religion 2221b, 2222a
  World War II 2222b
Moron 1952c
Moroni, Giambattista tab 107
  The Tailor tab 111
Moroni, Comoro Islands 2310c,
  2364c
Morpheus (myth) 1440c
Morphine 1824c
Morphology defined 1637b
Morrill, Lot tab 796
Morrill Act 888b, 1127a

Morris, Gouverneur (pol.) 314c
  Constitutional Convention
  2030b
  U.S. Constitution 809c
Morris, Lewis tab 803
Morris, Robert 314c
  Declaration of Independence
  tab 803
  U.S. Constitution 809c
Morris, Thomas tab 800
Morris, William 314c, 1105b, 1369a,
  tab 1477
  Arthurian legend 1395c
  printing 145b, 146a
  Sigurd the Volsung and the
  Fall of the Niblungs 1417b
Morris Brown College 662
Morris Harvey College 707
Morrison, Richard James tab 1463c
Morse, Samuel 314c, 2037c, 2039b
  painting tab 108
  telegraph 1151c, 1183a
Morse code 1183a
Mortality statistics 955a
  see also Death rate
Morte d'Arthur (bk., Malory)
  1360b, 1395c, 1411a, 1425b,
  tab 1466
  Holy Grail 1435a
  Lady of the Lake 1437c
Morte d'Arthur (poem, Tennyson)
  1397c
Mortgage 892a
  chattel 836b
Mortising (print.) 153a
Mortlake, England pottery tab 130
Morton, John Declaration of In-
  dependence tab 803
Morton, J. Sterling tab 797
Morton, Levi Parson 314c
  vice-presidency tab 801
Morton, Paul tab 796
Morton, William Thomas Green
  314c
Mosaic 76a
Moscherosch, Johann Michael tab
  1467
Moschus tab 1464
Moscow, Soviet Union 2254b, 2256a,
  2257a–2257b, 2258a–2258c,
  2262b, 2365a
  Lenin State Library tab 1463
Moscow Conference 2076b
Moscow Papyrus 1501a
Moseley, Henry Gwyn-Jeffreys 315a,
  1800a
Moselle River 2157b, 2337c
Moselle (wine) 723c
Moses 1458a
  law 813a
Moses, Anna Mary (Grandma
  Moses) 315a
Moses, Robert 315a
Moses (sculpt., Michelangelo)
  122a
Mosesh (chieftain) 2208b, 2208c
Moshi, Tanzania 2365a
Moshoeshoe II 2208c
Moskva River 2337c
Moslem League 892a
Moslems
  see Islam; Muslims
Mosley, Sir Oswald 315a
Mosques 78a
Mosquito 46b–46c
Mosquito Coast 2337c
Mosquito Indians 2227b–2227c
Mosquitoes public health 957b
Mossadegh, Mohammed 315a, 2189b
Mosses 1641a–1641c
  club 1642a
Mosslike plants 1641a–1641c
Mostaert, Jan tab 106
Mosul, Iraq 2190a, 2365a
Mosul rugs 1110c
Mote 507c
Motet 160c, 176b
Moth 46c
Mother Ann see Lee, Ann
Mother Goose Rhymes 408–412,
  1411a
Motif (motive) (mus.) 158c, 176b
Motion (law) 844b, 845b
Motion (mus.) 176b
Motion (phys.) 1875b
Motion, Laws of 1875c
  first 1804a, 1875c, 1879c
  second 1875c
  third 1876a
Motion pictures 1168a
  camera 1161b
  censors 1168b

cinematography 1161a
projectors 1161b
Motion sickness 942c
Motivation 1949a
  Freud, S. 1957b
Motley, John Lothrop tab 1475
Moto (mus.) 176c
Motorcycles 1170b
Motor end-plate 928a
Motors 1885b
  electric 1141c
Motor Vehicles 1169a
  accidents 954a
Mott, Lucretia 914a
Mottled enamel 959b
Moulmein, Burma 2365a
Moulouya River 2337c
Moulton, Forest Ray 454a
Moultrie, William 315a
Mound Builders pottery 128b
Mt. Angel College 694
Mount Hamilton, California tele-
  scope 1791b
Mount Holyoke College 674
Mount Mary College 708
Mount Mercy College 668, 697
Mount Palomar Observatory tele-
  scope 1791b
Mount of see under latter part of
  name, such as Olives, Mount
  of
Mount Rainier National Park 2019b
Mount Royal Tunnel 1226
Mt. Rushmore National Park 2016b
Mount Saint Agnes College 672
Mount Saint Mary College 682
Mount St. Mary's College 657
Mount Saint Mary's College 673
Mount St. Scholastica College 669
Mount Union College 691
Mount Vernon (Washington's
  home) 2030b
Mount Vernon Conference 786c
Mount Wilson Observatory tele-
  scope 1791b
Mountain ash 1680b
Mountain bluebird 1980c, 1988b
Mountain building 508a
Mountain climate 508a
Mountain laurel 1680b, 1993a, 1977c
Mountains 508a, 2337c
  formation of 455a
  see also under names of indi-
  vidual mountains
Mountbatten, Louis Alexander
  (1854–1921) 203c
Mountbatten, Louis (1900–) 315a,
  2185c
Moulouya River 2221c
Mouse see Mice
Mouse Tower 1440c
Moussorgsky, Modest 169a, tab 172a
Mouth 508a
Mouth (anat.) digestion 920b
Movable type (print.) 142b
Movement for the Social Evolution
  of Black Africa (MESAN) 2119b
Movement (mus.) 176c
Movements (plants) 1647b
Movies see Motion pictures
Moving stairway see Escalator
Mowat, Oliver 2117a
Mowbray, Harry S. tab 108
Mowgli (lit. char.) 1408a
Mozambique 2241c, 2317
  agriculture 2317b
  climate 2317c
  economy 2317a
  geography 2317a
  government 2317b
  history 2317b–2317c
  map Atlas-38
  people of 2317a
  religion 2317a
  slavery 3217c
Mozart, Wolfgang Amadeus 164b,
  tab 171c
  biography 315b
Mrs. Siddons (paint., Gains-
  borough) tab 111
Mrs. Siddons As Tragic Muse
  (paint., Reynolds) tab 112
Mrs. Warren's Profession (play)
  1370a
Mswati (Ngoni chief) 2267b
Muang Swa, Laos 2206c
Muchinga Mountains 2305a
Muck 508a, 751b
Mud cracks 508a

Mud Mountain Dam 1206
Mudflow 447b, 508a
Mudstone 508a
Mueller, Frederick H. *tab* 797
Mufti of Jerusalem 2193b
Muhammad 965a, 995a
  see also Mohammed
Muhammad Ahmad 1005b
Muhammad Ali 2281b
Muhammad al-Badr, Imam
  (Yemen) 2302c
Muhammad II, Sultan (Ottoman
  Empire) 1000a
Muhammad, Dost 2085c–2086a
Muhammad Ali Jinnah 2185b, 2185c
Muhammad bin Yusuf (Muham-
  mad V) 2222b
Muhammad Hatta 2188a
Muhammad Nadir 2086a
Muhammad Riza 2189b
Muhlenburg, Frederick Augustus
  (1750–1801 House of Repre-
  sentatives *tab* 802b
Mühlenberg, Heinrich Melchior
  315b
Muhlenberg College 697
Muir, John 315b, 775c, *tab* 1477
Mulambwa, Chief 2305b
Mulberry 1680b–1680c
Mulberry family 1680c
Mule 46c–47a
Mule frame (spinning) 1281c
Mulhouse, France 2149b
**Mulinu'u II, Fiame Mata'afa Fau-
  muina** 2302a
Mullein 1680c
Muller, Hermann Joseph 1858c
Mullet 47a
Mullins, Priscilla 1019a
Müller, Johannes Peter 1762b
Müller, Wilhelm (poet) *tab* 1473
Mullite 1201c
Muloch, Dinah Maria 1367c, 1462c,
  tab 1476
  John Halifax, Gentleman 1407c
Multiple personality 1957a
Multiple sclerosis 942c
Multiple stars 1790b
Multiplication 1516a
  algebra 1532c, 1534a
  algorithm 1519b
  definition 1605a
  facts *tab* 1513a
  fractions 1527c
  history 1510a
  justification of process *tab* 1517
Mumford, Lewis 315b, 1348b, 1377a
Mummer's Wife, The (nov.) 1369c
Mumps *tab* 947
Munch, Edvard *tab* 108
  biography 315b
München, Germany *see* Munich,
  Germany

Münchhausen, Karl Friedrich von
  1411a
Muncie, Indiana 1981c
Münchhausen (nov.) 1384c
Munchausen, Baron (lit. char.)
  1411a
Mundelein College 665
Muenster cheese *tab* 731b
Munich, Germany 2157c, 2158a,
  2365a, 2365c
  Oktoberfest il 2158
  State Library *tab* 1463
Municipal government 793c, 864a
Municipal University of Omaha
  681
Munin 1441b
Muñoz Marin, Luis 2003b
Muñoz Rivera, Luis 2003a, 2003b
Munro, H. H. *tab* 1463a
Muntz metal 1196a
Munz, Hope *tab* 1481
Moraes, Francisco de 1388b
Murano glass 134a, *tab* 135
Murat, Joachim 315b
Muratori, Ludovico 1387a
Murcia, Spain 2264a
Murder 892b
Mures, River 2243c
Murfree, Mary N. *tab* 1478
  pen name 1461c
Murfreesboro, Battle of 2049
Murger, Henri *tab* 1476
Murillo, Bartolomé *tab* 107
  biography 315c
  Immaculate Conception tab 109
Murillo, Pedro Domingo 2100c
Murmansk, Soviet Union 2365a
Murner, Thomas 1383c, *tab* 1466
Muroran, Japan 2365a
Murphy, Frank *tab* 796
  Supreme Court *tab* 802a
Murphy, John Francis *tab* 108
Murphy, William Parry 315c
Murray, Sir **James Augustus Henry**
  315c
Murray, Sir **John** (Eng. zool.) 462a
Murray, Lindley 315c
Murray, Phillip 315c
Murray, William H. H. nickname
  1461a
Murray State University 670
Murray-Darling rivers 2337c
Murry, Kathleen
  see Mansfield, Katharine
Musa, King 2215a, 2215b
Muscat and Oman 2222–2223, 2365a
  agriculture 2222c
  climate 2222c
  economy 2222c
  flag *il* 2183
  geography 2222c
  government 2222c

  history 2222c–2223a
  map 2222, *Atlas*-25
  people 2222c
  religion 2222b
Muscle Shoals 2020c
Muscles 927a
  contraction 927c
  energy production 927b
  muscular dystrophy 942c
  myathenia gravis 942c
  structure 927a
  tetany 945c
Muscovite (mineral) 453b, 508a
Muscovy *see* Russia; Soviet Union
Muscovy ducks 731c
Muscular dystrophy 942c
Muses 1440c
Museum of Fine Arts (Boson) *tab*
  110
Museums adult education 637c
  famous paintings *tab* 109–113
  *see also under names of individ-
  ual museums, such as* Louvre
Musgrave Mountains 2091b
Mushka (dog) 951b
Music 154–179
  acoustics 1895c
  careers 374b
  chords 1896c
  contrapuntal 160a
  folk 154c
  great names in *tab* 171–172
  kindergarten 401a
  romanticism 165a
  scales 1896c
Musical comedy 1376a
Musical Fund Society 169c
Musical instruments 154b
  Greece 157b
  keyboards 171a
  kindergarten 401b
  percussion 173a
  secular 159c
  sound 1894c, 1896a
  stringed 178b
Musk ox 47a–47b
Muskeg 508a
Muskegon, Michigan 1985c
Muskegon Heights, Michigan 1985c
Muskellunge *il* 1717
Muskingham River 2019c
Muskingum College 692
Muskmelon *see* Melon
Muskrat 47b
Muslim League 2185b, 2185c
Muslims
  architecture 78a
  in India 980c, 2180b–2180c
  in Spain 2264b–2264c
  see also Islam
Mussel 47b
Musserana *il* 32
Musset, Alfred de *il* 208, 1380c,
  1381a
  biography 315c

Mussolini, Benito 315c, 988c, 2096a,
  2096b, 2146b, 2154c, 2162c,
  2175b, 2196b, 2196c, 2246b,
  2262b
  centralization 862c
  corporative state 870c
  march on Rome 871c
  World War II 1028a–1028c
  writer and orator 1330c
  see also Fascism; Italy
Mussorgsky, Modest 316c
Mustard 1680c–1681a
Mustard family 1681a
Mutations 1853c, 1858a
  life, origin of 1839a, 1841a
Mute (mus.) 176c
Mutes (gram.)
  see Explosives (gram.)
Mutesa II, Edward Kabaka (king)
  (Uganda) 2280a, 2280b
Mutilation primitive culture 1930c
Mutiny on the Bounty (nov.) 1398a
Mutsuhito, Emperor (Japan) 316a,
  979a
Mutual assent (law) 818b
Mutualism (bio.) *see* Symbiosis
MVD 907b
Mwambutsa IV, Mwami 2108b
Mwanga, King (Uganda) 2280a
Mweru, Lake 2134c, 2305a, 2338a
My Bed is a Boat (nursery rhyme)
  414b
My Pedagogic Creed (bk.) 622c
My Shadow (nursery rhyme) 414c
Myasthenia gravis 942c
Mycelium 1846c
Mycenae (ancient city) sculpture
  116a
Mycology 1638a
Myiasis 957a
Myknos (Greece) *il* 2166
Myofibrils 927a
Myopia *see* Nearsightedness
Myriameter *tab* 1500
Myrmidons 1440c
Myron 116b
  biography 316a
Myrtle 1681a
Myrtle family 1681a–1681b
Mysteries of Udolpho (nov.) 1366c
Mystery plays Scandinavian *tab*
  1466
Mystic River 2005c
Mysticism 1620c
Mystic Marriage of St. Catherine
  (paint.) *tab* 112
Myth 1421a
Mythology 1421–1449
Myxedema 942c
Myxobacteriales 1844b

N

N.I.R.A. *see* National Industrial
  Recovery Act
N.R.A. *see* National Recovery
  Administration
Nabokov, Vladimir 316b, 1309b,
  tab 1481
Nabopolassar, King (Babylon)
  1016a
Nacala, Mozambique 2365b
Nadelman, Elie *tab* 125
Nadir 1793c, 1795c
Nadir Shah 2180c, 2189a–2189b
Naevius, Gnaeus 1354c
Nagasaki, Japan 2200c, 2201b, 2365b
  atomic bombing of 1028c, 2076c,
  1914c
Nagel, Charles *tab* 797
Nagoya, Japan 2198c, 2199a, 2365b
Nagpur, India 2365b
Nagy, Imre 2175c
Naha, Ryukyu Islands 2365b
Naharro, Bartolome de Torres
  see Torres Naharro
Nahum 1458b
Naiads 1440c

Nails (anat.) 918c
Nails (tool) 1252b
Nairobi, Kenya 2202b, 2365b–2365c
Naismith, James 1707a
Nájera, Manuel Gutiérrez 1393b
Najib, Muhammad 2281c
Namgyal, Maharajah Gyalsay
  Palden 2249c
Nan Mountains 2338a
Nan Ling Mountains 2124a
Nan Shan (mountains) 2123c
Nanchang, China 2365c
Nancy, France 2149a
Nanda dynasty 2779b
Nanking, China 2365c
Nanking, Treaty of (1842) 2128c
Nansen, Fridtjof 316b
Nantes, France 2149b
Nantes, Edict of *see* Edict of Nantes
Nanteuil, Robert 139c
Nantucket 2016c
Naoise 1430a
Napthalene 1203a
Napier, John 316b
  logarithms 1504c, 1604b, 1596a
Naples, Italy 2194a, 2195a, 2195c,
  2365c
  National Library *tab* 1463
Naples, Kingdom of 2195b

Napoleon I (Napoléon Bonaparte)
  316b, 1010a, 1010b, 1023c, 2098c,
  2122a, 2152c–2153a, 2195c, 2160c,
  2215c, 2218c, 2225b, 2240a,
  2268c, 2269a, 2270b, 2281b,
  2290c ,2297c
  archeological excavations 968c
  coup d'etat 871c
  dictatorship 987b
  Louisiana Purchase 2033a
  reparations 905b
  in Russia 1014b
  on St. Helena 2321a
  seizes Spanish throne 2265a
  sobriquets 1462b
  Toussaint L'Ouverture 354a
  at Waterloo 1023c–1024a
Napoleon II 317a
Napoleon III (Louis Napoleon),
  Emperor (France) 317a,
  2153b–2153c, 2196a, 2219b, 2300c
  coup d'etat 871c
Napoleonic Code *see* Code
  Napoleon
Napoleonic Wars 1006c, 1007a, *tab*
  1074
Napoli, Italy *see* Naples, Italy
Nappe 508b
Nara, Japan 2200a, 2365c–2366a
Narbada-Tapi River 2177c
Narcissism 1440c

Narcissus (myth) 1440c
Narcissus (flower) 1681b
  mythology 1440c
Narcotics 2128b, 2128c
Narcotics Control Act 899c
Narragansett Bay 1993c
Narration (writing) 1319a
Nasby, Petroleum V.
  see Locke, David
Naseberry 1691c
Naseby, Battle of 1016c
Nash, John (Amer. paint.) *tab* 109
Nash, Ogden 317a, 1376b
Nash, Paul *tab* 109
Nash, Walter 2227b
Nashe, Thomas 317a
Nashville, Tennessee 1994c, 1995a,
  2012a–2012b
Nashville, Battle of 2049, 2050b
Naso, Publius Ovidius *see* Ovid
Nassau, Bahamas 2307b
Nasser, Gamal Abdel 317a, 2247b,
  2247c, 2271c, 2281c
Nasson College 672
Nast, Thomas 317b
Nasturtium 1681b–1681c
Natchez Trace National Parkway
  896a
Nathan 1458b

Nathan, George Jean 317b
Nathan, Marshall I. 1890c, 1911a
Nathanael 1458b
Nathan der Weise (play) 1384a
Nation, Carry A. 317b
National Aeronautic Association of
   U.S.A. 1742a
National American Woman Suffrage
   Association 914b
National Association of Amateur
   Athletes of America 1703a
National Bank 599a
National banks 529c
National brand 599a
National Civil Service Reform
   League 2056a
National College of Education 665
National Collegiate Athletic
   Association 1703b
National Conference of Methodist
   Youth 1745a
National Congress of Parents and
   Teachers 1745b
National Council of Churches of
   Christ in the U.S.A. 1743b
National Council of Nigeria and
   Cameroons (NCNC) 2229c
National Council for Prevention of
   War 1745b
National Education Association
   1743c
National Exchange Club 1743c
National Federation of Business
   and Professional Women's
   Clubs 1746a
National Federation of Music Clubs
   1745a
National forests 896a
   see also under the names of in-
   dividual forests such as El-
   dorado National Forest
National Gallery (London) *tab* 111
National Gallery (Washington,
   D.C.) *tab* 113
National Geographic Society 1744a
National Guard 891c, 829b
National Health Service (Great
   Britain) 2292a
National Housing Act 882c
National Hydrocarbons Agency
   2194c
National income 599b
National Indonesian Party 2188a
National Industrial Recovery Act
   527a, 834c, 835a, 839a, 882c,
   885a, 2072c, 2073a
National Institute of Social
   Sciences 1745c
National Labor Board 839a
National Labor Relations Act
   (Wagner Act) 527b, 831b, 839a,
   892b, 908c, 910a, 913a, 2074a
National Labor Relations Board
   791b, 831b, 849b, 889b, 892b,
   913b, 2074a
National Labor Union 838a
National League of American Pen
   Women 1745
National Liberation Front (FLN)
   (Algeria) 2088b
National Library (Madrid) *tab* 1463
National Library (Naples) *tab* 1463
National Library (Paris) *tab* 1463
National Library (Vienna) *tab* 1463
National Maritime Union 882a
National Meteorological Center 478a
National monuments 896a
   see also under names of indi-
   vidual monuments, such as
   Devil's Tower National
   Monument
National Museum (Amsterdam)
   see Rijks Museum
National Park Service 896a
National Park System 775c, 896a
   conservation 777c
National parks 594c, 777c, 896a
   see also under the names of in-
   dividual parks, such as Yel-
   lowstone National Park
National Party (New Zealand)
   2227b
National Party (South Africa)
   2253b
National Power Authority 2194c
National Public Library
   (Leningrad) *tab* 1463
National Radical Union Party
   (Greece) 2167c
National Recovery Administration
   (N.R.A.) 834c, 898c, 2073a
National Research Council 1745c
National Rifle Association 1745c

National Road 2034a
National Revolutionary Movement
   (MNR) 2101a
National Revolutionary Party
   (PNR) 2219c
National Rwanda Union 2245c
National Safety Council 1745c
National Science Foundation 630a
National Security Act (1947) 893b,
   913a
   Air forces 850c
National Socialism
   see Nazi Party
National Socialist German Workers'
   Party *see* Nazi Party
National Society of Crippled
   Children and Adults 1743b
National Travelers Aid Association
   1746a
National Union and Progress Party
   (UPRONA) 2108b
National Unionist Party (Sudan)
   2266c
National University Extension
   Association 635a
National War College 913b
National Weather Service 477c
National Wildlife Federation 1746a
National Woman Suffrage Associa-
   tion 914a
Nationalism 892c
Nationalist China *see* China, Na-
   tionalist
Nationalist Party (Australia)
   2093c–2094a
Nationalist Party (China) 2126a,
   2130a
   see also China, Nationalist;
   Kuomintang
Nationalist Party (Puerto Rico)
   2003a–2003b
Nationality 892c
Nationalization 892c
Native oak 1981a
Native violet 1981a
Nativity (paint., Correggio)
   tab 184
NATO *see* North Atlantic Treaty
   Organization
Natong River 2203b–2203c
Nattier, Jean 85a, *tab* 107
Natural (mus.) 176c
Natural bridge 508b
Natural gas 508b, 1210a
   Alaska 1975a
   California 1977a
   energy consumption 1130a
   fuel 1137b
   Louisiana 1983c
   Montana 1988a
   Nebraska 1988b
   New Mexico 1990a
   Oklahoma 1992b
   Romania 2244a
   Soviet Union 2256b–2256c
   Spain 2263c
   sulfur 1224b
   Texas 1995a
   U.S. 2293c
   Venezuela 2297b
   West Virginia 1998c
   Wyoming 1999c
Natural History (bk., Pliny) 1357c
Naturalism
   English Art 85c
   French literature 1381c
   German literature 1385c
Naturalization 892c–893b
   citizenship 863c–864a
Natural keys (mus.) 176c
Natural logarithms 1604b
Natural resources conservation
   775a
Natural sciences 389c
Nature myths 1421b
Naumberg, Germany cathedral
   120c
Nauru 2223
   climate 2223a
   economy 2223a–2223b
   flag *il* 2183
   geography 2223a
   government 2223b
   history 2223b
   map *Atlas*-6
   people 2223a
   religion 2223a
   World War II 2223b
Nausicaa 1440c
Nautical mile 508b
Nautilus 47b–47c
Nautilus (submarine) 1167c, 1182b
   Fulton, Robert 1182c
Navajos music 170c

Naval Academy, (U.S.) *see* United
   States Naval Academy
Naval War College 629c
Navarino, Greece 2166a
Navassa Island 2001
Nave (arch.) 75c
Navigation international law 886a
Navigation Acts 2027a
Navigation canals 1160c
Navigation lock 1160c
Navigators Islands *see* Samoa
Navy aviation 1157a
Navy (U.S.) careers 388c
   education for 629c
   forms of address *tab* 1119
   space programs 1769a
   War of 1812 2034a
Navy, Department of the 893b
   establishment *tab* 797
   secretaries of *tab* 795–796
Nazareth 1458b
Nazareth, Israel 2366a
Nazareth College 676
Nazareth College 686
Nazareth College of Kentucky 670
Nazi Party 893c, 966a, 1015a, 2096a,
   2162a–2163a, 2175b
   end of 1028c
   Gestapo 881c
Ndola, Zambia 2366a
Neanderthals 1925a
   culture 1928b
Neap tide 508b
Neapolitan sixth (mus.) 1119c
Near East camel 19a
Near Eastern civilizations 972b, 981c
Near Island 2016a
Nearsightedness 942c
Nebel (mus.) 156a
Nebo, Mount 1458b
Nebraska 1988
   admitted to the Union 2053a
   agriculture 1988b
   budget system 858b
   capital punishment 860b
   census (1960) 1972
   climate 1988a
   colleges 681
   commercial law *tab* 826
   committees 866c
   congressional apportionment
     tab 853
   economy 1988b
   flag *il* 2010
   geography 1988a–1988b
   government 793a, 1988b
   initiative and referendum 884c
   legal holidays 841–842
   people 1988b
   public school enrollments
     tab 646
   public school expenditures
     tab 644
   student enrollment *tab* 645
Nebraska, University of 681
Nebraska Wesleyan University 681
Nebuchadnezzar, King (Babylon)
   317b, 996c–997a, 1003c, 1458b
   architecture 74b
   captures Jerusalem 1017a
   Jews 1629a
Nebula 1795c
   solar system 1781c, 1782a, 1785a
Nebular hypothesis 454a, 1784c
Necessity of Atheism, The (tract)
   1365a
Necho II, King (Egypt) 1003c
Neck (anat.) torticollis 945c
Neck (geog.) 508b
Neck cutoff 508b
Nectar (flower) 1645c
Nectar (myth) 1440c
Nectarine *see* Peach
Needham, J. T. 1844c
Needle (instr.) 137a
Needle bearings 1234a
Needlework Guild of America 1745a
Needles (pine) 1642c
Ne'eman, Yuval 1916a
Negative numbers 1532a
Negev Desert 2192a, 2338a
Negligence (law) 824b, 893c
Negotiable instruments 599b, 820c,
   821a
Negritos 1927a
Negro Congoids 1927a
   education 610b
   Fifteenth amendment 2053b
   Fourteenth Amendment 2051c
   music 170c
   slavery 829c
   suffrage 793b
   unemployment 610b

Colombia 2132b
   Ecuador 2144a
Negroids 1924c, 1925c
   Capoids 1927a
   Congoids 1927a
Negros (Philippine Islands) 2237c
Nehru, Jawaharlal 317c, 2185b,
   2185c, 2186a
Neichiang, China 2366a
Neisse River 2157a, 2238c
Nekrasov, Nikolay 1390a, *tab* 1476
Nekton 465a
Nelson, George (designer) furni-
   ture 1102a
Nelson, George (pol.) vice-presi-
   dential candidate *tab* 801
Nelson, John *tab* 795
Nelson, Horatio 317c
Nelson, Samuel Supreme Court
   tab 802a
Nelson, Thomas Jr. Declaration of
   Independence *tab* 803
Nelson, New Zealand 2226c
Nemean lion 1440c
Nemesis 1440c
Nenni, Pietro 2196c
Nennius
   History of the Britons 1425a
Neo-Destour Party (Tunisia) 2277b
Neodymium 1834
   atomic weight *tab* 1805
Neolithic Age 967b, 972b, 1928c
   art 83a
   dogs 1934a
Neon 1808b, 1834, 1906a
   atomic structure 1807b
   atomic weight *tab* 1805
   conductors 1882b
   electrons 1807a
   spark chamber 1914c
Neon lighting 1890a, 1906a
Neo-Platonism 1755a
Neoprene 1222a
Neoptolemus 1424a, 1445a
Neo-Thomism 623c
Nepal 2223–2224
   agricultre 2223c
   climate 2223c
   economy 2223c–2224a
   flag *il* 2183
   geography 2223b, 2223c
   government 2224a
   history 2224a–2224b
   map 2224, *Atlas*-29
   people of 2223c
   Rana rule 2224b
   religion 2223b, 2223c, 2224a
   sheep 57b–57c
Nephele 1424c
Nephron 925b
Nephrosis 945a
Nepos, Cornelius 1397b, *tab* 1464
Neptune (myth) 1440c, 1445a
Neptune (planet) *tab* 1782, 1783b
   albedo 1793b
   atmosphere 1840b
   Bode's law 1780c, *tab* 1781
   discovery of 1759c
Neptunium 1800a, 1834, 1911c
   atomic weight *tab* 1805
Nereid 1440c
Neri, Filippo *tab* 171b
Neritic 508b
Neritic zone (oceanog.) 1866a
Nero, Emperor (Rome) 317c,
   1016b
   music 157c
Neruda, Pablo 1893c
Nerva, Marcus 317c
Nerval, Gérard de 1381a
Nervous system 938a
   Bell, Charles 1947c
   disease 959c
   muscles 927c
   multiple sclerosis 942c
   neuralgia 945a
   neuritis 945a
   Parkinson's disease 945a
Nesiotes 116b
Nessus 1440c
Nestor 1441a
Nestorius 318a
Netherlands 2098a, 2224–2225
   agriculture 2224c
   Benelux customs union 998b
   cattle 20b
   cheese *tab* 731b
   economy 2224c–2225a
   European Common Market 877b
   flag *il* 2183
   history 2225a–2225c
   geography 2224c

government 2225a
independence 2225b
industry 2224c-2225a
Luxembourg and 2211b
map 2225, *Atlas-22*
map-making industry 779c
music 160a, *tab* 171b
people of 2224c
printing 144a
religion 2224c, 2225b
Triple Alliance (1668, 1717) 1022c
tulips 1697b
wine 723c
—History 2225a-2225c
American colonization *tab* 1060
Congress of Vienna 1023c
Delaware 2024c
English Dutch wars 999b
in Guyana 2171a
in Indonesia 2187c-2188a
mercantilism 986c
in Netherlands Antilles 2317c-2318a
New York 2024b
in Surinam 2323b-2323c
Triple Alliance (1668, 1717) 1022c
in the Virgin Islands 2004c
War of Liberation *tab* 1073
World War I 2225b
World War II 1028a, 2162c, 2225b-2225c, 2292a
see also Dutch art; Dutch language
Netherlands Antilles 2225a, 2225c, 2317-2318
agriculture 2318a
climate 2317c
economy 2318a
geography 2317c
government 2318a
history 2318a
Indians 2317c
map *Atlas-53*
people of 2317c-2318a
religion 2318a
slavery 2318a
Netherlands Guiana *see* Surinam
Netherlands New Guinea (West Irian) 2225c, *Atlas-30*
Nettle 1681c
Neufchâtel cheese *tab* 731b
Neuilly, Treaty of 2106a
Neuralgia 945a
Neumes 158b
Neurath, Otto 1619a
Neuritis 945a
Neurology psychiatry 1952b
Neurons 939a
Neuroses 1954a
Neurospora 1856a
Neurosurgeons 1952b
Neutra, Richard J. 81c, 82c
Desert House il 80
Neutrality 893c
Neutralization (chem.) 1817c
Neutrons 1803c, 1804c, 1881b, 1919a
chain reactions 1829a
characteristics of 1911a
magnetic moment 1915b
Neutron stars 1795c
Neutrophils 922b
Neva River 2338a
Nevada 1988-1989
agriculture 1988c
capital punishment 860b
census (1960) 1972
climate 1988c
colleges 681
commercial law *tab* 826
congressional apportionment *tab* 853
congressmen at large 855a
divorce 875b
economy 1988c-1989a
electoral votes 876c
flag *il* 2010
geography 1988b-1988c
government 1989a
initiative and referendum 884c
legal holidays 841-842
people of 1988c
public school enrollment *tab* 646
public school expenditures *tab* 644
recall 904b
student enrollment *tab* 645
Nevada, University of 681
Nevada Southern University 681
Neve 508b
Nevers, France pottery *tab* 130
Neville, Richard (1428-1471) *see* Warwick, 1st Earl of
Nevin, Ethelbert 170a
Nevinson, C. R. *tab* 109

Nevis Island 2321
New, Harry S. *tab* 796
New Atlantis (treatise) 1362a, 1426a
New Bedford, Massachusetts 1985b
New Britain, Connecticut 1978a
New Caledonia 2318
warfare 1937a
New Croton Dam 1205c
materials 1189c
New Deal 791a, 867b, 898b, 2072c, 2073
farm credit administration 878a
housing 883a
legislation 889a
opposition to 2074a
results of 2074a
social security 908c
Supreme Court 792b
unemployment 911c
New Delhi, India 2177a, 2366a
New England black widow 17a
catbird 20a
colonial education 615c
lobster 43b
see also under the individual states
New England Confederation 786b, 2025a, 2026b
New England Primer (bk.) 616a, 1372a
New France 2113a, 2113c-2114c
New Granada 2133a, 2133b, 2144b, 2234b, 2237a, 2297c
New Guinea 2186c, 2318
agriculture 2318c
azaleas 1650b
bird of paradise 17a
boa 17c
climate 2318b
daisy 1660c
deer 25b
economy 2318c
eucalyptus 1666b
geography 2318b-2318c
government 2318c
history 2318c
kangaroo 40c
opossum 48b-48c
parrot 49c
people of 2318b-2318c
pigeon 51b
rhododendron 1690a
tooth shells 63c
wallaby 65b-65c
World War I 2318c-2319c
New Guinea Island 2338a
New Hampshire 1989
agriculture 1989b
capital punishment 860b
census (1960) 1972
climate 1989a
colleges 682
history, colonial 2024c
commercial law *tab* 826
congressional apportionment *tab* 853
economy 1989b
flag *il* 2010
geography 1989a
government 793a, 1989b
labor legislation 832b
legal holidays 841-842
people 1989a-1989b
public school enrollments *tab* 646
public school expenditures *tab* 644
referendum 884c
student enrollment *tab* 645
U.S. Constitution 809c
New Hampshire, University of 682
New Haven, Connecticut 1978a
American revolution 2029
colonial history 2025a
Yale University Library *tab* 1463
New Hebrides 2319
New Holland *see* Australia
New Hope Church, Battle of 2049
New International Auxiliary Language *see* Novial
New Jersey 1989
agriculture 1989c
appointment 852b
capital punishment 860b
census (1960) 1972
child labor laws 831c
climate 1989c
colleges 682-683
history, colonial 2025a
commercial law *tab* 826
congressional apportionment *tab* 853
economy 1989c
fair employment laws 836c
flag *il* 2010
geography 1989a-1989c
government 1989c
holidays 841-842
labor legislation 833b

people 1989c
public school enrollment *tab* 646
public school expenditures *tab* 644
student enrollment *tab* 645
U. S. Constitution 787a, 809c
New Life (poem) 1386a
New London, Connecticut 1978a
New Market, Battle of 2049
New Mexico 1989-1990
acquired by U. S. 2040b
archeology 971a
agriculture 1990a
bighorn 16c
capital punishment 860b
census (1960) 1972
climate 1990a
colleges of 683
commercial law *tab* 826
Compromise of 1850, 2041a
congressional apportionment *tab* 853
congressmen at large 855a
economy 1990a
flag *il* 2010
geography 1989c-1990a
government 1990a
holidays 841-842
Indians 1990a
people of 1990a
public health 960c
public school enrollment *tab* 646
public school expenditures *tab* 644
student enrollment *tab* 645
yucca 1700c
New Mexico, University of 683
New Mexico Highlands University 683
New Mexico Institute of Mining and Technology 683
New Mexico State University 683
New moon 1796a
New Netherland 2024b
New Orleans, Louisiana 1983c, 2012b, 2018c, 2019c
climate 477a
government 864a
New Orleans, Battle of 2035a
New School for Social Research 686
New Spain 2218c
New Stone Age *see* Neolithic Age
New Sweden 2024c
New Testament 1450a
law 815a
New Way to Pay Old Debts (play) 1361a
New World Symphony (mus.) 168c
New Year's Day states celebrating 841a
New York 1990
agriculture 1990c
alewife 13a
appointment 852b
budget system 858b
capital punishment 860a
census (1960) 1972
climate 1990c
codes 865b
colleges 683-688
commercial law *tab* 826
commercial apportionment *tab* 853
departments 873b
economy 1990c
electoral votes 876c
fair employment laws 836c
flag *il* 2010
geography 1990b-1990c
government 1990c
governor's salary 881b
holidays 841-842
hornet 39a
labor legislation 832c
parks 895c
people of 1990c
physicians 960b
public school enrollment *tab* 646
public school expenditures *tab* 644
referendum 884c
skimmer birds 58b
starlings 60a
student enrollment *tab* 645
—History
colonial history 2024b
craft unions 838a
labor legislation 833b, 834a
U.S. Constitution 809c
New York, New York 1990c, 2012b, 2013
aldermen 851a
Board of Estimate 857c
boroughs 858a

commercial arbitration 854a
educational television 619a
first daily newspaper 1171a
housing 882b
proportional representation 902b
—Landmarks
Little Church Around the Corner 1092b
Public Library *tab* 1463
Wall Street 606b
New York Central and Hudson River Railroad 2062a
New York Gazette 1170c
New York Herald 1171a
New York Journal-American *tab* 1171
New York Mirror *tab* 1171
New York News *tab* 1171
New York Philharmonic Society 169c
New York Public Library *tab* 1463
New York State Barge Canal 1967c, 2013c
New York Stock Exchange
Kennedy, J. F. 2080c
stock-ticker 1182a
New York Times *tab* 1171
New York Tribune (news.)
linotype machine 146a
New York University 686
educational T.V. 619b
enrollment 629a
New York Weekly Journal 1170c
New Zealand 2225-2227
agriculture 2226a-2226b
araucaria 1649a-1649b
beech 1652a
black widow 17b
bluebells 1653b
bluegrass 1653c
buttercups 1655a
climate 2226a
Commonwealth status 1000c
in Cook Islands 2311a
daisy 1660c
deer 25b
economy 2226a-2226b
eggplant 1666a
falcon 33b
flag *il* 2184
fuchsia trees 1668a
gallinule 35a
geography 2225c-2226a
government 2226b-2226c
hare 38a
heron 38a
history 2226c-2227b
immigration 883c
jay 40b
kiwi 41b
League of Nations 1012c
myrtle species 1681a-1681b
in Nauru 2223b
in Niue 2319a
parrot 49c
partridge 49c
penguin 50b
people of 2226a
quail 53c
religion 2225c
salmon 55a-55b
sea lions 56c-57a
shrews 57c-58a
snipe 59a
squirrels 59c-60a
stork 60b-60c
swallow 61a
tanager birds 62a
teal ducks 62c
thrushes 63a
in Tokelau Islands 2324a
tortoises 63c-64a
trade 2226b
trap-door spiders 64a
trout 64b
World War I 2227a
World War II 2227b
Newark, New Jersey 1989c
government 864b
Newark College of Engineering 682
Newark State College 683
Newberry, Truman H. *tab* 796
Newberry College 699
Newbery, John 1411a
Newbold, Charles 720a
Newcomb, Simon 318a
Newcomb College 671
Newcomb pottery 131c, *tab* 132
Newcomes, The (nov.) 1367b
Newfoundland 2113b, 2114c, 2116b
auk 14c
cod 22b
exploratory period 2023a
fishing 2112b
grackle 36c

sharks 57b
yellowlegs 68b–68c
Newlands, John A. R. 1799c
Newlands Reclamation Act 868c, 904b
Newman, John Henry 318a, 1366b, *tab* 1474
nickname 1461b
Newman, Rhode Island American Revolution 2029
founding 2025b
navy 629c
Newport News, Virginia 1997c
Newspapers 1170c
careers 388a
largest American *tab* 1171
largest foreign *tab* 1170c
letterpress printing 142a
photoengraving 148b
Newt 47c
Newton, Sir Isaac 318a, 986c, *tab* 1468, 1758b, 1800b
astronomy 1781a, 1796c
calculus 1504b, 1602a
gravitation 1763c, 1781b, 1873b
inertia 1918b
laws of motion 1804a, 1875c
telescope 1791a
Nexo, Martin Andersen *tab* 1479
Ney, Michel 318b
Ngendandumwe, Pierre 2108b
Nguru, Nigeria 2229b
Ngwenya, Swaziland 2267c
Nhu, Ngo Dinh 2301a, 2301b
Niacin *tab* 919. 1821c, 1824c
pellagra 945a
Niagara Bridge 1197a
Niagara Falls 2019b
Niagara River 2006a, 2019b
Niagara University 686
Niam 1441c
Niamey, Niger 2228b, 2228c, 2366a
Nibelungenlied (epic) 1383b, *tab* 1465
Alberich 1423c
Atli 1426b
Balmung 1426c
Brunhild 1427c
Kriemhild 1437b
Nibelungs 1441a
Nibelungs 1441a
Nicaea, Council of 871b, 995c, 1016c, 1631b
Nicaragua 2000c, 2173b, 2227–2228, 2234c
agriculture 2227c
climate 2227b
economy 2227c
flag *il* 2184
geography 2227b
history 2228a–2228b
government 2227c–2228a
Indians 2227b–2227c
industry 2227c
League of Nations 1012c
map 2227, *Atlas*-55
people of 2227c–2227c
religion 2227b
trade 2227c
Walker, William 2042b
Walker's filibustering expedition 1006a
World War II 2228b
Nicaragua, Lake 2227b, 2227c, 2338a
Nice, France 2148b, 2366a
Nicene Creed 871b, 1016c
Niche (ecology) 1860c
Nicholas, Saint 1446c
Nicholas I, Czar (Russia) 318b, 2259c–2260a
Nicholas II, Czar (Russia) 318b, 1025b, 2260b–2261a
abdication 849a
Nicholas Nickleby (nov.) 1366c, 1411b
Nicholson, Ben *tab* 109, *tab* 125
Nicholson, Meredith *tab* 1479
Nicias 113a
Nickel 1194a
Nickel (chem.) 1834
alloys 1193a
atomic weight *tab* 1805
Cuba 2136c
ferromagnetism 1884a
French Guiana 2312c
New Caledonia 2318c
Soviet Union 2256b
U.S. 1967a
Nickel silver 1196a
Nickel-cadmium storage cell 1132a, 1883b
Nickeltype 153a
Nicknames
dictionary of 1461–1463
U. S. presidents *tab* 799

Nicodemus 1458b
Nicolle, Charles Jules Henri 318b
Nicolls, Richard 2024c
Nicosia, Cyprus 2138a, 2366a
Nicotine pesticides 741c
Nicotinic acid *see* Niacin
Niebuhr, Barthold Georg 318b
Niebuhr, Reinhold 318b
Niello design 139c
furniture 1096b
Niepce, Joseph Nicéphore 1172a
Nielsen, Carl *tab* 172b
Nietzche, Friedrich Wilhelm 318c, 1385a, *tab* 1478, 1620a
Niflheim 1441a
Niger 2228–2229
agriculture 2228c
climate 2228b–2228c
economy 2228c
flag *il* 2184
geography 2228b–2228c
government 2228c
history 2228c–2229a
map 2228, *Atlas*-37
people of 2228c
religion 2228b, 2228c
Niger Progressive Party 2229a
Niger River 2169c, 2214c, 2215a, 2228b, 2228c, 2229a, 2338a
Nigeria 878c, 2110b, 2229–2230a
agriculture 2229c
Commonwealth status 1000c
economy 2229b
flag *il* 2184
geography 2229a
government 2229b–2229c
history 2229c–2230a
independence 2229c–2230a
industry 2229b
map 2229, *Atlas*-37
people of 2229a–2229b
religion 2229a
rubber production 1221b
slavery 2229c
Nigger of the Narcissus (nov.) 1370a, 1411b
Night Before Christmas (poem) 416c
Night blindness 945a
Night-blooming cereus 1681c
Night Thoughts (poem) 1363b
Nighthawk 47c
Nightingale, Florence 318c
Nightingale 47c–48a
Nightjar 48a
Nightshade 1681c–1682a
Nihilism 893c, 894a
Niihau Island 1980b
Nijinsky, Vaslav 184a
biography 318c
Nike of Samothrace *see* Winged Victory
Nikitin, Ivan 1390a
Nikolayev, Andrian *tab* 1770
Nile River 2265c, 2280b, 2280c, 2281c, 2338a
catfish 20b
Niles, John M. *tab* 795
Niloak ware *tab* 132
Nimba Mountains 2208c, 2209a, 2338a
Nimbostratus clouds 470c
Nimbus (satellite) 1769c
Nimitz, Chester W. 318c
Nimrod 1458c
Nimue *see* Lady of the Lake (leg.)
Nina (ship) 2023a
Nineteen Eighty Four (1984) (bk.) 1371c
Nineveh (ancient city) 1458c
archeology 969a
glass *tab* 135
Ninghsien, China 2366a
Ningpo, China 2366a
Niobe 1441a
Niobium 1835
atomic weight *tab* 1805
Nirvana 980c
Nis, Yugoslavia 2366b
Nitrates 508b
Chile 2121c, 2122b
Nitric acid 1215c, 1817b, 1862b
etching 136c
oxidation-reduction reactions 1813b
rocket fuels 1766c
Nitrogen 1820c, 1835, 1862b
atomic weight *tab* 1805
atmosphere 468a
bacteria 1846a
boiling point *tab* 1902
chemical bonding 1809a
electrons 1807a

fertilizers 733a, *tab* 752c, 753b, *tab* 753
in plants 1646b
radiocarbon dating 1816c
soil 743b, 751b
Nitrogen cycle 1862b
Nitrogen dioxide oxidation-reduction reactions 1813b
Nitrogen-fixing bacteria 1646c, 1862b
Nitroglycerin 1207c
Nobel, A. 1766c
Niue 2319
Nix 1441a
Nixon, Richard M. 318c, 2079a
Nivation 508b
Nkrumah, Kwame 319a, 2164b–2164c, 2170b
Noah 1458c
Noailles, Comtesse de 1382b, *tab* 1480
Nobel, Alfred 1207c
Nobel, Alfred Bernhard 319a
dynamite 1766c
genetics 1858c
transistors 1890c
Nobelium 1835
atomic weight *tab* 1805
Noble, John W. *tab* 797
Nobre, Antonio 1388c
Nobunaga, Oda 2200b
No confidence, vote of 894a
Nobility forms of address *tab* 1120
Nocturn 176c
Nodes (astron.) 1795c
Nodier, Charles 1381a
Nodule 508b–508c
Noguchi, Isamu *tab* 125
Nolle prosequi 894a
Nolo contendere 894a
Nomads 769
political institutions 1937a
shelter 1930a
Nombre de Dios, Panama 2234b
Nominalism (philos.) 1620c
Nomination 894a
petition 898a
Nonagon 1606b
Nonahedron 1606c
Nonane 1820c
Nonconformity 508c
Nordic Council 2230c
Nondirective technique (psych.) 1952a
Nondurable goods 599b
Non-Euclidean geometry 1579c, 1604a
Nonferrous metals 1215c
Nonintercourse Act 2033c, 2034a
Nonpareil type 146c
Nonresistance 894b
Nora (lit. char.) 1401b
Noradrenalin (norepinephrine) 926a, 939a
Nordenfeldt, Thorsten 1182c
Nordhoff, Charles B. *Mutiny on the Bounty* 1398a
Norepinephrine *see* Noradrenalin
Norfolk, Virginia 1997c
Norfolk Island 2319
Norfolk island pine 1682a
Norge (airship) 1155a
Normal, Illinois 1981b
Normal curve 1597a
Normal school 616c
Normal solution (chem.) 1815b
Norman Conquest (England)
English language 1321b
English literature 1358c
feudalism 888a
Normandie (ship) 1180c
Normandy, Duke of (1027–1087) *see* William I, King (England)
Normandy, Duke of (1056–1100) *see* William II, King (England)
Normandy, France *il* 2149
Norns (myth) 1441a, 1432a
Norodom Sihanouk 2109b
abdiction 849a
see also Cambodia
Norris, Frank 319a, 1375b, *tab* 1479
Norris, George W. 910b
Norris-La Guardia Act 831a, 839b, 885a
Norsemen *see* Vikings
North, Christopher 1462b
North, Frederick 319a
North, Sir Thomas 1360b
North Adams, State College at 674
North Africa
cattle 20b
locust 43c

see also Algeria; Libya; Morocco; Tunisia
North America 2338b
archeology 971a
avocet 14c
bighorn 16c
black widow 17a
brown thrasher 18a
bufflehead 18b
bunting 18b
camel 19a
cankerworm 19a
cattle 20c
centipede 20c
coal 1202c
cony 23a
coyote 23c
crow 24c
culture region 768b–768c, 769a
dobsonfly 25b
duck 26a
economic geography 774c–775c
1440 World Map of 780
frog 35a
furs 738a
gallinule 35a
gar 35b
gecko 35b
goose 36b
grosbeak 37a
gull 37b
hare 38a
horseshoe crab 39c
hornet 39a
iguana 40b
jay 40b
junco 40b
kingbird 41a
kingfisher 41a
kinglet 41a
kinkajou 41b
lamprey 42a
lemming 42c
limpet 43a
lizard 43a
locust 43b
loon 43c
lynx 44b
magpie 44c
mallard 44c
map *Atlas*-64
merganser 45b
mole 46a
rice production 742b
Vikings 2023a
see also Canada, United States
North America Act (1867) 2116b
North Atlantic coast dogfish 25c
North Atlantic Ocean
alewife 13a
cod 22b
eels 26c
haddock 37c
ling 43a
mackerel 44b
see also Atlantic Ocean
North Atlantic Treaty Organization (NATO) 2118b, 2230c, 2231, 2078a
flag *il* 2184
purpose of 1016c
North Canadian River 2012c
North Carolina 1990–1991
agriculture 1991b
capital punishment 860b
census (1960) 1972
climate 1991a
colleges 688–690
history, colonial 2025b
commercial law *tab* 826
congressional apportionment *tab* 853
coquina 23a
economy 1991a
flag *il* 2010
geography 1991a
government 1991b
governor 881b
legal holidays 841–842
people of 1991a
public school enrollment *tab* 646
public school expenditures *tab* 644
restored to Union 2053c
secession 2045a
student enrollment *tab* 645
U. S. Constitution 809c
vegetable sponge 1698a
North Carolina, University of (Chapel Hill) 689
North Carolina, University of (Greensboro) 689
North Carolina College at Durham 689
North Carolina State University at Raleigh 689
North Central College 665
North Channel 2282a, 2338b

North Dakota 1991
agriculture 1991c
capital punishment 860a
census (1960) 1972
climate 1991b–1991c
colleges 690
commercial law *tab* 826
congressional apportionment *tab* 853
economy 1991c
flag *il* 2010
geography 1991b–1991c
government 1991c
legal holidays 841–842
people of 1991c
public school enrollment *tab* 646
public school expenditures *tab* 644
recall 904b
statehood 2058a
student enrollment *tab* 645
North Dakota, University of 690
North Dakota State University 690
North Georgia College 662
North German Confederation 2161b
North Island (New Zealand) 2225c, 2226a–2226b
North Korea *see* Korea, North
North Little Rock, Arkansas 1976a
North Peak 2019a
North Park College 665
North pole 508c
North Sea 2338b
North Temperate Zone
beaver 15c
North Texas State University 702
North Vietnam *see* Vietnam, North
Northeast Louisiana State College 671
Northeast Missouri State Teachers College 679
Northeastern State College 693
Northeastern University 674
Northern Arizona University 655
Northern Europe wildcat 19c
Northern Hemisphere eagle 26b
winds 474a
Northern Highlands 2333b–2333c
Northern Illinois University 665
Northern Ireland *see* Ireland, Northern
Northern lights 508c
see also Aurora borealis
Northern Michigan University 676
Northern Montana College 680
Northern Peoples' Congress (NPC) 2229c
Northern Rhodesia anthropology 1924c
see also Zambia
Northern Securities Company 2062a
Northern State College 699
Northampton, Assize of 855a
Northanger Abbey (nov.) 1366a
Northland College 708
Northmen *see* Vikings
Northrop, James L. 1287a
Northrop Institute of Technology 657
Northumbria, Kingdom of 2284a

Northwest Missouri State College 679
Northwest Nazarene College 663
Northwest Ordinance (1787) 2030b
civil rights 864c
education 629b
Northwest Passage 2023c, 2113b
Northwest Territories, Canada 2117a
map *Atlas*-59
Northwestern College 668
Northwestern State College 693
Northwestern State College of Louisiana 671
Northwestern University 665
Norton, Charles Eliot 319a
Norwalk, Connecticut 1978a
Norway 2230–2232
agriculture 2230b
climate 2230b
cod 22b
Congress of Vienna 1023c
under Danish crown 2142a
Denmark and 2230c–2231a
economy 2230b–2230c
fjords 2230a
flag *il* 2184
geography 2230a
government 2230c
hake 37c
history 2230c–2232a
in Iceland 2176c
independence 2231b–2231c
manufacturing 2230b
map 2230, *Atlas*-14–15
musicians *tab* 172a
people of 2230b
raids on the British Isles 2284a
rat 54a–54b
religion 2230a, 2230b, 2231a
in Svalbard and Jan Mayen Islands 2323c–2324a
Sweden and 2231a–2231b
trade 2230b–2230c
tuna 64b
Vikings 2230c, 2312a
World War I 2231c
World War II 1028a, 2162c, 2231c
Norway maple *il* 1664
Norway pine 1986a
Norwegian language classification 1333b
Norwegian Sea 2338b
Norwich University 704
Norwick, Connecticut 1978a
Nose (anat.) deviated septum 941b
Nose, The (story) 439c–442a
Nose cone 1779a
Nostradamus 319a
Notary public 894b
Notation (mus.) 176c
Notch 508c
Noteč River 2238c
Notker (Balbulus) 158c, *tab* 171b
Notker (Labeo) *tab* 1465
Notre Dame, Cathedral of (Paris)
architecture 985a
sculpture 120a
Notre Dame, University of 666
Notre Dame College 692
Notre Dame College of Staten Island 686
Notre-Dame de Paris (nov.) 1411b

Notus *see* Auster
Nouakchott, Mauritania 2216a, 2366b
Noue, François de la *see* La Noue, Francois de
Nouméa, New Caledonia 2318a, 2366c
Noumenon (philos.) 1618a
Nouns 1304a
forms and kinds 1304a
use 1303b
Nova (astron.) 1795c
Nova Scotia 2114c, 2115a–2115b, 2116a, 2116c
hummingbird 39c
menhaden 45b
Novalis *see* Hardenberg, Friedrich von
Novaya Zemlya Archipelago 2338b
Novel 1346a
American 1375c
Canadian 1390c
definition 1411b
development 1346a
French 1380b, 1382b
Italian 1387c
November Revolution (Russia) 2261b–2261c
Noverre, Jean Georges 183b, 185b
Novgorod, Soviet Union 2258a
Novi Sad, Yugoslavia 2366b
Novial (lang.) 1338c
Novikov, Nikolay 1389a
Novosibirsk, Soviet Union 2256a, 2366c
Novum Organum (bk.) 1348a, 1362a
Nowa Huta, Poland 2239b
Nox (myth) 1441a
Noyes, Alfred 319a, 1370c, *tab* 1480
Nozze di Figaro (opera) 164b
Ntare V, Mwame 2108b
Nu, U 2107c, 2108a
Nuba Mountains 2265c
Nubian Desert 2338b
Nuclear chemistry 1800c, 1828–1829
Nuclear energy conversion chart 1130
Japan 2199c
Nuclear engineering 1143c
Nuclear fision 1919a
reactions 1914c
Nuclear fusion 1919a
reactions 1914c
Nuclear physics 1911–1916
collectors 1943a
scatter experiment 1911c
Nuclear power 1143c
France 2155a
Japan 2199c
marine engineering 1167c
Soviet Union 2263a
Nuclear reactor 1144a, 1804b, 1829a
operation 1144c
types 1145b
Nuclear submarines 1182a
first 1182c
Nuclear testing Kennedy, J. F. 2081b
Nucleoli 1851b
Nucleons (phys.) 1911c
structure 1915b

Nucleophilic reagent 1823a
Nucleophilic substitution 1823a
Nucleotides 1825c, 1854b
Nucleus (bio.) genetics 1851b
microbiology 1842a
plant cell 1643b
Nucleus (phys.) 1881b, 1911a
atomic structure 1804c
chain reactions 1829a
fission 1914c
fusion 1914c
properties 1915a
Nudism primitive culture 1930b
Nuee ardente 508c
Nuku' Alofa, Tonga 2324a, 2366c
Number congruence 1530c
Numbers 1508a
algebra 1532a
binary system 1505b
definition 1605b
perfect 1606a
progression 1607a
Pythagoras 1613a
Pythagorean 1751b
sequence 1607a
systems 1509b, 1510, 1605b
Numbers, Book of (Bib.) 1458c
Numerical coefficient 1535b
Numerical value *see* Absolute Value
Numerology 1524c
Numismatics organizations 1745
Nunatak 508c
Núñez, Rafael 2133b
Núñez de Arce, Gaspar 1392b
Nuremberg, Germany *see* Nürnberg, Germany
Nurhachu 980a
Nürnberg, Germany 2366c
Dürer, Albrecht 143
War Crimes trials *il* 2162
Nursery rhymes 408–417
Mother Goose Tales 1411a
Nursing (career) 382c
Nut pine 1989c
Nutation (astron.) 1795c
Nuthatch 48a
Nutmeg 744b, 1682a
Nutria 48a–48b
Nutrients plant absorption of 1646a–1646b
Nutrition 919a
careers 390c
problems 955c
Nux vomica 1682a
Nyasa, Lake 2212b, 2338b
Nyasaland 2212c–2213a, 2243b
see also Malawi
Nyasaland African Congress (1944) 2213a
Nye, Bill (Edgar Wilson Nye) 1462c
Nye, Gerald P. 2076a
Nyerere, Julius 2273a
Nuku'alofa, Tonga *see* Nuku'Alofa
Nylon 1208c, *tab* 1219, 1220a, 1824c
Nymphenburg, Germany pottery *tab* 131
Nymphs (myth) 1441a
Nyx (myth) 1441a

O

O. Henry *see* Porter, William Sydney
Oahe Dam 1206
Oahu Island 1980a, 2008a
Oak 1682a–1682b, 1982a
live 1979c
native 1981a
red 1989b
white 1977c, 1984c
Oak Ridge, Tennessee 1995
Oakland, California 1976c, 2014a–2014b
Oakland University 676
Oakwood College 654
OAS *see* Organization of American States
Oases 508c, 2280b
Libya 2209c, 2210a

Oath 894b
Oats 740c
Argentina 2089c
Iowa 1982a
Minnesota 1986b
North Dakota 1991c
Poland 2239b
South Dakota 1994c
Sweden 2268a
U.S. 1968b–1968c, 2294a
Uruguay 2295a
Oats, Peas, Beans and Barley Grow (song) 421
Oaxaca, Mexico 2217b, 2217c
Ob River 2338b
Obadiah 1458c
Obbligato 176c
Oberlin College 692
Obermann (nov.) 1381a
Oberon (folklore) 1441a
Oberon (opera) 165c
Oberon (poem) 1384b
Obertass 182a

Oberth, Hermann 1765a
Obiter dicta 894b
Oblate 508c
Oblique angles 1601b, 1605b
Oblique triangles 1607c
Oblomov (nov.) 1389c
Oboe 176c, 1896b
Obote, Milton 2280a–2280b
Obregón, Alvaro 319b, 2219c
O'Brien, Lawrence F. *tab* 796
O'Brien, T. C. *tab* 801
Obsequent stream 508c
Obsidian 134a, 450c, 508c, 1937b
Obstetrics 382b
Obtuse angles 1601b
Obtuse triangles 1607c
O'Casey, Sean 319b
Occam, William of *see* Ockham, William
Occam's Razor *see* Parsimony, Law of
Occidental College 657

Occluded front 477a
Occultation (astron.) 1795c
Occupational therapy careers 382a, 383b
Occupational training 609c
Occupations *see* Career guidance
Ocean *see* Oceans
Ocean basins 759c
Ocean current 508c
Ocean depth zones 508c–509a
Ocean Island 2314a
Ocean Pond, Battle of *see* Olustee, Battle of
Oceanids 1441b
Oceanography 461–467, 509a, 1869c
bibliography 467c
careers 390b
history 461c
origin 461b
marine environment 1865c
tides 464a
Oceans 508c, 765b–765c

chemical nutrients 1866a
circulation 765c
climate 477c
composition 765b–765c
currents 461a, 465a
depths 462b
erosion 448b
organisms 1865c
waves 464b
*see also under the names of
the individual oceans, such
as* Pacific Ocean
Ocelot *see* Cat
Ochoa, Severo 1858c
Ochs, Adolph Simon 319b
Ochtman, Leonard *tab* 108
Ockham, William (William of
Occam) 1616a
O'Conor, Charles presidential can-
didate *tab* 801
Octagon 1606b
Octahedron 1606c
Octameter 1411b
Octane 1820b
Octave 176c
Octavia 319b
Octavian (Octavius) *see* Augustus,
Emperor
Octavius *see* Augustus, Emperor
Octonary number system 1605b
Octopus 48b
Odd Fellows (frat. organ.) 1745a
Odd function (math.) 1584c
Odd lot 599c
Odds (probability) 1597b
Ode 1344c, 1411b
Ode for St. Cecilia's Day (mus.)
163a
Ode to Sleep (poem) 1372b
Ode Written in 1746 (poem) 1364a
Oder River 2138c, 2157a, 2157b,
2238c, 2239a, 2239c, 2338b
Odessa, Soviet Union 2366c
Odessa, Texas 1995c
Odets, Clifford 319b
Odin 1441b
Odoacer 319b, 2195a
O'Donnell, Hugh 2191b
Odysseus (Ulysses) (myth) 1441b
Polyphemus 1444c
sirens 1447c
Odyssey (epic) 1343a, 1350c, 1411b,
tab 1463
Acheron 1422b
Aphrodite 1424b
Argus 1424c
Atlas 1426a
Calypso 1428a
Circe 1429a
Greek education 613a
Lotus Eaters 1438c
Odysseus 1441b
Shaw's translation 1351a
Oedipus 1441b
Sphinx 1447c
Oedipus Tyrannus (drama) 1352c
Oenone 1441c
Oenus 1425a, 1428a
Oersted, Hans Christian 1194c,
1760c, 1881a, 1884c
Offa II, King (Mercia) 2284a
Offenbach, Jacques *tab* 171c, 319b,
1381c
Offertory 176c
Office (gov.) 894b
Officer with Red Sash (paint.) *tab*
113
Officers of St. Adrien (paint.) *tab*
111
Officers of St. George (paint.) *tab*
111
Offset printing 149b, 153a, 1174a
duplicating 1164b
newspapers 1171a
Offshore bars (geol.) 449a
Offshore wind 509a
O'Flaherty, Liam 319b
Ogbomosho, Nigeria 2229b
Ogden, R. M. 1948a
Ogden, Utah 1996a, 2012b–2012c
Ogden River 2012c
Ogdensburg, New York 2020c
Ogier 1441c
Oglethorpe, James 319c, 2026a
Oglethorpe College 662
Ogooue River 2155b
Ogotai 2221a
Ogre 1441c
O'Hara, John 319c
Oh, Dear! What Can the Matter Be?
(song) 422

O'Higgins, Bernardo 2122a
Ohio 1991–1992
agriculture 1992a
capital punishment 860b
census (1960) 1972
climate 1992a
colleges of 690–692
commercial law *tab* 826
congressional apportionment
tab 853
congressmen at large 855a
economy 1992a
electoral votes 876c
flag *il* 2010
geography 1991c–1992a
government 1992a
initiative and referendum 884c
labor legislation 832c, 833c
legal holidays 841–842
people of 1992a
public school enrollment *tab*
646
public school expenditures *tab*
644
saltbush 1691c
Scarlet carnation 1991c
statehood 2030b, 2034a
student enrollment *tab* 645
Ohio Northern University 692
Ohio River 1962a, 1981a, 1983b,
1991a, 1991c, 2006b, 2011b,
2013a, 2015c, 2018c, 2019b–
2019c, 2020c, 2293a
salamanders 54c–55a
shad 57a–57b
Ohio University 692
Ohio Wesleyan University 692
Ohm (phys.) 1882c, 1919a
Ohm, Georg Simon 319c, 1882c
Ohmmeter 1248b
Ohm's law 1882c
Oil 509a, 762a
Alabama 1974b
Alaska 1975a
Angola 2306b
Arkansas 1976b
Bahrain 2096c, 2097a
Brunei 2309b
California 1977a
China 2125b
Colorado 1977b
Illinois 1981b
Indiana 1981c
Indonesia 2187a
Iran 2188a, 2189a, 2189b
Iraq 2189c, 2190a
Israel 2192b
Jan Mayen Island 2324a
Kentucky 1983a
Kuwait 2205b, 2205c
Libya 2210a
Louisiana 1983c
Mauritania 2216b
Mississippi 1987a
Mongolia 2220c
Montana 1988a
Muscat and Oman 2222c
Nebraska 1988b
Netherlands Antilles 2318a
New Guinea 2318c
New Mexico 1990a
Nigeria 2229b
North Dakota 1991c
Oklahoma 1992b
Pakistan 2232b
Qatar 2242b–2242c
Romania 2244a
Saudi Arabia 2246a, 2246c–2247a
South Dakota 1994c
South Yemen 2253c–2254a
Spain 2263c
Spanish Sahara 2323a
Svalbard Archipelago 2324a
Syria 2271a
Texas 1995c
Trinidad and Tobago 2275c
Turkey 2278a
U.A.R. 2280c
U.S.S.R. 2256b
U.S. 1967a, 2293c
Utah 1996b
Venezuela 771, 2297a–2297b, 2298
Wyoming 1999c
Oil *see also* Petroleum
Oil gas 1210b
Oil lamps 1140b
Oil Rivers Protectorate 2229c
Oil seeds 1934a
Oil of vitriol *see* Sulfuric acid
Oils
animal 732a
lubricants 1214b
plant 732a
Oireachtas 870a
Oiron pottery 1095c
Oisin 1441c
Oistrakh, David 319c
Ojeda, Alonso de 2023a
Okapi 48b

Okavango River 2101b, 2338b
Okayama, Japan 2366c
Okeechobee, Lake 2018a, 2019c,
2292c
O'Keeffe, Georgia *tab* 109, 319c
Okeghem, Johannes 160a, *tab* 171b
Okhotsk, Sea of 2338b–2338c
Okinawa Island 2003b
Oklahoma 1992
agriculture 1992b
armadillo 14b
bobwhite 17c
capital punishment 860b
census (1960) 1972
climate 1992b
colleges of 692–693
commercial law *tab* 826
congressional apportionment
tab 853
economy 1992b
flag *il* 2010
geography 1992b
government 1992b
initiative and referendum 884c
legal holidays 841–842
people of 1992b
public school enrollment *tab*
646
public school expenditures *tab*
644
student enrollment *tab* 645
tanager birds 62a
Oklahoma, University of 693
Oklahoma Baptist University 693
Oklahoma City, Oklahoma 1992a,
1992b, 2012c
Oklahoma City University 693
Oklahoma College of Liberal Arts
693
Oklahoma State University 693
Okra *see* Hibiscus
Olaf I (Olaf Trygvesson), King
(Norway) 320a
Olaf V, King (Norway and Den-
mark) 2231a, 2232a
Olafsson, Magnus *tab* 1467
Old age 959c
Old-age and Survivor Insurance
837c, 908b
Old-age pensions 897c
Old Buck *see* Buchanan, James
Old Buena Vista *see* Taylor,
Zachary
Old Bulgarian (lang.) *see* Old
Church Slavic
Old Bullion *see* Benton, Thomas
Hart (statesman)
Old Church Slavic (lang.) 1334a
Old Curiosity Shop (nov.) 1367a,
1411c
Old Deluder Satan Act 616a
Old Dominion College 705
Old English 1295a, 1296c, 1358b
cognates *tab* 1297b
literature 1358b
Old-Fuss-and-Feathers *see* Scott,
Winfield
Old Hickory *see* Jackson, Andrew
Old Man of the Sea (nov.) 1441c
Old Man with White Beard (paint.)
tab 110
Old Mortality (nov.) 1365c
Old Mother Goose (nursery rhyme)
410c
Old Mother Hubbard (nursery
rhyme) 410c
Old Noll *see* Cromwell, Oliver
Old Norse (lang.) 1336a
Old Public Functionary *see* Bu-
chanan, James
Old Rough-and-Ready *see* Taylor,
Zachary
Old Rowley *see* Charles II, King
(England)
Old Stone Age *see* Paleolithic Age
Old Testament (Bib.) 1450a, 1628c
Jewish law 813c
origin 973a
Old Wives' Tales (nov.) 1370b
Old Woman in Black Head-Dress
(paint.) *tab* 110
Old Woman Who Lived in a Shoe
(nursery rhyme) 409b
Old World
civet cat 22a
cobra 22a
deer 25b
Olds Motor Works 1169c
Oldstyle, Jonathan *see* Irving,
Washington
Old-style type 153a
Olduvai Gorge 1924c
Oleander 1682b
Oleoresinous varnish 1226c

Oleum 1224c
Olfaction *see* Smell
Oligarchy 784c
Oligocene Epoch *tab* 457, 458a,
509a
Oligopoly 539a, 599c
Oligotrophic waters 1866b
Olivant 1446a
Olive family 1682c
Oliver 1441c
Roland 1446a
Oliver, Isaac *tab* 107
Oliver Twist (nov.) 1411c, 1366c
Artful Dodger 1395b
Fagin 1403b
Olives 1682c
Greece 2165a
Italy 2194c
Lebanon 2207b
Portugal 2241b
Spain 2264a
Syria 2271a
Tunisia 2277a
Olives, Mount of 1458b
Olivet College 677
Olivet Nazarene College 665
Olivier, Sir Laurence 320a
Olivine 454a, 509a
Olmsted, Frederick Law 320a, 775b
Olney, Richard 320a, *tab* 796
Oltul River 2243c
Olustee, Battle of 2049
Olympia, Greece
Temple of Zeus 1876b
Olympia (paint.) *tab* 112
Olympia, Washington 1997c, 2012c
Olympias 320a
Olympic Mountains 1998a, 2016c–
2017a, 2019c
Olympic National Park 59c, 2019c
Olympic Peninsula 2019c
Olympio, Sylvanus 2275b
Olympus, Mount (Greece) 1442a
Olympus Mountains 2138a, 2338c,
2342a
Omaha, Nebraska 1988b, 2012c,
2019a
government 864b
Oman (sultanate) *see* Muscat and
Oman
Oman, Gulf of 2222c, 2338c
Omar I (Caliph) 320a, 994b–994c
Omar, Mosque of (Cairo) 78a
Omar Khayyám 320b, 982b, *tab*
1465
Rubaiyat, The 1416b
Omodeo, Giovanni *see* Amadeo,
Giovanni Antonio
Omo River 2146a
Omphale 1442a
Omuta, Japan 2366c
On Conciliation with America
(speech) 1364a
On the Fabric of the Human Body
(tract) 1759a
On Music (essay) 157b
On the Nature of Things (essay)
tab 1464
**On the Origin of Species by Means
of Natural Selection** (book)
see Origin of Species
**On the Revolutions of the Heav-
enly Orbs** (tract) 1756b
On Two Planets (novel) 1764c
Ona Indians 1930a
Onager *see* Ass
**One little, two little, three little
Indians** (nursery rhyme) 92c,
410c
One, two, buckle my shoe (nur-
sery rhyme) 411a
Onega, Lake 2338c
O'Neill, Eugene 320b, 1376c, *tab*
1480
Ah, Wilderness! 1394a
Emperor Jones 1402b
Strange Interlude 1418a
O'Neill, Hugh 2191b
Onganía, Juan 2091a
Onion 1682c
Onitsha, Nigeria 2366c
Onofri, Arturo 1388a
Onomatopoeia 1315c
Onondaga Lake 2015a
Onondaga ware *tab* 132
Onshore wind 509a
Ontario, Canada 2020c
pelican 50a–50b
Ontario, Lake 2017c, 2018a, 2019c,
2020b, 2115b

Oolite 509a
Oolong tea 745c
Ooze 509a
  diatomaceous 489c
  foraminiferal 497c
  globigerina 499b
Opal glass 133c
Oparin, Alexander I. 1840a
Open circuit 1917a
Open-door policy 2060a
Open-hearth process 1261c
Open score (mus.) 176c
Open shop 599c
Opera 176c
  American colonies 169c
  careers 374b
  grand opera 166b
  rise of 161b
  Wagner 166c
Opera House (Paris) 77c
Operant conditioning 1949b
Operating engineers
  careers 376c
Operation Bootstrap (Puerto Rico) 2002b
Operations research 547a
Operetta 176c
Ophelia (lit. char.) 1405b
Ophir 1458c
Ophiuchus (constellation) 1793b
Ophthalmology 382c
Opis dynasty 996c
Opitz, Martin 1383c, tab 1467
Opium 1825a, 2128b, 2128c
Opium War 2128c
Opossum 48b–48c
Oppenheimer, J. Robert 320b
Opporto, Portugal 723c
Ops 1442a
Option (finance) 600a
Optic, Oliver 320b, 1462c
Optic chiasma 928b
Optic nerve 928c
Optical axis 1908a
Optical glass 135c
Optical pyrometers 1898c
Optical squares see Penta prisms
Optical telescopes 1791a
Opticks (bk., Newton) 1759c
Optics 1870a, 1919b
  Ibn al-Haytham (Alhazen) 1754b
  image 1918b
  infinity 1918b
  lenses 1908a
  Newton 1759c
  prisms 1909a
  see also Light
Optometrists 382a
Opus (mus.) 176c
Oracle 1442a
Oradea, Romania 2366c
Oradea Mare, Romania 2366c
Oran, Algeria 2367a
Orange blossom 1979a
Orange Free State 2208b
Orange River 2208a, 2252a, 2338c
Orange, William of see William III, King (England)
Oranges 1682c–1683a
  Spain 2264a
  U.S. 2294a
Orangutan 48c, 1923c
Oratorio 161b, 176c
Orbegosa, Luís José 2237a
Orbital decay 1769b
Orbiter, Project see Project Orbiter
Orbits 1763b, 1779a, 1780a, 1795c
  aphelion 1778a
  apogee 1778a
  apsides 1793b
  artificial satellites 1769b, 1771a
  Kepler's laws 1781a
  parking orbit 1779b
  permanent orbit 1779b
  planets 1771a
Orcagna, Andrea tab 106, 121a, tab 125, 320b
Orchesography (bk.) 182a
Orchestra 176c
Orchid family 1683a
Ordeal of Richard Feveral (nov.) 1368a, 1411c
Order (bus.) 600a
Orders (plant) 1639a
Ordinal numbers 1508a
Ordinance of Laborers (England) 876a
Ordinance of 1787 see Northwest Ordinance
Ordinate (math.) 1602b

Ordos Desert 2124a, 2124b
Ordovician Period tab 456, 509a
Ore 509a
Ore Mountains 2338c
Ore treatment 1271a
Oreads (myth) 1442a
Oregon 1014b, 1992–1993
  admission to Union 2042c
  agriculture 1993a
  barberry 1651b
  boundary fixed 2040b
  capital punishment 860b
  census (1960) 1972
  climate 1992c
  colleges of 693–694
  commercial law tab 826
  congressional apportionment tab 853
  economy 1992c–1993a
  flag il 2010
  forests 896a
  geography 1992c
  government 1993a
  initiative and referendum 884c
  labor legislation 832c, 834a
  legal holidays 841–842
  oregon-grape 1683a
  people of 1992c
  pine trees 1686c
  pitcher plant 1687b
  public school enrollment tab 646
  public school expenditures tab 644
  recall 904b
  sequoia trees 1692b–1692c
  student enrollment tab 645
Oregon, University of 694
Oregon College of Education 694
Oregon-grape 1683a, 1992c
Oregon State University 694
Oregon Treaty (1846) 2115c, 2116c
O'Rell, Max see Blouet, Paul
Orem, Utah 1996a
Orestes 1442a
  Clytemnestra 1429b
  Iphigenia 1435c
Oreti River 2225c
Orfeo (opera) 161c, tab 1467
Orfeo ed Euridice (opera) 163b
Organ (mus.) 157c, 161a, 162a, 176c
Organ of Corti 937a
Organ point (mus.) 176c
Organic Act of Guam 2001b
Organic chemistry 1800c, 1818–1827
  growth of 1799b
Organic reactions 1822c
Organic rocks 449c
Organisms ecology 1860c
  evolution 1841b
  nature of first living 1841a
Organization of American States (OAS) 2138a, 2143b
  flag il 2184
Organs (anat.) 917a
Orient 2338c
  architecture 78a
  history 976–982
  literature outline tab 1464–1465
  music of 155a
  sculpture of 124b
Oriental Culture Region 769c–770c
Oriental rugs 1110b
Origen 320b
Origin of the Milky Way (paint.) tab 111
Origin of Species (bk.) 1348a, 1366c, 1411c
Original jurisdiction 792a
Origines (bk.) 1355b
Orinda see Philips, Katharine
Orinoco River 2132b, 2297a, 2338c
Oriole 48c
Orion (myth) 1442a
Orkhon River 2220b
Orkney Islands 1019c, 2282a, 2338c
Orlando (lit. char.) 1416a
Orlando, Vittorio Emanuele 1023a
Orlando, Florida 1979b
Orlando Furioso (poem) 1386c, tab 1466
Orlando Inamorato (story) 1386c
Orléans, Jean d' (1305–1408) tab 106
Orléans, Louis Philippe Albert d' see Paris, Count de
Orley, Bernard van tab 107
Orlich, Francisco 2136b
Orlon 1824c
Ormandy, Eugene 320b
Ormazd (Ahura Mazda) 1442a, 1627b

Ormolu 1097b
Ornamental notes (mus.) 176c
Ornithomimus il 27
Oro, John 1840c
Orogenesis 455a
Orogeny 509a
Orographic rain 509b
Orography 509b
Orontes River 2270c, 2338c
Orozco, José Clemente tab 108, 320c
Orozco, Pascual 2219b
Orpen, William tab 108
Orphans' Court (U.S.) 894c
Orpheus (myth) 1442a
  music 157a
Orphism 1628a
Orpine 1683a–1683b
Orpine family 1683b
Orr, James tab 802b
Orris root see ivy
Ortega y Gasset José 320c, 1392c
Orthoclase feldspar 453b, 497a
Ortuño, René Barrientos 2101a
Oruro, Bolivia 2100b
Orvieto, Italy sculpture 121a
Orwell, George 1371c
Osage Indians 1683b
Osage River 2018c
Osage-orange 1683b
Osaka, Japan 2198c, 2367a
Osborn, Henry Fairfield 320c
  Lucretius 1356b
  Our Plundered Planet 1348b
Osborne, John 320c
Oscan (lang.) 1335a
Oscar I, King (Sweden) 2269a
Oscar II, King (Sweden) 2269a
Oscar 1 (satellite) tab 1163
Oscar 2 (satellite) tab 1163
Oscar 3 (satellite) tab 1163
Osceola (Amer. Ind. chief) 320c
Oscilloscope 1249a
Oshogbo, Nigeria 2367a
Osier see Willow
Osiris 1442b, 1622b
Osler, Sir William 2082c
Oslo, Norway 2230a, 2230b, 2367a
Os Lusiadas (epic) 1388b
Osman, Aden Abdullah 2251b
Osmium 1835
  atomic weight tab 1805
Osmosis (plants) 1646b
Osmotic pressure 921c
Osorio, Oscar 2145c
Osprey 48c–49a
Ossa 1442b
Ossian 1364a
Ossification 917b
Ossoli, Marchioness see Fuller, Margaret
Ostade, Adrian van tab 107
Ostend Manifesto 2042a
Osteoarthritis 940b
Osteochondritis 945a
Osteomalacia 917c, 945a
Osteopathic physicians careers 382c
Osteoporosis 917c
Ostrava, Czechoslovakia 2367a
Ostrich 49a, il 11
Ostrovsky, Aleksandr 1390a
Oswald, Lee Harvey 321a, 2081c
Oswego tea 1683c
Otaru, Japan 2367a
Otello (opera) 167b
Otfried Gospel Book 1383a, tab 1465
Othello (play) 1411c
  Desdemona 1401a
Otho see Otto
Oti River 2163c
Otis, Elisha Graves 321a
Otis, James 321a, 1372c
Otolaryngology careers 382b
Otosclerosis 937b
Ottawa, Canada 2110a, il 2117, 2367b
Ottawa River 2020c
Ottawa University 669
Otter 49a
Otter Island 2019c
Otterbein College 692
Otto, King (Greece) 2166b, 2166c
Otto I, Emperor (Italy) 2195b
  King 2159b
  Holy Rom. emp. 321a, 984a
Otto II (Holy Rom. emp.) 321a

Otto III (Holy Rom. emp.) 321a
Otto, Nikolaus 1134b, 1169b
Otto cycle 1364b
Ottoman Empire tab 1045–1051, 1005c, 2088a, 2278c–2279a
  Battle of Lepanto 1013c–1014a
  in Lebanon 2207c–2208a
  rule of Bulgaria 2105c–2106a
Ottoman Turks 2278c–2279a
  capture Constantinople (1453) 1000a, 1001c
  Crusades 984b
  culture 982c
  in Cyprus 2138b
  in Egypt 2181a–2281b
  in Greece 2165c, 2166a
  in Hungary 2174c
  in Iraq 2190a
  in Libya 2210a–2210b
  in Muscat and Oman 2222c–2223a
  in Palestine 1017b
  in Qatar 2242c
  in South Yemen 2254a
  in Syria 2271b
  in Tunisia 2277b
  in Yemen 2302b–2302c
  in Yugoslavia 2304a–2304b
  World War I 995a
Otway, Thomas tab 1469
Ou River 2206a
Ouachita Baptist University 655
Ouachita Mountains 1976a, 1992b
Ouachita River 1976a
Ouagadougou, Upper Volta 2294a, 2367b
Oughtred, William 1236a, 1505a
Ouida 331c, 1462c
Oujda, Morocco 2367b
Ounce tab 1500
Our American Cousin (play) 2051a
Our Mutual Friend (nov.) 1367a
Our Plundered Planet (bk.) 1348b
Outcrop 509b
Outer Mongolia see Mongolia
Outer space 1779a
Outlier 509b
Outline of History (bk., Wells) 1370b, 1411c
Outlines (writing) 1319c
Outwash plain 449b, 509b
Ouwater, Aelbert van tab 106
Ovary (anat.) 926a
  menstrual cycle 926b
Overburden 509b
Overconvergence (vision) 1299b
Overhead (fin.) 600a
Overhead irrigation 740b
Overland Trail see Oregon Trail
Overmatter (print.) 153a
Overproduction 600a
Overrun (print.) 153a
Overtones 1918b
Overture (mus.) 176c, 178b
Ovid 1357b, tab 1464
  biography 321a
  metre 1344b
Oviedo, Spain 2264a
Ovule sac (flower) 1645c
Ovum 926c
Owen, Robert 321a
  socialism 908a
Owen Falls 2279c
Owen-Glass Act 879a
Owl 49a–49b
Owl and the Pussy Cat (poem) 414c
Owls, Order of (organ.) 1745b
Owyhee Dam 1206
Ox see Cattle
Oxalic acid 1817b
Oxalis 1683b–1683c
Oxbow 509b
Oxford, England 2367c
  Provisions of 2286a
Oxford Unversity
  Baskerville, John 144c
  Bodleian Library tab 1463
  representation in House of Commons 867c
  Press 146b
Oxidation (chem.) inorganic chemistry 1813a
Oxidation (geol.) zone of 520
Oxidation numbers 1813b
Oxidation-reduction reactions 1813a
Oxidizers 1779b
Oxygen 1808a, 1835
  atmosphere 468a

atomic weight *tab* 1805, 1806a
bacteria 1843b
boiling point *tab* 1902
chemical bonding 1809c
electrons 1807a
freshwater 1866c

ions 1809b
photosynthesis 1861b
plants 146b, 749c
respiration 922a
rockets 1766b
space travel 952c

sulfur 1821c
Oxysphere 509b
Oxytocin 925c
Oyashio 509b
Oyster plant *see* Salsify
Oysters 49b–49c, 2097a

Ozark Mountains 1987a
Ozark Plateau 1976a, 1992b
Ozarks 2019a
Ozone 468c, 763a–763b
Ozonosphere 763a–763b

P

P wave 511c
Paca, William *tab* 803
Pacassi, Nicolas 2095
Pace College 686
Pacheco Areco, Jorge 2296a
Pacific, University of the 657
Pacific cable 2062b
Pacific Cable Treaty 2069a
Pacific Culture Region 770c
Pacific Lutheran University 706
Pacific Ocean 2338c–2339a
    auk, 14c
    by-the-wind sailor 18c
    clam 22a
    cone shell 22c
    cowrie 22c
    crab 23c
    eagle 26b
    exploratory period 2023b
    frigate bird 34c
    loon 43c
    Marianas Trench 462b
    nautilus 47b–47c
    petrel 50c
    salmon 55a–55b
    sea horses 56c
    seals 56c
    smelt 59a
    sturgeon 60c
    swordfish 61c–62a
    tooth shells 63c
    tuna 64b
    whales 66c–67a
Pacific Union College 657
Pacific University 694
Pacifism 894c
Pack animals 1934b
Pack ice 509b
Pacuvius, Marcus 1354a, 1355b
Padang, Indonesia 2367c
Paderewski, Ignace Jan 321b, *tab* 172b
Paekche Kingdom 2204a, 2204b
Paeonius 116c
Paéz, José Antonio 2298a
Pagan, Burma 2107b
Paganini, Nicolò 166b, *tab* 171c
    biography 321b
Page, Thomas Nelson 1375a, *tab* 1478
    biography 321b
Paget's disease 945a
Pagliacci, I (opera) 167c
Pagnol, Marcel 321b
Pago Pago, Samoa 2000a, 2367c
Pago Pago, Tahiti 2301c
Pago Pago Bay 2000
Pahang River 2213b
Pahoehoe 509b
Pailleron, Edouard *tab* 1477
Pain 937c
Paine College 662
Paine, John K. 170a
Paine, Robert T. Declaration of Independence *tab* 803
Paine, Thomas 321b, 1167b, 1372c, *tab* 1470
    Common Sense 1348a
Painted Desert (Arizona) 1975
Painter, William 1416a
Painting 71a, 82–113
    Barbizon School 94a
    frames 1111c
    great painters *tab* 106–109
    Impressionism 94b, 1406c
    interior decoration 1111a
    leading galleries *tab* 109–113
    twentieth century 94c
Paints 1216a
    calcimine 1199a
    casein 727a
    colors 1907c
    lacquers 1213b

Paisiello, Giovanni 171c
Pakistan 981a, 2185c, 2232–2233
    agriculture 2232b–2232c
    CENTO 1000b
    climate 2232a
    Commonwealth status 1000c
    economy 2232b–2232c
    flag *il* 2184
    geography 2232a–2232b
    government 2232c
    history 2232c–2233c
    hyena 40a
    India and 2177a, 2185c–2186a, 2232c, 2233c
    industry 2232b
    manufacturing 2232c
    map 2233, *Atlas*-28–29
    people of 2232b
    religion 2232a, 2232b, 2232c
    SEATO 1021a
    trade 2232c
Pakistan Industrial Development Corporation 2232c
Palacio Valdés, Armando 1392b, *tab* 1478
Paladins 1442b
Palatal consonants 1294c
Palazzechi, Aldo 1388a
Pales (myth) 1442b
Palembang, Indonesia 2367b–2367c
Paleobotany 1638a, 1923b
Paleocene epoch *tab* 457, 458a, 509c
Paleogeography 509c
Paleolithic Age 967b, 971a, 972a, 1927c, 1928a
    art 71b, 82b
    mathematics 1501a
Paleontology 447a, 458, 509c, 1923b
Paleozoic Era *tab* 456, 458a, 509c
Palermo, Italy 2367c
Pales (myth) *see* Panamá
Palestine 1017a–1017c, 2192c–2193c, 1454c, 1458c
    archeology 970a
    Balfour Declaration 1017b
    British mandate 1017b, 1017c
    Ottoman Turks occupation of 1017b
    partitioned (1947) 1017b, 1017c
    religious shrines 1017
    Sennacherib 1459c
    see also Israel, Jordan
Palestrina, Giovanni da 160a, *tab* 171b
    biography 321c
Paley, William *tab* 1470
Palgrave, Sir Francis 321c
Pali (lang.) 1334a
Palisade 509c
Palisades Dam *tab* 1206
Palisades Interstate Park 895b
Palissy, Bernard 127b
Palissy, France
    pottery *tab* 130
Palladio, Andrea 76c, 1196b
Palladium (chem.) 1835
    atomic weight *tab* 1805
Palladium (myth) 1442b
Pallas (myth) 1442b
Pallavas 2180a
Pallavas Kingdom 2180a
Palm family 1683c–1684a
Palma, Jacopo (Palma Vecchio) *tab* 107
    biography 321c
Palmeirim de Inglaterra (nov.) 1388b
Palmer, A. Mitchell *tab* 796
Palmer, Erastus *tab* 125
Palmer, John McCauley
    presidential candidate *tab* 801
Palmerston, 3rd Viscount (Henry John Temple) 321c
Palmetto *see* Palm family
Palmgren, Selim *tab* 172b
Palmyra Island 2001
Palo Alto, Battle of (Mexican War) 2039c

Paloverde 1684a, 1975b
Paludal 509c
Palustrine 509c
Pamela (nov.) 1363c, 1412a
Pamir Mountains 2339a
Pampa 509c
Pampas 2339a
    Argentina 2089a
    grass 1683a
Pampero 509c
Pamphlets binding 87c
Pan (myth) 1432a, 1442b
    music 157a
Panama 2133a, 2133b, 2136a, 2234
    agriculture 2234b
    climate 2234a
    dog 25c
    economy 2234a–2234b
    flag *il* 2184
    gar 35b
    geography 2234a
    government 2234b
    history 2234b–2234c
    independence 2234c
    Indians 2234a, 2234c
    map 2234, *Atlas*-52
    marmoset 44c
    people of 2234a
    religion 2234a
    trade 2234b
    U.S. relations 2061b
    World War II 2234c
Panamá (Panama City), Panama 2234b, 2367c
Panama Canal 2001, 2097c, 2234a, 2234c
    U.S. history 2061b
Panama Canal Zone 521a, 2001–2002, 2234a, 2234b, 2234c, *see also* Canal Zone
Panama City *see* Panamá
Panama Congress of 1826 1017c
Panama Declaration 880c
Panama, Isthmus of 2339a
Pan American College 702
Pan American Conferences
    Bogota (1948) 1000b, 1017c, 2058a
    Buenos Aires (1910) 1017c
    first 1017c, 2058a
    Havanna (1928), 1017c
    Lima (1938) 1017c
    Mexico City (1901) 1017c
    Montevideo (1933) 1017c
    Rio de Janeiro (1906, 1943) 1017c
    Santiago (1923) 1017c
Pan-American Sanitary Bureau 960c
Pan-American Union 1017c
Panathenaea 1351a
Panay (Philippine Islands) 2237c, 2238a
Panchayat (legislative assembly) 2224a
Panchen Lama 979b
Pancreas 920c, 926a
    diabetes mellitus 941b
Pandarus 1442b
Pandit, Madame Vijaya Lakshmi 321c
Pandora 1442b
Pandya Kingdom 2179c
Pandyas 2180a
Panhandle 1992b
Panhandle Agricultural and Mechanical College 693
Panicale, Masolino da *see* Masolino da Panicale
Panic 600a
    (1837) 2038a
    (1873) 2054a
    (1893) 2058c
    (1907) 2062b
    (1929 Stock-Market Crash) 2071c–2072a
Panini *tab* 1464
Panjim, India 2367c
Panmunjom, Korea, armistice 2078b
Pannartz, Arnold 143c
Pannonia 2174b
Panpipe 157b

Pan-Slav Congress 2161a
Pansy *see* Violet
Pansy (pseud.) *see* Alden, Isabella Macdonald
Pantagruel 1378b
Pantheism 1613b, 1622b
Panther *see* Cat
Pantothenic acid *tab* 919
Panzini, Alfredo 1388a
Paolo, Giovanni da *tab* 106
    Life of St. John the Baptist *tab* 110
Papain 734c
Papal States 2195b, 2195c
Papandreou, Andreas 2167c
Papandreou, George 2167b, 2167c
Papaw 1684a
Papaya *il* 1661, 1684a–1684b
    Western Samoa 2301c
Papeete, Tahiti 2312c, 2367c
Papen, Franz von *tab* 1481
Paper 1272a
    business definition 600b
    etching 137c
    manufacture 148a, 1272b
    papyrus 142a
Paperhanger careers 376b
Paper mulberry 1684b
Papilla 918b
Papillary layer 918a
Papini, Giovanni 321c, 1388a
Paprika *see* Pepper, red
Papua 2319
Papuan languages 1337c
Papyrus 142a, 1272a, 1684b
    manuscripts 83a
Papyrus Ebers (bk.) *tab* 1463
Parables 1315a
Parabola 1593a
    conic section 1602c
Parabolic dune 509c
Paraboloid 1605c
Paracelsus, Philippus 1127a, 1798b
    biography 321c
Paradies und die Peri (oratorio) 166a
Paradise Lost (poem) 1344c, 1362b, 1412a
    Abdiel 1422b
    Beelzebub 1426c
    Belial 1426c
Paradise Regained (poem) 1362b, 1412b
Paradoxes Zeno 1502b
Paragraph 1318a
Paraguay 2090b, 2101a, 2104a, 2235–2236
    agriculture 2235b
    climate 2235a
    dog 25c
    economy 2235a–2235b
    flag *il* 2184
    geography 2235a
    government 2235b
    history 2235b–2236a
    independence 2235c
    Indians 2235a, 2235c
    industry 2235b
    League of Nations 1012c
    map 2235, *Atlas*-45
    osprey 48c–49a
    peccary 50a
    people of 2235a
    religion 2235a
    tapir 62b
    trade 2235b
    War of the Triple Alliance 2235c
    war with Bolivia 2236a
Paraguay River 2235a, 2235b, 2339a
Parallax 1788b, 1796a
Parallel circuit 1917a
Parallel Lives *see* Plutarch's Lives
Parallelism (math.) 1566a, 1576a
    Euclid 1505c
Parallel motion (mus.) 177a

Parallelogram method (phys.) 1874a
Parallelograms 1567c, 1605c
Paramaribo, Surinam 2323b, 2367c
Paramecium 1848a
Parameter 1605c
Parametric equations 1593b
Paramo 509c
Paraná Plateau 2235a
Paraná River 2089a, 2235a, 2235b, 2339a
Paranoia 1953c
Paraphrase (mus.) 177a
Parapsychology 1947a, 1952a
Parasympathetic nervous system 938a
Parasympathetic pathways 924a
Parathyroid glands 925c
Paratyphoid fever 956c
Parcae (myth) 1432a, 1440b, 1442b
Parcel post establishment 2062c
Parchment 142a
Pardo Bazán, Emilia 1392b
Pardo, Manuel 2237a
Pardon (law) 894c
Pardons, Board of 857c
Paré, Ambroise 322a
Parenchyma cells (anat.) 921a
Parenchyma tissue (plants) 1643c
Parent, Etienne 1391b
Parentheses 1314a
Paresis 1953c
Pareto, Vilfredo 538c
Paria, Gulf of 2339a
Parian ware 1929c
Paride ed Elena (opera) 163b
Parini, Giuseppe 1387a, tab 1470
Paris, Comte de 322a
Paris (myth) 1442c
  Helen of Troy 1434a
  Oenone 1441a
Paris, France 2148a, 2148b, 2367c
  commune 868a
  industrial district 2149a
  St. Bartholomew's Day massacre 997c, 1010c
—Landmarks
  National Library tab 1463
  Arc de Triomphe il 2153
  Eiffel tower il 2148
Paris, Convention of (1858) 2244c
Paris, Peace of (1763) 2290c
Paris Peace Conference (1919) 2068a
Paris, Treaty of 2217a
  (1229) 994b
  (1763) 2027a, 2114c
  (1783) 2115a, 2290c
  (1814) 2322b
  (1878) Universal Postal System 900a
  (1898) 2060a, 2238b
Paris, University of 613c
Parish schools 614c
Parity 600b
Park, Chung Hee 2205b
Park College 680
Parker, Alton B. 2062a
  presidential candidate tab 801
Parker, Dorothy 322a, 1376a
Parker, Gilbert tab 1479
Parker, Horatio W. 170a
Parker, Theodore tab 1475
Parkes process 1213c
Parkhurst, Helen 618c
Parking orbits 1777b, 1779b
Parkinson, James 322a
Parkinson's disease 945a
  liquid nitrogen 1903a
Parkman, Francis 322a, tab 1476
Parks 775a, 895a
  conservation 777c
Parks, National see National parks
Parlement of Foules (poem) 1359c, 1360a
Parley, Peter see Goodrich, Samuel G.
Parliament 896b
Parliament (Eng.) devolution 873c
  dissolution 874c
  House of Commons 867b
  House of Lords 890c
  subsidy 909b
Parliamentary law 842-848
  abuses 848c
  conduct of business 843a
  debate 844b
  model constitution and by-laws 848a
  motions 844a, 845b
  nominations 842c

officers 843a
order of business 844a
resolutions 844a
voting 845a
Parlors 1106c
Parmenides 322b, 1751b
  philosophy 1613b
Parmesan cheese tab 731b
Parnassians (lit.) 1381c
  influence in Latin America 1393b
Parnassus, Mt.
  mythology 1442c
  poetry 1381c
Parnell, Charles Stewart 322b, 2191c
Parochial schools 625b
Parody 1412b
Parole 896c
Paropamisus Mountains 2339a
Parotid glands 920b
Parr, Catherine 2288a
Parrington, Vernon L. 1377a
Parrot 49c
Parrot fever tab 947
Parry, Charles Hubert tab 172a
Parry, William Edward 322b
Parsecs 1786a, 1788b, 1796a
Parsifal (opera) 167a, 1442c
  Kundry 1437c
Parsimony, Law of 1620c
Parsing 1309b
Parsis 980c, 1627c
Parsley 1684c
Parsnip 1684c
Parsons, William Barclay 322b
Part (mus.) 177a
Part song (mus.) 177a
Parthenon 75a, 373b
  archeology 970c
  sculpture 116c
Parthians 969c
Participation in Adult Education (study) 635a
Participles 1306a, 1307c
Particle accelerators 1889c, 1919b
Partita 177a
Partnerships 822c, 823b
  dissolution 823b
  rights and duties 823a
Partridge 49c
Parts of speech 1304a
  adjectives 1305b
  adverbs 1308b
  conjunctions 1308c
  diagrams of 1309c
  interjections 1308c
  nouns 1304a
  prepositions 1308b
  pronouns 1304c
  verbs 1305b
Party government 896c
  see also Political parties
Party of the Hutu Emancipation Movement 2245c, 2246a
Par value 600b
Parzival (story) 1383b, tab 1465
Pasadena, California schools 627b
Pasadena College 657
Pascal, Blaise 1379a, tab 1468, 1505a
  adding machine 1236a, 1243a
  biography 322b
  theorem 1605c
  triangle 1606a
Pascoli, Giovanni 1387c
Pasque-flower see Anemone
Pass 509c
Passacaglia (mus.) 162a
Passage (mus.) 177a
Passaic, New Jersey 1989c
Passamaquoddy Bay 777b
Passionate Friends, The (nov.) 1370a
Passion-flower 1684c
Passover 1629c
Pasternak, Boris 322c, 1390b, tab 1481
Pasteur, Louis 322c, 1381c, 1762a
  bacteria 1844a
  spontaneous generation 1839b
Pasteurization 1844c
  public health 956b
Pastorale (mus.) 177a
Pastoral poetry 1345a
Pastoral Symphony (paint.) tab 112
Pastorelle (mus.) 159b
Pastor fido (drama) 1387a
Patagonia 2339a
  black widow 17a
Pataliputra, India 2179b, 2179c

Patan, Nepal 2223c
Patanjali 322c
Patapsco River 2005b
Pâte tendre (porcelain) 127a
Patent 897a
Patent Office 897a
Pater, Jean Baptiste tab 107
Pater, Walter 322c, 1366c, tab 1477
Pater noster lakes 509c
Paterson, William Supreme Court tab 802a
  U.S. Constitution 809c
Paterson, New Jersey 1989c
Paterson State College 683
Pathet Lao 2207a
Pathology 1638a
Patiner, Joachim de tab 107
Patmos (island) 1458c
Patna, India 2179c, 2367c
Paton, Alan tab 1481
Patrick, Saint 322c, 2191a
Patriots' Day 841c
Patroclus 1422c
Patronage-dividend plan 589b
Patterne, Sir Willoughby (lit. char.) 1412b
Patterson, Robert (Amer. general) 2045b
Patterson, Robert Porter tab 796
Patton, George S., Jr. 322c
Pauker, Ana 322c
Paul, Lewis 1281c
Paul, Saint see Paul of Tarsus, Saint
Paul, Prince (Yugoslavia) 2304b
Paul III, Pope 323a, 2246b
Paul VI, Pope 323a
Paul I, King (Greece) 323a, 2167b
Paul I, Czar (Russia) 323a
Paul of Tarsus, Saint 1458c, 1630c, 1631a,
  Menander 1353a
Paul and Virginia (nov.) 1380b, 1412b, tab 1470
Paulding, James Kirke tab 795, tab 1472
Pauling, Linus 323b, 1800a, 1856c
Paulo Afonso Falls 2339a
Paul Revere House 78b
Paulus, Lucius Aemilius 1000a
Pauper schools 616b
Pausanias 116b, 323b
Pause (mus.) 177a
Pavane 182a
Pavlov, Ivan P. 323b, 1949b
Pavlova, Anna 184a, 323b
Pawtucket, Rhode Island 1994a, 2013b-2013c
Pax (myth) 1443a
Payload rocket 1779b
Payne, Henry C. tab 796
Payne, John Barton tab 797
Payne, John Howard tab 1473
Payne-Aldrich Tariff Act 2062b
Paz Estenssoro, Victor 2101a
Pazzi Chapel 77b
Pchelka (dog) 951b
Pea 1684c-1685a
Pea family 1685a
Peabody, Elizabeth Palmer 323b
Peabody, George 323b
Peace Corps 2080b
Peacemaker, The (nickname) see Clay, Henry
Peach 1685a
  West Virginia 1998c
Peach blossom 1978a
Peafowl 50a
Peak 509c
Peale, Charles Wilson tab 107
Peale Island 2004c
Peale, Norman Vincent 323b
Peano, Giuseppe 1507b
Peanuts 740a, 1685a
  Alabama 2174b
  Chad 2120c
  farms 381b
  Gambia 2156a-2156b
  Georgia 1979c
  Guinea 2170a
  Indonesia 2187a
  Libya 2210a
  Mali 2215a
  Niger 2228c
  Nigeria 2229b
  North Carolina 1991b
  Oklahoma 1992b
  Portuguese Guinea 2320a
  Senegal 2248a
  Sudan 2266a

  Thailand 2273c
  Upper Volta 2294c
  Vietnam 2299b
  Virginia 1997c
  Zambia 2305b
Pear 1685a
Pearl of the Antilles see Cuba
Pearl Harbor, Hawaii 1980a, 2076b
  Japanese attack on 1028b, 2201b
Pearl of the Orient see Ceylon
Pearl River 2008b, 2128b, 2316b, 2328c
Pearls Qatar 2242b
  Trucial Oman 2276b
Pearson, Lester 323b, 2118b, 2118c
Peary, Robert E. 323c
Peas see Pea
Peasants' Revolt (England) 2287a
Pease porridge hot (nursery rhyme) 408b
Peat 509c, 751b, 1136c, 1201c
Pebble tools 1927c
Pebbles 509c
Pecan 1995b
  see also Hickory
Peccary 50a
Peck (meas.) tab 1500
Peckham, Rufus W. tab 802a
Pecos Bill 1443a
Pécs, Hungary 2174a, 2368a
Pedal (mus.) 177a
Pedal keys (mus.) 177a
Pedal point (mus.) see Organ point
Pedalfer 509c
Pederson, Christian tab 1466
Pediatrics careers 382b
Pediment 509c
Pedocal 509c
Pedology 510a
Pedrell, Felipe tab 172c
Pedro I, Emperor (Brazil) 323c, 2104a
  abdication 849a
Pedro II, Emperor (Brazil) 323c, 2104a-2104b
Peel, Sir Robert 323c
Peeping Tom (leg.) 1433b
Peepul see Fig
Peer Gynt (play) 1412b
  Grieg, E. 168b
Pegasus 1443b
Peggotty (lit. char.) 1396c
Pegmatite 510a
Péguy, Charles 1382c
Peg Woffington (nov.) 1367c
Peiping, China see Peking, China
Peirce, Charles Sanders 1619a
Peisistratus 1350c
  Aesop 1394a
Pekin ducks 731c
Peking, China 524a, 2123a, 2123b, 2127c, 2128a, 2129a, 2368a
  anthropology 1924a
Peking Gazette (news.) 978a
Peking man 1924b, 2126a
Pelagic 510a
Pelagic life 1865c
Pelargonium see Geranium
Peleus 1443b
Pelias 1443b
Pelican 50a-50b
  brown 1983c
Pelion 1443c
Pellagra 945a
Pelle's New Suit (story) 439
Pellico, Silvio 1387b, tab 1473
Peloponnesian War 963a, 1021c, tab 1071
Peloponnesos, Greece 2165a, 2339a
Pelops 1443c
Peltier, Jean C. A. 1146b
Peltier effect 1146b
Pelvis 917c
Pembroke College 698
Pembroke State College 689
Pathfinder, The (nickname) see Frémont, John C.
Pathfinder, The (nov.) 1409a
Pathological fracture 917c
Pathology careers 382b
Pen names
  dictionary of 1461-1463
Penalty (law) 897b
Penang, Malaysia 2213c
Penang Island 2213b

Penates (myth) 1443c, 1628b
Pendennis (nov.) 1367b, 1412b
Pendentives (arch.) 76a
Pendleton, George Hunt tab 801
Pendulums 1162a
Penelope (myth.) 1443c
Peneplain 448a, 510a
P'enghu Islands 2339b
Penguin il 28, 50b
Penicillin 1824c, 1847b
  discovery 251c
  Fleming, Alexander 1845c
Penis 926b
Penmanship see Handwriting
Penn, John tab 803
Penn, William 323c, 1016a, 2012c
  Delaware 2024c
  Pennsylvania 2025c
Penner Rivers 2339b
Pennine Mountains 2282a
Pennington, William House of
  Representatives tab 802b
Pennsylvania 1993
  agriculture 1993c
  apprenticeship 829b
  capital punishment 860b
  census (1960) 1973
  child labor laws 831c
  climate 1993b
  colleges of 694–698
  colonial history 2025c
  commercial law tab 826
  commonwealth 867c
  congressional apportionment
    tab 853
  Constitution (U.S.) 809c
  Dutchman's pipe vine 1665c
  economy 1993b–1993c
  electoral votes 876c
  flag il 2010
  geography 1993a–1993b
  government 1993c
  holidays 841–842
  labor legislation 832b, 833b
  Mason and Dixon Boundary
    Line 1016a
  mountain-laurel shrub 1680b
  people of 1993b
  pottery 128c
  public school enrollment tab
    646
  public school expenditures tab
    644
  student enrollment tab 645
  Whisky Insurrection 1024a–
    1024b
Pennsylvania, University of 697
Pennsylvania Farmer see Dickinson, John
Pennsylvania Magazine, The 1167b
Pennsylvania State House
  sculpture 124a
Pennsylvania State University 697
Pennsylvanian Period tab 456, 510a
Pennyroyal, see Mint
Pennyweight tab 1500
Penobscot Bay 1984
Penrod (nov.) 1412b
Pensacola, Florida 1979b
Pensées (bk.) 1379a
Pensions 897b
  Cleveland, Grover 2057a
  military 897b
  old-age 897c
Penta prisms 1909b
Pentagon (math.) 1606b
Pentahedron 1606a
Pentameter 1412b
Pentateuch 1458c
Pentatonic scale 154b, 155b, 177a
Pentaur (poem) tab 1463
Pentodes 1889a
Penumbra 1794a, 1797a
Peony 1685b, 1981c
People's Charter (Great Britain)
  863b, 1000b–1000c
People's Democratic Party (Sudan) 2266c
People's Liberation Army (Laos) 2207a
People's National Congress (PNC) (Guyana) 2171a
People's National Party (Jamaica) 2198b
People's Party (Austria) 2096b
People's Party (U.S.) see Populist Party
People's Progressive Party (PPP) (Guyana) 2171a, 2171b
Peoples' Socialist Community (Cambodia) 2109b
Peoria, Illinois 1981b
Pepin the Short (Pepin III), King 983b, 1000b, 2150a, 2195a

Pepper 744a, 1685b–1685c
Pepper, red 1685c–1686a
Pepper family 1685c
Pepperdine College 657
Peppergrass 1685c
Pepperidge see Tupelo
Peppermint see Mint
Peppertree 1686a
Pepsin 920c
Peptides 920c, 1841a
Pepusch, John tab 171c
Pepys, Samuel 323c
  diary 1362c, 1412c, tab 1468
Pepys' Diary 1362c, 1412c, tab 1468
Peralta Azurdía, Enrique 2169b
Per cent 1530c
Perception 1948c
  sociology 1942c
Perceval (leg.) see Percivale
Perch 50b
Perched water table 510a
Percivale (Perceval) (leg.) 1443c
  Chrétien de Troyes 1377c
Percolation 510b
Percussion (mus.) 177a
Percussion instruments 154b, 159c,
  177a, 1896a
Percy, Sir Henry 323c
Percy, Thomas (Bishop Percy)
  1364a, tab 1470
Pereda, José María de 1392b, tab
  1477
Père Goriot, Le (nov.) 1412c
Peregrinacao (nov.) 1388c
Peregrine Pickle (nov.) 1363c
Pereira de Souza, Washington Luís
  2104c
Perelman, Sidney Joseph 324a
Perennial plants 1644c
Pérez de Ayala, Ramón 1392c
Pérez Galdós, Benito 1392b, tab
  1478
Pérez Jiménez, Marcos 2298b
Perfect numbers 1524b, 1606a
Perfect power (math) 1606a
Performing arts careers 373c
Pergamum 117b
  Altar of Zeus 117c
Pergolesi, Giovanni tab 171c, 324a
Peri, Jacopo 161c, tab 171b, 1443c
Periander 324c
Pericles 974b
  biography 324a
  on education 613b
Peridotite 510b
Perigee 1778b, 1796a
Perigon 1601b
Perihelion 1763b, 1778b, 1796a
Period (astronomy) 1781a, 1796a
Period (geology) 510b
Period (music) 177a
Period (punctuation) 1312a, 1318a
Periodic law 1807c
Periodic system (chem.) 1799c
Periodicals see Magazines
Periodocity (math) trigonometry
  1583c
Peripheral nervous system 938a
  neuritis 945a
Periquillo sarniento, El (nov.)
  1393a
Peristaltic waves 920c
Periwinkle 50b, 1686a
Perjury 897c, 914a
Perkins, Frances 324a, tab 797
Perkins, Lawrence 618a
Perm, U.S.S.R. 2368c
Permafrost 510b, 1863c
Permalloy tab 1193
Permanent Court of International
  Justice (World Court) 853c,
  914b, 992a, 2069b, 2070c
  established 1013c
Permanent International Court of
  Arbitration (Hague Tribunal)
  853c, 854a, 2061c, 2069b
Permeability 510b
Permian Period tab 456c, 510b
Permutations 1606a
Pernicious anemia 920b
Perón, Juan D. 2090c–2091a
  biography 324a
Perosi, Lorenzo 167c
Perpendiculars 1606a
  postulates 1576a
Perrault, Charles 1379c, tab 1468
  Bluebeard 1427b
  Mother Goose Tales 1411a
Perrin, Pierre tab 171c

Perronet, Jean 1196c
Perry, Edgar A. see Poe, Edgar
  Allan
Perry, Matthew Calbraith 324a,
  2200c
  Japan 2042b
Perry, Oliver Hazard 324b, 2034c
Perryville, Battle of 2049
Persephone 1444a
Persepolis (anc. city) 74b
  archeology 969a
  palace 116a
Perseus 1444a
  Andromeda 1424a
  Medusa 1439a
Perseus with Head of Medusa
  (sculp.) 122a
Pershing, John Joseph 324b, 995b
  AEF (American Expeditionary
    Forces) 2066a
  Mexico 2064b
  World War I 2065c, 2066b
Persia 816–817, 981c, tab 1030–1031
  archeology 969a
  architecture 74b, 79a
  Battle of Marathon 1015b–1015c
  Biblical 1458c
  kings tab 1079
  lion 20a
  literature outline tab 1463–1466
  pottery tab 130
  religion 1627b
  sculpture 114b, 115b
  Syria 969c
  see also Iran
Persian Empire 2189a–2189b
Persian Gulf 2222b, 2222c, 2339b
Persian language 1334a
Persian rugs 1110b, 1111a
Persian Wars tab 1071
Persimmon 1686a
Persius, Aulus 1357c
Person (gram.) 1304c
Persona grata 898a
Persona non grata 898a
Personal disposable income 600b
Personality 1950c
Personality disorders 1954a
Personality tests 1950c
Personal property 898a
  caveat emptor 860c
  chattels 863b
  mortgage 892a
  replevin 906a
  sale of 823b
Personification 1315a
Personnel 578–582
  career 377b
Persuasion (nov.) 1366a
Perth, Australia 2093, 2368a
Perturbations (astron.) 1779b,
  1796a
Peru 2100b–2101a, 2122a, 2144b,
  2144c, 2236–2237
  agriculture 2236b, 2236c
  alpaca 13b
  art 971c
  chimney swift 21b
  church 877b
  cinchona 1658a–1658b
  climate 2236b
  coca 1658c
  economy 2236b–2236c
  flag il 2184
  four-o'clocks 1667c
  geography 2236a–2236b
  government 2236c
  history 2236c–2237b
  independence 2237a–2237b
  Indians 2236b, 2236c, 2237a
  industry 2236c
  map 2236, Atlas-50–51
  osprey 48c–49a
  people of 2236b
  religion 2236a, 2236b
  slavery 2237a
  trade 2236c
  war with Chile 2122c
Peru State College 681
Perugino, Il tab 106, 324b
Peruzzi, Baldassare 76c, 324b
Pesach see Passover
Pescadores Islands 2123b, 2339b
Peshawar, Pakistan 2368a–2368b
Pessoa, Fernando 1388c
Pest control 723a, 1868c
Pestalozzi, Johann 324b
Pesticides 740a
  pollution 776b, 1868c
Pétain, Henri Philippe 324b, 2154c
Petals (flower) 1645c
Peter, Saint 1458c, 1630c
Peter, King (Serbia) 2304b
Peter I (Peter the Great), Tsar

(Russia) 324b, 2259a–2259b
Peter I, King (Yugoslavia) 2304b
Peter II, King (Yugoslavia) 324c,
  2304b, 2304c
Peter V, King (Portugal) 2242a
Peter the Hermit (Peter of
  Amiens) 324c, 1002a–1002b
Peter Ibbetson (novel) 1412c, tab
  1477
Peter Pan (play) 1369c, 1412c
Peter, Peter, pumpkin-eater (nursery rhyme) 410b
Peter Piper (nursery rhyme) 412a
Peter Rabbit (story) 433–434
Peters, Samuel 2025a
Petiole (plant) 1645a
Pétion, Alexandre 2172b
Petitcodiac River
  tidal bore 464b
Petit Jehan de Saintré, Le (nov.)
  1378a
Petit jury 886c
Petit mal 941c
Petition (gov.) 898a
Petition, Right of see Right of
  petition
Petofi, Sandor tab 1476
Petrarch, Francesco 324c, 986a,
  1344b, 1386a, tab 1466
Petrassi, Goffredo tab 172a
Petrel 50c
Petrie, William Matthew Flinders
  1296a
Petrified Forest (Arizona) 1975b
Petrochemicals 1216c
Petrograd see Leningrad, Soviet
  Union; St. Petersburg, Russia
Petrography 510b
Petroleum 460b
  Canada 2112a
  Colombia 2132c
  drilling 1217c
  energy consumption 1130a
  Germany 2158b
  industry 1217
  lubricants 1214b
  offshore 1217c
  refining 1273a
  rise of industry 524b
  U.S. 460b
  see also Oil
Petroleum coke 1136c
Petroleum engineering 1218a
Petroleum jelly 1227a
Petroleum waxes 1227a
Petrology 447a, 510b
Petronius tab 1464
Petrucci, Ottaviano 160b, tab 171b
Pe-tsai see Mustard
Petunia il 1662, 1686a
Pevsner, Anton 123c
Pewee 50c
Pewter tab 1193
Pfaal, Hans see Poe, Edgar Allan
Pfeiffer College 689
Pfister, Albrecht 143c
pH 510c
Phaedo (Phaedon) 324c
Phaedra 1444a
Phaedrus 1394a
Phaethon 1444a
Phagocytosis 922b
Phalarope 50c–51a
Phanariots 2244b–2244c
Phaneritic 510b
Phanerozoic eon 510c
Phantom Ship (nov.) 1432b
Phaon 1444b
Pharaoh (title) 1459a
Pharisees 1629c
Pharmaceutical industry 1273c
Pharmacists 382b
Pharmacologists 390c
Pharsalia 1357c, tab 1464
Pharynx 1294a, 1295a
Phase (matter) changes 1899b
Phase diagrams 1873a
Pheasant 51a, 741c
  ring-necked 1994b
Phèdre (play) 1379a
Phenocryst 510c
Phenolics tab 1219
Phenology 510c
Phenolthalein 1817c
Phenomenology 1620b
Phenotype 1850c
Pheochromocytoma 945a

Pherecrates 1353a
Phetchabun Mountains 2273b
Phidias 116c
  biography 324c
Philadelphia, Pennsylvania 1993b, 2012c–2013c
  British occupation of 1014c
  Fairmount Park 895c
  founding 2025c
  library tab 1463
  rapid transit 1165b
  Revolutionary War 1014c
Philadelphia Bulletin tab 1171
Philadelphia Centennial Exposition 2055a
Philadelphia Enquirer tab 1171
Philadelphia and Lancaster Turn-pike Road 1180a
Philadelphia Society for Promoting Agriculture 719c
Philadelphus, King (Egypt) see Ptolemy II
Philander Smith College 655
Philemon 1426c
  epistle to 1459a
Philharmonic Hall (N.Y.) acoustics 1895b
Philip (apostle) 1459a
Philip, King (American Indian) 325a
Philip II (Philip Augustus), King (France) 325a, 984c, 2150c, 2286c
Philip IV (Philip the Fair), King (France) 984c, 2150c
Philip VI, King (France) 2150c, 2151b
Philip II, King (Macedonia) 325a, 1015a–1015b
  Philippics 1353c
Philip II, King (Spain) 325a, 2098c, 2211b, 2225b, 2242a, 2264c–2265a, 2288a, 2288b
  Invincible Armada 995c–996a
  tomb 77c
Philip IV, King (Spain)
  portrait (Velásquez) tab 111, 112
Philip V, King (Spain) 325a, 1392b, 1021a–1021b, 2152b, 2265a
Philip Augustus see Philip II, King (France)
Philip the Good of Burgundy 2211b
Philippics (speeches) 1353c
Philippine Islands see Philippines
Philippines 2214b, 2237–2238
  abacá 1648a
  agriculture 2237c
  climate 2237c
  cobra 22b
  economy 2237c–2238a
  eagle 26b
  falcon 33b
  flag il 2184
  flying lemur 34b
  geography 2237c
  government 794c, 2063b, 2238a
  history 2060b, 2238a–2238c
  independence 2238c
  kapok 1674b
  map Atlas-30–31
  oranges 1683a
  people of 2237c
  porcupine 52b–52c
  religion 2237b, 2238a
  sea cows 55b
  SEATO 1021a
  Spanish-American War 2060a
  trogons 64a–64b
  World War II 1028c, 2238b
Philippopolis see Plovdiv
Philips, Katharine 1462c
Philistines 1017a, 1459a
Phillip, Arthur 2092c
Phillips, John poetic style 1394c
Phillips, Stephen tab 1479
Phillips University 693
Phillips, Wendell 325a
Philo of Alexandria 1615b
Philo (Philo Judaeus) 325a
Philoctetes Paris 1442c
Philosopher's stone 1798
Philosophical Transactions 1167b
Philosophy 1611–1620
  bibliography 1620c
  German 1384–1385
  glossary 1620
  Greek 1353c
  history 963c, 965c, 1612b
  literary works 1348c
Phipps, William 2026c
Phlegethon 1444b
  Hades 1433c
Phloem (plants) 1643c

Phlogiston theory 1798c
Phlox il 1663, 1686a–1686b
Phnom Penh, Cambodia 2108b, 2368b
Phocion 325a
Phocylides 1351b
Phoebe 51a 290b
  see also Artemis
Phoebus Apollo see Apollo
Phoenicia 1000b, 1017c–1018b
  alphabet 972b, 1018a, tab 1294
  Assyrian conquest 1018c
  cedar trees 1018b
  civilization 973a
  glass tab 135
  maritime power 1018a
  textile industry 1018a
Phoenix (myth) 1444b
Phoenix, John see Derby, George Horatio
Phoenix, Arizona 1975b, 2013a
Phoenix Island 2000c
Phonetics 1293c
Phonograms 1296a
Phonographs 1171b
  records 1181b
Phonolaryngoscope 1293c
Phorminx 157b
Phormio (play) 1355b
Phorogenesis 510c
Phosphates 510c
  Christmas Island 2310b
  fertilizers 733a, tab 752, tab 753
  French Polynesia 2313a
  Gilbert and Ellice Islands 2314a
  Jordan 2201c
  Morocco 2221c
  Nauru 2223a, 2223b
  Senegal 2248a
  Spanish Sahara 2323a
  Togo 2275a
  Tunisia 2277a
  U.S. 1967b, 2293c
Phosphocreatine 927c
Phosphorescence 1906b, 1918a
Phosphoric acid 1817b
Phosphorus 450b, 1821a, 1835
  alloys 1193a
  atomic weight tab 1805
  body requirement 919c
  electrovalence 1809a
  fertilizers 733a, 753b
  plants 1646b
  soil 743b, 752a
Phospines 1821a
Photocells 1883b
  photoconductive 1890c
  photodiode 1890c
  semiconductors 1890c
Photochemistry 1800c
Photocomposition 1174b
Photoelectric cells 1274a, 1883b
Photoelectric devices 1274a
Photoelectric effect 1886c
  discovered 1761a
Photoengraving 148b, 149a, 153a
  color 149a
Photographic copying process 1164c
Photography 1171c
  archeology 967c
  careers 375b
  cinematography 1161a, 1595a
  color 1172b
  half-tone 148c
  telescopes 1792a
  xograph 1188b
Photogravure 86c, 153a
Photometers 1792c
Photometric units 1906c
Photons 1804b, 1904a, 1919c
Photoperiodism plants 1647b
Photosphere 1796b
Photosynthesis 461a, 749c, 1646b–1646c, 1825b, 1841c, 1861a
  bacteria 1843b
  marine environment 1865c
Phototropism plants 1647a
Photovoltaic cells 1274c, 1883c, 1890c
Phrase (gram.) 1309a
Phrase (music) 155b, 177a
Phreatic 511a
Phrixos 1424c, 1433b
Phrygian (lang.) 1334a
Phrygian (music) 177a
Phrynichus 1353a
Phyfe, Duncan 325b, 1101a
Phyllite 511a
Phylogenetic psychology 1951a
Physical anthropology 1923–1927
Physical chemistry 1800c, 1828
Physical education
  kindergarten 407b

recreation 1703–1740
Physical geography 757–766
  atmosphere 762–765
  biosphere 765–766
  earth 757–759
  hydrosphere 765
  lithosphere 759–762
Physical Geography of the Sea, The (bk.) 461c
Physical geology 447–451
Physical oceanography 461a, 464a
Physical sciences careers 390a
Physical therapy careers 383b
Physicians careers 382b
  U.S. statistics 960b
Physics 1869–1920
  bibliography 1920c
  careers 390a
  cryogenics 1902c
  electricity 1881–1890
  electronics 1886c
  glossary 1916–1920
  heat 1897b
  Hellenistic period 1753b
  history 1759c
  lasers 1910–1911
  light 1903b
  magnetism 1881–1890
  masers 1909–1910
  matter, properties of 1870–1873
  mechanics 1873–1880
  Newton, Isaac 1758c
  nuclear 1911–1916
  role of 1870b
  scope of 1869c
  semiconductors 1890–1893
  sound 1893–1897
Physiography 511a
Physiological psychology 1950c
  careers 383b
Physiology 917–945, 1637c
  bibliography 948
  hearing 1894a
Phytoplankton 461b, 465b, 1866a
Pi (math.) 1606b
  printing 153a
Piano 177a
Piast dynasty 2239c–2240a
Piatigorsky, Gregor 325b
Pica (print.) 153a
Picacho 511a
Picard, Henri 1282c
Picaresque novel 1391b
Picasso, Pablo 86c, 103b, tab 108
  biography 324b
  Portrait of Madame Z il 102
Piccard, Auguste 325b
Piccini, Niccolò 162c, tab 171c
Piccirilli, Attilio tab 125
Piccirilli, Furio tab 125
Piccolo 177b
Piccolpasso 127a
Pickerel il 1717
Pickering, Edward Charles 325b
Pickering, Timothy 325c, tab 795
Picketing 600b
Pickett, George Edward 325c, 2048c
Pickford, Mary 325c
Picktall, Marjorie 1390a
Pickwick Papers (nov.) 1366c, 1412c
  Sam Weller 1421a
Pico della Mirandola 325c
Pictographs 142a
  Chinese 977b
Picts 1019c, 2284a
Pictures of the Gone World (poems) 1376b
Pie plant 1690a
Pieck, Wilhelm 2163b
Pied Piper of Hamelin (leg.) 1444b
Piedmont 511a
Piedmont Plateau 1991a
Pierce, Charles Saunders 623c
Pierce, Franklin 325c, tab 798–799
  administration 2041b–2042b
  administration, events pareling tab 1064
  Cabinet tab 796–797
  election and inauguration tab 800
Pierné, Gabriel tab 172a
Pierre, South Dakota 1994b, 2018c, 2013a
Pierrepont, Edwards tab 796
Piers Plowman (poem) 1360a, 1413a, tab 1466
Pietà (sculp., Michelangelo) 122a
Pietermaritzburg, South Africa 2368b
Piezoelectric crystals 1897a
Piezoelectricity 1919b
Piezometric surface 511a

Pig see Swine
Pig iron 1212b
  coke 1203c
Pigalle, Jean Baptiste 122c, tab 125
Pigeons 51b, 742a
Pigments 1907c
Pignut see Hickory
Pika see Cony (zool.)
Pike (fish) 51b, il 1717
Pike, James Albert 326a
Pike, Zebulon Montgomery 326a
Pikeville College 670
Pilate, Pontius 326a, 1459a
Pilgrim geese 739a
Pilgrims 1018b–1019a, 2024b
Pilgrim's Progress (allegory) 1362c, 1394b, 1413a, tab 1468
  Vanity Fair 1420a
Pillars of Hercules 1434c
Pillow lavas 511a
Pilon, Germain 122b, tab 125
Pilot Knob, Battle of 2049
Pilsen, Czechoslovakia see Plzen
Pilsudski, Józef 2240b
Pimiento see Pepper, red
Pimpernel 1686b–1686c
Pinafore (operetta) 1369b
Pinchot, Gifford 775c
  Ballinger, R. 2062c
Pinckney, Charles C. 326a, 2032b
  presidential candidate tab 800
  U.S. Constitution 809c
Pinckney, Thomas presidential candidate tab 800
Pincushion distortion 1908c
Pindar 1344c, 1351c, tab 1464
  biography 326a
Pindus Mountains 2164c, 2339b
Pine 1686c, 1975c, 1990c
  Norway 1986a
  Ponderosa 1987c
  Southern 1974a
  white 1980c, 1984c
Pine Bluff, Arkansas 1976a
Pine family 1686c
Pineapple family 1687a
Pineapples 1686c–1687a
  Cook Islands 2311a
  Ivory Coast 2197a
  Martinique 2316c
  Puerto Rico 2002c
  Tonga 2324b
  U.S. 1968c
Pinel, Philippe 1954b
Pinero, Arthur Wing tab 1478
Pines, Isle of 2318a
Ping-Pong 1727b
Pink, ground see Phlox
Pink family 1687a
Pink and white lady's slipper 1986a
Pinkerton, Allan 326a
Pinkie: Mary Moulton-Barrett (paint.) tab 112
Pinkney, William tab 795
Piñon 1989c
Pins (tool) 1252c
Pint tab 1500
Pinta (ship) 2023a
Pintail 51c
Pinter, Harold 326b
Pinto, Fernão Mendes 1388c
Pinturicchio, Bernardino tab 106
Pinworms tab 947
Piombo, Sebastiano del see Sebastiano del Piombo
Pioneer III 952b
Pioneer V (satellite) tab 1772
Pioneers, The (nov.) 1409a
Pipal see Fig
Pipe lines natural gas 1210a
  petroleum 1218a
  water 1195b
Piper, John tab 109
Piper, The (poem) 416c
Pipsissewa 1678a
Piracy, stream 511a
Piraeus, Greece 2368b
Pirandello, Luigi 326b, 1387c
Piranesi, Giambattista tab 107, 326b
Piranha 51c
Pirates of Penzance, The (operetta) 1369b
Pirin Mountains 2105a
Pirithous 1428b
  Theseus 1448b
Piron, Alexis tab 1469

Pisa, Italy architecture 76b
Pisano, Andrea 121a, *tab* 125, 326b
Pisano, Giovanni 121a, *tab* 125
Pisano, Nicola (Niccoló) 121a, *tab* 125
  biography 326b
Pisano, Vittore *tab* 106
Pisemski, Aleksyey 1389c, 1390a
Pisistratus 326b
Pissarro, Camille 86b, *tab* 102, 1406c
  biography 326b
Pistachio 1678a
Pistil (flower) 1645c
Pistoja, Cino da *see* Cino da Pistoja
Pistols 1625a
Piston compressors 1242b
Piston, Walter 172c
Pit and the Pendulum, The (story) 1413a
Pitcairn Island 1398, 2319
Pitch (geol.) 511a
  coal 1203b
Pitch (music) 177b
Pitch (physics) 1893b, 1919b
Pitch Lake 2275c
Pitchblende *see* Uraninite
Pitcher, Molly *see* McCauley, Mary
Pitcher plant 1687b
Pitchstone 511a
Pithecanthropus 1924a
Pithecanthropus erectus 1924a
Pithecanthropus pekinensis *see* Peking Man
Pitman, Isaac 326c
Pitney, Mahlon *tab* 802a
Pitt, William (the Elder) 326c, 2290c
  nickname 1462b
Pitt, William (the Younger) 326c, 863a, 2290c
  prime minister 901a
Pitti Gallery *tab* 110
Pittsburgh, Pennsylvania 1993b, 2013a, 2019c
  French and Indian War 2027a
  transit expressway 1165c
Pittsburgh Landing, Battle of *see* Shiloh, Battle of
Pittsburgh, University of 697
  educational T.V. 619b
Pittsfield, Massachusetts 1985b
Pituitary gland 925c, 938c
  acromegaly 940a
  dwarfism 941b
  diabetes insipidus 941b
  gigantism 942a
Pit-viper 51c–52a
Pityriasis rosea 945a
Pius V, Pope 1014a
Pius IX, Pope 326c
Pius X, Pope 326c
Pius XI, Pope 326c
Pius XII, Pope 327a
Pixie 1444c
Pizarro, Francisco 327a, 2144b, 2234b, 2236c, 2237a
Pizarro, Gonzalo 2100c
Pizarro, Hernando 2100c
Pizzicato 177b
Placenta 926a
Placer deposit 511a
Placid, Lake 2016a
Plagal 177b
Plague *tab* 947
Plain 511a
  outwash 509b
Plain chant *see* Gregorian chant
Plain Tales from the Hills (stories) 1413a
Plains of Abraham battle 2027a
Plains Indians language 1935b
Plainsong 177b *see also* Gregorian chant
Plaintiff 898a
Planck, Max 1869c, 1904a
  biography 327a
Planck's constant 1909c
Plane geometry 1604a
Plane-tree family 1687b
Planers (machinery) 1265c, 1288c
Planetarium 1796b
Planetary configurations 1796b
Planetary probes 1771a, *tab* 1772
Planetary winds 511a
Planetoids 1793b
Planets 1763b, 1780a, *tab* 1782
  configurations 1796b
  estimated age 1784c
  Kepler, J. 1757b

Kepler's laws 1781a
  Newton's laws 1758c
  origin 454a
  Plato 1752a
Plankton 465b, 1865c
Planographic printing 148a
Planosol 511a
Planquette, Jean Robert *tab* 171c
Plantain family 1687c
Plantains Puerto Rico 2002c
Planters (mach.) 1251b
Plantin, Christophe 144a
Plants 766b, 1637–1700, 1859
  agronomy 749b
  algae 1639a–1640a
  alternation of generations 1641c–1642b
  angiosperms 1642c–1643b
  annual 1644c
  assimilation 1647a
  bacteria 1640c
  botany 1637–1639
  breeding 726a
  cells 1643b–1643c
  classification of 1638c–1639b
  club mosses 1642a
  cycado 1643b
  deciduous 1645a
  digestion 1646c
  diseases 1845a
  embryonic tissue 1643c
  fats and oils 732a
  fern allies 1641c–1642b
  ferns 1641c–1642b
  fertilizers 733a
  flowers 1645c–1646a
  food storage 1646c
  fruits 1646a
  fungi 1640a–1641a
  geological time *tab* 456–457
  germination 1647b–1647c
  gibberellic acid 738c
  ginkgo 1642b
  growth 1647b–1647c
  guard cells 1645b
  gymnosperms 1642c
  herbaceous stems 1644c
  herbicides 744c
  heredity 1858a
  history of, study of 1638a–1638c
  horsetails 1642a–1642b
  hydroponics 739c
  leaves 1644c–1645c
  lichens 1640c–1641a
  liverworts 1641c
  long-day 1647b
  main characteristics of 1637
  marine environment 1865c
  mosses 1641a–1641c
  mosslike 1641a–1641c
  nutrient absorption 1646a–1646b
  number of known forms of 1638c
  perennial 1644c
  permanent tissue 1643c–1644a
  photoperiodism 1647b
  photosynthesis 1646b–1646c, 1825b, 1861a
  physiology 1646a–1647c
  pollination 1645c–1646a
  respiration 1646c–1647a
  roots 1644a–1644b
  sand culture 739c
  seed 1642b–1643b, 1644a–1646a
  short-day 1647b
  slime molds 1640c
  stems 1644b–1644c
  stimulus and response 1647a–1647b
  structure of 1643b–1644a
  subterranean stems 1644c
  taxonomy 1638a–1638c
  thallophytes 1639b–1640a
  tissues 1643c–1644a
  transpiration 1646b
  tropisms 1647a–1647b
  viral diseases 1842c
  water absorption 1646a–1646b
  woody stems 1644c
  see also individual plants, such as Ferns
Plasma (blood) 922b
Plasma (physics) 1919b
Plasma-arc welding 1288a
Plaster of Paris gypsum 1212a
Plastics 1218c, *tab* 1219, 1220a
Plastids 1842a, 1858a
  plant 1643c
Plata, Rio De La 2339b
Plateau 511a
Plateau basalt 511a
Plate glass 135c
  resistivity 1882a
Platen, August von *tab* 1474
Plateresque style (arch.) 77a
Plates (print.) 153a
Platform (pol.) 899a
Platinum 1835

atomic weight *tab* 1805
Plato 974c, 975a, *tab* 1464, 1614a, 1615a
  Atlantis 1426a
  biography 327a
  education 622b
  literary style 1353c
  mathematics 1752a
  realism 1620c
  sobriquet 1461a
Platt, Thomas 2055c
Platt Amendment 902c, 2060b, 2137c
Platte River 1962a, 2018c
Plattsburg, N.Y. War of 1812 2034c
Platypus *see* Duckbill
Plautus, Titus Maccius 1353a, 1354b, 1355a, *tab* 1464
  biography 327b
Playa 511a
Playboy of the Western World (play) 1370c
Playfair, John 1566b
Playfair postulate 1566b
Playthings *see* Toys
Plea (law) 825c, 899a
Pleadings (law) 899b
Pleasure-pain principle 1957b
Pleasure Reconciled to Vertue (drama) 1410b
Plebiscite 899b
Plectrum 177b
Pléiade (lit. group) 1378b
Pleiades (astron.) 1787a
Pleiades (myth) 1444c
Pleistocene epoch *tab* 457, 458, 511a, 1348b, 1923c, 1924a
Plessy v. Ferguson (law case) 2078c
Pleura pleurisy 945a
  pneumothorax 945a
Pleurisy 945a
Pliny (the Elder) 327b, 452a, 1638a
  Natural History 1357c
Pliny (the Younger) 158a, 327b, 1358a
  Epistles tab 1464
Pliocene Epoch *tab* 457, 458, 511a
Ploesti, Romania 2244a, 2368b
Plotinus 327c, 1354a, *tab* 1464
Plougastel Bridge 1197, 1198a
Plovdiv, Bulgaria 2105a, 2368b
Plovers 52a–52b
Plows (mach.) 720a
  improvement of 720a
Plowshare, Project *see* Project Plowshare
Plucking 511b
Plum 1687c
Plumbers (career) 376b
Plumed Knight *see* Blaine, James Gillespie
Plural voting 899b
Pluralism (philos.) 1613b
Plurality (pol.) 899b
Plutarch 327c, 965c
  moon 1763a
Plutarch's Lives (bk.) 1354a, 1360b, 1397b, *tab* 1464
Pluto (myth) 1430c, 1433c, 1444c
Pluto (planet) 757a, *tab* 1782, 1783b
  albedo 1793b
  Bode's law 1780c, *tab* 1781
Plutonic rock 511b
Plutonium 1800a, 1835, 1911c
  atomic weight *tab* 1805
Plutus 1444c
Pluvial 511b
Pluvius 1444c
Plymouth, Eng. pottery 127c, *tab* 131
Plymouth, Massachusetts 1019a
Plymouth, Montserrat 2317a, 2368c
Plymouth Colony 2024a
  first winter at 1019a
  founded 1018b–1019a
  labor 827b
Plymouth Plantation, History of (bk.) *see History of Plymouth Plantation*
Plymouth Rock chickens eggs 732a
Plymouth State College 682
Plywood 1220b
Plzen, Czechoslovakia 2139a
PMC Colleges 697
Pneumatic tires 1277c
Pneumococcus 1843c, 1853c
Pneumonia *tab* 947
Pneumothorax 945a
P-N junctions 1890b, 1892a·
Po Hai (gulf) 2328c

see also Chihli, Gulf of
Po River 2194a
Po Valley 2194b–2194c
Pobedonostsev, Konstantin 2260a
Pocahontas 327c
Pocket veto 912a
Podzol 511b
Podzolic soils 743a
Poe, Edgar Allan *il* 208, 1346c, 1374b, *tab* 1475
  biography 327c
  Gold Bug 1404c
  Pit and the Pendulum, The 1413a
  pseudonyms 1462b, *tab* 1463a
  Raven, The 1414c
Poet Laureate 1413b
Poet-Naturalist *see* Thoreau
Poetics (Aristotle) 1353c
Poetry 1343–1346
  American 1376a
  biblical 1459a
  Canadian 1390c
  children's 412–417
  definition 1413c
  elegy 1351a
  epic 1350c–1351a
  Greek 1350–1354
  Greek music 156b
  Imagists 1371a
  kindergarten 400c
  lyric 1351b
  meter 1410b
  Mother Goose Rhymes 408–412
  Parnassian school 1381c
  sonnet 1417c
  Spanish 1391c
Poetry Society of America 1745b
Poincaré, Raymond 327c
Poinsett, Joel R. *tab* 795
Poinsettia 1687c
Point (geog.) 511b
Point (print.) 153a
Point Four Program 899b
Point Loma, California
  water conservation 777b
Pointe Noire, Congo (Brazzaville) 2134a
Pointe-à-Pitre, Guadaloupe 2315a, 2368c
Pointed arch 76c
Poison hemlock 1687c–1688a
Poison ivy 1688a, 1711c
Poison sumac 1712a
Poisoning 958b
Poitiers, Diane de 122b
Pokeweed family 1688a
Pol, Heinz *tab* 1481
Polabian (lang.) 1334a
Polacca 177b
Poland 2095c, 2163a, 2238–2240
  agriculture 2239a, 2239b
  climate 2239a
  cominform 866a
  communism 2238a, 2239b, 2239c, 2240c
  Congress of Vienna 1023c
  dances 181c
  economy 2239a–2239c
  flag *il* 2184
  flax 1667b
  geography 2238c–2239a
  government 2239c
  history 2239a–2240c
  independence 2240b
  industry 2239b–2239c
  League of Nations 1012c
  Little Entente 1014c–1015a
  map 2239, *Atlas*-8–9
  music 154c, *tab* 172a
  natural resources 2239a–2239b
  partitions 2240a
  people of 2239a
  religion 2238c, 2239a, 2240a, 2240c
  swan 61b–61c
  trade 2239c
  Versailles Treaty 1023a
  World War I 988c, 2240b
  World War II 1028a, 2154c, 2162c, 2239a, 2240b–2240c, 2292a
Polar coordinates 1593a, 1606b
Polar covalent bond 1810a
Polar easterlies 474a
Polar front 511b
Polar molecules 1810a
Polar Regions *see* Antarctica; Arctic
Polar wind 511b
Polaris (star) 1796c
Polarizability 1822a
Polarization 1905c
Polarized light 1905c
  uses 1906a
Polaroid 1905c

Polder 511b
Pole vault 1739b
Polecat 52b
Poles (geol.) 511b
Poles (phys.) 1883c
Poles, Celestial see Celestial poles
Police (careers) 388c
Police power 899b
Poliomyelitis tab 947, 1849c
  virus 1842b
Polish (lang.) 1334a
Polish Committee of National Liberation 2240c
Polish Corridor 2240b
Polish National Committee 2240b
Polish Rider, The (paint.) tab 111
Polish Succession, War of
  results of 1021b
Polish United Worker's Party 2239c
Politian, Angelo (Ambrogini) 327c, 1386b, tab 1466
Political Economy (bk.) tab 1475
Political parties 785a, 896b
  committees 866c
  organization tab 393
  platform 899a
  third parties 910c
  see also under names of various political parties
Political philosophy 1611c
Political and Social History of Modern Europe (Hayes) 1007b
Politics careers 390c, 392
  literary works 1348c
  primitive culture 1936c
  technology 1127c
Poliziano, Angelo see Politian
Polje 511b
Polk, James Knox 328a, tab 798–799, 873a
  administration 2039b–2040
  administration, events paralleling tab 1063
  Cabinet tab 795
  election and inauguration tab 800
  House of Representatives tab 802b
  Whig Party 914a
Pollaiuolo, Antonio tab 106, tab 125
  biography 328a
  Heracles and Hydra tab 110
Pollaiuolo, Piero tab 110
Pollination 726a, 1645c–1646a
  cross 1645c
  self 1645c
Pollock see Cod
Pollock, Jackson tab 109, 328a
Poll tax 899c
Pollution 776b, 1868c
Pollux see Castor and Pollux
Polly Put the Kettle On (nursery rhyme) 409b
Polo, Marco 328a, 979c, 2022c, 2127c
Polo (sport) 1727c
Polonaise (mus.) 177b
Polonium 1835
  atomic weight tab 1805
Polyandry 1936b, 1941b
Polybius 328a, 975a, 1151a, 1354a, tab 1464
Polybutadiene 1222b
Polycarp, Saint 328b
Polyclitus 116c, 328b
Polycythemia vera 945a
Polydorus 117c
Polyesters 1209a, tab 1219
Polyethylene tab 1219, 1219c
Polyeucte (poem) 1379a
Polygamy 1941b
Polygnotus 84a
Polygon method (phys.) 1874b
Polygonial ground 511b
Polygons 1606b
  regular 1574c
Polygyny 1936b, 1941b
Polyhedrons 1576a, 1599a, 1606c
Polyhvmnia 1444c
Polyisoprene 1222b
Polymers 1219c, 1824a
Polymorphism 1828c
Polynesians anthropology 1927b
  cooking 1933a
Polynices 1444c
  Antigone 1424b
  Eteocles 1431b
Polynomials 1535c
  adding 1535c
  algebra 1535b
  dividing 1536c
  multiplying 1536a

  subtracting 1536a
Polynucleotides 1841a
Polypeptides 1855a
Polyphase generators 1885c
Polyphemus 1444c
Polyphony 177b
  chords 161b
  Greek music 156c
Polypody family 1688b
Polypropylenes tab 1219
Polyrhythm 160c
Polysaccharides 1824a
Polystyrene tab 1219
Polytechnic Institute of Brooklyn 686
Polytheism 1622b
Polyunsaturated acids 732c
Polyuridylic acid 1855a
Polyxena 1445a
Pombal, Marquis of 2242a
Pomegranate 1688b
Pomelo see Grapefruit
Pomes 1646a
Pomona (myth) 1445a
Pomona College 658
Pompadour, Marquise de 328b
Pompeii 75b, 84b
Pompey (the Great) 328b
Ponce, Federico 2169a
Ponce, Puerto Rico 2002b, 2013b
Ponce Enríquez, Camilo 2144c
Ponce de León, Juan 2023a
  Fountain of Youth 1432b
Ponchielli, Amilcare 167c, tab 171c
Pond 511b
Pond lily see Waterlily
Ponderosa pine 1987c
Poniatowski, Stanislas 2240a
Pons, Lily 328c
Pons Amelius 1196b
Pons Sublicius 1196b
Ponselle, Rosa Melba 328c
Pont de la Concorde 1196c
Pontchartrain, Lake 2018a, 2019c, 2292c
Ponte Molle 1196b
Ponte Vecchio 1196c
Pontiac (Amer. Ind. chief) 328c
Pontifex, Ernest 1421a
Pontius Pilate 1630c
Pontoppidan, Henrik tab 1478
Pontormo, Jacopo da tab 107
Pony (animal) 739c
Pools (bus.) 600b
Poona, India 2368c
Poor Richard (lit. char.) see Saunders, Richard
Poor Richard's Almanac 1372c, 1413c
Poorten-Schwartz, J.M.W. van der see Maartens, Maarten
Pop! goes the weasel (nursery rhyme) 410c
Popcorn 729c
Pope, Alexander 328c, 1363a, tab 1469
  Essay on Man 1403a
Pope, John 2045c, 2048b
Popes forms of address tab 1119
  list of tab 1080
  Middle Ages 985b
  pardons 895a
Poplar 1688b
  tulip 1994c
Popocatépetl (mountain) 2217b–2217c
Popovich, Pavel R. tab 1770
Poppy family 1688c
Popular Action Party (PAP) (Peru) 2237b
Popular Democratic Party (Puerto Rico) 2003b
Population 1127c, 1859a
  stability 1859c
  United States (1960) 1970–1973
Population I (stars) 1787a
Population II (stars) 1787a
Population genetics 1858a
Population grouping 767c, 768c
Populist Party (People's Party) (U.S.) 899c, 2058b
  silver 2059b
Poquelin, Jean Baptiste see Molière
Porcelain 127a
  ceramics 126a
  Chinese 126c
  electrical 132c

  manufacture 1220c
  resistivity 1882a
Porcupine 52b–52c
Pore 511b
Pork wholesale cuts 735c
Porosity 511b
Porphyry 450c, 511b
Porpoise 52c
Porpora, Niccolò tab 171c
Porro prism 1909a
Port (geog.) see Ports
Port Arthur, Texas 1995c
Port Elizabeth, South Africa 2252b, 2368c
Port Etienne, Mauritania 2216a, 2216b
Port Gentil, Gabon 2155c
Port Harcourt, Nigeria 2229b, 2368c
Port Louis, Mauritius 2216c, 2368c
Port Moresby, Papua 2319b, 2368c
Port Royal, Nova Scotia founding 2023c
  King William's War 2026c
Port Royal Textbooks tab 1468
Port Said, United Arab Republic 2280c, 2369a
Port Sudan, Sudan 2369a
Port Victoria, Mahé 2322a, 2369a
Port wine 723c, 2241b
Portal circulatory system 924c
Portal vein 924c
Portales, Diego 2122a
Port-au-Prince, Haiti, 2171b, 2171c, 2368c
Port-de-France, Martinique 2316c
Porter, Cole 328c
Porter, David (1780–1843) 328c
Porter, David Dixon (1813–1891) 329a, 2050a
Porter, Fitz-John 2048a
Porter, James M. tab 795
Porter, Jane 1366a
  Scottish Chiefs 1416c
Porter, Katherine, Ann 329a, 1376a
Porter, Peter Buel tab 795
Porter, William Sydney 329a, 1375c, tab 1479
Porter ale 724a
Porthos 1396a
Portia Julius Caesar 1413c
Portia (lit. char.) Merchant of Venice 1410b
Portinari, Beatrice 1386a
Portinari, Candido tab 109
Portland, Maine 1984b, 2013b
Portland, Oregon 1992c, 2013b
  government 864b
Portland, University of 694
Portland cement 1189c, 1200a
Portland State College 694
Porto, Portugal 2368c, 2241b
Portobelo, Panama 2234b
Port-of-Spain, Trinidad and Tobago 2275b
Porto-Novo, Dahomey 2140b, 2140c, 2369a
Porto-Riche, Georges de 1382b
Portrait of the Artist As a Young Man (novel) 1371b
Portrait of Helena Fourment (paint.) tab 113
Portrait of Madame X (paint.) tab 112
Portrait of Madame Z (paint.) il 102
Portraiture sculpture 118a
Ports (geog.) harbors 1166b
Portsmouth, (N. H.) treaty 2062b
Portsmouth, R. I. founding 2025b
Portsmouth, Virginia 1997c
Portugal 874a, 2241–2242
  agriculture 2241b
  Angola 2306a–2307a
  Avis dynasty 2241c
  Bragança dynasty 2242a
  Brazil 2103b–2104b
  Cape Verde Islands 2309b–2309c
  climate 2241a
  economy 2241b
  Ethiopia 2146b
  exploration tab 1060
  flag il 2184
  geography 2241a
  government 2241b–2242b
  history tab 1044–1056, 2241c–2242b
  independence 2264b
  in Indonesia 2187c
  industry 2241b
  kingfisher 41a
  in Macao 2129a, 2316b–2316c

  map 2241, Atlas-12
  in Mozambique 2317a–2317c
  in Muscat and Oman 2222c–2223a
  natural resources 2241b
  New World 2023a
  in Nigeria 2229c
  people of 2241a–2241b
  in Portuguese Guinea 2319c–2320b
  in Portuguese Timor 2320b–2320c
  in Principe 2322a
  religion 2241a
  in Sao Tomé 2322a
  trade 2241b
  in Uruguay 2295c
  World War I 2242b
  World War II 2242b
  see also Portuguese literature
Portuguese Guinea 2241c, 2319–2320
  agriculture 2320a
  economy 2320a
  geography 2319c–2320a
  government 2320a
  history 2320a–2320b
  map Atlas-36
  people of 2320a
  slavery 2320a
Portuguese language 1335b
  punctuation 1314c
  study of 1331a
Portuguese India map 29
Portuguese literature 1388b–1389a
  outline tab 1466
Portuguese man-of-war 52c–53a, il 456
Portuguese Timor 2320
Portuguese West Africa see Angola
Portulaca see Purslane
Poseidon (myth) 1440c, 1445a, 1628a
  Andromeda 1424a
Posidonius 779a, 1354a
Position (mus.) 177b
Positrons 1916c, 1919c
Post, Emily 329a
Post, Wiley 329a
Post mills 1150b
Post Office Department 900a
  careers 377c
  censorship 862a
  clerks 378a
  divisions 875b
  establishment tab 797
  mail carriers 378a
  postmaster general tab 795–796, 900a
Posters
  commercial 136b
  lithography 141b
Postimpressionism 86b
Postlude 177b
Postman, The (song) 419
Post-mortem 900a
Postulates see Axioms
Posture (in writing) 1301b
Potala (Tibet) 979b
Potash 511b, 1220b
  fertilizers tab 752, 753b, tab 753
  Germany 2158b
  glassmaking 133a
  Jordan 2201c
  New Mexico 1990a
  U.S. 1967b, 2293c
Potassium 463b, 762a, 1835
  atomic weight tab 1805
  body requirement 919c
  chloride 733b
  fertilizers 733a, 753b
  glassmaking 133b
  plants 1646b
  potash 1220b
  soils 743b
Potato 1688b
  Argentina 2089c
  Germany 2158b
  Guam 2001a
  Idaho 1980c
  Ireland 2190c, 2191c
  Japan 2199b
  Maine 1984b
  Mississippi 1987a
  Niue 2319a
  North Dakota 1991c
  Peru 2236c
  Poland 2239b
  Rhode Island 1994a
  Romania 2244a
  Rwanda 2245c
  Sikkim 2249c
  Spain 2264a

Sweden 2268a
Switzerland 2270a
U.S. 2294a
Venezuela 2297b
Vermont 1997a
Vietnam 2299b
Washington 1998a
Western Samoa 2301c
Wyoming 1999c
Yugoslavia 2303b
Potato family 1688c
Potato War see Bavarian Succession, War of the
Potemkin, Grigori 329c
Potential difference 1919b
Potential energy 1877c, 1897b, 1918a
Potentiometer 1248c, 1817c, 1919b
Pothole 511b
Potiphar 1459a
Pot-marigold 1688c–1689a
Potomac River 1978c, 1984c, 1998, 2019c, 2293a
Potosí, Bolivia 2100b
Potpourri (mus.) 177b
Pots (ceramics) 126b
Potsdam, Germany 2163a, 2369a
Potsdam Agreement 2238c, 2239a
Potsdam Conference 880b
reparations 905c
Potter, Beatrice
Peter Rabbit 433a–434a
Potter, Edward C. tab 125
Potter, Paul tab 107
Potter's wheel 126b, 130a
Pottery tab 130–131, 1933a
American 128b
archeology 967b
ceramics 126a
eighteenth century 128c
Greek 126b
manufacture 1220b
Pott's fracture 917c
Poulenc, Francis 168b, tab 172a, 329b
Poulsen, Valdemar 1181a
Poultry Alabama 2174b
Arkansas 1976b
California 1977a
Delaware 1978c
farms 381a
Great Britain 2282c
Maine 1984b
manure tab 752, 753a
Maryland 1985a
Massachusetts 1985b
Mississippi 1987a
New Hampshire 1989b
New Jersey 1989c
New York 1990c
Ohio 1992a
products 735c
Rhode Island 1994a
U.S. 1968b, 2294a
Vermont 1997a
Virginia 1997c
Wallis and Futuna Islands 2324c
West Virginia 1998c
Western Samoa 2301c
Wyoming 1999c
Yugoslavia 2303c
Pound (weight) tab 1500, 1873b
Pound, Ezra 329b, 1376a, tab 1480
Pound-second 1879a
Pourbus, Pieter tab 107
Poussin, Nicolas tab 107, tab 112
biography 329b
Corot, influence on 86a
Shepherds in Arcadia tab 112
Powder metallurgy 1193c
Powell, Lake 1975b
Power (math.) algebra 1534c
Power (phys.) 1129–1150, 1878b
Power of attorney 900a
Power lines 1132c
Powers, Francis G. 2079b
Powers, Hiram 123c, tab 125
Powhatan (Amer. Ind. chief) 329b
Powys, Alyse G. 1371b
Powys, John Cowper 1371b
Powys, Llewelyn 1371b
Powys, Theodore Francis 1371b
Poyang, Lake 2339b
Poznan, Poland 2239c, 2369a, 2240
Pozzolana 1200a, 1204b
Practical geometry 1556a
Practice and procedure (law) 900a
Prado tab 111
Praeterita (bk.) 1366b
Pragmatic Sanction 1019a
Pragmatism 1612a, 1619a
Prague, Czechoslovakia 2138c, 2139a, 2369a

Praha see Prague
Praia, Cape Verde Islands 2309b, 2369a
Prairie 511b
conservation 1868a
geography 1865a
Prairie chicken see Grouse
Prairie dog 53a
Prairie State see Illinois
Prairie View Agricultural & Mechanical College 702
Prajadhipok, King (Thailand) 329b
abdication 849a
Prakit (lang.) 1334a
Praseodymium 1836
atomic weight tab 1805
Praslin Island 2322a
Pratt, Edward J. 1390c
Pratt, John 1188a
Pratt Institute 686
Pravda circulation tab 1170c
Praxiteles 117a
biography 329c
Nicias 113c
Prayer rugs 1109c
Praying mantis il 29, 53a
Precambrian 511c
Precedent (law) 900b
Precentor (mus.) 177b
Precession (astron.) 1796c
Précieuses Ridicules, Les (play) 1379b
Precious stones see Gems
Precipice 511c
Precipitation 473b, 511c, 764a–764c
measurement 473c
types 473b
Precognition (parapsych.) 1952a
Predis, Ambrogio de tab 106
Preferential voting 900b
Preferred stock 545b, 600c
Pregnancy 926c
eclampsia 941b
morning sickness 942c
placenta 926a
public health 959a
tests 926c
Prehistoric archeology 967a, 1923a, 1927–1929
abrasives 1192a
art 71b, 1928a
painting 82b
Prelude (mus.) 177b
Prelude, The (poem) 1612a
Préludes, Les (mus.) 166b
Prempeh I, King (Ashanti) 2164b
Prendergast, Maurice 104c, tab 108
biography 329c
Prepositions 1308b
idioms 1316c
use of 1303c
Pre-Raphaelites 1369a
Presbyterian College 699
Prescott, William H. 329c, tab 1474
Presentation of Christ in the Temple (paint.) tab 112
Preservation (food) 1239a
Presidency (U.S.)
Constitution 787b, 789c
election 810b
forms of address tab 1120
minimum age 850b
oath of office 808c
power 789a
separation of powers 907c
succession 859c
term 811b
veto 912a
Presidential Range 2019b
Presidential Succession Act (1886) 2056b, (1947) 2056b
Presidential Succession Act (1947) 2056b
Presidents (U.S.) tab 798–799
administrations 2031–2082
ancestry tab 798
birthplaces tab 798
burial places tab 799
cabinets tab 795–797
elections and inaugurations tab 800–801
events paralleling administrations tab 1061–1070
parents of tab 798
sobriquets of tab 799
writings of tab 799
see also under names of individual presidents, such as Washington, George
Press, Freedom of the see Freedom of the press
Pressburg, Czechoslovakia see Bratislava

Pressey, Sidney 620a
Pressure
root (plant) 1646b
Pressure gradient 511c
Preston, Margaret J. tab 1476
Preston, William tab 796
Pretender, The Young see Stuart, Charles Edward
Pretoria, South Africa 2251c, 2252b, 2369a
Pretorius, Andries Wilhelmus Jacobus 329c
Prevailing wind 511c
westerlies 474a
Prévost, Abbé 329c, 1380b, tab 1469
Prévost, Marcel tab 1479
Prévost, Pierre 1906c
Prezzolini, Giuseppe 1388a
Priam 1445a
Pribilof Islands 998c, 2019c
Price, Leontyne 329c
Price Administration, Office of 894c
Price cutting 600c
Price index 600c
Price stability 528a
Prickly heat 945b
Pride and Prejudice (nov.) 1366a, 1413c
Priestley, Joseph 329c, 749b, 1798c
Primary (astronautics) 1779b
Primary cells (elec.) 1883c
Primary colors 1907a
Primary elections 900c, 901a
candidates 860a
Primary groups 1939c
Primates anthropology 1923c
Primavera (paint.) il 96, tab 110
Prime Minister 901a
Prime mover 1145c
Prime numbers 1523b, 1606c
Primitive animism 1947b
Primitive culture 1929c
agriculture 1934a
art 1937c,
dance 180a
education 612a
initiation rites 1939a
law 813a, 1937a
music 154b
mutilation 1930c
religion 1621c, 1937b
technology 1929c
Primo de Rivera, Miguel 2265b
Primogeniture 888a, 901b
Primrose 1689a
Primrose, Archibald Philip see Rosebery, 5th Earl of
Primrose family 1689a
Prince (title) forms of address tab 1120
Prince, Morton 1954b
Prince, The (bk.) 1386b
Prince and the Pauper, The (nov.) 1414a
Prince Edward Island 2110c, 2116b, 2116c
Princess (title) forms of address tab 1120
Princess, The (poem) 1368c, 1414a
Princesse de Clèves, La (nov.) tab 1468
Princeton, Battle of 2028b, 2029
Princeton University 683
Mather, Cotton 1372b
Principe Islands 2241c, 2322
Principia College 665
Principia mathematica philosophiae naturalis (bk.) 1619a, 1758b
Principles of Psychology, The (bk.) 1948a
Printed circuit 1919b
Printing 142–153, 1173c, 1931–1942
binding 150c
bronzing 150b
collotype 150a
Colonial America 145a
dictionary of printers' terms 150–153
die cutting 150b
electrotyping 148b
embossing 150b
gravure method 149c
Gutenberg Bibles 143b
history of 142a
invention of 978a
linotype 147a
lithography 141a
monotype 147a
newspapers 1171a
offset 149b
paper making 148a
photoengraving 148b
planographic 149a

proofreader's marks 147
stereotyping 148b
thermography 150b
type composition 1174b
typesetting 146c
type sizes 146c
Printing press 143a, 148a
introduction of 1360a
Printing Types (bk.) 146b
Prints (art) 136a
block 140c
collecting of 141c
woodcuts 139c
Printz, Johan 2024c
Prior, Matthew 1363b
Priority 600c
Prisms (math.) 1577c
Prisms (phys.) 1909a
systems 1909b
Prisoner of Chillon, The (poem) 1365a, 1399a
Pritchett, Victor Sawdon 1371c
Prithvi, Narayan 2224a
Private brand 600c
Private law 901b
Private schools 625b
Privet 1689a
Privilege (law) 901b
Privy Council (Eng.) 871a, 889b
Privy seal 901b
Prize courts 901b
Prize law 901b
Probability 548a, 1597a, 1606c
Probate court 901c
Probation 901c
Procaryotic cells 1842b
Process (law) 901c
Process cheese 731b
Procession in Piazzo of San Marco (paint.) tab 112
Proclamation of 1763 2114c
Proclus 1566b
Proconsul (anthrop.) 1923c
Procrustes 1448a
Procter, Bryan W. 1461c
Proctor, A. Phimister tab 125
Proctor, Henry 2034b
Proctor, Redfield tab 796
Prodicus of Ceos 1614a
Producers radio and TV careers 378b
Production 555–559
economics 601a
engineering 1274c
Proetus 1426c
Professional schools 628c
Profile (geol.) 511c
Profit 601a
Profit sharing 601a
Profitable Book (law bk.) 817b
Profundal zone 1866c
Progesterone 926
Program music 165b, 177b
Programing see Programming
Programmed learning 620a
Programming
computers 1243b
radio-TV careers 378b
Progression (math.) 1607a
Progression (music) 177b
Progressive education 622c
Progressive Party (Iceland) 2177a
Progressive Party (Togo) 2275b
Progressive Party (U.S.) 901c, 2063a
Bull Moose Party 858b
Progressive People's Party (Gambia) 2156c
Prohibition local option 890b
public opinion 812c
U.S. 787b, 811b–811c, 2068b
Prohibition Party 901c
Project Apollo 1777c
Project Bumper 1769a
Project Gemini 1770b, 1777c
Project Mercury 1770b
Project Orbiter 1769a
Project Plowshare 1829a
Project Rover 1767b
Project Vanguard 1769a
Projective geometry 1505a, 1607a
Projective tests 1950c
Projectors (cameras) 1161b
Prokofiev, Sergei S. 169b, tab 172
biography 330a
Proletariat 901c

Prometheus (myth) 1414a, 1445a
Prometheus Bound (play) 1414a, 1352b
  story 1445a
Prometheus Unbound (poem) 1414a, 1365b
Promethium 1800a, 1809b, 1836
  atomic weight *tab* 1805
Prominences 1793c
Promised Land *see* Canaan
Promissory notes 601a, 821a
Promontory (geog.) 511c
Promontory, Utah 1177a
Promotion (bus.) 601a
Pronghorn 53a–53b
Pronouns 1304c
  agreement with antecedent 1317c
Proof (print.) 147b, 153a–153b
  author's 150b
Proofreading 147b
  symbols 147
Prop roots 1644b
Propaganda 902a
Propane 1210c
Propellants solid 1766c
Propeller turbine 1148b
Proper fractions 1604a
Propertius, Sextus 1357b
Property taxes 534c
Property eminent domain 876c
  partnership 823a
  personal 823b
  real estate 824b
Prophecy (Bib.) 1459b
Prophet Elijah, The (paint.) *tab* 109
Prophets Judaism 1629a
Propolis 724c
Proportion (math.) 1530a
Proportional representation 902a
Proposition (debating) 1328a
Proprietary schools 636c
Proprioceptors 937b
Propylaea (Athens) 75a
Prorogation 902b
Prose 1346a–1347, 1414a
  Greek 1353a
Prose de l'âne (song) 159b
Proserpina (myth) 1445a
Proses (mus.) 158c
Prosperity business cycles 601b
Prospero 1418b
  Ariel 1425a
Prostate gland 926b
Protactinium *tab* 1836
  atomic weight *tab* 1805
Protection 902b
Protectorate 902c
Proteins 919b, 1824b, 1825a, 1853c
  genetics 1855a, 1856c
Proteoses 920c
Proterozoic Era 458a
Protest (law) 601b
Protestantism church music 160b
  education 614c
  founding 986b
  literature 1347c
  philosophy 1612c
  Reformation 1631c
Proteus 1445a
Prothrombin 921c, 922c
Protium 1806a
Protocol 902c
Protogenes 330a
Proton transfer theory 1817c
Protons 1870b, 1881b, 1803c, 1804c
  characteristics 1911b
  definition 1919b
Protoplanets 1796c
Protoplasm 1643b
Protoplasts 1842a
Protozoa 465b, 1848a
Proudhon, Pierre Joseph 330a, 851c, 908a, 909c
Proust, Marcel 330a, 1382c, *tab* 1480
Provençal (lang.) 1335b
Proverbs 1414a, 1422a
Proverbs, Book of (Bib.) 1459b
Providence, Rhode Island 1993c, 1994a, 2013b–2013c
Providence College 698

Providence Plantations 2025b
Province (geog.) 902a
Provo, Utah 1996a
Provolone *tab* 731b
Prudentius *tab* 1465
Prudhomme, Sully *see* Sully-Prudhomme
Prud'hon, Pierre-Paul *tab* 108
Prune *see* Plum
Prussia 2095b, 2153c, 2160b–2160c, 2161a–2161b, 2175a
  Battle of Leipzig 1014b
  Congress of Vienna 1023c
  historical outline *tab* 1052, *tab* 1054
  Holy Alliance 1010a–1010b
  kings of *tab* 1078
Prut River 2243c, 2339b
Prynne, Hester (lit. char.) 1416b
Psalmbooks 161c
Psalms 177c
  hymns 158a
Psalms, Book of (Bib.) 1459b
Psalter 160c, 162a
Psaltery 156a, 159c
Psammetich II, King (Egypt), 1003c
Pseudonyms dictionary 1461–1463
Pseudopodia 1848a
Psittacosis 1843a
Psoriasis 945b
Psyche (myth) 1445a
Psychiatry 1947a, 1952–1958
  bibliography 1958c
  careers 383a
  character disorders 1954a
  growth of 1954a
  mental health 959b
  neuroses 1954a
  psychoses 1953a
  see also Psychology
Psychic research 1947a, 1952a
Psychoanalysis 1947a, 1957a
Psychobiology 1958c
Psychological field theory 1948b
Psychology 1947–1958
  anthropology 1923b
  bibliography 1958c
  careers 383a
  color 1104c
  fields 1951b
  history 1947a
  mental health 959b
  schools of 1947c
  see also Psychiatry
Psychometry (parapsych.) 1952a
Psychoneuroses *see* Neuroses
Psychophysics 1951a
Psychoses 1953a
Psychosomatic disorders 1954a
Psychotherapy 1947a
Psychrometer 470a, 511c
Ptah 1622b
Ptarmigan 53b
Ptolemy (geographer) 779a–779b
Ptolemy (Claudius Ptolemaeus) 330b, 1503a, 1756c
  Almagest tab 1464
Ptolemy I (Ptolemy Soter), King (Egypt) 330b, 994b, 1003c–1006a, 2281a
Ptolemy II (Ptolemy Philadelphus), King (Egypt) 330b, 994b
Ptolemy III, King (Egypt) 330b
Ptolemy XIII, King (Egypt) 1005a
Ptolemy XIV, King (Egypt) 1005a
Public Assistance, Bureau of 908b
Public debt 902a
Public domain 903a
Public health 954–960
  agencies 960c
  disease control 955b
  kindergarten 402c, 404a
Public Health Organization (League of Nations) 1013b
Public Health Service education 630a
Public interest 903b
Public opinion 812c
Public Parks and the Enlargement of Towns (bk.) 775b
Public relations careers 377b
Public Works Administration 2073b
Publick Occurrences (newspaper) 1170c

Public schools 625b
  adult education 636a
  districts 633b
  enrollments *tab* 646
  estimated expenditures (1963–64) *tab* 644
  organization 626c
Public speaking 1326–1328
  Greece 1353b
Public utilities 601b, 903b
Public Utility Holding Company Act 879c, 907b
Public works 903c
Publicity 601b
Publishing 1173c
  books 1160a
  careers 388a
  see also Printing
Puccini, Giacomo 167c, *tab* 172a
  biography 330b
Puck (folklore) 1445b
Puck of Pook's Hill (stories) 1414a
Puddingstone *see* Conglomerate
Pudd'nhead Wilson (bk.) 1419a
Puebla, Mexico 2218a
  pottery 128b, *tab* 131
Puebla, Battle of 2219b
Pueblo, Colorado 1977b
Puerto Barrios, Guatemala 2369b
Puerto Montt, Chile 2121b
Puerto Rico 2002–2003
  agriculture 2002b
  child labor laws 831c, 832a
  climate 2002a
  commercial law *tab* 826
  commonwealth 867c
  economy 2002b–2002c
  geography 2002a
  government 793c, 2002c–2003a
  history 2003a–2003b, 2060b
  holidays 841–842
  Indians in 2003a
  labor legislation 832c
  map *Atlas*-57
  people of 2002a–2002b
  pineapples 1686c–1687a
  Spanish-American War 2060a
  U.S. control 2003a–2003b
Puffin 53b
Puget, Pierre 122c, *tab* 125
Puget Sound 1998a, 2014c, 2020a
Puget Sound, University of 706
Pulaski, Casimir 330b
Pulci, Luigi 1386c
Pulitzer, Joseph 330b
Pullman, George Mortimer 330c
Pullman strike 2058c
  injunction 885a
Pulmonary artery 923b, 924c
Pulmonary circulatory system 924c
Pulmonary embolism 945b
Pulmonary vein 923b, 924c
Pulp cavity 920b
Pulse 924a
Pulse radar 1176c
Pultowa, Battle of 1002c
Puma *see* Cat
Pumice 134a, 450c, 511c
Pumpkin 1689a
Pumps 1275a
Puna 511c
Punch (print.) 153b
Punch and Judy (puppet show) 1414a
Punched card system 1164a, 1236b
Punctuation apostrophe 1314b
  brace 1314a
  brackets 1314a
  colon 1312c
  comma 1313a
  dash 1313c
  diacritical marks 1314a
  exclamation point 1312b
  foreign composition 1312c
  hyphen 1314b
  parentheses 1314a
  period 1312a
  question mark 1312b
  quotation marks 1312c
  semicolon 1313a
Punic Wars *tab* 1071
  battle of Cannae 1000a
  Second 1000a, 1014c, 1016b
Punishment (law) 813a, 903c
Punjab 981a

Punta Arenas, Chile 2121b
Pupil (anat.) 928b
Pupin, Michael 330c
Puranas (lit.) *tab* 1463
Purcell, Henry 161c, 171c
  biography 330c
Purchasing 553–554
  careers 377c
Purdue University 619a, 666
Pure Food and Drug Act 904a, 956b, 2062a
Pure Food, Drug, and Cosmetic Act 904a
Pure food laws 904a
Pure mathematics 1601
Purismo movement (lit.) 1387b
Puritans 1362a, 1632a
  education 615c
Purkinje, Johannes 1762b
Purple 1907c
Purple finch 1989a
Purple Land, The (bk.) 1414b
Purple lilac 1989a
Purple violet 1989b
Purpura 945b
Pus 922b
Pusan, South Korea 2203c
Pushkin, Aleksandr *il* 208, 1389b, *tab* 1474
  biography 330c
Purslane 1689b
Puss in Boots (play) *tab* 1472
Pussley 1689b
Pussy-cat, Pussy-cat (nursery rhyme) 410a
Pussy willow *see* Willow
Put (fin.) 601b
  see also Call (fin.)
Putnam, Israel 330c
Puvis de Chavannes, Pierre *tab* 108
Puyallup River 2015a
Pu-yi, Henry (Hsuan T'ung), Emperor (China) 276c
  abdication 849a
Puzzled Centipede (rhyme) 417c
Pye, Henry James 1413b
Pyeshkov, A. M. *see* Gorky, Maxim
Pygmalion (myth) 1445b
Pygmalion (play) 1414b
Pygmies anthropology 1924c
  Congoids 1927a
  fire 1930a
Pylades 1435c
Pynchon, William 330c
Pyongyang, North Korea 2203b, 2203c, 2369b
Pyorrhea 920b
Pyramidal cells 939a
Pyramiding (fin.) 601c
Pyramids (arch.)
  Egypt 74a, 973a
Pyramids (geom.) 1578a
Pyramus 1445b
Pyrenees Mountains 2148a, 2263b, 2339b
Pyrethrum 741c
Pyridoxine *see* Vitamin B$_6$
Pyrite 453c, 511c
  Korea, North 2203c
Pyroclastic rock 511c
Pyrola family 1689b
Pyrometallurgy 1215c, 1216a
Pyrometer 511c
Pyroxene 453b, 511c
Pyrrha 1430a
Pyrrho of Elia 1615b
Pyrrhotite 511c
Pyrrhus, King (Epirus) 331a, 2086a
Pyruvic acid 1897c
Pythagoras 331a, 974c, 1502a, 1557b, 1751c
  musical scale 157a, 1896b
  philosophy 1613a
Pythagorean theorem 1571a, 1607a
Pytheas 331a
Pythias Damon 1429c
Python (myth) 1445c

Q

Q (pseud.) *see* Quiller-Couch, Arthur
Q fever *tab* 947, 1846c
Qahtan al-Shaabi 2254a
Qairouan, Tunisia 2277a
Qajar dynasty 2189b
Qanat 511c
Qaramanli dynasty 2210b
Qasim, Abdel Karim 2190b
Qat 2302a
Qatar 2242
  climate 2242b
  economy 2242b–2242c
  flag *il* 2184
  geography 2242b
  government 2242c
  history 2242c
  map *Atlas*-25
  oil 2242b–2242c
  people of 2242b
  religion 2242b
Qattara Depression 2339b
Quad (print.) 153b
Quad folder (print.) 153b
Quadratic equations 1544c, 1548c
  functions 1592a
Quadrature 512a
Quadrilateral 1606b
Quadrille 177c
Quagmire 512a
Quail 53c
Quaker Poet *see* Whittier, John Greenleaf
Quakers Colonial Pennsylvania 2025c
  pacifism 894b
Qualitative analysis 1800c, 1827a

Quality control 1275c
Quality Street (play) 1414b
Quantitative analysis 1800c, 1827a
Quantity theory of money 531b, 601c
Quantum 1904a, 1919b
  masers 1919a
Quantum mechanics 1804b
Quantum number electrons 1806c
Quantum theory history 1870a
  light 1903c
Quarks (phys.) 1911b, 1917c
Quarrying 512a, 1275b
Quart *tab* 1500
Quarter horses 739b
Quartet (music) 177c
Quartz 453b, 512a, 1220c
  hardness *tab* 1192b
  light 1905c
  ultrasonics 1897a
Quartz glass 133a
Quartzite 451a, 512a
Quasar 1796c
Quasi contracts 824a
Quasimodo, Salvatore 1388a, *tab* 1481
Quasi-optical propagation (radio) 1175c
Quaternary Period *tab* 457, 458a, 512a
Quatrain 1414b
Que Que, Rhodesia 2369b
Quebec, Canada 2020c, 2113c, 2115a, 2369b
  capture by English 2027a
  founding 2023c
  kittiwake 41b
Quebec Act of 1774 2115a
Quebec Bridge 1197
Quebracho (bot.) 1209c
Queen forms of address *tab* 1120

Queen, Ellery *tab* 1463a
Queen Anne furniture 1100a
Queen Anne's War 1021b, *tab* 1073
  United States 2026c
Queen Ann's lace *see* Carrot
Queen of the Antilles *see* Jamaica
Queen of the Danube *see* Budapest
Queen Elizabeth (ship) 1180c
Queen Elizabeth's Virginal Book (mus.) 161a
Queen of Hearts (nursery rhyme) 412b
Queen Mab (poem) 1365a
Queen Mary (ship) 1180c
Queen Mother forms of address *tab* 1120
Queen Victoria (bk.) 1397b
Queens College 689
Queensberry, 8th Marquis of (John Sholto Douglas) *see* Douglas
Queensland, Australia 2318c, 2319c
Queiroz, José María Eça de *see* Eça de Queiroz
Quemoy 2131c
Quental, Antero T. de 1388c
Quentell, Heinrich 143c
Quentin Durward (nov.) 1365c, 1414b
Quercia, Jacopo della 121b, *tab* 125
  biography 331a
Quern 1933b
Query (print.) 153b
Quesada, Gonzalo Jiménez de *see* Jiménez de Quesada
Question mark 1312b
Quételet, Adolphe 1506c
Quetta, Pakistan 2369b
Quetzal *see* Trogon

Quevedo y Villegas, Francisco Gómez de 1391c, *tab* 1467
Quezon, Manuel 2238b
Quezon City, Philippines 2237b, 2369b–2369c
Quicklime 1214a
Quicksand 512a
Quicksilver *see* Mercury (chem.)
Quiller-Couch, Arthur 1395a
  pseudonym *tab* 1463a
Quinary system 1512a
Quince 1689b
Quincy, Josiah 331a
Quincy College 665
Quinet, Edgar 1381b
Quinine 1824c
Quintal *tab* 1500
Quintana, Manuel José 331a
Quintet (mus.) 177c
Quintilian 1357c, *tab* 1464
  biography 331a
  on Latin authors 1356b
Quire 153b
Quiroga, Horacio 1393c
Quisling, Vidkun 2231c
Quita Sueño Bank 2003
Quito, Ecuador 2143c, 2144a, 2369c
Quo Vadis (nov.) 1414b
Quo warranto 904a
Quorum 844a
Quoin (print.) 153b
Quoits (game) 1726b
Quorum 904a
Quotas (immigration) 851a, 883c, 884a
Quotation (bus.) 601c
Quotation marks 1312c
Quotient 1603a
Quran *see* Koran
Quyen, Ngo 2300a

R

Ra (anc. deity) 1445b, 1622c
Raabe, Wilhelm 1385b
Rabab (mus. instr.) 155b, 159c
Rabat, Morocco 2221b, 2221c, 2369c
Rabbit 53c, 2091c–2092a
Rabeh (warlord) 2121a
Rabelais, François 331b, 1378b, *tab* 1466
Rabies *tab* 947, 958a
Raborn, William F. 862b
Raby, 1st Baron *see* Strafford, 1st Earl of
Racan, Honoré de *tab* 1467
Raccoon 53c–54a
Race (geog.) 512a
Race horses 1983b
Races (anthrop.) 1925b
  adaptation 1927b
  classification 1925b
Rachmaninoff, Sergei 169a, *tab* 172a
  biography 331b
Racine, Jean Baptiste 331b, 1379a, *tab* 1468
Racine, Wisconsin 1999a
Racing track and field 1737b
Racoon River 2007a
Radama I, 2212a
Radar 1889b
  weather forecasting 478a
Radcliffe, Ann Ward 1366a
Radcliffe College 675
Radek, Karl 331b
Radford College 705
Radharkrishnan, Sarvepalli 2186b
Radial drainage pattern 512a
Radial engines 1135b
Radiance 1907a
Radiant energy 1796c, 1906c
  sun 1782c
Radiation 512a, 1869a, 1870b
  conversion chart 1130
  cosmic 952a, 1917c
  food preservation 737a
  heat 1900c
  nuclear chemistry 1828c

  public health 958a
  solar flare 952a
  space biology 951c
Radiation detectors 1275c
Radical Socialist Party (France) 2154b–2154c
Radicals (algebra) 1547a, 1607a
  simplification 1547c
Radicals (chem.) 1811c
Radicals (pol.) 904a
Radio 1174c, 1889a
  careers 378b
  communications 1151c
  crystal rectifiers 1890b
  receiver 1176c
  repairmen 386c
  transmitter 1176b
  wave propagation 1175a
Radio biology 722c
Radio compass 1163c
Radio stars 1796c
Radio telescopes 1786a, 1792c, 1796c
Radio waves 1792c
Radioactive age determination 512a
Radioactive decay 454b, 512a, 1919c
  half-life 1918b
Radioactive isotopes 1829b
Radioactivity 512a, 1870a
  discovered 1914a
Radiocarbon dating 454c
Radiography 1288c
Radioisotope tracers 1829b
Radiolaria 1848b
Radiolarian ooze 512a
Radiology careers 382b
Radiometric units 1906c
Radiosonde 512b
Radish 1689b
Radium 1836
  atomic weight *tab* 1805
Radius 1571b
Radon 1808b, 1836
  atomic structure 1807b
  atomic weight *tab* 1805
  ion 1809b
Raeburn, Henry *tab* 107
  biography 331b
  Master William Blair tab 112
Raetian (lang.) 176c, *see* Ladin
Raffaello *see* Raphael

Raff, Joachim *tab* 172a
Raffia *see* Palm
Raffles, Sir Stamford 2250c
Rafts 1934c
Ragas (mus.) 155b
Ragnarok (myth) 1445c
Ragweed 1689c
Rahab 1459b
Rahman al-Iryani, Abdul 2302c
Rahu (myth) 1445c
Rail 54a
Railroad engineering 1179a
Railroad signaling 1179b
Railroads 1153a, 1176c, 2092b
  Canada 2112c, 2115c, 2116c
  cars 1178c
  history 524a
  Liberia 2209a
  locomotive 1178a
  rails 1178c
  tracks 1179a
  U.S. 2022b, 2038a
Railroads War Board 2066a
Rail-splitter, The *see* Lincoln, Abraham
Railways *see* Railroads
Raimondi, Marcantonio *tab* 107
Rain 473b, 512b, 763c, 764a–764c
  orographic 509b
  shadow 512b
Rain (poem) 414c
Rain forests 1859c, 1863c, 1864c
Rain, Rain, Go Away (nursery rhyme) 408b
Rain shadow 512a
Rainbow 512b
Rainbow trout *il* 1717
Rainey, Henry T. House of Representatives *tab* 802b
Rainier III, Prince 2220b
Rainier, Mt. 1998a, 2016c, 2019a, 2019b
Rainmaker Mountain 2000
Rainmaking 474c
Raised beach 512b
Raisin in the Sun (play) 1377a
Rajang River 2213b
Rajputs, the 2180a, 2180b, 2180c
Rake 512b

Rakosi, Mátyás 2175b
Raleigh, Sir Walter 1022c, 1360b, *tab* 1466, 2171a
  biography 331b
  explorations 2023c
Raleigh, North Carolina 1990c, 1991a, 2013c
  Civil War 2050c
Rall, Colonel 2028b
Ralph Roister Doister (play) 1360c, *tab* 1466
Rama (myth) 1449a
Ramadan (month) 982a
Ramapithecus 1923c
Ramayana (epic) 1344a, 1414c, *tab* 1464
Rambaud, Alfred Nicolas 331b
Rambler, The (essays) 1363b, 1414c
Rambouillet, Marquise de 1378c
Rameau, Jean *tab* 171c
Ramée, Marie Louise de la *see* Ouida
Ramgoolam, Seewoosagur 2217b
Ramie *see* Nettle
Ramírez, Pedro 2090c
Ramona (nov.) 1374c, 1414c
Ramp 512b
Rampur, India 2369c
Ramsay, William 331c
Ramses I, King (Egypt) 331c, 1003c
Ramses II, King (Egypt) 331c, 1003c
Ramses III, King (Egypt) 331c
Ramsey, Alexander *tab* 796
Ranat (mus.) 155b
Ranches 381a
Ranchi, India 2369c
Rand 512b
Randall, Alexander *tab* 796
Randall, James Ryder 1374b
Randall, Samuel Jackson House of Representatives *tab* 802b
Randolph, Edmund Jennings 331c, *tab* 795, 2031a
Randolph, John 331c
Randolph, Peyton Continental Congress *tab* 802b
Randolph-Macon College 705

Randolph-Macon Woman's College 705
Range 512b
Range management (conservation) 1868a
Ranger, Henry Ward *tab* 108
Ranger III (spacecraft) *tab* 1772
Ranger IV (spacecraft) *tab* 1772
Ranger V (spacecraft) *tab* 1772
Ranger VII (spacecraft) *tab* 1772
Rangitaiki River 2225c
Rangoon, Burma 2106b, 2106c, 2369c–2370a
Rank, Otto 1958a
Ranke, Leopold von 332a, 1385a
Rankin, Jeanette 332a
Rankine, William J. M. 1190c
Rankine cycle 1901b
Rankine scale 1898c
Rape *see* Mustard
Rape of the Bucket (poem) 1387a, *tab* 1467
Rape of the Lock (poem) 1363a
Rape of Lucrece (poem) 1361c
Raphael *tab* 76c, *tab* 107, *tab* 111
  Alba Madonna tab 113
  biography 332a
  Madonna of the Candelabra tab 109
  Sistine Madonna tab 110
  Transfiguration tab 112
Rapid 512b
Rappahannock (river) Civil War 2050a
Ras Taffari 2146b
Rashid al-Din 332a
Rasmussen, Knud Johan V. 332a
Raspberry 1689c
Raspe, Rudolph Erich 1411b
Rasputin, Grigori E. 332a, 2260c–2261a
Rasselas (tale) 1363c, 1414c
Ras Shamra (anc. city) 969c
Rat 54a–54b
Rat Island 2016a
Ratio 602a, 1530a, 1607a
Rational numbers 1605b
Rationalism (philos.) 1617a
Rats diseases 957c
  ecology 1859b
Rats, Lice and History (bk.) 1348b
Rattlesnakes *il* 32, 1711c
Rauch, Christian Daniel *tab* 125
  biography 332a
Ravel, Maurice 168b, *tab* 172a
  biography 332a
Raven *see* Crow
Raven, The (poem) 1414c
Ravenna, Italy 2195a
  cathedral 1192
  painting 84b
Ravine 512b
Rawalpindi, Pakistan 2232a, 2370a
Rawlins, John *tab* 796
Rawlinson, George 332b
Rawlinson, Sir Henry Creswicke 332a, 969a
Raverat, Gwendolen *tab* 1481
Ray 54b
Ray, John 332b, 1638a, 1638c
Ray, Man 332b
Rayburn, Samuel T. 332b, *tab* 802b
Rayleigh, 3rd Baron (John William Strutt) 332b
Raymond of Poitiers (myth) 1439b
Raynal, Guillaume T. F. 332c
Raynaud's disease 945b
Rayon 1208c 1219b
Re (Egy. deity) *see* Ra
Reaction series 512b
Reaction turbines 1148b, 1150a
Read, A. C. 1156a
Read, George Declaration of Independence *tab* 803
  U.S. Constitution 809c
Read, Thomas Buchanan 332c, *tab* 1476
Reade, Charles 332c, 1367b, *tab* 1475
  Cloister and the Hearth 1399b
Reader's Digest (magazine) circulation 1167b
Reading, 1st Marquis of (Rufus Daniel Isaacs) 332c
Reading 1299–1301
  first grade 1300c
  kindergarten 400b
  learning 1299a–1301b
  pre-primer level 1299b
  test 1301a
Reading, Pennsylvania 1993b

Real image (optics) 1908a
Real numbers 1547a, 1605b
Real property 824b
  chattels 863b
  wills 825b
Realism 1415a
  American art 104b
  education 623b
  French literature 1381b
  German literature 1385a
  glossary 1620c
  Greek sculpture 117a
  painting 86a
  Portuguese literature 1388c
Reality principle (psych.) 1957b
Ream (print.) 153b
Reaper 720b
Reasoning 1950a
Réaumur, René Antoine Ferchault de 332c, 1920a
Réaumur scale 1920a
Rebab *see* Rabab
Rebecca (lit. char., Scott) 1407a, 1415a
Rebecca of Sunnybrook Farm (bk.) 1415a
Rebellion 904a
Rebikov, Vladimir I. 169b
Rebora, Clemente 1388a
Recall (gov.) 904a
Recall (psych.) 1950a
Receipt 602a
Recent (geol.) 512b
Reception (law) 904b
Recession (econ.) 602a
Recessive traits 1850c
Recife, Brazil 2370a
Reciprocal equations 1603b
Reciprocal Tariff Act 902c
Reciprocal Trade Agreements Act 902c
Reciprocity 904b
Reciprocity Agreement (1911) 2117c
Reciprocity Treaty (1854) 2115c, 2116b
Recitative (mus.) 177c
Reclamation 904b
Reclamation Act 888b, 2062b
Reclamation, Bureau of 888b
Reclamation, land *see* Land reclamation
Recognition (psych.) 1950a
Recon 1855c
Reconstruction (U.S.) 2051c, 2052c
  events during *tab* 1065–1066
  literature 1374c
Reconstruction Act 2052a
Reconstruction Finance Corporation 867a, 904c, 2072a
Reconstructionism (educ.) 624b
Recorder (law) 904c
Recording 1889b, 1895a
Recreation 1703–1740
Rectangle 1605c
Rectangular coordinate system 1553c, 1593a
Rectangular drainage pattern 512b
Rectification (elec.) 1919c
Rectifiers (elec.) 1890b, 1892b, 1919c
Recto (print.) 153b
Rectocele 945b
Rectum 920c
Recurved spit (geol.) 512b
Recuyell of the Historyes of Troye (bk.) 1360b
Red 1104b, 1907c
  color vision 928c
  political meaning 904c
Red and yellow soils 512b
Red Badge of Courage (nov.) 1415a
Red blood cells 922a
  anemia 940a
  polycythemia vera 945a
  sickle cell anemia 945c
Red Book of Hergest (lit.) 1395c
Red brass 1196a
Red clay 512b
Red clover 1996b
Red Cross, American 1745b
Red fuming nitric acid *see* RFNA
Red Guards 2125b, 2131a
Red maple 1993c
Red oak 1989b
Red River 1962a, 1968a, 1986b, 1991b, 1992b, 1995b, 2007b, 2018c, 2020a, 2116c
  length of 2020b
Red (Hong) **River** 2298c, 2299a, 2339b

Red River of the North 2339b
Red Sea 2339b–2339c
  Biblical 1459b
  sea cows 55b
Red shift 1794a
Red snapper *il* 1717
Red soil 750a
Red Wing 332c
Red-banded leafhopper *il* 29
Redbud 1689c, 1992a
Redfield, Edward Willis *tab* 108
Redfield, William Charles 332c
Redfield, William Cox *tab* 797
Red-figured ware 84a, 126b
Redi, Francesco 1839a
Redlands, University of 658
Redon, Odilon *tab* 108, 332c
Redstart 54b–54c
Redstone arsenal 1769a
Redstone (rocket) 1769a
Reducing agent (chem.) 1813b
Redwood *il* 1664
  forests 1976c
  see also Sequoia
Reed, John 332c
Reed, Stanley Supreme Court *tab* 802c
Reed, Thomas Brackett 904a
  House of Representatives *tab* 802b
Reed, Walter 332c, 2060b
Reed 1690a
Reed College 694
Reed instruments (mus.) 177c
  physics 1896b
Reed organ (mus.) 177c
Reef 512c
Reel (dance) 181c
Reentry (astronautics) 1769c
Reference marks 153b
Referendum 884b, 889b
  definition 904c
Reflecting telescopes 1791a, 1797b
  largest 1791b
Reflection (light) 1904a
  law of 1904a
  prisms 1909a
Reflex angle 1601b
Reflex camera 1237b
Reflexes 939b
Reforestation 904c
Reform Bill of 1832 1014c
Reform Bills (Eng.) 987b
Reformation 2287c–2288a
  education 614b
  England 1015a
  German literature 1383b
  Germany 2160a–2160b
  history outline *tab* 1044–1049
  literature 1383c
  music 160b
  Sweden 2268c
  Switzerland 2270b
Refracting telescopes 1791a, 1797b
  largest 1791b
Refraction 1828b, 1904b, 1919c
  index of 1904c
  law of 1904c
Refractory 512c
Refrain (mus.) 177c
Refrigeration 1276a, 1902a
  careers 380a
  engineers 379c
  food poisoning 956b
  food preservation 737a
  repairmen 386a
Refrigerators 1260a
Refugee Settlement Commission (League of Nations) 1013b
Refutation (debating) 1328b
Reg 512c
Regan (lit. char.) 1405a, 1408b
Regelation 512c
Regency furniture 1097c,
Regensburg, Berthold von *tab* 1465
Regent 904c
Regents, Board of (N.Y.) 904c
Regents of St. Elizabeth's Hospital (paint.) *tab* 111
Reger, Max 167c, *tab* 172a
Regimen 512c
Regina, Canada 2370a
Regional economics 602a
Regional enteritis 945b
Regional metamorphism 512c
Regis College (Colo.) 659
Regis College (Mass.) 675
Register (mus.) 177c
Register (print.) 153b
Registered nurses 382c

Registration (voting) 905a
Regnard, Jean François *tab* 1469
Régnier, Henri de 1382b
Rêgo, José Lins do 1393c
Regolith 512c
Regosols 512c
Regression (astron.) 1796c
Regression (psych.) 1957b
Regular polygons 1606b
Regular polyhedrons 1606c
Regulation (econ.) 602a
Regulator Movement, The 2026b
Regulus, Marcus Atilius 332c
Regur 512c
Rehabilitation careers 383b
Rehoboam 1459b
Reich 905a
Reichstag 874a
Reid, Whitelaw *tab* 801
  pseudonym 1461a
Reims Cathedral 76c
  architecture 985a
  sculpture 120a
Reindeer *see* Deer
Reindeer Lapps 1927b
Reiner, Fritz 333a
Reinforcement (light) 1905a
Reinforcement (psych.) 1949c
Reinhardt, Max 333a
Reinken, Johann 163a, *tab* 171c
Rejuvenation 512c
Relapsing fever *tab* 947
Relative key (mus.) 177c
Relative time 512c
Relativity, Theory of 1870b
Relay (satellite) 1769c, *tab* 1163
Relay races 1737b
Relief (econ.) 905a
Relief (geog.) 512c
Relief printing *see* Letterpress printing
Relief sculpture 116a
  Rome 118b
Religio Medici (bk.) 1347a, 1362a
Religion 1621–1634
  Arab world 1632c
  bibliography 1634c
  dance 181a
  definition 1621a
  pacifism 894c
  philosophy 1612a
  primitive 1937b
  state 909b
  see also under the names of individual countries, such as Panama, religion and under the names of various religions
Religion and the Rise of Capitalism (bk.) 1348b
Religions U.S. 1966b
Reliques of Ancient English Poetry (poems) 1364a, *tab* 1470
Remarque, Erich Maria 333a, 1385c, *tab* 1481
Rembrandt *tab* 107, *tab* 110, *tab* 112
  Anatomy Lesson tab 111
  Aristotle Contemplating the Bust of Homer tab 112
  biography 333a
  etching 136b
  Portrait of His Mother tab 113
  Saskia tab 109
  Self-Portrait il 89
  Syndics of the Cloth Hall tab 109
Remington, Frederic 333a
Remington and Sons typewriters 1188a
Reminiscences (bk., Carlyle) 1366a
Remson, Ira 745a
Remus (myth) 1446a
Renaissance 965a, 985c, 1415a, 2022c
  architecture 76c–77c
  art 72a
  dance 182c
  education 614a
  English literature 1360b
  French literature 1378a
  furniture 1094c
  German literature 1383b
  history outine *tab* 1042–1045
  Italian 2195a
  Italian literature 1386b
  literature 1344b
  map-making 779c
  philosophy 1616a
  Portuguese literature 1388b
  sculpture 114a, 121b–122b
  Spanish literature 1391a
Renan, Joseph Ernest 1381b, *tab* 1476

Renard, Charles 1155a
Reni, Guido *tab* 107
  biography 333b
Rennie, John 1196c
Rennin 727a
Reno, Nevada 1988c, 2013c
Renoir, Pierre Auguste 86b, *tab* 108
  biography 333b
  Impressionism 1406c
  Madame Charpentier and Children tab 112
  Two Little Circus Girls tab 110
Rensselaer, Van *see* Van Rensselaer
Rensselaer Polytechnic Institute (R.P.I.) 686
Rent 602a
Reorganization (bus.) 602a
Repairmen careers 385c
Reparations 905b
Reparations Commission (World War I) 1023a
Repeal (law) 905c
Repeat (mus.) 177c
Replevin (law) 906a
Reply to Hayne (D. Webster) 2037c
Repplier, Agnes *tab* 1479
Report on the Affairs of British North America (Durham) 1001a
Report on the Affairs of British North America (Lambton) 2116a
Representation of Soul and Body (oratorio) 161c
Representative money 598c
Repression (psych.) 1957a
Reprieve 906a
Reproductive system female 926b
  male 926b
Republic (gov.) 784c, 906a
Republic of *see under the latter part of the name, such as* South Africa, Republic of
Republic, The (Plato) 1353c
Republic River 1977b
Republican Party 906a
  Democratic Party 872c
  Jefferson, Thomas 2031b
  rise of 2042b
  third parties 910c
Republican Peoples Party (Turkey) 2279b
Repulsion (phys.) magnets 1883c
  static electricity 1881b
Requiem (mus.) 177c
Requiem (poem) 1368b
Requisition 906b
Resaca de la Palma, Battle of 2039f
Rescue, The (nov.) 1370a, 1415a
Reserve (fin.) 602b
Reserve Banks 879a
Reservoirs 1221a
Residual soil 512c
Resist (print.) 150a, 153b
Resistance (phys.) 1919c
  measurement 1882c
Resistance (psych.) 1957c
Resistance furnaces 1248a
Resistance thermometers 1898c
Resistance welding 1287c
Resistivity (phys.) 1882a
Resistors (elec.) 1919c
Resita, Romania 2244a
Resonance 1893c
Respighi, Ottorino 168a, *tab* 172a
  biography 333b
Respiration 921c
  plants 1646c–1647a
  see also Breathing
Respiratory diseases 955a
Response conditioning 1949b
  plants 1647a–1647b
Restraint of trade 906c
Restrepo, Carlos Lleras 2133c
Rests (mus.) 177c
Resumption Act 2054b
Resurrection (nov., Tolstoy) 1389c
Retail 602b
Retail stores 602b
  careers 389b
Retention (memory) 1950a
Reticular layer 918a
Reticulate 1642c
Reticuloendothelial system 921a, 924c
Retina 928b
  detachment 937a
Retroactive inhibition 1950a
Retrograde motion 1796c

Retro-rocket 1779b
Return of the Native (nov.) 1368a, 1415a
Return of the Prodigal Son (paint.) *tab* 110
Reuben (Bib.) 1459b
Réunion 2320
Reuter, Fritz 1385a, *tab* 1475
Reuther, Walter P. 333b
Reval, Estonia *see* Tallinn
Revelations, Book of 1459b
Revenue Act (1932) 910b
Reverberation time 1192c
Revere, Paul 333b, 960c
  public health 960c
Reversed stream 512c
Reverted image 1909a
Revolt of Islam (poem) 1365b
Revolution (astron.) 1781a, 1796c
Revolution (geol.) 512c
Revolution *see* Industrial Revolution
Revolution (pol.) 906c, 987a
  see also under names of individual revolutions, such as American Revolution
Revolution of 1917 1025b
Revolutionary Party (Guatemala) 2169c
Revolvers 1255a
Rewards and Fairies (bk.) 1415b
Rey, Jean 1125a, 1798c
Reykjavik, Iceland 2176a, 2370a
Reynard the Fox (fables) 1377c, 1445c
Reynolds, Joshua 104a, *tab* 107, 1103b
  biography 333b
  Lord Heathfield tab 111
  Mrs. Siddons tab 112
Reynolds Metal Company Detroit building *il* 79
Reza Shah Pahlavi 982b
Reza'iyeh, Iran 2370a
RFNA 1766c, 1779a
Rh factor 922c
Rhadamanthus 1445c
Rhapsodie Nègre (mus., Powell) 265c, 1421c
Rhapsody (mus.) 177c
Rhazes 728c
Rhea (myth) 1429c, 1445c
Rhee, Syngman 333b, 2205a, 2205b
Rheinberger, Joseph 167b
Rheingold *see* Rhinegold
Rhenish (wine) 723c
Rhenium 1836
  atomic weight *tab* 1805
Rhetoric (bk., Quintilian) *tab* 1464
Rhetorical question *see* Interrogation (figure of speech)
Rheumatic fever 945b, *tab* 947
Rheumatoid arthritis 940b
Rhind Papyrus 1501b, 1556c
Rhine River 2148a, *il* 2157, 2157b, 2210b–2210c, 2269b, 2339c
Rhine (wine) *see* Rhenish
Rhinegold (Rheingold) (leg.) 1445c
Rhinegold, The (Das Rheingold) (opera) 167a
  Alberich 1423c
  Freya 1432c
Rhinoceros 54c
Rhizobium 1846a
Rhizomes (plant) 1644c
Rhode, Gilbert 1102a
Rhode Island 1993–1994
  agriculture 1994a
  appointment 852b
  bobwhite 17c
  capital punishment 860a
  census (1960) 1973
  climate 1994a
  child labor laws 831c
  colleges 698
  colonial government 785a
  colonial history 2025b
  commercial law *tab* 826
  congressional apportionment *tab* 853
  Constitution (U.S.) 809c
  economy 1994a
  geography 1993c–1994a
  government 1994a
  holidays 841–842
  labor legislation 833c, 836c
  people of 1994a
  public school expenditures *tab* 644
  public school enrollment *tab* 646
  student enrollment *tab* 645
Rhode Island, University of 698

Rhode Island College 698
Rhode Island Reds (chickens) 1993c
  eggs 732a
Rhode Island School of Design (R. I. S. D.) 698
Rhodes, Cecil John 333b, 2212c, 2243b, 2253a, 2305c
Rhodes 2164c
  sculpture 117b
Rhodesia and Nyasaland, Federation of 2243b
  see also Malawi; Rhodesia; Zambia
Rhodesia 2242–2243
  agriculture 2243a
  climate 2243a
  economy 2243a
  flag *il* 2184
  geography 2242c–2243a
  government 2243a–2243b
  history 2243b
  independence 2292b
  map 2243, *Atlas*-40–41
  people of 2243a
  religion 2242c
  Southern *see* Southern Rhodesia
Rhodium 1836
  atomic weight *tab* 1805
Rhododendron 1690a, 1998b
Rhodope Mountains 2105a
Rhomboidal prism 1909b
Rhombus 1605c, 1567c
Rhone River 2148a, 2149b, 2269b, 2339c
Rhubarb 1690a
Rhyme 1315c, 1415b
  development 1344b
  music 158c
Rhyolite 512c
Rhythm 154a, 177c
  Greek music 157a
  poetry 1351a
  prosody 1415b
Ria coast 512c
Rib cage 917c
Ribault, Jan 2025b
Ribbed vault 76c
Ribbentrop, Joachim Von 333c
Ribeiro, Aquilino 1389a
Ribera, José *tab* 107, 333c
  Martyrdom of St. Bartholomew tab 111
Ribicoff, Abraham B. *tab* 797
Riboflavin *see* Vitamin B$_2$
Ribonuclease 1855a
Ribonucleic acid (RNA) 1841a, 1842c, 1853c, 1855a
  code words *tab* 1855
Ribosomes 1855a
Rice, Elmer 333c
Rice 742a, 1690a–1690b
  Arkansas 1976b
  British Honduras 2308a
  Brunei 2309b
  Burma 2107a
  China 2125b
  Comoro Islands 2310c
  Fiji Islands 2312b
  gibberellic acid 738c
  Guam 2001a
  Guyana 2170b, 2170c
  India 2178b
  Indonesia 2187a
  Iraq 2189c
  Italy 2194b–2194c
  Japan 2199b
  Korea, South 2203c
  Laos 2206b
  Liberia 2209a
  Louisiana 1984a
  Madagascar 2212a
  Malawi 2212c
  Malaysia 2213b
  Mali 2215a
  Mauritania 2216a
  Mexico 2218a
  New Caledonia 2318b
  Pakistan 2232b
  Panama 2234b
  Paraguay 2235b
  Peru 2236c
  Philippines 2237c
  Portugal 2241b
  Portuguese Guinea 2320a
  producing areas 742b
  Niger 2228c
  Senegal 2248a
  Sierra Leone 2248c
  Spain 2264a
  Surinam 2323b
  Swaziland 2267a
  Taiwan 2125c
  Tanzania 2272a
  Texas 1995c
  Thailand 2273c
  Togo 2275a

U.A.R. 2280c
U.S. 1966b
Uruguay 2295a
Venezuela 2297b
Vietnam 2299b
Rice University 702
Richard, Duke (York) 2287b
Richard I, King (England) *tab* 171b, 1020a
  biography 333c
  reign of 2285b–2285c
Richard II, King (England) 333c
  literature of reign 2287a
Richard III, King (England) 333c, 2287b
Richard the Lion-hearted *see* Richard I
Richard Yea-and-Nay (bk.) 1370c
Richards, Ivor Armstrong 334a
Richards, Theodore William 334a
Richardson, Henry Hobson 78c
Richardson, Jack 1377a
Richardson, John 1390c
Richardson, Sir Owen W. 334a
Richardson, Samuel 1346a, 1363c, *tab* 1469
  biography 334a
  Pamela 1412a
Richardson, William *tab* 796
Richelieu, Duc de (Cardinal Richelieu) 334a, 2114a, 2151c
  French Academy 1378c
Richelieu River 2020c
Richepin, Jean *tab* 1478
Richmond, Virginia 2013c, 1997a–1997c
  capitol 78c
  Civil War 2050c
  Confederacy 2045a
Richmond, University of 705
Richter, Jean Paul 334a, 1384c, *tab* 1471
Richter magnitude scale 512c
Rickenbacker, Edward V. 334a
Rickets 945b
Rickettsiae 1846b
Rickettsial pox *tab* 947
Ricotta cheese *tab* 731b
Ride a Cockhorse (nursery rhyme) 408b
Rider College 683
Ridge 512c
Ridgway, Matthew 334a
  Korean War 1012a
Ridpath, John Clark 334b
Riel, Louis 334b, 2116c, 2117a
Riemann, Georg 1506a, 1558a, 1580c
Rienzi, Cola di (Niccolo Gabrini) 334b, 1462b
Rienzi (opera) 166c
Riete, Vittorino *tab* 172a
Rif Atlas Sea 2221b–2221c
Rif Mountains 2222b
Rifles 1254c, *il* 1719–1722
Rift 512c
Rift body 513a
Riga, Latvia 2370a, 2240b
Rigaud, Hyacinthe *tab* 107
Rigel (star) *tab* 1786
  temperature 1789a
Right-angle prism 1909a
Right angles 1601b, 1606a
Right of assembly 810a, 854c
Right of Petition 810a, 898a
Rights of Man (pamphlet) 1372c
Right triangles 1607c
  trigonometric functions 1607c
Rigid airships 1155a
Rigoletto (opera) 167b
Rig-Veda (Hindu scriptures) 1420b, *tab* 1463, 1624a
  language 1334a
Riis, Jacob August 334b
Riisager, Knudage *tab* 172b
Rijks Museum (Amsterdam) *tab* 109
Riksdag (Swed. gov.) 874a
Rila Mountains 2105a
Riley, James Whitcomb 334b, 1374c, *tab* 1478
  pseudonyms 1462b
Rilke, Rainer Maria 334b, 1385c, *tab* 1480
Rill 513a
Rimbaud, Arthur 334b, 1382a
Rime of the Ancient Mariner (poem) 1394c
Rimmer, William *tab* 125

Rimski-Korsakov, Nikolay 169a, *tab* 172a, 184a
  biography 334b
Rinaldo (opera) 162c
Rinaldo and Armida (paint.) *tab* 110
Rinehart, William Henry *tab* 125
  biography 334c
Ring and the Book (poem) 1415b
Ring-a-ring of Roses (nursery rhyme) 408c
Ring des Nibelungen (opera, Wagner) 167a
  Brunhild 1428a
  Gunther 1433c
  Hagen 1433c
Ringling Brothers 334c
Ring-necked pheasant 741c, 1994b
Rinuccini, Ottavio 161c
Rio de Bayanón (river) 2002a
Rio de Janeiro, Brazil 2102a–2102c, *il* 2103, 2370a
  Pan American Conferences (1906, 1943), 1017c
Rio de Janeiro Protocol (1942), 2144c
Río Grande de Arecibo (river) 2002a
Río Grande de Lóiza (river) 2002a
Rio Grande (river) 1990a, 1995b, 2220a, 2005a, 2007a, 2020a, 2293a
  length of 2020a–2020b
Río de la Plata (river) 2002a
Río Ulúa (river) 2172c
Rion River 2254c
Riot 906c
Riot Act 907a
Rip current 513a
Rip saws 1288c
Rip Van Winkle (story) 1415c
Riparian 513a
Ripon College 708
Ripple mark 513a
Rise 513a
Rise of American Civilization (bk.) 1348c
Rise of Silas Lapham (nov.) 1375a
Risk 602c
Risorgimento 1387b
Ristoro d'Arezzo 1386a
Ritardando (mus.) 177c
Rites 1937b
Rittenhouse, David 334c
Rittenhouse, William 1272c
Rivals, The (play) 1364a, 1415c
  Mrs. Malaprop 1410a
Rivas, Duke of 1392b
River engineering 1179c
Rivera, Diego *tab* 108
  biography 334c
Rivera, Julio Adalberto 2145c
Rivera y Orbaneja, Miguel Primo de 334c
Rivers 513a, 2339c–2340a
  delta 449a
  erosion 448a
  see also under names of individual rivers, such as Mississippi
Riverside Press 148a
Rivets 1252c
Rivier College 682
Riviera 2340a
Riyadh, Saudi Arabia 2246b, 2370b
Riza Shah 2189b
Rizal, José 2238a–2238b
Rizzio, David 334c
RNA *see* Ribonucleic acid
Ro (lang.) 1338b
Road Inquiry, Office of 1180a
Road Town, British Virgin Islands 2309a, 2370b
Roadrunner 1989c
Roads 1152c, 1179c
Roadtown *see* Road Town
Roanoke, Virginia 1997c
Roanoke College 705
Roanoke Island 2023c
Roaring forties 513c
Rob Roy (1671–1734) *see* MacGregor, Robert
Robalo *il* 1717
Robbery 907a
Robbia, Andrea della 122a, *tab* 125
Robbia, Giovanni della 122a
Robbia, Luca della 121c, *tab* 125, 127a, *tab* 130
  biography 334c
Robbia ware 113c, 122a
Robbins, Jerome 184c

Robeiro, Júlio 1393c
Robert I, King (Scotland) 214b, 1020a, 2286b
  legend 1427c
Robert II, King (Scotland) 1020a
Robert III, King (Scotland) 1020a
Robert VI, King (Scotland) 1020a
Robert, Louis 148b
Robert, Nicholas 1272a
Roberts, Elizabeth Madox 334c
Roberts, Frederick ("Bobs") 334c
Roberts, Owen J. Supreme Court *tab* 802a
Roberts, Mt. 2008c
Roberts Wesleyan College 686
Roberval, Giles Personne de 334c
Roberval, Sieur de 2023b
Robeson, George *tab* 796
Robeson, Paul 335a
Robespierre, Maximilien de 335a, 1006c, 1007b, 1008c, 1010c, 2152c
  guillotined 1008a
  nickname 1462b
Robin 54c, 1977c, 1985c, 1999c
Robin Goodfellow 1445b
Robin Hood 1445c
  Allan-a-Dale 1423c
  Friar Tuck 1432c
  Little John 1438b
  Maid Marian 1438c
Robin's Father (play) 1371b
Robinson, Boardman *tab* 108
Robinson, Edwin Arlington 335a, 1376a, *tab* 1479
  Arthurian legend 1395c
Robinson, James Harvey 335a
Robinson, Joseph Taylor 335a
  vice-presidential candidate *tab* 801
Robinson, Theodore *tab* 108
Robinson, William 1179b
Robinson Crusoe (bk.) 1415c
Robinson-Patman Act 879c
Rob Roy (nov.) 1366a
Roc 1446a
Rochambeau, Comte de 335a
  American Revolution 2030a
Roche, Josephine 335a
Roche, Mazo de la *see* De la Roche, Mazo
Roche moutonnee 513a
Rochefoucauld, François de la *see* La Rochefoucauld, François de
Rochelle salts 1897a
Roche's limit 1783b, 1796c
Rochester, Edward Fairfax (lit. char.) 1416a
Rochester, New York 1990c, 2013c
  government 864b
Rochester, University of 686
Rochester Institute of Technology 686
Rock 447a, 449c, 513a
  economic geology 459
  geologic time 455b
  impermeable 503a
  intrusive 503b
  metamorphic 506c
  mineral content 453b
  paleontology 458a
  platonic 511b
  pyroclastic 511c
  quarrying 1275b
  sedimentary 514a
Rock of Chickamauga *see* Thomas, George Henry
Rock flour 513a
Rock glacier 513a
Rock gypsum 1212a
Rock Island, Illinois 1981b, 1982b
Rock mantle 513a
Rock salt 513a
Rock slide 513a
Rock wool 513a, 1202b
Rock-a-by Lady from Hushaby Street (poem) 415c
Rockefeller, John Davison 335a
Rockefeller, Nelson A. 335b
Rocker (art instr.) 139a
Rocket engines 1767c, 1768a
  fuel systems 1766b
  missile 1779a
  specific impulse 1766a
  sustainer 1779c
Rocket fuels
  liquid 1764a, 1766b
  solid 1766c
  specific impulse 1766a
Rocket into Interplanetary Space, The (bk.) 1765a
Rocket propulsion 1765b

Rockets 1764a
  atomic 1767b
  Congreve 1764b
  definition 1779b
  fuel systems 1766b
  gravity 949a
  history 1764a
  mass ratio 1765b
  staging 1765c
  ullage 1779c
  Vernier 1779c
Rock-fill dams 1205c
Rockford, Illinois 1981b
Rockford College 665
Rockhurst College 680
Rockne, Knute 335b
Rock-stratigraphic unit 513a
Rocky Mountain College 681
Rocky Mountain columbine 1977a
Rocky Mountain spotted fever *tab* 947
  immunization 1849c
Rocky Mountains 1977a–1977b, 1980c, 1987c, 1988b, 1990a, 1992b, 1995c, 1996a, 1998b, 1998c, 1999b, 2006a, 2016a, 2019a, 2020b, 2111a, 2111c, 2292c
  deer 25b
  gar 35b
  goat 36a
  Lewis and Clark Expedition 1014a
  locust 43c
  perch 50b
  pine trees 1686c
  prairie dog 53a
  ptarmigan 53b
  sheep 57b–57c
  tanager birds 62a
  tent caterpillars 62c–63a
Rocky River Bridge 1197a
Rod (anat.) 928b
Rod (meas.) *tab* 1500
Rodents diseases 957b
Roderick Random (nov.) 1363c
Rodin, Auguste 123a, *tab* 125
  biography 335c
Rodney, Caesar *tab* 795, *tab* 803
Rodney, Daniel *tab* 800
Rodney, George Brydges 335b
Rodó, José Enrique 1393a
Rodrigues de Montalvo, García *see* Montalvo, García Rodrigues de
Rodrigues Island 2216c
Roebling, John Augustus 335b, 1197a
Roebling, Washington A. 1191a, 1197a
Roentgen, Wilhelm Konrad 335b, 1240c, 1290b
Roentgen rays *see* X rays
Roger de Coverley (lit. char.) 1363b, 1400a
Rogers, Bruce 146b
Rogers, Carl R. 1952a
Rogers, John (sculp.) *tab* 125
Rogers, Randolph *tab* 125
Rogers, Will (William Penn Rogers) 335c
Rogers, William Pierce *tab* 796
Rogers, Mt. 1997b
Rogers Act 870b, 874b
Roger's Pass Tunnel *tab* 1226
Roggeveen, Jacob 2301c
Rohe, Mies van der *see* Mies van der Rohe
Rojas Pinilla, Gen. Gustavo 2133b–2133c
Rojas-Zorrilla, Francisco de 1392c
Rokel River 2248b
Roland 1446a
  Oliver 1441c
Roland de la Platière, Jean Marie 335c
Role (soc.) 1946a
  kinship 1936a
Rolfe, John 335c
Rolland, Romain 335c, 1382c, *tab* 1479
Roller bearing 1234a
Rolling (metal) 1268b
Rollins, Carl 146b
Rollins College 661
Romains, Jules 1382c, *tab* 1480
  biography 335c
Roman de Renart (bk.) *see* Reynard the Fox
Roman art 71b
  architecture 75b
  color 1103c
  furniture 1093c

glass *tab* 135
  painting 84b
  pottery 126b, *tab* 130
  sculpture 113a, 114a, 117c
Roman Catholic Church 1630c, 2235a, 2240c
  censorship 861a
  Counter-Reformation 1632b
  divorce 875b
  education 613c, 614c, 625c
  established church 877b
  heresies 994b, 995c, 1008c–1009a
  Middle Ages 982b, 985a
  papal rivalry 1001a
  popes *tab* 1080
  Vatican City 2296a–2296c
  Vatican Council 871b
  see also headings starting Church
Roman de la Rose (poem) 1359c, *tab* 1465
Roman Empire 972a, 976a, 995a, 999c, 1015a, 1016b, 1016c, 1019c, *tab* 1034–1036, 2150a, 2195a–2195b
  Barbarian invasion *tab* 1072
  British Isles 2283c–2284a
  Christianity 1016c, 1631a
  conquest of Greece 994a
  decline of 997c, 1016a
  Egypt 1005a
  feudalism 1006a
  Germany 2159a
  Greece 994a, 2165b
  rivalry with Carthage 1000a, 1000b
  Second Punic War 1000a
  slavery 964c
  see also Rome—Ancient
Roman Forum *see* Forum, Roman
Roman History (bk.) *tab* 1464
Roman law 814a–815b, 2285b
  beginning of 1002c
  citizenship 863c
  Licinian Rogations 1014c
  origins 1002c
  reception 904b
Roman literature *see* Latin literature
Roman numerals 1510a
Roman Republic 1001a
  censorship 860c
  decemvirate 1002c
  Licinian-Sextian Laws 1014c
  patrician-plebeian strife 1014c
  slavery 1014c
Roman type (print.) 153b
Roman y Reyes, Victor Manuel 2228b
Romance (lit.) 1416a
Romance (mus.) 177c
Romance languages 1331a
Romance of Love and Youth (paint.) *tab* 111
Romanes, George John 335c
Romanesque Period (art) architecture 71b, 71c
  influence in U.S. 78c
  sculpture 119a
Romania 2243–2245
  agriculture 2244a, 2245a
  Cominform 866a
  communism 2243a, 2244a, 2244b, 2245a–2245b
  economy 2244a–2244b
  flag *il* 2184
  geography 2243c
  government 2244b
  history 2244b–2245b
  independence 2244c–2245a
  industry 2244a
  League of Nations 1012c
  Little Entente 1014c–1015a
  map 2244, *Atlas-18–19*
  natural resources 2244a
  people of 2243c–2244a
  Phanariot rule 2244b–2244c
  religion 2243c
  trade 2244a–2244b
  World War I 1025a, 2245a
  World War II 2245a
Romanian language 1335c
  study of 1331a
Romano, Giulio *tab* 107, 335c
Romano cheese *tab* 731b
Romanov, Czar Alexis 2258c, 2259c
Romanov, Czar Michael 2258c
Romanov family 2258c–2261a
Romanticism 1416a
  English literature 1358a, 1364b
  French art 85c
  French literature 1380c
  German literature 1384c
  Italian literature 1387b
  music 165a
  Portuguese literature 1388c
  Spanish literature 1392b

Romberg, Sigmund 335c
Rome, Italy 2193c, 2194a, 2195a, 2296a, 2370b
  see also Vatican City
—Ancient 975b
  aqueducts 1195b
  archeology 971a
  bridges 1196b
  cement 1199c
  census 862a
  dance 181b
  dictator 873c
  education 613b
  emperors tab 1079
  government 975b
  history outline tab 1030–1033
  music 157c
  numbers 1510a
  proletariat 901c
  religion 1628b
  Romulus 1446a
  wars tab 1072
  see also Roman art
  see also Roman Empire
Rome, New York 1990c
Romeo and Juliet (Shakespeare) 1416a
Rommel, Erwin 336a, 1028b
Romney, George (artist) tab 107, tab 111
  color 1103b
  Lady Hamilton tab 111
  The Misses Beckford tab 112
Romola (nov.) 1368a, 1416a
Romulus 1446a
Roncador Cay 2003
Rondeau (lit.) 1345b
Rondel (lit.) 1345b
Rondo (mus.) 177c
Ronsard, Pierre de 1378b, tab 1466
Roofs 1198c
Rookwood pottery 131c, tab 132
Rooms dining room 1107c, 1108a
  living room 1106c
  modern 1106a
Roosevelt, (Anna) Eleanor 336b
  White House 1109a
Roosevelt, Franklin Delano 336a, 775c, tab 798–799, 1002c, 2172b, 2238b
  administrations 706, 2072b–2076
  administrations, events paralleling tab 1068, tab 1069
  air transport 1156b
  Atlantic Charter meeting 996a
  birthday 841a
  Cabinet tab 796–797
  Democratic Party 873b
  election and inauguration tab 801
  foreign policy 880c
  Four Freedoms of 996a
  labor legislation 831a
  relief agencies 905a
  TVA 910b
  United Nations 990a
  veto 912b
Roosevelt, Theodore 336b, 775c, tab 798–799, 849b, 867b, 2143a, 2234c, 2260b
  administrations 2061–2063a
  administrations, events paralleling tab 1067
  Cabinet tab 796–797
  conservation 868c
  election and inauguration tab 801
  land policies 888b
  Nobel Prize 2062b
  Progressive Party 858b, 901c
  Republican Party 906b
  Rough Riders 2060a
Roosevelt, Theodore, Jr. 336c
Roosevelt University 665
Root, Elihu 336c, tab 796
  World Court 2069b, 2072b
Root (gram.) 1297a
Root (music) 177c
Root cap (plant) 1644a–1644b
Root hairs 1644b
Roots (plant) 1644a–1644b
  aerating 1644b
  aerial 1644b
  pressure 1646b
  prop 1644b
  specialized 1644b
  structure of 1644a–1644b
  systems 1644b
  ventitious 1644b
Root-Takahira note 2062b
Ropak 513a
Rope 1276b
Roper, Daniel Calhoun tab 797
Roper, Sylvester 1169a
Ropy lava 513a
Roque (game) 1714b
Roquefort cheese tab 731b

Rore, Cyprian de 162a, tab 171b
Rorschach test 1950c
Rosa, Salvator tab 107, 1387a
  biography 336c
Rosalind (lit. char.) 1416a
Rosario, Argentina 2089b
Rosary College 665
Rosas, Juan Manuel de 2090b
Roscius, Quintus 336c
Rose il 1663, 1690b, 1990b
  wild 1982a
  wild prairie 1991b
Rose family 1690b–1690c
Rose Island (atoll) 2000a
Rose Polytechnic Institute 666
Rose quartz 1220c
Rosecrans, William 336c
Roseau, Dominica 2311a
Roseau, Windward Islands 2370b
Rosebery, Earl of 1001a
Rosegger, Peter tab 1478
Rosemary 1690c
Rosemont College 697
Rosenwald, Julius 336c
Rose-of-China, see Hibiscus
Rose-of-Sharon 1690c
Roses, Wars of the tab 1072–1073, 2287b
Rosetta Stone 968c, 1004
Rosh Hashanah 1629c
Rosin 1221a, 1896a
Ross, Betsy 337a
Ross, George tab 803
Ross, James tab 800
Ross, Sir James Clark 337a
Ross, Nellie Tayloe 337a
Ross, Robert War of 1812, 2034c
Ross, Sir Ronald 337a
Ross Dam 1206
Ross Sea 2340a
Rosselli, Cosimo tab 106
Rossellino, Antonio tab 125
Rossellino, Bernardo 121c, tab 125
Rossetti, Christina 337a, tab 1477
  Sing-Song 415a
Rossetti, Dante Gabriel 337a
  paintings tab 108
  poetry 1369a, tab 1476
Rossetti, William 337a
Rossi-Forel intensity scale 513a
Rossini, Gioacchino Antonio 166c, tab 171c
  biography 337a
Rostand, Edmond 337a, 1382b, tab 1479
  Cyrano de Bergerac 1400b
Roswitha 1383a
Roszak, Theodore tab 125
Rotary compressors 1242c
Rotary engine 1135c
Rotary fault 513a
Rotary International 1745c
Rotary press 153b
Rotary wing aircraft 1158c
Rotation (astron.) 1781a, 1797a
Rotenone 741c
Rothamsted Experiment Station 749c
Rothenstein, Sir William tab 108
Rotherham plow 719c
Rothschild, James (1792-1868) 337b
Rothschild, Karl (1788-1855) 337a
Rothschild, Meyer Amschel (1743-1812) 337a
Rothschild, Meyer Amschel (1773-1855) 337a
Rothschild, Nathan Meyer (1777-1836) 337a
Rothschild, Salomon (1774-1855) 337a
Rotogravure 150a, 153b
Rotterdam, Netherlands 2224c, 2225a, 2370b, 2370c
Rouault, Georges 103b, tab 108, 337b
  Holy Face, The il 93
Roubaix, France 2149a
Rouen, France
  pottery tab 130
Rouget de Lisle, Claude 337b, 1380c, tab 1471
Rough Riders 2060a
Round (mus.) 177c
Round and Round the Village (song) 421
Roundheads 1019b
Round Table (Arthurian leg.) 1446a
Rousseau, Henri 337b

Rousseau, Jean Jacques tab 171c, 986c, 1007a, 1380a, tab 1470
  biography 337b
  Confessions 1396a
  education 623b
  pseudonym 1462b
Rousseau, Theodore 86a, tab 108
Routers 1289b
Routing (print.) 153b
Rouvroy, Claude Henri de see Saint-Simon, Comte de
Rouvroy, Louis de see Saint-Simon, Duc de
Rover, The (nov.) 1370a
Rover, Project see Project Rover
Rowan, see Mountain ash
Rowe, Nicholas Poet Laureate 1413b
Rowena (lit. char.) 1416b
Rowing 1728a, 1934c
Rowley Poems 1364a
Row, Row, Row Your Boat (song) 419
Roxanne (lit. char.) 1400b
Roxas, Manuel 2238c
Royal Academy of the Dance 182c
Royal Arcanum (frat.) 1745c
Royal Dutch Shell Company 2318a
Royal Gallery of Fine Arts (Venice) tab 112
Royal Museum (Antwerp) tab 109
Royal Museum (The Hague) tab 111
Royal Niger Company 2229c
Royal Society 1127a
Royal William (steamship) 2038a
Royal Worcester (china) 127c, tab 131
Royall, Kenneth C. tab 796
Royalty (payment) 602c, 1160a
Royce, Josiah 337c
Ruanda-Urundi 2108b, 2245c
Ruapehu, Mount 2225c
Rub a dub dub (nursery rhyme) 411a
Rubáiyát (poem) 1416b
  FitzGerald, Edward 1369b
Rub Al Khali Desert 2340a
Rubato (mus.) 177c
Rubber 1221b
  Brunei 2309b
  Ceylon 2119c, 2120a
  Congo 2135c
  Indonesia 2187a
  Liberia 2209a
  Malaysia 2213b, 2214a
  manufacturing 1276c
  molecular structure 1824c
  New Guinea 2318c
  Nigeria 2229b
  Papua 2319b
  producing areas 1277a
  rocket fuels 1767a
  Singapore 2250b
  synthetic 1221c, 1222a, 2199c
  Thailand 2273c
  Vietnam 2299b
  vulcanization 1278a
Rubber plant see Fig
Rubber tree 1690c
Rubbra, Edmund tab 172b
Rubel, Ira W. 149b
Rubens, Peter Paul 146a, tab 107, tab 111, tab 112
  Adoration of the Magi tab 109
  biography 337c
  Isabella Brant tab 113
Rubidium tab 1836, 1886a
  atomic weight tab 1805
  electrons 1807a
Rubinstein, Anton 169a, tab 172a
  biography 337c
Rubinstein, Artur 337c
Rubinstein, Nikolai tab 172a
Ruby, Jack 2081c
Ruby in etching 138a
Ruby glass 133c
Rucellai, Giovanni 337c
Rucellai Palace (Florence) 77b
Ruckert, Friedrich tab 1473
Rudagi tab 1465
Rudder 1728
Rude, François tab 125
  Arc de Triomphe 122c
Rudolf, Lake 2202b, 2340a
Rudolf I (of Hapsburg) (Holy Rom. emp.) 337c, 2159c
Rudolphine Tables (astron.) tab 1466
Rue 1690c–1691a
Rue family 1691a
Rueda, Lope de 1392a
Rueda, Salvador 1392b

Ruffini, Paolo 1506c
Ruffled grouse 1993a
Rufiji River 2272a, 2340a
Rufus of Ephesus 338a
Rugby 1714c
Rugs 1109c
Ruisdael, Jacob van see Ruysdael, Jacob van
Ruiz, José Martínez 1392b
Ruiz, Juan tab 1466
Rules (print.) 153b
Rules of Life for Monks (St. Benedict) 998b
Rum 724b, 2097a
  Montserrat 2317a
Rumba 182b
Rumford, Count (Benjamin Thompson) 1760b, 1898a
  biography 352a
Ruminants bacteria 1846b
Rumsey, James 1234b
Run (mus.) 177c
Run in (print.) 153b
Runeberg, Johan Ludvig tab 1474
Runic Inscriptions (lit.) tab 1465
Running head (print.) 153b
Runnymede, England 2285c
Runoff 513a
Ruodlieb (bk.) 1383a
Rural Credits Act 2063c
Ruse, Bulgaria 2105a, 2370b
Rush 1691a
Rush, Benjamin 338a
  Declaration of Independence tab 803
Rush, Richard tab 795, tab 800
Rush, William tab 125
Rusk, Dean 338a, tab 796
Rusk, Jeremiah M. tab 797
Ruskin, John 78c, 1105b, 1358a, 1366b, tab 1476
  biography 338a
  essay 1402c
  pseudonym 1462b
  Sesame and Lilies 1417a
Russell, Bertrand 338a, 1619a
Russell, George William 1370c, tab 1479
Russell, Henry Norris 1790a
Russell, John (1st Earl Russell of Kingston) 338b
Russell, John (Amer. states.) tab 801
Russell, Lillian 338b
Russell Sage College 686
Russia tab 1038–1058
  ballet 184a
  Bolsheviks 858a
  Congress of Vienna 1023c
  Constitutional Democrats 860a
  Duma 2260b–2260c
  established church 877b
  history 2257c–2261b
  Holy Alliance 1010a–1010b
  horse 39b
  in Iran 2189b
  in Korea 2204c, 2205a
  lemming 42c
  Mongolia 2221a, 2221b
  music 154c, 169a, tab 172a
  Napoleon I 1014b
  pelagic sealing 998c
  in Poland 2240a–2240b
  religion 2258a
  revolution (1917) 2261a–2261b
  in Romania 2244b–2245a
  rulers tab 1079
  Russo-Japanese War tab 1075
  serfdom 2258c–2259a
  treaty with China (1896) 2129b
  war with Japan 2260b
  war with Turkey (1877) 2106a, 2166a–2166b
  World War I 999a–999b, 1024c–1025b, 2154b, 2161c, 2257b, 2260c–2261a
  see also Union of Soviet Socialist Republics (after 1917)
Russian language 1334b
  alphabet tab 1295, 1296a
Russian literature 1389–1390
Russian Revolution tab 1076
Russo-Japanese War (1904–1905) 2201a
Russo-Turkish War (1828–1829) 2244c
Russo-Turkish War (1877–1878) 2166c, 2244c–2245a
Rustic Wedding, The (paint.) tab 113
Rutabaga see Mustard
Rutgers—The State University 683
Ruth (Bib. bk.) tab 1464
Ruth (Bib. char.) 1459b

Ruth, "Babe" 338b
Ruthenian language *see* Ukrainian language
Ruthenium *tab* 1836
atomic weight *tab* 1805
Rutherford, Ernest 1800a, 1912a
biography 338b
Rutledge, Edward Declaration of Independence *tab* 803
Rutledge, John 338b
presidential candidate *tab* 800
Supreme Court *tab* 802a

U.S. Constitution 809c
Rutledge, Wiley B., Jr. Supreme Court *tab* 802a
Ruud, Sigmond 1731b
Ruwenzori, Mount 2134c
Ruwenzori Mountains 2279a, 2340a
Ruysdael, Jacob van *tab* 107, *tab* 110
biography 338a
The Mill tab 109
The Swamp tab 110
View of Haarlem tab 111

Wheatfields tab 112
Rwanda 2108b, 2245–2246
agriculture 2245c
economy 2245c
flag *il* 2184
geography 2245c
government 2245c
history 2245c–2246a
map 2245, *Atlas-39*
people of 2245b–2245c
religion 2245b

Rydberg, Abraham Victor *tab* 1476

Ryder, Albert 104c, *tab* 108, 338b
Rye 742b, 1691a
Germany 2158b
North Dakota 1991c
Poland 2239b
Sweden 2268a
U.S.S.R. 2257a
Rye, N.H. 2024c
Rye House Plot 1019b
Ryswick, Treaty of 2026c
Ryukyu Islands 2003, 2201b

S

S wave *see* earthquake
Sá de Miranda, Francisco de 1388b
Saadi (Sadi) (Muslik-ud-Din) 338c, *tab* 1465
Saar World War I 2068a
Saarinen, Eero 338c, 618a
Saarinen, Gottlieb Eliel 81c, 618a
biography 338b
Saavedra, Angel de *see* Rivas, Duke of
Saba Island 2317c
Sabah 2188b
see also North Borneo
Sabarmati River 2340a
Sabatini, Rafael 338c
Sabbah, Hasan ibn-al- *see* Hasan ibn-al-Sabbah
Sabine River 1983c, 1995c
Sable *see* Marten
Sabotage 907a
Sacajawea (Indian guide) *il* 1014
Saccharin 745a
Saccheri, Girolamo 1505c, 1580b
Sacchini, Antonio *tab* 171c
Sacco, Nicola 338c
Sachs, Hans 159c, *tab* 171b, 1383b, *tab* 1466
biography 338c
Meistersinger 1410b
Sackville, Thomas 1360c, *tab* 1466
blank verse 1397c
Sackville-West, Victoria 338c, 1371c, *tab* 1481
Sacramento, California 1976b, 2013c
proportional representation 902b
Sacramento River 1976c, 2013c
Sacramento State College 658
Sacraments 1632b
Sacred and Profane Love (paint.) *tab* 112
Sacred Heart Dominican College 702
Sacred War (339–338 B.C.) *tab* 1071
Sacrifice 1622a
Sacrifice of Abraham (paint.) *tab* 110
Saddle (geol.) 513b
Sade, Marquise de 338c
Sadducees 1629c
Sadi *see* Saadi
Sa'dis dynasty 2222a
Saemund the Wise 1402a
Saeverud, Harold *tab* 172b
Safes 1278a
Safety
labor legislation 835–836
Safety technician (careers) 380c
Safflower 1691a–1691b
Saffron *see* Crocus
Saga 1416b
Saga, Japan 2370c
Sagami Bay 2198c
Sagan, Françoise 338c
Sagauli, Treaty of 2224b
Sage 1691b
Sage, Margaret 338c
Sage, Russell 338c
Sagebrush 1619b, 1865a, 1988b
Sage of Monticello 309a *see* Jefferson, Thomas
Saginaw, Michigan 1985c
Sago Palm 1691b
Saguaro 1691b, 1975b

Saguenay River 2020c
Sahara elephant 33a
Sahara Desert 2087c, 2170a, 2209c, 2210a, 2214c, 2265c, 2340a
Saharan Atlas Mountains 2087b
Saifuddin, Sultan Omar Ali 2309
Saiga antelope 1867b
Saigon, South Vietnam 2298a, 2299b, 2370c
Sailfish *il* 1717
Sailing 1728b, 1934c
Sailor King *see* William IV, King (England)
Sailor's hornpipe 181c
Saint, Thomas 1278c
St. Ambrose College 668
St. Andrews Presbyterian College 689
St. Anselm's College 682
St. Antonio and Saints (paint.) *tab* 112
St. Augustine, Florida founding 2023c
Saint Augustine's College 689
St. Barbara (paint., Eyck.) *tab* 109
St. Benedict's College 669
St. Bernard College 654
St. Bernard Tunnel *tab* 1226
Saint of Bleeker Street, The (opera) 170c
St. Bonaventure University 686
Saint Cecilia Musical Society 169c, 1885c
St. Cecilia's Day (ode) 1362c
Saint Christopher (is.) 470a *see* Saint Kitts
St. Clair, Arthur 338c, 2032a
Continental Congress *tab* 802b
St. Clair, Lake 2018c
St. Cloud, Fr. porcelain 127a, *tab* 131
St. Cloud State College 678
St. Croix Island 2004b
St. Croix River 1986b, 1999a, 2018c
St. Denis, Ruth 184b
Saint-Denis, Réunion 2320c, 2370c
St. Dominique 2172a
Sainte-Beuve, Charles Augustin 339a, 1381c, *tab* 1474
Saint Edward's University 702
St. Elias Mountains 2016c, 2019a
St. Elmo's fire 513a
St. Etienne, France 2149c
St. Eustacious Island 2317c
Saint-Exupéry, Antoine de 339a
St. Francis Breaks With His Father (paint.) *il* 87
Saint Francis College 666, 686, 697
Saint Francis in Ecstasy (paint.) *tab* 111
St. Francis, Lake 2020b
St. Francis River 2020c
St. François Mountains 1987a
St. Gall (canton), Switz., referendum 884c
Saint-Gaudens, Augustus 123c, *tab* 125
biography 339a
St. George Fighting the Dragon (sculp.) 122b
St. George Island 2019c
St. George's, Grenada 2314c, 2370c
St. George's Channel 2282a
St. Germain, Treaty of 2095c, 2140a
St. Gotthard Tunnel 1226c
St. Helena Island 2321
St. Helier, Jersey Island 2310a
Saint Joan (play) 1370a

St. John, John P. presidential candidacy *tab* 801
St. John, New Brunswick *il* 2113
St. John City, Antigua 2307a, 2371a
Saint John College of Cleveland 692
St. John Fisher College 686
St. John Island 2004b
St. John, Lake 2110c
St. John River 2208c
Saint John's, Newfoundland 2371a
St. John's College 683
St. Johns River 2008b
St. John's University 678, 686
St. John the Baptist in the Wilderness (paint.) *tab* 110
St. Jones River 2007a
St. Joseph, Missouri 1987b
Saint Joseph's College 660, 667, 672, 697
Saint Joseph's College for Women 686
Saint-Just, Louis Antoine de 1008a
St. Kitts Island 2321
St. Laurent, Louis Stephen 339a, 2118b
St. Lawrence, Gulf of 2017c, 2110c
alewife 13a
St. Lawrence River 1990b, 2017c, 2018a, 2020b, 2020c, 2113c, 2115b
discovery 2023b
mackerel 44b
oyster 49b–49c
St. Lawrence Seaway 2078a, 2118b
St. Lawrence Seaway and Power Project 2020c
St. Lawrence University 687
St. Lawrence Valley 2110c, 2113c
St. Leger, Barry 2028b
St. Louis, Missouri 1987b, 2013c–2014a, 2018c
St. Louis Arch 1197a
Saint-Louis, Senegal 2247c, 2248a, 2371a
Saint Louis University 680
St. Lucia Island 2321
Indians 2321b
St. Luke Painting the Virgin (paint.) *tab* 110
St. Maarten Island 2317c
Saint-Marceaux, René de *tab* 125
St. Mark's Cathedral (Venice) 76a
St. Martin's College 706
St. Matthew Passion (mus.) 163b
St. Maurice River 2020c
Saint Mary of the Plains College 669
Saint Mary-of-the-Woods College 667
Saint Mary's College 667, 669, 678
St. Mary's Dominican College 671
St. Mary's Island 2156a
St. Mary's River 2014c
St. Mary's University of San Antonio, Texas 702
St. Michael's College 704
St. Mihiel (commune), France World War I 2066a
St. Nicholas (magazine) 1167b
St. Norbert College 708
St. Olaf College 678
St. Paul, Minnesota 1986a, 1986b, 2012a, 2018c
St. Paul Island 2019c
St. Paul River 2208c
Saint Paul's College 705
St. Peter, Lake 2020b
St. Peter Port, Guernsey Island 2310a

St. Petersburg, Florida 1979b, 2015a
St. Petersburg, Russia 740b, 2257a, 2259a, 2259b, 2261b
see also Leningrad, U.S.S.R.
St. Peter's (cathedral, Rome) architecture 77b
Saint Peter's College 683
Saint-Pierre, Bernardin de *see* Bernardin de Saint-Pierre
St. Pierre, St. Pierre and Miquelon 2321c
St. Pierre and Miquelon 2321
St. Procopius College 665
Saint-Saëns, Camille 168b, *tab* 172a, 339a
Saintsbury, George E. B. 339a
Saint's Everlasting Rest (treatise) *tab* 1468
Saint-Simon, Comte de 908a
Saint-Simon, Duc de 1379c, *tab* 1469
St. Sophia (Istanbul) *see* Santa Sophia
St. Thomas, University of 702
St. Thomas Island 2004b
St. Tome Island 2241c
St. Trophime, Church of (Arles) sculpture 119a
Saint Victor, Claude Niepce de 1172b
St. Vincent College 697
St. Vincent Island 2321
St. Vitus' dance *see* Chorea
Saint Xavier College 665
St. Yrieix-la-Perche, France kaolin *tab* 131
Sakai, Japan 2371a
Sakarya River 2278a
Sakhalin Island 2340a–2340b
Saki (pseud.) *see* Munro, H. H.
Sakiet-Sidi-Youssef, Tunisia 2277c
Sakishima Island 2003b
Sakkara, Pyramid of 373b, 1003a
Sakuma Dam *tab* 1206
Saladin 339a, 1002b, 1005a, 1017b
Saladin (Syrian officer) 2281a
Salamanca (prov.) Spain architecture 77b
church 76b
Salammbo (bk.) 1381c, *tab* 1476
Salamander 54c–55a
Salaries *see* Wages
Salazar, António de Oliveiria 339b, 2241b, 2242b
Sale, George *tab* 1469
Sale (bus.) 602c
career 389b
legal phases 823b
see also Selling
Salem, India 2371a
Salem, Massachusetts 2014b
colonial history 2024b
Salem, Oregon 1992c
Salem College (North Carolina) 689
Salem College (West Virginia) 707
Salem, State College at 675
Sales Act 849b
Sales management 602c
Sales promotion 602c
Sales tax 534b
Salesman (careers) 389b
Salesmanship 602c
Salic Law 1019b–1019c
Salieri, Antonio *tab* 171c
Salinator, Livius 1016a

Salinger, J. D. 399b, 1375c, *tab* 1481
Salinity 513b
Salisbury, 2nd Earl of (1428–1471) *see* Warwick, 1st Earl of (Richard Neville)
Salisbury, Rhodesia 2242c, 2371a
Salisbury Cathedral 76c
  painting *tab* 113
Salisbury State College 673
Saliva 920b
Salivary glands 920b
Salk, Jonas 339b
Sallust 1354b, 1356b, *tab* 1464
  biography 339b
Salmon 55a–55b, *il* 1717
Salmonella 956c
Salome 1459c
  John the Baptist 1456a
Salonika, Greece 2374c
Saloum River 2247c
Salpiglossis 1691b–1691c
Salsify 1691c
Salt 513b
  chemistry 1816c
  saline soil 751c
Salt (sodium chloride) 1222c, 1817c
  crystal structure 1870c
Salt dome 513b
Salt glacier 513b
Salt lake 513b
Salt Lake City, Utah 1996a–1996b, 2014b
Salt marsh 513b
Salt pan 513b
Salt plug 513b
Salt River 2013a
Salt water 463b
  groundwater 448b
  oceans and seas 448c
Saltation 513b
Saltbush 1691c, 1865a
Salton Sea 2020c
Salton Sink 2020c
Saltpeter 749b
  fertilizers 753a
  glassmaking 133b
Saltykov, Mikhail 1389c, *tab* 1476
Saluda Dam 1206
Salvador, Brazil 2103c, 2371b
Salvador, El *see* El Salvador
Salvation Army Booth, William 212a
Salve Regina College 698
Salverson, Laura G. *tab* 1480
Salvia *see* Sage
Salvini, Tommaso 1411c
Salween River 2106c, 2273a, 2340c
Salzburg, Austria 2371b
Sam Houston State College 702
Sam Sene T'ai 2206c
Samadhi 1624c
Samara, U.S.S.R. 2360c
Samara fruit 1646a
Samaria 1459c
Samarium *tab* 1836
  atomic weight *tab* 1805
Samarkand, U.S.S.R. 982c, 2371b
Samarkand rugs 1110c
Sama-Veda (Hindu liturgy) 1420b
Sambre River 2098a
Samford University 654
Samisen 155a
Sammartini, Giovanni 163b, *tab* 171c
Samnite Wars *tab* 1071
Samoa 2058a
  division 2060c
  see also American Samoa; Western Samoa
Samori ben Ture 2170a, 2170b
Samos 2164c
Sample (statistics) 1597a
Sampson, William Thomas 2060a
Samsara 1624c
Samson (Bib.) 1459c
Samson (oratorio, Handel) 163a
Samson Agonistes (poem) 1362b
Samudragupta 2179c
Samuel 1459c
Samurai 2200c
San Angelo, Texas 1995c
San Antonio, Texas 1995c, 2014b
San Antonio River 2014b
San Benito, Texas 1995c
San Bernardino (county), California 871c
San Bernardino Mountains 2017a, 2019a

San Blas Islands 2234c
San Cristóbal *see* Chatham Island
San Diego, California 2014b
San Diego, University of, College for Men 658
San Diego, University of, for Women 658
San Diego Mountains 1976c
San Diego State College 658
San Fernando Valley State College 658
San Francisco, California 1976c, 1980a, *il* 2014, 2014a, 2014b
  earthquake 2062b
  rapid transit 1165b
San Francisco, University of 658
San Gabriel Mountains 2019a
San Gabriel No. 1 Dam 1206
San Jacinto (frigate) 2045b
San Jacinto, Battle of 2219a
San Jacinto Day 841c
San Jacinto Mountains 2017a
San Joaquin River 1976c
San José, Costa Rica 2135b, 2135c, 2371b
San Jose State College 658
San Juan, Puerto Rico 2002a, 2002b, 2014c
San Juan Capistrano Mission 61a
San Juan Mountains 2020a
San Marco (cathedral, Venice) *see* St. Mark's Cathedral
San Marino 2246
  agriculture 2246a
  climate 2246a
  communism 2246b
  economy 2246a
  flag *il* 2184
  geography 2246b
  government 2246b
  history 2246b
  map 2246; *Atlas*-13
  people of 2246a
  religion 2246a
  World War I 2246b
  World War II 2246b
San Marino, San Marino 2246a
San Marino River 2246a
San Martín, José de 339c, 2122a, 2237a
San Martin, Mt. 2217b
San Petronio (Bologna) 121c
San Rafael Ranges 2017a
San Salvador 2023a
San Salvador, El Salvador 2144c, 2371b
Sana, Yemen 2302a, 2371b
Sanagha River 2340b
Sánchez, Florencio 1393c
Sánchez Cerro, Luis 2237b
Sanchez Hernandez, Fidel 2145c
Sancho I (Portugal) 2241c
Sancho II (Portugal) 2241c
Sancho Panza 1401c
Sanctions 907a
Sand, George 1381a, *tab* 1463a, *tab* 1474
  biography 339b
Sand 450a, 513b, 1222c
  brick 1196a
  erosion 447c
  glassmaking 133b
  soil 752b
Sand casting 1267b
Sand dollar *see* Sea urchin
Sand dune 513c
Sand Hills 1988a
Sand Island 2001b
Sand spout 513c
Sandalwood 1691c
Sandbar 513c
Sandburg, Carl 218a, 339c, 1376a, *tab* 1480
  Lincoln 1377a
Sando Bridge *tab* 1197, 1198a
Sandpiper 55b
Sand-Reckoner (bk.) 1502c
Sandstone 450a, 513c, 1223a
Sandstorm 513c
Sandwich Islands *see* Hawaii
Sandwich, Massachusetts glass 134c
Sanford, Edward Terry Supreme Court *tab* 802a
Sanford, Nathan *tab* 800
Sangamon River 2015a
Sangay (volcano) 2143c
Sänger, Eugen 1768a
Sanger, Margaret 339c
Sangha River 2133c
Sangue-de-bois *il* 28
Sanitary engineering 1223a

Sanjurjo, José 2265b
Sannazaro, Jacopo 1386c, *tab* 1466
Sannyasin 1624c
Sans serif (print.) 153b
Sanskrit 1296b, 1333c
Sanskrit Grammer (bk.) *tab* 1464
Sansovino, Andrea 125
Sansovino, Jacopo *tab* 125
Santa Anna, Antonio López de 339c, 2219a
  Mexican War 2040a
Santa Clara, University of 658
Santa Claus 1437a, 1446c
Santa Cruz, Andrés 2100c
Santa Cruz, Bolivia 2100b
Santa Cruz River 2015b
Santa Fe, New Mexico 1989c, 2014c
  archeology 971a
Santa Isabel, Equatorial Guinea 2311a, 2371c
Santa Isabel island *see* Ysabel
Santa Maria (ship) Columbus 2023a
Santa Marta, Colombia 2133a
Santa Monica Range 2017a
Santa Sophia (Hagia Sophia) (Istanbul) 1124c
  architecture 75c
Santana, Pedro 2143a
Santander, Francisco de Paula 2133a
Santander, Spain 2264a
Santayana, George 340a, *tab* 1479
Santiago, Chile 2121b, 2121c, 2371c
  Pan American Conference (1923) 1017c
Santiago, Cuba 2136c
  Spanish-American War 2060a
Santillana, Marqués de *see* Mendoza, Íñigo López de
Santo Domingo, Dominican Republic 2142c, 2371c
Santo Domingo (island) *see* Hispaniola
Santo Domingo (republic) *see* Dominican Republic
Santo Tomé de Guayana, Venezuela 2297b, 2371c
Santos-Dumont, Alberto 340a, 1155c
São Francisco River 2340b
São Paulo, Brazil 2102b, 2102c, 2371c
São Tomé, Sao Tomé 2322a, 2371c
São Tomé Island 2322
Saône River 2149b
Sapele, Nigeria 2371c
Sapodilla 1691c
Sapote 1691c
Sappho 974b, 1351c, 1352a, *tab* 1466
  biography 340a
  Phaon 1444b
Sapporo, Japan 2371c
Saprolite 513c
Sapropel 513c
Sapsago cheese *tab* 731b
Saqqara *see* Sakkara
Saraband 178a
Sarabande 182a
Saracen Wars *tab* 1072
Saracens historical outline *tab* 1037–1039
Sarah 1459c
Sarah Lawrence College 687
Sarajevo, Yugoslavia 1024c, 2303b, 2304b, 2371c
Saran (polymer) 1209a, 1824c
Saranac Lake 2016a
Saratoga, Battle of 2028b
Saratov, U.S.S.R. 2371c–2372a
Sarawak 2188b, 2213c
Sarcey, Francisque 1382a, *tab* 1476
Sarcina 1843b
Sarcodina 1848a
Sarcoidosis 945c
Sarcophagus of Alexander 117a
Sardinia 2193c, 2220b
  sheep 57b–57c
Sardinia, Kingdom of 2195c, 2196a
Sardou, Victorien 340a, 1381c, *tab* 1477
Sargasso Sea 465a, 1640a
Sargent, Epes 169c
Sargent, John Garibaldi *tab* 796
Sargent, John Singer *tab* 108
  biography 340a
  Portrait of Madame X *tab* 112
Sargon II 1459c
  palace 74b
Sarmiento, Domingo F. 2090a

Saros (astron.) 1794b
Saroyan, William 340a, *tab* 1481
Sarpedon 1431b
Sarpi, Pietro *tab* 1467
Sarsaparilla, *see* Smilax
Sarto, Andrea del *tab* 107
  biography 340a
  Madonna of the Harpies *tab* 110
Sartor Resartus (bk.) 1366a
Sartre, Jean-Paul 1348c, 1382b, *tab* 1481
  biography 340a
  philosophy 1620a
Saruk rugs 1110c
Saskia (paint.) *tab* 109
Sassafras 1692a
Sassafras Mountain 1994b
Sassandra River 2197a
Sassanid Dynasty 981c
Sassetta *tab* 106
Sassoferrato *tab* 107
Sassoon, Siegfried 1371a
  pen name 1462b
Sastrugi 513c
Satan 1430b, 1438c
  Bible 1459c
Satellites (artificial) 1769b, 2079a
  astronomical instruments 1792c
  communications 1162b
  definition 1779b
  first 1769b
  lasers 1911a
  Newton, I. 1763c
  permanent orbit 1779b
  planetary and lunar probes 1771a
  solar batteries 1883b
  solar cells 1146a
  U.S.S.R. 951a
  U.S. 952b
  weather 478a
Satellites (astron.) 1780a, 1784c, *tab* 1782
  definition 1779b
  formation 1782c
  Jupiter 1783a
  Kepler, J. 1763c
  Mars 1783a
  Roche's limit 1797a
  Saturn 1783b
Satie, Erik *tab* 172a
  biography 340b
Satin spar 1212a
Satire 1416c
  Latin literature 1354a
Satires (Juvenal) *tab* 1464
Satires (Lucilius) 1355b, *tab* 1464
Satiricon (Satyricon) (Petronius) 1357c, *tab* 1464
Sato, Eisaku 2201b, 2003c
Satori 1627b
Satrap 907a
Satpura Mountains 2340b
Satu-Mare, Romania 2372a
Saturated acids 732c
Saturation (chem.) 1815c
  zone of 520c
Saturday Evening Post circulation 1167b
Saturn (myth) 1446c
Saturn (planet) *tab* 1782, 1783b
  albedo 1793b
  atmosphere 1840b
  Bode's law *tab* 1781
  moons 1782a
  rings 1783b
  speed of orbit 1771b
Saturnian verse 1354c
Satyr 1446c
Satyricon (Petronius) *see* Satiricon
Saud, Abd al-Aziz ibn, King (Saudi Arabia) 340b, 2247b
Saud, Muhammad ibn 2247a–2247b
Saudi Arabia 995b, 2097a, 2205c, 2246–2247
  agriculture 2247a
  climate 2246c
  coffee trees 1659a
  economy 2246c–2247a
  flag *il* 2184
  geography 2246c
  government 2247a
  history 2247a
  map 2246, *Atlas*-25
  oil 2246a, 2246c–2247a
  people of 2246c
  religion 2346b, 2247a
Sauer River 2211a
Saul 1017a, 1459c
  David 1452c
Saul of Tarsus *see* Paul of Tarsus, Saint

Sault Ste. Marie, Michigan 2014c
Saunders, Richard *tab* 1463a
Saunders, William 747b
Saussure, Nicolas Théodore de 749b
Sava River 2303a, 2340b
Savai'i Island 2301b
Savanna 513c, 1864c
Savannah (ship) 1167c
Savannah, Georgia 1979c, 2014c
   American Revolution 2028c, 2029
   founding 2026a
Savannah River 1979c, 2014c, 2293a
Savannah State College 662
Savery, William 1099c
Saving 602c
Savings and loan associations 529b
Savings banks 529b, 585a
   postal 2062c
Savonarola, Girolamo 340b, 1386c, *tab* 1466
Savoy operas 1404c
Sawatch Mountains 1977b
Sawfly 55c
Saws 1288c
Sawyer, Charles W. *tab* 797
Saxhorn 178a
Saxifrage 1692a
Saxifrage family 1692
Saxo Grammaticus *tab* 1465
Saxons 2159a–2159c
Saxophone 178a
Sayan Mountains 2255a, 2340b
Sayyid Abd al-Rahman al Mahdi 2266c
Sayyid Ahmad Khan, Sir 2233a
Sayyid Ali al-Mirghani 2266c
Scabies 957c
Scalar quantity (phys.) 1873c
Scale insect 55c
Scalene triangles 1607c
Scales (mus.) 154a, 158b, 178a, 1896b
   Chinese 155a
   degree 174c
   Greek 157b
   Indian 155b
   major 176a
   minor 176b
Scallop 55c–56a
Scandinavia *tab* 1047–1057
   badger 15a
   goldeneye 36a
   grouse 37b
   kittiwake 41b
   lemming 42c
   music 168b
   see also Denmark
   see also Iceland
   see also Norway
   see also Sweden
Scandinavia Peninsula 2340b
Scandinavian languages 1336a
Scandinavian literature *tab* 1465–1481
   saga 1416b
Scandium 1836
   atomic weight *tab* 1805
   electrons 1807a
Scanning (television) 1186a
Scapula 917c
Scarcity 603a
Scarlatti, Alessandro 161c, *tab* 171c
   biography 340b
Scarlatti, Domenico 162b, *tab* 171c
   biography 340b
Scarlet fever *tab* 947
Scarlet Letter (bk.) 1416b
Scarron, Paul 340c, 1378c, *tab* 1467
Scattering experiment 1911c
Scaup 56a
Scena (mus.) 178a
Scenes from Clerical Life (bk.) 1368a
Sceptical Chymist, The (bk.) 1798c
Schadow, Johann 122c, *tab* 125
Schawlow, A. L. 1910b
Schecter v. U.S. 831c
Scheele, Karl Wilhelm 340c, 1171c, 1798c
Scheffel, Josef Victor von *tab* 1476
Scheherazade (lit. char.) 1395a
Scheidt, Samuel 162c, *tab* 171c
Schelde River 2098a, 2340b
Schelling, Ernest Henry *tab* 172c
Schelling, Friedrich Wilhelm Joseph von 1384c, *tab* 1472, 1618b
   biography 340c
Schenectady, New York 1990c, 2005a

King William's War 2026c
Scherzo (mus.) 178a
Schick, Bela 340c
Schick Gutiérrez, René 2228b
Schikaneder, Emanuel 164b
Schiller, Johann Christoph Friedrich von *il* 208, 340c, 1384a, *tab* 1471
Schirra, Walter M. *tab* 1770
Schist 451a, 513c
Schistosomiasis *tab* 947
Schizanthus *see* Butterfly-flower
Schizophrenia 1953a
Schlegel, August Wilhelm von 340c, 1384c, *tab* 1471
Schlegel, Friedrich von 1384c, *tab* 1472
Schleiermacher, Friedrich 341a, *tab* 1471
Schlemmer, Oskar *tab* 125
Schlesinger, Arthur Meier 341a
Schleswig (duchy) 2161a
Schley, Winfield Scott 341a, 2060a
Schleyer, Johann Martin 1338b
Schlick, Moritz 1619a
Schliemann, Heinrich 970c
Schlüter, Andreas 122c, *tab* 125
Schmidt telescope 1797b
Schmitt, Florent *tab* 172a
Schnabel, Artur 341a
Schnitzler, Arthur 341a, 1385c, *tab* 1479
Schoeffer, Peter 143b
Schoenbein, Christian F. 1207c
Schoenberg, Arnold 168a, *tab* 172a
   biography 341a
Schoenbrunn Castle 2095
Schofield, John McAllister 341a, *tab* 796
Schola cantorum 158b
Scholasticism 985a, 1615c
Schönberg, Arnold *see* Schoenberg, Arnold
Schongauer, Martin *tab* 106, 139c
   biography 341a
School for Scandal (play) 1364a
School of American Archaeology 971a
Schoolcraft, Henry Rowe 341b
Schools 609–643
   architecture 617c
   curriculum 638–643
   educational structure 625–637
Schopenhauer, Arthur 1385a, *tab* 1473
   biography 341b
   music 154a
   philosophy 1618b
Schottische 178a
Schreiner, Olive 1462a, *tab* 1463b
Schreker, Franz 168a, *tab* 172a
Schubert, Franz 165b, *tab* 172a
   biography 341b
Schulze, Johann Heinrich 1171c
Schuman, Frederick Lewis *tab* 1481
Schuman, William *tab* 172c, 341b
Schumann, Georg 167c
Schumann, Robert 165c, *tab* 172a
   biography 341c
Schumann-Heink, Ernestine 341c
Schurz, Carl 341c, 775b, *tab* 797
Schütz, Heinrich *tab* 171c
   biography 341c
Schuyler, Philip John 341c
   American Revolution 2028b
Schwab, Charles M. 341c, 524c
Schweitzer, Albert 341c
Schwellenbach, Lewis *tab* 797
Sciatica 945b
Science 1749–1958
   bibliography 1762c
   careers 389c
   Christian Era 1753c
   definition 1749a
   history of 1749–1762
   kindergarten 400a
   literary works 1348b, 1377c
   Medieval Era 1754c
   philosophy 1612a, 1616a
   seventeenth century 1125a
   sixteenth century 1125a
Science and Health (bk.) 1348a
Science of Life (bk.) 1370b
Scientific management 603a
Scientific method 1798c
Scientific Revolution 1756a
Scilly Islands 2340b
Scintillation (astron.) 1797a
Scintillation counters 1275c, 1914a
Scioto River 2006c
Sciotoville, Ohio bridge 1190c

Scipio (the younger) 342a
Scipio (the elder) 342a
Scissor-tailed flycatcher 1992a
Sclerenchyma tissue 1643c
Scleroderma 945b
Sclerophyll 1864a
Scoliosis 945b
Scootering (iceboating) 1726c
Scopas 117a
Score (mus.) 178a
Score (satellite) *tab* 1163
Scorel, Jan van *tab* 107
Scoria 450c, 513c
Scorpion *il* 29, 56a
Scot, Michael 342a
Scotland 1019c–1020b, 2282a, 2283c, 2284a
   assize 854c
   Battle of Bannockburn 1020a
   dances 181c
   feudalism 1006b, 1020a
   highlands 1019
   history outline *tab* 1042–1046
   House of Lords 891a
   independence wars 1020a
   industry 2283a
   kings *tab* 1080
   lavender industry 1675a
   map *Atlas*-10
   music 154c
   Revolution of 1688, 1020b
   Robert I 214b
   Roman Empire 1019c
   union with England 1020b
   whiskey 723c
   see also United Kingdom
Scots (tribe) 1019c, 2284a
Scott, Cyril 169b, *tab* 172b
Scott, Dred 342a
Scott, Léon 1171b
Scott, Robert Falcon 342a
Scott, Sir George Gilbert 342a
Scott, Sir Walter *il* 208, 1006b, 1364c, *tab* 1472
   biography 342a
   epithet *tab* 1463c
   pseudonyms 1461c
   —Works 1365c
      Abbot, The 1393a
      Ivanhoe 1407a
      Kenilworth 1408a
      Lady of the Lake 1408c
      Marmion 1410b
      Quentin Durward 1414b
      Talisman, The 1418a
      Waverley novels 1420c
Scott, Walter Dill 342a
Scott, Winfield 342b, 2034c
   Mexican War 2039c
   nickname 1462c
   presidential candidate *tab* 800, 2041b
Scottish Chiefs (bk.) 1366a, 1416c
Scottish language 1336a
Scour and fill 513c
Scourge of God *see* Attila
Scouring rushes *see* Horsetails
Scranton, Pennsylvania 1993b
Scranton, University of 697
Scree 513c
   see also Talus
Screen (print.) 153b
Screwpine 1692a
Screws 1252a, 1280c
Scriabin, Alexander 169b, *tab* 172b
   biography 342b
Scribe, Augustin Eugène 342b, 1381c, *tab* 1473
Scrimmage (football) 183c
Scripps College 658
Scripps, Edward Wyllis 342b
Script (print.) 153b
Scriptures, Holy *see* Bible
Scrooge 1399a
Scrotum 926b
Scrub (astronautics) 1779c
Scrub (botany) 513c, 1864a
Scrub typhus *tab* 947
Scruple (weight) *tab* 1500
Scuba diving 467a, 1246c
Scudder, Janet *tab* 125
Scudéry, Magdeleine 1378c, *tab* 1467
Sculling 1728a, 1934c
Sculpture 71a, 113–125
   history 114a
   materials and methods 113a
   objectives 114a
   polychromy 113a
   portraiture 118a
   relief sculpture 118b
   Renaissance 72a, 121b–122a
   Robbia school 121c
   sculptors *tab* 125

Scurvy 920b, 945b
Scylla 1428c, 1447a
   Glaucus 1433b
Scythians art 116a
   sculpture 114b
Sea (geog.) *see* Seas
Sea anemone 56a
Sea bass *il* 1717
Sea breeze 474a, 514a
Sea cow 56b
Sea cucumber 56b
Sea fan 56b–56c
Sea gull 56b
Sea horse 56c
Sea level 514a
Sea lily 56c
Sea lion 56c–57a
Sea mile 514a
Sea of Galilee *see* Galilee, Sea of
Sea of Japan 2198c
Sea of Lot *see* Dead Sea
Sea sickness 942c
Sea squirt *see* Tunicate
Sea stars 57a
Sea urchin 57a
Sea water 463b
   magnesium 1214c
   see also Starfish
Seafood 733c
   processing 734b
Seal 56c
Sealants 1199a
Seals (law) 907a
Seamounts 462c, 514a
Search warrant 914a
Sears, Roebuck Company 1101c
Seas 461–467, 513c–514a
   erosion 448b
   see also under names of individual seas
Seasons 758, 1797a
   Mars 1783a
Seasons (poem) 1363b
SEATO *see* Southeast Asia Treaty Organization
Seattle, Washington 1998a, 2014c, 2020a
   recall 904b
Seattle Pacific College 706
Seattle University 706
Seaton, Frederick A. *tab* 797
Sebaceous glands 918b
Sebastiano del Piombo *tab* 107
Sebring ware *tab* 132
Sebal palm 1979a
Sebum 918c
Secants 1607c
   calculus 1594a
   circle 1571b
Secchia Rapita (poem) *see* Rape of the Bucket (poem)
Secession 907a, 2043b
Second (mus.) 178a
Secondary boycott 603a
Secondary cells (elec.) 1883a
Secondary groups (soc.) 1939c
Secretariat (U.N.) 992a
Secretaries (careers) 386c
Secretary bird 57a
Secretary-General (U.N.) 992a
Secret City, The (bk.) 1371c
Secret police 907b
Secret Service 907b
Sectile minerals 453a
Securities 603a
Securities Act (1933) 907b
Securities and Exchange Commission 880a, 907b, 2073c
Securities Exchange Act (1934) 880a, 907b, 2073c
Security Council (U.N.) 991a
Sedan, Battle of 1003a, 2066b
Seddon, Richard 2227a
Sedge 1692b
Sedge family 1692b
Sedgwick, Theodore House of Representatives *tab* 802b
Sediment 463a
Sedimentary rocks 449c, 514a
Sedition 907c
Sedum *see* Orpine
See, Thomas Jefferson Jackson 342b
Seebeck, Thomas Johann 1146b, 1761a, 1883b
Seebeck effect 1146b
Seed coat 1646a

Seed plants 1642b–1643b, 1644a–1646a, 1934a
  anatomy of 1644a–1646a
  buds 1644c
  flowers 1645c–1646a
  leaves 1644c–1645a
  pollination 1645c–1646a
  roots 1644a–1644b
  stems 1644b–1644c
Seeds 1646a
  germination 1647b–1647c
Seeger, Alan 342b
Segantini, Giovanni tab 108
Sego lily 1996a
Segonzac, André Dunoyer de see Dunoyer de Segonzac
Ségou, Mali 2215a
Segregation, Law of (genetics) 1850b
Seguidillas 182a
Seicentisti (It. lit.) 1387a
Seiche 514a
Seidel, Emil tab 801
Seigniorage 602c
Seine River 2148a, 2340b
Seismicity 514a
Seismic sea wave 514a
Seismographs 460a, 514a, 1217c, 1278b
Seismology 514a
  careers 390b
Seistan March 2340c
Seizal, Portugal 2241b
Sekondi-Takoradi, Ghana 2372a
Selden, George Baldwin automobiles 1169b
Selective Service Act (1917) 892b, 2065c
Selective Service Act (1940) 892b
Selective Service Acts 868b
Selene 1425a, 1447a
  see also Luna
Selenga River 2220b, 2340c
Selenite 1212a
Selenium 1836
  atomic weight tab 1805
  cells 1274c
  glassmaking 133c
  rectifiers 1890b
Seleucid dynasty 2271b
Seleucus I 342b, 2271b
Self-heal 1692b
Self-pollination 1645c
Self-Portrait (Rembrandt) il 89, tab 111
Self-Portrait (Van Gogh) il 91
Selim I, Sultan (Turkey) 1005a
Seljuk Turks 982c, 1001c, 1002a
Selkirk, Alexander 342b, 1415c
Selkirk Mountains 2020b
Selling 603b
  careers 389b
  see also Sale
Selling agent 603b
Selma, Ala. 2082b
Semaphore 1151a
  railroad signaling 1179b
Semele 1447a
Semen 926b
Semiarid 514a
Semicircular canals 937b
Semicolon 1313a, 1318a
Semiconductor injection laser 1911a
Semiconductors 1890–1893, 1919c
  hole conduction 1918b
  portable use 1889c
  theory 1891a
  transistors 1890b
Semimetals 1919c
Semimicroanalysis 1827a
Seminal ducts 926b
Seminal vesicles 926b
Seminiferous tubules 926b
Seminole Indians 1660b
  Jackson, Andrew 2035c
  U.S. history 2037c
Semipermeable membranes (plant) 1646b
Semirigid airships 1155a
Semites 973a
Semitone (mus.) 178a
Semmelweiss, Ignaz Philipp 342b
Semmes, Raphael 342b
Sénancour, Etienne Pivert de 1381a
Senate (U.S.) 787b, 788a, 807a, 811a
  committees 866c
  duties and qualifications 810c
  forms of address tab 1119, tab 1120
  impeachment 884a
  minimum age 850b

Sendai, Japan 2372a
Sender, Ramón José 1392c
Seneca, Lucius Annaeus 342b, 976b, 1357c, tab 1464, 1615b
Seneca snakeroot 1692b
Senefelder, Aloys 141b, 149a
Senegal 2156c, 2247–2248
  agriculture 2248a
  climate 2247c
  economy 2248a
  flag il 2184
  geography 2247c
  government 2248a
  history 2248a–2248b
  independence 2248b
  map 2247, Atlas-36
  people of 2247c
  religion 2247c
Sénégal River 2169c, 2214c, 2215a, 2216a, 2247c, 2340c
Senegalese Progressive Union 2248b
Senfl, Ludwig 160c tab 171b
Seng River 2206a
Senghor, Léopold 2248b
Senile psychosis 1953c
Sennacherib, King (Assyria) 996c, 1459c
Sensation (psych.) 1948c
Sense and Sensibility (nov.) 1366a, 1416c
Sense organs 928a, 1947c
Senses 928a, 1948c
  brain center 938a
  hearing 937a
  pain 937c
  sight 928b
  smell 937b
  taste 937c
  touch 937c
Sensitive plant see Mimosa
Sentences (algebra) 1540b
  two variables 1549c
Sentences (gram.) 1308c
  composition of 1316c
  diagrams 1309c
Sentimental Journey (nov.) 1363c, 1417a
Sentimental Tommy (nov.) 1369c, 1417a
Seoul, South Korea 2203b, 2203c, 2372a
Sepals (flower) 1645c
Separation (law) 875b
Separation of powers 907c
Septa 1846c
Septicemia see Blood poisoning
Septuagint (Bib.) 1459c, tab 1464
Sequence (math.) 1607a
Sequence (mus.) 158c, 178a
Sequoia 1692b–1692c
Sequoia National Park 896a, 2019b
Seracs 514a
Serajevo, Yugoslavia see Sarajevo
Serao, Matilde 1387c, tab 1478
Seraphic Doctor see Bonaventura
Serbia 791c, 2161c, 2167a, 2304b, 2304c
  music 154c
  World War I 1024b–1024c, 2064c, 2291c
  see also Yugoslavia
Serbo-Croatian (lang.) 1334a
Serenades 159b, 178a
Sergeant, John tab 800
Sergeant at arms 907c
Sericulture 1223b
Series (geol.) 514a
Series (math.) 1607a
Series circuit 1917a
Series-parallel circuit 1917a
Serif (print.) 153c
Seringapatam, Battles of 1764b
Serkin, Rudolf 342c
Serpentine asbestos 1195c
Serpentine (mineral) 454a
Serra, Junípero 342c
Serra, Renato 1388a
Serrana Bank 2003
Serum sickness 945b
Service, Robert William 1390c, tab 1480
Serviceberry 1692c
Servicemen's Readjustment Act 838a
Servitude
  see Indentured labor
  see Slavery
Servomechanism 1278c
Sesame 1692c
  Nicaragua 2227c
  Sudan 2266a

Sesame and Lilies (lectures) 1402c, 1417a
Sessions, Roger tab 172c
Sestet (poetry) 1417a
Set (deity) 1447a, 1622b
Set (math.) 1507c, 1508a, 1540c, 1607b
Set (psych.) 1948a
Set (print.) 153c
Seth 1460a
Seti I, King (Egypt) 342c, 1003c
Seton, Ernest Thompson 342c
Seton Hall University 683
Seton Hill College 697
Settlement, Act of 856c
Seurat, Georges 86c, tab 108
  biography 342c
  Sunday at the Grande Jatte tab 110
Sevastopol, U.S.S.R. 2372a
774 (rocket) 1769a
Seven against Thebes 1431b
Seven Days' Battles 2048a
Seven Joys of the Virgin (paint.) tab 111
Seven Lamps of Architecture (bk.) 1366b
Seven Pines, Battle of 2048a, 2049
Seven Sacraments, The (paint.) tab 109
Seven Sleepers of Ephesus 1447a
Seven Weeks' War tab 1075, 2161b
Seven Wonders of the World see Wonders of the World
Seven Years' War tab 1073, 2027a, 2152b, 2290b
Seventh (mus.) 178a
Severn River 2282a, 2284a, 2340c
Severn Tunnel 1226
Severnaya Zemlya Islands 2340c
Sévigné, Marquise de 1379c, tab 1468
Seville, Spain 2263c, 2372a
  cathedral 76c
  oranges 1682c
Sèvres, Treaty of 2167a
Sèvres porcelain 127c, tab 131
  furniture 1097c
Sewage bacteria 1846a
  disposal 957a
  sanitary engineering 1223a
Sewall, Arthur tab 801
Sewall, Samuel 1372a, tab 1469
Seward, William Henry 342c, tab 796, 2053a
  Hampton Roads Conference 1009a–1009b
  Trent Affair 2045b
Seward Day 841c
Sewell, Anna
  Black Beauty 1397c
Sewing kindergarten 402b
  tufting 1283c
Sewing machines 1241b, 1278c
Sex
  Freud, S. 1957a
  genetics 1852b
Sexagesimal system 1501b
Sex-linkage (genetics) 1852a
Sextet 178a
Sextus Empiricus 1615b
Sexual Behavior in the Human Male (bk.) 1348b
Sexual system (plants) 1638b
Seychelles Archipelago 2322
Seyhan River 2278a
Seymour, Horatio 342c
  presidential candidate 2053a, tab 801
Seymour, Jane 2288a
  Holbein's portrait tab 113
Seyss-Inquart, Arthur 2096b
Sfax, Tunisia 2277a, 2372a
Sforza, Count Carlo 342c
Sforza, Lodovico 342c
Sforza family 2195b
Sforzando 178a
Sgambati, Giovanni 167c, tab 172a
Shabali River 2251a
Shabuoth 1629c
Shackleton, Sir Ernest Henry 342c
Shad 57a–57b
Shadwell, Thomas 1413b
Shafter, William Rufus 2060b
Shaftesbury, 1st Earl of 343a
  Achitophel 1362c, 1461a
Shah dynasty 2224a
Shah Jahan 2180c
  biography 343a
  Taj Mahal 78a
Shahn, Ben tab 109

Shahnamah (epic) 1417c
Shake (mus.) 178a
Shakespeare, William il 207, 1000a, 1020a, 1344a, 1361a, tab 1466, 1650a
  biography 343a
  nickname 1396b, 1461a
—**Plays**
  As You Like It 1395c
  Hamlet 1405b
  Henry IV 1405b
  Henry V 1405b
  King Lear 1408b
  Julius Caesar 1407c
  Macbeth 1409c
  Merchant of Venice 1410b
  Midsummer Night's Dream 1410c
  Othello 1411c
  Tempest, The 1418b
  Troilus and Cressida 1419b
  Twelfth Night 1419b
Shale 450a, 514a, 1223a
Shallot see Onion
Shamans 612a, 1937b
Shamash 1623a
Shamrock 1692c
Shang Dynasty 976c, 977c, 2126a
Shanghai, China 2123b, 2372a
Shankaracharya 343b
Shannon, Charles tab 108
Shannon, James tab 108
Shannon River 2340c
Shapero, Harold 170c
Shari River 2119a, 2327c
Sharistan rugs 1111a,
Shark 57b
Sharp, Becky see Becky Sharp
Sharp, William 1369b
  pseudonym 1462c
Sharp (mus.) 178a
Sharpeville, South Africa 2253b
Sharpsburg, Battle of see Antietam, Battle of
Sharqi Mountains 2207b
Shasta Dam 1206
Shasta, Mt. 2019b
Shashi River 2242c
Shastri, Lal Bahadur 343b, 2186b
Shaw, Anna Howard 343b, 914b
Shaw, George Bernard 1369c, tab 1478
  biography 343b
  Man and Superman 1410a
  pseudonyms 1461a, tab 1463c
  Pygmalion 1414b
  socialism 908a
Shaw, Henry Wheeler 1461b
Shaw, Leslie M. tab 796
Shaw, T. E. see Lawrence, Thomas Edward
Shaw University 689
Shawn, Ted 184b
Shays, Daniel 343c, 1020b–1020c
Shays' Rebellion 1020b–1020c
Shchedrin, N. see Saltykov, Mikhail
She Stoops to Conquer (play) 1363c, 1417a
Shearwater ware (U.S.) tab 132
Sheba, Queen of 1459b, 2146b
Sheep 57b–57c, 742c
  Afghanistan 2085b
  Albania 2086b
  Argentina 2089c
  Arizona 1975c
  Australia 2092b
  California 1977a
  Colorado 1977b
  diseases 45a
  Faeroe Islands 2311c
  Falkland Islands 2312a
  Great Britain 2282c
  Greece 2165a
  Greenland 2314b
  Ifni 2316a
  Iraq 2189c–2190a
  Isle of Man 2316b
  Lebanon 2207b
  Libya 2210a
  manure analysis tab 752c
  Mauritania 2216a
  Mongolia 2220c
  Montana 1988a
  Nepal 2223b
  New Mexico 1990a
  New Zealand 2226a–2226b
  Niger 2228c
  Ohio 1992a
  Pakistan 2232b
  Poland 2239b
  Rhodesia 2243a
  Romania 2244a
  Saudi Arabia 2247b

Somali Republic 2251a
South West Africa 2322c
South Yemen 2253c
Spanish Sahara 2323a
Tunisia 2277a
Turkey 2278a
U.S. 1968b, 1969a
Upper Volta 2294c
Uruguay 2295a
West Virginia 1998c
Wyoming 1999c
Yemen 2302a
Sheep laurel *see* Laurel
Sheet erosion 514a
Sheet lightning *see* Heat lightning
Sheeting 514a
Sheetwise (print.) 153c
Shellac 1226c
Shelley, Mary 343c, 1365b
Frankenstein 1404b
Shelley, Percy Bysshe 1365a, *tab*
1473
Adonais 1393c
biography 343c
Prometheus Unbound 1414c
Shelter 1930a, *see also* Housing
Shem 1460a
Shenandoah River 1998, 2019c
Shenandoah Valley Civil War
2048a, 2050c
Sheng (mus.) 155a
Shepard, Alan B. *tab* 1770, 2079b
Shepherd Boy, The (fable) 444b
Shepherd College 707
Shepherds in Arcadia (paint.) *tab*
112
Shepherd's Calendar (poem) 1345b,
1360c, *tab* 1466
Shepard's purse 1693a
Sher Shah 2180b, 2180c
Sheradizing 1267a
Sheraton, Thomas 1098b
Sheridan, Philip Henry 343c, 2050c
nickname 1462b
Sheridan, Richard Brinsley 1363c,
tab 1471
biography 343c
Rivals, The 1415c
Sherlock Holmes 1417a
Sherman, James Schoolcraft vice-
presidential candidate *tab*
801
Sherman, John 343c, *tab* 796
Sherman, Roger 344a
Declaration of Independence
tab 803
U.S. Constitution 809c
Sherman, William Tecumseh
2050a, 2050b, *tab* 796
biography 344a
march to the sea 2050b
Sherman Antitrust Act 526c, 539b,
906c, 2057c
Sherman Silver Purchase Act
689a, 2057c, 2059a
repeal 2058c
Shermarke, Abdi Rashid 2251b
Sherry 723c
Sheshonk, Prince (Egypt) 2281c
Shetland Islands 1019c, 2282a,
2340c
Shield (geol.) 514b
Shigella 956c
Shih Huang Ti 971a
Shiites 982a
Shikoku Island 2198b
Shillong, India 2372b
Shiloh (Bib.) 1460a
Shiloh, Battle of 1020c, 2045c, *tab*
2049
Shimer College 665
Shimizu Tunnel 122b, *tab* 1226
Shimonoseki, Japan 2372b
Shimonoseki, Treaty of (1895),
2129b
Shimonoseki Strait 2198c
Shinano River 2198c
Shiner *see* Minnow
Shingle (geol.) 514b
Shingles (disease) *tab* 947
Shinto 979a, 1627c
Ship of Fools (poem, Brant) 1383b,
tab 1466
Ship Rock (New Mexico) 451c
Ship worm 57c
Shipbuilding 1279a
Shippensburg State College 697
Shipping Board 2066a
Ships 1180b
etiquette 1116b
marine engineering 1167c
marine signaling 1168a

submarine 1182a
see also Shipbuilding
Shiras, George *tab* 802a
Shiraz, Iran 2372b
Shiraz rugs 1110c
Shire River 2212b, 2212c
Shirley, James *tab* 1467
Shirley, Thomas 1140b
Shirley (nov.) 1367c
Shirvan rugs 1110c
Shishakly, Adib 2271c
Shiva *see* Siva
Shizuoka, Japan 2372b
Shkodër, Albania 2372b
Shoal 514b
Shock (med.) 945b
Shockley, William 1283a, 1890b
Shoes manufacture 1280a
primitive 1930c
Shoestring Republic *see* Chile
Shofar 155c, 156b
Sholapur, India 2372b
Sholes, Christopher 1188c
Sholokhov, Mikhail A. 344a, *tab*
1481
Shooting star 1693a, 1795b
Shopping goods 603b
Shoreline 448c, 514b
Short (weight) *tab* 1500
Short haul 597b
Short letters (print.) 153c
Short story 1346c
American 1375c
Italian 1387c
Short ton *tab* 1500
Short wave radio 1175b
Shorter College 662
Shoshone Falls 2020c
Shostakovich, Dmitri 169b, *tab* 172b
biography 344a
Shotoku Taishi 978b
Shot-put 1738b
Shott 514b
Shoulder blade *see* Scapula
Shreveport, Louisiana 1983c
Shrew 57c–58a
Shrike 58a
Shrimp 58a
Shrimp Girl (paint.) *tab* 111
Shriners (Ancient Arabic Order
of the Nobles of the Mystic
Shrine) 1745c
Shriver, R. Sargent 2080b
Shropshire Lad, A. (poems) 1370c,
1417b, *tab* 1479
Shub-ad, Queen (Babylonia) 115c
Shull, George 721a
Shunt motors 1142a
Shute, Neville *tab* 1481
Shutter (camera) 1237a
Shuttle (badminton) 1704b
Shylock 1410b, 1417b
Si River 2340c
Siam *see* Thailand
Siam, Gulf of 2340c
Siamese-Burmese language 1333a
Sibelius, Jean 168c, *tab* 172b, 344a
Siberia 1020c–1021a, 2128a, 2254c,
2256b, 2257a, 2259b
dog 25c
eagle 26b
elephant 33a
goat 36a
perch 50b
phlox 1686a–1686b
pike 51b
tiger 20a
weasels 66c
wrens 68b
Sibiu, Romania 2372b–2372c
Siblings 1936a
Sibyls 1447a
Sicily 2193c
sculpture 119a
World War II 1028b–1028c
Sicily Island 2340c
Sickle cell anemia 945b, 1856c
genes 1858a
Sid (Sidhe) 1447b
Side stroke 1733c
Sidereal day 514b
Sidereal month 1795b
Sidereal time 1797b
Sidereal year 1797c
Sidi-Ifni, Ifni 2315c, 2372c
Sidon, Lebanon 2207b
Phoenicia 1018a, 1018b
Sidney, Sir Philip 344a, 1360c, *tab*
1466

pseudonym 1461a
sonnet 1344c
Sidra, Gulf of 2209b, 2210a, 2340c
Siebe, Augustus 1246b
Siege Perilous 1446b, 1447b
Siegfried (leg.) 1428a, 1447b
Siegfried (opera) 167a, 1447b
Siegfried I, Count 2211b
Siemering, Rudolf *tab* 125
Siena, Guido da *tab* 106
Siena, Italy
painters *tab* 106
Siena College 687
Siena Heights College 677
Sienkiewicz, Henryk 344a, *tab* 1478
Quo Vadis 1414c
Sierra 514b
Sierra, Gregorio *see* Martínez Si-
erra, Gregorio
Sierra de Bahoruco 2142c
Sierra de Gata 2263b
Sierra de Gaudarrama 2263b
Sierra de Gredos 2263b
Sierra Leone 2156c, 2248–2249
agriculture 2248c
climate 2248b
Commonwealth status 1000c
economy 2248c
flag *il* 2184
geography 2248b
government 2248c
history 2248c–2249b
independence 2249a–2249b
map 2248, *Atlas*-36
people of 2248b
religion 2248b
slavery 2248c
Sierra Leone Company 2249b
Sierra Leone People's Party 2249a,
2249b
Sierra Madre (Mexico) 2340c–2341a
Sierra Madre (Philippines) 2237c
Sierra Madre del Sur 2217c
Sierra Madre Occidental 2217b
Sierra Madre Oriental 2217b
Sierra Maestra 2136b–2136c
Sierra Morena 2263b
Sierra de Neiba 2142c
Sierra Nevada de Mérida 2296c
Sierra Nevada Mountains 1976c,
1988b, 2019a, 2019b, 2292c
sequoia trees 1692b–1692c
Sierra de los Organos 2136c
Sierra de Perijá 2296c
Sierra de Zacatecas 2217b
Sieyès, Emmanuel Joseph 1007b
Sight (physiol.) *see* Vision
Sight (song) 423
Sigismund Augustus 2240a
Sigma 7 (spacecraft) *tab* 1770
Sigma-minus (particle) 1916a
Signac, Paul 344a
Signature (mus.) 178b
Signature (print.) 153c
Signorelli, Luca *tab* 106
Sigurd (leg.) 1447b
**Sigurd the Volsung and the Fall
of the Niblungs** (epic, Morris)
1417b
Sihanouk, Prince Norodom 2109a,
2109b
Sikkim 2249–2250
agriculture 2249c
climate 2249b
economy 2249c
flag *il* 2184
geography 2249b
government 2249c
history 2249c–2250a
map 2249, *Atlas*-29
people of 2249b–2249c
religion 2249b
Sikorsky, Igor 344b, 1159a
Sikussak 514b
Silas (Bib.) 1460a
Silas Marner (nov.) 1368a, 1417b
Silesia 2160c
Silesius, Angelus *tab* 1468
Silhoutte, Etienne de 344b
Silhouette Island 2322a
Silica 514b, 1200a
glass 133a, 1211a
sands 1223a
Siliceous 514b
Silicon 514b, 1837, 1890a, 1892b
alloys 1193a
atomic weight *tab* 1805
Silicon carbide 1192b
hardness 1192c
Silicon solar cell 1890c
Silicosis 945c
Silk 1223b

history 1280b
India 2178c
Japan 2199b
manufacture 1280b
Vietnam 2299b
Silk screen printing 1174a
Silkworm 58a–58b, 1223b
cocoon 1223b
Sill 514b
Silla Kingdom 2204a, 2204b
Sills (geol.) 450c
Silone, Ignazio 344b, 1388b, *tab*
1481
Silt 514c, 752b
load 514c
Siltstone 514c
Silurian Period *tab* 456, 514c
Silva, José Asuncíon 1393b
Silva Quadros, Jânio da 2104c
Silver 1837
atomic weight *tab* 1805
Bland-Allison Act 2055b
coinage 865b
conductivity 1882a
Honduras 2173a
Mexico 2218a
Montana 1988a
Nicaragua 2227c
Panama 2234a
Peru 2237a
Romania 2244a
Sweden 2268a
Silver Age 1447b
Silver-cadmium cell 1132a
Silver foxes fur farming 738a
Silver King, The (play) 1369c
Silver Purchase Act *see* Sherman
Silver Purchase Act
Silver Spoon (nov.) 1410c
Silverfish *see* Bristletail
Silver-transfer process (duplicat-
ing) 1164c
Silver-zinc cell 1132a
Sima 514c
Simeon (Bib.) 1460a
Similarity (math.) 1569a
Simile 1314c
Simmons, Edward E. *tab* 108
Simmons College 675
Simms, William Gilmore 1373b, *tab*
1475
Simon (Bib.) 1460a
Simon, Jeanne Lucien *tab* 108
Simonides of Amorgus 1351b
Simonides of Ceos 1351b, *tab* 1464
Simoom, 514c
Simple fracture (med.) 917c
Simple Simon (nursery rhyme)
410a
Simplicissimus (nov.) *tab* 1468
Simplon Tunnel 1226c
Simpson, Sir James Young 344b
Simpson, Mrs. Wallis *see* Wind-
sor, Duchess of
Simpson College 668
Simultaneous equations 1550b,
1592a
problems 1552b
substitution 1551b
Sin (anc. deity) 1623a
Sinai, Mount 1460a
Sinai Peninsula 2192a, 2280b, 2280c,
2281c, 2341a
language 1296a
Sinanthropus *see* Peking man
Sinclair, Harry F. 2068c
Sinclair, May 1370c
Sinclair, Sir John 719c
Sinclair, Upton 344b, 1375c, *tab*
1463b
The Jungle 1348c
Sindbad the Sailor 1447b
Sinding, Christian 168b, *tab* 172b
Sines 1583a, *tab* 1589, 1607c
law of 1587b
Sing a song of sixpence (nursery
rhyme) 409c
Singalila Range 2249b
Singapore 2188b, 2250a, 2250b–2250c
agriculture 2250a
climate 2250a
Commonwealth status 1000c
economy 2250a–2250b
flag *il* 2184
geography 2250a
government 2250b
history 2250b–2250c
independence 2250c
industry 2250b
map *Atlas*-30
people of 2250a

religion 2250a
trade 2250b
World War II 1028c, 2250c
Singer, Izaac Merrit 344b, 1241b, 1279a
Singing careers 374b
Singjerli
archeology 970b
Singkep Island 2187a
Single tax 907c
Single-leaf piñon 1988b
Single-phase generators 1885c
Single-phase induction motor 1143b
Single-Speech Hamilton see Hamilton, William Gerard
Sing-Song (poem) 415a
Singspiel (mus.) 165b
Sining, China 2372c
Sinjohn, John see Galsworthy, John
Sinkhole 448b, 514c
Sinking fund 603c
Sinn Féin movement 2191c
Sinoauricular node 923b
Sino-Japanese Treaty 2069a
Sino-Japanese War (1894–1895) tab 1075, 2201b, 2129a
Sino-Japanese War (1937–1945) tab 1076, 2030c
Sinon 1449c
Sino-Tibetan languages see Indo-Chinese languages
Sintenis, Renée tab 125
Sinter 514c
Sintering 1193c
Sioux City, Iowa 1982b
Sioux Falls, South Dakota 1994c
Sioux Falls College 699
Siqueiros, David Alfaro tab 109
biography 344b
Sir Patrick Spens (ballad) 1396b
Sirens (myth) 1447c
Sirens (sound) 1896a
Siret River 2243c
Sirius (myth) 1447c
Sirius (star) tab 1786
Sirocco 514c
Sisal 733c, 1693a
Cayman Islands 2310a
Comoro Islands 2310c
Kenya 2202b
Mozambique 2317b
Tanzánia 2272b
Venezuela 2297b
Sisley, Alfred tab 108
Sismondi, Jean Charles tab 1472
Sistine Madonna (paint., Raphael) tab 110
Sistrum 155c
Sisyphus 1447c
Sitang River 2341c
Sitka spruce 1974c
Sittang River 2106c
Sitting Bull 344b
Sitwell, Dame Edith 344b
Siva (Shiva) 1447c, 1430b
Siwalik Mountains 2341a
Six Characters in Search of an Author (play) 1388a
Sixth (mus.) 178b
Sixtus IV, Pope
Melozzo da Forli tab 112
61 Cygni (star) tab 1786
Sjaelland see Zealand
Sjaelland Island 2141a
Sjogren, Emil 168b
Skagerrak Strait 2341a
Skalds 1417b, tab 1465
Skanderbeg 2087a
Skarn 514c
Skate see Ray
Skating 1729b–1730a
stunt races 1730a
Skeat, Walter W. 344b
Skeletal muscle 927a
Skeleton (human) 917c, il 1614, il 1619
Skelton, John 344c
Skeptics (philos.) 1615b
Sketch Book of Geoffrey Crayon, Gent 1373a, 1417c
Ichabod Crane 1400a
Legend of Sleepy Hollow 1409a
Sketches by Boz (bk.) 1366c
Skidmore College 687
Skiing 1730a
jumping 1731a
racing 1731a
Skijoring 1731a
Skilton, Charles Sanford 170c

Skim milk 727a
Skimmer 58b
Skin 918a
chilblain 941a
dermatitis 941b
eczema 941b
hives 942b
lichen planus 942c
pityriasis rosea 945a
prickly heat 945b
psoriasis 945b
scleroderma 945b
ulcers 945c
Skinner, John Stuart 719c
Skywaves (radio) 1175b
Skinner, B. F. 620b, 1949c
Skinner, Cornelia Otis 344c
Skopje, Yugoslavia 2303b, 2372c
Skuld 1441a
Skull 917c
Skunk 58b
Skunk cabbage 1693a
Skyscrapers 81b
Slack water 514c
Slag 753a
Slag-refining 1216a
Slag wool 1208b
Slaking 514c
Slander 889c
Slate 451a, 514c, 1223c
Slater, Samuel 344c, 523c, 1286c
Slavery 1002b, 1936a
Antigua 2307a
Bahamas 2307b
Barbados 2097b–2097c
Barbary States 997c
Bermuda 2307c
Brazil 2102c, 2103c, 2104a
British Virgin Islands 2309a
Congo (Brazzaville) 2134a
Cuba 2137b
Dahomey 2141a
Gabon 2155c
Gambia 2156c
Ghana 2164b
Great Britain 2290a, 2291a
Greece (ancient) 964c, 1010a
Guadeloupe 2315a
Guyana 2170c, 2171a
Haiti 2172a
history as justification of 964c
Jamaica 2198a
Kenya 2202c
Martinique 2316c
Mozambique 2317c
Netherlands Antilles 2318a
Nigeria 2229c
Peru 2237a
Portuguese Guinea 2320a
Roman Empire 964c, 1014c
Sierra Leone 2248c
Sudan 1005a
Tanzania 2272c–2273a
Trinidad and Tobago 2276a
—U.S.
829c, 1009b, 1022c–1023a, 2044b
Abolition Movement 2038b
Brown, John 2043a
Compromise of 1850 2041a
Constitution 810c
Emancipation Proclamation 2048b
Lincoln, Abraham 2044b
Missouri Compromise 2035c
Northwest Territory 2030b
Texas 2039b
Virgin Islands 2004b, 2004c
Slavic (Slavonic) languages 1334a, tab 1334
Slavophils (Russ. reformers) 1389b
Slavs anthropology 1927a
music 154c
Sleeping sickness tab 948
Sleeping Venus (paint.) tab 110
Sleet 473b, 514c
Sleipnir 1447c
Slick, Sam tab 1463b
Slickenside 514c
Slide rule 1236a, 1596c
Slidell, John 344c, 2045a
Slime molds 1640c
Slipped disc 945c
Slipper shell 58b–58c
Slippery Rock State College 697
Slipsheeting 153c
Slopes (math.) analytic geometry 1591b
Sloth 58c
Slough 514c
Slovak (lang.) 1334a
Slovakia 2139b–2140a
Slovene (Slovenian) (lang.) 1334a
Slue Foot Sue 1443a
Slug 58c–59a

Slur (mus.) 178b
Sluter, Claus 120b, tab 125
Small business proprietors 387c
Small Business Administration 904c
Small caps (print.) 153c
Small intestines 920c
Smallmouth black bass il 1717
Smallpox tab 948
immunity 1849a
Smeaton, John 1189c, 1201b
Smell (sense) 937b
Smelt 59a
Smetana, Bedrich (Friedrich) 168c, tab 172a
biography 344c
Smilax 1693a
Smith, Adam 344c, 523b, 867b, 986c, 987a, 1261a, 1364a, tab 1470
laissez-faire 598c
mercantilism 598b
Smith, Alfred Emanuel 344c
presidential candidacy tab 801, 2070b, 2071a
Roosevelt, F. D. 2072b
Smith, Caleb B. tab 797
Smith, Charles E. tab 796
Smith, David 124b, tab 125
Smith, Francis Hopkinson tab 1477
Smith, Goldwin 344c
Smith, Green Clay presidential candidacy tab 801
Smith, Hoke tab 797
Smith, Ian 2243b
Smith, James Declaration of Independence tab 803
Smith, Captain John 344c, 1372a, tab 1467
Virginia 2024a
Smith, Joseph 345a
Smith, Robert tab 795
Smith, Seba 1462a
Smith, Sydney 345a, tab 1472
Smith, William (pol.) tab 800
Smith, William Farrar (general) 1461a
Smith College 675
Smith-Connally Act 831b, 885a
Smith-Lever Act 721a
Smithson, James Macie 345a
Smog 468a, 514c, 777a
Smoke tree 1693a–1693b
Smollett, Tobias 345a, 1346a, 1363c, tab 1470
Smooth muscle 927a
Smuggling 908a
Smuts, Jan Christian 345a, 1012b, 2117c–2118a, 2253b
Smyrna rugs 1110c
Snake bites 1711a
Snake River 1980c, 1981, 1992c, 2017a, 2020c, 2293a
length of 2020b
Snakes poisonous in U.S. 1711c
Snapdragon 1693b
Snell's law 1904c
Snipe 59a
Snorri Sturluson 345a, tab 1465
Eddas 1402a
Snow 473c, 514c
glaciers 449a
measurement of snowfall 473c
Snow modeling 1731b
Snow plant 1693b
Snow tracking 1739b
Snowden, Philip 345a, 908a
Snowdrift 515a
Snowdrop 1693b
Snowfall 764a–764c
Snowfield 515a
Snowline 515a
Snowshoe hare 1859c
Snowshoeing 1731b
Snyder, John W. tab 796
Snyders, Frans tab 107
Soap 1224a
fats 732b
Soapberry 1693b–1693c
Soapberry family 1693c
Soapstone 515a
Soapwort see Bouncing bet
Sobaek Mountains 2341a
Sobhuza II, King (Swaziland) 2267b, 2267c
Sobieski, John see John III Sobieski
Sobrero, Ascanio 1207c
Sobriquets, dictionary of 1461–1463
of U.S. presidents tab 799
Socarrás, Carlos Prío 2137c

Soccer 1731c
Social anthropology 1929b
Social classes see Class (social)
Social Contract (Rousseau) 1380a
Social Credit Party (Canada) 2118b
Social dance 181b
Social Democrat Party (Austria) 2095c–2096b
Social Democrat Party (West Germany) 2163a
Social Democratic Party (Iceland) 2177a
Social Democratic Party (Madagascar) 2212b
Social insurance 603c
Social philosophy 1611c
Social psychology 1951c
careers 383b
Social Security Act 831b, 836–838, 897c, 905b, 908b, 2074a
Social Security Administration 908b
bureaus 908b
Social Statics (tract) 1348a
Social War (90–88 BC) tab 1071
Social welfare 908b
careers 379a
relief 905a
Social work career 379a
Socialism 908a
communism 868a
rise of 987c
syndicalism 909c
Socialist Party (France) 2154a, 2154b, 2155a
Socialist Party (Italy) 2196c
Socialist Party (Sweden) 2269a
Socialist Party (U.S.) 908a
Socialist Unity Party (Germany) 2158c
Society 1941c
organization of 1935c
stratification of 1943b
technology 1123a
Society of Antiquaries 968c
Society of Dilettanti 968c
Society of the Cincinnati 1743b
Society of Friends (Greek organization) 2165c
Society for the Abolition of Slavery 2248b
Society Islands 2312c–2313a
Sociology 1938–1946
American literature 1375c
bibliography 1946c
history of 1938c
Sociopaths 1954a
Socrates 345a, 345b, 974c, 1614a, 1752a
Soda ash (sodium carbonate) 133b, 1193b
Södermann, August 168b, tab 172a
Sodium 463b, 762a, 1808b, 1837
atomic weight tab 1805
body requirements 919c
chemical bonding 1809c
electrons 1807a
electrovalences 1809a
soil 752a
Sodium chloride see Salt
Sodium cyclamate 745a
Sodium hydroxide (caustic soda) 1193b, 1199b, 1817b
Sodium-vapor lamp 1906a
Sodom 1460a
Sodoma, II tab 106
Soekarno (Indon. pres.) see Sukarno
Soffici, Ardengo 1388a
Sofia, Bulgaria 2105a, 2372c
Softball 1732b
Soft coal 515a
Soft-ground etching 138b
Soft water 515a
Soglo, Christophe 2141a
Sohrab and Rustum (poem) 1366b, 1417c
Soil agronomy 749a
chemical additives 753a
characteristics of 762a–762b
classification 750a
definition 749c
fertility 750c
fertilizers 733a, 752c
improvement 752b
intrazonal 503b
organic content 751b
residual 512c
Soil analysis 752a
Soil conservation 754b
careers 381b
Soil Conservation Service 750b

Soil erosion 1867c
Soil mechanics building construction 1198b
Soil physics 749a
Soil profile 515b
Soils 515a, 743a, 762a–762c
 azonal 762a–762b
 chemical content 743a
 latosols 762b
 moisture 743b
 red 512b
 tillage 743c
 tropical 762c
 tundra 762b
 yellow 512b
Soil science 749a
 career 381b
Soil structure 752b
Soil surveys 750b
Soirées Canadiennes, Les (periodical) 1391b
Solar apex 1793b
Solar batteries 1883b
Solar cell 1145c
Solar constant 515b
Solar eclipse 1794a
Solar energy ecology 1861a
 photosynthesis 1861a
 regulating 475a
Solar flares 952a
Solar radiation 757c
Solar system 1763b, 1780a
 aphelion 1793b
 distance relationships 1780b
 gravity 1780a
 major members 1782b
 Milky Way 1785c
 minor members 1783c
 origin of 454a, 1784b
 planetary probes 1771a
 properties 1784c
 tides 464a
Solar time 1797b
Solar wind 1797a
Sole see Flatfish
Solenoids 1884b
Solder tab 1193
Soldering 1281b
 flux 1209b
Solfeggio 178b
Solicitor General 908c
Solid fuels 1767a
Solid geometry 1604a
 cone 1602b
 cylinder 1603a
Solid propellants 1766c, 1779c
 main types 1767a
Solidification 1899c
Solids 1803a, 1828b
 heat 1899c
 properties 1870b, 1871a
Solifluction 515c
Solís, Antonio de tab 1467
Solís, Juan Díaz de 2090a, 2295b
Soll und Haben (nov.) 1385a
Solmisation 158b
Solnhofen, Germany
 lithography 141b
Solo (mus.) 178b
Sologub, Fëdor 1390b
Solo Man (anthrop.) 1924a
Solomon, King (Israel) 1017a, 1018b, 1460a
Solomon Islands
 kingfisher 41a
 World War II 1028c
Solomon's seal 1693c
Solon 345b, 974b
Solovev, Vladimir 1390a
Solstices 1797a
Solubility 1815c
Solum 515b
Solute 1815a
Solutions (chem.) 1815c
Solvay, Ernest 1212a
Solvay process 1193b, 1212a
Solvents 1815b
 paints 1216b
Solyman (Turk. rulers) see Suleiman
Solzhenitsyn, Aleksandr 1390b
Somali Republic 2146c
Somali Republic 2146c, 2250–2251
 agriculture 2251a
 economy 2251a
 flag il 2184
 geography 2251a
 government 2251a–2251b
 history 2251b–2251c
 independence 2251b–2251c
 map 2251, Atlas-35
 people of 2251a
 the Protectorates 2251b

religion 2250c
Somali Youth League (SYL) 2251b
Somaliland 2196b
 ass 14b
 gazelle 35b
 kudu 41c
Somaliland, Italian see Italian Somaliland
Somes River 2243c
Somme River 2341a
Somnium (story) 1763b
Somoza, Anastasio 2136a, 2228b
Somoza, Luis 2228b,
Son of the Middle Border (bk.) 1374c
Sonar 1894a
Sonata 178b
 Haydn 164a
Sonatina 178b
Songhai empire 2228c
Songhai kings 2215b
Song of the Plow (poem) 1370c
Song of Roland tab 1465, see also Chanson de Roland, La
Song of the Shirt (poem) 1365b
Song of Songs (Song of Solomon; Canticles) 1452a, 1460a, tab 1464
 music 160c
Song of the Yarper (Egyptian) tab 1463
Songs 178b
 kindergarten 401c, 418–424
Songs Before Sunrise (poems) 1369a
Songs of Experience (poems) 1364b
Songs of Innocence (poems) 1364b
Songs Without Words (mus.) Mendelssohn 165c
Sonic boom 1154b
Sonnet 1344c, 1417c
Sonnets (Milton) 1362b
Sonnets (Shakespeare) 1361c
Sonnets from the Portuguese (Browning) 1368c, 1417c
Sonoma State College 658
Sons of Liberty 2026b
Sons of the American Revolution 1745c
Soo Canal 1967c
Soochow, China 2372c
Soong Ch'ing-ling 2130b
Sophists (philos.) 1614a
Sophocles 345b, 975a, 1352c, tab 1464
 Ajax 1423b
 Antigone 1424b
 pseudonym 1461a
Soprano 160b, 178b
Sopron, Hungary 2372c
Sorbian (lang.) see Wendish (lang.)
Sordello 345b
Sorel see Sheep sorrel
Sorel, Albert tab 1478
Sorel, Felicia 184c
Sorghum 1693c
 Kansas 1982c
 Nebraska 1988b
 Niger 2228c
 Senegal 2248a
 Somali Republic 2251a
 Swaziland 2267a
 Tanzania 2272a
 Texas 1995c
 Togo 2275a
 Upper Volta 2294c
Sorolla y Bastida, Joaquín tab 108
Sorrows of Young Werther (nov.) 1384b
Sortie of the Civic Guard (paint.) tab 109
Soto, Bernardo 2136a
Sotto voce 178b
Soudan colony 2215b
Sound 129c, 515c, 1893–1897
 acoustics 1894c
 hearing 1894a
 motion pictures 1161b
 recording 1181a
 velocity 1893b
 see also Phonetics
Sound waves 1893a
 ultrasonics 1897a
Sounding 515c
Sour soil see Acid soil
Sourou-Migan 2141a
Soursop see Custard-apple
Sousa, João da Cruz e 1393b
Sousa, John Philip 170a, tab 172c
 biography 345b
Sousse, Tunisia 2277a, 2372c–2373a
South, The University of the 701

South Africa 2251–2253
 agriculture 2252b
 aloe 1648c
 amaryllis 1648c
 banana species 1651a
 calla lily 1655c
 climate 2252a–2252b
 cobra 22b
 economy 2252b–2252c
 flag il 2184
 freesia 1667c
 fumatory plants 1668a
 gazelle 35b
 geography 2252a–2252b
 geraniums 1668c
 government 2252c
 hawkweed 1670c
 history 2253a–2253c
 hyacinth 1672c
 ice plant 1673a
 lobelia 1676b
 lobster 43c
 map 2252, Atlas-40–41
 milkweed 1679c
 national parks 896a
 people of 2252b
 phalarope 50c–51a
 poppy 1688b
 potatoes 1688c
 religion 2251c
 resigns from Commonwealth of Nations 1000c
 rhinoceros 54c
 in South West Africa 2322b–2323a
 trade 2252c
 woodpeckers 68a–68b
 World War I 2253b
South African War (1899–1902) 2267b
South America 2341a–2341b
 agouti 13a
 alpaca 13b
 anteater 13c
 armadillo 14b
 archeology 971c
 bobolink 17c
 camel 19a
 cattle 20c
 coot 23a
 cormorant 23b
 crocodile 24b, 24c
 culture region 768b–769a
 deer 25b
 dog 25c
 economic geography 971a–971c
 elephant 33a
 flamingo 33c
 fox 34c
 gallinule 35a
 guinea pig 37b
 guppy 37b–37c
 hare 38a
 heron 38c
 hummingbird 39c
 ibis 40b
 iguana 40b
 jaguar 19c
 llama 43b
 lovebird 44a
 lungfish 44a
 map Atlas-44–45
 marmoset 44c
 see also under names of individual countries, such as Brazil
South Bend, Indiana 1981c
South Carolina 1994
 agriculture 1994c
 appointment 852b
 capital punishment 860b
 census (1960) 1973
 climate 1994b
 colleges of 698–699
 commercial law tab 826
 congressional apportionment tab 853
 economy 1994b
 geography 1994a–1994b
 government 1994b
 holidays 841–842
 Huguenots in 1010c
 people of 1994b
 public school enrollment tab 646
 public school expenditures tab 644
 student enrollment tab 645
 vegetable sponge 1698a
 —History 2053c
 Civil War 2050c
 colonial period 2025b
 Constitution (U.S.) 809c
 secession 907a, 2043c
 tariff 2037b
South Carolina, University of 699
South Carolina Society for Promoting and Improving Agriculture 719c
South Carolina State College 699
South China Sea 2341b

South Dakota 1994
 agriculture 1994c
 capital punishment 860b
 census (1960) tab 1973
 climate 1994c
 colleges of 699–700
 commercial law tab 826
 congressional apportionment tab 853
 economy 1994c
 geography 1994b–1994c
 government 793b, 1994c
 holidays 841–842
 initiative and referendum 884c
 people of 1994c
 public school enrollment tab 646
 public school expenditures tab 644
 statehood 2058a
 student enrollment tab 645
South Dakota, University of 699
South Dakota State University 700
South Island 2225c, 2226
South Korea see Korea, South
South Orkney Island 2308a
South Platte River 1977b, 2006c
South Shetland Island 2308a
South Vietnam see Vietnam, South
South West Africa 2322–2323
 climate 2322c
 economy 2322c
 geography 2322c
 government 2322c
 history 2322c–2323a
 map Atlas-40–41
 people of 2322c
 World War I 2322c
South Yemen 2253–2254
 agriculture 2253c
 economy 2253c–2254a
 flag il 2184
 geography 2253c
 government 2254a
 history 2254a
 map 2253, Atlas-25
 people of 2253c
 religion 2253c
Southard, Samuel tab 795
Southeast Asia Treaty Organization (SEATO)
 flag il 2184
 members 1021a
 terms of 1021a
Southeast Missouri State College 680
Southeastern Louisiana College 671
Southeastern Massachusetts Institute (S.M.T.I.) 675
Southeastern State College 693
Southern Alps (New Zealand) 2225c
Southern California College 658
Southern California, University of 658
Southern Colorado State College 659
Southern Connecticut State College 660
Southern Hemisphere winds 474a
Southern Illinois University 665
Southern lights see Aurora australis
Southern Methodist University 702
Southern Missionary College 701
Southern Mississippi, University of 678
Southern Oregon College 694
Southern pine 1974a
Southern State College (Arkansas) 655
Southern State College (South Dakota 700
Southern University & Agricultural & Mechanical College 671
Southey, Robert 1364c, 1408c, tab 1472
 biography 345b
 nickname 1461b
 Poet Laureate 1413b
Southgate, J. H. tab 801
Southwark Bridge 1196c
Southwest Missouri State College 680
Southwest Texas State College 703
Southwestern College (Kansas) 669
Southwestern Louisiana, University of 671
Southwestern at Memphis 701
Southwestern University (Texas) 702
Soutine, Chaim tab 109
Souvanna Phouma 2207a
Soviet 908c

Soviet Union *see* Union of Soviet Socialist Republics
Sowbug 59a
Sowerby, Leo 170b
Soybeans 743c
  Arkansas 1976b
  Illinois 1981b
  Indiana 1981c
  Iowa 1982b
  Louisiana 1984a
  oil 732c
  Maryland 1985a
  Minnesota 1986b
  Mississippi 1987a
  Missouri 1987b
  Ohio 1992a
  South Carolina 1994b
  Thailand 2273c
  U.S. 1963b, 1968b–1968c
Spaak, Paul Henri 345b
Space (astron.) 1780a
Space (mus.) 178b
Space biology 949–953
Space medicine 949
Space science *see* Astronautics
Space stations 1777c
Space travel 1769, 2079a
  early literature 1763a
  life support 952c–953a
  manned flight 1770a
  planetary probes 1771a
Spacecraft atomic rockets 1767b
  manned flight 1770a
  lasers 1911a
  radio communication 1889b
  satellites, artificial 1769b
  solar cells 1146a
  U.S. space programs 1769a
Spade (tool) 719a
Spaight, Richard Dobbs 809c
Spain 2263–2265
  agriculture 2263c–2264a
  anchovy 13b
  in Bolivia 2100c
  chameleon 20c
  in Chile 2122a
  Civil War 2265b
  climate 2263b
  Cold War 2265b
  in Colombia 2133a
  Congress of Vienna 1023c
  in Cuba 2137a
  economy 2263c–2264a
  in El Salvador 2145b
  in Equatorial Guinea 2311b–2311c
  established church 877b
  expulsion of Moors 1009a
  feudalism 1006b
  flag *il* 2184
  geography 2263b
  in Gibraltar 2314a
  government 2264a–2264b
  in Guatemala 2168c
  in Haiti 2172a
  hazel trees 1671a
  history 2264b–2265c
  in Ifni 2315c–2316a
  industry 2263a
  League of Nations 1012c
  map 2263, *Atlas*-12
  in Mexico 2218b–2218c
  in Morocco 2222b
  Muslims in 2264b–2264c
  natural resources 2263a
  in Nicaragua 2228a
  oranges 1682c–1683a
  in Panama 2234c
  in Paraguay 2235c
  people of 2263b–2263c
  peppers 1685c
  in Peru 2237a
  in the Philippines 2238a–2238b
  in Puerto Rico 2003a
  religion 2263b, 2264c–2265a, 2265b
  sheep 57b–57c
  in Spanish Sahara 2323a–2323b
  in Uruguay 2295c
  in Venezuela 2297c
  in the Virgin Islands 2004c
  World War I 2265a
  World War II 2265b
—Arts
  Altamira 971a
  architecture 77a
  ceramics *tab* 130
  dance 181c, 182a
  furniture 1096b
  glass *tab* 135
  music 169b, *tab* 172a
  painting 85b, *tab* 107–109
  printing 144b
  sculpture 120b
  see also Spanish literature
—History *tab* 1038–1056, 2264b–2265c
  kings *tab* 1079
  mercantilism 986c
  Middle Ages 985c
  New World *tab* 1060, 2021b,

2023a
  Spanish-American War 2060a
Spalato, Yugoslavia *see* Split
Spallanzani, Lazarro 1839a, 1844c
Spalling 515c
Spandex fibers 1209a
Spanish (language) *see* Spanish language
Spanish-American War *tab* 880b, *tab* 1075, 2060a, 2137b–2137c, 2265a
  Puerto Rico 2003a
  United States 794c
Spanish Civil War *tab* 1076
Spanish language 1335b
  English derivatives *tab* 1297c
  punctuation 1312c, 1314c
  study 1331a
Spanish literature 1391–1392, 1465–1469
  Latin America 1393
Spanish moss 1693c–1694a
Spanish Sahara 2323a
Spanish Succession, War of the *tab* 1073, 2026c
  battle of Blenheim 998c–999a
  results of 1021a–1021b
Spanish Tragedy, The (play) 1360c
Spanish War Veterans, United 1745c
Spar (geol.) 515c
Spare (bowling) 1707c
Spark chamber 1914c
Spark plug 1136a
Sparkling wine 723c
Sparks, Jared 345c, *tab* 1473
Sparrow 59a–59b
Sparta, Greece 974b, 1021c
  education 613a
Sparta (ancient) Helots 1010a
Spartacus 345c
Spathic 515c
Speaker, Tristram E. 345c
Speaker (gov.) 908c
Speaker of the House 908c
  forms of address *tab* 1120
Specialization (labor) *see* Division of labor
Specialty goods 604a
Specialty shop 604a
Species 1638b, 1639a
Specific energy 1897b
Specific gravity 515c, 1880b, 1919c
Specific heat 1899a
Spectator, The (periodical) 1167b, 1347b, 1363b, 1417c
  essay 1402c
  Roger de Coverley 1400a
Spectrographs 1792c
Spectrophotometry 1827c
Spectroscopic parallaxes 1788c
Spectroscopy 1906b
Spectrum 1919c
  audiofrequency 1919c
  colors 1907c
  electromagnetic 1903c, 1919c
  thermal radiation 1906a
Spee, Friedrich von *tab* 1467
Speech 1935a
  irregularities 1298b
  learning 1298
  production 1293c–1295c
  public speaking 1326–1328
Speech, freedom of *see* Freedom of speech
Speech, parts of *see* Parts of speech
Speed 1920a
  Mach number 1918c
  ultrasonics 1897a
  see also Velocity
Speed, James *tab* 796
Speed the Plough (play) Mrs. Grundy 1405a
Speedwell 1698b
  see also Veronica
Speke, John Hanning 2280a
Speleology 515c
Spelling 1302c
Spellman, Francis Joseph 345c
Spelman College 662
Spemann, Hans 345c
Spencer, Gilbert *tab* 109
Spencer, Herbert 1366b, *tab* 1476, 1619c
  biography 345c
Spencer, John Canfield *tab* 795
Spencer, Niles *tab* 109
Spencer, Stanley *tab* 109
Spender, Stephen 345c
Spender, Stephen H. 1371c
Spengler, Oswald 345c, 963c

Decline of the West 1348c
Spenser, Edmund 1360c, *tab* 1466
  biography 345c
  Epithalamium 1402c
  Faerie Queen 1403b
  pastoral 1345b
Spenserian stanza 1360c
Sperm (spermatozoa) 926b
  genetics 1851b
  meiosis 1851c
Spermaceti wax 1227b
Spermatogenic cells 926b
Sphalerite 453c, 515c
Spheres of influence 909a
Spherical aberration 1908b
Spheroid 515c, 1603b
Sphinx (myth) 1447c
Sphinx at Giza (Egypt) 115a, 1003a
Spice Islands *see* Moluccas
Spicebush 1694a
Spices 744a
  Ceylon 2119c, 2120b
  Comoro Islands 2310c
  Grenada 2314c
  India 2178b
  Indonesia 2187a, 2187c
  St. Lucia 2321b
  St. Vincent 2321c
  Seychelles 2322b
  Sierra Leone 2248c
  Tanzania 2272b
Spielhagen, Friedrich 1385a, *tab* 1476
Spies, Johann 1403c
Spikenard 1694a
Spillway 515c
Spina bifida 945c
Spinach 1694a
Spinal cord 938a
Spinal disorders scoliosis 945b
  slipped disc 945c
  spina bifida 945c
Spinal nerves 938a
Spindle 1281b
Spindle tree *see* Euonymus
Spines (plant) 1645a
Spinets 161b
Spinning 1281b
Spinning wheels 1281b
Spirea 1694a
Spires (Speyer), **Diet of** 874a
Spinoza, Baruch (Benedict) 1616c, *tab* 1468
  biography 346a
Spiral springs 1282a
Spirilla 1843b
Spirit duplicating method 1164b
Spirit ground (etching) 138c
Spirit varnish 1226c
Spirits (drink) 723c
Spirits of hartshorn *see* Ammonia
Spirituals (songs) 170c
Spirochaetales 1844b
Spits (geol.) 449a, 515c
Spitsbergen Island 2230a
Splash erosion 515c
Splats (furniture) 1098a
Spleen 925a
Split, Yugoslavia 2373a
Spohr, Ludwig 165c, *tab* 172a
Spoils system 909a, 2037a
Spokane, Washington 1998a, 2014c–2015a
  government 864a
Spokane River 2014c
Spondee 1417c, 1344b
Spontaneous generation 1839a
Spontini, Gasparo 166c, *tab* 171c
Spoon River Anthology (poems) 1376a, 1417c
Sporades 2165a
Spores bacteria 1844a
  fungi 1847a
Sporozoa 1848c
Sports 1703–1740
  primitive culture 1937a
Sportsman's Sketches, A (bk.) 1389c
Spottsylvania Court House, Battle of 2050a
Spread (fin.) 604a
Spreckels, Claus 346a
Spring (geol.) 515c
Spring (mech.) 1281c
Spring (season) 1797a
Spring Arbor College 677
Spring Hill College 654
Spring tide 515c
Springfield, Illinois 1981a, 1981b,

2015a
Springfield, Massachusetts 1985b
Springfield, Missouri 1987b
Springfield, Ohio 1992a
Springfield College 675
Springs, South Africa 2373a
Springtail 59b–59c
Sprinting 1736c
Spruce 1694a–1694b
  Black Hills 1994b
  blue 1977a, 1996a
  sitka 1974c
Spruce Knob 1998b
Sprue 920b, 945c
Spur 515c
Spurge 1694b
Sputnik 1764c
Sputnik I 951a, 1769b
Sputnik II 951a, 1769b
Sputnik IV 951b
Sputnik V 951b, 1770c
Sputnik VI 951b
Sputnik VIII *tab* 1772
Sputnik IX 951b
Sputnik X 951b
Squabs 742a
Squall 515c
Squarcione, Francesco *tab* 106
Square (geometry) 1605c, 1567c
Square (measure)
  centimeter *tab* 1500
  foot *tab* 1500
  inch *tab* 1500
  kilometer *tab* 1500
  meter *tab* 1500
  mile *tab* 1500
  millimeter *tab* 1500
  rod *tab* 1500
  yard *tab* 1500
Square root 1546a
  computation 1547a
Squash 1694b
Squash rackets (game) 1732c
Squeers, Wackford 1411b
Squeteague 59c
Squibob *see* Derby, George Horatio
Squid 59c, 1865c
Squirrel 59c–60a
Squirrel-cage motors 1143b
Squirrel corn *see* Dutchman's breeches
Sri Lanka Freedom Party (SLFP) 2120b
Srinigar, India 2373a
Srivijaya Kingdom 2187b–2187c, 2213c
Stabat Mater (hymn) 178b
Staccato 178b
Stack 515c
Staël, Madame de 346a, 1380c, *tab* 1471
Staël, Nicolas de *tab* 109
Staff (mus.) 158b, 178b
Staff tree 1694b–1694c
Staffordshire, England
  pottery 128a, *tab* 130–131
Stages (geol.) 455b
Stahl, Georg Ernest 1798c
Stalactite 516a
Stalagmite 516a
Stained glass 134a
Stainless steel alloys *tab* 1193
Stalin, Joseph 988c, 1028b, 1028c, 2087b, 2175c, 2262a–2263a, 2304c, 2305a
  biography 346a
  Cominform 865c
  World War II 2076b
Stalin Peak 2337c
Stalingrad, U.S.S.R. 2376c
Stalky and Co. (story) 1418a
Stallings, Laurence 346b, *tab* 1480
Stalwarts 2055c
Stam, Mart 1101c
Stamboliski, Aleksandr 2106a
Stamens (flower) 1645c
Stamford, Connecticut 1978a
Stamford Bridge, Battle of 2284c
Stamp Act 786b, 2027b
Stamp Act Congress 786b, 2026b, 2027b
Stanbury, Henry *tab* 796
Standard of living 604a
Standard money 598c
Standard Oil Company 524b
  trust-busting 2057c, 525a, 2062a
Standard time 1797b
Standardbreds 739b

Standish, Myles (Miles) 346b, 1019a
Stanford, Charles Villiers *tab* 172a
Stanford, Leland 346b
Stanford University 658
 linear accelerator 1912c
Stanhope, Charles (3rd Earl)
 printing 148a
Stanhope, Lady Hester Lucy 346b
Stanhope, Philip Dormer *see* Chesterfield, 4th Earl of
Stanislas I, King (Poland) 1021b
Stanislaus State College 658
Stanley, Henry 2135a
Stanley, Sir Henry Morton 346b
Stanley, Wendell 1842c
Stanley, Falkland Islands 2312a, 2373a
Stanleyville, Congo 2134c, 2360a
Stanovoy Mountains 2254c
Stanton, Edwin McMasters 346b, *tab* 796, 2052b
Stanton, Elizabeth Cady 346c, 914a
Stanza 1418a
Stapes *see* Stirrup (anat.)
Staphylococcus 1843b
 food poisoning 956a, 941c
 infections 954b
Stapling 1252c
Starch 1824b, 919b
Stare decisis (law) 817b
Starfish *see* Sea star
Stark, John 346c
Starling 60a
Stars *tab* 1786, 1787c
 Cepheid variable 1786b
 constellations 1793c
 distances 1788a
 double 1790b
 forming of 1787a
 galaxy 1786c
 luminosity 1788c
 magnitude 1788b
 multiple 1790b
 neutron stars 1795c
 novas 1795c
 spectra 1789a
 temperature 1788c
 twinkling 1797a
Star Spangled Banner *tab* 1472, 2034c
 derivation 1352b
State (pol.) 1936c
 totalitarian 910c
State, The (bk., Wilson) 784a
State, U.S. Department of 909a
 establishment *tab* 797
 secretaries of *tab* 795–796
State College of Iowa 668
State government Board of Education 631a
 Department of Education 631c
 local school districts 633b
 political party organization *tab* 393
 public health 960b
State Library (Berlin) *tab* 1463
State Library (Munich) *tab* 1463
State religion 909b
State University at Albany 687
State University at Buffalo 687
State University at Stony Brook 687
State University College at Brockport 687
State University College at Buffalo 687
State University College at Cortland 687
State University College at Fredonia 687
State University College at Genesco 687
State University College at New Paltz 687
State University College at Oneonta 687
State University College at Oswego 687
State University College at Plattsburgh 687
State University College at Potsdam 687
Staten Island 1990b
States rights 990a
Statia (is.) *see* Saint Eustatius
Static electricity 1881a
Statics (phys.) 1875b
Stationary front 477a
Statistics 548a, 1506c, 1596c, 1607b
 career 385b
 mean 1604c
 median 1605a
 probability 1606c

Statius Caecilius *see* Caecilius Statius
Statuary 114a
 see also Sculpture
Status (soc.) 1945c
Statute (law) 909b
Statute of Apprentices 827a
Statute of Frauds 818c
Statute of Laborers (Eng.) 876a
Statute of Limitations 818c, 819a, *tab* 826
Statute mile 516a
Statute of Westminster (1931) 872a, 875b
Statutory law 815c, 816b
Staunton, Virginia
 government 864b
Steam engines 1901b, 1146a
 agriculture 721a
Steam heating 1258b
Steam locomotives 1178a
Steam power 1153a, 1189c
Steam turbines 1148c
Stedman, Edmund Clarence *tab* 1477
Stedman, Seymour *tab* 801
Steel 1194a, 1212c, 1261b
 architecture 82a
 Austria 2095a
 Belgium 2098b
 Bessemer process 1261b
 conductivity 1882a
 engravings 139b
 Germany 2161b
 Hong Kong 2315b
 India 2178c
 Indiana 1981c
 industry beginnings 524b
 Luxembourg 2211a–2211b
 Maryland 1985a
 open hearth process 1261c
 Pennsylvania 1993b
 U.S. 1967b
 see also Iron
Steele, Sir Richard 1167b, 1363b, 1358a, *tab* 1469
 biography 346c
 pseudonym 1461b
 Roger de Coverley 1400a
 Spectator, The 1417c
 Tatler, The 1418b
Steelhead trout *il* 1717
Steen, Jan *tab* 107
 biography 346c
Steer 727b
Steer, Philip *tab* 108
Steering committees 866c
Stefan's law 1788c
Stefansson, Vilhjalmur 346c
Steffens, Lincoln 346c
Stein, Baron Heinrich 2160c
Stein, Gertrude 346c, 1375c, *tab* 1480
Steinbeck, John 346c, *tab* 1481
Steiner, Rudolf 347a
Steinheim, Germany
 anthropology 1925a
Steinmetz, Charles Proteus 347a
Stella *see* Johnson, Esther
Stella, Joseph *tab* 109
Stem (gram.) 1297a
Stems (plant) 1644b–1644c
 aerial 1644b
 bulbs 1644c
 corms 1644c
 herbaceous 1644b, 1644c
 rhizomes 1644c
 subterranean 1644b, 1644c
 tubers 1644b, 1644c
 woody 1644b, 1644c
Stendhal 1381a, *tab* 1463b, *tab* 1472
 biography 347a
Stenographers (career) 386c
Stephanus *see* Estienne
Stephen, King (Hungary) 2174b
Stephen II, Pope 2195a
Stephen (the Martyr), (Saint) 1406a
Stephen, Sir Leslie 347a
Stephen F. Austin State College 703
Stephens, Alexander Hamilton 347a
 Confederacy 2043c
 Hampton Roads Conference, 1009a–1009b
Stephens, James 347a
Stephens College 680
Stephenson, George 347a
Stephenson, Robert 1178a, 1196c
Steppes 516a, 1865a, 2255b
Steradian 1907a
Stere *tab* 1500
Stereophonic sound 1181c, 1895a

Stereotypes 148b, 153c
Sterkfontein, South Africa
 Australopithecus 1924b
Sterling College 669
Sterling silver alloys *tab* 1193
Stern, Isaac 347a
Sterne, Laurence 1346a, 1363c, *tab* 1470
 biography 347a
 pen name *tab* 1463c
 Sentimental Journey 1417a
Sterne, Maurice *tab* 108
Sternum 917c
Sterope 1444c
Stesichorus 1351c
Stetson University 661
Stettinius, Edward R., Jr. *tab* 796
 United Nations *tab* 797
Steuart, House of *see* Stuart
Steuben, Friedrich Wilhelm von 347a, 2028c
Steuben glass 135a
Steubenville, Ohio 1992a, 1998b
Stevens, Alfred *tab* 108, *tab* 125
Stevens, John 347b
Stevens, Siaka 2249b
Stevens, Wallace 347b, 1376b
Stevens Dam *see* Mud Mountain Dam
Stevenson, Adlai E. (1835–1914) 347b, 2058b, 2078b, 2079a, 2080a
Stevenson, Adlai E. (1900–1965) 347b
 presidential candidacy *tab* 801
 United Nations *tab* 797
Stevenson, Andrew House of Representatives *tab* 802b
Stevenson, Robert Louis *il* 207, 1368a, *tab* 1478
 biography 347b
 writing style 1321a
—Works
 Child's Garden of Verses 414a, 1399a
 David Balfour 1400c
 Dr. Jekyll and Mr. Hyde 1401c
 essays 1402c
 Kidnapped 1408b
 Treasure Island 1419b
 Virginibus Puerisque 1420c
Stevenson, William 1360c
Stewart, House of *see* Stuart
Stewart, Albert *tab* 125
Stewart, G. T. *tab* 801
Stewart, Potter Supreme Court *tab* 802a
Stewart, Robert (1316–1390) *see* Robert II, King (Scotland)
Stewart, Robert (1739–1821) *see* Castlereagh, Lord
Stewart of Kyle, John *see* Robert II, King (Scotland)
Stewart Island 2225c
Stick (print.) 153c
Stick insect 60a
Stickleback 60b
Stiegel, Henry W. 134c
Stieglitz, Alfred *tab* 108
Stiernhielm, Georg *tab* 1467
Stigma (flower) 1645c
Stikine Mountains 2020b
Stillman College 654
Stilo, L. Aelius 1355c
Stilt 60b
Stimson, Henry Lewis 347c, *tab* 796
Stimulated emission of radiation 1909c
Stimulus conditioning 1949b
 plants 1647a–1647b
Sting rays 54b
Stipple engraving 139c
Stirling, Arthur *see* Sinclair, Upton
Stirling, Battle of 1020a
Stirrup (anat.) 937a, 1894b
Stoa of Attalus 970c
Stoat *see* Weasel
Stock 1694c
Stock, Frederick August 170b, *tab* 172c
Stock exchange 604b
 stock-ticker 1182a
 see also under individual stock exchanges, such as New York Stock Exchange
Stockholm, Sweden 2267, 2373a
Stockholm Harbor Bridge 1197
Stocks (fin.) 604b
 blue-sky laws 857b
 corporations 822b
 crash (1929) 2071c
 growth stock 593c
 over the counter 600a

 preferred stock 600c
 stock split 604c
 unlisted 605c
Stockton, Frank R. *tab* 1477
 Lady or the Tiger, The 1408c
 pseudonym 1462a
Stockton, Richard *tab* 800, *tab* 803
Stockton, Robert Field 2040a
Stockton and Darlington Railway 1176c
Stoddard, Lothrop *tab* 1480
Stoddard, Richard Henry 347c
Stoddert, Benjamin *tab* 795
Stoics (philos.) 975a, 976b, 1615b
Stoke-By-Nayland (paint.) *tab* 110
Stoke-on-Trent, England
 ceramics *tab* 132
Stoke-Poges churchyard 1402a
Stokowski, Leopold 347c
Stolen Bacillus, The (story) 1370a
Stolo, Caius Licinius 1014c
Stolypin, Peter A. 2260b–2260c
Stomach digestion 920b
Stomata (plant) 1645b
Stone (geol.) *see* Stones
Stone, Harlan Fiske 347c, *tab* 796, 2077a
 Supreme Court *tab* 802a
Stone, Irving 347c
Stone, Lucy 347c
Stone, Thomas *tab* 803
Stone Age *see* Mesolithic Age; Neolithic Age; Paleolithic Age
Stonecrop *see* Orpine
Stonecutters Island 2315c
Stonefly 60b
Stonehill College 675
Stone River, Battle of *see* Murfreesboro, Battle of
Stones 752b
Stones of Venice (bk.) 1366b
Stonewall Jackson *see* Jackson, Thomas J.
Stoneware 128b
Stoping 516a
Stops (gram.) *see* Explosives (gram.)
Stops (mus.) 178b
Storage batteries 1883a, 1131c
 automobiles 1131b
Storage cells 1883b
Stories
—Children's Stories 400c, 424–442
 Gingerbread Boy 427a
 kindergarten dramatization 399a
 Little Black Sambo 424b
 Little Pine Tree 425b
 Little Red Hen 424a
 Nose, The 439c
 Pelle's New Suit 439a
 Peter Rabbit 433a
 Straw, the Coal and the Bean, The 435b
 Three Bears 427c
 Three Little Pigs 426a
 Ugly Duckling 428b
—Short Stories 1346c
Stork 60b–60c
Storm, Edward *tab* 1471
Storm, Theodor 1385a, *tab* 1475
Storms 475a, 516a
 control of 475a
Storstrom Bridge 1197
Story, Joseph 347c
 Supreme Court *tab* 802a
Story, William W. *tab* 125
Story of the Glittering Plain (bk.) 146a
Stoss 516a
Stoss, Veit *tab* 125
Stourbridge Lion (locomotive) 1178a
Stout (beverage) 724c
Stout State University
 Barron County Campus 708
 Menomonie 708
Stoves 1259c
 electric 1259c
Stowe, Harriet Beecher *il* 207, 1346c, *tab* 1475
 biography 347c
 Uncle Tom's Cabin 1374b, 1419c,
Strabo 347c
Strachey, Lytton 347c, 1347a, 1397b
Stradella, Alessandro *tab* 171b
Straddle (fin.) 601c
Stradivarius, Antonius 347c
Strafford, 1st Earl of (Thomas Wentworth) 347c

Straight, Mrs. Willard 1744b
Straight angle 1601b
Strain (geog.) 516a
Strain (music) 178b
Strait 516a
  see also under names of individual straits
Strait of Malacca 2213a, 2213b
Strand 516a
Strange Case of Dr. Jekyll and Mr. Hyde *see* Doctor Jekyll and Mr. Hyde
Strange Interlude (play) 1418a
Strapwork (pattern) 1095b
Strasbourg, France 2149b
  cathedral 76c
  libraries *tab* 1463
  sculpture 120c
Strassburg, Gottfried von *see* Gottfried von Strassburg
Strath 516a
Stratification (geol.) 516a
  drift 516a
Stratification (soc.) 1943b
Stratigraphic time 516a
Stratigraphic trap 516a
Stratigraphy 516a
Stratocumulus clouds 470c
Stratoscope telescopes 1792c
Stratosphere 468b, 516a, 763a
  temperature 468c
Stratton Porter, Gene *see* Porter, Gene
Stratum 516a
Stratus clouds 470c
Straus, Oscar S. *tab* 797
Strauss, David Friedrich 348a
Strauss, Johann (1804–1849) *tab* 172a
  biography 348a
Strauss, Johann (1825–1899) 348a
Strauss, Richard *tab* 172a
  biography 348a
Stravinsky, Igor 169b, *tab* 172b
  biography 348a
Straw 1136c
Strawberry 1694c
Straw, the Coal and the Bean, The (story) 435b
Streak 516a
Stream capture 516b
Stream of consciousness 1418a
Streams 516a
  ephemeral 494a
  erosion 447c
  influent 503a
  insequent 503a
  insulated 503a–503b
  intermittent 503b
  interrupted 503b
  obsequent 508c
  reversed 512c
  subsequent 517a
  superimposed 517a
  Yazoo 520c
Streetcars 1165a
Streeter, Alson presidential candidacy *tab* 801
Strelka (dog) 951b
Strength 516b
Streptococci 1843b
  wound infections 954b
Streptomyces 1845c
Stresemann, Gustav 348a
Stress 516b
Stress-strain law 516b
Striae 516b
Striated muscle 927a
Strife (play) 1370b
Strike 516b
Strikes (baseball) 1704c
Strikes (bowling) 1707c
Strikes (labor) 604c, 838c, 2057a
  coal strike (1902) 2061a
  Pullman Company 2058c
  steel 2058b
  syndicalism 909c
  Taft-Hartley Act 2077b
Strindberg, Johan August 348a, *tab* 1478
Stringed instruments 154b, 159c, 178b, 1896a
String quartets 178b
  Haydn 164a
Striped bass *il* 1717
Striped marlin *il* 1717
Strip cropping 743c
Stroessner, Alfredo 2236a
Stroke (med.) 924b, 945c
  arteriosclerosis 940b
Strombolian phase *see* volcano
Strong, William *tab* 802a

Strontium 1837
  atomic weight *tab* 1805
Strophic poetry Greek 1351b
Strozzi Palace 77b
Structural engineering 1191a
Structural geology 447a, 516c
Structural isomerism 1819a
Structural mechanics 1190b
Structural school (psych.) 1948a
Structure 516c
Structures 1189–1227
Stuart, Alexander *tab* 797
Stuart, Charles Edward, Prince (England) 348a
  nickname *tab* 1463a
Stuart, Gilbert 104a, *tab* 107
  biography 348b
  Portrait of Washington tab 110
Stuart, James Ewell Brown 348b
Stuart, Mary, Queen (Scotland) *see* Mary (Queen of Scots)
Stuart family 1020a–1020b, 2288b–2290a
Stubble mulch 743c
Study in Scarlet (story) 1370a
Study of History, A (Toynbee) 1348c
Stultz, Wilmer 1156a
Sturgeon 60c
Sturluson, Snorri *see* Snorri Sturluson
Sturm und Drang (lit.) 1384a
Sturtevant, Edgar Howard 1294a
Stuttering 1298b
Stuttgart, West Germany 2373a–2373b
Stuyvesant, Peter 348b, 2024b
  Delaware 2024c
Style (flower) 1645c
Styx 1448a
  Charon 1428c
  Hades 1433c
Subaerial 516c
Subaqueous 516c
Subarctic 516c
Subbituminous coal 1202a
Subcutaneous tissue 919a
Subdominant (mus.) 178c
Subhumid 517a
Subirrigation 740b
Subject (grammar) 1319c
Subject (music) 178c
Sublimation 517a
Sublimation (chem.) 1803a, 1872c
Sublingual glands 920b
Sublittoral *see* ocean depth zones
Submarine canyon 517a
Submarine warfare World War I 1025a, 1025c
  World War II 1028a, 1028b
Submarines 1182a
  sonar 1894a
  World War I 2065a
Submaxillary glands 920b
Submediant (mus.) 178c
Subsequent stream 517a
Subsidence 517a
Subsidy 909b
Subsoil 517a
Subsonic speeds Mach number 1918c
Subsistence theory of wages 605a
Subsurface water 517a
Subterranean stems 1644b, 1644c
Subtonic (mus.) 178c
Subtraction 1517b, 1607b
  algebra 1533b
  algorithms 1520b
  fractions 1528c
  history 1510a
Subtropical 517a
Subways 1165a
  first in New York 1189c
Succession Wars *see under the individual wars, such as Austrian Succession*
Sucker 60c–61a
Sucre, Antonio José de 2100c, 2144b
Sucre, Bolivia 2100a, 2373b
Sudan 995b, 2265–2266
  agriculture 2266a
  British rule 1005b
  climate 2266a
  condominium 1005c
  economy 2266a–2266b
  flag *tab* 2184
  geography 2265c–2266a
  goat 36a
  government 2266b

history 2266b–2266c
  independence 2266a
  mahdi rebellion in 1005b
  map 2265, *Atlas-34–35*
  millet 1679c
  people of 2265c–2266a
  religion 2265c, 2266b, 2266c
  slavery 1005a
  World War II 2266c
Sudan grass 1694c
Sudanic languages 1337c
Sudbury, Canada 2373b
Sudermann, Hermann 1385b, *tab* 1478
Sudeten Mountains *see* Sudetes
Sudetes (mountains) 2138c, 2238c, 2341b
Sudras 612a
  India 980b
Sue, Eugène 348b, 1474
Suetonius (Gaius Suetonius Tranquillus) 348b, 1358b, *tab* 1464
Suez, United Arab Republic 2373b
Suez Canal 1005a, 2193c, 2214a, 2271b, 2280b, 2280c
  crisis of 1957–1958, 995b, 2118b
  nationalized 2281c
  opening of 2281b
  United Nations 993b
Suez Canal Company 2291b
Suffolk University 675
Suffrage
  Negro 793b
  U.S. 793b, 811a
  U.S.S.R. 870a
  see also Women—Suffrage
Sugar 744b
  Antigua 2307a
  Barbados 2097a, 2097c
  Brazil 2102c, 2103b, 2103c
  British Honduras 2308a
  Colombia 2132c
  Cuba 2136c, 2137a, 2137b
  Dominican Republic 2142c
  Fiji Islands 2312b
  French Guiana 2312c
  Guadaloupe 2315a
  Guyana 2170b, 2170c, 2171
  Haiti 2171c
  Hawaii 1980b
  human physiology 927b
  Idaho 1980c
  India 2178b
  Indonesia 2187a
  Ireland 2191a
  Jamaica 2197a, 2198a
  Louisiana 1984a
  Madagascar 2212a
  Martinique 2316c
  Mauritius 2217a
  Montserrat 2317a
  Mozambique 2317b
  Netherlands Antilles 2318a
  Nicaragua 2227c
  nutrition 919b
  Pakistan 2232b
  Panama 2234b
  Paraguay 2235b
  Peru 2236c
  processing 1282a
  producing areas 744c
  Puerto Rico 2002c
  Réunion 2320c
  Rhodesia 2243a
  St. Kitts-Nevis-Anguilla 2321b
  Surinam 2323b
  Swaziland 2267a
  Syria 2271a
  Taiwan 2125c
  Thailand 2273c
  Trinidad and Tobago 2275c
  Turkey 2278a
  Uganda 2279c
  U.A.R. 2280c
  U.S. 1968c, 2294a
  Venezuela 2297b
  Vietnam 2299b
  Virgin Islands 2004b
  Yugoslavia 2303b
Sugar Act (Eng. 1764) 2027b
Sugar apple *see* Custard-apple
Sugar beets 744c, 1282a
Sugar cane 744c, 1282a, 1694c–1695a
Sugar maple 1990b, 1996b, 1998b, 1999c
Suger, Abbé 348b
Suharto, General 2188b
Sui dynasty 2127b
Suicide 909c, 959c
  in U.S. 954b
Suite (mus.) 161b, 178c
Suk, Josef 168c, *tab* 172b
Sukarnapura, Indonesia 2373b
Sukarno, President (Indonesia) 2188a–2188b, 2214b
Sukhodol (nov.) 1390a
Sukhot'ai Kingdom 2274a

Sulaiman Mountains 2341b
Sulawesi Island 2186c, 2188b
Suleiman the Magnificent (Solyman, Sulayman) 348c, 982c, 2278c
Sulfonamides 1273c
Sulfur 463b, 1224a, 1821c, 1837
  atomic weight *tab* 1805
  crystalline forms 1828c
  electrovalence 1809a
  Italy 2194b
  Louisiana 1983c
  Mexico 2218a
  Nepal 2223c
  in plants 1646b
  Poland 2239b
  soils 743b
  Sweden 2268a
  Texas 1995c
  U.S. 1967b, 2293c
  Venezuela 2297b
Sulfur dioxide chemical bonding 1810a
Sulfur Trioxide chemical bonding 1810a
Sulfuric Acid 1224b, 1817b
Sulla, Lucius Cornelius 348c
Sullivan, Sir Arthur 169b, *tab* 172a, 1369b, 1404c
  biography 348c
Sullivan, Harry Stack 1958b
Sullivan, John L. 348c
Sullivan, Louis 81b
  biography 348c
Sully, Thomas *tab* 108
  biography 348c
Sully-Prudhomme, René François Armand 348c, 1381c, *tab* 1477
Sulphur *see* Sulfur
Sul Ross State College 703
Sultaniyeh (tomb) 78a
Sulte, Benjamin 1391a
Sulzberger, Arthur Hays 348c
Sumac 1695a
Sumac family 1695a
Sumak rugs 1110c
Sumanguru (leader) 2215a
Sumarokov, Aleksandr 1389a
Sumatra 2186c, 2187a, 2188a–2188b
  dog 25c
  maple trees 1678a–1678b
  orangutan 48c
  rabbit 53c
  rhinoceros 54c
  trogons 64a–64b
Sumerians 969b
  architecture 74a
  furniture 1093b
Summa Theologica (Aquinas) 1347b, 1755c
Summer 1797a
Summerfield, Arthur E. *tab* 796
Summons (law) 909c
Sumner, Charles 348c
Sumner Tunnel *tab* 1226
Sumter, South Carolina government 864b
Sun 757c–758a, 1780a, 1782b
  chromosphere 1793c
  Copernicus 1756c
  earth relationships 757b–757c
  estimated age 1784c, 1790c
  matter 1780a
  photosphere 1796b
  planets, origin of 454a
  solar flare 952a
  star 1790c
  sunspots 1797a
  temperature 1789a
  see also under headings beginning with Solar
Sun Valley, Idaho 1980c
Sun Yat-sen 2129b, 2129c, 2130a, 2130b
  biography 348c
Sunay, Cevdet 2279b
Sunday legal phases 819a
Sundew 1695a
Sundew family 1695a–1695b
Sundiata (leader) 2215a
Sunfish 61a, *il* 1717
Sunflower, Mt. 1982c
Sunflowers 1695b
  wild 1982b
Sung Dynasty 978b, 2127c
Sungari River 2124a, 2341b
Sunlight 1782c, 1907b
Sunnites 982a
Sunset Cox *see* Cox, Samuel S.
Sunspots 1797a
Superconductivity 1903a
Superego 1957c
Superimposed stream 517a

Superior, Lake 1985c, 1999a, 2017c, 2020c, 2110c
Superior, Wisconsin 1986b, 1999a
Superiors (print.) 153c
Supernovas 1795c
Superposition, Law of 455b
  see also Law of superposition
Supersonic speed 1897a
  Mach number 1918c
Supertonic (mus.) 178c
Supper at Emmaus (paint.) *tab* 112
Supplication Day 842b
Supply and demand 537b, 605a
Supralittoral see Ocean depth zones
Supreme Court (U.S.) 791c, 808c, 809a, 869a
  advisory opinion 850a
  appeal 852a
  civil rights 864c
  Dred Scott Decision 2042b
  forms of address *tab* 1119
  justices of *tab* 802a
  labor legislation 833a–834b
  powers of 792a
  reorganization 2074b
Supreme Soviet 869c
Surabaja, Java 2373b–2373c
Surat, India 2373c
Surf 517a
Surface chemistry 1800c
Surface condensers 1244a
Surface tension 1828b
Surface wave 517a
Surinam (Dutch Guiana) 2225a, 2323
  minerals 453c
Surplus 605a
Surplus value 609a
Surrender of Breda (paint.) *tab* 111
Surrey, Earl of (1517–1547) 1006b
  see also Howard, Henry
Surrogate 909c
Suruga Bay 2198c
Surveying 1282b
Susa, Persia 74b
  sculpture 113a
Susanna (Bib.) 1460b
Suspended sentence (law) 909c
Suspension (mus.) 178c
Suspension bridges 1191a, 1197a
Susquehanna River 1984c, 2008a
Susquehanna University 697
Sussex (ship) 2065a
Sussex Kingdom 2284a
Sustainer engines 1779c
Susy-Q (dance) 182b
Sutherland, George Supreme Court *tab* 802a
Sutherland, Graham *tab* 109
Sutherland Waterfall 2341b
Sutter, John Augustus 349a
Sutton, W. S. 1851b
Suva, Fiji Islands 2312a, 2373c
Suvadiva 2214c
Svalbard Archipelago 2323–2324
  see also Spitsbergen
Svealand, Kingdom of 2268b
Svendsen, Johan 168b, *tab* 172b
Sverdlovsk, U.S.S.R. 2373c
Sverdrup, Johan 2231b
Svevo, Italo 1388a
Swains Island 2000a
Swale 517a
Swallow 61a
Swallow, Silas presidential candidate *tab* 801
Swallowtail 61b

Swamp, The (paint.) *tab* 110
Swamps 517a
  mangrove 506b
Swan, Sir Joseph Wilson 349a
Swan of Avon see Shakespeare, William
Swan Islands 2003
Swan Song (nov.) 1410c
Swans 61b–61c
Swanscombe England anthropology 1925a
Swanson, Claude A. *tab* 796
Swarming (bees) 724b
Swarthmore College 697
Swatow, China 2373c
Swayne, Noah Haynes Supreme Court *tab* 802a
Swaziland 2266–2267
  agriculture 2267a
  climate 2267a
  economy 2267a–2267b
  flag *il* 2184
  geography 2266c–2267a
  government 2267b
  history 2267b–2267c
  independence 2267b–2267c
  map 2267, *Atlas*-41
  people of 2267a
  religion 2266c
Sweat glands 918c
Sweden 2147b, 2267–2269
  agriculture 2268a
  architecture 78a
  Battle of Leipzig 1014b
  Congress of Vienna 1023c
  Danish crown 2142a
  economy 2268a–2268b
  established church 877b
  flag *il* 2184
  geography 2267c
  government 2268b
  history 2268b–2269b
  Kalmar Union 2268b–2268c
  kings *tab* 1080
  League of Nations 1012c
  map 2268, *Atlas*-14–15
  merchant shipping 2268b
  music 168b, *tab* 172b
  nightingale 47c–48a
  Norway and 2230c–2231a
  painters *tab* 108
  people of 2267c–2268a
  raids on the British Isles 2284a
  religion 2258b, 2267c, 2268c
  rugs 1109c
  trade 2268b
  Triple Alliance (1668) 1022c
  Vasa Kings 2268c
  Vikings 2268b
  World War I 2269a
  World War II 2269b
Swedenborg, Emanuel 349a, *tab* 1469
Swedish language 1336a
  classification 1333b
Swedish Nightingale see Lind, Jenny
Sweelinck, Jan 162a, *tab* 171c
Sweet, John E. 1215b
Sweet and Low (poem) 417b
Sweet bay see Laurel
Sweet Briar College 705
Sweet clover 1695b
Sweet gum 1695b–1695c
Sweet pea 1695c
Sweet potato 1695c
Sweet william see Pink
Sweeteners, artificial 745a
Sweetsop see Custard-apple
Swell 517a
Sweynheim, Konrad 143c
Swift, Gustavus 524a
Swift, Jonathan 1346a, 1363a, *tab* 1469

  biography 349a
  Drapier letters 1462a
  Gulliver's Travels 1405b
  pseudonyms 1461b, 1462a, *tab* 1463c
Swift Dam 1205c
Swifts 61c
Swimming 1729b
  strokes 1733c
Swinburne, Algernon 1369a, *tab* 1477
  Atalanta in Calydon 1425c
  biography 349a
Swine 61c, 745a
  breeds of 745b
  undulant fever 958a
  see also Hogs
Swing, The (poem) 414a
Swiss chard see Beet
Swiss cheese bacteria 1845b
Swiss Confederation see Switzerland
Switzerland 2269–2270
  agriculture 2269c–2270a
  appointment 852b
  Austro-Swiss War *tab* 1072
  beets 1652a
  cheese *tab* 731b
  climate 2269b
  economy 2269c–2270a
  flag *il* 2184
  geography 2269b
  government 2270a
  history 2270b–2270c
  independence 2270b
  industry 2270a
  Liechtenstein and 2210c–2211a
  literature outline *tab* 1470
  map 2269, *Atlas*-17
  music 160c, *tab* 171b
  natural resources 2269c
  neutrality 2270b–2270c
  painters *tab* 108
  people of 2269b–2269c
  referendum 884c
  religion 2269b, 2269c, 2270b
  trade 2270a
Sword dance 181c
Swordfish 61c–62a, *il* 1717
Swordtail 62a
Sycamore see Plane-tree family
Sydney, Australia 2092a, 2092c, *il* 2093, 2373c
Sydney, Nova Scotia 2373c
Sydney Harbor Bridge 1197
Syenite 517a
Sylla, Lucius Cornelius see Sulla, Lucius Cornelius
Sylvester II (pope) 1503c
Sylvius 1798b
Symbiosis 1859c
  bacteria 1846a
Symbolic logic 1507a, 1598a, 1611b, 1619a
Symbolic Logic (book, Boole) 1507a
Symbols (math.) 1604c, *tab* 1605a
Symbols (proofreading) 147
Symington, William 349a
Symmetrical fold 517a
Symonds, John Addington *tab* 1477
Sympathetic nervous system 938c
Sympathetic pathways 924a
Sympathetic strikes 605b
Sympathetic vibration 1893c
  hearing 1894c
Symphony 178b
  Haydn 164a
Synapse 939a
Synchrocyclotrons 1912c
Synchronous generators 1139a
Synchronous motors 1142c, 1885c
Synchronous satellites 1769c

Synchrotrons 1912c, 1919b
  largest 1912c
Syncline 451a, 517b
Synclinorium 517b
Syncom 1 (satellite) *tab* 1163
Syncom 2 (satellite) *tab* 1163
Syncom 3 (satellite) *tab* 1163
Syncopation 170c, 178c
Syndicalism 909c
Syndicate 605b
Syndics of the Cloth Merchants Guild (paint.) *tab* 109
Synecdoche 1315b
Synecology 1859a
Synge, John Millington 1370c, *tab* 1480
  biography 349a
Synodic month 1795b
Synoptic 517b
Syntax 1310–1311
  adjectives 1305b
  adverbs 1308b
  common errors 1311b
  conjunctions 1308c
  diagrams of sentences 1309c–1310a
  nouns 1304b
  prepositions 1308b
  pronouns 1305a
  verbs 1307c
Synthesis gas 1210b
Synthetic faults 517b
Synthetic products see under the latter part of the name, such as Fibers, Synthetic
Syphilis *tab* 948, 958b
  aneurysm 940b
Syr River 2341b
Syracuse (ancient) 1021b–1021c
Syracuse, New York 1990c, 2015a
  pottery 130a
Syracuse Museum of Fine Arts (N.Y.) ceramics 132a
Syracuse University 687
Syria 995b, 2190b, 2202a, 2270–2271
  agriculture 2271a
  archeology 969c, 970a
  ass 14b
  climate 2270c
  economy 2271a
  flag *il* 2184
  gazelle 35b
  geography 2270c
  government 2271a
  history 2271a–2271c
  independence 2271c
  industry 2271a
  map 2271, *Atlas*-25
  Ottoman Turks in 2271b
  people of 2270c–2271a
  religion 2270c, 2271b
  trade 2271a
  World War II 2271c
  —Ancient 969c, 970a
  biblical 1460b
  kings of *tab* 1080
  painting 84c
  pottery *tab* 130
  sculpture 119a
Syrian Desert 2270c
Syringa 1980c
  see also Lilac and Mock orange
Syrinx (mus.) 157a
Syrinx (myth) 1448a
  Pan 1442a
System 517b
Systems engineering 722c, 1283a
Systole 923b
Syzygy 517b
Szczecin, Poland 2239c, 2373c
Szeged, Hungary 2174a, 2373c
Szymanowski, Karol *tab* 172b

T

Tabard Inn 1360a
Tablatures (mus.) 160a
Table tennis see Ping-pong
Table Texts (math.) 1751a
Tableland 517b
Tablemounts 463a, 517b

Taboos 813a
Tabriz, Iran 982b, 2373c–2374a
Tabular pluton 517b
Tacitus, (Publius) **Cornelius** 963a, 965b, 965c, 1358a, 1397b, *tab* 1464
  biography 349b
Tacoma, Washington 1998a, 2015a, 2020a
  bridge 1191a
Taconic Mountains 1985a, 1996c
Taebaek Mountains 2203b, 2341b

Taegu, South Korea 2374a
Tafari see Haile Selassie I
Taft, Alphonso *tab* 79b
Taft, Lorado *tab* 125
Taft, Robert A. 349b, 2078a
Taft, William Howard 349b, 791c, *tab* 798–799, 1012b, 2173b, 2238b
  administration 2062b–2063a
  administration, events paralleling *tab* 1068
  Cabinet *tab* 796–797

  Cuba 2062a
  election and inauguration *tab* 801
  Philippines 2060c
  Supreme Court *tab* 802a
Taft Commission 2238b
Taft-Hartley Act 527b, 831b, 835b, 839b, 885a, 892c, 910a, 913a, 2077b
  hiring halls 882a
  mediation 891c
  right to work 602b

Tagore, Rabindranath 349b, *tab* 1479

Tagus River 2241a, 2241c, 2263b, 2341b–2341c
  bridge 1196c

Tahiti 2313

Tahoe, Lake 1988b, 2006a

Taiga 517b, 2255a
  geography 1863b

Taillefere, Germaine 349c

Tailor, The (paint.) *tab* 111

Taine, Hippolyte A. 349c, 1381b, *tab* 1476

Taipa Island 2316b

Taipei, Taiwan 2123a, 2374a

Taiping Rebellion 2128c

Taiwan 2128a
  agriculture 2125c
  climate 2125a
  economy 2125c
  geography 2124c–2125a
  government 2126c
  history 2131b–2131c
  invaded by Japan 2129a
  laurel 1675a
  loon 43c
  people of 2125a
  World War II 2131b

Taiyüan, China 2374a

Taj Mahal 980c
  architecture 78a

Tajumulco, Mt. 2168a

Takamatsu, Japan 2374a

Take (print.) 153c

Takkaze River 2146a

Takla Makan Desert 2123c, 2341c

Takoradi, Ghana 2164a

Talbot, Fox 148c

Talbot, William Henry Fox 349c, 1171c, 1172a

Talc (mineral) 453a, 517b
  hardness *tab* 1192b

Talcahuano, Chile 2121b 2122

Tale of a Tub (bk.) 1363c

Tale of Old Japan, A (poem) 1370c

Tale of Two Cities (nov.) 1367a, 1418a
  Sidney Carton 1398c

Tales from Shakespeare (bk.) 1365b

Tales of a Wayside Inn (poems) 1418a

Talisman, The (nov.) 1365c, 1418a

Talking *see* Speech

Talladega College 654

Tallahassee, Florida 1979a, 1979b, 2015a

Tallard, Camille de 998c

Talleyrand-Périgord, Charles Maurice de 349c, 1023c
  XYZ Affair 2032b

Tallinn, Soviet Union 2374a

Tallis, Thomas 161a, *tab* 171b, 349c

Tallow tree 1695c

Talmud *tab* 1464, 1629c

Talon, Jean 2114a, 2114b

Talus (geog.) 447b, 517b

Tam O'Shanter (poem) 1418b

Tamarack *see* Larch

Tamarand 1695c–1696a

Tamarisk 1696a

Tamayo, Rufino *tab* 109, 349c

Tambourine 178c

Tamburlaine (play) 1397c

Tamerlane 350a, 982c, 2085b, 2180b, 2221a

Tamiris, Helen 184

Tammany Hall 2054c

Tampa, Florida 1979b, 2015a

Tampa, University of 661

Tampere, Finland 2146c

Tampico, Mexico 2218a

Tan bark 1136c

Tana, Lake 2146a

Tana River 2341c

Tanager 62a

Tananarive, Madagascar 2211c, 2212a

Taney, Roger B. 350a, 792b, *tab* 795, *tab* 802a

T'ang Dynasty 978a, 2127b–2127c, 2300a

Tanganyika *see* Tanzania

Tanganyika, Lake 2134c, 2305a 2341c

Tanganyika African National Union (TANU) 2273a

Tangent *tab* 1589, 1607c
  calculus 1594a
  circle 1571b

Tangerine *see* Orange

Tangier, Morocco 2221b, 2221c, 2222b, 2374a
  anthropology 1925a

Tanglewood Tales (bk.) 1418b, 1421b

Tango 182a

Tanguy, Ives (Yves) *tab* 109
  biography 350a

Tanjore, India 2374a

Tanna Tunnel 1226

Tannhäuser (knight) 1448a

Tannhäuser (opera) 167a

Tannarive, Malagasy Republic 2374a

Tannin 1209c

Tanning 1209c

Tansman, Alexandre *tab* 172b

Tanta, United Arab Republic 2280c, 2374a

Tantalum 1837
  atomic weight *tab* 1805

Tantalus 1448a

Tanzania 2272–2273
  anthropology 1924a, 1927a
  climate 2272a
  Commonwealth status 1000c
  economy 2272a–2272c
  flag *il* 2184
  geography 2272a
  government 2272c
  history 2272c–2273a
  map 2272, *Atlas*-39
  people of 2272a
  religion 2272a
  slavery 2272c–2273a

Taoism 977a, 1623c, 2127b

Tao Te Ching (Tao Teh King) (rel. bk.) 977a, 1623c

Tapa Mountains 2341c

Tape recorder 1181a, 1895a

Tapestry Weavers, The (paint.) *tab* 111

Tapeworm 62a–62b, *tab* 948

Tapioca *see* Cassava

Tapir 62b

Tappan Zee Bridge *tab* 1197

Tap-root systems 1644b

Tar 1203a

Tarantella (dance) 178c, 182a

Taranto, Gulf of 2341c

Tarantula *il* 29, 62b

Tarawa, Gilbert and Ellice Islands 2314a, 2374b

Tarbagatap Mountains 2255a

Tarbell, Ida M. 350a

Targets archery 1704a

Tariff 605b, 876b, 902c, 910a
  Cleveland, Grover 2057a
  Dingley Bill 2059b
  McKinley Act 2057b
  Payne-Aldrich Act 2062b
  Smoot-Hawley Act 2071b
  Underwood Act 2063b
  Walker, Robert G. 2040c
  Wilson Bill 2058c
  see also Taxation

Tariq (Muslim general) 2314a

Tarija, Bolivia 2100a, 2100b

Tarkington, Booth 350a, *tab* 1479
  Monsieur Beaucaire 1411a
  Penrod 1412c

Tarkio College 680

Tarn 517b

Taro 1696a
  Western Samoa 2301c

Tarpon 62b–62c, *il* 1717

Tarquin (Lucuis Tarquinius Superbus) Cumaean sibyl 1447b

Tarragon 1696a

Tarsus, Turkey
  Paul 1460b

Tartaglia, Niccolò 1503a

Tartars *see* Tatars

Tartarus 1448a
  Hades 1433c

Tartary *see* Tatary

Tartini, Giuseppe *tab* 171c
  biography 350a

Taruc, Luis 2238b

Tartuffe (play) 1379b

Tashkent, U.S.S.R. 2256a, 2374b

Tashkent Agreement 2186b

Task, The (poem) 1364a

Tasman, Abel 2092c, 2226c

Tasmania 2091a, 2092a, 2092c, 2341c
  beech 1652a
  kangaroo 40c
  parks 896b
  shrews 57c–58a
  wombats 67c

Tasso, Torquato 1386c, *tab* 1467
  biography 350a

Jerusalem Delivered 1407b

Tassoni, Alessandro 1387a, *tab* 1467

Taste (sense) 937c

Taste (song) 424

Tatars 1021a

Tatary 979a

Tate, Nahum Poet Laureate 1413b

Tatler, The (periodical) 1167b, 1347b, 1363b, 1418b
  essay 1402c

Tattooing 1930c

Tatum, Edward Lawrie 1856c, 1858c

Taufa'ahau Tupou IV, King (Tonga) 2324b

Tauler, Johannes *tab* 1466

Taum Sauk Mountains 1987a

Taurus Mountains 2277c

Tawney, R. H. 1348b

Taxation 910a
  congressional power 811a
  Mellon Plan 2070a
  poll 899c
  single tax plan 907c
  structure of 534b
  see also Tariff

Taxes *see* Taxation

Taxonomy 1637b, 1638a–1638b, 1951a

Taygeta 1444c

Taylor, Bayard *tab* 1476

Taylor, Deems 170b, *tab* 172c
  biography 350b

Taylor, Frederick Winslow 1261a, 1266b

Taylor, George *tab* 803

Taylor, Jeremy 1362a, *tab* 1468
  biography 350b

Taylor, John W. House of Representatives *tab* 802b

Taylor, Zachary 350b, *tab* 798–799, 873a
  administration 2041a
  administration, events paralleling *tab* 1064
  Cabinet *tab* 796–797
  election and inauguration *tab* 800
  epithets 1462c
  Mexican War 2039c
  Whig Party 914a

Taylor University 667

Taylor ware *tab* 132

Tazewell, L. W. *tab* 800

Tbilsi, U.S.S.R. 2374b

Tchaikovsky, Petr Ilich 169a, *tab* 172a
  biography 350b

Tchelitchew, Pavel *tab* 109

Tcherepinin, Nicolai 169b

Tcherkess rugs 1110c

Tea 745c, 1696a–1696b
  Ceylon 2119c, 2120a, 2120b
  China 978a
  India 2178b
  Indonesia 2187a
  Kenya 2202b
  Malawi 2212c
  Mauritius 2217a
  Mozambique 2317b
  Pakistan 2232b
  picking (Ceylon) *il* 2120
  Uganda 2279c
  Vietnam 2299b

Tea family 1696b

Teachers colleges 628b

Teaching career in 378c
  first teacher training school 616c
  of languages 1331b
  of penmanship 1302c
  of reading 1299a
  of spelling 1303b
  parent-teacher relationship 403c
  teacher training 617c

Teaching machines 620a

Teak 1696b, 2107a

Teal 62c

Teapot Dome Scandal 2068c

Teapots 129a

Teasdale, Sara 350b, *tab* 1480

Teasel 1696b–1696c

Technetium 1837
  atomic weight *tab* 1805

Technical institutes 627c

Technological Revolution 987c

Technology 1123–1290
  agricultural advances 721a
  careers 380a
  development of 1124b
  nineteenth century 523c
  prehistoric 1927a
  primitive 1929b
  transportation 1153a
  twentieth century 525b.

Techtonic 517b

Tectono-physics 517b

Tecumseh 350b

Te Deum (canticle) 160c

Teeth human 920b
  public health 959b
  speech sounds 1294c

Tegner, Esaias *tab* 1472

Teguicigalpa, Honduras 2172c, 2173a

Tehachapi Mountains 2019a

Teheran Conference 2076b

Teheran, Iran 982b, 2188c, 2374b

Teheran rugs 1110c

Tehauntepec, Gulf of 2340c

Tejo River 2341b–2341c

Teju Lizard *il* 32

Tektite 517b

Tel Aviv, Israel 2192b, 2374b–2374c

Telegonus 1441b

Telegraph 1151c, 1182c
  invention 1183a, 1884b

Telemachus 1448a

Telemann, Georg Philipp *tab* 171c 350b

Telemaque (nov.) 1379c

Telemetry 1183b, 1889b

Teleology 1620c

Telephones 1151c, 1183–1185
  amplifiers 1889a
  careers 378a
  invention 1884b, 2054c
  laser 1910c
  recent developments 1185a
  switching 1184a
  television 1152b
  transmission 1184b
  types 1185a

Teleprinters 1183a

Telescopes 1791a, 1797a
  mounting 1792b
  radio 1796c
  size 1791a

Teletypewriters 1185b

Television 1152a, 1176a, 1185c, 1889b, 1906b
  camera tubes 1241a
  careers 378b
  cathode-ray tube 1240b
  educational 619a
  modulation 1186c
  picture tube 1187b
  repairmen 386b
  scanning 1186a

Telex 1183b

Telfair, Edward presidential candidate *tab* 800

Telford, Thomas 1152c, 1179c, 1191a, 1197a

Tell, William 1449b

Tell Atlas Mountains 2087b, 2276c–2277x

Teller, Edward 350b

Teller, Henry M. *tab* 797

Téllez, Gabriel *see* Tirso de Molina

Telluric current 517b

Tellurium 1837
  atomic weight *tab* 1805

Tellus 1432c

Telstar (satellite) 1152b, *tab* 1163, 1769c
  vacuum tubes 1284c

Tema, Ghana 2164a

Temora (poem) 1364a

Temperate zone 517b
  forests 1863b

Temperature 1897c, 1898a, 1919c
  absolute zero 1916b
  atmosphere 468b
  body temperature 918c
  boiling point 1916c
  freezing point 1918a
  measurement 469c
  thermocouples 1883b
  troposphere 468b
  weather forecasting 469a

Temperature gradient 517c

Temperature scales 1898b, 1919c

Temperley, H. W. V. 1023a

Tempest, The (play) 1418b
  Ariel 1395b, 1425a
  Caliban 1398b

Temple, Sir William 350c

Temple Buell College 659

Temples Egyptian 74a
  Greek 75a

Temple University 697

Tempo (mus.) 179a

Temuchin *see* Genghis Khan

Ten, Council of 1001b
Ten Commandments 1629a
Ten Years' War (1868–1878) 2137b
Tenant farming 380c
Tenant of Wildfell Hall (nov.) 1367c
Tendons 918a
Teniers, David (the Elder) 350c
Teniers, David (the Younger) tab 107
  biography 350c
Tennessee 1994–1995
  admission to Union 2032a
  agriculture 1995b
  arbor vitae 1649b
  budget system 858b
  capital punishment 860b
  census (1960) 1973
  climate 1995a
  colleges of 700–701
  commercial law tab 826
  congressional apportionment tab 853
  Constitutional Union Party 870b
  economy 1995a–1995b
  Fourteenth Amendment 2052a
  geography 1994c–1995a
  government 1995b
  holidays 841–842
  people of 1995a
  public school enrollment tab 646
  public school expenditures tab 644
  secession 2045a
  student enrollment tab 645
Tennessee, University of 701
Tennessee Agricultural & Industrial State University 701
Tennessee River 1020c, 1947a, 1962a, 1968a, 2006a, 2011a, 2019c, 2020c, 2293a
Tennessee Technological University 701
Tennessee Valley Authority (TVA) 849c, 876b, 888c, 898c, 903c, 910b, 1995a, 2011a, 2020c, 2073c
Tennessee walking horse 739c
Tennessee Wesleyan College 701
Tenniel, Sir John 350c, 1394a
Tennis 1734b
  doubles 1736a
Tennyson, Alfred 350c, 997c, 1358a, 1368c, tab 1475
  Arthurian legend 1395c
  blank verse 1397c
  Poet Laureate 1413b
—Poems
  Charge of the Light Brigade 1399a
  Enoch Arden 1402b
  Idylls of the King 1406b
  In Memoriam 1406c
  Princess, The 1414a
  Sweet and Low 417b
Tenochtitlán, Mexico 2218b, 2218c
Tenor 160b, 179a
Tenpins 1708a
Tenses (gram.) 1297a
Tent caterpillar 62c–63a
Tenth Muse (poem) tab 1468
Tents 1930a
  camping 1709c
Tenure of Office Act 2052b
Tepees 1710a
Tephra 517c
Terbium tab 1837
  atomic weight tab 1805
Terence 1353a, 1354b, 1355b, tab 1464
  biography 350c
Tereshkova, Valentina tab 1770
Terhune, Albert Payson 350c
Terminal velocity 1876b
Terminator (astron.) 1797c
Termite 63a
Tern 63a
Ternefine, Algeria
  anthropology 1924c
Terpander 157a
Terpsichore 1440c
Terra, Gabriel 2296a
Terra cotta 132c
  sculpture 113a
Terra Rosa 517c
Terraces (geol.) 517c
  unpaired 519b
  wave cut 449a
Terramycin 1824c
Terrapin see Tortoise
Terre Haute, Indiana 1981c
Terrigenous 517c

Territorial waters 517c
Territory 910c
Terry, Eli 1162b, 1229c
Terry, Ellen 350c
Tertiary period tab 457, 458a, 517c
Tertullian 351a, tab 1464
Teshu Lama see Panchen Lama
Tesla, Nikola 351a
Tess of the D'Urbervilles (nov.) 1368a, 1418b
Testicles (testes) 926a
  cryptorchidism 941b
Testing 621a
  intelligence 1950b
  personality 1950c
  scholastic aptitude 1952a
Testosterone 926a, 1824c
Tetanus tab 948, 954b
  immunization 954c, 1849c
Tetany 945c
Tethys 517c
Teton 517c
Teton Range 2020b
Tetrachord 157b, 179a
Tetracocci 1843b
Tetrahedron 1606c
Tetrameter 1418b
Tetrazzini, Luisa 351a
Tetrode 1889a
Teufelsdröckh, Herr (lit char.) tab 1463b
Teutonic languages see Germanic languages
Tewfik, Khedive (Egypt) 1005a
Texarkana, Arkansas 1976a, 1995c
Texas 1995, 2219a
  agriculture 1995c
  annexation 2039b
  bear grass 1651c
  capital punishment 860b
  census (1960) 1973
  cession 903b
  cinnamon 1658b
  climate 1995c
  colleges of 701–703
  commercial law tab 826
  Compromise of 1850 2041a
  congressional apportionment tab 853
  congressmen at large 855a
  coquina 23a
  cotton 730c
  county 871c
  economy 1995c
  electoral votes 876c
  gecko 35b
  geography 1995b–1995c
  government 1995c
  guayule 1670c
  holidays 841–842
  jaguar 19c
  lupine 1677a
  natural gas 1210a
  osage orange 1683b
  palms 1683c–1684a
  pit viper 51c–52a
  people of 1995c
  public school enrollment tab 646
  public school expenditures tab 644
  restored to Union 2053b
  secession 2043c
  student enrollment tab 645
  sunflowers 1695b
Texas, Republic of annexed 1964c
Texas, The University of 703
Texas, University of, at El Paso 703
Texas A. & M. University 703
Texas Christian University 703
Texas City, Texas 1995c, 2007b–2007c
Texas Lutheran College 703
Texas Southern University 703
Texas Technological College 703
Texas Wesleyan College 703
Texas Woman's University 703
Texcoco, Lake 2218b
Textbooks 616a
Textiles beginnings of industry 523c, 1018a
  cotton 730c
  dying 1247b
  felt 1208a
  fiber crops 733c
  fibers, synthetic 1208b
  wool 748a
Texture 517c
Thabit, Zaydibn 1408b
Thackeray, William Makepeace il 208, 1358a, 1367a, tab 1475
  biography 351a
  Henry Esmond 1405c
  Pendennis 1412b

pseudonym tab 1463b
  Vanity Fair 1420a
  Virginians, The 1420c
Thaddaeus 1460b
Thailand 2107a, 2109b, 2206b–2206c, 2273–2274
  agriculture 2273c
  civilization 981b
  climate 2273b
  communism 2274c
  economy 2273c–2274a
  flag il 2184
  geography 2273a–2273b
  government 2274a
  history 2274a–2274c
  industry 2273c–2274a
  map 2274, Atlas-30
  music 155a
  people of 2273b
  religion 2273a–2273b, 2274a
  rubber production 1221b
  SEATO 1021a
  trade 2274a
  World War I 1025a
  World War II 2274c
Thales 974c, 1611a, 1612c, 1751a
  biography 351a
  geometry 1501c, 1557a
Thalia 1440c
Thallium tab 1837
  atomic weight tab 1805
Thallophytes 1639b–1640a
Thames River 1977c, 2282a, 2341c
Thanatopsis (poem) 1374b, 1418c
Thanatos 1957b
Thanet, Octave see French, Alice
Thanglha Mountains 2341c
Thanglha Ri Mountain 2123c
Thanjavor, India 2374a
Thanksgiving Day 842c
  first 2024b
Thant, U 992b, 2078b
  biography 351b
Thar Desert 2342a
Tharaud brothers 1382c
Thasos (island) il 2167
Thatcher (wheat) 747c
Thaulow, F. tab 108
Thayer, Abbott H. tab 108
Theater etiquette 1113a
  Greek architecture 75a
Theater of the Absurd (lit.) 1376b
Theatre of Dionysus 1352b
Theiu-Tri, Emperor 2300c
Theme (mus.) 179a
Themis 1448a
Themistocles 351b
Theocracy 813c
Theocritus 1345b, 1354a, tab 1464
  biography 351b
  Idyls 1406b
Theodolite 517c
Theodora (508?–548) (emp.) 351b
Theodore I, Czar 2258c
Theodoric (the Great) 351b, 2195a
Theodorus 1614a
Theodosius I (Rom. emp.) 351b, 999c
Theodosius II (Rom. emp.) Seven Sleepers of Ephesus (myth) 1447a
Theognis 1351b
Theogony (rel. bk.) 1351a
Theological colleges 628c
Theology medieval 984c
Theophrastus 451c, 749b, 1638a
Theorems 1559a, 1607b
Theoretical geometry 1557a
Theotocopuli see El Greco
There Was a Crooked Man (nursery rhyme) 410c
There Was a Little Girl (nursery rhyme) 409b
Theremin, Leo 179a
Theremin (mus.) 179a
Theresa, St. 351b, 1392a
Thermal balance (global) 763b–763c
Thermal conductivity 1900b
Thermal equator 517c
Thermal gradient see Geothermal gradient
Thermal radiation 1906b
Thermal springs see Hot springs
Thermal stratification 518a
Thermionic emission 1886c
Thermit 1194b
Thermit welding 1287c
Thermoclines 1866c
Thermocouples 1146b, 1883b, 1898c
Thermodynamics 1870a, 1920a
  entropy 1918a

first law 1897c
  second law 1861c, 1900a
Thermoelectric devices 1891a
Thermoelectricity 1146b, 1883b
  discovered 1761a
Thermographs 469c, 518a
Thermography (print.) 150b
Thermometers 469b, 1898b, 1919c
  invention 468a
Thermopile 1883b
Thermoplastics 1219c
Thermopylae, Battle of 1021c
Thermoset plastics 1219c, 1220a
Theseus 1448a
Thesis (mus.) 179a
Thessaloníki, Greece 2374c
Thessaly, Greece il 2166
Thetis 1448b
  nereids 1440c
Thiamine see Vitamin B1
Thiard, Pontus de 1378b
Thibault, Jacques see France, Anatole
Thicket 518a
Thiel College 697
Thierry, Augustin 1381a, tab 1473
Thiers, Adolphe 2153c
Thiers, Louis A. 351c, tab 1474
Thiès, Senegal 2247c
Thiess, Frank tab 1480
Thieu, Nguyen Van 2301b
Thimbu, Bhutan 2099a
Thinker, The (sculp.) 123a
Thioalcohols 1832a
Thionville, France 2149a
Third Crusade 2285b
Third parties (gov.) 910c
Thirkell, Angela tab 1480
Thirty days hath September (nursery rhyme) 411a
Thirty Years' War tab 1073, 2151c, 2160b, 2288c
  causes of 999a
38th parallel 2203b, 2205a
Thisbe 1445b
This little pig (nursery rhyme) 408a
Thistle 1696c
Thomas (apostle) 1460b
Thomas, Ambroise tab 171c
Thomas, Arthur Goring 169b, tab 172a
Thomas, Dylan 351c, 1371c
Thomas, George Henry 2050b
  nickname tab 1463c
Thomas à Kempis 352a, tab 1466
  Imitation of Christ 1347b
Thomas, Lowell 351c
Thomas, Norman 351c, 908b
  presidential candidacy tab 801
Thomas, Philip tab 796
Thomas, Rodrigues 2320b
Thomas, Theodore 170a, tab 172c,
  biography 352a
Thomas Aquinas, Saint see Aquinas, Thomas
Thomas à Becket see Becket, Thomas à
Thomas More College 687
Thomashevsky, Boris 352a
Thomasius, Christian tab 1469
Thompson, Benjamin see Rumford, Count
Thompson, David 1390b
Thompson, Francis 352a, 1369b, tab 1479
Thompson, H. A. vice-presidential candidacy tab 801
Thompson, Homer Agora 970c
Thompson, Jacob 797
Thompson, Randall tab 172c
Thompson, Richard tab 796
Thompson, Smith Cabinet tab 795
  Supreme Court tab 802a
Thompson, Virgil 170b, tab 172c
Thompson, Wyville 462a
Thompson type caster 147b
Thomsen, Christian J. 1124b
Thomson, Elihu 352a
Thomson, James (1700–1748) 1363b, tab 1469
Thomson, James (1834–1882) 352a
Thomson, Sir Joseph John 352a, 1800a
  electrons 1886c
Thomson, Virgil 352b
Thor (myth) 1448b
Thor (rocket) 1769a

Thoreau, Henry David 352b, 775b, 1373b, *tab* 1475
  nickname *tab* 1463a
  nonresistance 894b
  Walden 1420c
Thorgilsson, Ari *tab* 1465
Thorium 1838
  atomic weight *tab* 1805
Thorn apple *see* Jimson weed
Thorndike, Ashley 352b
Thorndike, Edward Lee 352b
Thorndike, Lynn 352b
Thorn forest 518a
Thornton, Matthew *tab* 803
Thornycroft, Sir Hamo *tab* 125
Thoroughbreds 739b
Thorpe, Jim 352b
Thorp, John 1281c
Thorshavn, Faeroe Islands 2311c, 2374c
Thorvaldsen, (Albert) **Bertel** 122c, *tab* 125
  biography 352b
Thoth 1448b
Thothmes I, King (Egypt) 1003b
Thothmes II, King (Egypt) 1003c
Thothmes III (Thutmose), King (Egypt) 352b, 1003b, 1003c
Thousand Islands 2020b
Thousand and One Nights *see* Arabian Nights
Thracian (lang.) 1334a
Thraco-Phrygian language 1334a
Three Bears (story) 427c
Three Fates (sculp., Phidias) 116c
Three Little Kittens (nursery rhyme) 410c
Three Little Pigs (story) 426a–427b
Three Musketeers, The (bk.) 1418c
  d' Artagnan 1400c
Three Wise Men of Gotham (nursery rhyme) 411a
Three-color printing 1907c
Thresher (machine) 720c
Thrombin 922c
Thrombophlebitis 945c
Thromboplastin 922c
Thrombosis 945c
Through the Looking Glass (bk.) 1367c, 1394c
  Jabberwock 1407a
Throw 518a
Thrush 63a
  hermit 1996b
Thucydides 352c, 963a, 974c, *tab* 1464
  literary style 1353b
Thuille, Ludwig *tab* 172a
Thuku, Harry 2203a
Thulium 1838
  atomic weight *tab* 1805
Thunder 475b, 1895c
Thurber, Charles 1188a
Thurber, James Grover 352c
Thuringians 2159a
Thurman, A. G. *tab* 801
Thursday Thor 1448b
Thus Spake Zarathustra (bk.) 1348a, 1385a, *tab* 1478
Thutmose *see* Thothmes
Thyme 1696c
Thymine 1854b
Thymus 926a
Thyroid gland 925c
  cretinism 941b, 1953a
  hyperthyroidism 942b
  myxedema 942c
Thyroid hormone 1825b
Thyrotrophic hormone (TSH) 925c
Thyrsis (poem) 1402a
Tiamet 1430b
Tibaldi, Pellegrino 352c
Tibbett, Lawrence 352c
Tibbles, Thomas H. *tab* 801
Tiber River 2194a, 2342a
Tiberias, Lake *see* Galilee, Sea of
Tiberias, Sea of *see* Galilee, Sea of
Tiberius (Rom. emp.) 352c
Tibesti Mountains 2342a
Tibet 979a, 1021c–1022b, 2099a, 2107a, 2123a, 2123c, 2128a, 2186a
  climate 2124c
  communism 1022b
  lotus 1677a
  Nepalese invasions of 2224a
  1954 revolt 1022b
  religion 1022a–1022b
  rhubarb 1690a
  yaks 68b

Tibetans adaptation 1927b
  shelter 1930a
Tibullus, Albius 1357b
Tic douloureux *see* Trigeminal neuralgia
Tick 63b
Tick fever 727c
Ticknor, George *tab* 1473
Ticonderoga, New York
  American Revolution 2027a, 2028a, *tab* 2029
Tidal bore 464b, *see also* Bore
Tidal current 518a
Tidal day *see* Lunar day
Tidal flat 518a
Tidal marsh 518a
Tidal range 518a
Tidal wave 518b
Tidal waves (tsunami) 464b
Tide 518b
Tides 464a, 1797b
  neap 508b
  spring 515c
Tie (mus.) 179a
Tieck, Johann Ludwig 353a, 1384c, *tab* 1472
Tien Shan (mountains) 2123c, 2255a
Tientsin, China 2374c
Tientsin treaties 2129a
Tiepolo, Giovanni Battista *tab* 107
  biography 353a
  Jugurtha Before the Consul *tab* 109
  Rinaldo and Armida *tab* 110
Tierra caliente 518b
Tierra del Fuego hummingbird 39c
  Indians 1927c
Tierra Del Fuego Islands 2342a
Tiffany, Louis Comfort 134a
  biography 353a
Tiflis, U.S.S.R. 2374b
Tift College 662
Tiger 20a
Tight fold 518b
Tigris (river) 1460b, 2189c, 2342a
Tilak, Bal Gangadhar 2185b
Tilde (punct.) 1314c
Tilden, Samuel 353a
  presidential candidate *tab* 801, 2055a
Tilden, William T., Jr. 353a
Tilghman, Benjamin 1272a
Till (geol.) 449b, 518b
Till Eulenspiegel (Ger. lit.) *tab* 1466
Till plains (geol.) 449b
Tiller 1728b
Tillich, Paul 353a
Tillite 450a, 518b
Tilly, Johan Tserclaes, Count von 353b
Timber 1264c
Timber bridges 1196b
Timberline 518b
Timbre (mus.) 179a
Timbuktu, Mali *see* Tombouctou
Time 758a–758b
  clocks and watches 1162a
  geologic 454c, *il* 456–457, 498c–499a, 759b
  measurement 1797b, 1873b
Time (mus.) 179a
Time to Rise (rhyme) 414c
Time zones 758b
Time-stratigraphic unit 518b
Timing motors 1143c
Timisoara, Romania 2244a, 2374c
Timms Hill 1999a
Timor 2241c
Timor Island 2342a
Timothy (Bib.) 1460b
Timothy (plant) 1696c
Timpani (mus.) 176a
Timrod, Henry 353b, *tab* 1476
  pseudonym 1461a
Timur *see* Tamerlane
Tin 1194a, 1224c, *tab* 1838
  Alaska 1975a
  alloys 1193a
  atomic weight *tab* 1805
  Bolivia 2100b, 2101a
  bronze 1198a
  cassiterite 453c
  Great Britain 2282c
  Indonesia 2187a
  Malaysia 2213b
  Portugal 2241b
  Swaziland 2267a
  Thailand 2273c
  U.S. 1967a

Tint laying (print.) 153c
Tintoretto, Il *tab* 107, *tab* 112
  biography 353b
  Origin of the Milky Way tab 111
Tiny Tim 1399a
Tipis 1930a
Tippecanoe *see* Harrison, William Henry
Tippett, Michael *tab* 172b
Tiraboschi, Girolamo *tab* 1470
Tiradentes conspiracy 2103c
Tirana, Albania *see* Tiranë
Tiranë, Albania 2086a, 2374c
Tiros (satellites) 478a, 1769c
Tirpitz, Alfred von 353b
Tirso de Molina 1392a
Tiruchirappalli, India 2375a
Tissue (plant) 1643c–1644a
  bast 1643c
  collenchyma 1643c
  complex 1643c
  embryonic 1643c
  epidermal 1643c
  fibrous 1643c
  permanent 1643c–1644a
  sclerenchyma 1643c
  sieve 1643c
  simple 1643c
  soft 1643c
  stone 1643c
  vascular 1644a
Tissue (human) 917a
Tista River 2249b
Tisza River 2173c, 2174a, 2342a
Titanium 1194a, 1225b, *tab* 1838
  alloys 1193a
  atomic weight *tab* 1805
Titanium dioxide 1225b
Titano, Mt. 2246a
Titans (myth) 1448b
  Atlas 1426a
Titchener, Edward B. 1948a
Tithonus 1448b
Titian *tab* 106, *tab* 110–113
  biography 353b
Titicaca, Lake 2100a, 2342a
Titmarsh, Michael Angelo *see* Thackery, William Makepeace
Titmouse 63b
Tito (Josip Broz) 353b, 1028c, 2304a, 2304c
  Cominform 866a
Titov, Gherman 951c, 1170c, *tab* 1770
Titration 1817c
Titus, Emperor (Rome) 353b
Titus, Arch of 118b
Titus Livius *see* Livy
Titusville, Pennsylvania
  natural gas 1210a
  petroleum 1214b
Tiu 1448c
TNT 1821a
To Have and to Hold (nov.) 1418c
Toad 63b
Tobacco 746a, 1696c–1697a
  Albania 2086b
  Andorra 2088c
  Bulgaria 2105b
  Colombia 2132c
  Connecticut 1978a
  Cuba 2136c
  Dominican Republic 2142c
  Georgia 1997c
  farms 381b
  Greece 2165a
  India 2178a
  Indonesia 2187a
  Iraq 2189c
  Kentucky 1983b
  Lebanon 2207b
  Malawi 2212c
  Maryland 1985a
  Massachusetts 1985b
  Nicaragua 2227c
  Niger 2228c
  North Carolina 1991b
  Pakistan 2232b
  Paraguay 2235b
  Peru 2236c
  Portugal 2241b
  Puerto Rico 2002c
  Rhodesia 2243a
  Singapore 2250b
  South Carolina 1994b
  Swaziland 2267a
  Syria 2271a
  Tennessee 1995b
  Thailand 2273c
  Turkey 2278a
  Uganda 2279c
  U.S. 1966b, 1968c, 2294a
  Venezuela 2297b
  Vietnam 2299b

Virginia 1997c
West Virginia 1998c
Yemen 2302a
Yugoslavia 2303b
Zambia 2305b
Tobago *see* Trinidad and Tobago
Tobin, Maurice J. *tab* 797
Tobit (apocryphal bk.) 1460b
Tobogganing 1736b
Toccata (mus.) 162a, 179a
Toch, Ernst *tab* 172a
Tocharian (lang.) 1333c, 1334c
Tocqueville, Alexis Charles Henri de 353b, 1381b, *tab* 1481
Todd, Thomas Supreme Court *tab* 802a
Togliatti, Palmiro 2196c
Togo 2274–2275
  agriculture 2275a
  climate 2275a
  economy 2275a
  flag *il* 2184
  geography 2274c–2275a
  government 2275a
  history 2275a–2275b
  independence 2275b
  map 2275, *Atlas*-37
  people of 2275a
  religion 2274c
Togo Atakora Mountains 2274c–2275a
Togo Mountains 2163c
Toilet of Venus (paint.) *tab* 113
Tojo, Heihachiro 353b, 2076b
Tokay (wine) 723c
Tokelau Islands 2324
Tokugawa Era 2200b–2200c
Tokyo, Japan 2198b, 2198c, 2199a, 2375a
  monorail 1165b
Tokyo Bay 2198c
Toledo, Ohio 1991, 1992a
  proportional representation 902b
Toledo, Spain
  cathedral 76c
Toledo, University of 692
Toleration Act (Eng.) 909b
Toleration Act (Md.) 2024c
To Let (nov.) 1404a
Toller, Ernst 1385c, *tab* 1480
Tolstoy, Aleksyey 1390a, *tab* 1475
Tolstoy, Alexandra *tab* 1481
Tolstoy, Count Leo *il* 208, 1389c, *tab* 1476
  Anna Karenina 1395a
  biography 353c
  nonresistance 894b
Toltec Indians 971b, 2021a, 2218b
To market, to market (nursery rhyme) 408c
Tomato 1697a
Tombalbaye, François 2121a
Tombigbee River 1974a
Tombo Island 2170a
Tombolo 518c
Tombouctou (Timbuktu), Mali 2215a
Tom Brown's School Days (bk.) 1418c
Tombs ancient Egypt 74a
Tom Jones (nov.) 1363c, 1418c
Tomlin, Bradley Walker *tab* 109
Tommy and Grizel (nov.) 1419a
Tompkins, Daniel D. *tab* 800
Tom Sawyer (nov.) 1406a, 1419c
Tom Thumb 1448b
Tom-tom (mus.) 179a
Tom, Tom, the Piper's Son (nursery rhyme) 408c, 409a
Tonality (mus.) 154b
Tone (mus.) 154a, 158b, 179a
Tone color (mus.) 155a
Tone River 2198c
Tone, Wolfe 2191c
Tonga 2324
Tongatapu Islands 2324a
Tonghak movement 2204c
Tongue glossitis 942a
  speech sounds 1294c
  taste cells 937c
Tonic sol-fa (mus.) 179a
Tonka bean tree 1697a
Tonle Sap (lake) 2108c, 2342a
Tonnenberg, Battle of 1025b
Tonty, Henry de 353c
Tools 767b
  abrasives 1192a
  agricultural 719a
  in cultures 767c

machine tools 1265c
prehistoric 1927c
primitive 1929c
woodworking tools 1288b
Toombs, Robert 353c
Tooth see Teeth
Tooth decay 920b
Tooth shell 63b
Topaz (gem) hardness 1192b
Topeka, Kansas 1982b, 1982c, 2015b
Topelius, Zachris 1408a
Topers, The (paint.) tab 111
Topes (arch.) 78a
Topography 518b–518c
Topology (math.) 1506c, 1599a, 1607b
Tor 518c
Torah 612c, 1629b
Tordesillas, Treaty of 2103b, 2103c
Toreva-block slide 518c
Torfaeus, Thormod tab 1468
Torino, Italy 2375c
Tornadoes 475b, 518c
forecasting 478c
Toronto, Canada 2375a
Toronto Globe 2116a
Torque 1878c
Torquemada, Tomás de 353c
Torrent 518c
Torres, Luis Vaez de 2092c
Torres Naharro, Bartolomé de 1391c
Torres Strait 2342a
Torricelli, Evangelista 353c, 468a, 1125a
Torrid zone 518c
Torsion bars 1281c
Tort (law) 824a, 910c
Torticollis 945c
Tortoise 63b–64a
Tortoiseshell furniture design 1097b
Tory, Geoffroy 144a
Toscanini, Arturo tab 172a
biography 353c
Tostig, Earl (Northumbria) 2284c
Totalitarian state 910c
censorship 862a
Totemism 1622a
Toucan il 28, 64a
Toucey, Isaac tab 795, tab 796
Touch (game) kindergarten 424
Touch (mus.) 179a
Touch (sense) 937c
Tougaloo College 678
Toulouse, France 2148b, 2149b, 2375a
Toulouse-Lautrec, Henri de il 90, tab 108
biography 354a
Tourcoing, France 2149a
Touré, Sékou 2170b
Tourism 2088c
American Samoa 2000a
Antigua 2307a
Arizona 1975c
Bahamas 2307b
Bermuda 2307c
British Virgin Islands 2309a
Bulgaria 2105a
Canada 2112c
Cayman Islands 2310a
Channel Islands 2310b
Colombia 2132c
Cyprus 2138a
Denmark 2141c
Florida 1979b
Gibraltar 2314a
Hawaii 1980b
Idaho 1980c
Ireland 2191a
Isle of Man 2316b
Italy 2194b
Jamaica 2197a
Lebanon 2207c
Liechtenstein 2210c
Massachusetts 1985b
Monaco 2220a
Netherlands Antilles 2318a
Nevada 1988c
New Hampshire 1989b
Norfolk Island 2319b
Puerto Rico 2002b
St. Kitts-Nevis-Anguilla 2321b
San Marino 2246a
Spain 2263c
Trinidad and Tobago 2275c
U.A.R. 2280c
Vermont 1996c
Virgin Islands 2004b
Tourmaline light 1905c
Tourniquet 1711c
Tours, France 2375a–2375b
Tours, Battle of 983a, 1002c

Toussaint L'Ouverture, Pierre Dominique 354a, 2172a
Tower of Babel 997a
Tower of London (nov.) 1404c
Tower mills 1150b
Town meetings Colonial America 2026b
Town Mouse and the Country Mouse, The (story) 443a
Townes, Charles H. 1909c, 1910b
Townsend, Francis Everett 2074b
Townshend, Charles 719c
Townshend Acts 786b, 2027c
Township 793c
Towson State College 673
Toxemias 941b
Toxic goiter 942a
Toxic soils 751b
Toxin immunity 1849b
Toyama, Japan 2375b
Toynbee, Arnold 354a, 963c, 1348c
Toys 398c, 406–407
Trace elements soil 750c
Trachea 922a
Trachoma 928c, tab 948
Track and field events 1736c
Tracking (sport) 1739c
Traction 918a
Tractors 721a, 1170b
Tracy, Benjamin F. tab 796
Trade see Barter
see Commerce
Trade, Board of (Eng.) 857b
Trade associations 605b
Trade discount 605b
Trade Expansion Act 2080c
Trade unions 596a
Trade winds 474a, 518c, 2204b
Trademarks 605b
Traditional education 622b
Traffic management
industrial 377c
television 378b
Tragedy 1419a
Greek literature 1352b–1353a
Trajan, Emperor (Rome) 354a, 2244b, 2264b
Trajan, Arch of 118b
Trajan's Column 114a
sculpture 118b
Trams 1165a
Trance shamans 1937b
Tranquilizers 1273c
Transatlantic cable
first telephone 1184c
Trans-Bay Bridge San Francisco-Oakland Bay Bridge tab 1197
Trans-Canada Highway 2112c
Transcendentalism 1373b
Transducer 1146c
Transfiguration (paint., Raphael) tab 112
Transformers 1147a, 1885c
Transistors 1283a, 1890b, 1920a
discovery 1283a
junction 1892b
Transit (astron.) 1797b
Transit (satellite) 1769c
Transit (telescope) 1791c
Transit expressway 1165c
Transition (music) 179a
Transition temperature 1828c
Transjordan 2202a
see also Jordan
Transmission (light) 1904a
radio 1889a
Transmittance (parapsych.) 1952a
Transmitter (radio) 1176b
Transpiration 1646b, 1862c
Transportation 518c, 1151–1188
electric transmit 1165c
evolution of 1152c
in cultures 767c
primitive 1934b
travel etiquette 1116a
Transportation Act (1920) 527a
Transposition (mus.) 179a
Trans-Siberian railway 1021a
Transuranic elements 1911c
Transvaal anthropology 1924b
Transverse dune 518c
Transverse Valley 519a
Transylvania 2174c, 2244a, 2245a
Transylvania College 670
Transylvanian Alps 2243a
Trap-door spider 64a
Trapezoid 1568a
Trappist cheese tab 731b
Traps (hunting) 1933a

Traumatic experiences 1957a
Travel see Transportation
Travertine 519a
Traviata, La (opera) 167b
Travois 1934b
Treading water 1734a
Treadwell, Daniel 148a
Treason 911a
Treasure Island (bk.) 1368b, 1419b
Treasury, Department of the 911a, 2040c
bureaus 858c
divisions 875b
establishment tab 797
secretaries tab 795–796
subtreasury system 2038b
Treble 179a
Treble clef 179b
Tree, Sir Herbert Beerbohm 354a
Tree of heaven 1697a
Tree and the Reed, The (fable) 444a
Trees see under names of individual trees, such as Maple; Wattle
Treitschke, Heinrich von 354b, tab 1477
Trejos Fernández, José Joaquin 2136c
Trellis drainage pattern 519a
Trembling of a Leaf, The (bk.) 1371a
Tremolo 179b
Tremor 179a
Trench 519a
Trent (ship) 2045b
Trent, William P. 354b
Trent, Council of 1632b
Trent River 2282a
Trenton, New Jersey 1989b, 1989c, 2015b
pottery 129c, 130a
Trenton, Battle of 2029
Trenton State College 683
Trésaguet, Pierre 1153a, 1179c
Tres Marias Dam tab 1206
Trespass (law) 911a
Trevelyan, George Macaulay 354b
Trevithick, Richard 1169a, 1178a
Triad (mus.) 179b
Trial-and-error learning 1950a
Triangle (math.) 1606b
congruence 1564b
definition 1607c
Triangle (music) 179b
Trianon, Treaty of 2175a
Triassic period tab 457, 458a, 519a
Tribhuvana, King 2224b
Triborough Bridge (N.Y.) 1197
Tributary 519a
Tribute Money (paint.) tab 110
Tricalcium phosphate 733b
Tricarboxylic acid cycle 1825c
Trichinopoly, India 2375a
Trichinosis tab 948, 958a
Trichomonads 1848c
Trichonympha 1848c
Trieste, Italy 2196b, 2375b
UN administration 1022c
Triffin, Robert 536c
Trigeminal neuralgia 945c
Trigonometric functions tab 1589, 1607c
Trigonometric parallax 1788b
Trigonometry 1503a, 1504c, 1581–1589
sample applications 1588b
Trigonos 157c
Trilby (bk.) 1419b, tab 1477
Trill (mus.) 178a
Trillium 1697
Trimble, Robert 802a
Trimeter 1419b
Trinidad and Tobago 2097c, 2275–2276
agriculture 2275c
banana species 1651a
climate 2275b
Commonwealth status 1000c
economy 2275c
flag il 2184
geography 2275b
government 2275c–2276a
history 2276a–2276b
independence 2276b
Indians 2276a
industry 2276b
map 2275, Atlas-53
people of 2275b–2275c
religion 2275b
slavery 2276a

trade 2276b
Trinidad Mountains 2136c
Trinitario 726b
Trinitrotoluene see TNT
Trinity Bridge 1196c
Trinity Church (Boston) 78c
Trinity College (Oxford, England) 144c
Trinity College (Texas) 704
Trinity College (Vermont) 660
Trinity College (Washington) 661
Trinity Dam 1205c, tab 1206
Trinity River 2006c
Trinity University (Connecticut) 703
Trinomials (math.) 1535b
quadratic 1537b
Trio (mus.) 179b
Triodes 1152a, 1284a, 1889a
Triolet 1419b
Triple Alliance (1668) 1022c
Triple Alliance (1717) 1022c
Triple Alliance (1882) 988b, 1022c, 2196b
Triple Entente 988b, 2161c
Triple point (phys.) 1872c
Triplet (mus.) 179b
Triplet (verse) 1419b
Tripoli, Lebanon 2207b, 2375b
Tripoli, Libya 2209b, 2210a, 2375b
Tripoli wars 997c
Tripolitania 2209b, 2210a
Triptych 119a
Tristram (Tristan) 1435c
Tristram Shandy (bk.) 1363c
Tristan de Cunha Island 2321a
Tristan and Isolde (poem) tab 1465
Tristan und Isolde (opera) 167a, 1436a
Trisuli River 2223c
Tritium 1806a
atomic weight 1806a
Triton 1448c
Trivandrum, India 2375c
Trobriand Archipelago 2319c
Trochee 1419b
Trogon 64a–64b
Troilus and Cressida (play, Shakespeare) 1419b
Troilus and Criseyde (poem, Chaucer) 1359c, 1419b
Trojan Horse 1448c
Trojan War tab 1071, 1448c, 1449b
Troll (myth) 1448c
Trolley buses 1165a
Trollope, Anthony 1367c, tab 1475
biography 354c
Trombone 173c, 179b
Trondheim, Norway 2230b
Troodos Mountains 2342a
Tropes 1314b
Tropic of cancer 519a
Tropic of capricorn 519a
Tropic levels (ecology) 1861c
Tropical cyclone 519a
Tropical month 1795c
Tropical solis 762c
Tropical year 1797b
Tropical zone 519a
forests 1864b
Tropisms plants 1647a–1647b
Tropopause 468b, 763a
Troposphere 468a, 763a
See also Atmosphere
Trotsky, Leon (Lev) 354c, 1390b, 2261b, 2262a
Bolshevik 858a
Troubadours 159c, tab, 171b, 1398b, 1419b
Trough 519a
Trout 64b, il 1717
Trouvère 1419b
Trovatore, Il (opera) 167b
Troy (Ilium) (anc. city) 1435c
excavations 970c
literature 1343b
Trojan War 1448c
Troy, New York 1990c, 2005a
Troy State College 654
Troy system (meas.) tab 1500
Troyon, Constant tab 108
Trucial Coast see Trucial Oman
Trucial Oman 2276
area 2276b
climate 2276b
economy 2276b–2276c

flag *il* 2184
geography 2276b
government 2276c
history 2276c
map 2276, *Atlas-25*
people of 2276b
religion 2276b
Trucial States *see* Trucial Oman
Truck farms 381b
Truckee River 2013c
Trucks 1170b
Trudgen (swimming) 1734a
True Relation of Virginia, A (bk.)
tab 1467
Trujillo, Peru 2236b
Trujillo Molina, Rafael Leonidas
354c, 2143b
Truman, Harry S. 354c, *tab* 798–
799, 849b
administration 2077a–2078a
cabinet *tab* 796–797
dismisses MacArthur 1012a
election and inauguration *tab*
801
Korean War 1010c–1012c
Point Four 899b
Truman Doctrine 2077c, 2279a
Greece 2167b
Trumbull, John *tab* 107, 354b, 1372b
Trumbull, Jonathan (1710–1785)
354b
Trumbull, Jonathan (1740–1809)
House of Representatives *tab*
802b
Trumbull, Lyman 354c
Trump, J. Lloyd 618c
Trumpet 157c, 173c, 179b, 1896b
Trumpet creeper 1697a–1697b
Truncated cone 1602c
Truss (arch.) 73a, 1624c
Truss bridges 1196c
Trusteeship 891b, 911a
Trusteeship Council (U.N.) 911a,
991c
Trusts 605c
busting 2062a
Clayton Act 2063c
Trust Territory of the Pacific Is-
lands 2003–2004
climate 2003c
economy 2003c–2004a
geography 2003c
government 2004a
history 2004a
people of 2003c
Truth (logic) 1598b
Truth in Securities Act 2073c
Truth table 1598b
Tryggvesson, King Olaf (Norway)
2231a
Tryon, Dwight William *tab* 108
Trypanosomes 1848c
Tsangpo River 2327c
Tschaikovsky *see* Tchaikovsky
TSH *see* Thyrotrophic hormone
Tshombe, Moise 2135b
Tsinan, China 2375c
Tsinghai, Lake 2335b
Tsingtao, China 2375c
Tsingling Mountains 2342a–2342b
Tsiranana, Philibert 2212b
Tsitsihar, China 2375c
Tsunami 519a
see also Tidal waves
Tswana-speaking people 2101c
Tuaillon, Louis 122c, *tab* 125
Tuamotu Archipelago 2313a
Tuatha de Danann 1448c
Tub, The (paint., Degas) *il* 92
Tuba 157c, 173c, 179b, 1896b
Tubal-Cain (Bib.) 969b

Tube-nosed bird 64b
Tuberculosis *tab* 948
cattle 727c
immunization 1849c
Tuberose 1697b
Tubers (plant) 1644c
Tubman, William V. S. 2209b
Tucson, Arizona 1975c, 2015b–
2015c
Tucumán, Argentina 2089c
Tudor family 2287b–2288b
Tudor style (furniture) 1097a
Tu-Duc, Emperor 2300c
Tufa *see* Travertine
Tufting 1283c
Tufts University 675
Tugela Waterfalls 2342b
Tughluq dynasty 2180b
Tulane University 671
Tularemia *tab* 948, 958a
Tulip 1697b
Tulip poplar 1983a, 1994c
Tulip tree 1697b–1697c, 1981c
Tull, Jethro 719c
Tulliver, Maggie 1410c
Tulliver, Tom 1410c
Tully, Christopher 1281c
Tulsa, Oklahoma 1992b, 2015c–
2015c
Tulsa University 693
Tumbleweed 1697c
Tumen River 2203b–2203c, 2342b
Tumors 945c
fibroma 941c
lipoma 942c
melanoma 942c
pheochromocytoma 945a
Tuna 64b
Tundra 519a, 743a, 1863c, 2255a
soil 762b
Tung oil 732c
tree 1697c
T'ung-meng hui 2129c
Tungsten (wolfram) 1193a, 1838
atomic weight *tab* 1805
California 1977a
Korea, North 2203c
Korea, South 2203c
Nicaragua 2227c
Spain 2263c
Sweden 2268a
Thailand 2273c
Tungting, Lake 2342b
Tunicate 64b–64c
Tuning 179b
Tuning fork 179b, 1893c
Tunis, Tunisia 2276c, 2277a, 2375c
Tunisia 995b, 997a, 2196b, 2276–
2277
agriculture 2277a
climate 2277a
economy 2277a
flag *il* 2184
geography 2276c–2277a
government 2277a
history 2277b–2277c
independence 2277b–2277c
map 2277, *Atlas-34*
people of 2277a
religion 2276c
Tunkhannock Bridge 1197a
Tunku Abdul Rahman 2214b
Tunnard, John *tab* 109
Tunnels 1225c, 1226
construction 1225c
railroads 1179a
Tunnel diodes 1890c
Tupelo 1697c
Tupac Amaru 2237a
Tupi Indians 62a
Tupper, Sir Charles Hibbert 354c

Tura, Cosimo *tab* 106
Turbidity currents 463b, 519b
Turbines 1148b, 1901c
Turbo generators 1139b
Turbo-jets 1148c
Turbulent flow 519b
Turco - Mongol - Tungus languages
classification 1333a
Turenne, Vicomte de 354c
Turgenev, Ivan S. 354c, 1389c, *tab*
1475
Fathers and Sons 1403c
nihilism 894a
Turgot, Anne Robert Jacques 355a
Turin, Italy 2194a, 2194c, 2375c
Turkestan *see* Turkistan
Turkey 1000b, 1010b, 1012c, 1015a,
1016c, 2277–2279
agriculture 2278a
archeology 970b
climate 2278a
Crimean War 997c
Cyprus controversy 2138b
dictator 874a
economy 2278a–2278b
flag *il* 2184
geography 2277c–2278a
government 2278b
Greece and 2165c–2167a
hazel trees 1671a
hibiscus 1671c
history 2278b–2279b
map 2278, *Atlas-26*
Palestine and 2193b
people of 2278a
refugee resettlement (World
War I) 1013b
religion 2277c
Russo-Turkish War *tab* 1075
war with Russia 2106a, 2166a–
2166b
World War I 1017b, 1024c–1025a,
2066c, 2161c, 2279a
World War II 2279a
Young Turk Movement 2279a
Turkeys 64c, 746b
Minnesota 1986b
Turkic-Mongol Culture Region 769b
Turkish Islands 2167a
Turkish rugs 1110c
Turkistan (Turkestan) rugs 1110c
Turkmen anthropology 1927b
Turks culture 982b
Turks Islands
Turku, Finland 2146c
Turn (mus.) 179b
Turner, Frederick Jackson 355a
Turner, Joseph M. W. 86a, *tab* 108
biography 355a
Cologne, Evening tab 111
Turnip *see* Mustard
Turnover 605c
Turtle (animal) 63
see also Tortoise
Turtle (print.) 153c
Turtle (submarine) 1182c
Tuscaloosa, Alabama 1974b
Tusculum College 701
Tuskegee Institute 654
Tussaud, Madame 355a
Tutankhamen 83b, 355a, 1622c
tomb 74a, 969a
Tutti (mus.) 179b
Tutuila Island 2000
U.S. acquisition 2060c
Tuz, Lake 2342b
TVA *see* Tennessee Valley Au-
thority
TV Guide (magazine) circulation
1167b
Twachtman, John Henry 104c, *tab*
108
Twain, Mark (Samuel Clemens)
1375a, *tab* 1463c, *tab* 1477

biography 224c
printing machine 147a
—Novels
Huckleberry Finn 1405c
Innocents Abroad 1406c
Life on the Mississippi 1409a
Prince and the Pauper 1414a
Tom Sawyer 1419a
Tweed, William Marcy (Boss
Tweed) 355b, 2054c
Tweed Ring 2054c
Tweed River 2282a
Twelfth Night (play) 1419b
Viola 1420b
Twelve Caesars (biography) 1397b
Twelve Tables, Law of the (law
code) 814a
Twelve Tribes of Israel 1455b
Twice-Told Tales (bk.) 1419c
Twilight 519b
Twin Falls 2020c
Twins 1857a
Two Little Circus Girls (paint.) *tab*
110
Two Sicilies, Kingdom of the 2195b
Two Years before the Mast (bk.)
1373b, 1419c, *tab* 1475
Tydings-McDuffie Act 2238b
Tyler, John 355b, *tab* 798–799, 849b,
873a
administration 2039a
events paralleling administra-
tion *tab* 1063
Cabinet *tab* 795
election and inauguration *tab*
800
Tyler, Moses Coit *tab* 1477
Tyler, Wat 355b, 1359c
Tyler, Texas 1995c
Tympanums 120a
Tyndale, William 355b, 1360b, *tab*
1466
Tyndall John 355b, 1366c, *tab* 1476,
1839c
Tyner, James N. *tab* 796
Type (print.) 150c, 1174b
family 153a
height 153c
movable 142b
sizes 146c
Type casting 146c
Type setting 146c
Typewriters 1187c
composition 1174b
Typhoid fever *tab* 948, 956c
bacteria 1845a
immunization 1849c
Typhon 1447a, 1448c
Typhoon (short stories) 1419c
Typhoons 475b, 519b
Guam 2001a
Japan 2200b
Philippines 2237c
Typhus *tab* 948
immunization 1849c
Typists (career) 386c
Typograph (mach.) 147a
Typography 146–147
Typology 968c
Tyr 1448c
Tyranny 784c
Tyre, Phoenicia 1018a, 1018b
Tyrone Wars 2191b
Tyrrhenian Sea 2342b
Tyrtaeus 1351b
Tyutchev, Feodor 1389b
Tze Yang, China
anthropology 1924b
Tzitzi rugs 1110c
Tz'u-hsi, Dowager Empress
(China) 2129b

U

U Thant *see* Thant, U
U.A.R. *see* United Arab Republic
Ubangi River 2119a, 2133c, 2134a,
2134c, 2342b
Ubangis body mutilation 1930c

Ubangi-Shari 2119b, *see also* Cen-
tral African Republic
Uccello, Paolo *tab* 106
biography 355c
Udall, Nicholas 355c, 1360c
Udall, Stewart *tab* 797
Ufa, Bashkir 2375c
Uffizi Gallery (Florence) *tab* 110
Uganda 2279–2280
agriculture 2279c

ass 14b
climate 2279c
Commonwealth status 1000c
economy 2279c
flag *il* 2184
geography 2279b–2279c
government 2279c
history 2279c
map 2279, *Atlas-39*
people of 2279c
religion 2279b, 2280a

Uganda Agreement (1900) 2280a
Uganda People's Congress (UPC)
2280a
Ugly Duckling (fairy tale) 428b–
431a
UHF 1185c
Uhland, Johann Ludwig 1384c, *tab*
1473
Ujjain, India 2179c, 2375c
Ukelele 179b

Ukrainian language 175b, 1334b
Ulan Bator, Mongolia 2220b, 2220c, 2375c
Ulanova, Galina 355c
Ulan-Ude, U.S.S.R. 2375c
Ulate, Otilio 2136a
Ulbricht, Walter 2163b
Ulcerative colitis 941b
Ulcers 945c
Ulfilas 1336c, 1383a, tab 1464
Ullage rockets 1779c
Ultimate base level 519b
Ultramicroanalysis 1827a
Ultrasonic motor 1149a
Ultrasonics 1897a
Ultraviolet light 1903b
Ultra vires 911b
Ulysses (bk.) 1348c, 1371b
Ulysses (myth) see Odysseus
Umbilical cord (astronautics) 1779c
Umbra (astron.) 1794a, 1797a
Umbrella plant see Papyrus
Umbrian (lang.) 1335a
Umbrians tab 106
Umlauf, Charles tab 125
Umlaut 1314c
Umma Party (Sudan) 2266c
Umtali, Rhodesia 2376a
U. N. see United Nations
Unam sanctam (papal bull) 2150c
Unamuno, Miguel de 1392c, tab 1479
Uncle Remus (lit. char.) 1419c, tab 1463c
Uncle Sam (Samuel Wilson) 364c
Uncle Sam, personification of 1022c
Uncle Tom's Cabin (bk.) 1419c, 1374b, tab 1475, 2041b
Unconformity 519b
Unconscious
  Freud, S. 1957b
  Jung, C. G. 1958a
Underconvergence (vision) 1299c
Underground railroads 1022c–1023a
Understatement 1315c
Undertow 519b
Underwood, Oscar Wilder 355c
Underwood-Simmons Tariff Act 2063b
Underwriter 605c
Undset, Sigrid 355c, tab 1480
Undue influence (law) 820a
Undulant fever 958a
UNEF see United Nations Emergency Force
Unemployment 911b
  depression 2072a
Unemployment compensation 836c, 837a
UNESCO see United Nations Educational, Scientific, and Cultural Organization
Unfinished Symphony (Schubert) 165b
Ungaretti, Giuseppe 1388a
Ungava Bay 2342b
Unger, Karoline 164c
UNICEF see United Nations Children's Fund
Uniform Acts 816b
Uniform Sales Act 823b
Uniformitarianism 519b
Unimpaired terraces 519b
Union 596a
Union Act (1840) 2116a
Union Army 2045a
Union College 670, 681, 687
Union Pacific Railroad 888b, 2022b
  chartering 720c
  locomotive 1178b
Union Party 2050b
Union of South Africa see South Africa
Union of Soviet Socialist Republics 2096b, 2254–2263
  agriculture 2256c–2257a
  antelope 14a
  auk 14c
  Bulgaria and 2106a–2106b
  China 2131a
  chipmunk 21c
  climate 2255c
  coal 1202b
  Cold War 2262b–2262c
  communism 2257c
  Cuba and 2137a, 2138a
  Czechoslovakia and 2140a–2140b
  dances 181c
  economy 2256b–2257c
  education budget 611c

Finland and 2147b–2147c
Five-Year Plans 879c, 898a
flag il 2184
flax 1667b
geography 2254b–2255c
Germany, East, and 2163b
government 2257c
history tab 1057, 2261a–2263a
Hungary and 2175b–2175c
industry 2257a–2257c
Iron Curtain 886b, 2262c–2263a
Lend-Lease 889b
Manchurian treaty (1945) 1015b
map 2255, Atlas-20–21
mountain systems 2254c–2255a
music 169a, tab 172b
natural resources 2256b–2256c
nonaggression pact with Germany 2162c
nuclear power 2263a
occupation of Germany 2163a
people of 2255c–2256a
pigweed 1686b
pit-viper 51c–52a
Poland and 2240b, 2240c
religion 2254b
reparations 905c
Romania and 2245a–2245b
sheep 57b–57c
Soviets (workers' councils) 908c
space program 2263a
thistle 1696c
trade 2257c
Treaty of Brest-Litovsk, 999a–999b
U.S. and 2262b–2263a
vegetation zones 2255a–2255c
wool 748b
World War II 2154c, 2162c, 2163a, 2262b, 2292a
See also Russia (before 1917); Russian language; Russian literature
—Astronautics 2263a
communications satellites tab 1163
manned flights 1769b, tab 1770, 1770c
rockets 1764c, 1765b, 1768
—Government 881b, 2257c
All-Union Congress of Soviets 851a
centralization 862c
Cheka 863c
cominform 865c
communism 868a
constitution 857a, 869c, 870a
Council of Ministers 871b
Cuba 2081a
dictatorship 873c, 874a
economic control 876b
labor legislation 831a
nationalization 892c
secret service 907c
Supreme Soviet 872c
Union University 701
Union of Utrecht 2098c, 2225b
Unison (mus.) 179b
Unitarios 2090b
United Africa Company 2229c
United Arab Republic (UAR) 2280–2281, 2190b, 2208a
  agriculture 2280c
  climate 2280c
  economy 2280c–2281a
  flag il 2184
  geography 2280b–2280c
  government 2281a
  history 2281a–2281c
  Israel and 2190b, 2192a, 2192b, 2193b
  manufacturing 2280c
  map 2280, Atlas-34
  people of 2280c
  religion 2280c
  wars with Israel 2280b, 2280c, 2281c
  See also Egypt; Egypt (ancient); Syria
United Australia Party 2094a
United Fruit Company 2169a, 2169b, 2173b
United Gold Coast Convention (UGCC) 2164b
United Kingdom 2282–2292
  agriculture 2282c, 2290c
  climate 2282b
  deer 25b
  economy 2282c–2283b
  empire of 2283c
  flag il 2184
  geography 2282a–2282b
  government 2283b–2283c
  history 2283c–2292b
  industry 2291b, 2282c–2283a
  manufacturing 2282c
  map 2282, Atlas-10–11
  Norman conquest 2284c–2285a
  people of 2282b–2282c
  religion 2282a, 2282b–2282c, 2284a

slavery 2290a, 2291a
trade 2291b, 2283a–2283b
World War I 2291c
World War II 2292a
see also Great Britain
United Mine Workers pensions 897c
United National Independence Party (Zambia) 2305c
United National Party (UNP) 2120b–2120c
United Nations 880c, 990–993, 998b, 2077a, 2118b
  budget 990a
  in Cyprus 2138b
  disarmament 993c
  documents 993c
  growth 993b
  in Indian-Pakistani conflict 2177a, 2186a
  International Court of Justice 914b
  in Israel-Arab states conflicts 2193c
  Korean War 1010c–1012b
  military actions 993b
  official languages 990a
  origins and aims 990a
  principal organs 990c
  regulating principles 990b
  Relief and Rehabilitation Administration 1003a
  specialized agencies 992c
  trusteeships 911b
  U.S. representatives tab 797
  veto 912b
United Nations Charter 996a, 1013
United Nations Children's Fund (UNICEF) 992b
United Nations Educational, Scientific, and Cultural Organization (UNESCO) 993a
United Nations Emergency Force 993c
United Nations Food and Agriculture Organization see Food and Agriculture Organization
United Party of the Cuban Socialist Revolution (PURSC) 2137a
United Provinces of Central America 2136a, 2145b, 2169a, 2173a, 2228a
United States of America 2292–2294
  accidents 954a
  agricultural revolution 720c
  agriculture 1968b–1969a, 2293c–2294a
  air transport 1968a
  Alaska purchased from Russia 1964c
  alfalfa 1648b–1648c
  almonds 1648c
  Appalachian Zone 1961b–1962a
  arbor vitae 1649a
  arbutus 1649b
  artichokes 1649c
  badger 15a
  bald-cypress 1650b–1650c
  bass 15b
  bat 15b
  beaver 15c
  benefit of clergy 856b
  Bering Sea controversy 998c
  birch 1652c
  bittersweet 1652c–1653a
  bluebells 1653b
  bluefish 17b
  bluegrass 1653c
  bobolink 17c
  bobwhite 17c
  book sales 1160b
  brown thrasher 18a
  buckwheat 1654c
  bufflehead 18b
  bunting 18b
  Canada and 2115b, 2116a, 2116b, 2116c, 2117c, 2118b, 2118c, 2119a
  cardinal 19b
  carp 19b
  catbird 20a
  cattle 20b
  census 862b
  census (1960) 1970–1973
  Central Lowlands and Plains 1962a–1962b
  century plants 1657b–1657c
  chestnut trees 1657c
  chickadee 21a
  chimney swift 21b
  chinchilla 21b
  chipmunk 21c
  cicada 21c
  cigarettes produced 746b
  cinnamon 1658b
  cities of 2005–2015
  city planning 864b
  civil rights 866a
  Civil War 963b, 1002c–1003a, 1009a–1009b
  clam 22a

climate 1962c–1963b, 2293a–2293b
coal 1202b
cockroach 22b
college graduates 1127b
communication 1968a–1968b
conservation 775a
conterminous 1961a, 2292c
copper 1205a
crayfish 24a
Crédit Mobilier affair 1001b
creosote-bush 1659c
cricket 24b
Cuba and 2136b, 2136c, 2137a, 2137b–2138a
cuckoo 25a
cultural regions 1965a–1965b
currant 1660a–1660b
daisy 1660c
dams tab 1206
deer 25b
discovery of 1964a–1964b
divorce rate 1941c
dobsonfly 25b
in Dominican Republic 2143a–2143b
douglas fir 1665c
Dutchman's pipe vine 1665c
economic geography 1966c–1969c
economic regions 1967b–1967c
economy 2393c–2394b
education 610c, 615c, 625–637
eel 26c
eider 33a
elder trees 1666a
elm trees 1666a
energy consumption 1129c
ethnic groups 1966b
exploration of 1964a–1964b
explosives 1207c
falcon 33b
figs 1667a
finch 33b
fir trees 1667a–1667b
fishing 1969a, 2294a
flag il 2010, 2184
flamingo 33c
forests 1969a, 2294a
four-o'clocks 1667c
fox 34c
fuels 1967a
fumitory plants 1668a
gaillardia 1668b
gardenia 1668b
geographic problems 1969c
geography 2292c–2293b
goldeneye 36a
goldfinch 36a
government 2294b
grackle 36c
guava 1670c
guayule 1670c
hackberries 1670c
in Haiti 2172b
hare 38a
heron 38c
hibiscus 1671c
historical geography 1964–1965
holidays 841–842
holly 1672a
huckleberry 1672c
human geography 1965a–1966c
Iceland and 2176c
immigration 1965a
Indians 1963b, 1964a, 2293c
industry 1969a–1969b, 2294a
international trade 1969a–1969b
irrigation 740a
ivy 1673c
jujubes 1674a
junco 40b
junior colleges 628b, 711–716
kapok 1674b
Kentucky coffee tree 1674b
kite 41b
in Korea 2205a, 2205b
kudzu vines 1674b
kumquats 1674b
laburnum 1674c
land regions 1961a–1962c
larch 1674c–1675a
lavender 1675a
in Lebanon 2208a
life expectancy 954a
locoweed 1676c
lotus 1677a
Louisiana Territory purchased 1964b–1964c
lynx 44b
madroña 1677b
magnolia 1677b–1677c
manufacturing 1969a–1969b
map 2293, Atlas-60–61, 62–63
maple trees 1678a–1678b
marigolds 1678b–1678c
marsh marigolds 1678c
Mason and Dixon Line 1016a
melon 1679a
mesquite 1679a–1679b
metals 1967a–1967b
migrations 2021c
militia 891c
minerals 1966c–1967a, 1967b

minorities 891c–892a
mobility 1966a–1966b
mockingbird 46a
mongoose 46b
motor vehicles 1170b
mountain laurel 1680c
mountains 2019a
mulberry 1680b–1680c
mullet 47a
musk ox 47a–47b
myrtle wood 1681a
national parks 895b
natural features 2016–2020
Negroes 1966a
newspapers 1170c, tab 1171
Niagara Falls 2019b
in Nicaragua 2228a–2228b
night-blooming cereus 1681a
nighthawk 47c
oak 1682a–1682b
occupation of Germany 2163a
open door policy 2129c
oriole 48c
oswego tea 1683b
owl 49a–49b
oyster 49b–49c
palms 1683c–1684a
in Panama 2234c
paper mulberry 1684b
papyrus 1684b
parrot 49c
partridge 49c
passion-flowers 1684c
peccary 50a
Pelagic sealing 998c
pelican 50a–50b
people of 2293b–2293c
perch 50b
persimmon 1686a
petunias 1686a
pheasant 51a
in the Philippines 2238b
physical geography 1961–1963
pike 51b
Pilgrim settlement of 1018b–
  1019a
pine trees 1686c
pintail duck 51c
pit viper 51c–52a
plum trees 1687c
pokeweeds 1688a
poppy 1688b–1688c
population distribution 1965b–
  1966c
population growth 1964c–1965a
praying mantis 53a
ptarmigan 53b
quail 53c
rail bird 54a
rail transport 1968a
railroads 1176c
Reconstruction period 1019b
recreation 1969b
redstart 54b–54c
religion 1966b, 2292b, 2293c
respiratory diseases 955a
rhododendron 1690a
rice 1690a–1690b
rivers 2020a–2020b
road transport 1968a
roads 1180a
robin 54c
rubber consumption 1222b
sagebrush 1691b
salamanders 54c–55a
sandpipers 5b
sedge 1692b
sequoia trees 1692b–1692c
settlement of 1964b
shrews 57c–58a
size of 1961a
skunks 58b
slavery 1009b, 1022c–1023a
slugs 58c–59a
snipe 59a
soapberry 1693b–1693c
soil 751a, 1963c
sorghum 1693c
Spanish moss 1693c–1694a
sparrows 59a–59b
spruce trees 1694a–1694b
squash 1694b
squirrels 59c–60a
starlings 60a
stick insects 60a
stork 60b–60c
strawberries 1694c
sturgeon 60c
Sudan grass 1694c
Suez Canal crisis 2118b
sumac 1695a
sunflowers 1695b
swallow 61a
swallowtail butterflies 61b
swan 61b–61c
tanager birds 62a
tea consumption 746a
teal ducks 52c
tent caterpillars 62c–63a
termites 63a
territorial expansion 1964b–
  1964c
territories 2000–2004

territories of 2294b
thrushes 63a
titmouse 63b
tobacco 1696c–1697a
tortoises 63c–64a
trade 2294a–2294b
transportation 1967c–1968b
trap-door spiders 64a
Tripoli wars 997c
trogons 64a–64b
trout 64b
tulip tree 1697b–1697c
tung tree 1697c
turkey 64c
U.S.S.R. and 2262b–2263a
urban areas 1965c–1966a
vegetation 1963b–1963c
in Vietnam 230a, 2301a–2301b
Vikings in 1964a–1964b
vultures 65a–65b
walnut trees 1699a
war with Mexico 2219a
warblers 65c
waterlily 1699a
water supply 777a
water thrushes 66b
water transport 1967c–1968a
waxwings 66b–66c
weasels 66c
weather problems 1963b
weights and measures tab 1500
Western Cordilleran Region
  1962b–1962c
wheat 748a, 1699b–1699c
whippoorwills 67a–67b
Whisky Insurrection 1024a–
  1024b
whitefish 67b
wildcat 19c
wistaria 1700a
wolves 67b
woodcocks 67c–68a
woodpeckers 68a–68b
World War I 1025a–1025c, 2154b,
  2161c
yams 1700a–1700b
yellowlegs 68b–68c
yellowthroats 68c
yellowwoods 1700b–1700c
yucca 1700c
see also under the names of
  the individual states
—Arts see American architecture
see American art
see American literature
see American music
—Astronautics
communications satellites tab
  1163
satellites tab 1163
manned flights 1770, 1770a
rockets 1764a, 1768c, 1769a
space programs 1769a, 1777c
—Government and Law 785–811,
  815b, 816a, 881b
administrative agencies 791a
administrative divisions 875b
budget 858b
bureaus 858b
Cabinet 859
capital punishment 860a
censorship 861b
centralization and decentralization 862b
checks and balances 863c
child labor 831c
citizenship 863c
civil service 865a
coinage 865b
colonial period 785–786
commercial law tab 826
common law 867a
Congress 788c
constitution 868c
constitution text 806
copyright laws 870c
county 871c
dependencies 873b
diplomatic service 874b
economic control 876b
executive department 789b
events paralleling presidential
  administrations tab 1061–1070
federal government 878b
foreign policies 880b, 902b
governor 881b
immigration 851a, 883b
initiative and referendum 884c
internal revenue receipts 885c
labor legislation 831a
labor unions 838a
legislative department 787b
Lend-Lease 889b
local government 793c
municipal government 793c
nationalization 892a
naturalization 893a
party government 896c
planning 898b
political divisions 793c
presidential administrations
  2031–2082
public debt 902a

recall 904a
separation of powers 907c
socialism 908a
social security 837a
Social Security Act 837b
state government 792c–794a
subsidies 909c
syndicalism 909c
taxation 910a
territorial government 794a
woman suffrage 914a
workmen's compensation 835c
—History see American history
see Colonial America
—Resources and Industry
conservation 775a
cocoa 726c
cattle 727b
corn 729c
cotton 730c
dairy products 731b
fishing industry 734a
glass industry tab 135
grapes 739a
industrial progress tab 1061–
  1070
mineral products 460b
motion picture industry 1168a
natural gas 1210a
plastics 1219c
oats 741a
paper production 1273a
pharmaceutical industry 1273c
rice production 742b
soybeans 743c
sugar industry 744c
tobacco 746a
United States (ship) 1180c
United States Air Force see Air
  Force (U.S.)
United States Air Force Academy
  629c, 659, 1976, 1977b
United States Armed Forces Institute 636c
United States Army see Army
  (U.S.)
United States Atomic Energy Commission 1995b
United States Bank see Bank of
  the United States, Second
United States Coast Guard Acad-
  emy 630a, 660
United States Congress see Con-
  gress (U.S.)
United States Constitution see
  Constitution (U.S.)
United States Employment Service
  840b
United States Housing Authority
  882c
United States Intl. Univ. — Cali-
  fornia Western U. Campus
  658
United States Lawn Tennis Asso-
  ciation 1744c
United States Marine Corps see
  Marine Corps (U.S.)
United States Merchant Marine
  Academy 688
United States Military Academy
  629c, 668, 913b
United States Naval Academy 629c,
  673, 2005a
United States Olympic Association
  1745a
United States Polo Association
  1727c
United States presidents see Pres-
  idents (U.S.)
United States Public Health Ser-
  vice 960c
United States Senate see Senate
  (U.S.)
United States Steel Corporation
  524c
United States Supreme Court see
  Supreme Court (U.S.)
Unity Party (Togo) 2275b
Universal Copyright Convention
  870c
Universal gravitation, law of 1801a,
  1873b
Universal military training 911c
Universal Military Training Service
  Act 868c
Universal Postal Union 900a, 993a
Universal and Regional Library
  (Strasbourg) tab 1463
Universal time 1797b
Universities 629a, 654–708
adult education 635c
history 984c
University of see under the latter
  part of the name, such as
  California, University of
Unlike terms (math.) 1535c

Unruh, Fritz von tab 1480
Unsaturated acids 732c
Untermeyer, Louis 355c
Untermyer, Samuel 356a
Upanishads (bks.) tab 1464, 1627a
Updike, Daniel Berkeley 146b
Updike, John 356a, 1376a
Upholstery 1095c
Upolu Island 2301c
Upper case (print.) 150c, 153c
Upper Cave people 1924b
Upper Iowa University 668
Upper Paleolithic Age 1928b
Upper Volta 2294–2295
agriculture 2294c
economy 2294c
flag il 2184
geography 2294b
government 2294c
history 2294c–2295a
independence 2295a
map 2294, Atlas-36–37
people of 2294b
religion 2294b
Upsala College 683
Upshur, Abel P. tab 795
Ur (anc. city) 74b
archeology 969b
tablets 1510b
Uracil 1855a
Ural Mountains 2254b, 2254c,
  2342b–2342c
Ural River 2342b
Urania (myth) 1440c
Uraninite 453c
Uranium 1144a, tab 1838
atomic structure 1911c
atomic weight tab 1805, 1806a
electron cloud 1806a
fission reactions 1828c
Germany 2158b
Greenland 2314b
New Mexico 1990a
radioactive decay 454b
Romania 2244a
U.S. 2293c
uraninite 453c
Utah 1996b
Sweden 2268a
Wyoming 1999c
Uranium oxide glass 133c
Uranus (myth) 1448c
Uranus (planet) tab 1782, 1783b
albedo 1793b
atmosphere 1840b
Bode's law 1780c, tab 1781
Urban II, Pope 1001c, 1002a
Crusades 984a
Urban VIII, Pope 356a, 902a
Urban development 1153c
Urban economics 605c
Urbana, Illinois 1981b
Urbino, Duke of portrait tab 110
Urea 921a, 1818a
plastics tab 1219
Uremia 945c
Ureters 925b
Urethanes tab 1219, 1219c
Urethra 926b
Urey, Harold Clayton 356a, 1840a
Urfé, Honoré d' 1378c
Urga, Mongolia see Ulan Bator
Uriens 1440b
Urine 925b
Urmia, Iran 2370a
Urn-Burial (bk.) 1362a
Urquiza, Justo José de 2090b
Ursinus College 697
Ursuline College 670
Ursuline College for Women 692
Urth 1441a
Uruguay 2090b, 2295–2296
agriculture 2295b
climate 2295a
deer 25b
economy 2295a–2295b
flag il 2184
geography 2295a
government 2295b
history 2295b–2296a
independence 2295c
map 2295, Atlas-45
people of 2295a
religion 2295a
World War II 2296a
Uruguay River 2089a, 2342c
Usher, John Palmer tab 797
U.S.S.R. see Union of Soviet
  Socialist Republics
Ussuri River 2254c
Usuman dan Fodio 2228c–2229a

Usury 605a, 819b
  penalties *tab* 826
Utah 1996
  acquisition 2040b
  agriculture 1996b
  budget system 858b
  capital punishment 860b
  census (1960) *tab* 1973
  climate 1996a
  colleges of 703–704
  commercial law *tab* 826
  Compromise of 1850 2041a
  congressional apportionment *tab* 853
  divorce 875b
  economy 1996b
  geography 1996a
  government 1996b
  holidays 841–842
  initiative and referendum 884c
  mariposa lily 1678c
  people of 1996a–1996b
  public school enrollment *tab* 646
  public school expenditures *tab* 644
  student enrollment *tab* 645
Utah, University of 703

Utah State University 704
Utamaro 141a
Uterus 926c
  menstruation 926b
Uther (myth) 1448c
Utilitarianism (philos.) 1618b
Utley, Freda *tab* 1481
Uto-Aztecan languages 1338a
Utopia (bk.) 1360b, 1420a, *tab* 1466
Utopian literature *Erewhon* 1402c
  More, T. 1360b, 1420a
  Plato 1353c

Utrecht, Netherlands 2224c, 2225c
  printing 144a
Utrecht, Treaty of 2026c, 2114c, 2289c
Utrecht Canons As Pilgrims (paint.) *tab* 110
Utrecht Psalter 1192a
Utrillo, Maurice 103c, *tab* 109
  biography 356a
Uvala 519b
Uzbegs 1927b

V

V-2 (rocket) 1765c, 1768c
  fuels 1766b
  staging 1765c
Vaal River 2252a, 2342c
Vaccination 922c
  public health 955c
Vacuoles plant 1643c
Vacuum (physics) sound 1893b
Vacuum cleaners 1260b
Vacuum tubes 1284a
Vadose water 519b
Vaduz, Liechtenstein 2210a, 2210b, 2210c, 2376a
Vagantes (mus.) 159a
Vagina 926c
Vagus nerve 938a
Vai tribe 2209a
Vaihinger, Hans 356b
Vaiont Dam 1206c
Vaisyas (caste) India 980b
Valdemar IV, King (Denmark) *see* Waldemar IV
Valdés, Armando Palacio *see* Palacio Valdés, Armando
Valdivia, Pedro de 2122a
Valdosta State College 663
Vale 519b
Valen, Karstein *tab* 172b
Valence (chem.) 1809a
Valence band (elec.) 1891b
Valence electrons 1809a
Valence shell 1809a
Valencia, Spain 2263c, 2376a
  oranges 1683a
Valenciennes, France 2149a
Valentinus 356b
Valentinus, Basilius 1212a
Valera y Alcalá Galiano, Juan 1392b, *tab* 1476
Valera, Eamon de *see* De Valera, Eamon
Valera River 2088c
Valerian 1697c–1698a
Valerian family 1698a
Valery, Paul 1382a, *tab* 1480
  biography 356b
Valetta, Malta 2215b, 2376a
Valhalla 1448c
Vali 1423a
Valjean, Jean (lit. char.) 1409a
Valkyrie (opera) Siegfried 1447b
  see also Walküre, Die
Valkyries 1448c
Vallandigham, Clement L. 356b
Valley City State College 690
Valley Farm (paint.) *tab* 111
Valley Forge American Revolution 2028b
Valley train 519b
Valleys 518, 519b, 761b
  hanging 500c
  longitudinal 505c
  rift 513a
  transverse 519a
Valmiki 1414c
Valmy, Battle of 1002c, 1007c
Valois kings 2150c–2151b
Valparaiso, Chile 2121b, 2121c
Valparaiso University 667
Value (econ.) 606a
Valverde, Battle of 2049
Valves 1284b
Vampire 64c, 1448c

Van (in names) *see also* under latter part of name, such as Eyck, Jan van
Van, Lake 2342c
Van Allen, James A. 356b, 952b
Van Allen belts 952b
Van Alstyne, Frances Jane *see* Crosby, Fanny
Van Briggle, Artus 131c
  ceramics *tab* 132
Van Buren, Martin *tab* 798–799, 881a
  administration 2038
  Barnburners 856b
  biography 356b
  Cabinet *tab* 795
  Democratic Party 873a
  election and inauguration *tab* 800
  events paralleling administration *tab* 1063
Van de (in names) *see also* under latter part of name, such as Velde, Willem van de
Van de Graaff, Robert Jemison 1912b
Van de Graaff accelerators 1912b, 1919b
Van der (in names) *see also* under latter part of name, such as Waals, Johannes Diderik van der
Van der Rohe, Mies *see* Mies van der Rohe, Ludwig
Van Devanter, Willis Supreme Court *tab* 802c
Van Dine, S. S. *tab* 1463c
Van Doren, Carl Clinton 356c, *tab* 1480
Van Doren, Mark 356c, 1395a
Van Dyck, Sir Anthony *tab* 107
  Anna Wake tab 111
  biography 356c
  Cardinal Bentivoglio tab 110
  Lord Philip Wharton tab 113
  William II of Orange and His Bride tab 109
Van Dyke, Henry *tab* 1478
Van Eyck (Flem. painters) *see* Eyck
Van Gogh, Vincent 86c, *tab* 108, 262a
  Bedroom at Arles tab 110
  Self-Portrait il 91
Van Loon, Hendrik Willem 356c
Van Rensselaer, Stephen War of 1812 2034b
Vanadium 1838
  alloys 1193a
  atomic weight *tab* 1805
Vancouver, George 356b
Vancouver, Canada 2376a
Vancouver Island 2110c, 2342c
Vandals 2159a
Vandenberg, Arthur 356c
Vanderbilt, Cornelius 356c, 524a, 2228a
Vanderbilt University 701
Vanderlyn, John *tab* 108
Vane, Sir Henry 356c
Vänern, Lake 2267c, 2342c
Vanguard (rocket) fuels 1766b
Vanguard I (rocket) 1769b
Vanguard II (rocket) 1769c
Vanguard III (rocket) 1769c
Vanguard, Project *see* Project Vanguard
Vanilla 744b
  Dominica 2311b
  French Polynesia 2313a
  Madagascar 2212a
  see also Orchid family

Vanillin 1821b
Vanir 1448c
Vanity Fair (bk.) 1367b, 1420a
  Becky Sharp 1397a
  Rawdon Crawley 1400a
Van't Hoff, Jacobus Hendricus 1761c, 1799b
Vantongerloo, Georges *tab* 125
Vanua Levi Island 2312a
Vanzetti, Bartolomeo 338c
Vapor condenser 1244a
Vapor pressure 1828b
Vargas, Getulio 2104b–2104c
Variable (math.) 1607c
  algebra 1534b
Variations (mus.) 179b
Varicose veins 924b, 945c
Variety store 606b
Varna, Bulgaria 2105a, 2376a
Varnish 1216b, 1226c
  France 1098b
Varnum, J. B. House of Representatives *tab* 802b
Varro, Caius Terentius 1000a
Varro, Marcus Terentius 1356a, *tab* 1464
  biography 356c
Varuna 1624a
Varus, Publius Quintilius 357a, 1002c
Varve 519b
Vasa, Gustavus 2268c
Vasa Kings 2268c
Vasari, Giorgio 1386c, *tab* 1466
  biography 357a
Vasco da Gama *see* Gama, Vasco da
Vasconcelos, Jorge Ferreira de 1388b
Vascular bundles (plant) 1644c, 1645c
Vase painting 83c, 84a
Vasoconstriction 918c
Vasodilatation 918c
Vásquez, Horacio 2143b
Vassal (feudalism) 984a
Vassar College 688
  Phi Beta Kappa 1745b
Vatican City 2296a–2296c
  flag *il* 2184
  geography 2296b
  history 2296b
  popes *tab* 1080
Vatican Council (1870) 871b, 1632b
Vatican Gallery famous paintings *tab* 112
Vättern, Lake 2267c, 2268b, 2342c
Vauban, Marquis de 2152a
Vaud (canton), Switzerland referendum 884c
Vaughan, Henry 357a, *tab* 1468
Vaughan Williams, Ralph 169b, *tab* 172b, 357a
Vault (arch.) 73a, 76c
Vaux, France
  World War I 2066b
Vava'u Islands 2324a
Veblen, Thorstein 357a, *tab* 1478
Vecchio, Palma *see* Palma, Jacopo
Vector analysis 1507a
Vector quantity 1873c
Vedangas (treatises) *tab* 1464
Vedas (bks.) 980b, 1420a, *tab* 1463, 1624a
Vedder, Elihu *tab* 108
Veering 519b
Vega, Garcilaso de la *see* Garcilaso de la Vega
Vega, Lope de 1391a, *tab* 1467

Vega (star) *tab* 1786
Vegetable oils 732b
  paint 1216b
Vegetable sponge 1698a
Vegetables 746c
  farms 381a
  food manufacturing 736a
  waxes 1227a
Vegetarians 1862a
Veilchen, Das (song) 164b
Veins 519b
Veins (anat.) 924b
  thrombophlebitis 945c
  varicose veins 945c
Veins (plant) 1645a
Velasco Ibarra, José María 2144c
Velázquez, Diego 2137b
Velásquez, Diego Rodríguez de Carpio 357a
Velásquez, Diego Rodríguez de Silva y *tab* 107
  biography 357a
  Infanta Margarita tab 112
  Infanta Maria Theresa tab 116
  Infanta Margarita Theresa tab 113
  Juan, a Servant il 90
  Philip IV tab 111
  Prado, The tab 111
Veld 519c
Velde, Willem Van de *tab* 107
Veléz de Guevara, Luis 1391c
Vellum 142a
Velocity 519c, 1875a, 1920a
  acceleration 1916c
  see also Speed
Vena cavae 923a
Venation 1642c, 1645a
Vendôme, Louis Joseph 357b
Venereal diseases control 958c
  public health 958b
Venetian painting *tab* 106–107
Venetian Republic *see* Venice, Republic of
Venezuela 2133a, 2234c, 2296–2298
  agriculture 2297b
  climate 2297a
  dictator 874a
  economy 2297a–2297c
  flag *il* 2184
  geography 2296c–2297a
  government 2297c
  Hague Tribunal 2061a
  history 2297c–2298b
  independence 2297c–2298a
  industry 2297b
  map 2297, *Atlas-52–53*
  natural resources 2297b
  oil 771
  pelican 50a–50b
  people of 2297a
  pitcher plant 1687b
  religion 2296c, 2297a
  trade 2297b–2297c
Venezuela, Gulf of 2342c
Venice, Italy 2195b, 2376a
  glassmaking 134a, *tab* 135
  printing 144a
  sculpture 119a
Venice, Republic of 1001b, 2195b
Venizelos, Eleutherios 357b, 2166c, 2167a
Vent 519c
Ventifact 519c
Ventitious roots 1644b
Ventricles 923a
Ventspils, Latvia 2376a
Venus (myth) 1424b, 1448c
  see also Aphrodite

Venus (planet) 757a, *tab* 1782, 1782c
  albedo 1793b
  atmosphere 1840a
  Bode's law *tab* 1781
  orbit 1771b
  probes of 1771c
Venus and Adonis (poem, Shakespeare) 1361c
Venus de Milo (sculp.) 117b
Venus's-flytrap 1698a
Veracruz, Mexico 2217b, 2218a, 2219c
  U.S. history 2064b
Verbena 1698a–1998b
Verbs 1305b
  agreement with subject 1317b
  conjugation 1296c, 1306a
  irregular 1308a
  moods 1306–1307
  syntax 1307c
  use 1303b
Vercingetorix 357c
Vercors *tab* 1481
Verdad sospechosa, La (bk.) 1391a
Verdi, Giuseppe 167b, *tab* 171c
  biography 357c
Verdict 912a
Verdun, Treaty of 1023a, 2150b, 2159a
Vereeniging, South Africa 2376b
Verga, Giovanni 1387c, *tab* 1477
Vergil 1000b, 1356c, *tab* 1464
  Aeneid 1393b
  on agronomy 749b
  biography 357b
  eclogue 1402a
  epic 1402b
  epithet 1462c
  pastoral 1345b
Verhaeren, Emile 1382a
Verkhoyansk Mountains 2342c
Verlaine, Paul 1382a, *tab* 1478
  biography 357c
Vermeer, Jan 107, *tab* 112
  biography 357c
  Lace Maker tab 113
  Mistress and Maid tab 111
  Young Lady With Pearl Necklace tab 109
Vermont 1996–1997
  absent voting 849a
  admission to Union 2032a
  agriculture 1997a
  appointment 852b
  budget system 858b
  capital punishment 860b
  census (1960) 1973
  climate 1996b
  colleges of 704
  commercial law *tab* 826
  congressional apportionment *tab* 853
  council of censors 860c
  economy 1996c–1997a
  electoral votes 876c
  geography 1996c
  government 1997a
  holidays 841–842
  marble 1215b
  people of 1996c
  public school enrollment *tab* 646
  public school expenditures *tab* 644
  skiing 1996c
  student enrollment *tab* 645
Vermont, University of 704
Vernacular schools 614a
Vernal equinox 1794c
Verne, Jules 357c, *tab* 1476
Vernet, (Claude) Joseph *tab* 107
Vernier rockets 1779c
Veronese, Paul *tab* 107, *tab* 111
  biography 357c
  Finding Moses tab 110
  Marriage At Cana tab 112
Veronica 1698b
Verrazano, Giovanni da 2023b
  biography 357c
Verrazano-Narrows Bridge 1191a, 1197a
Verrocchio, Andrea del *tab* 106, *tab* 125
  biography 357c
  sculpture 121c
Vers libre 1420b
Versailles, Treaty of (1919) 994c, 999b, 1025c, 2068b, 2118a, 2130b, 2154b, 2176c, 2240b
  limitation of armaments 854a
  reparations 905c
  reparations demands 1023b–1023c
  terms of 1023a–1023c
Versailles Palace 77a, 2152a

Verse 1420b
  blank verse 1397c
  music 179b
  see also Poetry
Vértes Mountains 2173c
Verthandi 1441a
Vertigo 945c
Verwoerd, Hendrik 2253b
Vesalius, Andreas 357c, 1759a
Vesicle 519c
Vespasian (Rom. emp.) 357c
  sculpture 118a
Vespucci, Amerigo 2022c
  biography 357c
Vesta (myth) 1449a, 1628c
  Hestia 1435a
Vested interest 606b
Vesuvius, 451c, 2343a
Vesuvius, Mount 451c, 2343a
Vetch 1698b
Veterans organizations 1743b
  World War I 2070b
Veterans Administration 912a
Veterans Day 842c
Veterinarians (careers) 383c
Veto 912a
Vezelay, France
  sculpture 119b
VHF 1185c
Viaud, Louis M. J. *see* Loti, Pierre
Vibrato (mus.) 179b
Vibrio 956c
Viburnum 1698b–1698c
Vicar of Wakefield (nov.) 1363c, 1420b
Vicat, Louis J. 1191a, 1197a
Vice-Presidency (U.S.) 790c, 811b–811c
  Cabinet member 795
  candidates *tab* 800, *tab* 801
  Congress 807a
  forms of address *tab* 1120
Vicente, Gil 1388b, 1391c, *tab* 1466
Viceroyalty of Peru 2237a
Viceroyalty of Río de la Plata 2235c, 2237a
Vicksburg, Mississippi 2018c
Vicksburg, Battle of 2048c
Vico, Giovanni Battista 1387a, *tab* 1469
Victor Emmanuel II, King (Italy) 357c
Victor Emmanuel III, King (Italy) 358a, 2196b
Victor Emanuel, King (Sardinia) 2196a
Victoria, Queen (England) 358a
  reign of 2291a–2291b
  Victorian Age 1420b
Victoria, Canada 2376b
Victoria, Hong Kong 2315a
Victoria, Lake 2202b, 2272a, 2279a, 2279c, 2343a
Victoria Falls 2305a, 2343a
Victoria Nile River 2279b
Victoria Regina (play) censorship 861b
Victorian Age 1366a, 1420b
  culture 987c
  furniture 1100b
Vie de Marianne, La (bk.) 1380b
Viegues Island 2002a
Vieira, Antonio 1388c
Vien, Joseph *tab* 107
Vienna, Austria 2094b, 2376b
  National Library *tab* 1463
  porcelain 127c
  World War II 1028c
Vienna, Congress of 874c, 987b
  results of 1023c
Vienna, Treaty of 2220b
Vienna Award 2245a
Vienna Circle (philos.) 1619a
Vientiane, Laos 2206a, 2206c, 2376b
Viet Minh 2298c, 2301a
Viète, François 358a
Vietnam 2298–2301
  agriculture 2299b–2299c
  communism 2302a
  economy 2298b–2299c
  geography 2298c–2299a
  government 2299c
  history 981b, 2299c–2301b
  Johnson, Lyndon B. 2082c
  map 2299, *Atlas*-30
  people of 2299a–2299b
  religion 2298c, 2299a, 2300b, 2301b
  17th parallel 2301a
  skimmer birds 58b
  World War II 2300c–2301b

Vietnam, North
  climate 2299a
  economy 2299b
  flag *il* 2184
  geography 2299a
  government 2299b
  Indo-Chinese War *tab* 1077
  Johnson, Lyndon B. 2082c
  people of 2299b
  religion 2298c
Vietnam, South
  agriculture 2299b–2299c 2299c
  climate 2299a
  economy 2299b–2299c
  flag *il* 2184
  geography 2299a
  government 2299c
  people of 2299b
  religion 2298c
Vietnam War 2094a, 2109b, 2274c, 2301a–2301b
Vigano, Salvatore 183c
Vignola, Giacomo da 76c
  biography 358b
Vigny, Alfred de 1380c, *tab* 1474
  biography 358b
Viking (rocket) 1769a
  fuels 1766b
Vikings 2113b, 2142a, 2230c
  archeology 971a
  Iceland 2176b, 2176c
  Ireland 2191a
  North America 1964a–1964b
  Norway 2312a
  Sweden 2268b
Vila, New Hebrides 2319a, 2376b
Vilas, William Freeman *tab* 796, *tab* 797
Villa, Francisco (Pancho) 2064b, 2219b, 2219c
  biography 358b
Villa Borghese (Rome) paintings *tab* 112
Villa Madonna College 670
Villa Maria College 697
Village, The (bk.) 1390a
Village, The (poem) 1364b
Village Magistrate, The (sculp.) 114c
Village Wife's Lament, The (poem) 1370c
Villa-Lobos, Heitor *tab* 172c
Villanova University 698
Villard, Henry 358b
Villari, Pasquale 1387c
Villazón, Eleodoro 2101a
Ville d'Avray (paint.) *tab* 112
Villehardouin, Geoffroi de 1378a, *tab* 1465
Villette (bk.) 1367c
Villiers de L'Isle-Adam, Comte Philippe 358b
Villon, François 1378a, *tab* 1466
  biography 358b
Villon, Jacques *tab* 109
Vilna, Lithuania 2240b, 2376b–2376c
Vina (mus.) 155b
Vilnius *see* Vilna
Vincennes, France
  pottery *tab* 131
Vincennes, Indiana
  American Revolution 2029
Vincent, Jean Hyacinthe 358c
Vincent of Beauvais 358c
Vincent de Paul, Saint 358c
Vinci, Leonardo da *tab* 106, 228c, 1215c, 1386c
  Adoration of the Magi tab 110
  aircraft 1158c
  biography 358c
  camera obscura 1171c
  Madonna of the Rocks il 92, *tab* 111
  Mona Lisa tab 112
Vindhya Mountains 2343a
Vindhya-Satpura Mountains 2177b
Vinegar bacteria 1845b
Vinson, Frederick Moore 358c, *tab* 796
  Supreme Court *tab* 802a
Vinson Massif 2343a
Vinyls *tab* 1219
Viol (mus.) 159c, 179c
Viola (lit. char.) 1420b
Viola (musical instrument) 179c
Violet 1698c, 1989b, 1993, 1999c
  native 1981a
Violet shift 1794c
Violins 179c, 1896a
Viollet-le-Duc, Eugene 358c
Violoncello 179c
Viotti, Giovanni Battista *tab* 171c

Viper 64c–65a
Viral diseases animals 1842a
  incubation period 955a
  plants 1842c
Virgil *see* Vergil
Virgin and Child (paint., Fra Angelico) *tab* 109
Virgin and Child (paint., Weyden) *tab* 110
Virgin and Child With Chancellor Rolin (paint., Van Eyck) *tab* 112
Virgin, Child and Four Saints (paint., Titian) *tab* 110
Virgin and Donor (paint., Memling) *tab* 113
Virgin Islands 2004
  agriculture 2004b
  climate\ 2004b
  economy 2004b–2004c
  geography 2004b
  government 794b, 2004c
  history 2004c
  holidays 841–842
  people of 2004b
  slavery 2004b, 2004c
  World War II 2004c
Virgin Mary (Bib.) *see* Mary
Virgin Queen, The *see* Elizabeth I, Queen (England)
Virginal (mus.) 161a
Virginia 1997
  agriculture 1997c
  appointment 852b
  bluebells 1653b
  capital punishment 860b
  census (1960) 1973
  climate 1997b
  colleges of 704–705
  commercial law *tab* 826
  commonwealth 867c
  congressional apportionment *tab* 853
  economy 1997c
  flag *il* 2010
  geography 1997a–1997b
  government 1997c
  holidays 841–842
  opossum 48b–48c
  people of 1997c
  public school enrollment *tab* 646
  public school expenditures *tab* 644
  rail bird 54a
  student enrollment *tab* 645
  woodbine 1700a
—History
  Bacon's rebellion 997b
  Civil War 2045a
  colonial period 2023c, 2024a
  Constitutional Union Party 870b
  indentured servants 829a
  restored to Union 2053b
  secession 2045a
  U.S. Constitution 809c
Virginia, University of 78c, 705
Virginia creeper *see* Boston ivy
Virginia Military Institute 705
Virginia Parsons' Case 2026b
Virginia Polytechnic Institute 705
Virginia State College 705
Virginian, The (nov., Wister) 1420b
Virginians, The (nov., Thackeray) 1367b, 1420c
Virginibus Puerisque (essays) 1420c
Virgo Cluster (galaxies) *tab* 1785
Virion 1842b
Virtual image (optics) 1904b, 1908b
Virtuoso 179c
Virunga Mountains 2245b
Viruses 1841a, 1842b
  diseases 1842c
  genetics 1854c
  microbiology 1842a
Vischer, Peter 122b, *tab* 125
Visconti family 2195b
Viscosity 1871b
Viscount forms of address *tab* 1120
Viscountess forms of address *tab* 1120
Vishnu 1449a
Vishtasp, King 1627c
Vision astigmatism 940c
  color vision 928c
  farsightedness 941c
  glaucoma 942a
  light sensitivity 1906c
  nearsightedness 942c
  night blindness 945c
  physiology 928b
  visual defects 1299b

Vision (figure of speech) 1315a
Vision of St. Theresa (sculp.) 122c
Vision of Sir Launfal, The (poem) 1420c
Visit and search (law) 912b
Vistula River 2238c, 2239a, 2239c, 2343a
Visual arts 71a
Visurgis (river) see Weser River
Vita nuova (lit., Dante) see New Life
Vitalistic theory 1818a
Vital statistics 1859b
    infant mortality 958c
    life expectancy 954a
    maternal mortality 958c
Vitamin tab 919, 920a, 1273c, 1824b
    deficiency diseases 920a
    diet 956a
Vitamin A tab 919, 919b
Vitamin B₁ tab 919
    diseases 920b
Vitamin B₂ tab 919, 1824c
Vitamin B₆ tab 919
Vitamin B₁₂ tab 919, 920b
Vitamin C tab 919
    diseases 920b
    food additives 734c
Vitamin D tab 919, 920b, 925c
    bone 917c
Vitamin D₂ 1824c
Vitamin E tab 919
    food additives 734c
Vitamin K tab 919, 920a
Vitellius, Emperor (Rome)
    sculpture 118a
Viterbo College 708
Viti Islands see Fiji Islands
Viti Levu Island 2312a
Vittorini, Elio 1388b
Vitreous see Luster
Vitriol, Oil of see Sulfuric acid
Vitruvius Pollio, Marcus 358c
Vivace (mus.) 179c
Vivaldi, Antonio tab 171c, 358c

Vivarini, Antonio da Murano tab 106
    St. Antonio and Saints tab 112
Vivarini, Bartolommeo tab 106
Vivian (leg. char.) 1449a
Vladivostok, U.S.S.R. 1021a, 2376c
Vlaminck, Maurice de 103c, tab 108, 358c
Vlei 519c
Vlonë, Albania 2376c
Vocal cords 1293c
Vocal music 154b, 179c
Vocational education 617b, 626c
    Federal Board 2064a
    state board of education 631a
Vocational psychology 1952a
Vodka 724a
Voelter, Henry 148b
Vogel, Julius 2227a
Vogelweide see Walther von der Vogelweide
Voice 179c
    production 1293c
Voicing (mus.) 179c
Voiture, Vincent tab 1467
Volapük (lang.) 1338b
Volatilization 1216a
Volcanic material 761a
Volcanic rocks 450c
Volcanism see Vulcanism
Volcanoes 451b, 519c-520a, 761a
    Ecuador 2143a
    Hawaii 1980a, 2018b
    Iceland 2176a
    Japan 2198b-2198c
    lava 450c
    Madagascar 2211c
    Mauritius 2216c
    Mexico 2217b-2217c
    New Zealand 2225c
    Nicaragua 2227b
    Niger 2228b
    Panama 2234a
Volcanologists 390b
Vole 65a

Volga River 2256c, 2343a
    sturgeon 60c
Volgograd U.S.S.R. 2257, 2262b, 2376c
Volk, Douglas tab 108
Volleyball 1739c
Volney, Comte de 358c
Volstead, Andrew Joseph 358c
Volsunga Saga (myth) Brynhild 1428a
    Sigurd 1447b
Volt see Volts
Volta, Alessandro 1131c, 1183a, 1760b, 1814a, 1882c, 1883a
    biography 359
Volta Dam tab 1206
Volta Redonda, Brazil 2376c-2377a
Volta River 2163c, 2343a
Voltage 1132c, 1919b
    transformers 1886a
Voltaic cells 1814b, 1883a
Voltaic Democratic Union (VDU) 2295a
Voltaire 359a, 986c, 1007a, 1010b, 1380a, tab 1463c, tab 1469
Volte (dance) 182a
Volterra, Daniele da tab 107
Voltmeters 1918a, 1920b
Volts 1882c, 1920b
Volume (meas.) tab 1500
    geometry 1607c
Volume (sound) 1893b
    music 179c
Volumetric analysis 1827c
Voluntary (mus.) 179c
Voluntary chain (bus.) 587c
Voluntary muscles 927a, 928a
Volutes 75a
Von (in names) see also under latter part of name, such as Goethe, Johann Wolfgang von
Von Braun, Wernher 1768b, 1769a
    biography 213b
Vondel, Joost van den 359a
Vorländer, Karl 359a

Vorster, Balthasar 2253b
Vosges Mountains 2148a
Vosges Tunnel 1226
Voskhod (spacecraft) tab 1770
Vostok (ship) 1770c
Vostok I (spacecraft) 951b, tab 1770, 1770c
Vostok II (spacecraft) 951c, tab 1770
Vostok III (spacecraft) tab 1770
Vostok IV (spacecraft) tab 1770
Vostok V (spacecraft) tab 1770
Vostok VI (spacecraft) tab 1770
Voting 912c
    absentee ballot 849a
    ballot 855c
    bloc 857b
    constitutional amendment 811c
    cumulative 902b
    machine 1284c
    parliamentary law 845a
    plural 899b
    poll tax 899c
    preferential 900b
    proportional representation 902a
    registration 905a
    see also Elections
    see also Suffrage
Voting machine 856a
Voting Rights Act (1965) 2082b
Vouet, Simon tab 107, 1095c
Vrbas River 2303a
VTOL (aviation) 1158a
Vug 520a
Vuillard, Jean Edouard 103c
    biography 359a
Vulcan 1434b, 1449a
Vulcanism (volcanism) (geol.) 455a
Vulcanization (ind.) 1276c
Vulgarisms (lang.) 1321c
Vulgate Bible 871b, 1460c
Vulture 65a-65b

Vyshinsky, Andrei Y. 359a

W

Waals, Johannes Diderik van der 1813c
Wabash College 667
Wabash River 1981a, 2019b
WAC-Corporal rocket 1768c
    fuels 1766c
Wace (poet) 1425b
Waddington, William Henry 359b
Wade, Benjamin Franklin 359b
Wade-Davis Bill 2051b
Wade-Davis Manifesto 2051b
Wadi 520a
Wadi al Araba 2201c
Wadsworth, James J. United Nations tab 797
Wagering contracts 819a
Wages 606b, 834a, 836b
    Colonial America 827b
    minimum wage laws 833a
    N.R.A. codes 835a
Wages and Hours Act see Fair Labor Standards Act
Wages-fund theory 606b
Wagner, Richard 166c, 167a, 172a, 1385a, tab 1474
    biography 359b
Wagner, Robert F., Sr. 2074a
Wagner Act see National Labor Relations Act
Wagner College 688
Wagner-Peyser Act 840b
Wagstaff, Simon see Swift, Jonathan
Wahhabis 2247a-2247b
Wahlgren, Erik 971b
Wahoo (fish) il 152
Waikato River 2225c
Wainwright Building 81b
Waitaki River 2225c
Waitangi, Treaty of 2226c
Waite, Morrison R. 359b

Supreme Court tab 802a
Wakayama, Japan 2377a
Wake Forest College 690
Wake Island 2004
    government 794b
    World War II 2004c
Wake robin see Trillium
Waksman, Selman 1845c
Walachia 2165a, 2244b, 2244c
Walbrzych, Poland 2239c
Wald, Lillian D. 359b
Waldemar IV, King (Denmark) 1009c
Walden (bk.) 775b, 1373c, 1420c
Wales 2282a, 2283a
    House of Lords 891a
    industry 2283a
    music 154c
    see also United Kingdom
Walker, Frank C. tab 796
Walker, James B. presidential candidate tab 801
Walker, Robert J. tab 795
    tariff 2040c
Walker, William 1006a, 2042b, 2228a
    biography 359c
Walking 1934b
Walking contests 1737c
Walking fern 1698c
Walküre, Die (opera) 167a
    see also Valkyrie
Wall Street (N. Y.) 606b
Wall tent 1709c
Walla Walla College 706
Wallaby 65b-65c
Wallace, Alfred Russel 359c
Wallace, Frederick W. 1390c
Wallace, George 2082b
Wallace, Henry A. 359c, 721a, tab 797
    presidential candidate tab 801
    Progressive Party 901c
Wallace, Henry C. tab 797
Wallace, Lew 359c, 1375a, tab 1476
    Ben Hur 1397a
Wallace, Sir William 359c, 2286b
Wallace-Johnson, I. T. A. 2249a

Wallach, Otto 359c
Wallachia see Walachia
Wallenstein, Albrecht von 359c
Waller, Edmund 1362b, tab 1467
Walleyed pike il 1717
Wallis, John 360a, 1566b
Wallis and Futuna Islands 2324
Wallflower 1698c
Wallonia 2099b
Walls structural mechanics 1190c
Walnut 1698c-1699a
    furniture 1097b
Walnut family 1699a
Walnut Lane Bridge 1197a
Walpole, Horace 360a, 1364a, tab 1470
Walpole, Hugh Seymour 360a, 1371b
Walpole, Sir Robert 360a, 863a, 2290b
    cabinet 859a
    prime minister 901a
Walpurgis Night 1449a
Walrus 65c
Walrus Island 2019c
Walsh, Thomas James 360a
Walsh-Healey Act 836b
Walter, Archbishop Hubert 2285c
Walter, Bruno 360a
Walter, Thomas Ustick 360a
Walters Art Gallery tab 109
Walther, Johann 160c, tab 171b
Walther von der Vogelweide 159b, tab 171b, tab 1465
    biography 360a
Walton, Ernest Thomas Sinton 1912b
Walton, George tab 803
Walton, Izaak 360a, 1362a, tab 1467
Walton, William tab 172b
Waltz 179c, 182a
Wanamaker, John tab 796
Wanamaker, Rodman 1157a
Wandering Jew 1449a
Wang An-Shih 978b
Wang Mang 2127a

Wanganui, New Zealand 2226b
Wanganui River 2225c
Wangchuk, Ugyen 2099c
War see Warfare
War, Laws of 913b
War and Peace (bk.) 1389c
War Boards 2065c-2066a
War Department 913a
    establishment tab 797
    secretaries of tab 795-796
War in the Air, The (nov.) 1370a
War Labor Disputes Act see Smith-Connally Act
War of see also under the latter part of the name, such as Spanish Succession, War of the
War of Devolution 2152a
War of 1812 1022c, tab 1074, 2034b, 2115b
    international law 886a
    naval engagements 2034c
War of Restoration 2143a
War of the Austrian Succession 2195b
War of the League of Augsberg 2152a
War of the Pacific 2100c, 2122b, 2237a-2237b
War of the Polish Succession 2152b, 2195b
War of the Roses 2191a-2191b
War of the Spanish Succession 2152a-2152b, 2195b, 2225b
War of the Triple Alliance 2090b, 2235c
War Trade Board 2066a
Warbeck, Perkin 360a
Warbler 65c
Warburg, Otto Heinrich 360b
Warburg College 668
Ward, Artemus see Browne, Charles Farrar
Ward, Edward 1167b
Ward, Mrs. Humphry 360b, 1369c

Ward, John Quincy Adams 123c,
    tab 125
    biography 360b
Ward (law) 881c, 913c
Warehouse 606b
Warfare
    primitive 1937a
    rockets 1764a
    technology 1127c
Warm front 477a
Warneke, Heinze tab 125
Warner, Charles Dudley tab 1476
Warner, Olin tab 125
Warner, Seth 360b
Warner Pacific College 694
Warping 520a
Warrant (law) 913c
Warranties 823c
Warren, Earl 360b, tab 802a
Warren, Joseph 360b
Warren, Ohio 1992a
Warren, Robert Penn 360c
Wars see under the individual
    wars, such as Queen Anne's
    War
    see also Warfare
Warsaw Pact 2159a, 2239c
Warsaw, Poland 2238c, 2239a,
    2239c, 2377a
Warta River 2238c
Warton, Thomas Poet Laureate
    1413b
Warwick, 1st Earl of (Richard
    Neville) 318a
    epithet 1462b
Warwick, Rhode Island 1994a
    founding 2025b
Wash, Redburn see Shaw, G. B.
Wash and wear fabrics 1209a
Washburn, Elihu tab 796
Washburn University of Topeka 669
Washburne, Carleton 618c
Washing machines 1260a
Washington, Booker T. 360c
Washington, Bushrod tab 802a
Washington, George 360c, tab 798-
    799, 965a, 998a, 1024a
    administration 2031-2032
    administration, events parallel-
        ing tab 1061
    American Revolution 2028a,
        2029
    army 2027c
    birthday 841b
    Cabinet tab 795, 859b
    Constitution (U.S.) 809c
    Constitutional Convention 2030b
    election tab 800
    epithet 1462a
    Farewell Address 1403c
    foreign policy 880b
    French and Indian War 2026c
    inauguration tab 800
    portrait (Stuart) tab 110
    writings tab 1470
Washington 1997-1998
    agriculture 1998a
    capital punishment 860b
    census (1960) 1973
    climate 1998a
    colleges of 705-706
    commercial law tab 826
    congressional apportionment
        tab 853
    economy 1998a
    flag il 2010
    geography 1998a
    government 1998a
    holidays 841-842
    initiative and referendum 884c
    people of 1998a
    public school enrollment tab
        646
    public school expenditures tab
        644
    recall 904b
    rhododendron 1690a
    slugs 58c-59a
    statehood 2058a
    student enrollment tab 645
Washington, D.C. 1978-1979, 2019c,
    2292b
    census (1960) 1970
    climate 1978c
    economy 1979a
    electoral votes 876c
    flag il 2010
    government 1979a
    land despoilment 776c
    people of 1978c-1979a
    rapid transit 1165b
    War of 1812 2034c
Washington, Mt. 1989a, 2019b

Washington, Treaty of (1871) 853c,
    994a-994b, 2053c, 2116c
Washington case (law) 833a
Washington College 673
Washington Conference (1921-1922)
    854a, 2068c, 2201a
Washington and Jefferson College
    698
Washington and Lee University 705
Washington State University 706
Washington University 680
Washington, University of 706
Wasp 66a
Wassermann, August von 360c
Wassermann, Jakob 1385c, tab 1480
Wasteland, The (poem) 1348c,
    1376b
Watches 1162a
    repairmen 386c
Water 520a, 1195b, 1816b
    acid-base reactions 1816c
    agronomy 749b
    ancient scientific theory 1751b
    aqueducts 1195b
    atmosphere 468a, 469c
    atomic rockets 1767c
    bacteria 1845c
    chemical equations 1810c
    connate 486
    desalinization 1245b
    ecology 1862c, 1865a
    electrolytes 1882b
    fresh 498a
    ground 765a-766b
    hard 500c
    hygroscopic, defined 501c
    interstitial 503b
    ionization 1817a
    juvenile 504a
    low 505c
    meteoric 507a
    plant absorption of 1646a-1646b
    reservoir 1221a
    slack 514c
    soft 515a
    softening 1285b
    subsurface 517a
    treatment 1285a
    vadose 519b
    see also Water power, Water
        supply
Water Babies (bk.) 1368a, 1420c
Water boatman 66a
Water chestnut 1699a
Water clock 1162a
Water cycle 1862c
    see also Hydrologic cycle
Water flea 66a-66b
Water gap 520a
Water gas 1210b
Water glass 133a
Water Nymphs (sculp.) 122b
Water pollution 776b
Water power 1139c
    energy consumption 1130a
Water softeners 1285b
Water strider 66b
Water supply 956c
    pollution 776b
    purification 956c, 1845c
    shortage 777a
    U.S. 777a
Water table 448b, 520a
Water thrush 66b
Water transport 1152c
    canals 1160c
    harbors 1166b
    primitive 1934c
Water wheel 1150a
Water wheel generators 1139c
Waterbury, Connecticut 1978a
Watercress see Cress
Watered stock 606c
Waterfalls 520a, 2343a-2343b
    see also under the names of
        individual falls, such as Ni-
        agara Falls
Waterlily il 1662, 1699a
Waterlily family 1699a-1699b
Waterloo 1023c-1024a
Waterloo, Battle of 987b, 1002c
    casualties 1024a
    results of 1023c-1024a
Waterloo, Belgium 2153a
Waterloo, Iowa 1982b
Watermelon see Melon
Waterplantain 1699b
Waterplantain family 1699b
Waterproofing 1276c
Waters, territorial 517c
Watershed see Divide
Waterspout 520a
Waterton National Park 2020b

Watkins, Aaron tab 801
Watkins, Franklin C. tab 109
Watkins Glen 2017c
Watling Island (Bahamas)
    see San Salvador (is.,
    Bahamas)
Watson, Dr. 1417b
Watson, James 1854b, 1858c
Watson, John Broadus 360c
Watson, Thomas E. tab 801
Watson, Sir William tab 1479
Watson-Crick model (genetics)
    1854a
Watt, James 361a, 1230a
    boiler 1234b
    Industrial Revolution 829c
Watt (unit) 1906c, 1920b
Watteau, Jean Antoine 85a, tab
    107, tab 112
    biography 361a
Watterson, Henry 361a
Watt-hour meters 1249a
Wattle tree 1699b
Wattmeters 1249a
Watts, George Frederic 361a, tab
    108
Waugh, Evelyn 361a, 1371c, tab
    1481
Waugh, Frederick J. tab 108
Wave theory (light) 1903b
Wavelength 1920b
Waves (physics) spectrum 1919c
Waves (water) 464b
    erosion 448b
    surface 517a
    tidal 518b
Waves of the Sea and of Love
    (drama) tab 1473
Wax 1227a, 1267c
Wax engraving 153c
Wax mold (print.) 153c
Wax-flower 1699b
Waxwing 66b-66c
Way of All Flesh 1367c, 1420c
Way of Power (bk.) 2126b
Wayfaring-tree see Viburnum
Wayland Baptist College 703
Wayland the Smith 1449a
Wayne, Anthony 361b, 2032a
    sobriquet 1462c
Wayne, James M. tab 802a
Wayne State College 681
Wayne State University 677
Weakfish il 1717
Wealth 606c
Wealth Against Commonwealth
    525b
Wealth of Nations (bk.) 523b, 876b,
    987a, 1348a, 1364a
Weapons explosives 1766c
    guided missiles 1257b
Weasel 66c
Weather 468c, 519a
    control of 474c
Weather Bureau 477c
    careers 390b
    history 477c
    publications 478c
Weather forecasting 468a
    barometer 468c
    research 478b
Weather vanes see Wind vanes
Weathering 447a, 520a-520b
    chemical, defined 485b
    differential, defined 489c
    mechanical 506c
Weaver, James B. tab 801, 881c,
    899c, 2058b
Weaving 1286a
    looms 1287a
Webb, Beatrice 908a
Webb, George James 169c
Webb, Sidney J. 361b, 908a
Webb-Pomerene Act 879c
Weber, Karl Maria von 165b, 172a
    biography 361b
Weber, Max tab 109
    biography 361b
Weber (unit) 1884a
Weber River 2012b-2012c
Weber State College 704
Weber-Fechner law 1489a
Webster, Daniel 361b, tab 795, tab
    796, tab 1472, 2039a
    Ichabod 1374a
    epithet 1462a
    presidential candidate tab 800
    Reply to Hayne 2037c
    Whig Party 914a
Webster, John 1361c, tab 1467

Webster, Noah 361b
    copyright 870c
Webster College 680
Webster-Ashburton Treaty 2039a,
    2115c
Weckherlin, Georg tab 1467
Weddell Sea 2343b
Weddings etiquette 1117b
Wedekind, Frank 1385b, tab 1479
Wedgwood, Josiah 361c
Wedgwood, Thomas 1171c
Wedgwood china 128a
Wee Willie Winkie (nursery rhyme)
    409c, 1421a
Weekly Memorials for the Ingeni-
    ous 1167b
Weeks, John W. tab 796
Weeks, Sinclair tab 797
Weelkes, Thomas tab 171b
Weeping Philosopher see Hera-
    clitus
Weevil 66c
Wegener, Alfred 759c
Weidman, Charles 184c
Weierstrass, Karl T. 1507b
Weight 1919a
    Biblical tab 1460-1461
    units tab 1500
Weight throw 1739a
Weightlessness 949a, 1779c
Weill, Kurt tab 172a
    biography 361a
Weimar Republic 2161c-2162a
Weingartner, Felix von 361c
Weinman, Adolph tab 125
Weir, J. Alden tab 108
Weirton, West Virginia, 1992a,
    1998b
Weise, Christian tab 1468
Weizacker, Carl von 454b
Weizmann, Chaim 361c
Welding 520b, 1287b
    electronic 1889c
Welfare, Social see Social Welfare
Well 520b, see also Wells
Welland Ship Canal 1967c, 2115b
Weller, Sam 1421a
Welles, Gideon tab 796
Welles, (George) Orson 361c
Wellesley, Arthur see Wellington,
    1st Duke of
Wellesley College 675
Wellington, 1st Duke of (Arthur
    Wellesley) 308b, 1023c-1024a
    biography 361c
    sobriquet 1462b
Wellington, New Zealand 2225c,
    2226c, 2377a
Wells artesian 1195b
Wells, Herbert George 362a, 1370a,
    tab 1479
    Outline of History 1411c
Wells College 688
Welsbach, Carl Auer von 362a, 1140b
Welsbach mantle 1140b
Welsh, Jane 1366a
Welsh language 1336a
Welt 520b
Wendish (lang.) 1334a
Wentworth, Thomas (1593-1641)
    see Strafford, 1st Earl of
Wentworth, William Charles 362a
Wentworth grade scale 520b
Werewolf 1449b
Werfel, Franz 362a, 1385c, tab 1480
Werner, Alfred 362a
Werner, F. L. Zacharias tab 1471
Weser River 2157b, 2343b
Wesley, John 362a
Wesleyan College 663
Wesleyan University 660
Wessex Kingdom 2284a, 2284b
Wessex Tales 1421a
Wessin y Wessin, Elías 2143b
West, A. M. tab 801
West, Benjamin 104a, tab 107
    biography 362a
West, Rebecca 362a, 1371c, tab
    1480
    pseudonym tab 1463c
West, Roy O. tab 797
West Africa gorilla 36c
West Chester State College 698
West Delaware Aqueduct 1226c
West Georgia College 663
West Germany see Germany, West
West Gulf Coastal Plain 1976a

West Hopkinton, New Hampshire 1988
West Indies 1693c–1694a, 2343b
  agouti 13a
  arrowroots 1649c
  avocado 1650a–1650b
  balsa 1650c
  bigonias 1652b
  Brazil nuts 1654a
  breadfruits 1654b
  buccaneers 999b
  catalpa 1656a
  clove trees 1658c
  colonialism 999b
  cony 23a
  crocodile 24b
  cucumber 1660a
  custard-apples 1660b
  finch 33b
  grapefruit 1670a–1670b
  guava 1670c
  guppy 37b–37c
  historical outline *tab* 1061–1070
  horsetail 1672c
  ibis 40b
  iguana 40b
  lignum vitae 1675c
  lotus 1677a
  mahogany trees 1677c
  night-blooming cereus 1681a
  nutmeg 1682a
  orchid species 1683a
  passion-flowers 1684c
  rum 724c
  sapote 1691c–1692a
  sedge 1692b
  sisal 1693a
West Indies Associated States 2307a
West Irian 2186c, 2188b
West Liberty State College 707
West Palm Beach, Florida 1979b
West Point *see* United States Military Academy
West Texas State University 703
West Virginia 1998
  admission to Union 2045a, 2050a
  agriculture 1998c
  budget system 858b
  capital punishment 860b
  census (1960) 1973
  climate 1998b
  colleges of 706–707
  commercial law *tab* 826
  congressional apportionment *tab* 853
  economy 1998c
  geography 1998b
  government 1998c
  holidays 841–842
  labor legislation 832c
  people of 1998b
  public school enrollment *tab* 646
  public school expenditures *tab* 644
  rhododendron 1690a
  sandstone 1998c
  student enrollment *tab* 645
West Virginia Institute of Technology 707
West Virginia State College 707
West Virginia University 707
West Virginia Wesleyan College 707
Westcott, Edward Noyes
  David Harum 1401a
Westerlies 520b
Western Carolina College 690
Western College for Women 692
Western Cordilleran Region (U.S.) 1962b–1962c
Western Desert 2280b
Western Ghats 2177c, 2177b
Western hemlock 1997c
Western Illinois University 665
Western Island *see* Hebrides
Western Kentucky University 670
Western Maryland College 673
Western meadowlark 1982b, 1987c, 1988a, 1991b, 1992c
Western Michigan University 677
Western Montana College 681
Western New Mexico University 683
Western Reserve 692
Western Samoa 2301–2302
  agriculture 2301c
  climate 2301b
  Commonwealth status 1000c
  economy 2301c
  flag *il* 2184
  geography 2301b
  government 2301c
  history 2301c–2302a
  independence 2302a
  map *Atlas*-6
  people of 2301b–2301c
  religion 2301b

Western State College of Colorado 659
Western Togoland 2164b
Western Washington State College 706
Westfield, State College at 675
Westinghouse, George 362b
Westmar College 668
Westminster, Statute of 1001a
Westminster Abbey 76c
Westminster College 680, 698, 704
Westmont College 659
Westphalia, Peace of (1648) 2151c, 2160b, 2270b
Westphalia, Treaty of 2225b
Westport, Battle of 2049
Westward Ho! (nov.) 1367c–1368a, 1421a
Wet 520b
Wet cells 1131c
Weyden, Roger van der *tab* 106, 362b
  Christ Appearing to His Mother tab 112
  St. Luke Painting the Virgin tab 110
  The Seven Sacraments tab 109
Weyler y Nicolau, Valeriano 2059c, 2137b
Whale 66c–67a
Wharton, Edith 326b, *tab* 1479
What Every Woman Knows (play) 1369c
Wheat 747a, 1699b–1699c
  Albania 2086b
  Algeria 2087b
  Argentina 2089c
  Australia 2092a
  Bulgaria 2105b
  China 2125b
  farms 381a
  France 2148c
  Great Britain 2282c
  Idaho 1980c
  Ifni 2316a
  Illinois 1981b
  India 2178b
  Indiana 1981c
  Iran 2188c
  Iraq 2189c
  Ireland 2191a
  Isle of Man 2316b
  Italy 2194b–2194c
  Japan 2199b
  Jordan 2201c
  Kansas 1982c
  Mexico 2218a
  Missouri 1987b
  Montana 1988a
  Morocco 2221c
  Nebraska 1988b
  Niger 2228c
  North Dakota 1991c
  Ohio 1992a
  Oklahoma 1992b
  Oregon 1993a
  Pakistan 2232b
  Poland 2239b
  Romania 2244a
  San Marino 2246a
  South Dakota 1994c
  Spain 2264a
  Sweden 2268a
  Switzerland 2270a
  Syria 2271a
  Texas 1995c
  Tunisia 2277a
  Turkey 2278a
  U.A.R. 2280c
  U.S. 1968c, 2294a
  U.S.S.R. 2257a
  Uruguay 2295a
  varieties 747b
  Washington 1998a
  Wyoming 1999c
  Yugoslavia 2303b
Wheatfields (paint.) *tab* 112
Wheaton College (Illinois) 665
Wheaton College (Massachusetts) 675
Wheatstone, Charles 362b, 1920b, 1248b
Wheatstone bridge 1920b
Wheel invention 1152c
Wheel lock 1254c
Wheeler, Andrew C. pen names 1461c, 1462b
Wheeler, Burton K. *tab* 801
Wheeler, Joseph 362b
Wheeler, Wayne Bidwell 362b
Wheeler, William Almon 362b
  vice-presidency *tab* 801
Wheeler Peak 1990a
Wheeling, West Virginia 1998b, 2015c, 2019c
  proportional representation 902b

Wheeling College 707
Wheelock, Warren *tab* 125
Wheelock College 675
When the Wind Is in the East (nursery rhyme) 411a
Where Are You Going to? (song) 422
Where Go The Boats? (nursery rhyme) 414c, *il* 415
Whey 731c
Whig Party (U.S.) 906a, 914a, 2036b, 2039a
  Constitutional Union Party 870b
  Democratic Party 873a
  Free-Soil Party 881a
Whip (politics) 914a
Whipple, Squire 1190c
Whipple, William *tab* 803
Whippoorwill 67a–67b
Whipworms *tab* 948
Whirlpool 520b
Whirlwind 520b
Whisky 723c
  distilling, Kentucky 1983b
Whisky Insurrection 1024a–1024b
  see also Whisky Rebellion
Whisky Rebellion 662a, 2031b–2032a
Whisky Ring 2054b
Whistler, James Abbott McNeill 86b, *tab* 108
  biography 362c
  etching 136c
  Whistler's Mother tab 112
White, Byron *tab* 802a
White, E. B. 362b
White, Edward D. *tab* 802a
White, Gilbert *tab* 1470
White, Henry 362c
White, Hugh L. presidential candidate *tab* 800
White, John 2023c
  House of Representatives *tab* 802c
White, Peregrine 362c
White, Stanford 362c
White, William Allen 362c
White ants *see* Termites
White birch 1989a
White blood cells 922a, 925a
  agranulocytosis 940a
  leukemia 942c
  lmyphosarcoma 942c
White Cliffs of Dover
  protozoa (forminifera) 1848b
White Company, The (the story) 1370a
White dwarfs (stars) 1790a
White House (Washington, D.C.)
  interior decoration 1109a
White light 1907b
White marlin *il* 1717
White matter 938a
White Monkey, The (nov.) 1410c
White Mountains 1984a, 1989a, 1989b, 2016a, 2019b
White oak 1977c
White pepper 744a
White pine 1980c, 1984a, 1985c
White pine cone and tassel 1984a
White River 2008b, 2018c
White Volta River 2163c
Whiteface Mountain 1990b
Whitefish 67b
Whitefield, George 362c
Whitehall Palace 77b
Whitehead, Alfred North 362c, 1619a
  on education 611c
  Science and the Modern World 1348b
Whitehead, William Poet Laureate 1413b
Whitestone Bridge 1644c, *see* Bronx-Whitestone Bridge
Whiting, William F. *tab* 797
Whiting *see* Cod
Whitman, Marcus 362c
Whitman, Sarah Helen Power 363a
Whitman, Walt 1345a, 1374b, *tab* 1476
  biography 363a
  epithet 1462a
Whitman College 706
Whitney, Eli 363a, 720a, 1229c, 2032a
Whitney, William *tab* 796
Whitney, Mount 1976c, 2019a
Whittaker, Charles E. Supreme Court *tab* 802c
Whittier, John Greenleaf *il* 208, 1374a, *tab* 1475
  Barbara Frietchie 1396b
  biography 263a
  epithet *tab* 1463a

Whittier, Joseph Liberty Party 889c
Whittier College 658
Whitworth College 706
WHO *see* World Health Organization
Whole note (mus.) 179c
Whole numbers 1515b
Whole rest (mus.) 179c
Whole step (mus.) 179c
Wholesale Price index 531a
Wholesalers 606c
  salesmen 389c
Whooping cough *tab* 948
  bacteria 1845a
  immunization 1849c
Wichita, Kansas 1982c, 2015c
  power *tab* 1132b
Wichita Falls, Texas 1995c
Wichita Mountains 1992b
Wichita State University 669
Wickard, Claude *tab* 797
Wickersham, George W. *tab* 796, 2071c
Wickersham Commission 2071c
Wickham, Henry A. 1221b
Wickliff, Charles *tab* 795
Widgeon *see* Duck
Widor, Charles M. 168b
Widow (print.) 153c
Wieland, Christopher Martin 363a, 1384b, *tab* 1470
Wieland (nov.) *tab* 1472
Wien, Austria *see* Vienna
Wiener, Norbert 363b
Wien's law 1788c
Wiesbaden, West Germany 2377a
Wiggin, Kate Douglas 363b
  Rebecca of Sunnybrook Farm 1415a
Wiggins, Thomas 1461b
Wigglesworth, Michael 1372a, *tab* 1468
Wight, Isle of 2282a, 2343b
Wiglaf 1427a
Wigman, Mary 184c
Wilberforce, William 363b
Wilberforce University 692
Wilbur, Curtis *tab* 796
Wilbur, Ray Lyman *tab* 797
Wilcox, Ella Wheeler 363b
Wilcox, Stephen 1234b
Wild prairie rose 1991b
Wild rose 1982a
Wild sunflower 1982b
Wildcat 19c
Wildcat banks 2038a
Wilde, Oscar 363b, 1368b, *tab* 1478
  Lady Windermere's Fan 1408c
Wildebeest *see* Gnu
Wildenbruch, Ernest von *tab* 1478
Wilder, Thornton 363c, *tab* 1481
Wilderness, Battle of the 2050a
Wiley College 703
Wilhelm (German name) *see* William
Wilhelmina, Queen (Netherlands) 363c, 2225c
  abdication 849a
Wilkes, Charles 363c
Wilkes, John 363c
Wilkes College 698
Wilkes Island 2004c
Wilkes-Barre, Pennsylvania 1993b
Wilkins, George Hubert 363c
Wilkins, John 1763b
Wilkins, Maurice Hugh Frederick 1854b, 1858c
Wilkins, Roy 363c
Wilkins, William *tab* 795, *tab* 800
Wilkinson, James 364a
Will, Phillip 618a
Willaert, Adrian 162a, *tab* 171b
Willard, Emma 364a
Willamette Lowland 1992c
Willamette River 1992a, 2013b, 2014b
Willamette University 694
Willapa Hills 1998a
Willem (Dutch name) *see* William
Willemstad, Curaçao (Netherlands Antilles) 2317, 2377a
William, Duke of Normandy 2284c
William I (William the Conqueror), King (England) 1010a, 1020a, 1022a, 1024a, 1358c, 2098c, 2211b

biography 364a
census of England 862a
conquest of England 2284c–2285a
reign 2285a
William II, King (England) 364a, 2285a
William III (William of Orange), King (England) 1020b, 2026c, 2225b
biography 364b
Cabinet 859a
reign 2289c
William IV, King (England) 364a
epithet tab 1463a
William I, Emperor (Germany) 2161b–2161c
William II, Emperor (Germany) 2161b–2161c
abdication 849a
biography 364b
William I (William the Silent), Stadholder (Netherlands) 364b
William III (William of Orange), Stadholder (Netherlands) see William III, King (England)
William Carey College 679
William the Conqueror see William I, King (England)
William Jewell College 680
William the Lion, King (Scotland) 1020a
William of Malmesbury 1425a, tab 1465
William and Mary College
Phi Beta Kappa 1745b
William of Ockham see Ockham, William
William II of Orange and His Bride (painting) tab 109
William Penn College 668
William the Silent see William I, Stadholder (Netherlands)
William Smith College 688
William Tell see Tell, William
William the Testy see Kieft, William
William of Wied 2087a
William Woods College 680
Williams, Ben Ames tab 1481
Williams, Frederick B. tab 108
Williams, George Henry tab 796
Williams, Ralph Vaughan see Vaughan Williams, Ralph
Williams, Roger 364b, 2025b
Williams, Tennessee 364b, 1376b, tab 1481
Williams, William tab 803
Williams, William Carlos 364c
Williams Bay, Wisconsin
observatory 1791b
Williams College 675
Williamsburg, Virginia 1964a
Williamson, Hugh Constitution (U.S.) 809c
Willimantic State College 660
Willis, Nathaniel tab 1475
Willkie, Wendell 364c
presidential candidate tab 801, 906b
Williwaw 520b
Willow 1699c
Willow family 1699c
Willow goldfinch 1997c
Willow ptarmigan 1974c
Wills (law) real property 825b
Willy boy, Willy boy (nursery rhyme) 409a
Willy-willy 520b
Wilmington, Delaware 2015c
Wilmington, North Carolina 1991a
Wilmington College 692
Wilmot Proviso 2040c
Wilson, Alexander tab 1471
Wilson, Charles Erwin 364c
Cabinet tab 797
space program 1769b
Wilson, Charles Thomson Rees 1914b, 1917b
Wilson, Edmund 364c, 1377a
Wilson, Harold 364c, 2292b
Wilson, J. Arbuthnot see Allen, Grant
Wilson, James (Amer. farmer, pol.) tab 797
Wilson, James (Amer. jur.) 364c
Constitution (U.S.) 809c
Declaration of Independence tab 803
Supreme Court tab 802a
Wilson, John (1785–1854) see North, Christopher

Wilson, Richard tab 107
Wilson, Samuel 1022c
Wilson, William Bauchop tab 797
Wilson, William Lyne tab 796
Wilson, Woodrow 365a, tab 798–799, 874a, 897a, 2143a–2143b, 2172b, 2240b
administrations 2063–2068c
administrations, events paralleling tab 1068
Cabinet tab 796–797
Democratic Party 873a
election and inauguration tab 801
election of 1916 1025a
Federal Trade Commission 879c
foreign policy 880b
Fourteen Points 1025c, 2066c
League of Nations 1012b–1012c, 1013a
Progressive Party 901c
State, The 784a
Versailles 1023a
Wilson Bill 2058c
Wilson cloud chamber 1914b
Wilson College 698
Wilson-Gorman Tariff Bill 2059a
Wilson's Creek, Battle of 2049
Wilting point 520b
Wiman Choson, Kingdom of 2204a
Win, Ne 2108a
Winchester, James War of 1812 2034b
Winckelmann, Johann Joachim 365a, 1384a
Wind 473c, 520b–520c
Coriolis effect 473c
erosion 447c
global patterns of 763c–764a
katabatic 504a
measurement 474b
monsoons 474a
ocean currents 465a
offshore 509a
onshore 509a
planetary 511a
polar 511b
prevailing 511c
systems 474a
velocity 474c
Wind, The (nursery rhyme) 414a
Wind and the Sun, The (fable) 442a
Wind Cave National Park 2016b
Wind chill gap 520c
Wind gap 520c
Wind instruments 154b, 159c, 179c
Greek 157b
Wind rose 520c
Wind shadow 520c
Wind speed see Beaufort scale
Wind vanes 474b
Windaus, Adolf 365a
Windbreaks 1930a
Windhoek, South West Africa 2322b, 2377a–2377b
Windmills 1150b
Windom, William tab 796
Windows glass 135c
Windows (astronautics) 1771c
Windpipe (anat.) see Trachea
Winds trade 518c
Windsor, Duchess of (Mrs. Wallis Simpson) 242b
Windsor, Duke of (Edward VIII) 242b, 784a, 849a
Windsor, Connecticut, founding 2025a
Windward 520c
Windward Islands 2317c, 2321b
Wine 723b, 1933b
California 1977a
France 2148c
Greece 2165b
Italy 2194c
Portugal 2241b
Morocco 2221c
Tunisia 2277a
Yugoslavia 2303c
Wing, Simon presidential candidate tab 801
Winged Victory (sculp.) 117b
Winkelried, Arnold von 365a
Winnetka, Illinois
Crow Island School 618a
Winnetka Plan 618c
Winnipeg, Lake 2343b
Winnipeg, Canada 2377b
Winona State College 678
Winooski River 2012a
Winslow, C. E. A. 954a
Winslow, Edward 365a

Winston-Salem, North Carolina 1991a
Winston-Salem State College 690
Winter 1797a
Wintergreen 1699c
Winthrop, John 365a, 2024b
wages 827b
writings 1372a, tab 1467
Winthrop, Robert Charles House of Representatives tab 802b
Winthrop College 699
Wirt, William Department of Justice tab 795
presidential candidate tab 800
writing tab 1472
Wirtz, W. Willard tab 797
Wirz, Henry 994a
Wisconsin 1998–1999
agriculture 1999a–1999b
budget system 858b
capital punishment 860a
census (1960) 1973
climate 1999a
colleges of 707–708
commercial law tab 826
congressional apportionment tab 853
economy 1999a–1999b
fair-employment laws 836c
geography 1999a
government 1999b
holidays 841–842
labor legislation 833c
people of 1999a
pit-viper 51c–52a
public school enrollment tab 646
public school expenditures tab 644
recall 904b
statehood 2030b, 2040c
student enrollment tab 645
Wisconsin, The University of —
Madison 708
Milwaukee 708
Wisconsin River 2018c
Wisconsin State University —
Eau Claire 708
La Crosse 708
Oshkosh 708
Platteville 708
River Falls 708
Stevens Point 708
Superior 708
Whitewater 708
Wisdom Literature (Bib.) 1460c
Wisdom of Solomon (Apocrypha) 1460c
Wise, Stephen Samuel 365a
Wista River 2343b
Wister, Owen 365a, 1375a
Virginian, The 1420b
Wisteria 1699c–1700a
Witch 1449b
Witchdoctor 1437b
Witch-hazel 1700a
Witenagemot 1024b
Withersfield, Connecticut, founding 2025a
Witherspoon, John tab 803
Withholding tax 606c
Witness (law) 914a
wills 825b
Witte, Count Sergei 365b, 2260b
Wittenberg University 692
Wittgenstein, Ludwig 1619a
Witwatersrand Region 2343b
Wizard Island 2017a
Wizard of Menlo Park see Edison, Thomas A.
Wizard of the North see Scott, Sir Walter
Wobblies see International Workers of the World
Wodehouse, P. G. 365b
Woden see Odin
Wofford College 699
Wöhler, Friedrich 1799b, 1818a, 1824c
Wolcott, Oliver 365b
Declaration of Independence tab 803
Cabinet tab 795
Wolf see Wolves
Wolf, Friedrich August 365b
Wolf, Hugo 168a, tab 172a
biography 365b
Wolf Creek Dam tab 1206
Wolf-Ferrari, Ermanno 167c, tab 172a
Wolf in Sheep's Clothing (fable) 442a
Wolf spider il 29
Wolfe, James 365b, 2114c
Plains of Abraham 2027a

Wolfe, Thomas 365b, tab 1481
Wolff, Baron Christian von tab 1469
Wolfram (chem.) see Tungsten
Wolfram von Eschenbach 1377c, 1383b, 1395c, tab 1465
music 159b, tab 171b
Wolframite Portugal 2241b
Wolfsbane see Aconite
Wolgemut, Michael tab 106
Wollstonecraft, Mary (Mary Godwin) 261c
Wolsey, Archbishop Thomas 365b, 2287c
Wolverine 67b–67c
Wolves 67b
Woman in White (nov.) 1367c, tab 1476
Woman of No Importance, A (play) 1368b
Woman's Day (magazine) 1167b
Woman with a Parrot (paint.) tab 112
Wombat 67c
Women division of labor 1935c
Hebrew education 612c
House of Commons 867b
jury duty 887a
labor legislation 832a, 834b
legal status 818a
life expectancy (U.S.) 954a
minimum wage laws 833a
—Suffrage 914a
England 867c
U.S. 811b
Wonder Book (stories) 1421b
Bellerophon 1427a
Wonders of the World 74b
Altar of Zeus 117c
Wonsan, North Korea 2377b
Wood
finishing 1288a
fuel 1136c
furniture 1107a
paper industry 1272b
plywood 1220b
woodworking tools 1288b
see also Lumber, Timber
Wood engraving 148b, 153c
Wood, Grant tab 109, 1107a
Wood, Mrs. Henry East Lynne 1401c
Wood, Jethro 720a
Wood, Leonard 365b
Cuba 2060b
Wood sorrel see Oxalis
Woodall Mountain 1986c
Woodbine 1700a
Woodbury, Levi Cabinet tab 795
Supreme Court tab 954a
Woodcarving furniture 1096b
Woodchuck see Marmot
Woodcock 67c–68a
Woodcuts 136a, 139c, il 140
block prints 140c
history of printing 142b
Wooden Horse of Troy see Trojan Horse
Woodin, William H. tab 796
Woodlark Archipelago 2319b
Woodpecker 68a
Woodring, Harry A. tab 796
Woods, William B. Supreme Court tab 802a
Woods, Lake of the 2018b
Woodwind instruments 179c
Woody stems 1644b, 1644c
Wool 748a
Australia 2092a, 2092c–2093a
sheep 742c
Woolen fabrics Japan 2199c
Woolf, Leonard 1371b
Woolf, Virginia 365c, 1371b, tab 1480
Woollcott, Alexander 365c
Woolley, James G. presidential candidate tab 801
Woolman, John 1372c
Woolworth, Frank 365c
Worcester, England
pottery tab 131
Worcester, Massachusetts 1985b
Worcester, State College at 675
Worcester Polytechnic Institute 675
Word Over All (bk.) 1371c
Worde, Wynkyn de 144c
Words often misused 1322–1325
spelling 1303a
Wordsworth, William 1364b, 1408c, tab 1471

biography 365c
epithet 1461a
Intimations of Immortality
1406c
on Milton 1362b
Poet Laureate 1413b
Work, Hubert *tab* 796, *tab* 797
Work (phys.) 1877b
definition 1920b
Work-and-turn (print.) 153c
Workers Party (North Vietnam)
2299c
Workmen's Compensation 826b,
835c–836b
Works and Days (poem) 1351a
World 2343b–2343c
history outline *tab* 1027–1059
map *Atlas*-6–7
geophysical globe *il* 2181
see also Earth
World Bank *see* International
Bank for Reconstruction and
Development
World Court *see* Permanent Court
of International Justice
World Health Organization 960c,
993a
major health problems 955c
World Meteorological Organization
993a
World War I 988b, 994c, 995a, 999a,
1005c, 1017b, 1024b–1025c, *tab*
1054–1055, *tab* 1076, 2161c
airplanes 1156a
Argonne Forest 995b
armistice 2066c
Austria 2095b–2095c, 2175a
Austria-Hungary 2161c
Barbados 2097c
Belgium 2099a
Bolivia 2101a
Bulgaria 2161c
Burundi 2108b
Canada 2117c
causes of 1024b–1024c
Chile 2122b
China 2130a
countries involved in 1024c–
1025a
Cyprus 2138b
Czechoslovakia 2139c
Denmark 2142b
France 995b, 2154a–2154b
Germany 995b, 2095b–2095c,
2099a, 2154b
Great Britain 2154b, 2291c
Greece 2167a
Hungary 2175a
Italy 2161c, 2196b
Japan 2201a
Jordan 2202a
kingdoms dissolved 887c
Luxembourg 2211c
Marne battles 1015c
Netherlands 2225b
neutrality 893c
New Guinea 2318c, 2319c
New Zealand 2227a
Norway 2231c
Poland 2240b
Portugal 2242b
reparations 905b, 1002b, 1023c

Romania 2245a
Russia 2154b, 2161c, 2257b,
2260c–2261a
San Marino 2246b
scope of operations 1025b–1025c
South Africa 2253b
South West Africa 2322c
Spain 2265a
submarine warfare 1025a, 1025c
Sweden 2269a
Syria 2271b
Treaty of Brest-Litovsk, 999a–
999b
Turkey 2161c, 2279a
United States 2064c–2066c, 2154b,
2161c
Yugoslavia 2304b
World War II 988c, 1012c, 1016b,
1025c–1028c, *tab* 1076, 2162c–
2163a, 2279a, 2308c–2309a
airplanes 1156b
Argentina 2090c
Australia 2093b–2093c, 2094a
Austria 2096b, 2154c, 2162c
Belgium 2099a, 2162c
Brazil 2104b
Bulgaria 2106a
Burma 2107c
Cambodia 2109b
Canada 2118b, 2163a
Chad 2121a
Channel Islands 2310b
Chile 2122c
China 2130c
Congo (Brazzaville) 2134b
conscription 868b
Czechoslovakia 2140a, 2154c,
2162c
Denmark 2142b, 2162c
Dunkirk evacuation 1028b
end of 1028c
events leading to 1025c–1028c
Faeroe Islands 2312a
Finland 2147c
France 2154c–2155a, 2162c
Germany 2099a, 2154c–2155a
Gilbert Islands 2314b
Great Britain 2162c, 2163a, 2292a
Greece 2167a–2167b
Greenland 2314c
Guam 2001b
Hong Kong 2315c
Hungary 2175c
Iceland 2176c
India 2185b–2185c
Indonesia 2188a
Iran 2189b
Iraq 2190b
Italy 2196c
Jamaica 2198b
Japan 2188a, 2201b
kingdoms dissolved 887c
Laos 2207a
Lend-Lease 1028b
Liberia 2209b
Libya 2210b
Luxembourg 2211c
Malaysia 2214a
Maldive Islands 2214c
Malta 2216a
Mexico 2219c
Midway Islands 2001c
Mongolia 2221b
Morocco 2222b
Nauru 2223b
Netherlands 2162c, 2225b–2225c

New Guinea 2319c
New Zealand 2227b
Nicaragua 2228b
Norway 2162c, 2231c
Panama 2234c
Philippines 2238b
Poland 2154c, 2162c, 2239a,
2240b–2240c
Portugal 2242b
Portuguese Timor 2320c
reparations 905c
resettlement of DP's 1003a
Romania 2245a
Ryukyu Islands 2003c
St. Helena 2321a
San Marino 2246b
Singapore 2250c
Soviet Union 2154c, 2162c, 2163a
Spain 2265b
submarine warfare 1028a, 1028b
Sudan 2266c
Sweden 2269b
Syria 2271c
Taiwan 2131b
Thailand 2274c
unemployment 911c
United States 2076b
Uruguay 2296a
Vietnam 2300c–2301b
Virgin Islands 2004c
Wake Island 2004c
Wallis and Futuna Islands 2324c
War crimes trials 913c, *il* 2162
Yugoslavia 2304c
**World War Adjusted Compensation
Act** 2070b
World's Columbian Exposition
(World's Fair 1893) architec-
ture 78c
Worms, Diet of (1521) 874a
Wormwood 1700
Wotan
Brunnehilde 1428a
Wouk, Herman 365c
Wound-rotor motors 1143a
Wouwerman, Philips *tab* 107
WPA 2073b
Wrangel, Baron **Ferdinand** Petro-
vich von 365c
Wratten, Frank Charles Luther
1172b
Wren, Sir **Christopher** 77a, 78b,
1101a
biography 366a
Wren 68b
Carolina 1994a
Wrench fault 520c
Wrestling 1740a
Wright, Sir **Almroth** 366a
Wright, Frances 2128a
Wright, Frank Lloyd 81c, 82b
biography 366a
Guggenheim Museum *il* 79
Wright, Luke E. *tab* 796
Wright, Orville 366a, 1155c
Wright, Patience *tab* 125
Wright, Wilbur 366a, 1155c
Wright, Willard H. *see* Van Dine,
S. S.
Writing 1935b
ancient 972b
Chinese 977b

see also Cuneiform; Hierogly-
phics
Writing (composition) 1316–1320
careers 388a
Writing materials 142a
Writing (penmanship) *see* Hand-
writing
Wroclaw, Poland 2239c, 2377b
Wrotham, England
pottery *tab* 130
Wrought iron 1189b, 1194a, 1212b
alloys *tab* 1193
Wu, King 2126a
Wu Sheh Dam *tab* 1206
Wu Ti 2127a
Wuhan, China 2377b
Wundt, Wilhelm 366b, 1947c
Wuppertal, Germany 1165b
Würm Glacial Period 1925a
Wut'ai Mountains 2124a
Wuthering Heights (nov.) 1367c,
1421b, *tab* 1475
Wyandotte Constitution 2043a
Wyant, Alexander H. *tab* 108
biography 366b
Wyatt, James 366b, 1281c
Wyatt, Sir **Thomas** 366b, 1360b,
tab 1466
Wycherley, William 366b, *tab* 1468
Wycliffe, John 985c, 1360a, *tab*
1466
biography 366b
epithet 1462c
religious movement of 1015a
Wyeth, Andrew 104c, *tab* 109
biography 366c
Wylie, Philip 366c
Wynken, Blynken and Nod (nursery rhyme) 416a
Wynne, Robert J. *tab* 796
Wyoming 1999
agriculture 1999c
capital punishment 860b
census (1960) 1973
climate 1999c
colleges of 708
commercial law *tab* 826
congressional apportionment
tab 853
divorce 875b
economy 1999c
electoral votes 876c
geography 1999b–1999c
government 1999c
holidays 841–842
people of 1999c
public school enrollment *tab*
646
public school expenditures *tab*
644
statehood 2058a
student enrollment *tab* 645
swan 61b–61c
women suffrage 914b
Wyoming, University of 708
Wyss, Johann Rudolf 366c
Wythe, George Declaration of
Independence *tab* 803
Wyszynski, Cardinal **Stefan** 2240c

X

X-15 (plane) 1156c
XB-70 (plane) 1157a
Xavier, Francis, Saint *see* Fran-
cis Xavier

Xavier University 692
Xavier University of Louisiana 671
Xenolith 520c
Xenon 1808b, 1838
atomic structure 1807b
atomic weight *tab* 1805
Xenophanes 1351b, *tab* 1464, 1613b
Xenophon 366c, *tab* 1464
Anabasis 1394c

literary style 1353b
Memorabilia 1397b
sobriquet 1461a
Xerographic process 1164c
Xerosin 1845c
Xerxes I, King (Persia) 1015a,
1021c
biography 366c
Xograph 1188b

X-ray 1240c, 1290b, 1889c
space biology 952a
X-ray technicians (career) 384c
X-ray tubes 1241a, 1290b
Xylem (plants) 1643c
Xylophones 179c
XYZ Affair 2032b

Y

Yablonovvy Mountains 2254c
Yadavas, the 2180a

Yahoo 1421c
Yahya, Imam 2302c
Yajur-Veda (sacred bk.) 1420b
Yak 68b
Nepal 2223c
Yale, Elihu 367a

Yale, Linus 1264b
Yale University 660
archeological excavations 969c
library *tab* 1463
Yalta Conference 1028c, 2076c,
2262b

Yalu River 2203b, 2203c, 2343c
Yam family 1700a–1700b
Yamacraw Bluff, Georgia 2026a
Yamagata, Japan 2377b
Yamasaki, Minoru Reynolds Metal
Building *il* 79

Yamato clan 2200a
Yaméogo, Maurice 2295a
Yana River 2343c
Yangtze River 2123c, 2124a, 2124b, 2343c
Yankton College 700
Yaoundé, Cameroon 2109c, 2377b–2377c
Yard (meas.) *tab* 1500
Yardang 520c
Yarkand rugs 1110c
Yarn weaving 1286a
Yarrow 1700b
Yaws *tab* 948
Yazoo stream 520c
Ydígoras Fuentes, Miguel 2169b
Year 1797b
Year's at the Spring (poem) 416c
Yeast 748c, 1847b
    uses 1847b
Yeast (nov.) 1367c
Yeats, William Butler 1369c, 1370b, *tab* 1479
    biography 367a
    Deirdre 1430a
Yedo (Yeddo) *see* Tokyo
Yegorov, Boris B. *tab* 1770
Yellow 1104b, 1907c
    color vision 928c
    glass 133c
Yellow brass 1196a
Yellow fever *tab* 948, 2060b, 2137b
    virus 1843a
Yellow perch *il* 1717
Yellow River 759b, 2123c, 2126a, 2333c
    see also Hwang Ho
Yellow Sea 2343c
Yellow-dog contracts 606c, 831b, 839a, 1097b
Yellowfin tuna *il* 1717
Yellowhammer 1974a
Yellowlegs 68b–68c
Yellowstone National Park 896a, 2020b, 2020c
    obsidian 134a
Yellowstone River 2005c, 2018c
Yellowtail (fish) *il* 1717

Yellowthroat 68c
Yellowwood 1700b
Yemassee, The (nov.) 1373b
Yemen 995a, 995b, 2281c, 2302
    agriculture 2302a
    climate 2302a
    economy 2302a–2302b
    flag *il* 2184
    geography 2302a
    government 2302b
    history 2302b–2302c
    map 2302, *Atlas*-25
    people of 2302a
    religion 2302a, 2302b
Yenisey River 2254c, 2343c
Yerevan, U.S.S.R. 2377c
Yerkes, Charles Tyson 367a
Yerkes Telescope 1791b
Yermak 1021a
Yerovi Indaburu, Clemente 2144c
Yeshiva University 688
Yevtushenko, Yevgeni 367a, 1390b
Yew 1700b–1700c
Yggdrasil 1449c
Yi dynasty 2204b
Yiddish (lang.) 1337a
Yin dynasty 2126a
Yin Shan Mountains 2124a
Y.M.C.A. *see* Young Men's Christian Association
Y.M.H.A. *see* Young Men's Hebrew Association
Yoga 1624c
Yogurt 731c
Yoho National Park 2020b
Yokohama, Japan 2198c, 2200c
Yom Kippur 1629c
Yomiuri, Tokyo *tab* 1170c
Yonker Ramp and His Sweetheart (paint.) *tab* 112
Yorick (pen name) *see* Sterne, Laurence
York, Alvin C. 367b
York, Duke of (1633–1701) *see* James II, King (England)
York, England
    cathedral 76c

York, Pennsylvania 1993b
Yorktown, Battle of (American Revolution) 2028c, 2029, 2030a
Yosemite National Park 896a
Yoshihito, Emperor (Japan) 367b
Youlou, Fulbert 2134b
Young, Arthur 719c
Young, Brigham 367b
Young, Charles Augustus 367b
Young, Edward 367b, 1363b, *tab* 1469
Young, Francis Brett 367b
Young, Mahonri *tab* 125
    biography 367b
Young, Owen D. 367b, 1023b, 2072a
Young, Thomas (physician) 1761a, 1905a
Young Cardinal, The (paint.) *tab* 111
Young Lady With Pearl Necklace (paint.) *tab* 109
Young Men's Christian Association
    educational activities 637a
Young Men's Hebrew Association
    educational activities 637a
Young Misses, The (magazine) 1167b
Young Plan 905c, 1002b, 1023b, 2072a
Young Woman with a Water Jug (paint.) *tab* 112
Young Women's Christian Association educational activities 637a
Young Women's Hebrew Association 637a
Young-Helmholtz theory 928c
Younghusband, Sir Francis Edward 367c
Youngstown, Ohio 1992a
Youngstown University 692
Youth (bk.) 1421c
Youth's Companion (magazine) 1167b
Ypsilanti, Alexander 2165c–2166a
Ysaye, Eugène 367c
Ytterbium 1838

atomic weight *tab* 1805
Yttrium 1838
    atomic weight *tab* 1805
Yüan dynasty 2127c, 2221a
Yüan Shih-K'ai 367c, 2130a–2130b
Yucatán Peninsula 2217c, 2343c
    discovery 2023b
    flamingo 33c
    Mayas 2021a
    sapodilla 1691c
Yucca 1700c, 1989c
    see also Cassava
Yueh-chi 2085c
Yugoslavia 1015b, 2095c, 2167b, 2302–2305
    agriculture 2303b–2303c
    area 2302c
    climate 2303a
    Cominform 866a
    communism 2303b, 2303c–2304a, 2304c–2305a
    economy 2303b–2303c
    flag *il* 2184
    geography 2302c–2303a
    government 2303c–2304a
    history 2304a–2305a
    industry 2303c
    languages 1334a
    Little Entente 1014c–1015a
    map 2303, *Atlas*-18–19
    natural resources 2303b
    people of 2303a–2303b
    proportional representation 902b
    religion 2302c, 2304a
    trade 2303c
    World War I 2304b
    World War II 1028c, 2304c
Yukawa, Hideki 1915c
Yukon River 1975a, 2020c
    length of 2020b
Yukon Territory map *Atlas*-59
Yule *see* Christmas
Yung-lo 2127c
Yurts 1930a
Y.W.C.A. *see* Young Women's Christian Association
Y.W.H.A. *see* Young Women's Hebrew Association

Z

Zacchaeus 1460c
Zachau, Friedrich 162b, *tab* 171c
Zadkiel *tab* 1463c
Zaghul 1006a
Zagreb, Yugoslavia 2303b, 2377c
Zagros Mountains 2188c, 2189c, 2343c
Zama, Battle of 1016b
Zambales Mountains 2237c
Zambezi River 2242c–2243a, 2305a, 2317a, 2343c
    crocodile 24b
Zambia 2305
    agriculture 2305b
    anthropology 1924c
    climate 2305a
    Commonwealth status 1000c
    economy 2305b
    flag *il* 2184
    geography 2305a
    government 2305b
    history 2305b–2305c
    map 2305, *Atlas*-38–39
    people of 2305b
    religion 2305a
Zamboanga, Philippines 2377c
Zandonai, Riccardo 167c
Zamenhof, (Lazarus) Ludwig 1338c
Zamora, Treaty of 2241c
Zangwill, Israel 368a, *tab* 1479
Zanzibar *see* Tanzania
Zanzibar Nationalist Party (ZNP) 2272c
Zapata, Emiliano 368a, 2219b, 2219c
Zaporozhye, U.S.S.R. 2377c
Zaragoza, Spain 2263c
Zarathustra *see* Zoroaster
Zaria, Nigeria 2377c
Zarlino, Gioseffo *tab* 171b

Zauberflöte, Die (opera) 164b
Zauditu, Empress 2146b
Zealots (rel. group) 1629c
Zechariah 1460c
Zédé, Gustave 1182c
Zeeman, Pieter 368a
Zeiss, Carl 368a
Zeitblom, Bartholomäus *tab* 106
Zelaya, José Santos 2228a
Zen 1627b
Zend-Avesta (sacred bk.) *tab* 1463
Zenger, John Peter 861c, 1170c
Zenith 1793c, 1797c
Zeno of Citium 368a
    stoicism 1615b
Zeno of Elea 368a, 1502b, 1613b
Zenobia 368a
Zeolite 520c
Zephaniah 1460c
Zephyrus 1449c
Zeppelin, Ferdinand von 368a, 1155a
Zero (math.) 1607c
Zero angle 1601b
Zero G *see* Weightlessness
Zero oxidation state 1813a
Zesen, Philipp von *tab* 1468
Zeus 1437a, 1449c, 1628a
Zeus, Altar of (Pergamum) 117c
Zeus, Temple of (Olympia) 116b
Zeuxis 368b
Zhdanov, U.S.S.R. 2377c
Zhivkov, Todor 2106b
Zhukov, Georgi K. 368b
Zhukovski, Vasili Andreevich 1389a
Ziegfeld, Florenz 368b
Ziegler, Heinrich von *tab* 1469
Ziggurats 972c
Zigrosser, Carl 141c
Zilahy, Lajos *tab* 1480
Zimmerman Note 2065b
Zinc 1193, 1194a, 1838
    atomic weight *tab* 1805

Australia 2092b
    brass 1195c
    Congo (Kinshasa) 2134c
    electrochemistry 1814a
    food poisoning 956b
    galvanized iron 1227b
    Germany 2158b
    Great Britain 2282c
    Greenland 2314b
    Japan 2199c
    Korea, North 2203c
    Mexico 2218a
    Montana 1988a
    Morocco 2221c
    Peru 2236b
    Poland 2239b
    South West Africa 2322c
    Spain 2263c
    sphalerite 453c
    Sweden 2268a
    Tennessee 1995b
    Turkey 2278a
    U.S.S.R. 2256b
    Utah 1996b
    Yugoslavia 2303b
Zinc etching 153c
Zinc oxide glass 133a
Zinder, N. 1854a
Zinder, Niger 2228c
Zinjanthropus 1124b, 1924a
Zinnia *il* 1662, 1700c
Zinoviev, Grigori 368b
Zinsser, Hans 1348b
Zinzendorf, Nikolaus Ludwig von 368b
Ziolkovsky, Konstantin Eduardovitch 1764c
Zionism 2193a–2193b
    beginning of 1017c
Zipporah 1458a
Zirconium 1838
    atomic weight *tab* 1805
Zodiac 1751a
    signs 1797c
Zodiacal light 1797c
Zog I, King (Albania) 368b, 2087a

Zogolli, Ahmed bey 2087a
Zogu, Achmed 2087a
Zola, Emile 1382a, *tab* 1477
    biography 368c
Zola Dam 1206c
Zomba, Malawi 2212b, 2377c
Zone of aeration 520c
Zone of eluviation 520c
Zone of oxidation 520c
Zone of saturation 520c
Zones (geog.) 455b, 520c
Zoning (city planning) 864b
Zoology careers 390c
    see also Animals
Zooplankton 465b, 1861c
Zorach, William 124b, *tab* 125
    biography 368c
Zorathustra *see* Zoroaster
Zorn, Anders Leonhard *tab* 108
    biography 368c
Zoroaster 368c, 1627b
Zoroastrianism 981c, 1624c
    literature *tab* 1463
Zorrilla y Moral, José 1392b
Zschokke, Johann Heinrich Daniel *tab* 1472
Zsigmondy, Richard 368c
Zuider Zee Inlet 2334a
Zuloaga, Ignacio *tab* 108
Zulu wars 2291b
Zulus 2101c
Zurbarán, Francisco de *tab* 107
    A Franciscan tab 111
Zurich, Switzerland 2269c, 2270c, 2377c
Zvezdochkar (dog) 951b
Zweig, Stefan 1385c
Zwingli, Ulrich 368c, 2270b
Zworykin, Vladimir 1152a
Zygote (seed) 1646a, 1850b